W9-CTB-534

Preface

Merriam-Webster's Advanced Learner's English Dictionary is not only an entirely new dictionary created by the editorial staff of America's oldest dictionary publisher; it also marks the beginning of a new kind of publishing for this company. Over the past 160 years, Merriam-Webster has produced hundreds of dictionaries and other reference books, and many of those books have been useful to learners of English as a second or foreign language, but this dictionary is the first one that we have produced specifically to meet the needs of those learners. The creation of this dictionary reflects the reality that English has become an international language, and that American English, in particular, is now being used and studied every day by millions of people around the world. We believe that we have a unique opportunity to help students of English—in the U.S. and elsewhere—to understand our language and to use it more clearly and effectively.

This dictionary provides coverage of both American and British English. Its coverage of British English is current and comprehensive. Its coverage of American English is, we believe, unparalleled. The thousands of entries, senses, phrases, forms, and examples that are labeled *US* in this dictionary will provide learners with a clearer and more precise description of idiomatic American usage than has ever before been available in a dictionary of this kind.

The approximately 100,000 entries in this dictionary include a broad selection of words from all major areas of interest, including popular culture, business, sports, science, and technology, among others. Our main focus in choosing entries has been to include the language that people are most likely to need and encounter in their daily lives. The evidence used to make decisions about which words and senses to include was drawn, first of all, from our continually growing database of citation text, now numbering more than 100 million words. That evidence was augmented in essential ways by the resources that are available to us over the Internet, and in particular by the enormous databases of Lexis-Nexis, which provided editors with ready access to vast amounts of material from both American and British sources. Not so long ago dictionary editors had to rely entirely on evidence that had been painstakingly collected over a period of years by a program of reading. That program continues at Merriam-Webster, providing the basis of our citation database, and we continue to find great value in the traditional methods of evidence-gathering, but we also have fully embraced the power of the electronic tools that have become available in recent decades. The use of computers now makes it possible for dictionary editors to examine and describe language at a level of detail that was never before imaginable.

The definitions in this dictionary are written in simple language. In many cases, a single use of a word will be given more than one definition. Very often a word will be defined by a quite simple definition, followed by a definition that is perhaps somewhat less simple or that shows how the defined word is related to another word. For example, the verb *pioneer* is defined both as "to help create or develop (new ideas, methods, etc.)" and as "to be a pioneer in the development of (something)." The first definition can certainly stand alone, but the second definition enhances it by underscoring the close connection between the verb *pioneer* and the noun *pioneer*—a connection that native speakers are unconsciously aware of, but that learners may not sense so strongly. The inclusion of multiple definitions thus helps learners both to expand their vocabularies and to gain a fuller picture of a word's meaning by approaching it from a slightly different direction. Notes of various kinds are also used abundantly throughout the dictionary to clarify and emphasize aspects of usage that cannot be easily captured or expressed in a definition.

True fluency in any language, of course, is not acquired by memorizing dictionary definitions, but by hearing and seeing how words are used in combination with each other to express meaning. In writing this book we have devoted a great deal of care and attention to creating simple and accurate definitions, but our feeling throughout has been that the real heart of the dictionary is its examples. We know from experience that dictionary users, whether native speakers or learners, want more examples. They want examples for common words, and they want examples for difficult words. Although not every entry in this dictionary includes an example—there is usually very little value in providing an example for, say, a noun like *microchip* or *monoplane*—the great majority of the entries do, and a large percentage of them include more than one. There are more than 160,000 usage examples in this dictionary. A few of them are quotations taken from well-known works of American and British literature, but most are made-up examples, based on evidence of real English, that have been carefully written to show words being used in appropriate contexts which accurately reflect their uses in actual speech and writing.

A large number of the examples in this dictionary do not simply illustrate usage, they also explain it and expand upon it in other ways. Many examples include synonymous words or phrases shown within brackets, thus allowing the reader either to learn a new word or to have the connection between the meanings of words reinforced. Examples also often include glosses, so that phrases and compound terms whose meanings are not obvious can be explained clearly and simply. And we have very frequently explained the meaning of entire phrases and sentences by restating them with other, simpler words. Many examples also show how the same word can be used in slightly different ways—or how related words can be used in different ways—to say the same thing. We believe that such examples are of great value to the learner; they are the next best thing to having a native speaker available by your side to help clarify what you are seeing and hearing.

Any comprehensive dictionary contains an enormous amount of information, and dictionary editors have typically been required to use a variety of abbreviations and other shortcuts to fit all that information into the limited space available between the covers of a book. Two of our main goals in creating the entries for this dictionary were to keep the use of such shortcuts to a minimum and to employ conventions that are readily understandable. We set out to create a dictionary that could be easily used without frequent reference to explanatory materials. To achieve that, we have minimized the use of abbreviations and symbols (although we were not able to eliminate them entirely) and we have tried to use labels and notes whose meanings are immediately clear. We have also made every effort to organize entries in a way that allows users to find the information they want quickly. The most obvious convention we have adopted for this purpose is the use of blue text for examples. The blue text not only highlights the examples, it also makes it much easier to identify the other elements of an entry—the definitions, usages notes, and so on—and to navigate through long entries to find the particular information that you need.

It can sometimes be easy to forget that a large dictionary like this one has to be written word by word and line by line. Each definition, each example, each note that appears in this dictionary is the product of careful and strenuous thought by at least one person, and often by many people, since the nature of the writing and editing process is such that multiple stages of review are required before the work is truly finished. The names of the many people who worked on this book are listed in the following paragraphs.

The length of this project has meant that some of the people who were with us when it began had moved on to other parts of their lives by the time it ended. The Merriam-Webster editors credited here include both current and former staff members. Former Director of Defining E. Ward Gilman and former Editor in Chief Frederick C. Mish, both now retired, provided helpful suggestions when the project was in its initial planning stages, as did consultant Robert Ilson. President and Publisher John M. Morse was also involved in the initial planning of the project and provided support and encouragement throughout it.

The editors who had the first crack at creating entries included, in no particular order, Karen L. Wilkinson, Susan L. Brady, Thomas F. Pitoniak, Kathleen M. Doherty, Emily A. Brewster, G. James Kossuth, Emily B. Arsenault, Penny L. Couillard-Dix, Emily A. Vezina, Benjamin T. Korzec, Ilya A. Davidovich, Judy Yeh, Rose Martino Bigelow, Kory L. Stamper, Peter A. Sokolowski, Neil S. Serven, Deanna Stathis, Anne Eason, Joanne M. Despres, Rebecca Bryer-Charette, and myself. Dr. Ilson undertook a complete review of the work that was done at that early stage, and he made many valuable corrections and additions. He was particularly helpful in providing good examples and in augmenting our coverage of British English by identifying distinctions (often very subtle ones) between American and British usage.

The pronunciations throughout the dictionary were provided by Joshua S. Guenter. The essential task of checking and re-checking cross-references was handled by Maria Sansalone, Donna L. Rickerby, and Adrienne M. Scholz. The work of copyediting the entries that had been created by the definers was done by editors Wilkinson, Brady, Brewster, Couillard-Dix, Korzec, Yeh, Stamper, Sokolowski, Serven, Eason, Despres, Bryer-Charette, and me. The complexity of this project was such that an additional reviewing stage was added following copyediting. That work was done by editors Bryer-Charette, Korzec, Brewster, Stamper, Brady, Couillard-Dix, Wilkinson, and Madeline L. Novak. The responsibility for final review of the manuscript fell to me.

The proofreading of the galleys and page proofs was done by many of the editors mentioned above and by Anne P. Bello and Paul S. Wood. The primary proofreader for the in-house keying of revisions was Kathleen M. Doherty. Specialized editing assistance was provided by editors Wood and Doherty. Most of the illustrations that appear throughout were newly created for this book. The new black-and-white illustrations were drawn by Tim Phelps of Johns Hopkins Univ., and the color illustrations were researched and drawn by Merriam-Webster editor Diane Caswell Christian. Mark A. Stevens oversaw the creation of the new illustrations and planned the black-and-white illustrations along with Lynn Stowe Tomb, who also coordinated work with Mr. Phelps and converted the drawings to electronic form for typesetting. Freelancer Loree Hany and editors Jennifer N. Cislo and Joan I. Narmontas assisted in art research. The selection of the 3,000 entry words that are highlighted as being most important for learners to know was based in large part on initial recommendations provided by James G. Lowe and Madeline L. Novak. Additional research was carried out and final selections were made by John M. Morse. The Geographical Names section was prepared by Daniel J. Hopkins. The other back matter sections were prepared by Mark A. Stevens, C. Roger Davis, and outside contributor Orin Hargraves. Robert D. Copeland arranged for

Content Data Solutions, Inc., to convert the dictionary data files to a suitable format before typesetting them. The converted files were checked by Donna L. Rickerby. Daniel B. Brandon keyed revisions into the converted data files and contributed other technical help. Thomas F. Pitoniak directed the book through its typesetting stages. Project coordination and scheduling were handled by Madeline L. Novak, who was also chiefly responsible for the book's typography and page design.

Our notions about what this book could and should be continued to develop as we progressed through the different stages of editing, and many of the people named above made useful suggestions that led to changes, both minor and major, in the book's style and content. Further changes were implemented thanks to comments and suggestions from a group of consultants who reviewed a selection of entries at a fairly late stage in the project. We gratefully acknowledge the important contributions of those consultants, whose names are listed below.

We want first of all to express our thanks to Jerome C. Su, President of the Taiwan Association of Translation and Interpretation and Chair of Bookman Books, Taipei, Taiwan, for all of his advice and good suggestions at the reviewing stage and throughout the project. Our other consultants, all of whom provided us with carefully considered and valuable feedback, were Virginia G. Allen, author and educator, Ohio State Univ.; James H. Miller, ESL teacher; Elizabeth Niergarth, ESL instructor/consultant, Harvard Univ.; Susan Despres Prior, ESL teacher; Caroline Wilcox Reul, lexicographer and ESL teacher; Maggie Sokolik, Director, Technical Communication Program, College of Engineering, Univ. of California, Berkeley; Yukio Takahashi, English teacher, Sendai Shirayuri Gakuen High School, Sendai, Japan; Gregory Trzebiatowski, Headmaster, Thomas Jefferson School, Concepción, Chile (and his students Felipe Opazo, Paula Reyes, and Carolina Sanhueza); and Rob Waring, author and educator, Notre Dame Seishin Univ., Okayama, Japan.

All of the editors who worked on this book have of course had the experience of studying a foreign language, with varying degrees of success. This project has given us renewed opportunities to understand what it is like to approach English—with all its complexities, subtleties, and apparent inconsistencies—as a learner rather than as a native speaker, and that experience has reminded us again of just how challenging the task of learning a new language truly is. We hope and believe that *Merriam-Webster's Advanced Learner's English Dictionary* is a resource that will make that task easier for students of English.

Stephen J. Perrault
Editor

Using the Dictionary

Entries

The entries in the dictionary are arranged in alphabetical order according to their headwords.

Headwords are the boldface words at the beginning of an entry.

> **bane** /ˈbeɪn/ *noun* [*singular*] **:** a cause of trouble, annoyance, or unhappiness — usually used in the phrase ***the bane of*** • The ugly school uniforms were *the bane of* the students' lives. • She was *the bane of* my existence. [=she made my life very unhappy, difficult, etc.]

Dots within headwords show the places where you can break a word and add a hyphen if all of it will not fit at the end of a line of print or writing.

> **gar·gan·tuan** /gɑɚˈgænʧəwən/ *adj* [*more ~; most ~*] **:** very large in size or amount **:** GIGANTIC • a creature of *gargantuan* proportions • a *gargantuan* appetite

A blue underline highlights the headwords of **3,000 basic English words** selected by Merriam-Webster editors as being the most important for learners to know.

> **achieve** /əˈʧiːv/ *verb* **achieves; achieved; achiev·ing**
> **1** [+ *obj*] **:** to get or reach (something) by working hard • This year, our company was able to *achieve* [=*accomplish, attain*] all of its production goals. • He worked hard and *achieved* success. [=became successful]

You will sometimes find two or more headwords that are spelled exactly alike and that have small numbers attached to them. These entries are called **homographs**.

Homographs often are related words that have different parts of speech. For example, the noun *lecture* and the verb *lecture* are entered in this dictionary as separate homographs.

> **[1]lec·ture** /ˈlɛkʧɚ/ *noun, pl* **-tures** [*count*]
> **1 :** a talk or speech given to a group of people to teach them about a particular subject • a *lecture* about/on politics • She's planning to give/deliver a series of *lectures* on modern art. • Several hundred people are expected to attend the *lecture*.
> **2 :** a talk that criticizes someone's behavior in an angry or serious way • I came home late and got a *lecture* from my parents. • I gave her a *lecture* about doing better in school.
>
> **[2]lecture** *verb* **-tures; -tured; -tur·ing**
> **1** [*no obj*] **:** to give a talk or a series of talks to a group of people to teach them about a particular subject • She *lectures* (to undergraduates) on modern art at the local college. • She *lectures* in art at the local college.
> **2** [+ *obj*] **:** to talk to (someone) in an angry or serious way • They *lectured* their children about/on the importance of honesty. • I *lectured* her about doing better in school.

Some homographs are words that are spelled the same way but are not related at all. For example, there are two different nouns in English that are spelled *calf.* Those two nouns are not related to each other and are treated as separate entries in this dictionary.

> **[1]calf** /ˈkæf, *Brit* ˈkɑːf/ *noun, pl* **calves** /ˈkævz, *Brit* ˈkɑːvz/ [*count*]
> **1 :** a very young cow
> **2 :** the young of various other large animals (such as the elephant or whale)
> – compare [2]CALF
>
> **[2]calf** *noun, pl* **calves** [*count*] **:** the muscular back part of the leg below the knee — see picture at HUMAN — compare [1]CALF

Idioms and **phrasal verbs** are shown in alphabetical order at the end of the entry that they relate to.

pave /ˈpeɪv/ *verb* **paves; paved; pav·ing** [+ *obj*] : to cover (something) with a material (such as stone, tar, or concrete) that forms a hard, level surface for walking, driving, etc. ▪ The crew was *paving* the road. ▪ Some of the roads were *paved* over. ▪ The driveway is *paved* with concrete. ▪ a *paved* highway/road ▪ It was said that this country was so rich, the streets were ***paved with/in gold***.

pave over [*phrasal verb*] ***pave over (something) or pave (something) over disapproving*** : to cover (an area) with roads, parking lots, buildings, etc. ▪ All this beautiful farmland will be *paved over*.

pave the way for (something or someone) : to make it easier for something to happen or for someone to do something ▪ The discovery *paves the way for* the development of effective new treatments.

Some words are shown without definitions at the very end of an entry. The meaning of these words can be understood when you know the meaning of the main entry word that they are related to. For example, when a word ends in a suffix like *-ly* or *-ness*, you can understand the word's meaning by combining the meaning of the base word (the main entry) and the meaning of the suffix.

con·cise /kənˈsaɪs/ *adj* [*more* ~; *most* ~] : using few words : not including extra or unnecessary information ▪ a clear and *concise* account of the accident ▪ a *concise* summary ▪ a *concise* definition
– con·cise·ly *adv* **– con·cise·ness** *noun* [*noncount*]

Pronunciations

The **pronunciations** in this dictionary are written using the International Phonetic Alphabet (IPA). The symbols used are listed in a chart on page 22a.

Pronunciations are shown between a pair of slashes / / following the entry word. Only one pronunciation is given for most words. This is the most commonly used pronunciation.

fal·la·cious /fəˈleɪʃəs/ *adj* [*more* ~; *most* ~] *formal* : containing a mistake : not true or accurate ▪ a *fallacious* [=*false*] set of assumptions ▪ *fallacious* [=*misleading*] arguments
– fal·la·cious·ly *adv* **– fal·la·cious·ness** *noun* [*noncount*]

Additional pronunciations are shown when the word can be pronounced in different ways that are equally common.

apri·cot /ˈæprəˌkɑːt, ˈeɪprəˌkɑːt/ *noun, pl* **-cots** [*count*] : a small orange-colored fruit that is related to the peach and plum — see color picture on page C5

Pronunciations are not shown at every entry. If homographs have the same pronunciation, the pronunciation is written only at the first homograph (as the entries above for *calf* show). If the homographs are pronounced differently, a pronunciation is written at each homograph.

[1]**pres·ent** /ˈprɛznt̩/ *noun, pl* **-ents** [*count*] : something that you give to someone especially as a way of showing affection or thanks : GIFT ▪ a birthday/Christmas/anniversary/wedding *present* ▪ Here's a *present* for you from John. ▪ I gave/got her a book as a *present*. ▪ Did you wrap the *presents*? — compare [4]PRESENT

[2]**pre·sent** /prɪˈzɛnt/ *verb* **-sents; -sent·ed; -sent·ing**
1 [+ *obj*] : to give something to someone in a formal way or in a ceremony ▪ He *presented* the queen with a diamond necklace. ▪ He was *presented* with a medal at the ceremony. ▪ She *presented* a check for $5,000 to the charity.

Pronunciations are not usually shown for entries like *gag order* that are compounds of two or more words which have their own entries.

gag order *noun, pl* ~ **-ders** [*count*] *chiefly US, law* : an order by a judge or court saying that the people involved in a legal case cannot talk about the case or anything related to it in public ▪ The judge has issued a *gag order.* — called also (*Brit*) *gagging order*

Pronunciations are not shown for most undefined words that end in a common suffix, such as *-ly* or *-ness.* Pronunciations are also not shown for the plurals of nouns, the past tenses of verbs, etc., if they are formed in a regular way.

bar•ba•rous /ˈbɑɚbərəs/ *adj* [*more* ~; *most* ~]
1 : not polite or proper : very rude or offensive ▪ His behavior was *barbarous.* ▪ They used *barbarous* language.
2 : very cruel and violent ▪ It was a *barbarous* [=*barbaric*] crime. ▪ a *barbarous* custom
– bar•ba•rous•ly *adv* **– bar•ba•rous•ness** *noun* [*noncount*]

[1]**gab** /ˈgæb/ *verb* **gabs**; **gabbed**; **gab•bing** [*no obj*] *informal* : to talk a lot in an informal way usually about things that are not important or serious ▪ They stayed up late *gabbing* (away) on the phone. ▪ *gabbing* about the weather
– gab•ber *noun, pl* **-bers** [*count*] ▪ talk radio *gabbers*

When only the last part of a pronunciation is shown, the missing part can be found in a full pronunciation shown earlier in that same entry. In this example, only the last syllable is shown for the pronunciation of the plural *formulae.* The pronunciation of the first two syllables of *formulae* is the same as the pronunciation of the first two syllables of the singular *formula.*

for•mu•la /ˈfoɚmjələ/ *noun, pl* **-las** *also* **-lae** /-ˌliː/

Most of the pronunciations in this dictionary should be considered standard American pronunciations, showing how words are typically pronounced in many parts of the United States. For some words, a British pronunciation is also provided.

British pronunciations are shown when the most common British pronunciation is very different from the American pronunciation.

flask /ˈflæsk, *Brit* ˈflɑːsk/ *noun, pl* **flasks** [*count*]
1 : a container that is shaped like a flattened bottle and that is used to carry alcohol ▪ a *flask* of whiskey — called also *hip flask*
2 : a glass bottle used in scientific laboratories
3 *Brit* : THERMOS

Spelling

Some words can be spelled in different ways. These additional spellings are called **variants** and are entered after the main entry words and after either *or* or *also*.

The word ***or*** is used when the variant is as common as the main entry word.

han•kie *or* **han•ky** /ˈhæŋki/ *noun, pl* **-kies** [*count*] *informal* : HANDKERCHIEF

[1]**sa•vor** (*US*) *or Brit* **sa•vour** /ˈseɪvɚ/ *noun, pl* **-vors** *formal*
1 [*count*] : a good taste or smell — usually singular ▪ She enjoys the *savor* of a baking pie. ▪ There was a *savor* to the dish that I couldn't identify. ▪ a *savor* of mint ▪ an earthy *savor*
2 [*noncount*] *literary* : the quality that makes something interesting or enjoyable ▪ Without her love, life has lost its *savor* for me.

The word ***also*** is used when the variant is less common than the main entry word.

Ha•nuk•kah *also* **Cha•nu•kah** /ˈhɑːnəkə/ *noun, pl* **-kahs** [*count, noncount*] : an eight-day Jewish holiday that is celebrated in November or December

A label in parentheses ( ) after a headword tells you where that spelling is used. The example shown here indicates that the spelling *ampule* is used in U.S. English. Notice that the spelling *ampoule* does not have a *US* or *Brit* label. This means that it is common in both U.S. and British English.

am•pule (*US*) *or* **am•poule** /ˈæmˌpjuːl/ *noun, pl* **-pules** *or* **-poules** [*count*] **:** a small glass container used to hold a fluid that is injected into someone through a needle

The word ***chiefly*** is used to tell you that a word or variant is very common in a specified country or region but that it is also sometimes used in other countries or regions. The example shown here indicates that the British spellings *grey* and *greyish* are also sometimes used in U.S. English.

[2]**gray** (*US*) *or chiefly Brit* **grey** *noun, pl* **grays**
1 [*count, noncount*] **:** a color that is between black and white **:** a color that is like the color of smoke ▪ wearing *gray* ▪ shades of *gray* — see color picture on page C1
2 [*count*] **:** something (such as an animal) that is gray
– gray•ish (*US*) *or chiefly Brit* **grey•ish** /ˈgrejɪʃ/ *adj*

Definitions

The definitions in this dictionary are written in simple and clear language. If you are unsure about the meaning of a word that is used in a definition, you can look that word up at its own entry in the dictionary and find its meaning explained there.

Most definitions begin with a boldface colon.

gait /ˈgeɪt/ *noun, pl* **gaits** [*count*] **:** a particular way of walking ▪ He has an awkward *gait.* ▪ an easy/unsteady *gait*

Some definitions are written as notes that describe how a word or phrase is used. Those definitions begin with a dash.

earliest *noun*
at the earliest — used to indicate the earliest possible time when something will happen or be done ▪ The job will not be finished until next year *at the* (very) *earliest.* [=it will not be finished before next year] — compare LATEST

Some definitions are written as complete sentences and begin with the ✧ symbol.

[1]**gorge** /ˈgoɚʤ/ *noun, pl* **gorg•es** [*count*]
1 : a deep, narrow area between hills or mountains
2 ✧ If ***your gorge rises*** you feel sick, disgusted, or angry. ▪ My *gorge rises* [=I feel very angry] when I think of children living in such bad conditions. ▪ a disgusting odor that ***made my gorge rise*** [=made me feel like vomiting]

Synonyms and Antonyms

Synonyms are words that have the same meaning. A word that is shown in small capital letters in a definition is a synonym of the word that is being defined. The example shown here indicates that the word *seafarer* has the same meaning as *sailor.*

sea•far•er /ˈsiːˌferɚ/ *noun, pl* **-ers** [*count*] *old-fashioned* **:** someone who works or travels on a boat or ship on the sea **:** SAILOR

For some words, the only definition shown is a synonym. You can read a full definition by looking at the entry for the synonym.

dust•cart /ˈdʌstˌkaɚt/ *noun, pl* **-carts** [*count*] *Brit* **:** GARBAGE TRUCK

The synonyms of an entry are often shown at the end of the entry or sense in a **called also** note.

garbage truck *noun, pl* ~ **trucks** [*count*] *US* **:** a truck used to take away garbage that people put outside their houses, buildings, etc., in bags or cans — called also (*Brit*) *dustcart*; see picture at TRUCK

Synonyms are also frequently shown in square brackets within examples.

ram•bunc•tious /ræmˈbʌŋkʃəs/ *adj* [*more* ~; *most* ~] *US* **:** uncontrolled in a way that is playful or full of energy ▪ a class full of *rambunctious* [=*boisterous*, (*Brit*) *rumbustious*] children ▪ a *rambunctious* crowd/audience

Antonyms are words that have opposite meanings. When a word has an antonym, it is shown at the end of the entry or sense.

op•ti•mist /ˈɑːptəmɪst/ *noun, pl* **-mists** [*count*] **:** a person who usually expects good things to happen ▪ You have to be a bit of an *optimist* to start a business. ▪ Somehow he remained an *optimist* despite all that had happened to him. — opposite PESSIMIST

Examples

Examples of how a word is used are provided at most of the entries and are printed in blue.

flustered *adj* [*more* ~; *most* ~] **:** upset or nervous ▪ She seemed *flustered* when he asked about her past. ▪ Don't do anything to get him *flustered*. ▪ He was too *flustered* to speak.

Some examples have explanations that are given in square brackets.

ga•lore /gəˈloɚ/ *adj, always used after a noun, informal* **:** in large numbers or amounts ▪ The store promises bargains *galore* [=promises that there will be many bargains] during its weekend sale.

Some examples show different ways of saying the same thing.

[2]**game** *adj* **gam•er; -est**

1 : willing or ready to do something ▪ "Do you feel like going to the movies tonight?" "Sure, I'm *game*." ▪ They were *game* for anything. = They were *game* to try anything.

Many **common phrases** are highlighted in examples and are sometimes followed by explanations.

be•hav•ior (*US*) *or Brit* **be•hav•iour** /bɪˈheɪvjɚ/ *noun, pl* **-iors**

1 : the way a person or animal acts or behaves [*noncount*] I'm surprised by her bad *behavior* toward her friends. ▪ Students will be rewarded for good *behavior*. ▪ scientists studying the *behavior* of elephants ▪ normal adolescent *behavior* ▪ criminal *behavior* ▪ an interesting **pattern of behavior** = an interesting **behavior pattern** ▪ The children were all **on their best behavior** [=were all behaving very well and politely] at the museum. ▪ Inmates may be released from prison early **for good behavior**. [=because they have followed prison rules and have not caused problems]

Examples that show collocations and other common word groups are introduced by a brief note.

in•struct /ɪnˈstrʌkt/ *verb* **-structs; -struct•ed; -struct•ing** [+ *obj*] *formal*

1 : to teach (someone) a subject, skill, etc. — usually + *in* or *on* ▪ His friend *instructed* him *in* English. ▪ Many doctors are *instructing* their patients *on* the importance of exercise. ▪ She *instructed* us *on* how to interpret the text.

2 a : to give (someone) an order or command ▪ She *instructed* us that we were to remain in our seats. — usually followed by *to + verb* ▪ She *instructed* us *to remain* in our seats. — often used as *(be) instructed* ▪ We were *instructed to remain* in our seats. **b** *law* **:** to give an order or an explanation of a law to (a jury) ▪ The judge *instructed* the jury that they should disregard the testimony of the last witness.

3 *Brit* **:** to hire (a lawyer) to represent you in a legal case ▪ She advised him to *instruct* a solicitor.

Words that are shown in parentheses in an example are optional words, which means that they can be included or omitted without changing the basic meaning of the example.

[2]hiss *verb* **hisses; hissed; hiss•ing**
1 [*no obj*] : to produce a sound like a long "s" : to make a hiss ▪ The radiator *hissed* as it let off steam. ▪ a *hissing* noise
2 : to show that you dislike or disapprove of someone (such as a performer or speaker) by making a hiss [*no obj*] The audience booed and *hissed* (at him) when he came on stage. [+ *obj*] The audience *hissed* him off the stage.
3 [+ *obj*] : to say (something) in a loud or angry whisper ▪ "Leave me alone!" he *hissed.*

A slash / is used between words in an example or phrase when either of the words can be used in the same place in that example or phrase. Words separated by slashes in examples do not always have the same meaning.

cat•nap /ˈkætˌnæp/ *noun, pl* **-naps** [*count*] : a short period of sleep : a brief nap ▪ He took/had a *catnap.*
– cat•nap *verb* **-naps; -napped; -nap•ping** [*no obj*] ▪ She closed her eyes to *catnap* while her friend drove the car.

flu•o•res•cent /flʊˈrɛsn̩t/ *adj*
1 : producing light when electricity flows through a tube that is filled with a type of gas ▪ a *fluorescent* light/lamp
2 : very bright ▪ *fluorescent* colors/clothing ▪ *fluorescent* tape/paint

Forms and Tenses

When a noun, verb, adjective, or adverb has different forms or tenses, those forms or tenses are shown in boldface at the beginning of the entry immediately after the label *noun, verb, adj,* or *adv.*

A noun's ***plural form*** is shown when one or more of its senses can be plural. The abbreviation ***pl*** is used to mean *plural.* Often just the last part of the plural form is shown.

ho•tel /hoʊˈtɛl/ *noun, pl* **-tels** [*count*] : a place that has rooms in which people can stay especially when they are traveling : a place that provides food, lodging, and other services for paying guests ▪ check into a *hotel* ▪ check out of a *hotel*

ho•tel•i•er /hoʊˈtɛljɚ/ *noun, pl* **-iers** [*count*] : a person who owns or operates a hotel

When the plural form of a compound noun is shown, a special symbol ~ is used to represent the first word or words of the noun. In the example shown here, the plural form of the noun *flower bed* is *flower beds.*

flower bed *noun, pl* **~ beds** [*count*] : an area where flowers are planted

All verb entries show these three forms: the **present third-person singular** form, the **past tense,** and the **present participle.** [See pages 1936–38 for grammar help on verb tenses.] In many cases, only the last parts of the forms are shown.

[1]blink /ˈblɪŋk/ *verb* **blinks; blinked; blink•ing**

ga•lumph /gəˈlʌmf/ *verb* **-lumphs; -lumphed; -lumph•ing** [*no obj*] *informal* : to move in a loud and clumsy way ▪ I could hear him *galumphing* around in the attic.

When the **past participle** and the past tense of a verb are different, the past participle is also shown after the past tense.

[1]drive /ˈdraɪv/ *verb* **drives; drove** /ˈdroʊv/; **driv•en** /ˈdrɪvən/; **driv•ing**

Some **adjectives** and **adverbs** have **comparative** and **superlative** forms which are shown in boldface at the beginning of the entry. These forms are often created by adding ***-er*** or ***-est*** to the main entry word. The entry for *short* indicates that the comparative form is *shorter* and the superlative form is *shortest.* [See also *Grammatical Labels* (below) for more information about the treatment of comparative and superlative forms.]

> [1]**short** /ˈʃoɚt/ *adj* **short·er; -est**

Sometimes the comparative and superlative forms are very different from the main entry word.

> [1]**good** /ˈgʊd/ *adj* **bet·ter** /ˈbɛtɚ/; **best** /ˈbɛst/

When an entry has both an American and a British spelling, the forms and tenses are shown only for the American spelling in order to save space. For example, the entry for *harbor* shows only the American plural *harbors.* If you are using the British spelling, of course, the plural should be *harbours.*

> [1]**har·bor** (*US*) *or Brit* **har·bour** /ˈhɑɚbɚ/ *noun, pl* **-bors** [*count*]

Grammatical Labels

In addition to having a part of speech label, such as *noun, verb,* or *adj,* many entries include one or more **grammatical labels** which are shown in square brackets and which tell you the different forms or uses of a particular noun, verb, adjective, etc. When these labels appear at the beginning of the entry, they describe the entire entry. They can also appear at individual senses in an entry, and they can be used to introduce a particular example or group of examples.

Most nouns are labeled [*count*], [*noncount*], [*count, noncount*], [*singular*], or [*plural*]. [See pages 1927–28 for grammar help on nouns.]

An entry or sense for a noun is labeled **[*count*]** when it has both a singular and a plural form.

> **heart·beat** /ˈhɑɚtˌbiːt/ *noun, pl* **-beats** [*count*] **:** the action or sound of the heart as it pumps blood ▪ The patient had a rapid *heartbeat.* ▪ irregular *heartbeats*

An entry or sense for a noun is labeled **[*noncount*]** when it does not have a plural form and when it refers to something that cannot be counted.

> **heart·burn** /ˈhɑɚtˌbɚn/ *noun* [*noncount*] **:** an unpleasant hot feeling in your chest caused by something that you ate ▪ I like spicy food, but it gives me *heartburn.*

When a noun can be used as both a count and a noncount noun, it is sometimes given a **[*count, noncount*]** label.

> **sedge** /ˈsɛʤ/ *noun, pl* **sedg·es** [*count, noncount*] **:** a plant like grass that grows in wet ground or near water

An entry or sense for a noun that is always used in its plural form is labeled **[*plural*]**.

> **long johns** /ˈlɑːŋˌʤɑːnz/ *noun* [*plural*] **:** underwear that covers your legs and that is worn in cold weather — called also (*US*) *long underwear;* see color picture on page C12

An entry or sense for a noun that refers to one thing and is never used in a plural form is labeled **[*singular*]**.

> [2]**glow** *noun* [*singular*]
> **1 :** a soft and steady light ▪ We could see the *glow* of the lamp in the window. ▪ The town's lights cast a *glow* on the horizon.

Most **verbs** in this dictionary are labeled as either [+ *obj*] or [*no obj*] or both. Other types of verbs have these labels: [*modal verb*], [*linking verb*], or [*auxiliary verb*]. Verbs labeled [*phrasal verb*] are entered as phrases at the end of a verb entry. [See pages 1930–31 for grammar help on verbs.]

An entry or sense for a verb that has an object is labeled **[+ *obj*]**. A verb of this kind is known as a **transitive verb**.

[2]**graze** *verb* **grazes; grazed; grazing** [+ *obj*]
1 : to touch or hit (something) while moving past it • The car's wheel *grazed* the curb. • He was *grazed* by a bullet.

An entry or sense for a verb that does not have an object is labeled **[*no obj*]**. A verb of this kind is known as an **intransitive verb**.

[1]**gab** /ˈgæb/ *verb* **gabs; gabbed; gab•bing** [*no obj*] *informal* : to talk a lot in an informal way usually about things that are not important or serious • They stayed up late *gabbing* (away) on the phone. • *gabbing* about the weather
– **gab•ber** *noun, pl* **-bers** [*count*] • talk radio *gabbers*

An entry or sense that is labeled **[*linking verb*]** does not express action but is used to say that something exists or is in a particular state. It connects an object with an adjective or noun that describes or identifies a subject.

be•come /bɪˈkʌm/ *verb* **-comes; -came** /-ˈkeɪm/; **-come; -com•ing**
1 [*linking verb*] : to begin to be or come to be something specified • Although I've known him for years, we didn't *become* close friends until recently. • She won the election, *becoming* the first woman to be President of the nation. • They both *became* teachers.

An entry or sense that is labeled **[*auxiliary verb*]** is used with another verb in order to show the verb's tense, to form a question, etc.

be /ˈbiː/ *verb*...
10 [*auxiliary verb*] — used with the past participle of a verb to form passive constructions • The money *was found* by a child. • They *were* [=*got*] *married* by a priest. • Don't *be fooled* by what he says. • Please *be seated*. [=please sit down] • The election *was expected* to produce a very close result. • God *be praised*! [=let God be praised] • I *was surprised* by her rudeness.

An entry or sense that is labeled **[*modal verb*]** is used with another verb to express an idea about what is possible, necessary, etc.

[1]**can** /kən, ˈkæn/ *verb, past tense* **could** /kəd, ˈkʊd/ *present tense for both singular and plural* **can**; *negative* **can•not** /ˈkænɑt, kəˈnɑːt, *Brit* ˈkænət/ *or* **can't** /ˈkænt, *Brit* ˈkɑːnt/ [*modal verb*]
1 : to be able to (do something) • I don't need any help. I *can* do it myself. • I *can't* decide what to do. • All we *can* do [=the only thing we can do] now is wait. : to know how to (do something) • She *can* read, *can't* she? • I *can* whistle. : to have the power or skill to (do something) • A weight lifter *can* lift a very heavy weight. • She *can* play the piano. • Only Congress *can* do that. : to be designed to (do something) • a car that *can* hold five people [=a car that has enough room for five people] • How fast *can* [=*does, will*] the car go?

A verb that is labeled **[*phrasal verb*]** is a verb that is used with a preposition, an adverb, or both.

[2]**pal** *verb* **pals; palled; pal•ling**
pal around with [*phrasal verb*] *informal* ***pal around with (someone)*** *chiefly US* : to spend time with (someone) as a friend • She's been *palling around with* a girl she met at school.
pal up [*phrasal verb*] *chiefly Brit, informal* : to become friends with someone • They *palled up* when they were neighbors long ago. • He *pals up* with anyone who can help his career.

The **comparative** and **superlative** forms of some **adjectives** and **adverbs** are formed by adding the letters *-er* and *-est* at the end of the word or by changing the word completely. Other adjectives and adverbs are given their comparative and superlative forms by using the words *more* and *most.* [See pages 1931–34 for grammar help on adjectives and adverbs.]

When a word has comparative and superlative forms that use the words *more* and *most*, the word is given the label **[*more* ~; *most* ~]**. This label also means that an adjective or adverb can be used with words like *very* and *slightly*. The example shown here means that you can say that one thing is "more complicated" than another, that something is the "most complicated" one of a group, that something is "very complicated," etc.

com·pli·cat·ed /ˈkɑːmpləˌkeɪtəd/ *adj* [*more* ~; *most* ~] : hard to understand, explain, or deal with ▪ The game's rules are too *complicated*. ▪ a *complicated* situation ▪ a very *complicated* issue : having many parts or steps ▪ The machine has a *complicated* design. ▪ a *complicated* plan ▪ a *complicated* mathematical formula

Sometimes the comparative and superlative forms of an adjective or adverb can be formed in two different ways. The word ***or*** is included in the label when the *more/most* forms are as common as the *-er/-est* forms. When the *more/most* forms are much less common, ***also*** is used.

drea·ry /ˈdriri/ *adj* **drea·ri·er**; **-ri·est** [*or more* ~; *most* ~] : causing unhappiness or sad feelings : not warm, cheerful, etc. ▪ It was a gray, *dreary* morning. ▪ She longed to leave her *dreary* [=*gloomy, dismal*] hometown. ▪ The family struggled through *dreary* economic times.

[1]**small** /ˈsmɑːl/ *adj* **small·er**; **-est** [*also more* ~; *most* ~] **1** : little in size ▪ They live in a *small* house. ▪ a *small* glass of soda ▪ She moved to a *smaller* town. ▪ The toy is *small* enough to fit in my pocket. ▪ He has *small* hands. ▪ This room is a little *smaller* than that one.

Sometimes the label [*more* ~; *most* ~] is shown only at a specific sense. In the example shown here, the first sense of *muscular* cannot be used with words like *more, most,* and *very,* but the second sense can.

mus·cu·lar /ˈmʌskjələ/ *adj* **1** : of or relating to muscles ▪ *muscular* strength/weakness ▪ a *muscular* injury **2** [*more* ~; *most* ~] : having large and strong muscles ▪ a *muscular* athlete ▪ He has a *muscular* physique. ▪ His legs are very *muscular*.
– **mus·cu·lar·i·ty** /ˌmʌskjəˈlerəti/ *noun* [*noncount*]

When an adverb is shown at the end of the entry for an adjective that has a [*more* ~; *most* ~] label, the label is not repeated for the adverb, but it also describes how the adverb can be used. In the example shown here, both the adjective *querulous* and the adverb *querulously* can be used with words like *more, most,* and *very.*

quer·u·lous /ˈkweəjələs/ *adj* [*more* ~; *most* ~] *formal* : complaining in an annoyed way ▪ The child said in a *querulous* [=*whining*] voice that he didn't like carrots. ▪ *querulous* customers
– **quer·u·lous·ly** *adv* – **quer·u·lous·ness** *noun* [*noncount*]

Other Labels

Many entries include labels such as *formal, informal, US, Brit,* etc. [See page 21a for a list of the labels that are commonly used in this dictionary.]

When a label appears at the beginning of an entry, it describes the entire entry, including any undefined words that may appear at the end of the entry. In the example shown here, the label *formal* means that both senses of *mendacious* are formal, and that the adverb *mendaciously* and the noun *mendaciousness* are also formal words.

men·da·cious /mɛnˈdeɪʃəs/ *adj* [*more* ~; *most* ~] *formal* **1** : not honest : likely to tell lies ▪ a *mendacious* businessman **2** : based on lies ▪ The newspaper story was *mendacious* and hurtful. ▪ a *mendacious* political campaign
– **men·da·cious·ly** *adv* – **men·da·cious·ness** *noun* [*noncount*]

When a label is used at a specific part of an entry (such as a particular sense or example), it relates only to that specific part.

[1]**grit** /ˈgrɪt/ *noun* [*noncount*]
1 : very small pieces of sand or stone ▪ He shook out his shoes to remove the small rocks and *grit*.
2 *informal* : mental toughness and courage ▪ Through resourcefulness and *grit*, the pioneers survived the winter.

live·li·hood /ˈlaɪvliˌhʊd/ *noun, pl* **-hoods** : a way of earning money in order to live [*count*] Many fishermen believe that the new regulations threaten their *livelihoods*. [*noncount*] (*formal*) He claims he lost a source/means of *livelihood* when he was injured.

Cross-references

Many entries include notes that direct you to another entry or sense for additional information.

Compare notes are placed at the entries of words that are similar or that may be confused with each other.

[1]**can·ter** /ˈkæntɚ/ *noun, pl* **-ters**
1 [*singular*] : the way a horse moves when it is running fairly fast ▪ He set off ***at a canter*** towards the stable.
2 [*count*] : a ride or run at a canter — usually singular ▪ a *canter* through the fields — compare [1]GALLOP, [2]TROT

When two or more homographs have the same part of speech, a *compare* note is included at the end of each entry.

[3]**do** *noun, pl* **dos** [*count*] *informal*
1 : something that a person should do — usually used in the phrase ***dos and don'ts*** ▪ She told her daughter about the *dos and don'ts* of dating. [=about the things that she should and should not do when dating someone]
2 *US* : a way of cutting and arranging a person's hair : HAIRDO ▪ She was worried that the wind might mess up her *do*.
3 : a party or social gathering ▪ We threw a big *do* for her after graduation.
– compare [4]DO

[4]**do** /ˈdoʊ/ *or chiefly Brit* **doh** *noun* [*noncount*] : the first note of a musical scale ▪ *do*, re, mi, fa, sol, la, ti — compare [3]DO

See also notes often direct you to another entry that uses a form of the word you were looking up.

ef·face /ɪˈfeɪs/ *verb* **-fac·es**; **-faced**; **-fac·ing** [*+ obj*] *formal* : to cause (something) to fade or disappear ▪ coins with dates *effaced* by wear ▪ a memory *effaced* by time — see also SELF-EFFACING
– **ef·face·ment** /ɪˈfeɪsmənt/ *noun* [*noncount*]

See also notes can also direct you to a phrase that is defined at another entry.

die–hard /ˈdaɪˌhɑɚd/ *adj* [*more* ~; *most* ~] : very determined or loyal ▪ *die-hard* fans; *especially* : very loyal to a set of beliefs and not willing to change those beliefs ▪ a *die-hard* conservative — see also *die hard* at [1]DIE
– **die·hard** *noun, pl* **-hards** [*count*] ▪ a bunch of conservative *diehards*

And *see also* notes can direct you to a different part of the same entry.

[2]**act** *verb* **acts**; **act·ed**; **act·ing**…
6 [*no obj*] : to make something happen : to have a particular effect ▪ The chemical *acts* [=*works*] by destroying the cells in the brain. — often *+ on* ▪ These medicines *act on* [=*affect*] the heart. — see also ACT ON/UPON (below)
act on/upon [*phrasal verb*] ***act on/upon (something)*** : to use (something, such as a feeling or suggestion) as a reason or basis for doing something ▪ They never *acted on* the information they had. ▪ We were too late to *act upon* his suggestion. ▪ It's okay to feel angry or jealous, but you mustn't *act on* those feelings. — see also [2]ACT 6 (above)

A **see** cross-reference tells you that more information can be found at another entry.

dif•fer /ˈdɪfɚ/ *verb* **-fers**; **-fered**; **-fer•ing** [*no obj*] . . .
2 : to have opinions that don't agree ▪ We *differ* [=*disagree*] on/about/over how best to raise the money. — often + *with* ▪ They *differed with* each other on religious matters.
agree to differ see AGREE
beg to differ see BEG

key•hole /ˈkiːˌhoʊl/ *noun, pl* **-holes** [*count*] : the opening in a lock into which a key is placed — see picture at DOOR

Other Features

Differences between words that have the same meanings or very similar meanings are discussed in special ***synonyms*** paragraphs.

synonyms REMARK, OBSERVATION, and COMMENT mean something that is said or written and that gives an opinion. REMARK often suggests a quick thought or an informal judgment. ▪ He made a casual *remark* about the food. OBSERVATION often suggests an opinion expressed after looking closely at and thinking about something. ▪ She published her *observations* on whales after 10 years of study. COMMENT often suggests a remark that is meant to explain or criticize. ▪ I asked her to give me her *comments* on the book when she finished it.

Problems and questions that relate to the use of a particular word are discussed in ***usage*** paragraphs.

usage *Ain't* is usually regarded as an error, but it is common in the very informal speech of some people and it is also used in informal and humorous phrases. ▪ That joke just *ain't* funny. ▪ Say it *ain't* so! ▪ You *ain't* seen nothing yet! ▪ Two out of three *ain't* bad. ▪ If it *ain't* broke don't fix it! ▪ Things *ain't* what they used to be. ▪ *Ain't* that the truth?

Many entries include notes that begin with the symbol ✧ and explain the **origins** of a word or provide other kinds of information.

Scrooge *or* **scrooge** /ˈskruːʤ/ *noun, pl* **Scroog•es** *or* **scrooges** [*count*] *informal* : a selfish and unfriendly person who is not willing to spend or give away money — usually singular ▪ His boss is a real *Scrooge* who never gives people raises. ✧ ***Scrooge*** is from the name of Ebenezer Scrooge, the main character in the story *A Christmas Carol* by Charles Dickens.

PIN /ˈpɪn/ *abbr* personal identification number ✧ A personal identification number is a secret number that is used to get money from a bank account through a machine, to get personal information on a Web site, etc.

Labels Used in This Dictionary

Parts of Speech

(See pages 1927–35 for explanations and examples.)

abbr — abbreviation
adj — adjective
adv — adverb
combining form
conj — conjunction
definite article
indefinite article
interj — interjection
noun
prefix
prep — preposition
pronoun
suffix
verb

Grammatical Labels

(See pages 16a–18a for explanations and examples.)

for nouns: [*count*], [*noncount*], [*count, noncount*], [*singular*], [*plural*]
for verbs: [+ *obj*], [*no obj*], [*auxiliary verb*], [*linking verb*], [*modal verb*], [*phrasal verb*]
for adjectives and adverbs: [*more* ~; *most* ~], [*or more* ~; *most* ~], [*also more* ~; *most* ~]

Usage Labels

Regional Labels:

US — common only in American English
chiefly US — common in American English and sometimes used in British English
Brit — common only in British English
chiefly Brit — common in British English and sometimes used in American English

Status Labels:

slang — used in very informal, spoken English usually by a small group of people
offensive — likely to offend many people and usually avoided
obscene — very offensive in a way that many people find shocking
impolite — not used in polite speech and writing

Register Labels:

informal — used in informal speech and writing
formal — used in formal speech and writing
literary — used in novels, poetry, etc., and rarely used in ordinary speech and writing
old-fashioned — not often used today but used by people in the recent past or by older people
humorous — having a funny or amusing quality
technical — used by people who have special knowledge about a particular subject
disapproving — used to show that you do not like or approve of someone or some thing
approving — used to show that you like or approve of someone or something

Subject Labels

Labels like *medical, law,* and *baseball* are used to show the specific subject that a definition relates to.

Pronunciation Symbols

VOWELS

Note: when two symbols are separated by / in the list below (eɪ/ej, ʊ/ow, etc.), the second symbol is used when the sound occurs immediately before another vowel and the first symbol is used elsewhere. The symbols /ɑː iː uː/ are written as /ɑ i u/ when found in unstressed syllables.

æ	**ask, bat, glad**
ɑː	**cot, bomb, paw**
ɛ	**bet, fed**
ə	**about, banana, collide**
iː/iːj	**eat, bead, bee**
ɪ	**id, bid, pit**
ʊ	**foot, should, put**
uː/uːw	**boot, two, coo**
ʌ	**under, putt, bud**
ɚ/ər	**merge, bird, further**
eɪ/ej	**eight, wade, play**
aɪ/aj	**ice, bite, tile**
aʊ/aw	**out, gown, owl**
oɪ/oj	**oyster, coil, boy**
oʊ/ow	**oat, own, zone**
ɑɚ/ɑr	**car, heart, star**
eɚ/er	**bare, fair, wear**
iɚ/ir	**near, deer, mere**
oɚ/or	**boar, port, door**
uɚ/ur	**boor, tour**

Note: The symbols below are for vowels that occur in British English. British pronunciations are shown in this dictionary when the most common British pronunciation is very different from the American pronunciation.

ɒ	*British* **cot, bomb**
ɔː	*British* **caught, paw, port**
ɚː	*British* **merge, bird**
əʊ	*British* **oat, own, zone**
ɪə	*British* **near, deer**
ɛə	*British* **bare, fair**
ʊə	*British* **boor, tour**

CONSONANTS

b	**baby, labor, cab**
d	**day, kid, riddle**
ʤ	**just, badger, fudge**
ð	**then, either, bathe**
f	**foe, tough, buff**
g	**go, dagger, bag**
h	**hot, ahead**
j	**yes, vineyard**
k	**cat, flock, skin**
l	**law, hollow**
l̩	**pedal, battle, final**
m	**mat, hemp, hammer**
n	**new, tent, tenor, run**
n̩	**button, satin, kitten**
ŋ	**rung, hang, swinger**
p	**top, speed, pay**
r	**rope, arrive**
s	**sad, mist, kiss**
ʃ	**shoe, mission, slush**
t	**stick, late, later**
ʧ	**batch, nature, choose**
θ	**thin, ether, bath**
v	**vat, never, cave**
w	**wet, software**
z	**zoo, easy, buzz**
ʒ	**vision, azure, beige**

OTHER SYMBOLS

ˈ	high stress: **penmanship**
ˌ	low stress: **penmanship**
Brit	indicates British pronunciation
/	slash used in pairs to mark the beginning and end of a pronunciation or set of pronunciations /ˈpɛn/

A Dictionary of the English Language

A

¹a *or* **A** /ˈeɪ/ *noun, pl* **a's** *or* **as** *or* **A's** *or* **As**

1 : the first letter of the English alphabet [*count*] a word that begins with an *a* [*noncount*] a word that begins with *a*

2 : a musical note or key referred to by the letter A : the sixth tone of a C-major scale [*count*] play/sing an *A* [*noncount*] a song in the key of *A*

3 [*count*] **: a grade that is given to a student for doing excellent work** ▪ She got an *A* on the exam. ▪ He's an ***A student*** [=a student who gets A's for his schoolwork]

4 [*noncount*] **— used to refer to the first of two or more people, places, or things that are being considered** ▪ If *A*, B, and C divide the coins equally, how many does each person get?

an A for effort see EFFORT

exhibit A see ²EXHIBIT

***from A to Z* : including everything** ▪ The book is titled "Home Repairs *From A to Z*."

***from (point) A to (point) B* : from one place to another** ▪ I don't care about the scenery. I'm only interested in getting *from A to B*.

²a /ə, ˈeɪ/ *or* **an** /ən, ˈæn/ *indefinite article* ✧ *A* **is used before a consonant sound.** ▪ *a* door ▪ *a* human *An* **is used before a vowel sound.** ▪ *an* icicle ▪ *an* honor **Note that when a word begins with a vowel letter but is pronounced with a consonant sound, *a* is used.** ▪ *a* one ▪ *a* union **When an abbreviation begins with a consonant letter but is pronounced with a vowel sound, *an* is used.** ▪ *an* FBI investigation ▪ *an* LCD display **When a word begins with *h* but the first syllable of the word is not given primary stress, both *a* and *an* are used.** ▪ *a* historic ▪ *an* historic

1 — used before singular nouns when the person or thing is being mentioned for the first time ▪ There was *a* tree in the field. ▪ *A* man walked past him. ▪ I heard *a* shout. ▪ He bought *a* house, but this is not the house he bought. ▪ I ordered *an* apple and some cheese: I ate the apple but not the cheese.

2 a — used like *one* before number words like *hundred, thousand*, etc. ▪ *a* hundred and twenty people ▪ *a* million dollars ▪ *a* dozen doughnuts **b — used like *one* before number words like *third, fortieth*, etc.** ▪ This is *a* [=*one*] third the size of that. **c — used like *one* before units of weight, measurement, etc.** ▪ *a* pound or two [=one or two pounds] ▪ *a* week or two [=one or two weeks] ▪ *a* foot and *a* half of water = one and *a* half feet of water **d : one single : even one — used in negative constructions** ▪ They didn't charge me *a* penny. [=they didn't charge me anything at all] ▪ "Did she say anything about it?" "Not *a* word."

3 — used before a word or phrase that indicates a type or class of person or thing ▪ My uncle is *a* plumber. ▪ Copper is *a* metal. ▪ She's *a* very nice lady. **— often used before noncount nouns that are modified by an adjective or phrase** ▪ *a* torrential rain ▪ She has *a* warmth that puts people at ease. ▪ I've always had *a* fondness for chocolate.

4 — used like *any* to refer in a general way to people or things ▪ *A* person who is sick can't work well. [=people can't work well if they are sick]

5 — used before a proper noun to indicate limited knowledge about the person or thing being mentioned ▪ *A* Mr. Smith [=a man named Mr. Smith] called to ask about the job. ▪ Among the towns of the area there is *a* Newton, I believe.

6 a — used before a proper noun that is acting as an example or type ▪ the attractions of *a* Boston or *a* Cleveland ▪ His friends say he's *an* Einstein in regard to science. **b — used before the name of a day of the week to refer to one occurrence of it** ▪ My birthday falls on *a* Tuesday this year.

7 a — used before the name of a person (such as a famous artist) when the name is being used to refer to something (such as a painting) created by that person ▪ The museum recently purchased *a* Rembrandt. [=a painting by Rembrandt] ▪ My violin is *a* Stradivarius. **b — used before a family name to show that someone is a member of that family** ▪ Did you know that she's *a* Kennedy?

8 — used before a proper noun referring to a person or thing that has a particular quality ▪ *A* triumphant Ms. Jones greeted her supporters. [=Ms. Jones was triumphant when she greeted her supporters] ▪ We were met at the door by *an* embarrassed Mr. Brown. [=Mr. Brown was embarrassed when he met us at the door] ▪ We had *a* very mild January.

9 — used with words like *bit* and *little* to form phrases that describe quantity, amount, or degree ▪ She felt *a bit* tired. ▪ It's getting *a little* late.

10 — used in phrases that describe how often something occurs, how fast something is going, etc. ▪ They meet twice *a* week. [=twice each week] ▪ The car was traveling at a hundred miles *an* [=*per*] hour.

¹a- /ə/ *prefix*

1 : on : in : at ▪ *a*bed

2 : in (such) a state or condition ▪ *a*fire

3 : in (such) a manner ▪ *a*loud

4 *old-fashioned* **: in the act or process of** ▪ gone *a*-hunting [=gone hunting]

²a- *or* **an-** *prefix* **: not : without** ▪ *a*sexual

AA *abbr* **1** Alcoholics Anonymous **2** *Brit* Automobile Association

AAA *abbr, US* American Automobile Association

¹aah /ˈɑː/ *interj* **— used to express pleasure, surprise, or happiness** ▪ *Aah*, that feels good.

²aah *verb* **aahs; aahed; aahing** [*no obj*] *informal* **: to express amazement, joy, or surprise — used in the phrase *ooh and aah*** ▪ We all *oohed and aahed* at/over the fireworks.

— aah *noun, pl* **aahs** [*count*] ▪ the oohs and *aahs* of the crowd

aard·vark /ˈɑɚdˌvɑɚk/ *noun, pl* **-varks** [*count*] **: a large African animal that has a long nose and that eats ants and other insects**

AARP *abbr, US* American Association of Retired Persons

ab /ˈæb/ *noun, pl* **abs** [*count*] *informal* **: any one of the muscles that cover a person's stomach : an abdominal muscle — usually plural** ▪ an athlete doing exercises to tone his *abs*

ab. *abbr* about

aback /əˈbæk/ *adv* **: by surprise — used in the phrase *taken aback*** ▪ She was *taken aback* [=she was very surprised] by his rude response. ▪ He was *taken aback* [=*shocked, startled*] when he saw their house.

aba·cus /ˈæbəkəs/ *noun, pl* **-cus·es** *also* **-ci** /-ˌsaɪ/ [*count*] **: a device used for counting and calculating by sliding small balls or beads along rods or in grooves**

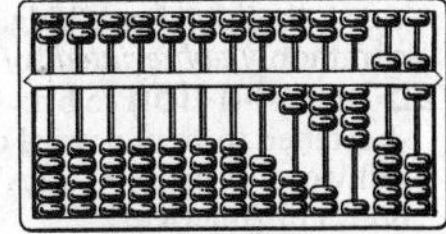

abacus

ab·a·lo·ne /ˌæbəˈlouni/ *noun, pl* **-nes** [*count, noncount*] **: a type of shellfish that is eaten**

A

as food and that has a shell that is lined with a hard white material (called mother-of-pearl)

[1]**aban·don** /əˈbændən/ *verb* **-dons; -doned; -don·ing** [+ *obj*]

1 a : to leave and never return to (someone who needs protection or help) ▪ The child had been *abandoned* (by his parents) as an infant. ▪ He *abandoned* his family. **b :** to leave and never return to (something) ▪ *abandon* property ▪ They *abandoned* the car on a back road. ▪ That house was *abandoned* years ago.

2 : to leave (a place) because of danger ▪ The approaching fire forced hundreds of people to *abandon* their homes. ▪ The officer refused to *abandon* his post. ✧ If you ***abandon ship***, you leave a boat or ship that is sinking. ▪ The captain gave the order to *abandon ship*. This phrase is sometimes used figuratively. ▪ The company is doing poorly, and many investors have decided to *abandon ship*. [=to sell their stock in the company]

3 : to stop supporting or helping (someone or something) ▪ The policy *abandons* the most vulnerable members of society. ▪ She *abandoned* the party not long after the election.

4 : to stop doing or having (something) **:** to give up (something) completely ▪ We *abandoned* hope of ever going back. ▪ He *abandoned* the principles that he once fought hard to defend. ▪ She had to *abandon* her plans for a vacation. ▪ Play was *abandoned* because of the bad weather.

abandon yourself to literary **:** to allow yourself to be fully controlled or affected by (something, such as a strong emotion) ▪ He *abandoned himself* to despair. [=he was overcome by despair]

– aban·don·ment /əˈbændənmənt/ *noun* [*noncount*] ▪ the *abandonment* of a child/home

[2]**abandon** *noun* [*noncount*] **:** a feeling or attitude of wild or complete freedom ▪ They all danced with (wild) *abandon*. ▪ She decided ***with reckless abandon*** [=in a very wild and reckless way] to quit her job and move to Tahiti.

aban·doned /əˈbændənd/ *adj*

1 a : left without needed protection or care ▪ an *abandoned* baby **b :** left by the owner ▪ an *abandoned* house/car **c :** no longer held or thought of **:** given up ▪ *abandoned* [=*forsaken*] hopes/dreams

2 [*more ~; most ~*] *literary* **:** wild and uncontrolled ▪ *abandoned* behavior ▪ He led a reckless and *abandoned* life and died young.

abase /əˈbeɪs/ *verb* **abas·es; abased; abas·ing**

abase yourself formal **:** to behave in a way that makes you seem lower or less deserving of respect ▪ politicians *abasing themselves* before wealthy businessmen

abashed /əˈbæʃt/ *adj* [*more ~; most ~*] **:** embarrassed or ashamed ▪ She seemed a little *abashed* when they asked about her job. — opposite UNABASHED

abate /əˈbeɪt/ *verb* **abates; abat·ed; abat·ing** [*no obj*] **:** to become weaker **:** to decrease in strength ▪ We waited for the wind/storm to *abate*. ▪ The excitement has *abated*.

– abate·ment /əˈbeɪtmənt/ *noun, pl* **-ments** [*noncount*] The violence has continued without *abatement*. [*count*] a ***tax abatement*** [=an amount by which a tax is reduced]

ab·at·toir /ˈæbəˌtwɑɚ/ *noun, pl* **-toirs** [*count*] *chiefly Brit* **:** SLAUGHTERHOUSE

ab·bess /ˈæbəs/ *noun, pl* **-bess·es** [*count*] **:** a woman who is the head of a convent

ab·bey /ˈæbi/ *noun, pl* **-beys** [*count*]

1 a : a monastery run by an abbot **b :** a convent run by an abbess

2 : a church that is connected to other buildings where monks or nuns live or once lived ▪ Westminster *Abbey*

ab·bot /ˈæbət/ *noun, pl* **-bots** [*count*] **:** a man who is the head of a monastery

abbr *or* **abbr.** *abbr* abbreviation

ab·bre·vi·ate /əˈbriːviˌeɪt/ *verb* **-ates; -at·ed; -at·ing** [+ *obj*] **:** to make (something) shorter ▪ He gave us an *abbreviated* [=*shortened*] account of his travels.; *especially* **:** to reduce (a word or name) to a shorter form ▪ You can *abbreviate* the word "building" as "bldg." ▪ "United States of America" is commonly *abbreviated* to/as "USA."

ab·bre·vi·a·tion /əˌbriːviˈeɪʃən/ *noun, pl* **-tions** [*count*] **:** a shortened form of a word or name that is used in place of the full word or name ▪ "USA" is an *abbreviation* of/for "United States of America."

[1]**ABC** /ˌeɪˌbiˈsiː/ *noun, pl* **ABCs** *or* **ABC's**

1 : the letters of the English alphabet [*plural*] (*US*) We learned our *ABC's*. [*singular*] (*Brit*) We learned our *ABC*.

2 : the most basic or important information about a subject [*plural*] (*US*) learning the *ABC's* of wine [*singular*] (*Brit*) learning the *ABC* of wine

(as) easy as ABC see [1]EASY

[2]**ABC** *abbr* **1** American Broadcasting Corporation ✧ ABC is one of the major television networks in the U.S. **2** Australian Broadcasting Corporation

ab·di·cate /ˈæbdɪˌkeɪt/ *verb* **-cates; -cat·ed; -cat·ing**

1 : to leave the position of being a king or queen [*no obj*] The king was forced to *abdicate*. [+ *obj*] The king *abdicated* the throne.

2 [+ *obj*] *formal* **:** to fail to do what is required by (a duty or responsibility) ▪ The government *abdicated* [=*abandoned*] its responsibility to provide a good education to all citizens.

– ab·di·ca·tion /ˌæbdɪˈkeɪʃən/ *noun, pl* **-tions** [*count, noncount*]

ab·do·men /ˈæbdəmən/ *noun, pl* **-mens** [*count*]

1 : the part of the body below the chest that contains the stomach and other organs — see picture at HUMAN

2 : the rear part of an insect's body

– ab·dom·i·nal /æbˈdɑːmənl/ *adj* ▪ *abdominal* pain/surgery ▪ *abdominal* muscles

ab·duct /æbˈdʌkt/ *verb* **-ducts; -duct·ed; -duct·ing** [+ *obj*] **:** to take (someone) away from a place by force ▪ He was *abducted* [=*kidnapped*] from his home. ▪ She claims that she was *abducted* by aliens. [=that she was carried away in a spaceship by creatures from another world]

– ab·duct·ee /ˌæbˌdʌkˈtiː/ *noun, pl* **-tees** [*count*] ▪ alien *abductees* [=people who say they were abducted by creatures from another world] **– ab·duc·tion** /æbˈdʌkʃən/ *noun, pl* **-tions** [*count*] *abductions* of children [*noncount*] an increase in the incidence of child *abduction* **– ab·duc·tor** /æbˈdʌktɚ/ *noun, pl* **-tors** [*count*] ▪ She managed to escape from her *abductors*.

abed /əˈbɛd/ *adv, literary* **:** lying in a bed ▪ Though it was long past sunup, she was still *abed*.

ab·er·rant /əˈbɛrənt/ *adj* [*more ~; most ~*] *formal* **:** different from the usual or natural type **:** unusual or abnormal ▪ *aberrant* behavior

ab·er·ra·tion /ˌæbəˈreɪʃən/ *noun, pl* **-tions :** something (such as a problem or a type of behavior) that is unusual or unexpected [*count*] For her, such a low grade on an exam was an *aberration*. [*noncount*] a study of sexual *aberration*

abet /əˈbɛt/ *verb* **abets; abet·ted; abet·ting** [+ *obj*] *formal* **:** to help, encourage, or support someone in a criminal act ▪ She *abetted* the thief in his getaway. ▪ Did he *abet* the commission of a crime? ▪ Their actions were shown to *abet* terrorism. ▪ She is charged with ***aiding and abetting*** [=helping and encouraging] the thief in his getaway.

abey·ance /əˈbejəns/ *noun*

in abeyance formal **:** in a temporary state of being stopped ▪ The plans are *in abeyance*. = The plans are being held *in abeyance*. [=the plans are not now being used]

ab·hor /əbˈhoɚ/ *verb, not used in progressive tenses* **-hors; -horred; -hor·ring** [+ *obj*] *formal* **:** to dislike (someone or something) very much ▪ They *abhor* [=*hate, loathe*] violence/racism. ▪ She simply *abhors* [=*despises*] exercise and hates to diet.

– ab·hor·rence /əbˈhorəns/ *noun* [*noncount*] ▪ their *abhorrence* of violence/racism

ab·hor·rent /əbˈhorənt/ *adj* [*more ~; most ~*] *formal* **:** causing or deserving strong dislike or hatred ▪ She finds violence in films *abhorrent*. ▪ It was an *abhorrent* crime. [=a contemptible crime] — sometimes + *to* ▪ The thought of failing is *abhorrent to* him. [=he hates the thought of failing]

abide /əˈbaɪd/ *verb* **abides; abid·ed; abid·ing**

1 [+ *obj*] **:** to accept or bear (someone or something bad, unpleasant, etc.) — usually used in negative constructions ▪ I can't *abide* his bad moods. [=(more commonly) I can't stand his bad moods; I hate his bad moods]

2 [*no obj*] *old-fashioned + literary* **a** *past tense also* **abode :** to stay or live somewhere ▪ *abide* in the house of the Lord **b :** to remain or continue ▪ a love that *abided* till the end of their lives

abide by [*phrasal verb*] ***abide by (something)*** **:** to accept and be guided by (something) **:** OBEY ▪ We have to *abide by* the rules. ▪ They promise to *abide by* our decision.

abid·ing /əˈbaɪdɪŋ/ *adj, always used before a noun* [*more ~; most ~*] *formal* **:** continuing for a long time **:** not changing ▪ She has an *abiding* [=*lasting*] love of art. ▪ They enjoyed an *abiding* [=*enduring*] friendship.

A

abil·i·ty /əˈbɪləti/ *noun, pl* **-ties** **:** the power or skill to do something [*count*] a young woman with many remarkable musical/artistic/athletic *abilities* — often followed by *to + verb* ▪ a teacher with an *ability to inspire* his students ▪ Does he have the *ability* [=*authority*] *to fire* employees? ▪ a writer's *ability* [=*capability, capacity*] *to interest* readers [*noncount*] a young woman of great musical/artistic/athletic *ability* ▪ She has shown some *ability* with foreign languages. ▪ He always works ***to the best of his ability*** [=as well as he can]

-abil·i·ty *also* **-ibil·i·ty** *noun suffix* **:** ability, fitness, or likeliness to act or be acted on in (such) a way ▪ read*ability* ▪ excit*ability* ▪ compati*bility* ▪ vis*ibility*

ab·ject /ˈæbˌʤɛkt/ *adj* [*more ~; most ~*]

1 : extremely bad or severe ▪ They live in *abject* misery/poverty. ▪ The project ended in *abject* [=*complete, utter*] failure.

2 a : very humble **:** feeling or showing shame ▪ He offered an *abject* apology. **b :** very weak **:** lacking courage or strength ▪ She thought he was an *abject* coward.

– ab·ject·ly /ˈæbˌʤɛktli/ *adv* ▪ *abjectly* apologetic

ab·jure /æbˈʤuɚ/ *verb* **-jures; -jured; -jur·ing** [+ *obj*] *formal* **:** to reject (something) formally ▪ He *abjured* [=*renounced*] allegiance to his native country.

ablaze /əˈbleɪz/ *adj, not used before a noun*

1 : in the process of burning **:** on fire ▪ The house was *ablaze.* ▪ Lightning set the building *ablaze.*

2 : glowing with light, color, or emotion — often + *with* ▪ The valley was *ablaze with* fall foliage. ▪ Her eyes were *ablaze* [=*blazing*] *with* anger.

able /ˈeɪbəl/ *adj*

1 *not used before a noun* **a :** having the power, skill, money, etc., that is needed to do something ▪ He will buy a new car as soon as he is *able.* — usually followed by *to + verb* ▪ He will buy a new car as soon as he is *able to do* so. ▪ Is he *able to swim*? [=can he swim?] ▪ They weren't *able to afford* a vacation. [=they were unable to afford a vacation] ▪ I was so tired that I was barely/hardly *able to get* out of bed. ▪ A weight lifter *is able to lift* [=can lift] a very heavy weight. **b :** not prevented from doing something **:** having the freedom or opportunity to do something ▪ Come for a visit when you are *able* (to). — usually followed by *to + verb* ▪ Will you be *able to visit* soon? ▪ We were *able to leave* at noon. **c —** used to say that the quality or condition of something makes something possible ▪ a car that *is able to hold* [=can hold] five people ▪ The car *wasn't able to be* repaired. [=could not be repaired]

2 ***abler; ablest*** [*also more ~; most ~*] **:** having skill or talent ▪ He turned out to be an *able* editor/leader/soldier. ▪ She is one of the *ablest* lawyers in the firm.

-able *also* **-ible** *adj suffix*

1 : fit for or worthy of being ▪ lov*able* ▪ collect*ible*

2 : likely to or capable of ▪ break*able* ▪ perish*able*

3 : having a certain quality ▪ knowledge*able* ▪ peace*able*

able–bod·ied /ˌeɪbəlˈbɑːdid/ *adj* [*more ~; most ~*] **:** having a healthy and strong body **:** physically fit ▪ We need several *able-bodied* men and women to help with the project.

ab·lu·tion /əˈbluːʃən/ *noun, pl* **-tions** [*count*] *formal* **:** the act of washing yourself — usually plural ▪ ritual *ablutions* before prayers ▪ (*humorous*) He performed his daily *ablutions* [=he washed himself] before having breakfast.

ably /ˈeɪbəli/ *adv* [*more ~; most ~*] **:** skillfully and well **:** in an able manner ▪ The chef was *ably* assisted by two helpers.

ab·nor·mal /æbˈnoɚməl/ *adj* [*more ~; most ~*] **:** different from what is normal or average **:** unusual especially in a way that causes problems ▪ *abnormal* behavior ▪ The results of the blood test were *abnormal.*

– ab·nor·mal·ly *adv* ▪ behave *abnormally* ▪ The cells grew *abnormally* quickly.

ab·nor·mal·i·ty /ˌæbnɚˈmæləti/ *noun, pl* **-ties :** something that is not usual, expected, or normal **:** something that is abnormal [*count*] The test results showed several genetic *abnormalities.* [*noncount*] There was some *abnormality* in his vision.

¹aboard /əˈboɚd/ *adv* **:** on, onto, or within a train, a ship, an airplane, etc. ▪ He climbed *aboard* just as the train was leaving. ▪ Everyone *aboard* was injured in the accident. ✧ ***All aboard!*** is a call for passengers to get onto a ship or train because it is ready to leave.

²aboard *prep* **:** on or into (a train, ship, etc.) ▪ We went *aboard* (the) ship. ▪ She got *aboard* [=*on board*] the train.

¹abode /əˈboud/ *noun, pl* **abodes** [*count*] *formal + humorous* **:** the place where someone lives — usually singular ▪ The cottage became their *abode* [=*home*] for the summer. ▪ Welcome to my humble *abode.* — often used in legal language ▪ How long has this been his principal ***place of abode***? [=the place where he usually lives] ▪ He has ***no fixed abode*** [=no home, no permanent address]

²abode *past tense of* ABIDE 2a

abol·ish /əˈbɑːlɪʃ/ *verb* **-ish·es; -ished; -ish·ing** [+ *obj*] **:** to officially end or stop (something, such as a law) **:** to completely do away with (something) ▪ *abolish* slavery/apartheid ▪ He is in favor of *abolishing* the death penalty.

ab·o·li·tion /ˌæbəˈlɪʃn̩/ *noun* [*noncount*] **:** the act of officially ending or stopping something **:** the act of abolishing something ▪ the *abolition* of a law; *specifically* **:** the act of abolishing slavery ▪ a proponent of *abolition*

ab·o·li·tion·ist /ˌæbəˈlɪʃnɪst/ *noun, pl* **-ists** [*count*] **:** a person who wants to stop or abolish slavery

A–bomb /ˈeɪˌbɑːm/ *noun, pl* **-bombs** [*count*] **:** ATOMIC BOMB

abom·i·na·ble /əˈbɑːmənəbəl/ *adj* [*more ~; most ~*] *formal* **:** very bad or unpleasant ▪ It was an *abominable* crime. ▪ We had *abominable* [=*terrible*] weather all week. ▪ His behavior was *abominable.*

– abom·i·na·bly /əˈbɑːmənəbli/ *adv* ▪ He behaved *abominably.*

abominable snowman *or* **Abominable Snowman** *noun* [*singular*] **:** a large hairy creature that walks on two feet like a man and that some people claim to have seen in the Himalayas — called also *yeti*; compare SASQUATCH

abom·i·nate /əˈbɑːməˌneɪt/ *verb* **-nates; -nat·ed; -nat·ing** [+ *obj*] *formal* **:** to feel great hatred for (someone or something) **:** ABHOR ▪ a politician who is revered by his supporters and *abominated* by his enemies

abom·i·na·tion /əˌbɑːməˈneɪʃən/ *noun, pl* **-tions** [*count*] **:** something that causes disgust or hatred ▪ Some people view the sculpture as art while others see it as an *abomination.*

¹ab·orig·i·nal /ˌæbəˈrɪʤənl/ *adj, always used before a noun*

1 : of or relating to the people and things that have been in a region from the earliest time ▪ *aboriginal* [=*native*] plant species ▪ *aboriginal* tribes/customs/art

2 : of or relating to the native people of Australia **:** of or relating to Australian aborigines ▪ the *aboriginal* peoples of Australia

²aboriginal *noun, pl* **-nals** [*count*] **:** ABORIGINE

ab·orig·i·ne /ˌæbəˈrɪʤəni/ *noun, pl* **-nes** [*count*]

1 : a member of the original people to live in an area ▪ North American *aborigines* [=*natives*]

2 *or* ***Aborigine*** **:** a member of any of the native peoples of Australia

abort /əˈboɚt/ *verb* **aborts; abort·ed; abort·ing**

1 [+ *obj*] **:** to end a pregnancy deliberately by causing the death of the fetus ▪ They decided to *abort* the pregnancy. ▪ *abort* a fetus

2 : to stop something before it is completed because of problems or danger [+ *obj*] *abort* the launch of a rocket ▪ *abort* a computer program ▪ I suggest that you *abort* the project. ▪ The mission had to be *aborted.* [*no obj*] When problems occurred during the launch, it was necessary to *abort.*

– aborted *adj* ▪ an *aborted* mission ▪ He made several *aborted* [=*abortive*] attempts to escape.

abor·tion /əˈboɚʃən/ *noun, pl* **-tions :** a medical procedure used to end a pregnancy and cause the death of the fetus [*count*] a doctor who performs *abortions* ▪ She chose to have/get an *abortion.* [*noncount*] demonstrators opposed to *abortion* ▪ *abortion* laws/rights

abor·tion·ist /əˈboɚʃənɪst/ *noun, pl* **-ists** [*count*] *disapproving* **:** a person who performs abortions

abor·tive /əˈboɚtɪv/ *adj* **:** failing to achieve the desired result **:** not successful ▪ He made several *abortive* [=*aborted*] attempts to escape. ▪ an *abortive* coup

abound /əˈbaund/ *verb* **abounds; abound·ed; abound·ing** [*no obj*] **:** to be present in large numbers or in great quantity ▪ a business in which opportunities *abound* [=a business in which there are many opportunities] ▪ They live in a region where oil *abounds.*

abound in/with [*phrasal verb*] ***abound in/with (something)*** **:** to be filled with (something) **:** to contain a very large amount of (something) ▪ They live in a region that *abounds in/with* oil. ▪ a stream *abounding in/with* fish

¹about /əˈbaut/ *adv*

1 a : almost or nearly ▪ We're *about* ready to go. ▪ I'm *about* starved. ▪ Are you *about* finished? ▪ This one is *about* as bad as that one. ▪ That's *about* all I know at this point. ▪ It's *about*

A

time to go. • That's *about* all the time we have. • We tried ***just about*** everything we could think of. • "Is there anything else to do?" "No, ***that's about it/all.***" [=that's it/all; there is nothing else to do] **b** — used to indicate that a number, amount, time, etc., is not exact or certain • The repair should cost *about* [=*approximately, roughly*] $200. • We should leave in *about* 10 minutes. • We got home at *about* 8 o'clock. = (*US*) We got home ***around about*** 8 o'clock. = (*Brit*) We got home ***round about*** 8 o'clock. [=it was approximately 8 o'clock when we got home]
2 : very close to doing something — followed by *to + verb* • He is *about to leave.* [=he will be leaving very soon] • We're *about to join* our friends for dinner. • Their daughter is *about to graduate* from college. — often used with *not* to stress that someone will not do something • I'm *not about to quit.* [=I am not going to quit; I will not quit]
3 *chiefly Brit* **a :** in many different directions • They wandered *about* [=*around*] for several hours. **b :** in many different places • People were standing *about* [=*around*], talking quietly in small groups. • His tools were scattered *about* [=*around*] carelessly. **c :** in or near a particular area or place • There was no one *about.* [=there was no one around; there was no one there]
4 : in the opposite direction • turn *about* [=(more commonly) *around*] • The captain ordered us to bring the ship *about.*

²about *prep*
1 a — used to indicate the object of a thought, feeling, or action • There has been a lot of anger *about* [=*concerning*] the decision. • We did something *about* the problems. • That's what I like *about* you. • What are you so pleased *about*? • I'm worried *about* her. • I forgot all *about* it. • There's a question *about* [=*as to*] how the problem should be fixed. **b** — used to indicate the subject of something said or written • I spoke *about* my past. • She told me all *about* her vacation. • What's he yammering *about* now? = (*Brit*) What's he ***on about*** now? • books *about* birds • a novel *about* Spain
2 : as part of (someone or something) • There is a mature wisdom *about* her. [=she has a quality of mature wisdom] • What was the most exciting thing *about* your vacation? [=what part of your vacation was most exciting?] • There's something weird *about* that guy. [=that guy is weird]
3 — used to indicate the most important or basic part or purpose of something • A good marriage is (all) *about* trust. [=trust is the most important part of a good marriage] • The work he does is all *about* helping young people.
4 : near or not far from (something) in time • a night *about* [=*around*] midsummer
5 a : in the area near to (something or someone) • Fish are abundant *about* [=*around*] the reefs. **b :** over or in different parts of (a place) • He traveled all *about* [=*around*] the country. • He's a well-known figure *about* [=*around, throughout*] the town. **c :** on every side of (something or someone) • A crowd gathered *about* [=*around*] him. • They wrapped the blanket *about* [=*around*] her.
6 a — used to say that something is done quickly or slowly • He was slow *about* doing his work. [=he did his work slowly] • If you're going to do that, you need to be quick *about* it. [=you need to do it quickly] **b** *chiefly Brit* **:** in the act or process of doing (something) • Do it well while you're *about* it. [=while you're at it] • He seems to know what he's *about.* [=to know what he's doing]
how about see ¹HOW
what about see ¹WHAT

³about *adj*
out and about see ¹OUT

about–face /əˈbaʊtˈfeɪs/ *noun, pl* **-fac·es** [*count*]
1 : the act of turning to face in the opposite direction • The soldiers were ordered to do an *about-face.*
2 : a complete change of attitude or opinion — usually singular • After saying that he didn't want the job, he did an *about-face* and accepted the offer.

about–turn /əˈbaʊtˈtən/ *noun, pl* **-turns** [*count*] *Brit* **:** ABOUT-FACE

¹above /əˈbʌv/ *adv*
1 : in or to a higher place • They stood under the tree and looked at the branches *above.* [=*overhead*] • The stars shone *above.* [=in the sky] • The stairs lead *above* [=*upstairs*] to the bedrooms. • up *above* and down below ✧ The opposite of every sense of *above* is *below.*
2 : in or to a higher rank or number • Students in the grade *above* [=in the next grade] study algebra. • Groups of six and *above* [=of six or more] need reservations. • a game that is suitable for children at/of age 10 and *above* [=*older*]
3 : above zero • Temperatures range from 5 below to 5 *above.*
4 : higher, further up, or earlier on the same page or on a preceding page **:** at a previous point in the same document • Write to us at the address shown *above.* [=at the above address] • Except as noted *above,* all the information can be verified. • the person named *above* = the *above*-named person
***from above* 1 :** from a higher place or position • It looks like a cross when viewed *from above.* **2 :** from someone with greater power or authority • waiting for orders *from above*

²above *prep*
1 : in or to a higher place than (something) **:** OVER • He raised his arms *above* his head. • They hung a mirror *above* the mantel. • We rented an apartment *above* a restaurant. — opposite BELOW
2 : greater in number, quantity, or size than (something) **:** more than (something) • Temperatures were *above* average all week. • men *above* 50 years old — opposite BELOW
3 a : to a greater degree or extent than (something) • She values her private time *above* her fame. **b :** in a higher or more important position than (something) • He puts his child's needs *above* his own. — opposite BELOW
4 : having more importance or power than (someone) **:** having a higher rank than (someone) • A captain is *above* a lieutenant. [=a captain outranks a lieutenant] • Who is *above* him in that department? — opposite BELOW
5 : too important for (something) **:** not able to be affected by (something) • She thinks that she's *above* criticism/suspicion. [=that she cannot be criticized/suspected] — see also *above the law* at LAW
6 : too good for (some type of behavior, work, etc.) • I thought you were *above* lying to people. [=I thought such dishonest behavior was beneath you] • He was not *above* cheating when it served his purposes. [=he would cheat when it served his purposes] • Does she think she's *above* that kind of work? [=does she think that kind of work is beneath her?]
7 : more loudly and clearly than (another sound) • I heard the whistle *above* [=*over*] the roar of the crowd.
***above all* :** as the most important thing **:** ESPECIALLY • *Above all,* we must consider what is best for the children.
***above and beyond* :** far beyond what is required by (something, such as a duty) • He went *above and beyond* the call of duty. [=he did more than his duty required him to do]
get above yourself *chiefly Brit* **:** to think you are more important than you really are • We are pleased by his success, but we worry that he might be *getting above himself.*
over and above see ²OVER

³above *adj* **:** mentioned at an earlier point in the same document **:** written above • You can contact me at the *above* address. [=at the address shown above]
the above* :** something that is mentioned at an earlier point in the same document • If any of *the above* is incorrect, please me know. • Contact any of *the above* [=any of the people mentioned above] for more information. • The correct answer is "none of the above.***"

above·board /əˈbʌvˌboəd/ *adj* [*more* ~; *most* ~] **:** open, honest, and legal • The committee tried to be fair and *aboveboard* in its hiring. • an *aboveboard* and responsible proposal • She acted in a completely ***open and aboveboard*** way.

above·ground /əˈbʌvˌgraʊnd/ *adj, US* **:** located or occurring above the ground • an *aboveground* swimming pool • *aboveground* nuclear tests — compare INGROUND, UNDERGROUND; see also *above ground* at ¹GROUND

ab·ra·ca·dab·ra /ˌæbrəkəˈdæbrə/ *interj* — used as a word with magical power by a performer doing a magic trick • The magician said "*Abracadabra!*" and the coin disappeared!

abrade /əˈbreɪd/ *verb* **abrades; abrad·ed; abrad·ing** [+ *obj*] **:** to damage (something) by rubbing, grinding, or scraping • skin *abraded* by shaving

abra·sion /əˈbreɪʒən/ *noun, pl* **-sions**
1 [*count*] **:** an injury caused by something that rubs or scrapes against the skin • She fell and suffered cuts, bruises, and *abrasions* [=*scrapes*] on her legs.
2 [*noncount*] **:** the act or process of damaging or wearing away something by rubbing, grinding, or scraping • *abrasion* of rocks by wind and water

¹abra·sive /əˈbreɪsɪv/ *adj* [*more* ~; *most* ~]
1 a : causing damage or wear by rubbing, grinding, or scraping **:** of or relating to abrasion • The waves had an *abrasive*

action on the rocks. **b :** having a rough quality • an *abrasive* surface **:** used for rubbing something to make it smooth or shiny • an *abrasive* material • an *abrasive* cleaner

2 : very unpleasant or irritating • He offended people with his *abrasive* [=*irritating, grating*] manner/personality. • *abrasive* [=*rude, offensive*] comments

– abra•sive•ly *adv* • an *abrasively* obnoxious manner/personality **– abra•sive•ness** *noun* [*noncount*]

²abrasive *noun, pl* **-sives** [*count*] **:** a substance that is used for rubbing something to make it smooth, shiny, or clean **:** an abrasive substance

abreast /əˈbrɛst/ *adv* — used to describe two or more people or things that are next to each other in a line • columns/rows of five men *abreast* = columns/rows of men five *abreast* • with seats two *abreast* on each side of the aisle

abreast of **1 :** next to (someone or something) • Another runner drew *abreast of* her. [=drew alongside her] **2 :** aware of or informed about (new occurrences, facts, etc.) • She is always *abreast of* the latest political news. • He likes to keep/stay *abreast of* the news.

abridge /əˈbrɪʤ/ *verb* **abridg•es; abridged; abridg•ing** [+ *obj*]

1 : to shorten (a book, a play, etc.) by leaving out some parts • *abridge* a dictionary by omitting rare/uncommon words — see also UNABRIDGED

2 *formal* **:** to lessen the strength or effect of (something, such as a right) • unlawful attempts to *abridge* [=*curtail, weaken*] freedom of speech

– abridged *adj* • an *abridged* dictionary • an *abridged* edition/version of a novel **– abridg•ment** *or* **abridge•ment** /əˈbrɪʤmənt/ *noun, pl* **-ments** [*count*] an *abridgment* of a book • an *abridgment* of their right to freedom of speech [*noncount*] a dictionary shortened by *abridgment*

abroad /əˈbrɑːd/ *adv*

1 : in or to a foreign country • an actress who is popular both here and *abroad* • both at home and *abroad* • He hopes to study/travel/work/go *abroad* next year. • The family came here ***from abroad*** [=from a foreign country] three years ago.

2 *formal* **:** going from one person to the next **:** talked about or known about by many people • There are rumors *abroad* that the company is in trouble. • A feeling of unease has been *abroad* these last few weeks.

3 *old-fashioned* **:** away from your home • She doesn't go walking *abroad* [=*outside*] at night.

ab•ro•gate /ˈæbrəˌgeɪt/ *verb* **-gates; -gat•ed; -gat•ing** [+ *obj*] *formal*

1 : to end or cancel (something) in a formal and official way • *abrogate* a law • *abrogate* a treaty

2 : to fail to do what is required by (something, such as a responsibility) • The company's directors are accused of *abrogating* their responsibilities.

– ab•ro•ga•tion /ˌæbrəˈgeɪʃən/ *noun, pl* **-tions** [*count, noncount*]

abrupt /əˈbrʌpt/ *adj* [*more* ~; *most* ~]

1 : very sudden and not expected • There was an *abrupt* change in the weather. • The road came to an *abrupt* end. • The storm caused an *abrupt* power failure.

2 a : talking to other people in a very brief and unfriendly way • He is friendly with customers but *abrupt* (in his dealings) with his employees. • She has an *abrupt* manner. **b :** rudely brief • an *abrupt* [=*curt, brusque*] reply

– abrupt•ly *adv* • The party ended *abruptly* when the police arrived. • She turned *abruptly* and walked away. • The land dropped off *abruptly*. **– abrupt•ness** *noun* [*singular*] There is an *abruptness* in her manner. [*noncount*] I was surprised by the *abruptness* of her manner.

abs *plural of* AB

ABS *abbr* antilock braking system

ab•scess /ˈæbˌsɛs/ *noun, pl* **-scess•es** [*count*] *medical* **:** a painful area of inflamed tissue that is filled with pus

– ab•scessed /ˈæbˌsɛst/ *adj* • an *abscessed* tooth [=an infected tooth that has caused an abscess in the gum]

ab•scond /æbˈskɑːnd/ *verb* **-sconds; -scond•ed; -scond•ing** [*no obj*] *formal*

1 : to go away or escape from a place secretly • The suspect *absconded* to Canada. • Several prisoners *absconded* from the jail.

2 : to go away and take something that does not belong to you — + *with* • a banker who *absconded with* all the money

– ab•scond•er *noun, pl* **-ers** [*count*]

ab•seil /ˈæbˌseɪl/ *verb* **-seils; -seiled; -seil•ing** [*no obj*] *chiefly Brit* **:** RAPPEL

ab•sence /ˈæbsəns/ *noun, pl* **-senc•es**

1 [*singular*] **:** a state or condition in which something expected, wanted, or looked for is not present or does not exist **:** a state or condition in which something is absent • There was an *absence* [=*lack*] of enthusiasm in the crowd. [=the crowd was not enthusiastic] • The products showed a remarkable *absence* of defects. • ***In the absence of*** reform [=without reform], progress was slow. • ***With the (continued) absence of*** rain [=because of the lack of rain], crops have begun to dry up.

2 [*count*] **a :** a failure to be present at a usual or expected place • He had many *absences* from work. • I expected to see her and was surprised by her *absence*. • He was ***conspicuous by his absence.*** [=it was very noticeable that he was not present] **b :** a period of time when someone is not present at a place, job, etc. • She returned to the company after a long/prolonged *absence*. — see also LEAVE OF ABSENCE ♦ The saying ***absence makes the heart grow fonder*** means that you tend to like someone better when that person goes away for a time. • She'll be away for a month, but you know what they say—*absence makes the heart grow fonder*.

in someone's absence **1 :** while someone is away • The study was completed *in her absence*. **2 :** in the place of someone who is not present • He was asked to speak *in his brother's absence*.

¹ab•sent /ˈæbsənt/ *adj*

1 : not present at a usual or expected place • They were talking about *absent* friends. [=friends who were not there] • an *absent* father who is not home most of the time • The soldier was ***absent without leave.*** [=*AWOL*; absent without having permission to be absent] • Most of the executives attended the meeting, but the company president was ***conspicuously absent.*** [=*conspicuous by his absence*; it was very noticeable that the company president was not there] — often + *from* • She was *absent from* work/school on three occasions.

2 : not present at all **:** not existing • a gene that occurs in mammals but that is *absent* in birds • a landscape in which vegetation is almost entirely *absent* — sometimes + *from* • Vegetation is almost entirely *absent from* the landscape.

3 *always used before a noun* **:** showing that a person is thinking about something else **:** showing a lack of attention to what is happening or being said • He made an *absent* reply to her question as he continued to watch the TV. • There was an *absent* [=*distracted*] look on her face.

– ab•sent•ly *adv* • He replied *absently* to her question.

²ab•sent /æbˈsɛnt/ *verb* **-sents; -sent•ed; -sent•ing**

absent yourself *formal* **:** to go or stay away from something • He *absented himself* from the meeting.

³ab•sent /ˈæbsənt/ *prep, US, formal* **:** in the absence of (something) **:** WITHOUT • *Absent* any objections, the plan will proceed. • *Absent* such an agreement we can go no further.

ab•sen•tee /ˌæbsənˈtiː/ *noun, pl* **-tees** [*count*] **:** a person who is not present in a usual or expected place **:** a person who is absent • There were 10 sick *absentees* that day.

absentee ballot *noun, pl* **~ -lots** [*count*] *US* **:** a vote that is submitted before an election by a voter who is not able to be present when the election occurs

ab•sen•tee•ism /ˌæbsənˈtiːˌɪzəm/ *noun* [*noncount*] **:** a tendency to be away from work or school without a good reason **:** the practice or habit of being absent from work or school • Her office has a high rate of *absenteeism*. [=people in her office are frequently absent from work]

absentee landlord *noun, pl* **~ -lords** [*count*] **:** someone who owns and rents property but does not live on or near the property and rarely visits it

absentia see IN ABSENTIA

ab•sent•mind•ed /ˌæbsəntˈmaɪndəd/ *adj* **:** tending to forget things or to not notice things **:** having or showing a lack of attention • Her *absentminded* husband forgot their anniversary. • She did the chores in an *absentminded* way.

– ab•sent•mind•ed•ly *adv* • Her husband *absentmindedly* forgot their anniversary. **– ab•sent•mind•ed•ness** *noun* [*noncount*] • She mislaid her keys in a fit of *absentmindedness*. [=*absence of mind*]

ab•sinthe *also* **ab•sinth** /ˈæbˌsɪnθ/ *noun* [*noncount*] **:** a green alcoholic drink that has a very strong and bitter flavor

ab•so•lute /ˈæbsəˌluːt/ *adj*

1 *always used before a noun* **:** complete and total • You can't predict the future with *absolute* certainty. • I have *absolute* faith/confidence in her ability to get the job done. • He swore an oath of *absolute* secrecy. • When it comes to using computers, I'm an *absolute* beginner. — often used informally to

A

make a statement more forceful • I swear that what I'm telling you is the *absolute* truth. • He was an *absolute* disgrace to his family. • That's *absolute* nonsense/rubbish! • (*US*) That restaurant serves the *absolute* best Mexican food I've ever eaten. [=that restaurant serves absolutely the best Mexican food I've ever eaten] — sometimes used with *the most* • That's *the most absolute* nonsense/rubbish I ever heard!
2 a : not limited in any way • a ruler with *absolute* power = a ruler whose power is *absolute* • *absolute* authority **b :** having unlimited power • The country is ruled by an *absolute* dictator/monarch. **c :** ruled by someone with unlimited power • The country is an *absolute* monarchy.
3 : not allowing any doubt • He says that he has *absolute* [=*certain*] proof that his client is innocent.
4 a : never changing : always true or real • You have the *absolute* right to remain silent. • an *absolute* requirement = a requirement that is *absolute* • *absolute* [=*unqualified*] freedom **b :** not depending on or compared with anything else • The company has grown ***in absolute terms***, but its share of the market is actually less than it was a few years ago.
– ab•so•lute•ness *noun* [*noncount*] • the *absoluteness* of the king's power • the *absoluteness* of his certainty

ab•so•lute•ly /ˈæbsəˌluːtli/ *adv*
1 : in an absolute way: such as **a :** completely or totally • He is *absolutely* certain who will win. • Let me make one thing *absolutely* clear. • Keep *absolutely* quiet during the movie. — often used to make a statement more forceful • We had an *absolutely* wonderful time. • I *absolutely* love the car. • His fans have gone *absolutely* crazy over his latest CD. • That restaurant serves *absolutely* the best food I've ever eaten. **b :** with unlimited power • The king ruled *absolutely*.
2 — used in speech as a forceful way of saying "yes" or of expressing agreement • "Would you like to see a movie tonight?" "*Absolutely*!" • "We all need to work harder." "*Absolutely*!" ✧ ***Absolutely not*** is used in speech as a forceful way of saying "no" or of expressing disagreement. • "Do you think he's right?" "*Absolutely not*!"

absolute zero *noun* [*noncount*] *technical* **:** the temperature that is believed to be the lowest possible temperature ✧ Absolute zero is equal to approximately -273.15°C or -459.67°F.

ab•so•lu•tion /ˌæbsəˈluːʃən/ *noun* [*noncount*] *formal* **:** the act of forgiving someone for having done something wrong or sinful : the act of absolving someone or the state of being absolved • He asked the priest to give/grant him *absolution* for his sins.

ab•solve /əbˈzɑːlv/ *verb* **-solves; -solved; -solv•ing** [+ *obj*] *formal*
1 : to make (someone) free from guilt, responsibility, etc. • He was *absolved* of the responsibility of repaying the loan. [=he was not required to repay the loan] • His youth does not *absolve* him from being guilty for these crimes. = His youth does not *absolve* him of guilt for these crimes.
2 : to give forgiveness to (someone who has sinned) or for (a sin) • He asked the priest to *absolve* him (of his sins). = He asked the priest to *absolve* his sins.

ab•sorb /əbˈsoɚb/ *verb* **-sorbs; -sorbed; -sorb•ing** [+ *obj*]
1 a : to take in (something, such as a liquid) in a natural or gradual way • A sponge *absorbs* water. • Plant roots *absorb* moisture. • a fabric that *absorbs* sweat — often used as *(be) absorbed* • Water *is absorbed* by plants through their roots. • nutrients that *are absorbed* into the body **b :** to draw in (heat, light, energy, etc.) • The walls are made of a material that *absorbs* sound. • *absorbing* heat from the sun
2 a : to learn (something) • She is good at *absorbing* information/knowledge. • He has retained the values that he *absorbed* as a young man. **b :** to take in and make (something) part of a larger group, country, etc. • a country that has *absorbed* many immigrants • smaller countries invaded and *absorbed* by/into bigger ones
3 : to take up the whole interest or attention of (someone) • His interest in photography *absorbs* him completely. • I was so *absorbed* by her story that I lost track of time. ✧ If you are ***absorbed in*** something, you are fully involved in it. • She was (completely) *absorbed in* [=*lost in*] thought. • He quickly found himself *absorbed in* [=*engrossed by*] the movie.
4 : to prevent (something harmful or unwanted) from passing through • The frame of the car *absorbed* the impact.
5 a : to accept or deal with (something that is difficult, harmful, etc.) • The company has had to *absorb* many setbacks in the past year. • The expenses were *absorbed* [=*borne*] by his family. **b :** to use up (something) • His work *absorbs* almost all of his time.
– ab•sorb•able /əbˈsoɚbəbəl/ *adj* [*more* ~; *most* ~] • nutrients *absorbable* by the body **– ab•sorb•er** *noun, pl* **-ers** [*count*] • a moisture *absorber* — see also SHOCK ABSORBER **– absorbing** *adj* [*more* ~; *most* ~] • The book includes an *absorbing* [=*engrossing, fascinating*] account of her childhood. **– ab•sorp•tion** /əbˈsoɚpʃən/ *noun* [*noncount*] • the *absorption* of water by a sponge • the *absorption* of nutrients by the body • heat/noise *absorption* • His *absorption* in his work was total. [=he was totally absorbed in his work; he gave all his attention to his work]

ab•sor•bent /əbˈsoɚbənt/ *adj* [*more* ~; *most* ~] **:** able to take in and hold liquid : able to absorb liquid • an *absorbent* cotton fabric • highly/very *absorbent* paper towels
– ab•sor•ben•cy /əbˈsoɚbənsi/ *noun* [*noncount*]

ab•stain /əbˈsteɪn/ *verb* **-stains; -stained; -stain•ing** [*no obj*]
1 : to choose not to do or have something — usually + *from* • He *abstained from* taking part in the discussion. • I need to *abstain from* eating [=I need to not eat] for at least 12 hours before my blood test. • *abstain from* (drinking) alcohol
2 : to choose not to vote • Ten members voted for the proposal, six members voted against it, and two *abstained*.
– ab•stain•er *noun, pl* **-ers** [*count*]

ab•ste•mi•ous /æbˈstiːmijəs/ *adj* [*more* ~; *most* ~] *formal* **:** not eating and drinking too much • She is known as an *abstemious* eater and drinker. • an *abstemious* diet
– ab•ste•mi•ous•ly *adv* **– ab•ste•mi•ous•ness** *noun* [*noncount*]

ab•sten•tion /əbˈstɛnʃən/ *noun, pl* **-tions :** the act or practice of abstaining: such as **a** [*noncount*] **:** the act of choosing not to do or have something • He started drinking again after a long period of *abstention*. [=*abstinence*] — usually + *from* • *abstention from* drugs and alcohol **b :** a formal refusal to vote on something [*count*] There were 10 ayes, 6 nays, and 2 *abstentions* when the vote was taken. [*noncount*] a high rate of voter *abstention*

ab•sti•nence /ˈæbstənəns/ *noun* [*noncount*] **:** the practice of not doing or having something that is wanted or enjoyable : the practice of abstaining from something • The program promoted sexual *abstinence* for young people. — often + *from* • *abstinence from* sex • He started drinking again after a long period of total/complete *abstinence from* alcohol.
– ab•sti•nent /ˈæbstənənt/ *adj* • He stopped drinking and has remained totally *abstinent*.

[1]ab•stract /æbˈstrækt, ˈæbˌstrækt/ *adj* [*more* ~; *most* ~]
1 : relating to or involving general ideas or qualities rather than specific people, objects, or actions • *abstract* thinking • *abstract* ideas/concepts such as love and hate • "Honesty" is an *abstract* word. • The word "poem" is concrete, the word "poetry" is *abstract*. — opposite [2]CONCRETE 2
2 *of art* **:** expressing ideas and emotions by using elements such as colors and lines without attempting to create a realistic picture • *abstract* art • an *abstract* painting/painter
– ab•stract•ly /æbˈstræktli/ *adv* • a child learning to think *abstractly* **– ab•stract•ness** /æbˈstræktnəs/ *noun* [*noncount*]

[2]ab•stract /ˈæbˌstrækt/ *noun, pl* **-stracts** [*count*]
1 : a brief written statement of the main points or facts in a longer report, speech, etc. : SUMMARY
2 : an abstract work of art (such as a painting) • an artist admired for his *abstracts*
***in the abstract* :** without referring to a specific person, object, or event : in a general way • thinking about freedom *in the abstract*

[3]ab•stract /æbˈstrækt/ *verb* **-stracts; -stract•ed; -stract•ing** [+ *obj*]
1 : to make a summary of the main parts of (a report, speech, etc.) : to make an abstract of (something) • *abstract* [=*summarize*] an academic paper
2 : to obtain or remove (something) *from* a source • Data for the study was *abstracted from* hospital records.
3 *chiefly Brit, humorous* **:** to steal (something) • She accused him of *abstracting* [=*pinching*] some money from her purse.

ab•stract•ed /æbˈstræktəd/ *adj* [*more* ~; *most* ~] *somewhat formal* **:** not paying attention to what is happening or being said : thinking of other things • She said hello but she seemed a bit *abstracted*.
– ab•stract•ed•ly *adv*

ab•strac•tion /æbˈstrækʃən/ *noun, pl* **-tions**
1 [*noncount*] **:** the act of obtaining or removing something from a source : the act of abstracting something • *abstraction* of data from hospital records

2 *formal* **:** a general idea or quality rather than an actual person, object, or event **:** an abstract idea or quality *[count]* "Beauty" and "truth" are *abstractions.* *[noncount]* the *abstraction* [=abstract quality] of his ideas

3 *[noncount] somewhat formal* **:** the state of someone who is not paying attention to what is happening or being said **:** an abstracted state ▪ She gazed out the window in *abstraction.*

ab·struse /əbˈstruːs/ *adj [more ~; most ~] formal* **:** hard to understand ▪ Her subject matter is *abstruse.* ▪ *abstruse* [=*obscure*] concepts/ideas/theories

– ab·struse·ly *adv* **– ab·struse·ness** *noun [noncount]*

ab·surd /əbˈsɚd/ *adj [more ~; most ~]* **:** extremely silly, foolish, or unreasonable **:** completely ridiculous ▪ an *absurd* situation ▪ The charges against him are obviously/patently *absurd.* ▪ an *absurd* idea/suggestion/argument ▪ *absurd* humor

the absurd **1 :** a state or condition of extreme silliness or foolishness **:** an absurd or ridiculous state ▪ Her ideas once seemed reasonable, but now they verge on *the absurd.* **2 :** things that are absurd ▪ a filmmaker who is fascinated with *the absurd*

– ab·sur·di·ty /əbˈsɚdəti/ *noun, pl* **-ties** *[noncount]* They laughed at the *absurdity* of the situation. *[count]* the *absurdities* of life **– ab·surd·ly** *adv* ▪ The directions were *absurdly* complicated. ▪ *absurdly* high prices

abun·dance /əˈbʌndəns/ *noun* **:** a large amount of something **:** an abundant amount of something *[singular]* The city has an *abundance* of fine restaurants. [=has many fine restaurants] ▪ a plant with an *abundance* of flowers *[noncount]* a plant known for the *abundance* of its flowers ▪ We are fortunate to live in a time of great *abundance.* [=a time when there is much food, money, etc.]

in abundance **:** in large amounts ▪ The city has fine restaurants *in abundance.* ▪ The flowers grew *in* great *abundance.*

abun·dant /əˈbʌndənt/ *adj [more ~; most ~]* **:** existing or occurring in large amounts ▪ Rainfall is more *abundant* in summer. ▪ It is the most *abundant* bird in the forest. ▪ an *abundant* supply of food ▪ He offers *abundant* evidence that he is right. ▪ a society *abundant* in things to buy/do

synonyms see PLENTIFUL

– abun·dant·ly *adv* ▪ flowers blooming/growing *abundantly* ▪ It is *abundantly* [=*extremely*] clear/obvious that this problem will not be easily solved.

¹abuse /əˈbjuːz/ *verb* **abus·es; abused; abus·ing** *[+ obj]*

1 : to treat (a person or animal) in a harsh or harmful way ▪ He *abused* [=*mistreated*] his wife both mentally and physically. ▪ *abuse* a dog ▪ He was accused of sexually/physically/psychologically *abusing* a child.

2 : to use or treat (something) in a way that causes damage ▪ He *abused* his body with years of heavy drinking. ▪ He had *abused* his first car by not taking care of it.

3 : to use (something) wrongly ▪ *abuse* [=*misuse*] a privilege ▪ She *abused* her friend's trust. ▪ a senator who *abuses* his power ▪ He *abused* my confidence by letting this secret be known.

4 : to use too much of (a drug, alcohol, etc.) ▪ a drug that is *abused* by many people ▪ He was known to *abuse* alcohol.

5 : to attack (someone) in words ▪ The fans were verbally *abusing* the referee.

– abused *adj* ▪ providing help for *abused* children/women **– abus·er** *noun, pl* **-ers** *[count]* ▪ a child *abuser* ▪ officeholders who are *abusers* of privilege ▪ alcohol/cocaine/drug/substance *abusers*

²abuse /əˈbjuːs/ *noun, pl* **abus·es**

1 : the act or practice of abusing someone or something: such as **a :** harmful treatment of a person or animal *[noncount]* He subjected his wife to physical and emotional *abuse.* ▪ child *abuse* ▪ sexual *abuse* *[plural]* The government has been accused of ***human rights abuses***. [=of violating the basic rights of people by treating them wrongly] **b** *[noncount]* **:** the use or treatment of something in a way that causes damage ▪ his *abuse* [=*mistreatment*] of his body through poor eating habits ▪ These toys can stand up to a lot of *abuse.* [=can be handled roughly without being damaged] **c :** the act or practice of using something wrongly *[noncount]* the governor's *abuse* [=*misuse*] of his power/privileges *[count]* the buying of votes and other election *abuses* **d** *[noncount]* **:** the act or practice of using too much of a drug, alcohol, etc. ▪ *abuse* of alcohol ▪ drug/substance *abuse*

2 *[noncount]* **:** harsh and insulting language ▪ She was subjected to every term of *abuse* her boss could think of. ▪ a torrent/stream of verbal *abuse* ▪ The prisoner hurled/shouted/screamed *abuse* at the judge.

abu·sive /əˈbjuːsɪv/ *adj [more ~; most ~]*

1 : using harsh and insulting language ▪ He spoke to her in an *abusive* manner. = He was *abusive* when he spoke to her. ▪ *abusive* language ▪ The fans yelled *abusive* comments to the referee. ▪ a verbally *abusive* fan

2 : using or involving physical violence or emotional cruelty ▪ an *abusive* parent ▪ protecting wives from *abusive* husbands ▪ people in *abusive* relationships

– abu·sive·ly *adv* ▪ The boss treated the staff *abusively.* **– abu·sive·ness** *noun [noncount]*

abut /əˈbʌt/ *verb* **abuts; abut·ted; abut·ting** *formal* **:** to touch along an edge *[+ obj]* Their property *abuts* [=*adjoins*] our property. = Their property and our property *abut* each other. [=their property is directly next to our property; an edge of their property touches an edge of our property] *[no obj]* Their property and our property *abut.* — often + *on* ▪ Their property *abuts on* our property.

– abut·ter /əˈbʌtɚ/ *noun, pl* **-ters** *[count]*

abut·ment /əˈbʌtmənt/ *noun, pl* **-ments** *[count] technical* **:** a heavy structure that supports something (such as a bridge) ▪ The car crashed into a bridge *abutment.*

a·buzz /əˈbʌz/ *adj, informal* **:** filled with excited talk about something — usually + *with* ▪ Washington is *abuzz with* [=is buzzing with] rumors of a scandal.

abys·mal /əˈbɪzməl/ *adj [more ~; most ~]* **:** extremely poor or bad ▪ They were living in *abysmal* ignorance/poverty. ▪ *abysmal* [=*horrible*] living conditions ▪ The team had an *abysmal* [=*awful*] record. ▪ Her grades were *abysmal.* [=*terrible*]

– abys·mal·ly *adv* ▪ *abysmally* ignorant ▪ The house is in *abysmally* poor condition.

abyss /əˈbɪs/ *noun, pl* **abyss·es** *[count]* **:** a hole so deep or a space so great that it cannot be measured ▪ the ocean's *abysses* ▪ I stood at the edge of the cliff and gazed down into the yawning/gaping *abyss.* [=*chasm*] — often used figuratively ▪ He says that there is a widening *abyss* between the rich and the poor. ▪ She was pulled down into an *abyss* of despair.

AC *abbr* **1** *US* air-conditioning ▪ an apartment equipped with *AC* **2** alternating current

aca·cia /əˈkeɪʃə/ *noun, pl* **-cias** *[count]* **:** a shrub or tree that grows in warm regions and that has white or yellow flowers

ac·a·de·mia /ˌækəˈdiːmijə/ *noun [noncount]* **:** the life, community, or world of teachers, schools, and education ▪ She found the business world very different from *academia.*

¹ac·a·dem·ic /ˌækəˈdɛmɪk/ *adj*

1 *usually used before a noun* **:** of or relating to schools and education ▪ She received awards for her *academic* achievements/accomplishments. ▪ I spent my *academic* career at one school. ▪ The board set tough *academic* standards for graduation. ▪ He was offered a teaching job and decided to return to *academic* life.

2 : having no practical importance **:** not involving or relating to anything real or practical ▪ His interest in sailing is purely *academic.* He's not a sailor himself. ▪ It was a question of only *academic* [=*theoretical*] interest.

3 *[more ~; most ~] chiefly Brit* **:** good at studying and at passing exams **:** good at academics ▪ He's not very *academic,* but he's good with his hands.

– ac·a·dem·i·cal·ly /ˌækəˈdɛmɪkli/ *adv* ▪ He did well enough *academically* to be accepted at many colleges. ▪ an *academically* gifted student

²academic *noun, pl* **-ics**

1 *[count]* **:** a person who is a teacher in a college or university ▪ The book appeals to *academics* and to the general public.

2 academics *[plural] chiefly US* **:** courses of study taken at a school or college ▪ She excelled at *academics.* ▪ He only cares about sports. He has no interest in *academics.*

academic year *noun, pl* **~ years** *[count]* **:** the time during a year when a school has classes ✧ In the U.S., the academic year usually begins in September and ends in May or June.

acad·e·my /əˈkædəmi/ *noun, pl* **-mies** *[count]*

1 a : a school that provides training in special subjects or skills ▪ a military/naval *academy* ▪ a riding/tennis *academy* **b** *US* **:** a private high school — used in proper names ▪ a student at Smith *Academy*

2 : an organization of people who work to support art, science, or literature — used in proper names ▪ the National *Academy* of Sciences ▪ a Fellow of the Royal *Academy*

Academy Award *trademark* — used for an award given by part of the U.S. film industry to the best actors, directors, etc., of the year

a cap·pel·la /ˌɑːkəˈpɛlə, *Brit* ˌækæˈpɛlə/ *adv* **:** without in-

A

strumental music • The choir sings *a cappella*.
– **a cappella** *adj* • *a cappella* singing/songs

ac·cede /æk'si:d/ *verb* **-cedes; -ced·ed; -ced·ing** [*no obj*] *formal*
1 : to agree to a request or a demand — usually + *to* • The government was forced to *accede to* their demands.
2 : to enter a high office or position • His son *acceded* upon the king's death. — usually + *to* • He ***acceded to the throne*** [=he became king] in 1838.

ac·cel·er·ate /ɪk'sɛləˌreɪt/ *verb* **-ates; -at·ed; -at·ing**
1 : to move faster : to gain speed [*no obj*] She stepped on the gas and the car *accelerated*. • The plane *accelerated* down the runway. [+ *obj*] She stepped on the gas and *accelerated* the car. — opposite DECELERATE
2 : to cause (something) to happen sooner or more quickly [+ *obj*] He says that cutting taxes will help to *accelerate* economic growth. • Conditions *accelerated* our departure. [=conditions caused us to depart sooner] [*no obj*] The rate of economic growth has continued to *accelerate*.
– **accelerated** *adj* • Changes have occurred at an *accelerated* pace/rate. • She's taking an *accelerated* course in English. [=a course in which English is taught at a faster pace than usual] – **accelerating** *adj* • an *accelerating* rate

ac·cel·er·a·tion /ɪkˌsɛlə'reɪʃən/ *noun*
1 : the act or process of moving faster or happening more quickly : the act or process of accelerating [*noncount*] The car delivers quick/rapid *acceleration*. • The car has good *acceleration*. [=the car is able to accelerate quickly] • There has been some *acceleration* in economic growth. [*singular*] There has been an *acceleration* in economic growth.
2 [*noncount*] *physics* **:** the rate at which the speed of a moving object changes over time

ac·cel·er·a·tor /ɪk'sɛləˌreɪtɚ/ *noun, pl* **-tors** [*count*]
1 : a pedal in a vehicle that is pressed down to make the vehicle go faster • hit/press the *accelerator* = step on the *accelerator* — called also (*US*) *gas pedal*; see picture at CAR
2 *technical* **:** a machine that causes charged particles (such as electrons and protons) to move at extremely high speeds • a particle *accelerator*

[1]**ac·cent** /'ækˌsɛnt, *Brit* 'æksənt/ *noun, pl* **-cents**
1 [*count*] **:** a way of pronouncing words that occurs among the people in a particular region or country • Regional *accents* are common in the U.S. • She spoke with an American/English *accent*. • The tourist had a foreign *accent*. • He has a heavy/thick southern *accent*. • a slight/light/faint *accent* • a French/German/Italian *accent*
2 [*count*] **:** greater stress or force given to a syllable of a word in speech • The word "before" has the *accent* on the last syllable. • Put the *accent* on the first syllable of the word.
3 [*count*] **a :** a mark (such as ˈ or ˌ) used to show the part of a word that should be given greater stress when it is spoken — called also *accent mark* **b :** a mark placed above a letter to show how it should be pronounced • The *accents* in the French word "émigré" show how the letter "e" should be pronounced. — called also *accent mark*
4 [*singular*] **:** special concern or attention : EMPHASIS — usually + *on* • This year's new TV shows put/place the/an *accent on* youth. • Our *accent* is *on* providing our customers with dependable service.
5 [*count*] **:** a small decorative object or detail that is different from the things that are around it • This type of plant is often used as a decorative *accent*. • used *accents* of bright colors in the new room • *accent* colors/lighting/plants

[2]**ac·cent** /'ækˌsɛnt, *Brit* ək'sɛnt/ *verb* **-cents; -cent·ed; -cent·ing** [+ *obj*]
1 : to give special attention to (something) • His speech *accented* [=*highlighted, emphasized*] positive parts of the plan.
2 : to say (part of a word) with greater stress or force • When you say "before," you should *accent* the second syllable. = You should *accent* the word "before" on the second syllable.

accented *adj* [*more* ~; *most* ~]
1 : pronounced with stress • an *accented* syllable
2 : spoken with a foreign accent • He spoke heavily/strongly/slightly *accented* English.

accent mark *noun, pl* ~ **marks** [*count*]
1 : [1]ACCENT 3a
2 : [1]ACCENT 3b

ac·cen·tu·ate /æk'sɛnʧəˌweɪt/ *verb* **-ates; -at·ed; -at·ing** [+ *obj*] **:** to make (something) more noticeable • He likes to wear clothes that *accentuate* his muscular build. • We felt that the article *accentuated* [=*emphasized*] the positive aspects of the program.
– **ac·cen·tu·ation** /ɪkˌsɛnʧə'weɪʃən/ *noun* [*noncount*]

ac·cept /ɪk'sɛpt/ *verb* **-cepts; -cept·ed; -cept·ing**
1 a : to receive or take (something offered) [+ *obj*] *accept* a gift • *accept* a proposal • *accept* a bribe • *accept* an assignment/invitation/offer • They offered him the job, and he *accepted it*. [*no obj*] They offered him the job, and he *accepted*. **b** [+ *obj*] **:** to take (something) as payment • The store doesn't *accept* credit cards. **c** [+ *obj*] **:** to be able or designed to take or hold (something) • a surface that will not *accept* ink • a computer program ready to *accept* commands
2 [+ *obj*] **:** to agree to (something) : to agree to receive or allow (something) • *accept* a telephone call • They *accepted* some applications and rejected others. • She's still trying to get her manuscript *accepted* for publication. • I *accept* your apology. • They refused to *accept* his resignation.
3 [+ *obj*] **a :** to think of (something) as true, proper, or normal • a word that has come to be *accepted* as standard • This treatment is now *accepted* by many doctors. • He refused to *accept* the decision. • I *accepted* his advice and joined the health club. • They *accepted* [=*believed*] her explanation. • The theory is widely *accepted* as correct. = It is widely *accepted* that the theory is correct. **b :** to stop denying or resisting (something true or necessary) • She found it difficult to *accept* change. • The truth is sometimes hard to *accept*. • He behaved badly, and now he has to *accept* the consequences. • He has to ***accept the fact that*** his baseball career is over. [=he has to admit that his baseball career is over] • He was unwilling to ***accept*** [=*believe*] ***that*** he could no longer play as he once had. **c :** to admit that you have or deserve (something, such as blame or responsibility) • *accept* blame • I *accept* responsibility for the accident. **d :** to be willing to have or experience (something) • To be a successful investor you have to *accept* some risk. • She *accepted* [=*took on, faced*] the challenge of starting her own business.
4 [+ *obj*] **a :** to allow (someone) to join a club, to attend a school, etc. • The club *accepted* her as a member but rejected her sister. • She was *accepted* at/by Georgetown University. **b :** to regard (someone) as belonging to a group • She felt that her in-laws had never really *accepted* her (as a member of the family). • She doesn't yet feel *accepted* (by her in-laws). • The new family was quickly *accepted* into the community.
– **accepted** *adj* • an *accepted* practice • an *accepted* definition • a widely *accepted* truth – **ac·cept·er** *or* **ac·cep·tor** /ɪk'sɛptɚ/ *noun, pl* **-ters** *or* **-tors** [*count*]

ac·cept·able /ɪk'sɛptəbəl/ *adj* [*more* ~; *most* ~]
1 : capable or worthy of being accepted • *acceptable* and unacceptable noise levels • an *acceptable* excuse • socially *acceptable* behavior — sometimes + *to* • We're trying to find a solution that will be *acceptable to* everyone.
2 : fairly good : SATISFACTORY • It was an *acceptable* performance, although not an outstanding one. • She plays an *acceptable* game of tennis.
– **ac·cept·abil·i·ty** /ɪkˌsɛptə'bɪləti/ *noun* [*noncount*] – **ac·cept·ably** /ɪk'sɛptəbli/ *adv*

ac·cep·tance /ɪk'sɛptəns/ *noun* [*noncount*]
1 : the act of accepting something or someone • *acceptance* of a gift • *acceptance* of the truth • *acceptance* of responsibility • her *acceptance* into the club • The university has sent me a letter of *acceptance*. • He delivered an ***acceptance speech*** after he was chosen as the party's presidential nominee.
2 : the quality or state of being accepted or acceptable • His theories have won/gained/found general/widespread *acceptance*. [=many people regard his theories as correct]

[1]**ac·cess** /'ækˌsɛs/ *noun* [*noncount*]
1 : a way of getting near, at, or to something or someone • All public buildings should provide wheelchair *access*. [=a way for people in wheelchairs to enter] • The cup holders are placed for easy *access*. [=so that they can be easily reached] — often + *to* • The town wants to increase public *access to* beaches. • A dirt road provides *access to* the home.
2 : a way of being able to use or get something • We have Internet *access* at the library. — usually + *to* • We have *access to* the Internet at the library. • I don't have *access to* a car right now. [=I don't have a car that I can use right now] • Patients need better *access to* medical care. • increasing children's *access to* education • They tried to gain illegal *access to* the company's network. — see also ACCESS TIME
3 : permission or the right to enter, get near, or make use of something or to have contact with someone — usually + *to* • They refused to give the police *access to* their home. • divorced parents who want increased/improved *access to* their children • Investigators are trying to ***gain/get access to*** his financial records. [=trying to get the right to see his financial

records] ▪ He was ***granted/denied access to*** the report. [=he was given/refused permission to see the report]

²access *verb* **-cess·es; -cessed; -cess·ing** [+ *obj*] **: to gain access to (something): such as a : to be able to use, enter, or get near (something)** ▪ The new system makes it easier to *access* the money in your bank account. ▪ Your favorite radio stations can be *accessed* at the touch of a button. **b : to open or load (a computer file, an Internet site, etc.)** ▪ The file loads every time you *access* the Web site. ▪ The file can be *accessed* by many users at the same time. ▪ She could work at home by remotely *accessing* the company's network. ▪ You'll need a password to *access* the database.

ac·ces·si·ble /ɪkˈsɛsəbəl/ *adj* [*more* ~; *most* ~]
1 : able to be reached or approached ▪ The inn is *accessible* by train and bus. ▪ The mall is *accessible* from the highway.
2 : able to be used or obtained — often + *to* ▪ The information should be *accessible* [=*available*] *to* all.
3 : easy to appreciate or understand ▪ His writing is more *accessible* now than it once was. [=is more easily understood now] ▪ It is a fascinating and *accessible* book. ▪ *accessible* art
4 *of a person* **: easy to speak to or deal with** ▪ You'll find that the teachers here are quite *accessible*.
— **ac·ces·si·bil·i·ty** /ɪkˌsɛsəˈbɪləti/ *noun* [*noncount*] ▪ the easy *accessibility* of the beach ▪ the *accessibility* of her art
— **ac·ces·si·bly** /ɪkˈsɛsəbli/ *adv* [*more* ~; *most* ~] ▪ He writes *accessibly* about complex topics.

ac·ces·sion /ɪkˈsɛʃən/ *noun, pl* **-sions** *formal*
1 [*noncount*] **: the act or process by which someone rises to a powerful and important position** ▪ the *accession* of Queen Elizabeth II **— often + *to*** ▪ Queen Victoria's *accession to* the crown/throne occurred in 1837. [=she became queen in 1837] ▪ upon his *accession to* the Supreme Court ▪ the king's *accession to* power
2 [*count*] **: something that is added to a collection at a museum** ▪ The museum has put its latest *accessions* [=*acquisitions*] on display.

ac·ces·so·rize (*US*) *or Brit* **ac·ces·so·rise** /ɪkˈsɛsəˌraɪz/ *verb* **-riz·es; -rized; -riz·ing : to add accessories to (something, such as clothing)** [+ *obj*] an outfit *accessorized* with a pair of diamond earrings [*no obj*] a stylish young woman who knows how to *accessorize*

ac·ces·so·ry /ɪkˈsɛsəri/ *noun, pl* **-ries** [*count*]
1 : something added to something else to make it more useful, attractive, or effective ▪ fashion/clothing *accessories* such as scarves, handkerchiefs, bracelets, and rings ▪ automotive *accessories* ▪ computer *accessories*
2 *law* **: someone who helps another person commit a crime** ▪ He is wanted as an *accessory* to murder. ▪ She was charged as an ***accessory before/after the fact*** [=someone who helps a criminal before/after a crime has been committed]

access time *noun* [*noncount*] *technical* **: the time required to get stored information from a computer memory**

ac·ci·dent /ˈæksədənt/ *noun, pl* **-dents** [*count*]
1 : a sudden event (such as a crash) that is not planned or intended and that causes damage or injury ▪ We got in a car *accident*. = We had a car *accident*. ▪ a traffic *accident* ▪ a fatal *accident* ▪ a motorcycle *accident* ▪ He was injured in an *accident* at work. ▪ The *accident* happened when her car slid on a patch of ice. ▪ Investigators are still trying to determine the cause of the *accident*. ▪ "I'm sorry that I broke the bowl." "That's OK. It was just an *accident*." = "That's OK. ***Accidents will happen***" ✧ An ***accident waiting to happen*** is a person or thing that is dangerous or unsafe. ▪ My brother is the clumsiest person I know. He's just an *accident waiting to happen*.
2 : an event that is not planned or intended : an event that occurs by chance ▪ Their meeting was an *accident*. ▪ It is just an *accident* that they arrived when they did. ▪ She says that her pregnancy was an *accident*. ▪ His wealth is a mere ***accident of birth*** [=he is wealthy only because he was born into a wealthy family] ▪ He says that no one is to blame for his illness. It was just an ***accident of nature*** [=something that happened naturally] ▪ It is ***no accident*** that the assistant he hired is so good-looking. [=he deliberately chose a good-looking person to be his assistant]
***by accident* : in a way that is not planned or intended** ▪ They met *by accident*. [=*by chance*] ▪ She says that she became pregnant *by accident*. [=*unintentionally*] ▪ Scientists discovered the vaccine almost/quite/entirely *by accident*. ▪ Did it happen *by accident* [=*accidentally*] or by design?

ac·ci·den·tal /ˌæksəˈdɛntḷ/ *adj* **: happening in a way that is not planned or intended : happening by accident** ▪ an *accidental* discovery of oil ▪ The timing of the announcement was purely *accidental*. **: happening as an accident** ▪ an *accidental* shooting ▪ The death was ruled *accidental*.
— **ac·ci·den·tal·ly** /ˌæksəˈdɛntḷi/ *adv* ▪ He *accidentally* deleted the file. ▪ The lock prevents the gate from opening *accidentally*. ▪ Did it happen *accidentally* [=*by accident*] or intentionally? ▪ He bumped into her ***accidentally on purpose*** [=he bumped into her on purpose but he tried to make it appear to be an accident]

accident–prone *adj* [*more* ~; *most* ~] **: tending to have many accidents** ▪ He is clumsy and *accident-prone*.

¹ac·claim /əˈkleɪm/ *noun* [*noncount*] **: strong approval or praise** ▪ Her performance in the ballet earned her critical *acclaim*. ▪ She deserves *acclaim* for all her charitable works.

²acclaim *verb* **-claims; -claimed; -claim·ing** [+ *obj*] **: to praise (someone or something) in a very strong and enthusiastic way** ▪ The critics have *acclaimed* her performance. **— often used as *(be) acclaimed*** ▪ Her performance *was acclaimed* by the critics. ▪ He has *been acclaimed* as one of the best players in the league.
— **acclaimed** *adj* [*more* ~; *most* ~] ▪ a critically *acclaimed* drama/performance ▪ a highly/hugely/widely *acclaimed* play ▪ the city's most *acclaimed* restaurants

ac·cla·ma·tion /ˌækləˈmeɪʃən/ *noun* [*noncount*]
1 : strong and enthusiastic approval or praise ▪ Her performance in the ballet earned her thunderous applause and shouts of *acclamation* from the audience. ▪ She has earned worldwide *acclamation* for her charitable works.
2 : a vote to accept or approve someone or something that is done by cheers, shouts, or applause — usually used in the phrase *by acclamation* ▪ The legislature passed the bill *by acclamation*. ▪ The president was elected *by acclamation*.

ac·cli·mate /ˈækləˌmeɪt, *Brit* əˈklaɪmət/ *verb* **-mates; -mat·ed; -mat·ing** *US* **: to adjust or adapt to a new climate, place, or situation — usually + *to*** [*no obj*] He was never really able to *acclimate to* the hot weather. [=to get used to the hot weather] ▪ The mountain climbers spent a few days *acclimating* [=becoming adjusted] *to* the high altitude. [+ *obj*] I *acclimated* myself *to* the hot weather. ▪ You might need to *acclimate* your plants *to* bright sunlight gradually. ▪ We took a few days to get *acclimated to* our new teacher.
— **ac·cli·ma·tion** /ˌækləˈmeɪʃən/ *noun* [*noncount*]

ac·cli·ma·tize *also Brit* **ac·cli·ma·tise** /əˈklaɪməˌtaɪz/ *verb* **-tiz·es; -tized; -tiz·ing : to adjust or adapt to a new climate, place, or situation : ACCLIMATE — usually + *to*** [*no obj*] The mountain climbers spent a few days *acclimatizing* [=becoming adjusted] *to* the high altitude. [+ *obj*] The mountain climbers spent a few days *acclimatizing* themselves *to* the high altitude.
— **ac·cli·ma·ti·za·tion** *also Brit* **ac·cli·ma·ti·sa·tion** /əˌklaɪmətəˈzeɪʃən, *Brit* əˌklaɪməˌtaɪˈzeɪʃən/ *noun* [*noncount*]

ac·co·lade /ˈækəˌleɪd/ *noun, pl* **-lades** [*count*] **: an award or an expression of praise** ▪ There is no higher *accolade* at this school than an honorary degree. **— often plural** ▪ She has been winning *accolades* [=she has been receiving praise] for her performances in small plays. ▪ The movie's special effects have drawn *accolades* from both fans and critics. [=have been praised by both fans and critics]

ac·com·mo·date /əˈkɑːməˌdeɪt/ *verb* **-dates; -dat·ed; -dat·ing**
1 [+ *obj*] **a : to provide room for (someone) : to provide a place to stay and sleep for (someone)** ▪ The hotel can only *accommodate* about 100 people. [=is only large enough for about 100 people] ▪ Over 600 people can be *accommodated* on the cruise ship. **b : to have room for (someone or something)** ▪ The ceilings were too low to *accommodate* his terrific height. ▪ The table *accommodates* [=*seats*] 12 comfortably. ▪ This ancient stadium could *accommodate* [=*hold*] up to 60,000 people.
2 [+ *obj*] *somewhat formal* **: to do something helpful for (someone)** ▪ They were kind enough to *accommodate* me with a ride to the train station. **: to provide what is needed or wanted for (someone or something)** ▪ I asked them for additional money, and they *accommodated* me with a loan. ▪ He would often change his schedule to *accommodate* his clients. ▪ New facilities are being added to *accommodate* the special needs of elderly residents.
3 : to get used to or become comfortable with something : to adapt or adjust *to* something [*no obj*] Smart investors quickly *accommodated to* the new market conditions. [+ *obj*] Smart investors quickly ***accommodated themselves to*** the new market conditions. = Smart investors quickly be-

A

came *accommodated to* the new market conditions.

accommodating *adj* [*more* ~; *most* ~] : willing to do what someone else wants or requests • The chef can be very *accommodating* [=*obliging*], often cooking meals that aren't even on the menu. • She seems less *accommodating* to the demands of her boss than she used to be.

ac·com·mo·da·tion /əˌkɑːməˈdeɪʃən/ *noun, pl* **-tions**
1 a accommodations [*plural*] *US* : a place (such as a room in a hotel) where travelers can sleep and find other services • We need overnight *accommodations* [=*lodging*] for four people. • They weren't sure if they could provide food and *accommodations* for the whole group. • The *accommodations* on board the boat are a bit cramped. **b** [*noncount*] *chiefly Brit* : a place where people can live, stay, or work • We need overnight *accommodation* [=*lodging*] for four people. • office *accommodation*
2 *formal* **a** : an agreement that allows people, groups, etc., to work together [*singular*] He hoped to reach an *accommodation* with the new owners. [*noncount*] Negotiators were convinced that *accommodation* with the union was possible. **b** : something done to provide what is needed or wanted for someone or something [*singular*] He changed his schedule as an *accommodation* to his clients. [*noncount*] Changes were made for the *accommodation* of differing viewpoints.

ac·com·pa·ni·ment /əˈkʌmpənimənt/ *noun, pl* **-ments**
1 : music played to support a person who is singing or playing a musical instrument [*noncount*] She sings without musical *accompaniment*. [*count*] — usually singular • She sang the song with a piano *accompaniment*. • She sang the song ***to the accompaniment of*** a piano. [=while a piano played]
2 [*count*] : something that is added to another thing to make it better or more appealing • A nice tie was a fine *accompaniment* to his new suit.; *especially* : something added to or served with food or a meal • This dish can be served as an *accompaniment* to/for most meat main dishes. • This wine is a good *accompaniment* for/of spicy foods.
3 [*count*] : something that is done or that happens at the same time as something else • She studied Italian as an *accompaniment* to her classes in art history. • She made the announcement ***to the accompaniment of*** loud applause. [=there was loud applause while she made the announcement]

ac·com·pa·nist /əˈkʌmpənɪst/ *noun, pl* **-nists** [*count*] : someone who plays a musical instrument while another person is singing or playing the main part : someone who plays an accompaniment • He will be her *accompanist* on the piano.

ac·com·pa·ny /əˈkʌmpəni/ *verb* **-nies; -nied; -ny·ing** [+ *obj*]
1 : to go somewhere with (someone) : to be a companion for (someone) • She will *accompany* me to the store. • Ten adults *accompanied* the class on their field trip. • Children under 17 must be *accompanied* by an adult to see this movie.
2 a : to go together with (something) : to be included with (something) • A delicious sauce *accompanied* the grilled fish. — often used as *(be) accompanied* • The text *is accompanied* by over 100 photographs and charts. **b** : to happen or occur at the same time as or along with (something) — usually used as *(be) accompanied* • Low rates of unemployment *are* often *accompanied* by high inflation. • The thunderstorm *was accompanied* by high winds.
3 : to play music with (someone who is singing or playing the main tune) : to perform an accompaniment for (someone) • He will be *accompanying* her on the piano.
– accompanying *adj* • Call the phone number in the *accompanying* booklet for further information.

accompli see FAIT ACCOMPLI

ac·com·plice /əˈkɑːmpləs/ *noun, pl* **-plic·es** [*count*] : a person who works with or helps someone who is doing something wrong or illegal • He was convicted as an *accomplice* to murder. • a murderer's *accomplice* • She was an unwitting *accomplice* to tax fraud. [=she didn't know that she was helping someone to commit tax fraud]

ac·com·plish /əˈkɑːmplɪʃ/ *verb* **-plish·es; -plished; -plish·ing** [+ *obj*] : to succeed in doing (something) • They have *accomplished* [=*done, achieved*] much in a very short period of time. • He finally felt like he had *accomplished* [=*done*] something important. • There are several different ways to *accomplish* the same task. • It's amazing what you can *accomplish* [=*do*] through/with hard work. • Exactly what he thought he would *accomplish* is unclear.
– ac·com·plish·able /əˈkʰɑmplɪʃəbəl/ *adj* [*more* ~; *most* ~]

accomplished *adj* [*more* ~; *most* ~]
1 : very skillful : having or showing the skill of an expert • an *accomplished* [=*expert*] pianist/artist/writer • She has the confidence of an *accomplished* athlete. • an *accomplished* [=*excellent*] performance
2 : very successful : having done or achieved many good or important things • He is one of the school's most *accomplished* graduates.

ac·com·plish·ment /əˈkɑːmplɪʃmənt/ *noun, pl* **-ments**
1 [*count*] : something done, achieved, or accomplished successfully • Her family is proud of all her academic *accomplishments*. • one of the greatest scientific *accomplishments* of the century
2 [*noncount*] : the successful completion of something : the act of accomplishing something • We celebrated the *accomplishment* of all our goals. • When the work was done, he had a sense of *accomplishment*. [=he felt that he had done something good] • a public official with a solid record of *accomplishment* [=of doing good things successfully]
3 : a special skill or ability gained by practice or training [*count*] Her knowledge of foreign languages is among her many *accomplishments*. [*noncount*] a young woman of *accomplishment* [=an accomplished young woman]

¹ac·cord /əˈkoəd/ *noun, pl* **-cords**
1 [*count*] : a formal or official agreement • The two sides were able to reach an *accord*. • a peace *accord*
2 [*noncount*] : a situation or state in which people or things agree • His ideas and mine were completely/fully ***in accord***. = His ideas were completely/fully ***in accord with*** mine. [=his ideas and mine agreed completely] • They dressed up for the festival *in accord with* [=*in accordance with*] the custom.
of its own accord ✧ If something happens *of its own accord*, it happens by itself without anyone causing it to happen. • The tree fell *of its own accord*.
of your own accord ✧ If you do something *of your own accord*, you do it because you want to, not because someone has asked you or forced you to do it. • They left *of their own accord*.
with one accord *chiefly Brit, formal* : all together • They rose *with one accord* from their seats.

²accord *verb* **-cords; -cord·ed; -cord·ing** [+ *obj*] *formal* : to give (something, such as special treatment or status) to someone or something • He was *accorded* certain favors because of his age. • Her students *accorded* her respect. = Her students *accorded* respect to her. = She was *accorded* respect by her students. • We *accord* great importance to education. [=we treat education as very important]
accord with [*phrasal verb*] ***accord with (something)*** : to be in agreement with (something) • His interpretation of the data did not *accord with* the facts. • His plans for the company did not *accord with* my own.

ac·cor·dance /əˈkoədns/ *noun*
in accordance with : in a way that agrees with or follows (something, such as a rule or request) • *In accordance with* your request, I am sending a copy of my book. • His funeral will be private, *in accordance with* his wishes. • The soldier said that he acted *in accordance with* his orders.

ac·cord·ing·ly /əˈkoədɪŋli/ *adv*
1 : in a proper or appropriate way : in a way that suits the facts, needs, or requirements of a situation • He knew his limitations and acted *accordingly*. • She is considered a manager and is paid *accordingly*. • The car is made with the best materials and is priced *accordingly*.
2 : as a result : THEREFORE • His campaign manager wanted to find out how people felt. *Accordingly* [=*consequently*], he took an opinion poll of the local voters.

according to *prep*
1 : as stated, reported, or recorded by (someone or something) • *According to* a recent survey, most Americans drive to work. [=a recent survey says that most Americans drive to work] • *According to* rumors I've heard, he was fired for stealing from the company.
2 : as directed or required by (rules, directions, etc.) • She always did everything *according to* the rules. • I cooked the rice *according to* the directions on the box. • Everything went ***according to plan***. [=everything went as it had been planned]
3 : in a way that is based on (something) • He arranged the books on the shelf *according to* [=*by*] their size. • He was paid *according to* how quickly he worked.

ac·cor·di·on /əˈkoɚdijən/ *noun, pl* **-ons** [*count*] : a musical instrument that is shaped like a box and that is held in your hands and played by pulling its sides apart and then pushing them together while pressing buttons and keys
– ac·cor·di·on·ist /əˈkoɚdijənɪst/ *noun, pl* **-ists** [*count*]

accordion

ac·cost /əˈkɑːst/ *verb* **-costs; -cost·ed; -cost·ing** [+ *obj*] : to approach and speak to (someone) often in an angry, aggressive, or unwanted way • He was *accosted* by three gang members on the subway. • She was so famous that people would *accost* her on the street and ask for an autograph.

¹ac·count /əˈkaʊnt/ *noun, pl* **-counts**
1 a [*count*] : a record of money that has been paid and money that has been received : BILL • the difference between the debit and credit sides of an *account* — see also EXPENSE ACCOUNT **b** ***accounts*** [*plural*] : records of income and expenses • We always keep very good *accounts.* • an *accounts* department • The company's *accounts* show a profit this year: our ***accounts receivable*** exceed our ***accounts payable***. [=the money owed to us exceeds the money we owe]
2 [*count*] : an arrangement in which a bank keeps a record of the money that a person puts in and takes out of the bank • We opened new *accounts* at a bank last week. • I took out my money and closed my *account.* • You can withdraw up to $1,000 a day from your *account.* • Every week, she puts/deposits a part of her paycheck into a separate *account.* • setting up a ***bank account*** • My wife and I keep our money in a ***joint account***. [=an account that both of us can use] — often used before another noun • Please enter your name and *account* number. • You can check your *account* balance [=the amount of money in your account] on the Internet. — see also CHECKING ACCOUNT, SAVINGS ACCOUNT
3 [*count*] : a company's record of the products or services used by a customer and of the money that the customer owes or has paid to the company • I don't have the money right now. Put it on my *account.* = Charge it to my *account.* • If you return the clothes, the store will credit your *account.* [=you will not have to pay for the clothes] • When do you intend to ***settle your account***? [=pay what you owe] — see also CHARGE ACCOUNT, CREDIT ACCOUNT ◊ In figurative use, to ***settle an account*** or to ***settle accounts with*** someone is to do something that brings a final end to an argument, disagreement, etc. • She's decided to *settle accounts with* her old political rivals.
4 [*count*] : a business arrangement in which a person or company regularly buys products or services from a particular company • She makes sure that all of the company's *accounts* [=*customers, clients*] make the necessary payments. • We just lost the Smith *account.* • That company was one of our biggest/best *accounts.* • She will be our ***account manager***. [=the person who manages our account]
5 [*count*] : an arrangement in which a person uses the Internet or e-mail services of a particular company • I use two separate e-mail *accounts.*
6 [*count*] : a description of an event or situation : a story or report about something • personal/firsthand/eyewitness *accounts* from the war • According to one *account,* the party was a complete disaster. — often + *of* • She gave the police a full/complete/detailed *account of* what happened. • We read an *account of* her trip to Paris. • a written *account of* his long and successful career
7 [*count*] : a list or description of facts • Our goal is to give an accurate *account* of the process. • an *account* of how the system works • The document is an *account* of the country's reasons for going to war.
8 [*count*] : a reason or explanation for an action • You will be asked to give an *account* of your actions. [=to explain the reasons for your actions] • He could give no *account* of what he did with the money. — often used in the formal phrase ***on that account*** • I hope we won't lose our friendship *on that account.* [=for that reason]
9 [*noncount*] *formal* : value or importance — used in the phrases ***of no account*** and ***of little account*** • He felt that his opinions were *of no account* to the others. [=he thought that the other people didn't care about his opinions] • It's *of little account* what I may think about it. — see also NO-ACCOUNT
bring/call (someone) to account : to require (someone) to explain and accept punishment or criticism for bad or wrong behavior • He was *called to account* by his boss for failing to spot the mistake in the company's records.
by/from all accounts : according to all of the different descriptions of something • *By all accounts,* the band put on a great show. [=everyone says that the band put on a great show] • She was, *by all accounts,* good at her job. • They seemed, *from all accounts,* to have a happy marriage.
by your own account : according to what you have said about your own life or experiences • *By her own account,* that was the worst performance of her career. [=she said that was her worst performance] • They had, *by their own account,* a wonderful time.
give a good account of yourself : to perform well especially in a competition • If I ever had to fight, I think I could *give a good account of myself.*
on account of : because of : for the reason of • The game was canceled *on account of* the rain. • They were treated badly *on account of* their beliefs. • *On account of* his bad behavior, he will not be allowed to play with the new toy.
on no account or ***not on any account*** *chiefly Brit* : for no reason : under no circumstances — used to say that something will not or should not happen • *On no account* should the children be left at home alone. • They said that *on no account* would they leave before the end of the game.
on someone's account : because of someone : in order to please someone • Don't leave *on our account.* [=because of us] • You didn't have to clean your room *on my account.* I don't care if your room is dirty.
on your own account **1** : by yourself : on your own : without the help of others • She bought the house entirely *on her own account.* • He left the company and went into business *on his own account.* **2** : for your own sake : in order to make a situation good for yourself • I'm doing it *on my own account,* not for anyone else.
take (something) into account or ***take account of (something)*** : to think about (something) before doing something (such as making a decision) : CONSIDER • Try to *take* our feelings *into account.* [=try to think about how we will feel] • Other issues must be *taken into account* before a choice can be made. • She did very well on the test when you *take into account* how little she studied. • She *takes no account of* my feelings. [=she doesn't consider how I feel] • The new health plan fails to *take account of* the fact that many people cannot pay for their medicine.
turn (something) to (good) account *formal* : to gain or profit from (something) : to take advantage of (something) • Is there a way to *turn* this situation *to good account*?

²account *verb* **-counts; -count·ed; -count·ing** [+ *obj*] *formal* : to think of (someone or something) in a specified way — usually used as ***(be) accounted*** • Their first project *was accounted* [=*considered*] a success.
account for [*phrasal verb*] **1 *account for (something)*** **a** : to give a reason or explanation for (something) • Eventually, you will need to *account for* your actions/behavior. • How do you *account for* [=*explain*] your success? ◊ The informal saying ***there's no accounting for taste*** means that there is no way to understand why some people like something while other people do not. • I don't see why they liked the movie, but *there's no accounting for taste.* **b** : to be the cause of (something) • The disease *accounted for* over 10,000 deaths last year. • These new features *account for* the computer's higher price. • The disease cannot be *accounted for* [=*explained*] by genetics alone. There must be other causes as well. **c** : to make up or form (a part of something) • Women *account for* [=*constitute, compose*] only 25 percent of our employees. **d** *US* : to think about (something) before doing something : to take (something) into consideration • The researchers failed to *account for* the fact that most of the students were poor. **2 *account for (someone or something)*** **a** : to show what happened to (someone or something) • We have to *account for* the time [=to say how much time] we spend on each activity. • I'll have to *account for* the money I spent.: to know the location of (someone or something) • The government couldn't *account for* millions of dollars of the taxpayers' money. • Is everyone *accounted for*? [=do we know where everyone is?] • ***All present and accounted for***. [=everyone who is supposed to be here is here] **b** : to destroy or kill (someone or something) • Enemy fighters have *accounted for* most of our bombers, Sir; *also, chiefly Brit* : to defeat or beat (someone or something) • We *accounted for* [=*dispatched*] the challengers 3–2.

A

ac·count·able /əˈkaʊntəbəl/ *adj, not used before a noun*
1 : required to explain actions or decisions to someone — usually + *to* ▪ Political leaders need to be *accountable to* the people they represent. ▪ a powerful businessman who seems to think that he's *accountable* [=*answerable*] *to* no one
2 : required to be responsible for something ▪ If anything goes wrong I will hold you personally *accountable*! — often + *for* ▪ They hold you *accountable for* your mistakes. ▪ Each child is *accountable* [=*responsible*] *for* his or her own behavior.
– ac·count·abil·i·ty /əˌkʰæʊntəˈbɪləri/ *noun* [*noncount*] ▪ We now have greater *accountability* in the department. [=people in the department can now be held more responsible for what happens] ▪ corporate *accountability*

ac·coun·tant /əˈkaʊntn̩t/ *noun, pl* **-tants** [*count*] **:** someone whose job is to keep the financial records of a business or person

ac·count·ing /əˈkaʊntɪŋ/ *noun* [*noncount*] **:** the skill, system, or job of keeping the financial records of a business or person — often used before another noun ▪ an *accounting* firm ▪ traditional *accounting* methods

ac·cou·tred *or* **ac·cou·tered** /əˈku:təd/ *adj, literary* **:** provided with equipment or clothing ▪ The knight's horse was properly *accoutred* for battle.

ac·cou·tre·ment *or US* **ac·cou·ter·ment** /əˈku:trəmənt, əˈku:təmənt/ *noun, pl* **-ments** [*count*] **:** a piece of clothing or equipment that is used in a particular place or for a particular activity — usually plural ▪ The room had a fully stocked bar and all the *accoutrements* of a first-class hotel.

ac·cred·it /əˈkrɛdət/ *verb* **-its; -it·ed; -it·ing** [+ *obj*]
1 : to say that something is good enough to be given official approval ▪ The association only *accredits* programs that meet its high standards. ▪ The program was *accredited* by the American Dental Association.
2 : to give (someone) credit for something **:** CREDIT ▪ The invention of scuba gear is *accredited* to Jacques Cousteau.
3 : to send (someone, such as an ambassador) to act as an official representative ▪ *accredit* an ambassador to France
– ac·cred·i·ta·tion /əˌkrɛdəˈteɪʃən/ *noun* [*noncount*] ▪ The school/hospital lost its *accreditation*. ▪ the *accreditation* of an ambassador **– accredited** *adj* ▪ an *accredited* college/hospital ▪ She was enrolled at an *accredited* law school.

ac·cre·tion /əˈkri:ʃən/ *noun, pl* **-tions**
1 [*noncount*] **:** a gradual process in which layers of a material are formed as small amounts are added over time ▪ rocks formed by the slow *accretion* of limestone — often used figuratively ▪ The gradual *accretion* of detail creates a complex and moving story.
2 [*count*] **:** something that has grown or accumulated slowly **:** a product or result of gradual growth ▪ strangely shaped limestone *accretions* ▪ There was an *accretion* of ice on the car's windshield.

ac·crue /əˈkru:/ *verb* **-crues; -crued; -cru·ing** *formal*
1 : to increase in value or amount gradually as time passes **:** to grow or build up slowly [*no obj*] I'll get back all the money I invested, plus any interest and dividends that have *accrued*. — often + *to* ▪ interest and dividends that have *accrued to* me [+ *obj*] investments that have *accrued* interest and dividends
2 [*no obj*] **:** to come to or be given to someone — usually + *to* ▪ the advantages/benefits that *accrue to* us [=that we receive] as members of a free society
– ac·cru·al /əˈkru:wəl/ *noun, pl* **-als** [*count*] an *accrual* of interest [*noncount*] money gained by *accrual* of interest **– accrued** *adj* ▪ I'll get back all the money I invested, plus any *accrued* interest and dividends.

ac·cu·mu·late /əˈkju:mjəˌleɪt/ *verb* **-lates; -lat·ed; -lat·ing**
1 [+ *obj*] **:** to gather or acquire (something) gradually as time passes ▪ She has slowly *accumulated* [=*amassed*] a fortune. ▪ You can *accumulate* [=*earn*] bonus points by participating in surveys. ▪ The police have been *accumulating* [=*collecting*] evidence of his guilt.
2 [*no obj*] **:** to increase gradually in amount as time passes ▪ A large amount of debris has *accumulated* [=*collected*] at the construction site. ▪ Evidence of his guilt is *accumulating*.
– ac·cu·mu·la·tion /əˌkju:mjəˈleɪʃən/ *noun, pl* **-tions** [*noncount*] the *accumulation* of evidence against him [*count*] The company's goal was a slow, steady *accumulation* of profits. ▪ The disease is caused by *accumulations of* fat in the kidneys.

ac·cu·mu·la·tive /əˈkju:mjələtɪv/ *adj* **:** growing or increasing over time **:** CUMULATIVE ▪ The *accumulative* effect of his injuries forced him to retire.

ac·cu·ra·cy /ˈækjərəsi/ *noun*
1 : freedom from mistake or error **:** the quality or state of being accurate **:** CORRECTNESS [*noncount*] Each experiment is performed twice to ensure *accuracy*. ▪ The police questioned the *accuracy* of his statement. ▪ He could not say with any *accuracy* what he had seen. [*singular*] She shot free throws with an *accuracy* of 80 percent. [=80 percent of her free throws were accurate/successful]
2 [*noncount*] **:** the ability to work or perform without making mistakes ▪ Several managers have tried to increase the speed and *accuracy* of the workers.

ac·cu·rate /ˈækjərət/ *adj* [*more* ~; *most* ~]
1 : free from mistakes or errors ▪ The model is *accurate* down to the tiniest details. ▪ an *accurate* account/record/report/description ▪ Her novel is historically *accurate*. ▪ He needed a more *accurate* [=*precise*] term to describe the procedure. ▪ an *accurate* throw/shot [=a throw/shot that does not miss its target] — opposite INACCURATE
2 : able to produce results that are correct **:** not making mistakes ▪ an *accurate* reporter ▪ an *accurate* measuring device ▪ The machines were not yet *accurate* enough to give useful results. — opposite INACCURATE
– ac·cu·rate·ly *adv* ▪ It is very difficult to *accurately* predict the weather. ▪ The book's title does not *accurately* reflect its subject.

ac·cursed /əˈkəst, əˈkəsəd/ *adj, old-fashioned*
1 : having very bad luck **:** placed under a curse ▪ an *accursed* [=*cursed*] team that can't seem to win a game
2 : very bad **:** greatly or strongly disliked ▪ I couldn't wait to get out of that *accursed* [=*cursed, damned*] place.

ac·cu·sa·tion /ˌækjəˈzeɪʃən/ *noun, pl* **-tions :** a claim that someone has done something wrong or illegal **:** a charge that someone has committed a fault or crime [*count*] Investigators have made/brought/leveled *accusations* of corruption against a group of former officials. ▪ The police are investigating serious *accusations* of wrongdoing. ▪ He denied/rejected the *accusation* that he had lied to the police. ▪ a false *accusation* [*noncount*] There was a hint/tone of *accusation* in his voice when he asked her where she had been.

ac·cu·sa·tive /əˈkʰju:zətɪv/ *noun* [*noncount*] *grammar* **:** the form of a noun or pronoun when it is the direct object of a verb or the object of a preposition ▪ a noun in the *accusative* — called also *objective*; compare NOMINATIVE
– accusative *adj* ▪ the *accusative* case

ac·cu·sa·to·ry /əˈkju:zəˌtori, *Brit* əˈkju:zətri/ *adj* [*more* ~; *most* ~] **:** accusing or blaming someone **:** assigning blame or fault ▪ He pointed an *accusatory* finger at the suspect. ▪ The book has a harsh, *accusatory* tone.

ac·cuse /əˈkju:z/ *verb* **-cus·es; -cused; -cus·ing** [+ *obj*] **:** to blame (someone) for something wrong or illegal **:** to say that someone is guilty of a fault or crime ▪ He was unjustly *accused*. — often + *of* ▪ He was *accused of* stealing the money. ▪ His children have *accused* him *of* neglect. ▪ You can't *accuse* him *of* being rude: he's always extremely polite. ▪ She has been *accused of* murder. = She ***stands accused of*** murder. — sometimes used humorously ▪ No one could ever *accuse* him *of* being overly modest. [=he is not modest]
– ac·cus·er *noun, pl* **-ers** [*count*] ▪ She deserves the chance to meet/confront her *accuser*. **– accusing** *adj* [*more* ~; *most* ~] ▪ She gave him a very *accusing* look. ▪ The governor ***pointed an accusing finger at*** the legislature [=said the legislature was to blame] for failing to approve her budget.
– ac·cus·ing·ly /əˈkʰju:zɪŋli/ *adv* ▪ She looked at him *accusingly*. ▪ "What did you do?" he asked *accusingly*.

accused *noun*
***the accused* :** a person who is charged with a crime ▪ *The accused* was found not guilty. **:** a group of people who are charged with a crime ▪ *The accused* were found not guilty.

ac·cus·tom /əˈkʌstəm/ *verb* **-toms; -tomed; -tom·ing** [+ *obj*] **:** to cause (someone) to become adjusted to or familiar with something — + *to* ▪ trying to gradually *accustom* the students *to* their new surroundings ▪ The time he spent in the army has *accustomed* him *to* rising early in the morning. ▪ He'll have to ***accustom himself to*** life in a new country. [=he will have to become adjusted to life in a new country]

ac·cus·tomed /əˈkʌstəmd/ *adj* [*more* ~; *most* ~]
1 : familiar with something so that it seems normal or usual — + *to* ▪ She is *accustomed to* [=*used to*] life/living on the farm. ▪ We have become/grown/gotten more *accustomed to* their traditions and routines. ▪ He is *accustomed to* doing

what he wants to do. [=he usually does what he wants to do]
2 *always used before a noun, formal* **: usual or regular** • at her *accustomed* [=*customary*] lunch hour • She arrived early enough to get her *accustomed* seat in the front row.

[1]**ace** /ˈeɪs/ *noun, pl* **ac·es** [*count*]
1 : a playing card with one large figure in its center that can be the card with either the highest or lowest value • the *ace* of spades/diamonds/hearts/clubs — see picture at PLAYING CARD
2 : a person who is very skilled at something • a computer *ace* • the *ace* of the team's pitching staff [=the best pitcher on the team] — often used before another noun • an *ace* mechanic/reporter
3 : a point scored on a serve that an opponent fails to hit in tennis • She won the match by scoring more than 30 *aces*.
4 *US* **: a score of one on a hole in golf : HOLE IN ONE** • He got/shot/scored an *ace* on the eighth hole.
an ace in the hole (*US*) *or chiefly Brit* ***an ace up your sleeve*** ✧ If you have *an ace in the hole* or *an ace up your sleeve*, you have a powerful and often secret weapon, advantage, etc., that you can use if it is needed. • The mayor's popularity among elderly voters gives him an *ace in the hole* for the coming election.
hold all the aces **: to have a strong advantage over others in a contest, competition, etc.** • As the strike continues into its second week, it appears that the company *holds all the aces* in its negotiations with the strikers.
within an ace of *informal* **: very near to (doing something)** • They were/came *within an ace of* winning the championship. [=they almost won the championship]

[2]**ace** *verb* **aces; aced; ac·ing** [+ *obj*]
1 *US, informal* **: to earn a very high grade on (an examination) : to get a grade of A on (an examination)** • He *aced* the test. • She *aced* her entrance exams. **: to perform very well on (a test or challenge)** • He *aced* his annual physical.
2 : to score an ace against (an opponent in tennis) • He *aced* his opponent on the last point of the match.
3 *US* **: to score an ace on (a hole in golf)** • She *aced* the 14th hole. [=she had a hole in one on the 14th hole]

acer·bic /əˈsɚbɪk/ *adj* [*more* ~; *most* ~] *somewhat formal* **: expressing harsh or sharp criticism in a clever way** • *acerbic* comedy • an *acerbic* playwright • the film's most *acerbic* critics • his *acerbic* wit
– acer·bi·cal·ly /əˈsɚbɪkli/ *adv*

acet·amin·o·phen /əˌsiːtəˈmɪnəfən/ *noun* [*noncount*] *US* **: a medicine that is used to relieve pain and fever**

acet·y·lene /əˈsɛtl̩ən/ *noun* [*noncount*] **: a gas that burns with a very hot flame which is used to melt and connect pieces of metal**

[1]**ache** /ˈeɪk/ *verb* **aches; ached; ach·ing** [*no obj*]
1 : to produce a dull continuous pain : to hurt in a way that is constant but not severe • Her muscles were *aching* from shoveling snow. • After running the marathon, his body *ached* for a week. • The candy's so sweet that it makes my teeth *ache*. — often used figuratively • His heart *ached* [=he felt sad and sorry] for the children begging on the streets.
2 : to want or desire something or someone very much — often + *for* • After years of war, most people are *aching* [=*longing, yearning*] *for* peace. • Her heart *ached for* him. — often followed by *to* + *verb* • I've been *aching to see* you.

[2]**ache** *noun, pl* **aches** [*count*] **: a pain that is not sharp but continues for a long time** • He had a dull *ache* in his back from lifting boxes all day. • muscle *aches* — often used in combination with parts of the body • a head*ache* • a stomach*ache* • tooth*aches* — often used figuratively • She looked through the old pictures with a dull *ache* in her heart. ✧ ***Aches and pains*** are many small pains that happen at the same time and make people feel uncomfortable. • Symptoms of the flu include fever, general *aches and pains*, and sore throat. • the many *aches and pains* of old age
– achy /ˈeɪki/ *adj* **ach·i·er; -est** • My feet are tired and *achy* from walking all day.

achieve /əˈʧiːv/ *verb* **achieves; achieved; achiev·ing**
1 [+ *obj*] **: to get or reach (something) by working hard** • This year, our company was able to *achieve* [=*accomplish, attain*] all of its production goals. • He worked hard and *achieved* success. [=became successful] • a diet that *achieves* dramatic results • With much practice, she has *achieved* a high level of skill. • They *achieved* high scores on their math tests.
2 [*no obj*] **: to become successful : to reach a goal** • We give students the skills they need in order to *achieve* in college.
– achiev·able /əˈʧiːvəbəl/ *adj* [*more* ~; *most* ~] • *achievable* goals

achieve·ment /əˈʧiːvmənt/ *noun, pl* **-ments**
1 [*count*] **: something that has been done or achieved through effort : a result of hard work** • The discovery of DNA was a major scientific *achievement*. • It was a great/extraordinary/remarkable *achievement*. • Getting the project done on time was a real *achievement*.
2 [*noncount*] **: the act of achieving something** • a high level of artistic *achievement* [=*accomplishment*] **: the state or condition of having achieved or accomplished something** • Tests measure students' academic *achievement*. [=measure how much the students have learned] • The students were awarded (with) certificates of *achievement*. [=documents saying that they reached an academic goal] • Repairing the car by himself gave him a real ***sense of achievement*** [=a proud feeling of having done something difficult and worthwhile]

achiev·er /əˈʧiːvɚ/ *noun, pl* **-ers** [*count*] **: a person who achieves success : a successful person** • Both of his brothers are *achievers*. = Both his brothers are ***high achievers***. [=both his brothers are hardworking and successful] • a ***low achiever*** [=an unsuccessful person who does not work hard] — see also OVERACHIEVER, UNDERACHIEVER

Achil·les' heel /əˈkɪliz-/ *noun, pl* ~ **heels** [*count*] **: a fault or weakness that causes or could cause someone or something to fail** • I'm trying to lose weight, but ice cream is my *Achilles' heel*. • This year, the team's *Achilles' heel* is its pitching. [=the team could fail because of its poor pitching]

Achilles tendon *noun, pl* ~ **-dons** [*count*] *medical* **: the body part that joins the muscles of the lower leg to the bone of the heel**

achoo /əˈʧuː/ *interj* — **used to represent the sound of a sneeze**

[1]**ac·id** /ˈæsəd/ *noun, pl* **acids**
1 *chemistry* **: a chemical with a sour taste that forms a salt when mixed with a base** [*count*] the *acids* in your stomach [*noncount*] the kinds of *acid* found in your stomach ✧ An acid has a pH of less than 7. Very strong acids are able to burn holes in things. — compare [1]BASE 6, PH
2 [*noncount*] *slang* **: LSD** • His friend ***dropped acid*** [=took LSD] at the concert.

[2]**acid** *adj* [*more* ~; *most* ~]
1 *always used before a noun* **: of, relating to, or having the qualities of an acid** • He washes his windows with an *acid* solution of vinegar and water. • an *acid* [=*sour*] taste • This kind of plant grows well in *acid* [=*acidic*] soil. • Their pizza gives me ***acid indigestion*** [=a burning feeling in the stomach]
2 : sharp, strong, and critical in tone • He made some very *acid* [=*biting, caustic*] comments. • *acid* remarks
– acid·i·ty /əˈsɪdəti/ *noun* [*noncount*] • They measured the *acidity* of the soil. • the *acidity* [=*tartness, sourness*] of lemon juice **– ac·id·ly** *adv* • She *acidly* refers to her former husband as "that little man."

acid·ic /əˈsɪdɪk/ *adj* [*more* ~; *most* ~]
1 : having a very sour or sharp taste • an *acidic* sauce/wine
2 : containing acid • The soil in our garden is very *acidic*. • the *acidic* water of a polluted lake — compare ALKALINE

acid·i·fy /əˈsɪdəˌfaɪ/ *verb* **-fies; -fied; -fy·ing** *technical* **: to cause (something) to become acidic** [+ *obj*] Pollution *acidified* the soil. [*no obj*] Pollution caused the soil to *acidify*.
– acid·i·fi·ca·tion /əˌsɪdəfəˈkeɪʃən/ *noun* [*noncount*]

acid rain *noun* [*noncount*] **: rain that contains dangerous chemicals because of smoke from cars and factories** • trees damaged by *acid rain*

acid test *noun* [*singular*] **: a difficult situation or task that shows if someone or something is good enough to succeed** • The new team faced its first *acid test* when it played the national champions. — compare LITMUS TEST

ac·knowl·edge /ɪkˈnɑːlɪʤ/ *verb* **-edg·es; -edged; -edg·ing** [+ *obj*]
1 : to say that you accept or do not deny the truth or existence of (something) : ADMIT • They *acknowledged* that the decision was a mistake. • Do you *acknowledge* that you caused this mess? • I *acknowledge* (the fact) that I hurt you, and for that I am sorry. • They readily/openly/grudgingly *acknowledged* their mistake. • She won't *acknowledge* responsibility for her actions. • He refuses to *acknowledge* the authority of the court. [=he denies that the court has authority]
2 : to regard or describe (someone or something) as having or deserving a particular status • They *acknowledge* him as their leader. = They *acknowledge* him to be their leader. — usually used as *(be) acknowledged* • She *is* widely/generally *acknowledged* as one of the world's best chefs. [=many people regard her as one of the world's best chefs] • Her pastries

A

are acknowledged to be the best. ▪ This part of the city *is acknowledged* to have the best restaurants.
3 : to tell or show someone that something (such as a letter or message) has been received ▪ He quickly *acknowledges* all of my e-mails when he receives them. ▪ Please *acknowledge* receipt of this letter. ▪ She *acknowledged* the gift with a card. ▪ She *acknowledged* his greeting with a smile.
4 : to show that someone has been seen and recognized **:** to look at or talk to (someone) ▪ She walked right by me without even *acknowledging* me. ▪ The players *acknowledged* their fans by waving their hands and blowing kisses into the crowd. ▪ He refuses to ***acknowledge her existence/presence.***
5 : to express thanks or appreciation for (something or someone) ▪ In their paper, they *acknowledge* the important work done by past scholars. ▪ They *acknowledge* past scholars for the important work they have done.
– acknowledged *adj* ▪ the *acknowledged* leader of a political party ▪ an *acknowledged* master of the art

ac·knowl·edg·ment *also* **ac·knowl·edge·ment** /ɪkˈnɑːlɪʤmənt/ *noun, pl* **-ments**
1 : the act of acknowledging something or someone: such as **a :** the act of showing that you know, admit, or accept that something exists or is true *[count]* The killer's apology was an *acknowledgment* [=*admission*] of his guilt. = The killer's apology was an *acknowledgment* that he was guilty. ▪ The day passed without any *acknowledgment* that it was their wedding anniversary. [=no one mentioned that it was their wedding anniversary] ▪ They made several public *acknowledgments* of their company's mistake. *[noncount]* He paid the fine without *acknowledgment* of his guilt. **b :** the act of praising or thanking someone for an action or achievement *[count]* Special *acknowledgments* will be made at the end of the meeting. *[noncount]* He has finally received the *acknowledgment* he deserves for his charitable work. ▪ They presented him with an award ***in acknowledgment of*** his charitable work.
2 *acknowledgments* *[plural]* **:** a section of a book, article, etc., in which people are thanked for their help ▪ He's the first person mentioned in the book's *acknowledgments*.
3 *[count]* **:** a usually written statement saying that a letter or message was received ▪ We sent an *acknowledgment* that we received their letter. ▪ He never received an *acknowledgment* of his payment.

ac·me /ˈækmi/ *noun [singular]* **:** the highest point of something ▪ He was struck down by illness at the *acme* [=*height*] of his fame. [=when he was most famous] ▪ His fame was at its *acme*.

ac·ne /ˈækni/ *noun [noncount] medical* **:** a condition in which the skin on a person's face, neck, etc., has many small, swollen spots (called pimples) ▪ a teenager with bad *acne*

ac·o·lyte /ˈækəˌlaɪt/ *noun, pl* **-lytes** *[count]*
1 *formal* **:** someone who follows and admires a leader ▪ a popular professor dining with a few of her *acolytes*
2 : someone who helps the person who leads a church service

acorn /ˈeɪˌkoɚn/ *noun, pl* **acorns** *[count]* **:** the nut of the oak tree

acorn squash *noun, pl* ~ **squash·es** *[count, noncount] US* **:** a vegetable that is somewhat round with a pointed end and has dark skin and yellow or orange flesh — see color picture on page C4

acous·tic /əˈkuːstɪk/ *also US* **acous·ti·cal** /əˈkuːstɪkəl/ *adj*
1 : of or relating to sound or to the sense of hearing ▪ the *acoustic* properties/characteristics of a room ▪ *acoustic* vibrations
2 a *of a musical instrument* **:** not having its sound changed by electrical devices ▪ an *acoustic* guitar ▪ *acoustic* instruments **b :** made with or using acoustic instruments ▪ She loves listening to *acoustic* folk music. ▪ an *acoustic* performance of a rock-and-roll song ▪ *acoustic* musicians
– acous·ti·cal·ly /əˈkuːstɪkli/ *adv* ▪ an *acoustically* perfect room

acous·tics /əˈkuːstɪks/ *noun*
1 *[plural]* **:** the qualities of a room (such as its shape or size) that make it easy or difficult for people inside to hear sounds clearly **:** acoustic qualities ▪ We love performing in this room because of its great *acoustics*. ▪ The *acoustics* in the school's auditorium are terrible.
2 *[noncount]* **:** the science that studies sounds ▪ *Acoustics* is a challenging subject.

ac·quaint /əˈkweɪnt/ *verb* **-quaints; -quaint·ed; -quaint·ing** *[+ obj] formal* **:** to cause (someone) to know and become familiar *with* something ▪ He *acquainted* the new employee *with* her duties. [=he told her about her duties] ▪ This class is designed to *acquaint* students *with* the region's most important writers. ▪ The lawyer took a few days to ***acquaint herself with*** [=to learn about] the facts of a case.

ac·quain·tance /əˈkweɪntn̩s/ *noun, pl* **-tanc·es**
1 *[count]* **:** someone who is known but who is not a close friend ▪ Is he an *acquaintance* of yours? [=have you met him?] ▪ She ran into an old *acquaintance* at the grocery store. ▪ My wife and I met through a mutual *acquaintance*. [=a friend introduced us to each other] ▪ a casual *acquaintance* ▪ friends and *acquaintances*
2 *[noncount] formal* **:** the state of knowing someone in a personal or social way **:** the state of knowing someone as an acquaintance ▪ our family's close *acquaintance* with our neighbors ▪ It's a pleasure to ***make your acquaintance.*** [=(less formally) it's nice to meet you] ▪ She ***made the acquaintance of*** [=she met] a man from the city. ▪ She ***struck up an acquaintance with*** a man from the city. ▪ a doctor ***of my acquaintance*** [=a doctor that I know] ▪ He seemed cold ***on/at first acquaintance*** [=when I first met him], but later I realized that he was just shy. ▪ He seemed cold at first, but ***on closer/further acquaintance*** I realized that he was just shy.
3 : knowledge about something — + *with [singular]* She has only a nodding/slight/superficial *acquaintance with* the facts of the case. [=she knows only a little about the facts of the case] ▪ He has ***more than a passing acquaintance with*** wine. [=he knows a lot about wine] *[noncount]* While he has some *acquaintance with* the subject, he is not an expert.
– acquaintanceship *noun, pl* **-ships** *[count]* An *acquaintanceship* grew between the two men. *[noncount]* Her long *acquaintanceship* [=*acquaintance*] with sorrow began when her young husband died.

acquaint·ed *adj, not used before a noun*
1 *formal* **:** having knowledge about something **:** having seen or experienced something — + *with* ▪ Are you *acquainted with* the facts in this case? [=do you know the facts?] ▪ I am (well) *acquainted with* his books. [=I have read his books]
2 : having met **:** knowing each other in a personal or social way ▪ Are you two *acquainted*? [=have you met before?] ▪ The two actors are intimately/casually *acquainted*. [=they know each other intimately/casually] ▪ Let's take a walk and ***get acquainted.*** ▪ I'll go get us some drinks while you two ***get better acquainted.*** [=while you two talk to each other and get to know each other better] — often + *with* ▪ It took him a few months to *get/become acquainted with* the other students.

ac·qui·esce /ˌækwiˈɛs/ *verb* **-esc·es; -esced; -esc·ing** *[no obj] formal* **:** to accept, agree, or allow something to happen by staying silent or by not arguing ▪ They demanded it, and he *acquiesced*. — often + *in* ▪ We cannot *acquiesce in* the killing of innocent people. — often + *to* ▪ She *acquiesced to* her husband's plans.
– ac·qui·es·cence /ˌækwiˈɛsn̩s/ *noun [noncount]* ▪ I was surprised by his *acquiescence* to their demands.

ac·qui·es·cent /ˌækwiˈɛsn̩t/ *adj [more ~; most ~] formal* **:** tending to accept or allow what other people want or demand ▪ The *acquiescent* girl became a strong assertive woman.

ac·quire /əˈkwajɚ/ *verb* **-quires; -quired; -quir·ing** *[+ obj]*
1 *formal* **:** to get (something) **:** to come to own (something) ▪ They're planning to *acquire* [=*buy*] a new home in the country. ▪ He *acquired* [=*got, inherited*] a small fortune after the death of her parents. ▪ The two ships were *acquired* by the navy after the war. ▪ The team *acquired* three new players this year. **:** to come to have (something) ▪ She dreamed of *acquiring* [=*gaining, getting*] control of the company. ▪ When I saw her next she had somehow managed to *acquire* a few cuts and bruises. [=she had a few cuts and bruises] ▪ The old word has *acquired* a new meaning. ▪ This apparently minor event has *acquired* increasing significance in recent weeks.
2 : to gain (a new skill, ability, etc.) usually by your own effort ▪ She quickly *acquired* [=*gained*] fluency in French. ▪ He is studying the way that language is *acquired* by children. ▪ *acquire* knowledge ▪ He has ***acquired a reputation*** as a careful/careless worker. [=people regard him as a careful/careless worker] ✧ When people ***acquire a taste for*** something, they like something that they did not like before. ▪ Although he usually avoided unusual foods, he eventually began to *acquire a taste for* raw fish. ✧ An ***acquired taste*** is something or someone that is not easily or immediately liked. ▪ Brussels sprouts are an *acquired taste* for many people. ▪ I admit that she is something of an *acquired taste*, but I think her art is wonderful.

acquired immune deficiency syndrome *noun* [*noncount*] *medical* : AIDS

ac·qui·si·tion /ˌækwəˈzɪʃən/ *noun, pl* **-tions**
1 [*noncount*] : the act of getting or acquiring something: such as **a** : the act or process of gaining skill, knowledge, etc. ▪ the *acquisition* of knowledge ▪ foreign language *acquisition* **b** : the act of obtaining money, possessions, etc. ▪ the *acquisition* of wealth ▪ the country's *acquisition* of new ships
2 [*count*] : something (such as a company or valuable property) that is acquired ▪ The big company's newest *acquisition* is a small chain of clothing stores. ▪ The museum has put its latest *acquisitions* on display.

ac·quis·i·tive /əˈkwɪzətɪv/ *adj, formal + disapproving* : having a strong desire to own or acquire more things ▪ our increasingly competitive and *acquisitive* [=*greedy*] society
– ac·quis·i·tive·ness *noun* [*noncount*]

ac·quit /əˈkwɪt/ *verb* **-quits**; **-quit·ted**; **-quit·ting** [+ *obj*]
: to decide that someone is not guilty of a crime ▪ The jury *acquitted* the defendant because there wasn't enough evidence to convict him of the crime. ▪ She was *acquitted* of the murder of her husband. = She was *acquitted* of murdering her husband. — compare ¹CONVICT
acquit yourself : to act or behave in a specified way — used to express approval or (less commonly) disapproval of someone's behavior or performance ▪ The soldiers *acquitted themselves* well/honorably in battle. ▪ The young actress *acquitted herself* extremely well/capably in her first film. ▪ He *acquitted himself* poorly in handling the controversy.

ac·quit·tal /əˈkwɪtl/ *noun, pl* **-tals** : the act of deciding that a person is not guilty of a crime : the act of acquitting someone [*noncount*] The case resulted/ended in *acquittal* of the defendant. ▪ Several jurors voted for *acquittal*. [*count*] The case resulted/ended in an *acquittal* of the defendant.

acre /ˈeɪkɚ/ *noun, pl* **acres** [*count*] : a measure of land area in the U.S. and Britain that equals 4,840 square yards (about 4,047 square meters) ▪ The house sits/is on two *acres* of land. ▪ They own hundreds of *acres* of farmland. — sometimes used figuratively ▪ a cheap stunt that got them *acres* of free publicity [=a great amount of free publicity]

acre·age /ˈeɪkərɪʤ/ *noun* [*noncount*] : land measured in acres ▪ A large portion of the park's *acreage* is forest.

ac·rid /ˈækrəd/ *adj* [*more* ~; *most* ~] : bitter and unpleasant in taste or smell ▪ Thick, *acrid* smoke rose from the factory.

ac·ri·mo·ni·ous /ˌækrəˈmoʊnijəs/ *adj* [*more* ~; *most* ~] *formal* : angry and bitter ▪ an *acrimonious* debate ▪ *acrimonious* disputes between nations ▪ He went through an *acrimonious* divorce.
– ac·ri·mo·ni·ous·ly *adv* ▪ The issue was *acrimoniously* debated.

ac·ri·mo·ny /ˈækrəˌmoʊni, *Brit* ˈækrəməni/ *noun* [*noncount*] *formal* : angry and bitter feelings ▪ The dispute began again with increased *acrimony*.

ac·ro·bat /ˈækrəˌbæt/ *noun, pl* **-bats** [*count*] : someone who entertains people (as at a circus) by performing difficult and often dangerous acts (such as swinging from a bar or walking on a rope high in the air)
– ac·ro·bat·ic /ˌækrəˈbætɪk/ *adj* [*more* ~; *most* ~] ▪ *acrobatic* skill ▪ an *acrobatic* feat ▪ The goalie is famous for her *acrobatic* saves. [=saves that involve difficult and skillful movements] **– ac·ro·bat·ical·ly** /ˌækrəˈbætɪkli/ *adj*

ac·ro·bat·ics /ˌækrəˈbætɪks/ *noun* [*plural*] : difficult and dangerous acts done by an acrobat ▪ The circus performers' *acrobatics* were spectacular!; *also* : difficult or dangerous acts, movements, etc., done by another kind of performer ▪ aerial *acrobatics* [=spectacular movements performed while flying] ▪ The singer's vocal *acrobatics* are impressive. — sometimes used figuratively ▪ It makes sense, but only after some complicated mental *acrobatics*.

ac·ro·nym /ˈækrəˌnɪm/ *noun, pl* **-nyms** [*count*] : a word formed from the first letters of each one of the words in a phrase ▪ The North Atlantic Treaty Organization is known by the *acronym* "NATO."

¹**across** /əˈkʰrɑːs/ *prep*
1 a : from one side to the other side of (something) ▪ We took a ferry *across* the river. ▪ We saw them walking *across* the street. ▪ She reached *across* the table to shake his hand. ▪ They traveled back and forth *across* the border. ▪ Airplanes flew *across* the sky above us. ▪ She slapped him right *across* the face. [=she slapped his face] **b** : on the other side of (something) ▪ He was seated *across* the table from me. ▪ Our grandparents live *across* the street (from us). ▪ The accident happened just *across* the state line.
2 : so as to reach or spread over or throughout (something) ▪ A smile spread *across* her face. ▪ Looking out *across* the ocean, he saw land. ▪ The sun's light spread *across* the mountains. ▪ The disease spread quickly *across* the country.
3 : in every part of (a country, region, etc.) ▪ The movie is now showing in theaters *across* [=*throughout*] America. ▪ Newspapers (all) *across* the world reported the story. ▪ We could hear the bells all *across* town.

²**across** *adv*
1 : from one side to the other ▪ The streams are small enough to jump *across*. ▪ They walked *across* to the other side of the street. ▪ They reached *across* and shook each other's hand.
2 : in a measurement from one side to the other side ▪ At its widest point, the pond measures 150 feet *across*. ▪ The hole was 10 feet *across*. [=10 feet wide]
3 : on the opposite side ▪ I saw them crossing the street and I waited until they were safely *across*.
across from : on the opposite side from (someone or something) ▪ She sat (directly) *across from* me at the table. ▪ The restaurant is (just) *across from* the high school.

across–the–board *adj, always used before a noun* : affecting everyone or everything in a group ▪ *across-the-board* price increases ▪ an *across-the-board* tax cut — see also *across the board* at ¹BOARD

acryl·ic /əˈkrɪlɪk/ *noun, pl* **-ics**
1 [*noncount*] : a material that is made from a chemical process and that is used for making many different products (such as clothing and paints) — often used before another noun ▪ *acrylic* fabrics ▪ *acrylic* paint
2 ***acrylics*** [*plural*] : paints that contain an acrylic substance and that are used by artists ▪ a painting done in *acrylics*

¹**act** /ˈækt/ *noun, pl* **acts**
1 [*count*] : something that is done ▪ His first official *act* [=*action*] as President was to sign the bill. ▪ We were grateful for her many *acts* of kindness. ▪ an *act* of bravery = a brave *act* ▪ criminal/illegal/unlawful/wrongful *acts* — see also SEX ACT
✧ An ***act of God*** is a natural event (such as a storm or earthquake) that cannot be controlled by people. ▪ The company cannot be held responsible in cases of bad weather or other *acts of God*.
2 [*count*] : a law made by a group of legislators ▪ The program was created by (an) *act* of Congress/Parliament. ▪ legislative *acts* ▪ the Civil Rights *Act* of 1964
3 [*count*] : one of the main divisions of a play or opera ▪ Please read *act* II, scene 1 of Shakespeare's *Romeo and Juliet*. ▪ In the first/opening *act*, two characters are talking in a restaurant. ▪ a play in three *acts* = a three-*act* play
4 [*count*] **a** : one of the performances in a show ▪ a circus/magic *act* **b** : a show that a person or group performs often ▪ He has a great stand-up/comedy *act*. [=*routine*] ▪ She took her *act* on the road. [=she traveled and performed her act in different places] **c** : a person or group that performs in shows ▪ a two-person comedy *act* from New York City ▪ The band was one of this summer's most successful live *acts*. ✧ A ***balancing act*** or ***juggling act*** is an attempt to do several different things or deal with several different situations at the same time. ▪ It's a difficult *balancing act*, but many students hold full-time jobs while attending school. ▪ Working and raising children can be a real *juggling act* for parents. — see also CLASS ACT, *a hard/tough act to follow* at FOLLOW
5 [*singular*] : a way of behaving that is not honest or sincere ▪ He said he was sorry, but I realize now that it was all just an *act*. ▪ He wasn't really sorry. He was just ***putting on an act***.
clean up your act see *clean up* at ²CLEAN
get into the act *or* ***get in on the act*** : to start to participate in an activity ▪ We started selling them last year, and now other stores are *getting into the act*. [=now other stores are also selling them]
get your act together see *get together* at GET
in the act (of doing something) : while doing something ▪ When they arrived, I was just *in the act* of starting to make dinner. ▪ He tried to rob a bank and was ***caught in the act***. = He was *caught in the act* of robbing a bank.

²**act** *verb* **acts**; **act·ed**; **act·ing**
1 [*no obj*] : to do something : to take action ▪ Think before you *act*. ▪ He knew he had to *act* quickly/fast. ▪ The government was slow to *act*. ▪ The firefighters *acted* with great courage. = They *acted* courageously. ▪ She *acted* on behalf of her father, who was not at the meeting. ▪ I believe that the killer *acted* alone. ▪ She had *acted* in self-defense when she killed

her attacker. • We were *acting* in the best interests of our children. • If he refuses to cooperate, he'll be *acting* against his own (best) interests. [=he'll be acting in a way that is harmful to himself] • We must *act* soon to end this crisis.

2 [*no obj*] **: to behave in a particular way** • She learned at an early age how to *act* properly in social situations. • People are always telling me how I should *act* and what I should say. • I noticed that the dog was *acting* funny/differently/strangely this morning. • *acting* more naturally/aggressively/responsibly • She's been *acting* kind of crazy lately. • Please learn the new rules and ***act accordingly.*** [=follow the new rules] ✧ To ***act the part*** is to behave the way that people in a particular role usually behave. • Now that he's rich he certainly *acts the part*. [=behaves like a rich person] ✧ To ***act your age*** is to behave the way that people your age should behave and not to behave like a younger person. • John, *act your age*. You're not a kid anymore. ✧ To ***act like*** a particular kind of person or thing is to behave the way that person or thing behaves. • You two are *acting like* children. • It's time you start *acting like* a man. • I'm sorry about yesterday. I *acted like* a fool/jerk. — see also ²ACT 3c (below)

3 a [*no obj*] **: to behave in a way that is not sincere or honest** • Stop *acting*. We know you're guilty. **b** [*linking verb*] **: to pretend to be something** • Stop *acting* innocent. • She was terribly nervous, but she *acted* confident. • I know you're bored, but can you at least try to *act* interested. • He did his best to *act* excited. • There she goes, offering advice and *acting* the expert. [=pretending to be an expert] • If anybody asks you where I am, ***act dumb.*** [=pretend that you do not know] **c** [*no obj*] **: to pretend that something is true — usually used in the phrases *act as if, act as though,* and (*chiefly US*) *act like*** • She *acted as if* nothing had happened. • We *acted as though* we knew what was going on. • I tried to *act like* it didn't bother me, but it did. • Even if you don't like your gift, you should *act like* you do. • I didn't *act like* it, but I really was happy. — see also *act like* at ²ACT 2 (above)

4 : to perform the words and actions of a character in a play, movie, etc. : to perform as an actor [*no obj*] It had always been his dream to *act*. • She can sing, dance, and *act*. • As a child, she began *acting* in television commercials. • Both actors have agreed to *act* in the movie. [+ *obj*] He'll be *acting* the part of Romeo in tonight's play. • The role of Romeo was wonderfully *acted* by Mr. Jacob Smith. • a beautifully *acted* movie [=a movie in which the acting is excellent]

5 [*no obj*] **: to do the work of a particular kind of person or thing : to perform a certain function or role — + *as*** • A young man *acted* [=*served*] *as* our guide through the city. • She'll be *acting as* her own attorney during the court trial. • She agreed to *act as* his secretary. • The trees *act as* a source of shade and protection from the wind.

6 [*no obj*] **: to make something happen : to have a particular effect** • The chemical *acts* [=*works*] by destroying the cells in the brain. — often + *on* • These medicines *act on* [=*affect*] the heart. — see also ACT ON/UPON (below)

act on/upon [*phrasal verb*] ***act on/upon (something)*** **: to use (something, such as a feeling or suggestion) as a reason or basis for doing something** • They never *acted on* the information they had. • We were too late to *act upon* his suggestion. • It's okay to feel angry or jealous, but you mustn't *act on* those feelings. — see also ²ACT 6 (above)

act out [*phrasal verb*] **1 a : to behave badly especially because you are feeling painful emotions (such as fear or anger)** • What can parents do when their kids start *acting out*? **b *act out (something) or act (something) out* : to show that you are feeling (a painful emotion) by acting in ways that are not good or acceptable** • children *acting out* their emotions in inappropriate ways • He tries not to *act out* his anger/frustrations. **2 *act out (something) or act (something) out* a : to perform (a play, a character in a movie, etc.)** • plays *acted out* on stage • She skillfully *acted out* the role of a young queen. **b : to do and say the things that happen in (a movie, past event, etc.)** • At their last party, they *acted out* [=*reenacted*] scenes from old movies. • The children were *acting out* what they saw on television. • adults *acting out* their childhood dreams/fantasies [=doing the things they wanted to do when they were children]

act the fool see ¹FOOL

act up [*phrasal verb*] **1 : to behave badly : to act in a way that is not polite or acceptable** • The kids are *acting up* [=*misbehaving*] again. • The book gives advice to parents whose children *act up*. **2** *of a machine* **: to not work properly** • The camera started *acting up* [=*malfunctioning*] after I dropped it. **3** *of a disease* **: to become worse and to start causing pain or physical problems** • His asthma *acts up* when it's cold outside. • Whenever it rains, my arthritis starts *acting up*.

ACT *abbr* **American College Test** ✧ **The *ACT* is a test that some U.S. students take as a part of applying to colleges.**

¹act·ing /ˈæktɪŋ/ *adj, always used before a noun* **: performing a job for a short time : holding a temporary position** • The college's *acting* president will be replaced with a permanent one next fall.

²acting *noun* [*noncount*] **: the art or profession of performing the role of a character in a play, movie, etc. : the art or profession of an actor** • *Acting* is my life! • Her *acting* is unusually good in this film. • a new style of *acting* **— often used before another noun** • She's been taking *acting* classes. • his successful *acting* career

ac·tion /ˈækʃən/ *noun, pl* **-tions**

1 [*count*] **: something that a person or group does** • As its first official *action* [=*act*], the committee elected Ms. Jones as its president. • He was critical of the government's *actions* before the war. • a military *action* against another country • criminal/illegal *actions* • She tried to explain/defend/justify her *actions*. • I accept full responsibility for my *actions*. **— often used with *take*** • The school has been asked to *take* certain *actions* to fix the problem. • This is just one of the many *actions* that they could have *taken*. ✧ **The saying *actions speak louder than words* means that the things that you do are more important than the things that you say.** • They say they want peace, but *actions speak louder than words*.

2 [*noncount*] **: things done to achieve a particular purpose** • The situation demanded immediate *action*. • The problem may require military *action*. • The school took disciplinary *action* against the drunken students. • They decided that no further *action* was necessary. • We need to agree on a ***plan of action.*** [=need to agree on what we will be doing] • What's the best ***course of action***? [=what's the best way to proceed?] • The protesters criticized the administration's ***lack of action*** [=*inaction*] on many issues. **— often used with *take*** • We were ready to *take action*. [=to do something] • Because the company failed to *take action* [=failed to act], many people were hurt. • The company *took* no *action*. • The police are now *taking* appropriate *action*. • She's ***all talk and no action.*** [=she says that she will do things, but she does not do them] ✧ **A *man of action* or *woman of action* is a man or woman who works in an active way to do things.** • He was a scholar and thinker but was also a *man of action*. — see also AFFIRMATIVE ACTION, POLITICAL ACTION COMMITTEE

3 [*noncount*] **: fighting that happens in a war** • His unit first ***saw action*** [=fought in a battle] on June 20th. • soldiers who were killed or wounded ***in action*** [=*in battle*] • soldiers who are ***missing in action*** [=soldiers who cannot be found after a battle and might have been killed, captured, or wounded] — see also IN ACTION (below)

4 *the action* : the most exciting or interesting activities that are happening in a particular place • The new theater places the audience closer to the center/middle of *the action*. • I moved to New York City to be (a) part of *the action*. • Downtown is ***where the action is.*** [=downtown is a very active and exciting place]

5 [*noncount*] **a** *informal* **: a chance or opportunity to make money** • Do any of you guys want to ***get in on the action***? [=participate in a plan to make money] ✧ ***A piece of the action*** **or (*chiefly US*) *a cut of the action* or (*chiefly Brit*) *a slice of the action* is a portion or share of the money that can be earned from something.** • He saw that his friends were making money illegally, and he wanted to get *a piece of the action*. **b** *slang, sometimes offensive* **: sexual activity** • I met a girl who was ready for some *action*.

6 [*noncount*] **: the events that happen in a story, movie, etc.** • Most of the play's *action* takes place in a restaurant. • the *action* [=*plot*] of the novel

7 [*noncount*] **: events that happen quickly and that cause feelings of danger and excitement** • The movie is two hours of nonstop *action*. [=*excitement*] • We went out looking for *action*. • That's when the *action* really starts. **— often used before another noun** • *action* movies • the film's final *action* sequence — see also LIVE ACTION

8 — used as a director's command to start filming part of a movie or television show • Lights, camera, *action*!

9 *law* **: the process of having a court of law make a decision about an argument** [*count*] The court dismissed the *action*. [=*case, lawsuit*] • She brought/filed an *action* against the company for damages. • ***civil actions*** [=lawsuits about a person's rights] [*noncount*] They are threatening/considering

legal *action*. ▪ bringing/taking *action* against companies for damages — see also CLASS ACTION
10 [*noncount*] **: a process in which one thing causes a change in another thing** ▪ the *action* [=*effect*] of certain chemicals on the brain ▪ The medicine blocks the *action* of these proteins. [=it stops the proteins from working] ▪ The cave was formed by the *action* of an underground river.
11 : the way that something works or moves [*noncount*] Food is swallowed by the *action* of the tongue. ▪ the *action* of the heart ▪ the mechanical *action* of a pulley ▪ the drill's twisting *action* ▪ a single-*action* revolver [*singular*] The gears meshed with a smooth *action*.
in action **: in the act of doing something : performing a usual job or function** ▪ We came to the court to see our country's judicial system *in action*. [=*at work*] ▪ The fans have come to see their favorite players *in action*. ▪ After a two year break from baseball, he's finally ***back in action***. [=he's playing baseball again] — see also ACTION 3 (above)
into action **: to an active state** ▪ They had already put the plan *into action*. [=started using the plan] ▪ Firefighters are ready to ***leap/spring/swing into action*** [=quickly start working] at a moment's notice. ✧ **When people or things are *called into action*, they are asked to start working or doing a particular task.** ▪ As a doctor, she can be *called into action* at any time of the day. ▪ Our military unit was *called into action* at the start of the war.
out of action **: unable to perform a usual job or function : not in action** ▪ He broke his leg and the doctors say that he'll be *out of action* [=*out of commission*] for at least a month. ▪ His broken leg will ***put/keep him out of action*** for at least a month.

ac·tion·able /ˈækʃənəbəl/ *adj*
1 *law* **: giving a reason to bring an action or a lawsuit against someone** ▪ Firing people because of their age is *actionable*.
2 *chiefly US, formal* **: able to be used as a basis or reason for doing something** ▪ We've received *actionable* information that the men are hiding in these mountains.

action figure *noun, pl* ~ **-ures** [*count*] **: a small usually plastic doll** ✧ *Action figures* are made to look like superheroes, soldiers, robots, etc.

action–packed *adj* [*more* ~; *most* ~] **: filled with action, danger, and excitement** ▪ an *action-packed* adventure movie

action replay *noun, pl* ~ **-plays** [*count*] *Brit* **:** INSTANT REPLAY ▪ see the winning goal again in an *action replay*

action verb *noun, pl* ~ **verbs** [*count*] *grammar* **: a verb that expresses action** ▪ "Drive" in "We often drive past their house" and "think" in "Let's think about the problem" are both *action verbs*. — compare LINKING VERB

ac·ti·vate /ˈæktəˌveɪt/ *verb* **-vates; -vat·ed; -vat·ing** [+ *obj*]
1 : to make (something) active or more active: such as a : to cause (a device) to start working ▪ Touch the screen to *activate* the system. ▪ *activate* and then deactivate a mechanism ▪ A loud alarm was *activated* [=*set off*] when he opened the door. ▪ The camera is *activated* by pushing a button. ▪ The bomb was *activated* by remote control. **b** *chemistry* **: to cause (a chemical reaction or natural process) to begin** ▪ Sunlight *activates* a chemical reaction in the plant's leaves. ▪ vitamins that *activate* the growth of new cells
2 *chiefly US* **: to order (soldiers) to serve in a war** ▪ The President has *activated* the reserves. ▪ *activate* the troops ▪ Our military unit was *activated* [=*called into action*] soon after the start of the war.
– ac·ti·va·tion /ˌæktəˈveɪʃən/ *noun* [*noncount*]

ac·tive /ˈæktɪv/ *adj*
1 [*more* ~; *most* ~] **: doing things that require physical movement and energy** ▪ We stay/keep *active* during the cold winter months by skiing and ice skating. ▪ Despite her age, she has been able to maintain her *active* [=*busy*] lifestyle. ▪ Cats are most *active* [=*energetic, lively*] at night.
2 [*more* ~; *most* ~] **a : involved in the activities of a group or organization** ▪ We are *active* members of our church. ▪ While many give money to the organization, only a few are *active* participants. **: participating in an action or activity** ▪ She was politically *active* as a volunteer for her state representative. — often + *in* ▪ They were *active in* the antiwar movement of the 1960s. ▪ *active in* women's causes **b : involving action or participation** ▪ They take an *active* interest in their children's education. ▪ He has taken/played a more *active* role in the production of this album.
3 : marked by regular action or use ▪ the bank's *active* and inactive accounts ▪ He became ***sexually active*** [=he began having sex] at the age of 21.
4 *of a volcano* **: likely to explode violently or produce fire and hot liquid rock : capable of erupting** ▪ Most volcanoes on this island are still *active* but a few are inactive.
5 *of a disease* **: becoming worse or continuing to have bad effects** ▪ *active* tuberculosis ▪ The disease remains *active* throughout the patient's life.
6 : having a chemical effect especially on the body ▪ The medicine has two *active* ingredients. ▪ the *active* ingredient in/of marijuana
7 a *US* **: involving service in the military as a main job** ▪ After two years of ***active duty*** [=two years of being a full-time member of the military] she entered the reserves. ▪ She was ***on active duty*** for two years. **b : involving fighting in a war as a member of the military** ▪ He saw no ***active service*** [=he did not fight in any battles] during his time in the army. ▪ He was ***on active service*** in three separate wars. ▪ soldiers returning home from *active service*
8 *grammar* **a** *of a verb or voice* **: showing that the subject of a sentence is the one doing the action expressed by the verb** ▪ "Picked" in "I picked the apples" is an *active* verb because it shows that the subject "I" is the one who picked the apples. ▪ "Hits" in "She hits the ball" is *active*, while "hit" in "The ball was hit" is passive. ✧ **The *active voice* is a way of writing or speaking that uses active verbs.** ▪ The sentence "The birds are singing" is written in the *active voice*. — compare PASSIVE **b** *of a verb* **: expressing action rather than describing the state of something** ▪ Words like "walk," "sing," and "eat" are *active* verbs. ▪ In the sentence "Look at this picture," the verb "look" is *active*.
– ac·tive·ly *adv* ▪ They participate *actively* in their church. ▪ *actively* involved in a conversation

ac·tiv·ist /ˈæktɪvɪst/ *noun, pl* **-ists** [*count*] **: a person who uses or supports strong actions (such as public protests) to help make changes in politics or society** ▪ Antiwar *activists* were protesting in the streets. ▪ an environmental *activist* ▪ political *activists*
– ac·tiv·ism /ˈæktɪˌvɪzəm/ *noun* [*noncount*] ▪ political *activism*

ac·tiv·i·ty /ækˈtɪvəti/ *noun, pl* **-ties**
1 [*noncount*] **: the state of being active** ▪ The holidays always set off a lot of *activity* in our home. **: behavior or actions of a particular kind** ▪ the sexual *activity* of married couples ▪ The police are now monitoring criminal/gang/drug *activity* in the area. ▪ There has been an increase in the city's (level of) economic *activity*. ▪ She gets at least 30 minutes of physical *activity* every day. ▪ The instruments are used to detect volcanic *activity* on the island.
2 [*count*] **: something that is done as work or for a particular purpose — usually plural** ▪ Grandma needs help with her everyday/daily *activities*. ▪ business *activities* ▪ political *activities* ▪ They were accused of financing the group's illegal *activities*.
3 [*count*] **: something that is done for pleasure and that usually involves a group of people** ▪ We planned an *activity* for the children. **— usually plural** ▪ The camp offers hiking, swimming, and other recreational *activities*. ▪ social *activities*

ac·tor /ˈæktɚ/ *noun, pl* **-tors** [*count*] **: a person who acts in a play, movie, etc.**

> ***usage* Actor is often used to refer specifically to a man or boy who acts.** ▪ He's a talented *actor*, and his wife is a well-known actress. ***Actor* can also refer to a woman or girl, and many women now prefer this use.** ▪ His wife is also an *actor*. **The plural form *actors* is used for groups that include both men and women.** ▪ She and her husband are both talented *actors*.

ac·tress /ˈæktrəs/ *noun, pl* **-tress·es** [*count*] **: a woman or girl who acts in a play, movie, etc. : a female actor** ***usage*** see ACTOR

ac·tu·al /ˈæktʃəwəl/ *adj*
1 : real and not merely possible or imagined : existing in fact ▪ The movie is based on *actual* events. [=on events that really happened] ▪ They signed the agreement in the spring, but the *actual* sale wasn't made until that summer. ▪ You deposit money in a bank account but the *actual* money is not held there. ▪ He looks younger, but he is ***in actual fact*** almost 60 years old. [=he is actually almost 60 years old]
2 : known to be correct or precise : not false or apparent ▪ The woman's *actual* [=*exact*] age is unknown. ▪ The *actual* cost of the repair was much higher than the estimate.
3 — used for emphasis ▪ This is the *actual* [=*very*] room in which my grandfather was born.

ac·tu·al·i·ty /ˌæktʃəˈwæləti/ *noun, pl* **-ties**

A

1 [*noncount*] : the quality or state of being actual or real ▪ It was hard to accept the *actuality* [=*reality*] of the disease.
2 [*count*] : something that is actual or real ▪ the *actualities* [=*realities*] of war ▪ The *actuality* was quite different from the theory.
in actuality : in truth — used to stress that something is true when it is different from what was believed or expected ▪ He gave me what turned out to be, *in actuality* [=*in reality, in fact*], only a copy of the original. ▪ I thought they just arrived, but *in actuality* they'd been here for an hour.

ac·tu·al·ly /ˈækʧəwəli/ *adv*
1 — used to refer to what is true or real ▪ I don't know what *actually* [=*really*] happened. ▪ After all these months, it's hard to believe that we're *actually* [=*really, truly*] finished.
2 — used to stress that a statement is true especially when it differs in some way from what might have been thought or expected ▪ We'd *actually* planned to leave early, but we were delayed. ▪ I wasn't worried about being late. *Actually*, I didn't want to go at all. ▪ I didn't think I'd like the movie, but it was *actually* pretty good. ▪ I was shocked to learn he could *actually* fly a plane. ▪ I could hardly believe it when she *actually* apologized to me. ▪ "I like your new glasses." "Thanks, but *actually* I've had them for almost a year."

ac·tu·ary /ˈækʧəˌweri, *Brit* ˈækʧuəri/ *noun, pl* **-ar·ies** [*count*] : a person whose job is to tell insurance companies how much they should charge people for insurance based on risks
– **ac·tu·ar·i·al** /ˌækʧəˈwerijəl/ *adj* ▪ *actuarial* calculations

ac·tu·ate /ˈækʧəˌweɪt/ *verb* **-ates; -at·ed; -at·ing** [+ *obj*]
1 *technical* : to make (a machine or electrical device) move or operate ▪ The pump is *actuated* by the windmill.
2 *formal* : to cause someone to do something or to act in a certain way — usually used as *(be) actuated* ▪ He had *been actuated* [=*motivated*] by greed when he made his decision. = His decision had *been actuated* by greed.

acu·ity /əˈkju:wəti/ *noun* [*noncount*] *formal* : the ability to see, hear, or understand something easily ▪ mental/visual/political *acuity* [=*acuteness*] ▪ her *acuity* [=*keenness, sharpness*] of perception

acu·men /əˈkju:mən/ *noun* [*noncount*] : the ability to think clearly and make good decisions ▪ Her political *acumen* won her the election. ▪ a lack of business/financial *acumen*

acu·pres·sure /ˈækjəˌprɛʃɚ/ *noun* [*noncount*] : a method of relieving pain or curing illness by pressing on particular points on a person's body with the fingertips or thumbs — compare ACUPUNCTURE

acu·punc·ture /ˈækjəˌpʌŋkʧɚ/ *noun* [*noncount*] : a method of relieving pain or curing illness by placing needles into a person's skin at particular points on the body — compare ACUPRESSURE
– **acu·punc·tur·ist** /ˈækjəˌpʌŋkʧərɪst/ *noun, pl* **-ists** [*count*]

acute /əˈkju:t/ *adj* **acut·er; -est** [*or more* ~; *most* ~]
1 : very serious or dangerous : requiring serious attention or action ▪ an *acute* [=*critical, severe*] fuel shortage ▪ an *acute* crisis ▪ the *acute* phase [=the most important and dangerous phase] of the struggle for independence
2 *usually used before a noun* : having or showing an ability to think clearly and to understand what is not obvious or simple about something ▪ an *acute* observation/understanding ▪ an *acute* observer ▪ an *acute* sense of humor ▪ It's a politically *acute* film that does not oversimplify the issues.
3 : very strong and sensitive : highly developed ▪ *acute* [=*keen*] hearing/vision ▪ *acute* awareness
4 : strongly felt or experienced ▪ *acute* distress/embarrassment
5 *medical* **a** : very sharp and severe ▪ *acute* pain/infection ▪ *acute* symptoms **b** : becoming very severe very quickly ▪ an *acute* disease ✧ A hospital or doctor who specializes in ***acute care*** works with patients who have diseases or problems that require immediate care. ▪ an *acute care* hospital — compare CHRONIC
6 *mathematics* : ending in a sharp point : measuring less than 90 degrees ▪ an *acute* angle — compare OBTUSE
7 *of an accent mark* : having the form ´ ▪ The word "café" is written with an *acute* accent over the "e." — compare ²GRAVE 3
– **acute·ly** *adv* ▪ I am *acutely* aware of these problems. ▪ The patient was *acutely* ill. – **acute·ness** *noun* [*noncount*] ▪ the *acuteness* of the fuel shortage

ad /ˈæd/ *noun, pl* **ads** [*count*] : ADVERTISEMENT ▪ I saw your *ad* in the newspaper. ▪ radio/television *ads* ▪ (*chiefly US*) She works for an ***ad agency*** [=*advertising agency*] in New York. — see also WANT AD

AD *or chiefly US* **A.D.** *abbr* — used to refer to the years since the birth of Christ ▪ 550 *A.D.* = *A.D.* 550 ▪ the first century *A.D.* ▪ in the year 823 *A.D.* ✧ *A.D.* stands for the Latin phrase *anno Domini*, which means "in the year of the Lord." — compare B.C., B.C.E., C.E.

ad·age /ˈædɪʤ/ *noun, pl* **-ag·es** [*count*] : an old and well-known saying that expresses a general truth ▪ My mother always used to remind us of the (old) *adage*, "If you can't say something nice, don't say anything at all."

¹**ada·gio** /əˈdɑ:ʤijoʊ/ *adv* : in a slow manner : SLOWLY — used as a direction in music
– **adagio** *adj*

²**adagio** *noun, pl* **-gios** [*count*] : a piece of music that is played or performed slowly and gracefully

Ad·am /ˈædəm/ *noun*
not know (someone) from Adam see ¹KNOW

ad·a·mant /ˈædəmənt/ *adj* [*more* ~; *most* ~] : not willing to change an opinion or decision : very determined ▪ She is an *adamant* [=*strong*] defender of women's rights. ▪ We've tried to talk him into coming with us, but he's *adamant* about staying here. ▪ an *adamant* refusal
– **adamance** *or* **adamancy** *noun* [*noncount*] ▪ the *adamancy* of her refusal – **ad·a·mant·ly** *adv* ▪ He's *adamantly* opposed to coming with us.

Adam's apple *noun, pl* ~ **apples** [*count*] : the lump that sticks out in the front of a person's neck, that is usually larger in men than in women, and that moves when a person talks or swallows

adapt /əˈdæpt/ *verb* **adapts; adapt·ed; adapt·ing**
1 : to change your behavior so that it is easier to live in a particular place or situation [*no obj*] When children go to a different school, it usually takes them a while to *adapt*. — usually + *to* ▪ These fish all *adapt* easily *to* colder water. ▪ She has *adapted to* college life quite easily. [+ *obj*] She has ***adapted herself to*** college life quite easily.
2 [+ *obj*] : to change (something) so that it functions better or is better suited for a purpose ▪ The teachers *adapted* [=*modified*] the curriculum so that students of all abilities will benefit from it. ▪ The camera has been *adapted* for underwater use. ▪ The clock was *adapted* to run on batteries.
3 [+ *obj*] : to change (a movie, book, play, etc.) so that it can be presented in another form ▪ He *adapted* the novel for the stage. [=he rewrote the novel as a play] ▪ The movie was *adapted* from the book of the same title. ▪ *adapting* the movie for television

adapt·able /əˈdæptəbəl/ *adj* [*more* ~; *most* ~] : able to change or be changed in order to fit or work better in some situation or for some purpose : able to adapt or be adapted ▪ an *adaptable* tool that combines a screwdriver, a corkscrew, and pliers ▪ very *adaptable* animals — often + *to* ▪ These plants are all easily *adaptable to* colder climates. ▪ The computer program is *adaptable to* the needs of individual users.
– **adapt·abil·i·ty** /əˌdæptəˈbɪləti/ *noun* [*noncount*]

ad·ap·ta·tion /ˌæˌdæpˈteɪʃən/ *noun, pl* **-tions**
1 [*count*] : something that is adapted; *especially* : a movie, book, play, etc., that is changed so that it can be presented in another form ▪ His stage *adaptation* of the novel was a success. ▪ The film is an *adaptation* of a book of the same title.
2 [*count*] : a change in a plant or animal that makes it better able to live in a particular place or situation ▪ The insect's evolutionary *adaptations* enable it to be almost invisible even when sitting in the middle of a leaf.
3 [*noncount*] : the process of changing to fit some purpose or situation : the process of adapting ▪ a tool designed for easy *adaptation*

adapt·er *also* **adap·tor** /əˈdæptɚ/ *noun, pl* **adapters** *also* **adaptors** [*count*] : a device that is used to connect two pieces of equipment that were not designed to be connected

add /ˈæd/ *verb* **adds; add·ed; add·ing**
1 [+ *obj*] **a** : to put (something) with another thing or group of things ▪ She's planning to *add* some new flowers to the garden. ▪ The company is *adding* over 200 jobs this year. ▪ This winter, he *added* skiing to his list of favorite sports. **b** : to mix or combine (an ingredient) with other ingredients ▪ *Add* (in) a little more salt and pepper. ▪ I *added* (in) just a dash/pinch of flour. ▪ *Add* one cup of sugar to the mixture. ▪ Next, *add* the remaining butter to the pan. **c** : to include (something) with something else ▪ It took us four hours to get there, if you *add* (in) the time we stopped to eat.
2 [+ *obj*] : to cause something to have (a usually good quality

A

or characteristic) • In this dish, fresh herbs *add* lots of color and flavor. • As an employee, she will *add* [=*bring*] great value to your company. • We can help you *add* excitement to your vacation. • The historical details *add* depth/richness/weight to his story. • She *adds* a certain amount of experience and authority to the project.

3 : to put (two or more numbers or amounts) together to find a total or sum [+ *obj*] When you *add* three and/to seven, you get ten. • *Add* these three numbers together. [*no obj*] schoolchildren learning how to *add* [=to perform addition] and subtract — **opposite** SUBTRACT

4 [+ *obj*] **: to say or write (something more or extra)** • That's all I have to say. Do you have anything (else/more) to *add*? = Is there anything (else/more) you would like to *add*? • "They all went to the bar," he said. "But I didn't go with them," he quickly *added*. • He was quick to *add* that he didn't go with them. = He ***hastened to add*** that he didn't go with them. • It was a long project and, ***I might add***, an expensive one.

add insult to injury see [2]INSULT

add on [*phrasal verb*] ***add (something) on*** or ***add on (something)*** **: to put (something) with another thing or group of things** • We're going to *add on* a new garage. — **often + to** • We're *adding* a new garage *on to* our house. • They're *adding* $200 *on to* what we already have to pay. ✧ **The phrase** *add on to* **is also written as** *add onto*. • We're *adding* a new garage *onto* our house.

add to [*phrasal verb*] ***add to (something)*** **: to make (something) larger, better, or greater** • He bought another rare coin to *add to* his collection. • Her research has greatly *added to* our knowledge of the subject. • She's been able to *add to* her savings [=to save more money] this year. • This movie will *add to* his fame. [=it will make him more famous] • The loud music *added to* the confusion. [=it made the confusion greater] • We hope this *adds to* your enjoyment of the play. • The funny characters really *add to* the story. [=they make the story better] ✧ **Phrases like** ***add to this/that*** **and** ***added to this/that*** **are often used informally to introduce a statement about something that makes a thing or situation better, worse, more important, etc.** • We were given little time to finish. *Add to this* the fact that nobody helped us, and you can understand why we were angry. • We were short of money. *Added to that*, we were lost!

add up [*phrasal verb*] **1 a : to be added together and equal the expected or correct total — usually used in negative constructions** • The numbers just don't *add up*. [=they don't equal the expected total] **b : to make sense : to seem to be logical or true** • They must be lying; their story just doesn't *add up*. **c : to slowly increase and become a large number or amount** • A cup of coffee may only cost a dollar, but those dollars *add up* quickly. • I'm saving a little money each month. Eventually it'll *add up*. • The hours that I spend traveling to work really *add up*. **2 *add (something) up*** or ***add up (something)*** **: to put together or count (the number or amount of something) to find the total** • Start by *adding up* how much money you have, and then *add up* your costs. • Let's *add up* all of the money we saved. • When you *add* it all *up*, he's spent over half of his life in jail. **3 *add up to (something)* a : to have (a number) as a total** • The amount of money she spends on coffee *adds up* to $2.75 a day. • That *adds up to* more than a thousand dollars a year. **b : to produce (a specified result)** • These plans should *add up to* a very exciting vacation. • With these three bands playing together, it all *adds up to* one of the year's best rock concerts. • All of the team's hard work didn't *add up to* a win.

– added *adj* • The historical details provide *added* [=*additional*] depth/richness/weight to his story. • *added* value • an *added* attraction/advantage

ADD *abbr* **attention deficit disorder**

ad·den·dum /əˈdɛndəm/ *noun, pl* **-den·da** /-ˈdɛndə/ *or* **-den·dums** [*count*] **: something that is added; *especially* : a section of a book that is added to the main or original text** • The letters are included as an *addendum* to the biography.

ad·der /ˈædɚ/ *noun, pl* **-ders** [*count*] **: a poisonous snake found in Europe**

ad·dict /ˈædɪkt/ *noun, pl* **-dicts** [*count*]

1 : a person who is not able to stop taking drugs : a person who is addicted to drugs • The clinic provides counseling for (drug) *addicts*. • a heroin/cocaine/crack *addict*

2 *informal* **: a person who likes or enjoys something very much and spends a large amount of time doing it, watching it, etc.** • a television *addict* [=*junkie*] • basketball *addicts*

ad·dict·ed /əˈdɪktəd/ *adj* [*more ~; most ~*] **: having an addiction: such as a : unable to stop using a harmful substance (such as a drug) — usually + to** • He's *addicted to* heroin/nicotine. **b : unable to stop doing something that is harmful** • a severely *addicted* smoker — **usually + to** • He's *addicted to* smoking. **c : having an unusually great interest in something or a need to do or have something — usually + to** • He's *addicted to* (playing/watching) basketball. • She's *addicted to* television.

ad·dic·tion /əˈdɪkʃən/ *noun, pl* **-tions**

1 : a strong and harmful need to regularly have something (such as a drug) or do something (such as gamble) [*count*] He has a drug *addiction*. — **often + to** • an *addiction to* pain medication • an *addiction to* playing the lottery [*noncount*] His life has been ruined by heroin *addiction*.

2 [*count*] **: an unusually great interest in something or a need to do or have something** • He devotes his summers to his surfing *addiction*. — **often + to** • She has an *addiction to* mystery novels.

ad·dic·tive /əˈdɪktɪv/ *adj* [*more ~; most ~*] **: causing addiction: such as a : causing a strong and harmful need to regularly have or do something** • highly *addictive* drugs like crack and heroin **b : very enjoyable in a way that makes you want to do or have something again** • the *addictive* thrill of surfing • These candies are *addictive*.

ad·di·tion /əˈdɪʃən/ *noun, pl* **-tions**

1 [*noncount*] **: the act or process of joining something to something else : the act or process of adding something — often + of** • The soup was thickened by the *addition of* cream in the last stage of cooking. • The town welcomed the *addition of* three new computers to the library.

2 [*noncount*] *mathematics* **: the act or process of adding numbers** • The children learned *addition* and subtraction.

3 [*count*] **: something or someone more that is included : something or someone that is added** • The museum's collection includes several new *additions*. — **usually + to** • an *addition to* the family [=a new member of the family, such as a newborn baby] • The sculpture is the newest *addition to* the museum's collection.

4 [*count*] *US* **: a part of a building that is built after the original part has been completed** • The *addition* expands the kitchen and adds a second bathroom.

in addition **: as something more — used for adding information to a statement** • The city has the largest population in the country and *in addition* [=*also, additionally*] is a major shipping port. • Sandwiches were served, and several salads *in addition*.

in addition to **: along with or together with (something or someone)** • *In addition to* soup, several salads were served. • There were six people at the meeting *in addition to* me.

ad·di·tion·al /əˈdɪʃənl/ *adj* **: more than is usual or expected** • Larger windows will require *additional* work, but the *additional* light they will provide may be worth the extra trouble. • There's an *additional* [=*extra*] fee/charge for returning the car a day late. • The memory on this computer has the *additional* [=*added*] advantage of being expandable.

– ad·di·tion·al·ly /əˈdɪʃənli/ *adv* • The restaurant has a large menu; *additionally* [=*in addition*], there are several special dishes that are prepared each day.

ad·di·tive /ˈædətɪv/ *noun, pl* **-tives** [*count*] **: something (such as a chemical) that is added in small amounts to a substance to improve it in some way** • a gasoline *additive* to reduce pollution • food *additives*

ad·dle /ˈædl/ *verb* **ad·dles; ad·dled; ad·dling** [+ *obj*] **: to make (someone's mind or brain) unable to think clearly** • It's a dangerous poison that's strong enough to *addle* the brain. • Their brains were *addled* with/by fear/drugs.

– addled *adj* • I needed a moment to clear my *addled* [=*confused*] brain/mind. • an *addled* old man

add–on /ˈædˌɑːn/ *noun, pl* **-ons** [*count*] **: an extra part or device that can be added to something else to improve it** • He has all the latest *add-ons* for his computer. • I knew the base price for the car, but with the *add-ons* I wanted, the final price was quite a bit higher. — **often used before another noun** • *add-on* components • *add-on* equipment

[1]**ad·dress** /əˈdrɛs/ *verb* **-dress·es; -dressed; -dress·ing** [+ *obj*]

1 : to write on an envelope, package, letter, etc., the name and address of the person or business it is being sent to • I've *addressed* the letter, but it still needs a stamp. • The package is sealed; it just needs to be *addressed*. • We spent the afternoon *addressing* invitations to all our friends. • The letter was

A

returned because it had been *addressed* incorrectly.
2 a : to speak to (a person or group) ▪ She ignored most of the people at the table, *addressing* only the man who was sitting next to her. ▪ One of the characters *addresses* the audience directly throughout the play. **b :** to use a specified name or title when speaking or writing to (someone) — *+ as* ▪ As children, we *addressed* him *as* "sir" [=we called him "sir"] even though he was only a few years older than us. ▪ You should *address* the queen *as* "Your Majesty." **c :** to direct (spoken or written words) *to* someone ▪ She *addressed* her comments *to* the man [=she spoke to the man] who was sitting next to her. ▪ Most of the speaker's remarks were *addressed to* those with experience in the industry.
3 : to give a formal speech to (a group of people) ▪ Before the awards were given, the mayor *addressed* the crowd.
4 *formal* **:** to give attention to (something) **:** to deal with (a matter, issue, problem, etc.) ▪ We're all curious about how the mayor plans to *address* the issue. ▪ Air pollution is one of the many problems being *addressed* by the scientists at the conference. ▪ The principal held a meeting to *address* the students' concerns. ✧ If you ***address yourself to*** an issue or problem you give your attention to it. ▪ The governor is *addressing himself to* the problem of underfunded schools.

²ad·dress /əˈdrɛs, ˈæˌdrɛs/ *noun, pl* **-dress·es** [*count*]
1 a : the words and numbers that are used to describe the location of a building and that are written on letters, envelopes, and packages so that they can be mailed to that location ▪ Write your name, *address*, and phone number in the spaces provided. ▪ Our *address* [=the address of our home] is 82 Third Street. ▪ Please deliver the package to my work *address*. [=the address of the building where I work] ▪ I forgot to put the ***return address***[=the address of the person sending the letter] on the envelope. — see picture at MAIL **b :** the letters, numbers, and symbols that are used to direct an e-mail message or to show the location of a site on the Internet ▪ an e-mail *address* ▪ a Web *address*
2 : a formal speech ▪ We listened to the President's inaugural *address* on the radio. ▪ She was asked to give/deliver a formal *address* at the ceremony. — see also KEYNOTE ADDRESS, PUBLIC ADDRESS SYSTEM
form/term of address **:** a word, name, or title that is used when speaking or writing to someone ▪ "Honey" is an affectionate *term of address* in U.S. English.

address book *noun, pl* **~ books** [*count*]
1 : a small book in which you write the names, addresses, and telephone numbers of people you know
2 : a place on a computer or other device for storing e-mail addresses, phone numbers, etc.

ad·dress·ee /ˌæˌdrɛˈsiː/ *noun, pl* **-ees** [*count*] **:** the person to whom mail is addressed ▪ The *addressee* no longer lives here, so I've returned the letter to the post office.

ad·duce /əˈduːs, *Brit* əˈdjuːs/ *verb* **-duc·es; -duced; -duc·ing** [*+ obj*] *formal* **:** to mention or provide (something, such as a fact or example) as evidence or proof to support an argument ▪ The evidence the author has *adduced* [=*put forth*] is rather weak.

ad·e·noids /ˈædəˌnɔɪdz/ *noun* [*plural*] **:** a mass of tissue in the back of the throat that can become swollen and make it difficult to breathe
— ad·e·noi·dal /ˌædəˈnɔɪdl/ *adj* ▪ an *adenoidal* voice [=a nasal voice, a voice that sounds odd or unattractive because it seems to be spoken through the nose]

¹adept /əˈdɛpt/ *adj* [*more ~; most ~*] **:** very good at doing something that is not easy ▪ He's *adept* in several languages. ▪ politically *adept* — usually *+ at* ▪ She's *adept at* fixing flaws in the system. ▪ He was *adept at* (using) computers.
— adept·ly *adv* ▪ He switched *adeptly* between English and Italian. **— adept·ness** *noun* [*noncount*] ▪ her *adeptness* at fixing flaws

²ad·ept /ˈæˌdɛpt/ *noun, pl* **-epts** [*count*] **:** a highly skilled or well-trained person **:** someone who is adept at something ▪ a computer *adept* ▪ an *adept* at chess

ad·e·quate /ˈædɪkwət/ *adj* [*more ~; most ~*]
1 : enough for some need or requirement ▪ Be sure to allow *adequate* [=*sufficient, enough*] time for the paint to dry. ▪ The garden hasn't been getting *adequate* water. ▪ The food was ***more than adequate***for the six of us.
2 : good enough **:** of a quality that is good or acceptable ▪ Millions of people lack *adequate* [=*sufficient*] health care. ▪ The school lunch should be *adequate* to meet the nutritional needs of growing children. ▪ The machine does an *adequate* job. ▪ The tent should provide *adequate* protection from the elements. ▪ The quality of his work was perfectly *adequate*. **:** of a quality that is acceptable but not better than acceptable ▪ Your grades are *adequate* but I think you can do better. ▪ The quality of his work was only/merely/barely *adequate*. — opposite INADEQUATE
— ad·e·qua·cy /ˈædɪkwəsi/ *noun* [*noncount*] ▪ Environmentalists doubt the *adequacy* of the regulations. [=doubt that the regulations are adequate] **— ad·e·quate·ly** *adv* ▪ Are you *adequately* prepared for the exam?

ad·here /ædˈhiɚ/ *verb* **-heres; -hered; -her·ing** [*no obj*] **:** to stick to something **:** to attach firmly to something ▪ The stamp failed to *adhere*. — usually *+ to* ▪ The stamp failed to *adhere to* the envelope. ▪ The mud *adhered to* his shoes.
adhere to [*phrasal verb*] ***adhere to (something)*** **:** to act in the way that is required by (something, such as a rule, belief, or promise) ▪ They will *adhere to* the terms of the contract. ▪ Certain standards must be *adhered to* by all members. ▪ She *adheres to* [=*follows*] a strict vegetarian diet.

ad·her·ence /ædˈhirəns/ *noun* [*noncount*] **:** the act of adhering; *especially* **:** the act of doing what is required by a rule, belief, etc. — usually *+ to* ▪ The school requires *adherence to* a strict dress code. ▪ *adherence to* religious laws — compare ADHESION

ad·her·ent /ædˈhirənt/ *noun, pl* **-ents** [*count*] **:** a person who is loyal to a leader, group, or religion ▪ *adherents* of Islam/Judaism/Buddhism ▪ one of Freud's *adherents* [=someone who agrees with Freud's theories] **:** a person who adheres to or supports a system or set of principles ▪ an *adherent* of free trade

ad·he·sion /ædˈhiːʒən/ *noun, pl* **-sions**
1 [*noncount*] **:** the act of adhering; *especially* **:** the act of sticking or attaching to something ▪ the *adhesion* of the coating ▪ the *adhesion* of the mud to my shoes — compare ADHERENCE
2 [*count*] *medical* **:** a condition in which body tissues that are supposed to be separate grow together because of swelling after surgery ▪ postoperative *adhesions*

¹ad·he·sive /ædˈhiːsɪv/ *adj* [*more ~; most ~*] **:** designed to stick to something ▪ Cover the cut with an *adhesive* bandage. ▪ *adhesive* tape

²adhesive *noun, pl* **-sives** [*count*] **:** a substance (such as glue or cement) that is used to make things stick together ▪ You'll need a strong *adhesive* to attach the boards.

ad hoc /ˈædˈhɑːk/ *adj*
1 : formed or used for a special purpose ▪ The mayor appointed an ***ad hoc committee***to study the project.
2 : made or done without planning because of an immediate need ▪ We had to make some *ad hoc* changes to the plans. ▪ We'll hire more staff on an *ad hoc* basis.
— ad hoc *adv* ▪ The decisions were made *ad hoc*.

¹adieu /əˈduː, əˈdjuː/ *interj, formal + literary* **:** goodbye or farewell ▪ *Adieu*, my friends.

²adieu *noun, pl* **adieus** *or* **adieux** /əˈduː, əˈdjuː/ [*count*] *formal + literary* **:** an expression of good wishes when someone leaves **:** FAREWELL ▪ She bid/wished me *adieu*.

ad in·fi·ni·tum /ˌædˌɪnfəˈnaɪtəm/ *adv* **:** without an end or limit **:** FOREVER ▪ We don't have to debate the issue *ad infinitum*, do we? ✧ *Ad infinitum* is a Latin phrase that means "to infinity."

adi·os /ˌɑːdiˈoʊs, *Brit* ˌædiˈɒs/ *interj, US, informal* **:** GOODBYE ▪ *Adios*! We'll see you tomorrow.

adj *abbr* adjective

ad·ja·cent /əˈʤeɪsn̩t/ *adj* **:** close or near **:** sharing a border, wall, or point ▪ The other group is meeting in the *adjacent* room. [=the room that is next to this room] ▪ Their property and our property are *adjacent*. [=are next to each other] ▪ The dialect is spoken in New York City and *adjacent* [=*nearby*] areas. — often *+ to* ▪ We're meeting in the room *adjacent to* [=*next to*] this one. ▪ Their property and our property are *adjacent to* each other.

ad·jec·tive /ˈæʤɪktɪv/ *noun, pl* **-tives** [*count*] **:** a word that describes a noun or a pronoun ▪ The words *blue* in "the blue car," *deep* in "the water is deep," and *tired* in "I'm very tired" are *adjectives*. — abbr. *adj*
— ad·jec·ti·val /ˌæʤɪkˈtaɪvəl/ *adj* ▪ an *adjectival* phrase
— ad·jec·ti·val·ly *adv* ▪ Use the word *adjectivally*.

ad·join /əˈʤoɪn/ *verb* **-joins; -joined -join·ing** *of a building, room, area of land, etc.* **:** to be next to or joined with something [*+ obj*]Her office *adjoins* the library. ▪ The two rooms *adjoin* each other. [*no obj*]The two rooms *adjoin*.
— adjoining *adj* ▪ We reserved *adjoining* rooms at the hotel.

ad·journ /əˈʤɚn/ *verb* **-journs; -journed; -journ·ing :** to end something (such as a meeting or session) for a period of time [+ *obj*] The chairperson has *adjourned* the meeting. • Court is *adjourned* until 10:00 tomorrow. • This meeting is *adjourned.* [*no obj*] The meeting *adjourned* at 4:00. • Congress will not *adjourn* until the budget has been completed.

adjourn to [*phrasal verb*] ***adjourn to (a place)*** **:** to leave one place and go to (another place) after the end of a meeting, discussion, etc. • After the ceremony, we *adjourned to* the garden where lunch was served. — often used humorously • Are we done here? Good, let's *adjourn to* the bar.

– ad•journ•ment /əˈʤənmənt/ *noun, pl* **-ments** [*count*] a six-hour meeting with only two brief *adjournments* [*noncount*] The *adjournment* of Congress will be delayed until the budget is complete.

ad•judge /əˈʤʌʤ/ *verb* **-judg•es; -judged; -judg•ing** [+ *obj*] *formal* **:** to consider or judge (something) in a specified way • The critics have *adjudged* [=(more commonly) *deemed, judged*] the play a success. • The court *adjudged* the contract to be fraudulent.

ad•ju•di•cate /əˈʤuːdɪˌkeɪt/ *verb* **-cates; -cat•ed; -cat•ing** *formal* **:** to make an official decision about who is right in a dispute [+ *obj*] The board will *adjudicate* claims made against teachers. • The case was *adjudicated* in the state courts. [*no obj*] The board will *adjudicate* when claims are made against teachers.

– ad•ju•di•ca•tion /əˌʤuːdɪˈkeɪʃən/ *noun* [*noncount*] • the process of *adjudication* • The case is under *adjudication.* **– ad•ju•di•ca•tor** /əˈʤuːdɪˌkeɪtɚ/ *noun, pl* **-tors** [*count*]

[1]ad•junct /ˈæˌʤʌŋkt/ *noun, pl* **-juncts** [*count*]

1 : something that is joined or added to another thing but is not an essential part of it • Massage therapy can be used as an *adjunct* along with the medication. — usually + *to* • The Web site is designed as an *adjunct to* the book.

2 *grammar* **:** a word or phrase (such as an adverb or prepositional phrase) that provides added information about the meaning of a verb in a sentence by expressing a relation of time, place, manner, etc. • In "They ate heartily," the word *heartily* is an *adjunct* and in "We left at noon," the phrase *at noon* is an *adjunct.*

[2]adjunct *adj, always used before a noun*

1 : added or joined in order to be used with something • massage therapy as an *adjunct* treatment

2 : added to a teaching staff for only a short time or in a lower position than other staff • *adjunct* faculty • an *adjunct* professor

ad•jure /əˈʤuɚ/ *verb* **-jures; -jured; -jur•ing** [+ *obj*] *formal* **:** to urge or command (someone) to do something • He *adjured* his followers to remain faithful to the cause.

ad•just /əˈʤʌst/ *verb* **-justs; -just•ed; -just•ing**

1 [+ *obj*] **a :** to change (something) in a minor way so that it works better • The car is easier to drive since the clutch was *adjusted.* • I *adjusted* the volume on the radio. **b :** to change the position of (something) • He *adjusted* his glasses/tie. • She *adjusted* the car seat so she could reach the pedals.

2 : to change in order to work or do better in a new situation [*no obj*] Going to a new school can be difficult, but the kids will eventually *adjust.* — often + *to* • The kids will eventually *adjust to* the new school. • Our eyes gradually *adjusted to* the darkness of the cave. • It's hard to *adjust to* the idea that she's gone. [+ *obj*] It's hard to ***adjust myself to*** the idea that she's gone. — see also WELL-ADJUSTED

3 : to make an amount or number more exact by considering other information — usually + *for* [+ *obj*] He actually makes less money now than he did 10 years ago, when you *adjust* his salary *for* inflation. [=when you calculate what his salary would be without inflation] [*no obj*] He makes less money now, when you *adjust for* inflation, than he did 10 years ago.

– ad•just•able /əˈʤʌstəbəl/ *adj* • an *adjustable* strap/wrench/waistband **– ad•just•er** *noun, pl* **-ers** [*count*] — see also INSURANCE ADJUSTER, LOSS ADJUSTER

ad•just•ment /əˈʤʌstmənt/ *noun, pl* **-ments**

1 : a small change that improves something or makes it work better [*count*] The engine only needed a minor *adjustment.* • She made some slight *adjustments* to the recipe. [*noncount*] The engine only needed minor *adjustment.*

2 : a change that makes it possible for a person to do better or work better in a new situation [*count*] Moving from the city to the country requires an *adjustment.* [*noncount*] We went through a period of *adjustment* at the new school.

3 : the act or process of changing or adjusting something (such as a number) [*count*] The figures were calculated with no *adjustments* for inflation. [*noncount*] The figures were calculated with no *adjustment* for inflation.

ad•ju•tant /ˈæʤətənt/ *noun, pl* **-tants** [*count*] **:** an army officer who helps the commanding officer and is responsible for written communications

ad–lib /ˈædˈlɪb/ *verb* **-libs; -libbed; -lib•bing :** to make up words or music in a performance instead of saying or playing something that has been planned **:** IMPROVISE [*no obj*] The actor forgot his lines, so he *ad-libbed.* • a comedian who is admired for his ability to *ad-lib* [+ *obj*] The actor *ad-libbed* his lines. • She *ad-libbed* the guitar solo. • *ad-lib* a joke

– ad–lib *noun, pl* **-libs** [*count*] • Some of the best jokes in the movie were *ad-libs.* **– ad–lib** *adj* • an *ad-lib* joke **– ad–lib** *adv* • did the whole dialogue *ad-lib*

ad•man /ˈædˌmæn/ *noun, pl* **ad•men** /-ˌmɛn/ [*count*] *somewhat informal* **:** a man who writes or sells advertisements

ad•min /ˈædˌmɪn/ *noun* [*noncount*] *Brit, informal* **:** ADMINISTRATION • You'll have to go see the people in *admin.* • She has a job in *admin.*

ad•min•is•ter /ədˈmɪnəstɚ/ *verb* **-ters; -tered; -ter•ing**

1 [+ *obj*] **:** to manage the operation of (something, such as a company or government) or the use of (something, such as property) • As a cost-saving measure, voters have elected to have the two towns *administered* jointly. • The UN personnel are there to help *administer* the territory. • She's been hired to *administer* the fund.

2 [+ *obj*] **:** to provide or apply (something, such as justice) **:** to put (something) into effect • *administer* justice [=give fair rewards and punishments in legal disputes and for crimes] • *administer* punishment

3 [+ *obj*] **:** to give or present (something) officially or as part of a ceremony • The assistant will *administer* the test. • *administer* an oath • a priest to *administer* the sacraments

4 [+ *obj*] **:** to give (a drug, medicine, or treatment) to someone • The doctor will *administer* the anesthesia before the surgery begins. • The drug is *administered* by injection.

5 [*no obj*] **:** to give needed help or care to others — + *to* • *administer* [=(more commonly) *minister*] *to* an ailing friend • *administer to* the needs of the poor

ad•min•is•tra•tion /ədˌmɪnəˈstreɪʃən/ *noun, pl* **-tions**

1 a [*noncount*] **:** the activities that relate to running a company, school, or other organization • He works in hospital *administration.* [=his work involves management of a hospital] • She has a degree in business *administration.* **b** [*count*] **:** a group of people who manage the way a company, school, or other organization functions • The editorial criticizes the college's *administration* for not taking a stand on the issue.

2 *or* ***Administration*** [*count*] **a :** a government or part of a government that is identified with its leader (such as a U.S. president or British prime minister) • We studied U.S. foreign policy in/during the Reagan *Administration.* [=during the time when Reagan was President] • the Thatcher *administration* • Her lecture compared the policies of this *administration* to the previous one. • *Administration* officials refused to comment. • At first, the *administration* denied the allegations. **b :** a U.S. government department • The drug has been approved by the U.S. Food and Drug *Administration.*

3 [*noncount*] **:** the act or process of providing or administering something • the *administration* of justice • oral *administration* of the drug

ad•min•is•tra•tive /ədˈmɪnəˌstreɪtɪv/ *adj* **:** of or relating to the management of a company, school, or other organization • She has an *administrative* job. • *administrative* tasks/duties • an *administrative* assistant

– ad•min•is•tra•tive•ly *adv*

ad•min•is•tra•tor /ədˈmɪnəˌstreɪtɚ/ *noun, pl* **-tors** [*count*] **:** a person who administers something: such as **a :** a person whose job is to manage a company, school, or other organization • a hospital *administrator* **b :** a person who controls the use of something (such as property or money) • Her eldest son will act as the *administrator* of the estate.

ad•mi•ra•ble /ˈædmrəbəl/ *adj* [*more* ~; *most* ~] **:** deserving to be admired **:** very good • The film does an *admirable* [=*excellent*] job of depicting life in the 1940s. • Loyalty was her most *admirable* quality. • Their motives were *admirable.*

– ad•mi•ra•bly /ˈædmrəbli/ *adv* • He managed the crisis *admirably.*

ad•mi•ral /ˈædmrəl/ *noun, pl* **-rals** [*count*] **:** a high-ranking officer in the navy

Ad•mi•ral•ty /ˈædmrəlti/ *noun*

the Admiralty **:** a government department formerly in charge of the British Navy

A

ad•mi•ra•tion /ˌædməˈreɪʃən/ *noun* **:** a feeling of great respect and approval [*noncount*] She looked at them in *admiration*. ▪ I have/feel great *admiration* for her courage. ▪ We were filled with *admiration* for him. ▪ She earned/won the *admiration* of her coworkers. [*singular*] I have/feel a great *admiration* for her courage.

ad•mire /ədˈmajɚ/ *verb* **-mires; -mired; -mir•ing** [+ *obj*]
1 : to feel respect or approval for (someone or something) ▪ I *admired* the way he handled the crisis. = I *admired* how he handled the crisis. ▪ We all *admire* her courage. = We all *admire* her for her courage. = She is much *admired* for her courage.
2 : to look at (something or someone) with enjoyment ▪ We gazed out the window and *admired* the scenery.
– ad•mir•er *noun, pl* **-ers** [*count*] ▪ an *admirer* of modern art ▪ a beautiful woman who has many *admirers* **– admiring** *adj* [*more* ~; *most* ~] ▪ She received many *admiring* glances as she walked into the room. **– ad•mir•ing•ly** /ədˈmaɪrɪŋli/ *adv*

ad•mis•si•ble /ədˈmɪsəbəl/ *adj* **:** able to be admitted or allowed; *especially* **:** able to be allowed or considered in a legal case ▪ *admissible* evidence ▪ The judge decided that the confession was *admissible* in court. — opposite INADMISSIBLE

ad•mis•sion /ədˈmɪʃən/ *noun, pl* **-sions**
1 [*noncount*] **:** the act of admitting or allowing something ▪ the *admission* of evidence in a court of law
2 [*count*] **:** a statement or action by which someone admits a weakness, fault, etc. ▪ His statement was interpreted as an *admission* of failure/weakness. ▪ an *admission* of error/defeat ▪ her *admission* of guilt = her *admission* that she was guilty ▪ ***By his own admission***, he is a terrible cook. [=he admits that he is a terrible cook]
3 a [*noncount*] **:** the right or permission to enter a place ▪ He tried to get into the theater but was refused *admission*. [=he was not allowed to enter] **b** [*noncount*] **:** the right or permission to join a club, group, etc. ▪ They opposed the *admission* of women into/to the club. ▪ She was unable to gain *admission* into/to the club. = She was denied *admission* into/to the club. **c :** the act or process of accepting a patient in a hospital for treatment [*noncount*] He died several hours after *admission* to the hospital. [=after being admitted to the hospital] ▪ Her injuries were serious enough to require hospital *admission*. ▪ The patient was unconscious on (his) *admission* to the hospital. [=when he was admitted to the hospital] [*count*] a large number of hospital *admissions* **d :** the act or process of accepting someone as a student at a school [*noncount*] The school's standards of *admission* are high. ▪ He submitted an application for *admission* to the school. [*count*] college/university *admissions* ▪ The school has a policy of ***open admissions***. [=a policy of accepting all students who want to go to the school] — often used before another noun ▪ an *admission(s)* exam ▪ an ***admissions officer*** [=an official at a school who is in charge of admitting students]
4 : the cost of entering a theater, sports stadium, museum, etc. [*noncount*] *Admission* (to the museum) is free on Tuesdays. ▪ A movie will be shown in the auditorium tomorrow night. *Admission*: $5 for adults, $2 for children. ▪ The museum offers reduced *admission* for young children. ▪ Her performance by itself was ***worth the price of admission***. [*count*] Reduced *admissions* are available for young children. — often used before another noun ▪ an *admission* fee/charge

ad•mit /ədˈmɪt/ *verb* **-mits; -mit•ted; -mit•ting** [+ *obj*]
1 : to say usually in an unwilling way that you accept or do not deny the truth or existence of (something) ▪ He *admitted* (to me) that he didn't know the answer. ▪ You know you're wrong. Why don't you *admit* it? [=why don't you say that you're wrong?] ▪ You know you're wrong! *Admit* it! ▪ He finally *admitted* his mistake. [=he stopped denying that he had made a mistake] ▪ I hate to *admit* it, but he's right. ▪ He *admitted* his guilt. = He *admitted* that he was guilty. = He *admitted* being guilty. ▪ I didn't think I'd like the movie, but I ***have to admit*** that it was good. = The movie was good, I *have to admit* (it). = The movie was good, I ***must admit***. ▪ She has refused to ***admit defeat***. [=to admit that she has been defeated] — see also ADMIT TO (below)
2 : to let in (someone or something): such as **a :** to allow (someone) to enter a place ▪ This ticket *admits* one person. ▪ He *admitted* them into his office. **b :** to allow (someone) to join a club, group, etc. ▪ They refused to *admit* her to/into the club. **c :** to accept (someone) as a patient in a hospital ▪ The patient was very sick when she was *admitted* to the hospital. ▪ He was *admitted* last night for chest pains. **d** *law* **:** to allow (something) to be considered as evidence in a legal case ▪ The judge decided to *admit* the evidence.
admit of [*phrasal verb*] ***admit of (something)*** *formal* **:** to allow or permit (something, such as an answer or solution) ▪ a question that *admits of* two possible answers
admit to [*phrasal verb*] ***admit to (something)*** **:** to admit (something) **:** to acknowledge the truth or existence of (something) ▪ He reluctantly *admitted to* knowing her. [=he admitted knowing her] ▪ He *admitted to* his guilt. = He *admitted to* being guilty. — see also ADMIT 1 (above)
– admitted *adj, always used before a noun* ▪ He is an *admitted* liar. [=he has admitted that he lied] **– ad•mit•ted•ly** /ədˈmɪtədli/ *adv* ▪ The movie was a success. *Admittedly*, it cost much more than expected. [=I admit that it cost much more than expected]

ad•mit•tance /ədˈmɪtn̩s/ *noun* [*noncount*] *formal* **:** permission to enter a place or to become a member of a club, group, etc. **:** permission to be admitted **:** ADMISSION ▪ gain *admittance* ▪ He tried to enter the restaurant but was refused *admittance*. ▪ They opposed the *admittance* of women into the club. ▪ The sign said "No *Admittance*."

ad•mix•ture /ædˈmɪkstʃɚ/ *noun, pl* **-tures** [*count*]
1 *technical* **:** something added by mixing ▪ an alloy that includes a small *admixture* of silver
2 : something formed by mixing **:** MIXTURE — not used technically ▪ Her feelings about starting the business were an *admixture* of fear and excitement.

ad•mon•ish /ædˈmɑːnɪʃ/ *verb* **-ish•es; -ished; -ish•ing** [+ *obj*] *formal*
1 : to speak to (someone) in a way that expresses disapproval or criticism — often + *for* ▪ His mother *admonished* him *for* shouting. ▪ We were *admonished for* arriving late.
2 : to tell or urge (someone) to do something ▪ She *admonished* [=*urged*] them to keep trying. ▪ They *admonished* [=*encouraged*] her to control her spending. ▪ They were *admonished* to take advantage of the opportunity.
– ad•mon•ish•ment /ædˈmɑːnɪʃmənt/ *noun, pl* **-ments** [*count, noncount*]

ad•mo•ni•tion /ˌædməˈnɪʃən/ *noun, pl* **-tions** *formal* **:** a criticism or warning about behavior [*count*] a stern *admonition* ▪ an *admonition* to be careful [*noncount*] He offered words of advice and *admonition*.
– ad•mon•i•to•ry /ədˈmɑːnəˌtʰori, *Brit* ədˈmɒnətri/ *adj* ▪ *admonitory* remarks

ad nau•se•am /ædˈnɑːzijəm/ *adv* — used to say that something happens or is done so many times or for such a long time that it makes people annoyed, disgusted, etc. ▪ We debated the issue *ad nauseam* without reaching an agreement.
✧ *Ad nauseam* is a Latin phrase that means "to sickness."

ado /əˈduː/ *noun* [*noncount*] **:** foolish or unnecessary talk, trouble, or activity — often used with *much* ▪ There has been *much ado* about the need for campaign reform. ▪ The controversy turned out to be *much ado* about nothing.
without further ado **:** without waiting any longer **:** right away ▪ *Without further ado*, I'd like to introduce our speaker.

ado•be /əˈdoʊbi/ *noun* [*noncount*] **:** a type of brick made of a mixture of mud and straw that is dried by the sun ▪ The house was built of *adobe*. — often used before another noun ▪ *adobe* bricks/walls/houses

ad•o•les•cence /ˌædəˈlɛsn̩s/ *noun* [*noncount*] **:** the period of life when a child develops into an adult ▪ Their children are on the verge of *adolescence*. ▪ He struggled through his *adolescence*. ▪ in early/late *adolescence*

ad•o•les•cent /ˌædəˈlɛsn̩t/ *noun, pl* **-cents** [*count*] **:** a young person who is developing into an adult **:** a young person who is going through adolescence ▪ Their children are now *adolescents*. ▪ a troubled *adolescent*
– adolescent *adj* ▪ an *adolescent* boy/girl

adopt /əˈdɑːpt/ *verb* **adopts; adopt•ed; adopt•ing**
1 : to take a child of other parents legally as your own child [*no obj*] They were unable to have children of their own, so they decided to *adopt*. [+ *obj*] They decided to *adopt* a child. ▪ He was *adopted* as an infant.
2 [+ *obj*] **a :** to begin to use or have (a different manner, method, etc.) ▪ Their boss has recently *adopted* a friendlier manner. [=has started behaving in a friendlier way] ▪ Did he *adopt* your point of view? ▪ We *adopted* some of the local customs. **b :** to begin to use (a name that is not your real or original name) ▪ The author Samuel Clemens *adopted* the name "Mark Twain." **c :** to live in (a country that is not your original country) and regard it as your home ▪ He was born in England but he has *adopted* Canada as his home.

3 [+ *obj*] : to accept or approve (something, such as a proposal) in a formal or official way • The assembly *adopted* a new constitution. • The resolution was unanimously *adopted* by the Senate.
4 [+ *obj*] *chiefly Brit* : to select (someone) officially as a candidate • The party *adopted* [=*selected, chose*] her as its candidate for mayor.
– **adopted** *adj* • an *adopted* child [=a child who has been adopted] • She is their *adopted* daughter. • "Mark Twain" was the ***adopted name*** of Samuel Clemens. • Canada is his ***adopted country.***

adop•tion /əˈdɑːpʃən/ *noun, pl* **-tions** : the act or process of adopting someone or something: such as **a** : the act or process of adopting a child [*noncount*] They chose *adoption* because they couldn't have children of their own. • children who are available for *adoption* • an *adoption* agency • She decided to ***put/give the baby up for adoption.*** [=to make it possible for other people to adopt the baby] [*count*] Our lawyer has handled many *adoptions.* **b** [*noncount*] : the act or process of beginning to use something new or different • our *adoption* of local customs • the company's *adoption* of new technology **c** [*noncount*] : the act or process of giving official acceptance or approval to something • the unanimous *adoption* of the resolution by the Senate

adop•tive /əˈdɑːptɪv/ *adj, always used before a noun* — used to describe a parent who has adopted a child • She is their adopted daughter, which makes them her *adoptive* parents. [=the parents who adopted her]

ador•able /əˈdorəbəl/ *adj* [*more* ~; *most* ~] : very appealing or attractive : very lovable • He is an *adorable* [=*delightful*] child. • They live in an *adorable* little cottage.
– **ador•ably** /əˈdorəbli/ *adv* • an *adorably* cute child

ad•o•ra•tion /ˌædəˈreɪʃən/ *noun* [*noncount*] : strong feelings of love or admiration • They looked at the baby in/with *adoration.* • The doctor has earned the *adoration* of his patients.

adore /əˈdoə/ *verb* **adores; adored; ador•ing** [+ *obj*]
1 : to love or admire (someone) very much • She *adores* her son. • He's a good doctor. All his patients *adore* him.
2 : to like or desire (something) very much : to take great pleasure in (something) • He *adores* [=*loves*] chocolate. • They *adored* shopping in all the boutiques.
– **adoring** *adj* • a star athlete and his *adoring* fans [=his fans who adore him]

adorn /əˈdoən/ *verb* **adorns; adorned; adorn•ing** [+ *obj*] *somewhat formal* : to make (someone or something) more attractive by adding something beautiful : DECORATE • Her paintings *adorn* the walls. — often + *with* • They *adorned* themselves *with* jewelry. • She wore a dress *adorned with* lace and silk flowers. • The walls are *adorned with* her paintings.

adorn•ment /əˈdoənmənt/ *noun, pl* **-ments**
1 [*noncount*] : the act or process of making someone or something attractive by decorating : the act or process of adorning someone or something • the *adornment* of the walls with her paintings
2 : something added to make a person or thing more attractive [*count*] Her room doesn't have any unnecessary *adornments.* [*noncount*] The entrance to the building has little *adornment.*

adren•a•line *or chiefly Brit* **adren•a•lin** /əˈdrɛnələn/ *noun* [*noncount*] : a substance that is released in the body of a person who is feeling a strong emotion (such as excitement, fear, or anger) and that causes the heart to beat faster and gives the person more energy • It was a thrilling experience that really got our *adrenaline* going. [=got us very excited] ✧ If you experience a ***rush of adrenaline*** or an ***adrenaline rush,*** you feel very excited and full of energy. • I felt a *rush of adrenaline* as I walked onto the stage.

adrift /əˈdrɪft/ *adj*
1 *of a boat* : floating on the water without being tied to anything or controlled by anyone • We could see a ship *adrift* [=*drifting*] in the storm. • The canoe was set/cast *adrift* from its moorings.
2 : without guidance, purpose, or support • She was alone and *adrift* in the city. • Many workers were ***cast adrift*** by massive layoffs.
3 *Brit* : behind by a specified amount in a race, competition, etc. • He was eight points *adrift* (of the leader).
come adrift *chiefly Brit* : to become loose or unattached • One of the straps on her dress *came adrift.*

adroit /əˈdroɪt/ *adj* [*more* ~; *most* ~] : very clever or skillful • an *adroit* negotiator • She is *adroit* at handling problems.
– **adroit•ly** *adv* • She managed the situation *adroitly.*
– **adroit•ness** *noun* [*noncount*]

ad•u•la•tion /ˌæʤəˈleɪʃən/ *noun* [*noncount*] : extreme admiration or praise • The rugby player enjoyed the *adulation* of his fans. • a writer who inspires *adulation* in her readers

[1]**adult** /əˈdʌlt, ˈæˌdʌlt/ *noun, pl* **adults** [*count*] : a fully grown person or animal • Her books appeal both to children and to *adults.* • Children must be accompanied by an *adult* in the museum. • Only *adults* can purchase alcohol. • This film is for *adults* only. Minors are not admitted. • People who are close friends as children aren't always friends as *adults.* • studying interactions between young birds and *adults*

[2]**adult** *adj, always used before a noun except in sense 2*
1 : fully grown and developed • an *adult* student/learner • *adult* birds • I've worked here all of my ***adult life.*** [=I've worked here since I became an adult] • preparing children for *adult life*
2 [*more* ~; *most* ~] : mature and sensible : not childish • We need to approach this in an *adult* way. • an *adult* decision/choice/responsibility
3 : of or intended for adults • *adult* literacy • *adult* learning
4 : dealing with sexual material • *adult* bookstores/movies
– **adult•hood** /əˈdʌltˌhʊd/ *noun, pl* **-hoods** [*noncount*] preparing children for *adulthood* [*count*] preparing children for their *adulthoods*

adult education *noun* [*noncount*] : a course of study for adults : CONTINUING EDUCATION • The university offers a popular program of *adult education.*

adul•ter•ate /əˈdʌltəˌreɪt/ *verb* **-ates; -at•ed; -at•ing** [+ *obj*] : to make (something, such as a food or drink) impure or weaker by adding something of poor quality • The company is accused of *adulterating* its products with cheap additives.
– **adulterated** *adj* • *adulterated* food – **adul•ter•a•tion** /əˌdʌltəˈreɪʃən/ *noun* [*noncount*]

adul•ter•er /əˈdʌltərə/ *noun, pl* **-ers** [*count*] : a married person who has sex with someone who is not that person's wife or husband : a person who commits adultery

adulter•ess /əˈdʌltərəs/ *noun, pl* **-ess•es** [*count*] : a married woman who has sex with a man who is not her husband : a woman who commits adultery

adul•tery /əˈdʌltəri/ *noun* [*noncount*] : sex between a married person and someone who is not that person's wife or husband • He found out that his wife had committed *adultery.* • She accused her husband of *adultery.*
– **adul•ter•ous** /əˈdʌltərəs/ *adj* • an *adulterous* affair/relationship – **adul•ter•ous•ly** *adv*

adv *abbr* adverb

[1]**ad•vance** /ədˈvæns, *Brit* ədˈvɑːns/ *verb* **-vanc•es; -vanced; -vanc•ing**
1 **a** [*no obj*] : to move forward • The car *advanced* slowly down the street. • The sun slowly *advanced* across the sky. • She opened the door and *advanced* cautiously into the room. • Enemy soldiers are ***advancing on*** the city. [=they are approaching the city in order to attack it] **b** [+ *obj*] : to move (someone or something) forward • *advance* the hands of a clock • *advance* a pawn [=move a pawn forward in a game of chess] • The film is *advanced* by an electric motor. • The team *advanced* the ball steadily down the field.
2 [*no obj*] : to go forward : to make progress • Our understanding of this disease has *advanced* rapidly in recent years. • The team did not *advance* beyond the first round of the play-offs. • The company tries to keep up with *advancing* technology. : to continue in a process of development, aging, etc. • As he *advanced* in age and stature he *advanced* in knowledge. • Their children are *advancing* toward maturity.
3 : to increase in amount or rate [+ *obj*] These measures are intended to keep landlords from *advancing* [=*raising*] rents unfairly. [*no obj*] Wages have continued to *advance.* • Some stock prices have *advanced* while others have declined. • Loss of memory is often a sign of *advancing* age.
4 [+ *obj*] **a** : to help the progress of (something) • heroes whose sacrifices *advanced* the cause of freedom • Volunteers have been raising money to *advance* the work of the society. • They used propaganda to *advance* their cause. • He was *advancing* his own interests at the expense of his friend's. : to cause or help (something) to go forward or continue • *advance* a plot **b** : to make (something) higher or better : to cause improvement to (something) • The success of this novel will help to *advance* [=*enhance*] his reputation/status.
5 **a** [+ *obj*] : to raise (someone) to a higher rank or position • He was *advanced* [=*promoted*] from clerk to assistant manager. **b** [*no obj*] : to rise to a higher rank or position • The fam-

A

ily has *advanced* to a position of influence in the community. ▪ He *advanced* quickly through the ranks. ▪ She has continued to *advance* steadily in her career.

6 [+ *obj*] **: to give money to someone as a loan or before the usual time** ▪ *advance* a loan to someone = *advance* someone a loan ▪ *advance* an employee a week's pay ▪ His publisher *advanced* him $100,000 on/for his new book.

7 [+ *obj*] **: to suggest or propose (something) for consideration or acceptance** ▪ *advance* a new plan/theory ▪ *advance* an argument ▪ Many theories were *advanced* and rejected.

8 [+ *obj*] **a : to cause (something) to occur more quickly** ▪ a chemical used to *advance* the ripening of fruit **b : to make (something) earlier** ▪ *advance* the date of the meeting

– ad•vanc•er *noun, pl* **-ers** [*count*] ▪ There were more *advancers* [=stocks that increased in value] than decliners in the stock market yesterday.

²**advance** *noun, pl* **-vances**

1 : forward movement [*noncount*] trying to halt the enemy's *advance* [*count*] trying to halt the enemy's *advances*

2 : progress in the development or improvement of something [*count*] recent *advances* in medicine ▪ a big/dramatic/huge/major/significant *advance* in technology ▪ The new system represents a considerable *advance* over the old one. ▪ There have been few *advances* made in the treatment of this disease. [*noncount*] There has been little *advance* made in the treatment of this disease. ▪ policies that are important for economic *advance* [=*advancement*]

3 [*count*] **: a rise in price, value, or amount** ▪ The workers won wage *advances*. ▪ a yearlong *advance* in stock prices

4 [*count*] **: the act of speaking to someone in an effort to start a sexual relationship — usually plural** ▪ Her unfriendly look discourages *advances*. ▪ She rebuffed/rejected his *advances*. ▪ He is accused of making unwelcome sexual *advances* to female coworkers.

5 [*count*] **: money given to someone as a loan or before the usual time of payment** ▪ I need an *advance* on my salary. ▪ He was given a $100,000 *advance* on/for his new book. ▪ a cash *advance*

in advance **: before something happens** ▪ He knew about the change two weeks *in advance*. [=two weeks before the change occurred] ▪ There was no way to know *in advance* [=*ahead of time*] that these problems would occur. **: before a future event or time** ▪ We made reservations *in advance*. ▪ You should call *in advance* to make an appointment. ▪ Thank you *in advance* for your help. **— often + *of*** ▪ They began to make preparations several days *in advance of* [=*before, ahead of*] her arrival.

³**advance** *adj, always used before a noun*

1 : made, sent, or provided at an early time ▪ an *advance* payment ▪ an *advance* warning ▪ an *advance* copy of a new book

2 : going or placed before others ▪ an *advance* guard ▪ an *advance* scout ▪ (*US*) an ***advance man/woman/team*** [=a man, woman, or group whose job is to go to a place and make preparations for someone (such as a politician or an entertainer) who is coming to visit that place at a later time]

ad•vanced /əd'vænst, *Brit* əd'vɑ:nst/ *adj* [*more* ~; *most* ~]

1 : beyond the basic level ▪ *advanced* mathematics ▪ She's taking an *advanced* course in English. = She's taking a course in *advanced* English. ▪ The school has courses for elementary, intermediate, and *advanced* students. ▪ The book explains both basic and *advanced* techniques. ▪ The job requires someone with an ***advanced degree***. [=a degree (such as a master's degree or a PhD) that is higher than a bachelor's degree]

2 : far along in a course of progress or development: such as a : having developed more than others ▪ a highly *advanced* civilization [=a modern civilization] ▪ an *advanced* society **b : having or using new and modern methods** ▪ *advanced* technology ▪ technologically *advanced* weapons ▪ The system has many *advanced* features. **c : having reached a bad state or condition** ▪ The house was in an *advanced* state of disrepair. [=the house was in very poor condition] ▪ The disease is in an *advanced* stage. ▪ an *advanced* form of cancer **d : far along in a process of aging** ▪ She began painting ***at an advanced age***. [=she began painting when she was old] ▪ He is rather ***advanced in age/years***. [=rather old] ▪ a man/woman ***of advanced age/years*** [=an old man/woman]

Advanced level *noun, pl* ~ **levels** [*count*] *Brit* **: A LEVEL**

ad•vance•ment /əd'vænsmənt, *Brit* əd'vɑ:nsmənt/ *noun, pl* **-ments : the act of advancing: such as a : the act of moving forward** [*noncount*] They have been unable to slow the *advancement* [=*advance*] of the enemy troops. ▪ A motor inside the camera is used for *advancement* of the film. [*count*] troop *advancements* [=(more commonly) *advances*] **b : the act or result of making something better, more successful, etc.** [*noncount*] She contributed greatly to the *advancement* of the new organization. ▪ working for the *advancement* of learning/science/truth ▪ The program supports economic *advancement* in rural areas. [*count*] There have been many recent *advancements* [=*advances, improvements*] in this technology. ▪ This new method is a great *advancement* over past techniques. **c : the act of being raised to a higher rank or position** [*noncount*] The job offers many opportunities for professional *advancement*. ▪ His *advancement* [=*promotion*] to captain came last year. ▪ He is being considered for *advancement*. ▪ career *advancement* ▪ social *advancement* [*count*] a series of rapid career *advancements*

ad•van•tage /əd'væntɪʤ, *Brit* əd'vɑ:ntɪʤ/ *noun, pl* **-tag•es**

1 [*count*] **a : something (such as a good position or condition) that helps to make someone or something better or more likely to succeed than others** ▪ Higher ground gave the enemy the/an *advantage*. ▪ He has/enjoys an unfair *advantage* over us because of his wealth. ▪ His plan has the *advantage* of being less expensive than other options. ▪ He lacked the *advantages* of an advanced education. ▪ Speed is an *advantage* in most sports. ▪ The company's only *advantage* over the competition is its location. ▪ Applicants for this job will find that previous experience is an *advantage*. ▪ The union should be ***at an advantage*** [=should have an advantage] in the negotiations. **b : a good or desirable quality or feature** ▪ Being able to set your own schedule is one of the *advantages* of owning a business. ▪ Among the *advantages* of a small college is its campus life. **— opposite DISADVANTAGE**

2 [*noncount*] **: benefit or gain** ▪ There isn't any *advantage* in/to leaving early. ▪ She used her position for personal *advantage*. [=for personal gain; to help herself] ▪ The error was ***to our advantage***. [=we were helped by the error] **— opposite DISADVANTAGE** ✧ If you ***turn/use something to your advantage*** or ***to good advantage***, you use something in a way that is helpful to you. ▪ Is there a way to *turn this situation to our advantage*? [=is there a way to exploit this situation?; is there a way to take advantage of this situation?]

3 [*noncount*] *tennis* **: the first point won after the score is tied at 40–40 — used to announce the person who has won the point** ▪ *Advantage* Mr. Jones.

take advantage of **1 : to use (something, such as an opportunity) in a way that helps you : to make good use of (something)** ▪ We *took advantage of* the warm weather and did some yard work. ▪ They are *taking advantage of* an opportunity to travel. ▪ You should *take* (full) *advantage of* this opportunity while you can. **2 a : to ask for or expect more than is fair or reasonable from (someone) : to treat (someone who is generous or helpful) unfairly** ▪ After a while, I began to think she was *taking advantage of* me. **b : to use (something) unfairly for personal gain** ▪ He *took advantage of* [=*exploited*] my lack of knowledge. ▪ She *took advantage of* our generosity.

to advantage **: in an attractive and appealing way** ▪ The display shows off the collection *to* (good/best) *advantage*.

ad•van•taged /əd'væntɪʤd, *Brit* əd'vɑ:ntɪʤd/ *adj* [*more* ~; *most* ~] **: having or providing the things (such as money and education) that are considered necessary for a good position in society : having or providing advantages over other people : PRIVILEGED** ▪ *advantaged* children ▪ He comes from an *advantaged* community/background. ▪ an *advantaged* position

ad•van•ta•geous /ˌæd,væn'teɪʤəs/ *adj* [*more* ~; *most* ~] **: helpful or favorable : giving an advantage to someone** ▪ He found it *advantageous* [=*beneficial*] to arrive early. ▪ These changes will be *advantageous* to you. [=will help you] ▪ Her experience placed her in an *advantageous* position to apply for the job. **— opposite DISADVANTAGEOUS**

– ad•van•ta•geous•ly *adv* ▪ Where can we invest the money most *advantageously*?

ad•vent /'æd,vɛnt/ *noun*

1 [*singular*] **: the time when something begins or arrives : the first appearance of something** ▪ the *advent* of spring ▪ the *advent* of the printing press ▪ the *advent* of personal computers

2 *Advent* [*noncount*] *in the Christian religion* **: the period of time beginning four Sundays before Christmas** ▪ Our church is holding some special services during *Advent*.

ad•ven•ture /əd'vɛnʧɚ/ *noun, pl* **-tures**

1 [*count*] **: an exciting or dangerous experience** ▪ The field trip was an *adventure* for the students. ▪ He told us about his

camping *adventures*. — often used before another noun ▪ an *adventure* story/novel
2 [*noncount*] **: danger or excitement** ▪ He has a strong spirit/sense of *adventure*. [=he enjoys doing dangerous and exciting things] ▪ They were looking for *adventure*.

adventure playground *noun, pl* ~ **-grounds** [*count*] *Brit* **: an outdoor area that has objects on which children can climb and play**

ad·ven·tur·er /əd'vɛntʃərɚ/ *noun, pl* **-ers** [*count*]
1 : someone who likes dangerous or exciting experiences : a person who looks for adventures
2 *somewhat old-fashioned* **: a person who tries to become wealthy or powerful by doing things that are illegal or dishonest** ▪ corporate *adventurers*

ad·ven·ture·some /əd'vɛntʃɚsəm/ *adj* [*more* ~; *most* ~] *chiefly US* **: liking to do dangerous and exciting things : seeking adventure** ▪ an *adventuresome* [=*adventurous*] explorer

ad·ven·tur·ism /əd'vɛntʃəˌrɪzəm/ *noun* [*noncount*] *disapproving* **: an attitude or way of behaving that involves attempting to gain an advantage by doing things that are regarded as foolish or risky** ▪ military *adventurism*
– ad·ven·tur·ist /əd'vɛntʃərɪst/ *noun, pl* **-ists** [*count*]

ad·ven·tur·ous /əd'vɛntʃərəs/ *adj* [*more* ~; *most* ~]
1 a : not afraid to do new and dangerous or exciting things ▪ The island attracts *adventurous* travelers. ▪ He is an *adventurous* cook who is always trying new recipes. **b : exciting or unusual** ▪ Her design is an *adventurous* departure from what we usually see. ▪ The restaurant offers an *adventurous* [=*innovative*] menu.
2 : full of danger and excitement ▪ They have an *adventurous* lifestyle. ▪ an *adventurous* trip/vacation

ad·verb /'ædˌvɚb/ *noun, pl* **-verbs** [*count*] **: a word that describes a verb, an adjective, another adverb, or a sentence and that is often used to show time, manner, place, or degree** ▪ In "arrived early," "runs slowly," "stayed home," and "works hard" the words "early," "slowly," "home," and "hard" are *adverbs*.
– ad·ver·bi·al /æd'vɚbijəl/ *adj* ▪ an *adverbial* phrase ▪ In some sentences the word "likely" is *adverbial* rather than adjectival. ▪ the *adverbial* suffix "-ly" **– ad·ver·bi·ally** *adv*

ad·ver·sar·i·al /ˌædvɚ'serijəl/ *adj* [*more* ~; *most* ~] *formal* **: involving two people or two sides who oppose each other** ▪ The two men have always had an *adversarial* relationship. [=they have always opposed each other; they have always treated each other as adversaries] ▪ an *adversarial* system of justice with prosecution and defense opposing each other

ad·ver·sary /'ædvɚˌseri, *Brit* 'ædvəsri/ *noun, pl* **-sar·ies** [*count*] *formal* **: an enemy or opponent** ▪ His political *adversaries* tried to prevent him from winning the nomination.

ad·verse /æd'vɚs, 'ædˌvɚs/ *adj* [*more* ~; *most* ~] **: bad or unfavorable : not good** ▪ *adverse* criticism/remarks ▪ He had an *adverse* reaction to the medicine. [=he reacted badly to the medicine; the medicine had a bad effect on him] ▪ Many fear that budget cuts will have an *adverse* [=*damaging*] effect on education. ▪ *adverse* circumstances/conditions/weather ▪ The drug has no *adverse* [=*harmful*] side effects.
– ad·verse·ly *adv* ▪ Sales were *adversely* affected by the bad weather. ▪ Staff changes could affect the project *adversely*.

ad·ver·si·ty /æd'vɚsəti/ *noun, pl* **-ties : a difficult situation or condition : misfortune or tragedy** [*noncount*] He showed courage in the face of *adversity*. ▪ We had to learn to deal with *adversity*. [*count*] They overcame many *adversities*.

ad·vert /'ædˌvɚt/ *noun, pl* **-verts** [*count*] *Brit, informal* **:** ADVERTISEMENT ▪ I saw your *advert* in the newspaper.

ad·ver·tise /'ædvɚˌtaɪz/ *verb* **-tis·es; -tised; -tis·ing**
1 : to make the public aware of something (such as a product) that is being sold [+ *obj*] They are *advertising* the new edition of the book. ▪ The vacation was *advertised* as a week in paradise. ▪ It turned out to be exactly as *advertised*. [*no obj*] Business increased after we began to *advertise* on the radio. ▪ If you want to attract customers, it pays to *advertise*.
2 : to make a public announcement (in a newspaper, on the Internet, etc.) about something that is wanted or available [*no obj*] The company is *advertising* for a secretary. [+ *obj*] We *advertised* the job in the paper.
3 [+ *obj*] **: to cause people to notice (something)** ▪ You don't have to *advertise* [=*draw attention to*] the fact that we arrived late. ▪ She *advertised* her presence by wearing a skimpy dress.
– ad·ver·tis·er *noun, pl* **-ers** [*count*] ▪ television *advertisers* [=companies that advertise on television]

ad·ver·tise·ment /ˌædvɚ'taɪzmənt, *Brit* əd'vɜ:təsmənt/ *noun, pl* **-ments**
1 [*count*] **: something (such as a short film or a written notice) that is shown or presented to the public to help sell a product or to make an announcement** ▪ The *advertisement* will appear in three magazines. ▪ He learned about the job from an *advertisement* in the newspaper. ▪ a television/radio *advertisement* — often + *for* ▪ I saw an *advertisement for* a new car on TV last night. — called also *ad, (Brit) advert*
2 [*count*] **: a person or thing that shows how good or effective something is** — + *for* ▪ The rusted car on the lot was not much of an *advertisement for* the car dealership. ▪ Successful graduates are a good *advertisement for* a school.
3 [*noncount*] **: the act or process of advertising** ▪ The company has spent a lot of money on *advertisement*.

ad·ver·tis·ing /'ædvɚˌtaɪzɪŋ/ *noun* [*noncount*]
1 : published or broadcast advertisements ▪ These is a lot of *advertising* in that magazine.
2 : the business of creating advertisements ▪ He is looking for a job in *advertising*. ▪ She works for an ***advertising agency*** [=(*chiefly US*) *ad agency*] in New York.

ad·vice /əd'vaɪs/ *noun* [*noncount*] **: an opinion or suggestion about what someone should do** ▪ My *advice* is to sell your old car and get a new one. ▪ Take my *advice* and sell your old car. ▪ He needs *advice* from an expert. ▪ She's been giving him some expert *advice* about investing. ▪ "May I ask your *advice* about/on something?" "Certainly. I'm always happy to give *advice* when asked for it." ▪ Let me offer you a bit/piece/word of *advice*. = Let me offer you some *advice*. ▪ I took/followed my doctor's *advice* and lost some weight. = I lost some weight ***on the advice of*** my doctor.

advice column *noun, pl* ~ **-umns** [*count*] *US* **: an article in a newspaper or magazine that offers advice to people who write to ask for help with a problem — called also (*Brit*) *agony column***
– advice columnist *noun, pl* ~ **-nists** [*count*]

ad·vis·able /əd'vaɪzəbəl/ *adj* [*more* ~; *most* ~] **: wise, sensible, or reasonable** ▪ The restaurant is very popular so it is *advisable* to make reservations if you go. [=it's a good idea to make reservations] ▪ My doctor said it was *advisable* for me to lose weight. — opposite INADVISABLE
– ad·vis·abil·i·ty /ədˌvaɪzə'bɪləti/ *noun* [*noncount*] ▪ I question the *advisability* of going into the park alone at night.

ad·vise /əd'vaɪz/ *verb* **-vis·es; -vised; -vis·ing**
1 a : to give an opinion or suggestion to someone about what should be done : to give advice to (someone) [+ *obj*] I strongly *advise* you to sell your old car. ▪ We *advised* them to save their money. ▪ My doctor *advised* me to lose some weight. ▪ She *advises* the President on foreign affairs. ▪ Our lawyer ***advised us against*** buying that house. [=she told us that we shouldn't buy that house] [*no obj*] We were thinking of buying that house, but our lawyer ***advised against*** it. **b** [+ *obj*] **: to recommend or suggest (something)** ▪ I *advise* selling your old car. ▪ We were thinking of buying that house, but our lawyer *advised* caution. [=said that we should be cautious] ▪ He *advises* patience/restraint when dealing with children. — see also ILL-ADVISED, WELL-ADVISED
2 [+ *obj*] *formal* **: to give information to (someone)** ▪ The police *advised* them of their rights. [=the police told them what their legal rights were] ▪ She says she was never *advised* [=*informed, told*] about the new procedures. ▪ We *advised* [=*apprised*] them of the danger. ▪ The boss asked us to ***keep him advised*** about/on how the project is going.
– ad·vis·er *also* **ad·vi·sor** /əd'vaɪzɚ/ *noun, pl* **-visers** *also* **-visors** [*count*] ▪ a financial/legal/medical *adviser* ▪ She's an *adviser* to the President on foreign affairs.

ad·vis·ed·ly /əd'vaɪzədli/ *adv, formal* **: in a deliberate way** ▪ They have misled us—and I use the word "misled" *advisedly*.

ad·vise·ment /əd'vaɪzmənt/ *noun*
take (something) under advisement *US, formal* **: to consider (something) carefully** ▪ Thank you for your suggestion. We'll *take* the matter *under advisement*.

[1]**ad·vi·so·ry** /əd'vaɪzəri/ *adj* **: having the power or right to make suggestions about what should be done : able to give advice** ▪ He attended a meeting of the *advisory* committee/board/panel. ▪ She is acting in an *advisory* role/capacity in the administration.

[2]**advisory** *noun, pl* **-ries** [*count*] *US* **: a report that gives information or a warning about something** ▪ We heard a weather *advisory* saying that heavy rains are expected tonight. ▪ a traffic *advisory*

ad·vo·ca·cy /'ædvəkəsi/ *noun* [*noncount*] **: the act or process of supporting a cause or proposal : the act or process of**

advocating something ▪ She is known for her *advocacy* of birth control. [=she is known for advocating/supporting birth control]

[1]**ad•vo•cate** /ˈædvəkət/ *noun, pl* **-cates** [*count*]
1 a : a person who argues for or supports a cause or policy ▪ a birth control *advocate* = an *advocate* of birth control [=a person who advocates birth control] ▪ a passionate/impassioned *advocate* of civil rights **b** *US* **:** a person who works for a cause or group ▪ a women's health *advocate* = an *advocate* for women's health ▪ She works as a consumer *advocate*.
2 : a person who argues for the cause of another person in a court of law **:** LAWYER

[2]**ad•vo•cate** /ˈædvəˌkeɪt/ *verb* **-cates; -cat•ed; -cat•ing** [+ *obj*] **:** to support or argue for (a cause, policy, etc.) ▪ He *advocates* traditional teaching methods. ▪ They *advocate* abolishing the income tax. = They *advocate* that the income tax should be abolished. ▪ The plan is *advocated* by the president.

adze *also* **adz** /ˈædz/ *noun, pl* **adz•es** [*count*] **:** a cutting tool that has a thin curved blade and that is usually used for shaping wood

ae•gis /ˈiːʤəs/ *noun* [*singular*] *formal* **:** the power to protect, control, or support something or someone — used in the phrase ***under the aegis of*** ▪ Their rights are protected *under the aegis* [=*authority*] *of* the law. ▪ The issue will be decided *under the aegis of* an international organization.

ae•on *chiefly Brit spelling of* EON

aer•ate /ˈeəˌeɪt/ *verb* **-ates; -at•ed; -at•ing** [+ *obj*] **:** to put air or a gas into (something, such as soil or a liquid) ▪ You should *aerate* the soil before planting the seeds.
– aer•a•tion /ˌeəˈeɪʃən/ *noun* [*noncount*] ▪ the *aeration* of soil

[1]**ae•ri•al** /ˈerijəl/ *adj*
1 : performed in the air ▪ the spectacular *aerial* acrobatics of the circus performers
2 : performed using an airplane ▪ *aerial* combat ▪ an *aerial* attack ▪ *aerial* photography **:** taken or seen from an airplane ▪ *aerial* photographs ▪ an *aerial* view

[2]**aerial** *noun, pl* **-als** [*count*]
1 *chiefly Brit* **:** ANTENNA 2 ▪ a broken radio *aerial*
2 : a difficult movement of the body performed by an athlete (such as a skier) in the air ▪ She tried a new *aerial* in her last competition.

ae•rie (*US*) *or chiefly Brit* **ey•rie** /ˈeri/ *noun, pl* **-ries** [*count*]
1 : the nest of a bird (such as an eagle or hawk) built high up on a cliff or on the top of a mountain
2 : a room or building built high up so that people inside can see things happening below them

aero- *also* **aer-** *combining form*
1 : air ▪ *aerobic* ▪ *aero*dynamics ▪ *aerate*
2 : gas ▪ *aero*sol
3 : dealing with airplanes or flying ▪ *aero*nautics

aer•o•bat•ics /ˌerəˈbætɪks/ *noun* [*plural*] **:** difficult and exciting movements of an airplane often performed for entertainment ▪ loops, spins, and other *aerobatics*
– aer•o•bat•ic /ˌerəˈbætɪk/ *adj* ▪ *aerobatic* maneuvers

aer•o•bic /ˌeəˈoʊbɪk/ *adj*
1 *of exercise* **:** strengthening the heart and lungs by making them work hard for several minutes or more ▪ *aerobic* exercises like running and swimming ▪ an *aerobic* workout
2 *technical* **:** using oxygen ▪ *aerobic* organisms such as bacteria — opposite ANAEROBIC

aer•o•bics /ˌeəˈoʊbɪks/ *noun* [*noncount*] **:** a system of exercises often done by a group of people while music is playing **:** a system of aerobic exercises ▪ an instructor teaching *aerobics* — often used before another noun ▪ an *aerobics* class; *also* [*plural*] **:** aerobic exercises ▪ She does *aerobics* three days a week.

aero•dy•nam•ics /ˌeroʊdaɪˈnæmɪks/ *noun*
1 [*noncount*] **:** a science that studies the movement of air and the way that objects (such as airplanes or cars) move through air ▪ She has a degree in *aerodynamics*.
2 [*plural*] **:** the qualities of an object that affect how easily it is able to move through the air ▪ Its improved *aerodynamics* give the car more speed and better gas mileage.
– aero•dy•nam•ic /ˌeroʊdaɪˈnæmɪk/ *adj* ▪ the airplane's *aerodynamic* shape/design **– aero•dy•nam•ic•al•ly** /ˌeroʊdaɪˈnæmɪkli/ *adv*

aero•nau•tics /ˌerəˈnɑːtɪks/ *noun* [*noncount*] **:** a science that deals with airplanes and flying ▪ the history of *aeronautics*
– aero•nau•ti•cal /ˌerəˈnɑːtɪkəl/ *adj* ▪ an *aeronautical* engineer [=a scientist who designs and builds airplanes]

aero•plane /ˈerəˌpleɪn/ *noun, pl* **-planes** [*count*] *Brit* **:** AIRPLANE

aero•sol /ˈerəˌsɑːl/ *noun, pl* **-sols :** a substance (such as hair spray or medicine) that is kept in a container under pressure and that is released as a fine spray when a button is pressed [*count*] chemicals used in *aerosols* [*noncount*] a can of *aerosol* — often used before another noun ▪ an *aerosol* container/can/spray

aero•space /ˈeroʊˌspeɪs/ *noun* [*noncount*] **:** an industry that deals with travel in and above the Earth's atmosphere and with the production of vehicles used in such travel ▪ a career in *aerospace* — often used before another noun ▪ The airplane was designed using the latest in *aerospace* technology. ▪ *aerospace* companies ▪ the *aerospace* industry

aes•thete *also US* **es•thete** /ˈɛsˌθiːt, *Brit* ˈiːsˌθiːt/ *noun, pl* **-thetes** [*count*] *formal + sometimes disapproving* **:** a person who recognizes and values beauty in art, music, etc. ▪ He regards art critics as a bunch of pretentious *aesthetes*.

[1]**aes•thet•ic** *also US* **es•thet•ic** /ɛsˈθɛtɪk, *Brit* iːsˈθɛtɪk/ *adj* **:** of or relating to art or beauty ▪ There are practical as well as *aesthetic* reasons for planting trees. ▪ the statue's *aesthetic* [=*artistic*] beauty ▪ making *aesthetic* improvements to the building ▪ *aesthetic* values/ideals
– aes•thet•i•cal•ly *also US* **es•thet•i•cal•ly** /ɛsˈθɛtɪkli, *Brit* iːsˈθɛtɪkli/ *adv* ▪ the garden's *aesthetically* pleasing design

[2]**aes•thet•ic** *also US* **es•thet•ic** *noun, pl* **-ics**
1 [*count*] **:** a set of ideas or opinions about beauty or art — usually singular ▪ The design of the building reflects a modern/traditional/old-fashioned *aesthetic*.
2 *aesthetics* a [*noncount*] **:** the study of beauty especially in art and literature ▪ *Aesthetics* is an important part of Greek philosophy. **b** [*plural*] **:** the artistic or beautiful qualities of something ▪ the *aesthetics* of the gemstones
– aes•thet•i•cism *also US* **es•thet•i•cism** /ɛsˈθɛtəˌsɪzəm, *Brit* iːsˈθɛtəˌsɪzəm/ *noun* [*noncount*] ▪ the *aestheticism* of the region

afar /əˈfaə/ *adv*
***from afar* :** from a great distance ▪ Their fans come *from afar* [=from far away] to watch them play. ▪ the Earth as it is seen/viewed *from afar* ▪ He loved/worshipped/admired her *from afar*. [=without telling her]

AFC *abbr, US* American Football Conference ✧ The *AFC* and the NFC make up the NFL.

af•fa•ble /ˈæfəbəl/ *adj* [*more* ~; *most* ~] *formal* **:** friendly and easy to talk to ▪ a lively, *affable* young fellow ▪ an *affable* host
– af•fa•bil•i•ty /ˌæfəˈbɪləti/ *noun* [*noncount*] **– af•fa•bly** /ˈæfəbli/ *adv* ▪ We were greeted *affably* by our host.

af•fair /əˈfeə/ *noun, pl* **-fairs**
1 *affairs* [*plural*] **:** work or activities done for a purpose **:** commercial, professional, public, or personal business ▪ The group conducts its *affairs* [=*business*] in private. ▪ We were told to arrange/settle our *affairs*. = We were told to put our *affairs* in order. ▪ handling/managing someone else's *affairs* ▪ They seem to be quite pleased with the current/present ***state of affairs*** [=*situation*] ▪ She's the company's director of ***public affairs*** [=the person who manages a company's relationship with the public] ▪ She's an expert in ***foreign affairs*** [=events and activities that involve foreign countries] ▪ ***world/international affairs*** [=events and activities that involve different nations] ▪ After the war, the government focused on its own ***domestic affairs*** ▪ They accused the U.S. of interfering in the ***internal affairs*** of other nations.
2 [*count*] **:** a matter that concerns or involves someone ▪ This has nothing to do with you. It's not your *affair*. [=*business, concern*] = It's none of your *affair*. [=*business*] ▪ How I choose to live is my *affair*, not yours.
3 [*count*] **:** a secret sexual relationship between two people **:** LOVE AFFAIR ▪ adulterous/extramarital *affairs* between married men and single women — often used in the phrase ***have an affair*** ▪ She divorced her husband after she discovered that he was *having an affair*. — often + *with* ▪ She *had an affair with* a coworker.
4 [*count*] **a :** a social event or activity ▪ He wants to make their wedding day an *affair* to remember. [=a special event] ▪ a simple/elaborate *affair* ▪ We were invited to a black-tie *affair* [=a party in which men wear tuxedos and women wear fancy dresses] at the governor's mansion. **b :** an event or series of events that usually involves well-known people ▪ the famous hostage *affair* of the late 1970s ▪ The public has shown little interest in the whole *affair*. — often used with

proper names • the Iran-Contra *affair* [=*scandal*]
5 [*count*] *informal* : something made or produced : an object or thing • The only bridge across the river was a flimsy *affair* of ropes and rotten wood.

af·fect /əˈfɛkt/ *verb* **-fects; -fect·ed; -fect·ing** [+ *obj*]
1 : to produce an effect on (someone or something): such as **a :** to act on (someone or something) and cause a change • His decisions could *affect* [=*influence*] the lives of millions of people. • The accident will *affect* [=*influence*] the value of the car. • We learned about the way the oceans are *affected* by the moon. • This medication may *affect* your ability to drive a car. [=this medicine may make it dangerous for you to drive a car] • This new evidence will *affect* the outcome of the trial. • The news could adversely *affect* [=could hurt] her chances of becoming the next president. • We kept the change from *affecting* [=*harming*] our friendship. • The incident really *affected* my opinion of him. **b :** to cause strong emotions in (someone) • The criticism *affected* [=*bothered, upset*] her deeply/greatly. • The entire town was *affected* by their deaths. [=everyone in the town felt sad about their deaths] • We were all greatly *affected* by the terrible news. [=we were all very upset by the terrible news] **c :** to cause a change in (a part of the body) • Paralysis *affected* his limbs. = His limbs were *affected* by/with paralysis. [=his limbs were paralyzed] • The disease can *affect* your muscles. • drugs that *affect* the nervous/immune system **d :** to cause illness in (someone) • The condition *affects* about five million adults each year. • a serious disease primarily/mainly *affecting* women over the age of 40 • Only men appear to be *affected* by the disease.

> ***usage*** Do not confuse the verbs *affect* and *effect*. *Affect* means to act on or change someone or something. • Rain *affected* [=*influenced*] their performance. *Effect* means to cause something to happen. • The new president *effected* [=*made, caused*] many changes to/in the company's policies. Note that the verb *affect* and the noun *effect* are used in contexts that are similar. • The weather *affected* our plans. = The weather had an *effect* on our plans. [=the weather caused us to change our plans]

2 *formal* **:** to pretend that a false behavior or feeling is natural or genuine • She *affected* indifference [=she pretended that she did not care], though she was deeply hurt. • He *affected* (a look of) surprise. [=he pretended to be surprised] • She *affects* [=*feigns*] a warm friendly manner. • He *affected* [=*faked*] a French accent.

af·fec·ta·tion /ˌæˌfɛkˈteɪʃən/ *noun, pl* **-tions :** an unnatural form of behavior that is meant to impress others [*count*] His French accent is just an *affectation*. [*noncount*] speaking without *affectation*

af·fect·ed /əˈfɛktəd/ *adj* **:** not natural or genuine • an *affected* [=*fake, phony*] French accent
– af·fect·ed·ly *adv*

af·fect·ing /əˈfɛktɪŋ/ *adj* [*more* ~; *most* ~] **:** causing a feeling of sadness or sympathy • He begins his book with an *affecting* description of his difficult childhood. • a powerful, *affecting* [=*moving, touching*] performance
– af·fect·ing·ly *adv* • He described her death *affectingly*.

af·fec·tion /əˈfɛkʃən/ *noun, pl* **-tions**
1 : a feeling of liking and caring for someone or something [*noncount*] She has/feels deep *affection* for her parents. • Their *affection* for each other is obvious. = Their mutual *affection* is obvious. • He shows great *affection* for his grandchildren. • feelings of love and *affection* • He now looks back on those years with great *affection*. • "darling" and other ***terms of affection*** [=words and names that friends and lovers say to each other to show their affection] [*singular*] She developed a deep *affection* for that country and its people.
2 ***affections*** [*plural*] **:** feelings of love **:** a person's romantic feelings • The two women competed for the *affections* [=*love, heart*] of the same man. • She's been ***the object of his affections*** since they were children. [=he has loved her since they were children]

af·fec·tion·ate /əˈfɛkʃənət/ *adj* [*more* ~; *most* ~] **:** feeling or showing love and affection • You were lucky to have such *affectionate* [=*loving*] parents. • an *affectionate* nickname
– af·fec·tion·ate·ly *adv* • His family *affectionately* refers to him as "the baby."

af·fi·da·vit /ˌæfəˈdeɪvət/ *noun, pl* **-vits** [*count*] *law* **:** a written report which is signed by a person who promises that the information is true • We have a signed *affidavit* stating that the two men were seen entering the building.

¹af·fil·i·ate /əˈfɪliˌeɪt/ *verb* **-ates; -at·ed; -at·ing** [+ *obj*] **:** to closely connect (something or yourself) with or to something (such as a program or organization) as a member or partner • Their group does not ***affiliate itself*** with/to any political party. — often used as *(be) affiliated* • Their group *is* not *affiliated* with/to any political party. • The medical school *is affiliated* with/to several hospitals.
– affiliated *adj* • the medical school and its *affiliated* hospitals • the television network's *affiliated* stations

²af·fil·i·ate /əˈfɪlijət/ *noun, pl* **-ates** [*count*] **:** an organization (such as a television station) that is a member of a larger organization (such as a national network) • the network's local *affiliates* • Two of the company's regional *affiliates* lost money in the past year.

af·fil·i·a·tion /əˌfɪliˈeɪʃən/ *noun, pl* **-tions :** the state of being affiliated to something: such as **a :** the state of being closely associated with or connected to an organization, company, etc. [*count*] The medical school has an *affiliation* to/with several hospitals. [*noncount*] proposing the *affiliation* of the medical school to/with several hospitals **b** [*count*] **:** the state of belonging to a particular religious or political group — usually plural • They agreed not to discuss their political *affiliations*.

af·fin·i·ty /əˈfɪnəti/ *noun, pl* **-ties** *formal*
1 : a feeling of closeness and understanding that someone has for another person because of their similar qualities, ideas, or interests [*singular*] They had much in common and felt a close *affinity* (for/to/with each other). • There's always been an *affinity* between us. [*noncount*] He never felt any *affinity* with the other kids in his neighborhood.
2 [*singular*] **a :** a liking for or an attraction to something • We share an *affinity* for foreign films. [=we both like foreign films] **b :** a quality that makes people or things suited to each other • Fish and white wine have a natural *affinity* for/to each other. [=fish and white wine taste good together]
3 : the state of being similar or the same [*noncount*] the *affinity* of all human beings with one another = the *affinity* between all human beings [*count*] Are there any *affinities* [=*similarities*] between the two styles of painting?

af·firm /əˈfɚm/ *verb* **-firms; -firmed; -firm·ing** [+ *obj*]
1 *formal* **:** to say that something is true in a confident way • We cannot *affirm* that this painting is genuine. • The two men *affirm* that they are innocent. = The two men *affirm* their innocence. [=they say they are not guilty] • They neither *affirmed* nor denied their guilt. ***synonyms*** see ASSERT
2 *formal* **:** to show a strong belief in or dedication to (something, such as an important idea) • laws *affirming* the racial equality of all peoples • They continued to *affirm* their religious beliefs. • *affirm* life — see also LIFE-AFFIRMING
3 *law* **:** to decide that the judgment of another court is correct • The decision was *affirmed* by a higher court. • The court *affirmed* his conviction. [=the court agreed that he was guilty]
– af·fir·ma·tion /ˌæfɚˈmeɪʃən/ *noun* [*noncount*] the *affirmation* of guilt/innocence • When asked if the statement was true, he nodded his head in *affirmation*. [*count*] The ceremony was an *affirmation* of their religious beliefs.

¹af·fir·ma·tive /əˈfɚmətɪv/ *adj, formal* **:** saying or showing that the answer is "yes" rather than "no" • She gave an *affirmative* answer, not a negative answer.
– af·fir·ma·tive·ly *adv* • She answered (the question) *affirmatively*.

²affirmative *noun*
in the affirmative *formal* **:** with a reply that means "yes" • He answered (the question) *in the affirmative*. [=he said "yes"] — compare *in the negative* at ²NEGATIVE

affirmative action *noun* [*noncount*] *chiefly US* **:** the practice of improving the educational and job opportunities of members of groups that have not been treated fairly in the past because of their race, sex, etc. — called also *(Brit) positive discrimination*

¹af·fix /əˈfɪks/ *verb* **-fix·es; -fixed; -fix·ing** [+ *obj*] *formal* **:** to attach (something) *to* something else • Please *affix* a stamp *to* [=put a stamp on] this letter. • She *affixed* her signature *to* the document. [=she signed the document]

²af·fix /ˈæˌfɪks/ *noun, pl* **-fix·es** [*count*] *grammar* **:** a letter or group of letters added to the beginning or end of a word to change its meaning **:** a prefix or suffix

af·flict /əˈflɪkt/ *verb* **-flicts; -flict·ed; -flict·ing** [+ *obj*] *formal* **:** to cause pain or suffering to (someone or something) • The disease *afflicts* an estimated two million people every year. — usually used as *(be) afflicted* • Much of the region *is*

A

afflicted by hunger and poverty. — often + *with* ▪ Most patients/people who *are afflicted with* the disease die within one year. ▪ people *afflicted with* cancer

af·flic·tion /əˈflɪkʃən/ *noun, pl* **-tions** *formal*

1 [*count*] **: something (such as a disease) that causes pain or suffering** ▪ She lost her sight and is now learning to live with her/the *affliction*. ▪ He died from a mysterious *affliction*.

2 [*noncount*] **: the state of being affected by something that causes suffering** ▪ her *affliction* with polio

af·flu·ent /ˈæfluwənt/ *adj* [*more* ~; *most* ~] **: having a large amount of money and owning many expensive things : RICH, WEALTHY** ▪ an *affluent* country ▪ an *affluent* suburb/neighborhood/community ▪ *affluent* families ▪ His family was more *affluent* than most.

– **af·flu·ence** /ˈæfluwəns/ *noun* [*noncount*] ▪ They rose from poverty to *affluence*. [=they were poor and became rich]

af·ford /əˈfoɚd/ *verb* **-fords; -ford·ed; -ford·ing** [+ *obj*]

1 : to be able to pay for (something) ▪ We were too poor to *afford* a doctor. ▪ He'll be able to *afford* a house next year. ▪ Don't spend more than you can *afford*. ▪ They couldn't *afford* new coats for the children. — **often followed by** *to* + *verb* ▪ They couldn't *afford to buy* new coats for the children. ▪ Don't spend more than you can *afford to (spend)*.

2 : to be able to do (something) without having problems or being seriously harmed ▪ We can *afford* waiting a while longer. — **usually followed by** *to* + *verb* ▪ We can *afford to wait* a while longer. — **usually used in negative constructions** ▪ She's already too thin. She can't *afford to lose* any more weight. = She can ***ill afford*** *to lose* any more weight.

3 *formal* **: to supply or provide (something needed or wanted) to someone** ▪ All of the rooms *afford* views of the lake. ▪ He was *afforded* the opportunity to work for a judge.

– **af·ford·abil·i·ty** /əˌfoɚdəˈbɪləti/ *noun* [*noncount*] ▪ the *affordability* of health care – **af·ford·able** /əˈfoɚdəbəl/ *adj* [*more* ~; *most* ~] ▪ a more *affordable* car ▪ *affordable* housing [=housing that is not overly expensive] ▪ an *affordable* price

af·for·es·ta·tion /æˌforəˈsteɪʃən/ *noun* [*noncount*] *chiefly Brit* **: the act or process of planting a forest**

af·fray /əˈfreɪ/ *noun, pl* **-frays** [*count*] *chiefly Brit, law, formal* **: a noisy fight between two or more people in a public place** ▪ a shooting *affray*

¹af·front /əˈfrʌnt/ *noun, pl* **-fronts** [*count*] *formal* **: an action or statement that insults or offends someone** ▪ He regarded her rude behavior as a personal *affront*. — **often +** *to* ▪ Her remarks were an *affront to* all of us. ▪ The test was an *affront to* our intelligence. [=the test was too simple]

²affront *verb* **-fronts; -front·ed; -front·ing** [+ *obj*] *formal* **: to do or say something that shows a lack of respect for (someone or someone's feelings)** — **usually used as** *(be) affronted* ▪ He *was affronted* [=*insulted, offended*] by her rude behavior.

af·ghan /ˈæfˌgæn/ *noun, pl* **-ghans** [*count*] *chiefly US* **: a blanket made of wool or cotton knitted in patterns**

Af·ghan /ˈæfˌgæn/ *noun, pl* **-ghans** [*count*]

1 : a person born, raised, or living in Afghanistan

2 : AFGHAN HOUND

– **Afghan** *or* **Af·ghani** /æfˈgæni, *Brit* æfˈgɑːni/ *adj* ▪ *Afghan* citizens ▪ *Afghani* children

Afghan hound *noun, pl* ~ **hounds** [*count*] **: a type of tall thin dog with long soft hair**

afi·cio·na·do /əˌfɪʃijəˈnɑːdoʊ/ *noun, pl* **-dos** [*count*] **: a person who likes and knows a lot about something** ▪ an *aficionado* of poetry ▪ sports *aficionados*

afield /əˈfiːld/ *adv* **: away from home : away from here or there — used with** *far, farther,* **or** *further* ▪ People came/traveled from as *far afield* as New York to see the show. ▪ He didn't want to go any *farther/further afield*. — **often used figuratively** ▪ Her question took us *far afield* from our original subject.

afire /əˈfajɚ/ *adj, not used before a noun* **: burning : on fire : AFLAME** ▪ The house was *afire*.

– **afire** *adv* ▪ They set the house *afire*.

aflame /əˈfleɪm/ *adj, not used before a noun* **: burning : on fire** ▪ In a few minutes, the entire town was *aflame*. [=*afire, ablaze*] — **often used figuratively** ▪ Their hearts were *aflame*. [=filled with love and excitement] ▪ The fields are *aflame* with flowers of every color.

– **aflame** *adv* ▪ The roof was set *aflame* by lightning.

afloat /əˈfloʊt/ *adj, not used before a noun*

1 : floating on water ▪ Our boat remained/stayed *afloat* through the storm. ▪ It's the largest ship *afloat*.

2 : having enough money to continue : able to continue without suffering financial failure ▪ The inheritance kept them *afloat* for years. ▪ trying to keep the business *afloat* ▪ struggling to stay *afloat*

aflut·ter /əˈflʌtɚ/ *adj, not used before a noun* **: nervously excited** ▪ Her heart was *aflutter* at the thought of his return.

afoot /əˈfʊt/ *adj, not used before a noun* **: developing or happening now : in progress** ▪ Plans were *afoot* to begin construction on the bridge. ▪ Something strange was *afoot*. ▪ There's trouble *afoot*.

afore·men·tioned /əˈfoɚˈmɛnʃənd/ *adj, always used before a noun, formal* **: mentioned before : spoken about or named earlier** ▪ The *aforementioned* book is the author's most famous work.

afore·said /əˈfoɚˌsɛd/ *adj, always used before a noun, formal* **: said or named before : AFOREMENTIONED — often used in legal contexts** ▪ Based on the *aforesaid* reasons, the court has come to its decision.

afore·thought /əˈfoɚˌθɑːt/ *adj* **: thought about or planned beforehand**

with malice aforethought see MALICE

afoul of /əˈfaʊləv/ *adv*

fall/run afoul of *chiefly US* **: to get into trouble because of (the law, a rule, etc.)** ▪ After leaving home he *fell afoul of* the law. [=he got into trouble for breaking the law; he was arrested for committing a crime] ▪ an investor who has *run afoul of* stock market rules

afraid /əˈfreɪd/ *adj, not used before a noun*

1 [*more* ~; *most* ~] **: feeling fear: such as a : worried that something will cause pain or injury** ▪ Don't be *afraid* [=*frightened, scared*]—the dog won't hurt you. — **often +** *of* ▪ I don't like tall buildings because I'm *afraid of* heights. [=of being high up in the air] ▪ He's *afraid of* snakes. ▪ All the kids at school were *afraid of* him. **b : nervous about doing something — often +** *of* ▪ She's *afraid of* failing/failure. ▪ He wasn't *afraid of* saying what he thought. ▪ Don't be *afraid of* [=don't worry about] what everyone else thinks. — **often followed by** *to* + *verb* ▪ He wasn't *afraid to say* what he thought. ▪ I wanted to visit her, but I was *afraid to ask*. ▪ Don't be *afraid to take* risks. **c : nervous or worried that something might happen** ▪ She's *afraid* (that) she might fail. ▪ We were all *afraid* (that) she wouldn't live. ▪ I'm *afraid* (that) everyone will laugh at me. ▪ I was *afraid* (that) you would say "no."

2 — used in the phrase *I'm afraid* as a polite way of showing that you are sorry about a disappointing, negative, or critical statement ▪ I'm sorry, but *I'm afraid* (that) I won't be able to come to your party. ▪ She tries hard, but *I'm afraid* that her work just isn't very good. ▪ I'm *afraid* that I still don't understand the problem. ▪ This is only the beginning of the battle, *I'm afraid*. ▪ Most of us worked very hard, but she, ***I'm afraid to say*** [=*I'm sorry to say; I regret to say*], did no work at all. ▪ "Is it raining?" "***I'm afraid so***." = "*I'm afraid* it is." [=yes, it is] ▪ "Can you come to our party?" "***I'm afraid not***." = "*I'm afraid* I can't." [=no, I can't come]

3 — used with *not* to say that someone is willing to do something; often + *of* ▪ She's *not afraid of* hard work. = She's *not afraid of* working hard. [=she's willing to work hard; she works hard] ▪ You *can't be afraid of* getting dirty in this job. [=you have to be willing to get dirty in this job] — **often followed by** *to* + *verb* ▪ She's *not afraid to work* hard. ▪ He's *not afraid to admit* his mistakes.

afraid for **: feeling fear or worry about (something or someone)** ▪ I'm *afraid for* the children. ▪ They were *afraid for* their lives. [=they feared for their lives; they were afraid that they might die] ▪ He's *afraid for* his job. [=he's worried that he might lose his job]

afresh /əˈfrɛʃ/ *adv* **: from a new beginning** ▪ Let's stop now and start *afresh* [=*again, anew*] in the morning. ▪ The author makes her readers look *afresh* at an old subject. [=she makes them think about an old subject in a new/fresh way]

Af·ri·can /ˈæfrɪkən/ *noun, pl* **-cans** [*count*]

1 : a person born, raised, or living in Africa

2 : a descendant of Africans

– **African** *adj* ▪ *African* history/countries

Af·ri·can–Amer·i·can /ˌæfrɪkənəˈmerɪkən/ *noun, pl* **-cans** [*count*] **: an American who has African and especially black African ancestors** ✧ Many people prefer the term *African-American* rather than *black* when referring to Americans of African descent.

– **African–American** *adj* ▪ *African-American* scientists ▪ *African-American* culture

African violet *noun, pl* ~ **-lets** [*count*] **:** a tropical plant from Africa that is grown indoors for its purple, pink, or white flowers — see color picture on page C6

Af·ri·kaans /ˌæfrɪˈkɑːns/ *noun* [*noncount*] **:** a language based on Dutch that is spoken in South Africa

Af·ri·ka·ner /ˌæfrɪˈkɑːnɚ/ *noun, pl* **-ners** [*count*] **:** a person born, raised, or living in South Africa whose first language is Afrikaans and whose ancestors were Dutch

Af·ro /ˈæfroʊ/ *noun, pl* **-ros** [*count*] **:** a hairstyle in which very curly hair is shaped into a smooth round ball — see picture at HAIR ✧ *Afros* were often worn by black people in the 1970s.

Afro- *combining form* **:** African (and) • *Afro*-American

Af·ro–Amer·i·can /ˌæfrowəˈmerəkən/ *noun, pl* **-cans** [*count*] **:** AFRICAN-AMERICAN • an *Afro-American*
– **Afro–American** *adj*

[1]**aft** /ˈæft, *Brit* ˈɑːft/ *adv* **:** towards or at the back part of a boat, ship, or airplane • We stood on the ship's deck facing *aft.* • The plane's exits are located fore and *aft.* • There is an exit located just ***aft of*** [=behind] the wing. — compare [2]FORE

[2]**aft** *adj* **:** located at the back of a boat, ship, or airplane • the ship's fore and *aft* cabins • The fore and *aft* exits can both be used in an emergency. — compare [3]FORE

[1]**af·ter** /ˈæftɚ, *Brit* ˈɑːftə/ *adv* **:** following in time **:** at a later time • Dinner was at six and we arrived shortly *after.* [=*thereafter*] • He returned 20 years *after.* [=*later*] • Don't tell them until *after.* • I expected her then, but she arrived the week *after.* • He ate lunch and left just/right/immediately *after.* • I saw her again the day *after.* [=the following day] • He vowed to love her forever/ever *after.* [=from that time on, forever]

[2]**after** *prep*

1 a : at a time following (something or someone) **:** later than (something or someone) • We arrived shortly *after* six o'clock. • He returned *after* 20 years. • before, during, and *after* the war • He left just/right/immediately/soon/shortly *after* nightfall/dark. • Night fell, and soon *after* that [=soon afterward] he left. • He finished the exam *after* me. • I stood up *after* the judge (did). [=the judge stood up before I (did)] • Call me *after* your arrival. • She was going to arrive tomorrow but I'm now expecting her the day *after* tomorrow instead. • She hasn't lived there since (the time) *after* the war. • They earned $30,000 *after* (paying) taxes. • He left *after* an hour. • Let's get going! It's *after* [=*past*] 12 (o'clock). • The job got easier ***after a while.*** [=after some time had passed] **b** *US* — used to describe a time following a specified hour • It's 20 (minutes) *after* 12. [=it's 20 past 12; it's 12:20]

2 a : following and because of (something) • *After* all our advice, she's certain to do better. [=she's certain to do better because we have given her our advice] **b :** following and in spite of (something) • Even *after* all our advice, she still did badly! [=she did badly even though we gave her our advice] • How can you say that *after* what happened last night?

3 a : following (something or someone) in order or in a series • It's the highest mountain *after* Mount Everest. • You'll see my house just before the bank and *after* the school. • The number 2 comes before 3 and *after* 1. [=2 comes between 1 and 3] • My name is listed *after* yours. • You go first and I'll go/follow *after* you. • The children marched out ***one after the other*** in single file. ✧ The phrase ***after you*** is used as a polite way of saying that someone should go ahead of you or do something before you do it. • *After you,* Madam! ✧ In British English, you can say ***after you with*** something to ask the person who is using something to let you use it next. • *After you with* the pencil, please. [=I would like to use the pencil when you have finished using it] **b —** used in phrases to describe something that happens many times or for a long period of time • They have suffered misfortune *after* misfortune. [=they have suffered a long series of misfortunes] • Wave *after* [=*upon*] wave was beating against the shore. • She does her job ***day after day*** without complaining. • He's done the same thing ***time after time.***

4 : trying to catch or get (something or someone) • The dog ran *after* the ball. [=the dog ran to get the ball] • The police went/chased *after* the escaped criminal. • The police are *after* him. [=are trying to catch him] • What do you think he's *after* with all his questions? [=what is he trying to achieve by asking his questions?] ✧ If people are ***after you*** to do something, they want you to do it and they tell you to do it repeatedly. • Mom was *after me* to clean my room. [=Mom repeatedly told me to clean my room]

5 : following the actions or departure of (someone) • She called/shouted *after* him as he walked away. [=she called/shouted at/toward him as he walked away] • They made a mess and didn't clean up *after* themselves. [=they didn't clean up the mess they made] • If you make a mess, don't expect me to clean up *after* you.

6 a : with the name of (someone or something) • He was called George *after* his father. • She was named *after* her grandmother. [=she was given the same name as her grandmother] • The game rugby was named *after* Rugby School in England, where it began. **b :** in the manner of (someone or something) • a building patterned *after* [=*on*] a cathedral • (*formal*) a story *after* (the manner of) Hemingway

7 : in a lower or less important position than (something) • They put quality *after* quantity. [=they cared more about quantity than about quality]

8 : about or concerning (someone or something) • I met one of your old friends and she was asking/inquiring *after* you. [=she was asking about you; she was asking how you are] • She was asking *after* your health.

after all **1 :** in spite of what was said **:** even though the opposite was expected • They decided to go *after all.* • It didn't rain *after all.* **2 —** used to emphasize something that needs to be considered • It's only Tuesday, *after all.* We have plenty of time. • You should apologize to her. *After all,* she is your best friend.

[3]**after** *conj* **:** later than the time that **:** later than when • He returned *after* 20 years had passed. • The defendant stood up *after* the judge did. [=the judge stood up before the defendant did] • Don't tell them until *after* they've had dinner. • He left just/right/immediately/soon/shortly *after* the show ended. • Call me *after* you arrive. • He finished the exam *after* I did. • It happened not long *after* he graduated from college.

[4]**after** *adj, always used before a noun, old-fashioned + literary* **:** later in time • in *after* [=*later*] years

af·ter·birth /ˈæftɚˌbɚθ, *Brit* ˈɑːftəˌbəːθ/ *noun* [*singular*] *medical* **:** the tissues that come out of the body of a woman after she gives birth to a baby

af·ter·care /ˈæftɚˌkeɚ, *Brit* ˈɑːftəˌkeə/ *noun* [*noncount*] **:** the care, treatment, etc., given to people after they leave a place (such as a hospital or prison) — often used before another noun • *aftercare* services

af·ter·ef·fect /ˈæftɚrɪˌfɛkt, *Brit* ˈɑːftərɪˌfɛkt/ *noun, pl* **-fects** [*count*] **:** an effect that occurs after time has passed — usually plural • He's suffering the *aftereffects* of his injury.

af·ter·glow /ˈæftɚˌgloʊ, *Brit* ˈɑːftəˌgləʊ/ *noun* [*singular*]

1 : a glowing light remaining in the sky after the sun has set • the *afterglow* of the sunset

2 : a happy feeling that remains after a successful or emotional event • the party's *afterglow* • We basked in the *afterglow* [=enjoyed the happiness and satisfaction] of the victory.

af·ter·life /ˈæftɚˌlaɪf, *Brit* ˈɑːftəˌlaɪf/ *noun* [*singular*] **:** a life that some people believe exists after death • Does he believe in an *afterlife*? — often used with *the* • She believes she will meet her ancestors in *the afterlife.*

af·ter·math /ˈæftɚˌmæθ, *Brit* ˈɑːftəˌmæθ/ *noun, pl* **-maths** [*count*] **:** the period of time after a bad and usually destructive event — usually singular • In the *aftermath* of the fire, many people were in need of shelter. • The country is rebuilding its economy in the *aftermath* of the war. • The children struggled through their parents' divorce and its *aftermath.*

af·ter·noon /ˌæftɚˈnuːn, *Brit* ˌɑːftəˈnuːn/ *noun, pl* **-noons** [*count*] **:** the middle part of the day **:** the part of the day between noon and evening • morning, *afternoon,* evening, and night • I'll see you again tomorrow *afternoon.* • It was early/late *afternoon* when I left. • She spent the/her *afternoon* at the library. • She came home the next/following *afternoon.* [=during the afternoon of the next day] • I remember the many rainy *afternoons* I spent reading at the library. • She doesn't have class on Friday *afternoons.* • It took us all *afternoon* to get there. • It's going to be a long *afternoon* listening to lectures. • We went for a walk ***this afternoon.*** [=during the afternoon today] — often used before another noun • an *afternoon* drive • *afternoon* tea • Our garden gets plenty of *afternoon* sun. [=the sun shines on the garden in the afternoon] — see also GOOD AFTERNOON

af·ter·noons /ˌæftɚˈnuːnz, *Brit* ˌɑːftəˈnuːnz/ *adv, US* **:** in the afternoon • He works *afternoons* in a convenience store.

af·ters /ˈæftɚz, *Brit* ˈɑːftəz/ *noun* [*noncount*] *Brit, informal* **:** DESSERT • What's for *afters*? • *Afters* is ice cream tonight.

af·ter–sales /ˈæftɚˌseɪlz, *Brit* ˈɑːftəˌseɪlz/ *adj, always used before a noun, Brit* **:** provided to customers after a sale has been made ▪ *after-sales* service and maintenance

af·ter–school /ˈæftɚˌskuːl, *Brit* ˈɑːftəˌskuːl/ *adj, always used before a noun* : happening or done after the end of the school day ▪ She started an *after-school* job so she could buy a car. ▪ *after-school* activities/programs

af·ter·shave /ˈæftɚˌʃeɪv, *Brit* ˈɑːftəˌʃeɪv/ *noun, pl* **-shaves** [*count, noncount*] : a pleasant-smelling liquid that some men put on their faces after they have shaved

af·ter·shock /ˈæftɚˌʃɑːk, *Brit* ˈɑːftəˌʃɒk/ *noun, pl* **-shocks** [*count*] : a smaller earthquake that occurs after a larger one ▪ The first *aftershock* came just minutes after the earthquake. — often used figuratively ▪ He still suffers from the *aftershocks* of being laid off.

af·ter·taste /ˈæftɚˌteɪst, *Brit* ˈɑːftəˌteɪst/ *noun* [*singular*] : a taste that remains after something is eaten or drunk ▪ The wine has a smooth/fruity/sweet *aftertaste*. — often used figuratively ▪ The experience left me with a bitter *aftertaste*. [=I felt bitter after the experience]

af·ter·thought /ˈæftɚˌθɑːt, *Brit* ˈɑːftəˌθɔːt/ *noun, pl* **-thoughts** [*count*] : something done or said after other things because it was not thought of earlier ▪ Then I remembered, almost as an *afterthought*, to feed the cat. ▪ The fact was hidden deep in the report, almost as an *afterthought*. ▪ The lounge was added to the office as an *afterthought*.

af·ter·ward /ˈæftɚwɚd, *Brit* ˈɑːftəwəd/ *or* **af·ter·wards** /ˈæftɚwɚdz, *Brit* ˈɑːftəwədz/ *adv* : at a later time : after something has happened ▪ You'll feel better *afterward*. ▪ He found out about it long *afterward*. ▪ *Afterward*, she got a promotion. ✧ In U.S. English, *afterward* is more common than *afterwards*. In British English, *afterwards* is more common.

af·ter·word /ˈæftɚˌwɚd, *Brit* ˈɑːftəˈwɜːd/ *noun, pl* **-words** [*count*] : a final section that comes after the main part of a book ▪ The novel has a foreword by an eminent critic and an *afterword* by the author herself.

again /əˈgɛn/ *adv*

1 : for another time : one more time ▪ Please, come see us *again*. ▪ Spring is beginning *again*. ▪ It was nice to see my friends *again*. ▪ She wants to prove that she can do it *again*. ▪ Things are back to normal *again*. ▪ I will never be so foolish *again*. = ***Never again*** will I be so foolish. ▪ When we heard the news, we all said, "Oh no! ***Not again***!" ▪ She demonstrated ***yet again*** her remarkable artistic talents. ▪ It'll just be the same thing ***all over again***. ▪ I told him ***over and over again*** to be careful. = I told him ***again and again*** to be careful. [=I told him many times to be careful] ▪ She returned to the bookstore *again and again*. [=repeatedly, many times]

2 : to a previous position or place ▪ We flew from Boston to Chicago and back *again*. [=back to Boston] ▪ When he stood up, he got so dizzy that he had to sit down *again*.

3 — used to introduce a thought or possibility that differs from a preceding one ▪ He might go, and *again* he might not. — usually used in the phrase ***then again*** ▪ He might go, and *then again*, he might not. ▪ *Then again*, perhaps they were right.

4 — used to introduce a statement that repeats and stresses something previously said ▪ *Again*, this is a serious problem.

5 — used to ask someone to repeat something because you did not hear or understand it clearly ▪ What was your name *again*?

6 — used in phrases like (*chiefly US*) ***half again as much*** and (*chiefly Brit*) ***half as much again*** to compare two amounts ▪ My ticket costs *half again as much* as your ticket. [=(for example) my ticket costs $15 and your ticket costs $10]

(every) now and again see EVERY

now and again see [1]NOW

once again see [1]ONCE

time and again see [1]TIME

against /əˈgɛnst/ *prep*

1 a : in opposition to (someone or something) ▪ Everyone was *against* them. [=everyone opposed them] ▪ We must continue the struggle for justice and *against* injustice. ▪ She voted *against* the proposal. ▪ You're either for/with me or *against* me! [=you either support me or oppose me] ▪ He spoke *against* appeasing the enemy. ▪ The U.S. fought *against* Germany in World Wars I and II. = The U.S. and Germany fought *against* each other in World Wars I and II. ▪ Some people were for the proposal but others were *against* it. ▪ There's a law *against* doing that. ▪ His parents were angry when they learned he had borrowed the car ***against their wishes***. [=he borrowed the car even though they did not want him to] ▪ ***Against my advice***, she quit her job. [=she quit her job even though I advised her not to] ▪ He was being held ***against his will***. [=he was being kept in a place by force even though he wanted to leave] **b** : in competition with (someone or something) ▪ two runners racing *against* each other ▪ It's the Yankees *against* [=*versus*] the Red Sox tonight.

2 — used to indicate the person or thing that is affected or harmed by something ▪ He denies the charges that have been made *against* him. ▪ The evidence *against* him is very convincing. ▪ The war was a crime *against* humanity. ▪ Someone has been making threats *against* her.

3 : not agreeing with or allowed by (something, such as a law) ▪ You can't do that. It's *against* the law. [=the law does not allow it] ▪ Touching the ball with your hands is *against* the rules. ▪ I won't do it. It's *against* my principles. [=my principles don't allow it; I believe that it is wrong] ▪ They were acting *against* tradition. [=acting in a way that did not agree with tradition]

4 a : not helping or favoring (someone) ▪ Everything was/went *against* them. [=everything that happened was unfavorable to them] ▪ Her appearance is/counts *against* her. [=her appearance does not help her; people form a bad opinion of her because of her appearance] **b** : as a reason for disliking (someone or something) ▪ I ***have nothing against*** him. [=I don't dislike him; I have no reason for disliking him] ▪ We disagree about many things, but I don't ***hold it/that against*** you. [=I don't dislike you because of it/that]

5 — used to say that one thing is being compared with another ▪ Profits are up this year *against* last year. [=profits are higher this year than they were last year] ▪ The yen rose/fell *against* the dollar. ▪ a graph that plots height *against* weight ▪ We will weigh/balance the risk *against* the possible benefit. [=we will compare the risk with the possible benefit]

6 a : as a defense or protection from (something) ▪ He built a crude hut as a shelter *against* [=*from*] the cold. ▪ injections *against* flu **b** : in preparation for (something) ▪ saving *against* [=*for*] an uncertain future

7 — used to describe hitting or touching something or someone ▪ I accidentally knocked/hit my head *against* the shelf. ▪ The waves were beating *against* [=*on*] the shore. ▪ She accidentally brushed *against* him as she walked by. ▪ The ladder was leaning *against* the wall. ▪ She was resting her head *against* the side of the chair.

8 : in a direction opposite to the movement of (something) ▪ They were sailing *against* the wind. ▪ swimming *against* the current/tide

9 : with the background of (something) ▪ The tree looked beautiful when viewed *against* the dark sky. ▪ Her colorful coat stood out *against* the dull colors of the room.

10 : as a charge on (something) ▪ The purchase was charged *against* [=*to*] her account. [=the amount of money needed for the purchase was added to the amount owed in her account]

as against see [2]AS

over against see [2]OVER

up against see [2]UP

agape /əˈgeɪp/ *adj, not used before a noun* : having the mouth open because of wonder, surprise, or shock ▪ He stood there with his mouth *agape*. [=with his mouth gaping] ▪ The crowd stared *agape* at the accident scene.

ag·ate /ˈægət/ *noun, pl* **-ates** [*count*] : a very hard stone used especially in jewelry that has colors arranged in stripes or in patches

[1]**age** /ˈeɪʤ/ *noun, pl* **ag·es**

1 a : the amount of time during which a person or animal has lived [*count*] What is your *age*? [=how old are you?] ▪ The *age* of the student was 20. = The student's *age* was 20. ▪ Some people are reluctant to reveal their *ages*. ▪ She died tragically at a young *age*. ▪ Exercise is good for a man (of) your *age*. ▪ The treatment depends on the sex and *age* of the patient. ▪ He joined the company ***at the age of*** 35. [=when he was 35 years old] ▪ She died at the ***ripe old age*** of 90. ▪ You're too old to behave so foolishly. You should know better ***at your age***. [=a person as old as you are should know better] ▪ You should learn to ***act your age***. [=to act in a way that is appropriate for a person of your age] ▪ She showed remarkable musical talent ***at/from an early age***. [=she showed talent when she was young] ▪ The movie appeals to people ***of all ages***. ▪ The book is popular among men/women ***of a certain age***. [=men/women who are not young anymore] ▪ Her ***age is catching up to her***. = She is starting to ***feel her age***. [=she is starting to feel old] ▪ He left home ***at the tender age*** of 18. [=when he was only 18 years old] ▪ He learned to paint ***in his old age***. [=when he was old] ▪ Our son is small ***for his age***. [=he's smaller than most children are at his age] [*noncount*] Their son needs to spend more time with children his own

age. ▪ a group of children ranging in *age* from 8 to 11 ▪ When you're my *age* [=when you're as old as I am] you'll realize that life isn't always fair. ▪ She became involved with a man twice her *age*. ▪ More people now live to extreme old *age*. [=live to be extremely old] ▪ The program is for people over/under *age* 50. ▪ groups of people classified by race and *age* ▪ The student was 20 years ***of age***. [=was 20 years old] ▪ He joined the company ***at age*** 35. — often used before another noun ▪ The movie appeals to people of all *age* groups. ▪ He was over the *age* limit. [=he was too old] — see also MIDDLE AGE, OLD AGE, SCHOOL AGE **b :** the amount of time during which a thing has existed [*count*] What is the *age* of your car? ▪ The car is in good condition *for its age*. [=considering how old it is] [*noncount*] The magazines were sorted by *age*.
2 : the time of life when a person does something or becomes legally able to do something [*count*] The voting *age* is 18. [=people are allowed to vote when they are 18 years old] ▪ He was past the *age* for military service. [*noncount*] Her parents are approaching retirement *age*. ▪ young people who have not yet reached drinking *age* ▪ students of college *age* = college-*age* students — see also AGE OF CONSENT
3 [*noncount*] **a :** the passage of time **:** the process of becoming old or older ▪ a tree weakened by *age* ▪ His skills haven't diminished with *age*. ▪ a wine that has improved with *age* ▪ "*Age* cannot wither her, nor custom stale her infinite variety." —Shakespeare, *Antony and Cleopatra* (1607) **b :** the condition of being old ▪ from youth to (old) *age* ▪ The building is showing signs of *age*. ▪ She died of old *age*.
4 [*count*] **:** a period of history — usually singular ▪ an airplane that became a symbol of the modern *age* ▪ a bygone/past *age* ▪ the great problems of our *age* ▪ It's hard to believe that such behavior is still tolerated ***in this day and age***. [=in current times; now] **:** a period of time that is associated with a particular thing or person ▪ People expect information instantly in this *age* of the Internet. ▪ the *age* of Columbus ▪ the machine *age* ▪ the *Age* of Discovery — see also BRONZE AGE, DARK AGES, GOLDEN AGE, ICE AGE, IRON AGE, NEW AGE, STONE AGE, *gilded age* at GILD
5 [*count*] *informal* **:** a long period of time ▪ It's been an *age* since we last saw them. — usually plural ▪ It's been *ages* since we last saw them. = We haven't seen them in/for *ages*. = It was *ages* ago when we last saw them.
come of age **:** to reach the age when you are considered an adult ▪ He received his full inheritance when he *came of age*. — often used figuratively. ▪ She *came of age* as an artist [=she developed fully as an artist] after she moved to New York. ▪ a political movement that has recently *come of age* [=has become fully formed and effective]
in a coon's age *or* ***in a dog's age*** *US, informal* **:** in a very long time ▪ We haven't seen them *in a coon's age*.

²age *verb* **ages; aged; ag·ing** *or chiefly Brit* **age·ing**
1 [*no obj*] **:** to become old or older ▪ As he *aged* he grew more and more bitter. ▪ You haven't *aged* a day since I saw you last! ▪ an *aging* population ▪ a book that has *aged* well [=a book that is still good or appealing although it is no longer new] ▪ She has *aged* gracefully. [=she has continued to be healthy and young looking as she has gotten older]
2 [+ *obj*] **:** to cause (someone or something) to become old or to appear to be old ▪ His troubles have *aged* him. ▪ Exposure to the sun has *aged* her skin.
3 *of food or drink* **:** to be stored for a period of time in order to gain desired qualities [*no obj*] The wine *ages* in oak barrels. [+ *obj*] The wine is *aged* in oak barrels. ▪ an *aged* cheese

-age /ɪʤ/ *noun suffix*
1 : action, process, or result of ▪ cover*age* ▪ break*age* ▪ wast*age*
2 : total amount or collection ▪ mile*age* ▪ acre*age*
3 : house or place of ▪ orphan*age* ▪ broker*age*
4 : state, status, or condition of ▪ bond*age* ▪ block*age*
5 : fee or charge ▪ post*age*

aged *adj*
1 /ˈeɪʤəd/ **:** very old ▪ an *aged* oak ▪ an *aged* man
2 /ˈeɪʤd/ *not used before a noun* **:** having reached a specified age ▪ a woman *aged* 40 [=a woman who is 40 years old] ▪ a child *aged* 10 ▪ a group of men *aged* between 20 and 30
the aged **:** old people ▪ providing help for *the aged* and the sick
– ag·ed·ness /ˈeɪʤədnəs/ *noun* [*noncount*]

ageing *chiefly Brit spelling of* AGING

age·ism /ˈeɪˌʤɪzəm/ *noun* [*noncount*] **:** unfair treatment of old people ▪ He accused his former employer of *ageism* when he lost his job to a younger man.
– age·ist /ˈeɪʤɪst/ *adj* ▪ an *ageist* attitude/society

age·less /ˈeɪʤləs/ *adj*
1 : not growing old or showing the effects of age ▪ *ageless* skin ▪ *ageless* beauty ▪ a seemingly *ageless* athlete
2 : lasting forever **:** ETERNAL, TIMELESS ▪ The movie retold an *ageless* legend. ▪ an *ageless* tradition ▪ *ageless* truths
– age·less·ly *adv* ▪ remains *agelessly* beautiful ▪ an *agelessly* romantic gesture **– age·less·ness** *noun* [*noncount*] ▪ the *agelessness* of her beauty

agen·cy /ˈeɪʤənsi/ *noun, pl* **-cies** [*count*]
1 : a business that provides a particular service ▪ an insurance/travel/employment *agency* ▪ a prominent ad *agency*
2 : a government department that is responsible for a particular activity, area, etc. ▪ federal law enforcement *agencies* ▪ the federal *agency* in charge of printing money ▪ various government *agencies*
through the agency of *formal* **:** by using the help or services of (something or someone) ▪ The treaty was ratified *through the agency of* a neutral country.

agen·da /əˈʤɛndə/ *noun, pl* **-das** [*count*]
1 : a list of things to be considered or done ▪ The committee set the *agenda* for the next several years of research. ▪ There are several items/issues/things on the *agenda* for tonight's meeting. ▪ What's the first/next item on the *agenda*? ▪ Such an idea has been high on the political *agenda* for some time.
2 : a plan or goal that guides someone's behavior and that is often kept secret ▪ He wants to push/promote his own *agenda* no matter what the others say. ▪ She had no ***hidden agenda***. [=she didn't have a secret plan]

agent /ˈeɪʤənt/ *noun, pl* **agents** [*count*]
1 : a person who does business for another person **:** a person who acts on behalf of another ▪ They worked with a travel *agent* to plan their vacation. ▪ The actor got a starring role through his (theatrical) *agent*. ▪ a ***literary agent*** [=a person who helps writers to get their works published] — see also FREE AGENT, INSURANCE AGENT, PRESS AGENT, REAL ESTATE AGENT
2 : a person who tries to get secret information about another country, government, etc. **:** SPY, SECRET AGENT ▪ a government *agent* — see also DOUBLE AGENT, SPECIAL AGENT
3 : a person or thing that causes something to happen ▪ They view themselves as *agents* of social change. [=people who cause social change to happen]
4 : something (such as a chemical) that is used to produce a particular effect or result ▪ The drug is an effective *agent* for the treatment of asthma. ▪ the main flavoring *agent* in the drink ▪ Cornstarch is used as a thickening *agent* in sauces.

agent pro·vo·ca·teur /ˈɑːˌʒɑːnproʊˌvɑːkəˈtɚ/ *noun, pl* **agents pro·vo·ca·teurs** *also* **agent provocateurs** /ˈɑːˌʒɑːnproʊˌvɑːkəˈtɚ/ [*count*] **:** a person employed to encourage people to break the law so that they can be arrested ▪ The government used *agents provocateurs* to try to undermine the opposition party.

age of consent *noun*
the age of consent **:** the age at which a person is considered old enough to agree to have sex or to get married

age–old /ˈeɪʤˈoʊld/ *adj, always used before a noun* **:** very old **:** having existed for a very long time ▪ an *age-old* [=*ancient*] conflict/debate/problem ▪ *age-old* rituals/ceremonies/traditions

ag·glom·er·a·tion /əˌglɑːməˈreɪʃən/ *noun, pl* **-tions** [*count*] *formal* **:** a large group, collection, or pile of different things ▪ This suburb has become just a vast *agglomeration* of houses, people, and cars.

ag·gran·dize·ment *also Brit* **ag·gran·dise·ment** /əˈgrændəzmənt/ *noun* [*noncount*] *disapproving* **:** advancement or increase in power or importance ▪ He acted only for his political advantage and personal *aggrandizement*. ▪ self-*aggrandizement*

ag·gra·vate /ˈægrəˌveɪt/ *verb* **-vates; -vat·ed; -vat·ing** [+ *obj*]
1 : to make (an injury, problem, etc.) more serious or severe ▪ She *aggravated* an old knee injury. ▪ They're afraid that we might *aggravate* an already bad situation. ▪ A headache can be *aggravated* by too much exercise. ▪ The symptoms were *aggravated* by drinking alcohol.
2 *informal* **:** to make (someone) angry **:** to annoy or bother (someone) ▪ All of these delays really *aggravate* me. ▪ Our neighbors were *aggravated* by all the noise.
– aggravating *adj* [*more* ~; *most* ~] ▪ It was an incredibly slow and *aggravating* process. ▪ He has some very *aggravating* [=*annoying, irritating*] habits. **– ag·gra·vat·ing·ly** *adv*

A

▪ an *aggravatingly* slow process

aggravated *adj*
1 [*more* ~; *most* ~] **:** annoyed or bothered ▪ I sometimes get very *aggravated* when she does that.
2 *always used before a noun, law* **:** made more serious by the use of violence or the threat of violence ▪ He was convicted of *aggravated* assault.

ag·gra·va·tion /ˌægrəˈveɪʃən/ *noun, pl* **-tions**
1 [*noncount*] **:** the act or result of making a condition, injury, etc., worse **:** the act or result of aggravating something ▪ trying to avoid the *aggravation* of an existing back problem
2 *informal* **:** something that annoys or bothers someone **:** something that aggravates someone [*noncount*] The weather was a source of *aggravation* for us. [=we were annoyed by the weather] ▪ I don't need all this *aggravation*. ▪ This car has caused me nothing but *aggravation*. ▪ Many talented people now feel that a career in politics isn't worth all the *aggravation*. [*count*] I don't need all these *aggravations*.

[1]**ag·gre·gate** /ˈægrɪˌgeɪt/ *verb* **-gates; -gat·ed; -gat·ing** *formal*
1 : to join or combine into a single group [+ *obj*] The Web site *aggregates* content from many other sites. [*no obj*] These insects tend to *aggregate* [=*congregate*] in dark, moist places.
2 [*linking verb*] **:** to equal a specified number or amount ▪ All together, they had profits *aggregating* [=*totaling*] more than 10 million dollars.
– **ag·gre·ga·tion** /ˌægrɪˈgeɪʃən/ *noun, pl* **-tions** [*count, noncount*]

[2]**ag·gre·gate** /ˈægrɪgət/ *noun, pl* **-gates** [*count*] *formal* **:** a total amount — usually singular ▪ We spent an *aggregate* of 30 million dollars in advertising during the last three years. ▪ They won the two games by an *aggregate of* 40 points.
in the aggregate *also* ***in aggregate*** *formal* **:** thought of as a whole **:** all together ▪ Dividends for the year amounted *in the aggregate* to 25 million dollars. ▪ The experience only becomes important when considered *in the aggregate*.
on aggregate *Brit, sports* **:** with the scores of a series of matches added together ▪ Our team won the same number of matches, but their team scored more goals so they won *on aggregate*.

[3]**ag·gre·gate** /ˈægrɪgət/ *adj, always used before a noun* **:** formed by adding together two or more amounts **:** TOTAL ▪ The university receives more than half its *aggregate* income from government sources. ▪ The team with the highest *aggregate* score wins.

ag·gres·sion /əˈgrɛʃən/ *noun* [*noncount*]
1 : angry or violent behavior or feelings ▪ He has a lot of pent-up *aggression*. ▪ a display of *aggression* ▪ behavior that is likely to provoke *aggression* ▪ dangerous dogs showing *aggression* toward people
2 : hostile action against another country, government, etc. ▪ military *aggression* ▪ The government says that it will view any attempt to fly over its territory as an ***act of aggression***.

ag·gres·sive /əˈgrɛsɪv/ *adj* [*more* ~; *most* ~]
1 : ready and willing to fight, argue, etc. **:** feeling or showing aggression ▪ He started to get *aggressive* and began to shout. ▪ an *aggressive* dog ▪ *aggressive* behavior
2 : using forceful methods to succeed or to do something ▪ an overly *aggressive* salesman ▪ an *aggressive* lawyer whose tactics have made people angry ▪ The team plays a very *aggressive* style of defense. ▪ The company took *aggressive* steps to prevent illegal use of their equipment. ▪ The publisher has been very *aggressive* in promoting the book. ▪ The city began an *aggressive* campaign to encourage recycling.
3 *medical* **a :** very severe ▪ an *aggressive* form of cancer **b :** very strong or intense ▪ *aggressive* chemotherapy
– **ag·gres·sive·ly** *adv* ▪ The company is *aggressively* promoting their products. – **ag·gres·sive·ness** *noun* [*noncount*]

ag·gres·sor /əˈgrɛsɚ/ *noun, pl* **-sors** [*count*] **:** a person or country that attacks another **:** a person or country that starts a fight or war ▪ Each country accused the other of being the *aggressor*.

ag·grieved /əˈgri:vd/ *adj*
1 [*more* ~; *most* ~] **:** feeling anger because of unfair treatment ▪ He felt *aggrieved* by their refusal to meet with him. ▪ an *aggrieved* victim
2 *law* **:** having suffered from unfair treatment ▪ The *aggrieved* party may cancel the contract.

aggro /ˈægroʊ/ *noun* [*noncount*] *Brit, informal*
1 : something that annoys or bothers someone **:** AGGRAVATION ▪ He's gotten nothing but *aggro* from his parents lately. ▪ They decided it wasn't worth the *aggro*.
2 : angry and violent behavior **:** AGGRESSION ▪ The police were there to prevent any *aggro*.

aghast /əˈgæst, *Brit* əˈgɑ:st/ *adj, not used before a noun* [*more* ~; *most* ~] **:** shocked and upset ▪ The news left her *aghast*. ▪ Critics were *aghast* to see how awful the play was. — often + *at* ▪ She was *aghast at* the news. ▪ Critics were *aghast at* how awful the play was.

ag·ile /ˈæʤəl/ *adj* [*more* ~; *most* ~]
1 : able to move quickly and easily ▪ She is the most *agile* [=*nimble*] athlete on the team. ▪ Leopards are very fast and *agile*. ▪ a car with *agile* handling [=a car that moves quickly and smoothly when the steering wheel is turned]
2 : quick, smart, and clever ▪ an *agile* mind ▪ an *agile* writer ▪ an *agile* thinker
– **ag·ile·ly** *adv* ▪ The cat jumped *agilely* out of the way. – **agil·i·ty** /əˈʤɪləti/ *noun* [*noncount*] ▪ the *agility* of a champion gymnast ▪ He has the *agility* of a mountain goat. [=he is very agile] ▪ mental *agility*

[1]**aging** *or chiefly Brit* **ageing** *adj* **:** becoming old **:** no longer young or new ▪ his *aging* parents ▪ an *aging* building

[2]**aging** *or chiefly Brit* **ageing** *noun* [*noncount*] **:** the act or process of becoming old or older ▪ premature *aging* of the skin ▪ a wine improved by *aging*

ag·i·tate /ˈæʤəˌteɪt/ *verb* **-tates; -tat·ed; -tat·ing**
1 [+ *obj*] **:** to disturb, excite, or anger (someone) ▪ If I talk about the problem with him it just *agitates* him even more.
2 [*no obj*] **:** to try to get people to support or oppose something ▪ Some members of the union have been *agitating* for a strike. ▪ *agitate* for equal rights ▪ A few local residents have been *agitating* against a military presence.
3 [+ *obj*] *technical* **:** to move or stir up (a liquid) ▪ water *agitated* by wind ▪ The mixture is heated and then *agitated*.
– **agitated** *adj* [*more* ~; *most* ~] ▪ I've never seen her so *agitated* before. ▪ The dog became very *agitated* during the storm. – **ag·i·tat·ed·ly** *adv* ▪ pacing back and forth *agitatedly* – **ag·i·ta·tion** /ˌæʤəˈteɪʃən/ *noun* [*noncount*] ▪ He spoke with increasing *agitation* about the situation. ▪ *agitation* for civil rights ▪ continuous *agitation* of the mixture

ag·i·ta·tor /ˈæʤəˌteɪtɚ/ *noun, pl* **-tors** [*count*]
1 *usually disapproving* **:** a person who tries to get people angry or upset so that they will support an effort to change a government, company, etc. ▪ The police arrested several antigovernment *agitators*.
2 : a device for stirring or shaking something in a machine (such as a washing machine)

agleam /əˈgli:m/ *adj, not used before a noun* **:** bright or shining with reflected light ▪ She spoke of all the possibilities, her eyes *agleam*. [=*gleaming*]

aglit·ter /əˈglɪtɚ/ *adj, not used before a noun* **:** sparkling brightly with reflected light ▪ The tree was all *aglitter* [=*glittering*] with Christmas decorations.

aglow /əˈgloʊ/ *adj, not used before a noun*
1 : glowing with light or color ▪ The lights of the city were *aglow* in the distance. ▪ The room was *aglow* with candlelight.
2 : very excited or happy **:** feeling or showing excitement and happiness ▪ The children were *aglow* with excitement. ▪ The town was *aglow* with pride.

AGM /ˌeɪˌʤi:ˈɛm/ *noun, pl* **AGMs** [*count*] *Brit* **:** a meeting that an organization has once every year to discuss business, elect officials, etc. ▪ The new Board was elected at our last *AGM*. [=(*US*) *annual meeting*] ✧ *AGM* is an abbreviation for "Annual General Meeting."

ag·nos·tic /ægˈnɑ:stɪk/ *noun, pl* **-tics** [*count*]
1 : a person who does not have a definite belief about whether God exists or not — compare ATHEIST
2 : a person who does not believe or is unsure of something ▪ She considered herself an *agnostic* on the truth of the theory. [=she was not sure if the theory was true or not] ▪ a political *agnostic* [=a person who lacks strong political beliefs]
– **agnostic** *adj* ▪ politically *agnostic* – **ag·nos·ti·cism** /ægˈnɑ:stəˌsɪzəm/ *noun* [*noncount*]

ago /əˈgoʊ/ *adv* **:** in the past **:** before the present time **:** before now ▪ "How long *ago* did she arrive?" "A few hours *ago*." ▪ That culture flourished here over 10,000 years *ago*. ▪ We met three months *ago* and we'll meet again three months from now. ▪ He long *ago* learned to be patient. ▪ I saw an interesting ad ***not long ago*** [=*recently*] for a new car. ▪ All the good tickets were sold a long time *ago*. = All the good tickets were sold (quite) ***some time ago***.

agog /əˈgɑ:g/ *adj, not used before a noun* **:** full of interest or excitement because of something ▪ The news has chemists *agog.* ▪ Her supporters were *agog* at the idea. ▪ The town is *agog* over the plan.

ag·o·nize *also Brit* **ag·o·nise** /ˈægəˌnaɪz/ *verb* **-niz·es; -nized; -niz·ing** [*no obj*] **:** to think or worry very much about something — usually + *about* or *over* ▪ She *agonized about* what she was doing. ▪ The coach *agonizes* for days *over* the choices he has to make. ▪ The architect *agonized over* every detail of the planning.

agonized *also Brit* **agonised** *adj* [*more ~; most ~*] **:** showing mental or physical pain or agony ▪ an *agonized* cry of despair

agonizing *also Brit* **agonising** *adj* [*more ~; most ~*] **:** very mentally or physically painful ▪ a long and *agonizing* battle with cancer ▪ She made the *agonizing* decision to cancel the trip. ▪ The *agonizing* wait was finally over. ▪ He was in *agonizing* pain.

– ag·o·niz·ing·ly *also Brit* **ag·o·nis·ing·ly** *adv* ▪ an *agonizingly* painful condition ▪ They moved at an *agonizingly* slow pace.

ag·o·ny /ˈægəni/ *noun, pl* **-nies :** extreme mental or physical pain [*noncount*] She was in terrible *agony* after breaking her leg. ▪ He died in *agony*. ▪ The medicine relieves the *agony* of muscle cramps very quickly. ▪ the *agony* of defeat ▪ It was *agony* to watch him suffer like that. [*count*] He suffered no ***agonies of guilt/remorse/regret*** over his decision. [=he did not feel guilty about his decision]

agony aunt *noun, pl* **~ aunts** [*count*] *Brit* **:** a person who writes an agony column ▪ Hundreds of people write in to the paper's *agony aunt* [=(*US*) *advice columnist*] every week.

agony column *noun, pl* **~ -umns** [*count*] *Brit* **:** ADVICE COLUMN

ag·o·ra·pho·bia /ˌægərəˈfoubijə/ *noun* [*noncount*] **:** a fear of being in open or public places ▪ a patient suffering from *agoraphobia* — compare CLAUSTROPHOBIA

– ag·o·ra·pho·bic /ˌægərəˈfoubɪk/ *adj* ▪ an *agoraphobic* patient **– agoraphobic** *noun, pl* **-bics** [*count*] ▪ a therapist who works with *agoraphobics*

agrar·i·an /əˈgrerijən/ *adj* [*more ~; most ~*] **:** of or relating to farms and farming ▪ a town founded in 1811 as an *agrarian* community ▪ an *agrarian* economy ▪ an *agrarian* society

agree /əˈgriː/ *verb* **agrees; agreed; agree·ing**

1 : to have the same opinion [*no obj*] We *agreed* about some things, but we disagreed about others. ▪ They *agreed* among themselves. ▪ She says that a change is needed, and I *agree* completely. ▪ I couldn't *agree* more. ▪ We can all *agree* on/about one thing: the current law needs to be changed. ▪ Some critics have called the movie a masterpiece, but not everyone *agrees*. ▪ The house is too big for one person, don't you *agree*? — often + *with* ▪ I *agree with* you. = I *agree with* what you say. [+ *obj*] I *agree* (that) the house is too big. ▪ We all *agree* (that) the law needs to be changed. ✧ When people ***are agreed***, they have the same opinion. ▪ We *are* all *agreed* that the law needs to be changed. [=we all agree that the law needs to be changed] ▪ Researchers *are* now *agreed* that the cause of the disease is genetic. ▪ "So we'll have to revise the schedule. *Agreed*?" [=are we agreed?] "*Agreed*." [=yes, we are agreed] ✧ When a person or thing ***is agreed to be*** something specified, people regard that person or thing as something specified. ▪ The movie *is* generally *agreed to be* a failure. [=most people think that the movie is a failure] ▪ She *is* widely *agreed to be* one of our best writers. ▪ Her first book *is* almost universally *agreed to be* her best.

2 : to say that you will do, accept, or allow something that is suggested or requested by another person [*no obj*] The reporter asked her for an interview, and she reluctantly *agreed*. [=she reluctantly said yes] — often + *to* ▪ He *agreed to* [=*consented to*] their proposal/plan. ▪ *agree to* a compromise ▪ She *agreed to* an interview. = She *agreed to* being interviewed. [+ *obj*] She asked if she could go with him, and he *agreed* that she could. — often followed by *to + verb* ▪ He *agreed to accept* their proposal. ▪ She reluctantly *agreed to be* interviewed. ▪ He readily *agreed to do* what they wanted him to do. ▪ They *agreed not to oppose* her nomination.

3 *of two or more people or groups* **:** to decide to accept something after discussing what should or might be done [*no obj*] — usually + *on* or *upon* ▪ The jurors were unable to *agree on* a verdict. [=to reach a verdict] ▪ *agree on* a plan ▪ They *agreed on* a fair division of the profits. ▪ The means of ending the dispute were finally *agreed upon*. ▪ They should accept the terms that were originally *agreed upon*. ▪ The price was *agreed upon* in advance. [+ *obj*] (*Brit*) ▪ The jurors were unable to *agree* a verdict. ▪ The means of ending the dispute were finally *agreed*. ✧ The forms ***agreed, agreed-upon***, and (less commonly) ***agreed-on*** are used as adjectives in both U.S. and British English. ▪ She paid him the *agreed* price. ▪ They met at the *agreed-upon* time.

4 [*no obj*] **:** to be alike **:** to resemble or match each other ▪ The accounts of the accident did not *agree* (with each other). ▪ The copies *agree* exactly with the originals. ▪ These results *agree* with earlier studies.

5 [*no obj*] *grammar* **:** to be alike in gender, number, case, or person ▪ A verb should *agree* with its subject. ▪ A verb and pronoun should *agree* in number.

6 [*no obj*] **:** to be suitable for or pleasing to someone — + *with* ▪ The climate *agrees with* you. [=the climate suits you] ▪ Spicy food doesn't *agree with* me. [=spicy food makes me feel unwell]

agree to disagree (*chiefly US*) *or chiefly Brit* ***agree to differ*** **:** to agree not to argue anymore about a difference of opinion ▪ He likes golf and his wife likes tennis, so when it comes to sports, they have *agreed to disagree*.

agree with [*phrasal verb*] ***agree with (something)*** **:** to regard (something) with approval ▪ Do you *agree with* capital punishment? — see also AGREE 1, 6 (above)

agree·able /əˈgriːjəbəl/ *adj* [*more ~; most ~*]

1 *somewhat formal + old-fashioned* **:** pleasing to the mind or senses **:** PLEASANT ▪ an *agreeable* taste ▪ He's a very *agreeable* young man. ▪ Traffic is one of the less *agreeable* aspects of city life. ▪ They spent an *agreeable* evening together. — opposite DISAGREEABLE

2 : ready or willing to agree **:** willing to do or allow something ▪ I suggested that we leave early, and she seemed *agreeable*. — usually + *to* ▪ She seemed *agreeable to* (the idea of) leaving early.

3 : able to be accepted **:** ACCEPTABLE — + *to* ▪ Is the schedule *agreeable to* you? [=do you agree to the schedule?]

– agree·able·ness *noun* [*noncount*] **– agree·ably** /əˈgriːjəbli/ *adv* ▪ an *agreeably* sweet taste ▪ They spent the evening together very *agreeably*.

agree·ment /əˈgriːmənt/ *noun, pl* **-ments**

1 [*noncount*] **a :** the act of agreeing ▪ Any changes to the plan require the *agreement* of everyone involved. ▪ We were surprised by his *agreement* to participate. [=we were surprised that he agreed to participate] ▪ She nodded her head ***in agreement***. [=to show that she agreed] **b :** a situation in which people share the same opinion **:** a situation in which people agree ▪ There is wide/widespread/universal *agreement* on this issue. ▪ Everyone seems to be ***in agreement*** [=seems to agree] about/on the need for reform, but there is much disagreement about how to achieve it. ▪ They have been unable to ***reach agreement*** about how to achieve reform.

2 [*count*] **a :** an arrangement, contract, etc., by which people agree about what is to be done ▪ I thought we had an *agreement*. ▪ a formal/contractual *agreement* ▪ Their *agreement* expires next year. ▪ He has to return the property under the terms of an *agreement* he has with the original owner. ▪ a peace *agreement* ▪ a trade *agreement* ▪ They have ***come to an agreement***. = They have ***reached an agreement***. **b :** a written record of such an agreement ▪ He signed an *agreement* to buy the property. — see also GENTLEMAN'S AGREEMENT

3 [*noncount*] *grammar* **:** the fact or state of being alike in gender, number, case, or person **:** the fact or state of agreeing grammatically ▪ The subject and the verb need to be ***in agreement*** (with each other).

ag·ri·busi·ness /ˈægrəˌbɪznəs/ *noun, pl* **-ness·es**

1 [*noncount*] **:** the business or industry of farming or agriculture **:** farming thought of as a large business ▪ a giant *agribusiness* corporation

2 [*count*] **:** a company engaged in agribusiness ▪ Several large *agribusinesses* own most of the farms around here.

ag·ri·cul·tur·al /ˌægrɪˈkʌltʃərəl/ *adj*

1 : of, relating to, or used in farming or agriculture ▪ *agricultural* machinery ▪ *agricultural* methods ▪ the state's main *agricultural* product ▪ rich *agricultural* land

2 : engaged in or concerned with farming or agriculture ▪ an *agricultural* society ▪ an important *agricultural* center ▪ a small *agricultural* community

– ag·ri·cul·tur·al·ly *adv*

ag·ri·cul·ture /ˈægrɪˌkʌltʃɚ/ *noun* [*noncount*] **:** the science or occupation of farming ▪ They cleared the land to use it for *agriculture*. — compare HORTICULTURE

– ag·ri·cul·tur·ist /ˌægrɪˈkʌltʃərəlɪst/ *or* **ag·ri·cul·tur·al·ist** /ˌægrɪˈkʌltʃərəlɪst/ *noun, pl* **-ists** [*count*] ▪ skilled *agriculturists*

A

agron·o·my /əˈgrɑːnəmi/ *noun* [*noncount*] **: a science that deals with the methods used by farmers to raise crops and care for the soil**
– **agron·o·mist** /əˈgrɑːnəmɪst/ *noun, pl* **-mists** [*count*]

aground /əˈgraʊnd/ *adv* **: on or onto the ground** ▪ The ship ran/went *aground* during the storm last night. [=the bottom of the ship struck and became stuck on the ground under the water] ▪ The boat ran *aground* on a reef.

ah /ˈɑː/ *interj* **— used to express pleasure, relief, etc.** ▪ *Ah*, I remember the good old days. ▪ *Ah*, that feels good. ▪ *Ah*, so that's where the idea came from! ▪ *Ah*, yes, now I remember.

aha /ɑˈhɑː/ *interj* **— used when something is suddenly seen, found, or understood** ▪ *Aha*! I knew it was you! ▪ *Aha*! So that's how it's supposed to work.

ahead /əˈhɛd/ *adv*
1 a : in or toward the front ▪ The road stretched *ahead* for many miles. ▪ Someone was standing in the road (up) *ahead*. ▪ We knew the way *ahead* [=*forward*] was difficult, but we persevered. ▪ "Full speed *ahead*!" shouted the captain. ▪ He was looking ***straight ahead*** [=directly forward] **b : to or toward the place where someone is going** ▪ I can't leave yet. You go on *ahead*. I'll catch up later. ▪ She was delayed at the airport so she sent her bags *ahead* to the hotel.
2 : in, into, or for the future ▪ We need to think/plan *ahead*. ▪ The past year has been successful and, looking *ahead*, we expect to do even better in the coming months. ▪ We have some hard work *ahead*. ▪ He expects to be very busy in the weeks *ahead*. ▪ We don't know what lies *ahead*. ▪ We'll pause now for a commercial. The weather report is just *ahead*. [=the weather report will be broadcast after the commercial]
3 : in the lead in a race or competition ▪ They were trailing by 5 points earlier in the game, but now they're *ahead* [=*winning*] by 7. ▪ They scored three runs to go *ahead* by two. ▪ a politician who is *ahead* in the polls ▪ We're winning now, but we have to work hard to stay/keep *ahead*.
4 : in or toward a better position ▪ I came out $20 *ahead* on the deal. [=I made a profit of $20 on the deal] ▪ He's very ambitious. He'll do anything to ***get ahead*** [=to become successful]
5 : at an earlier time ▪ She prepared most of the food *ahead*. [=*ahead of time*] ▪ make payments *ahead*

ahead of *prep*
1 : in, at, or to a place before (someone or something) ▪ She got *ahead of* me. ▪ Someone was standing in the road just a few yards (up) *ahead of* us. ▪ They went on *ahead of* us and by now are several miles *ahead of* us.
2 : in the future for (someone or something) ▪ We have some hard work *ahead of* us.
3 : having a lead or advantage over (a competitor) ▪ The polls show that he is *ahead of* the other candidates. ▪ The company is working hard to stay one step *ahead of* the competition. ▪ They were trailing us by 5 points earlier in the game, but now they're *ahead of* us by 7.
4 a : better than (something) ▪ The company's earnings are (way/far) *ahead of* forecasts. [=are (much) better than they were expected to be] **b : in a more advanced position than (someone or something)** ▪ He was a year *ahead of* me in school. [=he finished school a year before I did] ✧ **If you are *ahead of your time* or if your ideas, creations, etc., are *ahead of their time*, you are too advanced or modern to be understood or appreciated during the time when you live or work.** ▪ As a poet, he was *ahead of his time*. His poems, now regarded as classics, were unpopular when he wrote them.
5 : at an earlier time than (someone or something) : sooner than (someone or something) ▪ They arrived at the party a few minutes *ahead of* [=*before*] us. ▪ They're hoping to work out an agreement well *ahead of* [=*before*] the deadline. ▪ She prepared most of the food ***ahead of time*** [=*beforehand*] ▪ It looks like we can finish the project ***ahead of schedule*** [=earlier than planned]

ahem /əˈhɛm/ *interj* **— used in writing to represent a sound that is like a quiet cough that people make especially to attract attention or to express disapproval or embarrassment**

ahoy /əˈhoɪ/ *interj* **— used by a sailor who is calling out to a passing ship or boat** ▪ Ship *ahoy*! ▪ *Ahoy* there, mate!

AI *abbr* artificial intelligence

[1]**aid** /ˈeɪd/ *verb* **aids; aid·ed; aid·ing : to provide what is useful or necessary : HELP** [+ *obj*] They gave money in order to *aid* the cause. ▪ She *aided* them in their efforts. ▪ He jumped into the water to *aid* the drowning child. ▪ His position was *aided* [=*strengthened*] by the fact that he was right. ▪ a home run that was *aided* by the wind ▪ *aiding* the poor ▪ She *aided* the government in the attempt to fight illiteracy. ▪ She is charged with ***aiding and abetting*** [=helping and encouraging] the thief in his getaway. [*no obj*] **— usually + *in*** ▪ She *aided in* the attempt to fight illiteracy. ▪ His research *aided in* the discovery of a new treatment for cancer. ▪ The research *aided in* establishing new theories.

[2]**aid** *noun, pl* **aids**
1 [*noncount*] **: the act of helping someone : help or assistance given to someone** ▪ The teacher enlisted/sought the *aid* of several students for the project. [=the teacher asked several students to help with the project] ▪ The project was completed ***with the aid of*** several students. ▪ The work was done *with the aid of* a computer. ▪ I can no longer read ***without the aid of*** glasses. [=without using glasses] ▪ When the climbers became trapped by bad weather, a rescue party was sent ***to their aid*** [=was sent to help/rescue them]
2 [*noncount*] **a : something (such as money, food, or equipment) that is given by a government or an organization to help the people in a country or area where many people are suffering because of poverty, disease, etc.** ▪ The government has given millions of dollars in economic/foreign *aid* to these nations. ▪ humanitarian *aid* **— often used before another noun** ▪ international *aid* organizations ▪ an *aid* worker [=a person who goes to a foreign country to help the people there] **b : money that is given to a student to help pay for the cost of attending a school** ▪ She applied for financial/student *aid* in order to go to college.
3 [*count*] **a : something that provides help or assistance** ▪ The diagram is provided as an *aid* to understanding. ▪ The computer is an *aid* to keeping costs down. **b : a device, object, etc., that makes something easier to do** ▪ He teaches art with visual *aids*. ▪ *aids* to navigation = navigational *aids* ▪ instructional/learning *aids* ▪ a pill used as an *aid* for sleeping = a ***sleeping aid* — see also** FIRST AID, HEARING AID
4 [*count*] *chiefly US* **: a person whose job is to assist someone : AIDE** ▪ She works as a teacher's *aid*.
in aid of *chiefly Brit* **: in order to help (something or someone)** ▪ The event is being held *in aid of* charity. ▪ *in aid of* refugees ✧ **The informal British expression *What's (all) this/that in aid of?* is used to ask about the purpose of something.** ▪ "*What's all this rushing about in aid of*, then?" [=what's all this rushing about for?] "We're trying to get things ready for the boss's visit."

aide /ˈeɪd/ *noun, pl* **aides** [*count*] **: a person whose job is to assist someone : ASSISTANT** ▪ a nurse's *aide* ▪ a teacher's *aide* ▪ The senate office hired several congressional *aides*. ▪ a presidential *aide*

aide–de–camp /ˌeɪddɪˈkæmp, *Brit* ˌeɪddɪˈkɑːmp/ *noun, pl* **aides–de–camp** /ˌeɪdzdɪˈkæmp, *Brit* ˌeɪdzdɪˈkɑːmp/ [*count*] **: a military officer who assists another high-ranking officer**

AIDS /ˈeɪdz/ *noun* [*noncount*] **: a serious disease of the immune system that is caused by infection with a virus** ✧ ***AIDS*** **is an abbreviation for *acquired immune deficiency syndrome*.**

ail /ˈeɪl/ *verb* **ails; ailed; ail·ing**
1 [+ *obj*] **: to cause pain or trouble for (someone) : TROUBLE** ▪ This medicine is good for what/whatever *ails* you. ▪ His back was *ailing* him. **— often used figuratively** ▪ a discussion about what *ails* public education these days
2 [*no obj*] **: to suffer bad health** ▪ She has been *ailing* for years. **— often used figuratively** ▪ The company is *ailing* financially.
– **ailing** *adj* ▪ He has an *ailing* back/elbow/heart. ▪ her *ailing* husband ▪ in *ailing* health ▪ the *ailing* economy ▪ an *ailing* company

ai·le·ron /ˈeɪləˌrɑːn/ *noun, pl* **-rons** [*count*] *technical* **: a part of an airplane wing that can be moved up or down to cause the airplane to turn — see picture at** AIRPLANE

ail·ment /ˈeɪlmənt/ *noun, pl* **-ments** [*count*] **: a sickness or illness** ▪ She suffered from a chronic back *ailment*. ▪ a kidney/liver/lung/skin *ailment* ▪ The doctor treated him for a variety of *ailments*.

[1]**aim** /ˈeɪm/ *verb* **aims; aimed; aim·ing**
1 a : to point (a weapon) at a target [+ *obj*] He *aimed* the gun carefully before shooting. ▪ Don't *aim* that pistol at me! [*no obj*] He *aimed* carefully before shooting. ▪ Ready, *aim*, fire! **b : to point (a device) at something** [+ *obj*] *aim* a camera ▪ Try to *aim* the antenna in the right direction. ▪ She *aimed* the telescope at a point in the eastern sky. [*no obj*] She *aimed* at a point in the eastern sky. **c** [+ *obj*] **: to direct (something, such as a missile, a ball, a punch, or a kick) at a target** ▪ He *aimed* the stone at the dog but missed. ▪ The

throw from the shortstop was poorly/badly *aimed*. ▪ well-*aimed* and badly *aimed* kicks/punches
2 : to have a specified goal or purpose [*no obj*] If you want to be successful, you have to ***aim high***. [=you have to be ambitious] — often + *at* ▪ The movie *aims at* comedy [=the movie is intended to be a comedy], but it really isn't very funny. ▪ a political movement that *aims at* promoting world peace — often + *for* ▪ The movie *aims for* comedy. ▪ *aim for* a goal ▪ If you're trying to lose weight, you should give yourself a goal/target to *aim for*. [+ *obj*] — followed by *to* + *verb* ▪ a political movement that *aims to promote* world peace ▪ They *aim* [=*intend*] *to reform* the government. ▪ We *aim* [=*plan*] *to arrive* there at around noon. ▪ We *aim to please*.
3 [+ *obj*] **:** to direct (something) *at* a particular goal, group of people, etc. ▪ He *aimed* his criticism primarily *at* parents. — usually used as *(be) aimed* ▪ His criticism *was aimed* primarily *at* parents. ▪ The television program *is aimed* directly/primarily *at* children. [=is intended mainly for children] ▪ The new system *is aimed at* reducing costs. [=the purpose of the new system is to reduce costs] ▪ a political movement that *is aimed at* promoting world peace

²aim *noun, pl* **aims**
1 [*count*] **:** a goal or purpose ▪ a political movement whose *aim* is to promote world peace ▪ Our ultimate *aim* is to create something of lasting value. ▪ The book has two basic *aims*. ▪ She was unable to achieve her *aims*. ▪ I started this business ***with the aim of*** making a profit.
2 [*noncount*] **:** the ability to hit a target ▪ His *aim* was good. ▪ He fired at the target but his *aim* was off/bad and he missed.
take aim **1 :** to point a weapon at a target ▪ He *took* careful *aim* at the target. [=he aimed carefully at the target] **2** *US* **:** to have a specified goal or intention ▪ The runner ***took aim at*** setting a record. [=the runner's goal was to set a record] **3 :** to have something as the object of an action or effort ▪ Investigators are ***taking aim at*** [=*targeting*] health-care fraud. [=investigators are intending to punish/stop health-care fraud]

aim·less /ˈeɪmləs/ *adj* **:** not having a goal or purpose ▪ an *aimless* young person ▪ an *aimless* conversation
– aim·less·ly *adv* ▪ She liked to wander *aimlessly* around the park. ▪ driving around *aimlessly* **– aim·less·ness** *noun* [*noncount*] He lived a life of *aimlessness*. [*singular*] There was an *aimlessness* to his life.

ain't /ˈeɪnt/
1 : am not ▪ I *ain't* worried. **:** are not ▪ They *ain't* interested. **:** is not ▪ It's a free country, *ain't* it?
2 : have not ▪ Those people *ain't* got a clue. **:** has not ▪ Her husband left and she *ain't* never been the same.

> ***usage*** *Ain't* is usually regarded as an error, but it is common in the very informal speech of some people and it is also used in informal and humorous phrases. ▪ That joke just *ain't* funny. ▪ Say it *ain't* so! ▪ You *ain't* seen nothing yet! ▪ Two out of three *ain't* bad. ▪ If it *ain't* broke don't fix it! ▪ Things *ain't* what they used to be. ▪ *Ain't* that the truth?

¹air /ˈeɚ/ *noun, pl* **airs**
1 [*noncount*] **a :** the invisible mixture of gases (such as nitrogen and oxygen) that surrounds the Earth and that people and animals breathe ▪ These laws are meant to produce cleaner *air*. ▪ A delicious smell filled the *air*. ▪ I like to dine outdoors in the open *air*. ▪ cool/warm *air* ▪ fresh *air* ▪ a sudden gust of *air* [=*wind*] ▪ polluted *air* ▪ stale *air* ▪ the hot summer *air* ▪ He can't breathe! Everybody move back and give him some *air*! ▪ High in the mountains the *air* is thin and it can be hard to breathe. ▪ He pumped *air* into the bicycle tire. ▪ My keys seem to have vanished/disappeared ***into thin air***. [=to have vanished in a very sudden and mysterious way] ▪ He seemed to appear ***out of thin air***. [=in a very sudden and mysterious way] — see also *a breath of fresh air* at BREATH **b :** the space or sky that is filled with air ▪ land, water, and *air* ▪ The city is wonderful seen from the *air*. ▪ the fish of the sea and the birds of the *air* ▪ The balloon rose up into the *air* and then floated through/in the *air*. ▪ There has been heavy fighting on the ground and in the *air*.
2 [*noncount*] **:** methods of travel that involve flying ▪ travel ***by air*** [=by flying in airplanes] — often used before another noun ▪ an *air* attack ▪ *air* safety ▪ *air* travel/travelers
3 [*singular*] **:** a quality that a person or thing has ▪ a dignified *air* — often + *of* ▪ an *air of* dignity ▪ The new furniture has given the hotel an *air of* luxury. ▪ He has an *air of* mystery about him. [=he has a mysterious quality]
4 [*count*] *old-fashioned* **:** a song or tune ▪ a pleasing *air*
5 [*noncount*] *US* **:** AIR-CONDITIONING ▪ a house with central *air*
clear the air **:** to talk about problems, feelings, etc., in order to reach agreement or understanding ▪ They *cleared the air* (between them) by discussing their differences.
floating on air *or* ***walking on air*** **:** feeling very happy ▪ After he won the election, he was *walking on air*.
give yourself airs *or* ***put on airs*** **:** to act in a way that shows you think you are better than other people ▪ Some of her old friends have accused her of *putting on airs* since she became wealthy. ▪ She's very rich, but she doesn't *give herself airs*. ✧ In British English, the phrase ***airs and graces*** describes an overly superior or proud way of behaving. ▪ She's very rich, but she doesn't *give herself any airs and graces*. = She doesn't have any *airs and graces*. = She doesn't put on any *airs and graces*.
hang in the air see *hang in* at ¹HANG
in the air **1 :** felt or sensed by many people ▪ There was a great sense of anticipation *in the air* as game time approached. **2 :** expected to happen soon ▪ Many changes are *in the air*.
nose in the air see ¹NOSE
off the air *of a radio or television station, program, etc.* **:** not being broadcast ▪ The station is now *off the air*. ▪ They took him *off the air* because of his extreme views. ▪ It was my favorite show, but it ***went off the air*** [=stopped being broadcast] last year.
on the air *also* ***on air*** *of a radio or television station, program, etc.* **:** being broadcast ▪ The interview will be *on the air* tomorrow. [=the interview will air tomorrow; the interview will be broadcast tomorrow] ▪ an interview being shown *on air* ▪ a show that first ***came/went on the air*** [=started being broadcast] five years ago ▪ The President *went on the air* to defend his policies.
up in the air **:** not yet settled or decided ▪ Our vacation plans are still *up in the air*.
– air·less /ˈeɚləs/ *adj* ▪ a hot, *airless* room

²air *verb* **airs; aired; air·ing**
1 a : to place something in an open area where there is a lot of moving air to make it cool, dry, or clean [+ *obj*] *air* a blanket ▪ *air* damp clothing [*no obj*] The blankets were left outside to *air*. **b :** to allow air from the outside to enter something (such as a room) so that it becomes fresher or cleaner [+ *obj*] She opened the windows to *air* the room. — usually + *out* in U.S. English ▪ She opened the windows to *air out* the room. ▪ *air out* a closet [*no obj*] — usually + *out* in U.S. English ▪ She opened the windows to let the room *air out*.
2 [+ *obj*] **:** to make (something) known in public **:** to state (something) publicly ▪ The company had a meeting so that employees could *air* their complaints/grievances. ▪ publicly *airing* their differences ▪ Let's not ***air our dirty laundry*** [=discuss our problems, make our problems known] in public.
3 : to broadcast something on radio or television [+ *obj*] *air* a program ▪ The interview will be *aired* tomorrow. [*no obj*] The program *airs* daily. ▪ The interview will *air* tomorrow.

air bag *noun, pl* **~ bags** [*count*] **:** a bag that fills with air to protect a driver or passenger when a vehicle crashes

air ball *noun, pl* **~ balls** [*count*] *basketball* **:** a shot that completely misses the basket

air base *noun, pl* **~ bases** [*count*] **:** a place where military aircraft take off and land **:** a base of operations for military aircraft

air bed *noun, pl* **~ beds** [*count*] **:** AIR MATTRESS

air·borne /ˈeɚˌboɚn/ *adj*
1 : in the air **:** moving or being carried through the air ▪ Once the plane was *airborne* I loosened my seat belt. ▪ *airborne* dust particles
2 *of soldiers* **:** specially trained to jump from airplanes into enemy territory for battle ▪ Thousands of *airborne* troops parachuted behind enemy lines. ▪ *airborne* forces *also* **:** of or relating to airborne soldiers ▪ *airborne* combat ▪ *airborne* divisions/operations

¹air·brush /ˈeɚˌbrʌʃ/ *noun, pl* **-brush·es** [*count*] **:** a device that is used to spray a liquid (such as paint) onto a surface

²airbrush *verb* **-brush·es; -brushed; -brush·ing** [+ *obj*] **:** to paint or treat (something, such as a photograph) with an airbrush especially to make improvements ▪ That photograph must have been *airbrushed*. ▪ The model's blemishes were ***airbrushed out*** in the photograph. [=an airbrush was used to change the photograph so that the model's blemishes could not be seen] — sometimes used figuratively ▪ The au-

A

thorities tried to *airbrush out* their mistake and pretend it had never happened.

Air·bus /ˈeɚˌbʌs/ *trademark* — used for a jet plane that carries passengers for short distances

air conditioner *noun, pl* **~ -ers** [*count*] : a machine that is used to cool and dry the air in a building, room, etc.

air–con·di·tion·ing /ˌeɚkənˈdɪʃənɪŋ/ *noun* [*noncount*] : a system used for cooling and drying the air in a building, room, etc. ▪ She wanted her house to have *air-conditioning.* ▪ We bought a car with *air-conditioning.* — often used before another noun ▪ an *air-conditioning* system ▪ *air-conditioning* ducts/equipment — abbr. *AC*

– air–con·di·tioned /ˌeɚkənˈdɪʃənd/ *adj* ▪ an *air-conditioned* building/room/car

air·craft /ˈeɚˌkræft, *Brit* ˈɛəˌkrɑːft/ *noun, pl* **aircraft** [*count*] : a machine (such as an airplane or a helicopter) that flies through the air ▪ a new military *aircraft* ▪ a company that manufactures *aircraft* — often used before another noun ▪ an *aircraft* engine ▪ *aircraft* parts

aircraft carrier *noun, pl* **~ -ers** [*count*] : a military ship that has a large deck where aircraft take off and land

air·drop /ˈeɚˌdrɑːp/ *noun, pl* **-drops** [*count*] : the act or action of delivering supplies by parachute from an airplane during an emergency when other methods are not possible ▪ The group organized an *airdrop* of food for the refugees.

– air–drop /ˈeɚˌdrɑːp/ *verb* **-drops; -dropped; -drop·ping** [+ *obj*] ▪ Supplies were *air-dropped* to the refugees.

air–dry /ˈeɚˈdraɪ/ *verb* **-dries; -dried; -dry·ing** : to dry something by placing it in an open area where there is a lot of moving air [+ *obj*] *air-dry* a blanket [*no obj*] She let the blanket *air-dry* before she put it away.

air·fare /ˈeɚˌfeɚ/ *noun, pl* **-fares** [*count*] : the money a person pays to travel on an airplane ▪ round-trip *airfare*

air·field /ˈeɚˌfiːld/ *noun, pl* **-fields** [*count*] : a field or airport where airplanes take off and land ▪ a military *airfield*

air force *noun, pl* **~ forces** [*count*] : the part of a country's military forces that fights with airplanes ▪ the combined allied *air forces* — usually capitalized when a specific air force is being referred to ▪ the British *Air Force* ▪ She joined the (U.S.) *Air Force* after she graduated from high school.

air gun *noun, pl* **~ guns** [*count*] : a gun that uses air pressure to shoot small pellets

air·head /ˈeɚˌhɛd/ *noun, pl* **-heads** [*count*] *informal* : a silly and stupid person ▪ She is not the *airhead* you think she is.

air·ing /ˈerɪŋ/ *noun, pl* **-ings** : an occurrence in which something is aired: such as **a** [*singular*] : an occurrence in which something (such as an idea) is made known to many people so that it can be discussed ▪ His ideas deserve an *airing.* [=his ideas deserve to be aired] ▪ A full *airing* of the issue is scheduled. **b** [*count*] : an occurrence in which a radio or television program is broadcast ▪ The series had its first *airing* [=the series was first aired/broadcast] on a local channel. ▪ the *airing* [=*broadcast*] of a presidential debate **c** [*count*] : an occurrence in which fresh air is allowed to fill a place or to surround something ▪ give the room an *airing* [=air the room] by opening the windows

airing cupboard *noun, pl* **~ -boards** [*count*] *Brit* : a heated cupboard in which sheets, towels, clothes, etc., are kept warm and dry

air·lift /ˈeɚˌlɪft/ *noun, pl* **-lifts** [*count*] : an occurrence in which people or things are carried to or from a place by airplanes during an emergency when other methods are not possible ▪ an emergency *airlift* to deliver supplies to the famine victims

– airlift *verb* **-lifts; -lift·ed; -lift·ing** [+ *obj*] ▪ Soldiers were *airlifted* to the frontier's borders. ▪ The organization was *airlifting* supplies to the famine victims.

air·line /ˈeɚˌlaɪn/ *noun, pl* **-lines** [*count*] : a company that owns and operates many airplanes which are used for carrying passengers and goods to different places ▪ a major *airline* — often used before another noun ▪ an *airline* pilot ▪ *airline* passengers

air·lin·er /ˈeɚˌlaɪnɚ/ *noun, pl* **-ers** [*count*] : a large airplane used for carrying passengers

air lock *noun, pl* **~ locks** [*count*] : a small room that has two doors which can be sealed tightly so that no air enters or leaves and that is used for moving between two spaces with different air pressures in a submarine, spaceship, etc.

air·mail /ˈeɚˌmeɪl/ *noun* [*noncount*] : the system used for sending mail by aircraft ▪ The package was sent by/via *airmail.*; *also* : mail sent by using this system ▪ a bag of *airmail* — often used before another noun ▪ an *airmail* letter ▪ *airmail* postage

– airmail *verb* **-mails; -mailed; -mail·ing** [+ *obj*] ▪ He *airmailed* the letter/package to me. = He *airmailed* me the letter/package.

air·man /ˈeɚmən/ *noun, pl* **-men** /-mən/ [*count*] : a member of the air force with a rank below that of sergeant

air mattress *noun, pl* **~ -tress·es** [*count*] : a soft plastic case that can be filled with air and used as a bed — called also *air bed*; see picture at CAMPING

air·plane /ˈeɚˌpleɪn/ *noun, pl* **-planes** [*count*] *US* : a machine that has wings and an engine and that flies through the air ▪ traveling on/in an *airplane* = traveling by *airplane* — called also *plane,* (*Brit*) *aeroplane*

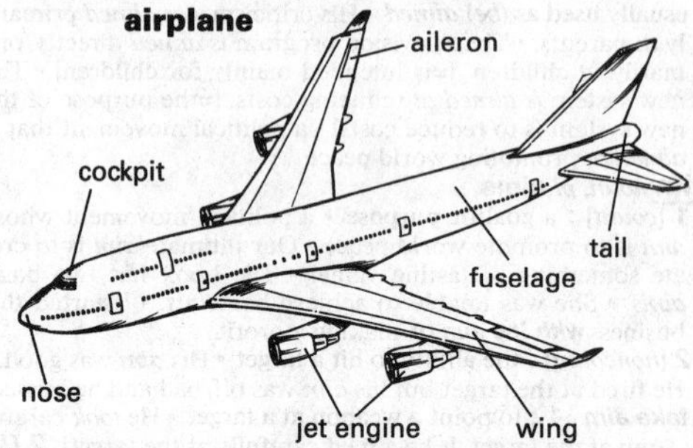

air·play /ˈeɚˌpleɪ/ *noun* [*noncount*] : time when a musical recording is played by a radio station ▪ Her latest record is getting a lot of *airplay.* [=is being played frequently on the radio] ▪ heavy/light *airplay*

air pocket *noun, pl* **~ -ets** [*count*] : a movement or condition of the air that causes an airplane to make a brief and sudden downward drop

air·port /ˈeɚˌpoɚt/ *noun, pl* **-ports** [*count*] : a place where aircraft land and take off and where there are buildings for passengers to wait in and for aircraft to be sheltered

air pump *noun, pl* **~ pumps** [*count*] : a pump used for removing air from or adding air to something (such as a tire)

air raid *noun, pl* **~ raids** [*count*] : an attack in which a place is bombed by military airplanes ▪ Much of the city was destroyed in an *air raid.* ▪ an *air-raid* shelter

air rifle *noun, pl* **~ rifles** [*count*] : a rifle that uses air pressure to shoot small pellets

air·ship /ˈeɚˌʃɪp/ *noun, pl* **-ships** [*count*] : a very large aircraft that does not have wings but that has a body filled with gas so that it floats and that is driven through the air by engines

air show *noun, pl* **~ shows** [*count*] : a public event at an airport where different kinds of aircraft are shown and pilots use their skills to fly in unusual and exciting ways

air·sick /ˈeɚˌsɪk/ *adj* [*more* ~; *most* ~] : feeling sick in the stomach while riding in an airplane because of its motion

– air·sick·ness *noun* [*noncount*]

air·space /ˈeɚˌspeɪs/ *noun* [*noncount*] : the space that is above a country and that is legally controlled by that country ▪ seeking permission to fly through U.S. *airspace*

air·speed /ˈeɚˌspiːd/ *noun, pl* **-speeds** [*count*] : the speed at which an aircraft moves through the air

air strike *noun, pl* **~ strikes** [*count*] : an attack in which military airplanes drop bombs ▪ The strategy calls for *air strikes* on key targets.

air·strip /ˈeɚˌstrɪp/ *noun, pl* **-strips** [*count*] : an area of land that is used as a runway for airplanes to take off and land

air·tight /ˈeɚˌtaɪt/ *adj*

1 : tightly sealed so that no air can get in or out ▪ Store the food in an *airtight* container.

2 : too strong or effective to fail or to be defeated ▪ an *airtight* argument ▪ The defendant had an *airtight* alibi.

air·time /ˈeɚˌtaɪm/ *noun* [*noncount*] : time during a radio or television broadcast : time when something is on the air ▪ The committee plans to buy radio/TV *airtime* for the campaign ads. ▪ The replay got a lot of *airtime.* [=the replay was broadcast frequently]

air–to–air /ˌeɚtəˈweɚ/ *adj* : shot from one flying airplane at another ▪ The enemy planes attacked our bombers with *air-to-air* missiles.

air traffic control *noun [noncount]*
1 : a system through which people on the ground give instructions by radio to aircraft pilots
2 : the people who give instructions to aircraft pilots by radio ▪ The pilot had permission to land from *air traffic control.*

air traffic controller *noun, pl* ~ **-lers** *[count]* **:** a person whose job is to give instructions to aircraft pilots by radio

air•waves /ˈeɚˌweɪvz/ *noun [plural]* **:** the signals used to broadcast radio and television programs ▪ The ads have begun to fill network *airwaves.* [=to appear frequently on network television] — usually used with *the* ▪ The ads have begun to fill *the airwaves.* ▪ The band's new recording ***hit the airwaves*** [=was broadcast for the first time] yesterday. ▪ news being broadcast ***on/over the airwaves***

air•way /ˈeɚˌweɪ/ *noun, pl* **-ways** *[count]*
1 *medical* **:** the area in the throat through which air passes to and from the lungs ▪ a patient with a partially blocked *airway* — often plural ▪ a patient with partially blocked *airways*
2 : a route along which airplanes regularly fly
3 — used in the names of some airlines ▪ British *Airways*

air•wor•thy /ˈeɚˌwɚði/ *adj [more ~; most ~]* **:** fit or safe for flying ▪ The agency considered the plane *airworthy.* ▪ an *airworthy* helicopter — compare ROADWORTHY, SEAWORTHY
– air•wor•thi•ness *noun [noncount]*

airy /ˈeri/ *adj* **air•i•er; -est**
1 : having a lot of open space through which air can move freely ▪ The room is open, light, and *airy.* ▪ an *airy* restaurant
2 : having a light or careless quality that shows a lack of concern ▪ He refused with an *airy* wave of his hand.
3 : very light or delicate ▪ an *airy* fabric
4 : high in the air **:** LOFTY ▪ The hawk gazed down from its *airy* perch.
– air•i•ly /ˈerəli/ *adv* ▪ He *airily* dismissed all advice. **– air•i•ness** /ˈerinəs/ *noun [noncount]* ▪ the *airiness* of the room

airy–fairy /ˈeriˈferi/ *adj [more ~; most ~] chiefly Brit, informal + disapproving* **:** not having substance or purpose **:** not practical ▪ a vague and *airy-fairy* fantasy/notion ▪ The idea sounded a bit *airy-fairy.*

aisle /ˈajəl/ *noun, pl* **aisles** *[count]* **:** a passage where people walk: such as **a :** a passage between sections of seats in a church, theater, airplane, etc. — see picture at THEATER ▪ The bride walked down/up the *aisle* to the altar. ▪ He likes to sit ***on the aisle.*** = He likes to sit in the ***aisle seat.*** [=he likes to sit in the seat next to the aisle] ▪ By the end of the concert, the people in the theater were ***dancing in the aisles.*** ✧ When the people of an audience are laughing a lot, they can be described as ***rolling in the aisles.*** ▪ a new comedy that has audiences *rolling in the aisles* all across the country **b :** a passage where people walk through a store, market, etc. ▪ supermarket *aisles*
walk down the aisle *also* ***go down the aisle*** *informal* **:** to get married ▪ She's been married twice before, and she's going to *walk down the aisle* again next week.

ajar /əˈʤɑɚ/ *adj, not used before a noun* **:** slightly open ▪ He left the door *ajar.* ▪ Her mouth was slightly *ajar.*

AK *abbr* Alaska

aka /ˌeɪˌkeɪˈeɪ/ *abbr* also known as — used to indicate another name that a person or thing has or uses ▪ Elvis Presley, *aka* "The King"

akim•bo /əˈkɪmboʊ/ *adj, not used before a noun*
1 *of the arms* **:** with the hands on the hips and the elbows turned outward ▪ She stood ***with arms akimbo.***
2 *of the legs* **:** spread apart in a bent position ▪ sitting ***with legs akimbo***

akin /əˈkɪn/ *adj, not used before a noun [more ~; most ~]* **:** similar or related ▪ The two languages are closely *akin.* — usually + *to* ▪ The two languages are closely *akin to* one another. ▪ a feeling *akin to* loneliness [=a feeling that resembles loneliness] ▪ To break your promise to him would be *akin to* betraying your friendship.

AL *abbr* Alabama

[1]**-al** *adj suffix* **:** of, relating to, or characterized by ▪ direction*al* ▪ fiction*al* ▪ operation*al*

[2]**-al** *noun suffix* **:** action **:** process ▪ rehears*al* ▪ withdraw*al*

à la /ˌɑːˌlɑː/ *prep* **:** in the manner or style of (someone or something) ▪ walking with a swagger *à la* John Wayne

al•a•bas•ter /ˈæləˌbæstɚ, *Brit* ˈæləˌbɑːstə/ *noun [noncount]* **:** a white stone that is used to make vases and decorations — often used before another noun ▪ an *alabaster* vase — sometimes used figuratively ▪ her *alabaster* skin [=her smooth and white skin]

à la carte /ˌɑːləˈkɑɚt/ *adv* **:** with a separate price for each item on the menu ▪ decided to order *à la carte*
– à la carte *adj* ▪ an *à la carte* menu

alac•ri•ty /əˈlækrəti/ *noun* **:** a quick and cheerful readiness to do something *[noncount]* She accepted the invitation ***with alacrity.*** [=very quickly and willingly] *[singular]* She accepted the invitation with an *alacrity* that surprised me.

à la mode /ˌɑːləˈmoʊd/ *adj, not used before a noun*
1 *US* **:** topped with ice cream ▪ apple pie *à la mode*
2 *old-fashioned* **:** stylish or fashionable ▪ a political movement that was once *à la mode*

[1]**alarm** /əˈlɑɚm/ *noun, pl* **alarms**
1 *[count]* **a :** a device that makes a loud sound as a warning or signal ▪ The *alarm* went off when he opened the door. ▪ a car *alarm* ▪ The whole town heard the *alarm.* ✧ In figurative usage, when ***alarm bells are ringing*** people are worried about a possible problem or danger. ▪ His long absence from school ***set (the) alarm bells ringing*** and we finally called the police. — see also BURGLAR ALARM, FALSE ALARM, FIRE ALARM, SMOKE ALARM **b :** ALARM CLOCK ▪ She set the *alarm* for six o'clock. ▪ The *alarm* went off at six o'clock.
2 *[noncount]* **:** a feeling of fear caused by a sudden sense of danger ▪ The rumors caused widespread *alarm* and concern. ▪ His parents have expressed *alarm* about/for his safety. ▪ The new developments are being viewed ***with alarm.*** ▪ She looked around ***in alarm*** when she heard the noise. ▪ There's ***no cause for alarm.*** [=there is no reason to be worried or afraid] ***synonyms*** see [1]FEAR
3 *[count]* **:** a warning of danger ▪ The dog's barking gave the *alarm* and the intruders were caught. ▪ A passerby saw the intruders and raised the *alarm.* ▪ They have ignored repeated *alarms* about the dangers of smoking. ▪ Economists have ***raised/sounded the alarm*** [=have warned people] about a possible recession. ▪ Economists have been ***raising/sounding alarms*** about a possible recession.

[2]**alarm** *verb* **alarms; alarmed; alarm•ing** *[+ obj]* **:** to cause (someone) to feel a sense of danger **:** to worry or frighten (someone) ▪ I didn't mean to *alarm* you. ▪ The rapid spread of the disease has *alarmed* many people.
– alarmed *adj [more ~; most ~]* ▪ I was *alarmed* to see how sick he is. ▪ Many people are *alarmed* about/at/by the rapid spread of the disease. **– alarming** *adj [more ~; most ~]* ▪ an *alarming* number of problems ▪ It is *alarming* to see how quickly the disease is spreading. ▪ The team lost with *alarming* frequency. **– alarm•ing•ly** /əˈlɑɚmɪŋli/ *adv*

alarm clock *noun, pl* ~ **clocks** *[count]* **:** a clock that can be set to sound an alarm at any desired time ▪ She set the *alarm clock* for six o'clock. ▪ The *alarm clock* went off at six o'clock.

alarm•ist /əˈlɑɚmɪst/ *noun, pl* **-ists** *[count]* **:** a person who spreads unnecessary fear about something that is not truly dangerous ▪ He wanted to alert people without sounding like an *alarmist.* ▪ He claims that *alarmists* have exaggerated the economy's problems.
– alarm•ism /əˈlɑɚˌmɪzəm/ *noun [noncount]* **– alarm•ist** *adj* ▪ an *alarmist* report ▪ *alarmist* critics

alas /əˈlæs/ *interj, old-fashioned + literary* — used to express sadness, sorrow, disappointment, etc. ▪ How did they fare? *Alas,* not very well. ▪ Life, *alas,* is all too short.

al•ba•tross /ˈælbəˌtrɑːs/ *noun, pl* **-tross•es** *[count]*
1 : a large white ocean bird that has very long wings
2 : a continuing problem that makes it difficult or impossible to do or achieve something ▪ Fame has become an *albatross* that prevents her from leading a normal and happy life. ▪ Fame has become ***an albatross around her neck.***

al•be•it /ɑlˈbiːjət/ *conj, formal* **:** even though **:** ALTHOUGH ▪ She appeared on the show, *albeit* briefly. ▪ It was an amazing computer, *albeit* expensive.

al•bi•no /ælˈbaɪnoʊ, *Brit* ælˈbiːnoʊ/ *noun, pl* **-nos** *[count]* **:** a person or animal born with a medical condition that results in very pale skin, white hair, and pink eyes
– al•bi•nism /ˈælbəˌnɪzəm/ *noun [noncount]* **– albino** *adj* ▪ an *albino* mouse

al•bum /ˈælbəm/ *noun, pl* **-bums** *[count]*
1 : a book with blank pages in which you put a collection of photographs, stamps, etc. ▪ a photo/stamp *album* ▪ I've been working on our wedding/family *album.* [=book of wedding/family photographs]
2 : a long musical recording on a record, CD, etc., that usually includes a set of songs ▪ She played a track from the group's latest *album.* ▪ a 2-CD *album* ▪ a pop/jazz/country *album* — compare [2]SINGLE 4

A

al·bu·men /æl'bju:mən, *Brit* 'ælbjumən/ *noun* [*noncount*] *technical* : the part of the inside of an egg that is clear before it is cooked and white after it is cooked : the white of an egg

al·che·my /'ælkəmi/ *noun, pl* **-mies**
1 [*noncount*] : a science that was used in the Middle Ages with the goal of changing ordinary metals into gold
2 : a power or process that changes or transforms something in a mysterious or impressive way [*noncount*] She practiced her *alchemy* in the kitchen, turning a pile of vegetables into a delicious salad. [*count*] The company hoped for some sort of economic *alchemy* that would improve business.
– al·che·mist /'ælkəmɪst/ *noun, pl* **-mists** [*count*]

al·co·hol /'ælkə,hɑ:l/ *noun, pl* **-hols**
1 : a clear liquid that has a strong smell, that is used in some medicines and other products, and that is the substance in liquors (such as beer, wine, or whiskey) that can make a person drunk [*noncount*] cough medicine that contains *alcohol* • drinks that are high in *alcohol* • There was a high level of *alcohol* in his blood at the time of the accident. • drug and *alcohol* abuse [*count*] a mixture of different *alcohols* — see also RUBBING ALCOHOL
2 [*noncount*] : drinks containing alcohol • The restaurant had a license to serve *alcohol*. • She doesn't drink *alcohol*.

1al·co·hol·ic /,ælkə'hɑ:lɪk/ *adj*
1 [*more ~; most ~*] : of, containing, or caused by alcohol • an *alcoholic* odor • *alcoholic* drinks/beverages • a slightly more *alcoholic* wine • *alcoholic* liver disease
2 : affected with alcoholism • She has an *alcoholic* uncle.
– al·co·hol·i·cal·ly /,ælkə'hɑ:lɪkli/ *adv*

2alcoholic *noun, pl* **-ics** [*count*] : a person who frequently drinks too much alcohol and is unable to live a normal and healthy life : a person who is affected with alcoholism • Her uncle is an *alcoholic*. • a recovering *alcoholic*

al·co·hol·ism /'ælkə,hɑ:,lɪzəm/ *noun* [*noncount*] : a medical condition in which someone frequently drinks too much alcohol and becomes unable to live a normal and healthy life

al·cove /'æl,koʊv/ *noun, pl* **-coves** [*count*] : a small section of a room that is set back from the rest of it

al den·te /ɑl'denteɪ/ *adj* : cooked but still firm • *al dente* carrots • *al dente* pasta = pasta *al dente*
– al dente *adv* • The pasta was cooked *al dente*.

al·der /'ɑ:ldɚ/ *noun, pl* **-ders** [*count*] : a type of tree or shrub that grows in wet ground in some northern countries

al·der·man /'ɑ:ldɚmən/ *noun, pl* **-men** /-mən/ [*count*]
1 : a member of a city government in the U.S., Canada, and Australia • the board of *aldermen*
2 : a senior member of an English town, county, or borough council who is elected by the other members — not used officially in Britain after 1974
– al·der·man·ic /,ɑ:ldɚ'mænɪk/ *adj*

ale /'eɪl/ *noun, pl* **ales** : an alcoholic drink that is similar to beer [*noncount*] a glass of *ale* [*count*] The bar serves two very different *ales*. — see also GINGER ALE

aleck see SMART-ALECK

ale·house /'eɪl,haʊs/ *noun, pl* **-hous·es** [*count*] *Brit, old-fashioned* : a place where people used to drink ale and beer

1alert /ə'lɚt/ *adj* [*more ~; most ~*] : able to think clearly and to notice things • An *alert* guard stopped the robbers. • The nurse kept/stayed *alert* for any change [=watched for any change] in the patient's condition. • He was tired and had trouble staying *alert* while he was driving. • She wasn't mentally *alert* enough to answer the questions. • an *alert* mind • An *alert* watchdog guarded the door. — often + *to* • The nurse should be *alert to* any change in the patient's condition. • He is *alert to* [=*aware of*] his duties as a father.
– alert·ly *adv* • A watchdog *alertly* guarded the door.
– alert·ness *noun* [*noncount*]

2alert *noun, pl* **alerts**
1 [*count*] : something (such as a message or loud sound) that tells people there is some danger or problem : an alarm or signal of danger • They sounded an *alert* when enemy planes were approaching the city. • Medical officials have put out an *alert* to hospitals to look out for the virus. • The government has issued a terrorism/security *alert*.
2 [*noncount*] : the state of being ready for something you have been warned about (such as an attack) — used with *on* • We need to be *on alert* for any sudden changes. • The attack could come at any time, so the soldiers need to be ***on full alert***. • The recently flooded community is again ***on high alert*** as more rain is expected. — see also RED ALERT
on the alert : looking for or expecting something (such as danger or an opportunity) • The soldiers need to be *on the alert* at all times. — often + *for* • When you're driving in winter you should always be *on the alert for* icy conditions. • I'm always *on the alert for* a good bargain.

3alert *verb* **alerts; alert·ed; alert·ing** [+ *obj*]
1 : to give (someone) important information about a possible problem, danger, etc. : to warn (someone) • Several neighbors *alerted* the authorities/police when they noticed strangers acting suspiciously. • The governor *alerted* island residents that a hurricane was coming.
2 : to make (someone) aware of something • The teacher *alerted* the students that tests would be given the next day. — often + *to* • A friend recently *alerted* me *to* the existence of a new museum in my city. • We need to *alert* the public *to* the dangers of these chemicals. [=we need to tell the public about the dangers of these chemicals]

A level *noun, pl* **A levels** [*count*] *Brit* : an advanced test in a particular subject that students in England, Wales, and Northern Ireland take usually at the age of 18 • The university requires at least three *A levels*. • She got an A in her *A levels* in maths, physics, and chemistry. — called also *Advanced level*; compare O LEVEL, S LEVEL

al·fal·fa /æl'fælfə/ *noun* [*noncount*] : a type of plant that is grown mostly as food for farm animals

al·fres·co /æl'freskoʊ/ *adv* : in the open air : OUTDOORS, OUTSIDE • an artist who likes to paint *alfresco* • We dined *alfresco*.
– alfresco *adj* • *alfresco* dining • an *alfresco* restaurant [=a restaurant with outdoor dining]

al·gae /'ælʤi/ *noun* [*plural*] : simple plants that have no leaves or stems and that grow in or near water • pond *algae* • seaweeds and other *algae*

al·ge·bra /'ælʤəbrə/ *noun* [*noncount*] : a branch of mathematics that uses numbers and letters that represent numbers
– al·ge·bra·ic /,ælʤə'brejɪk/ *adj* • *algebraic* equations/problems

al·go·rithm /'ælgə,rɪðəm/ *noun, pl* **-rithms** [*count*] *technical* : a set of steps that are followed in order to solve a mathematical problem or to complete a computer process

1ali·as /'eɪlijəs/ *adv* : also called : otherwise known as — used to indicate an additional name that a person (such as a criminal) sometimes uses • The thief was identified as John Smith, *alias* Richard Jones. [=John Smith, who is also known as Richard Jones]

2alias *noun, pl* **-as·es** [*count*] : an additional name that a person (such as a criminal) sometimes uses • a fugitive using several *aliases* • He was traveling ***under an alias***. [=he was traveling under an assumed name; he was using a name that was not his real name]

al·i·bi /'ælə,baɪ/ *noun, pl* **-bis** [*count*]
1 : a claim that you cannot be guilty of a crime because you were somewhere else when the crime was committed • Nobody could confirm his *alibi* that he was at the movies. • He has an ironclad/perfect *alibi*. [=an alibi that cannot be proved false]; *also* : evidence which shows that such a claim is true • Her doctor is her *alibi*: she was in surgery at the time of the murder.
2 : an excuse for not being somewhere or doing something • She made up an *alibi* for why she missed the meeting.

1alien /'eɪlijən/ *adj*
1 [*more ~; most ~*] : not familiar or like other things you have known : different from what you are used to • She felt lost in an *alien* [=*strange*] culture when she moved to the city. • an *alien* environment • Honesty seems to be an *alien* concept in that family. [=people in that family are not honest] — often + *to* • The whole idea of having a job was *alien* [=*unfamiliar, foreign*] *to* him.
2 : from another country : FOREIGN • *alien* residents
3 [*more ~; most ~*] : too different from something to be acceptable or suitable — + *to* • Such behavior is totally *alien to* the spirit of the religion. • ideas *alien to* [=*incompatible with*] democracy
4 : from somewhere other than the planet Earth • an *alien* spaceship • The movie is a story about an attack on Earth by an army of *alien* [=*extraterrestrial*] monsters.

2alien *noun, pl* **aliens** [*count*]
1 : a person who was born in a different country and is not a citizen of the country in which he or she now lives • *aliens* seeking asylum in the U.S. • ***illegal aliens*** [=foreign people who live in a country without having official permission to live there]
2 : a creature that comes from somewhere other than the

planet Earth ▪ The movie is about an invasion by *aliens*. [=*extraterrestrials*] ▪ He claims that he was captured by space *aliens*.

alien·ate /ˈeɪlijəˌneɪt/ *verb* **-ates; -at·ed; -at·ing** [+ *obj*]
1 : to make (someone) unfriendly **:** to cause (someone) to stop being friendly, helpful, etc., towards you ▪ He *alienated* most of his colleagues with his bad temper. ▪ Her position on this issue has *alienated* many former supporters.
2 : to cause (someone) to feel that she or he no longer belongs in a particular group, society, etc. — *+ from* ▪ Her position on this issue has *alienated* her *from* many voters. ▪ His drug problems have *alienated* him *from* his parents.
– alienated *adj* [*more* ~; *most* ~] ▪ He feels very *alienated* from his parents. ▪ *alienated* young people [=young people who do not feel that they have a part in society] **– alien·ation** /ˌeɪlijəˈneɪʃən/ *noun* [*noncount*] ▪ Her position on this issue has caused the *alienation* of many former supporters. ▪ His *alienation* from his parents stems from his drug problems. ▪ She has struggled with feelings of loneliness and *alienation* for much of her adult life.

[1]**alight** /əˈlaɪt/ *verb* **alights; alight·ed; alight·ing** [*no obj*] *somewhat formal*
1 *of insects, birds, etc.* **:** to stop on a surface after flying ▪ A butterfly *alighted* [=*landed*] on her hat.
2 : to step down from a boat, vehicle, etc. ▪ A group of tourists *alighted* from the boat/bus/train.
alight on/upon [*phrasal verb*] ***alight on/upon (something)*** **:** to see, notice, or think of (something) ▪ Her eye/eyes *alighted on* a strange man in the crowd. ▪ a speaker who easily *alights upon* topics that interest a wide audience

[2]**alight** *adj, not used before a noun*
1 : full of light **:** lighted up ▪ The sky was *alight* with stars. — often used figuratively ▪ a face *alight* with excitement ▪ The children laughed, their eyes *alight*.
2 *chiefly Brit* **:** on fire **:** ABLAZE, AFIRE ▪ Enemy soldiers set the building *alight*.

align /əˈlaɪn/ *verb* **aligns; aligned; align·ing**
1 : to arrange things so that they form a line or are in proper position [+ *obj*] The storekeeper carefully *aligned* [=*lined up*] the cans on the shelf. ▪ He *aligned* the two holes so he could put the screw through them. ▪ The text is *aligned* [=*in line*] with the bottom of the picture. ▪ The two parts of the machine are not properly *aligned*. [*no obj*] The two parts of the machine don't *align* [=*line up*] properly. ▪ The text *aligns* with the bottom of the picture.
2 [+ *obj*] **:** to change (something) so that it agrees with or matches something else ▪ The schools had to *align* their programs with state requirements.
3 : to join a group that is supporting or opposing something [+ *obj*] He has ***aligned himself with*** the protesters. [=he has joined the protesters] [*no obj*] She is *aligning* with other senators to oppose his nomination.

align·ment /əˈlaɪnmənt/ *noun, pl* **-ments**
1 [*noncount*] **:** the state or condition of being aligned: such as **a :** the state of being arranged in a line or in proper position ▪ wheel *alignment* ▪ planetary *alignment* ▪ The parts were not ***in alignment***. = The parts were ***out of alignment***. [=the parts were not aligned] **b :** the state or condition of agreeing with or matching something else ▪ The school has to bring its programs ***into alignment*** with state requirements. **c :** the state of being joined with others in supporting or opposing something ▪ Many people were surprised by his *alignment* with the protesters. [=his support of the protesters]
2 [*count*] **:** an arrangement of groups or forces ▪ New *alignments* have been created within the political party.

[1]**alike** /əˈlaɪk/ *adj, not used before a noun* [*more* ~; *most* ~] **:** similar in appearance, nature, or form ▪ The two cars are much *alike*. — often *+ in* ▪ He and his brother are *alike in* their beliefs. [=they have similar beliefs] ▪ two apples *alike in* shape

[2]**alike** *adv* [*more* ~; *most* ~] **:** in the same way ▪ We think *alike*. ▪ a film intended for parents and teenagers *alike* [=intended for both parents and teenagers]

al·i·men·ta·ry canal /ˌæləˈmentri-/ *noun, pl* **~ -als** [*count*] **:** the long tube in the body through which food passes after it is eaten ✧ The alimentary canal begins at the mouth and ends at the anus.

al·i·mo·ny /ˈæləˌmouni, *Brit* ˈæləməni/ *noun* [*noncount*] **:** money that a court orders someone to pay regularly to a former wife or husband after a divorce

A–line /ˈeɪˌlaɪn/ *adj, always used before a noun, of a piece of clothing* **:** having a wide bottom and a close-fitting top **:** shaped like the letter *A* ▪ an *A-line* skirt

A–list /ˈeɪˌlɪst/ *noun* [*singular*] **:** a list or group of people who are very well-known or respected ▪ She's new on the celebrity *A-list*. ▪ *A-list* celebrities

alive /əˈlaɪv/ *adj, not used before a noun*
1 : having life **:** living **:** not dead ▪ It feels great to be *alive*. ▪ The patient was barely *alive*. ▪ The sheriff was ordered to find the killer and bring him back *alive*. ▪ She must be the happiest woman *alive*. [=the happiest woman in the world] ▪ He managed to ***stay alive*** for a week without any food. ▪ The patient is being ***kept alive*** by artificial means.
2 a : continuing to exist ▪ an old tradition that is still *alive* ▪ We tried to keep the organization *alive* [=*active*] despite having fewer members. ▪ We need to keep hope *alive*. **b :** not yet defeated **:** still having a chance to win or succeed ▪ The legislation is still *alive* in the Senate. [=the legislation has not been defeated yet] ▪ The team needs to win tonight in order to stay *alive* in the play-offs.
3 [*more* ~; *most* ~] **a :** filled with life and energy ▪ I love to sail because it makes me feel so *alive*. — often *+ with* ▪ Her face was *alive with* joy/happiness. **b :** filled with activity — usually *+ with* ▪ flower gardens *alive with* bees [=filled with the activity of many bees] ▪ The city streets are *alive* [=*busy*] *with* shoppers.
alive and kicking **:** healthy and active ▪ She ran a marathon late in life, just to prove she was still *alive and kicking*. — often used figuratively ▪ After years of slow earnings, the industry is now *alive and kicking*.
alive and well **1 :** living and healthy ▪ She found out that her aunt is *alive and well* and living in Arizona. **2 :** still popular **:** continuing to be used ▪ Many of the old traditions are still *alive and well*.
alive to **:** aware of (something) **:** able to notice (something) ▪ Recovering from his illness has made him more *alive to* the beauty of life. ▪ We need to be *alive* [=*sensitive*] *to* new opportunities for our business to grow.
bring (something) alive **:** to make (something) seem more real or interesting ▪ The play *brings the old fairy tale alive*.
come alive **:** to become lively: such as **a :** to become excited and filled with energy ▪ The crowd *came alive* when the singer appeared on stage. **b :** to become filled with activity ▪ This neighborhood is quiet during the day, but it *comes alive* at night. **c :** to become exciting or appealing ▪ In her kitchen, Italian food *comes alive*.
eat (someone or something) alive see EAT
skin (someone) alive see [2]SKIN

al·ka·li /ˈælkəˌlaɪ/ *noun, pl* **-lies** *or* **-lis** *chemistry* **:** a substance that has a bitter taste and that forms a salt when mixed with an acid [*count*] strong *alkalis* [*noncount*] smaller amounts of *alkali* ✧ An alkali has a pH of more than 7.

al·ka·line /ˈælkəˌlaɪn/ *adj*
1 [*more* ~; *most* ~] **:** containing an alkali ▪ *alkaline* soil — compare ACIDIC
2 : having the qualities of an alkali ▪ *alkaline* conditions
– al·ka·lin·i·ty /ˌælkəˈlɪnəti/ *noun* [*noncount*]

[1]**all** /ˈɑːl/ *adj*
1 : the whole, entire, total amount, quantity, or extent of ▪ He stayed awake *all* night. [=the whole/entire night] ▪ She worked hard *all* day. [=throughout the entire day] ▪ I've been waiting *all* week to see her. ▪ He had to walk *all* the way home. ▪ She works *all* year round. ▪ He'll need *all* the help he can get. ▪ Someone took *all* the candy. ▪ It was one of the greatest victories of *all* time. [=one of the greatest victories ever] ▪ I think about her ***all the time***. [=I think about her constantly]
2 a : every member or part of — used with a plural noun or pronoun to mean that a statement is true of every person or thing in a group ▪ *All* my friends were there. ▪ a film suitable for *all* ages ▪ They *all* came late. ▪ We *all* need to work faster. ▪ I read *all* the magazines. = I read them *all*. ▪ *All* these eggs are ready. ▪ "'. . . *all* men are created equal . . .'" —*U.S. Declaration of Independence* (1776) ▪ She thinks *all* teenagers are alike. = She thinks teenagers are *all* alike. ▪ ***Not all*** teenagers are alike. = Teenagers are not *all* alike. ▪ They serve breakfast ***at all hours***. [=at any hour, at any time of day] ▪ They were up ***till/until all hours***. [=they were up very late] ▪ She has to deal with ***all kinds/sorts/types*** of people. [=with people of every kind/sort/type] **b :** the whole number or sum of — used with a plural noun or pronoun to mean that a statement is true of a group of people or things considered together ▪ It was great to see him again after *all* these years.
3 : any whatever ▪ His guilt is beyond *all* doubt. [=he is cer-

A

tainly guilty] • She denied *all* [=*any*] responsibility for the accident.

4 a : as much as possible of (something) — used to indicate the manner in which something is done • He spoke in *all* seriousness/innocence. [=he spoke in a completely serious/innocent way] **b :** having or showing only (some quality, feature, etc.) • The students became *all* attention [=became very attentive] when the teacher came in. • He was *all* smiles with the boss. [=he was smiling constantly when he was with the boss] • This drink is too strong: it's *all* alcohol! **c** — used to indicate that someone has or seems to have a lot of or too much of some physical feature • an actress who is *all* legs [=an actress who has very long legs] — see also *all ears* at [1]EAR, *all eyes* at [1]EYE, *all heart* at HEART, *all mouth* at [1]MOUTH, *all thumbs* at [1]THUMB

5 *US, chiefly Southern, informal* — used in speech to refer to a group of people or things • Who *all* is coming? [=who is coming?] • What *all* do we need to do? [=what are the things that we need to do?] — see also WHAT ALL, YOU-ALL

for all **:** in spite of (something) • *For all* his confident talk, he is actually very unsure of himself. • She still loves him, *for all* his faults.

of all (the) *informal* — used in phrases to express surprise, disapproval, anger, etc. • Who should I meet in New York but Max *of all* people! = *Of all the* people in New York, who should I run into but Max! [=I was very surprised to meet Max in New York] • Why did my car break down now *of all* times, when I can least afford it?! • "He actually called you a fool!" "***Of all the nerve!***" [=I am shocked and offended that he called me a fool]

[2]all *adv*

1 : entirely or completely • She sat *all* alone. • She has traveled *all* around the world. • This money will be *all* yours when I die. • He got *all* wet. • She had buttons *all* down the side of her dress. • I forgot *all* about paying the bill. • The noise continued *all* through the night. [=all night long, throughout the night] — often used to make a statement more forceful • I'm *all* in favor of trying again. • His criticisms were *all* out of proportion. • These problems have been occurring ***all too*** often. [=much too often]

2 : for each side or player — used to indicate a tie score • The score is 2 *all*. [=*apiece*] • The game ended in a 5-*all* draw. • We're tied at 3-*all* after seven innings.

3 *informal* **:** [1]VERY • The kids got *all* excited when they saw Santa Claus.

all along see [2]ALONG

all around (*US*) *or chiefly Brit* ***all round*** **1 :** in every way **:** from every point of view • It was a good deal *all around*: we made money and nobody lost out. **2 :** for everyone • Let's have drinks *all around*, bartender. — see also ALL-AROUND

all of **1 :** not more than — used to stress that an amount is surprisingly small • She learned to fly a plane when she was *all of* 16 years old. • The team scored *all of* six points the entire game. **2 :** as much as — used to stress that an amount is somewhat large • The prize is now worth *all of* 10 million dollars.

all over **1 a :** over an entire area • We looked *all over* [=*everywhere*] for you. **b :** in every part of (something) • The flower can be found *all over* the island in spring and early summer. • He's lived *all over* Texas. • In his office there are books piled ***all over the place***. [=*everywhere*] — see also ALLOVER **2** *informal* **:** very critical of (someone) • She was *all over* me for being late. **3** *informal* **:** crowding around, pushing against, or touching (someone) in a very eager or aggressive way • The band's fans were *all over* them. • Look at that young couple. They're *all over* each other! [=they are kissing, touching, etc., very passionately] • She tried to score, but the other team's defense was *all over* her. **4** *chiefly Brit, informal* **:** in every way • She's her mother *all over*. [=she's just like her mother] • Late again, is she? That's her *all over*. [=that's very typical of her]

all that **:** to a high degree — usually used in negative statements • I wasn't *all that* [=*very*] interested in the story. • The movie wasn't *all that* [=*so*] bad. — see also *all that* at [1]THAT

all the — used to give added force to a word like "more" or "better" • With the economy in such bad shape, it's *all the more* important [=it's even more important] that we correct these problems quickly. • If we arrive early, *all the better*. [=it will be even better if we arrive early]

all told **:** with everything considered or included **:** in all • *All told*, it took us three full days to get there. • There were seven of us *all told*.

go all out see [1]GO

not all there *informal* — used to describe a person who is somewhat strange or stupid • Her aunt is very sweet but *not all there* (mentally).

[3]all *pronoun*

1 : the entire number, quantity, or amount • *All* [=*everything*] that I have is yours. • *All* [=*everything*] will be explained soon. • She told us *all* about what happened. • Her other books were good, but this one is the best of *all*. • *All* are welcome! [=everyone is welcome] • We *all* enjoyed the movie. = *All* of us enjoyed the movie. • Many people were invited and *all* came. • His stories may be entertaining, but I don't think *all* (of them) are true. • Thanks to *all* who helped out. • *All* of this money will be yours when I die. • Not *all* of our students go on to college. • It ***was all (that) I could do*** to keep from laughing! [=I had a hard time trying not to laugh] • "Is there anything else to be done?" "No, ***that's all***." • He gave equal attention to ***one and all***. [=to everyone] • ***Come one, come all***. [=everyone is invited to come] ***usage*** see ALTOGETHER

2 : the only thing • That's *all* I can do to help. • *All* I know is that the game was canceled. I don't know why.

above all see [2]ABOVE

after all see [2]AFTER

All aboard! see [1]ABOARD

all in all *informal* **:** in a general way **:** when everything is thought of or considered • *All in all* [=*in general, generally, for the most part*], I like the way things have gone. • We did lose some money, but we got most of it back. So *all in all* things might have been a lot worse.

all's fair in love and war see [1]FAIR

all told **:** including everything or everyone — used to indicate a total • The cost of the repairs came to about $300 *all told*. [=*in all*] [=the total cost of the repairs was about $300]

and all **1 :** and everything else • What with the noise outside, the fire *and all*, we got hardly any sleep. • He endured everything, insults *and all*, without getting angry. **2** *Brit, informal* — used to emphasize a response • "It's really hot out!" "It is *and all*!" [=it certainly is]

at all — used to make a statement or question more forceful • He will go anywhere *at all* to get a job. • Did you find out anything *at all*? — used especially in negative statements • "Did she say anything?" "No, nothing *at all*." • I don't mind cooking *at all*. • It's not *at all* what you think it is. It's something else entirely. • I wasn't tired *at all*. = I wasn't *at all* tired. [=I wasn't even slightly tired] • This chair is not *at all* comfortable. • I didn't like it *at all*. • That is not *at all* likely.

✧ The phrase ***not at all*** is sometimes used as a polite response when someone thanks you. • "Thank you for all your trouble." "*Not at all*." • "That was very kind of you." "*Not at all*. It was the least I could do."

for all see [1]FOR

for all I know see [1]KNOW

for all (someone) cares see [2]CARE

give your all **:** to do or give as much as you can to achieve something, to support a cause, etc. • He *gave his all* for the cause. = He *gave his all* to help the cause. • You'll never succeed in this business unless you *give (it) your all*.

in all **:** including everything or everyone — used to indicate a total • There were about a thousand people at the concert *in all*. [=*all told*]

once and for all see [1]ONCE

that is all see [1]THAT

when all is said and done **:** after considering or doing everything — used for a final general statement or judgment • It won't be easy, but *when all is said and done*, we'll be glad we did it. • The candidates claim to have different views but, *when all is said and done*, they're very much alike.

all- *combining form*

1 : entirely **:** completely • an *all*-wool suit • an *all*-woman band

2 : including everything • an *all*-encompassing philosophy • Her *all*-consuming passion was music.

3 *US* **:** selected as the best at something (such as a sport) within an area or organization • an *all*-league halfback

Al·lah /ˈɑːlə, *Brit* ˈælə/ *noun* [*singular*] — used as the name of God in Islam

all–Amer·i·can /ˌɑːləˈmerəkən/ *adj*

1 : having qualities that are thought to be typical of people in the U.S. or that are widely admired in the U.S. • a wholesome *all-American* boy • her *all-American* optimism

2 *sports* **a :** selected as one of the best in the U.S. in a particular sport ▪ an *all-American* football player ▪ He was *all-American* twice when he played college football. **b :** having only all-American players ▪ an *all-American* football team
3 : consisting entirely of Americans or of American elements ▪ The tennis tournament will have an *all-American* final. [=both players in the final are American]
– all–American *noun, pl* **-cans** [*count*] ▪ He was an *all-American* in football.

all–around /ˌɑːləˈraʊnd/ *adj, always used before a noun, US*
1 : relating to or involving many different things ▪ The computer has good *all-around* performance. ▪ There has been an *all-around* improvement in his work recently. **:** considered in a general way ▪ He is an *all-around* good guy. ▪ She is a teacher, writer, and *all-around* nice woman.
2 : skillful or useful in many ways ▪ She's the best *all-around* player on the team. ▪ a good *all-around* pickup truck ▪ The encyclopedia is an excellent *all-around* resource.

al•lay /æˈleɪ/ *verb* **-lays**; **-layed**; **-lay•ing** [+ *obj*] *formal* **:** to make (something) less severe or strong ▪ Managers tried to *allay* [=*calm, ease*] fears that some workers would lose their jobs. ▪ The new advertising campaign is an attempt to *allay* the public's concerns/worries about the safety of the company's products. ▪ *allay* suspicions

all but *adv* **:** very nearly **:** ALMOST ▪ Without you the job would have been *all but* impossible. ▪ We had *all but* given up hope.

all clear *noun*
the all clear **:** a signal telling you that a situation is no longer dangerous ▪ "How will we know when it's safe to leave?" "I'll give you *the all clear* by blowing a whistle." ▪ Doctors have given her *the all clear* [=have told her that she is healthy] and she should be back at work next week.

all–day /ˈɑlˈdeɪ/ *adj, always used before a noun* **:** lasting throughout the day ▪ an *all-day* trip/event

al•le•ga•tion /ˌælɪˈgeɪʃən/ *noun, pl* **-tions** [*count*] **:** a statement saying that someone has done something wrong or illegal ▪ The police are investigating *allegations* that the mayor has accepted bribes. ▪ The mayor denies the *allegations* (that have been made) against him. ▪ There have been *allegations* of fraud in the city government. ▪ You're making a serious *allegation*. Do you have any proof?

al•lege /əˈlɛʤ/ *verb* **-leg•es**; **-leged**; **-leg•ing** [+ *obj*] **:** to state without definite proof that someone has done something wrong or illegal ▪ *allege* a person's guilt ▪ He *alleged* that the mayor has accepted bribes. ▪ The mayor is *alleged* to have accepted bribes. ▪ *allege* a conspiracy ▪ She *alleged* misconduct. = She *alleged* that there had been misconduct. ▪ You *allege* that she stole a large quantity of money. Do you have any proof?

al•leged /əˈlɛʤd/ *adj, always used before a noun*
1 : accused of having done something wrong or illegal but not yet proven guilty ▪ The *alleged* thief was arrested.
2 : said to have happened but not yet proven ▪ He denied the *alleged* conspiracy. ▪ *alleged* abuse
– al•leg•ed•ly /əˈlɛʤədli/ *adv* ▪ She *allegedly* stole the money. = *Allegedly*, she stole the money.

al•le•giance /əˈliːʤəns/ *noun, pl* **-gianc•es** *formal* **:** loyalty to a person, country, group, etc. [*noncount*] I pledge *allegiance* to my country. [=I promise to be loyal to my country] ▪ He owes *allegiance* to them for all the help they have given him. [*count*] Both candidates are working hard to convince voters to switch *allegiances*.
the Pledge of Allegiance see [1]PLEDGE

al•le•go•ry /ˈæləˌgori, *Brit* ˈæləgri/ *noun, pl* **-ries :** a story in which the characters and events are symbols that stand for ideas about human life or for a political or historical situation [*count*] the long poem is an *allegory* of/about love and jealousy [*noncount*] a writer known for his use of *allegory*
– al•le•gor•i•cal /ˌæləˈgorɪkəl/ *adj* [*more* ~; *most* ~] ▪ an *allegorical* poem**– al•le•gor•i•cal•ly** /ˌæləˈgorɪkli/ *adv*

[1]**al•le•gro** /əˈlegrou/ *adv, music* **:** in a quick and lively way ▪ a movement played *allegro*
– allegro *adj* ▪ an *allegro* movement

[2]**allegro** *noun, pl* **-gros** [*count*] **:** a piece of music that is played or performed in a quick and lively way ▪ The symphony's first movement is an *allegro*.

al•le•lu•ia /ˌæləˈluːjə/ *interj* **:** [1]HALLELUJAH
– alleluia *noun, pl* **-i•as** [*count*]

all–encompassing *adj* **:** including everything or everyone ▪ We're unlikely to find an *all-encompassing* solution.

Al•len wrench /ˈælən-/ *noun, pl* **~ wrenches** [*count*] *US* **:** a small tool that is used to turn a special type of screw — called also (*Brit*) *Allen key*

al•ler•gen /ˈælɚʤən/ *noun, pl* **-gens** [*count*] *medical* **:** a substance that causes an allergy ▪ common *allergens*, such as pollen
– al•ler•gen•ic /ˌælɚˈʤɛnɪk/ *adj* [*more* ~; *most* ~] ▪ a highly *allergenic* substance

al•ler•gic /əˈlɚʤɪk/ *adj*
1 : of or relating to an allergy ▪ an *allergic* reaction/response/condition
2 [*more* ~; *most* ~] **:** having an allergy ▪ an *allergic* person— usually + *to* ▪ I'm *allergic to* cats/nuts. ▪ people who are highly *allergic to* shellfish — often used figuratively in informal contexts ▪ My brother is *allergic to* hard work. [=my brother does not like hard work; my brother is lazy]

al•ler•gist /ˈælɚʤɪst/ *noun, pl* **-gists** [*count*] *medical* **:** a doctor who is an expert in the treatment of allergies

al•ler•gy /ˈælɚʤi/ *noun, pl* **-gies :** a medical condition that causes someone to become sick after eating, touching, or breathing something that is harmless to most people [*noncount*] Many people have some form of *allergy*. [*count*] food *allergies*— often + *to* ▪ I have an *allergy to* strawberries. I get a rash if I eat just one.— sometimes used figuratively in informal contexts ▪ My brother has an *allergy to* hard work. [=my brother does not like hard work; my brother is lazy]

al•le•vi•ate /əˈliːviˌeɪt/ *verb* **-ates**; **-at•ed**; **-at•ing** [+ *obj*] **:** to reduce the pain or trouble of (something) **:** to make (something) less painful, difficult, or severe ▪ The doctor tried to *alleviate* [=*relieve*] her symptoms/suffering. ▪ finding ways to *alleviate* stress ▪ The new tunnel should *alleviate* [=*lessen, reduce*] traffic on the bridge. ▪ government programs that are intended to *alleviate* [=*reduce*] poverty
– al•le•vi•a•tion /əˌliːviˈeɪʃən/ *noun* [*noncount*] ▪ the *alleviation* of suffering/poverty

al•ley /ˈæli/ *noun, pl* **-leys** [*count*] **:** a narrow street or passage between buildings ▪ a dark *alley*— see also BLIND ALLEY, BOWLING ALLEY
up someone's alley *also* ***down someone's alley*** *chiefly US, informal* **:** suited to someone's tastes or abilities ▪ A job like that would be ***right up my alley***! [=a job like that would suit me very well] ▪ I love books, so volunteering at the library is *right up my alley*. [=(*Brit*) *up my street*]

al•ley•way /ˈæliˌweɪ/ *noun, pl* **-ways** [*count*] **:** a passage between buildings **:** ALLEY

all–fired /ˈɑːlˌfajɚd/ *adj, always used before a noun, US, informal + somewhat old-fashioned* **:** extreme or excessive ▪ Why are you in such an *all-fired* hurry?
– all–fired *adv* ▪ I don't know why you're being so *all-fired* stubborn!

All Fools' Day *noun* [*singular*] **:** APRIL FOOLS' DAY

all fours *noun*
on all fours *of a person* **:** with the hands and knees on the ground ▪ The baby crawled away *on all fours*.

all get–out *noun, always used after an adjective*
as all get-out *US, informal* **:** very or extremely ▪ The café was (as) busy *as all get-out* [=was extremely busy] this afternoon.

al•li•ance /əˈlajəns/ *noun, pl* **-anc•es**
1 [*count*] **:** a union between people, groups, countries, etc. **:** a relationship in which people agree to work together ▪ We need to form/forge/encourage a closer *alliance* between government and industry. ▪ strengthen/weaken the *alliance* of western nations ▪ There has been a pattern of shifting *alliances* in the political world. ▪ The article condemns what some say is an ***unholy alliance*** between government and media.
2 [*noncount*] **:** the state of being joined in some activity or effort **:** the state of being allied ▪ two nations in close *alliance* (with each other) ▪ one nation working ***in alliance with*** another
3 [*count*] **:** a group of people, countries, etc., that are joined together in some activity or effort ▪ There is disagreement within the *alliance* about how to deal with this problem.

al•lied /əˈlaɪd, ˈæˌlaɪd/ *adj*
1 a : joined in a relationship in which people, groups, countries etc., agree to work together ▪ *allied* nations = nations that are *allied* to/with each other **b *Allied*** *always used before a noun* **:** of or relating to the nations that fought together against Germany in World War I and World War II ▪ *Allied* soldiers/troops/forces
2 *somewhat formal* **:** related or connected ▪ chemistry and *allied* subjects ▪ two families *allied* [=(more commonly) *joined*] by marriage

A

al·li·ga·tor /ˈæləˌgeɪtɚ/ *noun, pl* **-tors**
1 [*count*] : a large reptile that has a long body, thick skin, and sharp teeth, that lives in the tropical parts of the U.S. and China, and that is related to crocodiles
2 [*noncount*] : the skin of an alligator used for making shoes and other products — often used before another noun ▪ *alligator* shoes

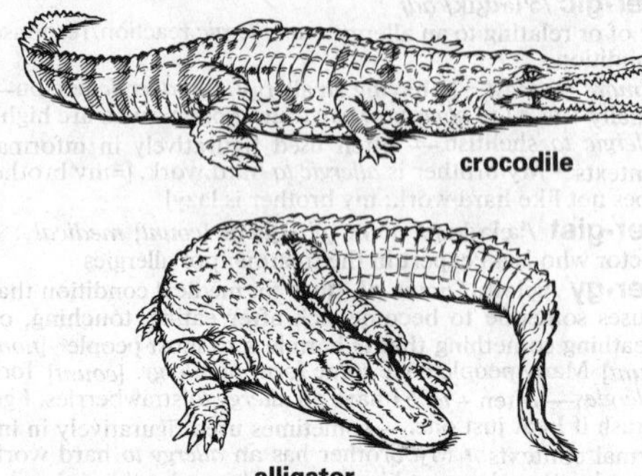

all–im·por·tant /ˌɑːlɪmˈpoɚtn̩t/ *adj* : very important ▪ an *all-important* question — often used in a humorous or exaggerated way ▪ She paused to consider the *all-important* issue of which shoes to wear.

all–in /ˌɑːlˈɪn/ *adj*
1 *informal* : very tired ▪ By the end of finals week, I was *all-in*. [=*exhausted*] — often written as two separate words ▪ You look *all in*.
2 *Brit* **a** : ALL-INCLUSIVE ▪ the *all-in* room rate **b** : allowing almost any technique or method ▪ *all-in* wrestling

all–in·clu·sive /ˌɑːlɪnˈkluːsɪv/ *adj* : including everything; *especially* : sold for one price that includes charges and fees that are often added separately ▪ The resort is *all-inclusive* so you don't worry about money while you're there.

al·lit·er·a·tion /əˌlɪtəˈreɪʃən/ *noun* [*noncount*] : the use of words that begin with the same sound near one another (as in *wild and woolly* or *a babbling brook*)
– **al·lit·er·a·tive** /əˈlɪtərətɪv/ *adj* ▪ an *alliterative* name like "Molly Mason"

all–night /ˈɑːlˈnaɪt/ *adj, always used before a noun*
1 : open for business throughout the night ▪ *an all-night* diner
2 : lasting throughout the night ▪ an *all-night* party

all–night·er /ˈɑːlˈnaɪtɚ/ *noun, pl* **-ers** [*count*] *informal* : a night during which someone works on something instead of sleeping ▪ I have to finish this by morning, so I guess tonight will be another *all-nighter*. ▪ He ***pulled an all-nighter*** [=he stayed up all night] to study for the exam.

al·lo·cate /ˈæləˌkeɪt/ *verb* **-cates; -cat·ed; -cat·ing** [+ *obj*] : to divide and give out (something) for a special reason or to particular people, companies, etc. ▪ *allocate* funds among charities ▪ Money from the sale of the house was *allocated* to each of the children. ▪ We need to determine the best way to *allocate* our resources. ▪ Have enough funds been *allocated* to finance the project?
– **al·lo·ca·tion** /ˌæləˈkeɪʃən/ *noun, pl* **-tions** [*noncount*] the *allocation* of funds ▪ asset *allocation* [*count*] asset *allocations*

al·lot /əˈlɑːt/ *verb* **-lots; -lot·ted; -lot·ting** [+ *obj*] : to give someone (an amount of something) to use or have ▪ Each speaker will be *allotted* 15 minutes. ▪ The newspaper will *allot* a full page to each of the three mayoral candidates.
– **allotted** *adj* ▪ Most of the students completed the exam in the *allotted* time.

al·lot·ment /əˈlɑːtmənt/ *noun, pl* **-ments**
1 [*count*] : an amount of something given to someone to use or have ▪ He complained that the 15-minute time *allotment* was too short.
2 [*noncount*] : the act of allotting something ▪ The *allotment* of a full page in the newspaper to each candidate is more than fair.
3 [*count*] *Brit* : a small area of land that a person can rent to use as a garden ▪ fresh tomatoes from my *allotment*

all–out /ˈɑːlˈaʊt/ *adj, always used before a noun*
1 : made or done with as much effort as possible ▪ an *all-out* attack/assault on poverty = an *all-out* effort to eliminate poverty — see also *go all out* at [1]GO
2 : fully developed ▪ an *all-out* [=*full-blown*] war

all·over /ˈɑːlˌoʊvɚ/ *adj, always used before a noun* : covering the whole surface of something ▪ a rug with an *allover* pattern — see also *all over* at [2]ALL

al·low /əˈlaʊ/ *verb* **-lows; -lowed; -low·ing** [+ *obj*]
1 a : to permit (something) : to regard or treat (something) as acceptable ▪ a religion that does not *allow* divorce ▪ They don't *allow* smoking in this hotel. ▪ I want to change my schedule, but my boss won't *allow* it. **b** : to permit (someone) to have or do something ▪ He *allowed* her to leave. [=he let her leave] ▪ My boss wouldn't *allow* me to change my schedule. ▪ They don't *allow* people to smoke in this hotel. ▪ He *allows* himself (to have) many luxuries. — used in the phrase ***allow me*** to make a polite offer to help someone ▪ *Allow me* to get/open the door for you. ▪ If you're going to remodel your kitchen, *allow me* to offer a few suggestions. **c** : to permit (someone) to go or come in, out, etc. ▪ Women were not *allowed* in/into the club. ▪ The hospital doesn't *allow* visitors after 8 p.m. ▪ Those children are too young to be *allowed* (to go) out at night.
2 a : to make it possible for someone or something to have or do something ▪ Her experience *allows* her to handle difficult situations easily. [=she can handle difficult situations easily because of her experience] ▪ Her schedule doesn't *allow* her any time to run errands. ▪ The system *allows* you to transfer data easily from one computer to another. **b** : to make it possible for something to happen ▪ Occasional gaps *allow* passage through the mountains. ▪ a password that *allows* access to the system ▪ The system *allows* the easy transfer of data from one computer to another. = The system *allows* data to be transferred easily from one computer to another. **c** : to fail to prevent something or someone from being, becoming, or doing something ▪ They *allowed* the garden to become overgrown with weeds. ▪ These conditions should never have been *allowed* to develop. ▪ I was surprised to see that she had *allowed* herself to become so fat. [=that she had become so fat]
3 : to include (a quantity of time, money, etc.) as an appropriate amount ▪ When you're planning your day you should *allow* an hour for lunch. ▪ Their parents *allowed* five dollars for each child as spending money. ▪ We need to *allow* (ourselves) enough time to get the job done properly.
4 a : to accept (something) ▪ The judge decided to *allow* the evidence. **b** : to admit (something) ▪ His job played a more important part in his life than his biographer *allows*. — usually + *that* or (*US, informal*) *as how* ▪ She *allowed that* the work was hard. = She *allowed as how* the work was hard. [=she admitted that the work was hard]
5 *sports* : to let an opposing team or player have or score (a goal, a hit, etc.) ▪ The pitcher *allowed* five hits and three runs in the first two innings. ▪ *allow* a goal ▪ The defense has not *allowed* a touchdown in the past three games.
allow for [*phrasal verb*] ***allow for (something)*** **1 a** : to think about or plan for (something that will or might happen in the future) ▪ When purchasing property, the company should *allow for* possible future growth/expansion. **b** : to consider (something) when you make a calculation ▪ The total distance, *allowing for* detours, is about 10 miles. ▪ If you *allow for* inflation, he's actually earning less money now than he was 10 years ago. [=the value of the money he earns now is less than that of the money he earned 10 years ago because of inflation] **2** : to make (something) possible ▪ The design of the system *allows for* [=*allows, permits*] easy upgrades.
allow of [*phrasal verb*] ***allow of (something)*** *formal* : to make (something) possible ▪ The evidence *allows of* [=*allows, permits*] two possible interpretations.
– **al·low·able** /əˈlawəbəl/ *adj* ▪ *allowable* behavior

al·low·ance /əˈlawəns/ *noun, pl* **-anc·es**
1 [*count*] **a** : an amount of money that is given to someone regularly or for a specific purpose ▪ a monthly *allowance* for household expenses ▪ a clothing *allowance* **b** *chiefly US* : a small amount of money that is regularly given to children by their parents ▪ Each of their children gets a weekly *allowance* of five dollars.
2 [*count*] **a** : an amount of something (such as time) that is allowed or available ▪ The schedule provides a generous *allowance* of time for sightseeing. [=provides a generous amount of time for sightseeing] **b** : an amount that is regarded as acceptable or desirable ▪ the recommended daily *allowance* of vitamin C **c** : an amount that is subtracted from the price of something ▪ When we bought our new car

we got a trade-in *allowance* of $2,000 on our old car. [=the price of our new car was reduced by $2,000 because we traded in our old car] **d** *Brit* : an amount of your earnings that you do not have to pay taxes on ▪ the ***tax allowance*** for married couples

3 a [*noncount*] : the act of thinking about or including something when you make a plan, calculation, etc. ▪ When you're comparing costs from different decades, you need to ***make allowance for*** inflation. [=you need to allow for inflation] ▪ His theory ***makes no allowance for*** [=does not allow for] the possibility that the disease may be genetic. **b** : the act of regarding bad behavior or a mistake as less serious or bad because of some special situation or condition [*noncount*] She performed poorly, but we should ***make some allowance for*** her inexperience. = Some ***allowance should be made for*** her inexperience. [=because she is inexperienced, we should not blame her too much for performing poorly] [*count*] They performed poorly, but *allowances should be made* for their inexperience.

4 [*noncount*] *formal* : the act of allowing something ▪ The lawyer protested the judge's *allowance* of the evidence.

al·loy /ˈæˌlɔɪ/ *noun, pl* **-loys** : a metal made by melting and mixing two or more metals or a metal and another material together [*count*] testing the properties of various *alloys* [*noncount*] a part made of aluminum *alloy*

– al·loy /əˈlɔɪ/ *verb* **-loys**; **-loyed**; **-loy·ing** [+ *obj*] ▪ Stainless steel is made by *alloying* steel with chromium.

all–pow·er·ful /ˈɑːlˈpawɚfəl/ *adj* : having complete power : able to do anything ▪ She believes in an *all-powerful* God. — often used in an exaggerated way to describe people or organizations that are very powerful ▪ the *all-powerful* committee ▪ an *all-powerful* leader

all–pur·pose /ˈɑːlˈpɚpəs/ *adj, always used before a noun* : suitable for many uses ▪ an *all-purpose* tool/knife/cleanser ▪ (*US*) *all-purpose* flour — compare GENERAL-PURPOSE

[1]all right *adv*

1 : fairly well : well enough ▪ She does *all right* in school. ▪ The engine was sputtering when I started it, but it's running/working *all right* now. ▪ "How's your father?" "He was pretty sick, but he's doing *all right* now."

2 : beyond doubt : CERTAINLY — used to stress that a preceding statement is true or accurate ▪ "Is this the one you wanted?" "Yes, that's it *all right*." [=that is indeed the one I wanted] ▪ "He seems pretty clever to me." "Oh, he's clever *all right*. A little *too* clever, if you ask me."

3 a — used to ask for or express agreement, acceptance, or understanding ▪ I'll meet you at 10 o'clock, *all right*? ▪ *All right*, I'll meet you at 10 o'clock. ▪ "I have to leave a little early today, *all right*?" "*All right*, that's fine." — often used in a way that shows annoyance or reluctance ▪ "Can we please go now?" "Oh, *all right*, if you insist." ▪ "Hurry up!" "*All right, all right*, I'm coming!" = "***All right already***, I'm coming!" **b** *chiefly US* — used to express pleasure or excitement ▪ "They won!" "*All right*! That's great!" **c** — used for emphasis at the beginning of a statement ▪ *All right*, let's suppose your theory is correct. What then? ▪ *All right* everyone, let's get started.

[2]all right *adj, not used before a noun except in sense 4*

1 : fairly good : SATISFACTORY ▪ The quality of his work is *all right* but not outstanding. ▪ Her first movie was pretty bad but her second one was *all right*.

2 a : acceptable or agreeable ▪ Whatever you decide to do is *all right* (with/by me). [=I will accept whatever you want to do] ▪ Is it *all right* to leave early? **b** : suitable or appropriate ▪ Is this movie *all right* for children?

3 a : not ill, hurt, unhappy, etc. ▪ He was very sick but now he's *all right* again. ▪ "Are you hurt?" "No, I'm *all right*." ▪ She was upset when her boyfriend left, but she's *all right* now. **b** : not marked by problems, danger, etc. — used to tell someone not to be worried or concerned ▪ Don't worry. Everything will be *all right*. ▪ "I'm so sorry that I'm late." "It's/That's *all right*. We still have plenty of time."

4 *informal* : likable, good, or honest ▪ He's an *all right* guy. ▪ I had my doubts about him at first, but I trust him now. He's *all right*.

a bit of all right see [1]BIT

all–round /ˈɑːlˈraʊnd/ *adj, always used before a noun, chiefly Brit* : ALL-AROUND ▪ a good *all-round* effort/athlete

all–singing, all–dancing *adj, always used before a noun, Brit, informal + humorous* — used in an exaggerated way to suggest that something (such as a machine that has many features) is like a large and expensive show that has many singing and dancing performers ▪ an *all-singing, all-dancing* stereo system

all·spice /ˈɑːlˌspaɪs/ *noun* [*noncount*] : a spice that is made from the berries of a tree and that is often used in baking

all–star /ˈɑːlˌstɑɚ/ *adj, always used before a noun* : including mostly or only performers who are famous or very skillful ▪ an *all-star* baseball team ▪ The movie boasts an *all-star* cast.

– all–star *noun, pl* **-stars** [*count*] ▪ He was selected as an *all-star*. [=a member of an all-star team]

all–terrain vehicle *noun, pl* **~ -hicles** [*count*] : a small open vehicle with three or four large wheels that is used to drive over very rough ground — called also *ATV*

all-terrain vehicle

all–time /ˈɑːlˌtaɪm/ *adj, always used before a noun* : more than all others have ever been ▪ It's my *all-time* favorite movie. ▪ The price of gasoline has hit an *all-time* high. [=the price is higher than it has ever been]

al·lude /əˈluːd/ *verb* **-ludes**; **-lud·ed**; **-lud·ing**

allude to [*phrasal verb*] ***allude to (something or someone)*** : to speak of or mention (something or someone) in an indirect way ▪ I'm interested in hearing more about the technology you *alluded to* a minute ago. ▪ She *alluded to* her first marriage/husband.

Do not confuse *allude* with *elude*.

al·lure /əˈluɚ/ *noun* [*noncount*] : power to attract : a quality that attracts people ▪ These rare books hold special *allure* for collectors. — often + *of* ▪ the *allure of* fame

al·lur·ing /əˈlurɪŋ/ *adj* [*more ~; most ~*] : very attractive : having a quality that attracts people ▪ an *alluring* offer/smile/aroma

al·lu·sion /əˈluːʒən/ *noun, pl* **-sions** : a statement that refers to something without mentioning it directly [*count*] The lyrics contain biblical *allusions*. — often + *to* ▪ She made an *allusion to* her first marriage, but said nothing more about it. [*noncount*] She made *allusion to* her first marriage.

Do not confuse *allusion* with *illusion*.

– al·lu·sive /əˈluːsɪv/ *adj* ▪ *allusive* lyrics

al·lu·vi·al /əˈluːvijəl/ *adj, geology* : made up of or found in the materials that are left by the water of rivers, floods, etc. ▪ an *alluvial* plain/deposit ▪ *alluvial* soil/diamonds

all–wheel drive *noun* [*noncount*] : a system that applies engine power directly to all four wheels of a vehicle together or separately ▪ a car with *all-wheel drive*

[1]al·ly /ˈæˌlaɪ/ *noun, pl* **-lies** [*count*]

1 a : a country that supports and helps another country in a war ▪ the nation's closest *ally* **b *the Allies*** : the nations that fought together against Germany in World War I or World War II ▪ fought with *the Allies* in World War II

2 : a person or group that gives help to another person or group ▪ She's counting on her *allies* in the state legislature. ▪ a powerful *ally* ▪ The teacher's union has found an unlikely *ally* in the company. [=the company supports the position that the union has taken and this was not expected]

[2]al·ly /əˈlaɪ/ *verb* **-lies**; **-lied**; **-ly·ing** : to join (yourself) with another person, group, etc., in order to get or give support — often + *with* or *to* [+ *obj*] She's *allied* herself *with* the moderates on this issue. ▪ countries *allying* themselves *with* the EU ▪ He'll even admit that he's hoping to *ally* himself *to* a wealthy family by marriage. [*no obj*] They've *allied with* their former enemies. — see also ALLIED

al·ma ma·ter /ˌælməˈmɑːtɚ/ *noun, pl* **~ -ters** [*count*] : the school, college, or university that someone attended ▪ I visited my old *alma mater* last week.

al·ma·nac /ˈɑːlməˌnæk/ *noun, pl* **-nacs** [*count*]

1 : a book published every year that contains facts about the movements of the sun and moon, changes in the tides, and information of general interest

2 : a book published every year that contains detailed information on a special subject ▪ an *almanac* of town news ▪ a hunter's *almanac*

al·mighty /ɑlˈmaɪti/ *adj*

1 *or* ***Al·mighty*** : having complete power ▪ *Almighty* God = God *Almighty*

2 *always used before a noun* : having a great deal of power or

A

importance ✧ This sense of *almighty* is often used to suggest that something has too much power over people. ▪ All he cares about is the *almighty* dollar. [=all he cares about is money]

3 *always used before a noun* **:** very great or loud ▪ The dishes fell down with an *almighty* crash. [=a mighty crash]

Almighty *noun*

the Almighty **:** GOD 1 ▪ worshipping *the Almighty*

al·mond /ˈɑːmənd/ *noun, pl* **-monds** [*count*] **:** a nut that has a sweet flavor; *also* **:** the tree that produces almonds — see picture at NUT

al·mo·ner /ˈælmənɚ/ *noun, pl* **-ners** [*count*] *Brit, old-fashioned* **:** a person whose job is to help people in hospitals with their financial and social problems

al·most /ˈɑːlˌmoust/ *adv* **:** only a little less than **:** NEARLY ▪ We're *almost* finished. ▪ Analysts predict that rates will rise by *almost* 40 percent. ▪ Goats will eat *almost* anything. ▪ He mentioned the prize *almost* as an afterthought. [=mentioned it in a way that made it seem like an afterthought] ▪ She's *almost* always late. ▪ in *almost* all cases = in *almost* every case ▪ I have ***almost no*** [=*hardly any*] money. ▪ She ***almost never*** [=*hardly ever*] misses a game. ▪ There's ***almost nothing*** [=*hardly anything*] in the fridge.

alms /ˈɑːmz/ *noun* [*plural*] *old-fashioned* **:** money, clothes, food, and other things given to poor people

alms·house /ˈɑːmzˌhaus/ *noun, pl* **-hous·es** [*count*] *in the past* **:** a building in which poor people were allowed to live for free

al·oe /ˈæloʊ/ *noun, pl* **-oes** [*count*] **:** a tropical plant that has heavy leaves which produce a thick liquid used in medicines, cosmetics, etc.

aloe vera /ˈæloʊˈverə/ *noun, pl* **~ veras** [*noncount*] **:** a thick liquid that is produced by a kind of aloe plant and used in medicines, cosmetics, etc. ▪ a skin cream that contains *aloe vera*; *also* [*count*] **:** the plant that produces this liquid

aloft /əˈlɑːft/ *adv* **:** in the air ▪ banners carried *aloft* ▪ The balloon stayed *aloft* for days.

alo·ha /əˈloʊˌhɑː/ *interj* — used in Hawaii to say hello or goodbye

¹alone /əˈloʊn/ *adj, not used before a noun*

1 a : without anyone or anything else **:** not involving or including anyone or anything else **:** separate from other people or things ▪ I was all *alone* [=*by myself*] in the office yesterday. ▪ This wine goes well with food, but is also very good *alone*. ▪ I got him *alone* and asked him what had really happened. ▪ She lived *alone* for many years. ▪ She doesn't mind being *alone* because she never feels lonely/lonesome. ▪ He was *alone* with his thoughts. **b :** without people that you know or that usually are with you ▪ This is the first time the couple has been out *alone* together since the birth of their child. [=the first time they have gone somewhere without their child] ▪ He traveled *alone* [=*by himself*] to visit his grandparents when he was only seven. ▪ She was nervous about being (all) *alone* in the city when she started her new job. ✧ If you are ***not alone*** when you do something, you are not the only person who is doing it. ▪ She's worried about losing her job, and she's *not alone*. [=other people are also worried about losing their jobs] ▪ He was *not alone* in calling for reform. Many people were demanding changes.

2 [*more ~; most ~*] **:** feeling unhappy because of being separated from other people ▪ He felt very *alone* when he went away to school.

²alone *adv*

1 : without help from anyone or anything else ▪ She raised six children *alone*. [=*on her own, by herself*] ▪ The police believe the criminal acted *alone*. ▪ Medication *alone* [=*by itself*] won't relieve the symptoms entirely.

2 : without another — used for emphasis ▪ The proof rests on one witness's statement *alone*. ▪ You *alone* [=only you] can decide what needs to be done. [=you are the only one who can decide] ▪ You *alone* are responsible. = The responsibility is yours *alone*. ▪ The blame is mine and mine *alone*. [=I am the only one who should be blamed]

3 : without including or needing anything more ▪ You can't rely on your looks *alone* [=you can't rely just on your looks]; you'll need to work very hard. ▪ The price *alone* is enough to discourage people. ▪ The special effects *alone* make the movie worth seeing.

go it alone **:** to do something by yourself ▪ If no one's willing to help me, I guess I'll just have to *go it alone*.

leave (someone or something) alone see ¹LEAVE

leave well enough alone see ¹LEAVE

let alone see ¹LET

stand alone see ¹STAND

¹along /əˈlɑːŋ/ *prep*

1 : in a line matching the length or direction of (something) ▪ We walked *along* the beach. ▪ We walked *along* (the side of) the road. ▪ The chairs were lined up *along* the wall. ▪ The ship sailed *along* the coast.

2 : at a point on (something) ▪ They have a house *along* [=*alongside*] the river. ▪ We drove to Boston and we stopped ***along the way*** for lunch.

²along *adv*

1 : in a forward direction ▪ We walked *along* beside the road. ▪ I was just walking *along*, minding my own business. ▪ The police told the people in the crowd to move *along*. ▪ We looked at the houses as we drove *along*.— often used figuratively ▪ Is there anything we can do to hurry this process *along*? [=to make this process go faster] ▪ He was rushing *along* through the speech. ▪ Her career was helped *along* by her wealthy uncle.

2 — used to say that someone or something is brought or taken with you when you go somewhere ▪ He brought his son *along* [=brought his son with him] when he went to the bank. ▪ We brought/took an extra battery *along* just in case we needed it.— often + *with* ▪ He brought his son *along with* him. ▪ The scenery was beautiful. I was glad that we had a camera *along with* us. [=I was glad that we brought a camera]

3 : at or to an advanced point ▪ Plans for a new stadium are already pretty far *along*. ▪ The morning was well *along* when we arrived. [=it was late in the morning when we arrived] ▪ people who are ***well/far along in years*** [=people who are old]

4 : at a particular place **:** here or there ▪ I'll be *along* [=I'll be there] to see him in a few minutes. ▪ We missed the first bus, but another one should be *along* [=should be here] soon.

5 : from one person to another ▪ Word was passed *along* that the attack was coming.

all along **:** during the entire time since something began ▪ I knew the truth *all along*. ▪ The police knew *all along* who was guilty.

along about *US, informal* **:** at a time near (a specified time) **:** ABOUT, AROUND ▪ He arrived in the city *along about* July 17. ▪ Our flight should be arriving *along about* 8:00.

along with **:** in addition to (something or someone) ▪ a plane carrying heavy radar equipment *along with* full fuel tanks **:** together with (something or someone) ▪ A bill came *along with* the merchandise. ▪ All my cousins were there *along with* my aunts and uncles. ▪ He worked *along with* several colleagues to finish on time.

¹along·side /əˈlɑːŋˈsaɪd/ *adv* **:** along or close at the side ▪ We waited for the other boat to come *alongside*.

alongside of *chiefly US, informal* **:** next to or together with (someone or something) **:** ALONGSIDE ▪ The police car pulled up *alongside of* our car. ▪ children working *alongside of* their parents

²alongside *prep*

1 : next to (someone or something) ▪ The children work *alongside* their parents in the field.

2 : along the side of (something) ▪ Bring the boat *alongside* the dock.

3 : at the same time as (something) **:** together with (something) ▪ one theory taught *alongside* the other ▪ The town grew up *alongside* the college.

aloof /əˈluːf/ *adj* [*more ~; most ~*]

1 : not involved with or friendly toward other people ▪ She remained *aloof* [=*distant*] despite their efforts to make friends. ▪ He held himself *aloof* from his coworkers. [=he was not warm or friendly toward them]

2 : not involved in or influenced by something ▪ They tried to keep/remain/stand *aloof* from the politics of the day.

– aloof·ness *noun* [*noncount*] ▪ She's been criticized for *aloofness* but she's really just very shy.

aloud /əˈlaud/ *adv* **:** in a way that can be clearly heard ▪ read *aloud* **:** in a voice that can be heard ▪ She wondered *aloud* [=*out loud*] where they'd gone.

al·paca /ælˈpækə/ *noun, pl* **-pac·as**

1 [*count*] **:** a South American animal that is related to the llama and has long woolly hair — see picture at LLAMA

2 [*noncount*] **:** wool of the alpaca or a cloth made of it

¹al·pha /ˈælfə/ *noun, pl* **-phas** [*count*] **:** the first letter of the Greek alphabet — Α or α

²alpha *adj, always used before a noun*

1 : having the most power in a group of animals or people ▪ a fight in the pack between a young wolf and the ***alpha male***

[=the dominant male] • the *alpha male/female* on the committee [=the most powerful man/woman on the committee]
2 — used to describe the first version of a product that is being developed and tested • the *alpha* version of the software • *alpha* testing — compare BETA

alpha and omega *noun*
the alpha and omega : the most important part of something • Money is *the alpha and omega* of his existence. [=money is the only thing that matters to him]

al·pha·bet /ˈælfəˌbɛt/ *noun, pl* **-bets** [*count*] : the letters of a language arranged in their usual order • The Roman *alphabet* begins with "A" and ends with "Z."

al·pha·bet·i·cal /ˌælfəˈbɛtɪkəl/ *also* **al·pha·bet·ic** /ˌælfəˈbɛtɪk/ *adj* : arranged in the order of the letters of the alphabet • an *alphabetical* list • The words in the dictionary are listed/shown ***in alphabetical order***.
– al·pha·bet·i·cal·ly /ˌælfəˈbɛtɪkli/ *adv* • The students are listed *alphabetically* by last name.

al·pha·bet·ize *also Brit* **al·pha·bet·ise** /ˈælfəbəˌtaɪz/ *verb* **-iz·es; -ized; -iz·ing** [+ *obj*] : to arrange (items) in alphabetical order • She *alphabetized* the books. [=put the books in order so that books with titles beginning with "A" came first, "B" second, etc.] • *alphabetize* the words on/in the list
– al·pha·bet·i·za·tion *also Brit* **al·pha·bet·i·sa·tion** /ˌælfəˌbɛtəˈzeɪʃən, *Brit* ˌælfəˌbɛˌtaɪˈzeɪʃən/ *noun* [*noncount*]

alphabet soup *noun* [*noncount*] : a type of soup for children with small noodles that are shaped like letters of the alphabet • a bowl of *alphabet soup* — often used figuratively to describe a confusing group of letters (such as abbreviations) that are used to refer to various organizations, items, etc. • the *alphabet soup* of government agencies

al·pha·nu·mer·ic /ˌælfənuˈmerɪk, *Brit* ˌælfənjuˈmerɪk/ *adj* : having or using letters and numbers • an *alphanumeric* system/keyboard
– al·pha·nu·mer·i·cal·ly /ˌælfənuˈmerɪkli, *Brit* ˌælfənjuˈmerɪkli/ *adv*

al·pine /ˈælˌpaɪn/ *adj*
1 : of or existing in high mountains and especially the Alps • an *alpine* meadow/lake • *alpine* flowers
2 : done in high mountains • *alpine* skiing/sports

al·ready /ɑːlˈrɛdi/ *adv*
1 : before this time : before now • They've *already* agreed to come. • I've *already* told him the news. = (*US, informal*) I *already* told him the news. : before that time • I'd *already* left by the time you called. • He acted as if he didn't *already* know. • Flight 102 will *already* have taken off by the time Flight 101 lands.
2 : so soon : so early • Have they arrived *already*?! I'm still not dressed! • Do you have to go *already*? • Is it *already* midnight? = Is it midnight *already*?
3 — used to describe a situation that exists now and that will continue to exist • The book is *already* available in Britain and should be in bookstores here next month. • The exhibit has *already* caused quite a stir.
4 *US, informal* — used to express impatience or annoyance • Answer the question, *already*! • Enough, *already*! • All right *already*!

al·right /ɑːlˈraɪt/ *adv or adj* : ALL RIGHT

> ***usage*** The spelling *alright* is less common than *all right* and is regarded by some people as an error. It occurs mainly in informal writing.

Al·sa·tian /ælˈseɪʃən/ *noun, pl* **-tians** [*count*] *Brit* : GERMAN SHEPHERD

al·so /ˈɑːlˌsoʊ/ *adv*
1 : in addition • She's a talented singer and *also* a fine actress. • Thomas Edison is best known for inventing the lightbulb, but he *also* invented the phonograph. • I don't think we should go out. Not only is it late, but it's *also* snowing.
2 : in a similar way • He saw something and she *also* saw it. [=she saw it too] • "I grew up in North Dakota." "Really? I'm *also* from North Dakota." [=I'm from North Dakota too] • My neighbors were *also* at the show that night.

al·so–ran /ˈɑːlˌsoʊˌræn/ *noun, pl* **-rans** [*count*] : a person who has taken part in an election or contest and did not win • He was an *also-ran* in last year's mayoral race.

al·tar /ˈɑːltɚ/ *noun, pl* **-tars** [*count*]
1 : a raised place on which sacrifices and gifts are offered in some religions — sometimes used figuratively • She sacrificed honesty ***on the altar of success***. [=she chose to be dishonest in order to achieve success]
2 : a platform or table used as a center of worship in Christian ceremonies and services
led to the altar ✧ If you are *led to the altar*, you get married. • They started a romance that eventually *led* (them) *to the altar*.
left at the altar ✧ If you are *left at the altar*, you do not get married because the person you were going to marry has decided against it at the last moment. • Her fiancé *left her at the altar*.

altar boy *noun, pl* ~ **boys** [*count*] : a boy who helps the priest during a Catholic service

al·ter /ˈɑːltɚ/ *verb* **-ters; -tered; -ter·ing**
1 : to change (something) [+ *obj*] Alcohol can *alter* a person's mood. • He *altered* his will to leave everything to his sister. • This one small event *altered* the course of history. [*no obj*] The place has *altered* in the 10 years since I left.
2 [+ *obj*] : to make a change to (a piece of clothing) so that it will fit better • I'll need to have/get the dress *altered* before the wedding.
3 [+ *obj*] *US* : to remove the sex organs of (an animal) so that the animal is unable to reproduce • They had the puppies *altered* [=*fixed*] before they were sold.
– altered *adj* • Later, we see this character again in a slightly *altered* form. • an *altered* state of consciousness

al·ter·a·tion /ˌɑːltəˈreɪʃən/ *noun, pl* **-tions** : the act, process, or result of changing or altering something [*noncount*] the *alteration* of the pattern • They did a good job on the dress *alteration*. [*count*] The addition of a glossary is the only significant *alteration* [=*change, modification*] to the book. • He made *alterations* in/to his will.

al·ter·ca·tion /ˌɑːltɚˈkeɪʃən/ *noun, pl* **-tions** [*count*] *formal* : a noisy or angry argument • She got into several *altercations* with the coach this season.

alter ego *noun, pl* ~ **egos** [*count*]
1 : a different version of yourself ✧ A character in a book or film is sometimes viewed as an author's *alter ego*. A role that an actor often plays is sometimes described as the actor's *alter ego*.
2 : a close friend who thinks or feels similarly to the way you think or feel • a trusted adviser who is the President's *alter ego*

[1]al·ter·nate /ˈɑːltɚˌneɪt/ *verb* **-nates; -nat·ed; -nat·ing** : to place or do (different things) so that one follows the other in a repeated series [+ *obj*] To make the appetizer, you should *alternate* layers of tomatoes and cheese. [=you should place a layer of tomatoes, then a layer of cheese, then a layer of tomatoes, etc.] • The poem/poet *alternates* fear and hope. — often + *with* • The necklace is made by *alternating* glass beads *with* shells. • The poem/poet *alternates* fear and hope *with* each other. = The poem/poet *alternates* fear *with* hope. [*no obj*] The light and dark woods *alternate* to form an elegant pattern around the window. — often + *with* • Light woods *alternate with* dark woods. — often + *between* • The poem *alternates between* fear and hope. • He *alternates between* riding his bike and taking the bus to work.
– alternating *adj* • To make the appetizer, you should use *alternating* layers of tomatoes and cheese. • The shirt has *alternating* red and yellow stripes. **– al·ter·na·tion** /ˌɑːltɚˈneɪʃən/ *noun, pl* **-tions** [*count, noncount*]

[2]al·ter·nate /ˈɑːltɚnət, *Brit* ɔːlˈtɜːnət/ *adj*
1 : occurring in or forming a repeated series • *alternate* sunshine and rain • *Alternate* shades of wood formed a pattern around the window.
2 — used to describe something that happens one time, does not happen the next time, happens again, etc. • The fair is held on *alternate* years. [=the fair is held every other/second year; the fair is held one year, not held the next year, held the following year, and so on] • She picks the children up from school on *alternate* days. [=(for example) she picks up the children on Monday, Wednesday, and Friday]
3 *chiefly US* : other than the usual : ALTERNATIVE • We took an *alternate* route because of the traffic. • Due to an emergency, the plane landed at an *alternate* airport.
– al·ter·nate·ly *adv* • The poem is *alternately* fearful and hopeful.

[3]al·ter·nate /ˈɑːltɚnət, *Brit* ˌɔːlˈtɜːnət/ *noun, pl* **-nates** [*count*] *US* : someone who is chosen to take another person's place if that person is not able to be present or to do a required job • The town has elected five councilors and two *alternates*. • an *alternate* juror

alternating current *noun* [*noncount*] : an electric current that changes its direction very frequently at regular intervals — abbr. *AC*; compare DIRECT CURRENT

A

[1]al·ter·na·tive /ɑlˈtɚnətɪv/ *adj*
1 *always used before a noun* **:** offering or expressing a choice • We have *alternative* [=*other*] plans in case the weather is bad. • an *alternative* explanation • We took an *alternative* route [=a different route] to avoid the traffic. • Scientists are developing an *alternative* approach to treating the disease.
2 : not usual or traditional • *alternative* rock music • He developed an *alternative* design for the new engine. • ***alternative medicine*** [=methods of healing or treating disease that are different from the usual methods taught in Western medical schools] — often used to describe something that is more natural or that causes less pollution than the usual product, method, etc. • *alternative* energy/fuel
3 : existing or functioning outside of the established society • an *alternative* newspaper • *alternative* lifestyles
– al·ter·na·tive·ly *adv* • We could meet at the library or, *alternatively*, we could all meet at my house.

[2]alternative *noun, pl* **-tives** [*count*] **:** something that can be chosen instead of something else **:** a choice or option • We decided to leave since our only other *alternative* was to wait in the rain. • They left me no *alternative* but to call the police. [=I had to call the police] • I was offered no *alternative.* • The menu offered several vegetarian *alternatives.* — often + *to* • We've been looking for *alternatives to* the usual treatment, but it seems there are few options.

al·ter·na·tor /ˈɑːltɚˌneɪtɚ/ *noun, pl* **-tors** [*count*] **:** a device that produces electricity (as in the engine of a vehicle) **:** a generator that produces alternating current — see picture at ENGINE

al·though /ɑlˈðoʊ/ *conj*
1 : despite the fact that **:** THOUGH — used to introduce a fact that makes another fact unusual or surprising • *Although* [=*while, even though*] he was hungry, he could not eat. • *Although* we rarely see each other, we're still very good friends. = We're still very good friends *although* we rarely see each other. • *Although* [=*while*] I'd love to have dinner with you tonight, I already have plans. • It feels as if I've known you forever *although* [=*even though*] we've only known each other for a day. • He's the basketball team's best player *although* he's the shortest one on the team. • *Although* (it is) small, the apartment is very expensive.
2 : BUT, HOWEVER, THOUGH — used when making a statement that differs from or contrasts with a statement you have just made • I don't believe we've met before, *although* I must say you do look very familiar. • I think his name is John, *although* I'm not completely sure about that. • I'd love to have dinner with you, *although* I can't. • The book had a good, *although* not great, plot.

al·tim·e·ter /ælˈtɪmətɚ/ *noun, pl* **-ters** [*count*] **:** an instrument used for measuring the altitude of something (such as an airplane or a mountain)

al·ti·tude /ˈæltəˌtuːd, *Brit* ˈæltəˌtjuːd/ *noun, pl* **-tudes :** the height of something (such as an airplane) above the level of the sea [*count*] We're now flying at an *altitude* [=*height*] of 10,000 feet. • the air temperature at different *altitudes* • Some visitors find it difficult to adjust to the city's high *altitude.* • plants found at higher/lower *altitudes* [=*elevations*] [*noncount*] The plane lost/gained *altitude* rapidly. • flying at low/high *altitude* • She trained for the race ***at altitude.*** [=at a high altitude, where the air is thin]

[1]al·to /ˈæltoʊ/ *noun, pl* **-tos** [*count*] *music* **:** a singing voice that is lower than the voice of a soprano and higher than the voice of a tenor; *also* **:** a singer having such a voice • She sang in her school choir as an *alto.* — compare BASS, SOPRANO, TENOR

[2]alto *adj, always used before a noun* **:** having a range that is lower than a soprano and higher than a tenor • an *alto* voice • He plays the *alto* sax/saxophone.

[1]al·to·geth·er /ˌɑːltəˈgɛðɚ/ *adv*
1 : completely and fully **:** TOTALLY, ENTIRELY • They had an *altogether* new idea. • It stopped raining *altogether.* • If we don't do something now, the forests may disappear *altogether.* • It's best to avoid the situation *altogether.* • That's an *altogether* different question. = That's a different question *altogether.* — often used with *not* • It is *not altogether* clear why she left. • He *didn't altogether* believe her story. — often used for emphasis before another adverb • This is an *altogether* more sensible solution. • I've said *altogether* [=*entirely*] too much on the subject already.
2 : with everything added together **:** when everything is added up • They spent a thousand dollars *altogether.* [=*in all*] • *Altogether* [=*all told*], we sold nearly 500 candy bars.
3 : in a general way **:** when everything is considered • *Altogether* [=*generally, on the whole, all in all*] I'd say this was our best vacation ever. • *Altogether,* their efforts were successful.

> ***usage*** Do not confuse the single word *altogether* with the two-word phrase *all together.* • We were *all together* [=all in a group, all with each other] for the whole day. • I tried to hold it *all together* with glue, but the pieces fell apart. • The detective put it *all together* [=figured out how the pieces of information related to each other] and solved the crime. • *All together* [=all at the same time] now, everybody, let's sing!

[2]altogether *noun*
in the altogether *informal + old-fashioned* **:** not wearing any clothes • posing *in the altogether* [=*nude, in the nude*]

al·tru·ism /ˈæltruːˌɪzəm/ *noun* [*noncount*] **:** feelings and behavior that show a desire to help other people and a lack of selfishness • charitable acts motivated purely by *altruism* • In one final act of *altruism,* she donated almost all of her money to the hospital.
– al·tru·is·tic /ˌæltruːˈɪstɪk/ *adj* [*more ~; most ~*] • His motives/reasons for helping the poor were not completely *altruistic.* [=he wanted to help himself in some way by helping the poor] • *altruistic* acts **– al·tru·is·tic·al·ly** /ˌæltruːˈɪstɪkli/ *adv*

alum /əˈlʌm/ *noun, pl* **alums** [*count*] *US, informal* **:** someone who attended or graduated from a particular school, college, or university **:** ALUMNUS, ALUMNA • a Harvard *alum*

alu·mi·num (*US*) /əˈluːmənəm/ *or Brit* **al·u·min·i·um** /ˌæljəˈmɪnijəm/ *noun* [*noncount*] **:** a silver metal that is strong and light and that is used for making many products — often used before another noun • *aluminum* cans • ***aluminum foil*** [=a very thin sheet of aluminum that is used for covering or wrapping food]

alum·na /əˈlʌmnə/ *noun, pl* **-nae** /əˈlʌmni/ [*count*] *chiefly US* **:** a woman who was a student at a particular school, college, or university • a group of Harvard *alumnae* — compare ALUMNUS, OLD GIRL

alum·nus /əˈlʌmnəs/ *noun, pl* **-ni** /əˈlʌmˌnaɪ/ [*count*] *chiefly US* **:** someone who was a student at a particular school, college, or university • Her parents are *alumni* of the state university. ✧ The plural form *alumni* usually refers to all of the men and women who are former students of a school, college, or university. • the college's *alumni* • the *alumni* association — compare ALUMNA, OLD BOY

al·ve·o·lar /ælˈviːjəlɚ/ *adj, technical* **:** of or relating to a speech sound that is made with the tip of the tongue touching the roof of the mouth near the front teeth • The word "two" begins with an *alveolar* sound.

al·ways /ˈɑːlˌweɪz/ *adv*
1 a : at all times **:** on every occasion **:** in a way that does not change • He *always* tries, but he doesn't *always* succeed. • It's *always* a pleasure to see you. • I can *always* tell when he's upset. • He's *always* [=*constantly*] looking for ways to make money. • She's almost *always* smiling. • This area is *always* filled with tourists. • You should *always* (remember to) wear your seat belt. • The holidays are *always* a very busy time for us. = (*less commonly*) The holidays *always* are a very busy time for us. • Things won't *always* go as planned. • You're *always* welcome to stay with us. — opposite NEVER **b :** at all times in the past • He has *always* been a good friend to me. • They didn't *always* get along so well. [=they get along now, but they didn't like each other in the past] • It hasn't *always* been easy for him. [=difficult or sad things have happened to him] • He could *always* make me angry. = He *always* could make me angry. [=he often made me angry]
2 : throughout all time **:** for a very long time: such as **a :** forever into the future • I'll remember you *always.* [=forever] • You'll *always* be my best friend. = You're my best friend, and you *always* will be. • Life won't *always* be this easy. **b :** forever in the past **:** from the beginning of the time that can be remembered • I've *always* loved you. • I *always* thought they'd get married some day, but they never did. • Isn't that what you've *always* wanted? • She *always* wanted to be famous. • It has *always* been my goal to have my own business. • He's *always* been a firm believer in hard work. = He's a firm believer in hard work, and he *always* has been.
3 : often, frequently, or repeatedly • We *always* tell people not to arrive too early. • My parents *always* told me not to speak to strangers. — often used to describe repeated behavior that is annoying • She's *always* calling me by the wrong name. • Must you *always* be so rude?! • He *always* tells such

funny stories. = He's *always* telling such funny stories.
4 — used to suggest another possibility ▪ If we don't win today, there's *always* tomorrow. [=we might win tomorrow] — usually used after *can* or *could* ▪ If she doesn't answer the phone now, you *can/could always* try (calling) again later. ▪ If you don't have enough money now, you *can always* use your credit card.
as always — used to say that something was expected because it always happens ▪ *As always,* dinner was delicious. [=dinner was delicious, as it always is] ▪ Your children, *as always,* were very well-behaved. [=your children were well-behaved, as they always are]

Alz·hei·mer's disease /ˈɑːlts͵haɪmɚz-/ *noun [noncount]* : a disease of the brain that causes people to slowly lose their memory and mental abilities as they grow old — called also *Alzheimer's*

am see BE

AM /ˈeɪ͵ɛm/ *noun [noncount]* : a system for sending radio signals in which the height of a radio wave is changed in order to send information in the form of sound ✧ *AM* is an abbreviation for *amplitude modulation.* — compare FM
– AM *adj* ▪ listening to my favorite *AM* station [=a radio station that sends sound using AM] ▪ Is this station *AM* or FM? ▪ *AM* radios

a.m. *or* **AM** *or Brit* **am** *abbr* in the morning — used with numbers to show the time of day ▪ She woke up at 6 *a.m.* and didn't go to bed until midnight. ▪ The class is held from 11:30 *a.m.* to/until 2:15 p.m. ▪ ***12 a.m.*** [=*midnight, one hour after 11 p.m.*] ✧ The abbreviation *a.m.* stands for the Latin phrase *ante meridiem,* which means "before noon." — compare P.M.

amal·gam /əˈmælgəm/ *noun, pl* **-gams**
1 *[count] formal* : a combination or mixture of different things — usually singular ▪ Several different styles of music come together in an unusual *amalgam.* — usually + *of* ▪ an *amalgam* [=*amalgamation*] *of* sweet and spicy flavors ▪ The language they speak is an *amalgam of* Spanish and English.
2 *[noncount] technical* : a mixture of mercury and other metals used for filling holes in teeth

amal·gam·ate /əˈmælgə͵meɪt/ *verb* **-ates; -at·ed; -at·ing** *[+ obj] formal* : to unite (two or more things, such as two businesses) into one thing ▪ They decided to *amalgamate* [=(more commonly) *merge*] the two companies. ▪ *amalgamating* different styles of music ▪ They *amalgamated* the hospital and/with the university. — often used as *(be) amalgamated* ▪ The hospital *was amalgamated with* the university.
– amal·gam·ation /ə͵mælgəˈmeɪʃən/ *noun [singular]* an *amalgamation* of different styles of music *[noncount]* the *amalgamation* of the two companies

amass /əˈmæs/ *verb* **amass·es; amassed; amass·ing** *[+ obj]* : to gather or collect (something, such as a large amount of money) especially for yourself ▪ By the time he was 21, he had already *amassed* [=*accumulated*] a great fortune. ▪ The police are *amassing* [=*gathering*] further evidence against him. ▪ They've *amassed* a wealth of information.

am·a·teur /ˈæmə͵tɚ/ *noun, pl* **-teurs** *[count]*
1 : a person who does something (such as a sport or hobby) for pleasure and not as a job ▪ She played soccer as an *amateur* before turning professional. ▪ These photos were taken by both *amateurs* and professionals.
2 : a person who does something poorly : a person who is not skillful at a job or other activity ▪ The people running that company are a bunch of *amateurs.* ▪ Only *amateurs* make this kind of mistake. ▪ He's a mere *amateur* when it comes to cooking. [=he doesn't know how to cook well]
– amateur *adj, always used before a noun* ▪ *amateur* photographers/athletes ▪ an *amateur* competition [=a contest for amateurs] ▪ They competed at the *amateur* level. **– am·a·teur·ism** /ˈæmə͵tə͵rɪzəm/ *noun [noncount]* ▪ a strong supporter of *amateurism* in sports ▪ the *amateurism* [=the lack of skill] of her writing style

amateur dramatics *noun [noncount] Brit* : COMMUNITY THEATER 1
– amateur dramatic *adj, Brit* ▪ the local *amateur dramatic* society

am·a·teur·ish /͵æməˈtərɪʃ/ *adj [more ~; most ~]* : lacking experience or skill ▪ His acting is hopelessly *amateurish.* = He's a hopelessly *amateurish* actor.
– am·a·teur·ish·ly *adv* ▪ He acts very *amateurishly.*

am·a·to·ry /ˈæmə͵tori, *Brit* ˈæmətəri/ *adj, literary* : of, relating to, or expressing sexual love ▪ a book of *amatory* [=*amorous*] poems ▪ their secret *amatory* relationship

amaze /əˈmeɪz/ *verb* **amaz·es; amazed; amaz·ing** : to surprise and sometimes confuse (someone) very much : to fill (someone) with wonder *[+ obj]* He has *amazed* audiences around the world with his magic tricks. ▪ It *amazes* me that no one noticed the error. ▪ I am always *amazed* by her garden's beauty. = Her garden's beauty ***never fails/ceases to amaze*** me. *[no obj]* Her garden's beauty *never fails/ceases to amaze.*

amazed *adj [more ~; most ~]* : feeling or showing great surprise ▪ The magician performed before a crowd of *amazed* spectators. ▪ There was an *amazed* expression on her face. ▪ His friends were *amazed* [=*stunned, dumbfounded*] when he said that he was getting married. — often + *that* ▪ We were *amazed* [=*astonished, astounded*] *that* no one was injured in the accident. ▪ I'm *amazed that* no one noticed the error. — often + *at* or *by* ▪ You'll be *amazed at* how easy it can be. ▪ They were *amazed at/by* the size of the place. — often followed by *to + verb* ▪ They were *amazed to discover* that their grandmother had been a professional dancer.

amaze·ment /əˈmeɪzmənt/ *noun [noncount]* : a feeling of being very surprised or amazed ▪ The garden's beauty filled me with *amazement.* [=*astonishment*] ▪ The crowd watched ***in amazement*** as the magician performed his tricks. ▪ I applied for the job, and, (much) ***to my amazement***, I was hired. [=I was very surprised to be hired] ▪ Much ***to the amazement of*** her family, she left school to pursue her acting career.

amazing *adj [more ~; most ~]* : causing great surprise or wonder : causing amazement ▪ She gave an *amazing* [=*wonderful*] performance in her first film. ▪ It's *amazing* [=difficult to believe] how/that many adults in this country don't know how to read. ▪ He showed an *amazing* lack of concern for others. ▪ The *amazing* thing is that no one knows where it came from. ▪ He has an *amazing* ability to learn new languages. ▪ Her grandmother was really an *amazing* woman. ▪ He's created an *amazing* number [=a surprisingly large number] of new designs for the spring.
– amaz·ing·ly *adv* ▪ an *amazingly* beautiful garden ▪ *Amazingly* (enough), the dog swam all the way across the lake.

am·a·zon /ˈæmə͵zɑːn/ *noun, pl* **-zons** *[count]*
1 ***Amazon*** : a member of a group of female warriors in stories told by the ancient Greeks
2 : a tall and strong woman ▪ I felt dwarfed, standing beside this redheaded *amazon.*

am·bas·sa·dor /æmˈbæsədɚ/ *noun, pl* **-dors** *[count]* : the highest-ranking person who represents his or her own government while living in another country ▪ Embassy officials met with the *ambassador.* — often + *to* ▪ She became the American *ambassador to* Italy [=she began representing America in Italy] several years ago. — often used figuratively ▪ a baseball player who has been a very effective *ambassador* [=*representative*] for his sport ▪ an *ambassador* of hope [=a person who tries to bring hope to another country or group of people] ▪ a ***goodwill ambassador*** [=a person who travels to different places to promote friendship and goodwill]
– am·bas·sa·do·ri·al /æm͵bæsəˈdorijəl/ *adj* ▪ his first *ambassadorial* assignment

am·ber /ˈæmbɚ/ *noun [noncount]*
1 : a hard orange-yellow substance that can be polished and used for jewelry and other decorations
2 : a dark orange-yellow color — see color picture on page C2
– amber *adj* ▪ the *amber* light of the late afternoon sun ▪ " . . . *amber* waves of grain . . . " —Katharine Lee Bates, "America the Beautiful" (1911)

am·bi·dex·trous /͵æmbɪˈdɛkstrəs/ *adj* : able to use both hands equally well ▪ an *ambidextrous* baseball player
– am·bi·dex·trous·ly *adv* **– am·bi·dex·trous·ness** *noun [noncount]*

am·bi·ence *or* **am·bi·ance** /ˈæmbijəns/ *noun [singular] formal* : the mood or feeling of a particular place ▪ They used soft music and candlelight to give the restaurant a romantic *ambience.* [=*atmosphere*] ▪ the *ambience* of a tropical island

am·bi·ent /ˈæmbijənt/ *adj*
1 *technical* : surrounding on all sides ▪ Keep the chemicals at an *ambient* temperature of 70°F. ▪ the *ambient* air quality ▪ the bright *ambient* light of the room
2 *of electronic music* : quiet and relaxing with melodies that repeat many times ▪ People shopped as *ambient* music played in the background. ▪ *ambient* instrumental music

am·bi·gu·i·ty /͵æmbəˈgjuːwəti/ *noun, pl* **-ties** : something that does not have a single clear meaning : something that is

A

ambiguous [*noncount*] You should remove *ambiguity* [=*vagueness*] from your essay by adding more details. ▪ ***moral ambiguity*** [=lack of certainty about whether something is right or wrong] [*count*] the *ambiguities* in his answers

am·big·u·ous /æmˈbɪgjəwəs/ *adj* [*more* ~; *most* ~]

1 : able to be understood in more than one way : having more than one possible meaning ▪ We were confused by the *ambiguous* wording of the message. ▪ He looked at her with an *ambiguous* smile. ▪ Due to the *ambiguous* nature of the question, it was difficult to choose the right answer. — opposite UNAMBIGUOUS ***synonyms*** see [1]OBSCURE

2 : not expressed or understood clearly ▪ He felt that his role in the company was becoming more *ambiguous*. [=*uncertain*] ▪ the *ambiguous* position of women in modern society

— am·big·u·ous·ly *adv* ▪ His answers were worded *ambiguously*, so no one could be sure what he meant.

am·bit /ˈæmbət/ *noun, pl* **-bits** [*count*] *formal* : the range or limit that is covered by something (such as a law) : SCOPE — usually singular ▪ I'm afraid your case doesn't ***fall within the ambit*** of our jurisdiction.

am·bi·tion /æmˈbɪʃən/ *noun, pl* **-tions**

1 [*count*] : a particular goal or aim : something that a person hopes to do or achieve ▪ My first *ambition* as a child was to be in the circus. ▪ The wife of a famous poet, she had literary *ambitions* of her own. [=she wanted to be a writer too] ▪ He has *ambitions* for an acting career. = He has *ambitions* to become an actor. = His *ambition* is to be/become an actor. ▪ She finally achieved/realized/fulfilled her ***life's ambition*** [=the thing she most wanted to do in her life] when she started her own business.

2 [*noncount*] : a desire to be successful, powerful, or famous ▪ He lacked *ambition* and couldn't compete with the others. ▪ With her talent and fierce *ambition* [=her very strong desire to succeed], she became a very successful actress.

3 [*noncount*] *US* : a desire to do things and be active — usually used in negative constructions ▪ I was tired and had no *ambition* [=*initiative, energy*], so I just spent the whole weekend watching TV.

am·bi·tious /æmˈbɪʃəs/ *adj* [*more* ~; *most* ~]

1 : having ambition : having a desire to be successful, powerful, or famous ▪ The company was created by two very *ambitious* young men in the early 1900s. ▪ *ambitious* politicians/lawyers ▪ He was very ***ambitious for*** his children but not for himself. [=he wanted his children to be successful but he didn't feel the need to be successful himself]

2 : not easily done or achieved : requiring or showing ambition ▪ This 500-page book is her most *ambitious* effort/project yet. ▪ Your plans for the future are very *ambitious*. ▪ It was too *ambitious* a task for just one person. ▪ *ambitious* goals

— am·bi·tious·ly *adv* ▪ She *ambitiously* worked her way to the top. **— am·bi·tious·ness** *noun* [*noncount*] ▪ the *ambitiousness* of the plan

am·biv·a·lent /æmˈbɪvələnt/ *adj* [*more* ~; *most* ~] : having or showing very different feelings (such as love and hate) about someone or something at the same time ▪ He felt *ambivalent* about his job. [=he both liked and disliked his job] ▪ He has an *ambivalent* relationship with his family. ▪ She has a deeply/very *ambivalent* attitude about/to/toward religion. ▪ The senator is *ambivalent* about running for president. [=the senator has not decided whether or not to run for president]

— am·biv·a·lence /æmˈbɪvələns/ *noun* [*noncount*] ▪ He feels some *ambivalence* about/toward/towards his job. **— am·biv·a·lent·ly** *adj* ▪ He spoke *ambivalently* about his feelings for his family.

am·ble /ˈæmbəl/ *verb, always followed by an adverb or preposition* **am·bles**; **am·bled**; **am·bling** [*no obj*] : to walk slowly in a free and relaxed way ▪ We *ambled* along as we talked. ▪ They *ambled* down/up/along the road. ▪ We spent the day *ambling* [=*strolling, sauntering*] through the park.

am·bu·lance /ˈæmbjələns/ *noun, pl* **-lanc·es** [*count*] : a vehicle used for taking hurt or sick people to the hospital especially in emergencies ▪ They called (for) an *ambulance*. ▪ She was taken ***by ambulance*** [=in an ambulance] to the hospital. ▪ (*disapproving*) She had a reputation for being an ***ambulance chaser***. [=a lawyer who gets clients by convincing accident victims that they should file a lawsuit about the accident]

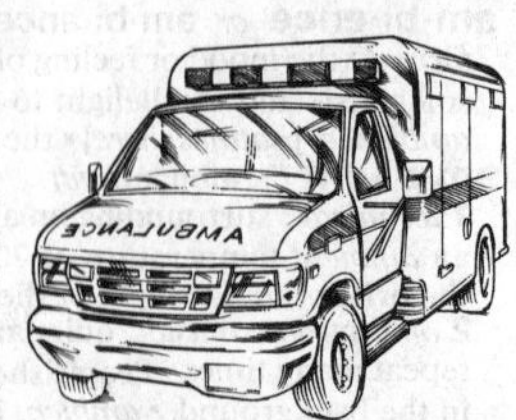

ambulance

[1]**am·bush** /ˈæmˌbʊʃ/ *noun, pl* **-bush·es**

1 [*count*] : an act of hiding, waiting for others to appear, and then suddenly attacking them : a surprise attack ▪ Many soldiers were killed in the *ambush*.

2 [*noncount*] : a hidden place from which a surprise attack can be made ▪ The soldiers were ***lying in ambush***, waiting for the enemy to approach. ▪ a snake ***waiting in ambush*** for its next meal

[2]**ambush** *verb* **-bush·es**; **-bushed**; **-bush·ing** [+ *obj*] : to attack (someone or something) by surprise from a hidden place ▪ We have reports of enemy soldiers *ambushing* civilians on this road. — often used as *(be) ambushed* ▪ He *was ambushed* and killed by robbers on his way home. — often used figuratively ▪ As she left the courthouse, she *was ambushed* by a group of reporters. ▪ Her book *was ambushed* [=criticized in a harsh and unfair way] by the critics.

ameba *variant spelling of* AMOEBA

ame·lio·rate /əˈmiːljəˌreɪt/ *verb* **-rates**; **-rat·ed**; **-rat·ing** [+ *obj*] *formal* : to make (something, such as a problem) better, less painful, etc. ▪ trying to *ameliorate* the suffering of people who have lost their jobs ▪ This medicine should help *ameliorate* the pain.

— ame·lio·ra·tion /əˌmiːljəˈreɪʃən/ *noun* [*noncount*]

amen /ɑˈmɛn, eɪˈmɛn/ *interj*

1 — used at the end of a prayer

2 — used to express agreement or approval ▪ People in the crowd shouted "*Amen*!" when the speaker said that change was needed. ▪ "I'll be glad when this winter is over." "***Amen to that***!" [=I agree very much with that]

ame·na·ble /əˈmiːnəbəl/ *adj*

1 [*more* ~; *most* ~] : willing to agree or to accept something that is wanted or asked for ▪ an *amenable* child — usually + *to* ▪ The children are generally *amenable to* our wishes. ▪ a government that is not *amenable to* change [=a government that resists change]

2 *formal* : able to be controlled, organized, or affected by something — + *to* ▪ The disease is not *amenable to* surgery. [=it cannot be fixed by surgery] ▪ data *amenable to* analysis [=data that can be analyzed]

amend /əˈmɛnd/ *verb* **amends**; **amend·ed**; **amend·ing** [+ *obj*]

1 : to change some of the words and often the meaning of (a law, document, etc.) ▪ The country's constitution was *amended* to allow women to vote. ▪ They voted to *amend* the law in 1920. — compare EMEND

2 : to change and improve (something, such as a mistake or bad situation) ▪ He tried to *amend* the situation by apologizing to me.

amend·ment /əˈmɛndmənt/ *noun, pl* **-ments**

1 [*count*] : a change in the words or meaning of a law or document (such as a constitution) ▪ constitutional *amendments* — often + *to* ▪ They proposed an *amendment to* the law. [=they officially suggested that a change be made to the law] ▪ an *amendment to* section 37(a) of the tax code ✧ The names of the amendments that have been made to the U.S. Constitution are usually capitalized. ▪ The first 10 *Amendments* to the Constitution of the United States are called the Bill of Rights. ▪ Our right to free speech is protected by the *First Amendment* (of the U.S. Constitution).

2 [*noncount*] : the act or process of changing the words or meaning of a law or document : the act or process of amending something ▪ rights that were granted by *amendment* of the Constitution

amends /əˈmɛndz/ *noun*

make amends : to do something to correct a mistake that you have made or a bad situation that you have caused ▪ She tried to *make amends* by apologizing to him. ▪ I'd like to *make amends* (to you) for my behavior last night.

ame·ni·ty /əˈmɛnəti/ *noun, pl* **-ties** [*count*] : something that makes life easier or more pleasant ▪ The hotel has every *amenity* you could want. — usually plural ▪ It offers all the *amenities* you would expect in a car of its size. ▪ The hotel has other *amenities* such as a restaurant, swimming pool, and exercise room. ▪ The government intends to provide the isolated town with ***basic amenities***. [=basic things such as roads, running water, and electricity] ▪ We have never really liked each other, but we ***observe the social amenities*** [=we behave with politeness towards each other] whenever we meet.

Am·er·asian /ˈæməˈreɪʒən/ *noun, pl* **-asians** [*count*] : a person who has one parent from the U.S. (such as a father who served in the armed forces) and one parent from Asia

[1]**Amer·i·can** /ə'merəkən/ *noun, pl* **-cans** [*count*]

1 : a person born, raised, or living in the U.S. ▪ *Americans* in all 50 states ▪ The President's speech began with the words "My fellow *Americans* . . ."

2 : a person born, raised, or living in North America or South America — see also NATIVE AMERICAN

[2]**American** *adj*

1 : of or relating to the U.S. or its citizens ▪ *American* culture/government/history ▪ the *American* people ▪ their *American* friends

2 : of or relating to North America, South America, or the people who live there ▪ the *American* continents ▪ a tropical *American* tree

(as) American as apple pie see APPLE PIE

Amer·i·ca·na /ə,merə'kɑːnə/ *noun* [*noncount*] **:** things produced in the U.S. and thought to be typical of the U.S. or its culture ▪ collectors of *Americana* ▪ handmade quilts and other pieces of *Americana*

American cheese *noun* [*noncount*] **:** a mild cheese made in the U.S. from cheddar cheese

American dream *noun*

the American dream *or* ***the American Dream*** **:** a happy way of living that is thought of by many Americans as something that can be achieved by anyone in the U.S. especially by working hard and becoming successful ▪ With good jobs, a nice house, two children, and plenty of money, they believed they were living *the American dream.*

American English *noun* [*noncount*] **:** the English language used in the U.S. ▪ There are many differences between British English and *American English.*

> ***usage*** The term *American English* is only used in the U.S. when it is being compared to some other kind of English. English speakers in the U.S. generally refer to the language they speak simply as *English.*

American football *noun* [*noncount*] **:** FOOTBALL 1a

American Indian *noun, pl* ~ **-ans** [*count*] **:** NATIVE AMERICAN ***usage*** see NATIVE AMERICAN

Amer·i·can·ism /ə'merəkə,nɪzəm/ *noun, pl* **-isms** [*count*] **:** a word or meaning that is common in U.S. English but is not common in the kinds of English spoken outside the U.S.

Amer·i·can·ize *also Brit* **Amer·i·can·ise** /ə'merəkə,naɪz/ *verb* **-iz·es; -ized; -iz·ing** [+ *obj*] **:** to make (something or someone) American **:** to cause (something or someone) to have American characteristics ▪ The editors of the book decided to *Americanize* the spelling.

– Amer·i·can·i·za·tion *also Brit* **Amer·i·can·i·sa·tion** /ə,merəkənə'zeɪʃən, *Brit* ə,mɛrəkə,naɪ'zeɪʃən/ *noun* [*noncount*] ▪ the *Americanization* of cultures around the world **– Americanized** *also Brit* **Americanised** *adj* [*more* ~; *most* ~] ▪ The longer she stays in the U.S., the more *Americanized* she becomes. ▪ an *Americanized* city

American League *noun*

the American League **:** one of the two major leagues in professional U.S. baseball ✧ In the American League, the designated hitter bats in place of the pitcher. — compare NATIONAL LEAGUE

American Revolution *noun*

the American Revolution **:** the war of 1775–83 in which 13 British colonies in North America broke free from British rule and became the United States of America — called also (*chiefly Brit*) *American War of Independence*

American Sign Language *noun* [*noncount*] **:** a kind of sign language used in the U.S. and Canada

Am·er·in·di·an /,æmə'rɪndijən/ *noun, pl* **-ians** [*count*] **:** NATIVE AMERICAN

– Amerindian *adj* ▪ *Amerindian* cultures/languages/population

am·e·thyst /'æməθəst/ *noun, pl* **-thysts**

1 [*count*] **:** a clear purple or bluish-purple stone that is used as a gem — see color picture on page C11

2 [*noncount*] **:** a medium purple color — see color picture on page C3

– amethyst *adj*

ami·a·ble /'eɪmijəbəl/ *adj* [*more* ~; *most* ~] **:** friendly and pleasant ▪ Everyone knew him as an *amiable* fellow. ▪ She had an *amiable* conversation with her friend.

– ami·a·bil·i·ty /,eɪmiə'bɪləti/ *noun* [*noncount*] the *amiability* of their conversation [*singular*] She has a warm *amiability.* **– ami·a·bly** /'eɪmijəbli/ *adv* ▪ They chatted *amiably* with one another.

am·i·ca·ble /'æmɪkəbəl/ *adj* [*more* ~; *most* ~] **:** showing a polite and friendly desire to avoid disagreement and argument ▪ The discussions were *amicable.* ▪ They reached an *amicable* agreement.

– am·i·ca·bil·i·ty /,æmɪkə'bɪləti/ *noun* [*noncount*] **– am·i·ca·bly** /'æmɪkəbli/ *adv* ▪ They met and settled the problem *amicably.*

amid /ə'mɪd/ *or* **amidst** /ə'mɪdst/ *prep* **:** in or into the middle of (something) ▪ It was hard to hear *amid* all the cheering. ▪ The investigation comes *amid* growing concerns. ▪ *Amid* such changes, one thing stayed the same. ▪ *Amidst* [=*during*] all the fighting there still remained a steady hope for peace. ▪ He managed to escape *amid* the confusion. ▪ There was a single dark bird *amid* a flock of white pigeons.

amid·ships /ə'mɪd,ʃɪps/ *adv* **:** in or near the middle of a ship ▪ The berths are located *amidships.*

ami·go /ə'miːgoʊ/ *noun, pl* **-gos** [*count*] *chiefly US, informal* **:** FRIEND ▪ What's new, *amigo*? ✧ *Amigo* is the Spanish word for "friend."

ami·no acid /ə'miːnoʊ-/ *noun, pl* ~ **acids** [*count*] *biology* **:** any one of many acids that occur naturally in living things and that include some which form proteins

Amish /'ɑːmɪʃ/ *adj* **:** of or relating to a Christian religious group whose members settled in America chiefly in the 18th century and continue to live in a traditional way on farms ▪ an *Amish* community/farmer

– Amish *noun* [*plural*] ▪ a tradition among the *Amish* ▪ the *Amish* who live nearby

[1]**amiss** /ə'mɪs/ *adj, not used before a noun* **:** not proper or correct **:** WRONG ▪ Something is *amiss* here. ▪ Some of his assumptions are *amiss.* ▪ The doctor's examination showed that nothing was *amiss.* ▪ A special award for her performance would not be *amiss.* [=would be proper]

[2]**amiss** *adv* **:** in the wrong way ▪ Now, don't take this remark *amiss.* [=don't misunderstand this remark] ▪ (*Brit*) A little more encouragement would not ***come/go amiss.*** [=would not be unwelcome; would be proper, helpful, or appropriate]

am·i·ty /'æməti/ *noun* [*noncount*] *formal* **:** a feeling of friendship **:** friendly relations between nations or groups ▪ an era of international *amity*

am·mo /'æmoʊ/ *noun* [*noncount*] *informal* **:** AMMUNITION ▪ The soldiers ran out of *ammo.*

am·mo·nia /ə'moʊnjə/ *noun* [*noncount*] **:** a colorless gas or liquid that has a strong smell and taste and that is used especially in cleaning products

am·mu·ni·tion /,æmjə'nɪʃən/ *noun* [*noncount*] **:** the objects (such as bullets and shells) that are shot from weapons ▪ The troops were supplied with weapons and *ammunition.* — often used figuratively ▪ She had the *ammunition* to prove her case. [=she had the evidence she needed to prove her case] ▪ His foolish statements provided his opponents with more *ammunition* to use against him in the campaign.

am·ne·sia /æm'niːʒə/ *noun* [*noncount*] *medical* **:** a condition in which a person is unable to remember things because of brain injury, shock, or illness

– am·ne·si·ac /æm'niːʒi,æk/ *adj* ▪ an *amnesiac* patient **– amnesiac** *noun, pl* **-acs** [*count*] ▪ a movie about a friendless *amnesiac* [=a person who has amnesia]

am·nes·ty /'æmnəsti/ *noun, pl* **-ties :** a decision that a group of people will not be punished or that a group of prisoners will be allowed to go free [*noncount*] The government gave/granted *amnesty* to/for all political prisoners. ▪ Illegal immigrants who came into the country before 1982 were granted/given *amnesty.* [*count*] — usually singular ▪ The government gave/granted a general *amnesty* to/for all political prisoners. ▪ The library declared an *amnesty* from fines for all books that are returned on Thursday.

– amnesty *verb* **-ties; -tied; -ty·ing** [+ *obj*] ▪ The government *amnestied* all political prisoners.

am·nio·cen·te·sis /,æmnijoʊ,sen'tiːsəs/ *noun, pl* **-te·ses** /-'tiː,siːz/ [*count*] *medical* **:** a test that is done to check for possible health problems in a baby that is not yet born

amoe·ba *also US* **ame·ba** /ə'miːbə/ *noun, pl* **-bas** *or* **-bae** /-,biː/ [*count*] **:** a tiny living thing that consists of a single cell

– amoe·bic *also US* **ame·bic** /ə'miːbɪk/ *adj*

amok *also* **amuck** /ə'mʌk/ *adv* **:** in a wild or uncontrolled manner — used in the phrase ***run amok*** ▪ After the attack, the looters were *running amok.* ▪ The virus *ran amok.* ▪ Conditions had allowed extremism to *run amok.*

among /ə'mʌŋ/ *also* **amongst** /ə'mʌŋst/ *prep*

1 : in or through (a group of people or things) ▪ The disease

A

spread quickly *among* the members of the community. ▪ The house is nestled *among* the trees. ▪ The ball was hidden *among* the leaves. ▪ There were ducks *among* the geese. ▪ There were several hecklers scattered *among* the crowd.

2 : in the presence of (a group of people) ▪ The leader was standing *among* [=*amidst*] his supporters. ▪ She enjoys spending time at home *among* [=*with*] family and friends. ▪ He lived *among* artists and writers. ▪ The people of the town were frightened to think that a killer might be living *among* them. ▪ Relax. ***You're among friends*** here. [=the people here are your friends] ✧ When people do something ***among themselves***, they do it as a group without involving others. ▪ The brothers are always quarreling *among themselves*. [=are always quarreling with each other] ▪ They were unable to agree *among themselves*. ▪ We were joking *among ourselves*.

3 — used to talk about the opinions, feelings, etc., of a group of people ▪ There is much unhappiness *among* voters. [=many voters are unhappy] ▪ attitudes that are common *among* older people [=attitudes that many older people have] ▪ There is debate *among* researchers about the causes of this disease. ▪ a TV show that is popular *among* young women ▪ He is known *among* his colleagues as a reliable worker.

4 — used to indicate the group of people or things involved in or affected by something ▪ The new policy has led to increased competition *among* local businesses. ▪ There has been a high rate of illness *among* the children in this community. ▪ No one *among* them expected to survive.

5 — used to say that a person or thing is part of a larger group ▪ He is *among* her greatest admirers. [=he is one of her greatest admirers] ▪ He can be counted *among* the greatest players in the game's history. ▪ *Among* his good qualities is honesty. ▪ He has many good qualities. Chief *among* them is his honesty. ▪ ***Among other things*** she was president of her college class. ▪ She met with the company's president and vice president, ***among others***.

6 — used to indicate the group of people or things being considered, compared, etc. ▪ They compared several new cars but found few differences *among* them. ▪ We were allowed to choose (from) *among* several options.

7 : in shares to each of (a group of people) ▪ The property was divided equally *among* the four survivors. [=each of the four survivors received an equal share of the property] ▪ The food was distributed *among* the people.

8 — used to describe someone who is unusual or excellent in some way ▪ He is an actor *among* actors. [=he is a great actor] ▪ He was a giant *among* men. [=he was very famous, powerful, successful, etc.]

amor·al /eɪˈmorəl/ *adj* [*more* ~; *most* ~] **:** having or showing no concern about whether behavior is morally right or wrong ▪ *amoral* politicians ▪ He is an *amoral*, selfish person pursuing his own goals. ▪ a cynical and *amoral* way of competing for business — compare IMMORAL, [1]MORAL
– amo·ral·i·ty /ˌeɪməˈræləti/ *noun* [*noncount*] ▪ sexual *amorality* [=amoral behavior] ▪ the *amorality* of his behavior
– amor·al·ly /ˌeɪˈmorəli/ *adv* ▪ behaving/acting *amorally*

am·o·rous /ˈæmərəs/ *adj* [*more* ~; *most* ~] **:** having or showing strong feelings of sexual attraction or love ▪ an *amorous* woman ▪ He has an *amorous* nature. ▪ She was feeling *amorous*. ▪ an *amorous* glance
– am·o·rous·ly *adv* **– am·o·rous·ness** *noun* [*noncount*]

amor·phous /əˈmoɚfəs/ *adj* [*more* ~; *most* ~] **:** having no definite or clear shape or form ▪ an *amorphous* shape ▪ *amorphous* [=*shapeless*] clouds ▪ an *amorphous* segment of society
– amor·phous·ly *adv* **– amor·phous·ness** *noun* [*noncount*]

am·or·tize *also Brit* **am·or·tise** /ˈæmɚˌtaɪz, *Brit* əˈmɔːˌtaɪz/ *verb* **-tiz·es; -tized; -tiz·ing** [+ *obj*] *business* **:** to pay money that is owed for something (such as a mortgage) by making regular payments over a long period of time ▪ *amortize* a debt/loan
– am·or·ti·za·tion *also Brit* **am·or·ti·sa·tion** /ˌæmɚtəˈzeɪʃən, *Brit* æˌmɔːtaɪˈzeɪʃən/ *noun* [*noncount*]

[1]**amount** /əˈmaʊnt/ *noun, pl* **amounts** [*count*]

1 : a quantity of something ▪ The drug is not being produced in adequate *amounts*. — usually + *of* ▪ They are not producing an adequate *amount of* the drug. [=they are not producing enough of the drug] ▪ A considerable/fair/great/large/tremendous *amount of* research went into the report. ▪ Be sure to add the right *amount of* salt. ▪ She spent amazing/enormous *amounts of* time planning her garden. ▪ There's a certain *amount of* truth to/in what you say. [=there is some truth in what you say] ▪ The new law limits the *amount of* money a candidate can spend. ▪ We have ***any amount of*** available resources. = We have a large *amount of* available resources. ▪ ***No amount of*** money can make up for their loss. [=money cannot make up for their loss]

2 : a quantity of money ▪ What is the *amount* to be paid? ▪ An *amount* was finally agreed upon. ▪ The new law limits the *amount* a candidate can spend. ▪ When he died we found he owed money ***to/in the amount of*** $250,000!

> ***usage*** *Amount* is chiefly used with noncount nouns. ▪ He lost a large *amount* of money. ▪ a minimum *amount* of effort ▪ They provided only a small *amount* of information. It is also sometimes used with plural count nouns, but this use is often criticized as an error. ▪ There were a large *amount* of mistakes. *Number* is the usual word in such contexts. ▪ a large *number* of mistakes ▪ an increasing *number* of problems

[2]**amount** *verb* **amounts; amount·ed; amount·ing**
amount to [*phrasal verb*] ***amount to (something)*** **1 :** to produce (a total) when added together ▪ The bill *amounted to* 10 dollars. ▪ They have debts *amounting to* thousands of dollars. ▪ The number of people taking part *amounted to* no more than a few hundred. **2 :** to turn out to be (something or someone important, impressive, etc.) ▪ The problems didn't ***amount to much***. [=the problems were not very bad] ▪ I don't think he'll ever ***amount to anything***. [=achieve success] **3 :** to be the same in meaning or effect as (something) ▪ acts that *amount to* treason ▪ Anything less than total victory would *amount to* failure/failing. [=would be the same as failure/failing]

amour /əˈmuɚ/ *noun, pl* **amours** [*count*] *literary* **:** a sexual relationship **:** a love affair; *especially* **:** a secret love affair ▪ memoirs devoted to accounts of his *amours*

amp /ˈæmp/ *noun, pl* **amps** [*count*]
1 : AMPERE ▪ a current of 15 *amps* = a 15-*amp* current
2 *informal* **:** AMPLIFIER ▪ He plugged his guitar into the *amp*.

am·per·age /ˈæmprɪʤ/ *noun* [*noncount*] *technical* **:** the strength of a current of electricity expressed in amperes

am·pere /ˈæmˌpiɚ, *Brit* ˈæmˌpeə/ *noun, pl* **-peres** [*count*] *technical* **:** a unit for measuring the rate at which electric current flows ▪ a current of 15 *amperes* — called also *amp*

am·per·sand /ˈæmpɚˌsænd/ *noun, pl* **-sands** [*count*] **:** a character & that is used for the word *and* ▪ Mr. & [=*and*] Mrs. Joe Smith

am·phet·amine /æmˈfɛtəˌmiːn/ *noun, pl* **-amines** [*count*] **:** a drug that causes the nervous system to become more active so that a person feels more energy and mental excitement

am·phib·i·an /æmˈfɪbijən/ *noun, pl* **-ans** [*count*]
1 : an animal (such as a frog or toad) that can live both on land and in water
2 : an airplane or vehicle that can be used both on land and water

am·phib·i·ous /æmˈfɪbijəs/ *adj*
1 : able to live both on land and in water ▪ *amphibious* plants/animals
2 : able to be used both on land and water ▪ *amphibious* airplanes/vehicles
3 : done by soldiers who are brought to land in special boats **:** carried out by land and sea forces acting together ▪ an *amphibious* assault/landing

am·phi·the·a·ter (*US*) *or chiefly Brit* **am·phi·the·a·tre** /ˈæmfəˌθiːjətɚ/ *noun, pl* **-ters** [*count*]
1 : a large building with seats rising in curved rows around an open space on which games and plays take place
2 : an area of level ground surrounded by hills ▪ a natural *amphitheater*

am·ple /ˈæmpəl/ *adj* **am·pler** /ˈæmplɚ/; **am·plest** /ˈæmpləst/ [*also more* ~; *most* ~]
1 a : having or providing enough or more than enough of what is needed ▪ There was *ample* room for a garden. [=there was plenty of room for a garden] ▪ They had *ample* money for the trip. ▪ The police found *ample* evidence of wrongdoing. ▪ There is *ample* parking at the stadium. ▪ You will have *ample* opportunity/time to finish the test. ▪ The light in the room is more than *ample*. ***synonyms*** see PLENTIFUL **b :** quite large ▪ There was room for an *ample* garden. ▪ an *ample* serving of pie
2 — used to describe a person's (especially a woman's) body as being large in usually an attractive way ▪ She has an *ample* figure. ▪ a woman with an *ample* bosom
– am·ply /ˈæmpli/ *adv* ▪ These facts *amply* demonstrate that

something is wrong. ▪ an *amply* stocked store ▪ You will be *amply* rewarded for your efforts. [=you will be given a large reward for your efforts]

am·pli·fi·er /ˈæmpləˌfajɚ/ *noun, pl* **-ers** [*count*] : a device that increases the strength of electric signals so that sounds played through an electronic system are louder ▪ He plugged his electric guitar into an *amplifier.* — called also (*informal*) *amp*

am·pli·fy /ˈæmpləˌfaɪ/ *verb* **-fies; -fied; -fy·ing** [+ *obj*]
1 a : to increase the strength of (an electric signal) ▪ *amplify* a weak radio signal ▪ a receiver that *amplified* the television signal **b :** to make (something, such as a musical instrument) louder by increasing the strength of electric signals ▪ *amplify* an electric guitar
2 *formal* **:** to give more information about (something, such as a statement) : to speak or write about (something) in a more complete way ▪ I'd like to *amplify* [=*expand on*] my earlier remarks by providing some illustrations.
3 : to make (something) stronger ▪ using spices to *amplify* the flavors of the food
– am·pli·fi·ca·tion /ˌæmpləfəˈkeɪʃən/ *noun, pl* **-tions** [*noncount*] songs played with and without *amplification* ▪ the *amplification* of a signal ▪ The new rules require some *amplification.* [*count*] He started the meeting with an *amplification* of the new rules.

am·pli·tude /ˈæmpləˌtuːd, *Brit* ˈæmpləˌtjuːd/ *noun, pl* **-tudes** [*count, noncount*] *technical* **:** a measurement that indicates the movement or vibration of something (such as a sound wave or a radio wave)

am·pule (*US*) *or* **am·poule** /ˈæmˌpjuːl/ *noun, pl* **-pules** *or* **-poules** [*count*] **:** a small glass container used to hold a fluid that is injected into someone through a needle

am·pu·tate /ˈæmpjəˌteɪt/ *verb* **-tates; -tat·ed; -tat·ing** [+ *obj*] *medical* **:** to cut off (part of a person's body) ▪ His arm/leg was badly injured and had to be *amputated.*
– am·pu·ta·tion /ˌæmpjəˈteɪʃən/ *noun, pl* **-tions** [*count, noncount*]

am·pu·tee /ˌæmpjəˈtiː/ *noun, pl* **-tees** [*count*] **:** a person who has had an arm or leg amputated

amuck *variant spelling of* AMOK

am·u·let /ˈæmjələt/ *noun, pl* **-lets** [*count*] **:** a small object worn to protect the person wearing it against bad things (such as illness, bad luck, etc.)

amuse /əˈmjuːz/ *verb* **amus·es; amused; amus·ing**
1 : to make someone laugh or smile : to entertain (someone) in a light and pleasant way [+ *obj*] His silly jokes *amused* the audience. = The audience was *amused* by his silly jokes. [=the audience found his silly jokes funny/entertaining/amusing] ▪ It *amuses* me to think of how he looked when I last saw him. ▪ That joke doesn't *amuse* me. [=I don't think that joke is funny] ▪ The loss did not *amuse* the coach. [=the coach was not happy about the loss] [*no obj*] a funny story that never fails to *amuse* — see also AMUSING
2 [+ *obj*] **:** to get the attention of (someone) in a pleasant way as time passes ▪ We need to find something to *amuse* [=*entertain, occupy*] the children. = We need to find something to keep the children *amused.* [=we need to find something for the children to do so that they aren't bored] ▪ He ***amused himself*** with a game of solitaire.
– amused *adj* [*more ~; most ~*] ▪ A faintly *amused* grin appeared on her face. ▪ She looked slightly/very *amused* by/at his appearance. ▪ I was *amused* to learn the whole story. ▪ The coach was not *amused* [=was not pleased/happy] after the loss.

amuse·ment /əˈmjuːzmənt/ *noun, pl* **-ments**
1 [*noncount*] **:** the feeling of being amused or entertained ▪ I'm reading this novel for *amusement.* ▪ People found great *amusement* in his strange behavior. = His strange behavior was a source of great *amusement.* [=people were very amused by his strange behavior] ▪ Several games were provided for the education and *amusement* of the children. ▪ Much ***to my amusement,*** his confident prediction of victory turned out to be completely wrong. [=I was amused when his prediction turned out to be completely wrong]
2 [*count*] **:** something (such as an activity) that amuses or entertains someone — usually plural ▪ plays, movies, and other *amusements* [=*entertainments*] ▪ He had no time for *amusements* and hobbies. ▪ The park had many *amusements,* including two roller coasters.

amusement arcade *noun, pl* **~ -cades** [*count*] *Brit* **:** ARCADE 3

amusement park *noun, pl* **~ parks** [*count*] **:** a place that has many games and rides (such as roller coasters and merry-go-rounds) for entertainment

amus·ing /əˈmjuːzɪŋ/ *adj* [*more ~; most ~*] **:** causing laughter or enjoyment : funny or enjoyable ▪ There are some *amusing* [=*funny*] twists to the story. ▪ a mildly *amusing* remark ▪ He's one of the most *amusing* people I know. ▪ It was *amusing* to hear her tell the story.
– amus·ing·ly *adv* ▪ an *amusingly* written story ▪ an *amusingly* named invention

an /ˈæn, ən/ *indefinite article* **:** ²A — used before words beginning with a vowel sound ▪ *an* oak ▪ *an* hour

an- see ²A-

¹-an *or* **-ian** *also* **-ean** *noun suffix* **:** someone or something that belongs to ▪ Americ*an* [=a person who lives in or is from America] ▪ Boston*ian* [=a person who lives in or is from Boston]

²-an *or* **-ian** *also* **-ean** *adj suffix*
1 : of or belonging to ▪ Americ*an*
2 : characteristic of : resembling ▪ Hercul*ean* [=resembling Hercules] ▪ Mozart*ean* [=characteristic of or resembling Mozart]

an·a·bol·ic steroid /ˌænəˈbɑːlɪk-/ *noun, pl* **~ -oids** [*count*] **:** a drug that is sometimes used illegally by athletes to help them become stronger and more muscular

anach·ro·nism /əˈnækrəˌnɪzəm/ *noun, pl* **-nisms** [*count*]
1 : something (such as a word, an object, or an event) that is mistakenly placed in a time where it does not belong in a story, movie, etc. ▪ The novel is full of *anachronisms.*
2 : a person or a thing that seems to belong to the past and not to fit in the present ▪ He's an old-fashioned politician who is seen by many of his colleagues as an *anachronism.*
– anach·ro·nis·tic /əˌnækrəˈnɪstɪk/ *adj* [*more ~; most ~*] ▪ a politician whose values seem somewhat *anachronistic*
– anach·ro·nis·ti·cal·ly /əˌnækrəˈnɪstɪkli/ *adv*

an·a·con·da /ˌænəˈkɑːndə/ *noun, pl* **-das** [*count*] **:** a large South American snake that squeezes its victims to death

anaemia, anaemic *chiefly Brit spellings of* ANEMIA, ANEMIC

an·aer·o·bic /ˌænəˈroʊbɪk/ *adj* **:** not aerobic: such as **a** *of exercise* **:** strengthening muscles by forcing them to work very hard for a brief time ▪ *anaerobic* sports/training ▪ Weight lifting is an *anaerobic* exercise. **b** *technical* **:** not using oxygen ▪ Some bacteria are aerobic and others are *anaerobic.*
– an·aer·o·bi·cal·ly /ˌænəˈroʊbɪkli/ *adv* ▪ exercising *anaerobically*

anaesthesia, anaesthetic, anaesthetist, anaesthetize *Brit spellings of* ANESTHESIA, ANESTHETIC, ANESTHETIST, ANESTHETIZE

an·a·gram /ˈænəˌgræm/ *noun, pl* **-grams** [*count*] **:** a word or phrase made by changing the order of the letters in another word or phrase ▪ The word "secure" is an *anagram* of "rescue."

anal /ˈeɪnl/ *adj*
1 *biology* **:** of, relating to, or located near the anus ▪ the *anal* area
2 [*more ~; most ~*] *informal* **:** extremely or overly neat, careful, or precise : ANAL-RETENTIVE ▪ He can be pretty *anal* about keeping his office neat.
– anal·ly *adv*

an·al·ge·sia /ˌænl̩ˈʤiːʒə/ *noun* [*noncount*] *medical* **:** the loss of the ability to feel pain while conscious

an·al·ge·sic /ˌænl̩ˈʤiːzɪk/ *noun, pl* **-sics** [*count*] *medical* **:** a drug that relieves pain ▪ a mild/powerful *analgesic* [=*painkiller*]
– analgesic *adj* ▪ a drug with *analgesic* [=*painkilling*] effects ▪ an *analgesic* drug

an·a·log (*chiefly US*) *or chiefly Brit* **an·a·logue** /ˈænəˌlɑːg/ *adj*
1 *technical* **:** of or relating to a device or process in which data is represented by physical quantities that change continuously ▪ Telephone lines carry data in *analog* form. ▪ It receives an *analog* video signal and converts it to a digital signal. ▪ an *analog* computer
2 *of a clock or watch* **:** having hour and minute hands ▪ an *analog* watch — compare DIGITAL 1

anal·o·gous /əˈnæləgəs/ *adj* [*more ~; most ~*] *formal* **:** similar in some way ▪ I could not think of an *analogous* situation. — usually + *to* ▪ I could not think of a situation *analogous to* this one. ▪ The telescope's lenses are *analogous* [=*comparable*] *to* a person's glasses. ▪ Think of the process as

A

analogous to [=*like*] riding a bike.
– **anal·o·gous·ly** *adv*

an·a·logue *or US* **an·a·log** /ˈænəˌlɑːg/ *noun, pl* **-logues** *or US* **-logs** [*count*] *formal* : something that is similar to something else in design, origin, use, etc. : something that is analogous to something else ▪ a modern *analog* to what happened before ▪ the synthetic *analog* of a chemical found in a tropical tree ▪ a meat *analogue* such as tofu

anal·o·gy /əˈnæləʤi/ *noun, pl* **-gies**
1 [*count*] : a comparison of two things based on their being alike in some way ▪ He ***drew/made an analogy*** between flying a kite and fishing. [=he compared flying a kite to fishing; he said that flying a kite was like fishing]
2 [*noncount*] : the act of comparing two things that are alike in some way ▪ coining new words by *analogy* to/with existing ones [=coining new words so that they are formed in a way similar to old ones] ▪ reasoning by *analogy*

anal–re·ten·tive /ˈeɪnl̩rɪˈtɛntɪv/ *adj* [*more* ~; *most* ~] : extremely or overly neat, careful, or precise ▪ My *anal-retentive* brother keeps records of everything that happens in his life.

anal·y·sis /əˈnæləsəs/ *noun, pl* **-y·ses** /-əˌsiːz/
1 a : a careful study of something to learn about its parts, what they do, and how they are related to each other [*count*] a scientific *analysis* of the data ▪ make/do/perform a chemical *analysis* of the soil ▪ a detailed *analysis* of the bone structure of horses [*noncount*] performing chemical *analysis* of the soil — see also SYSTEMS ANALYSIS **b** : an explanation of the nature and meaning of something [*count*] The newspaper printed an *analysis* of each candidate's positions. ▪ That's not a bad *analysis* of the situation. [*noncount*] It's a problem that requires careful *analysis*. ▪ a problem that ***defies analysis*** [=a problem that cannot be easily understood or explained]
2 [*noncount*] : PSYCHOANALYSIS ▪ He has been in/undergoing *analysis* for many years.
in the final analysis *also* ***in the last analysis*** : after considering everything — used for a final statement or judgment that is based on what is most important in a particular situation ▪ It was a difficult decision but, *in the final analysis*, it was the right choice.

an·a·lyst /ˈænələst/ *noun, pl* **-lysts** [*count*]
1 : a person who studies or analyzes something ▪ a financial/legal/political *analyst*
2 : PSYCHOANALYST ▪ My *analyst* felt that I was making good progress.

an·a·lyt·i·cal /ˌænəˈlɪtɪkəl/ *or* **an·a·lyt·ic** /ˌænəˈlɪtɪk/ *adj* [*more* ~; *most* ~]
1 : of or relating to the careful study of something : of or relating to analysis of something ▪ The office managers were asking for more *analytical* reports. ▪ *analytical* chemistry ▪ a powerful *analytical* tool to determine the nature and extent of climate change ▪ an *analytical* examination of the text
2 : having or showing skill in thinking or reasoning ▪ developing social and *analytical* skills in children ▪ She looked at the room with an *analytical* [=*critical*] eye and saw where the changes were made. ▪ She has a very quick *analytical* mind.
– **an·a·lyt·i·cal·ly** /ˌænəˈlɪtɪkli/ *adv*

an·a·lyze (*US*) *or Brit* **an·a·lyse** /ˈænəˌlaɪz/ *verb* **-lyz·es; -lyzed; -lyz·ing** [+ *obj*]
1 : to study (something) closely and carefully : to learn the nature and relationship of the parts of (something) by a close and careful examination ▪ *analyze* a problem ▪ The data was recorded and *analyzed* by computer. ▪ We took the sample to be chemically *analyzed* by a lab. ▪ Researchers are busy *analyzing* the results of the study. ▪ The bacteria were *analyzed* under a powerful microscope.
2 : to study the emotions and thoughts of (someone) by using psychoanalysis : PSYCHOANALYZE
– **an·a·lyz·able** (*US*) *or Brit* **an·a·lys·able** /ˈænəˌlaɪzəbəl/ *adj*

an·ar·chic /æˈnɑɚkɪk/ *adj* [*more* ~; *most* ~] : not following or having any laws or rules : wild and uncontrolled ▪ *anarchic* behavior ▪ *anarchic* confusion
– **an·ar·chi·cal·ly** /æˈnɑɚkɪkli/ *adv* ▪ behaving *anarchically*

an·ar·chism /ˈænɚˌkɪzəm/ *noun* [*noncount*] : a belief that government and laws are not necessary

an·ar·chist /ˈænɚˌkɪst/ *noun, pl* **-chists** [*count*] : a person who believes that government and laws are not necessary
– **an·ar·chis·tic** /ˌænɚˈkɪstɪk/ *adj* [*more* ~; *most* ~] ▪ *anarchistic* rebels

an·ar·chy /ˈænɚki/ *noun* [*noncount*] : a situation of confusion and wild behavior in which the people in a country, group, organization, etc., are not controlled by rules or laws ▪ *Anarchy* reigned in the empire's remote provinces. ▪ When the teacher was absent, there was *anarchy* in the classroom.

anath·e·ma /əˈnæθəmə/ *noun, formal* : someone or something that is very strongly disliked — usually + *to* [*noncount*] ideas that are *anathema to* me [=ideas that I strongly dislike] ▪ a politician who is *anathema to* conservatives/liberals [*singular*] ideas that are an *anathema to* me

anat·o·my /əˈnætəmi/ *noun, pl* **-mies**
1 *biology* **a** [*noncount*] : the study of the structure of living things ▪ We had to take a class on/in *anatomy*. ▪ a professor of *anatomy* **b** : the parts that form a living thing (such as an animal or plant) [*noncount*] the *anatomy* of birds ▪ human *anatomy* and physiology [*count*] learning about the *anatomies* of different types of birds
2 [*count*] *informal* : a person's body — usually singular ▪ She wore an outfit that showed off various parts of her *anatomy*.
3 [*noncount*] : the parts or causes that form or create something ▪ learning about the *anatomy* of an earthquake
4 [*singular*] : a close study of the causes or parts of something ▪ The book is an *anatomy* of life in the inner city.
– **an·a·tom·i·cal** /ˌænəˈtɑːmɪkəl/ *also US* **an·a·tom·ic** /ˌænəˈtɑːmɪk/ *adj* ▪ *anatomical* similarities between dinosaurs and birds ▪ the *anatomical* structure of the eye – **an·a·tom·i·cal·ly** /ˌænəˈtɑːmɪkli/ *adv* ▪ ***anatomically correct*** dolls [=dolls that have body parts like those of actual people] – **anat·o·mist** /əˈnætəmɪst/ *noun, pl* **-mists** [*count*] ▪ a noted *anatomist* [=a scientist who studies anatomy]

-ance /əns/ *noun suffix* : the action or process of doing something ▪ avoid*ance* ▪ perform*ance* ▪ accept*ance*

an·ces·tor /ˈænˌsɛstɚ/ *noun, pl* **-tors** [*count*]
1 : a person who was in someone's family in past times : one of the people from whom a person is descended ▪ My *ancestors* came to America during the 1800s. ▪ Her *ancestors* were great sea captains.
2 : an animal in the past from which a modern animal developed ▪ an ancient animal that was the *ancestor* of the modern horse
3 : something in the past from which something else has developed ▪ The museum included an exhibit showing *ancestors* of the modern computer. ▪ several languages that are derived from a common *ancestor* ▪ Latin is the *ancestor* of Italian and French.
– **an·ces·tral** /ænˈsɛstrəl/ *adj* ▪ We returned to our *ancestral* home [=the home of our ancestors] after many years.

an·ces·try /ˈænˌsɛstri/ *noun, pl* **-tries** : a person's ancestors : the people who were in your family in past times [*noncount*] They claim to be of noble *ancestry*. ▪ an Englishman of German *ancestry* = an Englishman who is German by *ancestry* ▪ a person of unknown *ancestry* ▪ She claims to be able to trace her *ancestry* all the way back to the earliest settlers. [*count*] They have different *ancestries*.

[1]an·chor /ˈæŋkɚ/ *noun, pl* **-chors** [*count*]
1 : a heavy device that is attached to a boat or ship by a rope or chain and that is thrown into the water to hold the boat or ship in place ▪ The ship ***dropped anchor*** in a secluded harbor. ▪ Several yachts stood/sat/rode ***at anchor*** [=were held in place by an anchor] in the harbor. ▪ The crew ***weighed anchor*** [=lifted the anchor] and prepared to sail.
2 a : a person or thing that provides strength and support ▪ a star quarterback who has been the *anchor* [=the most important part] of a football team's offense for many years ▪ He described his wife as the emotional *anchor* of his life. ▪ a local bank that has been the financial *anchor* of the community **b** : a large store that attracts customers and other businesses to an area (such as a shopping mall) ▪ an ***anchor store***
3 *chiefly US* : someone who reads the news on a television broadcast : an anchorman or anchorwoman ▪ a television news *anchor*

[2]anchor *verb* **-chors; -chored; -chor·ing**
1 : to keep a ship or boat from moving by using an anchor [+ *obj*] They *anchored* the ship in the bay. [*no obj*] The ship *anchored* in the bay.
2 [+ *obj*] : to connect (something) to a solid base : to hold (something) firmly in place — usually used as *(be) anchored* ▪ The cables of the bridge *are anchored* to the hillside. — often used figuratively with *in* ▪ Her authority *is anchored in* more than 20 years of experience.
3 [+ *obj*] : to be the strongest and most important part of (something) ▪ a star quarterback who has *anchored* the team's offense for many years

4 [+ *obj*] *US* : to read the news on (a television broadcast) : to be the anchorman or anchorwoman on (a news program) ▪ She *anchors* the nightly news broadcast.

an·chor·age /ˈæŋkərɪʤ/ *noun, pl* **-ag·es**
1 : a place where boats and ships are anchored [*count*] a safe/secluded *anchorage* [*noncount*] an area of safe *anchorage*
2 : something that provides a strong hold or connection [*noncount*] A heavy metal ring provides *anchorage* for the cable. [*count*] The ring serves as a secure *anchorage*.

an·cho·rite /ˈæŋkəˌraɪt/ *noun, pl* **-rites** [*count*] : a religious person who lives apart from other people

an·chor·man /ˈæŋkɚˌmæn/ *noun, pl* **-men** /-ˌmɛn/ [*count*] *chiefly US* : a man who reads the news and introduces the reports of other broadcasters on a television news program ▪ a network *anchorman*

an·chor·wom·an /ˈæŋkɚˌwʊmən/ *noun, pl* **-wom·en** /-ˌwɪmən/ [*count*] *chiefly US* : a woman who reads the news and introduces the reports of other broadcasters on a television news program ▪ a network *anchorwoman*

an·cho·vy /ˈænˌʧoʊvi/ *noun, pl* **an·cho·vies** *also* **ancho·vy** [*count*] : a small fish that has a salty flavor ▪ a salad topped with garlic and *anchovies* ▪ pizza with *anchovies*

an·cient /ˈeɪnʃənt/ *adj* [*more* ~; *most* ~]
1 : very old : having lived or existed for a very long time ▪ The people in the village still observe the *ancient* customs/traditions of their ancestors. ▪ a grove of *ancient* oak trees — often used in an exaggerated way to describe an old machine, person, etc. ▪ We got a ride in an *ancient* truck. ▪ an *ancient* barn ▪ I never thought I'd feel *ancient* at age 31. ▪ She finally decided to replace her *ancient* computer with something more modern and up to date.
2 : of, coming from, or belonging to a time that was long ago in the past ▪ The practice was more common in *ancient* times than it is now. ▪ life in *ancient* Egypt/Rome/Greece/China ▪ the gods of the *ancient* Romans ▪ *ancient* artifacts ▪ She studied both *ancient* and modern history. ✧ In informal use, something that happened long ago and that is not important any more is ***ancient history***. ▪ Our relationship is *ancient history*. ▪ Forget about the problems we've had in the past. They're *ancient history*. ***synonyms*** see [1]OLD
– an·cient·ly /ˈeɪnʃəntli/ *adv* ▪ a drink that was used *anciently* [=in ancient times] as a love potion

an·cients /ˈeɪnʃənts/ *noun*
the ancients : the people who lived in ancient times : the people of ancient Greece and Rome ▪ a temple built by *the ancients* ▪ the gods of *the ancients*

an·cil·lary /ˈænsəˌleri, *Brit* ænˈsɪləri/ *adj, formal* : providing something additional to a main part or function : EXTRA ▪ The company hopes to boost its sales by releasing *ancillary* products. ▪ *ancillary* services/expenses — sometimes + *to* ▪ These expenses are *ancillary to* the basic cost.

-an·cy /ənsi/ *noun suffix* : the quality or state of being (something) — used to form nouns from adjectives that end in *-ant* ▪ dorm*ancy* ▪ tru*ancy* ▪ buoy*ancy*

and /ˈænd, ənd, ən/ *conj*
1 — used to join words or groups of words ▪ We have ice cream *and* cake for dessert. ▪ He's feeling strong *and* healthy. ▪ She answered quickly *and* confidently. ▪ He swerved *and* avoided an accident. ▪ She's the club's secretary *and* treasurer. ▪ He walked into the room *and* sat down at the table. ▪ an actor who is tall, dark, *and* handsome
2 : added to : plus ▪ 2 *and* 2 equals 4.
3 a — used to describe an action that is repeated or that occurs for a long time ▪ The dog barked *and* barked. ▪ She cried *and* cried. **b** — used to repeat a word for emphasis ▪ You *and* you alone are responsible for correcting these errors. ▪ There were hundreds *and* hundreds of people there. ▪ The project is becoming more *and* more expensive. ▪ The work is getting harder *and* harder.
4 a — used to describe actions that occur at the same time ▪ They walked *and* talked. ▪ We sat *and* waited for hours. **b** — used to describe an action that occurs after another action ▪ They drove five miles *and* stopped to eat. ▪ He promised to come *and* didn't. **c** — used to describe an action that occurs after and is caused by another action ▪ I told him to go *and* he went.
5 — used after *go, come, try, write*, etc., to indicate the purpose of an action ▪ Why don't you go/come *and* see her? [=go/come to see her] ▪ I'll try *and* do it. [=I'll try to do it] ▪ Promise that you'll write *and* tell me [=write to tell me] about your vacation.
6 — used to indicate a choice ▪ You have to choose between him *and* me.
7 — used to start a new sentence or clause that continues or adds to a previous sentence or clause ▪ These problems have been occurring for many years, as everyone acknowledges. *And* of course they are going to continue unless something is done. ▪ Critics of the administration—*and* there many of them—have objected to the new plan. ▪ "Well, I've spoken to him . . ." "*And*?" "*And* he said yes!"
8 a — used after *hundred* and *thousand* when saying a number aloud ▪ a/one hundred *and* twenty-four [=124] ▪ two thousand *and* sixty-five [=2,065] **b** — used when saying aloud a number that is followed by a fraction ▪ seven *and* three quarters [=7¾] ▪ One *and* a half years have passed since then. = A year *and* a half has passed since then.
9 — used to indicate the point where two streets meet or cross ▪ a restaurant located at (the corner of) Main Street *and* First Avenue

an·dan·te /ˌɑːnˈdɑːnteɪ/ *noun, pl* **-tes** [*count*] : a musical composition or a part of a musical composition that is played somewhat slowly
– andante *adj or adv* ▪ an *andante* movement ▪ This piece should be played *andante*.

and·iron /ˈændˌajɚn/ *noun, pl* **-irons** [*count*] : either one of a pair of metal supports that hold the wood in a fireplace — usually plural

an·drog·y·nous /ænˈdrɑːʤənəs/ *adj* [*more* ~; *most* ~]
1 : having both male and female characteristics or qualities ▪ an *androgynous* rock star ▪ *androgynous* models/dancers
2 : suitable for both men and women ▪ *androgynous* clothes
– an·drog·y·ny /ænˈdrɑːʤəni/ *noun* [*noncount*]

an·droid /ˈænˌdrɔɪd/ *noun, pl* **-droids** [*count*] *in stories* : a robot that looks like a person

an·ec·dote /ˈænɪkˌdoʊt/ *noun, pl* **-dotes** [*count*] : a short story about an interesting or funny event or occurrence ▪ He told us all sorts of humorous *anecdotes* about his childhood.
– an·ec·dot·al /ˌænɪkˈdoʊtl/ *adj* [*more* ~; *most* ~] ▪ I enjoyed the book's *anecdotal* style. ▪ His conclusions are not supported by data; they are based only on ***anecdotal evidence***. [=evidence in the form of stories that people tell about what has happened to them] **– an·ec·dot·al·ly** *adv* ▪ *Anecdotally*, doctors report an increase in the disease.

ane·mia (*US*) *or Brit* **anae·mia** /əˈniːmijə/ *noun* [*noncount*] *medical* : a condition in which a person has fewer red blood cells than normal and feels very weak and tired — see also SICKLE-CELL ANEMIA

ane·mic (*US*) *or Brit* **anae·mic** /əˈniːmɪk/ *adj* [*more* ~; *most* ~]
1 *medical* : relating to or suffering from anemia ▪ The doctor told me I was slightly *anemic*.
2 : not strong, forceful, or impressive : WEAK ▪ The band played an *anemic* rendition of a classic love song. ▪ Investors are worried about the stock's *anemic* performance. ▪ Officials worried about *anemic* attendance at the shows. ▪ Sales rose an *anemic* 0.5 percent last quarter.
– ane·mi·cal·ly (*US*) *or Brit* **anae·mi·cal·ly** /əˈniːmɪkli/ *adv* ▪ The economy grew *anemically* last year.

anem·o·ne /əˈnɛməni/ *noun, pl* **-nes** [*count*]
1 : a type of garden plant that has white, purple, or red flowers
2 : SEA ANEMONE

an·es·the·sia (*US*) *or Brit* **an·aes·the·sia** /ˌænəsˈθiːʒə/ *noun* [*noncount*] *medical* : loss of feeling in a person's body or part of the body through the use of drugs ▪ The patient was given an injection to induce *anesthesia*. ▪ patients who are under ***general anesthesia*** [=patients who have been given drugs that make them unconscious and unable to feel pain] ▪ The doctor removed the mole while the patient was under ***local anesthesia***. [=the patient had been given drugs that took away feeling in only the part of the body where the doctor worked]

an·es·the·si·ol·o·gist /ˌænəsˌθiːziˈɑːləʤɪst/ *noun, pl* **-gists** [*count*] *US, medical* : a doctor who specializes in anesthesia and anesthetics : ANESTHETIST

an·es·thet·ic (*US*) *or Brit* **an·aes·thet·ic** /ˌænəsˈθɛtɪk/ *noun, pl* **-ics** [*count*] *medical* : a drug that causes a person to lose feeling and to feel no pain in part or all of the body ▪ The doctor gave him the stitches without an *anesthetic*. ▪ The surgery required a ***general anesthetic***. [=a drug that makes a person unconscious and unable to feel pain] ▪ a ***local anes-***

A

thetic [=a drug that makes a part of the body unable to feel pain]
– **anesthetic** (*US*) *or Brit* **anaesthetic** *adj* ▪ the *anesthetic* properties of a drug

anes·the·tist (*US*) *or Brit* **anaes·the·tist** /əˈnɛsθətɪst/ *noun, pl* **-tists** [*count*] *medical* : a doctor or nurse who gives an anesthetic to a patient

anes·the·tize (*US*) *or Brit* **anaes·the·tize** *or* **anaes·the·tise** /əˈnɛsθəˌtaɪz/ *verb* **-tiz·es**; **-tized**; **-tiz·ing** [+ *obj*] *medical* : to give drugs to (a patient) so that no pain can be felt : to give an anesthetic to (a patient) ▪ The doctor *anesthetized* the patient by/with an intravenous injection. ▪ She was *anesthetized* before the operation.

anew /əˈnuː, *Brit* əˈnjuː/ *adv, somewhat formal*
1 : over again : once more ▪ He demonstrated *anew* that he's not a good leader. ▪ These problems must be dealt with *anew*. ▪ The process begins *anew* each spring. ▪ Let's stop for now and start *anew* [=*afresh, again*] in the morning.
2 : in a new or different form ▪ The poem has been translated *anew* for this new book.

an·gel /ˈeɪnʤəl/ *noun, pl* **an·gels** [*count*]
1 : a spiritual being that serves especially as a messenger from God or as a guardian of human beings ▪ an *angel* from heaven ▪ a merciful *angel* = an *angel* of mercy ▪ the *angel* of death [=an angel that comes when someone dies] — see also GUARDIAN ANGEL
2 *informal* : a person (such as a child) who is very good, kind, beautiful, etc. ▪ Your son is such an *angel*! ▪ He's not a bad kid, but he's no *angel*. ▪ Be an *angel* and get me a cup of tea, would you?
– **an·gel·ic** /ænˈʤɛlɪk/ *adj* [*more ~; most ~*] ▪ a child's *angelic* face ▪ an *angelic* voice ▪ *angelic* behavior [=very good behavior] – **an·gel·i·cal·ly** /ænˈʤɛlɪkli/ *adv* ▪ an *angelically* behaved/beautiful child ▪ She smiled *angelically*.

angel food cake *noun, pl* **~ cakes** [*count, noncount*] *US* : a soft and light white cake — compare DEVIL'S FOOD CAKE

[1]an·ger /ˈæŋgɚ/ *noun* [*noncount*] : a strong feeling of being upset or annoyed because of something wrong or bad : the feeling that makes someone want to hurt other people, to shout, etc. : the feeling of being angry ▪ He couldn't hide his *anger* with/at us. ▪ You could hear the *anger* in his voice. ▪ The group expressed/vented its *anger* over/about the company's arrogance. ▪ He said that he had/felt no *anger* towards the person who shot him. ▪ He never raised his voice in *anger*. ▪ She was shaking/trembling in/with *anger*. ▪ He is not easily moved to *anger*. [=he does not become angry easily]

> ***synonyms*** ANGER, RAGE, FURY, and WRATH mean a strong feeling caused by displeasure. ANGER is a general word that applies to many different levels of emotion that may or may not be shown. ▪ She kept her *anger* inside herself. RAGE suggests loss of control because of great anger. ▪ They were screaming with *rage*. FURY suggests a violent anger. ▪ In their *fury* they smashed all the dishes. WRATH is a slightly old-fashioned word that suggests a desire to punish someone or to get revenge for something. ▪ In his *wrath* the king ordered the rebels executed.

[2]anger *verb* **-gers**; **-gered**; **-ger·ing** [+ *obj*] : to make (someone) angry ▪ They were shocked and *angered* by the company's arrogance. ▪ He was *angered* to learn that he had been fired. ▪ It *angered* me that she would say something like that. ▪ He's a gentle man who's not easily *angered*.

an·gi·na /ænˈʤaɪnə/ *noun* [*noncount*] *medical* : a heart disease that causes brief periods of intense chest pain ▪ an attack of *angina* = an *angina* attack — called also *angina pectoris*

anglais see COR ANGLAIS

anglaise see CRÈME ANGLAISE

[1]an·gle /ˈæŋgəl/ *noun, pl* **an·gles** [*count*]
1 a : the difference between the direction of two lines or surfaces that come together : the space or shape formed when two lines or surfaces meet each other ▪ The two lines form a sharp *angle*. = The two lines meet/intersect at a sharp *angle* (to each other). ▪ The two lines meet at a 30-degree *angle* to each other. = There is a 30-degree *angle* between the two lines. ▪ The lines are at sharp *angles* to each other. — see picture at GEOMETRY; see also RIGHT ANGLE **b** — used to describe a surface that is not level ▪ The hill slopes down/up at an *angle* of about 30 degrees. **c** — used to describe something that leans or goes to the side rather than straight up or directly forward ▪ The pole stood ***at an angle***. ▪ The road goes off ***at a sharp/slight angle*** to the right/left. ▪ The rays of light shone through the window *at an angle*.
2 : the position from which something is approached, looked at, etc. ▪ Critics love the clever camera *angles* the director used in the film. ▪ She took pictures of the same scene from several different *angles*. ▪ The soldiers were being attacked from every *angle*.
3 : a way of thinking about, describing, or discussing something ▪ We need to approach the problem from a new/different *angle*. ▪ They considered the question from all *angles*. ▪ The reporter tried to work that *angle* into his story.
4 *chiefly US, informal* **a** : a secret and often improper reason for doing something ▪ I don't trust that guy, but I can't figure out what his *angle* is yet. **b** : a clever and often improper way of doing or getting something ▪ a salesman who's always looking for an *angle* [=looking for a way to convince people to buy the things he is selling]

[2]angle *verb* **angles**; **an·gled**; **an·gling** /ˈæŋglɪŋ/
1 : to turn, move, or point something so that it is not straight or flat [+ *obj*] One spotlight was put high in the corner and *angled* [=*pointed*] down toward the floor. ▪ The seats in the theater were *angled* so that we were looking almost straight up. ▪ The road was *angled* down toward the river. [*no obj*] The road *angled* [=*sloped*] down toward the river.
2 [+ *obj*] : to present (something, such as a news story) in a particular way or from a particular point of view ▪ You should try to *angle* the story so that it appeals to younger readers. — often used as *(be) angled* ▪ The story *was angled* to appeal to younger readers.
– compare [3]ANGLE

[3]angle *verb* **angles**; **angled**; **angling** [*no obj*]
1 : to fish with a hook and line ▪ go *angling* for trout — see also ANGLER, ANGLING
2 *informal* : to try to get what you want in a clever or indirect way ▪ She's been *angling* to get a promotion. — usually + *for* ▪ She's *angling for* a promotion. ▪ They're all *angling for* a place on the committee.
– compare [2]ANGLE

angle bracket *noun, pl* **~ -ets** [*count*] : either one of a pair of punctuation marks ⟨ ⟩ used to enclose written material

an·gler /ˈæŋglɚ/ *noun, pl* **-glers** [*count*] : a person who catches fish for pleasure : FISHERMAN ▪ a skilled *angler*

An·gli·can /ˈæŋglɪkən/ *noun, pl* **-cans** [*count*] : a member of the Church of England
– **Anglican** *adj* ▪ an *Anglican* bishop ▪ the *Anglican* Church

An·gli·can·ism /ˈæŋglɪkəˌnɪzəm/ *noun* [*noncount*] : the beliefs and practices of the Church of England

an·gli·cize *also Brit* **an·gli·cise** /ˈæŋgləˌsaɪz/ *verb* **-ciz·es**; **-cized**; **-ciz·ing** [+ *obj*] : to make (something or someone) English or more English ▪ *anglicize* a French word/name ▪ the word's *anglicized* pronunciation/spelling ▪ The cookbook *anglicized* many exotic dishes to make them easier to prepare.
– **an·gli·ci·za·tion** *also Brit* **an·gli·ci·sa·tion** /ˌæŋgləsəˈzeɪʃən, *Brit* ˌæŋgləˌsaɪˈzeɪʃən/ *noun* [*noncount*]

an·gling /ˈæŋglɪŋ/ *noun* [*noncount*] : the activity or sport of fishing for pleasure ▪ an *angling* adventure/expedition in the mountains

An·glo /ˈæŋgloʊ/ *noun, pl* **An·glos** [*count*] *chiefly US* : a white person who lives in the U.S. and is not Hispanic ▪ a committee with a mixture of blacks, *Anglos*, and Hispanics — often used before another noun ▪ the town's *Anglo* population

An·glo- *combining form* : English or British ▪ *Anglo*-American ▪ *Anglo*phile

An·glo–Amer·i·can /ˌæŋgloʊəˈmerəkən/ *noun, pl* **-cans** [*count*] : an American whose family comes originally from England
– **Anglo–American** *adj*

An·glo·phile /ˈæŋgləˌfajəl/ *noun, pl* **-philes** [*count*] : a non-English person who greatly likes and admires England and English things

An·glo·phobe /ˈæŋgləˌfoʊb/ *noun, pl* **-phobes** [*count*] : a person who dislikes England and English things
– **An·glo·pho·bic** /ˌæŋgləˈfoʊbɪk/ *adj* [*more ~; most ~*]

An·glo·phone /ˈæŋgləˌfoʊn/ *adj* : having English as the main language ▪ the city's *Anglophone* population ▪ an *Anglophone* neighborhood in a French-speaking country
– **Anglophone** *noun, pl* **-phones** [*count*] ▪ a neighborhood that includes both *Anglophones* [=people who speak English as their main language] and Francophones

An·glo–Sax·on /ˌæŋgloʊˈsæksən/ *noun, pl* **-ons**

1 a [*count*] **:** a member of the Germanic people who conquered Britain in the fifth century A.D. **b** [*noncount*] **:** the language of the Anglo-Saxons **:** OLD ENGLISH ▪ There are many words from *Anglo-Saxon* that survive in English today.
2 [*count*] **:** a person whose ancestors were English
– Anglo–Saxon *adj* ▪ an *Anglo-Saxon* person ▪ a white *Anglo-Saxon* Protestant ▪ an *Anglo-Saxon* word

an•go•ra /æŋˈgorə/ *noun, pl* **-ras**
1 [*noncount*] **:** a kind of soft yarn or wool that is made from the hair of the Angora goat or the Angora rabbit — often used before another noun ▪ an *angora* scarf/sweater
2 [*count*] **:** a type of cat, goat, or rabbit that has long soft hair — usually used before another noun ▪ an *Angora* rabbit

an•gry /ˈæŋgri/ *adj* **an•gri•er; -est** [*also more ~; most ~*]
1 a : filled with anger **:** having a strong feeling of being upset or annoyed ▪ I've never seen her look so *angry*. ▪ An *angry* crowd gathered outside the courthouse. ▪ I was *angry* that he had forgotten my birthday. ▪ What made you so *angry*? ▪ He got/grew/became *angry* when he found out about their plans. — often + *at* or *with* ▪ He was *angry at/with* her for staying out so late. ▪ I was *angry at/with* him for forgetting my birthday. — often + *about* or *over* ▪ She's still *angry about/over* the way she's been treated. ▪ Students are *angry about/over* the increase in tuition. ▪ What is she so *angry* [=(*US*) *mad*] *about*? **b :** showing anger ▪ He sent an *angry* letter to the company president. ▪ They had an argument and exchanged some *angry* words. ▪ She gave me an *angry* look.
2 *literary* **:** seeming to show anger **:** threatening or menacing ▪ The sea/sky grew *angry*. [=*dark and stormy*] ▪ *angry* clouds
3 : very red and painful ▪ an *angry* rash/sore/scratch
– an•gri•ly /ˈæŋgrəli/ *adv* ▪ He slammed the door *angrily*. ▪ She glared at us *angrily*.

angst /ˈɑːŋst, ˈæŋst/ *noun* [*noncount*] **:** a strong feeling of being worried or nervous **:** a feeling of anxiety about your life or situation ▪ a film about teenage *angst*

an•guish /ˈæŋgwɪʃ/ *noun* [*noncount*] **:** extreme suffering, grief, or pain ▪ tears/cries of *anguish* ▪ He experienced the *anguish* of divorce after 10 years of marriage. ▪ mental *anguish* ▪ They watched ***in anguish*** as fire spread through the house.
– an•guished /ˈæŋgwɪʃt/ *adj* [*more ~; most ~*] ▪ She looked at me with an *anguished* expression. ▪ I will never forget their *anguished* cries.

an•gu•lar /ˈæŋgjələ/ *adj* [*more ~; most ~*]
1 : having little flesh so that the shapes of your bones can be seen **:** thin and bony ▪ He has an *angular* face. ▪ She's a tall, *angular* girl.
2 : having one or more angles ▪ The house is low and *angular*. ▪ an *angular* mountain peak
– an•gu•lar•i•ty /ˌæŋgjəˈlerəti/ *noun* [*noncount*]

¹an•i•mal /ˈænəməl/ *noun, pl* **-mals** [*count*]
1 : a living thing that is not a human being or plant ▪ people and *animals* ▪ the *animals* in the zoo ▪ the plants and *animals* of the forest ▪ She loves all kinds of *animals*. ▪ pigs, chickens, and other ***farm animals*** [=animals that live on a farm] — often used to refer specifically to mammals as distinguished from other living things (such as fish and birds) ▪ the plants, birds, and *animals* of the forest ▪ furry little *animals* ▪ wild/domestic *animals* — see also PACK ANIMAL, STUFFED ANIMAL
2 : any living thing that is not a plant ▪ Fish, birds, insects, reptiles, mammals, and human beings are all *animals*. ▪ Dogs, like humans, are ***social animals***. [=animals that live in groups] ▪ studying the habits of ***the human animal*** [=the habits of human beings; the habits of people in general]
3 : a person who behaves in a wild, aggressive, or unpleasant way ▪ He's a real *animal*. ▪ You're all behaving like a bunch of *animals*. — see also PARTY ANIMAL
4 *somewhat informal* **:** a person or thing of a particular kind ▪ You want someone who will love you and give you everything you want but ask nothing in return? Let's face it, there's ***no such animal***! [=there is no person who will do that] ▪ Everyone wants a computer that always works perfectly, but there's *no such animal*. ▪ The sport has changed. It's a very/completely ***different animal*** today. [=it's very/completely different today] ▪ His wife has always been a ***political animal***. [=has always been very interested in politics]

²animal *adj*
1 *always used before a noun* **a :** of or relating to animals ▪ studying *animal* behavior ▪ several different plant and *animal* species ▪ the other members of the ***animal kingdom*** [=a basic group of living things that includes all animals] ▪ She's a supporter of ***animal rights***. [=she believes that all animals should be treated in a fair and kind way] **b :** coming from the bodies of animals ▪ *animal* cells/bones/fat/skin ▪ milk, meat, and other *animal* products
2 : of or relating to the body and not to the mind ▪ Their attraction was *animal* [=*physical*] rather than intellectual or spiritual. ▪ *animal* instincts/passion/desires ▪ People were shocked by the *animal* brutality of the attack. ✧ ***Animal magnetism*** is a strong physical or sexual attractiveness. ▪ Women were drawn to his *animal magnetism*. [=*sex appeal*]

animal cracker *noun, pl* **~ -ers** [*count*] **:** a small cookie that is shaped like an animal

animal husbandry *noun* [*noncount*] **:** a kind of farming in which people raise animals for meat, milk, eggs, etc.

¹an•i•mate /ˈænəmət/ *adj, formal* **:** having life **:** alive or living ▪ The lecture was about ancient worship of *animate* and inanimate objects. — opposite INANIMATE

²an•i•mate /ˈænəˌmeɪt/ *verb* **-mates; -mat•ed; -mat•ing** [+ *obj*]
1 : to make (someone or something) lively or excited ▪ A smile *animated* [=*brightened*] his face. ▪ The writer's humor *animates* the novel.
2 : to make (something, such as a drawing) appear to move by creating a series of drawings, pictures, etc., and showing them quickly one after another **:** to make (something) appear to move by using the process of animation ▪ The film's very realistic dinosaurs were *animated* on computers.

an•i•mat•ed /ˈænəˌmeɪtəd/ *adj*
1 [*more ~; most ~*] **:** full of life and energy ▪ He became more *animated* [=*excited, lively*] as he described the project. ▪ She gave an *animated* description of the project. ▪ After dinner, the discussion got more *animated*.
2 : produced by the creation of a series of drawings, pictures, etc., that are shown quickly one after another **:** produced through the process of animation ▪ an *animated* film/cartoon ▪ Many movies for kids are *animated* rather than live-action. ▪ *animated* characters
– an•i•mat•ed•ly *adv* ▪ She spoke *animatedly* about her son's soccer game.

an•i•ma•tion /ˌænəˈmeɪʃən/ *noun, pl* **-tions**
1 [*noncount*] **:** a lively or excited quality ▪ He talked ***with animation*** [=in an excited or animated way] about his vacation.
2 a [*noncount*] **:** a way of making a movie by using a series of drawings, computer graphics, or photographs of objects (such as puppets or models) that are slightly different from one another and that when viewed quickly one after another create the appearance of movement ▪ The *animation* for the film took over two years to complete. ▪ The studio used computer *animation* for some of the special effects. — compare LIVE ACTION **b** [*count*] **:** a movie or brief scene that is made this way ▪ The Web site has hundreds of *animations* you can download.
— see also SUSPENDED ANIMATION

an•i•ma•tor /ˈænəˌmeɪtə/ *noun, pl* **-tors** [*count*] **:** a person who creates animated movies and cartoons

an•i•me /ˈænəˌmeɪ/ *noun* [*noncount*] **:** a style of animation that was created in Japan and that uses colorful images, strong characters, and stories that have a lot of action

an•i•mism /ˈænəˌmɪzəm/ *noun* [*noncount*] **:** the belief that all plants, animals, and objects have spirits

an•i•mos•i•ty /ˌænəˈmɑːsəti/ *noun, pl* **-ties :** a strong feeling of dislike or hatred [*noncount*] There has always been *animosity* [=*hostility*] between them. [=they have always disliked each other] ▪ He felt nothing but *animosity* toward his boss. [=he disliked his boss very much] [*count*] We put aside our personal *animosities* so that we could work together.

an•i•mus /ˈænəməs/ *noun, formal* **:** a strong feeling of dislike or hatred [*noncount*] my *animus* [=(more commonly) *animosity*] towards/against the organization [*singular*] She felt an *animus* against them.

an•ise /ˈænəs/ *noun* [*noncount*] **:** a plant with seeds that are used in cooking and to flavor candies and alcoholic drinks

ani•seed /ˈænəsˌsiːd/ *noun* [*noncount*] **:** the seed of the anise plant

an•is•ette /ˌænəˈsɛt/ *noun* [*noncount*] **:** a sweet alcoholic drink that is flavored with aniseed

an•kle /ˈæŋkəl/ *noun, pl* **an•kles** [*count*] **:** the joint where the foot joins the leg ▪ I hurt/twisted/sprained/broke my *ankle*. ▪ *ankle* boots [=boots that cover only the foot and ankle] — see pictures at FOOT, HUMAN

ankle sock *noun, pl* **~ socks** [*count*] **:** a short sock that reaches slightly above the ankle — called also (*US*) *anklet*; see color picture on page C13

A

an·klet /ˈæŋklət/ *noun, pl* **-klets** [*count*]
1 : a band, ring, or chain that is worn around the ankle — called also *ankle bracelet*
2 *US* **:** ANKLE SOCK

an·nals /ˈænəlz/ *noun* [*plural*]
1 : historical records — usually used in the phrase ***in the annals of*** ▪ This event will go down *in the annals of* sports/war/medicine. [=will be remembered as part of the history of sports/war/medicine] ▪ He became a major figure *in the annals of* justice.
2 : records of the activities of an organization — often used in the titles of publications ▪ She used a quote from the *Annals of Family Medicine.*

an·neal /əˈniːl/ *verb* **-neals; -nealed; -neal·ing** [+ *obj*] *technical* **:** to heat and then slowly cool (metal, glass, etc.) in order to make it stronger

[1]**an·nex** /əˈnɛks/ *verb* **-nex·es; -nexed; -nex·ing** [+ *obj*] **:** to add (an area or region) to a country, state, etc. **:** to take control of (a territory or place) ▪ The United States *annexed* Texas in 1845. ▪ The government planned to *annex* the islands.
— **an·nex·a·tion** /ˌæˌnɛkˈseɪʃən/ *noun, pl* **-tions** [*count, noncount*]

[2]**an·nex** (*chiefly US*) *or Brit* **an·nexe** /ˈæˌnɛks/ *noun, pl* **-nex·es** [*count*]
1 : a building that is attached to or near a larger building and usually used as part of it ▪ The addition will be used as an *annex* to the library. ▪ We store our old files in the *annex.*
2 *chiefly Brit* **:** a section or statement added at the end of a document **:** APPENDIX ▪ an *annexe* to the document

an·ni·hi·late /əˈnajəˌleɪt/ *verb* **-lates; -lat·ed; -lat·ing** [+ *obj*]
1 : to destroy (something or someone) completely ▪ Bombs *annihilated* the city. ▪ The enemy troops were *annihilated.*
2 : to defeat (someone) completely ▪ He *annihilated* his opponent in the last election.
— **an·ni·hi·la·tion** /əˌnajəˈleɪʃən/ *noun* [*noncount*] ▪ The regime is facing *annihilation.* ▪ the *annihilation* of the city

an·ni·ver·sa·ry /ˌænəˈvɚsəri/ *noun, pl* **-ries** [*count*] **:** a date that is remembered or celebrated because a special or notable event occurred on that date in a previous year ▪ the *anniversary* of the invasion/attack ▪ We are celebrating our fifth (wedding) *anniversary* this year. = We are celebrating the fifth *anniversary* of our wedding this year. ▪ The exhibit will close on the 100th *anniversary* of the artist's death. — often used before another noun ▪ an *anniversary* party/celebration/dinner

an·no·tate /ˈænəˌteɪt/ *verb* **-tates; -tat·ed; -tat·ing** [+ *obj*] **:** to add notes or comments to (a text, book, drawing, etc.) ▪ He *annotated* the text at several places. ▪ *annotate* a list
— **annotated** *adj* ▪ a fully *annotated* diagram

an·no·ta·tion /ˌænəˈteɪʃən/ *noun, pl* **-tions**
1 [*count*] **:** a note added to a text, book, drawing, etc., as a comment or explanation ▪ Without the *annotations,* the diagram would be hard to understand.
2 [*noncount*] **:** the act of adding notes or comments to something **:** the act of annotating something ▪ the author's *annotation* of the diagram

an·nounce /əˈnaʊns/ *verb* **-nounc·es; -nounced; -nounc·ing**
1 [+ *obj*] **:** to make (something) known in a public or formal way **:** to officially tell people about (something) ▪ The government *announced* a cut in taxes. ▪ They *announced* plans to move the company out of the state. ▪ The company president has *announced* her retirement. ▪ Their engagement was formally *announced* in the newspaper. — often + *that* ▪ The government *announced that* there would be a cut in taxes. ▪ A voice on the loudspeaker *announced that* the store was closing in 10 minutes. — sometimes used figuratively ▪ The sound of the door slamming *announced* his departure. [=I knew he had left when I heard the door slam]
2 [+ *obj*] **:** to say (something) in a loud and definite way ▪ When everyone was sitting down, she abruptly *announced* [=*declared*] (to us) her intention to quit school. ▪ He suddenly stood up and *announced,* "I'm leaving." = He suddenly stood up and *announced* that he was leaving.
3 [+ *obj*] **:** to say in a formal or official way that something or someone has arrived or is present or ready ▪ She *announced* dinner [=said that dinner was ready] promptly at six o'clock. ▪ Don't enter the president's office until you've been *announced.* [=until the president has been told that you are there] ▪ A man in a tuxedo *announced* each guest [=loudly told everyone the guests' names] as they arrived. ▪ We only had to wait a few minutes before our flight was *announced* [=*called*] over the loudspeaker.
4 [*no obj*] *US* **:** to say that you are a candidate for a political office ▪ He is expected to *announce* for President [=to say that he is going to run for President] tomorrow.
5 [+ *obj*] *US* **:** to describe (a sports event) on radio or television **:** to be the announcer for (a sports event) ▪ Do you know who's going to *announce* tonight's game?

an·nounce·ment /əˈnaʊnsmənt/ *noun, pl* **-ments**
1 [*count*] **:** a written or spoken statement that tells people about something **:** public or formal words that announce something ▪ Many people were surprised by the government's *announcement* that there will be a cut in taxes. ▪ I heard an *announcement* on the loudspeaker saying that the store was closing in 10 minutes. ▪ The company president ***made an announcement*** about the merger. ▪ He asked us to pay attention because he had an important ***announcement to make.*** ▪ I saw their ***wedding announcement*** in the newspaper. ▪ Our program will pause now for a brief ***commercial announcement.*** [=a television or radio commercial]
2 [*noncount*] **:** the act of officially telling people about something **:** the act of announcing something ▪ They have been very busy since the *announcement* of their wedding. ▪ We had to leave before the *announcement* of the winners. [=before the winners were announced]

an·nounc·er /əˈnaʊnsɚ/ *noun, pl* **-ers** [*count*]
1 : a person who gives information on television or radio ▪ He works part-time as an *announcer* for a local radio station.
2 : a person who gives information in a public place (such as a store or airport) especially using a loudspeaker ▪ The racetrack *announcer* said that the next race was about to start. ▪ a ***public address announcer*** [=a person who makes announcements over a public address system]
3 *US* **:** a person who describes a sports event for television or radio ▪ The *announcer* said that the catcher had injured his shoulder.

an·noy /əˈnoɪ/ *verb* **-noys; -noyed; -noy·ing** [+ *obj*] **:** to cause (someone) to feel slightly angry ▪ Her constant chatter *annoyed* [=*irritated*] all of us. ▪ I was *annoyed* [=*upset, bothered*] by his question.
— **annoyed** *adj* [*more ~; most ~*] ▪ She is *annoyed* at/with me. ▪ She looked at him with a very *annoyed* expression. ▪ He was *annoyed* (to realize) that he had forgotten his wallet. — **annoying** *adj* [*more ~; most ~*] ▪ He has several *annoying* [=*irritating*] habits. ▪ That noise is very *annoying.*
— **an·noy·ing·ly** *adv* ▪ She can be *annoyingly* sweet.

an·noy·ance /əˈnojəns/ *noun, pl* **-anc·es**
1 [*noncount*] **:** slight anger **:** the feeling of being annoyed ▪ She expressed *annoyance* at the slow service. ▪ They were late again, (much) ***to our annoyance.*** [=it annoyed us that they were late again] ▪ She shook her head ***in annoyance.*** [=in a way that showed she was annoyed]
2 [*count*] **:** something that causes feelings of slight anger or irritation **:** a source of annoyance ▪ The long wait at the restaurant was a minor *annoyance.* [=*nuisance*]

[1]**an·nu·al** /ˈænjəwəl/ *adj*
1 : happening once a year ▪ The *annual* meeting is in July. ▪ It's time for your *annual* [=*yearly*] checkup. ▪ The company's earnings for last year are published in the *annual* report.
2 : covering the period of a year ▪ We had more snow this year than the average *annual* amount. ▪ The company charges an *annual* fee of $45.
3 *always used before a noun, of a plant* **:** living for only one year or season **:** having a life cycle that is one year or season long ▪ *annual* plants/herbs/flowers — compare [1]BIENNIAL, [1]PERENNIAL
— **an·nu·al·ly** *adv* ▪ We meet *annually* [=*once a year*] in July. ▪ Their earnings increase *annually.* [=*every year*] ▪ A report of the company's earnings is published *annually.*

[2]**annual** *noun, pl* **-als** [*count*]
1 : a plant that lives for only one year or season ▪ We planted some *annuals* in front of the house. — compare [2]BIENNIAL, [2]PERENNIAL
2 : a book or magazine that is published once a year

an·nu·ity /əˈnuːəti, *Brit* əˈnjuːəti/ *noun, pl* **-ities** [*count*]
1 : a fixed amount of money that is paid to someone each year
2 : an insurance policy or an investment that pays someone a fixed amount of money each year ▪ Part of her retirement income will come from an *annuity.*

an·nul /əˈnʌl/ *verb* **-nuls; -nulled; -nul·ling** [+ *obj*] **:** to say officially that something is no longer valid **:** to make (something) legally void • Their marriage was *annulled.* • *annul* a contract/vote/election

– **an·nul·ment** /əˈnʌlmənt/ *noun, pl* **-ments** [*count*] They wanted an *annulment* of their marriage. [*noncount*] The couple has filed for *annulment.*

annum see PER ANNUM

An·nun·ci·a·tion /əˌnʌnsiˈeɪʃən/ *noun*

the Annunciation **:** March 25 celebrated as a Christian festival in memory of the announcement to the Virgin Mary that she would be the mother of Christ

an·ode /ˈæˌnoud/ *noun, pl* **-odes** [*count*] *technical* **:** the part of an electrical device (such as a battery) from which electrons leave — compare CATHODE

an·o·dyne /ˈænəˌdaɪn/ *adj* [*more* ~; *most* ~] *formal* **:** not likely to offend or upset anyone • an *anodyne* [=*innocuous*] question about the weather

anoint /əˈnoɪnt/ *verb* **anoints; anoint·ed; anoint·ing** [+ *obj*]

1 : to put oil on (someone) as part of a religious ceremony • The priest *anointed* them (with oil).

2 : to officially or formally choose (someone) to do or to be something • He *anointed* [=*named, designated*] her his successor. • The magazine *anointed* her the most popular actress of the year.

– **anoint·ment** /əˈnoɪntmənt/ *noun* [*noncount*]

anom·a·lous /əˈnɑːmələs/ *adj* [*more* ~; *most* ~] *somewhat formal* **:** not expected or usual • Researchers could not explain the *anomalous* test results.

– **anom·a·lous·ly** *adj*

anom·a·ly /əˈnɑːməli/ *noun, pl* **-lies** [*count*] *somewhat formal* **:** something that is unusual or unexpected **:** something anomalous • A storm like that is an *anomaly* for this area. [=a storm like that does not usually happen in this area] • We couldn't explain the *anomalies* in the test results. • The doctor detected an *anomaly* [=*irregularity*] in my heartbeat.

anon /əˈnɑːn/ *adv, literary* + *humorous* **:** in a short time **:** SOON • I will answer his letter *anon.*

ever and anon see EVER

anon. *abbr* anonymous; anonymously

an·o·nym·i·ty /ˌænəˈnɪməti/ *noun* [*noncount*] **:** the quality or state of being unknown to most people **:** the quality or state of being anonymous • They are trying to protect their child's *anonymity.* • She enjoyed the *anonymity* of life in a large city. • She agreed to speak to the reporter only ***on condition of anonymity.*** [=only if her name would not be revealed by the reporter]

anon·y·mous /əˈnɑːnəməs/ *adj*

1 : not named or identified • The donor wishes to remain *anonymous.* • An *anonymous* buyer purchased the painting.

2 : made or done by someone unknown • The college received an *anonymous* gift. • He made an *anonymous* phone call to the police. • The reporter got an *anonymous* tip.

3 [*more* ~; *most* ~] **:** not distinct or noticeable **:** lacking interesting or unusual characteristics • She works in an *anonymous* [=*bland, nondescript*] brick building. • His was just another *anonymous* face in the crowd.

– **anon·y·mous·ly** *adv* • They made the donation *anonymously.*

an·o·rak /ˈænəˌræk/ *noun, pl* **-raks** [*count*]

1 : a jacket that has a hood and that is long enough to cover your hips ✧ An anorak is usually worn to protect against wind and rain.

2 *Brit, informal* + *disapproving* **:** a person who is extremely interested in something that other people find boring • political *anoraks*

an·orex·ia /ˌænəˈrɛksijə/ *noun* [*noncount*] **:** a serious physical and emotional illness in which an abnormal fear of being fat leads to very poor eating habits and dangerous weight loss ✧ *Anorexia* most commonly affects teenage girls and young women. — called also *anorexia nervosa*; compare BULIMIA

– **an·orex·ic** /ˌænəˈrɛksɪk/ *adj* • an *anorexic* young woman

– **anorexic** *noun, pl* **-ics** [*count*] • She's an *anorexic.* [=a person suffering from anorexia]

¹an·oth·er /əˈnʌðɚ/ *adj*

1 : one more in addition • Should we open *another* bottle of wine? • Don't say *another* word. • It will take *another* two years [=an additional two years; two more years] to finish the building. • That's *another* way of saying the same thing. • As far as I'm concerned, "frugal" is just *another* word for "cheap." [="frugal" means the same thing as "cheap"] • We had dinner at ***another one*** of the city's many Italian restaurants. • This is ***yet another*** example of government waste. • If you ask me, he's ***just another*** overpaid athlete. [=he's one of many overpaid athletes]

2 : some other **:** different from the first or other one • We'll plan to meet again (at) *another* time. • We'll discuss this again on *another* occasion. • The view is very different when it is seen from *another* angle. • Please bring me *another* cup. This one is chipped. • Since his illness he has been *another* man. [=he has been very different from how he was before he became sick] • Tomorrow is *another* day. • the splendors of *another* age [=a past age] • I'm willing to help you, but if you're asking for money, that's ***another thing/matter/story.*** [=I'm willing to help you but that does not mean that I'm willing to give you money] • Complaining about problems is one thing, but finding solutions to them is ***another thing*** altogether/entirely. [=it is more difficult to find solutions to problems than to complain about them]

3 : similar or equal to a particular person or thing • He thought of himself as *another* Napoleon. [=as a person who was like Napoleon] • The city advertises itself as *another* Las Vegas.

²another *pronoun*

1 : one more of the same kind **:** another one • I've had one drink, but I think I'll have *another.* • One copy of the letter was sent out, and *another* was placed in the files. • One thief carried a gun, *another* (carried) a knife. • This cup is chipped. Could you please bring me *another*? • We had dinner at *another* of the city's many Italian restaurants.

2 : one that is different **:** someone or something else • She's not comfortable living in *another's* house. [=in another person's house] • Complaining about problems is one thing, but finding solutions to them is *another.* [=it is more difficult to find solutions to problems than to complain about them] • The family seems to move from one city to *another.*

3 — used in phrases with *one* or (less commonly) *some* to refer to something that is not specified • We all do foolish things ***at one time or another.*** [=*sometimes, on occasion*] • They had to change their plans ***for one/some reason or another.*** [=for some reason] • He vowed that he would succeed (in) ***one way or another.*** [=vowed that he would find a way to succeed] • a lock ***of one kind/sort/type or another*** [=some kind/sort/type of lock] • What with ***one thing and another,*** we still haven't finished. [=we still haven't finished because of various things that have happened] — see also ONE ANOTHER

one after another **1 :** in a continuing series • The buses kept arriving, *one after another.* • *One* person *after another* walked out of the concert. **2 :** each one in a continuing series • *One after another* of her friends got married and moved away.

A. N. Other /ˌeɪˌɛnˈʌðɚ/ *noun, Brit, informal* — used to refer to another person who is not known or named • The rumor was traced to Smith, Jones, and *A. N. Other.*

¹an·swer /ˈænsɚ, *Brit* ˈɑːnsə/ *noun, pl* **-swers**

1 [*count*] **a :** something you say or write when someone asks you a question • I asked him a simple question and he gave me a long and confusing *answer.* • I didn't believe her *answer.* • They wouldn't give me a straight *answer* to my question. • There will be a ***question and answer session*** [=a period of time when people can have their questions answered] following the speech. **b :** a response to a question that is meant to show whether or not you know something (such as a question asked as part of an exam) • I didn't know the right/correct *answer.* • That is the wrong/incorrect *answer.* **c :** the correct response to a question • Do you know the *answer* to this question? • He knew the *answers* to only 3 of the 10 questions. • The *answers* are listed in the back of the book.

2 : something you say or write as a reaction to something someone else has said or done [*count*] I sent a letter of complaint but I never got an *answer.* [=*response*] • I finally received an *answer* [=*reply*] to my letter. • When I say something to you I expect an *answer.* [=*response*] • I called out her name but I got no *answer.* [=*reply*] [*noncount*] ***In answer*** [=*in response*] to your request we are sending a catalog.

3 [*count*] **:** something you do in response to something that has happened **:** a reaction to something — usually singular • I called several times but there was no *answer.* [=no one answered the phone when I called] • I got no *answer* when I called. • I knocked on the door but there was no *answer.* [=no one opened the door when I knocked on it] • The company

A

had no *answer* when its competitors lowered their prices. • When she called him a liar, his only *answer* was to walk out. • Our team had no *answer* for the other team's strong offense. [=our team could not win because of the other team's strong offense]

4 [*count*] **:** a solution to a problem **:** something that makes a bad situation better • More money is not the *answer* (to our problems). • It's a very difficult problem, and I don't know what the *answer* is. • They don't have *answers* for everything. = They don't have an *answer* for everything. • For a tough issue like this there are no easy *answers*. • He thinks he ***has/knows all the answers***. [=he thinks that he knows the solution to every problem] ✧ Someone or something that is ***the answer to (all) your prayers*** provides you with something that you want or need. • If you've been wanting to get your schedule organized, this new software is *the answer to (all) your prayers*. • They were desperate to find a good lawyer, and they thought she might be *the answer to their prayers*.

5 [*count*] **:** something or someone that resembles a well-known or successful thing or person — + *to* • The program is television's *answer to* newsmagazines. [=the program is similar to a newsmagazine]

²answer *verb* **-swers; -swered; -swer·ing**

1 a : to say or write something when someone asks you a question **:** to give an answer to (a question) [+ *obj*] She *answered* all my questions. • He *answered* only three of the test questions correctly. [*no obj*] When the police asked him his name, he refused to *answer*. • She *answered* correctly/incorrectly. **b** [+ *obj*] **:** to say or write (something) as a reply • When asked if she would run for office, she *answered* that she hadn't decided. = When asked if she would run for office, she *answered* "I haven't decided." **c** [+ *obj*] **:** to reply to (someone) **:** to say or write something as a response to (someone) • When I ask you a question I expect you to *answer* me! • *Answer* me this: where have you put my money?

2 a : to write a response to a letter, e-mail message, etc. [*no obj*] I sent her a letter asking for her help, but she never *answered*. [+ *obj*] She never *answered* my letter. = She never *answered* me. **b :** to pick up (a ringing telephone) [*no obj*] The phone rang repeatedly, but no one *answered*. [+ *obj*] Would somebody please *answer* the phone? • *answer* a phone call **c :** to open a door when someone knocks on it [*no obj*] I knocked on the door but no one *answered*. [+ *obj*] No one *answered* the door.

3 : to act in response to (something) **:** to react to (something) by taking some action [+ *obj*] I got the job by *answering* a "help wanted" ad in the newspaper. • When the war began, thousands of young men *answered* the call to arms. [=thousands of young men joined the armed forces] • He *answered* her anger with indifference. [=he responded to her anger by acting indifferent] [*no obj*] The home team scored first but the visiting team *answered* quickly. [=the visiting team also scored soon after the home team scored]

4 [+ *obj*] **:** to say something in response to (something, such as an accusation) **:** to defend yourself against (something) • The police chief will appear in court today to *answer* charges of corruption. • *answer* criticism

5 [+ *obj*] **:** to be the same as (something) **:** to be in agreement with (something, such as a description) • The suspect *answered* [=*matched*] the description that had been given by the witness. — see also ANSWER TO 1 (below)

6 [+ *obj*] **:** to be what is needed for (something) • We don't have a sink, but this bucket will *answer* [=(more commonly) *serve*] the purpose. [=we can use this bucket as a sink] — see also ANSWER FOR 1c (below)

answer back [*phrasal verb*] **1** *somewhat informal* **:** to reply to someone especially in a rude way • impolite children who *answer back* [=*talk back*] when their teacher corrects them **2** ***answer (someone) back*** **:** to reply rudely to (someone) • He became angry when she *answered him back*.

answer for [*phrasal verb*] **1** ***answer for (something)*** **a :** to take responsibility for (something) • I can't *answer for* their safety. [=I can't promise that they will be safe] **:** to be responsible for (something) • The company will have to *answer for* any damage done by its employees. • She ***has a lot to answer for***. [=she is responsible for many bad things that have happened] **b :** to be punished for (something) • He must *answer for* his crimes. **c** *US* **:** to be used as (something) **:** to serve as (something) • The old bucket *answered for* a sink. [=the old bucket was used as a sink] — see also ²ANSWER 6 (above) **2** ***answer for (someone)*** **:** to say what someone else thinks **:** to give the opinion of (someone else) • I like the proposal myself, but I can't *answer for* my boss.

answer someone's prayers **:** to provide what someone hopes or prays for • They hoped that God would *answer their prayers* and restore their son's health. • *Their prayers were answered* when their son's health was restored.

answer to [*phrasal verb*] **1** ***answer to (something)*** **:** to be the same as (something) **:** to be in agreement with (something, such as a description) • The suspect *answers to* [=*answers, matches*] the description perfectly. — see also ²ANSWER 5 (above) **2** ***answer to (someone)*** **:** to be required to explain your actions to (someone) • He has to *answer to* a tough boss. **3** ***answer to a name*** ✧ If an animal, such as a dog, *answers to a name*, it responds when it is called by that name. • This dog *answers to the name* (of) "Rover." This phrase is also used to refer to the name used by a person. • My uncle's real name is "Edwin," but he doesn't *answer to that name*. He prefers to be called "Ed."

— an·swer·er /ˈænsərɚ/ *noun, pl* **-ers** [*count*]

an·swer·able /ˈænsərəbəl, *Brit* ˈɑːnsərəbəl/ *adj*

1 *not used before a noun* **a :** required to explain actions or decisions *to* someone • Political leaders need to be *answerable to* [=*accountable to*] the people they represent. • a powerful businesswoman who seems to think that she's *answerable to* no one **b :** responsible *for* something • The company is *answerable for* [=*accountable for*] any damage caused by its employees.

2 : capable of being answered • an easily *answerable* question

answering machine *noun, pl* ~ **-chines** [*count*] **:** a machine that answers the telephone and records messages left by the people who call • I haven't spoken to him yet, but he left a message on my *answering machine*.

answering service *noun, pl* ~ **-vices** [*count*] **:** a business that answers telephone calls and takes messages for the people and businesses that hire it • The doctor is not in the office now, but you can reach her *answering service* at this number if you have an emergency.

an·swer·phone /ˈænsɚˌfoun, *Brit* ˈɑːnsəˌfəun/ *noun, pl* **-phones** [*count*] *Brit* **:** ANSWERING MACHINE

ant /ˈænt/ *noun, pl* **ants** [*count*] **:** a kind of small insect that lives in an organized social group • a colony of *ants* = an *ant* colony — see color picture on page C10

ants in your pants *informal* **:** a strong feeling of wanting to be active and not wait for something **:** a feeling of excitement and impatience • a little kid with *ants in her pants*

¹-ant /ənt/ *noun suffix* **:** a person or thing that does a specified thing • assist*ant* • attend*ant* • immigr*ant* • cool*ant* • pollut*ant*

²-ant *adj suffix* **:** doing a specified thing or behaving in a specified way • propell*ant* • hesit*ant* • observ*ant*

ant·ac·id /æntˈæsəd/ *noun, pl* **-ids** [*count, noncount*] **:** medicine that prevents or lessens the pain caused by having too much acid in your stomach

an·tag·o·nism /ænˈtægəˌnɪzəm/ *noun, pl* **-nisms :** a strong feeling of dislike or hatred **:** a desire to oppose something you dislike or disagree with — often + *between* or *toward* [*noncount*] There is a long history of *antagonism* [=*hostility, enmity*] *between* the two nations. • The policy is creating *antagonism* [=*opposition*] *between* the staff and management. • I never felt any *antagonism* [=*animosity*] *toward* her. [*plural*] The region has a long history of ethnic *antagonisms*.

an·tag·o·nist /ænˈtægənɪst/ *noun, pl* **-nists** [*count*] **:** a person who opposes another person • He faced his *antagonist* [=(more commonly) *opponent, adversary*] in a series of debates.

an·tag·o·nis·tic /ænˌtægəˈnɪstɪk/ *adj* [*more* ~; *most* ~] **:** showing dislike or opposition **:** showing antagonism • They found it impossible to deal with such *antagonistic* groups. — often + *to* or *toward* • Many people are *antagonistic* [=*opposed, hostile*] *to* the idea of making major changes to the building. • The two groups have always been *antagonistic toward* each other. • She was *antagonistic toward* the media.

— an·tag·o·nis·tic·al·ly /ænˌtægəˈnɪstɪkli/ *adv* • Many people reacted *antagonistically* to her comments.

an·tag·o·nize *also Brit* **an·tag·o·nise** /ænˈtægəˌnaɪz/ *verb* **-niz·es; -nized; -niz·ing** [+ *obj*] **:** to cause (someone) to feel hostile or angry **:** to irritate or upset (someone) • He didn't mean to *antagonize* you. • Her comments *antagonized* many people.

ant·arc·tic *or* **Ant·arc·tic** /æntˈɑɚktɪk/ *adj, always used before a noun* **:** of or relating to the South Pole or the region around it • off the *antarctic* coast • The group is involved in

Antarctic exploration. • *Antarctic* waters — compare ARCTIC

Antarctic Circle *noun*

the Antarctic Circle : an imaginary line that goes around the Earth near the South Pole

[1]**an·te** /ˈænti/ *noun, pl* **an·tes** [*count*] : the amount of money that a player must bet at the beginning of play in a poker game — usually singular • The dealer called for a dollar *ante*. — see also PENNY-ANTE

raise the ante or up the ante : to increase an amount or level: such as **a** : to raise the cost or price • The popular actor first demanded twice the salary offered him but then kept *upping the ante*. **b** : to increase the risk or possible harm that could result from something — often + *on* • The new law *ups the ante on* [=increases penalties for] people who cheat on their taxes. **c** : to set a higher standard or goal — often + *on* • The film *ups the ante on* special effects.

[2]**ante** *verb* **antes; an·ted; an·te·ing** : to pay the amount of money required to start play in a poker game [*no obj*] Did everyone at the table *ante*? — usually + *up* • The dealer waited until everyone had *anted up* before he dealt the cards. [+ *obj*] Everyone *anted up* a dollar. — often used figuratively • Parents are usually expected to *ante up* [=*pay*] for their children's college education. • They had to *ante up* [=*pay*] $5,000 to attend the senator's banquet.

ante- *prefix*

1 : before or earlier • *ante*date • *ante*natal

2 : in front of • *ante*room

ant·eat·er /ˈæntˌiːtɚ/ *noun, pl* **-ers** [*count*] : an animal that has a very long nose and tongue and eats ants

an·te·bel·lum /ˌæntɪˈbɛləm/ *adj, always used before a noun, formal* : occurring in the southern U.S. during the time before the American Civil War • the *antebellum* South • *antebellum* society/houses

[1]**an·te·ced·ent** /ˌæntəˈsiːdənt/ *noun, pl* **-ents**

1 [*count*] *grammar* : a word or phrase that is represented by another word (such as a pronoun) • "John" is the *antecedent* of the pronoun "him" in "Mary saw John and thanked him."

2 [*count*] *formal* : something that came before something else and may have influenced or caused it • The events were *antecedents* of/to the war. [=the events helped to cause the war] • the *antecedents* of rap music [=music that came before and influenced rap music]

3 ***antecedents*** [*plural*] *formal* : the people in a family who lived in past times • He is proud of his Scottish *antecedents*. [=(more commonly) *ancestors*]

[2]**antecedent** *adj, formal* : earlier in time • These *antecedent* [=*prior, previous*] events affected the outcome of the war.

an·te·cham·ber /ˈæntɪˌʧeɪmbɚ/ *noun, pl* **-bers** [*count*] *formal* : ANTEROOM

an·te·date /ˈæntɪˌdeɪt/ *verb* **-dates; -dat·ed; -dat·ing** [+ *obj*] *formal*

1 : to give an earlier date rather than the actual date to (something) • *antedate* a check — opposite POSTDATE

2 : to be earlier or older than (something) : PREDATE • The church *antedates* the village itself. — opposite POSTDATE

an·te·di·lu·vi·an /ˌæntɪdəˈluːvijən/ *adj* [*more* ~; *most* ~] *formal* : very old or old-fashioned • an *antediluvian* automobile • He has *antediluvian* notions/ideas about the role of women in the workplace.

an·te·lope /ˈæntɪˌloʊp/ *noun, pl* **an·te·lopes** *or* **antelope** [*count*] : an animal in Africa and Asia that looks like a deer, has horns pointing up and back, and runs very fast

an·te·na·tal /ˌæntɪˈneɪtl/ *adj, always used before a noun, Brit, medical* : PRENATAL

an·ten·na /ænˈtɛnə/ *noun, pl* **-nae** /-ni/ *or* **-nas** [*count*]

1 : a thin sensitive organ on the head of an insect, crab, etc., that is used mainly to feel and touch things — sometimes used figuratively • a Senator with sensitive political *antennae* [=a Senator who is very aware of political issues and attitudes] ✧ The plural of *antenna* in this sense is usually *antennae*.

2 *chiefly US* : a device (such as a wire or a metal rod) for sending or receiving radio or television signals • a TV *antenna* [=(*chiefly Brit*) *aerial*] — see picture at CAR ✧ The plural of *antenna* in this sense is usually *antennas*.

an·te·ri·or /ænˈtirijɚ/ *adj, technical* : near or toward the front of something (such as the body) • the *anterior* part of the brain — opposite POSTERIOR

an·te·room /ˈæntɪˌruːm/ *noun, pl* **-rooms** [*count*] : a small room that is connected to a larger room and used as a place for people to wait before going into the larger room — called also *antechamber*

an·them /ˈænθəm/ *noun, pl* **-thems** [*count*]

1 : a formal song of loyalty, praise, or happiness • patriotic *anthems* — see also NATIONAL ANTHEM

2 : a song that is important to a particular group of people • teen *anthems*

— **an·the·mic** /ˌænˈθiːmɪk/ *adj* • an *anthemic* song/chorus

an·ther /ˈænθɚ/ *noun, pl* **-thers** [*count*] *technical* : the part of a flower that contains pollen

ant·hill /ˈæntˌhɪl/ *noun, pl* **-hills** [*count*] : a mound of dirt made by ants when building a nest

an·thol·o·gy /ænˈθɑːləʤi/ *noun, pl* **-gies** [*count*]

1 : a published collection of writings (such as poems or short stories) by different authors • an *anthology* of American poetry

2 : a collection of works of art or music • The band will be releasing an *anthology* of their earlier albums.

an·thra·cite /ˈænθrəˌsaɪt/ *noun* [*noncount*] : a hard type of coal that burns slowly without much smoke or flame

an·thrax /ˈænˌθræks/ *noun* [*noncount*] : a serious disease that affects animals (such as cattle and sheep) and sometimes people

an·thro·poid /ˈænθrəˌpɔɪd/ *adj, technical* : resembling a human being • *anthropoid* apes

— **anthropoid** *noun, pl* **-poids** [*count*] • gorillas and other *anthropoids*

an·thro·pol·o·gy /ˌænθrəˈpɑːləʤi/ *noun* [*noncount*] : the study of human races, origins, societies, and cultures

— **an·thro·po·log·i·cal** /ˌænθrəpəˈlɑːʤɪkəl/ *adj* • *anthropological* research — **an·thro·po·log·i·cal·ly** /ˌænθrəpəˈlɑːʤɪkli/ *adv* — **an·thro·pol·o·gist** /ˌænθrəˈpɑːləʤɪst/ *noun, pl* **-gists** [*count*]

an·thro·po·morph·ic /ˌænθrəpəˈmoɚfɪk/ *adj*

1 : described or thought of as being like human beings in appearance, behavior, etc. • a story in which the characters are *anthropomorphic* animals

2 : considering animals, objects, etc., as having human qualities • *anthropomorphic* beliefs about nature

an·ti /ˈænti, ˈænˌtaɪ/ *prep, informal* : opposed to (something or someone) : AGAINST • She's *anti* big corporations.

an·ti- /ˌænˌtaɪ, ˌænti; *sometimes* ˌæntɪ *before consonants*/ *prefix*

1 : opposite to something • *anti*climax • *anti*social

2 : against someone or something • *anti*government [=opposed to the government] • *anti*smoking • *anti*war — often used with a hyphen • *anti*-American • *anti*-poverty • *anti*-gun — opposite PRO-

3 : acting to prevent something • *anti*bacterial • *anti*freeze • *anti*theft

4 : fighting or defending against something • *anti*aircraft

an·ti·air·craft /ˌæntiˈeɚˌkræft, *Brit* ˌæntiˈeəˌkrɑːft/ *adj, always used before a noun* : used for defense against military aircraft • *antiaircraft* guns/missiles

an·ti·bac·te·ri·al /ˌænˌtaɪbækˈtirijəl/ *adj* : able to kill bacteria • *antibacterial* soap

an·ti·bi·ot·ic /ˌænˌtaɪbaɪˈɑːtɪk/ *noun, pl* **-ics** [*count*] *medical* : a drug that is used to kill harmful bacteria and to cure infections

— **antibiotic** *adj* • an *antibiotic* pill • *antibiotic* drugs

an·ti·body /ˈæntɪˌbɑːdi/ *noun, pl* **-bod·ies** [*count*] *medical* : a substance produced by the body to fight disease

an·tic /ˈæntɪk/ *adj* [*more* ~; *most* ~] : very playful, funny, or silly • an *antic* comedian • *antic* humor — see also ANTICS

an·tic·i·pate /ænˈtɪsəˌpeɪt/ *verb* **-pates; -pat·ed; -pat·ing** [+ *obj*]

1 : to think of (something that will or might happen in the future) : EXPECT • The cost turned out to be higher than *anticipated*. • They do not *anticipate* [=*foresee*] any major problems during construction. • The hotel *anticipated* my every need. [=I didn't have to ask for anything because they already provided it] • The author *anticipated* objections to his theory. • The organizers of the fair *anticipate* a large crowd. • I did not *anticipate* having to pay for your ticket. • The boxer tried to *anticipate* [=*predict*] his opponent's next move.

2 : to expect or look ahead to (something) with pleasure : to look forward to (something) • He eagerly *anticipated* her arrival.

3 *formal* : to do something before someone else • His use of composition *anticipated* later Renaissance paintings. = He *anticipated* later Renaissance painters in his use of composition.

an·tic·i·pa·tion /ænˌtɪsəˈpeɪʃən/ *noun* [*noncount*]

A

1 : a feeling of excitement about something that is going to happen • She had a feeling of great *anticipation* before her graduation ceremony. • He looked forward to the party with *anticipation*. • The actor's fans were trembling with/in *anticipation* [=*excitement*] when his limousine drove up.

2 : the act of preparing for something • They hired extra police officers ***in anticipation of*** a big crowd [=because they expected a big crowd] at the concert.

– **an·tic·i·pa·to·ry** /æn'tɪsəpə,tori, *Brit* æn,tɪsə'peɪtri, æn'tɪsəpətri/ *adj, formal* • the *anticipatory* excitement before a baseball play-off game • The town took *anticipatory* measures to prevent a flood.

an·ti·cli·max /,æn,taɪ'klaɪ,mæks/ *noun, pl* **-max·es** : something that is much less exciting or dramatic than it was expected to be : a dull or disappointing ending or result [*count*] The last chapter of the book was an *anticlimax*. [*noncount*] The movie ended in *anticlimax*.

– **an·ti·cli·mac·tic** /,æn,taɪ,klaɪ'mæktɪk/ *adj* • The last chapter of the book was *anticlimactic*. • The trial was *anticlimactic*, since it ended without a verdict.

an·ti·clock·wise /,æn,taɪ'klɑ:k,waɪz/ *adj or adv, Brit* : COUNTERCLOCKWISE

an·ti·co·ag·u·lant /,æn,taɪ,koʊ'ægjələnt/ *noun, pl* **-lants** [*count*] *medical* : a substance that prevents blood from forming clots

an·tics /'æntɪks/ *noun* [*plural*] *often disapproving* : funny or playful actions or behavior • I'm tired of his childish *antics*.

an·ti·cy·clone /,æntɪ'saɪ,kloʊn/ *noun, pl* **-clones** [*count*] *technical* : winds that turn around an area of high pressure and that often bring clear, dry air ✧ Anticyclones and cyclones turn in opposite directions.

– **an·ti·cy·clon·ic** /,æntɪsaɪ'klɑ:nɪk/ *adj*

an·ti·de·pres·sant /,æn,taɪdɪ'prɛsn̩t/ *noun, pl* **-sants** [*count*] *medical* : a drug that is used to relieve or prevent depression in a person

– **antidepressant** *adj* • *antidepressant* drugs/medication

an·ti·dote /'æntɪ,doʊt/ *noun, pl* **-dotes** [*count*]

1 : a substance that stops the harmful effects of a poison • There is no *antidote* to/for this poison.

2 : something that corrects or improves the bad effects of something • For him, racing motorcycles is a great *antidote* to boredom.

an·ti·freeze /'æntɪ,fri:z/ *noun* [*noncount*] : a substance that is added to the water in a vehicle's engine to prevent it from freezing

an·ti·gen /'æntɪʤən/ *noun, pl* **-gens** [*count*] *medical* : a harmful substance that causes the body to produce antibodies

an·ti·he·ro /'æn,taɪ,hiroʊ/ *noun, pl* **-roes** [*count*] : a main character in a book, play, movie, etc., who does not have the usual good qualities that are expected in a hero

an·ti·his·ta·mine /,æntɪ'hɪstə,mi:n/ *noun, pl* **-mines** [*count, noncount*] *medical* : a drug that is used to treat allergic reactions and colds

an·ti–in·flam·ma·to·ry /,æntijɪn'flæmə,tori, *Brit* ,æntijɪn'flæmətri/ *adj, medical* : used to control or reduce inflammation • *anti-inflammatory* drugs

– **anti–inflammatory** *noun, pl* **-ries** [*count*]

an·ti·lock /'æn,taɪ,lɑ:k/ *adj, always used before a noun* : made to keep the wheels of a vehicle from causing a skid when the vehicle stops suddenly • *Antilock* braking systems give the driver greater control during a sudden stop. • *antilock* brakes

an·ti·mo·ny /'æntə,moʊni, *Brit* æn'tɪməni/ *noun* [*noncount*] *technical* : a silvery-white metal that breaks easily and that is used especially in alloys

an·ti·ox·i·dant /,æntɪ'ɑ:ksədənt/ *noun, pl* **-dants** [*count*] : a substance that is added to food and other products to prevent harmful chemical reactions in which oxygen is combined with other substances

an·ti·pas·to /,æntɪ'pɑ:stoʊ, ,æntɪ'pæstoʊ, *Brit* 'æntɪ,pæstəʊ/ *noun* [*noncount*] : a plate of cold meat or vegetables that is served especially as the first course of a meal

an·tip·a·thy /æn'tɪpəθi/ *noun, pl* **-thies** *formal* : a strong feeling of dislike [*noncount*] There has always been strong *antipathy* between the two groups. • feelings of *antipathy* [*count*] The author's *antipathies* and prejudices are obvious. — often + *to* or *toward* • The author's *antipathy to/toward* other cultures is obvious.

– **an·ti·pa·thet·ic** /,æntɪpə'θɛtɪk/ *adj* • *antipathetic* views/feelings — often + *to* • He is *antipathetic to* change.

an·ti·per·son·nel /,æn,taɪpəsə'nɛl/ *adj, always used before a noun* : made to kill and injure people rather than to destroy buildings, vehicles, etc. • *antipersonnel* land mines

an·ti·per·spi·rant /,æntɪ'pəsprənt/ *noun, pl* **-rants** [*count, noncount*] : a substance that is used to prevent sweating — compare DEODORANT

An·tip·o·des /æn'tɪpə,di:z/ *noun*

the Antipodes *chiefly Brit* : Australia and New Zealand

– **an·tip·o·de·an** *or* **Antipodean** /æn,tɪpə'di:jən/ *adj* • *antipodean* destinations • her *Antipodean* friends [=friends from Australia or New Zealand] – **antipodean** *or* **Antipodean** *noun, pl* **-ans** [*count*]

[1]**an·ti·quar·i·an** /,æntə'kwerijən/ *noun, pl* **-ans** [*count*] : a person who collects, studies, or sells valuable old things — called also *antiquary*

[2]**antiquarian** *adj* : relating to the collection and study of valuable old things (such as old books) • *antiquarian* bookstores

an·ti·quary /'æntə,kweri, *Brit* 'æntəkwəri/ *noun, pl* **-quaries** [*count*] : ANTIQUARIAN

an·ti·quat·ed /'æntə,kweɪtəd/ *adj* [*more* ~; *most* ~] : very old and no longer useful, popular, or accepted : very old-fashioned or obsolete • *antiquated* [=*outmoded, outdated*] medical procedures • He has some pretty *antiquated* opinions about politics.

[1]**an·tique** /æn'ti:k/ *adj* : belonging to an earlier period, style, or fashion : old and often valuable • *antique* furniture • an *antique* clock/car ***synonyms*** see [1]OLD

[2]**antique** *noun, pl* **-tiques** [*count*] : art, furniture, jewelry, etc., that was made at an earlier time and is often valuable • She collects *antiques*. • That car is an *antique*. — often used before another noun • an *antique* collector/dealer/shop

an·tiq·ui·ty /æn'tɪkwəti/ *noun, pl* **-ties**

1 [*noncount*] : ancient times • Greek/Roman *antiquity* • The town dates from *antiquity*. • late *antiquity* • A palace stood here in *antiquity*.

2 [*noncount*] : very great age • a castle of great *antiquity* [=a very old castle]

3 ***antiquities*** [*plural*] : objects from ancient times • a museum of Roman *antiquities*

an·ti–Sem·ite /,æn,taɪ'sɛ,maɪt/ *noun, pl* **-ites** [*count*] : someone who hates Jewish people

an·ti–Se·mit·ic /,æn,taɪsə'mɪtɪk/ *adj* [*more* ~; *most* ~] : feeling or showing hatred of Jewish people • *anti-Semitic* literature • The group denied being *anti-Semitic*.

an·ti–Sem·i·tism /,æn,taɪ'sɛmə,tɪzəm/ *noun* [*noncount*] : hatred of Jewish people

an·ti·sep·tic /,æntə'sɛptɪk/ *noun, pl* **-tics** : a substance that prevents infection in a wound by killing bacteria [*count*] Clean the affected area with an *antiseptic*. [*noncount*] He applied *antiseptic* to the wound.

– **antiseptic** *adj* • *antiseptic* cream/lotion/soap

an·ti·so·cial /,æn,taɪ'soʊʃəl/ *adj* [*more* ~; *most* ~]

1 : violent or harmful to people • Crime is *antisocial*. • *antisocial* tendencies/attitudes/behavior

2 : not friendly to other people • My neighbor is *antisocial*. • She's not being *antisocial*; she's just shy at parties.

an·ti·tank /'æntɪ,tæŋk/ *adj, always used before a noun* : used to destroy or stop tanks • *antitank* weapons

an·tith·e·sis /æn'tɪθəsəs/ *noun, pl* **-e·ses** /-ə,si:z/ [*count*] *formal*

1 : the exact opposite of something or someone • poverty and its *antithesis* [=*opposite*], wealth — often + *of* • She is the *antithesis of* a politician. [=her character is the opposite of a politician's] • His lifestyle is the *antithesis of* healthy living.

2 : the state of two things that are directly opposite to each other — often + *of* or *between* • The poem reflects the *antithesis of/between* good and evil.

an·ti·thet·i·cal /,æntə'θɛtɪkəl/ *adj* [*more* ~; *most* ~] *formal* : directly opposite or opposed • the *antithetical* forces of good and evil — often + *to* • The court's ruling is *antithetical to* the very idea of democracy.

an·ti·trust /,æntaɪ'trʌst/ *adj, always used before a noun, law* : protecting against unfair business practices that limit competition or control prices • *antitrust* laws • an *antitrust* violation [=a violation of an antitrust law]

an·ti·vi·rus /,æntɪ'vaɪrəs/ *adj* : used to protect a computer from viruses • *antivirus* software

ant·ler /'æntlə/ *noun, pl* **-lers** [*count*] : the horn of a deer or similar animal

– **ant·lered** /'æntləd/ *adj* • a deer with an *antlered* head

an·to·nym /ˈæntəˌnɪm/ *noun, pl* **-nyms** [*count*] **:** a word with a meaning that is opposite to the meaning of another word • "Hot" and "cold" are *antonyms*. — compare SYNONYM

ant·sy /ˈæntsi/ *adj* **ant·si·er; -est** *chiefly US, informal*
1 : impatient and unable to keep still • The children were getting *antsy* [=*fidgety, restless*] on the trip in the car.
2 : nervous about what might happen • Investors are *antsy* [=*anxious*] as stock prices continue to decline.

anus /ˈeɪnəs/ *noun, pl* **anus·es** [*count*] **:** the opening between a person's buttocks through which solid waste passes from the body

an·vil /ˈænvəl/ *noun, pl* **-vils** [*count*] **:** a heavy iron block on which heated metal is shaped by hitting it with a hammer

anvil

anx·i·ety /æŋˈzajəti/ *noun, pl* **-et·ies**
1 : fear or nervousness about what might happen [*noncount*] feelings of anger and *anxiety* • She suffers from chronic/acute *anxiety*. • He suffers from test *anxiety*. [=excessive fear about taking tests] • He's been feeling a lot of *anxiety* about/over his new job. [*count*] — usually plural • modern *anxieties* about terrorism • She discussed her *anxieties* with her sister.
2 [*singular*] **:** a feeling of wanting *to do* something very much • She has always had an *anxiety to succeed*. [=she has always been anxious to succeed]

anx·ious /ˈæŋkʃəs/ *adj* [*more* ~; *most* ~]
1 a : afraid or nervous especially about what may happen **:** feeling anxiety • She feels *anxious* and depressed. • They are *anxious* [=*worried, concerned*] about their son's health. • People are *anxious* about the future. • They were *anxious* for their daughter. [=they were worried about what might happen to their daughter] • He was *anxious* that the weather would not improve in time for the party. **b :** causing or showing fear or nervousness • We experienced a few *anxious* moments as we waited to hear the results of the test. • It was an *anxious* night as she waited for her children to come home. • an *anxious* moment • He was waiting at the door with an *anxious* expression/look on his face.
2 : wanting or eager to do or have something very much especially because of fear or nervousness • He was *anxious* for more news. — often followed by *to + verb* • She was *anxious to succeed* in school. • It was snowing hard and we were *anxious to get* home. • We were *anxious to hear* the results.
– anx·ious·ly *adv* • Her parents waited *anxiously* for her to come home that night. **– anx·ious·ness** *noun* [*noncount*] • feelings of *anxiousness* [=(more commonly) *anxiety*]

¹any /ˈɛni/ *adj, always used before a noun*
1 — used to indicate a person or thing that is not particular or specific • Ask *any* man you meet, and he will tell you the same thing. • *Any* one of them could have answered the question. • You can return the product if *any* defect appears within the first six months. • *Any* plan (at all) is better than no plan. • *Any* [=*every*] child knows that. [=all children know that] • He is as good as *any* other pitcher in the league. • We can meet *any* day but Monday. • You could have seen him *any* afternoon last week. • The recipe uses a large amount of pepper, and ***not just any*** pepper, but a special blend imported from India. • You have to be a member to go there. They won't let ***just any*** person in.
2 — used to indicate an amount greater than zero or none; usually used in negative statements, in questions, and in statements with *if* or *whether* • You haven't eaten *any* salad. [=no salad has been eaten] • I can't find *any* stamps. • Don't pay *any* attention to him. • There is hardly *any* difference between the two teams. • They dropped by without *any* warning. • We don't want there to be *any* misunderstandings. • The company has denied *any* [=*all*] responsibility for the accident. • There are ***few if any*** [=few or no] details about the accident. • Do you have *any* money? • He asked if/whether you had *any* money. • If there are *any* errors, report them to me. = Report *any* errors to me. • If you can give me *any* help, I'd appreciate it. = I'd appreciate *any* help you can give me.

> ***usage*** *Some* is used instead of *any* in positive statements. • I have *some* money. It is sometimes used instead of *any* in questions and in statements with *if* or *whether*. • Do you have *some* money? • If I had *some* money, I would spend it on books.

any moment see MOMENT
any old see ¹OLD
at any cost see ¹COST
by any chance see ¹CHANCE
go to any length/lengths see LENGTH
in any case see ¹CASE
in any event see EVENT

²any *pronoun*
1 : any one of the people or things in a group • She asked if there were *any* present who needed assistance. • The movie's opening scene is as powerful as *any* I've ever watched. — often + *of* • *Any of* them could answer the question. • He is taller than *any of* the other boys.
2 : any amount • "I'd like some more coffee." "I'm sorry, but there isn't *any* left." • Is there *any* [=*some*] left? • I'll see if there's *any* [=*some*] left. — often + *of* • You have not eaten *any of* your salad.

³any *adv* **:** to the least amount or degree • The food there is never *any* good. • He won't be *any* happier there than he was here. • I could not walk *any* farther. • Do you want *any* [=*some*] more pizza? • I can't eat *any* more pizza. • If you want *any* [=*some*] more pizza, it's in the fridge. • (*US, informal*) You certainly aren't helping me *any*. [=*at all*] • We can't ignore these problems ***any longer***. [=*anymore*] [=we must stop ignoring these problems]

any·body /ˈɛniˌbɑːdi, ˈɛniˌbʌdi/ *pronoun*
1 : any person **:** ANYONE • Did *anybody* call? • I don't know how *anybody* can believe that. • I thought I heard someone outside, but when I looked there wasn't *anybody* there. [=no one was there] • An accident like that could happen to *anybody*. • You have to be a member to go there. They won't let ***just anybody*** in. • ***Everybody who's anybody*** [=every important or well-known person] was there. • She arrived 10 minutes before ***anybody else***. [=before any other person]
2 — used when asking a question that could be answered by any of the people in a group • Does *anybody* know where my keys are? [=do any of you know where my keys are?] • Would *anybody* like more coffee?

any·how /ˈɛniˌhaʊ/ *adv, informal*
1 : ANYWAY • It's OK if we don't go to the movie. I'm not that interested in seeing it *anyhow*. • What exactly did she mean by that *anyhow*?
2 *chiefly Brit* **:** in a way that is not organized or neat **:** in a careless way • The books were scattered *anyhow* [=*every which way*] around the office.

any·more /ˌɛniˈmoɚ/ *adv* **:** in the recent or present period of time • I never see them *anymore*. • She used to live there, but she doesn't live there *anymore*. [=she doesn't live there any longer; she doesn't live there now]

> ***usage*** *Anymore* is usually used in negative statements and in questions. • Does she live there *anymore*? In some parts of the U.S. it is also used informally in positive statements. • I've been seeing them a lot *anymore*. [=I've been seeing them a lot lately/recently] It is sometimes written *any more*. • She doesn't live there *any more*.

any·one /ˈɛniˌwʌn/ *pronoun*
1 : any person **:** ANYBODY • Did *anyone* call? • If *anyone* calls, take a message. • I don't know how *anyone* can believe that. • An accident like that could happen to *anyone*. • I thought I heard someone outside, but there wasn't *anyone* there. [=no one was there] • You have to be a member to go there. They won't let ***just anyone*** in. • ***Everyone who's anyone*** [=every important or well-known person] was there. • She arrived 10 minutes before ***anyone else***. [=before any other person]
2 — used when asking a question that could be answered by any one of the people in a group • Does *anyone* know where my keys are? [=do any of you know where my keys are?] • Would *anyone* like more coffee? — compare SOMEONE

any·place /ˈɛniˌpleɪs/ *adv, US* **:** ¹ANYWHERE 1 • I'll go *anyplace* you want. • I can't find my keys *anyplace*. • I'm happy here and I wouldn't want to live *anyplace* else.

any·thing /ˈɛniˌθɪŋ/ *pronoun*
1 : a thing of any kind • We were allowed to do *anything* we wanted to. • If you're not sure what to say, just say *anything* that comes to mind. • She didn't say *anything* at all. [=she said nothing at all] • That dog will eat almost/nearly/practically/virtually *anything*. • We didn't talk about *anything* much. • The new stadium is spectacular. There's never been *anything* like it. • She never does *anything* but complain. [=all she does is complain] • I'll do *anything* I can to help. • They were ready for *anything* (that might happen). • You can't tell him *any*-

A

thing about computers. He thinks he's an expert. • I can't think of her as *anything* but a good friend. [=I can only think of her as a good friend] • He'll do *anything* for a laugh. • I'd do/give *anything* to see her again. • He won't take *anything* from anyone. [=he won't allow anyone to mistreat him, to be rude to him, etc.] • She ate hardly *anything*. [=she ate almost nothing] • He said he was sorry, but that doesn't really mean *anything*. • I don't have *anything* against them. [=I don't have any reason for disliking them] • She thought it was funny but I didn't see *anything* funny about it. [=I didn't think it was funny at all] • They've been doing ***everything and anything*** to finish on time. = They've been doing ***anything and everything*** to finish on time. • The problems were caused by lack of time ***as much as anything***. • She dresses conservatively at work, but on the weekends, ***anything goes***. [=anything is acceptable; there are no rules that have to be followed]

2 : [1]SOMETHING — used in questions • Would you like *anything* else? • Is there *anything* wrong? • Is there *anything* (good/interesting) on TV tonight? • (*informal*) Do you want some pretzels ***or anything***? [=or a similar thing]

anything but : not at all • He looked *anything but* happy. [=he looked very unhappy] • Though he said he was happy, he looked *anything but* (happy). • This problem is *anything but* new.

anything like **1 :** at all like — used in negative statements • He doesn't look *anything like* his brother. **2** *or* ***anything near*** : in any way : at all — used in negative statements • He doesn't look *anything like* his brother. • The movie wasn't *anything like/near* what I expected it to be. [=the movie was completely different from what I expected it to be] • We don't have *anything like/near* enough time. [=we don't have nearly enough time]

as anything *informal* : as any person or thing — used to make a statement more forceful • He was (*as*) calm *as anything*. [=he was very calm] • It was as obvious *as anything* [=it was extremely obvious] that she didn't want to go.

for anything : for any reason — used in negative statements • I like my life, and I wouldn't change it *for anything*.

if anything see [1]IF

like anything *informal* : very much : very forcefully • It was raining *like anything*. [=it was raining very hard] • She was hoping *like anything* that the weather would be good.

more than anything : very much : very badly • I wanted to believe her *more than anything* [=I very much wanted to believe her], but I couldn't. • *More than anything* (in the world), I'd like to visit Paris again. [=the thing I most want to do is to visit Paris again]

any·time /ˈɛniˌtaɪm/ *adv* : at any time • You can call me *anytime*. I'm always home. • We should arrive *anytime* between 5 and 6 p.m. • The bus should be here *anytime* now. • Things will not improve ***anytime soon***. [=things will not improve in the near future] ✧ *Anytime* is sometimes used informally to say that you are willing to do something again at any time. • "Thanks for your help." "*Anytime*."

any·way /ˈɛniˌweɪ/ *adv*

1 : despite something that has been stated before • The road got worse, but they kept going *anyway*. • I didn't expect her to say "yes," but I asked her *anyway*. • It makes no difference what we say. She's going to do what she wants *anyway*. • He's far from perfect, but she loves him *anyway*.

2 — used to give added force to a question • How do they do it *anyway*? • What exactly does this mean *anyway*? • I can't believe he acted so rudely. Who does he think he is *anyway*?

3 — used to add something to a previous statement • It's too expensive, ***and anyway*** [=and besides], we don't have enough time to do it.

4 — used to correct or slightly change a previous statement • I've never known him to be sad—not this sad *anyway*. • The movie wasn't that bad. I liked it, *anyway*, even if no one else did. • For a brief time, *anyway*, they seemed to be happy. • The weather is expected to improve next week. *Anyway*, that's what I've heard.

5 — used to indicate that something stated before is not important • Don't worry about being late. It doesn't matter *anyway*.

6 — used to introduce a statement that begins a new subject or that goes on to the next important part of a story • So, *anyway*, what do you want to do next? • *Anyway*, I have to go now. I'm already late. • I must have fallen asleep at that point. *Anyway*, the next thing I knew, the phone was ringing.

any·ways /ˈɛniˌweɪz/ *adv, US, informal* : ANYWAY • Who does that guy think he is *anyways*? • You're late. *Anyways*, at least you showed up.

[1]**any·where** /ˈɛniˌweɚ/ *adv*

1 : in, at, or to any place • This type of plant can grow just about *anywhere*. • It's a small camera that you can take practically/virtually *anywhere*. • They gave her permission to go *anywhere* she wanted to. • This kind of thing could happen *anywhere*. • You can sit *anywhere* you like. • He seems to be at home *anywhere* in the world. • I can't find my keys *anywhere*. • I'd know/recognize her *anywhere*. • They produce some of the finest wines made *anywhere*. • He never walks *anywhere*. He always drives. • I'll take you *anywhere* you want to go. • I heard that she might be quitting, but she says she's not going *anywhere*. [=she says that she's staying] • This bird species is not found ***anywhere else*** in the world. [=the bird is not found at any other place in the world] • I wouldn't want to live *anywhere else*. • These plants don't grow ***just anywhere***. They need lots of sun. — often used figuratively • His career isn't ***going anywhere***. [=his career is not making progress; his career is not becoming more successful; his career is going nowhere] • It seemed like a good idea, but it never ***went anywhere***. [=it never produced any useful results] • We're working hard but we don't seem to be ***getting anywhere***. [=we don't seem to be making progress] • Arguing will not ***get us anywhere***. [=arguing will not help us solve the problem] • Our efforts to get more information didn't ***lead anywhere***. [=our efforts were not successful]

2 : [1]SOMEWHERE — used in questions • Did you go *anywhere* while on your vacation? • Have you been ***anywhere else*** in Europe?

3 — used to give added emphasis to *near* and *close* • The police wouldn't let us get *anywhere near* the accident scene. • The dog barks if you come *anywhere near* him. • The company hasn't come *anywhere near/close* to meeting its goals. • We're not *anywhere close* to being done. [=we're very far from being done] • The movie was not *anywhere near* as good [=the movie was not nearly as good] as I expected it to be.

4 — used to indicate a range of amounts, values, etc. • The house's value is estimated at *anywhere* from $200,000 to $220,000. • The plants can live *anywhere* between 50 and 100 years. • The procedure can take *anywhere* from/between two to four hours to complete.

[2]**anywhere** *noun* [*noncount*]

1 : any place — usually used after *from* • It's a short drive *from anywhere* in the region. — sometimes used figuratively • They live ***miles from anywhere***. [=they live in a place that is very far from other people]

2 : [2]SOMEWHERE — used in questions • Do you know *anywhere* I can buy cheap furniture? • Do you need *anywhere* to stay tonight?

AOB *abbr, Brit* any other business — used at the end of a list of things to be discussed in a business meeting to indicate that new topics may be introduced

A–OK /ˌeɪoʊˈkeɪ/ *adj, US, informal* : entirely good or satisfactory : perfectly OK • Everything is *A-OK*.

— **A–OK** *adv* • Everything is going *A-OK*.

A1 /ˈeɪˈwʌn/ *adj, informal + somewhat old-fashioned* : very good or excellent • The car's in *A1* condition.

aor·ta /eɪˈoɚtə/ *noun, pl* **-tas** [*count*] : the large artery that brings blood from the heart to the rest of the body

— **aor·tic** /eɪˈoɚtɪk/ *adj* • a tear in the *aortic* wall

apace /əˈpeɪs/ *adv* : at a fast speed or pace : QUICKLY • Development on the project continued/proceeded *apace*. • growing *apace*

apace with : going or advancing at the same rate as (something) • The company has been struggling to ***keep/stay apace with*** [=*keep up with*] the latest developments.

Apache /əˈpætʃi/ *noun, pl* **Apache** *or* **Apaches** [*count*] : a member of a Native American people of the southwestern U.S.

[1]**apart** /əˈpɑɚt/ *adv*

1 : separated by an amount of space • He stood with his feet planted far/wide *apart*. • with legs *apart* • They live five miles *apart* (from each other). • The garage stands *apart* from the house. [=the garage is separate from the house] • He stood *apart* while the other members of the team celebrated. • They started fighting and it took four people to pull them *apart* (from each other). [=to separate them] — often used figuratively • She tried to keep *apart* from [=to stay out of] family arguments. • She has a quality that sets her *apart* from other singers. [=that makes her different from other singers] • They were close friends once, but they have ***drifted/grown apart***. [=they are no longer close friends] • They are far *apart* on most issues. = They are ***worlds/poles apart*** on most issues.

[=they disagree very much on most issues] ▪ The neighborhood she lives in now is ***a world apart*** from [=is completely different from] the small town where she grew up.
2 : separated by an amount of time ▪ Their children were born two years *apart*.
3 : not together ▪ My wife and I are unhappy when we're *apart*. ▪ They separated and have been living *apart* for the past year.
4 : into parts or pieces ▪ He took the clock *apart*. ▪ The old couch is falling *apart*. = The old couch is ***coming apart at the seams***. ▪ blast/blow/break/fly *apart* ▪ cut/pry/pull *apart* ▪ rip/tear/split *apart*
5 — used to say that something is not included in a statement that follows ▪ A few minor flaws *apart* [=*aside*], the novel is excellent. [=except for a few minor flaws, the novel is excellent]
apart from **1 :** not including (something) : with the exception of (something) ▪ The potatoes were a little salty, but *apart from* [=*except for*] that, the food was very good. **2 :** other than (something) : BESIDES ▪ *Apart from* his work, his only real interest is baseball. ▪ The work has value in itself, ***quite apart from*** the good effects it produces. ▪ I don't like it. ***Apart from anything else***, it's too expensive. **3 :** separately from (something) ▪ This problem needs to be considered *apart from* the other issues.

²apart *adj, not used before a noun* **:** separate or different from others ▪ in a place *apart* ▪ a man *apart* ▪ Those athletes are ***a breed apart***. [=they are not like other people; they are a special type of people]
– apart·ness *noun* [*noncount*]

apart·heid /əˈpɑɚˌteɪt/ *noun* [*noncount*] **:** a former social system in South Africa in which black people and people from other racial groups did not have the same political and economic rights as white people and were forced to live separately from white people

apart·ment /əˈpɑɚtmənt/ *noun, pl* **-ments** [*count*]
1 *chiefly US* **:** a usually rented room or set of rooms that is part of a building and is used as a place to live ▪ We lived in an *apartment* for several years before buying a house. — compare CONDOMINIUM, ²FLAT
2 *Brit* **:** a large and impressive room or set of rooms — usually plural ▪ the Royal *apartments*

apartment building *noun, pl* **~ -ings** [*count*] *US* **:** a large building that has several or many apartments ▪ We lived in an *apartment building* for several years before buying a house. — called also *(US) apartment house, (Brit) apartment block, (Brit) block of flats*

ap·a·thet·ic /ˌæpəˈθɛtɪk/ *adj* [*more ~; most ~*] **:** not having or showing much emotion or interest ▪ Young people are becoming increasingly *apathetic*. ▪ a politically *apathetic* [=*indifferent, uninterested*] generation ▪ the *apathetic* attitude of the public ▪ As a teenager, he was *apathetic* about his future. [=he didn't care about his future] ▪ Surprisingly, most Americans are *apathetic* toward/about this important issue.
– ap·a·thet·ic·al·ly /ˌæpəˈθɛtɪkli/ *adv*

ap·a·thy /ˈæpəθi/ *noun* **:** the feeling of not having much emotion or interest : an apathetic state [*noncount*] People have shown surprising *apathy* toward/about these important social problems. ▪ Many commentators are surprised by the *apathy* [=*indifference*] of the country's voters. ▪ voter *apathy* ▪ a culture of *apathy* [=a culture in which people do not care about things] [*singular*] People have shown a surprising *apathy* toward/about these problems.

¹ape /ˈeɪp/ *noun, pl* **apes** [*count*]
1 : a type of animal (such as a chimpanzee or gorilla) that is closely related to monkeys and humans and that is covered in hair and has no tail or a very short tail
2 *informal* **:** a large and stupid or rude person ▪ Her boyfriend's some big *ape* she met at a party.
– apelike *adj* [*more ~; most ~*]

²ape *verb* **apes; aped; ap·ing** [*+ obj*] *often disapproving* **:** to copy or imitate (something or someone) ▪ After years of *aping* [=*mimicking*] the styles of famous artists, he has created his own unique way of painting. ▪ She *apes* the speech and manners of the rich.

³ape *adj*
go ape *informal* **1 :** to become very excited ▪ The kids *go ape* [=*go crazy, go wild*] whenever they hear that song. **2 :** to become very angry ▪ Mom really *went ape* [=*went ballistic, blew her top*] when I got home late.

aper·i·tif /əˌperəˈtiːf/ *noun, pl* **-tifs** [*count*] **:** an alcoholic drink that people drink before eating a meal ▪ They served us champagne as an *aperitif*.

ap·er·ture /ˈæpɚˌtʃɚ/ *noun, pl* **-tures** [*count*]
1 *formal* **:** a hole or small opening in something ▪ We entered the cave through a narrow *aperture*.
2 *technical* **:** an opening that controls the amount of light that passes through a lens (such as a camera lens) ▪ The photograph was taken using a fast shutter speed and a large *aperture*.

apex /ˈeɪˌpɛks/ *noun, pl* **apex·es** [*count*] **:** the top or highest point of something — usually singular ▪ the mountain's *apex* [=*peak, summit*] — usually used figuratively ▪ Tragically, she died at the *apex* [=*acme, high point*] of her career/fame. ▪ The excitement was about to reach its *apex*.

aphid /ˈeɪfəd/ *noun, pl* **aphids** [*count*] **:** a very small insect that harms plants

aph·o·rism /ˈæfəˌrɪzəm/ *noun, pl* **-risms** [*count*] **:** a short phrase that expresses a true or wise idea : ADAGE ▪ When decorating, remember the familiar *aphorism*, "less is more."
– aph·o·ris·tic /ˌæfəˈrɪstɪk/ *adj* [*more ~; most ~*] ▪ her *aphoristic* wisdom **– aph·o·ris·tic·al·ly** /ˌæfəˈrɪstɪkli/ *adj*

aph·ro·di·si·ac /ˌæfrəˈdiːziˌæk/ *noun, pl* **-acs** [*count*] **:** something (such as a food, drink, or drug) that causes or increases sexual desire
– aphrodisiac *adj* [*more ~; most ~*] ▪ an *aphrodisiac* drug

apiece /əˈpiːs/ *adv, always used after a noun* **:** for or to each person or thing : EACH ▪ They're selling tickets at/for 10 dollars *apiece*. [=each ticket costs 10 dollars] ▪ His shoes weigh four pounds *apiece*. ▪ She gave the kids a dollar *apiece*. [=she gave a dollar to each kid]

aplenty /əˈplɛnti/ *adj, always used after a noun* **:** in a large number or amount ▪ There are books *aplenty* on this subject. [=there are many books on this subject] ▪ We found mistakes *aplenty* in their story. ✧ *Aplenty* has an old-fashioned quality, but it is still commonly used today.

aplomb /əˈplɑːm/ *noun* [*noncount*] **:** confidence and skill shown especially in a difficult situation ▪ He showed/demonstrated great *aplomb* in dealing with the reporters. — usually used in the phrase ***with aplomb*** ▪ He's handled the reporters *with* great *aplomb*. [=in a confident and skillful way] ▪ She speaks French and German *with* equal *aplomb*.

apoc·a·lypse /əˈpɑːkəˌlɪps/ *noun* [*singular*] **:** a great disaster : a sudden and very bad event that causes much fear, loss, or destruction ▪ His book tells of an environmental *apocalypse*. ▪ fears of a nuclear *apocalypse* [=a disaster caused by nuclear weapons]
the apocalypse **:** the end or destruction of the world especially as described in the Christian Bible ▪ Some people be-

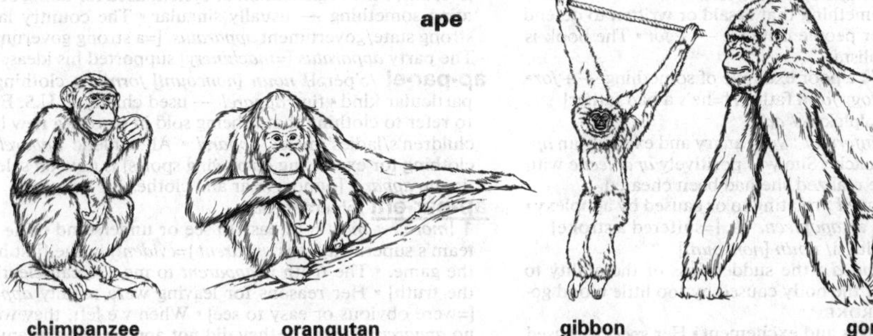

A

lieved *the apocalypse* would happen in the year 2000. • waiting for *the apocalypse*

apoc·a·lyp·tic /əˌpɑːkəˈlɪptɪk/ *adj* [*more* ~; *most* ~]
1 : of, relating to, or involving terrible violence and destruction • No one listened to her *apocalyptic* predictions/warnings. • a less *apocalyptic* view of the future • an *apocalyptic* battle
2 : of or relating to the end of the world • the *apocalyptic* destruction of the world
– **apoc·a·lyp·tic·al·ly** /əˌpɑːkəˈlɪptɪkli/ *adv*

apoc·ry·phal /əˈpɑːkrəfəl/ *adj* : well-known but probably not true • an *apocryphal* story/tale about the president's childhood

apo·gee /ˈæpəʤi/ *noun* [*singular*]
1 *formal* : the highest point of something • The style reached its *apogee* [=(more commonly) *apex*, *high point*] in the mid-1960s.
2 *technical* : the point in outer space where an object traveling around the Earth (such as a satellite or the moon) is farthest away from the Earth — compare PERIGEE

apo·lit·i·cal /ˌeɪpəˈlɪtɪkəl/ *adj* [*more* ~; *most* ~] : not political : not interested or involved in politics • Although both of her parents are politicians, she's completely *apolitical*. • an *apolitical* scientific journal
– **apo·lit·i·cal·ly** *adv*

apol·o·get·ic /əˌpɑːləˈʤɛtɪk/ *adj* [*more* ~; *most* ~] : feeling or showing regret : expressing an apology • We received an *apologetic* letter and a full refund from the company. • an *apologetic* smile • They were *apologetic* about the mistake. • She seemed almost *apologetic* about buying a new car.
– **apol·o·get·i·cal·ly** /əˌpɑːləˈʤɛtɪkli/ *adv* • He smiled *apologetically*. • "I'm sorry I'm late," she said *apologetically*.

apol·o·gist /əˈpɑːləʤɪst/ *noun, pl* **-gists** [*count*] : a person who defends or supports something (such as a religion, cause, or organization) that is being criticized or attacked by other people • the film industry's *apologists* [=people who write and speak in support of the film industry] — often + *for* • an *apologist for* the film industry

apol·o·gize *also Brit* **apol·o·gise** /əˈpɑːləˌʤaɪz/ *verb* **-gizes**; **-gized**; **-giz·ing** [*no obj*] : to express regret for doing or saying something wrong : to give or make an apology • He *apologized* to his wife and children for losing his temper. • I want to *apologize* (to you) for what I said. I didn't mean it, and I'm sorry if it hurt your feelings. • We *apologize* for the mistake and promise that it won't happen again. • She ***doesn't apologize for*** her lifestyle. [=she does not believe that her lifestyle is wrong]

apol·o·gy /əˈpɑːləʤi/ *noun, pl* **-gies**
1 a : a statement saying that you are sorry about something : an expression of regret for having done or said something wrong [*count*] The company issued/delivered an official *apology* to its customers for its error. • Please accept our sincerest/humblest *apologies* for any problems we may have caused. • I demand an *apology*! • I owe you an *apology*. = You deserve an *apology*. • a written *apology* • He made a public *apology* for his controversial remarks. • He refused to accept my *apology*. • She ***makes no apologies for*** her lifestyle. [=she does not believe that her lifestyle is wrong] • He ***offered no apology for*** his bad behavior. [=he didn't say he was sorry for acting badly] [*noncount*] We received a letter/note of *apology* from the company. • ***Without apology*** [=without excusing himself or saying he was sorry], he got up and left the room.
b ***apologies*** [*plural*] : an expression of regret for not being able to do something • Please give my *apologies* [=*excuses*] to your cousin. I'm sorry that I won't be able to come to the wedding. • I made my *apologies* and left.
2 [*count*] *formal* : something that is said or written to defend something that other people criticize — + *for* • The book is an *apology for* capitalism.
3 [*singular*] *informal* : a poor example of something — + *for* • He's a poor/sad *apology for* a father. [=he's a bad father]

ap·o·plec·tic /ˌæpəˈplɛktɪk/ *adj*
1 [*more* ~; *most* ~] *informal* : very angry and excited • an *apoplectic* basketball coach • She was positively *apoplectic* with anger/rage when she realized she had been cheated.
2 *medical, old-fashioned* : relating to or caused by apoplexy • The patient suffered an *apoplectic* fit. [=suffered a stroke]

ap·o·plexy /ˈæpəˌplɛksi/ *noun* [*noncount*]
1 *medical, old-fashioned* : the sudden loss of the ability to feel or move parts of the body caused by too little blood going to the brain : STROKE
2 *informal* : great anger and excitement • Her speech caused *apoplexy* among the audience members.

apos·tate /əˈpɑːˌsteɪt/ *noun, pl* **-tates** [*count*] *formal* : someone whose beliefs have changed and who no longer belongs to a religious or political group
– **apos·ta·sy** /əˈpɑːstəsi/ *noun* [*noncount*]

a pos·te·ri·o·ri /ɑˌpoʊˌstiriˈori/ *adj, formal* : relating to what can be known by observation rather than through an understanding of how certain things work • an *a posteriori* judgment/justification/explanation — compare A PRIORI
– **a posteriori** *adv* • You can't justify what you did *a posteriori*.

apos·tle /əˈpɑːsəl/ *noun, pl* **apos·tles** [*count*]
1 : any one of the 12 men chosen by Jesus Christ to spread the Christian religion • Christ's *apostles*
2 : someone who believes in or supports an idea, cause, etc. — often + *of* • *apostles* [=*adherents*, *advocates*] *of* peace and nonviolence • an *apostle of* democracy

ap·os·tol·ic /ˌæpəˈstɑːlɪk/ *adj*
1 : of or relating to the original 12 apostles
2 : of or relating to the pope : PAPAL • *apostolic* authority

apos·tro·phe /əˈpʰɑːstrəfi/ *noun, pl* **-phes** [*count*]
1 : the punctuation mark ' used to show that letters or numbers are missing (as when "did" and "not" are combined into "didn't" or when the date 1776 is written as '76) • In the contraction "can't," an *apostrophe* replaces two of the letters in the word "cannot."
2 : the punctuation mark ' used to show the possessive form of a noun (as in "Lee's book" or "the tree's leaves")
3 : the punctuation mark ' used to show the plural forms of letters or numbers (as in "dot your *i's* and cross your *t's*" or "in the 1960's")

apoth·e·cary /əˈpɑːθəˌkeri/ *noun, pl* **-car·ies** [*count*] : a person who prepared and sold medicines in past times

apo·the·o·sis /əˌpɑːθiˈoʊsəs/ *noun, pl* **-oses** /-ˌsiːz/ [*count*] *formal*
1 : the perfect form or example of something — usually singular • a dish that is the *apotheosis* of French cuisine
2 : the highest or best part of something — usually singular • His music reaches/achieves its *apotheosis* [=*peak*, *pinnacle*] in this album.

app /ˈæp/ *noun, pl* **apps** [*count*] *chiefly US, computers, informal* : APPLICATION 4 • a popular *app* — see also KILLER APP

ap·pall (*US*) *or Brit* **ap·pal** /əˈpɑːl/ *verb* **-palls**; **-palled**; **-pall·ing** [+ *obj*] : to cause (someone) to feel fear, shock, or disgust • The thought of war *appalls* me. • It *appalls* me to think of the way those children have been treated. — often used as *(be) appalled* • We *were appalled* at how long it took for our food to be served. = We *were appalled* that it took so long. • She *was appalled* by/at their behavior.

ap·pall·ing /əˈpɑːlɪŋ/ *adj* [*more* ~; *most* ~] : very bad in a way that causes fear, shock, or disgust • We drove by an *appalling* accident on the highway. • Your behavior has been *appalling*. [=*atrocious*, *outrageous*, *terrible*]
– **ap·pall·ing·ly** *adv* • *appallingly* bad treatment • an *appallingly* [=*dreadfully*] bad movie

ap·pa·rat·chik /ˌɑːpəˈrɑːʧɪk/ *noun, pl* **-chiks** [*count*] *disapproving* : a very loyal member of an organization (such as a company or political party) who always obeys orders • corporate/party/political *apparatchiks*

ap·pa·ra·tus /ˌæpəˈrætəs/ *noun, pl* **apparatus·es** *or* **apparatus**
1 : a tool or piece of equipment used for specific activities [*count*] She fell off a gymnastics *apparatus* and broke her leg. • an electrical *apparatus* [*noncount*] an expensive piece of *apparatus* [=*machinery*]
2 [*count*] : the organization or system used for doing or operating something — usually singular • The country lacks a strong state/government *apparatus*. [=a strong government] • The party *apparatus* [=*machinery*] supported his ideas.

ap·par·el /əˈperəl/ *noun* [*noncount*] *formal* : clothing of a particular kind • fine *apparel* — used chiefly in U.S. English to refer to clothing that is being sold in stores • a new line of children's/ladies'/men's *apparel* • All athletic *apparel* [=all clothing for exercising or playing sports] is now on sale. • intimate *apparel* [=underwear and clothes for sleeping]

ap·par·ent /əˈperənt/ *adj*
1 [*more* ~; *most* ~] : easy to see or understand • The other team's superiority was *apparent* [=*evident*] in the first half of the game. • The truth is *apparent* to me. [=I can clearly see the truth] • Her reasons for leaving were readily *apparent*. [=were obvious or easy to see] • When we left, they were in no *apparent* danger. [=they did not appear to be in any dan-

ger] ▪ From the beginning, it was *apparent* that she was not an ordinary child. ▪ It soon/quickly became *apparent* (to us) that something was wrong. ▪ He started yelling and throwing things ***for no apparent reason***

2 *always used before a noun* **: seeming to be true but possibly not true** ▪ We disagreed on the *apparent* meaning of the movie. ▪ He died of an *apparent* heart attack. [=it appears that a heart attack caused his death] ▪ What was the *apparent* cause of the accident?

ap·par·ent·ly /əˈperəntli/ *adv* **— used to describe something that appears to be true based on what is known** ▪ The window had *apparently* been forced open. ▪ We were surprised when their *apparently* [=*seemingly, ostensibly*] happy marriage ended after only two years. ▪ *Apparently*, he died of a heart attack. = He died of a heart attack, *apparently*. = He *apparently* died of a heart attack. [=it appears that a heart attack caused his death] ▪ "Did the bus leave without us?" "*Apparently* (so)." [=yes, that seems/appears to be the case] ▪ "Is the bus still here?" "*Apparently* not."

ap·pa·ri·tion /ˌæpəˈrɪʃən/ *noun, pl* **-tions** [*count*] *formal* **: a ghost or spirit of a dead person** ▪ People say there are ghostly *apparitions* [=*ghosts, phantoms*] in this house. ▪ a strange *apparition*

[1]ap·peal /əˈpiːl/ *noun, pl* **-peals**

1 [*noncount*] **: a quality that causes people to like someone or something** ▪ I can't understand the *appeal* of skydiving. [=I can't understand why some people like it] ▪ Music never held much *appeal* [=*attraction*] for him. ▪ Her jokes are quickly losing their *appeal*. ▪ The movie has great *appeal* to/for adults as well as children. [=adults and children like the movie] ▪ the wide/broad/mass/universal *appeal* of the artist's work **— see also** SEX APPEAL

2 [*count*] **a : a serious request for help, support, etc.** ▪ They made a desperate *appeal* [=*plea, entreaty*] for help. ▪ His *appeals* to his father for money were ignored. ▪ The mayor made an *appeal* to the people of the city to stay calm. **b : an attempt to make someone do or accept something as right or proper by saying things that are directed at a person's feelings, attitudes, etc. — + *to*** ▪ The author makes an *appeal to* the reader's emotions. ▪ an *appeal to* reason ▪ an *appeal to* the intellect **c : an organized effort to raise money** ▪ We made a donation during the school's annual *appeal*. ▪ She helped to organize/launch an *appeal* on behalf of the homeless.

3 : a process in which a decision is studied and accepted or rejected by a higher court or by someone in authority [*count*] My lawyer said the court's decision wasn't correct and that we should file for an *appeal*. ▪ lodge an *appeal* [*noncount*] Her conviction was thrown out ***on appeal*** [=a higher court decided that she should not have been convicted] ▪ The case is currently ***under appeal*** [=the case is currently being reviewed by a higher court] **— see also** COURT OF APPEALS

[2]appeal *verb* **-peals; -pealed; -peal·ing**

1 [*no obj*] **: to be liked by someone : to be pleasing or attractive *to* someone** ▪ The movie *appeals to* adults as well as (*to*) children. [=adults and children like the movie] ▪ music that *appeals to* a wide variety of people ▪ The idea of going to college *appealed to* him greatly. [=the idea was very appealing to him]

2 [*no obj*] **a : to ask for something (such as help or support) in a serious way** ▪ The government *appealed* for calm. ▪ desperate people who are *appealing* for help ▪ The government *appealed* to the people to stay calm. **b : to try to make someone do or accept something as right or proper by saying things that are directed at a person's feelings, attitudes, etc. — + *to*** ▪ We got them to join by *appealing to* their sense of duty and honor.

3 : to make a formal request for a higher court or for someone in authority to review and change a decision [*no obj*] He *appealed*, arguing that there was not enough evidence to convict him. ▪ She lost the case and *appealed* the following month. ▪ (*Brit*) We plan to ***appeal against*** the court's decision. [+ *obj*] (*US*) ▪ We plan to *appeal* the court's decision. ▪ The ruling can be *appealed* within 30 days. ▪ (*baseball*) The runner was called out at home plate but the manager *appealed* the umpire's decision.

ap·peal·ing /əˈpiːlɪŋ/ *adj* [*more* ~; *most* ~] **: having qualities that people like : pleasing or attractive** ▪ a book with an *appealing* title ▪ *appealing* colors ▪ It is an idea that most people will ***find appealing*** [=that most people will like] **— often + *to*** ▪ The offer is especially *appealing to* young people who are buying their first car. **— opposite** UNAPPEALING

— ap·peal·ing·ly *adv* ▪ Her idea was *appealingly* simple.

appeals court (*US*) *or chiefly Brit* **appeal court** *noun, pl* **~ courts** [*count*] *law* **:** COURT OF APPEALS 1

ap·pear /əˈpiɚ/ *verb* **-pears; -peared; -pear·ing**

1 [*linking verb*] *somewhat formal* **: to seem to be something : to make someone think that a person or thing has a particular characteristic :** LOOK, SEEM ▪ She *appears* angry. ▪ "Is she angry?" "So it *appears*." = "So it would *appear*." = "It *appears* so." ▪ "Is she pleased?" "It *appears* not." = "It would *appear* not." ▪ She *appears* a nice enough person. ▪ Although everything *appeared* normal to me [=although I thought everything was normal], something was wrong. ▪ Winning the election *appears* unlikely at this point. ▪ Things are not always as they *appear*. [=they are not always what you think they are] ▪ It *appears* to us [=we think] that something should be done. **— often followed by *to + verb*** ▪ She *appeared to be* angry. ▪ She *appears to be* a nice enough person. ▪ Everyone *appeared to have* a good time. = They all *appeared to enjoy* themselves.

2 [*no obj*] **: to become visible : to begin to be seen** ▪ One by one, the stars *appeared* in the sky. ▪ The sun began to *appear* from behind the clouds. ▪ The airplanes seemed to *appear* out of nowhere. ▪ Her grandfather often *appears* to her in her dreams. [=she often sees her grandfather in her dreams] ▪ The storm disappeared as suddenly as it had *appeared*. **— opposite** DISAPPEAR

3 [*no obj*] **: to arrive at a place : to show up** ▪ The cat *appears* at our kitchen door every morning. ▪ One of the guests *appeared* a few minutes late. ▪ He *appeared* a little before eight last night. **— opposite** DISAPPEAR

4 [*no obj*] **: to begin to exist** ▪ The disease first *appeared* in the late 1970s. ▪ This new technology first *appears* in Europe in the early 20th century. **— opposite** DISAPPEAR

5 [*no obj*] **: to be seen or heard by the public: such as a : to go where you can be seen to give a speech, answer questions, etc. — often + *before*** ▪ I was invited to *appear before* a meeting of teachers to talk about the school system. ▪ *appearing before* a group of reporters **b : to work as an actor or performer in a movie, on the radio, etc.** ▪ The two actors *appeared* [=*performed*] together in the film. ▪ He has *appeared* on many radio and television shows. ▪ She *appeared* in her first Broadway musical last year. ▪ Several guest musicians *appeared* on his latest album. **c : to be published or made available to the public** ▪ The story *appeared* on the front page of the newspaper. **— often + *in*** ▪ We got a lot of phone calls after the story *appeared in* the newspaper. ▪ Her papers have *appeared in* several different scientific journals. ▪ The book ***appeared in print*** [=was published] again a few years ago. ▪ The word first *appeared in print* in 1782.

6 [*no obj*] **: to go in front of a person or group that has authority (such as a judge or council) especially in order to answer questions** ▪ I *appeared* in front of the committee during its last meeting. ▪ She was instructed to *appear* in court the next morning. ▪ She *appeared* before the judge. ▪ He will be *appearing* as a witness at the trial.

ap·pear·ance /əˈpirəns/ *noun, pl* **-anc·es**

1 *somewhat formal* **: the way that someone or something looks** [*count*] The room has a neat/fresh/clean *appearance*. [=*look*] ▪ The general *appearance* of the house is quite good. ▪ The museum restored the painting to its original *appearance*. ▪ lotions that improve your skin's *appearance* and texture ▪ It minimizes the *appearance* of wrinkles. [=it makes wrinkles more difficult to see] ▪ You shouldn't judge a man by his *appearance*. ▪ Have you noticed any changes in her *appearance*? ▪ He's very proud of his ***physical appearance***. [=the way he looks] [*noncount*] He is still very youthful ***in appearance***. [=he still looks very young] ▪ They are very similar *in appearance*. [=they look the same]

2 [*count*] **: a way of looking that is not true or real** ▪ He appears to be happy, but *appearances* can be deceptive/deceiving. ▪ Their expensive home created a false *appearance* of success and happiness. ▪ The furniture ***has the appearance*** of being made by hand. [=the furniture was not made by hand but it looks/appears as if it was] ▪ ***Despite appearances***, her company is very successful. = ***Appearances to the contrary***, her company is very successful. [=her company is very successful even though it does not appear to be] ▪ She is only attending the banquet ***for the sake of appearances***. [=because people think that she should attend] ▪ He was, ***to/by all (outward) appearances***, a happily married man. [=he seemed to be a happily married man, but he wasn't] ▪ Their meetings tend to ***take on the appearance of*** [=to look like] family gatherings. ▪ His white beard ***gave him the appearance of*** an old

A

man. [=made him look like an old man] • The playground ***gives every appearance of*** being a safe place for children [=the playground appears to be a safe place for children], but a tragic accident occurred there recently.

3 [*count*] : the action of appearing : the fact that something or someone arrives or begins to be seen — usually singular • The *appearance* of buds on the trees tells us that spring has arrived. • We were surprised by the *appearance* of smoke in the distance. • I wasn't expecting him to come and was surprised by his sudden *appearance*. [=I was surprised when he suddenly appeared/arrived]

4 [*count*] : the time when something begins to exist or is seen for the first time — usually singular • The *appearance* [=*creation*] of the Internet has changed our culture in many ways. • The technology made its first *appearance* [=appeared for the first time] in the early 1980s. • Before the *appearance* of the telephone, people sent messages by telegraph.

5 [*count*] : an act of being seen or heard by the public as an actor, politician, athlete, etc. • He has announced that this will be his final/last *appearance* with the band. [=the last time that he will perform in public with the band] • This is her first *appearance* [=the first time that she has competed] at/in the national championships. — often used with *make* • She is *making* her first *appearance* at/in the national championships. • Tonight, he is *making* his first ***public appearance*** since winning the award. • He'll be *making* a special ***guest appearance*** [=performing as a guest] on the popular television show next fall.

6 [*count*] : the formal act of going in front of a person or group to speak, answer questions, etc. • One man has been convicted of the crime, and two others are awaiting ***court appearances***. [=waiting to go to court] — often + *before* • He is awaiting his *appearance before* a judge. • She made an *appearance before* Congress last year.

keep up appearances : to hide something bad by pretending that nothing is wrong • Although they were getting a divorce, my parents thought it was important to *keep up appearances*.

make an appearance or put in an appearance : to go to an event, gathering, etc., usually for a short period of time • The candidate *made an appearance* at the rally. • The governor *put in an appearance* at the party.

ap·pease /ə'pi:z/ *verb* **-peas·es**; **-peased**; **-peas·ing** [+ *obj*] *formal*

1 *often disapproving* : to make (someone) pleased or less angry by giving or saying something desired • They *appeased* the dictator by accepting his demands in an effort to avoid war. • Efforts to *appease* [=*pacify, placate*] the angry protesters were unsuccessful. • His critics were not *appeased* by this last speech. • They made sacrifices to *appease* the gods.

2 : to make (a pain, a problem, etc.) less painful or troubling • We had no way to *appease* our hunger. • She *appeased* [=*eased*] her guilty conscience by telling him the truth.

— ap·pease·ment /ə'pi:zmənt/ *noun* [*noncount*] • the *appeasement* of a dictator • *appeasement* of hunger

ap·pel·lant /ə'pɛlənt/ *noun, pl* **-lants** [*count*] *law* : someone who requests that a higher court review and change the decision of a lower court : someone who appeals a decision

ap·pel·late /ə'pɛlət/ *adj, always used before a noun, law* : having the power to review and change the decisions of a lower court • an *appellate* court • *appellate* judges

ap·pel·la·tion /ˌæpə'leɪʃən/ *noun, pl* **-tions** [*count*] *formal* : a name or title • an honorary *appellation*

ap·pend /ə'pɛnd/ *verb* **-pends**; **-pend·ed**; **-pend·ing** [+ *obj*] *formal* : to add (something) to a piece of writing — usually + *to* • Please read the notes *appended to* each chapter.

ap·pend·age /ə'pɛndɪʤ/ *noun, pl* **-ag·es** [*count*]

1 *medical* : a body part (such as an arm or a leg) connected to the main part of the body : LIMB

2 : something connected or joined to a larger or more important thing • The court system acts as an *appendage* to the government. • an *appendage* of a larger political party

ap·pen·dec·to·my /ˌæpən'dɛktəmi/ *noun, pl* **-mies** [*count*] *medical* : an operation to remove a person's appendix • The surgeon performed an *appendectomy* on her.

ap·pen·di·ci·tis /əˌpɛndə'saɪtəs/ *noun* [*noncount*] *medical* : a condition in which a person's appendix is painful and swollen • an attack of *appendicitis*

ap·pen·dix /ə'pɛndɪks/ *noun* [*count*]

1 *pl* ***-dix·es or -di·ces*** /-dɪˌsi:z/ : a section of extra information added at the end of a book • In your textbooks, turn to *Appendix* 3: Glossary of Terms. • The book has several *appendixes/appendices*.

2 *pl* ***-dixes*** : a small tube at the beginning of the large intestine that can be removed by surgery if it becomes infected — see picture at HUMAN

ap·per·tain /ˌæpə'teɪn/ *verb* **-tains**; **-tained**; **-tain·ing** [*no obj*] *formal* : to belong to or be connected or related to something : PERTAIN • the rights and privileges that *appertain* to marriage

ap·pe·tite /'æpəˌtaɪt/ *noun, pl* **-tites**

1 : a physical desire for food [*count*] He has a healthy/good/hearty *appetite*. • men with big/large/gargantuan *appetites* • Delicious smells from the kitchen ***whetted our appetites***. [=made us hungry] • That movie made me ***lose my appetite***. [=I no longer wanted to eat after seeing that movie] [*noncount*] Some common symptoms are tiredness, nausea, and loss of *appetite*. • I had no *appetite* and couldn't sleep.

2 [*count*] : a desire or liking for something • a healthy sexual *appetite* — usually + *for* • He has a voracious *appetite for* books/reading. • She has an *appetite for* adventure. [=she likes adventure; she likes to do adventurous things]

ap·pe·tiz·er *also Brit* **ap·pe·tis·er** /'æpəˌtaɪzɚ/ *noun, pl* **-ers** [*count*] : a small dish of food served before the main part of a meal

ap·pe·tiz·ing *also Brit* **ap·pe·tis·ing** /'æpəˌtaɪzɪŋ/ *adj* [*more ~; most ~*] : having a good smell or appearance that makes people want to eat • an *appetizing* [=*delicious, tasty*] meal • While the stew may not look very *appetizing*, it tastes wonderful. • an *appetizing* aroma — sometimes used figuratively • an *appetizing* [=*appealing*] display of merchandise

— ap·pe·tiz·ing·ly *also Brit* **ap·pe·tis·ing·ly** *adv*

ap·plaud /ə'plɑ:d/ *verb* **-plauds**; **-plaud·ed**; **-plaud·ing**

1 : to strike the hands together over and over to show approval or praise [*no obj*] The audience stood and *applauded* [=*clapped*] at the end of the show. [+ *obj*] Everyone *applauded* the graduates as they entered the auditorium. • The audience stood and *applauded* her performance.

2 [+ *obj*] : to express approval of or support for (something or someone) • They *applauded* [=*praised*] the change in policy. • We *applaud* the decision to lower taxes. • I *applaud* their efforts to clean up the city, but they must do more. • Although he didn't succeed in the end, he should be *applauded* [=*praised*] for his efforts. • Rather than being criticized for her honesty, she should be *applauded* for it.

ap·plause /ə'plɑ:z/ *noun* [*noncount*] : a show of approval or appreciation at a play, speech, sporting event, etc., in which people strike their hands together over and over • He accepted the award to thunderous *applause*. [=people applauded very loudly as he accepted the award] • The announcement was greeted with *applause* and cheers. • The audience burst into *applause*. [=began applauding/clapping loudly] • The audience gave the performers a big ***round of applause***. [=*hand*]

ap·ple /'æpəl/ *noun, pl* **ap·ples** : a round fruit with red, yellow, or green skin and firm white flesh [*count*] crisp juicy *apples* • a bad/rotten *apple* [=an apple that has rotted and cannot be eaten] [*noncount*] a piece of *apple* — often used before another noun • *apple* pie • *apple* juice • *apple* trees — see color picture on page C5 ✧ In figurative use, a ***bad apple*** or ***rotten apple*** is a bad member of a group who causes problems for the rest of the group. • A few *bad apples* cheated on the test, and now everyone has to take the test again. • One *rotten apple* ruined the day for the rest of us. — see also ADAM'S APPLE, CRAB APPLE

compare apples to apples/oranges see [1]COMPARE

the apple of someone's eye : a person or thing that someone loves very much • His daughter is *the apple of his eye*.

upset the apple cart see [2]UPSET

apple–cheeked /'æpəlˌʧi:kt/ *adj* : having red or pink cheeks • *apple-cheeked* youngsters

apple pie *noun, pl* **~ pies** [*count*] : a sweet pie made with apples

(as) American as apple pie : very or typically American • Baseball is *as American as apple pie*.

in apple-pie order *informal* : arranged neatly or perfectly : in perfect order • Everything in the cupboard was (arranged) *in apple-pie order*.

apple polisher *noun, pl* **~ -ers** [*count*] *US, informal + disapproving* : a person who tries to get the approval and friendship of someone in authority by praise, flattery, etc. • an executive surrounded by *apple polishers*

ap·ple·sauce /'æpəlˌsɑ:s/ *noun* [*noncount*] : a sweet sauce made from cooked apples

ap·pli·ance /ə'plajəns/ *noun, pl* **-anc·es** [*count*] : a machine (such as a stove, microwave, or dishwasher) that is powered by electricity and that is used in people's houses to perform a particular job • All household/domestic *appliances* are now on sale. • an *appliance* store

ap·pli·ca·ble /ˈæplɪkəbəl/ *adj* [*more* ~; *most* ~] **:** able to be applied or used in a particular situation • Businesses must comply with all *applicable* laws. — often + *to* • The rule is not *applicable* [=*relevant*] *to* this case. • This method is *applicable to* a variety of problems.

– ap·pli·ca·bil·i·ty /ˌæplɪkəˈbɪləti/ *noun* [*noncount*]

ap·pli·cant /ˈæplɪkənt/ *noun, pl* **-cants** [*count*] **:** someone who formally asks for something (such as a job or admission to a college) **:** someone who applies for something • successful college/job *applicants* • We interviewed 30 qualified *applicants* for the job.

ap·pli·ca·tion /ˌæpləˈkeɪʃən/ *noun, pl* **-tions**

1 a : a formal and usually written request for something (such as a job, admission to a school, a loan, etc.) [*count*] We've made an *application* for certification. [=we have applied to be certified] • Our loan *application* has been approved/denied. • Anyone interested in running for office must file/submit an *application* by August 1st. [*noncount*] If you'd like to be considered for the job, please send us a ***letter of application*** that gives your experience and qualifications. **b** [*count*] **:** a document that is used to make a formal request for something • Please fill out this *application*.

2 : the act of applying something: such as **a :** the act of putting something on a surface, a part of the body, etc. [*noncount*] The *application* of heat often helps sore muscles. • I prefer using the lotion because of its ease of *application*. [=because it is easy to apply] • Repeated *application* of fertilizer will help the grass become green and healthy. [*count*] Repeated *applications* of fertilizer will help the grass become green and healthy. • The cut should be treated with a generous/liberal *application* of ointment. **b :** the use of an idea, method, law, etc., in a particular situation or for a particular purpose [*noncount*] Strict *application* of the rules is necessary in this case. • the *application* of new information • learning about the creative *application* [=*use*] of new technology [*count*] He teaches his students about the practical *applications* [=*uses*] of technology. • I think it is a fair *application* of the law. • *applications* of science to everyday life **c** [*noncount*] **:** the use of a word, name, etc., to describe someone or something • the *application* of the term "baby boomer" to people who were born right after World War II

3 : the ability to be used for practical purposes [*noncount*] The technique has wide/limited *application*. [=it can/cannot be used for a large number of practical purposes] [*count*] The tool has a number of *applications*. = The tool has a wide range of *applications*.

4 [*count*] *computers* **:** a computer program that performs a particular task (such as word processing) • How many *applications* is your computer currently running? • *applications* software — called also (*chiefly US, informal*) *app*

5 [*noncount*] *formal* **:** effort made to work hard in order to complete something successfully • She succeeded because of *application* and intelligence.

ap·pli·ca·tor /ˈæpləˌkeɪtɚ/ *noun, pl* **-tors** [*count*] **:** a tool that is used to put something (such as paint or makeup) on a surface **:** a tool that is used to apply something • a paint *applicator*

ap·plied /əˈplaɪd/ *adj* **:** having or relating to practical use **:** not theoretical • a professor of *applied* science • *applied* linguistics/physics/psychology

ap·pli·qué /ˌæpləˈkeɪ, *Brit* əˈpliːkeɪ/ *noun, pl* **-qués :** a decoration that is sewn onto a larger piece of cloth [*count*] colorful *appliqués* [*noncount*] a strip of *appliqué*

– appliqué *verb* **-qués; -quéd; -qué·ing** [+ *obj*] • They *appliquéd* their sweaters with colorful strips.

ap·ply /əˈplaɪ/ *verb* **-plies; -plied; -ply·ing**

1 [*no obj*] **:** to ask formally for something (such as a job, admission to a school, a loan, etc.) usually in writing • For further information, *apply* to the address below. • I *applied* in writing to several different companies. • You must have a high school diploma for this job. High school dropouts ***need not apply.*** — often + *for* • I *applied for* several jobs and was offered one. • Anyone can *apply for* membership. • We *applied* to the bank *for* a loan. • To *apply for* our credit card, just fill out this form and send it to us. • Many high school students have begun ***applying for college.*** [=asking to be accepted as students at colleges or universities by filling out and sending applications] — sometimes followed by *to* + *verb* • Anyone can *apply to become* a member.

2 [+ *obj*] **:** to put or spread (something) on a surface, a part of the body, etc. • After *applying* a thin layer of paint to the wall and letting it dry, *apply* another coat. • We *applied* the ointment to the cut. • I washed my face and *applied* fresh makeup. • Fertilizer was *applied* to the lawn every two weeks.

3 [+ *obj*] **:** to cause (force, pressure, etc.) to have an effect or to be felt • He was able to stop the bleeding by *applying* pressure to the cut. [=by pressing on/against the cut] • He knows how to *apply* [=*use, exert*] pressure to get what he wants. • The police should have been able to deal with the situation without *applying* [=*using*] force.

4 [+ *obj*] **:** to use (an idea, method, law, etc.) in a particular situation • Try to solve the math problems by *applying* the formulas/methods that we learned in class. • They *applied* a new technique to solve an old problem. • We can handle these problems effectively if we *apply* the lessons learned from past experiences. • They *apply* what they learned in school to their everyday lives. • The law has not been *applied* fairly. [=has not been used in a fair way]

5 [+ *obj*] **:** to cause (the brakes of a vehicle) to work • Take your foot off the gas pedal and slowly *apply* the brakes.

6 [*no obj*] **:** to have an effect on someone or something • The rule no longer *applies*. • The same principle *applies* [=can be used] when you are trying to lose weight. — often + *to* • The ban *applies* [=*relates, pertains*] *to* all guns that are not used for hunting. • These rules *apply to* everyone in the school. [=everyone in the school must obey these rules] • This *applies* equally *to* men and (*to*) women. • The rule doesn't *apply to* you, so don't worry about it.

7 : to use a word, name, etc., to describe someone or something — usually + *to* [*no obj*] The term "baby boomer" usually *applies to* people who were born immediately after World War II. [+ *obj*] The author *applies* the name/label *to* corrupt politicians. — often used as *(be) applied* • The term "baby boomer" *is* usually *applied to* people who were born immediately after World War II.

apply yourself **:** to make yourself work hard in order to complete something successfully • If you *apply yourself*, you might be able to finish the project on time. • She *applied herself* to learning the language.

ap·point /əˈpoɪnt/ *verb* **-points; -point·ed; -point·ing** [+ *obj*]

1 : to choose (someone) to have a particular job **:** to give (someone) a position or duty • The President *appointed* [=*named, designated*] him (as) Secretary of Education. • She was *appointed* professor of chemistry at the university. • After his parents died, the boy's uncle was *appointed* as his guardian. • Every year, the group *appoints* three new members. • a committee *appointed* by Congress • the company's newly *appointed* assistant director • The defendant will be represented by a ***court-appointed attorney.*** [=a lawyer chosen by a court to defend someone who has been accused of a crime] — often + *to* • *appointing* women to positions of power • She was *appointed to* the position last year. — often followed by *to* + *verb* • He has been *appointed to serve* as president of the club. • A young lawyer was *appointed to represent* the accused man. — see also SELF-APPOINTED

2 *formal* **a :** to decide or establish (something) in an official way — usually used as *appointed* • She wasn't able to accomplish her *appointed* tasks. [=the things that she was supposed to do] • We will not deviate/stray from our *appointed* course. • doctors on their *appointed* rounds **b :** to decide (the time or place at which something will happen or be done) — usually used as *appointed* • We were all ready at the *appointed* time/hour. • on the *appointed* day • Call me when you reach the *appointed* place/location.

3 : to decorate and put furniture in (a room or space) — usually used as *(be) appointed* • Each suite *is appointed* with handmade furniture and original artwork. • We stayed in one of the hotel's beautifully *appointed* rooms. — see also WELL-APPOINTED

– ap·poin·tee /əˌpoɪnˈtiː/ *noun, pl* **-tees** [*count*] • presidential *appointees* [=people chosen by the President to fill a position] • He was a political *appointee*, not an elected official.

ap·point·ment /əˈpoɪntmənt/ *noun, pl* **-ments**

1 : an agreement to meet with someone at a particular time [*count*] I'm late for an *appointment*. • I have a doctor's *appointment* tomorrow morning at nine o'clock. • dental/dentist's *appointments* • She ***made an appointment*** (to meet) with her professor. • We are calling to ***confirm your appointment*** with Dr. Jones. = We are calling to make sure that you will

A

keep your appointment with Dr. Jones. [*noncount*] The museum is open to visitors ***by appointment*** only. [=you have to make an appointment to visit the museum]
2 [*noncount*] **: the act of giving a particular job or position to someone : the act of appointing someone** • The court ordered the *appointment* of an attorney to represent the child. • the *appointment* of a committee • the *appointment* of the new secretary of state • Did he get his job by *appointment* or election?
3 [*count*] **: a job or duty that is given to a person : a position to which someone is appointed** • He now holds an *appointment* from the President. • academic *appointments* • her *appointment* as ambassador to Spain

ap·por·tion /əˈpoɚʃən/ *verb* **-tions; -tioned; -tion·ing** [+ *obj*] *formal* **: to divide (something) *among* or *between* people** • The proceeds from the auction will be *apportioned among* the descendents. • *Apportion* the expenses *between* the parties involved. **: to give (a part of something) to a number of people** • The agency *apportions* water from the lake to residents. • Any attempt to ***apportion blame*** [=to say who should be blamed] so many years after the incident is pointless.
– ap·por·tion·ment /əˈpoɚʃənmənt/ *noun, pl* **-ments** [*noncount*] The *apportionment* of the expenses will take some time. [*count*] an *apportionment* of blame

ap·po·site /ˈæpəzət/ *adj* [*more ~; most ~*] *formal* **: very appropriate : suitable for the occasion or situation** • an *apposite* quotation • The poem was an *apposite* [=(more commonly) *apt*] choice for the ceremony. — often + *to* • Each panel member made remarks *apposite* [=*relevant, germane*] *to* the discussion.
– ap·po·site·ly *adv*

ap·po·si·tion /ˌæpəˈzɪʃən/ *noun* [*noncount*] *grammar* **: an arrangement of words in which a noun or noun phrase is followed by another noun or noun phrase that refers to the same thing** • In "my friend the doctor," the word "doctor" is ***in apposition*** to "my friend."

ap·prais·al /əˈpreɪzəl/ *noun, pl* **-als**
1 : the act of judging the value, condition, or importance of something : the act of appraising something [*noncount*] the *appraisal* of some jewelry [*count*] real estate *appraisals* • I made a quick *appraisal* of the situation and decided to leave right away. • Your annual job/performance *appraisal* [=*review, evaluation*] will be in July. [=your boss will meet with you to tell you if you are doing a good or bad job in July]
2 [*count*] **: something that states an opinion about the value, condition, or importance of something** • The book is an excellent *appraisal* of the influences that have shaped our government.

ap·praise /əˈpreɪz/ *verb* **-prais·es; -praised; -prais·ing** [+ *obj*]
1 : to say how much something is worth after you have carefully examined it : to give an official opinion about the value of (something) • She *appraised* the painting at $1.2 million. [=she said that the painting is worth $1.2 million] • The ring must be *appraised* by a jeweler before it can be insured. • *appraise* the house and property • What is the property's *appraised* value?
2 : to give your opinion about the condition, quality, or importance of (something or someone that you have studied or examined) • In the book, he *appraises* Hollywood's recent films and contrasts them with several independent films. • *appraising* recent political trends

Do not confuse *appraise* with *apprise*.

– ap·prais·er *noun, pl* **-ers** [*count*] • The *appraiser* gave us a detailed report on the value of the house and property.

ap·pre·cia·ble /əˈpriːʃəbəl/ *adj* **: large enough to be noticed or measured** • Researchers found that the chemical made no *appreciable* [=*noticeable, perceptible*] difference in the results. • *Appreciable* [=(more commonly) *significant*] numbers of these plants grow in this region.
– ap·pre·cia·bly /əˈpriːʃəbli/ *adv* • Her appearance has not changed *appreciably*. [=*significantly*]

ap·pre·ci·ate /əˈpriːʃiˌeɪt/ *verb* **-ates; -at·ed; -at·ing**
1 [+ *obj*] **: to understand the worth or importance of (something or someone) : to admire and value (something or someone)** • The company strives to make its employees feel *appreciated*. • Living in the city has taught me to *appreciate* the differences between people. • Those who *appreciate* fine wine will enjoy reading the restaurant's wine list.
2 [+ *obj*] **a : to be grateful for (something)** • I really *appreciated* the information you gave me. • I don't *appreciate* being ignored. [=I do not like to be ignored] • Your help the other day was greatly *appreciated*. **b** — used to make a polite request • I ***would appreciate it*** if you would tell your father to call me. [=please tell your father to call me]
3 [+ *obj*] **: to be aware of (something) : to recognize or understand (something)** • I'm not sure you *appreciate* [=*understand*] how crucial it is that we find these documents. • The tiny creature contributes to its ecosystem in ways we are only just beginning to *appreciate*. • I don't think you *appreciate* the complexity of the situation. • I *appreciate* what the artist is trying to do, but I think the painting fails to do it.
4 [*no obj*] **: to increase in value** • Given the history of the company, your investment should *appreciate* (in value) over time. • rapidly *appreciating* assets — opposite DEPRECIATE
– ap·pre·cia·tive /əˈpriːʃətɪv/ *adj* [*more ~; most ~*] • I'm very *appreciative* of your efforts on my behalf. [=I'm very grateful for your efforts] • She gave an *appreciative* nod. [=a nod that showed that she appreciated something]
– ap·pre·cia·tive·ly *adv* • She listened to the story, nodding *appreciatively*.

synonyms APPRECIATE, VALUE, PRIZE, TREASURE, and CHERISH mean to feel that something is important and worth treating with special care. APPRECIATE often suggests knowledge that makes it possible to enjoy or admire how excellent something is. • Over the years, I've come to *appreciate* fine wine. VALUE suggests that a thing is worth a lot simply because of what it is. • I *value* our friendship so much. PRIZE is used when you are very proud of something you have or own. • Despite the time and money it demands, he *prizes* that sailboat. TREASURE suggests that you enjoy having or owning something and are careful about keeping it in good condition. • You'll *treasure* these pictures. CHERISH describes a very strong love and desire to care for something or someone. • She *cherishes* her children above all.

ap·pre·ci·a·tion /əˌpriːʃiˈeɪʃən/ *noun, pl* **-tions**
1 [*noncount*] **: a feeling of being grateful for something** • You've been so generous, and I'd like to show my *appreciation* by cooking a meal for you. • We'd like to present you with this gift ***in appreciation of*** your hard work. [=to show that we are grateful for your hard work]
2 [*singular*] **: an ability to understand the worth, quality, or importance of something : an ability to appreciate something** • a music *appreciation* class [=a class that teaches people to understand and value music] — usually + *of* or *for* • She has developed an *appreciation of* exotic foods. • There is an increasing *appreciation for* video as an art form.
3 : full awareness or understanding of something — usually + *of* or *for* [*noncount*] She's shown little *appreciation for* the effort you've made. [*singular*] I'm not sure you have an *appreciation of* the complexity of the situation. • I've gained an *appreciation for* the skills involved in the game.
4 [*count*] **: a speech or piece of writing that praises something or someone** • She recently published an *appreciation* of an obscure sculptor who lived in the 17th century.
5 : an increase in the value of something [*singular*] He bought the statue because he believed there would be an *appreciation* in its value. • Based on the history of the company, you can expect a significant *appreciation* in your investment over a number of years. [*noncount*] There's been no *appreciation* in the stock's value. — opposite DEPRECIATION

ap·pre·hend /ˌæprɪˈhend/ *verb* **-hends; -hend·ed; -hend·ing** [+ *obj*] *formal*
1 *of police* **: to arrest (someone) for a crime : to catch (a criminal or suspect)** • Within hours, police had *apprehended* the thief.
2 *somewhat old-fashioned* **: to notice and understand (something) :** PERCEIVE • subtle differences that are difficult to *apprehend*

ap·pre·hen·sion /ˌæprɪˈhenʃən/ *noun, pl* **-sions**
1 : fear that something bad or unpleasant is going to happen : a feeling of being worried about the future [*noncount*] The thought of moving to a new city fills me with *apprehension*. • There is growing *apprehension* [=*fear*] that profits will be lower than expected. [*count*] He has *apprehensions* [=*misgivings*] about the surgery.
2 *formal* **: the act of apprehending someone or something: such as a : the act of arresting someone for a crime** [*noncount*] the sheriff's *apprehension* of the criminal = the criminal's *apprehension* by the sheriff [*count*] an increased number of *apprehensions* **b** [*noncount*] *somewhat old-fashioned* **: the act of noticing and understanding something** • the *ap-*

prehension [=*perception*] of danger

ap·pre·hen·sive /ˌæprɪˈhɛnsɪv/ *adj* [*more* ~; *most* ~] : afraid that something bad or unpleasant is going to happen : feeling or showing fear or apprehension about the future • He was quite *apprehensive* [=*fearful, uneasy*] about the surgery. • She gave me an *apprehensive* [=*anxious*] look.
– **ap·pre·hen·sive·ly** *adv* • She looked at me *apprehensively*. – **ap·pre·hen·sive·ness** *noun* [*noncount*]

[1]**ap·pren·tice** /əˈprɛntəs/ *noun, pl* **-tic·es** [*count*] : a person who learns a job or skill by working for a fixed period of time for someone who is very good at that job or skill • a carpenter's *apprentice* = an *apprentice* to a carpenter — often used before another noun • an *apprentice* carpenter

[2]**apprentice** *verb* **-tices; -ticed; -tic·ing**
1 [+ *obj*] : to make (someone) an apprentice — usually used as *(be) apprenticed* • He ***was apprenticed to*** a carpenter [=he became a carpenter's apprentice] at the age of 15.
2 [*no obj*] : to work as an apprentice • He *apprenticed* with a master carpenter for two years.

ap·pren·tice·ship /əˈprɛntəsˌʃɪp/ *noun, pl* **-ships** [*count*]
1 : a position as an apprentice • He obtained an *apprenticeship* with a carpenter.
2 : the period of time when a person is an apprentice • He served a two-year *apprenticeship*.

ap·prise /əˈpraɪz/ *verb* **-pris·es; -prised; -pris·ing** [+ *obj*] *formal* : to give information to (someone) : INFORM — usually + *of* • Please *apprise* me *of* any changes in the situation. = Please keep me *apprised of* any changes in the situation. [=please let me know if there are any changes in the situation]

Do not confuse *apprise* with *appraise*.

[1]**ap·proach** /əˈproʊʧ/ *verb* **-proach·es; -proached; -proach·ing**
1 a : to move or become near or nearer to something or someone [+ *obj*] The cat *approached* the baby cautiously. • We are *approaching* [=*nearing*] our destination. [*no obj*] The cat *approached* cautiously. • Ease off the gas pedal to slow down as the bend in the road *approaches*. **b** : to move or become near or nearer in time to something [+ *obj*] We are *approaching* the end of the fiscal year. • She is *approaching* retirement. [=she will soon be retiring from her job] [*no obj*] Your birthday is *approaching* fast. = Your birthday is fast *approaching*. [=your birthday is soon]
2 [+ *obj*] **a** : to get close to (an amount or level) • This weekend we're expecting temperatures *approaching* 100 degrees. • The success rates *approach* 90 percent. **b** : to be almost the same as (something or someone) • We were never treated with anything even remotely *approaching* rudeness. [=no one was at all rude to us] • He has a wild laugh that sometimes *approaches* hysteria. • a reproduction that *approaches* the quality of the original painting • When it comes to cooking Italian food, no one can *approach* her. [=no one is as good at cooking Italian food as she is]
3 [+ *obj*] : to start talking to (someone) for some purpose (such as to ask a question or make a request) • The supervisor is quite easy to *approach*, so don't hesitate to bring up any problems you have. • We were advised to never be too aggressive when *approaching* a potential client. — often used as *(be) approached* • He *was approached* about the job but he didn't take it. • I *was approached* by a young boy asking me to make a donation.
4 [+ *obj*] : to begin to deal with or think about (something) • When writing, consider the way your reader will *approach* the text. • She *approached* the problem from a different angle. • I will *approach* the idea with an open mind.

[2]**approach** *noun, pl* **-proaches**
1 [*count*] : a way of dealing with something : a way of doing or thinking about something • a traditional *approach* • trying a more healthy *approach* — often + *to* • I really admire your direct *approach to* the problem. • Some doctors are trying a radical new *approach to* cancer treatment.
2 [*singular*] : the act of moving or becoming near or nearer to someone or something : the act of approaching • The cat made a cautious *approach*. : an act or occurrence in which something comes nearer • The quiet afternoon was interrupted by the *approach* of a motorboat. • A loud growl warned us of the bear's *approach*. • With the *approach* of summer came longer, hotter days.
3 [*count*] : the act of speaking to someone for some purpose (such as to ask a question or make a request) — often plural • A group of businessmen has made *approaches* to the owners of the club with an offer to buy it.
4 [*count*] : a road or path that leads to a place • This road is the only *approach* to the cabin (that is) not blocked by snow.
5 [*singular*] : something that is similar *to* another thing • These potted herbs are the nearest *approach to* a garden I can manage.
6 [*count*] : the final part of a flight just before landing • The pilot lowered the landing gear as the plane began its *approach*. • The plane was ***on final approach***.

ap·proach·able /əˈproʊʧəbəl/ *adj*
1 [*more* ~; *most* ~] : easy to talk to or deal with • The supervisor is quite *approachable*, so don't hesitate to bring up any problems you have. • The topic is complex but the book itself is very *approachable*. — opposite UNAPPROACHABLE
2 *not used before a noun* : able to be reached or approached • The cabin is *approachable* from several directions.
– **ap·proach·abil·i·ty** /əˌproʊʧəˈbɪləti/ *noun* [*noncount*] • He's known for his *approachability*.

ap·pro·ba·tion /ˌæprəˈbeɪʃən/ *noun* [*noncount*] *formal* : praise or approval • The company has even received the *approbation* of its former critics.

[1]**ap·pro·pri·ate** /əˈproʊprijət/ *adj* [*more* ~; *most* ~] : right or suited for some purpose or situation • It's a formal occasion and *appropriate* attire/dress/clothing is expected. [=you are expected to wear formal clothing] • Red wine would have been a more *appropriate* choice with the meal. • We'll need to find an *appropriate* [=*suitable*] place to store the fuel. • Do you think the movie is *appropriate* for small children (to see)? = Do you think it's *appropriate* for small children to see the movie? • The movie is perfectly/entirely *appropriate* to/for people of all ages. — opposite INAPPROPRIATE
– **ap·pro·pri·ate·ly** *adv* • The dinner is formal, so please dress *appropriately*. • She met her husband, ***appropriately enough***, at a wedding. – **ap·pro·pri·ate·ness** *noun* [*noncount*] • He questioned the *appropriateness* of the movie for young children.

[2]**ap·pro·pri·ate** /əˈproʊpriˌeɪt/ *verb* **-ates; -at·ed; -at·ing** [+ *obj*]
1 : to get or save (money) for a specific use or purpose • The town has *appropriated* funds to repair the bridge and work should begin this summer.
2 : to take or use (something) especially in a way that is illegal, unfair, etc. • The economy has been weakened by corrupt officials who have *appropriated* the country's resources for their own use. • Elements of the design were *appropriated* from other architects. • The term "bad" has been *appropriated* by teenagers as a synonym for "good." — compare MISAPPROPRIATE

ap·pro·pri·a·tion /əˌproʊpriˈeɪʃən/ *noun, pl* **-tions** *formal*
1 [*noncount*] : the act of appropriating something: such as **a** : the act of getting or saving money for a specific use or purpose • the *appropriation* of funds to repair the bridge **b** : the act of taking or using something especially in a way that is illegal, unfair, etc. • The economy has been weakened by the *appropriation* of the country's resources by corrupt officials.
2 [*count*] : an amount of money that is used or provided by a government for a specific purpose • The library's *appropriation* (from the state) has decreased over the years.

ap·prov·al /əˈpruːvəl/ *noun, pl* **-als**
1 [*noncount*] : the belief that something or someone is good or acceptable : a good opinion of someone or something • children who never gained/won their parents' *approval* • He nodded in full *approval* of their decision. [=he nodded to show that he agreed with their decision] • I hope that these arrangements ***meet with your approval***. [=I hope that these arrangements are acceptable to you; I hope that you approve of these arrangements] • The governor's ***approval rating*** with the voters is going up. [=a larger number of voters say that the governor is doing a good job] — opposite DISAPPROVAL
2 : permission to do something : acceptance of an idea, action, plan, etc. [*noncount*] Do I have your *approval* to make the changes? • The change is subject to the committee's *approval*. [=the change must be approved by the committee] • The rally will be on May 19, provided the city gives its *approval*. • The company is seeking *approval* of the drug [=is seeking official permission to sell the drug] as a treatment for cancer. • The government has so far withheld *approval* of the drug. [*count*] We were required to get *approvals* at each stage of the project. — see also *seal of approval* at [2]SEAL
on approval ✧ If you buy something *on approval*, you can return it after using it for a period of time if you decide

A

that you do not want it. • We bought the new furniture *on approval.*

ap·prove /əˈpruːv/ *verb* **-proves; -proved; -prov·ing**
1 [*no obj*] **:** to believe that something or someone is good or acceptable • I don't care if all the other parents are letting their kids do it; I still don't *approve.* — often + *of* • I still don't *approve of* it. • I don't *approve of* the way he treats his wife. = I don't *approve of* him treating his wife the way he does. — opposite DISAPPROVE
2 [+ *obj*] **:** to officially accept (an idea, action, plan, etc.) • The state has *approved* the building plans, so work on the new school can begin immediately. • Your supervisor must *approve* the report before it can be sent. — often used as *(be) approved* • The drug is expected to *be approved* as a treatment for cancer by the end of the year. • Your application *has been approved.*

approved school *noun, pl* **~ schools** [*count*] *Brit* **:** a special school in past times for children who committed crimes

approving *adj* [*more ~; most ~*] **:** showing that you believe that something or someone is good or acceptable **:** showing approval • an *approving* nod/smile
– ap·prov·ing·ly /əˈpruːvɪŋli/ *adv* • She spoke *approvingly* of their efforts. • He nodded *approvingly.*

approx. *abbr* approximate; approximately

[1]**ap·prox·i·mate** /əˈprɑːksəmət/ *adj* **:** almost correct or exact • This is the *approximate* location of the ancient city. • her *approximate* age **:** close in value or amount but not precise • Can you give me the *approximate* cost of the repair?
– ap·prox·i·mate·ly *adv* • The repair should cost *approximately* [=*about, around, roughly*] $200.

[2]**ap·prox·i·mate** /əˈprɑːksəˌmeɪt/ *verb* **-mates; -mat·ed; -mat·ing**
1 a : to be very similar to but not exactly like (something) [+ *obj*] I've finally found a vegetarian burger that *approximates* the taste of real beef. • The colors in the pictures can only *approximate* the real thing. [*no obj*] (*chiefly Brit*) — + *to* • The colors in the pictures can only *approximate to* the real thing. **b** [+ *obj*] **:** to do or make a thing that is very similar to but not exactly like (something) • an Australian who can *approximate* a strong New York City accent
2 [+ *obj*] **:** to calculate the almost exact value or position of (something) • Students learned to *approximate* [=*estimate*] the distance between the Earth and the planets.

ap·prox·i·ma·tion /əˌprɑːksəˈmeɪʃən/ *noun, pl* **-tions** [*count*]
1 : an amount, figure, etc., that is almost correct and is not intended to be exact **:** an approximate amount, figure, etc. • These numbers are only *approximations* [=*estimates*] but they give us some idea of what we can afford. • This isn't an exact figure but I think it's a good/rough *approximation* of what the land is worth.
2 : something that is similar to something else • The color of the paint isn't the exact same color as the vase, but it's a close *approximation.* — usually + *of* or *to* • The astronauts train in a room that provides an *approximation of* conditions in space. • There's little more than a vague *approximation to* the truth in their story.

appt. *abbr* appoint; appointed; appointment

ap·pur·te·nance /əˈpɚtənəns/ *noun, pl* **-nanc·es** [*count*] *formal* **:** an object that is used with or for something — usually plural • an office equipped with all the *appurtenances* [=*accessories*] of the modern business world

Apr. *abbr* April

APR /ˌeɪˌpiːˈɑɚ/ *noun* [*singular*] *business* **:** the rate at which interest on a loan is calculated over the period of a year ✧ *APR* is an abbreviation of "annual percentage rate."

après–ski /ˌɑːˌpreɪˈskiː/ *noun* [*noncount*] **:** social activities after a day of skiing — often used before another noun • an *après-ski* party

apri·cot /ˈæprəˌkɑːt, ˈeɪprəˌkɑːt/ *noun, pl* **-cots** [*count*] **:** a small orange-colored fruit that is related to the peach and plum — see color picture on page C5

April /ˈeɪprəl/ *noun, pl* **Aprils :** the fourth month of the year [*noncount*] in (early/middle/mid-/late) *April* • early/late in *April* • We arrived on *April* the fourth. = (*US*) We arrived on *April* fourth. = We arrived on the fourth of *April.* [*count*] We have had snowstorms the last few *Aprils.* • The children have a week off from school every *April.* — abbr. *Apr.*

April Fools' Day *or* **April Fool's Day** *noun* [*singular*] **:** April 1 celebrated as a day on which people play tricks on each other — called also *All Fools' Day* ✧ A trick that is played on April Fools' Day is often called an ***April Fools' trick*** or ***April Fools' joke.*** A person who is tricked on April Fools' Day is sometimes called an ***April fool.***

a pri·o·ri /ˌɑːpriˈori/ *adj, formal* **:** relating to what can be known through an understanding of how certain things work rather than by observation • There's no *a priori* reason to think your expenses will remain the same in a new city. — compare A POSTERIORI
– a priori *adv*

apron /ˈeɪprən/ *noun, pl* **aprons** [*count*]
1 : a piece of clothing that is worn on the front of the body over clothes to keep them from getting dirty • a cook's *apron*
2 : the part of a stage that is in front of the curtain — called also *apron stage*
3 : the paved part of an airport where airplanes load or unload or are turned around

apron string *noun, pl* **~ strings** [*count*] **:** either one of a pair of strings that are attached to an apron and are used to keep it close to your body — usually used figuratively • At 38 years old, he's still ***tied to his mother's apron strings.*** [=he is still controlled by his mother] • The company has relied on government support, but the government is now threatening to ***cut the apron strings.*** [=to stop providing support]

apron

[1]**ap·ro·pos** /ˌæprəˈpoʊ/ *adj* [*more ~; most ~*] **:** suitable or appropriate • The ceremony concluded with the reading of an *apropos* poem. • The comment, though unexpected, was *apropos.*

[2]**apropos** *prep* **:** with regard to (something) **:** APROPOS OF • *Apropos* [=*concerning*] the proposed changes, I think more information is needed.

apropos of *prep* **:** with regard to (something) • *Apropos of* [=*concerning*] the proposed changes, I think more information is needed. • Her comment about the weather was ***apropos of nothing.*** [=did not relate to any previous topic]

apse /ˈæps/ *noun, pl* **aps·es** [*count*] **:** a part of a church that is shaped like a half circle and that is usually at the east end of the building

apt /ˈæpt/ *adj* **apt·er; apt·est** [*or more ~; most ~*]
1 : likely to do something **:** having a tendency to do something — followed by *to + verb* • Don't wake him; he's *apt to become* angry. • Adolescents are more *apt to take* risks than adults are.
2 : appropriate or suitable • an *apt* remark • "Stripe" is an *apt* name for the cat, since she has striped fur.
3 : quick to learn • a very *apt* student/pupil
– apt·ly *adv* • The cat is *aptly* named "Stripe." **– apt·ness** *noun* [*noncount*] • the *aptness* of the remarks

apt. *abbr* **1** apartment **2** aptitude

ap·ti·tude /ˈæptəˌtuːd, *Brit* ˈæptəˌtjuːd/ *noun, pl* **-tudes :** a natural ability to do something or to learn something [*count*] The new test is supposed to measure the *aptitudes* of the students. • Anyone who can speak five languages obviously has a great natural *aptitude* for (learning) languages. [*noncount*] She's shown great natural *aptitude for* (learning) languages. • a test of *aptitude* = an ***aptitude test*** [=a test that is designed to show how easily someone will be able to learn certain skills]

aqua /ˈɑːkwə/ *noun, pl* **aquas** [*count, noncount*] **:** a light greenish-blue color — see color picture on page C2
– aqua *adj*

aqua·ma·rine /ˌɑːkwəməˈriːn/ *noun, pl* **-rines**
1 [*count*] **:** a pale greenish-blue stone that is used in jewelry — see color picture on page C11
2 [*count, noncount*] **:** a pale greenish-blue color that is more blue than aqua
– aquamarine *adj*

aquar·i·um /əˈkwerijəm/ *noun, pl* **-i·ums** *or* **-ia** /-ijə/ [*count*]
1 : a glass or plastic container in which fish and other water animals and plants can live
2 : a building people can visit to see water animals and plants

aquarium

Aquar·i·us /əˈkwerijəs/ *noun, pl* **-us·es**
1 [*noncount*] **:** the 11th sign

of the zodiac that comes between Capricorn and Pisces and is symbolized by a person carrying a jug of water — see picture at ZODIAC
2 [*count*] : a person born under the sign Aquarius : a person born between January 20th and February 18th • She was born on February third, so she's an *Aquarius*.

aquat•ic /ə'kwɑ:tɪk/ *adj*
1 : living or found in or near water • *aquatic* animals/plants • *aquatic* environments
2 : of or relating to the animals and plants that live in or near water • *aquatic* biology • an *aquatic* biologist
3 : done in or on water • *aquatic* sports

aq•ue•duct /'ækwəˌdʌkt/ *noun, pl* **-ducts** [*count*] : a structure that looks like a bridge and that is used to carry water over a valley; *also* : a pipe or channel that is used to bring water to an area

aque•ous /'eɪkwijəs/ *adj, technical* : containing water or similar to water • an *aqueous* solution/fluid

aqui•fer /'ækwəfɚ/ *noun, pl* **-fers** [*count*] *technical* : a layer of rock or sand that can absorb and hold water • an underground *aquifer*

aq•ui•line /'ækwəˌlaɪn/ *adj* [*more ~; most ~*]
1 : curving like an eagle's beak • an *aquiline* nose
2 : like an eagle • an actor with *aquiline* features [=an actor whose face has an angular shape like an eagle's face]

aquiv•er /ə'kwɪvɚ/ *adj, not used before a noun* : shaking or trembling because of strong emotion : quivering • He was all *aquiver* with excitement/rage.

AR *abbr* Arkansas

-ar /ɚ/ *adj suffix* : of or relating to • molecul*ar* • circul*ar*

Ar•ab /'erəb/ *noun, pl* **-abs** [*count*]
1 : a member of the people who are originally from the Arabian Peninsula and who now live mostly in the Middle East and northern Africa
2 *Brit* : ARABIAN HORSE
– **Arab** *adj* • the *Arab* states • *Arab* history • an *Arab* scholar of the Arabic language

ar•a•besque /ˌerə'bɛsk/ *noun, pl* **-besques**
1 [*count*] : a complicated decorative design made with many lines that curve and cross each other
2 : a ballet position in which the dancer stands on one foot and holds one arm forward while the other arm and leg are held out behind [*count*] The students practiced their *arabesques*. [*noncount*] She held her arms in *arabesque*.
– **arabesque** *adj* • an *arabesque* pattern

Ara•bi•an /ə'reɪbijən/ *adj* : from or in Arabia • *Arabian* cities/scenery • the *Arabian* Desert : connected with the Arab people • *Arabian* history/culture/music

Arabian horse *noun, pl* **~ horses** [*count*] : a type of horse originally from Arabia

Ar•a•bic /'erəbɪk/ *noun* [*noncount*] : the language of the Arab people • fluent in *Arabic*
– **Arabic** *adj* • an Arab scholar of the *Arabic* language • *Arabic* literature/writing • the *Arabic* alphabet

Arabic numeral *noun, pl* **~ -rals** [*count*] : any one of the number symbols 1, 2, 3, 4, 5, 6, 7, 8, 9, and 0 — compare ROMAN NUMERAL

ar•a•ble /'erəbəl/ *adj*
1 [*more ~; most ~*] : suitable for farming : able to produce crops • The family is selling several acres of *arable* land.
2 *Brit* : of or relating to growing crops • *arable* farming • *arable* farmers

arach•nid /ə'ræknəd/ *noun, pl* **-nids** [*count*] *technical* : a kind of animal that has eight legs and a body formed of two parts • Spiders, scorpions, mites, and ticks are *arachnids*. — see color picture on page C10

ar•bi•ter /'ɑɚbətɚ/ *noun, pl* **-ters** [*count*]
1 : a person who is considered to be an authority on what is right, good, or proper — often + *of* • an *arbiter of* fashion/manners/grammar • He is regarded as an ***arbiter of taste*** in the world of jazz.
2 : a person who has the power to settle an argument between people • The mayor will act as the ***final arbiter*** in any disputes between board members.

ar•bi•trage /'ɑɚbəˌtrɑ:ʒ/ *noun* [*noncount*] *business* : the practice of buying something (such as foreign money, gold, etc.) in one place and selling it almost immediately in another place where it is worth more
– **ar•bi•tra•geur** /ˌɑɚbəˌtrɑ:'ʒɚ/ *also US* **ar•bi•trag•er** /'ɑɚbəˌtrɑ:ʒɚ/ *noun, pl* **-geurs** *also US* **-gers** [*count*]

ar•bi•trary /'ɑɚbəˌtreri, *Brit* 'ɑ:bətrəri/ *adj*
1 [*more ~; most ~*] : not planned or chosen for a particular reason • An *arbitrary* number has been assigned to each district. : not based on reason or evidence • I don't know why I chose that one; it was a completely *arbitrary* decision.
2 : done without concern for what is fair or right • Although *arbitrary* arrests are illegal, they continue to occur in many parts of the country.
– **ar•bi•trari•ly** /ˌɑɚbə'trerəli, *Brit* 'ɑ:bətrərəli/ *adv* • The number was *arbitrarily* chosen. – **ar•bi•trari•ness** /'ɑɚbəˌtrerinəs, *Brit* 'ɑ:bətrərinəs/ *noun* [*noncount*]

ar•bi•trate /'ɑɚbəˌtreɪt/ *verb* **-trates; -trat•ed; -trat•ing** : to settle an argument between two people or groups after hearing the opinions and ideas of both [*no obj*] The council will *arbitrate* among the interest groups. • *arbitrate* between managers and staff [+ *obj*] She will *arbitrate* the dispute.

ar•bi•tra•tion /ˌɑɚbə'treɪʃən/ *noun* [*noncount*] : a process of settling an argument or disagreement in which the people or groups on both sides present their opinions and ideas to a third person or group • Both parties have agreed to (go to) *arbitration*. • a dispute settled by *arbitration*

ar•bi•tra•tor /'ɑɚbəˌtreɪtɚ/ *noun, pl* **-tors** [*count*] : a person who is chosen to settle a disagreement between people or groups • Both sides agreed to accept a decision by an impartial *arbitrator*.

ar•bor (*US*) *or Brit* **ar•bour** /'ɑɚbɚ/ *noun, pl* **-bors** [*count*] : a wooden shelter in a garden that is shaped like an arch and that plants grow over

arbor

ar•bo•re•al /ɑɚ'borijəl/ *adj*
1 *formal + literary* : of or relating to trees • the forest's *arboreal* beauty
2 *technical* : living in or often found in trees • an *arboreal* monkey

ar•bo•re•tum /ˌɑɚbə'ri:təm/ *noun, pl* **-re•tums** *or* **-re•ta** /-'ri:tə/ [*count*] : a place where trees and plants are grown in order to be studied or seen by the public

[1]**arc** /'ɑɚk/ *noun, pl* **arcs** [*count*]
1 : a line or shape that is curved like part of a circle • He bent the twig into an *arc*. • The ball floated in a high *arc*. — see picture at GEOMETRY
2 *technical* : a brightly glowing electric current that flows across an open space between two points (such as two electrodes) • an electric *arc*

[2]**arc** *verb* **arcs; arced** /'ɑɚkt/; **arc•ing** /'ɑɚkɪŋ/ [*no obj*]
1 : to move or lie in a curving path : to follow an arc-shaped course • The arrow *arced* through the air. • A light *arced* across the sky. • The island chain *arcs* from north to south.
2 *technical* : to form an electric arc

ar•cade /ɑɚ'keɪd/ *noun, pl* **-cades** [*count*]
1 : a row of arches that are supported by columns
2 : an arched or covered passageway with many shops; *also, chiefly Brit* : a building that includes many shops • a ***shopping arcade***
3 : a place with many games that can be played by putting coins in them — often used before another noun • an ***arcade game*** — called also (*Brit*) *amusement arcade,* (*US*) *penny arcade*

ar•ca•dia *or* **Ar•ca•dia** /ɑɚ'keɪdijə/ *noun* [*noncount*] : a very pleasant and quiet place or scene

ar•cane /ɑɚ'keɪn/ *adj* [*more ~; most ~*] : secret or mysterious : known or understood by only a few people • an *arcane* scientific puzzle • an *arcane* ritual • a theory filled with *arcane* details

[1]**arch** /'ɑɚʧ/ *noun, pl* **arch•es** [*count*]
1 : a usually curved part of a structure that is over an opening and that supports a wall or other weight above the opening
2 : the raised area on the bottom of the foot that is formed by a curved section of bones — see picture at FOOT
3 : something that has a curved shape • There was a slight *arch* to her eyebrows. • an *arch* in the cat's back

[2]**arch** *verb* **arches; arched; arch•ing** : to bend into the shape of an arch : CURVE [+ *obj*] She *arched* her arm/back/neck. • The cat *arched* its back. • She *arched* her eyebrows in surprise. [*no obj*] A tree *arches* over the road. • She *arched* backward to begin the exercise.
– **arched** *adj* • the cat's *arched* back • her *arched* eyebrows • *arched* ceilings/doorway/gateway/roof/windows

[3]**arch** *adj* : having or showing an amused feeling of being superior to or knowing more than other people • an *arch* look •

a politician known for his *arch* humor • The novel is never mocking or *arch* in its tone.
– **arch·ly** *adv* • an *archly* playful reply • an essay with an *archly* comic title – **arch·ness** *noun [noncount]*

arch- /ˌɑɚʧ/ *prefix*
1 : main or chief • *arch*enemy • *arch*bishop • *arch*rival
2 : extreme • *arch*conservative

ar·chae·ol·o·gy *or chiefly US* **ar·che·ol·o·gy** /ˌɑɚkiˈɑːləʤi/ *noun [noncount]* : a science that deals with past human life and activities by studying the bones, tools, etc., of ancient people
– **ar·chae·o·log·i·cal** *or chiefly US* **ar·che·o·log·i·cal** /ˌɑɚkijəˈlɑːʤɪkəl/ *adj* • an *archaeological* site/dig – **ar·chae·o·log·i·cal·ly** *or chiefly US* **ar·che·o·log·i·cal·ly** /ˌɑɚkijəˈlɑːʤɪkli/ *adv* – **ar·chae·ol·o·gist** *or chiefly US* **ar·che·ol·o·gist** /ˌɑɚkiˈɑːləʤɪst/ *noun, pl* **-gists** *[count]*

ar·cha·ic /ɑɚˈkejɪk/ *adj*
1 : old and no longer used • the *archaic* word "methinks" • *archaic* spellings of words • *archaic* customs ***synonyms*** see [1]OLD
2 *[more ~; most ~]* : old and no longer useful : OUTDATED • The company needs to update its *archaic* computer systems.
3 : of or relating to ancient times • *archaic* art

ar·cha·ism /ˈɑɚkiˌɪzəm/ *noun, pl* **-isms** *[count]* : an old word or expression that is no longer used : an archaic word or expression • the *archaisms* "methinks" and "saith"

arch·an·gel /ˈɑɚʧˌeɪnʤəl/ *noun, pl* **-gels** *[count]* : an angel of the highest rank

arch·bish·op /ɑɚʧˈbɪʃəp/ *noun, pl* **-ops** *[count]* : the bishop of highest rank in a particular area

arch·bish·op·ric /ɑɚʧˈbɪʃəprɪk/ *noun, pl* **-rics** *[count]* : the rank of an archbishop or the area over which an archbishop has authority

arch·con·ser·va·tive /ɑɚʧkənˈsɚvətɪv/ *noun, pl* **-tives** *[count]* : a person who is extremely conservative in politics
– **archconservative** *adj*

arch·dea·con /ɑɚʧˈdiːkən/ *noun, pl* **-cons** *[count]* : a church official who assists a bishop

arch·di·o·cese /ɑɚʧˈdajəsəs/ *noun, pl* **-ces·es** *[count]* : the area an archbishop is in charge of : the diocese of an archbishop

arch·duch·ess /ɑɚʧˈdʌʧəs/ *noun, pl* **-ess·es** *[count]*
1 : a princess of the royal family of Austria
2 : the wife or widow of an archduke

arch·duke /ɑɚʧˈduːk, *Brit* ɑːʧˈdjuːk/ *noun, pl* **-dukes** *[count]* : a prince of the royal family of Austria

arch·en·e·my /ɑɚʧˈɛnəmi/ *noun, pl* **-mies** *[count]* : someone's main enemy • The two politicians were *archenemies*. • The country went to war with its *archenemy*.

archeology *chiefly US spelling of* ARCHAEOLOGY

ar·cher /ˈɑɚʧɚ/ *noun, pl* **-chers** *[count]* : a person who shoots with a bow and arrow

ar·chery /ˈɑɚʧəri/ *noun [noncount]* : the sport or skill of shooting with a bow and arrow — often used before another noun • an *archery* competition/contest • *archery* equipment

ar·che·type /ˈɑɚkɪˌtaɪp/ *noun, pl* **-types** *[count]* : a perfect example of something • He is the *archetype* of a successful businessman. • an *archetype* of the modern family
– **ar·che·typ·al** /ˌɑɚkɪˈtaɪpəl/ *adj [more ~; most ~]* • an *archetypal* businessman • an *archetypal* American town

ar·chi·pel·a·go /ˌɑɚkəˈpɛləˌgoʊ/ *noun, pl* **-goes** *or* **-gos** *[count]* : a group of islands

ar·chi·tect /ˈɑɚkəˌtɛkt/ *noun, pl* **-tects** *[count]*
1 : a person who designs buildings • a famous *architect*
2 : a person who designs and guides a plan, project, etc. — usually + *of* • He is the main/chief/principal *architect of* the country's foreign policy. • an *architect of* the peace proposal • She earned praise as the *architect of* a new school program.

ar·chi·tec·ture /ˈɑɚkəˌtɛkʧɚ/ *noun, pl* **-tures**
1 *[noncount]* : the art or science of designing and creating buildings • In college, he studied *architecture*.
2 *[noncount]* : a method or style of building • The *architecture* of the building is modern.
3 *[count] technical* : the way in which the parts of a computer are organized • different program *architectures*
– **ar·chi·tec·tur·al** /ˌɑɚkəˈtɛkʧərəl/ *adj* • *architectural* blueprints/designs/drawings/plans • an *architectural* detail/element/feature/style – **ar·chi·tec·tur·al·ly** *adv* • *architecturally* wonderful buildings

[1]**ar·chive** /ˈɑɚˌkaɪv/ *noun, pl* **-chives** *[count]* : a place in which public records or historical materials (such as documents) are kept • an *archive* of historical manuscripts • The original movie was stored in a film *archive*.; *also* : the material that is stored in an archive • He has been reading through the *archives* to research his article on the town's history.
– **ar·chi·val** /ɑɚˈkaɪvəl/ *adj* • *archival* resources/material

[2]**archive** *verb* **-chives; -chived; -chiv·ing** *[+ obj]* : to collect and store materials (such as recordings, documents, or computer files) so that they can be found and used when they are needed • The organization was devoted to cataloging and *archiving* printed materials on the labor movement. • She *archived* her e-mail messages in a folder on her hard drive. • a collection of *archived* articles

ar·chi·vist /ˈɑɚkəvɪst/ *noun, pl* **-vists** *[count]* : a person who has the job of collecting and storing the materials in an archive

arch·ri·val /ɑɚʧˈraɪvəl/ *noun, pl* **-vals** *[count]* : someone's chief rival or opponent • In baseball, the Boston Red Sox and the New York Yankees are *archrivals*.

arch·way /ˈɑɚʧˌweɪ/ *noun, pl* **-ways** *[count]* : a passage that goes under an arch; *also* : an arch over a passage

arc·tic /ˈɑɚktɪk/ *adj*
1 *or* ***Arctic*** *always used before a noun* : of or relating to the North Pole or the region around it • off the *arctic* coast • The group is involved in *Arctic* exploration. • *Arctic* waters — compare ANTARCTIC
2 : very cold • *arctic* temperatures

Arctic Circle *noun*
the Arctic Circle : an imaginary line that goes around the Earth near the North Pole

ar·dent /ˈɑɚdn̩t/ *adj [more ~; most ~]* : having or showing very strong feelings • She is an *ardent* [=*fervent*] believer in her religion. [=she believes very strongly in her religion] • an *ardent* [=*passionate*] admirer • *ardent* fans • *ardent* [=*amorous*] lovers
– **ar·dent·ly** *adv*

ar·dor *(US) or chiefly Brit* **ar·dour** /ˈɑɚdɚ/ *noun, pl* **-dors**
1 : a strong feeling of energy or eagerness *[noncount]* He preached with the *ardor* [=*fervor*] of a true believer. *[count]* the sudden *ardors* of youth
2 *[noncount]* : a strong feeling of love • young love, with all its *ardor* [=*passion*] and intensity

ar·du·ous /ˈɑɚʤəwəs/ *adj [more ~; most ~]* : very difficult • He went through a long and *arduous* training program. • *arduous* efforts • years of *arduous* study • an *arduous* chore/duty/job/task • an *arduous* journey across miles of desert
– **ar·du·ous·ly** *adv* • working *arduously* – **ar·du·ous·ness** *noun [noncount]*

are see BE

ar·ea /ˈerijə/ *noun, pl* **ar·eas**
1 *[count]* **a** : a part or section within a larger place : REGION • Settlers came to this *area* from the east. • The group visited the *area* during a hunting trip. • in the *area* surrounding the lake • The storm caused damage in many *areas* along the coast. • a bird found only in remote *areas* of the U.S. • in many *areas* of the world • He is the metropolitan *area's* most popular politician. • urban and rural *areas* • He lived in an unfashionable *area* of the city. • a residential *area* • One of our representatives will be in your *area* [=*neighborhood*] next week. **b** : a section of space within a building, room, etc. • She set aside a work *area* in the kitchen. • The dining *area* has extra windows. • We were asked to wait in the reception *area*. • The park had several picnic *areas*.
2 *[count]* : a part of the surface of something (such as a person's body or a piece of cloth) • Choose a small *area* of the fabric to test first. • The patient was having pain in the shoulder/abdominal *area*. = The patient was having pain in the *area* of the shoulder/abdomen.
3 *[count]* : a field of activity or study • The discovery has opened up new *areas* of/for research. • The budget continues to be a major *area* of concern. • a problem *area* • the whole *area* of foreign policy • She wants the government to provide more help in the *area* of health care. • Your question falls outside my *area* of expertise. • There are still some *areas* of disagreement between the two sides. — see also GRAY AREA
4 : the amount of space inside a shape, surface, region, room, etc. *[count]* The students learned how to calculate the *area* of a triangle. • a circle with an *area* of 500 square meters • The park has an *area* of 2 square miles. *[noncount]* a circle that is 500 square meters in *area* • *(chiefly US)* The nightclub provided enough *area* [=*room, space*] for a dance floor.
in the area of : close to (an amount) • The project will cost (somewhere) *in the area of* $50,000.

area code *noun, pl* ~ **codes** [*count*] : a number that represents each telephone service area in a country (such as the U.S. or Canada) — called also (*Brit*) *dialling code*

are·na /əˈriːnə/ *noun, pl* **-nas** [*count*]
1 : a building for sports and other forms of entertainment that has a large central area surrounded by seats • a basketball/hockey *arena*
2 : an area of activity, interest, or competition • Congress became an *arena* of opposing views. • the toughest political *arena* in the world • The economic *arena* has been dominated by that country.

arena football *noun* [*noncount*] *US* : a game that is like American football but that is played indoors on a shorter field

aren't /ˈɑɚnt, ˈɑrənt/
1 — used as a contraction of *are not* • We *aren't* ready to leave.
2 — used in questions as a contraction of *am not* • *Aren't* I included too? = I'm included too, *aren't* I? [=am I not also included?]

ar·gon /ˈɑɚˌgɑːn/ *noun* [*noncount*] : a chemical element that is a colorless gas and that is used in various products (such as lasers and some electric light bulbs)

ar·got /ˈɑɚgət, ˈɑɚgoʊ/ *noun, pl* **-gots** : the language used by a particular type or group of people [*noncount*] people communicating in criminal *argot* [=the language used by criminals] [*count*] groups communicating in their own secret *argots*

ar·gu·able /ˈɑɚgjuwəbəl/ *adj*
1 : not certain or clearly true : open to argument, dispute, or question • That word's pronunciation is *arguable*. • the *arguable* [=*questionable*] benefits of trying to follow every fad diet • That is an *arguable* point of view.
2 : possibly true — used to say that there are good reasons for believing that a statement is true • It is *arguable* that he's the best writer of his generation.

ar·gu·ably /ˈɑɚgjuwəbli/ *adv* : it can be argued — used to say that a statement is very possibly true even if it is not certainly true • He is *arguably* the best writer of his generation. [=he may well be the best writer of his generation] • It is *arguably* the busiest airport in the world.

ar·gue /ˈɑɚgju/ *verb* **-gues; -gued; -gu·ing**
1 a : to give reasons for or against something : to say or write things in order to change someone's opinion about what is true, what should be done, etc. [*no obj*] She *argued* against the proposed law. • The senator *argued* in favor of lowering taxes. • They *argued* (convincingly/persuasively) against cutting the budget. • He's always willing to *argue* for what is right. • *argue* for better funding [+ *obj*] She *argued* that the proposed law should be defeated. • He *argued* that it's far too early to make a decision. **b** [+ *obj*] : to cause (someone) to decide to do or not do something by giving reasons • They tried to *argue* their parents into getting a new car. [=to persuade their parents to get a new car] • No one can *argue* me out of doing this.
2 [*no obj*] : to disagree or fight by using angry words : QUARREL • Their neighbors *argued* (with each other) all the time. • They started *arguing* about/over politics/religion. • She would *argue* with anyone.
3 [*no obj*] : to express doubt or disagreement about something — + *with* • You ***can't argue with*** her success. [=you can't deny that she is successful]
4 a [*no obj*] : to show that something is or is not necessary, appropriate, etc. — usually + *for* or *against* • The result *argues for* a new approach. [=the result shows that we need a new approach] **b** [+ *obj*] *formal* : to give evidence of (something) • The facts *argue* [=*indicate, show*] his innocence.
argue the toss see ²TOSS
– ar·gu·er *noun, pl* **-ers** [*count*]

ar·gu·ment /ˈɑɚgjəmənt/ *noun, pl* **-ments**
1 a [*count*] : a statement or series of statements for or against something • They made a compelling/convincing/persuasive/strong *argument* for our participation. • The committee presented strong *arguments* against building a new school. • a lawyer's closing *argument* at the trial • His *argument* did not convince his opponents. **b** [*noncount*] : a discussion in which people express different opinions about something • Let us accept, for the sake of *argument*, that she is right. • Don't you want to hear both sides of the *argument*?
2 : an angry disagreement : QUARREL [*count*] They were always getting into *arguments* about/over politics. • There were many *arguments* about/over the new design. • They settled an *argument* that started in class. • I don't want to hear any *arguments* about whether you'll go. [*noncount*] I don't want to hear any *argument* about whether you'll go. • You'll get no *argument* from me. [=I won't disagree] • On that issue, there's no *argument*. [=*disagreement*]
3 [*singular*] : something which shows that something is or is not necessary, appropriate, etc. — usually + *for* or *against* • The result is an *argument for* a new approach. [=the result shows that we need to try a new approach]

ar·gu·men·ta·tion /ˌɑɚgjəmənˈteɪʃən/ *noun* [*noncount*] *formal* : the act or process of giving reasons for or against something : the act or process of making and presenting arguments • He tried to use *argumentation* to convince his opponents, rather than force.

ar·gu·men·ta·tive /ˌɑɚgjəˈmɛntətɪv/ *adj* [*more* ~; *most* ~] : tending to argue : having or showing a tendency to disagree or argue with other people in an angry way : QUARRELSOME • an *argumentative* person • He became more *argumentative* during the debate. • an *argumentative* essay
– ar·gu·men·ta·tive·ly *adv* **– ar·gu·men·ta·tive·ness** *noun* [*noncount*]

ar·gy–bar·gy /ˌɑɚʤiˈbɑɚʤi/ *noun, Brit, informal* : an argument or disagreement : SQUABBLE [*singular*] The tenants got into a bit of an *argy-bargy* with each other. [*noncount*] There's been a certain amount of *argy-bargy* between the tenants.

aria /ˈɑrijə/ *noun, pl* **ari·as** [*count*] : a song in an opera sung by one person

ar·id /ˈerəd/ *adj* [*more* ~; *most* ~]
1 : very dry : having very little rain or water • an *arid* desert • *arid* lands/regions
2 : lacking in interest and life • a dull and *arid* textbook
– arid·i·ty /əˈrɪdəti/ *noun* [*noncount*] • the *aridity* of the land

Ar·i·es /ˈeriz/ *noun, pl* **Aries**
1 [*noncount*] : the first sign of the zodiac : the sign of the zodiac that comes between Pisces and Taurus and has a ram as its symbol — see picture at ZODIAC
2 [*count*] : a person born under the sign of Aries : a person born between March 21 and April 19 • My friend is an *Aries* and I'm a Taurus.

aright /əˈraɪt/ *adv, old-fashioned + literary* : so as to be correct • His name was Jones, if I remember *aright*. [=*rightly, correctly*] • He tried to set/put things *aright*. [=*right, to rights*]

arise /əˈraɪz/ *verb* **aris·es; arose** /əˈroʊz/; **aris·en** /əˈrɪzn̩/; **aris·ing** [*no obj*]
1 a : to begin to occur or to exist • These problems *arise* when people try to avoid responsibility. • Questions have *arisen* concerning/about the company's financial records. • The sport *arose* in the 19th century. • The opportunity *arose* for a new position to be created. • A conflict *arose* because of a misunderstanding. • Jobs will be created ***as/when the need arises*** [=jobs will be created when they are needed] • ***Should the need arise***, he can defend himself. [=he can defend himself if it is necessary to do so] **b** : to begin at a source • Tumors *arose* in different areas of the skin. — usually + *from* • arteries that *arise from* the aorta • small roots *arising from* the stems • The disease probably *arose from* a virus. • The river *arises from* two main sources.
2 a : to get up from sleep or after lying down • He *arose* [=(more commonly) *rose*] refreshed after a good night's sleep. **b** : to stand up • He *arose* [=(more commonly) *rose*] from his chair.
3 : to move upward • Mist *arose* [=(more commonly) *rose*] from the valley.

ar·is·toc·ra·cy /ˌerəˈstɑːkrəsi/ *noun, pl* **-cies** [*count*] : the highest social class in some countries : the people who have special titles (such as *duke* and *duchess*), who typically own land, and who traditionally have more money and power than the other people in a society • a member of the *aristocracy*

aris·to·crat /əˈrɪstəˌkræt/ *noun, pl* **-crats** [*count*] : a member of an aristocracy • an *aristocrat* by birth
– aris·to·crat·ic /əˌrɪstəˈkrætɪk/ *adj* [*more* ~; *most* ~] • *aristocratic* titles like *duke* and *duchess* **– aris·to·crat·i·cal·ly** /əˌrɪstəˈkrætɪkli/ *adv*

arith·me·tic /əˈrɪθməˌtɪk/ *noun* [*noncount*]
1 : a branch of mathematics that deals with numbers and their addition, subtraction, multiplication, and division
2 : the act or process of calculating a number • a software program that will do the *arithmetic* for you
– ar·ith·met·ic /ˌerɪθˈmɛtɪk/ *or* **ar·ith·met·i·cal** /ˌerɪθˈmɛtɪkəl/ *adj* **– ar·ith·met·i·cal·ly** /ˌerɪθˈmɛtɪkli/ *adv*

A

Ark /ˈɑɚk/ *noun* [*singular*] *in the Bible* : the ship in which Noah and his family were saved from a great flood that God sent down on the world in ancient times • Noah's *Ark*

[1]**arm** /ˈɑɚm/ *noun, pl* **arms** [*count*]

1 : either one of the two long body parts that join the top of your body at the shoulder and that end at the hand or wrist • He has big, strong, muscular *arms.* • She broke her left *arm.* = Her left *arm* was/got broken. • He hurt his throwing/pitching *arm* [=the arm that he uses to throw/pitch a ball] in the last game. • She put/threw her *arms* around him. [=she hugged him] • She had a newspaper tucked under her *arm.* • He was carrying a bag of groceries in each *arm.* • He gave/offered his *arm* to her, and she took it. [=she held onto his arm] • She grabbed my *arm.* = She grabbed me by the *arm.* • He was standing there with his *arms* crossed/folded. • She stood with her *arms* outstretched. = She stood with her *arms* wide open. • She sat cradling the baby in her *arms.* • I've known her since she was ***a babe in arms***. [=a baby who is too young to walk and has to be held] • He ***took her in/into his arms*** [=he embraced her] and kissed her passionately. • She found him ***in the arms of*** [=being embraced by] another woman. • He showed up at the party with a young woman ***on his arm***. [=holding his arm] • He ***took her (by the) arm*** and they walked in to dinner. — see picture at HUMAN

2 : the part of a piece of clothing (such as a shirt or coat) that covers the arm : SLEEVE • The jacket's *arms* are too tight. = The jacket is too tight in the *arms.*

3 : a part of a piece of furniture (such as a chair or couch) that gives support for a person's arm • the *arm* of the sofa — see also [1]ARMCHAIR

4 a : a long thin piece that is connected to the main part of a machine, structure, etc., and that looks or moves like a human arm • the robot's mechanical *arm* • the machine's robotic *arm* • the *arm* of the record player **b :** a long and narrow area of water • an *arm* of the sea

5 : the part of a group or organization that performs a specific job or function — usually singular • the organization's political *arm* [=the part of the organization that deals with politics] • It is the most powerful *arm* [=*division*] of the organization. • the military *arm* of the government

6 *US, sports* : a person's ability to throw a ball — usually singular • Their pitcher's got a great *arm.* • a strong/weak *arm*

an arm and a leg informal : a very large amount of money • It's a reliable car, and it doesn't cost *an arm and a leg.* [=it isn't too expensive]

arm in arm : next to each other with the arm of one person linked at the elbow to the arm of another person • an elderly couple walking down the street *arm in arm*

a shot in the arm see [1]SHOT

as long as someone's arm see [1]LONG

at arm's length : from a distance that is the length of a person's arm • It's best to view the painting *at arm's length.* • holding a candle *at arm's length* ✧ To ***keep someone or something at arm's length*** is to avoid being very close to or friendly with someone or something. • Since going to college, he has *kept his old friends at arm's length.* • They no longer trust her and are *keeping her at arm's length.* • The government has *kept the group at arm's length* until now.

chance your arm see [2]CHANCE

give your right arm see [1]GIVE

the long arm of the law : the ability of the police to find and catch people who commit crimes • *The long arm of the law* finally caught up with him [=the police caught him] 30 years later. • So far, she's been able to escape *the long arm of the law.*

twist someone's arm see [1]TWIST

with open arms : in a very kind and friendly way • We were welcomed back ***with open arms***.

— compare [2]ARM

[2]**arm** *noun, pl* **arms**

1 [*count*] : a gun or other weapon that is used especially in a war — usually plural • The government was selling *arms* to other countries. • the right of individuals to carry/bear *arms* [=*firearms*] — often used before another noun • an *arms* agreement/deal • *arms* shipments • The United Nations lifted the *arms* embargo against the country. — see also ARMS RACE, FIREARM, SMALL ARMS

2 *arms* [*plural*] : COAT OF ARMS • the royal *arms* of Portugal

call to arms ✧ A *call to arms* is a request or command to become ready to fight. • The government issued a *call to arms.* The phrase is also used for something that tries to make people fight for a cause. • Her book is a political *call to arms.*

in arms ✧ If someone is your ***brother/sister/comrade in arms***, that person has helped you fight an enemy especially in a war. • He and I were *brothers in arms.* [=we fought in a war together]

lay down your arms : to put down your weapons and stop fighting • The soldiers refused to *lay down their arms.*

present arms military — used as a command to hold your rifle so that it points straight up in front of you as a sign of respect

take up arms : to pick up weapons and become ready to fight • They *took up arms* to defend their city. • The rebels are *taking up arms* against their own government.

under arms : serving in the military • the number of Americans now *under arms* around the world

up in arms : angry and ready to fight or argue • Voters were *up in arms* over the new taxes.

— compare [1]ARM

[3]**arm** *verb* **arms; armed; arm·ing**

1 : to provide (yourself, a group, a country, etc.) with weapons especially in order to fight a war or battle [+ *obj*] They *armed* the men for battle. • The group of fighters was *armed* by a foreign government. • The two countries have been *arming* themselves for years, but now they have agreed to disarm. — often + *with* • The government has *armed* its military *with* the best weapons. • She *armed* herself *with* a kitchen knife. [*no obj*] *arming* for battle • countries that are continuing to *arm* [=to produce and gather weapons] — opposite DISARM; see also [1]ARMED, UNARMED

2 [+ *obj*] : to provide (someone) *with* a way of fighting, competing, or succeeding • We *armed* ourselves *with* the tools we would need to survive in the forest. • They *arm* people *with* accurate information. • *arming* women *with* the right to vote

3 [+ *obj*] : to make (a bomb, weapon, etc.) ready for use • Once the bomb has been *armed*, we have five minutes to escape. — opposite DISARM

ar·ma·da /ɑɚˈmɑːdə/ *noun, pl* **-das** [*count*] : a large group of ships, boats, etc. • an *armada* of fishing boats

ar·ma·dil·lo /ˌɑɚməˈdɪloʊ/ *noun, pl* **-los** [*count*] : a small American animal that lives underground and whose head and body are protected by a hard shell

armadillo

Ar·ma·ged·don /ˌɑɚməˈgɛdn/ *noun* : a final destructive battle or conflict [*singular*] trying to avoid/avert the threat of a nuclear *Armageddon* [=a nuclear war that would destroy the world] [*noncount*] the threat of nuclear *Armageddon*

ar·ma·ment /ˈɑɚməmənt/ *noun, pl* **-ments**

1 [*noncount*] : the process of preparing for war by producing and obtaining weapons • The country's *armament* will take years. — opposite DISARMAMENT

2 *armaments* [*plural*] : military weapons that are used to fight a war • a small nation that is determined to have adequate *armaments*

ar·ma·ture /ˈɑɚməʧɚ/ *noun, pl* **-tures** [*count*] *technical*

1 : the part of an electric motor or generator that produces an electric current when it turns in a magnetic field

2 : a frame used by a sculptor to support a figure that is being modeled

arm·band /ˈɑɚmˌbænd/ *noun, pl* **-bands**

1 [*count*] : a band worn around the arm; *especially* : one that is worn around the upper part of a sleeve to show who you are or to show that you are in mourning

2 *armbands* [*plural*] *Brit* : WATER WINGS

[1]**arm·chair** /ˈɑɚmˌʧeɚ/ *noun, pl* **-chairs** [*count*] : a chair with supports for your arms

[2]**armchair** *adj, always used before a noun*

1 — used to describe people who like to read about or watch the dangerous or exciting activities of other people • an *armchair* adventurer • *armchair* tourists/travelers

2 — used to describe people who like to give opinions about matters they do not have to deal with themselves and do not have responsibility for • *armchair* strategists who second-guess generals

[1]**armed** /ˈɑɚmd/ *adj*

1 : involving the use of weapons • They planned an *armed* attack/assault on the country's capital. • the threat of *armed* conflict • *armed* uprisings • He's serving eight years for

armed robbery. [=robbery while carrying a gun or other weapon] — opposite UNARMED; see also ARMED FORCES
2 : carrying weapons • The building is surrounded by *armed* guards/soldiers. • an *armed* robber • He wasn't *armed* at the time. [=he wasn't carrying a gun] • The police said that the thieves should be considered ***armed and dangerous***. • a group of ***heavily armed*** men [=men who are carrying many dangerous weapons] • The police were ***armed to the teeth***. [=the police had many weapons] — often + *with* • The car was *armed with* explosives. • airplanes *armed with* bombs • The robber was *armed with* a knife. — opposite UNARMED
3 : having something that provides security or strength — usually + *with* • We went into the forest *armed with* food, extra clothes, and lots of bug spray. • journalists *armed with* cameras and notebooks • students *armed with* the knowledge they would need to succeed in the world
– compare ²ARMED

²**armed** *adj* **:** having arms of a specific kind or number — used in combination • a one-*armed* man • a long-*armed* boxer — compare ¹ARMED

armed forces *noun [plural]* **:** the military organizations (such as the army, navy, and air force) of a country • He has had a long career in the *armed forces*. • Will the new defense policy weaken the *armed forces*? • The *armed forces* oppose the policy. [=military leaders oppose it] — called also *armed services*

arm·ful /ˈɑɚmˌfʊl/ *noun, pl* **arm·fuls** *also* **arms·ful** /ˈɑɚmzˌfʊl/ *[count]* **:** an amount that can be carried in a person's arm or arms — usually + *of* • She returned from the library with an *armful of* books. • stacking *armfuls of* wood to bring in for the fireplace

arm·hole /ˈɑɚmˌhoʊl/ *noun, pl* **-holes** *[count]* **:** an opening for the arm in a piece of clothing

ar·mi·stice /ˈɑɚməstəs/ *noun, pl* **-stic·es** *[count]* **:** an agreement to stop fighting a war **:** TRUCE

Armistice Day *noun, pl* ~ **Days** *[count, noncount] US, old-fashioned* **:** VETERANS DAY — used before the official adoption of *Veterans Day* in 1954

arm·load /ˈɑɚmˌloʊd/ *noun, pl* **-loads** *[count]* **:** ARMFUL • an *armload* of clean clothes

ar·moire /ɑɚmˈwɑɚ/ *noun, pl* **-moires** *[count]* **:** a tall piece of furniture that usually has two doors and that is used to store things (such as clothes)

ar·mor *(US) or Brit* **ar·mour** /ˈɑɚmɚ/ *noun [noncount]*
1 : special clothing that people wear to protect their bodies from weapons • The officers are required to wear bulletproof body *armor*. ✧ *Armor* commonly refers to the heavy metal suits that men wore long ago when they fought in battles. • medieval suits of *armor* — see also *knight in shining armor* at ¹KNIGHT ✧ A ***chink/crack in someone's or something's armor*** is a weakness that might cause someone or something to fail or to be defeated. • They watched carefully for any *cracks in the other team's armor*. • The plan looks good, but we've found/discovered some *chinks in its armor*. • The scandal revealed/exposed a *chink in his* seemingly perfect *armor*.
2 a : a hard covering that protects something (such as a vehicle or an animal) • The shots penetrated/pierced the tank's *armor*. • an ***armor-plated*** vehicle [=a vehicle that is protected by armor; a vehicle that is covered in flat pieces of metal] • The armadillo's *armor* consists of a series of small, bony plates. — often used before another noun • The ship's hull is reinforced with ***armor plate/plating***. **b :** soldiers and vehicles (such as tanks) that are protected with armor • a weapon designed for use against enemy *armor*

ar·mored *(US) or Brit* **ar·moured** /ˈɑɚmɚd/ *adj*
1 : covered in flat pieces of metal **:** protected by armor • *armored* cars/trucks • a ship with an *armored* hull
2 a : having soldiers and vehicles that are protected with armor • Additional *armored* divisions were deployed to the eastern front. **b :** using soldiers and vehicles that are protected with armor • an *armored* assault/attack

ar·mor·er *(US) or Brit* **ar·mour·er** /ˈɑɚmərɚ/ *noun, pl* **-ers** *[count]* **:** a person or business that makes and repairs armor or weapons • The sword was made by a master *armorer*.

ar·mory *(US) or Brit* **ar·moury** /ˈɑɚməri/ *noun, pl* **-ies** *[count]*
1 : a supply of weapons • the nation's nuclear *armory* [=*arsenal*] — sometimes used figuratively • The professional artist has an *armory* [=(more commonly) *arsenal, battery, array*] of tools at her disposal.
2 : a place where weapons are kept • the site of a 19th-century *armory*; *especially, US* **:** a place where weapons are kept and where soldiers are trained • a National Guard *armory*
3 : a place where weapons are made

arm·pit /ˈɑɚmˌpɪt/ *noun, pl* **-pits** *[count]*
1 : the hollow area on a person's body beneath the place where the arm and the shoulder meet — called also *underarm*; see picture at HUMAN
2 *US, informal* **:** the worst area in a place • a city described as the *armpit* of America

arm·rest /ˈɑɚmˌrɛst/ *noun, pl* **-rests** *[count]* **:** the part of a seat in a car, an airplane, etc., that supports your arm

arms race *noun, pl* ~ **races** *[count]* **:** a situation in which countries that are enemies each try to build or collect weapons faster than the other can • a nuclear *arms race*

arm–twist·ing /ˈɑɚmˌtwɪstɪŋ/ *noun [noncount] informal* **:** the act of using pressure to make people do things that they do not want to do • There was a lot of political *arm-twisting* before the Senate vote. — see also *twist someone's arm* at ¹TWIST

arm wrestling *noun [noncount]* **:** a contest in which two people sit facing each other and join usually their right hands together and then try to force each other's arm down
– arm wrestler *noun, pl* ~ **wrestlers** *[count]*

ar·my /ˈɑɚmi/ *noun, pl* **-mies** *[count]*
1 a : a large group of soldiers organized to fight battles on land • the *armies* of Alexander the Great • raise an *army* **b :** the part of a country's military forces that includes soldiers who are trained to fight on land • He left home and joined the *army* after he graduated from high school. — usually capitalized when a specific army is being referred to • the U.S. *Army*, Navy, Air Force, and Marines • She's in the British *Army*. — often used before another noun • *army* officers/units/barracks
2 : a large number of people or things that are involved in some activity together • The company employs an *army* of lawyers to handle its legal affairs. • They sent in a whole *army* of trained technicians. • an *army* of ants • The organization was founded by a dedicated *army* of volunteers. — see also SALVATION ARMY

aro·ma /əˈroʊmə/ *noun, pl* **-mas** *[count]* **:** a noticeable and usually pleasant smell • the *aroma* of fresh-baked bread • The wine has a fruity *aroma*.

aro·ma·ther·a·py /əˌroʊməˈθɛrəpi/ *noun [noncount]* **:** the use of natural oils that have a pleasant smell to make a person feel better especially by rubbing the oils into the skin
– aro·ma·ther·a·pist /əˌroʊməˈθɛrəpɪst/ *noun, pl* **-pists** *[count]*

ar·o·mat·ic /ˌerəˈmætɪk/ *adj [more ~; most ~]* **:** having a noticeable and pleasant smell **:** FRAGRANT • *aromatic* herbs/oils • a highly *aromatic* stew

arose *past tense of* ARISE

¹**around** /əˈraʊnd/ *adv*
1 a : in a circle • The wheel went/turned *around* (and *around*). • We kept going *around* [=(*chiefly Brit*) *round*] in circles without getting anywhere. **b :** in, along, or through a curving path • The road goes *around* [=(*chiefly Brit*) *round*] by the lake. • Don't take the long way *around*: I know a shortcut. **c** *chiefly US* — used to indicate a measurement that is made along the outer surface of something circular • "How big *around* is the tree?" "It's five feet *around*." [=(*chiefly Brit*) *round*] [=the circumference of the tree is five feet]
2 — used to indicate that a number, amount, time, etc., is not exact or certain • The price of dinner was *around* [=(*chiefly US*) *about*] $50. • It lasted *around* [=(*chiefly US*) *about*] a century. • The repair should cost *around* [=*approximately, roughly*] $200. • We should leave in *around* 10 minutes. • We got home at *around* 8 o'clock. = (*US*) We got home ***around about*** 8 o'clock. [=it was approximately 8 o'clock when we got home]
3 a : in close from all sides so as to surround someone or something • People crowded *around* [=(*chiefly Brit*) *round*] to hear her. **b :** in many different directions • They wandered *around* [=(*chiefly Brit*) *about*] for several hours. • He entered the room and looked *around*. **c :** in or to many different places • People were standing *around* [=(*chiefly Brit*) *about*], talking quietly in small groups. • His tools were scattered *around* [=(*chiefly Brit*) *about*] carelessly. • She travels *around* [=(*chiefly Brit*) *about*] on business quite a lot. • This is a very interesting town: let me show you *around*. **d :** in or near a particular area or place • We went to the store, but there was no one *around*. [=there was no one there; (*chiefly Brit*) there was no one about] • Let's wait/stay/stick *around* awhile. • I'm

A

not sure where it is, but it must be *around* somewhere. • It's safer when there are other people *around*. • I'd like to speak to him if he's *around*. • So long, then! ***(I'll) See you around*** [=I'll see you later] **e : to a particular place** • Why don't you come *around* (to my house) for dinner?

4 : in the opposite direction • She turned (completely) *around*. [=(less commonly) *about*, (*chiefly Brit*) *round*]

5 — used with some verbs to indicate repeated or continued action or behavior that does not have a clear or definite purpose • He's always joking *around* when he should be serious. • Don't play/fool *around* with your food like that! • I was just standing *around*, waiting for the train to arrive.

6 — used to describe something that returns in a regular or repeated way • Winter has come *around* [=(*chiefly Brit*) *round*] again.

7 — used to describe how two things are arranged or ordered • You put the fork on the left and the knife on the right. They should be the other way *around*. [=(*chiefly Brit*) *round*] [=the fork should be on the right and the knife on the left] • You've got them the wrong way *around*. [=(*chiefly Brit*) *round*]

come around see [1]COME

[2]around *prep*

1 a : on all sides of (something or someone) • a house with trees (all) *around* [=(*chiefly Brit*) *round*] it • The people were seated *around* the table. • A crowd gathered *around* him. **b : so as to circle or surround (something or someone)** • He tied the rope *around* his waist. • They wrapped the blanket *around* [=*about*] her. **: moving so as to circle (something or someone)** • The Earth revolves/goes/moves *around* [=(*chiefly Brit*) *round*] the Sun. • We went all *around* the lake enjoying the different views. • They sailed *around* the world. **c : over or in different parts of (a place)** • He traveled (all) *around* [=(*chiefly Brit*) *round*] the country. • He's a well-known figure *around* the town. • We drove all *around* the town looking for him. • This is a very interesting town: let me show you *around* it. • We took a tour *around* New England. • You can find lots of good restaurants *around* here. • I help her out sometimes *around* the house. **d : on or to another side of (something)** • We were surprised by what we saw when we walked *around* the corner. • There's another door *around* the back of the house.

2 a : in the area near to (something or someone) • Fish are abundant *around* [=*about*, *near*] the reefs. • I'm not sure where it is, but it must be somewhere *around* here. = It must be *around* here somewhere. • I feel happier when I'm *around* her. • It happened in Naples—or (somewhere) *around* there. • I can tell from/by your accent that you're not from *around* here. • It's safer when there are other people *around* you. **b : near or not far from (something) in time** • The company was founded (at) *around* [=*about*] the turn of the century. • a night *around* [=*about*] midsummer

3 : so as to avoid or get past (something) • She went *around* the puddle to avoid getting dirty. • We found a way *around* their objections.

4 — used to indicate the central part or idea used for building or organizing something • a society built/organized *around* kinship ties

[3]around *adj, not used before a noun* **: existing or active** • She is among the most creative of the artists *around* [=*active*, *working*] today.

been around ✧ Something that has *been around* for a long time has existed or been available for a long time. • I'm surprised you haven't read that book yet. It's *been around* [=*been out*] for ages! A person who has *been around* has had a lot of different experiences and knows a lot about the world. • You're a man of the world: I can tell you've *been around*.

up and around see [2]UP

around–the–clock *adj, always used before a noun, chiefly US* **: happening or continuing all day and all night** • The prisoner requires *around-the-clock* [=*round-the-clock*, *constant*] surveillance. • *around-the-clock* care

arouse /əˈraʊz/ *verb* **arouses; aroused; arous·ing** [+ *obj*]

1 : to cause (an emotional or mental state) • He tried to sneak past without *arousing* suspicion. [=without causing people to become suspicious] • Their comments *aroused* our anger/curiosity. [=their comments made us angry/curious] • The report *aroused* a great deal of public interest/debate. • She *aroused* [=*inspired*] great loyalty in her friends and extreme hatred in her enemies.

2 : to excite (someone) sexually • The husky sound of her voice could always *arouse* him.

3 a : to wake (someone) from sleep • She was sleeping so soundly that we had difficulty *arousing* her. [=(more commonly) *waking her up*] • I was *aroused* [=*roused*, *awakened*] from a deep sleep by a loud noise outside my window. **b : to cause (someone) to become active, ready, or upset** • Their proposal is certain to *arouse* the opposition. • They get *aroused* [=(more commonly) *worked up*] over the slightest offense.

– arous·al /əˈraʊzəl/ *noun* [*noncount*] • sexual *arousal*

– arousing *adj* [*more* ~; *most* ~] • He found the idea very *arousing*. [=sexually exciting]

ar·peg·gio /ɑɚˈpɛʤijoʊ/ *noun, pl* **-gios** [*count*] *music* **: a chord in which the notes are played separately instead of at the same time** • The guitarist warmed up with a few simple *arpeggios*.

arr. *abbr* **1** arranged by • String Quartet No. 11 by Beethoven (*arr.* Mahler) **2** arrive, arrival • flight 206 *arr.* New York 12:30 p.m.

ar·raign /əˈreɪn/ *verb* **-raigns; -raigned; -raign·ing** [+ *obj*] *law* **: to state the charges against someone who is accused of a crime in a formal procedure before a judge — usually used as *(be) arraigned*** • He *was arraigned* on charges of manslaughter.

– ar·raign·ment /əˈreɪnmənt/ *noun, pl* **-ments** [*count*] Her *arraignment* is scheduled for two weeks from today. [*noncount*]The defendant failed to appear for *arraignment*.

ar·range /əˈreɪnʤ/ *verb* **-rang·es; -ranged; -rang·ing**

1 [+ *obj*] **a : to move and organize (things) into a particular order or position** • She *arranged* her pictures on her desk. • He *arranged* some fresh fruit neatly on a plate. • *arranging* flowers in a vase • The books were *arranged* according to their subject. = The books were *arranged* by subject. • We *arranged* and rearranged the order several times. **b : to give a particular order or position to the parts of (something)** • They *arranged* [=*organized*] the room around a fireplace. • She *arranged* her hair on top of her head.

2 : to organize the details of something before it happens : to plan (something) [+ *obj*]Don't worry: I'll *arrange* [=*take care of*, *deal with*] everything. • All of the details have been *arranged* [=*taken care of*, *dealt with*] in advance. • Please *arrange* a meeting with your partners. • *arrange* a funeral • I think we can *arrange* a deal. • Let's *arrange* our schedules so that we can meet for lunch. • They *arranged* their daughter's marriage when she was a child. [=they chose who she would marry] • You'll need to *arrange* transportation from the airport. [*no obj*] **— often + *for*** • You'll need to *arrange for* transportation from the airport. • She *arranged for* a car to pick us up at our house. • Can you *arrange for* us to meet your friend? **— often followed by *to + verb*** • I can *arrange to have* the day off from work. • They *arranged to meet* each other at the restaurant.

3 [+ *obj*] *music* **: to change (a song, a musical, etc.) so that it can be performed by particular voices or instruments** • He *arranged* her last two albums.

arranged marriage *noun, pl* ~ **-riages** [*count*] **: a marriage in which the husband and wife are chosen for each other by their parents**

ar·range·ment /əˈreɪnʤmənt/ *noun, pl* **-ments**

1 : the way that things or people are organized for a particular purpose or activity : the way that things or people are arranged [*noncount*]They changed the *arrangement* of furniture in the room. • the dictionary's alphabetical *arrangement* [=*ordering*] of words • the collection and *arrangement* of data [*count*]a chronological *arrangement* of historical events • We tried several different *arrangements* of the parts/components/elements. • Having my brother and his wife living nearby was an ideal *arrangement* for our family. • The family had very unusual living *arrangements*. • "What were your sleeping *arrangements*?" "I slept on the bed while he slept on the floor." • We'll have to change the seating *arrangements* for the dinner party.

2 : something that is done to prepare or plan for something in the future [*count*] **— usually plural** • She has her secretary handle all of her travel *arrangements*. • He helped his mother with his father's funeral *arrangements*. **— often used with *make*** • The city *made* special *arrangements* [=*preparations*] for the Queen's visit. • All of the *arrangements* have been *made* in advance. • They *made arrangements* to meet each other at the restaurant. • We provide breakfast and dinner, but you *make* your own *arrangements* for lunch. [*non-*

count] Her job includes *arrangement* of her boss's travel plans.
3 [*count*] **:** a usually informal agreement ▪ There was an unusual political *arrangement* between the two countries. ▪ business/financial *arrangements* ▪ I'm sure we can come to some *arrangement.* — often + *with* ▪ Our band has an *arrangement with* the club's manager. ▪ The company made an *arrangement with* the college to supply all of its computers.
4 [*count*] **:** something made by putting things together and organizing them ▪ a flower/floral *arrangement* = an *arrangement* of flowers
5 [*count*] *music* **:** a piece of music that has been changed so that it can be performed by particular types of voices or instruments ▪ orchestral/vocal *arrangements* ▪ an *arrangement* for the guitar ▪ a rock *arrangement* of an old blues song

ar·rang·er /əˈreɪnʤɚ/ *noun, pl* **-ers** [*count*]
1 : a person who changes pieces of music for particular voices or instruments **:** a person who arranges music ▪ a talented composer and *arranger*
2 : a person who arranges things ▪ a flower *arranger* ▪ a funeral *arranger* ▪ an *arranger* [=(more commonly) *organizer*] of political rallies

ar·rant /ˈerənt/ *adj, always used before a noun* [*more* ~; *most* ~] *somewhat old-fashioned + literary* **:** of the worst kind — used to make a statement more forceful ▪ This is *arrant* [=*utter, complete*] nonsense! ▪ an *arrant* fool

Do not confuse *arrant* with *errant.*

¹ar·ray /əˈreɪ/ *noun, pl* **-rays**
1 [*count*] **:** a large group or number *of* things — usually singular ▪ They offer a wide/vast/bewildering *array of* products and services. ▪ The car is available in an *array of* colors. [=in many different colors] ▪ We encountered a whole *array of* problems. [=many problems]
2 [*count*] *technical* **a :** a group of numbers, symbols, etc., that are arranged in rows and columns **b :** a way of organizing pieces of information in the memory of a computer so that similar kinds of information are together
3 [*count*] *technical* **:** a group of devices that together form a unit ▪ an antenna *array* ▪ an *array* of solar panels
4 [*noncount*] *formal + literary* **:** rich or beautiful clothing ▪ She was dressed in grand/glorious *array.*

²array *verb* **-rays; -rayed; -ray·ing** [+ *obj*] *formal*
1 : to place (a group of things) in a particular position so that they are in order or so that they look attractive — usually used as *(be) arrayed* ▪ The layers consist of bricks *arrayed* [=*arranged*] in regular patterns. ▪ The table *was arrayed* with all sorts of delicacies. [=there were all sorts of delicacies placed attractively on the table]
2 *literary* **:** to dress (someone, especially yourself) in fine clothing ▪ She *arrayed* herself in rich velvets and satins.
3 : to put (soldiers) in a place or position so that they are ready to attack ▪ They *arrayed* [=*deployed*] the troops along the hilltop. — usually used as *(be) arrayed* ▪ The troops *were arrayed* along the hilltop. ▪ The general surveyed the forces *arrayed* against him.

ar·rears /əˈriɚz/ *noun* [*plural*]
1 : money that is owed and that has not been paid when it should be ▪ He's been trying pay off the *arrears* on his mortgage. ▪ alimony/rent *arrears*
2 — used to describe a situation in which someone has failed to make a regular payment at the required time ▪ He is two months ***in arrears*** [=*behind*] with his mortgage payments. ▪ The account is two months *in arrears.* [=*overdue, delinquent*] ▪ He has fallen ***into arrears*** on his mortgage payments.
3 — used to describe a situation in which someone is paid money that was earned at an earlier time ▪ You will be paid interest on your investment ***in arrears.*** ▪ construction workers paid *in arrears* for their work

¹ar·rest /əˈrest/ *verb* **-rests; -rest·ed; -rest·ing** [+ *obj*]
1 : to use the power of the law to take and keep (someone, such as a criminal) ▪ The police *arrested* him on drug charges. ▪ The police officer said, "I'm *arresting* you in the name of the law." — often used as *(be) arrested* ▪ He *was arrested* for assault. ▪ She threatened to have him *arrested.* ▪ He got *arrested.* ✧ A person who is arrested by the police is taken to a police station or jail and kept there.
2 *formal* **:** to stop the progress or movement of (something) ▪ The medics were unable to *arrest* [=*stop*] the bleeding. ▪ The drugs can't *arrest* the disease's progress, but they can slow it down considerably. ▪ *arrested* development
3 *formal* **:** to attract and hold the attention of (someone or something) ▪ colors that *arrest* [=*catch*] the eye ▪ My attention was *arrested* [=*caught*] by a sudden movement.
– arresting *adj* [*more* ~; *most* ~] ▪ an *arresting* [=*eye-catching*] painting/image ▪ his most *arresting* novel yet

²arrest *noun, pl* **-rests**
1 : the act of legally taking and keeping someone (such as a criminal) **:** the act of arresting someone [*count*] The police are investigating the case but they have not yet made any *arrests.* [*noncount*] She was charged with resisting *arrest.* ▪ He has accused the police of wrongful *arrest.* [=of arresting someone who should not have been arrested] ▪ The information has led to the *arrest* of three suspects. ▪ The police placed/put her ***under arrest*** [=the police arrested her] — see also CITIZEN'S ARREST, FALSE ARREST, HOUSE ARREST
2 *medical* **:** an occurrence in which a part of the body suddenly stops working [*noncount*] The patient went into ***cardiac arrest*** [=the patient's heart stopped beating] [*count*] The hospital reported an increase in ***respiratory arrests.*** [=instances in which patients stopped breathing]

ar·riv·al /əˈraɪvəl/ *noun, pl* **-als**
1 : the act of coming to or reaching a place **:** the act of arriving [*noncount*] They were awaiting the *arrival* of guests. ▪ We checked into the hotel upon (our) *arrival.* ▪ The flight's estimated time of *arrival* is 11:30. = The flight's estimated *arrival* time is 11:30. ▪ When is the mail scheduled for *arrival*? [*count*] They track the number of airport *arrivals* and departures.
2 [*count*] **:** someone or something that has come to a place **:** someone or something that has arrived ▪ They were late *arrivals* at the party. ▪ Have you had a look at the bookstore's new *arrivals*? [=the books that have recently come to the bookstore] ✧ The phrase ***new arrival*** is often used to refer to a baby that has recently been born. ▪ Everyone gathered at the hospital to see the family's *new arrival.*
3 [*noncount*] **:** the time when something begins or happens ▪ They are eagerly awaiting the *arrival* of their wedding day. ▪ the changes that occur with the *arrival* of spring ▪ the *arrival* of new technology

ar·rive /əˈraɪv/ *verb* **-rives; -rived; -riv·ing** [*no obj*]
1 : to come to or reach a place after traveling, being sent, etc. ▪ He *arrived* home at six o'clock. ▪ We had some dinner before/on/upon/after *arriving* at the station. ▪ When do you expect them to *arrive* in Boston? ▪ Their flight is due to *arrive* at 11:30. ▪ The train from New York is now *arriving.* ▪ They *arrived* late at the party. ▪ The mail hasn't *arrived* yet. ▪ The new version of the software has finally *arrived* in stores.
2 a *of a day, season, time, etc.* **:** to happen or begin ▪ The day of their wedding has almost *arrived.* [=*come*] ▪ The time has *arrived* [=*come*] to address the problem. ▪ There's always a lot to do when spring *arrives.* **b** *of a baby* **:** to be born ▪ When is their baby expected to *arrive*?
3 *informal* **:** to become successful — used with a form of *have* ▪ After years of climbing the corporate ladder, he felt he *had* finally *arrived.*
arrive at [*phrasal verb*] ***arrive at (something)*** **:** to make or reach (something, such as a decision) after a lot of thought or effort ▪ She finally *arrived at* a decision. ▪ They've *arrived at* the conclusion that the plan won't work. ▪ I hope we can *arrive at* some sort of understanding/consensus.

ar·ro·gance /ˈerəgəns/ *noun* **:** an insulting way of thinking or behaving that comes from believing that you are better, smarter, or more important than other people [*noncount*] Her *arrogance* has earned her a lot of enemies. ▪ We were shocked by the *arrogance* of his comments. [*singular*] They have an *arrogance* about them. [=there is something in their behavior that seems arrogant]

ar·ro·gant /ˈerəgənt/ *adj* [*more* ~; *most* ~] **:** having or showing the insulting attitude of people who believe that they are better, smarter, or more important than other people **:** having or showing arrogance ▪ an *arrogant* young attorney ▪ She's first in her class, but she's not *arrogant* about it. ▪ an *arrogant* remark/attitude
– ar·ro·gant·ly *adv* ▪ She *arrogantly* dismissed their claims.

ar·ro·gate /ˈerəˌgeɪt/ *verb* **-gates; -gat·ed; -gat·ing** [+ *obj*] *formal* **:** to take or claim (something, such as a right or a privilege) in a way that is not fair or legal ▪ They've ***arrogated to themselves*** the power to change the rules arbitrarily. ▪ She *arrogated* the leadership role *to herself.*

ar·row /ˈeroʊ/ *noun, pl* **-rows** [*count*]
1 : a weapon that is made to be shot from a bow and that is usually a stick with a point at one end and feathers at the other end ▪ shoot an *arrow*

A

2 : a mark (such as →) that is shaped like an arrow and that is used to show direction • The *arrow* on the map points north. — see also STRAIGHT ARROW

ar·row·head /ˈeroʊˌhɛd/ *noun, pl* **-heads** [*count*] **:** a piece of stone or metal that forms the point of an arrow

ar·row·root /ˈeroʊˌruːt/ *noun* [*noncount*] **:** a powdery substance that is made from the root of a tropical plant and that is used in cooking to make liquids thicker

arse /ˈɑɚs/ *noun, pl* **ars·es** [*count*] *Brit, informal + offensive* **:** ²ASS 1

arse·hole /ˈɑɚsˌhoʊl/ *noun, pl* **-holes** [*count*] *Brit, informal + offensive* **:** ASSHOLE

ar·se·nal /ˈɑɚsənəl/ *noun, pl* **-nals** [*count*]

1 a : a collection of weapons • the nation's nuclear *arsenal* [=the nuclear weapons that the nation has] **b :** a place where weapons are made or stored • The city is home to a federal *arsenal.*

2 : a group of things or people that are available to be used • The computer comes equipped with an *arsenal* [=*battery, array*] of features. • Doctors have a broad *arsenal* of medicines to choose from. • the team's *arsenal* of veteran players

ar·se·nic /ˈɑɚsənɪk/ *noun* [*noncount*] **:** a poisonous chemical that is used especially to kill insects and weeds

ar·son /ˈɑɚsn̩/ *noun, pl* **-sons :** the illegal burning of a building or other property **:** the crime of setting fire to something [*noncount*] The cause of the fire has not yet been determined, but investigators suspect *arson.* • The town has suffered a rash of *arson* attacks. [*count*] The town has suffered a rash of *arsons.*

— ar·son·ist /ˈɑɚsn̩ɪst/ *noun, pl* **-ists** [*count*] • Investigators suspect that the fire was set by an *arsonist.*

art /ˈɑɚt/ *noun, pl* **arts**

1 [*noncount*] **:** something that is created with imagination and skill and that is beautiful or that expresses important ideas or feelings • a piece of modern/contemporary *art* • It's a remarkable picture, but is it *art*? — see also OP-ART, PERFORMANCE ART, POP ART, WORK OF ART

2 [*noncount*] **:** works created by artists **:** paintings, sculptures, etc., that are created to be beautiful or to express important ideas or feelings • the *art* [=*artwork*] of Salvador Dalí • The museum has a large collection of folk *art.* • African/Japanese/Mayan *art* — often used before another noun • *art* history • *art* objects • an *art* museum/gallery • an *art* collector/lover • She prefers *art* films to Hollywood blockbusters. — see also ARTS AND CRAFTS

3 [*noncount*] **:** the methods and skills used for painting, sculpting, drawing, etc. • He studied *art* in college. — often used before another noun • an *art* teacher/program

4 a [*count*] **:** an activity that is done to create something beautiful or to express important ideas or feelings • She studied the *art* of drawing/painting/dance. • dance, drama, and other *art* forms • the performing/visual/graphic *arts* — see also FINE ART **b** ***the arts*** **:** painting, sculpture, music, theater, literature, etc., considered as a group of activities done by people with skill and imagination • She's a patron of *the arts.* • He wants the government to increase its funding for *the arts.* — see also PERFORMING ARTS

5 [*count*] **:** a skill that someone learns through experience or study — usually singular • He never learned the *art* of making friends. [=he never learned how to make friends] • She's a master of the *art* of conversation. [=she is very good at conversation] • There's an *art* to cooking that comes only with practice. • Writing letters has become something of a ***lost art.*** [=not many people write letters any more] ✧ If you ***raise/elevate something to an art (form)*** you are known for doing something or having something (such as a personal quality). This phrase is often used in an ironic or joking way to describe qualities or abilities that are not admired. • He seems to have *elevated stupidity to an art form.* [=he is very stupid]

6 [*count*] **:** an activity that requires special knowledge or skill • Shipbuilding is both an *art* and a science. • the *art* of navigation — see also MARTIAL ART

7 ***arts*** [*plural*] **:** areas of study (such as history, language, and literature) that are intended to develop the mind in a general way **:** LIBERAL ARTS • a bachelor of *arts* • the College of *Arts* and Sciences

art de·co *or* **Art Deco** /ˌɑɚtˈdɛkoʊ/ *noun* [*noncount*] **:** a style of art, design, and architecture that uses bold lines and simple shapes ✧ Art Deco was popular in the U.S. and Europe in the 1920s and 1930s. • an *Art Deco* vase/building

artefact *chiefly Brit spelling of* ARTIFACT

ar·te·rio·scle·ro·sis /ɑɚˌtirijoʊskləˈroʊsəs/ *noun* [*noncount*] *medical* **:** a disease in which the walls of arteries become thick and hard so that it is difficult for blood to flow through them

— ar·te·rio·scle·rot·ic /ɑɚˌtiɚrijoʊskləˈrɑːtɪk/ *adj* • *arteriosclerotic* heart disease

ar·tery /ˈɑɚtəri/ *noun, pl* **-ter·ies** [*count*]

1 : any one of the tubes that carry blood from the heart to all parts of the body • coronary *arteries* • clogged *arteries* — compare VEIN

2 : a large road, river, railroad line, etc. • He favors local side roads over major *arteries.*

— ar·te·ri·al /ɑɚˈtʰirijəl/ *adj* • *arterial* walls/pressure/blood • *arterial* roads

ar·te·sian well /ɑɚˈtiːʒən-/ *noun, pl* **~ wells** [*count*] **:** a place in the ground where water flows up to the surface because of natural pressure

art·ful /ˈɑɚtfəl/ *adj* [*more ~; most ~*]

1 : done with or showing artistic skill • *artful* writing • an *artful* performance/arrangement

2 : good at getting or achieving things in ways that are clever and not noticeable • an *artful* negotiator **:** used to get or achieve things in ways that are clever and not noticeable • *artful* questioning ✧ This sense of *artful* is sometimes used in a disapproving way, especially in British English. • an *artful* [=*crafty, sly*] politician who seems to have deceived everyone • *artful* deception — compare ARTLESS

— art·ful·ly /ˈɑɚtfəli/ *adv* • an *artfully* arranged display **— art·ful·ness** *noun* [*noncount*]

art house *noun, pl* **~ houses** [*count*] **:** a movie theater that shows mostly foreign movies and movies that are made by small companies **:** a building where art films are shown — called also *art theater*

ar·thri·tis /ɑɚˈθraɪtəs/ *noun* [*noncount*] *medical* **:** a disease that causes the joints of the body to become swollen and painful — see also RHEUMATOID ARTHRITIS

— ar·thrit·ic /ɑɚˈθrɪtɪk/ *adj* [*more ~; most ~*] • painful *arthritic* fingers/joints • *arthritic* symptoms **— arthritic** *noun, pl* **-ics** [*count*] • medicines used for treating *arthritics* [=people who have arthritis]

ar·ti·choke /ˈɑɚtəˌʧoʊk/ *noun, pl* **-chokes** [*count*] **:** a vegetable with thick, pointed leaves ✧ The artichoke consists of a soft middle part surrounded by small, thick leaves. The middle, known as the *heart* of the artichoke, and the bottom part of the leaves are eaten after being cooked. — see color picture on page C4; see also JERUSALEM ARTICHOKE

¹ar·ti·cle /ˈɑɚtɪkəl/ *noun, pl* **-ti·cles** [*count*]

1 : a piece of writing about a particular subject that is included in a magazine, newspaper, etc. • a magazine/newspaper *article* • I just read an interesting *article* on/about the city's early history. • He has published numerous *articles* in scholarly journals. • an encyclopedia *article*

2 : a particular kind of object • an *article* [=*piece*] of clothing • domestic/household *articles* • *articles* [=*pieces*] of furniture — sometimes used figuratively • For many people it is an ***article of faith*** [=something that is believed without being questioned or doubted] that the economy will begin to improve soon. • A lot of people pretend to be cowboys, but he's ***the genuine article.*** [=he's a real cowboy]

3 : a separate part of a legal document that deals with a single subject • *Article* 3 of the U.S. Constitution • The company amended its *articles* of incorporation.

4 *grammar* **:** a word (such as *a, an,* or *the*) that is used with a noun to show whether or not the noun refers to a specific person or thing — see also DEFINITE ARTICLE, INDEFINITE ARTICLE

²article *verb* **-ticles; -ti·cled; -ti·cling** *Brit* **:** to work for a group of lawyers, architects, etc., while you are learning to become a lawyer, architect, etc. [*no obj*] He *articled* at the famous law firm many years ago. [*+ obj*] — usually used as *(be) articled to* • She *was articled to* a firm of engineers.

— articled *adj* • an *articled* clerk

¹ar·tic·u·late /ɑɚˈtɪkjələt/ *adj* [*more ~; most ~*]

1 : able to express ideas clearly and effectively in speech or writing • She's an intelligent and *articulate* speaker. • He was very *articulate* about his feelings on the subject. — opposite INARTICULATE

2 : clearly expressed and easily understood • an *articulate* argument/essay/speech • The baby is beginning to form *articulate* words and phrases. — opposite INARTICULATE

— ar·tic·u·late·ly *adv* • She spoke clearly and *articulately.* **— ar·tic·u·late·ness** *noun* [*noncount*]

²ar·tic·u·late /ɑɚˈtɪkjəˌleɪt/ *verb* **-lates; -lat·ed; -lat·ing**
1 [+ *obj*] **:** to express (something, such as an idea) in words ▪ He had some trouble *articulating* his thoughts. ▪ We disagree with the views *articulated* by the administration. ▪ a theory first *articulated* by ancient philosophers
2 : to say or pronounce (something, such as a word) in a way that can be clearly heard and understood [+ *obj*] She spoke slowly, *articulating* [=*enunciating*] each syllable. [*no obj*] Try to *articulate* [=*enunciate*] when delivering your speech.
3 [*no obj*] *technical* **:** to connect with a joint or something that is like a joint ▪ the bones that *articulate* with the clavicle

ar·tic·u·lat·ed /ɑɚˈtɪkjəˌleɪtəd/ *adj*
1 : connected by a joint ▪ dolls with *articulated* limbs [=arms and legs that can be moved because they are connected by joints] ▪ dinosaurs with *articulated* skulls
2 *of a vehicle* **:** having a front section connected to a large back section by means of a hinge or a joint that allows sharp turns ▪ an *articulated* bus ▪ (*Brit*) *articulated* lorries

ar·tic·u·la·tion /ɑɚˌtɪkjəˈleɪʃən/ *noun, pl* **-tions**
1 [*noncount*] *formal* **:** the act of articulating something: such as **a :** the act of expressing an idea, thought, etc., in words ▪ The book is the *articulation* of his vision. **b :** the act of saying or pronouncing something in a way that can be clearly heard and understood ▪ the *articulation* of consonants
2 [*count*] *medical* **:** a joint that allows connected parts (such as bones) to move ▪ the *articulations* between vertebrae

ar·ti·fact (*chiefly US*) *or chiefly Brit* **ar·te·fact** /ˈɑɚtɪˌfækt/ *noun, pl* **-facts** [*count*]
1 : a simple object (such as a tool or weapon) that was made by people in the past ▪ The caves contained many prehistoric *artifacts*. ▪ an *artifact* from the Colonial period
2 : an accidental effect that causes incorrect results — usually + *of* ▪ The drop in scores was merely an *artifact of* the way the test was administered.

ar·ti·fice /ˈɑɚtəfəs/ *noun, pl* **-fic·es :** dishonest or insincere behavior or speech that is meant to deceive someone [*noncount*] He spoke without *artifice* or pretense. [*count*] political/legal *artifices* ▪ The whole story was just an *artifice* to win our sympathy.

ar·ti·fi·cial /ˌɑɚtəˈfɪʃl/ *adj*
1 : not natural or real **:** made, produced, or done to seem like something natural ▪ *artificial* lighting/plants ▪ the world's first *artificial* heart ▪ This product contains no *artificial* colors/flavors/sweeteners—only natural substances are used.
2 : not happening or existing naturally **:** created or caused by people ▪ *artificial* price inflation ▪ The country's borders are *artificial*, and were set with no consideration for the various ethnic groups in the region.
3 [*more ~; most ~*] **:** not sincere ▪ an *artificial* smile ▪ Her concern seemed a bit *artificial*. [=*forced*]
– ar·ti·fi·ci·al·i·ty /ˌɑɚtəˌfɪʃiˈæləti/ *noun* [*noncount*] ▪ the *artificiality* of his manner/smile **– ar·ti·fi·cial·ly** *adv* ▪ *artificially* flavored/colored ▪ The building is *artificially* lit.

artificial insemination *noun* [*noncount*] *medical* **:** a medical process in which semen is used to make a woman or female animal pregnant without sexual intercourse ▪ children conceived through *artificial insemination*

artificial intelligence *noun* [*noncount*] *computers*
1 : an area of computer science that deals with giving machines the ability to seem like they have human intelligence
2 : the power of a machine to copy intelligent human behavior ▪ a robot with *artificial intelligence* — abbr. *AI*

artificial respiration *noun* [*noncount*] *medical* **:** a process in which air is forced into and out of the lungs of a person who has stopped breathing ✧ Artificial respiration can be done by pressing on the person's chest, by blowing into the person's mouth, or by using a special machine. — see also MOUTH-TO-MOUTH RESUSCITATION

ar·til·lery /ɑɚˈtɪləri/ *noun* [*noncount*]
1 : large guns that are used to shoot over a great distance ▪ The troops were being bombarded by *artillery*. — often used before another noun ▪ The troops were under heavy *artillery* fire. ▪ *artillery* shells — often used figuratively ▪ His first argument didn't work, so he brought out the ***heavy artillery***. [=he started using a different and more powerful argument]
2 : the part of an army that uses large guns to shoot over a great distance ▪ a captain in the *artillery* — often used before another noun ▪ *artillery* units

ar·ti·san /ˈɑɚtəzən, *Brit* ˌɑːtɪˈzæn/ *noun, pl* **-sans** [*count*] **:** a person who is skilled at making things by hand **:** CRAFTSPERSON ▪ They sell rugs made by local *artisans*.

art·ist /ˈɑɚtɪst/ *noun, pl* **-ists** [*count*]
1 : a person who creates art ▪ the great *artists* of the Renaissance ▪ a graphic *artist* **:** a person who is skilled at drawing, painting, etc. ▪ I can't draw at all, but both of my children are very talented *artists*. [=they draw very well]
2 : a skilled performer ▪ a jazz *artist* ▪ a trapeze *artist* ▪ famous ***recording artists*** [=singers and musicians who record their music]
3 : a person who is very good at something ▪ She's an *artist* in her field. [=she's very good at her job] ▪ a scam *artist* — see also RIP-OFF ARTIST

ar·tiste /ɑɚˈtiːst/ *noun, pl* **-tists** [*count*] *chiefly Brit* **:** a skilled performer **:** ARTIST

ar·tis·tic /ɑɚˈtɪstɪk/ *adj*
1 : relating to art or artists ▪ her *artistic* achievements ▪ a work of *artistic* value ▪ He shows real *artistic* talent.
2 [*more ~; most ~*] **:** having or showing the skill of an artist ▪ *artistic* creations ▪ She's an *artistic* person. [=a creative person] ▪ Both of my children are very *artistic*.
– ar·tis·ti·cal·ly /ɑɚˈtɪstɪkli/ *adv* ▪ an *artistically* arranged bouquet ▪ He's not *artistically* inclined. [=he doesn't have artistic skill]

art·ist·ry /ˈɑɚtəstri/ *noun* [*noncount*]
1 : artistic ability or skill ▪ We admired the singer's *artistry*.
2 : a quality that results from artistic ability or skill ▪ the *artistry* of her novel

art·less /ˈɑɚtləs/ *adj* [*more ~; most ~*] **:** not false or artificial **:** NATURAL ▪ the dancer's *artless* grace ▪ Her simple *artless* charm won us over instantly. — compare ARTFUL
– art·less·ly *adv* **– art·less·ness** *noun* [*noncount*]

art nou·veau *or* **Art Nouveau** /ˌɑɚtnuˈvoʊ/ *noun* [*noncount*] **:** a style of art, design, and architecture that uses curving lines and shapes that look like leaves and flowers ✧ Art Nouveau was popular in the U.S. and Europe in the late 1800s. ▪ an *Art Nouveau* lamp

arts and crafts *noun* [*plural*] **:** objects that are meant to be both useful and beautiful ▪ a shop that sells local *arts and crafts*, such as pottery and baskets **:** the activity of making such objects ▪ demonstrations of various *arts and crafts* ▪ the ***Arts and Crafts Movement*** [=a time when many people were working together to make arts and crafts popular] in the second half of the 19th century

art·sy /ˈɑɚtsi/ *adj* **art·si·er; -est** [*or more ~; most ~*] *chiefly US, informal + usually disapproving* **:** ARTY ▪ an *artsy* neighborhood ▪ Her boyfriend is the *artsy* type.

art theater *noun, pl* **~ -ter** [*count*] **:** ART HOUSE

art·work /ˈɑɚtˌwɚk/ *noun, pl* **-works**
1 : a painting, sculpture, photograph, etc., that is created to be beautiful or to express an important idea or feeling **:** an artistic work [*noncount*] A local painter was selling her *artwork* on the street. ▪ The walls of the restaurant are decorated in original *artwork*. ▪ Some of the children's *artwork* was hanging on the refrigerator. [*count*] The museum recently recovered two stolen *artworks*. ▪ contemporary *artworks*
2 [*noncount*] **:** drawings, photographs, etc., that are included in books, magazines, and other printed materials

arty /ˈɑɚti/ *adj* **art·i·er; -est** [*or more ~; most ~*] *informal + usually disapproving* **:** artistic in a way that seems insincere or too extreme ▪ some *arty* intellectual type who doesn't know the meaning of hard work ▪ a rock band with *arty* pretensions

aru·gu·la /əˈruːgələ, *Brit* əˈruːgjələ/ *noun* [*noncount*] *US* **:** a plant with strongly flavored leaves that are eaten in salads — called also (*Brit*) *rocket*

¹-ary *noun suffix* **:** thing or person belonging to or connected with ▪ mission*ary* ▪ revolution*ary*

²-ary *adj suffix* **:** of, relating to, or connected with ▪ diet*ary* ▪ legend*ary*

¹as /ˈæz, əz/ *adv*
1 : to the same degree or amount ▪ He has a lot of time but I don't have *as* much. [=I have less time than he has] ▪ He has many books, but I have ***just as*** many. [=I have the same amount of books that he has] ▪ He was angry, but she was *just as* angry.
2 *formal* — used to introduce an example ▪ various trees, *as* [=*such as*] oaks and pines

²as *conj*
1 a — used to make comparisons ▪ The fabric was soft *as* silk. [=the softness of the fabric was like the softness of silk] — usually used in the phrase ***as . . . as*** ▪ The fabric was *as* soft *as* silk. ▪ He is every bit *as* clever *as* she (is). ▪ There are *as* many books here *as* (there are) there. ▪ That was *as* deli-

A

cious a meal *as* your last one (was). = That was a meal *as* delicious *as* your last one (was). • *as* hard *as* a rock [=very hard] • *as* clear *as* crystal [=completely clear] • *as* white *as* snow [=snow-white, pure white] • He is *as* brave *as* he is loyal. • Her second book is twice *as* long *as* her first one. • He's not *as* old *as* he claims to be. — sometimes used in negative phrases with *so* • He's not *so* old *as* he claims to be. **b** — used in the phrase ***as . . . as*** to say when something should be done, how often something should happen, etc. • Come back *as* often *as* you like. • If you're going to look for a new job, you should do it ***as soon/early/quickly as possible.***

2 a : in the way that • The letter "k" is sometimes silent, *as* it is in "knee." • In the word "macho" the "ch" should be pronounced *as* (it is) in "China," not *as* (it is) in "Chicago." • Knowing him *as* I do [=because I know him well], I'm not surprised by his decision. • Do (it) *as* I do. • I'll do it *as* I planned (to). • Sometimes a noun comes from a verb (*as* "publisher" comes from "publish") and sometimes a verb comes from a noun (*as* "edit" comes from "editor"). • ***As it happens***, I know his brother. [=I happen to know his brother] • We planned a picnic but, ***as it happened***, it rained that day. [=it happened to rain that day] • We arrived late and, ***as it turned out***, all the tickets were already sold. [=we learned that all the tickets were already sold when we arrived late] • He seemed to be having a midlife crisis, *as* many men do. = ***As is the case*** with many men, he seemed to be having a midlife crisis. **b** — used to introduce a statement which indicates that something being mentioned was known, expected, etc. • He won the election, *as* you know. = *As* you know, he won the election. • *As* was only to be expected, the election was very close. • He is a foreigner, *as* is evident from his accent. • It rained that day, *as* often happens. • Just *as* I suspected/thought! You've been drinking! **c** — used in phrases with *same* • He works in the *same* building *as* my brother. [=he and my brother work in the same building] • I've got shoes the *same as* his. = I've got the *same* type of shoes *as* he has. [=my shoes and his shoes are the same] • He was fooled the *same as* I was. [=he and I were both fooled]

3 : while or when • She spilled the milk just *as* she was getting up. • I met him *as* I was leaving.

4 : regardless of the degree to which **:** THOUGH • Unaccustomed *as* I am to public speaking [=although I am unaccustomed to public speaking], I'd like to say a few words now. • Improbable *as* it seems, it's still true. = (*chiefly US*) *As* improbable *as* it seems, it's still true. [=although it seems improbable, it's still true] • ***Much as*** I respect him [=although I respect him very much], I still have to disagree with him on this point. = (*chiefly US*) ***As much as*** I respect him, I still have to disagree with him on this point. • ***Try as he might*** [=no matter how hard he tried], he couldn't do it.

5 *formal* **:** for the reason that **:** BECAUSE • She stayed home *as* she had no car. • *As* I'm a pacifist, I'm against all wars.

6 — used to indicate that one relationship is like another relationship • A puppy is to a dog *as* a kitten is to a cat. • Two is to four *as* eight is to sixteen.

7 — used with *so* or *such* to indicate the result or effect of something • The evidence is *such as* to leave no doubt of his guilt. [=the evidence leaves no doubt of his guilt] • He is *so* clearly guilty *as* to leave no doubt. — see also SO AS (below)

as against **:** in comparison to (something) • The government's foreign policy is approved by 54 percent of men *as against* 48 percent of women.

as for **:** with regard to **:** CONCERNING • He's here. *As for* the others, they'll arrive later. [=the others will arrive later] • He was a nice enough person, but *as for* his suggestions, I found them unhelpful.

as from *chiefly Brit* — used to indicate the time or date when something begins • The new law takes effect *as from* [=*as of*] July 1.

as if *or* ***as though*** **1 :** the way it would be if • The plane looked *as if* it was going to crash. • He was as sad *as if* he had lost his last friend. • The dog wagged its tail *as if* to say "Welcome back!" = The dog wagged its tail *as if* it was/were saying "Welcome back!" • The day seemed *as though* it would never end. = It seemed *as though* the day would never end. **2 :** as someone would do if • He ran *as if* ghosts were chasing him. • He had his hands together *as though* in prayer. **3** — used in spoken phrases to say that something is not true, will not happen, etc. • "She's afraid you might try to take the job yourself." "***As if I ever would!***" [=I never would] • "He'll never come back, you know!" "***As if I cared!***" [=I don't care] **4** ✧ The phrase *as if* is sometimes used informally as an interjection to say that something suggested or claimed is impossible or very unlikely. • "He thinks you like him." "*As if!*" [=I don't like him at all; there is no chance that I would like him]

as is *chiefly US* **:** in the present condition without any changes • The car is being sold *as is*. • She bought the clock at an auction *as is*.

as it is **1 :** in the present condition • Leave everything exactly/just *as it is*. [=how it is, the way it is] **2 :** with the situation that exists now • We have enough to do *as it is* [=*already*] without your latest orders!

as it were — used to say that a statement is true or accurate in a certain way even if it is not literally or completely true • His retirement was, *as it were* [=*so to speak*], the beginning of his real career.

as of — used to indicate the time or date when something begins • The new law takes effect *as of* July 1. • *As of* July 1, prices will rise.

as to **1 :** [2]ABOUT • I'm at a loss *as to* how to explain the error. [=I don't know how to explain the error] • There is disagreement *as to* the causes of the fire. • I remained uncertain *as to* the value of his suggestions. **2 :** ACCORDING TO, BY • The eggs are graded *as to* size and color.

as was *Brit, informal* **:** FORMERLY, ORIGINALLY — used after a former name • Myanmar—Burma *as was* [=Myanmar, which was formerly called Burma]

so as — used to indicate the purpose of something • He defended himself *so as* [=*in order*] to prove his innocence. — see also [2]AS 7 (above)

[3]as *prep*

1 — used to indicate how a person or thing appears, is thought of, etc. • They regarded/described the situation *as* (being) a disaster. • Don't think of it *as* (being) a setback—think of it *as* (being) a challenge! • Many people now regard him *as* a traitor.

2 — used to indicate the condition, role, job, etc., of someone or something • Then she spoke *as* a child [=she was a child when she spoke then], but now she is speaking *as* an adult. • He has a job *as* an editor. • The policeman disguised himself *as* a beggar. • Some people were surprised by his election *as* Governor. • The critics praised his performance *as* Othello. • I like her both *as* a poet and *as* a novelist. • *As* a pacifist, I'm against all wars. • Everyone rose ***as one***. [=everyone rose together]

ASAP *abbr* as soon as possible — used in informal contexts in both spoken and written English • Please come quickly. We need you here *ASAP*. • Write back *ASAP*.

as·bes·tos /æsˈbɛstəs/ *noun* [*noncount*] **:** a soft gray mineral that does not burn, that was used especially as a building material in the past, and that can cause serious diseases of the lungs when people breathe its dust

as·cend /əˈsɛnd/ *verb* **-cends; -cend·ed; -cend·ing**

1 *formal* **:** to go up **:** to rise or move toward the sky [*no obj*] They watched their balloons slowly *ascend* into the sky. • Divers must not *ascend* too rapidly/quickly to the water's surface. • She believed that when she died, her soul would *ascend* to heaven. [+ *obj*] Most people are able to *ascend* [=*climb*] the mountain in less than four hours. • She said goodnight and *ascended* [=*climbed*] the stairs to her room. — opposite DESCEND

2 [*no obj*] **:** to slope or lead upward • Several paths *ascend* to the top of the mountain. • stairs *ascending* to the attic — opposite DESCEND

3 [*no obj*] **:** to rise *to* a higher or more powerful position in a government, company, etc. • John Adams *ascended to* the presidency in 1797. • She worked as a clerk before *ascending to* her current position. • A new national government *ascended* [=*rose*] *to* power. [=it gained control of the country]

ascend (to) the throne **:** to become a king or queen • He *ascended the throne* after the death of his father. • In Shakespeare's play, Macbeth kills the king and *ascends to the throne*.

in ascending order ✧ If people or things are *in ascending order*, they are arranged in a series that begins with the least or smallest and ends with the greatest or largest. • The children were lined up *in ascending order* of height. • Test scores are listed *in ascending order* from lowest to highest.

as·cen·dance /əˈsɛndəns/ *noun* [*noncount*] *chiefly US*

1 : the act of rising or moving up **:** the act of ascending • Abraham Lincoln's *ascendance* [=(more commonly) *ascent, ascension*] to the presidency • her *ascendance* [=(more commonly) *ascent*] to/into heaven

2 : ASCENDANCY • gain/lose *ascendance*

as·cen·dan·cy *also* **as·cen·den·cy** /əˈsɛndənsi/ *noun* [*noncount*] *formal* : a position of power in which someone can control or influence other people ▪ the *ascendancy* of the government ▪ She gained (the) *ascendancy* in the debate.

[1]**as·cen·dant** /əˈsɛndənt/ *noun*
in the ascendant *formal* : becoming more powerful : gaining more power ▪ The President's party is no longer *in the ascendant*.

[2]**ascendant** *adj* [*more ~; most ~*] *formal*
1 : becoming more popular or successful ▪ the actress' *ascendant* [=*rising*] career
2 : more powerful or important than any other ▪ the *ascendant* [=*dominant*] beliefs at that time

as·cen·sion /əˈsɛnʃən/ *noun* [*singular*]
1 : the act of rising or ascending ▪ the *ascension* [=(more commonly) *ascent*] of a balloon; *especially* : the act of moving to a higher or more powerful position ▪ The play tells of his *ascension* to the presidency. ▪ the *ascension* of women in society
2 ***the Ascension*** : the Christian holiday that celebrates Jesus Christ's journey to heaven after his death

as·cent /əˈsɛnt/ *noun, pl* **-cents** [*count*]
1 : the act or process of ascending: such as **a** : the act or process of rising, moving, or climbing up — usually singular ▪ Fifty years ago, he made the first successful *ascent* of the mountain. [=he was the first person to climb the mountain] ▪ The climbers completed their *ascent* to the mountain on a rainy morning in April. ▪ The old elevator began its slow *ascent* to the top floor. ▪ The plane made a steep *ascent* to 30,000 feet. — opposite DESCENT **b** : the act or process of moving to a higher or more powerful position — usually singular ▪ the *ascent* and decline [=the rise and fall] of the world's great civilizations ▪ the new government's gradual/rapid *ascent* to power ▪ She began her *ascent* up the corporate ladder as a secretary. [=she started working as a secretary and gradually improved her career in business]
2 : a way of going up something : an upward slope, path, etc. ▪ They followed a steep *ascent* to the top of the hill.

as·cer·tain /ˌæsəˈteɪn/ *verb* **-tains; -tained; -tain·ing** [+ *obj*] *formal* : to learn or find out (something, such as information or the truth) ▪ They were unable to *ascertain* [=(more commonly) *determine*] the cause of the fire. ▪ The police are now attempting to *ascertain* his whereabouts. [=to find out where he is] ▪ Her doctors have been unable to *ascertain* [=*find out*] why she is ill. = Her doctors have been unable to *ascertain* the cause of her illness. ▪ The information can be *ascertained* by anyone with a computer.
– as·cer·tain·able /ˌæsəˈteɪnəbəl/ *adj* ▪ The cause of the fire was not readily/easily *ascertainable*.

as·cet·ic /əˈsɛtɪk/ *adj* [*more ~; most ~*] *formal* : relating to or having a strict and simple way of living that avoids physical pleasure ▪ an *ascetic* monk ▪ an *ascetic* scholar ▪ the *ascetic* [=*severe, austere*] life of monks ▪ an *ascetic* diet of rice and beans
– ascetic *noun, pl* **-ics** [*count*] ▪ She left the comforts of home to live the life of an *ascetic*. **– as·cet·i·cism** /əˈsɛtəˌsɪzəm/ *noun* [*noncount*] ▪ religious *asceticism*

ASCII /ˈæski/ *noun* [*noncount*] : a standard way of representing numbers and letters in a computer file so that they can be read by most computers ✧ The word *ASCII* comes from the initial letters of the words in the phrase *American Standard Code for Information Interchange*.

as·cot /ˈæˌskɑːt/ *noun, pl* **-cots** [*count*] *chiefly US* : a thin scarf worn by men that is folded into a loop under the chin

as·cribe /əˈskraɪb/ *verb* **-cribes; -cribed; -crib·ing**
ascribe to [*phrasal verb*] ***ascribe (something) to (something or someone)*** *formal* : to say or think that (something) is caused by, comes from, or is associated with (something or someone) ▪ They *ascribed* [=*attributed*] his illness *to* chemicals in his brain. [=they said his illness was caused by chemicals in his brain] ▪ The author *ascribes* the economy's success *to* the current government. [=the author credits the current government with the economy's success] ▪ She *ascribes* [=*assigns*] no importance *to* having lots of money. [=she does not believe that having lots of money is important] ▪ These poems are usually *ascribed to* Homer. [=most people believe that these poems were written by Homer] ▪ qualities that are usually *ascribed to* men [=qualities that many people think are typical of men]

asep·tic /eɪˈsɛptɪk/ *adj* [*more ~; most ~*] *medical* : free from germs that cause disease ▪ an *aseptic* wound

asex·u·al /eɪˈsɛkʃəwəl/ *adj*
1 : not having or including sex ▪ They had a completely *asexual* relationship.
2 *technical* : of or relating to a kind of reproduction that does not involve the combining of male and female cells ▪ *asexual* plants/organisms ▪ *asexual* reproduction
– asex·u·al·ly /eɪˈsɛkʃəwəli/ *adv* ▪ plants that reproduce *asexually*

[1]**ash** /ˈæʃ/ *noun, pl* **ash·es**
1 : the soft gray powder that remains after something (such as a cigarette or wood) has been completely burned and destroyed by fire [*noncount*] The town lay under a thick layer/blanket of *ash*. ▪ clouds of hot volcanic *ash* [*count*] The village was covered in *ashes*. ▪ cigarette *ashes*
2 ***ashes*** [*plural*] : the burned parts that remain when something is destroyed ▪ The city was reduced to *ashes* by the fire. = The city was burned to *ashes*. — often used figuratively ▪ Their happiness turned to *ashes*. [=their happiness was destroyed] ▪ The nation slowly rose from the *ashes* of war. = It slowly rose out of the *ashes* and began to rebuild itself. ▪ We sifted through the *ashes* of our ruined lives.
3 ***ashes*** [*plural*] : the remains of a dead human body after it has been burned or cremated ▪ the *ashes* of the dead ▪ She kept her dead mother's *ashes* in a jar above the fireplace. ▪ He asked to have his *ashes* scattered along the river.
sackcloth and ashes see SACKCLOTH
– compare [2]ASH

[2]**ash** *noun, pl* **ashes**
1 [*count*] : a type of tree that grows in northern parts of the world and that has thin gray bark and hard wood
2 [*noncount*] : the hard wood of an ash tree ▪ baseball bats made of *ash*
– compare [1]ASH

ashamed /əˈʃeɪmd/ *adj, not used before a noun* [*more ~; most ~*]
1 : feeling shame or guilt ▪ She was *ashamed* that she hit her brother. = She felt *ashamed* for/about hitting her brother. ▪ You ought to be *ashamed*! — often + *of* ▪ You ought to be *ashamed of* yourself! ▪ He was deeply *ashamed of* his behavior at the company party. ▪ I'm not *ashamed of* what I did. There's nothing to be *ashamed of*. ▪ I can't believe that you behaved so rudely. I'm *ashamed of* you!
2 : not wanting *to do* something because of shame or embarrassment ▪ I can't believe that you behaved so rudely. I'm *ashamed to be seen* with you! ▪ We were too *ashamed to go* back to school. [=we didn't go back to school because we were too embarrassed] ▪ I'm *ashamed* [=*embarrassed*] *to admit* it, but I still don't know how to ride a bicycle. = I'm *ashamed to say* I still don't know how to ride a bicycle.

ash–blond *or* **ash–blonde** /ˈæʃˈblɑːnd/ *adj* : pale blond or grayish blond ▪ *ash-blond* hair

ash can *noun, pl* **~ cans** [*count*] *US, old-fashioned* : GARBAGE CAN

ash·en /ˈæʃən/ *adj* [*more ~; most ~*] : having a pale light gray color because of sickness, fear, etc. ▪ His skin became *ashen*. ▪ She was *ashen* with fear.

ashore /əˈʃoɚ/ *adv* : on or to the shore of an ocean, sea, lake, or river ▪ We docked our boat and went *ashore* to visit the island. ▪ the seashells that wash *ashore* after a storm

ash·ram /ˈɑːʃrəm/ *noun, pl* **-rams** [*count*] : a place where a person or a group of people go to live separately from the rest of society and practice the Hindu religion

ash·tray /ˈæʃˌtreɪ/ *noun, pl* **-trays** [*count*] : a small dish or other small container that is used for throwing away used cigarettes and cigars and their ashes

Ash Wednesday *noun* [*noncount*] : the first day of the Christian holy period of Lent

[1]**Asian** /ˈeɪʒən/ *noun, pl* **Asians** [*count*] : a person born, raised, or living in Asia : a person whose family is from Asia ▪ There are many *Asians* living in South America.

> ***usage*** In U.S. English, *Asian* refers usually to a person from the countries of eastern Asia, such as China, Korea, and Japan. In British English, *Asian* often refers to a person from the countries of western Asia, such as India and Pakistan.

[2]**Asian** *adj* : of or relating to Asia or its people ▪ *Asian* cities/populations/immigrants ▪ *Asian* culture/philosophy/cooking

Asian–Amer·i·can /ˈeɪʒənəˈmerəkən/ *noun, pl* **-cans** [*count*] : an American who was born in Asia or whose family is from Asia
– Asian–American *adj* ▪ Most of the people who live in this neighborhood are *Asian-American*.

A

Asi·at·ic /ˌeɪʒiˈætɪk/ *adj, always used before a noun* **:** of or relating to Asia • *Asiatic* plants and animals • *Asiatic* countries • the *Asiatic* fleet of the U.S. Navy [=the ships of the U.S. Navy that are in Asia] ✧ *Asiatic* should not be used to describe people.

[1]aside /əˈsaɪd/ *adv*
1 : to or toward the side • He stepped *aside* and let her pass. • She drew *aside* the curtains. = She drew the curtains *aside.* • He threw/tossed his coat *aside.* • Please stand *aside.* • She laid/set the book *aside.* • He elbowed people *aside* as he moved through the crowd. • He took/drew her *aside* to speak to her privately. • Someone grabbed him and pulled/pushed him *aside.* — often used figuratively • Their objections were swept/brushed *aside.* [=were quickly dismissed or disregarded] • The old methods have been cast/thrown *aside* [=have been abandoned] in favor of new ones. • Leaving/Putting *aside* the question of money for the moment, we need to come up with a workable schedule.
2 — used with *put* or *set* to describe something that is being kept or saved for a future use • She's been *setting/putting* money *aside* [=has been saving money] for school. • The government has *set aside* a thousand acres for use as a park.
3 — used to say that something is not included in a statement that follows • Dangerous appearances *aside*, these animals are really very gentle and friendly. [=these animals are friendly despite their dangerous appearances] • Such minor problems *aside* [=except for such minor problems], the movie is a very entertaining thriller.
aside from *chiefly US* **1 :** not including (something) **:** with the exception of (something) • *Aside from* [=*apart from, except for*] a few pieces of bread, the food is gone. • The movie has been praised by most people, *aside from* a few critics who have called its happy ending trite and predictable. **2 :** in addition to (something) **:** BESIDES • *Aside from* being well written, the book is also beautifully illustrated

[2]aside *noun, pl* **asides** [*count*]
1 : a comment spoken by a character in a play that is heard by the audience but is supposedly not heard by other characters on stage
2 : a comment that is spoken quietly to someone so that it cannot be heard by other people who are present • She made a joke about the food in a muttered/whispered *aside* to her husband.
3 : a comment or discussion that does not relate directly to the main subject being discussed • The book includes several lengthy *asides* about the personal lives of scientists involved in the project. • In his speech he mentioned her contributions almost as an *aside*, despite the fact that she was the one who came up with the idea originally.

as·i·nine /ˈæsəˌnaɪn/ *adj* [*more* ~; *most* ~] *formal* **:** very stupid and silly • That is the most *asinine* [=*foolish, ridiculous*] joke I've ever heard. • a completely *asinine* question

ask /ˈæsk, *Brit* ˈɑːsk/ *verb* **asks; asked; ask·ing**
1 : to say or write something to someone as a way of gaining information **:** to request an answer to a question [*+ obj*] I need to *ask* a question. • I need to *ask* you a question. = (less commonly) I need to *ask* a question of you. • Are there any questions you would like to *ask* (me)? • Did you *ask* her yet? • "Have you seen the movie yet?" he *asked.* • a list of frequently *asked* questions — often + *about* • We always *ask* him *about* his mother. — often + *if* or *whether* • He *asked* (them) *if* they had seen the movie. • She *asked* (me) *if* I was worried. • They were *asked whether* they would like to buy the car. — often + *why, what,* etc. • You should *ask* (him) *why* he didn't come. • He always *asks* (her) *what* she thinks. • May I *ask what* time it is? • It's not polite to *ask how* much a person weighs. [*no obj*] "If you don't mind me/my *asking*, how old are you?" "I'm 35 years old. Why do you *ask*?" • Please don't *ask* again. • "Do they have any soda?" "I don't know. I'll go *ask.*" — often + *about* • I *asked about* her plans for the future. • The police were here *asking about* you.
2 : to tell someone in the form of a question that you want to be given something or that you want something to happen **:** to request something [*no obj*] If you want something to drink, just *ask.* [=just tell me that you want something to drink] • I would have given it to him, but he never *asked.* — often + *for* • Let's stop and *ask for* directions. • I'll have to *ask for* permission to leave. • She *asked for* their forgiveness/help. • She ate all of her food and *asked for* more. • His lawyers are *asking for* the case to be dismissed. [*+ obj*] We had to stop and *ask* directions. • May I *ask* the time? • Did you *ask* permission to leave? • She *asked* their forgiveness. — often + *for* • We had to *ask* someone *for* directions. • I *asked* her *for* permission. • She *asked* them *for* their forgiveness. — often + *if* or *whether* • He *asked if* he could use my telephone. • They *asked* us *whether* we might stay an extra day. — often + *that* • She *asked that* I not say anything about it. • His lawyers are *asking that* the case be dismissed. — often followed by *to + verb* • She *asked* (for permission) *to borrow* her father's car for the day. • I *asked* (for permission) *to leave* work early. • You should *ask* your teacher *to help* you. • Unhappy with the service, he *asked to see* the manager. • He *asked* me *to marry* him. • I'm sorry, but I need to *ask* you *to leave.* • She *asked* me not *to say* anything about it to anyone. • I wanted to say something about it, but she *asked* me not *to.*
3 [*+ obj*] **:** to invite (someone) to go somewhere or do something • He's *asking* just a few friends to the party. • I *asked* him to lunch. • They *asked* me over for dinner. ✧ To ***ask someone out*** is to ask someone to go on a date with you. • I *asked her out* (on a date), but she turned me down.
4 [*+ obj*] **a :** to believe that you should receive (something) from someone • She doesn't *ask* [=*expect, require*] a lot. She *asks* very little in return for her hard work. — often + *of* • The school *asks* much *of* its students. [=the school expects its students to do a lot] • He says that people *ask* too little *of* their politicians. • He was ready to go to war, should the government *ask* it *of* him. [=should the government ask him to go to war] **b :** to set (a specific amount of money) as a price • The dealer originally *asked* [=*wanted*] $20,000 for the car, but he sold it to me for $18,000. • They're asking [=*charging*] $100 or more per concert ticket. — see also ASKING PRICE
ask after [*phrasal verb*] ***ask after (someone or something)*** **:** to ask about (someone or something) • He *asked after* my wife's health. • He greeted us warmly and *asked after* our families. [=he asked how our families were]
ask around [*phrasal verb*] **:** to ask many people to tell you information about someone or something • Maybe you should *ask around* to find out more about this guy. • We usually *ask around* before trying a new restaurant.
ask for [*phrasal verb*] **1** ***ask for (someone)*** **:** to request to see or talk to (someone) • Unhappy with the service, he *asked for* the store manager. • There's someone on the phone *asking for* you. **2** ***ask for it informal*** **:** to behave in a way that makes someone want to hurt or punish you • You're *asking for it*, kid! If you keep misbehaving, you're going to get punished. • All right. You *asked for it!* **3** ***ask for trouble informal*** **:** to behave in a way that is likely to result in trouble • If you invest your money without doing careful research, you're just *asking for trouble.* — see also *ask for the moon* at [1]MOON
ask yourself ✧ To *ask yourself* something is to think about the true answer to a question. • *Ask yourself* what you would do in that situation. • Before buying an expensive item, he needs to *ask himself* if/whether he can afford it.
don't ask informal — used to say that something is too strange, embarrassing, or complicated to explain • "She married and divorced a man in the same day? How is that possible?" "*Don't ask.*"
don't ask me informal — used to say that you do not know the answer to a question • "Why are they having a company meeting?" "*Don't ask me.* I only work here." • *Don't ask me* why they're changing the system. I think it's fine the way it is.
for the asking ✧ If something is yours *for the asking*, you can have it if you want it or ask for it. • This job is hers *for the asking.* [=she can have the job if she wants it] • Our services are available/free *for the asking.* [=our services are available/free for anyone who wants them]
I ask you ✧ People use the phrase *I ask you* before or after a question when they want someone to agree or sympathize with them. • (Now) *I ask you*, is that fair? [=I don't think it's fair; do you?] • Look at that hat! Who would wear such a thing, *I ask you*?
if you ask me informal **:** in my opinion • She looks ridiculous in that hat, *if you ask me.*
who asked you? informal + impolite — used as a response when someone gives an opinion that is not wanted • "I think you should break up with that guy." "*Who asked you?*" [=*mind your own business*; I don't want to hear your opinion]

askance /əˈskæns/ *adv* **:** in a way that shows a lack of trust or approval • Most scientists ***looked askance at*** the new discovery. [=most scientists were doubtful about the new discovery] • Several people *looked at him askance* when he walked into the room. = Several people ***eyed him askance*** when he walked into the room.

askew /əˈskjuː/ *adv* [*more* ~; *most* ~] **:** not straight **:** at an angle ▪ The picture hung *askew* [=*crookedly*] on the wall.
– askew *adj, not used before a noun* ▪ His tie is slightly *askew* [=*crooked*] in this picture.

asking price *noun* [*singular*] **:** the price that is asked for by a person who is selling something ▪ The original *asking price* for/of the car was $20,000, but I was eventually able to buy it for $18,000. — compare SELLING PRICE

asleep /əˈsliːp/ *adj, not used before a noun*
1 : in a state of sleep **:** sleeping ▪ "Are you *asleep*?" "No, I'm awake." ▪ He tries to clean up the house while the kids are *asleep*. ▪ The cats are *asleep* on the floor. ▪ She was still *asleep* at noon. ✧ When people are ***fast asleep*** or ***sound asleep***, they are sleeping very deeply. ▪ It was late at night and everyone was *fast asleep*. ▪ One moment she was *sound asleep*, the next she was wide awake! ✧ If you are ***half asleep***, you are very tired and not completely awake. ▪ We were still *half asleep* when we went to school the next morning.
2 : lacking any feeling ✧ If a part of your body (such as a foot or leg) is *asleep*, it is not able to feel anything for a brief time, usually because you have kept it in an awkward position for too long. ▪ My foot's *asleep*.
fall asleep **:** to begin sleeping ▪ She *fell asleep* during the movie. ▪ I woke up and I couldn't *fall* back *asleep*. [=I couldn't go to sleep again]

asp /ˈæsp/ *noun, pl* **asps** [*count*] **:** a small poisonous snake from Egypt

as·par·a·gus /əˈsperəgəs/ *noun* [*noncount*] **:** a plant with long green stems and tiny leaves at one end that is cooked and eaten as a vegetable — see color picture on page C4

as·pect /ˈæˌspɛkt/ *noun, pl* **-pects**
1 [*count*] **:** a part of something ▪ Our proposal differs from theirs in one important *aspect*. [=*respect*] — usually + *of* ▪ Their religion affects almost/nearly/virtually every *aspect* [=*facet*] *of* their lives. ▪ Eating healthy foods is only/just one *aspect* [=*part*] *of* a healthy lifestyle. ▪ Nobody has discussed the most important *aspect of* the problem. ▪ Computers now influence all *aspects of* American life.
2 *formal* **:** the way a person, place, or thing appears [*singular*] The old house took on a dark and lonely *aspect* [=*appearance*] at night. [*noncount*] Their gods are primarily human in *aspect*. [=they look like humans]
3 [*singular*] *formal* **:** the direction that something (such as a room or building) faces or points towards ▪ The house has a southern *aspect*. [=a southern exposure; the front of the house faces the south] — sometimes used figuratively ▪ We studied the situation from every *aspect*. [=*angle*]
4 *grammar* **:** the characteristic of a verb that expresses the way an action happens ✧ A verb's *aspect* shows whether an action happens one time and stops quickly, happens repeatedly, or happens continuously. [*count*] The *aspect* of "sit" in "please sit down now" is different from the *aspect* of "sitting" in "I was sitting at my desk." [*noncount*] two verb forms differing in *aspect*

aspect ratio *noun, pl* **~ ratios** [*count*] *technical* **:** a number that compares the width and height of a movie or television picture

as·pen /ˈæspən/ *noun, pl* **-pens** [*count*] **:** a kind of tree whose leaves move easily when the wind blows

as·per·i·ty /əˈsperəti/ *noun* [*noncount*] *formal* **:** harshness of behavior or speech that expresses bitterness or anger ▪ He spoke about his ex-wife with *asperity*. [=*acrimony*]

as·per·sions /əˈspɚʒənz/ *noun*
cast aspersions *formal* **:** to say critical things about (someone or someone's character) **:** to criticize (someone) harshly or unfairly ▪ He tried to discuss his political opponents respectfully, without *casting aspersions*. — usually + *on* ▪ He tried to avoid *casting aspersions on* (the motives/integrity of) his political opponents.

as·phalt /ˈæsˌfɑːlt/ *noun* [*noncount*] **:** a black substance that is used for making roads

as·phyx·ia /æsˈfɪksijə/ *noun* [*noncount*] *medical* **:** the state of not being able to breathe ▪ The cause of death was *asphyxia*.

as·phyx·i·ate /æsˈfɪksiˌeɪt/ *verb* **-ates; -at·ed; -at·ing** [+ *obj*] **:** to cause (someone) to stop breathing and often to become unconscious and die ▪ The murder victim was *asphyxiated*.
– as·phyx·i·a·tion /æsˌfɪksiˈeɪʃən/ *noun* [*noncount*] ▪ The murder victim died of *asphyxiation*.

as·pic /ˈæspɪk/ *noun* [*noncount*] **:** a clear jelly that is usually served with cold meat or fish ▪ a serving of chicken in *aspic*

as·pi·rant /ˈæspərənt/ *noun, pl* **-rants** [*count*] *formal* **:** a person who tries to become something **:** a person who aspires to do or to be something ▪ a presidential *aspirant* = an *aspirant* to the presidency [=someone who wants to become president]

¹as·pi·rate /ˈæspəˌreɪt/ *verb* **-rates; -rat·ed; -rat·ing** [+ *obj*]
1 *linguistics* **:** to pronounce (a letter or word) with the sound of a breath or the letter "h" ▪ The letter "h" in "house" is *aspirated*, but the "h" in "hour" is not.
2 *medical* **:** to remove (liquid) from a person's body ▪ The doctor *aspirated* fluid from the cyst. = The doctor *aspirated* the cyst.
3 *medical* **:** to breathe (liquid, food, etc.) into your lungs ▪ She began coughing when she *aspirated* some orange juice.

²as·pi·rate /ˈæspərət/ *noun, pl* **-ates** [*count*] *linguistics* **:** the sound of the letter "h" ▪ The word "hour" is not pronounced with an *aspirate*.

as·pi·ra·tion /ˌæspəˈreɪʃən/ *noun, pl* **-tions**
1 [*count*] **:** something that a person wants very much to achieve ▪ I've never had any *aspiration* to become famous. [=I've never wanted to become famous] — usually plural ▪ What are your *aspirations* for the future? [=what do you want to accomplish in the future?] ▪ the different *aspirations* of the group's members ▪ She has political *aspirations*. [=she wants/aspires to be a politician] ▪ romantic/social/literary *aspirations*
2 [*noncount*] **:** the act of aspirating something: such as **a** *linguistics* **:** the act of pronouncing the sound of a breath or the letter "h" ▪ the *aspiration* of the letter "h" in "a house" **b** *medical* **:** the act of removing liquid from a person's body ▪ the *aspiration* of stomach fluids **c** *medical* **:** the act of breathing something into the lungs ▪ problems caused by the *aspiration* of fluids into the patient's lungs
– as·pi·ra·tion·al /ˌæspəˈreɪʃənəl/ *adj* [*more* ~; *most* ~] *Brit* ▪ *aspirational* [=*ambitious*] people ▪ *aspirational* brands/products [=brands/products that appeal to people who want to raise their social status] **– as·pi·ra·tion·al·ly** *adv*

as·pire /əˈspajɚ/ *verb* **-pires; -pired; -pir·ing** [*no obj*] **:** to want to have or achieve something (such as a particular career or level of success) — often + *to* ▪ Both young men *aspire to* careers in medicine. [=both young men want to have careers in medicine] ▪ She *aspires to* a more active role in her government. ▪ people who *aspire to* home ownership [=people who want to own their own homes] — often followed by *to* + *verb* ▪ He says he never *aspired to become* famous. ▪ little girls who *aspire to play* professional basketball
– aspiring *adj* ▪ an *aspiring* actor [=a person who wants to be an actor] ▪ an *aspiring* young writer

as·pi·rin /ˈæsprən/ *noun, pl* **aspirin** *or* **as·pi·rins :** a medicine that reduces pain and fever [*noncount*] *Aspirin* is effective in controlling headaches. ▪ an *aspirin* pill [*count*] I had a headache so I took a couple of *aspirins/aspirin*. [=a couple of aspirin pills]

¹ass /ˈæs/ *noun, pl* **ass·es** [*count*]
1 *old-fashioned* **:** a donkey
2 *informal* + *impolite* **:** a foolish, stupid, or stubborn person ▪ You can be such an *ass* sometimes! ▪ They act like a couple of pompous/pretentious *asses*. ▪ I ***made an ass of myself*** at the party. [=I behaved very foolishly at the party]
– compare ²ASS

²ass *noun, pl* **asses**
1 [*count*] *chiefly US, informal* + *impolite* **a :** the part of the body above the legs that is used for sitting **:** BUTTOCKS ▪ She slipped and fell flat on her *ass*. [=(*Brit*) *arse*] **b** — used in various phrases ▪ I've got to thank the soldiers who ***protected my ass*** [=*protected my life/hide/skin*] during the war. ▪ She ***saved your ass***. [=she saved you] ▪ I wish he'd admit to his mistakes instead of always trying to ***cover his ass***. [=to keep from being blamed or punished] ▪ ***Get your ass back here***! [=come back here] ▪ We don't have much time so you'd better ***move your ass***! = You'd better ***get your ass in gear***! [=you'd better start going/moving faster] ▪ "Are you sure you're going to win?" "***You (can) bet your ass*** [=you can be very certain] I'm going to win!" ▪ This comedian will make you laugh ***your asses off***. [=will make you laugh very hard] ▪ I work *my ass off* everyday to try to make ends meet. ▪ Work, ***my ass!*** [=what nonsense] You just sit in front of the TV all day. ▪ You've been (sitting) ***on your ass*** in front of the TV all day. ▪ It's time (for you) to ***get off your ass*** and do some work! ▪ She's always ***on my ass*** about getting a better job.

A

[=she's always telling me that I should get a better job] • That gray truck has been *on our ass* [=has been following us very/too closely] for the last mile. • Why can't you ***get off his ass***?! [=stop criticizing him] He's doing the best he can! — see also *haul ass* at [1]HAUL, *kick someone's ass* at [1]KICK, *kiss (my/someone's) ass* at [1]KISS

2 [*noncount*] *US, offensive* **a** : sexual intercourse • looking to get some *ass* **b** — used in the phrase ***piece of ass*** to refer to a person (especially a woman) in a sexual way • He described her as "a nice *piece of ass*." ✧ These uses of *ass* are very offensive and should be avoided.

– compare [1]ASS

as·sail /əˈseɪl/ *verb* **-sails; -sailed; -sail·ing** [+ *obj*] : to attack or criticize (someone or something) in a violent or angry way • The movie was *assailed* by critics. • politicians *assailed* by the media — often used figuratively • A horrible odor *assailed* our noses. [=we smelled a horrible odor] • We were *assailed* by doubts [=we were very doubtful] about the decision we'd made. • *assailed* by fears

as·sail·ant /əˈseɪlənt/ *noun, pl* **-ants** [*count*] *formal* : a person who attacks someone violently • She said that her *assailant* [=the person who attacked her] was wearing a mask.

as·sas·sin /əˈsæsn̩/ *noun, pl* **-sins** [*count*] : a person who kills someone (such as a famous or important person) usually for political reasons or for money : a person who assassinates someone • He's a hired *assassin*. [=someone hired to kill someone] • the President's would-be *assassin* [=the person who tried to kill the President] • John Wilkes Booth was the *assassin* of Abraham Lincoln.

as·sas·si·nate /əˈsæsəˌneɪt/ *verb* **-nates; -nat·ed; -nat·ing** [+ *obj*] : to kill (someone, such as a famous or important person) usually for political reasons • They discovered a secret plot/plan to *assassinate* the governor. • President John F. Kennedy was *assassinated* in 1963.

– **as·sas·si·na·tion** /əˌsæsəˈneɪʃən/ *noun, pl* **-tions** [*count*] an attempted *assassination* of the President [*noncount*] a leader whose life was tragically cut short by *assassination*

[1]**as·sault** /əˈsɑːlt/ *noun, pl* **-saults**

1 a [*noncount*] *law* : the crime of trying or threatening to hurt someone physically • He was accused of *assault*. = He was charged with *assault*. = *Assault* charges were brought against him. • She was wanted (by the police) for *assault* with a deadly weapon. • He was found guilty of ***sexual assault*** [=the crime of touching someone in an unwanted sexual way] — see also INDECENT ASSAULT **b** [*count*] : a violent physical attack • She was injured in a brutal *assault*.

2 [*count*] : a military attack • They launched several air *assaults* [=attacks using airplanes] against the enemy. • They got ready for an enemy *assault*. [=an attack by the enemy] — often + *on* • The enemy has launched an *assault on* the city. — often used figuratively • They saw the change as an *assault on* the values of their society. • They launched a fierce legal *assault* against the company. • The government is attempting an all-out/full-scale *assault on* the use of drugs.

under assault : being attacked or criticized • The city is *under assault* from enemy troops. • He came *under assault* for his unusual beliefs. [=he was severely criticized for his unusual beliefs] • Their personal freedoms are (coming) *under assault* by the government.

[2]**assault** *verb* **-saults; -sault·ed; -sault·ing** [+ *obj*] : to violently attack (someone or something) • He was arrested for *assaulting* a police officer. • She verbally *assaulted* one of her coworkers. • He had been sexually *assaulted* [=touched or hurt in a sexual way] as a young boy. • Enemy forces *assaulted* the city. — sometimes used figuratively • A terrible noise *assaulted* our senses. [=we heard a terrible noise]

assault and battery *noun* [*noncount*] *law* : the crime of threatening and physically hitting or attacking someone

assault course *noun, pl* ~ **courses** [*count*] *Brit* : OBSTACLE COURSE

assault rifle *noun, pl* ~ **rifles** [*count*] : a gun that can shoot many bullets quickly and that is designed for use by the military — called also *assault weapon*; see picture at GUN

as·say /æˈseɪ/ *verb* **-says; -sayed; -say·ing** [+ *obj*] *technical* : to test something (such as a metal or drug) to find out what it contains • They *assayed* the gold to determine its purity.

– **as·say** /ˈæˌseɪ/ *noun, pl* **-says** [*count*] • a gold *assay*

as·sem·blage /əˈsɛmblɪʤ/ *noun, pl* **-blag·es** [*count*] *formal* : a group of people or things • an *assemblage* [=*group*] of parents and teachers • an *assemblage* [=*set*] of tools

as·sem·ble /əˈsɛmbəl/ *verb* **-sem·bles; -sem·bled; -sem·bling**

1 [+ *obj*] : to collect (things) or gather (people) into one place or group • We'll need to *assemble* a list of songs for the concert. • She *assembled* all of her old photos into three albums. • Hundreds of notes and letters were *assembled* into a book. • A team of scientists was *assembled* to study the problem.

2 [*no obj*] : to meet together in one place • The U.S. Constitution gives people the right to *assemble* peacefully. • A crowd had *assembled* in front of the courthouse during the trial. • After dinner, the men would *assemble* in the living room to watch the game on TV. • The club *assembles* once a month to discuss upcoming activities.

3 [+ *obj*] : to connect or put together the parts of (something, such as a toy or machine) • Their father helped them *assemble* their new bicycles in the garage. • The cars are *assembled* on an assembly line.

as·sem·bly /əˈsɛmbli/ *noun, pl* **-blies**

1 [*noncount*] : the act of connecting together the parts of something (such as a machine) : the act of assembling something • The parts are made in this factory and then shipped to another country for *assembly*. • No *assembly* required. [=this product is already put together]

2 [*count*] : a group of people who make and change laws for a government or organization • the organization's general *assembly* • elected legislative *assemblies* • the New York State *Assembly* • the French National *Assembly*

3 [*count*] **a** : a group of people who have gathered together • an *assembly* of armed men **b** : a meeting of all the teachers and students of a school • School *assemblies* were usually held in the cafeteria.

4 [*noncount*] : the act of gathering together to talk about issues • Freedom of speech and freedom of *assembly* are protected by the U.S. Constitution.

assembly line *noun, pl* ~ **lines** [*count*] : PRODUCTION LINE

as·sem·bly·man /əˈsɛmblimən/ *noun, pl* **-men** /-mən/ [*count*] : a person (especially a man) who is a member of a legislative assembly

as·sem·bly·wo·man /əˈsɛmbliˌwʊmən/ *noun, pl* **-women** /-ˌwɪmən/ [*count*] : a woman who is a member of a legislative assembly

as·sent /əˈsɛnt/ *verb* **-sents; -sent·ed; -sent·ing** [*no obj*] *formal* : to agree to or approve of something (such as an idea or suggestion) especially after carefully thinking about it • The general proposed a detailed plan and the President *assented*. — often + *to* • She refused to *assent to* [=*agree to*] the new rules.

– **assent** *noun* [*noncount*] • A contract requires the *assent* [=*agreement, approval*] of both parties. • The leaders gave their *assent* [=*approval*] to the peace proposal.

as·sert /əˈsɚt/ *verb* **-serts; -sert·ed; -sert·ing** [+ *obj*]

1 : to state (something) in a strong and definite way • "Poverty is the city's most serious problem," the authors *assert*. = The authors *assert* that poverty is the city's most serious problem. • He *asserted* that there were spies in the government. • Despite the evidence against him, he has continued to *assert* his innocence. [=has continued to say that he is innocent]

2 : to demand that other people accept or respect (something) • She *asserted* her independence from her parents by getting her own apartment. • The boss was reluctant to *assert* his authority over his employees.

assert yourself **1** *of a person* : to speak or act in a strong and definite way • If you want people to listen to your opinions, you'll need to learn how to *assert yourself*. • The coach wants the players to *assert themselves* [=play more aggressively] on the field. **2** *of a thing* : to become apparent : to start to be clearly seen or known • Doubts about the value of the work began to *assert themselves*.

– **as·ser·tion** /əˈsɚʃən/ *noun, pl* **-tions** [*count*] I don't always agree with his *assertions* [=his strong statements] about politics. • an *assertion* of innocence [*noncount*] Getting her own apartment was the first step in the *assertion* of her independence.

synonyms ASSERT, DECLARE, AFFIRM, and AVOW mean to say something in a way that shows you feel strongly about it, usually when you expect someone to disagree or challenge you. ASSERT suggests that you are confident about what you are saying and that you do not need proof or evidence. • The group *asserts* that the smoking ban will negatively affect restaurant and bar owners. DECLARE is used when you are saying something in a public or open way. • She has *declared* her support for the candidate. AFFIRM is a formal word which suggests that you believe something because of evidence, experience, or faith. • He again *affirmed* his belief in the existence of an afterlife. AVOW is also formal and emphasizes that you are being honest or sincere. • Both *avowed* that they had nothing to do with the crime.

as•sert•ive /əˈsɚtɪv/ *adj* [*more* ~; *most* ~] **:** confident in behavior or style • an *assertive* attitude • Their daughter is an *assertive* little girl. • The country has adopted a more *assertive* [=*aggressive*] foreign policy. • If you want people to listen to your opinions, you'll need to learn to be more *assertive*. — sometimes used figuratively • a sauce with an *assertive* flavor [=a strong flavor] — see also SELF-ASSERTIVE
– **as•sert•ive•ly** *adv* • He walked *assertively* [=*confidently*] onto the stage. – **as•sert•ive•ness** *noun* [*noncount*] • the country's new *assertiveness* [=*aggressiveness*] in foreign policy • She is getting/undergoing ***assertiveness training*** [=training that teaches people to act more confidently]

as•sess /əˈsɛs/ *verb* **-sess•es**; **-sessed**; **-sess•ing** [+ *obj*]
1 : to make a judgment about (something) • The school will *assess* [=*evaluate*] the students' progress each year. • After the hurricane, officials *assessed* the town's need for aid. • *assess* a problem • We need to *assess* whether or not the system is working. • *assess* the situation/danger/impact/severity
2 : to officially say what the amount, value, or rate of (something) is • Damage to the boat was *assessed* at $5,000. • Their house is *assessed* [=*appraised, valued*] at $163,000.
3 a : to tax or charge (someone or something) **:** to require (a person, business, etc.) to pay a particular amount of money • The company was *assessed* $12 million in fines for polluting the river. **b :** to require a person, business, etc., to pay (a tax, fee, fine, etc.) • The bank *assesses* [=(more commonly) *charges, imposes*] a fee for replacing lost credit cards.
4 *US, sports* **:** to give (a player or team) a penalty during a game • He was *assessed* five fouls during the game.

as•sess•ment /əˈsɛsmənt/ *noun, pl* **-ments** *formal*
1 a : the act of making a judgment about something **:** the act of assessing something [*count*] The book is a careful *assessment* [=*appraisal, evaluation*] of the president's achievements. • The school uses a variety of tests for its annual student *assessments*. [=*evaluations*] [*noncount*] It's a difficult problem that requires careful *assessment*. **b** [*count*] **:** an idea or opinion about something • I don't agree with his *assessment* of the problem.
2 [*count*] **:** an amount that a person is officially required to pay especially as a tax • The owners claimed the tax *assessment* on their house was too high.

as•ses•sor /əˈsɛsɚ/ *noun, pl* **-sors** [*count*]
1 : a person whose job is to officially say how much something (such as a property) is worth especially so that it can be taxed according to that value • a tax *assessor*
2 *law* **:** a person who knows a lot about a particular subject and whose job is to give advice about that subject to a judge or other court official
3 : a person whose job is to officially say how well someone has done on a test, in a competition, etc.

as•set /ˈæˌsɛt/ *noun, pl* **-sets** [*count*]
1 : a valuable person or thing • Good looks can be an *asset* [=*advantage*] in an acting career. • The state's natural *assets* include mountains and beautiful lakes. — often + *to* • Good looks can be an *asset to* an actor. • She is a great *asset to* the team. [=she's a valuable member of the team]
2 : something that is owned by a person, company, etc. — usually plural • The company had to sell some of its *assets* to avoid bankruptcy. • a bank with billions of dollars in *assets* • business *assets* and liabilities • They bought the company and stripped it of its *assets*. [=they sold the property owned by the company]

as•set–strip•ping /ˈæˌsɛtˈstrɪpɪŋ/ *noun* [*noncount*] *chiefly Brit* **:** the practice of buying a company that is not successful at a low price and then selling its property (such as buildings or land) to make a profit

ass•hole /ˈæsˌhoul/ *noun, pl* **-holes** [*count*] *US, informal* + *offensive*
1 : ANUS
2 : a very stupid or annoying person • Her boyfriend is a real *asshole*. [=(*Brit*) *arsehole*]

as•sid•u•ous /əˈsɪʤəwəs/ *adj* [*more* ~; *most* ~] *formal* **:** showing great care, attention, and effort • They were *assiduous* in their search for all the latest facts and figures. • The project required some *assiduous* planning. • *assiduous* [=*diligent*] students
– **as•si•du•ity** /ˌæsəˈduːwəti, *Brit* ˌæsəˈdjuːwəti/ *noun* [*noncount*] • the *assiduity* [=*diligence*] of the students – **as•sid•u•ous•ly** *adv* • He worked *assiduously* [=*diligently*] to improve his grades. – **as•sid•u•ous•ness** *noun* [*noncount*] • the *assiduousness* [=*diligence*] of the students

as•sign /əˈsaɪn/ *verb* **-signs**; **-signed**; **-sign•ing** [+ *obj*]
1 : to give someone a particular job or duty **:** to require someone to do a particular task • They *assigned* me the job of cleaning the equipment. = They *assigned* the job of cleaning the equipment to me. = They *assigned* me to clean the equipment. • The teacher *assigned* us 50 math problems for homework! • Students will be *assigned* five books to read and must choose two additional books (to read).
2 : to send (someone) *to* a particular group or place as part of a job • She was *assigned to* the embassy in India. • The new teacher was *assigned to* the science laboratory. • *assigned to* a platoon/squadron
3 : to give out something **:** to provide someone with something • Parts in the play were *assigned* [=*given*] to each student. • They *assigned* me a secretary. = They *assigned* a secretary to me. [=they provided me with a secretary] • A section of the field was *assigned* [=*set aside*] for parking. • The plane landed at its *assigned* gate. • our *assigned* positions/seats
4 : to say that someone has (something, such as blame or responsibility) • He believes that they have *assigned* blame/responsibility to the wrong people.
5 : to give a particular value, identity, etc., to something • The computer program will *assign* a number to each image.
6 *law* **:** to officially give (property or a legal right) to someone else • She *assigned* her share of the estate to her brother.
– **as•sign•able** /əˈsaɪnəbəl/ *adj, chiefly law* • an *assignable* interest in the estate – **as•sign•or** /ˌæsəˈnoɚ/ *noun, pl* **-ors** [*count*] *law* • the property of the *assignor*

as•sig•na•tion /ˌæsɪgˈneɪʃən/ *noun, pl* **-tions** [*count*] *formal* **:** a meeting between lovers • a secret *assignation* [=*tryst*]

as•sign•ment /əˈsaɪnmənt/ *noun, pl* **-ments**
1 : a job or duty that is given to someone **:** a task someone is required to do [*count*] My *assignment* was to clean the equipment. = They gave me the *assignment* of cleaning the equipment. • The students were given a homework *assignment*. • The reporter's *assignment* is to interview the candidate. • The reporter is here on an *assignment*. [*noncount*] The reporter is here ***on assignment***
2 [*noncount*] **:** the act of assigning something or someone: such as **a :** the act of sending someone to a particular group or place as part of a job • The article discusses the recent *assignment* of senators to some of the more powerful committees. • her *assignment* to the embassy in India **b :** the act of giving a particular value, identity, etc., to something • the computer's *assignment* of a number to each image **c :** the act of saying that someone has something (such as blame) • the *assignment* of blame/responsibility **d** *law* **:** the act of officially giving property or a legal right to another person • the *assignment* of property
3 [*count*] **:** something (such as a particular position or seat) that is chosen for you to use or have • She asked if she could change her seating *assignment*.

as•sim•i•late /əˈsɪməˌleɪt/ *verb* **-lates**; **-lat•ed**; **-lat•ing**
1 [+ *obj*] **:** to learn (something) so that it is fully understood and can be used • Children need to *assimilate* new ideas/concepts. • There was a lot of information/material to *assimilate* at school.
2 a [+ *obj*] **:** to cause (a person or group) to become part of a different society, country, etc. • Schools were used to *assimilate* the children of immigrants. • She was thoroughly/completely *assimilated* to/into her new country. [=she had completely adapted to her new country] **b** [*no obj*] **:** to adopt the ways of another culture **:** to fully become part of a different society, country, etc. • They found it hard to *assimilate* to/into American society.
3 [+ *obj*] **:** to adopt (something) as part of a larger thing • The language is constantly *assimilating* new words. [=making new words part of itself; the language is constantly getting new words] • Many of these religious traditions have been *assimilated* into the culture.
– **as•sim•i•la•tion** /əˌsɪməˈleɪʃən/ *noun* [*noncount*] • a child's *assimilation* of concepts/ideas/information • Her *assimilation* into American society was complete.

[1]**as•sist** /əˈsɪst/ *verb* **-sists**; **-sist•ed**; **-sist•ing :** to give support or help **:** to make it easier for someone to do something

or for something to happen : HELP [+ *obj*] The device *assists* those who can't climb stairs. • The President was *assisted* by his advisers. • The President was *assisted* with his speech. = The President was *assisted* in writing his speech. • She *assisted* the boy with his homework. • Another doctor *assisted* him with the operation. [*no obj*] Another doctor *assisted* with the operation. • Federal agents are *assisting* with the investigation. • She *assisted* in making the decision. • The cream *assists* in the prevention of skin cancer.

[2]assist *noun, pl* **-sists** [*count*]
1 *US, somewhat informal* : an action that helps someone — usually singular • He wrote the story ***with an assist from*** [=*with the help/assistance of*] his friend. [=his friend helped him to write the story]
2 *sports* : an action (such as passing a ball or puck) that helps a teammate to score • He had 3 goals and 2 *assists* in the hockey game.

as•sis•tance /əˈsɪstəns/ *noun* [*noncount*] : the act of helping or assisting someone : help or support • Any *assistance* you can give me would be appreciated. • I'll be happy to provide you with whatever *assistance* you may need. • financial/cash *assistance* • The store salesperson asked her, "Do you need (any) *assistance*?" • She offered her *assistance*. • She asked, "Can I be ***of (any) assistance***?" [=can I help you?] • He wrote the story with his friend's *assistance*. = He wrote the story ***with the assistance of*** his friend. [=his friend helped him to write the story] • Nobody ***came to her assistance*** [=nobody helped her] when her car broke down. — see also DIRECTORY ASSISTANCE

[1]as•sis•tant /əˈsɪstənt/ *noun, pl* **-tants** [*count*]
1 : a person who helps someone; *especially* : a person whose job is to help another person to do work • a magician's *assistant* [=*helper*] • an *assistant* to the college president • an *assistant* to the store manager • a dental *assistant* [=a person whose job is to help a dentist] • a wealthy executive who has a personal *assistant* — see also PHYSICIAN'S ASSISTANT
2 : a person whose job is to help the customers in a store • She works as a ***sales assistant*** [=*salesclerk*] at Macy's. • (*Brit*) a ***shop assistant***

[2]assistant *adj, always used before a noun* : having the job of helping someone to do work : having a lower rank or position than others in a group, organization, etc. • an *assistant* store manager • an *assistant* editor

assistant professor *noun, pl* ~ **-sors** [*count*] : a teacher at a U.S. college or university who has a rank above an instructor and below an associate professor

assisted living *noun* [*noncount*] : a system that provides a place to live and medical care for people (such as elderly or disabled people) who need help with daily activities — often used in the form ***assisted-living*** before another noun • an *assisted-living* facility/residence

assisted suicide *noun, pl* ~ **-cides** : suicide with help from another person (such as a doctor) to end suffering from severe physical illness [*count*] a doctor who has been involved in several *assisted suicides* [*noncount*] an opponent of *assisted suicide*

assn. *abbr* association

assoc. *abbr* associate; associated; association

[1]as•so•ci•ate /əˈsoʊʃiˌeɪt/ *verb* **-ates; -at•ed; -at•ing**
1 [+ *obj*] : to think of one person or thing when you think of another person or thing — usually + *with* • I *associate* flowers *with* spring. • She will always *associate* that place *with* her youth. • People *associate* the company *with* televisions but it also makes computers. ✧ When one thing is ***associated with*** another, they happen together or are related or connected in some way. • There are several dangers/risks *associated with* [=*connected with*] that approach. • plants *associated with* the desert • He has symptoms *associated with* lung disease. • There are health problems that are often *associated with* poverty.
2 : to be together *with* another person or group as friends, partners, etc. [*no obj*] She *associates with* [=is friends with] some pretty strange people. • They denied *associating with* terrorists. [=they denied being involved with terrorists] [+ *obj*] He was *associated* [=*connected, identified*] *with* a group of radicals in the government. • I no longer wish to be *associated with* people like him. • She ***associates herself*** *with* some pretty strange people. ✧ If you ***associate yourself with*** something, such as a political movement, you show or say that you support and agree with it. • He was reluctant to *associate himself with* the government's position.

[2]as•so•ci•ate /əˈsoʊʃijət/ *noun, pl* **-ates** [*count*]
1 : a person who you work with or spend time with • business *associates* [=*colleagues*] • Her *associates* respected her for her hard work. • He is a known *associate* of criminals. [=he is known to associate with criminals; people know that he works with or spends time with criminals]
2 : a member of a group or organization who is at a level that is below the highest level • She started as an *associate* at the law firm. — sometimes used in the names of companies • He works for Jones and *Associates*, a consulting firm in Santa Fe.

[3]as•so•ci•ate /əˈsoʊʃijət/ *adj, always used before a noun* : having a rank or position that is below the highest level in a group, organization, etc. • He's an *associate* member of the club but he hopes to become a full member soon. • She was promoted from assistant editor to *associate* editor and may soon be promoted to senior editor.

associate professor *noun, pl* ~ **-sors** [*count*] : a teacher at a U.S. college or university who has a rank above an assistant professor and below a full professor

associate's degree *noun, pl* ~ **-grees** [*count*] : a degree that is given to a student who has completed two years of study at a junior college, college, or university in the U.S.

as•so•ci•a•tion /əˌsousiˈeɪʃən/ *noun, pl* **-tions**
1 [*count*] : an organized group of people who have the same interest, job, etc. • an athletic *association* [=*league*] • a baseball players' *association* [=*union*] • an *association* of local business leaders — see also PARENT-TEACHER ASSOCIATION, SAVINGS AND LOAN ASSOCIATION
2 : a connection or relationship between things or people [*count*] They denied having any *association* with terrorists. • They have a long *association* with the school and have donated millions of dollars to it. • a study examining the *association* [=*link*] between obesity and heart disease [*noncount*] The book was produced by the publisher ***in association with*** the museum that sponsored the exhibit. [=the publisher and the museum were both involved in making the book]
3 [*count*] : a feeling, memory, or thought that is connected to a person, place, or thing — usually plural • Chicago has pleasant *associations* for me because of the happy times I spent there. • His former school has only bad/negative *associations* for him. [=he has only unhappy memories of his former school]

Association football *noun* [*noncount*] *Brit, formal* : SOCCER

as•so•nance /ˈæsənəns/ *noun* [*noncount*] *technical* : the use of words that have the same or very similar vowel sounds near one another (as in "summer fun" and "rise high in the bright sky")

as•sort•ed /əˈsoətəd/ *adj* : including several kinds • a box of *assorted* cheeses • *assorted* colors/flavors/sizes/styles • She hangs around with rock stars, drug addicts, and *assorted* [=*various*] other oddballs.

as•sort•ment /əˈsoətmənt/ *noun, pl* **-ments** [*count*] : a group or collection of different things or people • an *assortment* of vegetables • The book has a wonderful *assortment* of characters. • You can choose from a wide *assortment* of options.

asst. *abbr* assistant • *asst.* coach • Dr. T. K. York, *Asst.* Professor

as•suage /əˈsweɪʤ/ *verb* **-suag•es; -suaged; -suag•ing** [+ *obj*] *formal* : to make (something, such as an unpleasant feeling) less painful, severe, etc. • The company tried to *assuage* [=*soothe, calm, ease*] investors' fears. • City officials needed to *assuage* [=*lessen, relieve*] neighbors' concerns about the new factory. • He couldn't *assuage* his guilt over the divorce. • trying to *assuage* [=*alleviate*] his hunger/thirst

as•sume /əˈsuːm/ *verb* **-sumes; -sumed; -sum•ing** [+ *obj*]
1 : to think that something is true or probably true without knowing that it is true • I *assumed* he was coming, so I was surprised when he didn't show up. • "Is he coming?" "So I *assume*." = "I *assume* so." • I think we can safely *assume* that he's coming. = I think it's safe to *assume* that he's coming. • She *assumed* from his expression that he was confused. • Let's *assume* [=*suppose*] (that) she rejects your invitation. What will you do then? = *Assuming* (that) she rejects your invitation, what will you do? [=what will you do if she rejects your invitation?] • We'll be arriving around noon. That's *assuming* that our flight is on time. • The study *assumes* that the problem develops after birth. [=the study does not consider the possibility that the problem may begin before birth]
2 a : to begin (a role, duty, etc.) as a job or responsibility •

She *assumed* the presidency. = She *assumed* the position of president. • *assume* [=*take*] office • The king *assumed* the throne when he was very young. **b :** to take or begin to have (power, control, etc.) in a job or situation • He is ready to *assume* [=*take*] control of the organization.
3 : to begin to have (a particular appearance or quality) • The last game of the season *assumes* much greater importance now. [=it becomes much more important now] • Their financial problems *assumed* huge proportions. [=grew to be very serious] • The sky gradually *assumed* [=*took on*] an otherworldly glow. • Under certain conditions, the chemical will *assume* the appearance of ice.
4 a : to make yourself have (an appearance that does not show your true feelings) in order to deceive someone • She immediately *assumed* a look of innocence. [=she had an expression on her face that made her look innocent, even though she wasn't] **b :** to place yourself in (a particular position or posture) • She *assumed* a sitting position [=she sat down] on the floor.
5 : to accept (a responsibility, debt, etc.) • When they purchased the company they had to *assume* [=*take on*] its debts. • *assume* liability • The city *assumes* greater financial risk with that plan.

assumed *adj* **:** not true or real • an *assumed* air of indifference • He traveled under an ***assumed name.*** [=he used a false name when he traveled]

as•sump•tion /əˈsʌmpʃən/ *noun, pl* **-tions**
1 [*count*] **:** something that is believed to be true or probably true but that is not known to be true **:** something that is assumed • I made the *assumption* that he was coming, so I was surprised when he didn't show up. • He will come home tomorrow. At least, that's my *assumption.* • Many scientific *assumptions* about Mars were wrong. • We are operating ***on/under/with the assumption*** that the loan will be approved. [=we are assuming that the loan will be approved; we are behaving as though we know that the loan will be approved] • I'm telling you our arrival time ***on the assumption that*** you will check to see whether or not our flight is on time before you come to the airport. • Her plan is based *on the* underlying *assumption that* the economy will improve in the near future.
2 [*noncount*] **:** the act of assuming something: such as **a :** the act of beginning a role, duty, etc. • her *assumption* of the presidency **b :** the act of taking or beginning to have power, control, etc., in a job or situation • the *assumption* of control/authority **c :** the act of accepting a responsibility, debt, etc. • the buyer's *assumption* of debt

as•sur•ance /əˈʃurəns/ *noun, pl* **-anc•es**
1 [*noncount*] **:** the state of being sure or certain about something • They lent us the money with the *assurance* that they would be repaid soon. • He has the *assurance* of continued support from his boss. — see also QUALITY ASSURANCE
2 [*noncount*] **:** a strong feeling of confidence about yourself or about being right • He spoke with quiet *assurance* about his future plans. — see also SELF-ASSURANCE
3 [*count*] **:** a strong and definite statement that something will happen or that something is true • She gave him every *assurance* that she would be there when he returned. — often plural • They sought *assurances* from the school that their children were safe. — see also LIFE ASSURANCE

as•sure /əˈʃuɚ/ *verb* **-sures; -sured; -sur•ing** [+ *obj*]
1 : to make (something) certain **:** ENSURE • He believed that hard work would *assure* his success. [=that hard work would make him sure to succeed] • We must *assure* that every child gets a proper education. = We must *assure* a proper education for every child. • Winning the Nobel Prize will *assure* [=*secure, guarantee*] her a place in history. ✧ To ***assure someone of doing something*** is to make it certain that someone will do something. • A victory in this game will *assure them of finishing* the season with a winning record.
2 : to tell someone in a very strong and definite way that something will happen or that something is true • I can *assure* you that you won't be disappointed. • She *assured* me (that) she was OK when I talked to her on the phone. • His boss *assured* him that he had her continued support. = His boss *assured* him of her continued support. = "You have my continued support," his boss *assured* him. • These mistakes won't happen again, ***I (can) assure you.***
assure yourself **:** to make yourself sure or certain about something • He tried opening the door to *assure himself* that it was locked. • They managed to be third in line, *assuring themselves* of good seats for the concert.

as•sured /əˈʃuɚd/ *adj*
1 : sure or certain to happen • Success is by no means *assured.* [=is definitely not certain] • an *assured* conclusion • Winners of the Nobel Prize have an *assured* place in history.
2 [*more ~; most ~*] **:** very confident **:** SELF-ASSURED • an *assured* voice/manner • His writing has become more *assured* as he has gotten older.
3 : sure that something is certain or true — used in the phrase ***rest assured*** • You can *rest assured* [=you can be sure] that these mistakes won't happen again. = *Rest assured,* these mistakes won't happen again.
assured of **:** certain to have or get (something) • They are not *assured of* being paid. [=it is not certain that they will be paid] • She is *assured of* (getting/having) a job when she gets out of college.

as•sur•ed•ly /əˈʃurədli/ *adv, formal*
1 : without doubt **:** CERTAINLY, DEFINITELY • The merger will almost *assuredly* lead to job layoffs. ✧ This sense of *assuredly* is commonly used with *most,* but it is not used with *more.* • He *most assuredly* [=very definitely] will not win.
2 [*more ~; most ~*] **:** in a way that shows that you are confident • She moved/walked *assuredly* [=*confidently*] across the platform to the microphone.

as•ter /ˈæstɚ/ *noun, pl* **-ters** [*count*] **:** a type of plant that is grown in gardens for its colorful flowers

as•ter•isk /ˈæstəˌrɪsk/ *noun, pl* **-isks** [*count*] **:** a symbol * that is used in printed text especially to tell someone to read a note that can be found at the bottom of a page
– asterisk *verb* **-isks; -isked; -isk•ing** [+ *obj*] • an *asterisked* note

astern /əˈstɚn/ *adv*
1 : in, at, or toward the back of a boat or ship **:** in, at, or toward the stern • The island lay *astern* (of us) [=the island was behind us] as we sailed east.
2 *of a boat or ship* **:** in a reverse direction • The ship went full speed *astern.*

as•ter•oid /ˈæstəˌrɔɪd/ *noun, pl* **-oids** [*count*] **:** any one of thousands of small planets that circle around the sun • Most *asteroids* are found between Mars and Jupiter.

asth•ma /ˈæzmə, *Brit* ˈæsmə/ *noun* [*noncount*] *medical* **:** a physical condition that makes it difficult for someone to breathe

asth•mat•ic /æzˈmætɪk, *Brit* æsˈmætɪk/ *adj, medical* **:** relating to or suffering from asthma • *asthmatic* symptoms • an *asthmatic* patient • an *asthmatic* cough
– asthmatic *noun, pl* **-ics** [*count*] • My son is an *asthmatic.*

astig•ma•tism /əˈstɪgməˌtɪzəm/ *noun* [*noncount*] *medical* **:** a problem with the eye that prevents a person from seeing clearly
– as•tig•mat•ic /ˌæstɪgˈmætɪk/ *adj* [*more ~; most ~*] • *astigmatic* eyes

astir /əˈstɚ/ *adj, not used before a noun, literary*
1 : in an active state • A breeze is *astir.* [=a breeze is blowing] — often + *with* • The air is *astir with* breezes.
2 : awake and out of bed • Nobody in the house was *astir.* [=*awake, up*]

as•ton•ish /əˈstɑːnɪʃ/ *verb* **-ish•es; -ished; -ish•ing :** to cause a feeling of great wonder or surprise in (someone) [+ *obj*] The garden *astonishes* [=*amazes*] anyone who sees it. • Despite the hype, there was nothing in the book to *astonish* readers. [*no obj*] The garden's beauty never fails to *astonish.*

astonished *adj* [*more ~; most ~*] **:** feeling or showing great surprise or wonder **:** AMAZED, ASTOUNDED • I was *astonished* by/at all the changes in the town's appearance. • I'm *astonished* that you could behave so selfishly. • They were *astonished* to see that their car had been stolen. • The announcement was greeted with *astonished* laughter.

as•ton•ish•ing /əˈstɑːnɪʃɪŋ/ *adj* [*more ~; most ~*] **:** causing a feeling of great surprise or wonder **:** causing astonishment **:** AMAZING, ASTOUNDING • He showed an *astonishing* lack of concern for others. • The truck can hold an *astonishing* amount of stuff. • She gave an *astonishing* performance in her first film.
– as•ton•ish•ing•ly *adv* • an *astonishingly* beautiful scene • *Astonishingly* (enough), the dog swam across the lake.

as•ton•ish•ment /əˈstɑːnɪʃmənt/ *noun* [*noncount*] **:** a feeling of being very surprised **:** AMAZEMENT • The garden's beauty filled me with *astonishment.* • A crowd watched ***in astonishment*** as he jumped from the bridge. • They discovered ***to their astonishment*** that their car had been stolen. • ***Much to the astonishment of*** her friends and family, she left school to pursue her acting career.

as•tound /əˈstaʊnd/ *verb* **-tounds; -tound•ed; -tound-**

ing [+ *obj*] : to cause a feeling of great surprise or wonder in (someone) : AMAZE, ASTONISH • The magician will *astound* you with his latest tricks. • What *astounds* me is that they never apologized.

astounded *adj* [*more* ~; *most* ~] : feeling or showing great surprise or wonder : AMAZED, ASTONISHED • She was *astounded* by/at the number of people in the room. • We were *astounded* to discover a valuable painting in the attic. • The *astounded* audience watched in amazement.

as•tound•ing /əˈstaʊndɪŋ/ *adj* [*more* ~; *most* ~] : causing a feeling of great surprise or wonder : AMAZING, ASTONISHING • Your ignorance is *astounding*. • He ate an *astounding* amount of food.

– **astoundingly** *adj* • *Astoundingly*, the school decided not to punish him. • an *astoundingly* successful businessman

as•tra•khan /ˈæstrəkən, *Brit* ˌæstrəˈkæn/ *noun* [*noncount*] : a type of curly black fur that comes from a young sheep; *also* : a cloth that resembles such fur

as•tral /ˈæstrəl/ *adj*

1 *technical* : of or relating to the stars • *astral* navigation

2 : involving a person's spirit rather than the body • She believes in ***astral projection***. [=the ability of a person's spirit to travel to distant places]

astray /əˈstreɪ/ *adv*

1 : off the right path or route — usually used with *go* • They marked the trail so hikers wouldn't *go astray*. [=become lost] • The rocket *went astray* after liftoff. • The letter *went astray*. [=was lost]

2 : away from what is right, good, or desirable — usually used with *go* or *lead* • Older students *led* him *astray*. [=made him behave badly] • The writer *goes* (badly) *astray* [=stops being correct or reasonable] when she blames the current government for these problems. • The President was *led astray* [=convinced to make a bad decision] by his advisers. • Their plans have *gone astray*. [=have failed]

astride /əˈstraɪd/ *prep* : with one leg or part on each side of (something) • She was sitting *astride* a horse. • The town lies *astride* a narrow river.

as•trin•gent /əˈstrɪnʤənt/ *adj* [*more* ~; *most* ~]

1 *medical* : causing body tissues (such as skin) to tighten — used to describe a liquid or lotion that makes the skin less oily or that helps to stop a cut from bleeding • *astringent* lotions

2 : having a sharp or bitter quality • an *astringent* taste

3 : very critical in a sharp and often clever way • Her speech included some *astringent* [=*caustic, biting*] comments about the other candidate. • an *astringent* critic of modern movies

– **as•trin•gen•cy** /əˈstrɪnʤənsi/ *noun* [*noncount*] • the *astringency* of her comments – **astringent** *noun, pl* **-gents** [*count*] *medical* • She used an *astringent* on her face. – **as•trin•gent•ly** *adv* • an *astringently* ironic writer

as•trol•o•gy /əˈstrɑːləʤi/ *noun* [*noncount*] : the study of how the positions of the stars and movements of the planets have a supposed influence on events and on the lives and behavior of people

– **as•trol•o•ger** /əˈstrɑːləʤɚ/ *noun, pl* **-gers** [*count*] • She consulted an *astrologer* to see if she would ever get married. – **as•tro•log•i•cal** /ˌæstrəˈlɑːʤɪkəl/ *adj* • *astrological* theories/beliefs/signs – **as•tro•log•i•cal•ly** /ˌæstrəˈlɑːʤɪkli/ *adv*

as•tro•naut /ˈæstrəˌnɑːt/ *noun, pl* **-nauts** [*count*] : a person who travels in a spacecraft into outer space

as•tro•nom•i•cal /ˌæstrəˈnɑːmɪkəl/ *also* **as•tro•nom•ic** /ˌæstrəˈnɑːmɪk/ *adj*

1 : of or relating to astronomy • *astronomical* research

2 : extremely large • The cost of the office building was *astronomical*. • We got an *astronomical* telephone bill this month.

– **as•tro•nom•i•cal•ly** /ˌæstrəˈnɑːmɪkli/ *adv* • The cost of health care has risen *astronomically*. • an *astronomically* large amount of money

as•tron•o•my /əˈstrɑːnəmi/ *noun* [*noncount*] : the scientific study of stars, planets, and other objects in outer space

– **as•tron•o•mer** /əˈstrɑːnəmɚ/ *noun, pl* **-mers** [*count*]

as•tro•phys•ics /ˌæstrəˈfɪzɪks/ *noun* [*noncount*] : the scientific study of the physical and chemical properties and structures of stars, planets, and other objects in outer space

– **as•tro•phys•i•cal** /ˌæstrəˈfɪzɪkəl/ *adj* – **as•tro•phys•i•cist** /ˌæstrəˈfɪzəsɪst/ *noun, pl* **-cists** [*count*]

As•tro•turf /ˈæstrəˌtʰɚf/ *trademark* — used for an artificial surface that resembles grass

as•tute /əˈstuːt, *Brit* əˈstjuːt/ *adj* [*more* ~; *most* ~] : having or showing an ability to notice and understand things clearly : mentally sharp or clever • He is an *astute* observer of the current political scene. • *Astute* readers will notice the error. • She made some *astute* [=*insightful*] observations about the movie industry. • His analysis of the battle was very *astute*.

– **as•tute•ly** *adv* • He invested his money *astutely*. [=*shrewdly*] – **as•tute•ness** *noun* [*noncount*] • political *astuteness*

asun•der /əˈsʌndɚ/ *adv, literary* : into parts : APART • He split the log *asunder* with an ax. — often used with *tear* • The government was *torn asunder* [=deeply divided] by scandal.

asy•lum /əˈsaɪləm/ *noun, pl* **-lums**

1 [*noncount*] : protection given by a government to someone who has left another country in order to escape being harmed • She asked for political *asylum*. • She was granted *asylum* after it was made clear that she would be killed if she returned to her native country. • *asylum* seekers

2 [*count*] *old-fashioned* : a hospital where people who are mentally ill are cared for especially for long periods of time : a mental hospital

asym•met•ri•cal /ˌeɪsəˈmɛtrɪkəl/ *or* **asym•met•ric** /ˌeɪsəˈmɛtrɪk/ *adj* [*more* ~; *most* ~] : having two sides or halves that are not the same : not symmetrical • an *asymmetrical* design

– **asym•met•ri•cal•ly** /ˌeɪsəˈmɛtrɪkli/ *adv* – **asym•me•try** /eɪˈsɪmətri/ *noun, pl* **-tries** [*noncount*] the *asymmetry* of the design [*count*] Doctors studied *asymmetries* in the brain.

asymp•tom•at•ic /ˌeɪˌsɪmtəˈmætɪk/ *adj, medical* : having or showing no symptoms of disease • You should continue to take the medication, even when you are *asymptomatic*. [=even when you do not have any pain or other signs that you are sick]

<u>**at**</u> /ˈæt, ət/ *prep*

1 — used to indicate the place where someone or something is • We're staying *at* a hotel. • The kitchen is *at* the back of the house. • He was sitting *at* the table. • They left for Cambridge early and arrived *at* [=*in*] Cambridge before noon. • The party will be *at* Susan's house. = The party will be *at* Susan's. • Ann works *at* [=*in*] a library. • We met *at* a party. • They live *at* opposite ends of town. • They met *at* [=*on*] a street corner in a town. • "Is your father *at* home?" [=is your father home?] "No, he's working late *at* the office." • She met us *at* the door. • He was standing *at* [=next to] the window. • There were 200 people *at* the wedding. [=200 people attended the wedding] • Their older son has graduated, but their younger son is still *at* school. [=is still attending school] • Who was *at* the controls when the accident occurred?

> The word ***at*** is used in speech in e-mail addresses. • "Can I e-mail you?" "Sure. Our e-mail address is 'comments *at* Merriam-Webster dot com.'" In writing, the symbol @ is used instead. • comments@Merriam-Webster.com

2 — used to indicate the person or thing toward which an action, motion, or feeling is directed or aimed • She pointed her gun *at* the target. • He's angry *at* his brother. • His anger is directed *at* his brother. • She shouted (words of) abuse *at* me. • He looked directly *at* me. • They laughed *at* him. • She grabbed *at* my arm. [=she tried to grab my arm] • He poked *at* his food.

3 — used to indicate something that is being tried or attempted • I made an attempt *at* persuading him to go. • I took a shot *at* doing it myself. [=I tried to do it myself]

4 : because of or in reaction to (something) • They laughed *at* my joke. • She's furious *at* how slowly the investigation is proceeding. — used to indicate the cause of an action, feeling, etc. • I was greatly surprised *at* [=*by*] the result. [=the result surprised me greatly] • He enlisted in the army *at* his father's urging. [=because his father urged him to] • She visited the museum *at* my suggestion. • They came here *at* our invitation. • You can act *at* your own discretion.

5 — used to indicate an activity • He's very serious when he's *at* work. [=when he's working] • children who are *at* play [=children who are playing] • She's good *at* (playing) chess. [=she plays chess well] • I'm bad *at* cooking. [=I'm a bad cook, I do not cook well] • She's doing very well *at* her studies.

6 — used to indicate a situation or condition • I'm not *at* liberty to discuss that. • *at* rest • two nations that are *at* war • people who are *at* risk • He is now *at* peace.

7 a — used to indicate position on a scale or in a series • The temperature is *at* 90 degrees. • He was driving *at* almost 80 miles an hour. **b** — used to indicate a rate • They sell *at* [=*for*] a dollar a dozen. [=each dozen costs one dollar]

A

8 — used to indicate an age or time ▪ He plans to retire *at* (age) 65. ▪ He called us *at* (about/exactly) 9 o'clock on July 24. ▪ *at* dawn/noon/sunset/night ▪ I still think of her *at* certain moments/times. ▪ He was president of the company *at* (the time of) his death.
9 — used to indicate the method by which something is done ▪ The property was sold *at* auction.
10 a — used in phrases like ***at best, at worst,*** etc., to indicate a possible result or condition that is considered best, worst, etc. ▪ The company will make a small profit *at best* this year. [=it is not possible that the company will earn anything better/more than a small profit] ▪ We might be 5 or 10 minutes late *at worst*. [=we will not be more than 5 or 10 minutes late] ▪ We should arrive by noon *at the latest*. [=we should not arrive later than noon] **b** — used in phrases like ***at its best, at its worst,*** etc., to indicate that something or someone is as good, bad, etc., as possible ▪ This is baseball *at its best*. ▪ He's often rude, and last night he was *at his worst*.
at it : doing some activity ▪ I didn't expect her to have started working yet, but she was already (hard) *at it* when I arrived. [=she was already working (hard) when I arrived] ▪ My neighbors are always arguing, and they were *at it* again last night. [=they were arguing again last night] ▪ Since we're cleaning the kitchen, we should wash the floor ***while we're at it***. [=we should wash the floor when we clean the kitchen] ▪ "I'm going to the store to buy a newspaper." "*While you're at it*, could you get some milk?"
at that see [1]THAT
where it's at see [1]WHERE
where (someone) is at see [1]WHERE

at·a·vis·tic /ˌætəˈvɪstɪk/ *adj, formal* : very primitive — used to describe feelings or qualities that human beings have had from the earliest times ▪ She thinks men have an *atavistic* desire to dominate any group. ▪ *atavistic* urges/instincts

ate *past tense of* EAT

ate·lier /ˌætl̩ˈjeɪ, *Brit* əˈtɛlijeɪ/ *noun, pl* **-iers** [*count*] : a room where an artist works

athe·ist /ˈeɪθijɪst/ *noun, pl* **-ists** [*count*] : a person who believes that God does not exist — compare AGNOSTIC 1
– athe·ism /ˈeɪθiˌɪzəm/ *noun* [*noncount*] **– athe·is·tic** /ˌeɪθiˈɪstɪk/ *adj* [*more ~; most ~*] ▪ *atheistic* beliefs

ath·lete /ˈæθˌliːt/ *noun, pl* **-letes** [*count*] : a person who is trained in or good at sports, games, or exercises that require physical skill and strength ▪ *Athletes* from around the world will be competing at the Olympics. ▪ amateur/professional *athletes* ▪ She was quite an *athlete* as a child.

athlete's foot *noun* [*noncount*] *medical* : a condition in which the skin between and around the toes cracks and peels

ath·let·ic /æθˈlɛtɪk/ *adj*
1 *always used before a noun* **a** : of or relating to athletes ▪ the national *athletic* association ▪ They each received an *athletic* scholarship to the school. **b** : of or relating to sports, games, or exercises ▪ Students can get discount tickets for all *athletic* events. ▪ His *athletic* career spanned three decades. ▪ the college's *athletic* department/director ▪ She has great *athletic* ability.
2 *always used before a noun* : used by athletes : used during or for sports, games, or exercises ▪ *athletic* socks/gear/shoes ▪ the school's *athletic* field
3 [*more ~; most ~*] **a** : strong and muscular ▪ She's tall and has an *athletic* build. **b** : active in sports, games, or exercises ▪ He's very *athletic*.
– ath·let·i·cal·ly /æθˈlɛtɪkli/ *adv* ▪ She's tall and *athletically* built.

ath·let·i·cism /æθˈlɛtəˌsɪzəm/ *noun* [*noncount*] : the ability to play sports or do physical activities well ▪ He's much admired for his *athleticism*. ▪ She has speed and *athleticism*.

ath·let·ics /æθˈlɛtɪks/ *noun*
1 [*plural*] *US* : sports, games, and exercises that require strength and skill : athletic activities ✧ *Athletics* is plural in form but is used with both plural and singular verbs. ▪ College *athletics* attract students from a variety of backgrounds. ▪ The coach believes high school *athletics* is in need of reform.
2 [*noncount*] *Brit* : TRACK AND FIELD

athletic supporter *noun, pl* **~ -ers** [*count*] *chiefly US* : JOCKSTRAP

at–home /ətˈhoʊm/ *adj, always used before a noun, US*
1 : made to be used in the home ▪ She uses an *at-home* blood test to monitor her blood levels. ▪ *at-home* exercise equipment
2 : happening at someone's home ▪ *at-home* entertainment ▪ one of the star's rare *at-home* interviews
3 : not employed outside the home ▪ an *at-home* [=(more commonly) *stay-at-home*] mother/father

-ation *noun suffix* : the action or process of doing something ▪ visit*ation* ▪ memoriz*ation*

atish·oo /əˈtɪʃu/ *interj, Brit* : ACHOO

-ative *adj suffix*
1 : relating to or connected with something ▪ authorit*ative*
2 : designed to do something ▪ prevent*ative* ▪ inform*ative*
3 : tending to do something ▪ talk*ative*

Atl. *abbr* Atlantic

At·lan·tis /ətˈlæntəs/ *noun* [*noncount*] : an island that according to legend sank to the bottom of the Atlantic Ocean long ago

at·las /ˈætləs/ *noun, pl* **-las·es** [*count*] : a book of maps ▪ a world *atlas* ▪ a road *atlas* of the U.S.

ATM /ˌeɪˌtiːˈɛm/ *noun, pl* **ATMs** [*count*] : a machine that people use to get money from their bank accounts by using a special card — often used before another noun ▪ *ATM* cards/machines ✧ *ATM* is an abbreviation of "automatic teller machine."

at·mo·sphere /ˈætməˌsfiɚ/ *noun, pl* **-spheres**
1 a [*singular*] : the whole mass of air that surrounds the Earth ▪ Experts have noticed changes in the *atmosphere*. ▪ Meteoroids burn up as they pass through Earth's *atmosphere*. **b** [*count*] : a mass of gases that surround a planet or star ▪ The planets have different *atmospheres*.
2 [*count*] : the air in a particular place or area — usually singular ▪ The waiting room's stuffy *atmosphere* made me feel a little sick. ▪ the moist *atmosphere* of the swamp
3 a [*count*] : the particular way a place or situation makes you feel — usually singular ▪ The inn has a romantic *atmosphere*. — often + *of* ▪ The relaxed *atmosphere of* the classroom was a stark contrast to the strict schools I'd gone to before. ▪ The news created an *atmosphere of* fear/excitement/confusion. **b** [*noncount*] : an interesting or pleasing quality or effect ▪ a country inn with lots of *atmosphere* ▪ The food was good but the restaurant has no *atmosphere*.

at·mo·spher·ic /ˌætməˈsfirɪk, *Brit* ˌætməˈsfɛrɪk/ *adj*
1 *always used before a noun* : of or relating to the atmosphere of the Earth or another planet ▪ *atmospheric* gases/conditions/pressure
2 : creating a pleasant or exciting mood or feeling ▪ *atmospheric* melodies

atoll /ˈæˌtɑːl/ *noun, pl* **atolls** [*count*] : an island that is made of coral and shaped like a ring

at·om /ˈætəm/ *noun, pl* **-oms** [*count*]
1 : the smallest particle of a substance that can exist by itself or be combined with other atoms to form a molecule ▪ carbon *atoms* ▪ an *atom* of hydrogen
2 : a very small amount of something ▪ The flu took every *atom* [=*bit*] of strength I had. ▪ There is not an *atom* of truth to what he said.

atom·ic /əˈtɑːmɪk/ *adj*
1 : of or relating to atoms ▪ *atomic* [=*nuclear*] physics/particles
2 : of, relating to, or using the energy that is produced when atoms are split apart ▪ *atomic* [=*nuclear*] weapons ▪ the *atomic* [=*nuclear*] age ▪ an *atomic* [=*nuclear*] reactor

atomic bomb *noun, pl* **~ bombs** [*count*] : a bomb that produces an extremely powerful explosion when atoms are split apart — called also *A-bomb, atom bomb*

atomic clock *noun, pl* **~ clocks** [*count*] : a special kind of clock that is extremely exact

atomic energy *noun* [*noncount*] *physics* : NUCLEAR ENERGY

at·om·iz·er /ˈætəˌmaɪzɚ/ *noun, pl* **-ers** [*count*] : a device that forces a liquid out of a very small hole so that it becomes a fine spray ▪ a perfume *atomizer*

aton·al /eɪˈtoʊnl/ *adj, music* : not written, played, or sung in a particular key ▪ *atonal* music/sounds

atone /əˈtoʊn/ *verb* **atones; atoned; aton·ing** [*no obj*] *formal* : to do something good as a way to show that you are sorry about doing something bad — usually + *for* ▪ He says that he volunteers at the homeless shelter as a way to *atone for* [=*make up for*] the sins of his youth.
– atone·ment /əˈtʰoʊnmənt/ *noun* [*noncount*] ▪ *atonement for* his sins

atop /əˈtɑːp/ *prep, chiefly US, somewhat old-fashioned + literary* : on top of ▪ The house sits *atop* a cliff overlooking the ocean.

A

atri•um /ˈeɪtrijəm/ *noun, pl* **atria** /ˈeɪtrijə/ *also* **atriums** [*count*]
1 : an open area inside a tall building that has windows to let light in from above
2 *technical* **:** one of two sections of the heart that take in blood from the veins — compare VENTRICLE

atro•cious /əˈtroʊʃəs/ *adj*
1 : very evil or cruel ▪ an *atrocious* period in the nation's history ▪ *atrocious* crimes.
2 : very bad ▪ *atrocious* [=*terrible, awful*] handwriting ▪ His performance was *atrocious.* [=*horrible*] ▪ *atrocious* [=*appalling*] behavior ▪ Isn't this weather *atrocious*? [=*awful*]
– atro•cious•ly *adv* ▪ The team played *atrociously* [=*horribly*] this season.

atroc•i•ty /əˈtrɑːsəti/ *noun, pl* **-ties :** a very cruel or terrible act or action [*count*] the *atrocities* of war ▪ *Atrocities* were committed by forces on both sides of the conflict. [*noncount*] Who could be capable of such *atrocity*?

¹at•ro•phy /ˈætrəfi/ *noun* [*noncount*] *medical* **:** gradual loss of muscle or flesh usually because of disease or lack of use ▪ The doctor is concerned about possible *atrophy* of the shoulder muscles. — often used figuratively ▪ emotional/intellectual *atrophy* [=loss of emotional/intellectual strength]

²atrophy *verb* **-phies; -phied; -phy•ing** [*no obj*] *medical* **:** to become weak from lack of use **:** to suffer from atrophy ▪ Her muscles *atrophied* during her illness. ▪ After her surgery, she received therapy to keep the muscles from *atrophying.*

att. *abbr* **1** attached **2** attention **3** attorney

at•tach /əˈtætʃ/ *verb* **-tach•es; -tached; -tach•ing**
1 a [+ *obj*] **:** to fasten or join one thing *to* another ▪ I've *attached* an application *to* the brochure for you. ▪ She *attached* a note *to* the package. ▪ I *attached* the file *to* the e-mail. — often used as *(be) attached* ▪ A hook *is attached to* the back of the picture frame. — often used figuratively ▪ The man *attached* the blame *to* the two boys. [=said the two boys should be blamed] ▪ The lawyer *attached* [=*added*] new conditions *to* the contract. ▪ The shy child *attached* herself *to* her mother [=stayed close to her mother] during the whole party. **b** [*no obj*] **:** to be or become joined or connected ▪ The handle *attaches* here on the top. — opposite DETACH
2 [+ *obj*] **a :** to associate or connect one thing with another — + *to* ▪ It's obvious in the way he dresses that he *attaches* great importance *to* appearance. [=he thinks appearance is very important] ▪ People *attach* different meanings *to* the poem. [=people understand the meaning of the poem in different ways] — often used as *(be) attached* ▪ Magical powers were once thought to *be attached to* the stone. [=the stone was once thought to have magical powers] ▪ Little credibility *was attached to* his story. [=people did not think that his story was very credible] **b :** to associate or connect (yourself) with someone or something — + *to* ▪ He *attached* himself *to* an older, wealthy woman. ▪ She *attached* herself *to* the cause. — often used as *(be) attached* ▪ His doctor *is attached to* the clinic. [=his doctor is associated with the clinic]

at•ta•ché /ˌætəˈʃeɪ, *Brit* əˈtæˌʃeɪ/ *noun, pl* **-chés** [*count*] **:** a person who works at an embassy as an expert on a particular subject ▪ a cultural/military *attaché*

attaché case *noun, pl* **~ cases** [*count*] **:** a small, thin suitcase that is used especially for carrying papers and documents

at•tached /əˈtætʃt/ *adj*
1 : connected or joined to something ▪ Please fill out the *attached* application. ▪ Please see the document *attached.* ▪ The house has an *attached* garage.
2 [*more ~; most ~*] **:** emotionally connected **:** having strong feelings of affection ▪ She's quite *attached* to her cousin. [=she likes her cousin very much] ▪ We both became very *attached* to the cat.

at•tach•ment /əˈtætʃmənt/ *noun, pl* **-ments**
1 [*count*] **:** an extra part that can be used with a machine to make it do a particular job ▪ The vacuum cleaner *attachments* help clean in tight spaces. ▪ I need a longer *attachment* for the drill.
2 : strong feelings of affection or loyalty for someone or something [*count*] — usually singular ▪ the baby's *attachment* to his mother ▪ They all have a deep *attachment* to the old house. [*noncount*] People need emotional *attachment.*
3 [*count*] **:** a document or file that is sent with e-mail ▪ I'll send the document as an *attachment* to my next e-mail.
4 a [*count*] **:** a part that is used to connect or attach something ▪ The *attachments* that connect the rack to the car are rusted and should be replaced. **b** [*noncount*] **:** the act of connecting or attaching something ▪ There are two brackets for *attachment* of the shelf.
on attachment *Brit* **:** working for a limited time in a particular place — usually + *to* ▪ She's *on attachment to* Australia for a month.

¹at•tack /əˈtæk/ *verb* **-tacks; -tacked; -tack•ing**
1 : to act violently against (someone or something) **:** to try to hurt, injure, or destroy (something or someone) [+ *obj*] He *attacked* the guard with a knife. ▪ Troops *attacked* the fortress at dawn. — often used as *(be) attacked* ▪ He *was attacked* by a dog. ▪ He *was attacked* from behind by two men. [*no obj*] Suddenly, the dog *attacked.* ▪ The troops *attacked* at dawn.
2 [+ *obj*] **:** to criticize (someone or something) in a very harsh and severe way ▪ The study has been *attacked* as unscientific. [=people have criticized the study by saying that it is unscientific] ▪ People are *attacking* the mayor for breaking campaign promises. ▪ The professor has been widely *attacked* for her position on the issue.
3 [+ *obj*] **a :** to begin to work on or deal with (something, such as a problem) in a determined and eager way ▪ We eagerly *attacked* the problem. [=we eagerly tried to solve the problem] **b :** to begin to eat (food) eagerly ▪ Did you see the way the kids *attacked* that pizza?
4 [+ *obj*] **:** to begin to harm, injure, or destroy (something) ▪ The virus *attacks* the body's immune system. ▪ A number of trees have been *attacked* by the disease. ▪ Insects have *attacked* the crops.
5 *sports* **:** to try to score points or goals by moving forward in a very forceful way [*no obj*] The team *attacked* from the outset, so it was no surprise that they won. [+ *obj*] The offense *attacked* the weak defensive line.
– at•tack•er *noun, pl* **-ers** [*count*] ▪ She was able to identify her *attacker,* and he was later brought to trial. ▪ The defense trapped the *attacker* and got the ball back.

²attack *noun, pl* **-tacks**
1 a [*count*] **:** a violent, harmful, or destructive act against someone or something ▪ dog/shark *attacks* = *attacks* by dogs/sharks ▪ One of the patients was the victim of a knife *attack.* [=an attack made using a knife] — often + *on* ▪ There have been a number of *attacks on* women on the campus. **b :** harmful or destructive action against something by a disease, insect, chemical, etc. [*noncount*] The immune system is the body's defense against *attack* by germs. [*count*] The spray protects plants from *attacks* by many common pests.
2 : an attempt by a military force to defeat an enemy **:** a military offensive [*count*] an air/ground *attack* = an *attack* made from the air/ground ▪ The surprise *attack* came at dawn. [*noncount*] There is a threat of nuclear *attack.*
3 [*count*] **:** strong or severe criticism ▪ There have been many *attacks* against the professor for her position on the issue. ▪ a verbal *attack* ▪ The newspaper editorial is an *attack* on policy-makers.
4 [*count*] **:** a sudden short period of suffering from an illness or of being affected by a strong emotion ▪ an asthma *attack* ▪ a panic/anxiety *attack* — often + *of* ▪ an *attack of* the flu ▪ an *attack of* food poisoning ▪ an *attack of* nerves/melancholy — sometimes used figuratively ▪ an *attack of* the giggles ▪ He had an unexpected *attack of* goodness and helped us out. — see also HEART ATTACK
5 [*count*] **:** an attempt to destroy or end something — often + *on* ▪ City leaders have called for an *attack on* poverty. ▪ Local schools are mounting an *attack on* racism.
6 : a method of dealing with something (such as a problem) [*count*] Each problem calls for a different *attack.* [*noncount*] The current approach isn't working. I think we need a new ***plan of attack*** [=a new idea of how to do what we are trying to do]
7 *sports* **a** [*count*] **:** an attempt by a player or group of players to score points, goals, or runs — usually singular ▪ They had a sustained *attack* but could not score. ▪ The players carried the *attack* deep into the opponent's side of the field. ▪ They won the game in the last two innings with an 8-hit *attack.* [=they won the game by getting eight hits in the last two innings] **b** *Brit* **:** the players on a team who try to score **:** OFFENSE [*singular*] The team's *attack* has been weakened by injury. [*noncount*] He will play ***in attack*** [=(*US*) *on offense*]
on the attack **:** making an attack ▪ The soldiers were *on the attack.* [=were attacking the enemy] ▪ The team was *on the attack* [=was aggressively trying to score] for most of the first half. ▪ The team ***went on the attack*** [=began to attack] and quickly scored a goal. ▪ The candidate *went on the at-*

tack and accused his opponent of lying. • Opponents of the project *went on the attack* and defeated the land sale.

under attack : being affected or hurt by an attack : being attacked • The troops were *under attack* [=were being attacked by the enemy] throughout the day. • The troops suddenly ***came under attack***. [=began to be attacked] • The new policy has *come under attack* [=has been strongly criticized] by environmentalists.

[3]**attack** *adj, always used before a noun* : designed for or used in a military attack • an *attack* helicopter/submarine • The bombers were in *attack* formation.

attack dog *noun, pl* ~ **dogs** *[count]*

1 : a dog that has been trained to attack people

2 : a person who is known for making very harsh and personal criticisms of other people • The charges against the candidate were made by one of the governor's *attack dogs*.

at·tain /əˈteɪn/ *verb* **-tains; -tained; -tain·ing** *[+ obj] somewhat formal*

1 : to accomplish or achieve (something) : to succeed in getting or doing (something) • a quest to *attain* enlightenment • She refused to let the injury keep her from *attaining* her goal of being in the Olympics.

2 : to grow or increase to (a particular amount, size, etc.) : REACH • This kind of tree can *attain* a height of 20 feet within just a few years. • The car can *attain* a top speed of 200 mph.

– at·tain·able /əˈteɪnəbəl/ *adj [more ~; most ~]* • Be sure that the goals you set are *attainable*. [=*achievable*]

at·tain·ment /əˈteɪnmənt/ *noun, pl* **-ments** *formal*

1 *[noncount]* : the state or condition of having gotten or done something difficult : the act of attaining something : ACHIEVEMENT • She values educational *attainment* above all else. — often + *of* • She is working toward the *attainment of* her goals. • the *attainment of* enlightenment

2 *[count]* : something that has been gotten, done, or achieved through effort : ACHIEVEMENT • Her scientific *attainments* have made her quite well-known in the field of biology.

[1]**at·tempt** /əˈtɛmpt/ *verb* **-tempts; -tempt·ed; -tempt·ing** *[+ obj]* : to try to do (something) : to try to accomplish or complete (something) • They've *attempted* a climb up Mount Everest once before. • She *attempted* suicide early in their marriage. — often followed by *to + verb* • Do not *attempt to repair* the equipment without the proper tools. • The book *attempts to prove* that they were not guilty.

– attempted *adj* • an *attempted* robbery/murder/suicide

> ***synonyms*** ATTEMPT, TRY, ENDEAVOR, and STRIVE mean to make an effort to do or accomplish something. ATTEMPT is a basic word that sometimes stresses the beginning of this kind of effort. • He will *attempt* to photograph the rare bird. TRY is very close to ATTEMPT but often stresses effort that is made to test or prove something. • The team is *trying* to determine which fuel is less efficient overall. ENDEAVOR is a more formal word that usually suggests a serious and continuing effort. • As a teacher, he *endeavors* to inspire a love of learning in his students. STRIVE suggests effort made over a long period of time in order to accomplish something difficult. • Despite setbacks, we must continue to *strive* for peace.

[2]**attempt** *noun, pl* **-tempts** *[count]*

1 : an act of trying to do something • In an *attempt* [=*effort*] to raise money, the school will begin charging admission to school concerts. • She failed her driving test on the first *attempt* but she succeeded on her second *attempt*. • We both ***made an attempt*** [=*tried*] to be friendly despite recent arguments. • He ***made no attempt*** to apologize. [=he did not try to apologize] • It was a successful *attempt at* climbing Mount Everest. = It was a successful ***attempt on*** Mount Everest. ✧ *Attempt* often suggests that the effort made was unsuccessful. • a suicide *attempt* • an assassination *attempt*

2 : something that results from trying to do something • Her *attempt* at a home-cooked meal consisted of frozen fish sticks and a can of soup.

an attempt on someone's life : an act of trying to kill someone : a usually unsuccessful effort to kill someone • Police report that there has been *an attempt on the actor's life*. • Someone ***made an attempt on her life***. [=someone tried to kill her]

at·tend /əˈtɛnd/ *verb* **-tends; -tend·ed; -tend·ing**

1 a : to go to and be present at (an event, meeting, etc.) *[+ obj]* My husband and I will both *attend* the banquet. • How many people *attended* the baseball game? • He won't be *attending* the conference. *[no obj]* How many people will be *attending*? • One hundred people *attended*. **b** *[+ obj]* : to regularly go to (classes, church services, etc.) • She *attends* a school in the city. • He'll be *attending* the university in the fall. • I am the first child in my family to *attend* college. • We *attend* the same church.

2 *[+ obj]* **a** : to help or care for (someone, such as a patient) • Each nurse *attends* 15 patients. **b** : to assist with (a birth) • A midwife *attended* the birth. — see also ATTENDING

3 *[+ obj] formal* : to go with or be with (someone) as a helper or adviser • ministers who *attend* the king • She's *attended* by several assistants.

attend to *[phrasal verb]* ***attend to (someone or something)***

1 : to deal with (something) • Please excuse me. I must *attend to* some business. = Please excuse me. I've got some business I must *attend to*. 2 : to give needed help or attention to (someone or something) • Volunteers *attend to* the park for the summer. • The hotel staff *attended to* my every need. • Please make sure that the guests are *attended to*.

at·ten·dance /əˈtɛndəns/ *noun, pl* **-danc·es**

1 : the number of people present at an event, meeting, etc. *[noncount]* The team wants to double *attendance* at its games this season. • *Attendance* is down so far this season. *[count]* Museum *attendances* in the city have been increasing in recent years.

2 *[noncount]* **a** : the act of being present at a place • *Attendance* (at all classes) is mandatory. **b** : a record of how often a person goes to classes, meetings, etc. • Her grades are good, but how's her *attendance*? • a student who has ***perfect attendance*** [=a student who has been present at every class] • The teacher ***takes attendance*** [=makes a record of who is present] every day.

in attendance 1 : present at an event, meeting, etc. • Everyone *in attendance* voted in favor of the measure. • A number of celebrities were *in attendance*. 2 : caring for or helping someone who is giving giving birth or getting medical treatment • Who was *in attendance* at the birth? • midwives/doctors *in attendance*

[1]**at·ten·dant** /əˈtɛndənt/ *noun, pl* **-dants** *[count]*

1 : an assistant or servant • a bride and her *attendants* [=*bridesmaids*] • the royal family's *attendants*

2 : an employee who serves or helps customers • gas station *attendants* • She let the parking *attendant* park her car. — see also FLIGHT ATTENDANT

[2]**attendant** *adj, formal* : coming with or following as a result • The town is trying to deal with the population boom and the *attendant* increase in traffic. — often + *on* or *upon* • the problems *attendant on/upon* the introduction of new technology

at·tend·ee /əˌtɛnˈdiː/ *noun, pl* **-ees** *[count]* : a person who is present at an event, meeting, etc., or at a particular place • There were 300 *attendees* at the conference.

at·tend·er /əˈtɛndɚ/ *noun, pl* **-ers** *[count] chiefly Brit* : ATTENDEE • They are frequent/regular *attenders* at the church.

at·tend·ing /əˈtɛndɪŋ/ *adj, always used before a noun, chiefly US* : serving as a doctor on the staff of a hospital who regularly visits and treats patients and is in charge of other staff members • an *attending* physician/surgeon

at·ten·tion /əˈtɛnʃən/ *noun, pl* **-tions**

1 : the act or power of carefully thinking about, listening to, or watching someone or something *[noncount]* We focused our *attention* on this particular poem. • My *attention* wasn't really on the game. • The game was boring and my *attention* began to wander. [=I was losing interest in the game and started thinking about other things] • You need to ***pay more attention*** in school. • Please give me your ***undivided/full/complete attention***. [=please listen carefully and concentrate on what I am saying and doing] • The movie ***keeps/holds your attention*** [=*interest*] right to the very end. — often + *to* • Her job requires careful *attention to* detail. • You need to ***pay more attention to*** the teacher. • ***Don't pay any attention to*** what the other kids say. [=ignore what the other kids say] • It's time to ***turn/give our attention to*** the next project. • ***Pay (close/careful) attention to*** what he says. *[count]* (*US*) Lately she's been focusing her *attentions* on making sales. ✧ This sense is sometimes used as an interjection. • *Attention*, please! [=please give me your attention]

2 *[noncount]* : notice, interest, or awareness • She likes all the *attention* she is getting from the media/press. • The actor avoids drawing *attention* to himself. • The book has received/attracted national *attention*. • The trial is getting a lot of public *attention*. • The children were competing for the teacher's

A

attention. ▪ A cat on a leash is sure to attract *attention*. ▪ Your hard work and dedication have not ***escaped my attention*** [=I have noticed your hard work and dedication] ▪ The book's title ***grabbed/caught my attention*** [=the title caused me to look at the book] ▪ He was trying to ***divert/distract attention*** away from his friend's mistake. [=he was trying to keep people from noticing or thinking about his friend's mistake] ▪ We tried to ***attract/get your attention*** [=we tried to get you to see us], but you didn't hear us calling you. ▪ Thank you for ***bringing the matter to my attention*** [=making me aware of the matter] ▪ It has been ***brought to my attention*** [=I've been made aware] that the meeting has been canceled. ▪ I would like to ***call/bring your attention to*** a problem we are having. ▪ It ***came to my attention*** [=I noticed] that several items were missing from my office. ▪ It has ***come to my attention*** [=I have been made aware] that some people were offended by my comments. ▪ He loves being the ***center of attention*** [=he loves being noticed and watched by many people]

3 [*noncount*] **:** special care or treatment ▪ Be sure the dog gets plenty of *attention*. ▪ The house is in good shape, but the porch needs some *attention*. ▪ The victim needed immediate medical *attention*.

4 attentions [*plural*] **:** acts of kindness, care, or courtesy **:** acts that show affection or admiration for someone ▪ She found his *attentions* flattering. ▪ She has been receiving unwanted *attentions* from a coworker.

5 [*noncount*] **:** the way a soldier stands with the body stiff and straight, the feet together, and both arms at the sides — often used as a command ▪ *Attention!*

at attention **1** *or* ***to attention*** **:** standing silently with the body stiff and straight, the feet together, and both arms at the sides ▪ (*US*) The troops ***stood at attention*** = (*Brit*) The troops stood ***to attention*** — compare *at ease* at [1]EASE **2 :** in a position that shows careful listening or attention ▪ The dog sat *at attention*, listening for something in the distance.

attention deficit disorder *noun* [*noncount*] *medical* **:** a condition in which someone (such as a child) has problems with learning and behavior because of being unable to think about or pay attention to things for very long — abbr. *ADD*

attention span *noun, pl* **~ spans** [*count*] **:** the length of time during which someone is able to think about or remain interested in something ▪ people with short *attention spans*

at·ten·tive /əˈtɛntɪv/ *adj* [*more* ~; *most* ~]

1 : thinking about or watching something carefully **:** paying careful attention to something ▪ *Attentive* [=*observant*] readers might notice some mistakes in the book. ▪ an *attentive* audience — often + *to* ▪ He's very *attentive to* details.

2 : very concerned about the needs of others ▪ The hospital is proud of its *attentive* staff. ▪ Our waiter was very *attentive*.

– at·ten·tive·ly *adv* ▪ The audience listened/watched *attentively*. **– at·ten·tive·ness** *noun* [*noncount*] ▪ We appreciated the *attentiveness* of the hospital staff.

at·ten·u·ate /əˈtɛnjəˌweɪt/ *verb* **-ates; -at·ed; -at·ing** [+ *obj*] *formal* **:** to make (something) weaker or less in amount, effect, or force ▪ Earplugs will *attenuate* the loud sounds of the machinery. ▪ an *attenuated* virus

– at·ten·u·a·tion /əˌtɛnjəˈweɪʃən/ *noun* [*noncount*]

at·test /əˈtɛst/ *verb* **-tests; -test·ed; -test·ing** *formal* **:** to show, prove, or state that something is true or real [*no obj*] — usually + *to* ▪ I can *attest to* the truth of his statement. ▪ The popularity of the treatment *attests to* its effectiveness. [=shows that it is effective] [+ *obj*] I can *attest* that what he has said is true. ▪ The certificate *attests* the authenticity of the painting. ▪ He was asked to *attest* [=*authenticate*] the will/signature. — often used as *(be) attested* ▪ The plant's presence in the ancient world *is attested* by fossils that have been found. ▪ the first *attested* written language

– at·tes·ta·tion /ˌæˌtɛsˈteɪʃən/ *noun, pl* **-tions** [*count*] the first *attestations* of written language [*noncount*] The signature required *attestation*.

at·tic /ˈætɪk/ *noun, pl* **-tics** [*count*] **:** a room or space that is just below the roof of a building and that is often used to store things

at·tire /əˈtajə/ *noun* [*noncount*] *formal* **:** clothing ▪ beach/business/golf *attire* ▪ Proper *attire* is required at the restaurant.

at·tired /əˈtajəd/ *adj, formal* **:** dressed in a particular way ▪ an elegantly *attired* gentleman ▪ Both were *attired* in the distinctive uniform.

at·ti·tude /ˈætəˌtuːd, *Brit* ˈætəˌtjuːd/ *noun, pl* **-tudes**

1 [*count*] **:** the way you think and feel about someone or something ▪ He has a positive/negative *attitude* about the changes. — often + *to, toward,* or *towards* ▪ I don't understand your *attitude to* money. ▪ She's studying how *attitudes toward* death vary from culture to culture. ▪ He wants to change the hostile *attitude* they have *toward* technology.

2 [*count*] **:** a feeling or way of thinking that affects a person's behavior ▪ He has an aggressive/rebellious *attitude*. [=he behaves toward other people in an aggressive/rebellious way] ▪ She's friendly and has a good *attitude*. ▪ You need to change your bad *attitude*. ▪ There's been a change/shift in his *attitude* since his accident. ▪ She has an ***attitude problem*** [=she is not friendly or cooperative]

3 *informal* **a :** a way of thinking and behaving that people regard as unfriendly, rude, etc. [*count*] I don't know what her problem is. She has a real *attitude*. ▪ I suggest you get rid of that *attitude* and shape up. [*noncount*] He was showing some *attitude* during practice today, so the coach benched him. **b** [*noncount*] **:** a strong, confident, or impressive quality ▪ a band/movie with *attitude*

4 [*count*] *formal* **:** a particular way of positioning your body ▪ She bowed her head in an *attitude* of prayer.

cop an attitude see [2]COP

at·ti·tu·di·nal /ˌætəˈtuːdənəl, *Brit* ˌætəˈtjuːdənəl/ *adj, formal* **:** relating to, based on, or showing a person's opinions and feelings ▪ *attitudinal* changes/judgments

attn. *abbr* attention

at·tor·ney /əˈtəni/ *noun, pl* **-neys** [*count*] *chiefly US* **:** LAWYER — see also DISTRICT ATTORNEY, POWER OF ATTORNEY, STATE ATTORNEY

attorney at law *noun, pl* **attorneys at law** [*count*] *chiefly US, formal* **:** LAWYER — used chiefly as a title ▪ John Smith, *Attorney at Law*

attorney general *noun, pl* **attorneys general** *or* **attorney generals** [*count*] **:** the chief lawyer of a country or state who represents the government in legal matters

at·tract /əˈtrækt/ *verb* **-tracts; -tract·ed; -tract·ing** [+ *obj*]

1 a : to cause (someone) to choose to do or be involved in something ▪ The company has a difficult time *attracting* good employees because of its poor pay and benefits. ▪ The chance to travel around the world *attracted* me to a career as a flight attendant. **b :** to cause (someone) to like or be interested in something — usually used as *(be) attracted* ▪ He *is attracted* to hockey because of the constant action of the game. ▪ I *was attracted* by the town's vibrant art community.

2 : to cause (someone or something) to go to or move to or toward a place ▪ The museum *attracts* visitors from all over the world. ▪ The smell of freshly baked cookies *attracted* the children (to the kitchen). ▪ The scent will *attract* certain insects. ▪ Certain insects are *attracted* by the scent.

3 : to cause sexual or romantic feeling in (someone or something) ▪ Short men *attract* her. ▪ Her bright blue eyes *attracted* me. ▪ The bird's colorful feathers are used to *attract* a mate. — often used as *(be) attracted* ▪ She *is attracted* to short men. ▪ I *was attracted* by her bright blue eyes. ▪ I felt very *attracted* to her. — see also *opposites attract* at [3]OPPOSITE

4 : to cause (a particular reaction) **:** to get or create (attention, notice, interest, etc.) ▪ The trial is *attracting* a lot of attention. ▪ Her comment *attracted* criticism. ▪ The bird uses its call to *attract* the attention of a mate.

5 *physics* **:** to pull (something) to or toward something else ▪ A magnet *attracts* iron.

at·trac·tion /əˈtrækʃən/ *noun, pl* **-tions**

1 [*count*] **a :** something interesting or enjoyable that people want to visit, see, or do ▪ The waterfall continues to be the main *attraction* at the park. ▪ The town's big *attraction* for movie lovers is the annual film festival. ▪ Buses take visitors to all the city's best ***tourist attractions*** [=things tourists usually like to see or do] ✧ A ***coming attraction*** is a movie, show, or other interesting thing that is going to happen or be available soon. ▪ Before the movie began, we saw previews of *coming attractions*. **b :** a performer who people want to see ▪ She is the star *attraction* of the show.

2 [*singular*] **:** a feeling that makes someone romantically or sexually interested in another person ▪ There's a strong sexual *attraction* between them. ▪ His *attraction* to her grew over the course of their time together.

3 : a feature or quality that makes someone or something interesting or enjoyable [*noncount*] A good relationship is based on more than just physical *attraction*. [*count*] I understand the *attraction* of skydiving, but I could never do it. ▪ What are the *attractions* of owning your own business?

4 *physics* : a force that pulls something to or toward something else [*noncount*] magnetic/gravitational *attraction* [*count*] *attractions* among particles — opposite REPULSION

at·trac·tive /əˈtræktɪv/ *adj* [*more* ~; *most* ~]
1 : having a pleasing appearance • an *attractive* flower arrangement • He has an *attractive* [=*charming*] smile.; *especially* : having a pleasing appearance that causes romantic or sexual feelings in someone : GOOD-LOOKING • An *attractive* woman greeted us at the door. • I've never really found him *attractive*. [=I have never been attracted to him]
2 : having a feature or quality that people like • It is a very *attractive* [=*appealing*] offer/proposition, but I can't accept it at this time. • The camera has many *attractive* features at a very *attractive* price. — often + *to* • His ideas are *attractive to* many people. [=many people like his ideas]
– at·trac·tive·ly *adv* • The flowers are *attractively* arranged. • an *attractively* priced camera **– at·trac·tive·ness** *noun* [*noncount*] • sexual/physical *attractiveness*

at·trib·ut·able /əˈtrɪbjutəbəl/ *adj, not used before a noun* : caused by a particular thing — + *to* • His health problems are *attributable to* a poor diet and lack of exercise.

[1]**at·trib·ute** /əˈtrɪˌbjuːt/ *verb* **-utes; -ut·ed; -ut·ing**
attribute to [*phrasal verb*] ***attribute (something) to (someone or something)*** **1** : to say that (something) is because of (someone or something) • He *attributes* his success *to* his coach. [=he credits his success to his coach] • His doctor *attributes* his health problems *to* a poor diet and a lack of exercise. **2** : to think of (something) as being a quality of (someone or something) • The study suggests that it is a mistake to *attribute* adult reasoning *to* children. • Is it right to *attribute* complex emotions *to* animals? • She *attributed* some importance *to* the research. **3** : to think of (something) as being made or created by (someone) • The poem is usually *attributed to* Shakespeare, but some scholars doubt that he wrote it.
– at·tri·bu·tion /ˌætrəˈbjuːʃən/ *noun, pl* **-tions** [*noncount*] The *attribution* of the poem to Shakespeare is questioned by some scholars. [*count*] The identified causes were later found to be mistaken *attributions*.

[2]**at·tri·bute** /ˈætrəˌbjuːt/ *noun, pl* **-butes** [*count*] : a usually good quality or feature that someone or something has • The interviewer asked me what I consider to be my best *attribute*. • Both candidates possess the *attributes* we want in a leader.

at·trib·u·tive /əˈtrɪbjətɪv/ *adj, grammar* : joined directly to a noun in order to describe it • "Red" in "red hair" is an *attributive* adjective. • In "airplane pilot" the noun "airplane" is *attributive*. — compare [3]PREDICATE
– at·trib·u·tive·ly *adv* • The noun "city" in "city streets" is used *attributively*.

at·tri·tion /əˈtrɪʃən/ *noun* [*noncount*] *formal*
1 *chiefly US* : a reduction in the number of employees or participants that occurs when people leave because they resign, retire, etc., and are not replaced • The staff has been thinned through *attrition*. [=the staff has become smaller because people have left] • *Attrition* is high among social workers because of the difficult work and poor pay. • a growing ***attrition rate*** = a growing ***rate of attrition*** — called also (*Brit*) *natural wastage*
2 : the act or process of weakening and gradually defeating an enemy through constant attacks and continued pressure over a long period of time — used especially in the phrase ***war of attrition*** • They can only gain victory by fighting a long *war of attrition*.

at·tune /əˈtuːn, *Brit* əˈtjuːn/ *verb* **-tunes; -tuned; -tun·ing** [+ *obj*] : to cause (a person, company, etc.) to have a better understanding of what is needed or wanted by a particular person or group — usually + *to* • It is important to *attune* the company *to* the needs of its customers. — often used as *(be) attuned* • The company *is attuned to* the needs of its customers. • He *is* more *attuned to* the political climate of the region.

atty. *abbr* attorney

atty. gen. *abbr* attorney general

ATV /ˌeɪˌtiːˈviː/ *noun, pl* **ATVs** [*count*] : ALL-TERRAIN VEHICLE

atwit·ter /əˈtwɪtɚ/ *adj, not used before a noun* : nervously excited • It was a book that set the publishing world all *atwitter*. [=caused excitement in the publishing world]

atyp·i·cal /eɪˈtɪpɪkəl/ *adj* : not typical : not usual or normal • an *atypical* case • This book is *atypical* of her previous work. [=is not like her previous work]
– atyp·i·cal·ly /eɪˈtɪpɪkli/ *adv* • We had an *atypically* [=*unusually*] leisurely lunch that afternoon.

au·ber·gine /ˈoʊbɚˌʒiːn/ *noun, pl* **-gines** [*count*] *Brit* : EGGPLANT

au·burn /ˈɑːbɚn/ *adj* : reddish brown • *auburn* hair

au cou·rant /ˌoʊkuˈrɑːnt/ *adj* [*more* ~; *most* ~]
1 : knowing about the newest information, trends, etc. • I try to stay *au courant* with the latest developments in the industry.
2 : stylish or current • *au courant* fashions

[1]**auc·tion** /ˈɑːkʃən/ *noun, pl* **-tions** : a public sale at which things are sold to the people who offer to pay the most [*count*] She bought the desk at an *auction*. • He made several bids at the *auction*. [*noncount*] The house is being sold ***at auction***. = The house is ***up for auction***. • She works as an auctioneer at an ***auction house***. [=a business that runs auctions]
on the auction block see [1]BLOCK

[2]**auction** *verb* **-tions; -tioned; -tion·ing** [+ *obj*] : to sell (something) at an auction • They *auctioned* a similar desk last year. • The house was *auctioned* last week. — often + *off* • The house was *auctioned off* last week.

auc·tion·eer /ˌɑːkʃəˈniɚ/ *noun, pl* **-eers** [*count*] : a person who runs an auction • The *auctioneer* started the bidding at $100.

au·da·cious /ɑˈdeɪʃəs/ *adj* [*more* ~; *most* ~] : very confident and daring : very bold and surprising or shocking • They have *audacious* plans for the new school. • This is her most *audacious* film so far. • She made an *audacious* decision to quit her job. • shockingly *audacious* behavior
– au·da·cious·ly *adv* • He *audaciously* disregarded all of their concerns. **– au·da·cious·ness** *noun* [*noncount*] • the *audaciousness* [=(more commonly) *audacity*] of their plans

au·dac·i·ty /ɑˈdæsəti/ *noun* [*noncount*] : a confident and daring quality that is often seen as shocking or rude : an audacious quality • I could not believe their *audacity*. • He ***had the audacity*** to suggest that it was all my fault.

au·di·ble /ˈɑːdəbəl/ *adj* [*more* ~; *most* ~] : heard or able to be heard • Her voice was barely *audible* over the noise. • He let out an *audible* sigh. • a clearly *audible* sound — opposite INAUDIBLE
– au·di·bil·i·ty /ˌɑːdəˈbɪləti/ *noun* [*noncount*] **– au·di·bly** /ˈɑːdəbli/ *adv* • He sighed *audibly*.

au·di·ence /ˈɑːdijəns/ *noun, pl* **-enc·es** [*count*]
1 : a group of people who gather together to listen to something (such as a concert) or watch something (such as a movie or play) : the people who attend a performance • The concert attracted a large *audience*. • The *audience* clapped and cheered. • an *audience* member = a member of the *audience*
2 : the people who watch, read, or listen to something • The film is intended for a young *audience*. [=is intended for young viewers] • Her books have reached an *audience* of millions. [=have been read by millions of people] • Her *audience* is made up mostly of young women.
3 : a formal meeting with an important person — usually singular • They were granted an *audience* with the Pope.

[1]**au·dio** /ˈɑːdiˌoʊ/ *adj, always used before a noun* : of or relating to the sound that is heard on a recording or broadcast • The school has new *audio* equipment. [=equipment used for recording sound or listening to recorded sound] • The *audio* portion of the broadcast was fine but the picture was poor. • They listened to an *audio* recording of the speech.

[2]**audio** *noun* [*noncount*] : the sound that is heard on a recording or broadcast • The picture was clear but the *audio* was very poor.

audio- *combining form* : relating to hearing or sound • *audio*visual

audio book *noun, pl* ~ **books** [*count*] : a recording of a book or magazine being read • I listen to *audio books* when I drive to work.

au·dio·tape /ˈɑːdijoʊˌteɪp/ *noun, pl* **-tapes** : tape on which sound is recorded [*noncount*] The program was recorded on *audiotape*. [*count*] a collection of *audiotapes* — compare VIDEOTAPE

au·dio·vi·su·al /ˌɑːdijoʊˈvɪʒəwəl/ *adj* : of, relating to, or using both sound and sight • The school will buy new *audiovisual* equipment. • *audiovisual* (teaching) aids — abbr. *AV*

[1]**au·dit** /ˈɑːdət/ *noun, pl* **-dits**
1 : a complete and careful examination of the financial records of a business or person [*count*] The *audit* showed that the company had mislead investors. • The Internal Revenue Service selected us for an *audit*. [*noncount*] You will need all your records if you are selected for *audit* by the IRS.
2 [*count*] : a careful check or review of something • Our local

A

power company will perform an energy *audit* [=*survey, inspection*] of our house. • Investigators called for an *audit* [=*review, analysis*] of flight safety standards.

²**audit** *verb* **-dits; -dit·ed; -dit·ing** [+ *obj*]
1 : to check the financial records of (a business or person) **:** to perform an audit on (a business or person) • They *audit* the company books every year. • The Internal Revenue Service *audited* him twice in 10 years.
2 *US* **:** to attend a course at a college or university without having to do any of the course work and without receiving credit • I *audited* an English literature class last semester.

¹**au·di·tion** /ɑˈdɪʃən/ *noun, pl* **-tions** [*count*] **:** a short performance to show the talents of someone (such as an actor or a musician) who is being considered for a role in a play, a position in an orchestra, etc. — often + *for* • *Auditions* will be held next week *for* the spring musical. • He went to an *audition for* a new TV show. • She had an *audition for* the starring role but wound up with a bit part.

²**audition** *verb* **-tions; -tioned; -tion·ing**
1 [*no obj*] *of a performer* **:** to try out for a role in a play or film, a position in an orchestra, etc. **:** to perform in an audition • When he came in to *audition*, he was very charming. — usually + *for* • She *auditioned for* the starring role.
2 [+ *obj*] **:** to test (someone) in an audition • They *auditioned* several girls for the role. • We will *audition* dancers today.

au·di·tor /ˈɑːdətɚ/ *noun, pl* **-tors** [*count*] **:** a person who checks the financial records of a company or person to make sure they are accurate **:** a person who audits accounts

au·di·to·ri·um /ˌɑːdəˈtorijəm/ *noun, pl* **-to·ri·ums** *also* **-to·ria** /-ˈtorijə/ [*count*]
1 *US* **:** a large room or building where people gather to watch a performance, hear a speech, etc.
2 : the part of a building (such as a theater) where an audience sits

au·di·to·ry /ˈɑːdəˌtori, *Brit* ˈɔːdətri/ *adj, technical* **:** relating to hearing or the ears • The patient has damage to the *auditory* nerve.

au fait /ˌoʊˈfeɪ/ *adj, not used before a noun, chiefly Brit* **:** completely familiar with or informed about something — usually + *with* • I'm not *au fait with* all the latest technology. • They're completely *au fait with* the situation.

Aug. *abbr* August

au·ger /ˈɑːgɚ/ *noun, pl* **-gers** [*count*] **:** a sharp tool that is used chiefly for making holes

aught /ˈɑːt/ *pronoun, literary + old-fashioned* **:** ANYTHING • ***For aught I know*** [=*for all I know*], he could have left an hour ago. [=I don't know when he left]

aug·ment /ɑgˈmɛnt/ *verb* **-ments; -ment·ed; -ment·ing** [+ *obj*] *formal*
1 : to increase the size or amount of (something) • The money *augmented* his fortune. • Heavy rains *augmented* the water supply. — often used as *(be) augmented* • The impact of the report *was augmented* by its timing. • The army *was augmented* by additional troops.
2 *US* **:** to add something to (something) in order to improve or complete it • Job training will *augment* [=*supplement*] the class work.
– aug·men·ta·tion /ˌɑːgmənˈteɪʃən/ *noun* [*noncount*]

au gra·tin /oʊˈgrɑːtn/ *adj* **:** covered with bread crumbs or cheese and then baked until brown • They served potatoes *au gratin* with the fish. • *au gratin* potatoes

au·gur /ˈɑːgɚ/ *verb* **-gurs; -gured; -gur·ing** *formal* **:** to show or suggest something that might happen in the future [*no obj*] The change *augurs* [=*bodes*] ill/badly for the success of the business. [=the change suggests that the business will not succeed] • The decision doesn't *augur* well. [+ *obj*] This bad news could *augur* [=*bode*] disaster for all of us.

au·gust /ɑˈgʌst/ *adj* [*more ~; most ~*] *formal* **:** having a formal and impressive quality • We visited their *august* mansion and expansive grounds. • The family claims an *august* lineage.

Au·gust /ˈɑːgəst/ *noun, pl* **-gusts :** the eighth month of the year [*noncount*] We are taking our vacation in *August*. • in (early/middle/mid-/late) *August* • early/late in *August* • We arrived on *August* the fourth. = (*US*) We arrived on *August* fourth. = We arrived on the fourth of *August*. [*count*] The last two *Augusts* have been very dry. — abbr. *Aug.*

auk /ˈɑːk/ *noun, pl* **auks** [*count*] **:** a black-and-white seabird of northern oceans

auld lang syne /ˌoʊldˌlæŋˈzaɪn/ *noun* [*singular*] **:** the good old times • They drank a toast to *auld lang syne*. ✧ *Auld lang syne* comes from the name of a Scottish song that is traditionally sung at midnight on New Year's Eve.

au na·tu·rel /ˌoʊˌnætəˈrɛl/ *adj* **:** in a natural state **:** without anything added • She wears makeup for special occasions, but otherwise prefers an *au naturel* look. • Some of the sunbathers were *au naturel*. [=*nude*]

aunt /ˈænt, ˈɑːnt/ *noun, pl* **aunts** [*count*] **:** the sister of your father or mother or the wife of your uncle • He has three *aunts* and two uncles. • This is my *Aunt* Mary.

aunt·ie /ˈænti, ˈɑːnti/ *noun, pl* **-ies** [*count*] *informal* **:** AUNT • The children were happy to see their *Auntie* Mary.

au pair /ˈoʊˈpeɚ/ *noun, pl* **~ pairs** [*count*] **:** a young person (usually a young woman) from a foreign country who lives with a family and helps to care for children and do housework in return for the opportunity to learn the family's language

au·ra /ˈorə/ *noun, pl* **-ras** [*count*] **:** a special quality or feeling that seems to come from a person, place, or thing — usually + *of* • His presence brought an *aura of* dignity to the proceedings. • The garden has an *aura* [=*atmosphere*] *of* mystery and romance.

au·ral /ˈorəl/ *adj* **:** relating to the ear or sense of hearing • visual and *aural* sensations
– au·ral·ly *adv* • The performance was both visually and *aurally* appealing.

au re·voir /ˌorəˈvwɑɚ/ *interj* **:** GOODBYE • *Au revoir*, my friends!

au·ro·ra aus·tra·lis /əˈrorəˈstreɪləs/ *noun* [*singular*] **:** SOUTHERN LIGHTS

au·ro·ra bo·re·al·is /əˈrorəˌboriˈæləs, *Brit* əˈrɔːrəˌbɔriˈeɪləs/ *noun* [*singular*] **:** NORTHERN LIGHTS

Aus. *abbr* Austria, Austrian

aus·pic·es /ˈɑːspəsəz/ *noun*
under the auspices of *formal* **:** with the help and support of (someone or something) • The donation was made *under the auspices of* the local historical society. • The research is being done *under the auspices of* the federal government.

aus·pi·cious /ɑˈspɪʃəs/ *adj* [*more ~; most ~*] *formal* **:** showing or suggesting that future success is likely • It was an *auspicious* [=*favorable, promising*] time to open a new business. • His acclaimed first novel was an *auspicious* debut. — opposite INAUSPICIOUS
– aus·pi·cious·ly *adv* **– aus·pi·cious·ness** *noun* [*noncount*]

Aus·sie /ˈɑːsi, *Brit* ˈɒzi/ *noun, pl* **-sies** [*count*] *informal* **:** a person who lives in or is from Australia **:** AUSTRALIAN
– Aussie *adj*

aus·tere /ɑˈstiɚ/ *adj* [*more ~; most ~*]
1 : simple or plain **:** not fancy • They chose *austere* furnishings for the office. • He was known for his *austere* style of writing.
2 *of a person* **:** having a serious and unfriendly quality • Her father was an *austere* [=*stern, unapproachable*] figure.
3 : having few pleasures **:** simple and harsh • They lived an *austere* life in the country.
– aus·tere·ly *adv* • an *austerely* furnished office

aus·ter·i·ty /ɑˈsterəti/ *noun, pl* **-ties**
1 [*noncount*] **:** a simple and plain quality **:** an austere quality • the *austerity* of the design • The *austerity* of their lifestyle was surprising.
2 [*noncount*] **:** a situation in which there is not much money and it is spent only on things that are necessary • They lived through years of *austerity* after the war. — often used before another noun • The government has announced a series of ***austerity measures***. [=things done to save money during difficult economic times] • an *austerity* program
3 ***austerities*** [*plural*] **:** things that are done to live in a simple and plain way • the *austerities* practiced by monks

Aus·tra·lian /ɑˈstreɪljən/ *noun, pl* **-lians** [*count*] **:** a person born, raised, or living in Australia
– Australian *adj* • an *Australian* writer • *Australian* history/English

Austrian /ˈɑːstrijən/ *noun, pl* **-ans** [*count*] **:** a person born, raised, or living in Austria
– Austrian *adj* • an *Austrian* custom • *Austrian* history

au·then·tic /əˈθɛntɪk/ *adj*
1 : real or genuine **:** not copied or false • We saw *authentic* examples of ancient Roman sculpture. • The document is *authentic*. • Experts have confirmed that the signature on the letter is *authentic*.
2 : true and accurate • The witness provided an *authentic*

record/report/account of what actually took place.
3 [*more ~; most ~*] **:** made to be or look just like an original • The actors were dressed in *authentic* medieval costumes. [=costumes that looked just like real medieval clothes] • She prepared a very *authentic* Mexican meal. • The building is an *authentic* reproduction of a colonial farmhouse.
– au·then·ti·cal·ly /əˈθɛntɪkli/ *adv* • *authentically* prepared Mexican food **– au·then·tic·i·ty** /ˌɑːˌθɛnˈtɪsəti/ *noun* [*noncount*] • We checked the *authenticity* of the signature.

au·then·ti·cate /əˈθɛntɪˌkeɪt/ *verb* **-cates; -cat·ed; -cat·ing** [+ *obj*] **:** to prove that something is real, true, or genuine **:** to prove that something is authentic • Experts *authenticated* the painting. • The signature has been *authenticated.*
– au·then·ti·ca·tion /əˌθɛntɪˈkeɪʃən/ *noun* [*noncount*] • *authentication* of the documents

[1]**au·thor** /ˈɑːθɚ/ *noun, pl* **-thors** [*count*]
1 : a person who has written something • The *author* of the article didn't check his facts.; *especially* **:** a person who has written a book or who writes many books • I enjoyed the book, but I can't remember the name of the/its *author.* • a best-selling *author* [=*writer*]
2 : a person who starts or creates something (such as a plan or idea) • She is the *author* of a plan for reforming the school system.

[2]**author** *verb* **-thors; -thored; -thor·ing** [+ *obj*] **:** to be the author of (something, such as a book) • He has *authored* [=*written*] several best-selling novels. • She *authored* [=*wrote*] several articles for the magazine.

au·thor·ess /ˈɑːθərəs/ *noun, pl* **-ess·es** [*count*] *somewhat old-fashioned* **:** a woman who is an author • a famous *authoress*

au·thor·i·tar·i·an /əˌθorəˈterijən/ *adj* [*more ~; most ~*] **:** expecting or requiring people to obey rules or laws **:** not allowing personal freedom • They had *authoritarian* parents. • an *authoritarian* government/regime
– authoritarian *noun, pl* **-ans** [*count*] • His father was an *authoritarian.* **– au·thor·i·tar·i·an·ism** /əˌθorəˈterijəˌnɪzəm/ *noun* [*noncount*] • Students protested against the government's *authoritarianism.*

au·thor·i·ta·tive /əˈθorəˌteɪtɪv/ *adj* [*more ~; most ~*]
1 : having or showing impressive knowledge about a subject • He is an *authoritative* [=*reliable, accurate*] source for information about Islamic art. • The book is an *authoritative* guide to the city's restaurants.
2 : having the confident quality of someone who is respected or obeyed by other people • His manner is polite but *authoritative.* • She addressed the group with an *authoritative* voice.
– au·thor·i·ta·tive·ly *adv* • She spoke *authoritatively* [=*with authority*] about the history of the building.

au·thor·i·ty /əˈθorəti/ *noun, pl* **-ties**
1 [*noncount*] **:** the power to give orders or make decisions **:** the power or right to direct or control someone or something • Only department managers have the *authority* [=*right, power*] to change the schedule. • Does he have the *authority* to do this? = (*US*) Does he have *authority* to do this? • This office has *authority* over personnel matters. [=this office has the power to make decisions about personnel matters] • You don't have *authority* over me. [=you don't have the power to give me orders] • The boss is not popular but his *authority* is unquestioned. • "Who gave him the *authority* to do this?" "He didn't do it ***on his own authority*** [=he didn't do it on his own]; he was acting ***under the authority of*** the company president." [=the company president gave him the power to do it] • No one ***in authority*** objected to the plan. = No one ***in a position of authority*** objected to the plan. [=no one with official power to make important decisions objected to the plan] • a ***figure of authority*** = an ***authority figure*** [=a person who has authority over other people] ***synonyms*** see [1]POWER
2 [*noncount*] **a :** the confident quality of someone who knows a lot about something or who is respected or obeyed by other people • She has an air of *authority.* • She spoke ***with authority*** [=*authoritatively*] about the history of the building. **b :** a quality that makes something seem true or real • His sincerity added much more *authority* [=*credibility*] to the story. • Her southern accent lent *authority* to her performance. • His opinions lacked *authority.*
3 ***authorities*** [*plural*] **:** people who have power to make decisions and enforce rules and laws • We reported the incident to hospital *authorities.* • Local *authorities* are investigating the accident. — often used with *the* • He complained to *the authorities* [=the police] about the disturbance.
4 [*count*] **:** a person who is an expert on a subject — usually + *on* • He is an *authority on* local history. [=he knows a lot about local history]
5 [*count*] **:** a government organization that has control of a specified activity or area • She is the director of the city's housing *authority.*
have it on good/excellent authority ✧ If you *have it on good/excellent authority* that something is true, you have been told that it is true by someone you trust and believe. • I *have it on good authority* that she is writing a novel.

au·tho·rize *also Brit* **au·tho·rise** /ˈɑːθəˌraɪz/ *verb* **-riz·es; -rized; -riz·ing** [+ *obj*]
1 : to give power or permission to (someone or something) • Only *authorized* personnel [=people who have been given special permission] can enter this area. — usually followed by *to* + *verb* • I *authorized* him *to use* my name. • She was *authorized* [=*empowered*] *to act* for her husband.
2 : to give legal or official approval to or for (something) • The city council *authorized* the sale of the land. • Who *authorized* the transfer of the funds? • an *authorized* biography
– au·tho·ri·za·tion *also Brit* **au·tho·ri·sa·tion** /ˌɑːθərəˈzeɪʃən/ *noun, pl* **-tions** [*noncount*] *Authorization* [=*permission*] is required to enter the building after hours. [*count*] I can't approve the request without a written *authorization.*

au·thor·ship /ˈɑːθɚˌʃɪp/ *noun* [*noncount*]
1 : the identity of the person who has written something • The novel is of unknown *authorship.* [=the author/writer of the novel is unknown]
2 : the job or profession of writing • His first attempt at *authorship* failed.

au·tism /ˈɑːˌtɪzəm/ *noun* [*noncount*] *medical* **:** a condition or disorder that begins in childhood and that causes problems in forming relationships and in communicating with other people
– au·tis·tic /ɑˈtɪstɪk/ *adj* • an *autistic* child **– autistic** *noun, pl* **-tics** [*count*] • Their child is an *autistic.*

au·to /ˈɑːtoʊ/ *noun, pl* **-tos** [*count*] *chiefly US* **:** AUTOMOBILE • a rusty *auto* — usually used before another noun • an *auto* accident/dealer/mechanic/show • *auto* parts/makers

auto- *combining form*
1 : self **:** same one • *auto*biography
2 : automatic **:** acting by itself • *auto*pilot

au·to·bi·og·ra·phy /ˌɑːtəˌbaɪˈɑːgrəfi/ *noun, pl* **-phies** [*count*] **:** a biography written by the person it is about • I read her *autobiography* last year.
– au·to·bi·og·ra·pher /ˌɑːtəˌbaɪˈɑːgrəfɚ/ *noun, pl* **-phers** [*count*] **– au·to·bio·graph·i·cal** /ˌɑːtəˌbajəˈgræfɪkəl/ *also* **au·to·bio·graph·ic** /ˌɑːtəˌbajəˈgræfɪk/ *adj* [*more ~; most ~*] • a very *autobiographical* novel [=a novel that is closely based on the life of the person who wrote it]

au·toc·ra·cy /ɑˈtɑːkrəsi/ *noun, pl* **-cies**
1 [*noncount*] **:** a form of government in which a country is ruled by a person or group with total power
2 [*count*] **:** a country that is ruled by a person or group with total power

au·to·crat /ˈɑːtəˌkræt/ *noun, pl* **-crats** [*count*] **:** a person who rules with total power
– au·to·crat·ic /ˌɑːtəˈkrætɪk/ *adj* [*more ~; most ~*] • The country is run by an *autocratic* government/ruler. • The company's employees disliked the new chairman's *autocratic* style.

[1]**au·to·graph** /ˈɑːtəˌgræf, *Brit* ˈɔːtəˌgrɑːf/ *noun, pl* **-graphs** [*count*] **:** the signature of a famous person • We asked her for her *autograph.* • He collects *autographs.* • There were several *autograph* seekers/hounds outside the theater. • I asked her to sign my ***autograph book.*** [=a book with blank pages for people to sign]

[2]**autograph** *verb* **-graphs; -graphed; -graph·ing** [+ *obj*] *of a famous person* **:** to write your signature in or on (something) • We asked her to *autograph* [=*sign*] her photograph/book.
– autographed *adj* • She gave him an *autographed* copy of the new novel. • an *autographed* photo

au·to·mak·er /ˈɑːtoʊˌmeɪkɚ/ *noun, pl* **-mak·ers** [*count*] *US* **:** a company that makes and sells cars **:** an automobile manufacturer • new models being offered by American *automakers* [=*carmakers*]

automata *plural of* AUTOMATON

au·to·mate /ˈɑːtəˌmeɪt/ *verb* **-mates; -mat·ed; -mat·ing** **:** to run or operate (something, such as a factory or system) by using machines, computers, etc., instead of people to do the work [+ *obj*] The company recently *automated* its filing

A

process. • a factory that has yet to be *automated* [*no obj*] a factory that has yet to *automate* • When companies *automate*, employees lose jobs.
– **automated** *adj* • an *automated* office system • a fully/highly *automated* factory • *automated* equipment/machinery – **au·to·ma·tion** /ˌɑːtəˈmeɪʃən/ *noun* [*noncount*] • the *automation* of the factory

automated teller *noun, pl* ~ **-ers** [*count*] *US* : ATM

automated teller machine *noun, pl* ~ **-chines** [*count*] *US* : ATM

[1]**au·to·mat·ic** /ˌɑːtəˈmætɪk/ *adj*
1 *of a machine or device* : having controls that allow something to work or happen without being directly controlled by a person • an *automatic* door [=a door that opens without being pushed] • an *automatic* coffeemaker [=a coffeemaker that can be programmed to start and shut off by itself] • I can't drive her car because it has a manual transmission instead of an ***automatic transmission***. [=a system that changes gears at different speeds without direct control by the driver]
2 *of a gun* : shooting many bullets very quickly when the trigger is pulled • an *automatic* machine gun • an *automatic* rifle/weapon — compare SEMIAUTOMATIC
3 [*more* ~; *most* ~] : happening or done without deliberate thought or effort • Without thinking, he gave an *automatic* reply. • She always has an *automatic* smile for everyone.
4 : always happening because of a rule, law, previous agreement, etc. • He had to pay a fine and serve an *automatic* 3-game suspension.
– **au·to·mat·i·cal·ly** /ˌɑːtəˈmætɪkli/ *adv* • The garage doors open *automatically*. • The fee will be *automatically* added to the bill. • Each individual winner *automatically* qualifies for the grand prize, which will be drawn at the end of the month. • She has her pay check *automatically* deposited.

[2]**automatic** *noun, pl* **-ics** [*count*]
1 : a gun that shoots many bullets very quickly : an automatic weapon
2 : a vehicle that changes gears by itself at different speeds : a car with automatic transmission • Will your next car be a manual or an *automatic*?

automatic pilot *noun, pl* ~ **-lots** [*count, noncount*] : AUTOPILOT

automatic teller *noun, pl* ~ **-ers** [*count*] *US* : ATM

automatic teller machine *noun, pl* ~ **-chines** [*count*] *US* : ATM

au·tom·a·ton /ɑˈtɑːmətən/ *noun, pl* **au·tom·a·tons** *or* **au·tom·a·ta** /-ətə/ [*count*]
1 : a machine that can move by itself; *especially* : ROBOT
2 : a person who acts in a mechanical or machinelike way • an unfeeling *automaton*

au·to·mo·bile /ˌɑːtəmoʊˈbiːl/ *noun, pl* **-biles** [*count*] *US* : a vehicle used for carrying passengers on streets and roads : CAR • He drives an expensive *automobile*. — often used before another noun • She was in an *automobile* accident. • *automobile* insurance • an *automobile* manufacturer

au·to·mo·tive /ˌɑːtəˈmoʊtɪv/ *adj, always used before a noun* : of, relating to, or concerned with cars and other vehicles • the *automotive* industry • The store stocks *automotive* parts.

au·ton·o·mous /ɑˈtɑːnəməs/ *adj* [*more* ~; *most* ~]
1 : existing or acting separately from other things or people : INDEPENDENT • *autonomous* [=*distinct, unrelated*] historical events • an *autonomous* [=*separate*] women's studies program • Many disabled children become *autonomous* [=*self-sufficient*] adults.
2 : having the power or right to govern itself • an *autonomous* region/republic/territory
– **au·ton·o·mous·ly** *adv* • elderly people who live *autonomously* • a region that operates *autonomously*

au·ton·o·my /ɑˈtɑːnəmi/ *noun* [*noncount*]
1 : the state of existing or acting separately from others : INDEPENDENCE • a teacher who encourages individual *autonomy*
2 : the power or right of a country, group, etc., to govern itself • The territory has been granted *autonomy*.

au·to·pi·lot /ˈɑːtoʊˌpaɪlət/ *noun, pl* **-lots** : a device that steers a ship, aircraft, or spacecraft in place of a person [*count*] an airplane equipped with an *autopilot* [*noncount*] The plane was flying ***on autopilot***. ✧ The phrase *on autopilot* is often used figuratively to describe a person who is doing something in a mechanical way without really thinking about it. • She performed her chores *on autopilot*. • He did his job as though he were *on autopilot*. — called also *automatic pilot*

au·top·sy /ˈɑːˌtɑːpsi/ *noun, pl* **-sies** [*count*] : an examination of a dead body to find out the cause of death • The coroner performed an *autopsy* on the murder victim's body.
– **autopsy** *verb* **-sies; -sied; -sy·ing** [+ *obj*] *US* • The body has not yet been *autopsied*.

au·tumn /ˈɑːtəm/ *noun, pl* **-tumns**
1 : the season between summer and winter [*count*] in the *autumn* of last year • a magnificent New England *autumn* • She went off to college in the *autumn* of 1999. [*noncount*] When *autumn* came he planted grass. • in early/late *autumn* — often used before another noun • *autumn* colors/foliage/leaves/trees • the *autumn* harvest • an early *autumn* chill in the air — called also (*US*) *fall*
2 [*count*] : the later part of someone's life or of something's existence • These songs were written in the *autumn* of his life. [=in his old age]

au·tum·nal /ɑˈtʌmnəl/ *adj* [*more* ~; *most* ~] : relating to, resembling, or associated with autumn • *autumnal* colors/foliage/leaves/trees • an *autumnal* harvest moon

[1]**aux·il·ia·ry** /ɑgˈzɪljəri/ *adj* : available to provide extra help, power, etc., when it is needed • a sailboat with an *auxiliary* engine • *auxiliary* fuel tanks • an *auxiliary* police force

[2]**auxiliary** *noun, pl* **-ries** [*count*]
1 : a group that provides help or assistance • She joined the women's *auxiliary*. [=a group of women who do work for a church, hospital, etc.]
2 : AUXILIARY VERB • a verbal *auxiliary*

auxiliary verb *noun, pl* ~ **verbs** [*count*] *grammar* : a verb (such as *have, be, may, do, shall, will, can,* or *must*) that is used with another verb to show the verb's tense, to form a question, etc. — called also *helping verb*

AV *abbr* audiovisual

[1]**avail** /əˈveɪl/ *verb* **avails; availed; avail·ing** *literary* : to be useful or helpful to (someone or something) [+ *obj*] Our best efforts *availed* [=*gained*] us nothing. • This knowledge *availed* her little. [=it was not very helpful or useful to her] [*no obj*] Our best efforts did not *avail*.
avail yourself of *formal* : to make use of (something) • They *availed themselves of* his services. [=they used his services]

[2]**avail** *noun* [*noncount*] : help toward reaching a goal • What I learned then is ***of little avail*** to me now. [=is not very helpful to me now] • Our best efforts were ***of no avail***. [=were not helpful] • They tried to discuss the issue calmly, but ***to no avail***. [=they were unable to discuss the issue calmly]

avail·able /əˈveɪləbəl/ *adj* [*more* ~; *most* ~]
1 : easy or possible to get or use • The family kept emergency supplies *available*. • The dress is also *available* in larger sizes. • The articles are *available* at any drugstore. • Fresh fruit is *available* during/through the summer. • The drug is readily/widely/easily *available* in Europe. • The report will soon be made *available* to the public. • I missed the plane, and the ***next available*** flight doesn't leave until tomorrow.
2 **a** : present or ready for use • All *available* resources were used. • She spent every *available* dollar on her hobby. • Parking is *available* for people staying at the hotel. • Tickets are *available* from the box office at the theater. **b** : present and able or willing to talk to someone • She was not *available* for comment, according to the newspaper. • The woman who answered the phone said, "I'm sorry, but Mr. Adams is not *available* right now. May I take a message?"
3 **a** : not being used or occupied by someone or something else • Toys covered every *available* space in the room. • the last *available* seat **b** : free to do something • We interviewed many *available* candidates for the job. • I'm *available* to give speeches. • We should go out for lunch. Are you *available* next Tuesday? **c** : not involved in a romantic relationship. • He wanted to ask her on a date, but wasn't sure if she was *available*. [=*single*] • a great way to meet *available* men/women/singles
– **avail·abil·i·ty** /əˌveɪləˈbɪləti/ *noun* [*noncount*] • The drug's lack of *availability* presents a serious problem for them. • She's the perfect candidate for the job, but I need to confirm her *availability*. [=I need to make sure she is available] • The *availability* of affordable housing attracted us to this town.

av·a·lanche /ˈævəˌlæntʃ/ *noun, pl* **-lanch·es**
1 [*count*] : a large amount of snow and ice or of dirt and rocks that slides suddenly down the side of a mountain • He was buried/trapped by an *avalanche*.
2 [*singular*] : a sudden great amount of something • an *avalanche* of words • an *avalanche* of praise/publicity

avant–garde /ˌɑːˌvɑːntˈgɑəd, *Brit* ˌævɒŋˈgɑːd/ *noun, pl*

A

avant–gardes [*count*] **:** a group of people who develop new and often very surprising ideas in art, literature, etc. • a literary *avant-garde* — often used with *the* • The book discusses the role of *the avant-garde* in the film industry.
– avant–garde *adj* [*more* ~; *most* ~] • *avant-garde* art • *avant-garde* artists/composers/writers • *avant-garde* films/theater **– avant–gard·ism** /ˌɑˌvɑntˈgɑɚdˌɪzəm, *Brit* ˌævɒŋˈgɑdˌɪzəm/ *noun* [*noncount*] • theatrical *avant-gardism* **– avant–gard·ist** /ˌɑːˌvɑːntˈgɑɚdɪst, *Brit* ˌævɒŋˈgɑːdɪst/ *noun, pl* **-ists** [*count*] • Some *avant-gardists* began experimenting with new film techniques.

av·a·rice /ˈævərəs/ *noun* [*noncount*] *formal + disapproving* **:** a strong desire to have or get money **:** GREED • The corporate world is plagued by *avarice* and a thirst for power. • He was driven by *avarice*.
– av·a·ri·cious /ˌævəˈrɪʃəs/ *adj* [*more* ~; *most* ~] • a spiteful and *avaricious* [=*greedy*] person

av·a·tar /ˈævəˌtɑɚ/ *noun, pl* **-tars** [*count*]
1 *Hinduism* **:** the human or animal form of a Hindu god on earth • an *avatar* of Vishnu
2 *formal* **:** someone who represents a type of person, an idea, or a quality • She has come to be regarded as an *avatar* of charity and concern for the poor.
3 *computers* **:** a small picture that represents a computer user in a game, on the Internet, etc. • She chose a penguin as her personal *avatar* in the chat room.

ave. *abbr* avenue

avenge /əˈvɛnʤ/ *verb* **aveng·es; avenged; aveng·ing** [+ *obj*] **:** to harm or punish someone who has harmed you or someone or something that you care about • The brothers vowed to *avenge* the death of their father. • They vowed to *avenge* their father by capturing and punishing his killer. • The team is out to *avenge* last week's defeat. [=to defeat the team that they were defeated by last week] • She vowed to ***avenge herself*** [=to get revenge], saying she would make him pay for what he had done to her.
– aveng·er *noun, pl* **-ers** [*count*] • the *avengers* of those who had been killed **– avenging** *adj* • saw herself as an *avenging* angel

av·e·nue /ˈævəˌnuː, *Brit* ˈævəˌnjuː/ *noun, pl* **-nues** [*count*]
1 a : a wide street • We drove down the *avenue*. — often used in names • Sixth *Avenue* in Manhattan • She grew up on Ledgelawn *Avenue*. **b** *chiefly Brit* **:** a path or driveway that leads to a house located off a main road • a magnificent tree-lined *avenue*
2 : a way of achieving something or of reaching a goal • We plan to pursue all available *avenues* to get our message to the public. • They have closed off that *avenue* of discussion. • a new *avenue* of research

aver /əˈvɚ/ *verb* **avers; averred; aver·ring** [+ *obj*] *formal* **:** to say (something) in a very strong and definite way • He *averred* that he was innocent. • "I am innocent," he *averred*.

[1]**av·er·age** /ˈævrɪʤ/ *noun, pl* **-ag·es**
1 : a number that is calculated by adding quantities together and then dividing the total by the number of quantities [*count*] The *average* of 16, 8, and 6 is 10. • Take all these temperatures and find their *average*. • An *average* of 2,000 people attended the show each night. [*noncount*] Prices have increased ***on average*** about eight percent. • *On average*, women live longer than men. • (*US*) He saves ***on the average*** about five percent of his income. — see also GRADE POINT AVERAGE, *the law of averages* at LAW
2 : a level that is typical of a group, class, or series **:** a middle point between extremes [*noncount*] His work has been better/worse than *average*. = His work has been ***above/below average***. [*count*] His work has been above the *average*.
3 [*count*] *baseball* **:** BATTING AVERAGE

[2]**average** *adj*
1 : calculated by adding quantities together and then dividing by the number of quantities • Take all these temperatures and find their *average* temperature. • The investment had a higher *average* return. • The *average* age of the company's employees is 36.
2 : ordinary or usual • The *average* woman lives longer than the *average* man. • Do you know what the *average* person earns? • an *average* day • the *average* American family/home buyer — often used informally with *your* • He's just *your average* guy. [=he is a typical or ordinary guy] • It wasn't *your average* snow storm. [=it was worse than an ordinary snowstorm] • He's not *your average* salesman. [=he is unusual]
3 a : not unusually large or small • Sales were about *average* for the industry on the whole. **b :** not unusually good or bad • *Average* grades are not good enough to get you into graduate school. • She was an *average* student. • She thought the performance was just *average*.

[3]**average** *verb* **-ages; -aged; -ag·ing** [+ *obj*]
1 : to have (a specified number) as an average • The children in that class *average* four feet in height. [=the average height of the children is 4 feet] • Her daily commute *averages* 40 minutes. [=the average length of her daily commute is 40 minutes] • We *average* six calls a day. [=we get six calls a day on average]
2 : to calculate the average of (something) • The teacher *averaged* the students' grades. • What figure do you get when you *average* the amount of rainfall for the last three months?
average out [*phrasal verb*] **1 :** to produce a result that is even and balanced when looked at over a period of time • The irregularities *averaged out* over the course of the study. • Sometimes you win, and sometimes you lose. It all *averages out* [=*evens out*] in the end. **2 *average out to (something)* :** to be equal to (a specified average amount) over a period of time • The gain *averaged out to* 20 percent.

averse /əˈvɚs/ *adj*
***averse to* :** having a clear dislike of (something) **:** strongly opposed to (something) • He seems to be *averse to* exercise. • No one is more *averse to* borrowing money than he is. — often used in negative statements • She is *not averse to* taking chances. [=she is willing to take chances]

aver·sion /əˈvɚʒən/ *noun, pl* **-sions :** a strong feeling of not liking something [*count*] deep *aversions* — often + *to* • He seems to have an *aversion to* exercise. [*noncount*] They regarded war with *aversion*.

avert /əˈvɚt/ *verb* **averts; avert·ed; avert·ing** [+ *obj*]
1 : to turn (your eyes, gaze, etc.) away or aside • She had to *avert* her eyes [=to look away] at the sight of the accident. • with *averted* eyes/gaze/glances
2 : to prevent (something bad) from happening • He sped up and *averted* an accident. • The diplomatic talks narrowly *averted* a war. • an attempt to *avert* a strike at the plant

avi·an /ˈeɪvijən/ *adj, technical* **:** of or relating to birds • *avian* species • *avian* behavior

avi·ary /ˈeɪviˌeri, *Brit* ˈeɪviəri/ *noun, pl* **-ar·ies** [*count*] **:** a place (such as a large cage or a building) where many birds are kept • The zoo has a new outdoor *aviary*.

avi·a·tion /ˌeɪviˈeɪʃən/ *noun* [*noncount*] **:** the business or practice of flying airplanes, helicopters, etc. • an expert in *aviation* • commercial/military *aviation* — often used before another noun • an *aviation* expert • the *aviation* industry

avi·a·tor /ˈeɪviˌeɪtɚ/ *noun, pl* **-tors** [*count*] **:** a person who flies an airplanes, helicopters, etc. **:** PILOT • a marine/naval *aviator*

aviator glasses *noun* [*plural*] **:** eyeglasses with light metal frames and large lenses

av·id /ˈævəd/ *adj* [*more* ~; *most* ~]
1 : very eager **:** ENTHUSIASTIC, KEEN • He is an *avid* admirer of horror movies. • They took an *avid* interest in politics. • an *avid* cook/dancer/fan/golfer/reader • some of the newspaper's most *avid* readers
2 : wanting something very much • He was *avid* for success. = He was *avid* to succeed.
– avid·i·ty /əˈvɪdəti/ *noun, pl* **-i·ties** [*noncount*] They pursued fame/wealth with *avidity*. [*singular*] an *avidity* for fame/wealth **– av·id·ly** *adv* • They are *avidly* interested in politics.

av·o·ca·do /ˌɑːvəˈkɑːdoʊ, *Brit* ˌævəˈkɑːdəʊ/ *noun, pl* **-dos** *also* **-does** [*count, noncount*] **:** a fruit with rough dark green or purple skin, smooth light green flesh, and a large seed in the middle — often used before another noun • an *avocado* tree • an *avocado* salad — called also (*Brit*) *avocado pear*; see color picture on page C5

av·o·ca·tion /ˌævəˈkeɪʃən/ *noun, pl* **-tions** [*count*] **:** an activity that you do regularly for enjoyment rather than as a job **:** HOBBY • He breeds dogs as an *avocation*. • My favorite *avocation* is reading.
– av·o·ca·tion·al /ˌævəˈkeɪʃənəl/ *adj* • She has an *avocational* interest in sports.

avoid /əˈvoɪd/ *verb* **avoids; avoid·ed; avoid·ing** [+ *obj*]
1 : to stay away from (someone or something) • Why do you keep *avoiding* me? • She took a detour to *avoid* the heavy traffic. • They successfully *avoided* each other for days.
2 : to prevent the occurrence of (something bad, unpleasant, etc.) • He tried hard to *avoid* accidents. • We need to *avoid* further delays. • *avoid* embarrassment • He was caught trying

A

to *avoid* arrest. ▪ in an effort to *avoid* confusion
3 : to keep yourself from doing (something) or participating in (something) ▪ I'm not going to be late if I can *avoid* it. ▪ How can I *avoid* paying too much tax? ▪ I am trying to *avoid* showing any hint of favoritism.
– avoid·able /əˈvoɪdəbəl/ *adj* ▪ It was a foolish and easily *avoidable* accident. ▪ an *avoidable* conflict/risk

avoid·ance /əˈvoɪdn̩s/ *noun* **:** the act of avoiding something [*noncount*] a writer known for *avoidance* of sentimentality [*count*] a complete *avoidance* of sentimentality

avow /əˈvaʊ/ *verb* **avows; avowed; avow·ing** [+ *obj*] *formal* **:** to declare or state (something) in an open and public way ▪ She *avowed* her innocence. = She *avowed* that she was innocent. ***synonyms*** see ASSERT

avow·al /əˈvaʊəl/ *noun, pl* **-als** [*count*] *formal* **:** an open and public statement ▪ I didn't believe her *avowal* of innocence. ▪ The couple exchanged *avowals* of love.

avowed /əˈvaʊd/ *adj, always used before a noun* **:** openly declared ▪ Their *avowed* aim/goal is to win the trophy. ▪ an *avowed* [=*self-proclaimed*] liberal/conservative
– avow·ed·ly /əˈvaʊədli/ *adv* ▪ She is *avowedly* [=*frankly, unabashedly*] conservative in her politics. ▪ an *avowedly* simple man

avun·cu·lar /əˈvʌŋkjələ/ *adj* [*more* ~; *most* ~] **:** like an uncle **:** kind or friendly like an uncle ▪ an *avuncular* shopkeeper ▪ a man known for his *avuncular* charm

aw /ˈɑː/ *interj, US + Scotland, informal* — used to express mild disappointment or sympathy ▪ *Aw* (shucks), I was hoping to play tennis today and now it's raining. ▪ *Aw*, that's too bad.

await /əˈweɪt/ *verb* **awaits; await·ed; await·ing** [+ *obj*]
1 : to wait for (someone or something) ▪ A crowd of people *awaited* the train. ▪ We're eagerly *awaiting* his arrival/answer. ▪ He was arrested and is now in prison *awaiting* trial. ▪ Her ***long-awaited*** new novel is finally being published.
2 : to be ready or waiting for (someone or something) ▪ A reward *awaits* you. ▪ Numerous requests *awaited* him. ▪ The same fate *awaits* us all.

[1]awake /əˈweɪk/ *verb* **awakes; awoke** /əˈwoʊk/; **awo·ken** /əˈwoʊkən/; **awak·ing** *somewhat formal* **:** to stop sleeping **:** to wake up [*no obj*] She fell asleep immediately but *awoke* an hour later. ▪ I *awoke* several times during the night. ▪ He *awoke* with a start. = He *awoke* suddenly. ▪ The baby *awoke* from his nap. [+ *obj*] The alarm *awoke* me early. ▪ They were *awoken* by a loud bang.
awake to [*phrasal verb*] ***awake to (something)* :** to become aware of (something) ▪ We finally *awoke to* the danger. ▪ How long will it take them to *awake to* their mistake?

[2]awake *adj, not used before a noun* **:** not asleep ▪ Drinking coffee keeps him *awake*. ▪ I am so tired I can barely stay *awake*. ▪ She was lying *awake*, tossing and turning. ▪ One moment she was sleeping soundly—the next she was wide *awake*.

awak·en /əˈweɪkən/ *verb* **-ens; -ened; -en·ing** *somewhat formal* **:** to stop sleeping **:** to wake up [*no obj*] She usually *awakens* several times during the night. [+ *obj*] A loud noise *awakened* her. — often used as ***(be) awakened*** ▪ I *was awakened* by the alarm clock. — often used figuratively ▪ Her arrival *awakened* [=*revived*] old memories. ▪ His interest *was awakened*. [=*aroused*]
awaken to [*phrasal verb*] ***awaken to (something) or awaken (someone or something) to (something)* :** to become aware of (something) or to make (someone or something) aware of (something) ▪ They finally *awakened to* the possibility of war. ▪ The book will *awaken* their minds *to* the beauty of nature.
– awakening *noun, pl* **-ings** [*count*] ▪ The group experienced a cultural/religious/spiritual *awakening*. ▪ Her arrival brought an *awakening* of old memories. ▪ He thinks he can get by without doing any work, but he is in for a ***rude awakening*** [=he will experience an unpleasant surprise; he will learn that he is mistaken]

[1]award /əˈwoəd/ *verb* **awards; award·ed; award·ing** [+ *obj*]
1 : to give (a reward or prize) to someone or something ▪ The judges will *award* a prize to the best speaker. ▪ The winner was *awarded* a gold medal. ▪ A prize will be *awarded* to the student who sells the most tickets.
2 : to officially decide that someone should get (something) ▪ The jury *awarded* damages to the defendant. ▪ The company is *awarding* the contract to the lowest bidder. ▪ He was *awarded* a patent for his invention.

[2]award *noun, pl* **awards** [*count*] **:** something (such as a prize) that is given to someone or something for being excellent or for doing something that is admired ▪ Will the film win any *awards* at the festival? ▪ She has won numerous *awards* for her books. ▪ an *awards* ceremony [=a ceremony at which awards are given out] ▪ an ***award-winning*** film/writer = an ***award-winner***

aware /əˈweə/ *adj* [*more* ~; *most* ~]
1 a *not used before a noun* **:** knowing that something (such as a situation, condition, or problem) exists ▪ Are you *aware* how important you are to me? — often + *of* ▪ She is acutely/keenly *aware of* the problem. ▪ I was not fully *aware of* the danger. ▪ He was made *aware of* the situation. — often + *that* ▪ He's not even *aware that* you are upset. ▪ You should be *aware that* the possibility/problem exists. **b :** feeling, experiencing, or noticing something (such as a sound, sensation, or emotion) — often + *of* ▪ Are you *aware of* any pain? [=have you noticed or felt any pain?] ▪ I became *aware of* a loud knocking sound. — often + *that* ▪ I was *aware that* he was following me. [=I had noticed that he was following me]
2 : knowing and understanding a lot about what is happening in the world or around you ▪ She is one of the most *aware* people I know. ▪ Students today are very *aware* about the environment. = Students today are very environmentally *aware*. ▪ Politically *aware* people [=people who know a lot about politics] will not be fooled by the government's latest pronouncements.
– aware·ness *noun* [*singular*] a heightened *awareness* about the problem ▪ They had an acute *awareness* of what was going on. [*noncount*] I admired her level of political *awareness*. ▪ He is trying to raise ***public awareness***.

awash /əˈwɑːʃ/ *adj, not used before a noun*
1 : flooded with or covered by water or another liquid ▪ The deck of the boat was almost *awash*. — usually + *with* or (*US*) *in* ▪ a floor *awash with/in* water — often used figuratively ▪ streets *awash in/with* litter [=streets covered with litter]
2 *US* **:** floating in a large amount of water or another liquid — + *in* ▪ The soup consisted of little bits of chicken *awash in* a tasteless broth. — often used figuratively ▪ He was *awash in* a sea of confusion. ▪ They were *awash in* debt.

[1]away /əˈweɪ/ *adv*
1 : from this or that place **:** in or to another place or direction ▪ She hopes to get *away* early. ▪ The family next door moved *away*. ▪ We rowed *away* from the shore. ▪ Roll up the rug and carry it *away*. ▪ He pulled his arm *away* from the hot stove. ▪ You should keep/stay *away* from the dog. It could be dangerous.
2 : toward another direction ▪ She turned her face *away*.
3 : in a safe or secure place ▪ The will was locked *away* in the safe. ▪ She stowed the luggage *away* in the overhead compartment.
4 : into a state of being completely gone ▪ The memory is fading *away*. ▪ He is wasting *away* from the disease. ▪ echoes dying *away*
5 : from someone's possession ▪ The family gave *away* a fortune to charity. ▪ They took *away* the one thing I cared about. ▪ The beautiful scenery took my breath *away*.
6 : without stopping or slowing down ▪ The clocks are ticking *away*. ▪ The water was bubbling *away*.
7 *sports* **:** on the field or court of an opponent ▪ The team played both (at) home and *away*. [=the team played both home games and away games]
far and away see [1]FAR

[2]away *adj*
1 *not used before a noun* **:** not at home or in a usual or expected place ▪ They are *away* for the weekend. ▪ "Where is he?" "He's *away* at the moment, but he'll be back soon." ▪ when I am *away* from home
2 *not used before a noun* — used to describe how distant something is in space or time ▪ The family went to a lake 10 miles *away*. ▪ They came from a continent *away*. ▪ The holiday season is two months *away*.
3 *always used before a noun* **:** played on the field or court of an opponent ▪ The team played both home games and *away* games.

[1]awe /ˈɑː/ *noun* [*singular*] **:** a strong feeling of fear or respect and also wonder ▪ It was a sight that filled me with *awe* and reverence. ▪ a person who inspires feelings of *awe* in others ▪ an ***awe-inspiring*** sight — often used after *in* ▪ We watched *in awe* as the building collapsed. ▪ They stared *in awe* at their hero. — often used in the phrase ***in awe of*** ▪ She is still *in awe of* her teacher. ▪ I stand *in awe of* their courage.

[2]awe *verb* **awes; awed; aw·ing** *[+ obj]* : to fill (someone) with awe ▪ Her style both *awes* and perplexes me. — often used as *(be) awed* ▪ He *was awed* [=*awestruck*] by the natural beauty of the place.
– **awed** *adj* ▪ a moment of *awed* surprise

awe·some /ˈɑːsəm/ *adj [more ~; most ~]*
1 : causing feelings of fear and wonder : causing feelings of awe ▪ the *awesome* sight of an erupting volcano ▪ one of the Earth's more *awesome* [=*awe-inspiring*] natural wonders ▪ It was an *awesome* responsibility. ▪ We had an *awesome* task ahead of us.
2 *informal* : extremely good ▪ We had an *awesome* time at the concert. ▪ She's an *awesome* singer. ▪ You did an *awesome* job on that project. ▪ The movie was totally *awesome*.
– **awe·some·ly** *adv* ▪ an *awesomely* destructive weapon ▪ an *awesomely* talented singer – **awe·some·ness** *noun [noncount]*

awe·struck /ˈɑːˌstrʌk/ *adj* : filled with feelings of fear and wonder : filled with awe ▪ *Awestruck* admiration showed on her face. ▪ They were *awestruck* by the sheer size of the project.

[1]aw·ful /ˈɑːfəl/ *adj [more ~; most ~]*
1 : extremely bad or unpleasant ▪ The music was *awful*. ▪ They heard the most *awful* sounds. ▪ *Awful* things began to happen. ▪ The weather was *awful*. ▪ He has some *awful* disease. ▪ That joke is just/pretty/really/truly *awful*. ▪ He's an *awful* person. ▪ That's an *awful* thing to say. ▪ She has *awful* manners. ▪ Who painted the house that *awful* color? ▪ I don't know what's wrong with me but I feel *awful*. [=very sick] ▪ I feel *awful* [=very sorry] about what happened.
2 *formal + old-fashioned* : causing feelings of fear and wonder : AWESOME ▪ The mountains have an *awful* majesty.
an awful lot *informal* **1** : a large amount ▪ They lost *an awful lot* of money. ▪ She does *an awful lot* of talking. **2** : very much ▪ I like him *an awful lot*. [=I like him a lot]
– **aw·ful·ness** *noun [noncount]* ▪ the sheer *awfulness* of it all ▪ the *awfulness* of the disease

[2]awful *adv, chiefly US, informal* : very or extremely : AWFULLY ▪ He was *awful* tired. ▪ We haven't heard from him in an *awful* long time. ▪ You've come an *awful* long way.

aw·ful·ly /ˈɑːfəli, ˈɑːfli/ *adv*
1 : very or extremely ▪ That's *awfully* nice of you. ▪ It turned out to be *awfully* difficult. ▪ The pie tasted *awfully* sweet. ▪ I'm *awfully* glad to see you. ▪ It's *awfully* cold out. ▪ You're *awfully* quiet today.
2 : in a very bad or unpleasant way ▪ He sings *awfully*.

awhile /əˈwajəl/ *adv* : for a while : for a short time ▪ I'm going to sit and rest *awhile*. ▪ The rumor had been around *awhile*.

awk·ward /ˈɑːkwəd/ *adj [more ~; most ~]*
1 a : not graceful : CLUMSY ▪ She is *awkward* at dancing. ▪ He had large feet and his walk was *awkward* and ungainly. ▪ an *awkward* movement ▪ The story contained some *awkward* writing. **b** : lacking skill ▪ She is an *awkward* writer.
2 : difficult to use or handle ▪ The machine is very *awkward* to operate. ▪ an *awkward* tool ▪ The box isn't heavy but it has an *awkward* shape and size. [=its shape and size make it difficult to carry]
3 a : not easy to deal with ▪ It was an *awkward* [=*embarrassing*] moment for everyone. ▪ I often find myself in *awkward* situations. ▪ He was put in the *awkward* position of having to write the memo. ▪ There was an *awkward* pause in the conversation. **b** : not socially graceful or confident : uneasy or uncomfortable ▪ I feel *awkward* (about) having to ask you to help. ▪ He feels *awkward* with/around strangers.
– **awk·ward·ly** *adv* ▪ The baby was crawling *awkwardly* on her hands and knees. ▪ He fell and landed *awkwardly*. ▪ an *awkwardly* written sentence – **awk·ward·ness** *noun, pl* **-ness·es** *[noncount]* A moment of *awkwardness* occurred after the introduction. ▪ the *awkwardness* of the writing *[count]* There was an *awkwardness* between us when we last saw each other.

awl /ˈɑːl/ *noun, pl* **awls** *[count]* : a pointed tool that is used for marking surfaces or for making small holes in leather, wood, etc.

aw·ning /ˈɑːnɪŋ/ *noun, pl* **-nings** *[count]* : a piece of cloth on a frame that sticks out over a door or window and provides shelter from sun, rain, snow, etc.

awoke *past tense of* [1]AWAKE

awoken *past participle of* [1]AWAKE

AWOL /ˈeɪˌwɑːl/ *adj* : absent from the armed forces without permission ▪ Three soldiers were *AWOL*. ▪ The soldiers ***went AWOL*** at the first chance; *broadly* : absent or missing ▪ The Senator has been *AWOL* for the last three votes. ▪ My keys have *gone AWOL*. I can't find them anywhere. ✧ *AWOL* comes from a phrase used in the military: *a*bsent *w*ithout *l*eave.

awning

– **AWOL** *noun, pl* **AWOLs** *[count]* ▪ Four *AWOLs* [=four soldiers who have gone AWOL] are still missing from their unit.

awry /əˈraɪ/ *adj or adv, not used before a noun*
1 : not working correctly or happening in the expected way : WRONG ▪ Something was dreadfully/terribly *awry*. — usually used in the phrase ***go awry*** ▪ Their plans *went awry*. ▪ Something had *gone* dreadfully/terribly *awry*.
2 : not straight or neat ▪ Her hair was all *awry*.

[1]ax *(US) or* **axe** /ˈæks/ *noun, pl* **ax·es** *[count]* : a tool that has a heavy metal blade and a long handle and that is used for chopping wood — see also ICE AX, PICKAX
ax to grind : a hidden and often selfish purpose for doing something. ▪ He had a political *ax to grind* with his opponent. ▪ She claims that she has no *ax to grind* in criticizing the proposed law.
escape the ax *informal* : to avoid being ended, eliminated, reduced, etc. ▪ The school program *escaped the ax* this year. [=the school program was not cut/eliminated this year]
get the ax *informal* : to lose your job : to be fired from your job ▪ The employees with less experience *got the ax*. [=were fired]
give (someone) the ax *informal* : to dismiss (someone) from a job : to fire (someone) ▪ His boss *gave him the ax*.
take the/an ax to *informal* : to eliminate (something) or reduce (something) severely ▪ Congress *took an ax to* the program. [=Congress made severe cuts in the program]

ax

[2]ax *or* **axe** *verb* **axes; axed; ax·ing** *[+ obj] informal*
1 : to cut or remove (something) ▪ The television program was *axed* [=*dropped*] from the new schedule.
2 : to fire (someone) ▪ The boss told him that he had been *axed*.

ax·i·om /ˈæksijəm/ *noun, pl* **-oms** *[count] formal* : a rule or principal that many people accept as true ▪ one of the key *axioms* of the theory of evolution

ax·i·om·at·ic /ˌæksijəˈmætɪk/ *adj, formal* : obviously true ▪ It is *axiomatic* that good athletes have a strong mental attitude. ▪ an *axiomatic* truth/assumption
– **ax·i·om·at·i·cal·ly** /ˌæksijəˈmætɪkli/ *adv*

ax·is /ˈæksəs/ *noun, pl* **ax·es** /ˈækˌsiːz/ *[count]*
1 : the imaginary straight line that something (such as the Earth) turns around ▪ the Earth's *axis* of rotation ▪ the spin of the Earth on its *axis*
2 : a straight line that divides a shape evenly into two parts — called also *axis of symmetry*

ax·le /ˈæksəl/ *noun, pl* **axles** *[count]* : a bar on which a wheel or a pair of wheels turns — see picture at CAR

[1]aye *also* **ay** /ˈaɪ/ *adv*
1 : [1]YES 1 — used especially in Scotland and in the language of sailors. ▪ The sailor said "*Aye, aye,* sir!" when the captain gave him a command.
2 — used to indicate a spoken yes vote ▪ All in favor, say "*aye*."

[2]aye *also* **ay** /ˈaɪ/ *noun, pl* **ayes** *[count]* : a yes vote ▪ We have six nays and 12 *ayes*, so ***the ayes have it***. [=the "yes" votes win] — compare [2]NAY, YEA

AZ *abbr* Arizona

aza·lea /əˈzeɪljə/ *noun, pl* **-leas** *[count]* : a type of bush that has colorful flowers that bloom in the spring

AZT /ˌeɪˌziːˈtiː, *Brit* ˌeɪˌzɛdˈtiː/ *noun [noncount] medical* : a drug used to treat AIDS

azure /ˈæʒə/ *noun, pl* **azures** *[count, noncount]* : the blue color of the sky
– **azure** *adj* ▪ the *azure* lake/sky/waters

B

b *or* **B** /ˈbiː/ *noun, pl* **b's** *or* **bs** *or* **B's** *or* **Bs**
1 : the second letter of the English alphabet [*count*] There are two *b's* in the word "abbey." [*noncount*] All of their children's names begin with *b*.
2 : a musical note or key referred to by the letter B **:** the seventh tone of a C-major scale [*count*] play/sing a *B* [*noncount*] a song in the key of *B*
3 [*count*] **:** a grade that is given to a student for doing good work • got a *B* in math • He's a ***B student*** [=a student who gets B's for his schoolwork]
4 [*noncount*] — used to refer to the second of two or more people, places, or things that are being considered • We chose option *B* over option A.
from (point) A to (point) B see [1]A

B.A. (*US*) *or* **BA** *abbr* bachelor of arts • He received a *B.A.* in philosophy from Tulane University. • She studied Spanish and economics and earned a *B.A.* degree.

baa /ˈbæ, ˈbɑː/ *noun* [*singular*] **:** the sound made by a sheep
– **baa** *verb* **baas; baaed; baa·ing** [*no obj*] • We heard a sheep *baaing* softly in the field.

[1]**bab·ble** /ˈbæbəl/ *verb* **bab·bles; bab·bled; bab·bling** [*no obj*]
1 a : to talk foolishly or too much • Pay no attention to her. She's just *babbling*. • He'll *babble* on about sports all night if you let him. • a *babbling* idiot **b :** to make speech sounds that do not make sense to the hearer • Her cousins were *babbling* in an unfamiliar dialect. • The baby *babbled* happily.
2 : to make the quiet sound of water flowing over rocks • a *babbling* brook
– **bab·bler** /ˈbæbələ/ *noun, pl* **bab·blers** [*count*]

[2]**babble** *noun* [*noncount*]
1 a : the confusing sound of many people speaking at the same time • a *babble* of voices **b :** talk that is silly or pointless • listening to their constant *babble*
2 : a quiet sound made by flowing water • the *babble* of a brook

babe /ˈbeɪb/ *noun, pl* **babes** [*count*]
1 : a very young child **:** BABY • a newborn *babe* • I've known her since she was ***a babe in arms*** [=a baby who is carried in the arms of an adult; an infant]
2 *slang* **a :** a sexually attractive person — usually used of young women • hot *babes* in bikinis ✧ This sense of *babe* is very informal and is sometimes considered offensive. **b** — used as an informal way of addressing a lover, friend, etc.; used especially by men to address women and by women to address men • Hey *babe*, how've you been? ✧ This sense of *babe* is very familiar in tone. Using *babe* to address someone you do not know well may cause offense.
babe in the woods *US* **:** a person who is innocent or who lacks experience • When I began my political career, I was a mere *babe in the woods*.

ba·bel *also* **Ba·bel** /ˈbeɪbəl/ *noun* [*singular*] **:** a confused mixture of sounds or voices — usually + *of* • a *babel of* languages • a *babel of* street sounds

ba·boon /bæˈbuːn/ *noun, pl* **-boons** [*count*] **:** a large African or Asian monkey

baboon

[1]**ba·by** /ˈbeɪbi/ *noun, pl* **-bies** [*count*]
1 a : a very young child • She had the *baby* yesterday. = She gave birth to the *baby* yesterday. • Are you expecting a *baby*? [=are you pregnant?] • I hear the *baby* crying. • The *baby* is just learning to crawl. — often used before another noun • a *baby* girl/boy • *baby* clothes • *baby* pictures • a *baby* monitor • (*US*) I gave my sister a ***baby shower.*** [=a party at which gifts are given to a woman who is pregnant] • She has a real ***baby face*** [=a face that resembles the face of a baby; a face that looks young and innocent] **b :** a very young animal • a bird and its *babies* — often used before another noun • a *baby* bird • a *baby* deer
2 a : the youngest member of a group • My sister is the *baby* of the family. — often used before another noun • my *baby* sister **b :** someone who is young in comparison with others • "Only 32? Oh, you're just a *baby*!" **c :** someone who behaves like a child; *especially* **:** someone who is afraid or who complains a lot • When it comes to getting shots, I'm a real *baby*. • Don't be such a *baby*—you'll get your turn.
3 *slang* **a :** a lover or sweetheart • Nothing's gone right since my *baby* went away. ✧ This sense of *baby* is common in song lyrics. **b** — used as an informal way of addressing a lover, friend, etc.; used especially by men to address women and by women to address men • I missed you, *baby*. ✧ This sense of *baby* is sometimes used in a very informal way by men to address an attractive woman. • Hey *baby*, nice car! Using *baby* to address someone you do not know well may cause offense.
4 : something that someone has created and developed with special personal attention or interest • This project is my *baby*.
hold the baby see [1]HOLD
throw out the baby with the bathwater *informal* **:** to get rid of something you want while trying to get rid of something you do not want • If you ignore her message because you don't like the way she presents it, you will be *throwing out the baby with the bathwater*.
– **ba·by·hood** /ˈbeɪbiˌhʊd/ *noun* [*noncount*] • We watched him grow from *babyhood* to adulthood. – **ba·by·ish** /ˈbeɪbijɪʃ/ *adj* [*more* ~; *most* ~] • *babyish* behavior/toys

[2]**baby** *adj, always used before a noun* **:** very small **:** much smaller than usual • a *baby* grand piano • *baby* carrots/vegetables • Take *baby* steps.

[3]**baby** *verb* **-bies; -bied; -by·ing** [+ *obj*]
1 : to treat (someone) like a baby **:** to be kind or too kind to (someone) • That boy will never learn to stand up for himself if you don't stop *babying* him. • I ***babied myself*** [=pampered myself] with a trip to the spa.
2 : to operate or treat (something) in a very careful and gentle way • *baby* a car • It looked like he was *babying* his injured foot.

baby blue *noun, pl* ~ **blues**
1 [*noncount*] **:** a very light blue color
2 *baby blues* [*plural*] *informal* **:** blue eyes • She gazed into his *baby blues*.
3 *baby blues* [*plural*] *informal* **:** a feeling of sadness that a woman has after giving birth to a baby • She had a bad case of the *baby blues*. — compare POSTPARTUM DEPRESSION
– **baby blue** *adj* • He was wearing *baby blue* pajamas.

baby boom *noun, pl* ~ **booms** [*count*] **:** a time when there is a great increase in the number of babies born • There was a *baby boom* in the U.S. after World War II.
– **baby boomer** *noun, pl* ~ **-ers** [*count*] • a television program that is popular among *baby boomers* [=people who were born during the baby boom after World War II]

baby buggy *noun, pl* ~ **-gies** [*count*]
1 *US* **:** BABY CARRIAGE
2 *Brit* **:** STROLLER

baby carriage *noun, pl* ~ **-riag·es** [*count*] *US* **:** a vehicle in which a baby lies while someone pushes it from place to place — called also (*US*) *baby buggy*, (*Brit*) *pram*

baby fat *noun* [*noncount*] *US* **:** the extra fat that a healthy baby or young child has • Their little boy still has his *baby fat*. — called also (*Brit*) *puppy fat*

ba·by–sit /ˈbeɪbiˌsɪt/ *verb* **-sits; -sat** /-ˌsæt/; **-sit·ting :** to take care of a child while the child's parents are away [+ *obj*] She *babysits* their kids on Saturday nights. [*no obj*] She *babysits* (for my wife and me) on Saturday nights.
– **ba·by·sit·ter** *noun, pl* **-ters** [*count*] • Did you pay the *babysitter*?

baby talk *noun* [*noncount*] **:** the speech used by very young children who are learning to talk or by adults who are speaking to young children

baby tooth *noun, pl* ~ **teeth** [*count*] **:** a tooth from the first set of teeth that a child develops — called also *milk tooth*

bac·cy /ˈbæki/ *noun* [*noncount*] *Brit, informal* **:** TOBACCO

bach·e·lor /ˈbætʃələ/ *noun, pl* **-lors** [*count*]
1 : a man who is not married; *especially* **:** a man who has

never been married • an ***eligible bachelor*** [=an unmarried man who is regarded as a desirable husband] • a ***confirmed bachelor*** [=a man who has been a bachelor for a long time and who shows no interest in marrying] • his apartment is a typical ***bachelor pad*** [=a typical apartment of an unmarried man] • They threw the groom a ***bachelor party***. [=a party for a man who is about to be married that is usually attended by men only]

2 : a person who has received a bachelor's degree • a *bachelor* of arts

– bach·e·lor·hood /ˈbætʃələˌhʊd/ *noun* [*noncount*]

bach·e·lor·ette /ˌbætʃələˈrɛt/ *noun, pl* **-ettes** [*count*] *US* **:** a woman who is not married • They threw the bride a ***bachelorette party***. [=a party for a woman who is about to be married that is usually attended by women only]

bachelor's degree *noun, pl* **~ -grees** [*count*] **:** a degree that is given to a student by a college or university usually after four years of study

ba·cil·lus /bəˈsɪləs/ *noun, pl* **-cil·li** /-ˈsɪˌlaɪ/ [*count*] *technical* **:** a straight rod-shaped bacterium that requires oxygen for growth; *also* **:** a bacterium that causes disease

[1]back /ˈbæk/ *noun, pl* **backs** [*count*]

1 a : the rear part of the body **:** the part of the body that is opposite to the stomach and chest and that goes from the neck to the top of the legs • She was carrying her little daughter on her *back*. • He injured his *back*. = He suffered a *back* injury. • She has a pain in the small of her *back*. • an aching *back* • I slapped/patted him on his/the *back* to congratulate him. • He broke his *back* [=*spine*] in a fall. • She stabbed/shot him in the *back*. • He was handcuffed with his hands behind his *back*. — see picture at HUMAN **b :** the part of an animal that is like a person's back • a bird with a spotted *back* • riding on the *back* of a horse/donkey/camel — see also HORSEBACK

2 a : the side or surface of something that is opposite the front or face **:** the rear side or surface of something — usually singular • the *back* of the head • the *back* of a mirror/spoon • the *back* of the hand/leg/foot • The book has fallen down the *back* of the couch. **b :** the side or surface of something (such as a piece of paper) that is not usually used or seen first — usually singular • She wrote something on the *back* of an envelope. • He signed his name on the *back* of the check. **c :** a place, position, or area that is at or near the rear of something — usually singular • He put the letter in the *back* of the drawer. • The kitchen is at/in the *back* of the house and the living room is at/in the front. • Since our plane was leaving soon we were moved to the front of the line while others remained at the *back*. • Please move to the *back* of the elevator to make room for others.

3 : the part of a chair or seat that supports a person's back • a comfortable chair with a padded *back*

4 a : the section of a book, magazine, etc., that includes the last pages — usually singular • There is an index in the *back* of the book. **b :** the part of a book's cover that can be seen when the book is on a shelf • The title of the book is shown on its *back*. [=*spine*]

5 *sports* **:** a player in some games (such as soccer and American football) who is positioned behind the front line of players • a defensive *back* — see also FULLBACK, HALFBACK, QUARTERBACK, RUNNING BACK

a pat on the back see [1]PAT

a stab in the back see [1]STAB

at/in the back of your mind **:** in the part of your mind where thoughts and memories are kept — used to describe ideas, memories, etc., that someone has but that are not usually thought about or not perfectly remembered • The thought of retiring and moving out into the country has been *in the back of her mind* for many years, and now she's finally doing it. • Somewhere *in the back of my mind* I knew I'd met him before.

back is to/against the wall ✧ When *your back is to/against the wall* or *you have your back to/against the wall* you are in a bad position in which you are forced to do something in order to avoid failure. • *With our backs to the wall* we made a last desperate effort to finish the project on time. • We knew that with so little time and money left to finish the project *we had our backs to the wall*.

back to back **1 :** with backs opposite or against each other • The soldiers stood *back to back*. **2 :** happening one after the other • She won the annual competition two times *back to back*. [=*in a row*] • He's had two victories *back to back*. • I've scheduled two appointments *back to back*. — see also BACK-TO-BACK

back to front *of a piece of clothing* **:** with the back where the front should be • He accidentally put the sweater on *back to front*. [=*front to back, backwards*]

behind someone's back **:** without someone's knowledge **:** in secret • You shouldn't gossip about people *behind their back(s)*. • If you have something to say, why not say it to my face instead of whispering it *behind my back*?! • She ***went behind his back*** and spoke directly to his supervisor.

break the back of **:** to get control of (something you are trying to stop or defeat) **:** to greatly weaken or subdue (something) • He says the government's new policies will *break the back of* inflation.

eyes in the back of your head see [1]EYE

get your back up **:** to become angry or annoyed and want to fight or argue • He *gets his back up* and becomes defensive whenever someone questions his work. — compare PUT SOMEONE'S BACK UP (below)

have someone's back see WATCH SOMEONE'S BACK (below)

in back **:** in an area at the back of something • There was only room for one passenger in front. The rest of us sat *in back*. [=*in the back*]

in back of *chiefly US* **:** directly behind (something or someone) • There's a small yard *in back of* the house.

on the back of **1 :** because of (something) • Profits have increased *on the back of* [=*on the strength of*] improved international sales. **2** *disapproving* **:** by using the efforts of (other people) • The company has achieved record profits *on the back of* cheap labor.

on/off your back ✧ Someone who is always or frequently criticizing you or telling you what to do is *on your back* and won't ***get off your back***. • He says his wife is always *on his back* about doing chores around the house. • *Get off my back*! I'm working as hard as I can! • My boss is always criticizing me. I wish I knew some way to *get him off my back*.

on your back ✧ If you are *(flat) on your back* you are lying with your back against the ground, on a bed, etc. • The accident left him (lying) *flat on his back* (in bed) for two weeks. This phrase is sometimes used figuratively. • The stock market has been *flat on its back* [=has been doing very poorly] in recent weeks.

out back (*US*) *or chiefly Brit* ***out the back*** *or* ***round the back*** **:** in the area behind something (such as a building) • In my youth we didn't have a toilet in the house but there was one *out back*.

put someone's back up **:** to offend or annoy someone **:** to make someone angry or ready to argue • I don't want to question his decision because that will just *put his back up*. — compare GET YOUR BACK UP (above)

put your back into **:** to work very hard at (something) **:** to put a lot of effort into (something) • If you want to get that floor clean you'll have to *put your back into* it. • You'll really have to *put your back into* this project if you want it to succeed.

scratch someone's back see [1]SCRATCH

see the back of ✧ In British English, to be ***glad/happy (etc.) to see the back of*** someone is to be glad to see someone finally going away. • He's done nothing but make trouble and I'll be *glad to see the back of* him! [=I'll be glad when he has gone]

stab (someone) in the back see [2]STAB

the shirt off your back see SHIRT

turn your back **:** to turn so that you are facing away from someone • He *turned his back* and walked away from me. — often + *on* • He *turned his back on* me and walked away. — often used figuratively • His former supporters have *turned their backs on* him. [=have abandoned him]

watch someone's back *or* ***have someone's back*** **:** to protect someone who is doing something that is dangerous or risky • The police officer's partner always *watches his back*. • Don't worry, ***I've got your back***.

watch your back ✧ If people tell you to *watch your back*, they are telling you to be careful. • I hear the boss is in a bad mood this morning, so you'd better *watch your back*.

– back·less /ˈbækləs/ *adj* • a *backless* evening gown

[2]back *adv*

1 a : in, toward, or at the back or rear • The soldiers moved *back* from the front lines. • The police asked the crowd to move/step *back* from the scene of the accident. • He left his friends two miles *back*. • She turned around and looked *back* toward him. • a chapter beginning several pages *back* **b :** to, toward, or in the place where someone or something was previously • He left his home and never went *back*. • I had to

B

go *back* (to the office) for some papers I had left behind. ▪ It's time to go *back* home. ▪ She took the book off the shelf and forgot to put it *back*. ▪ She left earlier but she should ***be back*** [=*return*] soon.

2 : in or into the past **:** backward in time ▪ In the opening chapter the author looks *back* on his youth. ▪ an event *back* in the last century; *also* **:** AGO ▪ It happened several years *back*. ▪ I met him in the city two days *back*.

3 a : to or toward a former state or condition ▪ He has decided to go *back* to private life. [=to return to private life] ▪ Good farming practices were needed to bring the fields *back* (to good condition). [=to restore the fields] **b :** in return or reply ▪ I gave the book to him and he gave it *back* (to me). ▪ He refused to give *back* the borrowed money. ▪ He hit his brother and his brother hit him right *back*. ▪ talk *back* ▪ She refused to take *back* her accusations. **c** — used to describe someone or something that is being held or kept from moving forward or happening ▪ He would have jumped if his friends had not held him *back*. ▪ He vowed that he wouldn't allow poverty to hold/keep him *back*. [=to keep him from succeeding] ▪ She struggled to hold *back* a laugh. [=to keep from laughing] ▪ Landslides set the construction job *back* many days. [=caused the construction job to be delayed many days] **d** — used to describe something that is being kept instead of being given or revealed ▪ They held *back* part of the money. ▪ keep *back* the truth

4 : to or at an angle ▪ The banks slant evenly *back* from the highway. ▪ The doctor told her to ***lie back*** on the couch. [=to lie down on the couch] ▪ When I get home from work I like to just ***sit/lean back*** on the couch and relax.

back of *US, informal* **:** on the rear side of (something) **:** BEHIND ▪ There's an old tractor out *back of* [=*in back of*] the barn.

get your own back see *get back* at GET

³back *adj, always used before a noun*

1 : of or relating to the back **:** located at the back ▪ the front door, not the *back* door [=the door at the back of a building] ▪ He keeps his wallet in his *back* pocket. ▪ She likes to sit in the front/first row, not the *back* [=*last*] row. ▪ We came in through the *back* entrance. ▪ the *back* pages [=the last pages] of the newspaper ▪ *back* teeth ▪ a *back* room

2 : far from a central or main area ▪ We drove on the *back* roads instead of the main roads. ▪ a *back* alley

3 : not yet paid **:** owed from an earlier time ▪ The company owes him several months in *back* pay. ▪ *back* rent

4 : published at an earlier time **:** no longer current ▪ a *back* issue/number of a magazine

5 *golf* — used to refer to the final 9 holes of an 18-hole golf course ▪ He was two over par on the front nine and three over par on the *back* nine.

⁴back *verb* **backs; backed; back·ing**

1 [+ *obj*] **a :** to give help to (someone) **:** SUPPORT ▪ I'm *backing* him (against the Establishment) in his struggle for reform. ▪ I'm *backing* him for President. **b :** to bet on (someone or something) ▪ She *backed* the winner of the race and won a lot of money. ▪ The pundits are all *backing* him to become the next President. [=the pundits all think that he will become the next President] **c :** to provide evidence that supports (something) ▪ She *backed* her argument with written evidence. **d :** to provide the money that is needed for (something) ▪ *back* a new company ▪ *back* a Broadway play **e :** to sing or play music that supports (a main singer or musical instrument) ▪ She *backed* the singer on the guitar. — often + *up* ▪ A guitarist *backed up* the singer. — see also BACK UP (below)

2 : to move backward [*no obj*] She *backed* into a parking space. ▪ She *backed* out of the garage. ▪ The dog kept growling but *backed* off/away cautiously. [+ *obj*] Could you *back* [=(more commonly) *back up*] your car a little to give me some room? — sometimes used figuratively ▪ The reporter ***backed her into a corner*** [=put her into a difficult position that was hard to get out of] with his probing questions.

3 [+ *obj*] **:** to provide (something) with a back ▪ *back* a skirt with stiff material

4 [*no obj*] **:** to have the back toward something ▪ The house fronts onto Main Street and *backs* onto/on the golf course. [=the back of the house faces the golf course]

back away [*phrasal verb*] **:** to move away from something or someone by walking backward ▪ The robber pointed a gun at the policeman and told him to *back away* slowly. — often + *from* ▪ The policeman slowly *backed away from* the robber. ▪ She *backed away from* the growling dog. — often used figuratively ▪ The government seems to be *backing away from* its earlier proposal. ▪ She has *backed away from* her controversial position on the death penalty.

back down [*phrasal verb*] **:** to stop arguing or fighting for something ▪ When threatened with a revolt of its own supporters, the government *backed down*. ▪ The strike is expected to continue because neither side is willing to *back down*. — often + *from* ▪ The government *backed down from* its position. ▪ He'll never *back down from* a fight.

back into [*phrasal verb*] ***back into (something)*** **:** to become involved in (something) without planning to become involved ▪ He *backed into* the antiques business almost by accident when he sold some old furniture he'd inherited.

back off [*phrasal verb*] **1 :** to stop arguing or fighting for something **:** to back down ▪ He has refused to *back off*. **2 :** to decide not to do something that you had agreed to do **:** to back out ▪ The deal fell through when investors *backed off*. **3 :** to stop bothering someone ▪ She was getting irritated, so I *backed off*.

back out [*phrasal verb*] **:** to decide not to do something that you had agreed to do ▪ The deal fell through when investors *backed out*. — often + *of* ▪ The investors *backed out of* the deal.

back up [*phrasal verb*] **1 a :** to move backward ▪ The car *backed up* slowly. ▪ Could you *back up* a little to give me some room? — sometimes used figuratively ▪ Wait, let's *back up* for a second. [=let's go back to what we were discussing earlier] **b** ***back (a vehicle) up*** *or* ***back up (a vehicle)*** **:** to move (a vehicle) backward ▪ Could you *back* your car *up* a little to give me some room? **2 a :** to become blocked so that movement or flow is slowed or stopped ▪ Traffic *backed up* for miles because of the accident. ▪ The drain *backed up* [=*clogged*] and had to be unclogged by a plumber. **b** ***back (something) up*** *or* ***back up (something)*** **:** to cause (something) to become blocked ▪ The accident *backed up* traffic for miles. = Traffic was *backed up* [=(*Brit*) *tailed back*] for miles because of the accident. ▪ The drain was *backed up*. **3** ***back (someone or something) up*** *or* ***back up (someone or something)*** **:** to give help or support to (someone or something) ▪ I'll *back* you *up* if I think you're right. ▪ She *backed* her argument *up* with written evidence. = Written evidence *backed* her argument *up*. ▪ It's time to *back up* your words with deeds! — see also ⁴BACK 1e (above) **4** ***back (something) up*** *or* ***back up (something)*** *computers* **:** to make a copy of (a computer file or data) to protect it from being lost ▪ Remember to *back up* your work before you log off. — see also BACKUP

back·ache /ˈbækˌeɪk/ *noun, pl* **-aches :** pain in the back [*count*] She has/gets frequent *backaches*. [*noncount*] a patient suffering from *backache* ▪ (*Brit*) She has/gets frequent *backache*.

back and forth *adv*

1 : toward the back and then toward the front **:** backward and forward ▪ The chair rocked *back and forth*.

2 : between two places or people ▪ The children were shuttled *back and forth* between school and home.

back–and–forth *noun* [*noncount*] **:** talk or discussion about something ▪ An agreement was finally reached after a lot of *back-and-forth* between the two sides.

back·bench /ˈbækˈbɛntʃ/ *noun, pl* **-bench·es** [*count*] *Brit* **:** a seat in the British Parliament that is held by an ordinary member ▪ the Prime Minister's supporters on the *backbenches* — often used before another noun ▪ *backbench* conservative MPs — compare FRONT BENCH

– back·bench·er /ˈbækˈbɛntʃɚ/ *noun, pl* **-ers** [*count*] ▪ Labour *backbenchers*

back·bit·ing /ˈbækˌbaɪtɪŋ/ *noun* [*noncount*] **:** unkind talk about someone who is not present ▪ petty *backbiting* among employees

back·board /ˈbækˌboɚd/ *noun, pl* **-boards** [*count*] *basketball* **:** the board behind the basket

back·bone /ˈbækˌboʊn/ *noun, pl* **-bones**

1 [*count*] **:** the row of connected bones that go down the middle of the back and protect the spinal cord — called also *spinal column, spine*; see picture at HUMAN

2 [*count*] **:** the most important or strongest part of something ▪ She is the *backbone* of the family.

3 [*noncount*] **:** strength and courage ▪ He showed some *backbone* by refusing to compromise his values.

back·break·ing /ˈbækˌbreɪkɪŋ/ *adj* [*more* ~; *most* ~] **:** involving very difficult physical work or effort ▪ *backbreaking* work

back burner *noun*

on the back burner *chiefly US* : in the position of something that will not receive immediate attention and action • She put her singing career *on the back burner* to pursue her dream of being a movie star. • The President has put tax reduction *on the back burner* because he has more urgent problems to deal with. — compare FRONT BURNER

back·chat /ˈbækˌtʃæt/ *noun* [*noncount*] *Brit, informal* : BACK TALK • Don't give me any *backchat*!

back·cloth /ˈbækˌklɑːθ/ *noun, pl* **-cloths** [*count*] *Brit* : BACKDROP

back·comb /ˈbækˌkoʊm/ *verb* **-combs**; **-combed**; **-comb·ing** [+ *obj*] *chiefly Brit* : to comb (hair) backwards : TEASE • She *backcombs* her hair.

back·date /ˈbækˌdeɪt/ *verb* **-dates**; **-dat·ed**; **-dat·ing** [+ *obj*]

1 : to give (something) an earlier date than the actual date : ANTEDATE • *backdate* a check

2 : to say that something began or became effective at a date earlier than the current date • an increase in salary *backdated* to the beginning of the year

back door *noun, pl* ~ **doors** [*count*] : a door at the back of a building — often used figuratively • He managed to get into the private club ***through the back door*** [=in a secret or indirect way] because he has a friend who works there.

back·door /ˈbækˈdoɚ/ *adj, always used before a noun* : done in a secret or indirect way • a *backdoor* tax increase

back·drop /ˈbækˌdrɑːp/ *noun, pl* **-drops** [*count*]

1 : a painted cloth that is hung across the back of a stage

2 : the scene or scenery that is in the background • The mountains provided a perfect *backdrop* for the wedding photos.

3 : the setting or conditions within which something happens • The novel unfolds against a *backdrop* of war. • The city provides the *backdrop* for the love story.

-backed *combining form*

1 : having a particular kind of back • a broad-*backed* weight lifter • a high-*backed* chair • a foam-*backed* mattress

2 : supported by a particular group, organization, etc. • a UN-*backed* peace plan • a government-*backed* antismoking campaign

back·er /ˈbækɚ/ *noun, pl* **-ers** [*count*] : a person or group that gives support to someone or something • the presidential candidate's *backers* • *backers* of the plan proposed by the committee

back·field /ˈbækˌfiːld/ *noun, pl* **-fields** *American football*

1 [*singular*] : the area of the field that is behind the line of scrimmage • a tackle made in the *backfield*

2 [*count*] : the players who line up behind the line of scrimmage • The team has a strong *backfield*.

back·fire /ˈbækˌfajɚ/ *verb* **-fires**; **-fired**; **-fir·ing** [*no obj*]

1 *of an engine or vehicle* : to make a loud sound when fuel is not burned properly • The car *backfired*.

2 : to have the opposite result of what was desired or expected • Our plans *backfired* (on us).

– **backfire** *noun, pl* **-fires** [*count*] • an engine *backfire*

back·gam·mon /ˈbækˌgæmən/ *noun* [*noncount*] : a board game for two players in which the players throw dice and try to move all of their pieces around and off the board

back·ground /ˈbækˌgraʊnd/ *noun, pl* **-grounds**

1 [*count*] **a** : the part of a scene or picture that is farthest from the viewer : the part of a scene that is behind a main figure or object in a painting, photograph, etc. • Objects in the foreground are drawn larger than those in the *background*. • a photograph of a house with mountains in the *background* • The mountains provided a perfect *background* [=*backdrop*] for the wedding photos. • *background* scenery **b** : a surface or color that is behind or around something (such as a printed design) • red letters printed on a white *background* • a *background* color

2 [*singular*] **a** : a position that attracts little attention • He was a shy man who always tried to keep/stay ***in the background*** [=tried to avoid attracting attention] • The war has pushed all other issues ***into the background*** [=has made all other issues less important] • An ethnic conflict that was simmering away *in the background* finally erupted into civil war. **b** — used to describe something that occurs without requiring attention while something else is also occurring • The software was automatically updated ***in the background*** while we continued to work on the data. **c** — used to describe something that is heard while something else is being listened to • It was hard to enjoy the music because I could hear a dog barking ***in the background***.

3 a [*count*] : the events and conditions that help to explain why something happens : the situation in which something occurs — usually singular • We learned about the social and economic *background* of the American Civil War. • The meetings took place ***against a background*** of increasing tension. **b** [*noncount*] : information needed to understand a problem or situation • Let me provide you with some *background* on this problem. — often used before another noun • *background* information

4 [*count*] : the experiences, knowledge, education, etc., in a person's past • What is your academic *background*? • We need to know more about his *background* before we hire him. • He and his wife come from similar social *backgrounds*. [=they were raised in similar social environments] • His writing is influenced by his ethnic *background*. — often used before another noun • They ran a *background* check to make sure the job candidate had no criminal record.

background music *noun* [*noncount*] : music that is played in a movie, television show, etc., to go along with and add to the story or mood

background noise *noun* [*noncount*] : undesired sound that is heard in a radio broadcast, a tape recording, etc. • The recording had a lot of *background noise*.

back·hand /ˈbækˌhænd/ *noun, pl* **-hands** [*count*] *sports*

1 : a way of hitting a ball in tennis and similar games in which the back of the hand holding the racket is turned in the direction of the ball • She has a good *backhand* but a weak forehand. — often used before another noun • a *backhand* shot

2 : a catch in baseball and similar games that is made on the side of the body that is opposite the hand being used — often used before another noun • The shortstop made a nice *backhand* catch on a line drive.

– **backhand** *verb* **-hands**; **-hand·ed**; **-hand·ing** [+ *obj*] • She *backhanded* the ball over the net. • The shortstop *backhanded* the ball and threw to first for the out.

back·hand·ed /ˈbækˈhændəd/ *adj* [*more* ~; *most* ~]

1 : not direct or sincere • We were disappointed by his *backhanded* apology. • She paid me a ***backhanded compliment*** [=a compliment that was not really a compliment at all] when she said my work was "surprisingly good." • He paid me a *backhanded compliment* [=an indirect compliment] by imitating my style.

2 *sports* : using or done with a backhand • a *backhanded* [=*backhand*] shot • a *backhanded* [=*backhand*] catch

back·hand·er /ˈbækˈhændɚ/ *noun, pl* **-hand·ers** [*count*]

1 *sports* : a backhanded shot • She hit a *backhander* into the net.

2 *Brit, informal* : [1]BRIBE

back·hoe /ˈbækˌhoʊ/ *noun, pl* **-hoes** [*count*] *US* : a large machine that digs into the ground with a metal scoop — see picture at CONSTRUCTION

back·ing /ˈbækɪŋ/ *noun, pl* **-ings**

1 [*count*] : something that forms a back • The tape has an adhesive *backing*.

2 [*noncount*] : support or aid • The project has received financial *backing* from several investors.

3 [*noncount*] : the music that is played along with someone who is singing or playing the main tune : the music that accompanies someone — often used before another noun • a *backing* group • *backing* music

back·lash /ˈbækˌlæʃ/ *noun, pl* **-lash·es** [*count*] : a strong public reaction against something • a *backlash* against feminism ✧ A backlash occurs when many people react to an event, movement, etc., in a way that is opposite to its intended effect.

back·log /ˈbækˌlɑːg/ *noun, pl* **-logs** [*count*] : a large number of jobs that are waiting to be finished • We have a huge *backlog* of orders to be filled.

back matter *noun* [*noncount*] : the pages at the end of a book following the main part • A list of geographical names appears in the *back matter* of the dictionary. — compare FRONT MATTER

back of beyond *noun*

the back of beyond *informal* : a place that is very far from other places and people : a remote place • He lives by himself in a cabin out in *the back of beyond*. [=*the boondocks*]

back–of–the–envelope *adj, always used before a noun, informal* : done to provide a rough idea of something • I can't tell you the exact amount, but my *back-of-the-envelope* [=*rough*] calculation indicates a cost of about $300,000.

back order *noun, pl* ~ **-ders** *chiefly US, business* : a prod-

B

uct that has been ordered but not sent to the customer because it is not yet available [*count*] The book I want to buy is a *back order* and won't be shipped for three weeks. [*noncount*] The book I want to buy is ***on back order*** and won't be shipped for three weeks.

– **back–or·der** *verb* **-ders; -dered; -der·ing** [+ *obj*] ▪ The book I want to buy has been *back-ordered* and won't be shipped for three weeks.

[1]**back·pack** /ˈbækˌpæk/ *noun, pl* **-packs** [*count*] *chiefly US* : a bag for carrying things that has two shoulder straps and is carried on the back — called also (*chiefly US*) *knapsack,* (*chiefly Brit*) *rucksack*; see picture at CAMPING

[2]**backpack** *verb* **-packs; -packed; -pack·ing** [*no obj*] : to hike or travel with a backpack ▪ After college, she *backpacked* through/around Europe. ▪ We're planning to ***go backpacking*** in a national park this summer.

– **back·pack·er** *noun, pl* **-ers** [*count*]

back passage *noun, pl* ~ **-sag·es** [*count*] *Brit* : the part of the body through which solid waste passes — used as a polite way to avoid saying the word "rectum"

back·ped·al /ˈbækˌpɛdl/ *verb* **-ped·als;** *US* **-ped·aled** *or chiefly Brit* **-ped·alled;** *US* **-ped·al·ing** *or chiefly Brit* **-ped·al·ling** [*no obj*] : to move backward with quick steps ▪ The outfielder *backpedaled* a few steps to catch the fly ball. — sometimes used figuratively ▪ When threatened with a revolt of its own supporters, the government *backpedaled* [=*retreated, backtracked*] from its previous position.

back·rest /ˈbækˌrɛst/ *noun, pl* **-rests** [*count*] : a support for a person to lean back against while sitting ▪ a chair with a cushioned *backrest*

back·seat /ˈbækˈsiːt/ *noun, pl* **-seats** [*count*] : a seat in the back of something (such as a car)

take a backseat : to be or become less important, active, or powerful — often + *to* ▪ He refuses to *take a backseat to* anyone. [=he refuses to let anyone have more power or control than he has]

backseat driver *noun, pl* ~ **-ers** [*count*]

1 : a passenger in a car who gives driving advice to the driver

2 : someone who gives unwanted advice or who tries to control something that is supposed to be controlled by another person ▪ Several members of the board of directors have accused him of being a *backseat driver.*

back·side /ˈbækˌsaɪd/ *noun, pl* **-sides** [*count*] *informal* : the part of the body that a person sits on : BUTTOCKS ▪ She slid down the snowy hill on her *backside.* [=*behind, bottom*]

back·slap·ping /ˈbækˌslæpɪŋ/ *noun* [*noncount*] : enthusiastic praise or congratulations ▪ We had expected the candidates to criticize each other, but instead they engaged in mutual *backslapping.*

– **back·slap·per** /ˈbækˌslæpɚ/ *noun, pl* **-pers** [*count*]

– **backslapping** *adj, always used before a noun* ▪ *backslapping* businessmen

back·slash /ˈbækˌslæʃ/ *noun, pl* **-slash·es** [*count*] : a mark \ that is used for separating written items in computer file names, commands, etc.

back·slide /ˈbækˌslaɪd/ *verb* **-slides; -slid** /-ˌslɪd/; **-slid·ing** [*no obj*] : to start doing something bad again after you have stopped it ▪ I was afraid of *backsliding* [=*relapsing*] into my old habits. ▪ Smokers who quit often *backslide* within a year.

– **back·slid·er** /ˈbækˌslaɪdɚ/ *noun, pl* **-ers** [*count*]

back·space /ˈbækˌspeɪs/ *noun, pl* **-spac·es** [*count*] : a key that is pressed on a typewriter or computer keyboard to move back toward the beginning of a line of text — usually singular ▪ press the *backspace*

– **backspace** *verb* **-spaces; -spaced; -spac·ing** [*no obj*] ▪ He *backspaced* to the beginning of the line.

back·spin /ˈbækˌspɪn/ *noun* [*noncount*] : a backward spinning motion of a ball ▪ put *backspin* on the ball — compare TOPSPIN

back·stab·bing /ˈbækˌstæbɪŋ/ *noun* [*noncount*] *US* : harmful and unfair things that are said or done to hurt the reputation of someone ▪ She was hurt by her former friend's *backstabbing.*

– **back·stab·ber** /ˈbækˌstæbɚ/ *noun, pl* **-bers** [*count*] ▪ She accused her former friend of being a *backstabber.*

– **backstabbing** *adj, always used before a noun* ▪ a *backstabbing* liar

back·stage /ˈbækˈsteɪʤ/ *adv* : behind the stage of a theater ▪ After the show, we went *backstage* to meet the band.

– **backstage** *adj, always used before a noun* ▪ the *backstage* [=*private*] lives of celebrities ▪ a ***backstage pass*** [=a card that gives permission to go backstage and usually to meet the performers]

back·stairs /ˈbækˌsteɚz/ *adj, always used before a noun, chiefly Brit, informal* : done in a secret and usually improper way ▪ a *backstairs* deal

back·stop /ˈbækˌstɑːp/ *noun, pl* **-stops**

1 [*count*] *baseball* **a** : a fence or screen that is placed behind the catcher to prevent the ball from rolling away ▪ The pitch got past the catcher and rolled all the way to the *backstop.* **b** *informal* : CATCHER ▪ a talented *backstop*

2 [*singular*] *Brit* : something that is kept so that it can be used if it is needed ▪ kept some gold as a *backstop* in case the value of the local currency collapsed

back·straight /ˈbækˌstreɪt/ *noun, pl* **-straights** [*count*] *Brit* : BACKSTRETCH

back·street /ˈbækˈstriːt/ *noun, pl* **-streets** [*count*] : a street that is away from the main streets ▪ a London *backstreet*

back·stretch /ˈbækˌstrɛʧ/ *noun, pl* **-stretch·es** [*count*] : the far side of a racetrack : the side of a track that is opposite to the homestretch ▪ The horses are in the *backstretch.* — called also (*Brit*) *backstraight*

back·stroke /ˈbækˌstroʊk/ *noun* [*singular*] : a way of swimming in which a person floats in the water facing upward while kicking the legs and rotating the arms ▪ She got into the pool and began to do the *backstroke.*; *also* : a race in which the swimmers do the backstroke ▪ She won the 50-meter *backstroke.*

back·swing /ˈbækˌswɪŋ/ *noun, pl* **-swings** [*count*] : a movement of the arm backwards before swinging something (such as a club, bat, or racket) ▪ a golfer with a short *backswing*

back talk *noun* [*noncount*] *US, informal* : rude speech in reply to someone who should be spoken to with respect ▪ Don't give me any *back talk*! — called also (*Brit*) *backchat*

[1]**back–to–back** *adj*

1 : facing in opposite directions and often touching at the back ▪ *back-to-back* seats

2 : coming one after another in time ▪ *back-to-back* victories ▪ *back-to-back* appointments — see also *back to back* at [1]BACK

– **back to back** *adv* ▪ They were standing *back to back.*

[2]**back–to–back** *noun, pl* **-backs** [*count*] *Brit* : a house that is connected in a row with other houses on each side and with a similar row of houses behind it

back·track /ˈbækˌtræk/ *verb* **-tracks; -tracked; -track·ing** [*no obj*]

1 : to go back over a course or path ▪ The hikers realized they had made a wrong turn and would have to *backtrack.*

2 : to return to something that was mentioned before ▪ Let me *backtrack* for a moment and pick up our previous conversation.

3 : to completely change what you think or say about something ▪ Voters lost confidence in him when he *backtracked* on the issues. [=when he reversed his position on the issues]

back·up /ˈbækˌʌp/ *noun, pl* **-ups**

1 a [*count*] : a person or thing that can be used to replace or support another person or thing ▪ His role on the team is to be a *backup* to the regular quarterback. ▪ We have an extra radio as a *backup* in case this one doesn't work. — often used before another noun ▪ a *backup* quarterback ▪ We need a ***backup plan*** in case of emergency. **b** [*noncount*] : help or support provided by additional people or things ▪ The policeman called for *backup* [=called for other police to come and help him] because the suspect was carrying a gun. ▪ We have an extra radio for *backup.* ▪ He provides *backup* for the regular quarterback.

2 [*count*] *US* : a situation in which the flow of something (such as traffic) becomes blocked ▪ There was a traffic *backup* [=(*Brit*) *tailback*] for miles on the road because of the accident. ▪ There was a *backup* [=*blockage*] in the drain.

3 [*noncount*] : a musical part that is sung to support the main singer ▪ She sang *backup* on his CD. — often used before another noun ▪ a *backup* singer

4 [*count*] : a copy of information stored on a computer ▪ Be sure to make a *backup* of your work. — often used before another noun ▪ a *backup* file/copy; *also* : the act or process of making such a copy ▪ It may take some time for the *backup* to be complete. — see also *back up* at [4]BACK

[1]**back·ward** (*chiefly US*) /ˈbækwɚd/ *or* **back·wards** /ˈbækwɚdz/ *adv*

1 : toward the back : to or toward what is behind ▪ a sudden movement *backward,* not forward ▪ I heard a noise behind me and glanced *backward.* ▪ He pushed the throttle *backward.* ▪ She took a small step *backward.* ▪ Can you skate *backward*?

2 : opposite to the usual way : in reverse ▪ Count *backward* from 10.

3 : toward the past ▪ a journey *backward* in time ▪ The narrative moves *backward* and forward in time.

4 : to or toward a less advanced state or condition : toward a worse state ▪ His new job, which paid less and had fewer responsibilities, felt like a step *backward.*

bend over backward *or* ***lean over backward*** *also* ***fall over backward*** **: to make a great effort to help someone or to reach agreement with someone** ▪ The salesman said he would *bend over backward* to make the deal. ▪ I've *leaned over backward* to please you—and you haven't even said thank you!

know something backward and forward see [1]KNOW

[2]**backward** *adj*

1 a : directed or turned toward the back ▪ a *backward* glance ▪ a *backward* baseball cap ▪ a sudden *backward* movement **b : done backward** ▪ a *backward* somersault

2 [*more ~; most ~*] **: behind others : not as advanced as others in learning or development** ▪ (*old-fashioned*) He was a *backward* pupil who struggled to keep up in school. ▪ a technologically *backward* village that has no running water

– back·ward·ly *adv* **– back·ward·ness** *noun* [*noncount*] ▪ the technological *backwardness* of the village

back·ward–look·ing /ˈbækwəd͵lʊkɪŋ/ *adj* [*more ~; most ~*] *disapproving* **: relating to the past** ▪ *backward-looking* [=*old-fashioned*] ideas/plans **: not planning for the future** ▪ *backward-looking* [=*hidebound*] engineers/politicians/industrialists— opposite FORWARD-LOOKING

back·wa·ter /ˈbæk͵wɑːtɚ/ *noun, pl* **-ters** [*count*]

1 : a part of a river where the water moves slowly because it is away from the main part of the river

2 : a quiet place (such as a town or village) where there is little activity, excitement, progress, etc. ▪ The once sleepy *backwater* is now a thriving city. ▪ a cultural *backwater*

back·woods /ˈbækˈwʊdz/ *noun* [*plural*] **: an area that is far from cities** ▪ She grew up in the *backwoods* of Maine. ▪ a *backwoods* politician [=a politician in a remote area far from cities]

back·woods·man /͵bækˈwʊdzmən/ *noun, pl* **-men** /-mən/ [*count*]

1 : a man who lives in the backwoods

2 *Brit* **: a male member of the House of Lords who rarely attends it and who typically lives in a rural area far from London**

back·yard /ˈbækˈjɑɚd/ *noun, pl* **-yards**

1 [*count*] **: an area in back of a house;** *especially, US* **: an area of grass behind someone's house** ▪ We spent the evening relaxing in the *backyard.*

2 [*noncount*] **: the general area near and around someone's home** ▪ For fun in the sun this summer, look no farther than your own *backyard.* [=*neighborhood*] ▪ Residents grew anxious when they learned the new prison would be located in their *backyard.* [=would be located near their homes]

– backyard *adj, always used before a noun* ▪ a *backyard* barbecue ▪ a *backyard* garden

ba·con /ˈbeɪkən/ *noun* [*noncount*] **: thin strips of salted and smoked meat from the sides and the back of a pig** ▪ We ate *bacon* and eggs for breakfast. ▪ a slice of *bacon* = (*Brit*) a rasher of *bacon* — often used before another noun ▪ *bacon* fat

bring home the bacon *informal* **: to earn the money that is needed to live** ▪ He worked hard all week to *bring home the bacon* for his family.

save someone's bacon see [1]SAVE

bacteria *plural of* BACTERIUM

bac·te·ri·ol·o·gy /bæk͵tiriˈɑːləʤi/ *noun* [*noncount*] **: the scientific study of bacteria**

– bac·te·ri·o·log·i·cal /bæk͵tirijəˈlɑːʤɪkəl/ *adj* **– bac·te·ri·ol·o·gist** /bæk͵tiriˈɑːləʤɪst/ *noun, pl* **-gists** [*count*]

bac·te·ri·um /bækˈtirijəm/ *noun, pl* **-te·ria** /-ˈtirijə/ [*count*] **: any one of a group of very small living things that often cause disease — usually plural** ▪ Keep the wound clean and dry to prevent the growth of *bacteria.*

– bac·te·ri·al /bækˈtirijəl/ *adj*

[1]**bad** /ˈbæd/ *adj* **worse** /ˈwɚs/; **worst** /ˈwɚst/

1 a : low or poor in quality ▪ a *bad* repair job ▪ *bad* work ▪ The house is in *bad* condition/shape. **b : not correct or proper** ▪ *bad* manners ▪ *bad* [=*incorrect, faulty*] grammar ▪ a letter written in *bad* French ▪ *bad* spelling ▪ a *bad* check [=a check that cannot be cashed]— see also BAD LANGUAGE

2 a : not pleasant, pleasing, or enjoyable ▪ He had a *bad* day at the office. ▪ I was having a *bad* dream. ▪ She made a very *bad* impression on her future colleagues. ▪ The food tastes *bad.* ▪ The flower smells *bad.* ▪ He has *bad* breath. [=breath that smells bad] ▪ We've been having *bad* weather lately. ▪ The medicine left a *bad* taste in his mouth. ▪ It feels *bad* [=*uncomfortable, painful*] to stretch out my arm. ▪ I look *bad* in this hat. = This hat looks *bad* on me. ▪ That hat doesn't look *bad* on you. [=that hat looks good on you] **b : having, marked by, or relating to problems, troubles, etc.** ▪ good and *bad* news ▪ They have remained together in good times and *bad* (times). ▪ It's a *bad* time for business right now. ▪ a *bad* omen ▪ *bad* luck/fortune ▪ Things are looking pretty *bad* for us at this point. ▪ I have a *bad* feeling about this.— see also BAD BLOOD, BAD NEWS **c : not adequate or suitable** ▪ I couldn't take a picture because the lighting was *bad.* ▪ It's a *bad* day for a picnic. ▪ She made a *bad* marriage. ▪ Is this a *bad* moment/time to have a word with you? **d : not producing or likely to produce a good result** ▪ a *bad* deal ▪ a *bad* risk ▪ a *bad* idea/plan ▪ The plan has its good points and its *bad* points. ▪ a ***bad debt*** [=a debt that will not be paid] ▪ a ***bad loan*** [=a loan that will not be repaid] **e : expressing criticism or disapproval** ▪ The movie got *bad* reviews.

3 a : not healthy : marked or affected by injury or disease ▪ His health is pretty *bad.* = He's in pretty *bad* health. ▪ The patient was pretty *bad* [=*ill, sick*] last week and even *worse* yesterday but is doing better now. ▪ He came home early because he was feeling pretty *bad.* [=he wasn't feeling well] ▪ My father has a *bad* back/leg. [=a back/leg that is always or often painful] ▪ She has *bad* eyesight/hearing. ▪ *bad* teeth **b : causing harm or trouble** ▪ a *bad* diet ▪ a *bad* influence ▪ ***bad cholesterol*** [=a type of cholesterol that can cause serious health problems when there is too much of it in your blood] — often + *for* ▪ Eating too much can be *bad for* you. = It can be *bad for* you to eat too much. ▪ Eating all that candy is *bad for* your teeth. ▪ Watching too much TV is *bad for* children.

4 a : not morally good or right : morally evil or wrong ▪ a *bad* person ▪ *bad* conduct/behavior ▪ a man of *bad* character ▪ *bad* intentions/deeds ▪ It's hard to tell the good guys from the ***bad guys*** in this movie.— see also BAD FAITH **b : not behaving properly** ▪ a *bad* dog ▪ I'm afraid your son has been a very *bad* [=*naughty*] boy.— see also BAD BOY

5 a : not skillful : not doing or able to do something well ▪ a *bad* musician ▪ a *bad* doctor ▪ She was pretty *bad* in that movie. [=she did not act well]— often + *at* ▪ a doctor who's *bad at* treating nervous patients ▪ He's very/really *bad at* expressing his true feelings. **b : having a tendency not to do something — +** ***about*** ▪ He's *bad about* getting to work on time. [=he often fails to get to work on time] ▪ I'm very *bad about* remembering people's birthdays. [=I often forget people's birthdays]

6 a : not happy or pleased : feeling regret or guilt about something ▪ I ***feel bad*** about what happened. [=I regret what happened] ▪ She *felt bad* that she forgot to call. = She *felt bad* about forgetting to call. **b : not cheerful or calm** ▪ She's in a *bad* mood. [=an angry mood] ▪ He has a *bad* temper. [=he's bad-tempered; he becomes angry easily]

7 : serious or severe ▪ She's in *bad* trouble. ▪ He has a *bad* cough/cold. ▪ That bruise looks *bad*: you'd better see a doctor about it. ▪ How *bad* is the pain?

8 : no longer good to eat or drink : not fresh ▪ the smell of *bad* fish ▪ Is the milk still good or has it ***gone bad***? [=*spoiled*]

9 bad·der; bad·dest *chiefly US, informal* **a : very good** ▪ He's the *baddest* guitar player you'll ever hear! **b : very tough or dangerous** ▪ Don't mess around with him. He's a *bad* dude.

a bad job see JOB

a bad lot see LOT

bad apple see APPLE

come to a bad end see [1]END

from bad to worse **: from a bad state or condition to an even worse state or condition** ▪ The company has been struggling for years, and things have recently gone *from bad to worse.*

in a bad way **: in a bad condition** ▪ Without enough funding, public services are *in a* pretty *bad way* right now. ▪ The patient was *in a bad way* last week but is doing better now.

in someone's bad books see [1]BOOK

not bad **: fairly good or quite good** ▪ All things considered, she's *not a bad* singer. [=she's a pretty good singer] ▪ "How are you?" "*Not* (too/so) *bad,* thanks. And you?"

B

too bad **1** — used to show that you are sorry or feel bad about something ▪ It's *too bad* [=*unfortunate*] that John and Mary are getting divorced. = It's *too bad* about John and Mary getting divorced. [=I'm sorry to hear that John and Mary are getting divorced] ▪ "I won't be able to come to the party." "(That's) *Too bad*. I was hoping you'd be there." **2** — used in an ironic way to show that you are not sorry or do not feel bad about something ▪ "But I need your help!" "(That's just) *Too bad*."

with bad grace see [1]GRACE

– bad·ness *noun* [*noncount*] ▪ the *badness* of his behavior ▪ the *badness* [=*severity*] of his injuries ▪ There's more goodness than *badness* in him.

[2]**bad** *adv* **worse; worst** *US, informal* : BADLY ▪ She was struggling when she first started the job, but she's not doing so *bad* now. [=she's doing fairly well now] ▪ He hasn't succeeded because he doesn't want it *bad* enough. ▪ He cut himself real *bad*. [=very badly] ▪ I need a vacation and I need it *bad*. [=I need it very much] ▪ "Is he in love with her?" "Oh yeah, he's ***got it bad***" [=he's extremely in love with her]

bad off US **1** : having little money ▪ They're pretty *bad off* [=they don't have enough money] now that he's lost his job. ▪ We're not rich, but we're not too *bad off* (for money). [=we're not poor] **2** : in a bad or difficult situation or condition ▪ When I heard how *bad off* they were, I asked if I could do anything to help. ▪ This state isn't too *bad off* compared to other parts of the country.

[3]**bad** *noun*

1 [*noncount*] : morally bad forces or influences : EVIL ▪ There's more good than *bad* in him. ▪ We need to teach our children the difference between good and *bad*.

2 ***the bad*** **a** [*singular*] : the unpleasant things that happen to people ▪ You have to ***take the good with the bad*** [=you have to accept the bad things that happen to you as well as the good things] **b** [*singular*] : things that are morally wrong ▪ teaching children the difference between the good and *the bad* **c** [*plural*] : morally bad people ▪ He believes that the good go to heaven when they die and *the bad* go to hell.

bad·ass /ˈbædˌæs/ *adj, always used before a noun, chiefly US, informal + sometimes offensive*

1 : likely to cause trouble : tough and dangerous ▪ a *badass* criminal

2 : very skillful or impressive ▪ a *badass* musician

– badass *noun, pl* **-ass·es** [*count*] He acted tough and thought of himself as a *badass*.

bad blood *noun* [*noncount*] : feelings of dislike between two people or groups ▪ There's been a lot of *bad blood* between them since their quarrel.

bad boy *noun, pl* **~ boys** [*count*] : a man who says or does things that shock other people; *especially* : a young and successful man who does things in a way that is very different from the usual way ▪ He has become known as the *bad boy* of the American television industry.

bad·die *or* **bad·dy** /ˈbædi/ *noun, pl* **-dies** [*count*] *informal* : a bad person in a book, movie, etc. : VILLAIN ▪ He plays one of the good guys in his latest film and defeats all the *baddies*. [=*bad guys*]

bade *past tense of* [1]BID

bad faith *noun* [*noncount*] : lack of honesty in dealing with other people ▪ She accused her landlord of *bad faith* [=*dishonesty*] because he had promised to paint the apartment but never did it. — compare GOOD FAITH

in bad faith : in a dishonest and improper way ▪ She signed the contract *in bad faith*. [=with no intention of doing what it said she would do]

badge /ˈbæʤ/ *noun, pl* **badg·es** [*count*]

1 : a small object (such as a tag, pin, or metal shield) that is worn or held up by a person so that it can be easily seen, that has writing (such as a person's name) and often a picture on it, and that shows who the person is ▪ The policeman flashed his *badge*. ▪ Don't forget to wear your name *badge*. ▪ The receptionist glanced at my visitor's *badge*.

2 : a cloth patch that can be sewn onto clothing and that is awarded to a person (such as a Boy Scout or Girl Scout) for doing something ▪ She earned 10 merit *badges* in scouting.

3 *Brit* : [1]BUTTON 2 ▪ She was wearing a *badge* that read "Support your local library."

4 : something that represents or is a sign of something else ▪ She viewed her failures as a *badge* of humanity. ▪ He wore his ethnic heritage as a ***badge of honor/pride*** [=he was proud of his ethnic heritage and did not try to hide it]

[1]**bad·ger** /ˈbæʤɚ/ *noun, pl* **-gers** [*count*] : a type of animal that lives in the ground and has short thick legs and long claws on its front feet

badger

[2]**badger** *verb* **-gers; -gered; -ger·ing** [+ *obj*]

1 : to bother or annoy (someone) with many comments or questions ▪ The celebrity was being *badgered* [=*pestered*] by reporters.

2 : to ask or tell someone again and again to do something ▪ He's been *badgering* [=*nagging, pestering*] me to clean the garage for months. ▪ She finally *badgered* me into cutting my hair.

bad·lands /ˈbædˌlændz/ *noun* [*plural*] : a region in the U.S. where weather has worn away rocks into strange shapes and where there are very few plants ▪ the *badlands* of South Dakota

bad language *noun* [*noncount*] : offensive language : dirty language ▪ She scolded the children for using *bad language*.

bad·ly /ˈbædli/ *adv* **worse** /ˈwɚs/; **worst** /ˈwɚst/

1 : in a bad manner ▪ We played *badly*. ▪ The car ran *badly*. ▪ He played *badly* but I played even *worse*. ▪ The failure reflects *badly* on the administration. ▪ The child behaved *badly*. ▪ a *badly* planned project

2 a : very much : to a great degree ▪ She wanted the job *badly*. ▪ I'm *badly* in need of a vacation. ▪ We miss you *badly*. **b** : severely or seriously ▪ Was she hurt *badly*? ▪ His fingers were *badly* frozen.

badly off **1** : having little money ▪ We were so *badly off* [=*poor, broke*] we couldn't afford a bus ticket. ▪ Thanks to the money my uncle left me, I'm not *badly off*. [=I'm pretty well off] **2** : in bad condition ▪ I felt unwell, but I wasn't so *badly off* that I had to stay home from work.

badly off for Brit : having a strong need for (something or someone) ▪ The team was *badly off for* young players.

not badly : fairly or quite well ▪ "How are you doing?" "*Not* too/so *badly*, thanks. And you?"

think badly of : to have a bad or low opinion of (someone) ▪ Will you *think badly of* me if I take the last cookie?

bad·min·ton /ˈbædˌmɪtn/ *noun* [*noncount*] : a game in which a light feathered object (called a shuttlecock) is hit over a net by players using light rackets — see picture at RACKET

bad–mouth /ˈbædˌmaʊθ/ *verb* **-mouths; -mouthed; -mouth·ing** [+ *obj*] : to say bad things about (someone or something) : to criticize (someone or something) ▪ She refuses to *bad-mouth* her colleagues.

bad news *noun* [*singular*] *informal* : a bad, unpleasant, or dangerous person or thing ▪ Stay away from him—he's *bad news*. ▪ "That drug is *bad news*," she warned.

bad–tempered *adj* [*more ~; most ~*] : easily annoyed or angered : ILL-TEMPERED ▪ a *bad-tempered* old man

[1]**baf·fle** /ˈbæfəl/ *verb* **baf·fles; baf·fled; baf·fling** [+ *obj*] : to confuse (someone) completely ▪ Her behavior *baffles* [=*bewilders*] me. ▪ I was *baffled* by many of the scientific terms used in the article.

– baffled *adj* [*more ~; most ~*] ▪ a *baffled* look [=a look that shows confusion] ▪ His explanation left me feeling even more *baffled* [=*confused*] than I had felt before. **– baf·fle·ment** /ˈbæfəlmənt/ *noun* [*noncount*] ▪ I couldn't hide my complete *bafflement* at her strange behavior. **– baffling** *adj* [*more ~; most ~*] ▪ It's completely *baffling* to me how she can behave like that! ▪ a *baffling* array of choices **– baf·fling·ly** /ˈbæflɪŋli/ *adv* [*more ~; most ~*] ▪ *bafflingly* strange behavior

[2]**baffle** *noun, pl* **baffles** [*count*] *technical* : a device (such as a wall or screen) that is used to control the flow of something (such as a fluid, light, or sound)

[1]**bag** /ˈbæg/ *noun, pl* **bags**

1 [*count*] **a** : a container made of thin material (such as paper, plastic, or cloth) that opens at the top and is used for holding or carrying things ▪ She packed her lunch in a paper *bag*. ▪ (*US*) a garbage/trash *bag* = (*Brit*) a rubbish *bag* ▪ (*US*) ***grocery bags*** = (*Brit*) ***carrier bags*** [=plastic or paper bags used for holding items bought at a store] **b** : a soft container carried by a woman and used to hold money and other small things (such as keys or makeup) ▪ She put the pencil in her *bag*. — see also HANDBAG, SHOULDER BAG **c** : a container used for carrying personal things (such as clothes) when you are going somewhere ▪ an overnight *bag* ▪ a gym

bag — usually plural ▪ We carried our *bags* [=*suitcases, luggage*] to the hotel room. ▪ She packed her *bags* and left.
2 [*count*] **:** the amount of something that is inside a bag ▪ We ate two *bags* [=*bagfuls*] of potato chips. ▪ a *bag* of apples/flour/fertilizer
3 ***bags*** [*plural*] **:** an area of swollen and often dark skin under a person's eyes ▪ a tired old man with *bags* under his eyes
4 [*singular*] **:** a collection of different things (such as ideas) ▪ They tried using their usual ***bag of tricks***. — see also GRAB BAG, MIXED BAG, RAGBAG
5 [*singular*] *informal + old-fashioned* **:** something that a person likes to do **:** something that a person does well ▪ Housecleaning isn't her *bag*. [=she doesn't like housecleaning] ▪ I've tried living in the city, but it's just not my *bag*.
6 [*count*] *baseball* **:** a square white bag that marks the position of first base, second base, and third base ▪ He slid into the *bag* and was safe at second base.
7 [*count*] *informal* — used as an insulting word for an old woman ▪ Shut up, you old *bag*!
8 ***bags*** [*plural*] *Brit, informal* **:** a large amount of something ▪ There's no need to hurry. We've still got *bags* [=*lots*] of time.
a bag of nerves see NERVE
bag and baggage *chiefly Brit* **:** with all of your possessions ▪ He got rid of the visitors, *bag and baggage*. [=*altogether, completely*]
hold the bag see [1]HOLD
in the bag *informal* **:** sure to happen ▪ Their success was *in the bag*. [=*guaranteed*] **:** certain to be successful ▪ We had the game *in the bag* [=*sewn up*] by the end of first half. ▪ She seemed to have the election *in the bag*. [=she seemed sure to win the election]
let the cat out of the bag see CAT

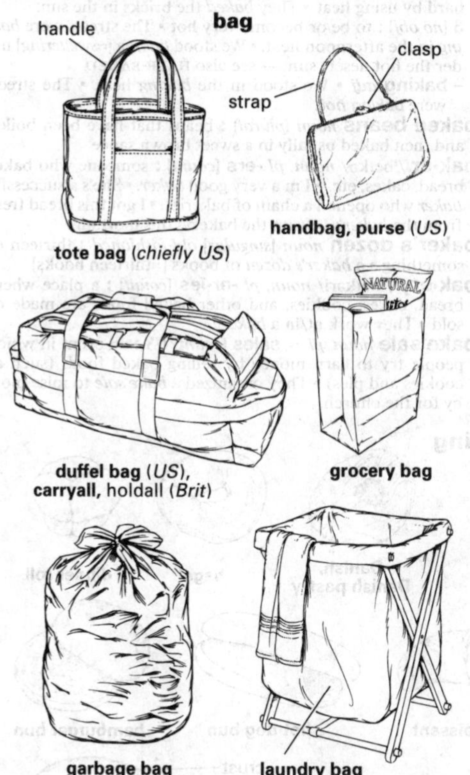

[2]**bag** *verb* **bags; bagged; bag·ging** [*+ obj*]
1 : to put (something) into a bag ▪ He got a job *bagging* groceries.
2 : to kill or catch (an animal) while hunting, fishing, etc. ▪ The hunters *bagged* five deer altogether. ▪ We *bagged* 10 fish today.
3 *informal* **:** to get (something desired) ▪ She's expected to *bag* the award for the team's most valuable player. ▪ I *bagged* the last seat so everyone else had to stand.
4 *US, informal* **:** to give up or leave (something) ▪ She decided to *bag* her job and move to the country. ▪ He finally *bagged* his acting career and went back to school.

ba·gel /ˈbeɪgəl/ *noun, pl* **-gels** [*count*] **:** a bread roll shaped like a ring — see picture at BAKING

bagful /ˈbægˌfʊl/ *noun, pl* **-fuls** [*count*]
1 : the amount that a bag can hold ▪ two *bagfuls* [=*bags*] of apples
2 : a large number or amount ▪ She always has a *bagful* of stories. ▪ a *bagful* of tricks

bag·gage /ˈbægɪʤ/ *noun* [*noncount*]
1 *chiefly US* **:** the bags, suitcases, and personal things that a person carries when traveling **:** LUGGAGE ▪ Please collect your baggage. — see also *baggage claim* at [2]CLAIM
2 : the feelings, beliefs, problems, or past events that can make life difficult for a person or group ▪ His difficult childhood left him with a lot of heavy/personal/emotional *baggage*. ▪ the cultural/political/historical *baggage* of the region
bag and baggage see [1]BAG

bag·gy /ˈbægi/ *adj* **bag·gi·er; -est** *of clothing* **:** very loose **:** not tight ▪ *baggy* jeans/sweaters ▪ These pants are too *baggy* at the knees.

bag lady *noun, pl* ∼ **ladies** [*count*] **:** a homeless woman who walks around the streets of a city carrying her possessions in a bag

bag lunch *noun, pl* ∼ **lunches** [*count*] *US* **:** a lunch that is made at home, packed inside a bag or box, and eaten at a job, at school, etc. ▪ Remember to bring a *bag lunch* to school tomorrow. — called also *box lunch*

bag of bones *noun* [*singular*] *informal* **:** a very thin person or animal ▪ I can't believe how thin he is. He's just a *bag of bones*.

bag·pipe /ˈbægˌpaɪp/ *noun, pl* **-pipes** [*count*] **:** a musical instrument that is played especially in Scotland and that has a bag, a tube for blowing air into the bag, and pipes where the air leaves and makes sounds ◊ The musical instrument is usually referred to by the plural *bagpipes*. ▪ He's learning to play the *bagpipes*. In U.S. English, the singular *bagpipe* is also used. ▪ We heard the sound of a *bagpipe*. In both U.S. and British English, *bagpipe* is sometimes used before another noun. ▪ *bagpipe* music

bagpipe

ba·guette /bæˈgɛt/ *noun, pl* **-guettes** [*count*] **:** a long, thin loaf of French bread

bah /ˈbɑː/ *interj, old-fashioned + humorous* — used to show dislike or disapproval of something ▪ *Bah*, humbug!

[1]**bail** /ˈbeɪl/ *noun* [*noncount*] **:** an amount of money given to a court to allow a prisoner to leave jail and return later for a trial

> The bail paid by a person accused of a crime is returned when the person comes back to court for a trial. To ***set bail*** is to decide how much money a person must pay in order to get out of jail until a trial. ▪ The judge/court *set bail* at $1 million. = The *bail* was *set* at $1 million. To ***grant bail*** or ***give bail*** is to allow a prisoner to pay money to leave jail until a trial. ▪ It is not clear whether the judge will *grant bail* in this case. If you are ***denied bail*** or ***held without bail***, a court will not allow you to pay money to leave jail until your trial. ▪ The two men are being *held without bail*. ▪ *Bail* was *denied*, and he was sent to prison to await his trial. If you are ***free on bail*** or ***out on bail*** or have been ***released/freed on bail***, you have paid the court money and are now out of jail and waiting for your trial. ▪ He is now *free on bail*. = He's *out on bail*. ▪ They were both *free/out on* $10,000 *bail*. [=they both paid the court $10,000 and promised to return for their trials] ▪ She was *released on* $5,000 *bail*. [=she left jail after paying the court $5,000] If you ***make bail*** or ***post bail***, you give enough money to the court and can leave jail until your trial. ▪ He didn't have enough money to *make bail* so he had to stay in prison until his trial. ▪ Someone *posted bail* for you. You're free to go. To ***jump bail*** or ***skip bail*** is to pay money to get out of jail and then not return for your trial. ▪ A day after he was released from jail, he decided to *jump bail* and leave the country. ▪ They *skipped bail* a week before the trial.

B

²bail *verb* **bails; bailed; bail·ing**
bail out [*phrasal verb*] **1** ***bail (someone) out or bail out (someone)*** : to make it possible for someone to leave jail by paying bail • She went to the jail to *bail out* her boyfriend. = She *bailed* him *out* of jail. **2** ***bail (someone or something) out or bail out (someone or something)*** : to help (someone) solve a problem or leave a difficult situation • They're always *bailing* their son *out* of trouble. : to help (a business, an organization, etc.) by giving or lending money • The federal government *bailed out* [=gave money to] their struggling company. • *bailing out* poor countries — see also BAILOUT
– compare ³BAIL

³bail *verb* **bails; bailed; bailing**
1 [+ *obj*] : to remove or throw water *from* or *out of* a boat • We used a bucket to *bail* water *out of* the canoe. = We used a bucket to *bail out* the canoe. • *bailing* water *from* the bottom of the boat
2 [*no obj*] *US, informal* : to leave a difficult situation • She *bailed* [=*bailed out*] when times got tough. [=she left when life became difficult] • I think we'd better *bail*. [=*bail out*]
bail out [*phrasal verb*] *chiefly US* **1** : to jump out of an airplane with a parachute • The pilot *bailed out* [=(*Brit*) *baled out*] just before the plane crashed. **2** : to leave or escape a harmful or difficult situation • Most investors have *bailed out* [=(*Brit*) *baled out*] of the business. • They *bailed out* [=*backed out*] of the deal.
– compare ²BAIL

bai·liff /ˈbeɪləf/ *noun, pl* **-liffs** [*count*]
1 *US* : an officer in a court of law who helps the judge control the people in the courtroom
2 *Brit* : someone hired by a sheriff to bring legal documents to people and to take away possessions when people cannot pay for them
3 *Brit* : someone who manages the land and property of another person : STEWARD

bail·out /ˈbeɪlˌaʊt/ *noun, pl* **-outs** [*count*] : the act of saving or rescuing something (such as a business) from money problems • government *bailouts* of large corporations — see also *bail out* 2 at ²BAIL

bairn /ˈbeən/ *noun, pl* **bairns** [*count*] *Scotland* : CHILD • a wee *bairn* [=a small child]

¹bait /ˈbeɪt/ *noun, pl* **baits** : something (such as a piece of food) that is used to attract fish or animals so they can be caught [*noncount*] We always use live *bait* [=worms that are alive] when we fish. • cheese used for/as *bait* in mousetraps • Wait until the fish ***takes the bait***. [*count*] a wide selection of lures and *baits* — often used figuratively • using bargains as *bait* for shoppers [=using bargains to attract shoppers] • The police waited for the bank robbers to *take the bait*. [=to be tricked into doing the thing that would cause them to be trapped or caught] • (*chiefly Brit*) The interviewer kept asking the politician whether he was lying, and he ***rose to the bait*** by getting angry.
fish or cut bait see ²FISH

²bait *verb* **baits; bait·ed; bait·ing** [+ *obj*]
1 : to put a piece of food on (a hook) or in (a trap) in order to attract and catch fish or animals • She *baited* the mousetraps with pieces of cheese. = She used cheese to *bait* the traps. • *baiting* hooks with live worms • a *baited* hook/trap
2 : to try to make (someone) angry by using criticism or insults • The interviewer kept *baiting* the politician by asking him whether he was lying. — see also RACE-BAITING
3 : to use dogs to make (an animal, such as a bear or bull) angry or afraid — used in combination • bear-*baiting* • bull-*baiting*

bait and switch *noun* [*singular*] *US* : a selling method in which a customer is attracted by the advertisement of a low-priced product but then is encouraged to buy a more expensive one

bake /ˈbeɪk/ *verb* **bakes; baked; bak·ing**
1 a : to make (food, such as bread and cake) by preparing a dough, batter, etc., and cooking it in an oven using dry heat [+ *obj*] I *baked* you a cake. = I *baked* a cake for you. • freshly *baked* bread [=bread that was baked recently] [*no obj*] He likes to *bake*. = He enjoys *baking*. [=he likes making pies, muffins, cookies, etc.] **b** : to cook (food) in an oven using dry heat [+ *obj*] *Bake* [=*roast*] the chicken for 30 minutes. • *baked* potatoes • She wrapped the fish in foil and *baked* it for 15 minutes. [*no obj*] — used in recipes • Wrap the fish in foil and *bake* for 15 minutes. **c** [*no obj*] : to be cooked in an oven • The turkey has been *baking* [=*roasting*] for an hour. • How long has the cake been *baking*?
2 [+ *obj*] : to make (something, such as clay or mud) dry and hard by using heat • They *baked* the bricks in the sun.
3 [*no obj*] : to be or become very hot • The streets were *baking* in the afternoon heat. • We stood *baking* [=*sweltering*] under the hot desert sun. — see also HALF-BAKED
– **baking** *adj* • We stood in the *baking* heat. • The streets were ***baking hot***.

baked beans *noun* [*plural*] : beans that have been boiled and then baked usually in a sweet brown sauce

bak·er /ˈbeɪkɚ/ *noun, pl* **-ers** [*count*] : someone who bakes bread, cakes, etc. • I'm a very good *baker*. • She's a successful *baker* who opened a chain of bakeries. • I got this bread fresh from the *baker's* [=from the bakery] this morning.

baker's dozen *noun* [*singular*] *old-fashioned* : thirteen of something • a *baker's dozen* of books [=thirteen books]

bak·ery /ˈbeɪkəri/ *noun, pl* **-er·ies** [*count*] : a place where bread, cakes, cookies, and other baked foods are made or sold • They work at/in a *bakery*.

bake sale *noun, pl* ~ **sales** [*count*] *US* : an event in which people try to earn money by selling baked foods (such as cookies and pies) • They organized a *bake sale* to raise money for the church.

baking

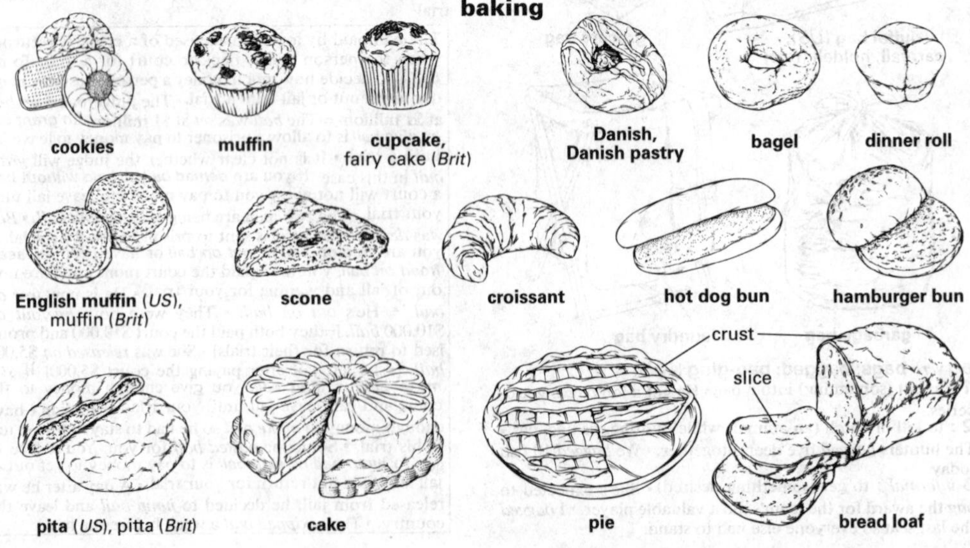

baking powder *noun* [*noncount*] **:** a white powder that is used to make baked foods (such as cakes and breads) light and fluffy ▪ The recipe calls for a teaspoon of *baking powder*.

baking sheet *noun, pl* ~ **sheets** [*count*] **:** a flat piece of metal used for baking things (such as cookies and biscuits) in an oven — called also (*chiefly US*) *cookie sheet*; see picture at KITCHEN

baking soda *noun* [*noncount*] **:** a kind of salt that is used to make baked foods (such as cookies and breads) light and fluffy ✧ *Baking soda* is one of the ingredients in baking powder. — called also *bicarb, bicarbonate of soda, sodium bicarbonate*

baking tray *noun, pl* ~ **trays** [*count*] *chiefly Brit* **:** BAKING SHEET

bal•a•cla•va /ˌbæləˈklɑːvə/ *noun, pl* **-vas** [*count*] **:** a warm hat that covers the head, neck, and most of the face

[1]**bal•ance** /ˈbæləns/ *noun, pl* **-anc•es**

1 [*noncount*] **a :** the state of having your weight spread equally so that you do not fall ▪ He held on to the rail for *balance*. = He held on to the rail to ***keep/maintain his balance***. ▪ She had trouble *keeping her balance* as the boat rocked back and forth. ▪ The skater suddenly ***lost his balance*** and fell. ▪ Another skater bumped into him and ***knocked/threw him off balance***. ✧ In figurative use, to ***knock/throw someone off balance*** or ***keep someone off balance*** is to make someone feel unsure about how to behave or what to expect. ▪ He was surprised and *thrown off balance* by her strong personality. ▪ The sudden change in the schedule *knocked me off balance*. ▪ The author *keeps* her readers *off balance* by always changing the subject. **b :** the ability to move or to remain in a position without losing control or falling ▪ Gymnasts need flexibility and *balance*. ▪ She has a good ***sense of balance***.

2 [*singular*] **:** a state in which different things occur in equal or proper amounts or have an equal or proper amount of importance ▪ To provide *balance* in her news story, she interviewed members of both political parties. ▪ Temperature changes could upset the delicate *balance* of life in the forest. ▪ To lose weight you need the proper/right *balance* of diet and exercise. ▪ The food had a perfect *balance* of sweet and spicy flavors. ▪ He needs to achieve/create/strike a better *balance* between his work life and his family life. [=he needs to spend less time at work and more time with his family] ▪ He's trying to keep his work life and his family life ***in balance***. = He's trying to keep his work life ***in balance with*** his family life. [=he's trying to give a proper of amount of time and attention to both his work life and his family life] ▪ It's important to keep your life *in balance*. ▪ His work life and his family life are ***out of balance***. = His work life is ***out of balance with*** his family life. ▪ If these ingredients are *out of balance* [=not used in good or correct amounts], the dish will not taste good. ▪ The death of his wife threw/sent his life *out of balance*.

3 a [*count*] **:** the amount of money in a bank account ▪ He has a comfortable/healthy/hefty bank *balance*. [=he has plenty of money in the bank] ▪ You must maintain a minimum *balance* of $1,000 [=you must keep at least $1,000] in your bank account. **b** [*count*] **:** the amount of money that still needs to be paid ▪ What are the unpaid *balances* on your credit cards? ▪ The bill was $500 and we've received $400, so the *balance* (of the bill) is $100. **c *the balance* :** something that remains or is left over after other things have been done or used ▪ We planned to stay there for *the balance* [=*the rest, the remainder*] of the summer. ▪ Although the beginning is funny, *the balance* of the book is very serious.

4 [*count*] **:** a device that measures weight and shows how heavy things are **:** SCALE — see also CHECKS AND BALANCES

in the balance ✧ If something (such as your future) ***hangs in the balance*** or ***is in the balance***, it is not certain but will soon be known or decided. ▪ Our future *hangs in the balance* as we await their decision. [=our future depends on their decision; their decision will control our future] ▪ With his job *in the balance*, he went to ask his boss for a raise.

on balance **:** with all things considered **:** in general ▪ The meeting went well *on balance*. ▪ Although our lives are difficult now, I believe that *on balance* we are becoming stronger people.

tip the balance see [1]TIP

[2]**balance** *verb* **-ances; -anced; -anc•ing**

1 : to make (something, such as a plate or your body) steady by keeping weight equal on all sides [+ *obj*] — usually + *on* ▪ The waiters *balanced* the food *on* large trays. ▪ She learned to walk while *balancing* a book *on* her head. ▪ Can you *balance* a spoon *on* your nose? [*no obj*] I find it difficult to *balance on* one foot. ▪ He had trouble *balancing on* his skis. ▪ He helped his daughter *balance on* her bicycle before she started peddling. — see also *balancing act* at [1]ACT

2 a [+ *obj*] **:** to adjust (an account or budget) so that the amount of money available is more than or equal to the amount of money that has been spent ▪ The legislature is still trying to *balance* the state's budget. ▪ a *balanced* budget **b :** to check and make adjustments to financial records so that they are accurate [+ *obj*] He *balances* his checkbook every month. ▪ The company hasn't done a good job *balancing* the books. [=keeping a record of the money it spends and earns] [*no obj*] Something's wrong: the books don't *balance*.

3 [+ *obj*] **:** to make (different or opposite things) equal in strength or importance ▪ She's able to *balance* her career with her family life. = She *balances* work and family. ▪ The group is *balanced* between new and old members. [=the group had an equal number of new and old members] — see also BALANCE OUT 2 (below)

4 [+ *obj*] **:** to make (a different or opposite thing) less powerful, noticeable, etc. ▪ Serve black coffee to help *balance* the sweetness of the dessert. ▪ His quickness will *balance* [=compensate for, make up for] the other fighter's greater strength. ▪ The movie's serious subject matter is *balanced* [=*offset*] with humor. ▪ His sadness was *balanced* by memories of happier days. — see also BALANCE OUT 1 (below)

5 [+ *obj*] **:** to think about (different things) and decide which is better or more important — usually + *against* or *with* ▪ Their fears must be *balanced* [=*weighed*] *against* the need for change. ▪ A national government must *balance* [=*compare*] the needs of individuals *with/against* the needs of the entire country. ▪ They'll have to *balance* the risks *with* the rewards. [=they'll have to decide if the possible good results are worth the possible bad results]

balance out [*phrasal verb*] **1 *balance out (something)*** *or* ***balance (something) out* :** to make (a different or opposite thing) less powerful, noticeable, etc. ▪ Serve black coffee to help *balance out* the sweetness of the dessert. ▪ His quickness will *balance out* [=compensate for, make up for] the other fighter's greater strength. ▪ The discount *balances out* the shipping charge. = The discount and the shipping charge *balance* each other *out*. [=the shipping charge and the discount together equal zero] — see also [2]BALANCE 4 (above) **2 :** to be or become equal or even ▪ The good times and the bad times *balanced out* [=*evened out*] in the end. — see also [2]BALANCE 3 (above)

balance beam *noun, pl* ~ **beams** [*count*] **:** a thick bar of wood raised above the floor that is used in gymnastics for displays of balance

bal•anced /ˈbælənst/ *adj* [*more* ~; *most* ~] **:** having good or equal amounts of all the necessary parts of something ▪ Most news articles gave a *balanced* [=*fair, unbiased*] account of the event. ▪ a *balanced* diet [=a diet having all the kinds of food needed to be healthy] ▪ Every morning she eats a *balanced* breakfast of toast, yogurt, and a glass of orange juice. — opposite UNBALANCED

balance of payments *noun* [*singular*] **:** the difference between the amount of money that a country spends and the amount it earns

balance of power *noun* [*singular*] **:** a state or situation in which two countries or groups (such as two political parties) have equal amounts of power — usually used with *the* ▪ Their party's loss of two members shifted/tipped *the balance of power* in the legislature. ✧ A group that ***holds the balance of power*** is able to control what happens by choosing to support either one of two larger groups that oppose each other.

balance of trade *noun* [*singular*] **:** the difference between the amount of money that a country spends on its imports and the amount that it earns from its exports ▪ Each nation tries to maintain a favorable *balance of trade* with other countries. [=they try to earn more from their exports than they spend on their imports]

balance sheet *noun, pl* ~ **sheets** [*count*] **:** a statement that shows the financial condition of a company at a particular time by listing the amount of money and property that the company has and the amount of money it owes

bal•co•ny /ˈbælkəni/ *noun, pl* **-nies** [*count*]

1 : a raised platform that is connected to the side of a building and surrounded by a low wall or railing ▪ We asked for a hotel room with a *balcony*. — see picture on next page

2 : a floor or seating area above the main floor of a th–

B

Our seats are on/in the *balcony*. = We have *balcony* seats. — see picture at THEATER

bald /ˈbɑːld/ *adj* **bald·er; -est**
1 a *of a person* : having no hair or very little hair on the head • a *bald* man • All of his uncles are completely *bald*. • He's already starting to ***go bald***. [=to become bald] • He had *gone* completely *bald* by the age of 30. **b** *of a part of the body* : not covered with hair • He covered his *bald* head with a baseball cap. • There's a *bald* spot on the top of his head. • There are *bald* patches in the cat's fur.
2 : not covered with trees and plants • a *bald* mountain top
3 *of a tire* : having a flat and smooth surface because of age and use • an old car with *bald* tires
4 : said or given in a very direct way without extra details or explanations • She repeated her *bald* assertion that her son was not guilty of the crime. • We need more than *bald* statements; we need evidence and proof. • the *bald* facts — compare BALD-FACED
— **bald·ly** *adv* • She *baldly* asserted that her son was not guilty. • To put it *baldly* [=to say it in a harsh and honest way], I don't like you. — **bald·ness** *noun* [*noncount*] • a medicine that treats *baldness* • I was surprised by the *baldness* of her assertion.

balcony 1

bald eagle *noun, pl* ~ **eagles** [*count*] : a very large bird of North America that has a white head and white tail feathers ✧ The bald eagle is a symbol of the U.S. — see color picture on page C9

bal·der·dash /ˈbɑːldəˌdæʃ/ *noun* [*noncount*] *old-fashioned + informal* : foolish words or ideas : NONSENSE • Frankly, I think that's absolute *balderdash*. [=*baloney, hogwash*] — sometimes used as an interjection. • *Balderdash*! That's not what happened!

bald–faced /ˈbɑːldˈfeɪst/ *adj* [*more* ~; *most* ~] *chiefly US*
1 : easy to see and understand as being bad • That's a *bald-faced* [=*barefaced, blatant*] lie!
2 : showing no guilt or shame : not hiding bad behavior • Don't believe her. She's a *bald-faced* [=*barefaced, blatant*] liar.

bald·ing /ˈbɑːldɪŋ/ *adj* : becoming bald • He wore a hat to cover his *balding* head. • a *balding* man

[1]**bale** /ˈbeɪl/ *noun, pl* **bales** [*count*] : a large amount of a material (such as hay or wool) that is pressed together tightly and often tied or wrapped • a *bale* of cotton/paper

[2]**bale** *verb* **bales; baled; bal·ing** [+ *obj*] : to press together and tightly tie or wrap (something, such as hay or paper) into a bale — compare [3]BALE

[3]**bale** *verb* **bales; baled; baling** [+ *obj*] *Brit* : [3]BAIL 1 • We used a bucket to *bale* water out of the canoe. = We used a bucket to *bale* out the canoe.
bale out [*phrasal verb*] *Brit* **1** : to jump out of an airplane with a parachute • The pilot *baled out* [=*bailed out*] just before the plane crashed. **2** : to leave or escape a harmful or difficult situation • The investors *baled out* [=*bailed out*] of the business. • They *baled out* [=*backed out*] of the deal.
— compare [2]BALE

bale·ful /ˈbeɪlfəl/ *adj* [*more* ~; *most* ~] *formal*
1 : threatening harm or evil • He turned and gave us a *baleful* [=*sinister*] glance/glare/look.
2 : harmful or deadly • the *baleful* effects/consequences of water pollution
— **bale·ful·ly** *adv* • He stared *balefully* at his opponent.

[1]**balk** *also Brit* **baulk** /ˈbɑːk/ *verb* **balks; balked; balk·ing** [*no obj*]
1 : to suddenly show that you do not want to do something : to refuse to do what someone else wants you to do • If this witness *balks* [=refuses to cooperate in court], our lawyers will not have enough evidence to win the case. — often + *at* • The public *balked at* the President's new tax plan. • He *balks at* sending his children to expensive private schools. [=he won't send his children to expensive private schools]
2 a *of a horse, mule, etc.* : to stop quickly and refuse to continue going • The horse *balked* and would not jump the fence. **b** *of an engine* : to fail to work in the usual or expected way • I turned the key, but the car's engine *balked*. [=refused to start]
3 *baseball, of a pitcher* : to stop suddenly after starting to throw a pitch : to commit a balk • The runner on third base tried to make the pitcher *balk*.

[2]**balk** *noun, pl* **balks** [*count*] *baseball* : an occurrence in which a pitcher stops suddenly or makes an illegal movement after starting to throw a pitch • He committed a *balk*. ✧ A pitcher can only commit a balk if there is a runner on first base, second base, or third base. When a balk occurs, the runner is allowed to go to the next base.

balky /ˈbɑːki/ *adj* **balk·i·er; -est** [*also more* ~; *most* ~] *chiefly US* : not doing what is wanted or expected • Several *balky* [=*stubborn*] congressmen have refused to support the President's tax plan. • a *balky* horse • a *balky* engine

[1]**ball** /ˈbɑːl/ *noun, pl* **balls**
1 [*count*] : a usually round object that is used in a game or sport or as a toy • a tennis/soccer *ball* • golf/billiard/bowling *balls* • a toy rubber *ball* • kick/throw/hit/catch/bounce/dribble the *ball*
2 [*count*] : something that has a round shape • a *ball* of string • She uses cotton *balls* to clean her face. • eating rice/melon *balls*
3 [*count*] : a round bullet shot out of an old-fashioned gun
4 [*count*] : the rounded part of the human foot that is at the bottom of the foot and behind the toes — usually plural • He stood on the *balls* of his feet. — see picture at FOOT
5 *informal + often offensive* **a** [*count*] : TESTICLE — usually plural • She kicked him in the *balls*. **b** ***balls*** [*plural*] : the courage that is needed to do something • You don't have the/enough *balls* [=*guts, nerve*] to fight me. **c** ***balls*** [*plural*] *Brit* : NONSENSE — often used as an interjection to express disapproval or annoyance
6 [*count*] **a** *sports* : a ball that is thrown or hit • She hit a high arching *ball* over the net. • I thought the *ball* [=serve] was good, but my opponent said it was out. — see also AIR BALL, CURVEBALL, FASTBALL, FLY BALL, GROUND BALL, *fair ball* at [1]FAIR, *foul ball* at [1]FOUL **b** *baseball* : a pitch that does not go through the proper area and that the batter does not swing at • The first pitch was a *ball* but the next two pitches were strikes.
carry the ball *US, informal* : to have the responsibility for doing something • No one else is available to make the arrangements, so it's up to you to *carry the ball*.

ball

golf ball tennis ball

cricket ball

baseball

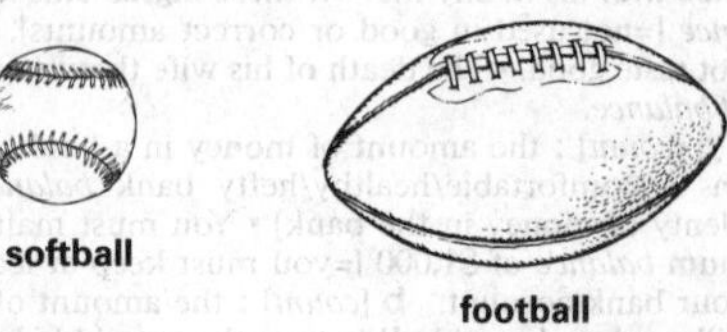
softball football

rugby ball

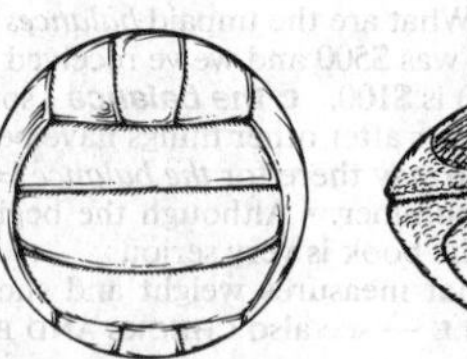
volleyball

soccer ball (*US*), football (*Brit*)

basketball

B

***drop the ball** US, informal* : to make a mistake especially by not doing something important • I think the mayor *dropped the ball* by not hiring more police officers.
***get/set/start the ball rolling** informal* : to begin an activity or process • She tried to *get the ball rolling* by asking him a few questions.
***keep the ball rolling** informal* : to cause an activity or process to continue • I've started the preparations for the party, but it's up to you to *keep the ball rolling.*
***keep your eye on the ball** informal* : to continue thinking about or giving attention to something important that you want to do or achieve • She really needs to *keep her eye on the ball* [=stay focused] if she wants to win the election.
***on the ball** informal* : mentally prepared : aware of what is happening and ready to do what is needed or wanted • With so many intelligent students, the teacher must always be *on the ball.* • Their lawyer was really *on the ball.*
play ball **1** : to begin or continue to play a game with a ball (such as baseball) • "Let's *play ball*!" shouted the umpire. • We went outside to *play* some *ball.* **2** : to do what other people want you to do : to cooperate or work with other people • He refused to *play ball* with the police.
the ball is in your court ✧ If *the ball is in your court,* you are the person who is expected or required to do something. • What do you think we should do now? *The ball is in your court.* • She's waiting for *the ball to be in her court.*
– compare [3]BALL

[2]**ball** *verb* **balls; balled; ball·ing** [+ *obj*] : to form (something) into a ball • I stood up quickly and *balled* my hands into fists. • He *balled* the letter in his hands and threw it in the trash. — often + *up* • He *balled up* the letter and threw it in the trash. • His clothes were *balled up* on the floor. • She lay in bed *balled up* [=*curled up*] under the blankets.

[3]**ball** *noun, pl* **balls** [*count*] : a large formal party for dancing • Cinderella went to the *ball* and danced with the prince. • They were invited to the governor's *ball.*
***have a ball** informal* : to have fun : to spend time in a very enjoyable way • Everyone *had a ball* at the party.
– compare [1]BALL

bal·lad /ˈbæləd/ *noun, pl* **-lads** [*count*]
1 : a slow popular song that is typically about love
2 : a kind of poem or song that tells a story (such as a story about a famous person from history) • a *ballad* about King Arthur

ball and chain *noun* [*singular*] : something that limits someone's freedom or ability to do things • Drugs are a *ball and chain* for many people. • (*old-fashioned*) He referred to his wife as "the *ball and chain.*"

bal·last /ˈbæləst/ *noun* [*noncount*] : heavy material (such as rocks or water) that is put on a ship to make it steady or on a balloon to control its height in the air — often used figuratively • His wife provided the *ballast* he needed in times of stress. [=his wife helped to keep him steady/stable in times of stress]

ball bearing *noun, pl* **~ -ings** [*count*]
1 : a part of a machine in which another part (such as a metal pole) turns easily ✧ A ball bearing is made up of several small metal balls that fit between two metal rings.
2 : one of the balls in a ball bearing

ball bearings

ball boy *noun, pl* **~ boys** [*count*] : a boy who picks up balls that go out of play during a game in tennis, baseball, etc.

bal·le·ri·na /ˌbæləˈriːnə/ *noun, pl* **-nas** [*count*] : a woman who is a ballet dancer — see also PRIMA BALLERINA

bal·let /bæˈleɪ, ˈbæˌleɪ/ *noun, pl* **bal·lets**
1 [*noncount*] : a kind of dancing that is performed on a stage and that uses dance, music, costumes, and scenery to tell a story • She does tap dancing and *ballet.* • a performance of *ballet* — often used before another noun • a *ballet* performance • He's taking *ballet* lessons. • a *ballet* dancer • *ballet* shoes
2 : a show in which ballet is performed [*count*] We are going to a *ballet* tonight. • This is one of my favorite *ballets.* [*noncount*] We enjoy going to the *ballet.* [=we enjoy going to ballet performances]
3 [*count*] : a group of dancers who perform ballets together — often used in names • the Royal *Ballet* • the New York City *Ballet*
– **bal·let·ic** /bæˈlɛtɪk/ *adj* [*more ~; most ~*] • *balletic* [=*graceful*] movements • She moved with *balletic* grace.

ball game *noun, pl* **~ games** [*count*]
1 : any game that is played with a ball • He was popular because he was good at *ball games.*
2 *US* : a baseball game • Dad took us to a *ball game.* • watching a *ball game* on TV
3 *informal* — used in phrases like ***a whole new ball game*** and ***a different ball game*** to describe a situation or activity that has changed • The sport of car racing is *a whole new ball game.* • Raising children is *a different ball game* now.

ball girl *noun, pl* **~ girls** [*count*] : a girl who picks up balls that go out of play during a game in tennis, baseball, etc.

bal·lis·tic /bəˈlɪstɪk/ *adj*
***go ballistic** informal* **1** : to become very angry • Dad *went ballistic* when he saw the dent in his car. **2** *US* : to become very excited • The crowd was *going ballistic.* [=*going wild*]

ballistic missile *noun, pl* **~ -siles** [*count*] : a weapon that is shot through the sky over a great distance and then falls to the ground and explodes • an intercontinental *ballistic missile*

bal·lis·tics /bəˈlɪstɪks/ *noun* [*plural*] : the science that studies the movement of objects (such as bullets or rockets) that are shot or forced to move forward through the air

ball of fire *noun, pl* **balls of fire** [*count*] *chiefly US, informal* : a person who is very active and has a lot of energy • That guy is a real *ball of fire.*

ball of wax *noun* [*singular*] *US, informal*
1 : a situation or set of conditions • He's a good amateur, but playing basketball at the professional level is an entirely different *ball of wax.* [=an entirely different thing]
2 : a collection of items or objects • He won the car, the furniture, and the tropical vacation—the ***whole ball of wax***! [=*everything*]

[1]**bal·loon** /bəˈluːn/ *noun, pl* **-loons** [*count*]
1 : a thin usually rubber bag that becomes larger when it is filled with air or gas • I blew up a *balloon* but then it burst. • brightly colored *balloons* and other party decorations — see also HOT-AIR BALLOON, TRIAL BALLOON
2 : a picture or space in a cartoon that contains words that are spoken or thought by a character
***go over like a lead balloon** (US) or Brit **go down like a lead balloon** informal, of a joke, suggestion, etc.* : to fail completely • He told a joke about his mother-in-law and it *went over like a lead balloon.* [=no one laughed at the joke] • My suggestion *went over like a lead balloon.* [=no one liked my suggestion]

[2]**balloon** *verb* **-loons; -looned; -loon·ing** [*no obj*] : to become bigger quickly • Their credit card debt *ballooned* to more than $5,000. • His weight *ballooned* to 300 pounds. = He *ballooned* to 300 pounds. • the *ballooning* costs of education • *ballooning* weight

bal·loon·ing /bəˈluːnɪŋ/ *noun* [*noncount*] : the activity or sport of riding in a hot air balloon • She's always wanted to ***go ballooning.***
– **bal·loon·ist** /bəˈluːnɪst/ *noun, pl* **-ists** [*count*] • an experienced *balloonist* [=a person who goes ballooning]

balloon payment *noun, pl* **~ -ments** [*count*] *US* : a final payment that is much larger than any earlier payment made on a debt • They agreed to pay $1,000 a year for five years and then make a *balloon payment* of $50,000 at the end of the term.

[1]**bal·lot** /ˈbælət/ *noun, pl* **-lots**
1 [*count*] : a ticket or piece of paper used to vote in an election • a paper *ballot* = (*Brit*) a ***ballot paper*** • The issue was ***on the ballot*** in November. [=people voted to support or oppose the issue in the November election] • I ***cast my ballot*** [=*voted*] for the new candidate. — see also ABSENTEE BALLOT
2 : a process that allows people to vote in secret so that other people cannot see their votes [*count*] They cast their votes in a ***secret ballot.*** [*noncount*] She was elected by *secret ballot.*
3 [*noncount*] **a** : the total number of votes in an election • He won 65 percent of the *ballot.* [=*vote*] **b** : an election • He claims that his opponent won by ***rigging the ballot.*** [=by rigging the election; by dishonestly controlling the results of the election]

[2]**ballot** *verb* **-lots; -lot·ed; -lot·ing** [+ *obj*] *chiefly Brit* : to ask (people) to decide something by voting — usually used as *(be) balloted* • Union members *were balloted* [=*polled*] about whether to accept the company's offer.

ballot box *noun, pl* ~ **boxes**
1 [*count*] : a box that holds the ballots used for voting in an election
2 [*singular*] : an act of voting using secret ballots • He'll never be able to win ***at the ballot box.*** [=in an election]
stuff the ballot box *US* : to vote more than once in an election in order to help someone win • Fans *stuffed the ballot box* for their favorite players.

bal·lot·ing *noun* [*noncount*] : an act or process of voting • The *balloting* [=*election, voting*] will not be secret. • the *balloting* for class president

[1]**ball·park** /ˈbɑːlˌpɑɚk/ *noun, pl* **-parks** [*count*] : a park in which baseball games are played : a baseball park or stadium • hit a home run out of the *ballpark*
in the ballpark *informal* : close to the correct or exact number, price, etc. • My first guess wasn't even *in the ballpark.* [=it was not close to being correct] • An offer of $5,000 would be *in the* (right) *ballpark* for this car. [=this car is worth about $5,000]

[2]**ballpark** *adj, always used before a noun* : not exact but close in number or amount : approximately correct • She gave us a *ballpark* price of $5,000. [=she said it could cost about $5,000] • We don't know exactly how many people live in this city, but a *ballpark* figure/estimate would be about two million.

ball·play·er /ˈbɑːlˌplejɚ/ *noun, pl* **-ers** [*count*] *US* : a baseball player • big-league *ballplayers*

ball·point pen /ˈbɑːlˌpoɪnt-/ *noun, pl* ~ **pens** [*count*] : a pen whose tip is a small metal ball that rolls on a writing surface — called also *ballpoint*; see picture at OFFICE

ball·room /ˈbɑːlˌruːm/ *noun, pl* **-rooms** [*count*] : a large room used for dances

ballroom dancing *noun* [*noncount*] : a style of dancing in which couples hold each other and use set moves to perform different kinds of formal dances (such as the polka, the tango, or the waltz)
– **ballroom dance** *noun, pl* ~ **dances** [*count*] • The waltz is a kind of *ballroom dance.*

balls /ˈbɑːlz/ *verb* **balls·es**; **ballsed**; **balls·ing**
balls up [*phrasal verb*] ***balls (something) up*** *or* ***balls up (something)*** *Brit slang, sometimes offensive* : to make mistakes in doing or making something • He *ballsed up* [=*fouled up, messed up*] everything and never got anything right. — see also BALLS-UP

balls–up /ˈbɑːlzˌʌp/ *noun, pl* **-ups** [*count*] *Brit slang, sometimes offensive* : a problem caused by mistakes or carelessness • He ***made a balls-up*** [=*made a mess*] of everything and never got anything right. — see also *balls up* at BALLS

ball·sy /ˈbɑːlzi/ *adj* **ball·si·er**; **-est** *informal, sometimes offensive* : very tough or brave • That was a *ballsy* [=*gutsy, nervy*] thing to say! • She's quite a *ballsy* lawyer. • a *ballsy* attempt to sneak out of the house

bal·ly·hoo /ˈbæliˌhuː/ *noun* [*noncount*] *informal* : talk or writing that is designed to get people excited or interested in something • Despite all of the *ballyhoo* [=*hype*], the group's new album is terrible.
– **ballyhoo** *verb* **-hoos**; **-hooed**; **-hoo·ing** [+ *obj*] • a much *ballyhooed* new album

balm /ˈbɑːm/ *noun, pl* **balms**
1 [*count, noncount*] : an oily substance that has a pleasant smell and that is used for healing, smoothing, or protecting the skin
2 [*singular*] : something that gives comfort or support • Art can be a *balm* to the soul. • She shows that laughter is a *balm* for difficult times.

balmy /ˈbɑːmi/ *adj* **balm·i·er**; **-est**
1 *of air, weather, etc.* : warm, calm, and pleasant • *balmy* [=*mild*] summer air • a *balmy* evening
2 *chiefly US, informal* : crazy or foolish • a *balmy* [=(*Brit*) *barmy*] idea that no one took seriously

ba·lo·ney /bəˈlouni/ *noun* [*noncount*]
1 *informal* : foolish words or ideas : NONSENSE • Don't believe all of that *baloney.* • He's been telling you a bunch/load of *baloney.* [=*hogwash, balderdash*] — sometimes used as an interjection. • *Baloney!* You've never been to the North Pole.
2 *US* : BOLOGNA • a *baloney* sandwich

bal·sa /ˈbɑːlsə/ *noun* [*noncount*] : the very light wood of a tropical American tree

bal·sam /ˈbɑːlsəm/ *noun* [*noncount*] : an oily substance with a pleasant smell that comes from different kinds of plants

balsam fir *noun, pl* ~ **firs** [*count*] : a small American evergreen tree

bal·sam·ic vinegar /bɑlˈsæmɪk-/ *noun* [*noncount*] : a type of Italian vinegar that has a dark color and a sweet taste

bal·us·ter /ˈbæləstɚ/ *noun, pl* **-ters** [*count*] : a short post that helps support a rail in a balustrade or similar structure

bal·us·trade /ˈbæləˌstreɪd/ *noun, pl* **-trades** [*count*] : a kind of low wall that is placed at the sides of staircases, bridges, etc., and that is made of a row of short posts topped by a long rail

bam /ˈbæm/ *noun, pl* **bams** [*count*] *informal* : a sudden loud noise • We heard a loud *bam.* — often used as an interjection to show that something has hit something or has happened suddenly • I was driving along when, *bam,* I hit a pothole. • Everything was fine, and then *bam,* the electricity went out.

bam·boo /bæmˈbuː/ *noun, pl* **-boos** : a tall plant with hard hollow stems that are used for building and to make furniture, tools, etc. [*noncount*] *Bamboo* grows in the grove near the house. [*count*] We cut down some *bamboos.*
– **bamboo** *adj* • The house is full of *bamboo* furniture. • The recipe is prepared with ***bamboo shoots.*** [=young bamboo plants]

bam·boo·zle /bæmˈbuːzəl/ *verb* **-boo·zles**; **-boo·zled**; **-boo·zling** [+ *obj*] *informal* : to trick or confuse (someone) • The salesperson *bamboozled* [=*deceived*] us into getting a more expensive item than we had planned to buy. • The quarterback was thoroughly *bamboozled* [=*confused*] by the defense.

[1]**ban** /ˈbæn/ *verb* **bans**; **banned**; **ban·ning** [+ *obj*]
1 : to forbid people from using (something) : to say that something cannot be used or done • The school *banned* that book for many years. • The city has *banned* smoking in all public buildings. • The drug was *banned* a decade ago. • The use of cell phones is *banned* in the restaurant.
2 : to forbid (someone) from doing or being part of something — usually + *from* • They *banned* [=*barred*] him *from* entering the building. = He was *banned from* entering the building. • She was *banned from* the team because of drug use.

[2]**ban** *noun, pl* **bans** [*count*] : an official rule saying that people are not allowed to use or do something • The city has imposed a smoking *ban* in all public buildings. — often + *on* • She challenged the *ban on* smoking. • They lifted the *ban on* the drug.

ba·nal /bəˈnæl, bəˈnɑːl, ˈbeɪnəl/ *adj* [*more* ~; *most* ~] : boring or ordinary : not interesting • He made some *banal* remarks about the weather. • The writing was *banal* but the story was good.

ba·nal·i·ty /bəˈnæləti/ *noun, pl* **-ties**
1 [*count*] : something that is boring or ordinary • The trip offers an escape from the *banalities* of daily life.; ***especially*** : an uninteresting statement : a banal remark • We exchanged *banalities* about the weather.
2 [*noncount*] : the quality of being ordinary or banal • The writing never rose above *banality.*

ba·nana /bəˈnænə, *Brit* bəˈnɑːnə/ *noun, pl* **-nan·as** [*count, noncount*] : a long curved fruit with a thick peel that is yellow when it is ripe • a bunch of *bananas* • peel a *banana* • (*US*) a ***banana peel*** = (*Brit*) a ***banana skin*** ✧ In British English *banana skin* is used figuratively to describe a foolish or embarrassing mistake or failure. • a director who has ***slipped on a banana skin*** [=who has failed in an embarrassing way] in her latest film — see color picture on page C5; see also SECOND BANANA

banana republic *noun, pl* ~ **-lics** [*count*] *disapproving + sometimes offensive* : a small, weak country usually in a tropical area

ba·nan·as /bəˈnænəz, *Brit* bəˈnɑːnəz/ *adj, not used before a noun, informal* : CRAZY • If you ask me, that guy is *bananas.* [=*nuts*] • You're ***driving me bananas*** [=*driving me crazy*] with all those questions. • All the noise *drove me bananas.*
go bananas *informal* : to become very excited or angry • The crowd *went bananas* [=*went crazy*] when the concert began.

banana split *noun, pl* ~ **splits** [*count*] : a dessert made with ice cream served on a sliced banana and usually covered with sweet sauces, fruits, nuts, and whipped cream

[1]**band** /ˈbænd/ *noun, pl* **bands** [*count*]
1 : a usually small group of musicians who play popular music together • The *band's* drummer is also the lead singer. • a rock-and-roll *band* • a jazz *band* — compare ORCHESTRA; see also BIG BAND, BRASS BAND, GARAGE BAND, MARCHING BAND, ONE-MAN BAND
2 : a group of people or animals • A *band* of scientists ques-

tioned the theory. • She photographed a *band* of gorillas. • a *band* of hunters from the tribe

3 : a flat, straight piece of material (such as plastic or metal) that forms a circle around something • A *band* of plastic holds the lid on the container. • They placed a metal *band* with an identification number on the bird's leg. • She lost her ***wedding band***. [=*wedding ring*] — see also ARMBAND, RUBBER BAND, SWEATBAND, WAISTBAND

4 : a strip of something that is different from what is around it : a thick line • The bird has black *bands* above its eyes. • The dress has an embroidered *band* at the hem. — often + *of* • There is a *band of* white near the hem of the dress. • A *band of* thunderstorms crossed the area late last night. • They left a narrow *band of* grass growing near the street.

5 *technical* **:** a range of frequencies over which radio signals are broadcast • The radio station broadcasts on the AM *band*.

6 *Brit* **:** a range or group between a lower and an upper limit : BRACKET • People in younger age *bands* may be in higher or lower tax *bands*.

to beat the band *US, informal* **:** in a very forceful or obvious way • He was snoring *to beat the band*. [=he was snoring very loudly]

[2]**band** *verb* **bands; band·ed; band·ing**

band together [*phrasal verb*] **:** to form a group in order to do or achieve something • They *banded together* for protection. • If we *band together*, we can meet the deadline.

[1]**ban·dage** /ˈbændɪʤ/ *noun, pl* **-dag·es** [*count*] **:** a covering (such as a strip of cloth) that protects or supports part of the body that has been hurt • He wrapped a *bandage* around his knee. • She put a *bandage* on/over the cut.

[2]**bandage** *verb* **-dag·es; -daged; -dag·ing** [+ *obj*] **:** to cover or wrap (something) with a bandage • She *bandaged* (up) their wounds. • He arrived with a *bandaged* ankle.

bandage

[1]**Band–Aid** /ˈbændˈeɪd/ *trademark* — used for a small bandage

[2]**Band–Aid** *adj, always used before a noun, disapproving* **:** able to help or improve something only for a short period of time • a *Band-Aid* solution to the problem

ban·dan·na *also* **ban·dana** /bænˈdænə/ *noun, pl* **-dan·nas** *also* **-dan·as** [*count*] **:** a square piece of cloth that is used as a head covering or worn around the neck

B and B *noun, pl* **B and Bs** [*count*] **:** BED-AND-BREAKFAST • We stayed at a nice *B and B* near the beach.

band·ed /ˈbændəd/ *adj* **:** having or marked by narrow strips of different color : having or marked by bands • a hawk with a *banded* tail • a *banded* rock

ban·dit /ˈbændət/ *noun, pl* **-dits** [*count*] **:** a criminal who attacks and steals from travelers and who is often a member of a group of criminals • They were two of the most famous *bandits* [=*outlaws, robbers*] of the 19th century. — see also ONE-ARMED BANDIT

– ban·dit·ry /ˈbændətri/ *noun* [*noncount*] • They were charged with *banditry* and smuggling.

band·lead·er /ˈbændˌliːdɚ/ *noun, pl* **-ers** [*count*] **:** a person who leads a band of musicians; *especially* **:** the leader of a band that plays jazz or dance music

band·mas·ter /ˈbændˌmæstɚ, *Brit* ˈbændˌmɑːstə/ *noun, pl* **-ers** [*count*] **:** BANDLEADER; *especially* **:** the leader of a brass band or a military band

ban·do·lier *or* **ban·do·leer** /ˌbændəˈliɚ/ *noun, pl* **-liers** *or* **-leers** [*count*] **:** a belt that is worn over the shoulder and across the body and that holds bullets

band saw *noun, pl* **~ saws** [*count*] **:** a type of powered saw that is used especially for making curved cuts in wood

bands·man /ˈbændzmən/ *noun, pl* **-men** [*count*] **:** a musician who plays in a brass band or military band

band·stand /ˈbændˌstænd/ *noun, pl* **-stands** [*count*]

1 : a covered outdoor platform on which a band or orchestra plays

2 *US* **:** a raised indoor platform on which a band or orchestra plays

band·wag·on /ˈbændˌwægən/ *noun, pl* **-ons** [*count*] **:** a popular activity, effort, cause, etc., that attracts growing support — usually singular • trying to get/keep a political *bandwagon* rolling • Local leaders ***jumped on the bandwagon*** in support of the legislation. • Many companies are ***getting/climbing on the bandwagon*** and offering flexible schedules to their employees.

band·width /ˈbændˌwɪdθ/ *noun, pl* **-widths** *technical* **:** a measurement of the ability of an electronic communications device or system (such as a computer network) to send and receive information [*count*] The modem has a *bandwidth* of 56 kilobits per second. [*noncount*] Graphics use more *bandwidth* than text does.

ban·dy /ˈbændi/ *verb* **-dies; -died; -dy·ing**

bandy about *also* ***bandy around*** [*phrasal verb*] ***bandy (something) about/around*** *or* ***bandy about/around (something)*** **:** to discuss or mention (something) in a casual or informal way • The candidate hasn't chosen a running mate yet, but some names have been *bandied about*. • The idea had been *bandied about* several years earlier.

bandy words *old-fashioned* **:** to say angry words in an argument : ARGUE • I don't want to *bandy words* with you.

bane /ˈbeɪn/ *noun* [*singular*] **:** a cause of trouble, annoyance, or unhappiness — usually used in the phrase ***the bane of*** • The ugly school uniforms were *the bane of* the students' lives. • She was *the bane of* my existence. [=she made my life very unhappy, difficult, etc.]

bane·ful /ˈbeɪnfəl/ *adj, formal + literary* **:** causing destruction or serious damage : bad or evil • The legislation could have a *baneful* effect on the poor. • the *baneful* consequences of war

[1]**bang** /ˈbæŋ/ *verb* **bangs; banged; bang·ing**

1 a [+ *obj*] **:** to cause or allow (something, such as part of your body) to hit something in a way that makes a loud noise • He accidentally *banged* his knee against the door. • He *banged* [=*bumped, struck*] his head getting out of the car. • She fell and *banged* her elbow. • She *banged* her fist on the table. • He *banged* his empty glass on the counter. **b :** to hit (something or someone) in a way that makes a loud noise [+ *obj*] His knee accidentally *banged* the door. • The chair fell over and *banged* the wall. [*no obj*] — usually + *into* or *against* • His knee accidentally *banged into* the door. • I thought the door was open and *banged* [=*bumped*] right *into* it. • The bird *banged into/against* the window. • One of the other players *banged into* her, knocking her to the ground.

2 : to use your hand or a tool to beat or hit (something) in a way that makes a loud noise [+ *obj*] He *banged* the drum. • She *banged* the table with her fist. [*no obj*] — + *on* • He *banged on* the drum. • She *banged on* the table. • Who is *banging* [=*pounding*] *on* the door? — see also *bang the drum for* at [1]DRUM

3 [*no obj*] **:** to make a sudden loud noise • I could hear the screen door *bang* [=*slam*] as he left. • The window suddenly *banged* shut. • The pipes *banged* as the heat came on.

4 [+ *obj*] *informal + offensive* **:** to have sex with (someone)

bang away [*phrasal verb*] *US, informal* **:** to work hard at something • We have to keep *banging away* if we want to finish on time. — often + *at* • The students are *banging away at* their homework.

bang heads together *informal* **:** to use angry or forceful methods to control or punish people • I am going to go in there and *bang* their *heads together* if they don't start behaving.

bang on about [*phrasal verb*] ***bang on about (something)*** *Brit, informal* **:** to talk about (something) repeatedly or for a long time • She's always *banging on about* [=*going on about*] the importance of a good diet.

bang out [*phrasal verb*] ***bang out (something)*** *or* ***bang (something) out*** *informal* **1 :** to produce (something) quickly • He *banged out* the speech in just a few hours. • The two sides are trying to *bang out* an agreement. **2 :** to play (a song, melody, etc.) loudly on a piano • She carelessly *banged out* a few melodies on the piano.

bang up [*phrasal verb*] **1** ***bang up (something or someone)*** *or* ***bang (something or someone) up*** *US, informal* **:** to injure or damage (something or someone) • She *banged up* [=*hurt*] her knee. • He *banged up* the car. • He was pretty badly *banged up* [=*injured*] in the accident. **2** ***bang up (someone)*** *or* ***bang (someone) up*** *Brit slang* **:** to put (someone) in prison • He got *banged up* [=*locked up*] for robbery.

[2]**bang** *noun, pl* **bangs**

1 a [*count*] **:** a sudden loud noise • I heard a loud *bang*. • The door slammed shut with a *bang*. **b** — used as an interjection to imitate a loud noise (such as the sound of a gun being fired) • "*Bang, bang*! You're dead." ✧ In British English the informal phrase ***bang goes*** is used when you are saying that something you wanted or planned has become impossible. •

The airport closed and *bang went* our holiday plans! [=our holiday plans were ruined because the airport closed]
2 [*count*] : a hard hit or blow • She got a nasty *bang* [=*bump*] on her head.
bang for the buck *also* ***bang for your buck*** *US, informal* — used to describe how much value is received when money is spent • This restaurant offers people the most *bang for the buck.* [=offers more than other restaurants for the same price] • He claims that the new stadium offers taxpayers too little *bang for the buck.* [=that the new stadium is not worth the tax money that is being spent on it]
get a bang out of *US, informal* : to enjoy (something) very much • You'll *get a bang out of* [=you'll like] this story. • She *got a bang out of* [=*got a kick out of*] watching her grandson at the beach.
with a bang : in a sudden and exciting way • The movie begins/starts *with a bang* and never slows down.

³bang *adv, Brit, informal* : exactly or directly • There it was—*bang* [=*right*] in front of us! • The show began *bang* on time. — see also *bang to rights* at ³RIGHT
bang on *Brit, informal* : exactly right • His explanation was *bang on.* [=*spot-on*]

bang·er /ˈbæŋɚ/ *noun, pl* **-ers** [*count*] *Brit, informal*
1 : SAUSAGE • We ordered ***bangers and mash.*** [=sausages and mashed potatoes]
2 : FIRECRACKER
3 : an old car that is in poor condition : JALOPY

ban·gle /ˈbæŋgəl/ *noun, pl* **ban·gles** [*count*] : a large stiff ring that is worn as jewelry around the arm, wrist, or ankle • She wore plastic *bangles* on both wrists. — see color picture on page C11

bangs /ˈbæŋz/ *noun* [*plural*] *US* : the front section of a person's hair when it is cut short and worn over the forehead • She wears her hair in *bangs.* = She has *bangs.* • She pushed her *bangs* off her forehead. — called also (*Brit*) *fringe*; see picture at HAIR

bang–up /ˈbæŋˌʌp/ *adj, always used before a noun, US, informal* : very good or excellent • We had a *bang-up* [=*fine, first-rate*] time at the party. • She did ***a bang-up job*** on/with the presentation.

ban·ish /ˈbænɪʃ/ *verb* **-ish·es; -ished; -ish·ing** [+ *obj*]
1 : to force (someone) to leave a country as punishment : EXILE • He was *banished* for life. • The dictator *banished* anyone who opposed him.
2 : to send (someone or something) away — often + *from* or *to* • He was *banished from* court. • They want to *banish* her *from* the sport. • She *banished* the dogs *to* the basement during the party. • The reporters were *banished to* another room.
3 : to cause (something) to go away : to get rid of (something) • His assurances *banished* [=*alleviated*] our fears. • She tried to *banish* all thoughts of him from her mind. [=she tried not to think about him] • They *banished* [=*eliminated*] red meat from their diet.
– ban·ish·ment /ˈbænɪʃmənt/ *noun* [*noncount*]

ban·is·ter *also* **ban·nis·ter** /ˈbænəstɚ/ *noun, pl* **-ters** [*count*] : a structure like a fence with a bar on top that is built along the side of a set of stairs • The children love to slide down the *banister.* • She held the *banister* tightly. — sometimes plural in British English • She held the *banisters* tightly.

ban·jo /ˈbænʤoʊ/ *noun, pl* **-jos** [*count*] : a musical instrument like a small guitar with a round body, a long neck, and four or five strings • I'm learning to play the *banjo.* = (*US*) I'm learning to play *banjo.* • a *banjo* player

¹bank /ˈbæŋk/ *noun, pl* **banks** [*count*]
1 : a business where people keep their money, borrow money, etc., or the building where such a business operates • Our paychecks are deposited in/into the *bank* automatically. • How much money do you have in the *bank*? • My cousin works in/at a *bank.* • I have to go to the *bank* today. — often used before another noun • *bank* customers • How much money do you have in your *bank* account? — see also SAVINGS BANK
2 : a small closed container in which money is saved • She saves all her change in a small *bank* on her desk. — see also PIGGY BANK
3 : a place where a particular thing is stored until it is needed • information stored in a computer's memory *banks* — see also BLOOD BANK, SPERM BANK
break the bank : to be very expensive or too expensive : to cost a lot of money — usually used in negative statements • Buy a car that's dependable but won't *break the bank.*
laugh all the way to the bank see ¹LAUGH
— compare ³BANK, ⁵BANK

²bank *verb* **banks; banked; bank·ing**
1 [*no obj*] : to have money in a bank : to use the services of a bank • We *bank* locally. • Where do you *bank*? [=which bank do you use?]
2 [+ *obj*] : to put (something, such as money) in a bank • *bank* a check
bank on [*phrasal verb*] ***bank on (something)*** : to feel confident or sure about (something) • We're *banking on* [=*counting on*] fair weather for the trip. • She may support us, but don't *bank on* [=*rely on, depend on*] it.
– compare ⁴BANK

³bank *noun, pl* **banks** [*count*]
1 : the higher ground that is along the edge of a river, stream, etc. • We sat on the *bank* of the river [=on the riverbank] to watch the boats. • The stream overflowed its *banks.*
2 a : a steep slope : the side of a hill • We planted bushes all along the *bank* in front of the house. • They climbed a steep *bank* to get to the terrace. — see also SANDBANK **b** : a small hill that is built next to a road along a curve in order to make driving on that section of road safer
3 : a thick mass of clouds or fog • a fog *bank* • A *bank* of dark clouds entered the region. — see also SNOWBANK
– compare ¹BANK, ⁵BANK

⁴bank *verb* **banks; banked; banking**
1 : to cause (something, such as an airplane) to tilt or lean to one side when turning [+ *obj*] The pilot *banked* the plane (to the right/left) and then leveled it out to land. [*no obj*] The pilot/plane *banked* (right/left) and then leveled out to land. • The motorcycle *banked* steeply as it went around the curve.
2 [+ *obj*] *US* : to cause (something, such as a ball) to bounce off a surface • The basketball player *banked* the ball off the backboard.
3 [+ *obj*] : to form (something) into a pile — often + *up* • *banking* sand *up* along the river to prevent flooding
4 [+ *obj*] : to cover (a fire) with fresh fuel in order to make it continue to burn — often + *up* • *bank up* a campfire
– compare ²BANK

⁵bank *noun, pl* **banks** [*count*] : a group or series of objects that are arranged close together in a row — usually + *of* • There is a *bank of* vending machines in the basement. • Several *banks of* lights hung above the stage. • a *bank of* file cabinets — compare ¹BANK, ³BANK

bank·able /ˈbæŋkəbəl/ *adj* [*more* ~; *most* ~] : certain to make a profit — used of people in the movie business • a *bankable* director [=a director who makes movies that earn a profit] • She is one of Hollywood's most *bankable* stars. [=if she is in a movie, the movie will make money]

bank·book /ˈbæŋkˌbʊk/ *noun, pl* **-books** [*count*] : a book in which a bank customer keeps a record of the money added to and taken from a bank account — called also *passbook*

bank card /ˈbæŋkˌkɑɚd/ *noun, pl* ~ **cards** [*count*]
1 *US* : a card (such as a credit card or debit card) that you get from your bank and that you use to pay for things or to get money from an ATM
2 *Brit* : CHEQUE CARD

bank draft *noun, pl* ~ **drafts** [*count*] : a check from one bank to another bank for money to be paid to a particular person or organization ✧ In order to write a bank draft to another bank, a bank must have money in an account at that bank.

bank·er /ˈbæŋkɚ/ *noun, pl* **-ers** [*count*] : a person who owns a bank or who has an important job in a bank

banker's card *noun, pl* ~ **cards** [*count*] *Brit* : CHEQUE CARD

bank holiday *noun, pl* ~ **-days** [*count*] *Brit* : LEGAL HOLIDAY

banking *noun* [*noncount*] : the business of operating a bank • They are both in *banking.* • He chose *banking* as a career. • the *banking* industry

banknote *noun, pl* **-notes** [*count*] : a piece of paper money : NOTE • a $10 *banknote*

bank rate *noun, pl* ~ **rates** [*count*] : the rate of interest that is charged by the banks in a particular country ✧ The bank rate is set by a country's main bank.

¹bank·roll /ˈbæŋkˌroʊl/ *verb* **-rolls; -rolled; -rol·ling** [+ *obj*] *chiefly US, informal* : to supply money for (a business, project, person, etc.) • His parents *bankrolled* [=*paid for*] his college education. • The company is *bankrolling* [=*financing*] the film.

²bankroll *noun* [*singular*] *chiefly US* : a supply of money •

B

They started the business with a fairly small *bankroll.*

[1]**bank·rupt** /ˈbæŋkˌrʌpt/ *adj*
1 : unable to pay debts ▪ a *bankrupt* company ▪ The lawsuit could leave them *bankrupt.* ▪ The company ***went bankrupt*** [=became unable to pay its debts]
2 — used to say that someone or something completely lacks a good or desired quality ▪ After 10 years in a bad marriage, she was *bankrupt* emotionally. [=empty of emotions; not able to feel emotions] ▪ a ***morally bankrupt*** politician [=an immoral politician; a politician who has no morals]

[2]**bankrupt** *verb* **-rupts; -rupt·ed; -rupt·ing** [+ *obj*] **:** to cause (a person, business, etc.) to be unable to pay debts **:** to make (someone or something) bankrupt ▪ Several risky deals *bankrupted* the company.

[3]**bankrupt** *noun, pl* **-rupts** [*count*] **:** a person, business, etc., that is unable to pay debts ▪ As a lawyer, she specialized in working with *bankrupts.*

bank·rupt·cy /ˈbæŋkˌrʌptsi/ *noun, pl* **-cies**
1 a [*noncount*] **:** the condition of being bankrupt **:** a condition of financial failure caused by not having the money that you need to pay your debts ▪ The company is facing *bankruptcy.* ▪ The company ***filed for bankruptcy*** [=officially asked to be legally recognized as bankrupt] in July. ▪ He ***declared bankruptcy*** [=formally said that he was bankrupt in a legal document] ▪ The company is now ***in bankruptcy*** [=has been officially recognized as bankrupt] ▪ The company was forced ***into bankruptcy*** — often used before another noun ▪ *bankruptcy* court/law ▪ a *bankruptcy* judge/lawyer **b** [*count*] **:** an occurrence in which a person, business, etc., goes bankrupt ▪ The number of *bankruptcies* was especially high last year.
2 [*noncount*] **:** the condition of completely lacking a good or desired quality ▪ Critics view the decision as an example of moral/ethical *bankruptcy* on the part of the administration.

[1]**ban·ner** /ˈbænɚ/ *noun, pl* **-ners** [*count*]
1 a : a large strip of cloth with a design, picture, or writing on it ▪ A *banner* was hung over the street advertising the local theater production. ▪ *Banners* were carried by members of each group marching in the parade. — often used figuratively ▪ Both candidates are running ***under the banner of*** "no new taxes." [=both candidates are using "no new taxes" as a slogan] ▪ a group of scientists gathering together *under the banner of* NASA [=in a meeting/event set up by NASA] ▪ changes made *under the banner of* "restoring order" [=for the officially stated purpose of restoring order] **b** *literary* **:** FLAG ▪ The Star-Spangled *Banner*
2 : words printed in large letters at the top of a newspaper's front page under the name of the newspaper — called also *banner headline*
3 : an advertisement that is across the top of a page on the World Wide Web — called also *banner ad*

[2]**banner** *adj, always used before a noun, US* **:** unusually good ▪ It was a *banner* year for the sales department. ▪ The team had a *banner* season last year.

bannister *variant spelling of* BANISTER

banns /ˈbænz/ *noun* [*plural*] **:** a public statement which announces that two people are going to be married ▪ The *banns* (of marriage) were posted in the church.

ban·quet /ˈbæŋkwət/ *noun, pl* **-quets** [*count*] **:** a formal dinner for many people usually to celebrate a special event ▪ They held a *banquet* in his honor. — often used before another noun ▪ a *banquet* hall/room/table
– ban·quet·ing /ˈbæŋkwətɪŋ/ *adj, always used before a noun, chiefly Brit* ▪ a *banqueting* hall/room/table

ban·shee /ˈbænˌʃiː/ *noun, pl* **-shees** [*count*] **:** a female spirit in Irish and Scottish stories who cries loudly to warn people that someone is going to die soon ▪ I heard someone wailing/screaming ***like a banshee***

ban·tam /ˈbæntəm/ *noun, pl* **-tams** [*count*] **:** a kind of small chicken

ban·tam·weight /ˈbæntəmˌweɪt/ *noun, pl* **-weights** [*count*] **:** a fighter in a class of boxers who weigh from 112 to 119 pounds (51 to 54 kilograms) — often used before another noun ▪ He won the *bantamweight* title. ▪ a *bantamweight* fighter

ban·ter /ˈbæntɚ/ *noun* [*noncount*] **:** talk in which people make jokes about each other in a friendly way ▪ two friends trading/exchanging lively/witty *banter* (with each other) ▪ I enjoyed hearing their good-natured *banter.*
– banter *verb* **-ters; -tered; -ter·ing** [*no obj*] ▪ two friends *bantering* with each other

ban·yan /ˈbænjən/ *noun, pl* **-yans** [*count*] **:** an Indian tree with long branches that send roots down to the ground forming secondary trunks — called also *banyan tree*

banyan

bap /ˈbæp/ *noun, pl* **baps** [*count*] *Brit* **:** BUN 1

bap·tism /ˈbæpˌtɪzəm/ *noun, pl* **-tisms :** a Christian ceremony in which a small amount of water is placed on a person's head or in which a person's body is briefly placed under water ✧ A baptism officially makes someone a member of the Christian Church. [*count*] There were over 100 *baptisms* at our church last year. [*noncount*] He received the sacrament of *baptism* as an infant. — often used figuratively ▪ The interview was a *baptism* into journalism for the young writer. [=it was the young writer's first experience as a journalist] ✧ A ***baptism of fire*** or (*chiefly US*) ***baptism by fire*** is a first experience that is very difficult or painful, such as the first time that soldiers are in a battle. ▪ He described his troop's *baptism of fire* on the front lines. ▪ Covering the disaster was a *baptism by fire* for the young reporter.
– bap·tis·mal /bæpˈtʰɪzməl/ *adj, always used before a noun* ▪ The priest stood at the *baptismal* font. ▪ a *baptismal* certificate

Bap·tist /ˈbæpˌtɪst/ *noun, pl* **-tists** [*count*] **:** a member of a Christian church in which members are baptized only as adults
– Baptist *adj* ▪ He attends the *Baptist* church. ▪ a *Baptist* preacher/service

bap·tize *also Brit* **bap·tise** /ˈbæpˌtaɪz, bæpˈtaɪz/ *verb* **-tiz·es; -tized; -tiz·ing** [+ *obj*]
1 : to perform the ceremony of baptism for (someone) ▪ The priest *baptized* the baby. ▪ She was *baptized* at the age of 20.
2 : to officially make someone a member of a specified Christian church through the ceremony of baptism — usually used as *(be) baptized* ▪ She *was baptized* a Catholic/Methodist when she was a teenager.
3 : to give (someone) a name through the ceremony of baptism — usually used as *(be) baptized* ▪ He *was baptized* [=*christened*] "John" when he was two months old.

[1]**bar** /ˈbɑɚ/ *noun, pl* **bars**
1 [*count*] **a :** a building or room where alcoholic drinks and sometimes food are served ▪ We went to a *bar* for a drink. — see also SPORTS BAR, TIKI BAR **b :** a counter where alcoholic drinks are served ▪ We sat at the restaurant's *bar* while we were waiting for a table. — see also CASH BAR, OPEN BAR, WET BAR **c :** a building or room where a particular food or drink is served ▪ a seafood *bar* ▪ a juice/coffee *bar* — see also SALAD BAR, SNACK BAR
2 [*count*] **:** a straight piece of metal, wood, etc., that is used as a tool, as part of a structure, or to keep people from entering or leaving through a door or window ▪ There were *bars* across all the windows. ▪ The door was secured with an iron *bar.* ▪ The pole-vaulter narrowly cleared the *bar.* [=the long bar that is set at a specific height and that a jumper tries to go over] ✧ In U.S. English, *bar* is used figuratively in phrases like ***raise/lower the bar*** and ***set the bar higher/lower*** to refer to changing the standard that is used to judge whether someone or something is good, successful, etc. ▪ The company's new software *raises the bar* for its competitors. [=the company's new software is very good and its competitors will have to produce better software to compete with it] ▪ Critics say that he has *lowered the bar* on what is considered acceptable behavior by politicians. [=he has caused people to accept worse behavior by politicians] — see also CROSSBAR, CROWBAR, PARALLEL BARS, UNEVEN BARS
3 [*count*] **:** a solid piece of something that is shaped like a rectangle ▪ She bought a chocolate/candy *bar.* ▪ a *bar* of soap
4 [*count*] **:** a straight line, stripe, or section that is longer than it is wide ▪ The bird's tail has an alternating series of white and black *bars.* [=*bands*] ▪ a ***menu bar*** [=a narrow section that is across the screen in a computer program and that shows the names of available menus] — see also BAR CODE, BAR GRAPH, TASK BAR, TOOLBAR
5 [*count*] *formal* **:** something that makes it difficult or impossible to do or achieve something — + *to* ▪ His poor attitude was a *bar to* his success. [=his poor attitude prevented him from succeeding]
6 ***the bar*** **a** *US* **:** the profession of a lawyer ▪ She is a member of *the bar.* [=she is a lawyer] ▪ the American *Bar* Association ▪ She has been ***called to the bar*** [=she has become a law-

yer] **b** *or* ***the Bar*** *Brit* : the profession of a barrister **c** *US* : the test that a person must pass in order to be a lawyer • She passed *the bar* on her first try. • *the bar* exam/examination

7 [*count*] *music* **a** : a line in written music that shows where a measure begins **b** : the beats between two bars in a piece of music • I'm not sure I know that song. Can you hum a few *bars*? [=*measures*]

behind bars : in jail • He has been *behind bars* for 10 years.

tend bar *US* : to work as a bartender : to prepare and serve drinks at a bar • He *tends bar* at the restaurant.

[2]**bar** *verb* **bars; barred; bar·ring** [+ *obj*]

1 : to put a bar or a set of bars in front of a door, window, etc., so that people cannot go in or out of it • He *barred* the door as soon as he got in. • All the windows and doors were *barred*. • a *barred* window

2 : to put something in a road, path, etc., so that people cannot get by • A herd of goats was *barring* the road. • obstacles *barring* our way

3 a : to prevent or forbid (someone) *from* doing something • Nothing *barred* them *from* meeting together. • The judge will *bar* the jurors *from* talking to reporters. • A federal court has *barred* the group *from* using the name. • Reporters were *barred* [=*excluded*] *from* the meeting. [=reporters were not allowed to go to the meeting] **b** : to prevent or forbid (something) • The decision *bars* the possibility of additional development in the area. • forms of punishment *barred* by the Constitution

no holds barred see [2]HOLD

[3]**bar** *prep*

1 — used in the phrase ***bar none*** to emphasize that a statement is completely true • She is the brightest student I've ever known, *bar none*. [=I have never known a student who is brighter than she is]

2 *Brit* : except for : BARRING • They have lost every match, *bar* one.

barb /ˈbɑɚb/ *noun, pl* **barbs** [*count*]

1 : a sharp point that sticks out and backward from the point of an arrow, a fishhook, etc.

2 : a clever insult or criticism • She directed/aimed a few *barbs* at reporters who had hounded her. • The candidates exchanged *barbs* during the debate.

bar·bar·i·an /bɑɚˈberijən/ *noun, pl* **-ans** [*count*]

1 : a member of a violent or uncivilized group of people especially in past times • The book describes tribes of *barbarians* massing on the borders of the Roman Empire. • The city was invaded by *barbarians*. — often used before another noun • *Barbarian* tribes invaded from the north. • a *barbarian* invasion/attack

2 : a person who does not behave in a proper way : a rude or uneducated person • The students behaved like *barbarians*. • He is well-spoken and polite but his father is a *barbarian*.

bar·bar·ic /bɑɚˈberɪk/ *adj*

1 : of or relating to barbarians • *Barbaric* tribes invaded the area.

2 [*more ~; most ~*] **a** : very rude or offensive : not polite or proper • His table manners are *barbaric*. **b** : very cruel • They considered the custom *barbaric*. • The treatment of the prisoners was positively *barbaric*.

– bar·bar·ic·al·ly /bɑɚˈberɪkli/ *adv*

bar·ba·rism /ˈbɑɚbəˌrɪzəm/ *noun, pl* **-risms**

1 : cruel and violent behavior [*noncount*] The *barbarism* of his dictatorship cannot be ignored. [*count*] Such *barbarisms* cannot be tolerated.

2 [*noncount*] : very rude behavior • acts of social *barbarism*

bar·bar·i·ty /bɑɚˈberəti/ *noun, pl* **-ties**

1 [*noncount*] : extreme cruelty : a very cruel and violent quality • The *barbarity* of the attack was horrifying. • The photos vividly capture the war's *barbarity*.

2 [*count*] : a cruel act • He is accused of inflicting unimaginable *barbarities* on his own people.

bar·ba·rous /ˈbɑɚbərəs/ *adj* [*more ~; most ~*]

1 : not polite or proper : very rude or offensive • His behavior was *barbarous*. • They used *barbarous* language.

2 : very cruel and violent • It was a *barbarous* [=*barbaric*] crime. • a *barbarous* custom

– bar·ba·rous·ly *adv* **– bar·ba·rous·ness** *noun* [*noncount*]

[1]**bar·be·cue** /ˈbɑɚbɪˌkjuː/ *noun, pl* **-cues**

1 [*count*] : a flat metal frame that is used to cook food over hot coals or an open fire • grill a steak on the *barbecue*

2 [*count*] : an outdoor meal or party at which food is cooked on a barbecue • We plan to have a *barbecue* for the whole family. — abbr. *BBQ*

3 [*noncount*] *chiefly US, informal* : food that has been cooked on a barbecue : barbecued food • She invited us over for some beer and *barbecue*. • He makes a ***barbecue sauce*** [=a spicy sauce that is usually eaten with barbecued food] that tastes great with chicken.

[2]**barbecue** *verb* **-cues; -cued; -cu·ing** : to cook (food) on a barbecue : to broil or roast (meat, fish, etc.) over hot coals or an open fire [+ *obj*] We *barbecued* chicken and ribs. [*no obj*] We *barbecue* often during the summer.

– barbecued *adj* • They served *barbecued* chicken/shrimp/pork at the cookout.

barbed /ˈbɑɚbd/ *adj*

1 : having a sharp point that sticks out and backward from a larger point : having a barb • a *barbed* fishhook

2 : expressing criticism in an unkind and often clever way • The candidates exchanged *barbed* comments during the debate.

barbed wire *noun* [*noncount*] : wire that has sharp points and that is often used for fences • a fence made of *barbed wire* = a *barbed-wire* fence — called also (*US*) *barbwire*

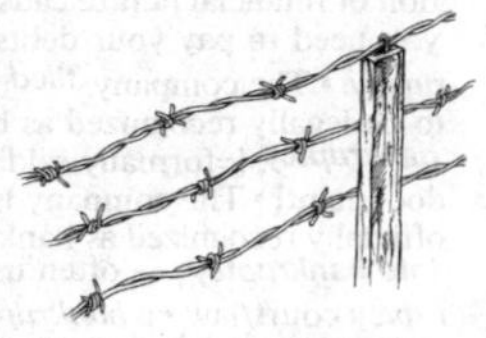
barbed wire

bar·bell /ˈbɑɚˌbɛl/ *noun, pl* **-bells** [*count*] : a metal bar with weights at each end that is used for exercise and in weight lifting — see picture at GYM

bar·ber /ˈbɑɚbɚ/ *noun, pl* **-bers** [*count*] : a person whose job is to cut men's hair • He goes to a *barber* downtown. • He went to the *barber's* [=(*chiefly US*) *barbershop*] to get a haircut.

bar·ber·shop /ˈbɑɚbɚˌʃɑːp/ *noun, pl* **-shops** [*count*] *chiefly US* : a place where a barber works

barbershop quartet *noun, pl* **~ -tets** [*count*] : a group of four male singers who sing in an old-fashioned style without instruments

bar·bie /ˈbɑɚbi/ *noun, pl* **-bies** [*count*] *chiefly Brit + Australia, informal* : [1]BARBECUE

bar·bit·u·rate /bɑɚˈbɪtʃərət/ *noun, pl* **-rates** [*count*] *medical* : any of various drugs that are used to calm people or to make them sleep

barb·wire /ˈbɑɚbˈwajɚ/ *noun* [*noncount*] *US* : BARBED WIRE • a *barbwire* fence

bar chart *noun, pl* **~ charts** [*count*] : BAR GRAPH

bar code *noun, pl* **~ codes** [*count*] : a group of thick and thin lines that is placed on a product so that a computer can get the price of the product and other information about it

50650
9 780877 799306
bar code

bard /ˈbɑɚd/ *noun, pl* **bards** [*count*] *old-fashioned + literary* : POET ✧ The poet and playwright William Shakespeare is sometimes called ***the Bard*** or ***the Bard of Avon***. • As *the Bard* says, "All the world's a stage."

[1]**bare** /ˈbeɚ/ *adj* **bar·er; bar·est**

1 a : not having a covering • There was a rug in the front room of the house, but the other floors were *bare*. • The walls were *bare*. • Do not let the *bare* wires touch. — sometimes used figuratively • He ***laid bare*** his soul. = He *laid* his soul *bare*. [=he revealed his most private thoughts and feelings] • The book is an attempt to ***lay bare*** [=*reveal, uncover*] the secrets of this very powerful political family. **b** : not covered by clothing, shoes, a hat, etc. • He covered her *bare* arms with his coat. • Her feet were *bare*. = She had *bare* feet. [=she wasn't wearing shoes or socks on her feet] • He had a glove on his left hand, but his right hand was *bare*. • His head is *bare*. [=he does not have a hat on] — see also *with your bare hands* at [1]HAND **c** : not covered by leaves, grass, trees, or plants • She likes the *bare* [=*naked*] branches of trees in the winter. • The ground was *bare* where the statue had stood for years. • The mountainside was ***laid bare*** by loggers. [=all the trees on the mountainside were cut down by loggers]

2 a : not containing anything : EMPTY • The cupboard was *bare*. • There was only one *bare* shelf. **b** : having little or no furniture • a *bare* room • Her office was pretty *bare*, having only one desk and one chair. • This is the *barest* room in the house.

3 *always used before a noun* **:** not having anything added or extra **:** including only what is most basic or needed • He only told me the *bare* facts about what happened. • We packed only the *bare* essentials for the hike. [=we packed only what we really needed for the hike] • They had only the *bare* [=*basic*] necessities (of life): food, water, and shelter. • He's lazy and only does the *bare* minimum of work. [=he does the least amount of work possible] • a *bare* majority [=the smallest possible majority] • She added the *barest* [=*smallest*] pinch of salt.

– bare•ness *noun* [*noncount*] • the *bareness* of the walls/land

[2]**bare** *verb* **bares; bared; bar•ing** [+ *obj*] **:** to remove the covering from (something) • He *bared* his chest to show the scar. • The dog growled and *bared* [=*exposed*] its teeth. • She was asked to ***bare (it) all*** for the magazine. [=she was asked to pose nude for the magazine] — sometimes used figuratively • She *bared* [=*revealed, told*] her fears to him. • He ***bared all*** [=told the whole story] in the interview. • He ***bared his soul*** to me. [=he told me his most private thoughts and feelings]

Do not confuse *bare* with *bear*.

bare•back /ˈbeɚˌbæk/ *adv* **:** without a saddle **:** on the bare back of a horse • We rode *bareback*.

– bareback *adj* • He likes *bareback* riding. • a *bareback* rider

bare bones *noun*

the bare bones **:** the most basic or important facts or parts of something • The company reduced the staff to *the bare bones*. [=the company's staff only includes people who are absolutely needed] — often + *of* • What are *the bare bones of* the story?

bare–bones *adj* [*more ~; most ~*] **:** including only what is most basic or needed • a *bare-bones* Web site • a *bare-bones* wedding ceremony • The hotel rooms are *bare-bones*.

bare•faced /ˈbeɚˈfeɪst/ *adj, always used before a noun* [*more ~; most ~*] *disapproving* **:** completely obvious • a ***barefaced lie*** • a ***barefaced liar***

bare•foot /ˈbeɚˌfʊt/ *or* **bare•foot•ed** /ˈbeɚˌfʊtəd/ *adv* **:** without shoes **:** with the feet bare • We walked *barefoot* in the stream.

– barefoot *or* **barefooted** *adj* • *barefoot* children • He was *barefoot*.

bare–hand•ed /ˈbeɚˌhændəd/ *adv* **:** with the hand or hands only **:** without using a tool, weapon, glove, etc. • She caught the ball *bare-handed*.

– bare–handed *adj* • She made a *bare-handed* catch.

bare•head•ed /ˈbeɚˈhɛdəd/ *adv* **:** without a hat **:** with the head bare • He left the house *bareheaded*.

– bareheaded *adj* • a *bareheaded* man

bare–knuck•le /ˈbeɚˈnʌkəl/ *also* **bare–knuck•led** /ˈbeɚˈnʌkəld/ *or* **bare–knuck•les** /ˈbeɚˈnʌkəlz/ *adj, always used before a noun* **:** without boxing gloves • a *bare-knuckle* fight/fighter • a *bare-knuckled* punch — often used figuratively • a *bare-knuckles* approach to doing business [=a very tough and aggressive approach to doing business] • *bare-knuckle* politics

bare•ly /ˈbeɚli/ *adv*

1 a : hardly or scarcely — used to say that something was almost not possible or almost did not happen • I *barely* recognized you with your hair cut short. • He could *barely* walk/read/write. • His voice was *barely* audible above the sound of the river. • The boat was *barely* visible off the coast. • We *barely* [=almost do not] have enough money to pay the bills. • I *barely* [=almost do not] have time to eat my lunch. • He *barely* made his flight. [=he almost was too late for his flight] **b** — used to say that someone or something only has a specified small size, age, length, etc. • The movie is (just) *barely* an hour long. • He's *barely* a teenager. • She's *barely* four feet tall. • *Barely* 50 percent of the population voted. **c** — used to say that something reached a specifed condition or happened only a short time before • The paint is *barely* dry. • They had *barely* [=*just*] set up the tents when it started to rain.

2 a : almost not at all • We *barely* spoke the entire time we were in the car. • I *barely* knew him. **b :** almost not • There are *barely* any new features in this software. • There is *barely* a difference between the two.

barf /ˈbɑɚf/ *verb* **barfs; barfed; barf•ing** [*no obj*] *US, informal* **:** VOMIT • The movie was so disgusting that it made me want to *barf*.

bar•fly /ˈbɑɚˌflaɪ/ *noun, pl* **-flies** [*count*] *US, informal* **:** a person who spends a lot of time drinking in bars

[1]**bar•gain** /ˈbɑɚgən/ *noun, pl* **-gains** [*count*]

1 : an agreement in which people or groups say they will do or give something in exchange for something else • I think everyone involved was satisfied with the *bargain* we made. • They've agreed to turn the land over to the state, and the state, as its part of the *bargain*, has agreed to keep it undeveloped. • The union is trying to ***strike a bargain*** [=reach an agreement, make a deal] with the company. • You're allowed to go to the football game tonight, but I expect you to ***keep your side of the bargain*** [=do what you agreed to do] and clean your room. — see also PLEA BARGAIN

2 : something that is bought or sold for a price which is lower than the actual value **:** something bought or sold at a good price • For that price, the suit is a (real) *bargain*. • I got a *bargain* on the plane tickets. = The plane tickets were a *bargain*. • She likes to hunt for *bargains* when she shops. — often used before another noun • *bargain* airplane tickets • The store has many items on sale at *bargain* prices.

drive a hard bargain ✧ If you *drive a hard bargain*, you do not agree easily to what other people want and are very determined to get what you want when you are discussing what will be done, especially in a business deal. • You *drive a hard bargain*, but I'll accept your terms.

in the bargain *or* ***into the bargain*** **:** in addition to what has been said **:** BESIDES • Locally grown food is fresher, and cheaper *in/into the bargain*. [=locally grown food is fresher and also cheaper]

[2]**bargain** *verb* **-gains; -gained; -gain•ing** [*no obj*] **:** to discuss an agreement or price in order to make it more appealing • The price listed is quite high, but the seller might be willing to *bargain*. • He was *bargaining* [=*haggling*] with the taxi driver over/about the fare. • Teachers are *bargaining* [=*negotiating*] for higher salaries.

bargain away [*phrasal verb*] ***bargain (something) away*** *or* ***bargain away (something)*** **:** to lose or give up (something) as part of an agreement • The employees on strike are concerned that the union will *bargain away* wage increases for other less desirable benefits.

bargain for/on [*phrasal verb*] ***bargain for/on (something)*** **:** to expect or plan on (something) • The Internet service is better than what we *bargained for*. [=better than we expected it to be] • No one *bargained for* the change in weather. = No one *bargained on* the weather changing. • They *bargained on* getting married after college. • He hadn't *bargained on* how his new position in the company would change the way people treated him. [=he was surprised by how his new position changed the way people treated him] • The job ended up being ***more than I had bargained for***. [=more difficult than I had expected] • I got *more than I bargained for* when I signed up as a volunteer. [=being a volunteer was harder than I expected]

– bar•gain•er *noun, pl* **-ers** [*count*] • He's a hard *bargainer*.

– bargaining *noun* [*noncount*] • After hours of hard *bargaining*, they came to an agreement. — often used before another noun • The larger corporation has more *bargaining* power. • They are in a good *bargaining* position. — see also COLLECTIVE BARGAINING, PLEA BARGAINING

bargain basement *noun, pl* **~ -ments** [*count*] **:** a section of a large store where products are sold at lower prices

bar•gain–base•ment /ˈbɑɚgənˈbeɪsmənt/ *adj, always used before a noun*

1 *of a price* **:** very low • I paid a *bargain-basement* price.

2 : having a low price or cost and often having poor quality • worthless *bargain-basement* products

bargaining chip *noun, pl* **~ chips** [*count*] **:** something that can be used to gain an advantage when you are trying to make a deal or an agreement • The workers used the threat of a strike as a *bargaining chip* in their negotiations for a new contract. — called also (*Brit*) *bargaining counter*

[1]**barge** /ˈbɑɚʤ/ *noun, pl* **barg•es** [*count*] **:** a large boat that has a flat bottom and that is used to carry goods in harbors and on rivers and canals

[2]**barge** *verb, always followed by an adverb or preposition* **barg•es; barged; barg•ing** [*no obj*] **:** to move or push in a fast, awkward, and often rude way • He came rushing down the stairs, *barging* into the crowd of people at the bottom. • She *barged* through the door without even knocking. • What makes him think he can *barge* in here [=enter suddenly and rudely] like that?

B

barge in on [*phrasal verb*] ***barge in on (something or someone)*** : to suddenly and rudely interrupt or disturb (something or someone) ▪ I was getting angry because she kept *barging in on* our conversation.

barge·pole /ˈbɑɚʤ͵poul/ *noun, pl* **-poles** [*count*] : a long pole that is used to guide or steer a barge
not touch (someone or something) with a bargepole see [1]TOUCH

bar graph *noun, pl* **~ graphs** [*count*] : a graph or chart that uses narrow columns of different heights to show and compare different amounts — called also *bar chart*

bar graph

bar·hop /ˈbɑɚ͵hɑp/ *verb* **-hops; -hopped; -hop·ping** [*no obj*] *US, informal* : to go to and drink at several bars in one evening ▪ They went *barhopping* downtown on Friday night.

ba·ris·ta /bəˈriːstə/ *noun, pl* **-tas** [*count*] : someone who makes and serves coffee and coffee drinks (such as cappuccino) to customers

[1]**bar·i·tone** /ˈberə͵toun/ *noun, pl* **-tones** [*count*] *music* : a man's singing voice that is higher than the voice of the bass and lower than the voice of the tenor; *also* : a singer who has such a voice ▪ He sang in his school choir as a *baritone*.

[2]**baritone** *adj, always used before a noun* : having a range that is higher than a bass and lower than a tenor ▪ a *baritone* voice ▪ a *baritone* saxophone

bar·i·um /ˈberijəm/ *noun* [*noncount*] : a chemical element that is a soft silver-white metal

[1]**bark** /ˈbɑɚk/ *verb* **barks; barked; barking**
1 [*no obj*] *of a dog* : to make a short loud sound ▪ The dog only *barks* when someone approaches the house.
2 : to shout or say (something) in a loud and angry way [+ *obj*] The captain *barked* orders/commands to the crew. ▪ "Come over at once!" he *barked* (at/to her). — often + *out* ▪ The captain *barked out* an order to the crew. [*no obj*] He was *barking* into the phone, giving orders to one of his employees. ▪ The captain *barked* at the crew.
barking up the wrong tree *informal* : trying to do something in a way that will not be successful ▪ If you are looking for money, you're *barking up the wrong tree.* [=you are asking the wrong person] ▪ She claims that researchers are *barking up the wrong tree* by focusing on conventional forms of treatment for the disease.

[2]**bark** *noun, pl* **barks** [*count*] : the short, loud sound made by a dog ▪ The dog gave a loud *bark.*; *also* : a similar sound ▪ The captain gave his orders with a sharp *bark.* ▪ The *bark* of the baby's cough woke the other children. ✧ If ***your bark is worse than your bite***, you appear to be more angry or dangerous than you really are. ▪ Don't get upset if the boss yells at you. *His bark is worse than his bite.* — compare [3]BARK, [4]BARK

[3]**bark** *noun, pl* **barks** : the outer covering of a tree [*noncount*] a piece of birch *bark* [*count*] She compared the *barks* of various trees. — compare [2]BARK, [4]BARK

[4]**bark** *or* **barque** /ˈbɑɚk/ *noun, pl* **barks** *or* **barques** [*count*] : a small sailing ship — compare [2]BARK, [3]BARK

bar·keep /ˈbɑɚ͵kiːp/ *also* **bar·keep·er** /ˈbɑɚ͵kiːpɚ/ *noun, pl* **-keeps** *also* **-keep·ers** [*count*] *US* : BARTENDER

bark·er /ˈbɑɚkɚ/ *noun, pl* **-ers** [*count*] *old-fashioned* : a person who stands at the entrance of a place where there is entertainment and tries to attract customers by shouting to them ▪ a carnival *barker*

barking *adj, Brit, informal* : BARKING MAD

barking mad *adj, Brit, informal* : completely crazy ▪ He was always rather strange, but he seems *barking mad* now.

bar·ley /ˈbɑɚli/ *noun* [*noncount*] : a kind of grain used for food and to make beer and whiskey; *also* : the plant on which this grain grows

barley sugar *noun, pl* **~ -gars** [*count, noncount*] *Brit* : a clear hard candy made from boiled sugar

barley wine *noun* [*noncount*] : a kind of strong ale

bar·maid /ˈbɑɚ͵meɪd/ *noun, pl* **-maids** [*count*] : a woman who serves drinks at a bar

bar·man /ˈbɑɚmən/ *noun, pl* **-men** /-mən/ [*count*] *chiefly Brit* : BARTENDER

bar mitz·vah /bɑɚˈmɪtsvə/ *noun, pl* **~ -vahs** [*count*] : a ceremony and celebration for a Jewish boy on his 13th birthday when he takes on the religious duties and responsibilities of an adult; *also* : a boy for whom a bar mitzvah is held — compare BAT MITZVAH

barmy /ˈbɑɚmi/ *adj* **barm·i·er; -est** [*also more ~; most ~*] *chiefly Brit, informal* : crazy or foolish ▪ a *barmy* [=(*chiefly US*) *balmy*] idea ▪ She's a little *barmy*. [=*loony*]
– bar·mi·ness *noun* [*noncount*]

barn /ˈbɑɚn/ *noun, pl* **barns** [*count*]
1 : a building on a farm that is used for storing grain and hay and for housing farm animals or equipment
2 *informal* : a large building that is usually bare and plain ▪ They live in a big *barn* of a house.

bar·na·cle /ˈbɑɚnɪkəl/ *noun, pl* **-na·cles** [*count*] : a kind of small shellfish that attaches itself to rocks and the bottoms of boats underwater
– bar·na·cled /ˈbɑɚnɪkəld/ *adj* ▪ *barnacled* rocks

barn burner *noun, pl* **~ -ers** [*count*] *US, informal* : a very exciting game, event, etc. ▪ The game should be a real *barn burner*.

barn dance *noun, pl* **~ dances** [*count*] : an informal social event at which people do traditional dances (such as square dances)

barn owl *noun, pl* **~ owls** [*count*] : a common kind of owl that nests in barns and other buildings

barn·storm /ˈbɑɚn͵stoɚm/ *verb* **-storms; -stormed; -storm·ing** *chiefly US* : to travel to different places to give speeches, perform shows, etc. [*no obj*] He spent the months leading up to the election *barnstorming* around/across the country. ▪ The national soccer team *barnstormed* through the country. [+ *obj*] They *barnstormed* the country.

barnstorming *adj, always used before a noun*
1 *chiefly US* : traveling to different places to give speeches, perform shows, etc. ▪ *barnstorming* politicians
2 *Brit* : very exciting and thrilling ▪ a *barnstorming* performance

[1]**barn·yard** /ˈbɑɚn͵jɑɚd/ *noun, pl* **-yards** [*count*] : an area of ground near a barn that usually has a fence around it

[2]**barnyard** *adj, always used before a noun*
1 : of or relating to a farm ▪ goats, pigs, and other *barnyard* animals
2 *US, informal* : not polite : somewhat crude or rude ▪ *barnyard* [=*earthy*] jokes/humor

ba·rom·e·ter /bəˈrɑːmətɚ/ *noun, pl* **-ters** [*count*]
1 : an instrument that is used to measure air pressure and predict changes in the weather
2 : something that is used to indicate or predict something ▪ The test is used as a *barometer* [=*standard*] to measure a student's reading level. ▪ Economists see housing prices as a *barometer* for inflation. [=economists use housing prices to predict inflation] — often + *of* ▪ A player's rookie season is not always a good/accurate *barometer of* his success in the league. ▪ Wealth is not a *barometer of* happiness.
– baro·met·ric /͵berəˈmetrɪk/ *adj, always used before a noun* ▪ *barometric* pressure

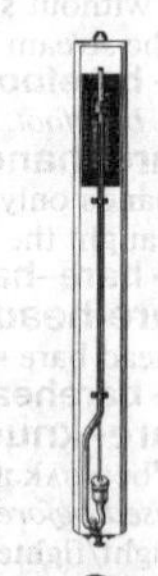

barometers

bar·on /ˈberən/ *noun, pl* **-ons** [*count*]
1 a : a man who is a member of a low rank of British nobility **b** : a man who is a member of various ranks of nobility in other countries
2 : a man who has a lot of power or influence in a particular industry ▪ a cattle/oil *baron* — see also ROBBER BARON

bar·on·ess /ˈberənəs/ *noun, pl* **-ess·es** [*count*]
1 a : a woman who is a member of a low rank of British nobility **b** : a woman who is a member of various ranks of nobility in other countries
2 : the wife or widow of a baron

bar·on·et /ˈberənət/ *noun, pl* **-ets** [*count*] : a man who is a member of the British nobility with a rank below a baron
– bar·on·et·cy /ˈberənətsi/ *noun, pl* **-cies** [*count*] ▪ He inherited the *baronetcy* [=the rank of a baronet] from his father.

ba·ro·ni·al /bəˈrounijəl/ *adj* : of or relating to a baron ▪ *baronial* privileges : suitable for a baron ▪ *baronial* [=*rich*] splendor ▪ a *baronial* estate [=a very large and impressive estate]

bar·ony /ˈberəni/ *noun, pl* **-on·ies** [*count*] : the rank of a baron ▪ He inherited the *barony* from his father.

B

ba·roque /bəˈrouk/ *adj*
1 : of or relating to a dramatic style of art and music that was common in the 17th and early 18th centuries and that featured many decorative parts and details • *baroque* paintings/music • a *baroque* cathedral • the *baroque* period
2 [*more ~; most ~*] : having many details or too many details • a somewhat *baroque* writing style • a book filled with *baroque* descriptions
– **baroque** *noun* [*noncount*] • The museum is exhibiting paintings from **the baroque**. [=the baroque period]

barque *variant spelling of* [4]BARK

bar·rack /ˈberək/ *verb* **-racks**; **-racked**; **-rack·ing**
1 *Brit* : to bother or interrupt (someone, such as a performer or speaker) by shouting comments or criticism [+ *obj*] The crowd *barracked* [=*heckled*] the visiting team. [*no obj*] The crowd *barracked* in protest as she gave her speech.
2 [*no obj*] *chiefly Australia* : to shout in support of a person or group — often + *for* • *barracking* [=*rooting, cheering*] *for* the home team
– **barracking** *noun* [*noncount*] She got a lot of *barracking* during her speech. [*singular*] She got quite a *barracking* during her speech.

bar·racks /ˈberəks/ *noun, pl* **-racks** [*count*] : a building or group of buildings in which soldiers live • The soldier was moved to a different *barracks*. • He was confined to *barracks* for insubordination.

bar·ra·cu·da /ˌberəˈkuːdə/ *noun, pl* **-da** *or* **-das** [*count*]
1 : a kind of fierce tropical fish that has strong jaws and sharp teeth • We fished for *barracuda*. — see color picture on page C8
2 *US, informal + disapproving* : someone who uses aggressive, harsh, and sometimes improper ways to achieve something • The company's lawyers are a bunch of *barracudas*.

[1]**bar·rage** /bəˈrɑːʒ, *Brit* ˈbæˌrɑːʒ/ *noun, pl* **-rag·es**
1 [*count*] : a heavy and continuous firing of weapons during a battle • The enemy laid down a *barrage* of machine-gun fire as our platoon approached the bridge. • artillery *barrages*
2 [*singular*] : a great amount of something that comes quickly and continuously — + *of* • He unleashed a *barrage of* insults. • The reports overwhelmed her with a *barrage of* questions. • a *barrage* [=*flood*] of phone calls
– compare [3]BARRAGE

[2]**barrage** *verb* **-rages**; **-raged**; **-rag·ing** [+ *obj*] *chiefly US* : to cause (someone) to receive a great amount of something : to direct a barrage of questions, comments, etc., at (someone) — usually used as *(be) barraged with* • The public *was barraged with* campaign ads in the months leading up to the election. • They *were barraged* [=*inundated, swamped*] *with* inquiries about the job. • The office *has been barraged* [=*flooded, inundated*] *with* phone calls.

[3]**bar·rage** /ˈbɑrɪʤ/ *noun, pl* **-rag·es** [*count*] : a barrier (such as a cement wall) that is built across a river or stream especially to increase the depth of water or change its direction — compare [1]BARRAGE

barred /ˈbɑəd/ *adj*
1 : covered by a bar or a set of bars • He looked out the *barred* windows of the jail.
2 : having bands or stripes of different color • a bird with a *barred* tail

[1]**bar·rel** /ˈberəl/ *noun, pl* **-rels** [*count*]
1 a : a round usually wooden container with curved sides and flat ends • Oak *barrels* are used for aging the wine. • an empty *barrel* **b** : the amount of something in a barrel • The price of oil is over 30 dollars a *barrel*. • They drank a whole *barrel* of beer. — see also PORK BARREL
2 : the part of a gun that the bullets go through when the gun is fired • the *barrel* of a gun • a rifle *barrel* — see picture at GUN; see also *lock, stock, and barrel* at [1]LOCK

barrel

a barrel of laughs *informal* : someone or something that is very funny — often used in negative statements or in an ironic way to describe someone or something that is not really funny • Several people have lost their jobs recently, so the office isn't exactly a *barrel of laughs* these days. • "Your boss is quite a kidder." "Oh yeah, he's a real *barrel of laughs*."
more fun than a barrel (full) of monkeys *US, informal + somewhat old-fashioned* : very funny and enjoyable • The ads say the movie will be *more fun than a barrel of monkeys*.
over a barrel : in a bad situation : in a situation where you are forced to do something you do not want to do • My landlord really has me *over a barrel*. I have to either pay double my rent or move somewhere else.
the bottom of the barrel see [1]BOTTOM
– **bar·reled** (*US*) *or Brit* **bar·relled** /ˈberəld/ *adj* — used in combination • a short-*barreled* shotgun [=a shotgun having a short barrel] — see also DOUBLE-BARRELED

[2]**barrel** *verb, always followed by an adverb or preposition* **-rels**; **-reled** *also* **-relled**; **-rel·ing** *also* **-rel·ling** [*no obj*] *US, informal* : to move very fast and often in an uncontrolled or dangerous way • The truck went *barreling* down Main Street. • She came running out of her office and went *barreling* past us down the hall.

bar·rel–chest·ed /ˈberəlˌʧɛstəd/ *adj, of a man* : having a large, round chest that usually suggests great strength • a big, *barrel-chested* football player

barrel organ *noun, pl* **~ -gans** [*count*] : a large musical instrument that is played by turning a handle and that was once commonly played by performers (called organ-grinders) on city streets — called also *hurdy-gurdy*

bar·ren /ˈberən/ *adj*
1 a : having very few plants : not suitable for plants • a *barren* [=*desolate*] landscape • a *barren* desert • Few creatures can thrive on these *barren* mountaintops. **b** : not producing fruit or not able to produce fruit • a *barren* tree • a *barren* orchard
2 *old-fashioned, of a woman or female animal* : not able to produce children or offspring : INFERTILE • a *barren* woman
3 [*more ~; most ~*] : not exciting or interesting • The book was good, but I found the *barren* lives of the characters depressing. • a very *barren* routine
4 : not producing good or useful things, ideas, etc. • an artist who is going through a *barren* period • a *barren* mind
barren of formal : not having (something) : WITHOUT • a hillside *barren of* trees
– **bar·ren·ness** *noun* [*noncount*] • the *barrenness* of the land/soil

bar·rette /bɑˈrɛt/ *noun, pl* **-rettes** [*count*] *US* : a decorative clip or bar that is used to hold a girl's or woman's hair in place — called also (*Brit*) *hair slide*; see picture at GROOMING

[1]**bar·ri·cade** /ˈberəˌkeɪd/ *noun, pl* **-cades** [*count*] : a temporary wall, fence, or similar structure that is built to prevent people from entering a place or area • The enemy broke through the *barricade*. • Police erected *barricades* to keep the crowds from approaching the crime scene.

[2]**barricade** *verb* **-cades**; **-cad·ed**; **-cad·ing** [+ *obj*] : to block (something) so that people or things cannot enter or leave • The police *barricaded* the crime scene. • They *barricaded* the door. • Ships *barricaded* the coastline.
barricade yourself ✧ If you *barricade yourself* in/inside something, you prevent other people from entering the place where you are by locking the door or by putting up a barricade. • Students *barricaded themselves* in the cafeteria to protest university policies.

bar·ri·er /ˈberijə/ *noun, pl* **-ers** [*count*]
1 : something (such as a fence or natural obstacle) that prevents or blocks movement from one place to another • Concrete *barriers* surround the race track to protect spectators. • The tree's roots serve/act as a *barrier* against soil erosion. • The mountain range forms a natural *barrier* between the two countries. • *barrier* beaches — see also BARRIER ISLAND, BARRIER REEF, CRASH BARRIER
2 a : a law, rule, problem, etc., that makes something difficult or impossible • Both leaders are in favor of removing trade *barriers*. • Cultural/social *barriers* have made it hard for women to enter many professions. • He argues that regulations should not be viewed as *barriers* to progress. **b** : something that makes it difficult for people to understand each other — often + *between* • The lecture was about finding ways to break through *barriers between* the social classes. • Age can be a big *barrier between* parents and children. • A ***language barrier*** existed *between* the two countries. [=people in the two countries did not understand each other because they spoke different languages]
3 : a level, amount, or number that is difficult to get past • His fastball broke the 100-mph *barrier*. [=he threw a baseball over 100 mph] • a price *barrier* [=a price that is regarded as a limit] — see also SOUND BARRIER

barrier island *noun, pl* ~ **islands** [*count*] : a long, sandy island that is near a shore

barrier reef *noun, pl* ~ **reefs** [*count*] : a long coral reef that is near a shore

B

bar·ring /ˈbɑrɪŋ/ *prep*
1 — used to say that something will happen unless something else happens • They'll be at sea for six months, *barring* medical emergencies. [=they'll be at sea for six months if there are no medical emergencies] • She's going to lose the election *barring* a miracle. [=unless a miracle occurs]
2 : other than (someone or something) : EXCEPT • No one, *barring* the magician himself, knows how the trick is done.

bar·rio /ˈbɑrijoʊ/ *noun, pl* **-rios** [*count*] : a neighborhood in a city or town in the U.S. in which many people who speak Spanish live ✧ *Barrio* is especially used for neighborhoods in the southwestern parts of the U.S.

bar·ris·ter /ˈberəstɚ/ *noun, pl* **-ters** [*count*] : a lawyer in Britain who has the right to argue in higher courts of law — compare SOLICITOR

bar·room /ˈbɑɚˌruːm/ *noun, pl* **-rooms** [*count*] : a place where alcoholic drinks are served : BAR — often used before another noun • a *barroom* brawl

bar·row /ˈberoʊ/ *noun, pl* **-rows** [*count*]
1 : WHEELBARROW
2 *chiefly Brit* : a cart with two wheels that is pushed or pulled and that is used for selling fruits, vegetables, etc., on the street

bar·tend·er /ˈbɑɚˌtɛndɚ/ *noun, pl* **-ers** [*count*] *US* : a person who serves drinks at a bar or restaurant
– bar·tend /ˈbɑɚˌtɛnd/ *verb* **-tends; -tend·ed; -tend·ing** [*no obj*] • He makes extra money by *bartending* on weekends.

[1]**bar·ter** /ˈbɑɚtɚ/ *verb* **-ters; -tered; -ter·ing** : to exchange things (such as products or services) for other things instead of for money [*no obj*] — often + *for* or *with* • The farmers *bartered for* supplies with their crops. • The town's people often *barter* [=*trade*] *with* the owner of the store. [+ *obj*] — often + *for* • They *barter* [=*trade*] eggs *for* cheese with the neighboring farm.

[2]**barter** *noun* [*noncount*]
1 : a system in which goods or services are exchanged for other goods or services instead of for money • The tribes use a system of *barter*. • a *barter* system
2 : goods or services that are exchanged for other goods or services • The explorers used blankets and other supplies for *barter* to get food from the native people.

ba·salt /bəˈsɑːlt/ *noun* [*noncount*] : a type of dark gray to black rock
– ba·sal·tic /bəˈsɑːltɪk/ *adj* • *basaltic* rock

[1]**base** /ˈbeɪs/ *noun, pl* **bas·es**
1 [*count*] : the bottom or lowest part of something : the part on which something rests or is supported — usually singular • The lamp has a heavy *base*. • He planted flowers around the stone's *base*. • Make sure the *base of* the stove rests evenly on the floor. • The climbers established a camp at the *base* of the mountain. = The climbers established a ***base camp***. — often used figuratively • Although I disagreed with the book's theoretical *base* [=*basis, foundation*], I couldn't really find fault with its logic. • The tour was informative, thanks to the guide's ***broad base of knowledge***.
2 [*count*] : something (such as a group of people or things) that provides support for a place, business, etc. — usually singular • At one time paper mills were the industrial *base* for the region. • The economic *base* of the village is tourism. [=tourism is the most important part of the village's economy] • The company has a solid ***customer base***. [=set of customers it can depend on] • The sport's ***fan base*** [=group of fans] is growing. — see also POWER BASE, TAX BASE
3 [*count*] : a main ingredient to which other things are added to make something — usually singular • The paint has a water *base*, not an oil *base*. • She uses chicken broth as the *base* of the soup.
4 a [*count*] : the main place in which a person works or lives or a business operates • He uses his home as the *base* for his accounting business. • The company's *base* is in London. = The company's ***base of operations*** is (in) London. [=the company's main offices are in London] • The band recently returned to its ***home base*** of Chicago after three months on tour. **b** : a place where a military force keeps supplies and where people in the military live and work [*count*] naval/military *bases* • the commander of the *base* = the *base* commander [*noncount*] The troops were ordered back to *base*. — see also AIR BASE
5 *baseball* : any one of the four places a runner must touch in order to score [*count*] He threw the ball to the wrong *base*. [*noncount*] There's a runner ***on base***. [=there's a runner on first, second, or third base] • The batter ***reached base*** on an error by the shortstop. — compare HOME PLATE; see also FIRST BASE, SECOND BASE, THIRD BASE
6 [*count*] *chemistry* : a chemical that reacts with an acid to form a salt ✧ A base has a pH higher than 7. — compare [1]ACID 1, PH
7 [*count*] *mathematics* : a number on which a system for counting and calculating is established — usually singular • Computers use a binary, or *base* 2, system, rather than the decimal, or *base* 10, system we usually use.
cover all the bases *also* ***cover every base*** : to do or include everything that needs to be done or included • The book is sometimes confusing because the writer tries too hard to *cover all the bases*. • They reviewed the contract to make sure that it *covered all the bases*.
off base *US, informal* **1** : not correct : wrong or mistaken • Her study proves that the theory is *off base*. • It turns out that the estimates were ***way off base***. [=very wrong] **2** : in an unprepared state • He was caught *off base* [=*off guard*] by the accusations. [=he was not prepared for the accusations]
touch all the bases *or* ***touch every base*** *chiefly US* : to cover all the bases; *especially* : to mention every subject or point that needs to be considered • She made sure that she *touched all the bases* in her report. • His opening remarks at the meeting *touched all the bases*.
touch base *informal* : to meet and talk as a way of learning about recent news • Let's get together for lunch next week to *touch base*. — usually + *with* • He attended the conference for a chance to *touch base with* other people in the computer industry.

[2]**base** *verb* **bases; based; bas·ing** [+ *obj*] : to have a particular place as the main place where a person works or lives or where a business operates • They are going to *base* their new company in Seattle. • The company has ***based itself*** in London. • Our tour group *based itself* in a hotel in the heart of the city. — often used as *(be) based* • The company *is based* in London. [=the company's main offices are in London] • The band *was based* in Chicago until recently. • a London-*based* company
base on/upon [*phrasal verb*] ***base (something) on/upon (something)*** : to form, make, or develop (something, such as an opinion, decision, or calculation) by using (something, such as information) as a basis, starting point, etc. • You've *based* your opinion *on* faulty information. = Your opinion is *based on* faulty information. [=the information that you used to form your opinion is wrong] • The interest rate is *based on* credit history. [=credit history is used to determine the interest rate] • The story is *based on* real-life events. [=the story was developed from real-life events] • The island's economy is *based on* tourism.

[3]**base** *adj*
1 ***bas·er; -est*** [*also more* ~; *most* ~] *formal + literary* : not honest or good • *base* motives • a *base* criminal
2 *technical, of a metal* : having low quality and value • Iron is a *base* metal.
– base·ly *adv* • He acted *basely*. **– base·ness** *noun* [*noncount*] • the *baseness* of his actions

base·ball /ˈbeɪsˌbɑːl/ *noun, pl* **-balls**
1 [*noncount*] : a game played on a large field by two teams of nine players who try to score runs by hitting a small ball with a bat and then running to each of the four bases without being put out • He likes playing *baseball*. • We watched *baseball* on TV last night. — often used before another noun • a *baseball* player/team/game • a *baseball* bat/card — see pictures at BAT, GLOVE
2 [*count*] : the ball used in baseball — see picture at BALL

baseball cap *noun, pl* ~ **caps** [*count*] : a rounded cap that fits close to the head and that has a long visor ✧ Baseball caps were originally worn only by baseball players as part of their uniform but are now worn by many people. — see picture at HAT

base·board /ˈbeɪsˌboɚd/ *noun, pl* **-boards** [*count*] *US* : a narrow board along the bottom of a wall that covers the area where the wall meets the floor — called also *(Brit) skirting board*

based *adj* — used to describe the base or basis of something

• a soundly *based* argument [=an argument that has a sound basis] — often used in combination • oil-*based* paints

base hit *noun, pl* ~ **hits** [*count*] *baseball* : a hit that allows a batter to reach a base safely : a single, double, triple, or home run • The pitcher gave up three *base hits* [=*hits*] in two innings.

base•less /ˈbeɪsləs/ *adj* : not based on facts : without a good reason • a *baseless* [=*unfounded*] accusation • The charges against him were found to be *baseless*.

base•line /ˈbeɪsˌlaɪn/ *noun, pl* **-lines** [*count*]
1 *technical* : information that is used as a starting point by which to compare other information • The experiment is meant only to provide a *baseline* for other studies. — often used before another noun • *baseline* data
2 : a line at either end of the playing area in games like basketball and tennis
3 *baseball* **a** : either one of the lines that lead from home plate to first base and third base **b** : BASE PATH

baseman see FIRST BASEMAN, SECOND BASEMAN, THIRD BASEMAN

base•ment /ˈbeɪsmənt/ *noun, pl* **-ments** [*count*] : the part of a building that is entirely or partly below the ground — see also BARGAIN BASEMENT

base on balls *noun, pl* **bases on balls** [*count*] *baseball* : a movement to first base that is awarded to a batter who does not swing at four pitches that are balls — called also *walk*

base path *noun, pl* ~ **paths** [*count*] : the area between two bases on a baseball field where a player must remain while running from one base to the other

base pay *noun, pl* ~ **pays** [*count, noncount*] : the amount of money paid to someone for work at a job that does not include any additional payments for bonuses, overtime, etc.

base runner *noun, pl* ~ **-ners** [*count*] *baseball* : a player who is on base or is trying to reach a base
– **base•run•ning** *noun* [*noncount*] • He is good at *baserunning*.

bases *plural of* ¹BASE *or of* BASIS

¹**bash** /ˈbæʃ/ *verb* **bash•es; bashed; bash•ing**
1 a [+ *obj*] : to cause or allow (something, such as part of your body) to hit something very hard or forcefully • She fell down and *bashed* [=*banged*] her knee against a rock. • I *bashed* my arm against the door. **b** : to hit (someone or something) very hard or forcefully [+ *obj*] Someone *bashed* him over/on the head with a chair. [*no obj*] The two cars *bashed* [=*crashed*] into each other. **c** [+ *obj*] : to hurt or damage (something) by hitting or beating • They tried to *bash* the door open/down. — often + *in* • He threatened to *bash* [=*beat, smash*] my head *in*.
2 [+ *obj*] : to criticize or attack (a person or group) • newspapers that use their editorial pages to *bash* [=harshly criticize] the president • groups accused of gay *bashing* [=criticizing or attacking gay people] • celebrity *bashing*
bash away [*phrasal verb*] *Brit, informal* : to work hard at something • The children are *bashing away* [=(*US*) *banging away*] at their homework.
bash on [*phrasal verb*] *Brit, informal* : to continue to work hard at something • You're not finished yet? Well, *bash on*. [=*press on*]
bash out [*phrasal verb*] ***bash out (something) or bash (something) out*** *Brit, informal* : to produce (something) quickly • He *bashed out* [=*banged out*] an angry letter to the editor.
bash up [*phrasal verb*] ***bash up (someone) or bash (someone) up*** *chiefly Brit, informal* : to attack (someone) • A group of older girls *bashed up* [=*beat up*] the sisters.
– **basher** *noun, pl* **-ers** [*count*] • celebrity *bashers* [=people who criticize celebrities]

²**bash** *noun, pl* **bashes** [*count*]
1 : a big or exciting party • We threw her a birthday *bash*.
2 : a hard and powerful hit or blow • She gave me a *bash* on the head.
have a bash at *Brit, informal* : to try or attempt (something) • I've never done it before, but I'll *have a bash at* it.

bash•ful /ˈbæʃfəl/ *adj* [*more* ~; *most* ~] : nervous or uncomfortable in social situations : afraid to talk to people because of a lack of confidence • She was very *bashful* [=*shy*] as a child. • *bashful* boys asking girls to dance • He looked at her with a *bashful* smile. [=a smile that showed he was feeling bashful] • Take another cookie if you like. Don't be *bashful*. [=*shy*]
– **bash•ful•ly** *adv* • He smiled *bashfully*. – **bash•ful•ness** *noun* [*noncount*]

¹**ba•sic** /ˈbeɪsɪk/ *adj* [*more* ~; *most* ~]
1 : forming or relating to the most important part of something • In this class, you will learn the *basic* principles of chemistry. • At its most *basic* level, the book is about a father's relationship with his children. • The *basic* difference between the two companies is their size. • The organization fights for *basic* human rights [=the rights that all people should have] throughout the world. • These ingredients are a *basic* part of Thai cooking. = These ingredients are ***basic to*** Thai cooking. • rights that are *basic to* all human beings
2 : forming or relating to the first or easiest part of something • We're learning *basic* [=*beginning*] English. • *basic* reading, writing, and mathematics • She lacks even the most *basic* skills necessary for the job.
3 : not including anything extra • That's just the *basic* salary without overtime or tips. • The motel is comfortable but pretty *basic*: you get the necessities all right, but no luxuries.

²**basic** *noun, pl* **-sics**
1 ***basics*** [*plural*] : the simplest and most important parts of something (such as a subject of study) • He's teaching me the *basics* of Japanese cooking. • the *basics* of computers = computer *basics*
2 [*noncount*] *chiefly US* : BASIC TRAINING • He starts *basic* in two months.
get/go back to (the) basics : to return to a simpler way of doing something or thinking about something • The restaurant is *getting back to basics* in terms of food, using fresh ingredients to make simple, good food.

BA•SIC /ˈbeɪsɪk/ *noun* [*noncount*] *computers* : a simple language used for programming computers • The program is written in *BASIC*.

ba•si•cal•ly /ˈbeɪsɪkli/ *adv*
1 : in a general or basic way — used to say that something is true or correct as a general statement even if it is not entirely true or correct • There are a few boring parts, but *basically* [=*generally, for the most part*], it's a very good book. • She's *basically* a good kid. • You're *basically* [=*fundamentally*] correct, but there's something you don't know. • There are *basically* two types of people: those who like chocolate and those who don't. • a *basically* healthy person • Children *basically* learn to speak by listening to their parents. • All people are *basically* the same. = *Basically*, all people are the same.
2 — used to show that a statement is expressing the most important reason for something • "Why don't you like him?" "*Basically*, I think he's crazy." • We'd like to buy a new car, but, *basically*, we just don't have enough money.
3 [*more* ~; *most* ~] : in a simple way • people who are trying to live more *basically* [=*simply*]

basic training *noun* [*noncount*] : the first few weeks of training for someone who has recently joined the military • Our son is in *basic training*.

ba•sil /ˈbæzəl, ˈbeɪzəl/ *noun* [*noncount*] : an herb that has a sweet smell and that is used in cooking — see color picture on page C6

ba•sil•i•ca /bəˈsɪlɪkə/ *noun, pl* **-cas** [*count*] : a large church that has a long central part that ends in a curved wall

bas•i•lisk /ˈbæsəˌlɪsk/ *noun, pl* **-lisks** [*count*] *in stories and legends* : a reptile that can kill people by breathing on them or looking at them

ba•sin /ˈbeɪsn̩/ *noun, pl* **-sins** [*count*]
1 a *chiefly Brit* : a kitchen sink **b** *Brit* : a large bowl that is used for mixing, cooking, or serving food **c** : the amount contained in a basin • a *basin* of cold water
2 : the area of land around a large river and the small rivers that flow into it • the drainage *basin* of a river • the Amazon *Basin*
3 : a large area of the earth's surface that is lower than the area around it • the Great *Basin* of the western U.S.
4 : an area of water where people keep their ships and boats when they are not sailing them • a yacht *basin*

ba•sis /ˈbeɪsəs/ *noun, pl* **ba•ses** /ˈbeɪˌsiːz/
1 : something (such as an idea or set of ideas) from which another thing develops or can develop [*count*] — usually singular • This principle forms the *basis* [=*base, foundation*] of the country's economic policies and will provide a firm *basis* for future development. • The actor's letters form the *basis* of the biography. [=the biography is based on the actor's letters; the most important information in the biography comes from the actor's letters] [*noncount*] These stories have very little *basis* [=*foundation*] in fact/reality. [=these stories are not based on or supported by facts/reality]
2 [*noncount*] : a reason for doing something • The judge

ruled that there is no legal *basis* [=*ground*] for a new trial. • The latest news at least provides some *basis* for hope. [=some reason to hope] • ***On what basis*** were the students chosen/selected? [=how were the students chosen/selected?; what was considered when the students were chosen/selected?] • Students were chosen/selected ***on the basis of*** [=*according to*] their grades and test scores. • Our decisions are made *on the basis of* the available information. [=we base our decisions on the available information] • The company does not hire employees *on the basis of* their race, sex, age, or religion.
3 [*singular*] **a** : a fixed pattern or system for doing something — used with *on* • He visits his grandmother ***on a regular basis***. [=*regularly*] • The company changes its Web site ***on a daily/weekly basis***. [=every day/week] • changes that occur ***on an hourly basis*** • They hired her ***on a trial/temporary basis***. • People are seated ***on a first-come, first-served basis***. [=the people who arrive first are given seats first] **b** — used to describe the way people act with each other • The two golfers still compete ***on a friendly basis***. [=in a friendly way] — see also *on a first-name basis* at FIRST NAME

bask /ˈbæsk, *Brit* ˈbɑːsk/ *verb* **basks; basked; bask·ing** [*no obj*]
1 : to lie or relax happily in a bright and warm place • We sat *basking* in the sun. • Tourists were *basking* on the beaches.
2 : to enjoy the attention and good feelings expressed by others • He stood before the audience, *basking* in their applause. • parents who ***bask in the reflected glory*** of their children [=parents who enjoy the attention people give them because of the success of their children]

bas·ket /ˈbæskɪt, *Brit* ˈbɑːskɪt/ *noun, pl* **-kets** [*count*]
1 a : a container usually made by weaving together long thin pieces of material • wicker/straw/wire *baskets* • a fruit *basket* = a *basket* filled with fruit • a laundry *basket* [=a basket that holds dirty clothes] • They brought their lunch in a picnic *basket*. — see also BREADBASKET, HANDBASKET, WASTEBASKET **b** : the amount contained in a basket • a *basket* [=*basketful*] of eggs

basket

2 *basketball* **a** : a net hanging from a thin metal ring that the ball must go through in order to score points • His shot missed the *basket* completely. **b** : a successful shot • She ***made/scored a basket***. [=she scored points by making a shot that went through the basket]
put all your eggs in one basket see ¹EGG
– basketful *noun, pl* **-fuls** [*count*] • a *basketful* of eggs

bas·ket·ball /ˈbæskɪtˌbɑːl, *Brit* ˈbɑːskɪtˌbɔːl/ *noun, pl* **-balls**
1 [*noncount*] : a game in which two teams of five players bounce a ball and try to score points by throwing the ball through one of the raised nets at each end of a rectangular court • She plays *basketball*. — often used before another noun • a *basketball* game/team/player/coach
2 [*count*] : a large rubber ball that is used in the game of basketball — see picture at BALL

basket case *noun, pl* **~ cases** [*count*] *informal*
1 : a person who is very nervous, tired, etc., and is not able to think or act normally • I was so worried about losing my job that I was a complete *basket case*.
2 : something (such as a company or a government) that is in very bad condition and close to failure • a business that was once very successful but is now a financial *basket case*

bas·ket·ry /ˈbæskɪtri, *Brit* ˈbɑːskətri/ *noun* [*noncount*]
1 : the art or craft of making baskets and other objects by weaving together long thin pieces of material
2 : baskets and other objects made by basketry • a collection of *basketry* — called also *basketwork*

bas·ket·work /ˈbæskɪtˌwək, *Brit* ˈbɑːskɪtˌwək/ *noun* [*noncount*] : BASKETRY 2

bas·ma·ti rice /ˌbɑːzˈmɑːtiː-, *Brit* ˌbæzˈmɑːtiː-/ *noun* [*noncount*] : a kind of long rice that is used especially in Indian and Middle Eastern cooking

bas mitz·vah /bɑsˈmɪtsvə/ *noun, pl* **~ -vahs** [*count*] : BAT MITZVAH

bas–re·lief /ˌbɑːrɪˈliːf/ *noun, pl* **-liefs** : a kind of sculpture in which shapes are carved so that they are only slightly higher than the flat background [*count*] the *bas-reliefs* on the building's façade [*noncount*] a façade decorated with flowers in *bas-relief* — often used before another noun • *bas-relief* carvings/sculptures

¹bass /ˈbeɪs/ *noun, pl* **bass·es** *music*
1 : low and deep sound : the lowest range of sounds used in music [*noncount*] Turn down the treble on your radio and turn up the *bass*. [*singular*] The song has a loud/heavy/booming *bass*. — compare TREBLE
2 [*count*] : the lowest male singing voice • He sings with/in a deep *bass*.; *also* : a singer who has such a voice • He's a *bass*. — compare ALTO, SOPRANO, TENOR
3 [*count*] **a** : a kind of guitar that usually has four strings and that makes low sounds [*count*] an electric/acoustic *bass* • She plays (the) *bass*. • a *bass* player — called also *bass guitar* **b** : DOUBLE BASS
– compare ³BASS

²bass /ˈbeɪs/ *adj, always used before a noun* : having or indicating a low sound or range • his deep *bass* voice • the sound of the *bass* drum • a *bass* clarinet • the *bass* clef

³bass /ˈbæs/ *noun, pl* **bass** : a kind of fish that people catch for food [*count*] She caught three *bass*. [*noncount*] We had *bass* for dinner. — see color picture on page C8 — compare ¹BASS

bas·set hound /ˈbæsət-/ *noun, pl* **~ hounds** [*count*] : a kind of dog that has short legs and long ears and that is used for hunting — called also *basset*

bas·si·net /ˌbæsəˈnɛt/ *noun, pl* **-nets** [*count*] : a small bed for a baby that looks like a basket and that usually has a hood or cover over one end

bass·ist /ˈbeɪsɪst/ *noun, pl* **-sists** [*count*] *music* : a person who plays a double bass or a bass guitar

bas·soon /bəˈsuːn/ *noun, pl* **-soons** [*count*] : a large musical instrument that is shaped like a tube, makes low sounds, and is played by blowing into a small, thin tube in its side — see picture at WOODWIND
– bas·soon·ist /bəˈsuːnɪst/ *noun, pl* **-ists** [*count*]

bas·tard /ˈbæstəd, *Brit* ˈbɑːstəd/ *noun, pl* **-tards** [*count*]
1 *informal* **a** *offensive* : a very bad or unpleasant man : a man who you strongly dislike or hate • You dirty *bastard*! **b** *sometimes offensive* : a man who you think is lucky, unlucky, etc. • Congratulations on getting the job, you lucky *bastard*! • His wife left him, the poor *bastard*. **c** *chiefly Brit, sometimes offensive* : something that is difficult or unpleasant • Life can be a real *bastard* sometimes.
2 *usually offensive* : a person whose parents were not married to each other : an illegitimate child — sometimes used before another noun • the *bastard* son of a wealthy noble ✧ This use of *bastard* was common in the past, but it is now usually avoided.

bas·tard·ize *also Brit* **bas·tard·ise** /ˈbæstəˌdaɪz, *Brit* ˈbɑːstəˌdaɪz/ *verb* **-iz·es; -ized; -iz·ing** [+ *obj*] *disapproving* : to produce a poor copy or version of (something) • It's a shame to see how Hollywood has *bastardized* the novel. • The restaurant serves a *bastardized* version of the classic French dish.

baste /ˈbeɪst/ *verb* **bastes; bast·ed; bast·ing** [+ *obj*]
1 : to pour hot juices, melted fat, etc., over (meat) while it is cooking • *Baste* the turkey every half hour.
2 : to sew together (pieces of cloth) with long, loose stitches • She *basted* the hem of the dress.

bas·tion /ˈbæstʃən, *Brit* ˈbæstiən/ *noun, pl* **-tions** [*count*] : a place or system in which something (such as an old-fashioned idea) continues to survive • The neighborhood is considered by many to be the city's last liberal/conservative *bastion*. [=the only place left in the city where liberal/conservative ideas are still accepted] • a *bastion* of racial inequality [=a system in which people of different races still do not have equal rights] • *bastions* of democracy

¹bat /ˈbæt/ *noun, pl* **bats** [*count*]
1 : a long rounded stick that is used to hit the ball in baseball • a baseball *bat*
2 : a long flattened stick that is used to hit the ball in cricket
3 *Brit* : PADDLE 2 • a table tennis *bat*
at bat *baseball* **1** — used to describe the player or team that is batting • He got a home run on his first time *at bat*. • It's the bottom of the first inning and the home team is *at bat*. [=is batting] **2** : the act of batting • She has two hits in three *at bats*.
go to bat *baseball* : to be the player or team that is batting • The visiting team *goes to bat* first. [=the visiting team bats first]
go to bat for *US, informal* : to try to help, support, or defend (someone or something) in an active way • Many of

his friends *went to bat for him* while he was under investigation for fraud.

off the bat *chiefly US, informal* : without any delay : IMMEDIATELY — usually used with *right* • I could tell it was fake ***right off the bat.*** [=*right away*]

off your own bat *Brit, informal* : through your own efforts • He didn't need my help—he made good *off his own bat.*

– compare [3]BAT

[2]**bat** *verb* **bats; bat·ted; bat·ting**

1 a [+ *obj*] : to hit (something, such as a ball) with a bat, club, etc., or with your hand • The ball was *batted* down. • a ***batted ball*** [=a ball that has been hit by a batter in baseball] **b** [*no obj*] : to try to hit a ball with a bat in baseball, cricket, or a similar game • It's your turn to *bat.* • She was *batting* when it began to rain. • Who's *batting*? = Who's ***up to bat?***

bat

cricket bat **baseball bat**

2 [*no obj*] *baseball* : to have a specified batting average • This year he's *batting* [=*hitting*] .300. [=his batting average is .300] • She has five hits in five at bats, so she's ***batting a thousand.*** [=her batting average is 1.000] ◊ In figurative use, to *bat a thousand* is to succeed in every attempt. This is an informal phrase that is used chiefly in U.S. English. • So far in her career, she's *batting a thousand.* [=she has succeeded in everything she has done in her career] • No one *bats a thousand* in this business.

bat around [*phrasal verb*] ***bat (something) around*** *or* ***bat around (something)*** *informal* : to think about or talk about (something, such as an idea) for a period of time • The plan was *batted around* for a while, but it was finally rejected. • We've been *batting* the idea *around* for a few years.

bat in [*phrasal verb*] ***bat in (a run)*** *also* ***bat (a run) in*** *baseball* : to hit the ball in a way that makes it possible for a run to score • He *batted in* 70 runs last year.

– compare [4]BAT

– **batting** *adj, always used before a noun* • *batting* practice • a *batting* coach • *batting* gloves/helmets

[3]**bat** *noun, pl* **bats** [*count*]

1 : an animal that has wings and a furry body like a mouse

2 *informal* : an unpleasant old woman • Don't take any notice of that ***old bat.***

bats in the/your belfry see BELFRY

(as) blind as a bat see [1]BLIND

like a bat out of hell *informal* : very quickly • He ran out of the house *like a bat out of hell.*

– compare [1]BAT

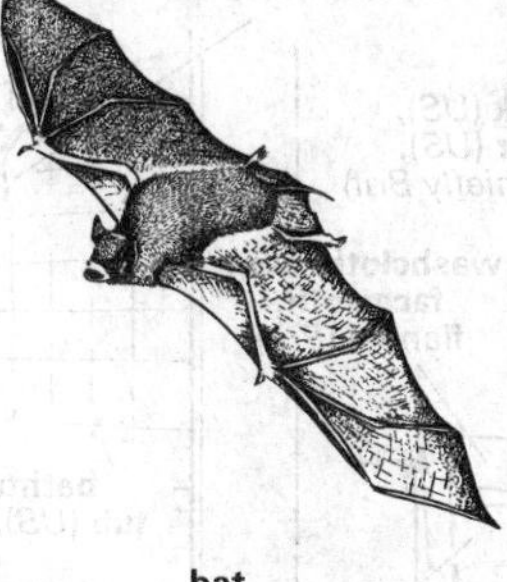

bat

[4]**bat** *verb* **bats; batted; batting**

[+ *obj*] : to close and open (your eyes or eyelashes) very quickly several times especially as a way of flirting • She smiled and *batted* her eyelashes at him.

not bat an eye/eyelash (*US*) *or Brit* ***not bat an eyelid*** *informal* : to show no surprise, fear, concern, etc. • He thought the news would make her upset, but she ***never batted an eye.*** [=she did not appear to be upset at all] • He listened ***without batting an eyelash.***

– compare [2]BAT

bat·boy /ˈbætˌbɔɪ/ *noun, pl* **-boys** [*count*] : a boy who takes care of the bats, balls, and other equipment used by a baseball team

batch /ˈbætʃ/ *noun, pl* **batch·es** [*count*]

1 : an amount of something that is made at one time • We baked two *batches* of cookies. • a fresh *batch* of salsa • mixing another *batch* of cement • Fry the potatoes ***in batches.*** [=fry one amount and then another amount and so on until all the potatoes have been fried]

2 : a group of people or things • They're hiring another *batch* of workers. • a new *batch* [=*bunch*] of television shows

3 *computers* : a set of jobs that a computer does together at one time — usually used before another noun • *batch* processing

bat·ed /ˈbeɪtəd/ *adj*

with bated breath : in a nervous and excited state because you do not know what will happen • They waited for the answer *with bated breath.* [=they nervously waited for the answer]

[1]**bath** /ˈbæθ, *Brit* ˈbɑːθ/ *noun, pl* **baths** /ˈbæðz, ˈbæθs, *Brit* ˈbɑːðz, ˈbɑːθs/

1 [*count*] **a** : the act of washing the body usually by sitting or lying in a container filled with water • Do you prefer *baths* or showers? • I was taking a *bath* when the phone rang. • (*chiefly Brit*) I was having a *bath.* • We tried giving the dog a *bath* in the bathtub. • a long hot *bath* • *bath* towels [=large towels used for drying yourself after a bath or shower] — see also BUBBLE BATH, SPONGE BATH, TURKISH BATH, TAKE A BATH (below) **b** : the water used for a bath • a *bath* of warm/hot water • I was in the *bath* when the phone rang. • Would you like me to ***draw/run a bath*** for you? [=to fill the bathtub with water for you?] **c** *chiefly Brit* : BATHTUB • He slipped and fell in the *bath.*

2 [*count*] *chiefly US* : BATHROOM — used when describing the number or kinds of bathrooms in a place • a room with a private *bath* • The house has three bedrooms and one and a half *baths.* [=one full bathroom and one bathroom with only a sink and a toilet] • a ***full bath*** [=a bathroom with a sink, toilet, and a bathtub or shower]

3 ***baths*** [*plural*] **a** : a public building where people in the past went to wash or soak their bodies • ancient Roman *baths* **b** *Brit, old-fashioned* : a public building with a swimming pool in it

4 [*count*] *technical* : a container filled with a liquid in which an object is placed to be cleaned, treated, etc. • She dipped the metal in a *bath* of acid. • a chemical *bath*

take a bath *US, informal* : to lose a large amount of money in a business deal • The movie studio *took a bath* on his last picture. — see also [1]BATH 1a (above)

– see also BLOODBATH

[2]**bath** *verb* **baths; bathed; bath·ing** *Brit*

1 [+ *obj*] : to wash (someone) in a container filled with water : to give a bath to (someone) • She *baths* [=(*US*) *bathes*] the baby in the kitchen sink.

2 [*no obj*] *formal* : to have a bath : to wash yourself in a bath • I usually *bath* [=(*US*) *bathe*] before going to bed.

[1]**bathe** /ˈbeɪð/ *verb* **bathes; bathed; bath·ing**

1 [*no obj*] *chiefly US* : to take a bath : to wash yourself in a bath • I always *bathe* [=(*Brit*) *bath*] in the morning.

2 [+ *obj*] *chiefly US* : to wash (someone) in a container filled with water : to give a bath to (someone) • We'll *bathe* [=(*Brit*) *bath*] the baby after she eats.

3 [*no obj*] *somewhat old-fashioned* : to swim for pleasure • We *bathed* [=*swam*] in the ocean. — see also SUNBATHE

4 [+ *obj*] : to wash or rinse (a part of the body) • If the chemical comes in contact with the eyes, *bathe* the eyes with water for 10 minutes.

5 [+ *obj*] : to cover (an area or surface) with light • The moon *bathed* the town in light. = The town was *bathed* in moonlight.

bathed in sweat : covered with sweat : very sweaty • He was *bathed in sweat* when he finished exercising.

– **bath·er** /ˈbeɪðɚ/ *noun, pl* **-ers** [*count*] • a beach crowded with *bathers* [=*swimmers*] – **bathing** *noun* [*noncount*] • a beach where *bathing* [=*swimming*] is not allowed • nude *bathing* • I like to ***go bathing*** [=*go swimming*] on summer mornings before breakfast. • a ***bathing cap*** [=a cap worn for swimming]

[2]**bathe** *noun, pl* **bathes** [*count*] *Brit* : the act of swimming for pleasure : SWIM • We went for a *bathe* in the sea.

bath·house /ˈbæθˌhaʊs, *Brit* ˈbɑːθˌhaʊs/ *noun, pl* **-hous·es** [*count*]

1 : a public building where people go to take baths, showers, etc.

2 *US* : a public building at a beach where people go to put on the clothes they use for swimming

bathing costume *noun, pl* **~ -tumes** [*count*] *Brit* : SWIMSUIT

bathing suit *noun, pl* **~ suits** [*count*] *chiefly US* : SWIMSUIT

bath mat *noun, pl* **~ mats** [*count*]

1 : a small rug outside a bathtub for people to stand on while they are drying themselves after a bath or shower — see picture at BATHROOM

B

2 : a rubber mat in a bathtub for people to stand on without slipping during a bath or shower

ba·thos /ˈbeɪˌθɑːs/ *noun [noncount] formal* **:** the sudden appearance of a silly idea or event in a book, movie discussion, etc., that is serious in tone ▪ The serious message of the film is ruined by the *bathos* of its ridiculous ending.

bath·robe /ˈbæθˌroʊb, *Brit* ˈbɑːθˌrəʊb/ *noun, pl* **-robes** *[count]* **:** a loose piece of clothing that wraps around your body and is worn especially before or after a bath — see color picture on page C12

bath·room /ˈbæθˌruːm, *Brit* ˈbɑːθˌruːm/ *noun, pl* **-rooms** *[count]*

1 : a room with a sink and toilet and usually a bathtub or shower ▪ Their house has three *bathrooms.* ✧ In U.S. English, a bathroom is mainly thought of as a room with a toilet. In British English, a bathroom is mainly thought of as a room with a bathtub or shower.

2 *US* **:** a room in a public place with a toilet and sink ▪ The restaurant has only one *bathroom.* ▪ a public *bathroom* [=*restroom, lavatory*]

***go to the bathroom** or **use the bathroom** US* **:** to use the toilet ▪ The little boy told his mother that he had to *go to the bathroom.* ▪ You should *use the bathroom* before we leave.

bath·tub /ˈbæθˌtʌb, *Brit* ˈbɑːθˌtʌb/ *noun, pl* **-tubs** *[count] chiefly US* **:** a large and long container in which people take baths or showers — called also *(chiefly Brit) bath, (US) tub*; see picture at BATHROOM

bath·water /ˈbæθˌwɑːtɚ, *Brit* ˈbɑːθˌwɔːtə/ *noun [noncount]* **:** water used for a bath

throw out the baby with the bathwater see ¹BABY

bat mitz·vah /bɑtˈmɪtsvə/ *noun, pl* **~ -vahs** *[count]* **:** a ceremony and celebration for a Jewish girl usually on her 13th birthday when she takes on the religious duties and responsibilities of an adult; *also* **:** a girl for whom a bat mitzvah is held — called also *bas mitzvah*; compare BAR MITZVAH

ba·ton /bəˈtɑːn, *Brit* ˈbæˌtɒn/ *noun, pl* **-tons** *[count]*

1 : a thin stick that is used by a music conductor to lead a band or orchestra

2 : a long thin stick with a ball at one end or both ends that is carried by someone who performs with or leads a marching band ▪ The majorette twirled the *baton.*

3 : NIGHTSTICK ▪ a policeman's *baton*

4 : a stick that is passed from one runner to the next runner in a relay race ▪ They practiced passing the *baton.* ▪ One of the runners dropped the *baton.* — sometimes used figuratively ▪ The chef recently ***passed the baton*** [=gave the job and responsibility that had been hers] to her young assistant.

bats·man /ˈbætsmən/ *noun, pl* **-men** *[count]* **:** a player who is batting especially in the game of cricket ▪ a skillful *batsman* ✧ The player who is batting in baseball is usually called the *batter*, but a batter who has been hit by a pitch is called a ***hit batsman.***

bat·tal·ion /bəˈtæljən/ *noun, pl* **-ions** *[count]*

1 : a large organized group of soldiers

2 : a large organized group of people who act together ▪ a *battalion* of angry protesters

¹bat·ten /ˈbætn̩/ *verb* **-tens; -tened; -ten·ing**

batten down *[phrasal verb]* **1 :** to prepare for possible trouble or difficulty ▪ The city is *battening down* for the weekend's scheduled protests. ▪ People are *battening down* in preparation for a hard winter. **2 *batten down (something)* or *batten (something) down* :** to tie, close, or cover (something) in order to prevent it from moving or becoming damaged ▪ Everything on the ship's deck was *battened down.* ▪ We were able to *batten down* the house just before the storm hit. **3 *batten down the hatches* :** to prepare a boat or ship for dangerous stormy weather by closing and covering the openings in the deck — often used figuratively ▪ As the economy grows worse, investors need to *batten down the hatches* and prepare for tough times ahead.

batten on *[phrasal verb]* ***batten on (something or someone)*** *Brit, formal + disapproving* **:** to live well or succeed by using (something or someone) ▪ someone who *battens on* the strength/generosity of others

²batten *noun, pl* **-tens** *[count]* **:** a long thin piece of wood that is used to connect and support other pieces of wood

¹bat·ter /ˈbætɚ/ *verb* **-ters; -tered; -ter·ing** *[+ obj]* **:** to hit (something or someone) forcefully many times in a way that causes much damage or injury ▪ Storms *battered* the shore. ▪ He forced his opponent into the corner and *battered* him with a series of hard punches. ▪ During the war, the city was *battered* by bombs. ▪ For thousands of years, these moun-

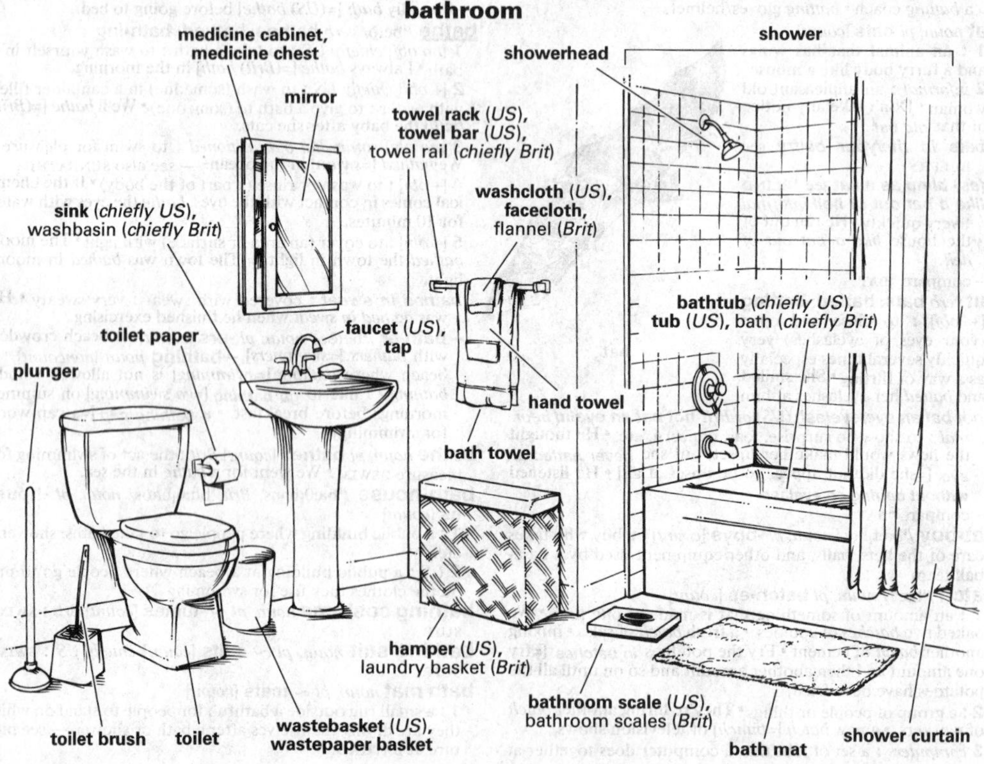

taintops have been *battered* by sun, wind, and rain. • Her ex-husband had *battered* her for many years. • children who are abused and *battered* by their parents • He tried to ***batter down*** [=*break down*] the door by kicking it. [=to force the door to open by kicking it hard] — often used figuratively • Businesses in the area have been *battered* [=badly damaged] by the bad economy. • a country *battered* by years of war and poverty • The team's confidence was *battered* by a series of losses. — see also BATTERED — compare [4]BATTER

– **bat·ter·er** *noun, pl* **-ers** [*count*]

[2]**batter** *noun, pl* **-ters**

1 : a mixture of different ingredients (such as flour, sugar, eggs, and oil) that is cooked and eaten [*count*] a thin pancake *batter* [*noncount*] cake *batter* — compare DOUGH

2 : a mixture of flour and a liquid (such as egg, oil, or water) that is used to cover food before it is fried [*count*] Dip the fish in a *batter* of flour, milk, and eggs. [*noncount*] The fish was coated with *batter* and then fried. • egg/beer *batter* – compare [3]BATTER

[3]**batter** *noun, pl* **-ters** [*count*] *baseball* **:** a player who is trying to hit the ball **:** a player who is batting • The pitcher walked the first *batter*. • He's a good fielder but a poor *batter*. [=*hitter*] • She's a right-handed/left-handed *batter*. — compare [2]BATTER

[4]**batter** *verb* **-ters; -tered; -tering** [+ *obj*] **:** to cover (food) in a batter and then fry it • *Batter* the fish and then fry it for 10 minutes. • lightly/thickly *battered* pieces of fish — compare [1]BATTER

battered *adj*

1 [*more* ~; *most* ~] **:** damaged by being used too much or in a careless way • He wore a very *battered* old hat and sunglasses. • We finally sold our *battered* truck and bought a new car.

2 : badly injured by being hit many times • The police took pictures of the victim's *battered* body. • the bruised and *battered* face of a boxer

3 : physically hurt by another person (such as a husband or parent) • a *battered* wife/woman • *battered* children

battering *noun* [*singular*] **:** an attack in which someone is badly injured by being hit many times • The victim suffered a vicious *battering*. — often used figuratively • The party is expected to ***take a battering*** [=to do very poorly] in the upcoming election. • markets that have recently *taken a battering*

battering ram *noun, pl* **~ rams** [*count*] **:** a large and heavy piece of wood or other material that is used to hit and break through walls and doors

[1]**bat·tery** /ˈbætəri/ *noun, pl* **-ter·ies**

1 [*count*] **:** a device that is placed inside a machine (such as a clock, toy, or car) to supply it with electricity • I bought new *batteries* for the flashlights. • a car *battery* • *battery*-powered computers • a ***dead battery*** = (*Brit*) a ***flat battery*** [=a battery that has no more electricity] — see picture at CAR

2 [*count*] **:** a usually large group of similar people, things, or ideas that work together, are used together, etc. • a *battery* of tests • The operation was performed by a *battery* of doctors.

3 [*count*] **:** a group of two or more big guns used by the military • an artillery *battery*

4 [*noncount*] *law* **:** the crime of hitting or touching someone in a way that is meant to cause harm or injury • He was found guilty of *battery*. — see also ASSAULT AND BATTERY

5 [*count*] *baseball* **:** the pitcher and catcher on a particular team

recharge your batteries see RECHARGE

[2]**battery** *adj, always used before a noun, Brit* **:** relating to or produced by a type of farming in which animals (such as chickens) are kept in small cages • a *battery* farm • *battery* chickens versus free-range chickens

batting average *noun, pl* **~ averages** [*count*] *baseball* **:** a number that shows how often a batter gets a base hit • an excellent hitter with a *batting average* above .300 • a low/high *batting average* — sometimes used figuratively • a movie director with a high *batting average* [=a director who has created many successful movies and few unsuccessful movies]

[1]**bat·tle** /ˈbætl/ *noun, pl* **bat·tles**

1 a : a military fight between groups of soldiers, ships, airplanes, etc. [*count*] That two-day conflict has become one of the most famous *battles* in history. • The *battle* continued late into the night. • the *battle* of Gettysburg [*noncount*] The men never spoke of the difficulties of *battle*. [=*war*] • Hundreds of dead soldiers lay on the ***field of battle***. [=the battlefield] • the brave warriors who died/fell ***in battle*** [=while fighting in a war] • Thousands of soldiers were willing to go ***into battle*** to fight the enemy. **b** [*count*] **:** a violent fight in which people use weapons • A police officer was injured in a gun *battle* that took place last night.

2 [*count*] **a :** a fight between people or groups in which each side tries to win a contest (such as a game or an election) or to gain control of something (such as a company) • The divorced couple is now in a fierce custody *battle* over their son. [=a legal fight about who their son will live with] • The company was involved in a legal *battle* with/against one of its employees. • He has been engaged in a ***running battle*** [=a fight or disagreement that continues for a long time] with the government over the amount of money he owes in taxes. — often + *for* • They are engaged in a *battle for* the presidency. [=a fight to win an election and become the president] • a *battle for* control of the land — often followed by *to* + *verb* • a *battle to control* the land ✧ A ***battle of wits*** is a contest in which each side tries to win by being smarter or cleverer than the other side. • In this movie, it's a *battle of wits* as the bank robbers try to outsmart the city's detectives. ✧ A ***battle of wills*** is a contest in which each side tries to win by refusing to stop trying. • The workers' strike became a difficult *battle of wills* between the company and the labor union. **b :** a fight between two different or opposite forces • the never-ending *battle* between/of good and evil • The comedy is a classic treatment of the ***battle of the sexes***. [=the struggle for power between women and men]

3 [*count*] **:** a long struggle to succeed or survive during a difficult situation • Last year, he lost his 10-year *battle* with/against AIDS. [=he died of AIDS after being sick with the disease for 10 years] • Starting her own business has proven to be an ***uphill battle***. [=a very difficult struggle] ✧ If you are involved in a ***losing battle*** you are trying to do something with little or no chance of success. • I tried to get him to change his mind, but it was a *losing battle*. [=he refused to change his mind] • She tried to stay awake but it was a *losing battle*. • a gardener ***fighting a losing battle*** against weeds

do battle **:** to fight or struggle • political opponents who have been *doing battle* [=*battling*] for years — usually + *with* • political opponents who have been *doing battle with* each other for years • soldiers *doing battle with* the enemy

half the battle **:** an important and necessary part of doing or achieving something • When you're opening a new restaurant, good advertising is *half the battle*. — often used with words like *only* and *just* to stress that something is not enough by itself to achieve a desired goal • If you want a career in show business, having talent is *only half the battle*—you also need to be lucky.

in the heat of (the) battle **:** while fighting in a battle • The soldier became confused *in the heat of battle*. — often used figuratively • He apologized to his wife for the angry things he had said to her *in the heat of battle*. [=while they were arguing]

join battle see JOIN

[2]**battle** *verb* **battles; bat·tled; bat·tling**

1 [*no obj*] **:** to fight with weapons • The army *battled* for control of the bridge. • The *battling* armies agreed to a truce.

2 [*no obj*] **a :** to try or struggle very hard *to do* something • The team *battled* [=*fought*] bravely *to win* their last game. • They *battled* [=*struggled*] *to keep* their son out of jail. **:** to struggle or fight *for* something • The two families have *battled for* control of the land for many years. **b :** to fight or argue with someone *over* something • The couple *battled* fiercely *over* how to spend their money.

3 [+ *obj*] **a :** to fight, compete, or argue with (someone or something) • The two teams are set to *battle* each other for the championship. • Members of both parties continue to *battle* the governor over her policies. **b :** to try to stop or defeat (something) • Hundreds of firefighters came to help *battle* the forest fire. • People often need help *battling* their drug and alcohol problems. • She's been *battling* cancer for 10 years. • *battling* the forces of evil

battle it out **:** to argue or fight • People were *battling it out* [=*fighting it out*] over parking spaces. • The two sides are now *battling it out* in the courtroom.

bat·tle–ax (*US*) *or Brit* **bat·tle–axe** /ˈbætlˌæks/ *noun, pl* **-ax·es** [*count*]

1 : an ax with a large blade that was used as a weapon in the past

2 *informal* + *disapproving* **:** an unpleasant older woman who speaks in an angry way and tries to control others

battle cruiser *noun, pl* **~ -ers** [*count*] **:** a ship that is used in fighting wars and that is lighter and faster than a battleship

battle cry *noun, pl* **~ cries** [*count*]

B

1 : a word, phrase, or sound that is shouted by soldiers in a battle : WAR CRY

2 : a phrase or saying that is used to make people support an idea, a cause, etc. • "Just Say No!" was the President's *battle cry* [=*rallying cry*] for stopping the use of illegal drugs.

battle fatigue *noun* [*noncount*] : a mental illness that is caused by the experiences of fighting in a war and that causes extreme feelings of nervousness, depression, etc. — called also *combat fatigue, shell shock*; compare POST-TRAUMATIC STRESS DISORDER

bat·tle·field /ˈbætl̩ˌfiːld/ *noun, pl* **-fields** [*count*]

1 : a place where a battle is fought • Hundreds of dead soldiers lay on the *battlefield*.

2 : an area of conflict or disagreement • a political *battlefield*

bat·tle·ground /ˈbætl̩ˌgraʊnd/ *noun, pl* **-grounds** [*count*] : BATTLEFIELD: such as **a :** a place where a battle is fought • an ancient *battleground* **b :** an area of conflict or disagreement • a political *battleground*

battle line *noun, pl* **~ lines** [*count*] : a line of soldiers who are fighting in a battle — usually used figuratively in phrases like ***the battle lines have been drawn*** to say that groups of people strongly disagree about an issue and are fighting or arguing with each other • When (the) *battle lines were drawn* over the issue of new taxes, she was quick to side with the governor.

bat·tle·ment /ˈbætl̩mənt/ *noun, pl* **-ments** [*count*] : a low wall at the top of a castle with open spaces for people inside to shoot through — usually plural • the castle's stone *battlements*

bat·tle·ship /ˈbætl̩ˌʃɪp/ *noun, pl* **-ships** [*count*] : a large ship that has many big guns and is used in fighting wars

bat·ty /ˈbæti/ *adj* **bat·ti·er; -est** *informal*

1 : foolish or silly • It's just another one of her *batty* [=*harebrained, nutty, wacky*] ideas.

2 : CRAZY • She's a little *batty*. • His bad jokes ***drive me batty***! [=make me feel angry or annoyed]

bau·ble /ˈbɑːbəl/ *noun, pl* **bau·bles** [*count*]

1 : an inexpensive piece of jewelry • shiny glass *baubles*

2 *Brit* **:** a shiny ball that is hung on a Christmas tree as a decoration

baulk *Brit spelling of* [1]BALK

baux·ite /ˈbɑːkˌsaɪt/ *noun* [*noncount*] *technical* : a soft substance that looks like clay and that is the source of aluminum

bawdy /ˈbɑːdi/ *adj* **bawd·i·er; -est** : dealing with sex in a way that is meant to be funny • *bawdy* [=*vulgar, lewd*] jokes • a *bawdy* film that is not appropriate for children

bawl /ˈbɑːl/ *verb* **bawls; bawled; bawl·ing**

1 [*no obj*] : to cry very loudly • He lay on his bed, *bawling* [=*sobbing, wailing*] uncontrollably. ✧ To ***bawl your eyes out*** is to cry loudly especially for a long time. • It's the saddest book I've ever read. I *bawled my eyes out* at the end.

2 *informal* : to say or shout (something) using a very loud voice [+ *obj*] "Get in the car!" he *bawled*. [*no obj*] The sergeant *bawled* [=*shouted, yelled*] at the soldier.

bawl out [*phrasal verb*] ***bawl out (someone)*** *or* ***bawl (someone) out*** *chiefly US, informal* : to yell at (someone) for doing something bad or wrong • His boss *bawled him out* for forgetting about the meeting.

[1]**bay** /ˈbeɪ/ *noun, pl* **bays** [*count*] : a large area of water that is part of an ocean or lake and partly surrounded by land • They went fishing in the *bay*. • She lives in California near San Francisco *Bay*. — see color picture on page C7 — compare [2]BAY, [3]BAY, [4]BAY, [5]BAY

[2]**bay** *noun, pl* **bays** [*count*]

1 : a section of a ship, airplane, etc., that is used for a special purpose (such as storing things) • a cargo *bay* on a ship • the airplane's bomb *bay* • an engine *bay*

2 : a section of a room or building • a barn with three *bays* — see also BAY WINDOW

— compare [1]BAY, [3]BAY, [4]BAY, [5]BAY

[3]**bay** *noun*

at bay : in the position of being unable to move closer while attacking or trying to approach someone — used with *keep* or *hold* • The soldiers *kept the attackers at bay*. [=they did not allow the attackers to come closer] • Armed with a gun, he *held the police at bay* [=he did not allow the police to arrest him] for 10 hours. — often used figuratively • Although the doctors had been able to *keep her illness at bay* [=to prevent her illness from becoming worse] for a few months, the disease soon began to spread again.

— compare [1]BAY, [2]BAY, [4]BAY, [5]BAY

[4]**bay** *noun, pl* **bays** [*count*] : a kind of European tree that has leaves which are used in cooking — see also BAY LEAF — compare [1]BAY, [2]BAY, [3]BAY, [5]BAY

[5]**bay** *noun, pl* **bays** [*count*] : a horse that is a reddish-brown color — compare [1]BAY, [2]BAY, [3]BAY, [4]BAY

— **bay** *adj, of a horse* • a *bay* [=reddish-brown] colt/mare

[6]**bay** *verb* **bays; bayed; bay·ing** [*no obj*]

1 : to bark with long sounds • The dog was *baying* [=*howling*] at the moon.

2 : to shout or cry out in a loud and often angry way • a *baying* crowd • an angry mob ***baying for blood*** [=angrily demanding or threatening violence]

bay leaf *noun, pl* **~ leaves** [*count*] : a dried leaf from the bay tree that has a sweet smell and is used in cooking

bay·o·net /ˈbejənət/ *noun, pl* **-nets** [*count*] : a long knife that is attached to the end of a rifle and used as a weapon in battle

— **bayonet** *verb* **-nets; -net·ed; -net·ing** [+ *obj*] • The soldier was *bayoneted* in the chest.

bay·ou /ˈbaju/ *noun, pl* **-ous** [*count*] : an area of water in the southern U.S. in which the water moves very slowly and is filled with many plants • Louisiana *bayous*

bay window *noun, pl* **~ -dows** [*count*] : a large window or set of windows that sticks out from the outside wall of a building — see picture at WINDOW

ba·zaar /bəˈzaɚ/ *noun, pl* **-zaars** [*count*]

1 : a type of market found especially in Middle Eastern countries that has rows of small shops which sell many different kinds of things

2 : an event at which things are sold to raise money for people or an organization • a charity *bazaar* • church *bazaars*

ba·zoo·ka /bəˈzuːkə/ *noun, pl* **-kas** [*count*] : a military weapon that rests on a person's shoulder and fires small rockets at tanks

BB /ˈbiːˌbiː/ *noun, pl* **BBs** [*count*] : a small metal ball that is fired from a BB gun

b–ball /ˈbiːˌbɑːl/ *noun* [*noncount*] *US, informal* : BASKETBALL

BBC *abbr* British Broadcasting Corporation ✧ The *BBC* is a radio and television company that is owned by the British government.

BB gun *noun, pl* **~ guns** [*count*] *chiefly US* : a gun that uses air pressure to fire small metal balls (called BBs)

BBQ *abbr* barbecue

BC *or chiefly US* **B.C.** *abbr* before Christ — used to refer to the years that came before the birth of Jesus Christ • 550 *B.C.* • in the fifth century *B.C.* [=between the years 499 and 400 *B.C.*] — compare A.D., B.C.E., C.E.

BCE *or chiefly US* **B.C.E.** *abbr* before the Christian Era; before the Common Era — used to refer to the years that came before the birth of Jesus Christ ✧ *B.C.E.* is now often used instead of *B.C.* especially in scientific writing. • 550 *B.C.E.* • in the fifth century *B.C.E.* [=between the years 499 and 400 *B.C.E.*] — compare A.D., B.C., C.E.

be /ˈbiː/ *verb, present first singular* **am** /ˈæm, əm/ *second singular* **are** /ˈaɚ, ɚ/ *third singular* **is** /ˈɪz, əz/ *pl* **are**; *past tense for first and third singular* **was** /ˈwəz/ *second singular* **were** /ˈwɚ/ *pl* **were**; *past participle* **been** /ˈbɪn, *Brit* ˈbiːn/ *present participle* **be·ing** /ˈbiːjɪŋ/

1 [*linking verb*] **a —** used to indicate the identity of a person or thing • Today *is* Wednesday. • John *is* my brother. • The first person I met *was* Susan. = Susan *was* the first person I met. • Who *are* you? • "There's someone at the door." "Who *is* it?" "It*'s* David." • Your responsibility *is* to keep this area clean. = Keeping this area clean *is* your responsibility. **b —** used to describe the qualities of a person or thing • My hands *are* cold. • He *is* 35 years old and six feet tall. • I*'m* hungry. • The leaves *are* green, and so *is* the grass. • The noise *was* very loud. • The way he behaves *is* foolish. • How foolish he *is*! • "*(Are)* You hungry?" "Yes, I *am*." • The book *is* about English grammar. • These people *are* with me. • The letter *is* for you. • They asked the students not to *be* late. = They asked that the students not *be* late. • Treat people with respect, whether they *are* rich or poor. = (formal) Treat people with respect, whether they *be* rich or poor. = (formal) Treat people with respect, *be* they rich or poor. • Our neighbors are *being* unusually friendly lately. • Don't *be* such a fool! [=don't act in such a foolish way] • ***To be*** perfectly/quite honest/frank (with you), I didn't like the movie. [=I am speaking honestly/frankly when I say that I didn't like the movie] • The book *is* mine. • I'd do it ***if I were you***. [=I think you should do it] **c** — used to indicate the condition of a person or thing • "Hi.

How *are* you?" "Fine, thanks. How *are* you?" • How *is* your father? = How *is* your father's health?
2 [*linking verb*] — used to indicate the group, class, category, etc., that a person or thing belongs to • I'*m* a doctor and my sister *is* a lawyer. • That fish *is* a trout. • The trout *is* a (kind of) fish. • Apes *are* mammals. • She'*s* a hard worker. [=she works hard] • What a fool he *is*! [=he is a fool] • *Being* an artist herself [=because she is an artist herself], she tends to look at other people's paintings very critically.
3 [*linking verb*] — used to indicate the place, situation, or position of a person or thing • The book *is* on the table. • "Where'*s* John?" "He'*s* in the living room." • The house *is* past the bridge. • It was great *being* here. = It was great *to be* here. • I must *be* on my way. [=I must go] • Here'*s* the book. = Here it *is*.
4 [*linking verb*] **a** — used in phrases with *there* to describe a situation, occurrence, etc. • *There is* a book on the table. [=a book is on the table] • *There are* concerts several times a week. [=concerts are held several times a week] • *There* will *be* concerts next week. • "*There's* someone at the door." "Who is it?" "It's John." **b** — used in phrases with *it* to indicate a time or place or to describe a current, past, or future condition • *It's* 12 o'clock. [=the time is 12 o'clock] • *It's* noon/early/late. • *It's* Wednesday today. [=today is Wednesday] • *It was* noon when we arrived. [=we arrived at noon] • *It was* here that I lost my way. [=I lost my way here] • *It's* raining. • *It's* hot out! • *It's* odd that he didn't see us. [=the fact that he didn't see us was odd]
5 [*linking verb*] — used to say how much something costs • "I like this painting. How much *is* it?" [=how much does it cost?] "*It's* 600 dollars." [=it costs 600 dollars]
6 [*linking verb*] — used to say that one amount or number is the same as another • Three plus two *is* [=*equals*] five.
7 [*no obj*] : to happen or take place • The concert *was* last night. • The concert *is* [=*will be*] tomorrow night. [=the concert will take place tomorrow night] • "When *was* the Battle of Waterloo?" "(It *was*) In 1815." • "When *is* Christmas?" "*It's* on a Wednesday this year."
8 [*no obj*] : to come or go — used in perfect tenses • She has already *been* [=*come*] and gone. • Have you ever *been* [=*gone*] to Rome? • I haven't *been* there for several years. • I've been waiting for you for half an hour. ***Where have you been***? [=where were you?; why weren't you here?] ✧ People who have ***been there, done that*** are bored about the idea of going somewhere or doing something because they have already done it before. This is an informal phrase that is often used in a joking way. • I suggested to my cousin that she go to Florida for her vacation, but she said, "*Been there, done that*."
9 [*no obj*] *somewhat formal* : to exist or live • I think, therefore I *am*. [=*exist*] • Once upon a time there *was* [=*lived*] a knight. • There once *was* a man who dwelt alone in a small village. • all the things that *are* [=*exist*] • "To *be*, or not to *be*: that is the question." —Shakespeare, *Hamlet* (1600)
10 [*auxiliary verb*] — used with the past participle of a verb to form passive constructions • The money *was found* by a child. • They *were* [=*got*] *married* by a priest. • Don't *be fooled* by what he says. • Please *be seated*. [=please sit down] • The election *was expected* to produce a very close result. • God *be praised*! [=let God be praised] • I *was surprised* by her rudeness.
11 [*auxiliary verb*] **a** — used with the present participle of a verb to express continuous action • They *are studying*. • I have *been sleeping*. • He *was reading*. • *Are* you *getting* hungry? • Our neighbors *are being* unusually friendly. **b** — used with the present participle of a verb to express future or later action • I'*m seeing* him tomorrow. [=I will see him tomorrow] • We *are leaving* soon. [=we will leave soon]
12 [*auxiliary verb*] **a** — used with *to + verb* to say what will happen or was going to happen in the future • The best *is* yet/still *to come*. [=the best has not yet happened] • No one realized that she *was* one day *to become* famous. [=that she would become famous one day] • She *was* not/never *to see* him again. [=she would never see him again] • There *are to be* two concerts next week. [=there will be two concerts next week] **b** — used with *to + verb* to say what should happen or be done • People like that *are to be* pitied, not hated. [=people like that should be pitied] • You *are* not (allowed) *to smoke* in here! • What *am* I *to do*? [=what should I do?] **c** — used in negative statements with *to + verb* to say what is or was possible • The truth of their argument *was not to be* denied. [=could not be denied] • You're not to blame: you *weren't to know* he'd be offended. [=you could not have known that he would be offended] • The book ***was nowhere to be found***. [=could not be found] **d** — used with *to + verb* to say that one thing must happen or be true so that another thing can happen or be true • He must study if he *is to pass* his exams. [=he must study in order to pass his exams]
13 [*auxiliary verb*] — used like *have* with the past participle of some verbs to form perfect tenses • He isn't here: he *is* [=*has*] gone. — now often considered archaic • Christ *is* risen. [=Christ has risen]
be yourself : to behave in a normal or natural way • You'*re* not *yourself* today. What's the matter? • I'll *be myself* again once I've had something to eat. • "How can I impress her?" "Just *be yourself*!"
leave (someone or something) be see [1]LEAVE
let (someone or something) be see [1]LET
the best is yet to be see [3]BEST
the powers that be see [1]POWER
to be sure see [1]SURE

be- *prefix*
1 : make : cause to be • *be*foul • *be*numb : treat as • *be*little • *be*friend
2 : about • *be*wail • *be*moan • *be*speak
3 : in a way that is easy to notice • *be*whiskered • *be*jeweled • *be*spectacled
4 : thoroughly : very much • *be*loved

[1]**beach** /ˈbiːʧ/ *noun, pl* **beach·es** [*count*] : an area covered with sand or small rocks that is next to an ocean or lake • We spent the day at the *beach*. • walking/lying on the *beach* • white, sandy *beaches* • private/public *beaches* — see color picture on page C7

[2]**beach** *verb* **beaches; beached; beach·ing** [+ *obj*]
1 : to cause (a boat or ship) to go out of the water and onto a beach • The pirates *beached* the ship on the island.
2 ✧ When a large ocean animal, such as a whale, is ***beached*** or has ***beached itself***, it has come out of the water onto land and is unable to return to the water. • People were trying to rescue a whale that had *beached itself* on the shore. • a *beached* whale

beach ball *noun, pl* ~ **balls** [*count*] : a large ball that is filled with air and made for use at the beach

beach buggy *noun, pl* ~ **-gies** [*count*] : DUNE BUGGY

beach·comb·er /ˈbiːʧˌkoumɚ/ *noun, pl* **-ers** [*count*] : a person who walks along beaches looking for things (such as seashells or items that can be sold)

beach·front /ˈbiːʧˌfrʌnt/ *noun, pl* **-fronts** [*count*] : an area of land that has a beach on one side • We went for a walk along the *beachfront*. — often used before another noun • *beachfront* properties

beach·head /ˈbiːʧˌhɛd/ *noun, pl* **-heads** [*count*] : a beach on an enemy's shore that an invading army takes and controls in order to prepare for the arrival of more soldiers and supplies — often used figuratively to mean a place or position that serves as a base for future action or progress • The company established a *beachhead* in New York City.

beach towel *noun, pl* ~ **-els** [*count*] : a large, usually brightly colored towel made for use at the beach

beach·wear /ˈbiːʧˌweɚ/ *noun* [*noncount*] : clothing made to be worn at the beach

bea·con /ˈbiːkən/ *noun, pl* **-cons** [*count*]
1 : a strong light that can be seen from far away and that is used to help guide ships, airplanes, etc.
2 : a radio signal that is broadcast to help guide ships, airplanes, etc. • a radio *beacon*
3 : someone or something (such as a country) that guides or gives hope to others • These countries are *beacons* of democracy. • Our nation should be a *beacon* of/for peace to people around the world. • This new medicine is a ***beacon of hope*** for/to thousands of people. [=this new medicine gives hope to thousands of people]
4 *in the past* : a fire built on a hill and used as a signal

bead /ˈbiːd/ *noun, pl* **beads** [*count*]
1 : a small, usually round piece of glass, wood, stone, etc., that has a hole through its center and that is put on a string with other similar pieces and worn as jewelry or that is sewn onto clothing • a string of *beads* • She was wearing *beads*. [=a necklace of beads] — see color picture on page C11
2 : a small, round drop of liquid (such as water or blood) • *Beads* of sweat began rolling/running down their faces.
draw a bead on *also US* ***get a bead on*** *or* ***take a bead on*** : to aim at (someone or something) • He lifted the rifle and carefully *drew a bead on* the target. — often used figuratively • The government is *drawing a bead on* inflation. [=is

targeting inflation] • It's hard to *get a bead on* [=to understand] the reasons for her decision.

bead·ed /ˈbiːdəd/ *adj*
1 : decorated with beads • fancy *beaded* dresses
2 : covered *with* small drops of sweat • Her forehead was *beaded with* sweat/perspiration.

bead·ing /ˈbiːdɪŋ/ *noun* [*noncount*] **:** beads that are sewn on a piece of clothing as decoration

bead·work /ˈbiːdˌwɚk/ *noun* [*noncount*] **:** BEADING • beautiful *beadwork*

beady /ˈbiːdi/ *adj* **bead·i·er; -est** *disapproving* — used to describe eyes that are small, round, and shiny and that usually suggest a bad quality (such as greed or dishonesty) • The workers were nervous because they knew the boss was watching them with his *beady* little eyes.

bea·gle /ˈbiːgəl/ *noun, pl* **bea·gles** [*count*] **:** a type of small dog used for hunting that has smooth black, brown, and white fur — see picture at DOG

beak /ˈbiːk/ *noun, pl* **beaks** [*count*]
1 : the hard usually pointed parts that cover a bird's mouth **:** BILL • the *beak* of a hawk — see picture at BIRD
2 *informal + humorous* **:** a person's nose • an actor with a big *beak*
– beaked /ˈbiːkt/ *adj* • a long-*beaked* bird

bea·ker /ˈbiːkɚ/ *noun, pl* **-kers** [*count*]
1 : a wide glass with a lip for pouring that is used especially in chemistry for holding and measuring liquids
2 *chiefly Brit* **:** a large drinking cup with a wide opening that is typically made of plastic or metal

be–all and end–all /ˈbiːˌɑːləndˈɛndˌɑːl/ *noun*
the be-all and end-all **:** the most important part of something or the reason for something • He acts as if making money is *the be-all and end-all* of human existence.

[1]**beam** /ˈbiːm/ *noun, pl* **beams** [*count*]
1 a : a line of light coming from a source (such as the sun or a headlight) • a bright *beam* of light • We saw the *beams* from their flashlights. • a laser *beam* — see also HIGH BEAM, LOW BEAM, SUNBEAM **b :** a line of energy, particles, etc., that cannot be seen • a *beam* of electrons • X-ray *beams*
2 : a long and heavy piece of wood or metal that is used as a support in a building or ship • the building's steel support *beams* • wood ceiling *beams* — see also BALANCE BEAM
off beam *Brit, informal* **:** incorrect or mistaken • My guess was way *off beam*. [=(*US*) *off base*]
on the beam *informal* **:** exactly correct • His description of the problem was right *on the beam*. [=(more commonly) *on the mark*]
– beamed *adj* • The living room has a *beamed* ceiling. [=a ceiling that is supported with wood or metal beams]

[2]**beam** *verb* **beams; beamed; beam·ing**
1 a [*no obj*] **:** to smile happily • She *beamed* as she told us the good news. • They stood *beaming* with satisfaction. **b** [+ *obj*] **:** to say (something) while smiling happily • "We're getting married!" he *beamed*.
2 : to send out beams of light or energy [*no obj*] Sunlight was *beaming* [=*shining*] through the window. [+ *obj*] The sun *beamed* its light through the window.
3 [+ *obj*] **:** to send out (information, television signals, etc.) through wires or the air • Pictures of the distant planet were *beamed* back to the Earth.
4 [+ *obj*] *in stories* **:** to send (someone) to another place instantly by using a special machine • The space explorers were *beamed* onto the surface of the planet.

[1]**bean** /ˈbiːn/ *noun, pl* **beans** [*count*]
1 a : a seed that is eaten as a vegetable and that comes from any one of many different kinds of climbing plants • We ate rice and *beans* for dinner. **b :** a part of a plant that contains very young seeds and that is eaten as a vegetable — see also GREEN BEAN, POLE BEAN, SNAP BEAN, STRING BEAN, WAX BEAN **c :** a plant that produces beans • We're growing tomatoes and *beans* in our garden this year.
2 : a seed that looks like a bean but that does not come from a climbing plant • coffee *beans* • cocoa *beans* • a vanilla *bean* — see also JELLY BEAN, JUMPING BEAN
a hill of beans see HILL
full of beans *informal* **1 :** full of energy and life • We were young and *full of beans*. • Although she's much older now, she's still *full of beans*. **2** *US* **:** not correct or truthful **:** full of nonsense • If that's what he's been saying, then he's *full of beans*.
not know beans about *US, informal* **:** to not know anything about (something) • He *doesn't know beans about* computers. [=he knows nothing about computers]
spill the beans *informal* **:** to reveal secret information • I tried to get him to tell me what he knew, but he refused to *spill the beans*.

[2]**bean** *verb* **beans; beaned; bean·ing** [+ *obj*] *informal* **:** to hit (someone) on the head with something • A kid in the back of the room *beaned* me with an eraser. [=threw an eraser that hit my head] • (*baseball*) The pitcher almost *beaned* the first batter. [=he threw a pitch that almost hit the batter's head]

bean·bag /ˈbiːnˌbæg/ *noun, pl* **-bags** [*count*]
1 : a small cloth bag that is filled with dried beans or small pieces of another material and used as a toy
2 : a large bag that is filled with small round pieces of material and used as a soft chair • a *beanbag* chair

bean counter *noun, pl* ~ **-ters** [*count*] *informal + disapproving* **:** a person who helps to run a business and who only cares about money • He blames corporate *bean counters* for causing thousands of workers to lose their jobs.

bean curd *noun* [*noncount*] **:** TOFU

bean·ie /ˈbiːni/ *noun, pl* **-ies** [*count*] **:** a small, round, tight-fitting hat or cap

bean·pole /ˈbiːnˌpoʊl/ *noun, pl* **-poles** [*count*] *informal + humorous* **:** a tall and thin person

bean sprouts *noun* [*plural*] **:** very young plants that come from bean seeds and that are used as a vegetable

[1]**bear** /ˈbeɚ/ *noun, pl* **bear** *or* **bears** [*count*]
1 : any one of a group of large and heavy animals that have thick hair and sharp claws and that can stand on two legs like a person • a mother *bear* and her cubs — sometimes used figuratively to describe a large man • a tall, friendly *bear* of a man • My father can be a grumpy old *bear* when he's tired. ✧ In informal British English, a person who becomes angry or annoyed very easily is ***(like) a bear with a sore head.*** • My father can be *like a bear with a sore head* when he's tired. — see also BLACK BEAR, GRIZZLY BEAR, POLAR BEAR, TEDDY BEAR
2 *finance* **:** a person who expects the price of stocks to go down and who sells them to avoid losing money • The *bears* outnumbered the bulls on Wall Street today. — compare BULL; see also BEAR MARKET
3 *US, informal* **:** something that is difficult to do or deal with • This oven is a *bear* to clean. [=this oven is very hard to clean]
loaded for bear see LOADED

bear

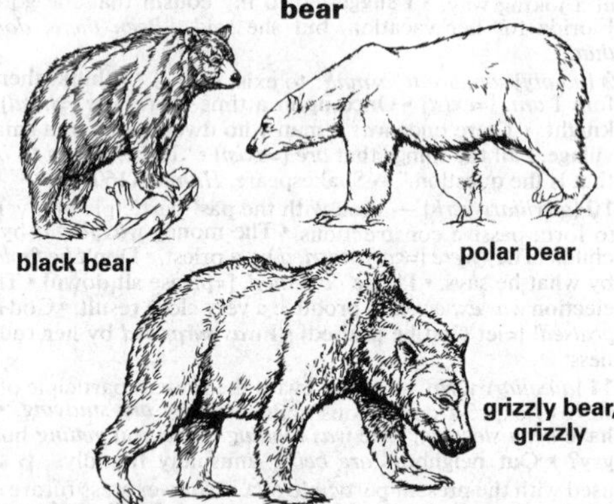

[2]**bear** *verb* **bears; bore** /ˈboɚ/; **borne** /ˈboɚn/; **bear·ing**
1 : to accept or endure (something) [+ *obj*] He *bore* [=*tolerated*] their insults patiently. — usually used in questions and negative statements with *can, can't, could,* and *couldn't* • He *could* hardly *bear* [=*stand*] the pain. • I *can't bear* cold weather. [=I strongly dislike cold weather] • I *couldn't bear* the suspense. • I *can't bear* it if/when people behave like that! • I *can't bear* doing this. = I can't *bear* to do this. • How *can* you *bear* to see him again after the way he's treated you? • I couldn't *bear* you to get the wrong idea. • I *couldn't bear* his behavior. = His behavior was ***more than I could bear.*** • I ***couldn't bear the thought/idea*** of moving again. [*no obj*] (*US*) — + *for* • I couldn't *bear for* you to get the wrong idea.
2 [+ *obj*] **:** to be worthy of (something) **:** to deserve or allow (something) • a joke too silly to *bear* repeating [=a joke that is too silly to be worth repeating] • It's so horrible it doesn't

bear thinking about! [=it's so horrible that I don't want to think about it] • a symphony that can *bear* comparison with Beethoven's best • a plan that will not *bear* [=*withstand*] close scrutiny/examination • suspicious behavior that ***bears watching*** [=that should be watched]

3 [+ *obj*] **:** to assume or accept (something, such as cost or responsibility) • The company agreed to *bear* the costs/expenses. • The criminals must *bear* full responsibility for the deaths of these innocent people. • Who will *bear* the blame for this tragedy?

4 [+ *obj*] *somewhat formal + literary* **:** to move while holding up and supporting (something) **:** CARRY • The demonstrators *bore* banners and sang songs. • They arrived *bearing* gifts. • The leaves were *borne* aloft/away by the wind. • disease-*bearing* germs [=germs that carry and spread diseases] • germ-*borne* diseases [=diseases that are carried and spread by germs] • He believes that citizens should have the right to ***bear arms*** [=to carry weapons] ◊ If something is ***borne in on/upon*** you, it is made very clear to you. This is a formal phrase. • It was *borne in on* us by the new evidence that prompt action was very important. [=the new evidence strongly indicated that prompt action was very important]

5 [+ *obj*] **a :** to have (something) as a feature or characteristic • His leg was badly injured in the accident and it still *bears* [=*shows*] the scars/wounds/marks. • His face *bears* marks/signs of suffering. • Your conclusion *bears* [=*has*] no relation to the evidence. • She ***bore a resemblance*** to her aunt. [=she looked like her aunt] **b :** to have a surface on which something is written, drawn, etc. • The cornerstone *bears* a Latin inscription. • a letter *bearing* the date of 1900 • a shield *bearing* strange symbols **c :** to have (a name, price, etc.) • He *bore* the name (of) John. • The store sells imported goods *bearing* [=*having, with*] high prices. **d :** to have or hold (a feeling) in the mind • She still *bears* a grudge against him. = She still *bears* him a grudge. • She says she *bears* him no resentment for the way he treated her. • I can't deny the love I still *bear* [=*feel*] for her.

6 [+ *obj*] **a** *formal* **:** to give birth to (a child) • She has *borne* three children. • She has *borne* her husband three children. **b :** to produce (something) • a bank account that *bears* interest = an interest-*bearing* bank account • a bush that *bears* red flowers • trees that *bear* fruit — see also BEAR FRUIT (below)

7 [+ *obj*] **:** to support the weight of (something) • How much weight is that wall able to *bear*?

8 [*no obj*] **:** to go, move, or turn in a specified direction • *Bear* south. • The road *bears* (to the) right. • When you get to the fork in the road, you should *bear* [=*turn*] left.

Do not confuse *bear* with *bare*.

bear down [*phrasal verb*] *US* **:** to use all of your strength and effort to do something **:** to try very hard to do something • The pitcher *bore down* and struck out the last batter. • If we're going to finish on time, we really have to *bear down*.

bear down on [*phrasal verb*] **1** ***bear down on (something)*** **:** to push or lean down on (something) • The old man *bore down* heavily *on* his cane. • She *bore down* hard *on* her pencil. **2** ***bear down on (someone)*** **:** to place pressure on (someone) • Don't let your problems *bear down* too hard *on* you. [=don't let your problems weigh you down] **3** ***bear down on (someone or something)*** **:** to approach or move toward (something or someone) quickly and in a frightening or impressive way • The enemy battleship *bore down on* us.

bear fruit **:** to produce a desired result or reward • All his plans have finally *borne fruit*. [=all his plans have finally been realized] — see also [2]BEAR 6b (above)

bear in mind see [1]MIND

bear on [*phrasal verb*] ***bear on (something)*** *formal* **1 :** to have an effect on (something) • Personal feelings did not *bear on* our decision. [=did not affect or influence our decision] **2 :** to apply or relate to (something) • What are the facts *bearing* directly *on* this matter?

bear out [*phrasal verb*] ***bear out (something or someone)*** *or* ***bear (something or someone) out*** **:** to show the correctness of (something or someone) • The facts *bore out* [=*confirmed*] her story. [=the facts showed that her story was true] • Research has fully *borne him out*. [=has shown that he was completely correct]

bear up [*phrasal verb*] **:** to not be overwhelmed during a time of trouble, pain, etc. • She's been going through a tough time, but she's *bearing up* pretty well. — often + *under* • She has found it hard to *bear up under* the strain.

bear with [*phrasal verb*] ***bear with (someone)*** **:** to be patient with (someone) • I'll have that information for you soon. Just *bear with* me for another minute or two.

bear witness see [1]WITNESS

bear yourself *formal* **:** to move, stand, or behave in a specified way • The soldier *bore himself* [=*carried himself*] stiffly upright. • The soldier never failed to *bear himself* [=*conduct himself, behave*] courageously on the battlefield. • He always *bore himself* [=*behaved*] like a gentleman.

bring (something) to bear **:** to cause (something) to have an effect or influence • The company's new president *brings* 30 years of experience *to bear*. • If we hope to resolve these issues, more resources must be *brought to bear*. — often used with *on* • They will *bring* their considerable skills/talent/experience/knowledge *to bear on* the problem. • The demonstrators will continue to ***bring pressure to bear on*** the government.

cross to bear see [1]CROSS

grin and bear it see GRIN

bear·able /ˈberəbəl/ *adj* [*more* ~; *most* ~] **:** possible to bear **:** able to be accepted or endured • He's in a great deal of pain, but the medication makes it *bearable*. — opposite UNBEARABLE

– bear·abil·i·ty /ˌberəˈbɪləti/ *noun* [*noncount*] **– bear·ably** /ˈberəbli/ *adv*

bear claw *noun, pl* **~ claws** [*count*] *US* **:** a filled pastry shaped to like a bear's foot

beard /ˈbiəd/ *noun, pl* **beards** [*count*]

1 : the hair that grows on a man's cheeks and chin • He grew a *beard* and mustache.

2 : the long hair that grows on the chin of some animals • the *beard* of a goat

– beard·ed /ˈbiədəd/ *adj* • a *bearded* college professor

bear·er /ˈberɚ/ *noun, pl* **-ers** [*count*]

1 : a person who bears or carries something • the *bearer* of a U.S. passport • The *bearers* [=*porters*] carried our baggage up the mountain. • the *bearer* of glad/bad tidings [=the person who brings good/bad news] • His nephew was the ***ring bearer*** [=the person who holds the rings until they are needed] at his wedding. — see also PALLBEARER, STANDARD-BEARER, TORCHBEARER

2 *finance* **:** a person who has a check or order for payment • The check was marked "payable to *bearer*."

bear hug *noun, pl* **~ hugs** [*count*] **:** a strong and rough hug **:** an act of showing affection by putting your arms around someone and squeezing very tightly • He gave his brother a *bear hug*.

bearing *noun, pl* **-ings**

1 [*singular*] *formal* **:** the way in which a person moves, stands, or behaves • a man of military/dignified/regal *bearing*

2 *formal* **:** a relation or connection — + *on* [*singular*] These facts have a direct *bearing on* the question. [=these facts relate to the question in a direct way] [*noncount*] Personal feelings ***had no bearing on*** our decision. [=personal feelings did not affect or influence our decision]

3 [*count*] *technical* **:** a machine part in which another part turns or slides — see also BALL BEARING

4 [*count*] *technical* **:** a measurement taken with a compass that indicates the direction or position of something • take/get a compass *bearing*

beyond bearing *or* ***past bearing*** *formal* **:** too painful, unpleasant, etc., to be accepted or endured • a grief that is almost *past bearing* [=*unbearable*]

get/find your bearings **:** to find out your position • Let's stop here and *find our bearings*. [=figure out exactly where we are] — often used figuratively • Our course for new employees will help you *get/find your bearings* at work.

B

lose your bearings **:** to become lost ▪ The ship *lost its bearings* in the fog. — often used figuratively ▪ I feel I've *lost my bearings* in life. [=I have become confused about my life; I do not know what I am doing or what I want to do in my life]

bear·ish /ˈberɪʃ/ *adj* [*more* ~; *most* ~]
1 : having qualities like a bear — used especially to describe a large man ▪ a grumpy, *bearish* old man
2 : expecting the price of stocks to go down ▪ *bearish* investors **:** characterized by falling stock prices ▪ The market has been *bearish* lately. — compare BULLISH
– bear·ish·ly *adv* **– bear·ish·ness** *noun* [*noncount*]

bear market *noun, pl* **~ -kets** [*count*] *finance* **:** a market (such as a stock market) in which prices are going down — compare BULL MARKET

bear·skin /ˈbeɚˌskɪn/ *noun, pl* **-skins** [*count*]
1 : the skin and fur of a bear — often used before another noun ▪ a *bearskin* rug
2 : a tall, black fur hat worn in ceremonies by some British soldiers

beast /ˈbiːst/ *noun, pl* **beasts** [*count*]
1 *old-fashioned* **:** an animal ▪ dogs and other four-footed *beasts* ▪ wild *beasts* ▪ the birds and *beasts* of the forest ▪ a conflict between man and *beast* [=between human beings and animals]; *especially* **:** a wild animal that is large, dangerous, or unusual ▪ They were attacked by a savage *beast*. ▪ a story about a mythical/imaginary *beast* [=*creature*] with two heads
2 *old-fashioned* **:** an unkind or cruel person ▪ He's a cruel, hateful *beast*! ▪ her *beast* of a husband [=her husband who is a beast]
3 *informal* **:** a person or thing of a particular kind ▪ Reading modern English is one thing, but understanding Shakespeare is an entirely ***different beast***. [=is an entirely different thing; is entirely different] ▪ a powerful political *beast* [=a powerful politician]

beast·ly /ˈbiːstli/ *adj* **beast·li·er; -est** [*also more* ~; *most* ~] *chiefly Brit* **:** very unpleasant ▪ We've been having such *beastly* [=*terrible*] weather lately. ▪ What a *beastly* habit! ▪ *beastly* behavior
– beast·li·ness *noun* [*noncount*]

beast of burden *noun, pl* **beasts of burden** [*count*] **:** an animal that people use to carry heavy things

¹beat /ˈbiːt/ *verb* **beat; beat·en** /ˈbiːtn̩/ *or chiefly US* **beat; beat·ing**
1 : to hit (something) repeatedly [+ *obj*] He *beat* the door with his fists. = He *beat* his fists against/on the door. ▪ He *beat* the dusty rug with a stick. = He *beat* a stick against the dusty rug. ▪ He *beat* the dust out of the rug with a stick. ▪ She used a hammer to *beat* the metal into shape. ▪ She used a hammer to *beat* the nail into the wall. ▪ The dented metal was *beaten* flat. ▪ The waves were *beating* the shore. [*no obj*] He *beat* at/against/on the door with his fists. ▪ The waves were *beating* on/against the shore. ▪ The rain *beat* on the roof.
2 [+ *obj*] **:** to hit (someone) repeatedly in order to cause pain or injury ▪ They *beat* him with clubs. ▪ He was *beaten* badly/savagely/brutally. ▪ a man accused of *beating* his wife ▪ They *beat* him to the ground. [=they hit him repeatedly and he fell to the ground] ▪ They threatened to ***beat the (living) daylights out of*** him. [=to beat him very badly] ▪ He was ***beaten to death***. — see also BEATING, BEAT UP (below), BEAT UP ON (below)
3 : to hit (a drum) repeatedly in order to produce music or a signal [+ *obj*] The drummer kept *beating* his drum. ▪ the sound of a *beaten* drum ▪ They *beat* (out) a message on their drums. ▪ The drum kept *beating* (out) its rhythm. [*no obj*] The drummer kept *beating*. ▪ The drum kept *beating*. ▪ the sound of a *beating* drum — see also *beat the drum for* at ¹DRUM
4 *cooking* **:** to stir or mix (something) in a forceful way [+ *obj*] She used a whisk to *beat* the eggs. ▪ The recipe says you should *beat* the eggs lightly/thoroughly/well. ▪ Slowly *beat* the sugar into the batter. = Slowly *beat* in the sugar. = Slowly *beat* the sugar in. [*no obj*] Separate out the egg whites and *beat* until stiff.
5 : to move (wings) with an up and down motion [+ *obj*] The bird was *beating* [=*flapping*] its wings. [*no obj*] the sound of *beating* wings
6 [*no obj*] *of the heart* **:** to make the regular movements needed to pump blood ▪ My heart was *beating* wildly/frantically with excitement and my pulse was racing! ▪ (*humorous*) We get free doughnuts? ***Be still, my beating heart***!
7 [+ *obj*] **a :** to defeat (someone) in a game, contest, etc. ▪ He gets very angry when I *beat* him at chess. ▪ We *beat* them 14 to 3. ▪ Our team was badly *beaten* in the championship game. ▪ She was narrowly *beaten* in the previous election, but she won this time. ▪ We *beat* them soundly/convincingly/comfortably/easily/badly. = (*US*) We ***beat the pants off*** them. ▪ They tried to lure away our customers by offering deep discounts, but we ***beat them at their own game***. [=we offered even deeper discounts than they did] ✧ People say ***if you can't beat them, join them*** or ***if you can't beat 'em, join 'em*** when they decide to do what other people are doing and to stop opposing them. **b :** to do better than (something) ▪ She managed to *beat* the old record by several seconds. ▪ We can still *beat* the deadline if we work quickly. ▪ His wonderful performance will be ***hard/tough to beat***. = His wonderful performance will ***take some beating***. [=it will be difficult for anyone to do better than his wonderful performance] ▪ Most new restaurants fail, but this one somehow managed to ***beat the odds***. [=this one succeeded even though it did not have a good chance of succeeding] ✧ People say ***can you beat that?*** when they are surprised or angry about something. ▪ *Can you beat that*?! A person like him being elected mayor! [=it is surprising or ridiculous to think that a person like him has been elected mayor] **c** *not used in progressive tenses* **:** to be better than (something) ▪ For sheer luxury ***you can't beat*** a nice hot bath. = For sheer luxury, ***nothing beats*** a nice hot bath. = For sheer luxury, a nice hot bath ***beats anything***. **d :** to control or overcome (something) ▪ By working together we can *beat* crime! ▪ (*US*) His favorite way of ***beating the heat*** [=remaining cool in hot weather] is to have a couple of cold beers. **e :** to be too difficult for (someone) ▪ This problem has *beaten* everyone. [=no one has been able to solve this problem] ✧ The informal expression ***(it) beats me*** means "I don't know." ▪ "How did she manage to fix the problem so quickly?" "*Beats me*." ▪ I don't believe anything he tells me. *It beats me* how people can continue to trust him.
8 [+ *obj*] **a :** to come, arrive, or act before (someone or something) ▪ I *beat* him narrowly to the finish line. [=I reached the finish line slightly before he did] ▪ I bet I can *beat* you to the front door! ▪ I wondered which of us would finish our work first, but she ***beat me to it*** by two days. [=she finished two days before I did] **b :** to avoid having problems with (something) by acting earlier ▪ We left early so that we could ***beat the traffic***. ▪ We got to the store when it opened and managed to ***beat the rush***.

beat a dead horse see ¹HORSE

beat a path **:** to make (a path) by walking over the ground many times ▪ They *beat a path* through the woods to the stream. — sometimes used figuratively ▪ If you work hard and well, success will ***beat a path to your door***. [=you will be very successful]

beat a retreat **:** to leave quickly ▪ A group of teenagers was causing trouble, but they ***beat a hasty retreat*** when the cops arrived.

beat around/about the bush see BUSH

beat back [*phrasal verb*] ***beat back (someone) or beat (someone) back*** **:** to force (someone) to go back or to retreat by fighting ▪ Our troops were *beaten back* by enemy forces.

beat down [*phrasal verb*] **1** *of the sun* **:** to shine down with great heat and strength ▪ The blazing sun was *beating down* on us mercilessly/relentlessly. **2** ***beat (something) down or beat down (something)*** **:** to hit (something, such as a door) so that it falls down ▪ The police had to *beat down* the door to get into the house. ▪ The storm *beat down* the crops. — often used figuratively ▪ Years of failure had *beaten* him *down*. [=had caused him to lose hope or spirit] **3** *chiefly Brit* **a** ***beat (someone) down or beat down (someone)*** **:** to cause (someone) to lower a price ▪ I *beat* her *down* from £30 to £15. **b** ***beat (a price) down or beat down (a price)*** **:** to cause someone to lower (a price) ▪ I *beat* her asking price *down* from £30 to £15.

beat it *informal* **:** to go away quickly ▪ The teenagers *beat it* when the cops arrived. — often used as a command ▪ Stop bothering me. *Beat it*! [=*get lost*]

beat off [*phrasal verb*] **1** ***beat off (someone or something) or beat (someone or something) off*** **:** to force (someone or something) to go away by fighting ▪ She managed to *beat off* her attacker. — sometimes used figuratively ▪ The company has managed to *beat off* [=*fight off*] its competitors and maintain control of the market. **2** *US, informal + impolite, of a man* **:** MASTURBATE

beat out [*phrasal verb*] **1** ***beat out (something) or beat (something) out*** **a :** to put out (a fire) by beating ▪ The fire was raging but we managed to *beat* it *out*. **b** *baseball*

: to turn (a ground ball) into a base hit by running fast to first base • He *beat out* a bunt. **2 *beat out (someone or something) or beat (someone or something) out US*** : to defeat or overcome (a person, team, etc.) • They were *beaten out* [=beaten] in the semifinals. • She thought she would get the job, but someone else *beat* her *out.* [=someone else got the job]

beat someone to the punch see ²PUNCH

beat the clock see ¹CLOCK

beat the rap see ¹RAP

beat up** [phrasal verb] **beat up (someone) or beat (someone) up : to hurt or injure (someone) by hitting • A gang of bullies threatened to *beat* him *up.* • He was *beaten up* badly by the bullies. — sometimes used figuratively • a politician who is getting *beat/beaten up* by liberal/conservative critics • He's been ***beating himself up*** [=he has been harshly blaming or criticizing himself] because of the failure of his marriage. — see also BEAT-UP

***beat up on** [phrasal verb] **beat up on (someone)** US, informal* : to hit (someone) repeatedly in order to cause pain or injury : to beat (someone) • A gang of bullies was *beating up on* him. — sometimes used figuratively • a politician who is getting *beat up on* by his critics

to beat the band see ¹BAND

– beat·able /ˈbiːtəbəl/ *adj* • an easily *beatable* opponent [=an opponent that can be easily defeated]

²beat *noun, pl* **beats**

1 a [*count*] : the act of beating • a single *beat* on a drum • a *beat* of the bird's wings • a single *beat* of his heart [=a single heartbeat] — see also *heart skipped a beat* at HEART **b** [*singular*] : a sound produced by beating • We could hear the steady *beat* of the waves against the shore. • They danced to the *beat* of the drums. • listening to the *beat* of his heart

2 a [*count*] : a loud or strong sound that occurs regularly in music or poetry • music that has four *beats* to a bar — see also DOWNBEAT **b** [*singular*] : the regular pattern of sounds in music or poetry : RHYTHM • She likes music with a Latin *beat.* • a pounding *beat* • The music had a steady *beat.*

3 [*count*] : a place or area that someone (such as a policeman) regularly goes to, walks through, or covers as part of a job — usually singular • The policeman was patrolling/pounding his/the *beat.* = The policeman was on his/the *beat.* • a reporter's *beat*

miss a beat** chiefly US* : to have difficulty in continuing : to stop or hesitate briefly • He answered their questions ***without missing a beat [=he answered all their questions very easily and without hesitating] • He answered all their questions and ***never missed a beat*** • He ***didn't miss a beat***

³beat *adj, not used before a noun, informal* : very tired : EXHAUSTED • Let me sit down. I'm absolutely *beat!*

beat·en /ˈbiːtn/ *adj, always used before a noun*

1 : formed into a desired shape by being hit with a hammer • *beaten* gold

2 *of a path, trail, etc.* : made smooth : walked on by many people • a *beaten* path

3 : having lost all hope or spirit • A failure at 50, he was a *beaten* [=*defeated*] man.

off the beaten track** or US **off the beaten path : in or to a place that is not close to the places where people usually go • The restaurant is a little *off the beaten track,* so it won't be crowded.

beat·er /ˈbiːtɚ/ *noun, pl* **-ers** [*count*]

1 : a device or tool that is used for beating something • a carpet *beater* — see also EGGBEATER, WORLD-BEATER

2 : someone who repeatedly hits another person • He is accused of being a wife *beater.* [=a man who beats his wife] • a child *beater*

3 *US, informal* : an old car that is in poor condition • driving a rusty old *beater*

be·atif·ic /ˌbiːjəˈtɪfɪk/ *adj, formal* : showing complete happiness • a *beatific* [=*blissful*] smile

be·at·i·fy /biˈætəˌfaɪ/ *verb* **-fies; -fied; -fy·ing** [+ *obj*] *in the Roman Catholic Church* : to give a dead person a title of honor for being very good and holy • She was *beatified* by the Pope one hundred years after her death.

– be·at·i·fi·ca·tion /biˌætəfəˈkeɪʃən/ *noun* [*noncount*]

beat·ing /ˈbiːtɪŋ/ *noun, pl* **-ings** [*count*] : the act of repeatedly hitting someone to cause pain or injury : the act of beating someone • He threatened to give the boys a (good) *beating* for stealing the apples. — often used figuratively • Our plans took a real *beating* from the review committee. [=the review committee strongly criticized our plans] • The reporters gave the politician quite a *beating* with all their hostile questions. • Many investors took quite a (bad) *beating* [=lost a lot of money] when the stock market crashed.

beat·nik /ˈbiːtˌnɪk/ *noun, pl* **-niks** [*count*] : a young person who was part of a social group in the 1950s and early 1960s that rejected the traditional rules of society and encouraged people to express themselves through art

beat–up /ˈbiːtˌʌp/ *adj* [*more ~; most ~*] *informal* : old and badly worn or damaged • a *beat-up* old car — see also *beat up* at ¹BEAT

beau /ˈboʊ/ *noun, pl* **beaux** /ˈboʊz/ *or* **beaus** [*count*] *old-fashioned* : a woman's male lover or friend : BOYFRIEND • She introduced us to her latest *beau.*

¹beaut /ˈbjuːt/ *noun, pl* **beauts** [*count*] *US + Australia + New Zealand, informal* : a very good or attractive thing or person • He just bought a new car—it's a real *beaut.* [=*beauty*] — often used in an ironic way to describe a bad thing or person • You've told lies before, but this one's a *beaut.* [=a very bad lie] • My boss is a real *beaut*—he complains about everything but never does any work himself.

²beaut *adj, Australia + New Zealand, informal* : excellent or beautiful • That new car of yours is *beaut!* • a *beaut* car

beau·te·ous /ˈbjuːtijəs/ *adj, literary* : BEAUTIFUL • a *beauteous* evening

beau·ti·cian /bjuˈtɪʃən/ *noun, pl* **-cians** [*count*] : a person whose job is to give beauty treatments to women by washing and cutting hair, applying makeup, etc. — called also (*US*) *cosmetologist*

beau·ti·ful /ˈbjuːtɪfəl/ *adj* [*more ~; most ~*]

1 : having beauty: such as **a** : very attractive in a physical way • a *beautiful* young woman/child • You have the most *beautiful* smile/eyes. **b** : giving pleasure to the mind or the senses • The film tells a *beautiful* story about two young lovers. • a *beautiful* song • a *beautiful* dress/color/garden/house • Our hotel room had a *beautiful* view of the ocean. • The sunsets here are absolutely *beautiful.*

2 : very good or pleasing : not having any bad qualities • We've been having such *beautiful* [=*excellent, fine*] weather lately. • a *beautiful* sunny day • What a *beautiful* day for a picnic! • They did a *beautiful* job [=an excellent job] fixing up the house. • a *beautiful* friendship/relationship • This is a *beautiful* example of early American poetry.

– beau·ti·ful·ly /ˈbjuːtɪfli/ *adv* • You sang *beautifully.* • a *beautifully* written poem

> ***synonyms*** BEAUTIFUL, PRETTY, LOVELY, and HANDSOME describe people and things that are pleasing to look at, hear, etc. BEAUTIFUL applies to things that give the greatest pleasure and cause people to feel strong emotions. • *beautiful* sunsets • a *beautiful* poem When used of a person, it usually describes a woman, girl, or small child. • She's the most *beautiful* woman I've ever met. • Their son was a *beautiful* baby. PRETTY often applies to small things that are attractive in a delicate way. • a *pretty* little dress with pink ribbons • He paints *pretty* pictures and sells them on the street. When used of a person, it almost always describes a woman or girl. • their *pretty* daughter • She looked very *pretty* in her new dress. LOVELY applies to things that make people feel strong emotions by being very graceful or delicate. • a *lovely* melody When used to describe a person's appearance, it almost always refers to a woman or girl. • They have two *lovely* daughters. It can also describe a person's character, and in this use it refers to both women and men. • My uncle is a *lovely* man. [=a very good man] HANDSOME applies to things that are attractive because they have a balanced design or shape. • a *handsome* house surrounded by gardens • She wore a *handsome* gray suit to the office. When used to describe a person, it usually refers to a man or boy. • their *handsome* son • a very *handsome* actor • He has a strong, *handsome* face. A woman who is described as *handsome* is attractive but usually not in a very delicate or feminine way.

beau·ti·fy /ˈbjuːtəˌfaɪ/ *verb* **-fies; -fied; -fy·ing** [+ *obj*] : to make (something) beautiful or more beautiful • Fresh flowers *beautify* every room.

– beau·ti·fi·ca·tion /ˌbjuːtəfəˈkeɪʃən/ *noun* [*noncount*] • the *beautification* of the city

beau·ty /ˈbjuːti/ *noun, pl* **-ties**

1 [*noncount*] : the quality of being physically attractive • Her *beauty* is beyond compare. [=she is very beautiful; no one is as beautiful as she is] — sometimes used before another noun • *beauty* products [=soaps, makeup, and other things

B

B

that help make people more physically attractive] • a *beauty* treatment
2 : the qualities in a person or a thing that give pleasure to the senses or the mind [*noncount*] the *beauty* [=*loveliness*] of the stars • We explored the natural *beauty* of the island. • I'm learning to appreciate the *beauty* of poetry. • We have different ideas/notions/conceptions of *beauty*. [=different opinions about what makes things beautiful] • "A thing of *beauty* is a joy for ever . . . " —John Keats, *Endymion* (1818) [*plural*] We explored the natural *beauties* of the island.
3 [*count*] **:** a beautiful woman • She was one of the great *beauties* of her time. • She was no *beauty*.
4 [*count*] *informal* **:** a very good thing **:** a very good example of something • That was a *beauty* of a fight. [=that was an excellent fight] • Dad and I went fishing and we caught a couple of *beauties*. — often used in an ironic way to describe a bad thing or person • That mistake was a *beauty*.
5 : a good or appealing part of something [*noncount*] The *beauty* of the game is that everyone can play. • No one knows when it's going to happen, and that's the *beauty* of it! [*count*] One of the *beauties* of the system is that it allows you to adjust the schedule easily.

beauty contest *noun, pl* ~ **-tests** [*count*] **:** a contest in which people judge a group of women or girls and decide which one is the most beautiful — called also *beauty pageant*

beauty mark *noun, pl* ~ **marks** [*count*] *US* **:** BEAUTY SPOT 1

beauty part *noun*
the beauty part *US, informal* **:** the best or most appealing part of something • There's plenty of food, and *the beauty part* is that it's all free!

beauty queen *noun, pl* ~ **queens** [*count*] **:** a woman or girl who is a winner of a beauty contest — sometimes used figuratively • She's fairly good-looking, but she's no *beauty queen*. [=she's not beautiful]

beauty salon *noun, pl* ~ **-lons** [*count*] **:** a shop where women get beauty treatments (such as haircuts) to make them more attractive — called also *beauty parlor, beauty shop*

beauty spot *noun, pl* ~ **spots** [*count*]
1 : a small dark mark (such as a mole) on a woman's face — called also (*US*) *beauty mark*
2 *Brit* **:** a beautiful place • a famous *beauty spot* by a mountain lake

¹bea·ver /ˈbiːvɚ/ *noun, pl* **beaver** *or* **bea·vers**
1 [*count*] **:** a small animal that has thick, brown fur and a wide, flat tail, that cuts down trees with its teeth, and that builds dams and underwater houses with mud and branches — often used before another noun • a *beaver* dam [=a dam built by beavers] • *beaver* ponds • *beaver* skins/pelts — see picture at RODENT
2 [*noncount*] **:** the fur of a beaver • a coat made of *beaver* — often used before another noun • a *beaver* coat • a *beaver* hat — see also EAGER BEAVER

²beaver *verb* **-vers; -vered; -ver·ing**
beaver away [*phrasal verb*] *informal* **:** to work in a very active and energetic way • They've been *beavering away* for hours. — often + *at* • They're still *beavering away at* the problem.

be·bop /ˈbiːˌbɑːp/ *noun* [*noncount*] **:** a fast and complex type of jazz music **:** BOP

be·calmed /biˈkɑːmd/ *adj, of a boat or ship* **:** not able to move because there is no wind • The ship was *becalmed* for nearly two days.

became *past tense of* BECOME

be·cause /bɪˈkɑːz, bɪˈkʌz/ *conj* **:** for the reason that • I ran *because* I was afraid. • We were late *because* our car wouldn't start. = *Because* our car wouldn't start, we were late. • "Why did you do it?" "*Because* she told me to."
because of **:** for the reason of • The picnic has been canceled *because of* [=*due to, on account of*] bad weather. • *Because of* this [=for this reason], only very rich people can afford to live on the island. • *Because of* you, we missed the bus. [=you caused us to miss the bus] • The accident happened *because of* [=*through*] carelessness.
just because **:** for the simple or single reason that • Don't get nervous *just because* the teacher might ask you a question. • We can't assume it will rain today *just because* it rained yesterday. • *Just because* your friends do it, that doesn't mean that you should do it, too.

¹beck /ˈbɛk/ *noun*
at someone's beck and call *or* ***at the beck and call of someone*** **:** always ready to do whatever someone asks • He expects his employees to be *at his beck and call* day and night. • She is *at the beck and call of* the committee. — compare ²BECK

²beck *noun, pl* **becks** [*count*] *Brit* **:** ²BROOK — compare ¹BECK

beck·on /ˈbɛkən/ *verb* **-ons; -oned; -on·ing**
1 : to signal (someone) with your arm or hand in order to tell that person to come closer or follow [+ *obj*] She was *beckoning* them in to shore. • He *beckoned* them over (to where he was). • She *beckoned* the waiter to come over. [*no obj*] She *beckoned* to the waiter to come over.
2 a [*no obj*] **:** to appear attractive or inviting • From the time he was a child, the wilderness *beckoned* to him. • New adventures were *beckoning*. • a *beckoning* smile **b** [+ *obj*] **:** to attract (someone or something) • The nature preserve *beckons* bird-watchers, who visit from around the world.
– beck·on·ing·ly *adv* [*more* ~; *most* ~] • She smiled *beckoningly*.

be·come /bɪˈkʌm/ *verb* **-comes; -came** /-ˈkeɪm/; **-come; -com·ing**
1 [*linking verb*] **:** to begin to be or come to be something specified • Although I've known him for years, we didn't *become* close friends until recently. • She won the election, *becoming* the first woman to be President of the nation. • They both *became* teachers. **:** to begin to have a specified quality • The book has *become* quite popular. • We *became* interested in the property last year. • The crackers had *become* stale. • It's *becoming* [=*getting*] quite cold in the evenings. • It eventually *became* clear that he had lied. • She's *become* [=*gotten*] somewhat cynical.
2 [+ *obj*] *formal* **a** *not used in progressive tenses* **:** to look attractive on (someone) **:** to be flattering to (someone) • That dress *becomes* you. **b :** to be suitable for (someone) **:** to be proper for (someone) • Though poor, he carried himself with a dignity *becoming* [=*befitting*] a king. • This kind of behavior hardly *becomes* a person of your age and position.
become of **:** to happen to • Whatever *became of* our old friend? I haven't heard from her in years. • I don't know what *became of* my keys. I can't find them anywhere.

be·com·ing /bɪˈkʌmɪŋ/ *adj* [*more* ~; *most* ~] *formal*
1 : causing someone to look attractive **:** having a flattering or attractive effect • That jacket is very *becoming* on you. • She's had her hair cut in a *becoming* new style.
2 : suitable or appropriate for a particular person or in a certain situation • She accepted the award with a *becoming* humility. — opposite UNBECOMING
– be·com·ing·ly *adv* • *becomingly* dressed

¹bed /ˈbɛd/ *noun, pl* **beds**
1 a : a piece of furniture that people sleep on [*count*] The room contains only a *bed* and a dresser. • There are two *beds* in the hotel room. • a hospital *bed* • a single *bed* [=a bed for one person] • a double *bed* [=a bed for two people] • He lay ***on the bed*** [=on top of the sheets, blankets, and bedspread] for a long time. • Don't forget to ***make the bed***. [=to neatly arrange the sheets, blankets, and bedspread on the bed so that the mattress is covered] • He became ill and ***took to his bed***. [=he went to lie in bed for a long time] [*noncount*] She usually ***goes to bed*** [=lies down in her bed to sleep] around 11:00. • It's time to ***get out of bed***. [=*get up*] • He lay/stayed ***in bed*** all morning. • The kids like to hear a story ***before bed***. [=before they go to sleep] • Have you ***put the children to bed***? [=have you prepared the children to go to sleep and put them in their beds?] • Come on, children. It's ***time for bed***. [=*bedtime, time to sleep*] **b** [*count*] **:** something that is used to sleep on • The blanket by the fireplace is the dog's *bed*. • Her *bed* was a mound of soft pine needles. — see also DEATHBED, SICKBED, SUNBED, WATER BED
2 — used in phrases that describe having sexual relations ✧ Someone who is ***good in bed*** is a skillful lover. When two people are ***in bed***, they are in the act of having sex. • She caught her husband and his secretary *in bed* together. = She caught her husband *in bed* with his secretary. To ***go to bed with*** someone is to have sex with someone. • She likes him as a friend, but she's not interested in *going to bed with* him. To ***get someone into bed*** is to get someone to have sex with you. • He has fantasies about *getting a fashion model into bed*. Phrases like these are also used figuratively. • a politician who is accused of being ***in bed with*** the oil industry [=of having an improperly close relationship with the oil industry] • The Communists and the Fascists *got into bed with* each other [=*joined forces*] to keep the liberals out of power.

3 [*count*] : a small area of ground specially prepared for plants • I'm planning on putting a *bed* of perennials in that corner of the yard. • a *bed* of flowers — see also BED OF ROSES, FLOWER BED, SEEDBED
4 [*count*] **a :** a flat pile or layer of something • a *bed* of coals **b :** a flat pile or layer of food that is placed on a dish with other food on top of it • grilled fish served on a *bed* of greens • a *bed* of rice
5 [*count*] **a :** the ground that is at the bottom of a sea, lake, etc. • seaweed growing on the ocean *bed* [=*floor*] **b :** an area of shallow water where something grows • an oyster *bed* [=an area where there are many oysters] — see also RIVERBED, SEABED
6 [*count*] *technical* : a layer of rock or some other material from inside the earth • fossil *beds* • a *bed* of shale
7 [*count*] : the platform or box in the back of some kinds of trucks • the *bed* of the truck • We loaded the equipment and put a cover over the truck *bed*. — see also FLATBED
die in (your) bed see [1]DIE
get up on the wrong side of the bed (*US*) *or chiefly Brit* ***get out of bed on the wrong side*** : to be in a bad mood throughout the day • Be careful when you talk to the boss. He *got up on the wrong side of the bed* this morning.
make your bed and lie in it ✧ Expressions like *you've made your bed, and now you must lie in it* mean that you have done something that causes problems and now you must accept and deal with those problems. • There's nothing we can do to help her. *She's made her bed and has to lie in it.*
marriage bed : a bed that married people share — sometimes used figuratively to refer to marriage in general or to the sexual relations that married people have • the sorrows of their *marriage bed*

[2]**bed** *verb* **beds; bed·ded; bed·ding** [+ *obj*]
1 *informal + old-fashioned* : to have sex with (someone) • He has fantasies about *bedding* a fashion model.
2 : to place (food) on a pile or layer of something else — usually used as *(be) bedded* • a mixture of scallops and lobster *bedded* on rice
bed down [*phrasal verb*] **1 :** to lie down somewhere for sleep • There were so many people that some of us had to *bed down* in the living room. **2** ***bed (someone or something) down or bed down (someone or something)*** : to provide (a person or animal) with a place to sleep • They *bedded* us *down* in the living room. • When the animals had been fed and *bedded down*, we went inside to eat dinner.

bed and board *noun* [*noncount*] *chiefly Brit* : food and a place to sleep • They provide *bed and board* [=*room and board*] for travellers.

bed–and–breakfast *noun, pl* **-fasts**
1 [*count*] : a house or small hotel in which someone can rent a room to sleep in for a price that includes breakfast the next morning • We stayed the night at a nice *bed-and-breakfast* near the beach. — called also *B and B*
2 [*noncount*] *chiefly Brit* : a service in which the price of a room also includes breakfast the next morning • a small hotel that offers *bed-and-breakfast* — called also *B and B*

be·daz·zle /bɪˈdæzəl/ *verb* **-daz·zles; -daz·zled; -daz·zling** [+ *obj*] : to thrill or excite (someone) very much • fans *bedazzled* by movie stars
— **be·daz·zle·ment** /bɪˈdæzəlmənt/ *noun* [*noncount*]

bed·bug /ˈbɛdˌbʌg/ *noun, pl* **-bugs** [*count*] : a very small insect that lives in dirty beds and that bites people and sucks their blood

bed·cham·ber /ˈbɛdˌʧeɪmbɚ/ *noun, pl* **-bers** [*count*] *literary* : BEDROOM • The queen was in her *bedchamber*.

bed·clothes /ˈbɛdˌkloʊz/ *noun* [*plural*] : [1]BEDDING 1

bed·cov·er /ˈbɛdˌkʌvɚ/ *noun, pl* **-cov·ers**
1 [*count*] : BEDSPREAD
2 ***bedcovers*** [*plural*] : [1]BEDDING 1

[1]**bed·ding** /ˈbɛdɪŋ/ *noun* [*noncount*]
1 : the sheets and blankets that are used on a bed
2 : something used for an animal's bed • Wash your cat's *bedding* regularly. • straw *bedding*

[2]**bedding** *adj, always used before a noun* : suitable for being planted in large groups in a flower bed • The flower makes an excellent ***bedding plant***.

be·deck /bɪˈdɛk/ *verb* **-decks; -decked; -deck·ing** [+ *obj*] : to decorate (someone or something) with things : to add decorative things to (something or someone) — usually used as *(be) bedecked* • She *was bedecked* in gold and jewels. • The hall *was bedecked* [=*decked*] with flowers.

be·dev·il /bɪˈdɛvəl/ *verb* **-ils;** *US* **-iled** *or Brit* **-illed;** *US* **-il·ing** *or Brit* **-il·ling** [+ *obj*] : to trouble (someone or something) in a constant or repeated way : to cause repeated problems for (someone or something) • The theory *bedevils* scientists, none of whom have been able to prove it true or false. • The project has been *bedeviled* by problems since its inception.

bed·fel·low /ˈbɛdˌfɛloʊ/ *noun, pl* **-lows** [*count*] : a person or thing that is associated or connected with another — used in phrases like ***strange bedfellows*** to describe people and things that are grouped or working together in a way that seems unlikely, unexpected, etc. • Politics makes *strange bedfellows*. [=people who are very different sometimes work together for political reasons]

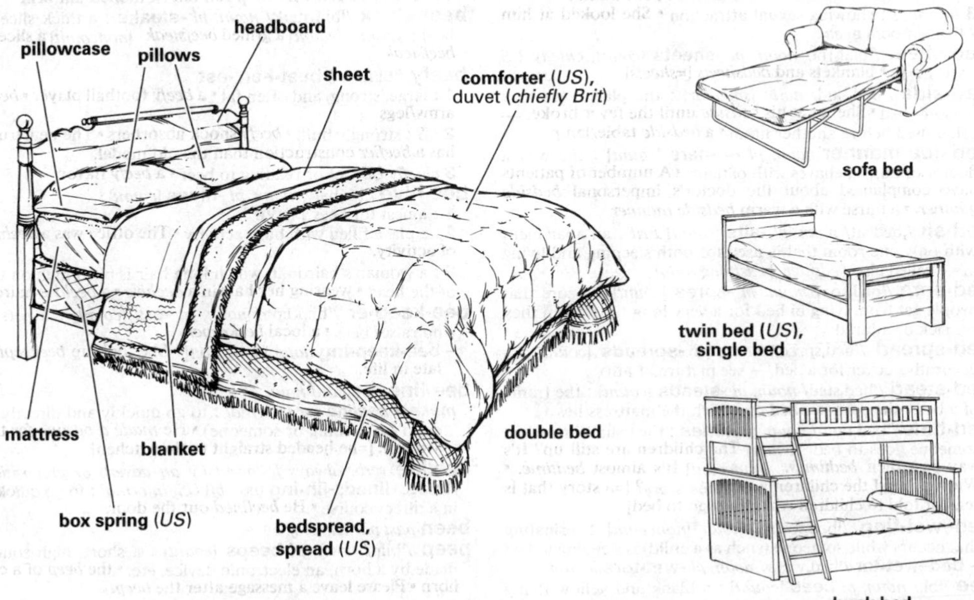

B

bed·head /ˈbɛd,hɛd/ *noun, pl* **-heads** [*count*] *Brit* : HEADBOARD

bed·lam /ˈbɛdləm/ *noun* [*noncount*] : a very noisy and confused state or scene • The park had never had so many visitors at one time. It was total/complete *bedlam.*

bed linens *noun* [*plural*] *chiefly US* : sheets and pillowcases for a bed — called also (*chiefly Brit*) *bed linen*

bed of roses *noun* [*singular*] : a place or situation that is pleasant or easy — usually used in negative statements • Grandfather liked to remind people not to expect things to be easy. "Life's no *bed of roses,*" he'd say.

Bed·ou·in /ˈbɛdəwən/ *noun, pl* **Bedouin** *or* **Bed·ou·ins** [*count*] : a member of an Arab tribe whose people live in the desert in tents

bed·pan /ˈbɛd,pæn/ *noun, pl* **-pans** [*count*] : a shallow pan used as a toilet by a person who is too ill to get out of bed — see picture at HOSPITAL

bed·post /ˈbɛd,poʊst/ *noun, pl* **-posts** [*count*] : any one of the four main supporting posts at each corner of an old-fashioned bed

be·drag·gled /bɪˈdrægəld/ *adj* [*more* ~; *most* ~] : wet or dirty from being in rain or mud • a *bedraggled* hitchhiker • She was *bedraggled* and exhausted.

bed rest *noun* [*noncount*] : rest while lying in a bed • The doctor prescribed *bed rest* for a month.

bed·rid·den /ˈbɛd,rɪdn/ *adj* : forced to stay in bed because of illness or weakness • *bedridden* patients

bed·rock /ˈbɛd,rɑːk/ *noun* [*noncount*]
1 : the solid rock that lies under the surface of the ground • They dug down for 10 feet before they hit *bedrock.*
2 : a strong idea, principle, or fact that supports something • His religious beliefs are/form the *bedrock* on which his life is based. — often used before another noun • *bedrock* beliefs/values

bed·roll /ˈbɛd,roʊl/ *noun, pl* **-rolls** [*count*] *US* : bedding materials that are rolled together so that they can be carried from one place to another

[1]**bed·room** /ˈbɛd,ruːm/ *noun, pl* **-rooms** [*count*] : a room used for sleeping • a house with three *bedrooms* = a 3-*bedroom* house • a spare/guest *bedroom* • a large ***master bedroom*** [=a large bedroom that is the main bedroom in a house]
– bedroomed *adj, Brit* — used in combination • a three-*bedroomed* house

[2]**bedroom** *adj, always used before a noun*
1 *US* : lived in by people who go to another town or city to work • They live in a ***bedroom community*** [=(*Brit*) *dormitory town*] just outside of the city.
2 : dealing with sexual relationships • The play is a *bedroom* farce about a middle-aged couple. • *bedroom* humor
3 *informal* : showing sexual attraction • She looked at him with ***bedroom eyes.***

bed·sheet /ˈbɛd,ʃiːt/ *noun, pl* **-sheets** [*count*] *chiefly US* : SHEET 1b • blankets and *bedsheets* [=*sheets*]

bed·side /ˈbɛd,saɪd/ *noun* [*singular*] : the place next to a person's bed • She sat at his *bedside* until the fever broke. — often used before another noun • a *bedside* table/lamp

bedside manner *noun, pl* ~ **-ners** [*count*] : the way a doctor or nurse behaves with patients • A number of patients have complained about the doctor's impersonal *bedside manner.* • a nurse with a warm *bedside manner*

bed·sit /,bɛdˈsɪt/ *noun, pl* **-sits** [*count*] *Brit* : an apartment with only one room that is used for both sleeping and living in — called also *bedsitter, bedsitting room*

bed·sore /ˈbɛd,soɚ/ *noun, pl* **-sores** [*count*] : a sore that people get from lying in bed for a very long time when they are sick or injured

bed·spread /ˈbɛd,sprɛd/ *noun, pl* **-spreads** [*count*] : a decorative cover for a bed — see picture at BED

bed·stead /ˈbɛd,stɛd/ *noun, pl* **-steads** [*count*] : the frame of a bed : the part of a bed on which the mattress lies

bed·time /ˈbɛd,taɪm/ *noun, pl* **-times** : the usual time when someone goes to bed [*count*] The children are still up? It's way past their *bedtimes.* [*noncount*] It's almost *bedtime.* • Will you read the children a ***bedtime story***? [=a story that is read or told to children when they go to bed]

bed–wet·ting /ˈbɛd,wɛtɪŋ/ *noun* [*noncount*] : urinating that occurs while someone (such as a child) is sleeping in bed
– bed–wet·ter /ˈbɛd,wɛtɚ/ *noun, pl* **-wet·ters** [*count*]

[1]**bee** /ˈbiː/ *noun, pl* **bees** [*count*] : a black and yellow flying insect that can sting and that is often kept in hives for the honey that it produces • flowers pollinated by *bees* and other insects • a swarm of buzzing/humming *bees* — sometimes used figuratively • My mom is a real ***busy bee*** around Christmastime. [=she is very busy and active] — see also BUMBLEBEE, HONEYBEE, KILLER BEE
(as) busy as a bee *informal* : very busy and active • My mom is (*as*) *busy as a bee* around Christmastime.
have a bee in your bonnet *informal* : to talk and think a lot about something • He always *has a bee in his bonnet* about safety.
the birds and the bees see BIRD
— compare [2]BEE

[2]**bee** *noun, pl* **bees** [*count*] *US* : a gathering of people for the purpose of spending time together while working on similar projects • a quilting *bee* — see also SPELLING BEE — compare [1]BEE

Beeb /ˈbiːb/ *noun*
the Beeb *Brit, informal* : the BBC • work for/at *the Beeb*

beech /ˈbiːʧ/ *noun, pl* **beech·es** *or* **beech**
1 [*count*] : a kind of tree that has smooth gray bark and small nuts — called also *beech tree*
2 [*noncount*] : the wood of the beech • a box made of *beech*

[1]**beef** /ˈbiːf/ *noun, pl* **beefs**
1 [*noncount*] : meat from a cow • a pound of *beef* • ground *beef* • I'm not eating as much *beef* as I used to. — often used before another noun • the *beef* industry • *beef* stew [=a stew made with beef]
2 [*count*] *informal* : COMPLAINT • My real *beef* is with the organization's president, not the group itself. • What's your *beef*?
3 [*noncount*] *informal* : muscles • a football player with a lot of *beef* and brawn [=a very muscular football player]

[2]**beef** *verb* **beefs; beefed; beef·ing** [*no obj*] *informal* : COMPLAIN • She's always *beefing* about something.
beef up [*phrasal verb*] ***beef (something) up*** *or* ***beef up (something)*** *informal* : to add weight, strength, or power to (something) • Security around the city will be *beefed up* during the event. • The medicine helps *beef up* the immune system.

beef·bur·ger /ˈbiːf,bɚgɚ/ *noun, pl* **-gers** [*count*] *chiefly Brit* : HAMBURGER

beef·cake /ˈbiːf,keɪk/ *noun, pl* **-cakes** *informal*
1 [*noncount*] : men who are muscular and attractive • He's not a great actor but he gets roles anyway because of all the moviegoers interested in *beefcake.* • *beefcake* photos/posters
2 [*count*] *US* : a muscular and attractive man • He's one of Hollywood's most celebrated *beefcakes.* — compare CHEESECAKE

Beef·eat·er /ˈbiːf,iːtɚ/ *noun, pl* **-ers** [*count*] : a guard at the Tower of London who wears an old-fashioned uniform

beef·steak /ˈbiːf,steɪk/ *noun, pl* **-steaks** : a thick slice of beef : STEAK [*count*] a grilled *beefsteak* [*noncount*] a slice of *beefsteak*

beefy /ˈbiːfi/ *adj* **beef·i·er; -est**
1 : large, strong, and often fat • a *beefy* football player • *beefy* arms/legs
2 *US* : strongly built • *beefy* shock absorbers • The new truck has a *beefier* construction than the old model.
3 *chiefly US* : of or relating to beef • a *beefy* flavor

bee·hive /ˈbiː,haɪv/ *noun, pl* **-hives** [*count*]
1 : a nest for bees : HIVE
2 : a place filled with busy activity • The office was a *beehive* of activity.
3 : a woman's hairdo in which long hair is piled high on top of the head • wearing her hair in a *beehive* • a *beehive* hairdo

bee·keep·er /ˈbiː,kiːpɚ/ *noun, pl* **-ers** [*count*] : a person who raises bees • a local *beekeeper*
– bee·keep·ing *noun* [*noncount*] • She took up *beekeeping* late in life.

[1]**bee·line** /ˈbiː,laɪn/ *noun*
make a beeline for *informal* : to go quickly and directly at or to (something or someone) • He *made a beeline for* the kitchen. [=he headed straight to the kitchen]

[2]**beeline** *verb, always followed by an adverb or preposition* **-lines; -lined; -lin·ing** [*no obj*] *US, informal* : to go quickly in a direct course • He *beelined* out the door.

been *past participle of* BE

[1]**beep** /ˈbiːp/ *noun, pl* **beeps** [*count*] : a short, high sound made by a horn, an electronic device, etc. • the *beep* of a car horn • Please leave a message after the *beep.*

[2]**beep** *verb* **beeps; beeped; beep·ing**

1 : to cause (a horn, an electronic device, etc.) to make a beep [+ *obj*] Why did you *beep* your horn at her? [*no obj*] She *beeped* at me first. • Something is *beeping* in the kitchen. • I could hear a *beeping* noise.

2 [+ *obj*] : to send a message to (someone) with a beeper • The doctor is not in the office today, but I can *beep* her for you. [=I can send the doctor a signal that will tell her to call the office]

beep·er /ˈbiːpɚ/ *noun, pl* **-ers** [*count*] *chiefly US* : PAGER

beer /ˈbiɚ/ *noun, pl* **beers**

1 : an alcoholic drink made from malt and flavored with hops [*noncount*] Would you like *beer* with dinner? • The pub brews its own *beer*. • a glass of *beer* • a *beer* mug [*count*] I'll have a *beer*, please. • a couple of cold *beers*

2 [*noncount*] : a drink made from roots or other parts of plants • a glass of birch/ginger *beer* — see also ROOT BEER

– beery /ˈbiri/ *adj* **beer·i·er; -est** • a *beery* flavor/smell • a *beery* tavern

beer belly *noun, pl* **~ bellies** [*count*] *informal* : a fat belly caused by drinking a lot of beer • a middle-aged man with a big *beer belly* — called also *beer gut*

beer mat *noun, pl* **~ mats** [*count*] *Brit* : a small piece of material placed under a glass of beer to protect the bar or table beneath it — compare COASTER

bee's knees *noun*

the bee's knees *informal + old-fashioned* : an excellent person or thing • She's *the bee's knees*. [=I like her very much]

bees·wax /ˈbiːzˌwæks/ *noun* [*noncount*] : wax made by bees that is used for making candles and other products

none of your beeswax *US, informal* — used as a way of telling someone that you won't provide information because it is private • "How old are you?" "That's *none of your beeswax*." [=*none of your business*]

beet /ˈbiːt/ *noun, pl* **beets** [*count*]

1 *US* **a** : a garden plant with thick leaves and a rounded red root • I've planted carrots, parsnips, and *beets* in the garden. — called also (*Brit*) *beetroot* **b** : the rounded red root of the beet plant that is eaten as a vegetable • sliced *beets* — called also (*Brit*) *beetroot*; see color picture on page C4

2 *Brit* : SUGAR BEET

beet red or red as a beet : red in the face especially from embarrassment • When she realized her mistake, she *turned beet red*. [=*blushed*]

¹bee·tle /ˈbiːtl/ *noun, pl* **bee·tles** [*count*] : a type of insect with wings that form a hard cover on its back when it is not flying

²beetle *verb, always followed by an adverb or preposition* **beetles; bee·tled; bee·tling** [*no obj*] *chiefly Brit, informal* : to move quickly • Everyone looked very busy, *beetling* [=*scurrying*] about the office. • Everybody *beetled* off home.

beetle–browed *adj* : having large and thick eyebrows • a *beetle-browed* old man

beet·root /ˈbiːtˌruːt/ *noun, pl* **-roots** [*count, noncount*] *Brit* : BEET 1

be·fall /bɪˈfɑːl/ *verb* **-falls; -fell** /bɪˈfɛl/; **-fall·en** /bɪˈfɑːlən/; **-fall·ing** [+ *obj*] *formal, of something bad or unpleasant* : to happen to (someone or something) • It's sad to think of the unhappy fate that *befell* him. • The drought was only one of many hardships to *befall* the small country.

be·fit /bɪˈfɪt/ *verb* **-fits; -fit·ted; -fit·ting** [+ *obj*] *formal* : to be suitable to or proper for (someone or something) • She has a mind for serious inquiry, as *befits* a scientist. • clothes *befitting* [=*fitting*] the occasion

– be·fit·ting·ly /bɪˈfɪtɪŋli/ *adv* [*more ~; most ~*]

¹be·fore /bɪˈfoɚ/ *adv*

1 : at an earlier time • Haven't we met *before*? • the night/day *before* • I've never seen her so happy *before*. [=I've never seen her as happy as she is now] • We haven't had these problems *before*. • Everything is just as (it was) *before*.

2 *formal + old-fashioned* : to or toward the place where someone is going : in advance • marching on *before* [=*ahead*]

²before *prep*

1 a : at a time preceding (something or someone) : earlier than (something or someone) • We arrived shortly *before* six o'clock. • *before* dinner • He left just *before* sunrise. • I've never seen her so happy *before* now. • Call me *before* your arrival. • She arrived the day *before* yesterday. • Why haven't you ever helped me *before* now/this? • I finished the exam *before* him. [=before he finished the exam] • You can go *before* me. [=before I go] • He's an electrician, like his father *before* him. [=his father was also an electrician] • They earned 50,000 dollars *before* (paying) taxes. **b** *US* — used to describe a time earlier than a specified hour • It's 20 (minutes) *before* 12. [=it's 20 of/to 12; it's 11:40]

2 : preceding (something or someone) in order or in a series • Your name is listed *before* mine. • You'll see my house just *before* the bank and after the school. • The number 2 comes *before* 3 and after 1. [=2 comes between 1 and 3]

3 a : in front of (someone or something) • The Great Plains stretched endlessly *before* them. • The championship fight took place *before* a crowd of thousands. : in the presence of (someone) • The defendant stood up *before* the judge. — see also *(right) before/in front of your (very) eyes* at ¹EYE **b** : being considered by (someone or something) • The case *before* the court involves a robbery. • the candidates *before* the voters • I have a proposal to put *before* [=*to*] the board. • The question *before* us is this: did he fall or was he pushed? **c** : in the future for (someone) : ahead of (someone) • They had no idea of the ordeal that lay *before* them.

4 a : in a higher or more important position than (something) • They put quantity *before* [=*above*] quality. [=they cared more about quantity than about quality] **b** : rather or sooner than • He vowed that he would choose death *before* dishonor. [=he would rather die than be dishonored]

5 *formal* : under the force of (something) • The tree fell *before* the force of the wind. [=the force of the wind caused the tree to fall]

³before *conj*

1 a : earlier than the time that : earlier than when • He left long *before* morning came. • The judge stood up *before* the defendant did. [=the defendant stood up after the judge did] • Say goodbye *before* you go. • Call me *before* you arrive. • *Before* [=*until*] she met him she had never been so happy. • I finished the exam *before* he did. • It was/happened not long *before* he arrived. • He left *before* I could thank him. [=I wasn't able to thank him because he left too soon] • I'll resign *before* I give in! [=I would rather resign than give in] — see also *before you know it* at ¹KNOW **b** : until the time that • It did not take long *before* he had earned their trust. [=he earned their trust quickly] • "I have promises to keep and miles to go *before* I sleep . . ." —Robert Frost, "Stopping by Woods on a Snowy Evening" (1923)

2 a — used to refer to something that might happen • Get out of there *before* you get dirty! [=get out of there because you will/might get dirty if you don't] • *Before* I forget, will you give me your telephone number? [=I'm asking for your telephone number now because I might forget to do it later] **b** — used to say that one thing must happen for another thing to happen or be possible • He must be convicted *before* he can be removed from office. • You must have completed an introductory class *before* you can take an advanced class.

be·fore·hand /bɪˈfoɚˌhænd/ *adv* : in advance : at an earlier or previous time • They'd agreed *beforehand* [=*ahead of time*] to leave early. • We paid for our tickets *beforehand*.

be·foul /bɪˈfawəl/ *verb* **-fouls; -fouled; -foul·ing** [+ *obj*] *formal* : to make (a substance, place, etc.) dirty : FOUL • pollutants that *befoul* the air and water

be·friend /bɪˈfrɛnd/ *verb* **-friends; -friend·ed; -friend·ing** [+ *obj*] : to become a friend to (someone) • He *befriended* the new student.

be·fud·dled /bɪˈfʌdl̩d/ *adj* [*more ~; most ~*] : unable to think clearly : very confused • Many people are totally *befuddled* by the tax code. • The paperwork left me completely *befuddled*.

beg /ˈbɛg/ *verb* **begs; begged; beg·ging**

1 : to ask people for money or food [*no obj*] A homeless man *begs* on that corner every day. • children *begging* for food [+ *obj*] children *begging* strangers for food • children *begging* food from strangers

2 a : to ask (someone) in a very serious and emotional way for something needed or wanted very much [+ *obj*] He *begged* the doctor for medicine. • He *begged* her for forgiveness. = He *begged* her to forgive him. • She *begged* him to read the story again. • I *beg* you to help them! = Help them, I *beg* you! • "Help them!" I *begged*. [*no obj*] — + *of* • (*formal*) I *beg of* you to help them! **b** : to ask for (something needed or wanted very much) in a very serious and emotional way [+ *obj*] He got down on his knees and *begged* forgiveness. = He got down on his knees and *begged* to be forgiven. • He *begged* that she would forgive him. • *begging* a favor of someone [*no obj*] He's too proud to *beg*. • He *begged* for forgiveness.

3 [*no obj*] *of a dog* : to sit up on the back legs with the front legs raised • "Does your dog know any tricks?" "She knows how to *beg*."

B

4 [+ *obj*] *of a thing* : to seem perfect for some purpose : to be very well suited for something — followed by *to + verb* • I couldn't resist cutting some of the flowers. They were just *begging to be made* into a bouquet. • a scene *begging to be photographed* [=a scene that should be photographed]

beg, borrow, or/and steal *informal* : to do whatever is necessary to get something that is wanted or needed • We'll have to *beg, borrow, or steal* the extra chairs we need for the party.

beg leave *formal + old-fashioned* : to ask for permission — followed by *to + verb* • We *beg leave to offer* our humble thanks. • I *beg leave to differ* with you, sir.

beg off [*phrasal verb*] *informal* : to say that you cannot do something that you have been asked to do or have agreed to do • He originally said he'd go to the party, but he later *begged off* (going), claiming he had to work that night.

beg the question **1** : to cause someone to ask a specified question as a reaction or response • The quarterback's injury *begs the question* of who will start in his place. • The tragic drowning *begs the question*: why are there no safe places in the area for children to swim? **2** *formal* : to ignore a question or issue by assuming it has been answered or settled • Their proposed solution *begs the question* of whether the changes in the town are actually a problem.

beg to differ : to politely disagree with someone • You say that the candidates are essentially the same, but I *beg to differ*. [=I do not agree]

beg your pardon ✧ The phrase *I beg your pardon* is used in polite speech to apologize when you have done something impolite or when you have made a mistake. • *I beg your pardon*. [=*sorry, excuse me*] I didn't mean to bump into you like that. • *I beg your pardon*. You're correct; the amount is 12 dollars. It can be used to show that you are annoyed or offended by something that another person has said. • "That boy isn't very bright." "*I beg your pardon*! That's my son!" It can also be used as a question when you have not heard or understood something clearly. • *I beg your pardon* [=*excuse me, sorry*]? What did you say? The shorter form ***beg pardon*** is also used informally this way. • "He's been in Haiti for the past two months." "*Beg pardon*? He's been in Hawaii?" "No, Haiti."

go begging *chiefly Brit* : to be something that few or no people want • With the poor economy, many expensive restaurants now have tables that *go begging*. [=tables that are empty because there are no customers] • If that last biscuit's (still) *going begging*, can I have it, please?

began *past tense of* BEGIN

be·get /bɪˈgɛt/ *verb* **-got** /-ˈgɑːt/ *also* **-gat** /-ˈgæt/; **-got·ten** /-ˈgɑːtn̩/ *or* **-got**; **-get·ting** [+ *obj*]

1 *formal* : to cause (something) to happen or exist • Violence *begets* [=*causes*] more violence.

2 *old-fashioned + literary* : to become the father of (someone) • He died without *begetting* an heir.

— be·get·ter *noun, pl* **-ters** [*count*]

¹beg·gar /ˈbɛgɚ/ *noun, pl* **-gars** [*count*]

1 : a person who lives by begging for money, food, etc.

2 *Brit, informal* : a person who is regarded as lucky, unlucky, lazy, etc. • I heard you won the contest! You lucky *beggar*! • He's a lazy *beggar*.

beggars can't be choosers ✧ The saying *beggars can't be choosers* means that people who need something must be satisfied with whatever they get even if it is not exactly what they wanted.

²beggar *verb* **-gars**; **-gared**; **-gar·ing** [+ *obj*]

1 *formal* : to make (someone or something) very poor • Years of civil war had *beggared* the country.

2 *chiefly Brit* — used in the phrases ***beggar belief*** and ***beggar description*** to talk about something that is very difficult to believe or describe • It almost *beggars belief* [=it is very hard to believe] that anyone can be so cruel. • a plot so complex that it *beggars description*

beg·gar·ly /ˈbɛgɚli/ *adj* [*more* ~; *most* ~] *formal* : very small or poor • She received a *beggarly* sum for her efforts.

be·gin /bɪˈgɪn/ *verb* **-gins**; **-gan** /-ˈgæn/; **-gun** /-ˈgʌn/; **-gin·ning**

1 a : to do the first part of an action : to start doing something [+ *obj*] They will *begin* construction on the new school soon. • I got the job and I *begin* work on Monday! • She'll *begin* the lecture at 10. • He plans to *begin* the project later this week. • They both *began* their careers at the local newspaper. • The university *began* accepting applications in November. • I had just *begun* eating when the phone rang. • She interrupted as soon as I *began* to speak. [*no obj*] He *began* by showing some photographs of his trip. = He *began* with some photographs of his trip. • Now that I've *begun*, I'll go on till I finish. • You'll have to *begin* again. [=start over] **b** [+ *obj*] : to start to work on, produce, or give attention to (something) • I *began* the quilt last month. • I *began* (reading) the book last week. • Schubert *began* more symphonies than he finished. **c** [+ *obj*] : to cause (something) to start • The chairman *began* the meeting at noon. • They *began* [=*founded*] the state's first traveling theater troupe. **d** [+ *obj*] : to start to have a feeling, thought, etc. — usually followed by *to + verb* • She *began to feel* dizzy soon after the accident. • I'm *beginning to think* the oversight was intentional. — sometimes + *-ing verb* • She *began feeling* dizzy soon after the accident.

2 : to start to happen, to exist, to be done, etc. [*no obj*] The meeting *began* [=*started*] in the morning and finished/ended at noon. • Construction on the new school will *begin* soon. • Our problems were just *beginning*. • When does the play *begin*? • The rain *began* around noon. • Let the games *begin*. • The American Civil War *began* in 1861 and ended in 1865. • His passion for music *began* at the age of six when he had his first piano lessons. [+ *obj*] — followed by *to + verb* • It's *beginning* [=*starting*] *to rain*. • The flowers on the trees are *beginning to bloom*.

3 [*no obj*] **a** : to have a particular starting point : to start at a specified place or in a specified way • "Where does the river *begin*?" "It *begins* in the mountains to the north." • The meeting *began* on a positive note. • The meeting *began* with an announcement. [=an announcement was made at the start of the meeting] • The English alphabet *begins* with A and ends with Z. • Each sentence should *begin* with a capital. • The season *began* with our team in last place but finished (up) with us in first place. • Her long career in advertising *began* at a small firm in Chicago. • Prices for the hotel rooms *begin* at 85 dollars. [=85 dollars is the lowest price for a hotel room; some rooms cost more than 85 dollars] • The road *begins* at the bottom of the hill and ends at the top of the hill. **b** : to have a specified quality, identity, job, etc., at the start — + *as* • What *began* [=*started*] *as* a simple idea has become a complicated project. • The town *began as* a small farming community. • He *began as* a clerk [=he was a clerk when he started working] and eventually became president of the company.

4 [+ *obj*] : to start speaking by saying (something) • "Allow me to introduce myself," he *began*.

5 — used in an exaggerated way to say that something is not possible • I ***can't even begin to describe*** how good the food was. [=the food was very good] • I ***can't begin to tell you*** how grateful I am for all your help. [=I am very grateful for all your help] • I ***can hardly begin to thank you*** for all you've done.

to begin with **1** : as the first thing to be thought about or considered • "I don't think we should buy the car." "Why not?" "*To begin with*, I'm not sure we can afford it." **2** : at the start : before the current time or situation • She has lost a lot of weight, and she wasn't very heavy *to begin with*. • She didn't like her job *to begin with*, [=*at first, initially*] but she got used to it eventually.

be·gin·ner /bɪˈgɪnɚ/ *noun, pl* **-ners** [*count*] : a person who is beginning something or doing something for the first time • a swimming class for complete *beginners* = a *beginner* class • The success of his first restaurant was just ***beginner's luck***. [=he succeeded because he was lucky, as beginners sometimes are]

¹be·gin·ning /bɪˈgɪnɪŋ/ *noun, pl* **-nings**

1 [*count*] : the point or time at which something begins : a starting point — usually singular • He has been working there since the *beginning* of the year. • A poem was recited at the *beginning* of the wedding ceremony. • It was clear ***from the (very) beginning*** that she would eventually succeed. • The company was very small ***in the beginning*** [=when it began], but it eventually became a giant corporation. • The argument marked ***the beginning of the end*** of their marriage. [=the argument was the start of a series of events that led to the end of their marriage]

2 [*count*] : the first part of something • Go back to the *beginning* of the song. • We were late, so we missed the *beginning* of the movie. • The changes that have been made so far are ***just/only the beginning***. There are many more changes still to come.

3 ***beginnings*** [*plural*] **a** : an early stage or period • I have the *beginnings* of a sore throat. [=my throat is starting to feel sore] **b** : the origins or background of a person or thing • He came from humble *beginnings.* • the company's modest *beginnings* in an old warehouse • The organization ***had its beginnings*** [=*began*] in a small Midwestern town.

²beginning *adj* : involving or learning about the simple or basic parts of a subject • *beginning* mathematics • The school has courses for *beginning* [=*elementary*], intermediate, and advanced students.

be·gone /bɪˈgɑːn/ *interj, old-fashioned + literary* — used to tell someone to go away • *Begone*!

be·go·nia /bɪˈgounjə/ *noun, pl* **-nias** [*count*] : a tropical plant that has shiny leaves and bright flowers

begot *past tense and past participle of* BEGET

begotten *past participle of* BEGET

be·grudge /bɪˈgrʌʤ/ *verb* **-grudg·es; -grudged; -grudg·ing** [+ *obj*]
1 : to think that someone does not deserve something • She's worked hard to get where she is. You shouldn't *begrudge* her the success she's earned. • After what he's been through, it's hard to *begrudge* him the money he has. : to regard (something) as not being earned or deserved • You shouldn't *begrudge* her success.
2 : to give or allow (something) in a reluctant or unwilling way • Many commuters *begrudge* every minute spent in traffic.

begrudging /bɪˈgrʌʤɪŋ/ *adj* [*more* ~; *most* ~] : said, done, or given in a reluctant way : GRUDGING • *begrudging* acceptance/admiration/respect
– be·grudg·ing·ly /bɪˈgrʌʤɪŋli/ *adv* • She agreed *begrudgingly.*

be·guile /bɪˈgajəl/ *verb* **-guiles; -guiled; -guil·ing**
1 [+ *obj*] : to trick or deceive (someone) • She was cunning enough to *beguile* her classmates into doing the work for her. • They were *beguiled* into thinking they'd heard the whole story.
2 : to attract or interest someone [*no obj*] Almost everything in the quaint little town *beguiles*, from its architecture to its art to its people. [+ *obj*] He *beguiled* the audience with his smooth and seductive voice. — often used as *(be) beguiled* • I *was beguiled* [=*charmed*] by his voice.
– beguiling *adj* [*more* ~; *most* ~] • a *beguiling* [=*charming*] melody • a *beguiling* temptress • The movie is a *beguiling* blend of humor and tragedy. **– be·guil·ing·ly** /bɪˈgaɪlɪŋli/ *adv* [*more* ~; *most* ~] • a *beguilingly* smooth and seductive voice

begun *past participle of* BEGIN

be·half /bɪˈhæf, *Brit* bɪˈhɑːf/ *noun*
on behalf of someone *or* ***on someone's behalf*** **1** : as a representative of someone • The teacher accepted the award *on behalf of the whole class.* • She's been elected to go before the town council *on behalf of the county's farmers.* **2** *or US* ***in behalf of someone*** *or* ***in someone's behalf*** : for the benefit of someone : in support of someone • She spoke *in behalf of the other candidate.* • They're willing to do anything *on their child's behalf.* • He argued before the court *on her behalf.* **3** : because of someone • Don't get up *on my behalf.*

be·have /bɪˈheɪv/ *verb* **-haves; -haved; -hav·ing**
1 : to act in an acceptable way : to act properly [*no obj*] If you can't *behave* in the store we'll have to leave. [+ *obj*] If you can't ***behave yourself*** in the store we'll have to leave. • I wish those children would *behave themselves.* — opposite MISBEHAVE
2 [*no obj*] : to act in a particular way • He *behaves* like a child! • *behave* well/generously
3 [*no obj*] *of a thing* : to function, react, or move in a particular way • The experiment tested how various metals *behave* under heat and pressure.

behaved *adj* : behaving in a certain way • a well-*behaved* child [=a child who behaves well; a polite child] • a very badly *behaved* little boy

be·hav·ior (*US*) *or Brit* **be·hav·iour** /bɪˈheɪvjɚ/ *noun, pl* **-iors**
1 : the way a person or animal acts or behaves [*noncount*] I'm surprised by her bad *behavior* toward her friends. • Students will be rewarded for good *behavior.* • scientists studying the *behavior* of elephants • normal adolescent *behavior* • criminal *behavior* • an interesting ***pattern of behavior*** = an interesting ***behavior pattern*** • The children were all ***on their best behavior*** [=were all behaving very well and politely] at the museum. • Inmates may be released from prison early ***for good behavior.*** [=because they have followed prison rules and have not caused problems] [*count*] An acceptable social *behavior* in one country may be unacceptable in another country. • Doctors are trying to educate people about *behaviors* that can put them at increased risk for skin cancer.
2 [*noncount*] : the way something (such as a machine or substance) moves, functions, or reacts • The experiment tested the *behavior* of various metals under heat and pressure.
– be·hav·ior·al (*US*) *or Brit* **be·hav·iour·al** /bɪˈheɪvjərəl/ *adj* • *behavioral* problems • *behavioral* patterns

be·head /bɪˈhɛd/ *verb* **-heads; -head·ed; -head·ing** [+ *obj*] : to cut off the head of (someone) especially as a punishment • Louis XVI was *beheaded* in 1793.

beheld *past tense and past participle of* BEHOLD

be·he·moth /bɪˈhiːməθ/ *noun, pl* **-moths** [*count*] : something very big and powerful • a corporate *behemoth* [=a giant corporation]

be·hest /bɪˈhɛst/ *noun*
at the behest of someone *or* ***at someone's behest*** *formal* : because of being asked or ordered by someone • A special meeting will be held *at the senator's behest.*

¹be·hind /bɪˈhaɪnd/ *adv*
1 a : in or toward the back • look *behind* • The older students entered the room first with the younger students following *behind.* **b** : in the place that someone is going away from • She ***stayed behind*** after the other guests left. • They ***left behind*** everything they owned when they fled the country. • We had to *leave* our family, friends, and neighbors *behind.* — often used figuratively • She has *left* her fears and doubts *behind.* [=she is no longer fearful and doubtful] • She wanted to ***leave the past behind*** [=forget about the past] **c** : later in time • "If Winter comes, can Spring be far *behind*?" —P. B. Shelley, "Ode to the West Wind" (1820)
2 : in a losing position in a race or competition • "How far *behind* was she?" "At least 50 yards (*behind*)." • We were ahead in the first half, but now we're *behind.* • We were *behind* by five runs. = We were five runs *behind.* • a politician who is *behind* in the polls • She was losing the race but she ***came from behind*** and is now in front.
3 a — used to describe something that is not happening or proceeding as quickly as it should • We're running about five minutes *behind* [=*late*] with tonight's schedule. **b** — used to describe someone who is not doing something (such as paying a debt) as quickly as required or expected • He got a bit *behind* [=*late*] in/with his payments. • He is *behind* in (paying) his rent.

²behind *prep*
1 : in or to a place at the back of or to the rear of (someone or something) • Look *behind* you. • He was standing in front of me and she was standing *behind* [=*in back of*] me. • The older students entered the room first with the younger students following *behind* them. • The house is *behind* some trees. [=there are some trees in front of the house] • The cat hid *behind* the couch. • The sun went/hid/was *behind* a cloud. — see also **behind the eight ball** at EIGHT BALL
2 : losing to (someone or something) in a race or competition • "How far *behind* the other runners was she?" "At least 50 yards (*behind* them)." • They were ahead of us by 5 points earlier in the game, but now they're *behind* us by 7. • The polls show that he is *behind* the other candidates. • The company is now *behind* the competition.
3 : in a less advanced position than (someone or something) • He was a year *behind* me in school. [=he finished school a year after I did] : not happening or proceeding as quickly as (someone or something) • He was *behind* the other students in his studies. • This year's sales have lagged considerably/significantly *behind* last year's sales. [=sales have not been as good this year as they were last year] • We're running about five minutes ***behind schedule.*** [=*late*]
4 a : in the past for (someone or something) • Those problems are *behind* us now. • Her best work is *behind* her. [=her best work was in the past] • He has many years of experience *behind* him. [=he has many years of experience in his past] **b** : out of the mind or thoughts of (someone) • Let's put our troubles *behind* us. [=let's stop thinking/worrying about our troubles]
5 a : providing the reason or explanation for (something) • We need to learn more about the conditions *behind* the strike. [=the conditions that led to the strike] • What was really *behind* his murder? [=what was the real reason for his murder?] **b** : responsible for (something) • We'll get to the bottom of this conspiracy and find out who's *behind* it!
6 a : in support of (someone or something) • Despite the

controversy, most of his supporters remain solidly *behind* him. • We're *behind* you all the way! • I encourage everyone to ***get behind*** these proposals. [=to support these proposals] **b :** with the support of (something) • They won the game 1–0 *behind* brilliant pitching. [=brilliant pitching made it possible for them to win the game 1–0]

behind bars see [1]BAR
behind the times see [1]TIME

[3]**behind** *noun, pl* **-hinds** [*count*] *informal* **:** the part of the body above the legs that is used for sitting **:** BUTTOCKS • kicked him in the *behind* • Get your *behind* over here right now! [=come here right now]

behind–the–scenes *adj, always used before a noun*
1 : working or happening privately without being known or seen by the public • There has been a lot of *behind-the-scenes* lobbying for more money. • She exerted a lot of *behind-the-scenes* influence when the project was being planned. • an effective *behind-the-scenes* operator
2 : revealing or reporting on things that usually happen privately without being known or seen by the public • The documentary provides a *behind-the-scenes* glimpse of Congress in action. • a *behind-the-scenes* account — see also *behind the scenes* at SCENE

be•hold /bɪˈhoʊld/ *verb* **-holds; -held** /bɪˈhɛld/; **-hold•ing** [+ *obj*] *formal + literary* **:** to look at (something) **:** to see (something) • Those who have *beheld* the beauty of the desert never forget it. • The huge crowd that gathered at the stadium was ***a sight/wonder to behold***. [=was a wonderful or impressive thing to see] — see also *lo and behold* at LO
– be•hold•er *noun, pl* **-ers** [*count*] • ***Beauty is in the eye of the beholder***. [=different people have different ideas about what is beautiful]

be•hold•en /bɪˈhoʊldən/ *adj*
beholden to *formal* **:** owing a favor or gift to (someone) **:** having obligations to (someone) • politicians who are *beholden to* special interest groups • She works for herself, and so is *beholden to* no one.

be•hoove (*US*) *or Brit* **be•hove** /bɪˈhu:v/ *or Brit* **be•hove** /bɪˈhoʊv/ *verb* **-hooves; -hooved; -hoov•ing** [+ *obj*] *formal* **:** to be necessary or proper for (someone) • He behaved with dignity, as *behooves* [=*befits*] a man of his age. ✧ The subject of *behoove* is usually the pronoun *it*. • It *behooves* a good citizen to obey the law. [=a good citizen should obey the law] • It ill *behooves* you to act so rudely. [=you should not act so rudely]

beige /ˈbeɪʒ/ *noun, pl* **beig•es** [*count, noncount*] **:** a light yellowish-brown color — see color picture on page C3
– beige *adj* • a *beige* skirt

[1]**be•ing** /ˈbi:jɪŋ/ *noun, pl* **-ings**
1 [*count*] **:** a living thing • a human/alien/mythical *being* • sentient/sexual *beings* — see also SUPREME BEING
2 [*noncount*] **:** the state of existing **:** EXISTENCE • philosophies of *being* • The story of how the university ***came into being*** [=began to exist; came to be] is quite fascinating. • a social movement that was ***brought into being*** in the 1960s
3 [*noncount*] *formal* **:** the most important or basic part of a person's mind or self • I knew it was true in the core of my *being*. • He loved music with his whole *being*. [=he deeply loved music]
with every fiber of your being see FIBER

[2]**being** *conj, informal* **:** SINCE — usually + *that* or *as* or *as how* • *Being that/as* it was too late to go home, we stayed the night at a hotel. • It should be her decision, *being as how* she's the one who's paying for it.

[3]**being** *present participle of* BE

be•je•sus /bɪˈdʒi:zəs/ *noun*
the bejesus *informal* — used for emphasis after words like *scare, frighten*, and *beat* • That movie scared *the bejesus* out of me. [=that movie scared me very badly] • They beat *the bejesus* out of the other team.

be•jew•eled (*US*) *or Brit* **be•jew•elled** /bɪˈju:ld/ *adj* **:** decorated with jewels • the *bejeweled* princess • a *bejeweled* sword — sometimes used figuratively • the city's *bejeweled* [=*sparkling*] skyline

be•la•bor (*US*) *or Brit* **be•la•bour** /bɪˈleɪbɚ/ *verb* **-bors; -bored; -bor•ing** [+ *obj*]
1 : to talk about (something) for too long **:** to repeat or stress (something) too much or too often • Her habit of *belaboring* the obvious makes her a very boring speaker. • Please don't *belabor* the point.
2 : to attack or criticize (someone) • He uses his newspaper column to *belabor* writers for even the most minor grammatical errors.

be•lat•ed /bɪˈleɪtəd/ *adj* [*more* ~; *most* ~] **:** happening or coming very late or too late • a *belated* birthday card • She received *belated* recognition for her scientific discovery.
– be•lat•ed•ly *adv* • She was *belatedly* recognized by the scientific community. **– be•lat•ed•ness** *noun* [*noncount*]

be•lay /bɪˈleɪ/ *verb* **-lays; -layed; -lay•ing** [+ *obj*] **:** to attach (a rope) to something so that it is secure • The climber *belayed* the rope. **:** to attach a secure rope to (a person) for safety • *belay* a climber

belch /ˈbɛltʃ/ *verb* **belch•es; belched; belch•ing**
1 [*no obj*] **:** to let out air from the stomach through the mouth very loudly • He *belched* loudly, and his girlfriend said, "That's disgusting!" — compare BURP
2 : to push or throw (something) out with force [+ *obj*] noisy trucks *belching* (out) black exhaust [*no obj*] black exhaust fumes *belching* (out) from noisy trucks • Smoke *belched* from the factory chimneys beside the river.
– belch *noun, pl* **belches** [*count*] • a rude *belch* • *belches* of smoke **– belch•er** *noun, pl* **-ers** [*count*]

be•lea•guer /bɪˈli:gɚ/ *verb* **-guers; -guered; -guer•ing** [+ *obj*] *formal* **:** to cause constant or repeated trouble for (a person, business, etc.) • the lack of funds that *beleaguers* schools — usually used as *(be) beleaguered* • The team has *been beleaguered* by errors. • a company *beleaguered* by debt
– beleaguered *adj* • an economically *beleaguered* city • a *beleaguered* politician [=a politician who is being criticized by many people]

bel•fry /ˈbɛlfri/ *noun, pl* **-fries** [*count*] **:** a tower or part of a tower where a bell or set of bells hangs
bats in the/your belfry *informal + old-fashioned* ✧ To have *bats in the belfry* or (*chiefly US*) *bats in your belfry* is to be crazy. • an old woman with *bats in her belfry* [=a crazy/batty old woman]

Bel•gian /ˈbɛldʒən/ *noun, pl* **-gians** [*count*]
1 : a person born, raised, or living in Belgium
2 : a person of Belgian descent
– Belgian *adj* • a *Belgian* couple and their children • *Belgian* beer/chocolate/linen

Belgian endive *noun, pl* ~ **-dives** [*count, noncount*] *chiefly US* **:** the leaves of a chicory plant that has been grown in darkness to make the leaves white instead of green

Belgian waffle *noun, pl* ~ **waffles** [*count*] *chiefly US* **:** a large waffle that is served usually with fruit and whipped cream

be•lie /bɪˈlaɪ/ *verb* **-lies; -lied; -ly•ing** [+ *obj*] *formal*
1 : to give a false idea of (something) • Her manner and appearance *belie* her age. [=she looks and acts like a much younger person than she really is] • a tree whose delicate beauty *belies* its real toughness
2 : to show (something) to be false or wrong • Their actions *belie* their claim to be innocent.

be•lief /bəˈli:f/ *noun, pl* **-liefs**
1 a : a feeling of being sure that someone or something exists or that something is true [*singular*] a heartfelt/deep/deep-seated/firm/strong/passionate *belief* — often + *in* • He says that he is given strength by his *belief in* God. • He has a strong *belief in* his ability to win. [=he is certain that he can win] • His family has an unshakable *belief in* his innocence. — often + *that* • It's my *belief that* the current policy is certain to fail. [=I believe that the current policy is certain to fail] • She bought the rug ***in the belief that*** [=because she believed that] it was a real antique, not a fake. • Many people arrived early ***in the mistaken/erroneous belief that*** [=because they mistakenly believed that] free tickets would be available. • There is a ***growing belief that*** [=an increasing number of people believe that] these policies will not succeed. [*noncount*] There is *growing belief that* these policies will not succeed. • ***Contrary to popular belief***, the economy has actually improved in recent months. [=the economy has improved although many/most people do not think that it has] — compare DISBELIEF **b** [*singular*] **:** a feeling that something is good, right, or valuable — + *in* • a *belief in* democracy • a judge who had a firm/strong *belief in* judicial restraint **c** [*singular*] **:** a feeling of trust in the worth or ability of someone — + *in* • He has a strong *belief in* himself. [=he strongly believes that he will succeed]
2 [*count*] **:** something that a person accepts as true or right **:** a strongly held opinion about something • He gets angry if anyone challenges his religious/political *beliefs*. • We challenged his *beliefs* about religion. • erroneous/mistaken/false *beliefs* • a system of *beliefs* = a *belief* system — compare UNBELIEF

3 [*noncount*] **:** the state of being accepted as true **:** the state of being believed ▪ a story that is ***worthy of belief*** [=a story that deserves to be believed, a believable story] ▪ a story that ***defies belief*** = (*chiefly Brit*) a story that ***beggars belief*** [=an unbelievable story]

beyond belief **:** not capable of being believed ▪ events that are *beyond belief* [=events that are unbelievable] ▪ She is beautiful *beyond belief.* [=she is unbelievably/extremely beautiful]

to the best of your belief ✧ If you say something is *to the best of your belief*, you mean that it agrees with what you know and believe to be true. ▪ *To the best of my belief* [=(more commonly) *to the best of my knowledge, as far as I know*], everyone arrived on time. [=I think that everyone arrived on time, but it is possible that someone arrived late and I don't know about it]

be·lieve /bəˈliːv/ *verb, not used in progressive tenses* **-lieves; -lieved; -liev·ing**

1 [+ *obj*] **a :** to accept or regard (something) as true ▪ The scientists *believed* the reports. ▪ Many people seem to *believe* that theory, but I find it hard/difficult to *believe.* ▪ You shouldn't *believe* everything you read. ▪ I knew that he was a liar and so I didn't *believe* a word he said. [=I didn't believe anything he said] ▪ I did not want to *believe* (that) it could happen. ▪ He says he'll help us, but I don't *believe* what he says. ▪ They were tricked into *believing* that he was a doctor. — opposite DISBELIEVE **b :** to accept the truth of what is said by (someone) ▪ He says he'll help us, but I don't *believe* him. — opposite DISBELIEVE

2 [+ *obj*] **:** to have (a specified opinion) **:** THINK ▪ I'm beginning to *believe* (that) this war will never end. ▪ I used to *believe* (that) I was the only one who felt that way but now I know (that) there are others like me. ▪ He clearly/firmly/honestly *believes* (that) it is possible. = He clearly/firmly/honestly *believes* it (to be) possible. ▪ He had reason to *believe* that they would accept his offer. = He had reason for *believing* that they would accept his offer. ▪ She was ***widely believed*** to be guilty. [=many people believed that she was guilty] ▪ We were ***led to believe*** it was true. [=we heard, saw, or read something that made us think it was true] ▪ "Has he accepted the job?" "***I believe so.***" = "***So I believe.***" ▪ "Has he accepted the job?" "***I believe not.***" = "***I don't believe so.***"

3 [*no obj*] **:** to regard the existence of God as a fact **:** to have religious beliefs ▪ She went to church because her family expected it, but she didn't really *believe.*

4 [*no obj*] **:** to have trust in the ability, worth, etc., of someone or something ▪ The team hasn't won a championship in many years, but their fans still *believe.* [=their fans still believe in them; their fans still believe that they will win]

5 *informal* — used for emphasis in phrases that express certainty, surprise, annoyance, etc. ▪ "Do you think they can win?" "***You/You'd better believe it!***" [=yes, I definitely think so] ▪ ***Believe me,*** he can really play the game. = ***Believe you me,*** he can really play the game. ▪ ***I can't believe*** how ugly that dress is. [=what an ugly dress] ▪ You broke the window? ***I can't believe*** you guys! [=I'm annoyed and shocked by what you did] How could you do such a thing? ▪ ***I can't believe*** [=I am amazed/surprised] that that terrible restaurant is still in business. ▪ That terrible restaurant is still in business, ***if you can believe it/that.*** ▪ ***Can/Would you believe it***?! That terrible restaurant is still in business. ▪ ***You won't believe*** what I just heard! [=you will be very surprised by what I just heard] ▪ ***You wouldn't believe*** how long it took us to get here. [=it took us a surprisingly long/short time to get here] ▪ ***I don't believe it!*** I swept the floor 10 minutes ago, and it's already dirty again! ▪ ***I could not believe*** my good fortune/luck. ▪ It's ***hard to believe*** that he's gone. ▪ His latest movie, ***believe it or not,*** is a romantic comedy about a group of lawyers. [=it is surprising but true that his latest movie is a romantic comedy about a group of lawyers] ▪ "I hear that their marriage is in trouble." "***Don't you believe it!*** [=that is completely untrue] They're the happiest couple I know!" ▪ "He says he's going to become a doctor." "***If you believe that, you'll believe anything!***" [=it would be very foolish to believe that he is going to become a doctor] ▪ "He says he's going to become a doctor." "***I'll believe that when I see it!***"

believe in [*phrasal verb*] **1 *believe in (something)*** **a :** to have faith or confidence in the existence of (something) ▪ Do you *believe in* ghosts? **b :** to have trust in the goodness or value of (something) ▪ She *believes in* (the value of) regular exercise. ▪ They *believed in* liberty for all. ▪ I *believe in* working hard to achieve success. ▪ She doesn't *believe in* using pesticides. [=she doesn't believe that it's right to use pesticides; she believes that pesticides do more harm than good] **2 *believe in (someone)*** **:** to have trust in the goodness or ability of (someone) ▪ Despite his problems, his parents still *believe in* him. ▪ She *believes in* herself and in her abilities.

can't believe your eyes/ears ✧ If you *can't believe your eyes/ears* or *can hardly/scarcely believe your eyes/ears*, you are very surprised at or upset by what you are seeing or hearing. ▪ I *could hardly believe my eyes* when I saw what he was wearing.

make believe **:** to act as though something that is not true or real is true or real **:** PRETEND ▪ When we were children we used to *make believe* (that) we were soldiers fighting in a war. ▪ He isn't really angry, he's just *making believe* (that he is). ▪ They want to *make believe* that everything is all right. — see also MAKE-BELIEVE

seeing is believing ✧ The expression *seeing is believing* means that when you actually see something, you have to believe that it exists or is true. ▪ I didn't think it could happen, but *seeing is believing.* [=I saw it happen, so now I believe it's possible]

– be·liev·able /bəˈliːvəbəl/ *adj* [*more* ~; *most* ~] ▪ The novel's ending is not very *believable.* ▪ His excuse was barely/scarcely *believable.* **– be·liev·ably** /bəˈliːvəbli/ *adv* ▪ The characters are all *believably* portrayed. **– be·liev·er** *noun, pl* **-ers** [*count*] ▪ a *believer* in religion ▪ devout *believers* ▪ She's a firm/great/strong *believer* in adult education. [=she firmly/strongly believes in the value of adult education; she thinks adult education is very useful and important] ▪ I was doubtful that he could run his own company, but he's ***made a believer out of me.*** = He's ***made me a believer.*** [=he's convinced me that he can run his own company]

be·lit·tle /biˈlɪtl/ *verb* **-lit·tles; -lit·tled; -lit·tling** [+ *obj*] **:** to describe (someone or something) as little or unimportant ▪ The critic *belittled* the author's work. ▪ Her detractors are in the habit of *belittling* her accomplishments.

– belittling *adj* [*more* ~; *most* ~] ▪ a very *belittling* description ▪ She did not mean to be *belittling* (about her predecessors). **– belittling** *noun* [*noncount*] ▪ his *belittling* of his opponents

bell /ˈbɛl/ *noun, pl* **bells** [*count*]

1 : a hollow usually cup-shaped metal object that makes a ringing sound when it is hit ▪ ring/sound/toll a *bell* ▪ We heard the church *bells* ringing. ▪ The school *bell* clanged. ▪ a dinner *bell* [=a bell that is rung to call people to dinner] ▪ The round ended when the *bell* sounded. ▪ the ***Liberty Bell*** [=a large bell in Philadelphia, Pennsylvania, that is a traditional symbol of U.S. freedom] — see also BELLS AND WHISTLES

2 : an electronic device that makes a ringing sound ▪ We rang the *bell* [=*doorbell*] twice, but no one came to answer the door. ▪ Warning/alarm *bells* went off. = Warning/alarm *bells* started to sound/ring. — sometimes used figuratively ▪ (Warning/alarm) *bells* went off (in my head) as I read her letter. [=there was something in her letter that alarmed me]

3 : something (such as a flower) that is shaped like a bell

(as) clear as a bell see [1]CLEAR

(as) sound as a bell see [3]SOUND

give (someone) a bell *Brit, informal* **:** to call someone on the telephone ▪ I'll *give you a bell* [=*give you a call*] tomorrow.

have/get your bell rung ✧ In informal U.S. and Canadian English, if you *have/get your bell rung*, you get hit hard on the head. ▪ The hockey/football player *had his bell rung* during the play.

ring a bell see [3]RING

bel·la·don·na /ˌbɛləˈdɑːnə/ *noun* [*noncount*]

1 : a poisonous plant that has reddish bell-shaped flowers — called also *deadly nightshade*

2 : a drug made from the belladonna plant

bell–bot·toms /ˈbɛlˈbɑːtəmz/ *noun* [*plural*] **:** pants with legs that become much wider at the bottom ▪ She was wearing (a pair of) *bell-bottoms.* — called also *flares*

– bell–bottom *adj* ▪ *bell-bottom* jeans/trousers

bell·boy /ˈbɛlˌbɔɪ/ *noun, pl* **-boys** [*count*] **:** BELLHOP

belle /ˈbɛl/ *noun, pl* **belles** [*count*] *old-fashioned* **:** a very attractive and popular girl or woman ▪ a Southern *belle* ▪ She was ***the belle of the ball.*** [=the most beautiful and popular woman at a dance, party, etc.]

bell·hop /ˈbɛlˌhɑːp/ *noun, pl* **-hops** [*count*] *chiefly US* **:** a boy or man who takes hotel guests to their rooms, carries luggage, etc. — called also *bellboy*

B

bel·li·cose /ˈbɛlɪˌkous/ *adj* [*more ~; most ~*] *formal* : having or showing a tendency to argue or fight • a *bellicose* general • *bellicose* [=*combative*] behavior • *bellicose* language/statements
— **bel·li·cos·i·ty** /ˌbɛlɪˈkɑːsəti/ *noun* [*noncount*]

[1]**bel·lig·er·ent** /bəˈlɪʤərənt/ *adj*
1 [*more ~; most ~*] : angry and aggressive : feeling or showing readiness to fight • a *belligerent* remark • He was drunk and *belligerent.*
2 *always used before a noun, formal* : fighting a war : engaged in a war • *belligerent* nations/states
— **bel·lig·er·ence** /bəˈlɪʤərəns/ *also* **bel·lig·er·en·cy** /bəˈlɪʤərənsi/ *noun* [*noncount*] — **bel·lig·er·ent·ly** *adv*

[2]**belligerent** *noun, pl* **-ents** [*count*] *formal* : a group or country that is fighting a war • An international group is trying to negotiate a cease-fire between the *belligerents.*

bel·low /ˈbɛlou/ *verb* **-lows; -lowed; -low·ing**
1 : to shout in a deep voice [*no obj*] He *bellowed* at/to/for her to come over at once. • He was *bellowing* into the phone, giving orders to one of his employees. [+ *obj*] The sergeant was *bellowing* orders. • "You're fired!" he *bellowed.*
2 [*no obj*] *of an animal* : to make a deep, loud sound • The bull *bellowed* angrily.
— **bellow** *noun, pl* **-lows** [*count*] • He let loose with an angry *bellow.* • a *bellow* of anger/rage • the *bellow* of a bull

bel·lows /ˈbɛlouz/ *noun* [*plural*] : a device that produces a strong current of air when its sides are pressed together • the *bellows* of an accordion ✧ *Bellows* is used with both plural and singular verbs. • *Bellows* were used to help start the fire. = A (pair of) *bellows* was used to help start the fire.

bell pepper *noun, pl* **~ -pers** [*count*] *chiefly US* : a large pepper with a mild flavor • a red/green *bell pepper*

bells and whistles *noun* [*plural*] *informal* : parts and features that are useful or appealing but not essential or necessary : FRILLS • The car was equipped with all the *bells and whistles* you could ask for.

bell·weth·er /ˈbɛlˈwɛðɚ/ *noun, pl* **-ers** [*count*] : someone or something that leads others or shows what will happen in the future • She is a *bellwether* of fashion. • High-tech *bellwethers* led the decline in the stock market. • a county that is a *bellwether* in national elections

[1]**bel·ly** /ˈbɛli/ *noun, pl* **bel·lies** [*count*]
1 a : a person's stomach or the part of the body that contains the stomach • My *belly* was full. • He got down on his *belly* to crawl. • They slid down the snowy hill on their *bellies.* • a kick in the *belly* [=*abdomen*] — see also BEER BELLY, POTBELLY **b** : the part of an animal's body that is like a person's belly • a horse's *belly* • a gray squirrel with a white *belly* — see also UNDERBELLY
2 : a curved or rounded surface or part • the *belly* of an airplane • the *belly* of a ship/violin
— **bel·lied** *adj* — used in combination • a red-*bellied* woodpecker — see also YELLOW-BELLIED

[2]**belly** *verb* **bel·lies; bel·lied; bel·ly·ing** : to cause (something, such as a sail) to curve or bulge outward [+ *obj*] The wind *bellied* (out) the sails of the ship. [*no obj*] The sails of the ship *bellied* [=*bulged*] out in the wind.
belly up to [*phrasal verb*] ***belly up to (someone or something)*** *US, informal* : to walk to or toward (someone or something) • The men *bellied up to* the bar.

[1]**bel·ly·ache** /ˈbɛliˌeɪk/ *noun, pl* **-aches** : a pain in the stomach : STOMACHACHE [*count*] He ate too much chili and it gave him a *bellyache.* [*noncount*] (*Brit*) • He ate too much chili and it gave him *bellyache.*

[2]**bellyache** *verb* **-aches; -ached; -ach·ing** [*no obj*] *informal* : to complain in an annoying way • He was *bellyaching* about how long it took to get a table at the restaurant.
— **bellyaching** *noun* • I'm tired of listening to his *bellyaching.*

belly button *noun, pl* **~ -tons** [*count*] *informal* : NAVEL

belly dance *noun, pl* **~ dances** [*count*] : a type of Middle Eastern dance done by a woman who makes rhythmic movements with her hips and belly
— **belly dance** *verb* **~ dances; ~ danced; ~ dancing** [*no obj*] — **belly dancer** *noun, pl* **~ -ers** [*count*] — **belly dancing** *noun* [*noncount*] • taught a class in *belly dancing*

belly flop *noun, pl* **~ flops** [*count*] *informal* : a poorly done dive in which the front of the body lands flat on the surface of the water • She did a *belly flop* into the pool.
— **belly flop** *verb* **~ flops; ~ flopped; ~ flopping** [*no obj*] • She *belly flopped* into the pool.

bel·ly·ful /ˈbɛliˌfʊl/ *noun* [*singular*] *informal* : a large amount of something • The movie provides a *bellyful* of laughs. — often used to express irritation or annoyance • I've ***had a bellyful of*** him and his advice. [=I'm sick of him and his advice; I do not want any more of his advice]

belly laugh *noun, pl* **~ laughs** [*count*] : a deep and loud laugh • He has an infectious *belly laugh.* • The show provided lots of *belly laughs.*

bel·ly–up /ˈbɛliˈʌp/ *adj*
go belly-up *informal* : to fail completely • The team *went belly-up* in the play-offs. • The business *went belly-up* [=went bankrupt] during the long recession.

be·long /bɪˈlɑːŋ/ *verb* **-longs; -longed; -long·ing** [*no obj*]
1 — used to say that someone or something should be in a particular place or situation • This book *belongs* [=*goes*] on the top shelf. • Put the groceries away where they *belong.* • Those kids really *belong* in school. [=they should be in school] • Does that item really *belong* on the list? • A dictionary *belongs* in every home. [=every home should have a dictionary] • A sick person *belongs* in bed. • A man with his abilities *belongs* in teaching. [=he should be a teacher] • Whales *belong* among the mammals, not fish. [=whales are mammals, not fish; whales are classified as mammals] • She and her husband are a perfect couple. They *belong* together. • They *belong* with each other.
2 : to be accepted and liked by the other people in a group • She was here for 15 years, but she never really *belonged.*
belong to [*phrasal verb*] **1** ***belong to (someone)*** : to be the property of (someone) : to be owned by (someone) • The money *belongs to* him. [=the money is his] • That watch *belongs to* me. • The house *belongs* not just *to* her, but *to* her husband as well. • His style *belongs* only *to* himself. [=no one else has his style] **2** ***belong to (something)*** **a** : to be a member of (a club, organization, etc.) • The family *belongs to* a country club. • Most of the company's employees *belong to* an HMO. **b** : to be included in (a category, group, etc.) • What family does that bird *belong to*? **c** : to be a part of (something) : to be connected with (something) • the parts *belonging to* the clock
— **belonging** *noun* [*noncount*] • The kindness that they showed to her when she first arrived gave her a real sense/feeling of *belonging.*

be·long·ings /bɪˈlɑːŋɪŋz/ *noun* [*plural*] : the things that belong to a person : POSSESSIONS • They gathered their *belongings* and left. • She left a pile of *belongings* next to her chair. • Be sure to take your ***personal belongings*** [=items that are yours and are small enough to be carried] with you when you get off the bus.

be·loved /bɪˈlʌvəd, bɪˈlʌvd/ *adj* [*more ~; most ~*] : very much loved : dearly loved • my own *beloved* grandmother • He is a *beloved* public figure. • an actor *beloved* by/of millions of fans • one of the city's most *beloved* buildings
— **beloved** *noun, pl* **-loveds** [*count*] *literary* • She saw her *beloved* [=the person she loved] approaching. ✧ The phrase ***dearly beloved*** is often used at the beginning of a Christian wedding ceremony to address the people who are there. • *Dearly beloved,* we are gathered here today . . .

[1]**be·low** /bɪˈlou/ *adv*
1 : in or to a lower place • The pencil rolled off the desk and fell to the floor *below.* • The pilot looked down at the sea far *below.* • We heard the elevator stop at the floor *below.* ✧ The opposite of every sense of *below* is *above.*
2 : on or to a lower deck on a ship or boat • They secured the goods on deck and went *below.* • The captain ordered the men *below.* [=ordered them to go below the main deck]
3 : in or to a lower rank or number • All personnel, captain and *below,* were ordered to report for duty. • The game is suitable for children at age 10 and *below.* [=*younger, under*]
4 : lower than zero • The temperature ranged from 5 *below* to 10 above. [=from –5 degrees to 10 degrees Fahrenheit]
5 : lower, further down, or later on the same page or on a following page : at a later point in the same document • The results of the test are discussed/explained/listed/shown *below.* • See the graph *below.*
from below : from a lower place • We heard voices calling *from below.* • I felt a draft *from below.*

[2]**below** *prep*
1 : in or to a lower place than (something) : BENEATH • Our apartment is *below* theirs. • She wore a skirt that reached *below* her knees. = The bottom of her skirt was *below* her knees. • We could see only clouds *below* us. • The diver descended *below* 25 meters. • The sun disappeared *below* the horizon. • a spot directly *below* us • the valley far *below* us •

just/slightly *below* the horizon ✧ The opposite of every sense of *below* is *above*.
2 : lower in number, amount, or size than (something) **:** less than (something) ▪ Temperatures were *below* average/normal all week. ▪ The game is suitable for children *below* [=*younger than, under*] the age of 10. ▪ She worked for wage rates *below* those of other workers.
3 : less important or powerful than (someone) **:** having a lower rank than (someone) ▪ A lieutenant is *below* a captain. [=a captain outranks a lieutenant] ▪ He ranks far *below* his superior.
4 : in a lower or less important position than (something) ▪ He puts his own needs *below* his child's needs.

[1]belt /ˈbɛlt/ *noun, pl* **belts** [*count*]
1 : a band of material (such as leather) that is worn around a person's waist ▪ I fastened/unfastened the buckle on my *belt*. = I buckled/unbuckled my *belt*. ▪ I tied the *belt* of my robe. — see color picture on page C14; see also BLACK BELT, GARTER BELT, SAFETY BELT, SEAT BELT
2 : a band that runs around wheels or other parts in a machine and that is used for moving or carrying something — see also FAN BELT
3 : a region that has a lot of a particular thing ▪ a *belt* of hilly land [=an area with many hills] ▪ a storm *belt* ▪ the farm/farming *belt* ▪ the corn/cotton *belt* [=a region with many farms growing corn/cotton] ▪ an asteroid *belt* ▪ (*chiefly US*) cities in the ***Rust Belt*** [=an area formerly known for industry and manufacturing] — see also BIBLE BELT, SUNBELT
below the belt *informal* **:** too harsh and unfair ▪ That remark was *below the belt*. = That remark really ***hit*** (him) ***below the belt***. ✧ The phrase *below the belt* comes from the sport of boxing, where it is against the rules to hit your opponent anywhere below the belt.
tighten your belt **:** to begin to spend less money **:** to make changes in order to save money ▪ Many companies are *tightening their belts* during the recession. — see also BELT-TIGHTENING
under your belt **:** as an achievement or as part of your experience ▪ She has a best-selling book *under her belt*. [=she has written a best-selling book] ▪ an actor who has several films *under his belt* [=who has appeared in several films] ▪ He finally has a full year of experience *under his belt*.
– compare [3]BELT
– belt·ed /ˈbɛltəd/ *adj* ▪ a *belted* coat/jacket/robe

[2]belt *verb* **belts; belt·ed; belt·ing**
1 [+ *obj*] **:** to fasten (something) with a belt ▪ His bathrobe was loosely *belted*.
2 [+ *obj*] *informal* **:** to hit (someone or something) hard ▪ He *belted* the ball down the fairway. ▪ *belt* a home run ▪ Some drunk got mad and threatened to *belt* me.
3 [+ *obj*] *informal* **:** to sing (a song) in a loud and forceful way — usually + *out* ▪ a singer *belting out* tunes at the top of her lungs
4 *always followed by an adverb* [+ *obj*] *US, informal* **:** to drink (something) quickly ▪ He *belted* down a shot of whiskey. ▪ *belting* back a drink
5 *always followed by an adverb or preposition* [*no obj*] *chiefly Brit, informal* **:** to move or go at a high speed ▪ The car was *belting* down/along the highway.
belt up [*phrasal verb*] *Brit* **1 :** to fasten a seat belt in a car or other vehicle ▪ When you're riding in a car, you should always *belt up* [=(*US*) *buckle up*] for safety. **2** *informal* **:** to stop talking ▪ Will you just *belt up* [=*shut up*] for once?

[3]belt *noun, pl* **belts** [*count*] *informal*
1 : a hard hit ▪ Some drunk got mad and threatened to give me a *belt*. [=*punch*]
2 *US, informal* **:** a drink of alcohol ▪ He had a few *belts* (of whiskey) before dinner.
– compare [1]BELT

belt·er /ˈbɛltɚ/ *noun, pl* **-ers** [*count*] *US, informal* **:** a singer with a powerful voice **:** a singer who belts out songs ▪ a legendary blues *belter*

belt–tight·en·ing /ˈbɛltˌtaɪtn̩ɪŋ/ *noun* [*noncount*] **:** a reduction in spending **:** changes that are made in order to save money ▪ The recession has caused many companies to do some *belt-tightening*. — often used before another noun ▪ a *belt-tightening* measure/move/policy — see also *tighten your belt* at [1]BELT

belt·way /ˈbɛltˌweɪ/ *noun, pl* **-ways**
1 [*count*] *US* **:** a highway that goes around a city ▪ an urban *beltway* — called also (*Brit*) *orbital*
2 ***the Beltway*** **:** the political and social world of Washington, D.C. ▪ politics inside *the Beltway* ▪ Her influence extends beyond *the Beltway*.
– Beltway *adj, always used before a noun* ▪ *Beltway* politicians/politics [=the politicians/politics of Washington, D.C.]

be·moan /bɪˈmoʊn/ *verb* **-moans; -moaned; -moan·ing** [+ *obj*] **:** to say that you are unhappy about (something) ▪ He *bemoans* the fact that the team lost again. ▪ an article *bemoaning* the decline in voter turnout **:** to complain about (something) ▪ Some critics are always *bemoaning* the state of the language.

be·muse /bɪˈmjuːz/ *verb* **-mus·es; -mused; -mus·ing** [+ *obj*] **:** to cause (someone) to be confused and often also somewhat amused — usually used as *(be) bemused* ▪ He thought of himself as an ordinary man, and he *was bemused* by all the attention that he was receiving.
– bemused *adj* [*more* ~; *most* ~] ▪ She had a *bemused* expression/smile on her face. **– be·mus·ed·ly** /bɪˈmjuːzədli/ *adv* She smiled *bemusedly*. **– be·muse·ment** /bɪˈmjuːzmənt/ *noun* [*noncount*] ▪ She smiled in/with *bemusement*.

[1]bench /ˈbɛntʃ/ *noun, pl* **bench·es**

bench

1 [*count*] **:** a long and usually hard seat for two or more people ▪ a park *bench*
2 ***the bench*** *law* **a :** the place where a judge sits in a court of law ▪ The lawyer asked if he could approach *the bench*. **b :** the position or rank of a judge ▪ her recent appointment to *the bench*
3 [*count*] **:** a long table for holding tools and work ▪ a carpenter's *bench*
4 *sports* **a** ***the bench*** **:** a long seat where the members of a sports team wait for a chance to play ▪ He spent most of his season on *the bench*. [=he did not play in many games] ▪ He plays better ***coming off the bench***. [=coming into the game after it has started] **b** [*count*] *chiefly US* **:** the players on a team who do not usually play at the start of a game **:** the reserve players on a team — usually singular ▪ The team's *bench* is deep. = The team has a deep *bench*. [=the team had many good players in addition to its main players] — often used before another noun ▪ a *bench* player [=a reserve player; a player who is part of a team's bench]

[2]bench *verb* **bench·es; benched; bench·ing** [+ *obj*] *US, sports* **:** to not allow (a player) to play in a game **:** to put (a player) on the bench ▪ The manager *benched* one of his most popular players. ▪ He was *benched* for several games by a leg injury. [=he was forced to miss several games because of a leg injury]

bench·mark /ˈbɛntʃˌmɑɚk/ *noun, pl* **-marks** [*count*] **:** something that can be used as a way to judge the quality or level of other, similar things ▪ a stock whose performance is a *benchmark* against which other stocks can be measured

bench press *noun, pl* **~ press·es** [*count*] **:** a lift or exercise in which a weight is raised by pushing your arms upward while you lie on a bench
– bench–press *verb* **-press·es; -pressed; -press·ing** [+ *obj*] ▪ He can *bench-press* 350 pounds.

bench seat *noun, pl* **~ seats** [*count*] **:** a long seat in a vehicle (such as a car) that goes across the full width of the passenger section

bench·warm·er /ˈbɛntʃˌwoɚmɚ/ *noun, pl* **-ers** [*count*] *US, sports* **:** a player who is not among the best players on a team and does not often play **:** a reserve player who is usually on the bench ▪ I played a little, but mostly I was a *benchwarmer*.

[1]bend /ˈbɛnd/ *verb* **bends; bent** /ˈbɛnt/; **bend·ing**
1 a [+ *obj*] **:** to use force to cause (something, such as a wire or pipe) to become curved ▪ *bend* a wire into a circle ▪ *bend* the cable around a wheel ▪ He *bent* the bow and shot an arrow from it. ▪ His glasses got *bent* when he dropped them. **b** [*no obj*] **:** to curve out of a straight line or position ▪ The road *bends* [=*curves, turns*] to the left. ▪ The trees were *bending* in the wind. ▪ The branch will *bend* before it breaks. ▪ The branches of the fruit tree were ***bending under their own weight***. [=were bending because they were so heavy] — sometimes used figuratively ▪ She refused to *bend* under pressure to change her decision. ▪ a politician accused of ***bending to the will*** of wealthy supporters [=being influenced

by wealthy supporters; doing the things that are wanted by wealthy supporters]

2 a [*no obj*] **:** to move your body so that it is not straight • She *bent* down/over/forward to pick up a piece of paper and then she straightened up again. • He *bent* back to look up at the ceiling. • *bend* to the left and then *bend* to the right • *bend* at the waist • He ***bent double*** with pain. [=he bent forward from the waist because he was in extreme pain] **b** [+ *obj*] **:** to move (part of your body, such as an arm or leg) so that it is not straight • *bend* a knee • *bend* a leg • *bend* an arm • *bend* [=*tilt*] your head ◇ In formal language, if you ***bend yourself to*** or ***bend your strength/energy/efforts (etc.) to/toward*** something (such as a job or task), you work hard in order to do it. • He has *bent himself* [=*applied himself*] *to* the task of making the company more efficient and profitable. • They are *bending their efforts toward* completing the job on time. • They *bent their minds* to [=gave a lot of thought to; thought hard about] the problem.

bend a rule **:** to not be strict or exact about following a rule • She's not really quite old enough to be admitted as a member, but she's very close, so I think we can *bend the rule(s)* a little in her case and let her in now.

bend over backward see [1]BACKWARD

bend someone's ear *informal* **:** to talk to someone for a long time • He didn't really care about me, he just wanted to *bend my ear* about his own problems.

bend (the) facts **:** to change facts in a dishonest way in order to deceive people • a journalist who has been accused of *bending the facts* in order to gain support for his political agenda

bend the truth **:** to say something that is not true or that misleads people but that is usually not regarded as a serious or harmful lie • When he tells people he's from Manhattan he's *bending the truth* a little since he really grew up in Brooklyn.

on bended knee *also* ***on bended knees*** **:** in a kneeling position : in the position of someone who is kneeling on one knee • He proposed to her *on bended knee*. = He got down *on bended knee* and proposed to her. — sometimes used figuratively • He was forced to ask for their help *on bended knee*. [=he was forced to beg for their help; he was forced to ask for their help in a very humble way]

[2]**bend** *noun, pl* **bends**

1 [*count*] **:** a curved part of something • a *bend* in a road/stream • They live just around/past the next *bend* (in the road). • the graceful *bends* [=curves] of the stairway

2 [*count*] **:** the act or process of bending something • a quick *bend* of the body • knee *bends*

3 ***the bends*** *medical* **:** a painful and dangerous condition caused by rising to the surface too quickly after being deep underwater — called also *decompression sickness*

around the bend (*chiefly US*) *or chiefly Brit* ***round the bend*** *informal* **1 :** CRAZY • The pressure of his job nearly drove him *around the bend*. • He almost went *around the bend*. • If you ask me, she's completely *round the bend*. **2** *US* **:** occurring soon • The end of summer is just/right *around the bend*. [=*around the corner*]

– bendy /ˈbɛndi/ *adj* **bend•i•er; -est** [*also more* ~; *most* ~] *chiefly Brit, informal* • a *bendy* [=*flexible*] toy • a *bendy* road [=a road with many curves]

bend•er /ˈbɛndɚ/ *noun, pl* **-ers** [*count*] *informal* **:** a period when someone gets very drunk • He ***went on a bender*** and was drunk all weekend. — see also FENDER BENDER

[1]**be•neath** /bɪˈniːθ/ *adv* **:** in or to a lower position : BELOW • the mountains and the towns *beneath* • the sky above and the earth *beneath* • an awning with chairs and tables *beneath* • The ground *beneath* is covered with flowers.

[2]**beneath** *prep*

1 a : in or to a lower position than (something or someone) : BELOW • the sky above us and the earth *beneath* us • just *beneath* the surface of the water • The painting is hanging on the wall with a plaque *beneath* it. — opposite ABOVE **b :** directly under (something or someone) • the ground *beneath* [=*underneath*] her feet • We had a picnic *beneath* a large tree. • The paper was hidden *beneath* a pile of books. • She wore a sweater *beneath* her coat.

2 : not worthy of (someone) : not good enough for (someone) • He won't do any work that he considers *beneath* him. [=work that he thinks is not good enough for a person of his social class] • She refused to marry *beneath* her. [=to marry someone with a lower social standing than hers] — opposite ABOVE

3 : under the pressure or influence of (something) • The chair sagged *beneath* [=*under, underneath*] his weight. [=his weight caused the chair to sag]

4 : hidden under (something) • He has a warm heart *beneath* [=*under, underneath*] his gruff manner.

from beneath **:** from a place below or under (something) • She gazed at us *from beneath* the brim of her hat.

bene•dic•tion /ˌbɛnəˈdɪkʃən/ *noun, pl* **-tions :** a prayer that asks for God's blessing [*count*] He dismissed the congregation with a *benediction*. [*noncount*] a prayer of *benediction*

ben•e•fac•tor /ˈbɛnəˌfæktɚ/ *noun, pl* **-tors** [*count*] **:** someone who helps another person, group, etc., by giving money • With the help of a rich *benefactor* he set up a charity. • an anonymous *benefactor*

ben•e•fac•tress /ˈbɛnəˌfæktrɪs/ *noun, pl* **-tress•es** [*count*] *somewhat old-fashioned* **:** a woman who helps another person, group, etc., by giving money : a female benefactor • a wealthy *benefactress*

be•nef•i•cent /bəˈnɛfəsənt/ *adj* [*more* ~; *most* ~] *formal* **:** doing or producing good • a *beneficent* leader • a humane and *beneficent* policy

– be•nef•i•cence /bəˈnɛfəsəns/ *noun* [*noncount*]

ben•e•fi•cial /ˌbɛnəˈfɪʃəl/ *adj* [*more* ~; *most* ~] **:** producing good or helpful results or effects : producing benefits • He hopes the new drug will prove *beneficial* to/for many people. • Regular exercise has many *beneficial* health effects. • They have a relationship that is *beneficial* to/for both of them. • Some insects are harmful but others are *beneficial*.

– ben•e•fi•cial•ly *adv*

ben•e•fi•ci•ary /ˌbɛnəˈfɪʃiˌeri, *Brit* ˌbɛnəˈfɪʃəri/ *noun, pl* **-ar•ies** [*count*]

1 : a person, organization, etc., that is helped by something : someone or something that benefits from something • Who will be the main *beneficiaries* of these economic reforms? [=who will be helped by these economic reforms?] • The college was a *beneficiary* of the private grant.

2 : a person, organization, etc., that receives money or property when someone dies • Her father named her the *beneficiary* of his life insurance policy. [=she will receive the money from her father's insurance policy if he dies] • She has made the school the sole *beneficiary* of/in her will. [=her will says that all her money and property should go to the school when she dies]

[1]**ben•e•fit** /ˈbɛnəˌfɪt/ *noun, pl* **-fits**

1 : a good or helpful result or effect [*count*] the *benefits* of fresh air and sunshine • A *benefit* of museum membership is that purchases are discounted. • There are many financial *benefits* to owning your own home. • She is just now starting to reap/enjoy the *benefits* of all her hard work. • The *benefits* of taking the drug outweigh its risks. [*noncount*] I see no *benefit* in changing the system now. • We're lucky to be able to get the full *benefit* of/from her knowledge. • These changes will be ***of benefit to*** all of you. [=will help/benefit all of you] • These changes will be ***to your benefit***. [=will help you] • I'm not doing it for myself; I'm doing it ***for your benefit***. [=to help you; for your sake] • Since he owns the land, he thinks he should be free to use it ***for his own benefit***. [=in a way that is helpful to him]

2 a : money that is paid by a company (such as an insurance company) or by a government when someone dies, becomes sick, stops working, etc. [*count*] He began collecting his retirement *benefits* when he was 65. • a disability *benefit* • (*Brit*) a family ***on benefits*** [=(*US*) *on welfare*; receiving money from the government because of a low income or lack of income] [*noncount*] He began collecting his retirement *benefit* when he was 65. • (*Brit*) He is on housing/unemployment *benefit*. — see also CHILD BENEFIT, DEATH BENEFIT, SICKNESS BENEFIT **b** [*count*] **:** something extra (such as vacation time or health insurance) that is given by an employer to workers in addition to their regular pay : FRINGE BENEFIT • The company provides health (insurance) *benefits*. • The job doesn't pay much, but the *benefits* are good. — often used before another noun • a company with a good *benefit* plan/package/program

3 [*count*] **:** a social event to raise money for a person or cause • The school is having/holding a *benefit* to raise money for a new gymnasium. • a charity *benefit* — often used before another noun • a *benefit* concert/dinner/event/performance

have the benefit of **:** to be helped by (something) : to be able to use (something) • Her judgment will be better when she *has the benefit of* more experience.

the benefit of the doubt ◇ When people give you *the bene-*

B

fit of the doubt, they treat you as someone who is honest or deserving of trust even though they are not sure that you really are. • He might be lying, but we have to give him *the benefit of the doubt* and accept what he says for now.

without the benefit of or US ***without benefit of*** : without the help of (something or someone) • The band had to perform *without benefit of* a rehearsal. • He was able to learn a great deal *without the benefit of* formal schooling. • You shouldn't try to handle this problem *without benefit of* a lawyer. • They lived together ***without (the) benefit of marriage***. [=without being married]

with the benefit of : with the help of (something) : by using (something) • *With the benefit of* hindsight, he saw where he had made a mistake. • She'll do better *with the benefit of* more experience.

²benefit *verb* **-fits**; **-fit·ed** *also* **-fit·ted**; **-fit·ing** *also* **-fit·ting**
1 [+ *obj*] : to be useful or helpful to (someone or something) • The new plan may *benefit* many students. • medicines that *benefit* thousands of people • These changes will *benefit* all of you. = All of you will be *benefited* by these changes. • The politician held a fund-raiser to *benefit* his campaign. • Some critics say that the tax cuts only *benefit* wealthy people.
2 [*no obj*] : to be helped • He'll *benefit* by having experiences I never did. — often + *from* • I *benefited from* the experience. • Many patients will *benefit from* the new drug. • All of you will *benefit from* these changes. • Some critics say that only wealthy people will *benefit from* the tax cuts.

be·nev·o·lent /bəˈnɛvələnt/ *adj* [*more* ~; *most* ~]
1 : kind and generous • a *benevolent* company/government • a gift from a *benevolent* donor
2 : organized to do good things for other people • He belonged to several *benevolent* societies and charitable organizations.
– be·nev·o·lence /bəˈnɛvələns/ *noun* [*noncount*] • The king's *benevolence* [=*kindness, generosity*] was known throughout the land. **– be·nev·o·lent·ly** *adv*

Ben·gali /bɛnˈgɑ:li/ *noun, pl* **-gal·is**
1 [*count*] : a person born or living in Bangladesh or in a state in northeastern India called West Bengal
2 [*noncount*] : a language spoken in Bangladesh and West Bengal
– Bengali *adj* • *Bengali* literature

be·night·ed /bɪˈnaɪtəd/ *adj* [*more* ~; *most* ~] *formal* : having no knowledge or education • These *benighted* [=*ignorant, unenlightened*] souls/people have so much to learn. • a strange, *benighted* country

be·nign /bɪˈnaɪn/ *adj*
1 *medical* **a** : not causing death or serious injury • a *benign* infection/disease **b** : without cancer : not cancerous • *benign* brain tumors • We were happy to hear that the tumor was *benign*. — opposite MALIGNANT
2 : not causing harm or damage • This chemical is environmentally *benign*. [=it does not hurt the environment] • He has a *benign* [=*harmless*] habit of biting his fingernails.
3 [*more* ~; *most* ~] : mild and pleasant • *benign* [=*favorable*] weather conditions • a *benign* climate
4 [*more* ~; *most* ~] : gentle and kind • a friendly, *benign* teacher
5 [*more* ~; *most* ~] : having or showing a belief that nothing bad will happen • She takes a *benign* view of her husband's spending habits. [=she does not worry about her husband's spending habits]
– be·nign·ly *adv* • He smiled *benignly* at his students.

¹bent /ˈbɛnt/ *adj* [*more* ~; *most* ~]
1 : having a shape that is changed by bending : not straight • a *bent* metal wire • *bent* arms/elbows • With your knees/legs slightly *bent*, bend forward and touch your toes. • He was ***bent double*** with pain. [=he was bending forward from the waist because he was in extreme pain]
2 *chiefly Brit, informal* : not honest • a *bent* [=*corrupt*] cop

bent on *also* ***bent upon*** : having a strong desire to do (something) • The doctors are *bent on* finding a cure. [=they are determined to find a cure] • She now seems *bent on* winning the competition. • They're *bent upon* destroying the world. — see also HELL-BENT

bent out of shape *US, informal* : very angry or unhappy • Don't get all *bent out of shape* [=*upset*]. Nothing bad happened!

²bent *noun, pl* **bents** [*count*] : an attraction to or an interest in a particular thing or activity • an organization with a strong religious *bent* : a natural talent or interest • students with a creative/scientific *bent* [=*leaning*]

³bent *past tense and past participle of* ¹BEND

be·numb /bɪˈnʌm/ *verb* **-numbs**; **-numbed**; **-numb·ing** [+ *obj*] *formal* : to make (someone) numb or unable to have emotions — usually used as *benumbed* • After years of war, they had become *benumbed* [=*numb*] to violence. [=violence no longer caused them to feel strong emotions]

ben·zene /ˈbɛn,zi:n/ *noun* [*noncount*] : a liquid chemical that is used to make plastics, fuel for automobiles, and other substances

be·queath /bɪˈkwi:θ, bɪˈkwi:ð/ *verb* **-queaths**; **-queathed**; **-queath·ing** [+ *obj*] *formal*
1 : to say in a will that (your property) will be given to (a person or organization) after you die • I *bequeath* this ring to my sister. = I *bequeath* my sister this ring. • He *bequeathed* his paintings to the museum.
2 : to give (ideas, knowledge, etc.) to (younger people) as part of their history • These stories were *bequeathed* [=*handed down, passed down*] to us by our ancestors. • Lessons of the past are *bequeathed* to future generations.

be·quest /bɪˈkwɛst/ *noun, pl* **-quests** [*count*] : the property or money that you promise in your will to give to another person or organization after you die • He made a *bequest* of his paintings to the museum.

be·rate /bɪˈreɪt/ *verb* **-rates**; **-rat·ed**; **-rat·ing** [+ *obj*] *formal* : to yell at (someone) : to criticize (someone) in a loud and angry way • She *berated* [=*scolded*] her son for coming home late.

be·reaved /bɪˈri:vd/ *adj, formal* : sad because a family member or friend has recently died • the *bereaved* parents/families of the victims

the bereaved : a bereaved person or group of people • The minister tried to comfort *the bereaved*.

be·reave·ment /bɪˈri:vmənt/ *noun, pl* **-ments** *formal*
1 [*noncount*] : the state of being sad because a family member or friend has recently died • a period of *bereavement*
2 : the death of a family member or friend [*noncount*] a period of grief after *bereavement* [*count*] people who have recently suffered *bereavements*

be·reft /bɪˈrɛft/ *adj* : sad because a family member or friend has died • the young soldier's *bereft* [=(more commonly) *bereaved*] mother

bereft of : not having (something that is needed, wanted, or expected) • They appear to be completely *bereft of* new ideas. [=to be completely without new ideas] • He was *bereft of* all hope. • a man *bereft of* reason

be·ret /bəˈreɪ/ *noun, pl* **-rets** [*count*] : a round hat with a tight band around the head and a top that is flat, soft, and loose — see picture at HAT

berk /ˈbək/ *noun, pl* **berks** [*count*] *Brit slang* : a stupid or foolish person • He was acting like a complete *berk*.

berm /ˈbəm/ *noun, pl* **berms** [*count*] *chiefly US* : a small hill or wall of dirt or sand • A landscaped *berm* [=a hill decorated with plants and flowers] separates the two roads.

Ber·mu·da shorts /bəˈmju:də-/ *noun* [*plural*] : short pants that reach down to the knees

ber·ry /ˈberi/ *noun, pl* **-ries** [*count*] : a small fruit (such as a strawberry, blueberry, or raspberry) that has many small seeds

ber·serk /bəˈsək, bəˈzək/ *adj* : crazy and violent especially because of anger • *berserk* behavior

go berserk **1** : to become very angry, crazy, and violent • A worker *went berserk* and killed his boss. **2** : to become very excited • The crowd was *going berserk*. [=*going wild*]

¹berth /ˈbəθ/ *noun, pl* **berths** [*count*]
1 : a place to sleep on a ship, train, etc. • a comfortable cabin with a deep *berth* • an upper/lower *berth*
2 : a place in the water near the shore where a ship stops and stays
3 *chiefly US* : a place or position on a team • She won an Olympic *berth*. = She earned a *berth* on her country's Olympic team. • He has a starting *berth* on the all-star team.

give (someone or something) a wide berth : to avoid or stay away from (someone or something) • I could see that she was in a bad mood, so I *gave her a wide berth*.

²berth *verb* **berths**; **berthed**; **berth·ing** : to bring (a ship) into a place where it can stop and stay : to bring (a ship) into a berth [+ *obj*] The ship was *berthed* at this pier. [*no obj*] The ship *berthed* at this pier.

be·seech /bɪˈsi:ʧ/ *verb* **-seech·es**; **-sought** /bɪˈsɑt/ *or* **-seeched**; **-seech·ing** [+ *obj*] *formal + literary* : to beg (someone) for something : to ask (someone) in a serious and emotional way to do something • I *beseech* you, let me live! [=please, don't kill me] • Oh, kind and gracious king, we *beseech* [=*implore, entreat*] you to set us free!

– beseeching *adj* [*more* ~; *most* ~] • She gave the king a *beseeching* look. **– be·seech·ing·ly** *adv*

be·set /bɪˈsɛt/ *verb* **-sets**; **-set**; **-set·ting** [+ *obj*] **:** to cause problems or difficulties for (someone or something) • A lack of money is the greatest problem *besetting* the city today. — usually used as *(be) beset* • He *was beset* by/with injuries this season. [=he suffered many injuries this season] • a city *beset* by/with economic problems

besetting sin *noun, pl* ~ **sins** [*count*] **:** a main or constant problem or fault • My *besetting sin* is a fondness for sweets.

be·side /bɪˈsaɪd/ *prep*

1 : by the side of (someone or something) **:** next to (someone or something) • She sat *beside* him during dinner. • The man *beside* her was wearing a brown suit and hat. • They were walking *beside* me. • Stand *beside* the statue and I'll take your picture. • Their house is *beside* a small lake.

2 : in comparison with (something) • These problems seem unimportant *beside* the potential benefits of the new system.

beside the point **:** not related to the main idea that is being discussed **:** not important • No one knows what we did, but that's *beside the point*. What we did was wrong.

beside yourself **:** not thinking clearly because you are feeling very strong emotions **:** in a state of extreme excitement • We were *beside ourselves* with anger/worry/embarrassment/joy. • He was *beside himself* [=very upset] after hearing the bad news.

[1]**be·sides** /bɪˈsaɪdz/ *prep*

1 : other than (someone or something) • There's no one here *besides* [=*except*] me. • Nothing *besides* [=*but*] a miracle could save them now. • The traffic was a little heavy but, *besides* [=*except for*] that, we had no problems getting here.

2 : in addition to (something) • She wants to learn other languages *besides* English and French. • *Besides* its famous cakes, the bakery also makes delicious breads and cookies. • These salads are delicious *besides* being healthy. • I'm not ready to get married yet. *Besides* which, I enjoy living alone.

[2]**besides** *adv*

1 : as well **:** ALSO • They serve pasta and many other foods *besides*.

2 : in addition to what has been said • The play is excellent, and *besides* [=(more formally) *furthermore, moreover*], the tickets don't cost much. • I'm not ready to get married yet. *Besides*, I enjoy living alone.

be·siege /bɪˈsiːʤ/ *verb* **-sieg·es**; **-sieged**; **-sieg·ing** [+ *obj*]

1 : to surround a city, building, etc., with soldiers and try to take control of it • The army *beseiged* the castle.

2 : to gather around (someone) in a way that is aggressive, annoying, etc. — usually used as *(be) besieged* • They *were besieged* by reporters while leaving the courthouse. • politicians *being besieged* by the media

3 : to overwhelm (someone) *with* too many questions or requests for things • Customers have *besieged* the company *with* questions. — usually used as *(be) besieged* • Every day, her office *is besieged* [=*bombarded*] *with* letters/questions/complaints about the problem.

be·smirch /bɪˈsmɚʧ/ *verb* **-smirch·es**; **-smirched**; **-smirch·ing** [+ *obj*] **:** to cause harm or damage to (the reputation of someone or something) • He has *besmirched* [=*sullied*] her reputation/name/honor by telling lies about her. [=he has caused people to have a low opinion of her]

be·sot·ted /bɪˈsɑːtəd/ *adj* [*more* ~; *most* ~] **:** loving someone or something so much that you cannot think clearly • her *besotted* lover • He was completely *besotted* with/by her. [=infatuated with her]

be·speak /bɪˈspiːk/ *verb* **-speaks**; **-spoke** /bɪˈspoʊk/; **-spo·ken** /bɪˈspoʊkən/; **-speak·ing** [+ *obj*] *formal* **:** to be evidence of (something) **:** to be a sign of (something) • Her newest album *bespeaks* a great talent for writing songs.

be·spec·ta·cled /bɪˈspɛktəkəld/ *adj* **:** wearing glasses • a *bespectacled* student

be·spoke /bɪˈspoʊk/ *adj* **:** made to fit a particular person **:** CUSTOM-MADE • a *bespoke* suit; *also* **:** producing clothes that are made to fit a particular person • a *bespoke* tailor

[1]**best** /ˈbɛst/ *adj, superlative form of* [1]GOOD *or of* [2]WELL

1 a : better than all others in quality or value • You should wear your *best* clothes tonight. • He took us to the (very) *best* restaurants in the city. • We ate the *best* food and drank the *best* wines. • You're our *best* customers. • His modesty and sense of humor are his *best* qualities. • Is that your *best* offer? • I've had the *best* time with you! [=I've had a very enjoyable time with you] • The *best* [=most valuable] things in life are free. • Which of these do you think tastes *best*? • Mary sends you her very *best* wishes/regards. • He's my ***best friend***. [=my closest/dearest friend] = He and I are ***best friends***. **b :** most skillful, talented, or successful • She's the *best* student in her class. • He won the award for *best* actor in a drama. • the team's *best* player

2 : most appropriate, useful, or helpful • She truly believes that this is the *best* way to solve the problem. • She's the team's *best* hope/chance for a medal. • She thought waiting was *best*. = She thought that the *best* thing to do was to wait. = She thought that it was *best* to wait. • It's *best* to leave early if you want to be sure of arriving on time. • We want to do what's *best* for you. • He's the *best* man for the job. • You should do whatever you think is the *best* thing to do. = You should do whatever you ***think best***. • We're making the ***best possible*** use of these materials.

best of all ✧ The phrase *best of all* is often used to refer to the most important or appealing part of something that has many good parts. • The machine is easy to use, easy to clean, and *best of all*, it's absolutely free when you order these books.

next best ✧ A person or thing that is *next best* is not as good as the best person or thing but is better than all others. • The shortstop is the best player on the team, and the catcher is the *next best* player. • We can't see each other often, but calling each other on the telephone is ***the next best thing***.

on your best behavior ✧ If you are *on your best behavior* you are behaving very politely and well. • Remember to be *on your best behavior* with your grandmother. • The children promised to be *on their best behavior*.

[2]**best** *adv, superlative form of* [1]WELL

1 : in the best way **:** in a way that is better than all others • The sauce is *best* served/eaten/enjoyed cold. • His cooking is *best* described as spicy. = It can *best* be described as spicy. **:** with the most success or benefit • They work *best* under pressure. • That's what we do *best*! • We need to think about how *best* to fix this problem. • This is a job *best* left to the professionals. [=it's better/best to allow professional workers to do this job] • Some things are *best* left unsaid. [=it's better/best not to talk about some things]

2 : to the greatest degree or extent **:** MOST • That's the one we liked (the) *best*. • The work should be done by the people who are *best* able to do it. • She's *best* suited to life in the city. • He is *best* known for his invention of the lightbulb. • The museum features some of the *best*-known examples of this style of painting. • the industry's *best*-kept secret

as best you can *or* ***the best (that) you can*** **:** as well, skillfully, or accurately as you can • She answered their questions *as best she could*. [=as well as she could] • You don't have to do it perfectly. Just do it *the best you can*.

had best ✧ If you *had best* do something, you should do it. • *You'd best* get ready for school. [=you'd better get ready for school; you should get ready for school] • *Had*n't you *best* get ready for school?

[3]**best** *noun* [*singular*]

1 ***the best*** **:** the best person or thing • Out of all of my workers, he's *the best*. • Our company is *the best* in the business. • Thanks, Dad. You're *the best*! • I have one more gift for you, and I saved *the best* for last. **:** the best group of people or things • Our store sells nothing but *the best*. = We sell only *the best*. [=the best products] • She's one of *the best* in the world. = She's among *the best*. • Bad things happen to *the best* of us. • They want *the best* for their children. • Even in *the best* of times, we had trouble paying our bills. • In *the best* of all possible worlds, no one would be without food and clean water. • He can compete ***with the best of them***. [=he can compete as well as anyone] • We were ***the best of friends***. [=we were very good friends] • I have a wonderful family and a great job, so I feel that I have ***the best of both worlds***. • Problems can occur even in/under ***the best of circumstances***. [=even if the situation is as good as possible] • All of the students are good, but these three are ***the best of the bunch***. [=the best ones in the group] — see also SUNDAY BEST

2 : someone's or something's most effective, capable, or successful condition — used in phrases like ***at your best*** and ***at its best*** • He's *at his best* in front of a live audience. • She's *at her best* in the morning. • This is democracy *at its best*.

3 : the highest level that you can do or achieve • Was that your *best*? = Was that the *best* you could do? • No one expects you to do the job perfectly. Just ***do your best***. = Just ***do the best you can***. [=do as well as you can] • He *did his best* to help them. • Her time in the race was a ***personal best***. [=it was the fastest time she had ever achieved]

(all) for the best : having or producing a better result — used to say that something will have a good result even though it was not the intended result • I won't be able to go, but maybe it's *all for the best*. I have a lot of work to do anyway.

(all) the best ✧ If you wish someone *(all) the best*, you hope that person will be happy and successful. • We wish you *all the best* in your new job.

at best — used to refer to a result, condition, etc., that is the best one possible even though it is not very good • The company won't make a profit this year. *At best*, they'll break even. • The work won't be finished for another three months *at best*.

best of luck see [1]LUCK

best (out) of three (five, seven, etc.) — used to say that the winner of a series of games will be the one who has won the most times after three (five, seven, etc.) games have been played

bring out the best in ✧ If someone or something *brings out the best in you*, that person or thing helps you to use or show your best qualities. • She seems to *bring out the best in him*. • Performing in front of an audience *brings out the best in me*. [=I perform better when I am in front of an audience]

feel your best : to feel very healthy • Exercise helps you look and *feel your best*. • I'm not *feeling my best* this morning. [=I'm not feeling very well this morning]

get the best of ✧ If an emotion or feeling *gets the best of you*, it causes you to do something that you should not do or that you are trying not to do. • I did get a little carried away. I guess the excitement *got the best of me*. [=*got the better of me*] • Their emotions have *gotten the best of them*.

know best or ***know what's best*** see [1]KNOW

look your best : to look very good : to look as attractive and pleasant as possible • Try to *look your best* when interviewing for a job.

make the best of **1** : to use (something) in an effective way • We may not get another chance, so we need to *make the best of* this opportunity. **2** : to deal with (a bad situation) as well as possible • Life is not very good right now—but let's try to ***make the best of it***. • We're trying to ***make the best (out) of a bad situation***. = *(Brit)* We're trying to ***make the best of a bad job***.

the best is yet to come/be — used to say that good things have happened but that even better things will happen in the future • Life is good now, but *the best is yet to come*.

to the best of my knowledge see KNOWLEDGE

to the best of your ability : as well as you are able to • Every game, we go out and play *to the best of our ability*.

to the best of your belief see BELIEF

[4]**best** *verb* **bests; best·ed; best·ing** [+ *obj*] : to do better than (someone or something) : to defeat or outdo (someone or something) • They were *bested* [=*beaten*] by their opponents in the opening game.

bes·tial /ˈbɛstʃəl/ *adj* [*more* ~; *most* ~] *formal* : resembling or suggesting an animal or beast : very cruel, violent, etc. • *bestial* behavior • *bestial* violence

bes·ti·al·i·ty /ˌbɛstʃiˈæləti/ *noun* [*noncount*]

1 : sex between a person and an animal

2 *formal* : a cruel and violent quality : a bestial quality • I was shocked by the *bestiality* of their behavior.

best man *noun* [*singular*] : the most important male friend or relative who helps a groom at his wedding • The groom asked his brother to be his *best man* and the bride asked her sister to be her maid of honor.

be·stow /bɪˈstoʊ/ *verb* **-stows; -stowed; -stow·ing** [+ *obj*] *formal* : to give (something) as a gift or honor • The university *bestowed* on/upon her an honorary degree.

be·strew /bɪˈstruː/ *verb* **-strews; -strewed; -strewn** *or* **-strewed; -strew·ing** [+ *obj*] : to cover (a surface) with something — usually used as *(be) bestrewn* • The path *was bestrewn* with flowers. [=flowers were strewed over the path]

be·stride /bɪˈstraɪd/ *verb* **-strides; -strode** /-ˈstroʊd/; **-strid·den** /-ˈstrɪdn̩/; **-strid·ing** [+ *obj*] *literary* : to sit or stand with one leg on either side of (something) : STRADDLE • a giant that *bestrode* the river — often used figuratively • the time when the Roman Empire *bestrode* the world [=had great power over the world]

best seller *noun, pl* ~ **-ers** [*count*] : a popular product (such as a book) that many people have bought • She has written several *best sellers*. • Her book is on the *best-seller* list.
— **best–sell·ing** /ˈbɛstˈsɛlɪŋ/ *adj* • his *best-selling* novel

[1]**bet** /ˈbɛt/ *noun, pl* **bets**

1 [*count*] : an agreement in which people try to guess what will happen and the person who guesses wrong has to give something (such as money) to the person who guesses right • He has a *bet* on the game. • "I'll bet five dollars that my team will beat your team." "Okay. It's a *bet*!" [=I agree to the bet] • He made a *bet* with his brother that he could finish his chores first. • He and his brother have a *bet* about who can finish his chores first. • He lost the *bet* and had to pay his brother five dollars. • His brother won the *bet*. • He paid his brother five dollars to ***settle the bet***.

2 [*count*] : the money or other valuable thing that you could win or lose in a bet • What's your *bet*? [=how much money do you want to risk?] • She placed/laid a $10 *bet* [=*wager*] on the number five horse.

3 [*singular*] : a choice made by thinking about what will probably happen • It's ***a good/safe/sure bet*** that they'll win. [=it is very likely that they will win] • I don't know what their decision will be, but ***my bet is*** that they'll approve the project. [=I think they'll approve the project] • If you want to get there early, your ***best/surest/safest bet*** is to take a different road. [=you are most likely to get there early if you take a different road]

all bets are off — used to describe a situation in which it is impossible to be sure about what will happen • *All bets are off* on the election: it's too close to call.

hedge your bets see [2]HEDGE

[2]**bet** *verb* **bets; bet** *also* **bet·ted; bet·ting**

1 : to make a bet : to risk losing something (such as money) if your guess about what will happen is wrong [+ *obj*] He *bet* $5 on the game. • I'll *bet* (you) a dollar that he makes the next shot. • I'll *bet* that he makes the next shot. • He always *bets* that the favorite will win. [*no obj*] He lost a lot of money by ***betting on*** college football and basketball. • He always *bets on* the favorite (to win). • I ***bet against*** the favorite and I lost. • I wouldn't *bet against* her. She's very likely to win this race.

2 [+ *obj*] : to risk losing (something) when you try to do or achieve something — usually + *on* • She's willing to *bet* [=*gamble, risk, stake*] everything *on* winning this election. • *(US, informal)* They want to start their own restaurant, but they're not willing to ***bet the farm on it***. [=they're not willing to risk losing everything they have]

3 [+ *obj*] : to make decisions that are based on the belief that something will happen or is true • Carmakers are *betting* that people will want to buy larger, more expensive cars this year. • We're *betting* (that) the price of houses will drop.

4 [+ *obj*] *informal* : to think that something will probably or certainly happen • I *bet* (that) it'll rain tomorrow. [=I think it'll rain tomorrow] • You can *bet* (that) he'll take the money. [=you can be sure that he'll take the money] • She says she'll quit her job, but I *bet* (you) she doesn't do it. [=I don't believe that she'll do it] : to think that something is probably or certainly true • I'd *bet* most people feel the same way. • I *bet* you that no one knows we're here. • I'll *bet* you've never seen one of these before. [=you've probably never seen one of these before] • I *bet* you were tired by the end of the trip. [=you must have been tired] • "He was so handsome in his new suit." "***I bet*** he was." = "***I'll bet*** he was." [=I'm sure he was] ✧ If you would ***bet your life*** or ***bet your bottom dollar*** that something will happen or that something is true, you are very sure about it. • "Are you sure he'll be there?" "Yes, I'd *bet my life* on it." [=I am entirely sure] • You can *bet your bottom dollar* he's going to be late! [=you can be sure he's going to be late]

5 *informal* — used in phrases like ***you bet, you can bet on it***, and ***you bet your life*** as an enthusiastic way of saying "yes" • "Would you like some cake?" "*You bet!*" • "Are you going to be there?" "*You bet* I'll be there!" [=I'll certainly be there] • "Are you going to be there?" "*You can bet on it!*" • "Will you be there?" "*You bet your life* I will!" — see also BETCHA

6 *informal* — used in phrases that express doubt about what will happen • "The economy will improve next year." "***I wouldn't bet on it*** if I were you." [=I'm doubtful that the economy will improve next year] • "The weather will be better tomorrow." "***Don't bet on it!***" • "The weather will be better tomorrow." "***Do you want to bet***?" = "***Wanna bet***?" [=I don't think that the weather will be better tomorrow]

— **betting** *adj* • I'm not a *betting* man myself. [=I'm not a man who likes to bet] — **betting** *noun* [*noncount*] • No *bet-*

B

ting [=*gambling*] is allowed in this state. • (*chiefly Brit*) The *betting* is that she'll win the election. [=most people think that she'll win the election]

be·ta /ˈbeɪtə, *Brit* ˈbiːtə/ *noun*
1 [*singular*] : the second letter of the Greek alphabet — B or β
2 [*noncount*] : a version of a product (such as a computer program) that is almost finished and that is used for testing • a program that is currently in *beta* — often used before another noun • the *beta* version of the software • a *beta* test • *beta* testing

be·ta–block·er /ˈbeɪtəˌblɑːkɚ, *Brit* ˈbiːtəˌblɒkə/ *noun, pl* **-ers** [*count*] *medical* : a drug that helps prevent heart attacks by lowering high blood pressure

be·ta–car·o·tene /ˈbeɪtəˈkerəˌtiːn/ *noun* [*noncount*] *technical* : a natural substance that is found in dark green and dark yellow fruits and vegetables and that helps your body grow and be healthy

bet·cha /ˈbɛʧə/ *informal* — used in writing to represent the sound of the phrase *bet you* when it is spoken quickly • *Betcha* I get home before you do! [=(I'll) bet you that I get home before you do] — used especially in the phrase ***you betcha*** as an enthusiastic way of saying "yes" • "Are you going to be there?" "*You betcha*!" [=*you bet*]

be·tel /ˈbiːtl/ *noun* [*noncount*] : the dried leaves of a climbing plant that are chewed by some people in southeastern Asia

betel nut *noun, pl* ~ **nuts** [*count*] : the seed of an Asian tree that is chewed with betel by some people in southeastern Asia

bête noire /ˌbɛtˈnwɑɚ/ *noun, pl* **bêtes noires** /ˌbɛtˈnwɑɚz/ [*count*] : a person or thing that someone dislikes very much • a politician who is the *bête noire* of liberal/conservative groups ✧ *Bête noire* is a French phrase that means "black beast."

be·tide /bɪˈtaɪd/ see *woe betide* at WOE

be·to·ken /bɪˈtoʊkən/ *verb* **-kens; -kened; -ken·ing** [+ *obj*] *formal* : to show (something) : to be a sign of (something) • His strong handshake *betokens* [=*indicates, bespeaks*] his self-confidence.

be·tray /bɪˈtreɪ/ *verb* **-trays; -trayed; -tray·ing** [+ *obj*]
1 : to give information about (a person, group, country, etc.) to an enemy • They *betrayed* their country by selling its secrets to other governments. • He was *betrayed* (to the authorities) by one of his students.
2 : to hurt (someone who trusts you, such as a friend or relative) by not giving help or by doing something morally wrong • She is very loyal and would never *betray* a friend. • He *betrayed* his wife with another woman. [=he was unfaithful to his wife] • She *betrayed* her own people by supporting the enemy. • I felt *betrayed*. [=I was hurt because someone betrayed me] • You've ***betrayed our trust*** [=we trusted you, but you did something very bad and hurt us] • I can't believe you lied to me. I feel as if you've ***betrayed our friendship*** [=you've betrayed me; you've treated me in a way that shows you are not really my friend]
3 a : to show (something, such as a feeling or desire) without wanting or trying to • Although he would not smile, his eyes *betrayed* his happiness. [=his eyes showed that he was happy] • She coughed, *betraying* her presence behind the door. • The expression on his face ***betrayed nothing*** [=the expression on his face did not show anything about what he was feeling or thinking] **b** : to reveal (something that should not be revealed) • *betray* a secret
4 : to do something that does not agree with (your beliefs, principles, etc.) • He felt that he would be *betraying* his principles if he accepted the money.
– be·tray·al /bɪˈtrejəl/ *noun, pl* **-als** [*count*] She divorced her husband after his *betrayal* (of her). [=after he had betrayed her] • He felt that accepting the money would be a *betrayal* of his principles. [*noncount*] acts of *betrayal* • feelings of anger, helplessness, and *betrayal* **– be·tray·er** /bɪˈtrejɚ/ *noun, pl* **-ers** [*count*] • a *betrayer* of his people

be·troth·al /bɪˈtroʊðəl/ *noun, pl* **-als** [*count*] *formal* + *old-fashioned*
1 : the act of promising to marry someone : ENGAGEMENT • They kept their *betrothal* a secret. [=they told no one that they were engaged to be married]
2 : an agreement that two people will be married in the future • They were both young at the time of their *betrothal*.

¹be·trothed /bɪˈtroʊðd/ *adj, formal* + *old-fashioned* : engaged to be married • a *betrothed* couple • She had been *betrothed* to the prince since she was a young girl.

²betrothed *noun* [*singular*] *formal* + *old-fashioned* : the person that someone has promised to marry • He spent the afternoon with his *betrothed*. [=*fiancée*]

¹bet·ter /ˈbɛtɚ/ *adj, comparative form of* ¹GOOD *or of* ²WELL
1 : higher in quality • Her second book is *better* than her first one. • This is one of the *better* [=*best*] restaurants in this part of town. • Her first book was good, but her second one is ***even better*** = Her second one is ***better still/yet*** • This one is ***no better*** than that one.
2 : more skillful • She's a *better* golfer than I am. • He's a *better* singer than he is an actor. • He's much *better* with children now that he's a father himself.
3 : more attractive, appealing, effective, useful, etc. • The weather is *better* today than it was yesterday. • They came up with a *better* solution to the problem. • I'd like to get a *better* [=more accurate and complete] understanding of the problem. • Don't you have something/anything *better* to do than to watch TV all day? • Her work wasn't that good at first, but it's getting *better*. • Her work just keeps getting ***better and better*** • There's ***nothing better*** than a cold drink of water when you're really thirsty. • My salary isn't very high, but it's ***better than nothing*** • "Suppose I move it a little to the left." "Yes, ***that's better*** It looks much *better* like that." • You could write to her, or, ***even/still better*** visit her in person. ✧ Someone or something that ***has seen/known better days*** was better in the past than now. • My old car *has seen better days*. ✧ People say ***the sooner the better***, ***the bigger the better***, ***the faster the better***, etc., when they want something to happen as soon as possible, to be as big as possible, to go as fast as possible, etc. • "They say the cold weather will end soon." "Well, *the sooner the better* as far as I'm concerned."
4 : more morally right or good : more deserving of praise • You're a *better* man than I am. • "It is a far, far *better* thing that I do, than I have ever done . . ." —Charles Dickens, *A Tale of Two Cities* (1859) • If you ask me, he's ***hardly/little/no better than*** a common criminal.
5 a : improved in health • I was sick but now I'm *better*. [=now I'm well] • I'm feeling all/completely *better*. • I'm somewhat/slightly *better* than (I was) yesterday, but I'm not fully recovered. • My cold is a little *better* today. [=my cold is not as bad today; my cold is less severe today] • I'm sorry to hear that you're sick. I hope you ***feel/get better*** soon. • He was feeling sick yesterday, and he's ***no better*** today. [=he's still feeling sick today] **b** : happier or more pleased • Your support makes me feel *better* about doing what I've done.
6 — used to suggest that something should or should not be done • It would be *better* for you to leave now [=you should leave now] if you want to get there on time. • It would be *better* not to wait too long.
better luck next time see ¹LUCK
the better part of see ¹PART

²better *adv, comparative form of* ¹WELL
1 : in a better way • "How is she doing in school?" "She did badly at first, but now she's doing much *better*." • She sings *better* than I do. • He sings *better* than he acts. • You could write to her, or, ***even/still better*** visit her in person. = You could write to her. *Even/Still better*, you could visit her in person. • "Instead of writing to her, I'm going to visit her in person." "***Even better***."
2 — used to suggest that something should or should not be done • Some things are *better* left unsaid. [=it is better not to say some things] • You would do *better* to leave now [=you should leave now] if you want to get there on time.
3 : to a higher or greater degree • He knows the story much *better* than you do. • Her paintings have become *better* known in recent years. • There's nothing I'd like *better* than to see you again.
4 : greater in distance or amount : MORE • It is *better* than nine miles to the next town. • It's *better* than an hour's drive to the lake.
had better ✧ If you *had better* do something, you should do it. • You'*d better* leave now or you might not get there on time. • *Had*n't you *better* leave now if you want to get there on time? • You'*d better* not do that or you'll get in trouble. [=you'll get in trouble if you do that] • I told him he'*d better* leave at once. • "Do you want to drive?" "I'*d better* not: I've had too much to drink." • "I'm sorry." "You'*d better* be!" • "Should I go there?" "You'*d better* not." In informal speech, *better* by itself is often used in this way without *had*. • "Do you want to drive?" "I *better* not." • I told him he *better* leave at once. • "Should I go?" "You *better*!" • "I'm sorry." "You *better* be!" • "Should I go?" "(You) *Better* not."

³better *noun* [*noncount*] : something that is better : better behavior • They've disappointed me. I expected *better* from them. [=I expected them to behave better] • They shouldn't treat him that way. He deserves *better*.

all the better* or *so much the better — used to say that something makes a situation, experience, etc., even better than it was • My daughter loves taking care of children. If she can earn money by doing it, *so much the better*!

for better or (for) worse : whether good or bad things happen : no matter what happens • We've made our decision and now we have to stick to it *for better or worse*.

for the better : so as to produce improvement • The new policy is a change *for the better*. [=the new policy is an improvement] • My father's health has recently ***taken a turn for the better***. [=has recently improved]

get the better of : to defeat or trick (someone) by being clever • It would be hard to *get the better of* someone as experienced as she is. ✧ If a feeling or emotion *gets the better of* you, it causes you to do something that you should not do or that you are trying not to do. • She knew she shouldn't open the package, but her curiosity finally *got the better of* her and she opened it. • He let his temper *get the better of* him. [=he lost his temper; he said or did something because of anger]

go one better see [1]GO

know better see [1]KNOW

think better of see [1]THINK

your betters *somewhat old-fashioned* : people who are more important than you or who have a higher social position than you • His parents always told him to respect *his betters*. • (*chiefly Brit*) You should respect ***your elders and betters***. [=people who are older and more important than you]

[4]**better** *verb* **-ters; -tered; -ter·ing** [+ *obj*]

1 : to make (something) better : IMPROVE • They are trying to *better* the lives/lot of working people. • He looked forward to *bettering* his acquaintance with the new neighbors. • The team has *bettered* its chances of winning the championship.

2 : to be or do better than (something or someone) : to improve on (something or someone) • I can *better* their offer. [=I can make you a better offer] • She *bettered* her previous performance. • He set a record that has never been equaled or *bettered*.

better yourself : to do things (such as improving your education) that will make you a better or more successful person • She was born poor but she has worked hard to *better herself*.

[5]**better** *variant spelling of* BETTOR

better half *noun, pl* ~ **halfs** [*count*] *old-fashioned + humorous* : someone's wife or husband • Please come to our party—and your *better half* is invited, too!

bet·ter·ment /ˈbɛtɚmənt/ *noun* [*noncount*] : the act or result of making something better : IMPROVEMENT • working for the *betterment* of the lives of working people

better off *adj, comparative form of* WELL-OFF

1 : having more money and possessions : more well-to-do • The *better off* he became, the less he thought about other people. • The *better-off* people live in the older part of town.

2 : in a better position • He'd be *better off* with a new job.

bet·tor *also* **bet·ter** /ˈbɛtɚ/ *noun, pl* **-tors** *also* **-ters** [*count*] : a person who makes a bet • Thousands of *bettors* were at the race track last weekend.

[1]**be·tween** /bɪˈtwiːn/ *prep*

1 : in the space that separates (two things or people) • The ball rolled *between* the desk and the wall. • He stood *between* his mother and his father. • The office has two desks with a table *between* them. • They put up a fence *between* their house and their neighbor's house. • There are fences *between* all the houses. — often used figuratively • a book that blurs the line/boundary *between* fact and fiction — often used in the phrase ***in between*** • There are fences *in between* all the houses.

2 : in the time that separates (two actions, events, etc.) • If you want to lose weight, you shouldn't eat *between* meals. • *Between* bites of food, they talked to their teacher. • The two days *between* Monday and Thursday are Tuesday and Wednesday. • We should arrive *between* 9 and 10 o'clock. — often used in the phrase ***in between*** • You shouldn't eat *in between* meals.

3 — used to indicate the beginning and ending points of a group of numbers, a range of measurement, etc. • a number *between* 1 and 20 • The package weighs somewhere *between* a pound and a pound and a half. — sometimes used in the phrase ***in between*** • a number *in between* 1 and 20

4 : in shares to each of (two or more people) • The property was divided equally *between* the son and the daughter. [=the son and the daughter received an equal share of the property] • His estate was divided *between* [=*among*] his four grandchildren.

5 — used to indicate two or more people or things that together produce a result or have an effect • She ate two hot dogs, and he ate three hot dogs, so *between* them they ate five hot dogs. • *Between* work and family life, she has no time for hobbies. [=because of all the time she spends on her work and family life, she has no time for hobbies]

6 — used to indicate two people or teams that are involved in a game, activity, etc. • There's a game tonight *between* the Red Sox and the Yankees. [=the Red Sox are playing a game against the Yankees tonight]

7 — used to indicate two or more people or things that are joined, related, or connected in some way • There are many relations/connections *between* linguistics, philosophy, and psychology. • There is a passageway *between* the two rooms. • the bond *between* friends • We used to love each other, but there's nothing *between* us now. [=we don't love each other now]

8 — used to indicate two or more people or things that are being considered, compared, etc. • They compared the cars but found few differences *between* them. • We were allowed to choose *between* two/several options. • There's not much to choose *between* the two cars. [=the two cars are very similar] • There is very little difference *between* the two cars.

9 — used to indicate movement from one place to another place • He flies *between* Miami and Chicago twice a week. • The airline provides service *between* New York and Paris.

10 : known only by (two people) • They shared a secret *between* them. • (Just) ***Between you and me***, I think he's wrong. [=I'm telling you that I think he's wrong, but you should not tell anyone else what I've told you] • What I'm going to tell you should remain a secret (just) ***between us/ourselves***.

[2]**between** *adv* : in the space separating two things or people • The office has two desks with a table *between*. — often used in the phrase ***in between*** • The office has two desks with a table *in between*.

betwixt and between see BETWIXT

few and far between see [1]FEW

be·twixt /bɪˈtwɪkst/ *prep, old-fashioned + literary* : BETWEEN

betwixt and between : in the middle : not completely one thing and not completely the other thing • Politically, my parents are *betwixt and between*. They're neither liberal nor conservative in their views.

[1]**bev·el** /ˈbɛvəl/ *noun, pl* **-els** [*count*]

1 : a slanted surface or edge on a piece of wood, glass, etc. • the *bevel* of the mirror

2 : a tool that is used to make a slanted surface or edge on a piece of wood, glass, etc.

[2]**bevel** *verb* **-els**; *US* **-eled** *or Brit* **-elled**; *US* **-el·ing** *or Brit* **-el·ling** [+ *obj*] : to cut or shape (a surface or edge) at an angle or slant • a tool that is used for *beveling* wood

– beveled (*US*) *or Brit* **bevelled** *adj* • a mirror with a *beveled* edge • The blade is *beveled* on one side.

bev·er·age /ˈbɛvrɪʤ/ *noun, pl* **-ag·es** [*count*] *somewhat formal* : something you can drink : a liquid for drinking • May I offer you a *beverage*? [=*drink*] • *Beverages* are listed on the back of the menu. • alcoholic/nonalcoholic *beverages*

bev·vy /ˈbɛvi/ *noun, pl* **-vies** [*count*] *Brit, informal* : an alcoholic drink • He'd had a few *bevvies* too many and was feeling none too clever.

bevy /ˈbɛvi/ *noun, pl* **-ies** [*count*] : a large group *of* people or things — usually singular • A *bevy of* girls waited outside.

be·wail /bɪˈweɪl/ *verb* **-wails; -wailed; -wail·ing** [+ *obj*] *literary + humorous* : to express great sadness or disappointment about (something) • Many people *bewailed* the changes to the historic building. • She *bewailed* [=*bemoaned*] the fact that he had such terrible table manners. • *bewail* your fate

be·ware /bɪˈweɚ/ *verb* : to be careful : to act in a way that shows you know that there may be danger or trouble — used only as *beware* or *to beware* [*no obj*] A ghostly voice cried "*Beware*!" • Let the buyer *beware*. • He told them *to beware*. — often + *of* • The sign said "*Beware of* the dog." [+ *obj*] The restaurant's food is excellent, but *beware* the chili if you don't like spicy food.

be·wil·der /bɪˈwɪldɚ/ *verb* **-ders; -dered; -der·ing** [+ *obj*] : to confuse (someone) very much • His decision *bewildered* [=*puzzled, perplexed*] her. — often used as *(be) bewildered* • She *was bewildered* by his decision. • I *was* completely/utterly

B

bewildered by the complex instructions.
– bewildered *adj* [*more* ~; *most* ~] ▪ He had a *bewildered* expression on his face. **– bewildering** *adj* [*more* ~; *most* ~] ▪ a *bewildering* number of choices **– be·wil·der·ing·ly** *adv* ▪ The instructions were *bewilderingly* complex. **– be·wil·der·ment** /bɪˈwɪldəmənt/ *noun* [*noncount*] ▪ She stared at them in *bewilderment* [=*confusion*] and shock.

be·witch /bɪˈwɪʧ/ *verb* **-witch·es**; **-witched**; **-witch·ing** [+ *obj*]
1 : to use magic to make someone do, think, or say something **:** to put (someone) under a spell ▪ People believed the girls had been *bewitched*.
2 : to attract or delight (someone) in a way that seems magical ▪ They were *bewitched* [=*enchanted, fascinated*] by her beauty.
– bewitching *adj* [*more* ~; *most* ~] ▪ She has a *bewitching* [=*captivating, charming*] smile. ▪ The painting was *bewitching*. [=*mesmerizing*]

¹be·yond /biˈɑːnd/ *adv*
1 a : on or to the farther part or side ▪ From the house we can see the valley and the hills *beyond*. ▪ We passed the hotel and drove a bit *beyond* to see the ocean. **b :** to or until a later time ▪ The children who are part of the study will be monitored through their school years and *beyond*.
2 : in addition ▪ The hostel provides the essentials but nothing *beyond*. [=*further, more, else*]

²beyond *prep*
1 : on or to the farther part or side of (something) **:** at a greater distance than (something) ▪ From the house we can see the valley and the mountains *beyond* it. ▪ The parking area is just *beyond* those trees. ▪ Our land extends *beyond* the fence to those trees. ▪ planets *beyond* our solar system
2 : outside the limits or range of (something) **:** more than (something) ▪ The job is *beyond* his ability. [=the job is too hard for him; he is not capable of doing the job well] ▪ Such a project is *beyond* the city's budget. [=the project is too expensive] ▪ The results were *beyond* our expectations. [=were better than we expected] ▪ His influence does not extend *beyond* this department. ▪ She became rich ***beyond her wildest dreams*** [=became very rich] ✧ If you ***live beyond your means***, you spend more money than you earn. ▪ We need to stop *living beyond our means* and start saving some money.
3 — used to say that something cannot be changed, understood, etc. ▪ The situation is ***beyond help*** [=the situation cannot be made better; nothing can help the situation] ▪ The city has changed ***beyond (all) recognition*** [=it has changed so much that it looks completely different] ▪ The circumstances are ***beyond our control*** [=we cannot control the circumstances] ▪ The stories she tells are ***beyond belief*** [=are not believable] ▪ His irresponsible actions are ***beyond comprehension/understanding*** [=cannot be understood] ✧ If something is ***beyond you***, you do not understand it. ▪ "Why is he going?" "It's *beyond me*." ▪ How she was able to afford the trip is *beyond me*.
4 : for a period of time that continues after (a particular date, age, etc.) ▪ The program is unlikely to continue *beyond* next year. [=it will probably end after next year] ▪ She plans to continue working *beyond* the usual retirement age.
5 : in addition to ▪ There were no other problems with the house *beyond* [=*besides*] the leaky roof. ▪ I knew nothing about him *beyond* [=*except*] what he told me.
above and beyond see ²ABOVE

BFA *abbr* bachelor of fine arts

bi- /baɪ/ *prefix*
1 : two ▪ *bi*partisan ▪ *bi*lateral ▪ *bi*lingual
2 a : coming or happening every two ▪ *bi*monthly **b :** coming or happening two times ▪ *bi*annual

bi·an·nu·al /baɪˈænjəwəl/ *adj, always used before a noun*
1 : happening twice a year **:** SEMIANNUAL ▪ The group holds *biannual* meetings in December and July.
2 : happening every two years **:** BIENNIAL ▪ The art show is a *biannual* event that won't happen again for two more years.
– bi·an·nu·al·ly *adv*

¹bi·as /ˈbajəs/ *noun, pl* **-as·es**
1 : a tendency to believe that some people, ideas, etc., are better than others that usually results in treating some people unfairly [*count*] The writer has a strong liberal/conservative *bias*. [=favors liberal/conservative views] ▪ ethnic and racial *biases* ▪ He showed a *bias* toward a few workers in particular. ▪ Do they have a *bias* against women/minorities? [*noncount*] The company was accused of racial/gender *bias*. ▪ The decision was made without *bias*. ▪ She showed no *bias* toward older clients.
2 : a strong interest in something or ability to do something ▪ a student with a strong *bias* towards the arts
on the bias **:** in a slanted directed — used to describe the way cloth is cut or sewn ▪ The material for the dress was cut *on the bias*.

²bias *verb* **-ases**; **-ased**; **-as·ing** [+ *obj*] **:** to have a strong and often unfair influence on (someone or something) ▪ I don't want to *bias* you against the movie, but I thought the book was much better. ▪ The circumstances could *bias* the results of the survey.

biased *adj* [*more* ~; *most* ~] **:** having or showing a bias **:** having or showing an unfair tendency to believe that some people, ideas, etc., are better than others ▪ She is too *biased* to write about the case objectively. ▪ an extremely *biased* statement ▪ He is *biased* against women/minorities. ▪ The judges of the talent show were *biased* toward musical acts.

bi·ath·lon /baɪˈæθlən/ *noun, pl* **-lons** [*count*] *sports* **:** an event in which athletes ski over the countryside and stop to shoot rifles at targets ▪ the Olympic *biathlon*
– bi·ath·lete /baɪˈæθˌliːt/ *noun, pl* **-letes** [*count*]

bib /ˈbɪb/ *noun, pl* **bibs** [*count*]
1 : a piece of cloth or plastic that is worn under a baby's chin while the baby is eating
2 : the part of a piece of clothing (such as an apron) that covers the area above a person's waist

bi·ble /ˈbaɪbəl/ *noun, pl* **bi·bles**
1 ***the Bible*** **a :** the book of sacred writings used in the Christian religion ✧ The Christian Bible contains the Old Testament and the New Testament. **b :** the book of sacred writings used in the Jewish religion ✧ The Jewish Bible contains the writings that also form the Christian Old Testament.
2 ***Bible*** [*count*] **:** a copy or edition of the Bible ▪ She gave each of her grandchildren a *Bible*.
3 [*count*] **:** a book, magazine, etc., that contains the most important information about a particular thing ▪ The book is famous among foodies—it's the gourmet's *bible*. ▪ The magazine is now considered the *bible* of the plastics industry.

Bible Belt *noun*
the Bible Belt **:** an area chiefly in the southern part of the U.S. where there are many people who have very strong and strict Christian beliefs

bib·li·cal /ˈbɪblɪkəl/ *adj* **:** relating to, taken from, or found in the Bible ▪ a *biblical* [=*scriptural*] passage ▪ *biblical* references ▪ The city was a center for trade in *biblical* times. [=during the time when some things written about in the Bible happened]

biblio- *prefix* **:** relating to books ▪ *biblio*graphy ▪ *biblio*phile

bib·li·og·ra·phy /ˌbɪbliˈɑːgrəfi/ *noun, pl* **-phies** [*count*]
1 : a list of books, magazines, articles, etc., about a particular subject ▪ The instructor provided the students with an excellent *bibliography* on local history.
2 : a list of the books, magazines, articles, etc., that are mentioned in a text ▪ The book includes a lengthy *bibliography*.
– bib·lio·graph·ic /ˌbɪblijəˈgræfɪk/ *also* **bib·lio·graph·i·cal** /ˌbɪblijəˈgræfɪkəl/ *adj* ▪ *bibliographic* information

bib·lio·phile /ˈbɪblijəˌfajəl/ *noun, pl* **-philes** [*count*] **:** a person who loves or collects books

bi·cam·er·al /baɪˈkæmrəl/ *adj, technical* **:** having two parts — used to describe a government in which the people who make laws are divided into two groups ▪ The U.S. has a *bicameral* legislature that is made up of the Senate and the House of Representatives.

bi·carb /baɪˈkɑəb/ *noun* [*noncount*] **:** BAKING SODA

bi·car·bon·ate of soda /baɪˈkɑəbəˌneɪt-/ *noun* [*noncount*] **:** BAKING SODA

bi·cen·te·na·ry /ˌbaɪsenˈtenəri, *Brit* ˌbaɪsenˈtiːnəri/ *noun, pl* **-ries** [*count*] *Brit* **:** BICENTENNIAL
– bicentenary *adj, always used before a noun* ▪ a *bicentenary* celebration/year

bi·cen·ten·ni·al /ˌbaɪsɛnˈtɛnijəl/ *noun, pl* **-als** [*count*] *US* **:** a 200th anniversary or its celebration ▪ The United States celebrated its *bicentennial* [=(*Brit*) *bicentenary*] in 1976. [=celebrated the fact that it was 200 years old] ▪ Next year is the *bicentennial* of the school's founding [=the year 200 years after the school was started] — compare CENTENNIAL
– bicentennial *adj, always used before a noun* ▪ a *bicentennial* [=(*Brit*) *bicentenary*] celebration/year

bi·cep /ˈbaɪˌsɛp/ *noun, pl* **-ceps** [*count*] **:** BICEPS ▪ She flexed her left *bicep*.

bi·ceps /ˈbaɪˌsɛps/ *noun, pl* **-ceps** [*count*] **:** a large muscle at the front of the upper arm — usually plural • His *biceps* were huge. — see picture at HUMAN; compare TRICEPS

bick·er /ˈbɪkɚ/ *verb* **-ers; -ered; -er·ing** [*no obj*] **:** to argue in a way that is annoying about things that are not important • She is always *bickering* with her mother. • They *bickered* about/over how to decorate the room.

— **bickering** *noun* [*noncount*] • I can't stand their constant *bickering*.

bi·coast·al /baɪˈkoustəl/ *adj* **:** relating to both the east and the west coasts of the U.S. • They're a *bicoastal* couple. [=one person lives on the east coast and the other person lives on the west coast] • a *bicoastal* flight/conference call

¹bi·cy·cle /ˈbaɪsɪkəl/ *noun, pl* **-cy·cles** [*count*] **:** a 2-wheeled vehicle that a person rides by pushing on foot pedals • She rode her *bicycle* [=*bike*] to school. • They toured Europe on *bicycles*. = They toured Europe by *bicycle*. • Let's go for a *bicycle* ride [=ride our bicycles for pleasure] after work tonight. — compare TRICYCLE, UNICYCLE

²bicycle *verb* **-cy·cles; -cy·cled; -cy·cling** [*no obj*] **:** to ride a bicycle • She *bicycles* [=*bikes*] to work every day.

— **bi·cy·cler** /ˈbaɪsɪklɚ/ *noun, pl* **-clers** [*count*] *US* • a group of *bicyclers* — **bicycling** *noun* [*noncount*] • *Bicycling* is his favorite sport. • Let's ***go bicycling*** after work tonight. — **bi·cy·clist** /ˈbaɪsɪklɪst/ *noun, pl* **-clists** [*count*] • A group of *bicyclists* rode by.

bicycle shorts *noun* [*plural*] **:** short pants that fit close to the body and that people sometimes wear when they ride a bicycle

¹bid /ˈbɪd/ *verb* **bids; bade** /ˈbæd, ˈbeɪd/ *or* **bid; bid·den** /ˈbɪdn̩/ *or* **bid; bid·ding**

1 *past tense and past participle* **bid** **a :** to offer to pay (a particular amount of money) for something that is being sold **:** to make a bid at an auction [+ *obj*] I'll *bid* $100 for/on the lamp but no higher. • The auctioneer said, "What am I *bid* [=*offered*] *for* this lamp?" [*no obj*] He plans to stop *bidding* if the bids go over $500. • She *bid* for/on a desk and a chair. • The two brothers *bid against* each other for the same chair. [=they each tried to buy the chair by repeatedly making higher bids than the other one had made] **b** [*no obj*] *US* **:** to offer to do work for a particular price • Several local companies are *bidding* for the same job. • His company *bid* on the snow removal contract.

2 *past tense and past participle* **bid :** to say how many points you are trying to win in a card game [+ *obj*] He *bid* two. [*no obj*] He *bid* and I passed.

3 [+ *obj*] *formal* **:** to order or command (someone) to do something • We did as we were *bid/bidden*. • She *bid/bade* them enter. [=told them to come in] — see also UNBIDDEN

4 [+ *obj*] *formal* **:** to express (greetings or good wishes) to (someone) **:** to say (something, such as "good morning," "good evening, etc.") to (someone) • They *bade* me farewell. = They *bade* farewell to me. [=they said goodbye to me] • She *bid* him good day.

bid fair **:** to seem likely • a movie that *bids fair* to become a big hit [=a movie that will probably be very successful]

bid up [*phrasal verb*] ***bid up (something) or bid (something) up*** **:** to raise the price of (something that is being sold) by repeatedly offering more money than other people • Several antique dealers *bid up* the best lots to shut out less experienced bidders. • Investors quickly *bid* stock prices *up* to record levels.

— **bid·der** *noun, pl* **-ders** [*count*] • Items will be sold to the highest *bidder*. [=to the person who offers to pay the most]

²bid *noun, pl* **bids** [*count*]

1 a : an offer to pay a particular amount of money for something • *Bids* for the painter's work have been quite high at recent auctions. • She had the highest *bid*. • He ***made a bid*** of $100 for the painting. • He *made* the opening *bid*. **b :** an offer to do a job for a particular price • The company is accepting *bids* for the renovation project.

2 : an attempt to win, get, or do something • The company is facing a ***takeover bid***. [=someone is trying to gain control of the company by buying most of its stock] — often + *for* • Two convicts made a dramatic *bid for* freedom but were soon recaptured. • They made a strong *bid for* the championship. • a *bid for* power/reelection — often followed by *to* + *verb* • They failed in their *bid to close* the school.

3 : a statement of how many points a player is trying to win in a card game

bid·da·ble /ˈbɪdəbəl/ *adj*

1 [*more ~; most ~*] *chiefly Brit* **:** willing to do whatever someone tells you to do **:** easily taught, led, or controlled • The children became less *biddable* as they grew older.

2 : available to be bid on • *biddable* items [=items that will be sold through bidding; items that will be sold to whoever will offer the most money] • a *biddable* job [=a job that people or companies can offer to do for a particular price]

bidding *noun* [*noncount*]

1 : the act of offering to pay a particular amount of money for something **:** the act of making bids at an auction • We expect to see heavy *bidding* on this item. [=we expect a lot of people to offer money for this item] • *Bidding* started at $1,000.

2 : the act of offering to do a job for a particular price • *Bidding* for the renovation project begins soon.

at someone's bidding also at the bidding of someone **:** as someone has told you or ordered you to do • He attended law school *at his father's bidding*. [=because his father told/wanted him to attend law school]

do someone's bidding also do the bidding of someone **:** to do what someone tells you or orders you to do • He was at the beck and call of powerful interest groups and was always willing to *do their bidding*.

bid·dy /ˈbɪdi/ *noun, pl* **-dies** [*count*] *informal + disapproving* **:** an old woman; *especially* **:** one who is silly or annoying • a couple of old *biddies*

bide /ˈbaɪd/ *verb* **bides; bid·ed; bid·ing**

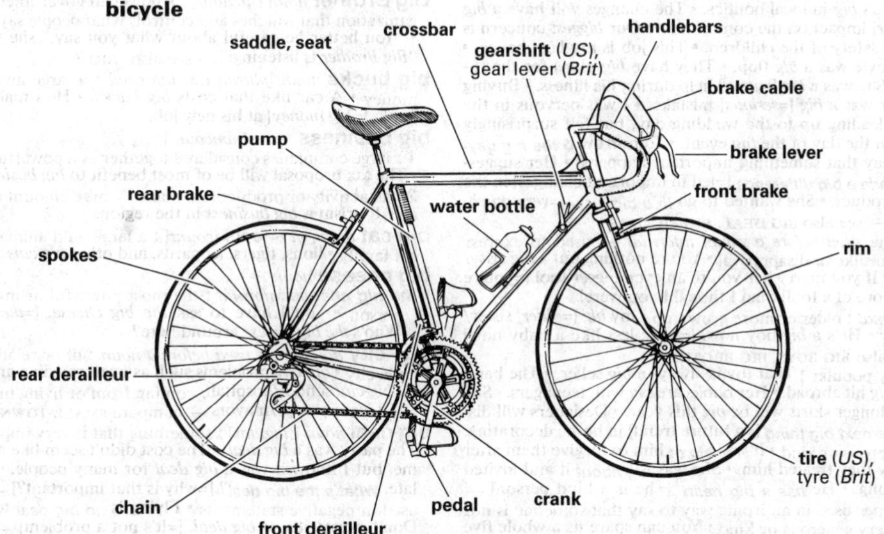

B

bide your time : to wait for the right time before you do something • He is *biding his time* [=waiting for the right opportunity] before asking his parents for a loan.

bi·det /bɪˈdeɪ/ *noun, pl* **-dets** [*count*] : a bowl like a small toilet with faucets that is used for washing your bottom

[1]**bi·en·ni·al** /baɪˈɛnijəl/ *adj, always used before a noun*
1 : happening every two years • The governor explained the *biennial* budget proposal. • a *biennial* show
2 *of a plant* : living for only two years or seasons : having a life cycle that is two years or seasons long • *biennial* plants/herbs/flowers — compare [1]ANNUAL, [1]PERENNIAL
– bi·en·ni·al·ly *adv* • The art show takes place *biennially.*

[2]**biennial** *noun, pl* **-als** [*count*] : a plant that lives for only two years or seasons : a biennial plant — compare [2]ANNUAL, [2]PERENNIAL

bier /ˈbiɚ/ *noun, pl* **biers** [*count*] : a table or platform on which a coffin or dead body is placed at a funeral

biff /ˈbɪf/ *verb* **biffs; biffed; biff·ing** [+ *obj*] *chiefly Brit, informal* : to hit (someone) hard especially with your hand or fist • She *biffed* [=*whacked*] him on the head.
– biff *noun, pl* **biffs** [*count*]

bi·fo·cal /ˈbaɪˌfoʊkəl, *Brit* baɪˈfəʊkəl/ *adj, of eyeglasses* : divided into two parts that help a person to see things that are nearby and things that are far away • *bifocal* lenses/glasses
– bi·fo·cals /ˈbaɪˌfoʊkəlz, *Brit* baɪˈfəʊkəlz/ *noun* [*plural*] • She wears *bifocals.* [=eyeglasses with bifocal lenses]

bi·fur·cate /ˈbaɪfɚˌkeɪt/ *verb* **-cates; -cat·ed; cat·ing** *formal* : to divide into two parts [*no obj*] The stream *bifurcated* into two narrow winding channels. [+ *obj*] *bifurcate* a beam of light
– bifurcated *adj* • a *bifurcated* stream **– bi·fur·ca·tion** /ˌbaɪfɚˈkeɪʃən/ *noun, pl* **-tions** [*count, noncount*]

[1]**big** /ˈbɪg/ *adj* **big·ger; -gest**
1 : large in size • a *big* house/room/field • a *big* glass of soda • He is a *big* [=*tall and heavy*] man. • She moved to a *bigger* city. • the *biggest* city in the state • The tent is *big* enough for 10 people. [=there is enough space in the tent for 10 people] • A ***great big*** [=*very large, huge*] truck pulled up beside us. • I can't understand her writing; she uses too many ***big words***. [=long words that many people don't know the meaning of] — see also *the big city* at CITY
2 : large in number or amount • He led a *big* group through the museum. • She was earning ***big money*** [=a lot of money] as a lawyer. — see also BIG BUCKS
3 : involving or including many people, things, etc. • She works for a *big* company. • He organized a *big* advertising campaign. • We had a *big* fund-raiser for the school.
4 *always used before a noun* **a** : tending to do something more often than most people • He's a *big* eater. [=he often eats large amounts of food] • She's a *big* shopper. [=she shops often] **b** : feeling or showing a lot of excitement or enthusiasm • I'm a *big* fan of their music. • He gave me a *big* smile/hug.
5 : important or significant • She became a *big* star in movies. • He's *big* in local politics. • The changes will have a *big* [=*major*] impact on the community. • Our *biggest* concern is for the safety of the children. • This job is my *big* chance. • The movie was a *big* flop. • They have *big* plans for the future. • She was a *big* [=*great*] help during his illness. • Buying this car was a *big* [=*serious*] mistake. • I was nervous in the weeks leading up to the wedding day, but felt surprisingly calm on the day of the *big* event. • Tomorrow is ***the big day***. [=the day that something important happens] • Her suggestion ***made a big difference*** [=led to important changes] in the final product. • She wanted to go ***in a big way***. [=*very much, badly*] — see also BIG DEAL, BIG PICTURE
6 *always used before a noun, informal* — used to express strong dislike or disapproval • You're nothing but a *big* sissy/bully! • If you marry her you're an even *bigger* fool [=you're even more of a fool] than I thought you were!
7 *informal* : older or more grown up • my *big* [=*older*] sister/brother • He's a *big* boy now. [=he is less like a baby now] — see also BIG BOYS, BIG BROTHER
8 : very popular • That toy is always a *big* seller. • The band was a *big* hit abroad. • Her books are *big* with teenagers. • She thinks longer skirts will be *big* this year. • Designers will discuss ***the next big thing*** [=a future trend] in home decorating.
9 : generous or kind • It was ***big of*** him to forgive them after the way they treated him. • She was ***big about*** it and invited him along. • He ***has a big heart***. [=he is a kind person] — sometimes used in an ironic way to say that someone is not being very generous or kind • You can spare us a whole five minutes of your time? Well, that's *big of you*! — see also BIG-HEARTED
10 : very strong, forceful, etc. • There was a *big* [=*powerful*] storm last night.
(as) big as life see [1]LIFE
big fish in a small/little pond see [1]FISH
big on informal : very enthusiastic about (something) • He's *big on* stamp collecting. [=he likes collecting stamps very much] • She's not (very) *big on* dancing.
big with child *old-fashioned* : pregnant and almost ready to give birth • a woman who was *big with child*
too big for your britches (*US*) *or chiefly Brit* ***too big for your boots*** *informal* : too confident or proud of yourself • I think the boss is growing *too big for his britches.*
– big·ness *noun* [*noncount*] • the *bigness* of the city

[2]**big** *adv*
1 : in a big way • They won/lost *big* [=they won/lost a large amount] at the casino.
2 : in a way that is meant to impress people • He ***talks big*** about his plans, but he hasn't done much yet.
go over big informal : to be successful or well-liked • Here's a recipe for healthy cookies that always *goes over big* with kids. [=that children like a lot]
make it big *or* ***hit it big*** *or* ***hit big informal*** : to become very successful • He always dreamed of *making it big* in the movie industry. • Her best friend *hit it big* playing the stock market.
think big : to think about doing things that involve a lot of people, money, effort, etc. : to think about doing big things • If we're going to start our own business, we should *think big.*

big·a·my /ˈbɪgəmi/ *noun* [*noncount*] : the crime of marrying one person while you are still legally married to another • He was accused of *bigamy.*
– big·a·mist /ˈbɪgəmɪst/ *noun, pl* **-mists** [*count*] • She found out that he was a *bigamist.* **– big·a·mous** /ˈbɪgəməs/ *adj* • a *bigamous* marriage

Big Apple *noun*
the Big Apple informal — used as a name for New York City • She moved to *the Big Apple* after she graduated.

big band *noun, pl* **~ bands** [*count*] : a large musical group that usually plays jazz music that people dance to

big bang *noun*
the big bang : a huge explosion that might have happened when the universe began • a few billion years after *the big bang* ✧ The scientific theory that the universe began with a huge explosion is called ***the big bang theory***.

big–boned *adj* **bigger–boned; biggest–boned** [*or more* ~; *most* ~] : having large bones : large but not fat • He is tall and *big-boned.* • a *big-boned* girl/gal

big boys *noun*
the big boys informal : the most powerful people or companies • He'll have to work pretty hard if he wants to compete with *the big boys* in the industry.

Big Brother *noun* [*singular*] : a powerful government or organization that watches and controls what people say and do • "You better be careful about what you say," she warned, "*Big Brother* is listening!" — see also [1]BIG 7

big bucks *noun* [*plural*] *US, informal* : a large amount of money • A car like that costs *big bucks.* • He's making *big bucks* [=*big money*] at his new job.

big business *noun* [*noncount*]
1 : large companies considered together as a powerful group • The tax proposal will be of most benefit to *big business.*
2 : an activity or product that makes a large amount of money • Tourism is *big business* in the region.

big cat *noun, pl* **~ cats** [*count*] : a large wild animal of the cat family • lions, tigers, leopards, and other *big cats*

big cheese *noun*
the big cheese informal : the most powerful or important person • You'll have to ask *the big cheese.* [=*the boss*] • Who's *the big cheese* around here?

big–city *adj, always used before a noun* : of or relating to a large city • *big-city* problems such as overcrowding and noise • a *big-city* school/hospital : coming from or living in a large city • *big-city* cops/mayors — compare SMALL-TOWN

big deal *noun* [*singular*] : something that is very important • The party was a *big deal.* • The cost didn't seem like much to me, but I know it was a *big deal* for many people. • So I'm late. ***What's the big deal***? [=why is that important?] — often used in negative statements • Flying is ***no big deal*** to him. • Don't worry, it's *no big deal.* [=it's not a problem] — some-

B

times used ironically as an interjection to say that something is not important to you • "She's going to be angry." "*Big deal*." [=*so what?*] • "You broke it!" "*Big deal*." [=I don't care]

make a big deal (out) of (something)** or **make (something) into a big deal : to treat (something) as very important or too important • The girl's song was far from perfect, but her parents *made a big deal of it*, and she was very happy. • Don't *make* such *a big deal (out) of* missing the bus: there'll be another one along in a minute.

big dipper *noun, pl* ~ **-pers**
1 ***the Big Dipper*** *US* : a group of seven stars in the northern sky that form a shape like a large dipper or ladle • We could see *the Big Dipper* [=(*Brit*) *the Plough*] in the northern sky. — compare LITTLE DIPPER
2 [*count*] *Brit, old-fashioned* : ROLLER COASTER 1

Big·foot *or* **big·foot** /ˈbɪg͵fʊt/ *noun* [*singular*] : SASQUATCH

big game *noun* [*noncount*] : large animals (such as elephants and tigers) that are hunted for sport • They traveled to Africa to hunt *big game*. • a *big-game* hunter

big·gie /ˈbɪgi/ *noun, pl* **-gies** [*count*] *informal* : someone or something that is very big or important • He met with some television *biggies*. • They've had problems before, but this one's a real *biggie*. • (*chiefly US*) "Sorry I'm late." "***No biggie***. [=it's not a problem] I'm not in a hurry."

big·gish /ˈbɪgɪʃ/ *adj* : somewhat big • He has a *biggish* [=*largish*] nose.

big government *noun* [*noncount*] *US* : government that has too much influence and power over citizens • a politician who promises to do away with high taxes and *big government*

big gun *noun*
the big guns *informal* : the most powerful people, companies, organizations, etc. • They called in *the big guns* to deal with the problem.

big–headed *adj*
1 : having a large head • a *big-headed* dinosaur
2 [*more* ~; *most* ~] *disapproving* : sure that you are better or more important than other people : CONCEITED • *big-headed* celebrities/politicians

big–hearted *adj* [*more* ~; *most* ~] : generous and kind • a *big-hearted* kid/person

big·horn sheep /ˈbɪg͵hoən-/ *noun, pl* ~ **sheep** [*count*] : a kind of wild sheep with long curved horns that lives in the mountains of western North America — called also *bighorn*

big house *noun*
the big house *US slang* : PRISON • He spent four years in *the big house*.

bight /ˈbaɪt/ *noun, pl* **bights** [*count*] : a curve in a coast or the bay formed by such a curve • the *Bight* of Benin • the Great Australian *Bight*

big league *noun*
the big leagues *US* : the two main U.S. baseball leagues (the American League and the National League) • He always dreamed of playing in *the big leagues*. [=*the major leagues*] — often used figuratively • She's in *the big leagues* now, working for a major law firm in a large city.
– **big–league** *adj, always used before a noun* • He hit a home run in his first *big-league* [=*major-league*] game. • *big-league* baseball • a *big-league* team – **big leagu·er** *noun, pl* ~ **-guers** [*count*] • He hopes to be a *big leaguer* [=*major leaguer*] some day.

big mouth *noun, pl* ~ **mouths** [*count*] *informal* : a person who cannot keep a secret or who talks too much • She's a *big mouth*. — used in phrases that describe a person who talks too much • Why did you have to ***open your big mouth*** and tell everyone our business? • Be careful of what you say around her—she ***has a big mouth***. [=she is likely to tell other people what you said]
– **big–mouthed** *adj* • The surprise was spoiled by my *big-mouthed* friend.

big name *noun, pl* ~ **names** [*count*] *informal* : a very famous person • There were many *big names* [=*celebrities*] at the party. • He is a *big name* in the business world. [=he is a famous businessperson]
– **big–name** *adj, always used before a noun* • a *big-name* movie star

big noise *noun, pl* ~ **noises** [*count*] *Brit, informal* : a powerful or important person : BIG SHOT — usually singular • She's a *big noise* in local politics.

big·ot /ˈbɪgət/ *noun, pl* **-ots** [*count*] *disapproving* : a person who strongly and unfairly dislikes other people, ideas, etc. : a bigoted person; *especially* : a person who hates or refuses to accept the members of a particular group (such as a racial or religious group) • He was labeled a *bigot* after making some offensive comments.

big·ot·ed /ˈbɪgətəd/ *adj* [*more* ~; *most* ~] *disapproving* : having or showing a strong and unfair dislike of other people, ideas, etc.; *especially* : hating or refusing to accept the members of a particular group • a *bigoted* neighbor • Many people found his *bigoted* comments offensive.

big·ot·ry /ˈbɪgətri/ *noun* [*noncount*] : bigoted acts or beliefs • a protest against *bigotry* • religious/racial *bigotry*

big picture *noun*
the big picture : everything that relates to or is involved in a situation or issue • We need to look at *the big picture* before we can work out specific details.

big screen *noun*
the big screen : movies and the movie industry especially when they are being compared to television • She was a star of *the big screen*. [=*the silver screen*] • The television show was adapted for *the big screen*. [=the television show was made into a movie]

big–screen *adj, always used before a noun*
1 : relating to movies or the movie industry • She worked on the novel's *big-screen* adaptation.
2 : having a large screen • a *big-screen* television

big shot *noun, pl* ~ **shots** [*count*] *informal* : a powerful or important person • All the corporate *big shots* are meeting this afternoon. • a *big shot* in local politics

big stick *noun, pl* ~ **sticks** [*count*] : a threat to use violence or force to make a person, group, country, etc., do something — usually singular • The organization wields a pretty *big stick* when it comes to fighting poverty. [=the organization is able to fight poverty because it can threaten to use force, such as legal action]

big–tick·et /ˈbɪgˈtɪkət/ *adj, chiefly US, informal* : having a high price : EXPENSIVE • *big-ticket* items like cars and appliances

big time *noun*
the big time : the highest or most successful level of an activity • He was a good basketball player but he never made (it to) *the big time*. • The group performed in small clubs for years before ***hitting the big time*** [=becoming very successful] with a record deal.

[1]**big–time** /ˈbɪg͵taɪm/ *adj, always used before a noun* : relating to or involved in the highest or most successful level of an activity • I covered *big-time* [=*major*] college sports for the newspaper. • He became a *big-time* racketeer.

[2]**big–time** *adv, chiefly US, informal* : in a big way : very much or very badly • The new show bombed *big-time*. [=the new show was very unsuccessful] • You owe me *big-time*.

big toe *noun, pl* ~ **toes** [*count*] : the largest toe on a person's foot

big top *noun* [*singular*] : a large circus tent — usually used with *the* • She dreamed of performing ***under the big top***. [=performing in/with the circus]

big wheel *noun, pl* ~ **wheels** [*count*]
1 *chiefly US, informal* : a powerful or important person : BIG SHOT • He's a *big wheel* in local politics.
2 *Brit* : FERRIS WHEEL

big·wig /ˈbɪg͵wɪg/ *noun, pl* **-wigs** [*count*] *informal* : a powerful or important person • corporate *bigwigs* [=*big shots*] • a *bigwig* in local politics

[1]**bike** /ˈbaɪk/ *noun, pl* **bikes** [*count*]
1 : BICYCLE • She rode her *bike* to school. • a *bike* path
2 : MOTORCYCLE — see also DIRT BIKE, MOTORBIKE

[2]**bike** *verb* **bikes; biked; bik·ing** [*no obj*] : to ride a bicycle • We *biked* to the park. • He *bikes* in the mountains.
– **biking** *noun* [*noncount*] • *Biking* is a great form of exercise. • We're planning to ***go biking*** tomorrow.

bik·er /ˈbaɪkɚ/ *noun, pl* **-ers** [*count*]
1 : a person who rides a motorcycle : MOTORCYCLIST
2 *chiefly US* : a person who rides a bicycle : BICYCLIST

bi·ki·ni /bəˈkiːni/ *noun, pl* **-nis** [*count*] : a piece of clothing in two parts that a girl or woman wears for swimming or for lying in the sun and that does not cover much of the body — see color picture on page C13

bi·la·bi·al /baɪˈleɪbijəl/ *noun, pl* **-als** [*count*] *linguistics* : a sound made by using both lips • English *bilabials* such as /b/, /p/, and /m/
– **bilabial** *adj* • a *bilabial* consonant

bi·lat·er·al /baɪˈlætərəl/ *adj* : involving two groups or countries • *bilateral* trade agreements • a *bilateral* treaty —

B

compare MULTILATERAL, UNILATERAL

bile /ˈbajəl/ *noun [noncount]*
1 : a yellow or greenish liquid that is made by the liver and that helps the body to digest fats
2 : anger or hatred • One writer objected to what she described as "the *bile* that is spewed from the newspaper's editorial page."

bilge /ˈbɪlʤ/ *noun, pl* **bilg·es**
1 *[count]* **:** the bottom part of the inside of a ship or boat • water in the *bilge*
2 *[noncount] informal* **:** foolish or worthless statements or information **:** NONSENSE • That magazine prints a lot of *bilge* about celebrities.

bi·lin·gual /baɪˈlɪŋgwəl/ *adj*
1 : able to speak and understand two languages • Several of the employees are *bilingual.* • He is *bilingual* in English and Japanese.
2 : using or expressed in two languages • a *bilingual* dictionary • She grew up in a *bilingual* community. • The town has an excellent *bilingual* education program. — compare MONOLINGUAL, MULTILINGUAL
– bilingual *noun, pl* **-guals** *[count]* • Several of the employees are *bilinguals.* **– bi·lin·gual·ism** /baɪˈlɪŋgwəˌlɪzəm/ *noun [noncount]* • She says her *bilingualism* [=her ability to speak two languages] has helped her in her career.

bil·ious /ˈbɪljəs/ *adj [more ~; most ~]*
1 : having or causing a sick feeling in the stomach **:** feeling or causing nausea • a *bilious* attack
2 : angry or bad-tempered • a *bilious* disposition
3 : very unpleasant to look at • a *bilious* [=*repulsive*] shade of green

bilk /ˈbɪlk/ *verb* **bilks; bilked; bilk·ing** *[+ obj] chiefly US, informal* **:** to cheat or trick (a person or organization) especially by taking money • They were convicted of *bilking* [=*defrauding, swindling*] the company (out) of a lot of money.

¹bill /ˈbɪl/ *noun, pl* **bills** *[count]*
1 : a document that says how much money you owe for something you have bought or used • He paid the telephone *bill.* • Did our water *bill* arrive yet? • I've been having a hard time paying the *bills* since I lost my job. [=paying what I owe for housing, heat, electricity, etc.] • The waiter gave us our *bill.* • I can't pay for it now: just put it on my *bill.* [=add the amount I now owe to what I already owe and I will pay the total amount later] — compare BILL OF SALE
2 : a written description of a new law that is being suggested and that the lawmakers of a country, state, etc., must vote to accept before it becomes law • They will introduce an antismoking *bill* in Congress. • The Senate passed/rejected the *bill.* • How does a *bill* become a law?; *also* **:** such a bill after it has become a law • the GI *bill* — see also BILL OF RIGHTS
3 *chiefly US* **:** a piece of paper money • He handed me a 5-dollar *bill.* • *bills* and coins — called also *(Brit) note*
4 : a written or printed advertisement that is used to announce a play, movie, or concert to the public and to list the names of the performers • Who is on the *bill*? [=who is performing?] • a ***double bill*** [=a concert that has two parts] featuring two of the world's best jazz trumpeters • The notice on the wall said "***Post No Bills.***" [=do not put any advertisements on the wall]
fill the bill *or* ***fit the bill*** **:** to be exactly what is needed **:** to be suitable • If you want to stay near the beach, this hotel will *fit the bill.*
foot the bill see ²FOOT
give (someone or something) a clean bill of health **:** to officially say that someone is healthy or that something is working correctly • The doctor *gave* him *a clean bill of health.* • The governor *gives* the program *a clean bill of health.*
– compare ³BILL

²bill *verb* **bills; billed; bill·ing** *[+ obj]*
1 : to send a bill to (someone or something) **:** to provide (a person, business, organization, etc.) with a statement that says how much money is owed for something that has been bought or used • They *billed* me for the repairs they made to the roof. • The company was *billed* for the deliveries.
2 : to describe (someone or something) *as* a particular thing so that people will like or want that person or thing — usually used as *(be) billed* • The city is *being billed* [=*advertised*] *as* one of the best places to live in the state. • She *was billed as* the next big movie star. — see also BILLING
3 : to officially say that someone is going *to do* something — usually used as *(be) billed* • Both writers *are billed to appear* at the conference.
– compare ⁴BILL

³bill *noun, pl* **bills** *[count]*
1 : a bird's beak • a duck's *bill* — see picture at BIRD
2 *US* **:** the part of a cap that sticks out in front **:** the visor of a hat
– compare ¹BILL

⁴bill *verb* **bills; billed; billing**
bill and coo *old-fashioned* **:** to kiss and talk quietly • A young couple sat together in the corner, *billing and cooing.*
– compare ²BILL

bill·board /ˈbɪlˌboɚd/ *noun, pl* **-boards** *[count]* **:** a large sign for advertisements that is next to a road, on the side of a building, etc. — called also *(Brit) hoarding*

¹bil·let /ˈbɪlət/ *noun, pl* **-lets** *[count]* **:** a private home where a soldier lives temporarily with the people who live there

²billet *verb* **-lets; -let·ed; -let·ing** *[+ obj]* **:** to put (someone, such as a soldier) in a private home to live there temporarily — usually used as *(be) billeted* • The soldiers *were billeted* [=*quartered, housed*] in houses throughout the town.

bill·fold /ˈbɪlˌfoʊld/ *noun, pl* **-folds** *[count] US* **:** a small folding case that holds paper money and credit cards **:** WALLET

bil·liards /ˈbɪljɚdz/ *noun [noncount]* **:** any one of several games that are played on a large table by hitting solid balls into one another with the end of a long stick ✧ The table used for some types of billiards has pockets at the corners and sides. — compare POOL, SNOOKER
– bil·liard /ˈbɪljɚd/ *adj, always used before a noun* • *billiard* balls • a *billiard* table

bill·ing /ˈbɪlɪŋ/ *noun [noncount]* **:** the things that are said or written to make people interested in a show, perfomer, etc. • The film didn't live up to its advance *billing.* [=it was not as good as people said it would be] ✧ The person who gets ***top/star billing*** for a play, movie, etc., is the most important or famous performer whose name is shown above the names of other performers in signs and advertisements. • She'll get *top billing* on her next film. • Both of the actors want *star billing.*

bil·lion /ˈbɪljən/ *noun, pl* **billion** *or* **bil·lions** *[count]*
1 : the number 1,000,000,000 **:** one thousand million • a/one/two *billion* (of them) • a hundred *billion* = 100 *billion* • several *billion* (of them) = (less commonly) several *billions* (of them) • hundreds of *billions* (of them) • a *billion* and one [=1,000,000,001] • a *billion* and a half = 1.5 *billion* [=1,500,000,000] • The company is worth *billions.* [=worth billions of dollars, pounds, euros, etc.]
2 : a very large amount or number • We could see a *billion* stars in the sky. • I've heard that excuse a *billion* times before. [=many, many times before] — often plural • We could see *billions* of stars. • ***billions and billions*** of stars
3 *Brit, old-fashioned* **:** the number 1,000,000,000,000 **:** TRILLION
– bil·lionth /ˈbɪljənθ/ *adj* • our (one) *billionth* customer • This is the *billionth* time I've seen this show. [=I've seen this show many times] **– billionth** *noun, pl* **-lionths** *[count]* • one *billionth* [=one of a billion equal parts] of a second

bil·lion·aire /ˌbɪljəˈneɚ/ *noun, pl* **-aires** *[count]* **:** a rich person who has at least a billion dollars, pounds, etc.

bill of exchange *noun, pl* **bills of exchange** *[count] business* **:** a document that tells a person or business to pay a particular amount of money to another person or business

bill of fare *noun, pl* **bills of fare** *[count] somewhat formal + old-fashioned* **:** a list of the things that are served at a restaurant **:** MENU • The *bill of fare* includes several soups.

bill of rights *or* **Bill of Rights** *noun [singular]* **:** a written statement that lists the basic rights of the citizens of a country • Certain freedoms are guaranteed to all Americans by ***the Bill of Rights.*** [=the first 10 amendments to the U.S. Constitution]

bill of sale *noun, pl* **bills of sale** *[count]* **:** a document saying that something has been sold to a new owner • Do you have the *bill of sale* for the car?

¹bil·low /ˈbɪloʊ/ *noun, pl* **-lows** *[count]*
1 : a moving cloud or mass of smoke, steam, etc. • *Billows* of smoke poured out of the burning building. • *billows* of fog
2 *literary + old-fashioned* **:** a large wave • the rolling *billows* of the sea

²billow *verb* **-lows; -lowed; -low·ing** *[no obj]*
1 : to move as a large cloud or mass • Clouds of smoke *billowed* (up) from the chimney.

2 : to be pushed outward by air ▪ sails *billowing* (out) in the breeze
3 *literary + old-fashioned* : to rise or roll in waves ▪ the *billowing* ocean

bil·ly club /ˈbɪli-/ *noun, pl* ~ **clubs** [*count*] *US* : NIGHTSTICK

billy goat *noun, pl* ~ **goats** [*count*] : a male goat — compare NANNY GOAT

bim·bo /ˈbɪmboʊ/ *noun, pl* **-bos** [*count*] *informal* : an attractive but stupid woman ▪ Her husband ran off with some *bimbo*.

bi·month·ly /baɪˈmʌnθli/ *adj*
1 : occurring every two months ▪ The group holds *bimonthly* meetings in January, March, May, and so on.
2 : occurring twice a month : SEMIMONTHLY ▪ The group holds *bimonthly* meetings on the first and third Tuesday of each month.
– **bimonthly** *adv*

[1]**bin** /ˈbɪn/ *noun, pl* **bins** [*count*]
1 : a box that is used for storing things ▪ a storage/laundry *bin* ▪ Put the old newspapers in the recycling *bin*.
2 *chiefly Brit* : a can for trash or garbage : DUSTBIN — see also BIN LINER, BINMAN

[2]**bin** *verb* **bins; binned; bin·ning** [+ *obj*] *Brit, informal* : to put (something) in the trash ▪ *binning* old newspapers

bi·na·ry /ˈbaɪnəri/ *adj, technical*
1 : relating to or consisting of two things or parts ▪ *binary* stars
2 : relating to or involving a method of calculating and of representing information especially in computers by using the numbers 0 and 1 ▪ *binary* digits/numbers

[1]**bind** /ˈbaɪnd/ *verb* **binds; bound** /ˈbaʊnd/; **bind·ing**
1 [+ *obj*] : to tie or wrap (something) with rope, string, etc. ▪ She *bound* her hair in a ponytail. ▪ The machine *binds* the hay into bales.
2 [+ *obj*] : to tie the hands or feet of a person to prevent escape or movement ▪ He *bound* the prisoner's wrists (together) with a rope. ▪ The captive was ***bound and gagged***. [=tied up and stopped from talking with something that covers the mouth] — sometimes used figuratively ▪ They are *bound* by their own inhibitions.
3 [*no obj*] *of clothing* : to prevent free movement by fitting too tightly ▪ He doesn't like to wear clothes that *bind*.
4 [+ *obj*] : to wrap or cover (something) with a bandage ▪ The doctor *bound* (up) the injured ankle.
5 [+ *obj*] : to make (someone) have to do something because of a promise, agreement, etc. ▪ He *bound* himself with an oath. — usually used as *(be) bound* ▪ By signing here, you agree to *be bound* by the terms of the contract. — see also [2]BINDING, [2]BOUND 5
6 [+ *obj*] : to make (something, such as an agreement) certain ▪ A handshake *binds* the deal.
7 [+ *obj*] : to cause (people) to be joined together closely ▪ the emotional ties that *bind* us ▪ different groups *bound* together by a common interest
8 : to cause (something) to form a mass that stays together [+ *obj*] The mayonnaise *binds* the salad together. [*no obj*] If you leave out the eggs, the dough won't *bind*.
9 *technical* : to combine with (something) by chemical forces [+ *obj*] cellulose *binds* water [*no obj*] particles that *bind* to/with one another
10 [+ *obj*] : to put a special decorative edge on (something, such as cloth or carpet) ▪ You need to *bind* the edges so it won't unravel.
11 [+ *obj*] : to put a cover or binding on (a book) ▪ This book was *bound* by hand. — see also [2]BOUND 6
bind over [*phrasal verb*] ***bind (someone) over*** 1 *US, law* : to require (someone) to appear in court ▪ He was *bound over* for trial. 2 *Brit, law* : to warn (someone) that if they break the law again they will be punished ▪ The shoplifters were simply *bound over*.

[2]**bind** *noun* [*singular*]
1 : a difficult situation ▪ Can you help me? I seem to have gotten myself into a (bit of a) *bind*.
2 *Brit* : an annoying problem : NUISANCE ▪ It's a real *bind* having to meet all these deadlines.

bind·er /ˈbaɪndɚ/ *noun, pl* **-ers** [*count*]
1 : a cover for holding together sheets of paper ▪ a loose-leaf *binder* — see also RING BINDER
2 : a material that is used to hold things together ▪ The egg in the recipe acts as a *binder*.
3 : a person or machine that puts books together
4 *US* : a temporary insurance contract that provides coverage until a policy is issued
5 *US* : a payment given to make an agreement official and legal ▪ She gave the lawyer 1,000 dollars as a *binder* when she signed the agreement to buy the house.

[1]**bind·ing** /ˈbaɪndɪŋ/ *noun, pl* **-ings**
1 [*count*] : the cover of a book ▪ a leather *binding*
2 : a narrow strip of cloth attached along the edge of something [*noncount*] a carpet edged with canvas *binding* [*count*] The *bindings* have started to come loose.
3 : a device that attaches a boot to a ski

[2]**binding** *adj* : forcing or requiring someone to do something because of a promise, agreement, etc. ▪ The contract is legally *binding*. ▪ The parties agreed to settle the dispute through ***binding arbitration***.

[1]**binge** /ˈbɪnʤ/ *noun, pl* **bing·es** [*count*] : a short period of time when you do too much of something ▪ a drinking/shopping *binge* — often used in the phrase ***go on a binge*** ▪ He *went on an* eating *binge*. [=he ate a lot in a short period of time] — often used before another noun ▪ *binge* drinking

[2]**binge** *verb* **binges; binged; binge·ing** *or* **bing·ing** [*no obj*] : to eat, drink, etc., too much in a short period of time : to go on a binge — often + *on* ▪ He *binges on* beer now and then.
binge and purge : to eat a lot of food and then force yourself to vomit so that you do not gain weight ▪ Her college roommate used to *binge and purge*.
– **bing·er** *noun, pl* **-ers** [*count*] ▪ He's a bit of a beer *binger*.

[1]**bin·go** /ˈbɪŋgoʊ/ *noun* [*noncount*] : a game in which players match numbered squares on a card with numbers that are called out until someone wins by matching five squares in a row ▪ She plays *bingo* twice a week. — often used before another noun ▪ *bingo* halls/parlors ▪ a *bingo* game

[2]**bingo** *interj*
1 — used to announce that you have won the game in bingo
2 — used to announce a successful result that is quick or unexpected ▪ Then, *bingo*! The idea hit me.
3 — used to indicate that another person's statement is correct ▪ "You mean he lied to us?" "*Bingo*!" [=*exactly*]

bin liner *noun, pl* ~ **-ers** [*count*] *Brit* : a plastic bag used in a garbage can

bin·man /ˈbɪn,mæn/ *noun, pl* **-men** /-,mɛn/ [*count*] *Brit* : GARBAGEMAN

bin·oc·u·lar /baɪˈnɑːkjələ/ *adj* : involving or designed for both eyes ▪ *binocular* vision ▪ a *binocular* microscope

bin·oc·u·lars /bəˈnɑːkjələz/ *noun* [*plural*] : a device that you hold up to your eyes and look through to see things that are far away ▪ a bird in a tree seen through (a pair of) *binoculars*

binoculars

bi·no·mi·al /baɪˈnoʊmijəl/ *noun, pl* **-als** [*count*] *mathematics* : an expression consisting of two terms connected by a plus sign or minus sign ▪ the *binomial* a + b
– **binomial** *adj* ▪ *binomial* expressions

bio- *combining form* : relating to life or living things ▪ *biosphere* ▪ *biochemistry*

bio·chem·is·try /,bajoʊˈkɛməstri/ *noun* [*noncount*] : the chemistry of living things ▪ the brain's *biochemistry* ▪ advances in the field of *biochemistry* ▪ a professor of *biochemistry*
– **bio·chem·i·cal** /,bajoʊˈkɛmɪkəl/ *adj* ▪ *biochemical* changes/processes – **bio·chem·ist** /,bajoʊˈkɛmɪst/ *noun, pl* **-ists** [*count*]

bio·de·grad·able /,bajoudɪˈgreɪdəbəl/ *adj* : capable of being slowly destroyed and broken down into very small parts by natural processes, bacteria, etc. ▪ *biodegradable* trash bags ▪ This plastic isn't *biodegradable*.

bio·di·ver·si·ty /,bajoudəˈvɚsəti/ *noun* [*noncount*] : the existence of many different kinds of plants and animals in an environment ▪ efforts to preserve *biodiversity*

bio·feed·back /,bajoʊˈfiːd,bæk/ *noun* [*noncount*] : the technique of controlling things in your body (such as heartbeats or brain waves) with your conscious mind

bio·graph·i·cal /,bajəˈgræfɪkəl/ *adj* : relating to or telling the story of a real person's life ▪ *biographical* information ▪ a *biographical* essay

bi·og·ra·phy /baɪˈɑːgrəfi/ *noun, pl* **-phies** [*count*] : the story of a real person's life written by someone other than that person ▪ a new *biography* of Abraham Lincoln — compare AUTOBIOGRAPHY
– **bi·og·ra·pher** /baɪˈɑːgrəfɚ/ *noun, pl* **-ers** [*count*] ▪ Lin-

coln's *biographers* [=people who wrote biographies of Lincoln]

bio·haz·ard /ˈbajoʊˌhæzəd/ *noun, pl* **-ards** [*count*] : a biological or chemical substance or situation that is dangerous to human beings and the environment ▪ The gasoline spill created a serious *biohazard.*

– **bio·haz·ard·ous** /ˌbajoʊˈhæzədəs/ *adj* ▪ *biohazardous* materials

bi·o·log·i·cal /ˌbajəˈlɑːʤɪkəl/ *adj*

1 : of or relating to biology or to life and living things ▪ *biological* processes ▪ *biological* research

2 : related through birth — used to distinguish the parents who gave birth to a child from the parents who later adopted the child ▪ an adopted child who finally found her *biological* mother

– **bi·o·log·i·cal·ly** /ˌbajəˈlɑːʤɪkli/ *adv* ▪ a *biologically* diverse region

biological clock *noun, pl* ~ **clocks** [*count*] : a system in the body that controls the occurrence of natural processes (such as waking, sleeping, and aging) — often used to describe a woman's desire to have children before she is too old ▪ She felt her *biological clock* ticking away and wanted to have a baby as soon as possible.

biological control *noun, pl* ~ **-trols**

1 [*noncount*] : a method of controlling harmful insects, diseases, etc., in an environment (such as a garden or a lawn) by using other insects or natural substances ▪ She practices *biological control* in her gardening.

2 [*count*] : an insect or a natural substance that is used to control control harmful insects, diseases, etc. ▪ She uses *biological controls* in her garden.

biological warfare *noun* [*noncount*] : the use of harmful living things (such as germs that cause disease) as weapons in a war

biological weapon *noun, pl* ~ **-ons** [*count*] : a harmful living thing (such as a germ that causes disease) used as a weapon in a war

bi·ol·o·gy /baɪˈɑːləʤi/ *noun* [*noncount*]

1 : a science that deals with things that are alive (such as plants and animals) ▪ advances in the field of *biology* ▪ a professor of *biology*

2 : the plant and animal life of a particular place ▪ the *biology* of the rain forest

3 : the processes that occur in a living thing ▪ human *biology* ▪ the *biology* of tumor cells

– **bi·ol·o·gist** /baɪˈɑːləʤɪst/ *noun, pl* **-gists** [*count*]

bi·on·ic /baɪˈɑːnɪk/ *adj, of body parts* : made stronger or more capable by special electronic devices — usually used figuratively ▪ a pitcher with a *bionic* arm [=a pitcher who throws extremely fast]

bio·pic /ˈbajoʊˌpɪk/ *noun, pl* **-pics** [*count*] *informal* : a biographical movie ▪ We watched a *biopic* about Beethoven.

bi·op·sy /ˈbaɪˌɑːpsi/ *noun, pl* **-sies** [*count*] *medical* : the removal of tissue, cells, or fluids from someone's body in order to check for illness ▪ a skin *biopsy*

bio·rhythm /ˈbajoʊˌrɪðəm/ *noun, pl* **-rhythms** [*count*] : a natural, repeated pattern of changes that occur in the body and that affect the way a person feels

bio·sphere /ˈbajəˌsfiə/ *noun* [*singular*] : the part of the Earth in which life can exist — usually used with *the* ▪ the effects of pollution on *the biosphere*

bio·tech /ˈbajoʊˌtɛk/ *noun* [*noncount*] : BIOTECHNOLOGY

bio·tech·nol·o·gy /ˌbajoutɛkˈnɑːləʤi/ *noun* [*noncount*] : the use of living cells, bacteria, etc., to make useful products (such as crops that insects are less likely to destroy or new kinds of medicine)

– **bio·tech·no·log·i·cal** /ˌbajoʊˌtɛknəˈlɑːʤɪkəl/ *adj*

bi·par·ti·san /baɪˈpɑətəzən, *Brit* ˌbaɪˌpɑːtəˈzæn/ *adj* : relating to or involving members of two political parties ▪ a *bipartisan* effort/commission ▪ The bill has *bipartisan* support.

– **bi·par·ti·san·ship** /baɪˈpɑətəzənˌʃɪp, *Brit* ˌbaɪˌpɑːtəˈzænˌʃɪp/ *noun* [*noncount*]

bi·ped /ˈbaɪˌpɛd/ *noun, pl* **-peds** [*count*] : a 2-footed animal ▪ Human beings are *bipeds.* — compare QUADRUPED

bi·plane /ˈbaɪˌpleɪn/ *noun, pl* **-planes** [*count*] : an old type of airplane that has two sets of wings with one placed above the other — compare MONOPLANE

bi·po·lar disorder /baɪˈpoulə-/ *noun* [*noncount*] *medical* : MANIC DEPRESSION

bi·ra·cial /baɪˈreɪʃəl/ *adj* : of, relating to, or involving people from two races ▪ a *biracial* coalition ▪ a *biracial* couple; *also* : having parents from two races ▪ *biracial* children

birch /ˈbəʧ/ *noun, pl* **birch·es**

1 a [*count*] : a type of tree that has outer bark which can be pulled off easily — called also *birch tree* **b** [*noncount*] : the hard, pale wood of the birch ▪ a cabinet made of *birch*

2 ***the birch*** *Brit* : the punishment of being hit with a birch stick ▪ In those days, schoolchildren got *the birch* when they misbehaved.

bird /ˈbəd/ *noun, pl* **birds** [*count*]

1 : an animal that has wings and is covered with feathers ▪ A large *bird* flew overhead. ▪ The *birds* were singing outside our window. ▪ a flock of *birds* — see color picture on page C9; see also BIRD OF PARADISE, BIRD OF PASSAGE, BIRD OF PREY

2 *informal* : PERSON ▪ He's a tough old *bird.* — see also RARE BIRD

3 *Brit, informal + sometimes offensive* : GIRL ▪ We met some smashing *birds* at the pub last night.

a bird in the hand is worth two in the bush ◊ The expression *a bird in the hand is worth two in the bush* means that it is better to hold onto something you have than to risk losing it by trying to get something better.

(as) free as a bird see [1]FREE

birds of a feather flock together see [1]FEATHER

for the birds *informal* : worthless or ridiculous ▪ This town is *for the birds.*

give (someone) the bird *informal* **1** *or* ***flip (someone) the bird*** *US* : to make an offensive gesture at someone by pointing the middle finger upward while keeping the other fingers folded down ▪ He *flipped them the bird.* [=*gave them the finger*] **2** *Brit* : to loudly shout at, laugh at, or boo someone (such as a performer) in order to show disapproval ▪ The audience *gave him the bird.*

kill two birds with one stone see [1]KILL

the birds and the bees *informal + humorous* : the facts about sex that are told to children ▪ He dreaded having to explain about *the birds and the bees* [=*the facts of life*] to his son.

the early bird catches/gets the worm see [2]EARLY

bird

bird·bath /ˈbədˌbæθ, *Brit* ˈbəːdˌbɑːθ/ *noun, pl* **-baths** [*count*] : a bowl that is filled with water and usually raised above the ground in a yard or garden so birds can bathe in it — see color picture on page C6

bird·brain /ˈbədˌbreɪn/ *noun, pl* **-brains** [*count*] *US, informal* : a stupid person ▪ Her brother's a real *birdbrain.*

– **bird·brained** /ˈbədˌbreɪnd/ *adj* ▪ her *birdbrained* brother

bird·cage /ˈbədˌkeɪʤ/ *noun, pl* **-cag·es** [*count*] : a cage for birds

bird dog *noun, pl* ~ **dogs** [*count*] *US* : a dog that has been trained to help people hunt birds — called also (*Brit*) *gun dog*

bird·er /ˈbədə/ *noun, pl* **-ers** [*count*] : BIRD-WATCHER

– **bird·ing** /ˈbədɪŋ/ *noun* [*noncount*] ▪ She goes *birding* [=*bird-watching*] with her friends.

bird·house /ˈbədˌhaʊs/ *noun, pl* **-hous·es** [*count*] : a small covered box that is made as a place for wild birds to nest

[1]**bird·ie** /ˈbədi/ *noun, pl* **-ies**

1 [*count*] : a small bird — used especially by children or when speaking to children ▪ Look at all the little *birdies.*

2 *golf* : a score of one stroke less than par on a hole [*count*] I made/scored a *birdie* on the fifth hole. [*noncount*] I made *birdie* on the fifth hole. — compare BOGEY, EAGLE

3 [*count*] *US* : SHUTTLECOCK

[2]**birdie** *verb* **bird·ies; bird·ied; bird·ie·ing** [+ *obj*] : to score a birdie on (a hole in golf) ▪ She *birdied* the second hole.

bird·like /ˈbədˌlaɪk/ *adj* [*more* ~; *most* ~] : resembling a bird ▪ a small, *birdlike* man ▪ *birdlike* features

bird·life /ˈbədˌlaɪf/ *noun* [*noncount*] : the birds that live in a particular place ▪ The rain forests are rich in *birdlife.* [=there are many birds in the rain forests]

bird of paradise *noun, pl* **birds of paradise** [*count*] : any one of many brightly colored birds that live in New Guinea and in nearby islands

bird of passage *noun, pl* **birds of passage** [*count*]
1 : a bird that travels from one location to another when the seasons change
2 *literary* **:** a person who wanders to many different places throughout life

bird of prey *noun, pl* **birds of prey** [*count*] : a bird that hunts and eats other animals • eagles, hawks, and other *birds of prey*

bird·seed /ˈbɚdˌsiːd/ *noun* [*noncount*] : seeds that are used for feeding birds

bird's–eye /ˈbɚdzˌaɪ/ *adj, always used before a noun* : seen from high above • We had a *bird's-eye* view/perspective of the city as we flew over it.

bird·song /ˈbɚdˌsɑːŋ/ *noun* [*noncount*] : the song of a bird or of many birds • The forest was filled with *birdsong*.

bird–watch·er /ˈbɚdˌwɑːʧɚ/ *noun, pl* **-ers** [*count*] : a person who watches and identifies wild birds — called also *birder*
– **bird–watch·ing** /ˈbɚdˌwɑːʧɪŋ/ *noun* [*noncount*] • She goes *bird-watching* [=*birding*] with her friends.

birth /ˈbɚθ/ *noun, pl* **births**
1 : the time when a baby comes out from the body of its mother [*count*] He was present at/for the *birth* of his daughter. • The hospital reported an increase in premature *births*. [*noncount*] Please indicate your date of *birth*. • the period from *birth* to adolescence • a disease that is present at *birth* • She's Canadian by *birth*. [=she was born in Canada] — often used before another noun • What was the baby's *birth* weight?
2 [*noncount*] **:** the beginning or origin of something • the *birth* of the solar system • the *birth* of the blues • We are witnessing the *birth* of a new era.
3 [*noncount*] — used to describe the kind of family a person comes from • a person of noble/low/humble *birth* [=*ancestry*]
give birth **1** *of a mother* **:** produce a baby from the body • Did she *give birth* in a hospital or at home? — usually + *to* • He was present when his wife *gave birth to* his daughter. • Our cat *gave birth to* four kittens. **2 :** to cause the beginning of something — + *to* • a revolution that *gave birth to* a new nation

birth canal *noun, pl* ~ **-nals** [*count*] : the part of a mother's body that a baby passes through when it is born

birth certificate *noun, pl* ~ **-cates** [*count*] : an official document that gives information about a person's birth (such as the person's name, the names of the parents, and the time and place where the birth occurred)

birth control *noun* [*noncount*] : things that are done to keep a woman from becoming pregnant • modern methods of *birth control* [=*contraception*] — often used before another noun • a *birth control* pill

birth·day /ˈbɚθˌdeɪ/ *noun, pl* **-days** [*count*]
1 : the day when someone was born or the anniversary of that day • Her *birthday* is September 30th. • Today is his 21st *birthday*. • Happy *Birthday*! — often used before another noun • a *birthday* party/gift
2 : the day when something began • The company just celebrated its 50th *birthday*.
birthday suit *informal + humorous* ✧ If you are wearing your *birthday suit*, you are naked. • We were standing there in nothing but our *birthday suits*.

birth father *noun, pl* ~ **-ers** [*count*] : the father of a child when the child is born : the natural father of a child who has been adopted

birth·ing /ˈbɚθɪŋ/ *noun* [*noncount*] : the act of giving birth • pregnancy and *birthing* • home *birthing* — often used before another noun • a *birthing* room/center • the *birthing* process

birth·mark /ˈbɚθˌmɑɚk/ *noun, pl* **-marks** [*count*] : an unusual mark that is present on the skin from the time when someone is born

birth mother *noun, pl* ~ **-ers** [*count*] : the mother of a child when the child is born : a woman who gave birth to a child who has been adopted

birth parent *noun, pl* ~ **-ents** [*count*] : the natural father or mother of a child who has been adopted

birth·place /ˈbɚθˌpleɪs/ *noun, pl* **-plac·es** [*count*] : the place where someone was born or where something began • He visited his grandmother's *birthplace*. • New Orleans is regarded as the *birthplace* of jazz.

birth·rate /ˈbɚθˌreɪt/ *noun, pl* **-rates** [*count*] : a number that shows how many babies are born in a particular place or during a particular time • nations with high *birthrates*

birth·right /ˈbɚθˌraɪt/ *noun, pl* **-rights** [*count*] : a right that you have because you were born into a particular position, family, place, etc., or because it is a right of all people • the freedom that is our *birthright*

B

bis·cuit /ˈbɪskət/ *noun, pl* **-cuits** [*count*]
1 *US* **:** a small, light roll that is eaten as part of a meal
2 *Brit* **:** COOKIE
take the biscuit *Brit, informal* **:** to win the prize — used to describe something that is extremely surprising, annoying, etc. • I've heard some silly excuses in my time, but this one really *takes the biscuit*! [=(*US*) *takes the cake*]

bi·sect /ˈbaɪˌsɛkt/ *verb* **-sects; -sect·ed; -sect·ing** [+ *obj*] : to divide (something) into two equal parts • Draw a line that *bisects* the angle. • The city is *bisected* by the highway.

bi·sex·u·al /baɪˈsɛkʃəwəl/ *adj*
1 : sexually attracted to both men and women • *bisexual* people • She's *bisexual*. — compare HETEROSEXUAL, HOMOSEXUAL
2 : having both male and female sex parts • a *bisexual* plant
3 : relating to or involving two sexes • *bisexual* reproduction
– **bisexual** *noun, pl* **-als** [*count*] • He identifies himself as a *bisexual*. – **bi·sex·u·al·i·ty** /ˌbaɪˌsɛkʃəˈwæləti/ *noun* [*noncount*]

bish·op /ˈbɪʃəp/ *noun, pl* **-ops** [*count*]
1 : an official in some Christian religions who is ranked higher than a priest and who is usually in charge of church matters in a specific geographical area • Roman Catholic *bishops* • the *Bishop* of New York
2 : a piece in the game of chess that moves across the board at an angle — see picture at CHESS

bish·op·ric /ˈbɪʃəprɪk/ *noun, pl* **-rics** [*count*]
1 : the area a bishop is in charge of : DIOCESE
2 : the position of bishop • He was elected to the *bishopric* at the turn of the century.

bis·muth /ˈbɪzməθ/ *noun* [*noncount*] : a grayish-white metallic element that is used in alloys and drugs

bi·son /ˈbaɪsn̩/ *noun, pl* **bison** *also* **bi·sons** [*count*] : a large, hairy wild animal that has a big head and short horns — called also (*US*) *buffalo*

bison

bisque /ˈbɪsk/ *noun, pl* **bisques** [*count, noncount*] : a thick, creamy soup • lobster *bisque*

bis·tro /ˈbiːstroʊ/ *noun, pl* **-tros** [*count*] : a small restaurant or bar • a trendy *bistro* • a *bistro* in Paris that serves veal chops and hearty stews

[1]**bit** /ˈbɪt/ *noun, pl* **bits**
1 [*count*] **:** a small piece of something • Put all the broken *bits* back together. — often + *of* • He ate every last/single *bit of* the food. [=he ate all of the food] • He ate only a couple of tiny little *bits of* bread and cheese and drank a drop or two of wine. • We need to get all the *bits of* dirt out of the carpet. • There were broken *bits of* glass all over the floor. — see also BITS AND PIECES (below)
2 [*count*] **a** *chiefly Brit* **:** a part of something (such as a book, play, etc.) • There are some good *bits* [=*parts*] near the end of the story: one is the *bit* where the hero and the heroine are nearly separated. **b** *chiefly US* **:** a brief comic performance or joke • The comedian did a funny *bit* about taking his daughter to the dentist. • a corny comedy *bit* **c :** a very short performance in a movie, play, etc. — usually used before another noun • a *bit* part/role • *bit* players
3 [*singular*] *informal* **:** all the things that are connected to an activity, a process, etc. • He says he's tired of his job, tired of driving to work every day, **the whole bit**. [=*everything*]
4 [*count*] *Brit* **:** an old coin with a specified small value • a threepenny *bit* — see also TWO BITS
a bit **1 :** a little : somewhat or rather • I let it bother me *a bit*. [=*slightly*] • His house is down the street *a bit* further. • There's *a bit* too much sugar in the dessert, which makes it *a bit* too sweet. • I'm feeling *a bit* better today. • It's *a bit* like driving a car. • This one is *a bit* bigger than that one. • At first, I was *a bit* confused. **2 :** a small amount or quantity : a little of something • They don't understand much—but they do understand *a bit*. • They saved money *a bit* at a time. • "How much cake is left?" "Only *a* (very little) *bit*." •

"How old is your daughter?" "She's two and *a bit.*" [=she's slightly older than two] — often + *of* ▪ They understand only *a bit of* [=*a little of*] what is going on. ▪ There's *a bit of* both brown sugar and molasses in these cookies. ▪ The job may cause you *a bit of* trouble. ▪ His mind's already made up. It won't do you *a bit of* good to argue. [=it won't do you any good to argue] **3 a :** a short period of time : a while ▪ Let's wait *a* (little/wee) *bit* longer. ▪ Repairs will begin in *a bit* more than a month. ▪ He left but came back after *a bit.* [=he came back soon] **b :** for a short period of time ▪ Please stay here with me *a bit.*

a bit much *informal* — used to describe a person or thing that is regarded as annoying, excessive, or unfair ▪ My mother thinks he's funny, but I find him *a bit much.* ▪ I find his constant joking *a bit much.* ▪ It was *a bit much* to expect us to wait that long. ▪ The hot weather is getting to be *a bit much.*

a bit of a/an *chiefly Brit* — used to make a statement or description less forceful or definite ▪ I had *a bit of a* shock when I saw him. [=I was somewhat shocked when I saw him] ▪ He's *a bit of a* rascal. [=he's something of a rascal] ▪ We had *a bit of a* laugh about it afterwards.

a bit of all right *Brit, informal* **:** someone or something very pleasing; *especially* **:** a sexually attractive person ▪ His girlfriend's *a bit of all right.*

a little bit see [3]LITTLE

bit by bit **:** by small steps or amounts : GRADUALLY ▪ The situation improved *bit by bit.* [=*little by little*] ▪ I got to know them *bit by bit.*

bits and pieces **1 :** small pieces ▪ There were broken *bits and pieces* of glass all over the floor. ▪ I finished the project ***in bits and pieces***[=a little at a time] during my spare time. **2** *or Brit* **bits and bobs :** things or objects of different kinds ▪ There are just a few *bits and pieces* of furniture in the office. ▪ No one knows exactly what happened. All we have is a few *bits and pieces* [=*odds and ends*] of information so far.

do your bit *chiefly Brit* **:** to do your share of a job or task ▪ We all have to *do our bit* [=*do our part*] to help out.

every bit **:** in every way ▪ The end of the movie was *every bit* [=*just*] as good as the beginning. ▪ This new project seems *every bit* as ambitious as the first one. ▪ He is *every bit* the high-powered businessman. ▪ You are *every bit* as deserving as she is.

not a/one bit *or* ***not (in) the least/smallest/slightest/tiniest bit*** **:** not at all ▪ It *didn't* interest me *a bit.* = It *didn't* interest me *one* (single/little) *bit.* ▪ I'm *not a bit* interested in this movie. = I'm *not the least bit* interested in this movie. ▪ That joke was *not a/one bit* funny. [=was not funny at all] ▪ We *weren't a bit* tired. [=we weren't tired at all]

not a bit of it *Brit, informal* — used to say that something expected or possible did not happen or is not true ▪ Am I tired? *Not a bit of it.* [=I am not tired at all] ▪ I thought she'd be angry, but *not a bit of it.* [=she wasn't angry at all]

quite a bit *or chiefly Brit* ***a good/fair bit*** **:** a fairly large amount : a lot ▪ He knows *quite a bit* [=*quite a lot*] more about it than I do. ▪ The wait was *quite a bit* [=*considerably*] longer than I thought it would be. ▪ She lost the race by *quite a bit.* ▪ We've been seeing *quite a bit* of each other lately. [=we've been spending a lot of time together lately] ▪ She'd already finished *a good bit* of the work before I returned. ▪ There's still *a fair bit* (of the cake) left.

take a bit of doing see DOING

to bits **1 :** to pieces : APART ▪ The ball hit the window and smashed it *to bits.* ▪ The bridge was blown *to bits* by the explosion. ▪ (*chiefly Brit*) The pie was ***falling to bits*** [=*falling apart*] as I tried to serve it. **2** *informal* **:** to a very great degree ▪ She was thrilled *to bits.* [=she was very thrilled]

— compare [2]BIT, [3]BIT

[2]bit *noun, pl* **bits** [*count*]

1 : the part of a tool (such as a drill) that is used for cutting, drilling, etc. — see picture at CARPENTRY

2 : a piece of metal that is put in the mouth of a horse and that is part of the device (called a bridle) that is used to control the horse — see picture at HORSE

champing/chomping at the bit **:** waiting in an impatient way to do something ▪ We've all been *champing at the bit* to get started on the project.

get/take the bit between your teeth **:** to start doing something in a very enthusiastic and determined way ▪ He can be lazy about doing his work, but when he *gets the bit between his teeth* there's no stopping him.

— compare [1]BIT, [3]BIT

[3]bit *noun, pl* **bits** [*count*] *computers* **:** a single unit of computer information that is represented as either 1 or 0 — compare BYTE; see also MEGABIT — compare [1]BIT, [2]BIT

[4]bit *past tense of* [1]BITE

[1]bitch /ˈbɪtʃ/ *noun, pl* **bitch·es**

1 [*count*] **:** a female dog

2 [*count*] *informal + offensive* **:** a very bad or unpleasant woman : a woman you strongly dislike or hate ▪ You stupid *bitch!* ▪ I hate that *bitch.*

3 [*singular*] *informal* **:** something that is very difficult or unpleasant ▪ Divorce is a *bitch.* ▪ That word is a *bitch* to spell. — see also SON OF A BITCH

[2]bitch *verb* **bitches; bitched; bitch·ing** [*no obj*] *informal + disapproving* **:** to complain about something in a repeated and annoying way ▪ He *bitched* constantly about his old car, but he doesn't like his new one either. ▪ Stop *bitching* at me.

bitch·in' /ˈbɪtʃən/ *adj* [*more* ~; *most* ~] *US slang* **:** very good or appealing : COOL ▪ a *bitchin'* car ▪ a *bitchin'* band

bitchy /ˈbɪtʃi/ *adj* **bitch·i·er; -est** [*also more* ~; *most* ~] *informal* **:** very unpleasant, unfriendly, or rude ▪ a *bitchy* salesclerk ▪ a *bitchy* attitude ▪ a *bitchy* comment

— **bitch·i·ly** /ˈbɪtʃəli/ *adv* — **bitch·i·ness** *noun* [*noncount*]

[1]bite /ˈbaɪt/ *verb* **bites; bit** /ˈbɪt/; **bit·ten** /ˈbɪtn̩/; **bit·ing** /ˈbaɪtɪŋ/

1 *of a person or animal* **a :** to press down on or cut into (someone or something) with the teeth [+ *obj*] He *bit* the apple. ▪ The hamster *bit* the child. ▪ She *bit* the cookie in half. ▪ Some people *bite* their nails when they feel nervous. — often + *off* ▪ The child *bit off* a corner of the cracker. [*no obj*] A wild animal may *bite* if it is frightened. — often + *down, into,* or *through* ▪ He accidentally *bit down* on his tongue. ▪ She had just *bitten into* her sandwich when the phone rang. ▪ The dog *bit through* its leash and ran off. ▪ Go talk to him. He ***won't bite.*** [=you should not be afraid to go talk to him] **b** *of an insect or snake* **:** to wound (someone) by pushing a stinger, fang, etc., into the skin [+ *obj*] The patient had been *bitten* by a poisonous snake. ▪ A mosquito *bit* me. [*no obj*] The mosquitoes are *biting* tonight. — sometimes used figuratively ▪ He was ***bitten by the travel bug.*** [=he became very interested in or excited about traveling]

2 [*no obj*] **:** to grab and hold something without slipping — usually + *into* ▪ The anchor *bit into* the ocean floor.

3 [*no obj*] **a** *of a fish* **:** to take a fishhook and bait into the mouth and usually to get caught ▪ Are the fish *biting* today? **b** *somewhat informal* **:** to respond to or accept something that is being offered ✧ Someone gets you to *bite* by offering something you want so that you will do something desired. ▪ We offered them a great deal, but they wouldn't *bite.* [=they wouldn't accept the deal] ▪ "I just heard the juiciest piece of gossip!" "OK, I'll *bite.* [=I'll ask the question you want me to ask] What is it?"

4 [*no obj*] *chiefly Brit* **:** to have a bad effect ▪ With the recession starting to *bite,* many government-funded programs have had to be eliminated.

5 [*no obj*] *US slang, impolite* **:** to be extremely bad ▪ This movie really *bites.* [=*sucks, stinks*] ▪ "They canceled the concert." "Man, ***that bites***!" [=(politely) that's awful]

bite back [*phrasal verb*] *informal* **1 :** to attack or criticize someone who has attacked or criticized you ▪ Weary of her rival's accusations, the candidate *bit back* [=*hit back, fought back*] with an aggressive ad campaign. — often + *at* ▪ She *bit back at* her rival with an aggressive ad campaign. **2** ***bite back (something) or bite (something) back*** **:** to stop yourself from saying (something) ▪ I attempted to smile sweetly while *biting back* angry comments.

bite off more than you can chew *informal* **:** to try to do too much : to take on more responsibility than you can handle ▪ I really *bit off more than I could chew* when I took on this project.

bite someone's head off *informal* **:** to yell at someone or to be very critical of someone especially very suddenly and without a good reason ▪ I asked him one simple question and he *bit my head off.*

bite the bullet *informal* **:** to do something unpleasant or painful because it is necessary even though you would like to avoid it ▪ We need to *bite the bullet* and make some budget cuts.

bite the dust *informal* **:** to die or stop functioning ▪ My old car finally *bit the dust* and I had to buy a new one.

bite the hand that feeds you *informal* **:** to harm someone who has helped or supported you ▪ He was reluctant to criticize his mentor for fear of *biting the hand that fed him.*

bite your tongue *also* ***bite your lip*** *informal* : to not speak : to stop yourself from saying something that you are tempted to say • I thought she was acting foolishly, but I *bit my tongue* [=*held my tongue*] and didn't say anything. — often used as a command • "I hope he gets hurt." "*Bite your tongue*! [=don't say that] That's a terrible thing to say!"

come back to bite you ✧ If something that you do *comes back to bite you*, it causes problems for you at a later time. • Their decision not to invest more money in new equipment may *come back to bite them* eventually.

hair of the dog that bit you see HAIR

once bitten, twice shy ✧ The expression *once bitten, twice shy* means that a person who has failed or been hurt when trying to do something is careful or fearful about doing it again.

– bit·er *noun, pl* **-ers** [*count*]

[2]**bite** *noun, pl* **bites**

1 [*count*] **a** : an act of biting • He ate the candy bar in three quick *bites*. • She gave her lip a gentle *bite*. • The fisherman felt a *bite* at the end of his line and reeled in a fish. **b** : the way the upper and lower teeth come together • My teenage daughter wears a special device at night to correct her *bite*. — see also OVERBITE

2 a [*count*] : the amount of food eaten with a bite • He took several *bites* (out) of the apple. • She didn't touch/eat a *bite*. [=she didn't eat anything] • I can't eat another *bite*. [=I'm completely full; I no longer feel any hunger] **b** [*singular*] *informal* : a small amount of food : a snack or a small informal meal • We grabbed a quick *bite* (to eat) before the show. • They've gone out for a *bite* (to eat).

3 [*count*] : a wound made by biting • Don't scratch that mosquito *bite*. — see also SNAKEBITE

4 [*noncount*] : a bad effect : a negative impact • Many agencies have been feeling the *bite* of budget cuts.

5 [*noncount*] **a** : a sharp feeling or taste • We felt the *bite* of the cold wind on our cheeks. • The soup has a peppery *bite*. **b** : a sharp quality in something written, spoken, or performed ✧ Something that has *bite* usually expresses criticism in a strong and often clever way. • satirical *bite* • the *bite* of his humor

your bark is worse than your bite see [2]BARK

– see also SOUND BITE

bite–size /ˈbaɪtˌsaɪz/ *also* **bite–sized** /ˈbaɪtˌsaɪzd/ *adj* : small enough to be eaten in one bite • *bite-size* pieces

bit·ing /ˈbaɪtɪŋ/ *adj* [*more ~; most ~*]

1 : unpleasantly cold • a *biting* wind • *biting* cold

2 : having a sharply critical and often clever quality • *biting* accusations • *biting* social commentary • *biting* wit

bit·map /ˈbɪtˌmæp/ *noun, pl* **-maps** [*count*] *computers* : an image which is stored as an arrangement of bits that represent each of the small dots that form the image

– bit·mapped /ˈbɪtˌmæpt/ *adj*

bitten *past participle of* [1]BITE

[1]**bit·ter** /ˈbɪtɚ/ *adj* [*more ~; most ~*] ✧ The form *bitterer* is almost never used to mean "more bitter," but the form *bitterest* is commonly used to mean "most bitter."

1 : having a strong and often unpleasant flavor that is the opposite of sweet • Cocoa beans have a *bitter* flavor. • The medicine had a *bitter* aftertaste.

2 : causing painful emotions • *bitter* disappointments • a *bitter* defeat : felt or experienced in a strong and unpleasant way • We were struck by the *bitter* irony of the situation. ✧ A ***bitter pill*** or ***a bitter pill to swallow*** is something that is difficult or painful to accept. • The defeat was a *bitter pill* for the team *to swallow*.

3 : angry and unhappy because of unfair treatment • His betrayal had made her *bitter*. • She was still *bitter* toward her ex-husband. • He's the *bitterest* man I know.

4 : feeling or showing a lot of hatred or anger • *bitter* enemies • a *bitter* argument • a *bitter* reply

5 : very cold • a *bitter* wind • *bitter* cold

to/until the bitter end : until the end of something that may be very bad, unpleasant, etc. • I knew she would stand by me *to the bitter end*. • He vowed that he would keep fighting *until the bitter end*.

– bit·ter·ly *adv* • We were *bitterly* disappointed. • He complained *bitterly* about the crowds. • *bitterly* cold **– bit·ter·ness** *noun* [*noncount*]

[2]**bitter** *noun, pl* **-ters**

1 bit·ters [*plural*] : a bitter alcoholic liquid that is used especially in mixed drinks • The cocktail recipe called for a dash of *bitters*.

2 *Brit* : a type of beer that has a slightly bitter flavor [*noncount*] a pint of *bitter* [*count*] a good selection of *bitters*

bittersweet *adj* [*more ~; most ~*]

1 : having both bitter and sweet flavors • *bittersweet* chocolate

2 : combining sadness and happiness • a *bittersweet* story • *bittersweet* memories

bit·ty /ˈbɪti/ *adj*

1 *chiefly US, informal* : very small • a little *bitty* [=*tiny*] room

2 *Brit, informal* : made up of many small parts that do not seem to fit together well • a *bitty* and uneven book

bi·valve /ˈbaɪˌvælv/ *noun, pl* **-valves** [*count*] *biology* : a sea animal that has a shell with two movable parts connected by a hinge • clams, mussels, oysters, and other *bivalves*

– bivalve *adj* • Clams and oysters are *bivalve* mollusks.

biv·ouac /ˈbɪvəˌwæk/ *noun, pl* **-ouacs** [*count*] : a temporary camp or shelter

– bivouac *verb* **-ouacs; -ouacked; -ouack·ing** [*no obj*] • The climbers *bivouacked* on a ledge of the cliff.

[1]**bi·week·ly** /baɪˈwiːkli/ *adj*

1 : happening every two weeks • The *biweekly* [=(*chiefly Brit*) *fortnightly*] sales meeting is scheduled for every other Tuesday.

2 : happening twice a week : SEMIWEEKLY • She attends *biweekly* classes and studies at the library every Saturday.

– biweekly *adv* • The class meets *biweekly*.

[2]**biweekly** *noun, pl* **-lies** [*count*] : a biweekly publication : a magazine or newspaper that is published every two weeks

biz /ˈbɪz/ *noun* [*singular*] *informal* : BUSINESS • the music *biz* • She left the farm for a career in ***show biz***. [=*show business*]

bi·zarre /bəˈzɑɚ/ *adj* [*more ~; most ~*] : very unusual or strange • His behavior was *bizarre*. • I just heard the most *bizarre* story. • She wore a *bizarre* outfit.

– bi·zarre·ly *adv* **– bi·zarre·ness** *noun* [*noncount*]

blab /ˈblæb/ *verb* **blabs; blabbed; blab·bing** *informal*

1 : to say something that was supposed to be kept secret [+ *obj*] Don't tell Mary. She'll *blab* it all over town. [*no obj*] "How did she find out about the surprise party?" "Tom *blabbed*."

2 [*no obj*] : to talk too much • He kept *blabbing* on and on about politics.

blab·ber·mouth /ˈblæbɚˌmaʊθ/ *noun, pl* **-mouths** [*count*] *informal* : someone who reveals secrets or talks too much

[1]**black** /ˈblæk/ *adj* **black·er; -est**

1 a : having the very dark color of coal or the night sky • *black* ink • a *black* dress **b** : very dark because there is no light • a *black* night

2 *or* ***Black*** : of or relating to a race of people who have dark skin and who come originally from Africa • *black* people • *black* culture ✧ In the U.S., the term *African-American* is often preferred over *black* when referring to Americans of African descent.

3 : very dirty • His hand were *black* with grime.

4 : served without cream or milk • *black* coffee

5 *literary* : evil or wicked • a *black* deed — see also BLACK ART, BLACK MAGIC

6 a : very sad or hopeless : BLEAK • The outlook was *black*. • When they heard the terrible news, they were filled with *black* despair. **b** : very tragic or unhappy • That was a *black* day in our country's history.

7 : marked by anger or hatred • A *black* [=very angry] look darkened his face. • *black* resentment • a *black* mood

8 — used to describe humor that deals with subjects which are usually regarded as very serious or unpleasant • The film is a *black* comedy set in a funeral home. • *black* humor

– black·ly *adv* • a *blackly* funny/comic/humorous movie **– black·ness** *noun* [*noncount*] • the *blackness* of the night

[2]**black** *noun, pl* **blacks**

1 : the dark color of coal or the night sky [*noncount*] The wall was painted in *black*. • the *black* of night [*count*] a mixture of grays and *blacks* — see color picture on page C1

2 [*noncount*] : black clothing • She was dressed in *black*.

3 [*count*] : a person belonging to a race of people who have dark skin : a black person ✧ The singular form *black* in this sense is rarely used and is often considered offensive. It should be avoided. The plural form *blacks* is commonly used to refer to black people as a group or community. • His policies are supported by both *blacks* and whites.

in the black : making a profit • The company is finally *in the black*. [=the company is profitable] — compare *in the red* at [2]RED

[3]**black** *verb* **blacks; blacked; black·ing** [+ *obj*]

B

1 *old-fashioned + literary* : to make (something) black • He *blacked* his boots with polish.
2 *Brit* : to refuse to work for or with (a business, employer, etc.) or to buy (goods, services, etc.) • Labor union members have *blacked* the company.
black out [*phrasal verb*] **1** : to suddenly become unconscious • What's the last thing you remember before you *blacked out*? [=*passed out, fainted*] **2** ***black (something) out or black out (something)*** **a** : to cover (something written) with a black or dark mark so that it cannot be read • Someone had *blacked out* certain sections of the newspaper. **b** : to cause (a place) to become dark • They *blacked out* the stage by turning off all the lights. **c** : to prevent the broadcast of (a televised sports event) — usually used as *(be) blacked out* • Last night's game *was blacked out* in this area, so I couldn't watch it. — see also BLACKOUT

black–and–blue /ˌblækənˈbluː/ *adj* : having dark marks (called bruises) on your skin because of being hit or injured • He beat me *black-and-blue*. [=he beat me until I was covered with bruises] • She had *black-and-blue* marks [=dark bruises] all over her legs.

black–and–white /ˌblækənˈwaɪt/ *adj*
1 : partly black and partly white in color • a *black-and-white* dog
2 : having, showing, or producing pictures that do not have colors except for black, white, and shades of gray • She loves to watch old *black-and-white* movies. • *black-and-white* wedding photos • a *black-and-white* television set • Did you put color or *black-and-white* film in the camera?
3 : involving a simple choice between things that are clearly opposite and especially between good and bad or right and wrong • You are oversimplifying things if you only look at the situation in *black-and-white* terms. • The truth is not always *black-and-white*.

black and white *noun*
in black and white **1** : in written or printed form • I want to see it *in black and white*. **2** : in a way that involves a simple choice between two opposite things (such as good and bad or right and wrong) • She sees everything *in black and white*. **3** : using equipment that produces only black-and-white pictures • a movie filmed *in black and white*.

black art *noun, pl* ~ **arts** [*count*] : a skill or ability that seems mysterious or magical — often used humorously • She's trying to master the *black art* of setting up a computer network.
the black arts : BLACK MAGIC • She practices *the black arts*.

black•ball /ˈblækˌbɑːl/ *verb* **-balls; -balled; -ball•ing** [+ *obj*] : to prevent (someone) from joining a group, club, etc., by voting against him or her — often used as *(be) blackballed* • He *was blackballed* by the fraternity.

black bear *noun, pl* ~ **bears** [*count*] : a North American bear that usually has black fur — see picture at BEAR

black belt *noun, pl* ~ **belts** [*count*] : an expert in a martial art such as karate or tae kwon do • She is a karate *black belt*.; *also* : the rank of such an expert • He has a *black belt* in judo.

black•ber•ry /ˈblækˌberi/ *noun, pl* **-ries** [*count*] : a black or dark purple berry that is sweet and juicy; *also* : the plant that blackberries grow on — see color picture on page C5

black•bird /ˈblækˌbɚd/ *noun, pl* **-birds** [*count*]
1 : any one of several American birds with males that are mostly black
2 : a common European bird with males that have black feathers and an orange bill

black•board /ˈblækˌboɚd/ *noun, pl* **-boards** [*count*] : a smooth, dark surface that is used for writing on with chalk in a classroom — called also (*chiefly US*) *chalkboard*

blackboard

black box *noun, pl* ~ **boxes** [*count*] : a device used in an airplane to record flight information (such as altitude or airspeed) or the voices of the pilots and crew • The *black boxes* were recovered from the crash site and provided useful information about the cause of the crash.

black death *noun*
the black death or the Black Death : a deadly disease (called bubonic plague) that spread through Asia and Europe in the 14th century

black•en /ˈblækən/ *verb* **-ens; -ened; -en•ing**
1 : to make something dark or black or to become dark or black [+ *obj*] Fire had *blackened* the field. [*no obj*] The sky *blackened* as the storm approached.
2 [+ *obj*] : to hurt the reputation of (someone or something) • Their false accusations failed to *blacken* my reputation/name/character. • a presidency *blackened* by scandal

black•ened /ˈblækənd/ *adj, of food* : coated with a mixture of hot spices and fried over very high heat • *blackened* tuna

black eye *noun, pl* ~ **eyes** [*count*] : a dark area of skin around the eye caused by being hit hard • He gave me a *black eye*. [=he punched me in the eye causing a dark bruise] — often used figuratively • The scandal gave the team a *black eye*. [=the scandal caused people to think badly of the team]

black–eyed pea /ˈblækˌaɪd-/ *noun, pl* ~ **peas** [*count*] *chiefly US* : a type of small, light bean that has a dark spot on it — called also (*chiefly Brit*) *black-eyed bean*, (*chiefly US*) *cowpea*

black–eyed Su•san /ˈblækˌaɪdˈsuːzən/ *noun, pl* ~ **-sans** [*count*] : a North American flower with yellow or orange petals and a dark center

black•fly /ˈblækˌflaɪ/ *noun, pl* **-flies** *or* **-fly** [*count*] : a small fly that bites

black gold *noun* [*noncount*] *informal* : PETROLEUM, OIL • After months of drilling, they finally hit/struck *black gold*.

black•guard /ˈblægɚd/ *noun, pl* **-guards** [*count*] *old-fashioned + literary* : a rude or dishonest man : a man who deserves to be hated • a cowardly *blackguard*

black•head /ˈblækˌhɛd/ *noun, pl* **-heads** [*count*] : a small, inflamed area on the skin with a dark spot in the middle

black hole *noun, pl* ~ **holes** [*count*] : an invisible area in outer space with gravity so strong that light cannot get out of it — often used figuratively • The project turned out to be a financial *black hole*. [=something that constantly uses up a large amount of money without producing a good result]

black ice *noun* [*noncount*] : a thin layer of ice on a paved road that is very difficult to see • Drivers should beware of *black ice*.

black•jack /ˈblækˌʤæk/ *noun, pl* **-jacks**
1 [*noncount*] : a card game in which the players try to get a score that is higher than that of the dealer but less than or equal to 21 — often used before another noun • a *blackjack* table [=a table at which blackjack is played in a casino] — called also (*US*) *twenty-one*
2 [*count*] : a small leather-covered metal club used as a hand weapon

black•leg /ˈblækˌlɛg/ *noun, pl* **-legs** [*count*] *Brit, disapproving* : a person who works while other employees are on strike : SCAB

¹black•list /ˈblækˌlɪst/ *noun, pl* **-lists** [*count*] : a list of people, organizations, etc., that are disapproved of or that are to be punished or avoided • He's on the FBI's *blacklist*. • The rental company has created a *blacklist* of bad drivers.

²blacklist *verb* **-lists; -list•ed; -list•ing** [+ *obj*] : to say that a person, company, etc., should be avoided or not allowed to do something : to place (someone or something) on a blacklist — often used as *(be) blacklisted* • In the 1950s, many Hollywood film actors *were blacklisted* for suspected involvement with the Communist Party.

black magic *noun* [*noncount*] : magic that is associated with the devil or with evil spirits : evil magic • He wore a special necklace to protect against *black magic*.

¹black•mail /ˈblækˌmeɪl/ *noun* [*noncount*]
1 : the crime of threatening to tell secret information about someone unless the person being threatened gives you money or does what you want • She was a victim of *blackmail*. — sometimes used figuratively • He used ***emotional blackmail*** to get what he wanted from her. [=he unfairly made her feel guilty or upset to get what he wanted]
2 : something (such as money) that is received through blackmail • The servant extorted *blackmail* from her employer.

²blackmail *verb* **-mails; -mailed; -mail•ing** [+ *obj*] : to use blackmail against (someone) • The old man was being *blackmailed* by his nephew.
— **black•mail•er** *noun, pl* **-ers** [*count*]

Black Ma•ria /-məˈrajə/ *noun, pl* ~ **Ma•rias** [*count*] *Brit, old-fashioned* : PATROL WAGON

black mark *noun, pl* ~ **marks** [*count*] : something that makes something else less perfect or less appealing • The suspension was a *black mark* on her record. • His habitual tardiness was a *black mark* against him.

black market *noun, pl* ~ **-kets** [*count*] : a system through which things are bought and sold illegally • The *black market* in prescription drugs is thriving. • They unloaded the stolen goods on the *black market.*
– black marketeer *noun, pl* ~ **-teers** [*count*]

black·out /ˈblæk,aʊt/ *noun, pl* **-outs** [*count*]
1 : a period when lights are kept off or are hidden from view to guard against enemy airplane attack in a war • the *blackouts* of World War II
2 : a period when lights are off because of an electrical power failure • She keeps flashlights and candles handy in case of a *blackout.* — compare BROWNOUT
3 : a sudden and temporary loss of consciousness, vision, or memory • He told his doctor he had been experiencing *blackouts.*
4 : a situation in which some kinds of information are deliberately kept from the public • The government imposed a news *blackout* during the war.
– see also *black out* at ³BLACK

black pepper *noun* [*noncount*] : a food seasoning that is made by grinding the dried berries of an Indian plant along with their hard, black covers — compare WHITE PEPPER

black power *or* **Black Power** *noun* [*noncount*] : the use of political and economic power by African-Americans especially as part of a social movement to promote equality and racial justice in the 1960s — often used before another noun • the *Black Power* movement of the 1960s

black pudding *noun, pl* ~ **-dings** [*count, noncount*] *Brit* : BLOOD SAUSAGE

black sheep *noun, pl* ~ **sheep** [*count*] : someone who does not fit in with the rest of a group and is often considered to be a troublemaker or an embarrassment • She was the *black sheep* of the family.

black·smith /ˈblæk,smɪθ/ *noun, pl* **-smiths** [*count*] : a person who makes or repairs things made of iron (such as horseshoes)

black spot *noun, pl* ~ **spots** [*count*] *Brit* : a dangerous place or a place where a particular problem or difficulty is very common • The intersection is a notorious (accident) *black spot.*

black–tie *adj* — used to describe a formal social event at which men wear black ties and tuxedos and women wear formal dresses • a *black-tie* dinner — compare WHITE-TIE

black·top /ˈblæk,tɑːp/ *noun* [*noncount*] *chiefly US*
1 : black material that is used for making roads • road crews laying down *blacktop*
2 : a surface that is covered with blacktop • cars lining the *blacktop*

black widow *noun, pl* ~ **-ows** [*count*] : a poisonous American spider ✧ The female black widow often kills and eats the male after they have mated. — called also *black widow spider*

blad·der /ˈblædɚ/ *noun, pl* **-ders** [*count*]
1 : the organ in the body that holds urine after it passes through the kidneys and before it leaves the body — see picture at HUMAN; see also GALLBLADDER
2 : a soft bag (such as the rubber bag inside a football) that is filled with water or air

blade /ˈbleɪd/ *noun, pl* **blades** [*count*]
1 : the flat sharp part of a weapon or tool that is used for cutting • a knife *blade* • the *blade* of an ax — see picture at CARPENTRY; see also RAZOR BLADE, SWITCHBLADE
2 : one of the flat spinning parts that are used on some machines to push air or water • a propeller *blade*
3 : the wide flat part of an oar or paddle
4 : the sharp metal piece on the bottom of an ice skate — see picture at SKATE
5 : a single piece of grass or a similar plant • a *blade* of grass
6 *literary* **a :** SWORD 1 • an opponent worthy of my *blade* **b :** SWORDSMAN • the best *blade* in the land
– see also SHOULDER BLADE

¹**blah** /ˈblɑː/ *adj* [*more* ~; *most* ~] *chiefly US, informal*
1 : not interesting or unusual : dull or boring • The hotel room was totally *blah.* • a *blah* winter day
2 : without energy or enthusiasm • She sat on the couch all day watching television and feeling *blah.*

²**blah** *noun, pl* **blahs** *informal*
1 ***the blahs*** *chiefly US* : a feeling of being bored, tired, etc. • She had a bad case of *the blahs.*
2 [*noncount*] : silly or meaningless talk ✧ *Blah* is usually repeated to suggest that what someone is saying is unimportant or boring. • He got tired of hearing his mother tell him to brush his teeth, clean his room, *blah, blah, blah.*

¹**blame** /ˈbleɪm/ *verb* **blames; blamed; blam·ing** [+ *obj*] : to say or think that a person or thing is responsible for something bad that has happened • Don't *blame* me. You are responsible for your own problems. • Don't *blame* me for your problems. = Don't *blame* your problems on me. • The company *blames* the poor economy for its financial losses. = The company *blames* its financial losses on the poor economy. • My father always *blames* everything on me. • I *blame* the poor harvest on the weather.
blame the messenger see MESSENGER
have yourself to blame ✧ If you ***have only yourself to blame*** or ***have no one to blame but yourself,*** then something is your fault and nobody else's. • She *has only herself to blame* for her money problems.
not blame ✧ If you say that you ***wouldn't/don't/can't blame someone*** or ***can hardly blame someone,*** you think that person has a good reason for doing something. • After the way he treated you, I *wouldn't blame you* [=I would completely understand] if you never spoke to him again. • You *can hardly blame her* for being angry.
to blame : responsible for something bad : deserving to be blamed for something. • Who's *to blame* for these problems? • He says he's not *to blame* for the delays. [=he did not cause the delays] • Poor communication is at least partly *to blame.* [=*at fault*]

²**blame** *noun* [*noncount*] : responsibility for something that fails or is wrong • It's not entirely his fault, but he's not completely free of *blame,* either. • He deserves *blame* [=deserves to be blamed] for his careless behavior. — usually used with *the* • *The blame* lies with me. [=I am at fault; I am to blame] • It's not fair—she gets the credit when things go well, and I get *the blame* when they fail. • Don't try to put/lay/pin *the blame* for your problems on me. • The coach ***took the blame*** for the defeat. [=the coach said he was responsible for the defeat] — see also *the finger of blame* at ¹FINGER

blame·less /ˈbleɪmləs/ *adj* [*more* ~; *most* ~] : not responsible for a problem, bad situation, etc. : free from blame or fault • The school is not *blameless* for the children's poor skills. • An investigation showed that police were *blameless* in the man's death. • a *blameless* [=*innocent*] life
– blame·less·ly *adv*

blame·wor·thy /ˈbleɪm,wɚði/ *adj* [*more* ~; *most* ~] *formal* : deserving blame : bad or wrong • His conduct was judged (to be) *blameworthy.* • Their failure to adequately inform participants of the risks was morally/ethically *blameworthy.*

blanch /ˈblæntʃ, *Brit* ˈblɑːntʃ/ *verb* **blanch·es; blanched; blanch·ing**
1 [+ *obj*] : to put (food items) in boiling water or steam for a short time • *Blanch* the potatoes before slicing them. • a cup of *blanched* almonds
2 [*no obj*] : to suddenly have less color in your face because you are afraid, embarrassed, etc. • She *blanched* and remained silent when the store owner accused her of taking the money. — often used figuratively • Military leaders *blanched* at the thought of being asked to accept further funding cuts. [=they reacted in a way that showed they did not want to accept further cuts]

blanche see CARTE BLANCHE

blanc·mange /bləˈmɑːndʒ/ *noun* [*count, noncount*] *Brit* : a cold, sweet dessert that looks like jelly formed into a shape

bland /ˈblænd/ *adj* **bland·er; -est**
1 : not interesting or exciting • a *bland* [=*dull, boring*] film • *bland* [=*uninteresting*] architecture
2 : lacking strong flavor • The vegetable soup was rather *bland.* • a *bland* diet = a diet of *bland* foods [=foods that are not spicy]
3 : showing no emotion, concern, etc. • a *bland* expression/face • The diplomat's *bland* statement did nothing to calm the situation.
– bland·ly *adv* **– bland·ness** *noun* [*noncount*] • the *blandness* of the film/food

blan·dish·ments /ˈblændɪʃmənts/ *noun* [*plural*] *formal* : nice things that you say or do to convince someone to do something • He found it hard to resist her *blandishments* and almost always ended up doing as she wished.

¹**blank** /ˈblæŋk/ *adj* **blank·er; -est**
1 a : without any writing, marks, or pictures • a *blank* sheet of paper • Leave that line *blank.* [=don't write on that line] • a book with *blank* pages • a *blank* wall — see also BLANK SLATE **b :** having empty spaces to be filled in with information : not yet written in or filled out • a *blank* passport appli-

cation/form • Sign your name on the ***blank line.*** [=a line that marks a place where you should write something] — see also BLANK CHECK

2 : without any recorded sound or information • a *blank* tape/disk/CD

3 : not showing any emotion • She gave me a *blank* look [=did not show any emotion or response] when I asked her where she had been. • a *blank* expression/stare

4 *always used before a noun* **:** stated in a very direct and certain way • I was surprised by her *blank* refusal to loan me the money. • a *blank* [=(more commonly) *flat*] denial — see also POINT-BLANK

go blank **1 :** to suddenly stop showing letters, images, etc. • The screen on my computer *went blank.* **2** ✧ If your ***mind goes blank***, you are unable to remember or think of something. • My *mind went blank* when I heard the question.

– blank·ly *adv* • She stared at him *blankly.* [=without any expression; her face showed no emotion] **– blank·ness** *noun* [*noncount*] • the wall's *blankness* = the *blankness* of the wall

²blank *noun, pl* **blanks**

1 [*count*] **:** an empty space on a document where you put information • The form has a *blank* for your signature. • Please ***fill in the blanks.*** [=put information in the blank spaces] — sometimes used figuratively • At the end of the movie, the narrator goes back and *fills in* (all) *the blanks.* [=the narrator provides missing information about the movie's plot]

2 [*singular*] **:** a period of time that you cannot remember anything about • He says that the first hour after the accident is a complete *blank.* [=he cannot remember anything that happened for an hour after the accident] ✧ If your ***mind is/draws a blank*** or if you ***draw a blank***, you are unable to remember or think of something. • I should know the answer, but my *mind's a blank.* • I *drew a blank* when I tried to remember his name.

3 [*count*] **:** a gun cartridge that is filled with powder but that does not contain a bullet • The actors are shooting/firing *blanks.*

³blank *verb* **blanks; blanked; blank·ing** [+ *obj*]

1 *US* **:** to keep (the opposing team) from scoring • The goalie *blanked* the Falcons for two periods in the hockey game.

2 *Brit slang* **:** to behave in an unfriendly way toward (someone you have been friendly with in the past) **:** to ignore or refuse to talk to (someone) • His former friends *blanked* [=*cut, snubbed*] him in the street after the scandal.

blank out [*phrasal verb*] ***blank out (something) or blank (something) out*** **1 :** to completely hide or cover (something) • They *blanked out* [=*blacked out*] parts of the document before making it public. **2 a :** to cause (something) to be forgotten • The injury *blanked out* parts of his memory. **b :** to completely forget (something) • She has *blanked out* [=*blocked out*] what happened that night.

blank check (*US*) *or Brit* **blank cheque** *noun, pl* ~ **checks** [*count*]

1 : a signed check that does not have the amount of money written on it yet

2 *informal* **:** complete control or freedom — often used in the phrase ***give/hand (someone) a blank check*** • The director had a lot of creative freedom on this project; the film's backers essentially *handed him a blank check.* [=let him direct the film exactly the way he wanted to]

¹blan·ket /ˈblæŋkət/ *noun, pl* **-kets** [*count*]

1 : a covering made of cloth that is used especially on a bed to keep you warm • a wool *blanket* • It's going to get cold tonight so you may need extra *blankets.* • an electric *blanket* [=a blanket warmed by electricity] • a ***beach blanket*** [=a blanket you sit on at the beach] — see picture at BED; see also SECURITY BLANKET

2 a : a mass *of* something that covers an area • a *blanket of* snow/fog/ice • a *blanket of* flowers/grass **b :** a general mood — usually singular • A *blanket* of gloom spread over the crowd when they realized their team would lose.

– see also WET BLANKET

²blanket *verb* **-kets; -ket·ed; -ket·ing** [+ *obj*] **:** to cover (something) • Ice was *blanketing* the bay. • The fields were *blanketed* with flowers. • Confetti *blanketed* the sidewalks.

³blanket *adj, always used before a noun* **:** affecting or applying to everyone or everything • a *blanket* amnesty for all illegal aliens • a *blanket* ban on use of the chemical • The witness was given *blanket* protection from prosecution. [=the witness would not be prosecuted for anything]

blank slate *noun, pl* ~ **slates** [*count*]

1 : someone or something that is still in an original state and that has not yet been changed by people, experiences, etc. • She viewed her students as *blank slates*, just waiting to be filled with knowledge.

2 : something that does not show or express anything • Her expression was a *blank slate.* [=it did not show any emotion]

blank verse *noun* [*noncount*] **:** poetry that is not rhymed but that has a regular rhythm • the *blank verse* of Shakespeare and Milton — compare FREE VERSE

¹blare /ˈbleɚ/ *verb* **blares; blared; blar·ing :** to make a loud and usually unpleasant sound [*no obj*] Rock music *blared* through the store from the loudspeakers. • Sirens *blared* all night. — often + *out* • Annoying commercials *blared out* from the television. [+ *obj*] Loudspeakers *blared* rock music through the store. — often + *out* • The television *blared out* annoying commercials.

²blare *noun* [*singular*] **:** a loud and usually unpleasant noise • the *blare* of electric guitars

blar·ney /ˈblɑɚni/ *noun* [*noncount*] *informal* **:** talk that is not true but that is nice and somewhat funny and that may be used to trick you • She was charmed by his *blarney.* • a tale with more than a hint of *blarney*

bla·sé /blɑˈzeɪ, *Brit* ˈblɑːˌzeɪ/ *adj* [*more* ~; *most* ~] **:** having or showing a lack of excitement or interest in something especially because it is very familiar • a *blasé* traveler • People get *blasé* about their hometown. • a *blasé* reaction

blas·pheme /blæsˈfiːm/ *verb* **-phemes; -phemed; -phem·ing** *formal* **:** to talk about God or religion in a way that does not show respect [*no obj*] He did not curse or *blaspheme.* • people who have *blasphemed* against God [+ *obj*] people who have *blasphemed* God

– blas·phem·er *noun, pl* **-ers** [*count*]

blas·phe·my /ˈblæsfəmi/ *noun, pl* **-mies**

1 [*noncount*] **:** great disrespect shown to God or to something holy • acts of *blasphemy* • commit *blasphemy* — often used figuratively • It's *blasphemy* to insult the local team.

2 [*count*] **:** something said or done that is disrespectful to God or to something holy • She was condemned by the church for uttering *blasphemies.*

– blas·phe·mous /ˈblæsfəməs/ *adj* [*more* ~; *most* ~] • *blasphemous* language • Religious leaders declared that the book was *blasphemous.* **– blas·phe·mous·ly** *adv*

¹blast /ˈblæst, *Brit* ˈblɑːst/ *noun, pl* **blasts** [*count*]

1 a : a mass of air that moves very quickly and forcefully • She opened the door and felt a cold *blast.* • a *blast* of wind **b :** a mass of water, gas, heat, etc., that moves very quickly and forcefully through the air • He was hit by a *blast* of water from the hose. • a *blast* of heat

2 : the loud sound made by a horn or a whistle • The driver gave a long *blast* on his horn. • the *blast* of the factory whistle • a bugle *blast*

3 : a powerful explosion • The bomb *blast* killed eight people. • a shotgun *blast*

4 : a sudden powerful force • She got a *blast* of reality when she returned to school in the fall. • a *blast* of criticism

5 *informal* **:** a very enjoyable and exciting experience • I had a *blast* at your party. • The wedding was a *blast.*

blast from the past *informal* **:** something that reminds you of an earlier time • Hearing that old song again was a real *blast from the past.*

full blast *informal* **:** with as much loudness or power as possible • The engines were running (at) *full blast.* • She turned up the heat *full blast.* • The stereo was ***going full blast.*** [=the stereo was very loud]

²blast *verb* **blasts; blast·ed; blast·ing**

1 a : to destroy, break apart, or remove (something) with an explosive [+ *obj*] Workers were *blasting* rock where the new highway will go. • The rock has been *blasted* away. [*no obj*] Workers were *blasting* (away) at the rock. **b** [+ *obj*] **:** to create (a space or opening) with explosives • The explosion *blasted* a hole in the side of the ship. • *blast* a tunnel

2 [+ *obj*] **:** to strongly criticize (someone or something) especially in public • The mayor was *blasted* by the local press. • The judge *blasted* the lawyers for delaying the trial. • Human rights groups have *blasted* the government for its treatment of political prisoners.

3 : to shoot (something or someone) with a weapon [+ *obj*] He *blasted* his rival with a pistol. • A gunship *blasted* enemy headquarters. • They *blasted* the enemy plane out of the sky. [*no obj*] Machine guns were *blasting.* • The soldiers were *blasting* (away) at the advancing enemy.

4 [+ *obj*] **:** to hit (something or someone) with a mass of wa-

ter, air, etc., that is moving forcefully • She *blasted* us with water from the hose. • They used an air hose to *blast* dust off the machine.
5 [+ *obj*] : to hit or kick (something) with great force • He *blasted* the puck past the goalie. • She *blasted* the ball over the fence for a home run.
6 : to make a loud and usually unpleasant sound : BLARE [*no obj*] Their music was *blasting* all night. • The television was *blasting* in the other room. [+ *obj*] A radio was *blasting* music in the next room.
blast off [*phrasal verb*] *of a missile, rocket, or spacecraft* : to leave the ground and begin flight • The rocket will *blast off* tomorrow morning. — see also BLASTOFF
– blast·er *noun, pl* **-ers** [*count*] • *Blasters* were hired to remove the rock. **– blasting** *noun* [*noncount*] • The actual construction of the road will begin after *blasting* is completed.

³blast *interj, informal* — used to express anger or annoyance • ***Blast it***! I forgot my keys!

blasted *adj, informal*
1 *always used before a noun* : very bad or annoying • I hate this *blasted* [=*damned*] weather.
2 : very drunk • He got totally *blasted* at the party.

blast furnace *noun, pl* **~ -naces** [*count*] : a large structure in which rock containing a metal is melted so that the metal can be separated from the rock

blast·off /ˈblæstˌɑːf, *Brit* ˈblɑːstˌɒf/ *noun, pl* **-offs** [*count*] : the time when a rocket, missile, etc., begins to rise into the air : LAUNCH • ten minutes until *blastoff* — see also *blast off* at ²BLAST

bla·tant /ˈbleɪtn̩t/ *adj* [*more* ~; *most* ~] : very obvious and offensive • a *blatant* lie • He showed a *blatant* disregard for the safety of other drivers. • a *blatant* [=*flagrant*] attempt to bribe the judge • *blatant* racial discrimination
– bla·tant·ly *adv* • She had *blatantly* copied the text from another book. • a *blatantly* false statement

blath·er /ˈblæðɚ/ *noun* [*noncount*] : foolish or dull talk or writing that continues for a long time • listening to a lot of *blather* from politicians about who's to blame for the bad economy
– blather *verb* **-ers; -ered; -er·ing** [*no obj*] • listening to politicians *blather* (on) about the bad economy **– blath·er·er** *noun, pl* **-ers** [*count*]

¹blaze /ˈbleɪz/ *noun, pl* **blaz·es**
1 [*count*] *somewhat formal* : an intense and dangerous fire • The family escaped the *blaze*. • Two people were injured in a restaurant *blaze* [=a fire in a restaurant] late last night.
2 [*singular*] : a very bright area of light or color • a shining *blaze* of light • a *blaze* of color in the autumn leaves
3 [*singular*] : a sudden appearance or expression *of* something : OUTBURST • a *blaze of* fury • a *blaze* of publicity/controversy ✧ A ***blaze of glory*** is a final important event just before someone or something is gone or dies. • The soldier went down in a *blaze of glory*. [=the soldier died doing something important and worthy of great respect]
4 ***blazes*** *informal* + *somewhat old-fashioned* — used to make a statement or question more forceful • It's ***hot as blazes***. [=it's very hot] • ***What in blazes*** are you doing? • (Just) ***Who the blazes*** do you think you are? • ***How the blazes*** am I going to do that?
– compare ³BLAZE

²blaze *verb* **blazes; blazed; blaz·ing** [*no obj*]
1 : to burn very brightly and intensely • A fire *blazed* in the stove.
2 a : to shine very brightly • The sun *blazed* down on us. **b** : to be extremely bright or colorful like fire • The field was *blazing* [=*ablaze*] with flowers. **c** *of the eyes* : to show anger • His ***eyes blazed*** with anger/fury.
3 : to shoot very quickly and constantly • The assassins rushed into the crowd, with their guns *blazing*. — often + *away* • The shooter was still *blazing away* with an automatic rifle.
4 : to move very quickly • A comet *blazed* across the sky. • He *blazed* past the other runners. • The team *blazed* through the tournament. [=they easily defeated every opponent]
– compare ⁴BLAZE

³blaze *noun, pl* **blazes** [*count*]
1 : a stripe of white fur on the center of an animal's face • a horse with a white *blaze*
2 : a mark made on a tree to show a trail • The trail was marked with yellow *blazes*.
– compare ¹BLAZE

⁴blaze *verb* **blazes; blazed; blazing**
blaze a trail **1** : to show a trail with marks on trees • We followed *a trail* that others had *blazed*. **2** : to be the first one to do something and to show others how to do it • The company *blazed a trail* with the first small computers. • She *blazed a trail* for other women in politics. — see also TRAILBLAZER
– compare ²BLAZE

blaz·er /ˈbleɪzɚ/ *noun, pl* **-ers** [*count*] : a jacket that is worn over a shirt and that looks like a suit jacket but is not part of a suit • He wore a blue *blazer* and khaki pants. • a wool skirt and matching *blazer*

blazing *adj* [*more* ~; *most* ~] : very hot, fast, or powerful • the *blazing* heat/sun • She runs with *blazing* speed.
– blaz·ing·ly *adv* • *blazingly* hot/fast

bla·zon /ˈbleɪzn̩/ *verb* **-zons; -zoned; -zon·ing** [+ *obj*] : EMBLAZON — usually used as *(be) blazoned* • T-shirts *blazoned* with the team's name [=T-shirts that have the team's name clearly printed on them]

bldg. *abbr* building

¹bleach /ˈbliːʧ/ *verb* **bleach·es; bleached; bleach·ing** [+ *obj*] : to remove color or dirt and stains from (hair, clothing, etc.) especially through the effect of sunlight or by using chemicals : to make (something) whiter or lighter in color • Those pants will look nicer if you *bleach* them. [=use bleach to make them cleaner and whiter] • bones *bleached* white by/in the sun • She *bleached* her hair blonde.

²bleach *noun* [*noncount*] : a strong chemical that is used to make something clean or white

bleach·ers /ˈbliːʧɚz/ *noun* [*plural*] *US* : a set of benches arranged like steps for people to sit on while they are watching a sporting event or performance • stadium *bleachers* — usually used with *the* • The ball bounced into *the bleachers*. • We cheered from our seats in *the bleachers*.
– bleach·er /ˈbliːʧɚ/ *adj, always used before a noun* • We cheered from our *bleacher* seats.

bleak /ˈbliːk/ *adj* **bleak·er; -est**
1 : not warm, friendly, cheerful, etc. • The weather is *bleak*. [=cold, rainy, dark, etc.] • a *bleak* landscape • a *bleak* [=*dismal*] movie about a prison • a *bleak* [=*dreary*] concrete building with few windows
2 : not hopeful or encouraging • The future looks *bleak*. [=*grim, depressing*] • Their chances of winning the game were *bleak*. [=it was not likely that they would win the game] • a *bleak* economic climate
– bleak·ly *adv* • He stared *bleakly* at the rubble. **– bleak·ness** *noun* [*noncount*] • the *bleakness* of the landscape

bleary /ˈbliri/ *adj* **blear·i·er; -est** : very tired and unable to see clearly • She looked at me with *bleary* eyes.
– blear·i·ly /ˈblirəli/ *adv* • She looked at me *blearily*.

bleary–eyed /ˈbliəˌaɪd/ *adj* [*more* ~; *most* ~] : having eyes that look very tired and watery • *bleary-eyed* travelers

bleat /ˈbliːt/ *verb* **bleats; bleat·ed; bleat·ing**
1 [*no obj*] : to make the sound that a sheep or goat makes • The lamb *bleated* as I approached.
2 *disapproving* : to speak or complain in an annoying way : WHINE [+ *obj*] "But why can't I go?" she *bleated*. [*no obj*] The labor union is always *bleating* about the management.
– bleat *noun, pl* **bleats** [*count*] • the *bleat* of a lamb

bleed /ˈbliːd/ *verb* **bleeds; bled** /ˈblɛd/; **bleed·ing**
1 [*no obj*] : to lose or release blood because of a cut, injury, etc. • She was *bleeding* from the/her face and hands. • Her lip is *bleeding*. • The man almost ***bled to death***. [=almost died because he lost too much blood]
2 [+ *obj*] : to remove blood from (a person) as part of a medical procedure that was done in past times • Doctors used to *bleed* their patients in an effort to cure them.
3 [+ *obj*] : to remove air or liquid from something • We *bled* air from the tank. • You'll need to *bleed* the car's brake lines.
4 [*no obj*] **a** *of dye, ink, paint, etc.* : to spread from one area into another • The shirt's colors might *bleed* [=*run*] if you wash it in hot water. **b** : to gradually spread into or become something else — usually + *into* • Her professional life had begun to *bleed* [=*seep*] *into* her personal life. • Reality *bleeds* [=*blends*] *into* fantasy as the story goes along.
5 [+ *obj*] *informal* : to take a lot of money from (someone) over a period of time • He complained that his ex-wife was *bleeding* him of all his money. • Many businesses complain that the new taxes are ***bleeding them dry***. [=are taking all their money] • The country has been ***bled white*** by a greedy dictator. [=all the country's money and resources have been used up by a greedy dictator]

B

6 [+ *obj*] *informal* : to lose (money) continually • The company was *bleeding* a million dollars a day.

your heart bleeds for see HEART

bleed·er /ˈbli:də/ *noun, pl* **-ers** [*count*] *Brit, informal*
1 *offensive* : a person (especially a man) who is very unpleasant • Don't let those *bleeders* grind you down.
2 *sometimes offensive* : a man who you think is lucky, unlucky, etc. • "I've won the lottery." "You lucky *bleeder*!"

¹bleed·ing /ˈbli:dɪŋ/ *noun* [*noncount*] : the process of losing blood • She pressed on the wound to stop the *bleeding*. • The procedure may cause ***internal bleeding*** [=loss of blood inside the body]

²bleeding *adj, always used before a noun, Brit, informal + offensive* — used to make an angry or critical statement more forceful • Our neighbor is a *bleeding* idiot. [=our neighbor is very stupid]

bleeding–heart *adj, always used before a noun, disapproving* : feeling too much sympathy for people in society who you think do not deserve sympathy or help • The conservative press calls him a ***bleeding-heart liberal***.

¹bleep /ˈbli:p/ *noun, pl* **bleeps** [*count*]
1 : a short, high sound made by an electronic device : BEEP • the *bleep* [=*beep*] of an answering machine
2 *US, informal* — used in place of an offensive word • What the *bleep* was that about?!

²bleep *verb* **bleeps; bleeped; bleep·ing**
1 [+ *obj*] *US* : to replace (offensive words on radio or television) with an electronic sound • They *bleeped* half the words in the interview! • The radio station *bleeped* (out) the swearwords.
2 [*no obj*] : to make a short, high sound : BEEP • The monitor *bleeped*.
3 [+ *obj*] *Brit* : BEEP 2 • The doctor is not in the office today, but I can *bleep* her for you.

bleep·er /ˈbli:pə/ *noun, pl* **-ers** [*count*] *Brit* : PAGER

¹blem·ish /ˈblɛmɪʃ/ *noun, pl* **-ish·es** [*count*]
1 : a mark that makes something imperfect or less beautiful : an unwanted mark on the surface of something • The cream is supposed to prevent *blemishes* on the skin. • The table had a few scratches and minor *blemishes*.
2 : a fact or event that causes people to respect someone or something less • The book fails to mention any of the organization's many *blemishes*. • The incident was/left a ***blemish on*** his record/reputation.

²blemish *verb* **-ishes; -ished; -ish·ing** [+ *obj*] : to make (something) imperfect or less beautiful : to hurt or damage the good condition of (something) • A series of burn marks *blemish* the table's surface. • The incident *blemished* his reputation. — usually used as *(be) blemished* • Her face *was* wrinkled and *blemished*. • His reputation *was blemished* [=*marred*] by the incident.

¹blend /ˈblɛnd/ *verb* **blends; blend·ed; blend·ing**
1 [+ *obj*] : to mix (things) thoroughly and usually with good results • *Blend* the fruit, yogurt, and milk (together). • *blend* caramel with chocolate • The music *blends* traditional and modern melodies. • She *blends* psychology and crime in her new novel.
2 [*no obj*] : to exist together as a combination • Psychology and crime *blend* (together) in her new novel. • The flavor of the sauce ***blends well*** with the fruit. [=the sauce and fruit taste good together]
blend in [*phrasal verb*] **1** : to look like what is around you • The fish settles on the sandy ocean bottom where it *blends in* perfectly. **2** : to look like you belong with a particular group • She tried to *blend in* by dressing like the other girls. — often + *with* • I've always found it difficult to *blend in with* my peers. **3** ***blend (something) in or blend in (something)*** : to add (something) to a mixture or substance and mix it thoroughly • Mix the first three ingredients together, then *blend in* the cream. • *Blend* the white paint *in* last.
blend into [*phrasal verb*] ***blend into (something)*** **1** : to gradually become the same as or part of (something) • One color *blends into* another. • where the city *blends into* the suburbs **2** : to look like (what is around you) • The animal's dark fur enables it to *blend into* its surroundings. **3** : to look like you belong in (something) • He tried to *blend into* the crowd. • A good journalist can easily *blend into* a community.
— **blending** *noun* [*singular*] • a *blending* of traditional French songs and punk rock • a seamless *blending*

²blend *noun, pl* **blends** [*count*] : something produced by mixing or combining different things • wool and cotton *blends* [=fabrics that are made of wool and cotton woven together] • a *blend* of cream and eggs • a *blend* of traditional and modern melodies

blended *adj*
1 : made from two or more kinds of a particular substance • *blended* tobacco/coffee • *blended* whiskies • *blended* fabrics
2 : made by mixing substances together • *blended* fruit drinks

blended family *noun, pl* **~ -lies** [*count*] : a family that includes children from a previous marriage of the wife, husband, or both parents

blend·er /ˈblɛndə/ *noun, pl* **-ers** [*count*] : an electric kitchen machine that is used to cut food and ice into very small pieces and to make soft foods (such as fruits) into a liquid — called also (*Brit*) *liquidizer*; see picture at KITCHEN

bless /ˈblɛs/ *verb* **bless·es; blessed** /ˈblɛst/; **bless·ing** [+ *obj*]
1 : to make (something or someone) holy by saying a special prayer • The priest *blessed* their marriage at the wedding. • The water for the baptism has been *blessed*.
2 : to ask God to care for and protect (someone or something) • The priest *blessed* the baby I held in my arms.
3 a — used in the phrase ***God bless*** to express good wishes or appreciation for someone or something • May *God bless* this country. • *God bless* modern medicine. [=thank God for modern medicine] — see also GOD BLESS YOU (below) **b** — used in phrases like ***bless his/her heart*** and ***bless him/her*** to express affection, appreciation, or understanding • She tries so hard, *bless her heart*. • My aunt Clare, *bless her*, watched the kids while we went out. • Our cousin, *bless his heart*, is just so disorganized. — see also BLESS YOU (below)
4 : to provide (a person, place, etc.) *with* something good or desirable • Nature has *blessed* the area *with* good soil and a sunny climate. — usually used as *(be) blessed* • I have *been blessed with* good health and a wonderful wife and children. • He *was blessed* [=*endowed*] *with* great speed as a runner.
5 : to give approval to (something) • The committee has not yet *blessed* the plan.
bless my soul *old-fashioned* — used in speech to express surprise • You decided to come see us after all. Well, *bless my soul*!
bless you or God bless you **1** — used in speech to express thanks or good wishes • "I'll be happy to help in any way I can." "Oh, *bless you*! That's very kind of you." **2** — said to someone who has just sneezed

bless·ed /ˈblɛsəd/ *adj* [*more ~; most ~*]
1 : having a sacred nature : connected with God : HOLY • the *blessed* Trinity
2 *always used before a noun* : very welcome, pleasant, or appreciated • The rain brought *blessed* relief from the heat. • He spent his weekend in *blessed* freedom.
3 *informal + somewhat old-fashioned* — used to make a statement more forceful • You don't know a *blessed* thing.
— **bless·ed·ly** *adv* • The park was *blessedly* free of crowds.
— **bless·ed·ness** *noun* [*noncount*] • eternal *blessedness* in heaven

blessing *noun, pl* **-ings**
1 [*noncount*] **a** : approval that allows or helps you to do something • He gave his *blessing* to the plan. [=he approved the plan] • Presumably he was acting with the government's *blessing*. • They got married without their parents' *blessing*. **b** : help and approval from God • We asked the Lord's *blessing* on us and on our project.
2 [*count*] : something that helps you or brings happiness — usually singular • My daughter is a *blessing* to me in my old age. • E-mail can be a *blessing* if you travel a lot in business. • It's a *blessing* that you came when you did. ✧ Something that is ***a blessing in disguise*** seems to be a bad thing at first but actually is a good thing. • Not getting the job turned out to be *a blessing in disguise*, since she got a much better job soon afterward. ✧ If something is ***a blessing and a curse*** or ***a mixed blessing*** there are both good and bad things about it. • Being famous can be *a blessing and a curse*. • The promotion was really a *mixed blessing* because I'm now so busy that I don't have time to spend the extra income.
3 [*count*] : a short prayer • He said a *blessing* before the meal.
4 [*noncount*] : the act of asking God to care for and protect someone or something • The priest performed the *blessing* of the fishing boats.
count your blessings : to make a special effort to appreciate the good things in your life • I try to remember to *count my blessings* every day.

blether *noun [noncount] Brit* : BLATHER

bleu see CORDON BLEU

blew *past tense of* [1]BLOW

[1]**blight** /ˈblaɪt/ *noun, pl* **blights**
1 [*count*] : a disease that makes plants dry up and die • potato *blight*
2 **a** [*count*] : something that causes harm or damage like a disease — usually singular • the *blight* of poverty in the city — usually + *on* • The abandoned factory is a *blight on* the neighborhood. **b** [*noncount*] : a damaged condition • the city's spreading urban *blight* • environmental *blight*

[2]**blight** *verb* **blights; blight·ed; blight·ing** [+ *obj*]
1 : to damage (plants) with a disease — usually used as *(be) blighted* • The apple trees *were blighted* by fungus.
2 : to damage (a thing or place) • Builders *blighted* the land with malls and parking lots.
– **blighted** *adj* • *blighted* areas of the city • a *blighted* industrial landscape

blight·er /ˈblaɪtɚ/ *noun, pl* **-ers** [*count*] *Brit, informal*
1 : a person (especially a man) who is unpleasant • Just tell the *blighter* to leave you alone.
2 : a man who you think is lucky, unlucky, etc. • I feel sorry for the little *blighter*.

Blighty /ˈblaɪti/ *noun* [*noncount*] *Brit slang* — used as a name for England or Britain • She's glad to be back in old *Blighty*.

bli·mey /ˈblaɪmi/ *interj, Brit, informal* — used to express surprise or amazement • "I've won the lottery." "*Blimey!* I can't believe it!"

blimp /ˈblɪmp/ *noun, pl* **blimps** [*count*] : a large aircraft without wings that floats because it is filled with gas — compare HOT-AIR BALLOON, ZEPPELIN

[1]**blind** /ˈblaɪnd/ *adj* **blind·er; -est**
1 : unable to see • a *blind* person • He was born *blind*. • She is *blind* in one eye. [=she can see with one of her eyes but not with the other] • She ***went blind*** [=she became unable to see] at age 67. — see also COLOR-BLIND
2 : unable to notice or judge something — usually + *to* • He is *blind to* his son's faults. • Each party was *blind to* the other's concerns.
3 **a** *usually disapproving* : accepting the actions or decisions of someone or something without any questions or criticism • *blind* loyalty/allegiance/obedience • I'm not sure *blind* faith [=unquestioning belief] in our leaders is wise. **b** — used to describe strong emotions that make someone unable to think clearly or to act reasonably • a *blind* fury/rage
4 : done in a way that prevents participants, judges, etc., from seeing or knowing certain things that might influence them • a *blind* taste test [=a test in which people taste something without knowing what it is, who made it, etc.] • a *blind* clinical trial for the new medicine • *blind* auditions — see also BLIND DATE, DOUBLE-BLIND
5 : difficult for a driver to see • a *blind* driveway/drive • a *blind* curve — see also BLIND SPOT
(as) blind as a bat *informal* : unable to see well at all : having very poor vision • Without glasses I'm *blind as a bat*.
love is blind see [1]LOVE
not a blind bit *Brit, informal* : not even a very small amount : not the slightest bit • I told them what I wanted, but they *didn't* take *a blind bit* of notice. [=they didn't notice at all; they did not listen to me] • It does *not* make *a blind bit* of difference what you do. [=it does not matter at all what you do]
the blind : blind people : people who are not able to see • The agency provides assistance to *the blind*. ✧ The expression ***the blind leading the blind*** is used informally to describe a situation in which someone who is not sure about how to do something is helping another person who also is not sure about how to do it. • I'll try to help, but it's *the blind leading the blind* because I've never done this before either.
turn a blind eye : to ignore a problem instead of dealing with it • Corruption in the police force is rampant, but authorities are *turning a blind eye*. — often + *to* • Colleges can't afford to *turn a blind eye to* alcohol abuse.
– **blind·ness** *noun* [*noncount*] • a leading cause of *blindness*

[2]**blind** *verb* **blinds; blind·ed; blind·ing** [+ *obj*]
1 : to cause (someone) to be unable to see : to make (someone) blind • The accident *blinded* me in one eye. = The accident left me *blinded* in one eye. • She was *blinded* as a child in a terrible fire.
2 : to cause (someone) to be unable to see for a short time • I was *blinded* by the sun as I came around the corner.
3 : to cause (someone) to be unable to think clearly or to act reasonably • He was *blinded* by love. — often + *to* • Greed *blinds* them *to* everything except money. [=greed causes them to think and care about only money]

[3]**blind** *noun, pl* **blinds**
1 [*count*] : something that is used to cover a window from the inside of a room; *especially* : a roll of cloth or plastic that is hung at the top of a window and pulled down over the window — usually plural • Raise/lower/open/close the *blinds*. — see picture at WINDOW; see also VENETIAN BLIND
2 [*count*] *US* : a place where hunters hide from animals while they are hunting • a duck *blind* [=a place to hide when hunting ducks] — called also (*chiefly Brit*) *hide*
3 [*singular*] : something that is used to trick people or to prevent people from noticing a particular thing • Some say the investigation is a *blind* to keep the public's attention off the governor.
draw the blinds on see [1]DRAW

[4]**blind** *adv*
1 : without seeing outside of an airplane : using only a plane's instruments • They had to ***fly blind*** through heavy smoke.
2 *informal* : to the degree that you are unable to think clearly or to act reasonably • He was ***blind drunk***.
rob someone blind see ROB

blind alley *noun, pl* ~ **-leys** [*count*] : a narrow path between two buildings that can only be entered at one end — often used figuratively • Police had been down several *blind alleys* [=they had tried several methods that did not produce useful results] in the murder investigation before they found the evidence they needed.

blind date *noun, pl* ~ **dates** [*count*] : an occasion for two people who do not know each other to meet and decide if they may want to have a romantic relationship • She went out on a *blind date* with her friend's cousin.

blind·er /ˈblaɪndɚ/ *noun, pl* **-ers**
1 ***blinders*** [*plural*] *chiefly US* : leather pieces that are placed on either side of a horse's head next to its eyes in order to keep the horse from seeing what is beside it • a horse wearing *blinders* — often used figuratively • Many parents ***put on blinders*** [=choose not to think about what might be happening] when their teenagers start staying out late. — called also (*chiefly Brit*) *blinkers*
2 [*singular*] *Brit, informal* : a very exciting or impressive performance or action in a game such as cricket or soccer • Their team ***played a blinder*** to beat us in the closing seconds of the match.

[1]**blind·fold** /ˈblaɪndˌfoʊld/ *verb* **-folds; -fold·ed; -fold·ing** [+ *obj*] : to cover the eyes of (a person) with a piece of cloth • The kidnappers tied him up and *blindfolded* him.

[2]**blindfold** *noun, pl* **-folds** [*count*] : a piece of cloth that covers the eyes

blindfolded *also* **blindfold** *adv* : with the eyes covered by a piece of cloth • He was led *blindfolded* into the woods. ✧ If you ***can do something blindfolded***, you can do it very well or easily because you have done it many times before. • She could find that house *blindfolded*.
– **blindfolded** *adj* • a *blindfolded* prisoner

blinding *adj* [*more* ~; *most* ~]
1 : very bright or strong • a *blinding* color • a *blinding* headache [=a very painful headache]; *especially* : so bright or strong that you cannot see • the *blinding* light of the sun in her eyes • a *blinding* snowstorm
2 : very fast • His *blinding* speed makes him a great player.
– **blind·ing·ly** /ˈblaɪndɪŋli/ *adv* • *blindingly* bright • *blindingly* fast

blind·ly /ˈblaɪndli/ *adv*
1 : without seeing • She stumbled *blindly* in the dark.
2 : without noticing or seeming to see anything • The frightened children ran *blindly* from the house. • He stared *blindly* [=*blankly*] at the wall.
3 : without thinking or questioning • They *blindly* followed their leaders. • They were taught not to *blindly* obey, but to consider carefully what they were being told to do.

blind·man's bluff /ˈblaɪndˈmænz-/ *noun* [*noncount*] : a game for children in which a player whose eyes are covered with a piece of cloth tries to catch and identify the other players — called also *blindman's buff*

blind·side /ˈblaɪndˌsaɪd/ *verb* **-sides; -sid·ed; -sid·ing** [+ *obj*] *US*
1 : to hit (someone who is facing in another direction) sud-

denly and very hard • The quarterback was *blindsided* just as he was about to throw a pass.

2 : to surprise or shock (someone) in a very unpleasant way • We were all *blindsided* by the news of her sudden death.

B

blind side *noun, pl* **~ sides** [*count*] **:** the side that is not the side you are facing • He was hit on his *blind side*.

blind spot *noun, pl* **~ spots** [*count*]

1 : an area around a car, truck, etc., that the driver cannot see • When driving on the highway, you need to make sure no one is in your *blind spot* before changing lanes.

2 : a tendency to ignore something especially because it is difficult or unpleasant • She has a *blind spot* concerning her son's behavior.

3 : a small area at the back of the eye that is not sensitive to light

¹blink /ˈblɪŋk/ *verb* **blinks; blinked; blink·ing**

1 : to close and then open your eyes very quickly [*no obj*] She *blinked* when the light flashed. • Her eyes *blinked* when the light flashed. [+ *obj*] She *blinked* her eyes when the light flashed. — compare WINK

2 [*no obj*] **:** to shine with a light that goes on and off • The red light was *blinking*. [=*flashing*]

3 [*no obj*] **:** to show that you are surprised or upset • Laura ***didn't (even) blink*** [=did not seem surprised or upset at all] when I told her that the car was gone. • She *didn't (even) blink* at the news.

4 [*no obj*] **:** to show weakness in an argument or disagreement **:** to show that you are willing to agree to or accept what someone else wants or says • When threatened, the government *blinked* [=*gave in*] and agreed to move the missiles. • Both sides in the dispute are determined not to *blink* first.

before you can blink *informal* **:** very quickly • This may hurt a little, but it'll be over *before you can blink*.

blink back tears *or* ***blink away tears*** **:** to prevent yourself from crying or to make your tears go away by blinking • He *blinked back* (his) *tears* as he told us the bad news.

²blink *noun, pl* **blinks** [*count*] **:** the act of closing and then opening your eyes very quickly **:** the act of blinking

in the blink of an eye **:** very quickly • He became famous, and then, *in the blink of an eye*, he was forgotten. • She reappeared *in the blink of an eye*.

on the blink *informal* **:** not working properly • The TV is *on the blink*.

blink·er /ˈblɪŋkɚ/ *noun, pl* **-ers**

1 [*count*] *US, informal* **:** a light on a car, truck, etc., that goes off and on and that is used as a warning or as a signal that the vehicle will be turning • Use your *blinker* [=*indicator*, (*US*) *turn signal*] when you turn.

2 ***blinkers*** [*plural*] *chiefly Brit* **:** leather pieces that are placed on either side of a horse's head next to its eyes **:** BLINDERS

blinking *adj*

1 : shining with a light that goes on and off • a *blinking* yellow light

2 *always used before a noun, Brit, informal* — used to make an angry or critical statement more forceful • Turn down that *blinking* music! It's driving me crazy!

blip /ˈblɪp/ *noun, pl* **blips** [*count*]

1 : a bright dot on the screen of an electronic device (such as a radar) • The approaching ship appeared as a *blip* on the screen. — often used figuratively • At that time, the organization was only a *blip* on the political radar screen. • As a football player he wasn't even a *blip* on the radar screen. [=he was not important; no one had noticed that he was or could become a good player]

2 : a very short high sound made by an electronic device • the *blips*, buzzes, and bleeps of a video game

3 : something that is small or unimportant or that does not last a long time • The company's financial problems were just a temporary *blip*.

bliss /ˈblɪs/ *noun* [*noncount*] **:** complete happiness • Their religion promises eternal *bliss* [=*joy*] in heaven. • marital/wedded/domestic *bliss* [=complete happiness in marriage] • Relaxing on the porch of our private villa was sheer *bliss*.

ignorance is bliss see IGNORANCE

bliss·ful /ˈblɪsfəl/ *adj* [*more* ~; *most* ~] **:** extremely or completely happy **:** full of or causing bliss • At first, their time together was *blissful*. • He sat there in a *blissful* state of comfort. • our *blissful* beach vacation • a *blissful* setting for a wedding • existing in ***blissful ignorance*** [=a state of not knowing and not wanting to know about unhappy things or possible problems]

— bliss·ful·ly *adv* • They were *blissfully* happy. • We were *blissfully* unaware/ignorant of the dangers ahead.

blis·ter /ˈblɪstɚ/ *noun, pl* **-ters** [*count*]

1 : a raised area on the skin that contains clear liquid and that is caused by injury to the skin • She developed a *blister* on her heel where her shoe rubbed against it.

2 : a raised area on a surface (such as a painted wall) that is filled with air

— blister *verb* **-ters; -tered; -ter·ing** [*no obj*] My feet started to *blister*. [=to form blisters] • The paint cracked and *blistered*. [+ *obj*] Her skin was *blistered* by the hot sun.

blis·ter·ing /ˈblɪstərɪŋ/ *adj* [*more* ~; *most* ~] **:** very harsh or powerful • *blistering* heat/sun • He received a *blistering* [=*scathing*] letter from his ex-wife. • a hockey player with a *blistering* slap shot

— blistering *adv* • a *blistering* hot day **— blis·ter·ing·ly** *adv* • a *blisteringly* hot day

blithe /ˈblaɪθ, ˈblaɪð/ *adj* **blith·er; -est**

1 : showing a lack of proper thought or care **:** not caring or worrying • He showed *blithe* disregard for the rights of others. • He was *blithe* about the risks to his health.

2 *literary* **:** happy and without worry **:** CAREFREE • a *blithe* spirit • *blithe* enjoyment

— blithe·ly *adv* • They *blithely* assumed there would be someone there to help them.

blith·er·ing /ˈblɪðərɪŋ/ *adj, informal* **:** very foolish or stupid • pages and pages of *blithering* nonsense • a ***blithering idiot***

blitz /ˈblɪts/ *noun, pl* **blitz·es** [*count*]

1 : a military attack in which many bombs are dropped from airplanes

2 a : a fast and powerful effort • The company is planning an advertising/marketing *blitz* for the new product. • a *blitz* of publicity • The movie flopped, despite the ***media blitz*** that accompanied its release. [=the movie failed even though a lot of information about it was on television, radio, in magazines, etc., all at once] **b** *Brit* **:** a sudden attack or effort to stop or end something — usually singular • a *blitz* on tax evaders • One of these days I'll ***have a blitz on*** the house. [=I will thoroughly clean the house]

3 *American football* **:** a play in which many defensive players rush toward the quarterback

— blitz *verb* **blitzes; blitzed; blitz·ing** [+ *obj*] The company has *blitzed* the country with advertising. • The linebackers *blitzed* the quarterback. [*no obj*] A linebacker *blitzed* from the right side.

blitzed /ˈblɪtst/ *adj, US slang* **:** very drunk • She was/got totally *blitzed* that night.

blitz·krieg /ˈblɪtsˌkriːg/ *noun, pl* **-kriegs** [*count*]

1 : a sudden and overwhelming military attack

2 : a fast and powerful effort **:** BLITZ • a promotional *blitzkrieg*

bliz·zard /ˈblɪzəd/ *noun, pl* **-zards** [*count*]

1 : a severe snowstorm that goes on for a long time • We were snowed in by a raging/fierce *blizzard*.

2 : a large amount of something that comes suddenly — usually singular • a *blizzard of* mail • The audience confronted him with a *blizzard of* questions.

bloat *noun* [*noncount*] *chiefly US* **:** too much growth • budget/bureaucratic *bloat* • The company became an example of corporate *bloat*. [=it became too big]

bloat·ed /ˈbloʊtəd/ *adj* [*more* ~; *most* ~] **:** very swollen **:** too full of liquid, gas, food, etc. • a *bloated* body • I felt *bloated* from eating too much. — often used figuratively • The government is *bloated* [=too large] and inefficient. • a *bloated* state budget • He has a *bloated* ego.

— bloat·ed·ness *noun* [*noncount*]

blob /ˈblɑːb/ *noun, pl* **blobs** [*count*] *somewhat informal*

1 : a usually small amount of something thick and wet • a *blob* of paint

2 : something that does not have a regular shape • That blue *blob* in the corner of the map is the lake we're headed for.

bloc /ˈblɑːk/ *noun, pl* **blocs** [*count*] **:** a group of people or countries that are connected by a treaty or agreement or by common goals • the communist *bloc* • a voting *bloc* in the senate

¹block /ˈblɑːk/ *noun, pl* **blocks**

1 [*count*] **:** a solid piece of material (such as rock or wood) that has flat sides and is usually square or rectangular in shape • a *block* of ice/cheese • a wall built out of concrete/cinder *blocks* • (*US*) kids playing with wooden *blocks* [=(*Brit*) *bricks*] — see also BUILDING BLOCK, CHOPPING BLOCK, STARTING BLOCK

2 [*count*] **a :** an area of land surrounded by four streets in a

city ▪ We took a walk around the *block*. ▪ She lived on our *block*. **b** *US* **:** the length of one city block ▪ The store is three *blocks* down on the right. ▪ Our hotel is a *block* from the ocean.
3 [*count*] **:** a large building divided into separate units (such as apartments or shops) ▪ an apartment *block* ✧ This sense of *block* is more common in British English than in U.S. English. ▪ a high-rise office *block* — see also BLOCK OF FLATS, CELLBLOCK, TOWER BLOCK
4 [*singular*] **:** something that stops the progress or achievement of something ▪ They put a *block* on future development of the area.
5 [*count*] *sports* **:** an action or movement that stops or slows down an opponent ▪ a shoulder *block* ▪ (American football) The lineman ***threw a block***. [=the lineman hit an opposing player to prevent him from making a tackle]
6 [*singular*] **:** something that stops a person from thinking about certain things ▪ a mental/emotional *block* — see also STUMBLING BLOCK, WRITER'S BLOCK
7 [*count*] **a :** a number of similar things that form a group ▪ We reserved a *block* of seats. ▪ She bought a large *block* of stock/shares in the company. **b :** an amount or section of something ▪ They played a half-hour *block* of music. ▪ We set aside a big *block* of time for the project. ▪ a *block* of text
chip off the old block see [1]CHIP
knock someone's block off see [1]KNOCK
new kid on the block see [1]KID
on the block *or* ***on the auction block*** **:** for sale at an auction ▪ Some valuable paintings went *on the block* today.; *broadly* **:** for sale ▪ Their business is now *on the block*.

[2]**block** *verb* **blocks; blocked; block•ing**
1 [+ *obj*] **a :** to be placed in front of (something, such as a road or path) so that people or things cannot pass through ▪ There's an accident *blocking* the road. ▪ The entrance was *blocked* by a gate. ▪ Blood clots have completely/partially *blocked* one of his arteries. — sometimes + *up* ▪ My nose is all *blocked* [=*stuffed*] *up*. ▪ Call a plumber. The sink pipe is *blocked* [=*clogged*] *up*. **b :** to place something in front of (something, such as a road) so that people or things cannot go into the area ▪ The protesters *blocked* the road with parked vehicles. — often + *off* ▪ Main Street has been *blocked off* [=*barricaded*] for the parade. ▪ The police *blocked off* the crime scene with yellow tape.
2 [+ *obj*] **a :** to stop (someone or something) from moving through or going by ▪ The ambulance was *blocked* by cars in the road. ▪ An accident was *blocking* traffic. **b :** to stop (something) from getting through to someone or something ▪ Could you move to the left, please. You're *blocking* my light. ▪ a shield that *blocks* the wind **c :** to be in front of (something) so that it cannot be seen ▪ The new building *blocks* [=*obstructs*] our view of the river.
3 [+ *obj*] **a :** to not allow (something, such as progress or an action) to occur ▪ Several senators are trying to *block* the passage of the bill. ▪ His vote *blocked* the treaty. ▪ The new law *blocks* the sale of liquor on Sundays. ▪ They made every effort to *block* her reelection. **b :** to be in the way of (something) ▪ *blocking* access to free health care
4 *sports* **:** to stop the movement of (an opponent, a shot, etc.). [+ *obj*] We practiced *blocking* our opponents. ▪ She *blocked* the shot! [*no obj*] He's getting better at *blocking*.
block in [*phrasal verb*] ***block in (someone or something)*** *or* ***block (someone or something) in*** **:** to put something in front of (someone or something) so that person or thing cannot leave ▪ My car is *blocked in*. = Somebody has *blocked my car in*. [=somebody has parked in a way that makes it impossible for me to move my car]
block out [*phrasal verb*] ***block out (something)*** *or* ***block (something) out*** **1 :** to hide or cover something so that it cannot be seen, felt, or heard ▪ Clouds *blocked out* the sun. ▪ We put on music to *block out* the sound of the traffic. **2 :** to force yourself not to think about (something) ▪ He tried to *block out* [=*forget*] the event. **:** to ignore (something) ▪ *blocking out* distractions
– block•er *noun, pl* **-ers** [*count*] ▪ He's one of the league's best *blockers*.

[1]**block•ade** /blɑˈkeɪd/ *noun, pl* **-ades** [*count*] **:** an act of war in which one country uses ships to stop people or supplies from entering or leaving another country ▪ a naval *blockade*

[2]**blockade** *verb* **-ades; -ad•ed; -ad•ing** [+ *obj*] **:** to place a blockade on (a port or country) **:** to stop people or supplies from entering or leaving (a port or country) especially during a war ▪ They *blockaded* the country's ports.

block•age /ˈblɑːkɪʤ/ *noun, pl* **-ag•es**
1 [*count*] **:** something that stops something (such as blood) from moving through something (such as a blood vessel) ▪ He had surgery to open up *blockages* in his arteries.
2 [*noncount*] **:** the state of being blocked ▪ trying to prevent *blockage* of the artery

block and tackle *noun* [*singular*] **:** a simple machine that is used to help lift heavy objects and that consists of rope and boxes containing pulleys

block•bust•er /ˈblɑːkˌbʌstɚ/ *noun, pl* **-ers** [*count*] **:** something that is very large, expensive, or successful ▪ a 900-page *blockbuster* of a novel ▪ The actor starred in a *blockbuster* [=a very successful movie] last year. — often used before another noun ▪ a *blockbuster* movie ▪ a *blockbuster* product

block•head /ˈblɑːkˌhɛd/ *noun, pl* **-heads** [*count*] *informal* **:** a stupid person ▪ Don't be such a *blockhead*!

block letters *noun* [*plural*] *chiefly US* **:** capital letters ▪ The message was written in *block letters*. — called also (*Brit*) *block capitals*

block of flats *noun, pl* **blocks of flats** [*count*] *Brit* **:** APARTMENT BUILDING

block party *noun, pl* ~ **-ties** [*count*] *US* **:** a party that is held outdoors for all the people who live in a neighborhood or city block

blocky /ˈblɑːki/ *adj* **block•i•er; -est :** short and thick ▪ a baseball player with a *blocky* [=(more commonly) *stocky*] body/build ▪ a shoe with a thick, *blocky* heel

blog /ˈblɑːg/ *noun, pl* **blogs** [*count*] **:** a Web site on which someone writes about personal opinions, activities, and experiences
– blog•ger *noun, pl* **-ers** [*count*] **– blog•ging** *noun* [*noncount*]

bloke /ˈbloʊk/ *noun, pl* **blokes** [*count*] *chiefly Brit, informal* **:** a man ▪ I'm just an ordinary *bloke*. [=*guy, fellow, chap*]

[1]**blond** *or* **blonde** /ˈblɑːnd/ *adj* **blond•er; -est**
1 : of a yellow or very light brown color ▪ long *blond* hair ▪ *blonde* curls/locks/braids ▪ She has *blonde* highlights in her hair. ▪ His hair was dyed/bleached *blond*.; *also* **:** having blond hair ▪ a *blond* actor ▪ She was *blonde* as a child. ✧ When used to describe a boy or man, the word is spelled *blond*. When used for a girl or woman, the word is often spelled *blonde*. ✧ A person with ***dirty blond*** hair has very dark blond hair that is almost light brown in color. — see also PLATINUM BLONDE, STRAWBERRY BLONDE
2 : of a very light color ▪ a table made of *blond* wood

[2]**blond** *or* **blonde** *noun, pl* **blondes** [*count*] **:** a person who has yellow or very light brown hair ✧ The word is spelled *blond* when used for a boy or man, and it is usually spelled *blonde* when used for a girl or woman. ▪ He's a tall, blue-eyed *blond*. ▪ She's a natural *blonde*. [=her hair has not been dyed blonde] ▪ a ***bottle/bleached/peroxide blonde*** [=someone whose hair has been made blond through the use of chemicals] — see also PLATINUM BLONDE, STRAWBERRY BLONDE

blood /ˈblʌd/ *noun* [*noncount*]
1 : the red liquid that flows through the bodies of people and animals ▪ The accident victim has already lost a lot of *blood*. ▪ the *blood* in your veins ▪ She ***donates/gives blood*** twice a year. [=twice a year she has blood taken out of her body so that it can be put into the body of a person who needs it] — see also BAD BLOOD, COLD-BLOODED, FULL-BLOODED, HOT-BLOODED, RED-BLOODED, WARM-BLOODED
2 — used to say that a person's ancestors were of a particular kind ▪ There's some Italian *blood* in her family. [=one or more of her family's ancestors was Italian] ▪ a man of royal *blood* [=a man with kings and queens in his family] — see also BLUE BLOOD, BLUE-BLOODED
3 : members of a team, company, or organization — usually used in the phrases ***new blood*** or ***young blood*** ▪ Our company could benefit from some *new blood*. [=new employees] ▪ We've just added some *young blood* to the team.
blood and guts see [1]GUT
blood is thicker than water ✧ The saying *blood is thicker than water* means that a person's family is more important than a person's other relationships or needs.
blood is up ✧ In British English, when you say that someone's *blood is up*, you mean that someone is angry and wants to fight or argue. ▪ It's best to avoid her when her *blood is up*.
blood on your hands ✧ If someone's *blood is on your hands*, you are responsible for that person's death. ▪ Her *blood is on your hands*!
by blood **:** by a relationship that connects two people through their natural parents, grandparents, etc. ▪ My aunt

and I are ***related by blood***. [=my aunt is the sister of one of my parents] • My aunt and I are not ***related by blood***. [=my aunt is/was married to the brother of one of my parents]

draw blood **1** : to take blood from a person's body for medical reasons • We need to *draw* some *blood* to test you for the virus. **2** : to cause blood to flow from a person's body • The punch to the nose *drew blood*. [=caused the nose to bleed] — sometimes used figuratively • Some politicians view debates as chances to *draw blood* from their opponents.

flesh and blood see [1]FLESH

in cold blood : in a deliberate way : following a plan • They were killed *in cold blood* by terrorists.

in your blood ✧ If something (such as an ability or activity) is *in your blood*, it is part of your nature and is often shared by your family members. • With two parents who are painters, art is *in her blood*.

make someone's blood boil : to make someone very angry • His hate-filled speeches *make my blood boil*! [=*make me see red*]

make someone's blood curdle or ***make someone's blood run cold*** : to cause someone to be very afraid or disgusted • The horrible news *made our blood run cold*. • a ghost story that will *make your blood curdle* • The mere sight of a cockroach *makes my blood curdle*.

out for blood ✧ If you are *out for blood* or *out for someone's blood*, you are very angry and you want to kill someone or to cause someone pain or discomfort. • Those soldiers were *out for blood*. • His ex-wife is *out for his blood*.

spill/shed blood : to kill people violently • The *blood* of too many young people *has been spilled/shed*.

sweat blood *informal* : to care a lot about something and work very hard for it • basketball players who *sweat blood* for their teams

taste blood *informal* : to experience pleasure as a result of defeating an opponent • She has *tasted blood* now, and can't wait to meet her rival on the court again.

blood bank *noun, pl* ~ **banks** [*count*] : a place where blood is stored so that it later can be given to people who are ill

blood·bath /ˈblʌdˌbæθ, *Brit* ˈblʌdˌbɑːθ/ *noun, pl* **-baths** [*count*] : a violent and cruel killing of many people • Thousands of people were murdered in the *bloodbath*. — sometimes used figuratively • The presidential race has become a political *bloodbath*.

blood brother *noun, pl* ~ **-ers** [*count*] : a man or boy who has promised to be loyal to another man or boy usually in a ceremony in which they mix their blood • He would never betray me—he's my *blood brother*.

blood cell *noun, pl* ~ **cells** [*count*] : a cell that is normally present in blood — see also RED BLOOD CELL, WHITE BLOOD CELL

blood clot *noun, pl* ~ **clots** [*count*] : a thick and sticky clump of dried blood that stops blood from flowing through a blood vessel in a person or an animal • She had a *blood clot* in her lungs. — called also *clot*

blood count *noun, pl* ~ **counts** [*count*] : the number of cells in someone's blood — usually singular • The patient has a low *blood count*.

blood·cur·dling /ˈblʌdˌkɚdlɪŋ/ *adj* [*more* ~; *most* ~] : causing great horror or fear • We heard *bloodcurdling* [=*horrifying*] stories about the war. • *bloodcurdling* [=*terrifying*] screams

blood doping *noun* [*noncount*] : an illegal method for temporarily improving an athlete's performance in a race or competition by increasing the number of red blood cells in the blood

blood feud *noun, pl* ~ **feuds** [*count*] : a very long fight between two families or groups in which each group kills members of the other group in order to punish the group for earlier murders

blood group *noun, pl* ~ **groups** [*count*] : BLOOD TYPE

blood heat *noun* [*singular*] *Brit* : the normal temperature of the human body ✧ In U.S. English, this temperature (98.6 degrees Fahrenheit or 37 degrees Celsius) is referred to as a person's normal ***body temperature***.

blood·hound /ˈblʌdˌhaʊnd/ *noun, pl* **-hounds** [*count*] : a large dog that has very long ears and a very good sense of smell and that is often used for finding people and for hunting

blood·ied /ˈblʌdid/ *adj* [*more* ~; *most* ~] : covered in blood : made bloody • Their faces were *bloodied* and bruised.

blood·less /ˈblʌdləs/ *adj* [*more* ~; *most* ~]
1 : done without killing people • He fought his ***bloodless*** battles in the courtroom. • They took control of the government in a *bloodless* coup.
2 : lacking feeling or emotion • Her speeches are dull and *bloodless*. • a bunch of *bloodless* numbers and statistics
3 : pale in color • His face was *bloodless* with fear.
– blood·less·ly *adv*

blood·let·ting /ˈblʌdˌlɛtɪŋ/ *noun, pl* **-tings**
1 [*noncount*] **a** : the former practice of taking some blood out of the bodies of sick people to heal them **b** : the practice of causing someone to bleed as part of a religious ceremony • They practiced ritual *bloodletting*.
2 [*noncount*] : the killing of people • They prayed for an end to the *bloodletting*. [=(more commonly) ***bloodshed***]
3 : the act of reducing the number of workers in a company [*noncount*] We survived last year's ***bloodletting***. [=we were able to keep our jobs] [*count*] a corporate ***bloodletting***

blood·line /ˈblʌdˌlaɪn/ *noun, pl* **-lines** [*count*] : the ancestors of a person or animal • her family's German ***bloodlines*** • the *bloodlines* of racehorses

blood·lust /ˈblʌdˌlʌst/ *noun* [*noncount*] : the desire to kill or to see people killed • soldiers inflamed by ***bloodlust***

blood money *noun* [*noncount*]
1 : money wrongly obtained by killing someone or because someone has died • the *blood money* earned by people who profited from the tragedy
2 : money paid to the family of a person who has been killed • They accepted *blood money* in exchange for the murderer's execution.

blood orange *noun, pl* ~ **-ang·es** [*count*] : an orange (sense 1) that is red inside the skin

blood platelet *noun, pl* ~ **-lets** [*count*] : PLATELET

blood poisoning *noun* [*noncount*] *medical* : a serious condition in which harmful bacteria spread throughout a person's blood

blood pressure *noun, pl* ~ **-sures** : the force with which blood moves through a person's body [*noncount*] The doctor says he has high *blood pressure*. • These drugs help lower *blood pressure*. [*count*] She has a *blood pressure* of 120/80.

blood–red *adj* : dark red like the color of blood • ***blood-red*** lips

blood relative *noun, pl* ~ **-tives** [*count*] *US* : someone who has the same parents or ancestors as you • Your sister is your *blood relative*, but your brother-in-law is not. — called also (*Brit*) *blood relation*

blood sausage *noun, pl* ~ **-sag·es** [*count*] : a very dark sausage that contains a lot of blood — called also *black pudding, blood pudding*

blood·shed /ˈblʌdˌʃɛd/ *noun* [*noncount*] : the killing of people especially in a war • Years of violence and ***bloodshed*** have left much of the country in ruins.

blood·shot /ˈblʌdˌʃɑːt/ *adj* [*more* ~; *most* ~] *of eyes* : having many red lines from lack of sleep, drunkenness, etc. • He had *bloodshot* eyes. = His eyes were ***bloodshot***.

blood sport *noun, pl* ~ **sports** [*count*] : a sport (such as hunting) in which birds or animals are killed

blood·stain /ˈblʌdˌsteɪn/ *noun, pl* **-stains** [*count*] : a spot of blood on something (such as a piece of clothing)
– blood·stained /ˈblʌdˌsteɪnd/ *adj* • a ***bloodstained*** carpet

blood·stock /ˈblʌdˌstɑːk/ *noun* [*noncount*] : horses that are bred for racing

blood·stream /ˈblʌdˌstriːm/ *noun* [*singular*] : the flow of blood that moves through the heart and body • The drug is now entering the ***bloodstream***.

blood·suck·er /ˈblʌdˌsʌkɚ/ *noun, pl* **-ers** [*count*]
1 : an animal (such as a leech or mosquito) that sucks the blood of other animals
2 *informal* : a person who unfairly takes or uses things that other people worked for • Our landlord, the ***bloodsucker***, just raised our rent again.
– blood·suck·ing /ˈblʌdˌsʌkɪŋ/ *adj, always used before a noun* • *bloodsucking* insects • our ***bloodsucking*** landlord

blood sugar *noun* [*noncount*] : the amount of sugar in your blood • As a diabetic, he needs his ***blood sugar*** to stay at the right levels.

blood test *noun, pl* ~ **tests** [*count*] : a test of the blood especially to learn if a person has any diseases or conditions (such as AIDS or high cholesterol) • He had a ***blood test***, and the doctor who did it said his cholesterol was too high.

blood·thirsty /ˈblʌdˌθɚsti/ *adj* [*more* ~; *most* ~] : eager to

hurt or kill : enjoying the sight of violence or bloodshed ▪ *bloodthirsty* soldiers
– **blood·thirst·i·ness** /ˈblʌd,θɚstinəs/ *noun [noncount]*

blood transfusion *noun, pl* ~ **-sions** *[count]* : a medical treatment in which someone's blood is put into the body of another person

blood type *noun, pl* ~ **types** *[count] chiefly US* : one of the eight different blood categories into which humans are separated ✧ These categories of blood are labeled A, B, AB, or O and each of these is either Rh-positive or Rh-negative. ▪ Her *blood type* is B negative. — called also *blood group*

blood vessel *noun, pl* ~ **-sels** *[count]* : a small tube that carries blood to different parts of a person or animal's body ✧ Arteries, veins, and capillaries are kinds of *blood vessels*.

[1]**bloody** /ˈblʌdi/ *adj* **blood·i·er; -est** *[also more ~; most ~]*
1 : bleeding or covered with blood ▪ He hit me and gave me a *bloody* nose. ▪ a *bloody* towel ▪ a *bloody* knife
2 : violent and causing the death or injury of many people ▪ a *bloody* battle/war/revolution — see also *scream bloody murder* at [1]SCREAM
3 *always used before a noun, Brit, informal + sometimes offensive* — used to make an angry or critical statement more forceful ▪ He's a *bloody* [=*damned*] fool! ▪ We had to read the whole *bloody* thing.
bloody hell *Brit, informal + offensive* — used to express anger or annoyance ▪ *Bloody hell* [=*damn it*]—I've lost my key again! ▪ How ***the bloody hell*** did you hear that?
– **blood·i·ly** /ˈblʌdəli/ *adv* ▪ The battle was won *bloodily*.

[2]**bloody** *adv, Brit, informal + sometimes offensive* : VERY, EXTREMELY — used to make an angry or critical statement more forceful ▪ a *bloody* awful mistake ▪ We all had a *bloody* good time. ▪ It was *bloody* marvellous! ▪ "Can I borrow your car again?" "***Not bloody likely!***" [=no, absolutely not]
bloody well *informal + sometimes offensive* — used before a verb to stress anger, annoyance, or disapproval ▪ I'm your father and you'll *bloody well* do as you're told!

[3]**bloody** *verb* **blood·ies; blood·ied; bloody·ing** *[+ obj]* : to make (something) bloody ▪ He hit me and *bloodied* my nose. — see also BLOODIED

Bloody Mary /-ˈmeri/ *noun, pl* ~ **Marys** *[count]* : an alcoholic drink made with vodka, tomato juice, and usually spices

bloody–mind·ed /ˌblʌdiˈmaɪndəd/ *adj [more ~; most ~] chiefly Brit, informal* : difficult to deal with : not willing to help others do things ▪ Stop being so *bloody-minded* and give me a hand here!
– **bloody–mind·ed·ness** *noun [noncount]*

[1]**bloom** /ˈbluːm/ *noun, pl* **blooms**
1 *[count]* : [1]FLOWER 1 ▪ The plant's purple *blooms* attract butterflies. ▪ He picked a red *bloom* [=*blossom*] for her hair.
2 *[count]* : a time period in which a plant has many open flowers ▪ roses with an early spring *bloom*
3 *[noncount]* : a state or time of beauty, health, and strength ▪ the *bloom* of youth
come in/into bloom see [1]COME
in bloom or in full bloom : having flowers ▪ The bushes should be *in bloom* [=*in flower; flowering; blooming*] soon. ▪ These plants are very fragrant when they are *in full bloom*.

[2]**bloom** *verb* **blooms; bloomed; bloom·ing** *[no obj]*
1 : to produce flowers ▪ trees that *bloom* [=*blossom, flower*] in the spring ▪ flowers *blooming* in the garden
2 : to change, grow, or develop fully ▪ Their love was just beginning to *bloom*. ▪ their *blooming* romance

bloom·er /ˈbluːmɚ/ *noun, pl* **-ers** *[count]*
1 : a plant that blooms at a specified time ▪ These plants are spring *bloomers*. [=they have flowers in the spring] ▪ plants that are early/late *bloomers*
2 *Brit, informal + somewhat old-fashioned* : an embarrassing mistake ▪ The politician's *bloomer* [=(*US*) *blooper*] was shown on every TV channel.
late bloomer *US* : someone who becomes successful, attractive, etc., at a later time in life than other people ▪ She was a *late bloomer* as a writer.

bloo·mers /ˈbluːmɚz/ *noun [plural]* : long and loose underpants worn by women and girls especially in the past

bloom·ing /ˈbluːmən/ *adj, always used before a noun, Brit, informal* — used to make an angry or critical statement more forceful ▪ We had to read the whole *blooming* thing! ▪ Don't be a *blooming* idiot!
– **blooming** *adv, Brit, informal* ▪ It's *blooming* marvellous!

bloop·er /ˈbluːpɚ/ *noun, pl* **-ers** *[count] US* : an embarrassing mistake usually made in public ▪ The politician's *blooper* [=(*Brit*) *bloomer*] was shown on every TV channel.

[1]**blos·som** /ˈblɑːsəm/ *noun, pl* **-soms** *[count]* : a flower especially of a fruit tree ▪ Her hair smelled of apple/cherry/orange *blossoms*. ▪ delicate pink *blossoms* [=*blooms*]

[2]**blossom** *verb* **-soms; -somed; -som·ing** *[no obj]*
1 : to produce flowers ▪ The trees have finished *blossoming*. [=*blooming, flowering*]
2 : to change, grow, and develop fully ▪ Their friendship began to *blossom* [=*bloom, flower, flourish*] during the summer. ▪ Their friendship *blossomed* into romance. ▪ Their business seemed to *blossom* [=*take off*] overnight. ▪ a *blossoming* romance ▪ a *blossoming* talent

[1]**blot** /ˈblɑːt/ *verb* **blots; blot·ted; blot·ting** *[+ obj]* : to dry (something, such as wet ink) by pressing a piece of cloth or paper over it ▪ Don't rub the wine stain. *Blot* it dry with a paper towel. ▪ *Blot* your lipstick with a tissue.
blot out *[phrasal verb]* ***blot out (something) or blot (something) out*** : to hide or block (something): such as **a** : to make (something) difficult to see ▪ Clouds *blotted out* the sun. **b** : to try to forget (an event or memory) ▪ *blotting out* memories of your childhood
blot your copybook *Brit, informal* : to harm your own reputation ▪ The star football player *blotted his copybook* by using bad language in an interview.

[2]**blot** *noun, pl* **blots** *[count]*
1 a : a spot or stain ▪ a *blot* of ink [=an ink blot] **b** : something that makes something else dirty or unattractive ▪ The tower is a *blot* on the landscape.
2 : a mark of shame or dishonor ▪ Slavery is a *blot* on the nation's history.

blotch /ˈblɑːtʃ/ *noun, pl* **blotch·es** *[count]* : a usually dark-colored spot especially on the skin ▪ She has brown *blotches* [=*splotches*] on her hands. ▪ *blotches* on the tree's leaves
– **blotched** /ˈblɑːtʃt/ *adj, Brit* ▪ leaves *blotched* with brown spots – **blotchy** /ˈblɑːtʃi/ *adj* **blotch·i·er; -est** *[or more ~; most ~]* ▪ *blotchy* skin

blot·ter /ˈblɑːtɚ/ *noun, pl* **-ters** *[count]*
1 : a large piece of blotting paper that is placed in a stiff frame on top of a desk
2 : a book used in a police station for writing down information about people or events ▪ a police *blotter*

blotting paper *noun [noncount]* : a soft, thick paper used to dry wet ink

blot·to /ˈblɑːtoʊ/ *adj [more ~; most ~] slang* : very drunk ▪ He came home *blotto* after the party. ▪ She got *blotto* on cheap wine.

blouse /ˈblaʊs/ *noun, pl* **blous·es** /ˈblaʊsəz/ *[count]* : an often somewhat formal shirt for women and girls ▪ She wore a *blouse* and a skirt to work. — see color picture on page C14

[1]**blow** /ˈbloʊ/ *verb* **blew** /ˈbluː/; **blown** /ˈbloʊn/; **blow·ing**
1 a *[no obj] of air, wind, etc.* : to move with speed or force ▪ The wind was *blowing* earlier but it's not *blowing* now. [=there was wind earlier but there isn't any wind now] ▪ The wind is *blowing* hard. = It's *blowing* hard outside. ▪ The storm is *blowing* hard/fiercely. = It's *blowing* up a storm. ▪ A cool breeze *blew* through the open window. ▪ The wind was *blowing* from the north. **b** *[+ obj]* : to cause (air or something carried by air) to move ▪ The fan *blew* the air. ▪ The fan *blew* the smoke out the window. **c** : to be moved or affected in a specified way by the wind *[no obj]* The door *blew* open/shut in the wind. ▪ The papers *blew* all over the place! ▪ The sign *blew* down/over. ▪ The leaves were *blowing* around in the wind. ▪ His hat *blew* off/away in the wind. *[+ obj]* The breeze *blew* my wet hair dry. ▪ The wind *blew* the door open/shut. ▪ The wind *blew* the sign down/over. ▪ The wind *blew* the ship off course. ▪ A gust of wind *blew* the papers all over the room. ▪ The wind *blew* his hat off/away.
2 a : to create a current of moving air by breathing *[no obj]* She *blew* on her fingers to warm them. ▪ He was *blowing* on his soup to cool it off. *[+ obj]* She *blew* air into the balloon. **b** *[+ obj]* : to produce or shape (something, such as a bubble) by blowing air ▪ The clown was *blowing* bubbles for the children. ▪ *blow* beautiful shapes out of glass = *blow* glass into beautiful shapes — see also GLASSBLOWING
3 a *[no obj] of a musical instrument, whistle, etc.* : to produce a loud sound ▪ The trumpet/whistle *blew* loudly. ▪ The siren *blew*. [=*sounded*] **b** *[+ obj]* : to play or produce a sound with (a musical instrument, whistle, etc.) ▪ *blow* a trumpet ▪ *blow* a whistle ▪ *blow* a siren
4 : to damage or destroy (something) with an explosion *[+ obj]* The terrorists rigged a bomb to *blow* [=(more commonly) *blow up*] the bridge. ▪ The explosion *blew* his leg off. = The

B

explosion *blew* off his leg. • The explosion *blew* out the window. • The burglar *blew* the safe open with dynamite. • The bomb *blew* the bridge to bits/smithereens. [=the bomb completely destroyed the bridge] [*no obj*] They ran away when they realized that the bridge was about to *blow*. [=(more commonly) *blow up, explode*] • The window *blew* out in the explosion. • The safe *blew* open when the burglar dynamited it. — sometimes used figuratively • The election has been *blown* wide open by the revelation that one of the candidates was lying. • The prosecution's case was *blown* apart by new evidence. — see also BLOW UP (below)

5 : to cause (a tire) to suddenly lose air and become flat [+ *obj*] He drove over a nail and *blew* a tire. — often + *out* • The car *blew out* a tire. [*no obj*] The car crashed because one of its tires had *blown*. — often + *out* • One of the car's tires *blew out*. — see also BLOWOUT 1

6 *of an electric fuse* **:** to melt and stop the flow of electricity when an electric current is too strong [*no obj*] The light went off because a fuse had *blown*. [+ *obj*] What *blew* the fuse? — see also *blow a fuse* at ¹FUSE

7 [+ *obj*] **:** to clear (your nose) by forcing air through it quickly • He ***blew his nose*** into his handkerchief.

8 [+ *obj*] *informal* **:** to spend or waste (a large amount of money) in a foolish way • He *blew* his whole paycheck on a horse that finished last.

9 [+ *obj*] *informal* **a :** to make a mistake in doing or handling (something) • The actress *blew* her lines. [=she said her lines incorrectly] **b :** to lose or miss (an opportunity) by acting in a stupid or clumsy way • He *blew* an opportunity to make a lot of money in the stock market. • I *blew* my chance for a big promotion. • They should have won the game but they ***blew it***. • "I have a job interview tomorrow." "Well, don't *blow it*." • I was late for the job interview and that *blew it* for me. [=that caused me not to get the job]

10 [+ *obj*] *US, informal* **:** to leave (a place) very quickly • Let's *blow* this joint. • He packed his bags and ***blew town*** [=*left town*] without even saying goodbye.

11 *always followed by an adverb or preposition* [+ *obj*] *US, informal* **:** to throw (a ball) with great force and speed • The pitcher *blew* a fastball by/past the batter.

12 *Brit, informal* — used to express surprise, annoyance, etc. • He washed the dishes? Well ***blow me down***! • ***Blow it***! I forgot to buy milk.

blow a gasket see GASKET

blow away [*phrasal verb*] ***blow (someone) away or blow away (someone) informal*** **1 :** to kill (someone) by shooting • a gangster who got *blown away* by a hit man **2 :** to impress (someone) in a very strong and favorable way • I was really *blown away* by her latest movie. **3** *US* **:** to defeat (someone) very badly • They *blew* their rivals *away* in the first game 34–7.

blow hot and cold **:** to change repeatedly from liking or favoring something to not liking or favoring it • Local residents have been *blowing hot and cold* on the question of whether to build a new school.

blow in [*phrasal verb*] *informal* **:** to arrive in a sudden or unexpected way • He just *blew in*, asking for a place to stay.

blow into [*phrasal verb*] ***blow into (a place) informal*** **:** to arrive at (a place) in a sudden or unexpected way • He just *blew into* town and needs a place to stay.

blown out of proportion see PROPORTION

blow off [*phrasal verb*] *US, informal* **1** ***blow (someone) off or blow off (someone)*** **a :** to refuse to notice or deal with (someone) **:** to ignore (someone) • I tried to say hello to him, but he just *blew* me *off*. **b :** to fail to meet (someone) at an expected time • He was supposed to meet me for lunch but he *blew* me *off*. **2** ***blow (something) off or blow off (something)*** **:** to fail to attend or show up for (something) • He *blew off* an official dinner.

blow off (some) steam see ¹STEAM

blow out [*phrasal verb*] **1** ***blow out or blow (something) out or blow out (something)*** **:** to go out or to cause (something, such as a candle) to go out by blowing • There was a sudden gust of wind and the candles *blew out*. • She *blew out* the candles on her birthday cake. • The wind *blew out* the candle. **2** *of a storm* **:** to come to an end **:** STOP • The storm eventually *blew out*. [=*blew over*] = The storm eventually ***blew itself out***. [=the storm eventually ended] — see also BLOWOUT

blow over [*phrasal verb*] *of a storm* **:** to come to an end **:** STOP • The storm eventually *blew over*. [=*blew itself out, ended*] — often used figuratively • The scandal *blew over* and was forgotten in a few months.

blow smoke see ¹SMOKE

blow (someone) a kiss see ²KISS

blow someone's brains out see ¹BRAIN

blow someone's cover see ²COVER

blow someone's mind see ¹MIND

blow the gaff see GAFF

blow the whistle see ¹WHISTLE

blow up [*phrasal verb*] **1** ***blow (something) up or blow up (something)*** **:** to fill (something) with air or gas **:** INFLATE • *blow up* a balloon • *blow up* a tire **2** ***blow up or blow (something) up or blow up (something)*** **a :** to explode or to cause (something, such as a bomb) to explode • The bomb *blew up*. • *blow up* a bomb **b :** to be destroyed or to destroy (something) by an explosion • The bridge *blew up* (in the explosion). • The soldiers *blew up* the bridge with a bomb. — sometimes used figuratively • The whole situation has ***blown up in his face*** [=has gone terribly wrong] and he may well be fired! **3 :** to become very angry • The boss *blew up* when the shipment arrived late. **4** ***blow (something) up or blow up (something)*** **:** to make (a photograph) larger • We had the photograph *blown up* for framing. **:** to make (something) seem larger or more important than it really is **:** EXAGGERATE • It was just a trivial mistake that got *blown up* into something much worse. [=got greatly exaggerated] **5** *of the wind, a storm, etc.* **:** to begin blowing • A wind *blew up* but quickly subsided. • A storm *blew up* suddenly. — see also BLOWUP

blow your cool see ³COOL

blow your own horn see ¹HORN

blow your own trumpet see ¹TRUMPET

blow your top or US blow your stack informal **:** to become very angry • Mom really *blew her top* when she found out I'd wrecked the car.

²blow *noun, pl* **blows** [*count*]

1 : a strong wind • If the weather reports are right, we're in for a good *blow* tonight. [=there will be a strong wind tonight; the wind will blow hard tonight]

2 : the act of blowing something (such as your nose) • He gave his nose a good *blow*. [=he blew his nose]

– compare ³BLOW

³blow *noun, pl* **blows** [*count*]

1 : a hard hit using a part of the body or an object • He delivered a mighty *blow* with a club. • a *blow* with a hammer = a hammer *blow* • I caught/got him with a heavy *blow* in the third round. = I landed a heavy *blow* on him in the third round. • The two boxers ***exchanged blows***. [=hit each other] • The boxer ***rained blows*** on his opponent's head. [=the boxer hit his opponent's head many times] • The falling tile struck him with a ***glancing blow*** on the head. [=hit his head with less than full force and fell off to one side] — see also BODY BLOW, LOW BLOW

2 a : something that is done to fight for or against something • They ***struck a blow*** for freedom and against tyranny. [=they did something that helped freedom and opposed tyranny] **b :** a sudden event that causes trouble, damage, sorrow, etc. • Hopes of peace received a mortal *blow* when negotiations were blocked. • The injury to their best player was a serious *blow* to the team's chances. [=the injury did serious harm to the team's chances] • The death of his wife was a terrible/shattering *blow* from which he never really recovered. • She was disappointed not to get the job, but the promise of another job ***cushioned/softened the blow***. [=the promise of another job made her disappointment less painful or severe]

come to blows **:** to begin fighting **:** to begin hitting each other • They almost *came to blows* during their argument.

deal a blow see ¹DEAL

– compare ²BLOW

blow–by–blow /ˈbloʊbaɪˈbloʊ/ *adj, always used before a noun* **:** describing each thing that happens in a series • He gave us a *blow–by–blow* account/description of the meeting.

blow–dried /ˈbloʊˌdraɪd/ *adj* **:** having blow-dried hair — sometimes used in a disapproving way in U.S. English to describe someone (such as a television personality) who has a neat appearance but is not very intelligent or interesting • a *blow-dried* newscaster

blow–dry·er /ˈbloʊˌdrajɚ/ *noun, pl* **-dry·ers** [*count*] **:** a handheld device that blows air and is used for drying hair • She dried her hair with a *blow-dryer*. — see picture at GROOMING

– **blow–dry** /ˈbloʊˌdraɪ/ *verb* **-dries; -dried; -dry·ing** [+ *obj*] She washed and *blow-dried* her hair. [*no obj*] Always brush or comb while you *blow-dry*. – **blow–dry** *noun, pl*

-dries [count] ▪ She gave her hair a quick *blow-dry*.

blow·er /ˈblowɚ/ *noun, pl* **-ers** [count] **:** a device that blows air ▪ a leaf *blower* [=a device that is used for clearing away leaves from the ground by producing a strong current of air] — see also SNOWBLOWER, WHISTLE-BLOWER

on the blower *Brit, informal + old-fashioned* **:** on the telephone ▪ When I finally got him *on the blower* [=(US) *on the horn*] he said he couldn't come.

blow·gun /ˈbloʊˌgʌn/ *noun, pl* **-guns** [count] **:** a long narrow tube that shoots out an arrow or dart when someone breathes into it quickly and forcefully

blow·hard /ˈbloʊˌhaɚd/ *noun, pl* **-hards** [count] *US, informal + disapproving* **:** a person who talks too much and who has strong opinions that other people dislike ▪ She's nice but her husband's a real *blowhard*. [=*windbag*]

blow·hole /ˈbloʊˌhoʊl/ *noun, pl* **-holes** [count]
1 : a hole that is on the top of a whale or related animal's head and is used by the animal for breathing
2 : a hole in the ice to which seals and other animals that are living in the water under the ice come to breathe

blow job *noun, pl* ~ **jobs** [count] *informal + offensive* **:** the act of stimulating a man's penis with the mouth for sexual pleasure

blow·lamp /ˈbloʊˌlæmp/ *noun, pl* **-lamps** [count] *Brit* **:** BLOWTORCH

blown *past participle of* ¹BLOW

blow·out /ˈbloʊˌaʊt/ *noun, pl* **-outs** [count]
1 : a sudden loss of air caused by a hole or cut in a tire ▪ The car crashed after one of its tires had a *blowout*. — see also ¹BLOW 5
2 *informal* **:** a large and informal social gathering **:** a big party ▪ We had a big *blowout* to celebrate his promotion.
3 *US, informal* **:** an easy victory **:** a game or contest in which the winner defeats the loser by a large amount ▪ The game was expected to be close but it turned out to be a *blowout*. ▪ a *blowout* game
– see also *blow out* at ¹BLOW

blow·sy *also* **blow·zy** /ˈblaʊzi/ *adj* **blow·si·er; -est** [*also more* ~; *most* ~] *of a woman* **:** not neat or clean in her clothing or appearance and usually fat ▪ a *blowsy* old woman

blow·torch /ˈbloʊˌtoɚʧ/ *noun, pl* **-torch·es** [count] *US* **:** a device that produces a very hot, narrow flame for doing work (such as melting metal to join pipes together) — called also *(Brit) blowlamp*

blow·up /ˈbloʊˌʌp/ *noun, pl* **-ups** [count]
1 : a photograph that has been made larger ▪ The *blowup* of the photograph was easy to frame.
2 a : an angry argument ▪ The two of them had a big *blowup* about something trivial. **b :** an occurrence in which someone becomes very angry **:** an angry outburst ▪ The coach's latest *blowup* occurred when one of his players arrived late. — see also *blow up* at ¹BLOW

blowy /ˈblowi/ *adj* **blow·i·er; -est :** BREEZY, WINDY ▪ a *blowy* March day

BLT /ˌbiːˌɛlˈtiː/ *noun, pl* **BLTs** [count] *US* **:** a bacon, lettuce, and tomato sandwich

¹**blub·ber** /ˈblʌbɚ/ *noun* [noncount] **:** the fat on whales and some other animals that live in the water

²**blubber** *verb* **-bers; -bered; -ber·ing** [*no obj*] **:** to cry in a noisy and annoying way ▪ Oh, stop *blubbering*, you big baby!

¹**blud·geon** /ˈblʌʤən/ *verb* **-geons; -geoned; -geon·ing** [+ *obj*]
1 : to hit (someone or something) very hard ▪ The victim was *bludgeoned* to death with a hammer.
2 : to use arguments or threats to force (someone) to do something ▪ He was *bludgeoned* [=*bullied*] into accepting the deal.

²**bludgeon** *noun, pl* **-geons** [count]
1 : a heavy stick that usually has one thick end and is used as a weapon
2 : something that is used to attack or bully someone ▪ the *bludgeon* of satire

¹**blue** /ˈbluː/ *adj* **blu·er; blu·est**
1 : having the color of the clear sky ▪ a *blue* house/car/shirt/pen ▪ his bright *blue* eyes ▪ the deep *blue* ocean — see also BABY BLUE, BLACK-AND-BLUE, COBALT BLUE, NAVY BLUE, ROYAL BLUE, SKY BLUE, TRUE-BLUE
2 : sad or unhappy ▪ Are you feeling *blue*? — see also BLUES

blue in the face ✧ If you do something until you are *blue in the face*, you do it for a very long time without having any success or making any difference. ▪ I talked to him until I was *blue in the face*, but he wouldn't listen to me.

blue with cold *or* ***blue from the cold*** *chiefly Brit, of a person or body part* **:** blue from being exposed to cold for too long ▪ Her hands and feet are *blue with cold*. ▪ He was shivering and *blue from the cold*.

go blue *Brit* **:** to turn blue from being cold or not breathing ▪ The baby stopped breathing and *went blue*.

talk a blue streak *US* **:** to talk rapidly and without stopping ▪ Sheesh! Your friend really *talks a blue streak*!

– **blue·ness** *noun* [noncount] ▪ the *blueness* of the ocean

²**blue** *noun, pl* **blues**
1 : the color of the clear sky [noncount] Her favorite color is *blue*. ▪ shades of *blue* ▪ He was dressed in *blue*. [=blue clothing] ▪ The sky was overcast, but here and there I could see a patch of *blue*. [=blue sky] [count] a mixture of *blues* and greens — see color picture on page C1
2 ***the blue*** *literary* **:** the sky or the sea ▪ They sailed off into *the blue*.

out of the blue **:** without warning **:** in a surprising or unexpected way ▪ Then, *out of the blue*, he sold his house and left the country.

blue baby *noun, pl* ~ **-bies** [count] **:** a baby that has bluish skin usually because its heart is not working correctly

blue·bell /ˈbluːˌbɛl/ *noun, pl* **-bells** [count] **:** a plant with blue flowers that are shaped like bells

blue·ber·ry /ˈbluːˌberi/ *noun, pl* **-ries** [count] **:** a small round fruit with blue, purple, or blackish skin ▪ We picked *blueberries*. ▪ a pie made with *blueberries* — often used before another noun ▪ *blueberry* muffins/pie ▪ a *blueberry* bush ▪ We went *blueberry* picking. — see color picture on page C5

blue·bird /ˈbluːˌbɚd/ *noun, pl* **-birds** [count] **:** a small North American bird that is mostly blue with a blue, brown, or orange belly — see color picture on page C9

blue blood *noun, pl* ~ **bloods**
1 [noncount] **:** membership in a royal or socially important family ▪ a woman of *blue blood*
2 [count] **:** a member of a royal or socially important family ▪ This is where the city's *blue bloods* like to gather.
– **blue–blood·ed** /ˈbluːˈblʌdəd/ *adj* [*more* ~; *most* ~] ▪ a *blue-blooded* family ▪ *blue-blooded* sports like golf and polo

blue book *noun, pl* ~ **books**
1 [singular] **:** a report that is published by the government ▪ The information is listed in the *blue book*.
2 [count] *US* **:** a thin booklet with a blue cover and empty pages that is often used for writing the answers to test questions in college
3 [singular] *US* **:** a book that lists the current value of items (such as used cars)

blue cheese *noun, pl* ~ **cheeses** [count, noncount] **:** a kind of cheese that is white with lines of blue mold and that has a strong flavor

blue–chip *adj, always used before a noun*
1 : valuable and likely to make a good profit **:** not likely to cause investors to lose money ▪ *blue-chip* companies/stocks
2 *chiefly US* **:** very good **:** EXCELLENT ▪ a *blue-chip* [=*first-class, first-rate*] artist/athlete/wine

blue–col·lar /ˈbluːˈkɑːlɚ/ *adj* **:** requiring physical work ▪ *blue-collar* jobs [=jobs making things in a factory, fixing machines, building things, etc.] **:** relating to or having jobs that require physical work ▪ *blue-collar* [=*working-class*] workers/families — compare PINK-COLLAR, WHITE-COLLAR

blue·fish /ˈbluːˌfɪʃ/ *noun, pl* **bluefish** [count] **:** a type of fish that lives in the ocean and is caught by people for food and for sport — see color picture on page C8

blue·grass /ˈbluːˌgræs, *Brit* ˈbluːˌgrɑːs/ *noun* [noncount] **:** a type of traditional American music that is played on stringed instruments (such as banjos and fiddles)

blue jay *noun, pl* ~ **jays** [count] **:** a common American bird that is mostly blue — see color picture on page C9

blue jeans *noun* [plural] **:** pants made of a strong blue cloth (called denim) ▪ He was wearing (a pair of) *blue jeans*. — see color picture on page C14

blue law *noun, pl* ~ **laws** [count] *US* **:** an old law that forbids people from doing certain things (such as working or selling alcohol) on Sundays

blue moon *noun*

once in a blue moon **:** very rarely ▪ It happens *once in a blue moon*.

blue·print /ˈbluːˌprɪnt/ *noun, pl* **-prints** [count]
1 : a photographic print that shows how something (such as a building) will be made ✧ Blueprints are often sheets of

blue paper with white lines on them. ▪ architectural *blueprints* — often used figuratively ▪ Each cell contains the organism's genetic *blueprint*.
2 : a detailed plan of how to do something ▪ a ***blueprint for*** success ▪ a *blueprint for* reforming the public school system

blue ribbon *noun, pl* ~ **-bons** [*count*] **:** a decorative piece of blue cloth that is given to the winner in a contest or competition ▪ Our pumpkin won the *blue ribbon* at the county fair this year. — called also (*Brit*) *blue rib·and* /ˈrɪbənd/

blue–ribbon *adj, always used before a noun* **:** made up of people who have special knowledge, abilities, etc. ▪ a *blue-ribbon* committee/panel

blues /ˈbluːz/ *noun*
1 *the blues* : a feeling of sadness or depression ▪ I've got (a case of) *the blues*. [=I have been feeling sad/depressed]
2 [*noncount*] **:** a style of music that was created by African-Americans in the southern U.S. and that often expresses feelings of sadness ▪ a band that plays *blues* and jazz — often used with *the* ▪ She sings *the blues*. — often used before another noun ▪ a *blues* singer — sometimes used figuratively ▪ He's been ***singing the blues*** [=feeling sad and discouraged] since he lost his job. — see also RHYTHM AND BLUES
– blue·sy /ˈbluːzi/ *adj* **blues·i·er; -est** ▪ *bluesy* music ▪ a band with a *bluesy* sound

blue·stock·ing /ˈbluːˌstɑːkɪŋ/ *noun, pl* **-ings** [*count*] *old-fashioned + often disapproving* **:** an educated woman who is interested in books and ideas

blue whale *noun, pl* ~ **whales** [*count*] **:** a very large bluish-gray whale ✧ The blue whale is the largest living animal.

[1]**bluff** /ˈblʌf/ *verb* **bluffs; bluffed; bluff·ing**
1 : to pretend that you will do something or that you know or have something in order to trick someone into doing what you want [*no obj*] Don't listen to his threats—he's just *bluffing*. [=he will not really do what he threatens to do] ▪ She says someone else has made her a higher offer, but I think she's *bluffing*. ▪ He's a terrible card player—you can always tell when he's *bluffing*. [=when he's pretending that he has better cards than he actually has] [+ *obj*] Don't listen to his threats—he's just *bluffing* you. ▪ I managed to ***bluff my way*** into the show without a ticket. [=I got into the show by bluffing] ▪ I *bluffed my way* through the interview.
2 [+ *obj*] *US* **:** to pretend to do or make (something) ▪ The catcher *bluffed* [=*faked, feigned*] a throw to first base.

[2]**bluff** *noun, pl* **bluffs** [*count*] **:** a false threat or claim that is meant to get someone to do something ▪ She says someone else has made her a higher offer, but I think it's just a *bluff*.
call your bluff ✧ If you have made a bluff or a threat and people *call your bluff*, they tell you to do the thing you have threatened to do because they do not believe that you will really do it. ▪ When she threatened to quit her job, her boss *called her bluff* and told her she could leave if she wanted to.
– compare [3]BLUFF

[3]**bluff** *noun, pl* **bluffs** [*count*] **:** a high, steep area of land **:** CLIFF ▪ They stood on the *bluffs* overlooking the Pacific Ocean. — compare [2]BLUFF

[4]**bluff** *adj* [*more* ~; *most* ~] **:** having a very open, honest, and direct way of talking that is friendly but not always polite ▪ a *bluff*, easygoing fellow

blu·ish /ˈbluːwɪʃ/ *adj* [*more* ~; *most* ~] **:** somewhat blue ▪ a *bluish* green [=a shade of green that is somewhat blue]

[1]**blun·der** /ˈblʌndɚ/ *verb* **-ders; -dered; -der·ing** [*no obj*]
1 : to move in an awkward or confused way ▪ We *blundered* along through the woods until we finally found the trail. ▪ Another skier *blundered* into his path. — often used figuratively ▪ a nation that is *blundering* into war
2 : to make a stupid or careless mistake ▪ The government *blundered* by not acting sooner.
– blundering *adj* ▪ a bunch of *blundering* idiots

[2]**blunder** *noun, pl* **-ders** [*count*] **:** a bad mistake made because of stupidity or carelessness ▪ The accident was the result of a series of *blunders*. ▪ a political/tactical *blunder*

blun·der·buss /ˈblʌndɚˌbʌs/ *noun, pl* **-bus·ses** [*count*] **:** an old-fashioned kind of gun with a wide opening at the end

[1]**blunt** /ˈblʌnt/ *adj* **blunt·er; -est** [*also more* ~; *most* ~]
1 : having a thick edge or point **:** not sharp ▪ scissors with *blunt* [=*rounded*] ends ▪ He was hit over the head with a ***blunt instrument*** [=an object without sharp edges or points] ✧ ***Blunt trauma*** is a serious injury caused by being hit by something that does not have sharp edges. ▪ She suffered *blunt trauma* to the head.
2 : saying or expressing something in a very direct way that may upset some people ▪ *blunt* language ▪ a *blunt* statement ▪ To be perfectly *blunt*, I find her annoying. ▪ He was *blunt* about needing more privacy.
– blunt·ly *adv* ▪ She *bluntly* refused their offer. ▪ To put it *bluntly*, I think he's out of his mind. **– blunt·ness** *noun* [*noncount*] ▪ He replied with characteristic *bluntness*.

[2]**blunt** *verb* **blunts; blunt·ed; blunt·ing** [+ *obj*] **:** to make (something) less sharp ▪ a weapon *blunted* by use — often used figuratively ▪ The stress and fatigue had *blunted* [=*weakened*] his reflexes. ▪ They tried to *blunt* [=*soften*] their criticism by praising her energy and enthusiasm.

[1]**blur** /ˈblɚ/ *noun, pl* **blurs**
1 [*count*] **:** something that you cannot see clearly — usually singular ▪ He passed by in a *blur* of motion. ▪ As the train sped on, everything outside the window was a *blur*. ▪ I looked out at the *blur* of faces in the audience. ▪ The letters are just a *blur* without my glasses.
2 [*singular*] **:** something that is difficult to remember ▪ The whole weekend is just a *blur* to me. [=I don't remember the events of the weekend very clearly]
– blur·ry /ˈblɚri/ *adj* **blur·ri·er; -est** [*or more* ~; *most* ~] ▪ a *blurry* image ▪ She's suffering from *blurry* vision. ▪ The letters are *blurry* [=*blurred*] without my glasses.

[2]**blur** *verb* **blurs; blurred; blur·ring**
1 [+ *obj*] **:** to make (something) unclear or difficult to see or remember ▪ a technique that *blurs* the edges of the image [=makes the edges of the image less sharp] ▪ The tears in my eyes *blurred* the words on the page. ▪ His novel is based on historical occurrences but it ***blurs the line/distinction between*** fact and fiction.
2 [*no obj*] **:** to become unclear or difficult to see or remember ▪ I was so tired that my vision/eyes started to *blur*. [=I was not able to see clearly] ▪ The two events have *blurred* together in my mind.
– blurred *adj* [*more* ~; *most* ~] ▪ The writing is *blurred* [=*blurry*] but I think I can read it. ▪ The patient's symptoms include *blurred* vision. ▪ a *blurred* memory

blurb /ˈblɚb/ *noun, pl* **blurbs** [*count*] **:** a short description that praises something (such as a book) so that people will want to buy it ▪ a *blurb* on a book jacket

blurt /ˈblɚt/ *verb* **blurts; blurt·ed; blurt·ing** [+ *obj*] **:** to say (something) suddenly and without thinking about how people will react ▪ "Gosh, you look awful!" she *blurted*. — usually + *out* ▪ He accidentally *blurted out* an obscenity. ▪ She *blurted out* the answer.

[1]**blush** /ˈblʌʃ/ *verb* **blush·es; blushed; blush·ing** [*no obj*]
1 : to become red in your face because you are ashamed, embarrassed, confused, etc. ▪ He *blushed* at the compliment. ▪ The unexpected attention made her *blush* (with embarrassment).
2 : to be embarrassed ▪ I *blush* to admit it, but you've caught me in an error.

[2]**blush** *noun, pl* **blushes**
1 [*count*] **:** the red color that spreads over your face when you are ashamed, embarrassed, confused, etc. ▪ The comment brought a *blush* to her cheeks.
2 [*count*] **:** a slight red or pink color ▪ The fruit is yellow, with a *blush* of pink.
3 [*noncount*] *US* **:** a cream or powder that some people put on their cheeks to make their cheeks pink or reddish ▪ She put on a little lipstick and *blush*. — called also (*chiefly Brit*) *blush·er* /ˈblʌʃɚ/
at first blush see [1]FIRST
spare someone's blushes see [2]SPARE

blush wine *noun, pl* ~ **wines** [*count, noncount*] **:** wine that has a pink color

[1]**blus·ter** /ˈblʌstɚ/ *verb* **-ters; -tered; -ter·ing**
1 : to speak in a loud and aggressive or threatening way [*no obj*] He brags and *blusters*, but he never really does what he says he'll do. [+ *obj*] "I don't want to hear it!" he *blustered*.
2 [*no obj*] *of wind* **:** to blow loudly and violently ▪ The wind *blustered* through the valley.
– blustering *adj* ▪ The storm brought *blustering* [=*blustery*] winds. ▪ a *blustering* bully

[2]**bluster** *noun* [*noncount*] **:** words that are loud and aggressive ▪ We were all tired of his macho *bluster*.

blus·tery /ˈblʌstəri/ *adj* [*more* ~; *most* ~] **:** blowing loudly and violently ▪ *blustery* winds

blvd. *abbr* boulevard ▪ The letter was addressed to him at 1066 Sunset *Blvd*.

B movie *noun, pl* ~ **-ies** [*count*] **:** a movie that costs little money to make and that is usually not considered to be very good

BO *abbr* body odor • She refused to wear deodorant and had horrible *BO.* [=her body smelled very unpleasant]

boa /ˈbowə/ *noun, pl* **boas** [*count*]
1 : BOA CONSTRICTOR
2 : a long scarf that is made of fur, feathers, or cloth • a pink feather *boa*

boa constrictor *noun, pl* ~ **-tors** [*count*] **:** a large brown snake that crushes the animals it eats by squeezing them with its body and that lives in the tropical regions of Central and South America

boar /ˈboɚ/ *noun, pl* **boars** [*count*]
1 : a male pig
2 : a wild pig — called also *wild boar*

[1]board /ˈboɚd/ *noun, pl* **boards**
1 [*count*] **:** a long, thin, flat piece of wood • They nailed some *boards* over the broken window. • Cut the *board* lengthwise.
2 [*count*] **a :** a flat piece of material (such as wood or cardboard) that is used for a special purpose • They covered the *board* in fabric and pinned some photographs to it. • the *board* that is used to play games like chess and checkers **b :** BULLETIN BOARD 1 • I saw a notice on the *board* calling for volunteers. — see also MESSAGE BOARD **c :** a large, smooth surface for writing on • Write the answers on the *board.* — see also BLACKBOARD, WHITEBOARD
3 [*count*] **a :** a group of people who manage or direct a company or organization • She sits on the bank's *board* of directors. = She's a *board* member at the bank. **b :** a group of people who have been chosen to learn information about something, to give advice, etc. • a member of the advisory *board* = a *board* member • She is on the town's planning/zoning *board.* • an investigative *board* [=(more commonly) *panel*] • The parole *board* has decided that the prisoner is not yet ready for release. — see also BOARDROOM, SCHOOL BOARD
4 [*noncount*] **:** daily meals that you pay for when you are paying to stay at a hotel, school, etc. • He's looking for a place that provides *board* and lodging in the city. • (*Brit*) A week at the hotel with ***half board*** [=some meals] is of course less expensive than a week with ***full board*** [=all meals] — see also ROOM AND BOARD
5 [*count*] **:** CIRCUIT BOARD
6 ***boards*** [*plural*] *US* **:** special tests that you take when you want to be accepted as a student at a college or medical school • Did you pass the *boards?*
7 ***the boards*** *US* **:** the low wooden wall that surrounds the playing surface in ice hockey • He crashed into *the boards.*
across the board **:** in a way that includes or affects everyone or everything • We've been forced to cut spending *across the board.* — see also ACROSS-THE-BOARD
go by the board *or US* ***go by the boards*** **:** to no longer be used or considered **:** to be discarded, rejected, or abandoned • Many of his original theories have *gone by the board* in recent years as new evidence has accumulated.
on board **1 :** in or on a train, boat, etc. **:** ABOARD • She got *on board* the train. • The ship's passengers are all *on board.* • Is all the equipment *on board* (the boat/train/bus/plane)? **2 :** included among the group of people who support a particular goal, project, etc. • They needed to get more senators *on board* for the bill to pass.
sweep the board see [1]SWEEP
take (something) on board *Brit* **:** to decide to accept or deal with (something, such as a suggestion or idea) • You will be pleased to note that we have *taken* your suggestions *on board* in formulating the present policy.
tread the boards see [1]TREAD

[2]board *verb* **boards; board·ed; board·ing**
1 a : to get into or onto (an airplane, a bus, a train, etc.) [+ *obj*] You must have a ticket in order to *board* the train. • The pirates tried to *board* the ship, but we fought them off. [*no obj*] We're supposed to *board* at 10:15. • Passengers may now *board.* **b :** to put or allow (someone) into or onto an airplane, a bus, a train, etc. [+ *obj*] We're now *boarding* all passengers. [*no obj*] The flight is about to begin *boarding.* • Passengers should remain in the *boarding* area.
2 [+ *obj*] **:** to cover or close (something) with pieces of wood • The caretaker *boarded* the window. — usually + *up* • The caretaker *boarded up* the window. • We decided to *board up* [=put boards over the windows and doors of] the old shed.
3 a [+ *obj*] **:** to provide (someone) with daily meals and a place to live in exchange for money • They *board* guests during the summer season. **b** [*no obj*] **:** to pay for daily meals and a place to live • Many students *board* at the college. — see also BOARDINGHOUSE, BOARDING SCHOOL

board·er /ˈboɚdɚ/ *noun, pl* **-ers** [*count*]
1 : a person who pays to live and have daily meals at another person's house or at a school • She decided to take in *boarders.* • Half of the students are *boarders.*
2 : a person who uses a snowboard • an amateur *boarder* [=*snowboarder*]

board game *noun, pl* ~ **games** [*count*] **:** a game (such as chess) that is played by moving pieces on a special board

board·ing·house /ˈboɚdɪŋˌhaʊs/ *noun, pl* **-hous·es** [*count*] **:** a house where people pay to live and have daily meals

boarding pass *noun, pl* ~ **passes** [*count*] *US* **:** a special piece of paper that you must have in order to be allowed to get onto an airplane • Please present your *boarding pass* to the flight attendant. — called also (*Brit*) *boarding card*

boarding school *noun, pl* ~ **schools :** a school where students can live during the school term [*count*] He attended a prestigious *boarding school* in Massachusetts. [*noncount*] She was sent to *boarding school* when she was nine.

board·room /ˈboɚdˌruːm/ *noun, pl* **-rooms** [*count*] **:** a room where the group of people who manage or direct a company or organization have meetings • The directors are meeting in the *boardroom.* — often used before another noun • There was lots of *boardroom* intrigue surrounding the appointment of a new CEO.

board·walk /ˈboɚdˌwɑːk/ *noun, pl* **-walks** [*count*] *chiefly US* **:** a wooden path along a beach ✧ A boardwalk can be on the ground or raised above the ground several feet.

[1]boast /ˈboʊst/ *verb* **boasts; boast·ed; boast·ing**
1 : to express too much pride in yourself or in something you have, have done, or are connected to in some way [*no obj*] They *boasted* to their friends about their son's salary. • She *boasted* of having won five games in a row. • That score is nothing to *boast* about. [=you shouldn't be proud of that score; that score is not very good] [+ *obj*] He liked to *boast* that he was the richest man in town. • "I've sold more paintings than you ever will," the artist *boasted.*
2 [+ *obj*] **:** to have (something that is impressive) • The museum *boasts* some of the rarest gems in the world. • The school *boasts* a number of Nobel laureates among its graduates.

[2]boast *noun, pl* **boasts** [*count*]
1 : a statement in which you express too much pride in yourself or in something you have, have done, or are connected to in some way • When he says he's the richest man in town, he's not just making an idle/empty *boast.* • We were offended by his *boast* that he would easily beat us.
2 : a reason to be proud **:** something impressive that someone or something has or has done • The museum's proudest *boast* is its collection of rare gems.
– boast·ful /ˈboʊstfəl/ *adj* [*more* ~; *most* ~] • a *boastful* person/remark **– boast·ful·ly** /ˈboʊstfəli/ *adv* **– boast·ful·ness** *noun* [*noncount*]

[1]boat /ˈboʊt/ *noun, pl* **boats** [*count*]
1 a : a small vehicle that is used for traveling on water • a fishing *boat* • He tied the *boat* to the dock. **b :** a vehicle of any size that is used for traveling on water • Cruise ships and other *boats* filled the harbor. • traveling ***by boat*** across the ocean — see picture on next page; compare SHIP
2 : a long and narrow container that is used for serving a sauce with a meal • a gravy/sauce *boat*
fresh/just off the boat *informal* **:** recently arrived in a country • My parents met in New York when my father was *fresh off the boat* from Italy.
in the same boat *informal* **:** in the same unpleasant or difficult situation **:** affected by the same problem • We're all *in the same boat.*
miss the boat *informal* **:** to fail to use an opportunity • If I don't act now I could *miss the boat* on this investment.
push the boat out *Brit, informal* **:** to spend a lot of money **:** to be extravagant • We're going to *push the boat out* and throw a big party to celebrate his recovery.
rock the boat *informal* **:** to cause trouble by changing or trying to change a situation that other people do not want to change • Don't *rock the boat.* • The system isn't perfect, but it's been this way for a long time and nobody wants to *rock the boat.*
– boat·ful /ˈboʊtfəl/ *noun, pl* **-fuls** [*count*] • a *boatful* [=(more commonly) *boatload*] of passengers

[2]boat *verb* **boats; boat·ed; boat·ing** [*no obj*] **:** to travel in a boat • We *boated* over to the island.

boat

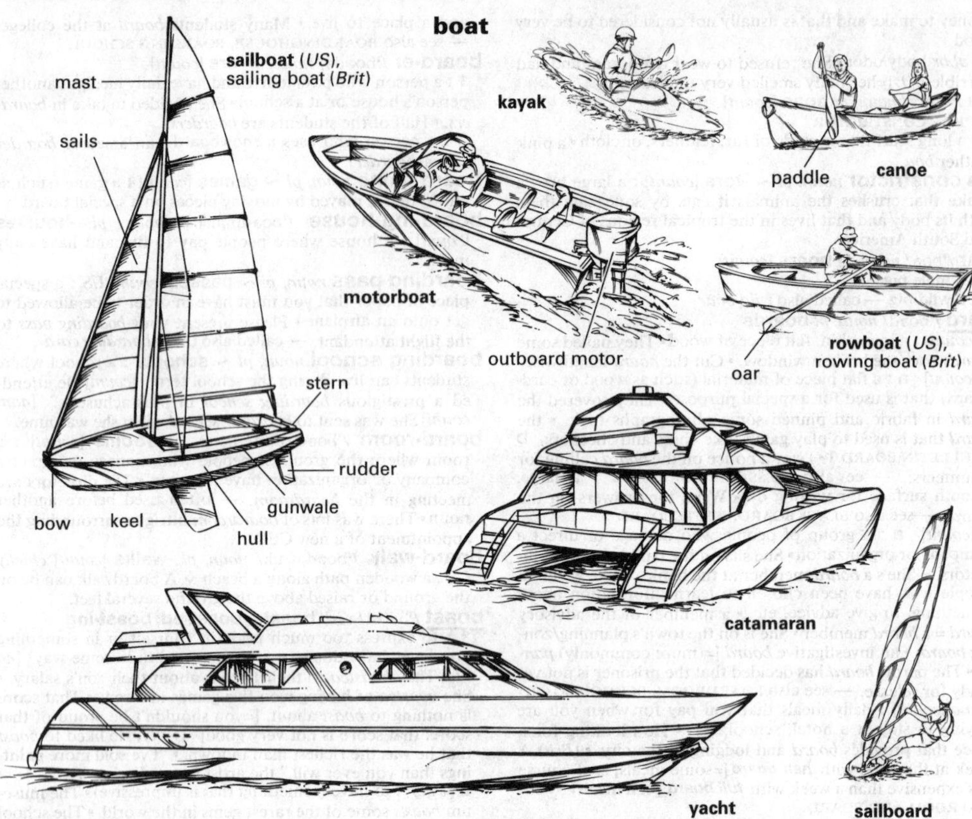

boat·er /ˈboʊtɚ/ *noun, pl* **-ers** [*count*]
1 : a person who travels in a boat • a favorite spot for pleasure *boaters*
2 : a stiff straw hat that has a brim and a flat top

boat·house /ˈboʊtˌhaʊs/ *noun, pl* **-hous·es** [*count*] **:** a small building that is used for storing boats near a river or lake

boating *noun* [*noncount*] **:** the activity of going or traveling in a boat for pleasure • She enjoys hiking, *boating*, and fishing. • We ***went boating*** on the lake. — often used before another noun • They own a store that sells *boating* equipment.

boat·load /ˈboʊtˌloʊd/ *noun, pl* **-loads** [*count*] **:** an amount or number that will fill a boat • a *boatload* of passengers — often used figuratively to refer to a very large number or amount • They made *boatloads* of money. = They made a *boatload* of money. • We bought souvenirs ***by the boatload***. [=in large numbers; we bought many souvenirs]

boat·man /ˈboʊtmən/ *noun, pl* **-men** /-mən/ [*count*] **:** a person (especially a man) who works on, rents, or operates boats; *especially* **:** a person who you pay to take you somewhere in a boat

boat people *noun* [*plural*] **:** people who leave their country in boats in order to get away from a dangerous situation

boat·swain *or* **bo·sun** /ˈboʊsn̩/ *noun, pl* **-swains** *or* **-suns** [*count*] **:** an officer on a ship whose job is to take care of the main body of the ship and all the ship's equipment

boat·yard /ˈboʊtˌjɑɚd/ *noun, pl* **-yards** [*count*] **:** a place where boats are built, repaired, stored, rented, or sold

[1]**bob** /ˈbɑːb/ *verb* **bobs; bobbed; bob·bing :** to move up and down quickly or repeatedly [*no obj*] A cork was *bobbing* in the water. • The bird's head *bobbed* up and down as it searched for food. [+ *obj*] The bird *bobbed* its head up and down as it searched for food.
bob for apples **:** to play a children's game in which you try to grab floating or hanging apples with your teeth
bob up [*phrasal verb*] *informal* **:** to appear suddenly or unexpectedly • The question *bobbed up* [=(more commonly) *popped up*] again.
– compare [4]BOB

[2]**bob** *noun, pl* **bobs** [*count*] **:** a quick up-and-down motion • He greeted us with a *bob* of his head. — compare [3]BOB, [5]BOB

[3]**bob** *noun, pl* **bobs** [*count*]
1 : a woman's or child's haircut in which the hair is all one length and usually at about the level of the person's chin • She had her hair cut in a *bob*.
2 : PLUMB BOB 1
3 : [2]FLOAT 1a
bits and bobs see [1]BIT
— compare [2]BOB, [5]BOB

[4]**bob** *verb* **bobs; bobbed; bob·bing** [+ *obj*]
1 : to cut (something, such as an animal's tail) shorter • They *bobbed* [=*cropped*] the horse's tail for the show.
2 : to cut (a person's hair) so that it is all one length and usually at about the level of the person's chin • I hadn't seen her since she *bobbed* her hair.
– compare [1]BOB

[5]**bob** *noun, pl* **bob** [*count*] *Brit, informal* **:** SHILLING • It costs five *bob*. • I'm always looking for ways to save ***a few bob***. [=some money] — compare [2]BOB, [3]BOB

Bob /ˈbɑːb/ *noun*
and Bob's your uncle *Brit, informal* — used to say that something is easy to do or use • Just complete the form, pay the fee, *and Bob's your uncle*! [=and there you go]

bob·bin /ˈbɑːbən/ *noun, pl* **-bins** [*count*] **:** a round object with flat ends and a tube in its center around which thread or yarn is wound

[1]**bob·ble** /ˈbɑːbəl/ *verb* **bob·bles; bob·bled; bob·bling**
1 [*no obj*] **:** to move up and down quickly or repeatedly • a doll with a head that *bobbles* [=*bobs*] up and down
2 [+ *obj*] *US* **:** to handle (something, such as a ball) in a clumsy or awkward way **:** to fail to catch (something) **:** FUMBLE • The catcher *bobbled* the ball.

[2]**bobble** *noun, pl* **bobbles** [*count*]
1 *US* **:** a mistake that occurs when a player fails to catch or handle the ball properly in baseball, football, etc. • a *bobble* that cost them the game — sometimes used figuratively • The show went well with only a minor *bobble*. [=*mistake*]
2 *chiefly Brit* **:** a small ball of fabric that is used for decora-

tion ▪ The curtains have a series of *bobbles* along the edge. ▪ a woolly hat with a *bobble* [=(*US*) *pom-pom*] on top

bob·by /ˈbɑːbi/ *noun, pl* **bob·bies** [*count*] *Brit, old-fashioned + informal* : POLICE OFFICER ▪ a *bobby* on his beat

bobby pin *noun, pl* ~ **pins** [*count*] *US* : a thin piece of metal that is bent so that the ends are close together and that is used for holding hair in place — called also (*Brit*) *hairgrip*; see picture at GROOMING

bobby socks *or* **bobby sox** *noun* [*plural*] *US* : girls' socks that cover the foot, ankle, and a small part of the lower leg

bob·cat /ˈbɑːbˌkæt/ *noun, pl* **-cats** [*count*] : a kind of large wild cat that has a short tail and that lives in North America

bob·sled /ˈbɑːbˌslɛd/ *noun, pl* **-sleds** [*count*] *US* : a small vehicle for two or four people that slides over snow and ice and is used for racing ▪ He drove a *bobsled* in the winter Olympics. — often used before another noun ▪ the *bobsled* competition ▪ an Olympic *bobsled* team — called also (*Brit*) *bobsleigh*
— **bob·sled·der** /ˈbɑːbˌslɛdɚ/ *noun, pl* **-ers** [*count*] ▪ an Olympic *bobsledder* — **bob·sled·ding** /ˈbɑːbˌslɛdɪŋ/ *noun* [*noncount*] ▪ He competed in *bobsledding* at the winter Olympics.

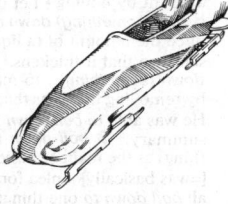

bobsled

bob·sleigh /ˈbɑːbˌsleɪ/ *noun, pl* **-sleighs** [*count*] *Brit* : BOBSLED
— **bob·sleigh·er** /ˈbɑːbˌslejɚ/ *noun, pl* **-ers** [*count*] — **bob·sleigh·ing** /ˈbɑːbˌslejɪŋ/ *noun* [*noncount*]

boc·cie *or* **boc·ci** *or* **boc·ce** /ˈbɑːʧi/ *noun* [*noncount*] *US* : a game in which players roll heavy balls across an area of ground and try to get each ball to stop as near as possible to a smaller ball

bod /ˈbɑːd/ *noun, pl* **bods** [*count*] *informal*
1 *chiefly US* : a person's body ▪ guys with hot *bods*
2 *Brit* : a person : FELLOW ▪ Some *bod* from the office rang you. ▪ He's a bit of an odd *bod*, but I quite like him.

bo·da·cious /boʊˈdeɪʃəs/ *adj* [*more* ~; *most* ~] *US, informal*
1 : very good or impressive ▪ a singer with a *bodacious* voice
2 : sexually attractive ▪ *bodacious* babes

bode /ˈboʊd/ *verb* **bodes; bod·ed; bod·ing** [+ *obj*] : to be a sign of (a future event or situation) ▪ This could *bode* disaster for all involved. ✧ If something ***bodes well*** or ***bodes ill***, it is a sign that something good or bad will happen. ▪ The news doesn't *bode well* for us. ▪ Her injury *bodes ill* for the team.

bod·ice /ˈbɑːdəs/ *noun, pl* **-ic·es** [*count*] : the upper part of a dress

¹bodi·ly /ˈbɑːdəli/ *adj* : relating to the body : having to do with a person's or animal's body ▪ *bodily* functions/fluids ▪ The victim suffered serious *bodily* injury/harm.

²bodily *adv*
1 : by moving someone's body ▪ The police removed them *bodily*. [=*forcibly*] ▪ The blast lifted him *bodily* into the air.
2 : as an entire structure rather than in pieces ▪ The house will have to be moved *bodily* to the new site.

body /ˈbɑːdi/ *noun, pl* **bod·ies**
1 [*count*] **a** : a person's or animal's whole physical self ▪ the human *body* ▪ a part of the *body* ▪ Her *body* is very muscular. ▪ A bird's *body* is covered in feathers. — often used before another noun ▪ *body* weight/fat ▪ *body* parts ▪ A person's normal ***body temperature*** [=(*Brit*) *blood heat*] is 98.6 degrees Fahrenheit or 37 degrees Celsius. **b** : a dead person or animal ▪ The *body* [=*corpse*] was shipped home for burial. **c** : the main physical part of a person or animal ▪ This species has a black *body* and a white head. ▪ She held her arms tightly against her *body*.
2 [*count*] : the part of a vehicle that does not include the engine, wheels, etc. ▪ There was extensive damage to the truck's *body*. ▪ The *body* of the bus is almost entirely rusted out.
3 [*count*] : the main or most important part of something written ▪ The (main) *body* of the text/letter is devoted to a description of the author's childhood home.
4 [*count*] : an object that is separate from other objects ▪ heavenly/celestial *bodies*, such as the moon, the planets, and the stars ✧ A ***foreign body*** is an object that is inside something (such as someone's body) where it should not be. ▪ The X-ray showed a *foreign body* in his stomach. ▪ Dust particles and other *foreign bodies* can irritate the eyes.
5 [*count*] : a large area of water — used in the phrase ***body of water*** ▪ This lake is the largest *body of water* in the state.
6 [*count*] : a group of people who are involved together in the same job, activity, etc. ▪ a *body* of troops ▪ the student *body* ▪ the state's legislative *body* [=the group of people who make the state's laws]
7 [*count*] : a group of things that are related or connected in some way ▪ They've accumulated quite a *body* of evidence. ▪ a writer with an impressive *body* of work
8 [*noncount*] *of wine* : a strong and appealing flavor ▪ a wine with full *body*
9 [*noncount*] *of hair* : a thick and appealing quality ▪ hair that lacks *body*
10 [*count*] : the section of a piece of clothing that covers the main part of a person's body ▪ the *body* of a wetsuit
11 [*count*] *old-fashioned* : a human being : PERSON — usually singular ▪ What's a *body* to do? ▪ It was just some poor *body* looking for work.
body and soul : with all of your energy and enthusiasm ▪ He devoted himself *body and soul* to the cause.
keep body and soul together : to have or get enough food and money to survive ▪ She *kept body and soul together* by working two jobs.
over my dead body *informal* — used to say that you are very determined to not let something happen ▪ "We're getting married." "*Over my dead body*!" ▪ I told her she could go with them *over my dead body*.

body bag *noun, pl* ~ **bags** [*count*] : a large bag that a dead person's body is put in to be carried or moved to another place

body blow *noun, pl* ~ **blows** [*count*] : a hard hit to a person's body — usually used figuratively to describe a sudden event or occurrence that causes severe trouble, damage, sorrow, etc. ▪ The economy has taken some serious *body blows* in the past few years. ▪ The latest attack has dealt a real *body blow* to the chances for peace.

body·build·ing /ˈbɑːdiˌbɪldɪŋ/ *noun* [*noncount*] : the activity of doing exercises (such as lifting weights) to make the muscles of your body larger and stronger ▪ She's been doing competitive *bodybuilding* for a few years now. — often used before another noun ▪ a *bodybuilding* competition
— **body·build·er** /ˈbɑːdiˌbɪldɚ/ *noun, pl* **-ers** [*count*] ▪ professional *bodybuilders*

body clock *noun, pl* ~ **clocks** [*count*] : a system in the body that controls when you need to sleep, eat, etc. ▪ It takes a while for my *body clock* to get adjusted when I fly from New York to London. — compare BIOLOGICAL CLOCK

body count *noun, pl* ~ **counts** [*count*] : the number of people killed in a war, disaster, etc. ▪ The rising *body count* fueled opposition to the war.

body double *noun, pl* ~ **doubles** [*count*] : a person who takes an actor's place in a movie or television show for certain scenes (such as sex scenes)

body·guard /ˈbɑːdiˌgɑɚd/ *noun, pl* **-guards** : a person or group of people whose job is to protect someone [*count*] They entered the building surrounded by *bodyguards*. [*noncount*] a member of the royal *bodyguard*

body language *noun* [*noncount*] : movements or positions of the body that express a person's thoughts or feelings ▪ We could tell from his *body language* that he was nervous.

body mass index *noun, pl* ~ **indexes** [*count*] : a measurement that shows the amount of fat in your body and that is based on your weight and height ▪ A person with a *body mass index* of more than 30 is considered to be obese.

body odor *noun* [*noncount*] : an unpleasant smell from the body of a person who has been sweating or is not clean — abbr. *BO*

body politic *noun*
the body politic *formal* : all the people in a particular country considered as a single group ▪ The article examines the language politicians use to appeal to *the body politic*.

body shop *noun, pl* ~ **shops** [*count*] : a place where the bodies of vehicles are repaired ▪ My car is at the *body shop* having the dent in the door fixed.

body stocking *noun, pl* ~ **-ings** [*count*] : a piece of clothing that fits tightly and covers the body from the neck to the ankles

body·suit /ˈbɑːdiˌsuːt/ *noun, pl* **-suits** [*count*] : a piece of clothing that fits tightly and covers the body except for the legs and sometimes the arms ▪ a gymnast's *bodysuit*

Boer /ˈboɚ/ *noun, pl* **Boers** [*count*] : a South African person

B

of Dutch descent : AFRIKANER

bof·fin /ˈbɑːfən/ *noun, pl* **-fins** [*count*] *chiefly Brit, informal* : a research scientist • Our *boffins* finally broke the enemy's code!

bof·fo /ˈbɑːfoʊ/ *adj* [*more* ~; *most* ~] *US slang* : extremely good or successful • a *boffo* idea • The store's been doing *boffo* business this year. [=the store has been very successful]

[1]**bog** /ˈbɑːg/ *noun, pl* **bogs** : an area of soft, wet land : MARSH [*count*] a kind of plant that commonly grows in *bogs* • a peat *bog* [*noncount*] areas of *bog* • *bog* plants/grasses — often used figuratively to refer to a situation that is complicated or difficult • a *bog* of anxiety/uncertainty — compare [3]BOG

– **bog·gy** /ˈbɑːgi/ *adj* **bog·gi·er; -est** [*or more* ~; *most* ~] • *boggy* soil

[2]**bog** *verb* **bogs; bogged; bog·ging**

bog down [*phrasal verb*] **1** ***bog (something) down*** *or* ***bog down (something)*** : to cause (something) to sink in wet ground • The mud *bogged down* the car. — usually used as *(be) bogged down* • The car got *bogged down* in the mud. — often used figuratively • It's easy to get *bogged down* in details. • The extra demand can *bog down* the system. **2** : to become stuck in wet ground • The car *bogged down* in the mud. — often used figuratively • The story *bogs down* after the second chapter. • The extra demand can cause the system to *bog down*.

[3]**bog** *noun, pl* **bogs** [*count*] *Brit slang* : a room with a toilet • go to the *bog* [=*bathroom, toilet*] • We've run out of ***bog paper***. [=*toilet paper*] — compare [1]BOG

[1]**bo·gey** *also* **bo·gie** *or* **bo·gy** /ˈbougi/ *noun, pl* **bo·geys** *also* **bo·gies**

1 *golf* : a score that is one more than the official standard score for a particular hole : a score of one stroke over par on a hole [*count*] He made/scored a *bogey* on the second hole. [*noncount*] He made *bogey* on the second hole. — compare BIRDIE, EAGLE; see also DOUBLE BOGEY

2 [*count*] : something that causes fear or worry • The administration is trying to protect the economy from the *bogey* of recession. [=the administration is worried that a recession might occur and is trying to prevent one]

3 [*count*] *Brit, informal* : BOOGER

[2]**bogey** *verb* **-geys; -geyed; -gey·ing** [+ *obj*] *golf* : to score a bogey on (a hole) • She birdied the first hole but *bogeyed* the second hole.

bo·gey·man /ˈbugiˌmæn/ *noun, pl* **-men** /-ˌmɛn/ [*count*]

1 : an imaginary monster that is used to frighten children • My aunt used to say to my sister and me, "The *bogeyman* will get you if you're bad."

2 : a person who is hated or feared by a group of people • a politician who is the familiar *bogeyman* of conservatives

bog·gle /ˈbɑːgəl/ *verb* **bog·gles; bog·gled; bog·gling** *informal*

1 [*no obj*] : to be unable to think clearly : to be amazed or overwhelmed • ***The mind boggles*** at what he has accomplished. = When I think of what he has accomplished, ***my mind boggles***. [=I am amazed by what he has accomplished]

2 [+ *obj*] : to make (the mind) unable to think clearly : to amaze or overwhelm (the mind) • ***It boggles the mind*** to think of what he has accomplished. = His accomplishments ***boggle my mind***. — see also MIND-BOGGLING

bog–standard *adj, Brit, informal* : having no special or interesting qualities : AVERAGE • a *bog-standard* speech • It's just a *bog-standard* school.

bo·gus /ˈbougəs/ *adj, informal* : not real or genuine : fake or false • It was just a *bogus* claim. • They conducted *bogus* experiments. • The evidence was completely *bogus*.

bo·he·mi·an /bouˈhiːmijən/ *noun, pl* **-ans** [*count*] : a person (such as an artist or writer) who does not follow society's accepted rules of behavior

– **bohemian** *adj* [*more* ~; *most* ~] • an artist known for his *bohemian* way of life • He lived in the *bohemian* part of the city. – **bo·he·mi·an·ism** /bouˈhiːmijəˌnɪzəm/ *noun* [*noncount*] • They followed a life of *bohemianism*.

[1]**boil** /ˈbojəl/ *verb* **boils; boiled; boil·ing**

1 a [*no obj*] : to become so hot that bubbles are formed in a liquid and rise to the top • Let the water *boil*. • Keep the temperature low enough so the mixture will not *boil*. • a pot of *boiling* water • The kettle (of water) is *boiling*. = The water in the kettle is *boiling*. • french fries cooked in *boiling* oil • Cook the mixture until the liquid has ***boiled away***. [=until the liquid has gone; until all of the liquid has turned into steam] **b** [+ *obj*] : to heat (a liquid or a container with liquid in it) so that bubbles are formed and rise to the top • *Boil* (up) some water. • Can you *boil* a kettle (of water) for tea?

2 : to cook (something) in water that is boiling [+ *obj*] *Boil* the eggs/vegetables. • Make sure you *boil* (up) a lot of potatoes. • *boiled* eggs/potatoes [*no obj*] He put some potatoes on to *boil*. [=he put a pot with potatoes and water in it on the stove and turned the burner on] • The pasta is *boiling*.

3 [*no obj*] : to feel a strong emotion (such as anger) — + *with* • The crowd *boiled* [=*seethed*] *with* anger.

a watched pot never boils ✧ The expression *a watched pot never boils* means that time passes very slowly when you are waiting for something to happen if that is the only thing you are thinking about.

boil down [*phrasal verb*] **1 a** : to become reduced in amount by boiling • Let the sauce *boil down* and thicken. **b** ***boil (something) down or boil down (something)*** : to reduce the amount of (a liquid) by boiling it • *Boil down* the sauce so that it thickens. **2** ***boil (something) down or boil down (something)*** : to make (something) short or simple by removing the parts that are not important or necessary • He was able to *boil down* [=*condense*] the report to a brief summary. **3** ***boil down to (something)*** : to have (something) as the main or basic part • His speech *boiled down to* [=was basically] a plea for more money. • Their objections all *boil down to* one thing: cost. • You can get advice from many sources, but it all *boils down to* common sense. [=you should be guided by common sense]

boil over [*phrasal verb*] **1** : to flow over the side of a container while boiling • The water in the pot is *boiling over*. = The pot (of water) is *boiling over*. **2 a** : to become violent or to lose control because of anger • He's so mad that he's ready to *boil over*. **b** : to change *into* something more violent • Their disagreement finally *boiled over into* a fight.

boil up [*phrasal verb*] : to grow toward a dangerous level • He could feel the anger *boiling up* inside him. [=he could feel himself becoming very angry] • Problems have been *boiling up* in the cities during the hot summer.

make someone's blood boil see BLOOD

[2]**boil** *noun, pl* **boils**

1 [*singular*] *of a liquid* : the act or state of boiling • (*US*) Bring the water to a *boil*. = (*chiefly Brit*) Bring the water to the *boil*. [=boil the water] • (*US*) The kettle on the stove came to a *boil*. = (*chiefly Brit*) The kettle on the stove came to the *boil*. [=the kettle began to boil] • She put the kettle (of water) ***on the boil***. [=she put the kettle on a hot burner so that the water in it would boil] • The mixture should be cooked at a ***slow boil***. [=with small bubbles rising slowly to the surface of the liquid] • Bring the pot to a ***rolling boil***. [=to a state where large bubbles rise quickly to the surface of the liquid]

2 [*count*] *US* : a dish of shellfish, vegetables, and spices that is cooked by boiling • a crab/shrimp *boil*; *also* : a party at which this dish is served • They invited their family and friends to a crab *boil* on the beach.

off the boil *Brit, informal* : into a state that is less good than before • After two hit singles, the band ***went off the boil***. [=the band was not as successful]

on the boil *Brit, informal* : in a state of activity or development • The deal is still *on the boil*. • kept their romance *on the boil*

– compare [3]BOIL

[3]**boil** *noun, pl* **boils** [*count*] : a painful, swollen area under the skin that is caused by infection — compare [2]BOIL

boiled sweet *noun, pl* ~ **sweets** [*count*] *Brit* : HARD CANDY

boil·er /ˈbɔɪlɚ/ *noun, pl* **-ers** [*count*]

1 : a large container in which water is heated to produce steam in an engine — see also DOUBLE BOILER

2 *chiefly Brit* : FURNACE b

boil·er·plate /ˈbɔɪlɚˌpleɪt/ *noun* [*noncount*] *US* : phrases or sentences that are a standard way of saying something and are often used • The last paragraph of the contract was legal *boilerplate*. [=the last paragraph was exactly the same as paragraphs in other contracts] — often used before another noun • a *boilerplate* speech that she has given many times

boiler room *noun, pl* ~ **rooms** [*count*]

1 : a room with equipment for heating a building or ship : a room in which a boiler is located

2 *US* : a room with many telephones that are used by people who call strangers and use dishonest or forceful methods to try to sell them something

boil·er·suit /ˈbɔɪlɚˌsuːt/ *noun, pl* **-suits** *Brit* : COVERALL

[1]**boil·ing** /ˈbɔɪlɪŋ/ *adj* : very hot • a *boiling* sun • a *boiling*

summer day • I'm *boiling* in this suit. • It is *boiling* in here.

[2]**boiling** *adv* : very or extremely • The sun was ***boiling hot.*** • He is ***boiling mad*** at how he was treated.

boiling point *noun, pl* ~ **points**
1 [*count*] : the temperature at which a liquid begins to boil • The *boiling point* of water is 212° Fahrenheit or 100° Celsius.
2 : the point at which people might do or say something violent or might take some definite or extreme action because of anger, disagreement, etc. [*count*] — usually singular • The incident brought tensions to a *boiling point.* • He sensed he had reached his *boiling point.* • (*chiefly US*) Tempers are reaching the *boiling point.* [*noncount*] (*Brit*) Tempers are reaching *boiling point.*

bois·ter·ous /ˈbɔɪstrəs/ *adj* [*more* ~; *most* ~] : very noisy and active in a lively way • A large and *boisterous* crowd attended the concert. • a *boisterous* drinking party • He had a big, *boisterous* [=*hearty*] laugh.
— **bois·ter·ous·ly** *adv* • They laughed *boisterously.*

bok choy (*US*) /ˈbɑːkˈʧoɪ/ *or Brit* **pak choi** /ˈpɑːkˈʧoɪ/ *noun* [*noncount*] : a type of cabbage originally from China that has green leaves with thick, white stems

[1]**bold** /ˈbould/ *adj* **bold·er; -est** [*also more* ~; *most* ~]
1 **a** : not afraid of danger or difficult situations • The area was settled by *bold* [=*brave, courageous*] pioneers. • Few politicians have been *bold* enough to oppose the plan to cut taxes. **b** : showing or needing confidence or lack of fear • It's a *bold* plan that might fail. • Hiring a novice was a *bold* move.
2 : very confident in a way that may seem rude or foolish • He punished the *bold* child for talking back. • He ***was/made so bold*** as to guarantee a victory. [=he confidently guaranteed a victory] • I'd like to offer a few criticisms, ***if I may be so bold.***
3 : very noticeable or easily seen • She wore a dress with *bold* stripes. • The painting is done in *bold* colors.
4 *literary* : very steep • *bold* cliffs
5 : BOLD-FACED 2 • The headline was printed in large, *bold* type/lettering.
(as) bold as brass : not afraid at all : very confident or bold • I was too nervous to do it, but my sister went right up to him *(as) bold as brass* and asked for his autograph.
— **bold·ly** *adv* • He was *boldly* direct. • a *boldly* original painting • a *boldly* striped shirt — **bold·ness** *noun* [*noncount*]

[2]**bold** *noun* [*noncount*] : BOLDFACE

bold·face /ˈbouldˌfeɪs/ *noun* [*noncount*] : letters that are printed in thick, dark lines • The headline was printed in *boldface.* — see picture at FONT

bold–faced /ˈbouldˈfeɪst/ *adj, chiefly US*
1 [*more* ~; *most* ~] *disapproving* : very obvious and showing no feeling of doing something wrong : BLATANT • a *bold-faced* lie • He is a *bold-faced* [=*bald-faced, barefaced*] liar.
2 *usually* ***bold·faced*** : having thick dark lines • The headline was printed in *boldfaced* [=*bold*] type. : printed in boldface • a *boldfaced* headline

bo·le·ro /bəˈlerou/ *noun, pl* **-ros** [*count*]
1 : a type of Spanish dance; *also* : the music for this dance
2 : a short jacket that does not close at the front

boll /ˈboul/ *noun, pl* **bolls** [*count*] : the part of the cotton plant that contains the seeds

bol·lard /ˈbɑːləd/ *noun, pl* **-lards** [*count*]
1 *Brit* : a post that prevents vehicles from going into an area where people can wait in the middle of a road
2 : a post around which a rope may be tied to keep a boat close to land

bol·lix /ˈbɑːlɪks/ *verb* **-lix·es; -lixed; -lix·ing** [+ *obj*] *US, informal* : to make mistakes in doing (something) : to upset or ruin (something) • That delay has *bollixed* our schedule. — usually + *up* • I *bollixed up* my income tax form and had to pay a penalty. • That one delay has *bollixed up* [=*messed up*] my whole week.

bol·locks /ˈbɑːləks/ *noun, Brit, informal + impolite*
1 [*noncount*] : foolish or untrue words or ideas : NONSENSE • They always say we talk *bollocks.* • It's all *bollocks.* I don't believe a word of it.
2 [*plural*] : TESTICLES • She kicked him in the *bollocks.*

boll weevil *noun, pl* ~ **-vils** [*count*] : a small insect that feeds on cotton plants

bo·lo·gna /bəˈlouni/ *noun* [*noncount*] : a wide cooked sausage that is cut into thin pieces and eaten in sandwiches • a slice of *bologna* • a *bologna* sandwich

bo·lo tie /ˈboulou-/ *or* **bo·la tie** /ˈboulə-/ *noun, pl* ~ **ties** [*count*] *US* : a string that is worn around the neck and is held in place by a decorative piece in the front — called also *bolo* ✧ Bolo ties are worn as neckties by men mainly in the western half of the U.S.

Bol·she·vik /ˈboulʃəˌvɪk, ˈbɑːlʃəˌvɪk/ *noun, pl* **-viks** [*count*] : a member of the political party that started to rule Russia in 1917 or a member of a similar political party : COMMUNIST
— **Bolshevik** *adj* • the *Bolshevik* leader • the *Bolshevik* revolution/state

bol·shie *or* **bol·shy** /ˈboulʃi, ˈbɑːlʃi/ *adj* [*more* ~; *most* ~] *Brit, informal* : refusing to obey or help • He turned *bolshie* and uncooperative. ✧ The word *bolshie* is a shortened form of *Bolshevik.*

[1]**bol·ster** /ˈboulstɚ/ *verb* **-sters; -stered; -ster·ing** [+ *obj*] : to make (something) stronger or better : to give support to (something) • She came with me to *bolster* my confidence. • a convincing argument that was *bolstered* by the speaker's reputation • He received news that *bolstered* [=*lifted*] his spirits. • She is thinking of ways to *bolster* her career/image.

[2]**bolster** *noun, pl* **-sters** [*count*] : a long bag of cloth completely filled with soft material : a long pillow or cushion

[1]**bolt** /ˈboult/ *noun, pl* **bolts**
1 [*count*] : a bright line of light that appears in the sky during a storm : a flash of lightning • a *bolt* of lightning = a lightning *bolt* — often used figuratively in the phrases ***a bolt from the blue*** and ***a bolt out of the blue*** • The news of his firing came as/like *a bolt from the blue.* [=like a bolt of lightning from the sky; it was surprising and unexpected]
2 [*count*] **a** : a sliding bar that is used to lock a door or window **b** : the part of a lock that is moved by a key — see also DEAD BOLT
3 [*count*] : a long, round piece of metal that has a wider part at one end and is like a screw at the other end ✧ A bolt and a nut are used together to hold something in place. — see picture at CARPENTRY; see also *nuts and bolts* at NUT
4 [*singular*] *Brit* : the act of running or moving quickly and suddenly in a particular direction or to a particular place • When he saw the police, he ***made a bolt for*** [=*made a dash for*] the door. • The thief ***made a bolt for it.*** [=ran away]
5 [*count*] : a large roll of cloth
6 [*count*] : a tube-shaped metal part inside a gun
7 [*count*] : a short, heavy arrow that is shot from a type of weapon (called a crossbow) used mainly in the past ✧ If you ***have shot your bolt***, you have done or used everything possible to try to do something, and there is nothing more that you can do. • The team had *shot its bolt* in the first quarter and didn't score again.

[2]**bolt** *verb* **bolts; bolt·ed; bolt·ing**
1 [*no obj*] **a** *always followed by an adverb, adjective, or preposition* : to move or go very suddenly and quickly from or to a particular place, position, or condition • He *bolted* up from the chair. • She *bolted* awake when the alarm sounded. • She *bolted* to her feet. • Reporters *bolted* [=*rushed*] for the door from which the mayor appeared. • The firefighters *bolted* [=*sprang*] into action. **b** : to run away suddenly and quickly • The horse *bolted* when it heard the gunfire. • He took the money and *bolted.*
2 *US* : to suddenly leave a political party, team, etc. [*no obj*] The coach *bolted* to a new team. [+ *obj*] Some unhappy members have threatened to *bolt* the party and support the opposition.
3 **a** : to fasten (something) tightly : to lock (something) with a bolt [+ *obj*] She closed and *bolted* the door. • Is the door *bolted*? [*no obj*] The door *bolts* on the inside. **b** [+ *obj*] : to attach (something) firmly : to attach (something) with a bolt • He *bolted* the panels together. • The bench was *bolted* to the floor.
4 [+ *obj*] : to eat (food) quickly • Mom told my brother not to *bolt* his food. — often + *down* • He *bolted down* his dinner and rushed out the door.

[3]**bolt** *adv* : with the back in a very straight position • She sat ***bolt upright***, staring straight ahead.

bolt–hole /ˈboultˌhoul/ *noun, pl* **-holes** [*count*] *Brit* : a safe or restful place : a place where you can hide or escape from something that is dangerous or unpleasant • They considered the inn a *bolt-hole* in times of stress.

[1]**bomb** /ˈbɑːm/ *noun, pl* **bombs**
1 **a** [*count*] : a device that is designed to explode in order to injure or kill people or to damage or destroy property • A *bomb* went off downtown. • The *bomb* is set to detonate at 3:00. = The *bomb* will blow up at 3:00. • Many *bombs* were dropped on the city during the war. • They hid/planted a

bomb in the building. ▪ a ***pipe bomb*** [=a bomb made from a piece of pipe] ▪ a ***suicide bomb*** [=a bomb carried by someone who plans to be killed by it when it explodes] — often used before another noun ▪ a *bomb* explosion/blast ▪ a ***bomb site*** [=a place where a bomb has exploded] ▪ Someone called in a ***bomb threat*** [=a message saying that a bomb is located in a particular place], so the building was evacuated. ▪ a ***bomb squad*** [=a group of people who have the job of preventing bombs from causing damage or injury] **b *the bomb*** : nuclear weapons ▪ countries that have *the bomb*
2 [*count*] *US, informal* : something that is a complete failure — usually singular ▪ The movie was a *bomb.* [=*flop*]
3 a *the bomb* *US slang* : something or someone that is very good ▪ Their new album is *the bomb.* [=their new album is great] **b** [*singular*] *Brit, informal* : something that is very successful ▪ The party ***went down/like a bomb*** [=the party was a success], and everybody enjoyed themselves.
4 [*count*] **a** *American football* : a long pass ▪ The quarterback threw a *bomb* to the wide receiver. **b** *basketball* : a long shot ▪ She's good at shooting three-point *bombs.* **c** *baseball* : a long home run ▪ He hit a three-run *bomb* over the left field wall.
5 [*singular*] *Brit, informal* : a large amount of money ▪ She paid a *bomb* for the car. ▪ I'm looking for a new computer that doesn't cost a *bomb.*
drop a bomb or drop the bomb *informal* : to do or say something that is very shocking and unexpected ▪ She *dropped a bomb* with her resignation. [=her resignation was a complete surprise] ▪ She *dropped the bomb* on her husband and asked for a divorce.

²bomb *verb* **bombs; bombed; bomb·ing**
1 [+ *obj*] : to attack (a place or people) with a bomb or many bombs ▪ The city was heavily *bombed* during the war. ▪ The planes flew 200 miles to *bomb* their target.
2 a [*no obj*] *informal* : to fail completely ▪ The plan *bombed* (out). ▪ The movie *bombed* at the box office. ▪ The play *bombed* on Broadway. ▪ He *bombed* at/in his first performance. **b** [+ *obj*] *US slang* : to fail (a test) ▪ I completely *bombed* my math exam.
3 *always followed by an adverb or preposition* [*no obj*] *informal* : to move or go very quickly ▪ A car was *bombing* down the highway. ▪ teenagers *bombing* around in a convertible
4 [+ *obj*] **a** *US, sports* : to hit (a ball) very hard ▪ He *bombed* a homer in the ninth inning. **b** *baseball* : to score many runs against (a pitcher) ▪ The relief pitcher was *bombed* in the ninth inning.
– bombing *noun, pl* **-ings** [*noncount*] The city was subjected to heavy *bombing* during the war. [*count*] The building was destroyed by repeated *bombings.* ▪ suicide *bombings* — often used before another noun ▪ a *bombing* attack/campaign

bom·bard /bɑmˈbɑɚd/ *verb* **-bards; -bard·ed; -bard·ing** [+ *obj*]
1 : to attack (a place) with bombs, large guns, etc. ▪ The navy *bombarded* the shore.
2 : to hit or attack (something or someone) constantly or repeatedly ▪ Scientists *bombarded* the sample with X-rays. ▪ The car was *bombarded* by rocks as it drove away from the angry crowd. — often used figuratively ▪ He is being *bombarded* by offers. ▪ We are constantly being *bombarded* by ads. ▪ The actress was *bombarded* with questions.
– bom·bard·ment /bɑmˈbɑɚdmənt/ *noun, pl* **-ments** [*count*] During the war, *bombardments* occurred every night. [*noncount*] The city was subjected to aerial *bombardment.* [=bombs were dropped on the city from airplanes]

bom·bar·dier /ˌbɑːmbəˈdiɚ/ *noun, pl* **-diers** [*count*]
1 *chiefly US* : the person in a military aircraft who controls when the bombs are dropped
2 : an officer who operates large guns and has a low rank in the British Army

bom·bast /ˈbɑːmˌbæst/ *noun* [*noncount*] *formal* : speech or writing that is meant to sound important or impressive but is not sincere or meaningful ▪ political *bombast*
– bom·bas·tic /bɑmˈbæstɪk/ *adj* [*more* ~; *most* ~] ▪ a *bombastic* speech/speaker **– bom·bas·ti·cal·ly** /bɑmˈbæstɪkli/ *adv*

bombed /ˈbɑːmd/ *adj, not used before a noun, US, informal* : affected by alcohol or drugs : very drunk or intoxicated ▪ He was *bombed* out of his mind. [=he was so drunk that he didn't know what he was doing]

bombed–out /ˈbɑːmdˈaʊt/ *adj*
1 : destroyed by bombs ▪ We passed many *bombed-out* buildings in the ruined city. ▪ The factory was completely *bombed-out* during the war.
2 : forced out of a house or a building by bombing ▪ *bombed-out* families/workers

bomb·er /ˈbɑːmɚ/ *noun, pl* **-ers** [*count*]
1 : a military aircraft designed for dropping bombs ▪ a *bomber* pilot
2 : a person who takes a bomb to a place so that it will explode there : a person who bombs a place ▪ a ***suicide bomber*** [=someone who takes a bomb to a place and expects to be killed by it when it explodes]

bomber jacket *noun, pl* ~ **-ets** [*count*] : a short jacket that is made of leather and fits closely around the waist

bomb·proof /ˈbɑːmˌpruːf/ *adj* : strong enough to protect someone or something from the force of bombs ▪ a *bombproof* bunker/shelter — sometimes used figuratively ▪ a *bombproof* investment [=a very safe investment]

bomb·shell /ˈbɑːmˌʃɛl/ *noun, pl* **-shells** [*count*]
1 : something that is very surprising or shocking — usually singular ▪ The book was a political *bombshell.* ▪ The news of his departure was a *bombshell.* ▪ She ***dropped a bombshell*** [=she surprised everyone] when she said she wouldn't run for reelection.
2 *informal* : a very attractive woman — usually used in the phrase ***blond/blonde bombshell*** to refer to an attractive woman with blonde hair ▪ She's a *blonde bombshell* who looks like a movie star of the 1950s.

bo·na fide /ˈboʊnəˌfaɪd, ˌboʊnəˈfaɪdi/ *adj*
1 : real or genuine ▪ She has established her position as a *bona fide* celebrity. ▪ His latest record was a *bona fide* hit.
2 *law* : made or done in an honest and sincere way ▪ a *bona fide* offer ▪ They have a *bona fide* claim for the loss.

bo·na fides /ˌboʊnəˈfaɪˌdiːz/ *noun* [*plural*] *formal* : evidence which shows that what you have said about yourself is true : evidence showing that you deserve a position or that you can be trusted ▪ She has worked hard to establish her *bona fides* with the company. [=to show the company that she can be trusted] ✧ *Bona fides* can be used with a singular or plural verb. ▪ The lawyer's *bona fides* was/were questioned.

bo·nan·za /bəˈnænzə/ *noun, pl* **-zas** [*count*]
1 : something that produces very good results for someone or something — usually singular ▪ The movie turned out to be a box-office *bonanza.* [=the movie made a great deal of money] ▪ The program has been a ratings *bonanza* for the network. [=the program has received very high ratings] ▪ The discovery proved to be a *bonanza* for scientists.
2 : a large amount *of* something valuable — usually singular ▪ Her research resulted in a *bonanza of* information.

bon ap·pé·tit /ˌboʊnæpəˈtiː/ *interj* — used to tell someone to enjoy a meal ✧ The phrase *bon appétit* comes from French.

bon·bon /ˈbɑːnˌbɑːn/ *noun, pl* **-bons** [*count*] : a type of candy that usually has a chocolate cover and a soft center ▪ chocolate *bonbons*

bonce /ˈbɑːns/ *noun, pl* **bonc·es** [*count*] *Brit slang* : a person's head ▪ a bald *bonce*

¹bond /ˈbɑːnd/ *noun, pl* **bonds**
1 [*count*] : something (such as an idea, interest, experience, or feeling) that is shared between people or groups and forms a connection between them ▪ the *bonds* of friendship ▪ a daughter's *bond* with her mother ▪ family/kinship *bonds* ▪ Recent events have helped to strengthen the *bonds* between our two countries. ▪ My roommate and I share a ***common bond*** because we both grew up in the Midwest. ▪ ***the bonds of holy matrimony*** [=the connection between two people who are married to each other]
2 [*count*] *finance* : an official document in which a government or company promises to pay back an amount of money that it has borrowed and to pay interest for the borrowed money ▪ She has invested most of her money in stocks and *bonds.* ▪ The city issued *bonds* [=the city created bonds and sold them to investors] to pay for the new school. ▪ municipal *bonds* [=bonds issued by a local government] — see also JUNK BOND, SAVINGS BOND
3 [*count*] *formal* : a chain or rope that is used to prevent someone from moving or acting freely — usually plural ▪ The prisoner was able to break free from the *bonds* that held him. — often used figuratively ▪ They struggled to free themselves from the *bonds* of oppression.
4 [*count*] : the condition of being held together or joined ▪

The glue provides a good/strong *bond* between the two pieces of wood.
5 [*count*] *chemistry* : a force that holds together the atoms in a molecule • chemical *bonds* — see also DOUBLE BOND, SINGLE BOND, TRIPLE BOND
6 [*count*] *formal* : a promise or agreement to do something • You can believe me when I say I'll help you. ***My word is my bond.*** [=I always do what I promise to do]
7 [*noncount*] *chiefly US, law* : the amount of money that someone promises to pay if a prisoner who is allowed to leave jail does not return later for a trial or to prison : an agreement to pay bail • The accused was released on $10,000 *bond.* [=the person accused of a crime was released from jail because someone promised to pay $10,000 if the accused person does not appear for the trial]
8 [*noncount*] : BOND PAPER • used high-quality *bond* for the letter

[2]bond *verb* **bonds; bond•ed; bond•ing**
1 a [+ *obj*] : to join (things) together • Heat was used to *bond* the sheets of plastic together. • The poster was *bonded* to the wall with glue/adhesive. **b** [*no obj*] : to join to something else • The pieces of wood *bonded* (to each other) well.
2 [*no obj*] : to form a close relationship with someone — often + *with* • We were strangers at first, but we *bonded* (*with* each other) quickly. • A new mother *bonds with* her baby.
– bonding *adj, always used before a noun* • a *bonding* agent [=a glue, an adhesive]

bond•age /ˈbɑːndɪʤ/ *noun* [*noncount*]
1 *formal + literary* : the state of being a slave : SLAVERY • He delivered the slaves from *bondage.* [=he freed the slaves] • a population held/kept in *bondage* — often used figuratively • He struggled in the *bondage* of drug addiction.
2 : sexual activity that involves tying a person up for pleasure

bonding *noun* [*noncount*] : the process of forming a close relationship with someone • mother-child *bonding* • He and his dad spent the weekend together for some ***male bonding.***

bond paper *noun* [*noncount*] : a paper that can be used for documents • printed the letter on *bond paper* — called also *bond*

bonds•man /ˈbɑːndzmən/ *noun, pl* **-men** /-mən/ [*count*] *chiefly US, law* : a person who agrees to make a payment if a prisoner who is released from prison does not return : a person who agrees to pay a bond

[1]bone /ˈboun/ *noun, pl* **bones**
1 [*count*] : any one of the hard pieces that form the frame (called a skeleton) inside a person's or animal's body • He broke a *bone* in his left arm. • The leg *bone* is connected to the knee *bone.* — sometimes used figuratively • He doesn't have a selfish/jealous *bone* in his body. [=he is not selfish/jealous at all] • My *bones* are aching from working in the garden. • My aching *bones*! [=my body is tired and sore] • I'll be glad to have a chance to ***rest my weary bones.*** • He ***knew in his bones*** [=*knew in his heart*; had a strong feeling] that he was wrong. • She ***felt in her bones*** [=she sensed very strongly] that nothing had changed. — see also BAG OF BONES, BARE BONES, FUNNY BONE
2 [*noncount*] : the hard material that bones are made of • a piece of *bone* • We are all made of flesh and *bone.* • The handle of the knife is made from *bone.*
bone of contention see CONTENTION
bone to pick *informal* : something to argue or complain about with someone — usually + *with* • I ***have a bone to pick with*** you!
bred in the bone see [1]BREED
close to the bone see [2]CLOSE
make no bones about : to be very sure and definite about (something) • *Make no bones about* the seriousness of the matter. • He *made no bones about* his plans to cut expenses. • ***Make no bones about it***—we will win.
off the bone : with the meat removed from the bone or bones • The pork is served *off the bone.*
on the bone : with the meat connected to the bone or bones • The ham was *on the bone.*
skin and bones see [1]SKIN
throw (someone) a bone *informal* : to offer (someone) something that is not very important or valuable especially to stop complaints or protests • The boss would not let his workers out early for the holiday but *threw them a bone* by buying lunch.
to the bone **1** : very much • We were frozen *to the bone.* [=we were very cold] • The threatening look in his eyes ***chilled me to the bone.*** [=made me feel very fearful] **2** : as much as possible • The company has cut costs *to the bone* in an effort to save money.
work your fingers to the bone see [1]FINGER
– bone•less /ˈbounləs/ *adj* • *boneless* ham [=ham from which the bone has been removed] • The chicken breast is *boneless.*

[2]bone *verb* **bones; boned; bon•ing** [+ *obj*] : to remove the bones from (a fish or meat) : DEBONE • *bone* a fish • *bone* a chicken breast
bone up [*phrasal verb*] *informal* **1** : to try to learn a lot of information quickly for a test, exam, etc. • She *boned up* [=*crammed*] for the exam. **2** : to study something again • He's going to *bone up* the night before the test. — usually + *on* • She *boned up on* the speech just before giving it. • I have to *bone up on* [=*brush up on*] my French for my trip.

[3]bone *adv, always used before an adjective* : extremely or very : completely or totally • *bone* tired/lazy/idle • The air is *bone* dry. — often used in combination • a *bone*-dry desert climate

bone–chill•ing /ˈbounˌʧɪlɪŋ/ *adj* [*more ~; most ~*]
1 : very cold • a *bone-chilling* wind
2 : causing strong feelings of fear, terror, etc. • a *bone-chilling* scream

bone china *noun* [*noncount*] : thin white plates, bowls, cups, etc., made from clay and crushed bones

boned /ˈbound/ *adj*
1 : having bones of a specified type — used in combination • She is a small-*boned* person. • a big-*boned* horse
2 : with the bones removed • *boned* chicken • a *boned* fish

bone•head /ˈbounˌhɛd/ *noun, pl* **-heads** [*count*] *informal* : a stupid or foolish person • I told him he was acting like a *bonehead.* [=*numbskull*] — often used before another noun • a *bonehead* [=*boneheaded*] decision
– bone•head•ed /ˈbounˈhɛdəd/ *adj* [*more ~; most ~*] • a *boneheaded* mistake **– bone•head•ed•ness** *noun* [*noncount*]

bone marrow *noun* [*noncount*] : a soft substance that fills the bones of people and animals — called also *marrow*

bone•meal /ˈbounˌmiːl/ *noun* [*noncount*] : bones that have been crushed or ground and that are added to soil to help plants grow better

bon•er /ˈbounɚ/ *noun, pl* **-ers** [*count*] *US, informal*
1 : a foolish or careless mistake • The manager pulled a *boner* [=made a stupid mistake] and lost the game.
2 *impolite* : an erection of the penis

bone•yard /ˈbounˌjaɚd/ *noun, pl* **-yards** [*count*] *US, informal* : CEMETERY

bon•fire /ˈbɑːnˌfajɚ/ *noun, pl* **-fires** [*count*] : a large outdoor fire

Bonfire Night *noun* [*count, noncount*] : the night of November 5th observed in Britain with fireworks and bonfires to celebrate the capture in 1605 of a group of people who planned to destroy the buildings of Parliament

[1]bong /ˈbɑːŋ/ *noun, pl* **bongs** [*count*] : a deep loud sound that is made by a large bell — compare [2]BONG

[2]bong *noun, pl* **bongs** [*count*] : a device that is used for smoking marijuana in which the smoke is passed through water : WATER PIPE — compare [1]BONG

bon•go /ˈbɑːŋgou/ *noun, pl* **-gos** [*count*] : one of a pair of small drums that are joined together and played with the hands — called also *bongo drum*; see picture at PERCUSSION

bon•ho•mie /ˌbɑːnəˈmiː, *Brit* ˈbɒnəmi/ *noun* [*noncount*] *formal* : a feeling of friendliness among a group of people • the *bonhomie* of strangers singing together around a campfire

bonk /ˈbɑːŋk/ *verb* **bonks; bonked; bonk•ing** [+ *obj*] *informal*
1 : to hit (someone or something) • He *bonked* him on the head. • The golf ball *bonked* the hood of the car.
2 *Brit* : to have sexual intercourse with (someone)

bonk•ers /ˈbɑːŋkɚz/ *adj, not used before a noun, informal* : CRAZY • You have to be *bonkers* to gamble that much. • I was ***driven bonkers*** by the noise.
go bonkers *informal* : to become very excited or angry • The fans *went bonkers* when their team won.

bon mot /ˌbɑːnˈmou/ *noun, pl* **bons mots** *or* **bon mots** /ˌbɑːnˈmou/ [*count*] *formal* : a clever remark : WITTICISM • She had a sparkling *bon mot* for every occasion. ✧ This term is from French and literally means "good word."

bon•net /ˈbɑːnət/ *noun, pl* **-nets** [*count*]
1 : a hat that ties under the chin ✧ Bonnets were worn by women in the past but are now only worn by babies.

B

2 *Brit* : [1]HOOD 2b • He lifted the car's *bonnet* to check the engine.
have a bee in your bonnet see [1]BEE

bon·ny *also* **bon·nie** /ˈbɑːni/ *adj* **bon·ni·er; -est** *chiefly Scotland* : very pretty or attractive • a *bonny* lass/baby

bon·sai /ˈbɑːnˌsaɪ/ *noun, pl* **bonsai**
1 [*count*] : a very small tree or bush that is grown in a pot by using special methods to control its growth
2 [*noncount*] : the art of growing bonsai

bonsai

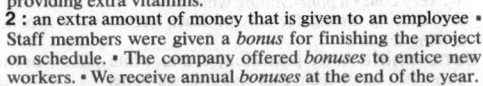

bo·nus /ˈboʊnəs/ *noun, pl* **-nus·es** [*count*]
1 : something good that is more than what was expected or required • As a *bonus* for good behavior you can stay up late. • The product has the ***added bonus*** of providing extra vitamins.
2 : an extra amount of money that is given to an employee • Staff members were given a *bonus* for finishing the project on schedule. • The company offered *bonuses* to entice new workers. • We receive annual *bonuses* at the end of the year.

bon vi·vant /ˌbɑːnviˈvɑːnt/ *noun, pl* **bons vi·vants** *or* **bon vi·vants** /ˌbɑːnviˈvɑnts/ [*count*] *formal* : a person who likes going to parties and other social occasions and who enjoys good food, wine, etc. — called also (*Brit*) *bon viveur*

bon voy·age /ˌbɑːnvoɪˈɑːʒ/ *noun* [*noncount*] : [2]FAREWELL 1 • The crowd waved *bon voyage* as the ship left the dock. — usually used to say that you hope someone who is leaving on a trip will have a good journey • People in the crowd shouted "*Bon voyage*!" as the ship left the dock. • *Bon voyage*. Have a safe trip. • We went with him to the station to ***wish/bid him bon voyage***.

bony /ˈboʊni/ *adj* **bon·i·er; -est** [*more* ~; *most* ~]
1 : resembling bone • a hard, *bony* substance
2 : full of bones • a *bony* piece of fish
3 : having large or noticeable bones • *bony* fingers/knees
4 : very thin • I used to be fat but my sister was always *bony*.

[1]**boo** /ˈbuː/ *noun, pl* **boos**
1 [*count*] : a sound that people make to show they do not like or approve of someone or something • A chorus of *boos* was heard after the shot missed the goal. • The announcement was greeted by/with a mixture of *boos* and cheers.
2 [*noncount*] *informal* : any sound at all — usually used in negative statements • He never said *boo* [=he never said anything], so I didn't even know he was there. ✧ A person who (*US*) ***wouldn't say boo*** or (*Brit*) ***wouldn't say boo to a goose*** is very quiet and shy.

[2]**boo** *interj*
1 — used to show dislike or disapproval of someone or something • The crowd shouted "*Boo!*" when the announcement was made. • *Boo*! Get off the stage. ✧ When people say "Boo!" with this meaning, they say it very slowly.
2 — used when a person frightens someone • My brother scared me when he jumped out from behind the door and shouted "*Boo!*" ✧ When people say "Boo!" with this meaning, they say it very quickly.

[3]**boo** *verb* **boos; booed; boo·ing** : to show dislike or disapproval of someone or something by shouting "Boo" slowly [*no obj*] Many people in the crowd *booed* when the announcement was made. [+ *obj*] Many people in the crowd *booed* the announcement, but a few people cheered it. • The crowd *booed* the singer off the stage. [=the crowd booed so much that the singer stopped singing and left the stage]
– booing *noun* [*noncount*] • The *booing* was so loud I could hardly hear the announcement.

[1]**boob** /ˈbuːb/ *noun, pl* **boobs** [*count*] *US, informal* : a stupid or foolish person • She's not the helpless *boob* she seems to be. • an incompetent *boob* — compare [2]BOOB, [3]BOOB

[2]**boob** *noun, pl* **boobs** [*count*] *informal + sometimes offensive* : a woman's breast • a woman with big *boobs* • She plans to have a ***boob job***. [=a surgical operation to increase the size of a woman's breasts] — compare [1]BOOB, [3]BOOB

[3]**boob** *noun, pl* **boobs** [*count*] *Brit, informal* : a foolish or careless mistake — compare [1]BOOB, [2]BOOB

[4]**boob** *verb* **boobs; boobed; boob·ing** [*no obj*] *Brit, informal* : to make a foolish or careless mistake • Officials really *boobed* [=(*chiefly US*) *goofed*] on handling the situation and made it worse.

boo–boo /ˈbuːˌbuː/ *noun, pl* **-boos** [*count*] *informal*
1 : a small injury (such as a bruise or scratch) — used especially by children or when speaking to children • She fell down and got a *boo-boo*. • Did you get a *boo-boo*?
2 : a foolish or careless mistake • I made a slight *boo-boo* when I added up the numbers. • a major diplomatic *boo-boo*

boob tube *noun, pl* ~ **tubes**
1 ***the boob tube*** *US, informal + often disapproving* : TELEVISION • They spent the evening in front of *the boob tube*. • What's on *the boob tube* tonight?
2 [*count*] *Brit* : TUBE TOP

[1]**boo·by** /ˈbuːbi/ *noun, pl* **-bies** [*count*] *chiefly Brit, informal* : a stupid or foolish person • a witless *booby* — compare [2]BOOBY

[2]**booby** *noun, pl* **-bies** [*count*] *US, informal + sometimes offensive* : a woman's breast — compare [1]BOOBY

booby hatch *noun*
the booby hatch *informal + often offensive* : a hospital for people who are mentally ill

booby prize *noun, pl* ~ **prizes** [*count*] *informal* : a prize that is given as a joke to the person who finishes last in a competition — usually singular • You came in last—you win/get the *booby prize*.

booby trap *noun, pl* ~ **traps** [*count*]
1 : a hidden bomb that explodes when the object connected to it is touched, moved, etc. • Someone had rigged a *booby trap* that blew up the car when the engine was started.
2 : a trap that is set as a joke to shock or frighten someone • We set a *booby trap* by balancing a bucket of water on top of the door so that it would fall on him when he came in.
– boo·by–trap *verb* **-traps; -trapped; -trap·ping** [+ *obj*] • Someone had *booby-trapped* the car. • His roommate *booby-trapped* the door. **– booby–trapped** *adj* • The house is *booby-trapped*. • a *booby-trapped* car

boog·er /ˈbʊgɚ/ *noun, pl* **-gers** [*count*] *US, informal* : a piece of mucus from the nose — used especially by children

boo·gey·man /ˈbʊgiˌmæn/ *noun, pl* **-men** /-ˌmɛn/ [*count*] *US*
1 : BOGEYMAN 1
2 : BOGEYMAN 2

[1]**boo·gie** /ˈbʊgi, *Brit* ˈbuːgi/ *noun* [*noncount*] : BOOGIE-WOOGIE

[2]**boo·gie** *also* **boo·gy** *or* **boo·gey** /ˈbʊgi, *Brit* ˈbuːgi/ *verb* **boo·gies** *also* **boo·geys; boo·gied** *also* **boo·geyed; boo·gy·ing** *also* **boo·gey·ing** [*no obj*] *informal*
1 : to dance especially to rock music • Everyone at the disco was just *boogying* (down) all night.
2 *US* : to move or go quickly • Let's *boogie* on out of here.

boo·gie–woo·gie /ˌbʊgiˈwʊgi, *Brit* ˌbuːgiˈwuːgi/ *noun* [*noncount*] : a style of playing a type of music similar to jazz (called the blues) on the piano with a fast, strong, steady beat

[1]**book** /ˈbʊk/ *noun, pl* **books**
1 [*count*] **a** : a set of printed sheets of paper that are held together inside a cover : a long written work • The shelves in his office are filled with *books*. • That's one of the best *books* I've read in a long time. • a novelist who has written some wonderful *books* • a *book* about plumbing • The library has many dictionaries and other reference *books*. • a hardcover/paperback *book* — sometimes used figuratively • You can learn many things by studying the great *book* of nature. [=by studying nature] **b** : a long written work that can be read on a computer : E-BOOK • an electronic *book*
2 [*count*] : a set of sheets of paper that are inside a cover and that you can write information on • an appointment *book* • an address *book* — see also NOTEBOOK
3 [*count*] : a major section of a long written work (such as the Bible) • the *books* of the Bible • a story that is told in the *Book* of Job — see also GOOD BOOK
4 [*count*] : a set of things held together inside a cover like the pages of a book • a *book* of stamps • a *book* of matches [=a matchbook] — see also CHECKBOOK
5 ***books*** [*plural*] **a** : the financial records of a business • The company's *books* [=*accounts*] show a profit. **b** : the official records of a business or organization • I'm sorry, but your name does not appear in/on our *books*.
6 ***the book*** *US, informal* : the knowledge or information that relates to a particular subject, person, etc. • *The book* on him is that he can't hit a curveball. [=people have seen and reported that he can't hit a curveball]
7 ***the book*** *informal* : PHONE BOOK • Give me a call if you need to. I'm in *the book*. [=my telephone number is listed in the telephone book]

a closed book : a person or thing that is difficult to understand • Even to his closest friends, he was always something of *a closed book.* — compare AN OPEN BOOK (below)
an open book : a person or thing that is easy to learn about and understand • My life is *an open book.* I have nothing to hide.
bring (someone) to book *chiefly Brit, formal* : to require (someone) to explain and accept punishment or criticism for bad or wrong behavior • The people responsible for these crimes must be *brought to book.* [=*brought to account*]
by the book : by following the official rules very strictly • My boss insists on doing everything *by the book.* • They ran all the investigations *by the book.*
cook the books see [2]COOK
every trick in the book see [1]TRICK
hit the books *informal* : to study or begin studying very intensely • I've got to *hit the books* all weekend if I'm going to pass this test.
in my book *informal* : in my opinion • She deserves credit, *in my book,* for much of the company's recent success. • He isn't even a good boss, at least not *in my book.*
in someone's bad books *chiefly Brit, informal* : in a state in which you are not liked or treated nicely by someone • He remains *in her bad books.* [=she is still displeased with him]
in someone's good books *chiefly Brit, informal* : in a state in which you are liked or are treated nicely by someone • He's trying to get back *in his boss's good books* by offering to work overtime.
one for the books : a very unusual, important, or surprising situation, statement, event, etc. • There have been a lot of scandals in local politics over the years, but this is *one for the books.*
on the books : part of the set of official laws • It's an outdated law that's still *on the books.*
read someone like a book see [1]READ
suit someone's book see [2]SUIT
throw the book at *informal* : to punish (someone) as severely as possible • The judge threatened to *throw the book at* him if he committed another offense. • I thought I would get off with just a warning, but they *threw the book at* me.
write the book on see WRITE

[2]**book** *verb* **books; booked; book·ing**
1 : to make arrangements so that you will be able to use or have (something, such as a room, table, or seat) at a later time [+ *obj*] We *booked* [=*reserved*] a hotel room. • They *booked* two seats at the theater. • They *booked* tickets for a direct flight from London to New York. • I *booked* a table at our favorite restaurant. [*no obj*] She *booked* through her travel agent. • We will need to *book* early. ♢ This sense is used in U.S. English, but it is more common in British English. In U.S. English, *reserve* or *make a reservation for* is more commonly used. ♢ When a hotel, restaurant, etc., is ***booked (up)***, ***booked solid***, or ***fully booked***, there are no more rooms, tables, etc., available. These forms are commonly used in both U.S. and British English. • The hotels in the city were *booked solid* for the conference. • The flight was *fully booked.* • The hotel was all *booked up* for the week.
2 [+ *obj*] : to make arrangements for (someone) to do, use, or have something at a later time • She *booked* me on a flight from Oslo to Paris. • He was *booked* to sail on Monday.
3 [+ *obj*] : to schedule a performance or appearance by (someone, such as a musician) • The band was *booked* to play at the reception. • *book* a singer
4 [+ *obj*] *law* : to write down in an official police record the name of (a person who is being charged with a crime) — usually used as *(be) booked* • She *was booked* on suspicion of murder.
5 [+ *obj*] *Brit, of a soccer referee* : to write down in an official book the name of (a player who has broken the rules in a game) — usually used as *(be) booked* • He *was booked* for a late tackle.
book in/into [*phrasal verb*] ***book in or book into (something)*** *Brit* : to arrive at and be given a room in a hotel, an inn, etc. • We *booked in* [=*checked in*] shortly after noon. • We *booked into* [=*checked into*] our hotel shortly after noon.
– book·able /ˈbʊkəbəl/ *adj, chiefly Brit* • *bookable* flights/seats • *bookable* hotel rooms

[3]**book** *adj, always used before a noun* : learned from reading books and not from experience • His schooling provided him with extensive *book* knowledge/learning. • She had plenty of *book* learning but no hands-on experience.

book·bind·ing /ˈbʊkˌbaɪndɪŋ/ *noun* [*noncount*] : the process or job of attaching the pages of a book together inside a cover
– book·bind·er /ˈbʊkˌbaɪndɚ/ *noun, pl* **-ers** [*count*]

book·case /ˈbʊkˌkeɪs/ *noun, pl* **-cases** [*count*] : a piece of furniture with shelves to hold books — see picture at LIVING ROOM

book club *noun, pl* **~ clubs** [*count*]
1 : an organization that sells books to its members at low prices
2 : a group of people who meet to talk about the books that they are reading

book·end /ˈbʊkˌɛnd/ *noun, pl* **-ends** [*count*] : something placed at the end of a row of books to hold them up • a pair of *bookends* shaped like horses • He used an empty flowerpot as a *bookend.*

book·ie /ˈbʊki/ *noun, pl* **-ies** [*count*] *informal* : BOOKMAKER • Their *bookie* is giving good odds.

book·ing /ˈbʊkɪŋ/ *noun, pl* **-ings**
1 : an arrangement for a person or group (such as a singer or band) to perform at a particular place [*count*] She has several concert *bookings* this fall. • The comedian missed some *bookings* because of illness. [*noncount*] All *booking* is done by the band's manager.
2 : an arrangement to have something (such as a room) held for your use at a later time [*count*] Our hotel register shows no *booking* [=(*US* more commonly) *reservation*] for you. • cruise ship *bookings* [*noncount*] Advance *booking* [=(*US* more commonly) *reservation*] is required. • *booking* fees • a *booking* agent
3 [*count*] *Brit, soccer* : the act of officially recording the name of a player who has broken the rules in a game

booking office *noun, pl* **~ -fices** [*count*] *Brit* : a place in a train station or bus station where people can buy tickets

book·ish /ˈbʊkɪʃ/ *adj* [*more ~; most ~*] *sometimes disapproving* : more interested in reading books and studying than doing more physical activities (such as sports) • Their teacher was a *bookish* fellow.
– book·ish·ness *noun* [*noncount*]

book·keep·er /ˈbʊkˌkiːpɚ/ *noun, pl* **-ers** [*count*] : a person whose job is to keep the financial records for a business
– book·keep·ing /ˈbʊkˌkiːpɪŋ/ *noun* [*noncount*] • He does the *bookkeeping.* • a *bookkeeping* error

book·let /ˈbʊklət/ *noun, pl* **-lets** [*count*] : a book with only a few pages that contains information on one subject • This *booklet* describes how to set up the DVD player. • The speaker handed out *booklets* [=*pamphlets*] on AIDS awareness.

book·mak·er /ˈbʊkˌmeɪkɚ/ *noun, pl* **-ers** [*count*] : a person who decides how likely it is that an event will occur (such as the winning of a race by a particular horse) and receives and pays off bets about it — called also (*informal*) *bookie*
– book·mak·ing /ˈbʊkˌmeɪkɪŋ/ *noun* [*noncount*]

[1]**book·mark** /ˈbʊkˌmɑɚk/ *noun, pl* **-marks** [*count*]
1 *or* ***book·mark·er*** /ˈbʊkˌmɑɚkɚ/ : something (such as a piece of paper) that is put in a book to show the place where you stopped reading
2 *computers* : something (such as a menu entry or icon) that allows you to go quickly and directly to something (such as an Internet site) that you have seen before

[2]**bookmark** *verb* **-marks; -marked; -mark·ing** [+ *obj*] *computers* : to create a computer bookmark for (something, such as an Internet site) • I *bookmarked* the site.

book·mo·bile /ˈbʊkmoʊˌbiːl/ *noun, pl* **-biles** [*count*] *US* : a large vehicle that contains many library books and that goes to different places so that people can borrow the books — called also (*Brit*) *mobile library*

book·plate /ˈbʊkˌpleɪt/ *noun, pl* **-plates** [*count*] : a piece of paper stuck on the inside front cover of a book that shows the name of the person who owns the book

book·sell·er /ˈbʊkˌsɛlɚ/ *noun, pl* **-ers** [*count*] : a person or company that sells books
– book·sell·ing /ˈbʊkˌsɛlɪŋ/ *noun* [*noncount*]

book·shelf /ˈbʊkˌʃɛlf/ *noun, pl* **-shelves** [*count*] : a shelf that is used for books

book·shop /ˈbʊkˌʃɑːp/ *noun, pl* **-shops** [*count*] : BOOKSTORE

book·stall /ˈbʊkˌstɑːl/ *noun, pl* **-stalls** [*count*] *Brit* : NEWSSTAND

book·store /ˈbʊkˌstoɚ/ *noun, pl* **-stores** [*count*] *chiefly US* : a store that sells books

book token *noun, pl* **~ -kens** [*count*] *Brit* **:** a card that can be used instead of money to pay for books **:** a gift certificate for buying books

book value *noun* [*noncount*] *finance* **:** the amount of money that something (such as a car) is officially worth based on its age, style, condition, etc. • I paid $4,100 for the car four years ago, but its *book value* is now under $500.

book•worm /ˈbʊkˌwɚm/ *noun, pl* **-worms** [*count*] **:** a person who likes to read books and who spends a lot of time reading and studying • She was always a *bookworm* when she was a kid.

[1]**boom** /ˈbuːm/ *verb* **booms; boomed; boom•ing**

1 a [*no obj*] **:** to make a deep and loud sound • the sound of the bass drum *booming* • His voice *boomed* out across the congregation. **b** [+ *obj*] **:** to say (something) in a deep and loud voice • She *boomed* commands from the stern of the ship. • "What's going on here?" he *boomed.*

2 [*no obj*] *of a business or industry* **:** to grow or expand suddenly • Housing construction has *boomed* in the past year. • Last year we almost had to close the store, but now business is *booming.*

[2]**boom** *noun, pl* **booms** [*count*]

1 : a deep and loud sound or cry • the *boom* of a gun • thunderous *booms* • the rhythmic *boom* of the waves — often used as an interjection to indicate that something has happened suddenly • The dance club was empty and then—*boom*!—a hundred people were there. — see also SONIC BOOM

2 : a rapid increase in growth or economic success • the population *boom* • the city's *boom* years **:** a rapid growth of business • a *boom* in tourism = a tourism *boom* • Housing costs have skyrocketed since the real estate *boom.* • a *boom* economy [=an economy experiencing a boom] — see also BABY BOOM, BOOMTOWN

– compare [3]BOOM

[3]**boom** *noun, pl* **booms** [*count*]

1 : a long pole attached to the bottom of a sailboat's sail

2 : a long pole used to hold a microphone in position from a distance

3 : a floating barrier used on a river, lake, or harbor to catch floating objects, to keep boats from entering, or to prevent an oil spill from spreading • Large *booms* were brought in to help contain the oil spill.

– compare [2]BOOM

boom box *noun, pl* **~ boxes** [*count*] **:** a large portable radio and often tape deck or CD player with two attached speakers

boom box

boom•er /ˈbuːmɚ/ *noun, pl* **-ers** [*count*] **:** a person born during a period of time when many babies were born **:** a person born during a baby boom • a television program that is popular among *boomers* [=*baby boomers*; people who were born during the baby boom after World War II]

[1]**boo•mer•ang** /ˈbuːməˌræŋ/ *noun, pl* **-angs** [*count*] **:** a curved, flat, wooden tool that can be thrown in such a way that it returns to the thrower ✧ *Boomerangs* were invented in Australia thousands of years ago and were originally used for hunting.

[2]**boomerang** *verb* **-angs; -anged; -ang•ing** [*no obj*] **:** to have an effect that is the opposite of the desired or expected effect **:** BACKFIRE • We thought that bringing the issue up would lessen tension, but that plan *boomeranged.* [=tension has increased] • His attempt to discredit his opponent *boomeranged* [=it affected him instead of his opponent] when people began questioning his motives.

boomerangs

boom•ing /ˈbuːmɪŋ/ *adj*

1 : growing or expanding very quickly • *booming* car sales • We're not benefiting from the country's *booming* economy.

2 : loud and low **:** having a low rumbling sound • Suddenly the children heard Grandpa's *booming* voice demanding that they get down from the roof.

3 : very forceful or powerful • a tennis player with a *booming* serve

boom•let /ˈbuːmlət/ *noun, pl* **-lets** [*count*] **:** a sudden and usually brief increase in business activity **:** a small boom • A few years ago, the town enjoyed a nice *boomlet,* but since then times have been tough.

boom•town /ˈbuːmˌtaʊn/ *noun, pl* **-towns** [*count*] **:** a town that experiences a sudden growth in business and population **:** a booming town • a former *boomtown*

boon /ˈbuːn/ *noun, pl* **boons** [*count*] **:** something pleasant or helpful **:** a benefit or advantage — usually singular • What at first looks like an inconvenience can be a *boon.* — usually + *for* or *to* • The new tax cut is a *boon for* homeowners. • Reliable daycare is a *boon to* working parents.

boon companion *noun, pl* **~ -ions** [*count*] *literary* **:** a close friend

boon•docks /ˈbuːnˌdɑːks/ *noun*

the boondocks US, informal **:** an area that is not close to any towns or cities • She grew up in *the boondocks* so city life came as a real shock to her.

boon•dog•gle /ˈbuːnˌdɑːgəl/ *noun, pl* **-dog•gles** [*count*] *US* **:** an expensive and wasteful project usually paid for with public money • Critics say the dam is a complete *boondoggle*—over budget, behind schedule, and unnecessary.

boon•ies /ˈbuːniz/ *noun*

the boonies US, informal **:** BOONDOCKS • The school is way out in *the boonies.*

boor /ˈbuɚ/ *noun, pl* **boors** [*count*] **:** a rude and rough person • I can't invite a *boor* like him to dinner! He'd offend the other guests.

Do not confuse *boor* with *bore.*

– **boor•ish** /ˈburɪʃ/ *adj* • *boorish* [=*rude, crude*] behavior • a *boorish* tyrant – **boor•ish•ly** *adv* • behaving *boorishly* – **boor•ish•ness** *noun* [*noncount*]

[1]**boost** /ˈbuːst/ *verb* **boosts; boost•ed; boost•ing** [+ *obj*]

1 : to increase the force, power, or amount of (something) • The farm has *boosted* [=*increased*] wheat production by 25 percent. • *boost* [=*raise*] prices • The article discusses a number of ways people can *boost* [=*strengthen*] their immune systems. • The company needs to find ways to *boost* [=*improve*] morale.

2 : to push or shove (something or someone) up from below • She *boosted* the boy onto his father's shoulders. — sometimes used figuratively • His work on the high-profile lawsuit has *boosted* him into the political arena.

[2]**boost** *noun, pl* **boosts** [*count*]

1 : an increase in amount • a *boost* in wheat production • a *boost* in sales • Exercise can sometimes provide a *boost* of energy. • After layoffs at the company, employees needed a *boost* in morale.

2 : help or encouragement • One company's innovation has proven to be a *boost* to the entire industry.

3 : a push upward • Give the boy a *boost* onto the stage, will you?

boost•er /ˈbuːstɚ/ *noun, pl* **-ers** [*count*]

1 : something that boosts someone or something: such as **a :** an action or substance that makes something stronger or more effective • These exercises are real metabolism *boosters.* • The herb is said to be an immune *booster.* [=something that strengthens a person's immunity to illness] **b :** something that helps or encourages someone or something • Music is my favorite mood *booster.* • A sincere compliment can be a true confidence *booster.* **c :** BOOSTER SHOT

2 *US* **:** someone who supports an idea or organization • The university has a number of wealthy *boosters* who contribute generously each year. • the football team's *boosters*

3 : part of a rocket that provides force for the launch and the first part of the flight • a new design for rocket *boosters*

– see also BOOSTER SEAT

boost•er•ism /ˈbuːstɚˌɪzəm/ *noun* [*noncount*] *US* **:** enthusiastic and usually excessive support for something or someone • Her article asserts that hometown *boosterism* keeps people from assessing the crime problem accurately. • nationalistic *boosterism*

booster seat *noun, pl* **~ seats** [*count*] **:** a high seat that raises a child to a higher position at a table, in a car, etc. — called also *booster chair,* (*Brit*) *booster cushion*

booster shot *noun, pl* **~ shots** [*count*] *chiefly US* **:** an extra amount of a substance (called a vaccine) that is injected with a needle into a person or animal to help protect against a particular disease • He had to get two *booster shots* at his latest checkup. • a tetanus *booster shot* — called also *booster*

B

[1]boot /ˈbu:t/ *noun, pl* **boots**
1 [*count*] : a covering usually of leather or rubber for the entire foot and the lower part of the leg • You'll need a pair of warm *boots* for winter. • It's been snowing, so you'd better wear your *boots*. • hiking *boots* [=boots worn for hiking] • riding *boots* [=boots worn for horseback riding] — see picture at SHOE; see also BOOTED, COWBOY BOOT, HOBNAIL BOOT, SKI BOOT
2 [*count*] : a forceful kick with the foot • She gave the ball a *boot*, and it landed on the other side of the field.
3 ***the boot*** *informal* : a sudden dismissal from a job • He ***got the boot*** [=*got fired*] for talking to the press about company secrets. • I heard they ***gave her the boot***. [=they fired her; they told her she could no longer work for them]
4 [*count*] *Brit* : the trunk of a car
5 [*count*] *US* : DENVER BOOT
as tough as old boots see [1]TOUGH
lick someone's boots see [1]LICK
the boot is on the other foot see [1]FOOT
to boot : BESIDES, ALSO • He's smart, funny, and handsome *to boot*.
too big for your boots see [1]BIG
to put the boot in *Brit, informal* **1** : to treat someone in a cruel or critical way **2** : to kick someone again and again
– see also BOSSY-BOOTS

[2]boot *verb* **boots; boot·ed; boot·ing**
1 [+ *obj*] : to kick (something) forcefully • She *booted* the ball across the field.
2 [+ *obj*] *informal* **a** : to force (someone) to leave a place or situation • He left public service after voters *booted* him from the mayor's office. [=he chose not to work for the government after he was not reelected as mayor] • Any players who start a fight will get *booted* from the game. — often + *out* • His wife *booted* him *out*. [=his wife made him leave their home] • He got *booted out* of office in the last election. **b** : to dismiss (someone) suddenly from a job • She got *booted* [=*fired*] in May and has been looking for work ever since.
3 : to start a computer [*no obj*] The new computer *boots* much more quickly than the old one did. — often + *up* • Did you *boot up* yet? [+ *obj*] You don't need all these applications to open every time you *boot* your computer. — often + *up* • She *booted up* the computer. — see also REBOOT
4 [+ *obj*] *US* : to lock a special device (called a Denver boot) onto one of the wheels of (a car) so that the car cannot be moved • His car was *booted* (by the police).

boot camp *noun, pl* **~ camps** [*count*] *US*
1 : a camp where people who have recently joined the U.S. Army, Navy, or Marine Corps receive their basic training
2 : a short but very difficult training program : a program or situation that helps people become much better at doing something in a short period of time • business *boot camp* • *boot camp* for artists

boot·ed /ˈbu:təd/ *adj* : wearing boots • She shoved her *booted* feet under the table.

bootee *chiefly Brit spelling of* BOOTIE

booth /ˈbu:θ, *Brit* ˈbu:ð/ *noun, pl* **booths** /ˈbu:ðz/ [*count*]
1 : a partially enclosed area or a small and usually temporary building where things are sold or displayed or services are provided • A local sheep farmer has a *booth* at the county fair and is selling wool yarn. • We got hot dogs at one of the food *booths*. • Someone at the ***information booth*** [=a booth at which general information about a place or event is provided] will be able to tell you where to find a bathroom.
2 a : a small area that is enclosed in order to provide privacy for one person • a voting *booth* — see also PHONE BOOTH, PHOTO BOOTH, POLLING BOOTH **b** : an enclosed area for some kinds of workers that provides shelter and keeps them separated from the public • a ticket *booth* • Traffic slowed as we approached the ***toll booth***. [=a booth at which drivers pay a fee for using a particular road or bridge] • Our seats at the baseball game were next to the ***broadcast booth***. [=a booth from which a radio broadcast is made]
3 *chiefly US* : a table in a restaurant between benches with high backs • They sat at/in a *booth* next to the window.

boo·tie *or chiefly Brit* **boo·tee** /ˈbu:ti/ *noun, pl* **boo·ties** *or* **boo·tees** [*count*]
1 : a short and thick sock for a baby
2 : a sock, slipper, or boot that covers the foot and ankle
3 : [2]BOOTY

[1]boot·leg /ˈbu:tˌlɛg/ *verb* **-legs; -legged; -leg·ging** [+ *obj*]
1 : to illegally copy (a video, CD, etc.) or illegally record (a live performance) • He *bootlegged* the show and gave copies to several friends. • *bootleg* a DVD • a *bootlegged* [=*pirated*] version of the movie
2 : to make or sell (alcoholic liquor) illegally • *bootlegging* moonshine
– **boot·leg·ger** *noun, pl* **-gers** [*count*] • a famous *bootlegger* during the Prohibition period

[2]bootleg *noun, pl* **-legs**
1 [*count*] : an illegal copy of a video, CD, etc., or an illegal recording of a live performance • She was arrested for selling *bootlegs* online. — often used before another noun • a *bootleg* album/DVD • selling *bootleg* copies of the concert
2 [*noncount*] : alcohol that is made or sold illegally — usually used before another noun • *bootleg* whiskey/bourbon

boot·lick·er /ˈbu:tˌlɪkɚ/ *noun, pl* **-ers** [*count*] *informal* + *disapproving* : a person who praises, helps, or obeys someone in order to gain favors or advantages — see also *lick someone's boots* at [1]LICK
– **boot·lick·ing** /ˈbu:tˌlɪkɪŋ/ *adj* • a *bootlicking* politician
– **bootlicking** *noun* [*noncount*] • His *bootlicking* [=*brownnosing*] disgusts me.

boot·straps /ˈbu:tˌstræps/ *noun*
by your own bootstraps : without help from other people : as a result of your own hard work • Despite many obstacles, she has pulled herself up *by her own bootstraps*.

[1]boo·ty /ˈbu:ti/ *noun* [*noncount*]
1 : money or goods stolen or taken in war • war *booty* [=*loot, plunder, spoils*]
2 : a valuable gain or prize • His *booty* from the auction included several rare antiques.
– compare [2]BOOTY

[2]booty *also* **boo·tie** /ˈbu:ti/ *noun, pl* **boo·ties** [*count*] *US slang* : BUTTOCKS • She was shaking her *booty*. — compare [1]BOOTY

[1]booze /ˈbu:z/ *noun* [*noncount*] *informal* : alcoholic drinks • We bought some chips and *booze* for the party.

[2]booze *verb* **booz·es; boozed; booz·ing** *informal* : to drink a lot of alcohol [*no obj*] He was out *boozing* with his friends. [+ *obj*] They ***boozed it up*** [=got drunk] the night before the wedding.

booz·er /ˈbu:zɚ/ *noun, pl* **-ers** [*count*] *informal*
1 : a person who drinks a lot of alcohol • an unapologetic *boozer*
2 *Brit* : PUB • They went into the *boozer* for a beer.

[1]bop /ˈbɑ:p/ *verb* **bops; bopped; bop·ping** [+ *obj*] : to hit (someone or something) especially in a playful way • She *bopped* him on the head. — compare [4]BOP

[2]bop *noun, pl* **bops** [*count*] : a hit that is not very forceful • She gave him a playful *bop* on the head. — compare [3]BOP

[3]bop *noun, pl* **bops**
1 [*noncount*] : a kind of jazz that uses complex melodies and harmonies and that often has a very quick tempo — called also *bebop*
2 [*count*] *Brit, informal* : DANCE • Are you up for a *bop*? [=would you like to dance?] They're playing my favorite song.
– compare [2]BOP

[4]bop *verb* **bops; bopped; bopping** [*no obj*] *informal*
1 : to go for only a short time • She'll be back in a few minutes. She just *bopped* [=*popped*] over to the store.
2 *US* : to walk or move like a person who is dancing to lively music • He was *bopping* down the street.
3 *Brit, informal* : to dance to popular music • I think we're going to ***go bopping*** tonight. Would you like to join us?
– compare [1]BOP

bor·age /ˈborɪʤ/ *noun* [*noncount*] : a type of European plant that has blue flowers and hairy leaves ✧ The leaves of this plant are used as medicine and in salads.

bo·rax /ˈboɚˌæks/ *noun* [*noncount*] : a mineral that is used especially for cleaning things

Bor·deaux /boɚˈdoʊ/ *noun, pl* **Bordeaux** [*count, noncount*] : a red or white wine from the Bordeaux region of France

bor·del·lo /boɚˈdɛloʊ/ *noun, pl* **-los** [*count*] *somewhat literary* : a building in which prostitutes are available : BROTHEL

[1]bor·der /ˈboɚdɚ/ *noun, pl* **-ders**
1 a [*count*] : a line separating one country or state from another • the *border* between Poland and Slovenia • He grew up in Malaysia, near the Indonesian *border*. • the *border* of Pennsylvania • the Florida–Georgia *border* • the contested northern *border* — often used before another noun • *border* guards • a *border* dispute • *border* crossings **b** [*count*] : a

boundary between places • They live just beyond the western *border* of the park. • the *border* of the Sahara **c** ***the border*** : a specific border • They've lived in southern Texas for years, but have never been south of *the border*. [=the U.S. border with Mexico] • She's from northern Montana, near *the border*. [=the U.S. border with Canada] • We crossed *the border* (into France) at Gavarnie.

2 [*count*] : a decorative design along the edge of something (such as a rug or wallpaper) • The quilt is quite plain except for its colorful *border*. • a broad red *border* on each plate • the photograph's white *border*

3 [*count*] : a narrow bed of plants along the edge of a garden or walk • He planted pansies in the *border*. • *border* plants

2border *verb* **-ders; -dered; -der·ing** [+ *obj*]

1 : to be next to (a country, state, or area) : to share a border with (a country, state, or area) • Slovenia *borders* Poland. • Their property *borders* the park.

2 : to form a border of (something) : to define the edge of (something) • Tall trees *border* the avenue. • Two rivers *border* the city. — usually used as *(be) bordered* • The neighborhood *is bordered* by Main Street on the north and the river on the south. • streets *bordered* by oak trees

3 : to put a border on (something) — usually used as *(be) bordered* • The scarf *is bordered* with gold stitching.

border on [*phrasal verb*] ***border on (something)*** **1** : to have a border on (something) : to lie on a boundary of (something) • The area my ancestors come from *borders on* the Atacama Desert. **2** : to be very like (something) : to come very close to being (something) • The play's dialog *borders on* [=*verges on*] the ridiculous. • an enthusiasm *bordering on* fanaticism

bor·der·land /ˈboɚdɚˌlænd/ *noun, pl* **-lands** [*count*]

1 : the land on either side of a border between countries • the Slovenian-Polish *borderlands* • a *borderland* province [=a province that is in a borderland]

2 : an unclear state or condition that is between two things and is like each of them in some ways • in the *borderland* between sleeping and waking • He describes adolescence as the tumultuous *borderlands* between childhood and adulthood.

1bor·der·line /ˈboɚdɚˌlaɪn/ *adj*

1 : having some but not all characteristics of something • In *borderline* cases like these, the best course of action is difficult to determine. • Two candidates for the job seem very good, and three others are *borderline*. [=three may or may not be suitable for the job]

2 : not quite as severe as what is usual or expected • As a *borderline* diabetic, Lara is able to control her blood sugar levels solely through diet. • *borderline* alcoholics

3 : existing at or near a border • a *borderline* town

2borderline *noun, pl* **-lines** [*count*] : the point at which one thing changes to another thing : the point *between* two different things • New technology in hearing aids makes the *borderline* [=*distinction*] *between* the deaf and hearing worlds less clear. • the *borderline between* fact and fiction

3borderline *adv* : almost or nearly • The movie is only *borderline* funny. • She was *borderline* suicidal.

1bore /ˈboɚ/ *verb* **bores; bored; boring** [+ *obj*] : to make (someone) tired and annoyed by being uninteresting or too much the same • He was *bored* by the lecture. = The lecture *bored* him. • Good writers will avoid *boring* their readers at any cost. • Eventually she got *bored* with the party and left. ✧ Someone or something that ***bores you stiff*** or ***bores you to death*** or ***bores you to tears*** is extremely boring. • I was *bored stiff* during the movie. • I was *bored to death* the whole time he was talking. • He *bores* us all *to tears* by telling the same stories over and over again. — compare 3BORE

– bored *adj* [*more* ~; *most* ~] • a few *bored* teenagers • I've never been so *bored*.

2bore *noun, pl* **bores** [*count*] : an uninteresting person or thing : a person or thing that makes people feel tired and annoyed • They're a bunch of *bores*! • The lecture was a total *bore*. — compare 4BORE, 5BORE

Do not confuse *bore* with *boor*.

3bore *verb* **bores; bored; bor·ing**

1 : to make (a hole, tunnel, etc.) in something with a tool or by digging [+ *obj*] My drill isn't powerful enough to *bore* a hole through that post. • She designs machines that are used to *bore* tunnels. [*no obj*] Along the trunk of the tree are holes where insects have *bored* into the tree. • *boring* deep into the earth — often used figuratively • The teacher's eyes *bored* into me. [=the teacher stared at me]

2 [*no obj*] : to move forward steadily • We *bored* through the crowd and finally got to the gate.

– compare 1BORE

4bore *noun, pl* **bores** [*count*]

1 : a hole made by boring — called also *borehole*

2 a : the space inside a gun barrel that is shaped like a tube **b** : the width of the inside part of a gun barrel • a .22 *bore* revolver

– compare 2BORE, 5BORE

5bore *noun, pl* **bores** [*count*] : a giant wave that rushes into a river or bay • a tidal *bore* — compare 2BORE, 4BORE

6bore *past tense of* 2BEAR

bore·dom /ˈboɚdəm/ *noun* [*noncount*] : the state of being bored • On days when few customers came to shop, Bob felt overwhelmed by *boredom*. • the *boredom* of a long car trip

bore·hole /ˈboɚˌhoʊl/ *noun, pl* **-holes** [*count*] : 4BORE 1; *especially* : a hole dug into the earth in order to find water or oil

bor·er /ˈborɚ/ *noun, pl* **-ers** [*count*] : an insect that digs holes in the woody parts of plants

bor·ing /ˈborɪŋ/ *adj* [*more* ~; *most* ~] : dull and uninteresting : causing boredom • a *boring* job/routine • I find her books totally *boring*.

born /ˈboɚn/ *adj*

1 *not used before a noun* : brought into life by the process of birth • She was *born* in a hospital. • He was *born* on a farm. • She was *born* in Nigeria in 1911. • The baby was *born* on July 31st. • Their second son was *born* prematurely. — see also FIRSTBORN, NEWBORN

2 : having certain qualities or characteristics from the time of birth • *born* blind/deaf • Both twins were *born* healthy. • The author Mark Twain was *born* Samuel Clemens. [=was named Samuel Clemens at birth] • She's a *born* teacher/leader. [=she was born with the qualities that make someone a teacher/leader] ✧ If you were ***born to do*** something or ***born to be*** something, you have natural qualities or talents that make you perfectly suited to do or be something. • She was *born to teach*. = She was *born to be* a teacher.

3 *not used before a noun* — used to describe the place where someone was born • He's American *born*. [=he was born in America] • He's Mexican ***born and bred***. = He was *born and bred* in Mexico. [=his birth and childhood took place in Mexico] — often used in combination • Maine-*born*

4 *not used before a noun* — used to describe the social conditions or situations that exist when people are born • Some are *born* in slavery, others *born* merely poor. • She was ***born to*** riches/wealth. = She was ***born into*** a rich/wealthy family. — see also HIGHBORN

5 *not used before a noun* : brought into existence • Her dream of owning farm was *born* when she visited the countryside as a child. • The wine is *born* [=*created*] from the union of two very different grapes. • a mentality *born* in the age of computers • Their relationship was ***born of necessity*** [=established because it was necessary in some way], but it has developed into a true and lasting friendship. • Church leaders assert that the recent unrest in the city is ***born out of*** [=has occurred because of] years of neglect of the city's poor neighborhoods.

born too late ✧ Someone who is said to be *born too late* seems to be better suited for life in an earlier time period. • John prefers early jazz music over the modern stuff. I guess he was *born too late*.

born with a silver spoon in your mouth ✧ If you were *born with a silver spoon in your mouth*, you were born into a very wealthy family.

in all your born days *informal + somewhat old-fashioned* : in your entire life — used to express how unexpected or unusual something is • I never saw anything like it *in all my born days*.

there's one born every minute *or* ***there's a sucker born every minute*** *informal* — used to say that there are many people in the world who are foolish and can be easily deceived

to the manner born see MANNER

to the manor born see MANOR

wasn't born yesterday ✧ Someone who *wasn't born yesterday* is unlikely to believe something that is not true or to trust someone who is not trustworthy. • He said he'd pay me back, but I'll believe it when I see it. I *wasn't born yesterday*.

born-again /ˌboɚnəˈgɛn/ *adj*

1 : having a new or stronger belief in the Christian religion •

The *born-again* actor often talks about his faith during interviews. • She's *born-again* now. • a ***born-again Christian***
2 : newly interested in and enthusiastic about something and eager to make other people think the way you do • a *born-again* fitness buff

[1]**borne** *past participle of* [2]BEAR

[2]**borne** /ˈboən/ *adj* : carried by : spread by — used in combination • water*borne* • It's an air*borne* virus.

bor·ough /ˈbɚrou/ *noun, pl* **-oughs** [*count*]
1 : a village, town, or part of a large city that has its own government ✧ Boroughs are found in a number of English-speaking countries. They are much more common in Great Britain than in the U.S. • the London *borough* of Brent
2 : one of the five main sections of New York City • the *borough* of Brooklyn

bor·row /ˈbɑrou/ *verb* **-rows; -rowed; -row·ing**
1 [+ *obj*] **a** : to take and use (something that belongs to someone else) for a period of time before returning it • Can I *borrow* your camera? [=will you lend me your camera] • The twins often *borrow* each other's clothes. • I'm *borrowing* a friend's car for the weekend. • He *borrowed* the book from the library. **b** : to take and use up (something) with the promise to give back something of equal value • Will you see if we can *borrow* a cup of sugar from the neighbors? • She *borrowed* $20 from me. ✧ When people borrow money from a bank they pay back the same amount over a number of months or years plus an added amount that is called *interest*. • He *borrowed* money from the bank to buy the car.
2 : to use (an idea, saying, etc.) that was thought up by someone else [+ *obj*] The speech was peppered with phrases *borrowed* from Winston Churchill. • She *borrowed* the technique from local artisans. • The company is ***borrowing a page from*** [=using a technique or idea first used by] its largest competitor. [*no obj*] He *borrows* heavily [=includes many ideas] from other philosophers in the book.
3 [+ *obj*] : to use (a word or phrase from another language) in a language • The English word "entrepreneur" was *borrowed* from (the) French.
4 [+ *obj*] *in subtracting from a number with two or more digits* : to take 1 from a digit and add it as 10 to the digit in the next lower place

beg, borrow, or/and steal see BEG

be living on borrowed time : to continue to be alive after you were expected to die • After his heart attack, my grandfather always felt that he was *living on borrowed time*.

– **bor·row·er** /ˈbɑrəwɚ/ *noun, pl* **-ers** [*count*] • Each *borrower's* payments will vary according to the terms of the loan. • the library's *borrowers* [=people who borrow books from the library]

bor·row·ing /ˈbɑrəwɪŋ/ *noun, pl* **-ings**
1 [*count*] : something that is borrowed; *especially* : a word or phrase from one language that is used in another language • He's compiling a list of Japanese *borrowings* in English.
2 [*noncount*] : the act of borrowing something • Students must have their own pencils. *Borrowing* is not allowed.; *especially* : the act of borrowing money • Economists predict that there will be increases in government *borrowing*.

borscht /ˈboɚʃt/ *noun* [*noncount*] : a soup made mainly of beets

Bor·stal /ˈboɚstl/ *noun, pl* **-stals** *Brit* : a special prison used for people who are too young to go to a regular prison [*noncount*] She was sent to *Borstal* for stealing cars. [*count*] He spent a year in a *Borstal*. ✧ The Borstal system is no longer in use.

bosh /ˈbɑːʃ/ *noun* [*noncount*] *Brit, informal + old-fashioned* : foolish words or ideas : NONSENSE • Don't believe a word she says—it's all *bosh*. — often used like an interjection • *Bosh*! That's absurd!

[1]**bos·om** /ˈbʊzəm/ *noun, pl* **-oms**
1 [*count*] **a** : a person's chest • He clutched the flowers to his *bosom*. **b** : a person's chest when it is thought of as the place where secret thoughts and feelings are kept • He never spoke of his childhood as an orphan, but kept dark memories of those days in his *bosom*.
2 [*count*] *somewhat old-fashioned* **a** : a woman's breasts • her large *bosom* **b** : one of a woman's breasts • a woman's *bosoms*
3 [*singular*] : the part of a piece of clothing that covers the chest • The shirt has a plain color and ruffles at the *bosom*.
4 [*singular*] : a safe and comfortable place or situation — usually + *of* • the *bosom of* your family • She found comfort in the *bosom of* the Church.

[2]**bosom** *adj, always used before a noun* : very close : very dear • They are *bosom* friends/buddies.

bos·omy /ˈbʊzəmi/ *adj, informal* : having large breasts • a *bosomy* waitress

[1]**boss** /ˈbɑːs/ *noun, pl* **boss·es** [*count*]
1 : the person whose job is to tell other workers what to do • Why don't you ask your *boss* for a raise? • Company policy says that vacation time must be cleared with your *boss*. [=*supervisor*] • my former *boss* • Jane started her own business so that she could ***be her own boss***. [=have no boss except for herself] — see also PIT BOSS
2 : a person who has a lot of power in an organization • a union *boss* • mafia *bosses* • the movie studio *boss* • During the campaign, no one was willing to stand up to the ***party boss***. [=the person with the most power in a political party or one branch of a political party]
3 : the person who has more power or control in a relationship • The two oldest children argued over who was *boss* for the entire hour their mother was out shopping. • He wants to show them who's (the) *boss*. [=who's in charge] — compare [4]BOSS

[2]**boss** *verb* **bosses; bossed; boss·ing** [+ *obj*] : to give orders to (someone) : to tell (someone) what to do — usually + *around* or (*Brit*) *about* • I wish he wouldn't let his father *boss* him *around* like that. • Don't *boss* me *around*!

[3]**boss** *adj, slang* : great or excellent • a *boss* new rock band

[4]**boss** *noun, pl* **bosses** [*count*] : a round raised decoration on a ceiling or shield — compare [1]BOSS

bos·sa no·va /ˌbɑːsəˈnouvə/ *noun, pl* **∼ -vas**
1 [*noncount*] : a kind of music that is originally from Brazil
2 [*count*] : a dance performed to bossa nova music

bossy /ˈbɑːsi/ *adj* **boss·i·er; -est** *informal* : tending too often to tell people what to do : often giving orders in a way that people do not like • His advice may be good, but he's much too *bossy*.
– **boss·i·ness** *noun* [*noncount*]

bossy–boots /ˈbɑːsiˌbuːts/ *noun, pl* **bossy–boots** [*count*] *Brit, informal* : a person who often tells other people what to do : a bossy person • Her mum is a real *bossy-boots*. — often used before another noun • her *bossy-boots* mum

Bos·ton cream pie /ˈbɑːstən-/ *noun, pl* **∼ pies** [*count*] *US* : a round cake that is filled with a custard or cream filling and usually frosted with chocolate

Boston lettuce *noun* [*noncount*] *US* : a kind of soft lettuce that is often used in salads

bosun *variant spelling of* BOATSWAIN

bo·tan·i·cal /bəˈtænɪkəl/ *adj, always used before a noun*
1 : of or relating to plants or the study of plants • *botanical* specimens
2 : made from or taken from plants • *botanical* extracts
– **bo·tan·i·cal·ly** /bəˈtænɪkli/ *adv*

botanical garden *noun, pl* **∼ -dens** [*count*] : a large usually public garden where plants are grown in order to be studied — called also *bo·tan·ic garden* /bəˈtænɪk-/

bot·a·ny /ˈbɑːtəni/ *noun* [*noncount*] : a branch of science that deals with plant life • She's studying *botany*. — often used before another noun • the university's *botany* department • She is taking a *botany* class.
– **bot·a·nist** /ˈbɑːtənɪst/ *noun, pl* **-ists** [*count*]

[1]**botch** /ˈbɑːʧ/ *verb* **botch·es; botched; botch·ing** [+ *obj*] : to do (something) badly : to ruin (something) because of carelessness or a lack of skill • The store *botched* the order—I received only half the books I paid for. • They clearly *botched* the investigation. • a *botched* robbery/experiment — sometimes + *up* • He really *botched up* [=*messed up*] the speech.

[2]**botch** *noun, pl* **botches** [*count*] : a bad job : a poorly done piece of work • a *botch* job • The plumbers ***made a botch of*** the pipes. [=the plumbers did a poor job with the pipes]

[1]**both** /ˈbouθ/ *adj* — used to indicate that two things or people are being referred to rather than just one • She put *both* feet in the stream. • *Both* countries have agreed to the treaty. • We went to *both* museums. • I found *both* these articles to be very helpful. • *both* his eyes • *Both* actors have appeared on Broadway before.

[2]**both** *pronoun* : each one of two things or people • I'd like *both*, please. • There were two paintings for sale, and he bought (them) *both*. • We *both* were tired. = We were *both* tired. = *Both* of us were tired. • Arabic and French are *both* spoken there. • He read *both* of the books. [=he read both books]

B

[3]both *conj* — used before two words or phrases connected with *and* to stress that each is included ▪ The show will be in *both* New York *and* London. ▪ She is *both* beautiful *and* charming. ▪ *Both* he *and* his wife play golf. ▪ This product can *both* clean *and* protect your floors.

[1]both·er /ˈbɑːðɚ/ *verb* **-ers; -ered; -er·ing**

1 [+ *obj*] **:** to cause (someone) to feel troubled, worried, or concerned ▪ He's so easygoing. Nothing seems to *bother* him. ▪ It didn't *bother* [=*trouble*] her in the least that she wasn't offered the job. ▪ It *bothers* [=*worries*] them that there's no hospital nearby. ▪ Something he said at the meeting has been *bothering* me. ✧ To ***not bother yourself about/with something*** or ***not bother your head about/with something*** is to not worry or be concerned about something. ▪ He decided he *wasn't* going to *bother himself about* the opinions of others. ▪ *Don't bother your head with* those questions right now.

2 [+ *obj*] **:** to annoy (someone) **:** to cause (someone) to feel annoyed ▪ It *bothers* [=*irks*] her when people throw trash on the ground. ▪ He's *bothered* [=*annoyed*] by drivers who don't use their turn signals. ▪ The entire car trip was filled with complaints like, "Mom, David keeps *bothering* me!" and "Will you tell him to quit *bothering* me?"

3 [*no obj*] **a :** to take the time to do something **:** to make an effort to do something ▪ Mother used to cook elaborate dinners, but with only herself to cook for, she doesn't *bother* anymore. ▪ "Should I call later?" "No, don't *bother*." — often followed by *to + verb* or by *-ing verb* ▪ Nobody *bothered* [=*took the trouble*] *to tell* me the school would be closed today. ▪ He never *bothered to explain* what happened. ▪ Don't *bother asking* him about it. He won't tell you anything. ▪ Why *bother talking* if no one is listening? ✧ If you ***can't be bothered*** to do something, you do not want to make an effort to do it or are not interested in doing it. ▪ The trick is somewhat dangerous, so if you *can't be bothered* to do it right, then don't even attempt it. ▪ I asked her to send a picture, but apparently she just *couldn't be bothered* (to send one). **b :** to be concerned *with* or *about* something ▪ I'm not going to *bother with* the details. ▪ We were told not to *bother about* the early data [=not to consider or use early data] when writing the report.

4 [+ *obj*] **:** to interrupt or talk to (someone who is working or who wants to be alone) ▪ Don't *bother* your mother right now. She's very tired. ▪ I hate to *bother* [=*trouble*] you, but I was wondering if you could help me with something. ▪ Sorry to *bother* [=*inconvenience*] you. I just had a quick question.

5 [+ *obj*] **a :** to make (someone) feel sick or uncomfortable ▪ He said his stomach was *bothering* him. ▪ Her arthritis has been *bothering* her. **b :** to cause a painful or unpleasant feeling in (part of someone's body) ▪ The camera strap *bothers* my shoulder. ▪ The bright light *bothered* her eyes.

6 *chiefly Brit, somewhat old-fashioned* — used as an interjection to express annoyance or frustration ▪ *Bother* this car! It won't start! ▪ Oh, *bother* (it). I forgot my keys.

[2]bother *noun*

1 [*singular*] **:** someone or something that is annoying or that causes trouble ▪ Replacing the windows could be more of a *bother* than it's worth. ▪ Sorry to be such a *bother* [=*nuisance*], but I was wondering if you could help me with something. ▪ I know what a *bother* driving into the city can be this time of day.

2 [*noncount*] **:** trouble or difficulty **:** INCONVENIENCE ▪ "Sorry to bother you." "That's okay, it's no *bother* at all." ▪ I considered replacing that part of the floor but decided it wasn't worth the *bother*. ▪ He doesn't want the *bother* of filling out all those forms again. ▪ Will you mail this for me? It will save me the *bother* of going to the post office.

both·er·ation /ˌbɑːðəˈreɪʃən/ *noun, pl* **-tions** [*count*] *old-fashioned* **:** something that is annoying **:** something that bothers you ▪ I hadn't realized what a *botheration* putting up a tent in the dark could be! — sometimes used as an interjection ▪ Oh *botheration*. The radio isn't working again.

both·er·some /ˈbɑːðɚsəm/ *adj* [*more* ~; *most* ~] **:** causing trouble or difficulty ▪ The injury isn't too bad. It's more *bothersome* [=*troublesome*] than painful.

[1]bot·tle /ˈbɑːtl̩/ *noun, pl* **bot·tles**

1 [*count*] **a :** a glass or plastic container that has a narrow neck and usually has no handle ✧ Bottles are usually used to store liquid or tablets. ▪ Shall I open another *bottle* of wine? ▪ There's a *bottle* of aspirin in the cabinet. ▪ empty soda *bottles* ▪ She kept a *bottle* [=a bottle of some strong alcoholic drink like whiskey] tucked away in the coat closet. ▪ Be sure to bring a ***water bottle*** [=bottle containing water] on your hike. ▪ Would you get me the ***bottle opener*** [=a tool used to remove metal tops from some bottles], please? **b :** the amount contained in a bottle ▪ We drank a *bottle* of wine.

2 ***the bottle*** **:** alcoholic drink ▪ He says he's lost too many years to *the bottle*, and that he's giving up alcohol. ▪ Her struggles with *the bottle* affected her entire family. ▪ I hear he's ***(gone) off the bottle*** [=stopped drinking alcohol] ▪ After his divorce he ***took to the bottle*** [=began to drink a lot of alcohol] ▪ When she gets depressed she ***hits the bottle*** [=begins drinking a lot of alcohol]

3 [*count*] **:** a special bottle for feeding babies that contains milk or a drink which contains milk ▪ Has the baby finished her *bottle* yet? ▪ (*US*) a baby *bottle* = (*Brit*) a baby's *bottle* ▪ raised on a *bottle* instead of breast milk — see also BOTTLE-FEED

4 [*noncount*] *Brit slang* **:** courage or strength of spirit ▪ I don't think he's got *bottle* [=*guts*] enough to confront them.

bring your own bottle (*US*) *or Brit* ***bring a bottle*** — used to tell the people who are invited to a party that they should bring their own alcoholic drinks

catch/capture lightning in a bottle see [1]LIGHTNING

– bot·tle·ful /ˈbɑːtl̩ˌfʊl/ *noun* [*singular*] ▪ a *bottleful* of water

[2]bottle *verb* **bottles; bot·tled; bot·tling** [+ *obj*]

1 : to put (something) into a bottle so that it can be sold or so that it is easier to use ▪ The restaurant *bottles* its own ginger ale. ▪ Near the top of the mountain, the climbers relied on *bottled* oxygen to breathe. ▪ *bottled* water ▪ ***bottled gas*** [=gas that is stored in containers for people to use in heating their homes or for cooking]

2 *Brit* **:** to put (fruit or vegetables) in a jar using a special procedure that preserves them ▪ At the end of summer we *bottle* [=(*US*) *can, preserve, put up*] tomatoes from the garden.

bottle out [*phrasal verb*] *Brit slang* **:** to become too afraid to do something **:** to lose your nerve ▪ I was going to ask him but then I *bottled out*. [=*chickened out*]

bottle up [*phrasal verb*] ***bottle (something) up*** *or* ***bottle up (something)*** **:** to keep (a feeling or emotion) inside of you instead of expressing it **:** to hide (a feeling or emotion) ▪ She's kept her feelings about the accident *bottled up* for too long. ▪ I know he's angry, but he *bottles* it *up* inside instead of talking to someone about it.

– bot·tler *noun, pl* **bot·tlers** [*count*] ▪ soft drink *bottlers* ▪ the region's best known wine *bottler*

bottle bank *noun, pl* ~ **banks** [*count*] *Brit* **:** a large container that people put empty bottles in so that the glass or plastic the bottles are made from can be used again

bottle blond *noun, pl* ~ **blonds** [*count*] **:** a person whose hair has been made blond by using chemicals

bot·tle–feed /ˈbɑːtl̩ˌfiːd/ *verb* **-feeds; -fed; -feed·ing** [+ *obj*] **:** to feed (a baby or young animal) with a bottle instead of from its mother's breast ▪ All her children were *bottle-fed*. ▪ We had to *bottle-feed* the kitten. — compare BREAST-FEED

bottle green *noun* [*noncount*] **:** a green color ✧ In the U.S., bottle green is usually a medium green color. In British English, it is usually a dark green color.

– bottle–green *adj*

bot·tle·neck /ˈbɑːtl̩ˌnɛk/ *noun, pl* **-necks** [*count*]

1 : a section of road or highway where the traffic moves very slowly ▪ Bridge construction has created a *bottleneck* on the southern part of Main Street.

2 : something that slows down a process ▪ All decisions must be approved by the committee, and this is where the company runs into *bottlenecks*.

bot·tle·nose dolphin /ˈbɑːtl̩ˌnoʊz-/ *noun, pl* ~ **-phins** [*count*] **:** a small gray whale that has a long nose — called also *bottle-nosed dolphin*

[1]bot·tom /ˈbɑːtəm/ *noun, pl* **-toms**

1 a [*count*] **:** the lowest part, point, or level of something — usually singular ▪ He's waiting at the *bottom* of the stairs. ▪ Our house is at the *bottom* of the hill. ▪ The top of the wall is painted and the *bottom* is covered in wood paneling. ▪ the *bottom* of the page/screen/list ▪ Please fill out this form and sign your name at the *bottom*. **b** [*count*] **:** the part of something that is below or under the other parts — usually singular ▪ the ship's *bottom* [=*underside*] ▪ The bowl was signed on the *bottom* [=*base*] by the artist. ▪ There's a small cut on the *bottom* [=*sole*] of his foot. **c** [*count*] **:** the lowest point or surface inside something **:** the part of something hollow that is furthest from the top — usually singular ▪ I think there is still a little sugar left in the *bottom* of the box/container. ▪ The pool is so deep I could not touch the *bottom*. ▪ One of

the drawers has a ***false bottom*** [=a panel that looks like the drawer's bottom but that can be removed to expose more space] **d** [*singular*] *chiefly Brit* : the part of something that is furthest away • We sailed to the *bottom* of the bay. • the *bottom* of the garden
2 [*count*] : the part of the body on which you sit : BUTTOCKS • The poor baby has a rash all over his little *bottom*.
3 a [*singular*] : a position of little power in a company or organization • The company's new CEO started at the *bottom* and worked her way up. **b** [*singular*] : a low rank or position • Why do I always find myself rooting for the team at the *bottom* of the league? • She graduated ***at the bottom of her/the class*** [=her grades were among the lowest in her graduating class] **c** [*noncount*] : the worst position, level, or condition • at the *bottom* of the pay scale • After weeks of losing value, the company's stocks have ***hit bottom*** [=reached the bottom; lost all value] • Jim has finally ***scraped bottom*** [=has finally reached the worst possible condition] — see also ROCK BOTTOM
4 a [*singular*] : the surface that is under a body of water • the *bottom* of the ocean • the sandy river/lake *bottom* **b bottoms** [*plural*] : the flat, low land along a river or stream : BOTTOMLAND • grazing in grassy river *bottoms*
5 [*count*] : a piece of clothing that is worn on the lower part of the body • a bikini *bottom* — often plural • pajama *bottoms* — see color picture on page C13
6 [*singular*] : the second half of an inning in baseball • They tied the score in the *bottom* of the ninth inning.
7 [*noncount*] *chiefly Brit* : the lowest gear of a car • Stay in *bottom* [=*bottom gear*] until you reach the top of the hill.
at bottom *chiefly Brit* : in reality : REALLY • The song is, *at bottom* [=*in truth*], a lullaby. • He is very shy, *at bottom*.
at the bottom of the pile see [1]PILE
be/lie at the bottom of *chiefly Brit* : to be the source or originator of (something) • I think I know who's *at the bottom of* [=*behind*] these pranks.
bottoms up *informal* — used as a toast or to tell people to finish their drinks • Here's to the groom-to-be! *Bottoms up*!
from the bottom of your heart see HEART
from top to bottom see [1]TOP
get to the bottom of : to find out the true reason for or cause of (something) • Police are working furiously to *get to the bottom of* this recent string of violent crimes.
the bottom drop/fall out ✧ If *the bottom drops/falls out* of something, it suddenly fails or becomes unable to continue in a normal and effective way. • Analysts warn that recent changes in the region may result in *the bottom dropping out* of the oil market. [=may cause the oil market to collapse] • When the accident happened, she felt *the bottom drop out* of her world. [=she felt her world collapse]
the bottom of the barrel : the lowest possible condition, level, etc. • After the divorce, Tim felt he had reached/hit *the bottom of the barrel*. • The excessive coverage of the scandal signals that the news media may have finally hit/reached *the bottom of the barrel*. • Salaries in the industry are scraping/hitting *the bottom of the barrel*. [=salaries in the industry are very low]
– bot·tomed /ˈbɑːtəmd/ *adj* • flat *bottomed* boats

[2]bottom *adj, always used before a noun*
1 : in the lowest position • the *bottom* rung of the ladder • the *bottom* drawer/shelf • her *bottom* lip • Somebody's fingerprints are all along the *bottom* edge of the photograph. — see also BOTTOM LINE
2 : living at the lowest level of an ocean or lake • *bottom* fish
bet your bottom dollar see [2]BET

[3]bottom *verb* **-toms; -tomed; -tom·ing**
bottom out [*phrasal verb*] : to reach a lowest or worst point usually before beginning to rise or improve • Real estate prices seem to have *bottomed out*, and sellers can expect to get higher prices in coming months. • The team *bottomed out* in last place.

bottom drawer *noun, pl* ~ **-ers** [*count*] *Brit* : HOPE CHEST

bottom feeder *noun, pl* ~ **-ers** [*count*]
1 : a fish that feeds at the bottom of a lake, pond, etc.
2 *US, disapproving* : someone who uses other people's troubles, weakness, etc., as an opportunity to make money • After his daughter's tragic death, he was hounded by media *bottom feeders* who demanded exclusive interviews.
3 *US, informal* : someone or something that has a very low status or rank • In a surprise upset, the all-star team lost to one of the league's *bottom feeders*.

bottom gear *noun* [*noncount*] *chiefly Brit* : low gear : a vehicle's lowest gear

bot·tom·land /ˈbɑːtəmˌlænd/ *noun, pl* **-lands** [*count*] : flat low land along a river or stream — usually plural • lush *bottomlands*

bot·tom·less /ˈbɑːtəmləs/ *adj*
1 a : having no bottom • a *bottomless* barrel [=a barrel that has no bottom because it has been removed] **b** : seeming to have no bottom or limit • a *bottomless* expense account • The diner serves *bottomless* cups of coffee. [=allows customers to have as much coffee as they like for one price]
2 : very deep • a *bottomless* pit

bottom line *noun*
1 *the bottom line* **a** : the most important part of something : the most important thing to consider • *The bottom line* [=all that matters] is that the product just wasn't practical. • If our flight is late, we will miss our connection. That's *the bottom line*. **b** : the final result or outcome • A student with special needs can stress a school's budget, but *the bottom line* is that the state must provide for the child's education.
2 [*singular*] : a company's profits or losses • How will these changes affect our *bottom line*? • He's always got his eye on the *bottom line*.
3 [*singular*] : the least amount of money you are willing to consider for something • He says his *bottom line* is $120,000.

bot·tom–up /ˈbɑːtəmˈʌp/ *adj* : progressing upward from the lowest levels : controlled or directed from the lower levels • *bottom-up* management — opposite TOP-DOWN

bot·u·lism /ˈbɑːʧəˌlɪzəm/ *noun* [*noncount*] : a serious illness that is caused by eating food that has not been preserved correctly and that is filled with bacteria

bou·doir /ˈbuːˌdwɑɚ/ *noun, pl* **-doirs** [*count*] *old-fashioned* : a woman's bedroom or private room for dressing or resting

bouf·fant /buˈfɑːnt, *Brit* ˈbuːˌfɒŋ/ *adj* : having a full and rounded shape • a *bouffant* skirt — usually used to refer to a hairstyle in which the hair is up and away from the head in a full, rounded shape • *bouffant* hairdos from the 1950s

bou·gain·vil·lea /ˌbuːgənˈvɪljə/ *noun, pl* **-leas** [*count, noncount*] : a tropical plant that has usually red or purple flowers

bough /ˈbaʊ/ *noun, pl* **boughs** [*count*] : a main branch of a tree

bought *past tense and past participle of* [1]BUY

bouil·la·baisse /ˌbuːjəˈbeɪs/ *noun*
1 [*count, noncount*] : a stew made with strong spices and two or more kinds of fish
2 [*singular*] : a mixture of different kinds of things • The book is a *bouillabaisse* [=(more commonly) *potpourri*] of stories and poems from around the world.

bouil·lon /ˈbuːlˌjɑːn, *Brit* ˈbuːˌjɒn/ *noun, pl* **bouillons** [*count, noncount*] : a clear liquid in which meat, chicken, fish, or vegetables have been cooked and which is eaten as soup or used to make sauces • beef *bouillon*

Do not confuse *bouillon* with *bullion*.

bouillon cube *noun, pl* ~ **cubes** [*count*] : a small cube of dried meat or vegetables that is used to add flavor to soup — called also (*Brit*) *stock cube*

boul·der /ˈbouldɚ/ *noun, pl* **-ders** [*count*] : a very large stone or rounded piece of rock

bou·le·vard /ˈbʊləˌvɑɚd/ *noun, pl* **-vards** [*count*] : a wide and usually important street that often has trees, grass, or flowers planted down its center or along its sides • walking down the *boulevard* — often used in names • Sunset *Boulevard* in Los Angeles — abbr. *blvd.*

[1]bounce /ˈbaʊns/ *verb* **bounc·es; bounced; bounc·ing**
1 a [+ *obj*] : to cause (a ball, rock, etc.) to hit against a surface and quickly move in a different and usually opposite direction • He was *bouncing* a tennis ball against/off the garage door. • *bouncing* the ball back and forth **b** [*no obj*] : to move in one direction, hit a surface (such as a wall or the floor), and then quickly move in a different and usually opposite direction — usually + *off* • The ball *bounced off* the wall. • A rock *bounced off* the road and hit our car's windshield. • The light will *bounce off* the mirror and shine into the next room.
2 a [*no obj*] : to move with a lot of energy and excitement • He *bounced* [=*bounded*] into the room to welcome his guests. • The kids are ***bouncing off the walls*** [=the kids are very/too excited and have a lot of energy] **b** : to move or jump up and down [*no obj*] The children love to *bounce* on the bed/trampoline. • The winner *bounced* up and down with delight.

B

• Her curls *bounced* as she jumped. [+ *obj*] He *bounced* the baby on his knee.

3 a [*no obj*] *of a check* : to be returned by a bank because there is not enough money in the bank account to pay the amount that is on the check • She gave me a check for 20 dollars, but the check *bounced*, and I never got the money. **b** [+ *obj*] : to write (a check) that is returned without payment by the bank • He *bounced* a 100-dollar check at the grocery store. • The store charges a $15 fee for a *bounced* check.

4 [*no obj*] : to go quickly and repeatedly from one job, place, etc., to another • He *bounces* back and forth between Miami and Houston. — often + *from* • *bouncing from* place to place • She *bounces from* one job to another. • Our teacher's always *bouncing from* one subject to another.

5 : to return (an e-mail) to the sender instead of delivering it [+ *obj*] I tried to send you an e-mail, but it got *bounced* back to me. [=the e-mail or computer system was not able to deliver it] [*no obj*] I tried to send you an e-mail but it *bounced*.

bounce around [*phrasal verb*] ***bounce (something) around*** *or* ***bounce around (something)*** *informal* : to talk about (something, such as an idea) in an informal way in order to get different opinions about it • We were *bouncing* some ideas *around* for the design of the book's cover.

bounce back [*phrasal verb*] : to return quickly to a normal condition after a difficult situation or event • She *bounced back* [=*recovered*] easily from her surgery. • After losing the first three games of the series, they *bounced back* to win their next eight games.

bounce into [*phrasal verb*] *Brit, informal* ***bounce (someone) into (something)*** : to force (someone) to decide to do (something) especially without having time to think about it • The voters were *bounced into* agreeing to the proposal.

bounce off [*phrasal verb*] ***bounce (something) off (someone)*** *informal* : to talk about (something, such as an idea) with (someone) in an informal way in order to get an opinion • I wanted to *bounce* some ideas *off* you before the meeting.

[2]**bounce** *noun, pl* **bounces**

1 [*count*] : the act or action of bouncing off the ground or another surface • The ball took a high *bounce* over the shortstop's head. • He caught the ball on the first *bounce*.

2 [*noncount*] **a** : the ability to move quickly in a different direction after hitting a surface : the ability to bounce • a basketball that has lost all its *bounce* **b** : a quality that makes a person's hair look healthy, full, and attractive : a bouncy quality • The shampoo promises to give limp hair lots of *bounce*.

3 [*singular*] : a sudden increase • Several companies showed a *bounce* [=*upswing, upsurge*] in earnings. • After the debates, she enjoyed a big *bounce* in the election polls.

4 : energy and liveliness [*noncount*] He may be 90 years old, but he still has plenty of *bounce* [=*spring*] in his step. [*singular*] There's still a *bounce* in his step.

bounc·er /ˈbaʊnsɚ/ *noun, pl* **-ers** [*count*]

1 : a person whose job is to force anyone who causes a problem in a bar, nightclub, etc., to leave that place

2 : a ball that bounces on the ground • The batter hit a *bouncer* to the shortstop.

bounce pass *noun, pl* ~ **passes** [*count*] *basketball* : a pass to a teammate that is made by bouncing the ball once

bounc·ing /ˈbaʊnsɪŋ/ *adj, always used before a noun* : very healthy and active • a *bouncing* baby boy

bouncy /ˈbaʊnsi/ *adj* **bounc·i·er**; **-est**

1 : able to bounce well • a *bouncy* rubber ball

2 : lively, cheerful, and full of energy • a *bouncy* host • *bouncy* dance music

3 : quickly returning to a full, rounded shape after being made flat • a *bouncy* [=*springy*] seat cushion • her curly, *bouncy* hair

– **bounc·i·ly** *adv* • *bouncily* energetic – **bounc·i·ness** *noun* [*noncount*] • the music's *bounciness*

[1]**bound** *past tense and past participle of* [1]BIND

[2]**bound** *adj*

1 *not used before a noun* : very likely or certain *to do* or *to be* something • It's *bound to rain* soon. • It's *bound to be* a great party. • I knew they would get married. It was *bound to happen*. • Everyone is *bound to make* mistakes sometimes. • Such a foolish plan is *bound to fail*.

2 : unlikely or unable to change, develop, move, etc., because of being held or controlled by something • an organization that is *bound* by tradition — often used in combination • a tradition-*bound* organization • a culture-*bound* philosophy — see also DESKBOUND, FOGBOUND, HOUSEBOUND, ICEBOUND, MUSCLE-BOUND, SNOWBOUND

3 : tied together with something (such as a string or rope) • a neatly/tightly/loosely *bound* stack of papers — see also [1]BIND 1, 2

4 *not used before a noun* : closely joined or connected to other people • She and I are *bound* (together) by our shared past. [=we are connected to each other because we have the same past] • family members *bound* by either blood or marriage — see also [1]BIND 7

5 *not used before a noun* : required by law or duty to do something • The state is legally *bound* [=*obligated*] to provide each child with an education. • He was ***duty bound*** [=it was his duty] to help. • I felt ***honor bound*** to defend them. [=I felt that I had to defend them because it was morally right] • (*chiefly Brit*) The experiment, I am ***bound to say*** [=*I must say/admit*], seems to have succeeded. — see also [1]BIND 5

6 : held together or covered with a particular type of material — often + *in* • books *bound in* leather/velvet — often used in combination • leather-*bound* books [=books with leather covers] • a spiral-*bound* notebook [=a notebook that has its pages held together with a curving wire] — see also [1]BIND 11

bound and determined : very determined • We were *bound and determined* to finish the project on time.

bound up : closely involved or associated : greatly affected • The fates of such projects are always *bound up* in politics. — usually + *with* • Their lives are closely *bound up with* their religion. • These societal changes are inextricably *bound up with* the development of new technologies.

I'll be bound *Brit, old-fashioned* — used to stress that you are sure of something you have said • It'll be dark soon, *I'll be bound*.

– compare [3]BOUND

[3]**bound** /ˈbaʊnd/ *adj* : going or planning to go to a specified place • We were homeward *bound*. [=we were going towards our home] • college-*bound* teenagers [=teenagers who are planning to go to college] — often + *for* • She got on a plane *bound for* [=going to] London. • He was *bound for* New York. • a ship *bound for* Africa — see also EASTBOUND, HOMEBOUND, INBOUND, NORTHBOUND, OUTBOUND, SOUTHBOUND, WESTBOUND — compare [2]BOUND

[4]**bound** *noun, pl* **bounds** [*count*] : a leap or long jump • He leapt over the puddle in/with a single *bound*.

by/in leaps and bounds see [2]LEAP

– compare [6]BOUND

[5]**bound** *verb, always followed by an adverb or preposition* **bounds**; **bound·ed**; **bound·ing** [*no obj*] : to move by jumping : to walk or run with long, energetic steps • She came *bounding* down the stairs. • We saw three deer *bound* over the fence into the woods. — compare [7]BOUND

[6]**bound** *noun, pl* **bounds**

1 ***bounds*** [*plural*] : the point at which something (such as an idea or someone's behavior) stops being good or acceptable : the limit of what is correct or proper • The play goes ***beyond the bounds*** of decency. = The play ***exceeds the bounds*** of decency. • ***within the bounds*** of reason = within reasonable *bounds* • The police officers ***exceeded/overstepped their bounds*** and broke the law.

2 [*count*] : something that shows where one area ends and another area begins — usually plural • the *bounds* [=(more commonly) *boundaries*] of the nature reserve

know no bounds : to have no limit • His generosity *knows no bounds*. [=he is extremely generous]

in bounds : inside the area where players or the ball must stay in sports like basketball and American football • The receiver was still *in bounds* when he caught the pass. • The referee said the ball landed *in bounds*.

out of bounds **1** : outside the area where players or the ball must stay in sports like basketball and American football • The ball was kicked *out of bounds*. • The player stepped *out of bounds* to avoid being hit. **2** : not good or acceptable • The teacher's comment was completely *out of bounds*. [=*unacceptable, inappropriate*] **3** — used to describe a place where people are not allowed to go • The auditorium is *out of bounds* for/to students during the renovations. **4** — used to describe something that people are not allowed to discuss or mention • The subject of politics is *out of bounds* [=*off limits*] when our family gets together.

– compare [4]BOUND

[7]**bound** *verb* **bounds**; **bounded**; **bounding** [+ *obj*] : to form a border around (an area) — usually used as *(be) bounded* • a quiet village *bounded* [=*surrounded, enclosed*] by mountains • The city *is bounded* by two major highways. — compare [5]BOUND

bound·ary /ˈbaʊndri/ *noun, pl* **-aries**
1 [*count*] : something (such as a river, a fence, or an imaginary line) that shows where an area ends and another area begins • Those two trees mark the *boundary* of our property. • The river forms the country's western *boundary.*
2 [*count*] : a point or limit that indicates where two things become different • at/on the *boundary* between fact and fiction
3 ***boundaries*** [*plural*] : unofficial rules about what should not be done : limits that define acceptable behavior • You need to set *boundaries* with your children. • Did he violate the *boundaries* of the doctor-patient relationship? • They're ***pushing the boundaries of*** [=doing things that are unusual in] traditional French cooking.
know no boundaries **1** : to be capable of affecting people everywhere • This is a disease that *knows no boundaries.* **2** : to have no limits • My admiration for him *knows no boundaries.* [=*knows no bounds*]

bound·less /ˈbaʊndləs/ *adj* : not limited in any way : having no boundaries • the *boundless* [=*limitless, endless*] sky • We were filled with *boundless* joy. • Her love for her family was *boundless.*
– bound·less·ly *adv* • a *boundlessly* generous person

boun·te·ous /ˈbaʊntijəs/ *adj* [*more* ~; *most* ~] *formal* : giving or providing many desired things : BOUNTIFUL • Together we give thanks for this *bounteous* harvest.

boun·ti·ful /ˈbaʊntɪfəl/ *adj, formal*
1 : giving or providing many desired things • this *bountiful* land • *bountiful* harvests
2 : given or existing in large amounts • a *bountiful* supply of water • a *bountiful* meal • *bountiful* baskets of fruit
– boun·ti·ful·ly *adv* • They were *bountifully* rewarded.

boun·ty /ˈbaʊnti/ *noun, pl* **-ties**
1 *literary* : good things that are given or provided freely and in large amounts [*noncount*] the *bounty* of nature = nature's *bounty* • summer's *bounty* of plump tomatoes [*singular*] The cottage is filled with a *bounty* of fresh flowers.
2 [*count*] : an amount of money given to someone as a reward for catching a criminal • A *bounty* of 500 dollars was put on his head. [=anyone who captured him would receive a 500-dollar bounty]

bounty hunter *noun, pl* ~ **-ers** [*count*] : someone who catches criminals who have not been caught by the police in exchange for a reward

bou·quet /boʊˈkeɪ, buːˈkeɪ/ *noun, pl* **-quets** [*count*]
1 : a group of flowers that are picked and often tied together • The bride carried a *bouquet* of white and red roses.
2 : a particular and usually pleasant smell of flowers or wine • The wine has a lovely *bouquet.*

bouquet gar·ni /-gɑəˈniː/ *noun, pl* **bouquets gar·nis** /-gɑəˈniː/ [*count*] : a bunch of herbs that are tied together or put in a cloth bag and cooked with food to add flavor but removed before the food is served

bour·bon /ˈbəbən/ *noun, pl* **-bons** : a type of American whiskey made from corn, malt, and rye [*noncount*] a glass of *bourbon* • I prefer *bourbon* to Scotch. [*count*] We'll have two *bourbons* [=two glasses of bourbon], please.

bour·geois /ˈbuəʒˌwɑː/ *adj*
1 : relating to or belonging to the middle class of society • the *bourgeois* class • *bourgeois* families/businessmen
2 [*more* ~; *most* ~] *disapproving* : having qualities or values associated with the middle class : too concerned about wealth, possessions, and respectable behavior • *bourgeois* life/culture/society • *bourgeois* attitudes/values • *bourgeois* materialism
– bourgeois *noun, pl* **bour·geois** /ˈbuəʒˌwɑːz/ [*count*] • He was a *bourgeois,* not a nobleman. • a philosopher who had no sympathy for the *bourgeois* — see also PETIT BOURGEOIS

bour·geoi·sie /ˌbuəʒˌwɑːˈziː/ *noun*
the bourgeoisie : the middle class of society : the social class of skilled workers, business and professional people, and government officials • members of *the bourgeoisie*

bout /ˈbaʊt/ *noun, pl* **bouts** [*count*]
1 : a period of time during which someone suffers from something (such as an illness or disease) — often + *of* • a *bout of* fever • She struggles with frequent *bouts of* depression. — often + *with* in U.S. English • She survived a 5-year *bout with* cancer. • a *bout with* the flu
2 : a short period of time during which something is done or happening • a drinking *bout* — often + *of* • a 4-hour *bout of* reading • a *bout of* unemployment
3 : a wrestling or boxing contest • He lost his *bout* [=*fight*] with the boxing champion.

bou·tique /buːˈtiːk/ *noun, pl* **-tiques** [*count*] : a small store that sells stylish clothing or other usually expensive things

bou·ton·niere /ˌbuːtṇˈiə, *Brit* buːˌtɒniˈeə/ *noun, pl* **-nieres** [*count*] *US* : a flower or small group of flowers that men sometimes wear on their jackets on special occasions (such as weddings) — called also (*Brit*) *buttonhole*

bo·vine /ˈboʊˌvaɪn/ *adj*
1 *technical* : relating to cows • a *bovine* illness • *bovine* growth hormones
2 *disapproving* : looking or acting like a cow • his round *bovine* face • She stared at us with a stupid, *bovine* expression.

[1]bow /ˈbaʊ/ *verb* **bows; bowed; bow·ing**
1 [*no obj*] : to bend forward at the neck or waist as a formal way of greeting someone or showing respect • He *bowed* politely and introduced himself to us. • You must *bow* (down) before the king. • a man *bowing* to kiss the hand of a woman • The men *bowed* and the women curtsied as the royal couple walked past. • She *bowed* down in front of the altar. — often + *to* • They *bowed to* each other and began talking. • She *bowed to* the audience and walked off stage.
2 [+ *obj*] : to turn (your head) down so that you are looking toward the ground • people *bowing* their heads in prayer • His head was *bowed* [=*lowered*] in shame. • We listened with *bowed* heads.
3 [*no obj*] : to stop trying to fight or resist something : to agree to do or accept something that you have been resisting or opposing — usually + *to* • The President *bowed* [=*gave in, yielded*] *to* political pressure. • They usually *bow to* his wishes. [=they usually do what he wants] • She finally ***bowed to the inevitable*** and accepted their decision.
bow and scrape : to treat someone who is powerful or wealthy in an extremely respectful way especially in order to get approval, friendship, etc. • She's disgusted by politicians who *bow and scrape* before wealthy contributors.
bow down to [*phrasal verb*] ***bow down to (someone or something)*** : to show weakness by agreeing to the demands or following the orders of (someone or something) • I will *bow down to* no one. [=I will take orders from no one; I will submit to no one] • The government is refusing to *bow down to* [=*give in to*] pressure to lift the sanctions.
bow out [*phrasal verb*] : to stop doing something : to stop being involved in a contest, an activity, etc. • He knew he would not win the election, so he decided to *bow out* of the presidential race. • He *bowed out* [=*left, withdrew*] gracefully. • She has *bowed out* of the restaurant business entirely.
– compare [5]BOW

[2]bow *noun, pl* **bows** [*count*] : the act of bending forward at the neck or waist in order to greet someone or show respect : the act of bowing • In some cultures it is polite to greet people with a *bow,* while in others a handshake is preferred. • He smiled and made/gave a *bow.*
take a bow : to bow towards an audience that is applauding for you • When the play has finished, the actors will line up to *take a bow.* — often used figuratively to say that someone deserves to be praised • The people who organized the festival should *take a bow* for its remarkable success.
– compare [3]BOW, [4]BOW

[3]bow /ˈbaʊ/ *noun, pl* **bows** [*count*] : the front part of a boat or ship • The deck was cleaned from *bow* to stern. [=from the front end to the back end] — see picture at BOAT; opposite [2]STERN — compare [2]BOW, [4]BOW

[4]bow /ˈboʊ/ *noun, pl* **bows** [*count*]
1 : a knot that is made by tying a ribbon or string into two or more loops and that is used for tying shoelaces or for decoration • She tied/wore a *bow* in her hair. — see also BOW TIE
2 : a weapon used for shooting arrows that is made of a long, thin piece of wood which is bent with its ends connected by a tight, strong string • They hunted with *bows* and arrows.
3 : a tool that is used for playing a violin or similar musical instrument and that is made of a thin stick of wood with its ends connected by stretched pieces of hair or fiber — see picture at STRINGED INSTRUMENT
– compare [2]BOW, [3]BOW

[5]bow *verb* **bows; bowed; bow·ing**
1 [+ *obj*] : to use a bow to play (a violin or similar musical instrument) • *bowing* or plucking the violin strings — see also BOWING
2 : to bend or curve [*no obj*] The wall *bows* out at the bottom. [+ *obj*] Years of riding horses has *bowed* his legs. • Peo-

ple with this disorder often have *bowed* legs. — see also BOWLEGGED
– compare ¹BOW

bowd·ler·ize *also Brit* **bowd·ler·ise** /ˈboʊdləˌraɪz, *Brit* ˈbaʊdləˌraɪz/ *verb* **-iz·es; -ized; -iz·ing** [+ *obj*] *usually disapproving* : to change (a book, play, movie, etc.) by removing parts that could offend people • *bowdlerize* a classic novel by removing offensive language
– **bowdlerized** *also Brit* **bowdlerised** *adj* • a *bowdlerized* version of the novel

bow·el /ˈbawəl/ *noun, pl* **-els**
1 [*count*] : the long tube in the body that helps digest food and carries solid waste out of the body • a disease of the *bowel* — often plural • a disease that affects the *bowels* ✧ To have a ***bowel movement*** or to ***move your bowels*** or (*Brit*) ***open your bowels*** is to pass solid waste from your body. • The patient made/had a normal *bowel movement.*
2 ***the bowels*** *literary* : the deep inner parts *of* something • They dug deep into *the bowels of* the earth. • The engine room is down in *the bowels of* the ship.

bow·er /ˈbawɚ/ *noun, pl* **-ers** [*count*] *literary* : a pleasant shady place in a garden or forest • resting in the shade of the *bower*

bow·ing /ˈbowɪŋ/ *noun* [*noncount*] : the style or technique for using a bow when playing a violin or similar musical instrument

¹bowl /ˈboʊl/ *noun, pl* **bowls**
1 [*count*] **a** : a round container that has tall, curving sides and that is used for preparing or serving foods and liquids • a soup/salad/pasta *bowl* [=a bowl used for serving or eating soup/salad/pasta] • the dog's water *bowl* — see picture at PLACE SETTING; see also MIXING BOWL, PUNCH BOWL **b** : the food or liquid served in a bowl • We gave the kittens a *bowl* [=*bowlful*] of milk. : the amount of food or liquid served in a bowl • I ate two *bowls* of soup for dinner. • May I have another *bowl* of ice cream?
2 [*count*] : a part of something that is shaped like a bowl: such as **a** : the bottom part of a toilet • a toilet *bowl* **b** : the deep, rounded part of a spoon **c** : the part of a pipe that holds tobacco
3 [*singular*] : a valley or area of land that is low and that has higher land around it • a town in the *bowl* of the mountains — see also DUST BOWL
4 [*singular*] *US* : a large stadium or theater that is shaped like a bowl — used in names • a concert at the Hollywood *Bowl*
5 [*count*] *American football* : a game that is played after the regular season between college teams that have been specially invited • college *bowl* games — usually used in names • the Orange *Bowl* — see also SUPER BOWL
6 a [*count*] : a ball used in the game of lawn bowling **b** ***bowls*** [*plural*] *Brit* : LAWN BOWLING

²bowl *verb* **bowls; bowled; bowl·ing**
1 [+ *obj*] : to roll (a ball) towards something especially in the game of bowling or lawn bowling • I don't think I can *bowl* a 12-pound ball.
2 a [*no obj*] : to play the game of bowling • We *bowl* every Thursday night. • Do you like to *bowl*? • I haven't *bowled* since I was a kid. **b** [+ *obj*] : to get (a score) in a game of bowling • She usually *bowls* around 150.
3 [+ *obj*] *cricket* **a** : to throw (a ball) to the batsman **b** : to force (a batsman) to leave the field by throwing a ball that hits the wicket behind the batsman • He was *bowled* (out) for 47.
4 *always followed by an adverb or preposition* [*no obj*] *chiefly Brit* : to move or go very quickly • We were *bowling* along the motorway in her new car.
bowl over [*phrasal verb*] **1** ***bowl (someone or something) over or bowl over (someone or something)*** : to hit and push down (someone or something) while quickly moving past • We were almost *bowled over* by the wind. **2** ***bowl (someone) over or bowl over (someone)*** : to surprise or impress (someone) very much • He was completely *bowled over* by the news. • She *bowled over* [=*amazed*] the judges with her excellent performance.

bow·leg·ged /ˈboʊˌlɛgəd/ *adj* : having legs that curve outward at the knee • He's short and *bowlegged.* • a *bowlegged* woman

bowl·er /ˈboʊlɚ/ *noun, pl* **-ers** [*count*]
1 : someone who plays the game of bowling • She's a great *bowler.* [=she bowls very well]
2 *cricket* : the player who throws the ball to the batsman
3 *chiefly Brit* : DERBY 4

bowl·ful *noun, pl* **-fuls** [*count*] : the amount of food or liquid that fits in a bowl • a *bowlful* of peanuts

bowl·ing /ˈboʊlɪŋ/ *noun* [*noncount*] : a game played by rolling a large, heavy ball down a smooth floor (called a lane) towards a set of pins in order to knock down as many pins as possible • She watches *bowling* on TV. • We're ***going bowling***. — often used before another noun • a *bowling* ball • a *bowling* lane — see also LAWN BOWLING

bowling alley *noun, pl* ~ **-leys** [*count*] : a room or building in which people play the game of bowling

bow·string /ˈboʊˌstrɪŋ/ *noun, pl* **-strings** [*count*] : the strong, tight string that is used on a bow for shooting arrows

bow tie *noun, pl* ~ **-ties** [*count*] : a narrow length of cloth that is worn by men around the neck and tied into a bow at the throat — see color picture on page C16; compare NECKTIE

bow window *noun, pl* ~ **-dows** [*count*] : a large window or set of windows that curves out from the outside wall of a building

bow·wow /ˈbaʊˌwaʊ/ *noun* [*noncount*] : the usual sound made by dog : a dog's bark ✧ *Bowwow* is a word used mainly by children. • "What does the doggy say?" "*Bowwow!*"

¹box /ˈbɑːks/ *noun, pl* **box·es**
1 [*count*] **a** : a container that is made of a hard material (such as wood, metal, or cardboard) and that usually has four straight sides • a cardboard *box* • She kept the letters in an old *box*. • empty pizza *boxes* • the cat's litter *box* • a *box* of tissues/matches/cigars/tools **b** : the amount of something inside a box • I ate an entire *box* of chocolates. • two *boxes* of cereal
2 [*count*] : a container used for holding mail or papers especially in an office • I'll put the messages in your *box*. • The letter was sent to a post office *box* in New York. — see also IN-BOX, MAILBOX, OUT-BOX
3 a [*count*] : a piece of electronic equipment that is contained inside a box • Where's the system's control *box*? • The cable *box* is on top of the TV. — see also BLACK BOX, GEARBOX **b** ***the box*** *Brit, informal* : a television • Let's turn on *the box* and watch the game.
4 [*count*] : a small area or section of seats that is separated from other seats inside a theater, stadium, or courtroom • She's sitting in the jury *box*. — see picture at THEATER; see also BOX SEAT, LUXURY BOX, PRESS BOX, SKYBOX
5 [*count*] : a closed shape with four sides on a piece of paper, a Web page, etc.: such as **a** : a square in which you make a mark (such as an X) to show that you choose something • If you are over 18 years old, check this *box*. • Put an X in the correct/appropriate *box*. **b** : a square or rectangle around special information in a document, book, etc. • For more information, see *box* A17.
6 [*count*] : an area on a sports field that is used for a special purpose; *especially* : one of six areas on a baseball field that are marked by lines and that show where the batter, pitcher, catcher, and coaches stand • He stepped out of the batter's *box* to take a practice swing. — see also PENALTY BOX
7 [*count*] *Brit* : ¹CUP 5
8 *chiefly Brit* : an area where two streets cross that is marked by painted lines to show where cars are not allowed to stop but can only pass through • The sign at the intersection said "Don't Block the *Box*." — called also (*Brit*) *box junction*
think outside the box ✧ If you *think outside the box*, your thoughts are not limited or controlled by rules or tradition, and you have ideas that are creative and unusual. • To solve this puzzle, you'll have to *think outside the box*.
– compare ²BOX

²box *verb* **boxes; boxed; box·ing** [+ *obj*] : to put (something) in a box • Can you *box* this for me? It's a gift. • The CDs are sold as a ***boxed set***. [=a set of things that are sold together in a box] — often + *up* • She was told to *box up* her things and go home.
box in [*phrasal verb*] ***box (someone or something) in*** : to surround (someone or something) and make movement difficult • The other bicyclists *boxed her in* and she couldn't move ahead. — usually used as *(be) boxed in* • We got *boxed in* and couldn't get out of our parking space. [=other cars were parked so close to our car that we could not move out of our parking space] — sometimes used figuratively • I feel *boxed in* by all these rules.
– compare ³BOX

³box *verb* **boxes; boxed; boxing** : to participate in the sport of boxing : to fight with the hands often while wearing very thick gloves [*no obj*] His father taught him how to *box* when he was 12. [+ *obj*] Who did he *box* in his first fight? — see also KICKBOXING, SHADOWBOX

box someone's ears *old-fashioned* : to hit someone on the sides of the head or on the ears • His mother threatened to *box his ears* if he misbehaved again.

– compare ²BOX

⁴box *noun, pl* **box·es** [*count, noncount*] : BOXWOOD 1 — compare ¹BOX

box·car /ˈbɑːksˌkɑɚ/ *noun, pl* **-cars** [*count*] *US* : a section of a train that has a roof and large, sliding doors and that carries goods and supplies rather than people • *boxcars* filled with lumber/televisions

box cutter *noun, pl* ~ **-ters** [*count*] : a small tool that is made for opening cardboard boxes and that has a very sharp blade that can be pushed in and out of its case

box·er /ˈbɑːksɚ/ *noun, pl* **-ers**

1 [*count*] : someone who participates in the sport of boxing

2 [*count*] : a type of dog that has a short, square face and a tail that is usually cut short when the dog is young — see picture at DOG

3 ***boxers*** [*plural*] : BOXER SHORTS

boxer shorts *noun* [*plural*] : loose shorts that are worn as underwear by men and boys • a pair of *boxer shorts* — see color picture on page C13; compare ²BRIEF 4

box·ing /ˈbɑːksɪŋ/ *noun* [*noncount*] : the sport of fighting someone with your hands while wearing very thick gloves — often used before another noun • a *boxing* glove • a *boxing* match • the heavyweight *boxing* champion of the world

Boxing Day *noun* [*count, noncount*] *chiefly Brit* : a holiday that is celebrated especially in England and Canada on the first day after Christmas that is not a Sunday

box junction *noun, pl* ~ **-tions** [*count*] *Brit* : ¹BOX 8

box lunch *noun, pl* ~ **lunches** [*count*] *US* : BAG LUNCH

box office *noun, pl* ~ **-fices**

1 [*count*] : an area in a theater where tickets are sold for a movie, play, etc. • The *box office* will open at 10:00 a.m.

2 [*singular*] — used to describe how many tickets have been sold for a movie, play, etc. • The movie did very well at the *box office*. [=many people bought tickets to see the movie] • It made over 100 million dollars at the *box office*. — often used before another noun • The movie is a *box office* hit/success. • a *box office* failure/flop

box room *noun, pl* ~ **rooms** [*count*] *Brit* : a room in a house where things are stored

box score *noun, pl* ~ **scores** [*count*] *US* : a small chart that shows the players, score, and other details of a baseball game • reading the *box scores* in the newspaper

box seat *noun, pl* ~ **seats** [*count*] : a seat in a small area or section of seats that is separated from the other seats a theater or stadium

box spring *noun, pl* ~ **springs** [*count*] *US* : a wide, flat box that is filled with metal springs and covered with cloth and that is put under a mattress for support — see picture at BED

box·wood /ˈbɑːksˌwʊd/ *noun, pl* **-woods**

1 *US* : an evergreen bush or small tree that has small dark leaves and that is used especially to make hedges or boundaries in gardens [*noncount*] a *boxwood* hedge [*count*] We planted a few *boxwoods*. — called also *box*

2 [*noncount*] : the tough, hard wood of the boxwood • a piece of *boxwood*

¹boy /ˈbɔɪ/ *noun, pl* **boys**

1 [*count*] **a** : a male child • It's a *boy*! She gave birth to a baby *boy* this morning. • a nine-year-old *boy* named David • Okay, *boys* and girls, it's time to play a game. • Ever since I was a (little/young) *boy*, I've wanted to fly airplanes. **b** : SON • Is this your little *boy*? • He's our oldest/youngest *boy*. • That's my *boy*! Good job, Son.

2 [*count*] **a** : a young man • a group of teenage *boys* • My parents want me to meet a nice *boy* and get married. • Don't be so hard on him. He's just a *boy*. • He's a *boy* genius. • a ***boy wonder*** [=a young man who has achieved many great things] **b** : a usually young man from a specified kind of place • city/country *boys* = *boys* from the city/country • a local/hometown *boy* • a poor *boy* from the north • a farm *boy* [=a young man who lives and works on a farm]

3 a ***the boys*** *informal* : the male friends or work partners of a man viewed as a group • Wait till *the boys* back home hear about this! • Our boss thinks of himself as just one of *the boys*. • He went out drinking with *the boys*. **b** [*singular*] *chiefly Brit, old-fashioned* : a man of any age ◊ The phrases ***my dear boy*** and ***old boy*** are used as friendly ways for one man to address another man. • Why, *my dear boy*, of course I want to see you. • Cheer up, *old boy*. — see also OLD BOY

4 [*count*] : a man or boy who does a particular job • a messenger *boy* ◊ *Boy* is often offensive in this sense when the person being described is an adult. — see also ALTAR BOY, BALL BOY, BATBOY, BELLBOY, BUSBOY, DELIVERY BOY, PAPERBOY

boys will be boys ◊ The expression *boys will be boys* is used to say that it is not surprising or unusual when men or boys behave in energetic, rough, or improper ways. • You shouldn't be too hard on them for staying out so late. *Boys will be boys*.

separate the men from the boys see ²SEPARATE

– see also BAD BOY, BIG BOYS, GOOD OLD BOY, POSTER BOY, PRETTY BOY

– **boy·hood** /ˈbɔɪˌhʊd/ *noun* [*noncount*] • the president's early *boyhood* — often used before another noun • his *boyhood* home [=where he lived when he was a boy] • *boyhood* heroes/friends – **boy·ish** /ˈbojɪʃ/ *adj* [*more* ~; *most* ~] • his *boyish* good looks • He has a *boyish* charm about him. • a *boyish* haircut • She's always had a *boyish* figure. – **boy·ish·ly** *adv* • a *boyishly* handsome actor – **boy·ish·ness** *noun* [*noncount*]

²boy *interj* — used as a way to express surprise or enthusiasm • *Boy*, I sure am hungry! • *Boy*, have I got a story for you! • There's a surprise? Oh, *boy*! What is it? • *Boy*, oh, *boy*. This is great!! • *Boy*, that test was really hard.

¹boy·cott /ˈbɔɪˌkɑːt/ *verb* **-cotts; -cott·ed; -cott·ing** [+ *obj*] : to refuse to buy, use, or participate in (something) as a way of protesting • plans to *boycott* American products • They *boycotted* the city's bus system. • The country's leaders *boycotted* [=did not attend] the event in protest. : to stop using the goods or services of (a company, country, etc.) until changes are made • We *boycotted* companies that were polluting the environment.

²boycott *noun, pl* **-cotts** [*count*] : an often organized act of boycotting something • the 1955 bus *boycott* — often + *of*, *against*, or *on* • the country's *boycott of* the Olympics • a *boycott against/on* the company's products

boy·friend /ˈbɔɪˌfrɛnd/ *noun, pl* **-friends** [*count*] : a man that someone is having a romantic or sexual relationship with • My *boyfriend* and I have only been dating for a couple of months. — compare GIRLFRIEND

Boy Scout *noun, pl* ~ **Scouts** [*count*] : a member of an organization for boys ages 11 to 17 ◊ Boy Scouts participate in group activities, learn skills, and are encouraged to have good morals and be good citizens. — called also *Scout*; compare CUB SCOUT, GIRL SCOUT

boy·sen·ber·ry /ˈbɔɪzn̩ˌberi, *Brit* ˈbɔɪzn̩bri/ *noun, pl* **-ries** [*count*] : a large reddish-black berry that has the flavor of a raspberry

bo·zo /ˈboʊzoʊ/ *noun, pl* **bo·zos** [*count*] *informal* : a stupid or foolish person • Some *bozo* forgot to shut the door.

Br *abbr* **1** Britain **2** British

bra /ˈbrɑː/ *noun, pl* **bras** [*count*] : a piece of clothing that is worn by women under other clothes to cover and support the breasts — called also *brassiere*; see color picture on page C13

¹brace /ˈbreɪs/ *verb* **brac·es; braced; brac·ing**

1 : to get ready for something difficult or unpleasant [*no obj*] (*chiefly US*) — usually + *for* • The town is *bracing for* a busy tourist season. • We *braced for* the storm. [+ *obj*] ***Brace yourself***. [=*prepare yourself*] I have some bad news. — usually + *for* • She *braced herself for* the news.

2 [+ *obj*] : to give added physical support or strength to (something) • He *braced* the gate with a piece of wood. • Steel columns *brace* the structure.

3 [+ *obj*] **a** : to support (yourself) by leaning against something or holding something • She ***braced herself*** with one hand and reached up with the other. — often + *against* • He *braced himself against* the wall. **b** : to place (something, such as your feet or hands) against something for support — usually + *against* • He *braced* his foot *against* the wall.

²brace *noun, pl* **braces**

1 [*count*] : a part that adds physical strength or support • We need to add some sort of *brace* to hold the shelf in place.

2 [*count*] **a** : a device that supports a part of the body • He could walk with *braces* on his legs. • She wears a back/neck *brace*. **b** : a device that is attached to teeth to make them straight • (*Brit*) He has a *brace* on his teeth. — plural in U.S. English • He has *braces* on his teeth. • She needed *braces* as a child.

B

B

3 [*count*] : either one of the marks { or } that are used as a pair around words or items that are to be considered together — usually plural • Computer codes appear within *braces.* — called also *curly brace, curly bracket*
4 braces [*plural*] *Brit* : SUSPENDERS
5 *pl* **brace** [*count*] : a pair of birds that have been hunted and killed • several *brace* [=(more commonly) *pairs*] of quail

brace·let /ˈbreɪslət/ *noun, pl* **-lets** [*count*] : a piece of jewelry worn on the wrist — see color picture on page C11

brac·ing /ˈbreɪsɪŋ/ *adj* [*more* ~; *most* ~] : pleasantly cool or cold • clean, *bracing* air — often used figuratively • Her honest remarks provided a *bracing* [=*refreshing*] change from the bland, political commentary.
– **brac·ing·ly** *adv* • *bracingly* cool breezes

brack·en /ˈbrækən/ *noun* [*noncount*] : a large plant that grows commonly in many places around the world : a large kind of fern

¹brack·et /ˈbrækət/ *noun, pl* **-ets** [*count*]
1 : an object that is attached to a wall and used to support or hold up something (such as a shelf) • The shelf is held up with two *brackets.* • There are wall *brackets* in the garage for the rakes and shovels.

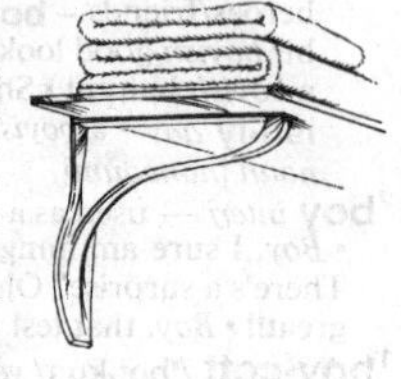
bracket

2 : a category that includes a certain range of incomes, ages, etc. • She is taller/shorter than average for her ***age bracket***. • He earned enough to put him in a higher ***tax bracket***. • She is now in a lower/higher ***income bracket*** than before.
3 a : either one of a pair of marks [ ] or ⟨ ⟩ used to enclose words or mathematical symbols — usually plural • The title appears in/within *brackets* at the top of the page. ✧ The marks [ ] are also called *square brackets* and the marks ⟨ ⟩ are also called *angle brackets*. **b** *Brit* : PARENTHESIS

²bracket *verb* **-ets**; **-et·ed**; **-et·ing** [+ *obj*]
1 : to place (words, symbols, etc.) within brackets • She *bracketed* (off) portions of the text. • *bracketed* information/text/material
2 : to be located at each side of (something) — usually used as *(be) bracketed* • The front door is *bracketed* [=*flanked*] by tall bushes.
3 : to put (two or more people or things) into the same category, group, etc. • Should Haydn and Mozart be *bracketed* (together/with each other)? = Should Mozart be *bracketed* (together) with Haydn?

brack·ish /ˈbrækɪʃ/ *adj* : somewhat salty • *brackish* water • a *brackish* pond

brag /ˈbræg/ *verb* **brags**; **bragged**; **brag·ging** : to talk about yourself, your achievements, your family, etc., in a way that shows too much pride [*no obj*] After winning the race, she couldn't stop *bragging.* • "I don't mean to *brag,*" he said, "but I'm an excellent cook." — often + *about* • She *bragged about* winning the race. • They're always *bragging about* their son's accomplishments. [+ *obj*] He *bragged* that his daughter was the best student in her class. • "I'm the fastest runner on the team," she *bragged.*

brag·ga·do·cio /ˌbrægəˈdoʊsiˌoʊ, ˌ/ *noun* [*noncount*] *literary* : the annoying or exaggerated talk of someone who is trying to sound very proud or brave • a loudmouthed braggart who hid his cowardice with *braggadocio*

brag·gart /ˈbrægət/ *noun, pl* **-garts** [*count*] : a person who brags a lot • a loudmouthed *braggart*

bragging rights *noun* [*plural*] *US* : a good reason to talk with pride about something you have done • She earned *bragging rights* for completing the project on time.

Brah·man *or* **Brah·min** /ˈbrɑːmən/ *noun, pl* **-mans** *or* **-mins** [*count*]
1 : a member of the highest priestly class of Hindu society
2 *usually* **Brahmin** *US, old-fashioned* : an educated person who belongs to a high social class • She was the daughter of a ***Boston Brahmin***.

¹braid /ˈbreɪd/ *noun, pl* **braids**
1 [*count*] *chiefly US* : an arrangement of hair made by weaving three sections together • She wore her hair in a long *braid.* [=(*chiefly Brit*) *plait*] — see picture at HAIR
2 [*noncount*] : a piece of cord or ribbon made of three or more strands woven together • a hat trimmed with *braid*

²braid *verb* **braids**; **braid·ed**; **braid·ing** [+ *obj*] : to form (something, such as hair) into a braid : to weave together (three or more strands or parts of something) • She *braids* her hair every morning. • They *braided* the ribbons.

braided *adj*
1 : formed with three or more parts woven together • *braided* [=(*chiefly Brit*) *plaited*] hair • a *braided* rug
2 : decorated with a piece of cord or ribbon made of three or more strands woven together : decorated with braid • a hat with *braided* trim

braille *or* **Braille** /ˈbreɪl/ *noun* [*noncount*] : a system of writing for blind people in which letters are represented by raised dots • a book made available in *braille* — often used before another noun • a *braille* book

¹brain /ˈbreɪn/ *noun, pl* **brains** [*count*]
1 : the organ of the body in the head that controls functions, movements, sensations, and thoughts • Scientists are learning more about how the human *brain* works. • The left and right sides of the *brain* have different functions. — often used before another noun • a *brain* injury/tumor • *brain* damage/surgery • *brain* cells/tissue
2 *informal* : the ability to think and reason : INTELLIGENCE • Don't be such an idiot—use your *brain.* [=*head*] • She has a good *brain.* [=she is smart] • I'm sorry—I don't know where my *brain* is today. [=I'm not thinking clearly today] • If he had ***half a brain*** [=if he was at all smart], he would have left a long time ago. — often plural • If he had any *brains,* he would have left a long time ago. • She has both *brains* and beauty.
3 *informal* : a very intelligent person • The other children always teased him about being such a *brain.* • She is one of the best *brains* [=*intellects, minds*] in the field. ✧ If you are ***the brains of/behind*** something, you are the person who thinks of plans or makes important decisions for a group. • She's *the brains of* this organization. • He was *the brains behind* the scheme.

beat/bash someone's brains out *or US* ***beat/bash someone's brains in*** *informal* : to hit someone on the head in a way that causes serious injury or death : to beat someone very badly • They threatened to *beat my brains in* if I ever came here again.

blow someone's brains out *informal* : to kill someone with a shot to the head : to shoot someone fatally in the head • When he refused to hand over the money, the robbers threatened to *blow his brains out.*

cudgel your brain/brains *informal* + *old-fashioned* : to think very hard : to rack your brain • I *cudgeled my brains* for a solution to the problem.

on the brain *informal* : always in your thoughts • I've had pizza *on the brain* all day. [=I've been thinking about pizza all day] • He's got sex *on the brain.* [=he's always thinking about sex]

pick someone's brain/brains *informal* : to talk to someone in order to get helpful information or advice • Do you have a moment? I need to *pick your brain* about a little situation that has come up.

rack your brain/brains see ²RACK

²brain *verb* **brains**; **brained**; **brain·ing** [+ *obj*] *informal* : to hit (someone) on the head very hard • The tree limb fell and nearly *brained* me.

brain·child /ˈbreɪnˌʧajəld/ *noun* [*singular*] : an idea, plan, or creation of one person • The museum is the *brainchild* of a wealthy art collector.

brain–dead /ˈbreɪnˌdɛd/ *adj*
1 *medical* : showing no sign of activity in the brain : having no brain function • Doctors determined that she was *brain-dead.*
2 *informal* : very stupid • You would have to be *brain-dead* not to see the problem. : not able to function normally • I'll be *brain-dead* in the morning if I don't get some sleep.

brain death *noun* [*noncount*] *medical* : the condition of having no brain function : the end of activity in the brain

brain drain *noun* [*singular*] : a situation in which many educated or professional people leave a particular place or profession and move to another one that gives them better pay or living conditions • Nothing has been done to stop the *brain drain* as more and more doctors move away from the area.

brain·i·ac /ˈbreɪniˌæk/ *noun, pl* **-acs** [*count*] *informal* : a very intelligent person • the class *brainiac* — often used before another noun • a *brainiac* scientist

brain·less /ˈbreɪnləs/ *adj* [*more* ~; *most* ~] *informal* : very stupid or silly • He thought most of his coworkers were

B

brainless. • The plot of the new movie is *brainless* and the acting is terrible.
– **brain·less·ly** *adv* – **brain·less·ness** *noun [noncount]*

brain·pow·er /ˈbreɪnˌpawɚ/ *noun [noncount]*
1 : the ability to think intelligently • The *brainpower* of the staff constitutes the company's greatest asset. • The product is supposed to boost your *brainpower.*
2 : people who are very intelligent • The company is increasing efforts to recruit scientific *brainpower.*

¹brain·storm /ˈbreɪnˌstoɚm/ *noun, pl* **-storms** *[count]*
1 *US* **:** an idea that someone thinks of suddenly — usually singular • Her latest *brainstorm* is to convert the garage into an apartment. — called also *(chiefly Brit) brain wave*
2 *Brit* **:** a temporary state of confusion **:** a period of unclear thinking • I'm sorry—I must have been having a *brainstorm* when I wrote that.

²brainstorm *verb* **-storms; -stormed; -storm·ing :** to try to solve a problem by talking with other people **:** to discuss a problem and suggest solutions *[no obj]* We need to *brainstorm* about this. *[+ obj]* They had a meeting to *brainstorm* some ideas.
– **brainstorming** *noun [noncount]* • We did some *brainstorming* and came up with some ideas. • We had a *brainstorming* session.

brain·teas·er /ˈbreɪnˌtiːzɚ/ *noun, pl* **-ers** *[count]* **:** a puzzle that is difficult to figure out or solve

brain trust *noun, pl* ~ **trusts** *[count] US* **:** a group of people who give advice to a leader about what should be done • The president's *brain trust* recommended the action. — called also *(Brit) brains trust*

brain·wash /ˈbreɪnˌwɑːʃ/ *verb* **-wash·es; -washed; -wash·ing** *[+ obj]* **:** to cause (someone) to think or believe something by using methods that make a person unable to think normally • Terrorists *brainwashed* the prisoners. • Does advertising *brainwash* children? — often + *into* • She was *brainwashed into* donating all her money to the cult.

brain wave *noun, pl* ~ **waves** *[count]*
1 : a pattern or cycle of electrical activity in the brain — usually plural • Do your *brain waves* change when you are sleeping?
2 *chiefly Brit* **:** ¹BRAINSTORM 1

brainy /ˈbreɪni/ *adj* **brain·i·er; -est** *[also more ~; most ~] informal* **:** very intelligent • a *brainy* child
– **brain·i·ness** *noun [noncount]* • She shouldn't hide her *braininess.*

braise /ˈbreɪz/ *verb* **brais·es; braised; brais·ing** *[+ obj]* **:** to cook (food) slowly in fat and a small amount of liquid in a covered pot • He *braised* the beef in a wine sauce.
– **braised** *adj* • *braised* chicken/cabbage

¹brake /ˈbreɪk/ *noun, pl* **brakes** *[count]*
1 : a device for slowing or stopping something (such as a wheel or vehicle) • She released the *brake* slowly. • Take your foot off the *brake.* — often plural • The car will need new *brakes* soon. • He ***slammed/jammed on the brakes*** [=he applied the brakes very quickly] to avoid hitting the other car. — often used before another noun • *brake* shoes/fluid • Take your foot off the *brake* pedal. • I didn't notice that the car in front of me had its *brake* lights on. — see picture at BICYCLE; see also DISC BRAKE, EMERGENCY BRAKE, HAND BRAKE, PARKING BRAKE
2 : something used to slow or stop movement or activity — usually + *on* • They plan to use interest rates as a *brake on* spending. [=as a way to slow down spending] • trying to ***put the brakes on*** crime

²brake /ˈbreɪk/ *verb* **brakes; braked; brak·ing** *[no obj]* **:** to use the brake on a vehicle • I had to *brake* suddenly when a cat ran in front of the car. • This car has excellent *braking.* [=it stops quickly and easily when the brakes are used]

bram·ble /ˈbræmbəl/ *noun, pl* **bram·bles** *[count]*
1 *US* **:** a rough bush or vine that usually has sharp thorns on its branches — usually plural • a field filled with *brambles*
2 *Brit* **:** BLACKBERRY

bran /ˈbræn/ *noun [noncount]* **:** the outer coat of the seed of a grain • The doctor told me to eat more *bran* because it is a good source of fiber. — often used before another noun • *bran* cereal/muffins [=cereal/muffins containing bran]

¹branch /ˈbræntʃ, *Brit* ˈbrɑːntʃ/ *noun, pl* **branch·es** *[count]*
1 : a part of a tree that grows out from the trunk • birds singing from the *branches* of a tree • A large (tree) *branch* fell into our yard during the storm. — see color picture on page C6
2 a : a local office or shop of a company or organization • The bank has a new *branch* in our area. • She works at the ***branch office*** downtown. **b :** a major part of a government — often + *of* • the executive/legislative/judicial *branch of* the United States government
3 : a part of an area of knowledge or study — often + *of* • Pathology is a *branch of* medicine.
4 : a part of a family that is descended from a particular family member in the past — often + *of* • We don't know much about that *branch of* the family.
5 : something that goes outward from a main line or source • Some of the river's smaller *branches* flooded after the heavy rains. • There was a problem with the railroad's ***branch line.***
root and branch see ¹ROOT
– **branched** /ˈbræntʃt, *Brit* ˈbrɑːntʃt/ *adj*

²branch *verb* **branch·es; branched; branch·ing** *[no obj]* **:** to divide into smaller parts **:** to separate into branches • The stream *branches* from the river near their house.
branch off *[phrasal verb]* **:** to separate from something and move in a different direction • The stream *branched off* to the left. — often + *from* • The stream *branches off from* the river near their house. • Streets *branch off from* both sides of the highway.
branch out *[phrasal verb]* **:** to begin to do more different kinds of activities or work • In the beginning the business was highly specialized, but it has since *branched out.* — often + *into* • The company specializes in casual clothing but it is *branching out into* formal wear.

¹brand /ˈbrænd/ *noun, pl* **brands** *[count]*
1 : a category of products that are all made by a particular company and all have a particular name • What *brand* are those jeans you are wearing? • The store sells a variety of shoe *brands.* • The company claims that its product is better than the ***leading brand.*** [=the brand that sells the most] — often + *of* • I'm trying a different *brand of* soap. • What is your favorite *brand of* soda? ✧ ***Brand loyalty*** is the tendency of a person to continue to buy a particular brand of something. • The company spends a lot of money on advertising to develop *brand loyalty.* — see also STORE BRAND
2 : a particular kind or type *of* something • I don't like his *brand of* humor. • a lively *brand of* theater
3 : a mark that is burned into the skin of an animal (such as a cow) to show who owns the animal

²brand *verb* **brands; brand·ed; brand·ing** *[+ obj]*
1 : to put a mark on the skin of (an animal) to show who owns it • They no longer *brand* their cattle.
2 : to describe or identify (someone or something) with a word that expresses strong criticism • They *branded* him a coward. [=they said he was a coward] — usually used as *(be) branded* • He *was branded* (as) a coward. • The newspaper *was branded* racist for publishing the article.

brand·ed /ˈbrændəd/ *adj, always used before a noun* **:** having a well-known brand name • She only buys *branded* [=*brand-name*] products.

bran·dish /ˈbrændɪʃ/ *verb* **-dish·es; -dished; -dish·ing** *[+ obj]* **:** to wave or swing (something, such as a weapon) in a threatening or excited manner • She *brandished* a stick at the dog. • I could see that he was *brandishing* a knife.

brand name *noun, pl* ~ **names** *[count]* **:** a name that is given to a product by the company that produces or sells it • The drug is sold under several *brand names.* • a trusted *brand name* — compare NAME BRAND

brand–name /ˈbrændˈneɪm/ *adj* **:** having a well-known brand name • I buy only *brand-name* [=*branded*] products.

brand–new /ˈbrændˈnuː, *Brit* ˈbrændˈnjuː/ *adj* **:** completely new • She bought a *brand-new* car. • They have a *brand-new* baby. • This concept is *brand-new*—no one has ever tried anything like it before.

bran·dy /ˈbrændi/ *noun, pl* **-dies** *[count, noncount]* **:** an alcoholic drink made from wine

brash /ˈbræʃ/ *adj* **brash·er; -est**
1 : confident and aggressive in usually a rude or unpleasant way • a *brash* young executive • She asks such *brash* questions.
2 : very strong or harsh • *brash* colors • *brash* lighting
– **brash·ly** *adv* • He *brashly* confronted his boss about a raise. – **brash·ness** *noun [noncount]*

brass /ˈbræs, *Brit* ˈbrɑːs/ *noun, pl* **brass·es**
1 *[noncount]* **:** a yellow metal that is made by combining copper and zinc • a candlestick made of *brass* — often used before another noun • a *brass* candlestick
2 : musical instruments (such as trumpets, trombones, and tubas) that are made of brass *[noncount]* The whole

B

orchestra—the strings, percussion, woodwinds, and *brass*—began to play. [*plural*] The *brasses* began to play. — often used before another noun • He's one of the best *brass* players in the orchestra. • a *brass* instrument • the orchestra's ***brass section*** [=the group of musicians in an orchestra who play brass instruments] — see also BRASS BAND
3 [*noncount*] : bright metal objects made of brass • polishing the *brass* and the silver
4 [*noncount*] *chiefly US, informal* : the people in the highest positions in an organization (such as the military or a business) • Navy *brass* [=*top brass*] met earlier today. — often used with *the* • *The brass* met earlier today. ✧ *Brass* is used with both plural and singular verbs in this sense. • *The* company *brass* have/has decided that no action is necessary at this time.
(as) bold as brass see [1]BOLD
get down to brass tacks *informal* : to start to discuss or consider the most important details or facts about something • We finally *got down to brass tacks* and decided to work out a schedule for the project.

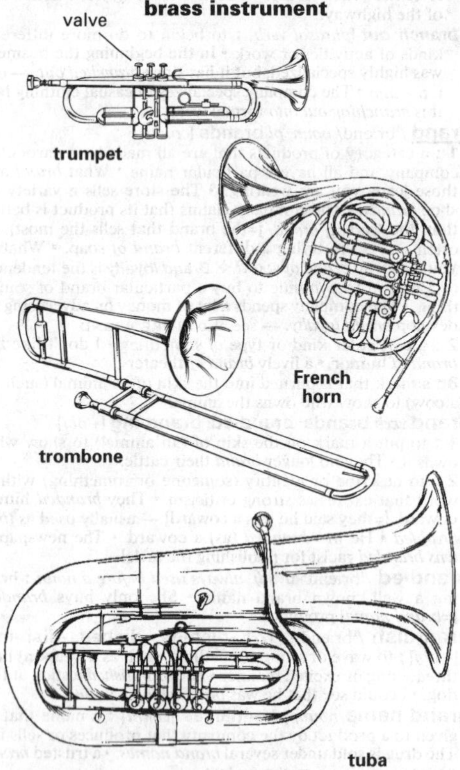

brass band *noun, pl* ~ **bands** [*count*] : a band (such as a marching band or a military band) in which most of the musicians play brass instruments (such as trumpets and trombones)
brassed off *adj* [*more* ~; *most* ~] *Brit, informal* : annoyed and unhappy • feeling a bit *brassed off*
bras•siere /brəˈziə, *Brit* ˈbræziə/ *noun, pl* **-sieres** [*count*] *formal* : BRA — see color picture on page C13
brass ring *noun*
the brass ring *US, informal* : a very desirable prize, goal, or opportunity • He made his first try for *the brass ring* when he ran for mayor a few years ago. — often used in phrases like ***grab the brass ring*** and ***go for the brass ring*** • She's decided to *go for the brass ring* and start her own business.
brassy /ˈbræsi, *Brit* ˈbrɑːsi/ *adj* **brass•i•er; -est**
1 : very confident and aggressive in a loud and sometimes annoying way • a *brassy* woman/reporter
2 : having a loud and often harsh sound • *brassy* music • a big, *brassy* voice
3 : resembling or suggesting brass • a *brassy* shine • *brassy* colors
— **brass•i•ly** /ˈbræsəli, *Brit* ˈbrɑːsəli/ *adv* — **brass•i•ness** *noun* [*noncount*]
brat /ˈbræt/ *noun, pl* **brats** [*count*] *informal*
1 *disapproving* : a child who behaves very badly : an annoying child • a bunch of ill-mannered little *brats* • He is a ***spoiled brat.***
2 *US* : the child of a person whose career is in the army, navy, etc. • I was an army/navy/military *brat.*; *also* : the child of a person whose career is in a specified field • His children are typical Hollywood *brats.*
— **brat•ty** /ˈbræti/ *adj* **brat•ti•er; -est** • a *bratty* child — **brat•ti•ness** *noun* [*noncount*]
bra•va•do /brəˈvɑːdoʊ/ *noun* [*noncount*] : confident or brave talk or behavior that is intended to impress other people • His stories are always told with *bravado.* • I remember his youthful *bravado.*
[1]**brave** /ˈbreɪv/ *adj* **brav•er; -est** : feeling or showing no fear : not afraid • He was a *brave* [=*courageous, fearless*] soldier. • She gave us a *brave* smile. • He lost his *brave* fight against the disease. • She tried to ***put on/up a brave face/front*** [=she tried to appear brave or calm] despite the pain of the injury.
the brave : brave people • the home of *the brave*
— **brave•ly** *adv* • He smiled *bravely* as he stepped in front of the cameras.
[2]**brave** *verb* **braves; braved; brav•ing** [+ *obj*] : to face or deal with (something dangerous or unpleasant) • We *braved* [=went out in] the rain without our umbrellas. • Thousands of fans *braved* rush-hour traffic to see the concert. • I had to ***brave the elements*** [=go out in bad weather] to get to work.
[3]**brave** *noun, pl* **braves** [*count*] *old-fashioned* : a Native American warrior
brave new world *noun* [*singular*] : a situation or area of activity that is created by the development of something completely new and different • The company was slow to enter the *brave new world* of computer technology. — often used to suggest that something is both new and possibly dangerous • Are we ready to face the *brave new world* of human cloning?
brav•ery /ˈbreɪvəri/ *noun* [*noncount*] : the quality that allows someone to do things that are dangerous or frightening : the quality or state of being brave : COURAGE • He received a medal for *bravery.* • She showed great *bravery.* • an act of *bravery* [=a brave act]
bra•vo /ˈbrɑːvoʊ/ *interj* — used to express approval of a performance • Shouts of "*Bravo!*" continued after the curtain fell.
bra•vu•ra /brəˈvjurə/ *noun* [*noncount*] : great skill and energy in doing something (such as performing on a stage) — usually used before another noun • a *bravura* performance
brawl /ˈbrɑːl/ *verb* **brawls; brawled; brawl•ing** [*no obj*] : to fight noisily in usually a public place • Fans were *brawling* in the streets after the game.
— **brawl** *noun, pl* **brawls** [*count*] • A *brawl* broke out among the fans after the hockey game. • a drunken street *brawl* • He was in a ***barroom brawl.*** [=a fight in a bar] — **brawl•er** *noun, pl* **-ers** [*count*] • Police arrested two of the *brawlers.*
brawn /ˈbrɑːn/ *noun* [*noncount*]
1 : muscular strength — usually used to compare physical strength to intelligence • When it comes to men, she prefers brains over *brawn.* [=she likes smart men better than muscular ones]
2 *Brit* : HEADCHEESE
— **brawny** /ˈbrɑːni/ *adj* **brawn•i•er; -est** • his *brawny* [=*muscular*] arms
bray /ˈbreɪ/ *verb* **brays; brayed; bray•ing**
1 [*no obj*] : to make the loud sound that a donkey makes • The donkey *brayed* loudly (at us) when we approached it. • a *braying* donkey
2 : to speak or laugh in a very loud and unpleasant way [*no obj*] My aunt *brayed* with laughter when I told her what had happened. • He *brayed* about what a great player he was. • a *braying* voice/laugh [+ *obj*] "I'm the best!" he *brayed.*
— **bray** *noun, pl* **brays** [*count*] • the *bray* of a donkey
[1]**bra•zen** /ˈbreɪzn/ *adj* [*more* ~; *most* ~] : acting or done in a very open and shocking way without shame or embarrassment • He exhibited a *brazen* disregard for other people's feelings. • a *brazen* lie
— **bra•zen•ly** *adv* • She *brazenly* ignored his orders. — **bra•zen•ness** *noun* [*noncount*]
[2]**brazen** *verb* **-zens; -zened; -zen•ing**
brazen it out : to continue in a confident way without showing shame or embarrassment • Despite the bad pub-

licity, the candidate decided to *brazen it out* and stay in the race.

bra·zier /ˈbreɪʒɚ, *Brit* ˈbreɪziə/ *noun, pl* **-ziers** [*count*]
1 : a container for holding burning coals
2 *chiefly US* **:** a device on which food is cooked over high heat

Bra·zil nut /brəˈzɪl-/ *noun, pl* ~ **nuts** [*count*] **:** a long, white nut that grows on a South American tree — called also (*Brit*) *Brazil*; see picture at NUT

[1]**breach** /ˈbriːʧ/ *noun, pl* **breach·es**
1 : a failure to do what is required by a law an agreement or a duty **:** failure to act in a required or promised way — usually + *of* [*count*] This is clearly a *breach of* the treaty. • He was fined for committing a ***breach of the peace*** [=for making a lot of noise or behaving violently in public; for disorderly conduct] • Many people consider her decision to be a ***breach of trust/confidence*** [*noncount*] They sued him for ***breach of contract*** [=for failing to do what the contract required] • The judge ruled that the doctor's actions were ***in breach of*** her contractual duty.
2 ✧ A ***breach of security*** or a ***security breach*** is an occurrence in which someone is able to get into a place that is guarded or is able to get secret information. • The break-in was a serious *breach of security*. • Allowing such information to be released to the public is considered a *security breach*.
3 [*count*] **:** a break in friendly relations between people or groups — often + *between* • The *breach between* them developed years ago. • The misunderstanding had caused a *breach between* the families. • The decision caused a *breach between* the two countries.
4 [*count*] **:** a hole or opening in something (such as a wall) made by breaking through it • They repaired a *breach* in the fence.
into the breach ✧ If you ***step/leap/jump (etc.) into the breach***, you provide help that is badly needed, such as by doing a job when there is no one else available to do it. • He *stepped into the breach* when the company needed new leadership.

[2]**breach** *verb* **breaches; breached; breach·ing** [+ *obj*]
1 : to fail to do what is required by (something, such as a law or agreement) **:** to break or violate (something) • He claims that the city *breached* an agreement by selling the property. • Is he going to *breach* his contract?
2 : to make a hole or opening in (something) • The army *breached* the castle wall.

[1]**bread** /ˈbrɛd/ *noun, pl* **breads**
1 : a baked food made from a mixture of flour and water [*noncount*] She bakes *bread* every day. • a loaf/slice/piece/hunk of *bread* [*count*] The bakery offers a nice selection of *breads* and pastries. — often used before another noun • *bread* crumbs • a *bread* knife [=a knife used for cutting bread]
2 [*noncount*] *old-fashioned, slang* **:** MONEY • I took the job because I needed to earn some *bread*. [=(more commonly) *dough*]
break bread **:** to have a meal together • He received an invitation to *break bread* with the president.
know which side your bread is buttered on *informal* **:** to know how to act or how to treat others in order to get what you want • He pretends to be impartial, but believe me, he *knows which side his bread is buttered on*.

[2]**bread** *verb* **breads; bread·ed; bread·ing** [+ *obj*] **:** to cover (food) with bread crumbs before cooking it • She *breaded* the pork chops before frying them.
– breaded *adj* • She served *breaded* pork chops.

bread and butter *noun* [*singular*] **:** a dependable source of income or success • Casual clothing has always been the company's *bread and butter*.

bread–and–butter *adj, always used before a noun*
1 : basic and important • *bread-and-butter* economic issues
2 : dependable as a source of income or success • the company's *bread-and-butter* products • His *bread-and-butter* pitch has always been his fastball.

bread·bas·ket /ˈbrɛdˌbæskət, *Brit* ˈbrɛdˌbɑːskət/ *noun, pl* **-kets** [*count*] **:** a region that provides large amounts of food • the *breadbasket* of the world • The area is becoming the nation's *breadbasket*.

bread·box /ˈbrɛdˌbɑːks/ *noun, pl* **-box·es** [*count*] *chiefly US* **:** a container in someone's kitchen where bread and other baked goods are stored to keep them fresh — often used informally to describe the size of something • The entire stereo system is not much ***bigger than a breadbox*** — called also (*Brit*) *bread bin*

bread·fruit /ˈbrɛdˌfruːt/ *noun, pl* **-fruit** [*count, noncount*] **:** a round fruit that resembles bread when it is baked

bread·line /ˈbrɛdˌlaɪn/ *noun, pl* **-lines**
1 [*count*] *chiefly US* **:** a line of people who are waiting to receive free food
2 ***the breadline*** *Brit* **:** the level of income at which someone is considered poor • people living below/near/on *the breadline* [=*the poverty line*]

breadth /ˈbrɛtθ/ *noun* [*noncount*]
1 : the distance from one side to the other side of something **:** WIDTH • We measured the height, *breadth*, and depth of each piece of furniture. • Its *breadth* is five feet. [=(more commonly) it's five feet wide] — see also HAIR'S BREADTH
2 : the quality of including many things **:** the wide scope or range of something • I admire his *breadth* of knowledge/experience/achievement. = I admire the *breadth* of his knowledge/experience/achievement.
the length and breadth of see LENGTH

bread·win·ner /ˈbrɛdˌwɪnɚ/ *noun, pl* **-ners** [*count*] **:** a person who earns money to support a family • He had always been the (family) *breadwinner*.

[1]**break** /ˈbreɪk/ *verb* **breaks; broke** /ˈbroʊk/; **bro·ken** /ˈbroʊkən/; **break·ing**
1 : to separate (something) into parts or pieces often in a sudden and forceful or violent way [+ *obj*] She *broke* the cup when she dropped it on the floor. • I *broke* the stick in two/half. = I *broke* the stick into two pieces. • *Break* the chocolate bar into pieces so that everyone can have some. • It is easiest to *break* a chain at its weakest link. [*no obj*] The cup *broke* (into bits/pieces) when it fell on the floor. • A chain will *break* at its weakest link.
2 : to cause (a bone) to separate into two or more pieces [+ *obj*] He fell and *broke* [=*fractured*] his collarbone. • He *broke* his arm in the accident. [=one of the bones in his arm was broken in the accident] • The fall *broke* his arm. [*no obj*] His arm *broke* in three places when he fell.
3 [*no obj*] **:** to open suddenly especially because of pressure from inside • The blister *broke*. • A bruise forms when a blood vessel *breaks* under the skin. — see also BREAK OPEN (below)
4 a [+ *obj*] **:** to cause (something, such as a machine) to stop working by damaging it • He *broke* his watch when he dropped it on the floor. • I'm afraid I've *broken* your phone. **b** [*no obj*] **:** to stop working because of being damaged • His watch *broke* when he dropped it on the floor. • The pump recently *broke*. — see also BREAK DOWN (below)
5 : to split or divide (something) *into* smaller units or parts [+ *obj*] The word "singing" can be *broken* (up) *into* the two syllables "sing-" and "-ing." • They *broke* the corporation (up) *into* several smaller companies. [*no obj*] The corporation *broke* (up) *into* several smaller companies. — see also BREAK INTO (below)
6 [+ *obj*] **a :** to go through or make a hole in (a surface, someone's skin, etc.) • There is no risk of infection if the dog's bite did not *break* [=*puncture*] the skin. • A large fish *broke* the surface of the water. **b :** to go through (something) by using force • Use a knife to *break* the seal. — usually used figuratively • The ceremony is to celebrate people who *broke* racial barriers in the music industry. — see also BREAK DOWN (below), BREAK THROUGH (below) **c :** to cut into and turn over the surface of (the ground, soil, etc.) • The farmer uses a plow to *break* the soil. — see also *break ground* at [1]GROUND
7 [+ *obj*] **:** to fail to do what is required by (a law, a promise, etc.) • She may not have *broken* the law, but she acted wrongly. • You *broke* your promise. • Students who *break* the rules will be punished. • He *broke* the contract by failing to make the payments on time. • You can get fined for *breaking* the speed limit. [=for driving faster than you are legally allowed to drive]
8 a : to destroy or defeat (something) by using force or pressure [+ *obj*] They kept putting pressure on him, but they couldn't *break* his spirit/determination/resistance. • They finally *broke* his will to resist. [*no obj*] His spirit/determination will never *break*. **b** [+ *obj*] **:** to defeat or ruin (someone) **:** to cause (someone) to fail or to stop trying or fighting • He swore that he would *break* his rivals/competitors. • They kept putting pressure on him, but they couldn't *break* him. • These huge losses are going to *break* [=*ruin*] me financially! • This film could ***make or break*** her career. [=the success or failure of her career could depend on the success or failure

B

of this film] — see also BREAK DOWN (below), MAKE-OR-BREAK **c** [*no obj*] **:** to lose your health, mental or physical strength, or control — usually + *under* • The witness *broke under* questioning. • I was afraid I would *break under* the strain of constant uncertainty. — see also BREAK DOWN (below) **d** [+ *obj*] **:** to train (a wild animal) to behave in a way that is useful to people • special equipment used to *break* horses

9 [+ *obj*] **a :** to cause the end of (something that is strong or that has continued for a long time) • A group of moderates from both parties are negotiating to *break* the deadlock in Congress. • Many people in the industry were very upset when the government *broke* the strike. • He decided to *break* all ties/links with them. [=to end all connections with them] • She scored a goal in the last minute of the game, *breaking* a 2–2 tie. • It's never easy to *break* [=*kick, give up*] a bad habit. **b :** to cause (someone) to give up a habit — + *of* • His friends have tried everything to *break* him *of* his smoking habit. [=have tried everything to make him stop smoking]

10 [+ *obj*] **a :** to interrupt (something) • The peaceful silence of the evening was *broken* by a sudden shout. • The commotion *broke* my train of thought. • The sudden noise *broke* my concentration. [=made it impossible for me to concentrate] • Sometimes I sing while I'm driving, just to *break* (up) the monotony of my commute. • The horizon line was *broken* only by a few stands of trees in the distance. • The planes ***broke formation*** [=stopped flying together in an organized group] and took off in different directions. — see also BREAK UP 4 (below) **b :** to cause (something, such as a curse or spell) to no longer be effective • a mystic who claimed to be able to *break* curses

11 [*no obj*] **:** to stop an activity (such as working) for a brief period of time • Let's *break* for lunch. [=let's take a break for lunch; let's temporarily stop working and eat lunch]

12 a [+ *obj*] **:** to tell (bad news) to someone in a kind or gentle way • I know she'll be very upset when she finds out she didn't get the job, so please try to *break* it to her gently. **b** [+ *obj*] **:** to make (something, such as news) publicly known for the first time • The local TV station was the first to *break* the news about the President's visit. **c** [*no obj*] *of news* **:** to become publicly known • The story *broke* yesterday. [=the story was reported for the first time yesterday] • People were shocked when (news of) the scandal first *broke*.

13 [+ *obj*] **:** to reduce the speed or force of (something) • The bushes beneath the window helped to ***break his fall***. [=helped make his fall less forceful] • She walked straight across the room without ***breaking (her) stride***. [=without pausing or slowing down]

14 [+ *obj*] **a :** to be higher or more than (a specified number, measurement, etc.) • The temperature is expected to *break* 90 (degrees Fahrenheit) today. **b :** to do better than (a record) • She ran a great race and almost *broke* the world record. [=she almost ran the race faster than anyone in the world has ever run it] • He set a record that may never be *broken*. **c :** to have a score that is lower than or higher than (a specified total) • golfers trying to *break* 90 [=to have a score below 90] • bowlers trying to *break* 200 [=to have a score above 200]

15 [+ *obj*] **a :** to find or provide an explanation or solution for (something, such as a criminal case) • The detective finally *broke* [=*solved*] the case. • The detective found the evidence that *broke* the case. **b :** to find the meaning of (a secret code) • A team of experts was finally able to *break* the code and decipher the meaning of the message.

16 [*no obj*] **a** *of the weather* **:** to change by becoming rainy, clear, cool, etc., after a long time • waiting for the weather to *break* • The heat wave should finally *break* [=*end*] tomorrow. **b** *of clouds* **:** to separate so that the sky or sun can be seen • The clouds *broke* and the fog dissipated, revealing blue sky above. **c** *of a storm* **:** to start suddenly • Everyone ran to get indoors when the storm *broke*. [=when it began to rain]

17 [*no obj*] *literary* **:** to begin when the sun rises • They left just as ***day was breaking***. [=just as the sun was rising] • The ***dawn was breaking***. — see also DAYBREAK

18 [*no obj*] **a :** to begin running quickly • Everyone *broke* [=*dashed, ran*] for cover. **b :** to stop fighting and run away • When the enemy charged, our troops *broke* and ran.

19 [+ *obj*] **a :** to give smaller bills or coins for (a large bill) • Can you *break* [=*change*] a $20 bill for me? **b :** to use (a large bill) to pay for something that costs much less than the value of the bill • I didn't want to *break* a $20 bill just to buy something for a dollar.

20 [*no obj*] *of a wave* **:** to curl over and fall onto or near land • the sound of waves *breaking* against/over/on the rocks

21 [*no obj*] **a** *of someone's voice* **:** to change sharply in tone or pitch because of strong emotion • Her voice was *breaking* with emotion as she said goodbye. **b** *of a boy's voice* **:** to change from the high voice of a boy to the lower voice of a man • an adolescent boy whose voice is *breaking*

22 [*no obj*] *sports, of a thrown or struck ball* **:** to turn or curve • The putt *broke* to the left as it neared the hole. • a pitch that *breaks* away from the batter • The pitcher threw a ***breaking ball***. [=a pitch that curves]

23 *tennis* **:** to win against (an opponent who is serving) [+ *obj*] The challenger *broke* the champion in the final set. = The challenger *broke* the champion's serve in the final set. [*no obj*] The challenger *broke* in the final set but the champion *broke* back to even the score.

24 [*no obj*] **:** to happen or develop • For the team to succeed, everything has to *break* right for them. [=for the team to succeed, they have to be lucky] • Things have been *breaking* [=*going*] well for the company in the past six months.

break a leg see [1]LEG

break a sweat see [2]SWEAT

break away [*phrasal verb*] **1 :** to get away from someone or something especially by using force or effort • Large pieces of the rock ledge have *broken away*. [=*broken free*] — usually + *from* • He *broke away* [=*broke free/loose*] *from* his captors and escaped. • She *broke away* [=*pulled away*] *from* the other runners to win the race. — often used figuratively • The company has *broken away from* the competition. • young people *breaking away from* traditional values **2 :** to separate or become separate from a larger group, country, etc. • Three members of the band *broke away* and formed their own group. — usually + *from* • a faction that has *broken away from* the main political party — see also BREAKAWAY

break bread see [1]BREAD

break camp see [1]CAMP

break cover see [2]COVER

break down [*phrasal verb*] **1 a** *of a machine* **:** to stop working properly • Our car *broke down* on the highway. • This old motorcycle is constantly *breaking down*. — see also [1]BREAK 4 (above) **b :** to fail or stop usually in a complete and sudden way • Negotiations have *broken down*. [=*collapsed*] • The government's argument *broke down* completely when new evidence came to light. • Their marriage had *broken down* [=*failed*], and there was nothing to do about it. **2 a :** to become overwhelmed by strong emotions • She *broke down* and started to cry. = She ***broke down in tears***. — see also [1]BREAK 8c (above) **b *break down or break (someone) down or break down (someone)*** **:** to lose or cause (someone) to lose strength or the ability to resist or fight • The prisoner finally *broke down* under intensive questioning. • She finally *broke down* and got a cell phone. [=she bought a cell phone after resisting the desire to buy one for a long time] • Intensive questioning finally *broke* the prisoner *down*. — see also [1]BREAK 8b (above) **3 *break down or break (something) down or break down (something)*** **a :** to become separated or to separate (something) into simpler substances • The foods you eat *break down* in the body's digestive system. • The body's digestive system *breaks* food *down*. • Water can be *broken down* into hydrogen and oxygen through electrolysis. = Water can *break down* into hydrogen and oxygen through electrolysis. **b :** to be able to be divided or to divide (something) *into* parts or groups • The report *breaks down into* three sections. = The report is *broken down into* three sections. [=the report has three sections] • The author has *broken down* the nation's history *into* three distinct periods. **4 *break (something) down or break down (something)*** **:** to use force to push (something) to the ground • *break* a door *down* • *break down* a barrier — sometimes used figuratively • They are working to *break down* legal barriers to integration. — see also BREAKDOWN

break even **:** to take in as much money as you spend **:** to operate without either a loss or a profit • After years of losing money the company is starting to *break even* and hopes to make a profit soon. — see also BREAK-EVEN

break faith with see FAITH

break free **:** to become able to move or escape by using force or effort • The prisoner struggled to *break free*. **:** to get away from someone or something that holds or limits you — often + *from* or *of* • She wanted to *break free from* the constraints of her middle-class life. • an animal struggling to *break free of* a trap

break from [*phrasal verb*] **break from (someone or something) :** to end a relationship, connection, or agreement with (someone or something) • She recently *broke from* [=*broke with*] the organization she helped found. • *breaking from* [=*breaking with*] tradition/stereotypes

break ground see ¹GROUND

break in [*phrasal verb*] **1 :** to enter a house, building, etc., illegally • Someone tried to *break in* while we were away. — see also BREAK INTO 1 (below), BREAK-IN **2 :** to interrupt or disturb someone or something • I was listening to my favorite radio program when a reporter *broke in* with news about a storm. • We were having a chat when he rudely *broke in* (on it). — see also BREAK INTO 4 (below) **3 break in** *or* **break (someone) in** *or* **break in (someone) :** to start or help (someone) to start a new activity, job, etc. • Baseball was very different when he first *broke in* [=started playing] as a catcher in 1962. • The job involves a wide variety of tasks, so we try to *break* new employees *in* gradually. • The band is *breaking in* a new backup singer. **4 break (something) in** *or* **break in (something) a :** to use (something, such as a new pair of shoes) for a period of time so that it becomes comfortable • The shoes were tight when she first got them, so she *broke* them *in* by wearing them around the house for a few days. **b :** to operate (a new machine) carefully for a period of time until it is ready for regular use • You shouldn't drive a new car too fast while you're *breaking* it *in*.

break into [*phrasal verb*] **break into (something) 1 :** to enter (a house, building, etc.) illegally and especially by using force • Someone tried to *break into* our house while we were away. — see also BREAK IN 1 (above) **2 :** to begin to do or have (something) suddenly • She *broke into* tears. [=she suddenly began to cry] • The audience *broke into* applause. [=the audience suddenly began applauding] • His face *broke into* a smile. [=he suddenly smiled] • The horse *broke into* a gallop. [=the horse suddenly began to gallop] • She *broke into* song. [=she suddenly began to sing] **3 :** to enter or get started in (something, such as a profession) • I knew her when she was a young actress trying to *break into* show business. **4 :** to interrupt (something) • The network *broke into* the program with a special news report. — see also BREAK IN 2 (above)

break loose 1 : to suddenly become loose **:** to suddenly stop being attached to something • One of the shutters *broke loose* during the storm. **2 :** to get away from someone or something by using force or effort • The prisoner *broke loose* [=*broke free*] and ran away. — often + *from* • The prisoner *broke loose from* the guards. • She wants to *break loose from* the constraints of her middle-class life. — see also *all hell breaks loose* at HELL

break new ground see ¹GROUND

break off [*phrasal verb*] **1 break off** *or* **break off (something)** *or* **break (something) off** *or* **break (something) off (something) :** to become separated or cause (something) to become separated because of force or violence • The piece of plaster *broke off* easily. • The handle *broke off* when I accidentally dropped the cup. • I accidentally *broke* the cup's handle *off*. = I accidentally *broke* the handle *off* the cup. • I *broke* [=*tore*] a piece of bread *off* (the loaf) and ate it. **2 break off** *or* **break off (something) :** to stop or end suddenly or cause (something) to stop or end suddenly • The speaker *broke off* (speaking) in the middle of a sentence. • At that point the recording suddenly *breaks off*. [=*ends*] • The two countries have *broken off* diplomatic relations. • The negotiations resumed soon after they were *broken off*. • They had a fight and *broke off* [=*called off*] their engagement.

break open [*phrasal verb*] **break open** *or* **break open (something)** *or* **break (something) open :** to open or to cause (something) to open suddenly • The pods *broke open* and the seeds scattered on the wind. • The police *broke open* the door. • The burglars *broke open* the locked safe. — see also ¹BREAK 3 (above)

break out [*phrasal verb*] **1 :** to begin happening suddenly • A fire *broke out* in the kitchen. • A riot *broke out* in the prison. • There is a danger that war could *break out* soon. **2 a :** to suddenly begin to have sweat, a rash, etc., on your skin • He **broke out in a sweat** [=he began to sweat] • Eating strawberries makes her **break out in hives** = Eating strawberries makes her *break out*. **b :** to appear on the skin suddenly • Sweat *broke out* on his forehead. • A rash *broke out* on her skin. **3 :** to escape from a prison, jail, etc. • Six prisoners were caught attempting to *break out*. — often + *of* • Six prisoners attempted to *break out of* the jail. — often used figuratively • The team is trying to *break out of* its slump. [=is trying to end its slump] • We need to *break out of* the financial rut we're in. **4 break (something) out** *or* **break out (something) :** to take (something) from the place where it is stored so that it can be used • We *broke out* the champagne to celebrate our victory. — see also BREAKOUT, OUTBREAK

break rank see ¹RANK

break someone's heart see HEART

break step see ¹STEP

break the back of see ¹BACK

break the bank see ¹BANK

break the ice see ¹ICE

break the mold see ¹MOLD

break through [*phrasal verb*] **break through** *or* **break through (something) 1 :** to use force to get through (something, such as a barrier) • The enemy attacked our defenses but they weren't able to *break through*. • The enemy finally *broke through* our defenses and defeated us. • The prisoners *broke through* the wall and escaped. — sometimes used figuratively • The organization is committed to *breaking through* the barriers of poverty. — see also ¹BREAK 6b (above) **2** *of the sun* **:** to shine through (clouds) • The sun finally began to *break through*. = The sun finally began to *break through* the clouds.

break up [*phrasal verb*] **1 break up** *or* **break (something) up** *or* **break up (something) a :** to separate into parts or pieces or cause (something) to separate into parts or pieces • The asteroid *broke up* [=*disintegrated*] when it hit the Earth's atmosphere. • Enzymes help *break up* protein molecules. • *break up* a large estate **b :** to end or cause (something) to end • The demonstration *broke up* when the police arrived. • The party began to *break up* shortly after midnight. • The police *broke up* the demonstration. • He got hurt while trying to *break up* a fight. • *break up* a terrorist organization **2 break up :** to end a romantic relationship, marriage, etc. • They dated for years but recently *broke up*. • I hear that he and his wife have *broken up*. = I hear that their marriage has *broken up*. — often + *with* • He *broke up with* his girlfriend. **3 break up** *or* **break (someone) up** *US, informal* **:** to begin laughing or cause (someone) to begin laughing suddenly and in a way that is difficult to control • I always *break up* [=*crack up*] when I hear that joke. • Everyone *broke up* [=*burst into laughter, busted out laughing*] when they saw what he was wearing. • That joke always *breaks me up*. [=*cracks me up*] **4 break (something) up** *or* **break up (something) a :** to change the regular quality or appearance of (something) • *break up* a dull routine • A chimney *breaks up* the line of the level roof. • *break up* a text with pictures — see also ¹BREAK 10 (above) **b :** to separate the parts of (something) so that it is not complete • The seller was unwilling to *break up* the dining room set by selling one of the chairs. • The owner *broke up* the team by trading many of the best players. **5 break up** *Brit, of a school* **:** to come to the end of a period of instruction (such as a term) • School *broke up* for the summer last Friday. — see also BREAKUP

break wind see ¹WIND

break with [*phrasal verb*] **break with (someone or something) :** to end a relationship, connection, or agreement with (someone or something) • He *broke with* his former friends and colleagues when he decided to support the conservative candidate. • a strong desire to *break with* tradition/the past • A number of people have *broken with* the church over this issue.

²**break** *noun, pl* **breaks**

1 [*count*] **a :** a crack, hole, etc., that is caused by damage, injury, or pressure • The tank is reinforced to prevent *breaks* and leaks. • The *break* [=*fracture*] in her arm will take months to heal. • Watch out for *breaks* [=(more commonly) *cracks*] in the ice. **b :** an opening or space *in* something • There was a *break* [=*gap*] *in* the clouds. **:** an opening that makes it possible for someone or something to enter or pass through something • There was a *break in* the hedge/fence. • We waited for a *break in* the traffic.

2 [*count*] **:** something that causes a change or interruption • She gets upset over any little *break* in her routine. [=anything that changes/interrupts her routine] • The fields extend for miles without a *break*.

3 [*count*] **a :** a time when something stops • It has rained for five days without a *break*. [=it has been raining constantly for five days] • We chatted during a *break* in the game. • It

B

rained all day. We waited for ***a break in the weather*** [=we waited for a time when the rain stopped], but it never came. **b :** a brief period of time during which someone stops an activity • I'm tired. Let's ***take a break***. [=let's stop doing whatever we are doing for a short period of time] • It was a long drive, but we *took* lots of *breaks*. [=we briefly stopped driving many times] • a ***bathroom break*** [=a brief period of time when you stop doing something in order to use a bathroom]; *especially* **:** a brief period of time during which a worker is allowed to rest, eat, etc., instead of working • All employees are entitled to two *breaks* during the workday. • We've been working all day without a *break*. • It's only five minutes until ***break time***. [=the time when workers are supposed to stop working for a brief period of time] — see also COFFEE BREAK, LUNCH BREAK **c :** a longer period of time when someone is not working or doing some other activity • The long weekend provided her with a much-needed *break* (from her job). **d :** a time when many people are not working or going to school because of a holiday, vacation, etc. • She went home to visit her parents during (the) winter *break*. • What are your plans for (the) Thanksgiving *break*? — see also SPRING BREAK

4 *[count]* **:** a planned interruption in a radio or television program • a *break* for a commercial = a commercial *break* • We'll be back with more after the *break*. — see also STATION BREAK

5 *[singular]* **:** a sudden fast run **:** DASH • The runner ***made a break for*** second base. [=the runner suddenly ran toward second base]; *especially* **:** a fast run by someone who is trying to escape • The prisoner *made a* (sudden) *break for* the door. • The prisoner ***made a break for it/freedom*** and got away. — see also JAILBREAK

6 *[count]* **:** a situation or event that is lucky or unlucky • a series of unlucky/bad *breaks* • Finding a hotel with a vacancy and low prices was a lucky/good *break* for us.; *especially* **:** a lucky situation or event that makes success possible • She's still hoping to get her big/lucky *break* in show business. • She got the *breaks* she needed to succeed. • She gets all the *breaks*. [=she is very lucky] • For the team to succeed, all the *breaks* will have to go their way. [=they will have to be lucky] • *(US)* I just can't seem to ***catch a break***. [=I am unlucky; I never have good luck] ✧ Informal expressions like ***those are the breaks*** and ***that's the breaks*** mean that something bad or unlucky should be thought of or accepted as the kind of thing that often happens to people. • I'm disappointed that I didn't get the job, but *those are the breaks*. I'll keep trying.

7 *[count]* **:** something that helps a particular person or group • Can you give me a *break* on the price? = Can I get a *break* on the price? [=can you lower the price for me?] • People with small children are being given a ***tax break***. [=are being required to pay less in taxes than other people]

8 *[singular]* **a :** a sudden ending of a relationship • The crisis has caused a *break* (in diplomatic relations) between the two countries. • If you don't want to keep dating him, you should just ***make a clean break*** [=you should end your relationship quickly] instead of dragging it out. • She talked about leaving her husband for years, but she never found the courage to ***make the break***. **b :** a change from what was done before — usually + *with* or *from* • We need to *make a clean break with* the past. [=we need to stop doing things as they were done in the past and start doing them in a completely new way] • The company has made a sharp *break with* tradition. • Her latest novel marks a complete *break with/from* her earlier fiction. [=her latest novel is completely different from her earlier fiction]

9 *[noncount] literary* — used in the phrase ***break of day*** to refer to the time of morning when the sun can first be seen • We left at (the) *break of day*. [=(more commonly) *dawn, sunrise, daybreak*]

10 *[count]* **:** a sharp change in the tone or pitch of someone's voice • There was a *break* [=(more commonly) *crack*] in her voice as she said goodbye.

11 *[noncount] sports* **:** a curve in the path of a thrown or hit ball • The batter was fooled completely by the *break* on the pitch. • The putt had a lot of *break*. [=the putt curved a lot]

12 *[count] tennis* **:** the act defeating an opponent who is serving • a service *break*

give me a break *informal* **1** — used to tell someone to stop bothering you or treating you unfairly • "Aren't you finished yet?" "*Give me a break*! I only started 10 minutes ago!" **2** — used to say that you do not believe or are disgusted about what someone has said or done • "He says he went Harvard." "*Give me a break*! I doubt he even graduated from high school!" • He wants more money? *Give me a break*! [=it's ridiculous/outrageous that he wants more money]

give (someone) a break **:** to stop treating (someone) in a strict or harsh way • Don't criticize him so much. He's doing the best he can. Why don't you *give him a break*?

break·able /ˈbreɪkəbəl/ *adj [more ~; most ~]* **:** possible to break **:** able to be broken • an easily *breakable* object • a world record that may not be *breakable* — opposite UNBREAKABLE

– breakable *noun, pl* **breakables** *[count]* • *Breakables* [=objects that can be broken easily; fragile objects] should be handled with care.

break·age /ˈbreɪkɪʤ/ *noun, pl* **-ag·es :** the act of breaking or being broken *[noncount]* The cups are very fragile and are prone to *breakage*. [=they break easily] • The pots are transported carefully to reduce the risk of *breakage*. • *breakage* of glass *[count]* The pots are transported carefully to reduce the number of *breakages*.

break·away /ˈbreɪkəˌweɪ/ *adj, always used before a noun* **:** having become separate from a larger group, country, etc. **:** having broken away • A *breakaway* faction formed a new party. • a *breakaway* republic/province — see also *break away* at ¹BREAK

break dancing *noun [noncount]* **:** a type of dancing in which a dancer performs very athletic movements that involve touching the ground with various parts of the body (such as the head or back)

– break dancer *noun, pl* **~ -ers** *[count]*

break·down /ˈbreɪkˌdaʊn/ *noun, pl* **-downs**

1 : a failure of a machine to function **:** an occurrence in which a machine (such as a car) stops working *[count]* We had a *breakdown* on the highway. [=our car broke down on the highway; our car stopped working on the highway] • The factory has had frequent equipment *breakdowns*. *[noncount]* Frequent equipment *breakdown* [=(more commonly) *failure*] has been a problem at the factory.

2 a *[count]* **:** the failure of a relationship or of an effort to discuss something • There has been a *breakdown* of/in negotiations. [=negotiations have broken down; negotiations have failed] • Both sides are to blame for the *breakdown* in communication. • The irretrievable *breakdown* of a marriage can be grounds for divorce. **b :** a failure that prevents a system from working properly *[count]* trying to prevent a *breakdown* of the health-care system *[noncount]* trying to prevent *breakdown* of the health-care system • Analysts predict that the country is headed for economic *breakdown*. [=*meltdown*]

3 *[count]* **:** a sudden failure of mental or physical health that makes someone unable to live normally • He suffered/had a *breakdown* after his wife died. • a total physical/mental *breakdown* [=*collapse*] — see also NERVOUS BREAKDOWN

4 : the process or result of showing the different parts of something in order to understand it more clearly *[count]* Doing/Providing a *breakdown* of the statistics into categories will take time. • I want a detailed *breakdown* of the statistics into categories. *[noncount]* The library's database enables *breakdown* by title, author, and genre.

5 *[noncount]* **:** the process or result of separating a substance into simpler parts • the *breakdown* of water into hydrogen and oxygen • observing cell/tissue/protein *breakdown* • a substance that resists *breakdown* — see also *break down* at ¹BREAK

breakdown lane *noun, pl* **~ lanes** *[count] US* **:** an area along the side of a highway where vehicles are able to stop for an emergency

breakdown truck *or* **breakdown lorry** *noun, pl* **~ trucks** *or* **~ lorries** *[count] Brit* **:** TOW TRUCK

break·er /ˈbreɪkɚ/ *noun, pl* **-ers** *[count]*

1 : someone or something that breaks something • a *breaker* of records = a record-*breaker* • a rule *breaker* — see also CIRCUIT BREAKER, ICEBREAKER

2 : a wave that is curling over and falling onto the shore, rocks, etc. **:** a breaking wave — usually plural • We could hear the *breakers* crashing on the shore.

break–even /ˈbreɪkˈiːvən/ *adj, always used before a noun* **:** having equal costs and income • After years of losing money the company has finally reached the ***break-even point*** [=the point at which the company earns as much as it spends] and we hope to make a profit soon. — see also *break even* at ¹BREAK

¹**break·fast** /ˈbrɛkfəst/ *noun, pl* **-fasts :** the first meal of the day *[count]* a big/good/hearty *breakfast* • a ***working/busi-***

ness breakfast [=a breakfast during which you talk with someone about business matters] • (*Brit*) a ***cooked breakfast*** [=a breakfast that includes cooked foods, such as eggs and meat] [*noncount*] I had pancakes for *breakfast.* • Did you have/eat *breakfast* before you left? • We relaxed/chatted/dawdled over *breakfast.* — often used before another noun • *breakfast* cereals • They sat at the *breakfast* table. — see also BED-AND-BREAKFAST, CONTINENTAL BREAKFAST

a dog's breakfast see [1]DOG

[2]**breakfast** *verb* **-fasts; -fast•ed; -fast•ing** [*no obj*] : to eat breakfast • We *breakfasted* on cereal and toast. • She likes to *breakfast* early.

break–in /ˈbreɪkˌɪn/ *noun, pl* **-ins** [*count*] : the act or crime of illegally entering a house, building, etc., especially by using force • There was an attempted *break-in* at our house while we were away. — see also *break in* at [1]BREAK

breaking and entering *noun* [*noncount*] *law* : the crime of illegally entering a house, building, etc., especially by using force • The thief was arrested and charged with *breaking and entering.*

breaking point *noun*

the breaking point (*US*) *or Brit* ***breaking point*** **1** : the time when a person can no longer accept or deal with a situation because of too much pressure or stress • My nerves were at *the breaking point.* = I had just about reached *the breaking point.* • My boss is pushing me to *the breaking point.* **2** : the time when a situation has become so difficult, dangerous, etc., that it cannot continue • Tensions between the two groups had reached *the breaking point.*

break•neck /ˈbreɪkˈnɛk/ *adj, always used before a noun* : very fast : dangerously fast • driving at *breakneck* speed

[1]**break•out** /ˈbreɪkˌaʊt/ *noun, pl* **-outs** [*count*] : an escape from a prison, jail, etc. — used especially to describe an escape by a group of prisoners • Police report that three people were killed during an attempted *breakout* (from the prison). • a prison *breakout* — see also *break out* at [1]BREAK

[2]**breakout** *adj, always used before a noun, US* : having, causing, or marked by sudden and great success that comes usually after a time without much success • The company had a *breakout* year last year, tripling its profits from the previous year. • an actor's *breakout* role [=the role that makes an actor famous and successful]

break•through /ˈbreɪkˌθru:/ *noun, pl* **- throughs** [*count*]

1 : a sudden increase in knowledge, understanding, etc. : an important discovery that happens after trying for a long time to understand or explain something • Researchers say they have made/achieved a major *breakthrough* in cancer treatment. • a scientific *breakthrough* • The police have announced a *breakthrough* in the murder case. — sometimes used before another noun • *breakthrough* ideas/products

2 : a person's first important success • This job could be the *breakthrough* she's been waiting for. — sometimes used before another noun • a *breakthrough* performance/role/album — see also *break through* at [1]BREAK

break•up /ˈbreɪkˌʌp/ *noun, pl* **-ups**

1 : the end of a relationship, marriage, etc. [*count*] Money problems often lead to marital *breakups.* • She's just gone through a bad/painful *breakup* with her boyfriend. [*noncount*] He began drinking heavily following the *breakup* of his marriage. • a couple heading for marital *breakup*

2 [*noncount*] : the separation of something into smaller parts or pieces • What caused the *breakup* of the Roman Empire? • the *breakup* of a monopoly • the *breakup* of an asteroid as it hits the Earth's atmosphere — see also *break up* at [1]BREAK

break•wa•ter /ˈbreɪkˌwɑ:tɚ/ *noun, pl* **-ters** [*count*] : a wall that is built out into the sea to protect a harbor or beach from the force of waves

bream /ˈbrɪm, ˈbri:m/ *noun, pl* **bream** [*count, noncount*] : a kind of fish that people catch for food

[1]**breast** /ˈbrɛst/ *noun, pl* **breasts**

1 [*count*] : either one of the two soft parts on a woman's chest that produce milk when she has a baby — often used before another noun • *breast* cancer • *breast* tissue/milk — see picture at HUMAN

2 [*count*] **a** *old-fashioned + literary* : the front part of a person's body between the neck and the stomach : CHEST • She clasped the child to her *breast.* [=*bosom*] • My *breast* heaved with emotion. **b** *literary* : the chest thought of as the place where emotions are felt • Dark thoughts lurked within his *breast.* [=*heart*]

3 a [*count*] : the front part of a bird's body below the neck • a bird with an orange *breast* — see picture at BIRD **b** : meat from the front part of a bird's or animal's body [*noncount*] I ordered the grilled *breast* of chicken. • a few slices of turkey *breast* • *breast* of lamb/veal [*count*] Do you prefer a *breast* or a leg?

4 [*count*] : the part of a piece of clothing that covers a person's chest • the *breast* of a jacket — usually used before another noun • He kept a watch in his *breast* pocket.

make a clean breast of : to speak openly and honestly about (something that you have previously lied about or kept secret) • I decided to *make a clean breast of* it/things and admit that I was to blame.

– breast•ed /ˈbrɛstəd/ *adj* — used in combination • a red-*breasted* bird [=a bird with a red breast] • bare-*breasted* women — see also DOUBLE-BREASTED, SINGLE-BREASTED

[2]**breast** *verb* **breasts; breast•ed; breast•ing** [+ *obj*] *formal* : to push against or move through (something) with your chest forward • I was at the race's finish line to see the winner *breast* the tape. — sometimes used figuratively • a boat *breasting* the waves

breast•bone /ˈbrɛstˌboʊn/ *noun, pl* **-bones** [*count*] : a flat, narrow bone in the middle of the chest to which the ribs are connected — called also *sternum;* see picture at HUMAN

breast–feed /ˈbrɛstˌfi:d/ *verb* **-feeds; -fed** /-ˌfɛd/; **-feed•ing** : to feed a baby from a mother's breast [*no obj*] mothers who *breast-feed* [+ *obj*] mothers who *breast-feed* [=*nurse, suckle*] their infants • Only one of her children was *breast-fed.* — compare BOTTLE-FEED

breast•plate /ˈbrɛstˌpleɪt/ *noun, pl* **-plates** [*count*] : a piece of metal that covers a person's chest and that was part of the protective clothing (called armor) that soldiers wore in the past

breast•stroke /ˈbrɛstˌstroʊk/ *noun* [*singular*] : a way of swimming in which the swimmer's face is in the water and the arms move in a large motion from front to back as the feet kick outward; *also* : a race in which the swimmers do the breaststroke • I'll be competing in the 50-meter *breaststroke.*

breath /ˈbrɛθ/ *noun, pl* **breaths**

1 [*noncount*] : the air that you take into your lungs and send out from your lungs when you breathe : air that is inhaled and exhaled in breathing • gum that freshens your *breath* • His *breath* smells like garlic. = He has garlic *breath.* • It's so cold outside that I can see my *breath.* • We could smell the alcohol ***on his breath.*** [=his breath smelled of alcohol] • He has ***bad breath.*** [=breath that smells unpleasant] — sometimes used before another noun • Would you like a *breath* mint? [=a candy used to make breath smell better] — see also BREATH TEST

2 a [*noncount*] : the ability to breathe freely • He was ***fighting/struggling for breath.*** [=he was having a lot of difficulty breathing] • My mad dash for the bus left me ***gasping for breath.*** ✧ To ***catch your breath*** or (*Brit*) ***get your breath back*** is to rest until you are able to breathe normally. • Give me a moment to *catch my breath.* ✧ If you are ***out of breath,*** you are breathing very hard because you have been running or doing hard physical work. • I'm a little *out of breath* from walking up all those stairs. ✧ Someone who is ***short of breath*** or who has ***shortness of breath*** has difficulty breathing in enough air especially because of a physical or medical condition. • The patient complains that he's *short of breath.* • The doctor asked if I had been experiencing *shortness of breath* lately. **b** [*count*] : an amount of air that you take into your lungs • I took/drew a long *breath* before speaking again. • The patient was only able to take shallow *breaths.* [=only able to take in small amounts of air] • ***Take a deep breath.*** [=breathe deeply; take a lot of air into your lungs] • (*US*) I've barely had time to (stop and/to) ***take a breath*** since they got here. = (*Brit*) I've barely had time to ***draw breath*** since they got here. [=I have not been able to pause and rest] • She recited the whole list ***in one breath.*** [=she recited it without stopping to breathe] • her ***last/dying breath*** [=the breath that she took just before she died] ✧ If you say two different things ***in the same breath,*** or if you say one thing and then something else ***in the next breath,*** it means that you say these things very close together. • It's unusual to hear "promotions" mentioned *in the same breath* as "layoffs." • She praises their work, then criticizes them *in the next breath.* [=then immediately criticizes them] ✧ If someone says that you are ***wasting your breath*** or tells you to ***save your breath*** or to ***not waste your breath,*** it means that the things you say will not make someone behave or think differently and that you should not bother to try. • He begged her to go with him, but she told him he was *wasting his breath*. • You're not going to get him to stop drinking, so *don't waste your breath*.

3 [*count*] **:** a slight breeze — usually singular • a hot day with scarcely a ***breath of wind***

4 [*singular*] **:** a very small amount of something • a faint *breath* [=*hint*] *of* scandal • There was never even the slightest *breath* [=*suggestion*] *of* suspicion.

a breath of fresh air **1 :** clean or cool outside air after you have been in a building for a period of time • We went outside to get *a breath of fresh air*. **2 :** someone or something that is different in a way that is interesting, exciting, enjoyable, etc. • His unusual outlook is *a breath of fresh air*. • After dealing for so long with a difficult boss, our new supervisor is *a breath of fresh air*.

hold your breath **1 :** to keep the air that you have breathed in your lungs for a short time instead of breathing out • How long can you *hold your breath*? **2** *informal* — used to say that you do not believe that something will happen soon or at all • He says he'll do it, but ***I'm not holding my breath***. [=I doubt he will do it] • "She promised to pay me tomorrow." "Well, ***don't hold your breath***." [=do not expect her to pay you tomorrow]

take your breath away ✧ Something that *takes your breath away* is extremely exciting, beautiful, or surprising. • The acrobatic skill of the dancers *took my breath away*.

under your breath ✧ If you say something *under your breath*, you say it quietly so that it is difficult to hear. • We heard her mutter something *under her breath*.

with bated breath see BATED

Breath·a·lyz·er (*chiefly US*) *or Brit* **Breath·a·ly·ser** /ˈbrɛθəˌlaɪzɚ/ *trademark* — used for a device that police use to test someone's breath in order to measure how much alcohol is in that person's blood

breathe /ˈbri:ð/ *verb* **breathes; breathed; breath·ing**

1 : to move air into and out of your lungs **:** to inhale and exhale [*no obj*] Relax and *breathe* deeply. • He was *breathing* hard from running. • The patient suddenly stopped *breathing*. • I can hardly *breathe* with all this smoke. [+ *obj*] He wants to live where he can *breathe* clean/fresh air.

2 a : to send (something) out from your lungs through your mouth or nose [+ *obj*] a dragon that *breathes* fire — often + *out* • *breathing out* [=*exhaling*] carbon dioxide [*no obj*] He *breathed* [=*blew*] on the glass and wiped it clean. — often + *out* • *Breathe out* through your nose. **b :** to take (something) into your lungs through your mouth or nose [+ *obj*] You shouldn't be *breathing* [=*inhaling*] those fumes. • People usually contract the virus by *breathing* contaminated air. — often + *in* • You shouldn't be *breathing in* those fumes. [*no obj*] *Breathe* deeply and then exhale. — usually + *in* • *Breathe in* through your nose.

3 [*no obj*] **:** to be alive • I'll never give up as long as I'm still *breathing*. • a living, *breathing* human being

4 [*no obj*] **:** to pause and rest before continuing • We had barely stopped to *breathe* before we were on the go again.

5 [+ *obj*] **:** to bring (something) *into* a thing • City leaders hope the project will *breathe* vitality/energy *into* the downtown. • Their leadership ***breathed new life into*** the movement. [=gave new energy to the movement]

6 [*no obj*] **:** to feel able to think or act freely • I need some room to *breathe*. = I need some *breathing* room/space.

7 [*no obj*] **a :** to allow air to pass through • a fabric that *breathes* **b :** to be cooled or refreshed by air that passes through clothing • Cotton clothing lets your skin *breathe*.

8 [+ *obj*] **:** to say (something) very quietly • "It's beautiful," she *breathed*. — usually used in the phrase ***breathe a word*** • Don't *breathe a word* of/about this to anyone! [=do not say anything about this to anyone]

9 [*no obj*] *of wine* **:** to develop a better flavor because of contact with air • Open the bottle a few minutes before you want to drink it so that the wine can *breathe*.

breathe a sigh of relief **:** to relax because something you have been worrying about is not a problem or danger anymore **:** to feel relieved • We all *breathed a sigh of relief* when we heard that they were safe.

breathe down someone's neck **1 :** to chase after someone closely • The cops were *breathing down our necks*. **2 :** to watch someone carefully and constantly • His parents are always *breathing down his neck*.

breathe easy *or* ***breathe easier*** *or* ***breathe easily*** *or* ***breathe freely*** **:** to feel relief from pressure, danger, etc. • I'll *breathe easier* once this whole ordeal is over. • You can *breathe easy* knowing that your children are safe.

breathe your last see [4]LAST

live and breathe ✧ If you *live and breathe* something, you spend a great deal of time, thought, or effort on that thing. • She *lives and breathes* music. • They *live and breathe* their work.

— breath·able /ˈbri:ðəbəl/ *adj* [*more ~; most ~*] • a *breathable* fabric [=a fabric that allows air to pass through]

— breathing *noun* [*noncount*] • Her *breathing* is heavy/shallow/labored. — often used before another noun • We'll begin with some *breathing* exercises. • He has *breathing* problems. — see also *heavy breathing* at [1]HEAVY

breath·er /ˈbri:ðɚ/ *noun, pl* **-ers** [*count*]

1 : a pause for rest **:** BREAK • Let's take a *breather*. • He decided to give them a *breather*.

2 : someone or something that breathes in a specified way • a mouth *breather* [=a person who breathes through the mouth rather than through the nose]

breath·less /ˈbrɛθləs/ *adj*

1 : unable to take enough air into your lungs **:** breathing very hard because you are trying to get more air • The workout left me *breathless*. [=(more commonly) *out of breath*]

2 a : full of emotion • They were *breathless* with anticipation. • I watched them in *breathless* wonder. • She describes the scene in *breathless* prose. **b :** very fast • He drove at a *breathless* pace. **c :** full of activity • a *breathless* schedule

— breath·less·ly *adv* • The hike left me panting *breathlessly*. • He *breathlessly* reported every detail of the accident.

— breath·less·ness *noun* [*noncount*] • She complained of *breathlessness*. [=(more commonly) *shortness of breath*]

breath·tak·ing /ˈbrɛθˌteɪkɪŋ/ *adj* [*more ~; most ~*]

1 : very exciting **:** THRILLING • The train raced past with *breathtaking* speed. • They gave a *breathtaking* performance. • The view of the mountains was *breathtaking*. • a scene of *breathtaking* beauty

2 : very great or surprising • his *breathtaking* ignorance • The scope of the error is *breathtaking*.

— breath·tak·ing·ly *adv* • a *breathtakingly* beautiful view

breath test *noun, pl* **~ tests** [*count*] **:** a test that is used by the police to measure how much alcohol a person has drunk

breathy /ˈbrɛθi/ *adj* **breath·i·er; -est :** spoken or sung with the sound of a person's breath • a *breathy* whisper • the singer's *breathy* voice/vocals

— breath·i·ly /ˈbrɛθəli/ *adv* • singing *breathily* **— breath·i·ness** /ˈbrɛθinəs/ *noun* [*noncount*]

bred *past tense and past participle of* [1]BREED

breech birth /ˈbri:ʧ-/ *noun, pl* **~ births** [*count*] **:** a birth in which a baby is born with the feet or buttocks coming out of the mother first instead of the head — called also *breech delivery*

breech·es /ˈbrɪʧəz/ *noun* [*plural*] **:** short pants that are fastened at or just below the knee • riding *breeches* ✧ Except for its modern use to describe pants that people wear when riding horses, *breeches* is an old-fashioned word. — compare BRITCHES

[1]**breed** /ˈbri:d/ *verb* **breeds; bred** /ˈbrɛd/; **breed·ing**

1 [+ *obj*] **:** to keep and take care of animals or plants in order to produce more animals or plants of a particular kind • He got into the business of *breeding* cattle. • The plants are *bred* to resist disease and drought. • dogs *bred* for hunting = dogs *bred* as hunters = dogs *bred* to hunt • wild horses ***bred to*** [=*mated to*] domestic horses [=wild horses and domestic horses brought together to produce horses that have qualities of both]

2 [*no obj*] **:** to produce young animals, birds, etc. **:** to produce offspring by sexual reproduction • low-lying areas where mosquitoes *breed* [=*reproduce*]

3 [+ *obj*] **:** to take care of and teach (a child who is growing up) • She believes that we are *breeding* a generation of children who know nothing about the history of their country. — usually used as *(be) bred* • children who *are bred* [=(more commonly) *raised, brought up*] in conditions of poverty and crime — see also BREEDING, ILL-BRED, WELL-BRED

4 [+ *obj*] **:** to cause or lead to (something) • Despair often *breeds* violence. • scandals that *breed* cynicism — see also *familiarity breeds contempt* at FAMILIARITY

bred in the bone — used to describe a personal quality that is a deep or basic part of someone's nature • His love of sports is *bred in the bone*. [=*ingrained*] — often used as *bred-in-the-bone* before another noun • He is a *bred-in-the-bone* conservative.

— breed·er *noun, pl* **-ers** [*count*] • cattle/dog *breeders* [=people who breed cattle/dogs]

B

²breed *noun, pl* **breeds** [*count*]
1 : a particular kind of dog, cat, horse, etc. **:** a kind of animal that has been produced by breeding ▪ The collie is a working *breed.* ▪ exotic *breeds* of cats ▪ different *breeds* of cattle
2 : a kind of person ▪ a new/different *breed* of athlete ▪ People like them are a ***dying breed.*** [=there are not many people like them anymore] ▪ Back then, stay-at-home dads were a ***rare breed.*** [=there were not many stay-at-home dads] — see also HALF-BREED

breeding *noun* [*noncount*]
1 : the process by which young animals, birds, etc., are produced by their parents — often used before another noun ▪ the *breeding* season
2 : the activity of keeping and caring for animals or plants in order to produce more animals or plants of a particular kind ▪ She became involved in the *breeding* of sled dogs. ▪ horse/dog/plant *breeding* — often used before another noun ▪ a *breeding* program
3 *somewhat old-fashioned* **:** the way a person was taught in childhood to behave ▪ His politeness shows good *breeding.* **:** good manners that come from being raised correctly ▪ a person who lacks *breeding*

breeding ground *noun, pl* **~ grounds** [*count*]
1 : a place where animals go to breed ▪ a *breeding ground* for seals
2 : a place or situation that helps or allows something to grow, develop, etc. ▪ The Gulf of Mexico is a *breeding ground* for hurricanes. ▪ The company's casual atmosphere serves as a *breeding ground* for innovation.

¹breeze /ˈbri:z/ *noun, pl* **breez·es**
1 [*count*] **:** a gentle wind ▪ a light/gentle/cool *breeze* ▪ The flag fluttered in the *breeze.*
2 [*singular*] *informal* **:** something that is easy to do ▪ The test was a *breeze.*
shoot the breeze see ¹SHOOT

²breeze *verb* **breezes; breezed; breez·ing** [*no obj*]
1 : to move quickly and confidently ▪ Look who just *breezed* in! ▪ He *breezed* past/by us without so much as a nod.
2 : to easily succeed at something ▪ She *breezed* through the test. ▪ The team *breezed* to victory. [=the team won easily]

breeze–block *noun, pl* **-blocks** [*count*] *Brit* **:** CINDER BLOCK

breeze·way /ˈbri:zˌweɪ/ *noun, pl* **-ways** [*count*] *US* **:** a narrow structure with a roof and no walls that connects two buildings (such as a house and garage)

breezy /ˈbri:zi/ *adj* **breez·i·er; -est**
1 : having strong winds **:** WINDY ▪ a *breezy* day ▪ a *breezy* beach
2 : informal and lively ▪ a *breezy* essay ▪ I enjoy the author's *breezy* style.
3 : relaxed in way that shows you are not concerned about or interested in something ▪ She listened to their complaints with *breezy* indifference.
– breez·i·ly /ˈbri:zəli/ *adv* ▪ He *breezily* dismissed our fears.

breth·ren /ˈbrɛðrən/ *plural of* BROTHER — used especially to begin to talk in a formal way to a group of people or to refer to the members of a particular group ▪ Welcome, *brethren.* ▪ our church *brethren*

brev·i·ty /ˈbrevəti/ *noun* [*noncount*] **:** the quality of being brief: such as **a :** the use of few words to say something ▪ I've omitted certain passages for the sake of *brevity.* [=because I want to be brief] ▪ The book's major flaw is its *brevity.* ▪ "*Brevity* is the soul of wit . . ." —Shakespeare, *Hamlet* (1600) **b :** the quality or fact of lasting only for a short period of time ▪ the *brevity* of youth

¹brew /ˈbru:/ *verb* **brews; brewed; brew·ing**
1 : to make (beer, ale, etc.) [*+ obj*] They *brew* the beer on the premises. ▪ The restaurant also *brews* its own ginger ale and root beer. [*no obj*] They've been *brewing* in the new brewery since March. ▪ *brewing* vats ▪ the *brewing* process
2 : to make (coffee, tea, etc.) [*+ obj*] I'll *brew* another pot of tea. — often *+ up* ▪ She *brewed up* some coffee while I cooked the bacon and eggs. [*no obj*] The coffee is *brewing.* [=the coffee is being brewed]
3 [*no obj*] **:** to start to form ▪ It feels like there's a storm *brewing.* ▪ Trouble is *brewing.*
– brew·er /ˈbru:wɚ/ *noun, pl* **-ers** [*count*] ▪ a *brewer* of fine ales

²brew *noun, pl* **brews**
1 *chiefly US* **:** a drink (such as beer or ale) that is made by brewing [*noncount*] a bottle of *brew* [*count*] I'll buy you a *brew.* ▪ a manufacturer of specialty *brews* ✧ A ***home brew*** is beer or ale that you make at home. ▪ Would you like to try one of my *home brews*?
2 a [*noncount*] *US* **:** COFFEE ▪ a perfect cup of *brew* **b** [*count*] *Brit* **:** a cup of tea ▪ time for a quick *brew*
3 [*count*] **:** a mixture of different things — usually singular ▪ a strange *brew* of jazz, classical, and bluegrass music ▪ Anger and desperation make for a dangerous *brew.* — see also WITCHES' BREW

brew·ery /ˈbru:wəri/ *noun, pl* **-er·ies** [*count*]
1 : a place where beer is made
2 : a company that makes beer

¹bri·ar *also* **bri·er** /ˈbrajɚ/ *noun, pl* **-ars** *also* **-ers** [*count*] **:** a wild plant that has many sharp points (called thorns) on its branches ▪ a thicket of *briars* — compare ²BRIAR

²briar *noun, pl* **-ers** *or* **-ars** [*count*] **:** a tobacco pipe that is made from the root of a European plant — called also *briar pipe* — compare ¹BRIAR

¹bribe /ˈbraɪb/ *noun, pl* **bribes** [*count*] **:** something valuable (such as money) that is given in order to get someone to do something ▪ I offered the children a *bribe* for finishing their homework. ✧ Usually a bribe is used to get someone to do something illegal or dishonest. ▪ a police officer accused of taking/accepting *bribes* ▪ They received more than $10,000 in *bribes.*

²bribe *verb* **bribes; bribed; brib·ing** [*+ obj*] **:** to try to get someone to do something by giving or promising something valuable (such as money) **:** to give or offer a bribe to (someone) ▪ She was arrested for attempting to *bribe* a judge. ▪ They *bribed* him to keep quiet about the incident. ▪ We *bribed* the children with candy.

brib·ery /ˈbraɪbəri/ *noun* [*noncount*] **:** the act or crime giving or accepting a bribe ▪ They were arrested on charges of *bribery.* — often used before another noun ▪ a *bribery* charge/conviction

bric–a–brac /ˈbrɪkəˌbræk/ *noun* [*noncount*] **:** small objects that are used for decoration and are not usually valuable ▪ shelves full of *bric-a-brac* [=*knickknacks*]

¹brick /ˈbrɪk/ *noun, pl* **bricks**
1 a [*count*] **:** a small, hard block of baked clay that is used to build structures (such as houses) and sometimes to make streets, paths, etc. ▪ a pile of *bricks* **b** [*noncount*] **:** blocks of baked clay used as building material ▪ a house made of *brick* ▪ Most of the buildings in the town are (made of) *brick.* — often used before another noun ▪ a *brick* wall/building/oven ▪ a *brick* sidewalk
2 [*count*] **a :** a block of something ▪ a *brick* of ice cream ▪ a glass *brick* **b** *Brit* **:** a child's toy block ▪ children playing with wooden *bricks*
3 [*count*] *informal + somewhat old-fashioned* **:** a helpful or dependable person ▪ He has been an absolute *brick.*
bricks and mortar *Brit* **:** houses and other buildings especially when people consider buying them because of their possible future value ▪ Market uncertainties have been driving the rush to invest in *bricks and mortar.* — see also BRICK-AND-MORTAR
drop a brick see ²DROP
like a ton of bricks *informal* **:** very hard or severely ▪ The loss of his job ***hit him like a ton of bricks.*** [=hit him very hard; made him very upset, unhappy, etc.] ▪ Our boss ***came down on us like a ton of bricks*** [=got very angry at us] when he found out we had missed the meeting.

²brick *verb* **bricks; bricked; brick·ing**
brick up [*phrasal verb*] ***brick (something) up*** *or* ***brick up (something)*** **:** to cover or block (something) with bricks ▪ They *bricked up* the windows.

brick–and–mortar *or* **bricks–and–mortar** *adj* — used to describe a traditional store or business that is in a building instead of on the Internet ▪ They have a Web site as well as several *brick-and-mortar* stores. — see also *bricks and mortar* at ¹BRICK

brick·bat /ˈbrɪkˌbæt/ *noun, pl* **-bats** [*count*] **:** a criticism or rude comment ▪ The candidates resorted to hurling *brickbats* at one another. ▪ For all the *brickbats* it has received, it's a good plan.

brick·lay·er /ˈbrɪkˌlejɚ/ *noun, pl* **-ers** [*count*] **:** a person whose job is to build things with bricks
– brick·lay·ing /ˈbrɪkˌlejɪŋ/ *noun* [*noncount*]

brick red *noun* [*noncount*] **:** a brownish-red color — see color picture on page C3
– brick red *adj* ▪ a *brick-red* scarf

B

brick•work /ˈbrɪkˌwɚk/ *noun* [*noncount*] : the part of something that is made with bricks • the building's decorative *brickwork* • Some of the *brickwork* is in need of repair.

brid•al /ˈbraɪdl/ *adj* : of or relating to a bride or a wedding • a *bridal* shop/gown • the ***bridal party*** [=the bride and groom and the people who stand with them during the wedding ceremony] • the hotel's ***bridal suite*** [=a special set of rooms for a couple who have just been married] • hosting a ***bridal shower*** [=a party for a woman who is about to be married]

bride /ˈbraɪd/ *noun, pl* **brides** [*count*] : a woman who has just married or is about to be married • a new *bride* • the mother of the *bride* — compare GROOM

bride•groom /ˈbraɪdˌgruːm, ˈbraɪdˌgrʊm/ *noun, pl* **-grooms** [*count*] : [1]GROOM 1 • the bride and *bridegroom*

brides•maid /ˈbraɪdzˌmeɪd/ *noun, pl* **-maids** [*count*] : a female friend or relative who helps a bride at her wedding • I was a *bridesmaid* in my sister's wedding. — compare BEST MAN, GROOMSMAN, MAID OF HONOR, MATRON OF HONOR

bride–to–be *noun, pl* **brides–to–be** [*count*] : a woman who is going to be married soon

[1]**bridge** /ˈbrɪʤ/ *noun, pl* **bridg•es** [*count*]
1 : a structure built over something (such as a river) so that people or vehicles can get across • a *bridge* connecting the island to the mainland • the Brooklyn *Bridge* • a ***railroad bridge*** [=a bridge for trains] — see also DRAWBRIDGE, FOOTBRIDGE, SUSPENSION BRIDGE
2 : something that joins or connects different people or things • Her work serves as a *bridge* between the past and the present. • They hope to ***build a bridge*** between the two cultures. [=they hope to help the people in the two cultures understand each other]
3 : the place on a ship where the ship is steered
4 a : the upper part of the nose • He broke ***the bridge of his nose*** **b :** the part of a pair of eyeglasses that rests on a person's nose
5 : the part of a guitar, violin, or similar musical instrument that raises the strings away from the surface
6 : part of a song that connects one section to the next section
7 : a false tooth or row of false teeth that fits between two real teeth
burn your bridges see [1]BURN
cross that bridge when you come to it ✧ If you say you will *cross that bridge when you come to it*, you mean that you will not worry about a possible problem until it actually happens. • I don't know how we'll pay the bills if you quit your job, but *we'll cross that bridge when we come to it.*
water under the bridge see WATER
– compare [3]BRIDGE

[2]**bridge** *verb* **bridges; bridged; bridg•ing** [+ *obj*] : to make a bridge over or across (something) — usually used figuratively • We hope to *bridge* the divisions between the two groups. — often used in the phrase ***bridge the gap*** • styles that *bridge the gap* between fashion and practicality • a book that attempts to *bridge the* generation *gap*

[3]**bridge** *noun* [*noncount*] : a card game for four players in two teams — compare [1]BRIDGE

bridge•head /ˈbrɪʤˌhɛd/ *noun, pl* **-heads** [*count*] : an area near the end of a bridge that is controlled by an army; *also* : any area that an army takes from an enemy and from which it can move forward to make an attack — sometimes used figuratively • The company views the project as a *bridgehead* into the Asian market.

bridge loan *noun, pl* ~ **loans** [*count*] *chiefly US* : money that a bank lends you for a short period of time until you receive the money that you are getting from another source (such as from selling your house) — called also (*Brit*) *bridging loan*

[1]**bri•dle** /ˈbraɪdl/ *noun, pl* **bri•dles** [*count*] : a device that fits on a horse's head and that is used for guiding and controlling the horse — see picture at HORSE

[2]**bridle** *verb* **bridles; bri•dled; bri•dling**
1 [+ *obj*] : to put a bridle on (a horse) — sometimes used figuratively • She was forced to *bridle* her anger.
2 [*no obj*] : to react in an angry way — usually + *at* • He *bridled at* their criticism of his methods.

bridle path *noun, pl* ~ **paths** [*count*] : a path that is used for riding horses

[1]**brief** /ˈbriːf/ *adj* **brief•er; -est**
1 : lasting only a short period of time • The meeting will be *brief.* • She worked there for only a *brief* period (of time) in the late 1980s. • They stopped by for a *brief* [=*quick*] visit.
2 : using only a few words • I promise to be *brief.* [=I promise to say what I need to say quickly] • She gave a *brief* [=*concise*] description/summary/history of the problem. • The essay is *brief* but thorough enough. • I'd like to say ***a brief word*** [=a few words] about the people who made this event possible. • a few *brief words* of caution/praise • I'd like to ***have a brief word*** with you. [=I would like to have a short conversation with you] — see also *in brief* at [2]BRIEF
3 *of clothing* : covering less of the body than is usual • *brief* skirts/shorts • a *brief* bikini

[2]**brief** *noun, pl* **briefs**
1 [*count*] : a brief statement or report • a news *brief*
2 [*count*] *US, law* : a document that states the facts a lawyer plans to use in a court case • a legal *brief*
3 [*count*] *chiefly Brit* : instructions that explain what a person is supposed to do • Her *brief* is to manage the company's sales department.
4 ***briefs*** [*plural*] : short underpants for men, women, or children that fit close to the body • a pair of *briefs* — see color picture on page C13; compare BOXER SHORTS
5 [*count*] *Brit, informal* : LAWYER • the defendant's *brief*
in brief : in a few words • Here is today's news *in brief.* [=here is a brief report of today's news] • Their conclusion, *in brief,* is that we need more funding.

[3]**brief** *verb* **briefs; briefed; brief•ing** [+ *obj*] : to give information or instructions to (someone) • The captain *briefed* the crew on the new safety procedures. • The President has been *briefed* by his advisers. — compare DEBRIEF
– briefing *noun, pl* **-ings** [*count*] • a military *briefing*

brief•case /ˈbriːfˌkeɪs/ *noun, pl* **-cas•es** [*count*] : a flat case that is used for carrying papers or books

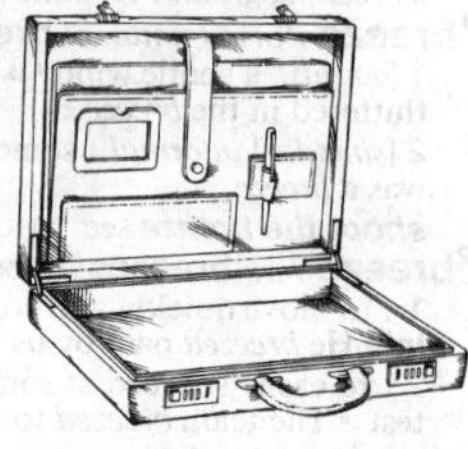
briefcase

brief•ly /ˈbriːfli/ *adv*
1 [*more* ~; *most* ~] : in only a few words : in a brief way • Several important issues are only *briefly* mentioned. • Please *briefly* describe/summarize your experience. • The party, ***to put it briefly,*** was a disaster. = *Briefly,* the party was a disaster.
2 : for a short period of time • They were *briefly* married. • We *briefly* considered canceling the trip.

brier *variant spelling of* [1]BRIAR

[1]**brig** /ˈbrɪg/ *noun, pl* **brigs** [*count*] : a ship with square sails and two masts — compare [2]BRIG

[2]**brig** *noun, pl* **brigs** [*count*] : a jail or prison of the U.S. Navy; *especially* : one that is on a ship — compare [1]BRIG

bri•gade /brɪˈgeɪd/ *noun, pl* **-gades** [*count*]
1 : a large group of soldiers that is part of an army ✧ A brigade is part of a division and is made up of regiments.
2 a : a group of people organized to act together • a fire *brigade* **b** *often disapproving* : a group of people who have the same beliefs • The morality *brigade* insists that the book be censored.

brig•a•dier /ˌbrɪgəˈdiɚ/ *noun, pl* **-diers** [*count*] : a British army officer who is in charge of a brigade; *also* : the rank of a brigadier

brigadier general *noun, pl* ~ **-rals** [*count*] : an officer in the U.S. Army, Air Force, or Marine Corps who is ranked above a colonel; *also* : the rank of a brigadier general

brig•and /ˈbrɪgənd/ *noun, pl* **-ands** [*count*] *formal + old-fashioned* : a robber who travels with others in a group : BANDIT

bright /ˈbraɪt/ *adj* **bright•er; -est**
1 : producing a lot of light • a *bright* light • The lighting was too *bright.* : filled with light • a *bright* room with lots of windows • It was a *bright,* sunny day.
2 : having a very light and strong color • The room was decorated in *bright* colors. • a *bright* red • *bright* blue eyes
3 a : able to learn things quickly : INTELLIGENT — used especially to describe a young person • a *bright* child • a *bright* young journalist **b :** showing intelligence : CLEVER • a *bright* idea — often used in a joking or ironic way to describe a foolish idea, action, etc. • Walking on the railroad bridge wasn't too *bright.* • Who's *bright* idea was it to leave the refrigerator open?
4 : happy and lively • a *bright* smile
5 : providing a reason for hope • a young actress with a

bright [=*promising*] future • *Brighter* days are ahead. [=things will improve in the future] • The prospects for the team are *bright*. [=*good*]

bright and early : very early • We will be getting up *bright and early* in the morning.

bright-eyed and bushy-tailed *informal* : happy and full of energy • He arrived all *bright-eyed and bushy-tailed*.

bright spot *informal* : a good thing that occurs during a bad or difficult time • Car sales were one of the few *bright spots* for the economy last year.

on the bright side — used to refer to the good part of something that is mostly bad • (*US*) He lost the race, but *on the bright side*, he didn't get hurt. • Your cat is very sick right now, but try to ***look on the bright side***. She can be treated with medicine.

– **bright·ly** *adv* • a candle glowing *brightly* • a *brightly* lit room • *brightly* colored toys • She smiled *brightly* [=*cheerfully*] at her daughter. – **bright·ness** *noun* [*noncount*] • You can adjust the light's *brightness*.

bright·en /ˈbraɪtn̩/ *verb* **-ens; -ened; -en·ing**

1 [+ *obj*] : to add more light to (something) • He *brightened* the picture on the television.

2 a [+ *obj*] : to make (something) more colorful or cheerful • Flowers can *brighten* any room. • The good news *brightened* her mood. — often + *up* • She always *brightens up* a party. • You really *brightened up* my day. **b** [*no obj*] : to become brighter or more cheerful • The sky *brightened* after the storm. • Her mood *brightened*. • Her eyes *brightened*. • Business prospects *brightened* last month. • Her face *brightened* in relief when she heard that he was not hurt.

brill /ˈbrɪl/ *adj, Brit, informal* : BRILLIANT 4 • We had a *brill* [=*great*] time.

bril·liance /ˈbrɪljəns/ *noun* [*noncount*] : the quality or state of being brilliant • The professor was known for his *brilliance*. • the *brilliance* of a diamond

bril·liant /ˈbrɪljənt/ *adj* [*more* ~; *most* ~]

1 : very bright : flashing with light • *brilliant* jewels • a *brilliant* star in the sky • a store decorated in *brilliant* colors

2 : very impressive or successful • He pitched a *brilliant* game. • She gave a *brilliant* performance. • a *brilliant* career

3 a : extremely intelligent : much more intelligent than most people • a *brilliant* scientist • She has a *brilliant* mind. **b** : showing extreme intelligence : extremely clever • a *brilliant* idea — often used in a joking or ironic way to describe a foolish idea, action, etc. • It was *brilliant* of you to leave your passport at home!

4 *Brit, informal* : very good : wonderful or excellent • Dinner was *brilliant*. • It is a *brilliant* [=*fabulous*] film. You really must see it. • We had a *brilliant* time at the circus.

– **bril·liant·ly** *adv* • a star shining *brilliantly* • *brilliantly* colored clothes • She acted *brilliantly* in her first film. • a *brilliantly* written essay

Bril·lo /ˈbrɪloʊ/ *trademark* — used for a steel wool pad filled with soap and used for scrubbing pots, pans, and other items

¹brim /ˈbrɪm/ *noun, pl* **brims** [*count*]

1 : the top edge of a glass or a similar container • He filled the glass ***to the brim*** [=to the top] • The glass was ***filled/full to the brim*** [=completely full] — often used figuratively • Her heart was *filled to the brim* with joy.

2 : the part of a hat that sticks out around the lower edge — see picture at HAT

– **brim·ful** /ˈbrɪmˌfʊl/ *adj* • The book is *brimful* of funny jokes. [=is filled with funny jokes] – **brimmed** /ˈbrɪmd/ *adj* • a *brimmed* hat — often used with another adjective • a wide-*brimmed* hat

²brim *verb* **brims; brimmed; brim·ming** [*no obj*] : to be completely filled *with* something • a boy *brimming* (over) *with* energy • Her heart was *brimming with* happiness. • The show *brims with* excitement. • Her eyes ***brimmed with tears*** [=tears filled her eyes]

brim·stone /ˈbrɪmˌstoʊn/ *noun* [*noncount*] *old-fashioned* : SULFUR — now usually used in the phrase ***fire and brimstone*** to refer to descriptions of hell • The preacher's sermons were full of *fire and brimstone*. [=the preacher's sermons warned of the punishment of hell]

brin·dled /ˈbrɪndl̩d/ *or* **brin·dle** /ˈbrɪndl̩/ *adj* : having faint dark streaks or spots on a gray or light brown background • a *brindled* cow

brine /ˈbraɪn/ *noun* [*noncount*]

1 : a mixture of salty water used especially to preserve or add flavor to food • The chicken was soaked in *brine* before it was roasted.

2 : the salty water of the ocean • ocean *brine* — see also BRINY

bring /ˈbrɪŋ/ *verb* **brings; brought** /ˈbrɑːt/; **bring·ing** [+ *obj*]

1 : to come with (something or someone) to a place • I'll *bring* a bottle of wine (with me) when I come to your party. • "Should I send you a check?" "Why not just *bring* me the money when you come?" • Have you *brought* the money with you from the bank? • She *brought* her boyfriend home to meet her parents. • You stay where you are and I'll *bring* you another drink. = I'll *bring* another drink to you.

2 : to cause (something or someone) to come • Her screams *brought* [=*attracted*] help. • Her screams *brought* the neighbors running. [=the neighbors ran to help her when they heard her screams] • Love of adventure *brought* her here before taking her to many other places. • This radio station *brings* you all the news as it happens.

3 : to cause (something) to exist, happen, or start • Can anything *bring* peace to this troubled region? • In this part of the country, winter *brings* snow (with it). • The tablets may *bring* (you) some relief. • Having a baby has *brought* great happiness into her life. • The sad story ***brought tears to our eyes*** [=made us cry] but its happy ending ***brought smiles to our lips*** [=made us smile]

4 *always followed by an adverb or preposition* : to cause (something or someone) to reach a specified state, place, condition, etc. • The dancer *brought* his hands up to his face. • (*US*) *Bring* the water to a boil. = (*Brit*) *Bring* the water to the boil. [=heat the water so that it boils] • The pilot *brought* them safely out of danger. • Winter snow *brought* traffic to a stop. • A few steps *brought* us to the front door. • The thrilling climax *brought* the audience to its/their feet. • This history book *brings* us up to the present day.

5 : to have (a particular talent, quality, etc.) when you start to do something (such as a job) — + *to* • She *brings* years of experience *to* the position. [=she comes to the position with years of experience] • He *brings* a rare talent for solving problems *to* his new job as company president.

6 *law* : to start a case against someone in a court of law • They threatened to *bring* [=*institute*] legal action against him. • They are going to ***bring charges against*** him. [=they are going to charge him with a crime]

7 : to cause (something) to reach a total — + *to* • Last week's sales figures *brought* our pretax profits for the year *to* just over $35,000,000. • The donation *brought* the fund *to* over a million dollars.

8 : to get (an amount of money) as a price : to be sold for (a price) • The painting ought to *bring* [=*fetch*] a high price.

> In addition to the phrases shown below, *bring* occurs in many idioms that are shown at appropriate entries throughout the dictionary. For example, *bring to bear* can be found at ²BEAR and *bring to an end* can be found at ¹END.

bring about [*phrasal verb*] ***bring about (something)*** *also* ***bring (something) about*** : to cause (something) • "What *brought about* the crisis?" "It was *brought about* by many factors."

bring around (*chiefly US*) *or chiefly Brit* ***bring round*** [*phrasal verb*]

1 ***bring (someone) around*** : to cause (someone) to come around: such as **a** : to cause (someone) to accept and support something (such as an idea) after opposing it • She still says she won't support us, but we'll *bring* her *around* eventually. [=we'll convince/persuade her to support us eventually] — often + *to* • I'm sure we can *bring* her *around to* our way of thinking. **b** : to cause (someone) to become awake again after being unconscious • The boxer was knocked out and it took the doctor several minutes to *bring* him *around*. [=bring him to] **c** : to come with (someone) for a social visit • Why don't you *bring* your friend *around* (to my house) after work today? **2** ***bring (something) around*** : to cause (something, such as a conversation) to go to a desired subject or area — + *to* • We gradually *brought* the conversation *around to* the subject of his unpaid bills.

bring back [*phrasal verb*] **1** ***bring (something or someone) back*** *or* ***bring back (something or someone)*** **a** : to come back with (something or someone) • What did you *bring back* (with you) from your vacation? • You promised to *bring back* a present for me. = You promised to *bring* me *back* a present. **b** : to cause (something or someone) to return • The death penalty was done away with in this area many years ago, but some people now want it to be *brought back*. ▪ The movie is a fantasy about a man who is *brought back* (to life) from the dead. ▪ The company is doing poorly, and its former president is being *brought back* to help solve its problems. **c :** to cause (something or someone) to return *to* a condition, subject, etc. ▪ That question *brings* us *back* (again) *to* the fundamental problem of world peace. ▪ We gradually *brought* the conversation *back to* the subject of his unpaid bills. **2** ***bring (something) back or bring back (something)*** **:** to cause (something) to return to someone's memory ▪ Seeing her again *brought back* a lot of happy memories. ▪ I had almost forgotten about the time we spent together, but seeing her again **brought it all back** (to me).

bring before [*phrasal verb*] ***bring (someone or something) before (someone or something)*** *formal* **:** to cause (someone or something) to come to (someone or something) for an official decision or judgment ▪ He was *brought* (up) *before* the judge on a charge of obstructing justice. ▪ The case was finally *brought before* the Supreme Court.

bring down [*phrasal verb*] **1** ***bring down (someone or something) or bring (someone or something) down*** **:** to cause (someone or something) to fall down onto the ground ▪ The deer was *brought down* by a single shot. ▪ The plane was *brought down* by enemy fire. — often used figuratively ▪ The government was *brought down* by a vote of no confidence. ▪ a famous politician who was *brought down* by scandal **2** ***bring (something) down or bring down (something)*** **:** to cause (something) to become lower ▪ Will anything ever *bring* house prices *down*? **3** ***bring (someone) down*** *informal* **:** to cause (someone) to become sad or depressed ▪ All this rainy weather is really *bringing* me *down*. [=getting me down]

bring forth [*phrasal verb*] ***bring (something) forth or bring forth (something)*** *somewhat formal* **:** to produce (something) ▪ The rosebushes *brought forth* an abundance of flowers. ▪ He was able to *bring forth* persuasive arguments in support of his position. **:** to cause (something) to occur or exist ▪ Her controversial comments *brought forth* [=*provoked*] strong reactions from the public.

bring forward [*phrasal verb*] ***bring (something) forward or bring forward (something)*** **1 :** to talk about or show (something) so that it can be seen or discussed by others ▪ The police have *brought* new evidence *forward*. **2 :** to make the time of (something) earlier or sooner ▪ We need to *bring* the meeting *forward* from Tuesday to Monday so that more people can attend.

bring in [*phrasal verb*] **1** ***bring in (someone) or bring (someone) in*** **:** to cause (someone) to become involved in a process, activity, etc. ▪ The company has decided to *bring in* outside experts to help on the project. **2** ***bring in (something) or bring (something) in*** **a :** to produce or earn (an amount of money) ▪ Each sale *brought in* $5. ▪ He works at a large company and *brings in* a good salary. **b** *law* **:** to report (an official decision) to a court ▪ The jury *brought in* [=*returned*] a verdict of not guilty. [=the jury said that the defendant was not guilty] **c** *chiefly Brit* **:** to introduce (a new law, rule, etc.) ▪ The government is going to *bring in* legislation to make such practices illegal. **3** ***bring in (someone or something) or bring (someone or something) in*** **:** to cause (someone or something) to come to a place ▪ The store is having a special sale in order to *bring in* [=*attract*] new customers/business. ▪ The police *brought* him *in* (to the police station) for questioning.

bring off [*phrasal verb*] ***bring (something) off also bring off (something)*** **:** to do (something difficult) **:** to achieve or accomplish (something) ▪ It's a challenging role. She's the only actress I know with enough talent to *bring* it *off*.

bring on [*phrasal verb*] **1** ***bring on (something) or bring (something) on*** **:** to cause (something) to appear or occur ▪ The crisis was *brought on* by many factors. **2** ***bring (something) on (someone)*** **:** to cause (something bad) to happen to (someone) ▪ You've *brought* nothing but shame *on* your family since the day you were born! ▪ I can't help thinking you've *brought* some of this trouble *on* yourself.

bring out [*phrasal verb*] **1** ***bring out (something) or bring (something) out*** **a :** to show (something) **:** to cause (something) to appear or to be more easily seen ▪ The debate *brought out* [=*highlighted*] the differences between the two candidates. ▪ That blue sweater really *brings out* the color in your eyes. ▪ Our school aims to *bring out* [=*develop*] the talents in each of our students. ▪ A crisis **brings out the best in** some people and **brings out the worst in** others. [=a crisis causes some people to behave very well and other people to behave very badly] **b :** to produce (something, such as a book) **:** to cause (something) to become available or to come out ▪ a writer who's expected to *bring out* a new novel next year **2** ***bring (someone) out in (something)*** *Brit* **:** to cause (someone) to begin to have (something, such as a rash) on the skin ▪ Eating strawberries *brings* me *out in* spots. [=eating strawberries makes me break out in spots]

bring round see BRING AROUND (above)

bring to [*phrasal verb*] ***bring (someone) to*** **:** to cause (someone) to become awake again after being unconscious ▪ The boxer was knocked out and it took the doctor several minutes to *bring* him *to*. [=bring him around]

bring together [*phrasal verb*] ***bring (people) together or bring together (people)*** **:** to cause (people) to join or meet **:** to cause (people) to come together ▪ She and her husband were *brought together* by a shared love of the natural world. ▪ The conference has *brought together* some of the world's leading experts on laser technology.

bring up [*phrasal verb*] **1** ***bring (someone) up or bring up (someone)*** **:** to take care of and teach (a child who is growing up) ▪ I was born and *brought up* [=*raised, reared*] in Chicago. ▪ My grandparents *brought* me *up* after my parents died. ▪ My parents *brought* me *up* to respect authority. [=my parents taught me to respect authority when I was a child] **2** ***bring (something) up or bring up (something)*** **a :** to mention (something) when talking **:** to start to talk about (something) ▪ We were waiting for a suitable moment to *bring up* [=*introduce, raise*] the subject of his unpaid bills. ▪ I wasn't going to talk about money, but since you've *brought* it *up*, I guess it's something we should really discuss. ▪ I'm glad you mentioned money. That *brings up* the question of how much we can afford to spend. **b** *computers* **:** to cause (something, such as a file or picture) to appear on a computer screen ▪ The system makes it easy to *bring up* (on the screen) information about any customer. **c :** [1]VOMIT ▪ The patient tried to eat some breakfast but immediately *brought* it back *up* again. **3** ***bring (someone) up*** **:** to cause (someone) to stop suddenly — used in phrases like **bring up short** and **bring up suddenly** ▪ He was just starting to argue when her scream *brought him up short*.

bring yourself **:** to force yourself *to do* something that you do not want to do — usually used in negative statements ▪ He knew that he should apologize, but he couldn't *bring himself to do* it.

– bring·er *noun, pl* **-ers** [*count*] ▪ a *bringer* of good news

bring–and–buy sale *noun, pl* **~ sales** [*count*] *Brit* **:** a sale to which people bring things for others to buy usually in order to raise money for charity

brink /ˈbrɪŋk/ *noun*

the brink **:** the edge at the top of a steep cliff — usually used figuratively to refer to a point that is very close to the occurrence of something very bad or (less commonly) very good ▪ He nearly lost everything because of his drug addiction, but his friends helped to pull him back from *the brink*. ▪ The two nations are **on the brink of** war. [=are very close to war] ▪ a city *on the brink of* financial disaster ▪ Doctors may be *on the brink of* finding a cure for this disease. ▪ a young actress who is *on the brink of* a brilliant career ▪ The other team **brought them to the brink of** defeat. [=came very close to defeating them] ▪ an animal that has been **brought/pulled back from the brink of** extinction

brink·man·ship /ˈbrɪŋkmənˌʃɪp/ *also chiefly US* **brinks·man·ship** /ˈbrɪŋksmənˌʃɪp/ *noun* [*noncount*] **:** the practice of causing or allowing a situation to become extremely dangerous in order to get the results that you want ▪ two nations caught up in nuclear *brinksmanship* ▪ engaging in political *brinkmanship*

briny /ˈbraɪni/ *adj* **brin·i·er; -est :** SALTY ▪ *briny* water ▪ oysters with a *briny* flavor

the briny *old-fashioned* **:** the sea ▪ out on *the briny*

brio /ˈbriːjoʊ/ *noun* [*noncount*] **:** great energy and confidence ▪ She sings with *brio*.

bri·oche /briˈoʊʃ/ *noun, pl* **brioches** [*count, noncount*] **:** a light, sweet type of bread

brisk /ˈbrɪsk/ *adj* **brisk·er; -est**

1 : moving or speaking quickly **:** quick and efficient ▪ a *brisk*, no-nonsense manager ▪ She answered the phone in a *brisk* voice.

2 : pleasantly cool or cold ▪ *brisk* autumn weather ▪ The wind was *brisk*.

3 a : done with quickness and energy ▪ They went for a *brisk*

walk in the woods. ▪ She walked at a *brisk* pace. **b** : very active and steady ▪ Business is *brisk* at the store. ▪ *brisk* economic growth ▪ There is a *brisk* market in old movie posters.
– **brisk·ly** *adv* ▪ The wind was blowing *briskly* off the ocean. ▪ The flowers have been selling *briskly*. – **brisk·ness** *noun* [*noncount*]

bris·ket /ˈbrɪskət/ *noun, pl* **-kets** [*count, noncount*] : beef from the chest of a cow

[1]**bris·tle** /ˈbrɪsəl/ *noun, pl* **bris·tles** [*count*] : a short, stiff hair, fiber, etc. ▪ a face covered with *bristles* ▪ the *bristles* of a brush
– **bris·tly** /ˈbrɪsli/ *adj* **bris·tli·er; -est** ▪ a *bristly* mustache

[2]**bristle** *verb* **bristles; bris·tled; bris·tling** [*no obj*]
1 *of hair* : to rise up and become stiff ▪ Electricity makes your hair *bristle*.
2 : to show signs of anger : to become angry — usually + *at* ▪ He *bristled at* the insult. ▪ She *bristled at* their criticism.
bristle with [*phrasal verb*] ***bristle with (something)*** **1** : to be covered with (something) ▪ a bush *bristling with* thorns ▪ The hillside *bristled with* soldiers. **2** : to be full of (something) ▪ The movie *bristles with* excitement. [=the movie is very exciting] ▪ He *bristles with* energy.

Brit /ˈbrɪt/ *noun, pl* **Brits** [*count*] *informal* : a British person

britch·es /ˈbrɪʧəz/ *noun* [*plural*] *chiefly US, informal + old-fashioned* : PANTS ▪ an old pair of *britches*
too big for your britches see [1]BIG

Brit·ish /ˈbrɪtɪʃ/ *adj* : of or relating to Great Britain and especially England ▪ *British* newspapers ▪ a *British* port
the British : the people of Great Britain and especially England ▪ talked about *the British*

British English *noun* [*noncount*] : the English language used in England

Brit·ish·er /ˈbrɪtɪʃɚ/ *noun, pl* **-ers** [*count*] *chiefly US, informal + old-fashioned* : a British person

British Summer Time *noun* [*noncount*] *Brit* : a period of the year between spring and fall when clocks in the United Kingdom are set one hour ahead of Greenwich mean time — called also (*Brit*) *Summer Time*; compare DAYLIGHT SAVING TIME

Brit·on /ˈbrɪtn̩/ *noun, pl* **-ons** [*count*] *somewhat formal* : a British person

brit·tle /ˈbrɪtl̩/ *adj* **brit·tler; brit·tlest** [*or more ~; most ~*]
1 : easily broken or cracked ▪ *brittle* glass ▪ *brittle* bones
2 : not strong : easily damaged ▪ The countries formed a *brittle* [=*fragile*] alliance.
3 : sharp in sound ▪ a *brittle* laugh ▪ a high, *brittle* voice
– **brit·tle·ness** /ˈbrɪtl̩nəs/ *noun* [*noncount*]

bro /ˈbroʊ/ *noun, pl* **bros** [*count*]
1 *informal* : BROTHER ▪ my big *bro*
2 *US slang* — used as a friendly way of addressing a man or boy ▪ Catch you later, *bro*.

[1]**broach** /ˈbroʊʧ/ *verb* **broach·es; broached; broach·ing** [+ *obj*] : to introduce (a subject, issue, etc.) for discussion ▪ She *broached* the idea of getting another cat.

[2]**broach** *noun, pl* **broaches** [*count*] : BROOCH

[1]**broad** /ˈbrɑːd/ *adj* **broad·er; -est**
1 a : large from one side to the other side : WIDE ▪ He has *broad* shoulders. ▪ a *broad* stripe ▪ *broad* prairies ▪ a *broad* avenue — opposite NARROW **b** *chiefly Brit* : having a specified width ▪ three metres *broad* [=*wide*]
2 : including or involving many things or people : wide in range or amount ▪ The store has a *broad* selection/variety of coats. ▪ a president with *broad* [=*widespread*] appeal ▪ There was *broad* agreement on the new government. ▪ There are three *broad* categories of industry in the region: computers, finance, and education. ▪ The conference was attended by ***a broad spectrum*** [=a range of many different kinds] of religious leaders. — opposite NARROW
3 : relating to the main parts of something : GENERAL ▪ the *broad* outlines of a problem ▪ discusses "family" in its *broadest* sense
4 : easily seen or noticed ▪ She gave him a *broad* [=*obvious*] hint. ▪ He speaks with a *broad* Midwestern accent.
in broad daylight : during the day when people and things can be easily seen rather than at night ▪ The crime was committed *in broad daylight*.
– **broad·ly** *adv* [*more ~; most ~*] ▪ He smiled *broadly* [=with a big smile] as he greeted us. ▪ The book is *broadly* [=*generally*] concerned with the oil industry. ▪ She *broadly* [=*obviously*] hinted that she wouldn't be coming back. ▪ a ***broadly based*** [=*broad-based*] political movement

[2]**broad** *noun, pl* **broads** [*count*] *US slang, old-fashioned + often offensive* : WOMAN ▪ a classy *broad*

broad·band /ˈbrɑːdˌbænd/ *noun* [*noncount*] : a fast electronic network that carries more than one type of communication (such as Internet and cable television signals)
– **broadband** *adj* ▪ *broadband* Internet access

broad–based /ˈbrɑːdˌbeɪst/ *adj* : involving or attracting many different types of people ▪ a *broad-based* environmental movement ▪ The show has a *broad-based* audience.

broad bean *noun, pl* **~ beans** [*count*] *chiefly Brit* : FAVA BEAN

broad–brush /ˈbrɑːdˌbrʌʃ/ *adj, always used before a noun* : relating to or involving the main or general parts of something rather than the details ▪ The book is a *broad-brush* treatment of the subject.

[1]**broad·cast** /ˈbrɑːdˌkæst, *Brit* ˈbrɔːdˌkɑːst/ *verb* **-casts; -cast; -cast·ing** [+ *obj*]
1 : to send out (signals, programs, etc.) by radio or television ▪ The station *broadcasts* the symphony live every Friday night. ▪ The interview was *broadcast* from London.
2 : to tell (something that is private or secret) to many people ▪ If you tell her anything about your personal life she'll *broadcast* it to everyone in the office.
3 : to throw (something, such as seeds) across a wide area of the ground ▪ *broadcast* fertilizer on the lawn
– **broad·cast·er** *noun, pl* **-ers** [*count*] ▪ radio/television *broadcasters* – **broadcasting** *noun* [*noncount*] ▪ She wants to have a career in *broadcasting*.

[2]**broadcast** *noun, pl* **-casts**
1 [*count*] : a radio or television program ▪ a live/recorded *broadcast* ▪ Did you hear the *broadcast* of last night's game?
2 [*noncount*] : the act of sending out radio or television signals : the act of broadcasting something ▪ The judge decided to allow *broadcast* of the trial. — sometimes used before another noun ▪ She wants to have a career in ***broadcast journalism***. [=a career in broadcasting]

broad·en /ˈbrɑːdn̩/ *verb* **-ens; -ened; -en·ing**
1 [+ *obj*] : to make (something) wider or more general ▪ They need to *broaden* their understanding of other cultures. ▪ The police have *broadened* the scope of the investigation. ▪ Travel can help to ***broaden your horizons/mind***. [=increase the range of your knowledge, understanding, or experience]
2 [*no obj*] : to become wider or more general ▪ The road *broadens* [=*widens*] near the airport. ▪ Her smile *broadened* when I told her the good news. ▪ The investigation has *broadened* to include the mayor's staff. ▪ His interests *broadened* to include art and music, not just sports.

broad jump *noun*
the broad jump *US* see LONG JUMP
– **broad jumper** *noun, pl* **~ -pers** [*count*]

broad–mind·ed /ˈbrɑːdˈmaɪndəd/ *adj* [*more ~; most ~*] : willing to accept opinions, beliefs, or behaviors that are unusual or different from your own ▪ Her mother was *broad-minded* about religion. ▪ a *broad-minded* view of racial issues
– **broad–mind·ed·ness** *noun* [*noncount*]

broad·sheet /ˈbrɑːdˌʃiːt/ *noun, pl* **-sheets** [*count*] *chiefly Brit* : a newspaper that has large pages and that usually deals with serious subjects — compare TABLOID

[1]**broad·side** /ˈbrɑːdˌsaɪd/ *noun, pl* **-sides** [*count*]
1 : a very strong and harsh spoken or written attack ▪ a *broadside* of criticism ▪ The senator delivered a *broadside* [=*blast*] against the President.
2 : an attack by a ship in which all the guns on one side of the ship are fired together

[2]**broadside** *adv*
1 : with the side facing forward ▪ Turn the ship *broadside*.
2 *chiefly US* : directly from the side ▪ The car was hit *broadside*.

[3]**broadside** *verb* **-sides; -sid·ed; -sid·ing** [+ *obj*] *US* : to hit (a vehicle) very hard from the side ▪ His car was *broadsided* by a truck as he was driving through the intersection.

broad·sword /ˈbrɑːdˌsoɚd/ *noun, pl* **-swords** [*count*] : a large, heavy sword that has a wide blade used for cutting

Broad·way /ˈbrɑːdˌweɪ/ *noun* [*noncount*] : a street in New York City where there are many theaters — used to refer to the world of the theater in New York City ▪ He's starring in a play on *Broadway*. ▪ She's a big star on *Broadway*. — often used before another noun ▪ a *Broadway* play/star — see also OFF-BROADWAY

bro·cade /broʊˈkeɪd/ *noun* [*noncount*] : a cloth with a raised design in gold or silver thread
– **bro·cad·ed** /broʊˈkeɪdəd/ *adj*

B

broc·co·li /ˈbrɑːkəli/ *noun [noncount]* **:** a common vegetable that has green branches and many small green or purple flowers — see color picture on page C4

bro·chure /broʊˈʃuɚ, *Brit* ˈbrəʊʃə/ *noun, pl* **-chures** *[count]* **:** a small, thin book or magazine that usually has many pictures and information about a product, a place, etc. • a travel *brochure*

[1]**brogue** /ˈbroʊg/ *noun, pl* **brogues** *[count]* **:** the way that English is pronounced in Ireland or Scotland **:** an Irish or Scottish accent • He spoke with an Irish *brogue*. — compare [2]BROGUE

[2]**brogue** *noun, pl* **brogues** *[count]* **:** a shoe decorated with small holes along the sides and at the toe — compare [1]BROGUE

broil /ˈbrojəl/ *verb* **broils; broiled; broil·ing** *US*
1 *[+ obj]* **:** to cook (food) directly over or under extremely high heat • *broil* a chicken • a *broiled* steak
2 *[no obj] informal* **:** to be extremely hot • The farm workers were *broiling* out in the hot sun.

broil·er /ˈbroɪlɚ/ *noun, pl* **-ers** *[count]*
1 *US* **:** a part of an oven that becomes very hot and that food is placed under to be broiled • Put the steaks under the *broiler*.
2 *chiefly US* **:** a young chicken that is suitable for broiling — compare FRYER, ROASTER

[1]**broke** *past tense of* [1]BREAK

[2]**broke** /ˈbroʊk/ *adj, not used before a noun, informal* **:** not having any money • She is *broke* and homeless. • Can I borrow 10 dollars? I'm *broke* until payday. • I'm ***flat broke*** = (*Brit*) I'm ***stony broke*** [=I have no money at all]
go broke *informal* **:** to spend or lose all of your money • He *went broke* after he lost his job. • The company could *go broke* if the economy doesn't improve soon.
go for broke *informal* **:** to do something that is dangerous or that could result in complete failure in order to try to achieve success • She decided to *go for broke* and start her own restaurant.
if it ain't broke, don't fix it *informal* — used to say that you should not try to change something that is working well

[1]**broken** *past participle of* [1]BREAK

[2]**bro·ken** /ˈbroʊkən/ *adj*
1 : separated into parts or pieces by being hit, damaged, etc. • The street was covered with *broken* glass. • a *broken* [=*cracked*] mirror • a *broken* bone • a *broken* leg/arm [=a leg/arm that has a broken bone]
2 : not working properly • a *broken* camera
3 : not kept or honored • a *broken* promise
4 : without hope or strength because of having suffered very much • a *broken* spirit • The failure of his business left him a *broken* man. • a *broken* heart
5 : spoken with many mistakes **:** not fluent • He spoke (in) *broken* English.
6 — used to describe a relationship (such as a marriage) that has ended • a *broken* marriage/engagement • a *broken* family [=a family in which the parents have divorced] • children from ***broken homes*** [=children whose parents are divorced]

broken–down *adj* **:** in a bad or weak condition because of being old, not well cared for, etc. • a *broken-down* car

bro·ken·heart·ed /ˈbroʊkənˈhɑɚtəd/ *adj* **:** filled with great sadness especially because someone you love has left you, has died, etc. **:** HEARTBROKEN • She was *brokenhearted* when her boyfriend left her.

[1]**bro·ker** /ˈbroʊkɚ/ *noun, pl* **-kers** *[count]* **:** a person who helps other people to reach agreements, to make deals, or to buy and sell property (such as stocks or houses) • a real estate *broker* • an insurance *broker* • a marriage *broker* [=a person who helps to arrange the marriages of other people] — see also PAWNBROKER, POWER BROKER, STOCKBROKER

[2]**broker** *verb* **-kers; -kered; -ker·ing** *[+ obj]* **:** to help people, countries, etc., to make a deal or to reach an agreement • *broker* a stock sale • The President has been trying to *broker* a peace treaty.

bro·ker·age /ˈbroʊkərɪʤ/ *noun, pl* **-ag·es** *[count]* **:** the business of a broker • one of the country's largest *brokerages* • She works for a *brokerage* firm.

brol·ly /ˈbrɑːli/ *noun, pl* **-lies** *[count] Brit, informal* **:** UMBRELLA

bro·mide /ˈbroʊˌmaɪd/ *noun, pl* **-mides**
1 *[count, noncount]* **:** a drug that makes a person calm
2 *[count]* **:** a statement that is intended to make people feel happier or calmer but that is not original or effective • His speech had nothing more to offer than the usual *bromides* about how everyone needs to work together.

bronc /ˈbrɑːŋk/ *noun, pl* **broncs** *[count] US, informal* **:** BRONCO

bron·chi·al /ˈbrɑːŋkijəl/ *adj* **:** relating to or involving the tubes that carry air into the lungs • a *bronchial* infection • *bronchial* tubes

bron·chi·tis /brɑnˈkaɪtəs/ *noun [noncount] medical* **:** an illness in which your bronchial tubes become sore or damaged and you cough a lot • acute/chronic *bronchitis*

bron·co /ˈbrɑːŋkoʊ/ *noun, pl* **-cos** *[count]* **:** a wild horse of western North America • a rodeo featuring ***bucking broncos***

bron·to·sau·rus /ˌbrɑːntəˈsorəs/ *noun, pl* **-rus·es** *[count]* **:** a very large dinosaur that had a long neck and tail

Bronx cheer /ˈbrɑːŋks-/ *noun, pl* ~ **cheers** *[count] US, informal* **:** a rude sound made to show that you dislike something **:** RASPBERRY

[1]**bronze** /ˈbrɑːnz/ *noun, pl* **bronz·es**
1 *[noncount]* **:** a metal that is made by combining copper and tin • a statue cast in *bronze*
2 *[count]* **a :** something (such as a statue) that is made of bronze • a *bronze* of the president **b :** BRONZE MEDAL • She won a *bronze* in skiing.
3 *[noncount]* **:** a yellowish-brown color — see color picture on page C2

[2]**bronze** *adj*
1 : made of bronze • a *bronze* statue
2 : having a yellowish-brown color • *bronze* curtains

Bronze Age *noun*
the Bronze Age **:** a period of time that began between 4000 and 3000 B.C. in which people used bronze to make weapons and tools • The artifact dates to *the Bronze Age*. • *The Bronze Age* preceded the Iron Age. • a *Bronze Age* weapon/tool — compare IRON AGE, STONE AGE

bronzed /ˈbrɑːnzd/ *adj*
1 : having skin that has been made brown by the sun **:** TANNED • a *bronzed* young swimmer • *bronzed* bodies
2 : covered with a material that makes something appear to be made of bronze • *bronzed* baby shoes

bronze medal *noun, pl* ~ **-dals** *[count]* **:** a medal made of bronze that is awarded as the prize for third place in a sports competition • The team won the *bronze medal* in basketball. — compare GOLD MEDAL, SILVER MEDAL

Bronze Star *noun, pl* ~ **Stars** *[count]* **:** a U.S. military award — called also *Bronze Star Medal*

brooch /ˈbroʊʧ/ *noun, pl* **brooch·es** *[count]* **:** a piece of jewelry that is held on clothing by a pin and worn by a woman at or near her neck — called also *broach*; see color picture on page C11

[1]**brood** /ˈbruːd/ *noun, pl* **broods** *[count]*
1 : a group of young birds (such as chickens) that were all born at the same time • a hen and her *brood* of chicks
2 *informal* **:** the children in someone's family • Mrs. Smith took her *brood* to church every Sunday.

[2]**brood** *verb* **broods; brood·ed; brood·ing** *[no obj]* **:** to think a lot about something in an unhappy way • He *brooded* over/about/on his mistake. • After the argument, she sat in her bedroom, *brooding*.
– brood·er *noun, pl* **-ers** *[count]*

brooding *adj [more ~; most ~]* **:** very serious and sad • a *brooding* artist • a *brooding* landscape/essay
– brood·ing·ly *adv*

broody *adj* **brood·i·er; -est**
1 : serious and sad **:** BROODING • a movie with a dark and *broody* atmosphere
2 a *of a hen* **:** ready to lay and sit on eggs • a *broody* hen **b** *Brit, informal, of a woman* **:** wanting to have a baby • a *broody* wife

[1]**brook** /ˈbrʊk/ *verb* **brooks; brooked; brook·ing** *[+ obj]* **:** to allow (something) to exist or happen — usually used with *no* • Their coach *brooks* [=*tolerates*] *no* disagreement. • a government that *brooks no* criticism

[2]**brook** *noun, pl* **brooks** *[count]* **:** a small stream • a babbling *brook*

broom /ˈbruːm/ *noun, pl* **brooms**
1 *[count]* **:** a brush that has a long handle and that is used for sweeping floors
2 *[noncount]* **:** a type of bush that has long, thin branches and yellow flowers

broom·stick /ˈbruːmˌstɪk/ *noun, pl* **-sticks** *[count]* **:** the handle of a broom

Bros. *abbr* brothers — used in company names • Smith *Bros*.

broth /ˈbrɑːθ/ *noun, pl* **broths** [*count, noncount*] : liquid in which food (such as meat) has been cooked ▪ chicken *broth*

broth·el /ˈbrɑːθəl/ *noun, pl* **-thels** [*count*] : a building in which prostitutes are available : BORDELLO

broth·er /ˈbrʌðɚ/ *noun, pl* **-ers** [*count*]
1 : a boy or man who has one or both of the same parents as you ▪ my little/younger *brother* ▪ her big/older *brother* ▪ Her *brother* was adopted. — compare BROTHER-IN-LAW, HALF BROTHER, STEPBROTHER
2 : a man who is from the same group or country as you ▪ his college fraternity *brothers* ▪ We must support our *brothers* and sisters fighting overseas.
3 *pl* ***broth·ers*** *or* ***breth·ren*** /ˈbrɛðrən/ : a male member of a religious group ▪ the *brothers* in a monastery — used especially as a title ▪ *Brother* John
4 *US, informal* : a black man — used especially by African-Americans
5 *US, informal* — used when talking to a man ▪ *Brother*, do you have an extra cigarette? ▪ *Brother*, you have got to relax.
6 *chiefly US, informal* — used as an interjection to express surprise or annoyance ▪ *Brother* was I ever sick. [=I was very sick] ▪ Oh, *brother*!

broom

broth·er·hood /ˈbrʌðɚˌhʊd/ *noun, pl* **-hoods**
1 [*noncount*] : feelings of friendship, support, and understanding between people ▪ the *brotherhood* of humankind
2 [*count*] : a group or organization of people who have the same interests, jobs, etc. ▪ the musical *brotherhood* — often used in the names of labor unions ▪ the International *Brotherhood* of Electrical Workers

broth·er–in–law /ˈbrʌðərənˌlɑː/ *noun, pl* **broth·ers–in–law** /ˈbrʌðɚzənˌlɑː/ [*count*]
1 : the brother of your husband or wife
2 : the husband of your sister

broth·er·ly /ˈbrʌðɚli/ *adj* [*more* ~; *most* ~] : showing or suggesting the love and closeness of a brother ▪ He gave his sister a *brotherly* hug. ▪ He received *brotherly* support from his fellow priests.
– **broth·er·li·ness** *noun* [*noncount*]

brought *past tense and past participle of* BRING

brou·ha·ha /ˈbruːˌhɑːˌhɑː/ *noun, informal + usually disapproving* : great excitement or concern about something [*singular*] A *brouhaha* erupted over her statements about the president. [*noncount*] There's been a lot of *brouhaha* about her statements.

brow /ˈbraʊ/ *noun, pl* **brows** [*count*]
1 : EYEBROW ▪ She raised her *brows* in surprise.
2 : FOREHEAD ▪ She wiped the sweat from her *brow*. — see also HIGHBROW, LOWBROW, MIDDLEBROW
3 : the upper edge of a steep slope ▪ the *brow* of a high hill
knit your brow see [1]KNIT

brow·beat /ˈbraʊˌbiːt/ *verb* **-beats**; **-beat**; **-beat·en** /-ˌbiːtn̩/; **-beat·ing** [+ *obj*] : to use threats or angry speech to make (someone) do or accept something ▪ His father likes to *browbeat* waiters and waitresses. — often + *into* ▪ He refuses to be *browbeaten into* making changes he thinks are not necessary.

[1]**brown** /ˈbraʊn/ *adj* **-er**; **-est**
1 : having a color like coffee or chocolate ▪ a *brown* cow ▪ The door was *brown*.
2 : having dark or tanned skin ▪ workers whose backs are *brown* from long hours in the sun

[2]**brown** *noun, pl* **browns** : a color like the color of coffee or chocolate [*noncount*] a shade of *brown* ▪ The room was decorated in *brown*. [*count*] a mix of *browns* and reds — see color picture on page C1
– **brown·ish** /ˈbraʊnɪʃ/ *adj* [*more* ~; *most* ~] ▪ *brownish* eyes

[3]**brown** *verb* **browns**; **browned**; **brown·ing** : to make (something) brown or to become brown especially by cooking or heating [+ *obj*] *Brown* the chicken in a pan with butter. ▪ lightly *browned* sausages ▪ Her skin was *browned* by the sun. [*no obj*] The chicken is *browning* in the oven.

browned off *adj* [*more* ~; *most* ~] *Brit, informal* : annoyed and unhappy about something ▪ feeling thoroughly *browned off*

brown·ie /ˈbraʊni/ *noun, pl* **-ies** [*count*]
1 ***Brownie*** : a member of an organization of Girl Scouts or Girl Guides for girls ages 7 through 10 — compare CUB SCOUT
2 : a short, square piece of rich, chocolate cake that often contains nuts

brownie points *noun* [*plural*] *informal* : praise, credit, or approval that a person gets from someone (such as a boss or a teacher) for doing something good or helpful ▪ He's trying to earn/win/get *brownie points* (from the boss) by offering to work more overtime.

brown·nose /ˈbraʊnˌnoʊz/ *verb* **-nos·es**; **-nosed**; **-nos·ing** [+ *obj*] *informal + disapproving* : to try to get the approval of (an important or powerful person) by praise, flattery, etc. ▪ He has been *brownnosing* everyone in the company just to get a bigger office.
– **brown·nos·er** *noun, pl* **-ers** [*count*] ▪ That girl is a *brownnoser*. – **brownnosing** *noun* [*noncount*] ▪ I can't stand his *brownnosing*.

brown·out /ˈbraʊnˌaʊt/ *noun, pl* **-outs** [*count*] *chiefly US* : a period when the amount of electricity in an area is reduced because there is not enough for everyone who needs it — compare BLACKOUT 2

brown·stone /ˈbraʊnˌstoʊn/ *noun, pl* **-stones**
1 [*noncount*] : a reddish-brown type of stone that is used for building
2 [*count*] *US* : a house that is covered with a layer of brownstone ▪ She lives in a beautiful *brownstone* in Manhattan.

brown sugar *noun* [*noncount*] : a type of sugar that is brown because it contains a dark syrup (called molasses)

browse /ˈbraʊz/ *verb* **brows·es**; **browsed**; **brows·ing**
1 : to look at many things in a store, in a newspaper, etc., to see if there is something interesting or worth buying [*no obj*] Several customers were *browsing* in the bookstore. — often + *through* ▪ He saw her *browsing through* the magazine section of the store. ▪ He was *browsing through* the want ads in the newspaper, looking for a job. [+ *obj*] He was *browsing* the want ads in the newspaper.
2 [+ *obj*] : to use a special program (called a browser) to find and look at information on the Internet ▪ *browse* [=*surf*] the Web/Internet
3 [*no obj*] *of an animal* : to eat grass, plants, etc. : GRAZE ▪ cows *browsing* in the pasture

brows·er /ˈbraʊzɚ/ *noun, pl* **-ers** [*count*]
1 : a person who looks at the things being sold in a store to see if there is something worth buying : a person who browses ▪ There were a few *browsers* in the bookstore.
2 : a computer program that is used to find and look at information on the Internet ▪ a Web *browser*

[1]**bruise** /ˈbruːz/ *noun, pl* **bruis·es** [*count*]
1 : a dark and painful area on your skin that is caused by an injury ▪ He had a bad *bruise* on his leg after he fell.
2 : a dark area on a plant or piece of fruit that has been damaged ▪ a *bruise* on an apple

[2]**bruise** *verb* **bruises**; **bruised**; **bruis·ing**
1 a [+ *obj*] : to cause a bruise on (part of a person's body, a piece of fruit, etc.) ▪ She *bruised* her knee when she fell. — often used as *(be) bruised* ▪ His arms and legs *were* badly *bruised* in the accident. **b** [*no obj*] : to get a bruise ▪ She *bruises* easily. [=she gets bruises from minor injuries that would not cause bruises in most people]
2 [+ *obj*] : to hurt (someone's confidence, feelings, etc.) through speech or actions ▪ I don't want to *bruise* anyone's feelings. — usually used as *(be) bruised* ▪ His ego *was* badly *bruised* when he lost the race. ▪ There were *bruised* feelings after he was thrown out of the band.
– **bruising** *noun* [*noncount*] I noticed some *bruising* on his back. [*singular*] His ego took a *bruising* when he lost.

bruis·er /ˈbruːzɚ/ *noun, pl* **-ers** [*count*] *informal* : a large, strong man ▪ That boy is going to be a *bruiser* when he grows up!

bruising *adj* [*more* ~; *most* ~] : extremely rough or painful ▪ a *bruising* campaign battle ▪ a *bruising* fight

brûlée see CRÈME BRÛLÉE

brunch /ˈbrʌntʃ/ *noun, pl* **brunch·es** [*count*] : a meal that combines breakfast and lunch and that is usually eaten in late morning

bru·nette *also* **bru·net** /bruˈnɛt/ *noun, pl* **-nettes** *also* **-nets** [*count*] : a person who has brown or black hair ▪ a beautiful *brunette* ✧ This word usually refers to a woman or a girl and is spelled *brunette*. When it refers to a man or a boy, it is usually spelled *brunet*.
– **brunette** *also* **brunet** *adj* ▪ *brunette* hair

brunt /ˈbrʌnt/ *noun*

the brunt of : the main force or effect of (something harmful or dangerous) ▪ Cities on the coast felt/bore *the brunt of* the storm. ▪ His troops took *the brunt of* the enemy attack. ▪ *The brunt of* his criticism was directed at the supervisors.

B

¹brush /ˈbrʌʃ/ *noun, pl* **brush·es** [*count*]
1 : a tool with many stiff hairs, fibers, etc., that is used for cleaning, smoothing, or painting something ▪ Use a wire *brush* to get the rust off the metal. — see picture at DUSTPAN; see also HAIRBRUSH, PAINTBRUSH, TOOTHBRUSH
2 a : an act of cleaning or smoothing something with a brush ▪ I gave my daughter's hair a quick *brush*. **b** : a quick, light movement ▪ She wiped the crumbs off the table with a *brush* of her hand.
(as) daft as a brush see DAFT
tar (someone) with the same brush see ²TAR
– compare ³BRUSH, ⁴BRUSH

²brush *verb* **brushes; brushed; brush·ing** [+ *obj*]
1 a : to clean or smooth (something) with a brush ▪ *brush* your teeth/hair **b** : to put (something) on or onto something with a brush ▪ *Brush* some butter onto the fish before cooking it.
2 : to remove (something) with a brush or with a quick movement of your hand, fingers, etc. ▪ *Brush* the dirt off your pants. ▪ The camera showed him *brushing* [=*wiping*] away a tear.
3 : to touch gently against (something) when going past it ▪ Leaves *brushed* my cheek. ▪ The two men ***brushed shoulders*** [=touched at the shoulders] as they walked past each other.
4 : to move quickly past someone without stopping or paying attention ▪ The governor *brushed* by/past the reporters.
brush aside [*phrasal verb*] ***brush (something) aside or brush aside (something)*** : to treat (something) as not important : to ignore or dismiss (something) ▪ He *brushed aside* [=*brushed off*] questions about his son's arrest.
brush off [*phrasal verb*] **1** ***brush (something) off or brush off (something)*** : to treat (something) as not important : to refuse to deal with or talk about (something) in a serious way ▪ The company *brushed off* [=*brushed aside*] reports that it couldn't pay its bills. **2** ***brush (someone) off or brush off (someone)*** : to respond to (someone) in a rude way that shows you are not interested in what is being asked for or suggested ▪ I asked him for some help, but he just *brushed* me *off*. — see also BRUSH-OFF
brush up [*phrasal verb*] ***brush up or brush up (something)*** : to improve your skill at (something) or increase your knowledge of (something) ▪ My Spanish is very rusty. I need to *brush up* before I go on my vacation to Mexico. ▪ I need to *brush up* my Spanish. — often + *on* ▪ I need to *brush up on* my Spanish.

³brush *noun, pl* **brushes** [*count*] : a situation in which you briefly experience or almost experience something bad, dangerous, exciting, etc. — + *with* ▪ As a teenager he had several *brushes with* the law. [=was in trouble with police several times] ▪ She had a *brush with* [=briefly saw or met] a famous actor at a restaurant in New York. ▪ Her *brush with* fame/greatness came when she sang the national anthem at the football game. ▪ He had a *brush with* death [=he almost died] when climbing the mountain. — compare ¹BRUSH, ⁴BRUSH

⁴brush *noun* [*noncount*]
1 : wood from small branches on a tree ▪ a pile of *brush*
2 : small bushes or trees ▪ a hillside covered with dense *brush* ▪ a lion hiding in the *brush* — see also UNDERBRUSH
– compare ¹BRUSH, ³BRUSH

brush–off /ˈbrʌʃˌɑːf/ *noun*
the brush-off *informal* : rude treatment or behavior by someone who is not interested at all in what another person wants or asks for ▪ I wanted to ask him about his decision but he ***gave me the brush-off***. ▪ I ***got the brush-off*** when I asked her for help. — see also *brush off* at ²BRUSH

brush·stroke /ˈbrʌʃˌstroʊk/ *noun, pl* **-strokes** [*count*] : the paint left on a painting by a movement of the artist's brush

brusque /ˈbrʌsk/ *adj* [*more ~; most ~*] : talking or behaving in a very direct, brief, and unfriendly way ▪ She asked for a cup of coffee and received a *brusque* reply: "We don't have any." ▪ The teacher was *brusque* and impatient.
– **brusque·ly** *adv* – **brusque·ness** *noun* [*noncount*]

brus·sels sprout *or* **Brus·sels sprout** /ˈbrʌsəl-/ *noun, pl* **~ sprouts** [*count*] : a small, green vegetable that looks like a very small cabbage — see color picture on page C4

bru·tal /ˈbruːtl̩/ *adj* [*more ~; most ~*]
1 : extremely cruel or harsh ▪ a *brutal* military dictatorship ▪ a *brutal* attack/murder/assault ▪ *brutal* winter weather ▪ Sailors sometimes faced *brutal* punishments like whipping. ▪ a *brutal* struggle for survival in the wilderness
2 : very direct and accurate in a way that is harsh or unpleasant ▪ The writer describes the dangers of drugs with *brutal* honesty. ▪ The movie is a *brutal* depiction of the war.
3 *informal* : very bad or unpleasant ▪ The traffic was *brutal* on the way to work. ▪ I had a *brutal* headache this morning.
– **bru·tal·ly** *adv* ▪ He was *brutally* murdered. ▪ He was *brutally* honest/frank in his criticism of my work.

bru·tal·i·ty /bruˈtæləti/ *noun, pl* **-ties** : cruel, harsh, and usually violent treatment of another person [*noncount*] police *brutality* ▪ the *brutality* of slavery [*count*] the *brutalities* of a prison

bru·tal·ize *also Brit* **bru·tal·ise** /ˈbruːtl̩ˌaɪz/ *verb* **-iz·es; -ized; -iz·ing** [+ *obj*]
1 : to cause (someone) to lose ordinary human kindness or feelings ▪ a young man *brutalized* by the experience of war
2 : to treat (someone) in a very harsh and usually violent way ▪ She claimed she had been sexually *brutalized*.
– **bru·tal·i·za·tion** *also Brit* **brutalisation** /ˌbruːtl̩əˈzeɪʃən/ *noun* [*noncount*]

¹brute /ˈbruːt/ *noun, pl* **brutes** [*count*] : a cruel, rough, or violent man ▪ Let go of me, you *brute*! ✧ *Brute* originally meant the same as *beast* but is used now to refer to a person who is like a beast.

²brute *adj, always used before a noun*
1 : very strong or forceful ▪ They used *brute* force to open the door. ▪ *brute* strength
2 : very harsh ▪ the *brute* fact of getting old ▪ *brute* necessity

brut·ish /ˈbruːtɪʃ/ *adj* [*more ~; most ~*] : cruel, violent, and stupid : resembling or suggesting a beast ▪ She is married to a *brutish*, drunken slob. ▪ *brutish* behavior
– **brut·ish·ness** *noun* [*noncount*]

BS *abbr, US*
1 *or* **B.S.** bachelor of science ▪ She received a *B.S.* in chemistry from Smith College. ▪ a *B.S.* degree
2 *informal + impolite* bullshit ▪ a load of *BS*

BSc *abbr, Brit* bachelor of science

bub /ˈbʌb/ *noun, pl* **bubs** [*count*] *US, informal + old-fashioned* : BUDDY — usually used to address someone ▪ Come on *bub*, let's get going.

¹bub·ble /ˈbʌbəl/ *noun, pl* **bubbles** [*count*]
1 a : a tiny, round ball of air or gas inside a liquid ▪ They saw air *bubbles* in the water. ▪ champagne *bubbles* **b** : a small ball of air in a solid substance ▪ There were *bubbles* in the ice. **c** : a very light ball of air inside a thin layer of soap ▪ soap *bubbles* ▪ The children were ***blowing bubbles***. [=were making soap bubbles by blowing air through a thin layer of soap]
2 : a period when many people invest money in something and cause its value to rise to a level that is much higher than its real value until finally its value drops very suddenly ▪ a stock market *bubble* ▪ The Internet stock *bubble* finally burst.
burst someone's bubble *informal* : to cause someone to suddenly realize that something is not really good, true, etc. ▪ I'm sorry to *burst your bubble*, but the job is not really that exciting.

²bubble *verb* **bub·bles; bub·bled; bub·bling** [*no obj*]
1 : to form or produce bubbles ▪ Water *bubbled* [=*boiled*] in the pot. ▪ Oil *bubbled* (up) through the ground.
2 : to flow with the quiet sound of water moving over rocks ▪ a *bubbling* brook
3 : to be very happy and excited — usually + *with* ▪ The children were *bubbling with* excitement. — often + *over* ▪ He was *bubbling over with* enthusiasm for the project.
4 *of emotions, feelings, etc.* : to exist in a constant way without being openly shown ▪ He seemed calm, but I could feel the tension that was *bubbling* beneath the surface.

bubble and squeak *noun* [*noncount*] *Brit* : a meal of potatoes, cabbage, and sometimes meat mixed together and fried

bubble bath *noun, pl* **~ baths**
1 [*count*] : a bath in which bubbles are made by a special type of soap ▪ She took a *bubble bath*.
2 [*noncount*] : the soap that is used to make bubbles in a bath ▪ She bought some *bubble bath*.

bubble gum *noun* [*noncount*] : a type of gum that you chew and that can be blown into large bubbles

bubble–gum *adj, always used before a noun* : intended to appeal to young teenagers ▪ *bubble-gum* music

¹bub·bly /ˈbʌbli/ *adj* **bub·bli·er; -est**

1 : full of bubbles • a *bubbly* liquid
2 : very happy, cheerful, and lively • She is pretty, *bubbly*, and smart. • *bubbly* music

[2]**bubbly** *noun [noncount] informal* : CHAMPAGNE • a glass of *bubbly*

bu·bon·ic plague /bjuːˈbɑːnɪk-/ *noun [noncount]* : a very serious disease that is spread especially by rats and that killed many people in the Middle Ages — compare BLACK DEATH

buc·ca·neer /ˌbʌkəˈniɚ/ *noun, pl* **-neers** *[count]*
1 : [1]PIRATE 1
2 : a person who tries to become wealthy or powerful by doing things that are illegal or dishonest • corporate *buccaneers*

[1]**buck** /ˈbʌk/ *noun, pl* **bucks** *[count]*
1 *informal* **a** : DOLLAR • I owe you a *buck*. • Those toys are five *bucks* apiece. **b** : MONEY • That car costs ***big bucks***. [=a lot of money] • I am just working hard, trying to ***make a buck***. [=to make money] • a ***fast/quick buck*** [=money earned or gotten quickly]
2 : a male animal (such as a male deer) — compare DOE • He's an outdoorsman who enjoys *buck* hunting.
3 *informal* : MAN • a veteran tennis star competing against an ambitious young *buck*
bang for the/your buck see [2]BANG
look/feel like a million bucks see MILLION
pass the buck : to avoid a responsibility by giving it to someone else • Stop trying to *pass the buck* and take responsibility for what you've done. • The federal government *passed the buck* to the state governments.
the buck stops here ✧ Expressions like *the buck stops here* are used to say that you accept a responsibility and will not try to give it to someone else. • I'm willing to accept the blame for what happened. ***The buck stops with me.***

[2]**buck** *verb* **bucks; bucked; buck·ing**
1 *[no obj] of a horse* : to jump violently into the air with the back bent upward • a *bucking* horse/bronco — sometimes used figuratively • The plane *bucked* when we went through some dark clouds.
2 *[+ obj]* : to oppose or resist (something or someone) • He is reluctant to *buck* [=*go against, defy*] the leaders of his own political party. • The local decline in crime *bucked* a nationwide trend. [=crime declined locally but is increasing nationally] • He was always trying to ***buck the system***. [=to oppose the rules of the system; to do things that were not allowed]
buck for *[phrasal verb]* ***buck for (something)*** *US, informal* : to try very hard or work very hard to get (something) • He is *bucking for* a promotion at work.
buck up *[phrasal verb] informal* **1** : to become happier or more confident • *Buck up*, buddy. You'll feel better soon. **2 *buck (someone) up or buck up (someone)*** : to cause (someone) to be happier or more confident : to cheer up (someone) • The shows were meant to *buck up* the soldiers. • trying to *buck up* [=*improve*] the morale of the troops

[1]**buck·et** /ˈbʌkət/ *noun, pl* **-ets**
1 *[count]* **a** : an open container with a handle that is used especially to hold and carry water and other liquids • a *bucket* and mop **b** : the amount contained in a bucket • a *bucket* [=*bucketful*] of water • We used two *buckets* of paint to paint the living room.
2 *[count]* : a large container that is part of a machine (such as a tractor) and that is used for digging or carrying dirt, rocks, and other material
3 ***buckets*** *[plural] informal* : a large amount especially of a liquid • The players were sweating *buckets*. [=were sweating very much] • crying *buckets* of tears • It's raining *buckets*. = The rain is coming down ***in buckets***. [=it's raining very hard]
4 *[count] basketball* : a successful shot : BASKET • She scored/sank five *buckets* in the last five minutes of the game.
a drop in the bucket see [1]DROP
kick the bucket see [1]KICK
– buck·et·ful /ˈbʌkətˌfʊl/ *noun, pl* **buck·et·fuls** /ˈbʌkətˌfʊlz/ *also* **buck·ets·ful** /ˈbʌkətsˌfʊl/ *[count]* • a *bucketful* [=*bucket*] of nails • She has *bucketfuls* [=*buckets*] of money.

bucket

[2]**bucket** *verb* **-ets; -et·ed; -et·ing**
bucket down *[phrasal verb] Brit, informal* : to rain very heavily • The rain is really *bucketing down*. = It's *bucketing down*. [=it's pouring]

bucket seat *noun, pl* ~ **seats** *[count]* : a low, separate seat for one person in a car or other vehicle

bucket shop *noun, pl* ~ **shops** *[count] Brit, informal* : a company that sells cheap airplane tickets

[1]**buck·le** /ˈbʌkəl/ *noun, pl* **buck·les** *[count]* : a metal or plastic device that is attached to one end of a belt or strap and that is used to connect it to the other end • a belt *buckle* — see picture at SHOE

buckle

[2]**buckle** *verb* **buckles; buck·led; buck·ling**
1 *[+ obj]* **a** : to fasten (something, such as a belt) with a buckle • *Buckle* your seat belt. **b** : to attach (something) with a buckle • She *buckled* the horses into their harness.
2 **a** *[no obj]* : to bend or collapse from pressure, heat, etc. • The pavement *buckled* in the heat. • I suddenly felt dizzy and my knees/legs *buckled*. [=my knees bent and I began to fall down] — often used figuratively • He finally *buckled* under the pressure/strain of his job. **b** *[+ obj]* : to cause (something) to bend or collapse • Heat *buckled* the pavement.
buckle down *[phrasal verb] informal* : to start to work hard • You had better *buckle down* if you want to get good grades.
buckle up *[phrasal verb] US* : to fasten your seat belt in a car or other vehicle • You should always *buckle up* [=*(Brit) belt up*] before you start driving.

buck naked *adj, informal* : completely naked : not wearing any clothes • He was standing in front of the window, *buck naked*.

buck private *noun, pl* ~ **-vates** *[count] US, informal* : a private in the U.S. Army or Marines — used to stress that a private has the lowest rank in the military • He enlisted as a *buck private* and rose through the ranks to become a general.

buck·shot /ˈbʌkˌʃɑːt/ *noun [noncount]* : small lead balls that are fired by a shotgun — called also *shot*

buck·skin /ˈbʌkˌskɪn/ *noun [noncount]* : a soft type of leather that is made especially from the skin of a deer or similar animal — often used before another noun • a *buckskin* jacket

buck teeth *noun [plural]* : upper teeth that stick out in the front of the mouth • She wore braces to fix her *buck teeth*.
– buck–toothed /ˈbʌkˌtuːθt/ *adj*

buck·wheat /ˈbʌkˌwiːt/ *noun [noncount]* : a plant with dark seeds that are used to make grain and flour; *also* : grain or flour made from the seeds of the buckwheat plant

bu·col·ic /bjuˈkɑːlɪk/ *adj, literary + formal* : of or relating to the country or country life : PASTORAL • a charming *bucolic* farmhouse • the *bucolic* English countryside

[1]**bud** /ˈbʌd/ *noun, pl* **buds** *[count]*
1 : a small part that grows on a plant and develops into a flower, leaf, or new branch • The bush has plenty of *buds* but no flowers yet. • flower *buds* ✧ If a plant is ***in bud*** it is beginning to grow buds. • The trees are *in bud* [=*budding*] now. — see color picture on page C6
2 *US, informal* : [1]BUDDY • Hey, *bud* [=*pal*], how's it going?
nip (something) in the bud see [1]NIP
— see also COTTON BUD, TASTE BUD

[2]**bud** *verb* **buds; bud·ded; bud·ding** *[no obj]* : to produce buds • The trees *budded* early this spring.

Bud·dhism /ˈbuːˌdɪzəm, ˈbʊˌdɪzəm/ *noun [noncount]* : a religion of eastern and central Asia that is based on the teachings of Gautama Buddha
– Bud·dhist /ˈbuːdɪst, ˈbʊdɪst/ *noun, pl* **-dhists** *[count]* • She and her husband are *Buddhists*. **– Buddhist** *adj* • *Buddhist* monks • a *Buddhist* temple

bud·ding /ˈbʌdɪŋ/ *adj*
1 : beginning to develop • the couples' *budding* romance • her *budding* career as a lawyer
2 *always used before a noun* : beginning to become successful • a *budding* singer/actor/writer

[1]**bud·dy** /ˈbʌdi/ *noun, pl* **-dies**
1 *[count] informal* : a close friend — used especially to describe men or boys who are friends • We've been *buddies* [=*pals, (chiefly Brit) mates*] since junior high school. • He's one of my old army *buddies*. • a *buddy* from college = a college *buddy*
2 *[singular] US, informal + sometimes impolite* — used to address a man who you do not know • Hey, *buddy*, do you know where Maple Street is?
3 *[count]* : a person who does some activity with you • His

B

fishing *buddy* just bought a new boat. • her drinking *buddies* [=the people who often drink alcohol with her]

the buddy system *US* : an arrangement in which two people help or protect each other • If your children walk to school, have them use the *buddy system*. [=have them walk with other children]

[2]**buddy** *verb* **buddies; bud·died; bud·dy·ing**

buddy up [*phrasal verb*] *US, informal* : to become friendly especially in order to get help or some advantage — often + *with* • New students are encouraged to *buddy up with* older students. — often + *to* • businessmen *buddying up to* [=*cozying up to*] politicians to get their support

[3]**buddy** *adj, always used before a noun, informal* : telling a story about a friendship between two usually male characters • a *buddy* movie/comedy

bud·dy–bud·dy /ˌbʌdiˈbʌdi/ *adj* [*more* ~; *most* ~] *US, informal* : very friendly or too friendly • She's been *buddy-buddy* [=*chummy*] with the band for several years. • He's a little too *buddy-buddy* with his professors.

budge /ˈbʌʤ/ *verb* **budg·es; budged; budg·ing**

1 : to move slightly — usually used in negative statements [*no obj*] Their horses refused to *budge*. • The door was stuck, and we couldn't even get it to *budge*. [+ *obj*] Could you try opening this jar for me? I can't *budge* the lid.

2 : to change your opinion or decision — usually used in negative statements [*no obj*] They wouldn't *budge* on the issue. = They refused to *budge*. • He wouldn't *budge* at all. = He wouldn't ***budge an inch***. [+ *obj*] We tried to change her mind, but we couldn't *budge* her.

bud·ger·i·gar /ˈbʌʤəriˌgɑɚ/ *noun, pl* **-gars** [*count*] : a small, usually light green and yellow bird that is often kept as a pet — called also *budgie*

[1]**bud·get** /ˈbʌʤət/ *noun, pl* **bud·gets**

1 a : an amount of money available for spending that is based on a plan for how it will be spent [*count*] What's the average weekly/monthly/annual *budget* for a family of five? • The film has a million-dollar *budget*. • He's been trying to live on a *budget* of less than $1,500 a month. • a movie with a big *budget* = a ***big-budget*** movie [=a movie that costs a lot of money to make] • a movie with a low/small *budget* = a ***low-budget*** movie [=a movie that does not cost a lot of money to make] [*noncount*] The project was completed on schedule and ***under budget***. [=it was completed for less money than had been planned] • We're still ***within budget***. [=we still are not spending more money than we planned to spend] • The director always goes ***over budget*** on his films. [=the director always spends more money than is planned] — often used before another noun • The governor will discuss the state's *budget* deficit/surplus. • a *budget* crisis • *budget* cuts **b** [*count*] : a plan used to decide the amount of money that can be spent and how it will be spent • We'll have to work out a *budget* so we can buy a new car. • The government may have to raise taxes to ***balance the budget***. [=to have enough money to provide the amount that is being spent] ✧ If you are ***on a budget***, you have planned how you will spend your money usually because you do not have a lot to spend and need to save money. • The store has great bargains for people *on a budget*. [=people who do not have much money to spend] • She started her business ***on a small/tight/shoestring budget*** [=she did not have much money when she started her business] and could not afford to overspend.

2 [*count*] : an official statement from a government about how much it plans to spend during a particular period of time and how it will pay for the expenses

– **bud·get·ary** /ˈbʌʤəˌteri, *Brit* ˈbʌʤətri/ *adj, formal* • *budgetary* plans/matters/issues/constraints/cuts

[2]**budget** *verb* **-gets; -get·ed; -get·ing**

1 [+ *obj*] : to plan to spend (an amount of money) for a particular purpose • They *budgeted* millions of dollars to make the film. • The project is *budgeted* at more than $100,000. • He *budgets* $50 for entertainment each month.

2 [*no obj*] : to make and follow a plan for spending your money • If we *budget* carefully, we will be able to go on the trip. • We're *budgeting* [=saving our money] for a new car.

3 [+ *obj*] : to plan how to use (something, such as your time) • I need to learn how to *budget* my time more wisely.

– **budgeting** *noun* [*noncount*] • Careful *budgeting* is essential to running a business.

[3]**budget** *adj, always used before a noun* : low in price : suitable for someone who is on a budget • *budget* hotels

bud·gie /ˈbʌʤi/ *noun, pl* **-gies** [*count*] *informal* : BUDGERIGAR

[1]**buff** /ˈbʌf/ *noun, pl* **buffs** [*count*] : a person who is very interested in something and who knows a lot about it • She's a tennis *buff*. [=*fan, enthusiast*] • history/movie/music *buffs* — compare [2]BUFF

[2]**buff** *noun* [*noncount*] : a light somewhat yellow or orange color — see color picture on page C2

in the buff *informal* : not wearing any clothes : NAKED • They sunbathe *in the buff*. [=*in the nude*]

to the buff *informal* : to a naked condition • They stripped down *to the buff*. [=they took all their clothes off]

– compare [1]BUFF

[3]**buff** *or* **buffed** /ˈbʌft/ *adj* [*more* ~; *most* ~] *US, informal* : having a strong, muscular body or form • a *buff* bodybuilder • He's at the gym every day trying to get *buff*. • the *buff* body of an athlete

[4]**buff** *verb* **buffs; buffed; buff·ing** [+ *obj*] : to make (a surface) smooth and shiny by rubbing it • The floors are waxed and *buffed* every year. • I *buffed* [=*shined*] my shoes. • She is going to the salon to get her nails *buffed*.

buff up [*phrasal verb*] ***buff up or buff (someone or something) up or buff up (someone or something)*** *informal* : to become stronger and more muscular or to make (someone or something) stronger and more muscular by exercising and weight lifting • She is *buffing up* for her role as a female boxer. • He *buffed* himself *up* by going to the gym every day. — often used as *buffed-up* • *buffed-up* bodies • a *buffed-up* actor/athlete

buf·fa·lo /ˈbʌfəˌloʊ/ *noun, pl* **buffalo** *or* **buf·fa·loes** [*count*]

1 *US* : BISON

2 : WATER BUFFALO

buffalo wing *noun, pl* ~ **wings** [*count*] *US* : a chicken wing that is fried and covered with a spicy sauce and that is usually served with blue cheese dressing ✧ Buffalo wings are named after the city of Buffalo, New York.

[1]**buff·er** /ˈbʌfɚ/ *noun, pl* **-ers** [*count*]

1 : something that gives protection by separating things : a protective barrier • Thick walls serve as a *buffer* from/against the sounds of the city. — often used figuratively • She had to act as a *buffer* between the two brothers, who wouldn't stop arguing. • It's important to save money as a *buffer* against times of illness or the loss of your job. — see also BUFFER STATE, BUFFER ZONE

2 *computers* : a place in the memory of a computer where information is stored for a short time

3 *chiefly Brit* : either one of two devices with metal springs that are connected to the front and back of railroad cars in order to reduce shock when the train hits things

hit the buffers or run into the buffers *Brit, informal* : to stop or fail • His acting career *hit the buffers*. • The project *ran into the buffers*.

– compare [3]BUFFER

[2]**buffer** *verb* **-ers; -ered; -er·ing** [+ *obj*]

1 : to protect (something) *from* something • The trees help *buffer* the house *from* the hot summer sun.

2 : to lessen the harmful effects of (something) • The wall *buffers* the noise of the traffic.

3 *computers* : to put (something, such as data) in a buffer

[3]**buffer** *noun, pl* **-ers** [*count*] *Brit, informal* : an old man • He's a harmless old *buffer*. — compare [1]BUFFER

buffer state *noun, pl* ~ **states** [*count*] : a country that is located between two larger countries that often fight with each other

buffer zone *noun, pl* ~ **zones** [*count*] : an area that keeps two things separated • There must be a 500-foot *buffer zone* between the river and the new buildings.

[1]**buf·fet** /bəˈfeɪ, *Brit* ˈbʊˌfeɪ/ *noun, pl* **-fets** [*count*]

1 : a meal for which different foods are placed on a table so that people can serve themselves • The restaurant offers a breakfast *buffet*. • There will be a cold *buffet* [=a meal of different cold foods set on a table] at the party. — often used before another noun • He went back to the *buffet* table for a second helping. • a *buffet* meal/lunch/dinner

2 *chiefly Brit* : a place in a train, a bus station, etc., where people can buy food and drinks — see also BUFFET CAR

3 *chiefly US* : a piece of furniture that is used in a dining room for holding dishes, silverware, etc. : SIDEBOARD

[2]**buffet** *verb* **-fets; -fet·ed; -fet·ing** [+ *obj*] : to hit (something) with great force many times • The waves *buffeted* [=*battered*] the shore. • The strong winds *buffeted* the ship. — often used as *(be) buffeted* • The island *was buffeted* by a tropical storm

last month. — often used figuratively • The city's schools are *being buffeted* by budget cuts.

buffet car *noun, pl* ~ **cars** [*count*] *Brit* : DINING CAR

buf•foon /bə'fu:n/ *noun, pl* **-foons** [*count*] : a stupid or foolish person who tries to be funny • Stop acting like a *buffoon*. • a ridiculous *buffoon*

– buf•foon•ery /bə'fu:nəri/ *noun* [*noncount*] • silly *buffoonery* [=foolish behavior that is meant to be funny]

¹bug /'bʌg/ *noun, pl* **bugs**

1 [*count*] *chiefly US, informal* : a usually small insect • There's a *bug* in my soup! • Close the door. You're letting the *bugs* in. — often used before another noun • Her legs were covered in *bug* bites. [=itchy or painful wounds from insects] • Use plenty of *bug* spray/repellent to keep the mosquitoes from biting you.

2 [*count*] : a usually mild illness (such as a cold) that can be passed from one person to another • He caught some kind of *bug* from the other kids at school. • There's been a nasty flu *bug* going around. • I picked up an intestinal/stomach *bug*.

3 [*count*] : a problem that prevents a computer program or system from working properly • We found/detected a *bug* [=*glitch*] in the program. • The software was full of *bugs*. • They've been trying to work/get the *bugs* out of the system. [=trying to fix the system's problems]

4 [*count*] : a small hidden microphone that is used to secretly listen to and record people : LISTENING DEVICE • The government planted/put a *bug* in her telephone/apartment.

5 ***the bug informal*** : a sudden, strong interest in a particular activity • He was first bitten by *the* acting *bug* [=he first became interested in acting] when he was 18. • *the* travel *bug*

²bug *verb* **bugs; bugged; bug•ging**

1 [+ *obj*] *informal* : to bother or annoy (someone) • Quit *bugging* me! • John, stop *bugging* your sister. • It really *bugs* me to see how he treats her.

2 [+ *obj*] : to put a hidden microphone in (a room, telephone, etc.) in order to secretly hear what people are saying • Is this phone *bugged*? • The cops *bugged* his apartment. • a *bugging* device

3 [*no obj*] *of the eyes* : to stick out more than is normal especially because of surprise or fear — usually + *out* • Their eyes were *bugging out* as if they saw a ghost. — see also BUG-EYED

bug off [*phrasal verb*] *US, informal* : to go away — used in speech as a rude or angry way to tell someone to leave you alone and to stop bothering you • She angrily told him to *bug off*.

bug out [*phrasal verb*] *US, informal* : to leave quickly • Wait here till we get back. Don't *bug out* (on us). — see also ²BUG 3 (above)

bug•a•boo /'bʌgəˌbu:/ *noun, pl* **-boos** [*count*] *US, often disapproving* : something that makes people very worried or upset • politicians complaining about that old *bugaboo*, high oil prices

bug•bear /'bʌgˌbeə/ *noun, pl* **-bears** [*count*] : something that causes problems or annoys people • The biggest *bugbear* of the skiing business is a winter with no snow.

bug–eyed /'bʌgˌaɪd/ *adj* : having eyes that stick far out of the head • The audience was *bug-eyed* with amazement.

¹bug•ger /'bʌgə/ *noun, pl* **-gers** [*count*] *informal*

1 : an annoying or difficult but usually small thing • I put down my keys, and now I can't find the *buggers*. • (*Brit*) The exam was a *bugger*. [=the exam was difficult]

2 *chiefly Brit* **a** *offensive* : a person (especially a man) who is strongly disliked • I can't stand that stupid *bugger*. **b** : an annoying or playful person or animal ✧ In this sense, *bugger* is an impolite word that is often used in a loving or friendly way. • Well, you're a cute little *bugger* [=*rascal*, *critter*, *guy*], aren't you! • You cheeky *bugger*!

²bugger *verb* **-gers; -gered; -ger•ing** [+ *obj*] *Brit*

1 *offensive* : to have anal sex with (someone)

2 *informal + impolite* — used as an interjection to express strong anger, surprise, etc. • *Bugger* [=*damn*] this machine! • *Bugger* it/me! • Well, I'll be *buggered*. [=*damned*] I can't believe you did it!

bugger about or bugger around [*phrasal verb*] *Brit, informal + impolite* **1** : to spend time in a useless or aimless way • We just *buggered about* [=*messed around*] all afternoon. **2** ***bugger (someone) about/around*** : to cause problems or trouble for (someone) • I don't like being *buggered about* by faceless bureaucrats with all their forms.

bugger off [*phrasal verb*] *Brit, informal + impolite* : to go away • She angrily told him to *bugger off*.

bugger up [*phrasal verb*] ***bugger up (something) or bugger (something) up*** *Brit, informal + impolite* : to make mistakes in doing or making (something) • The waiter *buggered up* [=*messed up*] our order.

bugger all *noun* [*noncount*] *Brit, informal + impolite* : nothing at all • They were wearing *bugger all*!

bug•gery /'bʌgəri/ *noun* [*noncount*] *Brit, law or slang* : anal sex : SODOMY

¹bug•gy /'bʌgi/ *noun, pl* **-gies** [*count*] : a light carriage that is usually pulled by one horse • He rode into town on his horse and *buggy*. — see also BABY BUGGY, BEACH BUGGY, DUNE BUGGY

²buggy *adj* **bug•gi•er; -est**

1 *US* : having many insects • It's too *buggy* out here—let's go inside. • a *buggy* swamp

2 *chiefly US, of a computer program, system, etc.* : having many problems or errors that prevent proper operation : having many bugs • *buggy* software • a *buggy* system

bu•gle /'bju:gəl/ *noun, pl* **bu•gles** [*count*] : a musical instrument like a trumpet that is used especially for giving military signals • blow a *bugle*

– bu•gler /'bju:glə/ *noun, pl* **-glers** [*count*] • He was a *bugler* in the army.

¹build /'bɪld/ *verb* **builds; built** /'bɪlt/; **build•ing**

1 : to make (something) by putting together parts or materials [+ *obj*] The house is *built* (out) of brick/logs. • The bridge was *built* in the 1890s. • The planes were *built* in Germany. • The organization helps *build* houses for poor families. • *building* more powerful machines/computers/weapons • A family of birds has *built* a nest on our roof. • She started *building* a fire in the fireplace. • He *built* a model airplane from a kit. • He *built* a dollhouse for the children. = He *built* the children a dollhouse. [*no obj*] You will need permission to *build* on your property.

2 [+ *obj*] : to develop or form (something) gradually • I've started *building* a collection of rare books. [=I've started collecting rare books] • They *built* the organization from scratch. = They *built* the organization from the ground/bottom up. • They are *building* a legal case against the tobacco industry. • scientists *building* theories about how the universe began • At college, you'll *build* friendships that will last a lifetime. • She *built* a successful career in advertising. • He has *built* a reputation as a talented artist. • *building* a more peaceful world [=making the world more peaceful] — often + *up* • *Building up* a successful business can take many years. • She has *built up* a large collection of awards. • We've been *building up* a savings account. — see also BUILD UP (below)

3 [+ *obj*] : to increase the amount of (something) • Lifting weights helps *build* muscle and increase strength. • These programs are designed to help *build* confidence in young women. • The advertisements are aimed at *building* support for political candidates. • They thought the army would *build* character in their son. [=would make their son become a better person] — often + *up* • She runs a little farther every day to *build up* (her) endurance. • *building up* momentum/stamina/energy • He's been trying to *build up* the courage/confidence to talk to her. • These exercises will help you *build up* your strength. — see also BUILD UP (below)

4 [*no obj*] : to grow or increase to a high point, level, number, etc. • The excitement was beginning to *build* before the game. • A crowd was *building* around the accident. • The story slowly *builds* to a climax. [=the story slowly reaches a climax] • Chemicals in the lake are *building* to dangerous levels. — often + *up* • As the water temperature rises, the pressure inside the pot begins to *build up*. • Their passion/anger/fear/hatred has been *building up* for years. — see also BUILD UP (below)

build around [*phrasal verb*] ***build (something) around (something)*** : to develop or organize (something) by using (something, such as an idea) as its main or central part • We *built* our program *around* the idea that people need love and support. • Their lives are *built around* their children. [=their children are the most important things in their lives] • The textbook *builds* lessons *around* grammar topics.

build in/into [*phrasal verb*] ***build in (something) or build (something) in or build (something) in/into (something)*** : to make (something) a part of (something else) • Carmakers are beginning to *build in* these new safety features as standard equipment. = Carmakers are *building* these new safety features *into* new cars as standard equipment. • We've *built* bookshelves *into* the wall. • These ideas are *built into*

B

the program/system/design. • There are special provisions for bonuses *built into* the contract. — see also BUILT-IN

build on/upon [*phrasal verb*] **1** ***build on/upon (something)*** : to use (something that has been done in the past) as a basis for further work, development, etc. • Each president *builds on/upon* the success of each past president. • These classes will help students *build on* what they already know. • *building upon* past experiences/successes **2** ***build (something) on/upon (something)*** : to develop or create (something) by using (something else) as its basis • He *built* [=*based*] his theory *on* recent studies. • She has *built* her reputation as a talented artist *on* the strength of her earlier paintings. • Their theory is *built upon* her research.

build onto [*phrasal verb*] ***build onto (something) or build (something) onto (something)*** : to add (a new room) to a structure that already exists • They *built* a new garage *onto* their house. • They *built onto* their house.

build up [*phrasal verb*] **1** : to increase gradually in amount as time passes : ACCUMULATE • They pick up the garbage that *builds up* [=*collects*] along the highway. • Dust has begun *building up* on his piano. • These dangerous chemicals are *building up* in our lakes and ponds. **2** ***build (something or someone) up or build up (something or someone)*** : to say many good things about (something or someone) • Political candidates are trying to *build* themselves *up* [=promote themselves] with public speeches and TV commercials. • The movie was *built up* so much [=we heard so many good things about the movie] that we were disappointed when we actually saw it. — see also [1]BUILD 2, 3, 4 (above), BUILDUP

[2]build *noun, pl* **builds** : the shape and size of a person's body [*count*] people with thin/slender/slight *builds* • He has a strong, muscular *build*. [=*physique*] [*noncount*] He is strong and muscular in *build*. • a man of average *build*

build·er /ˈbɪldɚ/ *noun, pl* **-ers** [*count*]

1 : a person or company that builds or repairs things (such as houses, ships, bridges, etc.) • The architect discussed her plans with the *builder* and the contractor. • We will have to get the *builders* to repair the wall. — see also SHIPBUILDER

2 : something that helps to develop or increase something • The army is said to be a character *builder*. • The experience was a real confidence *builder*.

build·ing /ˈbɪldɪŋ/ *noun, pl* **-ings**

1 [*count*] : a structure (such as a house, hospital, school, etc.) with a roof and walls that is used as a place for people to live, work, do activities, store things, etc. • My office is in that small brick *building*. • office/apartment *buildings* [=buildings with offices/apartments inside]

2 [*noncount*] : the act or process of making structures by putting together materials • We bought the land for *building*. — often + *of* • He planned the *building* [=*construction*] *of* the town's roads and bridges. • The *building of* the bridge took 10 years. — often used before another noun • *building* materials/supplies • a *building* contractor [=someone whose business is building structures] • the *building* site

building block *noun, pl* **~ blocks** [*count*] : an important part that is grouped together with many other similar things to form something larger — usually plural; usually + *of* • Families are the *building blocks of* our society. • Cells are the *building blocks* of the body.

building society *noun, pl* **~ -ties** [*count*] : a British business that is like a bank, that holds and invests the money saved by its members, and that provides loans and mortgages — compare SAVINGS AND LOAN ASSOCIATION

build·up /ˈbɪldˌʌp/ *noun, pl* **-ups**

1 : an increase in something that occurs as time passes [*count*] the country's military *buildup* [=an increase in the size of its military] • There is a big traffic *buildup* on the highway. — often + *of* • He had a *buildup of* fluid in the lungs. • a *buildup of* tension/pressure/stress [*noncount*] You should clean the mechanism regularly to prevent *buildup* of dirt.

2 : things that are said to cause people to feel excited about something (such as a future event) or someone (such as a performer) [*noncount*] After all the *buildup* [=*hype, publicity*], I expected the movie to be better than it actually was. [*count*] Both players were given big *buildups* before the game.

3 [*noncount*] : a series of things that lead to an important event or occurrence — + *to* • There have been many news stories during the *buildup to* the peace talks. • The story/movie/song has a great *buildup to* a terrific ending.

[1]built *past tense and past participle of* [1]BUILD

[2]built /ˈbɪlt/ *adj*

1 *not used before a noun* — used to say that someone or something has the right qualities *for* or *to do* something • He was *built for* fighting. • This horse is *built for* speed. • These chairs were *built for* comfort. • These tools are *built to last*. [=these tools will last a long time]

2 : made, formed, or shaped in a specified way • a powerfully *built* wrestler • a newly *built* house — often used in combination • a brick-*built* house [=a house built of bricks] • a Japanese-*built* car [=a car made in Japan] — see also CUSTOM-BUILT, JERRY-BUILT

built-in /ˈbɪltˈɪn/ *adj, always used before a noun*

1 : included as a part of something • His new watch has a *built-in* calculator. • a camera with a *built-in* flash • the car's *built-in* safety features • a *built-in* bookshelf [=a bookshelf that is built as part of a wall]

2 : forming a natural part of someone or something • All humans have a *built-in* ability to learn their native language. • Living in warmer climates has many *built-in* [=(more formally) *intrinsic, inherent*] advantages. — see also *build in/into* at [1]BUILD

built-up /ˈbɪltˈʌp/ *adj* [*more ~; most ~*] : having many buildings in a small area • Many people left the more heavily *built-up* areas of the city and moved to the suburbs.

bulb /ˈbʌlb/ *noun, pl* **bulbs** [*count*]

1 : LIGHT BULB • a 100-watt *bulb* • fluorescent *bulbs* — see also DIM BULB

2 : a rounded part of some plants that is under the ground and that grows into a new plant during the growing season • tulip *bulbs* — see color picture on page C6

3 : a part that has a rounded shape • the *bulb* of the thermometer/eyedropper

bul·bous /ˈbʌlbəs/ *adj* [*more ~; most ~*] : big and round often in an unattractive way • a big, *bulbous* nose

Bul·gar·i·an /ˌbʌlˈgerijən/ *noun, pl* **-ans**

1 [*count*] : a person born or living in Bulgaria

2 [*noncount*] : the chief language of the people of Bulgaria

– Bulgarian *adj* • She speaks with a *Bulgarian* accent.

[1]bulge /ˈbʌlʤ/ *noun, pl* **bulg·es** [*count*]

1 : a rounded lump on the surface of something • "What's in there?" he asked, pointing to the large *bulge* in my purse. • I'm exercising to get rid of this *bulge* around my middle.

2 : a sudden increase • a population *bulge*

[2]bulge *verb* **bulges; bulged; bulg·ing** [*no obj*]

1 : to stick out in a rounded lump • His face turned white and his eyes *bulged*. • middle-aged people *bulging* at the waist/middle — often + *out* • Her eyes *bulged out* (of her head).

2 : to be completely filled *with* something • Their bags *bulged with* books and papers. • The squirrel's cheeks were *bulging with* nuts. • a notebook *bulging with* ideas

– bulging *adj* • *bulging* biceps/muscles • big *bulging* eyes

bu·lim·ia /buˈliːmijə, *Brit* bjuˈlɪmiə/ *noun* [*noncount*] : a serious physical and emotional illness in which people and especially young women eat large amounts of food and then cause themselves to vomit in order to not gain weight — called also *bulimia nervosa*; compare ANOREXIA

– bu·lim·ic /buˈliːmɪk, *Brit* bjuˈlɪmɪk/ *adj* • She became *bulimic* in high school. **– bulimic** *noun, pl* **-ics** [*count*] • She's been a *bulimic* since high school.

[1]bulk /ˈbʌlk/ *noun*

1 ***the bulk*** : most of something : the largest part of something • We spent *the bulk* of the summer at the beach. • Farming makes up *the bulk* of the country's economy. • *The* great *bulk* of these people are extremely poor.

2 [*noncount*] : the large size of someone or something • Despite his *bulk*, he's a very fast runner. • The sheer weight and *bulk* of the car makes it safe to drive. [=the car is safe because it is heavy and large]

in bulk : in large containers or in large amounts • The restaurant buys rice and flour *in bulk*. [=it buys large bags of rice and flour]

[2]bulk *adj, always used before a noun* : of or relating to things that are sent or sold in large amounts • *bulk* foods • They sent *bulk* shipments of food to the country. • *bulk* prices/rates • *bulk* mailings/e-mail

[3]bulk *verb* **bulks; bulked; bulk·ing**

bulk large : to have great importance or influence • This is a problem that *bulks large* [=*looms large*] in the minds of many people.

bulk out [*phrasal verb*] ***bulk out (something) or bulk (something) out*** : to make (something) bigger or thicker by adding more material • He *bulked out* the report with lots of graphs and charts.

bulk up [*phrasal verb*] **1 :** to gain weight often by becoming more muscular • He's *bulked up* to 200 pounds. • She's been trying to *bulk up* at the gym. **2 a *bulk (someone) up* :** to cause (someone) to gain weight • They tried to *bulk* him *up* with pizza and hamburgers. **b *bulk up (something)*** *or* ***bulk (something) up* :** to make (something) bigger or thicker by adding more material • He *bulked up* the report with lots of graphs and charts.

bulk·head /ˈbʌlkˌhɛd/ *noun, pl* **-heads** [*count*] **:** a wall that separates the different parts of a ship or aircraft

bulky /ˈbʌlki/ *adj* **bulk·i·er; -est** [*also more ~; most ~*]
1 : large and difficult to carry or store • a *bulky* wool sweater • a big, *bulky* package
2 *of a person* **:** large and fat or muscular • a big, *bulky* football player
– bulk·i·ness *noun* [*noncount*]

[1]**bull** /ˈbʊl/ *noun, pl* **bulls** [*count*]
1 a : an adult male animal of the ox and cow family **b :** an adult male of some other large animals (such as elephants or whales) — often used before another noun • a *bull* elephant • a *bull* moose — compare CALF, COW; see also PIT BULL
2 *finance* **:** a person who tries to make money by buying stocks and selling them after their price has gone up : a person who expects the price of stocks to go up • The bears outnumbered the *bulls* on Wall Street today. — compare [1]BEAR; see also BULL MARKET
***a bull in a china shop* :** a person who breaks things or who often makes mistakes or causes damage in situations that require careful thinking or behavior • As a politician, he was *a bull in a china shop* and often had to apologize for his rough speech.
a red rag to a bull see [1]RED
***take the bull by the horns* :** to deal with a difficult situation in a very direct or confident way • She decided to *take the bull by the horns* and try to solve the problem without any further delay.
– compare [2]BULL, [3]BULL

[2]**bull** *noun* [*noncount*] *informal* **:** foolish or untrue words or ideas • That's a lot/load/bunch of *bull*! [=*nonsense*, (*offensive*) *bullshit*] — see also COCK-AND-BULL STORY; compare [1]BULL, [3]BULL

[3]**bull** *noun, pl* **bulls** [*count*] **:** an official command or statement written by the pope • A ***papal bull*** was issued in 1582. — compare [1]BULL, [2]BULL

bull·dog /ˈbʊlˌdɑːg/ *noun, pl* **-dogs** [*count*] **:** a short, strong, muscular dog with short hair, short legs, and a wide square head

bull·doze /ˈbʊlˌdouz/ *verb* **-doz·es; -dozed; -doz·ing** [+ *obj*]
1 a : to use a bulldozer to move, destroy, or knock down (something) • The crew is *bulldozing* the trees/forest/field. • Their houses were *bulldozed* (flat) to make room for a new school. **b :** to create (something, such as a road) by using a bulldozer • They *bulldozed* a road through the hills.
2 a : to force (something that others might not want to happen) to be done or accepted in an aggressive or harsh way • The governor *bulldozed* the law through the legislature. **b :** to force (someone) to do something • She *bulldozed* [=*bullied*] her partners into accepting the agreement even though they didn't like it.
***bulldoze your way* :** to move forward while forcing other people to move out of your way • They rudely *bulldozed their way* through the crowd. — often used figuratively • He *bulldozed his way* to the top and became the company's president.

bull·doz·er /ˈbʊlˌdouzɚ/ *noun, pl* **-ers** [*count*] **:** a powerful and heavy vehicle that has a large curved piece of metal at its front and that is used for moving dirt and rocks and pushing over trees and other structures — see picture at CONSTRUCTION

bul·let /ˈbʊlət/ *noun, pl* **-lets** [*count*]
1 : a small piece of metal or another material that is shot out of a gun • He was hit by a stray *bullet*. [=the bullet missed its target and hit him instead] • He was killed by an assassin's *bullet*. • He took a *bullet* to the head. [=he was shot in the head] — often used before another noun • There are *bullet* holes in the walls. • a *bullet* wound — see also MAGIC BULLET, RUBBER BULLET, SILVER BULLET
2 : a large dot in a document, book, etc., that brings attention to separate pieces of information in a list • *Bullets* were used to separate each item. — see also BULLET POINT
3 *US, sports* **:** a hit or thrown ball or puck that is moving very fast • The quarterback threw a *bullet* to the receiver.
bite the bullet see [1]BITE
dodge a/the bullet see [1]DODGE
sweat bullets see [1]SWEAT
– bul·let·ed /ˈbʊlətəd/ *adj* • a *bulleted* list

bul·le·tin /ˈbʊlətən/ *noun, pl* **-tins** [*count*]
1 : a quick announcement from an official source about an important piece of news • The television/radio program was interrupted for a news *bulletin*. • We've just received a (news) *bulletin*: the election has been decided!
2 : a short piece of writing that an organization publishes to give news about itself **:** NEWSLETTER • a church *bulletin*

bulletin board *noun, pl* **~ boards** [*count*]
1 *US* **:** a board on the wall of a classroom, office, etc., where things (such as written notices or pictures) are put so that they can be seen by many people • Our teacher put our pictures up on the *bulletin board*. — called also (*Brit*) *noticeboard*; see picture at OFFICE
2 : MESSAGE BOARD

bullet point *noun, pl* **~ points** [*count*] **:** an item in a list that has a large dot (called a bullet) in front of it to show that it is important

bul·let·proof /ˈbʊlətˌpruːf/ *adj* **:** made to stop bullets from going through • The car has *bulletproof* windows. • The police officer was wearing a *bulletproof* vest.

bull·fight /ˈbʊlˌfaɪt/ *noun, pl* **-fights** [*count*] **:** an event that is popular especially in Spain in which a person fights with and usually kills a bull for public entertainment
– bull·fight·er /ˈbʊlˌfaɪtɚ/ *noun, pl* **-ers** [*count*] **– bull·fight·ing** /ˈbʊlˌfaɪtɪŋ/ *noun* [*noncount*]

bull·finch /ˈbʊlˌfɪntʃ/ *noun, pl* **-finches** [*count*] **:** a small European bird

bull·frog /ˈbʊlˌfrɑːg/ *noun, pl* **-frogs** [*count*] **:** a large frog that makes a loud, deep sound

bull·head·ed /ˈbʊlˈhɛdəd/ *adj* [*more ~; most ~*] *chiefly US, disapproving* **:** not willing to change an opinion, plan, etc. : very stubborn in a foolish or annoying way • a *bullheaded* boss who won't take advice from anyone

bullhorn

bull·horn /ˈbʊlˌhoɚn/ *noun, pl* **-horns** [*count*] *US* **:** an electrical device that is used for making your voice much louder so that you can be heard over a large distance — called also (*Brit*) *loudhailer*; compare MEGAPHONE

bul·lion /ˈbʊljən/ *noun* [*noncount*] **:** bars of gold or silver • gold *bullion*

Do not confuse *bullion* with *bouillon*.

bull·ish /ˈbʊlɪʃ/ *adj* [*more ~; most ~*]
1 : hopeful or confident that something or someone will be successful **:** optimistic about the future of something or someone • Members of her party are *bullish* about her reelection. • They are *bullish* about the future of the product. — often + *on* • A lot of investors are *bullish on* the company's future.
2 : expecting the price of stocks to go up • *bullish* investors **:** characterized by rising stock prices • a *bullish* market — compare BEARISH

bull market *noun, pl* **~ -kets** [*count*] *technical* **:** a market (such as a stock market) in which prices are going up — compare BEAR MARKET

bull·ock /ˈbʊlək/ *noun, pl* **-ocks** [*count*] **:** a young bull that has had part of its sex organs removed so that it cannot breed

bull·pen /ˈbʊlˌpɛn/ *noun, pl* **~ pens** [*count*]
1 : a place on a baseball field where pitchers practice throwing the ball before they start pitching in a game • A relief pitcher is warming up in the *bullpen*.
2 : the pitchers on a baseball team who can replace another pitcher during a game • The team has a strong *bullpen*.

bull·ring /ˈbʊlˌrɪŋ/ *noun, pl* **-rings** [*count*] **:** a large circular area in which bullfights take place

bull session *noun, pl* **~ -sions** [*count*] *US, informal* **:** an informal conversation in which a group of people talk about something • The governor had a *bull session* with his staff.

B

bull's–eye /ˈbʊlzˌaɪ/ *noun, pl* **-eyes** [*count*]
1 : the small circle at the center of a target toward which people throw darts or shoot arrows or bullets — usually singular • Try to hit the *bull's-eye.* = Aim for/at the *bull's-eye.* — often used figuratively • Her comments about our problems ***hit the bull's-eye*** [=her comments were exactly correct]
2 : a shot that hits the center of a target — usually singular • You got/threw/shot/scored a *bull's-eye*!

¹bull•shit /ˈbʊlˌʃɪt/ *noun* [*noncount*] *informal + offensive* **:** foolish or untrue words or ideas • That's (a load of) complete/pure/total/utter *bullshit*! [=*nonsense, bull*] — often used before another noun • He told some *bullshit* story about how he sailed around the world.

²bullshit *verb* **-shits; -shit; -shit•ting** *informal + offensive* **:** to say foolish or untrue things to (someone) **:** to lie to (someone) [+ *obj*] Don't *bullshit* me. Tell me the truth! • He tried to ***bullshit his way*** through the interview. [=to fool the people who were interviewing him by saying things that were not true] [*no obj*] Stop *bullshitting* and tell me the truth.
– bull•shit•ter *noun, pl* **-ters** [*count*] • Don't believe him. He's just a *bullshitter.*

bull terrier *noun, pl* **~ -ers** [*count*] **:** a type of dog that is very strong and has short hair — compare PIT BULL

¹bul•ly /ˈbʊli/ *noun, pl* **bul•lies** [*count*] **:** someone who frightens, hurts, or threatens smaller or weaker people • *Bullies* would often pick on him or beat him up after school. • My sister was the school/class/neighborhood *bully.*

²bully *verb* **bullies; bul•lied; bul•ly•ing** [+ *obj*]
1 : to frighten, hurt, or threaten (a smaller or weaker person) **:** to act like a bully toward (someone) • A group of girls were *bullying* [=*picking on*] her at the playground. • He *bullied* his younger brothers.
2 : to cause (someone) to do something by making threats or insults or by using force — usually + *into* • His boss *bullied* him *into* working overtime. • The kids were often *bullied* [=*forced*] *into* giving up their lunch money.
– bullying *noun* [*noncount*] • *Bullying* is not tolerated at school. • verbal/political *bullying*

³bully *adj, informal* — used in phrases like ***bully for you*** to express approval or praise especially when the approval or praise is not sincere • She won? Well, *bully for her.*

bul•ly•boy /ˈbʊliˌbɔɪ/ *noun, pl* **-boys** [*count*] *chiefly Brit* **:** an aggressive or violent man • political *bullyboys* who threaten their opponents — often used before another noun • uses *bullyboy* [=*strong-arm*] tactics to get what he wants

bully pulpit *noun, pl* **~ -pits** [*count*] *US* **:** an important public position that allows a person to express beliefs and opinions to many people • She uses her position as a famous actress as a *bully pulpit.*

bul•rush /ˈbʊlˌrʌʃ/ *noun, pl* **-rush•es** [*count*] *Brit* **:** CATTAIL

bul•wark /ˈbʊlˌwɚk/ *noun, pl* **-warks** [*count*]
1 *formal* **:** something that provides protection for or against something • democratic principles that stand as a *bulwark* against tyranny • a *bulwark* of freedom [=something that protects freedom]
2 : a wall that is built for protection **:** RAMPART
3 : a wall that is part of a ship's sides and that is above the ship's upper deck — usually plural • the ship's high *bulwarks*

¹bum /ˈbʌm/ *noun, pl* **bums** [*count*]
1 *chiefly US, informal + disapproving* **:** a person who has no place to live and no job and who asks people for money • *Bums* [=*vagrants*] often sleep on the park's benches. • a deserted building where *bums* [=*derelicts*] sometimes sleep
2 *informal* **:** a person who is lazy or who does something badly • Get to work, you lazy *bum*! • "He didn't even bother to write." "What a *bum*!"
3 : a person who spends a lot of time relaxing and doing something fun rather than working • a beach *bum* [=a person who spends a lot of time at the beach] • a ski *bum*
– compare ⁵BUM

²bum *verb* **bums; bummed; bum•ming** [+ *obj*] *informal* **:** to get (something) for free by asking **:** to ask for and get (something) • Can I *bum* [=*hitch*] a ride with you? • She's always *bumming* cigarettes off people.
bum around *or Brit* ***bum about*** [*phrasal verb*] *informal* **1** ***bum around/about*** *or* ***bum around/about (a place)*** **:** to spend time relaxing in (a place) instead of working • I spent the whole day just *bumming around* the house. **2** ***bum around/about (a place)*** **:** to spend time living and traveling in (a place) without a job or much money • After graduation, she *bummed around* Mexico for a while.
– compare ³BUM

³bum *verb* **bums; bummed; bum•ming** *US, informal*
1 [+ *obj*] **:** to cause (someone) to feel sad or disappointed — usually + *out* • The news really *bummed* me *out.* = I was really *bummed (out)* by the news.
2 *always used in progressive tenses* [*no obj*] **:** to feel sad or disappointed about something • She's *bumming* because she can't go to the concert.
– compare ²BUM
– bummed *adj* [*more* ~; *most* ~] • He's pretty *bummed* about not getting the scholarship.

⁴bum *adj, always used before a noun, informal*
1 : of bad quality • We lost money thanks to your *bum* [=*bad*] advice. • *bum* luck • I got a *bum* deal on this car. [=this car is worth much less than what I paid for it] — see also *bum rap* at ¹RAP
2 : not legally acceptable **:** not valid • He's known for writing/passing ***bum checks*** [=checks that promise money he does not have; checks that bounce]
3 *US* **:** injured or damaged • He has a *bum* knee/ankle/leg. [=his knee/ankle/leg does not function properly, is painful, etc.]

⁵bum *noun, pl* **bums** [*count*] *chiefly Brit, informal* **:** the part of the body that you sit on **:** BUTTOCKS • He slipped and fell on his *bum.* [=*behind, backside, bottom*] • Get off your *bum* [=*butt*] and get to work!
get/put bums on seats *Brit, informal* **:** to attract people to see a movie, play, game, etc. • She has the looks and voice that really *get/put bums on seats.*
– compare ¹BUM

bum•ble /ˈbʌmbəl/ *verb* **bum•bles; bum•bled; bum•bling**
1 : to act, move, or speak in an awkward or confusing way [*no obj*] I *bumbled* around in search of my glasses. • He *bumbled* through the speech. [+ *obj*] He *bumbled* his way through the speech.
2 *US* **:** to do, make, or handle (something) badly [+ *obj*] I had one chance and I *bumbled* [=*bungled*] it. [*no obj*] Someone *bumbled* [=*blundered*] and told the story to the press.
– bum•bler /ˈbʌmblɚ/ *noun, pl* **-blers** [*count*] • an incompetent *bumbler* **– bumbling** *adj* • a *bumbling* attempt at a robbery • a *bumbling* robber/man

bum•ble•bee /ˈbʌmbəlˌbiː/ *noun, pl* **-bees** [*count*] **:** a large, hairy bee — see color picture on page C10

bumf *also* **bumph** /ˈbʌmf/ *noun* [*noncount*] *Brit, informal* **:** material that is not important or interesting • a lot of public relations *bumf* about the company's new products

bum•mer /ˈbʌmɚ/ *noun* [*singular*] *informal* **:** something that is unpleasant or disappointing • That was a real *bummer* of a movie. • You can't go? What a *bummer*!

¹bump /ˈbʌmp/ *verb* **bumps; bumped; bump•ing**
1 [+ *obj*] **a :** to hit (something, such as part of your body) against an object in a sudden and forceful way • I have a bruise from where I *bumped* my head. — often + *against* or *on* • He *bumped* his head *against* the shelf. • I fell and *bumped* my elbow *on* the floor. **b :** to hit and move (someone or something) • Be careful not to *bump* the vase. • You nearly *bumped* me off/over the edge! • The jolt *bumped* him right out of his seat. • He accidentally *bumped* [=*knocked*] my drink out of my hand when he passed by.
2 [*no obj*] **:** to move *into* or *against* (someone or something) in a sudden and forceful way • They *bumped into* us from behind. • The boat *bumped against* the pier. — often + *up* • The boat *bumped up against* the pier. — sometimes used figuratively • They're *bumping (up) against* the limits of technology. — see also BUMP INTO (below), BUMP UP (below)
3 [+ *obj*] **a :** to move (someone or something) to a different level, position, rank, etc. • The TV show will be *bumped* to a new time. • Increasing fuel costs are *bumping* the company's prices higher. **b :** to remove (someone or something) from a group or position • The loss *bumped* us out of first place. — often used as *(be) bumped* • The flight was overbooked, and I was the first to *be bumped.* [=my seat on the flight was the first seat to be given to someone else]
4 *always followed by an adverb or preposition* [*no obj*] **:** to move in an up and down motion over a rough surface • The truck *bumped* along the dirt road.
bump into [*phrasal verb*] ***bump into (someone)*** *informal* **:** to meet (someone) by chance **:** to see and usually talk to (someone you did not expect to see) • I *bumped into* [=*ran into*] a friend at the store. — see also ¹BUMP 2 (above)
bump off [*phrasal verb*] ***bump (someone) off*** *or* ***bump off (someone)*** *informal* **:** to murder (someone) • He knew too

much, so they *bumped* him *off*.

bump up [*phrasal verb*] ***bump up (something or someone) or bump (something or someone) up informal*** : to move (something or someone) to a higher level, position, rank, etc. • Prices are being *bumped up*. [=*raised*] • They're *bumping* her *up* [=promoting her] to district manager. — see also ¹BUMP 2 (above)

²bump *noun, pl* **bumps** [*count*]

1 : an area of skin that is raised because it was hit, injured, etc. • He wound up with a few minor *bumps* and bruises from the fight. • Feel this *bump* [=*lump*] on the back of my head. — see also GOOSE BUMPS

2 : a small raised area on a surface • The car hit a *bump* (in the road). — often used figuratively in U.S. English • His career hit a *bump* in the road. = His career hit a road *bump*. [=something happened that slowed the progress of his career] • When you're doing something for the first time, you're bound to hit a few *bumps* along the way. — see also SPEED BUMP

3 : an act of something hitting against something else • Did you feel/hear a *bump*? • The airplane landed ***with a bump***. [=the airplane went up again and then down when it hit the ground]

4 : the act of pushing the hips forward in a sexual way • a dancer doing the *bump* and grind — compare GRIND

¹bum·per /ˈbʌmpɚ/ *noun, pl* **-ers** [*count*] : a bar across the front or back of a car, truck, etc., that reduces the damage if the vehicle hits something • the car's front/rear *bumper* — see picture at CAR

²bumper *adj, always used before a noun*

1 : unusually large • We had a ***bumper crop*** of tomatoes this year.

2 : very good or successful • It's a *bumper* [=(more commonly) *banner*] year for tomatoes. • a *bumper* harvest/season

bumper car *noun, pl* **~ cars** [*count*] *chiefly US* : a small electric car that you drive around in a small area at an amusement park and use to try to hit other cars

bumper sticker *noun, pl* **~ -ers** [*count*] : a strip of paper or plastic that has a printed message and that is made to be stuck on the bumper of a car, truck, etc.

bumper–to–bumper *adj* : made up of long lines of cars that are very close to each other • *bumper-to-bumper* traffic • The cars on the highway were *bumper-to-bumper*. [=the cars were very close to each other]

bumph *variant spelling of* BUMF

bump·kin /ˈbʌmpkən/ *noun, pl* **-kins** [*count*] *informal* : a person who lives in the country far away from cities and who is regarded as stupid • country *bumpkins*

bump·tious /ˈbʌmpʃəs/ *adj* [*more ~; most ~*] *disapproving* : proud or confident in a loud and rude way that annoys other people • a *bumptious* young man • *bumptious* behavior

bumpy /ˈbʌmpi/ *adj* **bump·i·er; -est** [*or more ~; most ~*]

1 *of a surface* : having or covered with bumps • The road is very *bumpy*. • the *bumpy* skin of a cucumber — opposite SMOOTH

2 : having sudden up and down movements • The flight was very *bumpy*. • The road was rough so we had a *bumpy* ride. • a *bumpy* journey — opposite SMOOTH

3 : having a lot of problems • a *bumpy* relationship • The project got off to a *bumpy* [=*rocky*] start, but it's back on schedule now. • Production of the movie has been a *bumpy* ride. [=there have been a lot of problems during the production of the movie] — opposite SMOOTH

– bump·i·ness *noun* [*noncount*]

bum–rush /ˈbʌmˈrʌʃ/ *verb* **-rush·es; -rushed; -rush·ing** [+ *obj*] *chiefly US* : to attack or move toward (someone or something) in a forceful and violent way • They *bum-rushed* him from behind. • Angry spectators *bum-rushed* the stage.

bum's rush *noun*

the bum's rush *chiefly US, informal* : the act of forcing someone to leave a position or place • The mayor is likely to ***get the bum's rush*** in next year's election. • They ***gave him the bum's rush***.

bun /ˈbʌn/ *noun, pl* **buns**

1 [*count*] : a small, round or long bread for one person to eat • tuna salad served on a *bun* [=*roll*] • a hamburger/hotdog *bun*

2 [*count*] : a small, usually round sweet cake • cinnamon *buns* — see also STICKY BUN

3 [*count*] : a way of arranging long hair by twisting it into a round shape at the sides or back of the head • She wears her hair in a *bun*.

4 ***buns*** [*plural*] *US, informal* : the two soft parts of the body that you sit on : BUTTOCKS • This exercise will firm up your *buns*.

have a bun in the oven *informal* : to be pregnant • Rumor has it, she *has a bun in the oven*.

¹bunch /ˈbʌntʃ/ *noun, pl* **bunch·es**

1 [*count*] : a group of things of the same kind that are held or tied together or that grow together • a *bunch* of flowers/grapes • He always had a *bunch* of keys on his belt. • Dried herbs hung in *bunches* from the kitchen rafters.

2 [*count*] *somewhat informal* : a group of people or things that are together or are associated with each other in some way — usually singular • a nice *bunch* of people • A *bunch* of us are going out for lunch. • They're a pretty wild *bunch* (of people). • All his books are good, but this one is the best/pick of the *bunch*.

3 *chiefly US, somewhat informal* : a large amount : LOT [*singular*] Thanks a *bunch*. — usually + *of* • We spent a *bunch of* money on our vacation. • having a (whole) *bunch of* problems • What a *bunch of* nonsense! [*plural*] They make *bunches* [=*lots*] *of* money.

4 ***bunches*** [*plural*] *Brit* : a way of arranging hair by separating it into two sections and tying these at each side of the head • She wore her hair in *bunches*. [=*(US) ponytails*]

²bunch *verb* **bunches; bunched; bunch·ing**

1 a [+ *obj*] : to put (things or people) together in a group or bunch — usually + *together* or *up* • They *bunched* [=*grouped*] the rest *together* under the category of "Miscellaneous." • She had *bunched* [=*gathered*] her curly hair *up* into a messy ponytail. — often used as *(be) bunched* • The flowers *are bunched together* in one corner of the yard. • The words *were* all *bunched together* at the bottom of the page. **b** [*no obj*] : to form a group — usually + *together* • The baby birds *bunch* [=(more commonly) *huddle*] *together* for warmth.

2 *of clothing* : to form a group of tight folds on or around part of your body [*no obj*] The child's tights *bunched* at the ankles. — usually + *up* or *together* • The sweater's long sleeves kept *bunching up* around her wrists. [+ *obj*] — usually + *up* or *together*; usually used as *(be) bunched* • The tights *were bunched together* at the ankles. • The sweater's long sleeves kept getting all *bunched up* around her wrists.

buncombe *variant spelling of* BUNKUM

¹bun·dle /ˈbʌndəl/ *noun, pl* **bun·dles** [*count*]

1 a : a group of things that are fastened, tied, or wrapped together • He arrived with several *bundles* [=*packages, parcels*] under his arms. — often + *of* • a *bundle of* straw/newspapers/clothes **b** : a group *of* things that are together or are associated with each other in some way • Whoever picks the winning ticket will win a *bundle of* prizes.

2 *informal* : a person who has a lot of some quality or who is known for a particular kind of behavior — + *of* • You're just a *bundle of* contradictions! [=you say or do things that seem to go against other things you say or do] • She's a ***bundle of energy***. [=she's very energetic] • I was a ***bundle of nerves***. [=I was very nervous] ✧ The phrase ***(little) bundle of joy*** is used as a humorous or affectionate way of referring to a baby. • He's our *little bundle of joy*.

3 *informal* : a large amount of money • He made/lost a *bundle* on the stock market. • A reliable car doesn't have to cost a *bundle*. • They made *bundles* of money.

4 : a group of products or services that are sold together at a single price • software *bundles*

go a bundle on *Brit, informal* : to like or be interested (something) very much. — usually used in negative statements • I don't usually *go a bundle on* science fiction, but this book is really good.

²bundle *verb* **bun·dles; bun·dled; bun·dling**

1 [+ *obj*] : to fasten, tie, or wrap a group of things together : to make (a group of things) into a bundle • Someone had *bundled* the wet towels into a big pile. — usually + *up* or *together* • I *bundled* the papers *together*. • *Bundle up* the newspapers.

2 : to move or push (someone) *into* a place quickly [+ *obj*] She *bundled* the children *into* the car. [*no obj*] We all *bundled into* the car.

3 [+ *obj*] : to include (a product or service) with another product or service so that they are sold together • They've increased sales by *bundling* their most popular programs. • a computer that comes with *bundled* software — often + *with* • The software is *bundled with* the computer.

bundle off [*phrasal verb*] ***bundle (someone) off or bundle off (someone)*** : to send (someone) to a place quickly or sud-

B

denly ▪ He *bundled* the children *off* to school. ▪ She was *bundled off* to summer camp.

bundle up [*phrasal verb*] ***bundle up or bundle (someone) up or bundle up (someone)*** : to dress (yourself or someone else) warmly ▪ Be sure to *bundle up*. It's cold out there. ▪ She *bundled up* the children. ▪ He was (all) *bundled up* in a hat and scarf.

[1]**bung** /ˈbʌŋ/ *noun, pl* **bungs** [*count*]

1 : a piece of wood, rubber, etc., that is used to close or cover a hole in a barrel

2 *Brit, informal* : BRIBE ▪ thousands of pounds in illegal *bungs*

[2]**bung** *verb* **bungs; bunged; bung·ing** [+ *obj*] *Brit, informal* : to put (something) *in* or *into* a place in a quick and careless way ▪ Just *bung* [=*toss*] it *in* the oven for 20 minutes. ▪ *Bung* [=*throw*] all the ingredients *into* the bowl, stir a bit, and it's done.

bung up [*phrasal verb*] ***bung up (something) or bung (something) up*** *Brit, informal* : to block (something) so that liquid, air, etc., cannot move through it ▪ Leaves had *bunged up* [=*plugged up, stopped up*] the drain. ▪ My nose is (all) *bunged up*. [=*stuffed up*]

bun·ga·low /ˈbʌŋgəˌloʊ/ *noun, pl* **-lows** [*count*]

1 : a house that is all on one level

2 *US* : a house that has one main level and a second smaller level above

bun·gee cord /ˈbʌnʤi-/ *noun, pl* ~ **cords** [*count*] : a very strong rope that can be stretched and that has hooks on either end — called also *bungee*

bungee jump *verb* ~ **jumps**; ~ **jumped**; ~ **jumping** [*no obj*] : to jump from a very high place while you are attached to a strong, long rope that stretches and that keeps you from hitting the ground ▪ A few people were *bungee jumping* off the bridge while a crowd of people looked on.

– **bungee jump** *noun, pl* ~ **jumps** [*count*] ▪ She did her first *bungee jump* last summer. – **bungee jumper** *noun, pl* ~ **-ers** [*count*] – **bungee jumping** *noun* [*noncount*] ▪ He likes daring sports like *bungee jumping* and skydiving.

bun·gle /ˈbʌŋgəl/ *verb* **bun·gles; bun·gled; bun·gling** : to make mistakes in doing (something) : to not do (something) well or successfully [+ *obj*] The police *bungled* [=*botched*] the investigation and the crime was never solved. [*no obj*] The government *bungled* badly in planning the campaign.

– **bungle** *noun, pl* **bun·gles** [*count*] ▪ They blamed him for the *bungle*. – **bungled** *adj* ▪ a *bungled* robbery – **bungler** *noun, pl* **-glers** [*count*] ▪ hapless *bunglers* – **bungling** *adj* ▪ a *bungling* attempt at humor – **bungling** *noun* [*noncount*] ▪ The investigation was ruined by their *bungling*.

bun·ion /ˈbʌnjən/ *noun, pl* **-ions** [*count*] : a painful swelling on the side of the big toe

[1]**bunk** /ˈbʌŋk/ *noun, pl* **bunks** [*count*]

1 : either one of two single beds that are placed one above the other : either one of the beds in a bunk bed ▪ He sleeps in the top/bottom *bunk*.

2 : a narrow bed attached to a wall on a ship, train, etc.

– compare [3]BUNK, [4]BUNK

[2]**bunk** *verb* **bunks; bunked; bunk·ing** [*no obj*] *chiefly US* : to stay overnight at a place ▪ We'll *bunk* here for the night. ▪ She was able to *bunk* with friends. — compare [5]BUNK

[3]**bunk** *noun* [*noncount*] *informal* : foolish or untrue words or ideas : NONSENSE ▪ His story is pure *bunk*. [=*bunkum*] ▪ All that talk about ghosts is (just) a lot of *bunk*. — compare [1]BUNK, [4]BUNK

[4]**bunk** *noun*

do a bunk *Brit, informal* : to leave a place suddenly and without telling anyone ▪ They *did a bunk* to avoid paying the rent.

– compare [1]BUNK, [3]BUNK

[5]**bunk** *verb* **bunks; bunked; bunking**

bunk off [*phrasal verb*] ***bunk off or bunk off (something)*** *Brit, informal* : to not go to (school, work, etc.) ▪ We used to *bunk off* school as kids. : to leave early from school, work, etc. ▪ He *bunked off* early last Friday.

– compare [2]BUNK

bunk bed *noun, pl* ~ **beds** [*count*] : a type of bed for two people that has two single beds placed so that one is above the other — see picture at BED

[1]**bun·ker** /ˈbʌŋkɚ/ *noun, pl* **-kers** [*count*]

1 : a strong building that is mostly below ground and that is used to keep soldiers, weapons, etc., safe from attacks ▪ The ammunition is stored in concrete *bunkers*. — see also BUNKER MENTALITY

2 *golf* : an area on a golf course that is filled with sand : SAND TRAP ▪ a fairway *bunker*

3 : a container for holding coal, oil, etc., on a ship or outside a house ▪ a coal *bunker*

[2]**bunker** *verb* **-kers; -kered; -ker·ing** [+ *obj*]

1 *golf* : to hit (a golf ball) into a bunker ▪ She *bunkered* her tee shot. ▪ He ***was bunkered*** [=his ball was in a bunker] on the second hole.

2 : to place or store (coal, oil, etc.) in a bunker ▪ They *bunkered* just enough coal to get them to the port.

bunker mentality *noun* [*singular*] *disapproving* : a very defensive way of thinking by the members of a group who believe that they are being wrongly attacked or criticized by others ▪ Faced with the threat of scandal, the company adopted a *bunker mentality* and refused to talk with reporters.

bunk·house /ˈbʌŋkˌhaʊs/ *noun, pl* **-hous·es** [*count*] : a building in which workers sleep

bun·kum *also* **bun·combe** /ˈbʌŋkəm/ *noun* [*noncount*] *old-fashioned + informal* : foolish or untrue words or ideas : NONSENSE, BUNK ▪ What a load of *bunkum*!

bun·ny /ˈbʌni/ *noun, pl* **-nies** [*count*] *informal* : a rabbit; *especially* : a young rabbit — used especially by children or when talking to children ▪ Look at the cute little *bunny*! — called also *bunny rabbit*; see also DUST BUNNY

bunny slope *noun, pl* ~ **slopes** [*count*] *US* : a hill or part of hill that is not very steep and that is used by people who are learning how to ski — called also *bunny hill, (Brit) nursery slope*

Bun·sen burner /ˈbʌnsən-/ *noun, pl* ~ **-ers** [*count*] : a piece of equipment that produces a hot flame and that is used in scientific experiments

bunt /ˈbʌnt/ *verb* **bunts; bunt·ed; bunt·ing** *baseball* : to hit a baseball lightly with the bat so that the ball rolls only for a short distance [*no obj*] The batter *bunted* for a single. [+ *obj*] He *bunted* the ball toward third base.

– **bunt** *noun, pl* **bunts** [*count*] ▪ He dropped/laid (down) a *bunt*. – **bunt·er** *noun, pl* **-ers** [*count*] ▪ an expert *bunter*

[1]**bun·ting** /ˈbʌntɪŋ/ *noun* [*noncount*] : flags or decorations that are made of thin cloth or paper ▪ The city decorated its streets and buildings with *bunting*. — compare [2]BUNTING

[2]**bun·ting** *noun, pl* **-tings** [*count*] : any one of several small and often colorful birds — compare [1]BUNTING

[1]**buoy** /ˈbu:wi, ˈbɔɪ/ *noun, pl* **buoys** [*count*] : an object that floats on water in a lake, bay, river, etc., to show areas that are safe or dangerous for boats — see also LIFE BUOY

buoys

[2]**buoy** *verb* **buoys; buoyed; buoy·ing** [+ *obj*]

1 : to cause (someone) to feel happy or confident — usually used as *(be) buoyed* ▪ *Buoyed* by the success of her first novel, she began work on a second. — often + *up* ▪ He felt *buoyed up* by the support and encouragement of his friends and family.

2 : to lift or improve (something) ▪ The tax breaks should help to *buoy* the economy. — usually used as *(be) buoyed* ▪ His spirits *were buoyed* [=*uplifted, raised*] by the good news. — often + *up* ▪ The falling leaf *was buoyed up* by a current of air.

buoy·an·cy /ˈbojənsi/ *noun* [*noncount*]

1 a : the ability of an object to float in water or air ▪ the natural *buoyancy* of cork **b** : the power of a liquid to make someone or something float ▪ The swimmer is supported by the water's *buoyancy*.

2 : the ability of someone or something to continue to be happy, strong, etc., through difficult times ▪ We hope that the economy will maintain its *buoyancy*.

buoy·ant /ˈbojənt/ *adj* [*more* ~; *most* ~]

1 a : able to float ▪ Cork is very *buoyant*. ▪ a *buoyant* material **b** : able to cause things to float ▪ Warm air is more *buoyant* than cool air.

2 : happy and confident ▪ The actors were *buoyant* as they prepared for the evening's performance. ▪ in a *buoyant* mood

3 : able to stay at a regular or high level ▪ a *buoyant* economy/market

– **buoy·ant·ly** *adv* ▪ *buoyantly* cheerful/confident

bur *variant spelling of* BURR 1

bur·ble /ˈbɚbəl/ *verb* **bur·bles; bur·bled; bur·bling** [*no obj*]
1 : to make the quiet sound of water moving over rocks • We heard a fountain *burbling* [=*gurgling, bubbling*] nearby.
2 a : to talk foolishly or too much • He *burbled* [=(more commonly) *babbled, chattered, prattled*] on for hours about his trip. **b** *of a baby* **:** to make quiet and happy sounds • The baby *burbled* happily in her crib.

burbs /ˈbɚbz/ *noun*
the burbs *US, informal* **:** the area around a city in which many people live **:** the suburbs • They bought a house in *the burbs.*

[1]**bur·den** /ˈbɚdn̩/ *noun, pl* **-dens** [*count*]
1 : something heavy that is carried **:** LOAD • They feared the donkey would collapse under the extra *burden.* — see also BEAST OF BURDEN
2 : someone or something that is very difficult to accept, do, or deal with • a (heavy) *burden* of sorrow/guilt • She had to bear/shoulder the *burden* of caring for her aging parents. • The ***tax burden*** has been falling increasingly on the middle class. [=middle class people have been paying a greater portion of taxes] • The ***burden of proof*** is on the plaintiff, since the defendant is presumed innocent until proven guilty. [=the plaintiff must prove that the defendant is guilty] • the company's large ***debt burden*** [=the large amount of money that the company owes] — often + *on* • His illness has placed a huge financial *burden on* the family. • I'm sorry to be such a *burden on* you.
burden has been lifted from your shoulders/back see [1]LIFT

[2]**burden** *verb* **-dens; -dened; -den·ing** [+ *obj*] **:** to make (someone) hold or carry something heavy or accept or deal with something difficult **:** to put a heavy burden on (someone) • I don't wish to *burden* you with my problems. — usually used as *(be) burdened* • *Burdened* with supplies and equipment, she headed to the camp. • For the rest of his life he *was burdened* with the knowledge that he had done nothing to help them. • *burdened* [=weighed down] by guilt

bur·den·some /ˈbɚdn̩səm/ *adj* [*more ~; most ~*] **:** causing difficulty or worry • a *burdensome* task/load • The responsibility has become *burdensome.*

bu·reau /ˈbjɚroʊ/ *noun, pl* **-reaus** *also Brit* **-reaux** /ˈbjuəroʊz/ [*count*]
1 a : a government department or part of a government department in the U.S. • the Federal *Bureau* of Investigation • the Census *Bureau* **b :** an office of a newspaper, magazine, etc., that is not the main office but is in an important city • the newspaper's Washington/Moscow *bureau* **c :** an office or organization that provides services or information to the public • a credit/travel *bureau* • the local visitors' *bureau*
2 a *US* **:** a piece of furniture with several drawers in which clothes are kept **:** CHEST OF DRAWERS • The book is on top of my *bureau.* **b** *Brit* **:** WRITING DESK

bu·reau·cra·cy /bjʊˈrɑːkrəsi/ *noun, pl* **-cies**
1 [*count*] **:** a large group of people who are involved in running a government but who are not elected • state/city *bureaucracies*
2 [*noncount*] *often disapproving* **:** a system of government or business that has many complicated rules and ways of doing things • management by *bureaucracy* • She was fed up with all the red tape and *bureaucracy.* • Both candidates pledge to simplify the state's bloated *bureaucracy.*

bu·reau·crat /ˈbjɚrəˌkræt/ *noun, pl* **-crats** [*count*] *often disapproving* **:** a person who is one of the people who run a government or big company and who does everything according to the rules of that government or company **:** a person who is part of a bureaucracy • government *bureaucrats*

bu·reau·crat·ic /ˌbjɚrəˈkrætɪk/ *adj* [*more ~; most ~*] **:** using or connected with many complicated rules and ways of doing things **:** of, relating to, or like a bureaucracy or bureaucrat • a *bureaucratic* institution/organization • *bureaucratic* hassles/power/procedures
— bu·reau·crat·i·cal·ly /ˌbjɚrəˈkrætɪkli/ *adv*

bur·geon /ˈbɚʤən/ *verb* **-geons; -geoned; -geon·ing** [*no obj*] *formal* **:** to grow or develop quickly • The market for collectibles has *burgeoned* in recent years.
— burgeoning *adj* • a *burgeoning* industry/field/population

bur·ger /ˈbɚgɚ/ *noun, pl* **-gers** [*count*]
1 : HAMBURGER • a grilled *burger* • I'll have a *burger* with fries, please.
2 : a food that is like a hamburger but that is not made from beef • a turkey/tofu *burger* — see also VEGGIE BURGER

bur·gher /ˈbɚgɚ/ *noun, pl* **-ghers** [*count*] *old-fashioned* **:** a person who lives in a particular town or borough • the *burghers* of Vienna

bur·glar /ˈbɚglɚ/ *noun, pl* **-glars** [*count*] **:** a person who illegally enters a building in order to steal things **:** a person who commits burglary — see also CAT BURGLAR

burglar alarm *noun, pl* **~ alarms** [*count*] **:** a device that makes a loud noise (such as a ringing sound) if someone tries to enter a building by using force

bur·glar·ize /ˈbɚgləˌraɪz/ *verb* **-iz·es; -ized; -iz·ing** [+ *obj*] *US* **:** to illegally enter (a building) and steal things • They were caught *burglarizing* [=*burgling*] a jewelry store. • Their house was *burglarized.* = They were *burglarized.*

bur·glary /ˈbɚgləri/ *noun, pl* **-glar·ies :** the act of illegally entering a building in order to steal things [*count*] There have been a number of *burglaries* in the neighborhood in recent months. [*noncount*] He has been charged with attempted *burglary.*

bur·gle /ˈbɚgəl/ *verb* **bur·gles; bur·gled; bur·gling** [+ *obj*] **:** BURGLARIZE

bur·gun·dy /ˈbɚgəndi/ *noun, pl* **-dies**
1 ***Burgundy*** **:** a red or white wine made in Burgundy, France [*count*] a red/white *Burgundy* [*noncount*] a bottle of *Burgundy*
2 [*count, noncount*] **:** a reddish-purple color — see color picture on page C3
— burgundy *adj* • *burgundy* velvet • a deep *burgundy* color

buri·al /ˈberijəl/ *noun, pl* **-als**
1 : the act or ceremony of burying a dead person in a grave [*noncount*] They prepared the body for *burial.* [*count*] She wanted to give him a proper *burial.* • Did you attend the *burial?* — often used before another noun • a *burial* chamber/site • ancient *burial* rites/customs • an ancient ***burial ground*** [=an area of land where dead people were buried in ancient times]
2 [*noncount*] **:** the act of burying something in the ground • The law prohibits the *burial* of toxic substances without special permits.

bur·ka *or* **bur·qa** /ˈbuɚkə/ *noun, pl* **-kas** *or* **-qas** [*count*] **:** a long piece of clothing that covers the face and body and that is worn by some Muslim women in public places

bur·lap /ˈbɚˌlæp/ *noun* [*noncount*] *US* **:** a strong, rough fabric that is used mostly for making bags • The bag is made of *burlap.* — often used before another noun • a *burlap* bag — called also *(Brit) hessian*

bur·lesque /bɚˈlɛsk/ *noun, pl* **-lesques**
1 : a play, story, novel, etc., that makes a serious subject seem funny or ridiculous [*count*] The book is a *burlesque* of Victorian society. [*noncount*] a writer whose *burlesque* often bordered on cruelty
2 [*noncount*] **:** a kind of entertainment that was popular in the U.S. in the late 19th and early 20th centuries and that included funny performances, singing, dancing, etc., and sometimes performances in which women took off their clothes • Several important 20th-century performers got their start in *burlesque.*
— burlesque *adj* • *burlesque* dancers • a *burlesque* show

bur·ly /ˈbɚli/ *adj* **bur·li·er; -est** [*or more ~; most ~*] *of a man* **:** strong and heavy **:** HUSKY • a big, *burly* man

[1]**burn** /ˈbɚn/ *verb* **burns; burned** /ˈbɚnd/ *or* **burnt** /ˈbɚnt/; **burn·ing** ✧ The forms *burned* and *burnt* are used in both U.S. and British English. *Burned* is more common in U.S. English; *burnt* is more common in British English.
1 [*no obj*] **a** *of a fire or flame* **:** to give off heat, light, and gases • A flame is kept constantly *burning* at the monument. • A small fire *burned* brightly in the fireplace. **b** *always used in progressive tenses* **:** to contain a fire • There was a little stove *burning* in the front room. — see also BURNING
2 a *always used in progressive tenses* [*no obj*] **:** to be on fire **:** to have or produce a flame • I could smell smoke and knew that something was *burning.* • Be sure not to leave any candles *burning* when you go to bed. **b** [+ *obj*] **:** to set (something) on fire **:** to make (something) have or produce a flame • We came to the memorial to *burn* [=*light*] a candle for the victims of the accident.
3 a : to destroy or damage (something) by fire or heat [+ *obj*] I *burned* the letter when I had finished reading it. • The new town law makes it illegal to *burn* trash. • The wildfire has *burned* acres of forest. • Parts of the house were badly *burned* in the fire. • *burnt* pieces of wood [*no obj*] The wood *burned* slowly. • a material that *burns* easily ✧ A building or

B

other structure that ***burns to the ground*** or ***is burned to the ground*** is completely destroyed by fire. • The house (*was*) *burned to the ground* in the fire. **b** : to injure or damage (someone or a part of the body) by fire, heat, acid, etc. [+ *obj*] He was badly *burned* in the accident. • She *burned* her hand on the hot stove. = The hot stove *burned* her hand. • The hot sun *burned* her skin. • I ***burned myself*** on the iron. [=I injured part of my body with the hot iron] • Several people were trapped in the building and were ***burned to death***. [=were killed by fire] • The captives were ***burned alive***. [=killed by being set on fire] [*no obj*] She has to stay out of the sun because her skin *burns* easily. [=she gets sunburned easily] • Several people *burned to death* in the fire.

4 : to ruin (food) by cooking it too long or with too much heat [+ *obj*] I'm afraid I *burned* the potatoes. • She *burned* the toast. • *burnt* toast [*no obj*] The toast *burned*.

5 a *of an acid, chemical, etc.* : to damage (something) by causing a strong chemical reaction [+ *obj*] The acid *burned* his hand. [*no obj*] The acid *burned* into/through the metal. — sometimes used figuratively • Her words *burned* themselves into his memory. = Her words were *burned* into his memory. [=he always remembered her words] • The image is *burned* in my mind. [=I cannot forget the image] **b** [+ *obj*] : to produce (something, such as a hole) by fire, heat, acid, etc. • He dropped his cigarette and accidentally *burned* a hole in the carpet. • The acid *burned* a hole in the cloth. ✧ If you have money and you want to spend it, the money is ***burning a hole in your pocket***. • He just got his tax refund and has some extra cash *burning a hole in his pocket*.

6 *always used in progressive tenses* [*no obj*] : to be very hot • The pavement was *burning*. — see also BURNING

7 a : to have or produce an unpleasantly hot and painful feeling [+ *obj*] The hot peppers *burned* my mouth. • The cigarette smoke *burned* my throat and made my eyes water. [*no obj*] My mouth is still *burning* from the hot peppers. • The iodine *burned* a little when I put it on the cut. **b** [*no obj*] : to feel a pain that is like being injured by heat or fire • My nose was bright red and my ears were *burning* from the cold. **c** *always used in progressive tenses* [*no obj*] : to have a high fever • She was *burning* with fever. — often + *up* • I'm going to call the doctor: you're *burning up*! — see also BURN UP (below), BURNING

8 [*no obj*] **a** : to feel a strong emotion — often + *with* • She was *burning with* anger at his rudeness. [=she was very angry because of his rudeness] • As a young man he *burned with* ambition. [=he was very ambitious] — sometimes + *for* • She was *burning for* a chance to prove herself. [=she wanted very much to get a chance to prove herself] — sometimes followed by *to + verb* • She was *burning to prove* herself. **b** : to become hot and red because of a strong emotion • Her cheeks were *burning*. — often + *with* • Her cheeks were *burning with* shame. • His face *burned with* anger/embarrassment.

9 [+ *obj*] *US, informal* **a** : to cheat or deceive (someone) : to take advantage of (someone) — usually used as *(be) burned* • He doesn't like giving interviews because he's been/gotten *burned* by reporters in the past. [=reporters have treated him unfairly in the past] • He's *been burned* in love before. **b** : to make (someone) very angry • It really *burns* me to see people being treated so badly. — usually + *up* • His arrogance really *burns* me *up*! — see also BURN UP (below)

10 a [*no obj*] : to be used as fuel • Some kinds of coal *burn* better than others. **b** [+ *obj*] : to use (something) as fuel • This furnace *burns* oil/gas. — often + *up* • an engine that *burns up* more fuel **c** [+ *obj*] : to use (food, calories, etc.) as a source of energy • Our bodies *burn* food/calories. • exercising to *burn* fat [=exercising to lose fat by using it to produce energy] — often + *off* or *up* • exercising to *burn off/up* calories/fat • Your body *burns up* more oxygen when you are active than when you are resting. — see also BURN OFF (below), BURN UP (below)

11 [*no obj*] : to give off light : to shine or glow • There was a light *burning* in the window. • a star that *burns* brightly in the evening sky • Lanterns *burned* in the boats on the canal.

12 [+ *obj*] *computers* : to record information or music on a disk • *burn* a CD/DVD • You can buy the songs online and then *burn* them onto a CD.

burn away [*phrasal verb*] ***burn away or burn (something) away or burn away (something)*** : to be removed or to remove (something) by fire or heat • The outer layer of wooden shingles *burned away* quickly in the fire. = The fire quickly *burned* the outer layer of wooden shingles *away*.

burn down [*phrasal verb*] **1** ***burn down or burn (something) down or burn down (something)*** *of a building or other structure* : to be destroyed or to destroy (something) by fire • The hotel *burned down* [=*burned to the ground*] in 1922. = A fire in 1922 *burned down* the hotel. **2** ***burn down*** *of a fire* : to become smaller : to gradually produce less and less flame • We watched the fire as it slowly *burned down*.

burn off [*phrasal verb*] ***burn off or burn (something) off or burn off (something)*** **1** *US, of fog, smoke, etc.* : to go away because of the sun's heat • We waited for the fog to *burn off*. = We waited for the sun to *burn off* the fog. **2** : to be removed or to remove (something) by fire or heat • The hot sun had *burned* the paint *off* the sign years before. — see also [1]BURN 10c (above)

burn out [*phrasal verb*] **1** ***burn out or burn (itself) out*** *of a fire* : to stop burning • The campfire eventually *burned out*. = The campfire eventually *burned itself out*. — sometimes used figuratively • His anger finally *burned itself out*. [=he finally stopped being angry] **2** ***burn (a building) out or burn out (a building)*** : to destroy the inside of (a building) by fire • The apartment building was completely *burned out* by the fire. — see also BURNED OUT 1 **3** ***burn out or burn (something) out or burn out (something)*** : to stop working or cause (something) to stop working because of too much use or careless use • The engine *burned out*. • If you keep running the engine like that you're going to *burn it out*. **4** ***burn out or burn (someone) out also burn out (someone)*** : to become or cause (someone) to become very physically and emotionally tired after doing a difficult job for a long time : to suffer burnout or cause (someone) to suffer burnout • Teaching can be very stressful, and many teachers eventually *burn out*. = Teaching can be very stressful, and many teachers eventually *burn themselves out*. • All that hard work *burned her out* eventually. — see also BURNED OUT 2

burn rubber see [1]RUBBER

burn the candle at both ends : to do too much by being active late at night and during the day • She's going to wear herself out if she keeps *burning the candle at both ends*.

burn the midnight oil : to work or study until very late at night • The students have been *burning the midnight oil* as they prepare for their final exams.

burn through [*phrasal verb*] ***burn through (something)*** *informal* : to use all of (something) quickly • They've *burned through* 2 million dollars already, and the renovations are far from complete.

burn up [*phrasal verb*] ***burn up or burn (something) up or burn up (something)*** : to be destroyed or cause (something) to be destroyed by fire • Most asteroids *burn up* upon entering the Earth's atmosphere. • Wildfires have been raging across the region *burning up* acres of forest. — see also [1]BURN 7c, 9b, 10b, c (above)

burn your bridges *also Brit* ***burn your boats*** : to do something that makes you unable to go back to a previous situation • Even after leaving his job, he tried to stay on friendly terms with his former boss because he didn't want to *burn his bridges*.

crash and burn see [1]CRASH

money to burn see MONEY

– burn·able /ˈbɚnəbəl/ *adj* [*more ~; most ~*] • an easily *burnable* material

[2]**burn** *noun, pl* **burns**

1 [*count*] **a** : an injury caused by fire, heat, acid, etc. • He suffered severe/serious *burns* on both his legs in the accident. • a second-degree *burn* **b** : a burned area : a mark on the surface of something caused by a flame or fire • There's a small *burn* on the tabletop. • a *burn* mark

2 [*count*] : a painful red mark on the skin caused by rubbing against something • rope/friction *burns*

3 [*singular*] : a sharp, hot pain : a burning feeling • the *burn* of iodine on a cut • Continue doing the exercise until you feel the *burn* in your muscles.

do a slow burn *US, informal* : to slowly become very angry • The boss *did a slow burn* when he saw the expense report.

burned out *or* **burnt out** *adj*

1 *of a building* : having the inside destroyed by fire — usually hyphenated • an empty, *burned-out* building — see also *burn out* 2 at [1]BURN

2 [*more ~; most ~*] : suffering burnout : feeling very physically and emotionally tired after doing a difficult job for a long time • I was *burned out* after 25 years as a corporate lawyer. — usually hyphenated when used before a noun • a *burned-out* novelist — see also *burn out* 4 at [1]BURN

burn·er /ˈbɚnɚ/ *noun, pl* **-ers** [*count*]

1 a : the part of a furnace, stove, etc., where the flame or

heat is produced • (*chiefly US*) The stove has four *burners*. [=(*Brit*) *rings*] • The *burner* on the furnace isn't working. — see picture at KITCHEN **b :** a device that burns something • a propane/gas/oil *burner* : a device in which something is burned • an incense *burner* — see also BACK BURNER, BARN BURNER, BUNSEN BURNER, FRONT BURNER
2 *computers* : a device that is used to record information or music on a CD or DVD • The computer comes equipped with a CD *burner*.

burn·ing /ˈbɚnɪŋ/ *adj, always used before a noun*
1 : on fire : producing or having a flame • a *burning* fire/candle/city • She stared at the *burning* embers for a long time.
2 : very strong • a *burning* hatred of corruption • his *burning* [=*intense*] desire to succeed
3 a : very hot • *burning* sand/pavement • He has a *burning* fever. [=he has a very high fever] **b :** similar to the feeling caused by something hot • The medicine produced a *burning* sensation on my tongue. • Symptoms include itchy, *burning* eyes.
4 : very important • This is one of the *burning* issues/questions of our time.
– **burning** *adv* • The pavement was ***burning hot***. [=extremely hot] – **burning** *noun* [*noncount*] • a sensation of *burning* on my tongue • Who ordered the *burning* of the city? – **burn·ing·ly** *adv* • *burningly* hot/intense

bur·nish /ˈbɚnɪʃ/ *verb* **-nish·es; -nished; -nish·ing** [+ *obj*] *formal* : to make (something, such as metal or leather) smooth and shiny by rubbing it : POLISH — often used figuratively • She started a publicity campaign to help *burnish* [=*improve*] her image/reputation.
– **burnished** *adj* • *burnished* gold/leather

burn·out /ˈbɚnˌaʊt/ *noun, pl* **-outs**
1 a [*noncount*] : the condition of someone who has become very physically and emotionally tired after doing a difficult job for a long time • Teaching can be very stressful, and many teachers eventually suffer/experience *burnout*. • the *burnout* rate among teachers **b** [*count*] : a person who suffers burnout • a novel about academic *burnouts* — see also BURNED OUT, *burn out* 4 at [1]BURN
2 [*noncount*] : the time when a jet or rocket engine stops working because there is no more fuel available

burnt *past tense and past participle of* [1]BURN

burnt out *variant spelling of* BURNED OUT

burp *verb* **burps; burped; burp·ing**
1 [*no obj*] : to let out air from the stomach through the mouth with a sound • Say "excuse me" when you *burp*. — compare BELCH
2 [+ *obj*] : to help (a baby) let out air from the stomach especially by patting or rubbing the baby's back
– **burp** /ˈbɚp/ *noun, pl* **burps** [*count*] • He let out a *burp*. • a loud *burp* [=*belch*]

burqa *variant spelling of* BURKA

burr /ˈbɚ/ *noun, pl* **burrs** [*count*]
1 *also* **bur :** a rough covering of a nut or seed ✧ Burrs often have small hooks that stick to clothing and fur.
2 : a rough area on a piece of metal that is left after the metal is cut • a tool that can cut through steel leaving a smooth edge and no *burrs*
3 : a strong way of pronouncing *r* that is used by some speakers of English especially in northern England and in Scotland — usually singular • He speaks with a Scottish *burr*.
a burr in/under the saddle *US, informal* : someone or something that is a constant cause of trouble or annoyance • He was *a burr in the saddle* of the competition. • She's been *a burr under their saddle* for many years.

bur·ri·to /bəˈriːˌtoʊ/ *noun, pl* **-tos** [*count*] : a Mexican food that consists of a flour tortilla that is rolled or folded around a filling (such as meat, beans, and cheese)

bur·ro /ˈbɚroʊ/ *noun, pl* **-ros** [*count*] *chiefly US* : a small donkey

[1]**bur·row** /ˈbɚroʊ/ *noun, pl* **-rows** [*count*] : a hole or tunnel in the ground that an animal (such as a rabbit or fox) makes to live in or for safety

[2]**burrow** *verb* **-rows; -rowed; -row·ing**
1 : to make a hole or tunnel in the ground by digging — usually + *into* or *under* [*no obj*] The rabbit *burrowed into* the side of the hill. • The frogs *burrow under* the mud. [+ *obj*] The mole *burrowed* its way *under* the ground.
2 *always followed by an adverb or preposition* : to move or press under, through, or into something [*no obj*] She *burrowed* [=*snuggled*] deep under the blankets. • I *burrowed* [=(more commonly) *dug*] through my purse looking for change. [+ *obj*] The baby *burrowed* [=*nestled*] her head into/against her mother's chest.
– **burrowing** *adj* • *burrowing* animals/rodents [=animals/rodents that make holes or tunnels]

bur·sar /ˈbɚsɚ/ *noun, pl* **-sars** [*count*] : a person whose job is to manage the money of a school, college, or university : TREASURER

bur·sa·ry /ˈbɚsəri/ *noun, pl* **-ries** [*count*] *Brit* : an amount of money that a student is given to help pay for college or university study : a scholarship or grant

[1]**burst** /ˈbɚst/ *verb* **bursts; burst** *also* **burst·ed; burst·ing**
1 a [*no obj*] : to break open or into pieces in a sudden and violent way • The balloon *burst*. [=*popped*] • We could hear bombs *bursting* [=*exploding*] in the distance. • Two of the water pipes *burst*. **b** [+ *obj*] : to cause (something) to break open or into pieces • Be careful not to *burst* [=*pop*] the balloon. • He *burst* a blood vessel.
2 : to open suddenly [*no obj*] The doors suddenly ***burst open***. [+ *obj*] The cops *burst* the door *open*.
3 *always followed by an adverb or preposition* [*no obj*] : to come or go very quickly and suddenly • He *burst* into the room. • The sun *burst* through the clouds. • She *burst* through the door and yelled "Surprise!" • They just ***burst in on*** us [=they suddenly entered the room we were in] without even knocking on the door. ✧ To ***burst onto/on/upon the scene*** is to suddenly become very well known. • They *burst onto the* music *scene* in 1995 with a very successful debut album. • when the technology first *burst on the scene*
4 [+ *obj*] *of a river, stream, etc.* : to flow over the surrounding land because of a flood • The stream ***burst its banks***.
be bursting **1 :** to be filled *with* something • The crate *was bursting with* fruit. • The dish *is bursting with* flavors. • The kids *are* just *bursting with* energy/excitement. • Her parents *were* practically *bursting with* pride. **2 :** to want very much *to do* (something you are not yet able to do) • I'm *bursting to tell you* the news, but I have to talk to Ken first. **3** *Brit, informal* : to need to urinate very badly
be bursting at the seams : to be very full or crowded • The nightclub *was bursting at the seams*. • The garden *is bursting at the seams* with colorful flowers.
burst into [*phrasal verb*] ***burst into (something)*** : to begin to produce or do (something) suddenly • She *burst into* [=*broke into*] laughter/tears. • The house *burst into* flame(s). • The entire cast *burst into* [=*broke into*] song. • The audience *burst into* applause. • The flowers were *bursting into* bloom.
burst out [*phrasal verb*] **1** ***burst out (doing something)*** : to begin (doing something) suddenly • They both *burst out* [=*busted out*] laughing. **2** ***burst out (something)*** : to say (something) suddenly • Everyone *burst out* "Surprise!" as he walked through the door.
burst someone's bubble see [1]BUBBLE
fit to burst see [1]FIT

[2]**burst** *noun, pl* **bursts** [*count*]
1 : a short period of producing or doing something that begins suddenly • She ran hard in short *bursts* toward the end of the race. — often + *of* • a (sudden) *burst of* speed/laughter/energy • *Bursts of* machine-gun fire could be heard in the distance.
2 : an act of breaking open or into pieces • the *burst* of a bubble : the result of something breaking open or into pieces • The plumber fixed the *burst* [=(more commonly) *break*] in the water pipe.

bur·ton /ˈbɚtn̩/ *noun*
go for a burton *Brit, informal + old-fashioned* : to be lost, broken, or ruined • Our holiday plans have *gone for a burton*.

bury /ˈberi/ *verb* **bur·ies; bur·ied; bury·ing** [+ *obj*]
1 a : to put (a dead person or animal) in a grave • He was *buried* with full military honors. • Their ancestors are *buried* in the local cemetery. • cultures that *bury* their dead **b :** to have someone that you love or are related to die • He had three children by two wives and *buried* [=*outlived*] them all.
2 a : to hide (something) in the ground • The dog *buried* her bone. • He *buried* the money in the backyard. • the search for *buried* treasure **b :** to hide (something) so that it cannot be seen or is difficult to see • He has learned to *bury* his feelings. • She *buried* her face in her hands. • The disclaimer was *buried* in the fine print. • The newspaper covered the story, but it was *buried* in the back of section C.
3 : to cover (someone or something) with something • A blanket of snow had *buried* the first few flowers of spring.—

B

usually used as *(be) buried* • Three skiers were ***buried alive*** in a massive avalanche on Tuesday. — usually + *under* or *beneath* • The car *was buried under* the snow. • My shoes *were buried beneath* a pile of clothes.

4 : to push (something) *in* or *into* something • He *buried* his face/head *in* the pillow. • The splinter *buried* itself *in* my thumb. ✧ When you ***bury yourself in something***, you give it all of your attention and ignore everything else. • He *buried himself in* his studies.

5 : to stop being angry or upset about (something) • We've decided to *bury* our differences and start working together.

6 *sports, informal* **:** to make (a shot) in a very impressive way • He *buried* the jumper. [=he made the jump shot] • She *buried* [=*holed*] the putt.

7 *informal* **:** to defeat (a competitor) easily or completely • They *buried* the other team (by a score of) 15–2.

bury the hatchet see HATCHET

dead and buried see [1]DEAD

[1]**bus** /ˈbʌs/ *noun, pl* **bus·es** *also US* **bus·ses :** a large vehicle that is used for carrying passengers especially along a particular route at particular times [*count*] She boarded a *bus* in Nashville. [*noncount*] I usually go to work ***by bus*** = I usually ***take the bus*** to work. • Are you traveling by train or *by bus*? — often used before another noun • a *bus* driver • a *bus* station • waiting at the ***bus stop*** [=one of the places where a bus stops for passengers to get on or off] — see also SCHOOL BUS

[2]**bus** *verb* **buses** *also US* **busses; bused** *also US* **bussed; bus·ing** *also US* **bus·sing** [+ *obj*]

1 : to transport (someone) in a bus — often used as *(be) bused* • Students from the other college *were bused* in for the game. • The children *are bused* to school.

2 *US* **a :** to remove dirty dishes from (a table at a restaurant) • He *buses* tables at the local diner. **b :** to remove (something, such as dirty dishes) • We're supposed to *bus* [=*clear*] our own trays.

bus·boy /ˈbʌsˌbɔɪ/ *noun, pl* **-boys** [*count*] **:** a man or boy whose job is to remove dirty dishes, clean tables, etc., at a restaurant

bus·by /ˈbʌzbi/ *noun, pl* **-bies** [*count*] **:** a tall fur hat that is worn by some British soldiers

bush /ˈbʊʃ/ *noun, pl* **bush·es**

1 [*count*] **:** a plant that has stems of wood and is smaller than a tree • a rose/mulberry *bush* • The *bushes* [=*shrubs*] in my yard need to be trimmed.

2 [*count*] **:** a thick growth of hair or fur • a *bush* of hair

3 ***the bush*** **:** a large area (such as in Australia or Africa) that has not been cleared and that is not used for farming • She recently spent several weeks in *the bush*.

a bird in the hand is worth two in the bush see BIRD

beat around the bush or *Brit* ***beat about the bush*** **:** to avoid saying something by talking about other things • Stop *beating around the bush* and tell me why you're here.

bushed /ˈbʊʃt/ *adj, not used before a noun* [*more* ~; *most* ~] *informal* **:** very tired • That hike wore me out. I'm *bushed*. [=*beat, exhausted*]

bush·el /ˈbʊʃəl/ *noun, pl* **-els**

1 [*count*] **:** a unit for measuring an amount of fruit and grain that is equal to about 35.2 liters in the U.S. and to about 36.4 liters in the U.K. • a *bushel* of wheat/apples

2 ***bushels*** [*plural*] *US, informal* **:** a large amount *of* something • The company made *bushels* [=*lots*] *of* money last year.

hide your light under a bushel **:** to not tell others about your talents, successes, ideas, etc.

bush league *noun, pl* ~ **leagues** [*count*] *informal* **:** MINOR LEAGUE

– bush leaguer *noun, pl* ~ **-uers** [*count*]

bush–league /ˈbʊʃˌliːg/ *adj, US, informal* **:** of very low quality • *bush-league* customer service • a *bush-league* [=*unprofessional*] reporter

Bush·man /ˈbʊʃmən/ *noun, pl* **-men** /-mən/ [*count*] **:** a member of a group of people of southern Africa who live and hunt in a wild area (called the bush)

bush pilot *noun, pl* ~ **-lots** [*count*] *chiefly US* **:** a pilot who flies a small airplane into areas that are hard to reach

bush·whack /ˈbʊʃˌwæk/ *verb* **-whacks; -whacked; -whack·ing**

1 [*no obj*] **:** to clear a path through thick woods by cutting down bushes and low tree branches • The group *bushwhacked* through the jungle.

2 [+ *obj*] **:** to attack (someone) suddenly • He was *bushwhacked* [=*ambushed*] by enemy soldiers. • They used the controversy as an opportunity to *bushwhack* their political opponents.

bushy /ˈbʊʃi/ *adj* **bush·i·er; -est** [*also more* ~; *most* ~]

1 : very thick and full • a *bushy* beard • *bushy* hair/eyebrows • an animal with a *bushy* tail

2 *of a plant* **:** having a lot of branches and leaves • a *bushy* tree

bright-eyed and bushy-tailed see BRIGHT

– bush·i·ness *noun* [*noncount*] • the *bushiness* of his eyebrows

busi·ly /ˈbɪzəli/ *adv* **:** in a busy way • He was *busily* engaged in his work. • They are *busily* planning next year's event.

busi·ness /ˈbɪznəs/ *noun, pl* **-ness·es**

1 [*noncount*] **a :** the activity of making, buying, or selling goods or providing services in exchange for money • The store will be open for *business* next week. [=the store will be ready for customers next week] • The store has lost a significant amount of *business* since the factory closed. • Allowing customers to leave your store unsatisfied is bad (for) *business*. • The new Web site has been good for (attracting) *business*. • What line of *business* [=*work*] are you in? • She works in the publishing *business*. • the fashion/music/restaurant *business* • We ***do business with*** [=sell to or buy from] companies overseas. • David has decided to ***go into business*** with his brother. • Remember that your customers can ***take their business elsewhere*** [=your customers can go to another place to do business] • Their publishing company is ***the best in the business*** • a ***place of business*** [=a place, such as a store, bank, etc., where business is done] — often used before another noun • *business* opportunities/contacts/interests • The *business* world is responding to changes in technology. [=businesses are responding to changes in technology] • Someone will be available to answer your call during regular ***business hours*** [=the hours that the office is open to do business] • a ***business meeting*** [=a meeting at which matters of business are discussed] — see also AGRIBUSINESS, BIG BUSINESS, IN BUSINESS (below), OUT OF BUSINESS (below), SHOW BUSINESS **b :** work that is part of a job • Is your trip to Miami (for) *business* or pleasure? • I have to go to New York City on/for *business* next week. — sometimes used before another noun • a ***business trip*** [=a trip that is made in order to do business] • I am flying ***business class*** [=in a seating section of an airplane that is more expensive than the main section but less expensive than first class] from Tokyo to New York. **c :** the amount of activity that is done by a store, company, factory, etc. • *Business* has been slow/bad lately. [=there have been few customers, sales, etc., lately] • *Business* was good/booming. • They advertised to increase *business*. • How is *business*?

2 [*count*] **:** an organization (such as a store, company, or factory) that makes, buys, or sells goods or provides services in exchange for money • He has the skills necessary to run/operate/start a *business*. • The town is trying to attract new *businesses*. • local *businesses* • She joined the ***family business*** [=the business owned or operated by her family] after graduating from college. — sometimes used before another noun • I had lunch with some *business* associates. • In addition to being married, the two are also *business* partners. • The restaurant is in the ***business district*** [=the part of a city or town where there are many businesses] • the ***business community*** [=people involved in the upper levels of businesses]

3 [*singular*] **:** something that concerns a particular person, group, etc. **:** something that needs to be considered or dealt with • Do we have any other *business* we need to discuss? • Air quality is a serious *business*. [=air quality is something people should think about seriously] • What's this *business* [=*news*] I hear about you moving away? • Educating students is the *business* [=*responsibility*] of schools. • No, I didn't ask him what he wanted the car for. That's his *business*. • I won't answer that question. Who I choose to vote for is my *business*. • He's decided to ***make it his business*** [=make it his goal] to bring more affordable housing to the city. • "Who did you vote for?" "That's ***none of your business***" [=that's private information that you should not be asking about] • It's ***no business of yours*** who I voted for. ✧ The phrase ***mind your own business*** is used as an informal and often somewhat impolite way to tell someone to stop watching or asking about something that is private. • *Mind your own business* and let them talk alone. ✧ To say that you were ***minding your own business*** when something happened means that you were doing what you normally do and were not bothering anyone. • I was walking down the street, *minding my own business*, when all of a sudden some man started yelling at me. ✧ If you say something is ***nobody's business***, you mean that it is private and other people do not need to know about it. ▪ It's *nobody's business* what we were talking about. ✧ Someone who ***has no business doing something*** has no right to do it. ▪ You *have no business telling me* what I can and cannot wear! I'll wear whatever I like!

4 [*noncount*] : something that must be done ▪ I have some *business* in town Friday afternoon. [=I have to do something in town Friday afternoon] ▪ He had to leave the meeting early because he had to attend to some ***unfinished business***. [=something not done that needs to be done] ▪ Now that we've all introduced ourselves, let's ***get down to business***. [=start doing what needs to be done, start working] ▪ I was just ***going about my business*** [=doing what I usually do], when I heard a big crash. ▪ Sarah is good at ***taking care of business*** [=doing what needs to be done], so she's been put in charge of organizing the event. ▪ The church has hired someone to take care of the bills and ***all that business***. [=everything else that needs to be done] ▪ A public library is ***in the business of*** providing information to the public. [=the job/purpose of a public library is to provide information] ▪ I'm not *in the business of* lending money to people I hardly know. [=I don't lend money to people I hardly know]

5 [*singular*] : a matter, event, or situation — usually used after an adjective ▪ Divorce can be such a messy *business*. [=*affair*] ▪ The earthquake was a terrible *business*. ▪ Predicting how people will react to something is a tricky *business*. ▪ Investing all your money in one stock is (a) very risky *business*. ▪ "How long did the ceremony take?" "Oh, the whole *business* was over in less than an hour." ▪ Let's just forget about that *business* of me being unhappy with my job. — see also MONKEY BUSINESS

business as usual — used to say that something is working or continuing in the normal or usual way ▪ Much of the town lost electricity in the storm, but for people with generators it was *business as usual*. ▪ As the election nears, both political parties continue to blame each other for all the city's problems. In other words, it's *business as usual*.

business is business — used to say that in order for a business to be successful it is necessary to do things that may hurt or upset people ▪ I'm sorry I have to let you go, but understand that *business is business*.

in business **1** : operating as a business ▪ The hotel has been *in business* for over 150 years. ▪ Customer satisfaction is important if you want to stay *in business*. **2** *informal* : ready to begin doing or using something ▪ Just plug in the computer and you're *in business*! [=you will be able to use the computer] ▪ All the musicians have finally arrived, so we're *in business*! ▪ He quickly changed the tire, and was ***back in business*** [=ready to drive again] in 10 minutes.

like nobody's business *informal* : very well or quickly or in very large amounts ▪ She can design computer programs *like nobody's business*. ▪ It's been raining *like nobody's business*.

mean business : to be serious about doing something ▪ We thought he was joking at first, but then we saw that he really *meant business*.

out of business : closed down : no longer in business ▪ My favorite flower shop is *out of business*. ▪ Small grocery stores are being driven/forced/put *out of business* by large stores. [=small grocery stores cannot compete with large stores and so are closing permanently] ▪ The store has ***gone out of business***. [=has closed]

the business *Brit slang* : a very good or impressive person or thing ▪ Since he's won the tournament, he thinks he's *the business*. [=*the best*] ▪ You should see their new flat. It's *the business*.

business administration *noun* [*noncount*] : a program of studies in a college or university that teaches students how to run a business ▪ a degree in *business administration*

business card *noun, pl* ~ **cards** [*count*] : a small card printed with a person's name and information about that person's company and job ✧ People give business cards to anyone who they think might want to contact them about their business.

business end *noun*

the business end *informal* : the part of a tool, weapon, or instrument that is used most directly for the object's purpose ▪ the *business end* of a rifle [=the end where the bullets come out]

busi·ness·like /ˈbɪznəsˌlaɪk/ *adj* [*more* ~; *most* ~] : having or showing qualities that are considered good in business : serious, polite, and practical ▪ His *businesslike* approach to the dispute was very helpful. ▪ a *businesslike* manner

busi·ness·man /ˈbɪznəsˌmæn/ *noun, pl* **-men** /-ˌmɛn/ [*count*]

1 : a man who works in business especially in a high position
2 : a man who is good at dealing with business and financial matters ▪ I know it's hard for him to sell his paintings. He's always been a better artist than *businessman*.

busi·ness·per·son /ˈbɪznəsˌpɚsn̩/ *noun, pl* **busi·ness·peo·ple** /ˈbɪznəsˌpiːpəl/ [*count*] : a man or woman who works in business

business suit *noun, pl* ~ **suits** [*count*] *US* : a type of suit that is worn by some people who work in offices and that includes a matching coat and pants or skirt

busi·ness·wom·an /ˈbɪznəsˌwʊmən/ *noun, pl* **-wom·en** /-ˌwɪmən/ [*count*]

1 : a woman who works in business especially in a high position
2 : a woman who is good at dealing with business and financial matters ▪ Like many musicians, she's found that she has to be a *businesswoman* as well as a performer.

bus·ing /ˈbʌsɪŋ/ *noun* [*noncount*] *US* : the act or practice of bringing children by buses to a school that is far from the area where they live so that the school will have many children of different races

busk /ˈbʌsk/ *verb* **busks; busked; busk·ing** [*no obj*] *chiefly Brit, informal* : to play music in a public place in order to earn money from people who are passing by

– busk·er /ˈbʌskɚ/ *noun, pl* **-ers** [*count*]

bus·load /ˈbʌsˌloʊd/ *noun, pl* **-loads** [*count*] *chiefly US* : a large group of people that fills a bus ▪ a *busload* of tourists ▪ People came to the park by the *busload*. [=many busloads of people came to the park]

bus·man's holiday /ˈbʌsmənz-/ *noun* [*singular*] : a holiday that you spend doing the same kind of thing that you usually do for your job

¹bust /ˈbʌst/ *noun, pl* **busts** [*count*]

1 : a sculpture of a person's head and neck and usually a part of the shoulders and chest ▪ a marble/bronze *bust* ▪ a *bust* of Albert Einstein
2 a : a woman's breasts ▪ The neckline of the dress is meant to accentuate the *bust*. **b** : a measurement taken around a woman's chest and back ▪ *bust* size
– compare ³BUST

²bust *verb* **busts; bust·ed** *also Brit* **bust; bust·ing** [+ *obj*] *informal*

1 : to break (something): such as **a** : to cause (something) to stop working by damaging it ▪ He *busted* his watch when he fell. ▪ I think the camera is *busted*. **b** : to cause (something) to separate into parts or pieces ▪ *bust* a window
2 a : to arrest (someone) ▪ Police *busted* 12 gang members on weapons charges. ▪ She got/was *busted* for drug possession. **b** : to catch (someone) doing something wrong ▪ Two students got *busted* by the teacher for smoking in the bathroom.
3 *US, impolite* — used in phrases like ***bust your butt/ass*** to describe working very hard ▪ She's been *busting her butt* to finish the project on time.
4 *US* : to hit or punch (someone) ▪ I felt like *busting* him in the nose.

bust a/your gut see ¹GUT

bust out [*phrasal verb*] *informal* **1** ***bust out (doing something)*** : to begin (doing something) suddenly : to burst out (doing something) ▪ She just *busted out* laughing. **2** ***bust out (something) or bust (something) out*** : to take (something) from the place where it is stored so that it can be used ▪ He *busted out* [=*broke out*] the champagne. **3** : to escape from a prison, jail, etc. ▪ Two prisoners *busted out* of jail.

bust up [*phrasal verb*] *informal* **1** : to end your relationship with someone ▪ Their marriage *busted up* after three years. ▪ Didn't you hear? They *busted up*. [=(more commonly) *broke up, separated*] **2** ***bust up (something) or bust (something) up*** : to cause (something) to end ▪ His gambling problem *busted up* their marriage. ▪ Police hope to *bust up* the crime ring for good. ▪ The police *busted* the party *up*.

or bust *informal* — used to say that you will do everything possible to get somewhere ▪ The sign on the car said "New Orleans *or bust*!"

³bust *noun, pl* **busts** [*count*] *informal*

1 *US* : a complete failure : FLOP — usually singular ▪ The new product was a *bust*. ▪ Although critically acclaimed, the play has been a *bust*.

2 : an occurrence in which the police catch and arrest people committing a crime ▪ a big drug *bust*
— compare [1]BUST

[4]**bust** *adj*
go bust *informal* : to spend or lose all of your money : to go broke ▪ The company has *gone bust.*

bust·er /ˈbʌstɚ/ *noun, pl* **-ers**
1 [*count*] **a** : a person or thing that stops or prevents something — usually used in combination ▪ crime-*busters* [=people who stop crimes, who catch criminals, etc.] **b** : a person or thing that breaks something apart — usually used in combination ▪ The new drug acts as a clot-*buster.* [=it causes blood clots to break apart]
2 *US, informal + somewhat old-fashioned* — used to address a man who is behaving in a way you do not like ▪ Wait a minute, *buster.* You're trying to trick me, aren't you?

bus·tier /ˌbuːstiˈeɪ, *Brit* ˈbʌstiˌeɪ/ *noun, pl* **-tiers** [*count*] : a tight piece of clothing that covers the upper part of a woman's body and that is worn by itself or under other clothes

[1]**bus·tle** /ˈbʌsəl/ *verb* **bus·tles; bus·tled; bus·tling** [*no obj*]
1 : to move or go in a busy or hurried way ▪ She *bustled* around the kitchen getting ready for dinner guests.
2 : to have a lot of busy activity — often + *with* ▪ The pier is always *bustling with* people.
— bustling *adj* ▪ a *bustling* town/pier

[2]**bustle** *noun* [*noncount*] : noisy or busy activity ▪ The countryside seems very quiet after the ***hustle and bustle*** of the city. — compare [3]BUSTLE

[3]**bustle** *noun, pl* **bustles** [*count*] : a frame or pad worn in the past under a skirt or dress to hold it out from the body in the back — compare [2]BUSTLE

bust–up /ˈbʌstˌʌp/ *noun, pl* **-ups** [*count*] *informal*
1 : the end of a relationship, marriage, etc. : BREAKUP ▪ the *bust-up* of their marriage
2 *Brit* : a very bad argument or disagreement : a quarrel or fight ▪ They had a *bust-up* over money.

busty /ˈbʌsti/ *adj* **bust·i·er; -est** [*also more ~; most ~*] *informal, of a woman* : having large breasts ▪ a *busty* blonde

[1]**busy** /ˈbɪzi/ *adj* **bus·i·er; -est** [*also more ~; most ~*]
1 : actively doing something ▪ She's *busy* preparing for her test. ▪ Are you *busy*? Can I talk to you for a minute? ▪ I will be *busy* cleaning the house. ▪ I'm sorry I haven't called. I've been so *busy.* ▪ *busy* people who don't have time to cook ▪ I got enough work to keep me *busy* for a while. ▪ He is a very *busy* person. ▪ He's been *busy* in the kitchen all afternoon. ▪ She's ***as busy as a bee*** [=she's very busy] — often + *with* ▪ The actress is *busy with* a new film. [=is working on a new film] ▪ He keeps himself *busy with* volunteer work. ▪ She is *busy with* wedding plans.
2 a : full of activity or work ▪ My week has been so *busy*! ▪ They live/lead *busy* lives. ▪ Is there any time in your *busy* schedule for us to have lunch next week? **b** : full of people or things ▪ a *busy* street ▪ a *busy* store
3 *chiefly US, of a telephone or telephone line* : being used ▪ I tried calling her, but her line/phone is *busy.* [=(*chiefly Brit*) *engaged*] ✧ When you dial a telephone line that is already in use, you hear a sound that is called a ***busy signal.***
4 : full of many details ▪ I like the fabric, but I think the pattern is too *busy* for this dress. ▪ *busy* wallpaper
get busy : to start doing work ▪ We need to finish by 5 o'clock, so we'd better *get busy.*
— busi·ly /ˈbɪzəli/ *adv* ▪ She is *busily* preparing for her test. ▪ He is working *busily* in the kitchen. **— busy·ness** /ˈbɪzinəs/ *noun* [*noncount*] ▪ I don't like the *busyness* of stores around the holidays. ▪ the *busyness* of the pattern

[2]**busy** *verb* **bus·ies; bus·ied; busy·ing**
busy yourself : to make or keep yourself busy : to occupy (yourself) with work or an activity ▪ The children *busied themselves* with puzzles all day. ▪ He *busied himself* in the workshop building things.

busy·body /ˈbɪziˌbɑːdi/ *noun, pl* **-bod·ies** [*count*] *disapproving* : a person who is too interested in the private lives of other people ▪ The neighborhood *busybody* is telling everyone that the couple up the street is getting divorced.

busy·work /ˈbɪziˌwɚk/ *noun* [*noncount*] *US* : work that is given to you only to keep you busy ▪ Students were given *busywork* for the last few minutes of class.

[1]**but** /ˈbʌt, bət/ *conj*
1 — used to introduce a statement that adds something to a previous statement and usually contrasts with it in some way ▪ I don't know her, *but* my husband does. ▪ He wants to go to the movies, *but* I want to go to the museum. ▪ He plans to visit Boston and Chicago, *but* not New York. ▪ The book is not a biography at all *but* (instead is) a fictional account. ▪ It's not the music I don't like *but* (rather) the band themselves. ▪ She got the promotion not by luck *but* by hard work. ▪ The fighting has been going on for years. *But* to really understand the current situation, you have to look at the history of the region. ▪ She called his name, *but* he did not answer. ▪ He fell *but* (he) wasn't hurt/injured. ▪ I told him to stay, *but* he refused to. ▪ It might have been raining, *but* it was still a nice wedding. ▪ I'd love to come to the party, *but* [=*however*] I'll be away that weekend. ▪ I'm sorry, *but* I won't be able to help you. ▪ The dress is quite plain *but* (it's) pretty. ▪ They were polite, *but* not really friendly. ▪ Not only was it quite cold on our trip, *but* it rained the whole time too. ▪ I can't do it—*but* neither can you.
2 : other than : EXCEPT ▪ We had no choice *but* to leave. ▪ They've done nothing *but* argue all afternoon.
3 — used in speech at the beginning of a sentence that expresses surprise, shock, etc. ▪ *But* you promised (that) you would help me with this. ▪ *But* it's not fair for them to treat him this way! ▪ They've arrived? *But* I thought they were coming Tuesday.
4 — used with a repeated word for emphasis ▪ Nobody *but* nobody could solve the riddle.
but then **1** — used to introduce a statement that adds another and different thought to a preceding statement ▪ I'm surprised to hear that Tom has left the army. *But then* I suppose he never was the type to obey orders. ▪ I'm sure she would do a wonderful job on the project, *but then* I know she's very busy. — sometimes used to introduce an explanation for something ▪ His cakes are amazing—*but then* he did study with some of the best pastry chefs in the world. **2** — used to introduce a statement that tells about something different or surprising that happened next ▪ The team won the first two games, *but then* failed to win any of the next five. ▪ The disease was said to be untreatable, *but then* a new medication was introduced.

[2]**but** *prep* : other than (something or someone) : EXCEPT ▪ We had nothing *but* rain all week. [=it rained for the entire week] ▪ There was no one there *but* him. ▪ I didn't tell anyone *but* my sister. ▪ Who *but* you would think that? ▪ No one *but* you would try that. = No one would try that *but* you. ▪ I was anything *but* tired. [=I was not at all tired]
but for : if not for (something or someone) : without (something or someone) ▪ We would never have visited the town *but for* [=*except for*] the newspaper article about local artists. ▪ The score would have been higher *but for* some excellent goaltending.

[3]**but** *adv, formal*
1 : [2]ONLY ▪ They have *but* two weeks to get ready. — sometimes used for emphasis ▪ If they had *but* given me a chance, I know I could have done it. ▪ He was here *but* five minutes ago. ▪ She is still *but* a child. ▪ This new product offers many advantages: speed, convenience, and durability, ***to name but a few.***
2 — used in negative statements to say that something must happen ▪ Anyone who reads the book ***cannot but*** feel sympathy for him. [=must feel sympathy for him] ▪ I ***could not (help) but*** wonder [=I felt compelled to wonder, I could not help wondering] why she had lied. — see also ALL BUT

[4]**but** /ˈbʌt/ *noun, pl* **buts** [*count*] : a reason someone gives for not doing or agreeing with something — usually plural ▪ I want this done today, and I don't want to hear any *buts* about it. ▪ (*US*) As far as I'm concerned, she's the most qualified candidate, and there are ***no ifs, ands, or buts*** about it! = (*Brit*) There are ***no ifs and buts*** about it! [=it is certain that she is the most qualified candidate]

bu·tane /ˈbjuːˌteɪn/ *noun* [*noncount*] : a type of gas that is used in a liquid form as a fuel usually for cooking or heating

butch /ˈbʊʧ/ *adj* [*more ~; most ~*] *informal*
1 *sometimes offensive* : having a very masculine appearance and way of behaving — used especially to describe homosexual women and men
2 *of hair* : cut very short ▪ a *butch* haircut

[1]**butch·er** /ˈbʊʧɚ/ *noun, pl* **-ers** [*count*]
1 a : someone who cuts and sells meat in a shop **b** : someone who kills animals and prepares their meat to be eaten
2 : a shop that sells meat ▪ The town was small but had a grocery store and a *butcher* (store/shop).
3 : someone who kills a lot of people or animals in a brutal or cruel way ▪ They are a bunch of *butchers* [=*murderers*] who gained power by slaughtering their enemies.

4 *informal* : someone who does something very roughly and badly ▪ That surgeon is a *butcher*! [=a terrible surgeon]
have/take a butcher's *Brit, informal* : to look at something ▪ This may be what we need. *Have a butcher's.*

²**butcher** *verb* **-ers; -ered; -er·ing** [+ *obj*]
1 : to kill (an animal) and prepare its meat for sale ▪ They've hired someone to *butcher* the hogs.
2 : to kill (people or animals) in a brutal and cruel way ▪ Many innocent people were *butchered* under his regime.
3 *informal* : to do (something) very badly : to make a mess of (something) ▪ The band has *butchered* my favorite song.

butch·ery /ˈbʊtʃəri/ *noun* [*noncount*]
1 : the violent and cruel killing of many people ▪ the *butchery* of civilians during the war
2 : the work of a butcher : the job of preparing meat for sale

but·ler /ˈbʌtlɚ/ *noun, pl* **-lers** [*count*] : the main male servant in the home of a wealthy person

¹**butt** /ˈbʌt/ *noun, pl* **butts** [*count*]
1 *chiefly US, informal + sometimes impolite* : the part of the body you sit on : BUTTOCKS ▪ He slipped and landed on his *butt*. [=(*chiefly Brit*) *bum*] ▪ These exercises will make your *butt* firmer. ▪ Why don't you ***get off your butt*** and do something? [=why don't you stop being so lazy and do something?] — used in informal phrases where *ass* might also be used ▪ Get your *butt* over here! [=come over here now] ▪ She really saved my *butt*. [=she helped me out of a difficult situation] ▪ He worked his *butt* off [=he worked very hard] to finish on time.
2 : the thicker end of a weapon or tool ▪ the *butt* (end) of a rifle
3 **a** : the end part of a cigarette or cigar that is not smoked ▪ a cigarette *butt* **b** *informal* : a cigarette ▪ She went out to buy some *butts*.
kick butt see ¹KICK
– compare ²BUTT, ⁴BUTT, ⁶BUTT

²**butt** *noun, pl* **butts** [*count*] : a person who is treated badly or is made fun of — usually singular; + *of* ▪ As a child, she was a clumsy girl who was the *butt of* everyone's jokes. [=people made jokes about her because she was clumsy] — compare ¹BUTT, ⁴BUTT, ⁶BUTT

³**butt** *verb* **butts; butt·ed; butt·ing** : to hit or push (something) forcefully with the head [+ *obj*] A few punches were thrown, and then one boy *butted* the other before a teacher broke up the fight. ▪ She got *butted* by an angry goat. [*no obj*] We saw the goat *butt* against the gate until it opened.
butt heads *chiefly US, informal* : to disagree about how something should be done ▪ They've *butted heads* over the issue a number of times.
butt in [*phrasal verb*] *informal* : to get involved in something (such as a conversation or someone else's activities) especially in a rude way ▪ I realize you're trying to help, but I wish you wouldn't *butt in*. You're only making things worse. ▪ Sorry to *butt in* (on you) like this, but I need to ask you a question.
butt out [*phrasal verb*] *chiefly US, informal* : to stop being involved in something (such as a conversation or someone else's affairs) ▪ This has nothing to do with you! I wish you would just *butt out*! ▪ They told me to *butt out* of the conversation.
– compare ⁵BUTT

⁴**butt** *noun, pl* **butts** [*count*] : a forceful hit or push with the head ▪ a head *butt* in/to the ribs — compare ¹BUTT, ²BUTT, ⁶BUTT

⁵**butt** *verb* **butts; butted; butting** *US* : to place something right next to something else or to be right next to something else [+ *obj*] We laid the boards so that the ends were *butted* against the wall. [*no obj*] The floorboards are weakest where they *butt* (against each other). [=where they meet, where the ends of the boards touch each other] ▪ **The apartment building *butts* up against an old church.** — compare ³BUTT

⁶**butt** *noun, pl* **butts** [*count*] *Brit* : WATER BUTT — compare ¹BUTT, ²BUTT, ⁴BUTT

butte /ˈbjuːt/ *noun, pl* **buttes** [*count*] : a type of hill with a flat top and steep sides that is found in the southwestern U.S. — see color picture on page C7

¹**but·ter** /ˈbʌtɚ/ *noun, pl* **-ters**
1 [*noncount*] : a solid yellow substance made from milk or cream that is spread on food or used in cooking ▪ bread and *butter* ▪ Would you like some *butter* for your potato? ▪ Sauté the onions in melted *butter*. — see also BREAD AND BUTTER
2 [*count, noncount*] : a food made from cooked fruit or roasted nuts that have been ground up ▪ apple *butter* — see also PEANUT BUTTER
butter wouldn't melt in someone's mouth *chiefly Brit* — used to say that a person who appears to be innocent, sincere, or kind is really not
like a (hot) knife through butter see ¹KNIFE

²**butter** *verb* **-ters; -tered; -ter·ing** [+ *obj*] : to spread or put butter on (something) ▪ *butter* a piece of bread ▪ *buttered* toast
butter up [*phrasal verb*] ***butter up (someone)*** *or* ***butter (someone) up*** *informal* : to treat (someone) very well or kindly in order to get something ▪ He's busy *buttering up* potential clients.
know which side your bread is buttered on see ¹BREAD

but·ter·ball /ˈbʌtɚˌbɑːl/ *noun, pl* **-balls** [*count*] *US, informal + often impolite* : a person who is somewhat fat ▪ I was a little *butterball* when I was a child.

butter bean *noun, pl* ~ **beans** [*count*]
1 *US* : a kind of small, flat bean : a small lima bean
2 *Brit* : a lima bean that is dried before it is sold

but·ter·cream /ˈbʌtɚˌkriːm/ *noun* [*noncount*] : a soft mixture of butter and sugar that is used as a filling or frosting for cakes

but·ter·cup /ˈbʌtɚˌkʌp/ *noun, pl* **-cups** [*count*] : a wild plant that has small yellow flowers that are shaped like cups

but·ter·fat /ˈbʌtɚˌfæt/ *noun* [*noncount*] : the natural fat of milk from which butter is made

but·ter·fin·gers /ˈbʌtɚˌfɪŋgɚz/ *noun* [*singular*] *informal* : a person who often drops things ▪ I dropped my pen again. Why am I such a *butterfingers* today?
– **but·ter·fin·gered** /ˈbʌtɚˌfɪŋgɚd/ *adj* ▪ a *butterfingered* ballplayer

¹**but·ter·fly** /ˈbʌtɚˌflaɪ/ *noun, pl* **-flies**
1 [*count*] : a kind of insect that has a long thin body and brightly colored wings and that flies mostly during the day — see color picture on page C10; compare MOTH
2 [*count*] *often disapproving* : a person who goes to many parties and other social events ▪ a ***social butterfly***
3 [*singular*] : a way of swimming in which the swimmer's face is in the water and the arms move together in a circular motion while the legs kick up and down ▪ swimmers doing the *butterfly*; *also* : a race in which the swimmers do the butterfly ▪ They competed in the *butterfly*.
4 ***butterflies*** [*plural*] *informal* : a nervous feeling in your stomach ▪ Even experienced musicians sometimes get *butterflies* before a performance. ▪ I have *butterflies* in my stomach.

²**butterfly** *verb* **-flies; -flied; -fly·ing** [+ *obj*] : to cut (food) into two pieces that are joined along one edge so that it can be spread apart for cooking ▪ *Butterfly* the chicken before roasting. ▪ *butterflied* shrimp

butter knife *noun, pl* ~ **knives** [*count*] : a small knife with a rounded blade that is used especially for spreading butter on bread during a meal

but·ter·milk /ˈbʌtɚˌmɪlk/ *noun* [*noncount*] : the liquid that is left after butter has been made from milk or cream

but·ter·nut squash /ˈbʌtɚˌnʌt-/ *noun, pl* ~ **squash** *or* ~ **squashes** [*count, noncount*] : a large vegetable that has a pale, hard shell and yellow or orange flesh — see color picture on page C4

but·ter·scotch /ˈbʌtɚˌskɑːtʃ/ *noun* [*noncount*] : a hard candy made by boiling butter, sugar, and water — often used before another noun ▪ a *butterscotch* sauce ▪ *butterscotch* pudding

but·tery /ˈbʌtəri/ *adj* [*more* ~; *most* ~]
1 : resembling butter ▪ The cheese has a *buttery* flavor. ▪ a smooth, *buttery* texture
2 : containing or covered with butter ▪ *buttery* pastries/popcorn

but·tock /ˈbʌtək/ *noun, pl* **-tocks** [*count*] : either of the two soft parts of the body that a person sits on ▪ the baby's left/right *buttock* — usually plural ▪ The shirt is long enough to cover your *buttocks*. — see picture at HUMAN

¹**but·ton** /ˈbʌtn̩/ *noun, pl* **-tons** [*count*]
1 : a small, usually round piece of plastic, glass, metal, etc., that is sewn to a piece of clothing and is pushed through a loop or hole to fasten one part of the clothing to another part ▪ a skirt/coat *button* ▪ a dress with *buttons* down the back ▪ I lost a *button* on my jacket. ▪ He took off his tie and undid the top *button* of his shirt. — see color picture on page C5
2 *US* : a small, usually round sign that has a picture or words on the front and a pin on the back ✧ People pin buttons to their clothing to show support for a person or idea. ▪ She was

B

wearing a *button* that read "Support your local library." • a ***campaign button*** [=a button that shows support for someone's political campaign] — called also *(Brit) badge*

3 a : a small part of a machine that you push to make the machine work • the on/off *button* • Will you please push/press the 'play' *button* on the CD player? • With a fax machine, you can send a document across the country with the touch/push of a *button*. **b :** a small area on a computer screen that you click on to make the computer software do something • If the information on the registration form is correct, click the 'OK' *button*. — see also HOT BUTTON

(as) cute as a button *informal* : very cute • Your nephew is *cute as a button*!

on the button *US, informal* **1 :** exactly at the specified time • They arrived at noon *on the button*. [=*on the dot, precisely*] **2 :** perfectly accurate • Your guess was (right) *on the button*. [=*on the nose*]

push the right buttons *informal* : to do the things that are needed to produce a desired effect or result • The coach knows how to *push all the right buttons* to get his players ready for the game.

push your buttons *informal* : to do or say something just to make you angry or upset • Don't pay any attention to her. She's just trying to *push your buttons*. • Even though they're both adults now, Rita's brother still ***knows how to push her buttons***. [=he is easily able to annoy or frustrate her]

²button *verb* **-tons; -toned; -ton·ing**

1 [+ *obj*] : to attach (a button) by passing it through a hole • He rarely *buttons* the top button on his shirt.

2 [+ *obj*] : to close or fasten (something) with buttons • Will you *button* the baby's jacket for her? — often + *up* • Be sure to *button up* your coat before you go outside.

3 [*no obj*] : to have buttons for fastening • The skirt *buttons* on the side.

button it *informal + impolite* — used to tell someone to stop talking • She angrily told him to *button it*.

button your lip/lips or keep your lip/lips buttoned *US, informal* : to not talk about something • *Button your lip*. He's coming toward us. • Don't tell him what I said, please. You know he can't *keep his lips buttoned*.

but·ton–down /ˈbʌtn̩ˌdaʊn/ *adj, always used before a noun*

1 a *of a collar* : having the ends fastened to the shirt with buttons • The shirt has a *button-down* collar. **b** *of a shirt* : having a button-down collar • a *button-down* shirt

2 *or* **but·toned–down** /ˈbʌʔn̩dˌdaʊn/ [*more* ~; *most* ~] *often disapproving* : having a very traditional and formal way of dressing, behaving, etc. • a very *buttoned-down* [=*conservative*] businessman

but·toned–up /ˈbʌtn̩dˈʌp/ *adj* [*more* ~; *most* ~] : not friendly and open about showing feelings • a *buttoned-up* [=*reserved*] executive

¹but·ton·hole /ˈbʌtn̩ˌhoʊl/ *noun, pl* **-holes** [*count*]

1 : a hole in clothing through which a button is passed in order to fasten something

2 *Brit* : BOUTONNIERE

²buttonhole *verb* **-holes; -holed; -hol·ing** [+ *obj*] *informal* : to force (someone who is going somewhere) to stop and talk to you • I'm sorry I'm late. I was *buttonholed* by a coworker just as I was leaving my office.

button mushroom *noun, pl* ~ **-rooms** [*count*] : a small, white mushroom that is often eaten as a vegetable

button nose *noun, pl* ~ **noses** [*count*] : a small, rounded nose

¹but·tress /ˈbʌtrəs/ *noun, pl* **-tress·es** [*count*] : a structure built against a wall in order to support or strengthen it — see also FLYING BUTTRESS

²buttress *verb* **-tresses; -tressed; -tress·ing** [+ *obj*] : to support, strengthen, or defend (something) • The treaty will *buttress* the cause of peace. • The theory has been *buttressed* by the results of the experiment.

but·ty /ˈbʌti/ *noun, pl* **-ties** [*count*] *Brit, informal* : a sandwich

bux·om /ˈbʌksəm/ *adj, of a woman* : healthy and attractive with large breasts • a *buxom* blonde

¹buy /ˈbaɪ/ *verb* **buys; bought** /ˈbɑːt/; **buy·ing**

1 : to get (something) by paying money for it : PURCHASE [+ *obj*] I *bought* a computer. • I *bought* this hat for $10. • He *bought* the quilt from a local artist. • He *bought* dinner for us. = He *bought* us dinner. [*no obj*] Stock prices are low, so now is a good time to *buy*. — opposite SELL

2 [+ *obj*] *of money* : to be able to get something • A quarter won't *buy* (you) much these days. • Money can't *buy* love.

3 [+ *obj*] *informal* : to accept or believe (something) as true • He said it was a mistake, but I don't *buy* it.

4 [+ *obj*] *informal* : to give money to someone in order to get that person to do something illegal or dishonest for you : BRIBE — usually used as *(be) bought* • an honest policeman who can't *be bought* — see also BUY OFF (below)

5 [+ *obj*] : to get (something) by losing or giving up something — usually used as *(be) bought* • Peace *was* finally *bought*, but at the cost of many lives.

buy a pup see PUP

buy in [*phrasal verb*] ***buy in (something) or buy (something) in*** *Brit* : to buy a large amount of (something) • Be sure to *buy in* a lot of tinned food in case we're snowed up.

buy into [*phrasal verb*] ***buy into (something)*** **1 :** to pay money in order to own part of (something, such as a company or sports team) • Investors are *buying into* Internet companies. **2 :** to accept or believe (something) as true • The book teaches kids not to *buy into* the notion that money brings happiness.

buy it *or* ***US buy the farm*** *informal* : to die • I nearly *bought the farm* when my car skidded off the road.

buy off [*phrasal verb*] ***buy off (someone) or buy (someone) off*** : to give money to (someone) for illegal or dishonest help • Many believe that Jones *bought off* the police so that he would not be investigated for the murder. — see also ¹BUY 4 (above)

buy out [*phrasal verb*] ***buy out (someone) or buy (someone) out*** : to pay money to (someone) for his or her part of a company or team • She *bought out* her partners so that she could manage the company the way she wanted to. — see also BUYOUT

buy time : to get more time for someone or something • The medication won't cure the disease but it will *buy* patients some *time*. [=it will allow patients to live longer]

buy up [*phrasal verb*] ***buy up (something) or buy (something) up*** : to pay money for all or a large part of (something) • The company has *bought up* the old factories along the river and will convert them into apartments. • She is *buying up* all the artist's early work.

²buy *noun, pl* **buys** [*count*]

1 — used to describe something that is being sold • The toy is a popular *buy*. [=many people are buying the toy] • The shoes were a great *buy* [=*deal*] at 50 percent off the original price.

2 : an act of buying something • an undercover drug *buy* [=*purchase, deal*]

buy·er /ˈbajɚ/ *noun, pl* **-ers** [*count*]

1 : someone who buys something • The *buyer* and seller must agree on a price for the property. • He's trying to find a *buyer* for the restaurant.

2 : someone whose job is to choose and buy the goods that a store will sell

buyer's market *noun* [*singular*] : a situation in which many things of the same kind are for sale, prices are low, and buyers have an advantage over sellers — opposite SELLER'S MARKET

buying power *noun* [*noncount*] : PURCHASING POWER 1 • Inflation decreases consumer *buying power*. • a multinational corporation with a tremendous amount of *buying power*

buy·out /ˈbaɪˌaʊt/ *noun, pl* **-outs** [*count*] : the act of gaining control of a company by buying the parts of it you do not own • an employee/management *buyout* = a *buyout* by the employees/managers of the company — see also *buy out* at ¹BUY

¹buzz /ˈbʌz/ *verb* **buzz·es; buzzed; buzz·ing**

1 [*no obj*] **a :** to make the low, continuous sound of a flying insect (such as a bee) • a *buzzing* bee • Flies were *buzzing* around the picnic tables. **b :** to make a low, continuous sound • The doorbell *buzzed* loudly. **c :** to be filled with a low, continuous sound • My ears were still *buzzing* [=*ringing*] hours after the concert.

2 [*no obj*] : to be filled with activity, excitement, etc. • The hall *buzzed* with excitement as the audience waited for the show to start. • My mind is *buzzing* with ideas.

3 a : to send for or signal (someone) by using an electric device (called a buzzer) that produces a loud, low sound [+ *obj*] The nurse *buzzed* the doctor who was on duty. • She *buzzed* her secretary to say she was going out for lunch. [*no obj*] — often + *for* • The nurse *buzzed for* the doctor. **b** [+ *obj*] : to let (someone) go into or out of a place by using an electric device that produces a loud, low sound as it unlocks a door, gate, etc. • Ring the bell when you arrive and someone will *buzz* you into the building. • Let me *buzz* you out.

4 [+ *obj*] *US, informal* : to call (someone) on the telephone • *Buzz* me when you get there.
5 [+ *obj*] : to fly an airplane low over (something or someone) • The plane/pilot *buzzed* the people watching the show.
6 [*no obj*] : to go or move quickly • The host of the party was *buzzing* around the room talking to everyone.
buzz off *informal* — used as a rude or angry way to tell someone to go away • He told me to *buzz off.* • *Buzz off*, will you? I'm busy right now.
– buzzing *noun* [*noncount*] • hear the *buzzing* of bees

[2]**buzz** *noun, pl* **buzzes**
1 [*count*] **a** : the low, continuous sound made by a flying insect (such as a bee) • We heard the *buzz* of the bees as we walked through the garden. **b** : a low, continuous sound • When the machine is turned on, it makes a quiet *buzz*.
2 [*singular*] : a low sound caused by many people talking at the same time • There was a *buzz* of voices in the hall as the audience waited for the show to start.
3 *informal* **a** [*noncount*] : the things that are being said about something • What's the latest *buzz* about their marriage? • The *buzz* is that she turned down the job because the pay was too low. **b** : excited talk about something [*singular*] There's been quite a *buzz* about the new movie. • The team's new players are creating a *buzz* among baseball fans. [*noncount*] There's been a lot of *buzz* about the new movie.
4 [*singular*] *informal* **a** : a feeling of excitement • Kids love the new game, and adults get a *buzz* [=*kick*] out of it too. **b** : a feeling of being somewhat drunk or intoxicated • He had a *buzz* after only two drinks. — see also BUZZED
5 [*singular*] *informal* : a telephone call • ***Give me a buzz*** [=call me] when you get there.

buz•zard /ˈbʌzɚd/ *noun, pl* **-zards** [*count*]
1 *US* : a kind of large bird that eats animals that are already dead
2 *Brit* : a kind of large hawk

buzz cut *noun, pl* ~ **cuts** [*count*] *US* : CREW CUT — see picture at HAIR

buzzed *adj, informal* : slightly drunk or intoxicated • He was *buzzed* after only two drinks.

buzz•er /ˈbʌzɚ/ *noun, pl* **-ers** [*count*] : an electric device that makes a loud sound • Their team was ahead by two points when the *buzzer* signaled the end of the game.

buzz saw *noun, pl* ~ **saws** [*count*] *US* : CIRCULAR SAW

buzz•word /ˈbʌzˌwɚd/ *noun, pl* **-words** [*count*] : a word or phrase that becomes very popular for a period of time ✧ Buzzwords are often related to a particular business or field of study. • At that time, the new *buzzword* in the tourism industry was "ecotourism."

[1]**by** /ˈbaɪ, bə/ *prep*
1 : close to or next to (something or someone) : NEAR • She was standing *by* [=*beside*] the window. • His wife was sitting *by* him. • They have a house *by* the lake.
2 **a** : up to and beyond (something or someone) : PAST • The bus went right *by* him without stopping. **b** : at or to (someone's home) • Some friends stopped/came *by* our house for a chat. • Why don't you come *by* my place later?
3 **a** — used following a passive verb to indicate the person or thing that does something • The decision was made *by* the company president. [=the company president made the decision] • Coal has been replaced *by* oil. [=oil has replaced coal] • He was killed *by* a falling rock. [=a falling rock killed him] • I was greatly surprised *by* the result. [=the result surprised me greatly] **b** — used to indicate the thing that is used to do something • He opened the door *by* (using) force. [=he used force to open the door] • She succeeded *by* pure determination. **c** — used to indicate an action that is done for a particular purpose • You can reset the machine *by* pressing this button. [=you can press this button to reset the machine] • He began his speech *by* thanking the President and ended it *by* telling a joke.
4 — used to indicate the person who wrote or created something • a play (written) *by* William Shakespeare • This is a portrait of Gaugin (that was painted) *by* Van Gogh.
5 **a** — used to indicate the method used to go somewhere, send something, etc. • Some people came *by* [=*via*] train while others came *by* car. • He returned *by* [=*on, via*] the last train. • They sent him a message *by* [=*via*] e-mail. • We drove here *by* the back roads. **b** — used to indicate the method used to enter or leave a place • We entered *by* [=*through, via*] the front door.
6 **a** — used to indicate the name that is used for someone or something • The American writer Samuel L. Clemens was known *by* the name "Mark Twain." • Her full name is Elizabeth but she goes *by* (the nickname) "Lizzie." • The Federal Bureau of Investigation is usually referred to *by* its initials "FBI." **b** — used to indicate how someone is spoken to, identified, etc. • He called her ***by name.*** [=he used her name when he spoke to her] • I know her ***by sight*** but not *by name.* [=I know what she looks like but I don't know her name] **c** — used to introduce the name of someone or something important as proof that you are speaking the truth • I swear *by* [=in the name of] all that's sacred that everything I've said is true. — often used in phrases like ***by God*** to add emphasis • He always said he'd retire to Hawaii, and *by God*, he did it! **d** : when using (a specified word or phrase) • What do you mean *by* "acceptable levels?" [=what levels do you consider acceptable?] • She called my theory "interesting," but I don't know what she meant *by* that. [=I don't know whether she was being sincere, polite, etc.] • It's hard to know what the author intended *by* this phrase.
7 — used to indicate the part of something or of a person's body that is held, grasped, etc. • He grasped the shovel *by* the/its handle. [=he grasped the handle of the shovel] • She grabbed him *by* the arm. [=she grabbed his arm] • He held/took his daughter *by* the/her hand. [=he held/took his daughter's hand]
8 **a** : during the time of (day or night) • New York ***by night*** [=at night, during the night] is very different from New York ***by day.*** [=during the day] **b** — used to indicate the kind of light that occurs or is used when something is being looked at, read, etc. • The landscape looked very different when we saw it *by* daylight than it had *by* moonlight. • She was trying to read *by* the light of a single candle.
9 **a** : not later than (a specified time) : at, in, on, or before (a specified time) • We need to leave *by* noon at the latest. • They should be here *by* tomorrow. • I don't know where she is. She should have been back *by* now. • *By* this time next year she hopes to have a new job. • She's planning to get married next year, *by* which time she hopes to have a new job. **b** : during the time until (a specified time) • *By* 2000 the U.S. had been an independent country for more than 200 years.
10 **a** : in a way that agrees with or follows (something, such as a rule) • They didn't play *by* the rules. **b** : in a way that is based on (something) • You shouldn't judge other people *by* (their) appearances. **c** : according to (something) • *By* my watch it's nearly noon. [=my watch says that it's nearly noon]
11 **a** — used to indicate units of measurement or quantity • The eggs are sold *by* the dozen. • She gets paid *by* the hour. • They have been making progress *by* small degrees. **b** — used to indicate the number that multiplies or divides another number • multiply 8 *by* 12 • divide 10 *by* 4 **c** — used to indicate the numbers of a measurement • The room measures 15 feet *by* 20 feet.
12 — used to indicate an amount, length, etc. • The horse won the race *by* a nose. • She's taller than I am *by* several inches. [=she's several inches taller than I am] • The price has been increased *by* five dollars. • This one is better ***by far*** than that one. [=this one is much better than that one]
13 — used to indicate someone's job, origin, character, etc. • She's a lawyer *by* profession. • He's French *by* birth, although he has lived in America for many years. • I'm an optimist *by* nature. [=it is my nature to be optimistic]
14 **a** — used in phrases to describe the speed at which something happens or changes • The work is getting done ***bit by bit.*** [=the work is getting done gradually in small amounts] • He's getting better ***little by little.*** • His health is growing worse ***day by day.*** = His health is growing worse ***by the day.*** [=his health is growing worse every day] • The situation is getting more dangerous ***by the second/minute/hour.*** **b** — used in phrases to describe how a series of people or things proceed or are dealt with • They entered the room ***two by two.*** [=*two at a time*] [=two of them entered the room, then two more entered the room, etc.] • I solved the problems ***one by one.*** [=I solved the first problem, then the second one, etc.]
15 *informal* : in the opinion of (someone) • Whatever you want to do is ***fine/okay by me.*** [=I am willing to agree to whatever you want to do]
16 *somewhat formal* **a** : on behalf of (someone) • He always did right *by* his children. [=he always did the right things to help his children] **b** — used to indicate the husband or wife who is the parent of someone's child • He had two daughters *by* his first wife and a son *by* his second wife. [=his first wife was the mother of his two daughters and his second wife was the mother of his son] • She has two children *by* her first husband.

***by the by or by the bye** old-fashioned* — used to introduce a statement that provides added information or that mentions another subject • I recently met his wife who, *by the by* [=*by the way, incidentally*], is a well-known author.

by yourself : without others : ALONE • He sat (all) *by himself*, reading the newspaper. • The new law will help, but it can't solve the problem (all) *by itself*. • You shouldn't lift that heavy box (all) *by yourself*. Let me help you.

C

²by /ˈbaɪ/ *adv*

1 : ⁴PAST • The bus went right *by* without stopping. • We stood and applauded as the parade went/passed *by*. • The last few years have ***gone by*** [=have passed] so quickly.

2 — used with *put* to describe something that is being kept or saved for a future use • You should be *putting* some money *by* [=*aside*] for your old age. [=you should be saving some money for your old age]

3 : at or to someone's home • Some friends stopped/came *by* for a chat. [=some friends came by our house for a chat] • Why don't you come *by* later?

4 : close or near • He did it when nobody was *by*. [=(more commonly) *around*] • She lives ***close by***. [=*nearby*]

***by and by** literary + old-fashioned* : before too long : EVENTUALLY • I feel sure that we'll succeed *by and by*. [=*ultimately, in the end*]

by and large **1** : in a general way : in general • *By and large* [=*generally, for the most part*], I like the way things have gone. **2** : in most cases : in general • *By and large* [=*generally, usually*] it takes a month for the shipment to arrive.

¹bye /ˈbaɪ/ *interj, informal* : ¹GOODBYE • *Bye*. I'll see you tomorrow. — often + *now* • "See you later." "OK. *Bye now*."

²bye *noun, pl* **byes** [*count*] *sports* : a situation in which a player or team is allowed to go forward to the next level in a competition without having to play against and defeat an opponent • She got a *bye* into the second round of the tennis tournament.

bye–bye /ˈbaɪˌbaɪ/ *interj, informal* : ¹GOODBYE • *Bye-bye*! See you later! — often used by children or when speaking to children • Say/Wave *bye-bye*, darling: it's time to go home.

go bye-bye** informal* **1** *or Brit* ***go bye-byes : to go to bed — used when speaking to children • It's time to *go bye-bye*, darling: it's way past your bedtime! **2** *US* : to go away — used in imitation of children's speech • When the company went bankrupt, investors watched their money *go bye-bye*.

by–elec·tion /ˈbajəˌlɛkʃən/ *noun, pl* **-tions** [*count*] *Brit* : a special election that is held between regular elections to replace someone who has died or resigned from office

by·gone /ˈbaɪˌgɑːn/ *adj, always used before a noun* : gone by : from a time in the past • the *bygone* days of our ancestors • The stone wall is from a *bygone* age/era.

by·gones /ˈbaɪˌgɑːnz/ *noun*

let bygones be bygones : to forgive someone for something done to you or for a disagreement with you and forget about it • I know we've had our fights over the years, but I think it's time we *let bygones be bygones*.

by·law /ˈbaɪˌlɑː/ *noun, pl* **-laws** [*count*]

1 *US* : a rule that an organization (such as a club or company) makes and that its members must follow

2 : a law or regulation that is made by a local government and that applies only to the local area

by·line /ˈbaɪˌlaɪn/ *noun, pl* **-lines** [*count*] : a line at the beginning of a newspaper or magazine article that gives the writer's name

¹by·pass /ˈbaɪˌpæs, *Brit* ˈbaɪˌpɑːs/ *noun, pl* **-pass·es** [*count*]

1 : a road that goes around a blocked or very crowded area • The bridge is being rebuilt so we'll have to take the *bypass*.

2 *medical* : a procedure done to allow blood to flow past a blocked blood vessel to reach the heart • heart *bypass* surgery • a double/triple/quadruple *bypass* [=a procedure done when two/three/four blood vessels are blocked]

²bypass *verb* **-passes; -passed; -pass·ing** [+ *obj*]

1 : to go around or avoid (a place or area) • To *bypass* the city, take the highway that circles it. • Is there a way to *bypass* the bridge construction?

2 : to avoid or ignore (someone or something) especially to get something done quicker • He *bypassed* the manager and talked directly to the owner. • She managed to *bypass* the usual paperwork.

by–prod·uct /ˈbaɪˌprɑːdəkt/ *noun, pl* **-ucts** [*count*]

1 : something that is produced during the production or destruction of something else — often + *of* • The chemical is a *by-product of* the oil-refining process. • Carbon monoxide is a *by-product of* burning fuel.

2 : something that happens as a result of something else — often + *of* • The loss of jobs was an unfortunate *by-product of* the industry's switch to new technology.

by·stand·er /ˈbaɪˌstændɚ/ *noun, pl* **-ers** [*count*] : a person who is standing near but not taking part in what is happening • Two innocent *bystanders* were injured in the shooting.

byte /ˈbaɪt/ *noun, pl* **bytes** [*count*] : a unit of computer information that is equal to eight bits — see also GIGABYTE, KILOBYTE, MEGABYTE

by·way /ˈbaɪˌweɪ/ *noun, pl* **-ways**

1 [*count*] : a road that is not used very much • I prefer to take *byways* to town. • He's traveled ***the highways and byways*** of this country.

2 ***byways*** [*plural*] : the parts of a subject that are not commonly known • the *byways* of the art world • The book chronicles some of the interesting *byways* of legal history.

by·word /ˈbaɪˌwɚd/ *noun, pl* **-words** [*count*] : someone or something that is closely connected with a particular quality — usually singular; usually + *for* • The new luxury hotel is fast becoming a *byword for* hospitality. • Her name has become a *byword for* wit.

byz·an·tine /ˈbɪzənˌtiːn, *Brit* baɪˈzænˌtaɪn/ *adj* [*more ~; most ~*] *formal + disapproving* : very complicated, secret, and hard to understand • The company's *byzantine* accounting practices have gotten it into trouble with the government.

C

c *or* **C** /ˈsiː/ *noun, pl* **c's** *or* **cs** *or* **C's** *or* **Cs**

1 : the third letter of the English alphabet [*count*] The word "access" is spelled with two *cs*. [*noncount*] Many English words begin with *c*.

2 [*count*] : the Roman numeral that means 100 • CCV [=205]

3 : a musical note or key referred to by the letter C : the first tone of a C-major scale [*count*] play/sing a *C* [*noncount*] a song in the key of *C*

4 [*count*] : a grade that is given to a student for doing average work • She got a *C* on the exam. • He's a ***C student***. [=a student who gets C's for his schoolwork]

5 — used to refer to the third of three or more people, places, or things that are being considered • If A, B, and *C* divide the coins equally, how many does each person get?

c. *abbr* **1** *also* **ca.** circa — used to indicate that a date is not exact • *c.* 1600 = *ca.* 1600 [=approximately in 1600] **2** *US* cup • 2 *c.* flour

C *abbr* **1** Celsius **2** centigrade **3** copyright

CA *abbr* California

cab /ˈkæb/ *noun, pl* **cabs** [*count*]

1 : ¹TAXI • Do you want to catch/get a *cab*? [=to get a taxi to stop and give you a ride]

2 : the part of a truck, tractor, etc., in which the driver sits

ca·bal /kəˈbɑːl, *Brit* kəˈbæl/ *noun, pl* **-bals** [*count*] *formal + disapproving* : a small group of people who work together secretly • a *cabal* plotting to overthrow the government

ca·bana /kəˈbænə, *Brit* ˈkəˈbɑːnə/ *noun, pl* **-ban·as** [*count*] : a small, simple building that has a roof and usually walls and is often used by people at a beach or swimming pool

cab·a·ret /ˌkæbəˈreɪ/ *noun, pl* **-rets**

1 [*count*] : a restaurant where you can buy alcohol and see a musical show

2 [*count, noncount*] : entertainment provided at a such a restaurant — often used before another noun • a *cabaret* act/singer

cab·bage /ˈkæbɪʤ/ *noun, pl* **-bag·es**
1 [*count, noncount*] : a leafy vegetable that has several forms; *especially* : one that grows in a tight round shape (called a head) — see color picture on page C4
2 [*count*] *Brit, informal* : VEGETABLE 2

cab·bie *or* **cab·by** /ˈkæbi/ *noun, pl* **-bies** [*count*] *informal* : CABDRIVER

cab·driv·er /ˈkæbˌdraɪvɚ/ *noun, pl* **-ers** [*count*] : a person who drives a taxi

cab·in /ˈkæbən/ *noun, pl* **-ins** [*count*]
1 : a small, simple house made of wood • a *cabin* in the woods • a ***log cabin*** [=a cabin made of logs]
2 a : a room that you can sleep in on a ship or boat **b** : the part of an airplane in which the passengers sit • Don't unbuckle your seat belt until the flight attendant says it is safe to move around the *cabin*.

cabin cruiser *noun, pl* **~ -er** [*count*] : CRUISER 3

cab·i·net /ˈkæbnɪt/ *noun, pl* **-nets** [*count*]
1 : a piece of furniture that is used for storing things and usually has doors and shelves • a kitchen/medicine *cabinet* — see also FILE CABINET
2 *or* ***Cabinet*** : a group of people who give advice to the leader of a government • the British *cabinet* • a member of the President's *Cabinet* ♦ In British English, *cabinet* in this sense is sometimes used with a plural verb. • The *Cabinet* are meeting now.

cab·i·net·mak·er /ˈkæbnɪtˌmeɪkɚ/ *noun, pl* **-ers** [*count*] : a person who makes fine wooden furniture
– cab·i·net·mak·ing /ˈkæbnɪtˌmeɪkɪŋ/ *noun* [*noncount*]

cabin fever *noun* [*noncount*] : an unhappy and impatient feeling that comes from being indoors for too long • She suffered from *cabin fever* during the long winter. • a bad case of *cabin fever*

¹ca·ble /ˈkeɪbəl/ *noun, pl* **ca·bles**
1 a : a thick, strong rope made of wires that are twisted together [*count*] The bridge is held up by *cables*. [*noncount*] Their company supplied *cable* for the project. **b** [*count*] : a wire that moves a part in a machine • a brake *cable*
2 : a group of wires, glass fibers, etc., covered in plastic or rubber and used to carry electricity or electrical signals [*count*] battery *cables* • computer *cables* • a fiber-optic *cable* [*noncount*] We need more *cable* to hook up the computers.
3 [*count*] : a message sent by telegraph : TELEGRAM
4 [*noncount*] : CABLE TELEVISION • Does our hotel room have *cable*? • The game will be shown on *cable*. • *cable* news • the big *cable* networks/companies • a ***cable box*** [=a box that sends television signals from a cable into the television]

²cable *verb* **cables; ca·bled; ca·bling** : to send a message by telegraph : TELEGRAPH [+ *obj*] She *cabled* the news to the United States. • She *cabled* her parents for money. [*no obj*] The soldiers *cabled* back to headquarters.

cable car *noun, pl* **~ cars** [*count*]
1 : a vehicle that hangs in the air from a cable that pulls it up and down mountains • The skiers took a *cable car* to the top of the mountain.
2 : a vehicle that is pulled along tracks by a cable • Tourists packed the *cable cars* on the hilly streets of San Francisco.

cable modem *noun, pl* **~ -dems** [*count*] : a device that connects a computer to a network (such as the Internet) through the same kind of cable used for cable television

cable television *noun* [*noncount*] : a system in which television signals are sent through cables rather than through the air — called also *cable, cable TV*

ca·boo·dle /kəˈbuːdl/ *noun*
the whole (kit and) caboodle *US, informal* : EVERYTHING • Her father owned 5 houses and 12 cars, and when he died he left her *the whole caboodle*. • You can buy one of the books every month, or buy *the whole kit and caboodle* at the same time.

ca·boose /kəˈbuːs/ *noun, pl* **-boos·es** [*count*] *US* : a part of a train that is attached at the back end and is used by people who work on the train — called also (*Brit*) *guard's van*

ca·cao /kəˈkaʊ/ *noun* [*noncount*] : the dried seeds of a tropical tree that are used to make cocoa and chocolate • a farmer who grows *cacao* • a *cacao*-producing region — often used before another noun • *cacao* seeds/beans [=(more commonly) cocoa beans] • a *cacao* tree

cache /ˈkæʃ/ *noun, pl* **cach·es** [*count*]
1 : a group of things that have been hidden in a secret place because they are illegal or have been stolen • a weapons *cache* used by terrorists • Police found a *cache* of stolen cars in the woods.
2 *technical* : a part of a computer's memory where information is kept so that the computer can find it very quickly • Her new laptop has one megabyte of *cache*. — called also *cache memory*

ca·chet /ˌkæˈʃeɪ/ *noun* — used to say that someone or something is liked or respected by people [*noncount*] a movie director with great artistic *cachet* • social *cachet* [*singular*] His research in Antarctica gave him a certain *cachet* among other scientists.

cack–hand·ed /ˈkækˌhændəd/ *adj* [*more ~; most ~*] *Brit, informal* : clumsy or awkward • a *cack-handed* [=*hamhanded*] attempt at being funny

cack·le /ˈkækəl/ *verb* **cack·les; cack·led; cack·ling** [*no obj*]
1 *of chickens, geese, etc.* : to make loud, unpleasant sounds • The hens were *cackling* in the henhouse. • Geese *cackled* by the pond in the park.
2 : to laugh noisily • I could hear my aunts *cackling* in the next room.
– cackle *noun, pl* **cackles** [*count*] • a *cackle* of laughter/delight • the *cackle* of a chicken

ca·coph·o·ny /kæˈkɑːfəni/ *noun* [*singular*] : unpleasant loud sounds • The sounds of barking dogs and sirens added to the *cacophony* on the streets. — usually + *of* • a *cacophony of* voices
– ca·coph·o·nous /kæˈkɑːfənəs/ *adj* [*more ~; most ~*] • a *cacophonous* birthday party

cac·tus /ˈkæktəs/ *noun, pl* **cac·ti** /ˈkækˌtaɪ/ *or* **cac·tus·es** *also US* **cactus** [*count*] : a plant that lives in the desert and that has many sharp points (called spines) — see color picture on page C6

cad /ˈkæd/ *noun, pl* **cads** [*count*] *old-fashioned* : a rude and selfish man • He is a *cad*, not a gentleman.
– cad·dish /ˈkædɪʃ/ *adj* [*more ~; most ~*] • *caddish* behavior • her *caddish* husband

ca·dav·er /kəˈdævɚ/ *noun, pl* **-ers** [*count*] *formal* : a dead body : CORPSE

ca·dav·er·ous /kəˈdævərəs/ *adj* [*more ~; most ~*] : looking very thin and pale : resembling a corpse • A tall, *cadaverous* man led us into the library. • We saw a *cadaverous* [=*emaciated*] heroin addict sitting in the park.

¹cad·die *or* **cad·dy** /ˈkædi/ *noun, pl* **-dies** [*count*] : a person who carries a golfer's clubs on the golf course

²caddie *or* **caddy** *verb* **caddies; cad·died; cad·dy·ing** [*no obj*] : to carry a golfer's clubs on the golf course • I *caddied* for Mr. Brewer yesterday.

cad·dy /ˈkædi/ *noun, pl* **-dies** [*count*] : a small box or chest • an antique ***tea caddy*** [=a small box to keep tea in]

ca·dence /ˈkeɪdn̩s/ *noun, pl* **-denc·es**
1 : a regular beat or rhythm [*count*] the steady *cadence* of the drums [*noncount*] Oars moved back and forth in smooth *cadence*.
2 [*count*] : the way a person's voice changes by gently rising and falling while he or she is speaking • He speaks with a soft Southern *cadence*.
3 [*count*] : an ending part of a piece of music

ca·den·za /kəˈdɛnzə/ *noun, pl* **-zas** [*count*] : a difficult part of a piece of classical music that is performed by only one person near the end of the piece

ca·det /kəˈdɛt/ *noun, pl* **-dets** [*count*] : a student at a military school who is preparing to be an officer • a naval *cadet* — see also SPACE CADET

cadge /ˈkæʤ/ *verb* **cadg·es; cadged; cadg·ing** [+ *obj*] : to persuade someone to give you (something) for free • He spent his time trying to *cadge* [=*beg, bum, scrounge*] drinks from the customers. • She *cadged* money from her sister.

cad·mi·um /ˈkædmijəm/ *noun* [*noncount*] : a bluish-white metal that is used especially in protective coatings and in batteries

caesarean, caesarean section *variant spellings of* CESAREAN, CESAREAN SECTION

ca·fé *also* **ca·fe** /kæˈfeɪ, *Brit* ˈkæˌfeɪ/ *noun, pl* **-fés** *also* **-fes** [*count*] : a small restaurant where you can get simple meals and drinks (such as coffee)
sidewalk café *or Brit* ***pavement café*** : a café that has tables and chairs outside near the street

caf·e·te·ria /ˌkæfəˈtirijə/ *noun, pl* **-rias** [*count*] : a place (such as a restaurant or a room in a school) where people get food at a counter and carry it to a table for eating • a school *cafeteria*

caff /ˈkæf/ *noun, pl* **caffs** [*count*] *Brit, informal* : CAFÉ

C

caf·fein·at·ed /ˈkæfəˌneɪtəd/ *adj* : containing caffeine • *caffeinated* beverages — opposite DECAFFEINATED

caf·feine /kæˈfiːn, *Brit* ˈkæˌfiːn/ *noun* [*noncount*] : a substance that is found especially in coffee and tea and that makes you feel more awake • Her doctor told her to avoid *caffeine*. • ***caffeine-free***[=*decaffeinated*] coffee/soda

caf·fe lat·te /ˈkɑːferˈlɑːteɪ, *Brit* ˈkæferˈlæteɪ/ *noun, pl* ~ **-tes** [*count*] : a drink that is made by mixing a type of strong coffee (called espresso) with hot milk — called also *latte*

caf·tan *or* **kaf·tan** /ˈkæfˌtæn/ *noun, pl* **-tans** [*count*] : a long piece of clothing with long sleeves that is worn by men in countries that are just east of the Mediterranean Sea

cage /ˈkeɪʤ/ *noun, pl* **cag·es** [*count*] : a box made of wire or metal bars in which people keep animals or birds • a hamster/monkey/parrot *cage* — see also BIRDCAGE, RIB CAGE

rattle someone's cage *informal* : to make someone feel worried or upset • Don't worry about what he said. He was just trying to *rattle your cage*.

caged /ˈkeɪʤd/ *adj* : kept in a cage • a *caged* lion • He felt like a *caged* animal at his old job.

ca·gey *also* **ca·gy** /ˈkeɪʤi/ *adj* **ca·gi·er; -est**

1 : not willing to say everything that you know about something — often + *about* • Officials are *cagey about* saying who met with the mayor.

2 : careful to avoid being trapped or tricked • a *cagey* [=*crafty*] lawyer • *cagey* [=*savvy*] consumers • a *cagey* old farmer

3 : very clever • a *cagey* prisoner • a *cagey* move

— **ca·gi·ly** /ˈkeɪʤəli/ *adv* — **cag·i·ness** *noun* [*noncount*]

ca·hoots /kəˈhuːts/ *noun*

in cahoots *informal* : working together or making plans together in secret — usually + *with* • He was robbed by a man who was *in cahoots with* the bartender.

Cain see *raise Cain* at [1]RAISE

cairn /ˈkeən/ *noun, pl* **cairns** [*count*] : a pile of stones that marks a place (such as the place where someone is buried or a battle took place) or that shows the direction of a trail

ca·jole /kəˈʤoʊl/ *verb* **-joles; -joled; -jol·ing** [+ *obj*] : to persuade someone to do something or to give you something by making promises or saying nice things — often + *into* • She had to *cajole* [=*coax*] her husband *into* going with her. • My roommate *cajoled* me *into* lending him money for pizza. — often + *from* • My roommate *cajoled* [=*wheedled*] money *from* me. • The reporter *cajoled* information *from* the hospital staff.

[1]**Ca·jun** /ˈkeɪʤən/ *noun, pl* **-juns** [*count*] : a person from Louisiana whose ancestors were French Canadian

[2]**Cajun** *adj*

1 : made by or relating to the Cajuns • *Cajun* music • *Cajun* culture

2 : prepared in a cooking style developed by the Cajuns and usually including spicy seasonings • *Cajun* chicken • *Cajun* food/cuisine

[1]**cake** /ˈkeɪk/ *noun, pl* **cakes**

1 : a sweet baked food made from a mixture of flour, sugar, and other ingredients (such as eggs and butter) [*count*] I made/baked three *cakes* for the party. • He blew out the candles on his ***birthday cake*** • a ***wedding cake*** [*noncount*] a slice/piece of chocolate *cake* — often used before another noun • (*US*) a *cake* pan = (*Brit*) a *cake* tin • *cake* mix [=a combination of all the dry ingredients needed to make a cake] — see picture at BAKING; see also FRUITCAKE, POUND CAKE, SPONGE CAKE, TEA CAKE, UPSIDE-DOWN CAKE

2 [*count*] : a mixture of food that has been shaped into a ball or a flat round shape and baked or fried • crab/clam/rice *cakes* • potato *cakes* — see also FISH CAKE, PANCAKE

3 [*count*] : something that is shaped like a rectangular block • a *cake* of soap = a soap *cake*

4 [*noncount*] *US, informal* : something that is very easy to do • That test was *cake*. — see also PIECE OF CAKE

a slice of the cake *Brit* : a portion or share of something • My business partner agreed to split the profits equally, but I know he wanted a bigger *slice of the cake*. [=*piece/slice/share of the pie*]

have your cake and eat it too (*US*) *or Brit* ***have your cake and eat it*** : to have or enjoy the good parts of something without having or dealing with the bad parts • They seem to think they can *have their cake and eat it too* by having excellent schools for their son without paying high taxes.

icing on the cake see ICING

take the cake *chiefly US* : to win the prize in a contest — used to describe something that is extremely surprising, foolish, annoying, etc. • You've done some silly things, but this one really *takes the cake*! [=(*Brit*) *takes the biscuit*] [=this is the silliest thing you have ever done]

[2]**cake** *verb* **cakes; caked; cak·ing**

1 [+ *obj*] : to cover something with an outer layer that becomes hard as it dries — usually used as *(be) caked* • Mud *was caked* all over the sides of his truck. = The sides of his truck *were caked* [=*covered*] in/with mud.

2 [*no obj*] : to become dry and hard • The mud had *caked* on his boots.

cake·hole /ˈkeɪkˌhoʊl/ *noun, pl* **-holes** [*count*] *Brit, informal* : someone's mouth • Shut your *cakehole*! [=(*US*) *pie hole*]

cake·walk /ˈkeɪkˌwɑːk/ *noun* [*singular*]

1 : an easy contest to win • She expected the election to be a *cakewalk*.

2 : an easy task : PIECE OF CAKE • Reducing the state budget is not going to be a *cakewalk*.

cal·a·mine /ˈkæləˌmaɪn/ *noun* [*noncount*] : a pink liquid that is used to treat skin that is sore, itchy, sunburned, etc. — called also *calamine lotion*

ca·lam·i·tous /kəˈlæmətəs/ *adj* [*more* ~; *most* ~] *formal* : causing great harm or suffering : DISASTROUS • a *calamitous* oil spill • the *calamitous* state of the nation's economy

ca·lam·i·ty /kəˈlæməti/ *noun, pl* **-ties** *formal* : an event that causes great harm and suffering : DISASTER [*count*] floods, earthquakes, and other *calamities* • an economic *calamity* [*noncount*] He predicted *calamity* for the economy.

cal·ci·um /ˈkælsijəm/ *noun* [*noncount*] : a substance that is found in most plants and animals and that is especially important in people for strong healthy bones • Her doctor said she should eat more foods that are high in *calcium*, such as milk and cheese.

cal·cu·late /ˈkælkjəˌleɪt/ *verb* **-lates; -lat·ed; -lat·ing** [+ *obj*]

1 : to find (a number, answer, etc.) by using mathematical processes • *calculate* the volume of a cylinder • *calculate* mass/area/distance/speed • I need to *calculate* how long it will take me to drive to Chicago. • We *calculated* the cost of new carpeting for the whole house.

2 : to get a general idea about the value, size, or cost of (something) : ESTIMATE • We need to *calculate* our chances of success before we invest more money in the business.

cal·cu·lat·ed /ˈkælkjəˌleɪtəd/ *adj* [*more* ~; *most* ~] : carefully planned for a particular and often improper purpose • The TV ads were a *calculated* [=*deliberate*] attempt to deceive voters. ✧ A ***calculated risk*** is one that is accepted after careful thought about the possible good and bad results of a particular action. • The army took a *calculated risk* when it attacked the enemy's capital without using planes.

cal·cu·lat·ing /ˈkælkjəˌleɪtɪŋ/ *adj* [*more* ~; *most* ~] : carefully thinking about and planning actions for selfish or improper reasons • a cold and *calculating* [=*scheming*] criminal

cal·cu·la·tion /ˌkælkjəˈleɪʃən/ *noun, pl* **-tions**

1 : a process or result of calculating something [*count*] According to experts' *calculations*, that star will explode within two billion years. • The computer can do millions of *calculations* each second. [*noncount*] Careful *calculation* is required to determine the required amount of fuel.

2 : careful thought and planning that is done usually for selfish reasons [*count*] The book reveals the cold *calculations* that were behind the government's policies. [*noncount*] His positions are based on political *calculation* of what voters want to hear.

cal·cu·la·tor /ˈkælkjəˌleɪtɚ/ *noun, pl* **-tors** [*count*] : a small electronic device that is used for adding, subtracting, etc. • a ***pocket calculator***[=a calculator that can fit in a shirt pocket] — see picture at OFFICE

cal·cu·lus /ˈkælkjələs/ *noun* [*noncount*] : an advanced branch of mathematics that deals mostly with rates of change and with finding lengths, areas, and volumes

caldron *variant spelling of* CAULDRON

cal·en·dar /ˈkæləndɚ/ *noun, pl* **-dars** [*count*]

1 : a document, chart, etc., that shows the days, weeks, and months of a year • a wall/desk *calendar* • an appointment/engagement *calendar*

2 : a list or schedule of events or activities that occur at different times throughout the year • The university's academic *calendar* runs from September to May.

3 : a particular system for organizing the days of the year by month • the Jewish *calendar* • the Mayan *calendar*

calendar year *noun, pl* ~ **years** [*count*] : the period of time from January 1 to December 31 — compare FISCAL YEAR

[1]calf /ˈkæf, *Brit* ˈkɑːf/ *noun, pl* **calves** /ˈkævz, *Brit* ˈkɑːvz/ [*count*]
1 : a very young cow
2 : the young of various other large animals (such as the elephant or whale)
– compare [2]CALF

[2]calf *noun, pl* **calves** [*count*] : the muscular back part of the leg below the knee — see picture at HUMAN — compare [1]CALF

calf·skin /ˈkæf,skɪn, *Brit* ˈkɑːf,skɪn/ *noun* [*noncount*] : leather made from the skin of a calf • Her boots are made of *calfskin*. • *calfskin* gloves

cal·i·ber (*US*) *or Brit* **cal·i·bre** /ˈkæləbɚ/ *noun, pl* **-bers**
1 [*noncount*] : level of excellence, skill, etc. • The school will only hire teachers of the highest *caliber*. [=will only hire the best teachers] • I was impressed by the high *caliber* of the team's work. • It is exciting to meet a writer of his *caliber*. [=a writer as good/skillful as he is] • The two colleges are not of the same *caliber*. [=one of the colleges is better than the other]
2 [*count*] : a measurement of the width of a bullet or a gun barrel • a *.22-caliber* bullet [=a bullet that is 22 hundredths of an inch in diameter] • a high-*caliber* bullet

cal·i·brate /ˈkælə,breɪt/ *verb* **-brates; -brat·ed; -brat·ing** [*+ obj*]
1 : to adjust or mark (something, such as a measuring device) so that it can be used in an accurate and exact way • *calibrate* a thermometer
2 : to measure (something) in an exact and precise way • carefully *calibrate* the dosage of a medicine
– cal·i·bra·tion /,kæləˈbreɪʃən/ *noun, pl* **-tions** [*count, noncount*]

cal·i·co /ˈkælɪ,koʊ/ *noun, pl* **-coes** *or* **-cos**
1 [*noncount*] *US* : a light, printed cotton cloth
2 [*noncount*] *Brit* : a heavy, plain white cotton cloth
3 [*count*] *US* : a cat that has white, brown, and black fur — called also *calico cat*
– calico *adj* • a *calico* dress

cal·i·per (*US*) *or Brit* **cal·li·per** /ˈkæləpɚ/ *noun, pl* **-pers**
1 [*count*] : a tool that has two narrow legs which can be adjusted to measure the thickness or width of something — usually plural • a pair of *calipers*
2 *callipers* [*plural*] *Brit* : metal devices that are worn to support legs that have been weakened by injury or disease • recovered enough to walk without *callipers* [=(*US*) *braces*]

ca·liph *or* **ca·lif** /ˈkeɪləf/ *noun, pl* **-liphs** *or* **-lifs** [*count*] : an important Muslim political and religious leader

cal·is·then·ics (*chiefly US*) *or Brit* **cal·lis·then·ics** /,kæləsˈθɛnɪks/ *noun* [*plural*] : physical exercises that are done without special equipment • The players warmed up for the game by doing *calisthenics*.
– cal·is·then·ic (*chiefly US*) *or Brit* **cal·lis·then·ic** /,kæləsˈθɛnɪk/ *adj* • *calisthenic* exercises

[1]call /ˈkɑːl/ *verb* **calls; called; call·ing**
1 a *always followed by an adverb or preposition* : to speak in a loud voice [*no obj*] He *called* to passersby for help. • She *called* up to her husband, who was at the top of the stairs. • Her husband *called* back down to her. • She saw her friends across the street and *called* over/across to them. [*+ obj*] He *called* her name in his sleep. — see also CALL OUT 1 (below) **b** [*+ obj*] : to announce or read (something) in a loud voice • *call* the roll • *call* (off) a row of figures • They're *calling* [=*announcing*] our flight: it's boarding at gate 57. — see also CALL OUT 1 (below) **c** [*no obj*] *of a bird or animal* : to make the sound that is usual for a particular type of bird or animal • The birds were *calling* as the sun rose.
2 : to make a telephone call [*no obj*] I *call* once a week to talk to my parents. • Where are you *calling* from? • May I say who's *calling*? • Thank you for *calling*. • Please *call* back/again later. • She *called* long-distance. [*+ obj*] I try to *call* my parents at least once a week. • She *called* me long-distance. • I *called* the office to get some information. • Please *call* us back/again later. • Don't *call* us—we'll *call* you. • In an emergency you should *call* [=*dial*] 911. • *Call* me when you get back from your vacation. — see also CALL 3b (below), CALL IN 1 (below), CALL UP 1 (below)
3 [*+ obj*] **a** : to tell, order, or ask (someone or something) to come • I *called* the waiter over (to my table) and asked for the check, and then I *called* him back to order something else. • My dog comes running when he's *called*. • She was *called* to court to testify. • He was *called* to the office for an interview. • soldiers who have been *called* to active duty • He's not home because he was ***called away*** on business. **b** : to make a telephone call to tell, order, or ask (someone or something) to come • We had to *call* an ambulance. • He *called* a taxi but it still hasn't come. • He *called* a taxi for me. = He *called* me a taxi. — see also CALL 2 (above)
4 [*+ obj*] **a** : to give a name to (someone or something) • Her parents *called* [=*named*] her Katherine after/for her grandmother. • The immigrants settled along the river and *called* their new town "Brookhaven." **b** : to talk to or refer to (someone or something) with a specified name • Her name is Katherine but her friends all *call* her "Kitty." • This part of the city is *called* "The Old Town." • It's important to *call* things by their right names. • Human beings belong to a large group of animals *called* "mammals." • The other children ***called him (bad) names***. [=the other children spoke to him with cruel and insulting words in place of his name] — see also NAME-CALLING **c** : to regard or think of (someone or something) in a certain way • Some people say he's a good man, but I *call* him a fool. [=I consider him to be a fool] • She went out in the rain without an umbrella? I *call* that pretty foolish. • He's not what you would *call* a generous man. [=he's not a generous man] • Her sense of humor is what you might *call* subtle. [=she has a subtle sense of humor] • (You can) *Call* me foolish if you like, but I still think people are basically good. • It costs 99 cents: let's *call* it an even dollar for simplicity's sake. • You may not agree with him, but he ***calls them like he sees them***! [=he states his opinion in an open, honest, and direct way] • You did me a favor and I did you a favor, so let's ***call it even***.
5 [*+ obj*] : to give the order for (something, such as a meeting) • *call* [=*convene*] a meeting • *call* an election • The union has threatened to *call* a strike against the company. • The chairman ***called a halt to*** [=*stopped*] the discussion.
6 [*no obj*] : to make a brief visit • He *called* to pay his respects. • We're planning to *call* [=*stop*] at a friend's house on the way home. — see also CALL AT (below), CALL FOR 2 (below), CALL IN 2 (below), CALL ON 5 (below)
7 [*+ obj*] : to say or guess what the result of something will be • Nobody else thought the election would turn out as it did, but he *called* [=*predicted*] it exactly right! • You *called* it! [=you correctly said what would happen] • *call* the toss of a coin • We flipped a coin; he *called* heads, and heads it was! • The election is still ***too close to call***. [=the election is too close to say who will win]
8 [*+ obj*] *sports* **a** : to stop or cancel (something, such as a baseball game) because of bad conditions • The game was *called* on account of rain. **b** : to make an official ruling or decision about (something, such as a pitched ball or a player's action) • Only the umpire has the right to *call* balls and strikes. • The pitch was *called* a strike. [=the umpire said that the pitch was a strike] • The umpire *called* the runner safe/out. • *call* a serve in/out • She was *called* for being offside. [=the official said that she was offside] **c** *American football* : to say or decide what kind of play will be used • The quarterback *called* a running play.
9 *poker* : to require (a player) to show a hand by making an equal bet [*+ obj*] I *call* you. [*no obj*] I *call*.

call a spade a spade see SPADE

call at [*phrasal verb*] ***call at (a place)*** *of a boat or ship* : to stop at (a place) briefly • The ship *called at* the port.

call down [*phrasal verb*] ***call down (something)*** *or* ***call (something) down*** *literary* : to pray or ask God to do something to someone • He *called down* a blessing/curse on the king. [=he prayed that the king would be blessed/cursed]

call for [*phrasal verb*] **1** ***call for (something)*** **a** : to say or demand publicly that something is needed or should be done • The opposition has *called for* an investigation. • The government has *called for* [=*asked for*] calm and restraint. **b** : to indicate that something is needed or should be done • The plan *calls for* three windows to be added. • You've won! That *calls for* a celebration! [=we should celebrate because you've won] **c** : to require or demand (something) as necessary or proper • The job *calls for* typing skills. [=you must have typing skills to do the job] • Action is urgently *called for* [=*needed*] in order to avert catastrophe! • These new problems *call for* [=*require*] further investigation. • His rude behavior was ***not called for***. [=his behavior was uncalled-for/inappropriate] **2** ***call for (someone or something)*** : to go to a place to get (someone or something) • I'll *call for* you (at your house) after dinner.

call forth [*phrasal verb*] ***call forth (something)*** *or* ***call (some-***

C

thing) forth : to bring (a memory, image, etc.) into the mind ▪ These events *call forth* [=*elicit, evoke*] strong feelings.

call in [*phrasal verb*] **1 a :** to make a telephone call to a place (such as the place where you work) ▪ She ***called in sick*** yesterday. [=she telephoned the place where she works to say that she was sick and would not be coming to work] **b :** to make a telephone call to a radio or television program ▪ Thousands of people *called in* to make a donation. ▪ Many people have *called in* (to the show) with questions about the new law. — see also CALL-IN **c** ***call (something) in*** or ***call in (something)*** : to deliver (something, such as a message) by making a telephone call ▪ He *called in* an order for pizza. **2 :** to go in somewhere to make a visit — often + *on* ▪ I *called in on* an old friend [=I visited an old friend] while I was in New York on business. **3** ***call (something) in*** or ***call in (something)*** **a :** to say that something that has been given or sent should be returned ▪ The manufacturer has *called in* all its defective products. **b :** to demand payment of (a loan) ▪ The bank has *called in* the loan. **4** ***call (someone) in*** or ***call in (someone)*** : to ask for the help or services of (someone) ▪ They may have to *call in* a mediator to settle the strike. ▪ Rescue workers have been *called in* to help search for survivors.

call into action see ACTION

call into question also US ***call into doubt*** : to make people doubt something ▪ His report *calls into question* the earlier reports we had. [=his report makes us feel not certain that the earlier reports were true] ▪ This news *calls* her loyalty *into question*. [=makes people doubt that she is loyal]

call it a day/night : to stop an activity (such as work) for the remainder of the day or night ▪ We've done enough work for now: let's *call it a day*. ▪ It's getting late. I think we should *call it a night*.

call it quits see QUITS

call off [*phrasal verb*] **1** ***call off (something)*** or ***call (something) off*** : to stop doing or planning to do (something) ▪ We had to *call off* [=*cancel*] our trip. ▪ The police have decided to *call* the investigation *off*. [=to stop the investigation] **2** ***call off (someone or something)*** or ***call (someone or something) off*** : to cause or tell (a person or animal) to stop attacking, chasing, etc. ▪ The dog was barking and growling at me until its owner *called* it *off*.

call on/upon [*phrasal verb*] **1** ***call on/upon (someone or something)*** : to ask (someone or something) to do something : to say that someone or something should do something — followed by *to* + *verb* ▪ The opposition has *called on/upon* the governor *to resign*. [=the opposition has said that the governor should resign] ▪ You may be *called upon to do* several jobs. ▪ Universities are *called upon to produce* trained professionals. [=it is the job of universities to produce trained professionals] **2** ***call on/upon (someone)*** : to ask for help from (someone) ▪ Is there anyone you can *call on* in an emergency? **3** ***call on/upon (something)*** : to use (something, such as a talent or skill) ▪ She had to *call on/upon* all her reserves of strength and skill to meet the challenge. **4** ***call on (someone)*** : to ask for a response from (someone, such as a student) ▪ I was hoping the teacher wouldn't *call on* me, because I didn't know the answer. **5** ***call on (someone)*** : to make a brief visit to (someone) ▪ I'm planning to *call on* an old friend after I leave here. **6** ***call (someone) on (something)*** *US, informal* : to directly criticize (someone) for (something, such as bad behavior) ▪ He's incredibly rude, but no one ever *calls* him *on* it. [=no one ever tells him that he should stop being so rude]

call out [*phrasal verb*] **1** ***call out*** or ***call (something) out*** or ***call out (something)*** : to speak in a loud voice ▪ He *called out* to passersby for help. ▪ He *called out* in his sleep. **:** to say (something) in a loud voice ▪ He *called out* her name in his sleep. ▪ He *called out* a cry for help. **:** to announce or read (something) in a loud voice ▪ *call out* a number **2** ***call out (someone)*** or ***call (someone) out*** **a :** to order or tell (a group of people, such as soldiers) to come or go somewhere ▪ The governor has *called out* troops to help control the riot. ▪ Emergency workers were *called out* to help with efforts to control the flood. **b :** to order or tell (workers) to go on strike ▪ Factory workers are expected to be *called out* on strike if a new contract isn't signed by tomorrow.

call (someone) on the carpet see ¹CARPET

call (something) to order see ¹ORDER

call the shots see ¹SHOT

call the tune see ¹TUNE

call time see ¹TIME

call to account see ¹ACCOUNT

call to mind see ¹MIND

call up [*phrasal verb*] **1** ***call (someone) up*** or ***call up (someone)*** *chiefly US* : to make a telephone call to (someone) ▪ I haven't spoken to her in years, but I *called* her *up* last night and we talked for hours. ▪ *Call* me *up* when you get back from your vacation. ▪ I *called up* my doctor and made an appointment. **2** ***call (something) up*** or ***call up (something)*** **a :** to bring (something, such as a memory) into the mind ▪ The sound of the ocean *called up* [=*brought back*] memories of my childhood. **b :** to bring (strength, courage, etc.) from within yourself ▪ He will have to *call up* all his reserves of strength to meet this challenge. **c :** to get (something) from the memory of a computer and show it on the screen ▪ *call up* an old document for revision **3** ***call (someone) up*** or ***call up (someone)*** **a :** to order or tell (someone) to come or appear ▪ The prisoner was *called up* before a magistrate. **b :** to bring (an athlete) to a higher league ▪ a minor-league player who is being *called up* to the major leagues **c :** to order (soldiers) to come for active military duty ▪ *call up* the reserves — see also CALL-UP

call your bluff see ²BLUFF

²call *noun, pl* **calls**

1 [*count*] **:** an act of using the telephone : an act of calling someone on the telephone ▪ a phone/telephone *call* ▪ A local *call* costs less than a long-distance or an international *call*. ▪ If there are any *calls* for me during the meeting, say that I'll call back later. ▪ I got a *call* from my brother last night. ▪ incoming/outgoing *calls* ▪ "There's someone on the phone for you, sir." "Tell them I can't ***take their call*** now [=I can't speak to them on the phone now] but I'll ***return their call*** [=I'll call them back] as soon as I can." ▪ ***Give me a call*** when you get back from your trip. [=call me when you get back] — see also TOLL CALL, TRUNK CALL, WAKE-UP CALL

2 [*count*] **a :** an act of calling with the voice : a loud cry or shout ▪ He gave a *call* to passersby for help. **b :** the sound made by an animal or bird ▪ We heard a bird that had a very loud and unusual *call*. **c :** an imitation of the sound made by a bird or animal ▪ He's an expert at doing bird *calls*. **d :** a device that is used to imitate the sound made by a bird ▪ He has a large collection of duck *calls*. **e :** a loud sound or signal made with a musical instrument ▪ a bugle *call* ▪ the *call* of a trumpet

3 a [*count*] **:** a public request or statement that asks or tells people to do something ▪ The government has issued a *call* to its supporters to defend it and hopes they will answer/heed its *call*. ▪ issue a *call* = put out a *call* ▪ The campaigners renewed their *calls* for reform. ▪ Their *calls* have gone unheeded. ▪ The political party has issued a ***call to action***. — see also CLARION CALL, CURTAIN CALL, *call to arms* at ²ARM **b :** a request for something [*count*] We get many *calls* for Christmas stories. [*noncount*] There's ***not much call for*** ice cream at this time of year. [=not many people want ice cream at this time of year] ▪ There is ***very little call for*** his services during the summer. **c** [*noncount*] **:** a reason for doing something — used in negative statements to criticize someone's behavior ▪ There was ***no call for*** your rudeness. = There was *no call for* you to behave so rudely. [=you were wrong to behave so rudely; your rudeness was uncalled-for]

4 [*count*] **:** a brief visit ▪ I made/paid a brief social *call* on an old friend. = I paid an old friend a brief social *call*. ▪ The ship made a *call* at Newport [=the ship stopped briefly at Newport] before proceeding to New Orleans. ▪ The doctor was on a *call* when her patient came to the office. — see also HOUSE CALL, PORT OF CALL

5 [*count*] **:** something that is called or announced ▪ I flipped a coin, and the *call* was heads.; *especially* **:** an announcement telling passengers to get on a plane, train, etc., that will be leaving soon ▪ This is the last *call* for Flight 139, now boarding at Gate 57. = This is the last *call* for passengers to board Flight 139 at Gate 57. — see also LAST CALL

6 [*count*] **a :** a decision made by an official in a sports contest ▪ The runner was called out at home plate, and the manager came out to argue about the *call*. **b** *chiefly US* **:** a decision ▪ "Should we stay or go?" "I don't know. It's a tough *call* (to make)." ▪ I'll let you make the *call*. ▪ "How should we deal with this problem?" "I don't know: ***it's your call***." [=you can decide how we should deal with this problem] — see also CLOSE CALL, JUDGMENT CALL

7 [*singular*] **:** the appeal or attraction of something that makes a person want to go somewhere ▪ sailors who cannot resist the *call* of the open ocean ▪ He ***heard the call of the wild*** [=he felt the desire to go out to wild places far away

from most people] — see also CALL OF NATURE
8 [*count*] : something that requires a person's attention or effort — + *on* • There are many *calls* [=*demands*] *on* the time of a busy housewife. [=there are many things that a busy housewife must spend time doing]
at someone's beck and call see [1]BECK
on call : available to be called when needed : ready to come when needed • a doctor who is *on call* throughout the day

call·back /ˈkɑːlˌbæk/ *noun, pl* **-backs** [*count*]
1 : a return telephone call • She got constant *callbacks* from the salesman even after she asked him to stop calling.
2 : an official request or order for someone or something to return: such as **a** : a call for employees to come back to work • With the latest *callback*, the factory will employ 30,000 workers. **b** : a request to a worker to come back and fix problems • If he used better materials, he wouldn't have so many *callbacks*.

call box *noun, pl* ~ **boxes** [*count*]
1 *US* : a telephone that is located on the side of a road and that is used for reporting emergencies
2 *Brit* : a public telephone booth

call·er /ˈkɑːlɚ/ *noun, pl* **-ers** [*count*] : a person who calls: such as **a** : a person who makes a telephone call • The police have received information from an anonymous *caller*. **b** : a person who comes to visit someone • She's had several *callers* at her house in the past few days.

caller display *noun* [*noncount*] *Brit* : CALLER ID

caller ID *noun* [*noncount*] : a service that allows you to see who is calling before you answer a telephone call • a phone system with *caller ID* — called also *(Brit) caller display*

call forwarding *noun* [*noncount*] : a service that allows you to have a telephone call sent to a different number

call girl *noun, pl* ~ **girls** [*count*] : a prostitute who arranges to meet with men who call her on the telephone

cal·lig·ra·phy /kəˈlɪgrəfi/ *noun* [*noncount*] : the art of making beautiful handwriting • Arabic *calligraphy*
— **cal·lig·ra·pher** /kəˈlɪgrəfɚ/ *noun, pl* **-phers** [*count*]

call–in /ˈkɑːlˌɪn/ *noun, pl* **-ins** [*count*] *US* : a radio or television show in which telephone calls from members of the audience are included as part of the broadcast — usually used before another noun • a *call–in* radio show — called also *(chiefly Brit) phone-in*; see also *call in* 1b at [1]CALL

call·ing /ˈkɑːlɪŋ/ *noun, pl* **-ings** [*count*]
1 : a strong desire to spend your life doing a certain kind of work (such as religious work) • He had always felt a *calling* to help others. • He experienced a *calling* to enter the priesthood. • For Mary, teaching wasn't a job, it was a *calling*. [=*vocation*]
2 : the work that a person does or should be doing • She discovered architecture as her true *calling* [=*vocation*] while in college. • He feels he ***missed his calling*** [=did not have the career he should have] by not becoming a doctor.

calling card *noun, pl* ~ **cards** [*count*] *US*
1 : a plastic card that allows a person to charge telephone calls to an account — called also *phone card*
2 *old-fashioned* : a small card presented when making a formal visit to someone that has the name and sometimes the address of the visitor — often used figuratively to describe something that identifies a particular person or group • The young actor's bright smile is his *calling card*. — called also *(Brit) visiting card*

call letters *noun* [*plural*] : CALL SIGN

call number *noun, pl* ~ **-bers** [*count*] : a combination of numbers and letters that is used to show where a book is located in a library

call of nature *noun*
the call of nature *humorous* : the need to use a toilet • He had to leave suddenly to answer/obey *the call of nature*.

cal·lous /ˈkæləs/ *adj* [*more* ~; *most* ~] *disapproving* : not feeling or showing any concern about the problems or suffering of other people • a selfish and *callous* young man • a *callous* refusal to help the poor • a very *callous* remark
— **cal·lous·ly** *adv* • Some of us were treated *callously*.
— **cal·lous·ness** *noun* [*noncount*] • *callousness* toward the poor

cal·loused /ˈkæləst/ *adj* [*more* ~; *most* ~] : having hard and thick skin : having calluses • *calloused* hands/feet

cal·low /ˈkæloʊ/ *adj* **cal·low·er**; **-est** [*also more* ~; *most* ~] *often disapproving* — used to describe a young person who does not have much experience and does not know how to behave the way adults behave • a *callow* [=*immature*] youth • training *callow* [=*inexperienced*] recruits for the army
— **cal·low·ness** *noun* [*noncount*]

call sign *noun, pl* ~ **signs** [*count*] : a combination of letters and numbers that is used to identify someone or something in a radio broadcast

call–up /ˈkɑːlˌʌp/ *noun, pl* **-ups**
1 [*count*] *sports* **a** : a decision to bring an athlete to play in a higher league • a minor-league baseball player who is hoping for a *call-up* to the major leagues **b** : a player who is brought up to a higher league • The pitcher in tonight's game is a recent *call-up* from the minors.
2 : an order telling someone to report for military service [*count*] military *call-ups* [*noncount*] He opposes the *call-up* of more troops. — often used before another noun • They received their *call-up* notices. — see also *call up* at [1]CALL

cal·lus /ˈkæləs/ *noun, pl* **-lus·es** [*count*] : a hard and thickened area on the skin and especially on the hands or feet

call waiting *noun* [*noncount*] : a service that makes it possible for someone who is speaking on the telephone to receive another call without ending the first one • Do you have *call waiting*?

[1]**calm** /ˈkɑːm/ *adj* **calm·er**; **-est**
1 : not angry, upset, excited, etc. • The teacher asked us to remain/stay *calm* after the fire alarm went off. • The capital city was *calm* despite rumors of a possible terrorist attack. [=people in the city behaved in the usual way; there was not a lot of excited or fearful activity in the city] • Let's try to have a *calm* discussion about your grades. • My brother is always ***calm, cool, and collected***. [=he never gets very upset]
2 — used to describe weather that is not windy, stormy, etc. • a *calm* day • They're predicting *calm* winds today. • a *calm* sea [=a sea that has no waves or only very small waves]
— **calm·ly** *adv* [*more* ~; *most* ~] • The coach *calmly* told her players what to do next. — **calm·ness** *noun* [*noncount*] • I suddenly had a great feeling of *calmness*.

[2]**calm** *noun*
1 : a quiet and peaceful state or condition [*noncount*] After two days of violent protests, the mayor appealed/pleaded for *calm*. • The *calm* was broken by another terrorist bombing. • the *calm* of a church • Police tried to ***restore calm*** after the riot. [*singular*] A quiet *calm* settled over the city.
2 [*count*] : a peaceful mental or emotional state — usually singular • The coach was able to keep his *calm* during the game. • Everyone noticed her outward *calm* at the funeral.
the calm before the storm see [1]STORM

[3]**calm** *verb* **calms**; **calmed**; **calm·ing**
1 : to become or to cause (someone) to become less upset, emotional, excited, etc. [+ *obj*] The mayor tried to *calm* [=*quiet, settle*] the protesters. • His words were effective in *calming* her fears. — often + *down* • The mayor tried to *calm down* the crowd. [*no obj*] — + *down* • The mayor asked the protesters to *calm down* so he could speak. • He needs to *calm down* enough to tell police about the accident.
2 : to become or to cause (something) to become less active, violent, forceful, etc. [*no obj*] The winds *calmed* overnight. — usually + *down* • The winds *calmed down* overnight. • The dispute over the new factory has finally *calmed down*. [+ *obj*] The medicine helped *calm* her breathing. — often + *down* • We need to *calm* the situation *down* a little.

cal·o·rie /ˈkæləri/ *noun, pl* **-ries** [*count*] : a unit of heat used to indicate the amount of energy that foods will produce in the human body • foods with high/low *calories* • You should try to eat fewer *calories* [=eat less food with high calories] and exercise more. • a low-*calorie* diet • No dessert for me—I'm ***watching/counting my calories***. [=being careful not to eat too much]
— **ca·lo·ric** /kəˈlorɪk/ *adj* [*more* ~; *most* ~] • *caloric* intake/restriction/values • *caloric* foods [=foods that contain many calories] — **cal·o·rif·ic** /ˌkæləˈrɪfɪk/ *adj, technical* • the *calorific* content of fat

cal·um·ny /ˈkæləmni/ *noun, pl* **-nies** [*count*] *formal* : an untrue statement that is made to damage someone's reputation • They uttered *calumnies* against him.; *also* [*noncount*] : the act of making such statements • He was the target of *calumny* for his unpopular beliefs.

calve /ˈkæv/ *verb* **calves**; **calved**; **calv·ing** [*no obj*] *of a cow* : to give birth to a calf • The cow *calved* in the barn.

calves *plural of* CALF

Cal·vin·ism /ˈkælvəˌnɪzəm/ *noun* [*noncount*] : a Christian set of beliefs that is based on the teachings of John Calvin and that stresses God's power and the moral weakness of human beings

C

C

– **Cal·vin·ist** /ˈkælvənɪst/ *noun, pl* **-ists** [*count*] – **Calvinist** *adj* – **Cal·vin·ist·ic** /ˌkælvəˈnɪstɪk/ *adj*

ca·lyp·so /kəˈlɪpsoʊ/ *noun, pl* **-sos** [*noncount*] : a lively musical style from the West Indies that usually has humorous lyrics concerning current topics (such as politics); *also* [*count*] : a song of this style

cal·zone /kælˈzoʊn/ *noun, pl* **calzone** *or* **cal·zones** [*count*] *chiefly US* : a food originally from Italy that consists of baked or fried dough folded over and filled with tomato sauce, cheese, etc.

cam /ˈkæm/ *noun, pl* **cams** [*count*] *technical* : a part of a machine (such as an engine) that changes circular motion into another type of motion (such as forward motion)

ca·ma·ra·de·rie /kɑmˈrɑːdəri, *Brit* ˌkæməˈrɑːdəri/ *noun* : a feeling of good friendship among the people in a group [*noncount*] There is great *camaraderie* among the teammates. [*singular*] They have developed a real *camaraderie* after working together for so long.

cam·ber /ˈkæmbɚ/ *noun, pl* **-bers** [*count*] : a slight downward curve from the middle to the sides of a surface (such as a road)

cam·bric /ˈkeɪmbrɪk/ *noun* [*noncount*] : a light, thin, white linen or cotton cloth

cam·cord·er /ˈkæmˌkoɚdɚ/ *noun, pl* **-ers** [*count*] : a small video camera for personal use

came *past tense of* [1]COME

cam·el /ˈkæməl/ *noun, pl* **-els** [*count*] : a large animal of Africa and Asia that has a long neck and one or two large humps on its back and that is often used for desert travel
the straw that breaks the camel's back see STRAW

camel

Cam·em·bert /ˈkæməmˌbeɚ/ *noun* [*noncount*] : a type of soft yellow cheese from France

cam·eo /ˈkæmiˌoʊ/ *noun, pl* **-eos** [*count*]
1 : a small role in a movie, play, etc., that is performed by a well-known actor ▪ He has a brief *cameo* in the film. ▪ a *cameo* role
2 : a piece of jewelry that has a carved design shown against a background of a different color — see color picture on page C11

cam·era /ˈkæmrə/ *noun, pl* **-er·as** [*count*] : a device that is used for taking photographs or for making movies, television programs, etc.
off camera : away from a television or movie camera : not on television or in a movie ▪ He is a different person (when he's) *off camera*.
on camera : within the range of a television or movie camera : on television or in a movie ▪ He looks very relaxed (when he's) *on camera*. ▪ His attempt to break into the store was ***caught on camera***. [=a camera recorded his attempt to break into the store]

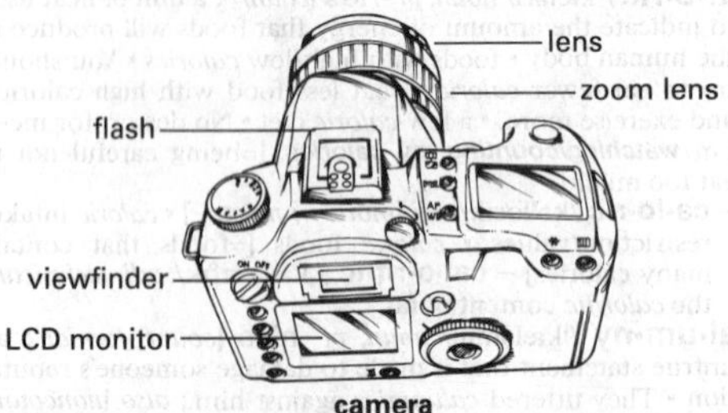

camera

cam·era·man /ˈkæmrəˌmæn/ *noun, pl* **-men** /-mən/ [*count*] : someone (especially a man) who uses a camera to film something (such as a movie or television show)

cam·era·per·son /ˈkæmrəˌpɚsn/ *noun, pl* **-peo·ple** /-ˌpiːpəl/ [*count*] : a cameraman or camerawoman

cam·era·wom·an /ˈkæmrəˌwʊmən/ *noun, pl* **-wom·en** /-ˌwɪmən/ [*count*] : a woman who uses a camera to film something (such as a movie or television show)

cam·i·sole /ˈkæməˌsoʊl/ *noun, pl* **-soles** [*count*] : a light piece of clothing for women that is worn on the top part of the body, does not have sleeves, and is often worn alone or under a blouse — see color picture on page C13

camo /ˈkæmoʊ/ *noun* [*noncount*] *US, informal* : [1]CAMOUFLAGE — often used before another noun ▪ a *camo* jacket ▪ *camo* pants

camomile *variant spelling of* CHAMOMILE

[1]**cam·ou·flage** /ˈkæməˌflɑːʒ/ *noun*
1 [*noncount*] **a** : a way of hiding something (such as military equipment) by painting it or covering it with leaves or branches to make it harder to see ▪ The army tanks were painted green and brown for *camouflage*. **b** : the green and brown clothing that soldiers and hunters wear to make them harder to see ▪ Troops in full *camouflage*. — often used before another noun ▪ a *camouflage* jacket ▪ *camouflage* pants ▪ *camouflage* gear
2 : something (such as color or shape) that protects an animal from attack by making the animal difficult to see in the area around it [*singular*] The rabbit's white fur acts as a *camouflage* in the snow. [*noncount*] Rabbits use their white fur as *camouflage* in the snow.
3 : behavior that is meant to hide something or convince another of something that is not true [*singular*] Her so-called charity work was a *camouflage* for her own self-interest. [*noncount*] His tough attitude served as *camouflage*.

[2]**camouflage** *verb* **-flag·es; -flaged; -flag·ing** [+ *obj*] : to hide (something) by covering it up or making it harder to see ▪ The swimming pool was *camouflaged* [=*hidden*] by a hedge. ▪ The makeup *camouflages* blemishes. ▪ *camouflaged* soldiers/animals ▪ She *camouflaged* [=*hid*] her feelings well. ▪ It was impossible to *camouflage* the facts.

[1]**camp** /ˈkæmp/ *noun, pl* **camps**
1 a : a place that is usually far away from cities and that has tents, small houses, etc., that people can live in for a short period of time [*count*] Fishing *camps* are located all along the river. ▪ army *camps* ▪ a refugee *camp* [*noncount*] The soldiers were confined to *camp*. ▪ The hikers decided to ***pitch/make camp*** just before sunset. ▪ They ***set up camp*** for the night. — see also BOOT CAMP, CONCENTRATION CAMP, DEATH CAMP, LABOR CAMP, PRISON CAMP **b** : a town that has been set up so people can live there and work nearby ▪ a logging/mining *camp*
2 a : a place usually in the mountains or by a lake where young people can do different activities during the summer [*noncount*] With the kids away at *camp*, the house is very quiet. ▪ The children have fond memories of ***summer camp***. [*count*] a music *camp* ▪ There are several ***day camps*** [=camps where children spend the day and then return home at the end of the day] in the area. — often used before another noun ▪ a *camp* counselor/director **b** : a place where athletes train before the beginning of a season [*count*] The sports writer visited a few ***training camps***. [*noncount*] Our star pitcher injured his arm in *camp* this spring.
3 [*count*] : a group of people who support or believe in certain ideas ▪ There are two proposals to consider, one from each *camp*. ▪ the Democratic/Republican *camp* ▪ Even within the conservative *camp*, there is quite a wide range of opinion. ▪ We are in the same *camp*. [=we have the same opinions, ideas, etc.]
break camp : to take down the tents and other parts of a camp in order to leave ▪ The soldiers *broke camp* at dawn.
– compare [3]CAMP

[2]**camp** *verb* **camps; camped; camp·ing** [*no obj*] : to sleep outdoors usually in a tent ▪ The hikers *camped* by the lake.
camp out [*phrasal verb*] **1** : to sleep outdoors usually in a tent ▪ We *camped out* [=*camped*] under the stars. ▪ Fans *camped out* [=spent the night outside] in huge numbers to purchase tickets in the morning. — see also CAMPOUT **2** *informal* **a** : to live in a place for a short period of time ▪ I *camped out* at a friend's apartment until I found a place of my own. **b** *US* : to stay in a place for a period of time ▪ He *camped out* in the library for the afternoon.
– compare [4]CAMP

[3]**camp** *noun* [*noncount*] — used of art and entertainment when qualities that are normally considered bad (such as excessive emotion and bad acting) are exaggerated so much that they become interesting and funny ▪ movie-goers who appreciate *camp* — compare [1]CAMP
– **camp** *adj* ▪ We went to see the movie for its *camp* value. ▪ The performance has become a *camp* classic. – **camp·i·ly** /ˈkæmpəli/ *adv* ▪ The movie was *campily* outrageous.

— **camp·i·ness** /ˈkæmpinəs/ *noun [singular]* ▪ the *campiness* of the movie — **campy** /ˈkæmpi/ *adj* **camp·i·er; -est** *US* ▪ a *campy* comedy/movie

[4]**camp** *verb* **camps; camped; camping**

camp it up *informal* : to act with exaggerated speech or gestures ▪ He really *camped it up* on stage.
— compare [2]CAMP

[1]**cam·paign** /kæmˈpeɪn/ *noun, pl* **-paigns** *[count]*
1 : a series of activities designed to produce a particular result ▪ an election *campaign* [=a campaign to win a political election] ▪ a presidential *campaign* ▪ The group launched/mounted/led a *campaign* to protect the area from commercial development. ▪ the *campaign* against drugs ▪ an expensive advertising *campaign* ▪ The university is organizing a *campaign* to attract a more diverse student population. — often used before another noun ▪ *campaign* contributions ▪ She kept/broke her *campaign* promises. ▪ a *campaign* slogan
2 : a series of military battles, attacks, etc., designed to produce a particular result in a war ▪ a bombing *campaign*

[2]**campaign** *verb* **-paigns; -paigned; -paign·ing** *[no obj]* : to lead or take part in a campaign to support or oppose someone or something or to achieve something ▪ She *campaigned* to save the town library. ▪ He *campaigned* hard to get more funding. ▪ a time when women were *campaigning* for the right to vote ▪ I *campaigned* for/against her when she ran for governor. ▪ He ***campaigned for president/governor/mayor.*** = He *campaigned* for the presidency/governorship/mayoralty. [=he tried to be elected president/governor/mayor]
— **cam·paign·er** *noun, pl* **-ers** *[count]* ▪ civil rights *campaigners* — **campaigning** *noun [noncount]*

cam·pa·ni·le /ˌkæmpəˈniːli/ *noun, pl* **-les** *[count]* : a tall tower with a bell in it

camp bed *noun, pl* ~ **beds** *[count] Brit* : COT 1

camp·er /ˈkæmpɚ/ *noun, pl* **-ers** *[count]*
1 : a person who sleeps outdoors, in a tent, or in a simple shelter usually for enjoyment for a short period of time ▪ Rangers warned *campers* that leaving food outside might attract bears. ▪ A careless *camper* accidentally started a fire in the woods. — see also HAPPY CAMPER
2 *US* : a type of vehicle or special trailer that people can live and sleep in when they are traveling or camping — called also *(Brit) camper van, (Brit) caravan*
3 : a young person who goes to a camp during the summer to do different activities

camp·fire /ˈkæmpˌfajɚ/ *noun, pl* **-fires** *[count]* : a fire that is built outdoors at a camp or picnic area ▪ We gathered around a *campfire* and shared stories.

Camp Fire girl *noun, pl* ~ **girls** *[count] US* : a girl who is a member of a national organization for young people from ages 5 to 18

camp follower *noun, pl* ~ **-ers** *[count]*
1 : a person who spends time with or near a group or person in order to gain some advantage ▪ media *camp followers* ▪ the famous boxer and his *camp followers*
2 : a person who follows a group of soldiers as they move to different areas and sells goods and services to them

camp·ground /ˈkæmpˌgraʊnd/ *noun, pl* **-grounds** *[count] chiefly US* : an area or place that is used for camping : a place where people can put up a tent or park a camper and that usually has toilets and showers for campers to use

cam·phor /ˈkæmfɚ/ *noun [noncount]* : a white substance with a strong smell that is used in medicine and to keep insects away

camping *noun [noncount]* : the activity of sleeping outdoors in a tent usually for enjoyment ▪ *Camping* is one of our favorite things to do. ▪ She likes to ***go camping*** on weekends.
— **camping** *adj* ▪ *camping* equipment/gear ▪ a *camping* trip

camp meeting *noun, pl* ~ **-ings** *[count] US* : a religious meeting that is held outdoors and is often attended by people who camp nearby

camp·out /ˈkæmpˌaʊt/ *noun, pl* **-outs** *[count] US* : an occasion when people go camping together ▪ our annual *campout* in Vermont — see also *camp out* at [2]CAMP

camp·site /ˈkæmpˌsaɪt/ *noun, pl* **-sites** *[count]*
1 *US* : a place where people can put up a tent ▪ The *campsite* includes a picnic table and a grill for cooking.
2 *Brit* : CAMPGROUND

cam·pus /ˈkæmpəs/ *noun, pl* **-pus·es** : the area and buildings around a university, college, school, etc. *[count]* Visitors crowded the *campus* on graduation day. ▪ Rallies were held on college/university *campuses* across the country. ▪ We

camping

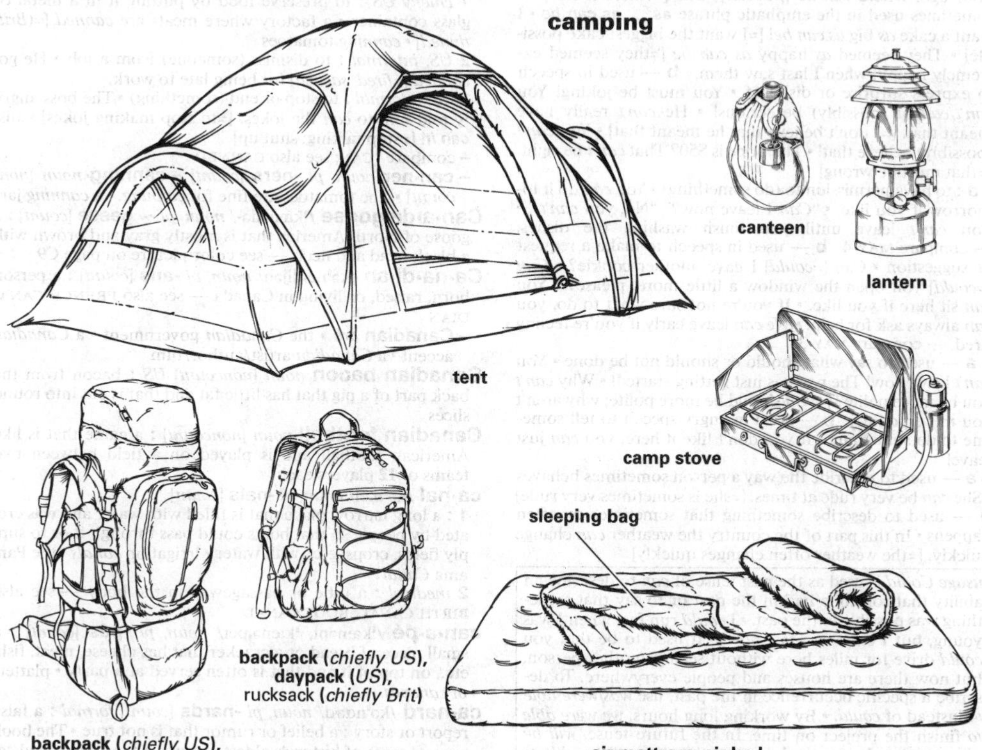

walked around the *campus* on our first day. [*noncount*] How do you like living ***on campus***? [=in the dormitories/housing provided by the school] • She prefers living ***off campus***. [=she prefers not living in the dormitories/housing provided by the school] • (*US, somewhat old-fashioned*) The quarterback of the football team is a real ***big man on campus***. [=he is important and well-known] — often used before another noun • *campus* events/life • *campus* politics

cam·shaft /ˈkæmˌʃæft, *Brit* ˈkæmˌʃɑːft/ *noun, pl* **-shafts** [*count*] *technical* **:** a metal shaft or bar to which a cam is attached — see picture at ENGINE

[1]**can** /kən, ˈkæn/ *verb, past tense* **could** /kəd, ˈkʊd/ *present tense for both singular and plural* **can**; *negative* **can·not** /ˈkænɑt, kəˈnɑːt, *Brit* ˈkænət/ *or* **can't** /ˈkænt, *Brit* ˈkɑːnt/ [*modal verb*]

1 : to be able to (do something) • I don't need any help. I *can* do it myself. • I *can't* decide what to do. • All we *can* do [=the only thing we can do] now is wait. **:** to know how to (do something) • She *can* read, *can't* she? • I *can* whistle. **:** to have the power or skill to (do something) • A weight lifter *can* lift a very heavy weight. • She *can* play the piano. • Only Congress *can* do that. **:** to be designed to (do something) • a car that *can* hold five people [=a car that has enough room for five people] • How fast *can* [=*does, will*] the car go? — sometimes used without a following verb • I visit her whenever I *can*. • I don't know if I'll be able to fix the problem, but I'll do what I *can*. • Please help us if you *can*.

2 — used to describe what someone sees, feels, thinks, etc. • "*Can* you see him yet?" "Yes, I *can* see him clearly." • I *can* barely hear you. • *Can* [=*do*] you remember/understand how to do it?

3 a — used to say that something is or is not possible • Do you think he *can* still be alive? [=do you think it is possible that he is still alive?] • I don't think he *can* still be alive. [=I think he must be dead] • These problems *can* be dealt with more easily at the local level. • You *can't* always get what you want in life. • At this time of year many birds *can* be found on the island. [=there are many birds on the island at this time of year] • If you don't tell me what the problem is, I *can't* help you. • You *can't* be very smart [=you aren't very smart] if you believe that! • He was supposed to be here an hour ago. ***Where can he (possibly) be***? [=where is he?] — sometimes used in the emphatic phrase ***as . . . as can be*** • I want a cake *as* big *as can be*! [=I want the biggest cake possible] • They seemed *as* happy *as can be* [=they seemed extremely happy] when I last saw them. **b** — used in speech to express surprise or disbelief • You must be joking! You *can't/cannot* (possibly) be serious! • He *can't* really have meant that. [=I don't believe that he meant that] • You *can't* (possibly) believe that! • The price is $50? That *can't* be right. [=that must be wrong]

4 a : to have permission to (do something) • You *can* do it tomorrow if you like. • "*Can* I leave now?" "No, you *can't*." • You *can't* leave until you finish washing the dishes. — compare MAY 4 **b** — used in speech to make a request or suggestion • Can [=*could*] I have another cookie? • *Can* [=*could*] you open the window a little more, please? • You *can* sit here if you like. • If you're not sure what to do, you *can* always ask for help. • We *can* leave early if you're feeling tired. — compare MAY 3

5 a — used to say what should or should not be done • You *can't* leave now! The party is just getting started! • Why *can't* you be more polite? [=you should be more polite; why aren't you more polite?] **b** — used in angry speech to tell someone to do something • If you don't like it here, you *can* just leave!

6 a — used to describe the way a person sometimes behaves • She *can* be very rude at times. [=she is sometimes very rude] **b** — used to describe something that sometimes or often happens • In this part of the country the weather *can* change quickly. [=the weather often changes quickly]

> ***usage*** *Could* is used as the past tense of *can* to describe an ability that someone had in the past or to say that something was possible in the past. • I *could* run fast when I was young, but I can't run fast now. • It used to be that you *could* drive for miles here without seeing another person, but now there are houses and people everywhere. To describe a specific occurrence in the past, use *was/were able to* instead of *could*. • By working long hours, *we were able to* finish the project on time. In the future tense, *will be able to* is used. • If you keep practicing, *you'll be able to* play the piano someday. • She believes that someday people *will be able to* vote at home on their computers. *Can* can be used to suggest something that might happen in the future. • If we save enough money, we *can* go to Hawaii for our vacation next year.

no can do *informal + humorous* — used in speech to say that you cannot do something that you have been asked or told to do • "Can you give me a ride to work tomorrow?" "Sorry—*no can do*. My car is in the shop."

– compare [3]CAN

[2]**can** /ˈkæn/ *noun, pl* **cans** [*count*]

1 a : a closed metal container that is usually shaped like a cylinder and that holds food or drink • Open a *can* [=(*Brit*) *tin*] of beans. • a *can* of tomatoes • a soda/beer *can* **b :** the food or drink that is in a can • He ate the whole *can* of beans.

2 a : a metal or plastic container that has a removable top and that is used for holding liquid, trash, etc. • a *can* of oil = an oil *can* • a garbage *can* • a trash *can* **b :** SPRAY CAN • a *can* of deodorant

can

can of worms* :** a complicated situation in which doing something to correct a problem leads to many more problems • We thought the project would be simple, but it turned out to be a real *can of worms*. • Our boss is reluctant to change the policy now because she doesn't want to ***open a can of worms.

carry the can *Brit, informal* **:** to accept blame or responsibility for something that you did not cause • He made the error, but she was left to *carry the can*. • Taxpayers will *carry the can* for the renovations.

in the can *of a film, recording, etc.* **:** completed and ready to be released • a movie that is *in the can*

the can *US, informal* **1 :** the part of the body that you sit on **:** BUTTOCKS • If you ask me, what he needs is a good kick in *the can*. **2 a :** a room with a toilet **:** BATHROOM • He locked himself in *the can* and wouldn't come out. **b :** TOILET • sitting on *the can* **3 :** a prison or jail • The cops threw him in *the can*.

– can·ful /ˈkænˌfʊl/ *noun, pl* **-fuls** • a *canful* of beans

[3]**can** /ˈkæn/ *verb* **cans**; **canned**; **can·ning** [+ *obj*]

1 *chiefly US* **:** to preserve food by putting it in a metal or glass container • a factory where meats are *canned* [=(*Brit*) *tinned*] • *canning* tomatoes

2 *US, informal* **:** to dismiss (someone) from a job • He got *canned* [=*fired, sacked*] for being late to work.

3 *US, informal* **:** to stop or end (something) • The boss angrily told him to *can* the jokes. [=to stop making jokes] • Just ***can it***! [=stop talking; shut up]

– compare [1]CAN; see also CANNED

– can·ner *noun, pl* **-ners** [*count*] **– canning** *noun* [*noncount*] • The tomatoes are fine for *canning*. • a *canning* jar

Can·a·da goose /ˈkænədə-/ *noun, pl* **~ geese** [*count*] **:** a goose of North America that is mostly gray and brown with a black head and neck — see color picture on page C9

Ca·na·di·an /kəˈneɪdijən/ *noun, pl* **-ans** [*count*] **:** a person born, raised, or living in Canada — see also FRENCH CANADIAN

– Canadian *adj* • the *Canadian* government • a *Canadian* accent • a *Canadian* artist/author/film

Canadian bacon *noun* [*noncount*] *US* **:** bacon from the back part of a pig that has little fat and that is cut into round slices

Canadian football *noun* [*noncount*] **:** a game that is like American football and is played on a field between two teams of 12 players each

ca·nal /kəˈnæl/ *noun, pl* **-nals** [*count*]

1 : a long narrow place that is filled with water and was created by people so that boats could pass through it or to supply fields, crops, etc., with water • irrigation *canals* • the Panama *Canal*

2 *medical* **:** a tube or passageway in the body — see also BIRTH CANAL, ROOT CANAL

can·a·pé /ˈkænəpi, ˈkænəˌpeɪ/ *noun, pl* **-pés** [*count*] **:** a small piece of bread or a cracker that has cheese, meat, fish, etc., on top of it and that is often served at a party • platters of *canapés*

ca·nard /kəˈnɑɚd/ *noun, pl* **-nards** [*count*] *formal* **:** a false report or story **:** a belief or rumor that is not true • The book repeats some of history's oldest *canards*. • the widespread *canard* that every lawyer is dishonest

ca•nary /kə'neri/ *noun, pl* **-nar•ies** [*count*] : a small usually yellow or green tropical bird that is often kept in a cage
like the cat that ate the canary see CAT

ca•nas•ta /kə'næstə/ *noun* [*noncount*] : a type of card game that is played with two decks of cards

can•can /'kæn,kæn/ *noun, pl* **-cans** [*count*] : a woman's dance of French origin that involves kicking the legs while holding up the front of a full skirt

can•cel /'kænsəl/ *verb* **-cels**; *US* **-celed** *or Brit* **-celled**; *US* **-cel•ing** *or Brit* **-cel•ling**
1 : to stop doing or planning to do (something) : to decide that something (such as a game, performance, etc.) will not happen [+ *obj*] The event was *canceled* at the last minute when the speaker didn't show up. ▪ We *canceled* our dinner reservation. ▪ My flight was *canceled* because of the storm. ▪ She *canceled* her appointment with the dentist. [*no obj*] I'm sorry, but I have to *cancel*. Can we meet next week?
2 : to cause (something) to end or no longer produce a certain effect : to stop (something) from being effective or valid [+ *obj*] He *canceled* his insurance policy last month. ▪ We *canceled* our magazine subscription when we moved. ▪ Please *cancel* my order. ▪ The bank *canceled* my credit card. [*no obj*] If you subscribe online, you can *cancel* at any time.
3 [+ *obj*] **:** to put a mark with a set of ink lines on something (such as a stamp) so that it cannot be used again ▪ a *canceled* stamp
cancel out [*phrasal verb*] ***cancel out (something) or cancel (something) out*** : to reduce the effect of (something) : to be equal to (something) in force or importance but have an opposite effect ▪ The costs *cancel out* the benefits. ▪ The two arguments ***cancel each other out***.

can•cel•la•tion *also US* **can•cel•a•tion** /,kænsə'leɪʃən/ *noun, pl* **-tions**
1 : a decision to stop doing or planning to do something : the act of canceling something (such as a game, performance, etc.) [*count*] The storm caused delays and flight *cancellations*. [*noncount*] In case of *cancellation*, the game will be played at a later date. [=if the game is canceled, it will be rescheduled for later]
2 : the act of causing something to end or no longer produce a certain effect : a decision to stop something from being effective or valid [*noncount*] Notice of *cancellation* should be given 30 days in advance. ▪ There is a fee for *cancellation*. [*count*] *Cancellations* increased when rates doubled. — often used before another noun ▪ *cancellation* fees ▪ The contract includes a *cancellation* clause.

can•cer /'kænsɚ/ *noun, pl* **-cers**
1 : a serious disease caused by cells that are not normal and that can spread to one or many parts of the body [*noncount*] breast/lung *cancer* ▪ He was diagnosed with *cancer*. ▪ She learned that she has *cancer*. ▪ Eating certain foods may help reduce the risk of *cancer*. [*count*] Advanced *cancers* are more difficult to treat. — often used before another noun ▪ *cancer* patients ▪ *cancer* prevention ▪ *cancer* treatments
2 [*count*] **:** something bad or dangerous that causes other bad things to happen — usually singular ▪ Her jealousy was a *cancer* that slowly destroyed her marriage. ▪ Drugs and violence have become a *cancer* in the city.
3 ***Cancer*** **a** [*noncount*] **:** the fourth sign of the zodiac that comes between Gemini and Leo and has a crab as its symbol — see picture at ZODIAC **b** [*count*] **:** a person born under the sign of Cancer : a person born between June 22nd and July 22nd ▪ I'm a Taurus, but my best friend is a *Cancer*.
– can•cer•ous /'kænsərəs/ *adj* ▪ a *cancerous* growth/lump ▪ The tumor is not *cancerous*.

can•de•la•bra /,kændə'lɑ:brə/ *noun, pl* **-bras** [*count*] : an object with several branches for holding candles or lights

can•de•la•brum /,kændə'lɑ:brəm/ *noun, pl* **-bra** /-brə/ *also* **-brums** [*count*] : CANDELABRA

can•did /'kændəd/ *adj* [*more ~; most ~*]
1 : expressing opinions and feelings in an honest and sincere way ▪ He was quite *candid* about his past. ▪ a *candid* confession ▪ a refreshingly/remarkably *candid* interview ▪ She gave us her *candid* opinion on the matter.
2 *photography* **:** showing people acting in a natural way because they do not know that they are being photographed ▪ a *candid* snapshot
– can•did•ly *adv* ▪ He stated his opinion *candidly*. ▪ She spoke *candidly* about some of the difficulties she had been experiencing. **– can•did•ness** *noun* [*noncount*] ▪ He responded to the question with surprising *candidness*. [=(more commonly) *candor*]

can•di•da•cy /'kændədəsi/ *noun, pl* **-cies** [*count, noncount*] : the position of a person who is trying to be elected : the state of being a candidate ▪ He withdrew his *candidacy* after the scandal damaged his reputation. — often + *for* ▪ She is expected to announce her *candidacy for* president.

can•di•date /'kændə,deɪt, 'kændədət/ *noun, pl* **-dates** [*count*]
1 : a person who is trying to be elected ▪ a presidential *candidate* ▪ the leading Democratic/Republican *candidates* — often + *for* ▪ a *candidate for* governor
2 a : a person who is being considered for a job, position, award, etc. ▪ *Candidates* can apply in person or send a resume. — often + *for* ▪ He seemed like an unlikely *candidate for* the job. ▪ Our son is a *candidate for* the Player of the Year award. **b :** a person who meets all the requirements for something — often + *for* ▪ She is a good *candidate for* laser surgery. [=she meets all the conditions to have laser surgery]
3 : a student in the process of meeting final requirements for a degree ▪ a Ph.D. *candidate* in linguistics ▪ The program has several doctoral *candidates*.
4 *Brit* **:** someone who is taking an exam ▪ Three out of four *candidates* passed the exam.

can•di•da•ture /'kændədə,ʧɚ/ *noun, pl* **-tures** [*count*] *Brit* : CANDIDACY

can•died /'kændid/ *adj, always used before a noun* : cooked in or covered with sugar ▪ *candied* fruit/ginger ▪ *candied* yams

can•dle /'kændl/ *noun, pl* **candles** [*count*] : wax that has been formed into a stick or another shape and has a string in the middle that can be burned
burn the candle at both ends see [1]BURN
hold a candle to : to be on the same level as or as good as (something or someone) — used in negative statements ▪ The new movie doesn't *hold a candle to* [=it is not as good as] the original version.
not worth the candle *chiefly Brit, old-fashioned* : not worth the necessary effort, cost, or trouble ▪ The car is so old that replacing the engine is *not worth the candle*. [=the effort isn't worth the cost]

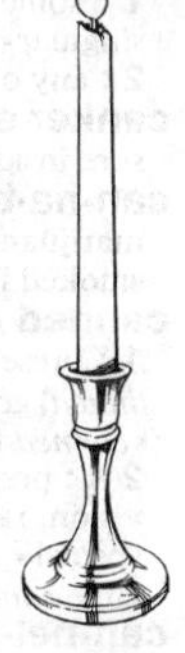
candle

can•dle•hol•der /'kændl,hoʊldɚ/ *noun, pl* **-ders** [*count*] *US* : CANDLESTICK

can•dle•light /'kændl,laɪt/ *noun* [*noncount*] : the light of a candle ▪ We dined/read ***by candlelight***.

can•dle•lit /'kændl,lɪt/ *adj* : lit with the light of candles ▪ a romantic *candlelit* dinner ▪ *Candlelit* tables [=tables with lit candles] created a warm atmosphere.

can•dle•stick /'kændl,stɪk/ *noun, pl* **-sticks** [*count*] : an object with a small hole in the middle for holding a candle ▪ a pair of *candlesticks*

can–do /'kæn'du:/ *adj, always used before a noun, informal* : having or showing an ability to do difficult things ▪ I admire her for her energy and *can-do* attitude. ▪ *can-do* spirit

can•dor (*US*) *or Brit* **can•dour** /'kændɚ/ *noun* [*noncount*] : the quality of being open, sincere, and honest ▪ She spoke with *candor* about racism. ▪ I was impressed by the *candor* of his statement.

can•dy /'kændi/ *noun, pl* **-dies** *US* : a sweet food made with sugar or chocolate [*noncount*] a box/bowl/piece of *candy* ▪ The children are fond of *candy*. [=(*Brit*) *sweets*] ▪ The cough syrup tastes like *candy*. [*count*] chewy *candies* — often used before another noun ▪ a *candy* bar — see also COTTON CANDY, ROCK CANDY

candy apple *noun, pl* **~ apples** [*count*] *US* : an apple that is covered with a sugary mixture that becomes hard

candy cane *noun, pl* **~ canes** [*count*] *US* : a stick of hard red and white candy with a curve at the top

candy floss *noun* [*noncount*] *Brit* : COTTON CANDY

candy–striped *adj* : having a pattern of colored stripes and white stripes that look like the stripes on some sticks of candy ▪ a *candy-striped* shirt

candy strip•er /-'straɪpɚ/ *noun, pl* **~ -ers** [*count*] *US* : a usually female teenage volunteer who works at a hospital ✧ The word comes from the candy striper's striped uniform, which looks like the stripes on some sticks of candy. Candy stripers are not as common in hospitals today as they once were, and they are less likely to wear the striped uniform.

[1]**cane** /'keɪn/ *noun, pl* **canes**

C

1 [*count*] : a short stick that often has a curved handle and is used to help someone to walk • a wooden *cane*
2 ***the cane*** : a form of punishment in which a person is hit with a cane or stick • In the past, some teachers would resort to *the cane* when students misbehaved.
3 [*noncount*] : the hard hollow stem of a plant (such as bamboo or reed) that is used to make furniture and baskets • The chair seat is made of *cane.* • woven strips of *cane*
4 [*count*] : SUGARCANE

[2]**cane** *verb* **canes; caned; can·ing** [+ *obj*] : to hit (someone) with a cane or stick as a form of punishment • In the past, some teachers would *cane* students who misbehaved.

cane sugar *noun* [*noncount*] : sugar from sugarcane

[1]**ca·nine** /ˈkeɪˌnaɪn/ *adj* : of or relating to dogs • *canine* behavior • *canine* loyalty • the police department's ***canine unit*** [=the part of a police department that has dogs that are trained for various purposes] • a ***canine companion*** [=a dog that is kept as a pet]

[2]**canine** *noun, pl* **-nines** [*count*]
1 *formal* : a dog • poodles and other *canines*
2 : a pointed tooth — called also *canine tooth*

can·is·ter /ˈkænəstɚ/ *noun, pl* **-ters** [*count*]
1 : a container with a lid that is used for keeping dry products • a flour/sugar/tea *canister*
2 : a plastic or metal container that is used for keeping a roll of film • a film *canister*
3 : a metal case that contains gas or chemical substances and that bursts when it is fired from a gun • tear gas *canisters*

can·ker /ˈkæŋkɚ/ *noun, pl* **-kers** [*count*]
1 : something that causes bad things to happen — usually singular • Poverty is the *canker* of this neighborhood.
2 : any of various plant diseases

canker sore *noun, pl* **~ sores** [*count*] *US* : a small painful sore inside the mouth — called also *mouth ulcer*

can·na·bis /ˈkænəbəs/ *noun* [*noncount*] : a drug (such as marijuana or hashish) that comes from the hemp plant and is smoked illegally

canned /ˈkænd/ *adj*
1 : preserved in a metal or glass container • *canned* [=(*Brit*) *tinned*] goods • *canned* food • *canned* soup • *canned* tomatoes • *canned* tuna • *canned* beans
2 a : prepared or recorded at an earlier time for use in television, radio, etc. • *canned* laughter **b** *US* : not original or special • a *canned* speech • The salesperson kept using the same *canned* phrases.

can·nel·lo·ni /ˌkænəˈlouni/ *noun* [*noncount*] : tubes of pasta that are filled with meat, fish, cheese, or vegetables and baked in a sauce

can·nery /ˈkænəri/ *noun, pl* **-ner·ies** [*count*] : a factory where food is put into cans

can·ni·bal /ˈkænəbəl/ *noun, pl* **-bals** [*count*] : a person who eats the flesh of human beings or an animal that eats its own kind
– **can·ni·bal·ism** /ˈkænəbəˌlɪzəm/ *noun* [*noncount*] – **can·ni·bal·is·tic** /ˌkænəbəˈlɪstɪk/ *adj*

can·ni·bal·ize *also Brit* **can·ni·bal·ise** /ˈkænəbəˌlaɪz/ *verb* **-iz·es; -ized; -iz·ing** [+ *obj*] : to remove parts from a machine, car, etc., to repair or build another one • He *cannibalized* one washing machine to fix another. • Many parts of the engine were *cannibalized* from older cars.

can·no·li /kəˈnouli/ *noun, pl* **cannoli** *or* **can·no·lis** [*count*] : a type of pastry filled with sweetened cheese

[1]**can·non** /ˈkænən/ *noun, pl* **can·nons** *or* **cannon** [*count*]
1 : a large gun that shoots heavy metal or stone balls and that was once a common military weapon — see also CANNON FODDER, LOOSE CANNON
2 : a large automatic gun that is shot from an aircraft

cannon

[2]**cannon** *verb, always followed by an adverb or preposition* **-nons; -noned; -non·ing** [*no obj*] *Brit* : to suddenly and forcefully hit or move into or against someone or something • The ball *cannoned* off the goalpost and into the net.

can·non·ade /ˌkænəˈneɪd/ *noun, pl* **-ades** [*count*] : an attack with cannons that continues for a long time • The French directed a *cannonade* at the British for three hours.

can·non·ball /ˈkænənˌbɑːl/ *noun, pl* **-balls** [*count*] : a heavy metal or stone ball that is shot from a cannon

cannon fodder *noun* [*noncount*] : soldiers who are sent into battle even though it is likely that they will die • The poorly trained forces are little more than *cannon fodder.* — sometimes used figuratively • The tabloids have been using her love life as *cannon fodder* for years.

can·not /ˈkænɑt, kəˈnɑːt, *Brit* ˈkænət/ — used as the negative form of *can* • We *cannot* [=*can't*] allow that to happen. • I *cannot* [=*can't*] believe that he would do such a thing.

> ***usage*** In speech, *can't* is much more common than *cannot.* In formal writing, *cannot* is much more common than *can't.*

can·ny /ˈkæni/ *adj* **can·ni·er; -est** : very clever and able to make intelligent decisions : SHREWD • a *canny* lawyer • *canny* investors/investments
– **can·ni·ly** /ˈkænəli/ *adv* – **can·ni·ness** /ˈkæninəs/ *noun* [*noncount*]

[1]**ca·noe** /kəˈnuː/ *noun, pl* **-noes** [*count*] : a long narrow boat that is pointed at both ends and that is moved by a paddle with one blade — see picture at BOAT

[2]**canoe** *verb* **-noes; -noed; -noe·ing** : to go or travel in a canoe [*no obj*] He *canoed* down the river to the camp. [+ *obj*] They *canoed* part of the Colorado River this summer.
– **canoeing** *noun* [*noncount*] • In the summers we like to swim and ***go canoeing.*** – **ca·noe·ist** /kəˈnuːwɪst/ *noun, pl* **-ists** [*count*] • an experienced *canoeist* – **canoer** *noun, pl* **-ers** [*count*] *US* • an experienced *canoer*

ca·no·la oil /kəˈnoulə-/ *noun* [*noncount*] *chiefly US + Canada* : a type of oil that is obtained from the seeds of a plant (called the rape plant) and used for cooking

[1]**can·on** /ˈkænən/ *noun, pl* **-ons** [*count*]
1 *formal* : an accepted rule or guide about how people should behave or about how something should be done • Anyone who violates every *canon* of decency as she has done should be dismissed immediately. • the *canons* of good taste • By the *canons* of science, the experiment was not valid.
2 a : a group of books, poems, plays, etc., that are traditionally considered to be very important • the *canon* of American literature = the American literary *canon* • She argues that the *canon* excludes too many women and minority writers. **b** : the group of books, poems, plays, etc., that a particular author is known to have written • the small *canon* of Alcott novels **c** : a list of books that are considered to be part of a religion's official text • writings that are outside the Jewish *canon*
3 : a piece of music in which the same melody is started at different times by each of the different groups of voices or instruments
– compare [2]CANON

[2]**canon** *noun, pl* **-ons** [*count*] : a Christian priest who works in a cathedral — compare [1]CANON

ca·non·i·cal /kəˈnɑːnɪkəl/ *adj* [*more* ~; *most* ~]
1 : connected with or allowed by the laws of the Christian church • *canonical* procedures
2 a : of or relating to the books that are considered to be part of a religion's official text • *canonical* scriptures • the Jewish *canonical* texts **b** : of or relating to the group of books, plays, poems, etc., that are traditionally considered to be very important • *canonical* literature
– **ca·non·i·cal·ly** /kəˈnɑːnɪkli/ *adv*

can·on·ize *also Brit* **can·on·ise** /ˈkænəˌnaɪz/ *verb* **-iz·es; -ized; -iz·ing** [+ *obj*] *in the Roman Catholic Church* : to officially give a dead person a special status as someone very holy : to declare (someone) to be a saint • She died 100 years ago and was *canonized* in Rome last year.
– **can·on·i·za·tion** *also Brit* **can·on·i·sa·tion** /ˌkænənəˈzeɪʃən, *Brit* ˌkænəˌnaɪˈzeɪʃən/ *noun* [*noncount*] • a saint's *canonization*

canon law *noun* [*noncount*] : the laws of a religion • a marriage valid under Catholic *canon law*

ca·noo·dle /kəˈnuːdl/ *verb* **-noo·dles; -noo·dled; -noo·dling** [*no obj*] *informal + old-fashioned* : to hug and kiss another person in a sexual way • Two lovers were *canoodling* on a park bench.

can opener *noun, pl* **~ -ers** [*count*] *chiefly US* : a device that is used in the kitchen to open cans of food — see picture at KITCHEN

can·o·py /ˈkænəpi/ *noun, pl* **-pies** [*count*]
1 : a piece of cloth that hangs over a bed, throne, etc., as a decoration or shelter • A *canopy* hung over the altar. • a ***canopy bed*** [=a bed that has a piece of cloth above it like a roof]

2 a : something that hangs or spreads out over an area • A crowd had gathered under the theater *canopy.* [=the part of the theater building that extends over the sidewalk] — sometimes used figuratively • the *canopy* of the sky **b :** the highest layer of branches in a forest or on a tree • the jungle's thick *canopy*
3 : a clear section that covers the part where the pilot sits in some airplanes
– can•o•pied /ˈkænəpid/ *adj* • a *canopied* bed/throne • a *canopied* forest

¹cant /ˈkænt/ *noun* [*noncount*] **:** words that are supposed to sound like serious statements about important issues (such as religion or morality) but that are not honest or sincere • I think the people are sick of hypocrisy and *cant* from their leaders.

²cant *verb* **cants; cant•ed; cant•ing :** to lean **:** to be positioned at an angle [*no obj*] The legs *cant* slightly to increase the chair's stability. [+ *obj*] — usually used as *(be) canted* • The legs of the chair *are canted* slightly to increase stability. • the chair's slightly *canted* legs

can't /ˈkænt, *Brit* ˈkɑːnt/ — used as a contraction of *cannot* • I *can't* do it. ***usage*** see CANNOT

can•ta•loupe *also* **can•ta•loup** /ˈkæntəˌloʊp, *Brit* ˈkæntəˌluːp/ *noun, pl* **-loupes** *also* **-loups** [*count, noncount*] **:** a type of large fruit (called a melon) that has a hard, rough skin and orange flesh — see color picture on page C5

can•tan•ker•ous /kænˈtæŋkərəs/ *adj* [*more* ~; *most* ~] **:** often angry and annoyed • a *cantankerous* [=*cranky*] old man

can•ta•ta /kənˈtɑːtə/ *noun, pl* **-tas** [*count*] **:** a piece of music for singers and instruments that usually has several parts (called movements) and often has a religious subject

can•teen /kænˈtiːn/ *noun, pl* **-teens** [*count*]
1 : a store in a camp, school, etc., in which food, drinks, and small supplies are sold
2 a *chiefly US* **:** a place where drinks and entertainment are provided for soldiers at a military base or camp **b** *chiefly Brit* **:** a place where food is served in a factory, school, etc. • the school *canteen* [=(*US*) *cafeteria*]
3 : a small container for carrying water or other liquids • a hiker's *canteen* — see picture at CAMPING
4 *Brit* **:** a box for storing knives, forks, spoons, etc.

¹can•ter /ˈkæntɚ/ *noun, pl* **-ters**
1 [*singular*] **:** the way a horse moves when it is running fairly fast • He set off ***at a canter*** towards the stable.
2 [*count*] **:** a ride or run at a canter — usually singular • a *canter* through the fields — compare ¹GALLOP, ²TROT

²canter *verb* **-ters; -tered; -ter•ing** [*no obj*]
1 *of a horse* **:** to run fairly fast **:** to run at a canter • The horses *cantered* across the grass.
2 : to ride on a horse that is running fairly fast **:** to ride a horse at a canter • We *cantered* off toward the lake.

can•ti•cle /ˈkæntɪkəl/ *noun, pl* **-ti•cles** [*count*] **:** a song that has words from the Bible and that is used in Christian church services

¹can•ti•le•ver /ˈkæntəˌliːvɚ/ *noun, pl* **-vers** [*count*] **:** a long piece of wood, metal, etc., that sticks out from a wall or other structure to support something above it (such as a balcony or bridge) • The porch is supported by steel *cantilevers.* • a ***cantilever bridge*** [=a bridge that uses cantilevers to support the main part]

²cantilever *verb* **-vers; vered; ver•ing**
1 [+ *obj*] **:** to support (something) with a cantilever — usually used as *(be) cantilevered* • *cantilevered* beams/floors
2 [*no obj*] *of a structure* **:** to extend out over an area • The balcony *cantilevers* over the terrace below.

can•to /ˈkæntoʊ/ *noun, pl* **can•tos** [*count*] **:** a major section of a long poem • the first *canto* of Dante's "Inferno"

can•ton /ˈkæntn̩/ *noun, pl* **-tons** [*count*] **:** one of the sections into which some countries (such as Switzerland) are divided

can•tor /ˈkæntɚ/ *noun, pl* **-tors** [*count*]
1 : a person who sings and leads people in prayer in a Jewish religious service
2 : a person who leads a group of singers in a church

Ca•nuck /kəˈnʌk/ *noun, pl* **-nucks** [*count*] *informal* **:** a person born, raised, or living in Canada **:** a Canadian

can•vas /ˈkænvəs/ *noun, pl* **-vas•es**
1 : a strong, rough cloth that is used to make bags, tents, sails, etc. [*noncount*] a tent made of *canvas* • a *canvas* chair/bag • *canvas* shoes [*count*] Use a *canvas* to cover the boat.
2 [*count*] **a :** a specially prepared piece of cloth on which a picture can be painted by an artist • a fresh/blank *canvas* **b :** a painting made on a piece of cloth • The museum has several *canvases* by Rubens.
under canvas chiefly Brit **:** in a tent • a night *under canvas* [=a night sleeping in a tent]

can•vass /ˈkænvəs/ *verb* **-vass•es; -vassed; -vass•ing**
1 a [+ *obj*] **:** to ask (the people in an area) what they think about a candidate, project, idea, etc. • A team of volunteers is *canvassing* the city for the Republican Party. • We go to every house to *canvass* voters. **b :** to talk to the people in an area in order to get them to support a candidate, project, idea, etc. [*no obj*] She is *canvassing* for one of the presidential candidates this year. [+ *obj*] The group has been *canvassing* neighborhoods to ask people to vote for him.
2 [+ *obj*] *somewhat formal* **:** to look at or consider (something) carefully • The company *canvassed* several sites for a new factory.
– can•vass•er *noun, pl* **-ers** [*count*] • a paid *canvasser* for a senate candidate

can•yon /ˈkænjən/ *noun, pl* **-yons** [*count*] **:** a deep valley with steep rock sides and often a stream or river flowing through it • the Grand *Canyon*

¹cap /ˈkæp/ *noun, pl* **caps** [*count*]
1 a : a small, soft hat that often has a hard curved part (called a visor) that extends out over your eyes • a Harvard University *cap* [=a cap that has the name or symbol of Harvard University on it] • a knit/knitted *cap* • his wool/tweed *cap* — see also BASEBALL CAP **b :** a covering for a person's head that is worn for a special purpose • a ***shower/bathing cap*** [=a head covering that people wear to keep their hair dry when they are showering/swimming] — see also THINKING CAP **c :** a hat that people with particular jobs wear while working • a painter's *cap* • a surgeon's *cap,* gown, and gloves
2 : a part or object that covers the end or top of something • a bottle *cap* • a lens *cap* • a pill bottle with a childproof *cap* • Put the *cap* back on the marker when you are done using it.
3 : a part that forms the top of something • a bird with a black *cap* [=a black section of feathers on the top of its head] • a ***mushroom cap*** [=the top part of a mushroom]
4 : a limit on the amount of money that can be spent, given, charged, etc., for something • a spending *cap* • a *cap* on political donations • a *cap* on doctor's fees
5 : a paper or metal container that holds an explosive substance • a blasting *cap*
6 *informal* **:** a capital letter — usually plural • e-mails written in all *caps* • She signed the letter with her name in *caps*: KIM.
7 : a hard substance that is shaped to look like a healthy tooth and used to cover a damaged tooth
8 *Brit, sports* **a :** an opportunity to play for your school or country • He won his first *cap* against Columbia when he was 22. **b :** a player chosen to play for a country's team
9 *Brit* **:** DIAPHRAGM 3
a feather in your cap see ¹FEATHER
cap in hand see ¹HAND
if the cap fits *or* ***if the cap fits, wear it*** *Brit* — used to say that something said about a person is true and the person should accept it as true • They may not like being called careless, but *if the cap fits, wear it.* [=(*US*) *if the shoe fits, wear it*]
tip your cap see ¹TIP

²cap *verb* **caps; capped; cap•ping** [+ *obj*]
1 : to cover the top or end of (something) • a pipe *capped* at one end • a mountain *capped* with snow = a snow-*capped* mountain **:** to put a cap on (something) • Be sure to *cap* the pen/marker when you are done using it.
2 a : to end (something) in usually an exciting or impressive way • The report *caps* a ten-year study of lung cancer among nonsmokers. — often + *off* in U.S. English • The band *capped off* the show with an extended version of their classic hit. • The victory *caps off* the career of a coach who's brought her team to the championships five times. **b :** to follow (something) with something that is better, worse, etc. • a concert *capped* by a fantastic fireworks display • The car was filthy when he returned it to me, and ***to cap it off*** [=*to top it off*], there was almost no fuel left in the tank.
3 a : to prevent (something) from increasing **:** to put an upper limit on (something) • If the teams don't *cap* player salaries, the league won't survive. • *capping* interest rates • The law would *cap* legal immigration. **b** *Brit* **:** to put a limit on the amount of money that can be spent by (a group) • The government wants to *cap* councils that spend too much.
4 : to cover (a tooth) with a hard material that is shaped to

look like a healthy tooth : to put a cap on (a tooth) • He had two of his teeth *capped.*

5 *Brit, sports* **: to choose (someone) to play for a national team — usually used as** *(be) capped* • He *was* first *capped* for Ireland at age 22.

ca·pa·bil·i·ty /ˌkeɪpəˈbɪləti/ *noun, pl* **-ties** [*count*] **: the ability to do something** • The device has the *capability* of recording two television channels at once. • That kind of job is beyond my *capability.* [=it is too difficult for me] • The company doesn't have any manufacturing *capability.* [=*capacity*] • The country's military *capability* is unclear. [=the country's ability to fight a war is unclear] • The country does not have ***nuclear capability***. [=does not have nuclear weapons] **— often plural** • Students are expected to participate in sports according to their *capabilities.* [=*abilities*] • a computer program's search *capabilities* • a cell phone with video game and Internet *capabilities*

ca·pa·ble /ˈkeɪpəbəl/ *adj*

1 : able to do something : having the qualities or abilities that are needed to do something — + *of* • a new train *capable of* (reaching) very high speeds • Many new cell phones are *capable of* connecting to the Internet. • He is not *capable of* making those medical decisions himself. [=he cannot make the decisions by himself because he cannot think clearly, he is too sick, etc.] • I don't believe that she's *capable of* murder. [=that she is the kind of person who could murder someone] • a storm *capable of* (causing) widespread destruction

2 [*more* ~; *most* ~] **: skilled at doing something : able to do something well** • She is one of the most *capable* [=*skilled*] and versatile actresses in Hollywood. • a *capable* student • a very *capable* pilot ✧ **Something that is in *capable hands* is being done or dealt with by someone who has the skill and knowledge to do it well.** • I will leave the store in your *capable hands* while I am gone.

– ca·pa·bly /ˈkeɪpəbli/ *adv* • He was assisted *capably* by one of the other students.

ca·pa·cious /kəˈpeɪʃəs/ *adj* [*more* ~; *most* ~] *formal* **: able to hold or contain a lot : large in capacity** • the museum's *capacious* [=*spacious*] rooms • The van is *capacious* [=*roomy*] enough to hold eight passengers easily.

– ca·pa·cious·ness *noun* [*noncount*]

ca·pac·i·tor /kəˈpæsətɚ/ *noun, pl* **-tors** [*count*] *technical* **: a device that is used to store electrical energy**

ca·pac·i·ty /kəˈpæsəti/ *noun, pl* **-ties**

1 a [*count*] **: the ability to hold or contain people or things — usually singular** • The restaurant has a large seating *capacity.* [=many people can sit in the restaurant; it has many seats] • What is the hard drive's storage *capacity*? **b : the largest amount or number that can be held or contained** [*count*] The nightclub has a 1,000-person *capacity.* • a bottle with a *capacity* of two liters [*noncount*] The prison has reached *capacity.* [=the prison is full] • The auditorium was ***filled to capacity***. [=was completely full]

2 : the ability to do something : a mental, emotional, or physical ability [*noncount*] Some species of birds do not have the *capacity* [=*ability*] to fly. • Does he have the *capacity* to handle this job? • The disease causes a deterioration of breathing *capacity.* [*count*] the machine's computational *capacities* [=*capabilities*] **— usually singular** • a character with a great *capacity* for love [=a character who is able to love people very deeply]

3 [*count*] **: a usually official position or job : ROLE** • He was acting in his *capacity* as judge. • She's worked for the company in various *capacities* over the years. [=she has had various jobs at the company] • serving in a supervisory *capacity*

4 [*noncount*] **: the amount of something that can be produced or managed by a factory, company, etc.** • a plan to double the factory's *capacity* • We can't hire more people because we lack the training *capacity.* • the nation's oil refining *capacity*; *also* **: the largest amount that a factory, company, etc., can produce or manage** • The factory is currently running at three-quarter *capacity.* [=the factory is producing three quarters of what it can produce] • The airport is not expected to reach *capacity* [=the highest number of planes it can deal with] for several years.

¹cape /ˈkeɪp/ *noun, pl* **capes** [*count*]

1 : a large area of land that sticks out into a sea, bay, etc. — often used in proper names • the *Cape* of Good Hope • *Cape* Cod

2 *US* **: a small house that has one or one-and-a-half levels and a steep roof — called also *Cape Cod cottage***

– compare ²CAPE

²cape *noun, pl* **capes** [*count*] **: a piece of clothing that does not have sleeves and that fits closely at the neck and hangs over the shoulders, arms, and back : a short cloak** • a superhero's mask and *cape* **— compare ¹CAPE**

– caped /ˈkeɪpt/ *adj* • a *caped* superhero

¹ca·per /ˈkeɪpɚ/ *noun, pl* **-pers** [*count*]

1 *informal* **: an illegal or improper activity that is usually seen as amusing or not very serious** • She has a long record of small-time *capers* [=*crimes*] that include everything from shoplifting to fraud. • a jewelry *caper* [=*theft, heist*]

2 : an amusing movie, story, etc., about tricks or crimes • a crazy *caper* about a bank robbery that goes wrong

3 : a lively jump or dance • He was so happy, he ***cut a caper*** [=did a short dance] on the steps of Town Hall.

– compare ²CAPER

²caper *noun, pl* **-pers** [*count*] **: a small flower bud that comes from a kind of bush and that is preserved in vinegar and used to flavor food** • a pasta salad made with artichokes, olives, and *capers* **— compare ¹CAPER**

³caper *verb* **-pers; -pered; -per·ing** [*no obj*] **: to jump around in a lively way** • a young goat *capering* in its pen

cap·il·lary /ˈkæpəˌleri, *Brit* kəˈpɪləri/ *noun, pl* **-lar·ies** [*count*] **: one of the many very small tubes that carry blood within the body : the smallest kind of blood vessel**

capita see PER CAPITA

¹cap·i·tal /ˈkæpətl/ *adj*

1 *of a letter* **: in the form A, B, C, etc., rather than a, b, c : UPPERCASE** • *capital* letters • a *capital* D • His handwritten *capital* S's look a lot like lowercase/small s's. **— sometimes used informally to give emphasis to a description** • He is conservative ***with a capital C***! [=he is very conservative] • The sauce is spicy *with a capital S.* [=it is very spicy]

2 : having the main offices of a government • the state's *capital* city

3 *of a crime* **: having death as a possible punishment** • Homicide that occurs during the course of an attempted kidnapping is a *capital* crime in some states. • *capital* murder/rape charges **— see also CAPITAL PUNISHMENT**

4 *chiefly Brit, old-fashioned* **: EXCELLENT** • a *capital* idea

²capital *noun, pl* **-tals**

1 [*noncount*] **a : money, property, etc., that is used to start or operate a business** • Does he have the *capital* to start a new business? **— see also VENTURE CAPITAL b : the money, property, etc., that a person or business owns** • *capital* accumulation = the accumulation of *capital* • Like most homeowners, her house is her biggest *capital* asset. **— sometimes used figuratively** • The governor wasted his political *capital* on an unpopular issue. • She's been accused of trying to ***make capital out of*** the tragedy. [=of trying to use the tragedy to her advantage; of trying to benefit from the tragedy] **— see also CAPITAL GAINS, CAPITAL GOODS, WORKING CAPITAL**

2 [*count*] **: a letter in the form A, B, C, etc. : a capital letter**

3 [*count*] **a : a city in which the main offices of a government are located : a capital city** • the state/provincial *capital* • Austin is the *capital* of Texas. • Beijing is China's *capital.* **b : the most important city for an activity or product** • New York City is the media *capital* of the United States. • This town is the region's cultural *capital.*

Do not confuse *capital* with *capitol.*

capital gains *noun* [*plural*] **: money that you get by selling property at a higher price than the price that you paid to buy it** • Stock sales resulted in millions of dollars in *capital gains* for the company. • the *capital gains* tax

capital goods *noun* [*plural*] *business* **: products (such as factory equipment and tools) that are used to make other products — compare CONSUMER GOODS**

capital–intensive *adj* [*more* ~; *most* ~] *business* **: requiring the payment or investment of a very large amount of money** • a *capital-intensive* industry • The airport expansion is a very *capital-intensive* project. **— compare LABOR-INTENSIVE**

cap·i·tal·ism /ˈkæpətəˌlɪzəm/ *noun* [*noncount*] **: a way of organizing an economy so that the things that are used to make and transport products (such as land, oil, factories, ships, etc.) are owned by individual people and companies rather than by the government — compare COMMUNISM, SOCIALISM**

¹cap·i·tal·ist /ˈkæpətəlɪst/ *also* **cap·i·tal·is·tic** /ˌkæpətəˈlɪstɪk/ *adj* **: of or relating to capitalism** • a *capitalist* society • *capitalist* values • *capitalist* ideology **: using capital-**

ism as an economic system • the world's *capitalist* nations

²**capitalist** *noun, pl* **-ists** [*count*]

1 : a person who has a lot of money, property, etc., and who uses those things to produce more money • a wealthy *capitalist*

2 : a person who believes that capitalism is the best kind of economic system

cap·i·tal·ize *also Brit* **cap·i·tal·ise** /ˈkæpətəˌlaɪz/ *verb* **-iz·es; -ized; -iz·ing** [+ *obj*]

1 a : to use a capital letter to write, print, or type (a letter of the alphabet) • Remember to *capitalize* the *I* in *Internet.* **b :** to begin (a word or name) with a capital letter • *Capitalize* the first word of your sentence. • She rarely *capitalizes* her name when she signs her e-mails.

2 a : to provide the money that is needed to start or develop (a business) • They're seeking investors (in order) to *capitalize* the business. • The venture was *capitalized* with a loan of one million dollars. **b :** to sell (something valuable, such as property or stock) in order to get money **:** to convert (something) into capital • You can *capitalize* your investment at any time.

capitalize on [*phrasal verb*] ***capitalize on (something)*** **:** to use (something, such as an event or situation) in a way that helps you **:** to get an advantage from (something) • They were able to *capitalize on* [=*take advantage of*] our mistakes. • She *capitalized on* her new fame by writing a book.

– cap·i·tal·i·za·tion *also Brit* **cap·i·tal·i·sa·tion** /ˌkæpətələˈzeɪʃən, *Brit* ˌkæpətəˌlaɪˈzeɪʃən/ *noun* [*noncount*] • Please check your spelling, punctuation, and *capitalization*. [=use of capital letters]

capital punishment *noun* [*noncount*] **:** punishment by death **:** the practice of killing people as punishment for serious crimes • an opponent of *capital punishment*

cap·i·tol /ˈkæpətḷ/ *noun, pl* **-tols**

1 [*count*] **:** the building in which the people who make the laws of a U.S. state meet • the dome of the state *capitol*

2 ***the Capitol*** **:** the building in which the U.S. Congress meets in Washington, D.C.

Do not confuse *capitol* with *capital*.

Capitol Hill *noun* [*singular*] **:** the group of people who make the federal laws in the United States **:** the U.S. Congress • The organization is lobbying *Capital Hill* to increase funding for AIDS research. ◇ The U.S. Congress is called *Capitol Hill* because that is the name of the area in Washington, D.C., where the Capitol building is located. • an apartment near/on *Capitol Hill*

ca·pit·u·late /kəˈpɪtʃəˌleɪt/ *verb* **-lates; -lat·ed; -lat·ing** [*no obj*] *formal*

1 : to stop fighting an enemy or opponent **:** to admit that an enemy or opponent has won **:** SURRENDER • The country still refuses to *capitulate* despite its weakening army and dwindling resources.

2 : to stop trying to fight or resist something **:** to agree to do or accept something that you have been resisting or opposing • The teacher refused to *capitulate*: no calculators were to be used during the exam. — often + *to* • The company *capitulated* [=*gave in*] *to* the labor union to avoid a strike. • Officials eventually *capitulated to* the protesters' demands.

– ca·pit·u·la·tion /kəˌpɪtʃəˈleɪʃən/ *noun, pl* **-tions** [*count, noncount*]

ca·pon /ˈkeɪˌpɑːn/ *noun, pl* **-pons** [*count*] **:** a male chicken whose sex organs have been removed

cap·puc·ci·no /ˌkæpəˈtʃiːnoʊ/ *noun, pl* **-nos :** a drink of strong coffee (called espresso) that has a bubbly layer of hot milk on top [*noncount*] She loves *cappuccino*. [*count*] We stopped for dessert and *cappuccinos*.

ca·price /kəˈpriːs/ *noun, pl* **-pric·es :** a sudden change [*count*] the *caprices* of the weather; *especially* **:** a sudden change in someone's mood or behavior [*count*] Employees have complained of being at the mercy of the manager's every whim and *caprice*. [*noncount*] policy changes that seem to be motivated by nothing more than *caprice*

ca·pri·cious /kəˈprɪʃəs/ *adj* [*more* ~; *most* ~] *formal*

1 : changing often and quickly • *capricious* weather/winds; *especially* **:** often changing suddenly in mood or behavior • employees who are at the mercy of a *capricious* manager

2 : not logical or reasonable **:** based on an idea, desire, etc., that is not possible to predict • The court ruled that the punishment was arbitrary and *capricious*.

– ca·pri·cious·ly *adv* • a manager who acts *capriciously*

– ca·pri·cious·ness *noun* [*noncount*]

Cap·ri·corn /ˈkæprɪˌkoɚn/ *noun, pl* **-corns**

1 [*noncount*] **:** the 10th sign of the zodiac **:** the sign of the zodiac that comes between Sagittarius and Aquarius and that has a goat as its symbol — see picture at ZODIAC

2 [*count*] **:** a person born under the sign of Capricorn **:** a person born between December 22 and January 19 • I'm a *Capricorn*. What are you?

ca·pri pants /kəˈpriː-/ *noun* [*plural*] **:** close-fitting women's pants that end above the ankle — called also *capris*; see color picture on page C14

cap·size /ˈkæpˌsaɪz/ *verb* **-siz·es; -sized; -siz·ing** *of a boat* **:** to turn over **:** to turn so that the bottom is on top [*no obj*] The canoe suddenly *capsized*. [+ *obj*] They were fooling around and accidentally *capsized* the canoe.

cap·stan /ˈkæpstən/ *noun, pl* **-stans** [*count*] **:** a machine that turns so that rope or a cable can wind around it and move or lift heavy weights (such as a ship's anchor)

¹**cap·sule** /ˈkæpsəl, *Brit* ˈkæpˌsjuːl/ *noun, pl* **-sules** [*count*]

1 a : a very small container that is filled with medicine and swallowed whole **b :** a small glass or plastic container that has something (such as a liquid) inside of it

2 : a small part of a spacecraft that is separate from the rest of the spacecraft and that is where people live and work – see also TIME CAPSULE

²**capsule** *adj, always used before a noun* **:** very short • a *capsule* [=*brief*] history of the world • *capsule* biographies

Capt. *abbr* captain

¹**cap·tain** /ˈkæptən/ *noun, pl* **-tains** [*count*]

1 : a person who is in charge of a ship or an airplane • The *captain* has turned off the "fasten seat belt" sign. • *Captain* Ahab

2 : an officer of high rank in some branches of the military • an army/navy *captain*

3 *chiefly US* **:** an officer of high rank in a police or fire department

4 : an athlete who is chosen to be the leader of a team • She was the *captain* of our team. = She was our team *captain*.

²**captain** *verb* **-tains; -tained; -tain·ing** [+ *obj*] **:** to be the captain of (something): such as **a :** to be in charge of (a ship or airplane) • The ship was *captained* by John Smith. **b :** to lead (a team) • She *captained* last year's team.

cap·tain·cy /ˈkæptənsi/ *noun, pl* **-cies**

1 : the position of being captain of a team [*noncount*] In college sports, *captaincy* is usually given to seniors. [*count*] He was promoted to a *captaincy*.

2 [*count*] **:** the period of time during which someone is a captain — usually singular • Under/during his *captaincy*, the team won nearly every game.

captain of industry *noun, pl* **captains of industry** [*count*] **:** someone who owns or manages a large, successful business or company

cap·tion /ˈkæpʃən/ *noun, pl* **-tions** [*count*] **:** a sentence or group of words that is written on or next to a picture to explain what is being shown • The *caption* on the picture says "This year's contest winners."

– caption *verb* **-tions; -tioned; -tion·ing** [+ *obj*] — usually used as *(be) captioned* • The picture *is captioned* "This year's contest winners."

cap·ti·vate /ˈkæptəˌveɪt/ *verb* **-vates; -vat·ed; -vat·ing** [+ *obj*] **:** to attract and hold the attention of (someone) by being interesting, pretty, etc. • The play has been *captivating* audiences for years. — often used as *(be) captivated* • We *were captivated* by her beauty.

captivating *adj* [*more* ~; *most* ~] **:** attractive and interesting in a way that holds your attention • a *captivating* [=*fascinating*] story • a *captivating* smile

¹**cap·tive** /ˈkæptɪv/ *adj*

1 : captured and kept in a prison, cage, etc. • The *captive* soldiers planned their escape. • *captive* animals • Enemy forces took/held them *captive*. [=took or kept them as prisoners]

2 *always used before a noun* **:** forced to watch or listen to something because you cannot leave • The passengers on the plane were a ***captive audience***. [=the passengers on the plane could not leave and had to listen to what was being said]

²**captive** *noun, pl* **-tives** [*count*] **:** someone who is captured and kept as a prisoner • They set their *captives* free.

cap·tiv·i·ty /kæpˈtɪvəti/ *noun* [*noncount*] **:** the state of being kept in a place (such as a prison or a cage) and not being able to leave or be free **:** the state or condition of being captive • The prisoners were released from *captivity*. • The lions were bred ***in captivity***. [=while living in a zoo]

C

cap·tor /ˈkæptɚ/ *noun, pl* **-tors** [*count*] **:** someone who has captured a person and is keeping that person as a prisoner • The men fought their *captors* and escaped.

[1]**cap·ture** /ˈkæpʧɚ/ *verb* **-tures; -tured; -tur·ing** [+ *obj*]
1 a : to take and hold (someone) as a prisoner especially by using force • They were *captured* by enemy soldiers. **b :** to catch (an animal) • using traps to *capture* mice
2 a : to get control of (a place) especially by using force • The city was *captured* by the Romans. **b :** to win or get (something) through effort • She *captured* 60 percent of the vote in the last election. • The company plans on *capturing* a larger segment of the market.
3 : to get and hold (someone's attention, interest, etc.) • The show has *captured* the attention/interest of teenagers. • The story ***captured our imaginations***. [=the story was very interesting and exciting]
4 : to describe or show (someone or something) in a very accurate way by using writing, painting, film, etc. • The story *captures* the essence of the holiday. • The biography *captured* her perfectly. • The beauty of the landscape was *captured* perfectly by the artist.
5 a : to record (something) in a picture, film, etc. • The robbery was *captured* (on film) by the security cameras. **b :** to get and put (information) into a form that can be read or used by a computer • The system is used to *capture* data relating to the buying habits of young people. • a digital camera that *captures* 1.2 million pixels
6 : to take (something, such as a chess piece) by following the rules of a game • In the game of chess, the goal is to *capture* your opponent's king.
capture lightning in a bottle see [1]LIGHTNING

[2]**capture** *noun* [*noncount*] **:** the act of capturing someone or something: such as **a :** the act of taking and holding someone as a prisoner or of being taken as a prisoner • They avoided/eluded/escaped *capture*. **b :** the act of getting control of something • the *capture* of the city by enemy forces **c :** the act of putting information in a form that a computer can use or read • data/image *capture*

car /ˈkɑɚ/ *noun, pl* **cars**
1 : a vehicle that has four wheels and an engine and that is used for carrying passengers on roads [*count*] I'll wait in the *car*. • He got into the *car* and drove away. • She bought a new *car*. • drive/park a *car* [*noncount*] We can go ***by car*** or by bus. [=we can travel in a car or in a bus] — often used before another noun • a *car* manufacturer/dealer/accident/crash — called also (*US*) *automobile*
2 [*count*] *US* **:** a separate section of a train • a railroad *car* • The train has 20 *cars*. [=(*Brit*) *carriages, coaches*] — see also CABLE CAR, DINING CAR, SLEEPING CAR, TROLLEY CAR

ca·rafe /kəˈræf/ *noun, pl* **-rafes** [*count*] **:** a glass container that has a wide mouth and that is used to serve drinks (such as water or wine) during a meal; *also* **:** the amount in a carafe • We drank a *carafe* of wine.

car·a·mel /ˈkɑɚməl, ˈkerəməl/ *noun, pl* **-mels**
1 : a light brown candy made from butter, sugar, and milk or cream [*noncount*] a piece of *caramel* [*count*] a bag of *caramels*
2 [*noncount*] **:** sugar that is cooked until it is burnt and that is used to give color and flavor to food — see also CRÈME CARAMEL
3 [*noncount*] **:** a light brown color

car·a·mel·ize *also Brit* **car·a·mel·ise** /ˈkɑɚməˌlaɪz, ˈkerəməˌlaɪz/ *verb* **-iz·es; -ized; -iz·ing**
1 : to cook (something, such as a fruit or vegetable) slowly until it becomes brown and sweet [+ *obj*] She *caramelized* the apples. • *caramelized* onions [*no obj*] The onions will take five minutes to *caramelize*.
2 : to change (sugar) into caramel by cooking it [+ *obj*] *Caramelize* two cups of sugar. [*no obj*] Continue stirring until the sugar *caramelizes*.

car·a·pace /ˈkerəˌpeɪs/ *noun, pl* **-pac·es** [*count*] *technical* **:** a hard shell on the back of some animals (such as turtles or crabs)

[1]**car·at** /ˈkerət/ *noun, pl* **-ats** [*count*] **:** a unit for measuring the weight of jewels (such as diamonds) that is equal to 200 milligrams

[2]**carat** *chiefly Brit spelling of* KARAT

[1]**car·a·van** /ˈkerəˌvæn/ *noun, pl* **-vans** [*count*]
1 a : a group of people or animals traveling together on a long journey especially through the desert **b :** a group of vehicles (such as cars or wagons) traveling together
2 *Brit* **:** CAMPER 2

[2]**caravan** *verb* **-vans; -vaned** *or* **-vanned; -van·ing** *or* **-van·ning** [*no obj*] *US* **:** to travel from one place to another in a group of vehicles • We *caravaned* to the campsite.

caravanning *noun* [*noncount*] *Brit* **:** the activity of taking a vacation in a trailer or camper • Camping and *caravanning* are popular in this area.

car·a·way /ˈkerəˌweɪ/ *noun* [*noncount*] **:** the seeds of a plant related to the carrot that are used to flavor foods • *caraway* seeds

carb /ˈkɑɚb/ *noun, pl* **carbs** [*count*] *US, informal* **:** CARBOHYDRATE • a diet low in *carbs* = a low-*carb* diet

car·bine /ˈkɑɚˌbiːn, ˈkɑɚˌbaɪn/ *noun, pl* **-bines** [*count*] **:** a short, light rifle

car·bo·hy·drate /ˌkɑɚboʊˈhaɪˌdreɪt/ *noun, pl* **-drates :** any one of various substances found in certain foods (such as bread, rice, and potatoes) that provide your body with heat and energy and are made of carbon, hydrogen, and oxygen [*count*] Pasta has a lot of *carbohydrates*. [=(*US*) *carbs*] • He's trying to lose weight by cutting down on *carbohydrates*. [=foods that contain a lot of carbohydrates] [*noncount*] a food that is low in protein but high in *carbohydrate*

car bomb *noun, pl* **~ bombs** [*count*] **:** a bomb that is hid-

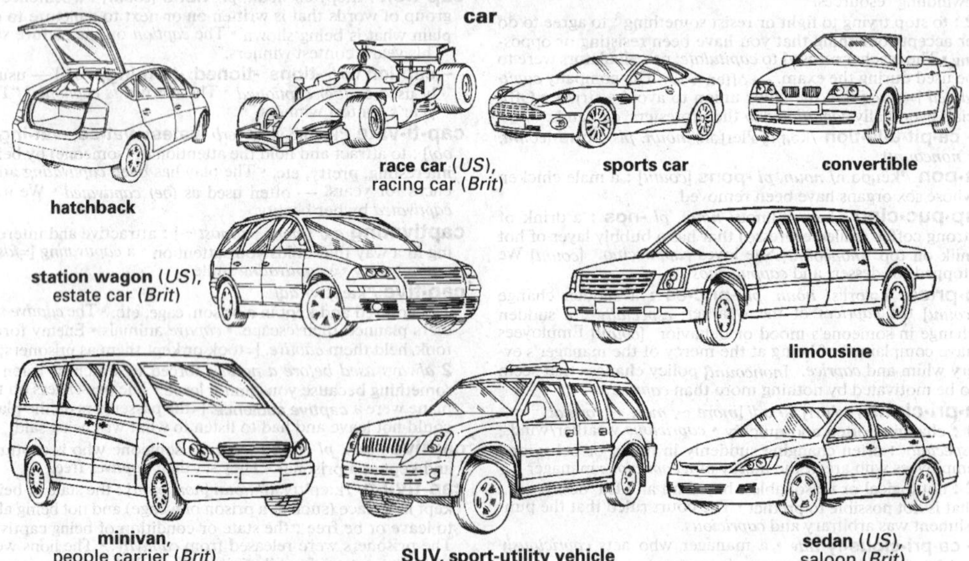

C

car

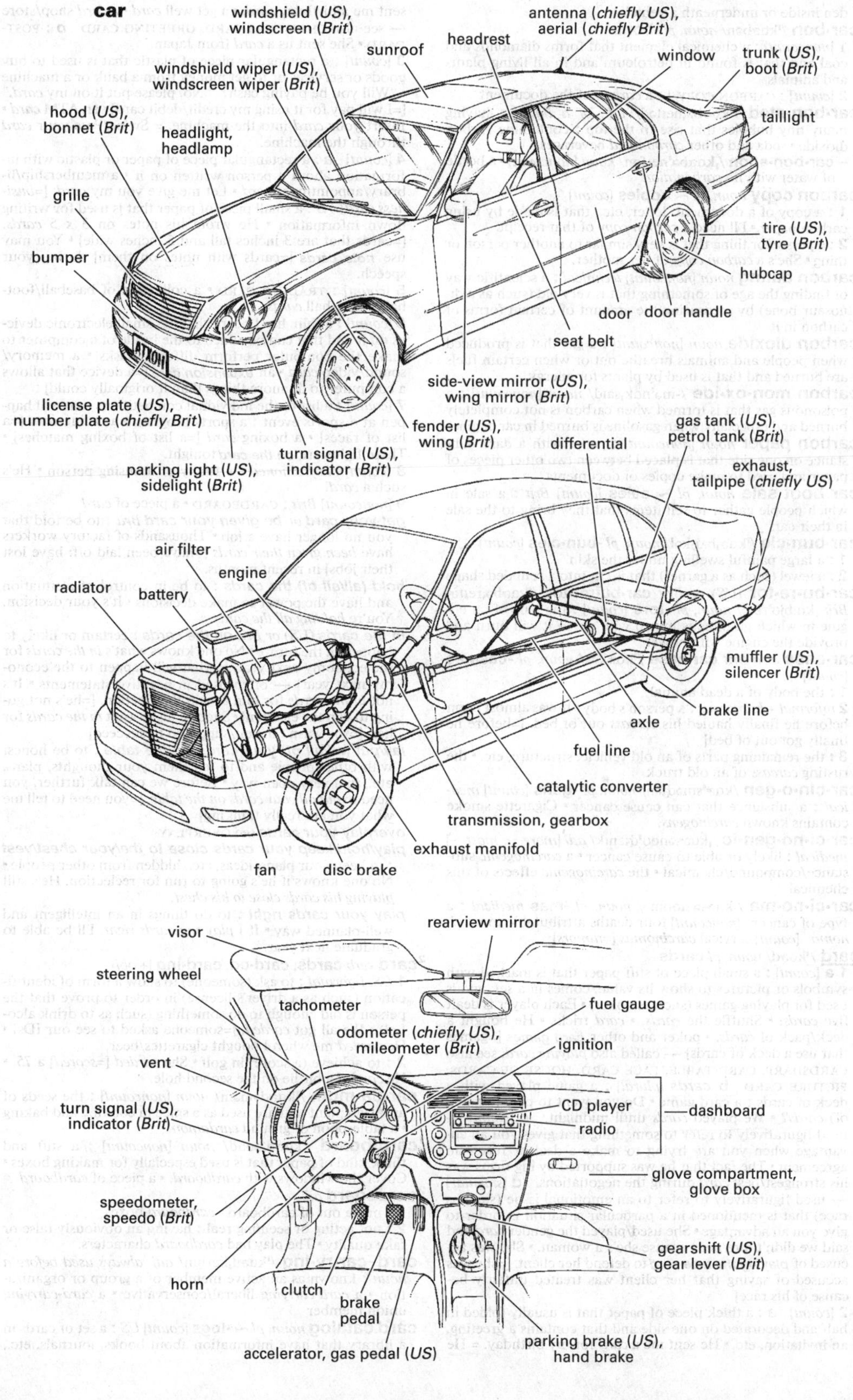

windshield (*US*),
windscreen (*Brit*)
sunroof
windshield wiper (*US*),
windscreen wiper (*Brit*)
hood (*US*),
bonnet (*Brit*)
headlight,
headlamp
grille
bumper
license plate (*US*),
number plate (*chiefly Brit*)
parking light (*US*),
sidelight (*Brit*)
turn signal (*US*),
indicator (*Brit*)
fender (*US*),
wing (*Brit*)
side-view mirror (*US*),
wing mirror (*Brit*)
seat belt
antenna (*chiefly US*),
aerial (*chiefly Brit*)
headrest
window
trunk (*US*),
boot (*Brit*)
taillight
tire (*US*),
tyre (*Brit*)
hubcap
door
door handle

air filter
engine
radiator
battery
fan
disc brake
exhaust manifold
transmission, gearbox
catalytic converter
fuel line
axle
brake line
differential
gas tank (*US*),
petrol tank (*Brit*)
exhaust,
tailpipe (*chiefly US*)
muffler (*US*),
silencer (*Brit*)

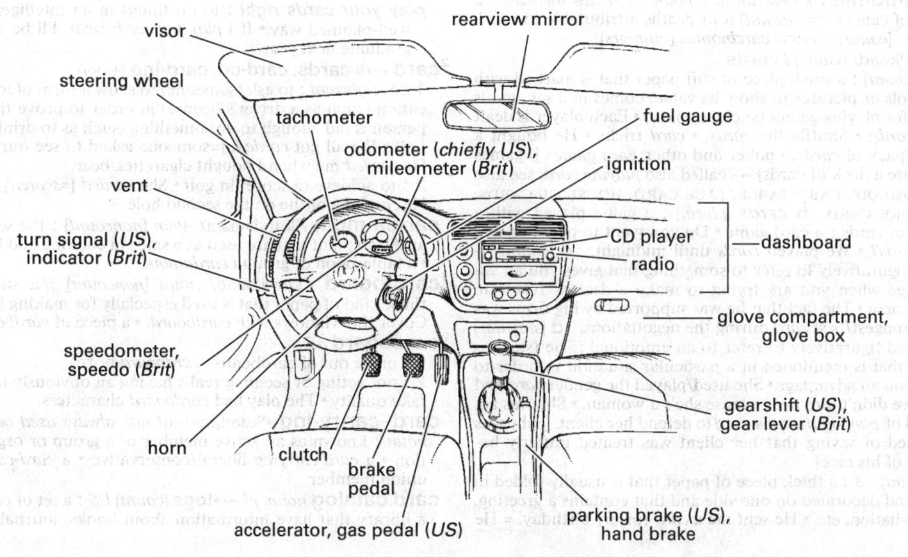

C

den inside or underneath a vehicle

car·bon /ˈkɑɚbən/ *noun, pl* **-bons**
1 [*noncount*] : a chemical element that forms diamonds and coal and that is found in petroleum and in all living plants and animals
2 [*count*] : CARBON COPY 1 ▪ a *carbon* of the document

car·bon·at·ed /ˈkɑɚbəˌneɪtəd/ *adj, of a liquid* : having many tiny bubbles that rise to the top : containing carbon dioxide ▪ soda and other *carbonated* beverages
– **car·bon·ation** /ˌkɑɚbəˈneɪʃən/ *noun* [*noncount*] ▪ a bottle of water with no *carbonation*

carbon copy *noun, pl* ~ **copies** [*count*]
1 : a copy of a document, letter, etc., that is made by using carbon paper ▪ I'll need a *carbon copy* of that receipt.
2 : a person or thing that is very similar to another person or thing ▪ She's a *carbon copy* of her mother.

carbon dating *noun* [*noncount*] *technical* : a scientific way of finding the age of something that is very old (such as a dinosaur bone) by measuring the amount of certain forms of carbon in it

carbon dioxide *noun* [*noncount*] : a gas that is produced when people and animals breathe out or when certain fuels are burned and that is used by plants for energy

carbon mon·ox·ide /-məˈnɑkˌsaɪd/ *noun* [*noncount*] : a poisonous gas that is formed when carbon is not completely burned and especially when gasoline is burned in car engines

carbon paper *noun* [*noncount*] : paper with a dark substance on one side that is placed between two other pieces of paper and used to make copies of documents

car boot sale *noun, pl* ~ **sales** [*count*] *Brit* : a sale in which people gather to sell items that they bring to the sale in their cars

car·bun·cle /ˈkɑɚˌbʌŋkəl/ *noun, pl* **-bun·cles** [*count*]
1 : a large painful swelling under the skin
2 : a jewel (such as a garnet) that is cut into a rounded shape

car·bu·re·tor (*US*) *or Brit* **car·bu·ret·tor** /ˈkɑɚbəˌreɪtɚ, *Brit* ˌkɑːbjʊˈrɛtə/ *noun, pl* **-tors** [*count*] : the part of an engine in which gasoline is mixed with air so it will burn and provide the engine with power

car·cass *also Brit* **car·case** /ˈkɑɚkəs/ *noun, pl* **-cass·es** [*count*]
1 : the body of a dead animal
2 *informal + humorous* : a person's body ▪ It was almost noon before he finally hauled his *carcass* out of bed. [=before he finally got out of bed]
3 : the remaining parts of an old vehicle, structure, etc. ▪ the rusting *carcass* of an old truck

car·cin·o·gen /kɑɚˈsɪnəʤən/ *noun, pl* **-gens** [*count*] *medical* : a substance that can cause cancer ▪ Cigarette smoke contains known *carcinogens.*

car·ci·no·gen·ic /ˌkɑɚsənoʊˈʤɛnɪk/ *adj* [*more ~; most ~*] *medical* : likely or able to cause cancer ▪ a *carcinogenic* substance/compound/chemical ▪ the *carcinogenic* effects of this chemical

car·ci·no·ma /ˌkɑɚsəˈnoʊmə/ *noun, pl* **-mas** *medical* : a type of cancer [*noncount*] four deaths attributable to *carcinoma* [*count*] cervical *carcinomas* [=*tumors*]

[1]**card** /ˈkɑɚd/ *noun, pl* **cards**
1 a [*count*] : a small piece of stiff paper that is marked with symbols or pictures to show its value, comes in a set, and is used for playing games (such as poker) ▪ Each player is dealt five *cards.* ▪ Shuffle the *cards.* ▪ *card* tricks ▪ He bought a deck/pack of *cards.* ▪ poker and other ***card games*** [=games that use a deck of cards] — called also *playing card*; see also CARDSHARP, CARD TABLE, FACE CARD, HOUSE OF CARDS, PICTURE CARD **b** ***cards*** [*plural*] : a game played with a deck of cards : a card game ▪ Do you want to play (a game of) *cards*? ▪ We played *cards* until midnight. **c** [*count*] — used figuratively to refer to something that gives you an advantage when you are trying to make a deal or reach an agreement ▪ The fact that he was supported by big firms was his strongest/best *card* during the negotiations. **d** [*singular*] — used figuratively to refer to an emotional issue (such as race) that is mentioned in a particular situation in order to give you an advantage ▪ She used/played the gender *card* and said we didn't hire her because she's a woman. ▪ She was accused of ***playing the race card*** to defend her client. [=she was accused of saying that her client was treated unfairly because of his race]
2 [*count*] **a** : a thick piece of paper that is usually folded in half and decorated on one side and that contains a greeting, an invitation, etc. ▪ He sent me a *card* for my birthday. = He sent me a birthday *card.* ▪ a get well *card* ▪ a *card* shop/store — see also CHRISTMAS CARD, GREETING CARD **b** : POSTCARD ▪ She sent us a *card* from Japan.
3 [*count*] : a rectangular piece of plastic that is used to buy goods or services or to get money from a bank or a machine ▪ "Will you be paying cash?" "No, please put it on my *card.*" [=I will pay for it using my credit/debit card] ▪ an ATM *card* ▪ Insert your *card* into the machine. = Swipe/Pass your *card* through the machine.
4 [*count*] **a** : a rectangular piece of paper or plastic with information about a person written on it ▪ a membership/library/appointment *card* ▪ Let me give you my *card.* [=*business card*] **b** : a small piece of paper that is used for writing down information ▪ He wrote his notes on 3 x 5 *cards.* [=cards that are 3 inches tall and 5 inches wide] ▪ You may use ***note cards*** [=cards with notes on them] during your speech.
5 [*count*] : TRADING CARD ▪ a collection of baseball/football/basketball *cards*
6 [*count*] : a thin, hard board that has small electronic devices on it and that can be added to the inside of a computer to make the computer perform different tasks ▪ a memory/sound/video *card* ▪ an ***expansion card*** [=a device that allows a computer to do more things than it originally could]
7 [*count*] : a list of the individual competitions that will happen at a sports event : a sports program ▪ a racing *card* [=a list of races] ▪ a boxing *card* [=a list of boxing matches] ▪ Three fights are ***on the card*** tonight.
8 [*count*] *old-fashioned* : a funny or amusing person ▪ He's such a *card*!
9 [*noncount*] *Brit* : CARDBOARD ▪ a piece of *card*

get your card *or* ***be given your card*** *Brit* : to be told that you no longer have a job ▪ Thousands of factory workers have *been given their cards* [=have been laid off; have lost their jobs] in recent months.

hold (all/all of) the cards : to be in control of a situation and have the power to make decisions ▪ It's your decision. You're *holding all the cards.*

in the cards (*US*) *or Brit* ***on the cards*** : certain or likely to happen in the future ▪ No one knows what's *in the cards* for the economy next year. [=what will happen to the economy next year] — often used in negative statements ▪ It's not *in the cards* for him to win the election. [=he's not going to win the election] ▪ Success just wasn't *in the cards* for her. [=she wasn't meant/supposed to succeed]

lay/put (all/all of) your cards on the table : to be honest with other people and to tell them your thoughts, plans, etc., in a very open way ▪ Before we can talk further, you need to *put all your cards on the table.* [=you need to tell me what you are really thinking]

overplay your cards see OVERPLAY

play/hold/keep your cards close to the/your chest/vest : to keep your plans, ideas, etc., hidden from other people ▪ No one knows if he's going to run for reelection. He's still *playing his cards close to his chest.*

play your cards right : to do things in an intelligent and well-planned way ▪ If I *play my cards right*, I'll be able to graduate next year.

[2]**card** *verb* **cards; card·ed; card·ing** [+ *obj*]
1 *US, informal* : to ask (someone) to show a form of identification (such as a driver's license) in order to prove that the person is old enough to do something (such as to drink alcohol) ▪ We all got *carded.* [=someone asked to see our IDs] ▪ He *carded* me when I bought cigarettes/beer.
2 : to achieve (a score) in golf ▪ She *carded* [=*scored*] a 75. ▪ He *carded* a birdie on the second hole.

car·da·mom /ˈkɑɚdəməm/ *noun* [*noncount*] : the seeds of an Asian plant that are used as a spice in cooking and baking ▪ a tablespoon of ground *cardamom*

[1]**card·board** /ˈkɑɚdˌboɚd/ *noun* [*noncount*] : a stiff and thick kind of paper that is used especially for making boxes ▪ Cover the windows with *cardboard.* ▪ a piece of *cardboard*

[2]**cardboard** *adj*
1 : made out of cardboard ▪ *cardboard* boxes
2 : not acting or seeming real : having an obviously false or fake quality ▪ The play had *cardboard* characters.

card–car·ry·ing /ˈkɑɚdˌkerijɪŋ/ *adj, always used before a noun* : known as an active member of a group or organization ▪ a *card-carrying* liberal/conservative ▪ a *card-carrying* union member

card catalog *noun, pl* ~ **-logs** [*count*] *US* : a set of cards in a library that have information about books, journals, etc., written on them and are arranged in alphabetical order — called also (*Brit*) *card index*

card·hold·er /ˈkaɚdˌhouldɚ/ *noun, pl* **-ers** [*count*] : someone who has a credit card • *Cardholders* are required to make a minimum payment each month.

car·di·ac /ˈkaɚdiˌæk/ *adj, always used before a noun, medical* : of or relating to the heart • *cardiac* problems/disease/surgery • *cardiac* patients [=people with heart disease or heart problems] • She went into ***cardiac arrest*** [=her heart stopped beating]

car·di·gan /ˈkaɚdɪgən/ *noun, pl* **-gans** [*count*] : a sweater that opens like a jacket and that is fastened in the front with buttons — called also (*US*) *cardigan sweater*; see color picture on page C15

[1]**car·di·nal** /ˈkaɚdənəl/ *noun, pl* **-nals** [*count*]
1 : a priest of the Roman Catholic Church who ranks immediately below the Pope • The Pope appointed two new *cardinals* this year. • *Cardinal* Newman
2 : a common North American bird ✧ The male cardinal is red and the female is mostly light brown. — see color picture on page C9

[2]**cardinal** *adj, always used before a noun, formal* : basic or most important • the *cardinal* principles of news reporting • My ***cardinal rule*** is to always be honest. • The ***cardinal points*** [=the four main directions] on a compass are North, South, East, and West.

cardinal number *noun, pl* ~ **-bers** [*count*] : a number (such as 1, 2, or 3) that is used in simple counting and shows quantity — compare ORDINAL NUMBER

cardinal sin *noun, pl* ~ **sins** [*count*] : a very bad or serious sin in Christianity — often used figuratively or humorously • Giving false information is a *cardinal sin* in news reporting. • He committed the *cardinal sin* of criticizing his boss.

card index *noun, pl* ~ **-dexes** [*count*] *chiefly Brit* : a set of cards that have information written on them and are arranged in alphabetical order; *especially* : CARD CATALOG

car·dio /ˈkaɚdijou/ *noun* [*noncount*] *US, informal* : any type of exercise that causes the heart to beat faster and harder for a period of time • After weightlifting, she does 40 minutes of *cardio*. — often used before another noun • *cardio* [=*cardiovascular*] exercises/fitness • a *cardio* workout

cardio- *combining form, medical* : heart : cardiac • *cardio*logy • *cardio*pulmonary [=relating to the heart and the lungs]

car·di·ol·o·gy /ˌkaɚdiˈɑːləʤi/ *noun* [*noncount*] *medical* : the study of the heart and of diseases that affect the heart • a doctor who specializes in *cardiology*
– **car·di·ol·o·gist** /ˌkaɚdiˈɑːləʤɪst/ *noun, pl* **-gists** [*count*]

car·dio·pul·mo·nary resuscitation /ˌkaɚdijouˈpʊlməˌneri-, *Brit* ˌkɑːdiəʊˈpʊlmənri-/ *noun* [*noncount*] *medical* : CPR

car·dio·vas·cu·lar /ˌkaɚdijouˈvæskjəlɚ/ *adj*
1 *medical* : of or relating to the heart and blood vessels • the *cardiovascular* system • *cardiovascular* disease
2 : causing the heart to beat faster and harder for a period of time • running, swimming, and other *cardiovascular* exercises • a *cardiovascular* workout

card·play·er /ˈkaɚdˌplejɚ/ *noun, pl* **-ers** [*count*] : someone who plays card games

card·sharp /ˈkaɚdˌʃaɚp/ *noun, pl* **-sharps** [*count*] : someone who makes money by cheating at card games — called also *card shark*

card table *noun, pl* ~ **tables** [*count*] : a small table that is used for playing card games and that often has legs that fold up

[1]**care** /ˈkeɚ/ *noun, pl* **cares**
1 [*noncount*] : effort made to do something correctly, safely, or without causing damage • She used *care* in selecting a doctor for her son. • a box marked "Handle With *Care*" [=handle carefully]
2 [*noncount*] **a** : things that are done to keep someone healthy, safe, etc. • The children have inadequate medical *care* and little formal education. • We need to provide poor people with better dental *care*. • He is ***under a doctor's care*** [=is being treated by a doctor] • The boys were ***in the care of*** [=being looked after by] their grandparents. — see also DAY CARE, HEALTH CARE, INTENSIVE CARE, PRIMARY CARE, *acute care* at ACUTE **b** : things that are done to keep something in good condition • She wrote a book about car *care*. • With proper *care*, the machine should last a decade or more. • She is an expert on skin/hair *care*. • She knows a lot about the ***care and feeding*** of horses. • These machines don't need a lot of *care and feeding*. [=*maintenance*]
3 [*count*] : something that causes you to feel worried or unhappy • He acts as if he doesn't have a *care* in the world. [=as if he has no worries] • She looks as if all the *cares* of the world are on her shoulders.
care of : at the address of • You can write to him *care of* his fan club. [=you can write to him by sending a letter to his fan club] — abbr. *c/o*
in/into care *Brit* — used to describe children who are being cared for by a government organization because their parents have died or are unable to care for them properly • The children had to be taken *into care* because of parental failure. • The youngest child was *in care* for several years.
take care : to be careful : to use caution • He *took care* not to upset anyone. • *Take care* when you cross the street. — often used informally to express good wishes when someone is leaving or at the end of a letter • I'll see you next week. *Take care*!
take care of **1** : to do the things that are needed to help or protect (someone) or to keep (something) in good condition : to care for (someone or something) • He *takes care of* [=*looks after*] his brother after school. • They *took care of* a ten-room house without help. • He is home *taking care of* a sick child. • Each worker *takes care of* [=is responsible for] three machines. • Their family doctor has been *taking care of* them for 20 years. • You really ought to *take* better *care of* yourself. If you don't get some rest and start eating better, you are bound to get sick. • I'm old enough to *take care of* [=*look out for*] myself. **2** : to deal with or do (something that requires effort or attention) • My assistant *takes care of* [=*makes*] all our travel arrangements. • Don't worry about that mess. I'll *take care of* it. [=I'll clean it up] • He offered to *take care of* [=*pay*] the bill.

[2]**care** *verb* **cares; cared; car·ing**
1 : to feel interest in something : to be interested in or concerned about something [*no obj*] He doesn't *care* if he gets fired. — often + *about* • I don't *care about* your little problems. • He *cares* deeply *about* religion. [+ *obj*] I *care* what happens to her.
2 [*no obj*] : to feel affection for someone • On Valentine's Day, send her flowers to show that you *care*. • I didn't know you *cared*.
3 [*no obj*] *somewhat formal* : to want *to do* something or *to be* something • I wouldn't *care* [=*like*] *to have* to make that decision. • I wouldn't *care to be* in your shoes right now. • I'm going for a walk. Would you *care to join* me? • He'll show the photos to anyone who *cares to see* them. • More factors influenced her decision than she *cares to admit*.
as if I cared *informal* — used in angry speech to say that you do not care at all about something • "She says she doesn't want to talk to you." "*As if I cared*!"
care a damn see [3]DAMN
care for [*phrasal verb*] **1** ***care for (someone or something)*** : to do the things that are needed to help and protect (a person or animal) : to look after (someone or something) • She *cares for* [=*takes care of*] elderly patients. • Who is *caring for* your son while you are at work? • I *cared for* his cat while he was away. **2** ***care for (someone)*** : to feel affection for (someone) • He sent flowers to show that he *cares for* you. • I got the feeling he never really *cared for* me. **3** ***care for (something)*** *somewhat formal* **a** : to like or enjoy (something) — often used in negative statements • I don't *care for* [=*like*] jelly beans. • He doesn't *care for* sports. • I don't *care for* your tone of voice. **b** : to want (something) • Would you *care for* some pie? • I don't *care for* any more coffee.
could/couldn't care less *informal* ✧ If you *could care less* (*US*) or *couldn't care less*, you are not at all concerned about or interested in something. • I *could care less* what happens. [=I don't care what happens] • He says he *couldn't care less* if he gets fired.
for all (someone) cares *informal* — used to say that someone does not care at all about something • *For all I care*, he can leave today. [=I don't care if he leaves today] • She could quit the whole thing, *for all he cares*.
see if I care *informal* — used in angry speech to say that you do not care at all about something • Go ahead and call her. *See if I care*!
what does (someone) care? *informal* — used to say that you do not think someone should have any interest in something • "She said we should go." "Well, *what does she care*?"
who cares? *informal* — used to stress that something is not

C

important. ▪ He can't carry a tune, but *who cares*? He's having fun and that's what matters. ▪ *Who cares* what she says? [=what she says is not important]

ca·reen /kəˈriːn/ *verb* **-reens; -reened; -reen·ing** [*no obj*] *US* : to go forward quickly without control ▪ The car *careened* [=*careered*] down the hill.

[1]**ca·reer** /kəˈriɚ/ *noun, pl* **-reers** [*count*]

1 : a job or profession that someone does for a long time ▪ I want to make teaching my *career*. = I want to have a *career* as a teacher. [=I want to be a teacher] ▪ She hopes to pursue a *career* in medicine. — often used before another noun ▪ He was a *career* diplomat/soldier. [=he was a diplomat/soldier for all or most of his working life]

2 : a period of time spent in a job or profession ▪ My *career* as a waitress lasted one day. ▪ During his long *career* in advertising he won numerous awards and honors.

[2]**career** *verb* **-reers; -reered; -reer·ing** [*no obj*] : CAREEN

ca·reer·ism /kəˈriɚˌɪzəm/ *noun* [*noncount*] *disapproving* : an attitude or way of behaving that involves trying to do whatever you can to make more money or get promoted at your job ▪ She was appalled by his *careerism*.

— **ca·reer·ist** /kəˈrirɪst/ *noun, pl* **-ists** [*count*] ▪ a ruthless *careerist*

care·free /ˈkeɚˌfriː/ *adj* [*more* ~; *most* ~] : having no worries or problems : free from care ▪ She has a *carefree* attitude toward life. ▪ They spent a *carefree* day at the lake.

care·ful /ˈkeɚfəl/ *adj* [*more* ~; *most* ~]

1 : using care ▪ He is a *careful* driver. ▪ You can never be too *careful* about these things. ▪ *Be careful*! The stove is hot! ▪ They are very *careful* with their money. [=they only spend what they can afford] ▪ She was *careful* of their feelings. ▪ The police were *careful* to leave the room exactly as they found it. — see also *(be) careful what you wish for* at [1]WISH

2 *always used before a noun* : made, done, or said with care ▪ Police made a *careful* examination of the scene. ▪ We kept *careful* [=*meticulous*] records of the project. ▪ They produced a *careful* study of the building.

— **care·ful·ly** *adv* ▪ He opened the door *carefully*. ▪ She *carefully* picked up the vase. ▪ Drive *carefully*. — **care·ful·ness** *noun* [*noncount*]

care·giv·er /ˈkeɚˌgɪvɚ/ *noun, pl* **-ers** [*count*] *US* : a person who gives help and protection to someone (such as a child, an old person, or someone who is sick) ▪ When she got sick her husband became her primary *caregiver*. — called also (*Brit*) *carer*

care·less /ˈkeɚləs/ *adj* [*more* ~; *most* ~]

1 : not using care : not careful ▪ He is a *careless* worker. ▪ She was *careless* with my things.

2 : done, made, or said without enough thought or attention ▪ It was a *careless* mistake. ▪ I made a *careless* [=*rude, thoughtless*] remark. ▪ a newspaper known for *careless* reporting

— **care·less·ly** *adv* ▪ She *carelessly* left the stove on. — **care·less·ness** *noun* [*noncount*] ▪ The mistake was the result of *carelessness*.

care package *noun, pl* ~ **-ages** [*count*] *US* : a package of useful or enjoyable items (such as candy or baked goods) that is sent or given as a gift to someone who is away from home

car·er /ˈkerɚ/ *noun, pl* **-ers** [*count*] *Brit* : CAREGIVER

[1]**ca·ress** /kəˈrɛs/ *noun, pl* **-ress·es** [*count*] : a gentle or loving touch ▪ She gave the baby's cheek a gentle *caress*.

[2]**caress** *verb* **-resses; -ressed; -ress·ing** [+ *obj*] : to touch (someone or something) in a gentle way ▪ She *caressed* the baby's cheek. ▪ A warm breeze *caressed* her face.

[1]**care·tak·er** /ˈkeɚˌteɪkɚ/ *noun, pl* **-ers** [*count*]

1 : a person who takes care of buildings or land while the owner is not there ▪ We have a *caretaker* who watches the place for us while we are away.

2 *chiefly US* : a person who gives physical or emotional care to someone (such as a child, an old person, or someone who is sick) ▪ I asked her *caretaker* [=*caregiver*] if there was anything I could do to help.

3 *Brit* : JANITOR

[2]**caretaker** *adj, always used before a noun* : doing a job for a short time before another is chosen to take the job officially ▪ a *caretaker* [=*interim, temporary*] government ▪ the *caretaker* President

care worker *noun, pl* ~ **-ers** [*count*] *Brit* : a person whose job is to give care to people who are ill, disabled, etc.

care·worn /ˈkeɚˌwoɚn/ *adj* [*more* ~; *most* ~] : looking sad, tired, or worried ▪ He has a *careworn* face. ▪ He looks tired and *careworn*.

car·fare /ˈkɑɚˌfeɚ/ *noun, pl* **-fares** [*count*] : the money a person pays to travel by bus, taxi, etc.

car·go /ˈkɑɚgoʊ/ *noun, pl* **-goes** *also* **-gos** : something that is carried from one place to another by boat, airplane, etc. [*count*] The ship was carrying a *cargo* of crude oil. [*noncount*] Workers unloaded *cargo* [=*freight*] quickly on the dock. — often used before another noun ▪ a *cargo* ship/plane ▪ Her new minivan has a lot of *cargo* space.

Ca·rib·be·an /ˌkerəˈbiːjən, kəˈrɪbijən/ *adj* : of or relating to the Caribbean Sea or its islands or to the people of the islands ▪ the *Caribbean* islands ▪ *Caribbean* food/customs

car·i·bou /ˈkerəˌbuː/ *noun, pl* **-bou** *or* **-bous** [*count*] : a large type of deer that lives in northern parts of the world ▪ a herd of *caribou* ✧ The word *caribou* is used especially to refer to these animals when they live in North America. The word *reindeer* is used for these animals when they live in other parts of the world. — see picture at DEER

[1]**car·i·ca·ture** /ˈkerɪkəˌʧɚ/ *noun, pl* **-tures** [*count*]

1 : a drawing that makes someone look funny or foolish because some part of the person's appearance is exaggerated ▪ An artist was doing *caricatures* in the park.

2 : someone or something that is very exaggerated in a funny or foolish way ▪ His performance in the film was a *caricature of* a hard-boiled detective. ▪ The interview made her into a *caricature of* a struggling artist.

— **car·i·ca·tur·ist** /ˈkerɪkəˌʧɚrɪst/ *noun, pl* **-ists** [*count*] ▪ an artist who's a talented *caricaturist*

[2]**caricature** *verb* **-tures; -tured; -tur·ing** [+ *obj*] : to do a caricature of (someone or something) : to draw or describe (someone or something) in a funny or exaggerated way ▪ The press *caricatured* him as clumsy and forgetful.

car·ies /ˈkeriz/ *noun* [*noncount*] *technical* : tooth decay

caring *adj*

1 [*more* ~; *less* ~] : feeling or showing concern for other people ▪ a *caring* parent/child/teacher ▪ a *caring* gesture

2 *always used before a noun, Brit* : of or relating to work that involves helping people ▪ the *caring* professions

car·jack·ing /ˈkɑɚˌʤækɪŋ/ *noun, pl* **-ings** [*count*] : the crime of using violence or threats to steal a car from its driver or to force the driver to take you someplace ▪ The police are investigating another *carjacking*.

— **car·jack** /ˈkɑɚˌʤæk/ *verb* **-jacks; -jacked; -jacking** [+ *obj*] ▪ She claimed to have been *carjacked*. — **car·jack·er** /ˈkɑɚˌʤækɚ/ *noun, pl* **-ers** [*count*] ▪ Police apprehended the *carjackers*.

car·load /ˈkɑɚˌloʊd/ *noun, pl* **-loads** [*count*] : the amount of people or things that will fit in a car : a car full of people or things ▪ She brought home a *carload of* books. ▪ People were arriving ***by the carload***.

car·mak·er /ˈkɑɚˌmeɪkɚ/ *noun, pl* **-ers** [*count*] : a company that makes and sells cars ▪ American *carmakers* [=(*US*) *automakers*] face stiff competition from Japan.

car·nage /ˈkɑɚnɪʤ/ *noun* [*noncount*] : the killing of many people ▪ Years of violence and *carnage* [=*bloodshed*] have left the country in ruins. ▪ Reporters described the highway accident as a scene of *carnage*.

car·nal /ˈkɑɚnl/ *adj, formal* : of or relating to the body : sexual or sensual ▪ *carnal* desires/pleasures — often used in the phrase ***carnal knowledge*** to refer to sexual intercourse ▪ *carnal knowledge* of a woman [=sexual intercourse with a woman]

car·na·tion /kɑɚˈneɪʃən/ *noun, pl* **-tions** [*count*] : a pink, white, yellow, or red flower that has a sweet smell ▪ The groom wore a *carnation* in his buttonhole. — see color picture on page C6

car·ni·val /ˈkɑɚnəvəl/ *noun, pl* **-vals**

1 *or* ***Carnival*** [*count, noncount*] : a festival held before Lent that includes music and dancing [=*count*] ▪ Will you be in town for (the) *Carnival* this year?

2 [*count*] *US* **a** : a form of entertainment that travels to different places and includes rides and games you can play to win prizes ▪ Are you going to the *carnival* [=(*Brit*) *funfair*] this weekend? **b** : an event where many people gather to celebrate something : FESTIVAL ▪ the school's annual winter *carnival*

3 [*count*] : a time or place that is exciting, lively, colorful, etc. ▪ That part of town is a *carnival* on Friday and Saturday nights. ▪ There is a *carnival* atmosphere in the office. ▪ The garden became a *carnival* of color.

car·ni·vore /ˈkɑɚnəˌvoɚ/ *noun, pl* **-vores** [*count*] : an animal that eats meat : a meat eater — sometimes used humor-

ously to refer to people who eat meat ▪ Many of my friends are vegetarians, but I'm a *carnivore*.
– **car·niv·o·rous** /kɑɚˈnɪvərəs/ *adj* ▪ a *carnivorous* animal

car·ob /ˈkerəb/ *noun* [*noncount*] : the fruit of a Mediterranean tree that can be prepared to taste similar to chocolate and is used in various foods — often used before another noun ▪ *carob* beans/pods ▪ *carob* powder

[1]**car·ol** /ˈkerəl/ *noun, pl* **-ols** [*count*] : a song sung during the Christmas season ▪ We sang our favorite *carols* while we decorated the tree. — called also *Christmas carol*

[2]**carol** *verb* **-ols**; *US* **-oled** *or chiefly Brit* **-olled**; *US* **-ol·ing** *or chiefly Brit* **-ol·ling** [*no obj*] : to go from place to place singing Christmas carols ▪ Last night, we went *caroling* with our friends.
– **carol·er** (*US*) *or chiefly Brit* **carol·ler** /ˈkerələ/ *noun, pl* **-ers** [*count*] ▪ Christmas *carolers* making their rounds

ca·rot·id artery /kəˈrɑːtəd-/ *noun, pl* ~ **-teries** [*count*] *medical* : either one of the two arteries in the neck that supply blood to the head

ca·rouse /kəˈraʊz/ *verb* **-rous·es**; **-roused**; **-rous·ing** [*no obj*] : to drink alcohol, make noise, and have fun with other people ▪ My brother and his friends went out *carousing* last night.

car·ou·sel *also* **car·rou·sel** /ˌkerəˈsɛl/ *noun, pl* **-sels** [*count*]
1 : MERRY-GO-ROUND 1 ▪ He loves to ride on the *carousel* at the park.
2 : a machine or device with a moving belt or part that carries things around in a circle ▪ the luggage *carousel* at the airport ▪ a dessert *carousel* ▪ a CD player with a six-disk *carousel*

[1]**carp** /ˈkɑɚp/ *verb* **carps**; **carped**; **carp·ing** [*no obj*] : to complain in an annoying way ▪ He's always *carping* about his boss. ▪ He's tired of always being *carped* at by his critics.
– **carping** *noun* [*noncount*] ▪ I'm tired of all his *carping*.
– **carping** *adj* ▪ *carping* critics

[2]**carp** *noun, pl* **carp** *or* **carps** [*count*] : a type of large fish that lives in rivers and lakes and is often used for food

car·pal tunnel syndrome /ˈkɑɚpəl-/ *noun* [*singular*] *medical* : a condition that causes pain and weakness in the wrist, hand, and fingers

car park *noun, pl* ~ **parks** [*count*] *Brit*
1 : PARKING LOT
2 : PARKING GARAGE

car·pen·ter /ˈkɑɚpəntɚ/ *noun, pl* **-ters** [*count*] : a person whose job is to make or fix wooden objects or wooden parts of buildings

car·pen·try /ˈkɑɚpəntri/ *noun* [*noncount*] : the skill or work of making or fixing wooden objects or wooden parts of buildings : the skill of a carpenter or the work done by a carpenter ▪ He learned *carpentry* from his father. ▪ When the *carpentry* is finished, the cabinets will be installed. — see picture on next page

[1]**car·pet** /ˈkɑɚpət/ *noun, pl* **-pets**
1 : a heavy fabric cover for a floor [*count*] We bought a new *carpet* for the bedroom. [*noncount*] Which brand of *carpet* did you choose? — compare RUG; see also MAGIC CARPET
2 [*count*] : a thick covering : a thick layer of something ▪ The ground was covered by a *carpet* of leaves/snow/grass.
call (someone) on the carpet *US, informal* : to criticize someone for doing something wrong ▪ He was/got *called on the carpet* for missing the deadline.
sweep (something) under the carpet see [1]SWEEP

[2]**carpet** *verb* **-pets**; **-pet·ed**; **-pet·ing** [+ *obj*]
1 : to put a carpet on the floor of a room ▪ We decided to *carpet* the bedroom. ▪ *carpet* the floor
2 : to cover (something) with a thick layer ▪ Leaves *carpeted* the lawn. = The lawn was *carpeted* with leaves.
3 *Brit, informal* : to criticize (someone) for doing something wrong — often used as *(be) carpeted* ▪ He *was carpeted* for missing the deadline.
– **carpeted** *adj* ▪ a *carpeted* room

car·pet·bag·ger /ˈkɑɚpətˌbægɚ/ *noun, pl* **-gers** [*count*] *disapproving*
1 : a person from the northern United States who went to the South after the American Civil War to make money
2 : a political candidate who runs for office in a place where he or she has lived only for a short time

carpet–bomb *verb* **-bombs**; **-bombed**; **-bomb·ing** [+ *obj*] : to drop many bombs in order to cause great destruction over (an area) ▪ a city that was *carpet-bombed* during World War II — often used figuratively ▪ Television viewers are being *carpet-bombed* with political advertisements as election day approaches.
– **carpet–bombing** *noun* [*noncount*] ▪ a city destroyed by *carpet-bombing*

car·pet·ing /ˈkɑɚpətɪŋ/ *noun, pl* **-ings**
1 [*noncount*] : carpets or the material used for carpets ▪ The house has ***wall-to-wall carpeting*** in the bedrooms.
2 [*count*] *Brit, informal* : an act of criticizing someone for doing something wrong ▪ The boss gave him a good *carpeting* [=*scolding*] for missing the deadline.

carpet slipper *noun, pl* ~ **-pers** [*count*] *Brit, old-fashioned* : SLIPPER

carpet sweeper *noun, pl* ~ **-ers** [*count*] : a device with a long handle and a rolling brush that is used for cleaning carpets

car pool *noun, pl* ~ **pools** [*count*] : a group of people who regularly share a car when they are going to and from their jobs or who take turns driving each other other's children to school, activities, etc.
– **car·pool** /ˈkɑɚˌpuːl/ *verb* **-pools**; **-pooled**; **-pool·ing** [*no obj*] ▪ She *carpools* to work every day with her neighbor. – **car·pool·er** *noun, pl* **-ers** [*count*]

car·port /ˈkɑɚˌpoɚt/ *noun, pl* **-ports** [*count*] : a shelter for a car that has open sides and that is usually attached to the side of a building — compare [1]GARAGE

car·riage /ˈkerɪdʒ/ *noun, pl* **-riag·es**
1 : a large vehicle with four wheels that is pulled by a horse and that carries people [*count*] They rode to the city in *carriages*. [*noncount*] They rode ***by carriage***. — called also *coach*
2 [*count*] : a wheeled structure that is used to carry and move something heavy (such as a large gun) ▪ an artillery *carriage*
3 [*count*] *US* : BABY CARRIAGE ▪ I took the baby to the park in the *carriage*.
4 [*count*] *Brit* : a separate section of a train ▪ a passenger *carriage* [=(*US*) *car*, (*Brit*) *coach*]
5 [*count*] : a moving part of a machine that supports or carries some other movable object or part ▪ a typewriter *carriage*
6 [*noncount*] *somewhat old-fashioned* : the way in which a person's body is positioned when the person is moving, standing, etc. ▪ a dancer noted for her elegant *carriage* [=*posture*]
7 [*noncount*] *Brit* : the process or cost of carrying or transporting goods ▪ the *carriage* of goods ▪ payment of *carriage* charges

car·ri·er /ˈkerijɚ/ *noun, pl* **-ers** [*count*]
1 : someone or something that carries something: such as **a** : MAIL CARRIER **b** : a container used to move something from one place to another ▪ I put the pet *carrier* in the car. ▪ The equipment comes with its own *carrier*. [=*carrying case*] **c** : AIRCRAFT CARRIER — see also PEOPLE CARRIER, PERSONNEL CARRIER
2 : a company that moves people or goods from one place to another ▪ The airline is the nation's largest *carrier*.
3 : a person or animal that can give a disease or a gene to others but is not affected by it ▪ Mosquitoes can be *carriers* of malaria.
4 *US* : a company that provides a specified service (such as insurance or long-distance telephone service) ▪ We switched to a different long-distance *carrier* to save money on our phone bill.
5 *Brit* : CARRIER BAG

carrier bag *noun, pl* ~ **bags** [*count*] *Brit* : a bag that a store gives you to carry any items you have bought there ▪ a plastic *carrier bag* from the supermarket

carrier pigeon *noun, pl* ~ **-geons** [*count*] : a type of pigeon that is trained to carry messages

car·ri·on /ˈkerijən/ *noun* [*noncount*] : the flesh of dead animals ▪ Vultures live chiefly on *carrion*.

car·rot /ˈkerət/ *noun, pl* **-rots**
1 : the long orange root of a plant that is eaten as a vegetable [*count*] She chopped some *carrots* for the soup. [*noncount*] He added some grated *carrot* to the soup. — see color picture on page C4
2 [*count*] *informal* : something that is offered as a reward or advantage to persuade a person to do something ▪ The company offered a *carrot* in the form of additional vacation time to workers who met their deadlines. ✧ This sense of *carrot* is often contrasted with *stick*, which suggests a punishment for not doing something. ▪ He'll have to choose between the *car-*

C

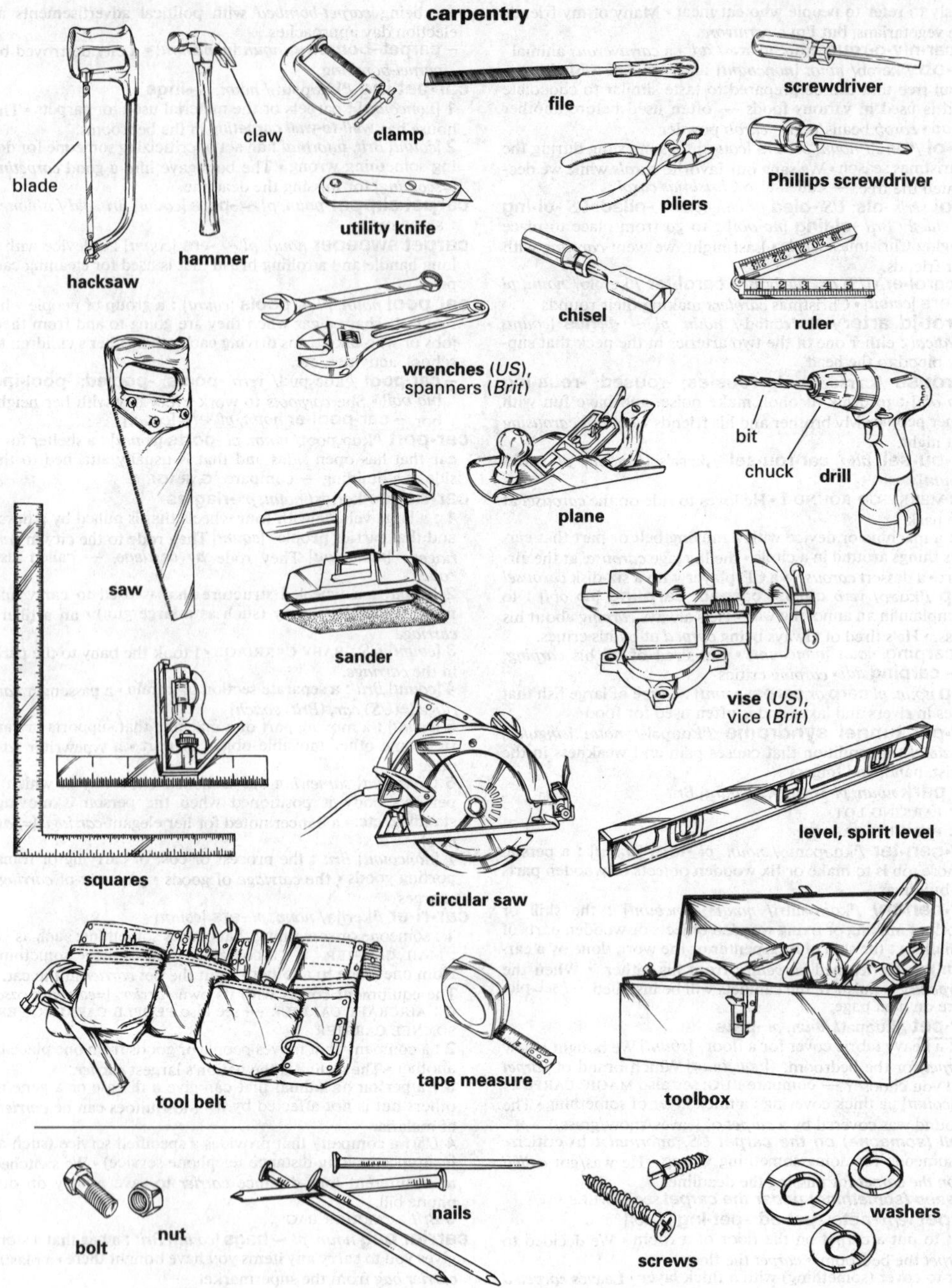

rot and the *stick*. • The administration was criticized for its *carrot-and-stick* approach to foreign policy.

car·rot·top /ˈkerət,tɑ:p/ *noun, pl* **-tops** [*count*] *informal* : a person with red hair : REDHEAD

[1]**car·ry** /ˈkeri/ *verb* **-ries; -ried; -ry·ing**

1 [+ *obj*] **:** to move (something) while holding and supporting it • She helped me *carry* [=*transport*] the boxes out to my car. • I'll *carry* your luggage to your room. • He was *carrying* his baby daughter in his arms. • For two months, I *carried* the book around with me everywhere I went. • The waitress *carried* away our empty dinner plates. • The wind *carried* the smoke away from the campsite. • These planes can *carry* up to 300 passengers. • a ship *carrying* thousands of gallons of oil — sometimes used figuratively • Your talent will *carry* you far. [=it will make you very successful] • She intended the play to *carry* audiences toward a sense of peace and understanding. • She still *carries* the memories of an unhappy childhood. • The song ***carries me back to*** [=it makes me remember] my first year of college.

2 [+ *obj*] **:** to contain and direct the flow of (water, electricity, etc.) • Oil is *carried* to the factory through these pipes. • We installed gutters that will *carry* water away from the house. • blood vessels that *carry* blood to the heart • These cables *carry* electricity to hundreds of homes. • The bridge *carries* traffic in two directions.

3 [+ *obj*] **:** to have (something) with you or on your body ▪ Do police officers *carry* guns when they're off duty? ▪ This bus driver doesn't *carry* change, so please have the exact fare ready. ▪ I always *carry* $20 in case of an emergency. ▪ tourists *carrying* cameras

4 [+ *obj*] **:** to be able to give (a disease or a gene) to others even though you may not be affected by it ▪ One percent of the population now *carries* the virus, and one in three will suffer symptoms of the disease.

5 [+ *obj*] **:** to be pregnant with (a baby) ▪ She's *carrying* her second child.

6 [+ *obj*] **:** to hold (your body or your head) in a particular way ▪ He's over 80 years old and still *carries* himself erect/upright like a soldier. ▪ Be proud of yourself. Walk tall and *carry* your head high! ▪ She always *carries* [=(more formally) *comports*] herself with dignity and grace.

7 [+ *obj*] **a :** to have (something) in a store and ready to be sold **:** to keep (something) in stock ▪ Our grocery store *carries* a good selection of wines. ▪ We no longer *carry* that brand. **b :** to have (someone or something) on a list or record ▪ The company *carries* nearly 200 employees on its payroll.

8 [+ *obj*] **a :** to have (something) as a quality or characteristic ▪ All of our products *carry* a lifetime guarantee. ▪ Your promises would ***carry more weight*** [=they would be more meaningful] if you didn't break them so often. **b :** to be marked or labeled with (something) ▪ Cigarettes are required to *carry* a government health warning. ▪ men who *carry* the physical scars of war

9 [+ *obj*] **:** to have (something) as a result or consequence ▪ Such crimes *carry* [=*entail, involve*] a heavy penalty. ▪ The surgery does *carry* certain risks. — often + *with* ▪ You must understand that the job *carries with* it great responsibility.

10 [+ *obj*] **:** to have (something) as a duty or responsibility ▪ I'm *carrying* a full course load this semester. ▪ He ***carries the weight of the world on his shoulders***. [=he feels much pressure because he has great responsibilities]

11 [+ *obj*] **:** to be responsible for the success of (something or someone) ▪ He's a player that's capable of *carrying* a team on his own. ▪ Her spectacular performance as Carmen *carried* the opera.

12 a [+ *obj*] **:** to make (something) continue ▪ They *carried* [=*took, extended*] the game into the 10th inning. ▪ The newspaper *carried* the story over to the following page. ▪ The design calls for the columns to be *carried* all the way up to the top of the building. ▪ *carrying* the war to another continent **b** [*no obj*] **:** to travel a long distance ▪ His deep voice *carries* well. ▪ Baseballs don't *carry* well in cold weather.

13 [+ *obj*] **:** to continue (something) beyond a normal or acceptable limit ▪ He realized that he had *carried* the joke too far and hurt her feelings. — see also *carry (something) to extremes* at [2]EXTREME

14 [+ *obj*] **:** to sing (a tune) correctly ▪ I've never been able to *carry* a tune.

15 [+ *obj*] **:** to present (a story, sports event, TV show, etc.) to the public ▪ Channel 9 will *carry* the game. ▪ Every local newspaper *carried* [=*ran*] the photograph. ▪ The trial was *carried* live [=broadcast as it was happening] on television.

16 a : to cause (a bill or an official proposal) to be passed or adopted [+ *obj*] — often used as *(be) carried* ▪ The bill *was carried* in the Senate by a vote of 75–25. [*no obj*] He called for a motion to stop debate, but the motion did not *carry*. ▪ The motion *carried* unanimously. [=everyone voted to pass it] **b** [+ *obj*] *chiefly US* **:** to win a majority of votes in (a state, legislature, etc.) ▪ The bill *carried* the Senate by a vote of 75–25. ▪ In the presidential election of 1936, Franklin D. Roosevelt *carried* [=*won, took*] all the states except Maine and Vermont.

17 [+ *obj*] **:** to move (a number) from one column to another when you are adding numbers together ▪ When you added these two numbers, you forgot to *carry* the 1.

be/get carried away **:** to be so excited that you are no longer in control of your behavior ▪ I shouldn't have behaved like that. I just *got carried away*. ▪ Just relax! There's no need to *get carried away*. ▪ They allowed themselves to *be carried away* by fear.

carry all/everything before you *literary* **:** to be completely successful ▪ This young boxer has the talent to *carry all before him*.

carry a torch for see [1]TORCH

carry coals to Newcastle see COAL

carry into effect see [1]EFFECT

carry off [*phrasal verb*] ***carry off (something)*** *or* ***carry (something) off*** **1 :** to do (something difficult) successfully **:** to achieve or accomplish (something) ▪ He tried to look cool but couldn't *carry it off*. [=*pull it off*] ▪ She's the only actress I know with enough talent to *carry this off*. **2 :** to win (something) ▪ We *carried off* the prize.

carry on [*phrasal verb*] **1 :** to continue to do what you have been doing ▪ I didn't mean to interrupt you—please *carry on*. ▪ She *carried on* as if nothing had happened. **:** to continue despite problems ▪ I know it's difficult, but you need to *carry on* as best you can. **2 :** to behave or speak in an excited or foolish way ▪ They laughed and *carried on* like they were old friends. ▪ We were embarrassed by the way he was *carrying on*. ▪ She's always *carrying on* [=talking in an excited way] about her neighbors. ▪ screaming, crying, and *carrying on* — see also CARRYINGS-ON, CARRY-ON **3** ***carry on (something)*** **a :** to manage or participate in (an activity) ▪ She *carried on* an affair with her boss. ▪ It's too noisy in here to *carry on* a conversation. ▪ The police are *carrying on* [=*conducting*] an investigation into his murder. ▪ *carrying on* a campaign against illegal drug use **b :** to continue doing (something) ▪ The money allows us to *carry on* our research. ▪ Although the teacher spoke to them, they just *carried on* [=*went on, kept on*] talking. **c :** to cause (something, such as a tradition) to continue ▪ We were the only ones left to *carry on* the tradition. ▪ *carrying on* the family name **4** ***carry on with (something)*** **:** to continue doing or participating in (an activity) ▪ Please *carry on with* what you were doing. ▪ They *carried on with* their conversation. **5** ***carry on with (someone)*** *chiefly Brit, old-fashioned* **:** to have an often immoral sexual relationship with (someone) ▪ I found out that he had been *carrying on with* [=(more commonly) *fooling around with*] my sister.

carry out [*phrasal verb*] ***carry (something) out*** *or* ***carry out (something)*** **1 :** to do and complete (something) ▪ We *carried out* several experiments to test the theory. ▪ An investigation *carried out* several years ago revealed no new information. **2 :** to act on (a promise, plan, etc.) **:** to do something that you said you would do or that someone has asked you to do ▪ She failed to *carry out* [=*fulfill*] her promise. ▪ The town has plans to build a new school, but it currently lacks the money to *carry* them *out*. ▪ You'll be paid when you've *carried out* [=*executed*] your instructions/orders/duties. — see also CARRYOUT

carry over [*phrasal verb*] **1 :** to continue to exist or be seen in another place or situation ▪ His unhappiness at home *carried over* into/to his work. ▪ Her abilities in singing didn't *carry over* to acting. **2** ***carry (something) over*** *or* ***carry over (something)*** **:** to cause or allow (something) to continue in another place or situation ▪ People can *carry* bad eating habits learned in childhood *over* to/into adulthood. — see also CARRYOVER

carry the ball see [1]BALL

carry the can see [2]CAN

carry the day see DAY

carry the torch see [1]TORCH

carry through [*phrasal verb*] **1 a :** to continue to exist or happen — usually + *to* ▪ The yellow and blue theme in the kitchen *carries through to* the rest of the house. ▪ Our conversation *carried through to* dessert. **b :** to continue to do something — usually + *to* ▪ Though extremely tired, she managed to *carry through to* the finish. **2** ***carry through with/on (something)*** *US* **:** to do (something that you said you would do) ▪ The mayor *carried through* [=*followed through*] *on* her promise to clean up the city. ▪ We're beginning to *carry through with* [=*carry out*] our plans. **3** ***carry (something) through*** **:** to successfully finish or complete (something that you have begun or said you will do) ▪ Whatever project you begin, you must *carry it through* to completion. **4 a** ***carry (someone) through*** **:** to help or allow (someone) to survive or continue ▪ We had enough supplies to *carry us through* (until spring). ▪ His faith *carried him through*. **b** ***carry (someone) through (something)*** **:** to help or allow (someone) to survive or continue during (a period of time) ▪ We had enough supplies to *carry us through* the winter. ▪ His faith *carried him through* a difficult time in his life. ▪ I borrowed a few more books to *carry me through* the summer.

fetch and carry see FETCH

[2]**carry** *noun, pl* **-ries** [*count*] *American football* **:** the act of running with the ball ▪ He averaged four yards per *carry* this season.

car•ry•all /ˈkeriˌɑːl/ *noun, pl* **-alls** [*count*] *US* **:** a large bag or carrying case — called also (*Brit*) *holdall*; see picture at BAG

car·ry–cot /ˈkeriˌkɑːt/ *noun, pl* **-cots** [*count*] *Brit* : a small bed that is used for carrying a young baby

carrying case *noun, pl* ~ **cases** [*count*] : a container that usually has a handle and that is made for carrying something with your hand ▪ The guitar had a plastic *carrying case*.

carryings–on *noun* [*plural*] : foolish, excited, or improper actions ▪ the questionable *carryings-on* of politicians ▪ the *carryings-on* of teenage boys — see also *carry on* at [1]CARRY

[1]**car·ry–on** /ˈkeriˌɑːn/ *noun, pl* **-ons**

1 [*count*] *US* : a small piece of luggage that a passenger can carry onto an airplane ▪ I packed the book in my *carry-on*.

2 [*singular*] *Brit, informal* : a moment of excitement or silly behavior ▪ She makes such a big *carry-on* [=*fuss, stir*] about everything. ▪ What a *carry-on*! — see also *carry on* at [1]CARRY

[2]**carry–on** *adj, always used before a noun* : small enough to be carried onto an airplane by a passenger ▪ *carry-on* baggage/luggage

car·ry·out /ˈkeriˌaʊt/ *noun, pl* **-outs** *chiefly US*

1 [*noncount*] : TAKEOUT 1 ▪ We ordered Chinese *carryout*.

2 [*count*] : TAKEOUT 2 ▪ She works in a Chinese *carryout*.

– carryout *adj, chiefly US* ▪ *carryout* food ▪ a *carryout* restaurant

car·ry·over /ˈkeriˌoʊvɚ/ *noun, pl* **-overs** [*count*] : something that existed in one time or place and continues in another ▪ His tendency to eat everything on his plate is a *carryover* [=*holdover*] from his childhood. ▪ superstitions that are *carryovers* from ancient times — see also *carry over* at [1]CARRY

car seat *noun, pl* ~ **seats** [*count*] : a special seat for a baby or a small child that can be attached to an automobile seat and that holds the child safely

car·sick /ˈkɑɚˌsɪk/ *adj* : feeling sick while riding in a car because of the movement of the vehicle

– car·sick·ness *noun* [*noncount*]

[1]**cart** /ˈkɑɚt/ *noun, pl* **carts** [*count*]

1 : a wagon with two wheels that is pulled by an animal (such as a horse or donkey)

2 : a small wheeled vehicle that is pushed: such as **a** *US* : a metal basket on wheels used to hold groceries while you are shopping ▪ a grocery *cart* — called also *shopping cart*, (*Brit*) *trolley* **b** *US* : a table with wheels used especially for serving food ▪ a dessert *cart* — called also (*Brit*) *trolley*

3 : GOLF CART

put the cart before the horse : to do things in the wrong order : to do something first instead of waiting until something else has been done ▪ People are *putting the cart before the horse* by making plans on how to spend the money before we are even certain that the money will be available.

upset the apple cart see [2]UPSET

[2]**cart** *verb* **carts; cart·ed; cart·ing** [+ *obj*]

1 : to carry or move (something) in a cart ▪ We *carted* some dirt to the garden.

2 : to carry or move (something) ▪ I *carted* all the books home. ▪ He *carted* the bags away.

3 : to take (someone) away by force — usually + *off* ▪ They *carted* him *off* to jail.

carte blanche /ˌkɑɚtˈblɑːnʃ/ *noun* [*noncount*] : permission to do something in any way you choose to do it ▪ We gave the decorator *carte blanche* to furnish the house.

car·tel /kɑɚˈtɛl/ *noun, pl* **-tels** [*count*] : a group of businesses that agree to fix prices so they all will make more money ▪ an illegal drug *cartel*

car·ti·lage /ˈkɑɚtəlɪʤ/ *noun* [*noncount*] : a strong but flexible material found in some parts of the body (such as the nose, the outer ear, and some joints) ▪ She fell and damaged some *cartilage* in her knee.

– car·ti·lag·i·nous /ˌkɑɚtəˈlæʤənəs/ *adj* ▪ *cartilaginous* tissue

car·tog·ra·pher /kɑɚˈtɑːgrəfɚ/ *noun, pl* **-phers** [*count*] : a person who makes maps

car·tog·ra·phy /kɑɚˈtɑːgrəfi/ *noun* [*noncount*] : the process or skill of making maps ▪ She studied *cartography* in college.

– car·tog·ra·phic /ˌkɑɚtəˈgræfɪk/ *adj* ▪ *cartographic* skills ▪ *cartographic* data

car·ton /ˈkɑɚtn̩/ *noun, pl* **-tons** [*count*]

1 : a light box or container usually made of cardboard or plastic ▪ She got a *carton* of ice cream out of the freezer. ▪ a *carton* of orange juice ▪ a milk *carton*

2 *US* : a box containing things that have been packed together so they can be sold or moved ▪ He bought a *carton* of cigarettes. ▪ Several *cartons* of books arrived yesterday.

car·toon /kɑɚˈtuːn/ *noun, pl* **-toons** [*count*]

1 a : a drawing in a newspaper or magazine intended as a humorous comment on something ▪ a political *cartoon* **b** : a series of drawings that tell a story : COMIC STRIP ▪ She enjoys reading the *cartoons* in the Sunday paper.

2 : a film or television show made by photographing a series of drawings : an animated film or television show ▪ The kids are watching *cartoons*. ▪ a *cartoon* character

3 *technical* : a design, drawing, or painting made by an artist as a model for the finished work

– car·toon·ist /kɑɚˈtuːnɪst/ *noun, pl* **-ists** [*count*]

car·tridge /ˈkɑɚtrɪʤ/ *noun, pl* **-tridg·es** [*count*]

1 : a tube which you put into a gun and which contains a bullet and explosive material

2 : a case or container that you put into a machine to make it work ▪ a video game *cartridge* ▪ The printer needs a new ink *cartridge*.

[1]**cart·wheel** /ˈkɑɚtˌwiːl/ *noun, pl* **-wheels** [*count*] : an athletic movement in which you move sideways by placing one hand and then the other on the ground, lifting your feet into the air, and then landing on one foot and then the other foot ▪ The children turned/did *cartwheels* and somersaults on the grass.

[2]**cartwheel** *verb* **-wheels; -wheeled; -wheel·ing** [*no obj*]

1 : to do a cartwheel ▪ She *cartwheeled* across the floor.

2 : to spin or turn over in a violent and uncontrolled way ▪ The car hit the pole and then *cartwheeled* across the road.

carve /ˈkɑɚv/ *verb* **carves; carved; carv·ing**

1 [+ *obj*] : to make (something, such as a sculpture or design) by cutting off pieces of the material it is made of ▪ We *carved* an ice sculpture. ▪ a *carved* object — often + *out of* or *from* ▪ He *carved* the sculpture *out of* marble. ▪ She *carves* figures *from* wood.

2 [+ *obj*] **a** : to cut (something, such as a pattern or design) into a surface — often + *into* or *on* ▪ He *carved* his name *on/into* the table. ▪ Their initials are *carved into* the tree. **b** : to create (something) by cutting into a surface — often + *out* ▪ The Colorado River *carved out* the Grand Canyon.

3 : to cut (cooked meat) into pieces or slices [+ *obj*] Who is going to *carve* the turkey? ▪ Would you *carve* me another slice of turkey, please? = Would you carve another slice of turkey for me? [*no obj*] He *carved* while I made the gravy.

4 [+ *obj*] : to create (a job, a fortune, a way of life, etc.) for yourself usually through hard work ▪ He *carved* a new life for himself after the divorce. — often + *out* ▪ She worked hard to *carve out* a career in education.

carved in stone see [1]STONE

carve up [*phrasal verb*] ***carve up (something)*** *or* ***carve (something) up*** *usually disapproving* : to divide something into small parts ▪ The once beautiful countryside has been *carved up* by developers.

– carv·er *noun, pl* **-vers** [*count*] ▪ a talented *carver*

carv·ing /ˈkɑɚvɪŋ/ *noun, pl* **-ings**

1 [*count*] : a carved object, design, or figure ▪ She bought a small wooden *carving* of a Buddha.

2 [*noncount*] : the act or skill of creating carved objects, designs, or figures ▪ an ancient people proficient in stone *carving* — see also WOOD CARVING

carving knife *noun, pl* ~ **knives** [*count*] : a sharp knife that is used to cut cooked meat

car wash *noun, pl* ~ **washes** [*count*]

1 : an area or building with equipment for washing cars ▪ a drive-through *car wash*

2 *US* : an event at which people pay to have their cars washed in order to raise money for some purpose ▪ Our church is having a *car wash* tomorrow from 9:00 a.m. to 3:00 p.m.

Ca·sa·no·va /ˌkæzəˈnoʊvə/ *noun, pl* **-vas** [*count*] : a man who has many lovers ▪ He has a terrible reputation as a *Casanova*.

[1]**cas·cade** /kæˈskeɪd/ *noun, pl* **-cades** [*count*]

1 : a small, steep waterfall; *especially* : one that is part of a series of waterfalls

2 : a large amount of something that flows or hangs down ▪ a *cascade* of water ▪ Her hair was arranged in a *cascade of* curls.

3 : a large number of things that happen quickly in a series ▪ That decision set off a *cascade of* events.

[2]**cascade** *verb* **-cades; -cad·ed; -cad·ing** [*no obj*] : to flow or hang down in large amounts ▪ The water *cascades* over the

rocks. • Her hair *cascaded* down around her shoulders.

[1]**case** /ˈkeɪs/ *noun, pl* **cas·es**

1 [*count*] : a situation or occurrence that is an instance or example of something • That was true in all three *cases*. [=*instances*] • We usually ask for a 100-dollar deposit, but ***in this case*** we'll make an exception. • They might not let you buy the tickets yet, ***in which case*** [=and if that is true] you should try again tomorrow. • It was a ***case of mistaken identity***. [=a situation in which someone or something is mistakenly thought to be someone or something else] • a ***classic case*** [=a typical example] of sibling rivalry

2 [*count*] : a situation that is being investigated or managed by someone (such as a police officer or social worker) in an official way • Her disappearance is a *case* for the police. • Detectives are on the *case*. • a murder/rape/kidnapping *case* • The abused child's *case* was turned over to state authorities.

3 [*count*] *grammar* : a form of a noun, pronoun, or adjective showing its relationship to other words in a sentence • The word "child's" in "a child's shirt" is in the possessive *case*.

4 *the case* : what actually exists or happens • A lot of people have had trouble working with him, and that was certainly *the case* with me. [=I also had trouble working with him] • She had expected him to come home, but that was not to be *the case*. [=but that didn't happen] • The doctor may or may not have been at fault, but ***whatever the case (may be)*** [=either way] the patient almost died. • ***Is it not the case*** [=isn't it true] that she took the car without permission?

5 [*count*] *law* : a situation that will be talked about and decided in court • a court *case* • a civil/criminal *case* • The lawyer agreed to take/handle the *case*. ✧ The phrase ***I rest my case*** can be used to say that you have finished an argument or to suggest that something proves that what you are saying is true. • I said that it wouldn't work and it didn't. *I rest my case*. — see also TEST CASE

6 [*count*] : a convincing argument • He makes a good *case* for cutting expenses.

7 [*count*] **a** : an occurrence of a disease or an injury • an AIDS *case* • He has a bad/severe/slight *case* of the flu. **b** : an occurrence of discomfort, fear, etc. • She had a bad *case* of the nerves/jitters/butterflies [=she was very nervous] before she gave her report.

8 [*singular*] : a particular person and his or her condition or character • You are a sad *case*. — see also BASKET CASE, HEAD CASE

in any case — used to indicate that something is true or certain regardless of what else has happened or been said • I'm not sure if I'll be at the next meeting, but I'll see you Sunday *in any case*. [=I may or may not see you at the next meeting, but I'll definitely see you Sunday] • *In any case*, you still owe me five dollars.

in case **1** : for the purpose of being ready for something that might happen • Bring an umbrella *in case* it rains. • We brought extra money ***just in case***. **2** — used to talk about something that might have happened or that might be true • Today is our anniversary, *in case* you've forgotten. • *In case* [=*if*] you're wondering, I'm looking for my glasses.

in case of : if (something) happens • That door is for use *in case of* [=*in the event of*] fire.

in that case : when that is considered : because of that • "The traffic could be heavy tomorrow." "*In that case*, we better leave early."

on/off your case *informal* ✧ Someone who is always or frequently criticizing you or telling you what to do is *on your case* and won't ***get off your case***. • Her brother is always *on her case* about the clothes she wears. • *Get off my case*! I'm working as hard as I can!

– compare [2]CASE

[2]**case** *noun, pl* **cases** [*count*]

1 : a box or container to hold something • a cigarette/pencil *case* — see also CARRYING CASE

2 : the contents of a box • They drank a *case* [=four six-packs; 24 bottles] of beer.

– compare [1]CASE

[3]**case** *verb* **cases**; **cased**; **cas·ing** [+ *obj*] : to study or watch (a house, store, etc.) with plans to rob it — often used in the phrase ***case the joint*** • A couple of robbers decided to *case the joint*.

case history *noun, pl* ~ **-ries** [*count*] : a record that shows a person's past illnesses, treatments, and other information for use by doctors, social workers, etc. • The patient's *case history* showed recurring fits of depression.

case in point *noun* [*singular*] : a specific example used to show that something you have said is true • He spends a lot of money on unnecessary things. A *case in point* is his collection of rare sports cars.

case law *noun* [*noncount*] : law that is based on decisions that judges have made in past cases • *Case law* says that a person has a right to privacy.

case·load /ˈkeɪsˌloʊd/ *noun, pl* **-loads** [*count*] : the number or amount of cases handled by a court, social worker, etc. • We have a heavy/light *caseload* today.

case·ment /ˈkeɪsmənt/ *noun, pl* **-ments** [*count*] : a window that opens on hinges like a door — called also *casement window*; see picture at WINDOW

case study *noun, pl* ~ **-ies** [*count*] : a published report about a person, group, or situation that has been studied over time • a *case study* of prisoners; *also* : a situation in real life that can be looked at or studied to learn about something • The company's recent history is a *case study* in bad management.

case·work /ˈkeɪsˌwɚk/ *noun* [*noncount*] : the work done by a social worker to help fix the problems of a person or family – **case·work·er** /ˈkeɪsˌwɚkɚ/ *noun, pl* **-ers** [*count*]

[1]**cash** /ˈkæʃ/ *noun* [*noncount*]

1 : money in the form of coins and bills • The vending machine only accepts *cash*. • The fine may be paid by check or in *cash*. • He offered to pay *cash* for the truck. — often used before another noun • *cash* payments/prizes/sums

2 : money along with other things (such as stocks) that can be quickly changed into money • The company has $4 million in *cash*.

[2]**cash** *verb* **cash·es**; **cashed**; **cash·ing** [+ *obj*] : to give or get cash for (a check) • The store wouldn't *cash* the check. • He *cashed* his paycheck at the bank.

cash in [*phrasal verb*] **1** ***cash in (something) or cash (something) in*** : to obtain money for (something that you own) • She *cashed in* her stocks. • *cash in* an insurance policy **2 a** ***cash in on (something)*** : to take advantage of something in order to make money • The magazine is planning to *cash in on* the hype surrounding the celebrity's wedding by publishing exclusive photos of the ceremony. • Carpenters *cashed in on* the construction boom. • stores *cashing in on* Christmas **b** ***cash in*** : to make money from something • He is going to *cash in* big [=make a lot of money] when he sells his house at the beach.

cash–and–car·ry /ˌkæʃn̩ˈkeri/ *noun, pl* **-ries** [*count*] : a store where businesses and other customers can pay cash for goods at low prices and take them away instead of having them delivered

– **cash–and–carry** *adj, always used before a noun* • items sold on a *cash-and-carry* basis

cash bar *noun, pl* ~ **bars** [*count*] : a place at a party where guests can buy drinks • They had a *cash bar* at their wedding reception.

cash card *noun, pl* ~ **cards** [*count*] *Brit* : a card that is used to get money from an ATM : an ATM card — compare BANK CARD

cash cow *noun, pl* ~ **cows** [*count*] : someone or something that makes a lot of money for a business, organization, etc. • The football team was a *cash cow* for the university. • The movie studio saw the actress as a *cash cow*.

cash crop *noun, pl* ~ **crops** [*count*] : a crop (such as tobacco or cotton) that is grown to be sold rather than for use by the farmer

cash desk *noun, pl* ~ **desks** [*count*] *Brit* : a checkout counter in a store : the place in a store where you pay for the things you are buying

cash dispenser *noun, pl* ~ **-ers** [*count*] *Brit* : ATM

cash·ew /ˈkæʃu, kəˈʃu/ *noun, pl* **-ews** [*count*] : a type of roasted nut that has a curved shape — called also *cashew nut*; see picture at NUT

cash flow *noun* : the movement of money in and out of a business [*singular*] We were able to maintain a steady *cash flow*. [*noncount*] The company is looking at new ways to generate *cash flow*.

[1]**cash·ier** /kæˈʃiɚ/ *noun, pl* **-iers** [*count*] : a person whose job is to take in or give out money in a store, bank, etc.

[2]**ca·shier** /kæˈʃiɚ/ *verb* **-shiers**; **-shiered**; **-shier·ing** [+ *obj*] : to remove (a person) from a position for doing something wrong • He was *cashiered* from the army.

cashier's check *noun, pl* ~ **checks** [*count*] : a check that is written by a bank and signed by a cashier — compare BANK DRAFT

cash machine *noun, pl* ~ **-chines** [*count*] *Brit* : ATM
cash•mere /ˈkæʒˌmiɚ, ˈkæʃˌmiɚ/ *noun* [*noncount*]
1 : fine wool from a kind of goat from India
2 : a soft fabric made from cashmere wool — often used before another noun • a *cashmere* sweater
cash•point /ˈkæʃˌpoɪnt/ *noun, pl* **-points** [*count*] *Brit* : ATM
cash register *noun, pl* ~ **-ters** [*count*] : a machine used in a store, restaurant, etc., that calculates the amount of cash due for a sale and has a drawer for holding money
cas•ing /ˈkeɪsɪŋ/ *noun, pl* **-ings** [*count*]
1 : a layer on the outside of something that covers and protects it • a sausage *casing* • a *casing* for a shotgun shell
2 : a frame around a door or window
ca•si•no /kəˈsiːnoʊ/ *noun, pl* **-nos** [*count*] : a building or room that has games (such as roulette or blackjack) for gambling
cask /ˈkæsk, *Brit* ˈkɑːsk/ *noun, pl* **casks** [*count*] : a container that is shaped like a barrel and is used for holding liquids • an oak *cask* for wine; *also* : the contents of a cask • They drank a *cask* of wine.
cas•ket /ˈkæskət, *Brit* ˈkɑːskət/ *noun, pl* **-kets** [*count*]
1 *chiefly US* : COFFIN
2 : a small chest or box for jewelry or other valuable things ✧ This sense is no longer common in U.S. English.
cas•sa•va /kəˈsɑːvə/ *noun, pl* **-vas** [*count, noncount*] : a tropical plant with thick roots that are used to make small white grains (called tapioca) that are used in cooking
cas•se•role /ˈkæsəˌroʊl/ *noun, pl* **-roles**
1 : food (such as meat, noodles, and vegetables) baked together and served in a deep dish [*count*] a seafood *casserole* [*noncount*] I made tuna *casserole* for dinner.
2 [*count*] : a deep dish used for baking • meat and noodles served in a *casserole* — called also *casserole dish*
cas•sette /kəˈsɛt/ *noun, pl* **-settes** [*count*] : a thin case that holds audio tape or videotape and in which the tape passes from one reel to another when being played • a *cassette* player/recorder • The songs are available on *cassette*. — see also VIDEOCASSETTE
cas•sock /ˈkæsək/ *noun, pl* **-socks** [*count*] : a long gown worn by a priest
[1]**cast** /ˈkæst, *Brit* ˈkɑːst/ *verb* **casts**; **cast**; **cast•ing** [+ *obj*]
1 a : to throw or move (something) in a forceful way • *cast* [=*throw, toss*] a stone • Seaweed was *cast* up by the waves. **b** : to throw (a fishing line, hook, etc.) into the water by using a fishing pole
2 a : to send or direct (something) in the direction of someone or something • He *cast* a glance toward the door. [=he glanced at the door] • The witch *cast* [=*put*] a spell on him. **b** : to send (something) out or forward • The fire *casts* [=*gives off*] a warm glow. • The tree *cast* a long shadow on the lawn. — often used figuratively • The trial *casts* a harsh light on [=reveals bad things about] the banking industry. • Their argument ***cast a pall*** on the party. [=gave the party an unhappy mood] • The incident ***casts doubt*** on her honesty.
3 : to make (a vote) formally • How many votes were *cast*? • *cast* a ballot
4 a : to assign roles for (a play, movie, etc.) to actors • *cast* a play **b** : to assign (an actor or actress) a role in a film, play, etc. • She was *cast* as a college professor who becomes a spy. — see also TYPECAST
5 a : to shape (a substance) by pouring it into a mold and letting it harden • The metal was *cast* into candlesticks. • molds used for *casting* steel **b** : to form (something, such as a sculpture) by casting metal, plaster, etc. • The statue will be *cast* in bronze.
6 : to arrange (something) into parts or into a proper form • He *cast* the story in the form of a diary.
7 : to talk about or think of (someone or something) in a particular way • The war was *cast* as a battle against terrorism. • Health care issues are often *cast* in economic terms.
cast about/around for [*phrasal verb*] ***cast about/around for (something)*** : to look in many places for (something) • They *cast about for* new ways to make money on the farm. • She is still *casting around for* [=*seeking*] someone to watch her son while she is at work.
cast a (dark) cloud see [1]CLOUD
cast adrift [*phrasal verb*] **1** ***cast (a boat) adrift*** : to cause (a boat) to float on the water without being tied to anything or controlled by anyone — often used as *(be) cast adrift* • a small lifeboat *cast adrift* in the open sea **2** ***cast (someone) adrift*** : to cause (someone) to float on the water in a boat that is not tied to anything or controlled by anyone — often used as *(be) cast adrift* • They *were cast adrift* in a small, leaky boat. — often used figuratively • I *was cast adrift* in a sea of confusion.
cast aside [*phrasal verb*] ***cast aside (something) or cast (something) aside*** : to stop thinking about (something) • She tried to *cast aside* her worries and enjoy the party.
cast aspersions see ASPERSIONS
cast away [*phrasal verb*] ***cast away (someone) or cast (someone) away*** : to leave (someone) alone somewhere (such as on an island) as a result of a storm, shipwreck, etc. — usually used as *(be) cast away* • The crew *was cast away* on a desert island. — see also CASTAWAY
cast caution to the wind see [1]CAUTION
cast light on see [1]LIGHT
cast lots see LOT
cast off [*phrasal verb*] **1** ***cast off (something) or cast (something) off*** : to get rid of (something) • The snake *casts off* [=*sheds*] its skin. • They wanted to *cast off* their fears. — see also CASTOFF, CAST-OFF **2** : to untie the rope that is holding a boat near the land • We decided to *cast off* and head out to sea. **3** : to remove stitches from a knitting needle in a way that does not cause them to become loose • When I finish this row, can you show me how to *cast off*?
cast on [*phrasal verb*] : to place stitches on a knitting needle • I was having trouble *casting on*, but I think I have it now.
cast out [*phrasal verb*] ***cast out (someone or something) or cast (someone or something) out*** : to force (someone or something) to go away • He was *cast out* of [=expelled from] the tribe. • They tried to *cast out* the spirits from the haunted house.
cast pearls before swine see PEARL
cast your eye over see [1]EYE
cast your lot see LOT
cast your mind back see [1]MIND
cast your net wide see [1]NET
the die is cast see [2]DIE
[2]**cast** *noun, pl* **casts**
1 [*count*] : the actors in a play, film, or television show • members of the *cast* = *cast* members • The show features ***an all-star cast*** [=a cast that includes many famous actors] • a strong ***supporting cast*** [=the actors other than the main stars] ✧ The phrase ***cast of characters*** is sometimes used to refer to a group of people who have important roles in a book, story, or event. • The *cast of characters* includes President Johnson and his top advisers during the Vietnam War.

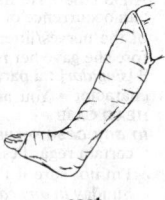

cast

2 [*count*] : a hard covering that is put on an arm, leg, etc., so that a broken bone can heal • She has a *cast* on her arm. — called also *plaster cast*
3 [*count*] : a container that is used to give its form or shape to something that is poured or pressed into it : MOLD; *also* : an object that is made by using such a container • They made a mask from a wax *cast* of her face.
4 [*singular*] *literary* : the shape or appearance of something • His face had a rugged *cast*.
5 [*singular*] : a slight bit of color • old photographs with a reddish *cast*
6 [*singular*] : a characteristic of a person or thing : a distinctive quality • She has a skeptical ***cast of mind***. [=she tends to be skeptical]
7 [*count*] : the act of throwing a fishing line into water with a pole
cas•ta•nets /ˌkæstəˈnɛts/ *noun* [*plural*] : a musical instrument that consists of two small, round parts that are clicked together by the fingers
cast•away /ˈkæstəˌweɪ, *Brit* ˈkɑːstəˌweɪ/ *noun, pl* **-aways** [*count*] : a person who is left alone in a place (such as an island) as a result of a storm, shipwreck, etc. — see also *cast away* at [1]CAST
caste /ˈkæst, *Brit* ˈkɑːst/ *noun, pl* **castes**
1 [*count*] : one of the classes into which the Hindu people of India were traditionally divided
2 : a division of society based upon differences of wealth, rank, or occupation [*count*] He was from a higher *caste*. [*noncount*] a system of *caste* = a *caste* system
cast•er (*US*) *or Brit* **cas•tor** /ˈkæstɚ, *Brit* ˈkɑːstə/ *noun, pl* **-ers** [*count*] : a small wheel attached to the bottom of some-

thing (such as a piece of furniture) to make it easier to move

cas·ti·gate /ˈkæstəˌgeɪt/ *verb* **-gates; -gat·ed; -gat·ing** [+ *obj*] *formal* : to criticize (someone) harshly • The author *castigated* the prime minister as an ineffective leader. — often + *for* • The judge *castigated* the lawyers *for* their lack of preparation. • He was *castigated* in the media *for* making millions of dollars while the company went bankrupt.

— **cas·ti·ga·tion** /ˌkæstəˈgeɪʃən/ *noun* [*noncount*]

cast·ing /ˈkæstɪŋ, *Brit* ˈkɑːstɪŋ/ *noun, pl* **-ings** [*count*] : something made from material that hardens in a mold • The workers make metal *castings* for truck engines.

cast iron *noun* [*noncount*] : a very hard type of metal that is made into different shapes by being melted and poured into special containers (called casts or molds) • The fence is made of *cast iron*.

cast–iron *adj*

1 : made of cast iron • a *cast-iron* stove

2 : very strong or tough • I have a *cast-iron* stomach. [=I can eat anything spicy, hot, etc.] • a *cast-iron* will

3 *Brit* : not likely to fail or be broken • You had better have a *cast-iron* [=(*US*) *airtight*] excuse for missing the meeting. • a *cast-iron* promise

cas·tle /ˈkæsəl, *Brit* ˈkɑːsəl/ *noun, pl* **cas·tles** [*count*]

1 : a large building usually with high, thick walls and towers that was built in the past to protect against attack

2 *informal* : a large expensive house • Millionaires built their *castles* along the lake.

3 : a piece in the game of chess that looks like a castle tower : ROOK — see picture at CHESS

castle in the air *also* ***castle in Spain*** : a dream, plan, or idea that can never become real — usually plural • He's just ***building castles in the air*** if he thinks he can open a restaurant without any money.

cast·off /ˈkæstˌɑːf, *Brit* ˈkɑːstˌɒf/ *noun, pl* **-offs** [*count*] : something or someone that is thrown out or replaced • The books were mostly *castoffs* from other schools. • He assembled a bunch of *castoffs* [=players fired by other teams] into a good football team. • a social *castoff* [=*reject*] — see also *cast off* 1 at [1]CAST

cast–off /ˈkæstˌɑːf, *Brit* ˈkɑːstˌɒf/ *adj* : thrown or given away • She had to wear her sister's *cast-off* clothes. • *cast-off* players — see also *cast off* 1 at [1]CAST

castor *Brit spelling of* CASTER

cas·tor oil /ˈkæstɚ-, *Brit* ˈkɑːstər-/ *noun* [*noncount*] : a thick oil made from a tropical plant and used in the past as a medicine

cas·trate /ˈkæˌstreɪt, *Brit* kæˈstreɪt/ *verb* **-trates; -trat·ed; -trat·ing** [+ *obj*] : to remove the testes of (a person or animal) • Farmers *castrated* the bull calf. • a *castrated* horse

— **cas·tra·tion** /kæˈstreɪʃən/ *noun* [*noncount*]

ca·su·al /ˈkæʒəwəl/ *adj*

1 *always used before a noun* : happening by chance : not planned or expected • a *casual* encounter on the sidewalk

2 [*more* ~; *most* ~] : designed for or permitting ordinary dress, behavior, etc. : not formal • *casual* clothes • a *casual* restaurant • The atmosphere at the meeting was quite *casual*.

✧ ***Casual days*** are days (such as ***casual Fridays***) when a company allows workers to dress in casual clothes.

3 [*more* ~; *most* ~] **a** : done without much thought, effort, or concern • She takes a *casual* [=*nonchalant*] approach to her homework. • He made a *casual* remark about her shoes. **b** : not involving a close or serious relationship • *casual* sex • They are only *casual* acquaintances. [=they know each other but not very well] • Their relationship was *casual*. **c** : having some interest but not a lot : not serious • He's a *casual* sports fan.

4 : happening at certain times but not on a regular basis • She found only *casual* work.

— **ca·su·al·ly** *adj* • I looked *casually* down at my watch. • He was dressed *casually* in jeans and a sweatshirt. — **ca·su·al·ness** *noun* [*noncount*]

ca·su·al·ty /ˈkæʒəwəlti/ *noun, pl* **-ties** [*count*]

1 : a person who is hurt or killed during an accident, war, etc. • a low number of *casualties* • The army suffered/took/sustained heavy *casualties* [=many soldiers were killed or wounded] in the town. • *casualty* rates [=the number of people or wounded killed each day]

2 : a person or thing that is harmed, lost, or destroyed : VICTIM — usually + *of* • The tree was a *casualty of* the high winds. • The factory was a *casualty of* the depression.

cat /ˈkæt/ *noun, pl* **cats** [*count*]

1 a : a small animal that is related to lions and tigers and that is often kept by people as a pet • I have two dogs and a *cat*. — often used before another noun • *cat* food — see also TOMCAT **b** : a lion, tiger, leopard, or similar wild animal

2 *old-fashioned slang* : a man • He's a cool *cat*. • You *cats* are crazy! — see also FAT CAT, HEPCAT, SCAREDY-CAT

Cat got your tongue? *informal* — used to ask someone why he or she is not saying anything • "You've been unusually quiet tonight," she said. "What's the matter? *Cat got your tongue*?"

curiosity killed the cat see CURIOSITY

fight like cats and dogs see [1]FIGHT

let the cat out of the bag : to reveal a secret • We wanted

cat

the party to be a surprise, but he *let the cat out of the bag.*
like something the cat brought/dragged/drug in ✧ If you look or feel *like something the cat brought/dragged/drug in,* you are very dirty or untidy. ▪ I need to take a shower—I look *like something the cat dragged in.*
like the cat that ate/got/swallowed the canary (*US*) *or Brit* ***like the cat that got the cream*** — used to say that someone looks very proud or satisfied about something he or she has done ▪ After pointing out his teacher's mistake, he smiled *like the cat that ate the canary.*
Look what the cat dragged in! *informal* — used to call attention to someone who has entered the room or area
rain cats and dogs see [2]RAIN
the cat's meow (*US*) *or* ***the cat's pajamas*** *or Brit* ***the cat's whiskers*** *old-fashioned + informal* — used to say that someone or something is very appealing ▪ That car is *the cat's meow.* [=I really like that car] ▪ Going to the movies was *the cat's pajamas* when I was a kid.
– cat·like /ˈkætˌlaɪk/ *adj* ▪ a *catlike* appearance ▪ *catlike* movements

cat·a·clysm /ˈkætəˌklɪzəm/ *noun, pl* **-clysms :** something that causes great destruction, violence, etc. [*count*] floods, earthquakes, and other *cataclysms* ▪ The country barely survived the *cataclysm* of war. [*noncount*] The revolution could result in worldwide *cataclysm.*
– cat·a·clys·mic /ˌkætəˈklɪzmɪk/ *adj* [*more* ~; *most* ~] ▪ a *cataclysmic* event

cat·a·comb /ˈkætəˌkoʊm, *Brit* ˈkætəˌkuːm/ *noun, pl* **-combs** [*count*] **:** an underground place where people are buried — usually plural ▪ ancient Roman *catacombs*

[1]**cat·a·log** (*chiefly US*) *or* **cat·a·logue** /ˈkætəˌlɑːg/ *noun, pl* **-logs** *or* **-logues** [*count*]
1 : a book containing a list of things that you can buy, use, etc., and often pictures ▪ She ordered clothes from a (mail-order) *catalog.* ▪ a college/course *catalog* — see also CARD CATALOG
2 : a group of similar or related things ▪ The band played many songs from their *catalog* of hits. ▪ a *catalog* of failures/disasters/mistakes

[2]**catalog** (*US*) *or* **catalogue** *verb* **-logs** *or* **-logues; -loged** *or* **-logued; -log·ing** *or* **-logu·ing** [+ *obj*] **:** to list or describe (something) in an organized way ▪ They use the computer to *catalog* books. ▪ The chart *catalogs* the results of each test.
– cat·a·log·er (*US*) *or* **cat·a·logu·er** *noun, pl* **-ers** [*count*] ▪ a book *cataloger*

cat·a·lyst /ˈkætələst/ *noun, pl* **-lysts** [*count*]
1 *technical* **:** a substance that causes a chemical reaction to happen more quickly
2 : a person or event that quickly causes change or action ▪ The bombing attack was the *catalyst* for war. ▪ She was proud to be a *catalyst* for reform in the government.

cat·a·lyt·ic converter /ˌkætəˈlɪtɪk-/ *noun, pl* ~ **-ers** [*count*] **:** a part of an automobile exhaust system that removes harmful chemicals — see picture at CAR

cat·a·ma·ran /ˌkætəməˈræn/ *noun, pl* **-rans** [*count*] **:** a boat with two hulls — see picture at BOAT

cat and mouse *noun* [*noncount*] **:** behavior that is like the way a cat chases a mouse or plays with a mouse before killing it — used especially to describe a situation in which someone says or does different things to deceive or control other people, to avoid being caught, etc.; usually used with *play* ▪ The governor has been *playing* (a game of) *cat and mouse* with the media, refusing to say definitely whether he will run for reelection. ▪ The thieves *played cat and mouse* with the police for several days before they were caught.
– cat–and–mouse *adj* ▪ a *cat-and-mouse* routine

[1]**cat·a·pult** /ˈkætəˌpʌlt/ *noun, pl* **-pults** [*count*]
1 a : an ancient weapon used for throwing large rocks **b** *Brit* **:** SLINGSHOT
2 : a device for launching an airplane from the deck of an aircraft carrier

[2]**catapult** *verb* **-pults; -pult·ed; -pult·ing**
1 [+ *obj*] **:** to throw (something) with a catapult ▪ They *catapulted* rocks toward the castle.
2 a [+ *obj*] **:** to cause (someone or something) to quickly move up or ahead or to a better position ▪ The publicity *catapulted* her CD to the top of the charts. ▪ The novel *catapulted* him from unknown to best-selling author. **b** [*no obj*] **:** to quickly move up or ahead **:** to quickly advance to a better position ▪ He *catapulted* to fame after his first book was published. ▪ Her career was *catapulting* ahead.

cat·a·ract /ˈkætəˌrækt/ *noun, pl* **-racts** [*count*]
1 *medical* **:** a condition in which a part of your eye (called the lens) becomes cloudy and you cannot see well — often plural ▪ His grandmother developed *cataracts.*
2 *literary* **:** a large waterfall

ca·tarrh /kəˈtɑɚ/ *noun, pl* **-tarrhs** [*count*] *medical* **:** a condition in which the nose and air passages become filled with mucus

ca·tas·tro·phe /kəˈtæstrəfi/ *noun, pl* **-phes :** a terrible disaster [*count*] The oil spill was an environmental *catastrophe.* ▪ Experts fear a humanitarian *catastrophe* if food isn't delivered to the refugees soon. ▪ a global/nuclear/economic *catastrophe* [*noncount*] an area on the brink of *catastrophe*
– cat·a·stroph·ic /ˌkætəˈstrɑːfɪk/ *adj* [*more* ~; *most* ~] ▪ The effect of the war on the economy was *catastrophic.* ▪ a *catastrophic* drought **– cat·a·stroph·i·cal·ly** /ˌkætəˈstrɑːfɪkli/ *adv* ▪ The dam failed *catastrophically,* flooding the entire valley.

cat·bird seat /ˈkætˌbɚd-/ *noun*
(sitting) in the catbird seat *US, informal* **:** in a very good position ▪ The team was *(sitting) in the catbird seat* after winning 10 games in a row.

cat burglar *noun, pl* ~ **-lars** [*count*] **:** a thief who enters buildings by climbing up a wall and going in through a window without being seen

cat·call /ˈkætˌkɑːl/ *noun, pl* **-calls** [*count*] **:** a sound or noise that someone (such as an audience member) makes toward a speaker, performer, athlete, etc., that he or she does not like ▪ The pitcher heard angry *catcalls* as he walked off the field.

[1]**catch** /ˈkætʃ, ˈkɛtʃ/ *verb* **catch·es; caught** /ˈkɑːt/; **catch·ing**
1 a : to use your hands to stop and hold (an object that is moving through the air) [+ *obj*] *Catch* the ball and throw it to first base. ▪ She *caught* the ball with one hand. ▪ I dropped the book but managed to *catch* it before it hit the ground. [*no obj*] I'll throw you the keys. Ready? *Catch!* **b** [+ *obj*] **:** to use your hands to grasp and hold onto (someone or something) ▪ He *caught* [=*grabbed, seized*] her by the wrist. ▪ He ***caught hold of*** her wrist.
2 [+ *obj*] **:** to capture and not allow (a person, animal, or fish) to escape ▪ The police are working hard to *catch* the criminals and put them in jail. ▪ "I bet you can't *catch* me!" she yelled to her brother. ▪ I once *caught* 10 fish in a single day. ▪ In the summer, we would *catch* fireflies and put them in jars. ▪ *catching* mice in traps ▪ lions *catching* their prey
3 [+ *obj*] **a :** to manage to find, meet, or reach (someone) at a particular time or in a particular state or condition ▪ I *caught* her just as she was leaving for work. ▪ I'm afraid you've *caught* me at a bad time. **b :** to find (someone who is doing something wrong) ▪ The police *caught* him trying to steal the painting. ▪ My teacher *caught* me cheating on a test. ▪ Her father *caught* her smoking in the basement. ▪ You'd never *catch* me doing that! [=I would never do that] ▪ They ***caught him in the act*** (of stealing the painting). = He was ***caught red-handed.***
4 [+ *obj*] **:** to affect (someone) in a sudden and surprising way ▪ They were ***caught unprepared*** by the crisis. = The crisis ***caught them unawares.*** [=they were not prepared when the crisis occurred] ▪ The announcement ***caught me by surprise.*** [=I was surprised by the announcement]
5 [+ *obj*] **a :** to suddenly stop (yourself) before you do something ▪ Luckily, he *caught* himself before he gave away the secret. **b :** to suddenly become aware that you are doing something ▪ He *caught* himself staring at her.
6 [+ *obj*] **:** to cause (someone) to be stopped, delayed, etc. — usually used as *(be/get) caught* ▪ We *got caught* in a rain storm and had to find shelter. ▪ I'm sorry I'm late. I *was caught* in traffic. ▪ We ***got caught up in*** traffic and were late for our flight. — see also CAUGHT UP IN 1 (below)
7 : to cause (something) to become stuck and unable to move [+ *obj*] I *caught* my sleeve on a nail. ▪ The kite got *caught* [=*tangled*] in the tree. ▪ She tried to stand up, but her foot was *caught* in the strap. [*no obj*] My sleeve *caught* on a nail.
8 [*no obj*] **:** to have the parts connect firmly ▪ I tried to lock the door, but the lock wouldn't *catch.*
9 [+ *obj*] **a :** to stop and hold (falling water) ▪ They kept a bucket outside to *catch* the rain. **b :** to become covered with (something that moves through the air) ▪ These curtains *catch* a lot of dust.
10 [+ *obj*] **a :** to hit or touch (someone or something) ▪ The bullet *caught* him in the leg. ▪ His last punch *caught* me in the jaw. ▪ Isn't it beautiful the way the setting sun *catches* the tips

of the trees? **b :** to be hit or touched by (something) ▪ He *caught* a bullet in the leg. ▪ The tips of the trees *catch* the light as the sun sets.

11 [+ *obj*] **:** to become affected with (a sickness or disease) ▪ We both *caught* [=*contracted*] the flu. ▪ I seem to *catch* a cold every winter. ▪ children *catching* colds from each other ✧ When people say that you will ***catch your death (of cold)***, they mean that you will become sick or catch a very bad cold. ▪ It's freezing! You'll *catch your death* if you go out without a coat! — see also CATCHING

12 [+ *obj*] **:** to begin to feel excitement or interest about something ▪ I haven't *caught* the holiday spirit yet this year. ▪ People are getting really interested in the sport. The whole country is starting to ***catch the fever.***

13 [+ *obj*] **:** to attract and hold (someone's attention, interest, etc.) ▪ I tried to *catch* the waiter's attention, but I guess he didn't see me. ▪ The show is more likely to *catch* the interest of an older audience. ▪ Her books have ***caught the imagination*** of children from around the world. [=children find her books very exciting and enjoyable] ✧ If someone or something ***catches your eye***, you notice that person or thing. ▪ There was one dress in particular that *caught my eye*. — see also EYE-CATCHING

14 [+ *obj*] **:** to see, smell, or notice (something) ▪ I *caught* [=*got*] a faint whiff of her perfume. ▪ While you're in Hollywood, you might ***catch a glimpse*** of some movie stars. ▪ I ***caught sight*** of his red shirt and started calling to him.

15 [+ *obj*] *informal* **:** to hear or understand (something) ▪ What was that again? I didn't quite *catch* [=*hear, get*] what you said. ▪ I didn't *catch* your name. ▪ Do you ***catch my drift?*** [=do you understand what I mean?]

16 [+ *obj*] **:** to become aware of (something, such as an illness) ▪ The disease is curable if *caught* [=*detected*] early.

17 [+ *obj*] **:** to have or do (something) ▪ You can *catch* [=*take*] a quick nap on the train.

18 [+ *obj*] **:** to get (something) through effort ▪ I managed to *catch* [=*get*] a ride into town with some friends.

19 [+ *obj*] *informal* **:** to meet with (someone) ▪ "See you soon." "Yup. ***Catch you later.***"

20 [+ *obj*] **:** to move fast enough to be next to or in front of (someone) ▪ She *caught* [=*overtook*] the leader in the final meters of the race. ▪ He left before I did so I had to hurry to *catch* him. [=to catch up with him]

21 [+ *obj*] **:** to get on a bus, train, etc., before it leaves ▪ If you miss the first bus, you can *catch* the next one in 15 minutes. ▪ If you'll excuse me, I have a plane to *catch*.

22 [+ *obj*] **:** to see or hear (a show, game, etc.) ▪ I only *caught* the last few minutes of the game. ▪ Did you *catch* the show on Channel 4 last night?

23 [+ *obj*] **:** to describe or show (someone or something) in an accurate way in art ▪ The new portrait *catches* her likeness perfectly. ▪ The novel successfully *catches* the atmosphere of 19th-century Paris.

24 [*no obj*] *baseball* **:** to play the position of catcher ▪ He *catches* for the New York Yankees. ▪ If you pitch, I'll *catch*.

catch at [*phrasal verb*] ***catch at (something)*** **:** to reach for and try to hold (something) ▪ The baby *caught at* my dress as I walked past.

catch fire **1** *or US* ***catch on fire*** **:** to begin to burn ▪ Newspaper *catches fire* [=*ignites*] easily. ▪ Their house *caught fire* and burned to the ground. ▪ Don't leave the towel on the stove. It could *catch fire*. **2 :** to become very popular or effective ▪ The idea failed to *catch fire*. ▪ The singer hasn't *caught fire* in this country yet. ▪ a new technology that has *caught fire* with the public

catch hell see HELL

catch it *chiefly Brit, informal* **:** to be punished or scolded ▪ He's really going to *catch it* [=(*US*) *catch hell*] (from his boss) if he comes in late again!

catch lightning in a bottle see [1]LIGHTNING

catch on [*phrasal verb*] **1 :** to become popular ▪ This trend is *catching on* with/among college students. ▪ Soccer is finally starting to *catch on* in America. **2 :** to learn or understand something ▪ Once you start playing the game, the kids will *catch on* pretty quickly. ▪ It took her a while to *catch on*, but she eventually got the joke.

catch out [*phrasal verb*] ***catch (someone) out*** *chiefly Brit* **:** to show that (someone) does not know something or is doing something bad ▪ She loved *catching* teachers *out* by asking tough questions. ▪ The police tried to *catch* him *out* in a lie.

catch (someone) dead see [1]DEAD

catch up [*phrasal verb*] **1 :** to move fast enough to join someone or something that is in front of you ▪ They went so fast we couldn't *catch up*. — often + *with* or *to* ▪ Slow down so that I can *catch up with* you. ▪ She ran as fast as she could, but she couldn't *catch up with* her brother. = (*US*) She couldn't *catch up to* him. — often used figuratively ▪ In order to *catch up with* its competitors in the industry, the company will need to start using more advanced technologies. ▪ She missed several months of school and may never *catch up with* the other children in her class. = (*US*) She may never *catch up to* them. **2 :** to learn about recent events ▪ We haven't seen each other in such a long time; we've got lots of *catching up* to do! ▪ *catching up* with old friends — often + *on* ▪ He reads the newspaper on Sunday mornings to *catch up on* the news. **3** ***catch up on (something)*** **:** to do (something) that you could have done earlier ▪ She has to *catch up on* her homework. ▪ I hope to *catch up on* some much-needed sleep this weekend. **4** ***catch (someone) up*** *Brit* **:** to join someone who is ahead of you ▪ He was ahead of me for most of the race, but I *caught him up* [=I caught up with him] at the end. ▪ Go on ahead: I'll *catch you up* later. **5** ***catch up with (someone)*** **a :** to begin to affect (someone) usually in a bad way ▪ All those late nights are really starting to *catch up with* me! ▪ Old age *catches up with* everyone in the end. **b :** to find and arrest (someone) ▪ The police eventually *caught up with* him in Texas. **c** *informal* **:** to meet with (someone) ▪ I've got to go. I'll *catch up with* you later.

catch your breath see BREATH

caught in the middle see [2]MIDDLE

caught short **1 :** not having enough of something ▪ Don't be *caught short*! Make sure you stock up on supplies before you set out on your trip. **2** *Brit, informal* **:** having a sudden urge to use the toilet

caught up in **1 :** involved in (a difficult or confusing situation) ▪ Several members of Congress were *caught up in* the scandal. ▪ How did you get *caught up in* this mess? — see also [1]CATCH 6 (above) **2 :** excited about something and having trouble thinking about anything else ▪ Everyone was *caught up in* the excitement. ▪ Try not to get too *caught up in* the moment.

– **catch·able** /ˈkætʃəbəl, ˈkɛtʃəbəl/ *adj* ▪ a *catchable* ball

[2]**catch** *noun, pl* **catch·es**

1 [*count*] **:** a hidden problem that makes something more complicated or difficult to do — usually singular ▪ The phone only costs $20, but there's a *catch*: you have to sign a two-year contract with the phone company. ▪ He said he would let me borrow his car, but I knew there had to be a *catch*. ▪ What's/Where's the *catch*?

2 a [*count*] **:** the act of stopping a moving object (such as a ball) and holding it in your hands **:** the act of catching something ▪ Great *catch*! ▪ The shortstop made a tough *catch*. **b** [*noncount*] **:** a game in which two or more people throw and catch a ball ▪ She used to play *catch* with her dad. ▪ Let's play a game of *catch*.

3 [*count*] **:** an amount of fish that has been caught ▪ a *catch* of about 20 fish ▪ She ordered the ***catch of the day.*** [=the fish offered on a particular day at a restaurant]

4 [*count*] *old-fashioned* **:** a person who would be very desirable as a husband or wife ▪ He was an excellent *catch*.

5 [*count*] **:** something that holds an object or stops the parts of an object from moving ▪ She fastened the *catch* on her purse. ▪ The *catch* on my grandmother's pin broke. ▪ a safety *catch* on a gun

6 [*singular*] **:** a short, sharp change or stop in a person's voice or breath while speaking ▪ I could hear the *catch* in his voice when he said his dead wife's name.

catch·all /ˈkætʃˌɑːl, ˈkɛtʃˌɑːl/ *noun* [*singular*] **:** something that holds or includes many different things ▪ They used the drawer as a *catchall* for kitchen items. ▪ "The arts" is a *catchall* for a variety of activities from painting to music. — often used before another noun ▪ a *catchall* phrase/term

catch·er /ˈkætʃɚ, ˈkɛtʃɚ/ *noun, pl* **-ers** [*count*]

1 : someone or something that catches something ▪ a dog *catcher* ▪ The cat is a good mouse *catcher*.

2 *baseball* **:** the player who plays behind home plate and catches the pitches thrown by the pitcher

catching *adj, not used before a noun* **:** able to be passed quickly from one person or animal to another **:** CONTAGIOUS ▪ "I have a cold." "Is it *catching*?" ▪ His enthusiasm is *catching*. — see also EYE-CATCHING

catch·ment area /ˈkætʃmənt-, ˈkɛtʃmənt-/ *noun, pl* ~ **areas** [*count*]

1 *technical* **:** the area from which water flows into a river, stream, etc.

C

2 *chiefly Brit* : the area that a school, hospital, etc., provides a service to

catch•phrase /ˈkæʧˌfreɪz, ˈkɛʧˌfreɪz/ *noun, pl* **-phras•es** [*count*] : a word or phrase that is easy to remember and is commonly used to represent or describe a person, group, idea, etc. ▪ popular *catchphrases* like "politically correct" ▪ The politician asked his writers to come up with new *catchphrases.* [=*slogans*]

catch–22 *or* **Catch–22** /ˈkæʧˌtwɛntiˈtu:, ˈkɛʧˌtwɛntiˈtu:/ *noun, pl* **-22's** *or* **-22s** [*count*] : a difficult situation for which there is no easy or possible solution ▪ I'm in a *catch-22*: to get the job I need experience, but how do I get experience if I can't get the job? — often used before another noun ▪ a *catch-22* dilemma/situation

catch–up /ˈkæʧˌʌp, ˈkɛʧˌʌp/ *noun*

play catch-up : to try to reach the same position, score, etc., as a competitor after you have fallen behind ▪ The team fell behind in the second inning and has had to *play catch-up* ever since. ▪ The company has been trying to *play* a difficult game of *catch-up* ever since its competitor introduced the new product. — see also *catch up* at [1]CATCH

catch•word /ˈkæʧˌwɚd, ˈkɛʧˌwɚd/ *noun, pl* **-words** [*count*] : CATCHPHRASE

catchy /ˈkæʧi, ˈkɛʧi/ *adj* **catch•i•er; -est** : appealing and easy to remember ▪ I can't think of a *catchy* name/title for my blog. ▪ The new slogan isn't as *catchy* as the old one. ▪ a *catchy* song/tune

cat•e•chism /ˈkætəˌkɪzəm/ *noun, pl* **-chisms**

1 [*noncount*] : a collection of questions and answers that are used to teach people about the Christian religion ▪ They went to school to learn their *catechism.* ▪ He taught *catechism* at Sunday school.

2 [*count*] : a book that explains the beliefs of the Christian religion by using a list of questions and answers

cat•e•gor•i•cal /ˌkætəˈgorɪkəl/ *also* **cat•e•gor•ic** /ˌkætəˈgorɪk/ *adj* : said in a very strong, clear, and definite way ▪ He issued a *categorical* denial about his involvement in the deal. ▪ a *categorical* statement

— **cat•e•gor•i•cal•ly** /ˌkætəˈgorɪkli/ *adv* ▪ She *categorically* denied the accusation. ▪ The statement is *categorically* false/untrue.

cat•e•go•rize *also Brit* **cat•e•go•rise** /ˈkætɪgəˌraɪz/ *verb* **-riz•es; -rized; -riz•ing** [+ *obj*] : to put (someone or something) into a group of similar people or things : to put (people or things) into categories ▪ This software lets you *categorize* your photographs in many different ways. ▪ Would you *categorize* [=*classify*] this book as science fiction? ▪ Their opinions can be *categorized* as conservative. ▪ Birds are *categorized* by type in this field guide.

— **cat•e•go•ri•za•tion** *also Brit* **cat•e•go•ri•sa•tion** /ˌkætɪgərəˈzeɪʃən, *Brit* ˌkætɪgəˌraɪˈzeɪʃən/ *noun, pl* **-tions** [*count, noncount*]

cat•e•go•ry /ˈkætəˌgori, *Brit* ˈkætəgri/ *noun, pl* **-ries** [*count*] : a group of people or things that are similar in some way ▪ The cars belong to the same *category.* ▪ Taxpayers fall into one of several *categories.* ▪ She competed for the award in her age *category.*

ca•ter /ˈkeɪtɚ/ *verb* **-ters; -tered; -ter•ing** : to provide food and drinks at a party, meeting, etc., especially as a job [*no obj*] The restaurant *caters* for parties/banquets/receptions. [+ *obj*] A local restaurant *catered* the banquet/meal/reception. ▪ The awards ceremony will be a *catered* event/affair.

cater to (*chiefly US*) *or chiefly Brit* ***cater for*** [*phrasal verb*] ***cater to/for (someone or something)*** : to provide what is wanted or needed by (someone or something) ▪ The inn *caters* exclusively *to* foreign tourists. ▪ The library *caters to* [=*serves*] scientists. ▪ That store *caters to* middle-class taste. ▪ The hotel *caters to* your every need. [=the hotel provides everything that you need] ▪ (*disapproving*) As a child he was spoiled by parents who *catered to* his every need.

— **ca•ter•er** /ˈkeɪtərɚ/ *noun, pl* **-ers** [*count*] ▪ a successful cook and *caterer* ▪ The party was serviced by the best *caterer* in the area. — **catering** *noun* [*noncount*] ▪ Who did the *catering* for the party? ▪ She runs a *catering* business.

cat•er•cor•ner /ˈkætiˌkoɚnɚ/ *adv, US* : KITTY-CORNER

cat•er•pil•lar /ˈkætɚˌpɪlɚ/ *noun, pl* **-lars** [*count*] : a small creature that is like a worm with many legs and that changes to become a butterfly or moth

cat•er•waul /ˈkætɚˌwɑ:l/ *verb* **-wauls; -wauled; -waul•ing** [*no obj*]

1 : to make a very loud and unpleasant sound ▪ Some animal was *caterwauling* in my backyard last night.

caterpillar

2 : to protest or complain noisily ▪ He continues to *caterwaul* about having to take the blame.

— **caterwaul** *noun, pl* **-wauls** [*count*]

cat•fight /ˈkætˌfaɪt/ *noun, pl* **-fights** [*count*] *informal* : an angry fight or argument between two women

cat•fish /ˈkætˌfɪʃ/ *noun, pl* **cat•fish** [*count, noncount*] : a type of fish that has a large head and long thin parts that look like a cat's whiskers around its mouth — see color picture on page C8

cat•gut /ˈkætˌgʌt/ *noun* [*noncount*] : a tough cord made from the intestines of animals (such as sheep) and used as strings for musical instruments, tennis rackets, etc.

ca•thar•sis /kəˈθɑɚsɪs/ *noun, formal* : the act or process of releasing a strong emotion (such as pity or fear) especially by expressing it in an art form [*noncount*] Acting is a means of *catharsis* for her. [*singular*] Painting/music/writing is a *catharsis* for me.

— **ca•thar•tic** /kəˈθɑɚtɪk/ *adj* [*more ~; most ~*] ▪ a *cathartic* experience

ca•the•dral /kəˈθi:drəl/ *noun, pl* **-drals** [*count*] : the main church of an area that is headed by a bishop

cathedral ceiling *noun, pl* **~ -ings** [*count*] : a high ceiling that has two sides that slant downwards from a pointed top

Cath•er•ine wheel /ˈkæθrɪn-/ *noun, pl* **~ wheels** [*count*] *Brit* : PINWHEEL 2

cath•e•ter /ˈkæθətɚ/ *noun, pl* **-ters** [*count*] *medical* : a thin tube that is put into the body to remove or inject a liquid or to keep a passage open

— **cath•e•ter•i•za•tion** *also Brit* **cath•e•ter•i•sa•tion** /ˌkæθətərəˈzeɪʃən, *Brit* ˌkæθətəˌraɪˈzeɪʃən/ *noun, pl* **-tions** [*noncount*] The patient underwent cardiac *catheterization.* [*count*] The surgeon has performed hundreds of *catheterizations* over the years.

cath•ode /ˈkæˌθoʊd/ *noun, pl* **-odes** [*count*] *technical* : the part of an electrical device (such as a battery) where electrons enter — compare ANODE

cathode–ray tube *noun, pl* **~ tubes** [*count*] : a large tube that shows a picture on a screen (such as a television or computer screen) — abbr. *CRT*

cath•o•lic /ˈkæθlɪk/ *adj*

1 *Catholic* : of or relating to the Roman Catholic Church ▪ a *Catholic* bishop/nun/priest ▪ My son goes to a local *Catholic* school. [=a school run by the Roman Catholic Church]

2 *formal* : including many different things ▪ She is a novelist who is *catholic* in her interests. ▪ He has *catholic* tastes in art and music. [=he likes many different things in art and music]

Cath•o•lic /ˈkæθlɪk/ *noun, pl* **-lics** [*count*] : a person who is a member of the Roman Catholic Church

Ca•thol•i•cism /kəˈθɑ:ləˌsɪzəm/ *noun* [*noncount*] : the Roman Catholic religion ▪ He converted to *Catholicism.*

cat•house /ˈkætˌhaʊs/ *noun, pl* **-hous•es** [*count*] *US slang* : a place where prostitutes are available : BROTHEL

cat•kin /ˈkætkən/ *noun, pl* **-kins** [*count*] : a bunch of flowers that grow in close rows on the branches of trees (such as willows or birches)

cat•nap /ˈkætˌnæp/ *noun, pl* **-naps** [*count*] : a short period of sleep : a brief nap ▪ He took/had a *catnap.*

— **cat•nap** *verb* **-naps; -napped; -nap•ping** [*no obj*] ▪ She closed her eyes to *catnap* while her friend drove the car.

cat•nip /ˈkætˌnɪp/ *noun* [*noncount*] : a type of mint that has a strong smell which is attractive to cats

CAT scan /ˈkæt-/ *noun, pl* **~ scans** [*count*] *medical* : a picture of the inside of a part of your body that is made by a computerized machine — called also *CT scan*

— **CAT scanner** *noun, pl* **~ -ners** [*count*]

cat's cradle *noun*

1 [*noncount*] : a game played with a string that is wrapped around your fingers in complex patterns

2 [*singular*] : something that is very complicated ▪ a *cat's cradle* of government regulations

cat's–eye /ˈkætsˌaɪ/ *noun, pl* **-eyes** [*count*]

1 : a jewel that has a pale stripe running down its middle which makes it look like the eye of a cat

2 *US* : a marble with round circles that look like eyes

Cats•eye /ˈkætsˌaɪ/ *trademark, Brit* — used for an object that is placed on the surface of a road and which reflects light from a car's headlights to make the road easier to see

cat·suit /ˈkætˌsuːt/ *noun, pl* **-suits** [*count*] : a tight piece of clothing that covers the body and legs and sometimes the arms

cat·sup /ˈkɛʧəp/ *noun* [*noncount*] *US* : KETCHUP

cat·tail /ˈkætˌteɪl/ *noun, pl* **-tails** [*count*] *US* : a tall plant that has long flat leaves and that grows in wet areas — called also (*Brit*) *bulrush*

cat·tery /ˈkætəri/ *noun, pl* **-ter·ies** [*count*] *chiefly Brit* : a place where cats are kept while their owners are away — compare KENNEL

cat·tle /ˈkætl̩/ *noun* [*plural*] : cows, bulls, or steers that are kept on a farm or ranch for meat or milk • a herd of *cattle* • His family used to raise *cattle*. • The people in the crowd were treated like *cattle* as they tried to leave the stadium. — often used before another noun • *cattle* feed • a *cattle* herd • the *cattle* industry • My uncle has a *cattle* ranch.

cattle call *noun, pl* ~ **calls** [*count*] *US, informal* : an audition for actors in a movie, television show, etc.

cattle guard *noun, pl* ~ **guards** [*count*] *US* : a set of bars placed over a shallow hole that is used to stop cattle from crossing a road — called also (*Brit*) *cattle grid*

cat·tle·man /ˈkætl̩mən/ *noun, pl* **-men** /-mən/ [*count*] *chiefly US* : a person who raises or takes care of cattle

cattle prod *noun, pl* ~ **prods** [*count*] : a device that is used to make cattle move by giving them an electric shock

cat·ty /ˈkæti/ *adj* **cat·ti·er; -est** *disapproving* : unkind or critical — used especially to describe a comment made by a woman • She said something *catty* about the way they were dressed. • *catty* comments/remarks
– **cat·ti·ly** /ˈkætəli/ *adv* – **cat·ti·ness** /ˈkætinəs/ *noun* [*noncount*]

cat·ty–cor·ner /ˈkætiˌkoɚnɚ/ *or* **cat·ty–cor·nered** /ˈkætiˌkoɚnɚd/ *adv, US* : KITTY-CORNER

CATV *abbr* cable television

cat·walk /ˈkætˌwɑːk/ *noun, pl* **-walks** [*count*]
1 : a narrow structure for people to walk on along a bridge or high up on the side of a building
2 : the raised structure that models walk along in a fashion show

Cau·ca·sian /kɑˈkeɪʒən, *Brit* kɔˈkeɪziən/ *noun, pl* **-sians** [*count*] : a person who has white or pale skin : a white person • The disease is largely associated with *Caucasians*.
– **Caucasian** *adj* • The police were looking for a *Caucasian* [=*white*] male.

¹cau·cus /ˈkɑːkəs/ *noun, pl* **-cus·es** [*count*]
1 : a meeting of members of a political party for the purpose of choosing candidates for an election • a presidential *caucus* [=a meeting to decide who the party's candidate for the presidential election will be]
2 : a group of people (such as members of the U.S. Congress) who meet to discuss a particular issue or to work together for a shared, usually political goal • the Congressional Arts *Caucus* • the National Women's Political *Caucus*

²caucus *verb* **-cuses; -cused; -cus·ing** [*no obj*] *US* : to meet in a caucus • Democrats/Republicans *caucused* last week to choose their candidates.

caught *past tense and past participle of* ¹CATCH

caul·dron *also US* **cal·dron** /ˈkɑːldrən/ *noun, pl* **-drons** [*count*] : a large pot • a witch's *cauldron* — often used figuratively • The area was a *cauldron* of violence. • a seething *cauldron* of intense emotions

cau·li·flow·er /ˈkɑːlɪˌflawɚ/ *noun, pl* **-ers** [*count, noncount*] : a vegetable that is grown for its head of white flowers — see color picture on page C4

cauliflower ear *noun, pl* ~ **ears** [*count*] : an ear that is permanently damaged and swollen after being hit many times

caulk /ˈkɑːk/ *verb* **caulks; caulked; caulk·ing** [+ *obj*] : to fill the cracks or holes in (something) with a substance that keeps out water • He carefully *caulked* the area around the windows.
– **caulk** *noun* [*noncount*] • He filled the cracks with *caulk*.

caus·al /ˈkɑːzəl/ *adj, formal*
1 : relating to or showing the cause of something • No *causal* connection/relationship between the events was found. • There is a *causal* link between poverty and crime.
2 : making something happen : causing something • The *causal* [=*causative*] agent of the disease is a fungus.
– **caus·al·ly** *adv* • The events are *causally* related.

cau·sal·i·ty /kɑˈzæləti/ *noun* [*noncount*] *formal*
1 : the relationship between something that happens or exists and the thing that causes it • Scientists found no *causality* between the events.
2 : the idea that something can cause another thing to happen or exist • the principle of *causality*

cau·sa·tion /kɑˈzeɪʃən/ *noun* [*noncount*] *formal*
1 : the act or process of causing something to happen or exist • the role of heredity in the *causation* of cancer
2 : the relationship between an event or situation and a possible reason or cause • He claimed that the accident caused his injury, but the court ruled that he did not provide sufficient evidence of *causation*.

caus·a·tive /ˈkɑːzətɪv/ *adj, formal* : making something happen or exist : causing something • A virus was found to be the *causative* agent of smallpox. • Speed was a *causative* factor in the accident. [=speed helped to cause the accident]

¹cause /ˈkɑːz/ *noun, pl* **caus·es**
1 [*count*] : something or someone that produces an effect, result, or condition : something or someone that makes something happen or exist • His symptoms had no apparent physical *causes*. • She is the *cause* of all their problems. • He died of/from ***natural causes***. [=he died because of old age or an illness] — often + *of* • The doctor determined the *cause of* death. • The exact *cause of* the accident/fire is not known.
2 : a reason for doing or feeling something [*noncount*] The medicine was prescribed without good *cause*. — often + *for* • There is some *cause for* concern. [=some reason to be concerned/worried] [*singular*] Their marriage was a *cause for* celebration. — see also PROBABLE CAUSE
3 [*count*] : something (such as an organization, belief, idea, or goal) that a group or people support or fight for • I can support a *cause* that means something to me. • I'm willing to donate money as long as it's for a good/worthy *cause*.
lost cause : a person or thing that is certain to fail • She decided her acting career was a *lost cause*. • I'm a *lost cause* when it comes to anything technical.
make/find common cause *formal* : to join together with someone in order to achieve a shared goal • He has *made common cause* with political rivals to defeat the proposed new law.

²cause *verb* **causes; caused; caus·ing** [+ *obj*]
1 : to make (something) happen or exist : to be the cause of (something) • He swerved and *caused* an accident. • The flood *caused* great hardship. • The illness is *caused* by a virus.
2 : to make (someone) feel, have, or do something • The flood *caused* the town great hardship. • You *caused* us a lot of extra work. — often followed by *to* + *verb* • His boss *caused* him *to resign*. [=his boss made him resign] • His nervous behavior *caused* me *to question* his innocence.

'cause /ˈkɑːz, kəz/ *conj* : BECAUSE — used in informal speech • "Why did he do that?" "*'Cause* I told him to."

cause cé·lè·bre *also* **cause ce·le·bre** /ˌkɑːzsəˈlɛbrə/ *noun, pl* **causes cé·lè·bres** *also* **causes ce·le·bres** /ˌkɑzːsəˈlɛbrə/ [*count*] *formal* : a legal case or an event that a lot of people become interested in — usually singular • The case became a *cause célèbre* for/among environmentalists.

cause·way /ˈkɑːzˌweɪ/ *noun, pl* **-ways** [*count*] : a raised road or path that goes across wet ground or water • The island is linked by a *causeway* to the mainland.

caus·tic /ˈkɑːstɪk/ *adj* [*more* ~; *most* ~]
1 : able to destroy or burn something by chemical action • The chemical was so *caustic* that it ate through the pipes.
2 : very harsh and critical • *caustic* film reviews • She wrote a *caustic* report about the decisions that led to the crisis. • *caustic* humor/wit
– **caus·ti·cal·ly** /ˈkɑːstɪkli/ *adv*

caustic soda *noun* [*noncount*] *chiefly Brit* : LYE

cau·ter·ize *also Brit* **cau·ter·ise** /ˈkɑːtəˌraɪz/ *verb* **-iz·es; -ized; -iz·ing** [+ *obj*] *medical* : to burn (something, such as a wound) with heat or a chemical substance in order to destroy infected tissue • The doctors *cauterized* the wound.
– **cau·ter·i·za·tion** *also Brit* **cau·ter·i·sa·tion** /ˌkɑːtərəˈzeɪʃən, *Brit* ˌkɔːtəˌraɪˈzeɪʃən/ *noun* [*noncount*]

¹cau·tion /ˈkɑːʃən/ *noun, pl* **-tions**
1 [*noncount*] : care taken to avoid danger or risk : a careful attitude or way of behaving • You should use *caution* when operating the electric saw. • He injected a note/word of *caution* in his talk. • Her financial adviser urged *caution* before investing in the project. • Investors should exercise *caution*. • The roads are slippery: drive with extreme *caution*.
2 : a warning telling someone to be careful [*count*] Her

C

comments were intended as a *caution* to us to protect our property. [*noncount*] A ***note/word of caution*** be sure that the electricity is off before you install the ceiling fan.

3 [*count*] *Brit, law* : a spoken official warning given to someone who has done something illegal but has not committed a serious crime ▪ She was given a *caution* by the magistrate.

throw/fling/cast caution to the wind : to stop being careful and do something that is dangerous or that might result in failure ▪ After thinking about it for years, he finally *threw/flung/cast caution to the wind*, quit his job, and started his own company.

²**caution** *verb* **-tions; -tioned; -tion·ing**

1 : to warn or tell (someone) about a possible danger, problem, etc. [+ *obj*] She *cautioned* me not to decide too quickly. = She *cautioned* (me) that I shouldn't decide too quickly. ▪ Officials are *cautioning* that the war may continue for years. ▪ "Don't decide too quickly," she *cautioned*. [*no obj*] — + *against* ▪ I would *caution against* getting involved with him.

2 [+ *obj*] *Brit, law* : to give a caution to (someone) ▪ He was *cautioned* for speeding.

cau·tion·ary /ˈkɑːʃəˌneri, *Brit* ˈkɔːʃənri/ *adj* : giving a warning about a possible danger, problem, etc. ▪ The story is a *cautionary* tale of what can happen when greed takes over.

cau·tious /ˈkɑːʃəs/ *adj* [*more* ~; *most* ~] : careful about avoiding danger or risk ▪ Any *cautious* tourist will guard her passport. ▪ You cannot be overly/too *cautious* when you're driving in snow. ▪ He answered the question with a *cautious* reply.

– **cau·tious·ly** *adv* [*more* ~; *most* ~] ▪ She *cautiously* moved down the dark hall. – **cau·tious·ness** *noun* [*noncount*] ▪ They proceeded with *cautiousness*. [=*caution*]

cav·al·cade /ˌkævəlˈkeɪd/ *noun, pl* **-cades** [*count*]

1 : a line of riders, vehicles, etc., moving along in the same direction ▪ The *cavalcade* arrived at the hotel. ▪ a *cavalcade* of antique cars

2 *literary* : a series *of* related things ▪ the *cavalcade of* years ▪ a *cavalcade of* natural disasters

cav·a·lier /ˌkævəˈliə/ *adj* [*more* ~; *most* ~] *disapproving* : having or showing no concern for something that is important or serious ▪ They are too *cavalier* in their treatment of others. ▪ The writer is very *cavalier* [=*careless*] about the truth. ▪ She has a *cavalier* attitude about/towards spending money. ▪ He has a *cavalier* disregard for the rights of others.

– **cav·a·lier·ly** *adv* ▪ He *cavalierly* disregarded their advice.

cav·al·ry /ˈkævəlri/ *noun* : the part of an army that in the past had soldiers who rode horses and that now has soldiers who ride in vehicles or helicopters [*noncount*] *Cavalry* is used to perform reconnaissance. [*plural*] The *cavalry* were brought in to support the mission. — often used before another noun ▪ *cavalry* forces/officers/troops — compare INFANTRY

cav·al·ry·man /ˈkævəlrimən/ *noun, pl* **-men** /-mən/ [*count*] : a soldier who is in the cavalry

¹**cave** /ˈkeɪv/ *noun, pl* **caves** [*count*] : a large hole that was formed by natural processes in the side of a cliff or hill or under the ground

²**cave** *verb* **caves; caved; cav·ing**

cave in [*phrasal verb*] **1 a** : to fall down or inward ▪ We need to keep the walls from *caving in*. [=*collapsing*] ▪ The roof *caved in* on them. **b** ***cave (something) in or cave in (something)*** : to cause (something) to fall down or inward ▪ The weight of the snow *caved in* the roof. **2** *informal* : to stop trying to resist or oppose something : to give in or submit to pressure ▪ We kept asking her to come and she finally *caved in*. ▪ He *caved in* to the pressure to resign. — sometimes used in U.S. English without *in* ▪ We kept asking her to come and she finally *caved*. — see also CAVE-IN

ca·ve·at /ˈkæviˌɑːt, *Brit* ˈkæviæt/ *noun, pl* **-ats** [*count*] *formal* : an explanation or warning that should be remembered when you are doing or thinking about something ▪ His investment advice comes with a *caveat*: that the stock market is impossible to predict with absolute accuracy.

ca·ve·at emp·tor /ˈkæviˌɑːtˈɛmptə/ *noun* [*noncount*] *law* : the principle that a person who buys something is responsible for making sure that it is in good condition, works properly, etc.

cave–in /ˈkeɪvˌɪn/ *noun, pl* **-ins** [*count*] : an occurrence in which something (such as the roof or walls of a building or cave) suddenly falls down or inward ▪ There are important safety procedures to prevent *cave-ins* in mines. ▪ They explored the area of the *cave-in*. — see also *cave in* at ²CAVE

cave·man /ˈkeɪvˌmæn/ *noun, pl* **-men** /-mən/ [*count*]

1 : a person who lived in a cave in ancient times

2 *informal* : a man who acts in a very rude and aggressive way

cav·er /ˈkeɪvə/ *noun, pl* **-ers** [*count*] : a person who explores caves : SPELUNKER

cav·ern /ˈkævən/ *noun, pl* **-erns** [*count*] : a large cave

cav·ern·ous /ˈkævənəs/ *adj* [*more* ~; *most* ~] *of a building or room* : resembling a large cave : very large ▪ We toured the *cavernous* airplane hangar. ▪ The dance was held in a *cavernous* hall. ▪ a *cavernous* auditorium

cav·i·ar /ˈkæviˌɑə/ *noun* [*noncount*] : the eggs of a large fish (such as the sturgeon) that are salted and eaten as food

cav·il /ˈkævəl/ *verb* **cav·ils**; *US* **cav·iled** *or Brit* **cav·illed**; *US* **cav·il·ing** *or Brit* **cav·il·ling** [*no obj*] *formal* : to complain about things that are not important ▪ I don't intend to *cavil* or compromise. ▪ A customer *caviled* about/over/at the price.

– **cavil** *noun, pl* **-ils** [*count*] The reviewer had only a few *cavils* [=small criticisms] about the book. [*noncount*] The need for these changes is ***beyond cavil*** [=cannot be doubted or argued about]

cav·ing /ˈkeɪvɪŋ/ *noun* [*noncount*] : the sport of exploring caves : SPELUNKING

cav·i·ty /ˈkævəti/ *noun, pl* **-ties** [*count*]

1 : a hole or space inside something ▪ Some birds nest in tree *cavities*. ▪ the abdominal/chest/nasal *cavity*

2 : a hole formed in a tooth by decay ▪ I had two *cavities* filled at the dentist's.

ca·vort /kəˈvoət/ *verb* **-vorts; -vort·ed; -vort·ing** [*no obj*]

1 : to jump or move around in a lively manner ▪ Otters *cavorted* in the stream.

2 : to spend time in an enjoyable and often wild or improper way — usually + *with* ▪ The governor has been criticized for *cavorting with* celebrities.

caw /ˈkɑː/ *noun, pl* **caws** [*count*] : the loud sound made by a crow or a similar bird

– **caw** *verb* **caws; cawed; caw·ing** [*no obj*] ▪ Crows *cawed* in the trees. – **cawing** *noun* [*noncount*] ▪ I heard the *cawing* of a crow.

cay /ˈkiː, ˈkeɪ/ *noun, pl* **cays** [*count*] : a low island made of sand or coral

cay·enne pepper /ˌkaɪˈɛn-, ˌkeɪˈɛn-/ *noun* [*noncount*] : a red powder that is made from hot peppers and that is used as a spice to give a hot taste to food ▪ a dash/pinch of *cayenne pepper*

CB /ˌsiːˈbiː/ *noun* [*noncount*] : a range of radio frequencies that people and especially truck drivers use to talk to each other over short distances often while driving — often used before another noun ▪ a *CB* radio; *also* : a radio that uses this range of frequencies ▪ We heard the truckers talking on the *CB*. ✧ *CB* is an abbreviation of "citizens band."

CBS *abbr* Columbia Broadcasting System ✧ CBS is one of the major television networks in the U.S.

¹**cc** *abbr* **1** cubic centimeter ▪ a 250*cc* engine **2** carbon copy — used to show that a copy of a business letter or an e-mail is also being sent to someone else ▪ to Meg Thomas, *cc* Ben Phipps

²**cc** /ˌsiːˈsiː/ *verb* **cc's; cc'd; cc'ing** [+ *obj*] : to send a copy of a business letter or an e-mail to someone in addition to the person addressed ▪ Please *cc* the letter to me. ▪ He *cc'd* the entire staff.

CCTV *abbr* closed-circuit television

¹**CD** /ˌsiːˈdiː/ *noun, pl* **CDs** : a small plastic disk on which information (such as music or computer data) is recorded [*count*] The singer released her new *CD* [=a new set of songs recorded on CDs for people to buy] last month. ▪ a four-*CD* set ▪ The car stereo includes a *CD* player. [*noncount*] The band's early albums are now available on *CD*. — called also *compact disc* — compare ²CD

²**CD** *noun, pl* **CDs** [*count*] : CERTIFICATE OF DEPOSIT — compare ¹CD

CD–ROM /ˌsiːˌdiːˈrɑːm/ *noun, pl* **-ROMs** : a small plastic disk on which large amounts of information (such as books, pictures, or computer programs) are stored in a form that cannot be changed [*count*] The dictionary comes with a free *CD-ROM*. [*noncount*] The dictionary is available on *CD-ROM*. ✧ *CD-ROM* is an abbreviation of "compact disc read-only memory." — see picture at COMPUTER

CE *or chiefly US* **C.E.** *abbr* Christian Era; Common Era — used to refer to the years that come after the birth of Jesus Christ ▪ the first century *C.E.* ▪ 883 *C.E.* ✧ *C.E.* has the same meaning as *A.D. C.E.* is now often used instead of *A.D.* especially in scientific writing. — compare A.D., B.C., B.C.E.

cease /ˈsiːs/ *verb* **ceas·es; ceased; ceas·ing** *formal*
1 [*no obj*] **:** to stop happening **:** to end ▪ The fighting along the border has temporarily *ceased*. ▪ The conversation abruptly *ceased*. [=*halted*] ▪ The noise *ceased* [=*stopped*] altogether. ▪ when the weary *cease* from their labors [=when people who are very tired stop working] ▪ The company was ordered by the court to ***cease and desist*** from selling the photographs. [=was ordered to immediately stop selling the photographs] — see also CEASE AND DESIST ORDER
2 [+ *obj*] **:** to stop doing (something) ▪ The factory *ceased* operations last year. ▪ The child would not *cease* his constant whining/complaining. ▪ The soldiers were ordered to ***cease fire***. [=to stop shooting their weapons] — often followed by ***to + verb*** ▪ The program would *cease to exist* without private funding. ▪ He had long *ceased to have* any regrets. ▪ Her courage ***never ceases to amaze*** me. [=I am always amazed by her courage] — see also CEASE-FIRE
wonders never cease see [1]WONDER

cease and desist order *noun, pl* ~ **-ders** [*count*] *law* **:** an official order to stop doing something immediately ▪ A *cease and desist order* was issued by the state.

cease–fire /ˈsiːsˈfajɚ/ *noun, pl* **-fires** [*count*] **:** an agreement to stop fighting a war for a period of time so that a permanent agreement can be made to end the war **:** TRUCE ▪ The countries each sent representatives to negotiate a *cease-fire*. ▪ a *cease-fire* agreement

cease·less /ˈsiːsləs/ *adj, somewhat formal* **:** seeming to never stop **:** continuous or constant ▪ her *ceaseless* efforts to build and improve the business ▪ his *ceaseless* complaints
– cease·less·ly *adv* ▪ He complained *ceaselessly*. [=*constantly, endlessly*]

ce·dar /ˈsiːdɚ/ *noun, pl* **-dars**
1 [*count*] **:** a very tall evergreen tree
2 [*noncount*] **:** the hard, reddish, and pleasant-smelling wood of a cedar ▪ a chair made of *cedar* — often used before another noun ▪ *cedar* shingles ▪ a *cedar* chest/closet

cede /ˈsiːd/ *verb* **cedes; ced·ed; ced·ing** [+ *obj*] *formal* **:** to give control of (something) to another person, group, government, etc. ▪ Russia *ceded* Alaska to the U.S. in 1867. ▪ The state had to *cede* [=*relinquish*] part of their territory. ▪ The country had no choice but to *cede* [=*surrender*] control of the canal. ▪ They *ceded* their authority.

ce·dil·la /sɪˈdɪlə/ *noun, pl* **-las** [*count*] **:** a mark ¸ placed under the letter *c* (as in *façade*) to show that it is pronounced like *s* and not *k* ✧ In English, the cedilla is mostly used in words that come from French.

ceil·ing /ˈsiːlɪŋ/ *noun, pl* **-ings** [*count*]
1 : the inside surface at the top of a room ▪ The house has low *ceilings*. ▪ a plaster *ceiling* ▪ a *ceiling* fan [=a fan that hangs from the ceiling of a room] — sometimes used figuratively ▪ a *ceiling* of stars/clouds — opposite FLOOR
2 : an upper limit — usually singular ▪ a price *ceiling* ▪ The government has put/set/imposed a *ceiling* on automobile emissions. ▪ Fuel prices are going ***through the ceiling***. [=fuel prices are quickly getting much higher] — opposite FLOOR; see also GLASS CEILING
3 *technical* **:** the greatest height at which an aircraft can fly ▪ The airplane has a *ceiling* of 32,000 feet.
hit the ceiling see [1]HIT
– ceilinged *adj* — used in combination ▪ a high-*ceilinged* room [=a room with a high ceiling]

ce·leb /səˈlɛb/ *noun, pl* **-lebs** [*count*] *informal* **:** CELEBRITY 2 ▪ Hollywood *celebs*

cel·e·brant /ˈsɛləbrənt/ *noun, pl* **-brants** [*count*] *formal*
1 a : a person who performs or leads a religious ceremony ▪ The bishop will be the main *celebrant*. ▪ the *celebrant* of the service/Mass **b :** a person who participates in a religious ceremony ▪ The *celebrants* lit their candles.
2 *US* **:** a person who celebrates something ▪ The city streets were crowded with *celebrants*. [=(more commonly) *revelers, celebrators*]

cel·e·brate /ˈsɛləˌbreɪt/ *verb* **-brates; -brat·ed; -brat·ing**
1 : to do something special or enjoyable for an important event, occasion, holiday, etc. [+ *obj*] We are *celebrating* my birthday by going out to dinner. ▪ The family gathered to *celebrate* Christmas. ▪ We are *celebrating* our anniversary next week. ▪ They are *celebrating* the birth of their third child. [*no obj*] We won! Let's *celebrate*!
2 [+ *obj*] *formal* **:** to praise (someone or something) **:** to say that (someone or something) is great or important ▪ The book *celebrates* the movies of the past. ▪ Her lecture *celebrated* the genius of the artist. ▪ We should *celebrate* diversity. ▪ He is *celebrated* for his contributions to modern science.
3 [+ *obj*] *formal* **:** to perform (a religious ceremony) ▪ A priest *celebrates* Mass at the church daily.
– cel·e·bra·tor /ˈsɛləˌbreɪtɚ/ *noun, pl* **-tors** [*count*] ▪ The dance floor was packed with *celebrators*. [=*revelers*] ▪ a *celebrator* of fine wine **– ce·leb·ra·to·ry** /ˈsɛləbrəˌtori, *Brit* ˌsɛləˈbreɪtri/ *adj* [*more* ~; *most* ~] *formal* ▪ The tone of the article was *celebratory*. ▪ a *celebratory* drink/dinner

celebrated *adj* [*more* ~; *most* ~] **:** known and praised by many people **:** FAMOUS ▪ He is one of today's most *celebrated* young writers. ▪ a *celebrated* book

cel·e·bra·tion /ˌsɛləˈbreɪʃən/ *noun, pl* **-tions**
1 [*count*] **:** a party or other special event that you have for an important occasion, holiday, etc. ▪ a victory/birthday/holiday *celebration* ▪ the town's bicentennial *celebrations*
2 [*noncount*] **:** the activity of doing special, enjoyable things for an important occasion, achievement, etc. **:** the activity of celebrating ▪ It was a night of *celebration*. ▪ We're having a dinner ***in celebration of*** their anniversary. [=as a way of celebrating their anniversary] ▪ Your promotion is (a) ***cause for celebration***.
3 [*count*] **:** the performance of a religious ceremony — usually singular ▪ a *celebration* of Mass

célèbre see CAUSE CÉLÈBRE

ce·leb·ri·ty /səˈlɛbrəti/ *noun, pl* **-ties**
1 [*noncount*] *formal* **:** the state of being famous or celebrated **:** FAME ▪ The actress lived a life of *celebrity*.
2 [*count*] **:** a person who is famous ▪ There were many *celebrities* at the party. ▪ She's become something of a ***local celebrity***. [=someone who everyone in the area knows or recognizes] — often used before another noun ▪ a *celebrity* chef [=a chef who is famous] ▪ *celebrity* interviews [=interviews with famous people]

cel·ery /ˈsɛləri/ *noun* [*noncount*] **:** a vegetable that is grown for its long light green stems ✧ Celery is eaten raw or cooked. ▪ a stalk of *celery* — see color picture on page C4

ce·les·tial /səˈlɛstʃəl, *Brit* səˈlɛstiəl/ *adj*
1 : of or relating the sky ▪ stars, planets, asteroids, and other *celestial* bodies ▪ Sailors still use *celestial* navigation. [=they still navigate by using the positions of the sun and stars in the sky]
2 : of or relating to heaven **:** HEAVENLY ▪ Angels are *celestial* beings. ▪ The late afternoon sunlight gave the room a *celestial* glow. ▪ *celestial* music

cel·i·bate /ˈsɛləbət/ *adj* — used to describe a person who is not married and does not have sex ▪ *celibate* monks and nuns ▪ They have chosen to lead *celibate* lives. ▪ He was *celibate* for many years following the death of his wife.
– cel·i·ba·cy /ˈsɛləbəsi/ *noun* [*noncount*] ▪ a vow of *celibacy*
– celibate *noun, pl* **-bates** [*count*] ▪ The monks and nuns are *celibates*.

cell /ˈsɛl/ *noun, pl* **cells** [*count*]
1 a : a room in a prison, jail, etc., where prisoners live or are kept ▪ a prison/jail *cell* ▪ The suspect was in the police station's holding *cell* overnight. **b :** a small room that one person (such as a monk or a nun) lives in
2 : any one of the very small parts that together form all living things ▪ blood/brain *cells* ▪ cancer *cells* — often used before another noun ▪ The nucleus splits during *cell* division. ▪ Her white blood *cell* count is low. ▪ the *cell* walls of plants
3 : any one of many similar sections that together form a larger structure ▪ a honeycomb *cell*
4 *technical* **a :** a container for holding substances that are used for producing electricity by chemical action ▪ dry *cell* battery ▪ a fuel *cell* **b :** a device for changing light (such as sunlight) into electricity ▪ a solar *cell*
5 : a small group of people who work together secretly as part of a larger organization or group ▪ terrorist *cells*
6 *US, informal* **:** CELL PHONE
7 *computers* **:** a space where information can be entered in an organized arrangement of rows and columns **:** a unit in a table or spreadsheet — see picture at TABLE
– celled /ˈsɛld/ *adj* — used in combination ▪ single-*celled* organisms

cel·lar /ˈsɛlɚ/ *noun, pl* **-lars** [*count*]
1 : the part of a building that is entirely or partly below the ground **:** BASEMENT ▪ The *cellar* has a dirt floor. — see also ROOT CELLAR
2 : the wines that are stored in a restaurant, in someone's

home, etc. : WINE CELLAR ▪ a restaurant with an impressive *cellar*

cellblock *noun, pl* **-blocks** [*count*] : a group of prison cells that make up a section of a prison

cel·list /ˈʧɛlɪst/ *noun, pl* **-lists** [*count*] : a person who plays the cello

cell·mate /ˈsɛlˌmeɪt/ *noun, pl* **-mates** [*count*] : someone who shares a prison cell with another prisoner

cel·lo /ˈʧɛloʊ/ *noun, pl* **-los** [*count*] : a large musical instrument like a violin that is held between the player's knees while the player sits — see picture at STRINGED INSTRUMENT

cel·lo·phane /ˈsɛləˌfeɪn/ *noun* [*noncount*] : a thin transparent material that is used for wrapping things ▪ He wrapped the gift basket in *cellophane*.

cell phone *noun, pl* ~ **phones** [*count*] *chiefly US* : a small telephone that people can take with them and use outside their homes ▪ Call me on my *cell phone*. — called also *mobile phone*, (*chiefly US*) *cellular phone*, (*US, informal*) *cell*, (*Brit*) *mobile*; see picture at TELEPHONE

cel·lu·lar /ˈsɛljələ/ *adj*

1 : of, relating to, or made of the cells of living things ▪ Researchers are observing the course of the disease at the *cellular* level. ▪ a *cellular* membrane

2 : relating to a system that uses radio waves instead of wires to send telephone signals ▪ a *cellular* network ▪ *cellular* telephone service

cellular phone *noun, pl* ~ **phones** [*count*] *chiefly US* : CELL PHONE

cel·lu·lite /ˈsɛljəˌlaɪt/ *noun* [*noncount*] : fat that is close to the surface of the skin and that makes the skin slightly bumpy

cel·lu·loid /ˈsɛljəˌlɔɪd/ *noun* [*noncount*]

1 : a tough kind of plastic that was used in the past to make photographic film and other products

2 : the film used to make movies ▪ The event was captured on *celluloid*. [=was filmed] — often used before another noun to refer to movies in general ▪ The new movie is about the *celluloid* stars of the past. ▪ a *celluloid* portrait of an aging athlete [=a movie about an aging athlete]

cel·lu·lose /ˈsɛljəˌloʊs/ *noun* [*noncount*] : a substance that is the main part of the cell walls of plants and that is used in making various products (such as paper)

Cel·si·us /ˈsɛlsijəs/ *adj* : relating to or having a scale for measuring temperature on which the boiling point of water is at 100 degrees and the freezing point of water is at 0 degrees ▪ the *Celsius* scale ▪ The temperature reached 23 degrees *Celsius*. — abbr. *C*; compare FAHRENHEIT

Celt /ˈkɛlt, ˈsɛlt/ *noun, pl* **Celts** [*count*]

1 : a member of a group of people (such as the Irish or Welsh) who lived in ancient Britain and parts of western Europe ▪ The *Celts* defended their lands against the Romans.

2 : a person whose ancestors were Celts

Celt·ic /ˈkɛltɪk, ˈsɛltɪk/ *adj* : of or relating to the Celts or their languages ▪ *Celtic* music/history ▪ *Celtic* languages

[1]**ce·ment** /sɪˈmɛnt/ *noun* [*noncount*]

1 a : a soft gray powder that is mixed with water and other substances to make concrete ▪ a bag of *cement* ▪ *cement* mix **b** : the hard substance that is made when cement is mixed with water and allowed to dry : CONCRETE ▪ There is a layer of *cement* under the bricks. ▪ *cement* blocks ▪ a *cement* floor

2 : a substance that is used to make things stick together : GLUE ▪ rubber *cement* — sometimes used figuratively ▪ Tradition is the *cement* that holds this community together.

[2]**cement** *verb* **-ments; -ment·ed; -ment·ing** [+ *obj*]

1 : to join (things) together with cement — usually used as *(be) cemented* ▪ The parts *are* then *cemented* together. ▪ A thick post *was cemented* to the floor.

2 : to make (something) stronger ▪ A win would *cement* her reputation as a strong competitor. ▪ The many hours they spent working together helped to *cement* their relationship. [=to make their relationship strong]

cement mixer *noun, pl* ~ **-ers** [*count*] : a truck that has a large container which turns when it is filled with wet cement so that the cement will not become hard — called also (*Brit*) *concrete mixer*; see picture at CONSTRUCTION

cem·e·tery /ˈsɛməˌteri, *Brit* ˈsɛmətri/ *noun, pl* **-ter·ies** [*count*] : a place where dead people are buried : GRAVEYARD

ceno·taph /ˈsɛnəˌtæf, *Brit* ˈsɛnəˌtɑːf/ *noun, pl* **-taphs** [*count*] : a special structure or statue that is built to remind people of a dead person who is buried somewhere else; *especially* : a structure built to honor the people who were killed in a war

[1]**cen·sor** /ˈsɛnsɚ/ *noun, pl* **-sors** [*count*] : a person who examines books, movies, letters, etc., and removes things that are considered to be offensive, immoral, harmful to society, etc. ▪ Government *censors* deleted all references to the protest.

[2]**censor** *verb* **-sors; -sored; -sor·ing** [+ *obj*] : to examine books, movies, letters, etc., in order to remove things that are considered to be offensive, immoral, harmful to society, etc. ▪ The station *censored* her speech before broadcasting it. ▪ His report was heavily *censored*. ▪ The government *censored* [=*removed*] all references to the protest.

Do not confuse *censor* with *censure*.

cen·so·ri·ous /sɛnˈsorijəs/ *adj* [*more* ~; *most* ~] *formal* : having or showing a tendency to criticize someone or something severely : very critical ▪ The stunt earned her the scorn of her *censorious* older sister. ▪ I was surprised by the *censorious* tone of the book review.

cen·sor·ship /ˈsɛnsɚˌʃɪp/ *noun* [*noncount*] : the system or practice of censoring books, movies, letters, etc. ▪ *censorship* of the press/media ▪ They oppose government *censorship*.

[1]**cen·sure** /ˈsɛnʃɚ/ *noun* [*noncount*] *formal* : official strong criticism ▪ The country faces international *censure* for its alleged involvement in the assassination.

[2]**censure** *verb* **-sures; -sured; -sur·ing** [+ *obj*] *formal* : to officially criticize (someone or something) strongly and publicly ▪ He was *censured* by the committee for his failure to report the problem.

Do not confuse *censure* with *censor*.

cen·sus /ˈsɛnsəs/ *noun, pl* **-sus·es** [*count*] : the official process of counting the number of people in a country, city, or town and collecting information about them ▪ According to the latest *census*, the racial makeup of the town has changed dramatically in the last 50 years. — often used before another noun ▪ *census* figures/data

cent /ˈsɛnt/ *noun, pl* **cents** [*count*] : a unit of money that is equal to $\frac{1}{100}$ of the basic unit of money in many countries : one percent of a dollar, euro, rupee, etc. ▪ A dime is worth 10 *cents*. ▪ The car isn't worth a *cent*. [=the car is not worth anything]

not one red cent *informal* : no money at all ▪ I would *not* pay *one red cent* for that car. [=I would not pay any money at all for that car]

two cents *US, informal* : someone's opinion about something ▪ He's always ready to offer his *two cents* on any topic, whether he knows anything about it or not. ▪ Can I ***put/throw in my two cents***? [=can I give my opinion?] ▪ If I can, I'd like to offer my ***two cents' worth***. [=my opinion]

cent. *abbr* century

cen·taur /ˈsɛnˌtoɚ/ *noun, pl* **-taurs** [*count*] : a creature in Greek mythology that is part human and part horse

cen·te·nar·i·an /ˌsɛntəˈnerijən/ *noun, pl* **-ans** [*count*] : a person who is 100 years old or older

cen·ten·a·ry /sɛnˈtɛnəri, *Brit* sɛnˈtiːnri/ *noun, pl* **-ries** [*count*] *Brit* : CENTENNIAL ▪ This year marks the *centenary* of the building's construction.

– centenary *adj, always used before a noun* ▪ a *centenary* year/celebration

cen·ten·ni·al /sɛnˈtɛniəl/ *noun, pl* **-als** [*count*] *US* : the 100th anniversary of something (such as an important event) ▪ We're celebrating the museum's *centennial* [=(*Brit*) *centenary*] this summer. [=celebrating the fact that it is 100 years old] ▪ Next year will be the *centennial* of the town's founding. [=the day/year 100 years after the town was officially begun] — compare BICENTENNIAL

– centennial *adj, always used before a noun* ▪ a *centennial* year/celebration

[1]**cen·ter** (*US*) *or Brit* **cen·tre** /ˈsɛntɚ/ *noun, pl* **-ters**

1 [*count*] : the middle point or part of something ▪ the *center* of the room/circle ▪ The candies have a soft *center*. [=*middle*] ▪ The staircase is in the *center* of the building. — often used before another noun ▪ the *center* aisle/lane

2 [*singular*] **a** : a person or thing that is causing a lot of interest, argument, etc. ▪ The proposed memorial has become a *center* of controversy. [=there is a lot of controversy about the proposed memorial] ▪ He likes to be the ***center of attention***. [=he likes to be noticed and watched by many people] **b** : the position of a person or thing that is causing a lot of interest, argument, etc. ▪ They are ***at the center of*** a furious debate over whether or not to expand the city's public transportation system. ✧ If you are ***at the center of things***, you are closely involved in things that are happening. ▪ He always likes to be *at the center of things.*

3 [*count*] : a building or set of buildings used by the people of a city, town, area, etc., for a particular purpose ▪ a communications/conference *center* ▪ a day-care *center* ▪ The vaccine is being tested at several medical *centers* around the country. — see also COMMUNITY CENTER

4 [*count*] : a place where a particular activity happens ▪ the financial/business/cultural *center* of the city ▪ The university is becoming a ***center of excellence*** for genetic engineering. [=becoming a place where genetic engineering is done very well] — see also NERVE CENTER, SHOPPING CENTER

5 [*count*] : an area where many people live ▪ a population/urban *center*

6 [*count*] : the main part of a town or city where there are many stores, restaurants, offices, etc. ▪ the town/city *center* ▪ efforts to rebuild the city's *center* [=*downtown*]

7 [*singular*] : the political position of people who support ideas that are not extreme : a moderate political position between the positions of people who are conservative and liberal ▪ The party's new policies show a shift toward the *center.* ▪ His political views are slightly ***right/left of center.*** [=are slightly conservative/liberal]

8 [*count*] *sports* : someone who plays a middle position on a team in sports like basketball, hockey, football, and soccer

front and center see ²FRONT

left, right, and centre see ²LEFT

²center (*US*) *or Brit* **centre** *verb* **-ters; -tered; -ter·ing**

1 [+ *obj*] : to place (something) in the middle of something ▪ *Center* the picture on the wall. — often used as *(be) centered* ▪ The sign *isn't centered.* Move it a little to the left. ▪ The pain *is centered* around/in his lower back.

2 a [*no obj*] : to be mainly concerned about or involved with someone or something — usually + *around, round, on,* or *upon* ▪ Her life *centers on/around* her children. [=her children are the most important part of her life] ▪ The story *centers on/upon* a teenage girl. ▪ The investigation has *centered* [=*focused*] mainly *on/upon* the alleged misuse of public funds. **b** [+ *obj*] : to cause (something) to be mainly concerned about or involved with something — usually + *around, round, on,* or *upon,* ▪ She *centers* her life *on/around* her children. = Her life is *centered on/around* her children. ▪ You should *center* your attention *on* the most important problems. ▪ The group is *centering* its efforts *on* getting food to the poor.

3 [+ *obj*] : to have the main or most important part of (something, such as an organization or activity) *in* or *at* a specified place — usually used as *(be) centered* ▪ an industry that *is centered in* the country's north ▪ The organization has members worldwide but *is centered in* Cairo. ▪ a series of arts events *centered at* the city park — see also CENTERED

cen·tered (*US*) *or Brit* **cen·tred** /ˈsɛntəd/ *adj*

1 : mainly concerned about or involved with something specified — used in combination with a noun ▪ a family-*centered* hotel ▪ a nature-*centered* religion — see also SELF-CENTERED

2 : having a specified kind of center — used in combination with an adjective ▪ a dark-*centered* flower

3 [*more* ~; *most* ~] : emotionally healthy and calm ▪ She struggled with depression for years, but she's more *centered* now and able to live a full life.

center field (*US*) *or Brit* **centre field** *noun* [*noncount*] : the part of the baseball outfield between right field and left field ▪ a fly ball to *center field*; *also* : the position of the player defending center field ▪ She used to be a shortstop but now she plays *center field.*

– **center fielder** (*US*) *or Brit* **centre fielder** *noun, pl* ~ **-ers** [*count*] ▪ a good *center fielder*

cen·ter·fold (*US*) *or Brit* **cen·tre·fold** *noun, pl* **-folds** /ˈsɛntəˌfoʊld/ [*count*]

1 : the pages that face each other in the middle of a magazine or newspaper

2 a : a picture of a person (such as a woman who is not wearing clothes) that is in the centerfold of a magazine **b** : a person whose picture is the centerfold of a magazine

center forward (*US*) *or Brit* **centre forward** *noun, pl* ~ **-wards** [*count*] : someone who plays in the middle of the front line of players in field hockey, soccer, and other sports

center ice (*US*) *or Brit* **centre ice** *noun* [*noncount*] : the middle section of an ice hockey rink ▪ She skated back to *center ice.*

center of gravity (*US*) *or Brit* **centre of gravity** *noun* [*singular*] : the point at which the entire weight of something can be balanced ▪ Its low *center of gravity* makes the car very stable.

cen·ter·piece (*US*) *or Brit* **cen·tre·piece** /ˈsɛntəˌpiːs/ *noun, pl* **-piec·es**

1 [*count*] : a decoration (such as a group of flowers) that is placed in the center of a table

2 [*noncount*] : the most important part of something — usually + *of* ▪ He made tax reform the *centerpiece of* his speech. ▪ Her voting record is the *centerpiece of* her campaign.

center stage (*US*) *or Brit* **centre stage** *noun* [*singular*]

1 : the middle section of a theater's stage ▪ The actor stood alone at *center stage.*

2 : a main or very important position ▪ As we wrap up work on the old project, a new one moves to *center stage.* ▪ The issue is expected to ***take center stage*** in the elections.

cen·ti- /ˈsɛntə/ *combining form*

1 : hundred ▪ *centipede*

2 : one hundredth part of something ▪ *centimeter*

cen·ti·grade /ˈsɛntəˌgreɪd/ *adj* : CELSIUS

cen·ti·gram /ˈsɛntəˌgræm/ *noun, pl* **-grams** [*count*] : a weight equal to ¹⁄₁₀₀ gram

cen·ti·li·ter (*US*) *or Brit* **cen·ti·li·tre** /ˈsɛntəˌliːtə/ *noun, pl* **-ters** [*count*] : a unit for measuring the volume of a liquid or gas that is equal to ¹⁄₁₀₀ liter or 10 cubic centimeters

cen·ti·me·ter (*US*) *or Brit* **cen·ti·me·tre** /ˈsɛntəˌmiːtə/ *noun, pl* **-ters** [*count*] : a length equal to ¹⁄₁₀₀ meter

cen·ti·pede /ˈsɛntəˌpiːd/ *noun, pl* **-pedes** [*count*] : a small creature that is like an insect and that has a long, thin body and many legs

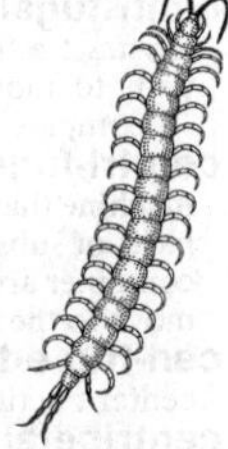
centipede

¹cen·tral /ˈsɛntrəl/ *adj*

1 *always used before a noun* : in the middle of something : located in the center of a thing or place ▪ The country is in *central* Africa. [=the area that is in the middle of Africa] ▪ The house has four rooms and a *central* chimney. ▪ City planners are looking for a *central* location for the new hospital.

2 : main or most important ▪ The novel's *central* [=*main*] character is an orphan. ▪ The professor has become a *central* [=*key*] figure in the controversy. ▪ The evidence was *central* to the defense's case. ▪ a *central* belief/claim

3 *always used before a noun* : controlling all other parts : having power over the other parts ▪ The country's schools are financed by both local and *central* governments. ▪ The *central* authority of the company's board is being challenged.

4 : designed to reach all parts of a building ▪ The apartment has both *central* air-conditioning and *central* heating.

– **cen·tral·i·ty** /sɛnˈtræləti/ *noun* [*noncount*] ▪ We should emphasize the *centrality* of this evidence to our case.

– **cen·tral·ly** /ˈsɛntrəli/ *adv* ▪ The new hospital will be *centrally* located.

²central *noun* [*singular*] *US, informal* : a place where an activity takes place or a group meets : a place that is a center for an activity or group ▪ The resort is party *central* for college students on spring break. [=college students on spring break have many parties at the resort] ▪ Our family room becomes kid *central* on weekends.

central bank *noun, pl* ~ **banks** [*count*] : a bank that does business with other banks and with the government and that controls a country's money supply and interest rates

– **central banker** *noun, pl* ~ **-ers** [*count*]

central casting *noun* [*noncount*] *informal* : the department at a movie company that chooses which actor will play each part ✧ Someone who is said to be ***from/out of central casting*** is a person whose appearance, behavior, or nature seem to be typical for their job or position. ▪ The physics professor looks like he's right *out of central casting*: his white hair is disheveled, his suit rumpled, and he looks a little lost.

central city *noun, pl* ~ **cities** [*count*] : the center part of a large city ▪ The *central city* is losing population, while the suburbs are expanding.

cen·tral·ism /ˈsɛntrəˌlɪzəm/ *noun* [*noncount*] : a way of organizing a political or educational system in which a single authority has power and control over the entire system

– **centralist** *adj*

cen·tral·ize *also Brit* **cen·tral·ise** /ˈsɛntrəˌlaɪz/ *verb* **-iz·es; -ized; -iz·ing** [+ *obj*]

1 : to bring (things that are in different places) together at a single point or place ▪ The city's hospitals hope to *centralize* [=*consolidate*] medical records in a single database. ▪ All shipping operations have been *centralized* at the Miami office.

2 : to bring (something) under the control of one authority ▪ *centralize* control ▪ The controversial reforms could be used to further *centralize* power in the hands of one party. ▪ a *centralized* authority/government — opposite DECENTRALIZE

– cen·tral·i·za·tion *also Brit* **cen·tral·i·sa·tion** /ˌsɛntrələˈzeɪʃən, *Brit* ˌsɛntrəˌlaɪˈzeɪʃən/ *noun* [*noncount*]

central locking *noun* [*noncount*] *Brit* **:** an electronic system that locks all the doors of a car at the same time

central nervous system *noun, pl* **~ -tems** [*count*] **:** the part of the nervous system that includes the brain and spinal cord

central processing unit *noun, pl* **~ units** [*count*] **:** CPU

central reservation *noun, pl* **~ -tions** [*count*] *Brit* **:** MEDIAN STRIP

centre *Brit spelling of* CENTER

-cen·tric /ˈsɛntrɪk/ *adj combining form*

1 : having (something) at the center ▪ The solar system is helio*centric*, meaning that the sun is at its center.

2 : having (something) as a central interest, influence, subject, etc. ▪ a Euro*centric* way of thinking [=a way of thinking that treats Europe and Europeans as most important] — sometimes hyphenated ▪ (*informal*) a kid-*centric* movie [=a movie for children]

cen·trif·u·gal /sɛnˈtrɪfjəgəl, *Brit* ˌsɛntrɪˈfjuːgəl/ *adj, technical* **:** moving away from a center **:** acting in a direction away from a center

centrifugal force *noun, pl* **~ forces** [*count, noncount*] *physics* **:** a force that causes an object moving in a circular path to move out and away from the center of its path — compare CENTRIPETAL FORCE

cen·tri·fuge /ˈsɛntrəˌfjuːʤ/ *noun, pl* **-fug·es** [*count*] **:** a machine that uses centrifugal force to separate substances or parts of substances ✧ A centrifuge spins substances inside a container around very fast, causing the heavier substances to move to the bottom or sides of the container.

cen·trip·e·tal /sɛnˈtrɪpətl/ *adj, technical* **:** moving toward a center **:** acting in a direction toward a center

centripetal force *noun, pl* **~ forces** [*count, noncount*] *physics* **:** a force that pulls an object moving in a circular path toward the center of its path — compare CENTRIFUGAL FORCE

cen·trist /ˈsɛntrɪst/ *noun, pl* **-trists** [*count*] **:** a person whose political opinions are not extreme **:** a person whose beliefs fall between those of liberals and conservatives ▪ The candidate hopes to appeal to *centrists* nationwide.

– centrist *adj* ▪ *centrist* political views

cen·tu·ry /ˈsɛnʧəri/ *noun, pl* **-ries** [*count*]

1 : a period of 100 years ▪ It took more than a *century* to complete the cathedral. ▪ This photograph was taken half a *century* [=50 years] ago. ▪ The herb has been used to treat headaches for *centuries*. [=hundreds of years] ▪ a *centuries*-old tradition

2 : a period of 100 years counted from the beginning of the Christian era ▪ Millions of people celebrated the beginning of the 21st *century* on January 1, 2000. ▪ the third *century* A.D. ▪ The pottery dates back to the sixth *century* B.C.E. ▪ When the prince got married, it was called the wedding of the *century*.

CEO /ˌsiːˌiːˈoʊ/ *noun, pl* **CEOs** [*count*] **:** the person who has the most authority in an organization or business ✧ *CEO* is an abbreviation of "chief executive officer."

ce·ram·ic /səˈræmɪk/ *adj* **:** made of clay that has been heated to a very high temperature so that it becomes hard ▪ a *ceramic* bead/bowl ▪ *ceramic* tiles

ce·ram·ics /səˈræmɪks/ *noun*

1 [*noncount*] **:** the art of making things out of clay ▪ She studied *ceramics* in Japan. ▪ a *ceramics* class

2 [*plural*] **:** things made out of hardened clay **:** ceramic objects ▪ the museum's collection of ancient Greek *ceramics*

ce·re·al /ˈsirijəl/ *noun, pl* **-als**

1 [*count*] **:** a plant (such as a grass) that produces grain that can be eaten ▪ Wheat and barley are common *cereals*.

2 : a breakfast food made from grain ✧ Cereal is usually eaten in a bowl with milk poured over it. [*noncount*] a bowl of *cereal* ▪ Some kinds of *cereal* have a lot of added sugar. [*count*] Some *cereals* have a lot of added sugar. ▪ breakfast *cereals*

cer·e·bel·lum /ˌserəˈbɛləm/ *noun, pl* **-lums** *or* **-la** /-lə/ [*count*] *medical* **:** the back part of the brain that controls balance and the use of muscles

ce·re·bral /səˈriːbrəl, ˈserəbrəl/ *adj*

1 *always used before a noun, medical* **:** of or relating to the brain ▪ the *cerebral* cortex/hemisphere ▪ a *cerebral* hemorrhage

2 [*more ~; most ~*] **:** related to the mind rather than to feelings **:** intellectual and not emotional ▪ He's a very *cerebral* comedian. ▪ The novel was a little too *cerebral* [=*highbrow*] for me.

cerebral palsy *noun* [*noncount*] *medical* **:** a disease that causes a person to have problems moving and speaking

ce·re·brum /səˈriːbrəm, ˈserəbrəm/ *noun, pl* **-brums** *or chiefly Brit* **-bra** /-brə/ [*count*] *medical* **:** the front part of the brain that is believed to be where thoughts occur

¹cer·e·mo·ni·al /ˌserəˈmounijəl/ *adj*

1 a : used in or done as part of a ceremony ▪ The tribe has different *ceremonial* masks for each ceremony. ▪ a *ceremonial* dance **b :** including a ceremony **:** marked by a ceremony ▪ a *ceremonial* occasion

2 : without real power or influence ▪ His new position is largely *ceremonial* because all the decisions are actually made by a committee.

– cer·e·mo·ni·al·ly *adv* ▪ The swords are now used only *ceremonially*. [=only as part of a ceremony]

²ceremonial *noun, pl* **-als** [*count*] **:** a special ceremony ▪ a number of religious *ceremonials*

cer·e·mo·ni·ous /ˌserəˈmounijəs/ *adj* [*more ~; most ~*] **:** formal and serious **:** suitable for a ceremony ▪ She read the announcement in a very *ceremonious* way. ▪ a *ceremonious* entrance — compare UNCEREMONIOUS

– cer·e·mo·ni·ous·ly *adv*

cer·e·mo·ny /ˈserəˌmouni/ *noun, pl* **-nies**

1 [*count*] **:** a formal act or event that is a part of a social or religious occasion ▪ graduation/wedding *ceremonies* ▪ There will be a *ceremony* honoring the town's veterans next week. — see also MASTER OF CEREMONIES

2 [*noncount*] **:** very polite or formal behavior ▪ With great *ceremony*, the children presented each of the visitors with a gift. ▪ He told them abruptly and ***without ceremony*** that they would have to leave.

stand on ceremony **:** to insist on doing the things that are usual or expected in polite or formal behavior — usually used in negative statements ▪ He doesn't *stand on ceremony*, he gets the job done.

cert /ˈsɚt/ *noun* [*singular*] *Brit, informal* **:** someone or something that is sure to be successful ▪ I've got a *cert* [=*sure thing*] for the next race. ▪ He's a ***dead cert*** [=*sure bet*] for player of the year.

¹cer·tain /ˈsɚtn̩/ *adj*

1 *not used before a noun* [*more ~; most ~*] **:** not having any doubt about something **:** convinced or sure ▪ Are you *certain* [=*sure*] you want to leave today? ▪ I feel less than *certain* about it. [=I am not sure about it] ▪ She's *certain* (that) she can do the job despite her lack of experience. ▪ I'm fairly *certain* that I'll be on time.

2 — used with *it* to say that something is known to be true or correct ▪ Although little is known about these ancient people, *it* is *certain* that they grew a number of crops. ▪ *It*'s not *certain* [=*definite*] that the company will lay off workers. [=the company may lay off workers, but it also may not] ▪ *It* seems *certain* that the jury will convict him.

3 — used to say that something will definitely happen or that someone will definitely do something ▪ Before the game was half over our team's defeat was nearly *certain*. ▪ Contact with the poison means *certain* death. ▪ Her victory seems *certain*. — often followed by *to + verb* ▪ As technology develops, the rates of success with the procedure are *certain to improve*. ▪ Health-care costs are *certain* [=*sure*] *to increase* in coming years. ▪ She is almost *certain to win*. ▪ He is ***all but certain to say*** no. [=he will almost surely say no]

4 *always used before a noun* — used to refer to something or someone that is not named specifically ▪ Each employee will receive a *certain* share of the profits. ▪ Building even a simple bookcase takes a *certain* amount of skill. [=takes some skill] ▪ *Certain* people are always late for dinner. ▪ On *certain* days there is no parking on the street. ▪ The new technology has *certain* limitations. ▪ Students must fulfill *certain* requirements to graduate. ▪ She's allergic to *certain* [=*particular*] foods. ▪ The contract can be extended ***under certain circumstances***. [=in some special cases] ▪ ***To a certain extent*** [=up to a point] he's right. ▪ The movie will appeal to people ***of a certain age***. [=people who are no longer young]

a certain **1** — used to refer to a quality that is noticed but that is difficult to explain or describe • She has *a certain* elegance about her. • The house has *a certain* charm. **2** *formal* — used with the name of a person you do not know • In 1889, *a certain* Mr. Kelly made a large donation to the church.

for certain : without a doubt : definitely or certainly • No one knows *for certain* what the outcome will be. • We'll need more than an hour to get there *for certain.* [=*for sure*]

make certain : to do something or find out something so that you have no doubt about whether something is true, correct, will happen, etc. • *Make certain* (that) you lock the door when you leave. = *Make certain* to lock the door when you leave. • We must *make certain* [=*make sure*] this doesn't happen again. • She *made certain* she thanked each of them for coming. — sometimes + *of* • *Make certain of* your flight times [=be sure that you definitely know your flight times] before you leave for the airport.

²**certain** *pronoun, formal* : certain ones : particular members of a group : SOME — + *of* • *Certain of* his assumptions are simply not true. • We know that *certain of* his classmates walk to school every day.

cer·tain·ly /ˈsɚtn̩li/ *adv*
1 : without doubt : DEFINITELY • It will *certainly* rain tomorrow. • This year's festival was *certainly* much better than last year's. • *Certainly* [=*surely*] you can do a better job than that! • I'm *certainly* going to try. • The new version is ***most certainly*** easier to use. • The snake that bit her was ***almost certainly*** poisonous. — sometimes used for emphasis • He didn't get the raise he was hoping for, but he's *certainly* not complaining. • I *certainly* didn't mean to offend anyone.
2 : of course — used to answer questions • "Can I speak to you for a moment?" "*Certainly.*" • "Did I offend you?" "Oh, ***certainly not***" [=no, you did not offend me at all] • "May I join you?" "You ***most certainly*** may."

cer·tain·ty /ˈsɚtn̩ti/ *noun, pl* **-ties**
1 [*noncount*] : the state of being or feeling certain about something • Scientists still do not know with any degree of *certainty* why the disease spread so quickly. • We cannot predict the outcome with absolute/any *certainty*. • There was no *certainty* that the package would arrive in time. • Her *certainty* about these complex moral issues is surprising. • It is difficult to say ***with certainty*** [=in a certain or definite way] which of the plays was written first.
2 [*count*] : something that is certain : a fact about which there is no doubt • We live in a world without *certainties*. [=a world in which things are not certain] • His victory in the election is ***almost a certainty***. [=it is nearly certain/definite that he will win the election]

cer·ti·fi·able /ˈsɚtəˌfajəbəl/ *adj*
1 *informal* : crazy or insane • Anyone who would run in front of a car like that is *certifiable*. • *certifiable* behavior
2 *always used before a noun, chiefly US* : real or genuine : AUTHENTIC • We called in a *certifiable* expert on legal issues. • A handful of cinema's *certifiable* masterpieces are in need of restoration. • a *certifiable* liar

cer·tif·i·cate /sɚˈtɪfɪkət/ *noun, pl* **-cates** [*count*]
1 : a document that is official proof that something has happened — see also BIRTH CERTIFICATE, DEATH CERTIFICATE, MARRIAGE CERTIFICATE
2 : a document that is official proof that you have finished school or a course of training • She has a *certificate* in midwifery. • He earned his teaching *certificate* last year.
3 : a document which shows that you own something • a stock *certificate* — see also GIFT CERTIFICATE

cer·tif·i·cat·ed /sɚˈtɪfɪˌkeɪtəd/ *adj, Brit* : CERTIFIED 1 • a *certificated* teacher

certificate of deposit *noun, pl* **certificates of deposit** [*count*] *chiefly US* : an official document in which a bank promises to pay a specified amount of interest when you deposit money in the bank for a specified period of time — called also *CD*

cer·ti·fi·ca·tion /ˌsɚtəfəˈkeɪʃən/ *noun, pl* **-tions**
1 [*noncount*] : the act of making something official : the act of certifying something • the *certification* of the vote • She had to wait until her *certification* as a nurse before she could start her new job.
2 : official approval to do something professionally or legally [*count*] The *certifications* of nine teachers were revoked. [*noncount*] instructor *certification* • The school offers scuba diving *certification*.

cer·ti·fied /ˈsɚtəˌfaɪd/ *adj*
1 : having met the official requirements that are needed to do particular type of work • a *certified* instructor • You must be *certified* in order to practice medicine. • The carpentry work must be done by someone who is *certified* for the job. • nationally *certified* [=(*Brit*) *certificated*] teachers • a ***board-certified*** doctor [=a doctor whose qualifications have been approved by an official group]
2 *chiefly US* **a** : officially approved as having met a standard • The food/restaurant is *certified* kosher. • *certified* organic vegetables **b** *informal* : real or genuine • a *certified* celebrity • Her boyfriend's a *certified* weirdo.

certified check (*US*) *or Brit* **certified cheque** *noun, pl* ~ **checks** [*count*] : a check that is guaranteed by a bank

certified mail *noun* [*noncount*] *US* : mail for which a person must sign an official document stating that it has been received • He sent the contract by *certified mail*. — called also (*Brit*) *recorded delivery*; compare REGISTERED MAIL

certified public accountant *noun, pl* ~ **-tants** [*count*] *US* : an accountant who has finished the schooling or tests required by law — abbr. *CPA* — called also (*Brit*) *chartered accountant*

cer·ti·fy /ˈsɚtəˌfaɪ/ *verb* **-fies; -fied; -fy·ing** [+ *obj*]
1 : to say officially that something is true, correct, or genuine • A judge must *certify* the contract. • The document has been *certified* by the court.
2 : to say officially that something or someone has met certain standards or requirements • The car dealer *certifies* each car before it is sold. • Has your doctor been *certified*?
3 *chiefly Brit* : to say officially that someone is insane and in need of treatment — often used as *(be) certified* • They *were* both *certified* and spent the next year in hospital.

cer·ti·tude /ˈsɚtəˌtuːd, *Brit* ˈsɜːtəˌtjuːd/ *noun* [*noncount*] : the state of being or feeling certain : freedom from doubt • moral *certitude*

cer·vi·cal /ˈsɚvɪkəl/ *adj, medical*
1 : of or relating to a cervix of the uterus • *cervical* cancer
2 : of or relating to the neck • *cervical* vertebrae

cervical smear *noun, pl* ~ **smears** [*count*] *Brit* : PAP SMEAR

cer·vix /ˈsɚvɪks/ *noun, pl* **-vi·ces** /-vəˌsiːz/ *or* **-vix·es** [*count*] *medical* : the narrow end at the opening of a woman's uterus

ce·sar·e·an *or* **cae·sar·e·an** /sɪˈzerijən/ *noun, pl* **-ans** [*count*] *medical* : CESAREAN SECTION
– cesarean *or* **caesarean** *adj* • a *cesarean* birth

cesarean section *also* **caesarean section** *noun, pl* ~ **-tions** [*count*] *medical* : a surgical operation for giving birth in which a cut is made in the mother's body so that the baby can be removed through the opening — called also *C-section*

ces·sa·tion /sɛˈseɪʃən/ *noun, pl* **-tions** *formal* : a stopping of some action : a pause or stop — often + *of* [*count*] With news of the treaty came a *cessation* of hostilities. [=fighting stopped when the treaty was announced] [*noncount*] Relapses after *cessation of* treatment are common.

ces·sion /ˈsɛʃən/ *noun, pl* **-sions** *formal* : the act of giving up something (such as power, land, or rights) to another person, group, or country [*count*] territorial *cessions* from one state to another • a temporary *cession* [=*yielding*] of local control [*noncount*] The law required *cession* of the land to the heirs.

cess·pit /ˈsɛsˌpɪt/ *noun, pl* **-pits** [*count*] *chiefly Brit* : CESSPOOL

cess·pool /ˈsɛsˌpuːl/ *noun, pl* **-pools** [*count*]
1 : an underground hole or container for holding liquid waste (such as sewage) from a building
2 : a place or situation that is very dirty, evil, or corrupt • The region had become a *cesspool* of pollution. • a *cesspool* of corruption — called also (*chiefly Brit*) *cesspit*

ce·ta·cean /sɪˈteɪʃən/ *noun, pl* **-ceans** [*count*] *technical* : a mammal (such as a whale, dolphin, or porpoise) that lives in the ocean
– cetacean *adj*

cf *abbr* compare — used to direct a reader to another idea, document, etc. • This article takes a new approach to the problems of today's inner cities. (*Cf* Smith's earlier article on the topic.) ✧ *Cf* comes from the Latin *conferre*, which means "to compare."

CFC *abbr* chlorofluorocarbon

CFO *abbr* chief financial officer

CFS *abbr* chronic fatigue syndrome

cg *abbr* centigram
ch *abbr* chapter
Cha·blis /ʃæˈbliː/ *noun, pl* **Chablis** [*count, noncount*] : a type of white wine from France
cha–cha /ˈtʃɑːˌtʃɑː/ *noun, pl* **-chas** [*count*] : a fast dance from Latin America — called also *cha-cha-cha*
chafe /ˈtʃeɪf/ *verb* **chafes; chafed; chaf·ing**
1 [*no obj*] : to become irritated or annoyed : to feel impatient — usually + *against, at,* or *under* • After working outdoors for years, he *chafed at* being stuck in an office all day. • Local builders are *chafing under* the new regulations. • She *chafed against* the strict policies of the school.
2 a : to cause soreness or damage by rubbing against something (such as your skin) [+ *obj*] When the strap is too tight, it *chafes* the baby's skin. [*no obj*] If my boots aren't laced up tight they *chafe.* **b** [*no obj*] : to become sore or damaged from rubbing • The baby's skin will *chafe* if the strap is too tight.
chaff /ˈtʃæf, *Brit* ˈtʃɑːf/ *noun* [*noncount*] : the seed coverings and other plant parts that cannot be eaten and are removed from grain
separate the wheat from the chaff see [2]SEPARATE
chaf·finch /ˈtʃæˌfɪntʃ/ *noun, pl* **-finches** [*count*] : a small European bird
chaf·ing dish /ˈtʃeɪfɪŋ-/ *noun, pl* ~ **dishes** [*count*] : a dish that is used for cooking or warming food at the table
cha·grin /ʃəˈgrɪn, *Brit* ˈʃægrɪn/ *noun* [*noncount*] : a feeling of being frustrated or annoyed because of failure or disappointment • The fact that he'd been unable to attend the funeral was a source of *chagrin* for Ted. • She had gained five pounds over the winter, much ***to her chagrin***. • He decided to get a tattoo, *to the chagrin* of his parents.
cha·grined *also* **cha·grinned** /ʃəˈgrɪnd, *Brit* ˈʃægrɪnd/ *adj* [*more* ~; *most* ~] *formal* : frustrated or annoyed : feeling chagrin • They were *chagrined* to find (that) no more rooms were available at the hotel.
[1]**chain** /ˈtʃeɪn/ *noun, pl* **chains**
1 a : a series of usually metal links or rings that are connected to each other in a line and used for supporting heavy things, for holding things together, for decoration, etc. [*count*] The neighbor's dog is kept on a *chain.* [=is connected to a chain that keeps it from getting away] • She wore a beautiful gold *chain* [=*necklace*] around her neck. • the ship's anchor *chain* • a bicycle *chain* [*noncount*] We'll need 25 feet of *chain* for the pulley. — see pictures on page C11 and at BICYCLE; see also CHOKE CHAIN, KEY CHAIN **b** [*count*] : a chain that is attached to the arms or legs of a prisoner — usually plural • The prisoners were kept ***in chains*** while being transferred to the new jail. — often used figuratively • The contract would keep the employees *in chains,* unable to leave the company for at least five years. — see also BALL AND CHAIN
2 [*count*] : a series or group of things or people that are connected to each other in some way • a *chain* of islands • The world's longest ***mountain chain*** [=group of mountains that form a long line] is the Andes. • The new book chronicles ***the chain of events*** leading up to the crime. • Protesters formed ***a human chain*** [=they stood next to each other with their arms linked] around the ancient tree to prevent it from being cut down. — see also DAISY CHAIN, FOOD CHAIN
3 [*count*] : a group of businesses (such as stores, restaurants, or hotels) that have the same name and basic appearance and sell the same products or services • They own a *chain* of organic grocery stores. • fast-food/clothing *chains; also* : the company that owns such a group of businesses • The hotel *chain* recently opened a new hotel in Hong Kong. — see also CHAIN STORE
4 [*count*] *Brit* : a number of people who each want to buy a house but must first sell their current house before moving to the next one — usually singular • Both houses are currently vacant so there is no *chain* to worry about.
pull the chain *Brit* : to flush a toilet
pull/yank someone's chain *US, informal* : to deceive someone in a friendly or playful way • I thought he really won the lottery but he was only *pulling my chain.* [=he was only playing a joke on me]
[2]**chain** *verb* **chains; chained; chain·ing** [+ *obj*] : to fasten, hold, or connect (someone or something) with a chain • She *chained* her bicycle to the post and went inside. — often used as *(be) chained* • The neighbor's dog *is* kept *chained* (up) in the yard. • The prisoners *were chained* together. — often used figuratively • Many office workers spend the day *chained* to the computer. [=they work with a computer all day] • He hopes to spend less time *chained* to his desk.
chain gang *noun, pl* ~ **gangs** [*count*] : a group of prisoners who are chained together while they do work outside the prison
chain letter *noun, pl* ~ **-ters** [*count*] : a letter that is sent to a certain number of people and that asks each of those people to send a copy of the letter to the same number of people
chain–link fence *noun, pl* ~ **fences** [*count*] : a fence of heavy steel wire that is woven to form a pattern of large diamond-shaped spaces
chain mail *noun* [*noncount*] : a kind of protective clothing (called armor) that is made up of many tiny metal rings that are linked together and that was worn by knights and soldiers in the Middle Ages
chain of command *noun, pl* **chains of command** [*count*] : a series of positions of authority or rank within an organization that are ordered from lowest to highest • In the United States, the President as the commander in chief is at the head of the military *chain of command.*
chain reaction *noun, pl* ~ **-tions** [*count*]
1 : a series of events in which each event causes the next one : a series of events caused by one single event • Increased oil prices could trigger a *chain reaction* in the economy.
2 *technical* : a chemical or nuclear change that causes other changes of the same kind to happen
chain saw *noun, pl* ~ **saws** [*count*] : a tool that cuts wood with a circular chain that is driven by a motor and made up of many connected sharp metal teeth

chain saw

chain–smoke /ˈtʃeɪnˌsmoʊk/ *verb* **-smokes; -smoked; -smoking** : to smoke cigarettes continuously one after another [*no obj*] He *chain-smokes* when he's under a lot of stress. [+ *obj*] She's been *chain-smoking* cigarettes for years.
– chain–smok·er *noun, pl* **-ers** [*count*]
chain store *noun, pl* ~ **stores** [*count*] : a store that has the same name and basic appearance as other stores that sell the same kind of goods and are owned by the same company
[1]**chair** /ˈtʃeɚ/ *noun, pl* **chairs**
1 [*count*] : a seat for one person that has a back and usually four legs • a *chair* by the window • We'll need a table and four *chairs* for the dining room. • Please ***pull up a chair*** [=bring a chair to where we are] and join us.
2 [*count*] **a :** the person who is the leader of a department at a college or university • He is now *chair* of the English department. **b :** the person who is the leader of a meeting, organization, committee, or event • She's *chair* of the school board this year. • Address any questions to the committee *chair.* — see also CHAIRMAN, CHAIRPERSON, CHAIRWOMAN
3 ***the chair*** *US, informal* : ELECTRIC CHAIR • a murderer who was sentenced/sent to *the chair*
[2]**chair** *verb* **chairs; chaired; chair·ing** [+ *obj*] : to be in charge of a meeting, organization, committee, or event : to be the chairperson of (something) • He's been chosen to *chair* the task force on school violence.
chair·lift /ˈtʃeɚˌlɪft/ *noun, pl* **-lifts** [*count*] : a series of seats that hang from a moving cable and that carry people (such as skiers) up and down a mountain
chair·man /ˈtʃeɚmən/ *noun, pl* **-men** /-mən/ [*count*]
1 : the person (especially a man) who is in charge of a meeting, committee, or event • He's the new *chairman* [=*chair, chairperson*] of the task force on school violence.
2 : the person who is in charge of a company or organization • the *chairman* of the airline company
chair·man·ship /ˈtʃeɚmənˌʃɪp/ *noun, pl* **-ships** [*count*] : the position of a chairperson : the position of being the leader of an organization, committee, etc. • He volunteered for the committee *chairmanship.* • She took over the *chairmanship* of the company from her father.
chair·per·son /ˈtʃeɚˌpɚsn̩/ *noun, pl* **-sons** [*count*] : the person who leads a meeting, organization, committee, or event : CHAIR • A new *chairperson* for the committee has not yet been appointed.
chair·wom·an /ˈtʃeɚˌwʊmən/ *noun, pl* **-wom·en** /-ˌwɪmən/ [*count*] : a woman who leads a meeting, organization, committee, or event : CHAIR

chaise longue /ˈʃeɪz-ˈlɑːŋ/ *noun, pl* **chaise longues** *or* **chaises longues** /ˈʃeɪzˈlɑːŋ/ [*count*]
1 : a long low chair with a back along half its length and one arm
2 *US* **:** a long chair with a back that can be moved so that you can sit up or lie down — called also (*US*) *chaise lounge*

chaise longue

cha·let /ʃæˈleɪ/ *noun, pl* **-lets** [*count*]
1 : a type of house that has a steep roof that extends past the walls • We stayed overnight at a ski *chalet*. ✧ Chalets were originally built in Switzerland and are common where there are mountains and a lot of snow.
2 *Brit* **:** a small house often in a group of similar houses where people go for vacations

chalet

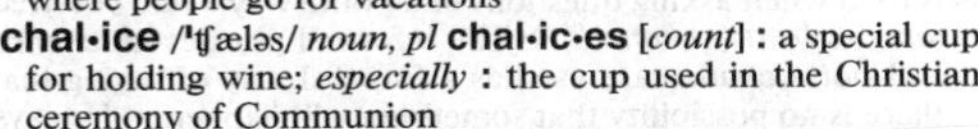

chal·ice /ˈʧæləs/ *noun, pl* **chal·ic·es** [*count*] **:** a special cup for holding wine; *especially* **:** the cup used in the Christian ceremony of Communion
poisoned chalice *chiefly Brit* **:** something that seems attractive at first but becomes unpleasant • Working as store manager was a *poisoned chalice* as it became more and more difficult to be the boss of her friends.

[1]**chalk** /ˈʧɑːk/ *noun, pl* **chalks**
1 [*noncount*] **:** a type of soft, light-colored rock ✧ Chalk is a kind of limestone.
2 a [*noncount*] **:** a substance that is made into white or colored sticks and used for writing or drawing • The teacher handed her a piece of *chalk* and asked her to write the answer on the chalkboard. • He put *chalk* marks on the stage to show the actors where they should stand. • a *chalk* drawing [=a drawing done with chalk] **b** [*count*] **:** a piece of chalk • They drew pictures on the sidewalk with colored *chalks*.
not by a long chalk *Brit* **:** not at all • Our work isn't done yet, *not by a long chalk*. [=(*US*) *not by a long shot*; we still have a lot more work to do]
– chalky /ˈʧɑːki/ *adj* **chalk·i·er**; **chalk·i·est** [*also more* ~; *most* ~] • *chalky* white [=the color of white chalk] • *chalky* soil [=soil that has chalk in it]

[2]**chalk** *verb* **chalks**; **chalked**; **chalk·ing** [+ *obj*]
1 : to write or draw (something) with chalk • She *chalked* a message on the side of the barn.
2 : to mark (something) with chalk • He *chalked* the stage to show the actors where they should stand.
chalk up [*phrasal verb*] ***chalk (something) up*** *or* ***chalk up (something)*** **1 :** to earn or achieve (something) **:** to accumulate (something) • As a runner, he's *chalked up* about 1,000 miles on the track. • The company has *chalked up* huge losses this quarter. **2** *Brit* **:** to charge (the cost of drinks or food) to your account to be paid for later • *Chalk up* these drinks to my account, please. **3** ***chalk (something) up to (something)*** *chiefly US* **:** to explain (something) by stating its cause **:** to say that (something) was caused by (something) • *Chalk* it *up* to bad timing. • Her early mistakes can be *chalked up* to inexperience.

chalk·board /ˈʧɑːkˌboɚd/ *noun, pl* **-boards** [*count*] *chiefly US* **:** BLACKBOARD

[1]**chal·lenge** /ˈʧæləndʒ/ *verb* **-leng·es**; **-lenged**; **-leng·ing** [+ *obj*]
1 : to say or show that (something) may not be true, correct, or legal **:** DISPUTE • A number of doctors are *challenging* the study's claims. • The new lawsuit *challenges* the lower court's decision. • The new data *challenges* many old assumptions. [=the new data gives people reasons to doubt many old assumptions]
2 a : to question the action or authority of (someone) • She's been *challenged* on her handling of the problem. • None of them were willing to *challenge* the referee on the call. **b** *law* **:** to question whether (someone) should serve on a jury • *challenge* a juror
3 : to test the ability, skill, or strength of (someone or something) **:** to be difficult enough to be interesting to (someone) • It's a game that will *challenge* a child's imagination. • The work doesn't *challenge* him anymore, and he's often bored.
4 : to invite (someone) to compete in a game, fight, etc. — usually + *to* • I *challenge* you *to* a game of chess. • The duke *challenged* him *to* a duel.
5 : to order (someone) to stop and prove who he or she is • The sentry *challenged* the stranger at the gate.
– chal·leng·er *noun, pl* **-ers** [*count*] • He hopes to be the governor's *challenger* in the next election. [=the candidate running against the governor] • The boxing match pitted the two-time champion against his *challenger*.

[2]**challenge** *noun, pl* **challenges**
1 : a difficult task or problem **:** something that is hard to do [*count*] The next major *challenge* for the company is to improve its distribution capabilities. • Teaching adolescents can be quite a *challenge*. • The band feels ready for new *challenges*. • If he takes on the new project he will face the greatest *challenge* of his career. • Passing the test was hardly a *challenge* [=was very easy] for her. • The coach is confident that you will ***rise to the challenge***. [=the coach is confident that you will succeed] • Management is seeking ways to better ***meet the challenge*** of future growth. [*noncount*] The ski slope offers a high degree of *challenge*.
2 [*count*] **:** an action, statement, etc., that is against something **:** a refusal to accept something as true, correct, or legal — often + *to* • The lawsuit is a *challenge to* the lower court's decision. • Both teachers have had to deal with many *challenges to* their authority.
3 [*count*] **a :** an invitation to compete in a game, fight, etc. • Do you accept my *challenge* to a game of chess? **b :** an attempt to defeat someone in a competition • The senator may face a *challenge* from within her own party.
4 [*count*] **:** an order to someone to stop and say who he or she is • The intruder fled at the sentry's *challenge*.

challenged *adj, chiefly US* **:** having a physical or mental problem that makes it difficult to do things as easily as other people do — used as a polite way to say that a person has a disability • She has worked as an advocate for the mentally and physically *challenged*. [=*disabled*] — sometimes used in a joking way • People call me short, but I prefer the term "vertically *challenged*."

chal·leng·ing /ˈʧæləndʒɪŋ/ *adj* [*more* ~; *most* ~] **:** difficult in a way that is usually interesting or enjoyable • I find the job *challenging* and fun. • Teaching is *challenging* but rewarding work. • It's a *challenging* book that requires careful reading. • The slope was *challenging* for even the most experienced climbers.
– chal·leng·ing·ly *adv*

cham·ber /ˈʧeɪmbɚ/ *noun, pl* **-bers** [*count*]
1 : a small space inside something (such as a machine or your body) • He put three bullets into the *chamber* of the gun. • the *chambers* of the heart
2 : a usually large room where members of a government group (such as a legislature) have meetings • We waited for the senator outside the Senate *chamber*.
3 : a group of people who form part of a government • The U.S. legislature is separated into two *chambers*: the Senate and the House of Representatives. • the upper and lower *chambers* of the British Parliament [=the House of Lords and the House of Commons] — see also CHAMBER OF COMMERCE
4 : a room where a judge goes to do official business or to discuss cases with lawyers outside of the courtroom — usually plural • the judge's *chambers*
5 *formal* + *old-fashioned* **:** a person's bedroom or other private room • the queen's personal *chambers* • a bridal *chamber* [=a bedroom used by two people who have just been married] • the temple's inner *chambers*
6 : a room used for a special purpose • the burial *chambers* inside an Egyptian pyramid • a torture *chamber* — see also GAS CHAMBER
– cham·bered /ˈʧeɪmbɚd/ *adj* • a six-*chambered* gun [=a gun with six chambers]

cham·ber·maid /ˈʧeɪmbɚˌmeɪd/ *noun, pl* **-maids** [*count*] **:** a woman who cleans bedrooms in hotels

chamber music *noun* [*noncount*] **:** classical music written for a small number of musicians

chamber of commerce *noun, pl* **chambers of commerce** [*count*] **:** a group of businesspeople who work together to try to help businesses in their town or city • The event is sponsored by your local *chamber of commerce*.

chamber orchestra *noun, pl* ~ **-tras** [*count*] **:** a small group of musicians who play classical music together

chamber pot *noun, pl* ~ **pots** [*count*] **:** a container that is kept in a bedroom and that is used as a toilet

cha·me·leon /kəˈmiːljən/ *noun, pl* **-leons** [*count*]
1 : a type of lizard that can change the color of its skin to look like the colors that are around it
2 *usually disapproving* **:** a person who often changes his or her beliefs or behavior in order to please others or to succeed • She's a political *chameleon.* [=she often changes her political beliefs]

C

cham·ois *noun, pl* **chamois**
1 /ʃæmˈwɑː/ [*count*] **:** a small animal that looks like a goat and that lives on mountains in Europe and western Asia
2 /ˈʃæmi/ **a** [*noncount*] **:** soft leather that is made from the skin of goats, sheep, or chamois — called also (*Brit*) *chamois leather* **b** [*count*] **:** a piece of chamois used especially for cleaning windows and cars • a bucket of water and a *chamois*
3 /ˈʃæmi/ [*noncount*] *US* **:** a type of cotton cloth that looks or feels like soft leather — often used before another noun • a *chamois* shirt

cham·o·mile *or* **cam·o·mile** /ˈkæməˌmajəl/ *noun* [*noncount*] **:** a plant that has a strong smell and small white and yellow flowers that are often used in making tea and medicine • *chamomile* tea

[1]**champ** /ˈʧæmp/ *noun, pl* **champs** [*count*] *informal* **:** CHAMPION • this year's national basketball *champs*

[2]**champ** *verb* **champs; champed; champ·ing :** to bite and chew on (something) in a noisy way **:** CHOMP [+ *obj*] He *champed* his pipe angrily. • The horse was *champing* its bit. [*no obj*] He *champed* on his pipe angrily.
champing at the bit **:** waiting in an impatient way to do something • We've all been *champing at the bit* to get started on the project.

cham·pagne /ʃæmˈpeın/ *noun, pl* **-pagnes** [*count, noncount*] **:** a French white wine that has many bubbles and that people often drink on special occasions

cham·pers /ˈʃæmpəz/ *noun* [*noncount*] *Brit, informal* **:** CHAMPAGNE • a glass of *champers*

[1]**cham·pi·on** /ˈʧæmpijən/ *noun, pl* **-ons** [*count*]
1 : someone or something (such as a team or an animal) that has won a contest or competition especially in sports • tennis *champions* • the heavyweight boxing *champion* of the world • Our team will play the defending/reigning/current *champions* next week. • the newly crowned national/world/Olympic *champions* — often used before another noun • a *champion* boxer/skier/swimmer • *champion* racehorses
2 : someone who fights or speaks publicly in support of a person, belief, cause, etc. • He was a *champion* for the working classes. — often + *of* • She was a lawyer and a *champion of* children's rights.

[2]**champion** *verb* **-ons; -oned; -on·ing** [+ *obj*] **:** to fight or speak publicly in support of (a person, belief, cause, etc.) • She is a lawyer who *champions* children's rights. • Our senator *championed* the idea of lowering taxes.

cham·pi·on·ship /ˈʧæmpijənˌʃıp/ *noun, pl* **-ships** [*count*]
1 : an important competition that decides which player or team is the best in a particular sport, game, etc. • the heavyweight boxing *championship* — often plural • We made it to the basketball *championships* this year, but we lost in the final game. — often used before another noun • a *championship* game/race/match/competition
2 : the title of champion in a sport or game • The team hasn't won a *championship* in 30 years. • This year she'll be defending the *championship.* = She'll try to win the *championship* again.

[1]**chance** /ˈʧæns, *Brit* ˈʧɑːns/ *noun, pl* **chanc·es**
1 : an opportunity to do something **:** an amount of time or a situation in which something can be done [*count*] I wanted to call you, but I never got/had the *chance* (to). • I go to the beach every *chance* I get. [=I go whenever I can] • This is the *chance* of a lifetime! • You missed your *chance.* • Everyone deserves a fair *chance* of winning the award. • If you give me a *chance,* I know I can do a good job. • He doesn't give ***second chances*** [=opportunities to try something again after failing one time] • If ***given half a chance*** [=if given some opportunity], she could show everyone how talented she is. — often followed by *to + verb* • Here's your *chance to try* something new. • Give me a *chance to explain.* • You have to give the wound a *chance to heal.* [=you have to allow time for the wound to heal] [*noncount*] We didn't have much *chance to talk* about it. ✧ To ***jump/leap/grab at the chance to do something*** is to have an opportunity to do something and to say in an excited way that you will do it or to do it in a very eager way. • She *jumped at the chance* to go to New York City. ✧ If you have a ***fighting chance*** to do something, you may be able to do it by making a great effort. • The patient still has a *fighting chance* to survive. • Their help gave us a *fighting chance* to finish the project on time.
2 : the possibility that something will happen [*count*] There's a good *chance* that we'll finish on time. • There's still a ***slim chance*** [=a small possibility] that we can win. • There's an ***outside chance*** [=a small possibility] that something could go wrong. • ***Chances are*** [=it is very likely that] she has already heard the news. — often + *of* • It increases/reduces the *chance of* getting the disease. • There's a 50 percent *chance of* rain this afternoon. • (*Brit, informal*) The challenger may not have much experience, but I still think he's ***in with a chance of*** winning. [=he has a possibility of winning] — often plural • What are the *chances* [=how likely is it] that we'll have nice weather today? • I think her *chances* of winning the election are good. • "How do you think the team will do this year?" "I ***like their chances***." [=I think they have a good chance of succeeding/winning] [*noncount*] If you are free tonight, is there any *chance* you could join me for dinner? — often + *of* • If you want to have any *chance of* getting the job, you'll have to dress nicely. • The prisoners had little/no *chance of* escape/escaping. ✧ The phrase ***by any chance*** is used when asking questions in a polite way. • Are you free tonight, *by any chance*? ✧ The informal phrases ***fat chance*** and ***not a chance*** are used as a forceful way of saying that there is no possibility that something will happen. • "He says that he'll get here on time." "*Fat chance*!" • "Do you think they'll win?" "*Not a chance*!" • *Fat chance* of that happening!
3 [*noncount*] **:** the way that events happen when they are not planned or controlled by people **:** LUCK • There is an element of *chance* [=*luck*] to winning a card game. • Which cards you're given is simply a matter of *chance.* • We planned for everything and ***left nothing to chance*** [=we prepared for everything possible] • That's not the kind of thing you want to ***leave to chance*** [=that's not the kind of thing you don't want to plan or prepare for] ✧ If something happens ***by chance***, people have not planned it or tried to make it happen. • *By* (pure/sheer) *chance,* I saw him again at the grocery store. • We found the house entirely *by chance.* ✧ The phrase ***as chance would have it*** is used to say that something happened because of good or bad luck. • Our car broke down on the road, but *as chance would have it* [=*as it turned out*], there was a garage nearby. ✧ A ***game of chance*** is a game (such as a dice game) in which luck rather than skill decides who wins. • *Games of chance* are illegal in some states.
chance would be a fine thing *Brit, informal* — used to say that something good or desirable is not likely to happen • This candidate promises to solve all the country's financial problems in six months. *Chance would be a fine thing*! [=if only that were possible]
on the off chance — used to talk about something that might happen or be true but that is not likely • I called his office *on the off chance* that he would still be there [=I called because I thought there was a slight chance that he would still be there], but he had already left.
stand a chance **:** to have a possibility of succeeding • The team *stands a chance* of doing well this year. • I think she ***stands a good chance*** of winning the election. — often used in negative statements • He ***doesn't stand a chance*** against the champion. • She ***stands no chance*** of winning. [=she has no chance of winning]
take a chance **:** to do something that could have either good or bad results • She's trying to find a publisher who will *take a chance* on her book. [=will publish her book without knowing for certain that it will succeed] • It might not work, but it's a *chance* we'll have to *take.* • I'm not willing to *take that chance.* • He said he couldn't afford to *take any chances.* • He's not afraid to ***take chances*** [=to do things that are risky or dangerous] • She ***was taking no chances*** = She ***wasn't taking any chances*** • "You might not succeed." "I know, but I'll ***take my chances*** anyway."

[2]**chance** *verb* **chances; chanced; chanc·ing**
1 [+ *obj*] **:** to accept the danger of (doing something) **:** RISK • We knew that the trip was dangerous, but we decided to *chance* it. [=we decided to go on the trip] • He couldn't *chance* playing with a broken toe.
2 [*no obj*] *formal* — used to describe something that happens because of luck or chance; followed by *to + verb* • It *chanced* [=(more commonly) *happened*] *to rain* that day. • We *chanced to arrive* at the same time. • a conversation that

chanced to take place outside my apartment

chance upon *also* **chance on** [*phrasal verb*] **chance upon/on (someone or something)** *formal* : to find (something) or meet (someone) by chance • She *chanced upon* an original copy of the book in her grandfather's attic. • We *chanced upon* a good restaurant.

chance your arm *Brit, informal* : to take a chance : to do something that could have bad results • The newspaper *chanced its arm* by printing the story.

[3]**chance** *adj, always used before a noun* : happening without being planned or controlled by people : happening by chance • It was a *chance* encounter/meeting between the two men. • a *chance* event/occurrence/discovery

chan·cel /ˈʧænsəl, *Brit* ˈʧɑːnsəl/ *noun, pl* **-cels** [*count*] : the part of a church that contains the altar and seats for the priest and choir

chan·cel·lery *or* **chan·cel·lory** /ˈʧænsələri, *Brit* ˈʧɑːnsələri/ *noun, pl* **-ler·ies** *or* **-lor·ies** [*count*]
1 : the department of a chancellor or the building where a chancellor's office is located • The prime minister will speak at the State *Chancellery* this afternoon.
2 : the people who work in the department of a chancellor • greeted by members of the *chancellery*

chan·cel·lor /ˈʧænsələ, *Brit* ˈʧɑːnsələ/ *noun, pl* **-lors** [*count*]
1 : the highest government official in Germany and Austria • Germany's *Chancellor* Helmut Kohl
2 a : the head of some U.S. universities • the new *chancellor* of the university **b** : the head of a British university who represents the school but who does not have many responsibilities
3 *Brit* : CHANCELLOR OF THE EXCHEQUER
4 : a judge in some U.S. courts

Chancellor of the Exchequer *noun, pl* **Chancellors of the Exchequer** [*count*] : an official in the British government who is in charge of taxes and the money that the government spends

chanc·er /ˈʧænsə, *Brit* ˈʧɑːnsə/ *noun, pl* **-ers** [*count*] *Brit, informal + disapproving* : someone who takes chances and often does improper things to get an advantage over other people

chan·cery /ˈʧænsəri, *Brit* ˈʧɑːnsəri/ *noun* [*singular*]
1 : a government office where public documents are kept
2 a : a type of court in the U.S. **b** ***Chancery*** : a part of the High Court in England and Wales
3 : the office of a group of people who represent their country in a foreign country : the office of an embassy

chancy /ˈʧænsi, *Brit* ˈʧɑːnsi/ *adj* **chanc·i·er; -est** [*also more ~; most ~*] *informal* : possibly having a bad result : involving chance or risk : RISKY • Building your own home is a *chancy* business. • Opening a new restaurant can be *chancy*.

chan·de·lier /ˌʃændəˈliə/ *noun, pl* **-liers** [*count*] : a large, decorated light that hangs from a ceiling and has branches for holding many light bulbs or candles • the dining room *chandelier* — see picture at LIGHTING

[1]**change** /ˈʧeɪnʤ/ *verb* **chang·es; changed; chang·ing**
1 a [*no obj*] : to become different • Her mood *changes* every hour. • He's *changed* in appearance. = His appearance has *changed*. • The leaves *change* (in color) from green to red in the fall. • The cars were stopped, waiting for the light/lights to *change* (from red to green). • My, how you've *changed*! • He *changed* from an optimist to/into a pessimist. • The town has *changed* little in recent years. • the *changing* times • the ever-*changing* [=constantly changing] fashions of teenagers **b** [*+ obj*] : to make (someone or something) different • These events have *changed* me in my attitude to/toward life. • He's *changed* his appearance with a new haircut. = His new haircut has *changed* his appearance. • You can't *change* human nature. • Life *changed* him from an optimist into a pessimist. • The leaves ***change color*** from green to red in the fall. — sometimes *+ up* in informal U.S. English • She *changed up* her daily routine. • We need to *change* things *up* a little. **c** [*no obj*] : to become something else — usually *+ to* or *into* • Winter *changed to/into* spring. • The magician made the rope *change into* a ribbon and then *change* back *into* a rope.
2 a : to replace one thing or person with another [*+ obj*] She *changed* her name when she got married. • We'll have a better view if we *change* our seats for better ones. [=if we move to better seats] • Could you *change* my appointment (from Monday) to Friday? • *change* a record/CD • France has *changed* its monetary unit from the franc to the euro. • She's thinking about *changing* jobs/dentists. [=about leaving her current job/dentist and going to a new one] • *change* the channel on the TV • ***change a (flat) tire*** [=replace a flat tire with one that is not flat] • Let's ***change the subject***. [=let's talk about a different subject] • I've ***changed my opinion/views*** on that subject. [=my opinion on that subject is different now from what it was before] • The police did not believe her because she had ***changed her story***. [=she said something different from what she had said before] [*no obj*] While watching TV, he would constantly *change* from one channel to another. • France has *changed* from the franc to the euro. • The U.S. has been slow to *change* to the metric system. **b** : to move from one position, place, etc., to another [*+ obj*] Mary *changed* [=*exchanged, switched*] places/seats with John. = John and Mary *changed* places/seats (with each other). • He may be rich and famous but I wouldn't *change* places with him for anything in the world. • He was opposed to the project at first, but then he ***changed sides*** and voted in favor of it. [*no obj*] Neither of them liked his seat so they *changed* with each other.
3 [*+ obj*] **a** : to exchange one kind of money for another kind • *change* money from dollars into pounds = *change* dollars into/for pounds **b** : to exchange a larger bill for an equal amount in smaller bills or coins • I need to *change* [=*break*] a $10 bill: can you give me a five and five ones?
4 a : to put on different clothes [*no obj*] Let me *change* out of this suit into something more comfortable. • Do they still *change* (to more formal clothes) for dinner? • I'll need a few minutes to *change* before we go out. [*+ obj*] I'll need a few minutes to ***change my clothes*** before we go out. **b** [*+ obj*] : to put clean clothes on (a baby) • ***change a baby*** = *change* a baby's diaper [=remove a baby's dirty diaper and replace it with a clean one] **c** [*+ obj*] : to put a fresh covering on (a bed) • ***change a bed*** = *change* the sheets on a bed [=remove dirty sheets from a bed and replace them with clean ones]
5 : to move from one plane, train, etc., to another in order to continue a journey [*+ obj*] We'll have to *change* planes in Chicago. [=we'll have to get on another plane in Chicago] [*no obj*] On the bus trip he had to *change* twice.

change around *or Brit* ***change round*** [*phrasal verb*] ***change (something) around/round or change around/round (something)*** : to change the order or positions of the parts of (something) • When I got back everything in my office had been *changed around*. • The schedule has been *changed around* a little.

change down [*phrasal verb*] *Brit* : to change to a lower gear in a motor vehicle : DOWNSHIFT • *Change down* to go uphill.

change gear/gears see [1]GEAR

change hands : to go from one owner to another • The property has *changed hands* many times in recent decades. [=the property has been sold many times] • The restaurant recently *changed hands*. [=the restaurant was recently bought by a new owner]

change horses in midstream see [1]HORSE

change over [*phrasal verb*] ***change over or change (something) over or change over (something)*** : to go from one system, method, etc., to another or to change (one system, method, etc.) to another • It will take a week to *change over* from the old computer network to the new one. • It will take a week to *change* the old computer network *over* to the new one. — see also CHANGEOVER

change someone's/your mind see [1]MIND

change up [*phrasal verb*] *Brit* : to change to a higher gear in a motor vehicle : UPSHIFT • *Change up* on the highway. — see also [1]CHANGE 1b (above)

change your tune see [1]TUNE

change your ways see [1]WAY

– chang·er *noun, pl* **-ers** [*count*] • a CD *changer* • a money *changer*

[2]**change** *noun, pl* **changes**
1 : the act, process, or result of changing: such as **a** : the act of becoming different or of causing someone or something to become different [*noncount*] There has been little if any *change* in her daily routine. • You shouldn't be afraid of *change*. *Change* is a natural part of life. • The terms of this contract are subject to *change* without notice. [=the terms can be changed at any time] [*count*] The years have brought many *changes* to the town's economy. • We need to make some *changes* in/to the system. • Many voters believe that it's time for a *change*. • We've had to make a slight *change* in the schedule. • There has been a *change* in/to our plans. = There's been a ***change of plan***. [=we have changed our plans] • ***a change for the better*** [=an improvement] • ***a change for***

C

the worse — see also SEA CHANGE **b** [*count*] : the act of replacing one thing with another ▪ a *change* of address/name ▪ *changes* of mood/attitude/tone ▪ I enjoy the ***change of seasons*** every year. [=I enjoy seeing the seasons change from winter to spring, etc.] ▪ The car needs an ***oil change***. [=needs to have the old, dirty oil removed and replaced with clean oil] **c** [*count*] : the act of moving from one plane, train, etc., to another in order to continue a journey ▪ If you take this flight you'll need to make a *change* (of planes) in Chicago. [=you'll need to change planes in Chicago]
2 [*singular*] : something that is different from what is usual or expected ▪ We've been so busy that a quiet day at home was a welcome *change*. ▪ We eat at home a lot, so dining out sometimes is/makes a nice *change*. ▪ (*chiefly Brit*) So you've done the cooking for once in your life! Well, that ***makes a change***! ▪ I've been stuck here in the city for months. I could really use ***a change of scene/scenery***. = (*chiefly Brit*) I could really use a ***change of air***. [=I would like to go somewhere else for a time] — see also FOR A CHANGE (below)
3 [*noncount*] **a** : smaller bills or coins that are given for a larger bill ▪ Have you got *change* for a $10 bill? **b** : the money returned when a payment is more than the amount needed ▪ It cost $9 and I gave you $10, so I should be getting $1 in *change*. ▪ "It costs $9." "Here's $10. You can ***keep the change***." ▪ (*US*) Can you ***make change*** for a twenty? [=can you give me change if I pay with a $20 bill?] **c** : money in the form of coins ▪ I've got a $10 bill and about $3 in *change*. [=*coins*] ▪ a pocketful of ***loose change*** ▪ The beggar asked us if we had any ***spare change***. [=a small amount of money that we did not need] — see also CHANGE PURSE, SMALL CHANGE **d** *US, informal* : MONEY — used in the phrase ***chunk of change*** ▪ She inherited a large/hefty/nice *chunk of change* [=a large amount of money] from her aunt.
4 [*count*] : a clean set of clothes that someone can wear if they are needed ▪ For a weekend in the country you'll need several *changes* of clothes. ▪ The only extra clothes he took with him were a pair of socks and a *change* of underwear.
5 [*count*] *baseball, informal* : CHANGEUP ▪ The batter struck out on a straight *change*.
6 ***the change*** *informal + old-fashioned* : CHANGE OF LIFE ▪ women who are going through *the change*
and change *US, informal* : and a very small additional amount ▪ There's only six minutes *and change* left in the game. [=there's only a little more than six minutes left in the game]
for a change : as something different from what is usual ▪ Let's eat out *for a change*. ▪ Why don't you help me out *for a change* instead of me always helping you?!
ring the changes see [3]RING

change·able /ˈʧeɪnʤəbəl/ *adj* [*more* ~; *most* ~]
1 : able to change or to be changed ▪ The terms of this contract are easily *changeable*.
2 : changing often or suddenly ▪ *changeable* weather ▪ *changeable* and unreliable people
– **change·abil·i·ty** /ˌʧeɪnʤəˈbɪləti/ *also* **change·able·ness** /ˈʧeɪnʤəbəlnəs/ *noun* [*noncount*] ▪ the *changeability* of the weather

change·less /ˈʧeɪnʤləs/ *adj* : never changing : always staying the same ▪ the *changeless* [=*unchanging*] rhythms of nature ▪ *changeless* [=*constant*] values
– **change·less·ly** *adv* – **change·less·ness** *noun* [*noncount*]

change·ling /ˈʧeɪnʤlɪŋ/ *noun, pl* **-lings** [*count*] *in stories* : a baby that is secretly left to replace another baby

change of heart *noun* [*singular*] : an important change in the way a person feels or thinks about something ▪ He had planned to retire but he had a sudden *change of heart* and decided to continue working.

change of life *noun*
the change of life *somewhat old-fashioned* : MENOPAUSE ▪ women approaching or going through *the change of life*

change of pace *noun, pl* **changes of pace** [*count*]
1 : a new activity or situation that comes after another activity or situation which has lasted for long time — usually singular ▪ He took a few days off work to give himself a welcome and much-needed *change of pace*.
2 *baseball* : CHANGEUP — usually singular ▪ The batter struck out on a *change of pace*.

change·over /ˈʧeɪnʤˌoʊvɚ/ *noun, pl* **-overs** [*count*] : a change from one condition, system, method, etc., to another ▪ Were there any problems during the *changeover* from the franc to the euro? — see also *change over* at [1]CHANGE

change purse *noun, pl* ~ **purses** [*count*] *US* : a very small bag for carrying coins

change·up /ˈʧeɪnʤˌʌp/ *noun, pl* **-ups** [*count*] *baseball* : a slow pitch that is thrown with the same motion as a fastball in order to fool the batter ▪ The batter struck out on a *changeup*.

changing room *noun, pl* ~ **rooms** [*count*] : a room where people can change their clothes in a public place (such as a store); *especially, Brit* : LOCKER ROOM

changing table *noun, pl* ~ **tables** [*count*] : a table used for changing a baby's clothes or diapers

[1]**chan·nel** /ˈʧænl/ *noun, pl* **-nels** [*count*]
1 : a television or radio station ▪ The TV program airs at 8:00 p.m. on *Channel* 5. ▪ Change the *channel*, please. ▪ What is your favorite radio *channel*? ▪ a movie/news/sports *channel*
2 a : a system used for sending something (such as information or supplies) from one place or person to another ▪ E-mail is a *channel* of communication. — often plural ▪ To make a complaint, you will need to go through (the) official/proper *channels*. ▪ the ordinary *channels* of trade ▪ the army's distribution/supply *channels* **b** : a way of expressing your ideas, feelings, etc., to other people ▪ Art provides a *channel* for creativity. ▪ Music became a *channel* for her emotions.
3 : a path, tube, or long narrow place where water flows ▪ A system of irrigation *channels* brings water to the fields.
4 : a deep part of a river, harbor, or other body of water where ships can go ▪ a narrow *channel* of the Mississippi River
5 : a narrow area of the sea between two large areas of land that are close together ▪ We took a ferryboat across the English *Channel* to France.

[2]**channel** *verb* **-nels**; *US* **-neled** *or Brit* **-nelled**; *US* **-nel·ing** *or Brit* **-nel·ling** [+ *obj*]
1 : to express (your ideas, thoughts, feelings, energy, etc.) through a particular behavior or action ▪ She's started *channeling* her anger towards me. — often + *into* ▪ His aggression was *channeled into* playing football. ▪ Actors learn how to *channel* their own emotions *into* their characters.
2 : to send (food, money, etc.) to someone or something ▪ He *channeled* millions of dollars into/to the program. — often + *through* ▪ Food, clothes, and money were *channeled through* churches to the poor people of the village.
3 : to carry and move (something, such as water) in or through a tube, passage, etc. ▪ Their irrigation system *channels* water to the corn fields.
4 : to allow (the spirit of a dead person) to enter your body in order to talk with living people ▪ She said that she was *channeling* my father and that he had a message for me.

channel surfing *noun* [*noncount*] : the activity of using a remote control to change television stations quickly as you look for something to watch — called also *channel-hopping*

[1]**chant** /ˈʧænt, *Brit* ˈʧɑːnt/ *verb* **chants**; **chant·ed**; **chant·ing**
1 : to say (a word or phrase) many times in a rhythmic way usually loudly and with other people [+ *obj*] The crowd began *chanting* her name. ▪ They *chanted* "Sara, Sara" until she came back on stage. [*no obj*] Protesters were *chanting* outside the governor's home.
2 : to sing words and especially religious prayers by using a small number of musical notes that are repeated many times [*no obj*] They were *chanting* in Arabic/Latin/Hebrew/Sanskrit. [+ *obj*] Priests *chanted* the Catholic Mass in Latin.

[2]**chant** *noun, pl* **chants**
1 [*count*] : a word or phrase that is repeated in a rhythmic way usually loudly and by a group of people ▪ Our *chant* was "Peace now, peace now!"
2 : a kind of singing using a small number of musical notes that are repeated many times [*count*] a religious *chant* [*noncount*] *Chant* is often used as a form of meditation and prayer. — see also GREGORIAN CHANT

chan·tey *or* **chan·ty** /ˈʃænti/ *noun, pl* **chan·teys** *or* **chan·ties** [*count*] *US* : SHANTY 2

Chanukah *variant spelling of* HANUKKAH

cha·os /ˈkeɪˌɑːs/ *noun* [*noncount*]
1 : complete confusion and disorder : a state in which behavior and events are not controlled by anything ▪ The loss of electricity caused *chaos* throughout the city. ▪ When the police arrived, the street was in total/complete/absolute *chaos*. ▪ The country had descended into economic *chaos*.
2 : the state of the universe before there was any order and before stars and planets were formed

cha·ot·ic /keɪˈɑːtɪk/ *adj* [*more* ~; *most* ~] : in a state of

complete confusion or disorder • a *chaotic* political race • After he became famous, his life became even more *chaotic*.
– **cha·ot·i·cal·ly** /keɪˈɑːtɪkli/ *adv*

chap /ˈʧæp/ *noun, pl* **chaps** [*count*] *chiefly Brit, informal + somewhat old-fashioned* : a man • He's a friendly sort of *chap*. [=*fellow, guy*] • Don't worry old *chap*. It'll be all right. — see also CHAPS

chap. *abbr* chapter

chap·ar·ral /ˌʃæpəˈræl/ *noun* [*noncount*] *US* : an area of dry land especially in southern California that is covered with bushes and short trees

chap·el /ˈʧæpəl/ *noun, pl* **-els**
1 [*count*] : a small church • a country *chapel* • a wedding *chapel* in Las Vegas
2 [*count*] : a room or small building that is used for private church services or prayer by a family or group • school/hospital/prison *chapels* • the family's private *chapel*
3 [*count*] : a room or area in a church that is used for prayer or small religious services • Church services will be held in the *chapel* this week.
4 [*noncount*] : Christian religious services held in a chapel • At our school, we always went to *chapel* twice a day.

¹chap·er·one *also* **chap·er·on** /ˈʃæpəˌroʊn/ *noun, pl* **-ones** *also* **-ons** [*count*]
1 *US* : someone (such as a teacher or parent) who goes with children on a trip or to a school dance to make sure that the children behave properly • I was a *chaperone* on one of my son's school trips.
2 : a person in the past who went with a young unmarried woman to social events in order to make sure that the woman behaved properly

²chaperone *also* **chaperon** *verb* **-ones** *or* **-ons**; **-oned**; **-on·ing** [+ *obj*] : to be a chaperone to or for (someone or something) • Two parents *chaperoned* the children. • My mom always *chaperoned* the school dances.

chap·lain /ˈʧæplən/ *noun, pl* **-lains** [*count*] : a priest or other Christian religious leader who performs religious services for a military group (such as the army) or for a prison, hospital, etc.

chap·lain·cy /ˈʧæplənsi/ *noun, pl* **-cies** [*count*]
1 : the position or work of a chaplain • He accepted the *chaplaincy*.
2 : the place where a chaplain works

chapped /ˈʧæpt/ *adj* [*more* ~; *most* ~] *of the skin or lips* : red, dry, and cracked usually because of cold air or wind • *chapped* lips/skin

chaps /ˈʃæps, ˈʧæps/ *noun* [*plural*] : leather coverings for the legs that cowboys and cowgirls wear over their pants when they ride horses • a pair of *chaps*

chap·ter /ˈʧæptɚ/ *noun, pl* **-ters** [*count*]
1 : one of the main sections of a book • *Chapter* three deals with the country's economy. • Please read the first two *chapters* of your textbook for our next class.
2 : a period of time that is very different from the period of time before it • Becoming a parent opened up a whole new *chapter* in my life. • a difficult *chapter* in European history
3 : the people in a certain area who make up one section of a large organization • local/regional *chapters* [=*branches*] of the American Red Cross
a chapter of accidents *Brit, informal* : a series of bad or unfortunate events
chapter and verse : exact information or details about something • He can give *chapter and verse* about/on the dangers of smoking.

¹char /ˈʧɑɚ/ *verb* **chars**; **charred**; **char·ring** : to burn or cook (something) until it is black [+ *obj*] Thousands of trees were *charred* in the fire. • Dad *charred* the hamburgers on the grill. [*no obj*] The hamburgers *charred* on the grill. — see also CHARRED — compare ²CHAR

²char *verb* **chars**; **charred**; **charring** [*no obj*] *Brit, old-fashioned* : to work as a cleaner especially in a large house or building — compare ¹CHAR

³char *noun, pl* **chars** [*count*] *Brit, old-fashioned* : CHARWOMAN

char·ac·ter /ˈkerɪktɚ/ *noun, pl* **-ters**
1 [*count*] : the way someone thinks, feels, and behaves : someone's personality — usually singular • He rarely shows his true *character*—that of a kind and sensitive person. • This is a side of her *character* that few people have seen. • the different aspects/facets of her *character* — often used before another noun • Certain *character* traits are helpful in the teaching profession. • Pride, his one *character* flaw, caused his downfall.
2 [*count*] : a set of qualities that are shared by many people in a group, country, etc. — usually singular • the *character* of the American people • the *character* of a nation • the French/Japanese/Mexican national *character*
3 a : a set of qualities that make a place or thing different from other places or things [*count*] the wine's distinctive *character* • the unique *character* of the town/city/region [*noncount*] The building is very simple in *character*. ✧ If something is ***in character with something else***, it has the same qualities or characteristics as something else. • This room is not really *in character with* the rest of the house. **b** [*noncount*] : the qualities or characteristics that make something interesting or special • The room lacks *character*. [=there's nothing special about the room] • Their house has a lot of *character*.
4 [*count*] : a person who appears in a story, book, play, movie, or television show • The film's main *characters* are a woman in her late 30s and her elderly neighbor. • She plays the film's lead/main/central *character*. • a fictional *character* [=a character in a work of fiction] • a popular cartoon *character* • the ***title character*** of the book *Tom Sawyer* [=the character named Tom Sawyer] — see also *cast of characters* at ²CAST
5 [*count*] *informal* **a** : a particular type of person • He's a strange/interesting *character*. **b** : a person who says or does funny or unusual things • That husband of yours is a real *character*! • She's quite a *character*.
6 [*noncount*] **a** : the good qualities of a person that usually include moral or emotional strength, honesty, and fairness • She's a kind and honest person of good *character*. • They believe that going to church will improve the moral *character* of their children. • He is admired for his ***strength of character*** in stressful situations. • Playing sports is seen as a way to ***build character*** in young people. = Playing sports is seen as ***character-building*** for young people. ✧ A ***test of (your) character*** is something that is difficult and that requires you to show that you are a good and emotionally strong person. • These past few days have been a real *test of my character*. **b** : the usually good beliefs or opinions that most people have about a particular person • They defended the *character* [=*reputation*] of their friend. • an attack on his *character*
7 [*count*] : a symbol (such as a letter or number) that is used in writing or printing • the Chinese *character* for "water" • The line is 30 *characters* long.
in character, out of character — used to say that some action or behavior is or is not like someone's usual way of behaving • It was entirely *in character* for a generous person like her to give him the money. • His rudeness was completely *out of character*. [=he is not usually rude]

character actor *noun, pl* ~ **-tors** [*count*] : an actor who is known for playing many different and unusual characters

character assassination *noun* [*noncount*] : the act of saying false things about a person usually in order to make the public stop liking or trusting that person • None of those rumors are true. She's been the victim of *character assassination*.

char·ac·ter·ful /ˈkerɪktɚfəl/ *adj* [*more* ~; *most* ~] *chiefly Brit* : having interesting or unusual qualities : having character • a *characterful* old house

¹char·ac·ter·is·tic /ˌkerɪktəˈrɪstɪk/ *adj* [*more* ~; *most* ~] : typical of a person, thing, or group : showing the special qualities or traits of a person, thing, or group • He responded to their comments with *characteristic* good humor. • the herb's *characteristic* flavor — often + *of* • Such behavior is not *characteristic of* a good neighbor.
– **char·ac·ter·is·ti·cal·ly** /ˌkerɪktəˈrɪstɪkli/ *adv* • She was *characteristically* modest when she accepted the reward.

²characteristic *noun, pl* **-tics** [*count*] : a special quality or trait that makes a person, thing, or group different from others • physical/genetic *characteristics* — often + *of* • What are some of the *characteristics of* this breed of dog? • the distinctive/unique *characteristics of* the population

char·ac·ter·i·za·tion /ˌkerɪktərəˈzeɪʃən, *Brit* ˌkærɪktəˌraɪˈzeɪʃən/ *noun, pl* **-tions**
1 *somewhat formal* : the act of describing the character or qualities of someone or something [*count*] The reporter was criticized for his *characterization* of the people of the town as poor and uneducated. [*noncount*] News reporting requires accurate *characterization*.
2 : the way a writer makes a person in a story, book, play, movie, or television show seem like a real person [*count*] The class discussed the author's *characterization* of the boy

as someone who wanted to be accepted by others. [*noncount*] The story has good *characterization.*

char•ac•ter•ize *also Brit* **char•ac•ter•ise** /ˈkerɪktəˌraɪz/ *verb* **-iz•es; -ized; -iz•ing** [+ *obj*] *somewhat formal*
1 : to describe the character or special qualities of (someone or something) • How would you *characterize* the situation/problem? • I would *characterize* this as a positive change for our company. • She had difficulty *characterizing* their relationship. • His personality is hard to *characterize*. • The newspaper article *characterizes* [=*portrays*] the people of the town as poor and uneducated.
2 : to be a typical feature or quality of (someone or something) • Humor and intelligence *characterize* [=*mark, distinguish*] his writing. • Farms and large flat fields *characterize* most of the area. • the beliefs that *characterized* Europe in the 15th century — often used as *(be) characterized* • The disease *is characterized* by a rise in blood pressure.

char•ac•ter•less /ˈkerɪktələs/ *adj* [*more* ~; *most* ~] **:** not having any interesting or unusual qualities **:** lacking character • rows of *characterless* houses • Their food is bland and *characterless.*

cha•rade /ʃəˈreɪd, *Brit* ʃəˈrɑːd/ *noun, pl* **-rades**
1 [*count*] **:** something that is done in order to pretend something is true when it is not really true • Her concern was just a *charade.* [=she pretended to be concerned but she was not] • We've grown tired of your *charades.* • an empty *charade*
2 ***charades*** [*plural*] **:** a game in which players try to guess a word or phrase from the actions of another player who is not allowed to speak • Let's play *charades*! • a game of *charades*

char•broil /ˈʧɑɚˌbrojəl/ *verb* **-broils; -broiled; -broil•ing** [+ *obj*] *US* **:** to cook (something) on a rack above charcoal • I am going to *charbroil* the chicken.
– charbroiled *adj* • *charbroiled* steak/chicken/salmon

char•coal /ˈʧɑɚˌkoʊl/ *noun* [*noncount*]
1 : a hard black material that is made by burning wood with a small amount of air ✧ *Charcoal* is burned for cooking food and is also made into sticks that are used for drawing pictures. • hamburgers cooked over *charcoal* • a *charcoal* grill • *charcoal* drawings
2 : a dark gray color — see color picture on page C2

chard /ˈʧɑɚd/ *noun* [*noncount*] **:** a plant with large leaves that are eaten as a vegetable — called also *Swiss chard*; see color picture on page C4

Char•don•nay /ˌʃɑɚdn̩ˈeɪ/ *noun, pl* **-nays** [*count, noncount*] **:** a type of dry white wine

[1]**charge** /ˈʧɑɚʤ/ *verb* **charg•es; charged; charg•ing**
1 [+ *obj*] **:** to give an amount of electricity to (something) **:** to put electricity into a battery so that a machine or device will run • We tried to *charge* the car's battery. • My cell phone needs to be *charged.* = The battery in my cell phone needs to be charged.
2 [+ *obj*] *formal* **:** to give a job or responsibility to (a person or group) **:** to make (a person or group) responsible for something — usually used as *(be) charged*; usually + *with* • The board *was charged with* deciding where to build a new school. • the department *charged with* helping war veterans
3 [+ *obj*] **a :** to formally accuse (someone) of a crime — usually + *with* • They *charged* him *with* theft. • She was *charged with* murder. **b :** to say that someone has done something wrong • The government *charged* that he had not paid taxes for five years. • It is not clear if he violated the rules, as his critics have *charged.* **c :** to say that a player has broken the rules in a game • The basketball player was *charged* with a foul.
4 a [+ *obj*] **:** to rush toward (a person, place, etc.) • The bull *charged* the matador. • Fans *charged* [=*rushed*] the stage but were stopped by the security guards. **b** [*no obj*] **:** to rush in a particular direction • People *charged* toward the stage. • She came *charging* into the room. • The bull *charged* right at me. • a *charging* rhinoceros
5 [+ *obj*] **:** to create a record of an amount of money that is owed • The clerk *charged* the purchase to my account. • The expenses were *charged* against the company's earnings.
6 a : to ask for money in return for providing or doing something [*no obj*] Do you *charge* for fixing flat tires? [+ *obj*] They *charge* a fee for late payment. • *charge* tuition **b** [+ *obj*] **:** to ask for (a specific amount of money) as a price, rate, or fee • The shop *charged* $100 for repairs. • The bank *charged* eight percent interest on the loan. **c** [+ *obj*] **:** to ask for payment from (a customer, client, etc.) • They *charged* me $500 to fix the engine. • She *charged* the city thousands of dollars for her work.

[2]**charge** *noun, pl* **charges**
1 [*count*] **a :** an amount of electricity • an electrical *charge* **b :** the amount of an explosive material (such as dynamite) that is used in a single blast • He set off a *charge* that destroyed the mountain. — compare DEPTH CHARGE
2 [*noncount*] **:** the responsibility of managing or watching over something • He has *charge* of the building. • He wanted to ***take charge*** [=*take control*] of the organization.
3 [*count*] **:** an amount of money that someone asks for in return for providing or doing something **:** the price charged for something • There is no *charge* for fixing the tire. • a delivery *charge* for the refrigerator • a monthly *charge* • an admission *charge* at the fair • The concert at the school is ***free of charge.*** [=costs nothing to attend] • A second member of your family can join ***at no charge.*** [=without paying] ***synonyms*** see [1]PRICE
4 [*count*] **a** *law* **:** a formal accusation that someone committed a crime • a *charge* of burglary • They dropped the *charges* against him. • She pleaded guilty to a lesser *charge.* • He decided not to ***bring/press charges.*** [=to formally accuse someone of a crime] • Will she ***face charges***? [=will she be charged?] **b :** a statement that criticizes someone or says that someone has done something wrong **:** an accusation or criticism • The senator rejects *charges* that he is too liberal. • She responded to the *charges* of plagiarism.
5 [*count*] *formal* **:** a person (such as a child) that another person must guard or take care of • She loved to play with her young *charges* at the day-care center.
6 [*count*] **:** a judge's instructions to a jury before it begins deciding a verdict • The judge delivered his *charge* to the jury.
7 [*count*] **:** an act of running or rushing forward especially in order to make an attack • a cavalry *charge* • Tennyson's poem "The *Charge* of the Light Brigade"
8 [*singular*] *US, informal* **:** a feeling of joy or excitement • The children ***got a charge out of*** [=were amused by] the juggler. • He *gets a charge out of* teasing his sister.
in charge **:** having control of or responsibility for something • She is *in charge* of hiring new employees. • I am not sure who is *in charge* at the restaurant.
reverse the charges see [1]REVERSE

charge•able /ˈʧɑɚʤəbəl/ *adj*
1 : able to be charged • The business lunch was *chargeable* to the company. • *chargeable* interest
2 : able to be treated as a crime • an act *chargeable* under federal law • a *chargeable* offense

charge account *noun, pl* ~ **-counts** [*count*] *US* **:** an arrangement in which a bank, store, etc., allows a customer to buy things with a credit card and pay for them later — called also *(Brit) credit account*

charge card *noun, pl* ~ **cards** [*count*] **:** CREDIT CARD

charged /ˈʧɑɚʤd/ *adj*
1 *technical* **:** having an amount of electricity • a *charged* particle
2 [*more* ~; *most* ~] **:** showing or causing strong feelings • The singer gave an emotionally *charged* interview. • a politically *charged* subject — often + *up* • The crowd was all *charged up* [=was very excited] during the game.

char•gé d'af•faires /ʃɑɚˌʒeɪdəˈfeɚ/ *noun, pl* **char•gés d'af•faires** /ʃɑɚˌʒeɪdəˈfeɚ/ [*count*]
1 : a person who takes the place of an ambassador when the ambassador is away
2 : a person with a lower rank than an ambassador who works as a diplomat in countries where no ambassador is assigned

charge nurse *noun, pl* ~ **nurses** [*count*] **:** a nurse who is in charge of one section of a hospital

charg•er /ˈʧɑɚʤɚ/ *noun, pl* **-ers** [*count*]
1 : a device that is used to add electricity to batteries
2 *literary* **:** a horse that a knight or soldier rides in battle

charge sheet *noun, pl* ~ **sheets** [*count*] *Brit* **:** RAP SHEET • The suspect already has a long *charge sheet.*

char•i•ot /ˈʧerijət/ *noun, pl* **-ots** [*count*] **:** a carriage with two wheels that was pulled by horses and was raced and used in battle in ancient times • a *chariot* race

char•i•o•teer /ˌʧerijəˈtiɚ/ *noun, pl* **-teers** [*count*] **:** a driver of a chariot

cha•ris•ma /kəˈrɪzmə/ *noun* [*noncount*] **:** a special charm or appeal that causes people to feel attracted and excited by someone (such as a politican) • The candidate was lacking in *charisma.* • His success is largely due to his *charisma.*

char•is•mat•ic /ˌkerəzˈmætɪk/ *adj*
1 [*more* ~; *most* ~] **:** having great charm or appeal **:** filled

with charisma • He is a *charismatic* leader.
2 — used to describe Christian religious groups whose members believe that they can communicate directly with God to receive help and guidance and the power to heal others • *charismatic* sects

char·i·ta·ble /ˈʧerətəbəl/ *adj*
1 : done or designed to help people who are poor, sick, etc. • She makes a *charitable* donation/contribution every year. • He performs *charitable* work to help the poor. • *charitable* organizations • They give money to *charitable* causes.
2 [*more* ~; *most* ~] **:** showing kindness in talking about or judging other people **:** not very critical • She has tried to be *charitable* about her sister's problems. • They tried to find a *charitable* explanation for his actions. [=an explanation that assumes that there was a good reason for his actions] • Half of the class has a chance at passing the test, and that is a *charitable* estimate.
– char·i·ta·bly /ˈʧerətəbli/ *adv* • His paintings could *charitably* be described as unique. [=they are unique even though they are not very good] • To put it *charitably*, she is not the most talented actress I've ever seen. [=she is not a talented actress]

char·i·ty /ˈʧerəti/ *noun, pl* **-ties**
1 [*noncount*] **:** the act of giving money, food, or other kinds of help to people who are poor, sick, etc. • The holidays are a time for *charity* and good will.; *also* **:** something (such as money or food) that is given to people who are poor, sick, etc. • She refused to accept *charity*. ✧ The phrase ***charity begins at home*** means you should take care of yourself and your family before helping others.
2 a [*count*] **:** an organization that helps people who are poor, sick, etc. • The dinner was held to raise funds for several *charities*. • She runs a local *charity* that gives books to children. **b** [*noncount*] **:** the organizations that help people in need • All the money will go to *charity*. — often used before another noun • a *charity* concert/dinner/event [=a concert/dinner/event held to raise money for a charity]

charity shop *noun, pl* ~ **shops** [*count*] *Brit* **:** a store that sells used clothes, goods, etc., in order to raise money for people who are poor, sick, etc. — compare THRIFT SHOP

char·la·tan /ˈʃɑɚlətən/ *noun, pl* **-tans** [*count*] **:** a person who falsely pretends to know or be something in order to deceive people • Some people thought he was a great leader, but others saw him as just a *charlatan*. [=*fake, fraud*]

Charles·ton /ˈʧɑɚlstən/ *noun*
the Charleston **:** a lively dance that became popular in the 1920s

char·ley horse /ˈʧɑɚli-/ *noun, pl* ~ **horses** [*count*] *US* **:** a painful cramp in the front of the thigh

¹charm /ˈʧɑɚm/ *noun, pl* **charms**
1 [*count*] **:** something that is believed to have magic powers and especially to prevent bad luck • He keeps a horseshoe as a good luck *charm*.
2 [*count*] **:** a small object that is worn on a chain or bracelet • a gold *charm* • a *charm* bracelet — see color picture on page C11
3 : a quality that causes someone or something to be very likeable **:** an attractive quality [*count*] He fell under the spell of her *charms*. • The resort has many *charms*. • The inn has a quaint *charm*. [*noncount*] The island possesses great *charm*. • The new curtains add *charm* to the room. • The seaside location is a big part of the house's *charm*. • He won her over with his *charm*.
the third time is the charm see ¹THIRD
work like a charm **:** to produce a desired result very easily and effectively **:** to work very well • The cleaning fluid *worked like a charm* on the carpet stain.
– charm·less *adj* [*more* ~; *most* ~] • The new building is completely *charmless*. [=*unattractive*]

²charm *verb* **charms; charmed; charm·ing** [+ *obj*]
1 : to put a spell on (someone or something) • The snake was *charmed* by the music.
2 a : to cause (someone) to like you or to do what you want by being nice, friendly, etc. • He was known for his ability to *charm* voters. • She *charmed* [=*captivated*] everyone with her warm smile. • He *charmed* the committee into approving his proposal. **b :** to attract (someone) by being beautiful or welcoming • I was *charmed* by the cozy country inn.
– charm·er *noun, pl* **-ers** [*count*] • Your little girl is a real *charmer*. [=she is sweet, cute, etc.] • a snake *charmer*

charmed /ˈʧɑɚmd/ *adj* [*more* ~; *most* ~] **:** very lucky **:** having good luck • She has always ***lived/led a charmed life***.

charmed circle *noun, pl* ~ **circles** [*count*] **:** a group of people who are special or powerful in some way • a famous writer and her *charmed circle* in Paris

charm·ing /ˈʧɑɚmɪŋ/ *adj* [*more* ~; *most* ~] **:** very pleasing or appealing **:** full of charm • a *charming* little café by the sea • a *charming* young man
– charm·ing·ly *adv* • a *charmingly* decorated room

charred /ˈʧɑɚd/ *adj* **:** made black from burning • The remains of the house were *charred*. • *charred* wood — see also CHAR

¹chart /ˈʧɑɚt/ *noun, pl* **charts** [*count*]
1 a : information in the form of a table, diagram, etc. • a *chart* showing the number of cars sold each month — see also BAR CHART, FLOW CHART, PIE CHART **b :** a record of information about a medical patient • The doctor consulted the patient's *chart*. — see picture at HOSPITAL
2 : a map of an area (such as the sky or ocean) used by pilots, sailors, etc.
3 : a list that shows which music recordings have sold the most during a recent period of time • a ***chart-topper*** [=a recording that is bought more than any other recording during a particular time] — usually plural; usually used with *the* • The record went to the top of *the charts*. • *the* country music *charts*

²chart *verb* **charts; chart·ed; chart·ing** [+ *obj*]
1 : to make a chart of (an area) • They *charted* the bay.; *also* **:** to mark (something) on a chart • They *charted* the course of the ship.
2 : to make a plan for (something) • She wanted to *chart* her own career path. • He will try to *chart* a new course for the company.
3 : to note the changes, progress, etc., in (something) • a book that *charts* [=*chronicles*] the rise and fall of the Roman Empire • analysts *charting* trends in the stock market

¹char·ter /ˈʧɑɚtɚ/ *noun, pl* **-ters** [*count*]
1 : a document issued by a government that gives rights to a person or group • The *charter* allows for unrestricted trading.
2 a : a document which declares that a city, town, school, or corporation has been established • the town *charter* • a corporate *charter* **b :** a document that describes the basic laws, principles, etc., of a group • the United Nations *Charter*

²charter *verb* **-ters; -tered; -ter·ing** [+ *obj*]
1 : to give a charter to (a government, corporation, etc.) • a royally *chartered* bank • The city was *chartered* in 1837.
2 : to hire (a ship, bus, etc.) for temporary use • The team *chartered* a plane. • *charter* a flight

³charter *adj, always used before a noun* **:** hired for temporary use • a *charter* flight • a *charter* plane

chartered *adj, always used before a noun, Brit* **:** allowed to work in a certain job because you have passed a test or qualified in some other way • a *chartered* engineer

chartered accountant *noun, pl* ~ **-tants** [*count*] *Brit* **:** CERTIFIED PUBLIC ACCOUNTANT

charter member *noun, pl* ~ **-bers** [*count*] *US* **:** FOUNDING MEMBER

charter school *noun, pl* ~ **schools** [*count*] *US* **:** a school that is established by a charter, is run by teachers, parents, etc., and uses tax money but does not have to be run according to the rules of a city or state

char·wom·an /ˈʧɑɚˌwʊmən/ *noun, pl* **-wom·en** /-ˌwɪmən/ [*count*] *old-fashioned* **:** a woman who cleans houses or office buildings

chary /ˈʧeri/ *adj* **char·i·er; -est :** cautious about doing something — + *about* or *of* • She is *chary about* spending money. • He is *chary of* expressing his emotions.

¹chase /ˈʧeɪs/ *noun, pl* **chas·es**
1 [*count*] **:** the act of following and trying to catch a person, animal, etc. • Police caught the bank robbers after a high-speed *chase* on the highway. • a car *chase*
2 [*singular*] **:** an eager attempt to get something • Though she has repeatedly failed to capture the world record, she refuses to give up the *chase*. [=she keeps trying] • He was always trying to find a new girlfriend and seemed to enjoy ***the thrill of the chase***. — see also WILD GOOSE CHASE
3 [*count*] *chiefly Brit* **:** STEEPLECHASE
cut to the chase **:** to go directly to the important points of a story, argument, etc., • She urged him to skip the details and *cut to the chase*. [=*get to the point*]
give chase **:** to chase someone or something • The officer saw the thief and *gave chase*. — often + *to* • Police *gave chase to* the suspect as he fled the scene.

²chase *verb* **chases; chased; chas·ing**

C

1 : to follow and try to catch (someone or something) [+ *obj*] The cops *chased* the thief. ▪ a child *chasing* a balloon [*no obj*] — + *after* ▪ My dog *chases after* butterflies.
2 a : to try very hard to get (someone or something) [+ *obj*] a journalist who is *chasing* a big story [*no obj*] — + *after* ▪ He's been *chasing after* the world record all season. **b** : to try to attract (someone) for a romantic or sexual relationship [+ *obj*] He was always *chasing* women half his age. [*no obj*] — + *after* ▪ He was always *chasing after* women half his age.
3 *always followed by an adverb or preposition* [+ *obj*] : to cause (someone or something) to go away ▪ She *chased* a dog off the lawn. ▪ He *chased* the kids away from his new car. ▪ She *chased* the cats out of her garden. ▪ Our last mayor was *chased* from office by political enemies. ▪ Her reassuring letter helped to *chase* away my fears.
chase down [*phrasal verb*] ***chase (someone or something) down*** *or* ***chase down (someone or something)*** **1** : to follow and catch (someone or something) ▪ Police *chased down* the robber in an alley. **2** : to search for and find (someone or something) ▪ I finally *chased down* [=*tracked down, found,* (*Brit*) *chased up*] that recipe I promised you.
chase up [*phrasal verb*] *Brit* **1** ***chase (something) up*** *or* ***chase up (something)*** : to search for and find (someone or something) ▪ Can you *chase up* those files for me? **2** ***chase (someone) up*** *or* ***chase up (someone)*** : to contact or find (someone) usually in order to get something ▪ His landlord had to *chase him up* for his rent.

chas·er /ˈʧeɪsɚ/ *noun, pl* **-ers** [*count*] : a different alcoholic drink that is drunk immediately after you have drunk a stronger or weaker one ▪ He ordered whiskey with a beer *chaser*. ▪ beer with a whiskey *chaser*

chasm /ˈkæzəm/ *noun, pl* **chasms** [*count*]
1 : a deep hole or opening in the surface of the earth : GORGE
2 : a major division, separation, or difference between two people, groups, etc. ▪ Leaders tried to bridge a *chasm* [=*split, divide*] between the two religious groups. ▪ a racial/cultural/economic *chasm*

chas·sis /ˈʧæsi, ˈʃæsi/ *noun, pl* **chas·sis** /ˈʧæsiz, ˈʃæsiz/ [*count*] : a frame upon which the main parts of an automobile are built

chaste /ˈʧeɪst/ *adj* **chast·er; -est** [*also more* ~; *most* ~]
1 *old-fashioned* : not having sex ▪ a *chaste* young woman
2 : morally pure or decent : not sinful ▪ a *chaste* kiss on the cheek
3 : simple or plain ▪ a *chaste* design
– chaste·ly *adj* ▪ a *chastely* dressed girl

chas·ten /ˈʧeɪsn̩/ *verb* **-tens; -tened; -ten·ing** [+ *obj*] : to cause (someone) to feel sad or embarrassed about something that has happened — usually used as *(be) chastened* ▪ He *was chastened* [=*humbled*] by his team's defeat.
– chastening *adj* [*more* ~; *most* ~] ▪ Having her proposal criticized was a *chastening* [=*humbling*] experience.

chas·tise /ʧæˈstaɪz/ *verb* **-tis·es; -tised; -tis·ing** [+ *obj*] *formal* : to criticize (someone) harshly for doing something wrong ▪ The waiter was *chastised* for forgetting the customer's order. ▪ The coach is always *chastising* the players for minor mistakes.
– chas·tise·ment /ʧæˈstaɪzmənt/ *noun* [*noncount*]

chas·ti·ty /ˈʧæstəti/ *noun* [*noncount*] : the state of not having sex with anyone : the quality or state of being chaste ▪ The priest took a ***vow of chastity*** [=made a promise never to have sex]

[1]chat /ˈʧæt/ *verb* **chats; chat·ted; chat·ting** [*no obj*]
1 : to talk with someone in a casual way ▪ We *chatted* about our plans for the summer. ▪ called him up to *chat*
2 : to talk over the Internet by sending messages back and forth in a chat room ▪ She stayed up all night *chatting* with her friends online.
chat up [*phrasal verb*] ***chat (someone) up*** *or* ***chat up (someone)*** *informal* : to talk informally with (someone, such as someone you are attracted to) ▪ He tried to *chat up* a girl at the dance.

[2]chat *noun, pl* **chats**
1 [*count*] : a light and friendly conversation ▪ We enjoyed a *chat* over coffee.
2 : a talk held over the Internet by people using a chat room [*count*] live *chats* [*noncount*] software used for e-mail and *chat* — often used before another noun ▪ *chat* sessions ▪ *chat* software — see also CHAT ROOM

châ·teau /ʃæˈtoʊ, *Brit* ˈʃætəʊ/ *noun, pl* **châ·teaus** *or* **châ·teaux** /ʃæˈtoʊz, *Brit* ˈʃætəʊz/ [*count*] : a castle or a large house especially in France

chat line *noun, pl* ~ **lines** [*count*] *Brit* : a telephone service that people call in order to speak with other people about a certain topic

chat room *noun, pl* ~ **rooms** [*count*] : a Web site or computer program that allows people to send messages to each other instantly over the Internet

chat show *noun, pl* ~ **shows** [*count*] *Brit* : TALK SHOW

chat·tel /ˈʧætl̩/ *noun, pl* **-tels** *old-fashioned* : something (such as a slave, piece of furniture, tool, etc.) that a person owns other than land or buildings [*count*] personal *chattels* [*noncount*] slaves treated as *chattel*

[1]chat·ter /ˈʧætɚ/ *verb* **-ters; -tered; -ter·ing** [*no obj*]
1 : to talk in a quick or casual way ▪ Children *chattered* in the middle of the playground. ▪ He was *chattering* [=*jabbering*] away on a cell phone.
2 : to make clicking sounds by knocking together rapidly ▪ My teeth were *chattering* from the cold.
3 : to make fast and usually high-pitched sounds ▪ Birds *chattered* in the trees.

[2]chatter *noun* [*noncount*]
1 : casual talk that is usually not important or interesting ▪ He couldn't stand their endless *chatter* [=*prattle*] about celebrities and movies. ▪ the *chatter* of schoolchildren
2 : a series of fast usually high-pitched sounds ▪ heard the *chatter* of squirrels

chat·ter·box /ˈʧætɚˌbɑːks/ *noun, pl* **-box·es** [*count*] *informal* : a person who talks a lot ▪ That little girl is a *chatterbox*.

chattering classes *noun*
the chattering classes *Brit, disapproving* : educated people who like to talk about politics, culture, society, etc.

chat·ty /ˈʧæti/ *adj* **chat·ti·er; -est**
1 : tending to talk a lot : fond of chatting ▪ a *chatty* neighbor ▪ I'm feeling *chatty* today.
2 : having an informal style that is similar to friendly speech ▪ a *chatty* book about his life in politics ▪ She writes with a *chatty* [=*casual*] style.
– chat·ti·ly /ˈʧætəli/ *adv* [*more* ~; *most* ~] ▪ She remarked *chattily* about the weather. **– chat·ti·ness** *noun* [*noncount*] ▪ He was known for his *chattiness*.

[1]chauf·feur /ˈʃoʊfɚ, ʃoʊˈfɚ/ *noun, pl* **-feurs** [*count*] : a person whose job is to drive people around in a car
– chauffeured *adj* ▪ We rented a *chauffeured* limousine. [=a limousine driven by a chauffeur]

[2]chauffeur *verb* **-feurs; -feured; -feur·ing**
1 : to drive (someone) around in a car as a job : to work as a chauffeur [*no obj*] He *chauffeurs* for a millionaire. [+ *obj*] He *chauffeurs* a millionaire.
2 [+ *obj*] : to drive (someone) in a car to a certain place ▪ She was *chauffeured* to the airport. ▪ He *chauffeured* his client to the hotel. ▪ They have to *chauffeur* [=*drive*] their children to soccer games every week.

chau·vin·ism /ˈʃoʊvəˌnɪzəm/ *noun* [*noncount*] *disapproving*
1 : an attitude that the members of your own sex are always better than those of the opposite sex ▪ ***male chauvinism*** [=a belief that men are superior to women]
2 : the belief that your country, race, etc., is better than any other ▪ American *chauvinism*

chau·vin·ist /ˈʃoʊvənɪst/ *or* **chau·vin·is·tic** /ˌʃoʊvəˈnɪstɪk/ *adj* [*more* ~; *most* ~] *disapproving* : believing that your country, sex, etc., is better than any other : showing or filled with chauvinism ▪ She called him a *chauvinist* pig. ▪ *chauvinist* attitudes
– chauvinist *noun, pl* **-ists** [*count*] ▪ a male *chauvinist*

chaw /ˈʧɑː/ *noun, pl* **chaws** *US, informal* : a piece or amount of chewing tobacco [*count*] enjoyed a *chaw* of tobacco [*noncount*] a lump of *chaw*

[1]cheap /ˈʧiːp/ *adj* **cheap·er; -est**
1 a : not costing a lot of money ▪ I always buy the *cheapest* brand of cereal. ▪ a place where you can get a *cheap* [=*inexpensive*] meal ▪ Rent isn't *cheap* here. ▪ *cheap* imported goods — see also DIRT CHEAP **b** : of low quality : not worth a lot of money ▪ curtains made of *cheap* material ▪ He wears a *cheap* watch that's always breaking. ▪ *cheap* perfume
2 : charging low prices ▪ This gas station is *cheaper* than the one by the highway. ▪ We ate at a *cheap* [=*inexpensive*] restaurant.
3 : not willing to share or spend money ▪ He was too *cheap* [=*stingy*] to pay for the dinner. ▪ Don't be *cheap*—buy good quality tires for your car. — often + *with* ▪ My uncle is *cheap with* his money.

4 : not hard to do or get • It was a *cheap* [=*easy*] victory over a lousy team. • He likes to harass the neighbor's dog as a ***cheap thrill.*** [=a minor thing done for entertainment]
5 : having little or no self-respect : ashamed of being used, abused, etc., by other people • He felt *cheap* letting other people treat him like that.
on the cheap *informal* : at the lowest possible cost : in a cheap way • The movie was made *on the cheap*. • They built the house *on the cheap*.
– **cheap·ly** *adv* [*more* ~; *most* ~] • It is not easy to live *cheaply* in this city. • The radio was *cheaply* made and didn't last long. – **cheap·ness** *noun* [*noncount*] • The *cheapness* of the stock made it an appealing buy. • My mother-in-law's *cheapness* [=*stinginess*] can be annoying.

²cheap *adv* : at a low cost • They were able to build a house *cheap*. [=*cheaply*] • The film was made *cheap*. : for a low price • The house sold *cheap*.
come cheap : to be available at a low price — usually used in negative statements • His services don't *come cheap*. [=his services are not cheap; his services are expensive] • These materials don't *come cheap*.

cheap·en /ˈʧiːpən/ *verb* **-ens; -ened; -en·ing** [+ *obj*]
1 : to cause (something) to be of lower quality • Using plastic instead of steel will *cheapen* [=*lower*] the quality of the car. • products *cheapened* by sloppy workmanship
2 : to cause (something) to have or to seem to have less value, meaning, or importance • Using the national flag in advertising only *cheapens* it. • Poor marketing can *cheapen* a brand name. • I thought that the show *cheapened* the lives of the people it portrayed. • The wedding ceremony was *cheapened* by the best man's tasteless jokes.

cheap·ie /ˈʧiːpi/ *noun, pl* **-ies** [*count*] *informal* : something that is cheap and usually of low quality • Her first camera was a *cheapie*.
– **cheapie** *adj* • The camera was a *cheapie* model.

cheapo /ˈʧiːpoʊ/ *adj* [*more* ~; *most* ~] *informal* : ¹CHEAP • a *cheapo* radio • a *cheapo* horror film

cheap shot *noun, pl* ~ **shots** [*count*] *disapproving*
1 *sports* : an unfair hit made against an opponent • He took a *cheap shot* at the quarterback. • a *cheap shot* to the back of the head
2 : something that one person says about another that is not kind or fair : a critical and unfair comment • The remark about his weight was a *cheap shot*.

cheap·skate /ˈʧiːpˌskeɪt/ *noun, pl* **-skates** [*count*] *informal* : a person who does not like to spend money • He is a *cheapskate* [=*miser, skinflint*] who almost never gives tips.

¹cheat /ˈʧiːt/ *verb* **cheats; cheat·ed; cheat·ing**
1 [*no obj*] : to break a rule or law usually to gain an advantage at something • The players were accused of *cheating*. • I had to *cheat* in order to solve the puzzle. — often + *on* or *at* • She was caught *cheating on* a test. • They *cheated on* their taxes. • He *cheats at* cards.
2 [+ *obj*] **a** : to take something from (someone) by lying or breaking a rule • The store *cheats* its customers through false advertising. — usually + *out of* • He *cheated* [=*tricked, swindled*] the elderly couple *out of* their property. • I was *cheated out of* 20 dollars. **b** : to prevent (someone) from having something that he or she deserves or was expecting to get • They *cheated* him out of a fair deal. — usually used in the phrase *feel cheated* • Tourists *felt cheated* when they arrived and found out the cathedral was closed.
3 [+ *obj*] : to avoid (something bad, dangerous, etc.) by being clever or lucky • a heroin addict who has *cheated* death many times • They tried to ***cheat fate***. [=they took a risk and hoped be lucky]
cheat on [*phrasal verb*] ***cheat on (someone)*** *informal* : to break a promise made to (someone, such as your wife or husband) by having sex with someone else • He *cheated on* his wife/girlfriend.
– **cheat·er** *noun, pl* **-ers** [*count*]

²cheat *noun, pl* **cheats** [*count*] : a person who cheats • He's a liar and a *cheat*. [=*cheater*] • tax *cheats*

¹check /ˈʧɛk/ *verb* **checks; checked; check·ing**
1 : to look at (something) carefully to find mistakes, problems, etc., or to make sure there is nothing wrong with it [+ *obj*] Make sure to *check* your spelling. • She *checked* her makeup in the mirror. • We should *check* the equipment to make sure that it's working properly. • I *checked* the tires for wear. [=to see if they are worn down/out] • The guards *checked* my passport. [*no obj*] — + *for* • Be careful to *check for* any mistakes. • The border guards *checked* in my luggage *for* contraband. — see also CROSS-CHECK, DOUBLE-CHECK, SPOT-CHECK
2 **a** : to get information by looking at something, asking about something, etc. [+ *obj*] He *checked* his watch and saw that it was almost noon. • I'll just *check* the map to see where we are. • I'll *check* the newspaper to see when the movie starts. [*no obj*] We were out of milk last time I *checked*. [=*looked*] • "Do you have these shoes in a larger size?" "I don't know. Let me *check*." [=*take a look*] • I think the door is locked, but I'll have to *check* (to be sure). — often followed by *to* + *verb* • Did you *check to see* where the movie was playing? • I *checked to make sure* the door was locked. **b** : to look at or in (a place) in order to find or get something or someone [+ *obj*] If you're looking for a spoon, *check* the top drawer. • I *checked* his office but he wasn't there. [*no obj*] If you're looking for the umbrella, *check* in the closet. **c** [+ *obj*] : to find out if you have any (mail, messages, etc.) • Did you *check* the mail yet today? • She *checked* [=listened to] her phone messages when she got home. • He logged on and *checked* [=*read*] his e-mail.
3 : to talk *with* someone in order to get approval, information, etc., about something [*no obj*] I'll have to *check with* the manager before I can let you in. • *Check with* your doctor to find out which drugs are safe. [+ *obj*] I'm not sure when you should arrive. I'll have to *check* that *with* my wife.
4 [+ *obj*] **a** : to slow or stop (something or someone) from doing something • She started to speak but then *checked* [=*stopped*] herself. • The batter *checked* his swing. [=the batter started to swing and then stopped] **b** *hockey* : to stop or hit (an opponent) in order to steal the ball or puck, defend the goal, etc. • He was *checked* by the defender.
5 [+ *obj*] *US* **a** : to leave (something you own) with a worker at a restaurant, hotel, etc., who keeps it in a special area or room (called a checkroom) while you are there • I *checked* my hat and coat in the restaurant's checkroom. **b** : to give (your bags, suitcases, etc.) to a worker so that they can be loaded onto a plane or train • We *checked* our bags before boarding. **c** : to take (someone's bags, suitcases, etc.) to load them onto a plane or train • The airline *checked* our bags before we boarded. — see also CHECK IN 3 (below)
6 [+ *obj*] *US* : to mark (something) with a check (✔) to show that it has been done, approved, etc. • You should *check* [=(*chiefly Brit*) *tick*] each item on the list after you've completed it. — often + *off* • You should *check off* [=(*chiefly Brit*) *tick off*] each item on the list after you've completed it.
7 [*no obj*] *US, informal* : to be proven to be true, accurate, etc. — usually used in negative statements • Her story didn't *check*. [=the evidence did not support her story] — see also CHECK OUT 2 (below)
check back [*phrasal verb*] *informal* : to return to a place, person, etc., in order to try something again or to get additional information • We are not hiring today, but *check back* next month. • I'll ***check back with you*** [=talk to you again] in about a week.
check in [*phrasal verb*] **1** : to report to someone when you arrive at a place (such as an airport or convention) to let them know you are there • Passengers must *check in* one hour before the flight leaves. • Where do I have to *check in*?; *especially* : to arrive at and be given a room in a hotel, motel, etc. • *check in* [=*register*] at a hotel • Guests cannot *check in* before 4:00 PM. — see also CHECK-IN **2** *US, informal* : to talk with someone in order to report or find out new information • I'm just *checking in* to see how things are going. — usually + *with* • I have to go to a meeting now, but I'll *check in with* you later. **3** ***check (something) in*** or ***check in (something)*** : to leave or take bags, suitcases, etc., so that they can be loaded onto a plane or train • We *checked* our bags *in* at the station. • The airline *checked in* our luggage.
check into [*phrasal verb*] ***check into (something)*** **1** : to arrive at and be given a room in (a hotel, motel, etc.) • We *checked into* a hotel. **2** : to look for information about (something) : to find out the truth about (something) by getting information • The police are *checking into* [=*checking on, checking up on*] his activities. [=the police are investigating his activities] • A problem like that should really be *checked into* carefully.
check off on [*phrasal verb*] ***check off on (something)*** *US, informal* : to give official approval for (something) • My boss will have to *check off on* [=*authorize, approve*] my decision.
check on [*phrasal verb*] ***check on (someone or something)*** **1** : to look at or examine (someone or something) to see if there are any problems • The nurse *checked on* the patients

regularly. **2 :** to look for information about (someone or something) : to find out the truth about (someone or something) by getting information ▪ The police are *checking on* [=*checking up on*] him. ▪ I asked the waiter to *check on* [=find out what was happening with] my order.

check out [*phrasal verb*] **1 a :** to leave and pay for your room at a hotel, motel, etc. ▪ We *checked out* (of the hotel) early. — see also CHECKOUT **b** *US, informal* **:** to die ▪ There are still a lot of things I want to accomplish in life before I finally *check out.* **2** *US, informal* **a :** to be proven to be accurate, true, etc. ▪ I didn't believe her at first, but her story *checked out.* ▪ The description *checked out* when we compared it with the photograph. [=we saw that the description was accurate when we compared it with the photograph] **b *check out (something) or check (something) out* :** to find out if (something) is true ▪ The police are still trying to *check out* [=*investigate, confirm*] his alibi. **3 *check out (something or someone) or check (something or someone) out* a :** to look at (something or someone) in order to find problems, mistakes, etc. ▪ We carefully *checked out* the car for defects. ▪ He had problems with his computer and asked the technician to *check* it *out.* ▪ He needs to get *checked out* by a doctor. **b** *informal* **:** to look at (someone or something that is attractive or interesting) ▪ When she walked into the room, all the guys were *checking* her *out.* ▪ Just *check out* his new car! ▪ We're going to the mall to *check out* that new clothing store. — often used in the phrase ***check it out*** to direct someone's attention to something ▪ *Check it out*—they've got that new book in stock. **4 *check out (something) or check (something) out* a :** to borrow (something) from a library ▪ He *checked out* [=*took out, borrowed*] a book on farming. **b** *US* **:** to add up the cost of the goods that someone buys in a store (such as a supermarket) and accept payment for them ▪ She got a job *checking out* groceries at the supermarket.; *also* **:** to pay for the goods that you buy in a store ▪ There was a long line of people waiting to *check out* their groceries. ▪ She was able to *check out* quickly using her debit card. — see also CHECKOUT

check over [*phrasal verb*] ***check (something or someone) over or check over (something or someone)* :** to look at (something or someone) in a careful way to find problems, mistakes, etc. ▪ *checking* the new cars *over* ▪ The doctors *checked* him *over* for bruises. ▪ Be sure to *check over* each item on the list for any mistakes. ▪ She *checked* herself *over* [=she looked at herself carefully] in the mirror before going to the party.

check through [*phrasal verb*] ***check through (something)* :** to look at the parts of (a group of things) ▪ I *checked through* all his letters but found nothing useful.

check up on [*phrasal verb*] ***check up on (someone or something)* :** to find or look for information about (someone or something) often in order to find out the truth ▪ My parents are always *checking up on* me. ▪ The police are *checking up on* his alibi.

– check·able *adj* ▪ an easily *checkable* fact

²check *noun, pl* **checks**

1 [*count*] **:** the act or process of looking at or examining something to find out information or see if there is anything wrong with it ▪ Please give the schedule a *check* to see if the times are correct. ▪ I gave the ingredients list a quick *check* to see if the cereal contained any sugar. ▪ She ran/did a quick *check* of the computer to make sure it was working properly. ▪ They did a ***sound check*** [=tested the sound equipment] before the concert. ▪ All government employees are subject to a ***security check.*** [=all government employees are investigated to see if they can be trusted] ▪ You should ***keep a close check on*** your blood pressure. [=you should watch your blood pressure closely] ▪ The police ***ran a check on*** the license plate and found out that the car had been stolen.

2 [*count*] **a :** something that stops or limits another thing — usually + *on* ▪ a system that acts/serves as a *check on* the governor's power [=a system that limits the governor's power] ▪ The store hired a guard to ***put a check on*** shoplifting. [=to reduce or stop shoplifting] ▪ The government has lowered interest rates in an attempt to *put a check on* inflation. — see also CHECKS AND BALANCES **b** *hockey* **:** an act of hitting or stopping a player in order to steal the ball or puck, defend a goal, etc. ▪ He was penalized for an illegal *check.* ▪ a hip *check* [=an act of hitting by bumping with the hips]

3 *US* ***check*** *or Brit* ***cheque*** [*count*] **:** a piece of paper that is used to make a payment to someone using the money in a bank account ▪ He made out the *check* to me and signed it, and I deposited it in my account. ▪ Do you want to pay in cash, by *check,* or by credit card? ▪ write/cash/draw a *check* — compare MONEY ORDER; see also BLANK CHECK, TRAVELER'S CHECK

4 [*count*] *US* **:** a bill for the food and drinks that are served in a restaurant ▪ She asked the waiter for the *check.*

5 a [*count*] *US* **:** a mark ✓ that is used to show that something (such as an item on a list) has been noted, done, etc. — called also (*US*) *check mark,* (*chiefly Brit*) *tick* **b** *informal* — used in speech to say that something has been noted, done, etc. ▪ "So you'll be here at 6 o'clock on the dot." "*Check.*" [=yes, I will be here at 6 o'clock] ▪ "Do you have the camera?" "*Check.*" "The umbrella?" "*Check.*"

6 [*count*] *US* **a :** a room in a restaurant, theater, etc., where you can leave something that you do not want to carry or wear ▪ He left his coat at the ***coat check.*** [=*checkroom, coatroom,* (*chiefly Brit*) *cloakroom*] ▪ a ***hat check*** ▪ When she was younger she worked as a ***coat-check/hat-check girl.*** [=a woman whose job is to take and return the things that people leave in a checkroom] **b :** a ticket that is given to you when you leave something (such as a hat or a coat) that you will return for later ▪ a baggage *check* — see also RAIN CHECK

7 [*noncount*] **:** a situation in the game of chess in which a player's king can be captured on the opponent's next turn and must be protected or moved ▪ He moved his bishop and said, "*Check!*" to show that my king was in *check.* — compare CHECKMATE

cut a check see ¹CUT

***in check* :** under control — used with *keep* or *hold* ▪ He's trying to *hold* his emotions *in check.* [=he is trying to control his emotions] ▪ The government has lowered interest rates in an attempt to *keep* inflation *in check.*

– compare ³CHECK

³check *noun, pl* **checks** [*count*] **:** a pattern of squares in different colors ▪ a fabric with a blue and yellow *check* — often used before another noun ▪ a *check* [=*checked, checkered*] fabric ▪ a tablecloth with a *check* [=*checked, checkered*] pattern — compare ²CHECK

check·book (*US*) *or Brit* **cheque·book** /ˈtʃɛkˌbʊk/ *noun, pl* **-books** [*count*] **:** a book containing checks for use with a checking account

checked *adj* **:** having a pattern made up of squares of different colors ▪ a *checked* shirt ▪ a *checked* [=*checkered*] pattern/fabric/tablecloth — see color picture on page C12

¹check·er /ˈtʃɛkɚ/ *noun, pl* **-ers** [*count*]

1 *US* **:** a person in a store whose job is to add up the cost of customers' purchases and take payment for them ▪ a grocery/supermarket *checker*

2 : someone or something that looks at things to find errors or problems ▪ She is a careful *checker* of details. ▪ a ***fact checker*** [=a person whose job is to make sure that the facts in a book, magazine, etc., are correct] ▪ The word processing software includes a ***grammar checker.*** [=a feature that finds grammatical errors] — see also SPELL-CHECKER

– compare ²CHECKER

²checker *noun, pl* **-ers** [*count*] *US* **:** any one of the round pieces that are used in the game of checkers — called also (*Brit*) *draught* — compare ¹CHECKER

check·er·board /ˈtʃɛkɚˌboɚd/ *noun, pl* **-boards** [*count*] *US*

1 : a board that is marked with squares of two different colors (such as white and black) and that is used in various games (such as checkers) — called also (*Brit*) *draughtboard*

2 : something that has a pattern or arrangement of squares that looks like a checkerboard ▪ The fields formed a *checkerboard* of light and dark squares. ▪ a *checkerboard* pattern

check·ered (*chiefly US*) *or Brit* **che·quered** /ˈtʃɛkɚd/ *adj*

1 : having a pattern made up of squares of different colors ▪ a *checkered* [=*checked*] pattern/fabric/tablecloth

2 a : including good parts and bad parts ▪ He has had a *checkered* career with many ups and downs. **b** [*more ~; most ~*] **:** including many problems or failures ▪ The senator has a ***checkered past.*** [=he has done bad things or been in trouble in the past] ▪ When it comes to labor relations, the company has a somewhat ***checkered history.*** [=the company has sometimes had problems with labor relations]

check·ers /ˈtʃɛkɚz/ *noun* [*noncount*] *US* **:** a game played on a board (called a checkerboard) by two players who each have 12 round pieces called checkers — called also (*Brit*) *draughts;* see also CHINESE CHECKERS

check–in /ˈtʃɛkˌɪn/ *noun, pl* **-ins**

1 [*noncount*] : the act or process of reporting that you have arrived at a hotel, an airport, etc. : the act or process of checking in ▪ *Check-in* was delayed.; *also* : the time when people are allowed to check in ▪ When is *check-in*? = When is *check-in* time?

2 [*count*] : the place where people go when they arrive at a hotel, airport, etc. ▪ When we got to the airport there was a long line at the *check-in*. — often used before another noun ▪ the *check-in* desk/counter — see also *check in* at [1]CHECK

checking account *noun, pl* ~ **-counts** [*count*] *US* : a bank account from which you can take money by writing checks — called also (*Brit*) *current account*

check·list /ˈtʃɛkˌlɪst/ *noun, pl* **-lists** [*count*]

1 : a list of things to be checked or done ▪ Before takeoff the pilot went down/through his *checklist* of safety precautions. ▪ I still have one thing left to do on my *checklist*.

2 : a list that includes many or all things of a certain kind ▪ a *checklist* of bird species

check mark *noun, pl* ~ **marks** [*count*] *US* : [2]CHECK 5a

check·mate /ˈtʃɛkˌmeɪt/ *noun, pl* **-mates** : a situation in chess in which a player loses the game because that player's king is in a position from which it cannot escape [*noncount*] a brilliant move that resulted in *checkmate* [*count*] The challenger can force a *checkmate* with his next move. — compare [2]CHECK 7, STALEMATE 2

– **check·mate** *verb* **-mates; -mat·ed; -mat·ing** [+ *obj*] ▪ The challenger *checkmated* the champion and won the tournament. ▪ His king was *checkmated*.

check·out /ˈtʃɛkˌaʊt/ *noun, pl* **-outs**

1 a : the action or an instance of leaving your room in a hotel, motel, etc., after you are finished staying there [*noncount*] She paid for the room at *checkout*. [*count*] an early *checkout* — often used before another noun ▪ the *checkout* desk **b** [*noncount*] : the time by which you must leave your room when you have finished staying in a hotel, motel, etc. ▪ When is *checkout*? = When is *checkout* time? ▪ *Checkout* is at 11:00. — see also *check out* 1a at [1]CHECK

2 [*count*] : the place or area where goods are paid for in a store (such as a supermarket) ▪ There was a long line at the *checkout*. — often used before another noun ▪ the *checkout* counter — see also *check out* 4b at [1]CHECK

check·point /ˈtʃɛkˌpoɪnt/ *noun, pl* **-points** [*count*] : a place where people, cars, etc., are searched by someone (such as a police officer) before being allowed to continue ▪ Our car was stopped at a police *checkpoint* before we were permitted to cross the border. ▪ a military/security *checkpoint*

check·room /ˈtʃɛkˌruːm/ *noun, pl* **-rooms** [*count*] *US* : a room in a restaurant, theater, etc., where you can leave something that you do not want to carry or wear while you are there ▪ I got my bag out of the *checkroom* when the performance ended. — called also (*chiefly Brit*) *cloakroom*, (*US*) *coatroom*; compare [2]CHECK 6

checks and balances *noun* [*plural*] : a system in which the different parts of an organization (such as a government) have powers that affect and control the other parts so that no part can become too powerful

check·up /ˈtʃɛkˌʌp/ *noun, pl* **-ups** [*count*] : an examination of a person made by a doctor to make sure the person is healthy ▪ She goes for a *checkup* every year. ▪ The doctor/dentist gave me a *checkup*.; *also* : an instance of looking at the parts of a machine to make sure it is working properly ▪ She brought in her car for a 30,000-mile *checkup*.

ched·dar /ˈtʃɛdɚ/ *noun, often* **Cheddar** [*noncount*] : a type of hard yellow, white, or orange cheese that is smooth

cheek /ˈtʃiːk/ *noun, pl* **cheeks**

1 [*count*] : the part of the face that is below the eye and to the side of the nose and mouth ▪ rosy/chubby *cheeks* ▪ He kissed her on the *cheek*. ▪ They were sitting/dancing/posing ***cheek to cheek*** [=with their cheeks touching] — see picture at FACE; see also TONGUE IN CHEEK

2 *Brit* : an attitude or way of behaving that is rude and does not show proper respect [*noncount*] He had the *cheek* [=*nerve*] to complain that our gift was cheap. [*singular*] He's got a *cheek* ignoring us like that.

3 [*count*] *informal* : one of the two parts of the body that a person sits on : BUTTOCKS

cheek by jowl : very close together ▪ We sat *cheek by jowl* [=*side by side*] with the city's elite. ▪ cheap knickknacks displayed *cheek by jowl* with fine antiques

turn the other cheek : to choose not to try to hurt or insult someone who has hurt or insulted you

cheek·bone /ˈtʃiːkˌboʊn/ *noun, pl* **-bones** [*count*] : a bone of the face that is located below the eye ▪ He suffered a broken *cheekbone*. ▪ She has high *cheekbones*, like her father.

cheeky /ˈtʃiːki/ *adj* **cheek·i·er; -est** *chiefly Brit, informal* : rude and showing a lack of respect often in a way that seems playful or amusing ▪ *cheeky* humor ▪ a *cheeky* grin

– **cheek·i·ly** /ˈtʃiːkəli/ *adv* – **cheek·i·ness** /ˈtʃiːkinəs/ *noun* [*noncount*]

cheep /ˈtʃiːp/ *verb* **cheeps; cheeped; cheep·ing** [*no obj*] *of a bird* : to make a quick high sound ▪ chicks *cheeping* for food

– **cheep** *noun, pl* **cheeps** [*count*] ▪ the *cheeps* of newly hatched chicks

[1]**cheer** /ˈtʃiɚ/ *noun, pl* **cheers**

1 [*count*] : a shout of praise or encouragement ▪ The audience let out a *cheer*. ▪ Loud *cheers* were coming from the bleachers. ▪ The star was greeted with *cheers*. ▪ ***Three cheers for*** our team! [=hooray for our team]

2 [*noncount*] *somewhat formal* : a happy feeling or attitude ▪ faces full of *cheer* ▪ Let's spread a little holiday *cheer*. ▪ ***Be of good cheer.*** [=be happy]

3 [*count*] : a special song or chant that is performed to encourage a team during a game in sports like American football and basketball ▪ The cheerleaders did/led a *cheer* for the home team. — see also BRONX CHEER

[2]**cheer** *verb* **cheers; cheered; cheer·ing**

1 a : to shout with joy, approval, or enthusiasm [*no obj*] The crowd *cheered* as he crossed the finish line. ▪ We were *cheering* for you all the way! [+ *obj*] The crowd *cheered* him as he crossed the finish line. ▪ Their fans *cheered* them to victory. **b** [+ *obj*] : to express enthusiastic approval of or support for (something) ▪ Supporters *cheered* the court's decision.

2 [+ *obj*] : to cause (someone) to feel happier or more hopeful ▪ Investors were *cheered* by good economic news.

cheer on [*phrasal verb*] ***cheer (someone) on*** or ***cheer on (someone)*** : to encourage (someone) with shouts or cheers ▪ Their fans *cheered* them *on* from the sidelines.

cheer up [*phrasal verb*] **1** ***cheer up*** or ***cheer (someone) up*** or ***cheer up (someone)*** : to become happier or to make (someone) happier ▪ They *cheered up* at the mention of her name. ▪ *Cheer up*—things will get better! ▪ We tried our best to *cheer* her *up*. **2** ***cheer (something) up*** or ***cheer up (something)*** : to make (something) more cheerful or pleasant ▪ Bright colors really *cheer up* a room.

cheer·ful /ˈtʃiɚfəl/ *adj* [*more* ~; *most* ~]

1 a : feeling or showing happiness ▪ a *cheerful* face/person ▪ She has a *cheerful* outlook on life. ▪ He seems a little more *cheerful* today. **b** : feeling or showing that you are willing to do something without complaining ▪ *cheerful* obedience

2 a : causing good feelings or happiness ▪ *cheerful* words/news **b** : bright and pleasant to look at ▪ *cheerful* colors ▪ a sunny *cheerful* room

– **cheer·ful·ly** *adv* ▪ He *cheerfully* admitted that he was wrong. ▪ She greeted us *cheerfully*. – **cheer·ful·ness** *noun* [*noncount*]

cheer·io /ˌtʃiriˈoʊ/ *interj, Brit, informal + somewhat old-fashioned* : [1]GOODBYE

cheer·lead·er /ˈtʃiɚˌliːdɚ/ *noun, pl* **-ers** [*count*]

1 : a person who is a member of a group (typically a group of young women) who shout out special songs or chants to encourage the team and entertain the crowd during a game in sports like American football and basketball

2 : a person who encourages other people to do or support something ▪ a politician who is a *cheerleader* for the government's new economic plan

– **cheer·lead·ing** *noun* [*noncount*] ▪ She participates in both soccer and *cheerleading* at school. — often used before another noun ▪ *cheerleading* tryouts/practice ▪ a *cheerleading* team/squad

cheer·less /ˈtʃiɚləs/ *adj* [*more* ~; *most* ~] : not causing happiness or warm feelings : bleak or gloomy ▪ a *cheerless* day/place ▪ The room was surprisingly bare and *cheerless*.

cheers /ˈtʃiɚz/ *interj*

1 — used as a toast to wish everyone happiness ▪ Drink up, everybody. *Cheers!*

2 *Brit* **a** — used as an informal way to say "thank you" **b** — used as an informal way to say "goodbye"

cheery /ˈtʃiri/ *adj* **cheer·i·er; -est** : having or causing happy feelings : CHEERFUL ▪ *cheery* words/colors

– **cheer·i·ly** /ˈtʃirəli/ *adv* – **cheer·i·ness** /ˈtʃirinəs/ *noun* [*noncount*]

cheese /ˈtʃiːz/ *noun, pl* **chees·es** : a yellow or white solid food that is made from milk [*noncount*] a piece of *cheese* ▪ Sprinkle the casserole with *cheese.* ▪ grated/melted *cheese* [*count*] imported *cheeses* ▪ a mild *cheese* — often used before another noun ▪ *cheese* sandwiches/omelets ▪ a *cheese* [=*cheesy*] sauce/spread

say cheese ✧ If you say the word "cheese" in an exaggerated way, you look like you are smiling, so someone who is taking your photograph and wants you to smile will tell you to *say cheese.*

– see also BIG CHEESE

cheese·burg·er /ˈʧiːzˌbɚgɚ/ *noun, pl* **-ers** [*count*] : a hamburger with a piece of cheese on top of the meat

cheese·cake /ˈʧiːzˌkeɪk/ *noun, pl* **-cakes**

1 [*count, noncount*] : a cake with a sweet filling usually made of cheese, eggs, and sugar

2 [*noncount*] *informal* : pictures of attractive young women who are wearing little clothing ▪ advertisers who rely on *cheesecake* to sell products — often used before another noun ▪ *cheesecake* photos/posters/calendars — compare BEEFCAKE

cheese·cloth /ˈʧiːzˌklɑːθ/ *noun* [*noncount*] : a very thin cotton cloth that is used especially in preparing food

cheesed off /ˌʧiːzdˈɑːf/ *adj* [*more ~; most ~*] *Brit, informal* : angry or annoyed ▪ feeling a bit *cheesed off*

cheese·steak /ˈʧiːzˌsteɪk/ *noun, pl* **-steaks** [*count*] *US* : a sandwich made with thin slices of beef and melted cheese

cheesy /ˈʧiːzi/ *adj* **chees·i·er**; **-est**

1 a : resembling cheese; *especially* : looking or smelling like cheese ▪ a *cheesy* texture/odor **b** : containing cheese ▪ a *cheesy* sauce

2 *informal* : of poor quality : lacking style or good taste ▪ a *cheesy* [=*cheap, shabby*] motel ▪ a *cheesy* movie ▪ *cheesy* [=*corny*] pop songs

chee·tah /ˈʧiːtə/ *noun, pl* **-tahs** [*count*] : a large wild cat that lives in Asia and Africa and that can run very fast — see picture at CAT

chef /ˈʃɛf/ *noun, pl* **chefs** [*count*]

1 : a professional cook who usually is in charge of a kitchen in a restaurant ▪ The hotel's *chef* trained at the finest culinary institutes in Europe. ▪ He's the ***head chef*** at a five-star restaurant. ▪ a ***celebrity chef*** with her own TV show

2 : a person who prepares food for people to eat : COOK ▪ My friend is an excellent *chef.*

[1]chem·i·cal /ˈkɛmɪkəl/ *adj*

1 : of or relating to chemistry ▪ a *chemical* analysis ▪ *chemical* elements/bonds ▪ They studied the compound's *chemical* structure/composition/properties. ▪ a *chemical* laboratory

2 : working by means of chemicals ▪ *chemical* pesticides/weapons/agents — see also CHEMICAL WARFARE

– **chem·i·cal·ly** /ˈkɛmɪkli/ *adv* ▪ The wood is *chemically* treated. ▪ drugs that are *chemically* related

[2]chemical *noun, pl* **-cals** [*count*] : a substance (such as an element or compound) that is made by a chemical process ▪ toxic/hazardous/industrial *chemicals*

chemical engineering *noun* [*noncount*] : a type of engineering that deals with the use of chemistry in industry

– **chemical engineer** *noun, pl* **~ -neers** [*count*]

chemical reaction *noun, pl* **~ -tions** [*count*] : REACTION 5a

chemical warfare *noun* [*noncount*] : the use of chemical substances (such as poisonous gases) as weapons in a war

che·mise /ʃəˈmiːz/ *noun, pl* **-mis·es** [*count*]

1 : a piece of clothing that looks like a light, loose dress and that is worn by women as underwear or in bed

2 : a loose dress that hangs straight

chem·ist /ˈkɛmɪst/ *noun, pl* **-ists** [*count*]

1 : a person who studies or does research in the science of chemistry

2 *Brit* : PHARMACIST

chem·is·try /ˈkɛməstri/ *noun* [*noncount*]

1 : a science that deals with the structure and properties of substances and with the changes that they go through ▪ a professor of *chemistry* — see also INORGANIC CHEMISTRY, ORGANIC CHEMISTRY

2 : the structure and properties of a substance : the way a substance changes and reacts with other substances ▪ studying the *chemistry* of gasoline/iron ▪ blood/body *chemistry*

3 a : a strong attraction between people ▪ They tried dating, but there was no *chemistry* between them. **b** : the way the people in a group work together and feel about each other ▪ the *chemistry* of the office ▪ The team lacks *chemistry.*

chemistry set *noun, pl* **~ sets** [*count*] : a set of equipment that a child can use to learn about chemistry by doing simple experiments

che·mo·ther·a·py /ˌkiːmoʊˈθerəpi/ *noun* [*noncount*] *medical* : the use of chemicals to treat or control a disease (such as cancer) ▪ She underwent (a course of) *chemotherapy.*

che·nille /ʃəˈniːl/ *noun* [*noncount*] : a thick, soft cloth ▪ a *chenille* bedspread

cheque *Brit spelling of* [2]CHECK 3

cheque·book *Brit spelling of* CHECKBOOK

cheque card *noun, pl* **~ cards** [*count*] *Brit* : a card that you show when you pay for something with a cheque to prove that the bank will pay the amount of the cheque

che·quered *Brit spelling of* CHECKERED

cher·ish /ˈʧerɪʃ/ *verb* **-ish·es**; **-ished**; **-ish·ing** [+ *obj*]

1 : to feel or show great love for (someone or something) ▪ She *cherishes* her friends/family. ▪ a book *cherished* by many ***synonyms*** see APPRECIATE

2 : to remember or hold (an idea, belief, etc.) in a deeply felt way ▪ I will always *cherish* that memory.

– **cherished** *adj* [*more ~; most ~*] ▪ a *cherished* friend ▪ my most *cherished* and deeply held beliefs

Cher·o·kee /ˈʧerəki/ *noun, pl* **-kee** *or* **-kees** [*count*] : a member of a Native American people originally from Tennessee and North Carolina

cher·ry /ˈʧeri/ *noun, pl* **-ries**

1 a [*count*] : a small round fruit that is usually red or black — see color picture on page C5 **b** [*count*] : a tree on which this fruit grows — called also *cherry tree* **c** [*noncount*] : the wood of a cherry tree ▪ The kitchen cabinets are made of *cherry.* — called also *cherry wood*

2 [*noncount*] : a bright red color — called also *cherry red*; see color picture on page C3

– **cherry** *adj* ▪ *cherry* juice/pie ▪ a *cherry* table [=a table made of cherry wood] ▪ *cherry* [=*red*] lips

cherry bomb *noun, pl* **~ bombs** [*count*] *US* : a round firecracker that makes a loud noise when it explodes

cher·ry–pick /ˈʧeriˌpɪk/ *verb* **-picks**; **-picked**; **-pick·ing** : to pick or accept the best people or things in a group [+ *obj*] Hollywood's biggest stars can *cherry-pick* the best projects and directors. [*no obj*] elite colleges that can *cherry-pick* from the best students available

cherry tomato *noun, pl* **~ -toes** [*count*] : a very small red or orange tomato or a plant that produces such tomatoes

cher·ub /ˈʧerəb/ *noun* [*count*]

1 *pl* ***cherubs or cherubim*** : a type of angel that is usually shown in art as a beautiful young child with small wings and a round face and body

2 *pl* ***cherubs*** : someone (such as a child) who is thought of as being like a small angel ▪ My little *cherub*! — sometimes used in combination ▪ a *cherub*-faced toddler

– **che·ru·bic** /ʧəˈruːbɪk/ *adj* ▪ a child with a *cherubic* face

cher·vil /ˈʧɚvəl/ *noun* [*noncount*] : an herb that is often used in cooking and salads

chess /ˈʧɛs/ *noun* [*noncount*] : a game for two players in which each player moves 16 pieces across a board and tries to place the opponent's king in a position from which it cannot escape ▪ We played (a game of) *chess.* — often used before another noun ▪ a *chess* player/champion ▪ a *chess* match/tournament

chess·board /ˈʧɛsˌboɚd/ *noun, pl* **-boards** [*count*] : a board used in chess that has 64 squares in two colors

chess·man /ˈʧɛsˌmæn/ *noun, pl* **-men** /-mən/ [*count*] : any of the playing pieces used in chess : a chess piece

chest /ˈʧɛst/ *noun, pl* **chests** [*count*]

1 : a container (such as a box or case) for holding things or moving them from place to place ▪ a linen *chest* ▪ a tool *chest* ▪ a treasure *chest* ▪ a ***medicine chest*** [=a cabinet on a bathroom wall that is used for storing medicine and small items] — see also CHEST OF DRAWERS, HOPE CHEST, WAR CHEST

2 : the front part of the body between the neck and the stomach ▪ He has a broad *chest.* ▪ The pain is in my upper *chest.* — often used before another noun ▪ the *chest* cavity ▪ a *chest* X-ray ▪ She's been complaining of *chest* pains. — see picture at HUMAN

close to your chest see [2]CLOSE

get (something) off your chest : to tell someone about something that has been making you upset or unhappy ▪ You've been a little cold to me lately. Is there something you'd like to *get off your chest*?

– **chest·ed** /ˈʧɛstəd/ *adj* — used in combination ▪ flat-*chested* ▪ bare-*chested*

¹**chest·nut** /ˈʧɛsˌnʌt/ *noun, pl* **-nuts**
1 a [*count*] : a type of tree that produces large, sweet nuts that can be eaten — called also *chestnut tree* **b** [*count*] : the nut of a chestnut tree ▪ roasted *chestnuts* — see picture at NUT **c** [*noncount*] : the wood of a chestnut tree — see also HORSE CHESTNUT, WATER CHESTNUT
2 [*count*] : a brown or reddish-brown horse

²**chestnut** *adj* : of a reddish-brown color ▪ *chestnut* hair ▪ a *chestnut* stallion

chest of drawers *noun, pl* **chests of drawers** [*count*] : a piece of furniture that contains drawers for storing clothes — called also (*US*) *bureau*

chev·ron /ˈʃɛvrən/ *noun, pl* **-rons** [*count*]
1 : a shape, pattern, or object in the form of a V or an upside-down V
2 : a piece of cloth that is shaped like a V and that is worn on the sleeve of a military or police uniform to show a person's rank

¹**chew** /ˈʧuː/ *verb* **chews; chewed; chew·ing**
1 a : to use your teeth to cut food into small pieces before you swallow it [+ *obj*] We were taught to *chew* our food thoroughly before swallowing. [*no obj*] He *chews* with his mouth open. **b** : to bite on (something) repeatedly with the teeth [+ *obj*] You're not allowed to *chew* gum in class. ▪ *chew* tobacco ▪ Stop *chewing* [=*biting*] your nails. [*no obj*] A mouse *chewed* through the cord. — often + *on* ▪ The dog was *chewing on* a bone.
2 [+ *obj*] : to make (something, such as a hole) by chewing ▪ The dog *chewed* a hole in the rug.
bite off more than you can chew see ¹BITE
chew off [*phrasal verb*] ***chew off (something) or chew (something) off*** : to remove (something) by chewing ▪ The dog *chewed* the doll's eyes *off*.
chew on [*phrasal verb*] ***chew on (something)*** *informal* : to think about (something) ▪ *Chew on* it for a while before you decide. ▪ That should give you *something to chew on*. — see also ¹CHEW 1b (above)
chew out [*phrasal verb*] ***chew (someone) out or chew out (someone)*** *US, informal* : to speak in an angry and critical way to (someone) ▪ I got *chewed out* [=*reprimanded*] for leaving early. ▪ The coach *chewed* him *out*.
chew over [*phrasal verb*] ***chew (something) over or chew over (something)*** *informal* : to think about (something) ▪ He *chewed* the problem *over* in his mind. ▪ *Chew it over* for a while before you decide.
chew the fat also chew the rag *informal* : to talk together in a friendly and casual way ▪ They would sit for hours and *chew the fat*. [=*chat, shoot the breeze*]
chew up [*phrasal verb*] ***chew (something) up or chew up (something)*** **1** : to destroy (something) by chewing it ▪ My new puppy *chewed up* my shoes. **2** *informal* : to destroy or defeat (someone or something) ▪ The truck *chewed up* the grass. ▪ The gears got all *chewed up*. ▪ They *chewed up* the competition. ▪ Don't mess with her—she'll ***chew you up and spit you out***.
– **chew·able** /ˈʧuːwəbəl/ *adj* ▪ *chewable* vitamins – **chew·er** *noun, pl* **-ers** [*count*] ▪ gum *chewers*

²**chew** *noun, pl* **chews** [*count*]
1 : the act of chewing something ▪ a quick *chew*
2 : something that a person or animal chews ▪ a *chew* of tobacco ▪ a rawhide *chew*

chewing gum *noun* [*noncount*] : a type of soft candy that you chew on but do not swallow ▪ a piece/stick of *chewing gum*

chewing tobacco *noun* [*noncount*] : a type of tobacco that is chewed rather than smoked

chew toy *noun, pl* **~ toys** [*count*] *US* : a toy that is designed to be chewed by a dog

chewy /ˈʧuːwi/ *adj* **chew·i·er; -est** [*also more ~; most ~*] : requiring a lot of chewing ▪ *chewy* meat ▪ a *chewy* candy/cookie

Chey·enne /ʃaɪˈæn/ *noun, pl* **-ennes** [*count*] : a member of a Native American people of the western U.S.

Chi·an·ti /kiˈɑːnti, *Brit* kiˈænti/ *noun, pl* **-tis** [*count, noncount*] : a dry red wine from Italy

¹**chic** /ˈʃiːk/ *adj* [*more ~; most ~*] : following the current fashion or style : fashionable and appealing ▪ *chic* clothes ▪ The café has a *chic* new look. ▪ She looked very *chic*.

²**chic** *noun* [*noncount*] : fashionable style ▪ French *chic* ▪ It's the height of *chic* this year.

chi·ca·nery /ʃɪˈkeɪnəri/ *noun* [*noncount*] *formal* : actions or statements that trick people into believing something that is not true : deception or trickery ▪ He wasn't above using *chicanery* to win votes.

Chi·ca·na /ʧɪˈkɑːnə/ *noun, pl* **-nas** [*count*] : an American woman or girl whose parents or grandparents came from Mexico
– **Chicana** *adj* ▪ a *Chicana* writer

Chi·ca·no /ʧɪˈkɑːnoʊ/ *noun, pl* **-nos** [*count*] : an American (especially a man or boy) whose parents or grandparents came from Mexico
– **Chicano** *adj* ▪ *Chicano* artists ▪ the *Chicano* community

chi·chi /ˈʃiːˌʃiː/ *adj* [*more ~; most ~*] *usually disapproving* : fashionable or showy especially in a way that is meant to impress people or to attract attention ▪ a *chichi* restaurant/nightclub

chick /ˈʧɪk/ *noun, pl* **chicks** [*count*]
1 : a baby bird ▪ eagle *chicks*; *especially* : a baby chicken ▪ a mother hen and her *chicks*
2 *informal* : a woman or girl ▪ a cute *chick* ✧ This sense of *chick* is somewhat old-fashioned and is now sometimes considered offensive.

chick·a·dee /ˈʧɪkəˌdiː/ *noun, pl* **-dees** [*count*] : a common, small American bird — see color picture on page C9

¹**chick·en** /ˈʧɪkn̩/ *noun, pl* **-ens**
1 a [*count*] : a bird that is raised by people for its eggs and meat **b** [*noncount*] : the meat of the chicken used as food ▪ We had *chicken* for dinner. ▪ fried/roasted/grilled *chicken* — often used before another noun ▪ *chicken* soup/broth ▪ *chicken* salad
2 [*count*] *informal* : a person who is afraid : COWARD ▪ It's just a spider, you *chicken*! ▪ Don't be such a big *chicken*.
count your chickens ✧ If you ***count your chickens*** or (*US*) ***count your chickens before they hatch*** or (*Brit*) ***before they're hatched***, you believe that something you want to happen will definitely happen before you know for certain that it really will. ▪ Don't *count your chickens before they hatch*—we don't know yet if she will accept our offer.

your chickens come home to roost see ²ROOST
— see also SPRING CHICKEN

²chicken *adj, not used before a noun* [*more* ~; *most* ~] *informal* : too afraid to do something • He's too *chicken* [=*cowardly*] to stand up to them. • You're *chicken*, aren't you?

³chicken *verb* **-ens**; **-ened**; **-en·ing**
chicken out [*phrasal verb*] *informal* : to decide not to do something because you are afraid • He was going to ask her on a date, but he *chickened out* at the last minute.

chicken–and–egg *adj* — used to describe a situation in which it is difficult to tell which of two things happened first • a *chicken-and-egg* situation/dilemma

chicken feed *noun* [*noncount*] *informal* : an amount of money that is too small to be considered important • The project cost almost a million dollars, which isn't exactly *chicken feed*. • Ten bucks? That's *chicken feed*!

chick·en–fried steak /ˈʧɪkənˈfraɪd-/ *noun, pl* ~ **steaks** [*count, noncount*] *US* : a steak that is coated with flour, fried, and served with gravy

chicken pox *noun* [*noncount*] : a disease that often affects children and that causes a fever and red spots on the skin

chick·en·shit /ˈʧɪkn̩ˌʃɪt/ *adj* [*more* ~; *most* ~] *US slang, offensive* : weak and cowardly • That guy likes to make threats but he's too *chickenshit* to act on them.
— **chickenshit** *noun, pl* **-shits** *US slang, offensive* [*count*] a bunch of *chickenshits*. [=*cowards*] [*noncount*] a load of *chickenshit* [=*nonsense, bullshit*]

chicken wire *noun* [*noncount*] : a type of strong wire that is used especially to make fences

chick flick *noun, pl* ~ **flicks** [*count*] *informal* : a movie that is intended to appeal to women

chick·pea /ˈʧɪkˌpiː/ *noun, pl* **-peas** [*count*] : a pale round seed that is cooked and eaten as a vegetable — called also (*US*) *garbanzo*, (*US*) *garbanzo bean*

chic·o·ry /ˈʧɪkəri/ *noun, pl* **-ries** [*count, noncount*] : a European plant that has bitter-tasting leaves that are often used in salads ✧ The dried, ground root of the chicory plant is sometimes used as a flavoring in or substitute for coffee. — compare BELGIAN ENDIVE

chide /ˈʧaɪd/ *verb* **chides**; **chid·ed** /ˈʧaɪdəd/; **chid·ing** /ˈʧaɪdɪŋ/ [+ *obj*] : to express mild disapproval of (someone) : to scold (someone) gently • She *chided* us for arriving late. • "You really should have been here on time," she *chided*.

¹chief /ˈʧiːf/ *noun, pl* **chiefs** [*count*] : the person who is the leader of a group of people, of an organization, etc. • She's the *chief* of surgery [=the doctor who is in charge of the surgical department] at the hospital. • the police *chief* = the *chief of police* • the fire *chief* [=the head of a department of firefighters] • an Indian *chief* [=the leader of a tribe of Native Americans]

²chief *adj, always used before a noun*
1 : highest in rank or authority • the *chief* engineer on the project • the company's *chief* executive — see also COMMANDER IN CHIEF, EDITOR IN CHIEF
2 : most important : MAIN • Her job is their *chief* source of income. • their *chief* accomplishment • our *chief* competitor • He has many concerns, *chief* among them his health.

chief constable *noun, pl* ~ **-stables** [*count*] *Brit* : a police officer who is in charge of a police force

chief executive *noun, pl* ~ **-tives** [*count*]
1 : CEO
2 a : the president of a country • The President is the *chief executive* of the U.S. **b** : the governor of a U.S. state

chief executive officer *noun, pl* ~ **-cers** [*count*] : CEO

chief justice *or* **Chief Justice** *noun, pl* ~ **-tices** [*count*] : the most important and powerful judge of a court of law and especially of the U.S. Supreme Court

chief·ly /ˈʧiːfli/ *adv* : mainly or mostly — used to identify the most important part of something, reason for something, etc. • We're *chiefly* concerned with protecting the environment. • His greatest works—*chiefly* those written between 1640 and 1685—are still read today. • an animal that hunts *chiefly* by smell • The disease occurs *chiefly* in children. • The rock is composed *chiefly* of quartz.

chief of staff *noun, pl* **chiefs of staff** [*count*]
1 : a person of high rank in the U.S. Army, Navy, Air Force, or Marines who advises the person in charge of military operations — see also JOINT CHIEFS OF STAFF
2 : a person of high rank who advises a leader (such as the U.S. President) on important matters • the White House *Chief of Staff*

chief of state *noun, pl* **chiefs of state** [*count*] : a person who is formally recognized as the leader of a country • a meeting with foreign chiefs of state

chief·tain /ˈʧiːftən/ *noun, pl* **-tains** [*count*] : a leader of a tribe or clan

chif·fon /ʃɪˈfɑːn, ˈʃɪˌfɑːn/ *noun* [*noncount*] : a very thin cloth made especially of silk • a *chiffon* dress/scarf

chig·ger /ˈʧɪgɚ/ *noun, pl* **-gers** [*count*] *US* : a small insect that bites people and causes painful swelling on the skin

chi·gnon /ˈʃiːnˌjɑːn/ *noun, pl* **chi·gnons** [*count*] : a way of arranging a woman's hair by twisting it into a round shape at the back of the head or neck

Chi·hua·hua /ʧəˈwɑːwɑ/ *noun, pl* **-huas** [*count*] : a type of very small dog with large ears and usually short hair — see picture at DOG

chil·blain /ˈʧɪlˌbleɪn/ *noun* [*count*] : a red and painful swollen area on the feet, hands, etc., that is caused by being exposed to cold — usually plural

child /ˈʧajəld/ *noun, pl* **chil·dren** /ˈʧɪldrən/ [*count*]
1 : a young person • the birth of a *child* • She's pregnant with their first *child*. • a play for both *children* and adults • I went there once ***as a child*** [=when I was a child] — often used before another noun. • a *child* prodigy • a *child* actor • *child* development • *child* psychologists
2 : a son or daughter • All of their *children* are grown now. • an elderly couple and their adult *children*
3 : an adult who acts like a child : a childlike or childish person • I'm a *child* when it comes to doing taxes. [=I need to be told or shown what to do] • Men are such *children* sometimes.
4 : a person who has been strongly influenced by a certain place or time or by the events happening during that time • She's a *child* of her time. • a *child* of the Depression
children should be seen and not heard — used to say that children should be quiet and well-behaved
with child *old-fashioned* : PREGNANT • She found herself *with child*. [=she discovered that she was pregnant]
— see also BRAINCHILD

child·bear·ing /ˈʧajəldˌberɪŋ/ *noun* [*noncount*] : the process of giving birth to children • women who delay *childbearing*
— **childbearing** *adj* • women of *childbearing* age [=women who are old enough to give birth to children]

child benefit *noun, pl* ~ **-fits** [*count*] *Brit* : money that the government pays to families with children

child·birth /ˈʧajəldˌbɚθ/ *noun, pl* **-births** : the act or process of giving birth to children [*count*] the total number of *childbirths* [=(more commonly) *births*] [*noncount*] advocates of natural *childbirth*

child·care /ˈʧajəldˌkeɚ/ *noun* [*noncount*] : the things that are done to take care of children especially when their parents are away or at work • The cost of *childcare* can be expensive. • *Childcare* is available for children under five. — often used before another noun • *childcare* centers/workers

child·hood /ˈʧajəldˌhʊd/ *noun, pl* **-hoods** : the period of time when a person is a child [*noncount*] I remember this place from (my) *childhood*. • diseases that can occur in *childhood* [*count*] Both men had unhappy *childhoods*. — often used before another noun • *childhood* heroes/friends/memories • my *childhood* home — see also SECOND CHILDHOOD

child·ish /ˈʧaɪldɪʃ/ *adj* [*more* ~; *most* ~] : of a child or typical of a child • She has a *childish* face. • a letter written in *childish* scrawl • He opened the gifts with *childish* delight. ; *especially, disapproving* : having or showing the unpleasant qualities (such as silliness or lack of maturity) that children often have • a *childish* prank • We're tired of their *childish* games. • I find his humor very *childish*. — compare CHILDLIKE
— **child·ish·ly** *adv* • a *childishly* simple idea — **child·ish·ness** *noun* [*noncount*] • She was annoyed by the *childishness* of his behavior.

child·less /ˈʧajəldləs/ *adj* : having no children • *childless* couples
— **child·less·ness** *noun* [*noncount*]

child·like /ˈʧajəldˌlaɪk/ *adj* [*more* ~; *most* ~] : resembling or suggesting a child : like that of a child • a *childlike* drawing/voice • a grown woman with a *childlike* face ; *especially* : having or showing the pleasing qualities (such as innocence) that children often have • *childlike* faith/enthusiasm • We gazed at it in *childlike* wonder. • She took a *childlike* glee in describing every detail. — compare CHILDISH

child·mind·er /ˈʧajəldˌmaɪndɚ/ *noun, pl* **-ers** [*count*] *Brit*

: a person who is paid to take care of children usually in his or her home while the parents are at work • a registered *childminder*

[1]**child·proof** /ˈʧajəldˌpru:f/ *adj* [*more* ~; *most* ~]
1 : made so that a child cannot open it • a *childproof* bottle
2 : made safe for children • a *childproof* home [=a home where dangerous objects, chemicals, etc., have been removed or placed where children cannot get them]

[2]**childproof** *verb* **-proofs**; **-proofed**; **-proof·ing** [+ *obj*] : to make (a place) safe for children • The article has tips on how to *childproof* a home.

child–rearing *noun* [*noncount*] : the process of taking care of and raising children • Her husband is actively involved in *child-rearing*. — often used before another noun • *child-rearing* practices/methods

children *plural of* CHILD

child's play *noun* [*noncount*] : something that is very easy to do • Landing a job should be *child's play* for someone with his skills.

child support *noun* [*noncount*] : money that a former husband or wife must pay regularly to help raise a child — called also (*Brit*) *maintenance*

chili (*US*) *or Brit* **chil·li** *also US* **chile** /ˈʧɪli/ *noun, pl* **chil·ies** *also* **chil·es** *or Brit* **chil·lies**
1 [*count, noncount*] : a small pepper with a very hot flavor — called also *chili pepper*
2 [*noncount*] : a spicy dish made of ground beef, hot peppers or chili powder, and usually beans • a bowl of *chili* — called also *chili con car·ne* /-ˌkɑ:nˈkaəni/

chili dog *noun, pl* ~ **dogs** [*count*] *US* : a hot dog with chili on top of it

chili powder (*US*) *or Brit* **chilli powder** *noun* [*noncount*] : a dry powder that is made of chilies and other spices and that is used to give food a hot flavor

chili sauce *noun* [*noncount*] *US* : a spicy sauce that is made with tomatoes and hot red and green peppers

[1]**chill** /ˈʧɪl/ *noun, pl* **chills**
1 [*singular*] : a cold feeling : a degree of cold that can be felt and that is usually unpleasant • There was a *chill* in the autumn air. • He closed the windows to keep out the *chill*. • I'll turn on the heat for a bit, just to ***take the chill off***. [=raise the temperature slightly to a comfortable level] — see also WINDCHILL
2 [*count*] **a** : a feeling of being cold • Her symptoms include *chills* and a fever. **b** : an illness that makes you feel cold • He ***caught a chill*** that turned into a bad cold.
3 [*count*] : a sudden feeling of fear • I feel a *chill* (of fear) every time I look at the photograph. • The novel's final scene ***gave him the chills***. • Her words ***sent chills down my spine***.
4 [*singular*] **a** : a cold and unfriendly quality • I felt the *chill* of my opponent's stare. **b** : a change that causes less friendly relations between people, countries, etc. • There has been a *chill* in diplomatic relations. [=diplomatic relations have grown colder]

[2]**chill** *verb* **chills**; **chilled**; **chill·ing**
1 a [+ *obj*] : to make (someone or something) cold or cool • *Chill* the dessert for one hour before serving it. — often used as *(be) chilled* • The spectators *were chilled* by the cold wind. • *chilled* wine • a *chilled* soup • I *was **chilled to the bone/marrow***. [=very cold] **b** [*no obj*] : to become cold or cool • Let the dessert *chill* for one hour before serving it.
2 [+ *obj*] : to cause (someone) to feel afraid • Here's a ghost story that will *chill* you. • Her screams ***chilled me to the bone/marrow***. • a horrible sight that ***chilled my bones/blood***
3 [*no obj*] *informal* **a** : to become more relaxed : to become less tense, anxious, or angry • He thinks his parents are way too uptight and says they should just *chill*. — often + *out* • They should just *chill out*. — often used as a command • *Chill* (*out*), man. **b** : to spend time in a relaxed manner • I decided to stay home and *chill*. — often + *out* • She's been *chilling out* with her girlfriends.

[3]**chill** *adj, somewhat formal* : unpleasantly cold : CHILLY • The nights grew *chill*. • The *chill* weather kept us indoors. • a *chill* wind

chilli *chiefly Brit spelling of* CHILI

chill·ing /ˈʧɪlɪŋ/ *adj* [*more* ~; *most* ~] : very disturbing or frightening • a *chilling* tale
– **chill·ing·ly** *adv* • *chillingly* cruel • a *chillingly* accurate description of the murderer

chilly /ˈʧɪli/ *adj* **chill·i·er**; **-est** [*also more* ~; *most* ~]
1 : noticeably cold • a *chilly* morning • a *chilly* breeze • It's a little *chilly* outside.
2 : feeling cold • I was getting *chilly*. • You must be *chilly* without a coat on.
3 : noticeably unfriendly • They gave him a *chilly* reception.
– **chill·i·ness** *noun* [*noncount*] the *chilliness* of the air [*singular*] She felt a *chilliness* in his voice.

[1]**chime** /ˈʧaɪm/ *noun, pl* **chimes** [*count*]
1 : a device that produces a sound like the sound made by a set of bells • The clock *chime* struck four. — usually plural • We bought a set of door *chimes*. — see also WIND CHIME
2 : the sound made by a set of bells • the *chime* of church bells — usually plural • We awoke to the *chimes* of a nearby church.

[2]**chime** *verb* **chimes**; **chimed**; **chim·ing**
1 [*no obj*] : to make the sound of a ringing bell • The door bell *chimed*.
2 *of a clock* : to make a ringing sound that indicates the time [+ *obj*] The clock *chimed* midnight. [*no obj*] The clock *chimed*.
3 [*no obj*] : to agree : to be in harmony • The music and the mood *chimed* well together. — often + *with* • His opinion doesn't *chime with* mine.
chime in [*phrasal verb*] **1** : to add your comment or opinion to a conversation or discussion that you have been listening to • He kept *chiming in* with his opinions. • "He left hours ago," Janet *chimed in*. **2** : to be in agreement or harmony *with* something • The illustrations *chimed in* perfectly *with* the story.

chi·me·ra /kaɪˈmirə/ *noun, pl* **-ras** [*count*]
1 ***Chimera*** : a monster from Greek mythology that breathes fire and has a lion's head, a goat's body, and a snake's tail
2 *formal* : something that exists only in the imagination and is not possible in reality • Economic stability in that country is a *chimera*.
– **chi·mer·i·cal** /kaɪˈmerəkəl/ *adj* [*more* ~; *most* ~] • *chimerical* [=*imaginary*] dreams of economic stability

chi·mi·chan·ga /ˌʧimiˈʧɑ:ŋgə/ *noun, pl* **-gas** [*count*] : a food that consists of a tortilla which is wrapped around a filling (such as seasoned meat) and deep-fried

chim·ney /ˈʧɪmni/ *noun, pl* **-neys** [*count*]
1 : a part of a building through which smoke rises into the outside air; *especially* : the part that sticks up above the roof — see picture at HOUSE; see also *smoke like a chimney* at [2]SMOKE
2 : a tall narrow opening through a large piece of rock (such as a cliff) that can be used for climbing the rock

chimney breast *noun, pl* ~ **breasts** [*count*] *Brit* : a part of a wall that extends out into a room to cover a chimney

chim·ney·piece /ˈʧɪmniˌpi:s/ *noun, pl* **-piec·es** [*count*] *Brit* : MANTELPIECE 1

chimney pot *noun, pl* ~ **pots** [*count*] *chiefly Brit* : a clay or metal pipe on top of a chimney

chimney stack *noun, pl* ~ **stacks** [*count*] *Brit*
1 : the part of a chimney that is above the roof of a building
2 : SMOKESTACK

chimney sweep *noun, pl* ~ **sweeps** [*count*] : a person who cleans the insides of chimneys

chimp /ˈʧɪmp/ *noun, pl* **chimps** [*count*] : CHIMPANZEE

chim·pan·zee /ˌʧɪmˌpænˈzi:/ *noun, pl* **-zees** [*count*] : an intelligent animal that is a type of ape and that lives mostly in trees in Africa — see picture at APE

chin /ˈʧɪn/ *noun, pl* **chins** [*count*] : the part of the face below the mouth and above the neck — see picture at FACE; see also DOUBLE CHIN
keep your chin up : to stay cheerful and hopeful during difficult times • He's still *keeping his chin up* despite all his health problems. • (*Keep your*) *chin up*! Everything will work out for the best.
take it on the chin *informal* **1** *US* : to be badly damaged or affected by something : to be hit hard by something • Many investors *took it on the chin* yesterday as the stock market dropped sharply. **2** *Brit* : to accept something difficult or unpleasant without complaining • The criticism was harsh but he *took it on the chin* and didn't try to blame anyone else.

chi·na /ˈʧaɪnə/ *noun* [*noncount*]
1 : a hard white material that is made of baked clay and used to make plates, bowls, etc. • This vase is (made of) *china*. — often used before another noun • a *china* teapot — see also BONE CHINA
2 : plates, bowls, cups, etc., that are made of china • She uses her good *china* when she has company for dinner.
a bull in a china shop see [1]BULL

Chi·na·town /ˈʧaɪnəˌtaʊn/ *noun, pl* **-towns** : the area of a city where many Chinese people live [*noncount*] We had dinner in *Chinatown*. [*count*] — usually singular ▪ There is a *Chinatown* in San Francisco.

chi·na·ware /ˈʧaɪnəˌweɚ/ *noun* [*noncount*] : CHINA 2

chin·chil·la /ʧɪnˈʧɪlə/ *noun, pl* **-las**

1 [*count*] : a small South American animal that has soft gray fur

2 [*noncount*] : the fur of a chinchilla ▪ The collar of the coat is *chinchilla*.

C

[1]**Chi·nese** /ʧaɪˈniːz/ *noun*

1 ***the Chinese*** : the people of China : Chinese people ▪ the customs of *the Chinese*

2 [*noncount*] : any one of a group of closely related languages that are spoken in China ▪ He is learning to speak *Chinese*.

[2]**Chinese** *adj* : of or relating to China, its people, or their languages ▪ *Chinese* history/food ▪ She is *Chinese*. ▪ The custom is *Chinese*. ▪ the *Chinese* writing system

Chinese cabbage *noun* [*noncount*]

1 : BOK CHOY

2 : a type of cabbage from Asia that has a long head and pale, wrinkled leaves

Chinese checkers (*US*) *or Brit* **Chinese chequers** *noun* [*noncount*] : a game in which players move marbles from one hole to another across a playing surface that is shaped like a star

Chinese whispers *noun* [*noncount*] *Brit* : a situation in which a piece of information is passed from one person to the next and is changed slightly each time it is told

[1]**chink** /ˈʧɪŋk/ *noun, pl* **chinks** [*count*]

1 : a small crack : a narrow opening or space — usually + *in* ▪ We peeked through a *chink in* the fence.

2 *chiefly Brit* : a small amount of light shining through a crack ▪ a *chink* of daylight

chink in someone's or something's armor see ARMOR

— compare [2]CHINK

[2]**chink** *noun, pl* **chinks** [*count*] : the short sharp sound made when objects made of metal or glass hit each other ▪ We heard the *chink* of coins from the slot machine. ▪ the *chink* [=*clink*] *of* her glass against mine — compare [1]CHINK

Chink /ˈʧɪŋk/ *noun, pl* **Chinks** [*count*] *informal + offensive* : a Chinese person ✧ The word *Chink* is very offensive and should be avoided.

chi·nos /ˈʧiːnoʊz/ *noun* [*plural*] : pants that are made of a somewhat stiff fabric and that are usually very light brown in color

chintz /ˈʧɪnts/ *noun* [*noncount*] : a shiny cotton fabric with a flowery pattern printed on it — often used before another noun ▪ *chintz* curtains ▪ a *chintz* sofa

chintzy /ˈʧɪntsi/ *adj* **chintz·i·er; -est** [*also more ~; most ~*]

1 *US, informal* **a** : not showing good taste : not tasteful or stylish ▪ The decorations were very *chintzy*. [=*tacky*] **b** : poorly or cheaply done or made : of low quality ▪ *chintzy* toys ▪ a *chintzy* low-budget film

2 *US, informal* : not willing to spend money or give anything away : stingy or cheap ▪ The boss is *chintzy* about raises.

3 *chiefly Brit* : decorated in or covered with chintz ▪ a *chintzy* cottage ▪ *chintzy* furniture

chin–up /ˈʧɪnˌʌp/ *noun, pl* **-ups** [*count*] *US* : PULL-UP

chin–wag /ˈʧɪnˌwæg/ *noun* [*singular*] *Brit, informal* : a friendly conversation : CHAT ▪ My mother and aunt were having a *chin-wag* in the kitchen.

[1]**chip** /ˈʧɪp/ *noun, pl* **chips** [*count*]

1 : a small piece that has been broken off from something larger ▪ wood *chips* ▪ *chips* of stone

2 : a place where a small piece of something has broken off ▪ The cup has a *chip* in/on it.

3 : a small piece of candy or chocolate used in baking ▪ chocolate *chips* ▪ ***chocolate chip cookies*** [=cookies with small bits of chocolate in them]

4 **a** : a thin, hard, and usually salty piece of food ▪ tortilla *chips*; *especially, US* : POTATO CHIP ▪ a bag of *chips* — see also CORN CHIP **b** *Brit* : FRENCH FRY — see also FISH AND CHIPS

5 : a small, flat, round piece of plastic that is used to represent an amount of money in gambling games like poker — see also BARGAINING CHIP

6 : a very small piece of hard material (called silicon) in a computer or other device that contains many electronic circuits ▪ computer/silicon *chips* — see also MICROCHIP

7 *US, informal* : a piece of dried waste matter from an animal ▪ buffalo/cow *chips*

8 : CHIP SHOT 1, 2

chip off the old block *informal* : someone who looks or behaves like his or her parent ▪ His son is a real *chip off the old block*.

have a chip on your shoulder *informal* : to have an angry or unpleasant attitude or way of behaving caused by a belief that you have been treated unfairly in the past ▪ He *has had a chip on his shoulder* ever since he didn't get the promotion he was expecting.

let the chips fall where they may *US, informal* : to allow events to happen without trying to change them ✧ This phrase usually suggests that you are willing to accept a result, whatever it may be. ▪ I will run the best campaign I can, then *let the chips fall where they may*.

when the chips are down *informal* : in a difficult situation : when things are not good ▪ True friends will stand by you *when the chips are down*.

[2]**chip** *verb* **chips; chipped; chip·ping**

1 **a** [+ *obj*] : to break off a small piece from (something) ▪ I bit into something hard and *chipped* my tooth. ▪ He fell and *chipped* a bone in his knee. ▪ She *chipped* a nail. [=she broke a small piece of hardened nail polish off a fingernail] ▪ a *chipped* cup/tooth **b** [*no obj*] : to break or come off in small pieces ▪ China *chips* easily. ▪ The paint had *chipped* off/away.

2 **a** *always followed by an adverb or preposition* [+ *obj*] : to break off (something) especially with a tool ▪ He *chipped* away the ice from the car's windshield. ▪ The sculptor *chipped* away/off bits of stone. ▪ The geologist *chipped* [=*cut*] the specimen out of the rock face. **b** [*no obj*] : to hit something with a tool in order to break off small pieces — usually + *away* ▪ The sculptor ***chipped away at*** the stone/marble. — often used figuratively ▪ There have been endless efforts to *chip away at* [=gradually reduce] social prejudice. ▪ His failures *chipped away at* his self-confidence.

3 : to hit or kick (a ball) so that it goes a short distance : to hit or kick a chip shot [+ *obj*] The golfer *chipped* the ball onto the green. ▪ She *chipped* the soccer ball over the goalie's head. ▪ He *chipped* a pass to his teammate. [*no obj*] The golfer *chipped* onto the green. ▪ She *chipped* in for par. [=she made a par by hitting a chip shot that went into the hole]

chip in [*phrasal verb*] **1** ***chip in or chip in (something)*** : to give something (such as money) to help a person, group, or cause ▪ We all *chipped in* [=*contributed*] to buy him a gift. ▪ If we all *chip in* [=*help (out)*], the work will get done quickly. ▪ We each *chipped in* 10 dollars. **2** *chiefly Brit* : to add your comment or opinion to a conversation or discussion ▪ "He left hours ago," Sue *chipped in*. [=*chimed in*]

chip·board /ˈʧɪpˌboɚd/ *noun* [*noncount*]

1 : PARTICLEBOARD

2 *US* : a type of cardboard made from paper that had been thrown away

chip·munk /ˈʧɪpˌmʌŋk/ *noun, pl* **-munks** [*count*] : a small North American animal that is related to the squirrel — see picture at RODENT

chip·o·la·ta /ˌʧɪpəˈlɑːtə/ *noun, pl* **-tas** [*count*] *Brit* : a small thin sausage

chipped beef *noun* [*noncount*] *US* : smoked dried beef that is sliced thin

[1]**chip·per** /ˈʧɪpɚ/ *adj* [*more ~; most ~*] *informal + somewhat old-fashioned* : cheerful and lively ▪ My, you're looking *chipper* this morning. ▪ She greeted me in a *chipper* voice.

[2]**chipper** *noun, pl* **-pers** [*count*] : a piece of equipment that is used to cut wood (such as tree branches) into small pieces ▪ a wood *chipper*

chip·py *also* **chip·pie** /ˈʧɪpi/ *noun, pl* **-pies** [*count*] *Brit, informal* : CHIP SHOP

chip shop *noun, pl* **~ shops** [*count*] *Brit* : a restaurant that sells fish and chips and other fried foods for people to take away and eat somewhere else

chip shot *noun, pl* **~ shots** [*count*]

1 *golf* : a very short shot that is made from an area near the green ▪ She hit a *chip shot* onto the green.

2 *soccer + rugby* : a short kick that lifts a ball high in the air ▪ He kicked a *chip shot* over the goalie's head.

3 *American football* : a short and easy field goal

chi·rop·o·dist /kəˈrɑːpədɪst/ *noun, pl* **-dists** [*count*] *chiefly Brit* : PODIATRIST

chi·ro·prac·tic /ˈkaɪrəˌpræktɪk/ *noun* [*noncount*] : a method of treating people who are sick or in pain by pushing and moving bones in the spine and joints

— **chiropractic** *adj* ▪ *chiropractic* care ▪ *chiropractic* adjustments of/to the spine — **chi·ro·prac·tor** /ˈkaɪrəˌpræktɚ/

noun, pl **-tors** [*count*] ▪ My sister goes to a *chiropractor* for her back pain.

chirp /ˈʧɚp/ *verb* **chirps**; **chirped**; **chirp·ing**
1 [*no obj*] **:** to make a short high-pitched sound ▪ The birds were *chirping* in the trees. ▪ We heard the crickets *chirping*.
2 [+ *obj*] **:** to say (something) in a cheerful and lively way ▪ "Good morning!" she *chirped*.
– chirp *noun, pl* **chirps** [*count*] ▪ the *chirps* of the birds

chirpy /ˈʧɚpi/ *adj* **chirp·i·er**; **-est** [*or more* ~; *most* ~] *informal* **:** cheerful and lively ▪ a *chirpy*, bright-eyed student
– chirp·i·ly /ˈʧɚpəli/ *adv* **– chirp·i·ness** /ˈʧɚpinəs/ *noun* [*noncount*]

chir·rup /ˈʧɚrəp/ *verb* **-rups**; **-ruped**; **rup·ing** [*no obj*] **:** CHIRP
– chirrup *noun, pl* **-rups** [*count*]

[1]**chis·el** /ˈʧɪzl/ *noun, pl* **-els** [*count*] **:** a metal tool with a flat, sharp end that is used to cut and shape a solid material (such as stone, wood, or metal) — see picture at CARPENTRY

[2]**chisel** *verb* **-els**; *US* **-eled** *or Brit* **-elled**; *US* **-el·ing** *or Brit* **-el·ling** [+ *obj*] **:** to cut or shape (something) with a chisel ▪ She *chiseled* the stone/wood/marble. ▪ He *chiseled* off a corner of the block. ▪ Letters were *chiseled* into a wall.

chis·eled (*US*) *or Brit* **chis·elled** /ˈʧɪzl̩d/ *adj* [*more* ~; *most* ~]
1 : having an attractive well-formed shape — used especially to describe a man's face and its features ▪ a handsome actor's *chiseled* face/jaw/nose
2 : having a strong, muscular body or form ▪ a *chiseled* bodybuilder ▪ He has the *chiseled* body of an athlete.

chit /ˈʧɪt/ *noun, pl* **chits** [*count*] **:** an official note that shows an amount of money that is owed or gives someone permission to have or do something

chit·chat /ˈʧɪtˌʧæt/ *noun, informal* **:** friendly conversation about things that are not very important [*noncount*] We exchanged some *chitchat* about the weather. [*singular*] I just had a *chitchat* [=*chat*] with my neighbor.
– chitchat *verb* **-chats**; **-chat·ted**; **-chat·ting** [*no obj*] ▪ I was just *chitchatting* [=*chatting*] with my neighbor.

chit·ter·lings *or* **chit·lins** /ˈʧɪtlənz/ *noun* [*plural*] *chiefly US* **:** the intestines of hogs eaten as food

chi·val·ric /ʃəˈvælrɪk/ *adj* **:** of or relating to the knights who fought in the Middle Ages ▪ *chivalric* adventures/codes

chiv·al·rous /ˈʃɪvəlrəs/ *adj* [*more* ~; *most* ~]
1 : behaving in an honorable or polite way especially toward women ▪ a kind and *chivalrous* man
2 : showing respect and politeness especially toward women ▪ *chivalrous* behavior ▪ a *chivalrous* act
– chiv·al·rous·ly *adv* ▪ He acted *chivalrously*.

chiv·al·ry /ʃɪvəlri/ *noun* [*noncount*]
1 : the system of values (such as loyalty and honor) that knights in the Middle Ages were expected to follow ▪ Medieval *chivalry* ▪ the knight's code of *chivalry*
2 : an honorable and polite way of behaving especially toward women ▪ He paid her fare as an act of *chivalry*.

chive /ˈʧaɪv/ *noun, pl* **chives**
1 [*count*] **:** a plant that is related to the onion
2 ***chives*** [*plural*] **:** the long thin leaves of the chive plant that are cut into small pieces and used for flavoring food ▪ Do you want *chives* on your baked potato?
– chive *adj, always used before a noun* ▪ *chive* sauce/butter

chiv·vy /ˈʧɪvi/ *verb* **chiv·vies**; **chiv·vied**; **chiv·vy·ing** [+ *obj*] *Brit, informal* **:** to try to make (someone) do something more quickly especially in an annoying way ▪ The parents *chivvied* the children along. ▪ They *chivvied* us to finish the job quicker.

chlo·ride /ˈkloɚˌaɪd/ *noun, pl* **-rides** [*count, noncount*] *technical* **:** a chemical compound of chlorine with another element or group ▪ sodium *chloride*

chlo·ri·nate /ˈklorəˌneɪt/ *verb* **-nates**; **-nat·ed**; **-nat·ing** [+ *obj*] *technical* **:** to add chlorine to (something, such as water) ▪ *chlorinated* water
– chlo·ri·na·tion /ˌklorəˈneɪʃən/ *noun* [*noncount*] ▪ *Chlorination* will kill the bacteria in the water.

chlo·rine /ˈkloɚˌiːn/ *noun* [*noncount*] **:** a chemical that in its natural form is a greenish-yellow gas and has a strong smell ✧ Chlorine in a liquid or solid form is often added to water (such as the water in a swimming pool) to keep it clean.

chlo·ro·flu·o·ro·car·bon /ˌklorouˌflorouˈkɑɚbən/ *noun, pl* **-bons** [*count*] *technical* **:** a gas that was once commonly used in various products (such as aerosols) but that is believed to cause damage to the ozone layer in the Earth's atmosphere ▪ Many nations have banned the production of *chlorofluorocarbons*. — abbr. *CFC*

chlo·ro·form /ˈklorəˌfoɚm/ *noun* [*noncount*] **:** a colorless poisonous liquid ✧ In the past, chloroform was used to make patients unconscious during medical operations. It is now usually used to dissolve other substances.
– chloroform *verb* **-forms**; **-formed**; **-form·ing** [+ *obj*] ▪ The doctor *chloroformed* the patient.

C

chlo·ro·phyll /ˈklorəˌfɪl/ *noun* [*noncount*] **:** the green substance in plants that makes it possible for them to make food from carbon dioxide and water

choc /ˈʧɑːk/ *noun, pl* **chocs** [*count*] *Brit, informal* **:** CHOCOLATE 2 ▪ a box of *chocs*

chock·a·block /ˈʧɑːkəˌblɑːk/ *adj, not used before a noun* **:** very full — usually + *with* ▪ The shelves are *chockablock with* books.

chock–full *or* **chock·ful** /ˈʧɑːkˈfʊl/ *adj, not used before a noun* **:** completely full — usually + *of* ▪ This book is *chock-full of* good information.

choc·o·hol·ic *also* **choc·a·hol·ic** /ˌʧɑːkəˈhɑːlɪk/ *noun, pl* **-ics** [*count*] *informal* **:** a person who likes to eat chocolate very much

choc·o·late /ˈʧɑːklət/ *noun, pl* **-lates**
1 [*noncount*] **:** a food that is made from cacao beans and that is eaten as candy or used as a flavoring ingredient in other sweet foods ▪ a bar of *chocolate* ▪ *chocolate*-covered raisins ▪ The cake recipe calls for four squares of *chocolate*. — see also DARK CHOCOLATE, HOT CHOCOLATE, MILK CHOCOLATE, WHITE CHOCOLATE
2 [*count*] **:** a candy made or covered with chocolate ▪ She gave me a box of *chocolates* for my birthday.
3 [*noncount*] **:** a dark brown color — called also *chocolate brown*; see color picture on page C3
– chocolate *adj* ▪ a *chocolate* cake with *chocolate* frosting ▪ *chocolate* ice cream ▪ *chocolate* sauce/milk **– choc·o·laty** *also* **choc·o·lat·ey** /ˈʧɑːkləti/ *adj* [*more* ~; *most* ~] ▪ a *chocolaty* flavor

chocolate–box *adj, always used before a noun, Brit, informal* **:** pretty in a way that seems too perfect to be true or real ▪ a *chocolate-box* house

choc·o·la·tier /ˌʧɑːkləˈtiɚ/ *noun, pl* **-tiers** [*count*] **:** a person who makes or sells chocolate candy

Choc·taw /ˈʧɑːktɑ/ *noun, pl* **-taws** [*count*] **:** a member of a Native American people of Mississippi, Alabama, and Louisiana

[1]**choice** /ˈʧoɪs/ *noun, pl* **choic·es**
1 [*count*] **:** the act of choosing **:** the act of picking or deciding between two or more possibilities ▪ He knew he had to make a *choice*. [=choose one thing or another] ▪ He has some important *choices* to make. ▪ You made a good/bad *choice*. ▪ She was faced with a difficult *choice*. ▪ You can either accept the job or not. It's your *choice*. ▪ I read about the various options so that I could make an informed *choice*.
2 : the opportunity or power to choose between two or more possibilities **:** the opportunity or power to make a decision [*singular*] Given the *choice*, I'd rather stay home tonight. ▪ He had no *choice* in the matter. = He did not have a *choice* in the matter. ▪ You leave me (with) no *choice*. ▪ They gave/offered me a *choice* between an automatic or standard transmission. [*noncount*] A flexible health insurance plan gives patients more *choice* about doctors and coverage. ▪ He had little *choice* in the matter. = He did not have much *choice* in the matter. — see also HOBSON'S CHOICE
3 a : a range of things that can be chosen [*singular*] — often + *of* ▪ The plan has a wide *choice of* options. [=there are many options that can be chosen] ▪ You have the *choice of* coffee or tea. [*noncount*] The menu does not have much *choice*. [=*selection*] ▪ (*chiefly Brit*) Customers are ***spoiled for choice*** [=customers have a lot of choices] when buying a new car. **b** [*count*] **:** one of the things that you can choose ▪ She wanted pizza, but that wasn't a *choice*. [=*option*] ▪ There is a wide range of *choices*. ▪ Other *choices* on the menu looked equally tempting. — see also MULTIPLE-CHOICE
4 [*count*] **:** the person or thing that someone chooses ▪ He is happy with his *choice*. ▪ She is my first *choice* for the job. [=she is the one I most want for the job] ▪ I don't like her *choice* of friends. ▪ Selling our car was the right *choice*.
by choice *also* ***out of choice*** ✧ If you do something *by choice* or *out of choice*, you choose to do it. ▪ I live here *by choice*. [=I live here because I want to] ▪ No one forced them to do it. They acted *out of choice*.
of choice **:** favorite or most liked **:** chosen most often ▪

C

Wine was his beverage *of choice*.

of your choice ✧ A person or thing *of your choice* is a person or thing that you have chosen. ▪ They said I could bring a guest *of my choice* to the party. ▪ The meal is served with a beverage *of your choice*.

[2]**choice** *adj, always used before a noun* **choic•er; -est**

1 : very good ▪ The store sells only the *choicest* [=*best*] fruits.

2 *US, of meat* **:** of a quality that is good but not the best ▪ *Choice* beef is not as expensive as prime beef.

3 *of words or phrases* **:** carefully chosen especially for the purpose of expressing anger or disapproval ▪ I had a few *choice* words for him. [=I said a few angry words to him]

choir /ˈkwajɚ/ *noun, pl* **choirs** [*count*]

1 : a group of singers especially in a church

2 : the part of a church where the singers sit

preach to the choir see PREACH

choir•boy /ˈkwajɚˌbɔɪ/ *noun, pl* **-boys** [*count*] **:** a boy who is a member of a church choir

choir•mas•ter /ˈkwajɚˌmæstɚ, *Brit* ˈkwajəˌmɑːstə/ *noun, pl* **-ters** [*count*] **:** the director of a choir

[1]**choke** /ˈʧoʊk/ *verb* **chokes; choked; chok•ing**

1 [*no obj*] **:** to become unable to breathe usually because something gets stuck in your throat or because the air is not good for breathing ▪ Chew your food well so you don't *choke*. ▪ She *choked* to death. = She died by *choking*. ▪ We were *choking* on fumes.

2 [+ *obj*] **a :** to cause (someone) to stop breathing by squeezing the throat ▪ The murderer *choked* his victim (to death). **b :** to make (someone) unable to breathe in a normal way ▪ The thick smoke was *choking* me. ✧ If you or your voice is ***choked with emotion, rage, etc.***, you are feeling emotion in such a strong way that it is hard for you to talk. ▪ When she was presented with the award, she was so *choked with emotion* that she couldn't say her thank-you speech.

3 [+ *obj*] **:** to stop (something) from growing or developing ▪ The flowers were *choked* by the weeds. — often + *out* ▪ The flowers were *choked out* by the weeds.

4 [+ *obj*] **:** to fill (something) completely so that movement is stopped or slowed ▪ Leaves *choked* [=*clogged, blocked*] the drain. ▪ The streets were *choked* with traffic. — often + *up* ▪ Logs were *choking up* the stream.

5 [*no obj*] *informal* **:** to fail to do something well because you are very nervous ▪ When the pressure was on, the tennis star *choked* and lost the match.

choke back [*phrasal verb*] ✧ If you are ***choking back tears, rage, anger, etc.***, you are finding it very hard not to cry or express emotion. ▪ He was *choking back tears* as he talked about his late wife. ▪ She struggled to *choke back her anger* as she listened to their criticisms.

choke down [*phrasal verb*] ***choke down (something) or choke (something) down*** *informal* **:** to eat (something) with difficulty or without enjoyment ▪ The meal was overcooked, but I managed to *choke down* a few bites.

choke off [*phrasal verb*] ***choke off (something) also choke (something) off*** **1 :** to make (something) smaller, weaker, or less powerful **:** to cause (something) to slow down or stop ▪ Rising interest rates may *choke off* consumer spending. ▪ Attempts have been made to *choke off* debate on the issue. **2 :** to prevent (something) from flowing or getting through ▪ A growth on the artery wall is *choking off* the blood supply.

choke out [*phrasal verb*] ***choke (something) out or choke out (something)*** **:** to say (something) with difficulty because of strong emotion ▪ She tearfully *choked out* an apology.

choke up [*phrasal verb*] **1** ✧ If you ***choke up*** or ***get/become (all) choked up***, you are almost crying and have trouble talking because of strong emotion. ▪ He *chokes up* whenever he tries to talk about the accident. ▪ She *got all choked up* when she saw her daughter in her wedding dress. **2** *baseball* **:** to move your hands to a higher position on a baseball bat — often + *on* ▪ He *choked up on* the bat and took a short swing.

[2]**choke** *noun, pl* **chokes** [*count*] **:** a part in a vehicle that controls the flow of air into the engine

choke chain *noun, pl* **~ chains** [*count*] **:** a chain for controlling a dog that is put around the dog's neck and that tightens when the end of the chain is pulled — called also *choke collar*

choke hold *noun, pl* **~ holds** [*count*] *chiefly US*

1 : a method of holding someone by putting your arm around the person's neck with enough pressure to make breathing difficult or impossible ▪ He put the suspect in a *choke hold*. = He used/placed a *choke hold* on the suspect.

2 : a force or influence that stops something from growing or developing **:** STRANGLEHOLD — usually singular ▪ The state has a *choke hold* on the city's finances. ▪ The tariffs have put a *choke hold* on the economy.

chok•er /ˈʧoʊkɚ/ *noun, pl* **-ers** [*count*]

1 : a necklace that fits closely around the neck

2 *informal* **:** a person who fails to do something because of nervousness **:** a person who chokes ▪ They called him a *choker* when he missed the shot that would have won the game.

chol•era /ˈkɑːlərə/ *noun* [*noncount*] **:** a serious disease that causes severe vomiting and diarrhea and that often results in death

cho•ler•ic /ˈkɑːlərɪk/ *adj* [*more ~; most ~*] *formal* **:** made angry easily **:** HOT-TEMPERED ▪ a *choleric* temperament

cho•les•ter•ol /kəˈlɛstəˌrɑːl/ *noun* [*noncount*] **:** a substance that is found in the bodies of people and animals ▪ Did your doctor check your *cholesterol*? ▪ She is on medication to lower her *cholesterol*. = She is on medication to lower her ***cholesterol level***. [=to lower the amount of cholesterol in her blood] ▪ My doctor told me that ***high cholesterol*** [=having too much cholesterol in your blood] can lead to serious medical problems such as heart attacks and strokes.

chomp /ˈʧɑːmp/ *verb* **chomps; chomped; chomp•ing** *informal* **:** to chew or bite on something [*no obj*] — often + *on* ▪ He was *chomping on* a bagel. ▪ The dog ***chomped down on*** its bone. — often + *away* ▪ The children were sitting at the table, happily *chomping away*. ▪ The bug ***chomped away at*** the leaf. — sometimes used figuratively ▪ Lawmakers have been *chomping away at* the state budget. [+ *obj*] They were *chomping* burgers at a picnic.

chomping at the bit **:** waiting in an impatient way to do something ▪ We've all been *chomping* [=*champing*] *at the bit* to get started on the project.

choo choo /ˈʧuːˌʧuː/ *noun, pl* **~ choos** *informal*

1 [*count*] **:** [1]TRAIN 1 — used by young children or by adults speaking to young children ▪ Here comes the *choo choo*! — called also *choo choo train*

2 [*noncount*] **:** the sound a train makes — used by young children or by adults speaking to young children

choose /ˈʧuːz/ *verb* **choos•es; chose** /ˈʧoʊz/; **cho•sen** /ˈʧoʊzn̩/; **choos•ing**

1 : to decide that a particular person or thing is the one that you want [+ *obj*] The political party *chose* a leader. ▪ They *chose* her as the team captain. ▪ We've *chosen* a different time to go. ▪ He was *chosen* because he's qualified for the job. ▪ She was *chosen* from a long list of people. ▪ He *chose* his words carefully. ▪ Which shirt would you *choose*? [*no obj*] How do I *choose* when there's so much available? ▪ Let everyone *choose* for themselves. ▪ You can *choose* from among a number of alternatives. ▪ You'll have to *choose* between the two of them. ▪ There are several books available to *choose* from.

2 : to make a choice about what to do **:** DECIDE [+ *obj*] — usually followed by *to + verb* ▪ They *chose to go* by train. ▪ They *chose* not *to believe* it. ▪ They *chose to keep* quiet. ▪ She *chooses to work* in the city. [*no obj*] You can do as you *choose*. [=you can do what you want to do]

choose sides **:** to divide a group into two teams that will play against each other ▪ When we *chose sides* in gym class, I was always the last person to be picked to be on a team. — often used figuratively ▪ They are forcing us to *choose sides* in the dispute.

pick and choose see [1]PICK

– choos•er *noun, pl* **-ers** [*count*] ▪ a careful *chooser* — see also *beggars can't be choosers* at BEGGAR

choosy *also* **choos•ey** /ˈʧuːzi/ *adj* **choos•i•er; -est** [*also more ~; most ~*] **:** very careful in choosing **:** liking only certain things ▪ She's pretty *choosy* [=*picky*] about her clothes/friends. ▪ You can't be too *choosy* if you want a job right away. ▪ We could afford to be as *choosy* as we wanted to be.

[1]**chop** /ˈʧɑːp/ *verb* **chops; chopped; chop•ping** [+ *obj*] **:** to cut (something) into pieces by hitting it with the sharp edge of an ax, knife, etc. ▪ She's in the kitchen *chopping* vegetables. ▪ They *chopped* wood for the fireplace. — often used figuratively ▪ They intend to *chop* [=*lower*] prices for the sale. ▪ Our budget was *chopped* [=*cut*] in half. [=it is now half of what it was]

chop and change *Brit, informal* **:** to keep changing your mind, your way of doing something, etc. ▪ You have to make a decision and stick with it. You can't *chop and change* all the time.

chop down [*phrasal verb*] ***chop (something) down** or **chop down (something)*** : to cut (a tree, bush, etc.) at the bottom so that it falls to the ground ▪ He *chopped* the tree *down.* ▪ She *chopped down* some thick grape vines.

chop off [*phrasal verb*] ***chop (something) off** or **chop off (something)*** : to remove (something) by cutting ▪ She'd had her ponytail *chopped off.* ▪ He used his knife to *chop off* a hunk of bread.

chop up [*phrasal verb*] ***chop (something) up** or **chop up (something)*** : to cut (something) into small pieces ▪ She *chopped up* the nuts and added them to the cookie dough.

– **chopped** *adj* ▪ two cups of *chopped* onions

[2]**chop** *noun, pl* **chops** [*count*]

1 : a small piece of meat that usually includes a bone from an animal's side ▪ lamb/pork *chops*

2 a : the act of hitting something with the sharp edge of an ax, knife, etc. ▪ He cut off the branch with a single *chop.* **b** : the act of hitting someone or something with the side of your hand ▪ He broke the boards with a ***karate chop.***

for the chop *Brit, informal* — used to say that someone is going to lose a job or that something is being stopped or canceled ▪ More than 100 jobs are *for the chop.* [=are going/likely to be eliminated] ▪ social programs that are *for the chop* [=(*US*) *on the chopping block*]

get the chop *Brit, informal* : to lose your job ▪ The employees with less experience *got the chop.* [=were fired; got the ax]

give (someone) the chop *Brit, informal* : to take someone's job away ▪ His boss *gave him the chop.* [=his boss fired him; his boss gave him the ax]

chop–chop /ˌtʃɑːpˈtʃɑːp/ *interj, informal* — used to tell someone to hurry ▪ Let's go! *Chop-chop!*

chop house /ˈtʃɑːpˌhaʊs/ *noun, pl* ~ **hous·es** [*count*] *chiefly US, informal* : a restaurant that serves steaks, chops, and other meats — compare STEAK HOUSE

chopped liver *noun* [*noncount*] *US slang* : someone or something that is not important or appealing ▪ "Wow, she's gorgeous!" "And what am I . . . *chopped liver?*"

chop·per /ˈtʃɑːpɚ/ *noun, pl* **-pers**

1 [*count*] : someone or something that chops something ▪ a food/wood *chopper*

2 [*count*] *informal* : HELICOPTER ▪ The sound of *choppers* filled the sky. ▪ a *chopper* pilot

3 [*count*] *chiefly US, informal* : a motorcycle that has a front wheel which is farther forward than the handlebars — called also *chopper bike*

4 ***choppers*** [*plural*] *chiefly US slang* : TEETH ▪ The dentist checked my *choppers* and said they look fine.

chopping block *noun, pl* ~ **blocks** [*count*] *US* : a hard wooden block on which things (such as meat, wood, or vegetables) are chopped or cut — compare CUTTING BOARD

on the chopping block *informal* : likely to be fired, removed, etc. ▪ There were several government programs *on the chopping block.* [=several government programs that were going to be cut/eliminated]

chopping board *noun, pl* ~ **boards** [*count*] *chiefly Brit* : CUTTING BOARD

chop·py /ˈtʃɑːpi/ *adj* **chop·pi·er; -est**

1 : rough with small waves ▪ The lake was *choppy.* ▪ *choppy* conditions/seas/waters

2 : marked by sudden stops and starts : not connected smoothly ▪ She tended to write in short *choppy* sentences. ▪ The video appeared *choppy* and jerky. ▪ He walked with quick *choppy* strides.

– **chop·pi·ness** *noun* [*noncount*]

chops /ˈtʃɑːps/ *noun* [*plural*]

1 a : the part of an animal's face that covers the jaws ▪ The dog was licking its *chops.* **b** *informal* : a person's jaw ▪ I'm going to break/bust your *chops* if you do that again. — often used figuratively ▪ My brother likes to ***bust my chops.*** [=he teases me; he criticizes me in a playful way]

2 *chiefly US, informal* : skill or excellence in a particular field or activity (such as acting or playing music) ▪ It's a challenging role that will give him a chance to show off his acting *chops.* [=to show his talents as an actor]

lick your chops see [1]LICK

chop·stick /ˈtʃɑːpˌstɪk/ *noun, pl* **-sticks** [*count*] : either one of a pair of thin sticks that are used especially by people in Asia to pick up and eat food

chop su·ey /ˌtʃɑːpˈsuːwi/ *noun* [*noncount*] : a combination of vegetables and meat or fish that is served with rice ✧ Chop suey is mainly served in Chinese restaurants and was probably invented in the U.S. by Chinese immigrants to suit American tastes.

chopsticks

cho·ral /ˈkorəl/ *adj* : of or relating to a choir or chorus ▪ a *choral* group ▪ *choral* singing : sung by a choir or chorus ▪ *choral* music

cho·rale /kəˈræl, *Brit* kɒˈrɑːl/ *noun, pl* **-rales** [*count*]

1 : a song that is sung in a church service by a large group of singers

2 : a chorus or choir

[1]**chord** /ˈkoɚd/ *noun, pl* **chords** [*count*] : a group of three or more musical notes that are played or sung at the same time — compare [2]CHORD

[2]**chord** *noun, pl* **chords** [*count*] *mathematics* : a straight line that joins two points on a curve

strike/touch a chord ✧ If something *strikes/touches a chord* in/with you, you think that it is true and have strong feelings about it. ▪ Her comments about political corruption clearly *struck a chord* with many voters.

– compare [1]CHORD

chore /ˈtʃoɚ/ *noun, pl* **chores** [*count*]

1 : a small job that is done regularly ▪ The children were each assigned different household *chores.* ▪ farm *chores* ▪ I liked the simple *chore* of bringing in the firewood.

synonyms see [1]TASK

2 : a dull, unpleasant, or difficult job or experience ▪ Doing taxes can be a real *chore.* ▪ That movie is a *chore* to sit through.

cho·reo·graph /ˈkorijəˌgræf, *Brit* ˈkɒrijəˌgrɑːf/ *verb* **-graphs; -graphed; -graph·ing** [+ *obj*] : to decide how a dancer or group of dancers will move during a performance ▪ She was hired to *choreograph* the ballet routines. — often used figuratively ▪ He carefully *choreographed* the meeting. [=he arranged the details of the meeting very carefully] ▪ The group had *choreographed* all aspects of the banquet.

– **cho·re·og·ra·pher** /ˌkoriˈɑːgrəfɚ/ *noun, pl* **-phers** [*count*]

cho·re·og·ra·phy /ˌkoriˈɑːgrəfi/ *noun* [*noncount*] : the art or job of deciding how dancers will move in a performance ▪ She studied *choreography.* ▪ He has an interest in *choreography.*; *also* : the movements that are done by dancers in a performance ▪ a show with excellent *choreography*

– **cho·re·o·graph·ic** /ˌkorijəˈgræfɪk/ *adj*

cho·ris·ter /ˈkorəstɚ/ *noun, pl* **-ters** [*count*] : a singer in a choir

cho·ri·zo /tʃəˈriːzoʊ/ *noun, pl* **-zos** [*count, noncount*] : a spicy pork sausage

chor·tle /ˈtʃoɚtl/ *verb* **chor·tles; chor·tled; chor·tling** : to laugh because you are amused or pleased by something [*no obj*] She *chortled* [=*chuckled*] with delight. [+ *obj*] He *chortled*, "You're going to love this."

– **chortle** *noun, pl* **chortles** [*count*] ▪ The gift was received with *chortles* of delight.

[1]**cho·rus** /ˈkorəs/ *noun, pl* **-rus·es** [*count*]

1 a : a group of singers and dancers in an ancient Greek play who take part in or talk about the things that are happening on stage **b** : a group of singers and dancers in a modern play, musical show, etc. **c** : a large group of singers : CHOIR

2 a : a part of a song that is repeated between verses : REFRAIN **b** : a piece of music that is sung by a large group of singers ▪ Handel's "Hallelujah *Chorus*"

3 a : a sound made by many people or animals at the same time ▪ We awoke to a *chorus* of birdsong. ▪ The announcement was met by a loud *chorus* of boos. [=people booed when they heard the announcement] **b** : a group of people or animals that are all heard at the same time ▪ The President's policies have been questioned by a growing *chorus* of critics. ▪ a *chorus* of frogs

in chorus : all together : all at the same time ▪ The phones in the room rang *in chorus.*

[2]**chorus** *verb* **-ruses; -rused; -rus·ing** [+ *obj*] : to say (something) all together : to say (something) in chorus ▪ The class *chorused* "Good morning!"

chorus girl *noun, pl* ~ **girls** [*count*] : a girl or young woman who sings or dances in a chorus

chose *past tense of* CHOOSE

[1]**chosen** *past participle of* CHOOSE

[2]**cho·sen** /ˈtʃoʊzn̩/ *adj* : selected to do or receive something special ▪ Only ***the/a chosen few*** will get to go on the trip.

[=only a few people will get to go]

¹chow /ˈtʃaʊ/ *noun* [*noncount*] *informal* : FOOD 1 ▪ Ample *chow* will be available. ▪ Let's grab some *chow*.

²chow *verb* **chows; chowed; chow·ing**
chow down [*phrasal verb*] *US, informal* : EAT 1 ▪ It's time to *chow down*. — often + *on* ▪ The kids *chowed down on* hamburgers and french fries.

C

chow chow /ˈtʃaʊˌtʃaʊ/ *noun, pl* ~ **chows** [*count*] : a type of dog that has thick fur and a short curled tail — called also *chow*

chow·der /ˈtʃaʊdɚ/ *noun, pl* **-ders** [*count, noncount*] : a thick soup or stew made of seafood or corn with potatoes and onions and milk or tomatoes ▪ a bowl of clam *chowder*

chow·der·head /ˈtʃaʊdɚˌhɛd/ *noun, pl* **-heads** [*count*] *US, informal* : a stupid person ▪ Any *chowderhead* [=*idiot, knucklehead*] could have told you the answer.
– **chowd·er·head·ed** /ˈtʃaʊdɚˌhɛdəd/ *adj* [*more* ~; *most* ~]

chow·hound /ˈtʃaʊˌhaʊnd/ *noun, pl* **-hounds** [*count*] *US, informal* : a person who likes to eat ▪ My dad doesn't eat much, but my brother is a real *chowhound*. [=*a big eater*]

chow mein /tʃaʊˈmeɪn/ *noun* [*noncount*] : a combination of meat, mushrooms, and vegetables with fried noodles that is served in Chinese restaurants in the U.S. — compare LO MEIN

Christ /ˈkraɪst/ *noun* [*singular*] : JESUS CHRIST
– **Christ·like** /ˈkraɪstˌlaɪk/ *adj* – **Christ·ly** *adj*

chris·ten /ˈkrɪsn̩/ *verb* **chris·tens; chris·tened; chris·ten·ing** [+ *obj*]
1 : to baptize (someone) ▪ He was *christened* when he was three months old.
2 a : to name (someone) at baptism ▪ They *christened* the baby Anna. **b** : to officially give (something, such as a ship) a name in a ceremony that often involves breaking a bottle of champagne ▪ The politician was chosen to *christen* a new ship. **c** : to give (someone or something) a nickname or an unofficial title ▪ The newspaper has *christened* her as the reigning Queen of Tennis.
3 : to use something for the first time ▪ They *christened* the new ball park with a win.

Chris·ten·dom /ˈkrɪsn̩dəm/ *noun* [*noncount*]
1 : people who are Christians
2 : the part of the world where most people are Christians — sometimes used in the old-fashioned phrase ***in all of Christendom*** ▪ You will not find a better man *in all of Christendom*. [=*anywhere*]

chris·ten·ing /ˈkrɪsənɪŋ/ *noun, pl* **-ings** [*count*]
1 : the ceremony of baptizing and naming a child ▪ The whole family was invited to the *christening*.
2 : the official ceremony in which something (such as a ship) is named ▪ a ship's *christening*

¹Chris·tian /ˈkrɪstʃən/ *noun, pl* **-tians** [*count*] : a person who believes in the teachings of Jesus Christ

²Christian *adj*
1 : of or relating to Jesus Christ or the religion based on his teachings ▪ *Christian* scriptures ▪ *Christian* ethics ▪ a *Christian* burial
2 : of, relating to, or being Christians ▪ a *Christian* country ▪ a *Christian* household ▪ Many of my friends are *Christian*.
3 [*more* ~; *most* ~] : treating other people in a kind and generous way ▪ He showed a very *Christian* concern for others.

Christian era *noun* [*noncount*] : the time starting from the birth of Jesus Christ — abbr. *CE*

Chris·ti·an·i·ty /ˌkrɪstʃiˈænəti/ *noun* [*noncount*] : the religion that is based on the teachings of Jesus Christ

Christian name *noun, pl* ~ **names** [*count*] : a person's first name : the name given to a person when the person is born or christened ▪ Her *Christian name* is Anna.

Christ·mas /ˈkrɪsməs/ *noun, pl* **-mas·es** : a Christian holiday that is celebrated on December 25 in honor of the birth of Jesus Christ or the period of time that comes before and after this holiday [*noncount*] We're spending *Christmas* with my parents. [*count*] We had a very happy *Christmas* this year. ▪ I wish you all a merry *Christmas*. — often used before another noun ▪ a *Christmas* present ▪ She finished her *Christmas* shopping. ▪ What are you serving for *Christmas* dinner? ▪ the rush of the ***Christmas season*** [=the time of year when people are getting ready for Christmas]

Christmas cake *noun, pl* ~ **cakes** [*count, noncount*] *Brit* : a cake that contains nuts and fruits and that is served at Christmas

Christmas card *noun, pl* ~ **cards** [*count*] : a greeting card sent at Christmastime

Christmas carol *noun, pl* ~ **-ols** [*count*] : ¹CAROL

Christmas cracker *noun, pl* ~ **-ers** [*count*] *Brit* : a paper tube that has a toy or other small object inside it and makes a loud sound when its ends are pulled apart

Christmas Day *noun, pl* ~ **Days** [*count, noncount*] : the day on which Christmas is celebrated : December 25

Christmas Eve *noun, pl* ~ **Eves** [*count, noncount*] : the day before Christmas : December 24

Christmas pudding *noun, pl* ~ **-dings** [*count*] *Brit* : PLUM PUDDING

Christmas stocking *noun, pl* ~ **-ings** [*count*] : STOCKING 3

Christ·mas·sy *also* **Christ·masy** /ˈkrɪsməsi/ *adj* [*more* ~; *most* ~] : typical of or suitable for Christmas ▪ The house looks more *Christmassy* now that the decorations are up.

Christ·mas·time /ˈkrɪsməsˌtaɪm/ *noun* [*noncount*] : the time of year when people get ready for and celebrate Christmas : Christmas day and the days and weeks before it ▪ It's fun to be in a large city at *Christmastime*. [=during the Christmas season]

Christmas tree *noun, pl* ~ **trees** [*count*] : an evergreen tree that is decorated in people's houses at Christmastime ▪ We hung the lights on the *Christmas tree*.

chro·mat·ic /kroʊˈmætɪk/ *adj, music* : of or relating to a musical scale that has all semitones ▪ *chromatic* harmonies/notes ▪ the *chromatic* scale — compare DIATONIC
– **chro·mat·i·cal·ly** /kroʊˈmætɪkli/ *adv*

chrome /ˈkroʊm/ *noun* [*noncount*] : a type of metal that is used to cover other metals in order to make them shiny

chro·mi·um /ˈkroʊmijəm/ *noun* [*noncount*] : a blue-white metallic element that is combined with other metals and used to cover other metals with a shiny surface

chro·mo·some /ˈkroʊməˌsoʊm/ *noun, pl* **-somes** [*count*] : the part of a cell that contains the genes which control how an animal or plant grows and what it becomes
– **chro·mo·som·al** /ˌkroʊməˈsoʊməl/ *adj* ▪ a test to detect *chromosomal* abnormalities

chron·ic /ˈkrɑːnɪk/ *adj*
1 *medical* : continuing or occurring again and again for a long time ▪ a *chronic* disease ▪ He suffers from *chronic* arthritis/pain. ▪ *chronic* health problems — compare ACUTE
2 a : happening or existing frequently or most of the time ▪ *chronic* [=*habitual*] lateness ▪ a *chronic* need for attention ▪ Inflation has become a *chronic* condition in the economy. ▪ *chronic* warfare **b** : always or often doing something specified ▪ He is a *chronic* complainer/grumbler. [=he complains/grumbles all the time] ▪ a *chronic* gambler/offender
3 *Brit, informal* : very bad ▪ Don't bother seeing that film—it's *chronic*.
– **chron·i·cal·ly** /ˈkrɑːnɪkli/ *adv* ▪ She has a *chronically* bad knee. ▪ He is *chronically* short of money.

chronic fatigue syndrome *noun* [*noncount*] *medical* : an illness that makes you feel very tired for a very long time and that often includes other symptoms such as headaches and weakness — abbr. *CFS*

¹chron·i·cle /ˈkrɑːnɪkəl/ *noun, pl* **-i·cles** [*count*] : a description of events in the order that they happened : HISTORY ▪ early medieval *chronicles* ▪ a *chronicle* of the American Civil War ▪ a *chronicle* of the President's years in office

²chronicle *verb* **-icles; -i·cled; -i·cling** [+ *obj*] : to describe a series of events in the order that they happened ▪ The book *chronicles* the events that led to the American Civil War. ▪ She intends to *chronicle* the broad social changes that have occurred in this part of the country. ▪ a magazine that *chronicles* the lives of the rich and famous
– **chron·i·cler** *noun, pl* **-clers** [*count*]

chro·no·graph /ˈkrɑːnəˌgræf/ *noun, pl* **-graphs** [*count*] : a device (such as a stopwatch) that is used for measuring and recording time in a very exact way

chro·no·log·i·cal /ˌkrɑːnəˈlɑːdʒɪkəl/ *adj*
1 : arranged in the order that things happened or came to be ▪ His art is displayed in roughly *chronological* order. ▪ a *chronological* account of their trip ▪ a *chronological* list/table
2 : using time as a measurement ▪ His ***chronological age*** is five, but his mental age is three. [=he is five years old but he thinks and behaves like a three-year-old]
– **chron·o·log·i·cal·ly** /ˌkrɑːnəˈlɑːdʒɪkli/ *adv* ▪ The book treats the subject *chronologically*. ▪ The events were discussed *chronologically*.

chro·nol·o·gy /krəˈnɑːləʤi/ *noun, pl* **-gies**
1 a [*noncount*] : the order in which a series of events happened • We tried to reconstruct the *chronology* of the accident. **b** [*count*] : a record of the order in which a series of events happened • The book provides a *chronology* of the events leading up to the American Civil War.
2 [*noncount*] : a science that deals with measuring time and finding out when events happened

chro·nom·e·ter /krəˈnɑːmətɚ/ *noun, pl* **-ters** [*count*] : a watch or clock that measures time very exactly

chrys·a·lis /ˈkrɪsələs/ *noun, pl* **chry·sal·i·ses** *also* **chrys·a·lid·es** /krɪˈsæləˌdiːz/ [*count*] *biology*
1 : a moth or butterfly at the stage of growth when it is turning into an adult and is enclosed in a hard case
2 : a hard case that protects a moth or butterfly while it is turning into an adult — compare [1]COCOON 1

chry·san·the·mum /krɪˈsænθəməm/ *noun, pl* **-mums** [*count*] : a plant that has brightly colored flowers and that is often grown in gardens; *also* : the flower of this plant — called also (*US*) *mum*; see color picture on page C6

chub·by /ˈʧʌbi/ *adj* **chub·bi·er; -est** : somewhat fat • He was always *chubby* as a child. • a baby with *chubby* [=*plump, full*] cheeks
– **chub·bi·ness** /ˈʧʌbinəs/ *noun* [*noncount*]

[1]**chuck** /ˈʧʌk/ *verb* **chucks; chucked; chuck·ing** [+ *obj*] *informal*
1 : to throw or toss (something) • Someone *chucked* a snowball at me. • She *chucked* the papers into the wastebasket.
2 : to get rid of (something) • You can save some of it, but *chuck* the rest. — sometimes + *out* • She finally *chucked out* her old college notebooks. — see also CHUCK OUT (below)
3 : to give up (something) • He decided to *chuck* [=*abandon, leave*] his career/job. — often + *in* • He grew tired of his job and decided to just ***chuck it (all) in***. [=quit, give it up]
4 : to touch or tap (someone) in a light and gentle way • He affectionately *chucked* her under the chin.
chuck out [*phrasal verb*] ***chuck (someone) out*** *or* ***chuck out (someone)*** : to force (someone) to leave • If they don't pay their rent, the landlord will have to *chuck* them *out*. • He was *chucked out* of the bar for being too noisy. — see also [1]CHUCK 2 (above)

[2]**chuck** *noun, pl* **chucks**
1 [*noncount*] : a piece of beef that comes from the area of a cow's neck and shoulders • I'll get some *chuck* for dinner. • a *chuck* roast
2 [*count*] : a part of a machine that holds something so that it does not move • To remove the drill bit, loosen the *chuck*. — see picture at CARPENTRY

chuck·hole /ˈʧʌkˌhoʊl/ *noun, pl* **-holes** [*count*] *US* : a hole in a road : POTHOLE

chuck·le /ˈʧʌkl̩/ *verb* **chuck·les; chuck·led; chuck·ling** [*no obj*] : to laugh in a quiet way • She *chuckled* at the memory of what he had said.
– **chuckle** *noun, pl* **chuckles** [*count*] • I got a *chuckle* out of the joke. • He said it with a *chuckle*. = He gave a *chuckle* when he said it.

chuck·le·head /ˈʧʌkl̩ˌhɛd/ *noun, pl* **-heads** [*count*] *US, informal* : a stupid person • Who was the *chucklehead* [=*idiot*] who came up with this idea?
– **chuck·le·head·ed** /ˈʧʌkl̩ˌhɛdəd/ *adj* [*more* ~; *most* ~] • He made a *chuckleheaded* decision.

chuck wagon *noun, pl* ~ **-ons** [*count*] *US, old-fashioned* : a wagon carrying a stove and food for cooking for a group of people (such as cowboys)

chuffed /ˈʧʌft/ *adj* [*more* ~; *most* ~] *Brit, informal* : very pleased : DELIGHTED • She's (feeling) quite/very *chuffed*.

[1]**chug** /ˈʧʌg/ *verb, always followed by a preposition or adverb* **chugs; chugged; chug·ging** [*no obj*] : to move or go while making a sound like the engine on a train • The train *chugged* up the hill. • The boats were *chugging* across the bay. • The car *chugged* down the street. — sometimes used figuratively • Business is *chugging* along quite nicely. — compare [2]CHUG

[2]**chug** *verb* **chugs; chugged; chugging** [+ *obj*] *US, informal* : to drink all the beer, soda, etc., in a can or bottle without stopping • He *chugged* a few beers at the party. — compare [1]CHUG

chug·a·lug /ˈʧʌgəˌlʌg/ *verb* **-lugs; -lugged; -lug·ging** [+ *obj*] *US, informal* : [2]CHUG • He *chugalugged* a few beers.

[1]**chum** /ˈʧʌm/ *noun, pl* **chums** [*count*] *informal + old-fashioned* : a close friend • They were talking together like a couple of old *chums*. [=*pals*] — compare [3]CHUM

[2]**chum** *verb* **chums; chummed; chum·ming** [*no obj*] *chiefly US, informal* : to spend time with someone as a friend — usually + *around* • a politician who is often seen *chumming around* [=*palling around*] with celebrities
chum up [*phrasal verb*] *Brit, informal* : to become friendly — often + *to* • businessmen *chumming up to* [=(*US*) *buddying up to*] politicians to get their support
– compare [4]CHUM

[3]**chum** *noun* [*noncount*] : pieces of fish thrown off a boat as bait to attract other fish — compare [1]CHUM

[4]**chum** *verb* **chums; chummed; chum·ming** [*no obj*] *US* : to throw pieces of fish off a boat as bait to attract other fish — often + *for* • They were ***chumming for*** sharks. [=throwing chum into the water to attract sharks]— compare [2]CHUM

chum·my /ˈʧʌmi/ *adj* **chum·mi·er; -est** [*also more* ~; *most* ~] *informal + old-fashioned* : very friendly • She was getting *chummy* with the reporters.

chump /ˈʧʌmp/ *noun, pl* **chumps** [*count*] *informal* : a person who is easy to trick : a stupid or foolish person • Don't be a *chump*.

chump change *noun* [*noncount*] *US, informal* : a small amount of money : an amount of money that is not important or impressive • His share of the profits was *chump change*. [=his share of the profits was not very big]

chunk /ˈʧʌŋk/ *noun, pl* **chunks** [*count*]
1 : a thick piece of something • She cut the fruit into large *chunks*. • *chunks* of meat/ice/wood/pineapple
2 *somewhat informal* : a large amount or part of something • She spends a good *chunk* of her day on the phone. • He devoted a large *chunk* of time to the project. • (*US*) He spent a big/hefty ***chunk of change*** [=a lot of money] on that car.

chunky /ˈʧʌŋki/ *adj* **chunk·i·er; -est**
1 : heavy, thick, and solid • She wore *chunky* earrings. • The shoes have *chunky* heels.
2 a : somewhat fat • She was a bit *chunky* [=*chubby, overweight*] as a child. **b** : having a short and strong body • an athlete with a *chunky* build • a *chunky* [=*stocky*] defensive lineman
3 : full of chunks : containing many solid pieces • *chunky* peanut butter

church /ˈʧɚʧ/ *noun, pl* **church·es**
1 a [*count*] : a building that is used for Christian religious services • This is the oldest *church* in town. • They would like to be married in a *church*. — often used before another noun • *church* bells/weddings/services **b** [*noncount*] : religious services held in a church • They ***go to church*** [=attend church services] every Sunday. • I didn't see you ***at/in church*** last Sunday.
2 *or* ***Church*** [*count*] : a particular Christian group • He is a member of the Catholic/Baptist/Anglican *Church*. • What *church* do you belong to?
3 [*noncount*] : the Christian religion seen as an organization : the institution of the Christian religion • the *church's* attitude toward divorce • the separation of *church* and state

church·go·er /ˈʧɚʧˌgowɚ/ *noun, pl* **-ers** [*count*] : someone who regularly goes to church
– **church·go·ing** *adj* • *churchgoing* people – **church·going** *noun* [*noncount*] • a decline in *churchgoing*

church·man /ˈʧɚʧmən/ *noun, pl* **-men** [*count*]
1 : a man who is a priest, minister, etc. : CLERGYMAN
2 : a man who is a member of a church

Church of England *noun*
the Church of England : the official state church in England

church·war·den /ˈʧɚʧˌwoɚdn̩/ *noun, pl* **-dens** [*count*] *Brit* : someone who is in charge of the property and money of an Anglican church

church·wom·an /ˈʧɚʧˌwʊmən/ *noun, pl* **-wom·en** /-ˌwɪmən/ [*count*] : a woman who is a member of a church

church·yard /ˈʧɚʧˌjaɚd/ *noun, pl* **-yards** [*count*] : a piece of land that belongs to and is usually close to a church and that is often used as a place to bury people

churl·ish /ˈʧɚlɪʃ/ *adj* [*more* ~; *most* ~] *formal* : not polite : RUDE • It would be/seem *churlish* not to congratulate him. • *churlish* behavior

[1]**churn** /ˈʧɚn/ *verb* **churns; churned; churn·ing**
1 : to stir or mix something (such as water or mud) with force [+ *obj*] The motorboats *churned* the water. — often + *up* • The horse's hooves *churned up* the sod. [*no obj*] The water *churned* all around us.
2 [*no obj*] : to move in a circle : TURN • The wheels/gears began to slowly *churn*.

3 [+ *obj*] : to make (butter) by stirring or shaking cream in a churn • He showed them how to *churn* butter.
4 [*no obj*] : to experience a lot of confused activity • My mind was *churning* as I tried to think of what to say. • Her emotions were *churning* inside her. ✧ If your ***stomach churns*** or something ***churns your stomach***, you feel sick from nervousness, disgust, etc. • Just thinking about the test made my *stomach churn*. • The violence in the movie *churned my stomach.*
churn out [*phrasal verb*] ***churn out (something) or churn (something) out*** *informal + often disapproving* : to produce (something, especially something of low quality) quickly as part of a continuous process • He *churns out* [=*grinds out*] a new novel every year. • the latest graduates *churned out* by the college

[2]**churn** *noun, pl* **churns** [*count*] : a container in which cream is stirred or shaken to make butter

chute /ˈʃuːt/ *noun, pl* **chutes** [*count*]
1 : a narrow tube or passage that things and people go down or through • She dropped the towels into the laundry *chute*. • a mail *chute* • children sliding down a water *chute* • The skiers came racing down the *chute*.
2 *informal* : [1]PARACHUTE • His *chute* opened automatically.
out of the chute *US, informal* : since the very beginning • He was successful (right) *out of the chute*.

chut·ney /ˈʧʌtni/ *noun, pl* **-neys** [*count, noncount*] : a thick sauce that is made from fruits, vinegar, sugar, and spices

chutz·pah /ˈhʊtspə/ *noun* [*noncount*] *approving* : personal confidence or courage that allows someone to do or say things that may seem shocking to others • It took a lot of *chutzpah* [=*nerve*] to stand up to him the way she did.

CIA *abbr* Central Intelligence Agency • The group is being investigated by the *CIA*. • a *CIA* agent ✧ The Central Intelligence Agency is a part of the U.S. federal government that is responsible for collecting information about other countries or foreign groups.

ciao /ˈʧaʊ/ *interj, informal* : [1]GOODBYE — usually spoken • "See you later." "*Ciao*."

ci·ca·da /səˈkeɪdə, səˈkɑːdə/ *noun, pl* **-das** [*count*] : a large insect ✧ The male cicada makes a loud, high-pitched sound. — see color picture on page C10

ci·der /ˈsaɪdɚ/ *noun, pl* **-ders** [*count, noncount*] : a drink made from apples • a cup of apple *cider* ✧ In U.S. English, *cider* when used by itself usually refers to a drink that does not contain alcohol. In British English, *cider* refers to an alcoholic drink, which is usually called "hard cider" in U.S. English.

cider vinegar *noun* [*noncount*] : a type of vinegar that is made from apple cider

cig /ˈsɪg/ *noun, pl* **cigs** [*count*] *informal* : CIGARETTE

ci·gar /sɪˈgaɚ/ *noun, pl* **-gars** [*count*] : a roll of tobacco leaves that is longer and thicker than a cigarette and that is smoked
close but no cigar see [2]CLOSE

cigar

cig·a·rette /ˌsɪgəˈrɛt/ *noun, pl* **-rettes** [*count*] : a small roll of paper that is filled with cut tobacco and smoked • a pack of *cigarettes* — often used before another noun • a *cigarette* butt/holder/lighter • *cigarette* smoke

cigarette paper *noun, pl* ~ **-ers** [*count*] : a small, thin piece of paper that is used for making a cigarette

cig·gie *or* **cig·gy** /ˈsɪgi/ *noun, pl* **-gies** [*count*] *Brit, informal* : CIGARETTE

ci·lan·tro /sɪˈlɑːntroʊ, sɪˈlæntroʊ/ *noun* [*noncount*] *US* : leaves of the coriander plant that are used in cooking especially in Asian and Mexican food — see color picture on page C6

C in C *abbr* commander in chief

[1]**cinch** /ˈsɪnʧ/ *noun, pl* **cinch·es**
1 [*singular*] *informal* : something that is very easy to do • This recipe is a *cinch*. • This dish is a *cinch* to make.
2 [*singular*] *chiefly US, informal* — used to say that something will certainly happen or that someone will easily do something • It's a *cinch* that he'll win the election. = He's a *cinch* to win the election.
3 [*count*] *US* : a strap that holds a saddle on a horse

[2]**cinch** *verb* **cinches; cinched; cinch·ing** [+ *obj*] *US*
1 : to fasten (something, such as a belt or strap) tightly around someone or something • He *cinched* his belt. • The coat is *cinched* at the waist. • The rider *cinched* the saddle.
2 *informal* : to make (something) certain to happen • The candidate *cinched* the nomination by winning the major primary elections. • The home run *cinched* the victory.

Cinco de Mayo /ˌsɪŋkoʊdəˈmajoʊ/ *noun* [*noncount*] *US* : a Mexican and Mexican-American holiday on May 5 that celebrates the Mexican army's victory over the French in 1862

cin·der /ˈsɪndɚ/ *noun, pl* **-ders** [*count*] : a very small piece of burned material (such as wood or coal) • *Cinders* from the campfire floated through the air. • The house was ***burned to a cinder***. [=was completely destroyed by fire]

cinder block *noun, pl* ~ **blocks** [*count*] *US* : a block that is made of cement and coal cinders and that is used in building — called also (*Brit*) *breeze-block*

Cin·der·el·la /ˌsɪndəˈrɛlə/ *noun, pl* **-las** [*count*] ✧ *Cinderella* is the name of a girl in a fairy tale who is treated badly by her stepmother and stepsisters but who marries a prince in the end.
1 : someone or something that is ignored but that deserves attention or credit • a company that is the *Cinderella* of the computer industry
2 *chiefly US* : someone or something (such as a sports team) that is not expected to do well but that succeeds or wins in a very exciting way • The team is the *Cinderella* of the tournament. — often used before another noun • a *Cinderella* team that surprisingly took the championship • Their win was a classic ***Cinderella story***.

cin·e·ma /ˈsɪnəmə/ *noun, pl* **-mas**
1 [*noncount*] **a** : the film industry • She had a long career in (the) *cinema*. **b** : the art or technique of making movies • a student of French *cinema*
2 [*count*] *chiefly Brit* : a movie theater • We drove by the *cinema* to see what was playing. • They are ***going to the cinema*** [=(*US*) *going to the movies*] tonight.

cin·e·mat·ic /ˌsɪnəˈmætɪk/ *adj* : of or relating to movies • a common *cinematic* [=*film*] technique • the actor's first *cinematic* [=*movie*] role • a director who has produced some great *cinematic* moments
– cin·e·mat·i·cal·ly /ˌsɪnəˈmætɪkli/ *adv* • *Cinematically*, the film was excellent, but it failed at the box office.

cin·e·ma·tog·ra·phy /ˌsɪnəməˈtɑːgrəfi/ *noun* [*noncount*] : the art, process, or job of filming movies : motion-picture photography • The film's *cinematography* is breathtaking. • Who did the *cinematography* for this film?
cin·e·ma·tog·ra·pher /ˌsɪnəməˈtɑːgrəfɚ/ *noun, pl* **-phers** [*count*] • He was one of the best *cinematographers* in the movie industry.

cin·na·mon /ˈsɪnəmən/ *noun* [*noncount*] : a sweet spice made from the bark of an Asian tree and used in cooking and baking • two teaspoons of *cinnamon* — often used before another noun • a *cinnamon* roll/stick

ci·pher *also chiefly Brit* **cy·pher** /ˈsaɪfɚ/ *noun, pl* **-phers**
1 *technical* : a way of changing a message to keep it secret : CODE [*count*] a *cipher* that can't be decoded [*noncount*] The message was written in *cipher*. [=the message was coded]
2 [*count*] *formal + disapproving* : a person who has no power or is not important • She was nothing more than a *cipher*.

cir·ca /ˈsɚkə/ *prep, formal* : about or around • He was born *circa* 1600. — abbr. *c., ca.*

cir·ca·di·an /sɚˈkeɪdijən/ *adj, always used before a noun, technical* : relating to the regular changes in a person or thing that happen in 24-hour periods • *circadian* rhythms in activity

[1]**cir·cle** /ˈsɚkəl/ *noun, pl* **circles** [*count*]
1 a : a perfectly round shape : a line that is curved so that its ends meet and every point on the line is the same distance from the center • She drew a *circle* around the correct answer. — see picture at GEOMETRY **b** : a path that goes around a central point • She walked (around) ***in a circle*** — often used figuratively • We've been walking/driving ***in circles***[=along the same path or course] for hours! • We've been trying to decide how to improve the system, but we just keep ***going around in circles*** [=we are not making any progress toward making a decision] • I feel like I have been ***running around in circles*** with this project. • The company has come up with some new products that will ***run circles around*** the competition. [=that will be much better than the competition; that will easily beat the competition] • Those little kids can *ski circles around* me. [=can ski much better than I can] — see also FULL CIRCLE, TRAFFIC CIRCLE, VICIOUS CIRCLE, WINNER'S CIRCLE

2 a : an arrangement of people or things that forms a circle ▪ She arranged the stones in a *circle*. = She made a *circle* out of/with the stones. ▪ a *circle* of stones ▪ We formed a *circle* around the campfire. **b** : something that is shaped like part of a circle ▪ He looked old and tired, with dark *circles* under his eyes.
3 : a group of people who do something together, are friends, belong to the same profession, etc. ▪ a sewing *circle* ▪ She has a large/wide *circle* of friends. ▪ the family *circle* [=the people in a family] ▪ She is well-known in banking/literary/professional/political *circles*. — see also CHARMED CIRCLE, INNER CIRCLE
4 *chiefly Brit* : a balcony or upper level of seats in a theater

²circle *verb* **cir·cles; cir·cled; cir·cling**
1 a : to form a circle around (something) [+ *obj*] There are trees *circling* [=*encircling, surrounding*] our little house. ▪ He *circled* his arms around his wife's waist. [*no obj*] His arms *circled* around his wife's waist. **b** [+ *obj*] : to draw a circle around (something) ▪ She *circled* the correct answer.
2 : to move or go around (someone or something) in a circle [+ *obj*] The pilot *circled* the airport before landing. ▪ We had to *circle* [=go around] the block again to find the house. [*no obj*] The hawk *circled* overhead. ▪ The halfback *circled* to the left. ▪ I ***circled back*** [=*returned*] to the house to get my briefcase.
circle the/your wagons see WAGON

cir·clet /ˈsɚklət/ *noun, pl* **-clets** [*count*] : a band made of metal, flowers, etc., that is usually worn on the head

cir·cuit /ˈsɚkət/ *noun, pl* **-cuits** [*count*]
1 : a series of performances, sports events, lectures, etc., that are held or done at many different places — usually singular ▪ She will be on a lecture *circuit* [=she will be traveling from place to place giving lectures] promoting her new book. ▪ He is one of the most popular drivers on the (racing) *circuit*. ▪ the women's tennis *circuit*
2 : a path or trip around something ▪ It takes a year for the Earth to make one *circuit* around the sun. — often + *of* ▪ She made a *circuit of* the museum.
3 : the complete path that an electric current travels along ▪ electric/electronic *circuits* ▪ a 120-volt *circuit* — see also CLOSED-CIRCUIT, INTEGRATED CIRCUIT, PRINTED CIRCUIT, SHORT CIRCUIT
4 *US, law* **a** *or* ***Circuit*** : a legal district that is established within a state or within the federal judicial system ▪ She was appointed chief judge for the *circuit*. ▪ The case will be heard by a court in the Third *Circuit*. **b** ***Circuit*** : a court of appeals for a particular circuit in the federal judicial system ▪ The Second *Circuit* ruled today against the plaintiff.

circuit board *noun, pl* **~ boards** [*count*] : a board that has many electrical circuits and that is used in a piece of electronic equipment (such as a computer)

circuit breaker *noun, pl* **~ -ers** [*count*] : a switch that automatically stops the flow of electricity to a place or device if the current becomes too strong or another dangerous problem occurs

circuit court *noun, pl* **~ courts** [*count*] *US, law* : a court of law that meets at two or more places within a particular area

circuit judge *noun, pl* **~ judges** [*count*] *US, law* : a judge who hears and tries cases in a circuit court

cir·cu·i·tous /sɚˈkju:wətəs/ *adj* [*more ~; most ~*] *formal*
1 : not straight, short, and direct ▪ He took a *circuitous* [=*roundabout*] route to town.
2 : not said or done simply or clearly ▪ a *circuitous* explanation ▪ Their logic seems a bit *circuitous*.
– cir·cu·i·tous·ly *adv*

cir·cuit·ry /ˈsɚkətri/ *noun* [*noncount*] : a system or group of electric circuits ▪ computer *circuitry*

¹cir·cu·lar /ˈsɚkjəlɚ/ *adj*
1 [*more ~; most ~*] : shaped like a circle or part of a circle ▪ a *circular* [=*round*] table ▪ They have a *circular* driveway. [=their driveway is curved like part of a circle] ▪ That planet has a more *circular* orbit than our planet does.
2 : moving or going around in a circle ▪ *circular* motion ▪ A *circular* [=*spiral*] staircase leads up to the loft.
3 [*more ~; most ~*] : incorrectly using a statement that may not be true to prove an idea or thought that would be false if the original statement was not true ▪ He used *circular* logic/reasoning/thinking. ▪ a *circular* argument/explanation
– cir·cu·lar·i·ty /ˌsɚkjəˈlerəti/ *noun* [*noncount*] ▪ the *circularity* of her argument

²circular *noun, pl* **-lars** [*count*] : a printed sheet (such as an advertisement) that is given or sent to many people at the same time ▪ According to the *circular*, eggs are on sale this week.

circular file *noun, pl* **~ files** [*count*] *US, informal + humorous* : WASTEBASKET ▪ I tossed/threw his letter in the *circular file*. [=I threw away his letter]

circular saw *noun, pl* **~ saws** [*count*] : a tool used for cutting wood that has a sharp round blade which is spun quickly by a motor — see picture at CARPENTRY

cir·cu·late /ˈsɚkjəˌleɪt/ *verb* **-lates; -lat·ed; -lat·ing**
1 : to move without stopping though a system, place, etc. [*no obj*] Blood *circulates* through the body. ▪ Steam *circulates* in the pipes. [+ *obj*] A pump *circulates* the water through the filter. ▪ Fans *circulate* the air.
2 a [*no obj*] : to go or spread from one person or place to another ▪ Rumors are *circulating* around town. ▪ The report *circulated* among the students. **b** [+ *obj*] : to cause (something) to go or spread from one person or place to another ▪ Stories were *circulated* about mismanagement. ▪ He is *circulating* a petition asking for a new election.
3 [*no obj*] : to go from group to group at a party or social gathering in order to talk to different people ▪ She *circulated* among her guests.

cir·cu·la·tion /ˌsɚkjəˈleɪʃən/ *noun, pl* **-tions**
1 [*noncount*] **a** : the movement of blood through the body that is caused by the pumping action of the heart ▪ He has bad *circulation* in his legs. ▪ The drug improves blood *circulation*. **b** : movement of air, water, etc., through the different parts of something ▪ The attic has poor air *circulation*. ▪ the *circulation* of ocean waters ▪ Let's open the windows to get some *circulation* in here.
2 [*noncount*] : the act of passing something (such as money, information, etc.) from person to person or place to place ▪ This memo is not meant for *circulation*.: the state of being passed from person to person or place to place ▪ The coins have recently entered *circulation*. ▪ That rumor has been ***in circulation*** [=has been going around] for a long time. ▪ The magazine has been taken ***out of circulation***. [=the magazine will no longer be made and sold]
3 [*noncount*] : the state of being actively involved in social activities (such as parties or dates) ▪ She's finally getting ***back in/into circulation*** after her divorce. [=she has started dating and going out again after her divorce] ▪ He'll be ***out of circulation*** [=unable to go out socially] for a while after the surgery.
4 [*count*] : the average number of copies of a newspaper, magazine, etc., that are sold over a particular period ▪ The newspaper has the largest *circulation* in the country. ▪ The magazine has a weekly *circulation* of about 70,000 subscribers nationwide.

cir·cu·la·to·ry /ˈsɚkjələˌtori, *Brit* ˌsɜ:kjəˈleɪtri, ˈsɜ:kjələtri/ *adj, always used before a noun, medical* : of or relating to the circulation of blood through the body ▪ the *circulatory* system ▪ *circulatory* failure/problems

cir·cum·cise /ˈsɚkəmˌsaɪz/ *verb* **-cis·es; -cised; -cis·ing** [+ *obj*]
1 : to cut off the skin (called the foreskin) at the end of the penis of (a man or boy) — often used as *(be) circumcised* ▪ He *was circumcised* in accordance with religious practice.
2 : to cut off the clitoris or outer sexual organs of (a woman or girl) — often used as *(be) circumcised* ▪ Most of the girls in the village *were circumcised*.
– cir·cum·ci·sion /ˈsɚkəmˌsɪʒən/ *noun, pl* **-sions** [*noncount*] *Circumcision* is an important rite in some religions. [*count*] How many *circumcisions* has he performed?

cir·cum·fer·ence /sɚˈkʌmfrəns/ *noun, pl* **-enc·es**
1 : the length of a line that goes around something or that makes a circle or other round shape [*count*] Calculate the circle's *circumference*. ▪ What is the *circumference* of the Earth at the equator? [*noncount*] The circle is 38 inches in *circumference*. — see picture at GEOMETRY
2 [*count*] : the outer edge of a shape or area ▪ The fence marks the *circumference* of the field.

cir·cum·flex /ˈsɚkəmˌflɛks/ *noun, pl* **-flex·es** [*count*] : a mark ˆ used in some languages (such as French) to show how a vowel should be pronounced

cir·cum·lo·cu·tion /ˌsɚkəmloʊˈkju:ʃən/ *noun, pl* **-tions** *formal* : the use of many words to say something that could be said more clearly and directly by using fewer words [*noncount*] He was criticized for his use of *circumlocution*. [*count*] I'm trying to avoid *circumlocutions* in my writing.

cir·cum·nav·i·gate /ˌsɚkəmˈnævəˌgeɪt/ *verb* **-gates; -gated; -gat·ing** [+ *obj*] *formal* : to travel all the way

around (something) in a ship, airplane, etc. • The ship *circumnavigated* the world.
— **cir·cum·nav·i·ga·tion** /ˌsɚkəmˌnævəˈgeɪʃən/ *noun* [*count, noncount*]

cir·cum·scribe /ˈsɚkəmˌskraɪb/ *verb* **-scribes; -scribed; -scrib·ing** [+ *obj*]
1 *formal* : to limit the size or amount of (something) — usually used as *(be) circumscribed* • His role as president *was* carefully *circumscribed* by the board. • plants that are found only in a *circumscribed* [=*limited*] area
2 *technical* : to draw a shape around (another shape) • The circle is *circumscribed* by a square.

cir·cum·spect /ˈsɚkəmˌspɛkt/ *adj* [*more* ~; *most* ~] *formal* : thinking carefully about possible risks before doing or saying something • They are *circumspect* [=*cautious*] in all their business dealings.
— **cir·cum·spec·tion** /ˌsɚkəmˈspɛkʃən/ *noun* [*noncount*] • a scholar known for her *circumspection* — **cir·cum·spect·ly** /ˈsɚkəmˌspɛktli/ *adv*

cir·cum·stance /ˈsɚkəmˌstæns/ *noun, pl* **-stanc·es**
1 [*count*] : a condition or fact that affects a situation • I can't imagine a *circumstance* in/under which I would do that. — usually plural • If our business is to survive, we must be able to adapt to changing *circumstances*. • It is impossible ***under these circumstances*** to meet our deadline. • Do not, ***under any circumstances***, open that door. = ***Under no circumstances*** are you to open that door. [=no matter what happens, do not open that door] • Due to ***circumstances beyond our control*** [=things that have happened that we cannot change or influence], the flight is canceled. • There is nothing we can do ***under the circumstances*** [=in this specific situation] • ***Given the circumstances***, I think we did well. [=when you consider how everything went, I think we did well]
2 circumstances [*plural*] : the way something happens : the specific details of an event • The *circumstances* of his death are suspicious.
3 : an event or situation that you cannot control [*noncount*] She says that her client is ***a victim of circumstance*** and should not be blamed for the accident. [*plural*] He was ***a victim of circumstances***
4 circumstances [*plural*] : the conditions in which someone lives • Their *circumstances* changed dramatically after she lost her job. • I don't know anything about his ***financial circumstances*** [=about how much money he has] • They have been forced to live in ***reduced circumstances*** [=to live with less money]
pomp and circumstance see POMP

cir·cum·stan·tial /ˌsɚkəmˈstænʃəl/ *adj* [*more* ~; *most* ~]
1 *law* : based on information which suggests that something is true but does not prove that it is true • The evidence is purely *circumstantial*. • The case against him is *circumstantial*.
2 *formal* : providing or including the details of a particular situation or event • a *circumstantial* account of the meeting

cir·cum·vent /ˌsɚkəmˈvɛnt/ *verb* **-vents; -vent·ed; -vent·ing** [+ *obj*] *formal* : to avoid being stopped by (something, such as a law or rule) : to get around (something) in a clever and sometimes dishonest way • We *circumvented* the problem by using a different program. • He found a way to *circumvent* the law.
— **cir·cum·ven·tion** /ˌsɚkəmˈvɛnʃən/ *noun* [*noncount*] • The *circumvention* of tax laws is illegal.

cir·cus /ˈsɚkəs/ *noun, pl* **-cus·es** [*count*]
1 : a traveling show that is often performed in a tent and that typically includes trained animals, clowns, acrobats, etc. • He worked for a small *circus*. • We're going to the *circus*. • She always wanted to join the *circus*. [=to become a performer in a circus] — often used before another noun • *circus* clowns/animals/performers
2 *informal* : a situation or event that is very busy, lively, and confusing and that attracts a lot of attention — usually singular • The town meeting quickly became a *circus*. • The trial has become a ***media circus*** — see also THREE-RING CIRCUS
3 *Brit* : a circular area where several streets meet — usually used in proper names • Piccadilly *Circus* in London
4 : a large outdoor theater in ancient Rome where shows and sports events were held • the *Circus* Maximus

cir·rho·sis /səˈroʊsəs/ *noun* [*noncount*] *medical* : a serious disease of the liver that can be caused by drinking too much alcohol

cir·rus /ˈsirəs/ *noun* [*noncount*] *technical* : a thin type of cloud that forms high in the sky

cissy *Brit spelling of* SISSY

cis·tern /ˈsɪstɚn/ *noun, pl* **-terns** [*count*] : a container that holds a supply of water: such as **a** *US* : an underground container that is used for collecting and storing rainwater **b** *Brit* : a tank that holds the water for a toilet **c** *Brit* : a tank on the roof of a building that holds water for the building

cit·a·del /ˈsɪtədl/ *noun, pl* **-dels** [*count*] : a castle or fort that in past times was used to protect the people of a city if the city was attacked • We visited a medieval *citadel* in Italy. — often used figuratively • The magazine has become a *citadel* [=*stronghold*] of liberalism/conservatism. • the *citadels* of power ✧ In the U.S., ***The Citadel*** is the name of a well-known military college.

ci·ta·tion /saɪˈteɪʃən/ *noun, pl* **-tions** [*count*]
1 *US* : an official order to appear before a court of law : SUMMONS • He was issued a *citation*. • He received a *citation* for reckless driving.
2 : a formal public statement that praises a person for doing something good or brave • gave her a *citation* for bravery
3 : a line or short section taken from a piece of writing or a speech • She includes *citations* [=*quotations*] from the article in her report.

cite /ˈsaɪt/ *verb* **cites; cit·ed; cit·ing** [+ *obj*]
1 : to write or say the words of (a book, author, etc.) : QUOTE • The article *cites* several experts on the subject.
2 : to mention (something) especially as an example or to support an idea or opinion • The museum had often been *cited* as an example of successful fund-raising. • He *cited* evidence suggesting she was in the area when the crime was committed.
3 *law* : to order (someone) to appear before a court of law • She was *cited* for reckless driving.
4 : to officially and publicly honor (someone) for something done • She was *cited* for bravery.

cit·i·zen /ˈsɪtəzən/ *noun, pl* **-zens** [*count*]
1 : a person who legally belongs to a country and has the rights and protection of that country • She was a United States *citizen* but lived most of her life abroad. • a group of Japanese *citizens* • I've been treated like a ***second-class citizen*** [=someone who is not given the same rights as other people]
2 : a person who lives in a particular place • the *citizens of* Boston — see also SENIOR CITIZEN

cit·i·zen·ry /ˈsɪtəzənri/ *noun, pl* **-ries** [*count*] *formal* : all the citizens of a place — usually singular • an educated *citizenry* • the *citizenry* of Boston

citizen's arrest *noun, pl* **~ -rests** [*count*] : an arrest made by a citizen rather than by the police

citizens band *noun* [*noncount*] : CB

cit·i·zen·ship /ˈsɪtəzənˌʃɪp/ *noun* [*noncount*]
1 : the fact or status of being a citizen of a particular place • She applied for Polish *citizenship*. • He was granted U.S. *citizenship*. • the rights of *citizenship* • She has ***dual citizenship*** [=she is a citizen of two countries]
2 : the qualities that a person is expected to have as a responsible member of a community • The students are learning the value of good *citizenship*. • She is an example of what true *citizenship* is all about. [=her behavior is an example of how a good citizen should act]

cit·ric acid /ˈsɪtrɪk-/ *noun* [*noncount*] : an acid that occurs naturally in the juices of oranges, lemons, limes, etc., and that can also be made from sugar

cit·ron /ˈsɪtrən/ *noun, pl* **-rons** [*count*] : a fruit that is like a large lemon

cit·ro·nel·la /ˌsɪtrəˈnɛlə/ *noun* [*noncount*] : an oil that smells somewhat like lemons and that is used in candles, lamps, etc., to keep bugs away • a *citronella* candle

cit·rus /ˈsɪtrəs/ *noun, pl* **citrus** *or* **cit·rus·es** [*count*] : a juicy fruit (such as an orange, grapefruit, or lemon) that has a thick skin and that comes from a tree or shrub that grows in warm areas — often used before another noun • *citrus* trees/fruits/farmers
— **cit·rusy** /ˈsɪtrəsi/ *adj* [*more* ~; *most* ~] • a *citrusy* flavor

city /ˈsɪti/ *noun, pl* **cit·ies**
1 [*count*] : a place where people live that is larger or more important than a town : an area where many people live and work • major/big *cities* like London, Tokyo, and Rome • ancient/modern *cities* • the *city* of Boston • *city* dwellers/streets • a *city* government • We spent the weekend in the *city*. [=in the nearest big city] ✧ This sense is sometimes used in the name of a city. • New York *City* • Mexico *City* • Kansas *City*
2 a [*count*] : the people in a city — usually singular • I think

the entire *city* has heard the news by now. • The whole *city* was excited about the football game. **b *the city*** : the government of a city • *The city* is working to make the streets safer. • a lawsuit against *the city*
3 *the City* : the section of London that is Great Britain's financial and business center
4 [*noncount*] *chiefly US, informal* — used to describe a place where there is a lot of a particular thing or activity • Their house was pet *city*. [=there were a lot of pets in their house] • It was celebration *city* [=there was a lot of celebration going on] at campaign headquarters last night!
the big city — used to refer to a particular city without naming it • I grew up on a farm, so my move to *the big city* was a big change. • life in *the big city* — see also BIG-CITY

city centre *noun, pl* ~ **centres** [*count*] *Brit* : the main or central part of a city : the part of a city where there are tall buildings, stores, offices, etc. — compare DOWNTOWN, TOWN CENTRE

city council *noun, pl* ~ **-cils** [*count*] : the group of people who make and change the laws of a city • He's running for *city council*.

city desk *noun, pl* ~ **desks** [*count*]
1 *US* : the area in a newspaper's office where stories about local news are written and edited
2 *Brit* : the area in a newspaper's office where stories about financial news are written and edited

city editor *noun, pl* ~ **-tors** [*count*]
1 *US* : a newspaper editor who is responsible for stories about local news
2 *Brit* : a newspaper editor who is responsible for financial news

city father *noun, pl* ~ **-thers** [*count*] *somewhat old-fashioned* : someone who works for a city government — usually plural • The *city fathers* have banned smoking in public places.

city hall *or* **City Hall** *noun, pl* ~ **halls** *or* ~ **Halls** *US*
1 [*count*] : a city government's main building — usually singular • The mayor will be giving a speech on the steps of *City Hall* this afternoon.
2 [*noncount*] : the government of a city • You can't fight *city hall*. [=the city government always wins]

city·scape /ˈsɪtiˌskeɪp/ *noun, pl* **-scapes** [*count*]
1 : the area where a city is and the way it looks • The *cityscape* is cluttered with factories. • the *cityscape* of Philadelphia
2 : a picture that shows part or all of a city • a photographer who does mostly *cityscapes*

city slicker *noun, pl* ~ **-ers** [*count*] *informal + often disapproving* : someone who lives in a city and does not understand what life outside a city is like • *city slickers* who've never seen a real farm

city–state /ˈsɪtiˌsteɪt/ *noun, pl* **-states** [*count*] : a state that has its own government and consists of a city and the area around it • the *city-states* of ancient Greece

city·wide /ˈsɪtiˌwaɪd/ *adj* : including or involving all parts of a city • a *citywide* blackout • The ban on smoking in public places is *citywide*.

civ·et /ˈsɪvət/ *noun, pl* **-ets**
1 [*count*] : a wild animal that is like a cat and that has a long body, short legs, and a long tail ✧ Civets live in parts of Africa, southern Europe, and Asia. — called also *civet cat*
2 [*noncount*] : a substance from the body of the civet that has a strong smell and is sometimes used to make perfume

civ·ic /ˈsɪvɪk/ *adj, always used before a noun*
1 : of or relating to a city or town or the people who live there • Recent improvements to the downtown area are a point of *civic* pride. • the library association and other *civic* groups/organizations/institutions • *civic* leaders
2 : relating to citizenship or being a citizen • Voting is your *civic* duty/responsibility.

civic center (*US*) *or Brit* **civic centre** *noun, pl* ~ **-ters** [*count*]
1 *US* : a large public building for sports events, concerts, etc.
2 *Brit* : a section of a city or town where the public buildings are

civ·ic–mind·ed /ˌsɪvɪkˈmaɪndəd/ *adj* : tending to do things that help your city or town and the people who live there • Town officials are hoping that some *civic-minded* person will volunteer to organize the parade. • *civic-minded* businesses/organizations/individuals
– civ·ic–mind·ed·ness *noun* [*noncount*]

civ·ics /ˈsɪvɪks/ *noun* [*noncount*] *chiefly US* : the study of the rights and duties of citizens and of how government works • Students will be studying *civics* this semester. — often used before another noun • a *civics* class/project

civ·il /ˈsɪvəl/ *adj*
1 *always used before a noun* : of or relating to the people who live in a country • *civil* liberties/duties • a period of *civil* unrest [=a time when groups of people in a country fight one another] — see also CIVIL DISOBEDIENCE, CIVIL WAR
2 *always used before a noun* : of or relating to the regular business of the people in a city, town, state, etc. : not connected to the military or to a religion • They got married in a *civil* ceremony at city hall. • *civil* institutions
3 *not used before a noun* [*more* ~; *most* ~] : polite but not friendly : only as polite as a person needs to be in order to not be rude • It was hard to be *civil* when I felt so angry. • She was barely *civil* to me. — opposite UNCIVIL
4 [*more* ~; *most* ~] : caring about art, science, government, people's well-being, etc. • She argues that a *civil* [=(more commonly) *civilized*] society takes care of its weakest members. — opposite UNCIVIL
5 *always used before a noun, law* : relating to laws that describe a person's rights rather than to laws about crime • The couple filed a *civil* suit against the company that made the crib. • *civil* cases • rules of *civil* procedure — compare [1]CRIMINAL 2; see also CIVIL LAW, CIVIL LIBERTY, CIVIL RIGHTS
– civ·il·ly /ˈsɪvəli/ *adv* • The couple couldn't even discuss things *civilly* [=*politely*] anymore. • "Thank you for helping me, sir," she said *civilly*.

civil defense (*US*) *or Brit* **civil defence** *noun* [*noncount*] : a group of people who are not part of the military but are trained to protect and help people if an enemy attacks their country or if there is a natural disaster (such as a flood or earthquake) • She's in training to be part of the local *civil defense*. • the head of *civil defense*

civil disobedience *noun* [*noncount*] : refusal to obey laws as a way of forcing the government to do or change something • In an act of *civil disobedience*, the family sent its tax money to an antiwar organization. • A student organization is encouraging *civil disobedience* as a way to get the university to change its policies.

civil engineering *noun* [*count*] : a type of engineering that deals with the science of designing and building roads, bridges, large buildings, etc. • He has a degree in *civil engineering*.
– civil engineer *noun, pl* ~ **-neers** [*count*]

ci·vil·ian /səˈvɪljən/ *noun, pl* **-ians** [*count*] : a person who is not a member of the military or of a police or firefighting force • The bomb injured 12 *civilians*.
– civilian *adj, always used before a noun* • *civilian* casualties • She left the army and began a *civilian* career as an airplane mechanic for a commercial airline.

ci·vil·i·ty /səˈvɪləti/ *noun, pl* **-ties** *formal*
1 [*noncount*] : polite, reasonable, and respectful behavior • Everyone should be treated with *civility*. [=*courtesy, politeness*] • codes/standards of *civility*
2 *civilities* [*plural*] : polite actions and words • They greeted each other with the usual exchange of *civilities*.

civ·i·li·za·tion *also Brit* **civ·i·li·sa·tion** /ˌsɪvələˈzeɪʃən, *Brit* ˌsɪvɪˌlaɪˈzeɪʃən/ *noun, pl* **-tions**
1 [*noncount*] : the condition that exists when people have developed effective ways of organizing a society and care about art, science, etc. • modern *civilization* • the impact of technical advancements on *civilization*
2 : a particular well-organized and developed society [*count*] ancient/modern *civilizations* [*noncount*] We are studying ancient Greek/Egyptian *civilization*.
3 [*noncount*] : all the societies of the world • a book about life on the planet after wars have destroyed *civilization*
4 [*noncount*] *informal* : a place that has the things that modern cities and towns have : a place where there is electricity, hot water, etc. • He was sick of camping with his family and wanted to get back to *civilization* and his video games.

civ·i·lize *also Brit* **civ·i·lise** /ˈsɪvəˌlaɪz/ *verb* **-liz·es; -lized; -liz·ing** [+ *obj*]
1 : to teach (a person or group of people) to behave in a way that you think is more polite and gentle • Her parents hoped that boarding school might *civilize* her some. • a teacher who had a *civilizing* influence on the students
2 : to make (something) more gentle, fair, reasonable, etc. • He is credited with *civilizing* the treatment of people with mental illnesses. • efforts to *civilize* the health-care system
3 : to cause (a group of people) to have a more highly organized and modern way of living • They believed it was their

duty to *civilize* the native people.

civilized *also Brit* **civilised** *adj* [*more* ~; *most* ~]

1 : marked by well-organized laws and rules about how people behave with each other • A *civilized* society must respond to crime with fairness and justice. • a more *civilized* culture • a person known throughout the ***civilized world*** [=everywhere people live in well-organized and developed societies] — opposite UNCIVILIZED

2 : polite, reasonable, and respectful • Stop yelling. We have to be more *civilized* about this. • a *civilized* conversation • Try to act like a *civilized* human being! • *civilized* behavior — opposite UNCIVILIZED

3 a : pleasant and comfortable • With my new job, I'll be able to start my day at a more *civilized* hour. [=at a time that is not so early in the morning] • a *civilized* way to spend the evening **b :** showing concern for what is correct according to social rules • They lived in a more *civilized* era. [=a time when people were more concerned with what was proper] — opposite UNCIVILIZED

civil law *noun* [*noncount*] **:** laws that deal with the rights of people rather than with crimes — compare CRIMINAL LAW

civil liberty *noun, pl* ~ **-ties** [*count*] **:** the right of people to do or say things that are not illegal without being stopped or interrupted by the government • Freedom of speech is a *civil liberty*. — usually plural • Opponents said the law would threaten *civil liberties*.

civil marriage *noun, pl* ~ **-riages** [*count*] **:** a marriage performed by a person (such as a justice of the peace) who is not a religious leader • a mayor who has officiated at several *civil marriages* this year

civil rights *noun* [*plural*] **:** the rights that every person should have regardless of his or her sex, race, or religion • Martin Luther King, Jr., fought for *civil rights*. • The U.S. *civil rights* movement achieved equal rights legislation for African-Americans.

civil servant *noun, pl* ~ **-vants** [*count*] **:** a person who works for the government **:** a person who works in the civil service

civil service *noun*

the civil service **:** the part of a government that takes care of the government's basic business **:** the administrative part of a government — often used before another noun • a *civil service* employee • the *civil service* system • I took the *civil service* exam. [=I took a test to get a job in the civil service]

civil union *noun, pl* ~ **unions** [*count*] *US* **:** a legal relationship between two people of the same sex that gives them some of the same rights and responsibilities that married people have

civil war *noun, pl* ~ **wars :** a war between groups of people in the same country [*count*] a region that has had many *civil wars* [*noncount*] The country is on the brink of *civil war*. ✧ *Civil war* is capitalized when it refers to a specific war. • the Spanish/American/Greek *Civil War* • a *Civil War* battlefield [=a battlefield of the American Civil War]

civ·vies /ˈsɪviz/ *noun* [*plural*] *informal* **:** clothing worn by people who are not on military duty **:** clothing that is not part of a military uniform • I didn't recognize the general in his *civvies*.

civ·vy street /ˈsɪvi-/ *noun* [*noncount*] *Brit, informal* **:** civilian life **:** life outside the military • He was trying to make some money in *civvy street*.

CJD *noun* [*noncount*] **:** CREUTZFELDT-JAKOB DISEASE

cl *abbr* centiliter

clack /ˈklæk/ *verb* **clacks; clacked; clack·ing :** to make or cause something to make a short sharp sound or series of short sharp sounds [*no obj*] I heard her heels *clacking* down the hall. • An old fan *clacked* (away) somewhere in another room. [+ *obj*] He *clacked* his teeth together.

– clack *noun, pl* **clacks** [*count*] — usually singular • the *clack* of typewriter keys • the *clack* of her heels

[1]**clad** /ˈklæd/ *adj* [*more* ~; *most* ~] *literary + formal* **1 :** covered with something specified — usually used in combination • ivy-*clad* buildings • snow-*clad* mountains

2 — used to describe the way someone is dressed • graduating students *clad* in black robes • scantily *clad* dancers — often used in combination • denim-*clad* cowboys • the team's red-*clad* fans

[2]**clad** *past tense and past participle of* CLOTHE

clad·ding /ˈklædɪŋ/ *noun* [*noncount*] *chiefly Brit* **:** SIDING 1

[1]**claim** /ˈkleɪm/ *verb* **claims; claimed; claim·ing** [+ *obj*]

1 : to say that (something) is true when some people may say it is not true • The man *claimed* (that) he was a long-lost relative. • They *claim* (that) the drug prevents hair loss. • She *claims* (that) the landlord owes her money. — often followed by *to + verb* • He *claims to know* nothing about the robbery. • He *claims to be* an expert.

2 a : to say that you have (something) • He *claims* a connection to British royalty. • The organization *claims* 10,000 members. • He *claimed* ignorance of the robbery. [=he said that he had no knowledge about the robbery] **b :** to say that (something) belongs to you or that you deserve (something) • The terrorist group *claimed* responsibility for the attack. • New Yorkers proudly *claim* the artist as one of their own. • Both of them *claimed* credit for the idea. • No one ever *claimed* authorship for the poem.

3 : to say that you have a legal right to be given (something) • You should *claim* compensation for the hours you worked. • No heirs came forward to *claim* the inheritance. • They *claimed* asylum. • You can *claim* these expenses as tax deductions. [=you can say that you should be able to pay less money in taxes because of these expenses]

4 : to take (something that belongs to you or that you deserve) • She *claimed* her baggage and left the airport. • The exiled king returned to *claim* his rightful place on the throne.

5 — used to say that someone's attention, time, etc., is being given to something • An urgent message *claimed* [=*required, demanded*] his attention. • This issue has already *claimed* too much of our time. [=we have already spent too much time on this issue]

6 : to cause the end of someone's life • The accident *claimed* seven victims. [=seven people were killed in the accident] • the fatal illness that ***claimed her life*** [=caused her death]

– claim·able /ˈkleɪməbəl/ *adj* • *claimable* expenses

[2]**claim** *noun, pl* **claims** [*count*]

1 : a statement saying that something happened a certain way or will happen a certain way **:** a statement saying that something is true when some people may say it is not true • She makes the *claim* that sea levels will actually go down. • He made false *claims* about his past job experience. • The book makes some extravagant *claims*. [=it includes statements that many people will not agree with] • She disputes/denies the *claim* [=she says it isn't true] that she was unfaithful to her husband. • I make no *claim* to be an expert. [=I don't say that I am an expert]

2 : an official request for something (such as money) that is owed to you or that you believe is owed to you • You'll need to file an insurance *claim* to pay for the damage. • make a *claim* on your insurance policy • All *claims* must be made in writing. • Please fill out this ***claim form***. [=a document with information about why you should be given money]

3 : a right to have something — usually + *on* or *to* • The bank has a *claim on/to* their house and land. • The book would have little *claim on* our attention if not for the fact that its story is true. • the family's *claim to* the name ✧ To ***lay claim to (something)*** is to say that it belongs to you or that you have a right to it. • She *laid claim to* the ring. • The community *lays claim to* (the honor of) being the oldest city in the country. [=it claims to be the oldest city in the country]

4 : an area of land that you take as your own often for a specified use • a mining/timber *claim*

baggage claim or baggage claim area **:** the area in an airport or bus station where you pick up your luggage after traveling • Call when your plane gets in and I'll meet you at (the) *baggage claim*. • at the *baggage claim area*

claim to fame **:** something that someone or something is famous for or that makes someone or something important or interesting • His *claim to fame* is the invention of the stapler. • The restaurant's *claim to fame* is its barbecue sauce.

stake (out) a claim see [2]STAKE

claim·ant /ˈkleɪmənt/ *noun, pl* **-ants** [*count*] *formal* **:** a person who believes that he or she has a right to something (such as an amount of money) **:** a person who claims something • They are *claimants* to the dead man's estate. • *Claimants* will need to fill out the appropriate paperwork. • a dispute between two *claimants* to the throne

clair·voy·ance /ˌkleəˈvojəns/ *noun* [*noncount*] **:** an ability to communicate with dead people, to predict future events, or to know about things that you did not actually see happen or hear about • I don't believe in *clairvoyance*, but I can't explain how he knew those things about my grandmother.

– clair·voy·ant /ˌkleəˈvojənt/ *adj* • *clairvoyant* powers • a *clairvoyant* man/woman **– clairvoyant** *noun, pl* **-ants**

[*count*] ▪ psychics and *clairvoyants*

[1]clam /ˈklæm/ *noun, pl* **clams**

1 [*count*] **:** a type of shellfish that lives in sand or mud, has a light-colored shell with two parts, and is eaten both cooked and raw ▪ steamed *clams* ▪ *clam* chowder — see color picture on page C8

2 clams [*plural*] *US slang, somewhat old-fashioned* **:** dollars ▪ He won 20 *clams* [=(more commonly) *bucks*] playing poker.

(as) happy as a clam *US, informal* **:** very happy ▪ She spent the afternoon reading and was *as happy as a clam*.

[2]clam *verb* **clams; clammed; clam·ming**

clam up [*phrasal verb*] *informal* **:** to stop talking ▪ They *clammed up* when the detectives started asking questions. **:** to refuse to talk ▪ A bunch of people saw what happened, but they all *clammed up* about it.

clam·bake /ˈklæmˌbeɪk/ *noun, pl* **-bakes** [*count*] *US* **:** an outdoor party especially on a beach where clams and other foods are cooked and eaten

clam·ber /ˈklæmbɚ/ *verb, always followed by an adverb or preposition* **-bers; -bered; -ber·ing** [*no obj*] **:** to climb or crawl in an awkward way ▪ The children *clambered* over the rocks. ▪ We *clambered* up the steep hill. ▪ The passengers *clambered* aboard.

clam·my /ˈklæmi/ *adj* **clam·mi·er; -est :** unpleasantly wet and cold ▪ His hand was cold and *clammy*. ▪ *clammy* air

– clam·mi·ness *noun* [*noncount*] ▪ the *clamminess* of the air

[1]clam·or (*US*) *or Brit* **clam·our** /ˈklæmɚ/ *noun*

1 : a loud continuous noise (such as the noise made when many people are talking or shouting) [*singular*] A *clamor* outside woke them in the night. ▪ a *clamor* of voices ▪ a *clamor* of bells [*noncount*] city streets filled with *clamor*

2 : a loud or strong demand *for* something by many people [*singular*] a public *clamor for* an arrest in the case [*noncount*] There is growing *clamor for* reform.

[2]clamor (*US*) *or Brit* **clamour** *verb* **-ors; -ored; -or·ing** [*no obj*]

1 *always followed by an adverb or preposition* **:** to be loud and noisy ▪ The children *clamored* around them, singing songs and laughing.

2 : to ask for or demand something in a loud way ▪ Everyone *clamored* to know what he had decided to do. — usually + *for* ▪ Fans *clamored for* autographs outside the stadium. ▪ People were *clamoring for* news about the trial.

– clam·or·ous /ˈklæmrəs/ *adj* [*more ~; most ~*] ▪ a *clamorous* [=*noisy*] restaurant ▪ *clamorous* customers/children

[1]clamp /ˈklæmp/ *noun, pl* **clamps** [*count*]

1 : a device that holds or presses parts tightly together ▪ a hose *clamp* — see picture at CARPENTRY

2 *Brit* **:** DENVER BOOT

[2]clamp *verb* **clamps; clamped; clamp·ing** [+ *obj*]

1 : to hold or press (things or parts of a thing) tightly together with a device **:** to fasten or tighten (something) with a clamp ▪ The surgeon *clamped* the vein. ▪ He *clamped* the two pieces of wood together.

2 : to press or squeeze (something) ▪ The bit was *clamped* firmly between the horse's teeth. ▪ He *clamped* his mouth shut and refused to speak.

3 *Brit* **:** [2]BOOT 4

clamp down on [*phrasal verb*] ***clamp down on (someone or something)*** **:** to try harder to punish (people who are doing something that is not legal or proper) ▪ Customs officials are *clamping down on* [=*cracking down on*] smugglers. ▪ The school should *clamp down on* students who cut classes. **:** to work harder to stop (a crime) ▪ The state is *clamping down on* [=*cracking down on*] drug trafficking. — see also CLAMPDOWN

clamp on [*phrasal verb*] *chiefly US* ***clamp (something) on (something or someone)*** **:** to officially set (a limit, rule, punishment, etc.) for (someone or something) ▪ The mayor *clamped* [=*imposed*] a curfew *on* the area after the riots. ▪ The new law *clamps* limits *on* the amount of money candidates can spend on election campaigns.

clamp·down /ˈklæmpˌdaʊn/ *noun, pl* **-downs** [*count*] **:** an increased effort to make sure that people obey laws and rules — usually singular ▪ a security *clampdown* in the city's subway system — usually + *on* ▪ a *clampdown on* drug trafficking ▪ a *clampdown* [=*crackdown*] *on* weapons smugglers — see also *clamp down on* at [2]CLAMP

clan /ˈklæn/ *noun, pl* **clans** [*count*]

1 : a large group of people who are related ▪ The tribe is divided into *clans*. ▪ rival *clans* ✧ People in clans often have the same last name. ▪ the McDonald *clan*

2 *informal* **:** a large family ▪ The whole *clan* gets together for the holidays.

3 *informal* **:** a group of people who are similar or who are interested in the same thing ▪ the country club *clan* [=people who are members of country clubs]

clan·des·tine /klænˈdɛstən/ *adj, formal* **:** done in a private place or way **:** done secretly ▪ a *clandestine* [=*secret*] meeting ▪ a *clandestine* marriage ▪ the spy's *clandestine* [=*covert*] operation

– clan·des·tine·ly *adv* ▪ spies working *clandestinely* [=*in secret, covertly*]

clang /ˈklæŋ/ *verb* **clangs; clanged; clang·ing :** to make or cause (something) to make the loud, ringing sound of metal hitting against something [*no obj*] His fork *clanged* against the plate. ▪ The bells *clanged*. ▪ The pots *clanged* together. ▪ The prison door *clanged* shut. [+ *obj*] children *clanging* cowbells ▪ The guard *clanged* the door shut.

– clang *noun, pl* **clangs** [*count*] — usually singular ▪ a dull *clang* ▪ the *clang* of cymbals **– clanging** *noun* [*singular*] ▪ the *clanging* of pots and pans in the kitchen

clang·er /ˈklæŋɚ/ *noun, pl* **-ers** [*count*] *Brit, informal* **:** a bad and embarrassing mistake **:** BLUNDER ▪ a verbal *clanger* ▪ They lost the game after a defensive *clanger*. — see also *drop a clanger* at [2]DROP

clank /ˈklæŋk/ *verb* **clanks; clanked; clank·ing :** to make or cause (something) to make the loud, sharp sound of metal hitting against something solid [*no obj*] The radiator hissed and *clanked*. ▪ The empty can *clanked* along the sidewalk. ▪ the factory's *clanking* machinery [+ *obj*] a ghost *clanking* its chains

– clank *noun, pl* **clanks** [*count*] — usually singular ▪ The hammer fell with a *clank* on the floor. ▪ We heard the *clank* of chains. **– clanking** *noun* [*singular*] ▪ We heard the *clanking* of chains.

clan·nish /ˈklænɪʃ/ *adj* [*more ~; most ~*] *often disapproving* **:** not showing interest in people who are not part of your group or who are not similar to you ▪ a *clannish* fishing community ▪ The college faculty can be pretty *clannish*, so it's difficult to be an outsider there.

clans·man /ˈklænzmən/ *noun, pl* **-men** /-mən/ [*count*] **:** a person (especially a man) who is a member of a clan (sense 1)

clans·wom·an /ˈklænzˌwʊmən/ *noun, pl* **-wom·en** /-ˌwɪmən/ [*count*] **:** a woman who is a member of a clan (sense 1)

[1]clap /ˈklæp/ *verb* **claps; clapped; clap·ping**

1 : to hit the palms of your hands together usually more than once ✧ People often clap to show approval or pleasure. [*no obj*] They cheered and *clapped* [=*applauded*] for the band. ▪ She *clapped* in delight when she heard the news. ▪ The audience *clapped* to the beat of the music. [+ *obj*] *Clap* your hands! ▪ The conductor *clapped* her hands twice, and the musicians stopped talking and prepared to play.

2 [+ *obj*] **:** to suddenly put the palm of your hand on someone or something ▪ He *clapped* his friend on the shoulder. ▪ He *clapped* his hand over his mouth when he realized what he had said.

3 [+ *obj*] **:** to quickly or forcefully put someone or something in a place or position ▪ He *clapped* his hat on his head and went out the door. ▪ He *clapped* the book shut. [=he closed the book quickly or forcefully] ▪ She *clapped* a muzzle on the dog. ▪ The prisoners were *clapped* in irons/chains.

4 : to hit (something, such as two hard surfaces) together in a way that makes a loud noise [+ *obj*] She *clapped* [=*banged*] the two boards together. [*no obj*] The tree branches *clapped* against the house.

5 [+ *obj*] *informal* **:** to suddenly put (someone) in prison, jail, etc. ▪ The police *clapped* him in jail for drug smuggling.

clap eyes on see [1]EYE

– clapping *noun* [*noncount*] ▪ The *clapping* [=*applause*] increased as the lead actors bowed to the audience.

[2]clap *noun, pl* **claps**

1 [*count*] **a :** a sound made by clapping your hands ▪ a series of drum beats and hand *claps* **b :** a loud, sharp sound ▪ The board fell with a *clap* on the floor. ▪ a *clap* of thunder

2 [*count*] **:** a friendly hit with the palm of your hand — usually singular ▪ He gave his friend a *clap* on the back.

3 [*singular*] *Brit* **:** the act of hitting the palms of your hands together again and again to show approval or pleasure ▪ They gave the speaker a long *clap*. [=*round of applause*] — compare [3]CLAP

C

C

[3]clap *noun*
the clap *slang* : GONORRHEA ▪ He got *the clap.*
– compare [2]CLAP

clap·board /ˈklæbɚd, ˈklæpˌboɚd/ *noun, pl* **-boards** *chiefly US*
1 [*count*] : a narrow board that is thicker at one edge than at the other and that is used to cover the outsides of buildings — called also (*Brit*) *weatherboard*
2 [*noncount*] : a set of narrow boards covering the outside of a building ▪ the house's decaying *clapboard*
– clapboard *adj, always used before a noun* ▪ *clapboard* siding ▪ a *clapboard* house/building [=a house/building that is covered in clapboards]

clapped–out /ˌklæptˈaʊt/ *adj, Brit, informal* : old or damaged from being used too much ▪ a *clapped-out* [=*worn-out*] car/machine ▪ *clapped-out* [=*tired, hackneyed*] clichés

clap·per /ˈklæpɚ/ *noun, pl* **-pers** [*count*] : a metal ball that hangs inside a bell and hits the inside of the bell to make it ring
like the clappers *Brit, informal* : very fast ▪ We drove/ran *like the clappers.*

clap·trap /ˈklæpˌtræp/ *noun* [*noncount*] *informal* : words, ideas, etc., that are very foolish or stupid : NONSENSE ▪ His entire speech was nothing but *claptrap.* ▪ I'm tired of hearing all that *claptrap* about how hard her life is. ▪ romantic *claptrap*

clar·et /ˈklerət/ *noun, pl* **-ets** [*count, noncount*]
1 : a type of red wine made in Bordeaux, France
2 : a dark purplish-red color
–claret *adj* ▪ a *claret* gown ▪ a *claret*-colored coat

clar·i·fy /ˈklerəˌfaɪ/ *verb* **-fies; -fied; -fy·ing** [+ *obj*] : to make (something) clear or clearer: such as **a** : to make (something) easier to understand ▪ Can you *clarify* exactly what it is you're proposing? ▪ Her explanation did not *clarify* matters much. ▪ The president was forced to *clarify* his position on the issue. ▪ The committee *clarified* the manager's duties. **b** : to make (a liquid) purer or easier to see through ▪ a substance used to *clarify* wine
– clar·i·fi·ca·tion /ˌklerəfəˈkeɪʃən/ *noun, pl* **-tions** [*noncount*] Your argument needs some *clarification.* [*count*] The newspaper printed a *clarification* [=a statement making the facts clearer] about yesterday's story. **– clarified** *adj* ▪ *clarified* butter [=butter that is made purer by a process that involves heating it] **– clar·i·fi·er** /ˈklerəˌfajɚ/ *noun, pl* **-ers** [*count*] ▪ water *clarifiers*

clar·i·net /ˌklerəˈnɛt/ *noun, pl* **-nets** [*count*] : a musical instrument that is shaped like a tube and that is played by blowing into the top of the tube through a special mouthpiece — see picture at WOODWIND
– clar·i·net·ist *or* **clar·i·net·tist** /ˌklerəˈnɛtɪst/ *noun, pl* **-ists** *or* **-tists** [*count*]

clar·i·on call /ˈklerijən-/ *noun, pl* **~ calls** [*count*] : a strong request for something to happen — usually singular ▪ He used his speech to sound a *clarion call* for affordable health care. ▪ the leader's *clarion call* to action

clar·i·ty /ˈklerəti/ *noun* [*noncount*] : the quality of being clear: such as **a** : the quality of being easily understood ▪ The essays are edited for *clarity.* ▪ There is a lack of *clarity* in many legal documents. **b** : the quality of being expressed, remembered, understood, etc., in a very exact way ▪ She remembered what happened that day with surprising *clarity.* ▪ I'm looking for greater *clarity* about what is expected of our students. ▪ The committee lacked ***clarity of purpose.*** [=the committee did not have a clearly stated purpose] ▪ a ***moment of clarity*** [=a time when you suddenly understand something] **c** : the quality of being easily seen or heard ▪ The *clarity* of the photographs was amazing. ▪ The DVD has excellent *clarity* of sound. ▪ visual *clarity* **d** : the quality of being easily seen through ▪ the *clarity* of the lake's water ▪ glass with exceptional *clarity* **e** : a lack of marks or spots ▪ The vitamin is believed to improve skin *clarity.*

[1]clash /ˈklæʃ/ *verb* **clash·es; clashed; clash·ing**
1 [*no obj*] : to be in a situation in which you are fighting or disagreeing : to come into conflict with someone ▪ Police and protesters *clashed* yesterday. ▪ The brothers often *clash* [=*argue*] over politics. — often + *with* ▪ Protesters *clashed with* the police yesterday.
2 [*no obj*] **a** : to look bad or ugly together ▪ Some colors *clash.* ▪ The sofa and the chair *clash.* ▪ She wore *clashing* colors. — often + *with* ▪ This shirt *clashes with* these pants. **b** : to be very different in a way that makes being or working together difficult ▪ Their personalities *clash.* ▪ *clashing* personalities/ideas — often + *with* ▪ So many of his ideas *clash with* mine.
3 : to make or cause (something) to make the loud sound of a metal object hitting another metal object [*no obj*] The cymbals *clashed.* ▪ Their swords *clashed.* [+ *obj*] She ended the song by *clashing* the cymbals.
4 [*no obj*] *of events* : to happen at the same time so that you cannot do or see both — usually + *with* ▪ The time of the picnic *clashes* [=(more commonly) *conflicts*] *with* another picnic I'm invited to.

[2]clash *noun, pl* **clashes** [*count*]
1 **a** : a short fight between groups of people ▪ Hundreds were killed in ethnic *clashes* in the region last month. — often + *between* or *with* ▪ *Clashes* broke out *between* the police and protesters. ▪ Several protesters were injured in a recent *clash with* the police. ▪ violent *clashes between* the factions **b** : an argument or disagreement between people — often + *between* or *with* ▪ a *clash between* the two leaders ▪ The company has had many *clashes with* environmentalists.
2 : a difference that makes it difficult for people or things to be together or work together ▪ a *clash* of opinions/cultures ▪ We have a personality *clash.* [=we often annoy each other or disagree; we do not get along] — often + *of* ▪ a *clash* of opinions/cultures
3 : a loud sound made by hitting a metal object against another metal object ▪ the *clash* of swords/cymbals
4 : a situation in which two events happen at the same time so that you cannot do or see both ▪ The date of the debate had to be changed because of scheduling *clashes.* [=(more commonly) *conflicts*]

[1]clasp /ˈklæsp, *Brit* ˈklɑːsp/ *noun, pl* **clasps** [*count*]
1 : a device for holding together objects or parts of something (such as a purse, necklace, belt, etc.) ▪ Can you fasten the *clasp* on this bracelet for me? ▪ a tie *clasp* — see color picture on page C11
2 : a strong hold with your hands or arms — usually singular ▪ She took her son's hand in a gentle/firm *clasp.*

[2]clasp *verb* **clasps; clasped; clasp·ing** [+ *obj*]
1 : to fasten (something) with a clasp ▪ She *clasped* her purse shut. ▪ He *clasped* the keys to his belt.
2 : to hold (someone or something) tightly with your hands or arms ▪ He *clasped* her hand gently/firmly. ▪ She *clasped* her son in her arms. ▪ She *clasped* her hands tightly in her lap. = Her hands were *clasped* tightly in her lap. [=she held her hands tightly together in her lap]

[1]class /ˈklæs, *Brit* ˈklɑːs/ *noun, pl* **class·es**
1 **a** [*count*] : a group of students who meet regularly to be taught a subject or activity ▪ There are 20 students in the *class.* ▪ Several people in the *class* are absent today. ✧ In U.S. English, *class* is used with a singular verb. ▪ The *class* is going on a field trip. In British English, *class* can also be used with a plural verb. ▪ The *class* are going on a field trip. **b** [*count*] : a series of meetings in which students are taught a particular subject or activity : a course of instruction ▪ This *class* is really difficult. ▪ He will be teaching an American history *class* next semester. ▪ The college offers *classes* in computer programming and engineering. ▪ She is ***taking a class*** on psychology. ▪ *taking* dance *class* ▪ What *classes* are you *taking* this semester? **c** : one of the meetings in which students are taught a particular subject or activity [*count*] I have an English *class* this morning. ▪ My *class* got out early today. ▪ I have already missed two *classes.* ▪ Read chapters 10 through 20 for the next *class.* [*noncount*] I'm late for *class.* ▪ Let's meet after *class.* ▪ *Class* starts at 8:00 a.m. ▪ What did you learn in *class* today? ▪ He got in trouble for talking during/in *class.* **d** [*count*] *US* : a group of students who finish their education at a particular school at the same time : students who graduate together ▪ She's a member of the *class* of 2006. ▪ the freshman *class* [=the group of students who are freshmen this year and will eventually graduate together] ▪ She's running for *class* president.
2 **a** [*count*] : a group of people in a society who are at the same economic and social level ▪ the ruling/professional *class* ▪ the higher/lower social *classes* — often used before another noun ▪ *class* distinctions ▪ a *class* struggle **b** [*noncount*] : the way people in a society are divided into different social and economic groups ▪ a discussion about *class* and race
3 [*noncount*] **a** : a quality that makes something or someone seem special and attractive ▪ The hotel has *class.* [=it is very elegant] ▪ The candles on the table added a ***touch of class.*** — see also FIRST-CLASS, HIGH-CLASS, WORLD-CLASS **b** : a quality that makes someone seem very good, kind, etc.

• She showed a lot of *class* by donating her prize money to charity. — see also CLASS ACT, CLASSY
4 [*count*] **a** : a group of people or things that are similar in some way • Do you have a license to drive this *class* of vehicle? • a new *class* [=*kind, type*] of nuclear submarine • There are many good players here, but she is in a different *class* altogether. [=she is far better than the other good players] ✧ If you are ***in a class by yourself*** or ***in a class of your own***, you are very different from others in a good or bad way. • There have been a lot of corporate scandals but this one is *in a class by itself*. [=worse than all the others] • As an architect, she is *in a class by herself*. [=she has exceptional talent as an architect] **b** : one of the sections of seats on an airplane, train, etc. • I am traveling ***business class***. [=in a section of an airplane that is more comfortable and expensive than the main section but less comfortable and expensive than first class] — see also FIRST CLASS, SECOND CLASS, THIRD CLASS, TOURIST CLASS
5 [*count*] *Brit* : one of the levels of a university degree

²class *verb* **classes; classed; class•ing** [+ *obj*] : to decide that (someone or something) belongs to a particular group : CLASSIFY — usually used as *(be) classed*; often + *as* • The animal has *been classed as* a fish by some scientists and as a reptile by others. • He *was classed as* a part-time worker.

class act *noun, pl* **~ acts** [*count*] *informal* : someone who is admirable and usually very fair or polite • She's a real *class act* on and off the soccer field.

class action *noun, pl* **~ -tions** [*count*] *US, law* : a lawsuit in which many people join together to sue because they all say they were harmed by the same person or group
– class–action *adj, always used before a noun* • a *class-action* suit against a car company

class–conscious *adj* [*more ~; most ~*] : having or showing a lot of awareness about which economic or social level a person is in : thinking that a person's economic or social class is important • She was never very *class-conscious*, so it surprised her when her classmates talked about the "rich kids" and "poor kids" on campus. • We live in a *class-conscious* society.
– class–consciousness *noun* [*noncount*]

¹clas•sic /ˈklæsɪk/ *adj* [*more ~; most ~*]
1 a — used to say that something has come to be considered one of the best of its kind • *classic* novels/movies • a *classic* case study on hysteria • He collects *classic* cars. **b** — used to say that something is an example of excellence • His winning goal was *classic*. **c** — used to describe something that has been popular for a long time • *classic* board games • The recipe is a new version of a *classic* dish. • a radio station that plays *classic* rock [=rock music from the past that is still popular]
2 : having a graceful design with simple lines • She prefers *classic* furniture designs. • It's a *classic* suit that won't go out of style. • I like the car's *classic* contours.
3 : very typical • The battle was a *classic* example/case of poor planning. • a *classic* error • (*informal*) She lost the tickets? How *classic*. [=it is not surprising that she lost the tickets; she often loses things]

²classic *noun, pl* **-sics**
1 [*count*] : something that has been considered to be excellent for a long time • That car is a *classic*. • film/literary *classics* • I like to read ***the classics***. • Their latest album is ***destined to become a classic***. [=it is very good and will still be admired many years from now]
2 ***classics*** [*noncount*] : the study of the literature, language, and culture of ancient Greece and Rome • He teaches *classics* at the local university. • She studied *classics* in college. • an interest in the *classics*
3 [*count*] : a traditional event • The football game is a Thanksgiving *classic*.

clas•si•cal /ˈklæsɪkəl/ *adj*
1 [*more ~; most ~*] : of a kind that has been respected for a long time • the *classical* [=*traditional*] idea of beauty • *classical* ballet
2 : of or relating to the ancient Greek and Roman world and especially to its language, literature, art, etc. • the *classical* [=*ancient*] and medieval worlds • *classical* literature/art • the *classical* tradition • a *classical* scholar
3 : relating to music in a European tradition that includes opera and symphony and that is generally considered more serious than other kinds of music • *classical* music/composers
4 : teaching ideas about literature, art, science, etc., rather than practical skills • a *classical* curriculum/education
5 : very typical : CLASSIC • a *classical* example of propaganda • the *classical* symptoms of the disease
– clas•si•cal•ly /ˈklæsɪkli/ *adv* • a *classically* trained actress [=an actress who was trained in traditional methods of acting] • a *classically* furnished house • Symptoms *classically* include fatigue and muscle soreness.

clas•si•cism /ˈklæsəˌsɪzəm/ *noun* [*noncount*] *formal*
1 : the ideas and styles that are common in the literature, art, and architecture of ancient Greece and Rome • Roman *classicism* • a return to *classicism* in modern architecture
2 : a traditional style of art, literature, music, architecture, etc., that is usually graceful and simple with parts that are organized in a pleasing way • French *classicism* • *classicism* in literature • the *classicism* of the building

clas•si•cist /ˈklæsəsɪst/ *noun, pl* **-cists** [*count*] *formal*
1 : an expert in ancient Greek and Roman language, literature, art, architecture, or culture
2 : someone who prefers a traditional and usually graceful and simple style in art, literature, music, architecture, etc. : a person who favors classicism

clas•si•fi•ca•tion /ˌklæsəfəˈkeɪʃən/ *noun, pl* **-tions**
1 [*noncount*] : the act or process of putting people or things into groups based on ways that they are alike • a system of *classification* • the *classification* of diseases/drugs • biological *classification* • the *classification* of new species
2 [*count*] : an arrangement of people or things into groups based on ways that they are alike • job *classifications* for government workers • racial/ethnic *classifications*

¹clas•si•fied /ˈklæsəˌfaɪd/ *adj*
1 : arranged in groups with similar things • a *classified* directory
2 : kept secret from all but a few people in the government • *classified* documents • The memo is *classified*. • The part of the report that includes *classified* information was removed before the report was made public.

²classified *noun, pl* **-fieds** [*count*] : a small advertisement that is grouped with others that are like it in a special section of a newspaper or magazine or on a Web site — usually plural • I've been looking through the *classifieds* for a car I can afford. • job/online *classifieds* — called also *classified ad, classified advertisement, (Brit) small ad*; compare WANT AD

clas•si•fy /ˈklæsəˌfaɪ/ *verb* **-fies; -fied; -fy•ing** [+ *obj*]
1 : to arrange (people or things) into groups based on ways that they are alike • Students will be learning about the ways scientists *classify* animals. • The online system can *classify* books by subject. — often used as *(be) classified* • Drugs *are classified* into different categories. • *classified* according to size/weight
2 : to consider (someone or something) as belonging to a particular group • As a singer, she is hard to *classify*. = It is hard to *classify* her as a singer [=to decide what type of singer she is] — often + *as* • The movie had some funny parts, but I wouldn't *classify* it as a comedy. — often used as *(be) classified* • The vehicle *is classified* as a truck.
– clas•si•fi•able /ˌklæsəˈfajəbəl/ *adj* [*more ~; most ~*] • She's one of those singers who are not easily *classifiable*.

class•ism /ˈklæsˌɪzəm, *Brit* ˈklɑːsˌɪzəm/ *noun* [*noncount*] : unfair treatment of people because of their social or economic class • a society plagued by racism and *classism*
– class•ist /ˈklæsɪst, *Brit* ˈklɑːsɪst/ *adj* [*more ~; most ~*] • *classist* views

class•less /ˈklæsləs, *Brit* ˈklɑːsləs/ *adj*
1 : without social or economic classes : not grouping people according to their social or economic level • the goal of a *classless* society
2 : not connected to a particular social or economic class • *classless* foods like pizza and ice cream
3 : rude in a way that is annoying • *classless* behavior
– class•less•ness *noun* [*noncount*]

class•mate /ˈklæsˌmeɪt, *Brit* ˈklɑːsˌmeɪt/ *noun, pl* **-mates** [*count*] : a member of the same class in a school, college, or university ✧ *Classmate* can refer to someone who is taking the same class as you or to someone who will graduate from your school or college in the same year as you. • We were *classmates* in high school. • She invited all of her *classmates* to her birthday party.

class•room /ˈklæsˌruːm, *Brit* ˈklɑːsˌruːm/ *noun, pl* **-rooms** [*count*] : a room where classes are taught in a school, college, or university

class•work /klæsˌwək, *Brit* ˈklɑːsˌwəːk/ *noun* [*noncount*] : the part of a student's work that is done in a class and not

C

at home ▪ All of the students have finished their *classwork* for today. — compare HOMEWORK

classy /ˈklæsi, *Brit* ˈklɑːsi/ *adj* **class·i·er; -est** [*or more ~; most ~*]

1 : having qualities that make someone or something special and attractive ▪ a *classy* [=*fancy, high-class, upscale*] hotel ▪ the *classiest* nightclub in Madrid ▪ The spa boasts some very *classy* clients.

2 : showing impressive character : very good, kind, etc. ▪ a *classy* guy ▪ Donating her salary bonus to charity was a really *classy* thing to do.

– class·i·ness *noun* [*noncount*] ▪ the hotel's *classiness*

clat·ter /ˈklætɚ/ *verb, always followed by an adverb or preposition* **-ters; -tered; -ter·ing** [*no obj*] **:** to make a quick series of short loud sounds ▪ The shutters *clattered* against the house. ▪ He heard dishes *clattering* in the kitchen. ▪ The box dropped and dozens of marbles *clattered* across the floor. ▪ The wagon *clattered* down the road.

– clatter *noun, pl* **-ters** [*count*] — usually singular ▪ the *clatter* of dishes **– clattering** *noun* [*singular*] ▪ the *clattering* of dishes

clause /ˈklɑːz/ *noun, pl* **claus·es** [*count*]

1 *grammar* **:** a part of a sentence that has its own subject and verb ▪ The sentence "When it rained they went inside" consists of two *clauses*: "when it rained" and "they went inside."

2 : a separate part of a legal document ▪ a *clause* in a will/contract — see also GRANDFATHER CLAUSE

claus·tro·pho·bia /ˌklɑːstrəˈfoʊbijə/ *noun* [*noncount*]

1 : a fear of being in closed or small spaces ▪ She doesn't go in elevators because of her *claustrophobia*. — compare AGORAPHOBIA

2 : an unhappy or uncomfortable feeling caused by being in a situation that limits or restricts you ▪ the *claustrophobia* of small-town life

claus·tro·pho·bic /ˌklɑːstrəˈfoʊbɪk/ *adj* [*more ~; most ~*]

1 *of a room, space, etc.* **:** not having enough space for people to feel comfortable : causing claustrophobia ▪ The theater can be a little *claustrophobic* when it's full.

2 : having a fear of being in closed or small spaces : having claustrophobia ▪ She doesn't go in elevators because she is *claustrophobic*.

3 : not having or providing enough freedom ▪ a very *claustrophic* relationship

– claus·tro·pho·bi·cal·ly /ˌklɑːstrəˈfoʊbɪkli/ *adv* ▪ a *claustrophobically* small room

clav·i·chord /ˈklævəˌkoɚd/ *noun, pl* **-chords** [*count*] **:** a musical instrument that is similar to a piano and was played mostly in the past before the piano was invented

clav·i·cle /ˈklævɪkəl/ *noun, pl* **clav·i·cles** [*count*] *medical* **:** COLLARBONE — see picture at HUMAN

[1]**claw** /ˈklɑː/ *noun, pl* **claws** [*count*]

1 : a sharp curved part on the toe of an animal (such as a cat or bird) ▪ The eagle was carrying a mouse in its sharp *claws*. ▪ the bear's *claws* — often used figuratively ▪ They've only been dating for a few months and already she's ***got her claws into*** him! [=she already has control over him] ▪ (*chiefly Brit*) The press has been *getting its claws into* him. [=has been attacking/criticizing him] ▪ They're still trying to ***get their claws on*** her money. [=to get her money]

2 : a body part of an animal (such as a lobster or crab) that is used for gripping and holding things

3 : a part on a tool or machine that is used for gripping, digging, etc. ▪ The excavating machine's *claw* dug into the earth. ▪ the *claw* of a hammer — see picture at CARPENTRY — see also BEAR CLAW

– clawed /ˈklɑːd/ *adj* ▪ a *clawed* foot

[2]**claw** *verb* **claws; clawed; claw·ing :** to scratch, grip, or dig with claws or fingers [*no obj*] — usually + *at* ▪ The cat *claws at* the door when she wants to go outside. ▪ The dog was *clawing at* the dirt. ▪ She desperately *clawed at* her attacker's face. [+ *obj*] How can we stop the cat from *clawing* the drapes/curtains? ▪ The dog *clawed* a hole in the carpet. ▪ She tried to *claw* his face with her fingernails.

claw back [*phrasal verb*] ***claw (something) back*** *or* ***claw back (something)*** *chiefly Brit* **:** to get back (something, such as money or business) by acting in a forceful way or by doing something that requires a lot of effort ▪ With budget cuts looming, the government is trying to *claw back* some of the money it promised to state agencies.

***claw your way* :** to move ahead slowly by grabbing onto things ▪ The climbers *clawed their way* up the steep terrain. — often used figuratively ▪ The company is *clawing its way* out of bankruptcy. ▪ He *clawed his way* to the top of his profession.

claw hammer *noun* **~ -mers** [*count*] **:** a hammer with a head that is curved and partially split in the back so that it can be used for pulling out nails

clay /ˈkleɪ/ *noun, pl* **clays** [*count, noncount*] **:** a heavy, sticky material from the earth that is made into different shapes and that becomes hard when it is baked or dried ✧ Clay is used to make pots, bricks, tiles, etc. — often used before another noun ▪ a *clay* pot/pipe/tablet

feet of clay see [1]FOOT

– claylike *adj* [*more ~; most ~*] ▪ a *claylike* substance

clay·ey /ˈkleji/ *adj* **:** containing a lot of clay ▪ a *clayey* soil

clay pigeon *noun, pl* **~ -geons** [*count*] **:** a circular object made of baked clay that people throw into the air and shoot at to practice their shooting skills

[1]**clean** /ˈkliːn/ *adj* **clean·er; -est**

1 : free from dirt, marks, etc. : not dirty ▪ a *clean* floor ▪ This table isn't *clean*. There's a sticky spot where something spilled. ▪ He keeps a very *clean* house. ▪ The janitor does a good job of keeping the office *clean*. ▪ *clean* laundry/socks/towels/sheets ▪ I wiped the baby's face *clean*.

2 : tending to keep clean ▪ He's a *clean* young man. ▪ Cats are very *clean* animals.

3 a : free from pollution or other dangerous substances ▪ *clean* air/water **b :** not causing pollution ▪ Solar power provides *clean* energy. ▪ a *clean* fuel

4 a : not yet used ▪ a *clean* [=*blank, fresh*] piece/sheet of paper **b** *of a document* **:** not having any mistakes ▪ We need a ***clean copy*** of the document.

5 : not infected ▪ a *clean* wound

6 : pleasingly simple ▪ I like the *clean* simplicity of the chair's design. ▪ She wore a formal wool suit with ***clean lines***.

7 : having edges that are straight and smooth ▪ a *clean* cut ▪ The vase was broken, but it was a *clean* break and easily repaired with a little glue.

8 : completely and quickly done ▪ The bank robbers made a *clean* getaway. ▪ When he left home, he made a ***clean break*** with the past. [=he completely separated himself from everything that had been part of his life]

9 *sports* **:** done in a skillful and impressive way without mistakes or awkwardness ▪ a *clean* dive/catch/hit ▪ The gymnast made a *clean* landing.

10 : not showing evidence of any broken rules or laws ▪ She has a *clean* driving record. — see also CLEAN SLATE (below)

11 a : not connected with or involving anything illegal or morally wrong ▪ a *clean* candidate ▪ They believe in hard work and *clean* living. ▪ The party was good, *clean* fun. **b :** not referring to anything sexual or offensive ▪ Only *clean* jokes, please. There are children here. ▪ *clean* language

12 *not used before a noun* **:** no longer using drugs : not addicted to drugs ▪ He's been *clean* for five years. ▪ *clean* and sober

13 *not used before a noun, informal* **:** not carrying any weapons, drugs, etc. ▪ All visitors to the prison are searched to make sure they're *clean*. ▪ I checked her; she's *clean*.

clean as a whistle see [1]WHISTLE

clean slate *also Brit* ***clean sheet*** **1 :** a person's record (as from a school or a job) that shows no evidence of any problems, broken rules, etc. : a clean record ▪ Everyone who comes to this school starts with a *clean slate*. **2** ***clean sheet*** *Brit* **:** a game in which the opposing team is prevented from scoring ▪ The team's star goalie has had five *clean sheets* [=(*US*) *shutouts*] this season. [=has prevented the other team from scoring in five games]

clean sweep **1 :** a victory in which one side or team wins every game, contest, etc. ▪ The Red Sox won the series in a *clean sweep*. ▪ The election was a *clean sweep* for local Democratic candidates. **2 :** a complete change in something ▪ The new governor has made a *clean sweep* of the staff in the governor's mansion. [=the new governor completely replaced the former governor's staff]

come clean *informal* **:** to tell the truth about what happened : to stop hiding the truth ▪ Eventually she *came clean* and helped the police recover the goods she'd stolen. ▪ He's finally *come clean* about his role in the scandal.

give (someone or something) a clean bill of health see [1]BILL

keep your nose clean see [1]NOSE

make a clean breast of see [1]BREAST

wipe the slate clean see [1]WIPE

– clean·ness /ˈkliːnnəs/ *noun* [*noncount*] ▪ the *cleanness* of the image

²clean *verb* **cleans; cleaned; clean·ing**
1 a : to make (something) clean **:** to remove dirt, marks, etc., from (something) [+ *obj*] The carpet needs to be *cleaned.* ▪ *clean* your fingernails ▪ clean [=*brush*] your teeth ▪ *clean* [=*wash*] the windows [*no obj*] They divide household duties so that she *cleans* and her husband cooks. — see also CLEAN UP 1a (below) **b** [*no obj*] **:** to become clean ▪ The pan has a surface that *cleans* easily. [=that is easy to clean]
2 [+ *obj*] **:** to make (something, such as a room) neat and orderly ▪ *Clean* your room. — see also CLEAN OUT 1 (below), CLEAN UP 1b (below)
3 [+ *obj*] **:** to remove the organs from the inside of (an animal) before cooking ▪ They *cleaned* the fish and cooked them on the campfire. ▪ skin and *clean* a rabbit/deer
clean house see ¹HOUSE
clean out [*phrasal verb*] **1** ***clean (something) out or clean out (something)*** **:** to remove unwanted things from (a room, closet, etc.) ▪ We spent the weekend *cleaning out* the garage. [=clearing unwanted items from the garage] ▪ I need to *clean out* my purse. **2** ***clean (someone or something) out or clean out (someone or something) informal*** **:** to steal or take everything from (someone or something) ▪ The thieves broke in and *cleaned out* the store. ▪ She fell for the scheme and was *cleaned out.* [=all her money was taken] **3** ***clean (someone) out or clean out (someone) informal*** **:** to use up all or most of someone's money ▪ Buying the house really *cleaned* us *out.* Now we're broke.
clean up [*phrasal verb*] **1** ***clean (something) up or clean up (something)*** **a :** to remove (dirt, spilled substances, etc.) ▪ Would you mind *cleaning up* the spilled milk? ▪ It will only take a moment to *clean* this mess *up.* **b** *or* ***clean up*** **:** to make (a room or space) clean and orderly ▪ Would you mind helping me *clean up* the kitchen after dinner? ▪ We stayed late to help them *clean up.* ✧ To ***clean up after*** someone is to make a place clean after someone has made it dirty or messy. ▪ His mother is always *cleaning up after* him. ▪ You should learn to *clean up after* yourself. **c :** to remove pollution from (something) ▪ The city has *cleaned up* the bay in recent years. — see also CLEANUP **2** ***clean up or clean (yourself) up*** **:** to make yourself clean **:** to wash your face and hands ▪ I'm sure you'll want to *clean up* after a full day of traveling. ▪ I just need a few minutes to *clean myself up* before dinner. ▪ The children are inside getting *cleaned up.* **3** ***clean (something) up or clean up (something)*** **a :** to remove whatever is illegal or immoral from (something) ▪ The new mayor has really *cleaned up* city hall. [=has made the city government less corrupt] **b :** to make (something) clearer or more acceptable ▪ We were able to *clean up* the sound on the recording using special equipment. ▪ He's *cleaned up* his image since his early rock music days. **4** ***clean (something) up or clean up (something) informal*** **:** to eat all of (something) ▪ The teenagers *cleaned up* [=(more commonly) *polished off*] the pizza in a matter of minutes. **5** ***informal*** **:** to make a large amount of money ▪ She really *cleaned up* last year in the stock market. **6** ***clean up your act informal*** **:** to behave in a way that is more acceptable ▪ After years of drug abuse, she finally got treatment and *cleaned up her act.*
clean your plate **:** to eat all the food on your plate ▪ The children were not allowed to have dessert until they had *cleaned their plates.* ***usage*** see CLEANSE

³clean *adv, informal* **:** all the way **:** completely or entirely ▪ Somehow, the top of the machine came *clean* off. ▪ The nail went *clean* through the wall. ▪ The fish were jumping *clean* out of the water.

⁴clean *noun* [*singular*] *informal* **:** an act of removing dirt from something ▪ She gave the tub a good *clean.* [=she cleaned the tub thoroughly]

clean–cut /ˈkliːnˈkʌt/ *adj* [*more ~; most ~*] **:** having a neat appearance that suggests you are someone who does not break rules or cause trouble ▪ a polite, *clean-cut* young man

clean·er /ˈkliːnɚ/ *noun, pl* **-ers**
1 [*count*] **:** a person whose job is to clean something ▪ street/window *cleaners* ▪ They have hired a ***house cleaner.*** [=a person whose job is to keep the rooms in a house or apartment clean]
2 [*count*] **:** a substance used for cleaning things ▪ He recommends using baking soda as a general household *cleaner.*
3 [*count*] **:** a device or machine used for cleaning things ▪ an air *cleaner* — see also PIPE CLEANER, VACUUM CLEANER
4 ***the cleaners or the cleaner's*** **:** a shop where clothes are cleaned **:** DRY CLEANER ▪ I took my suit to *the cleaners.*
take (someone) to the cleaners informal **:** to get all or most of someone's money or possessions usually in a dishonest or unfair way ▪ I heard that his ex-wife really *took him to the cleaners* [=*cleaned him out*] in the divorce.

cleaning *noun* [*noncount*] **:** the act or process of cleaning something ▪ She needs someone to help her with the *cleaning* [=*housecleaning*] while she is recovering from surgery.

cleaning lady *noun, pl* **~ ladies** [*count*] **:** a woman whose job is to clean offices or houses — called also *cleaning woman*

cleaning person *noun, pl* **~ -sons** [*count*] **:** a woman or man whose job is to clean offices or houses

clean·li·ness /ˈklɛnlinəs/ *noun* [*noncount*]
1 : the state of being clean ▪ The restaurant's kitchen is regularly inspected for *cleanliness.*
2 : the practice of keeping yourself and your surroundings clean ▪ the virtues of *cleanliness* and honesty

clean·ly /ˈklɛnli/ *adv* [*more ~; most ~*] **:** in a clean manner: such as **a :** easily and completely ▪ A sharp knife will cut through the skin of a tomato *cleanly.* **b :** without causing pollution ▪ This fuel burns more *cleanly* than other fuels.

clean room *noun* **~ rooms** [*count*] **:** a room that is kept extremely clean so that certain products can be made in it ▪ The microchips are manufactured in a *clean room.*

cleanse /ˈklɛnz/ *verb* **cleans·es; cleansed; cleans·ing** [+ *obj*] **:** to make (someone or something) clean ▪ The cut should be *cleansed* gently with mild soap and water. ▪ *cleansed* of all impurities — see also ETHNIC CLEANSING

> ***usage*** The verbs *clean* and *cleanse* both mean "to make (something or someone) clean." *Cleanse* usually refers to making the body or part of the body clean. ▪ *cleansing* the skin ▪ The herb is believed to *cleanse* the body of toxins. It can also refer to making a person's mind, soul, reputation, etc., clean. ▪ The ceremony is meant to *cleanse* people of their guilt and sin. ▪ Try to *cleanse* your mind through meditation. *Clean* is more common than *cleanse* and its use is less specific.

cleans·er /ˈklɛnzɚ/ *noun, pl* **-ers :** a substance (such as a powder or cream) that is used for cleaning something [*count*] a skin *cleanser* [*noncount*] Sprinkle some *cleanser* on the floor and let it sit for a while before you start scrubbing.

clean–shaven *adj, of a man* **:** having a shaved face **:** having no beard or mustache ▪ The waiters were *clean-shaven.*

¹clean·up /ˈkliːnˌʌp/ *noun, pl* **-ups** [*count*] **:** the process of cleaning something ▪ The children helped with the *cleanup* [=helped to clean up] after the meal. — often used before another noun ▪ The *cleanup* costs of the oil spill will be in the millions of dollars. ▪ The company's *cleanup* efforts have been applauded by the town.

²cleanup *adj, always used before a noun* **:** fourth in the batting order of a baseball team ▪ a *cleanup* hitter
– cleanup *adv* ▪ He's batting *cleanup.*

¹clear /ˈkliɚ/ *adj* **clear·er; -est** [*also more ~; most ~*]
1 : very obvious **:** not causing or allowing doubt ▪ The show was a *clear* failure. [=it was clearly a failure; there is no doubt that the show was a failure] ▪ There are *clear* differences between the two candidates. ▪ She's the *clear* favorite to win the election. ▪ I'm not completely happy with the plan, but I see no *clear* alternative. ▪ He was the *clear* winner. ▪ It has become *clear* [=*evident*] to me that changes are necessary. ▪ She has made it abundantly/painfully/very *clear* that she does not support us. ▪ It's not *clear* how much longer we'll have to wait. ▪ She made (it) *clear* to me that she was unhappy. [=she told/showed me in a very definite way that she was unhappy] ▪ "Changes will have to be made." "Yes, that's *clear.*" ▪ The sign said/read "Keep Out" ***as clear as day/daylight/anything.*** [=the sign very clearly said "Keep Out"] — sometimes used in spoken phrases that express anger ▪ I want this work finished by this afternoon. ***Do I make myself clear***? [=do you understand me?] ▪ The work needs to be finished by this afternoon. ***Is that clear***? ▪ ***Let's get one thing perfectly clear***: I want this work finished by this afternoon.
2 : easily understood ▪ She's a *clear* writer. [=she writes clearly] ▪ Her writing has a *clear* style. ▪ a *clear* definition/explanation ▪ a *clear* message ▪ The instructions weren't very *clear* about when we were supposed to begin. ▪ (*informal*) The explanation was ***as clear as mud.*** [=extremely unclear]
3 a : free from doubt or confusion ▪ I think I have a *clear* understanding of the problem. ▪ Are you *clear* on/about what you need to do? [=do you understand what you need to do?]

• He has *clear* ideas about what he hopes to accomplish. **b : able to think in an accurate way without confusion** • She's a *clear* thinker. • This job requires someone with a ***clear head*** [=someone who can think clearly] — see also CLEAR-HEADED

4 : easily seen : having small parts and details that can be easily seen and identified • This picture is blurry, but that one is *clear*. • Our TV has a beautifully *clear* picture/image.

5 : easily heard • a very *clear* sound **: easily heard and understood** • *clear* pronunciation • The teacher has a very *clear* speaking voice.

6 : easily seen through • *clear* [=*transparent*] glass • a *clear* liquid • a glass of cool, *clear* water • *clear* plastic bags • *clear* soup/broth • *clear* air • The water in the lake is ***crystal clear.*** = The water in the lake is (as) ***clear as crystal***

7 : not blocked by anything • I had a *clear* view of the accident. [=I was able to see the accident clearly] • The aisles must be kept *clear* during the show. [=no people or things can be in the aisles during the show] • a *clear* path **: not covered by anything** • You should keep your work area *clear*. — **often + *of*** • You should keep your work area *clear of* clutter. • Don't try to cross the street until it's *clear of* traffic. [=until there is no traffic on the street] — see also CLEAR OF (below), *the coast is clear* at [1]COAST, *clear sailing* at SAILING

8 *of weather or the sky* : not having any clouds, fog, etc. • It was a beautifully *clear*, sunny day. • a *clear* blue sky • You can see thousands of stars on a *clear* night.

9 a : free of marks or spots • an actress with beautifully/perfectly *clear* healthy skin **b : having a distinct and bright color** • She has *clear* blue eyes. **c *medical* : free of abnormal signs or symptoms** • After treatment, all his tests were *clear*. [=his tests did not show any problems]

10 : free from feelings of guilt or blame — used with *conscience* • The accident wasn't my fault. My *conscience* is *clear*. = I have a *clear conscience*. ✧ If your conscience is *clear*, you do not feel guilty because you do not believe that you have done anything wrong.

11 *finance* — used to describe the amount that remains after costs, taxes, etc., have been paid • We made a *clear* [=*net*] profit of $500.

12 : not having any planned or scheduled activities • Wednesday afternoon is *clear* [=*free*], so let's meet then. • I like to keep my schedule *clear* on Friday afternoons.

***(as) clear as a bell* : very clear** • It was *clear as a bell* that morning—not a cloud in the sky. • The water was *as clear as a bell*. • *Clear as bell*, I heard him say my name. • a sound *as clear as a bell*

***clear of* : away from (something dangerous, harmful, etc.)** • Keep/Stay *clear of* [=*out of*] trouble! • Stand *clear of* the closing doors! • We'll pick up speed once we get *clear of* the heavy traffic. — see also [1]CLEAR 7 (above)

see your way clear see [1]SEE

steer clear (of) see [2]STEER

– clear·ness *noun* [*noncount*] • I was impressed by the *clearness* [=(more commonly) *clarity*] of his explanation. • the *clearness* of the water

[2]clear *verb* **clears; cleared; clear·ing**

1 [*no obj*] **: to become clear: such as a *of weather or the sky* : to change so that there are no clouds, fog, etc.** • The sky *cleared* after the rain. • The weather is cloudy now, but it's *clearing* gradually. — see also CLEAR UP (below) **b *of clouds, fog, smoke, etc.* : to go away** • The clouds *cleared* (from the sky) after the rain. • The morning fog gradually *cleared*. • When the smoke *cleared*, we could see that the building had been completely destroyed. **c *of a liquid* : to change by becoming easier to see through : to become transparent or more transparent** • The water *cleared* after the mud had settled. **d *of the skin* : to become free of marks or spots** • My skin *cleared* when I started using the cream. — see also CLEAR UP (below) **e** ✧ When your ***head clears*** or when something ***clears your head***, you become more awake or alert and are able to think in a normal way without confusion. • My *head cleared* after a good night's sleep. = A good night's sleep *cleared my head*. [=I was able to think clearly again after a good night's sleep] **f** ✧ When your ***vision/eyesight clears*** you become able to see things correctly. • When I woke up everything was blurry at first, but then my *vision* gradually *cleared*.

2 a [*+ obj*] **: to remove something entirely from an area or place** • He used a shovel to *clear* the snow off/from the driveway. = He used a shovel to *clear* the driveway of snow. • They *cleared* timber from/off the land. • She *cleared* everything out of the closet. • I'll *clear* those books out of the/your way. • She *cleared* [=*removed*] the dishes from the table. = She ***cleared the table*** (of dishes). **b : to cause the people in an area or place to leave** [*+ obj*] *clear* a room of unwanted visitors = *clear* unwanted visitors from a room • The alarm *cleared* [=*emptied*] the room (of people). [*no obj*] The room *cleared* quickly when the alarm sounded. [=the people in the room left quickly when the alarm sounded] **c** [*+ obj*] **: to leave (an area or place) so that it is empty** • The police ordered the crowd to *clear* the area.

3 [*+ obj*] **: to make (a path, road, open space, etc.) by removing things that block or cover an area or surface** • The guide *cleared* a path for us through the jungle. • I *cleared* a space on the desk for my new computer.

4 [*+ obj*] **: to go over, under, or past (something) without touching** • The horse *cleared* [=jumped over] the fence easily. • The pole-vaulter *cleared* 15 feet on his first try. • The boat's sail just/narrowly *cleared* [=passed under] the bottom of the bridge.

5 [*+ obj*] **: to prove that (someone) is not guilty of a crime** • The investigation *cleared* him officially of all the charges against him. • He says he's innocent and he wants an opportunity to ***clear himself.*** = He wants an opportunity to ***clear his name*** [=to prove that he is innocent]

6 [*+ obj*] **a : to get approval for (something)** • You should *clear* the article with your boss before trying to get it published. **b : to give approval for (something)** • Her boss *cleared* [=*approved*] the article for publication. **c : to say that (someone) has official permission to do something** • The head of the agency has *cleared* her to see classified information. • The flight/plane/pilot was *cleared* to land. = The flight/plane/pilot was *cleared* for landing. [=the flight/plane/pilot was given official permission/clearance to land] • We were *cleared* (to go) through customs. = We ***cleared customs*** **d : to be passed or officially approved by (a group)** • The bill has finally *cleared* the Senate. [=the Senate has finally passed the bill]

7 [*+ obj*] ***finance*** **a : to pay all the money that is owed for (a debt or loan)** • *clear* a debt **b : to gain (an amount of money) after paying all costs, taxes, etc.** • After paying our expenses we *cleared* almost 1,000 dollars on the deal. • *clear* a profit **c** ✧ When a ***check clears*** or ***is cleared***, it goes through the process of being reviewed and accepted by a bank, and the money for the check is taken from the bank's account. • Checks can take up to four days to *clear*. = Checks can take up to four days to *be cleared*. • The check failed to *clear*. [=the check bounced]

clear away [*phrasal verb*] ***clear (something) away or clear away (something)*** **: to remove (something) from an area or surface** • Just give me a moment to *clear away* all these papers, then we can sit down at the table. — **sometimes used figuratively** • They had a long talk and were able to *clear away* [=*clear up, resolve*] all their misunderstandings.

clear off [*phrasal verb*] **1 *clear off (something) or clear (something) off (something)* : to remove things from (an area or surface)** • It took her a few minutes to *clear off* the dinner table. • It took her a few minutes to *clear* the dishes *off* the dinner table. • I'll *clear off* my desk so that you can use it. **2 *chiefly Brit, informal* a : to go away or run away : to leave quickly** • When we heard the night watchman, we *cleared off* as quickly as we could. • I told him to *clear off* [=*get lost*] and leave me alone. **b *clear off (a place)* : to leave (a place) quickly** • I ordered the hikers to *clear off* [=*get off*] my land at once.

clear out [*phrasal verb*] **1 : to leave quickly** • He *cleared out* without paying his rent. **2 *clear (something) out or clear out (something)* : to remove unwanted things from (an area or place)** • *clear out* a cluttered closet — see also CLEAROUT

clear the air see [1]AIR

clear the deck/decks see [1]DECK

clear up [*phrasal verb*] **1 : to become clear: such as a *of weather or the sky* : to change so that there are no clouds, fog, etc.** • The sky *cleared up* after the rain. • It's cloudy now, but it's *clearing up* gradually. **b *of the skin* : to become free of marks or spots** • My skin *cleared up* when I started using the cream. **2 *clear up or clear (something) up or clear up (something)* : to go away or cause (something) to go away** • My symptoms *cleared up* once I started using the cream. • The cream has *cleared up* my symptoms. **3 *clear (something) up or clear up (something)* a : to make (something) clear by explaining it** • *clear up* a mystery **b : to cause the end of (something) by talking about it or dealing with it** • We need to *clear up* [=*resolve*] these

misunderstandings. ▪ If we try I'm sure we can *clear up* these problems quickly. **4** *Brit* **:** to make an area clean or tidy ▪ Let's *clear up* [=*clean up, tidy up*] before we leave.
clear your throat **:** to make a noise in your throat for attention or to be able to speak more clearly ▪ He *cleared his throat* and began to speak.

³clear *adv*
1 : in a clear manner — used in the phrase ***loud and clear*** ▪ "Can you hear me now?" "*Loud and clear.*" [=I can hear you very clearly]
2 *chiefly US, informal* **:** all the way **:** completely or entirely ▪ We drove *clear* across the state. ▪ The ball rolled *clear* across the street.
free and clear see ²FREE

⁴clear *noun*
in the clear **:** free from guilt or suspicion ▪ The investigation/jury considered all the charges against him and concluded that he was *in the clear.* [=that he was not guilty] ▪ He's not *in the clear* yet. The police still consider him a suspect.

clear·ance /ˈklirəns/ *noun, pl* **-anc·es**
1 a : an official decision saying that someone has permission to do something [*noncount*] You'll have to get *clearance* [=*approval*] from management to go ahead with the project. ▪ The documents are only available to people with ***security clearance*** [=special permission given only to people who are approved to know or see secret things] from the government. [*count*] She has a *security clearance* that allows her to see the classified information. **b :** official permission for an aircraft, pilot, etc., to do something [*noncount*] The pilot got *clearance* to land. ▪ That flight has not received *clearance* for landing/takeoff. [*count*] a *clearance* for landing/takeoff
2 : the amount of space between two things [*noncount*] There was only 10 inches of *clearance* between the car and the side of the tunnel. [*count*] The car has a ***road/ground clearance*** of seven inches. [=the bottom of the car is seven inches above the road/ground] ▪ a bridge with a 100-foot *clearance* above the water
3 [*noncount*] **:** the act or process of removing things (such as trees or old buildings) from an area ▪ the *clearance* of forests for farming ▪ slum *clearance* to make room for new housing

clearance sale *noun, pl* **~ sales** [*count*] **:** a sale in which prices are lowered in order to sell things quickly and make room for new items ▪ The store is having/holding a *clearance sale* this weekend.

¹clear–cut /ˈkliɚˈkʌt/ *adj* [*more ~; most ~*] **:** very obvious and sharp ▪ a *clear-cut* distinction **:** free from doubt or uncertainty **:** very definite ▪ a *clear-cut* victory/decision ▪ The difference between their views on this issue is not *clear-cut.*

²clear–cut /ˈkliɚˌkʌt/ *noun, pl* **-cuts** [*count*] *US* **:** an area of land in which all the trees have been cut down ▪ The law limits the size of *clear-cuts.*

³clear–cut *verb* **-cuts; -cut; -cut·ting** [*+ obj*] *US* **:** to cut down all the trees in (an area) ▪ Ten years ago the lumber company *clear-cut* this hillside.
– clear–cutting *noun* [*noncount*] ▪ *Clear-cutting* has led to mudslides in many regions.

clear–eyed /ˈkliɚˌaɪd/ *adj* [*more ~; most ~*] **:** having or showing an ability to think clearly ▪ She provided a *clear-eyed* [=*clear-sighted, clearheaded*] assessment of the problem.

clear·head·ed /ˈkliɚˌhɛdəd/ *adj* [*more ~; most ~*] **:** having or showing an ability to think clearly ▪ He remains calm and *clearheaded* in tense situations. ▪ a *clearheaded* analysis
– clear·head·ed·ly *adv* **– clear·head·ed·ness** *noun* [*noncount*]

clear·ing /ˈklirɪŋ/ *noun, pl* **-ings**
1 [*noncount*] **:** the act or process of making something clear or of becoming clear ▪ the *clearing* of the table ▪ the *clearing* of wood and brush from part of the forest
2 [*count*] **:** an open area of land in which there are no trees ▪ We found a *clearing* in the forest.

clearing bank *noun, pl* **~ banks** [*count*] *Brit* **:** any bank that uses a clearinghouse

clear·ing·house /klirɪŋˌhaʊs/ *noun, pl* **-hous·es** [*count*]
1 : a business that banks use to exchange checks and money between them
2 : an organization that collects and gives out information about a specific thing ▪ an online *clearinghouse* for information on museums around the world

clear·ly /ˈkliɚli/ *adv* [*more ~; most ~*]
1 : in a clear manner **:** in a way that is easy to see, hear, or understand ▪ You should try to speak more *clearly.* ▪ She writes very *clearly.* ▪ The mountain was *clearly* visible in the distance.
2 : in a way that is certain **:** without doubt **:** OBVIOUSLY ▪ The project was *clearly* a failure. [=the project was a clear failure] ▪ The problem is very *clearly* getting worse. ▪ *Clearly,* a new approach is needed. = A new approach is *clearly* needed. [=it is clear that a new approach is needed] ▪ "A new approach is needed." "*Clearly.*" ▪ "The current method isn't working." "*Clearly* not."

clear·out /ˈkliɚˌaʊt/ *noun, pl* **-outs** [*count*] *Brit* **:** the act of removing all unwanted material from a place ▪ We gave the house the first thorough *clearout* it's had/gotten for years. — see also *clear out* 2 at ²CLEAR

clear–sight·ed /ˈkliɚˌsaɪtəd/ *adj* [*more ~; most ~*] **:** having or showing an ability to think clearly ▪ He provided a *clear-sighted* [=*clear-eyed, clearheaded*] appraisal of the problem. ▪ a *clear-sighted* commentator
– clear–sight·ed·ness *noun* [*noncount*]

clear·way /ˈkliɚˌweɪ/ *noun, pl* **-ways** [*count*] *Brit* **:** a major road on which cars are not usually allowed to stop

cleat /ˈkliːt/ *noun, pl* **cleats**
1 [*count*] **:** a metal or wooden object that is attached to something (such as a boat or dock) and around which a rope can be tied
2 a [*count*] **:** a piece of rubber, wood, or metal that is fastened to the bottom of a shoe or boot to prevent slipping — usually plural ▪ *cleats* on a football shoe **b** ***cleats*** [*plural*] *US* **:** shoes that have cleats on them ▪ a football player wearing *cleats*

cleav·age /ˈkliːvɪʤ/ *noun, pl* **-ag·es**
1 [*noncount*] *informal* **:** the space between a woman's breasts especially when it can be easily seen ▪ The dress is cut low enough to reveal a lot of *cleavage.*
2 : a division between two things or groups [*noncount*] the *cleavage* between the rich and poor [*count*] social *cleavages*
3 [*count*] *technical* **:** the act of splitting apart ▪ the *cleavages* of an egg as an embryo develops

¹cleave /ˈkliːv/ *verb* **cleaves; cleaved** /ˈkliːvd/ *also* **cleft** /ˈklɛft/ *or* **clove** /ˈkloʊv/; **cleaved** *also* **cleft** *or* **clo·ven** /ˈkloʊvən/; **cleav·ing** *formal + literary*
1 a : to split (something) by hitting it with something heavy and sharp [*+ obj*] The ax easily *cleaves* the log. [*no obj*] The wood is old and *cleaves* [=*splits*] easily. **b :** to pass easily and quickly through (something) [*+ obj*] The bow of the ship *cleaved* the water. ▪ The darkness was *cleft* by the lantern's beam. [*no obj*] The ship's bow *cleaved* through the water.
2 [*+ obj*] **:** to separate (something) into parts ▪ The country was *cleaved* [=*divided*] in two by civil war.
– compare ²CLEAVE

²cleave /ˈkliːv/ *verb* **cleaves; cleaved** /ˈkliːvd/ *or* **clove** /ˈkloʊv/; **cleaved; cleav·ing**
cleave to [*phrasal verb*] *formal + literary* **1** ***cleave to (someone)*** **:** to stay very close to (someone) ▪ children *cleaving to* their families **2** ***cleave to (something)*** **:** to stick closely to (something) — usually used figuratively ▪ He continued to *cleave to* the beliefs of his childhood.
– compare ¹CLEAVE

cleav·er /ˈkliːvɚ/ *noun, pl* **-ers** [*count*] **:** a heavy knife with a wide blade used for cutting up large pieces of meat

clef /ˈklɛf/ *noun, pl* **clefs** [*count*] *music* **:** a sign that is placed at the beginning of a line of written music to show the pitch of the notes ▪ the treble/bass *clef*

cleft /ˈklɛft/ *noun, pl* **clefts** [*count*]
1 : a narrow space in the surface of something ▪ The river begins as a trickle of water from a *cleft* in the rock.
2 : a narrow area that looks like a small dent in someone's chin ▪ He has a distinctive *cleft* in his chin.
– cleft *adj* ▪ The plant has deeply *cleft* leaves. ▪ a *cleft* chin

cleft lip *noun, pl* **~ lips** [*count*] *medical* **:** a split in the upper lip that some people are born with

cleft palate *noun, pl* **~ -ates** [*count*] *medical* **:** a split in the roof of the mouth that some people are born with

clem·a·tis /ˈklɛmətəs/ *noun, pl* **-tis·es** [*count, noncount*] **:** a climbing plant that has large pink, purple, red, or white flowers

clem·en·cy /ˈklɛmənsi/ *noun* [*noncount*] **:** kind or merciful treatment of someone who could be given harsh punishment ▪ The judge ignored the prisoner's pleas for *clemency.* [=*mercy*] ▪ The President has granted *clemency* to several people this month.

clem·ent /ˈklɛmənt/ *adj* [*more ~; most ~*] *formal* **:** not too hot or too cold ▪ The country is known for its *clement*

[=(more commonly) *mild*] weather. — compare INCLEMENT

clem·en·tine /ˈklɛmənˌtiːn/ *noun, pl* **-tines** [*count*] : a kind of orange that is small and sweet

clench /ˈklɛntʃ/ *verb* **clench·es; clenched; clench·ing**
1 : to set (something) in a tightly closed position [*+ obj*] He *clenched* his teeth and continued to look straight ahead. ▪ He *clenched* his fists in anger. ▪ She was angry and spoke quietly through *clenched* teeth. [*no obj*] His jaw/fists *clenched* and unclenched as he listened to the speech.
2 [*+ obj*] **:** to hold (something) tightly ▪ She danced alone, with a rose *clenched* in her teeth. ▪ He was *clenching* a cigarette in his teeth.

clere·sto·ry /ˈkliɚˌstori/ *noun, pl* **-ries** [*count*] *technical* **:** the upper part of a wall that rises above a roof and that has windows

cler·gy /ˈklɚdʒi/ *noun* [*plural*] **:** people (such as priests) who are the leaders of a religion and who perform religious services ▪ Local *clergy* have been invited to participate in an interfaith service. ▪ a member of the *clergy* ✧ *Clergy* is used most often to refer to priests and ministers in a Christian church. — compare LAITY

cler·gy·man /ˈklɚdʒimən/ *noun, pl* **-men** /-mən/ [*count*] **:** a man who is a member of the clergy especially in a Christian church

cler·gy·per·son /ˈklɚdʒiˌpɚsn/ *noun, pl* **-sons** [*count*] **:** a person who is a member of the clergy especially in a Christian church

cler·gy·wom·an /ˈklɚdʒiˌwʊmən/ *noun, pl* **-wom·en** /-ˌwɪmən/ [*count*] **:** a woman who is a member of the clergy especially in a Christian church

cler·ic /ˈklerɪk/ *noun, pl* **-ics** [*count*] **:** a member of the clergy in any religion

cler·i·cal /ˈklerɪkəl/ *adj*
1 : of or relating to a clerk or office worker ▪ She spent the summer doing *clerical* work for a lawyer. ▪ a member of our *clerical* staff ▪ The mistake was due to a *clerical* error.
2 : of or relating to members of the clergy ▪ *clerical* celibacy ▪ a ***clerical collar*** [=a narrow and stiff white collar that is worn by some clergy]

[1]**clerk** /ˈklɚk, *Brit* ˈklɑːk/ *noun, pl* **clerks** [*count*]
1 : a person whose job is to keep track of records and documents for a business or office ▪ a bank/office *clerk* ▪ a ***law clerk*** [=a person whose job is to assist a judge]
2 : an elected or appointed official whose job is to take care of official papers and business for a court or government ▪ Have the court *clerk* file your request with the judge. ▪ a ***city/town clerk*** [=a person whose job is to record what happens at city or town meetings and to keep special information about the city or town]
3 *US* **a :** a person who works in a store ▪ He works as a *clerk* in a local pet store. ▪ a grocery *clerk* ▪ a sales *clerk* at a women's clothing store **b :** a person who works at the main desk of a hotel assisting the people who are staying there ▪ a ***hotel clerk*** = a ***desk clerk***

[2]**clerk** *verb* **clerks; clerked; clerk·ing** [*no obj*] *US* **:** to work as a clerk — usually used of law clerks ▪ After graduating from law school, she *clerked* for a judge for several years.

clev·er /ˈklɛvɚ/ *adj* **clev·er·er; -est** [*also more* ~; *most* ~]
1 : intelligent and able to learn things quickly ▪ A few *clever* [=*smart, bright*] students have started a business recycling old computers. ▪ Some cats are *clever* enough to figure out how to operate doorknobs.
2 : showing intelligent thinking ▪ a *clever* design/invention ▪ That's the *cleverest* idea I've heard yet! ▪ She found a *clever* hiding place for the letter. — often used in a joking or ironic way to describe a foolish idea, action, etc. ▪ Whose *clever* idea was it to leave the window open?
3 : funny in a way that shows intelligence ▪ I enjoyed the play's *clever* [=*witty*] dialogue.
4 *Brit, informal* **:** talking in a rude way that is meant to show you are smart ▪ Don't you start getting *clever* [=(*US*) *fresh*] with me! [=don't speak to me in a disrespectful way]
5 : good at doing things with your hands **:** SKILLFUL ▪ Even as a little boy playing with blocks he was *clever* with his hands. ▪ a *clever* machinist
6 *Brit, informal* — used in various negative expressions to suggest that someone is not feeling well ▪ I'd had a few drinks and wasn't ***feeling very clever***. ▪ For someone who hasn't been ***feeling too clever*** lately, he just played a great round of golf.
too clever by half *chiefly Brit, informal* **:** clever in a way that is annoying or that causes problems ▪ an arrogant politician who is *too clever by half* ▪ a complex computer program that is *too clever by half*
— **clev·er·ly** *adv* ▪ a *cleverly* designed gadget ▪ *cleverly* written dialogue — **clev·er·ness** *noun* [*noncount*] ▪ the *cleverness* of the idea ▪ a cat's *cleverness*

clever dick *noun, pl* ~ **dicks** [*count*] *Brit, informal + disapproving* **:** a person who is clever in a way that is annoying — called also *clever clogs*

cli·ché /kliˈʃeɪ, ˈkliːˌʃeɪ/ *noun, pl* **-chés** [*count*]
1 : a phrase or expression that has been used so often that it is no longer original or interesting ▪ a speech filled with *clichés* about "finding your way" and "keeping the faith"
2 : something that is so commonly used in books, stories, etc., that it is no longer effective ▪ The macho cop of Hollywood movies has become a *cliché*.
— **cli·chéd** /kliˈʃeɪd/ *adj* [*more* ~; *most* ~] ▪ a *clichéd* phrase ▪ The movie's characters are *clichéd* and uninteresting.

[1]**click** /ˈklɪk/ *verb* **clicks; clicked; click·ing**
1 a [*+ obj*] **:** to cause (something) to make a short, sharp sound ▪ He *clicked* his heels together and saluted the officer. ▪ *click* your tongue/fingers **b** [*no obj*] **:** to make a short, sharp sound **:** to make a click ▪ Her heels *clicked* on the marble floor. ▪ a *clicking* noise/sound ▪ Press the door until you hear the latch *click*. ▪ The last piece of the puzzle *clicked* [=*snapped*] into place.
2 *computers* **:** to press a button on a mouse or some other device in order to make something happen on a computer [*+ obj*] To open the program, point at the icon and *click* the left mouse button. ▪ *click* the icon [*no obj*] *Click* here to check spelling in the document. — often *+ on* ▪ *Click on* the icon to open the program. ▪ I got to the Web site by *clicking on* a link at another site. — see also RIGHT-CLICK
3 [*no obj*] *informal* **:** to become friends **:** to like and understand each other ▪ They met at a party and *clicked* [=*hit it off*] right away. ▪ I know him fairly well, but we've never really *clicked*.
4 [*no obj*] *informal* **:** to get the attention or interest of people — usually *+ with* ▪ This is the issue that has really *clicked with* the voters this year.
5 [*no obj*] *informal* — used to describe what happens when you suddenly understand or remember something ▪ I worked on the problem for days, until finally one day something *clicked* and I knew what I had to do.
— **click·able** /ˈklɪkəbəl/ *adj, computers* ▪ The names in the list are all *clickable*. [=you can click on the names with your mouse to cause something to happen] ▪ a *clickable* image on a Web page

[2]**click** *noun, pl* **clicks** [*count*]
1 : a short, sharp sound ▪ the *click* of her heels on marble ▪ There was a *click* as the door closed behind him.
2 : the act of selecting something on a computer screen by pressing a button on a mouse or some other device ▪ You can order movie tickets on the Internet with just a few *clicks* of your mouse.

click·er /ˈklɪkɚ/ *noun, pl* **-ers** [*count*] *chiefly US, informal* **:** REMOTE CONTROL

cli·ent /ˈklajənt/ *noun, pl* **-ents** [*count*]
1 : a person who pays a professional person or organization for services ▪ a lawyer's *clients* ▪ The accountant is meeting with another *client* right now, but she'll be able to see you later this afternoon.
2 : a customer in a shop or hotel ▪ the spa's wealthy *clients*
3 *computers* **:** a computer in a network that uses the services provided by a server

cli·en·tele /ˌklajənˈtɛl/ *noun* [*singular*] **:** the group of people who are regular customers at a particular business ▪ The restaurant generally attracts an older *clientele*. ▪ the boutique's wealthy *clientele*

client state *noun, pl* ~ **states** [*count*] **:** a country that depends on another country for military, economic, or political support

cliff /ˈklɪf/ *noun, pl* **cliffs** [*count*] **:** a high, steep surface of rock, earth, or ice ▪ Standing at the edge of the *cliff*, we watched the waves crash on the shore far below. ▪ rock climbers scaling steep *cliffs* — see color picture on page C7

cliff–hang·er /ˈklɪfˌhæŋɚ/ *noun, pl* **-ers** [*count*] **:** a story, contest, or situation that is very exciting because what is going to happen next is not known ▪ The election was a real *cliff-hanger*. No one knew who was going to win until the very end.

cli·mac·tic /klaɪˈmæktɪk/ *adj* [*more* ~; *most* ~] **:** most exciting and important **:** forming a climax ▪ At the *climactic* moment, the main character of the novel finds herself face to face with the thief. ▪ the movie's *climactic* chase scene

Do not confuse *climactic* with *climatic*.

cli·mate /ˈklaɪmət/ *noun, pl* **-mates** [*count*]
1 a : a region with particular weather patterns or conditions ▪ living in a cold/dry/mild/hot *climate* ▪ These trees only grow in humid *climates.* **b :** the usual weather conditions in a particular place or region ▪ The country's *climate* is ideal for growing grapes. ▪ the humid *climate* of Malaysia ▪ increasing concerns about ***climate change*** [=changes in the Earth's weather patterns]
2 : the usual or most widespread mood or conditions in a place ▪ A *climate* of fear prevails in the city. ▪ the country's changing economic/political *climate* ▪ The company is trying to develop a positive *climate* for innovation.
– cli·mat·ic /klaɪˈmætɪk/ *adj* ▪ The *climatic* conditions in the region make it an ideal place to grow grapes.

Do not confuse *climatic* with *climactic*.

cli·ma·tol·o·gy /ˌklaɪməˈtɑːləʤi/ *noun* [*noncount*] **:** the scientific study of climates
– cli·ma·tol·o·gist /ˌklaɪməˈtɑːləʤɪst/ *noun, pl* **-gists** [*count*]

[1]**cli·max** /ˈklaɪˌmæks/ *noun, pl* **-max·es** [*count*]
1 a : the most exciting and important part of a story, play, or movie that occurs usually at or near the end ▪ The movie's *climax* is a fantastic chase scene. ▪ At the novel's *climax*, the main character finds herself face to face with the thief. **b :** the most interesting and exciting part of something **:** the high point ▪ the tournament's *climax* ▪ the *climax* of her career ▪ The protest in May was the *climax* of a series of demonstrations in the nation's capital.
2 : the most intense point of sexual pleasure **:** ORGASM ▪ able/unable to reach *climax*

[2]**climax** *verb* **-maxes; -maxed; -max·ing**
1 a [*no obj*] **:** to reach the most exciting or important part in something ▪ The movie *climaxes* with a fantastic chase scene. **b** [+ *obj*] **:** to occur at the end as the most exciting or important part of (something) ▪ The May protest *climaxed* a series of demonstrations in the nation's capital.
2 [*no obj*] **:** to have an orgasm ▪ able/unable to *climax*

[1]**climb** /ˈklaɪm/ *verb* **climbs; climbed; climb·ing**
1 [+ *obj*] **:** to move or go up (something) using your feet and often your hands ▪ *climb* a ladder/tree ▪ *climb* the stairs
2 : to go up mountains, cliffs, etc., as a sport [+ *obj*] He dreams of *climbing* Kilimanjaro. ▪ It took them six days to *climb* the mountain. [*no obj*] She has *climbed* seriously for several years now.
3 *always followed by an adverb or preposition* [*no obj*] **:** to move yourself in a way that usually involves going up or down ▪ The actors were *climbing* down from the stage. ▪ He *climbed* over the fence. ▪ The passengers of the sailboat *climbed* aboard. ▪ The pilot *climbed* into the cockpit. ▪ I think she *climbed* in through the window. ▪ He *climbed* out of the car with a box in his hands. ▪ The players *climbed* into their uniforms [=put on their uniforms] and headed for the field.
4 a [*no obj*] **:** to go higher **:** to go upward ▪ The plane rapidly *climbed* up above the clouds. ▪ We watched the smoke *climb* [=*rise*] into the night sky. ▪ The trail *climbs* steeply as it nears the summit of the mountain. **b :** to move to a higher position in a ranking or list [*no obj*] The book has *climbed* to number 2 on the bestsellers list. [+ *obj*] Their second album is *climbing* the charts. **c :** to move to a social or professional position that is more respected or powerful [*no obj*] The book describes how the senator *climbed* [=*rose*] to power. [+ *obj*] He was hired right out of business school and started ***climbing the corporate ladder***.
5 [*no obj*] **:** to increase in amount, value, or level ▪ Divorce rates have *climbed* in recent decades. ▪ The company's earnings have *climbed* 13 percent this year. ▪ The temperature keeps *climbing*.
6 *of plants* **:** to grow up or over something [+ *obj*] There is ivy *climbing* the walls of the old building. [*no obj*] a ***climbing plant*** [=a plant that attaches itself to something, such as a wall, as it grows up it]
climb down [*phrasal verb*] *chiefly Brit* **:** to admit that you have made a mistake and change your position or opinion ▪ His statement is seen as an attempt to *climb down* [=*back away*] from the strong denial he made yesterday. — see also CLIMBDOWN
climbing the walls *informal* **:** feeling very anxious or frustrated because you have a lot of energy but are unable to do something you want to do ▪ Being stuck at home all weekend had me *climbing the walls.*
– climbing *noun* [*noncount*] ▪ She enjoys mountain *climbing.* ▪ We're going to ***go climbing*** this weekend. — see also ROCK CLIMBING

[2]**climb** *noun, pl* **climbs** [*count*] **:** the act of climbing: such as **a :** the act or process of climbing a mountain, hill, etc. ▪ It's a 20-minute *climb* to the ridge from here. ▪ He's planning to attempt one of the most difficult *climbs* in South America this summer. **b :** the act or process of moving upward ▪ The plane made a steep *climb* [=*ascent*] to 30,000 feet. **c :** the act or process of going to a higher level or position ▪ The book chronicles her *climb* [=*ascent*] to political power. ▪ The book made a rapid *climb* to the top of the best-seller list.

climb·down /ˈklaɪmˌdaʊn/ *noun* [*singular*] *Brit* **:** an act of admitting that you have made a mistake and are changing your position or opinion ▪ His statement is seen as a *climbdown* from the strong denial he made yesterday. — see also *climb down* at [1]CLIMB

climb·er /ˈklaɪmɚ/ *noun, pl* **-ers** [*count*]
1 : someone who climbs mountains, cliffs, etc., as a sport ▪ a mountain *climber*
2 : an animal that climbs a lot or very well ▪ Chimpanzees are excellent *climbers* and spend a lot of their lives in trees.
3 : a plant that grows up walls, poles, etc., ▪ *climbers* like clematis and ivy
– see also SOCIAL CLIMBER

climbing frame *noun, pl* **~ frames** [*count*] *Brit* **:** PLAY STRUCTURE

climbing wall *noun, pl* **~ walls** [*count*] **:** a wall that is specially designed to be climbed and that is used to develop the skills needed for climbing mountains and cliffs

clime /ˈklaɪm/ *noun, pl* **climes** [*count*] *literary* **:** a climate **:** a place with a particular climate — usually plural ▪ They traveled south in search of warmer *climes.*

[1]**clinch** /ˈklɪnʧ/ *verb* **clinch·es; clinched; clinch·ing**
1 [+ *obj*] **a :** to make (something) certain or final ▪ His home run *clinched* the victory. ▪ The new evidence *clinches* the case. ▪ Her work on the project should *clinch* her a promotion. ▪ The photos of the city have *clinched* it for me. I have to visit Prague. **b :** to make certain the winning of (something) ▪ If they win tonight's game they'll *clinch* the pennant.
2 [*no obj*] **:** to hold each other closely during a fight ▪ The boxers *clinched.*

[2]**clinch** *noun, pl* **clinches** [*count*] **:** a position in which two people (such as two boxers) are holding each other very closely ▪ The referee told the boxers to break their *clinch.* ▪ The movie ended with the hero and heroine locked in a passionate *clinch.* [=(more commonly) *embrace*]

clinch·er /ˈklɪnʧɚ/ *noun* [*singular*] *informal* **:** a fact or statement that makes something certain or final ▪ This delicious soup is bound to impress guests. And here's the *clincher*: it's very easy to make. [=the fact that the soup is easy to make makes it especially appealing]

cling /ˈklɪŋ/ *verb* **clings; clung** /ˈklʌŋ/; **cling·ing** [*no obj*]
1 : to hold onto something or someone very tightly ▪ The children *clung* together under the little umbrella waiting for the storm to pass. — usually + *to* or *onto* ▪ The little cat *clung to* the narrow branch. ▪ The boy *clung onto* his mother's hand as they walked through the crowd. ▪ The little boy *clung to* his mother when it was time for her to leave.
2 *often disapproving* **:** to stay very close to someone for emotional support, protection, etc. ▪ a *clinging* child — usually + *to* ▪ parents who *cling to* their children instead of allowing them to be independent ▪ He *clung to* his friends for support.
3 : to stick to something or someone — usually + *to* ▪ The shirt *clung to* his wet shoulders.
4 : to continue to believe in or depend on something — + *to* ▪ He is still *clinging to* the idea that his marriage can be saved.
5 : to try very hard to keep something that you are in danger of losing — usually + *to* ▪ an aging leader *clinging to* power
– clingy /ˈklɪŋi/ *adj* **cling·i·er; -est** ▪ a *clingy* dress ▪ He was a *clingy* child.

cling film *noun* [*noncount*] *Brit* **:** PLASTIC WRAP

clin·ic /ˈklɪnɪk/ *noun, pl* **-ics** [*count*]
1 : a place where people get medical help ▪ The *clinic* is offering free screening for diabetes. ▪ a family-planning *clinic* ▪ He checked into a drug rehab *clinic.*
2 : an event at which a doctor is available to talk to people about a particular health matter ▪ The hospital is holding/having a pain *clinic* on Tuesday night for anyone interested in learning how to deal with chronic pain.

3 : a meeting during which a group of people learn about a particular thing or work on a particular problem ▪ a reading *clinic* ▪ A local club is giving a fishing *clinic* on Saturday.

4 : a place where professional services are offered to people for a lower cost than is usual ▪ A legal *clinic* in the city provides poor families with advice on legal matters.

put on a clinic *US, informal* : to perform or play extremely well ▪ The quarterback really *put on a clinic* in the second half, throwing four touchdown passes.

C

clin·i·cal /ˈklɪnɪkəl/ *adj*

1 *always used before a noun* : relating to or based on work done with real patients : of or relating to the medical treatment that is given to patients in hospitals, clinics, etc. ▪ Both experimental and *clinical* evidence show that the treatment is effective. ▪ She enjoys her *clinical* practice but is looking forward to working in a laboratory. ▪ Three hundred patients were involved in the ***clinical study***. ▪ a drug that is undergoing ***clinical trials*** [=scientific tests to see the effect of a drug by using it with real patients] ▪ He's a ***clinical psychologist*** [=a psychologist who works with patients] and professor of psychology at the university.

2 : requiring treatment as a medical problem ▪ ***Clinical depression*** [=depression that is a medical condition] is more serious than the occasional bouts of sadness that most people deal with.

3 *always used before a noun* : of or relating to a place where medical treatment is given : of or relating to a clinic ▪ *clinical* offices ▪ She has been the *clinical* director [=the director of a clinic] here for five years.

4 [*more* ~; *most* ~] : not showing emotion or excitement ▪ Her voice was calm, almost *clinical* [=*cold*], as she told us what happened.

5 : very exact or skillful ▪ He did the work with *clinical* precision.

– **clin·i·cal·ly** /ˈklɪnɪkli/ *adv* ▪ *clinically* depressed patients

cli·ni·cian /klɪˈnɪʃən/ *noun, pl* **-cians** [*count*] : a person (such as a doctor or nurse) who works directly with patients rather than in a laboratory or as a researcher

¹**clink** /ˈklɪŋk/ *verb* **clinks**; **clinked**; **clink·ing** : to make or cause (something) to make a short, sharp sound that is made when glass or metal objects hit each other [*no obj*] The bottles *clinked* together. [+ *obj*] When she'd completed the toast, they *clinked* glasses.

– **clinking** *noun* [*noncount*] ▪ I could hear the *clinking* of glasses coming from the dining room.

²**clink** *noun, pl* **clinks** [*count*] : a short, sharp sound made when glass or metal objects hit each other ▪ the *clink* of glasses — compare ³CLINK

³**clink** *noun*

the clink *slang* : a jail or prison ▪ I spent a night in *the clink*. [=in jail]

– compare ²CLINK

clink·er /ˈklɪŋkɚ/ *noun, pl* **-kers** [*count*] *US, informal*

1 : something that fails completely ▪ All his recent movies have been real *clinkers*. [=*flops*]

2 : a wrong note in a musical performance ▪ Somebody in the orchestra hit a *clinker*.

¹**clip** /ˈklɪp/ *noun, pl* **clips** [*count*]

1 : a usually small piece of metal or plastic that holds things together or keeps things in place ▪ hair *clips* ▪ a tie *clip* [=a piece of metal that holds together the ends of a necktie] ▪ He uses a money *clip* instead of a wallet. — see also PAPER CLIP

2 : a container that is filled with bullets and that is placed inside a gun so that the bullets can be fired ▪ an ammunition *clip*

– compare ³CLIP

²**clip** *verb* **clips**; **clipped**; **clip·ping**

1 [+ *obj*] : to hold (two or more things) together with a clip ▪ *clip* the papers together

2 : to attach (something) *to* or *onto* something else with a clip [+ *obj*] He *clipped* the keys *to* her belt. ▪ *Clip* this microphone *onto* your shirt. [*no obj*] The radio *clips to/onto* a belt.

– compare ⁴CLIP

³**clip** *noun, pl* **clips**

1 [*count*] : a short section of a movie, TV show, etc. ▪ Here's a *clip* from his new movie. ▪ video/audio *clips*

2 [*count*] *US* : an article that has been cut out of a newspaper or magazine : CLIPPING ▪ a pile of press *clips* about her son

3 [*singular*] : the speed at which something happens ▪ The market is growing at a *clip* [=*rate*] of five percent a year. ✧ If something moves or happens ***at a fast/rapid/steady/good clip***, it moves or happens quickly. ▪ The train was moving *at a good clip*.

4 [*singular*] *US, informal* : one time or instance ▪ He makes up to $1,000 a *clip*. — usually used in the phrase ***at a clip*** ▪ She can bicycle 30 miles *at a clip*.

5 [*singular*] *Brit, informal* : a quick and painful hit with the hand ▪ She gave him ***a clip round the ear***. [=she hit him on the ear]

– compare ¹CLIP

⁴**clip** *verb* **clips**; **clipped**; **clipping** [+ *obj*]

1 : to make (something) shorter or neater by cutting off small pieces ▪ She's outside *clipping* [=*trimming*] the hedges/bushes. ▪ *clipping* the tips of their cigars ▪ closely *clipped* grass ▪ The bird's wings have been *clipped* so that it can't fly away. — see also *clip someone's wings* at ¹WING

2 : to cut (an article, a picture, etc.) out of a newspaper or magazine ▪ She *clipped* (out) several recipes from the magazine. ▪ *clipping* coupons

3 : to hit the side of (something) while going past it ▪ The car skidded off the road and *clipped* a tree.

– compare ²CLIP

clip·board /ˈklɪpˌboɚd/ *noun, pl* **-boards** [*count*]

1 : a small board that has a clip at the top for holding papers

2 : a feature of a computer program that holds a copy of some data (such as words or a picture) and allows the user to move the data to another document or program ▪ Copy the sentence to the *clipboard* and paste it in a new document.

clip–clop /ˈklɪpˌklɑːp/ *noun* [*noncount*] : the sound made by a horse that is walking on a hard surface ▪ the slow *clip-clop* of the horses as the parade passed by

– **clip–clop** *verb* **-clops**; **-clopped**; **-clop·ping** [*no obj*] ▪ The horse-drawn carriage *clip-clopped* down the street.

clip joint *noun, pl* ~ **joints** [*count*] *slang* : a business (such as a bar or nightclub) that makes its customers pay too much money

clip–on /ˈklɪpˌɑːn/ *adj, always used before a noun* : attached to something with a clip ▪ a *clip-on* necktie ▪ *clip-on* earrings

clipped *adj* [*more* ~; *most* ~] — used to describe speech that is fast, that uses short sounds and few words, and that is often unfriendly or rude ▪ She answered their questions in a *clipped* voice/tone. ▪ the police officer's *clipped* speech

clip·per /ˈklɪpɚ/ *noun, pl* **-pers** [*count*]

1 : a device used for cutting something ▪ a hedge *clipper* — usually plural ▪ fingernail *clippers* ▪ wire *clippers* ▪ hedge *clippers* ▪ She cut his hair with electric *clippers*.

2 : a person who clips something ▪ a coupon *clipper*

3 : a very fast type of sailing ship that was used especially in the 1800s

clip·ping /ˈklɪpɪŋ/ *noun, pl* **-pings** [*count*]

1 *chiefly US* : something (such as an article or a picture) that has been cut out of a newspaper or magazine ▪ a newspaper/magazine *clipping* ▪ an old news *clipping* — called also *press clipping*, (*Brit*) *cutting*

2 : a small piece that has been cut off of something ▪ a fingernail *clipping* — usually plural ▪ grass *clippings*

clique /ˈklɪk, ˈkliːk/ *noun, pl* **cliques** [*count*] *disapproving* : a small group of people who spend time together and who are not friendly to other people ▪ high school *cliques*

– **cliqu·ish** /ˈklɪkɪʃ, ˈkliːkɪʃ/ *also* **cliqu·ey** /ˈklɪki, ˈkliːki/ *adj* [*more* ~; *most* ~] ▪ The students in the high school are very *cliquish* and unfriendly. ▪ *cliquish* attitudes

cli·to·ris /ˈklɪtərəs/ *noun, pl* **-ri·ses** [*count*] : a female sexual organ that is small, sensitive, and located on the outside of the body in front of the opening of the vagina

– **cli·to·ral** /ˈklɪtərəl/ *adj*

Cllr *abbr, Brit* councillor

¹**cloak** /ˈkloʊk/ *noun, pl* **cloaks**

1 [*count*] : a piece of clothing that is used as a coat, that has no sleeves, and that is worn over the shoulders and attached at the neck

2 [*singular*] : a thing that hides or covers someone or something ▪ The soldiers began their attack under (the) *cloak* of darkness. ▪ Their plans were shrouded in a *cloak* of secrecy.

²**cloak** *verb* **cloaks**; **cloaked**; **cloak·ing** [+ *obj*] *literary*

1 : to cover (someone or something) — usually used as *(be) cloaked* ▪ a field *cloaked* in snow

2 : to hide or disguise (something) — usually used as *(be) cloaked* ▪ His caring personality *was cloaked* [=*hidden, concealed*] by shyness. — usually + *in* ▪ The plans *were cloaked* [=*shrouded*] *in* secrecy. ▪ a company *cloaked in* mystery

– **cloaked** *adj* ▪ A *cloaked* figure [=a person wearing a cloak] entered the room.

cloak–and–dagger *adj* : relating to or showing actions or behavior in which people or governments try to protect their important secrets or try to learn the secrets of others ▪ a *cloak-and-dagger* novel ▪ *cloak-and-dagger* [=*undercover, secret*] operations

cloak·room /ˈkloʊkˌruːm/ *noun, pl* **-rooms** [*count*]
1 *Brit* : a room in a public building that has toilets and sinks ▪ The ladies' *cloakroom* [=(*US*) *bathroom, restroom*] is down the hall.
2 *chiefly Brit* : CHECKROOM ▪ We left our things in the *cloakroom*.

¹clob·ber /ˈklɑːbɚ/ *verb* **-bers; -bered; -ber·ing** [+ *obj*] *informal*
1 : to hit (someone) very hard ▪ Some guy was *clobbering* [=*beating*] him in the parking lot. ▪ If you say anything I'll *clobber* you.
2 : to defeat (a person or team) very easily in a competition ▪ We *clobbered* them in our last game. ▪ She was/got *clobbered* in the election. [=she lost by a large number of votes]
3 : to have a very bad effect on (someone or something) ▪ Businesses are being/getting *clobbered* by the bad economy.

²clobber *noun* [*noncount*] *Brit, informal* : someone's clothes, supplies, or equipment ▪ Just dump your *clobber* anywhere.

¹clock /ˈklɑːk/ *noun, pl* **clocks**
1 [*count*] : a device that shows what time it is and that is usually placed in a room or attached to a wall ▪ She looked/glanced at the *clock* on the wall. It was now 2:30. ▪ the hands/face of the *clock* ▪ a digital *clock* — often used before another noun ▪ a *clock* tower [=a tower with a clock on at least one of its sides] ▪ a *clock* face — compare WATCH; see also ALARM CLOCK, ATOMIC CLOCK, BIOLOGICAL CLOCK, BODY CLOCK, CUCKOO CLOCK, GRANDFATHER CLOCK
2 ***the clock*** : a clock that is used in sports and that shows how much time remains for a particular part of a game ▪ They were winning by 2 points with 10 seconds (left) on *the clock*. ▪ They stopped *the* (game) *clock* with eight seconds remaining. ✧ In U.S. English, to ***eat up the clock*** or ***run out the clock*** or ***kill the clock*** is to keep control of the ball or puck near the end of a game so that your opponent will not have a chance to score. ▪ We kept moving the ball to try to *eat up the clock*. ▪ If we can *run out the clock*, we can keep our lead and win. — see also SHOT CLOCK
3 ***the clock*** : TIME CLOCK ▪ I punched *the clock* at 8:45 and started working right away.
4 ***the clock*** *chiefly Brit, informal* : a device that shows how far a vehicle has traveled : ODOMETER ▪ a car with 100,000 miles ***on the clock***
against the clock **1** : in order to do or finish something before a particular time ▪ On our last project, we were working/racing *against the clock*. ▪ It was a race *against the clock* to finish the job on time. **2** ✧ If a race is *against the clock*, the time of each racer is measured and the racer with the fastest time wins. ▪ One by one the skiers sped downhill, racing *against the clock*.
around the clock *also* ***round the clock*** : throughout the entire day and night : every hour of the day ▪ Our stores are now open *around the clock*. [=our stores are open 24 hours a day] ▪ Reporters worked *around the clock* to cover the story.
beat the clock : to do or finish something quickly before a particular time ▪ In a desperate attempt to *beat the clock*, I raced to mail my tax return before midnight.
put/turn back the clock *also* ***put/turn the clock back*** : to return to a condition that existed in the past ▪ This new decision has effectively *turned back the clock* on 20 years of progress. ▪ I wish that we could *turn back the clock* and start all over again.

²clock *verb* **clocks; clocked; clock·ing**
1 [+ *obj*] **a** : to measure the amount of time it takes for (a person) to do something or for (something) to be completed — usually + *at* ▪ She *clocked* [=*timed*] her first mile *at* 5 minutes and 20 seconds. ▪ He *clocked* me *at* 30 seconds. **b** : to finish a race in (an amount of time) ▪ He *clocked* 3 hours and 15 minutes in his last marathon.
2 a [+ *obj*] : to measure or show (the speed of something) with a measuring device ▪ His fastest pitch was *clocked* at 91 miles per hour. ▪ The cop said she *clocked* me going 95 miles per hour. **b** [*no obj*] : to have a particular speed or to continue for a particular amount of time — + *in* ▪ The movie *clocked in* at just under three hours. [=the movie was almost three hours long]
3 [+ *obj*] *informal* : to hit (someone or something) very hard ▪ I was so angry I wanted to *clock* him.
4 [+ *obj*] *Brit, informal* : to look at or notice (someone or something) ▪ Just *clock* [=*get a load of*] that new motor of his.
clock in/on [*phrasal verb*] *chiefly Brit* : to record on a special card the time that you start working ▪ What time did you *clock on*? ▪ I *clocked in* [=(*US*) *punched in*] 10 minutes late.
clock off/out [*phrasal verb*] *chiefly Brit* : to record on a special card the time that you stop working ▪ What time did you *clock off* yesterday? ▪ I *clocked off* [=(*US*) *punched out*] 10 minutes late.
clock up [*phrasal verb*] ***clock up (something)*** *chiefly Brit* : to gain or reach (a particular number or amount) ▪ Our company *clocked up* a record number of sales this year.

clock radio *noun, pl* ~ **-dios** [*count*] : a radio that includes a clock and that can be set so that the radio turns on at a particular time

clock·wise /ˈklɑːkˌwaɪz/ *adv* : in the direction that the hands of a clock move when you look at it from the front ▪ Turn the screw *clockwise* to tighten it. — opposite COUNTERCLOCKWISE
– clockwise *adj* ▪ in a *clockwise* direction

clock·work /ˈklɑːkˌwɚk/ *noun* [*noncount*]
1 : the system of moving wheels inside something (such as a clock or an old-fashioned toy) that makes its parts move ▪ the *clockwork* inside a mechanical toy soldier
2 — used to describe something that happens or works in a very regular and exact way ▪ Every morning, ***like clockwork***, customers line up outside the front door of the bakery. ▪ Their wedding went (off) *like clockwork*. [=their wedding went very smoothly; everything in the wedding happened the way they planned] ▪ The birds return each year, (as) ***regular as clockwork***. — often used before another noun ▪ The work was done with *clockwork* precision. ▪ They return with *clockwork* regularity. ▪ a *clockwork* operation

clod /ˈklɑːd/ *noun, pl* **clods** [*count*]
1 : a lump of dirt or clay
2 *informal* : a person who is stupid and dull ▪ Her husband's such a *clod*.
– clod·dish /ˈklɑːdɪʃ/ *adj* [*more* ~; *most* ~] ▪ his typically *cloddish* behavior

clod·hop·per /ˈklɑːdˌhɑːpɚ/ *noun, pl* **-ers** [*count*] *informal*
1 : a person from the country who is clumsy or who has bad manners
2 : a large heavy shoe or boot — usually plural ▪ a pair of old *clodhoppers*

¹clog /ˈklɑːg/ *verb* **clogs; clogged; clog·ging** : to slowly form a block in (something, such as a pipe or street) so that things cannot move through quickly or easily [+ *obj*] The sink was *clogged* by/with dirt and grease. ▪ Traffic starts *clogging* (up) the streets at around five o'clock. ▪ Something's *clogged* (up) the pipes. [*no obj*] The drain *clogs* easily because the opening is so small. ▪ His arteries *clogged* (up) again five years after his surgery. — often used figuratively ▪ There are too many legal cases *clogging* up the court system.
– clogged *adj* ▪ a *clogged* pipe ▪ *clogged* pores ▪ *clogged* arteries ▪ *clogged* blood vessels

²clog *noun, pl* **clogs** [*count*]
1 : a shoe or sandal that has a thick usually wooden sole ▪ a pair of *clogs* — see picture at SHOE
2 : something that blocks or clogs a pipe ▪ There's a *clog* in the kitchen sink. ▪ a liquid chemical that gets rid of *clogs*

clois·ter /ˈklɔɪstɚ/ *noun, pl* **-ters** [*count*]
1 : a place where monks or nuns live : a monastery or convent
2 : a covered path or hall with arches that is on the side of a building (such as a monastery or church) and that has one open side usually facing a courtyard

cloister

clois·tered /ˈklɔɪstɚd/ *adj* [*more* ~; *most* ~] : separated from the rest of the world ▪ She leads a private, *cloistered* life in the country. : protected from the problems and concerns of everyday life ▪ He spent most of his adult life *cloistered* in universities.

clomp /ˈklɑːmp/ *verb* **clomps; clomped; clomp·ing** [*no obj*] *chiefly US* : to walk with loud, heavy steps ▪ He was *clomping* [=*clumping*] around in his big rubber boots.

C

[1]clone /ˈkloʊn/ *noun, pl* **clones** [*count*]
1 *biology* **:** a plant or animal that is grown from one cell of its parent and that has exactly the same genes as its parent ▪ the *clone* of an adult female sheep
2 : a product (such as a computer) that is a copy of another product produced by a well-known company ▪ a company that manufactures computer *clones* = a *clone*-maker
3 : a person or thing that appears to be an exact copy of another person or thing ▪ I am not a *clone* [=*duplicate*] of my father. He and I are very different people.

[2]clone *verb* **clones; cloned; clon·ing :** to make an exact copy of (a person, animal, or plant) **:** to make a clone of (something or someone) [+ *obj*] Do you think scientists should *clone* humans? [*no obj*] a plant produced by *cloning*

[1]close /ˈkloʊz/ *verb* **clos·es; closed; clos·ing** ✧ The opposite of *close* is *open* in every sense except senses 3b and 9.
1 : to move (a door, window, etc.) so that things cannot pass through an opening **:** SHUT [+ *obj*] Please *close* the door. ▪ We had better *close* the windows; it looks like it's going to rain. ▪ I forgot to *close* the gate. ▪ She was having trouble *closing* the drawer. ▪ *Close* the lid on the box tightly. [*no obj*] The door opened and *closed* so quietly that I didn't notice he had come in the room. ▪ The box's lid *closed* with a bang.
2 [+ *obj*] **:** to cover the opening of (something) **:** SHUT ▪ Remember to *close* the box of cereal when you're done.
3 a : to bring together the parts or edges of (something open) [+ *obj*] Please *close* your books and put them under your desks. ▪ *Close* your mouth. ▪ *Close* your eyes and go to sleep. ▪ I *closed* my fists and got ready to fight. ▪ *close* an umbrella [*no obj*] This suitcase just won't *close*! ▪ Her eyes *closed*, and she drifted off to sleep. ▪ My throat *closed* and I felt like I couldn't breathe. **b :** to bring together the edges of (a wound) so that it can heal [+ *obj*] It took 10 stitches to *close* the wound on his head. [*no obj*] The cut eventually *closed* [=*closed up, healed over*] on its own.
4 : to not allow (a road, park, etc.) to be used for a period of time [+ *obj*] The city *closed* [=*closed off*] the beach during the storm. ▪ They *closed* the bridge to traffic. [=they did not allow cars to use the bridge] [*no obj*] The park *closes* every evening at dusk.
5 a : to stop the services or activities of (a business, school, etc.) for a period of time [+ *obj*] They *closed* the school today because of the storm. ▪ We'll be *closing* the theater while we make the necessary repairs. [*no obj*] The store *closes* for lunch from 1 to 2 p.m. ▪ The airport *closed* for two hours yesterday due to icy conditions. ▪ The bank *closes* at noon on Saturdays. ▪ What time does the library *close*? **b :** to stop the services or activities of (a business, school, etc.) permanently [+ *obj*] They *closed* [=*closed down, shut down*] the school/factory/office last year. [*no obj*] The restaurant has *closed* for lack of business. ▪ The play *closed* [=it stopped being performed] after 112 performances.
6 : to end (something) [+ *obj*] The minister *closed* [=*concluded*] the services with a short prayer. ▪ She *closed* the meeting by thanking everyone for their help. ▪ Investigators *closed* the case after concluding that his death was an accident. [*no obj*] The services *closed* [=*concluded*] with a short prayer. ▪ I'd like to *close* by thanking you all for your help.
7 [+ *obj*] **:** to stop keeping money in (an account at a bank) ▪ I *closed* [=*closed out*] my savings account and opened up a new one at another bank.
8 [+ *obj*] **:** to end the use of (a file, document, or program) on a computer ▪ Remember to save the file before *closing* it.
9 [+ *obj*] **:** to formally accept (an agreement) ▪ They just *closed* a deal to take ownership of a new restaurant. ▪ the custom of *closing* a deal by shaking hands — see also CLOSE ON (below)
10 [*no obj*] **:** to reach a specified price or level at the end of the day ▪ The stock opened at $19 a share and *closed* at $22. ▪ Stocks opened weak but *closed* strong.
11 : to reduce the amount of distance or difference between two things, people, or groups [+ *obj*] The challenger has *closed* [=*narrowed*] the champion's lead to within two points. ▪ *closing* the distance to the lead runner ▪ These changes will help ***close the gap*** between the richest and the poorest countries. [*no obj*] She has *closed* to within two points of the champion.

close down [*phrasal verb*] **1 a :** to permanently stop operating **:** CLOSE ▪ The factory *closed down* in the 1980s. **b** *Brit* **:** to stop broadcasting from a radio or television station for the day ▪ We're *closing down* for the night: tune in again tomorrow morning! **2** ***close down (something)*** *or* ***close (something) down*** **:** to permanently stop the services or activities of (a business, school, etc.) ▪ They *closed down* [=*closed, shut down*] the school due to financial problems. — see also CLOSEDOWN

close in [*phrasal verb*] **:** to come or move nearer or closer ▪ The storm is *closing in* [=*approaching*] fast. ▪ Enemy troops are *closing in* all around us! ▪ The lions *closed in* for the kill. ▪ I felt that the world was *closing in* around me. ▪ The air became colder as night/darkness *closed in*. [=as darkness fell, as the night became dark] — often + *on* ▪ The fire was *closing in on* their neighborhood. ▪ The camera slowly *closed in on* the actor's face. ▪ Police were *closing in on* the two men. ▪ Researchers are *closing in on* [=they are close to finding] a cure for the disease. ▪ She's *closing in on* 40. [=she is almost 40 years old]

close off [*phrasal verb*] ***close off (something)*** *or* ***close (something) off*** **:** to not allow (something) to be used for a period of time **:** CLOSE ▪ The city *closed off* the beach to tourists. ▪ *closing off* a road with barriers ▪ Half of the museum was *closed off* while they made the changes. — sometimes used figuratively ▪ He *closes* himself *off* to new experiences. [=he does not allow himself to have new experiences]

close on [*phrasal verb*] ***close on (something)*** *US* **:** to formally and legally agree to and complete (an important financial arrangement, such as the purchase of a house) ▪ We're going to *close on* our house next Friday. ▪ They *closed on* the deal. — see also [1]CLOSE 9 (above)

close out [*phrasal verb*] ***close out (something)*** **1** *US* **:** to quickly sell (all of a particular type of product in a store) at a lower price ▪ We're *closing out* our entire stock of children's clothing! Come and pick up some bargains! — see also CLOSEOUT **2 :** to stop keeping money in (a bank account) ▪ She withdrew all her money and *closed out* [=*closed*] her account. **3 :** to end (something) in a specified way ▪ The team *closed out* the series with a 2–1 win over New York. ▪ She *closed out* her remarkable career with a final grand performance.

close ranks see [1]RANK

close the door on see DOOR

close up [*phrasal verb*] **1 a :** to close and lock all the doors of a building usually for a short period of time ▪ Businesses *closed up* [=*closed*] early so employees could attend the parade. ▪ We've *closed up* for the day. Please come back tomorrow. **b** ***close (something) up*** *or* ***close up (something)*** **:** to close and lock all the doors of (a house, store, etc.) ▪ They *closed up* the house and left town. ✧ To ***close up shop*** is to go out of business forever or stop performing all services or activities for a period of time. ▪ Rather than *closing up shop* entirely, the company laid off half of its workers. ▪ The restaurant has already *closed up shop* for the winter. **2 :** to move closer together ▪ The troops *closed up* and prepared to begin the attack. **3** *of a wound* **:** to become completely healed ▪ The cut eventually *closed up* [=*closed*] on its own. **4 :** to become quiet **:** to stop talking about your thoughts or emotions with other people ▪ She *closes up* when people ask her about her parents. **5** ***close (something) up*** *or* ***close up (something)*** **:** to bring (people or things) closer together ▪ *Close up* the spaces between the lines.

close your doors see DOOR

close your eyes to see [1]EYE

[2]close /ˈkloʊs/ *adj* **clos·er; -est**
1 : near in space **:** not far away or distant ▪ We're not there yet, but we're getting *close*. ▪ We stood *close* together to stay warm. — often + *to* ▪ New York is much *closer to* Chicago than it is *to* Los Angeles. ▪ Don't get too *close to* the fire. ▪ Stay *close to* me, children! ▪ Let's try to sit *close to* the front. ▪ The trees were planted ***in close proximity to*** [=*near*] the building. ▪ The gun is made for shooting ***at close range***. [=from a short distance] ▪ We were able to observe their behavior ***at close quarters***. [=from a short distance] ▪ Over 200 people lived ***in close quarters*** [=very close together] on the ship. — see also *close encounter* at [2]ENCOUNTER
2 : near in time ▪ Christmas is getting *closer* and will soon be here. ▪ She had her two children very *close* together. [=her second child was born soon after her first] — often + *to* ▪ You shouldn't snack so *close to* dinnertime. ▪ It's getting *close to* midnight. ▪ My birthday is *close to* Thanksgiving.
3 *not used before a noun* **:** very similar **:** almost the same ▪ Their daughters are *close* in age. ▪ *close* in size and shape — often + *to* ▪ a sound *close to* the sound of breaking glass ▪ He bears a ***close resemblance to*** his father. [=he looks very much like his father]
4 *not used before a noun* **:** almost correct ▪ "I'd guess that

you're 29 years old." "You're *close*. I'm 30." • It's not exactly right, but it's *close*. • You're way off! Not even *close*! [=you are completely wrong] ✧ The informal phrase ***close but no cigar*** is used to say that a guess was almost correct or that an effort was almost good enough. • "Was I right?" "*Close, but no cigar*." • We were *close but no cigar*.
5 a — used to say that someone or something has almost reached a particular condition; + *to* • He was *close to* death when they brought him to the hospital. • These rare birds are *close to* extinction. • His reply left her *close to* tears. [=his reply almost made her cry] **b** : almost *doing* something — + *to* • She was *close to* crying. • The bridge came dangerously *close to* collapsing. [=the bridge almost collapsed]
6 — used to say that something bad almost happened • That was *close*! We almost missed our plane. • That was a ***close one***. [=*close call, close shave*] — see also *too close for comfort* at [1]COMFORT
7 — used to describe the people you are most directly related to (such as your parents, children, sisters, brothers, etc.) • She had no *close* relatives nearby. • We're only inviting *close* family members to our wedding. — compare DISTANT
8 — used to describe people who know each other very well and care about each other very much • They were *close* friends in high school, but they've since grown apart. • My sister and I have always been very *close*. • We have a very *close* relationship. — often + *to* • We've always felt very *close to* each other. • He's very *close to* his grandparents.
9 : connected in a direct way • Sources *close* to the president say that he is willing to make a deal. • She stays in *close* touch/contact with her friends back home. • Authorities claim he has *close* ties to terrorist organizations. — sometimes used figuratively • This idea lies *close* to the heart of Democracy. [=it has an important connection to Democracy] • Animal rights is a cause that is ***close to my heart***. [=I care very much about animal rights]
10 : very careful, complete, or precise • It's important to pay *close* attention to the details. • Take a *closer* look at the evidence. • On *closer* examination, it appeared that something was missing. • We worked under the *close* supervision of a trained professional. • a *close* study of the Greek classics • a *close* reading of a text • Keep (a) ***close watch*** on the baby. = Keep a ***close eye*** on the baby. [=watch the baby closely]
11 — used to describe a race, contest, game, etc., in which one person, group, or team defeats the other or is leading the other by only a small amount • That was a *close* game. We only beat them by one point. • It was the *closest* election in recent history. • a *close* race • At this point, the election is ***too close to call***. [=it is not clear who will win] ✧ When you are ***a close second***, there is a small difference between you and the winner. • Vanilla is the most popular flavor while chocolate is/finishes/runs *a close second*. • She won the race while her teammate came in *a close second*. [=her teammate finished soon after her]
12 : very short or near to the skin • a *close* haircut/shave
13 : fitting tightly : having no extra space • I think there's enough room in the car for all of us, but it'll be a *close* [=*tight*] fit. — see also CLOSE-FITTING
14 : warm in an uncomfortable way : not having enough fresh air • It's very *close* in here: let's open a window.
close to home ✧ If something is *close to home*, it affects you in a strong and personal way. • I'm a teacher, so their criticisms of our educational system hit *close to home*. • People are usually not concerned about crime until it comes *close to home*. [=until it affects them directly]
close to the bone ✧ If something is *close to the bone*, it is very honest and deals with sensitive issues that can shock people or hurt their feelings. • His joke about racism in America cut pretty *close to the bone*.
close to the edge see [1]EDGE
close to the mark see [1]MARK
close to your chest or *US* ***close to the vest*** ✧ If you hold, keep, or play something *close to your chest* or *close to the vest*, you do not tell other people about it. • It's better to hold such information *close to the vest*. • She tends to keep her opinions *close to her chest*.
– close·ly *adv* [*more* ~; *most* ~] • Don't drive too *closely* behind the car in front of you. • The houses on our street are crowded very *closely* together. • She *closely* resembles her mother. • The suspects were watched *closely* by the police. • We've been studying their behavior very *closely*. • *closely* related family members **– close·ness** *noun* [*noncount*] • the *closeness* of the election results • the *closeness* felt by a parent and child

[3]close /ˈklous/ *adv* **clos·er; -est** : at or to a short distance or time away • Don't drive so *close* to the car in front of you. • He told me to stay/keep *close* as we walked through the crowd. • Come *close*, everyone. • Look *close* [=*closely*] and tell me what you see. • She drew me *close* (to her) and held me. • The time for a decision is drawing *closer*. • My teammate came in third, and I finished ***close behind***. • They sat ***close together*** at the dinner table.
close at hand : near in time or place • I always keep a few tissues *close at hand* [=near me] just in case. • The time for us to leave was *close at hand*.
close by : at a short distance away • Don't worry: if anything happens I'll be (standing) *close by* (you). • They're building a school *close by*.
close on *Brit* : almost or nearly • We walked for *close on* [=*close to*] five miles.
close to **1** : almost or nearly • They spent *close to* half a million dollars on the project. • Our company employs *close to* a thousand workers. • I haven't seen her in *close to* a year. • I sat there for *close to* an hour. **2** *Brit* : from a short distance • She's even more beautiful when seen *close to*. [=*close up*]
close up or ***up close*** : from a short distance : at close range • You have to look at the painting *close up* to really appreciate its detail. • It looks very different *up close*. — see also CLOSE-UP
come close **1** : to almost do something • We didn't win, but we *came close*. — often + *to* • The band *came* very *close to* breaking up. • We *came close to* winning the championship this season. **2** : to be similar to something or as good as expected • She said they taste just like real hot dogs, but they don't even *come close* (to the real thing).
cut it close see [1]CUT

[4]close /ˈklouz/ *noun* [*singular*] *formal* : the end of an activity or a period of time • Students vote for their favorite teacher at the *close* of each year. • At the *close* of trading, the stock market was two percent lower than yesterday. • As the year ***drew to a close***, the debate over the new project grew more intense. • The war finally appears to be ***coming to a close***. • She ***brought*** the show ***to a close*** with a performance of her most famous song. — see also COMPLIMENTARY CLOSE — compare [5]CLOSE

[5]close /ˈklous/ *noun, pl* **clos·es** [*count*] *Brit*
1 : the area and buildings that are around a cathedral • a cathedral *close*
2 : a road that is closed at one end — used in street names • Turn into Bloomhill *Close*.
— compare [4]CLOSE

close call /ˈklous-/ *noun, pl* **~ calls** [*count*] : an escape that was almost not successful • We nearly didn't get out of the burning building. It was a pretty *close call*, let me tell you! — called also *close shave*

close–cropped /ˈklousˌkrɑːpt/ *adj* : cut very short • his *close-cropped* hair • the *close-cropped* grass of the golf course

closed /ˈklouzd/ *adj*
1 : covering an opening • All the windows in the house are *closed*. [=*shut*] : having an opening that is covered • Keep your eyes *closed*. • He looked at me through half-*closed* eyes. • a *closed* container • a *closed* umbrella
2 : not operating or open to the public • The store is *closed* for lunch between 1 and 2 p.m. • The beach is *closed* this time of night. • These restrooms are *closed* for cleaning. • a *closed* road/bridge
3 a : having ended : not being worked on anymore • The case is *closed*. **b** : no longer able to be discussed • The question is *closed*. • The chairman declared the discussion *closed* and allowed no further speeches.
4 : including only people from a particular group • There was a *closed* circle of advisers protecting the President. • clubs with *closed* memberships
5 : happening in private : not allowing the public to participate or know what is being said or done • The meeting was *closed* to the public. • The Prime Minister said that today's *closed* meeting with the President was particularly constructive. • a *closed* session of Congress
6 : not willing to listen to or accept different ideas or opinions • *closed* societies • I had a ***closed mind*** at first, but now I understand the need for change.
behind closed doors : in a private room or place : in private • All of their meetings are held *behind closed doors*. • They seemed like the perfect couple, but you never know

what goes on *behind closed doors*. • The decisions are made *behind closed doors*.

with your eyes closed see [1]EYE

closed–cap·tioned /ˈklouzdˈkæpʃənd/ *adj, of a television show or movie* **:** having written words that appear on the screen to describe what is being said for people who do not hear well and that can only be seen if you are using a special device

– closed–cap·tion·ing /ˈklouzdˈkæpʃənɪŋ/ *noun [non-count]*

closed–cir·cuit /ˈklouzdˈsɚkət/ *adj, always used before a noun* — used to describe a television system that sends its signal through wires to a limited number of televisions • The store uses *closed-circuit* television to monitor the activities of shoppers.

closed–door /ˈklouzdˈdoɚ/ *adj, always used before a noun* **:** held secretly or privately • The council held a *closed-door* session in Washington. • *closed-door* meetings

closed–mind·ed /ˈklouzdˈmaɪndəd/ *adj [more ~; most ~] chiefly US, disapproving* **:** not willing to consider different ideas or opinions **:** having or showing a closed mind • He's becoming increasingly *closed-minded* in his old age. • a *closed-minded* refusal to listen — opposite OPEN-MINDED

– closed–mind·ed·ly *adv* **– closed–mind·ed·ness** *noun [noncount]*

closed–mouthed /ˈklouzdˈmauθt/ *adj [more ~; most ~] US* **:** CLOSE-MOUTHED • He remains *closed-mouthed* about his plans.

close·down /ˈklouzˌdaun/ *noun, pl* **-downs**

1 *[count] chiefly Brit* **:** an occurrence or situation in which work is stopped for a long time or permanently in a business, factory, etc. **:** SHUTDOWN • plant *closedowns* • a government *closedown*

2 *[singular] Brit* **:** the end of television or radio broadcasts for the day — see also *close down* at [1]CLOSE

close–fit·ting /ˈklousˈfɪtɪŋ/ *adj [more ~; most ~] of clothes* **:** fitting tightly to the body **:** not baggy or loose • a *close-fitting* pair of pants

close–knit /ˈklousˈnɪt/ *adj [more ~; most ~]* — used to describe a group of people who care about each other and who are very friendly with each other • a *close-knit* family • *close-knit* communities/towns

close–mind·ed /ˈklouzˈmaɪndəd/ *adj [more ~; most ~] US* **:** CLOSED-MINDED • *close-minded* people • a very *close-minded* attitude

close–mouthed /ˈklousˈmauθt/ *adj [more ~; most ~] US* **:** not saying very much especially about a secret or about a particular subject • *close-mouthed* officials • They've been *close-mouthed* [=*secretive*] about the settlement.

close·out /ˈklouzˌaut/ *noun, pl* **-outs** *[count] US*

1 a : a sale in which a store tries to sell all of its products because the store is going out of business • a store *closeout* **b :** a sale to sell all of the old models of a product so that a store can sell the new models

2 : a product that is being sold at a closeout • a store that sells *closeouts* — see also *close out* at [1]CLOSE

clos·er /ˈklouzɚ/ *noun, pl* **-ers** *[count] baseball* **:** a pitcher who specializes in finishing games

close–set /ˈklousˈsɛt/ *adj [more ~; most ~] of eyes* **:** close together • her *close-set* eyes

close shave *noun, pl* **~ shaves** *[count]* **:** CLOSE CALL • I've had a few *close shaves* in my lifetime, but this one was the scariest.

[1]**clos·et** /ˈklɑːzət/ *noun, pl* **-ets**

1 *[count] chiefly US* **:** a usually small room that is used for storing things (such as clothing, towels, or dishes) • The sheets and blankets are in the hall *closet*. • He has a *closet* full of new clothes. • broom/coat *closets* • a ***walk-in closet*** [=a large closet usually for clothes] — see also WATER CLOSET

2 *[noncount]* **:** a state in which someone will not talk about something or admit something; *especially* **:** a state in which someone will not admit being a homosexual — usually used in the phrases ***in the closet*** or ***out of the closet*** • He's still *in the closet*. [=he has not told people that he is gay] • She ***came out of the closet*** in college.

skeleton in the/your closet see [1]SKELETON

[2]**closet** *adj, always used before a noun* **:** hiding the fact that you are a particular type of person • She's a *closet* racist. [=she does not want people to know that she is a racist] • Some people think he's a *closet* homosexual.

[3]**closet** *verb* **-ets; -et·ed; -et·ing** *[+ obj]*

1 : to put (yourself) in a room in order to be alone • He *closeted* himself in his apartment for several days.

2 : to bring (someone) into a room in order to talk privately — usually used as *(be) closeted* • The manager *was closeted* with one of her employees for several hours.

close–up /ˈklousˌʌp/ *noun, pl* **-ups :** a photograph or movie picture taken very close to an object or person *[count]* "Move in for a *close-up*," said the film's director. • a *close-up* of her face *[noncount]* The scene was shot ***in close-up***.

– close–up /ˌklousˈʌp/ *adj, always used before a noun* • Get a *close-up* shot of them kissing.

[1]**clos·ing** /ˈklouzɪŋ/ *noun, pl* **-ings** *[count]*

1 : a situation or occurrence in which a business or organization shuts down and stops its operations • factory/plant/store *closings* • the *closing* of the local school/hospital

2 : the last part of a letter or speech • a very brief/abrupt *closing*

3 : a meeting in which the owners of a house formally give ownership of the house to other people • We met with our lawyer before the *closing* on our new house. • ***closing costs*** [=the extra amounts of money that people need to pay when they buy a house]

in closing formal **:** at the end of a speech, letter, etc. • "Thank you all for your help, and for making the fair such a big success," she said *in closing*. — used to introduce the final remarks in a speech, letter, etc. • *In closing* [=*in conclusion*], I would like to make one final point.

[2]**closing** *adj, always used before a noun* **:** forming the last part or end of something • the book's *closing* chapters/pages/lines • the *closing* days/years of his life • In her *closing* arguments, the lawyer repeated that her client was not guilty. • his *closing* remarks in the debate • the *closing* ceremonies of the Olympics • His name's listed in the movie's *closing* credits.

closing date *noun, pl* **~ dates** *[count] Brit* **:** the last day that something (such as applying for a job or entering a contest) can be done **:** DEADLINE • The *closing date* for entries is October 1st.

closing price *noun, pl* **~ prices** *[count]* **:** the price of a stock or bond at the end of a day • the previous day's *closing price*

closing time *noun [noncount]* **:** the time when businesses (such as banks and bars) close for the day

clo·sure /ˈklouʒɚ/ *noun, pl* **-sures**

1 *[count]* **:** a situation or occurrence in which something (such as a business or factory) closes forever • business *closures* [=*closings*] • a school *closure* = the *closure* of a school • The government forced the *closure* of the factory.

2 *[noncount]* **a :** a feeling that something has been completed or that a problem has been solved • I need to talk to him and get some *closure* on this issue. **b :** a feeling that a bad experience (such as a divorce or the death of a family member) has ended and that you can start to live again in a calm and normal way • Going to the memorial service for his late wife made it possible for him to achieve *closure*. • We all felt a sense of *closure* after our sister's murderer was sent to jail. • trying to bring *closure* to the victim's family

3 *[count]* **:** the way that something (such as a jacket) is closed together — usually singular • The coat has a zipper *closure*. [=the coat is closed with a zipper]

[1]**clot** /ˈklɑːt/ *noun, pl* **clots** *[count]*

1 : BLOOD CLOT • We were told that his stroke was caused by a *clot* in his brain.

2 *Brit, informal* **:** a stupid person • That stupid little *clot*!

[2]**clot** *verb* **clots; clot·ted; clot·ting :** to become thick and partly solid **:** to develop clots *[no obj]* medications that prevent blood from *clotting* *[+ obj]* substances that help to *clot* blood

– clotted *adj* • *clotted* blood • *clotted* arteries [=arteries that are blocked by blood clots] — sometimes used figuratively • The streets are *clotted* [=*clogged*] with traffic. — see also CLOTTED CREAM **– clotting** *noun [noncount]* • I take a drug to prevent (blood) *clotting*.

cloth /ˈklɑːθ/ *noun, pl* **cloths** /ˈklɑːðz, ˈklɑːθs/

1 : material that is made by weaving together threads of cotton, wool, nylon, etc., and that is used to make clothes, sheets, etc. *[noncount]* a piece of *cloth* [=*fabric*] *[count]* The dress is made out of a beautiful silk *cloth*. — often used before another noun • *cloth* napkins/diapers • a *cloth* bag

2 *[count]* **:** a piece of cloth that is used for a particular purpose (such as cleaning things) • Wipe the surface with a clean dry *cloth*. • a damp/wet *cloth* — see also DISHCLOTH, FACE-

CLOTH, LOINCLOTH, TABLECLOTH, WASHCLOTH

3 ***the cloth*** **:** Christian priests and ministers **:** CLERGY • He has great respect for *the cloth.* • ***a man of the cloth*** [=a priest or minister]

cut from the same cloth ✧ If people or things are *cut from the same cloth*, they are very similar to each other. • Our mothers were *cut from the same cloth.* • The country's new president is *cut from the same cloth* as his predecessor.

out of whole cloth US, informal ✧ If something is created *out of whole cloth*, it is invented in order to trick someone into believing something. • He would make up stories *out of whole cloth* just to stir up trouble.

clothe /ˈkloʊð/ *verb* **clothes; clothed** *also* **clad** /ˈklæd/; **cloth·ing** [+ *obj*]

1 : to provide (someone) with clothes • the cost of feeding and *clothing* your children

2 *formal* **:** to dress (someone) *in* a particular type of clothing • people who *clothe* themselves *in* designer fashions [=people who wear expensive clothes]

clothed *adj*

1 : wearing clothes • He fell into the swimming pool fully *clothed.* • scantily *clothed* [=(more commonly) *clad*] young women — often + *in* • The men were *clothed* entirely *in* black. • She answered the door *clothed* only *in* her bathrobe.

2 : covered *in* something • The land is *clothed in* dense green forests. • a bird *clothed in* bright yellow feathers

clothes /ˈkloʊz/ *noun* [*plural*] **:** the things that people wear to cover their bodies and that are usually made from cloth • heavy winter *clothes* [=*clothing*] • I need some new *clothes* for the summer. • My sister and I borrow each other's *clothes* all the time. • Always wear your best *clothes* for interviews. • dress *clothes* [=fancy or formal things to wear] • work *clothes* [=items that are appropriate to wear at work] • He changed his *clothes.* • I bought a new *clothes* dryer/washer. • a *clothes* hamper — see also *plain clothes* at [1]PLAIN ***synonyms*** see CLOTHING

clothes hanger *noun, pl* **~ -ers** [*count*] **:** COAT HANGER

clothes·horse /ˈkloʊzˌhoɚs/ *noun, pl* **-hors·es** [*count*] *informal + sometimes disapproving* **:** a person who likes to wear stylish clothing • My teenage daughter's a real *clotheshorse.*

clothes·line /ˈkloʊzˌlaɪn/ *noun, pl* **-lines** [*count*] **:** a piece of rope or a wire that people hang wet clothes on to dry

clothes·pin /ˈkloʊzˌpɪn/ *noun, pl* **-pins** [*count*] *US* **:** a small object used for holding clothes on a clothesline — called also (*Brit*) *clothes peg*

clothespin

cloth·ier /ˈkloʊðjɚ/ *noun, pl* **-iers** [*count*] *somewhat old-fashioned* **:** a person or business that makes or sells clothing • the city's finest *clothiers*

cloth·ing /ˈkloʊðɪŋ/ *noun* [*noncount*] **:** the things that people wear to cover their bodies • an expensive article/item/piece of *clothing* • winter *clothing* • women's/men's/children's *clothing* [=*clothes*] • We're collecting food and *clothing* for the poor. • Only people wearing protective *clothing* may enter the room. — often used before another noun • *clothing* stores • a *clothing* company/manufacturer • the *clothing* industry — see pictures of clothing starting on page C13

a wolf in sheep's clothing see [1]WOLF

> ***synonyms*** CLOTHING and CLOTHES both refer to the things that people wear to cover their bodies. *Clothing* tends to be used when discussing a particular type of clothes or talking about clothes in general. • a shop that sells vintage *clothing* • Food, *clothing*, and shelter are things that every person needs. *Clothes* is usually used when you are talking about the things that someone is wearing. • I need to put on some clean *clothes.* • He's wearing fancy *clothes* today. *Clothing* is somewhat more formal than *clothes* and is not used in speech as often as *clothes.* There is no singular form of *clothes*, but you can talk about *an article/piece/item of clothing* if you want to refer to one thing that you wear.

clotted cream *noun* [*noncount*] **:** a very thick kind of cream that is made and eaten especially in England

[1]**cloud** /ˈklaʊd/ *noun, pl* **clouds** [*count*]

1 : a white or gray mass in the sky that is made of many very small drops of water • The sun is shining and there's not a *cloud* in the sky. • a rain *cloud* • flying high above the *clouds* • It stopped raining and the sun poked through the *clouds.* • Thick ***cloud cover*** [=a large number of clouds in the sky] hid the moon. — see also MUSHROOM CLOUD, STORM CLOUD

2 a : a large amount of smoke, dust, etc., that hangs in the air • a *cloud* of cigarette smoke • *clouds* of steam/gas • dust *clouds* **b :** a large number of things (such as insects) that move together through the air in a group • a *cloud* [=*swarm*] of bees

3 : a feeling or belief that a person or organization has done something wrong • The company remains ***under a cloud of suspicion***. [=people believe the company did something wrong] • The team has been ***under a cloud*** since its members were caught cheating. • There's ***a cloud of controversy/uncertainty/doubt*** hanging over the election.

cast a (dark) cloud **:** to cause people to stop trusting something • The scandal *cast a cloud* over his presidency. [=people thought the President did something wrong] • Several problems have *cast a cloud* on the program's future.

cloud on the horizon **:** a problem that could appear in the future • The only *cloud on the horizon* for the team is the age of its key players.

every cloud has a silver lining see SILVER LINING

in the clouds ✧ If you are *in the clouds* or you ***have your head in the clouds***, you spend too much time thinking about love or about ideas that are not practical. • Since he met Sara, he's been walking around *with his head in the clouds.*

on cloud nine informal **:** very happy • He's been *on cloud nine* ever since she agreed to marry him.

[2]**cloud** *verb* **clouds; cloud·ed; cloud·ing**

1 [+ *obj*] **:** to confuse (a person's mind or judgment) • The alcohol must have ***clouded my judgment***. [=made me unable to think clearly] • greed ***clouding the minds*** of men

2 [+ *obj*] **:** to make (something, such as an issue or situation) difficult to understand • These new ideas only *cloud* the issue further.

3 [+ *obj*] **:** to affect (something) in a bad way • a scandal that continues to *cloud* [=*tarnish, taint*] his reputation • The final years of her life were *clouded* by illness.

4 [*no obj*] *of the sky* **:** to become covered with clouds — usually + *over* • The sky had *clouded over*, and it was beginning to rain.

5 [+ *obj*] **:** to cover or fill (a room, the sky, etc.) with large amounts of smoke, dust, etc. • The room was *clouded* with cigarette smoke. • smog *clouding* the sky

6 [+ *obj*] **:** to cover (glass, a window, etc.) with many very small drops of water • Steam *clouded* [=*fogged up*] the bathroom mirror. • *clouding* the camera lens

7 [*no obj*] *of a person's face or eyes* **:** to show that someone is worried or unhappy • Her face *clouded* with concern. • Her eyes *clouded* over with tears.

cloud·burst /ˈklaʊdˌbɚst/ *noun, pl* **-bursts** [*count*] **:** a brief time when it rains very hard **:** a sudden downpour • A *cloudburst* caused the river to flood.

cloud–cuckoo–land *noun* [*noncount*] *chiefly Brit, informal* **:** LA-LA LAND 1 • If he really thinks he can win the election, he's living in *cloud-cuckoo-land.* [=he's crazy or foolish]

cloud·less /ˈklaʊdləs/ *adj* **:** without clouds • a *cloudless* [=*clear*] blue sky

cloudy /ˈklaʊdi/ *adj* **cloud·i·er; -est** [*also more ~; most ~*]

1 : having many clouds in the sky • Tomorrow will be *cloudy* and cold. • a *cloudy* day • *cloudy* weather **:** covered with clouds • partly *cloudy* skies

2 : not clean or clear • a puddle of *cloudy* [=*dirty, murky*] water • *cloudy* eyes

– cloud·i·ness *noun* [*noncount*] • We'll have clear skies in the morning with increasing *cloudiness* in the afternoon.

[1]**clout** /ˈklaʊt/ *noun, pl* **clouts**

1 [*noncount*] **:** the power to influence or control situations • She used her political *clout* to have another school built. • the country's economic/financial *clout*

2 [*count*] *chiefly Brit, informal* **:** a hit especially with the hand — usually singular • When she was naughty, she would get a *clout* from her mother.

[2]**clout** *verb* **clouts; clout·ed; clout·ing** [+ *obj*]

1 *baseball* **:** to hit (the ball) very hard • He *clouted* 19 home runs last year.

2 *chiefly Brit* **:** to hit (someone or something) hard especially with your hand • He'll *clout* me around the head if he finds out what I've done.

[1]**clove** /ˈkloʊv/ *noun, pl* **cloves** [*count*] **:** any one of the small sections that are part of a large head of garlic • a garlic *clove*

C

= a *clove* of garlic — see color picture on page C4 — compare ²CLOVE

²**clove** *noun, pl* **cloves** [*count*] : a small, dried flower bud that is used in cooking as a spice • two teaspoons of ground *cloves* • Add four whole *cloves*. — compare ¹CLOVE

³**clove** *past tense of* CLEAVE

cloven *past participle of* ¹CLEAVE

cloven hoof *noun, pl* ~ **hooves** *also* ~ **hoofs** [*count*] : a foot of some animals (such as sheep, goats, or cows) that is divided into two parts

clo•ver /ˈkloʊvɚ/ *noun, pl* **-vers** : a small plant that has usually three leaves on each stem and that usually has round flowers that are white, red, or purple [*noncount*] a field of *clover* [*count*] It's good luck to find a ***four-leaf clover***. [=a clover with four leaves instead of three]

¹**clown** /ˈklaʊn/ *noun, pl* **clowns** [*count*]
1 : someone who performs in a circus, who wears funny clothes and makeup, and who tries to make people laugh • a circus *clown* • Those big shoes make you look like a *clown*! • a rodeo *clown* [=a person in a rodeo who dresses like a circus clown] — sometimes used before another noun • She came dressed in a *clown* suit/costume. • a big red *clown* nose
2 : someone who often does funny things to make people laugh • His classmates remember him as ***the class clown***. [=a student who tried to make other students laugh] • He was always ***playing the clown***. [=trying to make people laugh]
3 *informal* : a rude or stupid person • Who's the *clown* standing in the middle of the road? • those *clowns* at the state capital

clown

²**clown** *verb* **clowns; clowned; clown•ing** [*no obj*] : to act like a clown : to say funny things or act in a silly way — often + *around* • Stop *clowning around*. We've got work to do.

clown•ish /ˈklaʊnɪʃ/ *adj* [*more* ~; *most* ~] : like a clown • his *clownish* red nose : acting in a silly or funny way • *clownish* behavior • her *clownish* coworkers

cloy•ing /ˈklojɪŋ/ *adj* [*more* ~; *most* ~] *disapproving* : too sweet, pleasant, or emotional • a *cloying* romantic comedy • After a while, the softness of his voice becomes *cloying*.
– cloy•ing•ly *adv* • a *cloyingly* sweet wine • *cloyingly* cute pink dresses

¹**club** /ˈklʌb/ *noun, pl* **clubs**
1 [*count*] **a** : a group of people who meet to participate in an activity (such as a sport or hobby) • an exclusive social/men's *club* • Do you belong to any *clubs*? • My friends and I formed/started a chess *club*. [=a group of people who play chess together] • She's the *club* president. = She's the president of the *club*. — see also FAN CLUB, GLEE CLUB, GOLF CLUB 2 **b** : the place where the members of a club meet • I'll see you at the *club*. — see also COUNTRY CLUB, HEALTH CLUB
2 [*count*] : a sports team or organization • the president of a major-league baseball *club* • He spent five years with the *club*. • a ball *club* • a boxing/football/hockey *club*
3 [*count*] : an organization in which people agree to buy things (such as books or CDs) regularly in order to receive a benefit (such as lower prices) • Join our movie *club* now and receive four free DVDs. — see also BOOK CLUB
4 [*count*] : a business that provides entertainment (such as music, dancing, or a show) and that usually serves food and alcohol : NIGHTCLUB • a dance *club* • jazz *clubs* • comedy *clubs* [=clubs in which people perform comedy shows] • They went ***club-hopping***. [=they went to several different clubs in one night] — often used before another noun • *club* owners • *club* music [=dance music that is played in clubs] — see also STRIP CLUB
5 [*count*] : a special metal stick used for hitting a golf ball : GOLF CLUB • I just bought a new set of *clubs*.
6 [*count*] : a heavy usually wooden stick that is used as a weapon • In battle, they used swords and wooden *clubs*. — see also BILLY CLUB
7 a [*count*] : a playing card that is marked with a black shape that looks like three round leaves • one heart, two diamonds, and two *clubs* — see picture at PLAYING CARD **b** ***clubs*** [*plural*] : the suit in a deck of playing cards that consists of cards marked by a black shape that looks like three round leaves • the nine of *clubs* — compare DIAMOND, HEART, SPADE
8 [*count*] *informal* : CLUB SANDWICH • She ordered a turkey *club* with French fries.
in the club *Brit, informal* : PREGNANT
join the club *also* ***welcome to the club*** *informal* — used to say that the problems or feelings someone is having are problems or feelings that you have had yourself • If you don't understand the rules, *join the club*: no one else does either! — often used to suggest that a person's problems or feelings are not unusual and do not deserve much sympathy • So you think you deserve to be paid more money for your work? Well, *join the club*. [=lots of people think they deserve more money] • "My son won't do what I tell him to do." "*Join the club*. I can't get my daughter to obey me, either."

²**club** *verb* **clubs; clubbed; club•bing** [+ *obj*] : to hit (a person or animal) with a heavy stick or object • They *clubbed* him with a baseball bat. • He was *clubbed* to death. [=killed by being hit him with a heavy object]
club together [*phrasal verb*] *Brit* : to combine your money with the money of other people ✧ If a group of people *club together* to do something, each member of the group gives some money to pay for something. • We *clubbed together* to buy him a new watch.

club•bing /ˈklʌbɪŋ/ *noun* [*noncount*] : the activity of going to nightclubs in order to dance, drink alcohol, etc. • a night of *clubbing* — often used in the phrases ***go clubbing*** or ***go out clubbing*** • Friday night, we *went out clubbing* in the city.
– club•ber /ˈklʌbɚ/ *noun, pl* **-bers** [*count*] • A line of *clubbers* [=people who go to nightclubs] was waiting at the door.

club•by /ˈklʌbi/ *adj* **club•bi•er; -est** *US* : friendly only to people who belong to a high social class • the restaurant's *clubby* [=*exclusive, elite*] atmosphere • the *clubby* world of New York's social elite
– club•bi•ness *noun* [*noncount*]

club•foot /ˈklʌbˌfʊt/ *noun, pl* **-feet** [*count*] : a foot that does not have a normal shape : a badly twisted or deformed foot that someone is born with; *also* [*noncount*] : the medical condition of having such a foot • *clubfoot* and other major birth defects
– club–foot•ed /ˈklʌbˌfʊtəd/ *adj*

club•house /ˈklʌbˌhaʊs/ *noun, pl* **-hous•es** [*count*]
1 : a building used by a club for its activities
2 : a building that has lockers and showers and that is used by a sports team
3 : a building at a golf course that usually has a locker room, a store that sells golf equipment, and a restaurant

club sandwich *noun, pl* ~ **-wiches** [*count*] : a sandwich that has three slices of bread with two layers of meat (such as turkey) and other cold foods (such as lettuce, tomato, and mayonnaise) between them

club soda *noun* [*noncount*] *US* : SODA WATER

¹**cluck** /ˈklʌk/ *noun, pl* **clucks** [*count*]
1 a : a short, low sound that is made by a chicken **b** : a short, low sound that is used to show disapproval or sympathy • *clucks* of disapproval
2 *US, informal* : a stupid or foolish person • Don't be such a ***dumb cluck***.

²**cluck** *verb* **clucks; clucked; cluck•ing**
1 [*no obj*] *of a chicken* : to make a low sound • The hen *clucked* at her chicks.
2 : to make a low sound with the tongue [*no obj*] The driver *clucked* at the horses to get them moving. • She *clucked* in sympathy/disappointment. [+ *obj*] He *clucked* his tongue.
3 [*no obj*] *informal* : to talk about something in an excited and often disapproving way • Commentators have been *clucking* over/about his lack of experience.
– clucking *noun* [*noncount*] • the *clucking* of chickens in the coop

¹**clue** /ˈkluː/ *noun, pl* **clues**
1 [*count*] : something that helps a person find something, understand something, or solve a mystery or puzzle • The book gives the reader plenty of *clues* to solve the mystery. • Science gives us *clues* about the origin of the universe. • "Guess who I met today." "Can you give me a *clue*?" • It gives a *clue* as to how to proceed. • a crossword puzzle *clue*
2 [*singular*] *informal* : an understanding of something : knowledge about something : IDEA • Get a *clue*! [=don't be so stupid or clueless] — usually used in negative statements • I had no *clue* what he meant. [=I didn't understand what he

meant at all] • He doesn't have a *clue* when it comes to fixing cars. [=he knows nothing about fixing cars] • Do you have any *clue* about what's going on here? • When it comes to computers, I don't have a *clue*. [=I'm clueless]

²clue *verb* **clues; clued; clue·ing** *or* **clu·ing**

clue in [*phrasal verb*] ***clue (someone) in*** *also* ***clue in (someone)*** *informal* : to give information to (someone) • The public should be *clued in* to what's happening. [=should be told about what's happening] — often + *on* • She'll *clue* you *in on* the latest news. — often used as *clued in* • He's totally *clued in on* [=he knows a lot about] the latest computer developments.

clued up *adj* [*more* ~; *most* ~] *Brit, informal* : having a lot of information about something • He's totally *clued up* [=*clued in*] (*on/about* the latest computer developments).

clue·less /ˈkluːləs/ *adj* [*more* ~; *most* ~] *informal* : not having knowledge about something : unable to understand something • When it comes to computers, I'm *clueless*. • her *clueless* kid brother • They were *clueless* about what to do.

¹clump /ˈklʌmp/ *noun, pl* **clumps** [*count*]
1 a : a small ball or mass of something • a *clump* of roots/grass/mud **b** : a group of things or people that are close together • There is a *clump* of bushes/trees at the edge of the field. • a *clump of* spectators
2 : a loud, heavy sound made by footsteps • I could hear the *clump* of his footsteps as he came down the stairs.

²clump *verb* **clumps; clumped; clump·ing**
1 : to form a mass or clump [*no obj*] The virus causes the cells to *clump* (together). [+ *obj*] The virus *clumps* the cells together.
2 [*no obj*] : to walk with loud, heavy steps • I could hear him *clumping* [=*clomping*] down/up the stairs.

clumpy /ˈklʌmpi/ *adj* **clump·i·er; -est** [*also more* ~; *most* ~] : having many small clumps • *clumpy* soil

clum·sy /ˈklʌmzi/ *adj* **clum·si·er; -est** [*also more* ~; *most* ~]
1 : moving or doing things in a very awkward way and tending to drop or break things • I'm sorry about spilling your wine—that was very *clumsy* of me. • I have very *clumsy* hands and tend to drop things. • He is very *clumsy*. = He is a very *clumsy* person.
2 : badly or awkwardly made or done • She made a *clumsy* attempt at a joke.
3 : hard to use : awkward to handle • a *clumsy* tool
– clum·si·ly /ˈklʌmzəli/ *adv* • They dealt with the situation *clumsily*. **– clum·si·ness** /ˈklʌmzinəs/ *noun* [*noncount*] • It was my own *clumsiness* that caused the accident.

clung *past tense and past participle of* CLING

clunk /ˈklʌŋk/ *noun, pl* **clunks** [*count*] : a loud, dull sound that is made when a heavy object hits another object or a surface • The book hit the floor with a loud *clunk*.
– clunk *verb* **clunks; clunked; clunk·ing** [*no obj*] The car door *clunked* shut. [+ *obj*] The ball *clunked* [=*hit*] him on the head.

clunk·er /ˈklʌŋkɚ/ *noun, pl* **-ers** [*count*] *chiefly US, informal*
1 : an old car or machine that does not work well • My first car was an old *clunker* that kept breaking down.
2 : something that is a complete failure • That joke was a real *clunker*. • The director's recent films have all been *clunkers*.

clunky /ˈklʌŋki/ *adj* **clunk·i·er; -est** [*also more* ~; *most* ~] *informal*
1 : large and awkward in form or appearance • *clunky* shoes
2 : old and not working well • I drive a *clunky* old station wagon. • a *clunky* old computer
3 : badly or awkwardly made or done • His act was full of *clunky* one-liners. • *clunky* dialogue

¹clus·ter /ˈklʌstɚ/ *noun, pl* **-ters** [*count*] : a group of things or people that are close together • a flower *cluster* • a *cluster* of cottages along the shore • A small *cluster* of people had gathered at the scene of the accident. • *clusters* of grapes

²cluster *verb, always followed by a preposition or adverb* **-ters; -tered; -ter·ing** [*no obj*] : to come together to form a group • The children *clustered* around the storyteller.

cluster bomb *noun, pl* ~ **bombs** [*count*] : a type of bomb that is dropped from an airplane and that contains many small bombs

¹clutch /ˈklʌʧ/ *verb* **clutch·es; clutched; clutch·ing**
1 [+ *obj*] : to hold onto (someone or something) tightly with your hand • I had to *clutch* the counter to keep from falling. • The child *clutched* her mother's hand firmly. • He had a book *clutched* in his hand.
2 [*no obj*] : to try to hold onto someone or something by reaching with your hand — usually + *at* • She *clutched at* his shoulder.
clutch at straws see STRAW

²clutch *noun, pl* **clutches** [*count*]
1 : the act of holding or gripping something or someone tightly — usually plural • She struggled to escape his *clutches*. [=he was holding her and she struggled to get away] • The hawk had the mouse ***in its clutches***. [=in its claws] — often used figuratively • They were powerless to oppose them. He had them *in his clutches*. [=he had control of them]
2 a : a pedal that is pressed to change gears in a vehicle • I have to learn how to let the *clutch* out smoothly. — see picture at CAR **b** : the part of a vehicle that is controlled by a clutch • The car needs a new *clutch*.
3 : CLUTCH BAG
in the clutch *US* : in a very important or critical situation especially during a sports competition • He is known for his ability to come through *in the clutch*. • She scored a basket *in the clutch*.
– compare ⁴CLUTCH

³clutch *adj* [*more* ~; *most* ~] *US*
1 *always used before a noun* : happening during a very important or critical time especially in a sports competition • She scored a *clutch* basket. • a *clutch* hit/play/goal • a *clutch* performance/situation
2 : able to perform well in a very important or critical situation especially in a sports competition • He is a *clutch* hitter/player. = He is *clutch*.

⁴clutch *noun, pl* **clutches** [*count*]
1 a : a group of eggs that is laid by a bird at one time • a *clutch* of eggs **b** : a group of young birds produced by a single group of eggs • a *clutch* of chicks
2 : a small group of things or people • a *clutch* of buildings/onlookers
– compare ²CLUTCH

clutch bag *noun, pl* ~ **bags** [*count*] : a small bag that women use especially on formal occasions : a small handbag

¹clut·ter /ˈklʌtɚ/ *verb* **-ters; -tered; -ter·ing** [+ *obj*] : to fill or cover (something) with many things : to fill or cover (something) with clutter • Tools *cluttered* the garage. • The garage was *cluttered* with tools. • Try to avoid *cluttering* your desk with books and papers. — often + *up* • Too many signs were *cluttering up* the street corner.
– cluttered *adj* [*more* ~; *most* ~] • a very *cluttered* attic/desk/office/room

²clutter *noun* [*noncount*] : a large amount of things that are not arranged in a neat or orderly way : a crowded or disordered collection of things • There's a lot of unnecessary *clutter* in the house. • a pile of *clutter* • desktop *clutter*

Clydes·dale /ˈklaɪdzˌdeɪl/ *noun, pl* **-dales** [*count*] : a type of very large, heavy horse that is used to pull wagons

cm *abbr* centimeter

Cmdr. *abbr* commander

c'mon /kəˈmaːn/ *informal* — used in writing to represent the sound of the phrase *come on* when it is spoken quickly • *C'mon*, everybody, let's go! — see *come on* 3 at ¹COME for situations in which *c'mon* is used

CNN *abbr* Cable News Network

C–note /ˈsiːˌnoʊt/ *noun, pl* **-notes** [*count*] *US, informal* : a 100-dollar bill

co. *abbr* **1** company **2** county

CO *abbr* **1** Colorado **2** commanding officer

c/o *abbr* care of ♢ This abbreviation is used in addresses when you are sending a letter or package to a person by using someone else's address or the address of a company. • The letter was addressed to "John Smith c/o Merriam-Webster, Inc."

co- *prefix*
1 : with : together • *co*exist
2 : associated with another • *co*worker • *co*author • *co*pilot

¹coach /ˈkoʊʧ/ *noun, pl* **coach·es**
1 [*count*] **a** : a person who teaches and trains an athlete or performer • a track/tennis star who has been working with a new *coach* • a vocal/voice/drama *coach* **b** : a person who teaches and trains the members of a sports team and makes decisions about how the team plays during games • a football/basketball/soccer *coach*
2 [*count*] *Brit* : a private teacher who gives someone lessons in a particular subject
3 : a large four-wheeled vehicle that is pulled by horses : CARRIAGE [*count*] In those days, people usually traveled long distances in *coaches*. [*noncount*] traveling ***by coach***

C

— see also STAGECOACH
4 *chiefly Brit* **:** a large bus with comfortable seating that is used for long trips [*count*] The company hired two *coaches* for the trip. [*noncount*] We traveled ***by coach*** to London. — often used before another noun ▪ a *coach* driver/tour/party
5 [*noncount*] *US* **:** the section of least expensive seats on an airplane or train ▪ We reserved two seats in *coach*. ▪ I usually ***fly coach***, but on this trip I'm flying first-class. — often used before another noun ▪ *coach* fares/passengers/seats
6 [*count*] *Brit* **:** a separate section of a train ▪ a passenger *coach* [=(*US*) *car*, (*Brit*) *carriage*]

²coach *verb* **coaches; coached; coach·ing**
1 a : to teach and train (an athlete or performer) [+ *obj*] She *coaches* young actors/singers. ▪ He *coaches* the tennis star. [*no obj*] He *coaches* in singing. **b :** to teach, train, and direct (a sports team) [+ *obj*] He has *coached* the team for several years. ▪ She *coached* the U.S. gymnastics team at the Olympics. ▪ He *coaches* football and basketball. [=he coaches football and basketball teams] [*no obj*] He has *coached* at the college level for many years.
2 [+ *obj*] *chiefly Brit* **:** to teach (a student) privately rather than in a class
3 [+ *obj*] **:** to give (someone) instructions on what to do or say in a particular situation ▪ The lawyer admitted to *coaching* the witness. ▪ It was clear that the witness had been *coached* by her lawyer on how to answer the questions.
– **coaching** *adj* ▪ a *coaching* job/career ▪ the team's *coaching* staff – **coaching** *noun* [*noncount*] ▪ She got into *coaching* a couple years ago. ▪ He can pass the test with a little *coaching*. ▪ The lawyer's *coaching* helped the witness.

coach·able /ˈkoʊʧəbəl/ *adj* [*more* ~; *most* ~] **:** capable of being easily taught and trained to do something better ▪ The player/singer is very *coachable*.

coach·load /ˈkoʊʧˌloʊd/ *noun, pl* **-loads** [*count*] *Brit* **:** a large group of people that fills a coach (sense 4) ▪ two *coachloads* [=(*chiefly US*) *busloads*] of tourists

coach·man /ˈkoʊʧmən/ *noun, pl* **-men** /-mən/ [*count*] *in the past* **:** a man whose job was driving a carriage pulled by horses

co·ag·u·late /koʊˈægjəˌleɪt/ *verb* **-lates; -lat·ed; -lat·ing :** to become thick and partly solid [*no obj*] The blood *coagulated*. ▪ The eggs *coagulate* when heated. [+ *obj*] The medicine helps *coagulate* blood.
– **co·ag·u·la·tion** /koʊˌægjəˈleɪʃən/ *noun* [*noncount*]

coal /ˈkoʊl/ *noun, pl* **coals**
1 [*noncount*] **:** a black or brownish-black hard substance within the earth that is used as a fuel ▪ a bin of *coal* ▪ The furnace burns *coal*. ▪ a lump of *coal* — often used before another noun ▪ a *coal* bin/mine/bed/stove ▪ the *coal* industry
2 [*count*] **a :** a piece of coal or charcoal especially when burning ▪ When the *coals* are red, they are very hot. **b** *US* **:** a glowing piece of wood from a fire **:** EMBER ▪ I toasted one last marshmallow over the *coals* of the campfire.
carry/take coals to Newcastle *Brit* **:** to take something to a place where it is not needed because a large amount of it is already there
haul/rake (someone) over the coals *informal* **:** to criticize (someone) very severely ▪ I arrived late for the meeting and was immediately *hauled over the coals* by my boss.

co·a·lesce /ˌkowəˈlɛs/ *verb* **-lesc·es; -lesced; -lesc·ing** [*no obj*] *formal* **:** to come together to form one group or mass ▪ a group of young reformers who gradually *coalesced* into a political movement ▪ The ice masses *coalesced* into a glacier over time.
– **co·ales·cence** /ˌkowəˈlɛsn̩s/ *noun* [*noncount*] a glacier formed by *coalescence* of ice masses [*singular*] a *coalescence* of forces

coal·face /ˈkoʊlˌfeɪs/ *noun, pl* **-fac·es** [*count*] *Brit* **:** the place inside a mine where the coal is cut out of the rock
at the coalface *Brit* **:** at the place where the actual work of an activity is done ▪ teachers working *at the coalface* in inner-city schools

coal·field /ˈkoʊlˌfiːld/ *noun, pl* **-fields** [*count*] **:** a large area where there is a lot of coal under the ground

co·a·li·tion /ˌkowəˈlɪʃən/ *noun, pl* **-tions**
1 [*count*] **:** a group of people, groups, or countries who have joined together for a common purpose ▪ The groups united to form a *coalition*. ▪ A multiparty *coalition* ruled the country. ▪ a *coalition* of businesses — often used before another noun ▪ *coalition* forces ▪ a *coalition* government/party
2 [*noncount*] **:** the action or process of joining together with another or others for a common purpose ▪ The group is working ***in coalition with*** other environmental groups.

coal tar *noun* [*noncount*] **:** a black, sticky liquid made from coal that is used as a fuel and to make various products (such as soap)

coarse /ˈkoɚs/ *adj* **coars·er; -est** [*also more* ~; *most* ~]
1 : made up of large pieces **:** not fine ▪ *coarse* sand/salt
2 : having a rough quality ▪ *coarse* wild grass ▪ The dog has a thick, *coarse* coat. ▪ The fabric varies in texture from *coarse* to fine. ▪ He has *coarse* hands.
3 : rude or offensive ▪ a *coarse* joke ▪ *coarse* behavior ▪ *coarse* [=*vulgar*] language
– **coarse·ly** *adv* ▪ *coarsely* chopped vegetables ▪ *coarsely* ground pepper – **coarse·ness** *noun* [*noncount*] ▪ We were shocked by the *coarseness* of his behavior.

coars·en /ˈkoɚsn̩/ *verb* **-ens; -ened; -en·ing**
1 a [+ *obj*] **:** to make (something) rough or rougher ▪ *Coarsen* [=*roughen*] the surface with a file before you apply the glue. ▪ Her hands were *coarsened* by years of hard work. **b** [*no obj*] **:** to become rough or rougher ▪ His hands *coarsened* [=*roughened*] from years of hard work.
2 a [+ *obj*] **:** to cause (someone or something) to become rude or offensive ▪ He was *coarsened* by his time in prison. ▪ offensive words that *coarsen* the English language **b** [*no obj*] **:** to become rude or offensive ▪ The book describes how popular culture has *coarsened* in recent decades.

¹coast /ˈkoʊst/ *noun, pl* **coasts**
1 : the land along or near a sea or ocean [*count*] sea/rocky *coasts* [=*shores*] ▪ the west/east *coast* ▪ He lives on the *coast*. [*noncount*] We drove along a long stretch of *coast*. [=*shore*]
2 ***the Coast*** *US, informal* **:** the area along or near the Pacific Ocean ▪ He's flying out to *the Coast* tomorrow.
from coast to coast **:** from one coast to the other coast of a country or continent ▪ They traveled *from coast to coast* across the U.S. ▪ The space shuttle launch was on television stations *from coast to coast*. [=throughout the country] — see also COAST-TO-COAST
the coast is clear ◊ When *the coast is clear* you can go somewhere or do something without being caught or seen because no one is in the area. ▪ OK, *the coast is clear*—you can come out now!
– **coast·al** /ˈkʰoʊstl̩/ *adj* ▪ *coastal* areas/regions/waters ▪ *coastal* mountains

²coast *verb* **coasts; coast·ed; coast·ing** [*no obj*]
1 a : to move forward using no power or very little power ▪ The car *coasted* to a stop. ▪ The airplane *coasted* down the runway. **b :** to move downhill by the force of gravity ▪ The children *coasted* on sleds down the snowy hill. ▪ They came *coasting* down the hill on bicycles.
2 : to progress or have success without special effort ▪ After taking a big lead, the team *coasted* to victory. ▪ He was accused of trying to *coast* through school. ▪ She decided she could *coast* along without a job for the next few months. ▪ The company is *coasting* on its good reputation.

coast·er /ˈkoʊstɚ/ *noun, pl* **-ers** [*count*]
1 : a small, flat object on which a glass, cup, or dish is placed to protect the surface of a table ▪ Set the glass on a *coaster*.
2 *chiefly US* **:** ROLLER COASTER 1
3 : a ship that sails along a coast or that is used in trade between ports of the same country

coast guard (*US*) *or Brit* **coast·guard** *noun, pl* ~ **guards**
1 *US* ***the Coast Guard*** *or Brit* ***the Coastguard*** **:** an organization that has the job of guarding the area along a country's coast and helping people, boats, and ships that are in danger on the sea ◊ The U.S. Coast Guard is a military organization. ▪ Their son joined *the Coast Guard* last year. — often used before another noun ▪ *Coast Guard* officials
2 [*count*] *Brit* **:** a member of the Coastguard

coast·guards·man /ˈkoʊstˌgɑɚdzmən/ *noun, pl* **-men** /-mən/ [*count*] *US* **:** a member of the Coast Guard

coast·line /ˈkoʊstˌlaɪn/ *noun, pl* **-lines :** the land along the edge of a coast [*count*] a rocky/sandy *coastline* [=*shoreline*] ▪ The plane flew along the eastern *coastline*. [*noncount*] miles of beautiful *coastline*

coast–to–coast /ˌkoʊstəˈkoʊst/ *adj*
1 : going across an entire nation or continent from one coast to another ▪ a *coast-to-coast* flight/broadcast
2 *US, informal* **a :** going from one end of a playing surface (such as a basketball court) to the other ▪ a *coast-to-coast* play **b :** resulting from a coast-to-coast play ▪ a *coast-to-coast* layup
– **coast–to–coast** *adv* ▪ The event was televised *coast-to-coast*.

[1]**coat** /ˈkoʊt/ *noun, pl* **coats** [*count*]
1 a : an outer piece of clothing that can be long or short and that is worn to keep warm or dry ▪ She put on her *coat,* hat, and gloves, and then she went outside. ▪ a winter/fur/wool *coat* **b** *chiefly US* **:** a piece of clothing that is worn over a shirt as part of a suit **:** JACKET ▪ He was wearing a *coat* and tie. ▪ a ***sport coat***
2 : the outer covering of fur, hair, or wool on an animal ▪ The dog has a thick/smooth/shaggy *coat.*
3 : a thin layer of paint covering a surface ▪ a *coat* of paint ▪ The house needed three *coats* to cover the original paint.
– coatless *adj* ▪ a shivering, *coatless* child

[2]**coat** *verb* **coats; coat·ed; coat·ing** [+ *obj*] **:** to cover (something or someone) with a thin layer of something ▪ Rock dust *coated* his hair. ▪ My shoes are *coated* with mud. ▪ Ice *coated* the deck. ▪ *Coat* the chicken with flour.

coat hanger *noun, pl* **~ -ers** [*count*] **:** a device that is used for hanging clothes in a closet **:** HANGER

coat hanger

coat·ing /ˈkoʊtɪŋ/ *noun, pl* **-ings** [*count*] **:** a thin layer or covering of something ▪ The fabric has a *coating* that prevents liquids from soaking through. ▪ A light *coating* of snow had fallen. ▪ There was a *coating* of ice on the pond.

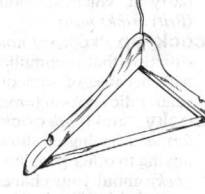

coat of arms *noun, pl* **coats of arms** [*count*] **:** a special group of pictures that belong to a person, family, or group of people and that are shown on a shield

coat·rack /ˈkoʊtˌræk/ *noun, pl* **-racks** [*count*] **:** a stand or pole that has pegs, hooks, or hangers that can be used for hanging coats and other clothes

coat·room /ˈkoʊtˌruːm/ *noun, pl* **-rooms** [*count*] *chiefly US* **:** CHECKROOM

coat·tail /ˈkoʊtˌteɪl/ *noun, pl* **-tails**
1 [*count*] **:** a long piece of cloth that hangs down at the back of a man's formal coat — usually plural ▪ He caught his *coattails* in the door.
2 ***coattails*** [*plural*] **:** the help or influence of another person's work, ideas, or popularity ▪ They were elected to Congress by ***riding (on) the coattails*** of the President. = They were swept into office ***on the coattails*** of the President. [=they were elected because they belong to the same political party as the President, who is very popular]

co·au·thor /ˈkoʊˈɑːθɚ/ *noun, pl* **-thors** [*count*] **:** someone who writes a book, article, etc., with another person ▪ He and his colleague were the *coauthors* of the study.

coax /ˈkoʊks/ *verb* **coax·es; coaxed; coax·ing** [+ *obj*]
1 : to influence or persuade (a person or animal) to do something by talking in a gentle and friendly way ▪ It took almost an hour to *coax* the cat down from the tree. — often + *into* ▪ He wanted to stay home, but I *coaxed* him *into* going out. ▪ Can we *coax* her *into* singing? — sometimes followed by *to* + *verb* ▪ The ad *coaxes* customers *to try* the new product.
2 : to get (something) by talking in a gentle and friendly way ▪ She tried to *coax* a raise from her boss. ▪ He was unable to *coax* an answer out of her.
3 : to cause (something) to do something by making a careful and continual effort ▪ He *coaxed* the fire to burn by blowing on it. ▪ The plant is difficult to *coax* into bloom.
– coaxing *noun* [*noncount*] ▪ He agreed to go after a little gentle *coaxing.*

co·ax·i·al cable /koʊˈæksijəl-/ *noun, pl* **~ cables** [*count*] *technical* **:** a type of electric cable that is used to send telegraph, telephone, and television signals

cob /ˈkɑːb/ *noun, pl* **cobs** [*count*]
1 : CORNCOB ▪ She used a knife to cut the corn from the *cob.* ▪ We had ***corn on the cob.***
2 : a type of horse that has short legs
3 : a male swan

co·balt /ˈkoʊˌbɑːlt/ *noun* [*noncount*] **:** a hard, shiny, silver-white metal that is often mixed with other metals

cobalt blue *noun* [*noncount*] **:** a deep blue color — see color picture on page C2

cob·ber /ˈkɑːbɚ/ *noun, pl* **-bers** [*count*] *Australia + New Zealand, informal* **:** a male friend ▪ remembering his mates and *cobbers* back home

[1]**cob·ble** /ˈkɑːbəl/ *verb* **cob·bles; cob·bled; cob·bling** [+ *obj*]
1 : to make (something) by putting together different parts in a quick way — usually + *together* or *up* ▪ The diplomats rushed to *cobble together* a treaty. ▪ The speech was *cobbled together* from papers and lectures. ▪ They worked quickly to *cobble up* a temporary solution.
2 *old-fashioned* **:** to make or repair (shoes) ▪ expensive leather shoes *cobbled* in Italy

[2]**cobble** *noun, pl* **cobbles** [*count*] **:** COBBLESTONE ▪ a street paved with *cobbles*

cobbled *adj* **:** covered with cobblestones ▪ a *cobbled* street

cob·bler /ˈkɑːblɚ/ *noun, pl* **-blers**
1 [*count*] *old-fashioned* **:** a person who makes or repairs shoes
2 [*count, noncount*] *US* **:** a dessert made of cooked fruit covered with a thick crust ▪ peach *cobbler*

cob·ble·stone /ˈkɑːbəlˌstoʊn/ *noun, pl* **-stones** [*count*] **:** a round stone that is used in paving streets
– cob·ble·stoned /ˈkɑːbəlˌstoʊnd/ *adj* ▪ *cobblestoned* streets

co·bra /ˈkoʊbrə/ *noun, pl* **-bras** [*count*] **:** a very poisonous snake found in Asia and Africa

cobra

cob·web /ˈkɑːbˌwɛb/ *noun, pl* **-webs** [*count*] **:** the threads of old spider webs that are found in areas that have not been cleaned for a long time ▪ Dirt and *cobwebs* filled the corners of the room. ▪ The barn is filled with *cobwebs.* — sometimes used figuratively ▪ She took a walk to ***clear the cobwebs*** from her mind. [=to clear her mind]
– cob·webbed /ˈkɑːbˌwɛbd/ *adj* ▪ a *cobwebbed* attic

co·caine /koʊˈkeɪn/ *noun* [*noncount*] **:** a powerful drug that is used in medicine to stop pain or is taken illegally for pleasure — called also (*informal*) *coke*

coc·cyx /ˈkɑːksɪks/ *noun, pl* **coc·cy·ges** /ˈkɑːksəˌʤiːz/ *also* **coc·cyx·es** /ˈkɑːksɪksəz/ [*count*] *technical* **:** the small bone at the end of the spine **:** TAILBONE

co·chlea /ˈkoʊklijə, ˈkɑːklijə/ *noun, pl* **co·chle·as** *or* **co·chle·ae** /ˈkoʊkliˌiː, ˈkɑːkliˌiː/ [*count*] *technical* **:** the part of the inner ear that contains the endings of the nerve that carries information about sound to the brain
– coch·le·ar /ˈkoʊklijɚ, ˈkɑːklijɚ/ *adj* ▪ the *cochlear* canal/duct/nerve ▪ a ***cochlear implant*** [=an electronic device that allows people with hearing loss to hear some sounds]

[1]**cock** /ˈkɑːk/ *noun, pl* **cocks** [*count*]
1 : an adult male chicken **:** ROOSTER ▪ The *cock* was crowing.
2 : a device for stopping or slowing the flow of a liquid or gas through a pipe **:** STOPCOCK
3 *informal + impolite* **:** PENIS
cock of the walk ✧ A man who is described as *(the) cock of the walk* is very proud and successful or acts in a very proud way. ▪ He was strutting around like *the cock of the walk* after he got a promotion.

[2]**cock** *verb* **cocks; cocked; cock·ing** [+ *obj*]
1 : to pull back the hammer of (a gun) to get ready to shoot ▪ He *cocked* the pistol/weapon.
2 : to pull or bend back (something) to get ready to throw or hit a ball ▪ The quarterback was tackled just as he *cocked* his arm to throw the ball. ▪ The hitter stood with the bat *cocked,* waiting for a pitch.
3 : to turn, tip, or raise (part of your body or face) upward or to one side ▪ He *cocked* his head to one side. ▪ She *cocked* an eyebrow in disbelief. ▪ The dog sat with one ear *cocked.* ✧ If you ***cock an ear/eye*** or ***cock your ear/eye,*** you listen to or look at someone or something with a lot of attention. ▪ If the politicians would *cock an ear* to/toward what voters are saying, they'd realize that the new law isn't working.
4 : to move (a hat) so that it is tilted on your head ▪ His hat was *cocked* to one side.
cock a snook at *Brit, informal* **:** to show that you do not respect or value (something) ▪ He never misses a chance to *cock a snook at* [=*thumb his nose at*] modern art.
cock up [*phrasal verb*] *Brit, informal* **1 :** to make a mistake **:** to do something incorrectly ▪ Someone had *cocked up* [=*screwed up, messed up*] badly, and the party was a disaster. **2** ***cock up (something) or cock (something) up*** **:** to make mistakes in doing or making (something) ▪ Someone

had *cocked up* [=*screwed up, messed up*] the arrangements. — see also COCK-UP
– see also HALF-COCKED

cock·ade /kɑˈkeɪd/ *noun, pl* **-ades** [*count*] : a decoration that is worn on a hat especially as part of a uniform to show a person's status, rank, etc.

cock–a–doo·dle–do /ˌkɑːkəˌduːdlˈduː/ *noun* [*singular*] : the loud sound that a rooster makes ▪ I was awakened by the rooster's *cock-a-doodle-do* at dawn.

cock–a–hoop /ˌkɑːkəˈhuːp/ *adj, not used before a noun* [*more* ~; *most* ~] *chiefly Brit, informal* : very excited and happy about something done ▪ The team was *cock-a-hoop* about/over winning the game.

cock·a·ma·my *or* **cock·a·ma·mie** /ˌkɑːkəˈmeɪmi/ *adj* [*more* ~; *most* ~] *US, informal* : ridiculous or silly ▪ Who dreamed up this *cockamamie* idea/scheme? ▪ What *cockamamie* excuse will he come up with this time?

cock–and–bull story /ˈkɑːkənˈbʊl-/ *noun, pl* ~ **stories** [*count*] *informal* : a ridiculous story that is is used as an explanation or excuse ▪ Do you think I'm going to fall for that *cock-and-bull story*?

cock·a·tiel /ˈkɑːkəˌtiːl/ *noun, pl* **-tiels** [*count*] : a type of small parrot from Australia that has a yellow head and is often kept as a pet

cock·a·too /ˈkɑːkəˌtuː/ *noun, pl* **-toos** [*count*] : a type of large parrot from Australia that has a large colorful bunch of feathers on top of its head

cocked hat /ˈkɑːkt-/ *noun, pl* ~ **hats** [*count*] *old-fashioned* : a hat with the edges turned up on two or three sides
into a cocked hat *informal* **1** *US* : into a state of confusion, ruin, etc. ▪ The discovery has knocked/thrown all our old assumptions *into a cocked hat.* [=has completely destroyed all our old assumptions] **2** *Brit* — used to say that one person or thing is much better than another ▪ The old design was good, but this new one knocks/beats it *into a cocked hat.*

cock·er·el /ˈkɑːkərəl/ *noun, pl* **-els** [*count*] : a young male chicken

cocker spaniel *noun, pl* ~ **-iels** [*count*] : a type of small dog that has long ears and long fur — see picture at DOG

cock·eyed /ˈkɑːkˌaɪd/ *adj* [*more* ~; *most* ~] *informal*
1 : turned or tilted to one side : not straight ▪ The windows of the house look *cockeyed.* ▪ a *cockeyed* grin
2 : crazy or foolish ▪ Where did you get those *cockeyed* ideas? ▪ She is full of *cockeyed* optimism.

cock·fight /ˈkɑːkˌfaɪt/ *noun, pl* **-fights** [*count*] : a fight between roosters that people watch for entertainment
– **cock·fight·ing** /ˈkɑːkˌfaɪtɪŋ/ *noun* [*noncount*] ▪ Many countries have outlawed *cockfighting.*

cock·le /ˈkɑːkəl/ *noun, pl* **cock·les** [*count*] : a type of shellfish with a shell that has two parts and is shaped like a heart
warm the cockles of your heart ✧ If something *warms the cockles of your heart*, it makes you have warm and happy feelings. ▪ It is a story with a happy ending to *warm the cockles of your heart.*

cock·le·shell /ˈkɑːkəlˌʃɛl/ *noun, pl* **-shells** [*count*] : the shell of a cockle

cock·ney *or* **Cock·ney** /ˈkɑːkni/ *noun, pl* **-neys**
1 [*count*] : a person from the East End of London
2 [*noncount*] : the way of speaking that is typical of cockneys
– **cockney** *adj* ▪ He has a *cockney* accent. ▪ *cockney* slang

cock·pit /ˈkɑːkˌpɪt/ *noun, pl* **-pits** [*count*] : the area in a boat, airplane, etc., where the pilot or driver sits — see picture at AIRPLANE

cockpit voice recorder *noun, pl* ~ **-ers** [*count*] : a device that records the voices of the pilots and crew in the cockpit of an airplane ✧ If an airplane crashes, its cockpit voice recorder can be used to help find out what caused it to crash.

cock·roach /ˈkɑːkˌroʊʧ/ *noun, pl* **-roach·es** [*count*] : a black or brown insect that is sometimes found in people's homes — called also (*US*) *roach*; see color picture on page C10

cock·suck·er /ˈkɑːkˌsʌkɚ/ *noun, pl* **-ers** [*count*] *informal + offensive* : a very stupid or annoying person (especially a man) ✧ This is a very offensive word that should be avoided.

cock·sure /ˈkɑːkˈʃuɚ/ *adj* [*more* ~; *most* ~] : having or showing confidence in a way that is annoying to other people ▪ a *cocksure*, know-it-all attitude ▪ *cocksure* arrogance

cock·tail /ˈkɑːkˌteɪl/ *noun, pl* **-tails**
1 [*count*] : an alcoholic drink that is a mixture of one or more liquors and other ingredients (such as fruit juice) ▪ We had *cocktails* before dinner. — often used before another noun ▪ a *cocktail* waiter/waitress/bar ▪ a *cocktail* glass ▪ A ***cocktail hour*** [=an hour when people drink cocktails] preceded the dinner.
2 [*count*] : a mixture of different things ▪ The disease is being treated with a *cocktail of* powerful drugs. ▪ a dangerous *cocktail of* chemicals — see also MOLOTOV COCKTAIL
3 [*count, noncount*] : a small dish of a particular food that is served usually at the beginning or end of a meal ▪ a shrimp *cocktail* ▪ fruit *cocktail*

cocktail dress *noun, pl* ~ **dresses** [*count*] : a usually short dress that is suitable for formal occasions

cocktail lounge *noun, pl* ~ **-lounges** [*count*] : a room in a hotel, restaurant, etc., where cocktails and other drinks are served

cocktail party *noun, pl* ~ **-ties** [*count*] : a usually formal party at which alcoholic drinks are served — called also (*Brit*) *drinks party*

cock–up /ˈkɑːkˌʌp/ *noun, pl* **-ups** [*count*] *Brit, informal* : a situation that is complicated, unpleasant, or difficult to deal with because of someone's mistake ▪ an administrative/bureaucratic *cock-up* [=*mess*] — see also *cock up* at ²COCK

cocky /ˈkɑːki/ *adj* **cock·i·er; -est** [*also more* ~; *most* ~] *informal* : having or showing confidence in a way that is annoying to other people ▪ a *cocky* young athlete ▪ Don't get too *cocky* about your chances of getting the job.
– **cock·i·ly** /ˈkɑːkəli/ *adv* ▪ She's *cockily* confident about getting the job. – **cock·i·ness** /ˈkɑːkinəs/ *noun* [*noncount*]

co·coa /ˈkoʊkoʊ/ *noun, pl* **-coas**
1 [*noncount*] : a brown powder made from roasted cocoa beans that is used to give a chocolate flavor to foods ▪ The recipe calls for three tablespoons of *cocoa.* — called also *cocoa powder*
2 [*count, noncount*] : a hot drink of milk or water mixed with cocoa ▪ a cup of *cocoa*

cocoa bean *noun, pl* ~ **beans** [*count*] : the seed of a tropical tree (called the cacao) that is used in making cocoa, chocolate, and cocoa butter

cocoa butter *noun* [*noncount*] : a pale fat made from cocoa beans that is used in making chocolate and in various products (such as soaps and skin lotions)

co·co·nut /ˈkoʊkəˌnʌt/ *noun, pl* **-nuts**
1 [*count*] : a large fruit that has a thick shell with white flesh and liquid inside it and that grows on a palm tree — see color picture on page C5
2 [*noncount*] : the white flesh of a coconut ▪ The pastry is covered with shredded *coconut.* ▪ a piece of *coconut*

coconut milk *noun* [*noncount*] : the liquid that is inside a coconut

coconut oil *noun* [*noncount*] : an oil taken from coconuts that is used especially in making soaps and food products

coconut shy *noun* [*noncount*] *Brit* : an outdoor game in which players throw balls at coconuts set up on poles in order to knock them down

¹co·coon /kəˈkuːn/ *noun, pl* **-coons** [*count*]
1 : a covering usually made of silk which some insects (such as caterpillars) make around themselves to protect them while they grow
2 : something that covers or protects a person or thing ▪ The child was wrapped in a *cocoon* of blankets. ▪ The movie star was surrounded by a protective *cocoon of* bodyguards.

²cocoon *verb* **-coons; -cooned; -coon·ing**
1 [+ *obj*] : to cover or protect (someone or something) completely — usually used as *(be) cocooned* ▪ We *were* comfortably *cocooned* in our sleeping bags.
2 [*no obj*] *chiefly US* : to spend time at home instead of going out for other activities ▪ Americans are spending more time *cocooning* at home in recent years.
– **co·coon·ing** /kəˈkuːnɪŋ/ *noun* [*noncount*] ▪ Americans are doing more *cocooning* in recent years.

cod /ˈkɑːd/ *noun, pl* **cod** [*count, noncount*] : a large fish that lives in the northern Atlantic Ocean and is often eaten as food

COD *or* **C.O.D.** *abbr* cash on delivery; collect on delivery — used to indicate that payment must be made when something is delivered ▪ The merchandise was shipped *C.O.D.*

co·da /ˈkoʊdə/ *noun, pl* **-das** [*count*] *formal*
1 : an ending part of a piece of music or a work of literature or drama that is separate from the earlier parts ▪ The movie's

coda shows the main character as an adult 25 years later.
2 : something that ends and completes something else — often + *to* ▪ In a fitting *coda to* his career, he served as ambassador to China.

cod·dle /ˈkɑːdl/ *verb* **cod·dles; cod·dled; cod·dling** [+ *obj*] *disapproving* **:** to treat (someone) with too much care or kindness ▪ She *coddles* [=*pampers*] her children. ▪ The judges were accused of *coddling* criminals.

[1]**code** /ˈkoʊd/ *noun, pl* **codes**
1 [*count*] **a :** a set of laws or regulations ▪ the state's criminal *code* ▪ the tax *code* ▪ the city's plumbing/electrical/building *codes* ▪ The school has a ***dress code*** [=rules about what a person can wear] — see also PENAL CODE **b :** a set of ideas or rules about how to behave ▪ a moral *code* ▪ Everyone in the organization has to follow its *code* of ethics. ▪ The army has a strict *code* of conduct/behavior.
2 a : a set of letters, numbers, symbols, etc., that is used to secretly send messages to someone [*count*] The enemy was unable to break/crack the army's secret *code*. [*noncount*] The message was sent in *code*. — see also MORSE CODE **b** [*count*] **:** a set of letters, numbers, symbols, etc., that identifies or gives information about something or someone ▪ Every item in the store has a product *code*. ▪ Enter your security *code* to access the computer. ▪ Each employee is given a ***code number***. — see also AREA CODE, BAR CODE, DIALLING CODE, POSTCODE, ZIP CODE
3 [*noncount*] **:** a set of instructions for a computer ▪ He was hired to write programming *code*. ▪ lines of *code*

[2]**code** *verb* **codes; cod·ed; cod·ing** [+ *obj*]
1 : to put (a message) into the form of a code so that it can be kept secret ▪ The message was *coded*. ▪ The general sent a *coded* message. — compare DECODE
2 : to mark (something) with a code so that it can be identified ▪ Each product has been *coded*. ▪ The trails on the mountain are all ***color coded*** [=each trail is marked by a particular color]
3 : to change (information) into a set of letters, numbers, or symbols that can be read by a computer ▪ Programmers *coded* the data.

co·deine /ˈkoʊˌdiːn/ *noun* [*noncount*] **:** a drug used to reduce pain

code name *noun, pl* **~ names** [*count*] **:** a name that is used to keep someone's or something's real name a secret ▪ Every secret agent has a *code name*.
– code–name /ˈkoʊdˌneɪm/ *verb* **-names; -named; -nam·ing** [+ *obj*] ▪ The military operation is *code-named* "Clean Sweep."

co·de·pen·den·cy /ˌkoʊdɪˈpɛndənsi/ *noun* [*noncount*] **:** a psychological condition in which someone is in an unhappy and unhealthy relationship that involves living with and providing care for another person (such as a drug addict or an alcoholic)
– co·de·pen·dent /ˌkoʊdɪˈpɛndənt/ *adj* ▪ the *codependent* spouse of an alcoholic **– codependent** *noun, pl* **-dents** [*count*] ▪ providing help for *codependents*

cod·er /ˈkoʊdɚ/ *noun, pl* **-ers** [*count*] **:** a computer programmer

code word *noun, pl* **~ words** [*count*] **:** a word or phrase that has a secret meaning or that is used instead of another word or phrase to avoid speaking directly ▪ The *code word* "conflict" has been used for what some people are calling a war.

cod·ger /ˈkɑːʤɚ/ *noun, pl* **-gers** [*count*] *informal* **:** an old man ▪ Her father is a feisty old *codger*.

cod·i·cil /ˈkɑːdəsəl, *Brit* ˈkəʊdəsɪl/ *noun, pl* **-cils** [*count*] *law* **:** a document that adds or changes something in a will

cod·i·fy /ˈkɑːdəˌfaɪ/ *verb* **-fies; -fied; -fy·ing** [+ *obj*]
1 : to put (laws or rules) together as a code or system ▪ The convention *codified* the rules of war.
2 : to put (things) in an orderly form ▪ The author tries to *codify* important ideas about language.
– cod·i·fi·ca·tion /ˌkɑːdəfəˈkeɪʃən/ *noun, pl* **-tions** [*count, noncount*]

cod–liver oil *noun* [*noncount*] **:** an oil from the liver of cod that is used in medicine as a source of vitamin A and D

cods·wal·lop /ˈkɑːdzˌwɑːləp/ *noun* [*noncount*] *Brit, informal* **:** NONSENSE ▪ That is a load of *codswallop*.

[1]**co·ed** /ˈkoʊˌɛd/ *noun, pl* **-eds** [*count*] *US, somewhat old-fashioned* **:** a female student at a college that has both male and female students

[2]**coed** *adj*
1 : COEDUCATIONAL ▪ a *coed* university/dormitory ▪ The college became/went *coed* this year.
2 *US* **:** having or including both men and women ▪ The softball team is *coed*. ▪ a *coed* health club

co·ed·u·ca·tion·al /koʊˌɛʤəˈkeɪʃənl/ *adj, formal* **:** having both male and female students ▪ a *coeducational* institution

co·ef·fi·cient /ˌkowəˈfɪʃənt/ *noun, pl* **-cients** [*count*]
1 *mathematics* **:** a number by which another number or symbol is multiplied ▪ 5 is the *coefficient* of *y* in the term 5*y*.
2 *physics* **:** a number that is used to measure some property or characteristic of a substance ▪ a *coefficient* of friction ▪ the metal's *coefficient* of expansion

co·equal /koʊˈiːkwəl/ *adj, formal* **:** equal with each other ▪ *coequal* branches of government

co·erce /koʊˈɚs/ *verb* **-erc·es; -erced; -erc·ing** [+ *obj*]
1 : to make (someone) do something by using force or threats — usually + *into* ▪ He was *coerced into* signing the confession. ▪ Soldiers *coerced* the residents *into* giving them food. ▪ The singer was *coerced into* a contract with the record company.
2 : to get (something) by using force or threats ▪ A confession was *coerced* from the suspect by police.
– co·er·cion /koʊˈɚʒən, koʊˈɚʃən/ *noun* [*noncount*] ▪ They used *coercion* to obtain the confession.

co·er·cive /koʊˈɚsɪv/ *adj* [*more* ~; *most* ~] *formal* **:** using force or threats to make someone do something **:** using coercion ▪ *coercive* measures/techniques/policies
– co·er·cive·ly *adv*

co·ex·ist /ˌkoʊɪgˈzɪst/ *verb* **-ists; -ist·ed; -ist·ing** [*no obj*]
1 : to exist together or at the same time ▪ They found proof that dinosaurs and turtles *coexisted* (with each other). ▪ The species *coexist* in the same environment.
2 : to live in peace with each other ▪ Can the two countries peacefully *coexist*?
– co·ex·is·tence /ˌkoʊɪgˈzɪstəns/ *noun* [*noncount*] ▪ the *coexistence* of dinosaurs and turtles ▪ The countries live in peaceful *coexistence*.

C of C *abbr* Chamber of Commerce

C of E *abbr* Church of England

cof·fee /ˈkɑːfi/ *noun, pl* **-fees**
1 : a dark brown drink made from ground coffee beans and boiled water [*noncount*] a cup of *coffee* ▪ iced/decaffeinated *coffee* ▪ I'll make/brew some *coffee*. [*count*] Would you like another *coffee*? [=another cup of coffee] — often used before another noun ▪ a *coffee* cup ▪ *coffee* mugs ▪ *coffee* ice cream [=ice cream that has the flavor of coffee]
2 [*noncount*] **:** coffee beans ▪ I bought a pound of *coffee*.
wake up and smell the coffee see [1]WAKE

coffee bar *noun, pl* **~ bars** [*count*] **:** a place where coffee and usually other drinks and refreshments are sold

coffee bean *noun, pl* **~ beans** [*count*] **:** the bean of a tropical tree or bush from which coffee is made

coffee break *noun, pl* **~ breaks** [*count*] **:** a short period of time in which you stop working to rest and have coffee or some other refreshment

coffee cake *noun, pl* **~ cakes** [*count*] *US* **:** a sweet, rich bread usually made with fruit, nuts, and spices and often eaten with coffee

cof·fee·house /ˈkɑːfiˌhaʊs/ *noun, pl* **-hous·es** [*count*] **:** a business that sells coffee and usually other drinks and refreshments

coffee machine *noun, pl* **~ machines** [*count*]
1 : a machine that you can buy cups of coffee from
2 *Brit* **:** COFFEEMAKER

cof·fee·mak·er /ˈkɑːfiˌmeɪkɚ/ *noun, pl* **-ers** [*count*] **:** a small electrical machine that makes coffee — see picture at KITCHEN

cof·fee·pot /ˈkɑːfiˌpɑːt/ *noun, pl* **-pots** [*count*] **:** a pot that is used for making and pouring coffee

coffee shop *noun, pl* **~ shops** [*count*] **:** a small restaurant that serves coffee and other drinks as well as simple foods ▪ We bought a muffin at the hotel's *coffee shop*.

coffee table *noun, pl* **~ tables** [*count*] **:** a long, low table that is usually placed in front of a sofa in someone's home — see picture at LIVING ROOM

coffee–table book *noun, pl* **~ books** [*count*] **:** a large expensive book with many pictures that is typically placed on a table for people to look at in a casual way

cof·fer /ˈkɑːfɚ/ *noun, pl* **-fers**
1 [*count*] **:** a box for holding money or other valuable things
2 ***coffers*** [*plural*] **:** money that is available for spending ▪ the city's *coffers* [=*treasury*] ▪ corporate *coffers* [=*funds*]

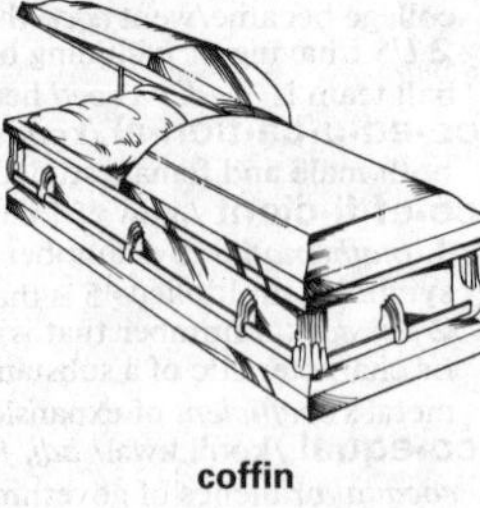
coffin

C

cof·fin /ˈkɑːfən/ *noun, pl* **-fins** [*count*] **:** a box in which a dead person is buried

a nail in the/someone's coffin see ¹NAIL

cog /ˈkɑːg/ *noun, pl* **cogs** [*count*]
1 a : any one of the small parts that stick out on the outer edge of a wheel or gear and that allow it to turn along with another wheel or gear **b :** COGWHEEL
2 : someone or something that is thought of as being like a part of a machine ▪ He was an important *cog* on that championship team. — often used to describe someone who is regarded as an unimportant part of a large business or organization ▪ My brother is just a minor *cog* in the Hollywood machine. He works as an electrician for a film studio. ▪ He's just ***a cog in the machine***.

co·gent /ˈkoʊʤənt/ *adj* [*more ~; most ~*] *formal* **:** very clear and easy for the mind to accept and believe ▪ She offers some *cogent* [=*convincing, persuasive*] reasons for building new schools. ▪ a *cogent* [=*reasonable*] argument
– **co·gen·cy** /ˈkoʊʤənsi/ *noun* [*noncount*] ▪ I was impressed by the *cogency* of his arguments. – **co·gent·ly** *adv*

cog·i·tate /ˈkɑːʤəˌteɪt/ *verb* **-tates; -tat·ed; -tat·ing** [*no obj*] *formal* **:** to think carefully and seriously about something ▪ I was *cogitating* about/on my chances of failing.
– **cog·i·ta·tion** /ˌkɑːʤəˈteɪʃən/ *noun* [*noncount*] a problem that requires further *cogitation* [=*thought*] [*count*] the *cogitations* of his mind

co·gnac /ˈkoʊnˌjæk, ˈkɑːnˌjæk/ *noun, pl* **-gnacs** [*count, noncount*] **:** a kind of brandy that is made in France

cog·nate /ˈkɑːgˌneɪt/ *adj, linguistics* **:** having the same origin ▪ English "eat" and German "essen" are *cognate*. ▪ Spanish and French are *cognate* languages.
– **cognate** *noun, pl* **-nates** [*count*] ▪ "Eat" and "essen" are *cognates*.

cog·ni·tion /kɑːgˈnɪʃən/ *noun* [*noncount*] *technical* **:** conscious mental activities **:** the activities of thinking, understanding, learning, and remembering ▪ disabilities affecting *cognition* and judgment

cog·ni·tive /ˈkɑːgnətɪv/ *adj, technical* **:** of, relating to, or involving conscious mental activities (such as thinking, understanding, learning, and remembering) ▪ *cognitive* development/psychology/impairment
– **cog·ni·tive·ly** *adv* ▪ *cognitively* impaired

cog·ni·zance *also Brit* **cog·ni·sance** /ˈkɑːgnəzəns/ *noun* [*noncount*] *formal* **:** knowledge or awareness of something ▪ They seemed to have no *cognizance* of the crime.
take cognizance of **:** to notice or give attention to (something) ▪ He should *take cognizance of* those who disagree with his theory.

cog·ni·zant *also Brit* **cog·ni·sant** /ˈkɑːgnəzənt/ *adj, not used before a noun* [*more ~; most ~*] *formal* **:** aware of something ▪ He is *cognizant* of his duties as a father.

cog·no·scen·ti /ˌkɑːnjəˈʃɛnti/ *noun*
the cognoscenti **:** the people who know a lot about something ▪ *the* jazz *cognoscenti* ▪ *the cognoscenti* of the art world

cog·wheel /ˈkɑːgˌwiːl/ *noun, pl* **-wheels** [*count*] **:** a wheel with cogs **:** GEAR

co·hab·it /koʊˈhæbət/ *verb* **-its; -it·ed; -it·ing** [*no obj*] *formal* **:** to live together and have a sexual relationship ▪ They *cohabited* in a small apartment in the city.
– **co·hab·i·ta·tion** /koʊˌhæbəˈteɪʃən/ *noun* [*noncount*]

co·here /koʊˈhiə/ *verb* **-heres; -hered; -her·ing** [*no obj*] *formal* **:** to be combined or united in a logical and effective way ▪ There are several themes in the story but they never *cohere* (with one another).

co·her·ent /koʊˈhirənt/ *adj* [*more ~; most ~*]
1 : logical and well-organized **:** easy to understand ▪ He proposed the most *coherent* plan to improve the schools. ▪ a *coherent* argument/essay
2 : able to talk or express yourself in a clear way that can be easily understood ▪ The drunk man was not *coherent*. [=*understandable*]
3 : working closely and well together ▪ They are able to function as a *coherent* group/team.
– **co·her·ence** /koʊˈhirəns/ *noun* [*noncount*] ▪ His films are confusing and have little *coherence*. ▪ You make some interesting points, but the essay as a whole lacks *coherence*. [=it moves in a disorganized or confusing way from one idea to another] ▪ The team lacks *coherence*. – **co·her·ent·ly** *adv* ▪ The student has trouble expressing his ideas *coherently*. ▪ They work *coherently* together.

co·he·sion /koʊˈhiːʒən/ *noun* [*noncount*] **:** a condition in which people or things are closely united **:** UNITY ▪ There was a lack of *cohesion* in the rebel army. ▪ social *cohesion*

co·he·sive /koʊˈhiːsɪv/ *adj* [*more ~; most ~*]
1 : closely united ▪ Their tribe is a small but *cohesive* group.
2 : causing people to be closely united ▪ Religion can be used as a *cohesive* social force.
– **co·he·sive·ly** *adv* – **co·he·sive·ness** *noun* [*noncount*]

co·hort /ˈkoʊˌhoət/ *noun, pl* **-horts** [*count*]
1 *often disapproving* **:** a friend or companion ▪ The police arrested the gang's leader and his *cohorts*.
2 *technical* **:** a group of people used in a study who have something (such as age or social class) in common ▪ Depression was a common problem for people in that age *cohort*.

coif /ˈkwɑːf/ *verb* **coifs; coiffed** *also* **coifed; coif·fing** *also* **coif·ing** [+ *obj*] **:** to cut and arrange someone's hair — usually used as *coiffed* ▪ a carefully *coiffed* man ▪ her perfectly *coiffed* hair

coif·fure /kwɑˈfjuə/ *noun, pl* **-fures** [*count*] *formal* **:** a way of cutting and arranging someone's hair **:** HAIRDO ▪ a fancy/stylish/elaborate *coiffure*

¹coil /ˈkojəl/ *verb* **coils; coiled; coil·ing :** to wind (something) into circles [+ *obj*] She *coiled* the loose thread around her finger. ▪ The cat *coiled* herself (up) into a ball on the rug. ▪ A long scarf was *coiled* around her neck. [*no obj*] The cat *coiled* up into a ball. ▪ The snake *coiled* around its prey.
– **coiled** *adj* ▪ *coiled* wire

²coil *noun, pl* **coils** [*count*]
1 : a long thin piece of material (such as a wire, string, or piece of hair) that is wound into circles ▪ a *coil* of wire
2 *technical* **:** a wire wound into circles that carries electricity
3 : INTRAUTERINE DEVICE

¹coin /ˈkoɪn/ *noun, pl* **coins** [*count*] **:** a small, flat, and usually round piece of metal issued by a government as money ▪ gold/silver/copper *coins* ▪ I have a dollar in *coins*.
the other/opposite/flip side of the coin **:** a different way of looking at or thinking about a situation ▪ The economy is improving, but *the other side of the coin* is that inflation is becoming a bigger problem.
toss/flip a coin **:** to decide something by throwing a coin up in the air and seeing which side is shown after it lands ▪ Let's *toss a coin*. Heads, we don't go; tails, we do.
two sides of the same coin **:** two things that are regarded as two parts of the same thing ▪ These problems may seem unrelated but they are really *two sides of the same coin*.

²coin *verb* **coins; coined; coin·ing** [+ *obj*]
1 : to create (a new word or phrase) that other people begin to use ▪ The coach *coined* the phrase "refuse to lose." ▪ William Shakespeare is believed to have *coined* many words. ✧ The phrase ***to coin a phrase*** is sometimes used in a joking way to say that you know you are using a very common expression. ▪ The couple lived happily ever after, *to coin a phrase*.
2 : to make (money in the form of coins) ▪ The nation plans to *coin* more money.
coin it *or* ***coin money*** *Brit, informal* **:** to earn a lot of money quickly or easily ▪ They are really *coining it/money* with their new CD.

coin·age /ˈkoɪnɪʤ/ *noun, pl* **-ag·es**
1 a [*noncount*] **:** the act of creating a new word or phrase that other people begin to use ▪ "Blog" is a word of recent *coinage*. [=a word that was recently created] **b** [*count*] **:** a word that someone has created ▪ The word "blog" is a recent *coinage*.
2 [*noncount*] **a :** money in the form of coins ▪ *Coinage* was scarce in the colonies. ▪ an expert in Chinese *coinage* **b :** the act or process of creating coins ▪ the *coinage* of money

co·in·cide /ˌkowənˈsaɪd/ *verb* **-cides; -cid·ed; -cid·ing** [*no obj*]
1 : to happen at the same time as something else ▪ The earthquakes *coincided*. — often + *with* ▪ The population increase *coincided with* rapid industrial growth. ▪ The parade is scheduled to *coincide with* the city's 200th birthday.
2 : to agree with something exactly **:** to be the same as some-

thing else ▪ The goals of the business partners *coincide*. — often + *with* ▪ Her job *coincided* well *with* her career goals.

co·in·ci·dence /koʊˈɪnsədəns/ *noun, pl* **-denc·es**
1 : a situation in which events happen at the same time in a way that is not planned or expected [*noncount*] It was mere/pure/sheer *coincidence* that brought them together so far from Chicago. ▪ ***By coincidence***, every man in the room was named Fred. ▪ Our meeting happened *by coincidence*. [=*by chance*] [*count*] "I'm going to Boston this weekend." "What a *coincidence*! I am too." ▪ It was no *coincidence* that he quit his job at the bank a day after the robbery. ▪ a series of strange *coincidences* ▪ By a fortunate/happy *coincidence*, we arrived at the theater at the same time.
2 [*singular*] *formal* **:** the occurrence of two or more things at the same time ▪ Scientists have no explanation for the *coincidence* of these phenomena.
3 [*singular*] *formal* **:** the state of two or more things being the same — often + *of* ▪ There is a *coincidence of* interests between the companies. [=the companies share the same interests]

co·in·ci·dent /koʊˈɪnsədənt/ *adj, formal* **:** happening at the same time ▪ *coincident* events — usually + *with* ▪ Animal hibernation is *coincident with* the approach of winter.

co·in·ci·den·tal /koʊˌɪnsəˈdɛntl/ *adj* [*more* ~; *most* ~] **:** happening because of a coincidence **:** not planned ▪ The fact that he and his boss went to the same college was purely/entirely/completely *coincidental*. ▪ a *coincidental* meeting
– co·in·ci·den·tal·ly *adv* ▪ Not *coincidentally*, they were both graduates of the same college.

co·i·tus /ˈkowətəs/ *noun* [*noncount*] *technical* **:** SEXUAL INTERCOURSE
– co·i·tal /ˈkowətəl/ *adj*

co·jo·nes /kəˈhoʊˌneɪs/ *noun* [*plural*] *US slang*
1 : boldness or courage needed to do something ▪ You don't have the/enough *cojones* [=*guts, nerve*] to fight me.
2 : a man's testicles ▪ threatened to kick him in the *cojones*

[1]coke /ˈkoʊk/ *noun* [*noncount*] **:** a black material made from coal that is used as fuel for heating — compare [2]COKE

[2]coke *noun* [*noncount*] *informal* **:** COCAINE ▪ He had a great career before he started snorting/using/taking *coke*. — compare [1]COKE

Coke /ˈkoʊk/ *trademark* — used for a cola drink

coke·head /ˈkoʊkˌhɛd/ *noun, pl* **-heads** [*count*] *informal* **:** a person who uses cocaine as an illegal drug **:** a cocaine addict

col. *abbr* column

Col. *abbr* colonel

co·la /ˈkoʊlə/ *noun, pl* **-las** [*count, noncount*] **:** a sweet brown drink that contains many bubbles ▪ a glass of *cola*

col·an·der /ˈkɑːləndɚ/ *noun, pl* **-ders** [*count*] **:** a bowl that has many small holes and that is used for washing or draining food — see picture at KITCHEN

[1]cold /ˈkoʊld/ *adj* **cold·er; -est**
1 : having a very low temperature ▪ The water was too *cold* for swimming. ▪ The weather has been unusually *cold* this spring. ▪ a country with a *cold* climate ▪ It was a long, *cold* winter. ▪ It's *cold* outside, but the wind makes it feel even *colder*. ▪ It's bitterly/freezing *cold* out there! ▪ a *cold*, rainy day ▪ metal that is *cold* to the touch ▪ Her hands were icy *cold*. = They were as *cold* as ice.
2 : having a feeling of low body heat ▪ Are you *cold*? I could turn up the temperature if you'd like.
3 a *of food* **:** not heated ▪ a bowl of *cold* cereal ▪ He ate *cold* pizza for breakfast. ▪ We were happy to eat a hot meal rather than *cold* sandwiches. ▪ *cold* meats **b** *of drinks* **:** served at a very low temperature or with ice ▪ They're serving coffee, tea, and *cold* drinks. ▪ a *cold* glass of milk ▪ a *cold* beer
4 : not appealing or pleasant **:** causing a cold or unhappy feeling ▪ the *cold* gray sky ▪ the harsh *cold* lights of the hospital
5 : not friendly or emotional **:** lacking emotional warmth ▪ Why is he so *cold* and distant toward me? ▪ She gave me a *cold* stare and turned away. ▪ I got a *cold* reception when I came home.
6 : not changed or affected by personal feelings or emotions ▪ Like them or not, these are the *cold* facts! ▪ It's time they took a *cold*, hard look at the situation.
7 : learned or memorized exactly — used with *have* ▪ Keep repeating the lines until you *have* them (down) *cold*. [=until you have memorized them perfectly]
8 : unconscious or sleeping very deeply ▪ He passed out *cold*. — usually used in the phrase ***out cold*** ▪ She was *out cold* by eight o'clock. — see also *knock cold* at [1]KNOCK
9 : not fresh or strong **:** no longer easy to follow ▪ The dogs picked up a *cold* scent. ▪ The police had been hot on the trail of the escaped prisoners, but then the trail went *cold*.
10 : not close to finding something or solving a puzzle — used especially in children's games ▪ You're getting warmer! You're getting hot! Oh, now you're getting *colder*!
11 : not having success or good luck ▪ The team was hot in the first half, but their shooting turned *cold* in the second half. [=they missed a lot of shots in the second half]
blow hot and cold see [1]BLOW
cast a cold eye on see [1]EYE
in cold blood see BLOOD
in the cold light of day **:** in the day when things can be seen clearly rather than at night ▪ The house that had looked so sinister at night seemed much less frightening *in the cold light of day*. — sometimes used figuratively ▪ She forced me to look at myself *in the cold light of day*, and I didn't like what I saw.
leave you cold ✧ Something that *leaves you cold* does not interest or excite you. ▪ His movies *leave me cold*.
make someone's blood run cold see BLOOD
pour/throw cold water on see WATER
– cold·ly *adv* ▪ "Your application has been denied," he said *coldly*. ▪ She looked at me *coldly* and turned away. **– cold·ness** *noun* [*noncount*] ▪ the icy *coldness* of winter ▪ Why does he treat me with such *coldness* and reserve?

[2]cold *noun, pl* **colds**
1 [*noncount*] **:** a cold condition ▪ I mind *cold* more than heat. ▪ They died of exposure to *cold*. ▪ She was shivering with *cold*. [=because she was cold]
2 ***the cold*** **:** cold weather ▪ *The cold* really sets in around late November and doesn't let up until April. ▪ I stood there shivering in *the cold*. ▪ He waited outside for her in *the* bitter *cold*. ▪ Come in out of *the cold*.
3 [*count*] **:** a common illness that affects the nose, throat, and eyes and that usually causes coughing, sneezing, etc. ▪ It's not the flu, it's just a *cold*. ▪ He got/caught a *cold*. = He came down with a *cold*. = (*Brit*) He went down with a *cold*. ▪ the ***common cold*** — often used before another noun ▪ the *cold* virus ▪ *cold* symptoms/remedies — see also HEAD COLD
blue with cold, blue from the cold see [1]BLUE
come in from the cold **:** to become part of a group or of normal society again after you have been outside it ▪ a former spy who has *come in from the cold*
leave (someone) out in the cold **:** to leave (someone) in a bad position **:** to not give (someone) the rights or advantages that are given to others ▪ The changes benefit management but *leave the workers out in the cold*.

[3]cold *adv*
1 *chiefly US* **a :** in a very clear, complete, and definite way ▪ She turned their offer down *cold*. [=*flat*] **b :** in a sudden way ▪ He was telling me a story but stopped *cold* [=*abruptly*] when the door opened.
2 : without practicing or preparing before doing something ▪ She was asked to perform the song *cold*.

cold–blood·ed /ˈkoʊldˈblʌdəd/ *adj*
1 [*more* ~; *most* ~] **:** showing no sympathy or mercy ▪ *cold-blooded* [=*ruthless*] murderers **:** done in a planned way without emotion ▪ a *cold-blooded* killing
2 [*more* ~; *most* ~] **:** based on facts **:** not affected by emotions ▪ A *cold-blooded* [=*cold-eyed, dispassionate*] assessment of the situation showed that we had to take harsh measures.
3 *biology* **:** having cold blood **:** having a body temperature that is similar to the temperature of the environment ▪ Reptiles are *cold-blooded*. — compare WARM-BLOODED
– cold–blood·ed·ly *adv* **– cold–blood·ed·ness** *noun* [*noncount*]

cold call *noun, pl* **~ calls** [*count*] **:** a telephone call made by a business to try to sell something ✧ *Cold calls* are made to people who have not been contacted before and have not asked to be called.
– cold–call *verb* **-calls; -called; -call·ing** [+ *obj*] ▪ I *cold-called* the people on the list.

cold cash *noun* [*noncount*] **:** money that a person has and can use immediately ▪ He paid $500 for it in *cold cash*. [=in cash and not with a check or credit card]

cold·cock /ˈkoʊldˈkɑːk/ *verb* **-cocks; -cocked; -cock·ing** [+ *obj*] *US, informal* **:** to hit (someone) very hard **:** to knock out (someone) with a hard punch ▪ He got *coldcocked* by some guy in a bar.

cold comfort *noun* [*noncount*] **:** something that is good for a situation but does not make someone happy because the whole situation is still bad ▪ The good news about the economy is *cold comfort* to people who have lost their jobs.

cold cream *noun [noncount]* **:** a cream that people use to clean the face or soften the skin ▪ She uses *cold cream* to remove her eye makeup.

cold cuts *noun [plural] chiefly US* **:** cold cooked meats (such as turkey, roast beef, or ham) that have been cut into thin slices

cold–eyed /ˈkouldˈaɪd/ *adj [more ~; most ~]*
1 : not affected by emotions ▪ Unlike her sentimental sister, she has a *cold-eyed* [=*cold-blooded, dispassionate*] view of reality. ▪ a *cold-eyed* analysis of the data
2 : having a cold or unfriendly appearance ▪ a *cold-eyed* businessman

cold feet *noun [plural]* **:** a feeling of worry or doubt that is strong enough to stop you from doing something that you planned to do ▪ He was going to ask her to marry him, but he got *cold feet* and couldn't do it.

cold fish *noun, pl* **~ fish** *[count]* **:** a cold and unfriendly person ▪ She's a lovely person, but her husband's a bit of a *cold fish*.

cold frame *noun, pl* **~ frames** *[count]* **:** a small wooden or metal frame covered with glass or plastic that is used for growing and protecting plants in cold weather

cold front *noun, pl* **~ fronts** *[count]* **:** the front edge of a moving mass of cold air ▪ A *cold front* will move in tomorrow, bringing with it clear skies. — compare WARM FRONT

cold·heart·ed /ˈkouldˈhɑɚtəd/ *adj [or more ~; most ~]* **:** lacking kindness, sympathy, or sensitivity ▪ She's a beautiful but *coldhearted* [=*heartless*] woman. ▪ a *coldhearted* criminal ▪ People are criticizing the government's *coldhearted* plans to stop funding programs for the poor. ▪ a *coldhearted* refusal — opposite WARMHEARTED
– cold·heart·ed·ly *adv* **– cold·heart·ed·ness** *noun [noncount]*

cold shoulder *noun*
the cold shoulder **:** cold and unfriendly treatment from someone who knows you ▪ He ***got the cold shoulder*** from his former boss when he saw him at a restaurant. ▪ Most of the other professors ***gave him the cold shoulder***.
– cold–shoul·der *verb* **-ders; -dered; -der·ing** *[+ obj]* ▪ He was *cold-shouldered* by his former boss.

cold sore *noun, pl* **~ sores** *[count]* **:** a small sore area around or inside the mouth that is caused by a virus

cold storage *noun [noncount]* **:** the state of being kept in a cold place for later use ▪ food that has been taken out of *cold storage* — often used figuratively ▪ They put/kept the project ***in cold storage*** until funds were obtained for it.

cold sweat *noun [singular]* **:** a condition in which someone is sweating and feeling cold at the same time because of fear, illness, etc. ▪ The patient feels faint and is in a *cold sweat*. ▪ I break out in a *cold sweat* when I think about asking my boss for a pay raise.

cold turkey *noun [noncount] informal* **:** the act of stopping a bad habit (such as taking drugs) in a sudden and complete way ▪ I tried lots of ways to stop smoking, even *cold turkey*.
– cold turkey *adv* ▪ Instead of trying to quit *cold turkey*, why don't you slowly decrease the amount that you smoke? ▪ Some people have to ***go cold turkey*** to stop.

cold war *noun, pl* **~ wars**
1 ***the Cold War*** **:** the nonviolent conflict between the U.S. and the former U.S.S.R. after 1945 ▪ the era of *the Cold War*
2 *[count]* **:** a conflict or dispute between two groups that does not involve actual fighting ▪ the *cold war* between the party's more liberal and conservative members
– cold–war *or* **Cold–War** *adj, always used before a noun* ▪ *cold-war* diplomacy ▪ the *Cold-War* era

cold warrior *noun, pl* **~ -riors** *[count]* **:** a person who supported or participated in the Cold War between the U.S. and the U.S.S.R.

cole·slaw /ˈkoulˌslɑː/ *noun [noncount]* **:** a salad made with chopped raw cabbage

col·ic /ˈkɑːlɪk/ *noun [noncount]*
1 : a sharp sudden pain in the stomach
2 : a physical condition in which a baby is very uncomfortable and cries for long periods of time
– col·icky /ˈkɑːlɪki/ *adj [more ~; most ~]* ▪ a *colicky* baby

col·i·se·um /ˌkɑːləˈsiːjəm/ *noun, pl* **-ums** *[count] chiefly US* **:** a large stadium or building for sports or entertainment

co·li·tis /kouˈlaɪtəs/ *noun [noncount] medical* **:** an illness that causes pain and swelling in the colon

col·lab·o·rate /kəˈlæbəˌreɪt/ *verb* **-rates; -rat·ed; -rat·ing** *[no obj]*
1 : to work with another person or group in order to achieve or do something ▪ The two companies agreed to *collaborate*. — often + *on* or *in* ▪ They *collaborated on* a book about dogs. ▪ The pair *collaborated* with each other *on* the film. ▪ Several doctors *collaborated in* the project. — sometimes followed by *to + verb* ▪ They *collaborated to write* a book.
2 *disapproving* **:** to give help to an enemy who has invaded your country during a war ▪ He was suspected of *collaborating* with the occupying army.
– col·lab·o·ra·tion /kəˌlæbəˈreɪʃən/ *noun, pl* **-tions** *[count]* The book is the product of a *collaboration* between two writers. = The book is a *collaboration* between two writers. ▪ an artistic *collaboration* *[noncount]* The writers worked in *collaboration* to produce the book. ▪ He worked in close *collaboration* with French scientists. ▪ He was accused of *collaboration* with the enemy.

col·lab·o·ra·tive /kəˈlæbərətɪv/ *adj* **:** involving or done by two or more people or groups working together to achieve or do something ▪ a *collaborative* project/study/effort ▪ *collaborative* research
– col·lab·o·ra·tive·ly *adv* ▪ They worked *collaboratively* on the project.

col·lab·o·ra·tor /kəˈlæbəˌreɪtɚ/ *noun, pl* **-tors** *[count]*
1 : a person who works with another person or group in order to achieve or do something ▪ She thanked her *collaborators* on the project.
2 : a person who helps an enemy who has invaded his or her country during a war ▪ He was accused of being a Nazi *collaborator*. [=someone who collaborated with the Nazis in World War II]

col·lage /kəˈlɑːʒ/ *noun, pl* **-lag·es**
1 a *[count]* **:** a work of art that is made by attaching pieces of different materials (such as paper, cloth, or wood) to a flat surface ▪ We made *collages* in art class. **b** *[noncount]* **:** the art or method of making collages ▪ an artist known for her use of *collage*
2 *[count]* **:** a collection of different things ▪ The album is a *collage* of several musical styles.

col·la·gen /ˈkɑːləʤən/ *noun [noncount]* **:** a substance that occurs naturally in the bodies of people and animals and is often put into creams and other products that are sold to make a person's skin smoother and less wrinkled

[1]**col·lapse** /kəˈlæps/ *verb* **-laps·es; -lapsed; -laps·ing**
1 *[no obj]* **:** to break apart and fall down suddenly ▪ The bridge/building *collapsed*. ▪ The roof *collapsed* under a heavy load of snow. ▪ The chair he was sitting in *collapsed*.
2 *[no obj]* **a :** to fall down or become unconscious because you are sick or exhausted ▪ He *collapsed* on stage during the performance and had to be rushed to the hospital. **b :** to completely relax the muscles of your body because you are very tired, upset, etc. ▪ She came home from work and *collapsed* on the sofa. ▪ The crying child ran to his mother and *collapsed* in her arms.
3 *[no obj]* **a :** to fail or stop working suddenly **:** to break down completely ▪ The civilization *collapsed* for reasons that are still unknown. ▪ He warned that such measures could cause the economy to *collapse*. ▪ Negotiations have completely *collapsed*. **b :** to lose almost all worth **:** to become much less valuable ▪ The country's currency *collapsed*. ▪ Oil prices had *collapsed*.
4 *[no obj] medical* **:** to become flat and empty ▪ a blood vessel that *collapsed* ▪ a *collapsed* lung
5 : to fold together *[no obj]* The stroller *collapses* easily. *[+ obj]* You can *collapse* the stroller easily and store it in the trunk of your car.
– col·laps·ible /kəˈlæpsəbəl/ *adj* ▪ a *collapsible* chair/table/stroller

[2]**collapse** *noun, pl* **-lapses**
1 : a situation or occurrence in which something (such as a bridge, building, etc.) suddenly breaks apart and falls down *[count]* — usually singular ▪ a fatal bridge *collapse* ▪ The earthquake caused the *collapse* of several homes. ▪ the *collapse* of the roof *[noncount]* The structure is in danger of *collapse*.
2 : a situation or occurrence in which someone suddenly falls down or becomes unconscious because of being sick or exhausted *[count]* — usually singular ▪ After her *collapse* she was rushed to the hospital. ▪ He suffered a *collapse* at work. *[noncount]* She was on the verge of *collapse*.

3 : a situation or occurrence in which something (such as a system or organization) suddenly fails : a complete failure or breakdown [*count*] — usually singular • the *collapse* of the Soviet Union • the *collapse* of negotiations • She moved to the city after the *collapse* of her marriage. [*noncount*] The country has endured civil war and economic *collapse*.
4 : a situation or occurrence in which something loses almost all of its worth or value [*noncount*] The country's currency is in danger of *collapse*. [*count*] — usually singular • a *collapse* in the value of their currency

[1]**col·lar** /ˈkɑːlɚ/ *noun, pl* **-lars** [*count*]
1 : a part of a piece of clothing that fits around a person's neck and is usually folded down • He wore a shirt with a tight-fitting *collar*. • She grabbed me by the *collar*. • He ***loosened his collar***. [=unbuttoned the top button of his shirt] — see color picture on page C14; see also BLUE-COLLAR, PINK-COLLAR, WHITE-COLLAR
2 : a band of leather, plastic, etc., worn around an animal's neck • I bought a new *collar* for the dog. — see also FLEA COLLAR
3 *technical* : a ring or band used to hold something (such as a pipe or a part of a machine) in place
hot under the collar see [1]HOT

[2]**collar** *verb* **-lars; -lared; -lar·ing** [+ *obj*] *informal*
1 : to catch or arrest (someone) • The police *collared* the guy a few blocks from the scene.
2 : to stop (someone) in order to talk : to force (someone) to have a conversation • He *collared* me on my way out the door.

col·lar·bone /ˈkɑːlɚˌboʊn/ *noun, pl* **-bones** [*count*] : a bone that connects the shoulder to the base of the neck — called also *clavicle*; see picture at HUMAN

col·lard greens /ˈkɑːlɚd-/ *noun* [*plural*] *US* : the dark green leaves of a plant that is grown especially in the southern U.S. ✧ Collard greens are cooked and eaten as a vegetable. — see color picture on page C4

col·late /kəˈleɪt, ˈkoʊˌleɪt/ *verb* **-lates; -lat·ed; -lat·ing** [+ *obj*]
1 : to gather together information from different sources in order to study it carefully • They are still *collating* the data.
2 : to arrange (sheets of paper) in the correct order • The photocopier will *collate* the pages of the report.
– **col·la·tion** /kəˈleɪʃən/ *noun, pl* **-tions** [*count, noncount*]

[1]**col·lat·er·al** /kəˈlætərəl/ *noun* [*noncount*] : something that you promise to give someone if you cannot pay back a loan • She put up her house as *collateral* for the loan. [=she agreed that she would give up her house if she did not repay the loan]

[2]**collateral** *adj, formal* : related but not in a direct or close way • *collateral* relatives • the *collateral* effects of the government's policies

collateral damage *noun* [*noncount*] : deaths, injuries, and damage to the property of people who are not in the military that happens as a result of the fighting in a war

col·league /ˈkɑːˌliːg/ *noun, pl* **-leagues** [*count*] *somewhat formal* : a person who works with you : a fellow worker • A *colleague* of mine will be speaking at the conference.

[1]**col·lect** /kəˈlɛkt/ *verb* **-lects; -lect·ed; -lect·ing**
1 [+ *obj*] **a** : to get (things) from different places and bring them together • They hope to *collect* over 1,000 signatures on the petition. • He *collected* stories from all over the world. • They *collected* information about the community. • We *collected* soil samples from several areas on the site. **b** : to get (one or more things) from a place • We *collected* our baggage from/at the baggage claim at the airport. • I left my suit at the cleaners and I have to *collect* it today.
2 : to get (similar things) and bring them together as a hobby [+ *obj*] He *collects* postage stamps. • She enjoys *collecting* antique teapots. [*no obj*] He has an impressive stamp collection, though he has been *collecting* for only a few years.
3 [+ *obj*] : to get control of (your thoughts, emotions, etc.) • I took a minute to *collect* my thoughts. • She stopped briefly to *collect* [=*calm*] herself.
4 **a** [+ *obj*] : to ask for and get (money that someone owes you) • I *collected* the rent from the tenants. • The city *collects* property taxes. **b** : to be given or paid (money) [+ *obj*] She *collects* social security benefits. [*no obj*] — + *on* • He is *collecting on* his disability insurance.
5 : to ask people to give (money or other things) to a group that helps people, a political candidate, etc. [+ *obj*] She has begun *collecting* contributions from supporters. — often + *for* • We *collected* $5,000 *for* the hospital. [*no obj*] I am *collecting for* the local women's shelter.
6 : to come together in a large amount as time passes [*no obj*] Junk started *collecting* in the attic soon after they moved in. • Dust had *collected* on the dashboard. • Snow was *collecting* on the driveway. [+ *obj*] Garbage can *collect* germs. — see also *collect dust* at [1]DUST
7 [+ *obj*] : to go somewhere in order to get (someone you will bring or take to another place) • She *collected* [=*picked up*] the children after school. • I'm going to *collect* him from the airport.
collect up [*phrasal verb*] ***collect up (something)*** or ***collect (something) up*** *Brit* : to gather (things) together • I *collected up* [=*picked up*] the dishes and brought them to the kitchen. • The children *collected* their toys *up* and put them away.

[2]**collect** *adj, US, of a telephone call* : paid for by the person who is receiving the call • a *collect* phone call • The operator asked me if I would accept a *collect* call from John Smith.
– **collect** *adv* • You can call me *collect*. [=you can call me and reverse the charges]

col·lect·ed /kəˈlɛktəd/ *adj*
1 *always used before a noun* : brought together in a group • the *collected* works of Shakespeare
2 *not used before a noun* [*more* ~; *most* ~] : calm and in control of your emotions • She seemed completely cool, calm, and *collected* during her speech.

[1]**col·lect·ible** *or chiefly Brit* **col·lect·able** /kəˈlɛktəbəl/ *adj* [*more* ~; *most* ~] : good for a collection : considered valuable by collectors • The shop sells antiques and various *collectible* items. • That kind of toy is very *collectible* [=popular with collectors] right now.

[2]**collectible** *or chiefly Brit* **collectable** *noun, pl* **-ibles** [*count*] : something that is considered valuable by collectors and usually kept as part of a group of similar things : a collectible thing • She displays her *collectibles* in a glass case.

col·lec·tion /kəˈlɛkʃən/ *noun, pl* **-tions**
1 : the act or process of getting things from different places and bringing them together [*noncount*] a system of tax *collection* • The technology makes data *collection* easier. [*count*] There will be a trash *collection* this week.
2 [*count*] : a group of interesting or beautiful objects brought together in order to show or study them or as a hobby • The museum's *collection* is one of the best in the country. • his baseball card *collection* — often + *of* • He has a huge *collection of* CDs. • She has an impressive *collection of* modern art. • He has quite a *collection of* exercise equipment. — sometimes used figuratively • She has acquired quite a *collection of* friends/contacts/experiences/stories.
3 [*count*] : a request for money in order to help people or to pay for something important • We ***took up a collection*** for the school renovations.; *also* : the money collected in this way • Ten percent of the *collection* goes to the city's shelters for homeless people. — often used before another noun • a *collection* plate/box
4 [*count*] : a group of clothes that a fashion designer has created • a fashion show featuring his spring *collection*
5 [*count*] : a group of different writings that are brought together in one book • You should consider publishing these stories as a *collection*. — often + *of* • I have a *collection of* her short stories.

[1]**col·lec·tive** /kəˈlɛktɪv/ *adj, always used before a noun* : shared or done by a group of people : involving all members of a group • We made a *collective* decision to go on strike. • The incident became part of our *collective* memory. • a *collective* effort • the *collective* wisdom of generations • a ***collective noun*** [=a noun like "team" or "flock" that refers to a group of people or things]
– **col·lec·tive·ly** *adv* • the group of languages known *collectively* as Romance languages

[2]**collective** *noun, pl* **-tives** [*count*] : a business or organization that is owned by the people who work there; *also* : the people who own such a business or organization

collective bargaining *noun* [*noncount*] : talks between an employer and the leaders of a union about how much a group of workers will be paid, how many hours they will work, etc. • The next round of *collective bargaining* is scheduled for September. — often used before another noun • the *collective bargaining* process • *collective bargaining* talks • a *collective bargaining* agreement

collective farm *noun, pl* ~ **farms** [*count*] : a farm that is run by several farmers and controlled by the government

col·lec·tiv·ism /kəˈlɛktɪˌvɪzəm/ *noun* [*noncount*] : a politi-

cal or economic system in which the government owns businesses, land, etc.
– **col·lec·tiv·ist** /kəˈlɛktɪvɪst/ *adj* ▪ *collectivist* ideology

collective noun *noun, pl* ~ **nouns** [*count*] *technical* : a word (such as *family* or *herd*) that names a group of people or things

col·lec·tor /kəˈlɛktɚ/ *noun, pl* **-tors** [*count*]
1 : a person who collects certain things as a hobby ▪ He is an avid stamp *collector.* ▪ The painting was purchased by a private *collector.*
2 : a person whose job is to collect something (such as trash or money) ▪ The trash *collectors* came early today. ▪ a tax/bill/debt *collector*

collector's item *noun, pl* ~ **items** [*count*] : an object that people want because it is rare or valuable ▪ Her paintings have become *collector's items.*

col·lege /ˈkɑːlɪʤ/ *noun, pl* **-leg·es**
1 : a school in the U.S. that you go to after high school : a school that offers courses leading to a degree (such as a bachelor's degree or an associate's degree) [*count*] She teaches art at a local *college.* ▪ He graduated from one of the country's best *colleges.* ▪ She attended a business *college.* [*noncount*] He attended *college* for several years, but didn't graduate. ▪ She dropped out of *college.* ▪ Where did you go to *college*? [=what college did you attend?] ▪ I went to Mount Holyoke *College.* ▪ When I was a junior ***in college,*** I spent a semester in Spain. — often used before another noun ▪ *college* students/courses/professors ▪ He is a *college* graduate. ▪ She was the first in her family to get a *college* education. ▪ a *college* campus ▪ *college* athletic programs — compare UNIVERSITY; see also COMMUNITY COLLEGE, JUNIOR COLLEGE, STATE COLLEGE
2 [*count*] : a part of an American university that offers courses in a specified subject — often + *of* ▪ He attended the university's *college of* dentistry/engineering/medicine.
3 a : a school in Britain that offers advanced training in a specified subject [*count*] an arts *college* ▪ the Edinburgh *College* of Art ▪ the London *College* of Fashion [*noncount*] She is attending fashion *college.* **b** [*count*] : a separate part of a large British university where students live and take courses ▪ Balliol *College* at Oxford
4 [*count*] *formal* : an organized group of people who have similar jobs or interests ▪ She is a member of the American *College* of Cardiology. ▪ the *college* of cardinals — see also ELECTORAL COLLEGE

col·le·giate /kəˈliːʤət/ *adj* : of or relating to a college or its students ▪ *collegiate* athletics

col·lide /kəˈlaɪd/ *verb* **-lides; -lid·ed; -lid·ing** [*no obj*]
1 : to hit something or each other with strong force : to crash together or to crash into something ▪ Two football players *collided* on the field. — often + *with* ▪ Two football players *collided with* each other on the field. ▪ The car *collided with* a truck/tree.
2 — used of situations in which people or groups disagree or are very different from each other ▪ Their ideas for the company often *collide.* [=*clash*] ▪ Two worlds *collide* in a new novel about an American family living in Japan. — often + *with* ▪ The candidate's opinions sometimes *collided with* his party's agenda.

col·lie /ˈkɑːli/ *noun, pl* **-lies** [*count*] : a large type of dog with long hair and a long pointed nose

col·lier /ˈkɑːljɚ/ *noun, pl* **-liers** [*count*] *chiefly Brit, old-fashioned* : a coal miner

col·liery /ˈkɑːljəri/ *noun, pl* **-lier·ies** [*count*] *chiefly Brit* : a coal mine and the buildings that are near it

col·li·sion /kəˈlɪʒən/ *noun, pl* **-sions** [*count*] : an act of colliding: such as **a** : a crash in which two or more things or people hit each other ▪ The car was destroyed in the *collision.* ▪ There was nothing I could do to avoid a ***head-on collision.*** [=a crash of two vehicles that are moving directly toward each other] — often + *between* or *with* ▪ He was injured in a *collision between* a car and an SUV. ▪ She hurt her shoulder in a *collision with* another player. **b** : a situation in which people or groups disagree : a clash or conflict — often + *between* ▪ He reported on the latest *collision between* the two leaders.

collision course *noun*
on a collision course ◇ Two people or things that are *on a collision course* are moving and will crash into each other if one of them doesn't change direction. ▪ The two airplanes were *on a collision course.* ▪ The comet was *on a collision course* with the planet. — often used figuratively ▪ The decision put us *on a collision course* with economic disaster.

col·lo·cate /ˈkɑːləˌkeɪt/ *verb* **-cates; -cat·ed; -cat·ing** [*no obj*] *technical* : to appear often with another word ▪ The word "college" *collocates* with "student."

col·lo·ca·tion /ˌkɑːləˈkeɪʃən/ *noun, pl* **-tions**
1 [*noncount*] : use of certain words together ▪ patterns of *collocation*
2 [*count*] : a particular combination of words ▪ a common *collocation*

col·lo·qui·al /kəˈloʊkwijəl/ *adj* [*more* ~; *most* ~]
1 : used when people are speaking in an informal way ▪ a *colloquial* word/expression
2 : using an informal style ▪ a *colloquial* writer
– **col·lo·qui·al·ly** *adv* ▪ The phrase is used *colloquially* but not in writing. ▪ The drink is known *colloquially* as a "brown cow."

col·lo·qui·al·ism /kəˈloʊkwijəˌlɪzəm/ *noun, pl* **-isms** [*count*] : a word or phrase that is used mostly in informal speech : a colloquial expression ▪ His English is very good, but he has trouble understanding certain *colloquialisms.*

col·lude /kəˈluːd/ *verb* **-ludes; -lud·ed; -lud·ing** [*no obj*] : to work with others secretly especially in order to do something illegal or dishonest ▪ The two companies had *colluded* to fix prices. — often + *in* or *with* ▪ She *colluded in* misleading the public. ▪ He is accused of *colluding with* criminals.

col·lu·sion /kəˈluːʒən/ *noun* [*noncount*] : secret cooperation for an illegal or dishonest purpose ▪ The company was acting ***in collusion with*** manufacturers to inflate prices. — often + *between* ▪ She uncovered *collusion between* city officials and certain local businesses.

co·logne /kəˈloʊn/ *noun, pl* **-lognes** : a liquid that has a light, pleasant smell and that people put on their skin : a light kind of perfume that does not have a strong smell [*noncount*] She put on some *cologne* and combed her hair. ▪ a TV commercial for men's *cologne* [*count*] TV commercials for men's *colognes* — called also *eau de cologne*

[1]**co·lon** /ˈkoʊlən/ *noun, pl* **-lons** [*count*] *medical* : the main part of the large intestine ▪ He died of *colon* cancer. — see picture at HUMAN — compare [2]COLON

[2]**colon** *noun, pl* **-lons** [*count*] : the punctuation mark : used in writing and printing to direct attention to what follows it (such as a list, explanation, or quotation) — compare [1]COLON

col·o·nel /ˈkɚnl̩/ *noun, pl* **-nels** [*count*] : an officer of high rank in the army, air force, or marines : a military officer who ranks above a major ▪ He retired as a *colonel* in the air force.

[1]**co·lo·nial** /kəˈloʊnijəl/ *adj*
1 a : of or relating to a colony ▪ *colonial* possessions/administration ▪ a *colonial* city **b** : owning or made up of colonies ▪ The country was a *colonial* power. ▪ a *colonial* nation and its *colonial* empire
2 *or* ***Colonial*** : of or relating to the original 13 colonies forming the United States ▪ The book describes life in *Colonial* America. ▪ an example of *colonial* architecture/furniture ▪ The port had been very important in *colonial* times.
3 : in a style that was popular in the U.S. during the American colonial period (before 1776) ▪ They live in a *colonial* (style) house.

[2]**colonial** *noun, pl* **-nials** [*count*]
1 *or* ***Colonial*** : a two-story house built in a style that was first popular in the U.S. during the American colonial period (before 1776) ▪ They bought a *Colonial* on a quiet street.
2 : a person who is part of a colony : COLONIST ▪ increasing tension between *colonials* and the mother country

co·lo·nial·ism /kəˈloʊnijəˌlɪzəm/ *noun* [*noncount*] : control by one country over another area and its people
– **co·lo·nial·ist** /kəˈloʊnijəlɪst/ *noun, pl* **-ists** [*count*]
– **colonialist** *adj* ▪ the *colonialist* past

col·o·nist /ˈkɑːlənɪst/ *noun, pl* **-nists** [*count*]
1 : a person who lives in a colony
2 : a person who helps to create a colony ▪ British *colonists* settled the area in the 18th century.

col·o·nize *also Brit* **col·o·nise** /ˈkɑːləˌnaɪz/ *verb* **-niz·es; -nized; -niz·ing** [+ *obj*]
1 : to create a colony in or on (a place) : to take control of (an area) and send people to live there ▪ England *colonized* Australia. ▪ The area was *colonized* in the 18th century.
2 : to move into and live in (a place) as a new type of plant or animal ▪ Weeds quickly *colonized* the field. ▪ The island had been *colonized* by plants and animals.
– **col·o·ni·za·tion** *also Brit* **col·o·ni·sa·tion** /ˌkɑːlənə-

ˈzeɪʃən, *Brit* ˌkɒləˌnaɪˈzeɪʃən/ *noun* [*noncount*] • European *colonization* of Asia – **col•o•niz•er** *also Brit* **col•o•nis•er** *noun, pl* **-ers** [*count*] • Certain plants are prolific *colonizers.* • the influence of Dutch and French *colonizers*

col•on•nade /ˌkɑːləˈneɪd/ *noun, pl* **-nades** [*count*] **:** a row of columns usually holding up a roof • A *colonnade* surrounds the courtyard.

co•lo•nos•co•py /ˌkoʊləˈnɑːskəpi/ *noun, pl* **-pies** [*count*] *medical* **:** a medical procedure in which a special tube-shaped instrument is used to take pictures of the inside of someone's colon

col•o•ny /ˈkɑːləni/ *noun, pl* **-nies** [*count*]
1 a : an area that is controlled by or belongs to a country and is usually far away from it • Massachusetts was one of the original 13 British *colonies* that later became the United States. • a former French *colony* in Africa **b :** a group of people sent by a country to live in such a colony • a *colony* of settlers
2 : a group of plants or animals living or growing in one place • an ant *colony* • a *colony* of bacteria
3 : a group of people who are similar in some way and who live in a certain area • an artist *colony* • a leper *colony*; *also* **:** the land or buildings used by such a group

[1]**col•or** (*US*) *or Brit* **col•our** /ˈkʌlɚ/ *noun, pl* **-ors**
1 : a quality such as red, blue, green, yellow, etc., that you see when you look at something [*count*] The *color* of blood is red. • What *color* are your eyes? • What *color* paint shall we use? • Blue and green are my favorite *colors.* • The pillows are all different *colors.* [*noncount*] The room needs more *color.* • In early summer the garden is full of *color.* • She added *color* to her outfit with a bright scarf. • The leaves are starting to ***change color.*** [=turn from green to orange, yellow, red, etc.] • His eyes were bluish-green ***in color.*** • She used red peppers in the salad ***for color.*** [=to make it more colorful] — see pictures of colors starting on page C1
2 : something used to give color to something **:** a pigment or dye [*count*] She's using a new lip/nail *color.* • The *color* bled when I washed the shirt. [*noncount*] a brand of hair *color*
3 [*noncount*] **a :** the use or combination of colors • a painter who is a master of *color* **b** — used to describe a photograph, televison picture, etc., that includes colors and that is not black and white • The book includes over 100 photographs ***in (full) color.*** [=not black and white] — often used before another noun • a *color* photograph • *color* printing/television — see also *in living color* at LIVING
4 [*noncount*] **:** the color of a person's skin as a mark of race • discrimination on the basis of sex or *color* ✧ A person ***of color*** is a person who is not white. • The book is about her experience as a woman *of color* in a mostly white community.
5 [*noncount*] **:** a pink or red tone in a person's face especially because of good health, excitement, or embarrassment • His *color* is not good. [=he looks ill] • She has some good *color* in her cheeks. • He could feel the *color* rising in his cheeks. [=he could feel himself blushing] • The ***color drained from her face.*** [=the blood left her face; she became very pale]
6 colors [*plural*] **:** something (such as a flag) that shows that someone or something belongs to a specific group • The ship sails under Swedish *colors.*
7 [*noncount*] **:** interest or excitement • Her comments added *color* to the broadcast. [=made the broadcast more enjoyable or entertaining] — see also LOCAL COLOR, OFF-COLOR
a horse of a different color see [1]HORSE
***show your true colors* :** to show what you are really like **:** to reveal your real nature or character • He seemed nice at first, but he *showed his true colors* during the crisis.
with flying colors see [1]FLYING

[2]**color** (*US*) *or Brit* **colour** *verb* **-ors; -ored; -or•ing**
1 [+ *obj*] **:** to give color to (something) **:** to change the color of (something) • We *colored* the water with red ink. • Does she *color* [=*dye*] her hair?
2 : to draw with crayons, markers, colored pencils, etc. **:** to fill in a shape or picture using markers, crayons, colored pencils, etc. [*no obj*] The children were busy *coloring* in their coloring books. [+ *obj*] My nephew *colored* a picture for me. • The child *colored* the sky blue and the sun yellow. — see also COLOR IN (below)
3 [+ *obj*] **:** to change (someone's ideas, opinion, attitude, etc.) in some way • He never lets rumors *color* [=*influence, affect*] his opinion of anyone. — often used as *(be) colored* • Her judgment *was colored* by reports of the student's behavioral problems. • His feelings about divorce *are colored* by his own experience as a child.
4 [*no obj*] *literary* **:** to become red in the face especially because of embarrassment • She *colors* [=*blushes*] easily. — often + *at* • She *colored at* the mention of his name.
color in [*phrasal verb*] ***color in (something) or color (something) in* :** to add color to (a shape or picture) by using markers, crayons, colored pencils etc. • She *colored in* the picture. — see also [2]COLOR 2 (above)

col•or•ant (*US*) *or Brit* **col•our•ant** /ˈkʌlərənt/ *noun, pl* **-ants** [*count, noncount*] **:** COLORING 2

col•or•a•tion (*chiefly US*) *or Brit* **col•our•a•tion** /ˌkʌləˈreɪʃən/ *noun*
1 [*noncount*] *biology* **:** the color or patterns of color on an animal or plant • the bird's brilliant *coloration* [=*coloring*] • the *coloration* of a flower
2 : the colors of an object (such as a piece of artwork or furniture) [*noncount*] the bright yellow *coloration* of the curtains [*count*] wine glasses with circle designs and blue and green *colorations*
3 : a quality or characteristic [*noncount*] the novel's political *coloration* [*count*] He attempted to give a religious *coloration* to the war.

col•or•a•tu•ra /ˌkʌlərəˈturə, *Brit* ˌkɒlərəˈtʊərə/ *noun, pl* **-ras**
1 [*noncount*] **:** a style of singing usually in opera that contains a lot of high notes sung very fast • a performance without much *coloratura*
2 [*count*] **:** a singer who is able to perform this type of music — often used before another noun • a *coloratura* soprano • *coloratura* roles

col•or–blind (*US*) *or Brit* **col•our–blind** /ˈkʌlɚˌblaɪnd/ *adj*
1 : unable to see the difference between certain colors • Many *color-blind* people cannot distinguish between red and green.
2 : treating people of different skin colors equally **:** not affected by racial prejudice • The company claims to be *color-blind.* • *color-blind* policies
– color blindness (*US*) *or Brit* **colour blindness** *noun* [*noncount*] • He has a common form of *color blindness.*

co•lo•rec•tal /ˌkoʊloʊˈrɛktəl/ *adj, always used before a noun, medical* **:** of or relating to the lower part of the large intestine **:** of or relating to the colon and the rectum • *colorectal* cancer

col•ored (*US*) *or Brit* **col•oured** /ˈkʌlɚd/ *adj*
1 : having color **:** not black or white • We decorated the Christmas tree with *colored* lights. • *colored* glass/pencils
2 : influenced by a person's feelings or prejudices • He gave a ***highly colored*** account of the events.
3 *old-fashioned + sometimes offensive* **a :** of a race other than white; *especially* **:** [1]BLACK 2 • a *colored* man/woman/child • *colored* people/folks **b :** of or relating to people who are not white • The town she grew up in had a *colored* church and a white church. [=a church attended by black people and a church attended by white people]

col•or•fast (*US*) *or Brit* **col•our•fast** /ˈkʌlɚˌfæst, *Brit* ˈkʌləˌfɑːst/ *adj* **:** able to keep the same color even if washed, placed in light, etc. • a *colorfast* carpet • *colorfast* printing ink

col•or•ful (*US*) *or Brit* **col•our•ful** /ˈkʌlɚfəl/ *adj* [*more* ~; *most* ~]
1 : having a bright color or a lot of different colors **:** full of color • I wore a *colorful* outfit. • the bird's *colorful* feathers
2 : interesting or exciting • He gave a *colorful* account of his travels. • She has a *colorful* [=*bright, cheerful*] personality. • He was a ***colorful character.*** [=a very unusual person]
3 ✧ If you use ***colorful language*** you use words that are usually considered rude or offensive. • He's been known to use some *colorful language* when he starts talking about politics.
– col•or•ful•ly (*US*) *or Brit* **col•our•ful•ly** /ˈkʌlɚfli/ *adv* • The room was *colorfully* decorated.

color guard (*US*) *or Brit* **colour guard** *noun* [*count*] **:** a person in uniform who holds a flag in a ceremony or parade

col•or•ing (*US*) *or Brit* **col•our•ing** /ˈkʌlərɪŋ/ *noun, pl* **-ings**
1 [*noncount*] **:** the act of adding colors to something (such as a picture in a coloring book) • Her favorite activities include playing with stuffed animals and *coloring.*
2 : something that produces color [*noncount*] Our product contains no artificial *coloring* or flavoring. • She added some blue ***food coloring*** to the icing. [*count*] artificial *colorings* • (*US*) a variety of hair *colorings* [=(*Brit*) *colourants*]
3 [*noncount*] **a :** the color of a person's skin and hair • This scarf will look great with your *coloring.* • He has very light

C

coloring. **b** : the color of an animal or plant ▪ a bird's bright *coloring* [=*coloration*]
4 [*noncount*] : the way color is used ▪ His paintings are notable for their bright *coloring*.

coloring book (*US*) *or Brit* **colouring book** *noun, pl* ~ **books** [*count*] : a book of pictures that you color in with crayons, markers, etc. ▪ I bought my son a new *coloring book*.

col·or·ist (*US*) *or Brit* **col·our·ist** /ˈkʌlərɪst/ *noun, pl* **-ists** [*count*]
1 : a painter who uses color in interesting and effective ways
2 : a person who dyes people's hair

col·or·less (*US*) *or Brit* **col·our·less** /ˈkʌlələs/ *adj*
1 : lacking color ▪ a *colorless* liquid/gas
2 [*more* ~; *most* ~] : dull or boring : not interesting ▪ *colorless* writing

color line *noun, pl* ~ **lines** [*singular*] *US* : a set of customs or laws that does not allow black people to do the same things or be in the same places as white people ▪ Jackie Robinson broke American baseball's *color line*. [=he was the first black man to play professional baseball with white players] — called also (*Brit*) *colour bar*

color scheme (*US*) *or Brit* **colour scheme** *noun, pl* ~ **schemes** [*count*] : a particular combination of colors ▪ They chose an unusual *color scheme* for the living room.

co·los·sal /kəˈlɑːsəl/ *adj* : very large or great ▪ a *colossal* [=*gigantic*] statue ▪ Their business partnership turned out to be a *colossal* [=*massive*] failure. ▪ The meeting was a *colossal* [=*huge, enormous*] waste of time.

col·os·se·um /ˌkɑːləˈsijəm/ *noun, pl* **-ums**
1 ***Colosseum*** [*singular*] : an outdoor arena built in Rome in the first century A.D.
2 [*count*] *chiefly US* : a large stadium or building for sports or entertainment : COLISEUM

co·los·sus /kəˈlɑːsəs/ *noun, pl* **-los·si** /-ˈlɑːˌsaɪ/ [*count*]
1 : a huge statue ▪ an ancient Egyptian *colossus*
2 : a very large or important person or thing ▪ The building is a *colossus* of steel and glass. ▪ a corporate *colossus*

colour *Brit spelling of* COLOR

colour supplement *noun, pl* ~ **-ments** [*count*] *Brit* : a magazine printed in color that is added to a newspaper usually on a Saturday or Sunday

colt /ˈkoʊlt/ *noun, pl* **colts** [*count*]
1 : a young male horse — compare FILLY, FOAL
2 *Brit* : a member of a sports team for young people

col·um·bine /ˈkɑːləmˌbaɪn/ *noun, pl* **-bines** [*count, noncount*] : a plant that has flowers with five petals that are thin and pointed

Co·lum·bus Day /kəˈlʌmbəs-/ *noun* [*singular*] : the second Monday in October observed as a legal holiday in many states of the U.S. in honor of the arrival of Christopher Columbus in the Bahamas in 1492

col·umn /ˈkɑːləm/ *noun, pl* **-umns** [*count*]
1 : a long post made of steel, stone, etc., that is used as a support in a building ▪ a facade with marble *columns*
2 a : a group of printed or written items (such as numbers or words) shown one under the other down a page ▪ Add the first *column* of numbers. **b** : any one of two or more sections of print that appear next to each other on a page and are separated by a blank space or a line ▪ The article takes up three *columns*. ▪ The error appears at the bottom of the second *column*. — see picture at TABLE
3 : an article in a newspaper or magazine that appears regularly and that is written by a particular writer or deals with a particular subject ▪ a sports/gossip *column* ▪ She writes a weekly *column* for the paper. — see also ADVICE COLUMN
4 : something that is tall and thin in shape — often + *of* ▪ *Columns of* smoke rose from the chimneys. — see also STEERING COLUMN
5 : a long row of people or things — often + *of* ▪ a *column of* troops/cars

col·um·nist /ˈkɑːləmnɪst/ *noun, pl* **-nists** [*count*] : a person who writes a newspaper or magazine column ▪ a gossip/sports *columnist*

com /ˈkɑːm/ *abbr* commercial organization — used in an Internet address to show that it belongs to a company or business ▪ www.Merriam-Webster.*com* — compare DOT-COM

co·ma /ˈkoʊmə/ *noun, pl* **-mas** : a state in which a sick or injured person is unconscious for a long time [*count*] He went into a *coma*. ▪ She was in a *coma* for a year. [*noncount*] patients in (a state of) *coma*

Co·man·che /kəˈmænʧi/ *noun, pl* **Comanche** *or* **Co·man·ches** [*count*] : a member of a Native American people of the southwestern U.S.

co·ma·tose /ˈkoʊməˌtoʊs/ *adj* : in a coma ▪ She lay in a *comatose* state. ▪ *comatose* patients

¹comb /ˈkoʊm/ *noun, pl* **combs** [*count*]
1 a : a flat piece of plastic or metal with a row of thin teeth that is used for making hair neat — see picture at GROOMING **b** : a device that is used for separating or straightening fibers (such as wool fibers)
2 : a soft part on top of the head of some birds (such as chickens) ▪ Roosters have red *combs*.
3 : HONEYCOMB
go over/through with a fine-tooth comb see FINE-TOOTH COMB

²comb *verb* **combs; combed; comb·ing**
1 [+ *obj*] : to smooth, arrange, or separate (hair or fibers) with a comb ▪ Go *comb* your hair. ▪ He *combed* back his hair. ▪ The wool is *combed* before being spun into yarn.
2 : to search (something) very thoroughly in order to find something [+ *obj*] We *combed* the beach for shells. [*no obj*] — usually + ***through*** ▪ They got the information by *combing through* old records.
comb out [*phrasal verb*] ***comb out (hair) or comb (hair) out*** : to make (hair) neat and smooth with a comb ▪ She sat in front of the mirror *combing out* her hair. ▪ Her mother *combed* the tangles *out*.

¹com·bat /ˈkɑːmˌbæt/ *noun* [*noncount*] : active fighting especially in a war ▪ troops ready for *combat* ▪ Some of these soldiers have never seen *combat*. ▪ He was killed in *combat*. ▪ armed/unarmed *combat* — often used before another noun ▪ *combat* operations/missions ▪ *combat* boots ▪ a *combat* zone

²com·bat /kəmˈbæt/ *verb* **-bats; -bat·ed** *also* **-bat·ted; -bat·ing** *also* **-bat·ting** [+ *obj*]
1 : to try to stop (something) from happening or getting worse ▪ The drug helps *combat* infection. ▪ She dedicated her life to *combating* poverty. ▪ Exercise can help *combat* the effects of stress. ▪ The mayor pledged to *combat* crime.
2 *formal* : to fight against (someone) : to engage in combat against (an enemy) ▪ They have been *combating* the rebels for months.

com·bat·ant /kəmˈbætn̩t, *Brit* ˈkɒmbətənt/ *noun, pl* **-ants** [*count*] : a person, group, or country that fights in a war or battle ▪ Britain was a main/major *combatant* in World War II. — often used before another noun ▪ *combatant* ships/nations

combat fatigue *noun* [*noncount*] : BATTLE FATIGUE

com·bat·ive /kəmˈbætɪv, *Brit* ˈkɒmbətɪv/ *adj* [*more* ~; *most* ~] : having or showing a willingness to fight or argue ▪ a *combative* attitude/style ▪ When the police tried to arrest him, he became *combative*.
— **com·bat·ive·ness** *noun* [*noncount*] ▪ a lawyer known for his *combativeness*

com·bi·na·tion /ˌkɑːmbəˈneɪʃən/ *noun, pl* **-tions**
1 [*count*] : a result or product of combining two or more things or people ▪ Water is a *combination* of hydrogen and oxygen. ▪ The car's interior is available in various/different color *combinations*. ▪ It's an unusual *combination*. ▪ A *combination* of factors led to her decision. ▪ The milkshakes come in chocolate, strawberry, and vanilla, or any *combination* of these. ▪ He has the right *combination* of talent and experience. ▪ Together on one team they are a ***winning combination***. [=they work, perform, etc., very well together]
2 : an act of combining two or more things [*count*] The *combination* of these two chemicals can cause an explosion. [*noncount*] The drugs should not be taken ***in combination***. [=should not be taken together] ▪ It can be used by itself or ***in combination with*** [=*together with*] our other products.
3 [*count*] : a particular series of numbers or letters that is used to open a lock ▪ What is the *combination* to the safe?
4 — used to describe something that can be used in more than one way ▪ The tool is a *combination* jackknife and bottle opener. ▪ The book is a *combination* dictionary and thesaurus.

combination lock *noun, pl* ~ **locks** [*count*] : a lock that can only be opened by using a particular series of numbers of letters

combination therapy *noun, pl* ~ **pies** [*count, noncount*] *medical* : the use of more than one method and especially more than one drug to treat a disease

¹com·bine /kəmˈbaɪn/ *verb* **-bines; -bined; -bin·ing**
1 [+ *obj*] : to cause (two or more things) to be together or to work together ▪ We decided to *combine* both methods/techniques. ▪ The groups have *combined* forces to lobby for re-

form. — often + *with* • The drug may be *combined with* other treatments.

2 a [+ *obj*] **:** to mix (two or more things) together to form a single thing • *Combine* the ingredients (together) in a large bowl. • *combining* oxygen and/with hydrogen **b** [*no obj*] **:** to come together and form a single thing or group • Atoms *combine* [=*unite*] to form molecules. • The two companies *combined* [=*merged*] under his leadership.

combination lock

3 [+ *obj*] **:** to have (two or more different things) at the same time • a writer whose novels *combine* imagination and scholarship • She found it difficult to *combine* a career and family. • This method of payment *combines* the advantages of cash with the convenience of a check.

4 [*no obj*] **:** to act together • Many factors *combined* to cause the recession. • All of these elements *combine* to make a wonderfully entertaining movie.

[2]**com·bine** /ˈkɑːmˌbaɪn/ *noun, pl* **-bines** [*count*]

1 : a group of people or organizations that work together • The teams belong to a *combine* that scouts new players. • a political *combine*

2 : a machine that cuts crops (such as corn or wheat) and separates the seeds of the plant from the rest of the plant

com·bined /kəmˈbaɪnd/ *adj, always used before a noun*

1 : formed or produced by adding two or more things or amounts together • They've raised a *combined* total of one thousand dollars. • The *combined* population of the two cities is over half a million.

2 : acting together • She is suffering from the *combined* effects of stress and fatigue. • The company succeeded thanks to the *combined* efforts of all its employees.

combining form *noun, pl* **~ forms** [*count*] *linguistics* **:** a form of a word (such as *electro-* in *electromagnetic* or *mal-* in *malodorous*) that only occurs as a part of other words

com·bo /ˈkɑːmboʊ/ *noun, pl* **-bos** [*count*]

1 : a small musical group that plays jazz or dance music • a three-piece jazz *combo*

2 *informal* **:** a combination of different things • The carpet design comes in three different color *combos*. • a washer-dryer *combo* • I ordered the seafood *combo*. [=a dish that includes different kinds of seafood]

com·bus·ti·ble /kəmˈbʌstəbəl/ *adj* [*more ~; most ~*] **:** able to be burned easily • *combustible* gases/materials • The fuel is highly/very *combustible*. — sometimes used figuratively • a *combustible* situation [=a situation in which people are angry and could become violent]

– combustible *noun, pl* **-tibles** [*count*] • *combustibles* such as coal and gasoline

com·bus·tion /kəmˈbʌstʃən/ *noun* [*noncount*] *technical*

1 : the act of burning • *Combustion* may occur at high temperatures. — see also SPONTANEOUS COMBUSTION

2 *technical* **:** a chemical reaction that occurs when oxygen combines with other substances to produce heat and usually light • This ratio of air to fuel results in better *combustion*. — see also INTERNAL COMBUSTION ENGINE

combustion chamber *noun, pl* **~ -bers** [*count*] **:** a closed space inside an engine in which fuel is burned — see picture at ENGINE

[1]**come** /ˈkʌm/ *verb* **comes; came** /ˈkeɪm/; **come; com·ing** [*no obj*]

1 : to move toward someone or something • Please *come* here for a minute. I want to show you something. • Don't *come* near me. • She *came* quietly into the room. • He *came* home late again last night. • The dog began to growl as we *came* closer. • Here he *comes*. [=he is approaching us] • The captain of the ship invited us to *come* aboard. • The dog ***came running*** when she called it. [=the dog ran to her when she called it] • If you need me I'll *come running*. [=I'll come to you very quickly]

2 : to go or travel to a place • People *come* from all over the country to see him. • Some people *came* by car while others *came* by plane. • Why don't you *come* and/to stay with us for a while? • My parents are *coming* for a visit. = My parents are *coming* to visit. • I hope you'll *come* (to/and) visit us soon. • About a hundred people are *coming* to the wedding. • People *come* many miles to visit the shrine. • They *came* very far [=they traveled a long way] to see you. • My brother is ***coming down*** [=traveling south] to visit me this week, and I'll be going up to visit him next month. • She lives uptown and rarely *comes down* to this part of the city. • My parents are ***coming up*** [=traveling north] to visit me this weekend. • She lives downtown and rarely *comes up* to this part of the city. — often used figuratively • We've *come* so far [=we've made so much progress]; we can't stop now. • It's remarkable to think of how far she's *come* since she started her career. — see also COME A LONG WAY (below)

3 *of mail* **:** to be delivered to a place • Did/has the mail *come* yet? • The mail *comes* every day at four o'clock. • A letter *came* for you.

4 a : to have or form an opinion, attitude, etc., after time passes — followed by *to* + *verb* • I didn't like him at first, but I eventually *came to regard* him as a friend. • He has *come to be* considered one of the leading candidates for the job. • They *came to believe* that no one would help them. • She *came to be known* [=she became known] as the world's greatest dancer. • The food wasn't as good as I've *come to expect*. **b :** to do something specified — followed by *to* + *verb* • I don't know how he *came to acquire* the property. [=I don't know how he acquired the property] • How did you *come to have* such an idea? [=what caused you to have such an idea?] • How did she *come to be* there? [=why was she there?]

5 *always followed by an adverb or preposition* **:** to reach a specified level, part, etc. • Her dress *came* (down) to her ankles. • The water *came* almost up to the window.

6 [*linking verb*] **:** to reach a specified state or condition • My shoe *came* untied. • The screw *came* loose. • Things will *come* [=*become*] clear if we are patient. • The party suddenly ***came alive***. [=the party suddenly became lively] • The rent is ***coming due*** next week. [=the rent will be due next week]

7 a : to happen or occur • These changes couldn't have *come* at a better time. • I promise that no harm will *come* to you. [=I promise that you will not be harmed] • Her success *came* at a high price. [=she paid a high price for her success] • It's important for children to learn about the people and things that *came* before us. • Success didn't ***come easy*** for her. [=she did not achieve success easily] **b :** to arrive or happen after time has passed • The days will be longer when spring *comes*. = *Come* spring the days will be longer. • She'll be back in school *come* September. = She'll be back in school when September *comes*. • This war will end eventually, and when that day *comes*, we will all be profoundly thankful. • The time has *come* to stop hesitating and make a decision.

8 *not used in progressive tenses, of a product that is being sold* **a :** to be available • This model *comes* in several sizes. [=this model can be bought in several sizes] • a product that *comes* in a variety of colors and shapes • when the product first ***came on the market*** [=when the product was first being sold] **b :** to have something as a feature, quality, ability, etc. • The car *comes* (equipped/complete) with air-conditioning.

9 a : to have a specified position or place in a series • I don't know which *came* first. • The letter D *comes* after C and before E. • He cares about his job, but his family ***comes first*** [=his family is more important than his job] **b** *Brit* **:** to end a race or competition in a specified position • Joan won the race and her sister *came* [=*finished, came in*] second.

10 *somewhat old-fashioned* **a** — used in speech as a mild way to urge someone to do something or to become less upset, angry, etc. • *Come*, it's not that bad. I'm sure you'll feel better soon. • ***Come now***, there's no reason to be so upset. **b** — used in speech as a mild way to show that you do not approve of or agree with what someone has said • ***Come, come***. You know as well as I do that he never said that.

11 *informal* + *impolite* **:** to experience an orgasm

as . . . as they come — used to describe someone or something as very good, bad, etc. • Their daughter is *as clever as they come*. [=their daughter is very clever] • The movie was *as boring as they come*. [=the movie was extremely boring]

come about [*phrasal verb*] **1 :** to happen • Their meeting *came about* by accident/chance. • I don't know how it *came about* that she overheard our conversation. **2** *of a boat or ship* **:** to turn to a different direction • The captain gave the order to *come about*.

come a cropper see CROPPER

come across [*phrasal verb*] **1 :** to seem to have a particular quality or character **:** to make a particular impression • How did he *come across*? [=what kind of impression did he make?] — usually + *as* • He *comes across as* (being) a good speaker. [=he seems to be a good speaker; people think that he is a good speaker when they hear him talk] • He *came across as* a nice guy. [=he seemed to be a nice guy] **2 :** to be expressed to someone • She says she was trying to be helpful, but that's not what *came across* when I talked to her. [=I did not get the feeling that she was trying to be helpful when I talked to her] ▪ Her enthusiasm really *came across* [=*came through*] when she talked about her job. [=we could see that she was really enthusiastic when she talked about her job] **3** ***come across (something or someone)*** **:** to meet or find (something or someone) by chance ▪ Researchers have *come across* important new evidence. ▪ As I was walking through the town, I *came across* a group of street performers. **4** ***informal*** **:** to pay money that someone wants or demands ▪ They threatened to hurt him if he doesn't *come across* (with the money).

come adrift see ADRIFT

come after [*phrasal verb*] ***come after (someone)*** **:** to chase (someone) **:** to try to find or capture (someone you want to hurt or punish) ▪ They're worried that the government might be *coming after* them.

come again *informal* — used to ask someone to repeat something that was not heard or understood clearly ▪ "Her name is Hermione." "*Come again*? I didn't quite hear you." "I said her name is Hermione."

come along [*phrasal verb*] **1 :** to go somewhere with someone ▪ They asked me to *come along* (with them) on the trip. [=they asked me to go with them on the trip] ▪ I'm going to the museum tomorrow. Would you like to *come along*? **2 :** to make progress **:** to get better or to proceed in a desired way ▪ The project started slowly, but now the work is *coming along*. **:** to proceed in a specified way ▪ The work is *coming along* well. ▪ The investigation is *coming along* slowly, and there's still a lot more work to be done. **3 :** to happen or appear as someone or something that might be used, chosen, etc. ▪ She says she won't just marry the first man that *comes along*. ▪ An opportunity like this doesn't *come along* [=*occur*] too often.

come a long way **1 :** to rise to a much higher level of success **:** to become very successful ▪ He's *come a long way* from his days as a young reporter. Now he's one of the country's most respected journalists. **2 :** to make a great amount of progress ▪ Medicine has *come a long way* in recent years.

come and go **1** — used to talk about time that has passed ▪ More than a hundred years have *come and gone* since the day of that famous battle. **2** — used to talk about people who appear and then leave as time passes ▪ She's seen a lot of employees *come and go* during her time in the company. ▪ Politicians *come and go*. They all seem pretty much the same to me.

come apart **:** to break into parts or pieces ▪ an old house that is ***coming apart at the seams*** [=an old house that is in very bad condition] — often used figuratively ▪ a coalition that is *coming apart* ▪ Their marriage is *coming apart at the seams*. [=their marriage is failing]

come around *or chiefly Brit* ***come round*** [*phrasal verb*] **1 :** to start to accept and support something (such as an idea) after opposing it **:** to stop opposing or disagreeing with something or someone ▪ She still says she won't support us, but she'll *come around* eventually. [=she'll support us eventually] — often + *to* ▪ She'll *come around to* our side eventually. ▪ People are starting to *come around to* the idea. **2 :** to become conscious ▪ He took a bad fall and knocked himself out. When he *came around* [=*woke up*, *came to*], he didn't remember what had happened. **3 :** to go to visit someone ▪ Why don't you *come around* [=*come over*] (to my house) after work today? **4 :** to occur in the usual way as time passes ▪ I always feel a little sad when the end of the school year *comes around*. — see also *what goes around comes around* at [1]GO **5** *of a boat or ship* **:** to turn to a different direction ▪ The sailboat *came around* [=*came about*] and began to head east.

come as — used to describe the effect that something has when people first learn about it ▪ Their decision *came as* a surprise (to me). [=their decision was a surprise to me] ▪ It should *come as* no surprise that many people oppose the plan. ▪ It *came as* a shock to me [=I was shocked] to see how old he looks now. ▪ The news of her recovery *came as* a great relief to all of us.

come at [*phrasal verb*] **1** ***come at (someone)*** **a :** to move toward (someone) in a threatening or aggressive way ▪ They kept *coming at* me. **b :** to be directed at or toward (someone) ▪ The questions kept *coming at* him so quickly that he didn't know how to respond to them. **2** ***come at (something)*** **:** to begin to deal with or think about (something) ▪ We need to *come at* [=*approach*] these problems from a different angle.

come away from [*phrasal verb*] ***come away from (something)*** **:** to move away from (an area, place, etc.) ▪ The guard told him to *come away from* the door. — often used figuratively ▪ Most readers *come away from* the book feeling reassured. [=most readers feel reassured when they finish the book] ▪ It was a difficult experience, but she *came away from* it a stronger and more confident person.

come back [*phrasal verb*] **1 :** to return to a place ▪ I hope you'll *come back* and see us again soon. — sometimes used figuratively ▪ a decision that may ***come back to haunt us*** [=a decision that may cause problems for us in the future] **2 a :** to return to a former good condition **:** to become strong, successful, or effective again after a time of weakness, failure, etc. ▪ It can be difficult for an athlete to *come back* [=*recover*] from an injury like this. ▪ a species that was nearly extinct but that has been *coming back* **b :** to become popular or fashionable again ▪ Short skirts were out of fashion for many years, but now they're *coming back*. **c :** to be successful in a game, sport, etc., after being behind ▪ The team was trailing after the first half, but they *came back* and won in the second half. **3 :** to return to someone's memory — usually + *to* ▪ I had forgotten a lot of what I learned about music, but it's all *coming back to* me now. [=I am beginning to remember it now] **4 :** to make a reply or response — usually + *with* ▪ When questioned about his involvement, he *came back with* an angry denial. — see also COMEBACK

come between [*phrasal verb*] ***come between (people or groups)*** **:** to cause disagreement between (people or groups) ▪ We shouldn't let these problems *come between* us.

come by [*phrasal verb*] **1 :** to make a visit to someone ▪ Why don't you *come by* [=*come over*] for a while after dinner? **2** ***come by (something)*** **:** to get or acquire (something) ▪ I asked him how he *came by* the money, but he wouldn't tell me. ▪ A good job is ***hard to come by***. [=it's hard to get a good job]

come cheap see [2]CHEAP

come clean see [1]CLEAN

come close see [3]CLOSE

come down [*phrasal verb*] **1 a :** to move or fall downward ▪ The crowd erupted in applause as the curtain *came down*. ▪ One of the tree's branches *came down* during the storm. **b** *of rain, snow, etc.* **:** to fall from the sky ▪ She stood at the window, watching the rain *come down*. ▪ The rain was *coming down* in sheets. [=it was raining very heavily] **2 :** to go to a lower level ▪ Stock prices have continued to *come down* [=*fall*] this week. = Stocks have continued to *come down* in price this week. ▪ It's sad to see how he has ***come down in the world***. [=how he has fallen to a lower position or status after being wealthy, successful, etc.] — see also COMEDOWN **3 :** to decide or say in an official or public way that you support or oppose someone or something ▪ The committee ***came down in favor of*** the proposal. = The committee ***came down on the side of*** the proposal. [=the committee approved the proposal] ▪ Some of his former supporters have ***come down against*** him. **4** ✧ An announcement or decision that ***comes down*** is an announcement or decision from someone who has power or authority. ▪ Word *came down* that the strike was over. ▪ The decision *came down* in his favor. **5** ✧ Something that ***comes down from*** the past is something that has existed for a very long time. ▪ This is a story that has *come down* from ancient times. **6** ***informal*** **:** to stop feeling the effect of an illegal drug **:** to stop being high on a drug ▪ an addict who is *coming down* from heroin

come down on [*phrasal verb*] **1** ***come down on (someone)*** **:** to criticize or punish (someone) ▪ The governor has promised to ***come down hard on*** corrupt officials. [=to severely punish corrupt officials] ▪ Her boss *came down on* her pretty hard when she didn't finish the report on time. **2** ***come down on (something)*** **:** to make a strong effort to stop or oppose (something) ▪ The governor has promised to *come down hard on* corruption.

come down to [*phrasal verb*] ***come down to (something)*** **:** to have (something) as the most important part ▪ People talk about various reasons for the company's failure, but it all *comes down to* one thing: a lack of leadership. ▪ The election is going to *come down to* which candidate seems most trustworthy to the voters. [=the candidate who seems most trustworthy will win the election] ▪ It's nice to be rich, but ***when you come (right) down to it***, it's more important to be healthy and happy.

come down with [*phrasal verb*] ***come down with (an illness)***

: to begin to have or suffer from (an illness) ▪ She *came down with* [=*contracted*] measles. ▪ I think I may be *coming down with* [=*getting, catching*] a cold.

come forward [*phrasal verb*] : to say openly or publicly that you are the person who should get something or who can do something ▪ No one has yet *come forward* to claim the reward. ▪ Several people *came forward* to offer their assistance.

come from [*phrasal verb*] **1** ***come from (something)*** **a** : to have (a specified origin or source) ▪ Wine *comes from* grapes. [=wine is made from grapes] ▪ English words *come from* a wide variety of sources. **b** — used to describe a person's family ▪ She *comes from* a wealthy family. [=her family is wealthy] ▪ He *comes from* a long line of entertainers. [=the people in his family have been entertainers for many years] **c** : to be the result of (something) ▪ I'm not surprised that you don't feel well. That's what *comes from* not eating the right kinds of food. **2** ***come from (a place)*** : to be from (a place): such as **a** *of a person* : to have been born or raised in (a place) ▪ She *comes* (originally) *from* a small southern town. : to live in (a place) ▪ The people who attend the convention *come from* countries all around the world. — sometimes used figuratively ▪ (*informal*) I understand where you're *coming from*. [=I understand why you feel or think the way you do; I understand your point of view] **b** *of a thing* : to be produced in (a place) ▪ Where did this wine *come from*? [=where is this wine from?] ▪ There was a bad smell *coming from* the basement. ▪ A sob *came from* her throat. [=she sobbed] **3** ***come from (someone)*** : to be said or told by (someone) ▪ This information *comes from* a person I trust. ▪ (*informal*) Those comments are pretty surprising, ***coming from you***. [=it is surprising that you would make those comments]

come full circle see FULL CIRCLE

come hell or high water see HELL

come home to see [2]HOME

come in [*phrasal verb*] **1 a** : to enter a place ▪ Welcome. Please *come in*. **b** : to arrive at a place ▪ The store will have some exciting new products *coming in* next week. **2** : to be received ▪ The election results should start *coming in* soon. [=we should start receiving/getting the election results soon] ▪ The broadcast was *coming in* loud and clear. [=we could hear the broadcast very clearly] **3** : to end a race or competition in a specified position ▪ Joan won the race and her sister *came in* [=*finished*] second. ▪ He *came in* first/last. **4** : to have a particular role or function ▪ We're going to need someone to help with the cooking, and ***that's where you come in***. [=your job will be to help us with the cooking] **5** ✧ Something that ***comes in handy*** or (less commonly) ***comes in useful/helpful*** turns out to be useful when it is needed. ▪ A pocketknife can *come in handy*. ▪ A little extra money would *come in useful* right now.

come in/into bloom or ***come into flower*** *of a plant* : to begin to produce flowers : to start to bloom ▪ in early spring, when the forsythias are *coming into bloom* ▪ The lilacs have begun to *come into flower*.

come in for [*phrasal verb*] ***come in for (something)*** : to get or be given (something unpleasant, such as criticism) : to be subjected to (something) ▪ The government's policies are *coming in for* increasing criticism. [=more people are beginning to criticize the government's policies]

come in from the cold see [2]COLD

come in on [*phrasal verb*] ***come in on (something) informal*** : to become involved in (something) ▪ He says he'd like to *come in* (with us) *on* the deal.

come into [*phrasal verb*] ***come into (something)*** **1** : to enter (a place) ▪ Everyone watched her as she *came into* the room. **2** : to get (something) as a possession ▪ He *came into* a fortune when he inherited his father's estate. **3** : to be involved in (something) ▪ Deciding who to hire should be a business decision. You shouldn't allow personal feelings to *come into* it. [=you shouldn't allow personal feelings to affect your decision]

come into effect see [1]EFFECT

come into your own : to begin to have the kind of success that you are capable of having : to become very skillful, successful, etc. ▪ She has really started to *come into her own* recently. ▪ The company was struggling for many months, but now it really seems to be *coming into its own*.

come in/into view/sight : to appear : to begin to be seen ▪ Another ship suddenly *came into view*. ▪ As we turned the corner, the distant mountains *came in sight*.

come naturally see NATURALLY

come of [*phrasal verb*] ***come of (something)*** : to be the result of (something) ▪ the excitement that *comes of* meeting people who share your interests ▪ They had discussions about possible new products, but ***nothing came of it***. [=no new products resulted from their discussions]

come of age see [1]AGE

come off [*phrasal verb*] **1** ***come off*** or ***come off (something)*** : to stop being attached to something ▪ When I tried to pick up the suitcase, the handle *came off*. = The handle *came off* the suitcase. **2** : to produce a desired result : to succeed ▪ His plans to start his own business never *came off*. **3** : to happen ▪ The meeting *came off* as scheduled. [=the meeting happened when it was scheduled to happen] **4** : to do or perform well or badly ▪ She *came off* well in the contest. ▪ He *came off* badly/poorly in the debate. **5** : to seem to have a specified quality or character — usually + *as* ▪ He's really just shy, but he *comes off as* a little arrogant. [=he seems a little arrogant] ▪ He *came off as* a stuffy old man. **6** ***come off (something)*** **a** *US* : to have recently completed or recovered from (something) ▪ a company that is *coming off* a very successful year ▪ an athlete who is *coming off* a serious injury **b** : to have recently stopped using (an illegal drug) ▪ an addict who is *coming off* heroin **7** *US, informal* — used in phrases like ***where do you come off?*** to express anger or annoyance at what someone has said or done ▪ *Where do you come off* talking to me like that? [=you have no right to talk to me like that; how dare you talk to me like that?] ▪ I ***don't know where he comes off*** making those kinds of accusations. [=he has no right to make those kinds of accusations]

come off it informal : to stop talking or acting in a foolish way — usually used as an interjection ▪ "I could be a pro golfer if I really tried." "Oh, *come off it*! You're not even close to being that good!"

come on [*phrasal verb*] **1 a** : to happen or progress as time passes ▪ Darkness *came on* rapidly/gradually [=it rapidly/gradually became dark] as the sun went down. **b** : to begin to happen ▪ Rain *came on* toward noon. [=it began to rain when it was almost noon] ▪ I feel a headache *coming on*. ▪ It looks like it might be ***coming on to rain***. [=it looks like it might start to rain soon] **2 a** *of an electrical machine, light, etc.* : to begin to work or function ▪ The lights *came on* briefly and then went out again. **b** *of a TV or radio program* : to start ▪ That program you like is *coming on* in a few minutes. **3** *informal* **a** — used in speech to ask or urge someone to do something ▪ "I don't feel like going out tonight." "Oh, *come on*! It'll do you good to get out of the house for a while." ▪ "I don't think I can go any further." "*Come on*! You can do it if you keep trying!" **b** — used in speech to tell someone to hurry or to go faster ▪ *Come on*, let's go. **c** — used in speech to express surprise, disbelief, etc. ▪ "I think she could win the election." "*Come on*! She doesn't have a chance!" **4** : to have or seem to have a certain quality or nature ▪ He *comes on* [=*comes across*] as a conservative.

come on strong **1** : to be very forceful or too forceful in talking to someone or dealing with someone ▪ She didn't like him because she felt that he *came on* too *strong*. **2** : to become stronger or more successful in a continuing contest, race, etc. ▪ The team was playing poorly in the early part of the season, but it has been *coming on strong* lately. ▪ a political candidate who has been *coming on strong* in the polls as the day of election draws closer

come on to [*phrasal verb*] **1** ***come on to (someone) informal*** : to show sexual interest in (someone) : to try to start a sexual relationship with (someone) ▪ She complained that her boss has been *coming on to* her. **2** ***come on to (something)*** *Brit* : to start to talk about or deal with (something) ▪ We'll *come on to* [=*come to, get to*] that question later.

come out [*phrasal verb*] **1** : to become available : to begin to be produced or sold ▪ A new magazine is *coming out* next week. ▪ The book/movie *comes out* next month. **2 a** : to become obvious : to be clearly shown ▪ His pride *came out* in his refusal to accept help. [=his refusal to accept help showed his pride] **b** : to become known ▪ The truth finally *came out*. [=people finally learned the truth] ▪ It *came out* that he had known about these problems all along, but he hadn't said anything. **3** : to say something openly ▪ Why don't you just *come out* and say what you really think? **4** : to say publicly that you support or oppose someone or something ▪ She ***came out in favor of*** the proposal. ▪ Some of his former supporters have ***come out against*** him. **5** : to say openly that you are a homosexual

• Many gay entertainers have been reluctant to *come out*. • Last year she *came out* (as a lesbian) to her parents. [=she told her parents that she is a lesbian] **6 a :** to appear after being hidden • The rain stopped and the sun/moon/stars *came out* as the clouds cleared away. **:** to appear in the open • animals that only *come out* at night **b** *of a flower* **:** to open **:** to blossom • in the spring, when the flowers are beginning to *come out* (in bloom) **7 a :** to end or finish in a specified way • How did the game *come out*? [=*turn out*] [=who won the game?] • Everything *came out* [=*ended up, turned out*] all right. • She expects to *come out* ahead in the end. • He's confident that he'll *come out* a winner. • He's confident that he'll ***come out on top*** [=that he'll win] when all the votes have been counted. **b** *of a photograph* **:** to produce a good picture • Those pictures I took at the game yesterday didn't *come out*. **c —** used to describe the quality that something has when it is finished • The picture *came out* blurry. • The brownies *came out* a little too dry. **8 :** to be said, expressed, or understood in a particular way • That's not what I meant to say. It didn't *come out* right. • He was trying to make a joke, but it *came out* wrong.

come out of [*phrasal verb*] ***come out of (something)*** **1 :** to result from (something) • It's hard to see how anything good can *come out of* this. **2 :** to go through the experience of (something) • I was lucky to *come out of* [=*come through*] the accident alive. **3** ✧ To ***come out of nowhere*** is to be very surprising and unexpected or to become successful, popular, etc., in a very sudden and surprising way. • That question *came out of nowhere*. • a company that has *come out of nowhere* to become one of the leaders in the industry — see also *come out of left field* at LEFT FIELD

come out with [*phrasal verb*] ***come out with (something)*** **1 :** to say or express (something, such as an idea) • She *came out with* a new proposal. • He's always saying ridiculous things. You never know what he'll *come out with* next. • Why don't you just *come out with* it and say what you really think? **2 :** to publish or produce (something that will be sold to the public) • a publisher that is *coming out with* a new series of children's books • a car company that is *coming out with* several new models next year

come over [*phrasal verb*] **1 :** to make a social visit to someone • Why don't you *come over* [=*come around*] (to my place) after work? **2 :** to change from one side to the other in a disagreement, competition, etc. — usually + *to* • I've been trying to persuade her to *come over to* our side, but I haven't convinced her yet. **3** *Brit, informal* **:** BECOME • He suddenly *came over* all bashful. [=he suddenly became very bashful] **4** ***come over (someone)*** **:** to affect (someone) in a sudden and strong way • A sudden feeling of dread *came over* me. [=I felt a sudden feeling of dread] • He's behaving so strangely. I don't know what's *come over* him lately. [=I don't know what has caused him to behave so strangely]

come round see COME AROUND (above)

come through [*phrasal verb*] **1 :** to succeed in doing something **:** to do what is needed or expected • an athlete who is known for *coming through* in the clutch • "I managed to get the tickets." "Great! I knew you'd *come through*." **2 a :** to be received and understood • The message *came through* loud and clear. • The signal wasn't *coming through*. [=we weren't receiving the signal] **b :** to be expressed to someone • Her enthusiasm really *came through* [=*came across*] when she talked about her job. [=we could see that she was really enthusiastic when she talked about her job] **3 :** to be given or made official in a formal and final way • We're still waiting for approval of our loan application to *come through*. **4** ***come through (something)*** **:** to have the experience of living through (something) • It was a very difficult illness, but he *came through* it in pretty good shape.

come to [*phrasal verb*] **1 :** to become conscious • He took a bad fall and knocked himself out. When he *came to* [=*woke up, came around*], he didn't remember what had happened. **2** ***come to (something)*** **a :** to reach (a place) while traveling • We *came to* a fork in the road. **b :** to reach (a particular point or step in a process) • Deciding to buy a new car was easy. Now we *come to* the hard part: finding the money. • I can't believe that it has *come to* this. **c :** to approach or reach (a specified condition) • The water *came* slowly *to* a boil. [=the water slowly began to boil] • The project suddenly ***came to a stop/halt***. [=the project suddenly stopped] • The work has finally ***come to an end***. [=has finally ended] — see also *come to a bad end* at [1]END **d :** to result in (something) — usually used in negative statements • His ambitious plans never *came to* much. • She talked about learning to fly, but it all ***came to nothing*** in the end. [=she never did learn to fly] **e :** to make or reach (something, such as a decision or an agreement) after thinking or talking • The two sides finally *came to* an agreement/understanding after many hours of discussion. • I've been thinking about what to do next, and I've *come to* a decision. [=I've made a decision] • I've ***come to the conclusion*** [=I've decided] that we need to try a different method. **3** ✧ People say that they ***don't know what the world is coming to*** or they ask ***What is the world coming to?*** when they are shocked or disgusted by something that has happened in the world. • I *don't know what the world is coming to* when so many poor children have to go to bed hungry every night. **4** ✧ The phrase ***when it comes to*** is used to identify the specific topic that is being talked about. • *When it comes to* playing chess, he's the best I know. **5** ✧ The phrase ***if it comes to that*** means "if that is necessary." • I'm willing to pay more money *if it comes to that*. **6** ***come to (an amount)*** **:** to produce (an amount) when added together • The bill *came to* [=*amounted to*] 10 dollars. **7** ***come to (someone)*** **:** to be thought of by (someone) **:** to occur to (someone) • The answer suddenly *came to* me. [=I suddenly thought of the answer] **8** ✧ Something that is ***coming to*** you is something that is owed to you. • I have another dollar *coming to* me. [=I am owed another dollar] • He wants all the credit that's *coming to* him. [=he wants all the credit that he deserves] ✧ If you ***get what's coming to you***, you get the punishment that you deserve. • He's a dirty cheat, and I'm going to see that he *gets what coming to him*. ✧ If you ***have it coming (to you)*** you deserve to get something bad, such as punishment. • I'm not sorry to hear that he lost his job. He *had it coming*.

come to blows see [3]BLOW

come together [*phrasal verb*] **1 :** to join or meet • the place where two rivers *come together* **2 :** to form a group • People from many different areas have *come together* to try to find a solution. **3 :** to begin to work or proceed in the desired way • The project started slowly, but everything is finally starting to *come together* now.

come to grief see GRIEF

come to grips with see [2]GRIP

come to life see [1]LIFE

come to light see [1]LIGHT

come to mind see [1]MIND

come to pass *formal + literary* **:** to happen • Many of the things he predicted have *come to pass*.

come to rest see [2]REST

come to terms see [1]TERM

come to think of it — used in speech to say that you have just remembered or thought of something • The meeting is next Tuesday, which, *come to think of it*, is also the date of my doctor's appointment.

come to your senses see [1]SENSE

come true see [1]TRUE

come under [*phrasal verb*] ***come under (something)*** **1 :** to be subjected to (something) • The troops were resting when they suddenly *came under* attack. [=when they were suddenly attacked] • His policies have been *coming under* attack/criticism/fire from conservatives. [=conservatives have been attacking/criticizing his policies] • Many people feel that their civil rights are *coming under* threat. [=are being threatened] • Some of the governor's recent proposals are now *coming under* increased scrutiny. [=people are now looking more closely and critically at the proposals] • The school is *coming under* pressure to change its policies. **2 :** to be affected, controlled, or influenced by (something) • an area that has *come under* the control of rebel forces [=an area that is now controlled by rebel forces] • He was 30 years old when he first *came under* the care of a psychiatrist. [=when he first began to be treated by a psychiatrist] • Many young people have *come under* his influence. [=many young people have been influenced by him] • areas that *come under* his authority **3 —** used to identify the group or category that something belongs to • These matters *come under* the heading of classified information.

come up [*phrasal verb*] **1 :** to move near to someone or something **:** to approach someone or something • He *came* (right) *up* (to me) and introduced himself. **2 a :** to be mentioned or thought of • That issue never *came up*. [=*arose*] • A question has *come up* about the budget. • I was surprised when his name *came up* as a possible candidate for the job. **b :** to occur in usually a sudden or unexpected way • She seems to be ready to deal with any problem that may *come up*. [=arise] • Something has *come up* and I won't be able to attend the meeting. • We need to be ready to take action if an opportunity *comes up*. **3** *of the sun or moon* **:** to become visible in the sky : to rise • She was already awake when the sun *came up*. **4** *of a plant* **:** to first appear above the ground • in the spring, when the daffodils and tulips are *coming up* **5 :** to finish in a specified condition or state • I flipped the coin and it *came up* heads/tails. • The shot ***came up short***. [=the shot did not go far enough] **6 :** to move up in rank or status • an officer who ***came up from/through the ranks*** [=who started as an ordinary soldier and rose to become an officer] **7** ✧ Something that is ***coming up*** will happen soon or will appear soon. • With the election *coming up*, both candidates are spending all their time on the campaign trail. • Our interview with the mayor is *coming* (right) *up* after this commercial. • "I'd like a turkey sandwich and a glass of lemonade, please." "***Coming right up***!" [=the sandwich and lemonade will be served to you very quickly]

come up against [*phrasal verb*] ***come up against (something)*** **:** to be stopped or slowed by (something) • The proposal has *come up against* some opposition. [=there is some opposition to the proposal]

come up empty **:** to fail to get or find something or someone • The police searched the area for clues but *came up empty*. [=they did not find any clues]

come upon [*phrasal verb*] *somewhat formal* **1** ***come upon (someone or something)*** **:** to meet or find (someone or something) by chance • As they turned the corner, they *came upon* an unexpected scene. • While researching the town's history, she *came upon* some surprising new information about its first mayor. **2** ***come upon (someone)*** *of a feeling* **:** to affect (someone) suddenly • An urge to travel suddenly *came upon* him. [=he suddenly felt an urge to travel]

come up to [*phrasal verb*] ***come up to (something)*** **:** to be as good as (something) • The movie didn't *come up to* our expectations. [=was not as good as we expected it to be]

come up with [*phrasal verb*] ***come up with (something)*** **:** to get or think of (something that is needed or wanted) • We finally *came up with* a solution (to our problem). • He *came up with* an interesting new method of improving the factory's efficiency. • He'll be in a lot of trouble if he doesn't *come up with* the money he owes.

come what may **:** regardless of what happens • He promised to support her, *come what may*.

easy come, easy go see [2]EASY

first come, first served see [2]FIRST

how come see [1]HOW

to come **:** existing or arriving in the future • No one knows what will happen in the days *to come*. • There will be more trouble *to come*.

[2]**come** *noun* [*noncount*] *impolite* **:** SEMEN

come·back /ˈkʌmˌbæk/ *noun, pl* **-backs** [*count*]

1 a : a return to a former good position or condition • The species was nearly extinct but is now ***making/staging a comeback***. **b :** a return to being popular or fashionable • Short skirts were out of fashion for many years, but now they're ***making/staging a comeback***. **c :** a new effort to win or succeed after being close to defeat or failure • The team was trailing after the first half, but they ***made/staged a comeback*** and won in the second half. • The team ***mounted a comeback*** in the second half of the season.

2 : a quick reply or response • She seemed to have a clever *comeback* [=*retort*] for everything I said. — see also *come back* at [1]COME

co·me·di·an /kəˈmiːdijən/ *noun, pl* **-ans** [*count*]

1 : a person who performs in front of an audience and makes people laugh by telling jokes or funny stories or by acting in a way that is funny : an actor who plays roles that make people laugh

2 : a person who is funny or makes people laugh • You'll like my friend. He's a real *comedian*.

co·me·dic /kəˈmiːdɪk/ *adj, always used before a noun* [*more ~; most ~*] **:** of, relating to, or like a comedy • She has a lot of *comedic* talent. • a drama with *comedic* elements

co·me·di·enne /kəˌmiːdiˈɛn/ *noun, pl* **-ennes** [*count*] **:** a woman who is a comedian

come·down /ˈkʌmˌdaʊn/ *noun, pl* **-downs** [*count*] **:** a situation in which a person falls to a lower level of importance, popularity, etc. : a fall in status or position • For a man who was once a very popular actor, working in a nightclub is quite a *comedown*. — see also *come down* 2 at [1]COME

com·e·dy /ˈkɑːmədi/ *noun, pl* **-dies**

1 [*count*] **:** a play, movie, television program, novel, etc., that is meant to make people laugh • The new *comedy* is the network's most popular television show. — see also MUSICAL COMEDY, SITUATION COMEDY

2 [*noncount*] **:** things that are done and said to make an audience laugh : comic entertainment • The movie includes a lot of physical *comedy*. • She had always dreamed of a career in *comedy*. [=a career as a comedian] — often used before another noun • *comedy* clubs • a *comedy* show

3 [*noncount*] **:** the funny or amusing part of something : HUMOR • We couldn't help laughing out loud at the *comedy* of the situation.

comedy of manners *noun, pl* **comedies of manners** [*count*] **:** a humorous play, movie, novel, etc., about the way a particular group of people behave

come–hith·er /kəmˈhɪðɚ/ *adj, always used before a noun* **:** attracting someone especially in a sexual way • She gave him a *come-hither* look.

come·ly /ˈkʌmli/ *adj* **-li·er; -est** [*also more ~; most ~*] *old-fashioned + literary* **:** pleasing in appearance : pretty or attractive — used to describe a girl or woman • a *comely* young lady

come–on /ˈkʌmˌɑːn/ *noun, pl* **-ons** [*count*]

1 *informal* **:** something that a person says or does to try to start a sexual relationship with someone • When he told her she looked familiar, she assumed it was just a *come-on* and ignored him. — see also *come on to* at [1]COME

2 : something that is done to get customers for a business • This special sale is a *come-on* to bring in new customers.

com·er /ˈkʌmɚ/ *noun, pl* **-ers** [*count*]

1 a : a person who goes to a place to take part in an activity — usually plural • The class is open to all *comers*. **b :** a person who arrives at a place • We're giving free T-shirts away to the first *comers*. — see also LATECOMER, NEWCOMER

2 *US, informal* **:** someone who is making progress quickly and is likely to be successful • She's regarded as a *comer* in political circles. • a young *comer*

com·et /ˈkɑːmət/ *noun, pl* **-ets** [*count*] **:** an object in outer space that develops a long, bright tail when it passes near the sun

come·up·pance /kəmˈʌpəns/ *noun* [*singular*] **:** punishment that someone deserves to receive • One of these days, he'll ***get his comeuppance*** for treating people so arrogantly.

[1]**com·fort** /ˈkʌmfɚt/ *noun, pl* **-forts**

1 [*noncount*] **:** a state or situation in which you are relaxed and do not have any physically unpleasant feelings caused by pain, heat, cold, etc. • These boots provide warmth and *comfort* in the coldest temperatures. • The car's seats are designed for *comfort*. • The suites combine *comfort* with convenience. • The drug gave some *comfort* to the patient. • I found a cozy chair where I could read ***in comfort***. • We like to watch movies ***in the comfort of our own home***. [=in our own home where we can relax and be comfortable]

2 [*noncount*] **:** a state or feeling of being less worried, upset, frightened, etc., during a time of trouble or emotional pain • He turned to her for *comfort* and support when he lost his job. • We found little/no *comfort* in their words. [=their words did not make us feel better] • If it is any *comfort* to you, I've made the same mistake myself. = It might give you *comfort* to know that I've made the same mistake myself. • I ***take comfort*** in the knowledge that I'm not alone. [=I feel less worried/upset because I know that I am not alone] — see also COLD COMFORT

3 [*count*] **:** a person or thing that makes someone feel less worried, upset, frightened, etc. • They were great *comforts* to each other during that difficult time. — usually singular • Her grandchildren were always a great *comfort* to her. • It's a *comfort* to know that you are nearby.

4 ***comforts*** [*plural*] **:** the things that make you more comfortable and that make your life easier and more pleasant • domestic *comforts* • a country inn with all ***the comforts of home*** — see also CREATURE COMFORT

5 [*noncount*] **:** a state or situation in which you have all the money and possessions that you need • They lived a life of *comfort* and ease.

too close for comfort *also* ***too near for comfort*** ✧ Something or someone that is *too close/near for comfort* is close enough to make you feel nervous, worried, or upset. • That bus came a little *too close for comfort*! • When we went out for drinks together, I realized we were getting *too close for* *comfort*. [=we were getting closer than I wanted to be]

[2]**comfort** *verb* **-forts; -fort·ed; -fort·ing** [+ *obj*] **:** to cause (someone) to feel less worried, upset, frightened, etc. **:** to give comfort to (someone) ▪ She did her best to *comfort* [=*console*] the crying child. ▪ Our family was *comforted* by the outpouring of support from the community. ▪ We can *comfort* ourselves with the thought that the worst is over.
– comforting *adj* [*more* ~; *most* ~] ▪ Knowing that I can rely on your help is a *comforting* thought. = It is *comforting* to know that I can rely on your help. **– com·fort·ing·ly** *adv* ▪ a *comfortingly* familiar face

com·fort·able /ˈkʌmftəbəl/ *adj* [*more* ~; *most* ~]
1 a : not causing any physically unpleasant feelings **:** producing physical comfort ▪ a *comfortable* chair/bed ▪ a *comfortable* home ▪ *comfortable* clothes ▪ a *comfortable* temperature ▪ These shoes aren't very *comfortable* for walking. ▪ I can't seem to find a *comfortable* position in this chair. **b** *not used before a noun* **:** not having any physically unpleasant feelings **:** experiencing physical comfort ▪ Are you *comfortable* enough in that chair? ▪ The nurse turned the patient on his side and asked him if he was *comfortable*. ▪ I was just getting *comfortable* when the phone rang.
2 a : allowing you to be relaxed **:** causing no worries, difficulty, or uncertainty ▪ a *comfortable* routine ▪ They stayed at a *comfortable* distance from the crowd. ▪ She walked along at a *comfortable* [=*easy*] pace. ▪ The team has a *comfortable* 6–0 lead. [=a large lead that makes a victory seem certain] ▪ It was a *comfortable* victory. [=an easy victory that was never in doubt] **b :** feeling relaxed and happy **:** not worried or troubled ▪ He is most *comfortable* working outdoors. [=working outdoors suits him best] — often + *with* ▪ I'm not very *comfortable with* the idea of flying. ▪ I felt *comfortable* with her as soon as I met her. [=it was easy to talk and do things together]
3 : having or providing enough money for everything you need to live well ▪ He has a *comfortable* job/income. ▪ She makes a *comfortable* living as a journalist. ▪ They enjoy a *comfortable* lifestyle.
– com·fort·ably /ˈkʌmftəbli/ *adv* ▪ The suit fits *comfortably*. ▪ Is everyone seated *comfortably*? ▪ They have enough money to live *comfortably*. = They are ***comfortably off***.

com·fort·er /ˈkʌmfətə/ *noun, pl* **-ers** [*count*]
1 : someone who helps you to feel less worried, upset, frightened, etc. **:** someone who comforts you ▪ He was her longtime confidant and *comforter*.
2 *US* **:** a thick bed covering that is filled with a soft light material (such as feathers) ▪ a down *comforter* — see picture at BED

comfort food *noun, pl* ~ **foods :** food that is satisfying because it is prepared in a simple or traditional way and reminds you of home, family, or friends [*count*] Pot roast and fried chicken are my favorite *comfort foods*. [*noncount*] a restaurant that serves *comfort food*

comfort zone *noun, pl* ~ **zones** [*count*] **:** a place, situation, or level where someone feels confident and comfortable ▪ He pushes the players to perform beyond their *comfort zone*. ▪ I need to expand my *comfort zone* and try new things.

com·fy /ˈkʌmfi/ *adj* **-fi·er; -est** [*also more* ~; *most* ~] *informal* **:** physically comfortable ▪ a big, *comfy* armchair ▪ Is everybody *comfy*?

[1]**com·ic** /ˈkɑːmɪk/ *adj*
1 : of or relating to a comedy ▪ a *comic* actor/writer
2 : causing laughter or amusement ▪ a *comic* monologue ▪ The drama has some *comic* moments. ▪ His *comic* timing is impeccable. ▪ The scene was included for *comic* effect.

[2]**comic** *noun, pl* **-ics**
1 [*count*] **:** a person who performs in front of an audience and makes people laugh by telling jokes or funny stories or by acting in a funny way **:** COMEDIAN ▪ a talented *comic*
2 *US* **a** [*count*] **:** COMIC STRIP — sometimes used before another noun ▪ the *comic* section of the newspaper **b** ***the comics*** **:** the comic strips in a newspaper **:** the part of a newspaper that has comic strips ▪ Did you read *the comics* [=*the funnies*] today?
3 [*count*] *chiefly Brit* **:** COMIC BOOK

com·i·cal /ˈkɑːmɪkəl/ *adj* [*more* ~; *most* ~] **:** causing laughter especially by being unusual or unexpected ▪ a *comical* performance ▪ I must have looked *comical* in that big hat. ▪ The way they argue is almost *comical*. ▪ There's nothing *comical* [=*funny*] about someone getting hurt.
– com·i·cal·ly *adv* ▪ *comically* inappropriate remarks

comic book *noun, pl* ~ **books** [*count*] **:** a magazine that is made up of a series of comic strips — often used as *comic-book* before another noun ▪ *comic-book* heroes

comic strip *noun, pl* ~ **strips** [*count*] **:** a series of cartoon drawings that tell a story or part of a story

comic strip

[1]**com·ing** /ˈkʌmɪŋ/ *adj, always used before a noun*
1 : happening soon or next ▪ The company has many plans for the *coming* year. ▪ An official announcement will be made in the *coming* days.
2 : becoming more important or popular ▪ new technology that's considered the *coming* [=*up-and-coming*] thing/trend in the industry
coming attraction see ATTRACTION

[2]**coming** *noun, pl* **-ings** [*count*] **:** the time when something begins — usually singular ▪ We eagerly awaited the *coming* [=*arrival*] of spring. — see also SECOND COMING
comings and goings **:** the activity of people arriving at and leaving a place ▪ He sat in the café watching the *comings and goings* of the customers.

coming–of–age *noun* [*noncount*] **:** the time when a person becomes an adult ▪ The film is about a young man's *coming-of-age*. — often used figuratively ▪ The album marked her *coming-of-age* as a singer. [=the album showed that she had developed her talents fully as a singer] — see also ***come of age*** at [1]AGE

com·ma /ˈkɑːmə/ *noun, pl* **-mas** [*count*] **:** a punctuation mark , that is used to separate words or groups of words in a sentence

[1]**com·mand** /kəˈmænd/ *verb* **-mands; -mand·ed; -mand·ing**
1 : to give (someone) an order **:** to tell (someone) to do something in a forceful and often official way [+ *obj*] She *commanded* us to leave. ▪ Military leaders *commanded* the troops to open fire. ▪ She *commanded* that work on the bridge cease immediately. [*no obj*] We had no choice but to do as they *commanded*.
2 [+ *obj*] **:** to have authority and control over (a group of people, such as soldiers) ▪ He *commands* a platoon of 60.
3 [+ *obj*] **a :** to deserve or be able to get or receive (something) ▪ She has a reputation that *commands* attention/respect. [=people give her respect/attention because of her reputation] ▪ With his skills and experience, he can *command* a high salary. **b :** to have and be able to use or control (something) ▪ The company *commands* much power and influence in the business world. ▪ They *command* many resources.
4 [+ *obj*] *formal* **:** to be in a place in which you can clearly see (something) ▪ Their house is on a hill that *commands* an excellent view of the valley.

[2]**command** *noun, pl* **-mands**
1 : an order given to a person or animal to do something [*count*] We are expected to obey his *commands*. ▪ She shouted out *commands* to the crew. ▪ Begin on/at my *command*. ▪ We started to teach the dog simple *commands* like "sit" and "lie down." ▪ The dog will only attack ***on my command*** [=will only attack when I tell it to] [*noncount*] The soldiers marched ***on command*** [=they marched when they were ordered to march] — see also ***your wish is my command*** at [2]WISH
2 [*count*] **:** an instruction in the form of a code or signal that tells a computer to do something ▪ You can perform several actions with keyboard *commands*. ▪ The system recognizes voice *commands*.
3 [*noncount*] **a :** the power that someone (such as a military officer) has to give orders and to control a group of people ▪ He was relieved of his *command* after being charged with misconduct. ▪ He has *command* of 100 troops. = He has 100 troops ***under his command*** ▪ Who is the officer ***in command of*** the unit? — see also CHAIN OF COMMAND ***synonyms*** see [1]POWER **b :** control of something (such as a situation, activity, or feeling) ▪ I assumed *command* of the business after my father's death. ▪ He immediately took *command* of the situation. ▪ She seems to be ***in (full) command of*** the situation. [=she seems to have complete control of the situation] ▪ He finally felt *in command of* his life. ▪ She stayed *in com-*

mand of herself [=she did not lose control of her emotions] during the trial.

4 [*singular*] **: knowledge and skill that allows you to do or use something well — + *of*** • She has a good *command of* French. [=she speaks French well] • His *command of* the piano is impressive.

5 [*count*] **: a group of people or an area that is under the control of a military officer** • He is an officer in the Middle East *command.* • He quickly earned the respect of his *command.*

6 [*count*] **: a group of military officers of high rank who give orders** • The order came down from Naval *Command.* — see also HIGH COMMAND, SECOND-IN-COMMAND

at your command **: available for your use** • They used every resource *at their command.* [=*at their disposal*] • If you need anything, please ask me. I am *at your command.* [=I am available to help you at any time]

com•man•dant /ˈkɑːmənˌdɑːnt, *Brit* ˌkɒmənˈdænt/ *noun, pl* **-dants** [*count*] **: an officer who is in charge of a group of soldiers in the military**

com•man•deer /ˌkɑːmənˈdiɚ/ *verb* **-deers; -deered; -deer•ing** [+ *obj*] *formal* **: to take (something, such as a vehicle or building) by force especially for military purposes** • The soldiers *commandeered* civilian vehicles to help transport the injured.

com•mand•er /kəˈmændɚ/ *noun, pl* **-ers** [*count*]

1 : a person who is in charge of a group of people • the platoon/battalion *commander* • the city's police *commander* — often used as a title • *Commander* John/Jane Smith

2 : an officer of high rank in the U.S. Navy, the U.S. Coast Guard, or the British Royal Navy

commander in chief *noun, pl* **commanders in chief** [*count*] **: a person who is in charge of all the armed forces of an entire country** • The President exercised his power as *commander in chief* to deploy forces in the region.

com•mand•ing /kəˈmændɪŋ/ *adj*

1 [*more ~; most ~*] **: having a powerful or important quality that attracts attention, respect, etc.** • He is a *commanding* figure in American literature. [=he is an important and respected figure in American literature] • He has a very *commanding* voice/manner. • He has a ***commanding presence*** when he speaks. [=he attracts attention when he speaks]

2 *always used before a noun* [*more ~; most ~*] **: very likely to result in victory in a race, competition, etc.** • She holds a ***commanding lead*** in the polls. • Our team was in a ***commanding position*** as the game neared its end.

3 *always used before a noun* **: allowing you to see an area very well** • The castle is in a ***commanding position*** at the top of the hill. • The hill provides a ***commanding view*** of the surrounding countryside.

commanding officer *noun, pl* **~ -cers** [*count*] **: an officer who is in charge of a group of people in the military or of a military camp or base** • He reported the incident to his *commanding officer.*

com•mand•ment /kəˈmændmənt/ *noun, pl* **-ments** [*count*] **: an important rule given by God that tells people how to behave** • a *commandment* from God • the Ten *Commandments* in the Bible • the First *Commandment*

com•man•do /kəˈmændoʊ/ *noun, pl* **-dos** *or* **-does** [*count*] **: a soldier who is trained to carry out surprise attacks on an enemy** • an army *commando* — often used before another noun • a *commando* raid/force

command performance *noun, pl* **~ -mances** [*count*] **: a special performance of a concert, play, etc., that is done at the request of an important person (such as a king)**

com•mem•o•rate /kəˈmɛməˌreɪt/ *verb* **-rates; -rat•ed; -rat•ing** [+ *obj*]

1 : to exist or be done in order to remind people of (an important event or person from the past) • The festival *commemorates* the town's founding. • The plaque *commemorates* the battle that took place here 200 years ago.

2 : to do something special in order to remember and honor (an important event or person from the past) • Each year on this date we *commemorate* our ancestors with a special ceremony. • All of the director's films will be shown to *commemorate* [=*observe*] the 50th anniversary of his death.

com•mem•o•ra•tion /kəˌmɛməˈreɪʃən/ *noun, pl* **-tions : something (such as a special ceremony) that is intended to honor an important event or person from the past** [*count*] Several well-known celebrities attended the *commemoration.* [*noncount*] A service was held ***in commemoration of*** the battle. [=was held to commemorate the battle]

com•mem•o•ra•tive /kəˈmɛmrətɪv/ *adj* **: intended to honor an important event or person from the past** • a *commemorative* postage stamp • a *commemorative* ceremony

com•mence /kəˈmɛns/ *verb* **-menc•es; -menced; -menc•ing** *formal* **: to begin** [*no obj*] The festivities will *commence* with a parade. • Their contract *commences* in January. • They *commenced* to argue. = They *commenced* arguing. [+ *obj*] The court *commenced* criminal proceedings. • The country has *commenced* preparations for war.

com•mence•ment /kəˈmɛnsmənt/ *noun, pl* **-ments** *formal*

1 [*noncount*] **: the time when something begins : BEGINNING** — usually + *of* • They awaited the *commencement of* the trial. • It's the first attempt at peace since the *commencement* [=*start*] *of* hostilities.

2 *US* **: a ceremony during which degrees or diplomas are given to students who have graduated from a school or college** [*noncount*] the week before *commencement* [=*graduation*] [*count*] A poet will speak at the *commencement.* — often used before another noun • a *commencement* speech/address/ceremony • *commencement* exercises

com•mend /kəˈmɛnd/ *verb* **-mends; -mend•ed; -mend•ing** [+ *obj*] *formal*

1 : to praise (someone or something) in a serious and often public way • He *commended* her honesty. • His poetry is highly *commended* by other writers. — often + *for* • He *commended* her *for* her honesty. • They should be *commended for* their bravery.

2 : to mention (someone or something) as deserving attention or approval : RECOMMEND • I *commend* this book to anyone interested in learning more about American history. • Their theory ***has much to commend it*** [=there are many good things about it] • His ideas are not likely to ***commend themselves to*** most voters. [=most voters will not like and approve of his ideas]

com•mend•able /kəˈmɛndəbəl/ *adj* [*more ~; most ~*] *formal* **: deserving praise and approval** • a *commendable* effort • Your honesty is *commendable.*

– com•mend•ably /kəˈmɛndəbli/ *adv* • He did a *commendably* thorough job.

com•men•da•tion /ˌkɑːmənˈdeɪʃən/ *noun, pl* **-tions** *formal*

1 [*noncount*] **: the act of praising or approving of someone or something** • words of *commendation* [=*approval, praise*] • Their hard work deserves *commendation.*

2 [*count*] **: something (such as an official letter) that praises someone publicly** • The President issued a *commendation* praising the volunteers for their exceptional work during the relief effort. — often + *for* • He was awarded a *commendation for* bravery.

com•men•su•rate /kəˈmɛnsərət/ *adj, formal* **: equal or similar to something in size, amount, or degree** • The increase in demand caused a *commensurate* [=*proportionate*] increase in prices. • Her new position came with a *commensurate* level of responsibility. — often + *with* • The punishment should be *commensurate with* the offense.

– com•men•su•rate•ly *adv* • a luxury hotel with *commensurately* high prices

[1]**com•ment** /ˈkɑːˌmɛnt/ *noun, pl* **-ments**

1 a : a spoken or written statement that expresses an opinion about someone or something [*count*] The most frequent *comment* was that the service was slow. • I find your *comments* offensive. • I'd like to begin with a few general *comments.* • We have no further *comments.* [=we have nothing more to say] • *Comments* or suggestions can be sent to our main Web address. • She heard him making rude *comments* [=*remarks*] about the neighbors. • We haven't gotten any *comments* on/about the new design. • I'd appreciate your *comments on* this issue. • We've received positive *comments* from many of our readers. [*noncount*] She couldn't be reached for *comment.* • We let the remark pass without *comment.* [=we did not respond to the remark] ✧ The phrase ***no comment*** is used to tell someone (such as a reporter) that you do not wish to answer a question. • "Did you know the defendant well?" "*No comment.*" ***synonyms*** see [1]REMARK

b [*count*] **: a written note that explains or discusses the meaning of something (such as a piece of writing)** • The new edition includes the translator's *comments.*

2 [*noncount*] **: spoken or written discussion about something (such as an event in the news)** • The radio program offers news and *comment.* • The trial drew widespread *comment.*

3 [*count*] **: something that shows or makes a statement about the true state or condition of something — usually singular;**

+ *on* ▪ Their case is a sad *comment* [=*commentary*] *on* the current state of the justice system. ▪ She sees the film as a *comment on* modern values.

[2]**comment** *verb* **-ments; -ment·ed; -ment·ing :** to make a statement about someone or something **:** to make a comment [*no obj*] When asked about his involvement in the scandal, he refused/declined to *comment*. — usually + *on* ▪ Several people have *commented on* my new dress. ▪ He declined to *comment on* the matter. [+ *obj*] She *commented* that the service seemed slow. ▪ "The service seems slow today," she *commented*. [=*remarked*]

C

com·men·tary /ˈkɑːmənˌteri, *Brit* ˈkɒməntri/ *noun, pl* **-taries**

1 : spoken or written discussion in which people express opinions about someone or something [*noncount*] The television show features political *commentary* by well-known journalists. ▪ The magazine includes humor and social *commentary*. [*count*] The book is a *commentary* on her experiences abroad. ▪ I like listening to his social *commentaries*.

2 : a spoken description of an event (such as a sports contest) as it is happening [*noncount*] He provided *commentary* during the game. [*count*] The major television stations provided ***running commentaries*** on the election results.

3 [*count*] **:** something that shows or makes a statement about the true state or condition of something — usually singular; + *on* ▪ The students' poor performance on the tests is a sad *commentary* [=*comment*] *on* the current state of education in this country.

com·men·tate /ˈkɑːmənˌteɪt/ *verb* **-tates; -tat·ed; -tat·ing** [+ *obj*] **:** to provide a description on a radio or television program of an event (such as a sports contest) as it is happening ▪ He will be *commentating* on tomorrow night's game.

com·men·ta·tor /ˈkɑːmənˌteɪtɚ/ *noun, pl* **-tors** [*count*]

1 : a person who discusses important people and events on television, in newspapers, etc. ▪ a political *commentator* ▪ social *commentators*

2 : a person who provides a description on a radio or television program of an event (such as a sports contest) as it is happening ▪ a sports *commentator* ▪ (*US*) a ***color commentator*** [=a person whose job is to make interesting comments on a radio or television broadcast about the things that are happening in a sports contest]

com·merce /ˈkɑːmɚs/ *noun* [*noncount*] **:** activities that relate to the buying and selling of goods and services ▪ interstate *commerce* [=*trade*] ▪ major centers of *commerce* ▪ He was the Secretary of *Commerce* under the last President. — see also CHAMBER OF COMMERCE

[1]**com·mer·cial** /kəˈmɚʃəl/ *adj*

1 : related to or used in the buying and selling of goods and services ▪ *commercial* property/regulations/vehicles ▪ a *commercial* airliner ▪ The city wanted to encourage *commercial* rather than residential development along the river. [=the city wanted businesses rather than apartments or houses to be built along the river] ▪ a *commercial* and industrial city [=a city with many businesses and factories]

2 [*more* ~; *most* ~] **a :** concerned with earning money ▪ Their music is too *commercial*. ▪ *commercial* artists **b** *always used before a noun* **:** relating to or based on the amount of profit that something earns ▪ The play was a *commercial* success but an artistic failure. [=the play earned a lot of money but did not show artistic skill]

3 *always used before a noun* **:** paid for by advertisers ▪ *commercial* television/broadcasting ▪ The average American sees and hears thousands of *commercial* messages each day.

— com·mer·cial·ly *adv* ▪ He produced several *commercially* successful films. ▪ *commercially* available software ▪ The album did well *commercially*. [=the album earned a lot of money; many people bought the album]

[2]**commercial** *noun, pl* **-cials** [*count*] **:** an advertisement on radio or television ▪ a *commercial* for a new kind of soap ▪ We'll be back after the ***commercial break***. [=the time when advertisements are broadcast during a radio or television program]

com·mer·cial·ism /kəˈmɚʃəˌlɪzəm/ *noun* [*noncount*] *disapproving* **:** the attitude or actions of people who are influenced too strongly by the desire to earn money or buy goods rather than by other values ▪ the *commercialism* of modern society ▪ the increasing *commercialism* of the Christmas holiday

com·mer·cial·ize *also Brit* **com·mer·cial·ise** /kəˈmɚʃəˌlaɪz/ *verb* **-iz·es; -ized; -iz·ing** [+ *obj*]

1 *disapproving* **:** to use (something) as an opportunity to earn money — usually used as *(be) commercialized* ▪ She hates to see Christmas *commercialized*. ▪ The beach resort *has been commercialized* and has none of its original charm.

2 *business* **:** to make (something) available to customers ▪ The company hopes to *commercialize* the drug next year.

— com·mer·cial·i·za·tion *also Brit* **com·mer·cial·i·sa·tion** /kəˌmɚʃələˈzeɪʃən, *Brit* kəˌmɜːʃəˌlaɪˈzeɪʃən/ *noun* [*noncount*] ▪ the *commercialization* of Christmas

com·mie *or* **Com·mie** /ˈkɑːmi/ *noun, pl* **-mies** [*count*] *chiefly US, informal + disapproving* **:** COMMUNIST

com·min·gle /kəˈmɪŋgəl/ *verb* **-min·gles; -min·gled; -min·gling** *formal* **:** to join or mix together **:** COMBINE [*no obj*] Fact and fiction *commingle* in the story. [+ *obj*] He *commingled* his personal funds with money from the business. — often used as *(be) commingled* ▪ Fact and fiction *are commingled* in the story.

— commingling *noun* [*noncount*] ▪ the *commingling* of fact and fiction

com·mis·er·ate /kəˈmɪzəˌreɪt/ *verb* **-ates; -at·ed; -at·ing** [*no obj*] *formal* **:** to express sadness or sympathy for someone who has experienced something unpleasant ▪ Friends called to *commiserate* [=*sympathize*] when they heard that he had to cancel the trip. ▪ The players *commiserated* over/about their loss in the championship game. — often + *with* ▪ The players *commiserated with* each other.

— com·mis·er·a·tion /kəˌmɪzəˈreɪʃən/ *noun, pl* **-tions** [*noncount*] Friends offered words of *commiseration*. [*plural*] It's still not clear whether congratulations or *commiserations* are in order.

com·mis·sary /ˈkɑːməˌseri, *Brit* ˈkɒməsri/ *noun, pl* **-saries** [*count*] *US* **:** a store that sells food and basic household supplies on a military base or in a prison

[1]**com·mis·sion** /kəˈmɪʃən/ *noun, pl* **-sions**

1 [*count*] **:** a group of people who have been given the official job of finding information about something or controlling something **:** COMMITTEE ▪ She served on the city's water *commission*. ▪ the Federal Elections *Commission* ▪ Both states set up *commissions* to examine their public schools.

2 : an amount of money paid to an employee for selling something [*count*] She gets a *commission* for each car she sells. [*noncount*] She sells cars ***on commission***. [=she receives an amount of money for each car that she sells] ▪ The salespeople in that store all work *on commission*.

3 [*noncount*] *formal* **:** the act of committing a crime ▪ a weapon used in the *commission* of a crime

4 : a request or order for someone to do something for money [*count*] He received a *commission* from the king to paint the queen's portrait. [*noncount*] an artist working ***on commission*** [=an artist doing work that has been specifically requested or ordered]

5 [*count*] **:** a position of high rank in the military ▪ He received his *commission* in the Army as a colonel.

in commission *or* ***into commission*** **:** able to function properly **:** ready for use ▪ The Internet connection is back *in commission*. [=is working again]

out of commission **:** not able to function properly ▪ The elevator/doorbell was *out of commission*. [=*broken, out of order*] — often used figuratively ▪ He was *out of commission* [=unable to work, travel, etc.] for three days with the flu.

[2]**commission** *verb* **-sions; -sioned; -sion·ing** [+ *obj*]

1 a : to order or request (something) to be made or done ▪ A portrait of the queen was *commissioned*. ▪ The magazine *commissioned* a story about the world's best beaches. ▪ The report on poverty was *commissioned* by the governor. **b :** to order or request (someone) to make or do something ▪ The king *commissioned* the artist to paint his portrait.

2 : to make (someone) an officer in the military ▪ She was *commissioned* in the Navy as a captain.

3 : to make (a ship) officially active and ready for use ▪ The ship was *commissioned* in 2004. — opposite DECOMMISSION

— commissioned *adj* ▪ The ship remained a *commissioned* ship for more than 30 years. [=the ship was officially in use for more than 30 years] ▪ a ***commissioned officer*** [=a military officer of high rank; an officer whose rank is higher than sergeant]

com·mis·sion·aire /kəˌmɪʃəˈneɚ/ *noun, pl* **-aires** [*count*] *chiefly Brit, old-fashioned* **:** DOORMAN

com·mis·sion·er /kəˈmɪʃənɚ/ *noun, pl* **-ers** [*count*]

1 : a member of a commission **:** one of a group of people who have been given the official job of finding information about something or controlling something ▪ the city's library *commissioners*

2 : an official who is in charge of a government department or part of a government department • the mental health *commissioner* • the police *commissioner*

3 *US* : an official who is in charge of a major professional sport (such as baseball, football, or hockey) • The baseball *commissioner* decided to suspend the players for 10 games.

com·mit /kəˈmɪt/ *verb* **-mits; -mit·ted; -mit·ting**

1 [+ *obj*] : to do (something that is illegal or harmful) • *commit* [=*perpetrate*] a crime • *commit* suicide/murder/rape/adultery • The massacre was *committed* by the rebel army.

2 [+ *obj*] : to decide to use (a person, money, etc.) for some particular purpose or use — often + *to* or *for* • The army *committed* two divisions *to* the battle. • The city *committed* millions of dollars *for* the housing project.

3 : to say that (someone or something) will definitely do something : to make (someone or something) obligated to do something [+ *obj*] I've *committed* myself to a meeting on Thursday. = I'm *committed* to a meeting on Thursday. [=I have said that I will definitely go to a meeting on Thursday] • The contract *commits* the company to finishing the bridge by next fall. • He keeps delaying his decision because he doesn't want to ***commit himself*** [*no obj*] Many companies are reluctant to *commit* to the new technology. [=to say that they will definitely use it] • They have not yet *committed* to a particular course of action.

4 : to decide to give your love, support, or effort to someone or something in a serious or permanent way [*no obj*] My girlfriend just can't seem to *commit*! [+ *obj*] He won't *commit* himself to a long-term relationship. • Many local officials have not yet *committed* themselves to a presidential candidate. • They are *committing* themselves to the pursuit of truth.

5 [+ *obj*] : to cause (someone) to be put in a prison or a mental hospital — usually used as *(be) committed* • She *was committed* to a state mental hospital.

6 [+ *obj*] *Brit, law* : to order (someone) to be tried in a court of law • The magistrate *committed* him to stand trial at the Bristol Crown Court.

commit (something) to memory : to learn (something) so that you remember it perfectly : to memorize (something) • I *committed* the poem *to memory*.

commit (something) to paper/writing : to write (something) down • She *committed* her thoughts *to writing*.

com·mit·ment /kəˈmɪtmənt/ *noun, pl* **-ments**

1 [*count*] : a promise to do or give something • We've got *commitments* from several charities to donate food and clothing. • the government's *commitment* of troops to the region • I can't coach my daughter's basketball team. I have too many *commitments* already. [=I have too many things that I have promised to do] • It's been a struggle to balance my professional and family *commitments*. [=to do both what I have promised to do for my job and what I have promised to do for my family] • The church has a *commitment* to helping the poor. • Getting a dog is a ***big commitment*** [=something that requires you to do a lot] • Opening your own business requires a significant ***financial commitment*** [=it requires you to spend a lot of money over a long time]

2 : a promise to be loyal to someone or something [*count*] — usually + *to* • She isn't ready to make a lifelong *commitment to* another person. • Are you willing to make a *commitment to* our cause? • He questions the company's *commitment to* safety. [*noncount*] He's afraid of *commitment*. [=he's afraid of committing himself to a serious relationship with one person]

3 [*noncount*] : the attitude of someone who works very hard to do or support something • Some of his teammates said he showed a lack of *commitment* (to the team). • The boss noticed her strong *commitment* to her work. • No one doubts your *commitment* to the cause.

com·mit·tal /kəˈmɪtl/ *noun, pl* **-tals** [*count*]

1 *formal* : the act of burying someone's body in a grave • a funeral service, followed by *committal* in the family plot • a private *committal* service = a private service of *committal*

2 *chiefly Brit, law* : the act or process of ordering someone to be put in a prison or a mental hospital • She argued against the *committal* of the defendant to a mental hospital. • *committal* proceedings

committed *adj* [*more* ~; *most* ~] : willing to give your time, energy, etc., to something : LOYAL, DEDICATED • We're very *committed* to the cause. • a *committed* environmentalist • *committed* [=*faithful*] Christians • I'm not married but I'm in a ***committed relationship*** [=I'm in a serious and lasting romantic relationship with someone]

com·mit·tee /kəˈmɪti/ *noun, pl* **-tees** : a group of people who are chosen to do a particular job or to make decisions about something [*count*] the Senate Judiciary *Committee* • the Olympic *Committee* • We're waiting for recommendations from the advisory/ethics *committee*. • a planning/congressional/legislative *committee* [*noncount*] management by *committee* • The bill has been referred back to *committee*. — see also SCHOOL COMMITTEE, SUBCOMMITTEE

com·mode /kəˈmoud/ *noun, pl* **-modes** [*count*]

1 : a low piece of furniture with drawers or sometimes a door and shelves

2 a : a chair with a hole in the seat and a pot underneath that is used as a toilet **b** *US* : TOILET • There are towels in the cabinet above the *commode*.

com·mod·i·fy /kəˈmɑːdəˌfaɪ/ *verb* **-fies; -fied; -fy·ing** [+ *obj*] *disapproving* : to treat (something that cannot be owned or that everyone has a right to) like a product that can be bought and sold • Do we really want to *commodify* our water supply? • I feel like our culture is being *commodified*.

– com·mod·i·fi·ca·tion /kəˌmɑːdəfəˈkeɪʃən/ *noun* [*noncount*] **– commodified** *adj* • our increasingly *commodified* culture

com·mo·di·ous /kəˈmoudijəs/ *adj* [*more* ~; *most* ~] *formal* : having a lot of space • a *commodious* apartment/room/house

com·mod·i·ty /kəˈmɑːdəti/ *noun, pl* **-ties** [*count*]

1 : something that is bought and sold • agricultural *commodities* like grain and corn • Oil is a *commodity* in high demand. • *commodity* prices

2 : something or someone that is useful or valued • Patience is a rare *commodity*. • an actor who is a ***hot commodity*** [=who is very popular] in Hollywood right now

com·mo·dore /ˈkɑːməˌdoə/ *noun, pl* **-dores** [*count*]

1 : a high-ranking officer in the navy

2 : the person who is in charge of a yachting or boating club

[1]com·mon /ˈkɑːmən/ *adj*

1 : belonging to or shared by two or more people or groups • They have a *common* ancestor. • The people on the island have a sense of *common* identity. • a *common* goal/interest • The pool at the condominiums is ***common property*** [=the pool is owned by all of the condominium owners] • The organization works for the ***common good*** [=the public good; the advantage of everyone] • He was chosen as the leader by ***common consent*** [=everyone agreed that he should be the leader] — see also COMMON GROUND, *common knowledge* at KNOWLEDGE

2 ***commoner; -est*** [*or more* ~; *most* ~] **a** : done by many people • It is *common* practice for one town's fire department to help another town when there is a big fire. • a *common* spelling mistake **b** : occurring or appearing frequently : not rare • a *common* [=*widespread*] disease • Buffalo were once a *common* [=*familiar*] sight on the American plains. • Electric windows are a *common* feature in new cars. • "Smith" is a *common* name. • The problem is *common* to laptop computers. = It's *common* for laptop computers to have this problem. • I think some of the most *common* flowers are also some of the prettiest.

3 : of a type that is regularly seen and not considered special or unique • the *common* housefly • cures for ***the common cold***

4 a : without special rank or status • a *common* soldier • You're nothing but a *common* [=*ordinary*] thief! **b** : not having power, wealth, or high status • My parents were *common* [=*ordinary, regular*] folk. • the *common* people • the *common* man — see also COMMON SENSE

5 : expected from polite and decent people • He didn't even have the *common* decency to apologize. • It is *common* courtesy to say "thank you."

6 ***commoner; -est*** [*or more* ~; *most* ~] *Brit, old-fashioned* + *disapproving* : of or belonging to a low social class • His manners are very *common*. • She thought him *common* and uneducated.

common-or-garden *chiefly Brit, informal* : not unusual : GARDEN-VARIETY • This is not just your *common-or-garden* nightclub.

– com·mon·ly *adv* [*more* ~; *most* ~] • He is *commonly* believed to be the discoverer of electricity. • a medicine *commonly* used to treat the flu • *commonly* held beliefs/notions • The kangaroo is *commonly* associated with Australia.

– com·mon·ness /ˈkɑːmənnəs/ *noun* [*noncount*] • The team showed a *commonness* of purpose. • the *commonness* of the name "Smith"

C

²common *noun, pl* **-mons**

1 [*count*] : a public area or park usually in the center of a town or city ▪ the town *common* ▪ Boston *Common*

2 commons *US* : a place where meals are served at a school, college, etc. [*singular*] a **dining commons** [*plural*] The campus has several *dining commons.*

3 the Commons : HOUSE OF COMMONS

in common : shared together ▪ Intersecting lines have one point *in common.* ✧ People who have something *in common* share interests, beliefs, attitudes, opinions, etc. ▪ We have *a lot* (of things) *in common* (with each other). ▪ You're a musician too? I guess we have a lot *in common.* ▪ She's very nice, but we have **nothing in common.** ✧ Things that have something *in common* share features or characteristics. ▪ The cameras have/share some basic features *in common.* ▪ The two cultures have a lot *in common* (with each other). ▪ The film has more *in common* with the director's earlier works than with his most recent projects. ▪ (*formal*) The town, **in common with** [=*like*] others in the region, depends on the tourism industry.

com·mon·al·i·ty /ˌkɑːməˈnæləti/ *noun, pl* **-ties** *formal*

1 [*noncount*] : the fact of sharing features or qualities ▪ *commonality* of origin

2 [*count*] : a shared feature or quality ▪ *commonalities* among the various religions [=features or qualities that the religions have in common] ▪ The plans share important *commonalities.* ▪ We have/share a *commonality* of purpose. [=our purpose is the same]

common denominator *noun, pl* **~ -tors** [*count*]

1 *mathematics* : a number that can be divided by each of the denominators of a group of fractions ▪ 36 is a *common denominator* of ¼ and ⅓.

2 : something (such as a feature or quality) that is shared by all the members of a group of people or things ▪ Drugs seem to be the *common denominator* in these crimes. — see also LOWEST COMMON DENOMINATOR

com·mon·er /ˈkɑːmənɚ/ *noun, pl* **-ers** [*count*] : a person who is not a member of the nobility ▪ a prince who married a *commoner*

Common Era *noun* [*noncount*] : CHRISTIAN ERA

common ground *noun* [*noncount*] : something that people agree about even if they disagree about other things ▪ Hunters and environmentalists found *common ground* in their opposition to the new law.

common law *noun* [*noncount*] : the laws that developed from English court decisions and customs and that form the basis of laws in the U.S.

com·mon–law /ˈkɑːmənˌlɑː/ *adj, always used before a noun* — used to describe a relationship between a man and a woman that is considered to be a marriage because the man and woman have lived together for a long period of time ▪ a *common-law* marriage ▪ his *common-law* wife ▪ her *common-law* husband

common market *noun, pl* **~ -kets** [*count*] : a group of countries that allows free trade among its members

common noun *noun, pl* **~ nouns** [*count*] : a word (such as "singer," "ocean," or "car") that refers to a person, place, or thing but that is not the name of a particular person, place, or thing — compare PROPER NOUN

¹com·mon·place /ˈkɑːmənˌpleɪs/ *adj* [*more ~; most ~*] : happening or appearing in many places and not unusual : very common or ordinary ▪ Drug use has become *commonplace* at rock concerts. ▪ He photographed *commonplace* objects like lamps and bowls. ▪ Much of her writing was *commonplace* [=*unoriginal, unremarkable*] and boring.

²commonplace *noun, pl* **-plac·es** [*count*] *formal*

1 : an idea, expression, remark, etc., that is not new or interesting ▪ It is a *commonplace* that we only use a small part of our brain's capacity.

2 : something that happens or appears in many places and is not unusual ▪ We now accept cell phones and laptop computers as *commonplaces* of everyday life.

common room *noun, pl* **~ rooms** [*count*] : a room that may be used by all members of a group of people in a school, residential community, etc.

common sense *noun* [*noncount*] : the ability to think and behave in a reasonable way and to make good decisions ▪ You really should go to see a doctor if your leg hurts that much. It's just *common sense!* ▪ Obey the laws and use *common sense* when operating your boat. ▪ She's very smart but she doesn't have a lot of *common sense.*

– com·mon·sense *adj, always used before a noun* ▪ He says there are *commonsense* solutions to social problems. ▪ *commonsense* wisdom

common touch *noun*

the common touch : the ability of someone in a position of power or authority to attract the support of ordinary people ▪ He is a politician with *the common touch.*

com·mon·weal /ˈkɑːmənˌwiːl/ *noun* [*noncount*] *old-fashioned + formal* : the happiness, health, and safety of all of the people of a community or nation ▪ a President who promotes the *commonweal* [=*common good*]

com·mon·wealth /ˈkɑːmənˌwɛlθ/ *noun, pl* **-wealths**

1 [*count*] : a group of countries or states that have political or economic connections with one another — often + *of* ▪ a *commonwealth of* states

2 a the Commonwealth : a U.S. state — used officially of Kentucky, Massachusetts, Pennsylvania, and Virginia ▪ *the Commonwealth* of Kentucky **b** [*count*] : a political unit that is like a U.S. state but that pays no federal taxes and has only a representative in Congress who does not vote — used officially of Puerto Rico and of the Northern Mariana Islands

3 the Commonwealth : the countries that were once part of the British Empire

com·mo·tion /kəˈmoʊʃən/ *noun* : noisy excitement and confusion [*noncount*] I went outside to see what all the *commotion* [=*hubbub*] was about. [*singular*] There was a sudden *commotion* when the actress entered the restaurant.

com·mu·nal /kəˈmjuːnl, ˈkɑːmjənl/ *adj*

1 a : shared or used by members of a group or community ▪ a *communal* meal/bathroom ▪ The tribe lived in *communal* huts. ▪ *communal* property **b** : relating to or involving members of a commune (sense 1) ▪ a *communal* living arrangement ▪ *communal* life ▪ a *communal* farm

2 [*more ~; most ~*] : relating to a situation in which you are doing something with other people ▪ the *communal* experience of riding on the train ▪ a *communal* atmosphere

3 *formal* : involving people from different racial or cultural groups ▪ *communal* violence

– com·mu·nal·ly *adv* ▪ Nuns live *communally.*

¹com·mune /kəˈmjuːn/ *verb* **-munes; -muned; -mun·ing** [*no obj*] *formal* : to communicate *with* someone or something in a very personal or spiritual way ▪ *commune with* God ▪ a psychic who *communes with* the dead — often used figuratively ▪ I like to be outside to *commune with* nature. [=to spend time experiencing and appreciating nature]

²com·mune /ˈkɑːmˌjuːn/ *noun, pl* **-munes** [*count*]

1 : a group of people who live together and share responsibilities, possessions, etc. ▪ He's living in a religious *commune.* ▪ hippie *communes*

2 : the smallest division of local government in some countries especially in Europe

com·mu·ni·ca·ble /kəˈmjuːnɪkəbəl/ *adj, medical* : able to be passed to another person ▪ *communicable* [=*infectious*] diseases ▪ There is no evidence that the virus is *communicable.* [=*contagious, catching*]

com·mu·ni·cant /kəˈmjuːnɪkənt/ *noun, pl* **-cants** [*count*] : a person who is a member of a usually specified Christian church ▪ He was a *communicant* of Holy Cross Church.

com·mu·ni·cate /kəˈmjuːnəˌkeɪt/ *verb* **-cates; -cat·ed; -cat·ing**

1 : to give information about (something) to someone by speaking, writing, moving your hands, etc. [*+ obj*] He was asked to *communicate* the news to the rest of the people. ▪ His book *communicates* [=*conveys*] the harsh realities of war. ▪ She *communicated* her ideas to the group. [*no obj*] Good teachers *communicate* effectively. ▪ She likes to *communicate* [=(more informally) *keep in touch*] with her sister through/by/via e-mail. ▪ The two computers are able to *communicate* directly with one another. ▪ The pilot *communicated* with the airport just before the crash.

2 : to get someone to understand your thoughts or feelings [*no obj*] The couple has trouble *communicating.* ▪ the challenge of getting the two groups to *communicate* with each other [*+ obj*] We *communicate* a lot of information through body language. ▪ He *communicated* his dissatisfaction to the staff. ▪ If you're excited about the product, your enthusiasm will *communicate* itself to customers.

3 [*+ obj*] *medical* : to pass (a disease) from one person or animal to another ▪ One monkey *communicated* [=*transmitted, spread*] the disease to the others. ▪ The disease is *communicated* through saliva.

4 [*no obj*] *formal, of rooms, parts of a building, etc.* : to have openings to each other • The rooms *communicate* [=*connect*] through a secret passage.

– com·mu·ni·ca·tor /kəˈmjuːnəˌkeɪtɚ/ *noun, pl* **-tors** [*count*] • The president was an effective *communicator*. • a good/poor *communicator*

com·mu·ni·ca·tion /kəˌmjuːnəˈkeɪʃən/ *noun, pl* **-tions**
1 [*noncount*] **:** the act or process of using words, sounds, signs, or behaviors to express or exchange information or to express your ideas, thoughts, feelings, etc., to someone else • human *communication* • nonverbal *communication* • He is studying insect *communication*. • Parents need to have good *communication* with their children. [=they need to be able to understand and be understood by their children] • *communication* problems/skills • There was a breakdown in *communication* between members of the group. • (*formal*) We are ***in communication*** by e-mail. [=we are communicating with each other by e-mail] • television and other means of ***mass communication***
2 [*count*] *formal* **:** a message that is given to someone **:** a letter, telephone call, etc. — usually singular • The captain received an important *communication*.
3 *communications* [*noncount*] **a :** the ways of sending information to people by using technology • radio/wireless/electronic *communications* • *Communications* is a growing industry. • *communications* systems/technology • a ***communications satellite*** [=a satellite that is used to send signals for television, radio, etc., to people around the world] **b :** the study of how information is sent to people by using technology • He majored in *communications* in college.

com·mu·ni·ca·tive /kəˈmjuːnəˌkeɪtɪv, kəˈmjuːnəkətɪv/ *adj, formal*
1 [*more ~; most ~*] **:** willing to talk to people • He wasn't very *communicative*. [=*talkative*]
2 : relating to communication • *communicative* disorders

com·mu·nion /kəˈmjuːnjən/ *noun, pl* **-nions**
1 *Communion* [*noncount*] **:** a Christian ceremony in which bread is eaten and wine is drunk as a way of showing devotion to Jesus Christ • She went to the front of the church for *Communion*. • take/receive *Communion* • celebrate *Communion* — called also *Holy Communion, the Eucharist*
2 [*noncount*] *formal* **:** a close relationship with someone or something — usually + *with* • He sat alone on the mountain, in *communion with* the wilderness.
3 [*count*] *formal* **:** a group of Christians who have the same beliefs • the Anglican *communion* [=*denomination*] • Christian *communions*

com·mu·ni·qué /kəˈmjuːnəˌkeɪ/ *noun, pl* **-qués** [*count*] *formal* **:** an official announcement about a usually very important piece of news • The news station received a *communiqué* [=*bulletin*] after the bombing.

com·mu·nism *or* **Communism** /ˈkɑːmjəˌnɪzəm/ *noun* [*noncount*] **:** a way of organizing a society in which the government owns the things that are used to make and transport products (such as land, oil, factories, ships, etc.) and there is no privately owned property — compare CAPITALISM, SOCIALISM

com·mu·nist *or* **Communist** /ˈkɑːmjənɪst/ *noun, pl* **-nists** [*count*] **:** a person who believes in communism or is a member of a political party that supports communism

– communist *or* **Communist** *adj* • *communist* ideology/leaders • a *communist* country • the *Communist* Party

com·mu·ni·ty /kəˈmjuːnəti/ *noun, pl* **-ties**
1 [*count*] **:** a group of people who live in the same area (such as a city, town, or neighborhood) • a respectable member of the *community* • The festival was a great way for the local *community* to get together. • Many *communities* are facing budget problems. • People in the *community* wanted better police protection. • a rural *community* • *community* leaders
2 [*count*] **:** a group of people who have the same interests, religion, race, etc. • an artistic/business/medical *community* • the town's Jewish *community* • ethnic/religious *communities* • the scientific *community*
3 [*count*] **:** a group of nations — usually singular • the international *community*
4 [*noncount*] **:** a feeling of wanting to be with other people or of caring about the other people in a group • The school encourages a sense/feeling of *community* in its students. • *community* spirit
5 [*count*] *biology* **:** a group of animals or plants that live in the same place • a *community* of bacteria

community center (*US*) *or Brit* **community centre** *noun, pl* **~ -ters** [*count*] **:** a building or group of buildings where there are classes and activities for the people who live in a community

community college *noun, pl* **~ -leges** [*count*] *US* **:** a school that you go to after high school **:** a school that offers courses leading to an associate's degree ✧ A community college offers two years of studies similar to those in the first two years of a four-year college.

community service *noun* [*noncount*] **:** work that is done without pay to help people in a community ✧ People do community service because they want to or because a court of law has ordered them to do it as a form of punishment for a crime. • She was sentenced to 100 hours of *community service*.

community theater *noun, pl* **~ -ters** *US*
1 [*noncount*] **:** the activity of acting in or producing a play in the theater for enjoyment and not as a job • She spends her free time acting in *community theater*. • He's done school plays and *community theater*. • a *community theater* group/production — called also (*Brit*) *amateur dramatics*
2 [*count*] **:** a small theater where community theater is performed • performing at the/a local *community theater*

com·mu·ta·tion /ˌkɑːmjəˈteɪʃən/ *noun, pl* **-tions** [*count*] *law* **:** a change of a punishment to a less severe one • He appealed for a *commutation* of his death sentence to life imprisonment.

[1]com·mute /kəˈmjuːt/ *verb* **-mutes; -mut·ed; -mut·ing**
1 [*no obj*] **:** to travel regularly to and from a place and especially between where you live and where you work • He *commutes* to work every day by train. • She *commutes* 400 miles a week. — compare TELECOMMUTE
2 [*+ obj*] *law* **:** to change (a punishment) to a less severe one • The judge *commuted* his death sentence to life imprisonment.

– com·mut·er /kəˈmjuːtɚ/ *noun, pl* **-ers** [*count*] • busy *commuters* on their way to work • a *commuter* train

[2]commute *noun, pl* **-mutes** [*count*] **:** the journey that you make when you travel to or from a place that you go to regularly (such as the place where you work) — usually singular • She has a long *commute* to work/school. • There is always a lot of traffic on my morning *commute*.

comp /ˈkɑːmp/ *noun, pl* **comps** [*count*] *US, informal* **:** something that is given to someone (such as a customer) for free • The tickets were *comps*.

– comp *verb* **comps; comped; comp·ing** [*+ obj*] • They *comped* us the tickets. [=they gave us the tickets for free] • Our meals were *comped*.

[1]com·pact /kəmˈpækt/ *adj* [*more ~; most ~*]
1 a : smaller than other things of the same kind • The camera is *compact*. • The drill has a *compact* design. • a ***compact car*** **b :** using little space and having parts that are close together • the apartment's *compact* floor plan • The cabin was *compact* but perfectly adequate.
2 : closely or firmly packed or joined together • *compact* dirt
3 *of a person or animal* **:** short but solid and strong • He is *compact* and muscular. • He has a *compact* body.

– com·pact·ly *adv* • The crib folds *compactly* for traveling. [=the crib can be folded so that its parts are close together] • a *compactly* built hockey player • *compactly* designed computers **– com·pact·ness** /kəmˈpæktnəs/ *noun* [*noncount*] • The computer offers power as well as *compactness*. [=it is both powerful and small]

[2]com·pact /kəmˈpækt/ *verb* **-pacts; -pact·ed; -pact·ing** **:** to press (something) so that it is harder and fills less space [*+ obj*] Tractors had *compacted* [=*compressed*] the soil. [*no obj*] The snow had *compacted* into a hard icy layer.

– com·pact·ed *adj* • *compacted* snow/soil **– com·pac·tor** *also* **com·pact·er** /kəmˈpæktɚ/ *noun, pl* **-tors** *also* **-ters** [*count*] • a ***trash compactor*** [=a machine that presses trash together]

[3]com·pact /ˈkɑːmˌpækt/ *noun, pl* **-pacts** [*count*]
1 : a small flat case containing powder or makeup for a woman's face — see picture at GROOMING
2 *US* **:** a small car • a new line of *compacts* [=*compact cars*] — compare SUBCOMPACT
— compare [4]COMPACT

[4]com·pact /ˈkɑːmˌpækt/ *noun, pl* **-pacts** [*count*] *formal* **:** an agreement between two or more people or groups • States created a *compact* to control milk prices. — compare [3]COMPACT

compact disc *noun, pl* **~ discs** [*count*] **:** CD

com·pa·dre /kəmˈpɑːdreɪ/ *noun, pl* **-dres** [*count*] *chiefly*

US, informal : a close friend : BUDDY • How are you doing, *compadre*?

com•pan•ion /kəmˈpænjən/ *noun, pl* **-ions** [*count*]

1 a : a person or animal you spend time with or enjoy being with • She has been my closest *companion* since childhood. • his longtime *companion* • The old dog had been her ***constant companion*** for over 12 years. [=had been with her most of the time for 12 years] — sometimes used figuratively • Pain was his *constant companion.* [=he felt pain all the time] **b :** someone you are with • my dinner *companion* [=the person I was eating dinner with] • traveling *companions*

2 a : something that is meant to be used with something else — often + *to* • The book is a *companion to* the television series with the same name. • The book is the *companion* volume *to* his previous book on jazz. • The table is a ***companion piece*** to the two chairs. **b** — used in the titles of books that give information about a particular subject • The Gardener's *Companion*

3 : a person who is paid to live with and help someone who is older or sick • We've hired a *companion* for my elderly mother.

com•pan•ion•able /kəmˈpænjənəbəl/ *adj* [*more* ~; *most* ~] *formal + literary* **:** FRIENDLY • a *companionable* young man • *companionable* laughter

– **com•pan•ion•ably** /kəmˈpænjənəbli/ *adv* • chatting/talking *companionably*

com•pan•ion•ship /kəmˈpænjənˌʃɪp/ *noun* [*noncount*] **:** the good feeling that comes from being with someone else • She missed her husband's *companionship* after he died. [=she missed being with her husband] • He had only a dog for *companionship.* [=his only companion was his dog]

com•pan•ion•way /kəmˈpænjənˌweɪ/ *noun, pl* **-ways** [*count*] **:** a stairway on a ship that connects one deck to another

com•pa•ny /ˈkʌmpəni/ *noun, pl* **-nies**

1 [*count*] **:** a business organization that makes, buys, or sells goods or provides services in exchange for money • He runs his own trucking *company.* • She joined the *company* last year. • record/insurance/computer *companies* • The *company* is based in Paris. — often used before another noun • *company* policy/profits • the *company* director • *company* executives/officials

2 [*noncount*] **:** the state or condition of being with another person • I enjoy her *company.* [=I enjoy being with her] • I would love for you to come over. I could really use the *company.* [=I really want to spend time with someone; I do not want to be alone] • I turned the radio on ***for company.*** [=so that I wouldn't be lonely] • I felt nervous being ***in the company of*** [=*around, with*] such important people. • (*chiefly Brit*) She arrived ***in company with*** the mayor. [=she was with the mayor when she arrived] • I'll ***keep you company*** [=I'll stay with you] while you wait for your mom. • He has been ***keeping company with*** [=associating with] a gang of known criminals. • (*chiefly Brit*) The children have no idea how to behave ***in company.*** [=with a group of people] • It's not something you should talk about ***in polite company.*** [=in formal settings; with people you do not know well] — see also *in mixed company* at MIXED

3 [*noncount*] **a :** someone or something you spend time with or enjoy being with • He's good *company.* [=he's enjoyable to be around] • I'm lousy *company* tonight. [=I'm not enjoyable to be around tonight; I'm in a bad mood] • Her dogs/sisters/books/thoughts are her only *company* these days. **b :** the people you spend time with • You can tell a lot about people by the ***company they keep.*** • She's been ***keeping bad company.*** [=spending time with people who are not morally good] ✧ If you are ***in good company*** or have ***plenty of company,*** you are in the same situation or have the same problem or opinion as many other people. • If you're confused about the new system, you're *in good company.* [=other people are also confused] • Do you know now what you will do when you retire? If not, you have *plenty of company.* • If you think health-care costs are out of control, you've got *plenty of company.*

4 [*noncount*] **:** guests or visitors especially at your home • We are having *company* for dinner. [=guests or visitors will be eating dinner with us at our home] • Are you expecting *company*?

5 [*count*] **a :** a group of soldiers • the soldiers of *Company* C **b :** the officers and crew of a ship • the ship's *company*

6 [*count*] **:** a group of actors, dancers, singers, etc., who perform together • a theater/ballet *company*

7 [*noncount*] **:** people who are not named but are part of a group • the law firm of Smith and *Company* • (*informal*) John and *company* got to the party pretty late.

part company see ²PART

two's company, three's a crowd — used to say that a third person is not welcome when two people (such as two lovers) want to be alone with each other • Well, I'll leave you two lovebirds alone. *Two's company, three's a crowd.*

company car *noun, pl* ~ **cars** [*count*] **:** a car that an employer gives an employee to use for driving that relates to the employee's work

com•pa•ra•ble /ˈkɑːmpərəbəl/ *adj* [*more* ~; *most* ~] — used to say that two or more things are very similar and can be compared to each other • A *comparable* refrigerator today would cost a lot more than the one I bought 10 years ago. • The two houses are *comparable* in size. • Their salaries are *comparable* with those of other managers. • The school's test scores were *comparable* [=*close*] to the national average. • The situations aren't at all *comparable.* [=*alike*]

– **com•pa•ra•bil•i•ty** /ˌkɑːmpərəˈbɪləti/ *noun* [*noncount*]

– **com•pa•ra•bly** /ˈkɑːmpərəbli/ *adv* • The two cars are *comparably* equipped. [=they have similar features]

¹com•par•a•tive /ˌkəmˈperətɪv/ *adj, always used before a noun*

1 : seeming to be something when compared with others • She is a *comparative* [=*relative*] newcomer to the industry. [=she is not really a newcomer but is much more of a newcomer than many others] • We dropped anchor in the *comparative* [=*relative*] safety of the harbor. [=the harbor was not completely safe but it was safer than the area outside the harbor]

2 : involving the act of looking at the ways that things are alike or different • She did a *comparative* study of classical and modern art. • I'm taking a class in *comparative* anatomy/literature. • a *comparative* analysis of the roles of women in different cultures

3 *grammar* **:** of or relating to the form of an adjective or adverb that is used to indicate more of a particular quality • The *comparative* form of "happy" is "happier"; the *comparative* form of "good" is "better"; the *comparative* form of "clearly" is "more clearly." — compare SUPERLATIVE

²comparative *noun, pl* **-tives** [*count*] **:** the comparative form of an adjective or adverb **:** the form of an adjective or adverb that is used to indicate more of a particular quality • "Taller" is the *comparative* of "tall." — compare SUPERLATIVE

com•par•a•tive•ly *adv* **:** when measured or judged against something else **:** in comparison with something else • These prices are *comparatively* [=*relatively*] high. • a *comparatively* [=*relatively*] small amount ✧ The phrase ***comparatively speaking*** is used to suggest that what is being said involves a comparison to something else. • *Comparatively speaking,* the movie wasn't bad. [=the movie was better than some other movie]

¹com•pare /kəmˈpeɚ/ *verb* **-pares; -pared; -par•ing**

1 [+ *obj*] **:** to say that (something) is similar *to* something else • The poet *compared* [=*likened*] his sweetheart *to* a beautiful rose. • The singer's voice has been *compared to* that of Elvis.

2 [+ *obj*] **:** to look at (two or more things) closely in order to see what is similar or different about them or in order to decide which one is better • We each did the homework assignment, then *compared* answers. • I *compared* several bicycles before buying one. • For our assignment we must ***compare and contrast*** the two poets. [=say what is similar and different about them]

3 [*no obj*] **:** to be as good or as bad as something else **:** to be on the same level or in the same category as something else — usually + *with* or *to* • He says skiing is fun enough but it can't *compare with* snowboarding. [=he says skiing is fun but snowboarding is better] • Spraining an ankle hurts but doesn't *compare to* breaking a leg. [=breaking a leg is worse than spraining an ankle]

4 [*no obj*] **:** to seem better or worse in comparison to something else **:** to be good or bad when measured against something else • How do the restaurants *compare*? — usually + *with* or *to* • How does your new job *compare to* the last one? [=is your new job better or worse than the last one?] • Her scores *compare* well *with* those of the rest of the class.

compare apples and/to/with apples **:** to compare things that are very similar • The article *compares apples to apples,* grouping wines of the same variety and price together.

compare apples and/to/with oranges **:** to compare things that are very different • To compare large trucks with compact cars is to *compare apples with oranges*.

compared to** or **compared with : in relation to (something else) : measured or judged against (something else) • I'm a slob *compared to* my roommate. • This rain is nothing *compared to* what we got yesterday. [=yesterday's rain was worse than today's rain] • Today's quiz was easy *compared with* the last one.

compare notes : to talk to someone about something that you and that person have each done, experienced, etc. • The parents *compared notes* on raising children. • I phoned a coworker after the meeting to *compare notes*.

[2]**compare** *noun*

beyond compare** also **without compare : better or greater than any other : having no equal • The singer's voice is *beyond compare*. • beauty *beyond compare*

com·par·i·son /kəmˈperəsən/ *noun, pl* **-sons**

1 : the act of looking at things to see how they are similar or different [*count*] a *comparison* of the data from the two studies [*noncount*] a wine that ***stands/bears comparison*** with [=it is as good as] wines that are much more expensive

2 : the act of suggesting that two or more things are similar or in the same category [*count*] the *comparison* of monkeys to humans • I don't think *comparisons* of her situation and/with mine are appropriate. [*noncount*] His poetry ***evokes/invites comparison with*** [=it is similar to] the work of Robert Frost.

by/in comparison : when compared with another : when looked at or thought about in relation to someone or something else • Yesterday's weather was very cold. Today's weather is mild *by comparison*. — often + *with* • He's a well-behaved child *in comparison with* his brother.

draw a comparison** or **draw comparisons : to say that two or more things or people are similar • The brochure *draws a comparison* between the hotel and a medieval palace. • The writer *draws* unflattering *comparisons* between the mayor and a dictator.

make a comparison** or **make comparisons **1 :** to say that two or more things or people are similar • His work has been widely praised. *Comparisons have been made* to the great painters of past centuries. **2 :** to look at similarities and differences between two or more things or people • The Web site allows consumers to *make* direct *comparisons* between competing products.

no comparison — used to suggest that two or more things are very different • There's really *no comparison* between the two models. [=one is much better than the other]

comparison shop *verb* **~ shops; ~ shopped; ~ shopping** [*no obj*] : to compare items while shopping in order to see which one is the best or has the lowest price • The Internet allows consumers to *comparison shop* with ease.

– comparison shopper *noun, pl* **~ -ers** [*count*]

com·part·ment /kəmˈpɑɚtmənt/ *noun, pl* **-ments** [*count*]

1 : an enclosed space or area that is usually part of something larger and is often used to hold a specific thing • The suitcase has a zippered *compartment* for personal items. • The refrigerator has a separate *compartment* for meats.

2 : one of the separate areas of an automobile, train, or airplane • the baggage *compartments* • the passenger *compartment* • the engine *compartment* — see also GLOVE COMPARTMENT

– com·part·men·tal /kəmˌpɑɚtˈmɛntl̩/ *adj* • a *compartmental* design **– com·part·ment·ed** /kəmˈpɑɚtˌmɛntəd/ *adj* • *compartmented* metal trays [=metal trays that have separate compartments]

com·part·men·tal·ize *also Brit* **com·part·men·tal·ise** /kəmˌpɑɚtˈmɛntəˌlaɪz/ *verb* **-iz·es; -ized; -iz·ing** [+ *obj*] *somewhat formal*

1 : to separate (something) into sections or categories • He *compartmentalizes* his life by keeping his job and his personal life separate.

2 : to separate (two or more things) from each other • The company has *compartmentalized* its services.

3 : to put (something) in a place that is separate from other things • A soldier must be able to *compartmentalize* [=*isolate*] his emotions to focus on the mission.

– com·part·men·tal·i·za·tion *also Brit* **com·part·men·tal·i·sa·tion** /kəmˌpɑɚtˌmɛntələˈzeɪʃən, *Brit* kəmˌpɑːtˌmɛntəˌlaɪˈzeɪʃən/ *noun* [*noncount*] • the *compartmentalization* of ideas/responsibilities **– com·part·men·tal·ized** *adj* [*more ~; most ~*] • a *compartmentalized* box • a *compartmentalized* life

com·pass /ˈkʌmpəs/ *noun, pl* **-pass·es**

compass

1 [*count*] : a device that is used to find direction by means of a needle that always points north • He always carries a *compass* when he walks in the woods. • Guests arrived from all ***points of the compass***. [=*directions*]

2 [*count*] : something that helps a person make choices about what is right, effective, etc. • His religion is the *compass* that guides him. • Interest rates serve as a *compass* for determining whether to buy or sell stocks. • The character in the movie had no ***moral compass*** to tell him that stealing was wrong.

3 [*count*] **a :** a tool that consists of two pointed sticks joined at the top and that is used for measuring distances — often plural • a pair of *compasses* [=*dividers*] **b :** a tool that consists of a pen or pencil attached to a pointed stick and that is used for drawing circles

4 [*noncount*] : a specialized area of knowledge, skill, experience, etc. — often used after *beyond* or *within* • That topic falls *beyond the compass* [=*beyond the scope*] of my research.

com·pas·sion /kəmˈpæʃən/ *noun* [*noncount*] : a feeling of wanting to help someone who is sick, hungry, in trouble, etc. • He felt *compassion* for the lost child. • She shows *compassion* to the sick. • She had the *compassion* to offer help when it was needed most.

com·pas·sion·ate /kəmˈpæʃənət/ *adj* [*more ~; most ~*] : feeling or showing concern for someone who is sick, hurt, poor, etc. : having or showing compassion • a very *compassionate* person • a *compassionate* act

– com·pas·sion·ate·ly *adv*

compassionate leave *noun* [*noncount*] *chiefly Brit* : a period of time when a person is allowed to stay home from work because a family member is sick or has died • He has three days of *compassionate leave* for the funeral.

com·pat·i·ble /kəmˈpætəbəl/ *adj* [*more ~; most ~*]

1 : able to exist together without trouble or conflict : going together well • *compatible* colors • two people with *compatible* personalities • My roommate and I are very *compatible*. [=we get along very well] • Our tastes are not *compatible*. [=we like very different things] • a policy that is *compatible* with my beliefs [=that agrees with my beliefs] — opposite INCOMPATIBLE

2 *of devices and especially computers* : able to be used together • *compatible* computers • *compatible* systems • This printer is *compatible* with most PCs. — opposite INCOMPATIBLE

– com·pat·i·bil·i·ty /kəmˌpætəˈbɪləti/ *noun* [*noncount*]

com·pa·tri·ot /kəmˈpeɪtrijət, *Brit* kəmˈpætriət/ *noun, pl* **-ots** [*count*]

1 : a person from the same country as someone else • We watched our *compatriots* compete in the Olympics.

2 *US* : a friend or colleague : someone who belongs to the same group or organization as someone else • the famous actor and his theater *compatriots*

com·pel /kəmˈpɛl/ *verb* **-pels; -pelled; -pel·ling** [+ *obj*]

1 : to force (someone) to do something • Illness *compelled* him to stay in bed. • Public opinion *compelled* [=*obliged*] her to sign the bill. • I ***feel compelled*** to leave. [=I feel that I must leave]

2 : to make (something) happen : to force (something) • We took steps to *compel* their cooperation.

com·pel·ling /kəmˈpɛlɪŋ/ *adj* [*more ~; most ~*]

1 : very interesting : able to capture and hold your attention • The novel was so *compelling* that I couldn't put it down.

2 : capable of causing someone to believe or agree • *compelling* evidence • He made a *compelling* argument.

3 : strong and forceful : causing you to feel that you must do something • I would need a very *compelling* reason to leave my job. • She had a *compelling* need to share what she had heard. • a *compelling* desire

– com·pel·ling·ly *adv* • The novel was *compellingly* written.

com·pen·di·um /kəmˈpɛndijəm/ *noun, pl* **-ums** [*count*] : a collection of things (such as photographs, stories, facts, etc.) that have been gathered together and presented as a group especially in the form of a book • a one-volume *compendium* of information • He published a *compendium* of folk tales.

com·pen·sate /ˈkɑːmpənˌseɪt/ *verb* **-sates; -sat·ed; -sat·ing** *somewhat formal*

1 [*no obj*] : to provide something good as a balance against something bad or undesirable : to make up *for* some defect

C

or weakness ▪ His enthusiasm *compensates for* his lack of skill. ▪ The price of the item has been reduced to *compensate for* a defect.

2 [+ *obj*] **: to give money or something else of value to (someone) in return for something (such as work) or as payment for something lost, damaged, etc.** ▪ *compensate* workers for their labor ▪ She was not *compensated* for the damage done to her car.

– com·pen·sa·to·ry /kəm'pɛnsə,tori, *Brit* kəm'pɛnsətri, kɒmpən'seɪtri/ *adj* ▪ a *compensatory* refund ▪ The patient sued for ***compensatory damages*** [=money awarded to a victim to make up for an injury, damage, etc.]

com·pen·sa·tion /,kɑmpən'seɪʃən/ *noun, pl* **-tions**

1 a [*noncount*] **: something that is done or given to make up for damage, trouble, etc.** ▪ The court awarded the victims millions of dollars in *compensation*. ▪ She offered to pay for lunch as *compensation* for keeping me waiting. — see also WORKERS' COMPENSATION **b** [*count*] **: something good that acts as a balance against something bad or undesirable** ▪ Moving to the coast had some drawbacks, but there were also *compensations*.

2 [*noncount*] *US* **: payment given for doing a job** ▪ annual *compensation* ▪ executive *compensation*

com·pete /kəm'pi:t/ *verb* **-petes; -pet·ed; -pet·ing** [*no obj*]

1 : to try to get or win something (such as a prize or reward) that someone else is also trying to win : to try to be better or more successful than someone or something else ▪ Thousands of applicants are *competing* for the same job. ▪ She *competed* against students from around the country. ▪ We are *competing* with companies that are twice our size. ▪ Did you *compete* in the track meet on Saturday?

2 : to try to be noticed, accepted, or chosen over something else ▪ The radio and the television were both on, *competing* for our attention. ▪ *competing* teams/products/theories

can't compete — used to say that one person or thing is much better than another ▪ Store-bought cookies *can't compete* with homemade ones. [=homemade cookies are much better than store-bought cookies]

com·pe·tence /'kɑ:mpətəns/ *noun* [*noncount*] **: the ability to do something well : the quality or state of being competent** ▪ He trusts in the *competence* of his doctor. ▪ Students must demonstrate *competence* in all subjects. [=must show that they have learned all subjects] — opposite INCOMPETENCE

com·pe·ten·cy /'kɑ:mpətənsi/ *noun, pl* **-cies**

1 [*noncount*] **:** COMPETENCE ▪ Critics have questioned the director's *competency*.

2 [*count*] *formal* **: an ability or skill** — usually plural ▪ The task is well within the range of her *competencies*. [=she is able to do the task]

com·pe·tent /'kɑ:mpətənt/ *adj* [*more ~; most ~*]

1 : having the necessary ability or skills : able to do something well or well enough to meet a standard ▪ a *competent* [=*capable*] teacher ▪ She is a *competent* [=*adequate*] portrait painter but she excels with landscapes. — opposite INCOMPETENT

2 *law* **: able to take part in a trial** ▪ The defendant was declared *competent* to stand trial. ▪ a *competent* witness — opposite INCOMPETENT

– com·pe·tent·ly *adv* ▪ He answered all our questions *competently*.

com·pe·ti·tion /,kɑ:mpə'tɪʃən/ *noun, pl* **-tions**

1 [*noncount*] **a : the act or process of trying to get or win something (such as a prize or a higher level of success) that someone else is also trying to get or win : the act or process of competing** ▪ The school fosters an atmosphere of *competition* rather than cooperation. [=it encourages students to compete against each other instead of work together] ▪ There will be intense/fierce *competition* for the top spots. [=many people will be trying to get the top spots] ▪ These products are ***in competition*** with each other. [=these products are competing with each other] **b : actions that are done by people, companies, etc., that are competing against each other** ▪ Prices are lower when there is *competition* among/between the stores. — often + *from* ▪ The industry has been affected by *competition from* new technologies. ▪ We're up against some stiff/tough *competition from* our rivals. ▪ Downtown stores are looking for new ways to attract customers in the face of *competition from* the stores at the mall.

2 *the competition* : a person or group that you are trying to succeed against : a person or group that you are competing with ▪ He sized up *the competition*. [=looked at who he was competing against] ▪ Don't let *the competition* know our trade secrets. ✧ Someone or something that ***has no competition*** is much better than others. ▪ In my opinion, this restaurant *has no competition*.

3 [*count*] **: a contest in which people try to win by being better, faster, etc., than others : an event in which people compete** ▪ They had/held/staged a *competition* to see who could sell the most lemonade. ▪ a gymnastics/dance/talent *competition* ▪ She won/lost the *competition*.

com·pet·i·tive /kəm'pɛtətɪv/ *adj* [*more ~; most ~*]

1 : of or relating to a situation in which people or groups are trying to win a contest or be more successful than others : relating to or involving competition ▪ *competitive* sports ▪ It is a very *competitive* job market. [=a situation in which a lot of people are trying to get jobs] ▪ The new technology gave them a *competitive* advantage/edge. [=a better chance than others of winning or succeeding]

2 : having a strong desire to win or be the best at something ▪ She is a very *competitive* player. ▪ He has a *competitive* nature. [=he likes to compete and to win]

3 : as good as or better than others of the same kind : able to compete successfully with others ▪ We offer great service at *competitive* rates. [=rates that are close to those of other companies] ▪ You need a degree to be *competitive* in today's job market. ▪ a *competitive* team [=a team with a good chance to win]

– com·pet·i·tive·ly *adv* ▪ Our products are *competitively* priced. **– com·pet·i·tive·ness** *noun* [*noncount*]

com·pet·i·tor /kəm'pɛtətɚ/ *noun, pl* **-tors** [*count*] **: someone who is trying to win or do better than all others especially in business or sports : someone who is competing** ▪ We offer better rates than our *competitors*. ▪ There were more than 500 *competitors* in the race. ▪ She is a fierce *competitor*. [=she is someone who tries very hard to win]

com·pi·la·tion /,kɑ:mpə'leɪʃən/ *noun, pl* **-tions**

1 [*count*] **: a group of things (such as songs or pieces of writing) that have been gathered into a collection** ▪ The CD is a *compilation* of greatest hits. ▪ a video *compilation*

2 [*noncount*] **: the act or process of gathering things together** ▪ the slow *compilation* of data

com·pile /kəm'pajəl/ *verb* **-piles; -piled; -pil·ing** [+ *obj*]

1 a : to create (a CD, book, list, etc.) by gathering things (such as songs or pieces of writing or information) ▪ He *compiled* a book of poems. ▪ She *compiled* a list of names. **b : to put together (various songs, pieces of writing, facts, etc.) in a publication or collection** ▪ They took the best submissions and *compiled* them in a single issue of the magazine. ▪ We *compiled* our findings in the report.

2 *computers* **: to change (computer programming instructions) into a form the computer can understand and use** ▪ a *compiled* program

– com·pil·er /kəm'pailɚ/ *noun, pl* **-ers** [*count*]

com·pla·cen·cy /kəm'pleɪsn̩si/ *noun* [*noncount*] **: a feeling of being satisfied with how things are and not wanting to try to make them better : a complacent feeling or condition** ▪ The public was lulled into *complacency*. ▪ The stock market crash rattled/shattered/shook our *complacency*. [=took away our feeling that everything was fine]

com·pla·cent /kəm'pleɪsn̩t/ *adj* [*more ~; most ~*] *disapproving* **: satisfied with how things are and not wanting to change them** ▪ The strong economy has made people *complacent*. ▪ We have grown too *complacent* over the years. ▪ a *complacent* [=*self-satisfied*] smirk ▪ We can't afford to be *complacent* about illiteracy.

– com·pla·cent·ly *adv*

com·plain /kəm'pleɪn/ *verb* **-plains; -plained; -plain·ing**

1 [*no obj*] **: to say or write that you are unhappy, sick, uncomfortable, etc., or that you do not like something** ▪ He works hard but he never *complains*. ▪ If you're unhappy with the service, you should *complain* to the manager. — often + *about* or *of* ▪ Customers are sure to *complain about* the price increase. ▪ In her letters, she *complains of* loneliness. [=she says that she is lonely] ▪ She *complained of* a sore throat. [=she said she had a sore throat] ▪ "How are you feeling?" "I ***can't complain***." [=I am not unhappy or ill; I am fine]

2 [+ *obj*] **: to say (something that expresses annoyance or unhappiness)** ▪ The students *complained* that the test was too hard. ▪ "These shoes are too tight," he *complained*.

– com·plain·er *noun, pl* **-ers** [*count*] ▪ He's a chronic *complainer*. [=he complains constantly or often] **– com·plain·ing·ly** /kəm'pleɪnɪŋli/ *adv*

com·plain·ant /kəmˈpleɪnənt/ *noun, pl* **-ants** [*count*] *law* : a person who makes a formal charge in court saying that someone has done something wrong ▪ The judge ruled in favor of the *complainant.* [=*plaintiff*]

com·plaint /kəmˈpleɪnt/ *noun, pl* **-plaints**
1 a [*count*] : a statement that you are unhappy or not satisfied with something ▪ We lodged a *complaint* with the hotel manager. [=we complained to the hotel manager] ▪ The board has received a number of *complaints* about the new policy. ▪ The company has a system to handle customer *complaints.* **b** [*noncount*] : the act of saying or writing that you are unhappy or dissatisfied with something ▪ She did her chores without *complaint.* [=without complaining] ▪ a letter of *complaint* [=a letter in which you complain about something] ▪ You have no ***grounds for complaint*** [=no reasons to complain]
2 [*count*] : something to be unhappy about : something that people complain about ▪ The lack of parking spaces is a common *complaint* among the city's residents. ▪ The lack of financial support is our biggest/only *complaint.* ▪ I have no *complaints* with/about the service. [=I am happy with the service]
3 [*count*] : a pain or sickness in the body : a symptom of a disease ▪ He is being treated for a stomach *complaint.* ▪ Shortness of breath was a common *complaint* among the patients.
4 [*count*] *law* : a formal charge saying that someone has done something wrong ▪ He filed a *complaint* against his employer. ▪ The court dismissed her *complaint.*

com·plai·sant /kəmˈpleɪsnt, *Brit* kəmˈpleɪznt/ *adj* [*more* ~; *most* ~] *formal* : willing or eager to please other people ▪ a *complaisant* young man : easily convinced to do what other people want ▪ He was too *complaisant* [=*compliant*] to say no to his brother's demands.
– **com·plai·sance** /kəmˈpleɪsn̩s, *Brit* kəmˈpleɪzn̩s/ *noun* [*noncount*] ▪ He took advantage of her *complaisance.*

¹com·ple·ment /ˈkɑːmpləmənt/ *noun, pl* **-ments** [*count*]
1 : something that completes something else or makes it better ▪ The scarf is a perfect *complement* to her outfit.
2 : the usual number or quantity of something that is needed or used ▪ a full *complement* of farm animals ▪ her usual *complement* of attendants ▪ a ship's *complement* of officers
3 *grammar* : a word or group of words added to a sentence to make it complete ▪ "President" in "they elected her president" and "to work" in "he wants to work" are different kinds of *complements.*

Do not confuse *complement* with *compliment.*

²com·ple·ment /ˈkɑːmpləˌmɛnt/ *verb* **-ments; -ment·ed; -ment·ing** [+ *obj*] : to complete something else or make it better ▪ The shirt *complements* the suit nicely. ▪ a delicious dinner *complemented* by a splendid dessert ▪ The soup and salad *complement* each other well.

Do not confuse *complement* with *compliment.*

com·ple·men·ta·ry /ˌkɑːmpləˈmɛntəri/ *adj* [*more* ~; *most* ~]
1 : completing something else or making it better : serving as a complement ▪ She wore a new outfit with a *complementary* scarf.
2 — used of two things when each adds something to the other or helps to make the other better ▪ The print and online publications are *complementary,* not competitive. ▪ The company owes its success to the *complementary* talents of its co-owners.
3 : going together well : working well together ▪ My spouse and I have *complementary* goals. ▪ *complementary* flavors
4 : not traditional : ALTERNATIVE ▪ ***complementary medicine*** [=*alternative medicine*; methods of healing or treating disease that are different from the usual methods taught in Western medical schools]

Do not confuse *complementary* with *complimentary.*

complementary angles *noun* [*plural*] *mathematics* : two angles that add up to 90 degrees

complementary color *noun* [*count*] *technical* : one of two colors (such as red and green) that are very different from each other and produce a dull color (such as brown or gray) when they are mixed together

¹com·plete /kəmˈpliːt/ *adj* **-plet·er; -est** [*or more* ~; *most* ~]
1 : having all necessary parts : not lacking anything ▪ a *complete* [=*entire; whole*] set of encyclopedias ▪ He spoke in *complete* sentences. ▪ This list of names is not *complete.* [=it is missing some names] ▪ She gave us a *complete* [=*thorough*] description of the events. — often used in book titles ▪ The *Complete* Works of Charles Dickens ▪ The *Complete* Guide to Organic Gardening — opposite INCOMPLETE
2 : not limited in any way ▪ She wants *complete* [=*total, absolute*] control of all aspects of the project. ▪ He gave the car a *complete* overhaul. [=made repairs to almost every part of the car] ▪ They sat in *complete* silence. — often used for emphasis ▪ The movie was a *complete* [=*total*] failure.
3 *not used before a noun* : not requiring more work : entirely done or completed ▪ By autumn, the road construction should be *complete.* [=*finished*] — opposite INCOMPLETE
4 *American football, of a forward pass* : caught by the player the ball was thrown to ▪ The pass to the receiver was *complete* for a gain of 10 yards.
complete with : having or including (something good or desirable) ▪ a birthday cake *complete with* candles ▪ The school has built a new sports complex, *complete with* a skating rink. ▪ The car ***comes complete with*** [=*includes*] air-conditioning and a CD player.
– **com·plete·ly** *adv* ▪ Her news took me *completely* by surprise. ▪ I *completely* agree. ▪ We are *completely* different. [=we are different in every way] – **com·plete·ness** *noun* [*noncount*]

²complete *verb* **-pletes; -plet·ed; -plet·ing** [+ *obj*]
1 : to finish making or doing (something) : to bring (something) to an end or to a finished state ▪ I have *completed* my research. = My research is now *completed.* ▪ We *completed* the job. ▪ The project took four months to *complete.* ▪ He has *completed* the ninth grade. [=he has satisfied all the requirements for the ninth grade] ▪ I *completed* the form. [=I wrote all the required information on the form]
2 : to make (something) whole or perfect ▪ Her latest purchase *completes* her collection. ▪ The new baby *completed* their family.
3 *American football* : to throw (a forward pass) to a teammate who catches it ▪ The quarterback *completed* 12 out of 15 passes.

com·ple·tion /kəmˈpliːʃən/ *noun, pl* **-tions**
1 [*noncount*] : the act or process of completing or finishing something : the state of being complete or finished ▪ He will receive his degree upon *completion* of his studies. ▪ The project is ***near completion*** [=almost finished]
2 [*count*] *American football* : a forward pass made to a teammate who catches it ▪ The quarterback has 11 *completions* in 20 attempts for 80 yards.

¹com·plex /kɑmˈplɛks, *Brit* ˈkɒmˌplɛks/ *adj*
1 [*more* ~; *most* ~] : having parts that connect or go together in complicated ways ▪ a *complex* system ▪ The house's wiring is *complex.*
2 [*more* ~; *most* ~] : not easy to understand or explain : not simple ▪ a *complex* problem ▪ The situation is more *complex* than you realize. ▪ Her poetry is too *complex* [=*complicated*] for my taste.
3 *grammar* : consisting of a main clause and one or more additional clauses ▪ a *complex* sentence
– **com·plex·ly** *adv* ▪ The rules are *complexly* written.

²com·plex /ˈkɑːmˌplɛks/ *noun, pl* **-plex·es** [*count*]
1 : a group of buildings, apartments, etc., that are located near each other and used for a particular purpose ▪ a sports *complex* ▪ an industrial/apartment *complex*
2 : an emotional problem that causes someone to think or worry too much about something ▪ She has a *complex* about her appearance. — see also INFERIORITY COMPLEX, OEDIPUS COMPLEX
3 : a group of things that are connected in complicated ways ▪ a *complex* [=*system*] of welfare programs ▪ a *complex* of protein molecules

com·plex·ion /kəmˈplɛkʃən/ *noun, pl* **-ions** [*count*]
1 : the color or appearance of the skin especially on the face ▪ She has a dark/fair/light/ruddy *complexion.* ▪ a glowing *complexion* ▪ All of the children had healthy *complexions.*
2 : the general appearance or character of something ▪ The *complexion* of the neighborhood has changed over the years.
put a new/different complexion on : to change the appearance of (something) : to cause (something) to be seen or thought about in a new way ▪ That information *puts a* whole *new complexion on* the case.
– **com·plex·ioned** /kəmˈplɛkʃənd/ *adj* — usually used in combination ▪ a fair-*complexioned* child [=a child with light-colored skin]

com·plex·i·ty /kəmˈplɛksəti/ *noun, pl* **-ties**

C

C

1 [*noncount*] : the quality or state of not being simple : the quality or state of being complex ▪ He was impressed by the *complexity* of the music. ▪ The diagram illustrates the *complexity* of the cell's structure. ▪ He doesn't grasp/understand the *complexity* of the situation.

2 [*count*] : a part of something that is complicated or hard to understand — usually plural ▪ the *complexities* of the English language

com·pli·ance /kəmˈplajəns/ *noun* [*noncount*] *formal* : the act or process of doing what you have been asked or ordered to do : the act or process of complying ▪ She was rewarded for her *compliance*. ▪ There has been a low/high rate of *compliance* with the new law.

in compliance with : in the way that is required by (a rule, law, etc.) ▪ *In compliance with* a court order, the company has ceased operations. ▪ The workers were not *in* full *compliance with* the rules. [=were not following the rules exactly]

com·pli·ant /kəmˈplajənt/ *adj*

1 [*more* ~; *most* ~] : willing to do whatever you are asked or ordered to do : ready and willing to comply ▪ I asked him for a favor, and he was *compliant*. ▪ a *compliant* young reporter ▪ a *compliant* servant

2 : agreeing with a set of rules, standards, or requirements ▪ The student's shirt was not *compliant* with the school's dress code. ▪ The software is *compliant* with the latest standards.

com·pli·cate /ˈkɑːmpləˌkeɪt/ *verb* **-cates; -cat·ed; -cat·ing** [+ *obj*]

1 : to make (something) more difficult or less simple ▪ Changing jobs now would *complicate* her life. ▪ This *complicates* things. [=this makes the situation more difficult] ▪ To *complicate* matters further, his train is running late. [=his train is running late, which makes the situation even more complicated or difficult]

2 : to cause (a medical problem) to become more dangerous or harder to treat ▪ a disease *complicated* by infection

com·pli·cat·ed /ˈkɑːmpləˌkeɪtəd/ *adj* [*more* ~; *most* ~] : hard to understand, explain, or deal with ▪ The game's rules are too *complicated*. ▪ a *complicated* situation ▪ a very *complicated* issue : having many parts or steps ▪ The machine has a *complicated* design. ▪ a *complicated* plan ▪ a *complicated* mathematical formula

com·pli·ca·tion /ˌkɑːmpləˈkeɪʃən/ *noun, pl* **-tions** [*count*]

1 : something that makes something harder to understand, explain, or deal with ▪ The negotiations stalled when *complications* arose.

2 *medical* : a disease or condition that happens in addition to another disease or condition : a problem that makes a disease or condition more dangerous or harder to treat ▪ Pneumonia is a common *complication* of AIDS. ▪ She experienced *complications* during her pregnancy. ▪ The patient died of *complications* from surgery.

com·plic·it /kəmˈplɪsət/ *adj, formal* : helping to commit a crime or do wrong in some way ▪ He was *complicit* in the cover-up. [=he helped with the cover-up]

com·plic·i·ty /kəmˈplɪsəti/ *noun* [*noncount*] *formal* : the act of helping to commit a crime or do wrong in some way ▪ There's no proof of her *complicity* in the murder. ▪ He acted with his brother's *complicity*.

[1]**com·pli·ment** /ˈkɑːmpləmənt/ *noun, pl* **-ments**

1 [*count*] : a remark that says something good about someone or something ▪ She gave/paid me a *compliment*. [=she said something nice about me] ▪ He told her he admired her paintings and she returned/repaid the *compliment* by saying that she was a fan of his sculptures. ▪ I received a nice *compliment* yesterday. [=someone said something nice about me yesterday] ▪ I'll take that as a *compliment*. [=I'll regard what was said as praise, whether or not the speaker meant it as praise] ▪ When I called you a perfectionist, I meant it as a *compliment*. [=I wanted what I said to be understood as praise] ▪ She is always ***fishing for compliments***. [=she is always trying to get people to say nice things about her]

2 [*count*] : an action that expresses admiration or approval ▪ When customers recommend our company to friends and family members, we consider that to be the highest/best *compliment* we can get.

3 ***compliments*** [*plural*] — used politely to express praise, welcome, or good wishes to someone ▪ Our *compliments* to the chef! [=we praise the chef for preparing a fine meal] ▪ Please accept this gift with our *compliments*. ▪ A free sample is enclosed with the *compliments* of the manufacturer. ✧ The phrase ***compliments of*** is often used to identify the giver of something that has been provided for free. ▪ We were served free drinks, *compliments of* [=provided without charge by] the casino. *Compliments of* is also used in a joking way to refer to the source of something that is not wanted. ▪ I woke up with a stiff neck, *compliments of* that uncomfortable mattress in their guest room. [=sleeping on the uncomfortable mattress gave me a stiff neck] ▪ He received an audit, *compliments* of the IRS.

Do not confuse *compliment* with *complement*.

[2]**com·pli·ment** /ˈkɑːmpləˌmɛnt/ *verb* **-ments; -ment·ed; -ment·ing** [+ *obj*] : to say nice things about (someone or something) : to pay a compliment to (someone or something) ▪ She *complimented* my outfit. — often + *on* ▪ We *complimented* the pianist *on* his performance.

Do not confuse *compliment* with *complement*.

com·pli·men·ta·ry /ˌkɑːmpləˈmɛntəri/ *adj*

1 : expressing praise or admiration for someone or something ▪ She made *complimentary* remarks about his work.

2 : given for free ▪ They handed out *complimentary* brochures. ▪ *complimentary* tickets ▪ The restaurant offers valet parking as a *complimentary* service.

Do not confuse *complimentary* with *complementary*.

complimentary close *noun, pl* ~ **closes** [*count*] *US* : the words (such as *sincerely yours*) that come before the signature of a letter

com·ply /kəmˈplaɪ/ *verb* **-plies; -plied; -ply·ing** [*no obj*] : to do what you have been asked or ordered to do ▪ I asked the waitress to refill my coffee cup and she happily *complied*. ▪ There will be penalties against individuals who fail to *comply*. — often + *with* ▪ You still have not *complied with* our request. [=have not done what we requested you to do] ▪ We have *complied with* federal law [=we have done what federal law requires] every step of the way. ▪ The devices *comply with* [=are in agreement with] industry standards.

[1]**com·po·nent** /kəmˈpoʊnənt/ *noun, pl* **-ments** [*count*] : one of the parts of something (such as a system or mixture) : an important piece of something ▪ the *components* of an electric circuit ▪ He sells spare computer *components*. ▪ The interview is a key *component* in the hiring process. ▪ Hard work has been a major *component* of his success.

[2]**component** *adj, always used before a noun* : helping to make up the whole of something (such as a system or a mixture) : forming or being a part of something ▪ the *component* parts of a machine

com·port /kəmˈpoɚt/ *verb* **-ports; -port·ed; -port·ing**

comport with [*phrasal verb*] ***comport with (something)*** *US, formal* : to be in agreement with (something) ▪ Her actions *comport with* [=*match*] her ideals.

comport yourself *formal* : to behave in a certain way — used especially in situations where the behavior is admirable or appropriate ▪ He *comported himself* with dignity. ▪ She *comported herself* well during the crisis.

com·port·ment /kəmˈpoɚtmənt/ *noun* [*noncount*] *formal* : the way in which someone behaves ▪ the *comportment* of a gentleman

com·pose /kəmˈpoʊz/ *verb* **-pos·es; -posed; -pos·ing**

1 [+ *obj*] : to come together to form or make (something) ▪ Minorities *composed* [=*made up*] about a third of the attendees at the conference. — usually used as *(be) composed of* ▪ a stew *composed of* [=made from/with] many ingredients ▪ Our group *is composed of* [=is made up of; consists of] travelers from 7 countries. ▪ The clouds *are composed of* water vapor.

2 a [+ *obj*] : to create and write (a piece of music or writing) ▪ *compose* a song/symphony ▪ *compose* music ▪ She *composed* a letter to her sister. **b** [*no obj*] : to practice the art of writing music ▪ He is in his studio *composing*.

3 [+ *obj*] : to arrange the appearance of (something, such as a picture or image) in an orderly or careful way ▪ an elegantly *composed* photograph

4 [+ *obj*] **a** : to make (yourself) calm ▪ Take a moment to *compose* yourself before you pick up the phone. **b** : to gain control of (your emotions) ▪ She sat quietly on the bench outside the courthouse, trying to *compose* her feelings.

com·posed /kəmˈpoʊzd/ *adj* [*more* ~; *most* ~] : calm and in control of your emotions : not feeling or showing anger, fear, etc. ▪ He had told us he felt nervous about the performance, but he seemed perfectly *composed* when he walked onto the stage. ▪ They tried to remain *composed* throughout the ordeal.

com·pos·er /kəmˈpoʊzɚ/ *noun, pl* **-ers** [*count*] : a person who writes music ▪ She prefers Mozart and Beethoven to modern *composers.*

¹com·pos·ite /kəmˈpɑːzət, *Brit* ˈkɒmpəzɪt/ *adj* : made of different parts or elements ▪ a *composite* photograph ▪ a *composite* material

²composite *noun, pl* **com·pos·ites** [*count*]
1 : something that is made up of different parts ▪ a *composite* of minerals ▪ a *composite* of diverse communities
2 *US* : a drawing of someone who is wanted by the police that is made using descriptions given by witnesses ▪ He spotted a man who resembled the police *composite.*

com·po·si·tion /ˌkɑːmpəˈzɪʃən/ *noun, pl* **-tions**
1 [*noncount*] : the way in which something is put together or arranged ▪ the painting's unique *composition* : the combination of parts or elements that make up something ▪ Each rock has a slightly different *composition.* [=*makeup*] ▪ the changing *composition* of the country's population ▪ the *composition* of a chemical compound
2 [*count*] : a piece of writing ▪ Is this poem an original *composition?* [=did you write this poem yourself?]; *especially* : a brief essay written as a school assignment ▪ The teacher reminded us to hand in our *compositions* at the end of class.
3 [*count*] : a written piece of music and especially one that is very long or complex ▪ a famous classical *composition*
4 [*noncount*] : the art or process of writing words or music ▪ She studies musical theory and *composition.*

¹com·post /ˈkɑːmˌpoʊst, *Brit* ˈkɒmˌpɒst/ *noun* [*noncount*] : a decayed mixture of plants (such as leaves and grass) that is used to improve the soil in a garden ▪ a ***compost heap*** = (*chiefly US*) a ***compost pile*** [=a pile of plant materials that are kept in a garden and allowed to decay to create compost]

²compost *verb* **-posts; -post·ed; -post·ing** [+ *obj*] : to change (plant materials) into compost ▪ We *compost* leaves in our backyard.

com·po·sure /kəmˈpoʊʒɚ/ *noun* [*noncount*] : calmness especially of mind, manner, or appearance ▪ She never loses her *composure.* [=she always appears calm] ▪ He kept/maintained his *composure.* ▪ After the initial shock she regained/recovered her *composure.* ▪ He answered with *composure.*

com·pote /ˈkɑːmˌpoʊt/ *noun, pl* **-potes** [*count, noncount*] : a dessert made of fruits cooked with sugar ▪ blueberry *compote*

¹com·pound /ˈkɑːmˌpaʊnd/ *noun, pl* **-pounds** [*count*]
1 : something that is formed by combining two or more parts; *especially, technical* : a substance created when the atoms of two or more chemical elements join together ▪ chemical/organic *compounds* ▪ a *compound* of sodium and chlorine ▪ The metal reacts with the gas to form a *compound.*
2 : a word formed by combining two or more words ▪ "Rowboat," "high school," and "light-year" are *compounds.* — compare ⁴COMPOUND

²com·pound /kɑːmˈpaʊnd/ *verb* **-pounds; -pound·ed; -pound·ing**
1 [+ *obj*] : to make (something, such as an error or problem) worse : to add to (something bad) ▪ He *compounded* [=*exacerbated*] his mistake by announcing it to the whole table.
2 *finance* : to pay interest on both an amount of money and the interest it has already earned [+ *obj*] The interest is *compounded* at regular intervals. [*no obj*] The interest *compounds* quarterly.
3 [+ *obj*] : to form (something) by combining separate things ▪ *compound* a medicine — usually used as *(be) compounded* ▪ an attitude ***compounded of*** [=*made up of*] equal parts greed and arrogance

³com·pound /ˈkɑːmˌpaʊnd/ *adj*
1 : made up of two or more parts ▪ a *compound* leaf ▪ a *compound* microscope
2 a : made by combining two or more words ▪ "Steamboat" is a *compound* noun. **b** : consisting of two or more main clauses ▪ "I told him to leave and he left" is a *compound* sentence.

⁴com·pound /ˈkɑːmˌpaʊnd/ *noun, pl* **-pounds** [*count*] : an enclosed area that contains a group of buildings ▪ a prison *compound* — compare ¹COMPOUND

compound fracture *noun, pl* **~ -tures** [*count*] *medical* : a broken bone in which a part of the bone sticks out through the skin

compound interest *noun* [*noncount*] *finance* : interest paid both on the original amount of money and on the interest it has already earned — compare SIMPLE INTEREST

com·pre·hend /ˌkɑːmprɪˈhɛnd/ *verb* **-hends; -hend·ed; -hend·ing** [+ *obj*] *somewhat formal* : to understand (something, such as a difficult or complex subject) ▪ He is able to fully *comprehend* [=understand completely] what is happening and react appropriately. — often used in negative statements ▪ They are unable to *comprehend* what had happened. ▪ We can scarcely *comprehend* how it all ended. ▪ I find his attitude impossible/difficult to *comprehend.*

com·pre·hen·si·ble /ˌkɑːmprɪˈhɛnsəbəl/ *adj* [*more ~; most ~*] *somewhat formal* : able to be understood ▪ a *comprehensible* [=*intelligible*] explanation ▪ They spoke in barely *comprehensible* slang. [=slang that was extremely difficult to understand] — opposite INCOMPREHENSIBLE
— **com·pre·hen·si·bil·i·ty** /ˌkɑːmprɪˌhɛnsəˈbɪləti/ *noun* [*noncount*] — **com·pre·hen·si·bly** /ˌkɑːmprɪˈhɛnsəbli/ *adv*

com·pre·hen·sion /ˌkɑːmprɪˈhɛnʃən/ *noun* : ability to understand [*noncount*] He has not the slightest *comprehension* of the subject. [=he does not understand the subject at all] ▪ The students showed excellent reading/language *comprehension.* ▪ The war caused suffering ***beyond comprehension.*** [=suffering that is impossible to imagine] ▪ mysteries that are ***beyond our comprehension*** [=mysteries that we cannot understand] [*singular*] I don't have a clear *comprehension* [=*understanding*] of how it works.

¹com·pre·hen·sive /ˌkɑːmprɪˈhɛnsɪv/ *adj* [*more ~; most ~*]
1 : including many, most, or all things ▪ a *comprehensive* list ▪ *comprehensive* insurance [=insurance that covers all kinds of risks] ▪ a *comprehensive* [=*thorough*] course of study
2 *Brit* : of or relating to a comprehensive school ▪ *comprehensive* education
— **com·pre·hen·sive·ly** /ˌkɑːmprɪˈhɛnsɪvli/ *adv* ▪ Each patient was *comprehensively* [=*completely, thoroughly*] evaluated. ▪ Trade was *comprehensively* regulated by the authorities. ▪ (*Brit*) The team was *comprehensively* [=*soundly*] beaten/defeated. — **com·pre·hen·sive·ness** *noun*

²comprehensive *noun, pl* **-sives** [*count*] *Brit* : COMPREHENSIVE SCHOOL

comprehensive school *noun, pl* **~ schools** [*count*] *Brit* : a school in Britain for children of all different levels of ability who are over the age of 11 ▪ Some of his friends attended the local *comprehensive school.*

¹com·press /kəmˈprɛs/ *verb* **-press·es; -pressed; -press·ing**
1 : to press or squeeze (something) so that it is smaller or fills less space [+ *obj*] *compress* the air in a closed chamber ▪ She *compressed* her lips. [*no obj*] Her lips *compressed* into a frown. ▪ a material that *compresses* easily
2 [+ *obj*] : to make (something) shorter or smaller ▪ *compress* a chapter ▪ The author *compressed* [=*condensed*] 80 years of history into 15 pages.
3 *computers* : to reduce the size of (a computer file) by using special software [+ *obj*] *compress* a digital photograph [*no obj*] This type of file *compresses* easily. — opposite DECOMPRESS
— **compressed** *adj* ▪ a bottle of *compressed* air — **com·press·ible** /kəmˈprɛsəbəl/ *adj* [*more ~; most ~*] ▪ This type of file is easily *compressible.* — **com·pres·sion** /kəmˈprɛʃən/ *noun* [*noncount*] ▪ *compression* of air ▪ file/data *compression*

²com·press /ˈkɑːmˌprɛs/ *noun, pl* **-press·es** [*count*] : a folded cloth that is pressed against a part of the body to reduce pain or stop bleeding from an injury ▪ a cold *compress*

com·pres·sor /kəmˈprɛsɚ/ *noun, pl* **-sors** [*count*] : a machine that compresses air or gas

com·prise /kəmˈpraɪz/ *verb* **-pris·es; -prised; -pris·ing** [+ *obj*]
1 : to be made up of (something) : to include or consist of (something) ▪ Each army division *comprised* 4,500 troops. ▪ The play *comprises* three acts.
2 : to make up or form (something) ▪ Nine players *comprise* [=*make up*] a baseball team. ▪ Plants *comprise* [=*constitute, form*] the bulk of their diet. — often used as *(be) comprised* ▪ The play ***is comprised of*** [=*is composed of*] three acts.

¹com·pro·mise /ˈkɑːmprəˌmaɪz/ *noun, pl* **-mis·es**
1 : a way of reaching agreement in which each person or group gives up something that was wanted in order to end an argument or dispute [*noncount*] the art of political *compromise* ▪ To avoid an argument, always be ready to seek *compromise.* [*count*] Both boys will have to ***make compromises*** if they are to share the room. [=they will each have to give up something in order to get along] ▪ The two sides were unable

to ***reach a compromise*** [=unable to come to an agreement] — often used before another noun • a *compromise* agreement/amendment/verdict/measure
2 [*count*] : something that combines the qualities of two different things — often + *between* • The style is a happy *compromise between* formal and informal.
3 : a change that makes something worse and that is not done for a good reason [*noncount*] a director who will not tolerate artistic *compromise* [*count*] She says that accepting their proposal would be a *compromise* of her principles.

²compromise *verb* **-mises; -mised; -mis·ing**
1 [*no obj*] : to give up something that you want in order to reach an agreement : to settle differences by means of a compromise • The two sides were unwilling/unable to *compromise*. — often + *on* • They are unwilling to *compromise* (with each other) *on* this issue.
2 [+ *obj*] : to expose (something) to risk or danger : ENDANGER • We can't reveal that information without *compromising* national security.
3 [+ *obj*] : to damage or weaken (something) : IMPAIR • a dangerous drug that can further *compromise* an already weakened immune system
4 [+ *obj*] : to damage (your reputation, integrity, etc.) by doing something that causes people to lose respect for you • He refused to do anything that might *compromise* his reputation/integrity/principles. • She had already ***compromised herself*** by refusing to answer their questions.
– com·pro·mis·er *noun, pl* **-ers** [*count*]

compromising *adj* [*more* ~; *most* ~] : revealing something that is improper or embarrassing • a *compromising* letter/situation • He and his secretary were caught in a ***compromising position*** [=they were caught having sexual relations]

comp·trol·ler /kənˈtroʊlɚ/ *noun, pl* **-lers** [*count*] : a person who is in charge of the financial accounts of a company or organization : CONTROLLER

com·pul·sion /kəmˈpʌlʃən/ *noun, pl* **-sions**
1 [*count*] : a very strong desire to do something • I gave in to one of my *compulsions* and ordered the chocolate dessert. — often followed by *to* + *verb* • He felt a *compulsion to say* something.
2 [*noncount*] **a** : the act of using force or pressure to make someone do something • We should be able to get them to cooperate without using *compulsion*. • legal *compulsion* **b** : the state of being forced to do something • He was acting ***under compulsion*** [=he was being forced to act] • Their children read only *under compulsion*. [=only when they are forced] • We are ***under no compulsion*** to decide immediately. [=we are not required to decide immediately]

com·pul·sive /kəmˈpʌlsɪv/ *adj* [*more* ~; *most* ~]
1 a : caused by a desire that is too strong to resist : impossible to stop or control • *compulsive* behavior **b** : not able to stop or control doing something • a *compulsive* gambler/liar
2 *chiefly Brit* : very interesting • Her most recent article made *compulsive* [=*compelling*] reading.
– com·pul·sive·ly *adv* • He cleans *compulsively*. • a *compulsively* readable story **– com·pul·sive·ness** *noun* [*noncount*]

com·pul·so·ry /kəmˈpʌlsəri/ *adj*
1 : required by a law or rule • *compulsory* [=*mandatory*] education/retirement
2 : having the power of forcing someone to do something • a *compulsory* law
– com·pul·so·ri·ly /kəmˈpʌlsərəli/ *adv*

com·punc·tion /kəmˈpʌŋkʃən/ *noun, pl* **-tions** : a feeling of guilt or regret : REMORSE [*noncount*] a brutal murderer who killed without *compunction* • He feels/has no *compunction* about his crimes. [*count*] (*chiefly US*) • He has no *compunctions* about his crimes.

com·pu·ta·tion /ˌkɑːmpjʊˈteɪʃən/ *noun, pl* **-tions** : the act or process of computing or calculating something : CALCULATION [*noncount*] methods used for the *computation* of taxes [*count*] simple mental *computations* • The solution required a series of *computations*.
– com·pu·ta·tion·al /ˌkɑːmpjʊˈteɪʃənl/ *adj* • a *computational* model

com·pute /kəmˈpjuːt/ *verb* **-putes; -put·ed; -put·ing** [+ *obj*] : to find out (something) by using mathematical processes : CALCULATE • *compute* a batting average • *compute* your income tax ✧ In informal U.S. English, something that ***does not compute*** does not make sense. • She said they made a mistake but that *does not compute*. [=does not seem true or possible]
– com·put·able /kəmˈpjuːtəbəl/ *adj*

com·put·er /kəmˈpjuːtɚ/ *noun, pl* **-ers** [*count*] : an electronic machine that can store and work with large amounts of information • He works all day on/with a *computer*. • a personal/desktop/laptop *computer* — often used before another noun • a *computer* program/game/virus • *computer* software

com·put·er·ize *also Brit* **com·put·er·ise** /kəmˈpjuːtəˌraɪz/ *verb* **-iz·es; -ized; -iz·ing** [+ *obj*]
1 : to use a computer to make, do, or control (something) • We plan to *computerize* our billing system.
2 : to provide (something) with computers • The office is being *computerized*.
3 : to put (something) into a form that a computer can use • Libraries are *computerizing* their records.
– com·put·er·i·za·tion *also Brit* **com·put·er·i·sa·tion** /kəmˌpjuːtərəˈzeɪʃən, *Brit* kəmˌpjuːtəˌraɪˈzeɪʃən/ *noun* [*noncount*] • the *computerization* of patient records
– computerized *also Brit* **computerised** *adj* • a *computerized* billing system • a *computerized* office/database

computer science *noun* [*noncount*] : the study of computers and their uses • She has a degree in *computer science*.
– computer scientist *noun, pl* ~ **-tists** [*count*]

computing *noun* [*noncount*] : the use of computers • business *computing*
– computing *adj* • *computing* power • a *computing* system

com·rade /ˈkɑːˌmræd, *Brit* ˈkɒmˌreɪd/ *noun, pl* **-rades** [*count*]
1 : a close friend you have worked with, been in the military with, etc. • He enjoys spending time with his old army *comrades*. • He spoke fondly of his old ***comrades in arms*** [=the people he fought with or worked together with to achieve something]
2 ***Comrade*** — used as a title for a member of a communist party
– com·rade·ly *adj* • a warm and *comradely* feeling **– com·rade·ship** /ˈkɑːmˌrædˌʃɪp, *Brit* ˈkɒmˌreɪdˌʃɪp/ *noun* [*noncount*]

¹con /ˈkɑːn/ *noun, pl* **cons** [*count*] *informal* : a dishonest trick that is done to get someone's money • It was not a good investment but a *con* [=*swindle, scam*] to rob them of their savings. — called also (*US*) *confidence game,* (*US*) *con game,* (*Brit*) *confidence trick,* (*Brit*) *con trick* — compare ³CON, ⁴CON

²con *verb* **cons; conned; con·ning** [+ *obj*] *informal* : to deceive or to trick (someone) : to persuade (someone) by telling lies • We don't like being *conned*. [=*swindled*] • They are accused of *conning* retirees out of their savings. [=of deceiving retired people in order to take their savings] • She was *conned* into volunteering. • He *conned* his way into the job. [=he lied about his qualifications to get the job]

³con *noun, pl* **cons** [*count*] *informal* : a person in prison : CONVICT • a tough *con* • an ***ex-con*** [=a former prisoner] — compare ¹CON, ⁴CON

⁴con *noun, pl* **cons** [*count*]
1 : a person who is opposed to something • When the new law was proposed, we began hearing arguments from both the pros and the *cons*. [=from the people who supported it and the people who opposed it]
2 : an argument against something • Each technology has its ***pros and cons*** [=has its good parts and its bad parts] : a reason for not doing something • They carefully considered the *pros and cons* of starting their own business. [=considered the arguments for and against starting their own business] • Buying a home can be risky, but the pros outweigh the *cons*. [=the advantages outweigh the disadvantages]
– compare ¹CON, ³CON

⁵con *adv* : against something • A lot has been written ***pro and con*** about the new law. [=both for and against the new law]

con artist *noun, pl* ~ **-tists** [*count*] : a person who tricks other people in order to get their money • The couple lost their savings to a *con artist* who told them he was an investment broker. — called also *con man,* (*US*) *confidence man*

con·cat·e·na·tion /kɑnˌkætəˈneɪʃən/ *noun, pl* **-tions** [*count*] *formal* : a group of things linked together in a series • An extraordinary *concatenation* of factors led to his victory.

con·cave /ˌkɑːnˈkeɪv/ *adj* [*more* ~; *most* ~] : having a shape like the inside of a bowl : curving inward • a *concave* lens — opposite CONVEX

con·cav·i·ty /kɑnˈkævəti/ *noun, pl* **-ties**
1 [*noncount*] : the quality or state of being concave : the quality of being curved inward • the *concavity* of the lens

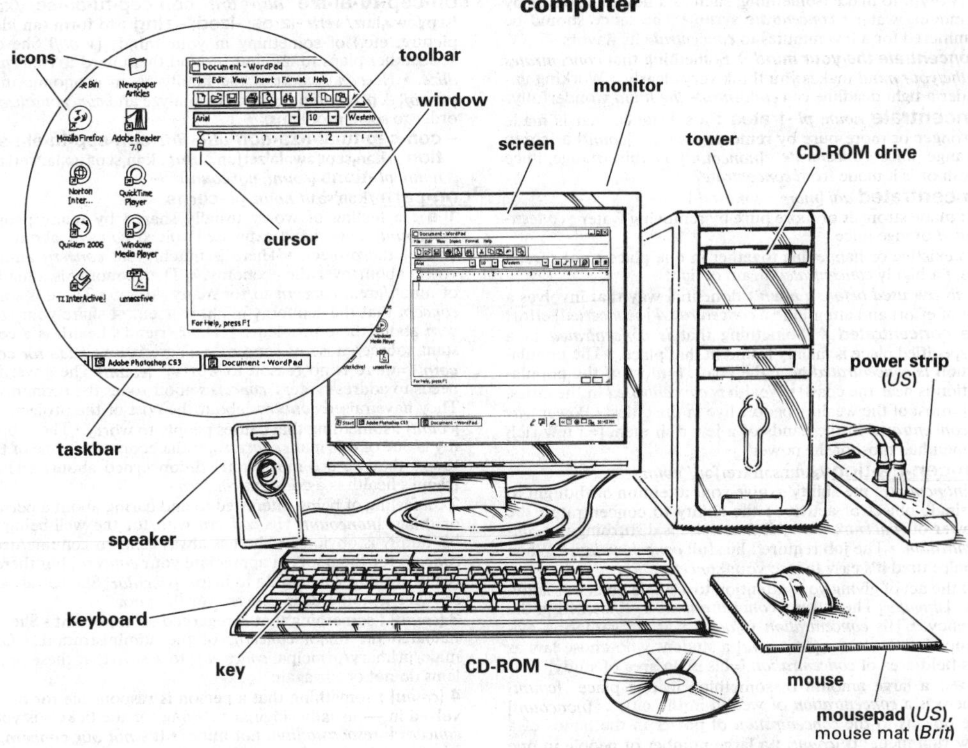

2 [*count*] : a shape that is curved inward : a concave shape • The lower back forms a *concavity*. • The large *concavities* along the wall of the restaurant are like private rooms.

con·ceal /kən'si:l/ *verb* **-ceals; -cealed; -ceal·ing** [+ *obj*]
1 : to hide (something or someone) from sight • The sunglasses *conceal* her eyes. • The controls are *concealed* behind a panel. • The defendant is accused of attempting to *conceal* evidence. — opposite REVEAL
2 : to keep (something) secret • The editorial accused the government of *concealing* the truth. • She could barely *conceal* her anger. — opposite REVEAL
– concealed *adj* • He was carrying a *concealed* [=*hidden*] weapon. • a *concealed* compartment **– con·ceal·ment** /kən'si:lmənt/ *noun* [*noncount*] • *concealment* of evidence

con·ceal·er /kən'si:lɚ/ *noun* [*noncount*] : a type of makeup that is used to hide small marks or dark areas on your face

con·cede /kən'si:d/ *verb* **-cedes; -ced·ed; -ced·ing**
1 [+ *obj*] **:** to say that you accept or do not deny the truth or existence of (something) : to admit (something) usually in an unwilling way • I *concede* that the work has been slow so far, but it should speed up soon. • When she noted that the economy was actually improving, he grudgingly/reluctantly *conceded* the point. [=he admitted that she was right] • "Your plan might work," she *conceded*, "but I still think mine is better." • It is generally *conceded* [=*acknowledged, agreed*] that they are the superior team. [=most people agree that they are the superior team]
2 : to admit that you have been defeated and stop trying to win [*no obj*] Although it seems clear that he has lost the election, he still refuses to *concede*. [+ *obj*] He's not ready to *concede* the election. • They were forced to ***concede defeat*** [=to admit that they were defeated]
3 [+ *obj*] **:** to give away (something) usually in an unwilling way • The former ruler was forced to *concede* power to a new government. • The company says that workers are not *conceding* enough in negotiations.
4 [+ *obj*] *sports* **:** to allow an opponent to score (a point, goal, etc.) • The team has not *conceded* [=*allowed*] a goal this half.

con·ceit /kən'si:t/ *noun, pl* **-ceits**
1 [*noncount*] **:** too much pride in your own worth or goodness • His *conceit* has earned him many enemies.
2 [*count*] *literary* **:** an idea that shows imagination • an artistic *conceit* • a clever *conceit*

con·ceit·ed /kən'si:təd/ *adj* [*more* ~; *most* ~] **:** having or showing too much pride in your own worth or goodness • a brilliant but *conceited* [=*vain*] musician
– con·ceit·ed·ly *adv* **– con·ceit·ed·ness** *noun* [*noncount*]

con·ceiv·able /kən'si:vəbəl/ *adj* **:** able to be imagined **:** imaginable or possible • They discussed the question from every *conceivable* angle. • It is *conceivable* that she will refuse to go.
– con·ceiv·ably /kən'si:vəbli/ *adv* • *Conceivably*, the date could be moved up a week. • We could *conceivably* [=*possibly*] finish tomorrow.

con·ceive /kən'si:v/ *verb* **-ceives; -ceived; -ceiv·ing**
1 : to think of or create (something) in the mind [+ *obj*] *conceive* an idea • a writer who has *conceived* [=*imagined*] an entire world of amazing creatures • When the writer *conceived* this role, he had a specific actor in mind to play the part. • The system was *conceived* [=*invented*] by a Swedish engineer. • As *conceived* by the committee, the bill did not raise taxes. [*no obj*] — + *of* • They *conceived of* [=*thought of, regarded*] her as a genius. • I can't *conceive of* [=*imagine*] a reason for not supporting this policy.
2 : to become pregnant [*no obj*] a woman who has been unable to *conceive* [+ *obj*] a woman who has been unable to *conceive* a child

[1]con·cen·trate /'kɑ:nsənˌtreɪt/ *verb* **-trates; -trat·ed; -trat·ing**
1 [*no obj*] **:** to think about something **:** to give your attention to the thing you are doing, reading, etc. • All that noise makes it hard to *concentrate*. • The student has difficulty *concentrating*. — often + *on* • All that noise makes it hard to *concentrate on* the book I'm trying to read. • We need to *concentrate* [=*focus*] *on* this problem. • We need to *concentrate on* finding ways to work more efficiently. • He thought about becoming a lawyer, but he has decided to *concentrate on* a medical career instead. [=he has decided to direct his efforts toward a medical career instead]
2 [+ *obj*] **:** to cause (attention, efforts, strength, etc.) to be used or directed for a single purpose — usually + *on* • She is *concentrating* her attention *on* her studies. [=she is giving her attention to her studies] • We need to *concentrate* our efforts *on* finding ways to work more efficiently.

3 [+ *obj*] **:** to make (something, such as a liquid) stronger by removing water ▪ *concentrate* syrup ▪ The sauce should be simmered for a few minutes to *concentrate* its flavors.

concentrate the/your mind ✧ Something that *concentrates the/your mind* makes you think very clearly. ▪ Working under a tight deadline can *concentrate the mind* wonderfully.

²**concentrate** *noun, pl* **-trates :** a substance that is made stronger or more pure by removing water [*count*] a frozen orange juice *concentrate* [*noncount*] Is this orange juice fresh or is it made from *concentrate*?

concentrated *adj* [*more* ~; *most* ~]

1 **:** made stronger or more pure by removing water ▪ *concentrated* orange juice

2 **:** existing or happening together in one place **:** not spread out ▪ a highly *concentrated* beam of light

3 *always used before a noun* **:** done in a way that involves a lot of effort and attention ▪ a *concentrated* [=*concerted*] effort

be concentrated ✧ Something that *is concentrated* in a specified place is mainly found in that place. ▪ The population *is concentrated* near the coast. [=most of the population is near the coast] ▪ Wealth *is concentrated* in the cities. [=most of the wealthy people live in the cities] ▪ Power *was concentrated* in the hands of a few rich men. [=a few rich men had most of the power]

con·cen·tra·tion /ˌkɑːnsənˈtreɪʃən/ *noun*

1 [*noncount*] **:** the ability to give your attention or thought to a single object or activity **:** the ability to concentrate ▪ the power of *concentration* ▪ All that noise is disturbing my *concentration*. ▪ The job required her full *concentration*. ▪ When you're tired it's easy to lose your *concentration*.

2 **:** the act of giving your attention to a single object or activity [*singular*] There was a *concentration* on ethics within the agency. ▪ His *concentration* [=*focus*] was on gathering evidence for the trial. [*noncount*] a student who chose law as his field/area of *concentration* [=his main area of study]

3 **a :** a large amount of something in one place [*count*] There is a *concentration* of wealth in the cities. [*noncount*] He objects to the *concentration* of power in the hands of a few rich men. **b** [*count*] **:** a large number of people in one place ▪ Officials are expecting a heavy/high *concentration* of tourists [=are expecting many tourists] for the festival.

4 [*count*] **:** the amount of an ingredient in a mixture ▪ Contaminants were found in low *concentrations*. [=*amounts*] ▪ measuring the *concentration* of salt in a solution ▪ They detected high *concentrations* of pollutants in the water.

concentration camp *noun, pl* ~ **camps** [*count*] **:** a type of prison where large numbers of people who are not soldiers are kept during a war and are usually forced to live in very bad conditions

con·cen·tric /kənˈsɛntrɪk/ *adj* **:** having the same center ▪ *concentric* circles

¹**con·cept** /ˈkɑːnˌsɛpt/ *noun, pl* **-cepts** [*count*] **:** an idea of what something is or how it works ▪ She is familiar with basic *concepts* of psychology. ▪ not a new *concept* ▪ a *concept* borrowed from computer programming ▪ She seems to be a little ***unclear on the concept*** of good manners. [=she seems not to understand what good manners are]

²**concept** *adj, always used before a noun*

1 **:** organized around a main idea or theme ▪ a ***concept album*** [=a collection of songs about a specific theme or story]

2 **:** created to show an idea ▪ a ***concept car*** [=a car built to test or show a new design]

con·cep·tion /kənˈsɛpʃən/ *noun, pl* **-tions**

1 [*noncount*] **:** the act or process of conceiving something: such as **a :** the process of forming an idea ▪ He directed the project from *conception* to production. ▪ the *conception* of a new device **b :** the process that occurs within a woman's body when she becomes pregnant ▪ the moment of *conception*

2 **:** an idea of what something is or should be **:** CONCEPT [*count*] They have a clear *conception* of how the process works. ▪ a child's *conception* of responsibility ▪ They have very different *conceptions* of the proper role of government. [*noncount*] He has ***no conception of*** the problems we have to face. [=he does not understand or realize the problems we have to face]

con·cep·tu·al /kənˈsɛptʃəwəl/ *adj* **:** based on or relating to ideas or concepts ▪ a *conceptual* framework/model ▪ The plans have both *conceptual* and practical difficulties. ▪ ***conceptual art*** [=art that expresses an idea]

– con·cep·tu·al·ly *adv* ▪ The software is *conceptually* similar to an earlier product but is much easier to use.

con·cep·tu·al·ize *also Brit* **con·cep·tu·al·ise** /kənˈsɛptʃəwəˌlaɪz/ *verb* **-iz·es; -ized; -iz·ing :** to form (an idea, picture, etc.) of something in your mind [+ *obj*] She described her plans to me, but I found them hard to *conceptualize*. ▪ He *conceptualizes* the family as an economic unit. [*no obj*] A programmer needs to analyze and *conceptualize* in order to solve problems.

– con·cep·tu·al·i·za·tion *also Brit* **con·cep·tu·al·i·sa·tion** /kənˌsɛptʃəwələˈzeɪʃən, *Brit* kənˌsɛptʃuəˌlaɪˈzeɪʃən/ *noun, pl* **-tions** [*count, noncount*]

¹**con·cern** /kənˈsən/ *noun, pl* **-cerns**

1 **a :** a feeling of worry usually shared by many people [*noncount*] They have expressed/voiced *concern* about the cost of the project. ▪ There is much/great *concern* among voters about/over the economy. = The economy is a matter of much/great *concern* to/for many voters. ▪ There is some *concern* that the economy might worsen. ▪ I share your *concern* about these problems. ▪ Their friend's health is a constant source/cause of *concern*. ▪ There is no ***cause for concern***. [=there is no reason to worry] [*count*] The governor needs to address voters' *concerns* about/over the economy. ▪ They have raised *concerns* about the cost of the project. **b** [*count*] **:** something that causes people to worry ▪ The economy is one of our main *concerns*. [=the economy is one of the things that we are most worried/concerned about] ▪ Their friend's health is a constant *concern*.

2 **:** a feeling of being interested in and caring about a person or thing [*noncount*] His *concern* with/for the well-being of his family is obvious. ▪ She has always shown genuine/deep *concern* for the poor. ▪ I appreciate your *concern*, but there's really nothing you can do to help. [*singular*] She has always shown a genuine/deep *concern* for the poor.

3 [*count*] **:** something that is regarded as important ▪ She articulated the major *concerns* of the administration. ▪ Our main/primary/principal *concern* is to assure that these problems do not occur again.

4 [*count*] **:** something that a person is responsible for or involved in — usually singular ▪ Paying for the tickets is your *concern* [=*responsibility*], not mine. ▪ It's ***not our concern***. = It's ***none of our concern***. = It's ***no concern of ours***. [=it's not our business; it doesn't involve/concern us]

5 [*count*] *formal* **:** a business or company ▪ a banking *concern* ▪ a ***going concern*** [=a successful business]

²**concern** *verb* **-cerns; -cerned; -cern·ing** [+ *obj*]

1 **:** to relate to (something or someone) **:** to be about (something or someone) ▪ The novel *concerns* three soldiers. ▪ This study *concerns* the noise levels in cities.

2 **:** to affect or involve (someone) **:** to be the business or interest of (someone) ▪ The problem *concerns* [=*affects*] us all. ▪ This conversation doesn't *concern* you. ✧ The phrase ***To whom it may concern*** is used at the beginning of a formal letter (such as a letter written to a company) when the name of the person who will read the letter is not known.

3 **:** to make (someone) worried **:** to cause concern for (someone) ▪ Our mother's illness *concerns* us.

concern yourself **:** to become involved or interested in something **:** to give your attention to something ▪ She can handle the problem alone. There's no need for you to *concern yourself*. ▪ There's no need for you to *concern yourself* with/in her problem. ▪ They shouldn't *concern themselves* with/about small details.

concerned *adj* [*more* ~; *most* ~]

1 **:** feeling worry or concern ▪ The school's decision is being questioned by a group of *concerned* parents. ▪ Her family was very *concerned* for/about her safety. ▪ Voters are deeply *concerned* about the economy. ▪ I was *concerned* (to hear) that they stayed out too late.

2 **a :** having an interest or involvement in something ▪ a discussion that will be of interest to everyone *concerned* ▪ The lawyers called a meeting of all the ***concerned parties***. ▪ She was more ***concerned with*** [=*interested in*] flirting than with getting the job done. ▪ (*chiefly Brit*) She was ***concerned to*** show that she could do the job. [=she thought it was important to show that she could do it] **b :** having a relation to something ▪ The memo is chiefly ***concerned with*** hiring policies. [=the memo chiefly concerns hiring policies; the memo is chiefly about hiring policies]

as far as (someone) is concerned **:** in the opinion of (someone) ▪ *As far as I'm concerned* [=in my opinion], everything he says is a lie. ▪ *As far as she's concerned*, he is perfect.

as far as (something) is concerned **:** about (something) **:** with regard to (something) ▪ He has no worries *as far as* *money is concerned.* [=he has no worries about money] ▪ *As far as the weather is concerned* [=*as for the weather*], we've been having nothing but rain for the past week.

concerning *prep* : relating to (something or someone) : ABOUT ▪ news *concerning* friends ▪ There is some confusion *concerning* [=*regarding*] his current whereabouts.

con·cert /ˈkɑːnsɚt/ *noun, pl* **-certs** [*count*] : a public performance of music ▪ a rock *concert* ▪ a classical *concert* ▪ The orchestra will be giving/having/holding a free *concert.* — sometimes used before another noun ▪ a live *concert* performance ▪ a *concert* pianist ▪ a *concert* hall

in concert **1** *formal* : TOGETHER ▪ The FBI and the local police acted *in concert* to solve the murder. — often + *with* ▪ The FBI acted *in concert with* the local police to solve the murder. **2** : performing at a concert ▪ I went to hear them ***in concert.*** [=in a public performance]

con·cert·ed /kənˈsɚtəd/ *adj, always used before a noun* : done in a planned and deliberate way usually by several or many people ▪ They made a *concerted* effort to make her feel welcome. ▪ a *concerted* action/campaign ▪ a *concerted* attack

con·cert·goer /ˈkɑːnsɚtˌgowɚ/ *noun, pl* **-goers** [*count*] : a person who often goes to concerts or who is at a particular concert ▪ a large crowd of *concertgoers*

[1]**con·cer·ti·na** /ˌkɑːnsɚˈtiːnə/ *noun, pl* **-nas** [*count*] : a musical instrument that resembles a small accordion and that is played by pressing the ends together

[2]**concertina** *verb* **-nas; -naed; -na·ing** [*no obj*] *Brit* : to fold or collapse together ▪ The car *concertinaed* on impact.

con·cert·mas·ter /ˈkɑːnsɚtˌmæstɚ, *Brit* ˈkɒnsətˌmɑːstə/ *noun, pl* **-ters** [*count*] *chiefly US* : a musician who is the leading violin player and the assistant conductor of an orchestra — called also (*Brit*) *leader*

con·cer·to /kənˈʧeɚˌtoʊ/ *noun, pl* **-ti** /-ˌtiː/ *or* **-tos** [*count*] : a piece of music for one or more main instruments with an orchestra ▪ a violin *concerto*

con·ces·sion /kənˈsɛʃən/ *noun, pl* **-sions**

1 [*count*] : the act of conceding something: such as **a** : the act of giving up something or doing something in order to reach agreement ▪ The company has been unwilling to ***make concessions*** (to the strikers) during negotiations. **b** : the act of admitting that you have been defeated in a contest ▪ We are waiting for his *concession* of the election. ▪ The candidate made an emotional ***concession speech*** when it was clear that he had lost.

2 [*count*] : something that you allow or do to end a conflict or reach an agreement ▪ The strikers have won/gained/secured some important/major *concessions* from the company.

3 [*count*] : something that is done because a particular situation makes it necessary or desirable — + *to* ▪ Her sensible shoes are a *concession to* comfort. [=she wears sensible shoes because they are comfortable] ▪ He takes afternoon naps now in/as a *concession to* his old age.

4 *US* **a** [*count*] : the right to sell something or do business on property that belongs to the government or to another company or person ▪ a mining *concession* **b** [*count*] : a small business or shop where things are sold in a public place (such as a sports stadium) ▪ He runs a *concession* that sells hot dogs and hamburgers at the ballpark. ▪ We got hot dogs at the ***concession stand.*** **c** ***concessions*** [*plural*] : things sold at a concession stand ▪ He has a license to sell *concessions* at the ballpark.

5 [*count*] *Brit* : a special lower price or rate ▪ tax *concessions* [=tax breaks] ▪ student *concessions* [=*discounts*]

con·ces·sion·aire /kənˌsɛʃəˈneɚ/ *noun, pl* **-aires** [*count*] : a person or business that has been given the right to sell something on property owned by someone else : a person or business that has been given a concession (sense 4a)

conch /ˈkɑːŋk, ˈkɑːnʧ/ *noun, pl* **conchs** /ˈkɑːŋks/ *or* **conch·es** /ˈkɑːnʧəz/ [*count*] : a type of shellfish that lives in a large shell which has the form of a spiral; *also* : the shell of a conch

con·cierge /ˌkɑːnsiˈeɚʒ/ *noun, pl* **-cierg·es** [*count*]

1 : a person in an apartment building especially in France who takes care of the building and checks the people who enter and leave

2 *chiefly US* : an employee at a hotel whose job is to provide help and information to the people staying at the hotel

con·cil·i·ate /kənˈsɪliˌeɪt/ *verb* **-ates; -at·ed; -at·ing** [+ *obj*] *formal* : to make (someone) more friendly or less angry ▪ The company's attempts to *conciliate* the strikers have failed.
— **con·cil·i·a·tion** /kənˌsɪliˈeɪʃən/ *noun* [*noncount*] — **con·cil·i·a·tor** /kənˈsɪliˌeɪtɚ/ *noun, pl* **-tors** [*count*]

con·cil·ia·to·ry /kənˈsɪlijəˌtori, *Brit* kənˈsɪliətri/ *adj* [*more ~; most ~*] : intended to make someone less angry ▪ a *conciliatory* note/message/statement ▪ She tried to sound *conciliatory* in discussing the current controversy.

con·cise /kənˈsaɪs/ *adj* [*more ~; most ~*] : using few words : not including extra or unnecessary information ▪ a clear and *concise* account of the accident ▪ a *concise* summary ▪ a *concise* definition
— **con·cise·ly** *adv* — **con·cise·ness** *noun* [*noncount*]

> ***synonyms*** CONCISE, TERSE, SUCCINCT, LACONIC, and PITHY mean expressing or stating an idea by using only a few words. CONCISE is the most general of these words and suggests a lack of extra or unnecessary information. ▪ She provided a *concise* description of the problem. TERSE suggests that you are using very few words in a way that may seem rude. ▪ "I'm not interested" was his *terse* reply. SUCCINCT suggests that the words you use are clear and helpful in explaining something. ▪ The article provides a *succinct* overview of the region's history. LACONIC suggests the use of words that may seem rude, indifferent, or mysterious. ▪ an aloof and *laconic* stranger ▪ She is known for her *laconic* style of writing. PITHY suggests the skillful or meaningful use of a small number of words. ▪ a comedy sharpened by *pithy* one-liners ▪ *pithy* prose

con·clave /ˈkɑːnˌkleɪv/ *noun, pl* **-claves** [*count*] *formal* : a private or secret meeting or group ▪ a *conclave* of bishops

con·clude /kənˈkluːd/ *verb* **-cludes; -clud·ed; -clud·ing**

1 a [*no obj*] : to stop or finish : to come to an end ▪ The investigation has not yet *concluded.* : to end in a particular way or with a particular action ▪ The meeting *concluded* at noon. ▪ The chairman *concluded* by wishing us all a happy holiday. **b** [+ *obj*] : to cause (something) to stop or finish ▪ *conclude* [=*end*] a speech : to end (something) in a particular way or with a particular action ▪ We *concluded* the meeting on a happy note. ▪ The chairman *concluded* his speech by wishing us all a happy holiday.

2 [+ *obj*] : to form or state (an opinion) : to decide (something) after a period of thought or research ▪ We *conclude* from our review of the evidence that they are right. ▪ Many studies have *concluded* that smoking is dangerous. ▪ The speech, many historians *concluded,* was the most important of his career.

3 [+ *obj*] : to complete (something, such as a business deal) : to bring about (something) as a result ▪ Their effort to *conclude* an agreement was a success. ▪ *conclude* a sale

concluding *adj* : coming at the end of something : FINAL ▪ the book's *concluding* chapter ▪ the *concluding* [=*last*] days of the campaign ▪ a *concluding* remark

con·clu·sion /kənˈkluːʒən/ *noun, pl* **-sions**

1 [*count*] : a final decision or judgment : an opinion or decision that is formed after a period of thought or research ▪ What is your *conclusion*? [=what do you conclude?] ▪ The evidence does not support the report's *conclusions.* ▪ The evidence points/leads to the inescapable *conclusion* that she was negligent. ▪ The logical/obvious *conclusion* is that she was negligent. ▪ What led/brought you to that *conclusion*? ▪ After thinking about it, we ***came to the conclusion*** [=we decided] that we shouldn't go. ▪ Scientists haven't yet ***reached a conclusion*** [=made a judgment/decision] on/about the causes of this illness. ▪ They haven't yet ***arrived at a conclusion.*** ▪ Is it possible to ***draw conclusions*** [=make judgments] from this evidence? ✧ To ***jump/leap to conclusions*** is to make judgments too quickly before knowing all the facts. ▪ The evidence suggests that he's to blame, but let's be careful not to *jump to conclusions.* He may have a good explanation for what happened. ▪ We should hear his explanation before we ***jump to the conclusion*** that he's to blame.

2 [*count*] : the last part of something : END — usually singular ▪ Many people were upset at the *conclusion* of the meeting. [=when the meeting concluded/ended] ▪ a satisfactory *conclusion* to the negotiations ▪ The *conclusion* of her speech contained some surprising news. ▪ The strike has finally ***reached its conclusion.*** [=has finally ended] ▪ At this point, his victory seems to be a ***foregone conclusion.*** [=his victory seems certain; there seems to be no doubt that he will win]

3 : the act of concluding or finishing something or the state of being finished [*singular*] We had hoped for a quick *conclusion* of/to the war. [=had hoped that the war would end quickly] ▪ The case was finally ***brought to a conclusion*** [=was finally concluded] last week. [*noncount*] the *conclusion* of a business deal ▪ The case was finally ***brought to conclusion*** last week.

in conclusion — used to introduce the final comments at the end of a speech or a piece of writing • *In conclusion,* I would like to thank you for inviting me to speak tonight.

con·clu·sive /kənˈkluːsɪv/ *adj* [*more ~; most ~*] : showing that something is certainly true • *conclusive* evidence/proof — opposite INCONCLUSIVE
– **con·clu·sive·ly** *adv* • They proved *conclusively* that they can compete with the best teams. – **con·clu·sive·ness** *noun* [*noncount*]

C

con·coct /kənˈkɑːkt/ *verb* **-cocts; -coct·ed; -coct·ing** [+ *obj*]
1 : to make (a food or drink) by mixing different things together • The drink was first *concocted* by a bartender in New York. • She *concocted* a stew from the leftovers.
2 : to invent or develop (a plan, story, etc.) especially in order to trick or deceive someone • They had *concocted* [=*devised*] a scheme/plan to steal money from the company. • He *concocted* [=*fabricated, invented*] an elaborate excuse for why he couldn't come in to work today.

con·coc·tion /kənˈkɑːkʃən/ *noun, pl* **-tions** [*count*] : something (such as a food or drink) that is made by mixing together different things • Would you like to try my new *concoction?*

[1]**con·com·i·tant** /kənˈkɑːmətənt/ *adj, formal* : happening at the same time as something else • The drug's risks increase with the *concomitant* use of alcohol. — often + *with* • changes that are *concomitant with* population growth
– **con·com·i·tant·ly** *adv*

[2]**concomitant** *noun, pl* **-tants** [*count*] *formal* : something that happens at the same time as something else : a condition that is associated with some other condition • hunger, a lack of education, and other *concomitants* of poverty

con·cord /ˈkɑːnˌkoɚd/ *noun* [*noncount*]
1 *formal* : a state in which people or things agree with each other and exist together in a peaceful way • They lived in peace and *concord.* [=*harmony*]
2 *grammar* : a state in which the different parts of a sentence or phrase agree with each other • grammatical *concord* • subject and verb *concord* [=(more commonly) *agreement*]

con·cord·ance /kənˈkoɚdəns/ *noun, pl* **-anc·es**
1 [*noncount*] *formal* : a state in which things agree and do not conflict with each other • There is little *concordance* between the two studies. • The witness's testimony was not ***in concordance with*** [=did not agree with] the rest of the evidence.
2 [*count*] : an alphabetical list of all of the words in a book or in a set of works written by an author • a *concordance* of Shakespeare's plays

con·cord·ant /kənˈkoɚdənt/ *adj, formal* : in agreement : having the same characteristics • All three tests have *concordant* results. — often + *with* • His views are *concordant with* those of the president.

con·course /ˈkɑːnˌkoɚs/ *noun, pl* **-cours·es** [*count*] : a large open space or hall in a public building • the *concourse* of the bus terminal • an airport *concourse*

[1]**con·crete** /ˈkɑːnˌkriːt/ *noun* [*noncount*] : a hard, strong material that is used for building and made by mixing cement, sand, and broken rocks with water • slabs of *concrete* — see also REINFORCED CONCRETE

[2]**con·crete** /kɑnˈkriːt/ *adj*
1 : made of concrete • a *concrete* floor/wall • *concrete* blocks • *concrete* structures
2 [*more ~; most ~*] : relating to or involving specific people, things, or actions rather than general ideas or qualities • It's helpful to have *concrete* examples of how words are used in context. • The police suspected that he was guilty, but they had no *concrete* evidence against him. [=the police had no clear and definite proof that he committed the crime] • *concrete* facts • Does anyone have any *concrete* [=*specific*] suggestions for how we can fix this? • We hope the meetings will produce *concrete* results. — opposite ABSTRACT
– **con·crete·ly** *adv* • Countries must deal with the problem more *concretely.* [=countries must develop more specific ideas for how they will deal with the problem] – **con·crete·ness** *noun* [*noncount*]

[3]**con·crete** /ˈkɑːnˌkriːt/ *verb* **-cretes; -cret·ed; -cret·ing** [+ *obj*] *Brit* : to cover or form (something) with concrete • They *concreted* (over) their drive.

concrete jungle *noun, pl* **~ jungles** [*count*] *informal* : a modern city or part of a city regarded as an unpleasant place filled with large, ugly buildings — usually singular • I finally got out of the *concrete jungle* and moved to the country.

concrete mixer *noun, pl* **~ -ers** [*count*] *Brit* : CEMENT MIXER

con·cu·bine /ˈkɑːŋkjʊˌbaɪn/ *noun, pl* **-bines** [*count*] : an unmarried woman who has sex with a man and lives with the man and his wife or wives ✧ *Concubines* were common in many different societies in the past. • the king's *concubines*

con·cur /kənˈkɚ/ *verb* **-curs; -curred; -cur·ring** [*no obj*] *formal* : to agree with someone or something • We *concur* that more money should be spent on education. • "I think more time is needed." "I *concur.*" — often + *with* • She *concurred with* the judge's ruling. = She *concurred with* the judge.

con·cur·rence /kənˈkɚrəns/ *noun, pl* **-renc·es** *formal*
1 [*noncount*] : the state of agreeing with someone or something : AGREEMENT • The bill was passed with the full *concurrence* of the Senate. [=everyone in the Senate agreed to pass the bill]
2 [*count*] : a situation in which two or more things happen at the same time : a situation in which things are concurrent — usually singular • an unlikely *concurrence* of events

con·cur·rent /kənˈkɚrənt/ *adj, formal* : happening at the same time • the *concurrent* use of two medications • He's currently serving two *concurrent* life sentences for murder.
– **con·cur·rent·ly** *adv* • The two sentences will be served *concurrently.*

con·cuss /kənˈkʌs/ *verb* **-cuss·es; -cussed; -cuss·ing** [+ *obj*] : to cause (someone) to suffer a concussion — often used as *(be) concussed* • He lay *concussed* on the ground.

con·cus·sion /kənˈkʌʃən/ *noun, pl* **-sions** : an injury to the brain that is caused by something hitting the head very hard [*count*] (*US*) • She suffered a severe *concussion* after falling on the ice. [*noncount*] (*Brit*) • He went to hospital with *concussion.*

con·demn /kənˈdɛm/ *verb* **-demns; -demned; -demn·ing** [+ *obj*]
1 : to say in a strong and definite way that someone or something is bad or wrong • We strongly *condemn* this attack against our allies. • The government *condemns* all acts of terrorism. • The country *condemns* the use of violence on prisoners. • The school *condemns* cheating, and any student caught cheating will be expelled. — often + *for* • People are *condemning* him *for* supporting the old government. • Voters *condemned* her *for* lying about her past. — often + *as* • They were *condemned as* criminals/heretics/rebels/traitors. • The policy was *condemned as* racist.
2 a : to give (someone) a usually severe punishment — usually + *to* • The jury quickly convicted her and *condemned* [=*sentenced*] her *to* death. — often used as *(be) condemned* • She *was condemned to* death. • a *condemned* man [=a man who has been sentenced to death] **b :** to cause (someone) to suffer or live in difficult or unpleasant conditions — + *to* • His lack of education *condemned* him *to* a life of poverty. — often used as *(be) condemned* • She *was condemned to* [=forced to live] a life of loneliness and suffering.
3 : to close (a building, house, etc.) for not being safe or clean enough for people to use • City officials *condemned* our apartment building and forced us to leave. — often used as *(be) condemned* • The houses *were condemned* after floods caused extensive damage. • The *condemned* building was torn down.

con·dem·na·tion /ˌkɑːndəmˈneɪʃən/ *noun, pl* **-tions :** a statement or expression of very strong and definite criticism or disapproval [*noncount*] The plan has drawn *condemnation* from both sides. [*count*] The government's statement was a *condemnation* of all acts of terrorism.

con·den·sa·tion /ˌkɑːndənˈseɪʃən/ *noun, pl* **-tions**
1 [*noncount*] : small drops of water that form on a cold surface • When we heat the house in the winter, *condensation* forms on the windows. • *Condensation* dripped from the air conditioner.
2 [*noncount*] *technical* : the process by which a gas cools and becomes a liquid • the processes of evaporation and *condensation*
3 a [*noncount*] : the act or process of making something (such as a piece of writing) shorter : the act or process of condensing something • The editor found *condensation* of the play very difficult. **b** [*count*] : a piece of writing that has been made shorter : a condensed piece of writing • a *condensation* of one of Shakespeare's plays

con·dense /kənˈdɛns/ *verb* **-dens·es; -densed; -dens·ing**
1 [+ *obj*] : to make (something) shorter or smaller by removing parts that are less important • The information is collect-

ed and then passed on to the CEO in *condensed* form. ▪ a *condensed* [=*abridged*] version of the story — often + *to* or *into* ▪ We've *condensed* the most important news down *to* a few paragraphs. ▪ Every week, they *condense* several hours of videotape *into* a one half-hour TV show. ▪ The book *condenses* nearly 50 years of history *into* 200 pages.
2 [*no obj*] **:** to change from a gas into a liquid ▪ The cooler temperatures cause the gas to *condense into* a liquid. ▪ Moisture in the air *condenses* to form tiny drops of water.
3 [+ *obj*] **:** to remove water from (something) to make it thicker ▪ *Condense* the milk by cooking it slowly. ▪ a can of ***condensed soup*** [=soup that has had much of the water removed and that is served by heating it with milk or water]

condensed milk *noun* [*noncount*] **:** canned milk with sugar added and much of the water removed ▪ a can of sweetened *condensed milk* — compare EVAPORATED MILK

con·dens·er /kənˈdɛnsɚ/ *noun, pl* **-ers** [*count*] *technical*
1 : a device used for changing a gas into a liquid ▪ a steam *condenser*
2 : a device used for storing electrical energy

con·de·scend /ˌkɑːndɪˈsɛnd/ *verb* **-scends; -scend·ed; -scend·ing** [*no obj*] *formal + disapproving*
1 : to show that you believe you are more intelligent or better than other people ▪ The author treats her readers as equals and never *condescends* (to them).
2 : to do something that you usually do not do because you believe you are too important to do it — usually followed by *to + verb* ▪ She *condescends to speak* to me only when she needs something.

condescending *adj* [*more ~; most ~*] *disapproving* **:** showing that you believe you are more intelligent or better than other people ▪ She spoke to us in a *condescending* [=*patronizing*] tone. ▪ His comments were offensive and *condescending* to us. ▪ a *condescending* attitude
– con·de·scend·ing·ly *adv*

con·de·scen·sion /ˌkɑːndɪˈsɛnʃən/ *noun* [*noncount*] **:** the attitude or behavior of people who believe they are more intelligent or better than other people ▪ The author discusses the politics of the region without *condescension*. [=without suggesting that he is more intelligent than the readers]

con·di·ment /ˈkɑːndəmənt/ *noun, pl* **-ments** [*count*] **:** something (such as salt, mustard, or ketchup) that is added to food to give it more flavor

¹con·di·tion /kənˈdɪʃən/ *noun, pl* **-tions**
1 [*noncount*] **:** a way of living or existing ▪ Happiness is the state or *condition* of being happy. ▪ The need to be loved is simply part of ***the human condition***. [=being human]
2 : the state in which something exists **:** the physical state of something [*count*] The museum restores paintings to their original *conditions*. [=the museum makes the paintings look the way they were originally] [*noncount*] The car is in excellent/perfect (physical) *condition*. ▪ Both clocks are still in good working *condition*. [=both clocks still work well]
3 [*singular*] **:** the physical or mental state of a person or animal ▪ The driver was taken to the hospital where he was reported to be in (a) good/stable/critical *condition*. ▪ Their weakened *condition* makes them more likely to get sick. ▪ He can't drive in that *condition*. [=he is too drunk, ill, upset, etc., to drive] ▪ The players are all in excellent physical *condition*. [=*shape*] ✧ If you are ***in no condition to do something***, you are not physically or mentally able to do it. ▪ I was *in no condition to go* to work yesterday. [=I was too sick to go to work] ▪ He is *in no condition to drive*. [=he is too drunk, ill, etc., to drive] ✧ If you are ***in condition*** or ***in good/excellent (etc.) condition***, you are strong and healthy. ▪ She was running every evening to stay/keep *in condition*. ▪ The players are all *in good condition*. ✧ If you are ***out of condition*** or ***in poor/bad (etc.) condition***, you are not strong and not ready to work or play a sport. ▪ He's overweight and *out of condition*. ▪ She hasn't been taking care of herself and is *in poor condition*.
4 [*count*] **:** a sickness or disease that a person has for a long time ▪ He was born with a serious heart *condition*. ▪ hereditary/genetic *conditions* ▪ The *condition* is often fatal. ▪ Her medical *condition* made it impossible for her to walk.
5 ***conditions*** [*plural*] **a :** the situation in which someone or something lives, works, etc. ▪ The organization is working to improve *conditions* for the poor by providing them with jobs, health care, and better housing. ▪ They need better living *conditions*. ▪ Companies must provide safe working *conditions* for their employees. ▪ This type of plant can live in very dry *conditions*. ▪ Both teams had trouble with the difficult playing *conditions*. ▪ dangerous driving *conditions* **b :** the things that affect the way something is or happens **:** the characteristics of a situation ▪ The President discussed the social and economic *conditions* of the country. ▪ New policies have made *conditions* more favorable for small businesses. ▪ Scientists controlled the *conditions* of the experiment. ▪ Under certain *conditions* [=in certain circumstances], it is possible to take the test at a later date. ▪ I will only take the job under the right set of *conditions*. **c :** the type of weather that occurs at a particular time ▪ weather/atmospheric *conditions* ▪ The area is experiencing cold/dry *conditions*. ▪ severe drought *conditions*
6 [*count*] **:** something that you must do or accept in order for something to happen ▪ The buyer must meet the terms and *conditions* of the contract. ▪ It was a *condition* of employment that I join the union. [=I had to join the union in order to get the job] ▪ You can go ***on one condition***: you have to finish your homework. [=you can go only if you finish your homework] ✧ If you agree to do something ***on (the) condition that*** something happens, you will do it only if that thing happens. ▪ She spoke *on the condition that* she not be identified. = She spoke ***on condition of anonymity***. ▪ He taught me the trick *on condition that* I never tell anyone else how to do it.
7 [*count*] **:** something that must happen or exist in order for something else to happen — usually + *for* or *of* ▪ Hard work is a necessary *condition for/of* success.
under no condition — used to say that something is definitely not allowed ▪ *Under no condition* are you to answer the phone. [=you are not to answer the phone at all]

²condition *verb* **-tions; -tioned; -tion·ing** [+ *obj*]
1 : to train or influence (a person or an animal) to do something or to think or behave in a certain way because of a repeated experience — often used as *(be) conditioned* ▪ an experiment in which mice are *conditioned* to press a button in order to receive food ▪ People have *been conditioned* to expect immediate results. ▪ *conditioned* behavior/responses/reflexes
2 : to make (something, such as hair or leather) softer and less dry by applying a liquid ▪ She shampoos and *conditions* [=uses conditioner on] her hair daily.
be conditioned on/upon *formal* — used to say that something will happen only if something else also happens ▪ Payment *is conditioned on/upon* completion of the project. [=if you complete the project, you will be paid]

¹con·di·tion·al /kənˈdɪʃənl/ *adj*
1 — used to describe something (such as an agreement) that will happen only if something else also happens ▪ She had a *conditional* agreement with her father that she could use the car if she paid for the gas. ▪ a *conditional* sale of land — often + *on* or *upon* ▪ Our agreement is *conditional on/upon* your raising the needed money. — compare UNCONDITIONAL
2 *grammar* **:** showing or used to show that something is true or happens only if something else is true or happens ▪ "If she speaks, you must listen" is a *conditional* sentence. ▪ The sentence contains the *conditional* clause "if she speaks."
– con·di·tion·al·ly *adv* ▪ The company has *conditionally* agreed to sell 20 percent of its stock.

²conditional *noun, pl* **-als** *grammar*
1 [*count*] **:** a word, clause, or sentence that shows that something is true or happens only if something else is true or happens ▪ The clause "if she speaks" is a *conditional*.
2 ***the conditional*** **:** the mood or form that is used to say that something is true or happens only if something else is true or happens ▪ *The conditional* is often marked by the word "if."

con·di·tion·er /kənˈdɪʃənɚ/ *noun, pl* **-ers** [*count, noncount*]
1 : a thick liquid that you put on your hair after washing it to make it softer and less dry
2 *Brit* **:** FABRIC SOFTENER
– see also AIR CONDITIONER

con·di·tion·ing /kənˈdɪʃənɪŋ/ *noun* [*noncount*]
1 *chiefly US* **:** the process of becoming stronger and healthier by following a regular exercise program and diet ▪ the team's excellent physical *conditioning* ▪ aerobic *conditioning* [=*training*] — often used before another noun ▪ After a three week *conditioning* program, he was ready to compete. ▪ strength and *conditioning* workouts
2 : the act or process of training a person or animal to do something or to behave in a certain way in a particular situation ▪ social *conditioning* ▪ With the proper *conditioning*, the horse will learn to trust and obey its handler.
– see also AIR-CONDITIONING

C

con·do /ˈkɑːndoʊ/ *noun, pl* **-dos** [*count*] *US* : CONDOMINIUM

con·do·lence /kənˈdoʊləns/ *noun, pl* **-lenc·es** : a feeling or expression of sympathy and sadness especially when someone is suffering because of the death of a family member, a friend, etc. [*noncount*] The governor issued a statement of *condolence* to the victims' families. ▪ a letter of *condolence* [*plural*] We wish to express/offer/send our sincere *condolences* to your family. ▪ Please accept my *condolences*.

con·dom /ˈkɑːndəm/ *noun, pl* **-doms** [*count*] : a thin rubber covering that a man wears on his penis during sex in order to prevent a woman from becoming pregnant or to prevent the spread of diseases — called also *rubber, (Brit) sheath*

con·do·min·i·um /ˌkɑːndəˈmɪnijəm/ *noun, pl* **-ums** [*count*] *chiefly US*
1 : a room or set of rooms that is owned by the people who live there and that is part of a larger building containing other similar sets of rooms — compare APARTMENT
2 : a building that contains condominiums

con·done /kənˈdoʊn/ *verb* **-dones; -doned; -don·ing** [+ *obj*] : to forgive or approve (something that is considered wrong) : to allow (something that is considered wrong) to continue ▪ a government that has been accused of *condoning* racism — often used in negative statements ▪ We cannot *condone* [=*excuse*] that kind of behavior.

con·dor /ˈkɑːnˌdoɚ/ *noun, pl* **-dors** [*count*] : a very large black bird from South America or a related bird from North America

con·du·cive /kənˈduːsɪv, *Brit* kənˈdjuːsɪv/ *adj, not used before a noun* [*more* ~; *most* ~] *formal* : making it easy, possible, or likely for something to happen or exist — + *to* ▪ The school tries to create an atmosphere (that is) *conducive to* learning. [=an atmosphere that makes learning easier] ▪ Hot, dry weather is *conducive to* the spread of forest fires.

[1]**con·duct** /kənˈdʌkt/ *verb* **-ducts; -duct·ed; -duct·ing**
1 [+ *obj*] : to plan and do (something, such as an activity) ▪ The police are *conducting* an investigation into last week's robbery. ▪ scientists *conducting* research/experiments ▪ I like the way the company *conducts* business. ▪ The magazine *conducted* a survey. ▪ Who will be *conducting* the meeting? ▪ The committee is expected to *conduct* hearings in May.
2 : to direct the performance of (musicians or singers) [+ *obj*] He *conducts* the choir with great skill and emotion. ▪ *conducting* the music of Mozart [*no obj*] She *conducts* extremely well.
3 *always followed by a preposition or adverb* [+ *obj*] *formal* : to guide or lead (someone) through or around a place ▪ Our guide slowly *conducted* us through the museum. ▪ Our guide *conducted* us along the path.
4 [+ *obj*] *technical* : to allow (heat or electricity) to move from one place to another ▪ Metals *conduct* electricity well.
conduct yourself : to behave especially in a public or formal situation ▪ The way you *conduct yourself* in an interview often determines whether or not you get the job. ▪ She *conducted herself* as a professional and earned the respect of her coworkers. ▪ I don't approve of the way he *conducts himself*.

[2]**con·duct** /ˈkɑːnˌdʌkt/ *noun* [*noncount*] *somewhat formal*
1 : the way that a person behaves in a particular place or situation ▪ A panel investigated her *conduct* and she was subsequently fired. ▪ His personal *conduct* reflected poorly on the company. [=he behaved in a way that made the company look bad] ▪ professional/sexual *conduct*
2 : the way that something is managed or directed — + *of* ▪ Laws and regulations control the *conduct* [=*management*] *of* business and trade.

con·duc·tion /kənˈdʌkʃən/ *noun* [*noncount*] *technical* : the movement of heat or electricity through something (such as metal or water) ▪ the *conduction* of electricity

con·duc·tiv·i·ty /ˌkɑːnˌdʌkˈtɪvəti/ *noun* [*noncount*] *technical* : the ability to move heat or electricity from one place to another : the power to conduct heat or electricity ▪ measuring the *conductivity* of different metals
– **con·duc·tive** /kənˈdʌktɪv/ *adj* [*more* ~; *most* ~] ▪ Copper is a *conductive* material.

con·duc·tor /kənˈdʌktɚ/ *noun, pl* **-tors** [*count*]
1 : a person who stands in front of people while they sing or play musical instruments and directs their performance
2 : a person who collects money or tickets from passengers on a train or bus — called also *(Brit) guard*
3 : a material or object that allows electricity or heat to move through it ▪ Metal is a good *conductor* of electricity.

con·duc·tress /kənˈdʌktrəs/ *noun, pl* **-tress·es** [*count*] : a woman who is a conductor

con·duit /ˈkɑːnˌduːwət, *Brit* ˈkɒndɪt/ *noun, pl* **-duits** [*count*]
1 *technical* : a pipe or tube through which something (such as water or wire) passes
2 *formal* : someone or something that is used as a way of sending something (such as information or money) from one place or person to another ▪ The council serves as a *conduit* [=*channel*] of information between the school and the children's parents. — often + *for* ▪ a port that has been a *conduit for* the trade of illegal weapons

[1]**cone** /ˈkoʊn/ *noun, pl* **cones** [*count*]
1 : a shape that has a pointed top and sides that form a circle at the bottom
2 : a hard and dry part that is the fruit of a pine tree or other evergreen plant and contains many seeds
3 a : something that looks like a cone ▪ He scooped out the popcorn with a paper *cone*. — see also TRAFFIC CONE **b** : the top of a volcano
4 : a thin crisp cookie that is usually shaped like a cone and that is used to hold ice cream ▪ Would you like your ice cream in a dish or a *cone*? ; *also* : a cone filled with ice cream ▪ I'd like two ***ice-cream cones*** please. — see also SNOW CONE

[2]**cone** *verb* **cones; coned; coning**
cone off [*phrasal verb*] ***cone off (something)*** *Brit* : to close off (a road or part of a road) with traffic cones ▪ The road was partially *coned off* while the repairs were being made.

con·fec·tion /kənˈfɛkʃən/ *noun, pl* **-tions** [*count*] : a very sweet food ▪ an assortment of delicious cakes and other *confections* — often + *of* ▪ a *confection of* cream, chocolate, and nuts — sometimes used figuratively ▪ a delightful literary *confection*

con·fec·tion·er /kənˈfɛkʃənɚ/ *noun, pl* **-ers** [*count*] : a person or business that makes or sells confections (such as chocolates and candies)

confectioners' sugar *noun* [*noncount*] *US* : POWDERED SUGAR

con·fec·tion·ery /kənˈfɛkʃəˌneri, *Brit* kənˈfɛkʃənri/ *noun* [*noncount*] *somewhat formal* : sweet foods (such as fudge and candy) — often used before another noun ▪ a *confectionery* shop

con·fed·er·a·cy /kənˈfɛdərəsi/ *noun, pl* **-cies**
1 [*count*] : a group of people, countries, organizations, etc., that are joined together in some activity or effort ▪ a *confederacy* of native tribes
2 ***the Confederacy*** : the group of 11 southern states that separated themselves from the U.S. during the American Civil War ▪ the last state to join *the Confederacy*

con·fed·er·ate /kənˈfɛdərət/ *noun, pl* **-ates** [*count*]
1 *formal* : a person who helps someone do something ▪ He turned to his *confederates* [=*allies, accomplices*] for help.
2 ***Confederate*** : a soldier, citizen, or supporter of the Confederacy during the American Civil War ▪ the Yankees and the *Confederates*

Con·fed·er·ate /kənˈfɛdərət/ *adj* : of or relating to the Confederacy of the American Civil War ▪ *Confederate* states/soldiers/money ▪ the *Confederate* flag/army

con·fed·er·a·tion /kənˌfɛdəˈreɪʃən/ *noun, pl* **-tions** [*count*] : a group of people, countries, organizations, etc., that are joined together in some activity or effort ▪ a loose *confederation* [=*coalition*] of businesses

con·fer /kənˈfɚ/ *verb* **-fers; -ferred; -fer·ring** *formal*
1 [*no obj*] : to discuss something important in order to make a decision ▪ The lawyer and judge *conferred* about the ruling. — often + *with* ▪ I'll *confer with* [=*consult*] my wife and let you know what we decide.
2 [+ *obj*] : to give (something, such as a degree, award, title, right, etc.) to someone or something — usually + *on* or *upon* ▪ The university will *confer* an honorary degree *on* the governor. ▪ The law *conferred upon* people over the age of 18 the right to vote.

con·fer·ee /ˌkɑːnfəˈriː/ *noun, pl* **-ees** [*count*] *US, formal* : someone who participates in a conference — usually plural ▪ *Conferees* from the Senate and the House will begin debating the issue next week.

con·fer·ence /ˈkɑːnfərəns/ *noun, pl* **-enc·es**
1 [*count*] : a formal meeting in which many people gather in order to talk about ideas or problems related to a particular topic (such as medicine or business) usually for several days ▪ The organization held/hosted its annual *conference* in New York this year. ▪ national *conferences* on women's health ▪ an

international peace *conference* [=a meeting in which leaders of many countries talk about peace] • a *conference* of foreign ministers — sometimes used before another noun • a *conference* center [=a large building where conferences are held]
2 : a formal meeting in which a small number of people talk about something [*count*] Our boss called a *conference* to discuss the new changes. [*noncount*] He spent an hour ***in conference*** with the president. — often used before another noun • a *conference* room/table — see also CONFERENCE CALL, NEWS CONFERENCE, PRESS CONFERENCE
3 [*count*] *US* **:** a group of sports teams that play against each other and that are part of a larger league of teams • a football *conference* • the champions of the American Football *Conference* — often used before another noun • the *conference* champions/championship

conference call *noun, pl* **~ calls** [*count*] **:** a telephone call in which someone talks to several people at the same time

con·fer·ment /kənˈfɚmənt/ *noun* [*noncount*] *formal* **:** the act of giving something (such as a degree, award, title, or right) to someone **:** the act of conferring something • the *conferment* of degrees/privileges

con·fess /kənˈfɛs/ *verb* **-fess·es; -fessed; -fess·ing**
1 : to admit that you did something wrong or illegal [*no obj*] He *confessed* after being questioned for many hours. — often + *to* • He's still refusing to *confess to* the murder. • No one *confessed to* taking the pen. • She *confessed to* having lied to me in the past. [=she told me that she lied to me] [+ *obj*] She *confessed* [=*admitted*] that she stole the necklace. • He willingly *confessed* his crime/guilt.
2 : to talk about or admit something that makes you embarrassed, ashamed, etc. [+ *obj*] He *confessed* (that) he got lost and had to ask for directions. • I have to *confess* that I was afraid at first. • I must *confess* [=I am a little embarrassed to say] that I know nothing about computers. • He never *confessed* his love for her. [=he never told her that he loved her] [*no obj*] — usually + *to* • She *confessed to* a love of trashy romance novels. [=she admitted that she loves trashy romance novels] • I *confess to* being a little unsure about what to do.
3 : to tell (your sins) to God or to a priest [+ *obj*] I *confessed* my sins to the priest. [*no obj*] I haven't *confessed* [=gone to confession] in three months.
– confessed *adj* • a *confessed* murderer — see also SELF-CONFESSED

con·fes·sion /kənˈfɛʃən/ *noun, pl* **-sions**
1 [*count*] **:** a written or spoken statement in which you say that you have done something wrong or committed a crime • She went to the police station and made/gave a full *confession*. • a written/signed *confession*
2 [*count*] **:** the act of telling people something that makes you embarrassed, ashamed, etc. • I have a *confession* to make: I have never done this before. • a *confession* of weakness/failure/error
3 a [*count*] **:** the act of telling your sins to God or to a priest • The priest will hear *confessions* after mass today. **b** [*noncount*] **:** the activity of telling a priest your sins • I haven't ***gone/been to confession*** in three years.
4 [*count*] **:** a formal statement in which you express your religious beliefs • a *confession* of faith

¹con·fes·sion·al /kənˈfɛʃənl/ *noun, pl* **-als** [*count*] **:** a private place inside a church where a priest hears confessions

²confessional *adj* [*more ~; most ~*] **:** telling private information about a person's life • *confessional* interviews of famous actors • *confessional* poetry/writing

con·fes·sor /kənˈfɛsɚ/ *noun, pl* **-sors** [*count*] **:** a priest who listens to a person's confession

con·fet·ti /kənˈfɛti/ *noun* [*noncount*] **:** small pieces of brightly colored paper that people often throw at celebrations (such as weddings and parties)

con·fi·dant /ˈkɑːnfəˌdɑːnt/ *noun, pl* **-dants** [*count*] **:** a trusted friend you can talk to about personal and private things • He is a trusted *confidant* of the president.

con·fi·dante /ˈkɑːnfəˌdɑːnt/ *noun, pl* **-dantes** [*count*] **:** a woman who is a trusted friend **:** a female confidant • She was her closest friend and *confidante*.

con·fide /kənˈfaɪd/ *verb* **-fides; -fid·ed; -fid·ing** [+ *obj*] **:** to tell (something that is secret or private) to someone you trust • He *confided* that he was very unhappy with his job. — often + *to* • She *confided to* me that she couldn't read. • He *confided* his secret *to* a friend. — see also CONFIDING
confide in [*phrasal verb*] ***confide in (someone)*** **:** to tell personal and private things to (someone) • She often *confides in* me. • He had no one to *confide in*.

con·fi·dence /ˈkɑːnfədəns/ *noun, pl* **-denc·es**
1 [*noncount*] **:** a feeling or belief that you can do something well or succeed at something • The class gave me more *confidence*. • He lacked the *confidence* to succeed. • The experience gave her the *confidence* to start her own business. • Good grades boosted/bolstered her *confidence*. • It takes time to build/gain *confidence* when you are learning a new skill. • He's brimming with *confidence*. = He's full of *confidence*. • They have an air of *confidence* about them. — often + *in* • He has a lot of *confidence in* himself. — see also SELF-CONFIDENCE
2 [*noncount*] **:** a feeling or belief that someone or something is good or has the ability to succeed at something • The candidate has won/lost the *confidence* [=*trust*] of voters. • She has done little to gain/earn their *confidence*. • There is a recent increase in ***consumer confidence***. [=the good feelings that people have about the economy] — often + *in* • They have complete/full *confidence in* their coach. • His parents had *confidence in* their son's ability to succeed. • The case inspired/restored *confidence in* our system of justice. • Recent scandals have undermined *confidence in* the city's public officials. — see also VOTE OF CONFIDENCE, VOTE OF NO CONFIDENCE
3 [*noncount*] **:** the feeling of being certain that something will happen or that something is true • School officials express *confidence* that the problem will soon be resolved. • We still can't talk about the future with any degree of *confidence*. [=we don't know what will happen in the future] • We have ***every confidence*** [=we are sure] that you'll make the right decision.
4 [*noncount*] **:** a relationship in which you tell personal and private information to someone • Doctors cannot betray the *confidence* of their patients. [=cannot reveal their patients' personal information to other people] • She accused him of a betrayal/breach of *confidence*. • He told me ***in confidence*** that he didn't know how to read. • Your personal information will be kept ***in strict/strictest confidence***. [=no one will be told your personal information] ✧ If you ***take someone into your confidence***, you tell someone secrets or private information about your life. • She *took me into her confidence* and told me all about her health problems.
5 [*count*] **:** a secret that you tell someone you trust • close friends sharing *confidences* • She accused him of betraying a *confidence*. [=she said that he told her secret to other people]

confidence game *noun, pl* **~ games** [*count*] *US* **:** ¹CON

confidence man *noun, pl* **~ men** [*count*] *US* **:** CON ARTIST

confidence trick *noun, pl* **~ tricks** [*count*] *Brit* **:** ¹CON

confidence trickster *noun, pl* **~ -ers** [*count*] *Brit* **:** CON ARTIST

con·fi·dent /ˈkɑːnfədənt/ *adj* [*more ~; most ~*]
1 a : having a feeling or belief that you can do something well or succeed at something **:** having confidence • The class made me more *confident* (about myself). • a *confident* young businesswoman • I am *confident* about my ability to do the job. • The players seem more relaxed and *confident* this season. • He has become more *confident* in his Spanish-speaking skills. — see also OVERCONFIDENT, SELF-CONFIDENT **b :** showing that you have confidence • a *confident* smile • They have a *confident* air about them. • His voice sounded *confident*.
2 *not used before a noun* **:** certain that something will happen or that something is true • We are *confident* that conditions will improve soon. • He seemed *confident* of success. [=sure that he would succeed]
– con·fi·dent·ly *adv* • "I know the answer," she said *confidently*. • We can *confidently* state that the product is safe.

con·fi·den·tial /ˌkɑːnfəˈdɛnʃəl/ *adj*
1 [*more ~; most ~*] **:** secret or private • These documents are completely/strictly *confidential*. • *confidential* medical records • Someone was leaking *confidential* information [=telling secrets] to the press.
2 [*more ~; most ~*] **:** showing that you are saying something that is secret or private • "I have something to tell you," John said in a *confidential* tone/voice. • Her voice was quiet and *confidential*.
3 *always used before a noun* **:** trusted with secret or private information • She worked as a *confidential* secretary to the mayor for many years.
– con·fi·den·tial·ly *adv* • Students can *confidentially* report any problems they see in their schools. • He leaned

forward *confidentially* and began telling his story. • *Confidentially*, I don't think she's very good at her job.

con·fi·den·ti·al·i·ty /ˌkɑːnfəˌdɛnʃiˈæləti/ *noun [noncount]* **: the quality or state of being private or confidential** • All medical records are treated with complete *confidentiality*. [=are kept completely private] • The doctor committed a ***breach of confidentiality*** [=the doctor told another person private information about a patient]

C

con·fid·ing /kənˈfaɪdɪŋ/ *adj [more ~; most ~]* **: showing that you trust someone not to tell secret or private information** • He spoke in a *confiding* voice. • They've developed a very *confiding* relationship over the years.

– con·fid·ing·ly *adv*

con·fig·u·ra·tion /kənˌfɪgjəˈreɪʃən, *Brit* kənˌfɪgəˈreɪʃən/ *noun, pl* **-tions** *[count]*

1 : the way the parts of something are arranged • a truck's gear *configuration* • airplane seating *configurations* • the *configuration* [=layout] of the room

2 *computers* **: the way a computer system or program is prepared for a particular use** • We'll have to change the *configuration* of the system to accommodate the new server.

con·fig·ure /kənˈfɪgjɚ, *Brit* kənˈfɪgə/ *verb* **-ures; -ured; -ur·ing** *[+ obj] technical* **: to arrange or prepare (something) so that it can be used** • The instructions tell you how to *configure* the kit correctly. • The plane is *configured* for military use. • *configure* a computer • The system is *configured* [=set up] to allow access only to people who know the password.

con·fine /kənˈfaɪn/ *verb* **-fines; -fined; -fin·ing** *[+ obj]*

1 : to keep (someone or something) within limits : to prevent (someone or something) from going beyond a particular limit, area, etc. — usually + *to* • Please *confine* [=restrict, limit] your comments *to* 200 words. • The cancer was *confined to* the lung. [=the cancer was only in the lung; the cancer had not spread to any other parts of the body] • We must *confine* ourselves *to* the agenda we've agreed on for this meeting. [=we must only talk about what is on the agenda] • The town would like to *confine* commercial development *to* an area by the highway. • Students need not *confine* themselves *to* a single area of study. • The city's poverty is not *confined to* just one neighborhood.

2 : to keep (a person or animal) in a place (such as a prison) — usually used as *(be) confined* • Violent criminals *are* sometimes *confined* for life. • a camp where prisoners *were confined* during the war **— often + *to* or *in*** • She *was confined to* a psychiatric hospital for a year. • The bull *was confined in* a pen behind the barn.

3 : to force or cause (someone) to stay in something (such as a bed or wheelchair) — usually used as *(be) confined* • I regularly visit a sick neighbor who *is confined* at home. [=who cannot leave home because of being sick] **— often + *to*** • He *was confined to* a wheelchair. • She *was confined to* bed for a week with the flu.

confined *adj [more ~; most ~] of a space or area* **: very small** • She gets uncomfortable in *confined* spaces.

con·fine·ment /kənˈfaɪnmənt/ *noun [noncount]*

1 : the act of confining someone or something : the state of being confined • the *confinement* of violent criminals [=the act of keeping violent criminals in prison] • years of *confinement* • his *confinement* to a wheelchair [=his state of being forced to stay in a wheelchair] • The dog was kept ***in confinement*** until it was determined to be healthy. — see also SOLITARY CONFINEMENT

2 *old-fashioned* **: the time when a woman is giving birth to a baby** • He remained with his wife during her *confinement*.

con·fines /ˈkɑːnˌfaɪnz/ *noun [plural] formal* **: the limits or edges of something** • He is probably somewhere within the *confines* [=(more commonly) borders] of the city. • The children were told not to venture beyond the *confines* of the camp. • There is no room for negotiation within the *confines* of this contract. • the narrow *confines* of academia

confining *adj [more ~; most ~]* **: limiting or preventing movement or freedom** • She thinks the corporate world is dull and *confining*. [=restrictive] • This coat feels too *confining*. [=tight]

con·firm /kənˈfɚm/ *verb* **-firms; -firmed; -firm·ing**

1 *[+ obj]* **: to state or show that (something) is true or correct** • The tests *confirmed* the doctors' suspicions of cancer. • The attack *confirmed* her worst fears about the neighborhood. • Police would not *confirm* [=verify] reports of a shooting. • The award *confirmed* her status as one of the great movie actresses. • Medical tests *confirmed* (that) he did not have a heart attack.

2 : to tell someone that something has definitely happened or is going to happen : to make (something) definite or official *[+ obj]* The dentist's office called to *confirm* your appointment for tomorrow. • Please *confirm* [=acknowledge] receipt of the shipment. • *confirm* a hotel reservation *[no obj]* We have a reservation for you for tomorrow night. Please call to *confirm*.

3 *[+ obj] formal* **: to make (something) stronger or more certain : to cause (someone) to believe (something) more strongly** • Her parents' attitude only *confirmed* [=strengthened, reinforced] her resolve to get her own apartment. **— often + *in*** • She was *confirmed in* her determination to get a higher-paying job.

4 : to give official approval to (something or someone) *[+ obj]* They voted to *confirm* [=ratify] the treaty. • The Senate has *confirmed* him as a Supreme Court justice. *[no obj]* The Senate is expected to vote to *confirm*.

5 *[+ obj]* **: to make (someone) a full member of a church or synagogue : to administer confirmation to (someone) — usually used as *(be) confirmed*** • Our son will *be confirmed* in the spring. • What year *were* you *confirmed*?

– con·firm·able /kənˈfɚməbəl/ *adj [more ~; most ~]* • Reports of a battle in the city were not *confirmable* today. • The judicial nominee should be easily *confirmable*.

con·fir·ma·tion /ˌkɑːnfɚˈmeɪʃən/ *noun, pl* **-tions**

1 *[noncount]* **: proof which shows that something is true or correct** • Reporters awaited *confirmation* from the army about the battle. • We don't have independent *confirmation* of the facts. • Final *confirmation* came only after the investigation was completed. **— often + *of*** • The customs officers will need to see *confirmation* [=proof] *of* your identity. • *confirmation of* a scientific theory

2 : a response which shows that information is received and understood; *especially* : a response that makes a purchase, appointment, etc., definite or official *[count]* You will receive an e-mail *confirmation* of your order. *[noncount]* You will receive *confirmation* of your order by e-mail. • waiting for written *confirmation*

3 *[noncount]* **: the act of giving official approval to something or someone** • Many senators are opposed to his *confirmation* as a federal judge. **— often used before another noun** • Senate *confirmation* hearings • the *confirmation* process

4 : a ceremony in which someone becomes a full, adult member of a religion *[noncount]* They are preparing for *confirmation*. *[count]* He attended both of his children's *confirmations*.

con·firmed /kənˈfɚmd/ *adj, always used before a noun* **: not likely to change** • a *confirmed* [=habitual, chronic] optimist • a *confirmed* baseball fanatic • a ***confirmed bachelor*** [=a man who seems happy to remain unmarried]

con·fis·cate /ˈkɑːnfəˌskeɪt/ *verb* **-cates; -cat·ed; -cat·ing** *[+ obj]* **: to take (something) away from someone especially as punishment or to enforce the law or rules** • Guards *confiscated* knives and other weapons from the prisoners. • The police have the authority to *confiscate* [=seize] the drug dealer's property. • The teacher *confiscated* all cell phones for the duration of the field trip.

– con·fis·ca·tion /ˌkɑːnfəˈskeɪʃən/ *noun [noncount]* • the *confiscation* of terrorists' assets

con·fla·gra·tion /ˌkɑːnfləˈgreɪʃən/ *noun, pl* **-tions** *[count] formal*

1 : a large destructive fire • a massive *conflagration*

2 : a war or conflict • The treaty is the latest attempt to resolve the ten-year *conflagration*. • a regional *conflagration*

¹con·flict /ˈkɑːnˌflɪkt/ *noun, pl* **-flicts**

1 : a struggle for power, property, etc. *[count]* an armed *conflict* • violent border *conflicts* • a *conflict* between two gangs *[noncount]* years of armed *conflict* [=battle] • recent violent *conflict* in the region • *conflict* between (forces of) good and evil

2 : strong disagreement between people, groups, etc., that results in often angry argument *[noncount]* Everyone in my family always tries to avoid *conflict*. • There was inevitable *conflict* over what to name the group. *[count]* They're having serious *conflicts* over the budget. • A few students are being trained to resolve *conflicts* [=arguments, disputes] between other students.

3 : a difference that prevents agreement : disagreement between ideas, feelings, etc. *[count]* I don't see any *conflicts* between the theories. • exploring the character's ***inner conflicts*** [=ideas, feelings, etc., that disagree with one another] *[noncount]* You'll need to resolve the *conflict* between your parents' plans for you and your own ambitions. — see also CONFLICT OF INTEREST

4 [*count*] *chiefly US* **:** a situation in which you are unable to do something because there is something else you have already agreed to do at that same time ▪ He has a *conflict* and can't attend tomorrow's meeting. ▪ a scheduling *conflict*

come into conflict **1 :** to be different in a way that prevents agreement ▪ Unfortunately, their goals for the project *came into conflict.* — often + *with* ▪ There are cases in which these rules *come into conflict with* [=*contradict*] one another. **2 :** to enter a situation in which there is a struggle for power, property, etc. — often + *with* ▪ groups *coming into conflict with* neighboring tribes

in conflict **1 :** different in a way that prevents agreement ▪ They're *in conflict* over which car to buy. [=they disagree about which car to buy] — usually + *with* ▪ The law is *in conflict with* [=does not agree with] the state's constitution. ▪ Her ideas were *in* direct *conflict with* those of her professor. **2 :** in a struggle for power, property, etc. ▪ The two clans were *in* constant *conflict* (with one another).

²con·flict /kən'flɪkt/ *verb* **-flicts; -flict·ed; -flict·ing** [*no obj*]

1 : to be different in a way that prevents agreement **:** to say or express opposite things ▪ Their versions of what happened *conflict.* [=do not agree] ▪ Their goals for the project *conflict.* [=*clash, disagree*] ▪ Reports *conflicted* on how many people were involved. — often + *with* ▪ His statement *conflicts with* the facts. ▪ Their research *conflicts with* [=*contradicts*] what other scientists have found.

2 : to happen at the same time as something else — usually + *with* ▪ The appointment *conflicts with* an important meeting I have to go to.

– conflicting *adj* ▪ We heard *conflicting* reports about how many people were involved. ▪ the candidates' *conflicting* views ▪ our *conflicting* schedules

con·flict·ed *adj* [*more* ~; *most* ~] *chiefly US* **:** having or showing feelings that disagree with one another ▪ She was still *conflicted* about her ex-husband's remarriage. ▪ the novel's *conflicted* characters

conflict of interest *noun, pl* **conflicts of interest** [*count*] *formal* **:** a problem caused by having official responsibilities that involve things that might be helpful or harmful to you ▪ Critics say the senator created a *conflict of interest* when she recommended a change to the law that could benefit her husband's company.

con·flu·ence /'kɑːnˌfluːwəns/ *noun* [*singular*]

1 *technical* **:** a place where two rivers or streams join to become one ▪ the Mississippi River's *confluence* with the Missouri River

2 *somewhat formal* **:** a situation in which two things come together or happen at the same time — usually + *of* ▪ a *confluence of* musical styles ▪ a rare *confluence* of events

con·form /kən'foəm/ *verb* **-forms; -formed; -form·ing** [*no obj*]

1 : to be similar to or the same as something — usually + *to* or *with* ▪ The animals' behavior *conforms to* a common pattern. ▪ Our budget numbers *conform with* official estimates.

2 : to obey or agree with something ▪ There are new security rules and all airlines are required to *conform.* [=(more commonly) *comply*] — usually + *to* or *with* ▪ The building doesn't *conform to* local regulations. ▪ She refuses to *conform to* society's traditional image of a mother. ▪ Employees have to *conform with* company rules. ▪ The priest's teachings do not *conform with* church doctrine.

3 : to do what other people do **:** to behave in a way that is accepted by most people ▪ Most teenagers feel pressure to *conform.*

con·for·ma·tion /ˌkɑːnˌfoə'meɪʃən/ *noun, pl* **-tions** *technical* **:** the way in which something is formed or shaped [*noncount*] The dogs will be judged on *conformation* tomorrow. [*count*] protein *conformations*

con·form·ist /kən'foəmɪst/ *noun, pl* **-ists** [*count*] *often disapproving* **:** a person who behaves in a way that is considered acceptable by most people and who avoids doing things that could be considered different or unusual **:** a person who conforms ▪ They went from being angry punk rockers to bland *conformists.* ▪ They like to travel, but they're *conformists* who go to only the most popular destinations. — opposite NONCONFORMIST

– conformist *adj* [*more* ~; *most* ~] ▪ a *conformist* society [=a society in which everyone behaves the same way] ▪ *conformist* attitudes

con·for·mi·ty /kən'foəməti/ *noun* [*noncount*]

1 : behavior that is the same as the behavior of most other people in a society, group, etc. ▪ religious *conformity* ▪ mindless *conformity* ▪ The corporate culture demands a certain *conformity* of appearance. ▪ *conformity* [=*obedience*] to social customs

2 : the fact or state of agreeing with or obeying something — usually + *to* or *with* ▪ the building's *conformity to* state specifications ▪ The state's traffic laws were changed to bring them into *conformity with* the rest of the country. ▪ We removed our shoes, ***in conformity with*** tradition.

con·found /kən'faʊnd/ *verb* **-founds; -found·ed; -found·ing** [+ *obj*]

1 : to surprise and confuse (someone or something) ▪ The strategy *confounded* our opponents. ▪ The murder case has *confounded* investigators. — often used as *(be) confounded* ▪ Investors *were confounded* by the conflicting reports.

2 : to prove (someone or something) wrong ▪ The school's team *confounded* all predictions and won the game. ▪ The success of the show *confounded* critics.

3 *informal + old-fashioned* — used as an interjection to express anger or annoyance ▪ ***Confound it!*** I can't find my keys!

confounded *adj, always used before a noun, informal + old-fashioned* **:** very bad or annoying ▪ I can't close this *confounded* window!

con·front /kən'frʌnt/ *verb* **-fronts; -front·ed; -front·ing** [+ *obj*]

1 a : to oppose or challenge (someone) especially in a direct and forceful way ▪ They *confronted* the invaders at the shore. — often used as *(be) confronted* ▪ He *was confronted* by a security guard when he tried to leave the store. ▪ The mayor *was confronted* by a group of angry protesters. **b :** to directly question the action or authority of (someone) ▪ She *confronted* him about his smoking. ▪ No one was willing to *confront* [=*challenge*] the company president on that point.

2 a : to deal with (something, such as a problem or danger) ▪ Firemen regularly *confront* danger. ▪ They *confronted* [=(more commonly) *encountered*] many obstacles along the way.; *especially* **:** to deal with (something) in an honest and direct way ▪ The country is reluctant to *confront* its violent past. ▪ The treatment center helps people *confront* [=*face*] their addictions. ▪ *confront* an illness ▪ It's better to *confront* [=*address*] a problem than to avoid it. **b :** to force (someone) to see or deal with (something, such as a problem) in a direct way ▪ The photographs *confront* the viewer with images of desperate poverty. ▪ I *confronted* her with the evidence. — often used as *(be) confronted* ▪ The country again finds itself *confronted* by water shortages. ▪ They *were confronted* with many problems during the project. **c :** to be a problem for (someone or something) ▪ We know of the financial problems *confronting* [=*facing*] local schools.

con·fron·ta·tion /ˌkɑːnfrən'teɪʃən/ *noun, pl* **-tions :** a situation in which people, groups, etc., fight, oppose, or challenge each other in an angry way [*count*] There were several violent *confrontations* between rival gangs. ▪ He would prefer not to have a *confrontation* with the authorities. ▪ a series of *confrontations* between residents and police [*noncount*] We want cooperation, not *confrontation.* ▪ We seek to avoid military *confrontation* at all costs.

con·fron·ta·tion·al /ˌkɑːnfrən'teɪʃənl/ *adj* [*more* ~; *most* ~] **:** challenging or opposing someone especially in an angry way ▪ a *confrontational* interview ▪ I think we should take a less *confrontational* approach. ▪ She's become increasingly *confrontational* with her parents and teachers. — opposite NONCONFRONTATIONAL

con·fuse /kən'fjuːz/ *verb* **-fus·es; -fused; -fus·ing** [+ *obj*]

1 : to make (someone) uncertain or unable to understand something ▪ The city's winding streets *confuse* [=*perplex*] most visitors. ▪ The general was trying to *confuse* the enemy. — often used as *(be) confused* ▪ She *was confused* by many of the scientific terms in the article.

2 : to make (something) difficult to understand ▪ Stop *confusing* [=*blurring*] the issue. ▪ The new evidence only *confused* matters further.

3 : to mistakenly think that one person or thing is another person or thing **:** to mistake (one person or thing) for another ▪ I always *confuse* [=(*informal*) *mix up*] your car and mine. ▪ You must be *confusing* me with someone else. ▪ Some people *confuse* money with happiness. [=think that having a lot of money will make them happy]

con·fused /kən'fjuːzd/ *adj* [*more* ~; *most* ~]

1 : unable to understand or think clearly ▪ I've never been so *confused.* ▪ We're *confused* about what to do next.
2 : difficult to understand : not clearly organized, expressed, etc. ▪ He gave a *confused* speech denying the accusations. ▪ My feelings were hopelessly *confused.* [=*jumbled*]
– con·fused·ly /kən'fju:zədli/ *adv*

confusing *adj* [*more* ~; *most* ~] **:** difficult to understand ▪ I find the whole political situation so *confusing!* [=*perplexing*] ▪ The instructions were *confusing.* ▪ The city's winding streets are *confusing* to most visitors. ▪ *confusing* terms
– con·fus·ing·ly *adv* ▪ The city's streets are *confusingly* arranged. ▪ Even more *confusingly,* they have the same first name.

con·fu·sion /kən'fju:ʒən/ *noun, pl* **-sions**
1 : a situation in which people are uncertain about what to do or are unable to understand something clearly [*noncount*] The detour caused much *confusion.* [=the detour confused many people; the detour made many people uncertain about which roads to use] ▪ There is still some *confusion* as to the time of the meeting. ▪ There is a great deal of *confusion* about how the system works. ▪ Changing the name of the company will only lead to *confusion.* [=make people uncertain] [*count*] the anxieties and *confusions* of teenage life
2 [*noncount*] **:** the feeling that you have when you do not understand what is happening, what is expected, etc. ▪ Her *confusion* was obvious. ▪ He stared in *confusion* and disbelief.
3 [*noncount*] **:** a state or situation in which many things are happening in a way that is not controlled or orderly ▪ a scene of *confusion* ▪ There was total/mass *confusion* when the truck hit the restaurant.
4 [*noncount*] **:** the act of mistakenly thinking that one person or thing is another ▪ Write clearly on the labels to avoid *confusion.* ▪ *Confusion* between/of the words "affect" and "effect" is common.

con·ga /'kɑ:ŋgə/ *noun, pl* **-gas**
1 [*singular*] **:** a dance in which people follow each other in a long, curving line ▪ a ***conga line*** [=a line of people dancing the conga]
2 [*count*] **:** a tall drum that is shaped like a barrel and played with the hands — called also *conga drum;* see picture at PERCUSSION

con game *noun, pl* ~ **games** [*count*] *US* **:** [1]CON

con·geal /kən'ʤi:l/ *verb* **-geals; -gealed; -geal·ing** [*no obj*] *of a liquid* **:** to become thick or solid ▪ The gravy began to *congeal* in the pan. — often used figuratively ▪ His anger *congealed* into bitterness.
– congealed *adj* ▪ *congealed* fat/blood

con·ge·nial /kən'ʤi:nijəl/ *adj* [*more* ~; *most* ~] *somewhat formal*
1 a : suitable or appropriate ▪ The town is a *congenial* place for raising children. ▪ We studied in the *congenial* atmosphere of the library. — often + *to* ▪ a style *congenial to* modern tastes ▪ The library offers an atmosphere *congenial to* learning. **b :** pleasant and enjoyable ▪ He found the work to be *congenial.*
2 : very friendly ▪ a *congenial* [=*genial*] host/companion ▪ She was *congenial* and easygoing.
– con·ge·ni·al·i·ty /kən,ʤi:ni'æləti/ *noun* [*noncount*] ▪ The club encouraged *congeniality* among its members. ✧ Someone who is described as ***Miss Congeniality*** or ***Mr. Congeniality*** is a very friendly person who could win a contest for having the best personality. These phrases are often used in a negative or ironic way to say that someone is not friendly. ▪ The teacher wasn't exactly *Miss Congeniality.* [=she was very unfriendly]

con·gen·i·tal /kən'ʤɛnətəl/ *adj*
1 : existing since birth ▪ *congenital* blindness/heart disease ▪ a *congenital* defect ▪ The irregularity in my backbone is probably *congenital.*
2 *always used before a noun, informal* **:** naturally having a specified character ▪ He's a *congenital* liar. [=he's a liar by nature; he has always lied a lot and is likely to continue to lie]
– con·gen·i·tal·ly *adv*

con·gest·ed /kən'ʤɛstəd/ *adj* [*more* ~; *most* ~]
1 : too full or crowded with something (such as vehicles or people) ▪ *congested* highways/stores ▪ The house was located in a *congested* area. [=an area with a lot of traffic] ▪ Traffic still gets *congested* because of the bridge construction.
2 *of a part of the body* **:** blocked with fluid (such as blood or mucus) ▪ a *congested* nose [=a nose blocked with mucus]
– con·ges·tion /kən'ʤɛsʧən/ *noun* [*noncount*] ▪ nasal *congestion* ▪ traffic/airport *congestion*

con·glom·er·ate /kən'glɑ:mərət/ *noun, pl* **-ates**
1 [*count*] **:** a large business that is made of different kinds of companies ▪ a news and entertainment *conglomerate* ▪ Our small company must compete with the big *conglomerates.*
2 [*count, noncount*] *technical* **:** a kind of rock that is made from many stones of different sizes held together with hardened clay

con·glom·er·a·tion /kən,glɑ:mə'reɪʃən/ *noun, pl* **-tions**
1 [*count*] **:** a group or mixture of different things ▪ a *conglomeration* of shops and restaurants ▪ microscopic *conglomerations* of proteins
2 [*noncount*] **:** a process in which different things come together to form a single thing ▪ phases of *conglomeration* ▪ the age of ***corporate conglomeration*** [=a time when many conglomerates are being formed]

con·grats /kən'græts/ *noun* [*plural*] *informal* **:** CONGRATULATIONS ▪ *Congrats* on your promotion!

con·grat·u·late /kən'grætʃə,leɪt, kən'grædʒə,leɪt/ *verb* **-lates; -lat·ed; -lat·ing** [+ *obj*]
1 : to tell (someone) that you are happy because of his or her success or good luck ▪ *congratulate* the winner ▪ I'd like to *congratulate* you on/for your success. ▪ She *congratulated* us on our test results. ▪ You are ***to be congratulated*** [=you should be congratulated; you deserve praise] on/for your excellent work.
2 : to feel pleased with (yourself) ▪ She *congratulated* herself for getting the best grade in her class.

con·grat·u·la·tion /kən,grætʃə'leɪʃən, kən,grædʒə'leɪʃən/ *noun, pl* **-tions**
1 *congratulations* [*plural*] **a :** a message telling someone that you are happy because of his or her success or good luck : words that congratulate someone ▪ Let me offer you my *congratulations* for/on being elected. ▪ Please send her my *congratulations.* **b —** used to tell someone that you are happy because of his or her success or good luck ▪ "I got promoted!" "*Congratulations!*" — often + *on* ▪ *Congratulations on* your promotion! ▪ *Congratulations on* a job well done.
2 *formal* **:** the act of telling someone that you are happy because of his or her success or good luck : the act of congratulating someone [*plural*] I sent her a letter/message of *congratulations.* [*noncount*] a letter/message of *congratulation*

con·grat·u·la·to·ry /kən'grætʃələ,tori, kən'grædʒələ,tori, *Brit* kən,grætʃə'leɪtri/ *adj* [*more* ~; *most* ~] *formal* **:** showing someone that you are happy because of his or her success or good luck : expressing congratulations ▪ The team got a *congratulatory* phone call from the president. ▪ a *congratulatory* handshake — see also SELF-CONGRATULATORY

con·gre·gant /'kɑ:ŋgrigənt/ *noun, pl* **-gants** [*count*] *chiefly US* **:** a person who is part of a congregation : a person who is attending religious services or who regularly attends religious services ▪ A small number of *congregants* had assembled for Midnight Mass. ▪ The church depends on the financial support of its *congregants.*

con·gre·gate /'kɑ:ŋgrɪ,geɪt/ *verb* **-gates; -gat·ed; -gat·ing** [*no obj*] **:** to come together in a group or crowd ▪ Students began to *congregate* [=*assemble*] in the hall. ▪ It's a place where the homeless *congregate.* ▪ Skiers *congregated* around the lodge's fireplace.

con·gre·ga·tion /,kɑ:ŋgrɪ'geɪʃən/ *noun, pl* **-tions** [*count*]
1 : the people who are attending a religious service ▪ The priest addressed the *congregation.*
2 : the people who regularly attend religious services ▪ She is a member of a small *congregation.*

con·gre·ga·tion·al /,kɑ:ŋgrɪ'geɪʃənl/ *adj*
1 : involving or done by the people who attend religious services : relating to a congregation ▪ *congregational* singing
2 *Congregational* : relating to a group of Christian churches that believe that the people who attend each church should make their own decisions, rules, etc. ▪ a *Congregational* church
– Con·gre·ga·tion·al·ist /,kɑ:ŋgrə'geɪʃənəlɪst/ *noun, pl* **-ists** [*count*] ▪ an active *Congregationalist* **– Congregationalist** *adj* ▪ a *Congregationalist* minister

con·gress /'kɑ:ŋgrəs, *Brit* 'kɑ:ŋ,grɛs/ *noun, pl* **-gress·es**
1 [*count*] **:** a formal meeting in which representatives or experts discuss important matters, make decisions, etc. ▪ a Communist Party *congress* ▪ an annual academic *congress*
2 a : the group of people who are responsible for making the laws of a country in some kinds of government [*count*] She was recently elected to the country's *congress.* ▪ the *congresses* of Mexico and Chile [*noncount*] acts of *congress* **b *Congress*** [*singular*] **:** a particular congress; *especially* **:** the

congress of the United States that includes the Senate and the House of Representatives • The bill easily passed both houses of *Congress*. • *Congress* is not currently in session.
3 [*singular*] — used in the names of some political parties • the Indian National *Congress*
– **con·gres·sion·al** /kən'grɛʃənl/ *adj* • a *congressional* committee • *congressional* investigators

con·gress·man /'kɑːŋgrəsmən/ *noun, pl* **-men** /-mən/ [*count*] : someone (especially a man) who is a member of a congress and especially of the U.S. House of Representatives • a former *congressman* who is now a senator • *Congressman* Smith

con·gress·wom·an /'kɑːŋgrəsˌwʊmən/ *noun, pl* **-wom·en** /-ˌwɪmən/ [*count*] : a woman who is a member of a congress and especially of the U.S. House of Representatives • a former *congresswoman* • *Congresswoman* Jones

con·gru·ent /kən'gruːwənt, 'kɑːŋgruːwənt/ *adj* [*more* ~; *most* ~]
1 *mathematics* : having the same size and shape • *congruent* triangles
2 *formal* : matching or in agreement with something • Their goals are not *congruent* with the goals of the team.
– **con·gru·ence** /kən'gruːwəns, 'kɑːŋgruːwəns/ *noun* [*noncount*]

con·i·cal /'kɑːnɪkəl/ *adj* [*more* ~; *most* ~] : shaped like a cone • a *conical* cap • The tree has a *conical* shape.

con·i·fer /'kɑːnəfə/ *noun, pl* **-fers** [*count*] *biology* : a bush or tree (such as a pine) that produces cones and that usually has leaves that are green all year • Most *conifers* are evergreen.
– **co·nif·er·ous** /koʊ'nɪfərəs/ *adj* • *coniferous* trees • *coniferous* and deciduous forests

conj *abbr* conjunction

[1]**con·jec·ture** /kən'ʤɛkʧə/ *noun, pl* **-tures** *formal* : an opinion or idea formed without proof or sufficient evidence : GUESS [*count*] The biography includes *conjectures* about the writer's earliest ambitions. • a *conjecture* about the extent of the injury [*noncount*] Your plan is based on (nothing more than) *conjecture*. • Most of the book is *conjecture*, not fact. • The criminal's motive remains a matter of *conjecture*. [=people can only guess about the criminal's motive; no one knows the criminal's motive]
– **con·jec·tur·al** /kən'ʤɛkʧərəl/ *adj* [*more* ~; *most* ~] • Most of the book is *conjectural*.

[2]**conjecture** *verb* **-tures; -tured; -tur·ing** *formal* : to form an opinion or idea without proof or sufficient evidence [+ *obj*] Some have *conjectured* that the distant planet could sustain life. [*no obj*] We only *conjecture* about his motives.

con·join /kən'ʤoɪn/ *verb* **-joins; -joined; -join·ing** *formal*
1 [*no obj*] : to join together • The two rivers eventually *conjoin*.
2 [+ *obj*] : to join (two or more people or things) together • their attempts to *conjoin* two very different concepts

conjoined twin *noun, pl* ~ **twins** [*count*] : either one of a pair of twins who are born with their bodies joined together in some way • She gave birth to *conjoined twins*. — called also *Siamese twin*

con·ju·gal /'kɑːnʤɪgəl/ *adj* [*more* ~; *most* ~] *formal* : relating to marriage or to a married couple • *conjugal* bliss/happiness ✧ *Conjugal* is often used to refer to the sexual relationship between a married couple. • *conjugal* relations • The prisoner is allowed ***conjugal visits*** from his wife. [=visits in which he is able to have sexual relations with his wife]

con·ju·gate /'kɑːnʤəˌgeɪt/ *verb* **-gates; -gat·ed; -gat·ing** [+ *obj*] *grammar* : to list the different forms of a verb that show number, person, tense, etc. • Can you *conjugate* the verb "to go"?

con·ju·ga·tion /ˌkɑːnʤə'geɪʃən/ *noun, pl* **-tions**
1 [*noncount*] : the way a verb changes form to show number, person, tense, etc. : the way a verb is conjugated • a lesson on French verb *conjugation*
2 [*count*] : a group of verbs that change in the same way to show number, person, tense, etc. : a set of verbs that are conjugated in the same way • Latin *conjugations*

con·junc·tion /kən'ʤʌŋkʃən/ *noun, pl* **-tions** [*count*]
1 *grammar* : a word that joins together sentences, clauses, phrases, or words • Some common *conjunctions* are "and," "but," and "although."
2 *formal* : a situation in which two or more things happen at the same time or in the same place • an unfortunate *conjunction* [=*concurrence*] of events
in conjunction with *formal* : in combination with : together with • The concert will be held *in conjunction with* the festival. • The medicine is typically used *in conjunction with* other treatments.

con·junc·ti·vi·tis /kənˌʤʌŋktə'vaɪtəs/ *noun* [*noncount*] *medical* : a disease that causes the eye to become pink and sore — called also *pinkeye*

con·jure /'kɑːnʤə, *Brit* 'kʌnʤə/ *verb* **-jures; -jured; -jur·ing** [+ *obj*]
1 : to make (something) appear or seem to appear by using magic • a magician who *conjures* live doves from silk scarves — usually + *up* • In the movie she has the power to *conjure up* storms, fires, and earthquakes.
2 a : to make you think of (something) • The title of the book *conjures* [=*evokes*] images of politics, protest, and war. — usually + *up* • The photos *conjure up* memories of a simpler time. • For many, the word "Greenland" *conjures up* images of vast, icy plains. **b** : to create or imagine (something) • The students *conjured* a clever scheme to raise the money they needed. — usually + *up* • Her imagination *conjured up* a summer scene.
a name to conjure with *chiefly Brit* — used to say that someone is an important person • He has become *a name to conjure with* in the business world.

con·jur·er *or* **con·ju·ror** /'kɑːnʤərə, *Brit* 'kʌnʤərə/ *noun, pl* **-ers** *or* **-ors** [*count*] : a person who performs magic tricks

[1]**conk** /'kɑːŋk/ *noun, pl* **conks** [*count*] *Brit slang* : [1]NOSE • a big *conk*

[2]**conk** *verb* **conks; conked; conk·ing** [+ *obj*] *informal* : to strike or hit (someone or something) hard • He *conked* his brother on the head with the toy.
conk out [*phrasal verb*] *informal* **1** *of a machine* : to stop working properly • My car's engine *conked out* [=(more commonly) *broke down*] this morning. **2** : to fall asleep • I *conked out* early last night.

con man *noun, pl* ~ **men** [*count*] : CON ARTIST

con·nect /kə'nɛkt/ *verb* **-nects; -nect·ed; -nect·ing**
1 a [+ *obj*] : to join (two or more things) together • Can you *connect* the hose to the sprinkler? • *Connect* the cable to the battery. • A hallway *connects* the two rooms. • It's the major highway *connecting* the two towns. • A common theme *connects* the stories. — often used as *(be) connected* • The two rooms *are connected* by a hallway. • The stories *are connected* by a common theme. • They *are* somehow *connected* to the royal family. [=they are related in some way to the royal family] • people *connected* by a common language • The schools *are* closely *connected*. [=they are closely involved with one another] **b** [*no obj*] : to join with or become joined to something else • The two bones *connect* at the elbow. • The hose *connects* easily to the sprinkler. • The bedroom *connects* to the kitchen. — opposite DISCONNECT
2 [+ *obj*] **a** : to think of (something or someone) as being related to or involved with another person, thing, event, or idea • People usually *connect* [=*associate*] clowns with the circus. • I never *connected* you with that group of people. — often used as *(be) connected* • In my mind, the two places *are connected*. [=I think of the two places as being related to each other] **b** : to show or prove that a person or thing is related to or involved with something • Police were unable to *connect* [=*link*] her to the crime. • There's no evidence *connecting* the company directly to the scandal. — often used as *(be) connected* • Many people still believe she *is* somehow *connected* to the crime.
3 : to join or become joined to something (such as a system or network) through a telephone, computer, or other device — usually + *to* [*no obj*] Guests can *connect to* the Internet from their hotel rooms. • The computer *connects to* the fax machine. [+ *obj*] "Operator, can you *connect* me to the front desk?" [=can you link my telephone with the telephone at the front desk so that I can talk to the person there?] — opposite DISCONNECT
4 [*no obj*] — used to say that an airplane, train, etc., stops at a particular place where passengers get onto another airplane, train, etc., in order to continue their journey • Our flight to New York *connects* in Chicago. • We leave from Boston and then *connect* in New York with a flight bound for China. • I took an early flight to *connect* with a train to the coast. • passengers *connecting* to/with international flights
5 [*no obj*] *chiefly US, informal* : to have or share a feeling of affection and understanding • We really *connected* on our first date. • She truly *connects* with her audience in concert.
6 [*no obj*] *chiefly US, sports* : to make a successful shot, hit, or throw • He *connected* for a home run. • She failed to *con-*

C

nect on the shot. = The shot failed to *connect.* [=the shot missed]

connect the dots *chiefly US, informal* **: to learn or understand how different things are related** ▪ The information about these events is not new but no one had ever *connected the dots* until today.

connect up [*phrasal verb*] ***connect up (something) or connect (something) up*** **: to join or link (a device, piece of equipment, etc.) to something** ▪ I'm having trouble *connecting* the speakers *up* to the TV. ▪ An electrician will be *connecting up* the new lights tomorrow. [=joining the lights to a source of electricity]

– con•nect•able /kəˈnɛktəbəl/ *adj* [*more* ~; *most* ~] ▪ The devices are *connectable.* [=they can be connected] **– con•nect•ing** *adj* ▪ I missed my *connecting* flight in Detroit.

connected *adj*

1 : joined or linked together ▪ a series of *connected* rooms

2 : having useful social, professional, or commercial relationships ▪ a politically *connected* businessman [=a businessman who has relationships with people who have political power] — see also WELL-CONNECTED

con•nect•ed•ness /kəˈnɛktədnəs/ *noun* [*noncount*] **: the state of being closely joined or linked especially in an emotional way** ▪ She has a strong feeling of *connectedness* to her hometown. ▪ *connectedness* with nature

con•nec•tion /kəˈnɛkʃən/ *noun, pl* **-tions**

1 [*count*] **: something that joins or connects two or more things** ▪ The state plans to improve roads that serve as *connections* between major highways. ▪ pipe/hose *connections*

2 [*noncount*] **: the act of connecting two or more things or the state of being connected** ▪ There is a fee for *connection* to the town's water supply. ▪ All classrooms will be wired for *connection* to the Internet.

3 [*count*] **a : a situation in which two or more things have the same cause, origin, goal, etc.** ▪ *connections* between thought and language ▪ Investigators found no *connection* between the two fires. ▪ The school has no *connection* with the museum. ▪ Evidence suggests there's a *connection* between the languages. ▪ I'm not sure I see the *connection.* ▪ Our family feels a deep *connection* to the land. **b : a situation in which one thing causes another** ▪ the *connection* between smoking and lung cancer ▪ The study suggests a *connection* between small class sizes and higher reading scores.

4 [*count*] **a : something that allows you to become connected to a system, network, etc., through a telephone, computer, or other device** ▪ a high-speed Internet *connection* ▪ The company provides telephone *connections* for most of the city's residents. ▪ I can't hear you very well. We must have a ***bad connection.*** [=a problem with the way our phones are connected] **b : a place where two parts or wires meet and touch** ▪ an electrical *connection* ▪ I fixed the loose *connection* and now the speaker works fine.

5 [*count*] **: a train, bus, or airplane that you get onto after getting off another train, bus, or airplane as part of the same journey** ▪ We fly out of Oslo and then have a *connection* [=connecting flight] in London. ▪ We don't have a direct flight to Boston. We have to make a *connection* in Chicago.

6 [*count*] **a : a relationship between people who are part of the same family, who do business together, etc.** ▪ He has no *connection* with his former law firm. ▪ They are proud of their *connection* to the royal family. ▪ Family *connections* can make getting a job much easier. **b : a shared feeling of affection and understanding** ▪ We didn't know each other for very long, but we had a real *connection.* ▪ They're working hard to make an emotional *connection* with their adopted children. ▪ a performer's *connection* with the audience

7 [*count*] **a : a powerful person who you know and who can help you — usually plural** ▪ She has some *connections* in the banking industry. **b** *informal* **: a person who sells something illegal** ▪ a drug *connection*

in connection with **: in relation to (something) : for reasons that relate to (something) — used especially in journalism** ▪ Police arrested four men *in connection with* the robbery.

make a/the connection **: to understand that there is a relationship between two or more things** ▪ It didn't take long for us to *make the connection* between the missing money and our partner's new car.

con•nec•tive /kəˈnɛktɪv/ *noun, pl* **-tives** [*count*] *grammar* **: a word (such as *and*) that connects words or groups of words**

connective tissue *noun, pl* **~ -sues** [*count, noncount*] *medical* **: the parts of the body (such as ligaments, tendons, and cartilage) that support and hold together the other parts of the body (such as muscles, organs, and bones)**

con•nec•tor /kəˈnɛktɚ/ *noun, pl* **-tors** [*count*]

1 : a device or a part of a device that connects two computers, pieces of equipment, etc. ▪ an electrical *connector*

2 : a road that connects two places, roads, etc. ▪ The road is a major *connector* from the highway to the town's commercial district. ▪ Take the airport *connector* from the main highway. ▪ a *connector* road/highway/bridge

con•ning tower /ˈkɑːnɪŋ-/ *noun, pl* **~ -ers** [*count*] **: a raised structure on the deck of a submarine**

con•nip•tion /kəˈnɪpʃən/ *noun, pl* **-tions** [*count*] *US, informal* **: behavior that shows that you are suddenly very angry, upset, etc.** ▪ Mom really had/threw a *conniption* [=*fit*] when I told her I got arrested. ▪ He ***goes into conniptions*** [=becomes very upset] if you disagree with him about politics.

con•nive /kəˈnaɪv/ *verb* **-nives; -nived; -niv•ing** [*no obj*] *disapproving* **: to secretly help someone do something dishonest or illegal** ▪ She *connived* [=*conspired*] with him to fix the election. ▪ He accused his opponents of *conniving* [=secretly working together] to defeat the proposal.

– con•niv•ance /kʰəˈnaɪvəns/ *noun* [*noncount*] ▪ He stole millions of dollars with the *connivance* of his partner.

conniving *adj* [*more* ~; *most* ~] *disapproving* **: acting in a dishonest way : using or controlling other people for selfish reasons** ▪ He plays a *conniving* swindler who charms people into giving him money.

con•nois•seur /ˌkɑːnəˈsɚ/ *noun, pl* **-seurs** [*count*] **: a person who knows a lot about something (such as art, wine, food, etc.) : an expert in a particular subject** ▪ wine *connoisseurs* ▪ She is a *connoisseur* of African art.

– con•nois•seur•ship /ˌkɑːnəˈsɚˌʃɪp/ *noun* [*noncount*]

con•no•ta•tion /ˌkɑːnəˈteɪʃən/ *noun, pl* **-tions** [*count*] **: an idea or quality that a word makes you think about in addition to its meaning** ▪ a word with negative/positive *connotations* ▪ For many people, the word "fat" has negative *connotations.* ▪ The word "childlike" has *connotations* of innocence. — compare DENOTATION

con•note /kəˈnoʊt/ *verb* **-notes; -not•ed; -not•ing** [+ *obj*] *formal, of a word* **: to make you think about (something) in addition to the word's meaning** ▪ The word "childlike" *connotes* innocence. ▪ For her, the word "family" *connotes* love and comfort. — compare DENOTE 1

con•quer /ˈkɑːŋkɚ/ *verb* **-quers; -quered; -quer•ing** [+ *obj*]

1 : to take control of (a country, city, etc.) through the use of force ▪ The city was *conquered* by the ancient Romans. ▪ Napoleon *conquered* vast territories. ▪ a *conquered* city

2 : to defeat (someone or something) through the use of force ▪ They *conquered* all their enemies. — see also *divide and conquer* at ¹DIVIDE

3 : to gain control of (a problem or difficulty) through great effort ▪ She has been unable to *conquer* [=*overcome*] her fear of heights. ▪ He finally *conquered* his drug habit. ▪ Scientists believe the disease can be *conquered.*

4 : to become successful in (a place, situation, etc.) ▪ She has *conquered* Hollywood and now has her sights set on Broadway. ▪ The company hopes to *conquer* new markets abroad.

5 : to succeed in climbing (a mountain) ▪ He was one of the first climbers to *conquer* Mount Everest.

– conquering *adj, always used before a noun* ▪ the *conquering* nation/hero **– con•quer•or** /ˈkɑːŋkərɚ/ *noun, pl* **-ors** [*count*] ▪ the Roman *conquerors* ▪ William the *Conqueror*

con•quest /ˈkɑːnˌkwest/ *noun, pl* **-quests**

1 : the act of taking control of a country, city, etc., through the use of force [*count*] tales of the ancient army's *conquests* ▪ the Norman *Conquest* [=the conquest of England by the Normans in 1066] [*noncount*] tales of military *conquest*

2 [*count*] **: a country, city, etc., that an army has taken control of through the use of force** ▪ Napoleon's *conquests*

3 [*count*] **: a person someone has succeeded in having a romantic and especially a sexual relationship with** ▪ She was one of his many *conquests.* ▪ people who boast about their sexual/amorous *conquests*

4 [*noncount*] **: success in defeating or dealing with something difficult or dangerous — usually + *of*** ▪ the *conquest of* space/nature/disease

con•quis•ta•dor /kɑnˈkiːstəˌdoɚ, *Brit* kɒnˈkwɪstədɔː/ *noun, pl* **con•quis•ta•do•res** /kɑnˌkiːstəˈdoriz, *Brit* kɑnˌkwɪstəˈdɔːreɪz/ *or* **con•quis•ta•dors** [*count*] **: a leader in the Spanish conquests of America, Mexico, and Peru in the 16th century**

con·science /ˈkɑːnʃəns/ *noun, pl* **-scienc·es**
1 : the part of the mind that makes you aware of your actions as being either morally right or wrong [*count*] — usually singular • You should decide what to do according to your own *conscience*. • Her *conscience* was bothering her, so she finally told the truth. • He doesn't seem to have a *conscience*. [=doesn't seem to know or care about what is morally right] • I cannot do anything that is/goes against my *conscience*. [=that I believe is morally wrong] • After searching my *conscience*, I realized that I could not accept their offer. • At least now I can face him with a ***clear conscience***. [=without guilt] • She had a ***guilty/troubled conscience***. [=she had a feeling of guilt about something she had done] • I urged the senator to ***vote his conscience*** [=vote as he felt he should], even if it was at odds with the party line. [*noncount*] The issue is a ***matter of (individual) conscience***. [=something that people must decide about according to what they believe is morally right] • I can't work for a company that has no ***social conscience***. [=a company that does not care about important social issues] — see also PRISONER OF CONSCIENCE
2 [*noncount*] **:** a feeling that something you have done is morally wrong • She felt a pang/prick of *conscience* [=*guilt*] about not inviting him. • The thief must have had an attack of *conscience*, because he returned the wallet with nothing missing from it.
in (all/good) conscience *formal* ✧ If you cannot do something *in (all/good) conscience*, you cannot do it because you think that it is morally wrong. • I cannot *in good conscience* allow this situation to continue. • She could not *in all conscience* remain silent.
on your conscience ✧ If something is *on your conscience*, it makes you feel guilty. • I have to tell you the truth, because I don't want this *on my conscience* any longer.

conscience–stricken *adj* **:** feeling very bad or guilty because of something you have done • the story of a *conscience-stricken* thief who repays all she's stolen

con·sci·en·tious /ˌkɑːnʃiˈɛnʧəs/ *adj* [*more* ~; *most* ~] **:** very careful about doing what you are supposed to do **:** concerned with doing something correctly • She has always been a very *conscientious* worker. • He was *conscientious* about following the doctor's orders.
— **con·sci·en·tious·ly** *adv* • He followed his doctor's orders *conscientiously*. — **con·sci·en·tious·ness** *noun* [*noncount*]

conscientious objector *noun, pl* ~ **-tors** [*count*] **:** a person who refuses to serve in the military because of moral or religious beliefs • He registered as a *conscientious objector*.
— **conscientious objection** *noun, pl* ~ **-tions** [*count, noncount*]

con·scious /ˈkɑːnʃəs/ *adj*
1 [*more* ~; *most* ~] **:** awake and able to understand what is happening around you • Is the patient *conscious* yet? • He was fully *conscious* when we found him. — opposite UNCONSCIOUS
2 *not used before a noun* [*more* ~; *most* ~] **:** aware of something (such as a fact or feeling) **:** knowing that something exists or is happening — usually + *of* or *that* • She was very *conscious of* how late it was. • We are *conscious of* the risks involved in the procedure. • He is *conscious of* being a role model for children. • I was *conscious of* the fact that I had to do well on the test to pass the course. • He was *conscious that* they were watching him closely. — opposite UNCONSCIOUS
3 : known or felt by yourself • *conscious* guilt • the capacity for *conscious* thought — opposite UNCONSCIOUS
4 [*more* ~; *most* ~] **:** caring about something specified • He is environmentally *conscious*. [=he thinks and cares about the health of the environment] • a cost-*conscious* shopper [=a shopper who is concerned about the price of things] — see also SELF-CONSCIOUS
5 : done after thinking about facts and reasons carefully • I made a *conscious* [=*deliberate*] effort/attempt to be more compassionate. • a *conscious* decision — opposite UNCONSCIOUS
— **con·scious·ly** *adv* • Becoming CEO of the company was a goal she had *consciously* pursued for 10 years. • someone who craves attention, whether *consciously* or unconsciously • I wasn't *consciously* aware of having laughed.

con·scious·ness /ˈkɑːnʃəsnəs/ *noun, pl* **-ness·es**
1 [*noncount*] **:** the condition of being conscious **:** the normal state of being awake and able to understand what is happening around you • She experienced a brief loss of *consciousness*. = She ***lost consciousness*** [=became unconscious] briefly. • He slowly ***regained consciousness*** [=became conscious again; woke up] after the surgery.
2 a : a person's mind and thoughts [*count*] — usually singular • The realization first entered my *consciousness* when I was a young child. • The memory was forever etched in her *consciousness*. [*noncount*] The medication caused her to enter an altered state of *consciousness*. — see also STREAM OF CONSCIOUSNESS **b** [*noncount*] **:** knowledge that is shared by a group of people • The events have become part of the national *consciousness*. • a crisis that has faded from the public *consciousness* [=that the public no longer remembers or thinks about]
3 : awareness or knowledge of something specified [*count*] — usually singular • a magazine that aims to raise the political *consciousness* of teenagers [=to make teenagers more aware of political issues] • I was impressed by his *consciousness* of our situation. • She developed a strong ***social consciousness***. [=she became aware of important social issues] [*noncount*] He hopes that he can raise public *consciousness* of the disease.

consciousness–raising *noun* [*noncount*] **:** the process of making people understand and be interested in important social or political issues — often used before another noun • a *consciousness-raising* group/effort

¹con·script /kənˈskrɪpt/ *verb* **-scripts; -script·ed; -script·ing** [+ *obj*] **:** to force (someone) to serve in the armed forces **:** DRAFT • The government is *conscripting* men for the army. • He was *conscripted* into the army.

²con·script /ˈkɑːnˌskrɪpt/ *noun, pl* **-scripts** [*count*] **:** a person who is forced to serve in the armed forces **:** DRAFTEE
— **con·script** /ˈkɑːnˌskrɪpt/ *adj, always used before a noun* • *conscript* soldiers • a *conscript* army [=an army made up of conscripts]

con·scrip·tion /kənˈskrɪpʃən/ *noun* [*noncount*] **:** the practice of ordering people by law to serve in the armed forces **:** DRAFT • young people who face *conscription* into the army • a campaign to end *conscription* [=(*US*) *the draft*]

con·se·crate /ˈkɑːnsəˌkreɪt/ *verb* **-crates; -crat·ed; -crat·ing** [+ *obj*]
1 : to officially make (something, such as a place or building) holy through a special religious ceremony — usually used as *(be) consecrated* • The church *was consecrated* in 1856. • The bones are buried in *consecrated* ground.
2 : to officially make (someone) a priest, bishop, etc., through a special religious ceremony — usually used as *(be) consecrated* • He *was* recently *consecrated* (as) a priest.
consecrate yourself *formal* **:** to officially promise that you will give your time and attention to something (especially a religion) • They *consecrated themselves* to the church.
— **con·se·cra·tion** /ˌkɑːnsəˈkreɪʃən/ *noun, pl* **-tions** [*count, noncount*] • the *consecration* of the church/bishop

con·sec·u·tive /kənˈsɛkjətɪv/ *adj* **:** following one after the other in a series **:** following each other without interruption • We had unusually cold temperatures for five *consecutive* [=*successive*] days. • The team has lost three *consecutive* games. [=three games in a row]
— **con·sec·u·tive·ly** *adv* • The prints are signed by the artist and numbered *consecutively*. [=the prints are each given a number 1, 2, 3, 4, etc.]

con·sen·su·al /kənˈsɛnʃəwəl/ *adj* **:** agreed to by the people involved **:** done with the consent of the people involved • *consensual* sex • a *consensual* decision/act • She claims their relationship was *consensual*.
— **con·sen·su·al·ly** *adv* • The decision was made *consensually*.

con·sen·sus /kənˈsɛnsəs/ *noun* **:** a general agreement about something **:** an idea or opinion that is shared by all the people in a group [*singular*] The (general) *consensus* (of the group) was to go ahead with the plan. • Scientists have not ***reached a consensus*** on the cause of the disease. [=scientists do not yet agree about the cause of the disease] • There is a ***growing consensus*** [=more and more people agree] about/on the need for further investigation. • What is the ***consensus of opinion*** among the experts? [=what do the experts all say?] [*noncount*] Everyone on the council seems to understand the need for *consensus*. • There is a lack of *consensus* among the citizens. • The decision was made ***by consensus***.

¹con·sent /kənˈsɛnt/ *verb* **-sents; -sent·ed; -sent·ing** [*no obj*] *formal* **:** to agree to do or allow something **:** to give permission for something to happen or be done • He was reluctant at first but finally *consented*. — often + *to* • He *consented*

C

to the plan. • Her father *consented to* the marriage. • She *consented to* a meeting. — sometimes followed by *to + verb* • The builder *consented to do* the repairs at no additional charge.

[2]consent *noun [noncount] somewhat formal*

1 : permission for something to happen or be done • He did not give his *consent* for the use of his name in the advertisement. • No one may use the vehicle without the *consent* of the owner. • Students must have the *consent* of their parents to go on the trip. = Students must have ***parental consent*** to go on the trip. • We need ***written consent*** [=a document giving permission] before we can publish the photograph. ✧ A ***consent form*** is a document that you sign in order to officially give your permission for something to happen or be done. • Patients must sign a *consent form* before having surgery. — see also AGE OF CONSENT, INFORMED CONSENT

2 : agreement about an opinion or about something that will happen or be done • This restaurant is, ***by common consent*** the best in the city. [=people agree that this restaurant is the best in the city] • The contract was canceled last month ***by mutual consent*** [=the people involved agreed to cancel the contract]

consenting adult *noun, pl* **~ adults** *[count] law* **:** a person who is legally considered old enough to decide to have sex **:** an adult who has consented to have sex

con·se·quence /ˈkɑːnsəˌkwɛns/ *noun, pl* **-quenc·es**

1 *[count]* **:** something that happens as a result of a particular action or set of conditions • The slightest error can have serious *consequences*. • What were the economic *consequences* of the war? • The decrease in sales was a *consequence* of some bad publicity about the company. • Some say many jobs will be lost as a *consequence* of the trade agreement. • He weighed/considered the *consequences* of making a career change. ✧ If you ***face/suffer the consequences*** of something, you deal with the results of something that you have done. • When he made the decision to leave, he knew he would have to *face the consequences*. • She *suffered the consequences* of her error.

2 *[noncount] formal* **:** importance or value • He was a man of *consequence*. [=he was an important man] • The outcome of the election will be of little *consequence* (to me). [=will not matter much to me] • The style you choose is of no *consequence*. • "What happened?" "Nothing of (any/great) *consequence*."

in consequence *or* ***as a consequence*** *formal* **:** as a result of something • She made some risky investments and *in consequence* [=*consequently*] lost a lot of money. = She lost a lot of money *in consequence* of some risky investments. • Hundreds of people became sick *as a consequence* [=*as a result*] of the poor sanitary conditions.

con·se·quent /ˈkɑːnsəkwənt/ *adj, always used before a noun, somewhat formal* **:** happening as a result of a particular action or set of conditions • Weather forecasters predict heavy rains and *consequent* flooding. • Falling sales and a *consequent* loss of profits forced the company to lay off more workers.

– con·se·quent·ly /ˈkɑːnsəˌkwɛntli/ *adv* • The state's economy was poor. *Consequently*, many college graduates were forced to move elsewhere in order to find jobs.

con·se·quen·tial /ˌkɑːnsəˈkwɛnʃəl/ *adj, formal*

1 *[more ~; most ~]* **:** IMPORTANT • There have been several *consequential* innovations in their computer software. • The change to the schedule is not *consequential*. — opposite INCONSEQUENTIAL

2 : happening as a result **:** CONSEQUENT • The company is considering layoffs but hopes to avoid a *consequential* loss in productivity. [=a loss in productivity because of the layoffs]

– con·se·quen·tial·ly *adv*

con·ser·van·cy /kənˈsɚvənsi/ *noun, pl* **-cies**

1 *[count]* **:** an organization that works to protect animals, plants, and natural resources especially by purchasing and caring for areas of land • The land was recently donated to a local *conservancy*. — usually used in the names of organizations • She works for the Nature *Conservancy*.

2 *[count] Brit* **:** a group of officials who control and protect a river or port

3 *[noncount]* **:** CONSERVATION • raising money for the *conservancy* of natural resources • water *conservancy*

con·ser·va·tion /ˌkɑːnsɚˈveɪʃən/ *noun [noncount]*

1 : the protection of animals, plants, and natural resources • wildlife *conservation* • They are trying to raise money for *conservation*. • the *conservation* of the environment — often used before another noun • a *conservation* commission • a local group's *conservation* efforts • the efforts of a local *conservation* group • The property borders a ***conservation area*** [=an area of land that is protected and that cannot be built on or used for certain purposes]

2 : the careful use of natural resources (such as trees, oil, etc.) to prevent them from being lost or wasted • water/forest/energy *conservation*

3 : the things that are done to keep works of art or things of historical importance in good condition • art *conservation* • She specializes in the *conservation* of furniture. • the *conservation* of religious shrines

con·ser·va·tion·ist /ˌkɑːnsɚˈveɪʃənɪst/ *noun, pl* **-ists** *[count]* **:** someone who works to protect animals, plants, and natural resources or to prevent the loss or waste of natural resources **:** a person who is involved in conservation

con·ser·va·tism /kənˈsɚvəˌtɪzəm/ *noun [noncount]*

1 : belief in the value of established and traditional practices in politics and society • political *conservatism* — compare LIBERALISM

2 : dislike of change or new ideas in a particular area • cultural/religious *conservatism*

[1]con·ser·va·tive /kənˈsɚvətɪv/ *adj*

1 *[more ~; most ~]* **:** believing in the value of established and traditional practices in politics and society **:** relating to or supporting political conservatism • a *conservative* newspaper columnist • *conservative* politicians/policies • She is a liberal Democrat who married a *conservative* Republican. — compare [1]LIBERAL

2 ***Conservative*** **:** of or relating to the conservative party in countries like the United Kingdom and Canada • *Conservative* voters/policies • the *Conservative* candidate

3 *[more ~; most ~]* **:** not liking or accepting changes or new ideas • He had some pretty *conservative* [=*traditional, conventional*] ideas about the way life should be. • She's more *conservative* now than she was in college.

4 *[more ~; most ~]* — used to describe a guess, estimate, etc., that is probably lower than the actual amount will be • He gave me a *conservative* estimate of how much repairs will cost. • She predicts that the total cost will be around 500 dollars, and that's a *conservative* guess. [=the total cost will probably be higher than that]

5 *[more ~; most ~]* **:** traditional in taste, style, or manners • Her taste in art is fairly *conservative*. • He is a *conservative* dresser. • a *conservative* suit

6 *[more ~; most ~]* **:** not willing to take risks • a *conservative* investor

7 *or* ***Conservative*** **:** accepting and following many of the traditional beliefs and customs of a religion • *Conservative* Judaism

– con·ser·va·tive·ly *adv* • The collection is *conservatively* valued at three million dollars. • He dresses *conservatively*.

[2]conservative *noun, pl* **-tives** *[count]*

1 : a person who believes in the value of established and traditional practices in politics and society **:** a person who is politically conservative • His message is being well received by *conservatives*. — compare [2]LIBERAL

2 ***Conservative*** **:** a member or supporter of a conservative political party in countries like the United Kingdom and Canada

con·ser·va·toire /kənˈsɚvəˌtwɑɚ/ *noun, pl* **-toires** *[count] Brit* **:** CONSERVATORY 1

con·ser·va·to·ry /kənˈsɚvəˌtori, *Brit* kənˈsɜːvətri/ *noun, pl* **-ries** *[count]*

1 *US* **:** a school in which students are taught music, theater, or dance • a theater *conservatory* • the Peabody *Conservatory* of Music

2 : a room or building with glass walls and a glass roof that is used for growing plants

[1]con·serve /kənˈsɚv/ *verb* **-serves; -served; -serv·ing** *[+ obj]*

1 : to keep (something) safe from being damaged or destroyed • The organization works to *conserve* [=*save*] our national forests/wildlife. • a scientist who is studying ways to *conserve* [=*preserve*] biological diversity

2 : to use (something) carefully in order to prevent loss or waste • With so little rain, everyone had to *conserve* water. • We need to *conserve* our natural resources. • Don't run around too much—you need to *conserve* your strength. • *conserving* fuel/energy

[2]con·serve /ˈkɑːnˌsɚv/ *noun, pl* **-serves** *[count, noncount]* **:** a sweet food made by cooking pieces of fruit with sugar

con·sid·er /kənˈsɪdɚ/ *verb* **-ers; -ered; -er·ing**

1 a : to think about (something or someone) carefully especially in order to make a choice or decision [+ *obj*] We are *considering* you for the job. ▪ She refused to *consider* my request. ▪ He seriously *considered* changing careers. ▪ The jury has *considered* the evidence and reached a verdict. ▪ The policy was well researched and well *considered*. ▪ Please *consider* what I've said. ▪ We never ***considered the possibility*** that the plan could fail. [*no obj*] He paused a moment to *consider* before responding. **b** [+ *obj*] **:** to think about (something that is important in understanding something or in making a decision or judgment) ▪ You have to *consider* that he is only three years old. ▪ When you *consider* how long she worked there, it's surprising that she would leave so suddenly. ▪ His achievements are very impressive when you ***consider the fact*** that he never graduated from high school.

2 [+ *obj*] **:** to think about (a person or a person's feelings) before you do something in order to avoid making someone upset, angry, etc. ▪ You have to learn to *consider* other people. ▪ You never *consider* my feelings.

3 [+ *obj*] **:** to think of or regard (someone or something) in a specified way ▪ I *consider* the price (to be) too high. ▪ We *consider* careful work (to be) essential. ▪ We *consider* it an honor to have you here with us tonight. ▪ a television program that is *considered* one of the best comedies ever ▪ He *considers* himself to be a great writer. ▪ ***Consider yourself lucky/fortunate*** that you survived the accident. [=you are lucky to have survived the accident]

4 [+ *obj*] *formal* **:** to look at (someone or something) carefully and thoughtfully ▪ He stepped back to *consider* the whole painting.

all things considered — used for saying that a statement is true when you think about all the good and bad parts or results of something ▪ *All things considered*, we're pleased with how the project turned out. ▪ It was a pretty good vacation, *all things considered*.

consider it done *informal* — used to say that you will gladly do something that someone has asked you to do ▪ "Can you mail this letter for me?" "*Consider it done*."

con·sid·er·able /kən'sɪdərəbəl/ *adj* [*more* ~; *most* ~] **:** large in size, amount, or quantity ▪ We received a *considerable* number of complaints. ▪ She was in *considerable* pain. ▪ We have already wasted a *considerable* amount of time and money. ▪ The murder trial attracted *considerable* public attention. ▪ Damage to the vehicle was *considerable*.

– con·sid·er·ably /kən'sɪdərəbli/ *adv* ▪ The house was *considerably* more expensive than what we could afford.

con·sid·er·ate /kən'sɪdərət/ *adj* [*more* ~; *most* ~] **:** thinking about the rights and feelings of other people **:** showing kindness toward other people ▪ She is one of the most *considerate* people I know. ▪ He was *considerate* and turned down the stereo when we asked him to. — often + *of* ▪ He is always *considerate of* other people's feelings. ▪ It was very *considerate of* you to offer to help. — opposite INCONSIDERATE

– con·sid·er·ate·ly *adv* ▪ He always treats people *considerately*.

con·sid·er·a·tion /kənˌsɪdə'reɪʃən/ *noun, pl* **-tions**

1 [*noncount*] **:** careful thought **:** the act of thinking carefully about something you will make a decision about ▪ You should give some serious *consideration* to your retirement plans. ▪ After careful *consideration*, he agreed to their requests. ▪ Her suggestion is still ***under consideration*** by the committee. [=the people on the committee are still thinking about and discussing her suggestion]

2 [*noncount*] **:** a desire to avoid doing something that will make another person sad, upset, angry, etc. ▪ Show/have some *consideration* and turn down that radio. — often + *for* ▪ He has no *consideration for* her feelings. ▪ Out of *consideration for* the victim's family, no photos will be shown.

3 [*count*] **:** something that you think about when you make a choice or decision ▪ Finding a house close to work was an important *consideration* for them. ▪ Economic/practical *considerations* forced her to delay her education. ▪ The tent weighs 10 pounds, which is no small *consideration* [=which is something that is important to think about] when you're going to be hiking.

4 *formal* **:** payment for something [*count*] — usually singular ▪ She offered to do the job for a small *consideration*. [*noncount*] He charged a small fee ***in consideration of*** [=as payment for] his many services.

take (something) into consideration **:** to think about (something) before you make a decision or form an opinion ▪ We will *take* your experience *into consideration* [=we will think about how much experience you have] when we decide who will get the job. ▪ Results of the study should be *taken into consideration* before the medication is prescribed to patients. ▪ When you ***take everything into consideration*** [=when you think about both the good and bad things], it really wasn't a bad deal. ▪ *Taking everything into consideration* [=*all things considered*], we're probably better off now.

con·sid·ered /kən'sɪdəd/ *adj, always used before a noun, formal* **:** resulting from careful thought ▪ It's my *considered* opinion that she was not guilty of the crime. ▪ Their actions were a *considered* response to the violence.

con·sid·er·ing /kən'sɪdərɪŋ/ *prep* **:** when you think about or consider (something) — used to indicate a fact or situation that is being thought of when a statement is made ▪ He did very well in the campaign, especially *considering* his lack of experience. ▪ *Considering* the damage to the car, it's a miracle that no one was hurt in the accident. — sometimes used informally in speech without a following object to suggest something that is being thought of without being specifically mentioned ▪ He didn't win, but he did very well, *considering*. [=he did well when you consider the situation or circumstances]

– considering *conj* ▪ He did well, *considering* (that) he had no experience. ▪ She surprised us when she left the company so suddenly, especially *considering* (that) she had worked here for 20 years.

con·sign /kən'saɪn/ *verb* **-signs; -signed; -sign·ing** [+ *obj*] *formal*

1 : to put (someone) in a usually unpleasant place or situation — + *to* ▪ Survivors described how they were *consigned to* labor camps. ▪ The accident left him *consigned* [=(more commonly) *confined*] *to* a wheelchair. ▪ When she first started working, she was *consigned to* a small, windowless office. — often used figuratively ▪ He was *consigned* by fate *to* a life of poverty.

2 : to put (something that is not wanted or used) in a place where old things are stored or thrown away — + *to* ▪ old clothes that have been *consigned to* the attic ▪ She *consigned* his letter *to* the wastebasket. [=she threw away his letter] — often used figuratively ▪ a political movement that has been *consigned to* the dustbin of history [=a political movement that has been forgotten] ▪ His career has been *consigned to* a mere footnote in the history books.

3 : to send (something) *to* a person or place to be sold ▪ She *consigned* the painting *to* an auction house. ▪ The goods were *consigned to* him.

con·sign·ment /kən'saɪnmənt/ *noun, pl* **-ments**

1 [*count*] **:** a quantity of goods that are sent to a person or place to be sold ▪ a *consignment* of books/goods/cars ▪ large *consignments* of grain

2 [*noncount*] **:** the act or process of sending goods to a person or place to be sold ▪ the *consignment* of goods

on consignment — used to describe a situation in which goods are sent to a person who pays only for what is sold and who may return what is not sold ▪ The goods were shipped/sold *on consignment*.

consignment store *noun, pl* **~ stores** [*count*] *US* **:** a store to which people bring items that they no longer want (such as old clothes, shoes, and equipment) to have them sold ✧ When an item at a consignment store is sold, the person who brought it to the store gets a portion of the money paid for it.

con·sist /kən'sɪst/ *verb, not used in progressive tenses* **-sists; -sist·ed; -sist·ing**

consist in [*phrasal verb*] ***consist in (something)*** *formal* **:** to have (something) as an essential or main part ▪ Happiness *consists in* being satisfied with what you have.

consist of [*phrasal verb*] ***consist of (something)*** **:** to be formed or made up of (specified things or people) ▪ Breakfast *consisted of* cereal, fruit, and orange juice. ▪ Coal *consists* mostly *of* carbon. ▪ His wardrobe *consists* almost entirely *of* jeans and T-shirts. ▪ The crowd *consisted* mainly/largely *of* teenage girls. ▪ The job mainly *consists of* classifying evidence. ▪ a museum with a collection *consisting* entirely *of* portraits

con·sis·ten·cy /kən'sɪstənsi/ *noun, pl* **-cies**

1 [*noncount*] **:** the quality or fact of being consistent: such as **a :** the quality or fact of staying the same at different times ▪ His statements on this subject have lacked *consistency*; *especially* **:** the quality or fact of being good each time ▪ He's a good pitcher, but he lacks *consistency*. [=his pitching is good in some games and bad in other games] ▪ Customers expect

C

consistency in the quality of service they receive. ▪ Practice will ensure greater *consistency* of performance. **b :** the quality or fact of having parts that agree with each other ▪ Her argument lacks *consistency*. [=her argument is not logical because its ideas do not agree with each other]

2 : the quality of being thick, firm, smooth, etc. [*count*] paints of varying *consistencies* — usually singular ▪ She mixed the dough to the right *consistency*. ▪ The batter should have/be the *consistency of* pudding. ▪ Boil the juice to the *consistency of* a thick syrup. [*noncount*] The paints vary in *consistency*.

con·sis·tent /kənˈsɪstənt/ *adj* [*more* ~; *most* ~]

1 a : always acting or behaving in the same way ▪ He is a *consistent* supporter of the museum. ▪ We need to be more *consistent* in handling this problem. ▪ Data from recent experiments show *consistent* results. [=results that do not change] **b :** of the same quality; *especially* **:** good each time ▪ His pitching has always been very *consistent*. [=*reliable*] ▪ Customers expect that the quality of service they receive will be *consistent*. — opposite INCONSISTENT

2 : continuing to happen or develop in the same way ▪ The pain has been *consistent*. ▪ Your grades have shown *consistent* improvement this school year. ▪ You need to exercise on a more *consistent* [=*regular*] basis. — opposite INCONSISTENT

3 : having parts that agree with each other ▪ Their descriptions of the accident were *consistent*. ▪ She is not being *consistent* in her argument. [=her argument includes parts that do not agree with one another] **: in agreement *with* something** ▪ His statements were not *consistent with* the truth. [=were not true] ▪ His symptoms are *consistent with* heart disease. [=the symptoms he has are symptoms of heart disease] ▪ The decision was *consistent with* the company's policy. — opposite INCONSISTENT

– con·sis·tent·ly *adv* ▪ The technique is now being used *consistently*. ▪ He *consistently* earned high grades all through high school. ▪ She has played *consistently* all season. ▪ The store has *consistently* low prices.

con·so·la·tion /ˌkɑːnsəˈleɪʃən/ *noun, pl* **-tions**

1 : something that makes a person feel less sadness, disappointment, etc. [*noncount*] His apology was of little/no *consolation* (to me). [=his apology did not make me feel much/any better] ▪ She found/took great *consolation* [=*comfort*] in all the cards and letters she received. ▪ ***If it's any consolation*** (to you) [=if it helps you to feel better], no one else got much of a raise this year, either. [*count*] His kind words were a *consolation* to/for me.

2 [*count*] **:** a contest in which people or teams that have previously lost compete against each other — usually used before another noun ▪ a *consolation* game/match/race

consolation prize *noun, pl* ~ **prizes** [*count*] **:** a prize that is given to someone who has not won a contest

con·so·la·to·ry /kənˈsoʊləˌtori, *Brit* kənˈsɒlətri/ *adj, formal* **:** intended to make someone who is sad or disappointed feel better ▪ *consolatory* words ▪ a *consolatory* pat on the shoulder

¹con·sole /kənˈsoʊl/ *verb* **-soles; -soled; -sol·ing** [+ *obj*] **:** to try to make (someone) feel less sadness or disappointment ▪ She *consoled* [=*comforted*] him after his wife died. ▪ Nothing could *console* her after his death. — often + *with* ▪ I *consoled* myself *with* the thought that things could be much worse.

– consolable *adj* [*more* ~; *most* ~] ▪ barely *consolable*
– consoling *adj* ▪ *consoling* words ▪ a *consoling* smile/hug

²con·sole /ˈkɑːnˌsoʊl/ *noun, pl* **-soles** [*count*]

1 : a flat surface that contains the controls for a machine, for a piece of electrical equipment, etc.

2 : a cabinet for a stereo or television that stands on the floor

con·sol·i·date /kənˈsɑːləˌdeɪt/ *verb* **-dates; -dat·ed; -dat·ing**

1 : to join or combine together into one thing [*no obj*] The two funds will *consolidate* into one. ▪ The two companies *consolidated*. [=*merged*] [+ *obj*] I *consolidated* my loans.

2 [+ *obj*] **:** to make (something, such as a position of power or control) stronger or more secure ▪ The team *consolidated* [=*strengthened*] their lead with another touchdown during the fourth quarter. ▪ The administration hopes that such measures will *consolidate* its position. ▪ Rebel forces have *consolidated* their hold on the region.

– con·sol·i·da·tion /kənˌsɑːləˈdeɪʃən/ *noun, pl* **-tions** [*count, noncount*] ▪ the *consolidation* of power

con·som·mé /ˌkɑːnsəˈmeɪ, *Brit* kənˈsɒmeɪ/ *noun* [*noncount*] **:** a clear soup that is usually made with seasoned meat

¹con·so·nant /ˈkɑːnsənənt/ *noun, pl* **-nants** [*count*]

1 : a speech sound (such as /p/, /d/, or /s/) that is made by partly or completely stopping the flow of air breathed out from the mouth

2 : a letter that represents a consonant; *especially* **:** any letter of the English alphabet except *a, e, i, o, u*, and sometimes *y* — compare VOWEL

²consonant *adj* [*more* ~; *most* ~]

1 *formal* **:** in agreement with something — often + *with* ▪ The decision was *consonant with* [=*consistent with*] the company's usual practice.

2 *music* **:** in harmony ▪ *consonant* chords — opposite DISSONANT

– con·so·nance /ˈkɑːnsənəs/ *noun, pl* **-nanc·es** [*noncount*] musical *consonance* ▪ His beliefs are ***in consonance with*** [=*agree with*] the political party's views. [*count*] the pleasing *consonances* of the symphony

¹con·sort /kənˈsoɚt/ *verb* **-sorts; -sort·ed; -sort·ing**

consort with [*phrasal verb*] ***consort with (someone)*** *formal* + *disapproving* **:** to spend time with (someone) ▪ There is evidence that he has *consorted with* criminals.

²con·sort /ˈkɑːnˌsoɚt/ *noun, pl* **-sorts** [*count*] *formal* **:** a wife or husband of a king, queen, emperor, etc.

con·sor·tium /kənˈsoɚʃəm, kənˈsoɚtijəm/ *noun, pl* **con·sor·tia** /-ʃə, -tijə/ *also* **con·sor·tiums** [*count*] **:** a group of people, companies, etc., that agree to work together ▪ A Japanese *consortium* invested millions in the technology. ▪ a *consortium* of universities/banks/newspapers

con·spic·u·ous /kənˈspɪkjəwəs/ *adj* [*more* ~; *most* ~]

1 : very easy to see or notice ▪ There were a number of *conspicuous* changes to the building. ▪ The sign was placed in a very *conspicuous* spot/position. ▪ The bird has a *conspicuous* red head. ▪ She felt very *conspicuous* in her pink coat. ▪ He was uncomfortable about his *conspicuous* weight gain. ▪ The President was ***conspicuous by his absence*** at the peace talks. [=his absence was very noticeable; people had expected him to be there and noticed that he wasn't] — opposite INCONSPICUOUS

2 : attracting attention by being great or impressive ▪ The business was a *conspicuous* success. ▪ *conspicuous* bravery

– con·spic·u·ous·ly *adv* ▪ The sign was placed very *conspicuously*. ▪ He was *conspicuously* [=*noticeably*] absent from the meeting. **– con·spic·u·ous·ness** /kənˈspɪkjəwəsnəs/ *noun* [*noncount*]

conspicuous consumption *noun* [*noncount*] **:** the act or practice of spending money on expensive things that are not necessary in order to impress other people ▪ a culture of *conspicuous consumption*

con·spir·a·cy /kənˈspirəsi/ *noun, pl* **-cies**

1 [*count*] **:** a secret plan made by two or more people to do something that is harmful or illegal ▪ The CIA uncovered a *conspiracy* against the government.

2 [*noncount*] **:** the act of secretly planning to do something that is harmful or illegal ▪ They were accused of *conspiracy* to commit murder.

conspiracy of silence *noun* [*singular*] **:** a secret agreement made between two or more people to not talk about something ▪ There seems to be a *conspiracy of silence* as far as his resignation is concerned.

conspiracy theory *noun, pl* ~ **-ries** [*count*] **:** a theory that explains an event or situation as the result of a secret plan by usually powerful people or groups ▪ *Conspiracy theories* sprung up soon after the leader's assassination.

– conspiracy theorist *noun, pl* ~ **-rists** [*count*] ▪ *Conspiracy theorists* believe the government is hiding evidence of UFOs.

con·spir·a·tor /kənˈspirətɚ/ *noun, pl* **-tors** [*count*] **:** a person who is involved in a secret plan to do something harmful or illegal **:** a person who is involved in a conspiracy

con·spir·a·to·ri·al /kənˌspirəˈtorijəl/ *adj*

1 : involving a secret plan by two or more people to do something that is harmful or illegal **:** of or relating to a conspiracy ▪ *conspiratorial* plots/plans

2 [*more* ~; *most* ~] **:** suggesting that something secret is being shared ▪ She gave me a *conspiratorial* smile/wink across the table. ▪ His voice became low and *conspiratorial*.

– con·spir·a·to·ri·al·ly *adv* ▪ He winked *conspiratorially*.

con·spire /kənˈspajɚ/ *verb* **-spires; -spired; -spir·ing** [*no obj*]

1 : to secretly plan with someone to do something that is harmful or illegal — often followed by *to* + *verb* ▪ They were accused of *conspiring to overthrow* the government. ▪ She *conspired* with him *to smuggle* the paintings out of the country. — often + *against* ▪ He thought that they were *conspiring against* him.

2 : to happen in a way that produces bad or unpleasant results — often followed by *to + verb* ▪ My illness and the bad weather *conspired to ruin* my vacation. ▪ Several things *conspired to force* them to change the policy. — often + *against* ▪ The organizer of the festival thinks the weather has *conspired against* him.

con·sta·ble /ˈkɑːnstəbəl, ˈkʌnstəbəl/ *noun, pl* **-stables** [*count*]

1 *US* **: a public official whose job is similar to that of a police officer but who is elected or appointed rather than hired**

2 *chiefly Brit* **:** POLICE CONSTABLE

con·stab·u·lary /kənˈstæbjəleri, *Brit* kənˈstæbjələri/ *noun, pl* **-lar·ies** [*count*] *Brit* **: the police force of a particular area**

con·stan·cy /ˈkɑːnstənsi/ *noun* [*noncount*] *formal*

1 : the quality of staying the same : lack of change ▪ the *constancy of* the Earth's rotation ▪ maintaining *constancy of* speed

2 : the quality of being loyal to a person or belief ▪ There was no doubt of his *constancy* [=*fidelity*] to his wife.

[1]**con·stant** /ˈkɑːnstənt/ *adj*

1 : happening all the time or very often over a period of time ▪ He suffers from *constant* headaches. ▪ The noise from the construction was *constant* [=*continuous*] from early morning until evening. ▪ Her *constant* chatter was a nuisance. ▪ The house is in *constant* need of repairs. ▪ The scar serves as a *constant* reminder of the accident. ▪ a problem demanding *constant* attention/care — **opposite** INCONSTANT

2 [*more ~; most ~*] **: staying the same : not changing** ▪ The equipment should be stored at a *constant* temperature. ▪ He kept the car's speed *constant*. ▪ She has struggled to maintain a *constant* weight. — **opposite** INCONSTANT

3 *formal + literary* **: always loyal** ▪ They remained *constant* friends throughout their lives. ▪ Their friendship was *constant*. — **opposite** INCONSTANT

– con·stant·ly *adv* ▪ He talked *constantly* all through the movie. ▪ They complained *constantly* about the noise.

[2]**constant** *noun, pl* **-stants** [*count*]

1 : something that stays the same : something that does not change ▪ Her job was the one *constant* in her life.

2 *technical* **: a quantity or number whose value does not change**

con·stel·la·tion /ˌkɑːnstəˈleɪʃən/ *noun, pl* **-tions** [*count*]

1 : a group of stars that forms a particular shape in the sky and has been given a name ▪ The *constellation* Ursa Major contains the stars of the Big Dipper.

2 *formal* **: a group of people or things that are similar in some way** ▪ A large *constellation* of relatives and friends attended the funeral. ▪ The patient presented a *constellation* of symptoms.

con·ster·na·tion /ˌkɑːnstəˈneɪʃən/ *noun* [*noncount*] *formal* **: a strong feeling of surprise or sudden disappointment that causes confusion** ▪ The candidate caused *consternation* among his supporters by changing positions on a key issue. ▪ Much to her parents' *consternation*, she had decided to not go to college. ▪ They stared at each other in *consternation* [=*dismay*], not knowing what to do.

con·sti·pat·ed /ˈkɑːnstəˌpeɪtəd/ *adj* **: unable to easily release solid waste from your body : unable to have a bowel movement easily**

con·sti·pa·tion /ˌkɑːnstəˈpeɪʃən/ *noun* [*noncount*] **: the condition of being unable to easily release solid waste from your body : the condition of being unable to have a bowel movement easily** ▪ A side effect of the drug is *constipation*.

con·stit·u·en·cy /kənˈstɪtʃəwənsi/ *noun, pl* **-cies** [*count*]

1 : a group of people who support or who are likely to support a politican or political party ▪ the governor's conservative/liberal *constituency* ▪ the party's core *constituencies* ▪ Analysts say she has a good chance of being elected because she appeals to a broad *constituency*. [=many different kinds of people like her and will vote for her]

2 a : the people who live and vote in an area ▪ The senator's *constituency* includes a large minority population. **b** *Brit* **: a voting area : a district with an elected representative** ▪ He was elected to represent a Liverpool *constituency*.

3 : a group of people who support, are served by, or are represented by an organization, business, etc. ▪ a corporation's *constituency*

[1]**con·stit·u·ent** /kənˈstɪtʃəwənt/ *noun, pl* **-ents** [*count*]

1 : any one of the people who live and vote in an area : a member of a constituency ▪ She's pledged to help her elderly *constituents*. ▪ Many senators have received calls from *constituents* who want them to vote in favor of the law.

2 : one of the parts that form something ▪ the chemical *constituents* of the liquid

[2]**constituent** *adj, always used before a noun* **: forming part of a whole** ▪ The company can be separated into several *constituent* parts/elements.

con·sti·tute /ˈkɑːnstəˌtuːt, *Brit* ˈkɒnstəˌtjuːt/ *verb* **-tutes; -tut·ed; -tut·ing** *formal*

1 *not used in progressive tenses* [*linking verb*] **: to make up or form something** ▪ Women *constitute* 70 percent of the student population at the college. ▪ Twelve months *constitute* a year. [=a year is made up of 12 months]

2 *not used in progressive tenses* [*linking verb*] **: to be the same as something : to be equivalent to something** ▪ The court determined that the search of their house *constituted* [=*amounted to*] a violation of their rights.

3 [+ *obj*] **: to establish or create (an organization, a government, etc.) — usually used as** *(be) constituted* ▪ The recently *constituted* government will hold elections in May.

con·sti·tu·tion /ˌkɑːnstəˈtuːʃən, *Brit* ˌkɒnstəˈtjuːʃən/ *noun, pl* **-tions**

1 [*count*] **a : the system of beliefs and laws by which a country, state, or organization is governed** ▪ The state's *constitution* has strict rules about what tax money can be used for. ▪ The right to free speech is guaranteed by the (U.S.) *Constitution*. ▪ Members of the club have drafted a new *constitution*. **b : a document that describes this system** ▪ The state's original *constitution* is on display at the museum.

2 [*count*] **: the physical health and condition of a person or animal** ▪ He has a robust/weak/tough *constitution*. ▪ Only animals with strong *constitutions* are able to survive the island's harsh winters.

3 [*noncount*] *formal* **: the form or structure of something** ▪ What is the molecular *constitution* of the chemical?

[1]**con·sti·tu·tion·al** /ˌkɑːnstəˈtuːʃənl̩, *Brit* ˌkɒnstəˈtjuːʃənl̩/ *adj*

1 *always used before a noun* **: of or relating to the system of beliefs and laws that govern a country : of or relating to a constitution** ▪ She is in favor of a *constitutional* amendment [=an amendment to the constitution] to overturn the unpopular law. ▪ *constitutional* law

2 : allowed by a country's constitution ▪ That kind of punishment is not *constitutional*. [=is not allowed by the constitution] ▪ the *constitutional* guarantee of free speech ▪ a *constitutional* right to vote — **opposite** UNCONSTITUTIONAL

3 a : of or relating to the health and strength of a person's body ▪ *Constitutional* symptoms of the disease include headache and fever. **b : of or relating to a person's basic nature or character** ▪ He has a *constitutional* dislike of controversy.

– con·sti·tu·tion·al·ly *adv* ▪ Free speech is a *constitutionally* guaranteed right in the U.S. ▪ He is *constitutionally* incapable of sitting still for more than a minute. [=it is not his nature to be able to sit still for more than a minute.]

[2]**constitutional** *noun, pl* **-als** [*count*] *old-fashioned* **: a brief walk that you take to improve your health** ▪ She's gone out for her morning *constitutional*.

con·sti·tu·tion·al·ism /ˌkɑːnstəˈtuːʃənəˌlɪzəm, *Brit* ˌkɒnstəˈtjuːʃənəˌlɪzəm/ *noun* [*noncount*] **: the belief that a government should be based on a constitution** ▪ the doctrine of *constitutionalism*

– con·sti·tu·tion·al·ist /ˌkɑːnstəˈtuːʃənəlɪst, *Brit* ˌkɒnstəˈtjuːʃənəlɪst/ *noun, pl* **-ists** [*count*]

con·sti·tu·tion·al·i·ty /ˌkɑːnstəˌtuːʃəˈnæləti, *Brit* ˌkɒnstəˌtjuːʃəˈnæləti/ *noun* [*noncount*] **: the state of being allowed by or in agreement with a constitution : the state of being constitutional** ▪ He questions the *constitutionality* of the proposed law.

constitutional monarchy *noun, pl* **~ -chies** [*count*] **: a system of government in which a country is ruled by a king and queen whose power is limited by a constitution**

con·strain /kənˈstreɪn/ *verb* **-strains; -strained; -strain·ing** [+ *obj*]

1 : to limit or restrict (something or someone) ▪ She believes that too much instruction *constrains* [=*limits*] an artist's creativity. ▪ People with criminal backgrounds are legally *constrained* [=*restricted*] from working for some government agencies. — often used as *(be) constrained* ▪ We *were constrained* [=*limited*] by the short amount of time we had. ▪ Teenagers often feel *constrained* [=*limited*] by rules.

C

2 *formal* **:** to use pressure to force (someone) to do something — usually used as *(be) constrained* ▪ She ***felt constrained*** [=(more commonly) *felt compelled*] to apologize for the harm she'd done.

constrained *adj* [*more ~; most ~*] *formal* **:** not done or happening naturally ▪ It was obvious from his *constrained* [=*forced*] smile that he was not enjoying himself. ▪ *constrained* behavior

con·straint /kən'streɪnt/ *noun, pl* **-straints**
1 [*count*] **:** something that limits or restricts someone or something ▪ Lack of funding has been a major *constraint* on the building's design. — usually plural ▪ Budget *constraints* [=*restrictions*] have forced me to revise my travel plans. [=I've changed my travel plans because I do not have enough money] ▪ Because of time *constraints* [=*limitations*], speeches will be limited to five minutes. ▪ Tradition puts/places/imposes *constraints* on [=puts limits on] people and their actions.
2 [*noncount*] **:** control that limits or restricts someone's actions or behavior ▪ They demand freedom from *constraint*. ▪ They refuse to work under *constraint* any longer.

con·strict /kən'strɪkt/ *verb* **-stricts; -strict·ed; -strict·ing**
1 a [*+ obj*] **:** to make (something) narrower, smaller, or tighter ▪ These shoes are too small and *constrict* [=*squeeze*] my feet. ▪ The drug is used to *constrict* blood vessels. **b** [*no obj*] **:** to become narrower, smaller, or tighter ▪ The drug causes the blood vessels to *constrict*. [=*contract*]
2 [*+ obj*] **:** to prevent or keep (something or someone) from developing freely ▪ The declining economy has *constricted* job opportunities. ▪ a life *constricted* by poverty and disease ▪ He ***felt constricted*** by their notions of what was proper.
– con·stric·tion /kən'strɪkʃən/ *noun, pl* **-tions** [*noncount*] The drug causes *constriction* of blood vessels. [*count*] *constrictions* in blood vessels

constrictor see BOA CONSTRICTOR

[1]**con·struct** /kən'strʌkt/ *verb* **-structs; -struct·ed; -struct·ing** [*+ obj*]
1 : to build or make (something physical, such as a road, bridge, or building) ▪ They plan to *construct* a barn behind the house. ▪ a newly *constructed* bridge/building ▪ The table is *constructed* [=*made*] of wood and steel.
2 : to make or create (something, such as a story or theory) by organizing ideas, words, etc. ▪ The author *constructs* all the stories around one theme. ▪ a well-*constructed* argument
3 *mathematics* **:** to draw (a shape) according to a set of instructions or rules ▪ *Construct* a triangle that has sides of equal length.
– con·struc·tor /kən'strʌktɚ/ *noun, pl* **-tors** [*count*] ▪ a *constructor* of sound arguments

[2]**construct** *noun, pl* **-structs** [*count*] *formal* **:** something (such as an idea or a theory) that is formed in people's minds ▪ He argues that time is a subjective *construct* with no objective existence. ▪ Class distinctions are a ***social construct***. [=an idea that has been created and accepted by the people in a society]

con·struc·tion /kən'strʌkʃən/ *noun, pl* **-tions**
1 [*noncount*] **a :** the act or process of building something (such as a house or road) ▪ *Construction* of the new bridge will begin in the spring. ▪ *Construction* on the bridge will occur daily from 8:00 p.m. to 4:00 a.m. ▪ The new school is now ***under construction***. [=is now being built] — often used before another noun ▪ *construction* costs/equipment/materials ▪ They haven't chosen a *construction* site for the building yet. [=they haven't decided where the building will be built yet] **b :** the business of building things (such as houses or roads) ▪ "What do you do for a living?" "I'm ***in construction.***" [=I do work that involves building things] ▪ the *construction* industry
2 [*noncount*] **:** the way something is built or made ▪ Note the similar *construction* of the buildings. ▪ I like these binoculars because of their sturdy *construction*. [=because they are strongly built]
3 [*count*] **:** the way words in a sentence or phrase are arranged ▪ Some people think it is wrong to end a sentence with a preposition, but the *construction* is quite common in English. ▪ That verb is commonly used in passive *constructions*. ▪ This word is used in positive/negative *constructions*.
4 [*noncount*] **:** the process of organizing ideas or thoughts into a new theory, statement, etc. ▪ His ideas were pivotal in the *construction* of a new way to understand time and space.
5 [*count*] *formal* **:** a way of understanding something ▪ Don't put a negative *construction* on what I said: [=don't understand what I said in a negative way] ▪ a broad/strict *construction* [=*interpretation*] of the Constitution

construction paper *noun* [*noncount*] *US* **:** a kind of thick paper that comes in many colors and is used especially by children in school to create art

con·struc·tive /kən'strʌktɪv/ *adj* [*more ~; most ~*] **:** helping to develop or improve something **:** helpful to someone instead of upsetting and negative ▪ I tried to offer *constructive* criticism/suggestions/comments. ▪ Your feedback was not very *constructive*. ▪ The program helps people recently released from prison figure out how they can play a *constructive* role in society.
– con·struc·tive·ly *adv*

con·strue /kən'struː/ *verb* **-strues; -strued; -stru·ing** [*+ obj*] *somewhat formal*
1 : to understand (an action, event, remark, etc.) in a particular way — usually *+ as* ▪ He *construed* my actions *as* hostile. — often used as *(be) construed* ▪ Her frustration *was construed* [=*perceived, interpreted*] *as* anger. — compare MISCONSTRUE
2 : to understand the meaning of (a word, phrase, or sentence) ▪ The way the court *construes* various words has changed over time.

con·sul /'kɑːnsəl/ *noun, pl* **-suls** [*count*]
1 : a government official whose job is to live in a foreign country and protect and help the citizens of his or her own country who are traveling, living, or doing business there — compare AMBASSADOR
2 : either one of two chief officials of the ancient Roman republic who were elected every year
– con·sul·ar /'kɑːnsəlɚ, *Brit* 'kɒnsjələ/ *adj* ▪ a *consular* official

con·sul·ate /'kɑːnsələt/ *noun, pl* **-ates** [*count*] **:** the building where a consul lives and works ▪ the Russian *consulate* in Washington, D.C.

con·sult /kən'sʌlt/ *verb* **-sults; -sult·ed; -sult·ing**
1 [*+ obj*] **:** to go to (someone, such as a doctor or lawyer) for advice **:** to ask for the professional opinion of (someone) ▪

construction

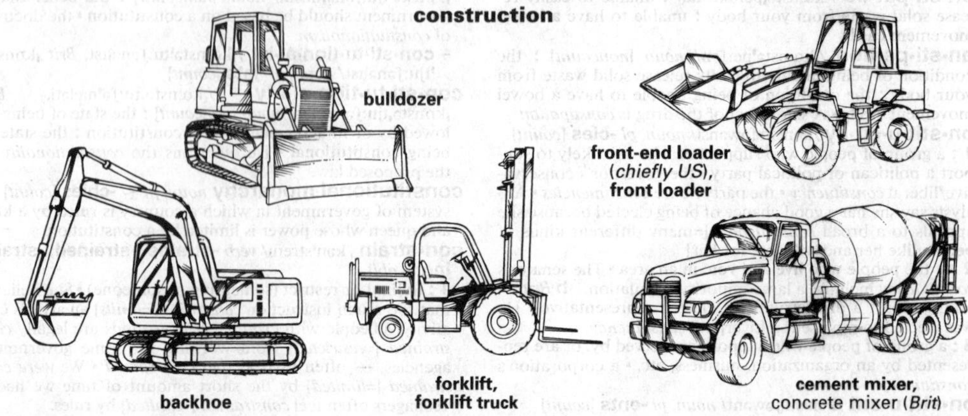

consult a lawyer/accountant about a business matter • You should not attempt these exercises without first *consulting* your doctor.
2 : to talk about something with (someone) in order to make a decision [+ *obj*] He made the decision without *consulting* me. • I expect to be *consulted* on important decisions. [*no obj*] — + *with* • I'll need to *consult with* my husband before I can sign the papers.
3 [+ *obj*] **:** to look for information in (something, such as a book or map) • *consult* a dictionary • I don't remember that part of the meeting; I'll have to *consult* my notes.
4 [*no obj*] *chiefly US* **:** to give professional advice to a person, organization, or company for a fee : to work as a consultant • She *consults* for a living.
– consulting *noun* [*noncount*] • Since she retired, she's done some *consulting* for the company. • He works for a *consulting* company. [=a company that gives professional advice to other companies for a fee]

con·sul·tan·cy /kənˈsʌltn̩si/ *noun, pl* **-cies** [*count*] **:** a company that gives professional advice to other companies for a fee : a consulting company • The company has hired an excellent marketing *consultancy.*

con·sult·ant /kənˈsʌltn̩t/ *noun, pl* **-ants** [*count*]
1 : a person who gives professional advice or services to companies for a fee • an advertising/management *consultant* • They've hired a computer *consultant* to assess how the company can upgrade its system.
2 *Brit* **:** a hospital doctor of the highest rank who is an expert in a particular area of medicine • a cardiology *consultant* [=*specialist*]

con·sul·ta·tion /ˌkɑːnsəlˈteɪʃən/ *noun, pl* **-tions**
1 [*count*] **:** a meeting in which someone (such as a doctor or lawyer) talks to a person about a problem, question, etc. • Many accountants offer a free *consultation* before charging for their work. • telephone *consultations* • After a series of *consultations* with doctors, a date for the operation was set.
2 : a discussion about something that is being decided [*count*] The group had a series of *consultations* with members of Congress. [*noncount*] The town decided to close the park without any *consultation* with town residents. • After *consultation* with the judge, lawyers decided to drop the case. • The book was chosen ***in consultation with*** [=after consulting] a panel of experts. • a *consultation* period/process
3 : the act of looking for information in a book, on a map, etc. [*noncount*] *Consultation* of city records confirms that she lived there in the 1950s. • Several dictionaries are available for *consultation*. [*count*] a quick *consultation* of the city records

con·sul·ta·tive /kənˈsʌltətɪv/ *adj, formal*
1 : giving advice • a *consultative* document
2 : having power only to give advice and not to make decisions • a *consultative* committee/council

consulting room *noun, pl* **~ rooms** [*count*] **:** a room where a doctor examines and talks to patients ✧ *Consulting room* is more common in British English than in U.S. English.

con·sum·able /kənˈsuːməbəl, *Brit* kənˈsjuːməbəl/ *adj* — used to describe products that need to be replaced after they have been used for a period of time • paper, pencils, and other *consumable* goods
– consumable *noun, pl* **-ables** [*count*] — usually plural • paper, pencils, and other *consumables*

con·sume /kənˈsuːm, *Brit* kənˈsjuːm/ *verb* **-sumes; -sumed; -sum·ing** [+ *obj*]
1 : to eat or drink (something) • The dogs *consume* [=*eat*] a bag of dog food each week. • They *consumed* [=*drank*] a lot of beer at the party. — sometimes used figuratively • He *consumes* [=*devours*] 10 novels a month. ***synonyms*** see EAT
2 : to use (fuel, time, resources, etc.) • The new lights *consume* less electricity. • She's making an effort to live more simply and *consume* less. • Most of our time was *consumed* [=*taken up*] by the search. • The car repair *consumed* [=*used up*] his entire paycheck. — see also TIME-CONSUMING
3 : to destroy (something) with fire • Hundreds of books were *consumed* in the fire. • Fire *consumed* the building.
4 : to take all of a person's attention, energy, time, etc. • Work on the project has *consumed* his attention for many months. = Work on the project has *consumed* him. — usually used as *(be) consumed* • The movie tells the story of a woman *consumed* by ambition/hatred. • He *was consumed* with/by jealousy.
– consuming *adj* • He has a *consuming* interest in politics. [=he is extremely interested in politics] • Her ***all-consuming*** passion was music. [=music was an interest that took all of her time and attention; music was the only thing she thought about]

con·sum·er /kənˈsuːmɚ, *Brit* kənˈsjuːmə/ *noun, pl* **-ers** [*count*] **:** a person who buys goods and services • Many *consumers* are still not comfortable making purchases on the Internet. — often used before another noun • *Consumer* spending is increasing. • *consumer* services • *consumer* demands/preferences

consumer durables *noun* [*plural*] *Brit* **:** DURABLE GOODS

consumer goods *noun* [*plural*] **:** products that people buy for personal use or for use at home • a range of *consumer goods*, from clothing to cameras to food

con·sum·er·ism /kənˈsuːməˌrɪzəm, *Brit* kənˈsjuːməˌrɪzəm/ *noun* [*noncount*] *often disapproving*
1 : the belief that it is good for people to spend a lot of money on goods and services
2 : the actions of people who spend a lot of money on goods and services • concerns about increasing *consumerism* among teenagers
– con·sum·er·ist /kənˈsuːmərɪst, *Brit* kənˈsjuːmərɪst/ *adj* • a *consumerist* culture

consumer price index *noun*
the consumer price index *US* **:** a list of prices of goods and services that shows how much prices have changed in a given period of time — abbr. *CPI* — called also *(Brit) retail price index*

[1]**con·sum·mate** /ˈkɑːnsəmət, kənˈsʌmət/ *adj, always used before a noun*
1 : very good or skillful • a *consummate* politician/actor/professional • She's a *consummate* storyteller. • He plays the piano with *consummate* skill.
2 : very bad • *consummate* cruelty/evil • a *consummate* liar
– con·sum·mate·ly *adv* • a *consummately* skillful pianist

[2]**con·sum·mate** /ˈkɑːnsəˌmeɪt/ *verb* **-mates; -mat·ed; -mat·ing** [+ *obj*] *formal*
1 : to make (a marriage or romantic relationship) complete by having sex • They were married for three months before the marriage was *consummated.* [=before they had sex]
2 : to make (something) perfect or complete • *consummate* an alliance • The bargaining process went on for a few days, but the deal was never *consummated.* • Their happiness was *consummated* when their son was born.
– con·sum·ma·tion /ˌkɑːnsəˈmeɪʃən/ *noun* [*noncount*] • Without *consummation*, the marriage can be annulled by the church. • the *consummation* of their happiness

con·sump·tion /kənˈsʌmpʃən/ *noun* [*noncount*]
1 : the act of eating or drinking something • alcohol/milk/chocolate *consumption* = the *consumption* of alcohol/milk/chocolate • Farms in the area grow food mostly for local *consumption.* [=they sell most of the food they grow to people who live nearby] • This food is not fit for human *consumption.* [=not fit to be eaten by people] • The doctor recommended that she reduce her *consumption* of sugar. [=that she eat less sugar]
2 : the use of something (such as fuel) • electricity/gas *consumption* = the *consumption* of electricity/gas • The jet's high fuel *consumption* makes it expensive to operate.
3 : use by a particular group of people • The governor said that the report was not for public *consumption.* [=it was not meant to be seen by the general public; it was intended only for a few people]
4 : the act of buying things • Rates of *consumption* typically rise as income increases. — see also CONSPICUOUS CONSUMPTION
5 *old-fashioned* **:** TUBERCULOSIS • He died of *consumption.*

con·sump·tive /kənˈsʌmptɪv/ *noun, pl* **-tives** [*count*] *old-fashioned* **:** a person who has tuberculosis • a hospital for *consumptives*
– consumptive *adj* • *consumptive* patients

cont. *also* **cont'd** *abbr* continued • *cont.* on page 15 • listings *cont'd* on pg. 4

[1]**con·tact** /ˈkɑːnˌtækt/ *noun, pl* **-tacts**
1 [*noncount*] **:** the state or condition that exists when two people or things physically touch each other : a state of touching • Physical *contact* between a mother and child is very important. • the point of *contact* between the bat and the ball [=the point where the bat and ball touch each other] • a disease that is spread by sexual *contact* • The players ***made contact*** [=touched or hit each other] and a foul was called. •

The train's wheels should ***make contact with*** [=*touch*] the track continuously. • Do not let your skin ***come in/into contact with*** [=*touch*] the acid. • The chemical kills germs ***on contact*** [=as soon as the chemical touches the germs]
2 a [*noncount*] **: the state or condition that exists when people see and communicate with each other** • The actor has had little *contact* with the public [=has not interacted much with the public] in recent years. • It was during that time that native people first ***came into/in contact with*** [=first saw and began communicating with] the settlers. • She joined a book club to get a little ***human contact*** [=interaction with other people] while the kids were in school. ✧ Your ***contact information*** is the information (such as your telephone number, address, or e-mail address) that tells someone how to communicate with you. • Don't forget to put your *contact information* on the application. ✧ If you are ***in contact*** with someone, you communicate with them sometimes. • "Are you *in contact* [=*in touch*] with them?" "No, I haven't been *in contact* with them for years. I don't even know where they live anymore." • We kept/stayed *in* close *contact* [=we communicated often] after college. • He's been *in* direct *contact* with the president. [=he has communicated directly with the president] • We'd lost touch, but a mutual friend put us *in contact* (with each other) again. ✧ If you ***lose contact*** with someone or something, you are no longer able to communicate with that person or thing. • I *lost contact* [=*lost touch*] with her years ago, but recently got her e-mail address through a mutual friend. • We *lost* radio *contact* with the ship for a short time. [=we could not communicate with the ship using their radio] ✧ If you ***make/establish contact***, you have succeeded in communicating with someone. • She's been trying to *make contact* with distant relatives. • The phone system wasn't working so we weren't able to *make contact*. • We were finally able to *establish contact* with them. **b** [*count*] **: an occurrence in which people communicate with each other** • *Contacts* between the two leaders have been frequent in recent weeks. — see also EYE CONTACT
3 [*count*] **: a person who you know and who can be helpful to you especially in business** • I applied for a job at that law firm because I have a *contact* there. • business *contacts* ✧ Someone who is listed as a ***contact*** in information from a company or organization is the person you can write to or call with questions about that company or organization.
4 [*count*] **:** CONTACT LENS • He lost one of his *contacts* in the swimming pool.
5 [*count*] **a : the connection of two objects (such as pieces of metal) that allows an electrical current to pass through them** • The *contact* must be maintained for the current to flow. **b : a part through which electricity passes from one object to another** • The camera's flash isn't working because the electrical *contacts* need to be cleaned.

²contact *verb* **-tacts; -tact·ed; -tact·ing** [+ *obj*] **: to call or write to (someone or something) : to communicate with (someone or something)** • For more information, *contact* the city's tourism office. • We were able to *contact* them by radio. • She *contacted* everyone on the list.

³contact *adj, always used before a noun*
1 *sports* **: allowing players to touch or hit each other** • Ice hockey is a *contact* sport.
2 : acting when physical contact occurs • *contact* insecticides/poisons

contact lens *noun, pl* **~ lenses** [*count*] **: a thin piece of round plastic that is worn on the eye to improve vision** • She wears *contact lenses* more often than glasses. — called also *contact*

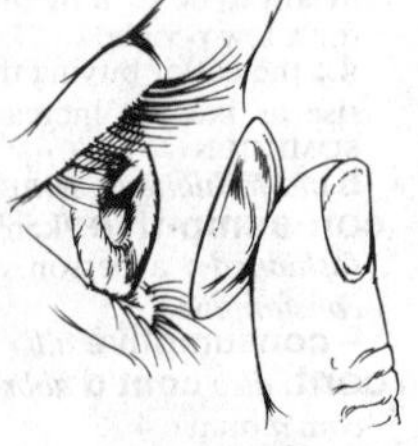
contact lens

con·ta·gion /kənˈteɪʤən/ *noun, pl* **-gions** *medical*
1 [*noncount*] **: the process by which a disease is passed from one person or animal to another by touching** • a disease that spreads by *contagion* • People have been warned to keep out of the area to avoid *contagion*.
2 [*count*] **: a disease that can be passed from one person or animal to another by touching : a contagious disease** • a deadly *contagion* — often used figuratively • The news created a *contagion* of fear that spread through the country.

con·ta·gious /kənˈteɪʤəs/ *adj* [*more ~; most ~*]
1 : able to be passed from one person or animal to another by touching • a *contagious* disease • It's a highly *contagious* virus. — compare INFECTIOUS
2 : having a sickness that can be passed to someone else by touching • I have a cold and I'm still *contagious*. • I'm sick, but the doctor says I'm not *contagious*.
3 : capable of being easily spread to others : causing other people to feel or act a similar way • She has a *contagious* smile. [=her smile makes other people smile; her smile makes other people happy] • *contagious* enthusiasm/laughter
– con·ta·gious·ly *adv* • a *contagiously* enthusiastic person
– con·ta·gious·ness *noun* [*noncount*]

con·tain /kənˈteɪn/ *verb* **-tains; -tained; -tain·ing** [+ *obj*]
1 : to have (something) inside • The box *contains* [=*holds*] an assortment of old papers. • The room was barely big enough to *contain* everyone who came to the meeting.
2 : to have or include (something) • The book *contains* over 200 recipes. • The article *contains* information on how to plan your retirement. • foods that *contain* a high level of fat • The movie *contains* something for both children and adults.
3 : to keep (something) from spreading : to keep (something) within limits • Firefighters *contained* the wildfires. • State health officials have succeeded in *containing* the virus.
4 : to keep (a feeling or yourself) under control • The children could barely *contain* their excitement as the day of the festival drew near. • When she saw that they were all safe, she could not *contain* herself [=control her feelings] and broke into tears of relief. — see also SELF-CONTAINED
– con·tain·able /kənˈteɪnəbəl/ *adj* • Health officials believe the virus is *containable* and are doing what they can to keep it from spreading. • barely *containable* excitement

con·tain·er /kənˈteɪnɚ/ *noun, pl* **-ers** [*count*]
1 : an object (such as a box or can) that can hold something • The tea leaves come in a small metal *container*. • bowls, boxes, jars, and other *containers*
2 : a large box that goods are placed in so that they can be moved from one place to another on a ship, airplane, train, or truck • The shipment of tools arrived at the dock in cargo *containers* yesterday.

container ship *noun, pl* **~ ships** [*count*] **: a large ship made to carry cargo containers** — see picture at SHIP

con·tain·ment /kənˈteɪnmənt/ *noun* [*noncount*]
1 : the act of preventing the spread of something • The company's hazardous waste *containment* plan is being reviewed. • trying to achieve cost *containment* [=trying to prevent costs from becoming too high]
2 : actions that are intended to keep an unfriendly government from getting more power • The government needs to adopt a *containment* strategy.

con·tam·i·nant /kənˈtæmənənt/ *noun, pl* **-nants** [*count*] **: something that makes a place or a substance (such as water, air, or food) no longer suitable for use : something that contaminates a place or substance** • a water *contaminant*

con·tam·i·nate /kənˈtæməˌneɪt/ *verb* **-nates; -nat·ed; -nat·ing** [+ *obj*] **: to make (something) dangerous, dirty, or impure by adding something harmful or undesirable to it** • The water was *contaminated* [=*polluted*] with chemicals. • Be careful not to allow bacteria to *contaminate* the wound. • Don't touch the microchip or the oil on your hands will *contaminate* it. • Make sure the white paint is not *contaminated* by any of the other colors. — often used figuratively • The election process has been *contaminated* by corruption. • Racist ideas have *contaminated* their minds.
– contaminated *adj* [*more ~; most ~*] • *contaminated* food/water **– con·tam·i·na·tion** /kənˌtæməˈneɪʃən/ *noun* [*noncount*] • *contamination* of the water by chemicals • Clean the wound and bandage it to prevent *contamination*.

cont'd see CONT.

con·tem·plate /ˈkɑːntəmˌpleɪt/ *verb* **-plates; -plat·ed; -plat·ing**
1 a [+ *obj*] **: to think deeply or carefully about (something)** • I stopped to *contemplate* [=*ponder*] what might have happened. • He *contemplated* the meaning of the poem for a long time. • Life without them is too awful to *contemplate*. [=too awful to even think about] **b** [*no obj*] **: to think deeply** • I'd like some time to just sit and *contemplate*.
2 [+ *obj*] **: to think about doing (something) :** CONSIDER • She's *contemplating* moving to the city. = She's *contemplating* a move to the city. • They're *contemplating* marriage. [=they're thinking about getting married]
3 [+ *obj*] **: to look carefully at (something)** • She stood and

quietly *contemplated* the scene that lay before her.

con·tem·pla·tion /ˌkɑːntəmˈpleɪʃən/ *noun* [*noncount*]
1 : the act of thinking deeply about something ▪ He made his decision after many hours of *contemplation*. [=*thought, consideration*] ▪ *contemplation* of the meaning of life
2 : the act of looking carefully at something ▪ He goes to the forest to spend time in *contemplation* of nature. ▪ She was lost in quiet *contemplation* of the scene.
in contemplation *formal* **: being thought about or considered** ▪ A lawsuit against the company is *in contemplation*.

con·tem·pla·tive /kənˈtɛmplətɪv, ˈkɑːntəmˌpleɪtɪv/ *adj*
1 [*more ~; most ~*] **: involving, allowing, or causing deep thought** ▪ She's in a *contemplative* mood today. [=she is quiet and thoughtful today] ▪ He has lived a quiet, *contemplative* life. ▪ a *contemplative* book
2 : devoted to religious thought and prayer ▪ She joined a *contemplative* order of nuns.
– con·tem·pla·tive·ly *adv*

con·tem·po·ra·ne·ous /kənˌtɛmpəˈreɪnijəs/ *adj, formal* **: existing or happening during the same time period** ▪ the *contemporaneous* publication of the two articles ▪ *contemporaneous* events in the past = events in the past that were *contemporaneous* with each other
– con·tem·po·ra·ne·ous·ly *adv* ▪ The articles were published *contemporaneously*. [=at the same time]

[1]con·tem·po·rary /kənˈtɛmpəreri, *Brit* kənˈtɛmpərəri/ *adj*
1 : happening or beginning now or in recent times ▪ *contemporary* [=*modern*] jazz/poetry/art/furniture ▪ The story is old, but it has importance to *contemporary* [=*current*] audiences.
2 : existing or happening in the same time period : from the same time period ▪ The book is based on *contemporary* accounts of the war. [=accounts of the war that were written when the war was happening]

[2]contemporary *noun, pl* **-rar·ies** [*count*] **: a person who lives at the same time or is about the same age as another person** ▪ He was a *contemporary* of George Washington. ▪ She is politically very different from most of her *contemporaries*.

con·tempt /kənˈtɛmpt/ *noun*
1 : a feeling that someone or something is not worthy of any respect or approval [*noncount*] He feels that wealthy people view/regard him with *contempt* because he is poor. ▪ He spoke with *contempt* in his voice. ▪ She has *contempt* for them. = She ***holds them in contempt***. [*singular*] She has displayed a profound *contempt* for her opponents.
2 : a lack of respect for or fear of something that is usually respected or feared [*noncount*] They have acted with *contempt* for public safety. [=they have completely ignored public safety] [*singular*] He has *contempt* for danger. [=he ignores danger; he is not afraid of doing things that other people are afraid to do]
3 [*noncount*] *law* **: speech or behavior that does not show proper respect to a court or judge** ▪ She was arrested for ***contempt of court***. ▪ He was ***held in contempt*** [=considered by the court to have broken the law by disobeying or disrespecting the judge] for his outbursts during the trial.
beneath contempt **: completely bad or worthless — used to describe someone or something that is too bad to deserve any respect** ▪ She's a liar who is *beneath contempt*.
familiarity breeds contempt see FAMILIARITY

con·tempt·ible /kənˈtɛmptəbəl/ *adj* [*more ~; most ~*] *somewhat formal* **: not worthy of respect or approval : deserving contempt** ▪ a *contemptible* [=*despicable*] lie ▪ I've never met a more selfish, *contemptible* person.
– con·tempt·ibly /kənˈtɛmptəbli/ *adv* ▪ a *contemptibly* selfish person

con·temp·tu·ous /kənˈtɛmptʃəwəs/ *adj* [*more ~; most ~*] *somewhat formal* **: feeling or showing deep hatred or disapproval : feeling or showing contempt** ▪ a *contemptuous* [=*disdainful*] attitude/smile/remark — often + *of* ▪ Scholars were *contemptuous* [=*scornful*] *of* the theory until recent scientific developments proved it possible.
– con·temp·tu·ous·ly *adv*

con·tend /kənˈtɛnd/ *verb* **-tends; -tend·ed; -tend·ing**
1 [+ *obj*] **: to argue or state (something) in a strong and definite way** ▪ These people *contend* that they have earned the right to the land. ▪ She *contends* [=*maintains, asserts*] the new law will only benefit the wealthy.
2 [*no obj*] **: to compete with someone or for something** ▪ A number of groups are *contending* (with each other) for power in the new government. **: to compete with a good chance of winning** ▪ The team is expected to *contend* for the championship this year.
contend with [*phrasal verb*] ***contend with (something)*** **: to deal with (something difficult or unpleasant)** ▪ Customers should not have to *contend with* the problems caused by these delays. ▪ He's had ***a lot to contend with*** recently. [=he's had many problems to deal with]

con·tend·er /kənˈtɛndɚ/ *noun, pl* **-ers** [*count*] **: a person who tries to win something in a contest;** ***especially*** **: a person who has a good chance of winning** ▪ There are several contestants, but only two real *contenders*. ▪ the top/leading presidential *contenders* ▪ This latest defeat means that she's no longer a *contender* for the world title.

[1]con·tent /ˈkɑːnˌtɛnt/ *noun, pl* **-tents**
1 ***contents*** [*plural*] **: the things that are in something** ▪ He poured/dumped/emptied the *contents* of the package/box/drawer onto the floor. ▪ The bedroom's *contents* have all been packed. ▪ The brochure describes the *contents* of the museum. ▪ a summary of the book's *contents* ✧ A ***table of contents*** is a list that is placed at the beginning of some books. It shows how the book is divided into sections and at which page each section begins. ▪ The stories included in the book can be found in the *table of contents*.
2 [*noncount*] **: the ideas, facts, or images that are in a book, article, speech, movie, etc.** ▪ In terms of *content*, the article is good, but it is written poorly. ▪ a summary of the book's *content* ▪ The children aren't allowed to watch movies with violent *content*. [=movies in which violent things happen] ▪ Some of the program's *content* may offend certain viewers.
3 [*noncount*] **: the amount of something that is in something else** ▪ This beer is low in alcohol *content*. [=does not have a lot of alcohol] ▪ the fat/fiber *content* of food
– compare [4]CONTENT

[2]con·tent /kənˈtɛnt/ *adj, not used before a noun* [*more ~; most ~*] **: pleased and satisfied : not needing more** ▪ The baby looks *content* in her crib. ▪ A fancy hotel is not necessary; I'd be *content* with a warm meal and a clean place to sleep. ▪ No, I don't want to play. I'm *content* to watch. ▪ Not *content* to stay at home, she set off to see the world at the age of 16. ▪ Polls show that voters are growing less and less *content* with the current administration.

[3]con·tent /kənˈtɛnt/ *verb* **-tents; -tent·ed; -tent·ing** [+ *obj*] *formal* **: to make (someone) pleased and satisfied : to make (someone) content** ▪ The toys *contented* the children, at least for a little while.
content yourself with **: to be satisfied with (something that is less than or different from what you really want) : to accept (something) as being enough** ▪ The rainy weather spoiled our plans for the beach, so we had to *content ourselves with* a relaxing day at home.

[4]con·tent /kənˈtɛnt/ *noun* [*noncount*] *literary* **: a feeling of being pleased and satisfied : the state of being content** ▪ He'd finished his dinner and now there was a look of perfect *content* [=(more commonly) *contentment*] on his face.
to your heart's content see HEART
– compare [1]CONTENT

con·tent·ed /kənˈtɛntəd/ *adj* [*more ~; most ~*] **: happy and satisfied : showing or feeling contentment** ▪ a *contented* smile ▪ He's a *contented* fellow. ▪ She felt peaceful and *contented*.
– con·tent·ed·ly *adv* ▪ smiled *contentedly*

con·ten·tion /kənˈtɛnʃən/ *noun, pl* **-tions**
1 [*count*] **: something (such as a belief, opinion, or idea) that is argued or stated** ▪ It is her *contention* [=she believes and says] that the new law will only benefit the wealthy. ▪ Evidence supports the *contention* [=*claim*] that the island was uninhabited before the 18th century.
2 [*noncount*] **: anger and disagreement** ▪ There has been too much *contention* [=*discord*] in this family in recent years. ▪ The main point of *contention* [=the point that is being argued over] is who has the rights to the land. ▪ That has been a source of *contention* for years. ▪ an issue that is still ***in contention*** [=that is still being argued about; that has not yet been decided] ✧ A ***bone of contention*** is something that causes anger and disagreement. ▪ The tariffs have been a *bone of contention* between the two nations.
3 [*noncount*] **: a situation in which you have a chance to win something that you are trying to win** ▪ This latest defeat means that she's now ***out of contention*** for the world title. [=there is no longer a chance that she will win the world title] ▪ He is ***in contention*** for the Olympic medal.

con·ten·tious /kənˈtɛnʃəs/ *adj* [*more ~; most ~*]
1 a : likely to cause people to argue or disagree ▪ I think it's wise to avoid such a highly *contentious* [=*controversial*] topic/

issue at a dinner party. **b : involving a lot of arguing** ▪ After a *contentious* debate, members of the committee finally voted to approve the funding. ▪ They have a *contentious* relationship. [=they argue with each other a lot]

2 : likely or willing to argue ▪ a *contentious* student ▪ The dispute involves one of the region's most *contentious* leaders.

– con·ten·tious·ly *adv* **– con·ten·tious·ness** *noun [noncount]*

con·tent·ment /kən'tɛntmənt/ *noun [noncount]* **: the state of being happy and satisfied : the state of being content** ▪ He believes that people can find peace and *contentment* in living simply. ▪ There was a look of perfect *contentment* on her face. ▪ a sigh of *contentment*

[1]con·test /'kɑːnˌtɛst/ *noun, pl* **-tests** *[count]*

1 : an event in which people try to win by doing something better than others ▪ a fiddle/fishing/singing *contest* [=*competition*] ▪ He won the *contest* for best photograph. = He won the *contest* to see who could take the best photograph. ▪ *Contest* winners receive a cash prize. ▪ Will you enter the *contest*? — see also BEAUTY CONTEST, POPULARITY CONTEST

2 : a struggle or effort to win or get something ▪ She hopes to win the *contest* for mayor. ▪ the presidential *contest* ▪ Democrats and Republicans are engaged in a *contest* for control of the House of Representatives.

no contest **1** *informal* **— used to say that someone or something is much better than another or can easily defeat another** ▪ When you compare the old version of the movie with the new one, it's *no contest*. The old one is much better. ▪ The last time I played him it was *no contest*. I won easily. **2** *US, law* **: a statement in a court of law in which someone who has been charged with a crime does not admit guilt but also does not dispute or argue with the charge** ▪ He pleaded *no contest* to (the charge of) driving while intoxicated.

[2]con·test /kən'tɛst/ *verb* **-tests; -test·ed; -test·ing**

1 *[+ obj]* **: to make (something) the subject of an argument or a legal case : to say that you do not agree with or accept (something)** ▪ Several of the dead man's relatives are *contesting* [=*disputing, challenging*] his will (in court). ▪ The losing candidate is *contesting* the results of the election. = (*US*) The losing candidate is *contesting* the election. ▪ The rule is being *contested* by a number of students at the university. [=students are formally complaining about the rule]

2 *[+ obj]* **: to try to win (something)** ▪ She plans to *contest* a seat in Congress next year. ▪ Both candidates have agreed to another debate before this hotly/bitterly *contested* election.

3 *[no obj]* **: to struggle or fight for or against something** ▪ *contesting* for power

con·test·ant /kən'tɛstənt/ *noun, pl* **-ants** *[count]* **: a person who takes part in a contest** ▪ The *contestant* who catches the most fish wins. ▪ The winning *contestants* will receive a cash prize. ▪ a game-show *contestant*

con·text /'kɑːnˌtɛkst/ *noun, pl* **-texts** *[count]*

1 : the words that are used with a certain word or phrase and that help to explain its meaning ▪ To really know a word, you must be able to use it ***in context*** [=in a sentence with other words] ◊ **If the words that someone has said are taken or quoted *out of context*, they are repeated without explaining the situation in which they were said so that their meaning is changed.** ▪ When taken *out of context*, his comments sound cruel, but he was really only joking. ▪ The actor claimed he'd been quoted *out of context*.

2 : the situation in which something happens : the group of conditions that exist where and when something happens ▪ We need to look at the event within the larger/broader *context* of world history. ▪ The book puts these events in their proper historical and social *contexts*. ▪ We need to consider these events ***in context***

– con·tex·tu·al /kɑn'tɛksʧəwəl/ *adj* ▪ *contextual* information ▪ To find the meaning of an unknown word you should look at the ***contextual clues*** provided by the words that are around it. **– con·tex·tu·al·ly** *adv*

con·tex·tu·al·ize *also Brit* **con·tex·tu·al·ise** /kən'tɛksʧəwəˌlaɪz/ *verb* **-iz·es; -ized; -iz·ing** *[+ obj] formal* **: to think about or provide information about the situation in which something happens** ▪ When the rebellion is historically *contextualized*, it becomes clear that there were many factors contributing to it.

– con·tex·tu·al·i·za·tion *also Brit* **con·tex·tu·al·i·sa·tion** /kənˌtɛksʧəwələ'zeɪʃən, *Brit* kənˌtɛksʧuəˌlaɪ'zeɪʃən/ *noun [noncount]* ▪ historical *contextualization*

con·tig·u·ous /kən'tɪgjəwəs/ *adj, formal* **— used to describe things that touch each other or are immediately next to each other** ▪ She's visited each of the 48 *contiguous* states in the U.S., but she hasn't been to Alaska or Hawaii yet. ▪ the mountains *contiguous* to/with our border

– con·ti·gu·i·ty /ˌkɑːntə'gjuːwəti/ *noun [noncount]* ▪ the *contiguity* of the lands

[1]con·ti·nent /'kɑːntənənt/ *noun, pl* **-nents**

1 *[count]* **: one of the great divisions of land (such as North America, South America, Europe, Asia, Africa, Australia, or Antarctica) of the Earth** ▪ the African *continent* = the *continent* of Africa

2 *the Continent* *chiefly Brit* **: the countries of Europe except for Great Britain and Ireland** ▪ The book provides information on hotels in Britain and on *the Continent*.

[2]con·ti·nent *adj, medical* **: able to control your bladder and bowels** ▪ Most children are *continent* by age three. — opposite INCONTINENT

– con·ti·nence /'kɑːntənəns/ *noun [noncount]* ▪ urinary *continence*

[1]con·ti·nen·tal /ˌkɑːntə'nɛntl/ *adj*

1 : of, relating to, or located on a continent ▪ *continental* glaciers [=glaciers that cover a large portion of a continent] ▪ the ***continental U.S.*** [=the part of the U.S. that is on the North American continent; the states of the U.S. except for Hawaii]

2 *Continental* : of or relating to the countries of Europe except for Great Britain and Ireland ▪ They will be touring *Continental* Europe. ▪ differences between Britain and its *Continental* neighbors

3 : characteristic of Europe ▪ The hotel combines American comfort with *continental* elegance.

[2]continental *noun, pl* **-tals** *[count] Brit, somewhat old-fashioned* **: a person from Continental Europe**

continental breakfast *noun, pl* **~ -fasts** *[count]* **: a light breakfast in a hotel, restaurant, etc., that usually includes baked goods, jam, fruit, and coffee — compare** ENGLISH BREAKFAST

continental drift *noun [noncount] technical* **: the very slow movement of the continents on the surface of the Earth**

continental shelf *noun, pl* **~ shelves** *[count] technical* **: the part of a continent that lies under the ocean and slopes down to the ocean floor**

con·tin·gen·cy /kən'tɪnʤənsi/ *noun, pl* **-cies** *[count]* **: something (such as an emergency) that might happen** ▪ In making our business plans, we tried to prepare for any *contingency* that might hurt sales. ▪ a ***contingency plan*** [=a plan that can be followed if an original plan is not possible for some reason] ▪ a ***contingency fund*** [=an amount of money that can be used to pay for problems that might happen]

contingency fee *noun, pl* **~ fees** *[count] US* **: a payment that you make to a lawyer only if the lawyer wins your case in court**

[1]con·tin·gent /kən'tɪnʤənt/ *adj, formal* **: depending on something else that might or might not happen — usually + *on* or *upon*** ▪ Our plans are *contingent on* the weather.

– con·tin·gent·ly *adv*

[2]contingent *noun, pl* **-gents** *[count]*

1 : a group of people who go to a place together, do something together, or share some quality, interest, etc. ▪ The group that makes up the largest *contingent* of voters in this area is the elderly. ▪ A *contingent* of reporters waited in front of the court for the defendant to appear.

2 : a group of soldiers who come from a particular army and are working together with soldiers from other armies ▪ A British *contingent* was sent to assist the security forces.

con·tin·u·al /kən'tɪnjuwəl/ *adj*

1 : happening without interruption : not stopping or ending ▪ This week we experienced days of *continual* sunshine. ▪ The country has been in a *continual* state of war since it began fighting for its independence.

2 : happening again and again within short periods of time ▪ The *continual* interruptions by the student were annoying the teacher.

– con·tin·u·al·ly *adv* ▪ He is *continually* experimenting with new recipes.

con·tin·u·ance /kən'tɪnjuwəns/ *noun, pl* **-anc·es** *formal*

1 *[noncount]* **: the act of continuing for a long period of time** ▪ They are making efforts to promote the *continuance* [=*continuation*] of good relations between the two countries.

2 *[noncount]* **: the period of time when something continues** ▪ No changes to the property are allowed during the *continuance* of the lease.

3 *[count] US, law* **: a legal decision that a court case will con-**

tinue at a later date ▪ The lawyer asked the judge for a *continuance.*

con·tin·u·a·tion /kənˌtɪnjəˈweɪʃən/ *noun, pl* **-tions**

1 [*count*] : something that starts where something else ends and adds to or continues the first part — usually + *of* ▪ This book is a *continuation of* her first novel. [=it continues the story where the first novel ended] ▪ The class is a *continuation of* the introductory class taught last semester. ▪ The road was built as a *continuation of* the state highway.

2 [*noncount*] : the act of continuing or of causing something to continue — usually + *of* ▪ His counselor felt the *continuation of* therapy would be worthwhile. [=felt that he should continue to receive therapy]

3 [*count*] : the act of beginning again after an interruption — usually singular; usually + *of* ▪ The *continuation of* the meeting was postponed until the next day.

con·tin·ue /kənˈtɪnju/ *verb* **-ues; -ued; -u·ing**

1 a : to do something without stopping : to keep doing something in the same way as before [*no obj*] The team will *continue* with their drills until the coach is satisfied with their performance. [+ *obj*] Do you plan to *continue* working after the baby is born? = Do you plan to *continue* to work? ▪ The world's population *continues* to grow. ▪ I *continue* to believe [=I still believe] that we can win this election. **b** [*no obj*] : to stay in a job or position — + *as* ▪ She has announced that she will *continue as* director [=stay in her job as the director] for another year.

2 [*no obj*] : to keep happening or existing : to remain active or in existence without changing or stopping ▪ The traditions will *continue* only as long as the next generations keep them alive. ▪ The good weather *continued* for several days. ▪ The lecture *continued* for another hour after we left.

3 [*no obj*] **a :** to go or move ahead in the same direction ▪ Exit the highway, take a right off the ramp, then *continue* down the street until you get to the first traffic light. ▪ *Continue* along this path until you come to the end. ▪ The boat *continued* downstream. **b :** to go onward : PROGRESS ▪ The plot gets more and more intricate as the story *continues.*

4 : to start again after an interruption or pause : RESUME [*no obj*] The article *continues* in the second section of the newspaper. ▪ The play *continued* after the intermission. ▪ We will *continue* on our journey in the morning. = Our journey will *continue* in the morning. [+ *obj*] The board *continued* their meeting after a short break. ▪ We will *continue* our journey in the morning. ▪ When Mom left the room, we *continued* arguing. ✧ When the words ***to be continued*** appear at the end of something (such as a story or television program), it has not really ended and will continue again at a later time.

5 : to begin speaking again after an interruption or pause [*no obj*] The teacher *continued* only when all the students were sitting quietly in their seats. [+ *obj*] "I understand what you're saying," she *continued,* "but I'm not convinced your idea will work."

– continuing *adj* ▪ We are thankful for your *continuing* [=*continued, ongoing*] support. ▪ I'm surprised by the film's *continuing* popularity.

continued *adj, always used before a noun* : lasting or happening for a long time without interruption ▪ Please accept our best wishes for your *continued* success. ▪ The colors of the paint will fade with *continued* exposure to the sun.

continuing education *noun* [*noncount*] : classes taken by adult students usually in the evenings — called also *continuing ed, adult education*

con·ti·nu·i·ty /ˌkɑːntəˈnuːwəti, *Brit* ˌkɒntəˈnjuːəti/ *noun, pl* **-ties**

1 [*noncount*] : the quality of something that does not stop or change as time passes : a continuous quality ▪ The new owners have ensured the *continuity* of the company's commitment to protecting the environment. [=have assured that the company's commitment will continue] ▪ The candidate attacked the incumbent for the lack of *continuity* [=*consistency*] in foreign policy under his presidency.

2 [*count*] *formal* : something that is the same or similar in two or more things and provides a connection between them ▪ The art historian is studying the *continuities* between the painter's works and those of her followers.

3 [*noncount*] : the arrangement of the parts in a story, movie, etc., in a way that is logical ▪ There's a problem with the movie's *continuity.*

con·tin·u·ous /kənˈtɪnjuwəs/ *adj*

1 [*more* ~; *most* ~] : continuing without stopping : happening or existing without a break or interruption ▪ The album is divided into different tracks, but it is really one *continuous* song. ▪ The fan keeps a *continuous* [=*uninterrupted*] stream of fresh air flowing through the car. ▪ a *continuous* line of traffic ▪ The batteries provide enough power for up to five hours of *continuous* use.

2 *grammar* : PROGRESSIVE 4 ▪ The phrases "am seeing," "had been seeing," and "is being seen" are all in *continuous* tenses.

– con·tin·u·ous·ly *adv* ▪ The volcano has been erupting almost *continuously* since 1980.

con·tin·u·um /kənˈtɪnjuwəm/ *noun, pl* **-ua** /-juwə/ *also* **-u·ums** [*count*] *formal* : a range or series of things that are slightly different from each other and that exist between two different possibilities ▪ His motives for volunteering lie somewhere on the *continuum* between charitable and self-serving. ▪ a *continuum* of temperatures ranging from very cold to very hot

con·tort /kənˈtoɚt/ *verb* **-torts; -tort·ed; -tort·ing** : to twist into an unusual appearance or shape [*no obj*] His body *contorted* with/in pain. [+ *obj*] The boy *contorted* his body to squeeze through the gate. ▪ Her face was *contorted* with/in rage/anger.

– contorted *adj* [*more* ~; *most* ~] ▪ the fossil's *contorted* limbs ▪ We could not follow her *contorted* [=*twisted, convoluted*] reasoning/logic.

con·tor·tion /kənˈtoɚʃən/ *noun, pl* **-tions** [*count*]

1 : the act of twisting something into an unusual shape : the act of contorting something ▪ The clown amused the children with funny facial *contortions.* ▪ The gymnast performed amazing *contortions* (with her body).— sometimes used figuratively ▪ His story was a blatant/obvious *contortion* [=(more commonly) *distortion*] of the truth.

2 : a difficult action ▪ The baby's mom went through the usual *contortions* to get him to eat.

con·tor·tion·ist /kənˈtoɚʃənɪst/ *noun, pl* **-ists** [*count*] : a performer who twists his or her body into unusual positions

con·tour /ˈkɑːnˌtuɚ/ *noun, pl* **-tours** [*count*] : the outline or outer edge of something ▪ He loved the sleek/smooth/flowing *contours* of the car. ▪ The map showed the *contour* of the coastline.

con·toured /ˈkɑːnˌtuɚd/ *adj*

1 : shaped to fit the outline of something (such as the human body) ▪ The car's *contoured* seats were very comfortable. ▪ a dress with a *contoured* waist

2 : having a smooth shape or outer edge ▪ a nicely *contoured* vase. ▪ the *contoured* wing of the aircraft ▪ the *contoured* hills of her native land

con·tra·band /ˈkɑːntrəˌbænd/ *noun* [*noncount*] : things that are brought into or out of a country illegally ▪ The border police searched the car for drugs and other *contraband.*

con·tra·bass /ˈkɑːntrəˌbeɪs/ *noun, pl* **-bass·es** [*count*] : DOUBLE BASS

con·tra·cep·tion /ˌkɑːntrəˈsɛpʃən/ *noun* [*noncount*] : things that are done to prevent a woman from becoming pregnant : BIRTH CONTROL

con·tra·cep·tive /ˌkɑːntrəˈsɛptɪv/ *noun, pl* **-tives** [*count*] : a drug or device (such as birth control pills or a condom) that is used to prevent a woman from becoming pregnant

– contraceptive *adj, always used before a noun* ▪ a *contraceptive* device/method/pill

[1]**con·tract** /ˈkɑːnˌtrækt/ *noun, pl* **-tracts** [*count*]

1 a : a legal agreement between people, companies, etc. ▪ The *contract* requires him to finish work by the end of the year. ▪ If he breaks the *contract* [=if he does not abide by the agreement], he will get sued. ▪ The company won a multi-million-dollar *contract* to build a new courthouse. = The company was awarded a multi-million-dollar *contract* to build a new courthouse. ▪ a marriage *contract* [=an agreement to marry someone]— often used before another noun ▪ *contract* negotiations ▪ *contract* law **b :** a document on which the words of a contract are written ▪ I tore up the *contract.* ▪ Have you signed the *contract* yet?

2 *informal* : an agreement to kill a person for money ▪ His enemies ***put/took out a contract on*** him. [=paid someone to kill him]

by contract : according to the terms stated in a contract : by a legal agreement ▪ We are bound *by contract* to pay the full price.

under contract : required to provide something (such as work or a service) according to the terms stated in a contract ▪ She is *under contract* with the TV station for three more years.

C

²con·tract /kənˈtrækt/ *verb* **-tracts; -tract·ed; -tract·ing**
1 a [+ *obj*] **:** to make (something) smaller or shorter • She *contracted* her lips into a frown. • *contract* a muscle **b** [*no obj*] **:** to become smaller • The muscle expands and then *contracts*. • The hot metal *contracted* as it cooled.
2 [+ *obj*] *somewhat formal* **:** to become ill with (a disease) • He *contracted* [=(more commonly) *caught*] a cold. • She *contracted* chicken pox. • They *contracted* malaria.
3 : to make an agreement by contract to work or to pay someone to work [*no obj*] The carpenter *contracted* (with them) to do the work on their house. [+ *obj*] We *contracted* [=*hired*] a lawyer.
4 /ˈkɑːnˌtrækt/ [+ *obj*] *formal* **:** to agree to (a marriage, an alliance, etc.) formally • a legally *contracted* marriage • The company *contracted* an alliance with a former competitor.
contract out /ˈkɑːnˌtrækt/ [*phrasal verb*] ***contract (something) out or contract out (something)*** **:** to agree by contract to pay someone to perform (a job) • The company *contracted out* its manufacturing jobs. [=the company paid another company to do its manufacturing jobs instead of doing them itself]

con·trac·tion /kənˈtrækʃən/ *noun, pl* **-tions**
1 [*noncount*] **:** the act or process of making something smaller or of becoming smaller • The hot metal undergoes *contraction* as it cools. • Two teams were eliminated in the *contraction* of the baseball league.
2 [*count*] *medical* **:** a movement of a muscle that causes it to become tight and that is sometimes painful; *especially* **:** a movement of muscles in the womb when a woman is giving birth to a child • She felt *contractions* every two minutes.
3 [*count*] **:** a short form of a word or word group that is made by leaving out a sound or letter • The word *don't* is a *contraction* of *do not*.

con·trac·tor /ˈkɑːnˌtræktɚ/ *noun, pl* **-tors** [*count*] **:** a person who is hired to perform work or to provide goods at a certain price or within a certain time • They hired a *contractor* to remodel the kitchen. • a building *contractor*

con·trac·tu·al /kənˈtræktʃəwəl/ *adj* **:** of or relating to the things that are required by a contract • They had to fulfill their *contractual* obligations/requirements before they could get paid.
– con·trac·tu·al·ly *adv* • The company is *contractually* obligated to pay the union.

con·tra·dict /ˌkɑːntrəˈdɪkt/ *verb* **-dicts; -dict·ed; -dict·ing** [+ *obj*]
1 a : to say the opposite of (something that someone else has said) **:** to deny the truth of (something) • *contradict* a rumor • He *contradicted* the charges of his critics. **b :** to deny or disagree with what is being said by (someone) • My sister doesn't like being *contradicted*.
2 : to not agree with (something) in a way that shows or suggests that it is false, wrong, etc. • She has made statements that *contradict* each other. [=statements that do not agree and that cannot both be true] • The evidence *contradicts* his testimony. [=the evidence does not support or agree with his testimony] • The mayor's actions in office *contradicted* the promises he made during the campaign.
contradict yourself **:** to say or do something that is opposite or very different in meaning to something else that you said or did earlier • The witness *contradicted herself* when she insisted she could identify the thief even though she had said that the night was too foggy to see clearly.

con·tra·dic·tion /ˌkɑːntrəˈdɪkʃən/ *noun, pl* **-tions**
1 : the act of saying something that is opposite or very different in meaning to something else [*count*] No one was surprised by the defendant's *contradiction* of the plaintiff's accusations. • Her rebuttal contained many *contradictions* to my arguments. [*noncount*] I think I can say ***without fear of contradiction*** [=I can say with absolute certainty] that this year has been very successful for our company.
2 : a difference or disagreement between two things which means that both cannot be true [*count*] There have been some *contradictions* in his statements. • There is a *contradiction* between what he said yesterday and what he said today. [*noncount*] Her statements are mired in *contradiction*. • What he said yesterday is ***in direct contradiction*** to what he said today.
contradiction in terms **:** a phrase that contains words which have very different or opposite meanings • I think "working vacation" is a *contradiction in terms*.

con·tra·dic·to·ry /ˌkɑːntrəˈdɪktəri/ *adj* [*more ~; most ~*] **:** involving or having information that disagrees with other information **:** containing a contradiction • The witnesses gave *contradictory* accounts/statements/descriptions of the accident. [=they described the accident in ways that did not agree with each other]

con·trail /ˈkɑːnˌtreɪl/ *noun, pl* **-trails** [*count*] **:** a stream of water or ice particles created in the sky by an airplane or rocket

con·tra·in·di·cat·ed /ˌkɑːntrəˈɪndəˌkeɪtəd/ *adj, medical* — used to say that something (such as a treatment, procedure, or activity) should not be done or used in a particular situation for medical reasons • Strenuous exercise is *contraindicated* for patients with severe heart conditions. [=patients who have severe heart conditions should not do strenuous exercise] • The drug is *contraindicated* in patients with certain allergies.

con·tra·in·di·ca·tion /ˌkɑːntrəˌɪndəˈkeɪʃən/ *noun, pl* **-tions** [*count*] *medical* **:** something (such as a symptom or condition) that is a medical reason for not doing or using something (such as a treatment, procedure, or activity) • The article stated that diabetes was not a *contraindication* to breastfeeding. [=it stated that women who have diabetes can breastfeed]

con·tral·to /kənˈtræltoʊ/ *noun, pl* **-tos** [*count*] **:** the lowest female singing voice — usually singular • a singer with a beautiful *contralto*; *also* **:** a female singer with such a voice • a duet performed by a soprano and a *contralto*

con·trap·tion /kənˈtræpʃən/ *noun, pl* **-tions** [*count*] **:** a piece of equipment or machinery that is unusual or strange • The people wondered how the *contraption* worked.

con·trar·i·an /kənˈtrerijən/ *noun, pl* **-ans** [*count*] **:** a person who takes an opposite or different position or attitude from other people • As an investor, he's a *contrarian*, preferring to buy stocks when most people are selling.
– contrarian *adj* [*more ~; most ~*] • a *contrarian* view/position/attitude

con·trari·wise /ˈkɑːnˌtreriˌwaɪz, kənˈtreriˌwaɪz/ *adv, formal* **:** in an opposite or very different way — used especially to introduce a statement that contrasts with a preceding statement • Her opponent has little knowledge of foreign policy. *Contrariwise*, she herself has many years of experience in this area.

¹con·trary /ˈkɑːnˌtreri, *Brit* ˈkɑːntrəri/ *noun*
on the contrary also quite the contrary — used to state that the opposite of what was said before is true • The test will not be easy; *on the contrary*, it will be very difficult. • The lecture was not boring. *Quite the contrary*, it was very informative and interesting.
the contrary **:** an opposite or different fact, event, or situation • He was sure his sister had made a mistake, but *the contrary* was true: she was right and he was wrong.
to the contrary **:** stating or proving the opposite of something • He was no fool, despite talk *to the contrary*. • Unless there is evidence *to the contrary*, we have to believe them.

²con·trary /ˈkɑːnˌtreri, *Brit* ˈkɑːntrəri/ *adj*
1 : exactly opposite to something else **:** entirely different from something else • The sisters gave *contrary* answers: one said "yes" and one said "no." • We had *contrary* opinions/views on the issue.
2 : against or opposed to something • Without *contrary* evidence, the jury will find her guilty. — often + *to* • Going over the speed limit is *contrary to* traffic laws. [=it is illegal; it is against the law]
3 : not favorable or helpful • The boat sailed against a *contrary* wind. • *Contrary* weather impeded the rescue efforts.
4 /kənˈtreri/ **:** unwilling to obey or behave well • a *contrary* child
contrary to **:** in a way or manner that is against (something) • *Contrary to* orders, he left the campsite. • ***Contrary to popular belief*** [=despite what many people believe], these animals are not really dangerous to humans.
– con·trar·i·ly /kənˈtrerəli/ *adv* • The child acted *contrarily*.
– con·trar·i·ness /kənˈtrerinəs/ *noun* [*noncount*] • the child's *contrariness*

¹con·trast /kənˈtræst, *Brit* kənˈtrɑːst/ *verb* **-trasts; -trast·ed; -trast·ing**
1 [*no obj*] **:** to be different especially in a way that is very obvious • Her black dress and the white background *contrast* sharply. — often + *with* • Her black dress *contrasts* sharply *with* the white background. • Her actions *contrasted with* her promises.
2 [+ *obj*] **:** to compare (two people or things) to show how they are different • We compared and *contrasted* the two

characters of the story. — often + *with* or *to* ▪ His essay *contrasted* his life in America *with/to* life in India.
– **contrasting** *adj* [*more* ~; *most* ~] ▪ He wore a dark suit with a necktie in a *contrasting* color. ▪ *contrasting* opinions/views/ideas – **con·trast·ing·ly** *adv*

[2]**con·trast** /ˈkɑːnˌtræst, *Brit* ˈkɒnˌtrɑːst/ *noun, pl* **-trasts**
1 [*count*] **: something that is different from another thing** — + *to* ▪ Today's weather is quite a *contrast to* yesterday's. [=today's weather is very different from yesterday's weather]
2 : a difference between people or things that are being compared [*count*] I observed an interesting *contrast* in/between the teaching styles of the two women. ▪ We talked about the *contrasts* between his early books and his later books. [=the ways in which his early and later books are different] [*noncount*] His comments were ***in stark/marked/sharp contrast with/to*** his earlier statements. [=his comments were very different from his earlier statements]
3 [*noncount*] **: the act of comparing people or things to show the differences between them** ▪ Careful *contrast* of the twins shows some differences. ▪ ***In contrast to/with*** last year's profits, the company is not doing very well. ▪ The queen's wit and humor made the prince seem dull ***by contrast***. ▪ They spent millions of dollars on advertising. ***By way of contrast***, our small company spent under 5,000 dollars.
4 [*noncount*] **: the difference between the dark and light parts of a painting or photograph** ▪ a painting with a lot of *contrast* ▪ She was wearing a black dress, so the photographer suggested using a white background for *contrast*.
– **contrasting** *adj* [*more* ~; *most* ~] ▪ They have very *contrasting* [=*different*] styles. – **con·tras·tive** /kənˈtræstɪv, *Brit* kənˈtrɑːstɪv/ *adj* [*more* ~; *most* ~] *formal* ▪ *contrastive* styles

con·tra·vene /ˌkɑːntrəˈviːn/ *verb* **-venes; -vened; -ven·ing** [+ *obj*] *formal* **: to fail to do what is required by (a law or rule) : VIOLATE** ▪ The overcrowded dance club *contravened* safety regulations.
– **con·tra·ven·tion** /ˌkɑːntrəˈvɛnʃən/ *noun, pl* **-tions** [*count*] Plagiarism is a *contravention* of school policy. [*noncount*] He cut off trade with the country ***in contravention of*** their treaty. [=he cut off trade in a way that was not allowed by the treaty]

con·tre·temps /ˈkɑːntrəˌtɑːn/ *noun, pl* **con·tre·temps** /ˈkɑːntrəˌtɑːnz/ [*count*] **: an unfortunate or embarrassing event, argument, or disagreement** ▪ The senator dismissed his disagreement with the President as a minor *contretemps*.

con·trib·ute /kənˈtrɪbjuːt/ *verb* **-utes; -ut·ed; -ut·ing**
1 : to give (something, such as money, goods, or time) to help a person, group, cause, or organization — usually + *to* or *toward* [+ *obj*] He *contributed* [=*donated*] 100 dollars *to* the charity. ▪ The volunteers *contributed* their time *towards* cleaning up the city. ▪ She *contributed* [=*added*] little *to* the discussion. [*no obj*] We're trying to raise money for a new school, and we're hoping that everyone will *contribute*. ▪ He did not *contribute to* the project.
2 [*no obj*] **: to help to cause something to happen** ▪ In order for the team to win, everyone has to *contribute*. — usually + *to* ▪ Many players have *contributed to* the team's success. ▪ Heavy drinking *contributed to* her death. [=heavy drinking helped to cause her death]
3 : to write (something, such as a story, poem, or essay) for a magazine [+ *obj*] He *contributed* many poems to the magazine. [*no obj*] Ten scientists *contributed* to the special edition of the journal.
– **contributing** *adj* ▪ The coach's positive attitude was a ***contributing factor*** to/in the team's success. [=the coach's positive attitude was a reason for the team's success] ▪ She has been a ***contributing writer/editor*** for the magazine for 10 years. – **con·trib·u·tor** /kənˈtrɪbjətə/ *noun, pl* **-tors** [*count*] ▪ She is a regular/frequent *contributor* to the magazine. ▪ a list of *contributors* who have donated more than one thousand dollars

con·tri·bu·tion /ˌkɑːntrəˈbjuːʃən/ *noun, pl* **-tions**
1 [*count*] **: something that is contributed: such as a : something that is given to help a person, a cause, etc.** ▪ She made a 100-dollar *contribution* [=*donation*] to breast cancer research. ▪ They thanked him for his *contribution* of time and money. ▪ He made an important *contribution* to the debate. **b : something that is done to cause something to happen** ▪ She's honored for her *contributions* [=*efforts, work*] towards finding a cure for AIDS. ▪ As mayor, he made many positive *contributions* to the growth of the city. **c : a piece of writing that is published as part of a larger work (such as a magazine, newspaper, or book)** ▪ a book of essays including *contributions* from several well-known political columnists
2 [*count*] **: a regular payment that is made to an employer or government for something (such as health insurance or a pension)**
3 [*noncount*] **: the act of giving something : the act of contributing** ▪ The money was raised by voluntary *contribution*.

con·trib·u·to·ry /kənˈtrɪbjəˌtori, *Brit* kənˈtrɪbjətri/ *adj, always used before a noun*
1 : helping to cause something ▪ Car exhaust is a major *contributory* factor in air pollution. [=car exhaust is a major cause of air pollution]
2 : paid for by both the employee and employer ▪ a *contributory* pension ▪ *contributory* insurance

con trick *noun, pl* ~ **tricks** [*count*] *Brit* **:** [1]CON

con·trite /ˈkɑːnˌtraɪt, kənˈtraɪt/ *adj* [*more* ~; *most* ~] *formal* **: feeling or showing regret for bad behavior** ▪ a *contrite* [=*remorseful*] criminal ▪ a *contrite* apology
– **con·trite·ly** *adv* ▪ "I should have been more careful," he said *contritely*.

con·tri·tion /kənˈtrɪʃən/ *noun* [*noncount*] *formal* **: the state of feeling sorry for bad behavior : the state of being contrite** ▪ Were her tears a true sign of *contrition*?

con·triv·ance /kənˈtraɪvəns/ *noun, pl* **-anc·es**
1 *usually disapproving* **a** [*count*] **: something that causes things to happen in a story in a way that does not seem natural or believable** ▪ The story is filled with ***plot contrivances*** that do not fit the ending. **b** [*noncount*] **: the use of contrivances in a story** ▪ He told the story honestly and without *contrivance*.
2 [*count*] **: a machine or piece of equipment made with skill and cleverness** ▪ modern *contrivances* [=*devices*] to cook food faster ▪ a clever *contrivance*
3 : a clever plan or trick [*count*] a *contrivance* to get out of doing the work [*noncount*] He convinced her to go without using *contrivance*.

con·trive /kənˈtraɪv/ *verb* **-trives; -trived; -triv·ing** [+ *obj*]
1 : to form or think of (a plan, method, etc.) ▪ The prisoners *contrived* a way to escape.
2 : to form or make (something) in a skillful or clever way ▪ Native Americans *contrived* [=*designed*] weapons out of stone, wood, and bone.
3 : to make (something) happen in a clever way or with difficulty ▪ He *contrived* a meeting with the president. — often followed by *to* + *verb* ▪ She *contrived* [=*managed*] *to make* it to the airport in time.

contrived *adj* [*more* ~; *most* ~] **: having an unnatural or false appearance or quality** ▪ The movie's *contrived* ending was a big disappointment. ▪ The results of the test seemed somewhat *contrived*.

[1]**con·trol** /kənˈtroul/ *verb* **-trols; -trolled; -trol·ling** [+ *obj*]
1 : to direct the behavior of (a person or animal) : to cause (a person or animal) to do what you want ▪ The parents could not *control* their child. ▪ The police *controlled* the crowd. ▪ The small boy could not *control* the big dog.
2 : to have power over (something) ▪ Her family *controls* the business. ▪ One country *controls* the whole island. ▪ The rebel army now *controls* nearly half the country.
3 a : to direct the actions or function of (something) : to cause (something) to act or function in a certain way ▪ The lights on stage are *controlled* by this computer. ▪ She struggled to *control* the cart as it rolled before her down the steep, bumpy road. **b : to set or adjust the amount, degree, or rate of (something)** ▪ He *controlled* the volume by turning the radio's knob. ▪ A thermostat *controls* the room's temperature. ▪ The dam *controls* the flow of the river.
4 : to limit the amount or growth of (something) ▪ The farmer used insecticides to *control* the pests. ▪ The state allowed hunting in the area to *control* the deer population. ▪ The government made new laws to *control* pollution. ▪ The firefighters worked all night to *control* the fire.
5 a : to keep (emotions, desires, etc.) from becoming too strong or from being shown ▪ Please *control* your temper. [=keep yourself calm] ▪ He tried hard to *control* his laughter. [=to avoid laughing] ▪ I was hungry, but I *controlled* my appetite [=I resisted the desire to eat] and waited for dinner. **b : to keep or make (yourself) calm especially when you are angry, upset, or excited** ▪ He couldn't *control* himself any longer.
– **con·trol·la·ble** /kənˈtrouləbəl/ *adj* [*more* ~; *most* ~] ▪ The temperature of the room is *controllable*. ▪ The lighter drill was more *controllable* than the heavier one.

[2]**control** *noun, pl* **-trols**

1 [*noncount*] : the power to make decisions about how something is managed or done • The city wanted local *control* of education. • The troops had no *control* [=*choice*] over where they would be stationed. • The tribes fought for *control* over the territory. • He ***took control*** of the family farm. • She hired an accountant to *take control* of her money. • Two-thirds of the market is ***in the control of*** three companies. [=is controlled by three companies] • He always wants to be ***in control.*** [=he wants to be the one who makes decisions] • The team is ***under the control of*** a new coach. [=a new coach is in charge of the team; the team has a new coach] • The weather is not ***in/under our control.*** = The weather is ***beyond our control.*** [=we cannot control the weather]

2 [*noncount*] : the ability to direct the actions of someone or something • He lost all muscle *control* in his left arm. • She no longer has *control* of her (mental) faculties. [=she is no longer able to think clearly or make rational decisions] • The soccer player showed good *control* of the ball. • a teacher with good *control* of her students • The driver ***lost control*** (of the car) and hit a tree. ✧ If you ***lose control*** or ***lose control of yourself***, you become very angry, upset, or excited. • He *lost control of himself* and yelled at his students. ✧ If people or things are ***out of control***, they cannot be handled or managed with success. • The car went *out of control* and crashed. • The child was *out of control*. She ran around the store screaming. • The campfire got *out of control* and started a forest fire. • The situation got *out of control*, and a fight started.

3 : an action, method, or law that limits the amount or growth of something [*count*] The farmer used an organic pest *control* on his crops. • To cut down on competition, the government passed price *controls* on prescription drugs. • The President wants stricter *controls* on immigration. [*noncount*] The two nations talked about arms *control*. [=control of the amount of weapons a country has] • population *control* — see also BIOLOGICAL CONTROL, BIRTH CONTROL, GUN CONTROL, QUALITY CONTROL, RENT CONTROL, *damage control* at [1]DAMAGE

4 [*count*] : a device or piece of equipment used to operate a machine, vehicle, or system • the volume *control* on a television • the *controls* of the aircraft • a car with manual *controls* • a *control* panel ✧ If you are ***at the controls***, you are controlling a vehicle. • The copilot was *at the controls* when the plane landed. — see also REMOTE CONTROL

5 [*singular*] : the group of people who direct or control something (such as the flight of an aircraft) • pilots communicating with air traffic *control* • a *control* tower/room — see also MISSION CONTROL

6 [*count*] : a person, thing, or group that is not treated with something that is being tested in an experiment in order to allow comparison with a treated person, thing, or group • The effects of the drug were clear when the test group was compared with the ***control group***.

in control **1** : having control of something • She will still be *in control* of the sales department. • He managed to stay *in control* of his emotions. **2** : not overly upset or excited : calm and able to think and act in a sensible way • In spite of the pressure to pass the test, he felt calm and *in control*.

under control : able to be handled or managed with success : not out of control • She remained calm and kept the situation *under control*. • A year after the divorce, he finally got his life back *under control*. [=he finally regained control of his life] • The firefighters got the fire *under control*. • You need to get your drinking/gambling/anger *under control*. • Don't worry—I have everything *under control*.

control freak *noun, pl* **~ freaks** [*count*] *informal* : a person who has a strong need to control people or how things are done • My boss is a real *control freak*.

con·trolled /kənˈtrould/ *adj*

1 [*more ~; most ~*] : not overly angry or emotional • Instead of arguing, they talked in a calm, *controlled* manner.

2 [*more ~; most ~*] : done or organized according to certain rules, instructions, or procedures • The test was done under *controlled* conditions. • The polar bears at the zoo live in a *controlled* environment.

3 — used to describe a drug that is illegal to have or use without permission from a doctor • a *controlled* drug/substance

con·trol·ler /kənˈtroulɚ/ *noun, pl* **-lers** [*count*]

1 : a person who is in charge of the money received and paid out by a business or college

2 : a person who directs the action of something • an air traffic *controller*

3 : a device or piece of equipment used to operate a machine, vehicle, or system • a volume *controller*

controlling *adj* [*more ~; most ~*]

1 : having a need to control other people's behavior • a *controlling* parent • She is very strict and *controlling*.

2 a : having the power to control how something is managed or done • The larger bank remained the *controlling* party when it took over the smaller banks. • *controlling* shareholders **b** : giving someone the power to control how something is managed or done • He paid over 40 million dollars for a *controlling* interest/share in the company.

con·tro·ver·sial /ˌkɑːntrəˈvɚʃəl/ *adj* [*more ~; most ~*] : relating to or causing much discussion, disagreement, or argument : likely to produce controversy • Abortion is a highly *controversial* subject/issue/topic. • a decision that remains *controversial* • He is a *controversial* author/director/figure.

— **con·tro·ver·sial·ly** *adv*

con·tro·ver·sy /ˈkɑːntrəˌvɚsi, *Brit* ˈkɒntrəˌvɜːsi, kənˈtrɒvəsi/ *noun, pl* **-sies** : argument that involves many people who strongly disagree about something : strong disagreement about something among a large group of people [*noncount*] The decision aroused/created much *controversy* among the students. • The new movie is a subject/topic of *controversy*. • There is *controversy* surrounding the team's decision to trade the star pitcher. • The *controversy* is over whether he should be fired or not. [*count*] A *controversy* arose over the new law.

con·tro·vert /ˈkɑːntrəˌvɚt/ *verb* **-verts; -vert·ed; -vert·ing** [+ *obj*] *formal* : to say or prove that (something) is untrue • The attorney offered evidence that *controverted* the plaintiff's allegations.

con·tus·ion /kənˈtuːʒən, *Brit* kənˈtjuːʒən/ *noun, pl* **-ions** [*count*] *medical* : an injury that usually does not break the skin : BRUISE • He suffered multiple *contusions* of the leg.

co·nun·drum /kəˈnʌndrəm/ *noun, pl* **-drums** [*count*] : a confusing or difficult problem • He is faced with the *conundrum* [=*dilemma*] of trying to find a job without experience. • an ethical *conundrum*

con·ur·ba·tion /ˌkɑːnəˈbeɪʃən/ *noun, pl* **-tions** [*count*] *chiefly Brit* : a large area consisting of cities or towns that have grown so that there is very little room between them • a *conurbation* of cities along the river

con·va·lesce /ˌkɑːnvəˈlɛs/ *verb* **-lesc·es; -lesced; -lesc·ing** [*no obj*] : to become healthy and strong again slowly over time after illness, weakness, or injury • She spent two months *convalescing* [=*recuperating, recovering*] at home after her surgery. • He is *convalescing* from his leg injuries.

con·va·les·cence /ˌkɑːnvəˈlɛsn̩s/ *noun* : the process or period of becoming well again after an illness or injury [*singular*] a prolonged *convalescence* • We visited her during her *convalescence* from surgery. [*noncount*] a period of *convalescence*

con·va·les·cent /ˌkɑːnvəˈlɛsn̩t/ *adj*

1 : going through the process of becoming well again after an illness or injury • the *convalescent* stage of his treatment • The nurse tended to the *convalescent* patients/soldiers.

2 : used for patients who are becoming well again after an illness or injury • He spent six months recuperating in a *convalescent* home/hospital. • a *convalescent* ward

— **convalescent** *noun, pl* **-cents** [*count*] • The nurse took care of the *convalescents*.

con·vec·tion /kənˈvɛkʃən/ *noun* [*noncount*] *technical* : movement in a gas or liquid in which the warmer parts move up and the colder parts move down • *convection* currents; *also* : the transfer of heat by this movement • foods cooked by *convection*

convection oven *noun, pl* **~ -ens** [*count*] : an oven with a fan that moves hot air around so that food cooks evenly

con·vene /kənˈviːn/ *verb* **-venes; -vened; -ven·ing** : to come together in a group for a meeting [*no obj*] The students *convened* [=*assembled*] in the gym. • We *convened* at the hotel for a seminar. • This class *convenes* twice a week. [+ *obj*] *convene* a meeting • A panel of investigators was *convened* by the president to review the case.

[1]**con·ve·nience** /kənˈviːnjəns/ *noun, pl* **-nienc·es**

1 [*noncount*] : a quality or situation that makes something easy or useful for someone by reducing the amount of work or time required to do something • An elevator was available for the shoppers' *convenience*. • I enjoy the *convenience* of living near a post office. • ***For your convenience***, we have added a feature that allows you to pay your bills over the Internet. — opposite INCONVENIENCE; see also MARRIAGE OF CONVENIENCE

2 [*noncount*] **:** a time that is appropriate for doing something or that is suitable for someone ▪ I'll be happy to meet with you ***at your convenience.*** [=at a time that is convenient for you; at a time that will not cause you too much trouble or effort] ▪ Please come to my office ***at your earliest convenience.***

3 [*count*] **:** something (such as a device) that makes you more comfortable or allows you to do things more easily ▪ Our hotel room was equipped with all the modern *conveniences.* ▪ They enjoyed the *conveniences* of flying first class.

²convenience *adj, always used before a noun* **:** designed for quick and easy preparation ▪ Frozen pizza is a popular *convenience* food. ▪ *convenience* snacks

convenience store *noun, pl* **~ stores** [*count*] *chiefly US* **:** a small store that is open for many hours of the day

con·ve·nient /kənˈviːnjənt/ *adj* [*more ~; most ~*]

1 : allowing you to do something easily or without trouble ▪ When is a *convenient* time for you to meet? ▪ The controls are located in a *convenient* spot on the dashboard. ▪ It might be more *convenient* to use a calculator, rather than adding the numbers yourself. ▪ a *convenient* method/way/means of cleaning windows — opposite INCONVENIENT

2 : located in a place that is nearby and easy to get to ▪ a *convenient* drugstore ▪ Schools, churches, and stores are all *convenient* from here.

3 : giving you a reason to do something that you want to do ▪ The power failure was a *convenient* excuse to leave work early. ▪ The economic recession gave lawmakers a *convenient* pretext for passing the bill.

– con·ve·nient·ly *adv* ▪ Several restaurants are *conveniently* located nearby.

con·vent /ˈkɑːnvənt/ *noun, pl* **-vents** [*count*] **:** a group of nuns who live together ▪ She joined a *convent.*; *also* **:** the house or buildings they live in — compare MONASTERY

con·ven·tion /kənˈvɛnʃən/ *noun, pl* **-tions**

1 [*count*] **:** a large meeting of people who come to a place for usually several days to talk about their shared work or other interests or to make decisions as a group ▪ We go to the weeklong annual teachers' *convention* every summer. ▪ He bought some new books at the science fiction *convention.* ▪ a constitutional *convention* [=a meeting in which political leaders create a constitution] ▪ The Democratic National *Convention* will meet next week to announce their party's candidate for president. ▪ The conference was held at the new ***convention center.*** [=a building or set of buildings designed to hold many people and meetings]

2 : a custom or a way of acting or doing things that is widely accepted and followed [*count*] It's important to follow the *conventions* of punctuation in a paper for school. ▪ They say school is just as important for teaching children social codes and *conventions* as for teaching math. ▪ Many sports shows have recently adopted the *conventions* of the talk show. [*noncount*] a poet who rebels against literary *convention* ▪ The award that ***by convention*** should have gone to the student with the highest grade went instead to the teacher's favorite. ▪ a director who has always ***defied convention*** [=done unexpected or unusual things] in his movies ▪ As ***a matter of convention***, the oldest members speak first.

3 [*count*] **:** a traditional or common style often used in literature, theater, or art to create a particular effect ▪ artistic *conventions* ▪ The director's use of the usual romantic *conventions* made the film boring and predictable. ▪ His latest novel uses the *conventions of* early 19th-century literature.

4 [*count*] *formal* **:** a formal agreement between two groups (such as countries or political organizations) ▪ an international *convention* banning the spread of nuclear weapons ▪ the United Nations *Convention* on the Law of the Sea

con·ven·tion·al /kənˈvɛnʃənl/ *adj*

1 *always used before a noun* **a :** used and accepted by most people **:** usual or traditional ▪ The number sign is the *conventional* symbol for labeling something measured in pounds. ▪ Today, many patients seek healing through both alternative medicine and ***conventional medicine.*** [=the usual methods of healing or treating disease that are taught in Western medical schools] **b :** of a kind that has been around for a long time and is considered to be usual or typical ▪ While microwaves heat up food more quickly, most food tastes better when it is cooked in a ***conventional oven.***

2 [*more ~; most ~*] **:** common and ordinary **:** not unusual ▪ Most of her books are *conventional* detective stories. ▪ His views on dating are more *conventional* than those of some of his friends.

3 *always used before a noun* **:** not nuclear ▪ *conventional* weapons ▪ *conventional* forces/warfare/war

– con·ven·tion·al·i·ty /kənˌvɛnʃəˈnæləti/ *noun* [*noncount*] ▪ The *conventionality* of his views on economics surprised us. **– con·ven·tion·al·ly** *adv* ▪ He's not *conventionally* attractive, but he has an interesting face that is not at all unpleasant to look at.

conventional wisdom *noun* [*noncount*] **:** opinions or beliefs that are held or accepted by most people ▪ *Conventional wisdom* in Hollywood says that a movie can't succeed unless it stars a famous actor or actress.

con·ven·tion·eer /kənˌvɛnʃəˈniə/ *noun, pl* **-eers** [*count*] *US* **:** a person who goes to a convention (sense 1)

con·verge /kənˈvəʤ/ *verb* **-verg·es; -verged; -verg·ing** [*no obj*]

1 : to move toward one point and join together **:** to come together and meet ▪ The two roads *converge* in the center of town. — opposite DIVERGE

2 : to meet or come together to form a crowd or group ▪ Students *converged* in the parking lot to say goodbye after graduation. — often + *on* ▪ Six police cars *converged on* the accident scene. ▪ Reporters from five different news sources *converged on* her after the game.

3 : to come together and have one interest, purpose, or goal ▪ Economic forces *converged* to bring the country out of a recession. ▪ Many companies are combining rapidly *converging* communication technology into one device that can act as a phone, take photographs, and send e-mail.

– con·ver·gence /kənˈvəʤəns/ *noun* [*noncount*] ▪ The *convergence* of political corruption and religious oppression led to civil war. **– con·ver·gent** /kənˈvəʤənt/ *adj* ▪ *convergent* lines ▪ The meeting focused on the companies' *convergent* interests.

con·ver·sant /kənˈvəsn̩t/ *adj, not used before a noun* [*more ~; most ~*]

1 *formal* — used to say that someone knows about something or has experience with it; + *with* ▪ He is (thoroughly) *conversant with* the facts of the case. ▪ They're *conversant with* the issues.

2 *US* **:** able to talk in a foreign language ▪ She's *conversant* in several languages.

con·ver·sa·tion /ˌkɑːnvəˈseɪʃən/ *noun, pl* **-tions**

1 : an informal talk involving two people or a small group of people **:** the act of talking in an informal way [*count*] a casual/telephone/private *conversation* ▪ He mentioned it during (the course of) our *conversation.* ▪ Do you remember our *conversation* about that new movie? ▪ The *conversation* turned to music. = Music became the topic of the *conversation.* ▪ We got into a long *conversation* about his behavior. ▪ I had a nice *conversation* [=(less formally) *chat*] with your mother. ▪ They were engaged in a lengthy *conversation* about politics. ▪ It was so noisy that we could hardly ***carry on a conversation.*** [=*talk*] ▪ a perfect spot to ***hold a quiet conversation*** [=*talk*] ▪ She often ***strikes up conversations*** with strangers. [=she often talks to strangers] [*noncount*] The topic came up in *conversation.* ▪ They were so deep in *conversation* that they barely noticed me. ▪ He kept trying to engage me in *conversation.* ▪ She's skilled in the art of *conversation.* ▪ an interesting topic of *conversation* ▪ "Where are you from?" he asked, trying to ***make conversation.*** [=start a conversation]

2 [*count*] **:** something that is similar to a spoken conversation ▪ We had a *conversation* by e-mail.

con·ver·sa·tion·al /ˌkɑːnvəˈseɪʃənl/ *adj* [*more ~; most ~*] **:** relating to or suggesting informal talk **:** relating to or suggesting conversation ▪ *conversational* skills ▪ The article is written in a *conversational* [=*informal*] style/tone. ▪ The class was in *conversational* French. [=the informal French that is used when people talk to each other]

– con·ver·sa·tion·al·ly *adv*

con·ver·sa·tion·al·ist /ˌkɑːnvəˈseɪʃənlɪst/ *noun, pl* **-ists** [*count*] **:** a person who likes or is good at conversation ▪ a good/lively/witty *conversationalist* ▪ She's not much of a *conversationalist.*

conversation piece *noun, pl* **~ pieces** [*count*] **:** something new or unusual that gives people a subject to talk about ▪ The exotic plant in our living room is a *conversation piece* that guests always ask about.

¹con·verse /kənˈvəs/ *verb* **-vers·es; -versed; -vers·ing** [*no obj*] *formal* **:** to talk usually informally with someone **:** to have a conversation ▪ They *conversed* quietly in the corner of the room. ▪ At home we often *converse* in Spanish. — often + *with* ▪ He knows enough German to *converse with* the locals.

[2]**con·verse** /ˈkɑːnˌvɚs/ *noun*

the converse formal : something that is the opposite of something else ▪ They need our help, but *the converse* is also true: we need their help as well.

[3]**con·verse** /kənˈvɚs, ˈkɑːnˌvɚs/ *adj, formal* : opposite or reverse ▪ One must also consider the *converse* case/problem. ▪ a *converse* effect

con·verse·ly *adv, formal* : in a way that is the opposite of something else ▪ Large objects appear to be closer. *Conversely*, small objects seem farther away.

con·ver·sion /kənˈvɚʒən, *Brit* kənˈvɜːʃən/ *noun, pl* **-sions**

1 a : the act or process of changing from one form, state, etc., to another — often + *to* or *into* [*count*] The company is undergoing a *conversion to* a new computer system. [*noncount*] They have suggested *conversion* of the old school *into* apartments. ▪ *Conversion to* gas heating will continue over the next few years. **b :** the act or process of changing from one religion, belief, political party, etc., to another — often + *to* [*count*] a *conversion* from Catholicism *to* Judaism [*noncount*] He is thinking about *conversion to* Buddhism.

2 [*count*] **a :** a successful attempt at scoring extra points in rugby or American football ▪ a 2-point *conversion* **b** *American football* : a successful attempt to move the ball forward 10 yards ▪ a third-down *conversion*

[1]**con·vert** /kənˈvɚt/ *verb* **-verts; -vert·ed; -vert·ing**

1 a [+ *obj*] : to change (something) into a different form or so that it can be used in a different way — usually + *to* or *into* ▪ The cells absorb light and *convert* it *to* energy. ▪ How do you *convert* pounds *to* grams? ▪ I need to *convert* my pesos back *into* dollars. [=I need to exchange my pesos for dollars] ▪ We *converted* the attic *into* a bedroom. **b** [*no obj*] : to change to a different system, method, etc. — usually + *to* ▪ The factory *converted to* newer machinery. **c** [*no obj*] : to change from one form or use to another — usually + *to* or *into* ▪ The sofa *converts* easily *into* a bed.

2 a [*no obj*] : to change from one religion, belief, political party, etc., to another — often + *to* ▪ He *converted to* Islam. **b** [+ *obj*] : to persuade (someone) to change from one religion, belief, political party, etc., to another — often + *to* ▪ The missionaries *converted* the native people to Christianity. ▪ They tried to *convert* us *to* their way of thinking. — see also *preach to the converted* at PREACH

3 a : to score extra points after a goal or touchdown in rugby or American football [*no obj*] They tried for two points but could not *convert*. [+ *obj*] (*rugby*) They failed to *convert* the try. **b :** to use (an opportunity, such as an opportunity to score points) successfully [+ *obj*] They had many chances to score but they couldn't *convert* their opportunities. [*no obj*] They had chances to score but couldn't *convert*.

[2]**con·vert** /ˈkɑːnˌvɚt/ *noun, pl* **-verts** [*count*] : a person who has changed to a different religion, belief, political party, etc. ▪ a religious *convert* ▪ I didn't think I'd like paying my bills online, but now I'm a *convert*.

con·vert·er *also* **con·vert·or** /kənˈvɚtɚ/ *noun, pl* **-ers** *also* **-ors** [*count*] *technical* : a piece of equipment that changes something (such as radio signals, radio frequencies, or data) from one form to another — see also CATALYTIC CONVERTER

[1]**con·vert·ible** /kənˈvɚtəbəl/ *adj* : able to be changed into another form ▪ a *convertible* sofa [=a sofa that converts into a bed] ▪ a *convertible* currency ▪ The bonds are *convertible* into stock.

– con·vert·ibil·i·ty /kənˌvɚtəˈbɪləti/ *noun* [*noncount*]

[2]**convertible** *noun, pl* **-ibles** [*count*] : a car with a roof that can be lowered or removed — see picture at CAR; compare HARDTOP

con·vex /kɑnˈvɛks, ˈkɑːnˌvɛks/ *adj* [*more ~; most ~*] : having a shape like the outside of a bowl : curving outward ▪ a *convex* lens/mirror — opposite CONCAVE

con·vex·i·ty /kənˈvɛksəti/ *noun, pl* **-ties** *technical*

1 [*noncount*] : the quality or state of being curved outward : the quality or state of being convex ▪ the *convexity* of the lens

2 [*count*] : a shape that is curved outward : a convex shape ▪ the *convexities* along the surface

con·vey /kənˈveɪ/ *verb* **-veys; -veyed; -vey·ing** [+ *obj*]

1 *formal* : to take or carry (someone or something) from one place to another : TRANSPORT ▪ The singer was *conveyed* from her hotel to the airport by limousine. ▪ They *conveyed* the goods by ship. ▪ The pipes *convey* water to the fields.

2 : to make (something) known to someone ▪ Words *convey* [=*communicate*] meaning. ▪ Mere words could not *convey* his joy. [=he could not express his joy in words] ▪ The painting *conveys* [=*expresses*] a sense/feeling of motion. ▪ Her appearance *conveys* self-confidence. ▪ The message *conveyed* a sense of urgency.

3 *law* : to change the ownership of (property) from one person to another ▪ He *conveyed* the estate to his son.

con·vey·ance /kənˈvejəns/ *noun, pl* **-anc·es** *formal*

1 [*noncount*] : the act of taking or carrying someone or something from one place to another ▪ the *conveyance* of goods/passengers

2 [*count*] : something that carries people or things from one place to another : VEHICLE ▪ public *conveyances*

3 [*noncount*] : the act of making something known to someone ▪ the *conveyance* of meaning

4 [*count*] *law* : a legal document that changes the ownership of property from one person to another

con·vey·anc·ing /kənˈvejənsɪŋ/ *noun* [*noncount*] *chiefly Brit, law* : the act or business of preparing deeds, leases, or other documents to change the ownership of property from one person to another

con·vey·or *also* **con·vey·er** /kənˈvejɚ/ *noun, pl* **-ors** *also* **-ers** [*count*] : someone or something that conveys something: such as **a :** a long strip of material (such as canvas or rubber, etc., that moves continuously and carries objects (such as packages or luggage) from one place to another — called also *conveyor belt* **b** *formal* : someone who makes something known to someone else ▪ the *conveyor* of good news

[1]**con·vict** /kənˈvɪkt/ *verb* **-victs; -vict·ed; -vict·ing** *law* : to prove that someone is guilty of a crime in a court of law [*no obj*] There is sufficient evidence to *convict*. [+ *obj*] He was *convicted* in federal court. ▪ The jury *convicted* them on three counts of fraud. ▪ Have you ever been *convicted* of a crime? ▪ a *convicted* criminal — compare ACQUIT

[2]**con·vict** /ˈkɑːnˌvɪkt/ *noun, pl* **-victs** [*count*] : a person who has been found guilty of a crime and sent to prison : PRISONER ▪ an escaped *convict*

con·vic·tion /kənˈvɪkʃən/ *noun, pl* **-tions**

1 *law* : the act of proving that a person is guilty of a crime in a court of law [*noncount*] She hopes to avoid *conviction*. [*count*] In light of the evidence, a *conviction* seems certain. ▪ He has three prior/previous drunk-driving *convictions*. ▪ *Convictions* for shoplifting have made it difficult for her to get a job.

2 a [*count*] : a strong belief or opinion ▪ religious *convictions* ▪ a person of deep *convictions* ▪ They share my strong/firm *conviction* that the policy is misguided. **b** [*noncount*] : the feeling of being sure that what you believe or say is true ▪ She spoke with *conviction*. ▪ His words lacked *conviction*.

con·vince /kənˈvɪns/ *verb* **-vinc·es; -vinced; -vinc·ing** [+ *obj*]

1 : to cause (someone) to believe that something is true ▪ He *convinced* me that the story was true. ▪ They *convinced* us of their innocence. ▪ I managed to *convince* myself that I was doing the right thing.

2 : to cause (someone) to agree to do something : PERSUADE ▪ We *convinced* them to go along with our scheme. ▪ I was unable to *convince* her to stay.

convinced *adj* [*more ~; most ~*]

1 *not used before a noun* : completely certain or sure about something ▪ I was never fully *convinced* of his innocence. [=I always believed that he might be guilty] ▪ You still don't sound *convinced*. ▪ She's still *convinced* that we're wrong. — opposite UNCONVINCED

2 *always used before a noun* : believing strongly in something ▪ a *convinced* Christian

convincing *adj* [*more ~; most ~*]

1 : causing someone to believe that something is true or certain ▪ Your argument/story isn't very *convincing*. ▪ They make a *convincing* case for reform. ▪ There is no *convincing* evidence to support his theory. — opposite UNCONVINCING

2 *of a victory* : easily achieved : clearly showing that one person or team is better than the other ▪ a *convincing* [=*decisive*] victory/win

– con·vinc·ing·ly *adv* ▪ She argued *convincingly* [=*persuasively*] that more money should be given to public schools. ▪ They won *convincingly*.

con·viv·i·al /kənˈvɪvijəl/ *adj* [*more ~; most ~*] *formal* : of or relating to social events where people can eat, drink, and talk in a friendly way with others ▪ a *convivial* [=*lively*] atmo-

sphere • a *convivial* gathering • a *convivial* [=*cheerful, friendly*] host
– **con•viv•i•al•i•ty** /kənˌvɪviˈæləti/ *noun* [*noncount*] • an atmosphere of *conviviality*

con•vo•ca•tion /ˌkɑːnvəˈkeɪʃən/ *noun, pl* **-tions** *formal*
1 [*count*] **a** : a large formal meeting of people (such as church officials) **b** *US* : a meeting of the members of a college or university to observe a particular ceremony (such as the beginning of the school year or the announcing of awards and honors) — often used before another noun • a *convocation* center • a *convocation* address/ceremony
2 [*noncount*] : the act of calling a group of people to a formal meeting • They called for the immediate *convocation* of the council.

con•voke /kənˈvoʊk/ *verb* **-vokes**; **-voked**; **-vok•ing** [+ *obj*] *formal* : to call a group of people to a formal meeting or convocation • The assembly was *convoked* for a special session. • They *convoked* a meeting of the delegates.

con•vo•lut•ed /ˈkɑːnvəˌluːtəd/ *adj* [*more* ~; *most* ~]
1 : very complicated and difficult to understand • *convoluted* logic • a *convoluted* plot • The argument was so *convoluted* [=*intricate, involved*] that most people missed the point.
2 *formal* : having many twists and curves • a *convoluted* structure

con•vo•lu•tion /ˌkɑːnvəˈluːʃən/ *noun, pl* **-tions** *formal*
1 : something that is very complicated and difficult to understand [*count*] I found it hard to follow the *convolutions* of the book's plot. [*noncount*] a plot full of *convolution* and confusion
2 [*count*] : a twist or curve — usually plural • the *convolutions* of the road

[1]**con•voy** /ˈkɑːnˌvoɪ/ *noun, pl* **-voys** : a group of vehicles or ships that are traveling together usually for protection [*count*] a military *convoy* • a long *convoy* of trucks • The President always travels in a *convoy*. • The United Nations is sending an ***aid/relief convoy***. [=a group of vehicles carrying food and supplies] [*noncount*] The ships were sailing ***in convoy***. [=together in a line]

[2]**convoy** *verb* [+ *obj*] *formal* : to travel with and protect (someone or something) • The tankers were *convoyed* by warships. • Police and FBI agents *convoyed* the President to the White House.

con•vulse /kənˈvʌls/ *verb* **-vuls•es**; **-vulsed**; **-vuls•ing**
1 a [*no obj*] *medical* : to have an experience in which the muscles in your body shake in a sudden violent way that you are not able to control : to experience convulsions • The patient reacted to the medication and began *convulsing*. **b** — used when something (such as laughter) causes a person's whole body to shake [*no obj*] The audience *convulsed* [=*shook*] with/in laughter. [+ *obj*] — usually used as *(be) convulsed* • The audience *was convulsed* with/by laughter.
2 [+ *obj*] *formal* : to affect (someone or something) suddenly and violently • The country was *convulsed* by war. • Riots *convulsed* the nation.

con•vul•sion /kənˈvʌlʃən/ *noun, pl* **-sions** [*count*]
1 a *medical* : a sudden violent shaking of the muscles in your body that you are unable to control — usually plural • The patient suffers from *convulsions*. • He suddenly went into *convulsions*. **b** : a sudden experience of something (such as laughter) that shakes or moves your body — usually plural • The joke sent the audience into ***convulsions of laughter***.
2 : a sudden change or disturbance that affects a country, organization, etc. — usually plural • an era of political *convulsions* [=*upheavals*] • The controversial exhibit caused *convulsions* in the artistic community.

con•vul•sive /kənˈvʌlsɪv/ *adj*
1 : involving or causing a sudden violent shaking of the muscles in your body that you are unable to control • a *convulsive* seizure/attack • a *convulsive* disorder
2 : causing the entire body to shake • *convulsive* laughter
– **con•vul•sive•ly** *adv* • His body shook *convulsively*. • They laughed *convulsively*.

coo /ˈkuː/ *verb* **coos**; **cooed**; **coo•ing**
1 [*no obj*] : to make the soft sound of a dove or pigeon; *also* : to make a similar sound • The baby *cooed* quietly in her crib. • The baby was making a *cooing* sound.
2 : to talk in a soft, quiet, and loving way [*no obj*] They all *cooed* over the baby pictures. [+ *obj*] "Oh, how sweet," she *cooed*.
– **coo** *noun, pl* **coos** [*count*] • We listened to the *coos* of the pigeons.

[1]**cook** /ˈkʊk/ *noun, pl* **cooks** [*count*] : someone who prepares and cooks food for eating at home, in a restaurant, etc. • He's a good *cook*. [=he cooks well]

[2]**cook** *verb* **cooks**; **cooked**; **cook•ing**
1 : to prepare (food) for eating especially by using heat [+ *obj*] *Cook* the onions over low/medium/high heat. • She *cooked* a great meal. • I'll *cook* dinner tonight. • The fish was *cooked* in a white wine sauce. • Carrots can be *cooked*, but they are often eaten raw. • a *cooked* chicken • Are the potatoes ***cooked through***? [=*done*] = Are the potatoes fully/thoroughly *cooked*? [*no obj*] We're too busy to *cook* at home. • He enjoys *cooking* on the weekends.
2 [*no obj*] : to go through the process of being cooked • The rice is still *cooking*, but it will be ready in 10 minutes.
3 [*no obj*] *informal* : to happen or take place • What's *cooking*? • There's something *cooking*, but he won't say what.
be cooking *informal* : to be performing or doing something well • The economy *is* really *cooking*. • That's it! ***Now you're cooking***!
cook someone's goose *informal* : to make it certain that someone will fail, lose, etc. • They were already trailing, and that last goal really *cooked their goose*. • ***Their goose was cooked*** after that last goal.
cook the books *informal* : to dishonestly change official records of how much money was spent and received • They *cooked the books* to drive up the company's stock prices.
cook up [*phrasal verb*] ***cook up (something) or cook (something) up*** **1** : to prepare (food) for eating especially quickly • I can *cook up* some hamburgers. **2** : to invent (something, such as an idea, excuse, etc.) to deal with a particular situation • They *cooked up* [=*devised, hatched*] a scheme to fool their neighbor. • You'll have to *cook* an excuse *up* quickly.

cook•book /ˈkʊkˌbʊk/ *noun, pl* **-books** [*count*] *chiefly US* : a book of recipes : a book of directions explaining how to prepare and cook various kinds of food — called also (*Brit*) *cookery book*; see picture at KITCHEN

cook•er /ˈkʊkɚ/ *noun, pl* **-ers** [*count*]
1 *US* : a piece of equipment that is used to cook food • a ***slow cooker*** [=an electric pot that slowly cooks food] • a ***rice cooker*** [=an electric pot that is used for cooking rice] • a ***pasta cooker*** [=a pot that is used for cooking pasta on a stove] — see also PRESSURE COOKER
2 *Brit* : a large piece of kitchen equipment that consists of an oven and a stove • a gas *cooker* [=(*US*) *range*]

cook•ery /ˈkʊkəri/ *noun* [*noncount*] : the art or activity of cooking food • Mexican *cookery* [=*cooking, cuisine*] • the basics of fish *cookery*

cookery book *noun, pl* ~ **books** [*count*] *Brit* : COOKBOOK

cook•ie /ˈkʊki/ *noun, pl* **-ies** [*count*]
1 *chiefly US* : a sweet baked food that is usually small, flat, and round and is made from flour and sugar • This recipe makes about two dozen *cookies*. • She put a batch of *cookies* into the oven. • chocolate chip *cookies* — often used before another noun • a *cookie* jar • *cookie* dough — see picture at BAKING; see also FORTUNE COOKIE
2 *informal* : PERSON • Don't worry about her—she's a ***tough cookie***. • You are one ***smart cookie***.
3 *computers* : a file that may be added to your computer when you visit a Web site and that contains information about you (such as an identification code or a record of the Web pages you have visited)
that's the way the cookie crumbles *informal* — used when something bad has happened to say that you must accept things the way they are • I'm disappointed that I didn't get the job but *that's the way the cookie crumbles*. [=*that's how it goes*]

cookie cutter *noun, pl* ~ **-ters** [*count*] *chiefly US* : a metal or plastic object that is pressed into the dough that is used to make cookies to give them a certain shape

cookie–cutter *adj, US, disapproving* : very similar to other things of the same kind : not original or different • a neighborhood of *cookie-cutter* houses • Opponents accused the candidate of taking a *cookie-cutter* approach to the problem. [=of not coming up with new ideas to deal with the problem]

cookie sheet *noun, pl* ~ **sheets** [*count*] *chiefly US* : BAKING SHEET

[1]**cooking** *noun* [*noncount*]
1 : the act of preparing and cooking food • I do most of the *cooking* in our house.
2 : food that is cooked • Don't you like my *cooking*? • a spice

used in Indian *cooking* [=*cuisine*] • delicious ***home cooking*** [=food cooked at home]

[2]**cooking** *adj, always used before a noun* **:** suitable for or used in cooking **:** involving or having to do with cooking • *Cooking* time is about 20 minutes. • *cooking* techniques/methods • *cooking* oil • I've been taking *cooking* classes.

cook–off /ˈkʊkˌɑːf/ *noun, pl* **-offs** [*count*] *US* **:** a competition in cooking

cook·out /ˈkʊkˌaʊt/ *noun, pl* **-outs** [*count*] *US* **:** a meal or party at which food is cooked and served outdoors • a backyard *cookout*

cook·stove /ˈkʊkˌstoʊv/ *noun, pl* **-stoves** [*count*] *US* **:** a usually old-fashioned stove that burns wood and can be used for cooking; *also* **:** a small stove that is used to cook food outdoors

cook·top /ˈkʊkˌtɑːp/ *noun, pl* **-tops** [*count*] *US* **:** a flat piece of equipment for cooking that is built into a kitchen countertop and that usually has four devices (called burners) that become hot when turned on — compare STOVETOP

cook·ware /ˈkʊkˌweɚ/ *noun* [*noncount*] **:** the pots, pans, etc., that are used in cooking • a set of *cookware* • stainless steel *cookware*

[1]**cool** /ˈkuːl/ *adj* **cool·er; cool·est**

1 [*or more* ~; *most* ~] **:** somewhat cold **:** not warm or hot • a *cool* breeze • The weather is *cool* today. • The surface is *cool* to the touch. • The plant grows best in *cool* climates. • I'm feeling a little *cool*. • a *cool* refreshing drink • It's *cooler* [=less warm or hot] in the shade. • This is the *coolest* [=least warm or hot] summer on record.

2 : made of a light, thin material that helps you stay cool • We changed into some *cooler* clothes.

3 [*or more* ~; *most* ~] **:** able to think and act in a calm way **:** not affected by strong feelings • It is important to ***keep a cool head*** in a crisis. = It is important to ***keep/stay cool*** in a crisis. [=it is important to remain calm in a crisis] • She remained ***calm, cool, and collected***. • He is a ***cool customer***. [=he is someone who remains calm and is not easily upset] ◊ If you are ***(as) cool as a cucumber***, you are very calm and able to think clearly often in a difficult situation. • Even in the emergency, she remained *as cool as a cucumber*. • The reporter was *cool as a cucumber* despite the confusion all around her.

4 [*or more* ~; *most* ~] **:** not friendly • a *cool* reply • He replied with a *cool* "I don't think so." • She was always *cool* toward strangers. • We were surprised by the *cool* reception we got.

5 [*or more* ~; *most* ~] *informal* **a :** very fashionable, stylish, or appealing in a way that is generally approved of especially by young people • *cool* sunglasses • The car has a *cool* new look. • You look *cool* in those jeans. • a magazine article about the *coolest* places to live/work — often used to show approval in a general way • Your brother is so *cool*. • That was a really *cool* [=*good, excellent*] movie. • "I got a job as a lifeguard this summer." "*Cool*." **b —** used to suggest acceptance, agreement, or understanding • "I'm sorry I'm late." "It's/That's *cool* [=*okay, all right*]—don't worry about it." • "Is getting together Friday *cool* with you?" "Yeah, I'm *cool* with that." • I thought she'd be mad, but she was *cool* about it.

6 *of a color* **:** suggesting cool things • Blue and green are *cool* colors, but red and orange are warm colors.

7 *informal* **—** used for emphasis in referring to a large amount of money • He's worth a *cool* million.

– cool·ish /ˈkuːlɪʃ/ *adj* • a *coolish* day • *coolish* colors • He was a little *coolish* towards us. **– cool·ly** *adv* • "Is that so?," she asked *coolly*. • My idea was received *coolly*. **– cool·ness** *noun* [*noncount*] • the *coolness* of the mountain air • I was surprised by his *coolness* towards us. • He always displays *coolness* under pressure.

[2]**cool** *verb* **cools; cooled; cool·ing**

1 a [+ *obj*] **:** to make (someone or something) cool • The fan *cools* the engine. • the *cooling* effect of the breeze • the car's *cooling* system — often + *off* or *down* • A swim *cooled* us *off/down* a little. • The rain should help to *cool* things *off/down*. **b** [*no obj*] **:** to become cool **:** to lose heat or warmth • Allow the cake to *cool* before slicing. • the *cooling* of the ocean waters — often + *off* or *down* • We went for a swim to *cool off/down*. • The weather has *cooled off/down* a little.

2 a [*no obj*] **:** to become less strong or intense especially in emotion • I took a break from the discussion to allow my anger to *cool*. • His interest in her has *cooled* somewhat. — often + *off* or *down* • You need to *cool off/down* before I talk to you. • Their relationship has *cooled off/down* a bit. **b** [+ *obj*] **:** to make (an emotion) less strong or intense • He couldn't *cool* [=*calm*] his anger. — often + *off* or *down* • You need to *cool off/down* your anger.

cool it *informal* **:** to stop being excited, angry, noisy, etc. • They were being too noisy, so he told them to *cool it*.

cool your heels *informal* **:** to wait for someone or something **:** to take a break from doing something or going someplace • Passengers had no choice but to *cool their heels* when their flight was delayed yet again.

[3]**cool** *noun*

keep your cool *also chiefly US* ***maintain your cool*** *informal* **:** to remain calm • He *kept/maintained his cool* [=he didn't get angry or upset] even though it was clear that he was being unfairly treated.

lose your cool *also US* ***blow your cool*** *informal* **:** to suddenly become very angry • She rarely *loses her cool*. [=she controls her feelings well] • He *lost his cool* and yelled at me. • After listening patiently, he finally *blew his cool*.

the cool **:** a cool time or place — usually + *of* • It was good to be outdoors in *the cool of* the evening/night. • We relaxed in *the cool of* an air-conditioned room.

[4]**cool** *adv, informal* **:** in a calm manner **:** in a way that does not seem unusual or excited • Here comes Mom. ***Act cool*** and she won't suspect a thing. • She didn't want to seem too eager, so she tried to ***play it cool*** [=to pretend to be calm even though she wasn't feeling calm]

cool·ant /ˈkuːlənt/ *noun, pl* **-ants** [*count, noncount*] **:** a liquid that is used to cool an engine or machine

cool·er /ˈkuːlɚ/ *noun, pl* **-ers** [*count*]

1 : a container for keeping food or drinks cool • The sodas are in the *cooler*. — called also *(Brit)* **cool bag**, *(Brit)* **cool box**

2 *US* **:** a cold drink that usually contains alcohol • a wine *cooler*

3 ***the cooler*** *informal + somewhat old-fashioned* **:** a prison or jail • They threw him in *the cooler*. [=(more commonly) *the slammer*]

cool·head·ed /ˈkuːlˌhɛdəd/ *adj* [*more* ~; *most* ~] **:** not easily excited **:** able to think and act in a calm way • a *coolheaded* leader

coo·lie /ˈkuːli/ *noun, pl* **-lies** [*count*] *offensive + old-fashioned* **:** an unskilled Asian worker who is paid low wages

cooling–off period *noun, pl* ~ **-ods** [*count*] **:** a period of time that must pass before you can do something or before an agreement becomes final • The law requires a *cooling-off period* between the time a gun is purchased and when it may be possessed. • The workers have agreed to a 30-day *cooling-off period* before they strike. • Once you join the pension plan, you have a 14-day *cooling-off period* within which to change your mind.

coon /ˈkuːn/ *noun, pl* **coons** [*count*] *US, informal* **:** RACCOON

in a coon's age see [1]AGE

coon·skin /ˈkuːnˌskɪn/ *noun, pl* **-skins** [*count, noncount*] **:** the skin and fur of a raccoon — often used before another noun • a *coonskin* cap/coat

[1]**coop** /ˈkuːp/ *noun, pl* **coops** [*count*] **:** a cage or small building in which chickens or other small animals are kept • a chicken *coop*

fly the coop see [1]FLY

[2]**coop** *verb* **coops; cooped; coop·ing**

coop up [*phrasal verb*] ***coop up (someone or something)*** *or* ***coop (someone or something) up*** **:** to keep (a person or animal) inside a building or in a small space especially for a long period of time — usually used as *(be) cooped up* • The children were cranky after *being cooped up* in the house all day. • The dog *is cooped up* in a cage.

co–op /ˈkoʊˌɑːp/ *noun, pl* **-ops** [*count*] **:** a business or organization that is owned and operated by the people who work there or the people who use its services **:** COOPERATIVE • a farmers' *co-op*

coo·per /ˈkuːpɚ/ *noun, pl* **-pers** [*count*] **:** a person who makes or repairs wooden casks or barrels

co·op·er·ate /koʊˈɑːpəˌreɪt/ *verb* **-ates; -at·ed; -at·ing** [*no obj*]

1 : to work together **:** to work with another person or group to do something • It will be much easier if everyone *cooperates*. • Several organizations *cooperated* in the relief efforts. • The country agreed to *cooperate* with the other nations on the trade agreement.

2 a : to be helpful by doing what someone asks or tells you to do • The mother asked the child to put on his pajamas, but the child refused to *cooperate*. • Witnesses were willing/unwilling to *cooperate.* — often + *with* ▪ They said they would *cooperate* fully *with* the investigation. ▪ He agreed/refused to *cooperate with* the police. **b :** to act in a way that makes something possible or likely : to produce the right conditions for something to happen ▪ We can barbecue on Sunday if the weather *cooperates.* [=if the weather is good enough]

co·op·er·a·tion /koʊˌɑːpəˈreɪʃən/ *noun [noncount]*
1 : a situation in which people work together to do something ▪ The report cited a lack of *cooperation* between state and local officials. ▪ The fair was organized in *cooperation* with local businesses. = The fair was organized with the *cooperation* of local businesses.
2 : the actions of someone who is being helpful by doing what is wanted or asked for ▪ Thank you for your *cooperation.* ▪ We are asking for your full *cooperation.*

[1]**co·op·er·a·tive** /koʊˈɑːprətɪv/ *adj [more ~; most ~]*
1 : willing to be helpful by doing what someone wants or asks for ▪ *cooperative* children ▪ The witness was very *cooperative.* — opposite UNCOOPERATIVE
2 : involving two or more people or groups working together to do something ▪ a *cooperative* [=*joint, combined*] effort/venture
3 : relating to a business or organization that is owned and operated by the people who work there or the people who use its services ▪ a *cooperative* store
– co·op·er·a·tive·ly *adv* ▪ The group acted *cooperatively.* ▪ a *cooperatively* owned store **– co·op·er·a·tive·ness** *noun [noncount]* ▪ He demonstrated his *cooperativeness* on many occasions.

[2]**cooperative** *noun, pl* **-tives** *[count]* **:** a business or organization that is owned and operated by the people who work there or the people who use its services ▪ the local farmers' *cooperative*

co–opt /koʊˈɑːpt/ *verb* **-opts; -opt·ed; -opt·ing** *[+ obj] formal*
1 : to cause or force (someone or something) to become part of your group, movement, etc. ▪ The national organization has *co-opted* many formerly independent local groups.
2 : to use or take control of (something) for your own purposes ▪ Advertisers *co-opted* the team's slogan. ▪ The candidate has been accused of *co-opting* his opponent's message to serve his own election campaign.

[1]**co·or·di·nate** /koʊˈoədəˌneɪt/ *verb* **-nates; -nat·ed; -nat·ing**
1 a : to make arrangements so that two or more people or groups of people can work together properly and well *[+ obj]* She'll be *coordinating* the relief effort. *[no obj]* You'll have to *coordinate* with the sales department. **b** *[no obj]* **:** to act or work together properly and well ▪ National and international relief efforts must *coordinate* if the operation is to be successful.
2 *[+ obj]* **:** to cause (two or more things) to be the same or to go together well : to cause (two or more things) to not conflict with or contradict each other ▪ We need to *coordinate* our schedules. ▪ Dancers need to *coordinate* their moves.
3 *[+ obj]* **:** to move (different parts of your body) together well or easily ▪ Since his illness, he has had trouble *coordinating* his arms and legs.
4 : to look good with another color, pattern, style, etc. *[no obj]* This color *coordinates* with your outfit. ▪ The shirt and pants are available in three *coordinating* styles/colors. ▪ *coordinating* patterns *[+ obj]* We *coordinated* the curtains and the fabric of the furniture.
– coordinated *adj [more ~; most ~]* ▪ a *coordinated* effort/attack ▪ I would take dance lessons, but I am not very *coordinated.* ▪ A more *coordinated* approach will improve productivity. — often used in combination ▪ a color-*coordinated* wardrobe ▪ a well-*coordinated* athlete

[2]**co·or·di·nate** /koʊˈoədənət/ *noun, pl* **-nates**
1 *[count] technical* **:** one of a set of numbers that is used to locate a point on a map, graph, etc. ▪ latitude and longitude *coordinates* ▪ We calculated its exact *coordinates.*
2 coordinates *[plural]* **:** articles of clothing that are made to be worn together ▪ *coordinates* in basic colors

coordinate clause *noun, pl* **~ clauses** *[count] grammar* **:** one of two or more clauses in a sentence that are of equal importance and usually joined by *and, or,* or *but* — compare MAIN CLAUSE, SUBORDINATE CLAUSE

coordinating conjunction *noun, pl* **~ -tions** *[count] grammar* **:** a conjunction (such as *and, or,* or *but*) that joins together words, phrases, or clauses of equal importance

co·or·di·na·tion /koʊˈoədəˈneɪʃən/ *noun [noncount]*
1 : the process of organizing people or groups so that they work together properly and well ▪ The new agency will oversee the *coordination* of the various departments. ▪ The manager is in charge of project *coordination.* ▪ There needs to be better *coordination* between departments. ▪ The FBI worked ***in coordination with*** local police. [=the FBI worked with local police]
2 : the process of causing things to be the same or to go together well ▪ the *coordination* of our schedules ▪ better *coordination* of the dancers' moves
3 : the ability to move different parts of your body together well or easily ▪ Playing sports improves strength and *coordination.* ▪ The illness causes a loss of *coordination.* ▪ poor *coordination*

co·or·di·na·tor /koʊˈoədəˌneɪtə/ *noun, pl* **-tors** *[count]* **:** a person who organizes people or groups so that they work together properly and well ▪ She is the program/project *coordinator.*

coot /ˈkuːt/ *noun, pl* **coots** *[count]*
1 : a type of black and gray bird that lives on or near the water
2 *US, informal* **:** a strange and usually old man ▪ Don't mind him—he's just a crazy old *coot.*

coo·tie /ˈkuːti/ *noun, pl* **-ties** *[count] US, informal* **:** a type of small insect that lives in people's hair ✧ *Cootie* is used especially by children. ▪ Don't touch him or you'll get *cooties!*

co–owner *noun, pl* **-ers** *[count]* **:** someone who owns something together with another person

[1]**cop** /ˈkɑːp/ *noun, pl* **cops** *[count] informal* **:** POLICE OFFICER ▪ He threatened to call the *cops* on us. — see also COPS AND ROBBERS, TRAFFIC COP
it's a fair cop *Brit, informal* — used to admit that you did something wrong and were caught fairly ▪ I'm annoyed about the speeding ticket, but *it's a fair cop.*
not much cop *Brit, informal* **:** not very good ▪ She's *not much cop* as an actress. ▪ I'm *not much cop* at sports.

[2]**cop** *verb* **cops; copped; cop·ping** *[+ obj]*
1 *US, informal* **:** to get (something desirable) ▪ I managed to *cop* an invitation. ▪ She *copped* [=*took*] first prize in the competition.
2 *US, informal* **:** to steal or take (something) from someone ▪ Somebody *copped* my watch. ▪ He *copped* the idea from me.
3 *chiefly Brit, informal* **:** to receive (something undesirable) ▪ They expected me to *cop* all the blame! ▪ He *copped* the full force of the blow.
cop a feel *US slang* **:** to touch someone in an unwanted and unexpected sexual way ▪ Some guy on the bus tried to *cop a feel!* [=some guy on the bus tried to grope me]
cop an attitude *US, informal* **:** to show that you believe you are more important or better than other people by behaving in a rude or unpleasant way ▪ The students tried to *cop an attitude* with the new teacher.
cop a plea *US, informal* **:** to admit to doing a less serious crime than the one you are accused of : to agree to a plea bargain ▪ Her lawyers convinced her to *cop a plea.*
cop hold of *Brit, informal* **:** to grab or take hold of (something) ▪ *Cop hold of* this part while I tighten the screw.
cop it *Brit, informal* **:** to be punished for doing something wrong ▪ When dad gets home, you're going to *cop it!* [=(*US*) *get it*]
cop off *[phrasal verb] Brit slang* **:** to have sexual intercourse *with* someone ▪ He *copped off with* one of the girls at the party.
cop out *[phrasal verb] informal* **1 :** to not do something that you are expected to do ▪ She said she would come, but then she *copped out* at the last minute. ▪ You'd better not *cop out* on me! **2 :** to fail to deal with a problem or situation ▪ He accused the mayor of *copping out* on the issue of homelessness. — see also COP-OUT
cop to *[phrasal verb]* ***cop to (something)*** *US slang* **:** to admit to doing (something) ▪ He agreed to *cop to* a misdemeanor.

co–pay /ˈkoʊˈpeɪ/ *noun, pl* **-pays** *[count]* **:** CO-PAYMENT

co–pay·ment /ˈkoʊˌpeɪmənt/ *noun, pl* **-ments** *[count]* **:** an amount of money that a person with health insurance is required to pay at the time of each visit to a doctor or when purchasing medicine

[1]**cope** /ˈkoʊp/ *verb* **copes; coped; cop·ing** *[no obj]* **:** to deal with problems and difficult situations and try to come up with solutions ▪ The trial has been difficult, but I'm learning to *cope.* — often + *with* ▪ You'll just have to *cope with* the situation. ▪ The book is about *coping with* stress. ▪ He says he can no longer *cope with* the demands of the job.

C

– **coping** *adj, always used before a noun* ▪ *coping* skills/strategies [=skills/strategies that help a person cope]

[2]**cope** *noun, pl* **copes** [*count*] : a long, loose piece of clothing that is worn by a priest on special occasions

copi·er /ˈkɑːpijɚ/ *noun, pl* **-ers** [*count*] : a machine that makes paper copies of printed pages, pictures, etc. — called also *copy machine, photocopier, photocopy machine*; see picture at OFFICE

co·pi·lot /ˈkoʊˌpaɪlət/ *noun, pl* **-lots** [*count*] : a pilot who helps the main pilot operate an airplane, helicopter, etc.

cop·ing /ˈkoʊpɪŋ/ *noun, pl* **-ings** [*count, noncount*] *architecture* : the top layer of a brick or stone wall that is usually higher on one end than the other to allow rain to be carried off easily

co·pi·ous /ˈkoʊpijəs/ *adj, always used before a noun* : very large in amount or number ▪ The storm produced a *copious* amount of rain. ▪ She sat in the front row and took *copious* notes during the lecture.

– **co·pi·ous·ly** *adv* ▪ a *copiously* illustrated book ▪ He wrote/drank *copiously*.

cop–out /ˈkɑːpˌaʊt/ *noun, pl* **-outs** [*count*] *informal + disapproving*

1 : an excuse for not doing something ▪ He played poorly and used his recent illness as a *cop-out*. ▪ She says she doesn't have the time, but that's just a *cop-out*. [=she really does have the time]

2 : something that avoids dealing with a problem in an appropriate way ▪ The ending of the book is a disappointing *cop-out*. — see also *cop out* at [2]COP

[1]**cop·per** /ˈkɑːpɚ/ *noun, pl* **-pers**

1 [*noncount*] : a reddish-brown metal that allows heat and electricity to pass through it easily ▪ The wires are (made of) *copper*. — often used before another noun ▪ *copper* wire/pipes ▪ a *copper* mine

2 [*noncount*] : a reddish-brown color — usually used before another noun ▪ *copper* hair ▪ *copper* skin — see color picture on page C2

3 [*count*] *chiefly Brit, informal* : a copper or bronze coin that has little value ▪ She gave the child a few *coppers*.

– compare [2]COPPER

– **cop·pery** /ˈkɑːpəri/ *adj* [*more ~; most ~*] ▪ *coppery* hair ▪ a *coppery* red

[2]**copper** *noun, pl* **-pers** [*count*] *chiefly Brit, informal* : POLICE OFFICER — compare [1]COPPER

copper–bottomed *adj* [*more ~; most ~*]

1 : having a copper coating on the bottom ▪ a *copper-bottomed* pan

2 *Brit, informal* : deserving to be trusted ▪ a *copper-bottomed* guarantee : certain to succeed ▪ The film is a *copper-bottomed* [=*surefire*] hit.

cop·per·head /ˈkɑːpɚˌhɛd/ *noun, pl* **-heads** [*count*] : a poisonous reddish-brown snake of the eastern and central U.S.

cop·pice /ˈkɑːpəs/ *noun, pl* **-pic·es** [*count*] : a group of small trees growing very close together

cops and robbers *noun* [*noncount*] : a children's game in which the players imitate the way police chase and shoot at criminals in movies, on television, etc.

copse /ˈkɑːps/ *noun, pl* **copses** [*count*] : COPPICE

cop shop *noun, pl* **~ shops** [*count*] *Brit slang* : POLICE STATION

cop·ter /ˈkɑːptɚ/ *noun, pl* **-ters** [*count*] *chiefly US, informal* : HELICOPTER

cop·u·la /ˈkɑːpjələ/ *noun, pl* **-las** [*count*] *grammar* : LINKING VERB

cop·u·late /ˈkɑːpjəˌleɪt/ *verb* **-lates; -lat·ed; -lat·ing** [*no obj*] *formal* : to have sexual intercourse ▪ Some animals have complex mating rituals before they *copulate*.

– **cop·u·la·tion** /ˌkɑːpjəˈleɪʃən/ *noun* [*noncount*]

[1]**copy** /ˈkɑːpi/ *noun, pl* **cop·ies**

1 [*count*] : something that is or looks exactly or almost exactly like something else : a version of something that is identical or almost identical to the original ▪ The paintings at the museum are originals, not *copies*. [=*reproductions*] — often + *of* ▪ Can you make me a *copy of* the letter/receipt? ▪ Be sure to make backup *copies of* any important files. ▪ I need 10 *copies* [=*photocopies*] *of* this page. ▪ It is a cheap *copy* [=*imitation, knockoff*] *of* a designer dress. ▪ It's an exact *copy* [=*replica, reproduction*] *of* a medieval sword. — see also CARBON COPY, HARD COPY

2 [*count*] : one of the many books, magazines, albums, DVDs, etc., that are exactly the same and are produced to be sold or given to the public ▪ The novel/album has sold more than a million *copies*. — often + *of* ▪ Here's a free *copy of* our catalog/brochure.

3 [*noncount*] : written information that is to be published in a newspaper, magazine, etc. ▪ She got a job writing advertising *copy*. ▪ All *copy* must be submitted by 5 p.m. ▪ Political scandals make ***good copy***. [=interesting news stories]

[2]**copy** *verb* **copies; cop·ied; copy·ing**

1 : to make a version of (something) that is exactly or almost exactly like the original : to make a copy or duplicate of (something) [+ *obj*] She *copied* the design on a piece of paper. ▪ *Copy* the file to your hard drive. ▪ Would you *copy* [=*photocopy*] these pages for me? ▪ The program allows you to ***copy and paste*** text. [=to copy text and insert it somewhere else in the document] [*no obj*] The page did not *copy* [=*photocopy*] well. ▪ The bills are designed to prevent *copying* by counterfeiters.

2 a : to write (something) down exactly as it appears somewhere else [+ *obj*] We caught him *copying* the answers out of the book. [*no obj*] We caught him *copying* out of the book. **b** [+ *obj*] : to use (someone else's words or ideas) as your own ▪ The speech was *copied* word for word.

3 [+ *obj*] **a** : to do the same thing as (someone) ▪ She's always *copying* [=*imitating*] her older sister. **b** : to make or do something the same way as (something else) ▪ His music was *copied* widely. ▪ Their competitors soon *copied* the idea.

copy down/out [*phrasal verb*] ***copy (something) down/out*** *or* ***copy down/out (something)*** : to write down (words that you are hearing or reading) ▪ Are you *copying* all of this *down*? ▪ I *copied out* the equations on a piece of paper.

copy·cat /ˈkɑːpiˌkæt/ *noun, pl* **-cats** [*count*]

1 *informal* : a person who does the same thing as someone else : a person who adopts the behavior, style, etc., of someone else ▪ She called me a *copycat* for wearing the same dress.

2 : something that is very similar to another thing ▪ The product has inspired a lot of *copycats*. [=*imitations*] — often used before another noun ▪ a *copycat* crime ▪ *copycat* drugs

copy editor *noun, pl* **~ -tors** [*count*] *US* : a person whose job is to prepare a book, newspaper, etc., for printing by making sure the words are correct — called also (*Brit*) *subeditor*

– **copy·ed·it** /ˈkɑːpiˌɛdət/ *verb* **-its; -it·ed; -it·ing** [+ *obj*] ▪ He *copyedits* the dictionary.

copy·ist /ˈkɑːpijɪst/ *noun, pl* **-ists** [*count*]

1 : someone who made copies of documents or maps by hand before printing became common

2 : someone who copies the style or design of something (such as a work of art or piece of clothing)

copy machine *or* **copying machine** *noun, pl* **~ -chines** [*count*] : COPIER

[1]**copy·right** /ˈkɑːpiˌraɪt/ *noun, pl* **-rights** : the legal right to be the only one to reproduce, publish, and sell a book, musical recording, etc., for a certain period of time [*count*] His family still holds the *copyright* to his songs. ▪ laws that protect *copyrights* [*noncount*] The book is under *copyright*.

[2]**copyright** *verb* **-rights; -right·ed; -right·ing** [+ *obj*] : to get a copyright for a book, musical recording, etc., for a certain period of time ▪ He has *copyrighted* all of his plays. ▪ These are *copyrighted* materials.

[3]**copyright** *adj, always used before a noun*

1 : of or relating to a copyright ▪ *copyright* law/infringement ▪ *copyright* protection ▪ The *copyright* date is 2005.

2 : not allowed to be copied without permission from the author, composer, etc. ▪ *copyright* material

copy·writ·er /ˈkɑːpiˌraɪtɚ/ *noun, pl* **-ers** [*count*] : someone whose job is to write the words for advertisements

coq au vin /ˌkoʊkoʊˈvæn/ *noun* [*noncount*] : chicken that is cooked in red wine

co·que·try /ˈkoʊkətri, *Brit* ˈkɒkətri/ *noun* [*noncount*] *literary* : the behavior of a coquette ▪ Her behavior was mistaken for *coquetry*. [=(more commonly) *flirtation*]

co·quette /koʊˈkɛt/ *noun, pl* **-quettes** [*count*] *literary + formal* : a woman who likes to win the attention or admiration of men but does not have serious feelings for them : FLIRT ▪ She was a bit of a *coquette*.

– **co·quett·ish** /koʊˈkɛtɪʃ/ *adj* [*more ~; most ~*] ▪ a *coquettish* grin/smile ▪ a *coquettish* young woman – **co·quett·ish·ly** *adv* ▪ She smiled *coquettishly* at him. – **co·quett·ish·ness** *noun* [*noncount*]

cor·a·cle /ˈkorəkəl/ *noun, pl* **-acles** [*count*] : a very small type of boat that has been used in parts of Great Britain since ancient times

cor·al /ˈkorəl/ *noun [noncount]*
1 : a hard material formed on the bottom of the sea by the skeletons of small creatures • brightly colored fishes swimming among the *coral*
2 : an orange pink color — see color picture on page C3
– coral *adj* • *coral* deposits

coral reef *noun, pl* **~ reefs** *[count]* **:** a long line of coral that lies in warm, shallow water

cor an·glais /ˌkorɑːŋˈgleɪ/ *noun, pl* **cors an·glais** /ˌkoɚzɑːŋˈgleɪ/ *[count] Brit* **:** ENGLISH HORN

[1]cord /ˈkoɚd/ *noun, pl* **cords**
1 : a long, thin material that is usually thicker than a string but thinner than a rope *[count]* She wore the key on a *cord* around her neck. • They used *cords* to tie the tent to the trees. *[noncount]* a piece of *cord* — see also BUNGEE CORD, RIP CORD
2 *[count]* **:** an electrical wire that is wrapped in a protective covering and used to connect a device to a power source • a telephone *cord* • a lamp *cord* • a power *cord* — called also *(Brit) flex*; see also EXTENSION CORD
3 *[count]* **:** a part of the body that is like a string or rope • a nerve *cord* — see also SPINAL CORD, UMBILICAL CORD, VOCAL CORDS
4 *[count] US* **:** an amount of wood that has been cut for burning in a fireplace, stove, etc. **:** a pile that contains 128 cubic feet of firewood • a *cord* of wood — compare CORDWOOD
5 ***cords*** *[plural]* **:** pants made of corduroy • a pair of black *cords [=corduroys]*

[2]cord *adj* **:** made of corduroy • a *cord* jacket

cord·age /ˈkoɚdɪʤ/ *noun [noncount]* **:** ropes or cords • a company that produced *cordage* for ships

[1]cor·dial /ˈkoɚʤəl, *Brit* ˈkɔːdiəl/ *adj [more ~; most ~]* **:** politely pleasant and friendly • We received a *cordial* greeting from our hostess at the party. • The two nations have maintained *cordial* relations.
– cor·di·al·i·ty /ˌkoɚʤiˈæləti, *Brit* ˌkɔːdiˈæləti/ *noun [noncount]* • They greeted the ambassador with *cordiality*.
– cor·dial·ly *adv* • You are *cordially* invited to attend the wedding of our daughter on May 14.

[2]cordial *noun, pl* **-dials** *[count, noncount]*
1 *US* **:** a sweet alcoholic drink **:** LIQUEUR
2 *Brit* **:** a drink of heavy fruit juice that is mixed with water

cord·less /ˈkoɚdləs/ *adj* **:** powered by a battery rather than by electricity through a cord • a *cordless* phone/drill

[1]cor·don /ˈkoɚdn/ *noun, pl* **-dons** *[count]* **:** a line of people or objects that are placed around or in front of a person or place to keep people away • A *cordon* of police kept protesters away from the building.

[2]cordon *verb* **-dons; -doned; -don·ing**
cordon off *[phrasal verb]* ***cordon off (something) or cordon (something) off*** **:** to prevent people from getting into (an area) by putting a line of people or objects around or in front of it • Police *cordoned off* the street.

cor·don bleu /ˌkoɚˌdɑːnˈbluː/ *adj* **:** having, showing, or requiring great skill at cooking • a *cordon bleu* chef • a *cordon bleu* meal

cor·du·roy /ˈkoɚdəˌroɪ/ *noun*
1 *[noncount]* **:** a strong cotton cloth with straight raised lines on it • a jacket made of *corduroy* — often used before another noun • a *corduroy* skirt
2 ***corduroys*** *[plural]* **:** pants made of corduroy • a pair of *corduroys [=cords]*

cord·wood /ˈkoɚdˌwʊd/ *noun [noncount] US* **:** wood used for fires that is piled or sold in cords (sense 4)

[1]core /ˈkoɚ/ *noun, pl* **cores** *[count]*
1 : the central part of a fruit (such as an apple) that contains the seeds • an apple *core* — see color picture on page C5
2 : the central part of something • the *core* of a golf ball • The pads have a foam *core*. • the engine *core* • the *core* of the galaxy • The Earth's *core* is very different from its crust. • the urban *core* [=the central part of a city]
3 : the most important or basic part of something • Lack of money is the *core* of the problem. • The *core* of the government's plan is to provide loans for small businesses. • voters who form the *core* of the party • The economy is at the very *core* of this year's election. — see also HARD CORE
4 *technical* **:** a part that has been removed from a material for scientific study • took a *core* sample of rock • an ice *core* from the glacier
5 *technical* **:** the place in a nuclear reactor where the reaction takes place • the reactor *core*
to the core **:** in a very complete or extreme way — used for emphasis • He is patriotic *to the core*. [=he is extremely patriotic] • Her family is English *to the core*. • He's ***rotten to the core***. [=he's a very bad/dishonest person] • They were ***shaken to the core***. [=extremely shaken/upset]

[2]core *adj, always used before a noun*
1 : most important or most basic • The company's *core* business is lending money. • Stealing would go against his *core* beliefs. [=his basic principles] • the *core* responsibilities of the police force • the *core* vocabulary of a language
2 : of or relating to the classes that all the students in a school are required to take or the skills that all students are required to learn • the *core* curriculum • *core* courses/subjects

[3]core *verb* **cores; cored; cor·ing** *[+ obj]* **:** to remove a core from (a fruit) • *core* an apple
– cor·er *noun, pl* **-ers** *[count]* • an apple *corer* [=a device that is used to remove the core from an apple]

co·ri·an·der /ˈkoriˌændɚ/ *noun [noncount]*
1 : a plant whose leaves and seeds are used in cooking
2 *chiefly Brit* **:** CILANTRO
3 : the dried seed of the coriander plant used as a flavoring — called also *coriander seed*

[1]cork /ˈkoɚk/ *noun, pl* **corks**
1 *[noncount]* **:** a material that is made from the soft bark of a kind of oak tree • a piece of *cork* • a *cork* bulletin board • shoes with *cork* heels
2 *[count]* **:** a piece of cork or another material (such as plastic) that is put in the end of bottle to close it • the *cork* of a wine bottle • She ***popped the cork*** on the champagne. [=she opened the bottle of champagne by removing the cork] • After their championship victory, the team was ready to *pop the cork*. [=to begin celebrating by opening and drinking bottles of champagne]
put a cork in it *chiefly US, informal* — used as a rude way to tell someone to stop talking and especially to stop complaining • Why don't you *put a cork in it*! [=*shut up*] I am sick of your whining!

[2]cork *verb* **corks; corked; cork·ing** *[+ obj]*
1 : to close (something, such as a bottle) with a cork • Please *cork* the wine. • a *corked* bottle of wine — opposite UNCORK; see also CORKED
2 : to put cork inside (something, such as a baseball bat) • a player who has been accused of illegally *corking* his bats • a *corked* bat

corked /ˈkoɚkt/ *adj, of wine* **:** having an unpleasant taste because of a damaged or decayed cork • *corked* wine

cork·er /ˈkoɚkɚ/ *noun, pl* **-ers** *[count] informal + old-fashioned* **:** a very good or amusing person or thing • Last week's episode was good, but this one is a real *corker*!

cork·ing /ˈkoɚkɪŋ/ *adj, informal + old-fashioned* **:** very good • an absolutely *corking* idea
– corking *adv* • a *corking* good story

cork·screw /ˈkoɚkˌskruː/ *noun, pl* **-screws** *[count]* **:** a tool that is used to pull corks from bottles

corkscrew

cor·mo·rant /ˈkoɚmərənt/ *noun, pl* **-rants** *[count]* **:** a type of dark-colored bird that has a long neck and that eats fish that it catches in the ocean

[1]corn /ˈkoɚn/ *noun [noncount]*
1 *US* **a :** a tall plant that produces yellow seeds (called kernels) that are eaten as a vegetable, used to produce many food products, and used as food for animals • driving past fields of *corn* — called also *(US) Indian corn, maize*; see color picture on page C4 **b :** the seeds of the corn plant eaten as a vegetable • a dish of buttered *corn* • a can of *corn* • We ate ***corn on the cob***. [=kernels still attached to the cob/corncob] — called also *(Brit) sweetcorn*
2 *Brit, somewhat old-fashioned* **:** a plant (such as wheat or barley) that produces seeds which are used for food; *also* **:** the seeds of such a plant **:** GRAIN
3 *US, informal* **:** something (such as writing, music, or acting) that is old-fashioned and silly or sentimental **:** some-

thing that is corny • The movie's humor is pure *corn.* [=is very corny]
– compare ²CORN

²**corn** *noun, pl* **corns** [*count*] : a painful hard spot on the skin of the foot — compare ¹CORN

corn•ball /ˈkoən,bɑːl/ *adj* [*more* ~; *most* ~] *US, informal* : old-fashioned and silly or sentimental : CORNY • a *cornball* musical about farmers • a *cornball* sense of humor

corn bread *noun, pl* ~ **breads** [*count, noncount*] : a kind of bread or cake that is made with cornmeal

corn chip *noun, pl* ~ **chips** [*count*] : a small, flat piece of fried cornmeal that is eaten cold as a snack

corn•cob /ˈkoən,kɑːb/ *noun, pl* **-cobs** [*count*] : the long, hard, center part of corn (sense 1) : the part of corn that the kernels grow on

corn dog *noun, pl* ~ **dogs** [*count*] *US* : a hot dog covered with a mixture of cornmeal that is fried and served on a stick

cor•nea /ˈkoənijə/ *noun, pl* **-neas** [*count*] *technical* : the clear outer covering of the eyeball
– **cor•ne•al** /ˈkoənijəl/ *adj*

corned beef *noun* [*noncount*] : beef that has been preserved in salt water • a slice of *corned beef* • a *corned beef* sandwich

¹**cor•ner** /ˈkoənə/ *noun, pl* **-ners** [*count*]
1 : the point or area where two lines, edges, or sides of something meet • the *corner* of a box/table/tablecloth • A post marks the *corner* of the property. • Write your name in the upper right-hand *corner* of the page. • He caught the ball in the *corner* of the end zone. • the northeast *corner* of the state • We sat at a table in a *corner* of the room.
2 a : the place where two streets or roads meet • a street *corner* • The hotel is at the *corner* of Fifth Avenue and 59th Street. • A group of teenagers were hanging around on the *corner.* • He went to the grocery store around/round the *corner* from the bank. **b** : a curve in a road • She knew there was a gas station just around the *corner.* [=after the curve] • The car took the *corner* [=drove around the curve in the road] too fast and went off the road. — see also (JUST) AROUND THE CORNER (below), TURN THE CORNER (below)
3 : the side of your mouth or eye • He said something out of the *corner* of his mouth to the person standing next to him. • There was a tear in the *corner* of her eye. • I saw something ***out of the corner of my eye.*** [=I saw something to the side of where I was looking]
4 : one of four parts of a boxing ring where the sides meet • The boxers returned to their *corners* when the round ended. — often used figuratively to describe people, groups, etc., that are opposing or fighting each other • In one *corner* you have the music industry, and in the other, those who want music but don't want to pay for it. ✧ Someone who gives you help and support is ***in your corner.*** • I am going to need you *in my corner* when I go to court.
5 a : a place that is private or secret or that few people know about or visit • They live in a quiet *corner* of the town. — often used figuratively • a memory that lies in some dark *corner* of his mind **b** : a place that is far away • His influence extends to every *corner* of the state. • She is famous in every *corner* of the world. [=throughout the world] • People came ***from the four corners of the earth*** [=*from everywhere; from all over*] to see the sight.
6 : a position that you cannot easily get out of : a difficult situation • The city is ***in a tight corner*** financially. [=is in a bad financial position] • The candidate ***backed/painted himself into a corner*** [=put himself in a bad position] by proposing a tax increase.
7 *soccer* : CORNER KICK
cut corners *often disapproving* : to save time or money by doing less than you usually do or than you should do • We don't have enough money to pay for everything, so we'll have to *cut corners* somewhere. • You should never *cut corners* on safety.
have/get a corner on : to have or get enough of (something) to be able to control its price • He *has a corner on* the silver market. — often used figuratively • He acts like he *has a corner on* new ideas. [=like he is the only person who has new ideas]
(just) around the corner : coming or happening very soon • The politicians say that a stronger economy is *just around the corner.* [=that the economy will become stronger very soon] • Summer vacation is *around the corner.*
turn the corner : to get past the most difficult area or period in something and begin to improve • The company claims it has *turned the corner* and will be profitable soon.

²**corner** *adj, always used before a noun* : located at a corner • a *corner* office • We ate in a *corner* booth at the restaurant. • a *corner* shop/store

³**corner** *verb* **-ners; -nered; -ner•ing**
1 [+ *obj*] **a** : to force (a person or animal) into a place or position from which escape is very difficult or impossible • Police *cornered* the suspect in a backyard. • A *cornered* animal can be dangerous. **b** : to force (someone who wants to avoid you or get away from you) to stop and talk with you • He *cornered* the actress and demanded her autograph. • The interviewer *cornered* the politician with some probing questions.
2 [+ *obj*] : to get control of a particular type of product that is being bought and sold — used in the phrase ***corner the market*** • They have *cornered the market* in wheat. = They have *cornered the* wheat *market.* — sometimes used figuratively • He acts as if he's *cornered the market* on new ideas.
3 [*no obj*] *of a vehicle* : to turn a corner • This car *corners* well.

corner kick *noun, pl* ~ **kicks** [*count*] *soccer* : a free kick from the corner of the field near the opponent's goal

cor•ner•stone /ˈkoənə,stoun/ *noun, pl* **-stones** [*count*]
1 : a stone that forms part of a corner in the outside wall of a building and that often shows the date when the building was built • Officials held a ceremony to lay the *cornerstone* for a new library.
2 : something of basic importance • Trust is the *cornerstone* of their relationship.

cor•net /koəˈnet, *Brit* ˈkɔːnɪt/ *noun, pl* **-nets** [*count*]
1 : a brass musical instrument that is similar to a trumpet but smaller
2 *Brit, old-fashioned* : an ice-cream cone

corn–fed /ˈkoən,fed/ *adj* : fed with grain • *corn-fed* pigs — sometimes used figuratively in U.S. English • a big, *corn-fed* farm boy • *corn-fed* [=*corny*] humor

corn•field /ˈkoən,fiːld/ *noun, pl* **-fields** [*count*] : a field in which corn is grown

corn•flakes /ˈkoən,fleɪks/ *noun* [*plural*] : toasted flakes made from kernels of corn (sense 1) and used as a breakfast cereal

corn flour *noun* [*noncount*] *Brit* : CORNSTARCH

corn•flow•er /ˈkoən,flawə/ *noun, pl* **-ers** [*count*] : a wild plant that usually has blue flowers

cor•nice /ˈkoənəs/ *noun, pl* **-nic•es** [*count*]
1 : the decorative top edge of a building or column
2 : a decorative strip of wood or some other material used at the top of the walls in a room

Cor•nish /ˈkoənɪʃ/ *adj* : of or relating to Cornwall or the people of Cornwall • the *Cornish* coast • *Cornish* miners • *Cornish* culture

Cornish pasty *noun, pl* ~ **-ties** [*count*] : a small pie that is filled with meat and vegetables

corn•meal /ˈkoən,miːl/ *noun* [*noncount*] : a coarse flour made from crushed corn (sense 1)

corn oil *noun* [*noncount*] : a type of oil made from corn (sense 1) and used in foods and soap

corn•pone /-ˈpoun/ *adj, US, informal* : of, relating to, or appealing to people who live on farms away from big cities • *cornpone* charm • *cornpone* humor

corn•rows /ˈkoən,rouz/ *noun* [*plural*] : a hair style in which hair is twisted together in tight rows that lie close to the skin — see picture at HAIR

corn•stalk /ˈkoən,stɑːk/ *noun, pl* **-stalks** [*count*] : the long stem of a corn plant (sense 1)

corn•starch /ˈkoən,stɑətʃ/ *noun* [*noncount*] *US* : a fine powder made from corn (sense 1) that is used in cooking especially to make liquids thicker • I used some *cornstarch* to thicken the gravy. — called also (*Brit*) *corn flour*

corn syrup *noun* [*noncount*] : a sweet, thick liquid made from corn (sense 1)

cor•nu•co•pia /,koənəˈkoupijə, ,koənjəˈkoupijə/ *noun, pl* **-pi•as**
1 [*count*] : a container that is shaped like a horn and is full of fruits and flowers
2 [*singular*] : a great amount or source of something • The market is/offers a *cornucopia* of fruits and vegetables. • The book includes a *cornucopia* of wonderful stories.

corny /ˈkoəni/ *adj* **corn•i•er; -est** *informal + usually disapproving* : old-fashioned and silly or sentimental • a *corny* joke • *corny* greeting cards

cor·ol·lary /ˈkorəˌleri, *Brit* kəˈrɒləri/ *noun, pl* **-lar·ies** [*count*] *formal* : something that naturally follows or results from another thing ▪ A *corollary* [=*result, by-product*] of increased poverty is more crime.
– corollary *adj* ▪ a *corollary* assumption

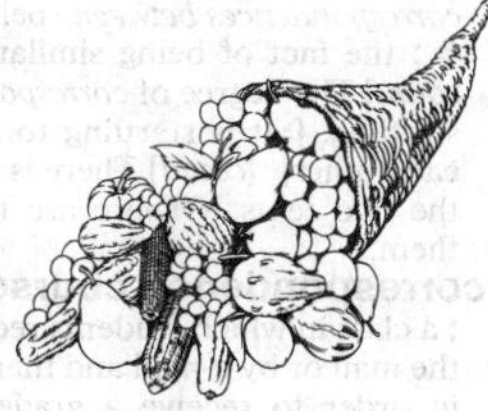
cornucopia

co·ro·na /kəˈrounə/ *noun, pl* **-nas** [*count*] *technical* : a bright circle seen around the sun or the moon

[1]**cor·o·nary** /ˈkorəˌneri, *Brit* ˈkɒrənri/ *adj* : of or relating to the heart and especially to the vessels that supply blood to the heart ▪ a *coronary* artery ▪ *coronary* surgery ▪ *coronary* heart disease ▪ ***coronary thrombosis*** [=a dangerous condition in which an artery to the heart is blocked by a blood clot]

[2]**coronary** *noun, pl* **-nar·ies** [*count*] *informal* : HEART ATTACK ▪ I almost had a *coronary* when I heard the news.

cor·o·na·tion /ˌkorəˈneɪʃən/ *noun, pl* **-tions** [*count*] : a ceremony in which a crown is placed on the head of a new king or queen ▪ the *coronation* of Queen Elizabeth

cor·o·ner /ˈkorənə/ *noun, pl* **-ners** [*count*] : a public official whose job is to find out the cause of death when people die in ways that are violent, sudden, etc. ▪ The *coroner* examined the body but found no evidence of foul play.

cor·o·net /ˌkorəˈnɛt, *Brit* ˈkɒrənɪt/ *noun, pl* **-nets** [*count*] : a small crown

Corp. *abbr* corporation ▪ Chrysler *Corp.*

corpora *plural of* CORPUS

cor·po·ral /ˈkoəpərəl/ *noun, pl* **-rals** [*count*] : an officer in the army or marines with a rank below sergeant — see also LANCE CORPORAL

corporal punishment *noun* [*noncount*] : punishment that involves hitting someone : physical punishment ▪ The school banned *corporal punishment* many years ago.

cor·po·rate /ˈkoəpərət/ *adj*
1 a : involving or associated with a corporation ▪ We have to change the *corporate* structure to survive. ▪ A bunch of *corporate* types in suits were sitting at the table in the conference room. ▪ *corporate* debt/bonds/taxes **b** : consisting of or including large corporations ▪ He is one of the most powerful men in *corporate* America. **c** *often disapproving* : produced by or associated with large corporations ▪ *corporate* rock music ▪ *corporate* art
2 : formed into a legal corporation ▪ The business is a *corporate* entity.

cor·po·ra·tion /ˌkoəpəˈreɪʃən/ *noun, pl* **-tions** [*count*] : a large business or organization that under the law has the rights and duties of an individual and follows a specific purpose ▪ He works as a consultant for/to several large *corporations*. ▪ a community development *corporation*

cor·po·re·al /koəˈporijəl/ *adj* [*more ~; most ~*] *formal* : having or consisting of a physical body or form ▪ *corporeal* existence ▪ the *corporeal* nature of matter — opposite INCORPOREAL

corps /ˈkoə/ *noun, pl* **corps** /ˈkoəz/ [*count*]
1 a : an organized part of the military — used in proper names ▪ the U.S. Marine *Corps* ▪ the Army *Corps* of Engineers ▪ the Signal *Corps* **b** : a large military group consisting of two or more divisions
2 : a group of people who are involved in some activity ▪ members of the press *corps* ▪ a *corps* of volunteers — see also DIPLOMATIC CORPS, PEACE CORPS

corpse /ˈkoəps/ *noun, pl* **corps·es** [*count*] : a dead body ▪ a battlefield strewn with *corpses*

cor·pu·lent /ˈkoəpjələnt/ *adj* [*more ~; most ~*] *formal* : fat ▪ a *corpulent* [=*obese*] man ▪ her large, *corpulent* body
– cor·pu·lence /ˈkoəpjələns/ *noun* [*noncount*]

cor·pus /ˈkoəpəs/ *noun, pl* **cor·po·ra** /ˈkoəpərə/ [*count*]
1 : a collection of writings, conversations, speeches, etc., that people use to study and describe a language ▪ a computerized *corpus* of English
2 : a collection of poems, paintings, songs, etc. ▪ the painter's *corpus* of work [=all the paintings the painter has done]
– see also HABEAS CORPUS

cor·pus·cle /ˈkoəˌpʌsəl/ *noun, pl* **-pus·cles** [*count*] *biology* : one of the cells that move in the body; *especially* : a blood cell ▪ a red/white blood *corpuscle*

[1]**cor·ral** /kəˈræl, *Brit* kəˈrɑːl/ *noun, pl* **-rals** [*count*] : an area that is surrounded by a fence and that is used for holding animals (such as cows and horses) on a farm or ranch

[2]**corral** *verb* **-rals; -ralled; -ral·ling** [*+ obj*] : to gather and put (cows, horses, etc.) into a corral ▪ *corralling* cattle — often used figuratively ▪ He *corralled* us all into his office for a quick meeting. ▪ *corralling* [=*collecting, gathering*] votes for next month's election

[1]**cor·rect** /kəˈrɛkt/ *adj*
1 : true or accurate : agreeing with facts : RIGHT ▪ What's the *correct* answer/response to this question? ▪ She is *correct* (in saying) that more money is needed. ▪ Yes, that's *correct.* ▪ Her watch never tells the *correct* time. ▪ an anatomically *correct* drawing of the human body
2 : having no errors or mistakes ▪ a grammatically *correct* sentence ▪ *correct* pronunciation/punctuation/spelling/usage
3 : proper or appropriate in a particular situation ▪ Did I give you the *correct* change? ▪ With the *correct* amount of water and sunlight, the plant will grow well. ▪ We're trying to find the *correct* [=*right*] way to deal with the problem. ▪ He was *correct* to do what he did. = He did the *correct* thing.
4 [*more ~; most ~*] *sometimes disapproving* : considered proper by people with a strict set of beliefs or values ▪ We need to find a more environmentally *correct* way of disposing these materials. [=a way that does not damage the environment] — see also POLITICALLY CORRECT
5 [*more ~; most ~*] *somewhat old-fashioned* : careful about behaving in a polite and socially accepted way ▪ a very *correct* young man
– cor·rect·ly *adv* ▪ You answered *correctly.* ▪ If I remember *correctly*, he was a good baseball player in high school. ▪ Did I spell your name *correctly*? **– cor·rect·ness** *noun* [*noncount*] ▪ anatomical *correctness* ▪ We question the *correctness* of his actions.

[2]**correct** *verb* **-rects; -rect·ed; -rect·ing**
1 [*+ obj*] : to change (something) so that it is right, true, proper, etc. : to make (something) correct ▪ a computer program that *corrects* [=*fixes*] spelling errors ▪ I hate it when she *corrects* my grammar. ▪ These errors are easily *corrected.* = These errors can be *corrected* easily. ▪ Please *correct* your essay for punctuation errors. ✧ To ***correct someone*** is to say that someone has made a mistake and to give the correct information. ▪ "I use the title 'Ms.' not 'Mrs.,'" she *corrected* him. ▪ He quickly *corrected* himself and said that it cost two dollars, not four. ▪ ***Correct me if I'm wrong***, but I think you owe me another dollar. [=do you owe me another dollar?] ✧ The phrase ***I stand corrected*** is a somewhat formal way of saying that you have learned that you were wrong about something. "He's four years old, not five." "Well, then, *I stand corrected.*" ▪ *I stand corrected.* The meeting is on Monday, not Tuesday as I'd thought.
2 [*+ obj*] : to mark the errors on (something that a person has written) ▪ Our teacher hasn't finished *correcting* our tests yet. ▪ He *corrects* papers with a red pen.
3 [*+ obj*] : to deal with or take care of (a problem, bad situation, etc.) successfully ▪ We are finding ways to *correct* this difficult situation. ▪ We'll *correct* the problem with the circuit as soon as possible. ▪ These medicines are used for *correcting* chemical imbalances in the brain. ▪ She's having surgery that will *correct* her vision. [=that will make her bad vision good/better]
4 : to make an amount or number more accurate by considering other information — usually *+ for* [*no obj*] The measurements are not accurate because I didn't *correct for* the change in temperature. [*+ obj*] We need to *correct* the measurements *for* the change in temperature.
– cor·rect·able /kəˈrɛktəbəl/ *adj* ▪ a *correctable* error ▪ a problem that is *correctable* by surgery

cor·rec·tion /kəˈrɛkʃən/ *noun, pl* **-tions**
1 [*count*] : a change that makes something right, true, accurate, etc. ▪ They ran/published a *correction* in today's paper. [=there was a statement in the newspaper saying that something printed in an earlier newspaper was not accurate] ▪ The teacher marked *corrections* on his students' tests. ▪ Please make *corrections* before handing in your compositions.
2 [*noncount*] : the act of making something (such as an error or a bad condition) accurate or better : the act of correcting something ▪ the *correction* of your mistakes ▪ people in need of vision *correction*
3 : the act or process of punishing and changing the behavior of people who have committed crimes [*noncount*] (*old-fashioned*) *correction* of criminals [*plural*] (*US*) — used to refer to government systems and actions that relate to pun-

ishing and dealing with criminals • The state's overall spending on *corrections* has increased rapidly in recent years. • the state Department of *Corrections* — often used before another noun • a *corrections* officer [=an official in a jail or prison]

– **cor·rec·tion·al** /kəˈrɛkʃənl/ *adj, always used before a noun, chiefly US* • the state's ***correctional facilities/institutions*** [=prisons or jails]

C

correction fluid *noun [noncount]* : a liquid used to cover typing or writing errors

¹cor·rec·tive /kəˈrɛktɪv/ *adj* : meant to correct a problem : intended to make something better • She had *corrective* surgery on her knee this past summer. • People with bad eyesight usually need to wear *corrective* lenses, such as eyeglasses or contact lenses.

²corrective *noun, pl* **-tives** *[count] formal* : something that helps to make a problem or bad situation better • The President's speech was intended to be a *corrective* [=*remedy*] to the country's feelings of fear and uncertainty.

¹cor·re·late /ˈkorəˌleɪt/ *verb* **-lates; -lat·ed; -lat·ing** *formal*

1 *[no obj]* : to have a close connection with something : to have a correlation to something ✧ If two things *correlate*, a change in one thing results in a similar or an opposite change in the other thing. • In general terms, brain size *correlates* with intelligence. [=a larger brain generally suggests greater intelligence] • Some studies have shown that the success of students *correlates* negatively with the number of students in a class. [=when more students are in a class, the students are less successful] • In this case, a difference in height *correlates* [=*corresponds*] to a difference in weight.

2 *[+ obj]* : to show that a close connection exists between (two or more things) • There is no evidence *correlating* height and intelligence.

be correlated : to have a close connection : to correlate • Brain size *is correlated* with intelligence.

²cor·re·late /ˈkorələt/ *noun, pl* **-lates** *[count] technical* : either one of two things that are closely connected or correlated with each other • brain size as a *correlate* of intelligence

cor·re·la·tion /ˌkorəˈleɪʃən/ *noun, pl* **-tions** : the relationship between things that happen or change together *[noncount]* the *correlation* of brain size and/with intelligence — often + *between* • the high/strong *correlation between* poverty and crime [=the fact that crime is more common when there is more poverty] *[count]* Researchers have found a direct *correlation between* smoking and lung cancer. • She says that there's no *correlation between* being thin and being happy.

cor·rel·a·tive /kəˈrɛlətɪv/ *adj, formal* : existing because something else exists : closely connected • a doctor's duties and a patient's *correlative* rights • As demand increases, we'll see a *correlative* increase in price.

– **correlative** *noun, pl* **-tives** *[count]*

cor·re·spond /ˌkorəˈspɑːnd/ *verb* **-sponds; -spond·ed; -spond·ing** *[no obj]*

1 : to be similar or equal *to* something • In some countries, the role of president *corresponds to* that of prime minister. • the joints on a horse that *correspond to* the human knees

2 : to have a direct relationship *to* or *with* something • Each number *corresponds to* a location on the map. • His statements do not *correspond to/with* the facts. [=do not match the facts] • We'll revise the schedule to *correspond with* the school calendar. — see also CORRESPONDING

3 *somewhat formal* : to write to someone or to each other • We haven't *corresponded* in years. [=we have not written letters/e-mails to each other for years] — often + *with* • She still *corresponded* regularly *with* friends she met in college.

cor·re·spon·dence /ˌkorəˈspɑːndəns/ *noun, pl* **-denc·es**

1 : the activity of writing letters or e-mails to someone *[noncount]* They communicated by telephone and *correspondence*. • E-mail *correspondence* has become extremely important for modern businesses. *[singular]* The two men began a *correspondence* that would continue throughout their lives.

2 *[noncount]* : the letters or e-mails that people write to each other • A book of the author's personal *correspondence* was published early last year. • A formal tone is always used in business *correspondence*. • I have a pile of *correspondence* [=letters from people] on my desk.

3 : a direct relationship *to* or *with* something or *between* two things *[noncount]* Note the *correspondence* of each number *to* a location on the map. • Sometimes there is little *correspondence between* the way a word is spelled and the way it is pronounced in English. *[count]* Sometimes there are few *correspondences between* spelling and pronunciation.

4 : the fact of being similar or equal to something *[noncount]* The degree of *correspondence* between the two texts is startling. [=it is startling to see how closely they resemble each other] *[count]* There is a close *correspondence* between the two texts. • There are many *correspondences* between them.

correspondence course *noun, pl* ~ **courses** *[count]* : a class in which students receive lessons and assignments in the mail or by e-mail and then return completed assignments in order to receive a grade • She took a *correspondence course* in world religions.

cor·re·spon·dent /ˌkorəˈspɑːndənt/ *noun, pl* **-dents** *[count]*

1 *somewhat formal* : someone who writes letters or e-mails to another person • When writing to business *correspondents*, use a formal tone.

2 : a person whose job is to send news to a newspaper, radio station, or television program often from different places around the world • We now turn to our political *correspondent* [=a person who sends news about politics] reporting from the nation's capital. • a war *correspondent* [=a reporter who sends news from places where there are wars] for an American newspaper • foreign *correspondents* [=reporters who send news from other countries]

corresponding *adj, always used before a noun*

1 : having the same characteristics as something else : matching something else • The store earned 20 percent more this month than it did in the *corresponding* [=*same*] month last year. • "Robert" is a boy's name, and the *corresponding* name for a girl is "Roberta."

2 : directly related to something • a test question and its *corresponding* chapter in the textbook • As the cost of steel goes up, expect to see a *corresponding* increase in building costs.

– **cor·re·spond·ing·ly** *adv* • As the cost of steel goes up, building costs will rise *correspondingly*.

cor·ri·dor /ˈkorədɚ, ˈkorəˌdoɚ/ *noun, pl* **-dors** *[count]*

1 : a long, narrow passage inside a building or train with doors that lead to rooms on each side • She slowly walked down the long, dark *corridor*. [=*hall, hallway*] • They pushed me down the hospital *corridor* to the operating room.

2 a : a long narrow piece of land • A *corridor* of land lies between the two mountain ranges. **b** : a narrow area of land that is known for something specified • a transportation *corridor*

the corridors of power see ¹POWER

cor·rob·o·rate /kəˈrɑːbəˌreɪt/ *verb* **-rates; -rat·ed; -rat·ing** *[+ obj] formal* : to support or help prove (a statement, theory, etc.) by providing information or evidence • Two witnesses *corroborated* [=*confirmed*] his story. — often used as *(be) corroborated* • The theory has *been corroborated* by recent studies.

– **corroborating** *adj* • No *corroborating* evidence was found. – **cor·rob·o·ra·tion** /kəˌrɑːbəˈreɪʃən/ *noun [noncount]* • the *corroboration* of his story – **cor·rob·o·ra·tive** /kəˈrɑːbəˌreɪtɪv, kəˈrɑːbərətɪv/ *adj* • *corroborative* evidence/testimony

cor·rode /kəˈroʊd/ *verb* **-rode; -rod·ed; -rod·ing**

1 : to slowly break apart and destroy (metal, an object, etc.) through a chemical process *[+ obj]* Rainwater may *corrode* the steel containers. • Over time, the pipes become *corroded* and need to be replaced. *[no obj]* After a few weeks in the ocean, the boat began to *corrode*.

2 *[+ obj]* : to gradually destroy or weaken (something) • Years of lies and secrets had *corroded* their relationship.

– **cor·ro·sion** /kəˈroʊʒən/ *noun [noncount]* • a material that is resistant to *corrosion* [=that cannot be corroded easily]

cor·ro·sive /kəˈroʊsɪv/ *adj [more ~; most ~]* : causing corrosion: such as **a** : causing damage to metal or other materials through a chemical process • highly *corrosive* chemicals/gases/liquids **b** : causing someone or something to become weak and damaged • the *corrosive* [=*destructive*] effects of drug use • She argues that racism is dangerous and *corrosive* to society.

cor·ru·gat·ed /ˈkorəˌgeɪtəd/ *adj* : having a wavy surface — used to describe thin sheets of material (such as metal or cardboard) that have a surface in which there are many folds that look like a series of waves • Their house had a dirt floor and a *corrugated* metal roof. • *corrugated* boxes = boxes made out of *corrugated* cardboard

¹cor·rupt /kəˈrʌpt/ *verb* **-rupts; -rupt·ed; -rupt·ing**

1 : to cause (someone or something) to become dishonest,

immoral, etc. [+ *obj*] He believes that violence on television and film is *corrupting* our children. [=teaching bad beliefs and behaviors to our children] • a politician *corrupted* by greed • music that *corrupts* the morals of children • *corrupting* the country's legal system [*no obj*] the *corrupting* influence/effects of power
2 [+ *obj*] : to change (something) so that it is less pure or valuable • He's convinced that the Internet is *corrupting* [=*ruining*] the English language. • Their idealism has been *corrupted* by cynicism.
3 [+ *obj*] : to change (a book, computer file, etc.) from the correct or original form • The file has been *corrupted* and no longer works properly. • *corrupted* databases/files • a *corrupted* version of the ancient text
– **cor·rupt·er** *noun, pl* **-ers** [*count*] • a *corrupter* of our nation's youth – **cor·rupt·ibil·i·ty** /kəˌrʌptəˈbɪləti/ *noun* [*noncount*] – **cor·rupt·ible** /kəˈrʌptəbəl/ *adj* [*more* ~; *most* ~] • young people who are easily *corruptible*

²corrupt *adj* [*more* ~; *most* ~]
1 a : doing things that are dishonest or illegal in order to make money or to gain or keep power • The country's justice system is riddled with *corrupt* judges who accept bribes. • *corrupt* politicians/officials • *corrupt* cops who sell drugs **b** : done or controlled by dishonest and immoral people • *corrupt* governments • the country's *corrupt* legal system
2 : dishonest, evil, or immoral • society's *corrupt* values
3 : changed or damaged : not in a correct or original form • a *corrupt* version of the text • The document is *corrupt*. • a *corrupt* computer file that no longer works properly
– **cor·rupt·ly** *adv* – **cor·rupt·ness** *noun* [*noncount*] • the *corruptness* of the local government

cor·rup·tion /kəˈrʌpʃən/ *noun, pl* **-tions**
1 [*noncount*] : dishonest or illegal behavior especially by powerful people (such as government officials or police officers) • There are rumors of widespread *corruption* in the city government.
2 : the act of corrupting someone or something [*noncount*] the mafia's *corruption* of public officials • *corruption* of the English language • computer software that is supposed to prevent the *corruption* of files • database *corruption* • the *corruption* of a text [*count*] file *corruptions*
3 [*count*] : something that has been changed from its original form — usually singular • The phrase "an apron" is a *corruption* of the original English phrase "a napron."

cor·sage /koɚˈsɑːʒ/ *noun, pl* **-sag·es** [*count*] : a flower or small group of flowers that a woman sometimes wears on her clothing or attached to her wrist on special occasions (such as weddings)

cor·sair /ˈkoɚˌseɚ/ *noun, pl* **-sairs** [*count*] *literary + old-fashioned* : ¹PIRATE 1

cor·set /ˈkoɚsət/ *noun, pl* **-sets** [*count*] : a tight, stiff piece of clothing worn by women under other clothing to make their waists appear smaller ✧ Corsets are no longer commonly worn.
– **cor·set·ed** /ˈkoɚsətəd/ *adj* • tightly *corseted* ladies

cor·tege *also* **cor·tège** /koɚˈtɛʒ, *Brit* kɔːˈteɪʒ/ *noun, pl* **-teg·es** *also* **-tèg·es** [*count*] : a line of people or cars moving slowly at a funeral • a funeral *cortege* [=*procession*]

cor·tex /ˈkoɚˌtɛks/ *noun, pl* **cor·ti·ces** /ˈkoɚtəˌsiːz/ *or* **cor·tex·es** [*count*] *medical* : the outer layer of an organ in the body and especially of the brain • the cerebral *cortex* • the brain's *cortex*
– **cor·ti·cal** /ˈkoɚtɪkəl/ *adj* • *cortical* thickness

cor·ti·sone /ˈkoɚtəˌsoʊn/ *noun* [*noncount*] *medical* : a hormone that is used to treat arthritis and other diseases

¹cosh /ˈkɑːʃ/ *noun, pl* **cosh·es** [*count*] *Brit* : a small, heavy weapon that is shaped like a stick
under the cosh *Brit, informal* : in a difficult situation • They put us *under the cosh* for most of the game.

²cosh *verb* **coshes; coshed; cosh·ing** [+ *obj*] *Brit, informal* : to hit (someone) with a cosh • He was *coshed* on the head.

co·sign /ˈkoʊˌsaɪn/ *verb* **-signs; -signed; -sign·ing** : to sign a document saying that you agree to share the responsibility for a loan or contract with another person [+ *obj*] My mother *cosigned* the loan on my car. • *cosign* a lease [*no obj*] She *cosigned* for my car.

co·sig·na·to·ry /koʊˈsɪgnəˌtori, *Brit* kəʊˈsɪgnətri/ *noun, pl* **-ries** [*count*] *formal* : COSIGNER

co·sign·er /ˈkoʊˌsaɪnɚ/ *noun, pl* **-ers** [*count*] : a person who signs an official document (such as a loan, contract, or law) with another person • Both senators are *cosigners* of the bill. : a person who cosigns something • My mother agreed to be a *cosigner* on my car loan.

co·sine /ˈkoʊˌsaɪn/ *noun, pl* **-sines** [*count*] *geometry* : the ratio between the long side (called the hypotenuse) and the side that is next to an acute angle in a right triangle

cos lettuce /ˈkɑːs-/ *noun* [*noncount*] *Brit* : ROMAINE

¹cos·met·ic /kɑzˈmɛtɪk/ *noun, pl* **-ics** [*count*] : a substance (such as a cream, lotion, or powder) that you put on your face or body to improve your appearance • Use a *cosmetic* to hide the scar. — usually plural • lipstick, nail polish, and other *cosmetics* • shopping for *cosmetics* [=*makeup*]

²cosmetic *adj*
1 *always used before a noun* : used or done in order to improve a person's appearance • *cosmetic* creams • Almond oil is sometimes used in *cosmetic* products. • medical procedures that are done for *cosmetic* purposes/reasons • She says she's never had/undergone **cosmetic surgery**. [=surgery done to improve a person's appearance]
2 : done in order to make something look better • The house just needs some paint and a few other *cosmetic* [=*decorative*] changes.
3 [*more* ~; *most* ~] : not important or meaningful • They made a few *cosmetic* [=*superficial*] changes to the deal, but they didn't change anything of real importance. • The changes were purely *cosmetic*.

cos·me·tol·o·gist /ˌkɑːzməˈtɑːləʤɪst/ *noun, pl* **-gists** [*count*] *US* : BEAUTICIAN

cos·me·tol·o·gy /ˌkɑːzməˈtɑːləʤi/ *noun* [*noncount*] *US* : the job or skill of giving beauty treatments to women by washing and cutting hair, applying makeup, etc. • a school of *cosmetology*

cos·mic /ˈkɑːzmɪk/ *adj*
1 *always used before a noun* : of or relating to the universe or outer space • *cosmic* theories • *cosmic* dust/radiation
2 : relating to spiritual matters • *cosmic* beauty/wisdom
3 [*more* ~; *most* ~] : very large or important • The discovery caused a *cosmic* shift in people's views of the world. • a book of *cosmic* [=*great, major, profound*] significance
– **cos·mi·cal·ly** *adv* • *cosmically* significant

cosmic ray *noun, pl* ~ **rays** [*count*] *technical* : a stream of energy that enters the Earth's atmosphere from outer space — usually plural

cos·mol·o·gy /kɑzˈmɑːləʤi/ *noun* [*noncount*] : the scientific study of the origin and structure of the universe
– **cos·mo·log·i·cal** /ˌkɑːzməˈlɑːʤɪkəl/ *adj* • *cosmological* data – **cos·mol·o·gist** /kɑzˈmɑːləʤɪst/ *noun, pl* **-gists** [*count*]

cos·mo·naut /ˈkɑːzməˌnɑːt/ *noun, pl* **-nauts** [*count*] : an astronaut in the space program of Russia or the former Soviet Union

¹cos·mo·pol·i·tan /ˌkɑːzməˈpɑːlətən/ *adj* [*more* ~; *most* ~]
1 : showing an interest in different cultures, ideas, etc. • *cosmopolitan* [=*worldly, sophisticated*] writers • Greater cultural diversity has led to a more *cosmopolitan* attitude among the town's younger generations. • the *cosmopolitan* taste/sophistication of the store's customers
2 : having people from many different parts of the world • It's one of the country's more *cosmopolitan* cities. • the community's *cosmopolitan* atmosphere
– **cos·mo·pol·i·tan·ism** /ˌkɑːzməˈpɑːlətəˌnɪzəm/ *noun* [*noncount*]

²cosmopolitan *noun, pl* **-ans** [*count*] : a person who has lived in and knows about many different parts of the world • a young *cosmopolitan*

cos·mos /ˈkɑːzməs, *Brit* ˈkɒzˌmɒs/ *noun, pl* **cosmos**
1 ***the cosmos*** : the universe especially when it is understood as an ordered system • the origins of *the cosmos*
2 [*count*] : a tall plant that has usually white, pink, or red flowers

cos·set /ˈkɑːsət/ *verb* **-sets; -set·ed; -set·ing** [+ *obj*] *formal* : to give (someone) a lot of care and attention or too much care and attention : PAMPER • The hotel *cossets* its guests with friendly service. • She had a safe, *cosseted* childhood.

¹cost /ˈkɑːst/ *noun, pl* **costs**
1 : the price of something : the amount of money that is needed to pay for or buy something [*count*] The original *cost* [=*price*] of the house was $200,000. • She attends college at a *cost* of $15,000 a year. • The average *cost* of raising a family has increased dramatically. • We offer services at a fraction of the *cost* of other companies. • bringing/driving down the *cost* of computers = lowering/reducing the *cost* of computers • The person at fault in the accident is expected to

bear the *cost* of repairs. [=is expected to pay for the repairs] [*noncount*] What's the difference in *cost*? ▪ We were able to update the room for very little *cost*. [=*money, expense*] ▪ They believe that everyone should have access to adequate medical care, regardless of *cost*. ***synonyms*** see [1]PRICE

2 [*count*] : an amount of money that must be spent regularly to pay for something (such as running a business or raising a family) ▪ The *cost* of doing business in this area is high. ▪ We need better *cost* control. ▪ The company needs to do some ***cost cutting***. [=needs to find ways to save money] — usually plural ▪ production/manufacturing/operating *costs* ▪ By keeping *costs* down, the company will make larger profits from its products. ▪ the firm's efforts to control *costs* ▪ Those are just some of the hidden *costs* [=*expenses*] of owning a house. ▪ The government covers most of the *costs* of the program. [=pays for most of the program] ▪ The family's medical *costs* have increased in the past year. ▪ The company has tried to ***cut costs*** [=spend less money] in several areas. — see also COST OF LIVING

3 : something that is lost, damaged, or given up in order to achieve or get something [*noncount*] Winning the war, he believes, was worth the *cost* in lives. — often used after *at* ▪ They had won the battle, but *at* what *cost*? Far too many people had died. ▪ He had achieved fame, but ***at a cost***; he'd lost many friends and no longer talked to anyone in his family. ▪ She completed the project on time but ***at the cost of*** her health. [=the work she did to complete the project on time damaged her health] ▪ He always says what he thinks, even *at the cost of* hurting someone's feelings. [*count*] What are the *costs* and benefits of the new law? ✧ To do something ***at all costs*** or (less commonly) ***at any cost*** is to do it even if you have to suffer, work very hard, lose everything you have, etc. ▪ She was determined to win *at all costs*. [=*no matter what*] ▪ Obscene language should be avoided *at all costs*. [=never use obscene words] ▪ He is determined to preserve his reputation *at any cost*.

4 *costs* [*plural*] : the money used to pay for a court case ▪ She was fined 50 dollars and ordered to pay court *costs*.

at cost *US* ✧ If you buy or sell something ***at cost***, you buy or sell it for the amount of money that was needed to make it or get it. ▪ We sold the books *at cost*. [=we sold the books for the same amount of money we paid to buy them; we did not make a profit from selling the books]

at no cost — used to say that something is free ▪ Improvements have been made *at no cost* to taxpayers. ▪ Club members can bring a friend *at no extra cost*.

count the cost see [1]COUNT

to your cost *chiefly Brit* : from your own bad experience ▪ I found out *to my cost* that he was a liar. [=I found out that he was a liar when I was hurt by his lies]

[2]**cost** *verb* **costs; cost; cost·ing** [+ *obj*]

1 a : to have (an amount of money) as a price ✧ If something ***costs*** a certain amount of money, you have to pay that amount of money in order to buy it, use it, or do it. ▪ Each ticket *costs* one dollar. ▪ How much does it *cost*? = What does it *cost*? ▪ This house *costs* more/less than most of the other houses in the area. ▪ It *costs* more than $300,000. ▪ (*informal*) New equipment ***costs money***. [=is expensive] ▪ (*informal*) I want a new car that doesn't ***cost an arm and a leg***. [=that is not too expensive] **b** : to cause (someone) to pay an amount of money ▪ The trip will *cost* you about $100 each way. ▪ The project will end up *costing* the government an estimated 3.5 billion dollars. ▪ It will *cost* you a lot of money, but it'll be worth it. ▪ (*informal*) I can get the part you need, but ***it'll cost you***. [=you will have to pay a lot of money for it] ✧ If something does not ***cost (you) a penny*** or (*US*) ***cost (you) a dime/nickel***, you do not need to pay any money for it; it is free. ▪ Come to my party. It won't *cost a dime*. = It won't *cost you a penny*.

2 a : to cause (someone) to lose something ▪ Her mistakes *cost* them the game. [=they lost the game because of her mistakes] ▪ The decision to drive that night nearly *cost* him his life. [=he almost died because of it] ▪ His frequent absences ended up *costing* him his job. ✧ If something ***costs you dearly/dear***, it causes you to lose something or to suffer a lot. ▪ Changing your mind now could *cost you dearly*. **b** : to cause (someone) to experience something unpleasant ▪ The error *cost* me a reprimand, but nothing more serious than that. ▪ a blunder that has *cost* her considerable embarrassment

3 *past tense* ***costed*** *Brit, business* : to determine how much money will be needed to pay for (something) — usually used as *(be) costed* ▪ The project *was* originally *costed* at 3 million pounds. — often + *out* ▪ The project has yet to *be costed out*. — see also COSTING

cost accounting *noun* [*noncount*] *business* : a system of recording and studying how much money a company spends

co·star /ˈkoʊˌstɑɚ/ *noun, pl* **-stars** [*count*] : one of two or more main actors in a movie, television show, or play ▪ the actress and her two *costars*

– **costar** *verb* **-stars; -starred; -star·ring** [+ *obj*] The film *costarred* Katharine Hepburn and Spencer Tracy. [*no obj*] He *costarred* in her most successful film.

cost–ben·e·fit /ˈkɑːstˈbɛnəˌfɪt/ *adj, always used before a noun, business* : of or relating to the study of how much money a company earns compared to how much money it spends ▪ *cost-benefit* analysis ▪ *cost-benefit* calculations

cost–ef·fec·tive /ˈkɑːstəˈfɛktɪv/ *adj* [*more* ~; *most* ~] : producing good results without costing a lot of money ▪ They need a more *cost-effective* [=*economical*] way to store data. ▪ It's just not *cost-effective* for us to have two cars.

– **cost–ef·fec·tive·ness** *noun* [*noncount*]

cost–ef·fi·cient /ˈkɑːstɪˈfɪʃənt/ *adj* [*more* ~; *most* ~] : COST-EFFECTIVE

cos·ter·mon·ger /ˈkɑːstɚˌmʌŋgɚ/ *noun, pl* **-gers** [*count*] *Brit, old-fashioned* : a person who sells fruit and vegetables outside rather than in a store

costing *noun, pl* **-ings** *Brit, business*

1 [*noncount*] : the process of determining how much money will be needed to pay for something ▪ *Costing* of the project will be completed early next month.

2 [*count*] : a plan or an estimate of how much money something will cost ▪ a lack of accurate financial *costings*

cost·ly /ˈkɑːstli/ *adj* **cost·li·er; -est** [*also more* ~; *most* ~]

1 : having a high price : costing a lot : EXPENSIVE ▪ *costly* jewelry ▪ We use less *costly* materials in our products. ▪ It was too *costly* to fix her car after the accident, so she decided to buy a new car instead.

2 : causing people to lose something or to suffer ▪ They won the game, but their best player was injured, so it was a *costly* victory. ▪ The decision to wait could be a *costly* mistake.

– **cost·li·ness** *noun* [*noncount*]

cost of living *noun, pl* **costs of living** [*count*] : the amount of money that is required in a particular area or society to pay for the basic things that people need (such as food, clothing, and housing) ▪ The city has one of the highest *costs of living* in the world. — usually singular ▪ Every year or so, we get a pay raise to compensate for the rising *cost of living*. ▪ The *cost of living* is much higher in that area.

cost price *noun* [*noncount*] *Brit* : the amount of money that is needed to make or get something that you are going to sell ▪ The company has agreed to sell the vaccine ***at cost price***. [=(*US*) *at cost*]

[1]**cos·tume** /ˈkɑːˌstuːm, *Brit* ˈkɒˌstjuːm/ *noun, pl* **-tumes** [*count*]

1 : the clothes that are worn by someone (such as an actor) who is trying to look like a different person or thing ▪ children in their Halloween *costumes* ▪ a colorful clown *costume*

2 : the clothes worn by a group of people especially during a particular time in the past ▪ a formal 18th-century Japanese *costume* ▪ The dancers were dressed in their ***national costumes***. [=the clothing that is traditional in their countries]

3 *Brit* : SWIMSUIT

in costume : wearing a costume ▪ If all the actors are *in costume*, we're ready to begin. ▪ The waiters were all *in* ancient Roman *costume*.

– **cos·tumed** /ˈkɑːˌstuːmd, *Brit* ˈkɒˌstjuːmd/ *adj* ▪ *costumed* actors

[2]**costume** *adj, always used before a noun* : involving people wearing costumes ▪ You're invited to a *costume* party! ▪ a *costume* ball ▪ ***costume dramas*** [=movies that are set in the past in which the actors are dressed like people from the past]

costume jewelry *noun* [*noncount*] : fancy jewelry that is usually made of inexpensive materials rather than real gold, diamonds, etc.

cos·tum·er /ˈkɑːˌstuːmɚ, *Brit* ˈkɒˌstjuːmə/ *noun, pl* **-ers** [*count*] *US* : a person or company that makes, rents, or sells costumes

cos·tu·mi·er /kɑˈstuːmiˌeɪ, *Brit* kɒˈstjuːmiə/ *noun, pl* **-ers** [*count*] *Brit* : COSTUMER

cosy *Brit spelling of* COZY

cot /ˈkɑːt/ *noun, pl* **cots** [*count*]

1 *US* : a narrow, light bed often made of cloth stretched over a folding frame — called also (*Brit*) *camp bed*

2 *Brit* : [1]CRIB 1a

cot death *noun, pl* ~ **deaths** [*count, noncount*] *Brit* : SUDDEN INFANT DEATH SYNDROME

co·te·rie /ˈkoutəri/ *noun, pl* **-ries** [*count*] *formal* : a small group of people who are interested in the same thing and who usually do not allow other people to join the group • her *coterie* of fellow musicians • His films are admired by a small *coterie* of critics.

co·til·lion /kouˈtɪljən/ *noun, pl* **-lions** [*count*] *chiefly US, formal* : a large formal party for dancing : BALL

cot·tage /ˈkɑ:tɪʤ/ *noun, pl* **-tag·es** [*count*] : a small house especially in the country • We rented a *cottage* for the weekend. • She owns a *cottage* at the beach.

cottage cheese *noun* [*noncount*] : a type of soft white cheese that has a mild flavor

cottage hospital *noun, pl* ~ **-tals** [*count*] *Brit* : a small hospital in the country

cottage industry *noun, pl* ~ **-tries** [*count*] : a system for making products to sell in which people work in their own homes and use their own equipment • weaving, pottery, and other *cottage industries*

cot·tag·er /ˈkɑ:tɪʤɚ/ *noun, pl* **-ers** [*count*] : a person who lives in a cottage

[1]**cot·ton** /ˈkɑ:tn̩/ *noun, pl* **-tons**

1 [*noncount*] : a soft, white material that grows on the seeds of a tall plant and that is used to make cloth • They are in the field picking *cotton*. • bales of *cotton*; *also* : the plants on which this material grows • He grows *cotton*. • fields of *cotton*

2 [*count, noncount*] : cloth that is made of cotton • shirts/sheets made from *cotton*; *also* : clothing that is made of this cloth • She doesn't wear *cotton* in the winter.

3 [*noncount*] *chiefly Brit* : yarn that is made of cotton

4 [*noncount*] *US* : COTTON WOOL

– **cotton** *adj* • *cotton* fabrics/dresses • The dress is *cotton*.

[2]**cotton** *verb* **-tons; -toned; -ton·ing**

cotton on [*phrasal verb*] *informal* : to begin to understand something : to catch on • It took a while, but they are finally starting to *cotton on*. — often + *to* • She *cottoned on to* the fact that I like her.

cotton to [*phrasal verb*] ***cotton to (someone or something)*** *US, informal* : to begin to like someone or something • We *cottoned to* our new neighbors right away. • He doesn't *cotton to* the idea of having children.

cotton ball *noun, pl* ~ **balls** [*count*] *US* : a small ball of cotton that can be used for a variety of purposes (such as removing makeup or cleaning a wound) and that is usually used once and then thrown away • a bag of *cotton balls* — called also (*Brit*) *cotton wool ball*

cotton bud *noun, pl* ~ **buds** [*count*] *Brit* : COTTON SWAB

cotton candy *noun* [*noncount*] *US* : candy made from sugar that is boiled, spun into a soft material using a special machine, and then wound around a stick — called also (*Brit*) *candy floss*

cotton gin *noun, pl* ~ **gins** [*count*] : a machine that separates the seeds of cotton plants from the cotton

cot·ton·mouth /ˈkɑ:tn̩ˌmauθ/ *noun, pl* **-mouths** [*count*] : WATER MOCCASIN

cottonmouth moccasin *noun, pl* ~ **-sins** [*count*] : WATER MOCCASIN

cot·ton–pick·ing /ˈkɑ:tn̩ˌpɪkən/ *adj, always used before a noun, US, old-fashioned + informal* — used to make a statement more forceful • She didn't do a *cotton-picking* [=*damned, darned*] thing all day. • Now wait one *cotton-picking* minute! • He is a *cotton-picking* [=*damned*] hypocrite.

cotton swab *noun, pl* ~ **swabs** [*count*] : a short stick that has round pieces of cotton at both ends — called also (*Brit*) *cotton bud*; compare Q-TIPS

cot·ton·tail /ˈkɑ:tn̩ˌteɪl/ *noun, pl* **-tails** [*count*] : a small rabbit with a white tail

cot·ton·wood /ˈkɑ:tn̩ˌwʊd/ *noun, pl* **-woods** [*count*] : a type of tree that grows in the U.S. and has seeds that look like they are covered with cotton

cotton wool *noun* [*noncount*] *Brit* : a mass of cotton that is used especially for cleaning the skin or wounds

cotton wool ball *noun, pl* ~ **balls** [*count*] *Brit* : COTTON BALL

cot·tony /ˈkɑ:tni/ *adj* [*more* ~; *most* ~] : like cotton : soft, fluffy, or covered with small soft hairs • The toys are stuffed with a *cottony* material. • *cottony* clouds • The flowers are small and *cottony*.

[1]**couch** /ˈkaʊʧ/ *noun, pl* **couch·es** [*count*]

1 : a long piece of furniture on which a person can sit or lie down : SOFA — see picture at LIVING ROOM

2 : a piece of furniture for a patient to lie on at a doctor's office • a psychiatrist's *couch*

[2]**couch** *verb* **couches; couched; couch·ing** [+ *obj*] *formal* : to say or express (something) in a particular way — usually used as *(be) couched*; usually + *in* • The letter *was couched in* polite terms.

couch potato *noun, pl* ~ **-toes** [*count*] *informal + disapproving* : someone who spends a lot of time sitting and watching television

cou·gar /ˈku:gɚ/ *noun, pl* **cou·gars** *also* **cougar** [*count*] : a large brownish cat that was once common in North and South America — called also *mountain lion*, (*US*) *panther*, *puma*; see picture at CAT

[1]**cough** /ˈkɑ:f/ *verb* **coughs; coughed; cough·ing** [*no obj*]

1 : to force air through your throat with a short, loud noise often because you are sick • She was *coughing* and sneezing all day. • The dust made him *cough*.

2 : to make a noise like that of coughing • The engine *coughed* and sputtered and then stopped.

cough up [*phrasal verb*] ***cough up (something) or cough (something) up*** **1** : to have (something, such as blood) come up through your throat and out of your mouth when you cough • He was *coughing up* blood. **2** *informal* : to give (something, such as money or information) to someone especially when you do not want to • We had to *cough up* an extra hundred dollars for the car rental. • The police made the suspect *cough up* the names of his accomplices. **3** *US, sports* : to fail to keep or hold (something) • The quarterback *coughed up* [=*fumbled*] the ball. • They *coughed up* [=*lost, gave up*] the lead in the second half.

[2]**cough** *noun, pl* **coughs** [*count*]

1 : a physical condition or illness that causes someone to cough • He has a *cough* and a cold. • They both have bad *coughs*. • He has a terrible **smoker's cough**. [=a cough caused by smoking] — see also WHOOPING COUGH

2 : an act of coughing or the sound made when someone coughs • I heard a *cough* from the back of the church. • He gave a *cough* [=he coughed] to get my attention. • dry/hacking *coughs*

cough drop *noun, pl* ~ **drops** [*count*] : a small piece of candy that contains medicine to prevent coughing

cough syrup *noun* [*noncount*] : a usually sweet liquid that contains medicine used to stop coughing — called also *cough medicine*, (*Brit*) *cough mixture*

could /ˈkʊd, kəd/ *verb* [*modal verb*]

1 — used as the past tense of *can* • When I was younger I *could* run fast, but I can't run fast now. • Years ago you *could* buy a record album for a quarter. • The car cost more than I *could* afford, so I bought a cheaper model. • From where we stood, we *could* see for miles. • She *could* be very rude at times. [=she was sometimes very rude] • He never *could* quite fit in with the group. • She said we *could* do whatever we wanted. [=she said, "You can do whatever you want."] • How *could* something like this happen? ***usage*** see [1]CAN

2 a — used to say that something is possible • You *could* [=*might, may*] be making the biggest mistake of your life! • This *could* be our only chance to get our of here. • His recovery *could* take months. • This medicine *could* help your cold. • The evidence is not conclusive, but he *could* (very well) be right. • This news *could* mean trouble. • Did you think he *could* still be alive? • That kind of thing *could* happen to anyone. • They *could* still succeed, although it's not likely. • I think he *could* be trying to cheat us. • Do you think he *could* [=*can*] really be serious? • *Could* this be our ride? [=is this our ride?] **b** — used with *have* to say that something was possible but did not actually happen • You *could have* been seriously hurt. • The accident *could have* been worse. • The movie *could have* been better. [=the movie wasn't very good] • They *could have* succeeded if they had worked harder. • The error *could* have lost the game for them. • We *could* just as easily *have* fixed the engine ourselves. **c** — used to talk about something that is not possible but that is hoped or wished for • We would go if only we *could*—but unfortunately we can't. • We would have gone if only we *could* have—but unfortunately we couldn't. • I wish I *could* fly! = (*formal*) Would that I *could* fly!

3 — used in speech to make a polite request or suggestion • *Could* you please pass me the salt? • *Could* [=*can*] I leave a little early today? • If you *could* come early, we would be pleased. • "*Could* I do it tomorrow instead of today?" "Yes,

you can." • *Could* I get you a cup of coffee? [=do you want a cup of coffee?] • If tape doesn't work, you *could* try glue. • "Where can I stay?" "Well, you ***could always*** stay with me."
4 — used to say that you are annoyed by something that was or was not done • He *could* have at least paid for dessert! • Why are you always late? You *could* try being on time for once! • If she wasn't going to make it, she *could* have called. • You *could* at least tell me why you were late!
5 — used in statements that express a strong emotional reaction • I *could* have died of embarrassment! [=I was very embarrassed] • I *could* just kill him! [=I am very angry at him] • When she told me I'd won, I *could* almost have hugged her! [=I felt like hugging her] • I'm so frustrated I *could* scream! [=I feel like screaming]
6 — used in statements that describe something as very bad, good, etc. • What *could* be better than this? • Registering *could* not be simpler. [=registering is very simple] • I *could* hardly be more pleased [=I'm very pleased] with the way things are going. • The situation ***couldn't be worse/better***. [=the situation is as bad/good as it can be] • I ***couldn't be happier*** [=I'm very happy] with the way our new kitchen looks.
could care less see [2]CARE
could do with ✧ If you *could do with* something, you need it or would be helped by getting or having it. • Is there a restaurant nearby? I *could do with* something to eat. • This room *could do with* a fresh coat of paint.

couldn't /ˈkʊdn̩t/ — used as a contraction of *could not* • I tried but I *couldn't* do it.
couldn't care less see [2]CARE

could've /ˈkʊdəv/ — used as a contraction of *could have* • I *could've* done it if I had more time.

cou·lis /kuˈliː/ *noun, pl* **cou·lis** /kuˈliːz/ [*count, noncount*] : a thick sauce made from vegetables or fruit • raspberry *coulis*

[1]**coun·cil** /ˈkaʊnsəl/ *noun, pl* **-cils** [*count*]
1 : a group of people who are chosen to make rules, laws, or decisions about something • The city *council* is considering a ban on smoking in restaurants. • the town/parish *council* • a national security *council* • a tribal *council*
2 : a group of people who provide advice or guidance on something • the governor's *council* on physical fitness • the king's *council*

Do not confuse *council* with *counsel.*

[2]**council** *adj, always used before a noun*
1 : of or relating to a council • a *council* member/meeting
2 *Brit* **:** provided by a local government council for people to live in for low rent • *council* estates/houses/flats

coun·cil·lor *or US* **coun·cil·or** /ˈkaʊnslɚ/ *noun, pl* **-cil·lors** *or US* **-cil·ors** [*count*] **:** a member of a council • a city *councillor*

Do not confuse *councillor* with *counselor.*

coun·cil·man /ˈkaʊnsəlmən/ *noun, pl* **-men** /-mən/ [*count*] *US* **:** a person (especially a man) who is a member of a council • a city *councilman*

council·wom·an /ˈkaʊnsəlˌwʊmən/ *noun, pl* **-wom·en** /-ˌwɪmən/ [*count*] *US* **:** a woman who is a member of a council • a town *councilwoman*

[1]**coun·sel** /ˈkaʊnsəl/ *noun, pl* **counsel**
1 [*noncount*] *formal* **:** advice given to someone • You were unwise to reject my *counsel.* • The student sought *counsel* from her teacher.
2 *law* **:** a lawyer who represents a person or group in a court of law [*noncount*] She is serving as *counsel* for the defendant. • On the advice of *counsel* [=because of the lawyer's advice], she refused to answer the question. [*count*] the company's chief/general *counsel* • a defense/legal *counsel* • All *counsel* are expected to obey the rules of the court.

Do not confuse *counsel* with *council.*

[2]**counsel** *verb* **-sels**; *US* **-seled** *or Brit* **-selled**; *US* **-sel·ing** *or Brit* **-sel·ling** [+ *obj*] *formal*
1 a : to give advice to (someone) • She *counseled* [=*advised*] him not to accept the offer. **b :** to listen to and give support or advice to (someone) especially as a job • He *counsels* people who are trying to quit drinking.
2 : to suggest or recommend (something) • The President's advisers *counseled* [=*advised*] restraint until the incident had been investigated.

counseling (*US*) *or Brit* **counselling** *noun* [*noncount*] **:** advice and support that is given to people to help them deal with problems, make important decisions, etc. • She is receiving *counseling* to cope with the death of her husband. • The college offers career *counseling.* • drug/debt *counseling*

coun·sel·or (*US*) *or chiefly Brit* **coun·sel·lor** /ˈkaʊnslɚ/ *noun, pl US* **-sel·ors** *or chiefly Brit* **-sel·lors** [*count*]
1 : a person who provides advice as a job **:** a person who counsels people • a marriage *counselor* • a school ***guidance counselor*** [=a person who gives students advice about school, college, etc.]
2 *US* **:** a person who is in charge of young people at a summer camp • He works as a camp *counselor.*
3 *US* **:** LAWYER • a ***counselor at law*** — often used as a form of address • I'd like to speak with you, *Counselor.*

Do not confuse *counselor* with *councillor.*

[1]**count** /ˈkaʊnt/ *verb* **counts; count·ed; count·ing**
1 a : to add (people or things) together to find the total number [+ *obj*] *Count* the plates on the table. • She made sure to *count* her change. • *Count* how many fingers I am holding up. • He *counted* seven deer in the field. • When it comes to books, I have ***too many to count***. [=I have a lot of books] • She is ***counting calories***. [=she counts the number of calories in the food she eats so that she won't eat too much] — often + *up* • She was *counting up* the money in the envelope. • All the votes were *counted up*, and he was the winner. [*no obj*] There are 10 days left until the end of school, *counting* from today. • Keep *counting* until there are no more left to count. • Don't interrupt me. I'm *counting.* **b** [*no obj*] **:** to say numbers in order • Can your daughter *count* yet? • The teacher taught the students to *count* by 10s. [=to say "10, 20, 30, etc."] — often + *to* or *up to* • My son can *count to* one hundred. • He *counted up to* 10 and then stopped.
2 [+ *obj*] **:** to include (someone or something) in a total • She *counts* [=*numbers*] several musicians among her friends. [=her friends include musicians] • There will be 150 people at the wedding, not *counting* children.
3 [*no obj*] **:** to be accepted or allowed officially • There was a penalty on the play, so the goal does not *count.* [=the goal is not allowed]
4 a [+ *obj*] **:** to consider or regard (someone or something) in a specified way • I *count* myself lucky. — often + *as* • I don't *count* him *as* my friend anymore. • She was *counted as* absent from school that day. **b** [*no obj*] **:** to be considered or regarded *as* something • A laptop computer *counts as* a piece of luggage on the plane. • The job is so easy that it hardly *counts as* work. [=it can hardly be considered to be work]
5 [*no obj*] **:** to have value or importance • Every vote *counts.* • He played well in the play-offs, when it really *counted.* [=*mattered*] — often + *for* • My effort in class has to *count for* something! • Her promises don't *count for* much. [=his promises don't have much value]
6 *always followed by an adverb or preposition* **:** to be considered in a specified way when a person or thing is being judged [*no obj*] His experience *counts* in his favor. [=his experience is a good thing that is in his favor] • His lack of experience *counts* against him. • A wrong answer on the quiz will not *count* against [=will not hurt] your final grade. [+ *obj*] They *counted* his lack of job experience against him. • A wrong answer on the quiz will not be *counted* against your final grade.
and counting **:** with more to come • He is 47 years old *and counting.* • They have been in business for 50 years *and counting.*
count down [*phrasal verb*] **1 :** to count numbers in a reverse order from higher numbers to lower ones • He *counted down* from 10 to 1. **2 *count down (something)* also *count (something) down* :** to pay close attention to the number of (days, miles, etc.) that remain until a particular moment or event is reached • He is *counting down* the days left in the school year. [=he is eagerly looking forward to the end of the school year] • We were *counting down* the miles as we approached our destination.
count heads **:** to count how many people are present at a place • The coach *counted heads* before the bus left.
count in [*phrasal verb*] ***count (someone) in*** **:** to plan to include (someone) in an activity **:** to consider (someone) as one of the people who will be doing something • "Do you want to go to the beach with us?" "Yes! *Count* me *in!*"
count off [*phrasal verb*] **1 :** to count numbers that are spaced a certain number apart • The students *counted off* by twos. [=counted 2, 4, 6, 8, etc.] **2 *count off (something)* or *count (something) off* :** to list (something) out loud • She *counted off* all the things she wanted to do.

count on/upon [*phrasal verb*] **1** ***count on/upon (someone)*** **a** : to trust (someone) : to rely or depend on (someone) to do something ▪ He isn't someone you can *count on* all the time. ▪ I am *counting on* you to help me through this difficult time. ▪ She is *counted on* [=*trusted*] as a leader. **b** : to expect (someone) to do something ▪ I wouldn't *count on* him to win the match. **2** ***count on/upon (something)*** : to expect (something) to happen ▪ My parents might loan me some money, but I can't *count on* it. ▪ She is *counting on* a big tax refund this year. ▪ The kids are *counting on* going to the movies. Don't disappoint them! ▪ They were not *counting on* getting a flat tire on the way to the restaurant.

count out [*phrasal verb*] **1** ***count (someone) out*** : to not include (someone) in an activity ▪ If you are looking for people to help you clean the house today, *count* me *out*. [=don't include me; I won't be helping you] **2** ***count (someone or something) out*** *or* ***count out (someone or something)*** : to decide that (someone or something) cannot win or succeed ▪ Don't *count out* our team just yet. They could still win.

count the cost : to feel the bad effects of a mistake, accident, etc. ▪ He was careless and now he's *counting the cost*. = Now he's *counting the cost* of his carelessness.

count toward/towards [*phrasal verb*] ***count toward/towards (something)*** *or* ***count (something) toward/towards (something)*** : to have value as a credit or payment in relation to (something) ▪ The credits you earned for this class *count toward* your degree. [=they are added to the total number of credits you have earned for your degree] — often used as *(be) counted toward/towards* ▪ Fifty dollars will *be counted towards* [=*credited to*] your next bill.

count your blessings see BLESSING

count your chickens before they hatch see [1]CHICKEN

stand up and be counted see [1]STAND

who's counting? *informal + humorous* — used to say that you do not care about how large a number is ▪ Tomorrow's my 80th birthday, but *who's counting*?

[2]**count** *noun, pl* **counts**

1 [*count*] **a** : an act or process of adding people or things together to find the total number : an act or process of counting — usually singular ▪ They completed the ballot *count* late last night. ▪ At (my) last *count* [=the last time I counted], I had 50 responses to the invitation. ▪ According to the last *count*, he still needs many more votes. ▪ The official *count* showed that 40 people were killed in the hurricane. ▪ The teacher took/did a quick *count* of the students. [=the teacher quickly counted the students] — see also HEAD COUNT **b** : the total number that is counted — usually singular ▪ The final *count* [=*tally*] of people at the conference was over 200. — see also BLOOD COUNT, BODY COUNT, POLLEN COUNT

2 [*singular*] : an act or process of saying numbers in order until a particular number is reached ▪ The boxer took an eight-*count* before getting up again. [=the referee counted to eight before the boxer got up again] — usually + *of* ▪ I'll give you a *count of* three to get out of here. = I'll give you ***until the count of*** three to get out of here. ▪ If you're not out of here ***by the count of*** three [=by the time I count to three], I'm calling the police. ▪ Jump off the diving board ***at the count of*** 10. [=when I say "10" after counting "one, two, three, . . . " etc.] ▪ Hold your breath ***for a count of*** 10. [=for the amount of time that it takes to count to 10]

3 [*count*] *law* : one of the crimes that someone is charged with — often + *of* ▪ She was charged with two *counts of* theft, and she was found guilty on both *counts*.

4 [*count*] : an idea or opinion that is expressed in a statement, argument, etc. ▪ The theory is wrong ***on all/several counts***. [=all/several parts of the theory are wrong] ▪ I agree with you ***on both counts***. [=I agree with both the points you have made]

5 ***the count*** *baseball* : the number of balls and strikes that have been pitched to a batter ▪ *The count* is two balls, two strikes. ▪ He was behind/ahead in *the count*. [=he had more/fewer strikes than balls against him] ✧ A ***full count*** is a situation in baseball in which a batter has three balls and two strikes.

down for the count (*US*) *or* ***out for the count*** *of a boxer* : knocked down and unable to get up again while the referee counts to 10 ▪ The boxer was *down for the count*. [=*knocked out*] — often used figuratively ▪ The company may be about to go *down for the count*. [=may be about to fail completely and go out of business] ▪ Two minutes after getting into bed, I was *out for the count*. [=I was sleeping deeply]

keep count : to remember or keep a record of a number or total ▪ He's has had so many different girlfriends lately that I no longer can *keep count*. ▪ She is *keeping count* [=*keeping track*] of the hours she spends watching TV.

lose count : to forget a number or total ▪ I've *lost count* [=*lost track*] of how many different girlfriends he's had. ▪ I was counting the money when he interrupted me and made me *lose count*.

– compare [3]COUNT

[3]**count** *noun, pl* **counts** [*count*] : a nobleman in some European counties who has a high rank similar to a British earl — compare [2]COUNT

count·down /ˈkaʊntˌdaʊn/ *noun, pl* **-downs** [*count*]

1 : the act of counting down the number of seconds that remain before something (such as the launch of a rocket) happens — usually singular ▪ Begin the *countdown*. ▪ The engineers stopped the *countdown* because something was wrong with the engine.

2 : the period of time before an important or special event — usually singular; usually + *to* ▪ the *countdown to* summer vacation ▪ the steady *countdown to* war

[1]**coun·te·nance** /ˈkaʊntn̩əns/ *noun, pl* **-nanc·es** [*count*] *formal + literary* : the appearance of a person's face : a person's expression ▪ The photograph showed his somber *countenance*.

[2]**countenance** *verb* **-nances**; **-nanced**; **-nanc·ing** [+ *obj*] *formal* : to accept, support, or approve of (something) ▪ The city would not *countenance* [=*permit*] a rock concert in the park. ▪ The leader did not officially *countenance* [=*encourage*] negotiations with the rebels.

[1]**count·er** /ˈkaʊntɚ/ *noun, pl* **-ers** [*count*]

1 : a piece of furniture with a flat surface that workers and customers stand on opposite sides of when doing business in a store, restaurant, etc. ▪ He walked up to the *counter* and ordered his food. ▪ There was a long line at the sales/checkout *counter*. ▪ I put my money down on the *counter*. ▪ She recognized the man ***behind the counter***. — see also LUNCH COUNTER

2 *US* **a** : a long, flat surface on which food is prepared in a kitchen ▪ a kitchen *counter* ▪ I wish my kitchen had more ***counter space***. [=I wish it had more counters or a bigger counter] — called also *countertop*, (*Brit*) *worktop*; see picture at KITCHEN **b** : a flat surface around a sink in a bathroom ▪ a bathroom *counter* — called also *countertop*

3 : a small object that is used in some board games

over the counter : without a special note (called a prescription) from a doctor ▪ The drug is available *over the counter*.

under the counter : secretly and usually illegally ▪ The workers were paid *under the counter*. [=*under the table*]

– compare [2]COUNTER, [4]COUNTER

[2]**counter** *noun, pl* **-ers** [*count*] : a person or device that counts something ▪ The *counter* records how many people visit the Web site. — see also BEAN COUNTER, GEIGER COUNTER — compare [1]COUNTER, [4]COUNTER

[3]**coun·ter** /ˈkaʊntɚ/ *verb* **-ters**; **-tered**; **-ter·ing**

1 a [*no obj*] : to do something in defense or in response to something — often + *with* ▪ She *countered with* some of the most brilliant chess moves ever seen. ▪ He *countered with* a punch to the other fighter's head. **b** [+ *obj*] : to make (something) less effective or ineffective ▪ This pill will *counter* [=*counteract*] the side effects of the other one.

2 : to say (something) in response to something that another person has said [+ *obj*] When they blamed him for the collapse of the bridge, he *countered* that his warnings about the bridge had been ignored. ▪ "I could say the same thing about you," she *countered*. [*no obj*] After she made her point, he could not *counter* with anything.

[4]**counter** *noun, pl* **-ters** [*count*] *formal* : something that is made or done as a defense against or response to something else : something that makes something else less effective or ineffective — usually singular; usually + *to* ▪ The policy is intended as a *counter* to efforts to decrease spending on education. — compare [1]COUNTER, [2]COUNTER

[5]**counter** *adv* : in a way that goes against or does not agree with something — + *to* ▪ The soldier acted *counter to* his orders. [=he did something that was against his orders] ▪ His theory ***ran counter to*** [=was opposed to; did not agree with] the beliefs of his time. ▪ Such behavior *runs counter to* the values of society.

coun·ter- /ˈkaʊntɚ/ *prefix*

1 : in a direction opposite to ▪ *counter*clockwise

2 : as a reaction against ▪ *counter*offensive

C

coun·ter·act /ˌkaʊntɚˈækt/ *verb* **-acts; -act·ed; -act·ing** [+ *obj*] **:** act against (something) **:** to cause (something) to have less of an effect or to have no effect at all ▪ The drug will *counteract* the poison. ▪ The new fees will *counteract* [=*offset*] state cuts in the school's budget.

coun·ter·at·tack /ˈkaʊntərəˌtæk/ *noun, pl* **-tacks** [*count*] **:** an attack that is made in response to an attack by an enemy or opponent ▪ They launched a fierce *counterattack* by air once the fog cleared. ▪ The team finally mounted a *counterattack* in the last quarter of the game.
– **counterattack** *verb* **-tacks; -tacked; -tack·ing** [*no obj*] The enemy *counterattacked* [=*retaliated*] at dawn. [+ *obj*] He quickly *counterattacked* his opponent.

coun·ter·bal·ance /ˌkaʊntɚˌbæləns/ *verb* **-anc·es; -anced; -anc·ing** [+ *obj*] *formal* **:** to have an effect that is opposite but equal to (something) **:** to balance (something) by being opposite ▪ Improved services for phone customers have been *counterbalanced* [=*offset*] by higher fees. ▪ The author's wry humor *counterbalances* the book's serious subject matter.
– **counterbalance** *noun, pl* **-anc·es** [*count*] ▪ The author's wry humor is a good *counterbalance* to the book's serious subject matter.

coun·ter·clock·wise /ˌkaʊntɚˈklɑːkˌwaɪz/ *adv, US* **:** in the direction opposite to movement of a clock's hands ▪ Turn the screw *counterclockwise* [=*(Brit) anticlockwise*] one full turn. — opposite CLOCKWISE
– **counterclockwise** *adj* ▪ a *counterclockwise* [=*(Brit) anticlockwise*] direction

coun·ter·cul·ture /ˈkaʊntɚˌkʌltʃɚ/ *noun, pl* **-tures** [*count*] **:** a culture with values and customs are very different from and usually opposed to those accepted by most of society ▪ the *counterculture* of the hippies; *also* **:** the people who make up a counterculture ▪ He was part of the antiwar *counterculture*. ▪ the drug *counterculture* — often used before another noun ▪ *counterculture* heroes/publications/struggles
– **coun·ter·cul·tur·al** /ˌkaʊntɚˈkʌltʃərəl/ *adj* ▪ *countercultural* movements/values/ideas

coun·ter·es·pi·o·nage /ˌkaʊntɚˈɛspijəˌnɑːʒ/ *noun* [*noncount*] *formal* **:** the activity of preventing or stopping enemies from spying ▪ He was involved in *counterespionage* against Germany in World War II.

¹coun·ter·feit /ˈkaʊntɚˌfɪt/ *verb* **-feits; -feit·ed; -feit·ing** [+ *obj*] **:** to make an exact copy of (something) in order to trick people ▪ They were *counterfeiting* money in his garage. ▪ He *counterfeited* [=*forged*] the documents.
– **counterfeiting** *noun* [*noncount*] ▪ He was sent to jail for *counterfeiting*. – **coun·ter·feit·er** *noun, pl* **-ers** [*count*]

²counterfeit *adj* **:** made to look like an exact copy of something in order to trick people ▪ *counterfeit* money/bills/currency ▪ The concert ticket is *counterfeit*.

³counterfeit *noun, pl* **-feits** [*count*] **:** something that is made to look like an exact copy of something else in order to trick people ▪ The 100-dollar bill turned out to be a *counterfeit*. [=*fake, phony*]

coun·ter·foil /ˈkaʊntɚˌfojəl/ *noun, pl* **-foils** [*count*] *chiefly Brit* **:** the part of a check, ticket, etc., that can be kept as a record when it is torn off **:** STUB

coun·ter·in·sur·gen·cy /ˌkaʊntərɪnˈsɚdʒənsi/ *noun, pl* **-cies** *formal* **:** action by a group, army, etc., against people who are fighting to take control of a government [*count*] The military has launched a *counterinsurgency*. [*noncount*] an expert in *counterinsurgency* — often used before another noun ▪ a *counterinsurgency* operation
– **coun·ter·in·sur·gent** *noun, pl* **-gents** [*count*] ▪ a band of *counterinsurgents*

coun·ter·in·tel·li·gence /ˌkaʊntərɪnˈtɛlədʒəns/ *noun* [*noncount*] *formal* **:** activity meant to hide the truth from an enemy or to prevent the enemy from learning secret information — often used before another noun ▪ *counterintelligence* agents/operations

coun·ter·in·tu·i·tive /ˌkaʊntərɪnˈtuːwətɪv, *Brit* ˌkaʊntərɪnˈtjuːətɪv/ *adj* [*more* ~; *most* ~] *formal* **:** different from what you would expect **:** not agreeing with what seems right or natural ▪ It may seem *counterintuitive*, but we do burn calories when we are sleeping. ▪ *counterintuitive* results

coun·ter·mand /ˈkaʊntɚˌmænd, *Brit* ˈkaʊntəˌmɑːnd/ *verb* **-mands; -mand·ed; -mand·ing** [+ *obj*] *formal* **:** to cancel (an order) especially by giving a new order ▪ Orders to blow up the bridge were *countermanded*.

coun·ter·mea·sure /ˈkaʊntɚˌmɛʒɚ/ *noun, pl* **-sures** [*count*] **:** an action or device that is intended to stop or prevent something bad or dangerous — usually plural ▪ new *countermeasures* against terrorism ▪ The army used electronic *countermeasures* to block enemy radar.

coun·ter·of·fen·sive /ˈkaʊntərəˈfɛnsɪv/ *noun, pl* **-sives** [*count*] **:** an attack made in order to defend against an enemy or opponent ▪ They mounted/launched a *counteroffensive* against the enemy.

coun·ter·of·fer /ˈkaʊntɚˌɑːfɚ/ *noun, pl* **-fers** [*count*] **:** an offer that is made by someone in response to a previous offer ▪ He turned down the deal and came back with a *counteroffer* asking for more money.

coun·ter·part /ˈkaʊntɚˌpɑɚt/ *noun, pl* **-parts** [*count*] **:** someone or something that has the same job or purpose as another ▪ The secretary of defense met with his *counterparts* in Asia to discuss the nuclear crisis. ▪ Metal tools replaced their stone *counterparts* many, many years ago. ▪ the lead actress and her male *counterpart*

¹coun·ter·point /ˈkaʊntɚˌpoɪnt/ *noun, pl* **-points**
1 *music* **a :** a combination of two or more melodies that are played together [*count*] a two-person *counterpoint* [*noncount*] The guitar and bass are played in *counterpoint*. **b** [*count*] **:** a melody played in combination with another
2 *formal* **:** something that is different from something else in usually a pleasing way [*count*] The dressing is a refreshing *counterpoint to* the spicy chicken. ▪ The painting is a pleasant *counterpoint to* his earlier works. [*noncount*] The music works in *counterpoint to* the images on the screen.

²counterpoint *verb* **-points; -point·ed; -point·ing** [+ *obj*] *formal* **:** to put two things together in a way that shows how different they are from each other **:** CONTRAST ▪ The violence of the movie is *counterpointed* by/with ironic humor.

coun·ter·pro·duc·tive /ˈkaʊntɚprəˈdʌktɪv/ *adj* [*more* ~; *most* ~] **:** not helpful **:** making the thing you want to happen less likely to happen ▪ His uncontrollable anger is very *counterproductive* to his attempt at saving his marriage. ▪ a *counterproductive* approach

coun·ter·rev·o·lu·tion /ˈkaʊntɚˌrɛvəˈluːʃən/ *noun, pl* **-tions :** action by a group, army, etc., that is done to overthrow a government that is in power because of an earlier revolution [*noncount*] The leader vowed to stop any attempt at *counterrevolution*. [*count*] Soldiers loyal to the President led the *counterrevolution*.
– **coun·ter·rev·o·lu·tion·ary** /ˈkaʊntɚˌrɛvəˈluːʃəˌneri, *Brit* ˈkaʊntəˌrɛvəˈluːʃənri/ *adj* ▪ *counterrevolutionary* forces
– **counterrevolutionary** *noun, pl* **-ar·ies** [*count*]

coun·ter·sign /ˈkaʊntɚˌsaɪn/ *verb* **-signs; -signed; -sign·ing** [+ *obj*] **:** to sign (a document) after another person has already signed it especially to show that it is valid or authentic ▪ The order has to be *countersigned* by a doctor.

coun·ter·ter·ror·ism /ˈkaʊntɚˈterəˌrɪzəm/ *noun* [*noncount*] **:** actions by a group, army, etc., that are done to prevent terrorist attacks and destroy terrorist networks — often used before another noun ▪ a *counterterrorism* agency
– **coun·ter·ter·ror·ist** /ˈkaʊntɚˈterərɪst/ *adj* ▪ *counterterrorist* strategy

coun·ter·top /ˈkaʊntɚˌtɑːp/ *noun, pl* **-tops** *US* **:** ¹COUNTER 2

coun·ter·vail·ing /ˌkaʊntɚˈveɪlɪŋ/ *adj, always used before a noun, formal* **:** having an equal but opposite effect ▪ *countervailing* influences ▪ The policy has many faults and many *countervailing* virtues.

coun·ter·weight /ˈkaʊntɚˌweɪt/ *noun, pl* **-weights** [*count*] **:** a weight that provides a balance against something of equal weight ▪ The crane has a heavy *counterweight* on the back. — often used figuratively ▪ Their liberal views act as a *counterweight* to/against the governor's conservatism.

count·ess /ˈkaʊntəs/ *noun, pl* **-ess·es** [*count*]
1 : the wife of a count or an earl
2 : a woman who has the rank of count or earl

count·less /ˈkaʊntləs/ *adj* **:** too many to be counted **:** very many ▪ He has written *countless* [=*numerous*] magazine and newspaper articles. ▪ There are *countless* reasons why that would not be a good idea. ▪ I've been there *countless* times.

count noun *noun, pl* ~ **nouns** [*count*] *grammar* **:** a noun (such as *bean* or *ball*) that has both a singular and plural form and can be used after a numeral, after words such as *many* or *few*, or after the indefinite article *a* or *an* — compare NONCOUNT NOUN

coun·tri·fied /ˈkʌntrɪˌfaɪd/ *adj* [*more* ~; *most* ~] *informal*
1 : suited to the country instead of the city ▪ a *countrified* man ▪ a restaurant with a *countrified* atmosphere
2 : played or sung like country music ▪ *countrified* rock

C

[1]**coun·try** /ˈkʌntri/ *noun, pl* **-tries**
1 a [*count*] : an area of land that is controlled by its own government : NATION • The two *countries* have a lot in common. • European/foreign *countries* • They drove across the *country* from California to New York. • They are living in different parts of the *country*. — see also MOTHER COUNTRY, OLD COUNTRY **b** ***the country*** : the people who live in a country • *The* whole *country* was stunned by the news. • The President has the support of most of *the country*.
2 [*noncount*] : an area or region that has a particular quality or feature or is known for a particular activity. • He moved to the north *country* to fish and hunt. • We went camping in the hill *country*. • They drove through miles of open *country*. • We took a trip to wine *country*. [=an area where grapes are grown and wine is made]
3 ***the country*** : land that is away from big towns and cities : COUNTRYSIDE • She lives out in *the country*. • They prefer *the country* to the city.
4 [*noncount*] : COUNTRY MUSIC • She loves *country* and rock.
across country **1** : from one side of a country to the other. • They drove *across country*. **2** : from one side of the countryside to the other • The river runs *across country*. : by a course going directly over the countryside rather than by roads • The group walked *across country*. — see also CROSS-COUNTRY
go to the country *Brit* : to call for a general election to be held • He *went to the country* and won.

[2]**country** *adj, always used before a noun*
1 : of, relating to, or characteristic of the country • a *country* town/road • *country* living/comforts • *country* folk
2 : of or relating to country music • a *country* singer • *country* radio

country and western *noun* [*noncount*] : COUNTRY MUSIC

country club *noun, pl* **~ clubs** [*count*] : a private club where people go for social events and to play golf, tennis, etc.

coun·try dance /ˈkʌntriˌdæns, *Brit* ˈkʌntriˌdɑːns/ *noun* [*noncount*] : a dance in which couples dance in long lines or circles
– country dancing *noun* [*noncount*]

country house *noun, pl* **~ houses** [*count*] : a large house in the country typically owned by someone who also has a home in a city

coun·try·man /ˈkʌntrimən/ *noun, pl* **-men** /-mən/ [*count*] *formal*
1 : a person who lives in or comes from the same country as you : COMPATRIOT • my fellow *countrymen*
2 *Brit* : a person who lives in the countryside

country mile *noun* [*singular*] *informal* : a long distance • He lives a *country mile* from the nearest store. • She beat the other swimmers by a *country mile*.

country music *noun* [*noncount*] : a style of music that developed in the southern and western U.S. and that often contains lyrics relating to the lives of people who live in the country

country rock *noun* [*noncount*] : a type of rock music that sounds similar to country music

country seat *noun, pl* **~ seats** [*count*] *chiefly Brit* : a large house that is built on a large piece of land

coun·try·side /ˈkʌntriˌsaɪd/ *noun* [*noncount*] : land that is away from big towns and cities • She lives in the *countryside*. [=*country*] • We took a long drive through the open *countryside*.

coun·try·wide /ˈkʌntriˈwaɪd/ *adj* : happening or existing in all parts of a country : NATIONWIDE • The murders attracted *countrywide* attention.
– countrywide *adv* • The company has opened several stores *countrywide*.

coun·try·wom·an /ˈkʌntriˌwʊmən/ *noun, pl* **-wom·en** /-ˌwɪmən/ [*count*]
1 : a woman born or living in the same country as someone else
2 *Brit* : a woman who lives in the countryside

coun·ty /ˈkaʊnti/ *noun, pl* **-ties** [*count*] : an area of a state or country that is larger than a city and has its own government to deal with local matters • the largest school district in the *county* — often used before another noun • the *county* sheriff • a *county* fair

county court *noun, pl* **~ courts** [*count*] : a court of law for cases within a county

county seat *noun, pl* **~ seats** [*count*] *US* : the town or city in a county where the government offices and buildings are located

county town *noun, pl* **~ towns** [*count*] *Brit* : COUNTY SEAT

coup /ˈkuː/ *noun, pl* **coups** [*count*]
1 : COUP D'ÉTAT • a military *coup* • a *coup* attempt
2 : an impressive victory or achievement that usually is difficult or unexpected • It was a major *coup* when they got the Vice President to appear on their show for an interview.

coup de grâce *or* **coup de grace** /ˌkuːdəˈgrɑːs/ *noun, pl* **coups de grâce** *or* **coups de grace** /ˌkuːdəˈgrɑːs/ [*count*] *formal*
1 : an action or event that finally ends or destroys something that has been getting weaker or worse • The legislature's decision to cut funding has administered the *coup de grâce* to the governor's proposal.
2 : a hit or shot that kills a person or animal that is suffering

coup d'état *or* **coup d'etat** /ˌkuːˌdeɪˈtɑː/ *noun, pl* **coups d'état** *or* **coup d'etat** /ˌkuːˌdeɪˈtɑː/ [*count*] : a sudden attempt by a small group of people to take over the government usually through violence • a military *coup d'état* • a bloody *coup d'état*

coupe (*US*) *or chiefly Brit* **cou·pé** /kuːˈpeɪ, ˈkuːp, *Brit* ˈkuːpeɪ/ *noun, pl* **coupes** [*count*] : a car that has two doors and that has room for four or sometimes only for two people — compare SEDAN

[1]**cou·ple** /ˈkʌpəl/ *noun, pl* **couples** [*count*]
1 : two people who are married or who have a romantic or sexual relationship • a happily married *couple* • "Are they a *couple*?" "No, they are just good friends." • Seventeen *couples* participated in the survey. • The romance had gone out of their relationship, so they signed up for ***couples therapy***. [=therapy in which a psychologist helps couples solve problems with their relationships]
2 : two people or things that are together : PAIR — usually used in the phrase ***in couples*** • The people were lined up *in couples*.
a couple *informal* **1** : two or a few of something • Can you give me *a couple* more examples? • This one costs *a couple* less dollars than that one. ✧ In informal U.S. English, *a couple* can be used like *a couple of* before a plural noun. • I lost interest in the book after *a couple* chapters. • We owned *a couple* dogs. • We stopped for *a couple* drinks after work. It is often used with periods of time and numbers. • I saw the movie *a couple* nights ago. • We met *a couple* years ago. • I took *a couple* weeks off. • *a couple* hundred people • *a couple* dozen **2** : two or a few • "How many drinks have you had?" "Oh, just *a couple*."
a couple of : two of or a few of : two (things) or a few (things) • It happened *a couple of* days ago. [=two days ago] • I only had *a couple of* sips. • Can you loan me *a couple of* dollars? • I have *a couple of* favorite restaurants I go to. • I'll be ready in *a couple of* minutes. [=I'll be ready soon] • Our schedule is booked solid for *the next couple of* weeks. [=for the next two weeks] • They've lost *the last/previous couple of* games.
– cou·ple·dom /ˈkʌpəldəm/ *noun* [*noncount*] • They are breaking up after eight years of *coupledom*. [=after eight years of being a couple]

[2]**couple** *verb* **couples; cou·pled; cou·pling** [*+ obj*]
1 : to join (two things) together : CONNECT • a device that makes it possible to *couple* the pieces • The coils are loosely/tightly *coupled*.
2 : to join (something) *to* something else : CONNECT • The wire is *coupled to* the terminal. • It took an hour to *couple* the trailer *to* the truck.
couple with [*phrasal verb*] ***couple (something) with (something)*** : to join or combine (something) with (something else) • The exhibit *couples* poems *with* paintings. — usually used as *(be) coupled with* • An oil spill *coupled with* [=*combined with, together with*] strong winds brought disaster. • The team's win, *coupled with* a loss by their rivals, put them in first place.
– cou·pler /ˈkʌplɚ/ *noun, pl* **-plers** [*count*] • The company manufactures trailer *couplers*. [=*couplings, hitches*]

cou·plet /ˈkʌplət/ *noun, pl* **-plets** [*count*] : two lines of poetry that form a unit • a rhyming *couplet* • a poem made up of six *couplets*

cou·pling /ˈkʌplɪŋ/ *noun, pl* **-plings** [*count*]
1 : a device that connects two parts or things • hose *couplings* [=*couplers*] • the *couplings* between railroad cars

2 *formal* : the act of having sex • erotic/illicit *couplings*
3 : the act of combining two things • a/the *coupling* of literature and science

cou·pon /ˈkuːˌpɑːn, ˈkjuːˌpɑːn/ *noun, pl* **-pons** [*count*]
1 : a usually small piece of printed paper that lets you get a service or product for free or at a lower price • Bring in this *coupon* for a free oil change. • I'm always clipping *coupons* from the newspaper to use at the grocery store. • The *coupon* is good for one free ice-cream cone.
2 *chiefly Brit* : a section of an advertisement that you can cut out and mail to a company in order to request information or to order a product or service • Send in this *coupon* for more information.

cour·age /ˈkərɪʤ/ *noun* [*noncount*] : the ability to do something that you know is difficult or dangerous • The troops showed great *courage* [=*bravery*] in battle. • She has the *courage* to support unpopular causes. • It takes *courage* to stand up for your rights. • I finally worked/got up the *courage* [=*nerve*] to tell him the bad news. • They showed great *courage* [=*fearlessness*] and determination. • Eventually she summoned (up) the *courage* to confront him. • They showed ***courage under fire.*** [=they were brave while they were being shot at or while they were being strongly criticized] • He has ***the courage of his convictions.*** [=he is not afraid to do what he believes is right]

cou·ra·geous /kəˈreɪʤəs/ *adj* [*more* ~; *most* ~] : very brave : having or showing courage • a *courageous* soldier • She was a *courageous* woman who wasn't afraid to support unpopular causes. • a *courageous* act/decision • a *courageous* [=*fearless*] companion
— **cou·ra·geous·ly** *adv* • They have fought *courageously* for their rights. — **cou·ra·geous·ness** *noun* [*noncount*] • a leader admired for his *courageousness*

cour·gette /kəˈʒɛt/ *noun, pl* **-gettes** [*count*] *Brit* : ZUCCHINI

¹cou·ri·er /ˈkərijə/ *noun, pl* **-ers** [*count*]
1 : a person whose job is to carry messages, packages, etc., from one person or place to another • A *courier* [=*messenger*] will deliver the photo this afternoon. • Police recently arrested a drug *courier* in our neighborhood. • He worked as a bicycle *courier* in the city. [=a courier who uses a bicycle]
2 : a business that is used to send messages, packages, etc. • The documents were sent by overnight *courier*.
3 *Brit* : a person who is employed by a travel company and whose job is to help people who are on holiday

²courier *verb* **-ers; -ered; -er·ing** [+ *obj*] *chiefly Brit* : to use a courier to send (a message, package, etc.) to a person or place • The package was *couriered* overnight to our offices.

¹course /ˈkoəs/ *noun, pl* **cours·es**
1 [*count*] **a** : the path or direction that something or someone moves along • the *course* of a river • a ship's *course* • The pilot brought the plane back ***on course.*** • The ship was blown ***off course*** by a storm. — often used figuratively • This win puts the team back *on course* for the championship. • The book is generally well written but it occasionally veers *off course.* [=it has some parts that do not seem to be about what the rest of the book is about] • a battle that altered/changed ***the course of history*** [=that changed the way things happened in the years that followed] — see also COLLISION COURSE **b** : a path or route that runners, skiers, bikers, etc., move along especially in a race • a cross-country/marathon/ski *course* — see also OBSTACLE COURSE, RACECOURSE
2 [*count*] **a** : a series of classes about a particular subject in a school • an introductory/training *course* • I'm taking a few writing *courses* [=*classes*] at the university. • She's taking a chemistry *course* this semester. — often used before another noun • *course* materials • *course* work/requirements • I have a light/full ***course load*** this semester. [=I am taking few/many classes this semester] **b** : a group of classes that lead to a degree (sense 5) • (*chiefly Brit*) She's beginning a four-year *course* in chemistry. [=(*US*) a four-year chemistry program] • Students earn the degree after a two-year ***course of study.*** — see also CORRESPONDENCE COURSE, CRASH COURSE, REFRESHER COURSE, SANDWICH COURSE, SURVEY COURSE
3 [*noncount*] : the normal or regular way that something happens over time • There is no cure, but the treatment will slow the *course* of the disease. • It's something you would never see in the normal/ordinary ***course of events.*** [=if things were happening as they usually happen] • payments made in the usual/normal/ordinary ***course of business*** [=as part of doing regular business] • The disease usually ***runs its course*** in a few days. [=develops in the usual way; begins, gets worse, and ends]
4 [*noncount*] — used to describe what happens during a period of time or when something is being done • They met 12 times during/in/over ***the course of*** a year. • facts discovered in *the course of* research • Things will get better ***in the course of time.*** [=things will get better as time passes]
5 [*count*] : a way of behaving or proceeding that you choose • Our wisest *course* is to retreat. • We're trying to determine the best ***course of action*** [=the best actions; the best things to do] at this point.
6 [*count*] *medical* : a series of medicines or medical treatments that are given to someone over a period of time • a new *course* of medication • The doctor prescribed a 10-day *course* of antibiotics. • a short/intensive *course* of therapy
7 [*count*] : a part of a meal that is served separately from other parts • We had salad for the first *course.* • You can choose what you want for the main *course.* • A different wine was served with each *course.* • a five-*course* dinner [=a dinner served in five separate parts]
8 [*count*] : GOLF COURSE • an 18-hole *course*
in due course : after a normal amount of time has passed : in the expected time • His discoveries led, *in due course,* to new forms of treatment. • The reasons will become apparent *in due course.* [=*eventually*]
let nature take its course see NATURE
of course **1** — used to show that what is being said is very obvious or already generally known • We're talking, *of course,* about what happened last night. • She was late and rude—so *of course* she didn't get the job. • *Of course,* it wasn't easy for me to admit I was wrong. • "Has the bus already left?" "*Of course.*" **2** — used informally to give permission or say yes in a way that shows you are very certain • "May I borrow this book?" "*Of course!*" [=*absolutely, certainly*] • "Will you go?" "*Of course!*" • "Are you angry with me for being late?" "***Of course not!***" [=I am not at all angry] • "Did you take the money?" "*Of course not!*" [=I definitely did not] **3** — used to stress that what you are saying is true and you feel no doubt about it • *Of course* we'll be there. We wouldn't miss it for the world! • *Of course* I don't hate you! How could you think such a thing? — see also *as a matter of course* at ¹MATTER
par for the course see PAR
pervert the course of justice see ¹PERVERT
stay the course see ¹STAY

²course *verb, always followed by an adverb or preposition* **courses; coursed; cours·ing** [*no obj*] : to move or flow quickly • the blood *coursing* through my veins • Tears were *coursing* down his cheeks.

¹court /ˈkoət/ *noun, pl* **courts**
1 a [*noncount*] : a formal legal meeting in which evidence about crimes, disagreements, etc., is presented to a judge and often a jury so that decisions can be made according to the law • *Court* is now in session. • *Court* is adjourned for the day. — often used before another noun • a *court* battle/fight • *court* cases/records/costs **b** : a place where legal cases are heard [*count*] There was a large group of protesters outside the *court.* • a lawyer who has appeared in *courts* around the country [*noncount*] His landlord threatened to ***take him to court.*** [=to start a lawsuit against him; to sue him] • The organization is prepared to ***go to court*** [=to start a lawsuit] to stop construction from proceeding. • They were able to settle/resolve the case ***out of court.*** [=without going to court] **c** [*count*] : an official group of people (such as a judge and jury) who listen to evidence and make decisions about legal cases • The case is before the state's highest *court.* • She's a judge on an appellate *court.* • state/federal *courts* • The prosecution has new evidence to submit to the *court.* • Please explain to the *court* what happened that night. • The *court* ruled/declared the law unconstitutional. • The *court* reversed/rejected the lower court's decision.
2 [*count*] : a large flat surface that is shaped like a square or rectangle and that is used for playing games like tennis and basketball • a basketball/tennis *court*
3 a : the place where the leader of a country and especially a king or queen lives and works [*count*] the *courts* of Europe [*noncount*] He spent a lot of time ***at court.*** **b** [*count*] : a king or queen and the people who live and work with him or her • The queen assembled her *court.* • a member of the king's *court*
4 [*count*] **a** — used in the names of short streets • My sister lives on Brynhurst *Court.* — abbr. *Ct.* **b** — used in the

names of apartment buildings or groups of apartment buildings ▪ I live in the Franklin *Court* apartments on Main Street. — see also MOTOR COURT **c** : COURTYARD ▪ the villa's inner *court* ▪ an interior *court* garden — see also FOOD COURT

hold court : to talk to a group of people who listen to what you say because it is funny or interesting ▪ The restaurant's owner was *holding court* at his usual table in the corner.

laugh out of court see [1]LAUGH

pay court to *formal + old-fashioned* : to give a lot of attention to (someone) in order to get approval, affection, etc. ▪ He does not approve of the young man who has *been paying court to* his daughter. [=who has been courting his daughter]

the ball is in your court see [1]BALL

the court of public/world opinion : the beliefs and judgment of most people ▪ The statement was quickly condemned in *the court of public opinion.* [=was condemned by the public]

[2]**court** *verb* **courts; court·ed; court·ing**

1 *somewhat old-fashioned* : to act in a way that shows that you want or intend to get married [*no obj*] The couple *courted* for two years before marrying. [+ *obj*] He was *courting* his college sweetheart.

2 *of an animal* : to perform the actions that lead to sexual activity [*no obj*] a pair of robins *courting* [+ *obj*] The male will sometimes *court* the female for hours.

3 [+ *obj*] : to give a lot of attention and praise to (someone) in order to get approval, support, etc. ▪ college teams *courting* high school basketball stars ▪ The government is *courting* [=*wooing*] investors from around the globe. ▪ The speech was clearly intended to *court* middle-class voters. ✧ If you ***court someone's favor*** or ***court favor with someone***, you try to get someone's approval. ▪ The company is *courting favor with* consumers by portraying itself as socially responsible.

4 [+ *obj*] : to act in a way that is likely to cause (something unpleasant) to happen to you ▪ Anyone who refuses to evacuate is ***courting disaster.*** [=*flirting with disaster*] ▪ They knew they were ***courting danger/trouble*** by accepting donations from a convicted felon.

court card *noun, pl* ~ **cards** [*count*] *chiefly Brit* : FACE CARD

cour·te·ous /ˈkɚtijəs/ *adj* [*more* ~; *most* ~] : very polite in a way that shows respect ▪ The clerks were helpful and *courteous.* ▪ a *courteous* manner — opposite DISCOURTEOUS

– **cour·te·ous·ly** *adv* ▪ He answered my questions *courteously.* – **cour·te·ous·ness** *noun* [*noncount*] ▪ I appreciated his *courteousness.*

cour·te·san /ˈkoɚtəzən, *Brit* ˌkɔːtəˈzæn/ *noun, pl* **-sans** [*count*] *old-fashioned* : a woman who has sex with rich or important men in exchange for money : a prostitute who has sex with wealthy and powerful men

[1]**cour·te·sy** /ˈkɚtəsi/ *noun, pl* **-sies**

1 [*noncount*] : polite behavior that shows respect for other people ▪ They treated us with *courtesy* and kindness. ▪ He didn't even have the ***common courtesy*** [=he was not even as polite as people can usually be expected to be] to say goodbye when he left.

2 [*count*] **a** : something that you do because it is polite, kind, etc. ▪ She did it as a *courtesy*, not because she had to. **b** : something that you say to be polite especially when you meet someone ▪ Everyone knows each other here, so we won't bother with the usual *courtesies.* ▪ They shook hands and exchanged *courtesies* before beginning their discussion.

courtesy of ✧ If you say that something has been provided ***through the courtesy of*** or ***(by) courtesy of*** a person, organization, business, etc., you are politely saying that they paid for it, gave it, or let it be used. ▪ The flowers were provided *through the courtesy of* a local florist. ▪ This program is brought to you *courtesy of* our sponsors. [=it has been paid for by our sponsors] The word ***courtesy*** is sometimes used informally by itself in this way. ▪ Photo *courtesy* Helen Jones. [=Helen Jones is allowing the photograph to be used] The phrase ***courtesy of*** is sometimes also used informally to indicate the cause of something. ▪ I have a bad cold now, *courtesy of* my brother. [=I have a bad cold that I caught from my brother]

[2]**courtesy** *adj, always used before a noun*

1 : done in order to be polite ▪ They paid a ***courtesy call*** on the ambassador. [=they visited the ambassador because it was the polite thing to do]

2 : provided for free ▪ Important visitors to the conference were provided with *courtesy* cars. ▪ He picked up the airport ***courtesy phone*** [=a telephone that customers can use to call the company that provides it] to call for a car.

courtesy title *noun, pl* ~ **titles** [*count*] : a polite and formal word that is used in place of someone's name or as part of someone's name ▪ the *courtesy titles* "Mr.," "Mrs.," "Ms.," "Dr.," etc. ▪ As a child, he was taught to address his elders with the *courtesy titles* "sir" and "ma'am."

court·house /ˈkoɚtˌhaʊs/ *noun, pl* **-hous·es** [*count*] *US* : a building in which legal cases are heard

court·ier /ˈkoɚtijɚ/ *noun, pl* **-iers** [*count*] : a member of a royal court (sense 3b)

court·ly /ˈkoɚtli/ *adj* **court·li·er; -est** [*or more* ~; *most* ~] : polite and graceful in a formal way ▪ *courtly* manners ▪ a *courtly* gentleman

– **court·li·ness** *noun* [*noncount*]

[1]**court–mar·tial** /ˈkoɚtˌmɑɚʃəl/ *noun, pl* **courts–martial** *also* **court–mar·tials**

1 : a military court : a court for people in the military who are accused of breaking military law [*noncount*] The officers will be tried by *court-martial.* [*count*] They will appear before a *court-martial.*

2 [*count*] : a trial in a military court ▪ The sergeant is facing a *court-martial* for failure to obey orders.

[2]**court–martial** *verb* **-tials;** *US* **-tialed** *or Brit* **-tialled;** *US* **-tial·ing** *or Brit* **-tial·ling** [+ *obj*] : to present evidence against (someone) in a military court : to put (someone) on trial in a military court ▪ He was *court-martialed* for failure to obey orders.

court of appeals (*US*) *or chiefly Brit* **court of appeal** *noun, pl* **courts of appeals** [*count*] *law*

1 : a court that studies the decisions made by a lower court and decides if they were correct — called also (*US*) *appeals court,* (*chiefly Brit*) *appeal court*

2 ***Court of Appeals*** *US* : any one of 13 courts in the U.S. below the Supreme Court ▪ the 9th/Ninth Circuit *Court of Appeals*

3 ***Court of Appeal*** *Brit* : the highest court in Britain below the House of Lords

court of law *noun, pl* **courts of law** [*count*] : [1]COURT 1a ▪ You have the right to a fair trial in a *court of law.*

court order *noun, pl* ~ **-ders** : a formal statement from a court that orders someone to do or stop doing something [*count*] He received a *court order* barring him from entering the building. [*noncount*] He is barred by *court order* from entering the building. ▪ The town is under *court order* to fix the problem.

court reporter *noun, pl* ~ **-ers** [*count*] : a person whose job is to write down exactly what is said and done during a legal trial

court·room /ˈkoɚtˌruːm/ *noun, pl* **-rooms** [*count*] : a room in which legal cases are heard

court·ship /ˈkoɚtˌʃɪp/ *noun, pl* **-ships**

1 *somewhat old-fashioned* : the activities that occur when people are developing a romantic relationship that could lead to marriage or the period of time when such activities occur [*count*] They had a two-year *courtship* before marrying. [*noncount*] the formalities of *courtship*

2 [*noncount*] : the behavior of animals that leads to sexual activity or the period of time when such behavior occurs ▪ The male of the species often displays aggression during *courtship.* — often used before another noun ▪ *courtship* behavior ▪ *courtship* displays/rituals

3 [*noncount*] : an attempt to convince someone to support you or to choose you or your organization ▪ the President's *courtship* of middle-class voters

court shoe *noun, pl* ~ **shoes** [*count*] *Brit* : [3]PUMP 1

court·side /ˈkoɚtˌsaɪd/ *noun* [*noncount*] *chiefly US* : the area at the edge of a tennis or basketball court ▪ Our seats were located a few rows (up) from *courtside.*

– **courtside** *adj* ▪ *courtside* seats – **courtside** *adv* ▪ We got to sit *courtside.* [=we got to sit in the seats that are closest to the court]

court·yard /ˈkoɚtˌjɑɚd/ *noun, pl* **-yards** [*count*] : an open space that is surrounded completely or partly by a building or group of buildings ▪ the palace *courtyards* ▪ The apartment overlooks a *courtyard.*

cous·cous /ˈkuːsˌkuːs/ *noun* [*noncount*] : a North African food that is made from wheat and is in the form of very small, round pieces; *also* : a dish of this food served with meat or vegetables ▪ lamb and vegetable *couscous*

cous·in /ˈkʌzən/ *noun, pl* **-ins** [*count*]

C

1 a : a child of your uncle or aunt — called also *first cousin*; see also SECOND COUSIN **b** : a person who is related to you but not in a close or direct way • Everyone came to the wedding, including a distant *cousin* no one had heard from in years. — see also KISSING COUSIN
2 : a person who is from another country but whose culture is similar to your own • our English *cousins*
3 : something that is similar or related to something else • The cricket is a *cousin* of the grasshopper. • hurricanes and their *cousins*, typhoons

cou·ture /kuˈtuɚ, *Brit* kuˈtjʊə/ *noun* [*noncount*] *somewhat formal*
1 : the business of designing, making, or selling women's clothes; *also* : women's clothes in general • The book discusses the relationship between culture and *couture*.
2 : HAUTE COUTURE • I can't afford to wear *couture*.

cou·tu·ri·er /kuˈturijə, *Brit* kuˈtjʊəriə/ *noun, pl* **-ers** [*count*] : a person or business that designs and makes clothes for women

[1]**cove** /ˈkoʊv/ *noun, pl* **coves** [*count*] : a small area of ocean that is partly surrounded by land : a small, sheltered inlet or bay • a coastline dotted with *coves* — compare [2]COVE

[2]**cove** *noun, pl* **coves** [*count*] *Brit, old-fashioned* : a man : CHAP • a genial *cove* — compare [1]COVE

cov·en /ˈkʌvən/ *noun, pl* **-ens** [*count*] : a group of witches

cov·e·nant /ˈkʌvənənt/ *noun, pl* **-nants** [*count*]
1 *formal* : a formal and serious agreement or promise • a *covenant* with God • the *covenant* of marriage
2 *law* : a formal written agreement between two or more people, businesses, countries, etc. • an international *covenant* on human rights • The restrictive *covenants* of the building development prohibit the construction of buildings over 30 feet tall.

[1]**cov·er** /ˈkʌvɚ/ *verb* **-ers; -ered; -er·ing**
1 : to put something over, on top of, or in front of (something else) especially in order to protect, hide, or close it [+ *obj*] The gardener *covered* the soil with mulch. • The furniture had been *covered* in a protective cloth. • Be sure to *cover* the pot. [=put a cover on the pot] • He *covered* his face with his hands. [=he put his hands over his face; he hid his face behind his hands] • We *covered* the stains on the wall with a fresh coat of paint. • You should *cover* your mouth when you cough. • She *covered* her head with a scarf. • tables *covered* with white linen • He wears a hair piece to *cover* [=*hide, conceal*] his bald spot. [*no obj*] — used in recipes and instructions • The recipe said: "Reduce heat. *Cover* [=put a cover/lid on the pot/pan] and continue cooking for another 10 minutes." • Place the seed in the hole and *cover* with soil.
2 [+ *obj*] **a** : to be spread over or on top of (something) • Water *covered* the floor. • Snow *covered* the hills. **b** : to be over much or all of the surface of (something) • Lakes *cover* much of the state. — usually used as *(be) covered* • Much of the state *is covered* with lakes. • The wall *is* completely *covered* with graffiti. • His legs *were covered* in mosquito bites.
3 [+ *obj*] : to pass over or through (an area, distance, etc.) • The hikers *covered* long distances every day. • The bird may *cover* thousands of miles during its migration.
4 [+ *obj*] **a** : to have (something) as a subject : to relate to or provide information about (a particular subject) • The course will *cover* the country's early history. • an exam *covering* a semester's worth of material • This material was *covered* in the book's first chapter. • We'd better get started because we have a lot (of information) to *cover* in one hour. **b** : to relate to or have an effect on (something) • The patent *covers* [=*applies to*] both kinds of devices/systems. • The term "house" *covers* a wide array of buildings. [=many different kinds of buildings can be called houses]
5 [+ *obj*] : to report news about (something) • He is an experienced journalist who has *covered* several presidential campaigns. • She *covers* political news for the network.
6 [+ *obj*] *of insurance* **a** : to protect (someone) by promising to pay for loss, damage, etc. : to provide financial protection to (someone) • The policy *covers* the traveler in any accident. **b** : to provide protection by promising to pay for (a problem, accident, etc.) : to provide financial protection against (something) • The policy *covers* water damage. • a policy *covering* loss by fire **c** : to provide payment for (something) • My health insurance doesn't *cover* this treatment/drug.
7 [+ *obj*] **a** : to have enough money for (something) • Your checking account balance will not *cover* the check. [=there is not enough money in your checking account to pay for the amount of the check] **b** : to pay for (something) • He has enough money to *cover* tuition, but he can't afford to buy the textbooks he needs. • This money should *cover* the cost of repairing the wall.
8 [+ *obj*] **a** : to guard or protect (something or someone) by being ready to shoot a gun or fire a weapon • The ships were *covering* approaches to the harbor. • Officer Blake's partner yelled "*Cover* me!" and ran for the door. **b** : to protect (yourself or someone else) from possible trouble or danger • He was trying to *cover* himself by lying about his involvement in the scandal. • (*US, informal* + *impolite*) He was trying to ***cover his ass/butt*** by lying.
9 [+ *obj*] **a** *sports* : to guard (an opponent) as part of your team's effort to prevent the other team from scoring • He was assigned to *cover* the tight end. **b** *baseball* : to be in a position to receive a throw to (a base) • The shortstop was *covering* second base. — see also *cover all the bases* at [1]BASE
10 [*no obj*] **a** : to help you by doing your job when you are away or not able to do it — + *for* • A coworker *covered for* me during my vacation. • She'll be out for a week, so the rest of us will have to *cover for* her. **b** : to hide the truth or lie for someone — + *for* • He *covered for* his friend, insisting that he hadn't seen him all day.
11 [+ *obj*] **a** : to be responsible for selling or providing something to all the people in (an area) for a company, organization, etc. • One salesperson *covers* the whole state. **b** : to provide something to (a group of people) • There should be enough of the vaccine to *cover* everyone.
12 [+ *obj*] : to record or perform (a song that was previously recorded by someone else) • The band has *covered* many hits from the 1980s.

cover up [*phrasal verb*] **1** ***cover up or cover (something) up or cover up (something)*** : to cover yourself, part of your body, etc., with something (such as clothing or a blanket) • She quickly *covered up* with a robe. • She quickly *covered* herself *up*. **2** ***cover (something) up or cover up (something)*** : to prevent people from learning the truth about (something, such as a crime) : to hide (something) • They tried to *cover up* the crime/mistake/problem/scandal. • I think they stole the money and then lied about it to *cover up* their guilt. — see also COVER-UP

cover your tracks see [1]TRACK

have (got) someone or something covered (*informal*) : to have done, gotten, or provided whatever is needed • Don't worry about a thing. We*'ve got you covered*. [=we have taken care of everything that you might need] • You don't need to buy soda for the party. We*'ve* already *got that covered*. [=we already have enough soda]

[2]**cover** *noun, pl* **-ers**
1 [*count*] : something that is put around or on top of another thing especially to protect, hide, or close it • She placed a *cover* over the pan so that the oil wouldn't spatter. • I put a *cover* on the sofa to protect it. • a mattress *cover* • I lifted the *cover* of the box and peaked inside. • He unscrewed the *cover* [=*top, lid*] of the jar.
2 [*count*] : a blanket or sheet on a bed — usually plural • She was in bed lying under the *covers*. • He threw off the *covers* and rose to begin the day.
3 [*count*] **a** : the outer part of a book or magazine • There's a picture of the author on the book's back/front *cover*. • The model appeared on the (front) *covers* of many weeklies. • She read the book ***from cover to cover***. [=she read all of the book] — see also COVER GIRL, COVER STORY **b** : the part of the case of a record album, CD, DVD, etc., that is seen from the outside • The singer is posing in jeans and cowboy boots on the album *cover*.
4 : something that covers the ground or the sky [*singular*] The ground was hidden under a *cover* of snow. • The moon was hidden behind a thick ***cloud cover***. [=behind thick clouds] [*noncount*] areas of light plant *cover* [=areas in which there are few plants] — see also GROUND COVER
5 [*noncount*] : a place or situation in which you are protected • The roof provided *cover* from the rain. • The soldiers sought *cover* behind the wall. • The officer ordered the soldiers to ***take cover*** as the enemy began shooting. • The hikers *took cover* under a tree and waited for the storm to pass. • The hikers ran/dashed/headed ***for cover*** as the storm approached. ✧ If you ***break cover***, you come out from a place where you have been safe or hidden. • The rabbit suddenly *broke cover* and ran across the field.
6 [*noncount*] : something that prevents actions, information, etc., from being seen or known • The crime was committed ***under (the) cover of darkness/night***. [=when it was dark; at night] • an official speaking to a reporter ***under cover of ano-***

nymity[=with the understanding that the reporter would not reveal the official's name]
7 [*count*] : something that is not what it seems to be but is actually used to hide something else — usually singular • The business was a *cover* for a criminal gang. • Her job as a consultant was just a *cover* for her true identity as a secret agent. • He acts tough, but that's just a *cover*. He's a real softy underneath. ✧ A person who is ***under cover*** has his or her true identity hidden. The phrase usually describes a person (such as a police officer) who pretends to be someone else in order to get information. • The policeman went *under cover* to collect more evidence. • The agent was working *under cover*. ✧ To ***blow someone's cover*** is to reveal someone's true identity. • The agent posed as a consultant until someone *blew her cover*. — see also UNDERCOVER
8 [*count*] : a recording or performance of a song that was previously recorded by someone else • a *cover* (version) of a popular song • a ***cover band***[=a band that plays songs previously recorded by other performers]
9 [*count*] *informal* : COVER CHARGE • The nightclub has a $5 *cover*.
10 [*noncount*] *Brit* : insurance coverage • a policy that provides *cover* [=(*US*) *coverage*] for loss by fire
11 [*noncount*] : protection from danger, an attack, etc. • They had to land in enemy territory without any ***air cover***. [=protection by military airplanes] • traveling with the benefit of ***diplomatic cover***[=the special protection that is given to a diplomat]
12 [*noncount*] *Brit* : work done by someone other than the person who usually does it • A small crew will provide emergency *cover* during the strike.
under separate cover : in a separate envelope • The manuscript is being sent to you *under separate cover*.

cov·er·age /ˈkʌvərɪʤ/ *noun, pl* **-ag·es**
1 [*noncount*] : the activity of reporting about an event or subject in newspapers, on television news programs, etc. • The issue is not getting much *coverage* in the mainstream press. • There was massive/extensive TV *coverage* of the funeral. • The network will have ***live coverage*** of the game. [=it will broadcast the game as it is happening]
2 [*noncount*] : discussion of a subject in a book, class, etc. • For more complete *coverage* of this issue, see Chapter Six. • The book gives full *coverage* to the history of the word.
3 *US* **a** [*noncount*] : the financial protection that is provided by an insurance policy • She has no insurance *coverage*. [=she does not have insurance] • affordable health/medical *coverage* [=insurance that will pay for medical care; health insurance] • My health insurance company has denied *coverage* for the treatment. [=it will not pay the cost of the treatment] **b** [*count*] : something that an insurance company will pay for : something that is covered by an insurance policy • Fire/liability insurance *coverages* varied. • optional/additional *coverages*
4 *chiefly US, sports* : the act of guarding an opponent as part of your team's effort to prevent the other team from scoring : the act of covering an opponent [*noncount*] He was responsible for *coverage* of the tight end. [*count*] The team uses a variety of defensive *coverages*.
5 [*noncount*] — used to describe how much of an area or surface is covered by something • Heavy cloud *coverage* is expected over the lake. • uniform paint *coverage* • There is no cell phone *coverage* in this valley. [=cell phone service is not available]

cov·er·all /ˈkʌvəˌɑːl/ *noun, pl* **-alls** [*count*] *US* : a piece of clothing that is worn over other clothes to protect them — usually plural • The mechanic was dressed in (a pair of) *coveralls*. [=(*Brit*) *overalls*]

cover charge *noun, pl* ~ **charges** [*count*] : an amount of money that must be paid to go into a nightclub or restaurant in addition to the charge for food and drink • The nightclub has a $5 *cover charge*.

covered *adj*
1 : having a cover or lid • a *covered* dish/container/jar/bowl
2 a : having a layer of something specified on top — usually used in combination • snow-*covered* hills • sugar-*covered* cookies **b** : having something specified over much or all of the surface — usually used in combination • a graffiti-*covered* wall • chocolate-*covered* pretzels
3 : having a roof • a *covered* walkway/entrance/porch • a *covered* bridge — see also COVERED WAGON
4 *US, insurance* : paid for by an insurance policy • *covered* medical expenses

covered wagon *noun, pl* ~ **-ons** [*count*] : a large wagon with a rounded top made of heavy cloth that was used in the past by people traveling to the western parts of North America

cover girl *noun, pl* ~ **girls** [*count*] : an attractive young woman whose picture is on the front of a magazine

cov·er·ing /ˈkʌvərɪŋ/ *noun, pl* **-ings** [*count*] : an object or substance that goes over or on top of something especially in order to hide or protect it • The ground was hidden under a *covering* [=*cover*] of snow. • floor/wall/window *coverings*

cov·er·let /ˈkʌvələt/ *noun, pl* **-lets** [*count*] : a decorative cover for a bed : BEDSPREAD

cover letter *noun, pl* ~ **-ters** [*count*] *US* : a letter that is sent with something to explain the reason for it or to give more information about it • Always include a *cover letter* with your résumé. — called also (*Brit*) *covering letter*

cover story *noun, pl* ~ **-ries** [*count*] : an important story or article that is the main subject shown on the cover of a magazine • The magazine recently did/had a *cover story* on/about diabetes.

co·vert /ˈkoʊvət/ *adj* [*more* ~; *most* ~] : made, shown, or done in a way that is not easily seen or noticed : secret or hidden • a *covert* glance/look • He has taken part in a number of *covert* military operations. • spy agencies taking *covert* action — opposite OVERT
– **co·vert·ly** *adv* – **co·vert·ness** *noun* [*noncount*]

cov·er–up /ˈkʌvəˌʌp/ *noun, pl* **-ups** [*count*]
1 : a planned effort to hide a dishonest, immoral, or illegal act or situation • The book describes the burglary and its ensuing *cover-up*. • The report exposes an attempted *cover-up* of the accident.
2 : an action or a way of behaving that is meant to prevent people from knowing about something • His brash manner is just a *cover-up* for his insecurity. — see also *cover up* at [1]COVER

cov·et /ˈkʌvət/ *verb* **-ets; -et·ed; -et·ing** [+ *obj*] : to want (something that you do not have) very much • All his life he has *coveted* [=*craved, desired*] success. • a *coveted* prize • His religion warns against *coveting* material goods.

cov·et·ous /ˈkʌvətəs/ *adj* [*more* ~; *most* ~] *formal* : feeling or showing a very strong desire for something that you do not have and especially for something that belongs to someone else • The expensive car drew many *covetous* looks. • They were *covetous* of his success. [=they envied his success]
– **cov·et·ous·ly** *adv* • They eyed her jewelry *covetously*.
– **cov·et·ous·ness** *noun* [*noncount*]

cov·ey /ˈkʌvi/ *noun, pl* **-eys** [*count*]
1 : a small flock of birds • a *covey* of quail
2 : a small group of people or things • A *covey* of schoolchildren approached. • A *covey* of reporters came to the event.

[1]**cow** /ˈkaʊ/ *noun, pl* **cows**
[*count*]
1 a : a large animal that is raised by people for milk or meat usually on a farm • horses, chickens, and *cows*; *especially* : the adult female of this animal • The *cows* need to be milked twice a day. — compare BULL, CALF **b** : an adult female of some other large animals (such as elephants, whales, and seals)

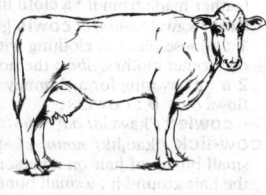

cow

2 *chiefly Brit slang, offensive* : a woman who is stupid or annoying • You stupid *cow*!
have a cow *slang* : to become very angry, upset, etc. • *Don't have a cow*! I said I'd take care of the problem and I will.
holy cow *informal* — used as an interjection to express surprise or excitement • *Holy cow*! That car almost ran into us!
till/until the cows come home *informal* : for a very long time • They'll be arguing about this *till the cows come home*.
– see also CASH COW, SACRED COW

[2]**cow** *verb* **cows; cowed; cow·ing** [+ *obj*] : to make (someone) too afraid to do something : INTIMIDATE • I refuse to be *cowed* by their threats. • They were *cowed* into silence by threats. [=they did not complain, publicly say anything, etc., because they had been threatened]

cow·ard /ˈkawəd/ *noun, pl* **-ards** [*count*] : someone who is too afraid to do what is right or expected : someone who is not at all brave or courageous • a proven *coward* who had deserted his troops

C

cow·ard·ice /ˈkawɚdəs/ *noun* [*noncount*] : fear that makes you unable to do what is right or expected : lack of courage ▪ soldiers accused of *cowardice* ▪ acts of *cowardice*

cow·ard·ly /ˈkawɚdli/ *adj* [*more ~; most ~*] : afraid in a way that makes you unable to do what is right or expected : lacking courage ▪ He insisted on avoiding a *cowardly* retreat. ▪ She made a *cowardly* decision to go along with the group. ▪ a *cowardly* thief ▪ a *cowardly* attack from behind
– **cow·ard·li·ness** *noun* [*noncount*]

cow·bell /ˈkaʊˌbɛl/ *noun, pl* **-bells** [*count*] : a bell that you hang around the neck of a cow so that you can tell where the cow is

cow·bird /ˈkaʊˌbɚd/ *noun, pl* **-birds** [*count*] : a brown and black North American bird that lays its eggs in the nests of other birds

[1]**cow·boy** /ˈkaʊˌbɔɪ/ *noun, pl* **-boys** [*count*]
1 : a man who rides a horse and whose job is to take care of cows or horses especially in the western U.S. ▪ a movie about *cowboys* in the old West ▪ He worked for several years as a *cowboy* on a ranch in Texas.
2 : a man who performs in a rodeo
3 *usually disapproving* : someone who has qualities that are commonly associated with the cowboys in movies; *especially* : someone who does things that other people consider foolish and dangerous ▪ political *cowboys* ▪ We've got a bunch of risk-taking *cowboys* running this project. — sometimes used before another noun ▪ *cowboy* diplomacy

[2]**cowboy** *verb* **-boys; -boyed; -boy·ing** [*no obj*] *US* : to work as a cowboy ▪ He *cowboyed* in Texas and Oklahoma.

cowboy boot *noun, pl* ~ **boots** [*count*] : a type of boot that has a thick heel and often a decorative design on the upper part and that is worn especially by cowboys and cowgirls — see picture at SHOE

cowboy hat *noun, pl* ~ **hats** [*count*] : a type of soft hat that has a wide brim and that is worn especially by cowboys and cowgirls — see picture at HAT

cow·er /ˈkawɚ/ *verb* **-ers; -ered; -er·ing** [*no obj*] : to move back or bend your body down because you are afraid ▪ They *cowered* at the sight of the gun. ▪ She was *cowering* in the closet. ▪ I *cowered* behind the door. ▪ *cowering* before a bully

cow·girl /ˈkaʊˌgɚl/ *noun, pl* **-girls** [*count*]
1 : a woman who rides a horse and whose job is to take care of cows or horses especially in the western U.S.
2 : a girl or woman who performs in a rodeo

cow·hand /ˈkaʊˌhænd/ *noun, pl* **-hands** [*count*] : [1]COWBOY 1

cow·herd /ˈkaʊˌhɚd/ *noun, pl* **-herds** [*count*] : a person whose job is to take care of cows especially in the western U.S.

cow·hide /ˈkaʊˌhaɪd/ *noun* [*noncount*] : the skin of a cow or leather made from it ▪ a cloth made of *cowhide*

cowl /ˈkawəl/ *noun, pl* **cowls** [*count*]
1 : a loose piece of clothing with a hood that a monk wears over other clothes; *also* : the hood itself
2 a : a covering for a chimney that controls the way smoke flows out **b** : COWLING
– **cowled** /ˈkawəld/ *adj* ▪ *cowled* monks

cow·lick /ˈkaʊˌlɪk/ *noun, pl* **-licks** [*count*] *chiefly US* : a small bunch of hair on a person's head that sticks up above the hair around it : a small bunch of hair that will not lie flat

cowl·ing /ˈkaʊlɪŋ/ *noun, pl* **-ings** [*count*] : a metal covering for the engine of an airplane

co·work·er /ˈkoʊˌwɚkɚ/ *noun, pl* **-ers** [*count*] : a person who works at the place where you work : someone you work with

cow·pat /ˈkaʊˌpæt/ *noun, pl* **-pats** [*count*] *chiefly Brit* : COW PIE

cow·pea /ˈkaʊˌpiː/ *noun, pl* **-peas** [*count*] *chiefly US* : BLACK-EYED PEA

cow pie *noun, pl* ~ **pies** [*count*] *chiefly US* : a piece of solid waste from a cow

cow·poke /ˈkaʊˌpoʊk/ *noun, pl* **-pokes** [*count*] *US, informal* : [1]COWBOY 1 ▪ a movie about a couple of old *cowpokes*

cow·punch·er /ˈkaʊˌpʌntʃɚ/ *noun, pl* **-ers** [*count*] *informal + old-fashioned* : [1]COWBOY 1

cow·rie *also* **cow·ry** /ˈkaʊri/ *noun, pl* **cow·ries** [*count*]
1 : a small snail that is found in warm seas
2 : the shiny and often brightly colored shell of the cowrie ✧ Cowrie shells have been used as money in Africa and other places.

cow·shed /ˈkaʊˌʃɛd/ *noun, pl* **-sheds** [*count*] : a building where cows are kept

cow·slip /ˈkaʊˌslɪp/ *noun, pl* **-slips** [*count*] : a wild plant with small yellow flowers that smell sweet

cox /ˈkɑːks/ *noun, pl* **cox·es** [*count*] : a person who steers a rowing boat in races
– **cox** *verb* **coxes; coxed; cox·ing** [+ *obj*] I'm not sure who will be *coxing* the boat in this race. [*no obj*] He *coxes* for the racing crew.

cox·swain /ˈkɑːksən/ *noun, pl* **-swains** [*count*]
1 : a person who is in charge of and usually steers a boat (such as a ship's lifeboat)
2 : COX

coy /ˈkɔɪ/ *adj* [*more ~; most ~*]
1 : having a shy or sweetly innocent quality that is often intended to be attractive or to get attention ▪ a *coy* flirt ▪ I didn't like her *coy* manner. ▪ a *coy* glance/smile
2 : not telling or revealing all the information that could be revealed ▪ He gave a *coy* answer. — often + *about* ▪ Both companies are being *coy about* the merger deal.
play coy *US* : to avoid giving a direct or complete answer ▪ When asked about his next book, he *played coy*.
– **coy·ly** *adv* ▪ She smiled *coyly*. ▪ She *coyly* refused to say anything more about it. – **coy·ness** *noun* [*noncount*]

coy·ote /kaɪˈoʊti/ *noun, pl* **coy·ot·es** *or* **coyote** [*count*] : a small wild animal that is related to dogs and wolves and that lives in North America — see picture at WOLF

[1]**co·zy** (*US*) *or Brit* **co·sy** /ˈkoʊzi/ *adj* **co·zi·er; -est** [*also more ~; most ~*]
1 a : small, comfortable, and warm ▪ a *cozy* restaurant/cottage ▪ The room was warm and *cozy*. — sometimes used in a joking or ironic way to describe a place that is not pleasant or comfortable ▪ She glanced around the cramped apartment and said, "Well, isn't this *cozy*?" **b** : friendly and pleasant ▪ We had a *cozy* dinner with the whole family. ▪ I spent a *cozy* evening reading in front of the fire. ▪ a *cozy* chat
2 *often disapproving* : suggesting or showing a closeness between two people, groups, businesses, etc. : very close ▪ He claims that there is a *cozy* arrangement/relationship between the police and the drug dealers. — often + *with* ▪ His political opponents accuse him of getting/being too *cozy with* powerful companies.
– **co·zi·ly** (*US*) *or Brit* **co·si·ly** /ˈkoʊzəli/ *adv* ▪ The children were snuggled *cozily* in their beds. – **co·zi·ness** (*US*) *or Brit* **co·si·ness** *noun* [*noncount*] ▪ We were charmed by the *coziness* of the little cottage.

[2]**cozy** (*US*) *or Brit* **cosy** *noun, pl* **-zies** [*count*] : a cloth cover that is placed over a teapot to keep the tea hot ▪ a tea *cozy*

[3]**cozy** (*US*) *or Brit* **cosy** *verb* **-zies; -zied; -zy·ing**
cozy up [*phrasal verb*] *informal* : to become or try to become friendly with someone in order to get help or some advantage — usually + *to* ▪ He has been *cozying up to* the boss lately in hopes of getting a promotion.

CPA *abbr* certified public accountant

CPI *abbr* consumer price index

Cpl. *abbr* corporal ▪ *Cpl.* Jones

CPR /ˌsiːˌpiːˈɑɚ/ *noun* [*noncount*] *medical* : a way of trying to save the life of someone who has stopped breathing and whose heart has stopped beating ▪ They pulled her out of the swimming pool and began *CPR*. ✧ *CPR* is an abbreviation for "cardiopulmonary resuscitation."

Cpt. *abbr* captain ▪ *Cpt.* Smith

CPU /ˌsiːˌpiːˈjuː/ *noun, pl* **CPUs** [*count*] *computers* : the part of a computer system that performs the computer's main functions and controls the other parts of the system — called also *processor* ✧ *CPU* is an abbreviation for "central processing unit."

[1]**crab** /ˈkræb/ *noun, pl* **crabs**
1 a [*count*] : a sea animal that has a hard shell, eight legs, and two large claws — see color picture on page C8; see also HERMIT CRAB, KING CRAB **b** [*noncount*] : the meat of a crab eaten as food ▪ We had *crab* for dinner.
2 *crabs* [*plural*] *medical* : a medical problem in which very small insects (called lice) live in the hair surrounding a person's sexual organs
3 [*count*] *US, informal* : an unhappy person who complains a lot : GROUCH ▪ I don't know why she's been such a *crab* lately.

[2]**crab** *verb* **crabs; crabbed; crab·bing** [*no obj*]
1 : to catch or try to catch crabs ▪ We *crabbed* in the bay on Saturday.
2 *US, informal* : to complain about something in a way that

annoys people ▪ He's been *crabbing* about the weather all afternoon.

– **crabbing** *noun [noncount]* ▪ We ***went crabbing*** in the bay on Saturday. ▪ I'm tired of listening to his *crabbing* about the weather.

crab apple *noun, pl* **~ apples** *[count]* : a small, sour apple or the kind of tree that produces it

crab·bed /ˈkræbəd/ *adj [more ~; most ~]*
1 : difficult to read or understand ▪ *crabbed* handwriting
2 : very negative : full of unhappy ideas ▪ Her *crabbed* [=*morose*] view of human nature makes it hard for her to trust people.

crab·by /ˈkræbi/ *adj* **crab·bi·er; -est** *[also more ~; most ~] informal* : unhappy and tending to complain a lot : GROUCHY ▪ She gets *crabby* if she doesn't get enough sleep. ▪ a *crabby* old man

crab·grass /ˈkræbˌgræs, *Brit* ˈkræbˌgrɑːs/ *noun [noncount] US* : a thick type of grass that often grows and spreads quickly in places where it is not wanted

crab·meat /ˈkræbˌmiːt/ *noun [noncount]* : the meat of a crab eaten as food ▪ mushrooms stuffed with *crabmeat*

[1]**crack** /ˈkræk/ *verb* **cracks; cracked; crack·ing**
1 : to break (something) so that there are lines in its surface but it is usually not separated into pieces *[+ obj]* The hailstones were big enough to *crack* some windows. ▪ He *cracked* his collarbone in a skiing accident. *[no obj]* The mirror/glass *cracked* when she dropped it. ▪ A piece of the statue *cracked* off. [=broke off]
2 *[+ obj]* : to hit or press (something) so hard that it breaks apart or opens suddenly ▪ Workers *cracked* the large rock into three pieces so it could be moved. ▪ The bird *cracked* the seed on a tree branch. ▪ a tool used for *cracking* nuts ▪ He ***cracked open*** the eggs.
3 *[+ obj]* : to hit (someone or something) hard and usually suddenly ▪ Someone *cracked* him over the head with a beer bottle. ▪ The baby *cracked* her chin pretty hard when she fell. ▪ He fell and *cracked* his elbow on/against the ice.
4 *[+ obj]* **a** : to open (a bottle or can) for drinking — usually + *open* ▪ He *cracked open* a beer. **b** : to open (a book) for studying or reading ▪ He hardly *cracked* a book his whole first semester of college. — usually + *open* ▪ It's a perfect day to relax and *crack open* a good book.
5 *[+ obj]* : to open (a safe) illegally without having a key, combination, etc. ▪ Any good thief could *crack* this safe.
6 *[+ obj]* **a** : to find an answer or solution to (something) ▪ Scientists have *cracked* [=*solved*] an ancient mystery using new technology. ▪ The police finally *cracked* [=*broke*] the case and arrested the murderer. **b** : to find the meaning of (a secret code) ▪ He was able to *crack* [=*break*] the enemy's secret code.
7 *[+ obj]* : to open (something, such as a door or window) a small amount — usually + *open* ▪ She *cracked open* the door and peeked into the room.
8 : to cause (something) to make a sudden loud sound *[+ obj]* When the sled dogs heard her *crack* the whip, they broke into a run. ▪ His habit of *cracking* his knuckles bothered her. *[no obj]* The sled dogs are trained to run when they hear the whip *crack*. — see also CRACK THE WHIP (below)
9 *[no obj] of a voice* : to change sharply in tone or pitch especially because of strong emotion ▪ Her voice *cracked* (with emotion) as she told them what had happened.
10 *[+ obj] informal* : to tell (a joke) ▪ The two of them *crack* jokes all the time. = The two of them are always *cracking* jokes.
11 *[no obj]* : to lose strength or the ability to resist or fight ▪ After hours of questioning by the police, the suspect finally *cracked*. [=finally told the police what they wanted to know] — often + *under* ▪ He *cracked under* the pressure/stress of the job.

a tough/hard nut to crack see NUT

crack a smile : to smile ▪ I tried to get him to laugh, but he never even *cracked a smile*.

crack down *[phrasal verb]* : to start to be strict about punishing people for doing something that is illegal or not allowed : to enforce a law or rule more strictly ▪ People have been violating this law for years, and now the government is finally starting to *crack down*. — often + *on* ▪ Authorities are *cracking down on* companies that pollute. — see also CRACKDOWN

crack into *[phrasal verb]* ***crack into (something)*** *informal* : to enter or get started in (something, such as a profession) ▪ Its not easy to *crack into* [=*break into*] professional football.

crack the whip : to force people to work very hard ▪ The team needs a coach who isn't afraid to *crack the whip*.

crack up *[phrasal verb] informal* **1** ***crack up*** *or* ***crack (someone) up*** *or* ***crack up (someone)*** : to begin laughing or cause (someone) to begin laughing suddenly and in a way that is difficult to control ▪ When we saw the picture, we both *cracked up*. ▪ That joke really *cracks* me *up*. [=I think that joke is very funny] **2** : to become mentally ill : to lose control of your thoughts and emotions so that you cannot continue to live in a normal way ▪ The stress was getting worse, and she felt herself *cracking up*. [=going crazy] **3** ***crack up*** *or* ***crack up (something)*** *also* ***crack (something) up*** *US, informal* : to damage (a vehicle) by crashing ▪ I *cracked up* [=*crashed*] on a curve in the road. ▪ I *cracked up* [=*crashed*] the car. — see also CRACK-UP **4** ✧ Something that is ***what/all/everything (etc.) it's cracked up to be*** is as good as people say it is. ▪ Is the movie really *all it's cracked up to be*? = Is it really *as good as it's cracked up to be*? This phrase is usually used in negative statements. ▪ The new restaurant *is not all it's cracked up to be*. When we went, the service was awful and our food was cold.

crack wise *US, informal* : to say something that is funny and smart : to make a wisecrack ▪ She's always *cracking wise*.

get cracking *informal* : to start doing something ▪ You ought to *get cracking* [=*get going; get moving*] on that assignment. [=you should start working on that assignment right away]

[2]**crack** *noun, pl* **cracks**
1 *[count]* : a thin line in the surface of something that is broken but not separated into pieces ▪ The *crack* runs all the way from the top of the wall to the bottom. ▪ an old patio with grass growing up through the *cracks* ▪ The vase has a few fine *cracks*, but it is still usable. — often + *in* ▪ There were *cracks in* the ice. ▪ There is a *crack in* the mirror/windshield/glass. ▪ Grass is growing up through the *cracks in* the old patio. — see also *crack in someone's or something's armor* at ARMOR
2 *[count]* : a very narrow space or opening between two things or two parts of something ▪ I could see them through the *crack* in the doorway. ▪ Light came through the *cracks* in the walls of the barn. ▪ Could you please open the window ***a crack***? [=open it slightly] It's getting hot in here.
3 *[count]* : a sudden loud, sharp sound — usually singular ▪ We heard a loud *crack* as the ice broke. ▪ The horse was frightened by the *crack* of the whip. ▪ a *crack* of thunder
4 *[count]* : a brief change in the sound of a person's voice especially because of strong emotion — usually singular ▪ There was a *crack* in her voice as she told us her story.
5 *[count]* : a weakness or problem ▪ Your theory/argument has a few *cracks*. — often + *in* ▪ The *cracks in* their relationship were becoming evident.
6 *[count] informal* : a joke or rude remark — often + *about* ▪ They're always making *cracks* [=*wisecracks*] *about* their teacher. ▪ I didn't appreciate your *crack about* my weight.
7 *[count]* : a hard and sudden hit — usually singular ▪ Someone gave him a *crack* on the head with a beer bottle.
8 *[count] informal* : an effort or attempt to do something — usually + *at* ▪ She succeeded in her first *crack at* writing a novel. ▪ If he's lucky, he'll get to ***take a crack at*** (a career in) professional baseball. ▪ Let me ***have a crack at*** it.
9 *[noncount]* : an illegal drug that is a form of cocaine ▪ He is addicted to *crack*. ▪ They were smoking *crack*. — called also *crack cocaine*

a fair crack of the whip *Brit, informal* ✧ If you are given *a fair crack of the whip*, you are given the same chance as other people to do something. ▪ They might have succeeded if they'd been given *a fair crack of the whip*.

at the crack of dawn : very early in the morning : at dawn ▪ We got up *at the crack of dawn* to go fishing.

fall through/between the cracks *also* ***slip through/between the cracks*** : to fail to be noticed or included with others ▪ Parents are concerned that children who have trouble in school will *fall through the cracks* in the school system. [=will not be given the help they need; will graduate without anyone noticing that they are unable to do the work] ▪ The program is meant to help workers who may have *slipped through the cracks* [=who may have not been included in other programs] because of their age.

[3]**crack** *adj, always used before a noun* : very good : of excellent quality or ability ▪ *crack* troops ▪ The company has a *crack* sales force. ▪ I hear she's become a ***crack shot***. [=a person who is very good at shooting a gun]

C

crack baby *noun, pl* **~ -bies** [*count*] *chiefly US* : a baby who is not strong and healthy at birth and whose mother used crack cocaine while she was pregnant

crack·brained /ˈkrækˈbreɪnd/ *adj* [*more ~; most ~*] *informal* : very silly or foolish • a *crackbrained* artist • They've devised some *crackbrained* [=*harebrained, crazy*] scheme.

crack cocaine *noun* [*noncount*] : ²CRACK 9

crack·down /ˈkræk,daʊn/ *noun, pl* **-downs** [*count*] : a serious attempt to punish people for doing something that is not allowed : an increased effort to enforce a law or rule • Companies that pollute are the target of a new *crackdown*. — often + *on* • There's been a federal *crackdown on* smuggling in recent years. — see also *crack down* at ¹CRACK

cracked /ˈkrækt/ *adj*
1 : having a crack or many cracks : having a damaged surface but usually not broken into pieces • a *cracked* windshield • The vase is *cracked* but it can still hold water.
2 : having deep lines in the surface • the *cracked* leather of the old chair • His hands were sore and *cracked* from working long hours in the cold. • Her lips are dried and *cracked*.
3 : broken into pieces • *cracked* wheat/pepper/corn
4 *not used before a noun, informal* : CRAZY • Don't pay any attention to her. She's a little *cracked*.

crack·er /ˈkrækɚ/ *noun, pl* **-ers** [*count*]
1 : a dry, thin baked food that is made of flour and water and is often eaten with cheese • a plate of cheese and *crackers* — see also ANIMAL CRACKER, GRAHAM CRACKER, OYSTER CRACKER, SODA CRACKER
2 : a person who can crack something (such as a safe or a secret code) • a safe *cracker* [=a criminal who can opens a safe illegally] • a code *cracker*
3 *chiefly Brit* : a colorful paper tube that holds small gifts and that opens with a loud noise when the ends are pulled ✧ Crackers are commonly used in Britain at Christmas. • a Christmas *cracker*
4 *Brit, informal* : a very good, amusing, or attractive person or thing • The match should be real *cracker*. • The guitarist played a *cracker* of a solo.
5 *US, informal + offensive* : a poor usually Southern white person

crack·er·jack /ˈkrækɚ,ʤæk/ *adj, always used before a noun, US, informal* : excellent or great • They did a *crackerjack* job.

crack·ers /ˈkrækɚz/ *adj, not used before a noun, chiefly Brit, informal* : CRAZY • This new computer program is driving me *crackers*! • I think he's gone a little *crackers*.

crack·head /ˈkræk,hɛd/ *noun, pl* **-heads** [*count*] *informal* : a person who smokes the illegal drug crack

crack house *noun, pl* **~ houses** [*count*] : a house or apartment where the illegal drug crack is made, used, or sold

crack·ing /ˈkrækɪŋ/ *adj, always used before a noun, Brit, informal* : very good or impressive • I think it's a *cracking* story. • The horses set off at a *cracking* [=very fast] pace around the track.
– cracking *adv, always used before a noun, Brit, informal* • I think it's a *cracking* good story.

crack·le /ˈkrækəl/ *verb* **crack·les; crack·led; crack·ling** [*no obj*] : to make a series of short, sharp noises • The logs *crackled* in the fire. • The leaves *crackled* under our feet. • a *crackling* fire — often used figuratively • The air *crackled* [=*sparkled*] with excitement as we prepared for the festival.
– crackle *noun, pl* **crackles** [*count*] • You could hear the *crackle* of distant gunfire.

crackling *noun, pl* **-lings**
1 [*count*] : a series of short, sharp noises — usually singular • We heard a *crackling* of leaves behind us.
2 [*count, noncount*] : the crisp skin of a roasted animal (such as a pig) eaten as food • pork/duck *cracklings*

crack·ly /ˈkrækəli/ *adj* [*more ~; most ~*]
1 : having or making a series of short, sharp noises • a *crackly* voice • the *crackly* sound of the old record
2 *US* : thin and easily cracked • The bread has a *crackly* [=*crisp*] crust.

crack·pot /ˈkræk,pɑːt/ *noun, pl* **-pots** [*count*] *informal* : a person who is crazy or very strange • Some *crackpot* in a clown suit is out there directing traffic.
– crackpot *adj, always used before a noun* • a *crackpot* philosophy/idea

crack–up /ˈkræk,ʌp/ *noun, pl* **-ups** [*count*] *US, informal*
1 : an accident in which a vehicle is badly damaged • She got into a *crack-up* on her way back from the city.
2 : NERVOUS BREAKDOWN • He had a *crack-up* in his late 50s and never quite recovered. — see also *crack up* at ¹CRACK

¹cra·dle /ˈkreɪdl/ *noun, pl* **cra·dles** [*count*]
1 : a bed for a baby that is usually designed to rock back and forth when pushed gently • She rocked the *cradle*. — sometimes used figuratively • He learned to play chess when he was barely out of the *cradle*. [=when he was very young]
2 *formal* : the place where something begins — usually singular; usually + *of* • the *cradle of* civilization/liberty
3 : something that is used to hold or support something else • She placed the phone back on its *cradle*. • A number of ships were resting in their *cradles* in the shipyard.
4 *Brit* : a platform designed to move up and down the sides of a building so that workers can paint, clean, etc.
from (the) cradle to (the) grave : from the beginning until the end of life • He led a life of hardship *from the cradle to the grave*. • The book describes her life *from cradle to grave*.
rob the cradle *US, informal* : to date or marry someone who is much younger than you • His friends accused him of *robbing the cradle* when they saw how young his girlfriend was.
– see also CAT'S CRADLE

²cradle *verb* **cra·dles; cra·dled; cra·dling** [+ *obj*] : to hold (something or someone) gently in your arms or hands • He *cradled* her face in his hands. • She was *cradling* the injured man's head in her arms. • *cradle* a baby

¹craft /ˈkræft, *Brit* ˈkrɑːft/ *noun, pl* **crafts**
1 [*count*] : an activity that involves making something in a skillful way by using your hands • The potter has been studying his *craft* [=*handicraft*] for two decades. • the *craft* of pottery/basketry
2 [*count*] : a job or activity that requires special skill • the *craft* of songwriting/acting • a photographer's *craft*
3 ***crafts*** [*plural*] : objects made by skillful use of the hands • The store sells *crafts* [=*handicrafts*] from around the world. • There's a ***crafts fair*** [=an event at which crafts are sold] at the school this Saturday. — see also ARTS AND CRAFTS
4 *pl* **craft** [*count*] **a** : a usually small boat • a fishing *craft* • We saw many fishing boats and ***pleasure craft*** [=boats used for pleasure rather than work] on the bay. **b** : an airplane, helicopter, or spacecraft • The *craft* landed safely despite engine trouble. — see also HOVERCRAFT, LANDING CRAFT

²craft *verb* **crafts; craft·ed; craft·ing** [+ *obj*] : to make or produce (something) with care or skill • The furniture is *crafted* from bamboo. • He is *crafting* a new sculpture. • beautifully *crafted* wine/shoes/stories • She *crafted* a strategy to boost the company's earnings.
– craft·er *noun, pl* **-ers** [*count*] • a *crafter* of arguments/fiction

crafts·man /ˈkræftsmən, *Brit* ˈkrɑːftsmən/ *noun, pl* **-men** /-mən/ [*count*]
1 : a person (especially a man) who makes beautiful objects by hand • Skilled *craftsmen* carved the enormous mantel. • He is a master *craftsman* who works with marble.
2 : a person (especially a man) who is very skilled at doing something • As a writer/photographer/musician, he has developed into a true *craftsman*.
– crafts·man·like /ˈkræftsmən,laɪk, *Brit* ˈkrɑːftsmən,laɪk/ *adj* [*more ~; most ~*] • his *craftsmanlike* approach to songwriting

crafts·man·ship /ˈkræftsmən,ʃɪp, *Brit* ˈkrɑːftsmən,ʃɪp/ *noun* [*noncount*]
1 : skillful work • The table is a fine piece of *craftsmanship*. • The poem is a fine example of literary *craftsmanship*.
2 : the quality of something made with great skill • The fine *craftsmanship* of the table is remarkable. • Critics have admired the *craftsmanship* of her poetry.

crafts·per·son /ˈkræfts,pɚsn, *Brit* ˈkrɑːfts,pəːsn/ *noun, pl* **-people** [*count*] : a person who makes beautiful objects by hand : a craftsman or craftswoman

crafts·wom·an /ˈkræfts,wʊmən, *Brit* ˈkrɑːfts,wʊmən/ *noun, pl* **-wom·en** /-,wɪmən/ [*count*] : a woman who makes beautiful objects by hand

crafty /ˈkræfti, *Brit* ˈkrɑːfti/ *adj* **craft·i·er; -est** [*also more ~; most ~*] : clever in usually a deceptive or dishonest way • a *crafty* schemer/plotter • a *crafty* scheme
– craft·i·ly /ˈkræftəli, *Brit* ˈkrɑːftəli/ *adv* • a *craftily* designed plan **– craft·i·ness** *noun* [*noncount*]

crag /ˈkræg/ *noun, pl* **crags** [*count*] : a high and very steep area of rock on a mountain or cliff • The goat stood on the mountain *crag*.

crag·gy /ˈkrægi/ *adj* **craggier; -est**

1 : having many crags ▪ a *craggy* island
2 : rough in a way that suggests strength ▪ a famous actor who is known for his *craggy* good looks ▪ his white hair and *craggy* face ▪ a *craggy* voice

[1]**cram** /ˈkræm/ *verb* **crams; crammed; cram·ming**
1 [+ *obj*] : to fill (something) so that there is no room for anything else : to fill (something) completely ▪ He *crammed* the suitcase with his clothes. ▪ Before the trip I *crammed* my head with information about Spain. ▪ Protesters *crammed* the streets. — often used as *(be) crammed* ▪ With so many guests, the house *was* really *crammed.* [=*packed*] ▪ The little store *is crammed* full of books. ▪ The museum felt *crammed* with statues. ▪ My schedule *is* totally *crammed* [=*full*] this week. Can we meet next week?
2 [+ *obj*] **a** : to push or force (someone or something) into a space that is tight or crowded — usually + *into* or *in* ▪ He tried to *cram* all his clothes *in/into* one suitcase. ▪ We can *cram* [=*pack, squeeze*] six people *into* my car. ▪ The instructor *crammed* a lot of information *into* one week. — see also CRAM IN (below) **b** [*no obj*] : to push or force yourself into a space that is tight or crowded — usually + *into* ▪ We all *crammed into* one car. ▪ Thousands of people *crammed into* the stadium.
3 **a** [*no obj*] : to prepare for a test, exam, etc., by learning a lot of information quickly — usually + *for* ▪ He's *cramming for* the exam tomorrow. **b** [+ *obj*] *chiefly Brit* : to prepare (someone) for a test, exam, etc., by teaching a lot of information quickly — usually + *for* ▪ The class *crams* students *for* the exam.
cram in [*phrasal verb*] ***cram in (someone or something)*** *or* ***cram (someone or something) in*** : to make a special effort to meet with (someone) or to do (something) although you are very busy ▪ I can *cram* you *in* this afternoon. ▪ We *crammed in* as much sightseeing as possible on our trip to New York City.

[2]**cram** /ˈkræm/ *noun, pl* **crams** [*count*] *US* : a quick period of study in order to learn a lot of information quickly for a test, exam, etc. — usually used before another noun ▪ We're having a ***cram session*** tonight to prepare for tomorrow's test. ▪ She's taking a ***cram course.*** ✧ A ***cram school*** is a school designed to help students prepare for exams and get into better schools. ▪ Like many Japanese students, she attends a *cram school* in the evening.

cram·mer /ˈkræmɚ/ *noun, pl* **-mers** [*count*]
1 *US* : a person who prepares for a test, exam, etc. by learning a lot of information quickly : a person who crams for a test ▪ a group of last-minute *crammers*
2 *Brit* : a special school or book that prepares people for a test, exam, etc., by teaching a lot of information quickly

[1]**cramp** /ˈkræmp/ *noun, pl* **cramps**
1 : a sudden painful tightening of muscle in a part of the body [*count*] (*US*) ▪ I got a *cramp* in my leg while running. [*noncount*] (*Brit*) ▪ I got *cramp* in my leg while running. — see also WRITER'S CRAMP
2 ***cramps*** [*plural*] *chiefly US* : sharp pains in the stomach and the area near it especially because of menstruation ▪ She gets bad *cramps* every month.
– crampy *adj* ▪ *crampy* abdominal pain

[2]**cramp** *verb* **cramps; cramped; cramp·ing**
1 **a** [+ *obj*] : to cause (a part of the body) to feel pain because of tight muscles : to cause a cramp in (your hand, foot, etc.) ▪ Writing for such a long time may *cramp* your hand. **b** [*no obj*] : to have a sudden painful tightening of muscles : to experience a cramp or cramps ▪ His leg was *cramping* so badly he could hardly move it. — often + *up* ▪ My hand kept *cramping up*.
2 [+ *obj*] : to prevent (something) from developing or growing freely ▪ The new regulations may *cramp* the company's financial growth.
3 [+ *obj*] : to prevent (someone) from behaving or expressing emotions freely — usually used as *(be) cramped* ▪ She felt *cramped* [=*hemmed in*] by the school's strict regulations. ✧ Someone or something that ***cramps your style*** prevents you from behaving the way you want. ▪ He's not used to formality and finds that formal settings *cramp his style*.
– cramping *noun* [*noncount*] ▪ The medication may cause abdominal *cramping*.

cramped *adj* [*more* ~; *most* ~]
1 **a** : not having enough space inside : too small and crowded ▪ The family has been living in the *cramped* apartment for three months. ▪ They have been working in *cramped* conditions. **b** : not having enough space to move freely : feeling crowded and uncomfortable ▪ We were pretty *cramped* inside the tiny cabin.
2 : small and having parts too close together ▪ It's impossible to read his *cramped* handwriting. ▪ The keyboard is too *cramped* to be used by someone with normal-sized hands.

cram·pon /ˈkræmˌpɑːn/ *noun, pl* **-pons** [*count*] : a piece of metal with sharp points on the bottom that is worn by mountain climbers on the bottom of boots to make it easier to walk on ice and snow — usually plural ▪ a pair of *crampons*

cran·ber·ry /ˈkrænˌberi, *Brit* ˈkrænbəri/ *noun, pl* **-ries**
1 [*count*] : a small, dark red berry or the plant that produces it — often used before another noun ▪ *cranberry* sauce/juice ▪ *cranberry* bogs — see color picture on page C5
2 [*noncount*] : a dark red color
– cranberry *adj* ▪ a *cranberry* [=dark red] sweater

[1]**crane** /ˈkreɪn/ *noun, pl* **cranes** [*count*]
1 : a big machine with a long arm that is used by builders for lifting and moving heavy things ▪ a ***crane operator*** [=a person who operates a crane]
2 : a type of tall bird that has a long neck and long legs and lives near water

[2]**crane** *verb* **cranes; craned; cran·ing** : to stretch out (your neck) in order to see better [+ *obj*] We *craned* our necks toward the stage. [*no obj*] Everyone in the crowd was *craning* forward (to see her).

crane fly *noun, pl* ~ **flies** [*count*] *Brit* : a type of fly that has a long thin body, two wings, and long legs — called also (*Brit*) *daddy longlegs*

cra·ni·al /ˈkreɪnijəl/ *adj, always used before a noun, medical* : of or relating to the bones of the head that cover the brain : of or relating to the skull or cranium ▪ *cranial* capacity/injuries

cra·ni·um /ˈkreɪnijəm/ *noun, pl* **-ni·ums** *or* **-nia** /-nijə/ [*count*] *technical* : SKULL

[1]**crank** /ˈkræŋk/ *noun, pl* **cranks** [*count*]
1 : a machine part with a handle that can be turned in a circular motion to move something ▪ To open the car window, turn the *crank* on the door.
2 *informal + usually disapproving* **a** : a person who has strange ideas or thinks too much about one thing ▪ He was dismissed as a *crank* until his article was published. ▪ Most people think she's just a harmless *crank.* **b** *US* : a person who is often angry or easily annoyed : GROUCH ▪ a bad-tempered old *crank*

[2]**crank** *verb* **cranks; cranked; crank·ing** [+ *obj*]
1 : to move (something) by turning a crank — usually + *up* or *down* ▪ Will you *crank up/down* [=*roll up/down*] the window?
2 *informal* : to increase (something) especially by a large amount ▪ He *cranked* the temperature to 75 degrees. — usually + *up* ▪ *Crank up* [=*turn up*] the volume. ▪ The company is looking for new ways to *crank up* production.
3 : to start or try to start (an engine) by using a crank or some other method to get it moving ▪ *Crank* the engine to see if it will start.
4 *US, informal* : to move (something) in a circular motion ▪ He *cranked* [=*turned*] the steering wheel quickly to the left.
crank out [*phrasal verb*] ***crank out (something)*** *or* ***crank (something) out*** *informal* : to produce (something) quickly or carelessly ▪ The factory *cranks out* hundreds of cars every day. ▪ Not many musicians are able to *crank out* an album in just six months. ▪ He *cranked out* the report in less than an hour.

[3]**crank** *adj, always used before a noun* : made or sent as a joke or to cause harm ▪ an anonymous *crank* call ▪ He received a threatening *crank* letter.

crank·case /ˈkræŋkˌkeɪs/ *noun, pl* **-cas·es** [*count*] *technical* : the part of an engine that contains the crankshaft — see picture at ENGINE

crank·shaft /ˈkræŋkˌʃæft, *Brit* ˈkræŋkˌʃɑːft/ *noun, pl* **-shafts** [*count*] *technical* : a long metal piece that connects a vehicle's engine to the wheels and helps turn them — see picture at ENGINE

cranky /ˈkræŋki/ *adj* **crank·i·er; -est** [*also more* ~; *most* ~] *informal*
1 *chiefly US* : easily annoyed or angered ▪ I've been *cranky* all day because I didn't get enough sleep. ▪ bored and *cranky* kids ▪ a *cranky* baby [=a baby that cries and wants a lot of attention]
2 *Brit* : strange or weird ▪ *cranky* ideas/theories
– crank·i·ness *noun* [*noncount*] ▪ I apologize for my *crankiness* yesterday.

C

cran•ny /ˈkræni/ *noun, pl* **-nies** [*count*] **:** a small opening or space • We saw strange, colorful creatures in the *crannies* of the reef while scuba diving. • We explored every *cranny* of the old castle. — sometimes used figuratively • The book explores every *cranny* of her life. — see also *every nook and cranny* at NOOK

[1]crap /ˈkræp/ *noun, informal + impolite*
1 [*noncount*] **:** something that is worthless, unimportant, or of poor quality • She treats him like (a piece of) *crap*. • We have a lot of *crap* [=*junk*] in the garage.
2 [*noncount*] **:** foolish or untrue words or ideas **:** NONSENSE • You don't believe all that *crap*, do you? • "Do you think they're telling the truth?" "No, I think they're ***full of crap***." • I heard what they said to you, and I think it's a ***load/pile of crap***. • (*US*) It's all a ***bunch of crap***. • ***Cut the crap*** [=stop lying] and tell me what really happened.
3 [*noncount*] **:** bad or unfair behavior or treatment • Do what I say, and don't ***give me any crap***. • He's a tough teacher who won't ***take crap*** from anyone. • I won't ***stand for your crap*** any longer. = I won't ***put up with your crap*** any longer.
4 a [*noncount*] **:** solid waste passed out of the body **:** FECES **b** [*singular*] **:** the act of passing solid waste from the body — used in the phrases ***take a crap*** and (*Brit*) ***have a crap***
5 — used for emphasis after words like *scare, frighten*, and *beat* • That movie ***scared the crap out of*** me. [=scared me very badly] • The boxer ***beat the crap out of*** his opponent.
give a crap **:** to care at all about someone or something • Who *gives a crap*? [=who cares?] — usually used in negative statements • She *doesn't give a crap* about us.
like crap **:** very badly • I sing *like crap*. [=I am a terrible singer] ✧ If you ***feel like crap***, you feel very sick, unhappy, etc. • I got drunk at the party, and the next morning I *felt like crap*. [=I felt sick]

[2]crap *verb* **craps; crapped; crap•ping** [*no obj*] *informal + impolite* **:** to pass solid waste from the body **:** DEFECATE • The puppy *crapped* on the floor.

[3]crap *adj, chiefly Brit slang, impolite* **:** of poor quality **:** not good • The DJ played some *crap* [=*crappy*] music. • I'm *crap* at golf. — compare [4]CRAP

[4]crap *adj, always used before a noun* **:** of or relating to the game of craps • a *crap* game/table — compare [3]CRAP

crap•o•la /ˌkræpˈoulə/ *noun* [*noncount*] *US slang*
1 : something that is useless or unimportant **:** CRAP • The furniture in the garage is *crapola*.
2 : foolish or untrue words or ideas **:** CRAP • Everything he says is just a bunch of *crapola*.

crap•per /ˈkræpɚ/ *noun*
the crapper *informal + impolite* **:** a toilet

crap•py /ˈkræpi/ *adj* **crap•pi•er; -est** *informal + impolite* **:** of poor quality **:** not good **:** LOUSY • *crappy* music/weather • I think that was the *crappiest* movie I've ever seen. • I felt *crappy* all day yesterday.

craps /ˈkræps/ *noun* [*plural*] **:** a game played for money with two dice • They were playing/shooting *craps* in the back of the room.

crap•shoot /ˈkræpˌʃuːt/ *noun, pl* **-shoots** [*count*] *US* **:** something that could produce a good or bad result — usually singular • Choosing a restaurant can be a real *crapshoot* when you're in an unfamiliar city.

[1]crash /ˈkræʃ/ *verb* **crash•es; crashed; crash•ing**
1 a [*no obj*] **:** to hit something hard enough to cause serious damage or destruction • Investigators are still trying to determine why the airplane *crashed*. [=why the airplane hit the ground] — often + *into* • The car *crashed into* the fence/wall/guardrail. • She *crashed into* another car. • A large meteorite may have *crashed into* the Earth 65 million years ago. **b** [+ *obj*] **:** to damage (a vehicle) by causing it to hit something • She *crashed* the car into a tree, but no one was hurt. • He has *crashed* two cars, a truck, and a motorcycle.
2 a *always followed by an adverb or preposition* [*no obj*] **:** to make a loud noise by falling, hitting something, etc. • We listened to the waves *crashing* against the shore. • The stuntman *crashed* through the window on a motorcycle. • The walls *crashed* down around them. • He came *crashing* [=*tearing*] through the woods. • The books *crashed* to the floor. • The whole stack of cans ***came crashing down***. [=fell down with a lot of noise and force] — sometimes used figuratively • The whole theory *came crashing down* when it was revealed that some of the supporting evidence had been falsified. • His world *came crashing down* when he lost his job. **b** [*no obj*] **:** to make a loud noise • The cymbals *crashed* and the trumpets blew. • Thunder *crashed* as the rain started to pour. **c** [+ *obj*] **:** to cause two things to hit against each other and make a loud noise • He *crashed* the cymbals together.
4 a [*no obj*] *of a computer* **:** to stop working suddenly • My computer keeps *crashing*. **b** [+ *obj*] **:** to cause (a computer) to stop working suddenly • This program always *crashes* my computer.
5 [*no obj*] *informal* **a :** to go to sleep • I was exhausted after the long flight, so I just checked into the hotel and *crashed*. **b :** to stay or live for a short time with someone • You can *crash* [=*sleep*] here tonight. • She's *crashing* with friends for a few days while her apartment is being repaired.
6 [*no obj*] *of a business, price, market, etc.* **:** to go down in value very suddenly and quickly • They lost thousands of dollars when the stock market *crashed*.
7 [+ *obj*] *informal* **:** to go to (a party) without being invited • He tried to *crash* the party but they wouldn't let him in.
8 [+ *obj*] *US, sports* **:** to move very quickly and forcefully toward (something, such as the goal in ice hockey) • The players *crashed* the net.
crash and burn *US, informal* **:** to fail completely • The company *crashed and burned* after only two years in business.
– crash•er *noun, pl* **-ers** [*count*] • a party *crasher*

[2]crash *noun, pl* **crashes** [*count*]
1 : an accident in which a vehicle is seriously damaged or destroyed by hitting something • He was injured in a car *crash*. • Investigators are still trying to determine the cause of the *crash*. • a train/airplane *crash* • An ambulance arrived at the *crash* site/scene within minutes.
2 : a very loud noise — usually singular • The pot/glass fell to the floor with a *crash*. • We listened to the *crash* of waves in the distance. • He ended the song with a *crash* of cymbals. • a *crash* of thunder
3 : an occurrence in which a computer suddenly stops working • I am always experiencing computer *crashes*.
4 : a sudden and extreme fall or drop in amount or value • They lost thousands of dollars in the stock market *crash*. • a species of fish that has undergone a population *crash*

crash barrier *noun, pl* **~ -ers** [*count*] *Brit* **:** GUARDRAIL

crash course *noun, pl* **~ courses** [*count*] **:** a class in which a lot of information is taught in a short period of time • Before her trip, she took a *crash course* in Russian culture and history at the local university. — sometimes used figuratively • Taking care of his sister's children was a *crash course* in parenting for him.

crash diet *noun, pl* **~ -ets** [*count*] **:** a way of losing a lot of weight very quickly by limiting how much you eat • He went on a *crash diet* and lost 20 pounds in a month.

crash helmet *noun, pl* **~ -mets** [*count*] **:** a very strong, hard hat that is worn to protect your head when you are riding a bicycle, motorcycle, etc.

crashing *adj, always used before a noun, informal* **:** very bad — used to make a negative statement more forceful • The book is a *crashing* bore. [=the book is extremely boring] • The movie was a *crashing* failure.
a crashing halt *chiefly US* **:** a complete and sudden end • When news of the scandal broke, her career came to *a crashing halt*. • Construction of the tunnel was brought to *a crashing halt* when the funds ran out.

crash–land /ˈkræʃˈlænd/ *verb* **-lands; -land•ed; -land•ing :** to land (an airplane, helicopter, etc.) in an unusual way because of an emergency [+ *obj*] The pilot *crash-landed* the plane in the field. [*no obj*] The pilot *crash-landed* in the field.
– crash landing *noun, pl* **~ -ings** [*count*] • The pilot had to make a *crash landing*.

crass /ˈkræs/ *adj* **crass•er; -est** [*also more ~; most ~*] *disapproving* **:** having or showing no understanding of what is proper or acceptable **:** rude and insensitive • A few people seemed shocked by her *crass* comments.
– crass•ly *adv* • They were joking *crassly* about her appearance. **– crass•ness** *noun* [*noncount*]

[1]crate /ˈkreɪt/ *noun, pl* **crates** [*count*]
1 a : a large wooden or plastic box used for moving things from one place to another • The bear arrived at the zoo in a *crate*. • packing/shipping *crates* • *crates* of apples/equipment **b :** a metal or plastic container that is used to hold bottles • Each milk *crate* holds nine bottles. **c :** the amount of something contained in a crate • They used a *crate* of oranges to make enough juice for everyone.
2 *old-fashioned* **:** an old car or airplane that is in bad condition • One day the old *crate* just wouldn't start.

[2]crate *verb* **crates; crat•ed; crat•ing** [+ *obj*] **:** to pack (something) in a crate • The equipment was *crated* today and will be shipped tomorrow. — often + *up* ▪ The bear was *crated up* and shipped to the zoo.

[1]**cra·ter** /ˈkreɪtɚ/ *noun, pl* **-ters** [*count*]

1 : a large round hole in the ground made by the explosion of a bomb or by something falling from the sky ▪ Scientists believe the enormous *crater* was created by the impact of a meteorite thousands of years ago.

2 : the area on top of a volcano that is shaped like a bowl ▪ We flew over the *crater* of the volcano in a helicopter.

– cratered /ˈkreɪtɚd/ *adj* ▪ a *cratered* moon/surface

[2]**crater** *verb* **-ters; -tered; -ter·ing** [*no obj*] *US, informal* **:** to fail or fall suddenly ▪ The deal *cratered* when neither party could agree on the final price. ▪ Stock prices *cratered* after the companies' merger.

cra·vat /krəˈvæt/ *noun, pl* **-vats** [*count*] **:** a short, wide piece of cloth that is worn around the neck by men with its ends tucked inside the collar of a shirt or sweater

crave /ˈkreɪv/ *verb* **craves; craved; crav·ing** [+ *obj*] **:** to have a very strong desire for (something) ▪ Like many celebrities, he *craves* attention. ▪ I was *craving* french fries, so I pulled into the nearest fast-food restaurant.

cra·ven /ˈkreɪvən/ *adj* [*more* ~; *most* ~] *formal* **:** having or showing a complete lack of courage **:** very cowardly ▪ a *craven* decision ▪ *craven* compromises

– cra·ven·ly *adv* ▪ He *cravenly* fled from the scene.

crav·ing /ˈkreɪvɪŋ/ *noun, pl* **-ings** [*count*] **:** a very strong desire for something ▪ I had/felt a sudden *craving* for french fries, so I pulled into the nearest fast-food restaurant.

craw /ˈkrɑː/ *noun, pl* **craws** [*count*] **:** an area in a bird's throat in which food can be kept **:** CROP

stick in your craw *informal* ✧ If something *sticks in your craw* you are very annoyed by it or cannot accept it because you think it is wrong or unfair. ▪ What really *sticks in my craw* is the way he acts as if he's done nothing wrong.

craw·dad /ˈkrɑːˌdæd/ *noun, pl* **-dads** [*count, noncount*] *US, informal* **:** CRAYFISH — used especially in the southern U.S.

craw·fish /ˈkrɑːˌfɪʃ/ *noun, pl* **crawfish** [*count, noncount*] *US* **:** CRAYFISH

[1]**crawl** /ˈkrɑːl/ *verb* **crawls; crawled; crawl·ing**

1 [*no obj*] **a :** to move on your hands and knees ▪ Does the baby *crawl* yet? ▪ We got down on our knees and *crawled* through a small opening. ▪ The baby *crawled* across the floor toward her mother. **b :** to move with the body close to or on the ground ▪ The soldiers *crawled* forward on their bellies. ▪ The snake *crawled* into its hole. ▪ There's a spider *crawling* [=moving forward on its legs] up the wall.

2 a [*no obj*] **:** to move slowly ▪ They're doing construction on the road, so traffic is *crawling*. ▪ I worked late into the night, and it was 2 a.m. before I finally *crawled* into bed. ▪ The bus *crawled* along the rough and narrow road. ▪ The days slowly *crawled* by. ▪ Traffic has ***crawled to a stop/standstill*** [=has come to a complete stop after moving very slowly] ▪ Work on the project has *crawled to a standstill*. **b** [+ *obj*] **:** to move slowly on, across, or through (something) ▪ We all got into the old truck and *crawled* the streets of the city looking for him.

3 [*no obj*] **:** to be full of many people, insects, animals, etc. — usually used in the phrase ***be crawling with*** ▪ The courthouse *is crawling* [=*teeming*] *with* reporters today. ▪ The table *was crawling with* ants.

4 [*no obj*] *Brit, informal + disapproving* **:** to be extremely nice to someone in order to get approval or some advantage for yourself ▪ He's been *crawling* [=*creeping*] to the boss for months, so it's no surprise he got a promotion.

come/go crawling to *informal* ✧ If you *come/go crawling (back) to* someone, you go to someone for help or approval in a way that shows you are weak or sorry for what you have done. ▪ Don't *come crawling to* me for help later if you aren't going to listen to me now. ▪ He's *gone crawling back to* his old girlfriend.

crawl out of the woodwork see WOODWORK

make your skin/flesh crawl ✧ If something *makes your skin/flesh crawl*, it causes you to have an uncomfortable feeling of fear or disgust. ▪ Just thinking about being down in that dark cave *makes my skin crawl*.

– crawl·er /ˈkrɑːlɚ/ *noun, pl* **-ers** [*count*] ▪ Both babies are *crawlers* now. — see also NIGHT CRAWLER

[2]**crawl** *noun* [*singular*]

1 : a very slow speed ▪ Near the construction site, traffic had slowed to a *crawl*. ▪ The bus was moving along at a *crawl*.

2 : a way of swimming in which the swimmer lies facing down in the water and moves first one arm over the head and then the other while kicking the legs ▪ Her strongest stroke is the *crawl*.

— see also PUB CRAWL

crawl space *noun, pl* ~ **spaces** [*count*] *US* **:** a space under the first floor or roof of a building that is not high enough to stand up in

cray·fish /ˈkreɪˌfɪʃ/ *noun, pl* **crayfish** [*count*] **:** an animal that looks like a small lobster and lives in rivers and streams — see color picture on page C8

cray·on /ˈkreɪˌɑːn/ *noun, pl* **-ons :** a stick of colored wax that is used for drawing [*count*] a box of *crayons* [*noncount*] The drawing is done in *crayon*. — often used before another noun ▪ *crayon* drawings

– crayon *verb* **-ons; -oned; -on·ing** [+ *obj*] Which one of you children *crayoned* the wall? [=drew on the wall with a crayon] [*no obj*] Which child *crayoned* on the wall?

craze /ˈkreɪz/ *noun, pl* **craz·es** [*count*] **:** something that is very popular for a period of time ▪ the latest dance/fashion/music *craze* — often + *for* ▪ I don't understand the current *craze for* low-fat diets.

crazed /ˈkreɪzd/ *adj* [*more* ~; *most* ~] **:** wild and uncontrolled ▪ a *crazed* killer ▪ The *crazed* look in his eyes frightened me. ▪ the *crazed* ramblings/rantings of a lunatic ▪ an addict *crazed* with drugs [=made crazy by drugs] ▪ The prisoner was *crazed* [=made crazy] by pain and fear.

[1]**cra·zy** /ˈkreɪzi/ *adj* **cra·zi·er; -est** [*also more* ~; *most* ~]

1 : not sane: such as **a** ***usually offensive*** **:** having or showing severe mental illness ▪ a hospital for *crazy* people ✧ This sense is no longer used in a serious way and is now usually considered offensive. The phrase *mentally ill* is preferred. **b :** unable to think in a clear or sensible way ▪ She's *crazy* with jealousy. ▪ He's been acting kind of *crazy* lately. **c** — used in the phrase ***drive/make (someone) crazy*** to describe annoying or bothering someone very much ▪ It *makes* me *crazy* [=I feel very annoyed] when people drive like that. ▪ That noise is *driving* me *crazy*. [=it is really annoying me] ▪ The kids were *driving* the teacher *crazy*. — see also STIR-CRAZY

2 : wild and uncontrolled ▪ He had a *crazy* [=*crazed, insane, wild*] look in his eyes.

3 : very foolish or unreasonable ▪ He likes to drive at *crazy* [=*insane*] speeds. ▪ There are a lot of *crazy* drivers on the streets. ▪ You are *crazy* to have paid so much for this car. ▪ You would be *crazy* not to accept their offer! ▪ What a *crazy* thing to do!

4 : very strange or unusual ▪ She likes *crazy* hair colors, like pink and blue. ▪ How do you think of all these *crazy* ideas? ▪ I love to listen to my uncle's *crazy* stories about his job.

5 : liking someone or something very much **:** very fond of or enthusiastic about someone or something ▪ She's *crazy* for anything having to do with Japanese animation. ▪ teenagers who are ***girl/boy crazy*** [=very interested in girls/boys] — often + *about* ▪ They are *crazy about* each other. [=they like each other a lot] ▪ He wasn't *crazy about* making the trip, but was glad he did in the end. ▪ She is *crazy about* baseball.

go crazy **1 :** to become mentally ill **:** to go insane ▪ She *went crazy* and started to think everyone was trying to kill her. — usually used in an exaggerated way ▪ I must be *going crazy*. I can't find my car keys anywhere. ▪ He kept honking his horn, and I thought I would *go* (completely) *crazy* if he didn't stop. **2 :** to act in a way that is out of control **:** to act wildly ▪ We were just talking when he suddenly *went crazy* and started screaming and breaking things. ▪ Everybody at the party was dancing and basically *going crazy*. ▪ The crowd *went crazy* [=became very excited] when the team won the championship.

like crazy *informal* **1 :** with a lot of energy and speed ▪ They've been working *like crazy* [=very hard] since dawn. **2 :** very quickly ▪ Cars were selling *like crazy*. ▪ He's been spending money *like crazy*. **3 :** very much ▪ When I broke my leg it hurt *like crazy*.

– cra·zi·ly /ˈkreɪzəli/ *adv* ▪ behaving *crazily* **– cra·zi·ness** *noun* [*noncount*] ▪ the *craziness* [=*insanity*] of war

[2]**crazy** *noun, pl* **-zies** [*count*] *chiefly US, informal* **:** a person who is crazy ▪ A bunch of *crazies* live there.

[3]**crazy** *adv, US, informal* **:** very or extremely ▪ I bought some *crazy* good/cheap stuff there.

crazy bone *noun, pl* ~ **bones** [*count*] *US* **:** FUNNY BONE

crazy golf *noun* [*noncount*] *Brit* **:** MINIATURE GOLF

crazy paving *noun* [*noncount*] *Brit* **:** many pieces of stone of different shapes and sizes that are placed together to form a path or other surface

crazy quilt *noun, pl* ~ **quilts** [*count*] *US*

1 : a covering for a bed that is made of many pieces of cloth in different sizes without a regular design
2 : a confused mix of things ▪ a *crazy quilt* [=*hodgepodge*] of regulations ▪ a *crazy quilt* of streets
– crazy–quilt *adj, always used before a noun* ▪ a *crazy-quilt* pattern ▪ *crazy-quilt* streets

creak /ˈkriːk/ *verb* **creaks; creaked; creak·ing** [*no obj*] **:** to make a long, high sound **:** to make a sound like the sound made by an old door when it opens or closes ▪ The door *creaked* open. = The door made a *creaking* sound as it opened. ▪ The old floorboards *creaked* under our feet. ▪ The porch roof *creaked* with the heavy weight of the snow.
– creak *noun, pl* **creaks** [*count*] ▪ We heard the *creak* of door as it opened.

creaky /ˈkriːki/ *adj* **creak·i·er; -est** [*also more ~; most ~*]
1 : making a creaking sound ▪ *creaky* floorboards
2 : no longer working well **:** old and in bad condition ▪ The new governor promises to work to revive the state's *creaky* economy. ▪ a computer system that is *creaky* with age

[1]**cream** /ˈkriːm/ *noun, pl* **creams**
1 [*noncount*] **:** the thick part of milk that rises to the top **:** the part of milk that contains fat ▪ Would you like some *cream* in your coffee? ▪ strawberries and *cream* ▪ hot chocolate with whipped *cream* — see also CLOTTED CREAM, HEAVY CREAM, SOUR CREAM, WHIPPING CREAM
2 : a food that is made with cream [*noncount*] *cream* of tomato soup ▪ a chocolate candy with a vanilla *cream* center [*count*] a box of coconut *creams* [=chocolate candies filled with a coconut and cream mixture] — see also CREAM CHEESE, CREAM OF TARTAR, CREAM PUFF, ICE CREAM
3 : a very thick liquid or soft substance that is rubbed into the skin to make it softer or is used as a medicine for the skin [*noncount*] The doctor prescribed a new *cream* for the rash. ▪ Do you have any ***hand cream***? [=*hand lotion*] [*count*] a cabinet full of special *creams* and pills — see also COLD CREAM, SHAVING CREAM, SUN CREAM
4 ***the cream*** **:** the best part of something ▪ a party attended by *the cream* of society — see also *the cream of the crop* at [1]CROP
5 [*count, noncount*] **:** a pale yellowish color that is close to white — see color picture on page C2
like the cat that got the cream see CAT
– cream *adj* ▪ a *cream* [=*cream-colored*] sweater

[2]**cream** *verb* **creams; creamed; creaming** [+ *obj*]
1 : to stir or mix (ingredients) until they are soft and smooth ▪ *Cream* the butter and sugar, and then add the eggs.
2 *US, informal* **a :** to defeat (a person or team) easily and completely — usually used as *(be/get) creamed* ▪ Our team *got creamed* in the play-offs. **b :** to hit (someone) very hard — usually used as *(be/get) creamed* ▪ She *was creamed* by another skier as she was coming down the slope. ▪ The surfer *got creamed* by a huge wave.
cream off [*phrasal verb*] ***cream off (someone or something) or cream (someone or something) off*** *chiefly Brit* **:** to remove (the best part) from something **:** to take (someone or something) away for yourself ▪ Most of the profit was *creamed off* by the government. ▪ The best students are *creamed off* to attend other schools.
– creamed *adj* ▪ *creamed* corn/spinach/onions [=corn/spinach/onions in a sauce made with cream]

cream cheese *noun* [*noncount*] **:** a soft white cheese made from milk and cream

cream–colored *adj* **:** having a pale yellowish color that is close to white ▪ The sheets are *cream-colored.*

cream·er /ˈkriːmɚ/ *noun, pl* **-ers**
1 [*count*] *US* **:** a small container that is used for serving cream ▪ a matching sugar bowl and *creamer*
2 [*count, noncount*] **:** a liquid or powder that is used instead of cream in coffee or tea ▪ a nondairy *creamer*

cream·ery /ˈkriːməri/ *noun, pl* **-er·ies** [*count*] **:** a place where butter and cheese are made or where milk and cream are prepared or sold

cream of tartar *noun* [*noncount*] **:** a type of white salt that is used especially in cooking and baking

cream puff *noun, pl* **~ puffs** [*count*] *US*
1 : a type of light pastry that is filled with whipped cream or a sweetened cream filling and often topped with chocolate — called also *(Brit) profiterole*
2 *informal* **:** a weak person **:** a person who can be easily controlled or defeated ▪ We'll never win with a bunch of *cream puffs* on our team!
3 *informal* **:** a used car that is in very good condition

cream soda *noun, pl* **~ -das** [*count, noncount*] **:** a type of sweet, bubbly soft drink that is flavored with vanilla

cream tea *noun, pl* **~ teas** [*count*] *Brit* **:** a small meal eaten in the afternoon that includes tea with scones, jam, and cream

creamy /ˈkriːmi/ *adj* **cream·i·er; -est** [*also more ~; most ~*]
1 a : made with cream or tasting like cream ▪ a rich, *creamy* flavor **b :** thick and smooth ▪ a *creamy* salad dressing ▪ The sauce has a smooth, *creamy* texture. ▪ Do you prefer *creamy* or crunchy peanut butter?
2 : smooth and soft ▪ She sings with a *creamy* voice.
3 : having a color like cream ▪ a *creamy* yellow ▪ *creamy* skin
– cream·i·ness *noun* [*noncount*] ▪ the *creaminess* of the sauce ▪ the *creaminess* of her skin

[1]**crease** /ˈkriːs/ *noun, pl* **creas·es**
1 [*count*] **a :** a line or mark made by folding, pressing, or crushing something (such as cloth or a piece of paper) ▪ He ironed his pants to make the *creases* sharp. ▪ a *crease* in the paper — see color picture on page C15 **b :** a line or fold in someone's skin **:** WRINKLE ▪ tiny *creases* at the corners of his eyes
2 ***the crease*** **:** an area around or in front of a goal in some games (such as hockey) ▪ Players from the opposing team may not enter *the crease.*
3 [*singular*] *Brit* **:** the line where the batsman stands in cricket ▪ The batsman moved out of the/his *crease.*

[2]**crease** *verb* **creases; creased; creas·ing**
1 [+ *obj*] **:** to fold, press, or crush (something, such as cloth or a piece of paper) so that a line or mark is formed **:** to put a crease in (something) ▪ a neatly *creased* pair of pants ▪ The pages of the book were stained and *creased.*
2 : to make a line or fold in (someone's skin) [+ *obj*] A frown *creased* [=*wrinkled*] his forehead ▪ Their faces were *creased* with worry. [=they had lines on their faces because they were worried] [*no obj*] She looked up, her face *creasing* into a smile.

cre·ate /kriˈeɪt/ *verb* **-ates; -at·ed; -at·ing** [+ *obj*]
1 : to make or produce (something) **:** to cause (something new) to exist ▪ Several new government programs were *created* while she was governor. ▪ The President has announced a plan to *create* new jobs. ▪ the scientists who *created* the world's first atomic bomb ▪ The machine *creates* a lot of noise. ▪ According to the Bible, the world was *created* [=*made*] in six days.
2 : to cause (a particular situation) to exist ▪ You *created* [=*made, caused*] this mess, and now you'll have to fix it. ▪ We need everyone's help in *creating* [=*developing*] a better society. ▪ It can be hard to *create* a balance between work and family. ▪ She *creates* a friendly and welcoming atmosphere for her guests. ▪ The advertisements are intended to *create* demand for the product.
3 : to produce (something new, such as a work of art) by using your talents and imagination ▪ He *creates* beautiful paintings. ▪ I've been *creating* music for over 30 years. ▪ She enjoys *creating* new dishes by combining unusual ingredients.
4 *chiefly Brit* **:** to give (someone) a new title or rank ▪ She was *created* (the) Duchess of Cornwall.

cre·a·tion /kriˈeɪʃən/ *noun, pl* **-tions**
1 [*noncount*] **:** the act of making or producing something that did not exist before **:** the act of creating something ▪ The play continues to entertain audiences 25 years after its *creation.* ▪ Job *creation* will be an important issue in next year's elections. ▪ These changes will lead to the *creation* of new businesses.
2 [*count*] **:** something new that is made or produced **:** something that has been created ▪ The company was largely the *creation* of one woman. ▪ his latest artistic *creation* ▪ Come taste our chef's delicious new *creations.* ▪ She's wearing one of her original fashion *creations.*
3 [*noncount*] **:** everything in the world ▪ How are humans different from the rest of *creation*? ▪ the whole of *creation* [=all of the world] ▪ They've traveled all over *creation.* [=they've traveled everywhere]
4 *or* ***Creation*** [*noncount*] **:** the act of making the world ▪ the biblical story of *Creation* ▪ *creation* myths [=stories about how people and the world were first created]

cre·a·tion·ism /kriˈeɪʃəˌnɪzəm/ *noun* [*noncount*] **:** the belief that God created all things out of nothing as described in the Bible and that therefore the theory of evolution is incorrect
– cre·a·tion·ist /kriˈeɪʃənɪst/ *noun, pl* **-ists** [*count*]

cre·a·tive /kri'eɪtɪv/ *adj*
1 [*more* ~; *most* ~] **:** having or showing an ability to make new things or think of new ideas ▪ He was more *creative* [=*imaginative*] than the other students. ▪ She's a very *creative* person. ▪ She has one of the most *creative* minds in the business. ▪ a burst of *creative* energy [=energy that you use to make or think of new things] ▪ They've come up with some *creative* new ways to make money. ▪ a *creative* solution to a difficult problem ▪ *creative* thinking
2 *always used before a noun* **:** using the ability to make or think of new things **:** involving the process by which new ideas, stories, etc., are created ▪ He teaches *creative* writing at the university. ▪ the first step in the *creative* process ▪ the show's *creative* director/team
3 *always used before a noun, usually disapproving* **:** done in an unusual and often dishonest way ▪ It turns out that the company's report of record profits last year was due to some ***creative accounting***.
– cre·a·tive·ly *adv* [*more* ~; *most* ~] ▪ Try to think more *creatively*. ▪ solving problems *creatively* **– cre·a·tive·ness** *noun* [*noncount*] ▪ I admire her *creativeness*. [=(more commonly) *creativity*]

cre·a·tiv·i·ty /ˌkriːˌeɪ'tɪvəti/ *noun* [*noncount*] **:** the ability to make new things or think of new ideas ▪ her intelligence and artistic *creativity*

cre·a·tor /kri'eɪtə/ *noun, pl* **-tors**
1 [*count*] **:** a person who makes something new ▪ the *creator* of the popular television show ▪ the Web site's *creators*
2 Creator [*singular*] **:** GOD 1 ▪ "... all men ... are endowed by their *Creator* with certain unalienable Rights ..." —*U.S. Declaration of Independence* (1776)

crea·ture /'kriːʧə/ *noun, pl* **-tures** [*count*]
1 a : an animal of any type ▪ rabbits, squirrels, and other furry *creatures* ▪ They say that these forests are filled with wild *creatures*. [=*beasts*] ▪ Few ***living creatures*** can survive without water. **b :** an imaginary or very strange kind of animal ▪ fantastic/mythical/legendary *creatures* [=*beasts, monsters*] ▪ strange sea *creatures* ▪ a giant hairy apelike *creature*
2 : a person usually of a specified type ▪ She's a *creature* of rare beauty. ▪ A social *creature* by nature, he loves working with people. ▪ The poor *creature* had no way to get home.
3 : a person or thing that is influenced or controlled by something specified — + *of* ▪ She's a *creature of* politics. ▪ The industry is still a *creature of* the 1930s. [=it began in the 1930s and has not changed] ▪ I'm a ***creature of habit*** [=I always do the same things in the same way]

creature comfort *noun, pl* ~ **-forts** [*count*] **:** something that makes life easier or more pleasant — usually plural ▪ a hotel with all the *creature comforts* [=*amenities*] of home

crèche /'krɛʃ/ *noun, pl* **crèch·es** [*count*]
1 *US* **:** a set of statues that represents the scene of Jesus Christ's birth and that is displayed during Christmas — called also (*chiefly Brit*) *crib*
2 *Brit* **:** a place where young children are cared for during the day while their parents are working **:** a day care center

cred /'krɛd/ *noun* [*noncount*] *informal* **:** the fact of being accepted and respected as a member of a social group or class ▪ geek/hipster *cred* ✧ *Cred* is an abbreviation of *credibility*. — see also STREET CRED

cre·dence /'kriːdn̩s/ *noun* [*noncount*]
1 : belief that something is true ▪ I ***place/put*** little ***credence in*** statistics. [=I generally do not believe statistics] ▪ Don't ***give credence to*** [=don't believe] their gossip.
2 : the quality of being believed or accepted as something true or real ▪ This new evidence gives/adds/lends (some) *credence* [=*credibility*] to their theory. [=makes their theory believable] ▪ The theory is gaining *credence* among scientists.

cre·den·tial /krɪ'dɛnʃəl/ *noun, pl* **-tials** [*count*]
1 : a quality, skill, or experience that makes a person suited to do a job ▪ My experience as a manager is my strongest *credential*. — usually plural ▪ What are your *credentials*? [=*qualifications*] ▪ her impressive academic/professional *credentials*
2 : a document which shows that a person is qualified to do a particular job ▪ (*US*) a teaching *credential* [=(more commonly) *certificate*] — usually plural ▪ The doctor showed us her *credentials*. ▪ press *credentials* [=documents which show that a person is a journalist]
– credentialed *adj, US* ▪ a *credentialed* teacher

cred·i·bil·i·ty /ˌkrɛdə'bɪləti/ *noun* [*noncount*] **:** the quality of being believed or accepted as true, real, or honest ▪ The new evidence lends *credibility* to their theory. ▪ a lack/loss of *credibility* ▪ The scandal undermined/damaged her *credibility* as an honest politician. ▪ In this instance, the lawyer's job is to make the jury doubt/question the witness's *credibility*. ▪ They doubted the *credibility* of the witness's story. [=they doubted that the story was true]

credibility gap *noun, pl* ~ **gaps** [*count*] **:** a situation in which the things that someone says are not believed or trusted because of the difference between what is said and what seems to be true ▪ There is a *credibility gap* between what the mayor says and what the people see happening in the city. ▪ The fact that the new estimates are so wildly different from the initial numbers has created a *credibility gap*.

cred·i·ble /'krɛdəbəl/ *adj* [*more* ~; *most* ~]
1 : able to be believed **:** reasonable to trust or believe ▪ Their story seemed *credible* [=*believable, plausible*] at first. ▪ We've received *credible* information about the group's location. ▪ *credible* evidence/witnesses
2 : good enough to be effective ▪ She does a *credible* job of playing the famous singer.
– cred·i·bly /'krɛdəbli/ *adv* ▪ She can talk *credibly* about the difficulties of being poor in this country.

¹cred·it /'krɛdɪt/ *noun, pl* **-its**
1 [*noncount*] **a :** money that a bank or business will allow a person to use and then pay back in the future ▪ banks that extend *credit* to the public ▪ Some banks will charge a fee if you go over your ***credit limit***. [=if you spend more money than the bank has agreed to let you use] ✧ If you buy something ***on credit***, you take it and promise to pay for it later. ▪ Back then, stores allowed their customers to buy food *on credit*. **b :** a record of how well you have paid your bills in the past ▪ How's your *credit*? ▪ Do you have good *credit*? [=have you paid back money you owe, paid your bills when they are due, etc.?] ▪ You need to have a strong ***credit history*** and a good job in order to get a mortgage.
2 [*count*] **a :** an amount of money that is added to an account ▪ A *credit* of $50 was added to your account. — opposite DEBIT **b :** an amount of money that is subtracted from the amount that must be paid ▪ Families with children in college will receive a ***tax credit*** this year. [=the amount that they owe in taxes will be reduced]
3 [*noncount*] **:** praise or special attention that is given to someone for doing something or for making something happen ▪ All the *credit* must go to the play's talented director. ▪ She's finally getting the *credit* she deserves. ▪ He shared the *credit* with his parents. ▪ You've got to give her *credit*; she knows what she's doing. — often + *for* ▪ They were given *credit for* the discovery. ▪ He didn't actually write the essay, but he got *credit for* it. ▪ You have to give us *credit for* trying. We did the best we could. ▪ She never took *credit for* her achievements. ▪ Party leaders took/claimed ***full credit for*** the country's progress. [=they claimed that they alone caused the country's progress] ✧ If you ***give credit where credit is due*** you praise someone who deserves to be praised. ▪ In receiving this award, I must *give credit where credit is due* and acknowledge all the people who helped me.
4 [*noncount*] **:** a good opinion that people have about someone or something ✧ Someone or something that ***brings credit to you*** or ***does you credit*** causes people to think of you in favorable way. ▪ She is a talented journalist who has *brought credit to* the newspaper. ▪ The fact that administrators fired the offending teacher immediately *does* the school *credit*. ✧ Something that is ***to your credit*** causes people to have a more favorable opinion of you. ▪ It's *to her credit* that she admitted her mistake. ▪ *To his credit*, Mr. Smith has offered to pay for the damages. ✧ Something that ***does you no credit*** causes people to have a less favorable opinion of you. ▪ It *does them no credit* to continue fighting over this issue.
5 [*singular*] **:** a source of honor or pride for someone or something — used in the phrase ***a credit to*** ▪ You are *a credit to* your family and your country. ▪ He's an excellent athlete and *a credit to* the sport.
6 *credits* [*plural*] **:** a list of the names of the people who have worked on or performed in a movie, television program, etc. ▪ the movie's opening/closing *credits* ▪ Her name was listed in the *credits*. ▪ We always stay to watch the *credits*.
7 a : a unit that measures a student's progress towards earning a degree in a school, college, etc. [*count*] So far, you've earned a total of 12 *credits*. [*noncount*] Our program gives academic *credit* for working with several social service organizations. **b** [*noncount*] **:** the amount of points earned for work done on a test, exam, project, etc. ▪ Students will only receive partial *credit* for correct answers that are not written as complete sentences. ▪ To earn ***full credit*** [=the total amount of points possible] you must include at least three

C

maps with your project. • Answer this last question correctly for ***extra credit.*** — sometimes used figuratively. • They deserve respect for making the event happen, and they get *extra credit* for doing it in a way that included everyone.

on the credit side **1** *chiefly Brit* : in the section of a financial record where credits are written • Enter these amounts *on the credit side.* **2** — used when mentioning the things that you like about something • *On the credit side,* the restaurant offers a wide range of choices.

²credit *verb* **-its; -it·ed; -it·ing** [+ *obj*]

1 a : to add (an amount of money) to a total • Your payment of $38.50 has been *credited* to your account. — opposite DEDUCT **b :** to add money to (an account) • The bank is *crediting* your account for the full amount. — opposite DEBIT

2 a : to give honor or recognition to (someone or something) for doing something or for making something happen • The team's players all *credit* their coach [=they say their coach is responsible] for helping them succeed. — often + *with* • She *credits* her family *with* her success. • He was *credited with* saving their lives. **b :** to say that (something) is because of someone or something : to give credit for (something) *to* someone or something • She *credits* [=*attributes*] her success *to* her family's support. • They *credited* the rescue *to* his quick thinking.

3 : to think of (someone) as having a particular quality or effect — usually used as *(be) credited* • She *is credited* as (being) the first woman to play the sport professionally.

4 *chiefly Brit* : to believe that (something) is true • It's hard to *credit* that anyone would want to buy this old car.

cred·it·able /ˈkrɛdətəbəl/ *adj* [*more* ~; *most* ~] : good enough to be praised • a *creditable* [=*estimable*] performance
— **cred·it·ably** /ˈkrɛdətəbli/ *adv* • He performed the part *creditably.*

credit account *noun, pl* ~ **accounts** [*count*] *Brit* : CHARGE ACCOUNT

credit card *noun, pl* ~ **cards** [*count*] : a small plastic card that is used to buy things that you agree to pay for later — called also *charge card*; compare DEBIT CARD

credit line *noun, pl* ~ **lines** [*count*] : LINE OF CREDIT

cred·i·tor /ˈkrɛdətɚ/ *noun, pl* **-tors** [*count*] : a person, bank, or company that lends money to someone • She owes thousands of dollars to *creditors.* — opposite DEBTOR

credit rating *noun, pl* ~ **ratings** [*count*] : a score or grade that a company or organization gives to a possible borrower and that indicates how likely the borrower is to repay a loan ✧ Credit ratings are based on how much money, property, and debt a borrower has and on how well the borrower has paid past debts.

credit union *noun, pl* ~ **unions** [*count*] : an organization that gives small loans to its members at low interest rates and that offers savings and checking accounts

cred·it·wor·thy /ˈkrɛdɪtˌwɚði/ *adj* [*more* ~; *most* ~] : considered able to repay borrowed money • *creditworthy* customers
— **cred·it·wor·thi·ness** *noun* [*noncount*] • the company's *creditworthiness*

cre·do /ˈkriːdoʊ/ *noun, pl* **cre·dos** [*count*] : an idea or set of beliefs that guides the actions of a person or group • Our *credo* [=*creed, philosophy*] is "better safe than sorry." • my personal *credo*

cre·du·li·ty /krɪˈduːləti, *Brit* krɪˈdjuːləti/ *noun* [*noncount*] *formal* : ability or willingness to believe something • Although most of the book is believable, its ending tests/strains *credulity.* [=its ending is difficult to believe; its ending does not seem true or possible]

cred·u·lous /ˈkrɛʤələs, *Brit* ˈkrɛdjʊləs/ *adj* [*more* ~; *most* ~] : too ready to believe things : easily fooled or cheated • Few people are *credulous* enough to believe such nonsense. • a *credulous* audience
— **cred·u·lous·ly** *adv* — **cred·u·lous·ness** *noun* [*noncount*]

creed /ˈkriːd/ *noun, pl* **creeds** [*count*]

1 : a statement of the basic beliefs of a religion • the religion's *creed* • people of different races and *creeds* [=religions]

2 : an idea or set of beliefs that guides the actions of a person or group • a political *creed* [=*credo*]

creek /ˈkriːk/ *noun, pl* **creeks** [*count*]

1 *US* : a small stream • The children waded in the *creek.*

2 *Brit* : INLET • The coast is dotted with tiny *creeks.*

up the creek *or* ***up the creek without a paddle*** *informal* : in a very difficult situation that you cannot get out of • If you hadn't helped us, we would've been *up the creek.*

creel /ˈkriːl/ *noun, pl* **creels** [*count*] : a basket that is used for carrying fish that have just been caught — see picture at FISHING

¹creep /ˈkriːp/ *verb* **creeps; crept** /ˈkrɛpt/; **creep·ing** [*no obj*]

1 : to move slowly with the body close to the ground • A spider was *creeping* [=*crawling*] along the bathroom floor. • She *crept* toward the edge of the roof and looked over.

2 *always followed by an adverb or preposition* **a :** to move slowly and quietly especially in order to not be noticed • I caught him *creeping* down the stairs to the kitchen. • She *crept* into bed next to her sleeping husband. **b :** to go or seem to go very slowly • The hours *crept* by as we waited for morning. • a train *creeping* through the town

3 *always followed by an adverb or preposition* : to appear gradually and in a way that is difficult to notice • The price of gasoline has *crept* back up to three dollars a gallon. • A few mistakes *crept* in during the last revision of the paper. • new words *creeping* into the language

4 *of a plant* : to grow along the ground or up a surface (such as a tree or wall) • ivy *creeping* up a wall • a *creeping* vine

5 *Brit, informal + disapproving* : to be extremely nice to someone in order to get approval or some advantage for yourself • He's been *creeping* (up) to the boss for months, so it's no surprise he got a promotion.

creep out [*phrasal verb*] ***creep (someone) out*** *or* ***creep out (someone)*** *US, informal* : to cause (someone) to have an uncomfortable feeling of nervousness or fear : to give (someone) the creeps • That guys really *creeps* me *out.* • I felt *creeped out* being alone in the office at night.

creep up on [*phrasal verb*] ***creep up on (someone)*** *informal* : to slowly and quietly move closer to (someone) without being noticed • We tried to *creep up on* [=*sneak up on*] them but they heard our footsteps. — often used figuratively • Old age *creeps up on* us. • The deadline had *crept up on* them.

make your skin/flesh creep ✧ If something *makes your skin/flesh creep,* it causes you to have an uncomfortable feeling of fear or disgust. • The thought of touching that slimy mess *makes my skin creep.*

²creep *noun, pl* **creeps** *informal*

1 [*count*] : a strange person who you strongly dislike • Leave me alone, you *creep!* [=*jerk, weirdo*]

2 ***the creeps*** : an uncomfortable feeling of nervousness or fear • I ***get the creeps*** every time he walks by. • I hate snakes. They ***give me the creeps.*** • That guy *gives me the creeps.*

creep·er /ˈkriːpɚ/ *noun, pl* **-ers** [*count*] : a plant that grows along the ground or up surfaces (such as trees or walls)

creepy /ˈkriːpi/ *adj* **creep·i·er; -est** [*or more* ~; *most* ~] *informal* : strange or scary : causing people to feel nervous and afraid • a *creepy* movie • a *creepy* old house • There's something *creepy* about that guy.
— **creep·i·ly** /ˈkriːpəli/ *adv* — **creep·i·ness** *noun* [*noncount*]

creepy–crawly /ˈkriːpiˈkrɑːli/ *noun, pl* **-lies** [*count*] *informal* : an unpleasant worm, insect, or spider • a basement full of *creepy-crawlies*

cre·mate /ˈkriːˌmeɪt, krɪˈmeɪt/ *verb* **-mates; -mat·ed; -mat·ing** [+ *obj*] : to burn (the body of a person who has died) • He wants to be *cremated* when he dies.
— **cre·ma·tion** /krɪˈmeɪʃən/ *noun* [*noncount*] • Some religions do not allow *cremation.*

cre·ma·to·ri·um /ˌkriːməˈtorijəm, *Brit* ˌkrɛməˈtɔːriəm/ *noun, pl* **-to·ria** /-ˈtorijə, *Brit* -ˈtɔːriə/ *or* **-to·ri·ums** [*count*] : CREMATORY

cre·ma·to·ry /ˈkriːməˌtori, *Brit* ˈkrɛmətri/ *noun, pl* **-ries** [*count*] *chiefly US* : a place where the bodies of dead people are cremated

crème an·glaise /ˌkrɛmɑŋˈgleɪz/ *noun* [*noncount*] : a sweet sauce made with cream that is usually served with desserts

crème brû·lée /ˌkrɛmbruˈleɪ/ *noun, pl* ~ **-lées** [*count, noncount*] : a sweet dessert made of a smooth, thick custard covered with a hard top of cooked sugar

crème car·a·mel /ˌkrɛmˌkerəˈmɛl/ *noun, pl* ~ **-mels** [*count, noncount*] : a sweet dessert made of a smooth, thick custard covered in a caramel sauce

crème de la crème /ˈkrɛmdəlɑˈkrɛm/ *noun*

the crème de la crème : the very best people or things in a group • These actors are *the crème de la crème* [=*the cream of the crop*] of American theater.

crème de menthe /ˈkrɛmdəˈmɛnθ, *Brit* ˈkrɛmdəˈmɒnθ/

noun [*noncount*] : a sweet and often green alcoholic drink with a mint flavor

crème fraîche /ˈkrɛmˈfrɛʃ/ *noun* [*noncount*] : a thick cream that is slightly sour and often served on fruit

cren•el•lat•ed /ˈkrɛnəˌleɪtəd/ *adj* : having open spaces at the top of a wall so that people can shoot guns and cannons outward ▪ the castle's *crenellated* walls ▪ a *crenellated* tower

Cre•ole /ˈkriːˌoʊl/ *noun, pl* **-oles**
1 [*count*] : a person who has African and French or Spanish ancestors; *especially* : such a person who lives in the West Indies
2 [*count*] : a person whose ancestors were some of the first people from France or Spain to live in the southeastern U.S. ✧ *Creoles* continue to have the same language and culture as their French or Spanish ancestors.
3 a [*noncount*] : a language that is based on French and that uses words from African languages ▪ Some people in Louisiana speak *Creole*. ▪ Haitian *Creole* [=a type of Creole spoken in Haiti] **b** ***creole*** [*count*] *linguistics* : a language that is based on one language but that has some words from another language

cre•ole *or* **Creole** /ˈkriːˌoʊl/ *adj*
1 : relating to people who are Creoles or to their language ▪ *Creole* music ▪ a *Creole* woman ▪ a *creole* word
2 — used to describe spicy food that is usually made with rice, okra, tomatoes, and peppers ✧ *Creole* is used for the traditional food of the Creoles from the southeastern U.S. ▪ He ordered the shrimp *creole*. ▪ *creole* dishes such as gumbo

cre•o•sote /ˈkriːjəˌsoʊt/ *noun* [*noncount*] : a brown, oily liquid used to keep wood from rotting
– **creosote** *verb* **-sotes; -sot•ed; -sot•ing** [+ *obj*] ▪ *creosoted* wood

crepe *or* **crêpe** /ˈkreɪp/ *noun, pl* **crepes** *or* **crêpes**
1 [*count*] : a very thin pancake
2 [*noncount*] : a thin often silk or cotton cloth that has many very small wrinkles all over its surface
3 [*noncount*] : a thin, hard type of rubber that has a bumpy surface and that is used especially for the bottoms of shoes ▪ *crepe*-soled shoes

crepe paper *noun* [*noncount*] : a type of colorful paper that has a wrinkled surface ✧ People often use colorful strips of crepe paper to make decoratations for a party, celebration, etc. ▪ a room decorated with balloons and strands of *crepe paper*

crept *past tense and past participle of* [1]CREEP

cre•scen•do /krəˈʃɛndoʊ/ *noun, pl* **-dos** *also* **-does** [*count*]
1 : a gradual increase in the loudness of a sound or section of music
2 : the highest or loudest point of something that increases gradually ▪ The excitement reaches its *crescendo* [=*climax, peak*] when he comes on stage. ▪ The noise rose to a *crescendo*.

cres•cent /ˈkrɛsn̩t/ *noun, pl* **-cents**
1 [*singular*] : the shape of the visible part of the moon when it is less than half full ▪ the *crescent* moon
2 [*count*] : a shape that is curved, wide at its center, and pointed at its two ends like a crescent moon ✧ The crescent is used as a symbol of Islam. — see also RED CRESCENT

crescent

cress /ˈkrɛs/ *noun, pl* **cress•es** [*count, noncount*] : a small plant that has spicy leaves that are eaten especially in salads — see also WATERCRESS

[1]**crest** /ˈkrɛst/ *noun, pl* **crests** [*count*]
1 : the highest part or point of something (such as a hill or wave) ▪ wave *crests* — usually + *of* ▪ The boat rose up on the *crest of* the wave. ▪ We stood on the *crest of* the hill/mountain. ▪ the *crest of* the flood — often used figuratively ▪ They're still riding the *crest of* the wave of their success. [=they are still very happy, excited, etc., because of their success] ▪ He was at the *crest of* his fame when he died tragically.
2 : a group of decorative feathers at the top of a bird's head; *also* : a decorative bunch of hair on the head of another animal
3 : a special symbol used especially in the past to represent a family, group, or organization ▪ her family's *crest* — compare COAT OF ARMS

[2]**crest** *verb* **crests; crest•ed; crest•ing**
1 [+ *obj*] : to reach the highest part or point of (a mountain, wave, etc.) ▪ We *crested* the hill and looked out around us.
2 [*no obj*] *US* : to rise to a high level before going back down ▪ The river *crested* [=reached its highest level] at 10 feet above its normal level. — often used figuratively ▪ His acting career *crested* in the mid-1940s.

crest•ed /ˈkrɛstəd/ *adj* : having a decorative bunch of feathers or hair : having a crest ▪ a *crested* bird

crest•fall•en /ˈkrɛstˌfɑːlən/ *adj* [*more* ~; *most* ~] : very sad and disappointed ▪ After losing its last game, the team was *crestfallen*. [=*dejected, depressed*] ▪ my *crestfallen* [=*downcast*] teammates

cre•tin /ˈkriːtn̩, *Brit* ˈkrɛtn̩/ *noun, pl* **-tins** [*count*] *informal* + *offensive* : a stupid or annoying person ▪ Let me know if these *cretins* [=*jerks, idiots*] bother you.
– **cre•tin•ous** /ˈkriːtnəs/ *adj* [*more* ~; *most* ~] ▪ a *cretinous* lout

Creutz•feldt–Ja•kob disease /ˈkrɔɪtsˌfɛltˈjɑːˌkoʊb-/ *noun* [*noncount*] *medical* : a disease of the brain that causes people to lose their memory, to no longer be able to control their muscles, and eventually to die — called also *CJD*

cre•vasse /krɪˈvæs/ *noun, pl* **-vas•ses** [*count*] : a deep, narrow opening or crack in an area of thick ice or rock

crev•ice /ˈkrɛvəs/ *noun, pl* **-ic•es** [*count*] : a narrow opening or crack in a hard surface and especially in rock

[1]**crew** /ˈkruː/ *noun, pl* **crews**
1 [*count*] **a** : the group of people who operate a ship, airplane, or train ▪ a skilled member of a ship's *crew* ▪ flight *crews* ▪ the flight's passengers and *crew* ▪ *crew* members **b** : the people who work on a ship except the officers and captain ▪ the ship's captain and *crew*
2 [*count*] : a group of people who do a specified kind of work together ▪ A construction *crew* will begin work on the house next week. ▪ the restaurant's kitchen *crew* ▪ television/news/film *crews* ▪ the film's camera *crew* ▪ We spoke with members of the show's original ***cast and crew***. [=actors and other people who work to produce a show] ▪ the driver's ***pit crew*** [=people who fix a race car during a race] ▪ one of the factory's ***crew chiefs*** [=people in charge of a group of workers] — see also GROUND CREW
3 [*singular*] *informal* : a group of people who are friends or who are doing something together ▪ He and his *crew* [=*gang*] used to hang out at the bowling alley. ▪ We were a ***motley crew*** [=an unusual mixed group] of musicians and athletes.
4 a [*count*] : a team that rows a boat in a race against other boats ▪ *Crews* from several colleges will be competing in today's race. **b** [*noncount*] *US* : the sport of racing in long, narrow boats that are moved by rowing with oars : ROWING ▪ In college, she participated in both *crew* and tennis.

[2]**crew** *verb* **crews; crewed; crew•ing** : to work as a member of a crew that operates a ship or airplane [*no obj*] She spent a couple of years *crewing* on a British ship. [+ *obj*] The ship was *crewed* by 12 men.

crew cut *noun, pl* ~ **cuts** [*count*] : a very short haircut usually for men or boys — called also (*US*) *buzz cut*; see picture at HAIR

crew•man /ˈkruːmən/ *noun, pl* **-men** [*count*] : a member of a crew: such as **a** : a person who helps operate a ship, airplane, or train ▪ Eight *crewmen* were wounded in the attack. **b** : a person who is part of a group of people who work together ▪ TV *crewmen*

crew neck *noun, pl* ~ **necks** [*count*]
1 : a plain, round neck on a T-shirt, sweater, etc. — often used before another noun ▪ a cotton *crew neck* sweatshirt
2 *usually* ***crewneck*** : a sweater with a crew neck

[1]**crib** /ˈkrɪb/ *noun, pl* **cribs** [*count*]
1 a *US* : a small bed with high sides for a baby — called also (*Brit*) *cot* **b** *Brit* : [1]CRADLE 1
2 *chiefly Brit* : CRÈCHE 1
3 : a long open box that holds food for farm animals
4 *informal* : something used for cheating on a test — usually used before another noun ▪ *crib* notes ▪ He got caught using a ***crib sheet***. [=a piece of paper with answers to test questions]
5 *US slang* : a usually small room, apartment, or house ▪ How about coming up to my *crib*? [=*place*]

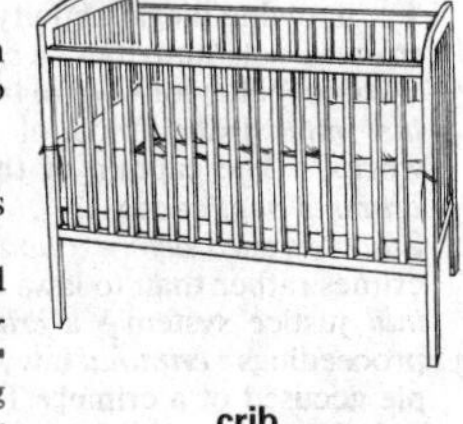
crib

[2]**crib** *verb* **cribs; cribbed; crib•bing** : to copy an idea, a piece of writing, etc., from someone else [+ *obj*] She *cribbed* a line or two from her favorite poet. [*no obj*] students *cribbing* off each other's papers

C

crib·bage /ˈkrɪbɪʤ/ *noun [noncount]* **:** a card game for two players in which a special board is used to count each player's points

crib death *noun, pl* **~ deaths** *[count, noncount] US* **:** SUDDEN INFANT DEATH SYNDROME

[1]**crick** /ˈkrɪk/ *noun, pl* **cricks** *[count]* **:** a sudden pain especially in your neck or back that is caused by tight muscles — usually singular; usually + *in* ▪ I got a *crick in* my neck from looking up at the stars too long.

[2]**crick** *verb* **cricks; cricked; crick·ing** *[+ obj] chiefly Brit* **:** to develop a crick in (your neck or back) ▪ He *cricked* his back sleeping on the sofa. ▪ a *cricked* neck

[1]**crick·et** /ˈkrɪkət/ *noun, pl* **-ets** *[count]* **:** a small black insect that jumps high and that makes loud, high-pitched noises — see color picture on page C10 — compare [2]CRICKET

[2]**cricket** *noun [noncount]* **:** a game played on a large field by two teams of 11 players who try to score runs by hitting a small ball with a bat and then running between two sets of wooden sticks — often used before another noun ▪ a *cricket* match — see pictures at BALL, BAT, GLOVE

not cricket *Brit, old-fashioned* **:** not fair, polite, or proper ▪ You can't keep ignoring her. It just *isn't cricket*.

– compare [1]CRICKET

crick·et·er /ˈkrɪkətɚ/ *noun, pl* **-ers** *[count]* **:** a person who plays cricket

cri·key /ˈkraɪki/ *interj, chiefly Brit* — used to express mild surprise ▪ *Crikey*, that was close!

crime /ˈkraɪm/ *noun, pl* **crimes**

1 *[count]* **:** an illegal act for which someone can be punished by the government ▪ Have you ever been convicted of a *crime*? = Were you ever found guilty of a *crime*? ▪ a very serious *crime* ▪ She paid dearly for her *crimes*. ▪ The punishment didn't fit the *crime*. [=the punishment was too mild/severe] ▪ evidence that helped them solve the *crime* ▪ a federal *crime* ▪ weapons used to ***commit crimes*** [=to do something illegal] ▪ I've *committed* no *crime*. = I haven't *committed* any *crime*. ▪ He was punished for a *crime* that he didn't *commit*. ▪ laws against ***hate crimes*** [=crimes that people commit because they hate the victim's race, religion, etc.] ▪ He thought he had committed a/the ***perfect crime***. [=a crime that leaves no evidence] — see also WAR CRIME, WHITE-COLLAR CRIME

2 *[noncount]* **:** activity that is against the law **:** illegal acts in general ▪ poverty and *crime* ▪ Hiring more police officers would help prevent/deter/reduce (the amount of) *crime* in our city. ▪ leaders who are tough on *crime* = leaders who work hard to fight *crime* ▪ He turned to a ***life of crime*** [=he became a criminal] as a teenager. ▪ He has links to ***organized crime***. [=a group of professional criminals who work together as part of a powerful and secret organization] ▪ the recent increase in ***violent crime*** — often used before another noun ▪ high *crime* rates ▪ *crime* novels/stories ▪ We found your wallet at the ***crime scene***. [=the place where a crime happened] ▪ a ***crime wave*** [=a sudden increase in the amount of crime in an area] ✧ Someone's ***partner in crime*** is a person who helps someone commit a crime. ▪ He was her *partner in crime* for most of the robberies.

3 *[singular]* **:** an act that is foolish or wrong ▪ It's a *crime* [=*sin*] to let food go to waste. ▪ Being single is not a *crime*. ▪ There's no greater *crime* than forgetting your anniversary.

crime against humanity **:** a very cruel or terrible illegal act that is directed against a group of people ▪ The country's former leader was tried for *crimes against humanity*.

[1]**crim·i·nal** /ˈkrɪmənl/ *adj*

1 : involving illegal activity **:** relating to crime ▪ committing *criminal* acts/activities ▪ a *criminal* organization ▪ a history of *criminal* behavior ▪ We're trying to understand how the ***criminal mind*** [=the mind of someone who commits crimes] works. ▪ The captain of the wrecked boat was accused of ***criminal negligence***.

2 *always used before a noun* **:** relating to laws that describe crimes rather than to laws about a person's rights ▪ the *criminal* justice system ▪ a *criminal* court/case/trial ▪ *criminal* proceedings ▪ *criminal* lawyers [=lawyers who represent people accused of a crime] ▪ The company brought/filed *criminal* charges against her. ▪ Using this drug is a *criminal* offense. [=it is illegal to use this drug] ▪ The police are conducting a *criminal* investigation. [=they are investigating a crime] — compare CIVIL 5; see also CRIMINAL LAW

3 *not used before a noun [more ~; most ~]* **:** morally wrong ▪ It's *criminal* that the government is doing nothing to stop the problem. — often used in a joking way to say that someone should not do something ▪ In my opinion, it would be *criminal* to miss seeing this movie. [=I think everyone should see this movie]

– crim·i·nal·i·ty /ˌkrɪməˈnæləti/ *noun [noncount]* ▪ the *criminality* of his actions **– crim·i·nal·ly** *adv* ▪ *criminally* liable/responsible

[2]**criminal** *noun, pl* **-nals** *[count]* **:** a person who has committed a crime or who has been proved to be guilty of a crime by a court ▪ She's a convicted *criminal*. ▪ violent/white-collar/common *criminals* ▪ a hardened *criminal* ▪ ***career criminals*** [=people who have committed many crimes throughout their lives]

crim·i·nal·ize *also Brit* **crim·i·nal·ise** /ˈkrɪmənlˌaɪz/ *verb* **-iz·es; -ized; -iz·ing** *[+ obj]* **:** to make (something) illegal ▪ a law that *criminalized* alcohol — opposite LEGALIZE

– crim·i·nal·i·za·tion *also Brit* **crim·i·nal·i·sa·tion** /ˌkrɪmənləˈzeɪʃən, *Brit* ˌkrɪmənˌlaɪˈzeɪʃən/ *noun [noncount]* ▪ the *criminalization* of alcohol

criminal law *noun [noncount]* **:** laws that deal with crimes and their punishments — compare CIVIL LAW

criminal record *noun, pl* **~ -cords** *[count]* **:** a known record of having been arrested in the past for committing a crime ▪ Do you have a *criminal record*? [=have you ever been arrested for a crime?] ▪ someone with no *criminal record* — called also *record*

crim·i·nol·o·gy /ˌkrɪməˈnɑːləʤi/ *noun [noncount]* **:** the study of crime, criminals, and the punishment of criminals ▪ a professor of *criminology*

– crim·i·nol·o·gist /ˌkrɪməˈnɑːləʤɪst/ *noun, pl* **-gists** *[count]*

[1]**crimp** /ˈkrɪmp/ *verb* **crimps; crimped; crimp·ing** *[+ obj]*

1 : to make the surface or edge of (hair, cloth, metal, etc.) have many small waves or folds ▪ She *crimps* her hair with a curling iron. ▪ *Crimp* the edges of the pie crust with a fork.

2 : to press (parts or pieces) tightly together ▪ *Crimp* the pieces of foil together.

3 *US* **:** to prevent (something) from happening or proceeding in the usual or desired way ▪ economic problems that have been *crimping* [=*putting a crimp in*] sales in the computer industry

[2]**crimp** *noun, pl* **crimps** *[count]* **:** a small wave or fold in the surface of something (such as hair or cloth)

put a crimp in *US* **:** to prevent (something) from happening or proceeding in the usual or desired way **:** to affect (something) badly ▪ The storm *put a crimp in* our travel plans. ▪ The extra expenses *put a crimp in* the company's budget.

crim·son /ˈkrɪmzən/ *noun [noncount]* **:** a deep purplish-red color — see color picture on page C3

– crimson *adj* ▪ a *crimson* dress

cringe /ˈkrɪnʤ/ *verb* **cring·es; cringed; cring·ing** *[no obj]*

1 : to feel disgust or embarrassment and often to show this feeling by a movement of your face or body ▪ Many English teachers *cringe* when their students use the word "ain't." ▪ I always *cringe* when I hear that song. ▪ Just the thought of eating broccoli makes me *cringe*.

2 : to make a sudden movement from fear of being hit or hurt ▪ The dog *cringed* at the noise.

[1]**crin·kle** /ˈkrɪŋkəl/ *verb* **crin·kles; crin·kled; crin·kling** **:** to form small, thin lines on the surface *[no obj]* The corners of his eyes *crinkle* when he smiles. *[+ obj]* an old *crinkled* newspaper — often + *up* ▪ She *crinkled up* her nose in disgust.

[2]**crinkle** *noun, pl* **crinkles** *[count]* **:** a small, thin line that appears on a surface — usually plural ▪ the *crinkles* at the corners of his eyes

– crin·kly /ˈkrɪŋkli/ *adj* **crin·kli·er; -est** *[also more ~; most ~]* ▪ dry, *crinkly* leaves ▪ the *crinkly* fabric of her dress

[1]**crip·ple** /ˈkrɪpəl/ *noun, pl* **crip·ples** *[count]*

1 *old-fashioned + offensive* **:** a person who cannot move or walk normally because of a permanent injury (such as a damaged leg or foot) or other physical problem ▪ He returned from war a *cripple*. ✧ *Cripple* is an old-fashioned word. People now usually use the less offensive term *disabled person*.

2 *informal* **:** a person who has emotional problems that prevent normal behavior with other people ▪ She's an emotional *cripple*. [=she's unable to express her emotions normally] ▪ social *cripples*

[2]**cripple** *verb* **cripples; crip·pled; crip·pling** *[+ obj]*

1 : to cause (a person or animal) to be unable to move or walk normally — usually used as *(be) crippled* ▪ Thousands of people have *been crippled* by the disease. ▪ The car accident left him *crippled*. [=*disabled*]

2 : to make (something) unable to work normally : to cause great damage to (something) • Higher taxes could *cripple* small businesses. • an economy *crippled* by inflation • The disease *cripples* the body's immune system. [=it makes the body unable to heal itself]

– crippling *adj* • *crippling* diseases • the *crippling* effects of the disease • the *crippling* effects of inflation

cri·sis /ˈkraɪsəs/ *noun, pl* **-ses** /-ˌsiːz/ : a difficult or dangerous situation that needs serious attention [*count*] the AIDS *crisis* • She was dealing with a family *crisis* at the time. • Most people blame the government for the country's worsening economic/financial/fiscal *crisis*. • last year's state budget *crisis* • an energy/fuel/water *crisis* [=a time when there is not enough energy/fuel/water] • a ***hostage crisis*** [=a situation in which someone is holding people as hostages] [*noncount*] In times of national *crisis*, we need strong leaders we can trust. • A year ago, both companies were ***in crisis***. — see also IDENTITY CRISIS, MIDLIFE CRISIS

¹crisp /ˈkrɪsp/ *adj* **crisp·er; -est**

1 a : dry, hard, and easily broken • the pie's deliciously *crisp* [=*crispy*] crust • a *crisp* cookie • The fish is fried until *crisp*. [=until its outer layer is brown and crunchy] • *crisp* bacon **b :** pleasantly firm and making a sharp sound when chewed or crushed • fresh, *crisp* lettuce • *crisp* celery

2 : clean, smooth, and somewhat stiff • I put on a *crisp* shirt and tie. • clean, *crisp* bedsheets • a *crisp* $100 bill

3 : having details that are easily seen or heard • *crisp* black-and-white photographs • The stereo's sound is *crisp* and clear.

4 : pleasantly cool, fresh, and dry • a *crisp* autumn day • *crisp* winter air • She chose a *crisp* white wine for dinner.

5 : moving or speaking quickly and directly • We were impressed by her *crisp*, businesslike manner. • He issued a series of *crisp* commands. • He responded with a *crisp* [=*terse*] "No. Thank you."

6 : done in a very confident and skillful way • a *crisp* tennis serve

– crisp·ly *adv* [*more* ~; *most* ~] • *crisply* fried fish • a *crisply* dressed man **– crisp·ness** *noun* [*noncount*] • the *crispness* of the vegetables

²crisp *noun, pl* **crisps**

1 [*count*] : a thin, hard, and usually salty piece of food • corn *crisps*; *especially, Brit* : POTATO CHIP — usually plural • a bag of *crisps*

2 [*count, noncount*] *US* : a dessert made of cooked fruit with a sweet, dry topping • a hot apple *crisp* — called also (*chiefly Brit*) *crumble*

to a crisp : to a state of being hard, dry, and easily broken • The toast had been ***burned to a crisp***.

³crisp *verb* **crisps; crisped; crisp·ing** : to make (something) crisp or to become crisp [+ *obj*] *Crisp* the celery in ice water. [*no obj*] The crust *crisped* (up) nicely in the oven.

crispy /ˈkrɪspi/ *adj* **crisp·i·er; -est** [*also more* ~; *most* ~] : pleasantly thin, dry, and easily broken • *crispy* [=*crisp*] crackers : having a pleasantly crisp outer layer • *crispy* fried chicken • Fry the potatoes until they are brown and *crispy*.

– crisp·i·ness *noun* [*noncount*] • the *crispiness* of the potatoes

¹criss·cross /ˈkrɪsˌkrɑːs/ *noun* [*singular*] : a pattern that is formed by lines crossing each other • She pointed toward the *crisscross* of trees that had fallen on the path.

– crisscross *adj* • a *crisscross* pattern on her dress

²crisscross *verb* **-cross·es; -crossed; -cross·ing**

1 : to form a pattern on (something) with lines that cross each other [+ *obj*] Several highways *crisscross* the state. [*no obj*] shoelaces that *crisscross* over the top of the shoe

2 [+ *obj*] : to go from one side of (something) to the other side and come back again • Tourists *crisscrossed* the lake from morning until night. • Scientists have been *crisscrossing* the country to collect data.

cri·te·ri·on /kraɪˈtirijən/ *noun, pl* **-te·ria** /-ˈtirijə/ [*count*] : something that is used as a reason for making a judgment or decision • High test scores are one *criterion* [=*standard*] used by universities to determine which students to admit. • What were the *criteria* used to choose the winner? — often + *for* • the university's *criteria for* admission • Our main *criterion for* hiring new employees is that they have a lot of past work experience.

crit·ic /ˈkrɪtɪk/ *noun, pl* **-ics** [*count*]

1 : a person who gives opinions about books, movies, or other forms of art • a film/theater/art *critic* • He is an influential literary *critic*. • *Critics* praised the book.

2 : a person who disapproves of someone or something : a person who criticizes someone or something • *Critics* of the new law say that it will not reduce crime. • The actor had to answer many charges from his *critics*. • He is a fierce/loud/outspoken *critic* of tax reform.

crit·i·cal /ˈkrɪtɪkəl/ *adj*

1 [*more* ~; *most* ~] : expressing criticism or disapproval • You're always so *critical*. • They are often *critical* of the mayor's policies. [=they often criticize the mayor's policies]

2 : of or relating to the judgments of critics about books, movies, art, etc. • The book received much *critical* acclaim. [=many critics said good things about the book] • *critical* writings/theory • The movie was a *critical* success [=critics liked the movie], but it didn't make much money.

3 : using or involving careful judgment about the good and bad parts of something • The program presents a *critical* analysis of the government's strategies. • She has a talent for *critical* thinking. • We need to look at these proposed changes ***with a critical eye*** before we accept them.

4 [*more* ~; *most* ~] : extremely important • We have reached a *critical* phase of the experiment. • It is absolutely *critical* [=*vital, essential*] for us to remain together. • This is a matter ***of critical importance*** to the future of our country.

5 [*more* ~; *most* ~] *medical* : relating to or involving a great danger of death • He suffered *critical* injuries in the accident. • The patient is in ***critical condition***. = The patient is *critical*. [=the patient is very sick or injured and may die] • a nurse who specializes in ***critical care*** [=the care of patients who are in critical condition] • patients who are ***on the critical list*** — sometimes used figuratively • a government program that is *on the critical list* [=that is in danger of failing or being eliminated]

– crit·i·cal·ly /ˈkrɪtɪkli/ *adv* • He spoke *critically* of the mayor's policies. [=he criticized the mayor's policies] • The movie was *critically* acclaimed. • She taught me to think *critically* about books. • This matter is *critically* important to the future of our country. • a *critically* ill person

critical mass *noun, pl* ~ **masses** [*count, noncount*]

1 *technical* : an amount of material (such as plutonium) that is large enough to allow a nuclear reaction to occur

2 : the size, number, or amount of something that is needed to cause a particular result • Production of the show stopped after complaints from viewers reached (a) *critical mass*.

crit·i·cism /ˈkrɪtəˌsɪzəm/ *noun, pl* **-cisms**

1 [*noncount*] : the act of expressing disapproval and of noting the problems or faults of a person or thing : the act of criticizing someone or something • There was much public *criticism* directed/leveled at the senator. • The new law attracted/drew widespread *criticism*. [=many people criticized the new law] • In this job you need to be able to take/face/accept *criticism*. • I asked my sister for some ***constructive criticism*** of my essay before I tried to revise it. — opposite PRAISE

2 [*count*] : a remark or comment that expresses disapproval of someone or something • I had one minor *criticism* about her design.

3 [*noncount*] : the activity of making careful judgments about the good and bad qualities of books, movies, etc. • literary *criticism*

crit·i·cize *also Brit* **crit·i·cise** /ˈkrɪtəˌsaɪz/ *verb* **-ciz·es; -cized; -ciz·ing**

1 : to express disapproval of (someone or something) : to talk about the problems or faults of (someone or something) [+ *obj*] His boss *criticized* him for his sloppy work habits. • The judge was widely/roundly *criticized* for his verdict. • The editor *criticized* the author's work as trite. [*no obj*] It seems as though all he ever does is *criticize*. — opposite PRAISE

2 [+ *obj*] : to look at and make judgments about (something, such as a piece of writing or a work of art) • He asked me to *criticize* [=*critique*] his drawings.

¹cri·tique /krəˈtiːk/ *noun, pl* **-tiques** [*count*] : a careful judgment in which you give your opinion about the good and bad parts of something (such as a piece of writing or a work of art) • She wrote a radical *critique* of the philosopher's early essays. • They gave a fair and honest *critique* of her art.

²critique *verb* **-tiques; -tiqued; -tiqu·ing** [+ *obj*] : to express your opinion about the good and bad parts of (something) : to give a critique of (something) • The class convened to *critique* the student's latest painting.

crit·ter /ˈkrɪtɚ/ *noun, pl* **-ters** [*count*] *US, informal* : a usually small creature or animal • The woods are filled with

C

skunks, raccoons, and other *critters.*

croak /ˈkroʊk/ *verb* **croaks; croaked; croak·ing**

1 [*no obj*] **:** to make the deep, harsh sound that a frog makes ▪ We could hear the frogs *croaking* by the pond.

2 : to say (something) in a rough, low voice that is hard to understand [*+ obj*] The man could only *croak* his name. [*no obj*] He tried to speak but could barely *croak.*

3 [*no obj*] *slang* **:** to die ▪ He had a heart attack and *croaked.*

– croak *noun, pl* **croaks** [*count*] ▪ the *croaks* of the frogs

croc /ˈkrɑːk/ *noun, pl* **crocs** [*count*] *informal* **:** CROCODILE 1

cro·chet /kroʊˈʃeɪ/ *noun* [*noncount*] **:** a method of making cloth or clothing by using a needle with a hook at the end to form and weave loops in a thread ▪ She learned basic *crochet* stitches from her mother. ▪ a *crochet* hook — see picture at SEWING

– crochet *verb* **-chets; -cheted; -chet·ing** [*+ obj*] She *crocheted* an afghan. [*no obj*] She enjoys *crocheting.*

– cro·chet·er /kroʊˈʃejɚ/ *noun, pl* **-ers** [*count*]

¹crock /ˈkrɑːk/ *noun, pl* **crocks**

1 [*count*] **:** a pot or jar made of baked clay ▪ chili served in a *crock*

2 [*singular*] *US, informal* **:** something that is impossible to believe because it is untrue or ridiculous ▪ We could tell that the salesman's claims about his product were a *crock.* ▪ She thinks horoscopes are a *crock.* ✧ This use of *crock* comes from its use in phrases with similar meanings such as ***a crock of baloney*** or (*offensive*) ***a crock of shit.***

– compare ²CROCK

²crock *noun, pl* **crocks** [*count*] *Brit, informal* **:** an old, ill, or unhappy person ▪ He's an old *crock* who complains about everything. — compare ¹CROCK

crocked /ˈkrɑːkt/ *adj, not used before a noun* [*more ~; most ~*] *US slang* **:** very drunk or intoxicated ▪ He was half-*crocked* when he came home.

crock·ery /ˈkrɑːkəri/ *noun* [*noncount*]

1 *US* **:** pots or jars made of baked clay used for cooking **:** EARTHENWARE

2 *chiefly Brit* **:** plates, dishes, and cups used in dining

croc·o·dile /ˈkrɑːkəˌdajəl/ *noun, pl* **-diles**

1 a [*count*] **:** a large reptile that has a long body, thick skin, and a long, thin mouth with sharp teeth and that lives in the water in regions with hot weather — see picture at ALLIGATOR **b** [*noncount*] **:** the skin of the crocodile used for making shoes and others products — often used before another noun ▪ a *crocodile* purse

2 [*count*] *Brit* **:** a line of people and especially of schoolchildren who are walking in pairs

crocodile tears *noun* [*plural*] **:** a false expression of sadness or regret about something ▪ The company shed/cried *crocodile tears* for the workers who were laid off. ✧ The phrase *crocodile tears* comes from the belief that crocodiles make false sounds of distress to attract the animals that they kill and eat.

cro·cus /ˈkroʊkəs/ *noun, pl* **-cus·es** [*count*] **:** a small purple, yellow, or white flower that blooms in the early spring

croft /ˈkrɑːft/ *noun, pl* **crofts** [*count*] *Brit* **:** a small farm usually with a house on it in Scotland

croft·er /ˈkrɑːftɚ/ *noun, pl* **-ers** [*count*] *Brit* **:** a person who owns or works on a croft

crois·sant /krəˈsɑːnt, *Brit* ˈkwɑːsɒŋ/ *noun, pl* **-sants** [*count*] **:** a type of roll that has a curved shape and that is usually eaten at breakfast — see picture at BAKING

crone /ˈkroʊn/ *noun, pl* **crones** [*count*] *literary* **:** a cruel or ugly old woman ▪ The old *crone* lived alone.

cro·ny /ˈkroʊni/ *noun, pl* **-nies** [*count*] *disapproving* **:** a close friend of someone; *especially* **:** a friend of someone powerful (such as a politician) who is unfairly given special treatment or favors ▪ The mayor rewarded his *cronies* with high-paying jobs after he was elected.

cro·ny·ism /ˈkroʊniˌɪzəm/ *noun* [*noncount*] *disapproving* **:** the unfair practice by a powerful person (such as a politician) of giving jobs and other favors to friends ▪ The mayor has been accused of *cronyism.*

¹crook /ˈkrʊk/ *noun, pl* **crooks** [*count*]

1 *informal* **a :** a dishonest person ▪ He thinks politicians are just a bunch of *crooks.* **b :** a criminal ▪ a small-time *crook*

2 a : the place where part of the body (such as an arm, leg, or finger) bends ▪ the *crook* of his arm **b :** a curved or hooked part of something ▪ The squirrel sat in the *crook* of the tree. ▪ the *crook* of the cane

3 : a long stick with one end curved into a hook that is used by a shepherd

by hook or by crook see ¹HOOK

²crook *verb* **crooks; crooked; crook·ing** [*+ obj*] **:** to bend (your finger, neck, or arm) ▪ He *crooked* his finger at us and led us to the table.

crook·ed /ˈkrʊkəd/ *adj* [*more ~; most ~*]

1 : not straight ▪ a *crooked* smile/grin **:** having bends and curves ▪ a *crooked* path

2 : not set or placed straight ▪ a *crooked* tooth ▪ The picture is *crooked.*

3 *informal* **a :** not honest ▪ *crooked* [=*corrupt, dishonest*] politicians **b :** done to trick or deceive someone ▪ a *crooked* card game

– crook·ed·ly *adv* ▪ The picture hung *crookedly.* **– crook·ed·ness** *noun* [*noncount*]

croon /ˈkruːn/ *verb* **croons; crooned; croon·ing :** to sing (a song) in a low soft voice [*+ obj*] *croon* a lullaby [*no obj*] The mother *crooned* as she rocked the baby.

croon·er /ˈkruːnɚ/ *noun, pl* **-ers** [*count*] **:** a male singer who sings slow, romantic songs in a soft, smooth voice

¹crop /ˈkrɑːp/ *noun, pl* **crops**

1 [*count*] **a :** a plant or plant product that is grown by farmers ▪ corn *crops* ▪ an apple *crop* ▪ Tobacco is their main *crop.* ▪ They sprayed the *crops* with a pesticide. — sometimes used before another noun ▪ *Crop* production was low last year because of the lack of rain. ▪ *crop* disease/damage — see also CASH CROP **b** [*count*] **:** the amount of a crop that is gathered at one time or in one season ▪ The second *crop* [=*harvest*] was not as good as the first. ▪ The drought caused a fall in this year's corn *crop.* [=the drought caused the amount of corn grown this year to be lower than it was last year] ▪ We produced a ***bumper crop*** of tomatoes [=a very large crop of tomatoes] this year.

2 [*singular*] **a :** a group of people who begin to do something at the same time ▪ The teachers got ready for a new *crop* of students. **b :** a group of things that happen or are produced at the same time ▪ a new *crop* of horror movies ✧ People or things that are ***the cream of the crop*** are the best of their kind or in their group. ▪ There were many good candidates for the job, but he was *the cream of the crop.*

3 [*count*] **:** a short whip used in horse riding ▪ a riding *crop* — see picture at HORSE

4 [*count*] **:** a short and thick quantity of hair on a person's head ▪ He has a thick *crop* of hair. ▪ a *crop* of red, curly hair

5 [*count*] **:** an area in the throat of a bird where food is stored for a time

²crop *verb* **crops; cropped; crop·ping**

1 [*+ obj*] **:** to cut off the upper or outer parts of (something) ▪ *crop* [=*trim*] a hedge [=make a hedge neat by cutting it] ▪ *crop* a dog's ears

2 [*+ obj*] **:** to cut off part of (a picture or photograph) ▪ The picture was *cropped* badly. ▪ We had to *crop* the image to fit it into the frame.

3 [*+ obj*] **:** to cut (someone's hair) short ▪ Her hair was *cropped* short. ▪ closely *cropped* hair

4 [*+ obj*] **:** to bite off and eat the tops of (grass or plants) ▪ The sheep were *cropping* the grass in the meadow.

5 [*no obj*] **:** to produce or make a crop ▪ The apple trees *cropped* well.

crop up [*phrasal verb*] **:** to come or appear when not expected ▪ New problems *crop up* every day. ▪ His name *crops up* frequently as a potential candidate.

crop circle *noun, pl* **~ circles** [*count*] **:** a large round shape or pattern in a field that is made by cutting or flattening grass or crops ✧ Some people believe that crop circles are made by creatures that come from another world.

crop·land /ˈkrɑːpˌlænd/ *noun, pl* **-lands :** land on which crops are grown [*plural*] plowing the *croplands* [*noncount*] acres of *cropland*

crop·per /ˈkrɑːpɚ/ *noun*

come a cropper *informal* **1 :** to fail completely in a sudden or unexpected way ▪ Her careful plan *came a cropper.* **2** *Brit* **:** to have a very bad fall ▪ He *came a cropper* on the ski slopes.

cro·quet /kroʊˈkeɪ, *Brit* ˈkrəʊkeɪ/ *noun* [*noncount*] **:** a game in which players use wooden mallets to hit balls through a series of curved wires that are stuck into the ground

cro·quette /kroʊˈkɛt/ *noun, pl* **-quettes** [*count*] **:** a roll or ball of meat, fish, or vegetables that is covered with egg and bread crumbs and fried in oil ▪ chicken *croquettes*

¹cross /ˈkrɑːs/ *noun, pl* **cross·es**

1 a [*count*] **: a long piece of wood with a shorter piece across it near the top that people were once fastened to and left to die on as a form of punishment** **b** ***the Cross*** **:** the cross on which Jesus Christ died **c** [*count*] **: an object or image in the shape of a cross that is used as a symbol of Christianity** ▪ a necklace with a gold *cross* — see also SIGN OF THE CROSS
2 [*count*] **: a decoration in the shape of a cross that is given to someone as an honor especially for military courage**
3 [*count*] **: a mark formed by two lines that cross each other** ▪ The teacher marked the absent students on her list with *crosses*. ▪ Those who could not write signed their names with a *cross*.
4 [*count*] **: a mixture of two different things, types, or qualities** ▪ Snowboarding is a *cross* between surfing and skiing. ▪ The play is a *cross* between comedy and romance. ▪ The dog is a *cross* of hunting dog and sheepdog.
5 [*count*] *boxing* **: a punch that goes over an opponent's punch** ▪ a right *cross*
6 [*count*] *soccer* **: a kick or hit of the ball that goes across the field from one side to another or to the middle of the field**
cross to bear **: a problem that causes trouble or worry for someone over a long period of time** ▪ We all have our *crosses to bear*. [=we all have problems to deal with] ▪ The loss was a heavy *cross to bear*. [=the loss was hard to deal with]

²cross *verb* **crosses; crossed; cross·ing**
1 : to go from one side of (something) to the other : to go across (something) [+ *obj*] We *crossed* the state border hours ago. ▪ The dog *crossed* the street. ▪ The highway *crosses* the entire state. ▪ He was the first runner to *cross* the finish line. [*no obj*] The train *crosses* through France.
2 : to go or pass across each other [*no obj*] the point at which two lines *cross* [=*intersect*] ▪ Put a nail where the boards *cross*. [+ *obj*] One line *crossed* the other.
3 [+ *obj*] **: to place one arm, leg, etc., over the other** ▪ *cross* your arms/legs/fingers ✧ If you ***cross your fingers*** or ***keep your fingers crossed***, you hope that you will be lucky and that something you want to happen will happen. ▪ I *crossed my fingers* and hoped that I would be chosen. ▪ *Keep your fingers crossed*. I just sent out my college applications.
4 [+ *obj*] **: to draw a line across (something)** ▪ Remember to *cross* your *t's*. [=to put a line across the top of the letter "t" when you write it] — see also *dot your i's and cross your t's* at ²DOT
5 [*no obj*] **: to pass in opposite directions** ▪ Our letters *crossed* in the mail. [=my letter was going to you while your letter was coming to me]
6 [+ *obj*] **: to turn (your eyes) inward toward your nose** ▪ He *crossed* his eyes.
7 [+ *obj*] **: to act against the wishes, plans, or orders of (someone)** ▪ My boss is usually nice, but she has a terrible temper and you don't want to *cross* her. — see also DOUBLE-CROSS, STAR-CROSSED
8 [+ *obj*] **a : to make two different kinds of animals breed together** ▪ The breeders *crossed* [=*crossbred, interbred*] the bison with domestic cattle. — often used figuratively to describe someone or something that combines the qualities of two different people or things ▪ As our leader, she was like a drill sergeant *crossed* with a camp counselor. **b : to mix two kinds of plants to form a new one** ▪ The farmers *crossed* two different types of corn together.
9 [*no obj*] *soccer* **: to kick or hit the ball sideways across the field** — + *to* ▪ He *crossed to* his teammate.
cross my heart ✧ The phrases ***cross my heart*** or ***cross my heart and hope to die*** are used in informal speech to stress that you are telling the truth and will do what you promise. ▪ I'll clean my room tomorrow—*cross my heart*. [=I promise that I'll clean my room tomorrow]
cross off [*phrasal verb*] ***cross (someone or something) off*** or ***cross off (someone or something)*** **: to draw a line through (a name or item on a list)** ▪ They *crossed off* the names of the people who had already been invited. ▪ We can *cross* her *off* our list of potential donors.
cross out [*phrasal verb*] ***cross (something) out*** or ***cross out (something)*** **: to draw a line through (something) to show that it is wrong** ▪ *cross out* a mistake
cross over [*phrasal verb*] ***cross over*** or ***cross over (something)*** **1 : to move or go from one side of (something) to the other** ▪ The deer *crossed over* to the other side of the river. ▪ The bridge *crosses over* the river. **2 : to change from one type of character or condition to another** ▪ People were *crossing over* to vote for the other party's candidate. [=people in one political party were voting for the other party's candidate] ▪ The singer *crossed over* from country to pop. [=the singer changed his style of music from country to pop] — see also CROSSOVER
cross paths ✧ When people ***cross paths*** or when their ***paths cross***, they meet each other at a time that was not planned or expected. ▪ After they left college, it was many years before they *crossed paths* again. = It was many years before their *paths crossed* again. ▪ I ***crossed paths with*** an old friend on a business trip.
cross someone's face **: to appear briefly on someone's face** ▪ A smile *crossed her face*.
cross someone's mind **: to come into someone's mind : to be thought of by someone** ▪ Losing never *crossed her mind*. [=she was sure that she would win] ▪ Did it ever *cross your mind* that I could be right?
cross swords **: to fight or argue** — often + *with* ▪ I didn't want to *cross swords with* him about who was right.
cross that bridge when you come to it see ¹BRIDGE
cross the line **: to go beyond what is proper or acceptable** ▪ Her criticism *crossed the line* from helpful to just plain hurtful. ▪ The magazine *crossed the line* when they printed the nude photos.
cross up [*phrasal verb*] *US* **1** ***cross (someone) up*** or ***cross up (someone)*** **: to make (someone) confused** ▪ The team *crossed up* their opponent by throwing the ball instead of running it. **2** ***cross (something) up*** or ***cross up (something)*** **: to ruin (something) completely** ▪ His failure to meet the deadline *crossed up* the deal.
cross yourself **: to make the sign of the cross on your head and chest** ▪ I *crossed myself* as I entered the church.
– cross·er *noun, pl* **-ers** [*count*]

³cross *adj* **cross·er; -est : annoyed or angry** ▪ I didn't mean to make you *cross*. ▪ I was *cross* with her for being so careless.
– cross·ly *adv* ▪ "Stop teasing your sister," she said *crossly*.

cross·bar /ˈkrɑːsˌbaɚ/ *noun, pl* **-bars** [*count*]
1 : a bar that joins two posts (such as goalposts in soccer or hockey)
2 : the bar that goes between the seat and the handlebars of a bicycle — see picture at BICYCLE

crossbones see SKULL AND CROSSBONES

cross·bow /ˈkrɑːsˌboʊ/ *noun, pl* **-bows** [*count*] **: a weapon that shoots arrows and that consists of a short bow attached to a longer piece of wood**

cross·breed /ˈkrɑːsˌbriːd/ *verb* **-breeds; -bred** /-ˌbrɛd/; **-breed·ing**
1 : to make two different kinds of animal breed together [+ *obj*] *crossbreed* [=*cross, interbreed*] sheep [*no obj*] Some birds may *crossbreed* [=*interbreed*] freely with other species.
2 [+ *obj*] **: to mix two kinds of plant to form a new one** ▪ *crossbreed* [=*cross*] wheat and rye
– crossbred *adj, always used before a noun* ▪ *crossbred* [=*hybrid*] sheep/roses **– crossbreed** *noun, pl* **-breeds** [*count*]

cross–check /ˈkrɑːsˌʧɛk/ *verb* **-checks; -checked; -check·ing** [+ *obj*] **: to use a different source or method to check (something, such as information or calculations)** ▪ I *cross-checked* the changes against the original copy. [=I looked at the original copy to make sure that the changes were correct] ▪ You should *cross-check* your answers with a calculator.
– cross–check *noun, pl* **-checks** [*count*]

¹cross–coun·try /ˈkrɑːsˈkʌntri/ *adj, always used before a noun*
1 : going or moving across a country ▪ a *cross-country* railroad ▪ a *cross-country* concert tour
2 : going over the countryside rather than by roads or over a track ▪ They ran in a *cross-country* race.
3 : relating to or used in a kind of skiing that is done over the countryside instead of down a mountain ▪ *cross-country* skiing ▪ *cross-country* skis ▪ a *cross-country* champion/competition — compare ²DOWNHILL 3
– cross–country *adv* ▪ We traveled *cross-country*.

²cross–country *noun* [*noncount*] **: cross-country skiing or racing** ▪ She has done *cross-country* for 10 years. ▪ He won a medal in *cross-country*.

cross·court /ˈkrɑːsˈkoɚt/ *adv* **: to or toward the opposite side of a tennis or basketball court** ▪ She hit/passed the ball *crosscourt*.
– crosscourt *adj, always used before a noun* ▪ a *crosscourt* pass/shot

cross–cul·tur·al /ˈkrɑːsˈkʌlʧərəl/ *adj* [*more* ~; *most* ~] **: relating to or involving two or more different cultures or**

countries ▪ a *cross-cultural* study ▪ a menu featuring *cross-cultural* cuisine

– cross–cul·tur·al·ly *adv*

cross·cur·rent /ˈkrɑːsˌkərənt/ *noun, pl* **-rents** [*count*] **:** a current of water that flows against or across the main current — sometimes used figuratively ▪ the political *crosscurrents* that interfere with the passing of laws

C

cross–curricular *adj, Brit* **:** relating to or involving different courses offered by a school ▪ *cross-curricular* activities

cross–dress·ing /ˈkrɑːsˌdrɛsɪŋ/ *noun* [*noncount*] **:** the act or practice of wearing clothes made for the opposite sex

– cross–dress·er /ˈkrɑːsˌdrɛsɚ/ *noun, pl* **-ers** [*count*]

cross–ex·am·ine /ˈkrɑːsɪgˈzæmən/ *verb* **-ines; -ined; -in·ing** [+ *obj*] *law* **:** to ask more questions of (a witness who has been questioned by another lawyer) ▪ The defendant's attorney *cross-examined* the witness and tried to show that his earlier testimony was false.

– cross–ex·am·i·na·tion /ˈkrɑːsɪgˌzæməˈneɪʃən/ *noun* [*noncount*] ▪ While he was under *cross-examination*, the defendant admitted that he had lied earlier in court.

– cross–ex·am·in·er /ˈkrɑːsɪgˈzæmənɚ/ *noun, pl* **-ers** [*count*] ▪ This lawyer is a tough *cross-examiner*.

cross–eyed /ˈkrɑːsˌaɪd/ *adj* [*more* ~; *most* ~] **:** having one or both eyes turned inward toward the nose ▪ a *cross-eyed* drunk ▪ He gave her a *cross-eyed* look.

– cross–eyed *adv* ▪ He looked at her *cross-eyed*.

cross–fer·til·ize *also Brit* **cross–fer·til·ise** /ˈkrɑːsˈfətəˌlaɪz/ *verb* **-iz·es; -ized; -iz·ing** [+ *obj*]

1 : to combine sex cells from (two separate plants) to produce a new plant ▪ Scientists *cross-fertilized* the two plants.

2 : to combine (two different ideas, style, etc.) in a good or creative way ▪ a musical style that *cross-fertilizes* jazz and rock

– cross–fer·til·i·za·tion *also Brit* **cross–fer·til·i·sa·tion** /ˈkrɑːsˌfətələˈzeɪʃən, *Brit* ˈkrɒsˌfɜːtəˌlaɪˈzeɪʃən/ *noun* [*noncount*]

cross·fire /ˈkrɑːsˌfajɚ/ *noun* [*singular*] **:** shots that come from two or more places so that the bullets cross through the same area ▪ Several civilians were killed in the *crossfire* during the battle. ▪ The war volunteers were at risk of being caught in the *crossfire*. — sometimes used figuratively ▪ She was caught in the *crossfire* between her quarrelling sisters. [=she became involved in the quarrel between her sisters and they became angry at her] ▪ a presidential candidate who has become caught in a political *crossfire* after making comments that angered both liberals and conservatives

cross·hair /ˈkrɑːsˌheɚ/ *noun, pl* **-hairs** [*count*] **:** a very thin wire or thread that is seen when you look into a microscope, telescope, etc., and that is used for precisely viewing or aiming at something

in the crosshairs **:** being aimed at by a gun (such as a rifle) that has an aiming device with crosshairs — often used figuratively ▪ The senator's voting record was *in the crosshairs* of his political rivals. [=was being targeted by his political rivals]

cross·hatch /ˈkrɑːsˌhætʃ/ *verb* **-hatch·es; -hatched; -hatch·ing** [+ *obj*] **:** to mark or draw (something) with sets of lines that cross each other ▪ The fields were *crosshatched* by plowed paths.

– crosshatching *noun* [*noncount*] ▪ The artist used *crosshatching* to fill in the shaded areas.

cross·ing /ˈkrɑːsɪŋ/ *noun, pl* **-ings** [*count*]

1 : a place where two things (such as a street and a railroad track) cross each other ▪ Stop at the railroad *crossing*. ▪ Federal agents questioned us at the border *crossing*. [=the place where people go across the border between two countries]

2 : a place where you can cross a street, stream, etc. ▪ a *crossing* for ferry boats — see picture at STREET; see also PEDESTRIAN CROSSING, PELICAN CROSSING, ZEBRA CROSSING

3 a : the act of going across something ▪ the *crossing* of a mountain range **b :** a voyage across water ▪ a weeklong *crossing* of the Atlantic Ocean

crossing guard *noun, pl* ~ **guards** [*count*] **:** a person whose job is to help people (such as schoolchildren) go across busy streets safely

cross–legged /ˈkrɑːsˌlɛgəd/ *adj* **:** having the legs crossed ▪ She curled up into a *cross-legged* position.

– cross–legged *adv* ▪ She sat *cross-legged*. ▪ The kids sat on the floor *cross-legged*. [=with their legs crossed and their knees spread wide apart]

cross·over /ˈkrɑːsˌouvɚ/ *noun, pl* **-overs** [*count*] **:** a change from one style or type of activity to another ▪ The actor made a smooth *crossover* to politics. ▪ a rock musician's *crossovers* into jazz and soul music — often used before another noun ▪ a successful *crossover* artist/star/celebrity ▪ a romantic movie that has *crossover* appeal to fans of science fiction — see also *cross over* at ²CROSS

cross·piece /ˈkrɑːsˌpiːs/ *noun, pl* **-piec·es** [*count*] **:** something (such as a piece of wood) that is placed or that lies across something else ▪ The carpenter attached a *crosspiece* to each side of the frame to give extra support to the roof.

cross–pol·li·nate /ˈkrɑːsˈpɑːləˌneɪt/ *verb* **-nates; -nat·ed; -nat·ing** [+ *obj*]

1 *botany* **:** to move pollen from one flower to another

2 : CROSS-FERTILIZE 2 ▪ *cross-pollinating* different musical styles

– cross–pol·li·na·tion /ˌkrɑːsˌpɑːləˈneɪʃən/ *noun* [*noncount*]

cross–pur·pos·es /ˈkrɑːsˈpɚpəsəz/ *noun*

at cross-purposes **:** in a way that causes confusion or failure because people are working or talking with different goals or purposes ▪ We'll never succeed together if we continue to work *at cross-purposes* (with each other). ▪ It became clear that they were talking *at cross-purposes*.

cross–re·fer /ˌkrɑːsrɪˈfɚ/ *verb* **-fers; -ferred; -fer·ring :** to direct a reader to more information that can be found in another place [+ *obj*] The entry for "gram" *cross-refers* you to a table of weights. [*no obj*] The entry *cross-refers* to a table of weights.

¹cross–ref·er·ence /ˈkrɑːsˈrɛfrəns/ *noun, pl* **-enc·es** [*count*] **:** a note in a book (such as a dictionary) that tells you where to look for more information ▪ The almanac includes *cross-references* to a map and timeline for each country.

²cross–reference *verb* **-ences; -enced; -enc·ing**

1 [+ *obj*] **:** to supply (something, such as a book) with cross-references ▪ The book is heavily *cross-referenced*.

2 : CROSS-REFER [*no obj*] The article on alligators in the encyclopedia *cross-references* to the entry on crocodiles. [+ *obj*] The census figures are *cross-referenced* to more detailed information about each state.

cross·road /ˈkrɑːsˌroud/ *noun, pl* **-roads** [*count*]

1 : a place where two or more roads cross ▪ Traffic was stopped at the *crossroad*. — often plural in form ▪ They arrived at a *crossroads* marked by a signpost. — often used figuratively to refer to a place or time at which a decision must be made ▪ The industry is at a critical *crossroad*. ▪ We've reached a *crossroads* [=*turning point*] in our relationship.

2 : a road that crosses a main road or that runs across land between main roads ▪ We turned onto a *crossroad*.

cross section *noun, pl* ~ **-tions**

1 : a view or drawing that shows what the inside of something looks like after a cut has been made across it [*count*] a detailed *cross section* of the human brain [*noncount*] The drawing showed the human brain ***in cross section***.

2 [*count*] **:** a small group that includes examples of the different types of people or things in a larger group ▪ The class surveyed a *cross section* of the student body. ▪ The people in our neighborhood are/form a representative *cross section* of American society.

– cross–sec·tion·al /ˈkrɑːsˈsɛkʃənəl/ *adj* ▪ a *cross-sectional* view of the brain

cross–stitch /ˈkrɑːsˌstɪtʃ/ *noun, pl* **-stitch·es** [*count*] **:** a stitch in the shape of an X ▪ The blouse had *cross-stitches* around the neckline.

cross·town /ˈkrɑːsˈtaun/ *adj, always used before a noun*

1 : located on different sides of a town or city ▪ The two schools were *crosstown* rivals in baseball.

2 : going across a town or city ▪ We rode a *crosstown* bus. ▪ *crosstown* traffic

– crosstown *adv* ▪ He drove *crosstown* to pick up his daughter.

cross·walk /ˈkrɑːsˌwɑːk/ *noun, pl* **-walks** [*count*] *US* **:** a marked path where people can safely walk across a street or road — called also *pedestrian crossing*; see picture at STREET

cross·wind /ˈkrɑːsˌwɪnd/ *noun, pl* **-winds** [*count*] **:** a wind that blows across the direction that something (such as an airplane) is moving in

¹cross·wise /ˈkrɑːsˌwaɪz/ *adv* **:** from one side or corner to the other **:** ACROSS ▪ Cut the potato *crosswise* rather than lengthwise into thin slices.

²crosswise *adj*

1 : going from one side or corner to another ▪ a *crosswise* cut

2 *US, informal* **:** involved in a conflict or disagreement ▪ He ***got crosswise*** with his boss and nearly lost his job.

cross·word puzzle /ˈkrɑːsˌwɚd-/ *noun, pl* ~ **puzzles** [*count*] : a puzzle in which words that are the answers to clues are written into a pattern of numbered squares that go across and down • My father does the *crossword puzzle* every morning. — called also *crossword*

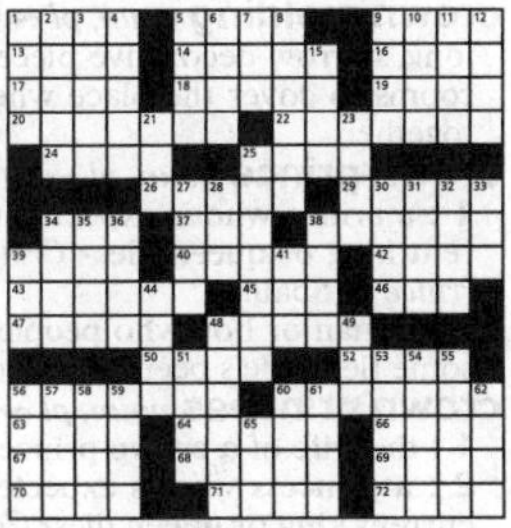

crossword puzzle

crotch /ˈkrɑːʧ/ *noun, pl* **crotch·es** [*count*] : the part of the body where the legs join together; *also* : the part of a piece of clothing that covers this part of the body • the *crotch* of the pants/shorts/pajamas — called also (*Brit*) *crutch* /ˈkrʌʧ/

crotch·et /ˈkrɑːʧət/ *noun, pl* **-ets** [*count*] *Brit* : QUARTER NOTE

crotch·ety /ˈkrɑːʧəti/ *adj* [*more* ~; *most* ~] : often annoyed and angry : GROUCHY • None of the students dared to talk back to the *crotchety* old teacher.

crouch /ˈkraʊʧ/ *verb* **crouch·es; crouched; crouch·ing** [*no obj*]
1 : to lower your body to the ground by bending your legs • She *crouched* down, trying to get a closer look at the spider. — see picture at POSITION
2 *of an animal* : to lie on the stomach close to the ground with the legs bent • The lion *crouched* in the tall grass, waiting to attack the gazelle.
– **crouch** *noun, pl* **crouches** [*count*] • The runner was in a tense *crouch*, waiting for the signal to start the race.
– **crouched** *adj* • a *crouched* position

croup /ˈkruːp/ *noun* [*noncount*] : a sickness that young children sometimes get that makes them cough a lot and have trouble breathing
– **croupy** /ˈkruːpi/ *adj* • a *croupy* cough

crou·pi·er /ˈkruːpijɚ/ *noun, pl* **-ers** [*count*] : a person whose job is to collect and pay out money in a casino

crou·ton /ˈkruːˌtɑːn/ *noun, pl* **-tons** [*count*] : a small piece of bread that is toasted or fried until it is crisp ✧ Croutons are usually served on salads or in soups.

[1]**crow** /ˈkroʊ/ *noun, pl* **crows** [*count*]
1 : a large black bird that has a loud and harsh cry — see color picture on page C9
2 ***Crow*** : a member of a Native American people of the western U.S.
as the crow flies : in a straight line • They live about three miles from here *as the crow flies*, though the actual drive is more like six (miles).
eat crow see EAT
– compare [2]CROW; see also JIM CROW

[2]**crow** *noun, pl* **crows** [*count*] : the loud, high sound a rooster makes or a similar sound • the cock's/rooster's loud *crow* • The boy gave a little *crow* of delight when he mastered the puzzle. — compare [1]CROW

[3]**crow** *verb* **crows; crowed; crow·ing**
1 [*no obj*] : to make the loud, high sound that a rooster makes or a similar sound • The cock/rooster *crowed* as the sun began to rise. • The boy *crowed* with delight.
2 : to talk in a way that shows too much pride about something you have done : to brag loudly or joyfully [*no obj*] The rest of us were sick of hearing her *crow* about/over her success. [+ *obj*] "I've won three times in a row," he *crowed*. = He *crowed* that he had won three times in a row.

crow·bar /ˈkroʊˌbaɚ/ *noun, pl* **-bars** [*count*] : a metal bar that has a thin flat edge at one end and is used to open or lift things

[1]**crowd** /ˈkraʊd/ *verb* **crowds; crowd·ed; crowd·ing**
1 a [+ *obj*] : to fill (something) so that there is little or no room for anyone or anything else : to take up much or most of the space in (an area or space) • College students *crowded* [=*packed*] the little bar on the night of the poetry reading. • Boxes *crowded* the floor of my apartment. • There are too many products *crowding* the market. • The hall was *crowded* [=*crammed, packed*] with scientists from around the world • streets *crowded* with traffic **b** [+ *obj*] : to push or force (something) *into* a small space • The club has been accused of *crowding* too many people *into* too small a space. **c** [*no obj*] : to move into a small space — + *into* or *onto* • The four of us *crowded into* a little booth at the restaurant. • We *crowded onto* the bus.
2 [+ *obj*] : to form a tight group around (something or someone) • Several horses were *crowding* [=*crowding around*] the water trough. • By the end of the 10th mile, three bicyclists were *crowding* the racer in front.
3 [+ *obj*] *chiefly US* : to stand very close or too close to (someone or something) • Please move back. You're *crowding* me. • (*baseball*) The batter was *crowding* the plate. — sometimes used figuratively • He said he broke up with his last girlfriend because she was beginning to *crowd* him. [=she was not allowing him enough privacy and independence]
crowd around/round [*phrasal verb*] ***crowd around/round*** or ***crowd around/round (something)*** : to form a tight group around (something or someone) • A small group of people *crowded around* the car. • When one of the protesters began to speak, the people *crowded around* (him) to hear what he had to say.
crowded together ✧ If a group of people or things are *crowded together*, they are next to and usually touching each other in a space that is too small. • We need to organize the closet so that the shoes aren't *crowded together*.
crowd in [*phrasal verb*] **1** : to move as a group into a small space • When we got to the elevator, everybody tried to *crowd in*. **2** *of thoughts, memories, etc.* : to come into your mind : to occupy your thinking — often + *on* • When I smell a pie baking, memories of childhood holidays *crowd in on* me. [=memories fill my mind]
crowd out [*phrasal verb*] ***crowd out (something or someone)*** or ***crowd (something or someone) out*** : to push, move, or force (something or someone) out of a place or situation by filling its space • The quick-growing grass is *crowding out* native plants. • She worries that junk food is *crowding* fruits and vegetables *out* of her children's diet.

[2]**crowd** *noun, pl* **crowds**
1 [*count*] : a large group of people who are together in one place • The President will address the *crowd* later. • The *crowd* is restless. = (*Brit*) The *crowd* are restless. • a *crowd* of kids/reporters/shoppers • The formerly unknown singer now regularly performs to *crowds* of 10,000 (people). • *Crowds* lined the street to watch the parade. • His speeches always ***draw a big/large crowd***. [=a lot of people come to hear him speak] • You can ***avoid the crowds*** by visiting a popular resort area in the off-season. • police trained in ***crowd control***
2 ***the crowd*** : ordinary people : people who are not special or unusual • kids trying to distinguish themselves from *the crowd* • She prefers to be ***one of the crowd***. [=she prefers to not to be noticed or treated in any special way] ✧ Someone who is ***just another face in the crowd*** is not famous or well-known. • Until her book became a best seller, she was *just another face in the crowd*. ✧ Someone or something that ***stands out from the crowd*** is unusual in a good way. • As a teacher, he always *stood out from the crowd*. • The high quality of these tools makes them *stand out from the crowd*. ✧ Someone who ***follows the crowd*** or ***goes with the crowd*** does whatever most other people are doing. • He was never one to *follow the crowd*, so we weren't surprised when he dropped out of college to start his own business.
3 [*singular*] : a group of people who spend time together or have something in common • Her parents are concerned that she's been hanging out with ***a bad crowd***. [=with people who do illegal or immoral things] — usually used with *the* • Her parents are concerned that she's been hanging out with *the* wrong *crowd*. • The new dance club caters to *the* under-18 *crowd*. [=to people who are less than 18 years old]
join the crowd **1** : to become part of a larger group : to do what most other people are doing • You can find a private hideaway or *join the crowd* at the beach. **2** *informal* — used to say that the problems or feelings that someone is having are problems or feelings that you have had yourself • If you don't understand the rules, *join the crowd* [=(more commonly) *join the club*]: no one else does either!
two's company, three's a crowd see COMPANY

crowded *adj* [*more* ~; *most* ~] : filled with too many people or things • a *crowded* bar/lobby/waiting room • The library was so *crowded* today! — often + *with* • The room was *crowded* [=*crammed, packed*] *with* people.

crowd–pleas·er /ˈkraʊdˌpliːzɚ/ *noun, pl* **-ers** [*count*] : a person, performance, or food that most people like • The play is a guaranteed *crowd-pleaser*. [=it is certain that many people will like the play]

– crowd–pleas•ing /ˈkraʊdˌpli:zɪŋ/ *adj* ▪ a *crowd-pleasing* show

[1]**crown** /ˈkraʊn/ *noun, pl* **crowns**

1 [*count*] **a** : a decorative object that is shaped like a circle and worn on the head of a king or queen for special ceremonies ✧ Crowns are usually made of gold or silver and decorated with jewels. **b** : a similar object worn by someone who is not an actual king or queen ▪ The winner of the beauty pageant walked down the runway wearing her sparkling *crown*. **c** : a ring of leaves or flowers worn on the head of someone who has won a game, contest, or award

2 ***the crown*** *or* ***the Crown*** : the government of a country that is officially ruled by a king or queen ▪ the blessing of *the* Spanish *crown* ▪ allegiance to *the crown* ▪ She was appointed by *the Crown*.

3 ***the crown*** : the position of power that a king or queen has ▪ When the king died childless, his brother assumed *the crown*. [=his brother became king]

4 [*count*] : something (such as a badge or decoration) in the shape of a king's or queen's crown ▪ a jacket with a *crown* insignia on the pocket

5 [*count*] : the title or position held by the person who has won a particular competition : CHAMPIONSHIP — usually singular ▪ If he loses this match, he'll lose the heavyweight boxing *crown*. [=he will no longer be the champion]

6 [*count*] : the part of a tooth that can be seen ▪ an artificial *crown* made of porcelain

7 [*count*] : the top of the head — usually singular ▪ She has a big bump on the *crown* [=*top*] of her head.

8 [*count*] : the part of a hat that covers the top of the head — usually singular ▪ The hat has a rounded *crown* and a wide brim. — see picture at HAT

9 [*count*] : the highest part of something (such as a tree or mountain) ▪ From the tower, we could see the *crowns* of the trees below.

10 [*count*] **a** : a unit of money used in several European countries ▪ Norwegian *crowns* **b** : an old British coin worth five shillings

– crown *adj, always used before a noun* ▪ a *crown* appointee [=someone appointed by the government of a king or queen]

[2]**crown** *verb* **crowns; crowned; crown•ing** [+ *obj*]

1 : to put a crown on (a new king, queen, etc.) : to give (someone) the power and title of a king or queen — usually used as *(be) crowned* ▪ She *was crowned* queen at the age of 18.

2 : to officially or formally give (someone) the title or position of a champion, winner, etc. ▪ The U.S. Open will *crown* a new champion Sunday. [=someone will be proclaimed champion at the U.S. Open championship] ▪ The magazine *crowned* her the new queen of rock-and-roll music.

3 : to end (something) in a successful and impressive way ▪ She *crowned* her long and distinguished career by designing the city's beautiful new bridge.

4 *literary* : to be on top of (something) : to form the top of (something) ▪ Snow *crowns* the mountain year-round. — usually used as *(be) crowned* ▪ The mountain *is crowned* with snow all year round. ▪ a hill *crowned* with yellow daffodils ▪ Her head *is crowned* by/with thick red hair.

5 : to put an artificial crown on (a tooth) ▪ I broke a tooth and I'll have to have it *crowned*.

6 *informal* : to hit (someone) on the head ▪ He got *crowned* with a beer bottle.

to crown it all *Brit* — used to indicate the last and usually worst thing in a series of bad things that have happened ▪ It rained, it snowed, and, *to crown it all* [=*to top it off*], our flight was canceled.

crown colony *noun, pl* **~ -nies** [*count*] : a colony (such as Gibraltar or the Falkland Islands) that is under the control of the British government

crowning *adj, always used before a noun* : greatest or most complete ▪ The bridge is the architect's *crowning* achievement. ▪ His refusal to see me was the *crowning* [=*worst, ultimate*] insult. ▪ The town's ***crowning glory*** is its old cathedral. [=the cathedral is the town's best feature] ▪ Her hair is her *crowning glory*.

crown jewel *noun, pl* **~ -els**

1 ***the crown jewels*** : the crown, scepter, and other jeweled objects that a king or queen uses on formal occasions

2 [*count*] : the most valuable or attractive thing in a collection or group ▪ The painting is the *crown jewel* of the museum's collection. ▪ one of the company's *crown jewels*

crown molding *noun, pl* **~ -ings** [*count, noncount*] *US* : a long, narrow decorative piece of wood that is used in some rooms to cover the place where the walls and ceiling come together

crown prince *noun, pl* **~ princes** [*count*]

1 : a prince who is expected to become king when the current king or queen dies ▪ *Crown Prince* George ▪ the *Crown Prince* of Spain

2 : a man or boy who people expect to become a leader in some field ▪ He's been heralded as the *crown prince* of jazz.

crown princess *noun, pl* **~ -cesses** [*count*]

1 : the wife of a crown prince

2 : a princess who is expected to become queen when the current king or queen dies ▪ *Crown Princess* Lydia

3 : a woman or girl who people expect to become a leader in some field ▪ She is ice-skating's new *crown princess*.

crow's–feet /ˈkroʊzˌfi:t/ *noun* [*plural*] : wrinkles around the outer corners of a person's eyes ▪ a new cream that is supposed to get rid of *crow's-feet*

crow's nest *noun, pl* **~ nests** [*count*] : a platform with short walls that is high on a ship's mast and from which you can see things (such as land and other ships) that are far away

CRT *abbr* cathode-ray tube

cru•cial /ˈkru:ʃəl/ *adj* [*more* ~; *most* ~] : extremely important ▪ Vitamins are *crucial* for maintaining good health. ▪ Eggs are a *crucial* [=*essential*] ingredient in this recipe. ▪ a *crucial* distinction/difference ▪ It's *crucial* that we arrive before 8 o'clock. ▪ Teachers are *crucial* to the success of the school. ▪ She played a *crucial* role in the meeting. ▪ Tonight's game is the *crucial* [=*decisive*] game of the series. [=whoever wins this game will win the series] ▪ a *crucial* decision

– cru•cial•ly *adv* ▪ *crucially* important

cru•ci•ble /ˈkru:səbəl/ *noun, pl* **-ci•bles** [*count*]

1 : a pot in which metals or other substances are heated to a very high temperature or melted

2 *formal + literary* : a difficult test or challenge ▪ He's ready to face the *crucible* of the Olympics.

3 *formal + literary* : a place or situation that forces people to change or make difficult decisions ▪ His character was formed in the *crucible* of war.

cru•ci•fix /ˈkru:səˌfɪks/ *noun, pl* **-fix•es** [*count*] : a model of a cross with a figure of Jesus Christ crucified on it ▪ He wears a *crucifix* on a chain around his neck.

cru•ci•fix•ion /ˌkru:səˈfɪkʃən/ *noun, pl* **-ions**

1 [*noncount*] : an act of killing someone by nailing or tying his or her hands and feet to a cross : an act of crucifying someone ▪ the *crucifixion* of the rebel Spartacus

2 ***the Crucifixion*** : the killing of Jesus Christ on a cross

cru•ci•form /ˈkru:səˌfoəm/ *adj* : in the shape of a cross ▪ a *cruciform* church

cru•ci•fy /ˈkru:səˌfaɪ/ *verb* **-fies; -fied; -fy•ing** [+ *obj*]

1 : to kill (someone) by nailing or tying his or her hands and feet to a cross ▪ Jesus Christ was *crucified*.

2 *informal* : to criticize (someone or something) very harshly ▪ They *crucified* her in the newspapers for having an affair.

crud /ˈkrʌd/ *noun* [*noncount*] *informal*

1 : a dirty or greasy substance ▪ I spent an hour scrubbing the *crud* off the old stove.

2 *chiefly US* : something unpleasant or worthless ▪ He complains that there's too much *crud* on TV these days.

crud•dy /ˈkrʌdi/ *adj* **crud•di•er; -est** *informal*

1 : dirty or greasy ▪ a *cruddy* old stove

2 *US* **a** : not of good quality ▪ They did a *cruddy* [=*lousy*] job with the repairs. **b** : not well or happy ▪ I ***felt cruddy*** [=*lousy, sick*] the day after the party. ▪ I ***feel cruddy*** [=*sorry, bad*] about what I said.

[1]**crude** /ˈkru:d/ *adj* **crud•er; crud•est** [*also more* ~; *most* ~]

1 : very simple and basic : made or done in a way that does not show a lot of skill ▪ *crude* tools ▪ a *crude* instrument/drawing ▪ They built a *crude* shelter out of branches.

2 : rude in a way that makes people uncomfortable; *especially* : talking about sexual matters in a rude way ▪ They tell a lot of *crude* [=*vulgar*] jokes.

3 : very simple and basic in a way that is true but not complete ▪ a *crude* summary of the country's history ▪ a *crude* theory ▪ a *crude* [=*rough*] estimate ▪ She first described the procedure in *crude* terms, and then went into more detail.

– crude•ly *adv* ▪ a *crudely* drawn picture ▪ To put it *crudely* [=*bluntly*], I just don't like you. **– crude•ness** *noun* [*noncount*] ▪ He doesn't appreciate the *crudeness* of their jokes.

[2]**crude** *noun* [*noncount*] : oil as it exists in the ground : petro-

leum that is not yet ready to be used as fuel — called also *crude oil*

cru·di·tés /ˌkruːdɪˈteɪ/ *noun [plural]* : pieces of raw vegetables (such as carrots and celery) that are served before a meal usually with a sauce for dipping

cru·di·ty /ˈkruːdəti/ *noun, pl* **-ties**
1 *[noncount]* : the quality or state of being crude ▪ the *crudity* of the drawing
2 *[count]* : something that is crude ▪ The movie's *crudities* were supposed to be funny, but they didn't make me laugh.

cru·el /ˈkruːl/ *adj, US* **cru·el·er** *or Brit* **cru·el·ler**; *US* **cru·el·est** *or Brit* **cru·el·lest** *[also more ~; most ~]*
1 — used to describe people who hurt others and do not feel sorry about it ▪ a *cruel* dictator/tyrant ▪ Children can be *cruel*, as any child who has been made fun of by others knows. ▪ He says he can't trust people who are *cruel* to animals. ▪ a *cruel* smile [=the smile of a cruel person]
2 : causing or helping to cause suffering : terrible and unfair ▪ a *cruel* joke ▪ It was a very *cruel* [=*hurtful*] thing to say. ▪ I thought it was rather *cruel* [=*unkind*] of them to give her all the dirty work. ▪ a *cruel* twist of fate ▪ Hunger is a *cruel* fact of nature. ▪ Life has dealt them some ***cruel blows*** in recent years. [=some very bad things have happened to them in recent years] ▪ The law forbids ***cruel and unusual punishment*** [=punishment that is very harsh and inappropriate for the crime]
– cru·el·ly *adv* ▪ treated *cruelly* ▪ He was *cruelly* beaten.

cru·el·ty /ˈkruːlti/ *noun, pl* **-ties**
1 *[noncount]* : a desire to cause others to suffer : the quality or state of being cruel ▪ a dictator/tyrant known for his *cruelty* ▪ The *cruelty* of children can be surprising.
2 a *[noncount]* : actions that cause suffering ▪ They protested against *cruelty* to animals. ▪ physical and emotional *cruelty*
b *[count]* : an act or occurrence that causes suffering — usually plural ▪ The prisoners endured awful *cruelties*. ▪ the *cruelties* of life/nature/war

cru·et /ˈkruːwət/ *noun, pl* **-ets** *[count]*
1 *US* : a small glass bottle that is used at the table during meals to hold vinegar, oil, or sauce
2 *Brit* : a container or set of containers used at the table during meals to hold salt, pepper, oil, etc.

[1]**cruise** /ˈkruːz/ *verb* **cruis·es; cruised; cruis·ing**
1 : to travel on a boat or ship to a number of places as a vacation *[no obj]* We *cruised* for a week down the Yangtze River. *[+ obj]* He dreams of *cruising* the Mediterranean.
2 *[no obj] of a car, airplane, etc.* : to move along at a steady speed ▪ The bus was *cruising* at 55 miles per hour. ▪ We were *cruising* along/down the highway. ▪ The plane was *cruising* at 30,000 feet.
3 : to drive or be driven slowly *[+ obj]* On Friday nights, teenagers *cruise* the main street in town to show off their cars. *[no obj]* A car *cruised* past us.
4 *[no obj]* : to do something easily : to easily succeed at something ▪ She *cruised* [=*waltzed, breezed*] through the exam. ▪ The team *cruised* to victory in the last game.
5 *[+ obj]* : to move around in (a place) without a specific purpose but usually with the hope of finding something interesting ▪ I *cruised* the mall for a couple hours on Saturday. — often used figuratively ▪ She spent hours *cruising* [=(more commonly) *surfing*] the Internet. ▪ He's always *cruising* the radio dial for new music.
6 *slang* : to go (somewhere) in search of a sexual partner *[+ obj]* They're out *cruising* bars. *[no obj]* a group of teenage guys out *cruising* for girls

[2]**cruise** *noun, pl* **cruises** *[count]* : a journey on a boat or ship to a number of places as a vacation ▪ We went on a weeklong *cruise* down the Yangtze River. ▪ They went on a *cruise* for their honeymoon. ▪ a Mediterranean *cruise* — sometimes used before another noun ▪ Which *cruise* line should I book my trip with? — see also CRUISE SHIP

cruise control *noun [noncount]*
1 : a device in a vehicle that a driver turns on to make the vehicle continue at whatever speed the driver has chosen
2 : a relaxed pace that does not require a lot of effort ▪ She admits that she's been doing the job so long that she's ***on cruise control*** [=she does not put a lot of effort into the job]

cruise missile *noun, pl* **~ -siles** *[count]* : a large military weapon that flies close to the ground and is directed to a specific place to explode

cruis·er /ˈkruːzə/ *noun, pl* **-ers** *[count]*
1 *US* : POLICE CAR
2 : a large and fast military ship
3 : a boat that has room to live on and that is used for pleasure — called also *cabin cruiser*

cruise ship *noun, pl* **~ ships** *[count]* : a large ship that takes many people on a cruise at one time : a large ship that stops at different ports and carries passengers who are traveling for pleasure — called also *cruise liner*; see picture at SHIP

cruising altitude *noun, pl* **~ -tudes** : the height in the sky at which an airplane stays for most of a flight *[noncount]* The pilot announced that we'd reached *cruising altitude*. *[count]* a *cruising altitude* of 40,000 feet

cruising speed *noun, pl* **~ speeds** : the speed at which an airplane, a boat, etc., usually moves when it is traveling at a fast speed for a long distance *[count]* The boat has a *cruising speed* of 25 knots. *[noncount]* The boat handled well at *cruising speed*.

crul·ler /ˈkrʌlə/ *noun, pl* **-lers** *[count] US* : a sweet food made from a piece of dough that has been twisted and fried

crumb /ˈkrʌm/ *noun, pl* **crumbs** *[count]*
1 : a very small piece of food ▪ He swept the *crumbs* from under the table. ✧ Crumbs are usually pieces of baked foods like bread or cake. They are sometimes used in cooking. ▪ The pie's crust is made with cookie *crumbs*. ▪ Coat the fish in bread *crumbs* before frying it.
2 *informal* : a very small amount of something — usually + *of* ▪ hoping for any *crumb of* affection ▪ They couldn't find a *crumb of* evidence against her.

[1]**crum·ble** /ˈkrʌmbəl/ *verb* **crum·bles; crum·bled; crum·bling**
1 *[+ obj]* : to break (something) into small pieces ▪ *Crumble* the cookies into small bits. ▪ The recipe calls for the herbs to be *crumbled*.
2 *[no obj]* : to separate into many small pieces : to fall apart ▪ The arch had *crumbled* [=*disintegrated*] under the weight of all those stones. ▪ bones so old they had *crumbled* to dust ▪ *crumbling* buildings/monuments/walls
3 *[no obj]* : to break down completely : to stop functioning ▪ Peace talks between the two parties have *crumbled*. [=*collapsed*] ▪ She was extremely depressed after her marriage *crumbled*. ▪ their *crumbling* marriage
that's the way the cookie crumbles see COOKIE

[2]**crumble** *noun, pl* **crumbles**
1 crumbles *[plural] US* : small pieces of something that has been crumbled ▪ *crumbles* of blue cheese
2 *[count, noncount] chiefly Brit* : [2]CRISP 2 ▪ an apple *crumble*

crum·bly /ˈkrʌmbəli/ *adj* **crum·bli·er; -est** : easily broken into small pieces ▪ *crumbly* soil ▪ a *crumbly* cheese

crumbs /ˈkrʌmz/ *interj, Brit, informal* — used to express surprise ▪ *Crumbs*! I can't believe he did it!

crum·my /ˈkrʌmi/ *adj* **crum·mi·er; -est** *informal*
1 : not pleasant ▪ We've had *crummy* [=*lousy*] weather all week.
2 : not of good quality ▪ The plumbers did a *crummy* [=*lousy*] job putting in the new sink. ▪ a *crummy* story
3 *chiefly US* : not well or happy ▪ I ***felt crummy*** [=*sick, lousy*] all day yesterday. ▪ I *feel crummy* [=*bad, sorry*] about the way I treated her.

crum·pet /ˈkrʌmpət/ *noun, pl* **-pets** *Brit*
1 *[count]* : a small round bread that has a smooth bottom and holes in the top and that is eaten hot with butter
2 *informal + sometimes offensive* : a sexually attractive person *[noncount]* He's looking for ***a bit of crumpet*** [=he's looking for an attractive woman to have sex with] *[count]* Because he is brainy as well as handsome, the actor is often referred to as "the thinking woman's *crumpet*."

crum·ple /ˈkrʌmpəl/ *verb* **crum·ples; crum·pled; crum·pling**
1 a *[+ obj]* : to press or squeeze (something) so that it is no longer flat or smooth ▪ She *crumpled* the piece of paper into a ball and tossed it into the garbage can. ▪ The car's fender was *crumpled* in the accident. ▪ a *crumpled* napkin/suit/bill — often + *up* ▪ He *crumpled up* the note and threw it away.
b *[no obj]* : to become wrinkled or bent : to stop being smooth or flat ▪ The fabric is stiff and does not *crumple* [=*wrinkle, rumple*] easily. ▪ Her ***face crumpled*** [=she looked like she was going to cry] when we told her that she couldn't come with us.
2 *[no obj]* : to suddenly bend and fall ▪ At the sight of blood, he *crumpled* to the floor.

crumple zone *noun, pl* **~ zones** *[count] technical* : the front part of a vehicle that is designed to bend easily in an accident so that the people inside are protected

C

[1]crunch /ˈkrʌnʧ/ *verb* **crunch·es; crunched; crunch·ing**
1 [*no obj*] **a :** to make the loud sound of something being crushed • The snow *crunched* underfoot. **b :** to move along a surface that makes the loud sound of something being crushed • We could hear the truck's tires *crunching* along the gravel road.
2 [+ *obj*] **:** to process (numbers, information, etc.) **:** to examine and analyze (numbers, information, etc.) • When she ***crunched the numbers***, she found that the business's profits were actually much lower than the company had said. — see also NUMBER CRUNCHER
crunch on [*phrasal verb*] ***crunch on (something)* :** to chew (a piece of food) in a way that makes a loud sound • She *crunched on* a carrot while watching TV. • *crunching on* potato chips

[2]crunch *noun, pl* **crunches**
1 a [*count*] **:** the sound made when something hard is being chewed or crushed **:** a crunching sound • the *crunch* of someone eating a carrot • We could hear the *crunch* of the truck's tires on the gravel road. **b** [*noncount*] **:** the quality of a food that produces a loud sound when it is chewed **:** a crunchy quality • The nuts give the salad *crunch*. [=the nuts make the salad somewhat crunchy]
2 ***the crunch* :** a very difficult point or situation • *The crunch* came when the computer stopped working. — see also CRUNCH TIME
3 [*count*] *US* **:** a situation in which there is not enough of something — usually singular • The city's budget *crunch* means that streets will not be repaired this spring. [=because the city does not have enough money, streets will not be repaired] • The project is facing a time *crunch*. • an energy *crunch* [=(more commonly) *crisis*]
4 [*count*] **:** a stomach exercise in which you lie on your back, raise the top part of your body until your shoulders are off the floor, and then lower it — usually plural • I try to do 50 *crunches* a day. — compare SIT-UP

crunch time *noun* [*noncount*] *informal* **:** the most important time in a game, event, etc. **:** a critical moment • The team had trained well, but at *crunch time* they just couldn't perform.

crunchy /ˈkrʌnʧi/ *adj* **crunch·i·er; -est :** having a hard texture and making a loud sound when chewed or crushed **:** not soft or mushy • *crunchy* chips/cereal/vegetables • *crunchy* snow • These cookies are very *crunchy*.

[1]cru·sade /kruˈseɪd/ *noun, pl* **-sades** [*count*]
1 ***Crusade* :** any one of the wars that European Christian countries fought against Muslims in Palestine in the 11th, 12th, and 13th centuries — usually plural
2 : a major effort to change something — usually + *for* or *against* • She has devoted herself to the *crusade for* equal rights for all people. • a *crusade* [=*campaign*] *against* crime/pollution • a politician conducting/waging a *crusade against* organized labor

[2]crusade *verb* **-sad·ed; -sad·ing** [*no obj*] **:** to take part in a major effort to change something — usually + *for* or *against* • She has *crusaded for* equal rights for all people. • They are *crusading* [=*campaigning*] *against* crime/pollution.
– cru·sad·er *or* **Crusader** *noun, pl* **-ers** [*count*] • human rights *crusaders* • the *Crusaders* of the Middle Ages

[1]crush /ˈkrʌʃ/ *verb* **crush·es; crushed; crush·ing** [+ *obj*]
1 : to press or squeeze (something) so hard that it breaks or loses its shape • Unfortunately some of the flowers got *crushed* when we were moving them. • *crushing* grapes • The bicycle was *crushed* under the truck's tires. • The machine *crushes* the cans so that they can be stored until they are recycled. • Her arm was *crushed* in the accident. • Several people were ***crushed to death*** [=killed by being crushed] as the crowd rushed for the exit doors.
2 : to break (something) into a powder or very small pieces by pressing, pounding, or grinding it • *Crush* the nuts and sprinkle them on top of the cake. • The rocks were *crushed* into dust. • *crushed* herbs/ice/garlic
3 : to defeat (a person or group that opposes you) by using a lot of force • The king sent out his special forces to *crush* [=*quash*] the rebellion.
4 : to make (someone) feel very unhappy, upset, etc. • The novelist was *crushed* by the editor's comments. • A string of bad luck had *crushed* his spirit. • He was *crushed* by regret. • She owed many people money, and felt *crushed* [=*overwhelmed*] by the debt.
– crush·er *noun, pl* **-ers** [*count*] • a garlic *crusher* • They used an electric *crusher* to crush the grapes.

[2]crush *noun, pl* **crushes**
1 [*count*] **a :** a strong feeling of romantic love for someone that is usually not expressed and does not last a long time ✧ The person who has a crush is usually young or is behaving or feeling like a young person. • a childhood *crush* • a ***schoolgirl crush*** [=romantic feelings felt by a schoolgirl or by someone who is being compared to a schoolgirl] — often + *on* • All through high school I had a *crush on* the art teacher. • I think he's got a *crush on* her. **b :** the person on whom you have a crush • Yesterday I saw my old high school *crush* for the first time in five years.
2 [*count*] **:** a crowd of people who are pressed close together • The *crush* in the train station is at its worst during the afternoon rush hour. • Outside the hotel stood a *crush* of reporters waiting for her arrival.
3 [*noncount*] *chiefly Brit* **:** a drink made from fruit juice • orange *crush*

crushing *adj* **:** very bad, harmful, or severe • The team suffered a *crushing* loss. • They are struggling to escape the *crushing* poverty they've known all their lives. • The news came as a *crushing* blow. • a *crushing* insult

crust /ˈkrʌst/ *noun, pl* **crusts**
1 : the hard outer surface of bread [*count*] Her children prefer to eat their sandwiches with the *crusts* [=the outer edges of the bread slices] cut off. • a crunchy/chewy *crust* [*noncount*] Her children prefer to eat their sandwiches with the *crust* cut off.
2 : the outside part of a pie **:** PIECRUST [*count*] Bake the pie until the *crust* [=*top*] is golden brown. [*noncount*] a pie with flaky *crust*
3 [*count, noncount*] **:** the bread that is used to make a pizza • He likes pizza with thin/thick *crust*. • She ate three slices of pizza, but left the *crusts* [=the thick, outer pieces of the crust] on her plate.
4 [*count, noncount*] **:** a hard layer on the surface of something • Our feet broke through the thin *crust* of ice and into the snow below. • the Earth's *crust*
earn a/your crust *Brit, informal* **:** to earn the money that you need to live **:** to earn a living • I'm really a poet, but I've got to *earn my crust* as an accountant.
– see also UPPER CRUST

crus·ta·cean /krəˈsteɪʃən/ *noun, pl* **-ceans** [*count*] *technical* **:** a type of animal (such as a crab or lobster) that has several pairs of legs and a body made up of sections that are covered in a hard outer shell ✧ Crustaceans usually live in the water.
– crustacean *adj*

crust·ed /ˈkrʌstəd/ *adj* **:** having a hard surface layer • *crusted* snow • mud-*crusted* shoes [=mud-encrusted shoes] — often + *with* • fish *crusted* with blackened spices

crusty /ˈkrʌsti/ *adj* **crust·i·er; -est**
1 : harsh and unfriendly • a *crusty* old man ✧ A crusty person often seems unfriendly at first but is really kinder and more caring than he or she seems. *Crusty* is usually used to describe old people.
2 *of food* **:** having a thick or crisp crust • a basket of warm, *crusty* bread
3 : having a crust **:** having a hard surface layer • We could see deer tracks in the *crusty* snow bank.
– crust·i·ness *noun* [*noncount*]

crutch /ˈkrʌʧ/ *noun, pl* **crutch·es** [*count*]
1 : a long stick with a padded piece at the top that fits under a person's arm — usually plural ✧ People who have difficulty walking often use crutches to help them walk. • He's able to walk short distances with *crutches* but prefers his wheelchair. • I was ***on crutches*** [=I was using crutches to walk] for six weeks after I broke my leg. — see picture at HOSPITAL
2 *usually disapproving* **:** something that a person uses too much for help or support • She eventually realized that alcohol had become a *crutch*. [=that she was drinking too much alcohol as a way of dealing with her problems]
3 *Brit* **:** CROTCH

crux /ˈkrʌks/ *noun*
***the crux* :** the most important part of something (such as a problem, issue, puzzle, etc.) — usually + *of* • *The crux of* the matter is that people are afraid of change. • It's taken a while to get to *the crux of* the problem, but I think I finally understand it.

[1]cry /ˈkraɪ/ *verb* **cries; cried; cry·ing**
1 : to produce tears from your eyes often while making loud sounds because of pain, sorrow, or other strong emotions [*no obj*] The baby is *crying*. Is she okay? • a *crying* baby •

Some people *cry* more easily than others. ▪ He *cried* silently while the song played. ▪ She *cried* all the way home from school that day. ▪ He *cried* (for) the whole day. ▪ She couldn't imagine why anyone would *cry* over a stupid movie. ▪ She was *crying* with relief/frustration/anger. ▪ The first day of camp, a number of children *cried* for their parents. [=cried because they wanted their parents] [+ *obj*] They *cried* tears of joy. ✧ If you **cry yourself to sleep**, you cry until you have fallen asleep. ✧ If you **cry your eyes out** or **cry your heart out**, you cry a lot. ▪ I *cried my eyes out* when I found out they had left without saying goodbye.

2 : to shout or say something loudly [+ *obj*] "We've won!" they *cried*. ▪ "Help," he *cried*, "Get a doctor! Quick!" ▪ I heard someone *cry* "Wait!" but the train pulled away anyway. [*no obj*] She *cried* [=*called out*] to the others to come and see what she'd found. — often + *for* ▪ I heard someone *crying for* help. — sometimes used figuratively ▪ Various groups have been *crying for* [=*calling for*] his resignation.

3 [*no obj*] *of a bird or animal* : to make the loud sound that is usual for a particular type of bird or animal ▪ She'd never heard the sound of sea gulls *crying* by the shore.

a shoulder to cry on see [1]SHOULDER

cry for [*phrasal verb*] ***cry for (something)*** : to need or require (something) very much ▪ This problem is *crying for* a solution. ▪ The old house is *crying for* a new coat of paint.

cry foul *chiefly US* : to complain that someone has done something that is not fair ▪ When Mika's parents gave her a new bicycle, her sisters *cried foul*.

cry off [*phrasal verb*] *Brit* : to say that you will not do something you have promised to do ▪ He said he would help me move into my new apartment but then he *cried off* [=*begged off*] at the last minute.

cry out [*phrasal verb*] **1** : to make a loud sound because of pain, fear, surprise, etc. ▪ She *cried out* in pain. **2** ***cry out or cry out (something)*** : to speak in a loud voice : to say (something) loudly or from a distance ▪ We could hear them on the shore *crying out* [=*calling out*] to us, so we waved. ▪ She *cried out* for help. ▪ "I'm stuck," she *cried out*. ▪ She *cried out* that she was stuck. **3** ***cry out against (something)*** : to say publicly that (something) is wrong or unfair : to protest (something) ▪ People around the world are *crying out against* the government's civil rights abuses. **4** — used to say that something clearly needs or should have a particular thing, person, use, etc.; often + *to be* ▪ A chair like this *cries out to be used* [=should definitely be used], not kept in some museum. ▪ The meal *cried out to be eaten* with a nice white wine. [=it was obvious that the meal should be served with a white wine] — often + *for* ▪ The meal *cried out for* a nice white wine. ▪ The job *cries out for* someone who's not afraid to take chances.

cry over spilled milk (*US*) *or chiefly Brit* ***cry over spilt milk*** *informal* : to be upset about something that has happened and that cannot be changed ▪ You made a mistake, but there's no use *crying over spilled milk*.

cry wolf : to make people think there is danger when there is really none ▪ News organizations have been warned not to *cry wolf*. If people hear too many warnings that turn out to be nothing, they won't listen to the important warnings when they come.

for crying out loud *informal* — used to show anger, annoyance, etc. ▪ Why won't they let me in? It's my house, *for crying out loud*!

– crying *noun* [*noncount*] ▪ We heard (the sound of) *crying* in the next room. ▪ a *crying* fit/jag/spell

[2]**cry** *noun, pl* **cries**

1 [*count*] : a loud sound that someone makes to express pain, hunger, sadness, etc. ▪ *cries* of pain ▪ The baby's *cry* woke me out of a deep sleep.

2 [*count*] : something that is said loudly : a shout or call ▪ There was a *cry* of "Fire" and we all rushed for the exits. ▪ The children were playing a game and their happy *cries* echoed through the house. — sometimes used figuratively ▪ The verdict has been met with *cries* of outrage. [=people are very angry and upset about the verdict] ▪ There have been loud *cries* [=*calls*] for his resignation from various groups. — see also HUE AND CRY

3 [*count*] : a loud sound made by an animal or bird ▪ the wild *cry* of a coyote ▪ The birds' loud *cries* [=*calls*] startled me.

4 [*singular*] : an act of crying or a period of time spent crying ▪ By the end of the movie, we'd all had a good *cry*. [=we had all cried for a while]

5 [*count*] : an act or way of behaving which shows that someone wants help, attention, etc. ▪ The doctor thinks the boy's bad behavior at school is ***a cry for help***.

6 [*count*] : a word or phrase that a group of people uses to express a common idea or goal or to unite them ▪ "Free speech" is the *cry* of the protesters. — see also BATTLE CRY, RALLYING CRY, WAR CRY

a far cry from : very different from (something or someone) ▪ The movie is *a far cry from* the book. ▪ He's *a far cry from* the idealistic young writer he once was.

in full cry **1** : full of anger, excitement, etc., especially in reaction to something ▪ The school's budget is being cut, and teachers and parents are *in full cry*. [=are very angry and upset] **2** *of hunting dogs* : in the act of chasing an animal : in full pursuit

cry·ba·by /ˈkraɪˌbeɪbi/ *noun, pl* **-bies** [*count*] *informal* : a person who cries easily or complains often ▪ "Don't be such a *crybaby*," she told her little sister.

cry·ing /ˈkrajɪŋ/ *adj*

a crying need : a very obvious need : a serious and important need ▪ There's *a crying need* for reform in this city.

a crying shame : a situation that makes you feel sad or disappointed ▪ It's *a crying shame* [=it's upsetting to me] that movies are often so violent these days. ▪ It'd be *a crying shame* to miss the beginning of the show.

cryo·gen·ics /ˌkrajəˈʤɛnɪks/ *noun* [*noncount*] *technical* : a science that deals with how very low temperatures are produced and how they affect other things

cry·on·ics /ˌkrajˈɑːnɪks/ *noun* [*noncount*] *medical* : a procedure in which a person's body is frozen just after he or she has died so that the body can be restored if a cure for the cause of death is found

crypt /ˈkrɪpt/ *noun, pl* **crypts** [*count*] : a room under a church in which people are buried after they have died

cryp·tic /ˈkrɪptɪk/ *adj* [*more* ~; *most* ~] : difficult to understand : having or seeming to have a hidden meaning ▪ a *cryptic* message/title/remark ▪ His instructions were *cryptic*. He said only to wait until we felt certain the answer was clear.

– cryp·ti·cal·ly /ˈkrɪptɪkli/ *adv* ▪ She smiled *cryptically*.

cryp·to- /ˌkrɪptoʊ/ *combining form* : hidden or secret ▪ a *crypto*-anarchist [=a person who does not seem to support anarchy but secretly holds anarchist beliefs]

cryp·to·gram /ˈkrɪptəˌgræm/ *noun, pl* **-grams** [*count*] : a message that is written in code

cryp·tog·ra·phy /krɪpˈtɑːgrəfi/ *noun* [*noncount*] : the process of writing or reading secret messages or codes ▪ Companies often use *cryptography* to protect private information.

– cryp·tog·ra·pher /krɪpˈtɑːgrəfə/ *noun, pl* **-phers** [*count*] ▪ He was hired as a *cryptographer* to break the enemy's secret code.

crys·tal /ˈkrɪstl/ *noun, pl* **-tals**

1 [*count*] : a small piece of a substance that has many sides and is formed when the substance turns into a solid ▪ ice/salt *crystals* ▪ a *crystal* of quartz ▪ the *crystal* structure of minerals

2 : a clear hard mineral that is either colorless or very light in color and that is used in making jewelry [*noncount*] a necklace made of *crystal* [*count*] Some of the *crystals* used in the necklace are a pale pink color.

3 [*noncount*] **a** : a special type of glass that is very clear ▪ The wine glasses are made of the finest *crystal*. — often used before another noun ▪ a *crystal* chandelier/vase **b** : objects made of this glass ▪ She inherited her mother's *crystal*. ▪ their wedding *crystal*

4 [*count*] *US* : the clear glass or plastic cover on a watch or clock ▪ I broke the *crystal* on my watch.

crystal ball *noun, pl* ~ **balls** [*count*] : a clear glass ball in which some people say they can see the future by using magic

crystal clear *adj*

1 : perfectly clear : able to be seen through completely ▪ *crystal clear* water

2 : perfectly easy to understand ▪ "Was my request clear?" "Yes, *crystal clear*." ▪ Eventually it became *crystal clear* that something had to change.

crys·tal·line /ˈkrɪstələn, *Brit* ˈkrɪstəˌlaɪn/ *adj*

1 : clear and shining like crystal ▪ the island's *crystalline* waters — sometimes used figuratively ▪ a singer with a *crystalline* voice [=a beautifully clear voice]

2 *technical* : made of or similar to crystal or crystals ▪ a *crystalline* solid ▪ the rock's *crystalline* structure

crys·tal·lize *also Brit* **crys·tal·lise** /ˈkrɪstəˌlaɪz/ *verb* **-liz·es; -lized; -liz·ing**

1 *technical* : to change into a solid form that is made up of crystals [*no obj*] Eventually the paint will start to *crystallize*.

C

• Certain conditions can cause carbon to *crystallize* into diamonds. [+ *obj*] Certain conditions can *crystallize* carbon into diamonds.
2 : to cause (something, such as an idea, belief, etc.) to become clear and fully formed [+ *obj*] The final paragraph of the essay *crystallizes* her theory. • He tried to *crystallize* his thoughts. [*no obj*] Her theory *crystallizes* in the final paragraph of the essay. • The plan *crystallized* slowly.
– crys·tal·li·za·tion *also Brit* **crys·tal·li·sa·tion** /ˌkrɪstələˈzeɪʃən, *Brit* ˌkrɪstəˌlaɪˈzeɪʃən/ *noun* [*noncount*] • the *crystallization* of the liquid • the *crystallization* of her theory

crystallized *also Brit* **crystallised** *adj* **:** covered in sugar • *crystallized* ginger/grapes

crystal meth *noun* [*noncount*] **:** an illegal drug in the form of crystals that causes you to feel more energetic and alert when you smoke it

C–sec·tion /ˈsiːˌsɛkʃən/ *noun, pl* **-tions** [*count*] *medical* **:** CESAREAN SECTION

ct. *abbr* carat

Ct. *abbr* court

CT *abbr* Connecticut

CT scan /ˈsiːˈtiː-/ *noun, pl* **~ scans** [*count*] *medical* **:** CAT SCAN

cub /ˈkʌb/ *noun, pl* **cubs** [*count*]
1 : a young animal that eats meat • a bear/fox/lion *cub*
2 *Cub Brit* **:** CUB SCOUT
– see also CUB REPORTER

cub·by /ˈkʌbi/ *noun, pl* **-bies** [*count*] **:** CUBBYHOLE

cub·by·hole /ˈkʌbiˌhoʊl/ *noun, pl* **-holes** [*count*]
1 : a small hole or space for storing things • The car has lots of *cubbyholes* for small items. • He keeps the key in a *cubbyhole* in his desk.
2 : a place (such as a room) that is very small • He worked in a *cubbyhole* under the stairs.

[1]**cube** /ˈkjuːb/ *noun, pl* **cubes** [*count*]
1 : an object that has six square sides • an ice *cube* • Cut the onion into half-inch *cubes*. — see picture at GEOMETRY
2 *mathematics* **:** the number that results from multiplying a number by itself twice • The *cube* of 2 [$=2^3$] is 8. [$=2 \times 2 \times 2 = 8$] — compare [1]SQUARE 3
3 *US, informal + humorous* **:** CUBICLE 1 • She decorated her *cube* with pictures of her children.

[2]**cube** *verb* **cubes; cubed; cub·ing** [+ *obj*]
1 : to cut (food) into small cubes • *Cube* the carrots and potatoes. • three slices of bread, *cubed*
2 *mathematics* **:** to multiply (a number) by itself twice — usually used as *cubed* • 2 *cubed* equals 8. [$=2 \times 2 \times 2 = 8$] — compare [3]SQUARE 3

cube root *noun, pl* **~ roots** [*count*] *mathematics* **:** a number that produces a specified number when it is multiplied by itself twice • The *cube root* of 8 is 2. — compare SQUARE ROOT

cu·bic /ˈkjuːbɪk/ *adj* [*more ~; most ~*]
1 — used to describe a measurement that is produced by multiplying something's length by its width and its height • one *cubic* centimeter [=a measure of volume that is one centimeter long, one centimeter wide, and one centimeter high] • three *cubic* feet of space — compare [2]SQUARE 2
2 : in the shape of a cube • *cubic* crystals/shapes • a *cubic* structure

cu·bi·cle /ˈkjuːbɪkəl/ *noun, pl* **-bi·cles** [*count*]
1 *chiefly US* **:** a work space in a large office with a desk that is usually surrounded by low walls • an office *cubicle*
2 *Brit* **:** a small space in a public room (such as a bathroom) that has walls for privacy • a shower/toilet *cubicle* [=(*US*) *stall*]

Cub·ism /ˈkjuːˌbɪzəm/ *noun* [*noncount*] **:** a style of art that originated in the early 20th century in which objects are divided into and shown as a group of geometric shapes and from many different angles at the same time
– Cub·ist /ˈkjuːbɪst/ *adj* • a *Cubist* painting • the *Cubist* movement **– Cubist** *noun, pl* **-ists** [*count*]

cub reporter *noun, pl* **~ -ers** [*count*] **:** a young newspaper reporter who does not have much experience

Cub Scout *noun, pl* **~ Scouts** [*count*] **:** a member of an organization of Boy Scouts for boys ages 7 through 10 — compare BROWNIE

[1]**cuck·old** /ˈkʌkəld/ *noun, pl* **-olds** [*count*] *old-fashioned* **:** a man whose wife has sex with someone else **:** a man's whose wife commits adultery

[2]**cuckold** *verb* **-olds; -old·ed; -old·ing** [+ *obj*] *old-fashioned*
1 : to have sex with someone other than (your husband) • There were rumors that his wife had *cuckolded* him.
2 : to have sex with the wife of (another man) • He was *cuckolded* by his best friend.

[1]**cuck·oo** /ˈkuːku, *Brit* ˈkʊku/ *noun, pl* **-oos** [*count*] **:** a type of bird that lays its eggs in the nests of other birds and that has a call that sounds like its name

[2]**cuckoo** *adj* [*more ~; most ~*] *informal + old-fashioned*
1 : silly or crazy • They told me that he's a little *cuckoo*. [=*nutty*] • a *cuckoo* idea
2 : very enthusiastic • I'm not *cuckoo* [=(more commonly) *wild, crazy*] about the idea.

cuckoo clock *noun, pl* **~ clocks** [*count*] **:** a clock that has a toy bird inside of it that comes out and makes a sound like a cuckoo to tell what time it is

cu·cum·ber /ˈkjuːˌkʌmbɚ/ *noun, pl* **-bers** [*count, noncount*] **:** a long vegetable with dark green skin and crisp flesh that is often used in salads or for making pickles — see color picture on page C4
(as) cool as a cucumber see [1]COOL

cud /ˈkʌd/ *noun* [*noncount*] **:** the food that an animal (such as a cow) brings back up from its stomach into its mouth to be chewed again • a cow chewing its *cud*

cud·dle /ˈkʌdl̩/ *verb* **cud·dles; cud·dled; cud·dling**
1 [+ *obj*] **:** to hold (someone or something) in your arms in order to show affection • He *cuddled* the puppy.
2 [*no obj*] **:** to lie or sit close together • Let's *cuddle* by the fire. — often + *up* • They *cuddled up* under the blanket. • They *cuddled up* to each other. • He *cuddled up* with a good book. [=he sat down in a comfortable position and began reading a good book]
– cuddle *noun, pl* **cuddles** [*count*] • She gave the children a *cuddle*.

cud·dly /ˈkʌdli/ *adj* **cud·dli·er; -est** *informal*
1 : having the soft or appealing quality of a thing or person that you would like to cuddle • *cuddly* teddy bears • He is so big and *cuddly*. • a soft, *cuddly* fabric
2 : designed to be easy to like and not to offend people • their *cuddly* brand of commercialism

[1]**cud·gel** /ˈkʌʤəl/ *noun, pl* **-gels** [*count*] **:** a short heavy club
pick/take up the cudgels for *somewhat old-fashioned* **:** to fight in defense or support of (someone or something) • She *took up the cudgels for* women's rights.

[2]**cudgel** *verb* **-gels;** *US* **-geled** *or Brit* **-gelled;** *US* **-gel·ing** *or Brit* **-gel·ling** [+ *obj*] **:** to hit (someone or something) with a club — usually used figuratively • a politician who is being *cudgeled* in the press for his failure to support tax cuts
cudgel your brain/brains see [1]BRAIN

[1]**cue** /ˈkjuː/ *noun, pl* **cues** [*count*]
1 : a word, phrase, or action in a play, movie, etc., that is a signal for a performer to say or do something • That last line is your *cue* to exit the stage.
2 : a sign that tells a person to do something • I'll take that yawn as my *cue* to leave. • Their silence was a *cue* for him to speak.
3 : something that indicates the nature of what you are seeing, hearing, etc. • The expressions on people's faces give us visual *cues* about their feelings. • auditory *cues*
on cue ◊ When something happens ***(right) on cue*** or ***as if on cue***, it happens at the exact moment you would expect it to. • She arrived *right on cue* at the mention of her name. • *As if on cue*, the entire group burst into laughter.
take a/your cue from **:** to do what is done or suggested by (someone or something) • *Take a cue from* the experts and get your taxes done early this year. • We should *take our cue from* their example.
– compare [3]CUE

[2]**cue** *verb* **cues; cued; cu·ing** [+ *obj*] **:** to give (someone) a signal to do something during a performance • *Cue* the band. • *Cue* the lights/sound. [=give a signal to the person running the lights/sound]

[3]**cue** *noun, pl* **cues** [*count*] **:** a long, thin stick that is used in playing pool, billiards, and snooker • a pool *cue* — compare [1]CUE

cue ball *noun, pl* **~ balls** [*count*] **:** the white ball that a player hits with the cue in pool, billiards, and snooker

cue card *noun, pl* **~ cards** [*count*] **:** a large card that can be seen by someone (such as an actor) who is performing or speaking on a stage or on television and that shows the words that the person is supposed to say

C

[1]cuff /ˈkʌf/ *noun, pl* **cuffs**
1 [*count*] **:** the part of a sleeve, glove, etc., that covers the wrist — see color picture on page C14
2 [*count*] *US* **:** a piece of cloth at the bottom of a pant leg that is folded up — called also (*Brit*) *turn-up*; see color picture on page C15
3 [*count*] **:** something that goes around a person's arm like the cuff of a sleeve ▪ She wore a *cuff* bracelet. ▪ The nurse put a blood-pressure *cuff* [=a cuff that measures blood pressure] on his arm. — see also ROTATOR CUFF
4 ***cuffs*** [*plural*] **:** HANDCUFFS ▪ The police led him away in *cuffs*.
off the cuff **:** without being prepared in advance **:** without planning or preparation ▪ He talked/spoke *off the cuff* about his work on the project. ▪ I had to give the speech *off the cuff*. — see also OFF-THE-CUFF
– cuffed *adj* ▪ a blouse with *cuffed* sleeves ▪ *cuffed* pants

[2]cuff *verb* **cuffs; cuffed; cuff·ing** [+ *obj*] **:** to put (someone) in handcuffs ▪ He was *cuffed* and led away. — compare [3]CUFF

[3]cuff *verb* **cuffs; cuffed; cuffing** [+ *obj*] **:** to hit (someone or something) with the palm of your hand ▪ She *cuffed* the boy on the head/ear. — compare [2]CUFF
– cuff *noun, pl* **cuffs** [*count*] ▪ She gave him a *cuff* on the head/ear.

cuff link *noun, pl* **~ links** [*count*] **:** a piece of jewelry that is used to fasten the cuff of a sleeve on a man's shirt — see color picture on page C11

cui·sine /kwɪˈziːn/ *noun, pl* **-sines**
1 : a style of cooking [*noncount*] I like gourmet/vegetarian/ethnic *cuisine*. ▪ a cooking method used in French *cuisine* [*count*] regional *cuisines* ▪ a *cuisine* based on local ingredients — see also HAUTE CUISINE, NOUVELLE CUISINE
2 [*noncount*] **:** food that is cooked in a particular way ▪ This restaurant is famous for its spicy *cuisine*.

cul–de–sac /ˈkʌldɪˌsæk/ *noun, pl* **cul–de–sacs** /ˈkʌldɪˌsæks/ *also* **culs–de–sac** /ˈkʌlzdɪˌsæk/ [*count*] **:** a street that is designed to connect to another street only at one end ▪ Our house is located on a quiet *cul-de-sac*.

cul·i·nary /ˈkʌləˌneri, *Brit* ˈkʌlənri/ *adj, always used before a noun* **:** used in or relating to cooking ▪ *culinary* herbs ▪ the *culinary* arts ▪ They serve a variety of *culinary* delights.

cull /ˈkʌl/ *verb* **culls; culled; cull·ing** [+ *obj*]
1 : to select or choose (someone or something) from a group ▪ Damaged fruits are *culled* (out) before the produce is shipped. — usually + *from* ▪ They've *culled* some of the best poems *from* her collected works. ▪ She *culled* the information *from* newspaper articles.
2 : to control the size of (a group of animals) by killing some animals ▪ He *culls* his herd annually. ▪ The town issued hunting licenses in order to *cull* the deer population.
– cull *noun, pl* **culls** [*count*] ▪ the annual *cull* of the herd

cul·mi·nate /ˈkʌlməˌneɪt/ *verb* **-nates; -nat·ed; -nat·ing**
1 [*no obj*] **:** to reach the end or the final result of something — usually + *in* or *with* ▪ She had a long acting career that *culminated in* two Oscar nominations. ▪ The investigation *culminated with* several arrests. ▪ Their efforts have *culminated in* the discovery of a new cancer treatment.
2 [+ *obj*] *somewhat formal* **:** to be the end or final result of (something) ▪ A bitter feud *culminated* months of tension.

cul·mi·na·tion /ˌkʌlməˈneɪʃən/ *noun* [*noncount*] **:** the end or final result of something ▪ This study is the *culmination* of years of research.

cu·lottes /kjuˈlɑːts/ *noun* [*plural*] **:** short pants for women or girls that are shaped like a skirt ▪ a pair of *culottes*

cul·pa·ble /ˈkʌlpəbəl/ *adj* [*more ~; most ~*] *formal* **:** deserving blame **:** guilty of doing something wrong ▪ They held her *culpable* for the accident. ▪ He's more *culpable* than the others because he's old enough to know better. ▪ (*law*) The defendant is charged with ***culpable negligence***. [=negligence that is regarded as a crime]
– cul·pa·bil·i·ty /ˌkʌlpəˈbɪləti/ *noun* [*noncount*] ▪ She refused to acknowledge her own *culpability*. **– cul·pa·bly** /ˈkʌlpəbli/ *adv* ▪ The defendant was *culpably* negligent.

cul·prit /ˈkʌlprət/ *noun, pl* **-prits** [*count*] **:** a person who has committed a crime or done something wrong ▪ The police eventually located the *culprits*. — often used figuratively ▪ Lack of exercise and poor diet are the chief/main/real *culprits* in heart disease.

[1]cult /ˈkʌlt/ *noun, pl* **cults** [*count*]
1 : a small religious group that is not part of a larger and more accepted religion and that has beliefs regarded by many people as extreme or dangerous ▪ a satanic *cult* ▪ *cult* members
2 : a situation in which people admire and care about something or someone very much or too much ▪ He criticizes the way journalists promote the ***cult of celebrity*** in modern America. [=the tendency of people to care too much about famous people] ▪ a ***cult of personality*** = a ***personality cult***
3 : a small group of very devoted supporters or fans ▪ a *cult* of admirers ▪ She has developed a *cult* following.
4 *formal* **:** a system of religious beliefs and rituals ▪ an ancient fertility *cult*

[2]cult *adj, always used before a noun* **:** very popular among a group of people ▪ a *cult* film/novel ▪ Her works have achieved *cult* status. ▪ The movie is a *cult* hit/classic/favorite.

cul·ti·vate /ˈkʌltəˌveɪt/ *verb* **-vates; -vat·ed; -vat·ing** [+ *obj*]
1 : to prepare and use (soil) for growing plants ▪ Prehistoric peoples settled the area and began to *cultivate* the land. ▪ Some of the fields are *cultivated* while others lie fallow.
2 a : to grow and care for (plants) ▪ a plant that is *cultivated* for its fruit ▪ They survived by *cultivating* vegetables and grain. **b :** to grow or raise (something) under conditions that you can control ▪ pearls from *cultivated* oysters
3 : to improve or develop (something) by careful attention, training, or study ▪ He has carefully *cultivated* his image/reputation. ▪ She *cultivated* a taste for fine wines.
4 : to try to become friendly with (someone) usually to get some advantage for yourself ▪ They're always looking for influential people to *cultivate* as friends.
– cul·ti·va·tion /ˌkʌltəˈveɪʃən/ *noun* [*noncount*] ▪ the *cultivation* of crops

cultivated *adj*
1 a : raised or grown on a farm or under other controlled conditions ▪ *cultivated* fruits/vegetables — compare WILD **b :** prepared and used for growing crops ▪ *cultivated* fields
2 [*more ~; most ~*] **:** having or showing good education, taste, and manners ▪ a very *cultivated* gentleman ▪ a person of *cultivated* [=*refined*] taste

cul·ti·va·tor /ˈkʌltəˌveɪtɚ/ *noun, pl* **-tors** [*count*]
1 : a person who prepares land for planting
2 : a tool or machine that is used to prepare the soil and kill weeds around growing plants

cul·tur·al /ˈkʌltʃərəl/ *adj* [*more ~; most ~*]
1 : of or relating to a particular group of people and their habits, beliefs, traditions, etc. ▪ *cultural* studies ▪ We studied our *cultural* heritage. ▪ There are some *cultural* differences between us.
2 : of or relating to the fine arts (such as music, theater, painting, etc.) ▪ We attended several *cultural* events over the weekend. ▪ The center provides a wide range of *cultural* activities. ▪ The city is the *cultural* center of the state.
– cul·tur·al·ly *adv* ▪ a *culturally* diverse population ▪ *culturally* defined social roles

[1]cul·ture /ˈkʌltʃɚ/ *noun, pl* **-tures**
1 a [*noncount*] **:** the beliefs, customs, arts, etc., of a particular society, group, place, or time ▪ a study of Greek language and *culture* ▪ today's youth *culture* ▪ Her art shows the influence of pop/popular *culture*. **b** [*count*] **:** a particular society that has its own beliefs, ways of life, art, etc. ▪ an ancient *culture* ▪ It's important to learn about other *cultures*.
2 [*count*] **:** a way of thinking, behaving, or working that exists in a place or organization (such as a business) ▪ The company's corporate/business *culture* is focused on increasing profits. ▪ There was a ***culture of success*** at the school. [=the school's policies and environment encouraged its students' success]
3 [*noncount*] **a :** artistic activities (such as music, theater, painting, etc.) ▪ an area that has been criticized for its lack of *culture* **b :** appreciation and knowledge of music, theater, painting, etc. ▪ She is a person of *culture*. [=a cultured person]
4 *technical* **a** [*noncount*] **:** the act or process or growing living material (such as cells or bacteria) in controlled conditions for scientific study ▪ Scientists have been refining techniques for the *culture* of living tissue. **b** [*count*] **:** a group of cells, bacteria, etc., grown in controlled conditions for scientific study ▪ bacterial/tissue *cultures*
5 [*noncount*] *technical* **:** the act or process of raising or growing plants, insects, etc., in controlled conditions ▪ bee *culture* ▪ the *culture* of grapes

[2]culture *verb* **-tures; -tured; -tur·ing** [+ *obj*] *technical* **:** to grow (something) in controlled conditions ▪ The virus is *cultured* in the laboratory from samples of infected tissue.

C

cultured *adj*
1 [*more* ~; *most* ~] **:** having or showing good education, tastes, and manners • a *cultured* person
2 **:** grown or made under controlled conditions • *cultured* cells/pearls

culture shock *noun* **:** a feeling of confusion, doubt, or nervousness caused by being in a place (such as a foreign country) that is very different from what you are used to [*noncount*] Foreign students often experience *culture shock* when they first come to the U.S. [*singular*] Moving to the city was a huge *culture shock* for him.

cul·vert /ˈkʌlvɚt/ *noun, pl* **-verts** [*count*] **:** a drain or pipe that allows water to flow under a road or railroad

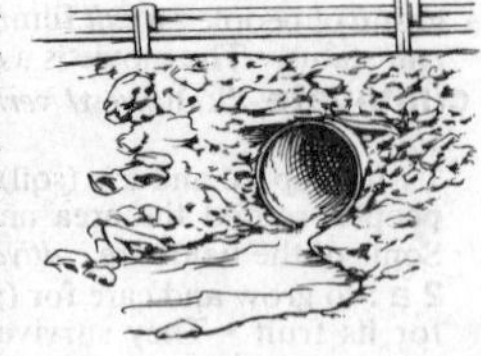
culvert

cum /ˈkʊm/ *conj* — used in hyphenated phrases to link nouns that describe a person or thing with two jobs, uses, etc. • He was hired as a cook-*cum*-dishwasher. • a patio-*cum*-sunroom

cum·ber·some /ˈkʌmbɚsəm/ *adj* [*more* ~; *most* ~]
1 **:** hard to handle or manage because of size or weight • a *cumbersome* package
2 **:** complicated and hard to do • The application process is *cumbersome* and time-consuming.
3 **:** long and difficult to read, say, etc. • a *cumbersome* name • Her expanded job title is really *cumbersome*.

cum·in /ˈkʌmən, ˈkju:mən/ *noun* [*noncount*] **:** dried seeds that are used as a spice in cooking and that come from a plant related to the carrot

cum lau·de /kʊmˈlaudə/ *adv, formal* **:** with honor — used in the U.S. to indicate that a student has graduated from a college or university at the third highest of three special levels of achievement • She graduated *cum laude*. — compare MAGNA CUM LAUDE, SUMMA CUM LAUDE

cum·mer·bund /ˈkʌmɚˌbʌnd/ *noun, pl* **-bunds** [*count*] **:** a wide piece of cloth (such as silk) that is worn around the waist beneath the jacket of a man who is formally dressed — see color picture on page C16

cu·mu·la·tive /ˈkju:mjələtɪv/ *adj* [*more* ~; *most* ~]
1 **:** increasing or becoming better or worse over time through a series of additions • the ***cumulative effect(s)*** of smoking on the body [=the effect(s) produced by smoking over a long period of time]
2 **:** including or adding together all of the things that came before • Their *cumulative* [=*total, overall*] scores will determine the winner.
– cu·mu·la·tive·ly *adv* • They have *cumulatively* spent more than a million dollars on the renovations.

cu·mu·lus /ˈkju:mjələs/ *noun, pl* **cu·mu·li** /ˈkju:mjəˌlaɪ/ [*count*] *technical* **:** a type of thick cloud that is rounded on top and has a flat base

cu·ne·i·form /kjuˈni:jəˌfoɚm, *Brit* ˈkju:nɪˌfɔ:m/ *adj* **:** relating to or written in a system of writing used in parts of the ancient Middle East • *cuneiform* characters/writing • an ancient *cuneiform* text
– cuneiform *noun* [*noncount*]

cun·ni·lin·gus /ˌkʌnɪˈlɪŋgəs/ *noun* [*noncount*] **:** the act of stimulating a woman's sexual organs with the mouth for sexual pleasure

[1]**cun·ning** /ˈkʌnɪŋ/ *adj* [*more* ~; *most* ~] **:** getting what is wanted in a clever and often deceptive way • a *cunning* criminal • She was *cunning* enough to fool me. • a *cunning* plan
– cun·ning·ly *adv* • They *cunningly* dodged our questions.

[2]**cunning** *noun* [*noncount*] **:** cleverness or skill especially at tricking people in order to get something • He may be a fraud, but you have to admire his *cunning*. • (*chiefly Brit*) He succeeded through a combination of charm and ***low cunning*** [=clever but morally bad and dishonest methods]

cunt /ˈkʌnt/ *noun, pl* **cunts** [*count*] *offensive + obscene*
1 **:** a woman's sexual organs
2 a *US* — used as an offensive way to refer to a woman **b** *Brit* — used as an offensive way to refer to a stupid or annoying person ✧ *Cunt* is an extremely offensive word in all of its uses and should be avoided.

[1]**cup** /ˈkʌp/ *noun, pl* **cups** [*count*]
1 a **:** a small round container that often has a handle and that is used for drinking liquids (such as tea and coffee) • a coffee *cup* • a paper/plastic *cup* — see picture at PLACE SETTING; see also TEACUP **b :** the liquid that is contained in a cup • How many *cups* (of water/coffee/tea) did you drink? • Would you like another *cup* of tea?
2 *US* **:** a unit of measurement that is used when you are cooking ✧ A cup is used to measure both dry and liquid ingredients. It is equal to half a pint or 237 milliliters. • two *cups* of flour • four *cups* of milk — see also MEASURING CUP
3 **:** a large gold or silver cup that is given as a prize for winning a competition or game • The winner will take home the *cup*. — used in the names of some sports competitions in which a cup is the prize • His goal is to win the America's *Cup*. • Our team won the Stanley *Cup*.
4 **:** something that is shaped like a cup • a custard *cup* — see also EGGCUP, SUCTION CUP
5 *chiefly US* **:** a food that is served in a cup or small bowl • a ***fruit cup*** [=a mixture of chopped fruits that is served usually as a dessert]
6 *US* **:** a hard piece of plastic that men and boys wear to protect and support their sexual organs while playing a sport • a protective *cup* — called also (*Brit*) *box*
7 **:** either one of the parts of a bra that cover the breasts — used especially to describe the size of a bra • a bra with C *cups* • She wears a B *cup*.
8 *US, golf* **:** the metal or plastic case that is placed in the hole on a putting green; *also* **:** the hole itself • The shot landed within inches of the *cup*.
in the cup of your hand ✧ If you hold something *in the cup of your hand*, you hold it in your palm with your hand curved like a cup. • He held the seeds *in the cup of his hand*. [=he cupped the seeds in his hand]
not your cup of tea ✧ If something is *not your cup of tea*, you do not like it very much or you are not very good at it. • I'm afraid that skiing just *isn't my cup of tea*. • She admits that stamp collecting *isn't everyone's cup of tea*.

[2]**cup** *verb* **cups; cupped; cup·ping** [+ *obj*]
1 **:** to curve (your hand) into the shape of a cup • He *cupped* his hands around his mouth and shouted at us. • I had to *cup* my hand to my ear in order to hear him.
2 **:** to put your hand in a curved shape around (something) • He *cupped* his mouth with his hands and shouted at us. • I sat with my chin *cupped* in my hand.

cup·board /ˈkʌbɚd/ *noun, pl* **-boards** [*count*]
1 **:** a piece of furniture used for storage that has doors and contains shelves • a jelly *cupboard* • kitchen *cupboards* [=*cabinets*] — see picture at KITCHEN
2 *US* **:** a small room with shelves where you keep cups, dishes, or food
3 *Brit* **:** a small room where things are stored **:** CLOSET
skeleton in the/your cupboard see [1]SKELETON

cup·cake /ˈkʌpˌkeɪk/ *noun, pl* **-cakes** [*count*] **:** a very small cake that is baked in a pan shaped like a cup — see picture at BAKING

cup·ful /ˈkʌpˌfʊl/ *noun, pl* **cup·fuls** /ˈkʌpˌfʊlz/ *also* **cups·ful** /ˈkʌpsˌfʊl/ [*count*] **:** the amount held by a cup • a *cupful* of sugar

cu·pid /ˈkju:pəd/ *noun, pl* **-pids**
1 ***Cupid*** [*singular*] **:** the god of sexual love in ancient Rome
2 [*count*] **:** a picture or statue of Cupid usually shown as a naked boy with wings who is holding a bow and arrow • a valentine decorated with hearts and *cupids*
play Cupid **:** to try to get two people to become romantically involved with each other • The movie is about a woman who *plays Cupid* with her brother and her best friend.

cu·pid·i·ty /kjuˈpɪdəti/ *noun* [*noncount*] *formal* **:** a strong desire for money or possessions **:** GREED • The evidence revealed the *cupidity* of the company's directors.

cu·po·la /ˈkju:pələ/ *noun, pl* **-las** [*count*]
1 **:** a rounded roof or part of a roof **:** DOME
2 *US* **:** a small structure that is built on top of a roof

cupola

cup·pa /ˈkʌpə/ *noun, pl* **-pas** [*count*] *Brit, informal* **:** a cup of tea • I could use a good *cuppa*.

cur /ˈkɚ/ *noun, pl* **curs** [*count*] *old-fashioned* **:** a dog that is a mix of different breeds **:** a low, bad, or disliked dog • a worthless *cur* [=*mutt, mongrel*]

cur·able /ˈkjurəbəl/ *adj* [*more* ~; *most* ~] : possible to cure • Most cases are *curable* with proper treatment. • a *curable* disease • Is the patient *curable*? — opposite INCURABLE

cu·rate /ˈkjurət/ *noun, pl* **-rates** [*count*] : a member of the clergy in certain churches (such as the Anglican church) who assists the priest in charge of a church or a group of churches

curate's egg *Brit* : something that has both good and bad parts or qualities • The concert was a bit of a *curate's egg*: good in some parts, bad in others.

cu·ra·tive /ˈkjurətɪv/ *adj* [*more* ~; *most* ~] : able to cure diseases or heal people • an herb believed to have *curative* powers/properties

cu·ra·tor /ˈkjurˌeɪtɚ, *Brit* kjʊˈreɪtə/ *noun, pl* **-tors** [*count*] : a person who is in charge of the things in a museum, zoo, etc.

[1]**curb** /ˈkɚb/ *noun, pl* **curbs** [*count*]

1 *US* ***curb*** *or Brit* ***kerb*** : a short border along the edge of a street that is usually made of stone or concrete • We sat on the *curb* eating our ice cream. — see picture at STREET

2 : something that controls or limits something else — usually plural • Many companies are protesting the new price/trade *curbs*. [=(more commonly) *checks, restrictions*] — often + *on* • government policies that are designed to put a *curb on* spending [=to limit/reduce spending]

[2]**curb** *verb* **curbs; curbed; curb·ing** [+ *obj*] : to control or limit (something) • The legislation is intended to *curb* price and wage increases. • pills designed to *curb* your appetite

curb·side (*US*) *or Brit* **kerb·side** /ˈkɚbˌsaɪd/ *noun, pl* **-sides** [*count*] : SIDEWALK — often used before another noun • a *curbside* vendor • *curbside* recycling programs

curd /ˈkɚd/ *noun, pl* **curds** : a thick substance that forms when milk becomes sour and that is used to make cheese [*plural*] The *curds* have separated from the whey. [*noncount*] The *curd* has separated from the whey. — see also BEAN CURD, LEMON CURD

cur·dle /ˈkɚdl/ *verb* **cur·dles; cur·dled; cur·dling** : to thicken and separate into liquids and solids : to form curds [*no obj*] The milk has *curdled*. [=the milk is sour] • Too much heat will make the custard *curdle*. [+ *obj*] Too much heat will *curdle* the custard.

make someone's blood curdle see BLOOD

[1]**cure** /ˈkjɚ/ *noun, pl* **cures** [*count*]

1 : something (such as a drug or medical treatment) that stops a disease and makes someone healthy again • The disease has no *cure*. [=the disease cannot be cured; the disease is incurable] — often + *for* • There is no *cure for* the common cold. • The drug was sold as a *cure for* a variety of ailments.

2 : something that ends a problem or improves a bad situation : SOLUTION • This is a problem that has no easy *cure*.— often + *for* • The highway construction program was presented as a *cure for* unemployment. • Exercise is a good *cure for* stress.

3 : the act of making someone healthy again after an illness • The doctors were unable to effect a *cure* because the disease had spread too far.

[2]**cure** *verb* **cures; cured; cur·ing**

1 [+ *obj*] **a** : to make (someone) healthy again after an illness • Her doctors have pronounced her *cured*. [=have said that she is no longer ill] — often + *of* • A team of doctors *cured* him *of* a rare blood disease. **b** : to stop (a disease) by using drugs or other medical treatments • Doctors *cured* his disease. • The infection can be *cured* with antibiotics.

2 [+ *obj*] : to provide a solution for (something) • Drinking won't *cure* [=*solve*] any of your problems.

3 [+ *obj*] : to cause (someone) to stop having a harmful habit, wrong idea, etc. : to make (someone) free *of* something • She was *cured of* any illusions she had about college after her first semester. • My wife *cured* me *of* most of my bad habits.

4 : to change something through a chemical or physical process so that it can be preserved for a long time [+ *obj*] *cure* bacon/meat • The fish was *cured* with salt. • olives *cured* in brine [*no obj*] The hay is *curing* in the sun.

5 [*no obj*] : to dry and become hard • It takes several days for concrete to *cure*. [=*harden, set*]

cure–all /ˈkjɚˌɑːl/ *noun, pl* **-alls** [*count*] : a cure or solution for any illness or problem • The drug is effective, but it is not a *cure-all*. — often + *for* • There is no *cure-all for* these problems.

cur·few /ˈkɚfju/ *noun, pl* **-fews**

1 a : an order or law that requires people to be indoors after a certain time at night [*count*] The teens were stopped by police for violating the *curfew*. • The city ordered/imposed a *curfew* soon after the rioting started. [*noncount*] The town was placed under *curfew*. **b** [*noncount*] : the period of time when such an order or law is in effect • No one is allowed on the streets during the *curfew*.

2 [*count*] *chiefly US* : the time set by a parent at which a child has to be back home after going out • He has a 10 o'clock *curfew*.

cu·rio /ˈkjɚriˌoʊ/ *noun, pl* **-ri·os** [*count*] : a small and unusual object that is considered interesting or attractive • She loves to browse the shops in small towns, looking for *curios*.

cu·ri·os·i·ty /ˌkjɚriˈɑːsəti/ *noun, pl* **-ties**

1 [*noncount*] : the desire to learn or know more about something or someone • Her natural *curiosity* led her to ask more questions. • The arrival of a construction crew at their house attracted/sparked/aroused the *curiosity* of their neighbors. • The movie failed to satisfy her *curiosity* about the assassination. • intellectual *curiosity* • He went into the store out of *curiosity*. [=because he was curious to see what was in the store]

◊ The expression ***curiosity killed the cat*** is used to warn people that too much curiosity can be dangerous.

2 [*count*] : something that is interesting because it is unusual • Tobacco was once a *curiosity* in Europe. • The antique shop was full of *curiosities*.

cu·ri·ous /ˈkjɚrijəs/ *adj* [*more* ~; *most* ~]

1 : having a desire to learn or know more about something or someone • The cat was naturally *curious* about its new surroundings. • They were *curious* to find out who won the game. • We're *curious* about why you never called us. • The *curious* [=*inquisitive*] reader can find more information in the back of the book. • I'm *curious* to know more about her.

2 : strange, unusual, or unexpected • She found a *curious* old clock in the attic. • That's *curious* [=*weird, strange, odd*]—I thought I left my keys right here. • The birds were engaged in some *curious* behavior. • Their music is a *curious* blend of disco and rock. • By a *curious* coincidence, they bought a house the same day their old one burned down. • The story of what really happened to them that day gets ***curiouser and curiouser***. [=stranger and stranger]

— **cu·ri·ous·ly** *adv* • She was *curiously* uninterested in what other people thought was important. • *Curiously* [=*strangely*] (enough), the dog returned to its home 70 miles away. • He looked at the strange object *curiously*.

[1]**curl** /ˈkɚl/ *verb* **curls; curled; curl·ing**

1 : to twist or form (something) into a round or curved shape [+ *obj*] The boy *curled* [=*wound*] the spaghetti around his fork. • She *curls* her hair every morning. • She took off her shoes and *curled* (up) her toes. • Can you *curl* your tongue? • The baby's fingers were tightly *curled*. • She *curled* (up) her legs under her. • The snake *curled* itself around its prey. [*no obj*] My hair *curls* naturally. • The cat *curled* into a ball and went to sleep.

2 [*no obj*] : to become curved or rounded • The old posters were *curling* (up) at the edges.

3 *always followed by a preposition or adverb* [*no obj*] : to move in curves or circles • We saw smoke *curling from* the cottage chimney. • A snake *curled around* his leg.

curl up [*phrasal verb*] : to lie or sit with your back bent forward and with your legs pulled up close to your body • She *curled up* on the couch for a nap. • It's a good night to stay home and *curl up* with a book and a cup of tea. — see also CURL 1, 2 (above)

curl your lip : to move the corner of your lip up in an expression that usually shows disgust or disapproval • She *curled her lip* when his name was mentioned. • Her *lip curled* in disgust.

make your hair curl see HAIR

make your toes curl see [1]TOE

[2]**curl** *noun, pl* **curls**

1 a [*count*] : a piece of hair that is formed into a round shape • Her daughter has cute blonde *curls*. • She likes to wear her hair in *curls*. **b** [*singular*] : the ability of hair to form curls • The conditioner will help you keep the *curl* of your hair. • His hair has a natural *curl*.

2 [*count*] : something that is curved or has a round shape • chocolate *curls* • a *curl* of smoke

3 [*count*] : an exercise in which a weight held in the hands is brought toward the shoulders and down again by bending either the wrists or the elbows • He did 12 wrist/bicep *curls*.

curl·er /ˈkɚlɚ/ *noun, pl* **-ers** [*count*]

1 : a small plastic or metal tube around which hair is wrapped to make it curl • Her hair was in *curlers*. [=*rollers*]

C

2 : a device that curls something ▪ an eyelash *curler*

cur·lew /ˈkəlu, *Brit* ˈkəlju/ *noun, pl* **cur·lews** *or* **cur·lew** [*count*] : a large brown bird with long legs and a long thin bill that lives near the water

cur·li·cue /ˈkəliˌkju:/ *noun, pl* **-cues** [*count*] : a decoratively curved line or shape ▪ round loops and *curlicues* ▪ *Curlicues* were carved into the wood.

curl·ing /ˈkəlɪŋ/ *noun* [*noncount*] : a game in which two teams of four players slide special stones over ice toward a circle

curling iron *noun, pl* ~ **irons** [*count*] *US* : a device with a long metal part that is heated to curl hair — called also (*Brit*) *curling tongs*

curly /ˈkəli/ *adj* **curl·i·er; -est** [*also more* ~; *most* ~]
1 : having curls ▪ She has *curly* hair and blue eyes.
2 : formed into a round shape ▪ *curly* french fries ▪ The dog's tail is *curly*.

curly brace *noun, pl* ~ **braces** [*count*] : [2]BRACE 3

curly bracket *noun, pl* ~ **-ets** [*count*] : [2]BRACE 3

cur·mud·geon /kəˈmʌʤən/ *noun, pl* **-geons** [*count*] *old-fashioned* : a person (especially an old man) who is easily annoyed or angered and who often complains ▪ a lonely old *curmudgeon*
— **cur·mud·geon·ly** *adj* [*more* ~; *most* ~] ▪ a *curmudgeonly* [=*bad-tempered*] old man

cur·rant /ˈkərənt/ *noun, pl* **-rants** [*count*]
1 : a small seedless raisin that is used in baking and cooking
2 : a small red, black, or white berry that is often used in making jams and jellies ▪ black/red *currants*

Do not confuse *currant* with *current*.

cur·ren·cy /ˈkərənsi/ *noun, pl* **-cies**
1 a : the money that a country uses : a specific kind of money [*count*] A new *currency* has been introduced in the foreign exchange market. ▪ foreign *currencies* [*noncount*] paper *currency* ▪ They were paid in U.S. *currency*. — see also HARD CURRENCY **b** [*noncount*] : something that is used as money ▪ Furs were once traded as *currency*.
2 [*noncount*] : the quality or state of being used or accepted by many people ▪ His ideas are gaining *currency* [=are becoming widely accepted] in the government. ▪ The word has not yet won/achieved widespread *currency*.
3 [*noncount*] : the quality or state of being current ▪ I'm not sure about the accuracy and *currency* of their information.

[1]**cur·rent** /ˈkərənt/ *adj* [*more* ~; *most* ~]
1 *always used before a noun* : happening or existing now : belonging to or existing in the present time ▪ the *current* month ▪ the magazine's *current* issue ▪ The dictionary's *current* edition has 10,000 new words. ▪ the *current* political crisis ▪ By *current* [=*present-day*] standards, they were very young when they got married. ▪ Who is your *current* employer? ▪ *current* trends/fashions ▪ *current* ideas about education
2 *not used before a noun, chiefly US* : aware of what is happening in a particular area of activity ▪ As a teacher I have to stay *current* [=*up-to-date*] in my field, which is biology. ▪ We need to keep *current* with the latest information.
— **cur·rent·ly** *adv* ▪ She is *currently* [=*presently*] living in Texas. ▪ The product is not *currently* available. ▪ *Currently* [=at the present time], police have no suspects in the case.

[2]**current** *noun, pl* **-rents**
1 [*count*] : a continuous movement of water or air in the same direction ▪ Strong *currents* pulled the swimmer out to sea. ▪ Air *currents* carried the balloon for miles.
2 : a flow of electricity [*count*] a strong/weak electrical *current* [*noncount*] The circuit supplies *current* to the saw. — see also ALTERNATING CURRENT, DIRECT CURRENT
3 [*count*] *formal* : an idea, feeling, opinion, etc., that is shared by many or most of the people in a group ▪ general *currents* in politics ▪ intellectual *currents* — often + *of* ▪ He is going against the *current of* public opinion. ▪ There was a *current of* discontent within the company.

Do not confuse *current* with *currant*.

current account *noun, pl* ~ **-counts** [*count*] *Brit* : CHECKING ACCOUNT

current events *noun* [*plural*] *chiefly US* : important events that are happening in the world ▪ She reads several newspapers so she can keep track of *current events*. ▪ Contestants are quizzed on *current events*. — called also *current affairs*

cur·ric·u·lum /kəˈrɪkjələm/ *noun, pl* **-la** /-lə/ *also* **-lums** [*count*] *formal* : the courses that are taught by a school, college, etc. ▪ the undergraduate/mathematics *curriculum* ▪ The college has a liberal arts *curriculum*.
— **cur·ric·u·lar** /kəˈrɪkjələ/ *adj, always used before a noun* ▪ *curricular* changes in the science program ▪ *curricular* materials — see also EXTRACURRICULAR

cur·ric·u·lum vi·tae /kəˈrɪkjələmˈvi:ˌtaɪ/ *noun, pl* ~ **vitae** [*count*] *chiefly Brit* : a short document that describes your education, work experience, etc. : RÉSUMÉ — called also *CV*, (*US*) *vita* ✧ In U.S. English, a person who is applying for a job as a scientist, doctor, or professor at a college or university is asked to submit a *curriculum vitae*. For other jobs, the usual word in U.S. English is *résumé*.

curried *adj, always used before a noun* : cooked with curry powder ▪ *curried* chicken

[1]**cur·ry** /ˈkəri/ *noun, pl* **-ries**
1 : a food, dish, or sauce in Indian cooking that is seasoned with a mixture of spices [*noncount*] We had chicken *curry* for dinner. [*count*] a delicious lamb *curry* — often used before another noun ▪ *curry* sauce/paste
2 [*noncount*] : CURRY POWDER ▪ The recipe calls for a tablespoon of *curry*.

[2]**curry** *verb* **-ries; -ried; -ry·ing**
curry favor *disapproving* : to try to get the support or approval of a person or group in order to get some advantage for yourself — often + *with* ▪ He is trying to *curry favor with* the voters by promising a tax cut if he's elected.

curry powder *noun* [*noncount*] : a mixture of spices that are used in Indian cooking to give a hot flavor to food

[1]**curse** /ˈkəs/ *noun, pl* **curs·es**
1 [*count*] : an offensive word that people say when they are angry : SWEARWORD ▪ I heard him utter a *curse* before the microphone was shut off.
2 [*count*] : magical words that are said to cause trouble or bad luck for someone or the condition that results when such words are said ▪ The witch pronounced a *curse* in some strange language. ▪ People believe that someone put a *curse* on the house. ▪ There is a *curse* on that old house. = That old house is under a *curse*.
3 [*count*] : a cause of trouble or bad luck ▪ His fame turned out to be a *curse*, not a blessing.
4 ***the curse*** *old-fashioned + informal* : MENSTRUATION

[2]**curse** *verb* **curses; cursed; curs·ing**
1 a [*no obj*] : to use offensive words when you speak ▪ He always starts *cursing* [=*swearing*] when he gets drunk. **b** [+ *obj*] : to say offensive words to (someone) ▪ She angrily *cursed* him [=swore at him] as he turned and walked away. **c** [+ *obj*] : to say or think bad things about (someone or something) ▪ He *cursed* himself for being so careless. ▪ She *cursed* her bad luck.
2 [+ *obj*] : to say words that are believed to have a magical power to cause trouble or bad luck for (someone or something) : to put a curse on (someone or something) ▪ In the book the evil witch *curses* the villagers.
curse out [*phrasal verb*] ***curse (someone) out*** *US, informal* : to say angry and offensive words to (someone) ▪ My boss *cursed* me *out*.

cursed /ˈkəsəd *before nouns*, ˈkəst *elsewhere*/ *adj*
1 : affected by a curse that causes bad things to happen ▪ Some people think the old house is *cursed*.
2 : affected by something bad ▪ The team has been *cursed* [=*plagued*] by injuries all year. ▪ a people *cursed* with famine
3 *always used before a noun, informal + old-fashioned* : annoying or unpleasant ▪ His *cursed* stupidity got him in trouble again. ▪ I can't get this *cursed* radio to work.

cur·sive /ˈkəsɪv/ *noun* [*noncount*] : a type of handwriting in which all the letters in a word are connected to each other ▪ He writes in *cursive* when he takes notes.
— **cursive** *adj* ▪ *cursive* handwriting

cur·sor /ˈkəsə/ *noun, pl* **-sors** [*count*] : a mark on a computer screen that shows the place where information is being entered or read — see picture at COMPUTER

cur·so·ry /ˈkəsəri/ *adj* [*more* ~; *most* ~] *formal + often disapproving* : done or made quickly ▪ Only a *cursory* inspection of the building's electrical wiring was done. ▪ The mayor gave a *cursory* glance at the report. ▪ Even the most *cursory* look at the organization's records shows problems.
— **cur·so·ri·ly** /ˈkəsərəli/ *adv* ▪ The battle is only mentioned *cursorily* in the book.

curt /ˈkət/ *adj* **curter; -est** [*also more* ~; *most* ~] : said or done in a quick and impolite way ▪ He gave only a *curt* reply to the question. ▪ a *curt* refusal ▪ a *curt* nod
— **curt·ly** *adv* ▪ He *curtly* dismissed the question. — **curt·ness** *noun* [*noncount*] ▪ I was offended by his *curtness*.

cur·tail /kɚˈteɪl/ *verb* **-tails; -tailed; -tail·ing** [+ *obj*] *formal* : to reduce or limit (something) • The new laws are an effort to *curtail* illegal drug use. • We have to severely/drastically *curtail* [=*cut back*] our expenses. • School activities are being *curtailed* due to a lack of funds.

– cur·tail·ment /kɚˈteɪlmənt/ *noun, pl* **-ments** [*count, noncount*]

¹cur·tain /ˈkɚtn̩/ *noun, pl* **-tains**

1 [*count*] : a piece of cloth that hangs down from above a window and can be used to cover the window • She opened/closed the curtains. • She drew/pulled the *curtains* (open/closed). — see picture at WINDOW

2 [*count*] : a piece of cloth or other material that is hung to protect or hide something • a shower *curtain* • *Curtains* separated the hospital beds. — see also IRON CURTAIN

3 a [*count*] : a very large piece of cloth that hangs at the front of a stage and that is raised when a performance begins and lowered when a performance ends • When the *curtain* rises after intermission, the set is bare and the main character finds himself alone. • As the *curtain* falls for the last time, we see a young woman holding a dying man in her arms. — often used figuratively • The ***curtain came down*** on his film career [=his film career ended] after a lifetime in show business. • His injury ***brought down the curtain*** on his remarkable career. = His injury ***brought the curtain down*** on his remarkable career. [=his injury ended his career] — see picture at THEATER **b** [*singular*] : the time when a curtain is raised or lowered at the beginning or end of a performance • The audience applauded enthusiastically after the ***final curtain***. [=after the curtain was lowered at the end of the performance] • ***Curtain times*** are 7:30 p.m. on Saturday and 2:00 p.m. on Sunday. [=the performance begins at 7:30 p.m. on Saturday and 2:00 p.m. on Sunday]

4 [*count*] : something that covers or hides something else — usually + *of* • A *curtain of* smoke hung at the edge of the forest. • It was hard to see their faces through the *curtain of* darkness.

be curtains for *informal* : to be the end, failure, or death of (someone or something) • It looks like *it's curtains for* the mayor after this election. [=the mayor will not be elected again] • If they don't win today's game, it'll ***be/mean/spell curtains for*** their hopes of winning the championship. [=their hopes will be ended]

²curtain *verb* **-tains; -tained; -tain·ing**

curtain off [*phrasal verb*] ***curtain (something) off*** or ***curtain off (something)*** : to separate or cover (something) by using a curtain • The booth was *curtained off* on three sides. • The back of the room was *curtained off* for privacy.

cur·tained *adj, always used before a noun* : decorated or covered with curtains • *curtained* windows • a *curtained* booth

curtain call *noun, pl* ~ **calls** [*count*] : the time when a performer returns to the stage at the end of a performance in response to the applause of the audience • The singer came back for one more *curtain call*.

cur·tain–rais·er /ˈkɚtn̩ˌreɪzɚ/ *noun, pl* **-ers** [*count*] : a short performance or event that comes before the main performance or event • The magic act was just a *curtain-raiser* for the circus performers.

curt·sy *also* **curt·sey** /ˈkɚtsi/ *noun, pl* **curt·sies** *also* **curt·seys** [*count*] : a formal way of greeting an important person (such as a king or queen) in which a woman shows respect by placing one foot slightly behind the other and bending her knees

– curtsy *also* **curtsey** *verb* **curtsies** *also* **curtseys; curtsied** *also* **curt·seyed; curt·sy·ing** *also* **curt·sey·ing** [*no obj*] • She *curtsied* before the queen.

cur·va·ceous /kɚˈveɪʃəs/ *adj* [*more* ~; *most* ~] *of a woman* : having an attractively curved body • a *curvaceous* young actress • a *curvaceous* figure

cur·va·ture /ˈkɚvəʧɚ/ *noun*

1 *technical* : the amount that something is curved [*count*] The lenses have different *curvatures*. — often + *of* • the *curvature of* the earth [*noncount*] The machine measures the eyeball's degree of *curvature*.

2 [*noncount*] *medical* : a condition in which your spine is curved in an abnormal way • a disease that can cause *curvature* of the spine

¹curve /ˈkɚv/ *noun, pl* **curves** [*count*]

1 : a smooth, rounded line, shape, path, etc. • The dog's tail has a slight *curve*. • There is a sharp/gentle *curve* coming up in the road.

2 *technical* : a curved line on a graph that shows how something changes or is affected by one or more conditions • the price *curve* in relation to inflation • the population growth *curve* — see also LEARNING CURVE

3 : a curving line or shape of the human body and especially of a woman's body — usually plural • The dress follows the *curves* of the body. • voluptuous *curves*

4 *baseball* : CURVEBALL • The pitcher threw him a *curve*. — often used figuratively • Life has ***thrown him some curves*** [=*thrown him some curveballs*] over the years but he's never given up. [=he has had some difficult and unexpected problems in his life] • The reporter *threw the actress a curve* [=surprised her with a difficult and unexpected question] when he asked about her past drug use.

ahead of the curve *chiefly US, approving* : faster about doing something than other people, companies, etc. • The company has been *ahead of the curve* in adopting new technologies. [=has adopted new technologies faster than other companies]

behind the curve *chiefly US, disapproving* : slower about doing something than other people, companies, etc. • We are *behind the curve* when it comes to advances in medicine. [=we have not been keeping up with the latest advances as well as others]

²curve *verb* **curves; curved; curv·ing**

1 [*no obj*] : to form a curve : to turn or change from a straight line, shape, or path to a smooth, rounded one • The tail *curves* over the dog's back. • The road *curves* to the left. • The fence *curves* in toward the side of the house. • The railing *curves* out near the observation platform. • a *curving* path

2 [+ *obj*] : to cause (something) to form a curve • He *curved* [=*bent*] the wire slightly.

curve·ball /ˈkɚvˌbɑːl/ *noun, pl* **-balls** [*count*] *baseball* : a pitch that is thrown with spin so that the ball curves in the air • The batter struck out on a *curveball*. — often used figuratively • Life has ***thrown him a few curveballs*** in recent years. [=he has had some difficult and unexpected problems in his life] — called also *curve*

curved *adj* [*more* ~; *most* ~] : having a rounded shape • a *curved* wall/blade • *curved* handlebars • The animal's horns are slightly *curved*.

curvy /ˈkɚvi/ *adj* **curv·i·er; -est** [*also more* ~; *most* ~] : having many curves • a *curvy* road • *curvy* lines

¹cush·ion /ˈkʊʃən/ *noun, pl* **-ions** [*count*]

1 : a soft object or part that is used to make something (such as a seat) more comfortable or to protect a surface from damage : a soft pillow, pad, etc. • a seat/sofa *cushion* • There is a *cushion* under the rug to protect the floor. • a *cushion* of air [=a layer of air that provides support or protection to something] — see picture at LIVING ROOM

2 : any one of the rubber parts that the ball bounces off along the inner edges of a billiard table

3 : something (such as an extra amount of money) that you can use to reduce the bad effect of something (such as an unexpected problem or expense) • We didn't have a financial *cushion* when my husband lost his job. — often + *against* • We use our savings as a *cushion against* major expenses.

4 : a lead in a game or competition that is large enough to allow the leader to feel confident about winning — usually singular • The team enjoyed a 6–0 *cushion* in the last inning.

²cushion *verb* **-ions; -ioned; -ion·ing** [+ *obj*] : to make (something, such as a fall or collision) less severe or painful : to soften or reduce the bad effect of (something) • The pile of leaves helped *cushion* his fall. • The tires help *cushion* the ride. [=help make the ride smoother] • The tax cut is meant to ***cushion the blow/impact*** of soaring gas prices. — often + *against* or *from* • The helmet *cushions* the head *against* violent collisions. • The tax cut should *cushion* the economy *from* the effect of soaring gas prices.

– cushioned *adj* • a *cushioned* seat/chair

cu·shion·ing /ˈkʊʃənɪŋ/ *noun* [*noncount*] : soft material that is used for comfort or protection • The padded insert in the sneaker provides extra *cushioning*.

cushy /ˈkʊʃi/ *adj* **cush·i·er; -est** [*also more* ~; *most* ~] *informal* : very easy and pleasant : involving little difficulty or effort • His uncle got him a *cushy* job in the city government.

cusp /ˈkʌsp/ *noun, pl* **cusps** [*count*] *technical* : a pointed end or part where two curves meet • the *cusp* of a tooth

on the cusp : at the point when something is about to change to something else • She is *on the cusp* [=*on the verge*] of being a star. • *on the cusp* between childhood and adolescence • I was born *on the cusp* between Leo and Virgo.

C

cus·pi·dor /ˈkʌspəˌdoɚ/ *noun, pl* **-dors** [*count*] *chiefly US* : SPITTOON

cuss /ˈkʌs/ *verb* **cuss·es; cussed; cuss·ing** [*no obj*] *US, informal* : to use offensive words when you speak : CURSE • She started to yell and *cuss* as soon as she saw him.

cuss out [*phrasal verb*] ***cuss (someone) out or cuss out (someone)*** *US, informal* : to say angry and offensive words to (someone) • He *cussed* me *out* for crashing his pickup truck. • We got *cussed out* [=*cursed out*] by the boss for missing the deadline.

cuss·word /ˈkʌsˌwɚd/ *noun, pl* **-words** [*count*] *US, informal* : an offensive word that people say when they are angry : CURSE, SWEARWORD

cus·tard /ˈkʌstɚd/ *noun, pl* **-tards** [*count, noncount*] : a type of sweet food that is made with eggs and milk

– cus·tardy /ˈkʌstɚdi/ *adj* [*more ~; most ~*] • a *custardy* dessert/filling

cus·to·di·al /ˌkʌˈstoudijəl/ *adj, always used before a noun*

1 *law* : having the responsibility for taking care of a child : having custody of a child • Her mother is the *custodial* parent.

2 *US* : relating to the care of a building, equipment, or land • *custodial* duties

3 *Brit, law* : involving punishment that requires a criminal to spend time in a prison • a ***custodial sentence***

cus·to·di·an /ˌkʌˈstoudijən/ *noun, pl* **-ans** [*count*]

1 *formal* : someone who keeps and protects something valuable for another person — often + *of* • The court appointed him *custodian of* the dead author's manuscripts. — often used figuratively • The museums are *custodians* of culture.

2 *US* : a person who cleans and takes care of a building : JANITOR • a school *custodian*

cus·to·dy /ˈkʌstədi/ *noun* [*noncount*]

1 *law* : the legal right to take care of a child (such as a child whose parents are divorced) • She has sole *custody* of her daughter. • The judge granted/awarded *custody* to the grandparents. • The parents have ***joint custody***. [=both parents have custody] • a bitter ***custody battle*** [=a legal fight between divorced parents about who will take care of a child]

2 : the state of being kept in a prison or jail — used after *in* or *into* • Several suspects in the killing are *in custody*. • He was taken *into* (police) *custody* last night and will be charged with murder today. • The witness is ***in protective custody***. [=is being kept in a safe place by the police]

3 *formal* : the act of protecting or taking care of something • The bank provides safe *custody* for valuables. — often + *of* • The artist's paintings are in the *custody of* the museum.

[1]**cus·tom** /ˈkʌstəm/ *noun, pl* **-toms**

1 : an action or way of behaving that is usual and traditional among the people in a particular group or place [*count*] tribal/local/family/ancient *customs* • social *customs* • an English/Indian *custom* • It is the *custom* for the bride to wear a white dress on her wedding day. [*noncount*] According to *custom*, the festivities begin at dusk. • It's a matter of *custom*.

2 [*singular*] : something that is done regularly by a person • She had breakfast in bed, as was her *custom*. [=*habit*]

3 *customs* [*plural*] **a** : taxes or fees that are paid to the government when goods come into or go out of a country — often used before another noun • *customs* duties **b** : the place at an airport, border, etc., where government officers collect customs on goods and look for things that people are trying to bring into a country illegally • We went through *customs* at the airport without any difficulty. • It took us a long time to ***clear customs*** at the border. — often used before another noun • a *customs* agent/officer/inspector

4 [*noncount*] *Brit, formal* : the practice of regularly going to the same shop or business to buy things or services • As new shops have opened people have been taking their *custom* [=*business*] elsewhere.

[2]**custom** *adj, always used before a noun, chiefly US*

1 : made to fit the needs or requirements of a particular person • *custom* furniture • The new kitchen will have *custom* cabinets. • *custom* designs • *custom* [=*custom-made*] clothes • a *custom* [=*custom-built*] home/motorcycle

2 : doing work that fits the needs or requirements of a particular person • a *custom* tailor • a *custom* furniture shop

cus·tom·ary /ˈkʌstəˌmeri, *Brit* ˈkʌstəmri/ *adj*

1 : usually done in a particular situation or at a particular place or time • He forgot the *customary* "thank you." • It is *customary* to hold the door open for someone who is entering a building behind you.

2 *always used before a noun* : usual or typical of a particular person • She dressed in her *customary* fashion. • He did the work with his *customary* efficiency.

– cus·tom·ar·i·ly /ˌkʌstəˈmerəli, *Brit* ˈkʌstəmrəli/ *adv* • *Customarily*, people wear black to funerals. • Our families *customarily* get together for a camping trip each summer.

cus·tom–built /ˈkʌstəmˈbɪlt/ *adj* : built to fit the needs or requirements of a particular person • a *custom-built* home • The car is *custom-built*.

cus·tom·er /ˈkʌstəmɚ/ *noun, pl* **-ers** [*count*]

1 : someone who buys goods or services from a business • She is one of our best/regular *customers*. • Remember, the *customer* is always right. [=never argue with a customer] — often used before another noun • The company has good/poor *customer* service. • *customer* satisfaction

2 *informal* : a person who has a particular quality • He is one tough/tricky *customer*. [=he is a tough/tricky person] • She's a pretty cool *customer*.

cus·tom·ize *also Brit* **cus·tom·ise** /ˈkʌstəˌmaɪz/ *verb* **-izes; -ized; -iz·ing** [+ *obj*] : to change (something) in order to fit the needs or requirements of a person, business, etc. • The telephone company has offered to *customize* a plan for our business. • The program can be *customized* to serve different purposes.

– cus·tom·iz·able *also Brit* **cus·tom·is·able** /ˌkʌstəˈmaɪzəbəl/ *adj* [*more ~; most ~*] • a *customizable* van • *customizable* software **– customized** *adj* • a *customized* van **– cus·tom·i·za·tion** *also Brit* **cus·tom·i·sa·tion** /ˌkʌstəməˈzeɪʃən/ *noun* [*noncount*] • software *customization*

cus·tom–made /ˈkʌstəmˈmeɪd/ *adj* : made to fit the needs or requirements of a particular person • All his clothes are *custom-made*. • *custom-made* curtains/furniture

[1]**cut** /ˈkʌt/ *verb* **cuts; cut; cut·ting**

1 a : to use a sharp tool (such as a knife) to open or divide (something, such as paper or wood) [+ *obj*] *Cut* the paper along/on the dotted line (with a pair of scissors). • *cutting* a piece of string • He uses the ax to *cut* wood. • The meat is so tender you can *cut* it with a fork. — sometimes used figuratively • The excitement/tension in the room was so thick ***you could cut it with a knife***. [=there was a lot of excitement/tension in the room] [*no obj*] *Cut* along/on the dotted line. • The saw easily *cuts* through metal. • She *cut* into the melon with a knife. **b** [+ *obj*] : to make a hole or wound in (a person's skin) • I *cut* myself while shaving. • I *cut* my finger on a sharp piece of metal. = A sharp piece of metal *cut* me (on the finger). • I had a *cut* finger. • We were fighting, and he tried to *cut* me with his knife. • Pieces of broken glass *cut* her face and arms. • He fell and *cut* his head open on a sharp rock. **c** [+ *obj*] : to make (a hole) in something by using a sharp tool • They *cut* a hole in the wall for the new window. • Doctors begin by *cutting* a small incision in the chest. • *Cut* several slits in the top of the crust to allow air to escape. **d** [+ *obj*] : to divide or separate parts of (something) by using a sharp tool • It's time to *cut* [=*slice*] the cake! • I'll *cut* the apple in half so you both can have some. • Would you *cut* me a slice of bread? = Would you *cut* a slice of bread for me? — often + *into* • Add one large onion that has been *cut into* one-inch pieces. • The chicken is *cut into* long strips and served on top of the salad. — often + *from* • Her walls were covered with pictures *cut from* magazines. • a piece of meat that is *cut from* the hind end of the animal — often + *off* • She was *cutting off* pieces of watermelon and giving them to the children.

2 [*no obj*] **a** : to be able to cut something • This knife doesn't *cut* well. **b** : to be able to be cut • Aluminum foil *cuts* easily with scissors.

3 [+ *obj*] : to make (hair, grass, etc.) shorter by using a sharp tool (such as scissors) • I *cut* my hair short for the summer. • Where'd you get your hair *cut*? • I need to *cut* [=*trim*] my nails; they're way too long. • She keeps her nails *cut* short. • The grass in our yard needs to be *cut*. [=*mowed*] • the smell of fresh-*cut* grass • The wood is already ***cut to size/length***. [=it has already been cut so that it is the proper size/length]

4 [+ *obj*] **a** : to give (hair or clothing) a certain style by cutting it — usually used as *(be) cut* • Her hair is light brown and *cut* in a short bob. • She was wearing a dress that *was cut* low at the neck. [=she was wearing a low-*cut* dress] **b** : to give (something) a new shape by using a sharp tool • a beautifully *cut* diamond

5 [+ *obj*] : to make or form (something) by cutting or removing material • We all *cut* [=*carved*] our names on/into the tree. • The stream *cuts* a path through the woods. • builders *cutting* new roads in the forest — often + *out* • At the center of the table was a statue *cut out* of ice.

6 [+ *obj*] **: to make the amount of (something) smaller : REDUCE** • Our benefits were recently *cut* at work. • The drug has been shown to *cut* the risk of heart attack by half. • In just three years, the mayor has *cut* the city's crime in half. • The President has promised to *cut* government spending. • *Cutting* taxes can have positive and negative effects on the economy. • measures that are designed to *cut* costs = cost-*cutting* measures • The company's expenses had been ***cut to the bone***. [=reduced to their lowest possible amount] — often + *off* • This route can *cut* as much as five minutes *off* your driving time. • The experience *cut* 20 years *off* (of) his life. [=shortened his life by 20 years] • We've *cut* 20 percent *off* the regular retail price.

7 [+ *obj*] **a : to make (a book, film, etc.) shorter by removing parts** • His article was *cut* [=*shortened*] by about 500 words. • The movie had to be *cut* because it was too long. **b : to remove (something) from a book, film, etc.** • The movie's director decided to *cut* [=*cut out, omit*] my part. — often + *from* • The director *cut* the scene *from* the final version of the film. • They decided to *cut* her report *from* the newscast. • About 500 words were *cut from* his article.

8 [+ *obj*] **: to remove (something) from a computer document in a way that allows you to move it to another part of the document or to another document** • After you select the text with your mouse, you can *cut* it and then paste it at the beginning of the paragraph. • You can ***cut and paste*** the picture into your file. — see also CUT-AND-PASTE

9 [+ *obj*] **: to remove (a plant or part of a plant) by cutting it** • It's illegal to *cut* [=*cut down*] trees in this forest. • We'll start *cutting* and harvesting the wheat next week. ✧ A ***cut flower*** is a flower that has been cut off the plant that it grew on. • He brought her a bouquet of *cut flowers*.

10 [+ *obj*] **: to cause (something) to no longer be connected** • The enemy has *cut* [=*severed*] our supply lines. • He wanted to *cut* all ties with his past and start a new life.

11 [+ *obj*] **: to allow (someone or something) to be free, loose, etc., by cutting something that stops movement** • They were trapped inside the crushed car and had to be ***cut free***. = They had to be *cut* from the car. • The boat was ***cut loose*** from the pier and allowed to drift away. — see also *cut loose* at [2]LOOSE

12 [+ *obj*] **: to remove (someone) from a team, organization, etc.** • I was on the team for two weeks before I got *cut*. — often + *from* • The coach *cut* two players *from* the team. • The band was *cut from* the show at the last minute.

13 : to divide (a pack of cards) into two piles [+ *obj*] You *cut* the deck and I'll deal. [*no obj*] You *cut* and I'll deal.

14 [+ *obj*] **: to divide (an area of land) into two parts** • The river *cuts* the city in half. • The mountain ridges are *cut* by deep valleys.

15 [*no obj*] **: to move or go *across* or *through* something** • Let's take a shortcut and *cut across* this field. • We *cut through* the park on our way home. • The boundary line between the two countries *cuts* directly *through* the group's traditional homeland. — often used figuratively to describe something that is not limited in the usual way • National security is an issue that *cuts across* party lines. [=an issue that is important to both political parties] • Child abuse *cuts across* all economic and racial lines/boundaries. [=it occurs in all economic and racial groups] • Her academic interests *cut across* [=involve or relate to] many disciplines.

16 [*no obj*] **a : to move quickly** • a fast ship *cutting* through the waves **b : to move suddenly in a different direction** • The driver *cut* across three lanes of traffic to get to his exit and nearly caused an accident. • (*American football*) The runner *cut* to his left to avoid being tackled.

17 [*no obj*] **: to move in front of other people in a line** • That guy *cut* to the head of the line. • She *cut* in front of us. = She *cut* ahead of us. — often + *in* • Our friends let us *cut in* in front of them. • Celebrities are allowed to ***cut in line*** at popular restaurants. • Hey, no *cutting* (*in line*)!

18 [+ *obj*] *chiefly US* **: to not go to (school or a class) when you should go to it** • We used to *cut* [=*skip*] school together and hang out at the beach. • She would take notes for me when I *cut* class.

19 [+ *obj*] *informal* **: to record (a song, album, etc.)** • She's in the studio *cutting* a new track/song for her next album. • Elvis Presley *cut* his first record in 1954.

20 [*no obj*] **: to suddenly move from one image or scene to another in a movie, television program, etc.** • The movie *cuts* quickly from one scene to the next. • The camera *cut* back to the actor's face. • To explain the present situation, the film *cuts* back to the hero's childhood. — often + *away* • They quickly *cut away* to the announcer when he appeared on stage.

21 [*no obj*] **: to stop filming a scene in a movie or television show — usually used as a command** • "*Cut!*" yelled the director.

22 [+ *obj*] **: to stop saying or doing (foolish or annoying things) — usually used in phrases like *cut the nonsense* and (less politely) *cut the crap*** • Let's *cut the nonsense* and get down to business. • *Cut the crap*, Jen! I know you're lying.

23 [+ *obj*] **: to stop (a motor) by moving a switch** • We *cut* the engine and drifted into shore. • I parked and *cut* the ignition. — often + *off* • The pilot *cut off* the engine after the plane had come to a stop.

24 [*no obj*] **: to go to or deal with something in a very direct way — usually + *to*** • Her question *cut to* the heart of the issue. • This research *cuts to* the very core of who we are as human beings. • Let me *cut to* the real reason why I'm here.

25 : to cause painful feelings or emotions [*no obj*] His words *cut* deeply. • The disappointment ***cut like a knife***. [+ *obj*] His harsh words *cut* me very deeply. • She was ***cut to the quick*** [=she was very badly hurt] by their insults.

26 [+ *obj*] **a** *US* **: to make (alcohol) less strong by adding water or another liquid** • They *cut* [=*diluted*] the wine with water. **b : to make (a drug, such as heroin) less strong by mixing it with another substance** • The substance is used to *cut* cocaine.

27 [+ *obj*] **: to cause (dirt, grease, etc.) to break apart and be removed** • soap that *cuts* grease and grime

cut a check *US* **: to write a check and give it to someone** • The company *cut* him *a check* and he cashed it.

cut a dash see [2]DASH

***cut a deal* : to make an agreement usually about business : to make a deal** • The band *cut a deal* with a recording company.

cut a figure ✧ If you ***cut a fine/dashing/heroic (etc.) figure***, you look very good and impressive. • He *cut a fine figure* in his officer's uniform.

***cut and run* : to leave quickly in order to avoid danger or trouble** • You can't just *cut and run* when your friends are in trouble.

cut a rug *old-fashioned slang* **: to dance in an energetic way** • He's not young anymore, but he can still *cut a rug* on the dance floor.

cut a tooth *of a baby* **: to have a tooth begin to come through the gums** • Their baby daughter *cut* her first *tooth* yesterday.

cut away [*phrasal verb*] ***cut away (something) or cut (something) away* : to remove (something that is not needed) by cutting** • They *cut away* [=*cut off*] a few of the tree's lower branches. — see also [1]CUT 20 (above), CUTAWAY

cut back [*phrasal verb*] **1 : to use less or do less of something** • We've been spending too much money and we need to *cut back* [=we need to spend less money] — often + *on* • I've been trying to *cut back on* smoking. • He's *cut back on* the time he spends in front of the TV. **2** ***cut (something) back or cut back (something)*** **a : to make (a plant) smaller or shorter by cutting its branches** • *Cut back* [=*prune*] the shrub in the late fall. **b : to reduce the size or amount of (something)** • We ran out of time and had to *cut back* our plans. • They've *cut back* my hours at work. — see also CUTBACK

***cut both ways* : to have both good and bad results, effects, etc.** • He knows that his extreme competitiveness *cuts both ways*. • These changes in the economy *cut both ways*.

cut corners see [1]CORNER

cut down [*phrasal verb*] **1 : to use less or do less of something** • I haven't been able to quit smoking completely, but at least I've *cut down*. [=*cut back*] — often + *on* • I've had to *cut down on* [=*reduce, cut back on*] the amount of money I spend on clothes. • She suggested he *cut down on* his drinking. • a building material that helps *cut down on* noise **2** ***cut (something) down or cut down (something)*** **a : to remove (a tree or bush) by cutting through its trunk or base** • Most of the tree was dead, so we had to *cut* it *down*. • Much of the forest has been *cut down* for firewood. **b : to reduce the size or amount of (something)** • We used a shortcut that *cut down* our traveling time by 15 minutes. • The machine significantly *cuts down* the amount of work necessary to harvest crops. **3** ***cut (someone) down or cut down (someone)* : to kill or wound (someone)** • She was *cut down* by a stray bullet. • The composer Schubert was *cut down* in his prime by illness. [=he died because of illness when he was in his prime]

cut from the same cloth see CLOTH

cut ice see [1]ICE

cut in [*phrasal verb*] **1 :** to join a conversation suddenly **:** INTERRUPT • We were trying to have a conversation, but she kept *cutting in*. • "What are you guys talking about?" he *cut in*. — often + *on* • He's always *cutting in on* our conversations. **2 :** to stop two people who are dancing and take the place of one of them • He went up to the dancing couple and said, "May I *cut in*?" **3** *of a machine* **:** to begin to work • Once the heater *cuts in* [=*kicks in*], it'll be a lot more comfortable in here. **4** ***cut (someone) in*** **:** to include (someone) in a group of people who are receiving money or other benefits • They'll help you start your business provided that you *cut* them *in* when you start making a profit. — often + *on* • They want you to *cut* them *in on* [=to give them some of] the profits. **5** ***cut (something) in*** *or* ***cut in (something)*** **:** to add (something, such as butter) to dry ingredients (such as flour) by making cutting motions with a knife or other sharp tool • After sifting the flour into a mixing bowl, use two knives to *cut in* the butter. — see also [1]CUT 17 (above)

cut into [*phrasal verb*] ***cut into (something)*** **:** to reduce the amount of (something) • Although it would *cut into* profits, we were forced to lower our prices. • The extra time I was spending at work was *cutting into* my time with my family.

cut it *informal* **1 :** to be able to do something well enough — usually used in negative statements • After two weeks at the new job, he decided that he just couldn't *cut it*. [=that he couldn't do the job well enough to succeed] • They didn't think that I would *cut it* as an actress. • Everyone's using bold colors to decorate their homes. Plain white walls just don't *cut it* anymore. [=plain white walls are not acceptable anymore] **2** ✧ People use the informal phrase ***any way you cut it*** to say that something is true no matter how you look at it or think about it. • *Any way you cut it*, it was a pretty good year for our company. • She's one of the world's best tennis players *any way you cut it*.

cut it close (*chiefly US*) *or chiefly Brit* ***cut it fine*** **:** to almost not be able to do something **:** to almost fail, lose, etc. • They ended up winning the game, but they really *cut it close* [=they almost lost the game] at the end • It's *cutting it* a bit *fine* to get to the station at 9:45 when the train leaves at 9:50!

cut off [*phrasal verb*] **1** *of a machine* **:** to stop working suddenly **:** to turn off • The engine suddenly *cut off*. [=*cut out*] • The air-conditioning *cut off*, and the room was silent. **2** ***cut (something) off*** *or* ***cut off (something)*** **a :** to remove (something) by cutting • *Cut off* dead flowers to promote new growth. • I had very long hair, but I *cut* most of it *off* in college. • He decided to *cut off* his beard. • He was running around ***like a chicken with its head cut off***. [=he was acting in a very excited and confused way] **b :** to stop or end (something) • They had a vote to *cut off* debate on the budget. • The organization *cut off* its ties with the country's government. • His family *cut off* all communication/contact with him after the incident. **c :** to stop people from seeing or using (something) **:** to block (something) • Their fence *cuts off* our view of the ocean. • Many of the town's roads were *cut off* when the river overflowed. • The army *cut off* all escape routes. **d :** to stop the movement or supply of (something) • The power was *cut off* to our apartment building. • The earthquake *cut off* our water supply. • They've decided to *cut off* funding/aid to the group. • His main source of income had been *cut off*. **3** ***cut (someone or something) off*** *or* ***cut off (someone or something)*** **:** to cause (someone or something) to be separate or alone — often + *from* • an island nation geographically *cut off from* the rest of the world • They are *cut off from* (contact with) the outside world. • She *cut* herself *off from* her family. • He's emotionally *cut off from* his wife. **4** ***cut (someone) off*** *or* ***cut off (someone)*** **a :** to stop (someone) from talking • I was in the middle of telling a story when she *cut* me *off* [=she interrupted me] to ask about dinner. • He spoke for 12 minutes until his teacher finally *cut* him *off*. ✧ If you ***get cut off*** when you are using the telephone, the telephone connection suddenly ends and you can no longer hear the other person. • I called him, but we *got cut off* [=we got disconnected; the telephone connection ended] two minutes into our conversation. **b** *US* **:** to drive in front of (someone in another vehicle) in a sudden and dangerous way • He shouted at a driver who *cut* him *off*. • Hey, that guy/car just *cut* me *off*! **c :** to move ahead and force (someone) to stop • "Sheriff, they're getting away!" "Don't worry, we'll take a shortcut and *cut* them *off*." **d :** to decide not to give money or property to (someone) after your death • In her will, she *cut off* her son without a cent/penny. • She *cut* him *off* completely. **e :** to refuse to allow (someone) to drink more alcohol • He's had too much to drink. We'd better *cut* him *off*. — see also [1]CUT 1d, 6 (above), CUTOFF

cut off your nose to spite your face see [1]NOSE

cut out [*phrasal verb*] **1** *of a machine* **:** to stop working suddenly • The plane's engines suddenly *cut out*. [=*cut off*] **2** *chiefly US* **:** to leave quickly and suddenly • We were in a hurry to get home, so we *cut out* before the performance ended. **3** *chiefly US* **:** to move out of a line of traffic • The other car/driver *cut out* from behind and sped ahead of us. **4** ***cut (something) out*** *or* ***cut out (something)*** **a :** to form (something) by cutting with a sharp tool • He got a piece of red paper and *cut out* a big heart. = He *cut* a big heart *out* of a piece of red paper. — sometimes used figuratively • She *cut out* [=*carved out*] a place for herself in history. [=she caused herself to be important in history] — see also [1]CUT 5 (above), CUTOUT **b :** to remove (something) by cutting • I *cut out* the recipe from a magazine. • *cutting out* newspaper articles • Doctors *cut out* the lump from her chest. **c :** to remove (something) from something • Fortunately, they *cut* [=*took*] that scene *out* of the movie. • He *cut out* sugar from his diet and began eating more fruits and vegetables. • I focused on my work and *cut out* everything else in my life. **d :** to stop doing (something) • I've cut down on the number of cigarettes I smoke, but I'd like to *cut out* [=*give up*] smoking altogether. • I told you to ***cut that out***! [=I told you to stop that] • That's enough, kids. I mean it! ***Cut it out***! **e** ✧ If your legs, feet, or knees are ***cut out from under you***, you are knocked down by something that hits your legs very hard. This phrase is often used figuratively. • When I learned that I was seriously ill, I felt like my feet were *cut out from under me*. • The financial legs had been *cut out from under* the program. [=the program lost money and could not do what it needed to do] **5** ***cut (someone) out*** *or* ***cut out (someone)*** **:** to cause (someone) to no longer be included in something • She *cut* all of her children *out* of her will and left everything to her grandchildren. • Don't *cut* me *out* of your life completely! • We can save money by ***cutting out the middleman*** and ordering our supplies directly from the manufacturer. **6** ✧ If you are ***cut out for (something)*** or ***cut out to do/be (something)***, you are naturally able or suited to do or be something. • Why do you think that you're *cut out for* this job? [=why would you be good at this job?] • I'm really not *cut out for* this kind of work. [=I'm not naturally good at it] • He's not *cut out to be* a teacher. = He's not *cut out to* teach. — see also *have your work cut out for you* at [2]WORK

cut short see [2]SHORT

cut (someone) dead **:** to pretend not to see (someone you know) **:** to deliberately ignore (someone) • When I saw her on the street yesterday, she *cut* me *dead*.

cut (someone) some slack see [2]SLACK

cut the Gordian knot see GORDIAN KNOT

cut the mustard see MUSTARD

cut through [*phrasal verb*] ***cut through (something)*** **:** to get through or past (something that blocks you or slows you down) quickly and directly • We were able to start the project once she told us how to *cut through* the red tape. • It took some time to *cut through* the lies and get to the truth. • *cutting through* all the nonsense — often + *to* • *cutting through to* the heart/essence of the problem — see also [1]CUT 15 (above)

cut to the chase see [1]CHASE

cut up [*phrasal verb*] **1** *US, informal* **:** to behave in a silly or rude way • I was sent to the principal's office for *cutting up* [=*clowning around*] in class. — see also CUTUP **2** ***cut (something) up*** *or* ***cut up (something)*** **:** to cut (something) into parts or pieces • He *cut up* the candy into little pieces and gave it to the child. — often + *into* • The area was *cut up* [=*divided*] *into* three separate farms. • They *cut up* the wood *into* small pieces. • We made sandwiches and *cut* them *up into* triangles. **3** ***cut (someone or something) up*** *or* ***cut up (someone or something)*** **a :** to hurt or damage (someone or something) by cutting • He got *cut up* pretty badly in the fight. • His face and arms were all *cut up*. **b** *informal* **:** to criticize (someone or something) in a harsh way • The critics really *cut up* his last play. **c** ✧ In informal British English, to be ***cut up about*** something is to be very sad or upset about something. • I was pretty *cut up*

about the way the critics treated my last play. • She's really *cut up about* losing her job.
cut up rough *Brit, informal* : to behave in an angry or violent way • He got drunk and started to *cut up rough.*
cut your losses see LOSS
cut your own throat see THROAT
cut your teeth — used to describe the things that people do when they are starting their careers • He *cut his teeth* performing at local bars and nightclubs. • She *cut her* political *teeth* [=she began her political career] as a volunteer during the 1992 presidential elections. — often + *on* • Many television and movie stars *cut their teeth on* soap operas.
fish or cut bait see ²FISH

²**cut** *noun, pl* **cuts** [*count*]
1 a : an opening or hole made with a sharp tool (such as a knife) • Make a few small *cuts* in the crust to let the air escape. • a two-inch *cut* in the cloth **b :** a wound on a person's body that is made by something sharp • She had a small *cut* [=*gash*] above her left eye. • He came home covered in *cuts* and bruises. • a deep/superficial *cut*
2 : an act of making something smaller in amount : REDUCTION • Further *cuts* in spending are needed. • He had to accept a *cut* in pay. = He had to accept a ***pay cut***. • a ***tax cut***
3 : the act of removing something from a book, movie, etc. • You'll have to make a few *cuts* in your manuscript if you want us to publish it.
4 : a version of a movie at a particular stage of being edited • Fortunately, that scene didn't make the film's final *cut*. [=that scene did not appear in the final version of the film] • I saw a ***rough cut*** [=a version that is not yet finished] of the movie. • a ***director's cut*** [=a special version of a movie that is created by the director and that usually includes scenes that are not included in other versions]
5 : a song on a record, tape, or CD • We listened to the same *cut* [=*track*] over and over.
6 : the shape and style of a piece of clothing • the *cut* of his pants
7 : the act or result of cutting someone's hair : HAIRCUT • I had a shampoo and a *cut*. — see also BUZZ CUT, CREW CUT
8 : a piece of meat that is cut from a particular part of an animal's body • a thick/tender/expensive *cut* of meat
9 : a part of something that is divided and shared among people — usually singular • We each got a *cut* [=*share*] of the profits. — see also *a cut of the action* at ACTION
10 : the act of reducing the size of a group (such as a group of competitors) by removing the ones that are not good enough or that have not done well enough — usually used with *make* or *miss* • He has to birdie the last hole in order to ***make the cut***. [=in order to have a score that is low enough to be among the players allowed to continue playing] • If he doesn't birdie this hole, he'll ***miss the cut***. • Only the best players are good enough to *make the cut* when the team is being chosen.
a cut above : better than other people or things • All of his books are good, but this one is *a cut above* (the rest). • She's *a cut above* the other competitors and should win easily.
cut and thrust *chiefly Brit* : the lively and exciting quality of an activity in which people compete or argue with each other • He has always enjoyed the *cut and thrust* of politics.

cut–and–dried /ˌkʌtn̩ˈdraɪd/ *also US* **cut–and–dry** /ˌkʌtn̩ˈdraɪ/ *adj* [*more* ~; *most* ~] : having a clear and definite quality that does not allow doubt or that cannot be changed • The situation wasn't as *cut-and-dried* as we had thought. • a *cut-and-dried* example • a *cut-and-dried* decision

cut–and–paste /ˌkʌtn̩ˈpeɪst/ *adj, always used before a noun* : made up of parts taken from many different sources • The book was an unprofessional *cut-and-paste* job.

cut·away /ˈkʌtəˌweɪ/ *adj* : having the top or outside removed so the inside parts can be seen • The diagram shows a *cutaway* view of an engine. — see also *cut away* at ¹CUT
– cutaway *noun, pl* **-aways** [*count*]

cut·back /ˈkʌtˌbæk/ *noun, pl* **-backs** [*count*] : the act of reducing the number or amount of something : REDUCTION — often + *in* • He is opposed to further *cutbacks* [=*cuts*] *in* military spending. — see also *cut back* at ¹CUT

cute /ˈkjuːt/ *adj* **cut·er; cut·est**
1 : having a pleasing and usually youthful appearance • What a *cute* [=*adorable*] little baby! • a *cute* [=*pretty*] pink dress • *cute* puppies • She's **as cute as a button**! [=she's very cute]
2 *chiefly US, informal* : attractive in a sexual way • Who's that *cute* [=*hot, sexy*] guy/girl you were with?
3 *chiefly US, informal* **a :** clever in an appealing way • a *cute* idea **b :** clever in a way that annoys people • Don't get *cute* [=*smart, fresh*] with me!
4 *chiefly US, informal* : trying too hard to be pleasant or likable • The movie's too *cute* [=*cutesy*] to be taken seriously.
– cute·ly *adv* • She was dressed *cutely* in a little pink outfit.
– cute·ness *noun* [*noncount*] • their annoying *cuteness*

cute·sy /ˈkjuːtsi/ *adj* **cute·si·er; -est** [*also more* ~; *most* ~] *informal + disapproving* : trying very hard or too hard to be appealing : too cute in an annoying way • *cutesy* cartoon characters • *cutesy* pop music

cut glass *noun* [*noncount*] : glass with patterns cut into its surface for decoration — often used before another noun • a *cut-glass* vase

cu·ti·cle /ˈkjuːtɪkəl/ *noun, pl* **-ti·cles** [*count*] : the layer of dead or hard skin around the base of a fingernail or toenail

cut·ie /ˈkjuːti/ *noun, pl* **-ies** [*count*] *informal* : an attractive person : a cute person • Her boyfriend's a real *cutie*.

cut·ie–pie /ˈkjuːtiˌpaɪ/ *noun, pl* **-pies** [*count*] *US, informal* : an attractive person : CUTIE — often used as an informal way of addressing a lover, a small child, etc. • Hey there, *cutie-pie*. [=*honey, sweetie*]

cut·lass /ˈkʌtləs/ *noun, pl* **-lass·es** [*count*] : a short, heavy sword with a curved blade that was used by sailors and pirates in the past

cut·lery /ˈkʌtləri/ *noun* [*noncount*]
1 *US* : sharp tools made of metal (such as knives and scissors) that are used for cutting things
2 : forks, spoons, and knives used for serving and eating food : SILVERWARE • plastic *cutlery*

cut·let /ˈkʌtlət/ *noun, pl* **-lets** [*count*] : a small, thin slice of meat • veal/chicken *cutlets*
2 *chiefly Brit* : chopped vegetables, nuts, etc., that are pressed together into a flat shape, covered with bread crumbs, and fried in oil • a nut *cutlet* • vegetable *cutlets*

cut·off /ˈkʌtˌɑːf/ *noun, pl* **-offs**
1 [*count*] : the act of stopping the movement or supply of something • a *cutoff* of the water supply
2 [*count*] : the time when something must be done or completed • The *cutoff* for new applications is next Wednesday.
3 *cutoffs* [*plural*] : short pants that are made from long pants by cutting off the legs at the knees or higher • a pair of *cutoffs*
– see also *cut off* at ¹CUT
– cutoff *adj, always used before a noun* • We are approaching the *cutoff* point of the negotiations but no agreement has been reached. • The *cutoff* date for new applications is next Wednesday. • She was wearing *cutoff* jeans/pants.

cut·out /ˈkʌtˌaʊt/ *noun, pl* **-outs** [*count*] : a shape or picture that is cut from a piece of paper, cardboard, etc. • a cardboard *cutout* of a famous actor — see also *cut out* at ¹CUT

cut–price /ˈkʌtˈpraɪs/ *adj, chiefly Brit* : CUT-RATE • a *cut-price* ticket

cut–rate /ˈkʌtˈreɪt/ *adj, chiefly US*
1 : selling goods or services at very low prices • *cut-rate* supermarkets • *cut-rate* airlines and hotels
2 *of a price* : very low • They sell wine at *cut-rate* prices.

cut·ter /ˈkʌtɚ/ *noun, pl* **-ters** [*count*]
1 : a person, machine, or tool that cuts something • a diamond *cutter* • a pizza *cutter* — sometimes plural • a pair of wire *cutters* — see also BOX CUTTER, COOKIE CUTTER
2 a : a boat on a ship that is used for carrying supplies or passengers to and from the shore **b :** a small sailing boat with one mast **c :** a small military ship • a Coast Guard *cutter*

cut·throat /ˈkʌtˌθroʊt/ *adj* [*more* ~; *most* ~] — used to describe a situation in which people compete with each other in an unpleasant and often cruel and unfair way • *cutthroat* [=*ruthless*] competition • It's a *cutthroat* business we're in.

cut–throat razor *noun, pl* **~ -zors** [*count*] *Brit* : STRAIGHT RAZOR

¹**cut·ting** /ˈkʌtɪŋ/ *noun, pl* **-tings** [*count*]
1 : a stem, leaf, or root that is cut from a plant and used to grow a new plant • Take some *cuttings* from the plant and put them in water.
2 *Brit* : CLIPPING 1 • She kept a collection of (press) *cuttings* about the war.

²**cutting** *adj* [*more* ~; *most* ~]
1 *always used before a noun* : used for cutting things • a *cutting* blade

C

C

2 a : unpleasantly cold • a raw *cutting* [=*biting*] wind **b** : causing great physical pain • a sharp, *cutting* [=*piercing, stabbing*] pain

3 : very harsh and critical : intended to hurt someone's feelings • He made a *cutting* remark about my family, and I haven't spoken to him since.

cutting board *noun, pl* ~ **boards** [*count*] *US* : a wooden or plastic board on which foods (such as meats and vegetables) are cut — called also (*chiefly Brit*) *chopping board*; see picture at KITCHEN; compare CHOPPING BLOCK

cutting edge *noun, pl* ~ **edges**

1 [*count*] : the sharp edge of something that is used to cut things • the *cutting edge* of a knife

2 ***the cutting edge*** : the newest and most advanced area of activity in an art, science, etc. • He's a director who tries to keep his films right on *the cutting edge*. — often + *of* • The research we're doing now is ***at/on the cutting edge of*** medical technology. • *the cutting edge of* youth culture

– cutting–edge *adj* [*more* ~; *most* ~] • *cutting-edge* technology

cutting room *noun, pl* ~ **rooms** [*count*] : a room where movies or television shows are edited and put into their final form — usually singular • He worked in the *cutting room*.

on the cutting-room floor : removed from a movie or television show • The scene ended up *on the cutting-room floor*. [=the scene ended up being removed] — often used figuratively • A lot of good ideas are rejected and end up *on the cutting-room floor*. [=end up not being used]

cut·up /ˈkʌtˌʌp/ *noun, pl* **-ups** [*count*] *US, informal* : a person who behaves in a silly way and tries to make other people laugh • In school he was always a/the *cutup*, telling jokes and acting silly. — see also *cut up* at [1]CUT

CV *noun, pl* **CVs** [*count*] : CURRICULUM VITAE

cwt *abbr* hundredweight

-cy /si/ *noun suffix*

1 : the state of having a particular quality • bankrupt*cy* • normal*cy* • accura*cy*

2 : the action or practice of a particular type of person • candida*cy* • pira*cy* • prophe*cy*

3 : the state of having a particular role or rank • occupan*cy* • captain*cy*

cy·an /ˈsaɪˌæn/ *noun* [*noncount*] *technical* : a greenish-blue color — see color picture on page C2

cy·a·nide /ˈsajəˌnaɪd/ *noun* [*noncount*] : a very poisonous chemical

cyber- /ˈsaɪbɚ/ *combining form* : computer • *cyber*café • *cyber*space

cy·ber·ca·fé /ˈsaɪbɚkæˈfeɪ, *Brit* ˈsaɪbəˈkæˌfeɪ/ *noun, pl* **-fés** [*count*] : a café or coffee shop where customers can use computers to search the Internet

cy·ber·net·ics /ˌsaɪbɚˈnɛtɪks/ *noun* [*noncount*] : the scientific study of how people, animals, and machines control and communicate information

– cy·ber·net·ic /ˌsaɪbɚˈnɛtɪk/ *adj* • *cybernetic* theory

cy·ber·punk /ˈsaɪbɚˌpʌŋk/ *noun* [*noncount*] : stories about future societies that are controlled by computer technology — often used before another noun • *cyberpunk* novels/authors

cy·ber·sex /ˈsaɪbɚˌseks/ *noun* [*noncount*] : activity in which people become sexually excited by sending messages about sex to each other over the Internet

cy·ber·space /ˈsaɪbɚˌspeɪs/ *noun* [*noncount*] : the online world of computer networks and the Internet • We send e-mails through *cyberspace*.

cy·borg /ˈsaɪˌboɚg/ *noun, pl* **-borgs** [*count*] *in stories* : a person whose body contains mechanical or electrical devices and whose abilities are greater than the abilities of normal humans

cy·cla·men /ˈsaɪkləmən, *Brit* ˈsɪkləmən/ *noun, pl* **cyclamen** *or* **cyclamens** [*count*] : a plant that has flowers with large white, pink, or red petals that hang downward

[1]**cy·cle** /ˈsaɪkəl/ *noun, pl* **cycles** [*count*]

1 : a set of events or actions that happen again and again in the same order : a repeating series of events or actions • the female menstrual *cycle* • These plants have a 2-year ***growth cycle*** [=the plants live and die within two years] — often + *of* • the annual *cycle of* the seasons • the *cycle of* life and death • World leaders must do more to stop/break this *cycle of* violence. — see also LIFE CYCLE

2 : a set of regular and repeated actions that are done by a machine as part of a longer process • We have to wait for the dishwasher's wash and dry *cycles* to end. • the spin *cycle* on a washing machine

3 *chiefly Brit* : a bicycle or motorcycle • He rode his *cycle* into town. — often used before another noun • a *cycle* lane/path/route

4 : a group of poems, plays, songs, etc., that relate to the same subject and that together form a larger work • a *cycle* of 15 poems • a song *cycle*

[2]**cycle** *verb* **cycles; cy·cled; cy·cling**

1 *US* : to go through a repeated process or to cause (something) to go through a repeated process [+ *obj*] The water is *cycled* back into/through the system after it has been used. [*no obj*] The water *cycles* back into/through the system.

2 [*no obj*] : to ride a bicycle • He *cycled* [=*biked, bicycled*] across town to the library.

– cy·clist /ˈsaɪkələst/ *noun, pl* **-clists** [*count*] • a group of *cyclists* [=*bicyclists*]

cy·clic /ˈsaɪklɪk, ˈsɪklɪk/ *or* **cy·cli·cal** /ˈsaɪklɪkəl, ˈsɪklɪkəl/ *adj* [*more* ~; *most* ~] : happening again and again in the same order : happening in cycles • *cyclic* changes in the weather • the *cyclical* nature of history

– cy·cli·cal·ly /ˈsaɪklɪkli, ˈsɪklɪkli/ *adv* • These events occur *cyclically*.

cycling *noun* [*noncount*] : the sport or activity of riding a bicycle • My doctor recommends aerobic activities such as running, *cycling*, [=*biking, bicycling*] and swimming. • He does a lot of *cycling*. • *cycling* shorts • The town is within easy *cycling* distance.

cy·clone /ˈsaɪˌkloʊn/ *noun, pl* **-clones** [*count*]

1 : an extremely large, powerful, and destructive storm with very high winds that turn around an area of low pressure — compare ANTICYCLONE

2 *chiefly US* : TORNADO

– cy·clon·ic /saɪˈklɑːnɪk/ *adj* • *cyclonic* winds

Cy·clops /ˈsaɪˌklɑːps/ *noun* [*singular*] : a giant man in stories told by the ancient Greeks who had a single eye in the middle of his forehead

cyg·net /ˈsɪgnət/ *noun, pl* **-nets** [*count*] : a young swan

cyl·in·der /ˈsɪləndɚ/ *noun, pl* **-ders** [*count*]

1 : a shape that has straight sides and two circular ends — see picture at GEOMETRY

2 : something that is shaped like a cylinder: such as **a** : a tube in which a piston of an engine moves • a four-*cylinder* engine — see picture at ENGINE **b** : the part of a gun that turns and that holds the bullets • the *cylinder* of a revolver

on all cylinders informal : with the greatest possible amount of effort, power, or speed : at full capacity or speed • The economy is ***running on all cylinders*** • The team didn't seem to be ***firing/hitting on all cylinders***.

cy·lin·dri·cal /səˈlɪndrɪkəl/ *adj* [*more* ~; *most* ~] : shaped like a cylinder • a *cylindrical* oil tank • a *cylindrical* tower

cym·bal /ˈsɪmbəl/ *noun, pl* **-bals** [*count*] : a musical instrument in the form of a slightly curved thin metal plate that is played by hitting it with a drumstick or with another cymbal and that makes a very loud metallic sound — see picture at PERCUSSION

cyn·ic /ˈsɪnɪk/ *noun, pl* **-ics** [*count*] : a person who has negative opinions about other people and about the things people do • He's too much of a *cynic* to see the benefits of marriage.; *especially* : a person who believes that people are selfish and are only interested in helping themselves • A *cynic* might think that the governor visited the hospital just to gain votes. • Reporters who cover politics often become *cynics*.

cyn·i·cal /ˈsɪnɪkəl/ *adj* [*more* ~; *most* ~]

1 : believing that people are generally selfish and dishonest • *Cynical* people say there is no such thing as true love. • People are so *cynical* nowadays. • She's become more *cynical* in her old age. — often + *about* • He's *cynical about* marriage. • Many young people today are *cynical about* politics.

2 : selfish and dishonest in a way that shows no concern about treating other people fairly • Some people regard the governor's visit to the hospital as a *cynical* attempt to win votes. • We live in a cruel, *cynical* [=*uncaring*] world.

– cyn·i·cal·ly /ˈsɪnɪkli/ *adv* • The character talks *cynically* about love.

cyn·i·cism /ˈsɪnəˌsɪzəm/ *noun* [*noncount*] : cynical beliefs : beliefs that people are generally selfish and dishonest • Nothing could change her *cynicism* about politics.

cy·no·sure /ˈsaɪnəˌʃuɚ/ *noun, pl* **-sures** [*count*] *formal* : a person or thing that attracts a lot of attention or interest • She was the ***cynosure of all eyes*** [=everyone was looking at her] as she walked into the room.

cypher *chiefly Brit spelling of* CIPHER

cy•press /ˈsaɪprəs/ *noun, pl* **-press•es** [*count, noncount*] : a tall and narrow evergreen tree

cyst /ˈsɪst/ *noun, pl* **cysts** [*count*] *medical* : a growth filled with liquid that forms in or on your body • an ovarian *cyst* [=a cyst on a woman's ovary]

cys•tic fi•bro•sis /ˈsɪstɪkfaɪˈbrousəs/ *noun* [*noncount*] *medical* : a very serious disease that usually appears in young children and that makes it hard to breathe and to digest food properly

cys•ti•tis /sɪˈstaɪtəs/ *noun* [*noncount*] *medical* : infection of the bladder

cy•tol•o•gy /saɪˈtɑːləʤi/ *noun* [*noncount*] *biology* : the study of plant and animal cells
– **cy•tol•o•gist** /saɪˈtɑːləʤɪst/ *noun, pl* **-gists** [*count*]

czar *also* **tsar** *or* **tzar** /ˈzɑɚ/ *noun, pl* **czars** *also* **tsars** *or* **tzars** [*count*]
1 : the title of the ruler of Russia before 1917 • Russia's *Czar* Nicholas II
2 *chiefly US* **a** : a very powerful person in a particular business or activity • a banking *czar* **b** — used as an unofficial title for the person who is in charge of a government office or department • The President has appointed a new drug *czar*. • the education/housing/terrorism *czar*

cza•ri•na *also* **tsa•ri•na** *or* **tza•ri•na** /zɑˈriːnə/ *noun, pl* **-nas** [*count*] : the wife of a Russian czar

czar•ist *also* **tsar•ist** *or* **tzar•ist** /ˈzɑrɪst/ *adj* : of or relating to the government of Russia when it was controlled by czars • *czarist* Russia • the *czarist* capital of St. Petersburg

Czech /ˈʧɛk/ *noun, pl* **Czechs**
1 [*count*] : a person born, raised, or living in Czechoslovakia or the Czech Republic • the customs of the *Czechs*
2 [*noncount*] : the Slavic language of the Czechs • He learned to speak *Czech*.
– **Czech** *adj* • the *Czech* people/language

D

d *or* **D** /ˈdiː/ *noun, pl* **d's** *or* **ds** *or* **D's** *or* **Ds**
1 : the fourth letter of the English alphabet [*count*] Many people who are learning to read confuse b's and *d's*. [*noncount*] names that start with *d*
2 : a musical note or key referred to by the letter D : the second tone of a C-major scale [*count*] play/sing a *D* [*noncount*] The song is in the key of *D*.
3 [*count*] : a grade that is given to a student for doing poor work • She got a *D* on her chemistry test.
4 : the Roman numeral that means 500 • CD [=400]

d. *abbr* died • Thomas Jefferson, *d.* 1826

D *abbr* Democrat

'd /əd *after* t *or* d; d *elsewhere*/ — used as a contraction of *had, would,* and *did* • When they arrived, we'*d* [=we had] already left. • If you'*d* [=you would] like to learn more, go to our Web site. • Where'*d* [=where did] he go?

DA *abbr* district attorney

[1]**dab** /ˈdæb/ *verb* **dabs; dabbed; dab•bing**
1 : to lightly touch (something) usually with quick, small motions [+ *obj*] She *dabbed* [=*patted*] her eyes with a handkerchief. [*no obj*] — usually + *at* • He politely *dabbed at* the corners of his mouth with his napkin.
2 [+ *obj*] : to put something on something with quick, small motions • He *dabbed* [=*daubed*] a little paint on the canvas. • She was *dabbing* [=*daubing*] her lips with dark red lipstick.

[2]**dab** *noun, pl* **dabs** [*count*]
1 : a quick, small touch • She gave her eyes a few *dabs* [=*pats*] with a handkerchief.
2 : a small amount of something • a *dab* of paint • You've got a *dab* of ice cream on your shirt. • a *dab* of butter/perfume — see also DAB HAND, SMACK-DAB

dab•ble /ˈdæbəl/ *verb* **dab•bles; dab•bled; dab•bling**
1 [*no obj*] : to take part in an activity in a way that is not serious — usually + *in* • She works as an accountant but *dabbles in* poetry. • He *dabbled in* politics as a college student.
2 : to play or move around in water [*no obj*] The ducks *dabbled* in the stream. [+ *obj*] She sat by the pool, *dabbling* her feet in the cool water.
– **dab•bler** *noun, pl* **-blers** [*count*] • a *dabbler* in politics

dab hand *noun, pl* ~ **hands** [*count*] *Brit, informal* : a person who is very good at doing something : EXPERT • He's a *dab hand* at cooking. • She's a *dab hand* in the kitchen. • She's always been a *dab hand* with a paint brush.

da•cha /ˈdɑːʧə/ *noun, pl* **-chas** [*count*] : a small Russian house in the countryside that is used especially in the summer

dachs•hund /ˈdɑːksˌhʊnt, *Brit* ˈdæksənd/ *noun, pl* **-hunds** [*count*] : a small type of dog that has a long body, very short legs, and long ears — see picture at DOG

Da•cron /ˈdeɪˌkrɑːn, ˈdæˌkrɑːn/ *trademark* — used for a type of cloth or thread that is made from an artificial material

dad /ˈdæd/ *noun, pl* **dads** [*count*] *informal* : a person's father • Her mom and *dad* both said she can't go.— often used as a form of address • *Dad*, can I borrow the car tonight?

dad•dy /ˈdædi/ *noun, pl* **-dies** [*count*] *informal* : a person's father — used especially by young children • Where's my *daddy*?— often used as a form of address • *Daddy*, can you read me a story?— see also SUGAR DADDY

dad•dy long•legs /ˌdædiˈlɑːŋˌlegz/ *noun, pl* ~ **-legs** [*count*]
1 *US* : a small insect that looks like a spider and that has a small round body and long thin legs — see color picture on page C10
2 *Brit* : CRANE FLY

dae•mon /ˈdiːmən/ *noun, pl* **-mons** [*count*]
1 : a creature in ancient Greek stories that is more powerful than a person but not as powerful as a god
2 : DEMON 1 • angels and *daemons*

daf•fo•dil /ˈdæfəˌdɪl/ *noun, pl* **-dils** [*count*] : a yellow flower that blooms in the spring and that has a center that is shaped like a long tube — see color picture on page C6

daf•fy /ˈdæfi/ *adj* **daf•fi•er; -est** [*also more ~; most ~*] *US, informal* : silly or strange often in a way that is funny • The actress is starring in a *daffy* new comedy this summer. • The book is filled with *daffy* characters.

daft /ˈdæft, *Brit* ˈdɑːft/ *adj* **daft•er; -est** [*also more ~; most ~*] *Brit, informal*
1 : strange often in a way that is funny • He's got a *daft* [=*silly, daffy*] sense of humor.
2 : crazy or foolish • Don't be *daft*! • Your idea seems a bit *daft* to me. • She looked at us as if we'd gone *daft*.
(as) daft as a brush : very silly or somewhat crazy • The professor is perfectly nice but she's *daft as a brush*.
– **daft•ly** *adv* – **daft•ness** *noun* [*noncount*]

dag•ger /ˈdægɚ/ *noun, pl* **-gers** [*count*] : a sharp pointed knife that is used as a weapon
at daggers drawn *chiefly Brit* : angry and ready to fight • political parties that are *at daggers drawn* (with each other)
look/shoot/stare daggers at : to look at (someone) in an angry way • They *looked daggers at* each other across the table.— see also CLOAK-AND-DAGGER

da•go *or* **Da•go** /ˈdeɪgoʊ/ *noun, pl* **-gos** [*count*] *informal + offensive* : a person who is from Italy, Spain, or Portugal ✧ The word *dago* is very offensive and should be avoided.

da•guerre•o•type /dəˈgeroʊˌtaɪp/ *noun, pl* **-types** [*count*] : an old type of photograph that was made on a piece of silver or a piece of copper covered in silver

dahl•ia /ˈdæljə, *Brit* ˈdeɪljə/ *noun, pl* **-ias** [*count*] : a type of plant that is grown in gardens and has large flowers with white, yellow, red, pink, or purple petals

[1]**dai•ly** /ˈdeɪli/ *adj, always used before a noun*
1 : happening, done, made, used, or existing every day • Television has become a part of our *daily* [=*day-to-day*] lives. • It has changed every aspect of *daily* life/existence. • I started eating healthier and added exercise to my *daily* routine/

schedule. ▪ *daily* activities such as eating breakfast and washing your face ▪ There's not enough water to meet the *daily* needs of the city's people. ▪ *daily* commuters ▪ He visits them ***on a daily basis***. [=every day] ▪ people working to earn their ***daily bread*** [=the food they need each day]
2 : published every day or every day except Sunday ▪ *daily* newspapers ▪ She reads the *daily* paper each morning.
3 : of or relating to one day ▪ Their average *daily* wage is only five dollars. ▪ She had been taking more than the recommended *daily* dose of the medicine. ▪ Our *daily* lunch specials [=the special lunch items offered on particular days of the week] are listed on the back of the menu.
– **daily** *adv* ▪ Take one pill/capsule twice *daily*. [=two times every day] ▪ The Web site is updated *daily*. [=every day]

[2]**daily** *noun, pl* **dai·lies**
1 [*count*] : a newspaper that is published every day or every day except Sunday ▪ the city's two largest *dailies*
2 dailies [*plural*] *US* : the first prints of a movie showing the scenes that are filmed each day ▪ The director watches the *dailies* [=*rushes*] every evening.
3 [*count*] *Brit, old-fashioned* : a person who you pay to clean your house and do other jobs for you every day — called also *daily help*

dain·ty /ˈdeɪnti/ *adj* **dain·ti·er; -est** [*also more ~; most ~*]
1 : small and pretty ▪ Her hair was decorated with *dainty* pink flowers. ▪ the girl's *dainty* little hands ▪ *dainty* teacups
2 : done with small and careful movements ▪ The dancers' *dainty* steps were followed by a series of leaps. ▪ She took a *dainty* sip of tea from her teacup.
3 *of food* : attractive and served in small amounts ▪ They served *dainty* sandwiches on silver trays. ▪ The food was served in *dainty* portions.
– **dain·ti·ly** *adv* ▪ She sipped *daintily* from her teacup.
– **dain·ti·ness** *noun* [*noncount*] ▪ He commented on the *daintiness* of my hands.

dai·qui·ri /ˈdækəri, ˈdaɪkəri/ *noun, pl* **-ris** [*count*] : an alcoholic drink that is usually made of rum, crushed fruit or fruit juice, and sugar ▪ frozen strawberry *daiquiris*

[1]**dairy** /ˈderi/ *noun, pl* **dair·ies** [*count*]
1 : a farm that produces milk
2 : a place where milk is kept and butter or cheese is made
3 : a company that sells milk and foods made from milk (such as butter and cheese)

[2]**dairy** *adj, always used before a noun*
1 : made from milk ▪ *dairy* products/foods such as cheese and ice cream : relating to foods made from milk ▪ You'll find yogurt in the *dairy* section of the grocery store.
2 : of or relating to a type of farming that deals with the production of milk and foods made from milk ▪ *dairy* farms/farmers ▪ *dairy* cows/cattle [=cows that are raised to produce milk] ▪ the *dairy* industry

dairy·ing /ˈderijɪŋ/ *noun* [*noncount*] : the business of managing a farm or company that produces or sells milk and foods made from milk

dairy·maid /ˈderiˌmeɪd/ *noun, pl* **-maids** [*count*] *old-fashioned* : a woman who works in a dairy

dairy·man /ˈderimən/ *noun, pl* **-men** /-mən/ [*count*] : a man who manages or works in a dairy

da·is /ˈdejəs/ *noun, pl* **-is·es** [*count*] : a raised platform in a large room or hall that people stand on when performing or speaking to an audience

dai·sy /ˈdeɪzi/ *noun, pl* **-sies** [*count*] : a type of white flower that has a yellow center
be pushing up daisies *informal + humorous* : to be dead ▪ We'll all *be pushing up daisies* by the time the government balances the budget.

daisy chain *noun, pl* **~ chains** [*count*]
1 : a string of daisies that you make by tying the stems together ▪ She wore a *daisy chain* around her neck.
2 : a group of things or people that are connected in a series ▪ a *daisy chain* of electronic devices ▪ The children linked arms forming a *daisy chain*.

Da·lai La·ma /ˌdɑːlaɪˈlɑːmə, *Brit* ˌdælaɪˈlɑːmə/ *noun, pl* **~ -mas** [*count*] : the spiritual leader of Tibetan Buddhism

dale /ˈdeɪl/ *noun, pl* **dales** [*count*] *old-fashioned* : VALLEY ▪ the beautiful hills and *dales* of our county

dal·li·ance /ˈdælijəns/ *noun, pl* **-anc·es** [*count*]
1 : an action that is not serious — often + *with* ▪ After a brief *dalliance with* acting, she pursued a law career.
2 *literary* : a romantic or sexual relationship that is brief and not serious ▪ He had *dalliances* [=(more commonly) *affairs*, (less formally) *flings*] with several women before he met his wife. ▪ sexual *dalliances*

dal·ly /ˈdæli/ *verb* **dal·lies; dal·lied; dal·ly·ing** [*no obj*] : to do something slowly or too slowly ▪ Don't *dally* [=*dawdle*] on the way home. ▪ Please don't *dally*. We need you here right away. ▪ The two of us *dallied* over our coffee that morning. — see also DILLYDALLY
dally with [*phrasal verb*] **1 *dally with (something)*** : to do or think about (something) in a way that is not serious ▪ He's been *dallying* [=*toying*] *with* the idea of running for office. **2 *dally with (someone)*** *old-fashioned* : to have a casual romantic or sexual relationship with (someone) ▪ a married man who has been *dallying with* another woman

dal·ma·tian *or* **Dal·ma·tian** /dælˈmeɪʃən/ *noun, pl* **-tians** [*count*] : a type of dog that has short white fur with many black or brown spots

[1]**dam** /ˈdæm/ *noun, pl* **dams** [*count*] : a structure that is built across a river or stream to stop water from flowing ▪ The government has plans to build a *dam* and flood the valley. ▪ There's a ***beaver dam*** [=a dam built by beavers] in the stream behind my house. — compare [3]DAM

[2]**dam** *verb* **dams; dammed; dam·ming** [+ *obj*] : to build a dam across (a river or stream) ▪ Beavers *dammed* the stream. — often + *up* ▪ They created a reservoir by *damming up* the river.

[3]**dam** *noun, pl* **dams** [*count*] *technical* : the female parent of some animals (such as horses) ▪ the foal's *dam* — compare [1]SIRE — compare [1]DAM

[1]**dam·age** /ˈdæmɪʤ/ *noun, pl* **dam·ag·es**
1 [*noncount*] : physical harm that is done to something or to someone's body ▪ The items were carefully wrapped to protect them from *damage* during shipping. ▪ The city sustained heavy *damage* during the war. ▪ water/sun/frost *damage* = *damage* caused by water/sun/frost ▪ Fortunately the boat suffered no serious *damage* in the storm. ▪ The fall caused/did considerable/extensive/severe *damage* to her knee. ▪ The disease is known to cause permanent/irreversible brain/liver/kidney *damage*. ▪ Few people were hurt during the storm, but ***property damage*** was great. [=many houses, cars, etc., were damaged or ruined] — see also COLLATERAL DAMAGE
2 [*noncount*] : emotional harm that is done to someone ▪ Traumatic events can cause serious psychological *damage*. [=can make someone mentally or emotionally unhealthy]
3 [*noncount*] : problems that are caused by a mistake, wrong action, etc. : bad or harmful effects on a situation, a person's reputation, etc. ▪ The scandal caused significant *damage* to her career. ▪ You've said enough. Please leave before you do any more *damage*. ▪ He tried to repair the *damage* by apologizing, but it was too late. ▪ He apologized, but the *damage* was already done.
4 *damages* [*plural*] *law* : an amount of money that a court requires you to pay to someone you have treated unfairly or hurt in some way ▪ The judge awarded her $5,000 ***in damages***. [=the judge said that the people who hurt her must pay her $5,000] — sometimes used in the form ***damage*** before another noun ▪ She won a $5,000 *damage* award.
5 *the damage* *informal* : the amount of money that something costs ▪ "***What's the damage?***" he asked the mechanic.
damage control *or Brit* ***damage limitation*** : things that are done or said to prevent a bad situation from becoming worse or to limit the bad effect of something ▪ The governor keeps making outrageous statements, forcing his staff to spend most of their time doing *damage control*.

[2]**damage** *verb* **damages; dam·aged; dam·ag·ing** [+ *obj*] : to cause damage to (something): such as **a** : to physically harm (something) ▪ Please return any items that are *damaged* during shipping. ▪ Many homes were *damaged* or completely destroyed in the fire. ▪ The fall severely *damaged* her knee. ▪ Smoking can seriously *damage* your lungs. ▪ badly *damaged* property ***synonyms*** see INJURE **b** : to cause problems in or for (something) : to have a bad effect on (a situation, a person's reputation, etc.) ▪ The scandal significantly *damaged* her career. ▪ This news will undoubtedly *damage* the governor's reputation. ▪ He was worried that his comments had seriously *damaged* their relationship. ▪ He's trying to repair his *damaged* reputation. — see also DAMAGED GOODS

damaged goods *noun* [*plural*]
1 : products that are broken, cracked, scratched, etc.
2 *informal* : a person who is considered to be no longer desirable or valuable because of something that has happened : a person whose reputation is damaged ✧ This sense of

damaged goods is used with a singular verb. ▪ She hasn't been charged with a crime, but politically she's *damaged goods* and will never get elected.

damaging *adj* [*more* ~; *most* ~] : causing or able to cause damage ▪ the *damaging* effects of the sun on your skin ▪ The storm may produce *damaging* winds. ▪ The chemical is *damaging* to the lungs. [=it will make a person's lungs less healthy] ▪ He says he has *damaging* information about the candidate. ▪ The evidence was very *damaging* to their case.

dam·ask /ˈdæməsk/ *noun, pl* **-asks** [*count, noncount*] : a thick usually shiny cloth that has patterns woven into it
– **damask** *adj* ▪ *damask* curtains ▪ The tablecloth is *damask*.

dame /ˈdeɪm/ *noun, pl* **dames** [*count*]
1 *US slang, old-fashioned* : WOMAN ▪ She's one classy *dame*. ▪ a dignified old *dame* ✧ *Dame* is sometimes used to refer to a woman in an offensive or negative way. ▪ He married some rich *dame* for her money. ▪ "Who's the *dame*?" he asked rudely.
2 *Brit* : a woman who has been given a title as an honor for something she has done ▪ She was made/created a *dame* the year before she died. — used as a title ▪ *Dame* Myra Hess — see also GRANDE DAME

dam·mit /ˈdæmət/ *informal + impolite* — used in writing to represent the sound of the phrase *damn it*
as near as dammit see [1]NEAR

[1]**damn** /ˈdæm/ *interj, informal + impolite* — used to show that you are angry, annoyed, surprised, etc. ▪ *Damn*! That really hurt! ▪ Well, *damn*. Why didn't you say you wouldn't be able to come? ▪ *Damn*! I had no idea you were planning a party for me!

[2]**damn** *verb* **damns; damned; damn·ing** [+ *obj*]
1 *informal + impolite* **a** — used to show that you are angry or annoyed at a person, thing, or situation ▪ *Damn* them! They've ruined everything! ▪ *Damn* this rain. We haven't had a nice day in weeks. ▪ ***Damn it!*** I forgot my keys! ▪ ***Damn it all!*** **b** — used to say in a forceful way that you do not care about something ▪ I'm going to do it, *damn* the consequences. = I'm going to do it, the consequences ***be damned***. [=I'm going to do it despite the possible consequences]
2 : to send (someone) to hell as punishment after death — usually used as *(be) damned* ▪ He said that they would *be damned* (to hell) for all eternity. [=that God would force them to be in hell forever] — sometimes used figuratively ▪ She *was damned* [=(more commonly) *doomed*] by her own lack of foresight.
3 : to say or think bad things about (someone or something) : to strongly criticize (someone or something) ▪ He *damned* them for their stupidity.
as near as damn it see [1]NEAR
damn with faint praise : to give praise without enthusiasm in a way that shows you really dislike someone or something
I'll be damned *informal + impolite* **1** — used to show that you are very surprised about something ▪ Well *I'll be damned*! Our team actually won! — often + *if* ▪ I spent an hour putting the machine together and *I'll be damned if* it didn't fall apart as soon as I tried to use it. [=I was very surprised that it fell apart] — sometimes shortened to ***damned if*** ▪ I told them they wouldn't enjoy the trip but *damned if* they didn't come anyway. **2** — used to say that you cannot or will not do something; + *if* ▪ *I'll be damned if* I can remember where I left my keys. [=I cannot remember where I left my keys] ▪ *I'll be damned if* I'm going to eat any more of that disgusting food. [=I will not eat any more of it]
the damned : the people who have been sent to hell as punishment after their death ▪ the souls of *the damned*
(you're) damned if you do and damned if you don't *informal* — used to say that you will be blamed or considered wrong no matter what you do
– **damning** *adj* [*more* ~; *most* ~] ▪ A *damning* piece of evidence showed that he had been at the crime scene.

[3]**damn** *noun* [*singular*] *informal + impolite* : anything at all — usually used in negative statements ▪ This computer's ***not worth a damn***. [=it has no value; it is worthless] ▪ His promises ***don't mean a damn***. [=don't mean anything] — see also TINKER'S DAMN
give a damn *also* ***care a damn*** : to care at all about someone or something — used in negative statements ▪ He doesn't *give a damn* what people think about him. ▪ Nobody *gives a damn* about us. ▪ I don't want to hear about her problems. I just don't *give a damn*. ▪ They don't seem to *care a damn* about their future.

[4]**damn** *also* **damned** *adj, always used before a noun, informal + impolite*
1 — used to show that you are angry, annoyed, surprised, etc. ▪ Turn the *damn* TV off and listen to me! ▪ The *damned* car won't start again. ▪ That's none of your *damn* business. ▪ The *damn* thing never worked right.
2 — used to make a statement more forceful ▪ If you believe that, you're a *damn/damned* fool. ▪ It's a *damn* shame that she couldn't afford to go to college. ▪ She's a *damned* liar! ▪ There's not a *damn* thing you can do about it. [=you cannot do anything about it] — see also DAMNEDEST

[5]**damn** *also* **damned** *adv, informal + impolite* : very or extremely ▪ That was a *damn* good movie. ▪ You did a *damned* fine job on that project. ▪ You'd better make *damn* sure that it doesn't happen again. ▪ "You seem angry." "You're *damn* right I am! That's for *damn* sure!" ▪ Some people just talk too *damn* much. [=talk far too much] ▪ The idea's pretty *damn* smart, if you ask me. ▪ He ***damn near*** killed us! [=he almost killed us] ▪ You know ***damn well*** what happened. ▪ You *damn well* better finish the job. [=you must finish the job] ▪ He does whatever he *damn/damned well* pleases. [=he does whatever he wants to do] — see also DAMNEDEST

dam·na·ble /ˈdæmnəbəl/ *adj* [*more* ~; *most* ~] *old-fashioned* : deserving strong criticism : very bad, wrong, annoying, etc. ▪ *damnable* lies ▪ *damnable* stupidity
– **dam·na·bly** /ˈdæmnəbli/ *adv* ▪ *damnably* difficult

dam·na·tion /dæmˈneɪʃən/ *noun* [*noncount*] : the state of being in hell as punishment after death ▪ The minister spoke about death and *damnation*. ▪ living in eternal *damnation*

[1]**damned·est** /ˈdæmdəst/ *adj, always used before a noun, chiefly US, informal + impolite* : most unusual or surprising ▪ It was the *damnedest* [=(more politely) *darnedest*] thing you ever saw. ▪ He said the *damnedest* thing the other day.

[2]**damnedest** *noun*
do your damnedest *or* ***try your damnedest*** *chiefly US, informal + impolite* : to try very hard to do something ▪ He's *doing his damnedest* to win. ▪ I'll *try my damnedest* [=*hardest, best*] to be there on time.

Damocles
sword of Damocles see SWORD

[1]**damp** /ˈdæmp/ *adj* **damp·er; -est** [*also more* ~; *most* ~] : somewhat or slightly wet ▪ Wipe up the mess with a *damp* cloth. ▪ Her forehead was *damp* with perspiration. ▪ My hair's still *damp* from the rain. ▪ a *damp* spring day ▪ *damp* [=*humid*] weather ***synonyms*** see MOIST
damp squib see SQUIB
– **damp·ness** *noun* [*noncount*]

[2]**damp** *noun* [*noncount*] : slight wetness in the air ▪ The books from her basement still smelled of *damp*. [=*dampness*] ▪ The boxes were left outside in the *damp*. ▪ the *damp* of the night

[3]**damp** *verb* **damps; damped; damp·ing** [+ *obj*]
1 : to make (something) somewhat or slightly wet : DAMPEN ▪ His hands were *damped* with sweat.
2 : to make (something) less strong or active ▪ Nothing could *damp* [=(more commonly) *dampen, depress*] his spirits.

damp·en /ˈdæmpən/ *verb* **-ens; -ened; -en·ing** [+ *obj*]
1 : to make (something) somewhat or slightly wet : to make (something) damp ▪ *Dampen* the spot with a wet cloth. ▪ The shower barely *dampened* the ground.
2 : to make (something) less strong or active ▪ We wouldn't let the bad weather *dampen* our excitement/enthusiasm/spirits. ▪ The experience *dampened* her interest [=made her less interested] in becoming a doctor.

damp·en·er /ˈdæmpənɚ/ *noun, pl* **-ers** [*count*] : something that reduces the force or effect of something ▪ a noise *dampener*
put a dampener on *Brit* : to make (something) less strong, active, or exciting : to put a damper on (something) ▪ His bad mood *put a dampener on* the celebration.

damp·er /ˈdæmpɚ/ *noun, pl* **-ers** [*count*]
1 : a flat piece of metal in a fireplace, furnace, etc., that controls the amount of air that can enter ▪ Close the *damper*.
2 : a small piece of wood inside a piano that is covered with cloth and that stops the movement of a piano string
put a damper on : to make (something) less strong, active, or exciting ▪ His bad mood *put a damper on* the celebration. ▪ The rain *put a damper on* our plans for a picnic. ▪ He was *putting* a bit of *a damper on* her spirits.

dam·sel /ˈdæmzəl/ *noun, pl* **-sels** [*count*] *old-fashioned* : a young woman who is not married ✧ The phrase ***damsel in distress*** is used often humorously in modern speech and writing to refer to a woman who needs to be rescued. ▪ The

D

novel comes complete with a knight in shining armor and a *damsel in distress.*

[1]**dance** /ˈdæns, *Brit* ˈdɑːns/ *verb* **danc·es; danced; danc·ing**

1 a [*no obj*] **:** to move your body in a way that goes with the rhythm and style of music that is being played ▪ He never learned how to *dance.* ▪ She has always loved to *dance.* ▪ I like the song but it's really hard to *dance* to. ▪ Would you like to *dance* with me? = (more formally) Shall we *dance*? ▪ We ***danced the night away.*** [=we danced the entire evening] **b** [+ *obj*] **:** to move with and guide (someone) as music plays **:** to dance with (someone) ▪ He *danced* her across the floor.
2 [+ *obj*] **:** to perform (a particular type of dance) ▪ *dancing* the waltz/polka/twist
3 [*no obj*] **:** to perform as a dancer ▪ She *dances* with a famous ballet company. ▪ She's a great actress, and she can *dance* and sing, too.
4 [*no obj*] **:** to move quickly up and down, from side to side, etc. ▪ We *danced* for joy when we heard the news. ▪ He sat watching the leaves *dancing* in the breeze. ▪ The boxer *danced* around his opponent.
dance to someone's tune **:** to do what someone wants or forces you to do ▪ The boss has got everyone *dancing to her tune.* ▪ The senators are *dancing to the tune of* the President.
– danc·er *noun, pl* **-ers** [*count*] ▪ I'm a terrible *dancer.* ▪ ballet *dancers* **– dancing** *adj* ▪ We're taking *dancing* lessons. ▪ *dancing* shoes **– dancing** *noun* [*noncount*] ▪ They went out for dinner and *dancing.* ▪ She's always loved *dancing.* ▪ Would you like to ***go dancing*** tonight? — see also BALLROOM DANCING, BREAK DANCING, LAP DANCING

[2]**dance** *noun, pl* **dances**

1 [*count*] **:** a series of movements that are done as music is playing **:** a way of dancing ▪ a slow *dance* ▪ They can do all the popular *dances.* ▪ The only *dance* he knows how to do is the twist. — often used before another noun ▪ a *dance* move ▪ *dance* classes ▪ It's the latest *dance* craze. — see also BARN DANCE, BELLY DANCE, LINE DANCE, SQUARE DANCE, TAP DANCE, WAR DANCE
2 [*count*] **:** an act of dancing ▪ How about one more *dance*? ▪ He stopped right in the middle of the *dance* to tie his shoe. ▪ Will you save a *dance* for me? [=will you dance with me during one song?] ▪ He did a celebration *dance* in the end zone after scoring the touchdown.
3 [*noncount*] **:** the art or activity of dancing ▪ She studied *dance* in college.
4 [*count*] **:** a social event at which people dance ▪ The church held a *dance* to raise money. ▪ Your father and I met at a *dance.* ▪ high school *dances*
5 [*count*] **:** a song or piece of music (such as a waltz) to which people dance ▪ The band can play all sorts of *dances.* — see also SONG AND DANCE
lead someone a (merry) dance see [1]LEAD

dance·able /ˈdænsəbəl, *Brit* ˈdɑːnsəbəl/ *adj* [*more* ~; *most* ~] **:** able to be used for dancing **:** having a rhythm and style that people can dance to ▪ a *danceable* song

dance card *noun, pl* ~ **cards** [*count*] *old-fashioned* **:** a card on which you write the names of people you are going to dance with at a social event — often used figuratively ▪ Her *dance card* has been filling up quickly. [=she has been busy going to parties, on dates, etc.]

dance floor *noun, pl* ~ **floors** [*count*] **:** an area where people can dance inside a restaurant, club, hall, etc.

dance hall *noun, pl* ~ **halls** [*count*] **:** a large building or room in which people pay to go dancing ▪ Their song is being played in *dance halls* across the country.

dan·de·li·on /ˈdændəˌlajən/ *noun, pl* **-ons** [*count*] **:** a very common wild plant that has bright yellow flowers

dan·der /ˈdændɚ/ *noun*

get someone's dander up *informal* **:** to cause someone to become angry ▪ Her rudeness really *got my dander up.*

dan·dle /ˈdændəl/ *verb* **dan·dles; dan·dled; dan·dling** [+ *obj*] *chiefly Brit* **:** to move (a baby) up and down in your arms or on your knee as a way of playing ▪ He was sitting in a corner *dandling* [=*bouncing*] his baby daughter on his knee.

dan·druff /ˈdændrəf/ *noun* [*noncount*] **:** very small white pieces of dead skin that form especially on a person's head ▪ The shampoo is supposed to help control *dandruff.*

[1]**dan·dy** /ˈdændi/ *adj* **dan·di·er; -est** *chiefly US, informal* + *somewhat old-fashioned* **:** very good ▪ This looks like a *dandy* [=*fine, splendid*] place to have lunch. ▪ We thought something was wrong, but he said everything was just ***fine and dandy.***

[2]**dandy** *noun, pl* **-dies** [*count*]

1 *old-fashioned* **:** a man who cares too much about his clothing and personal appearance
2 *chiefly US, informal* **:** something that is very good or impressive **:** a very good example of something ▪ Have you seen the new boat? It's a *dandy.* [=(more commonly) *beauty*] ▪ That was a *dandy* of a game.
– dan·dy·ish /ˈdændijɪʃ/ *adj, old-fashioned* ▪ He had a *dandyish* manner about him.

Dane /ˈdeɪn/ *noun, pl* **Danes** [*count*] **:** a person born, raised, or living in Denmark — see also GREAT DANE

[1]**dang** /ˈdæŋ/ *interj, US, informal* — used as a more polite form of *damn* ▪ *Dang*! That hurt! ▪ *Dang*! She sure looked surprised, didn't she?

[2]**dang** *verb, US, informal* — used as a more polite form of *damn* ▪ *Dang* them! They're late again! ▪ ***Dang it.*** It's raining! ▪ ***I'll be danged!*** You found it!

[3]**dang** *also* **danged** *adj, US, informal* — used as a more polite form of *damn* or *damned* ▪ Those *dang* kids stepped on our flowers! ▪ a *dang/danged* fool ▪ The whole *dang* city knows now. ▪ There's not a *dang* thing you can do about it.
– dang *also* **danged** *adv* ▪ What's so *dang/danged* funny, huh? ▪ She's too *dang* skinny. ▪ You know ***dang well*** where the key is. [=I am certain that you know where it is]

dan·ger /ˈdeɪnʤɚ/ *noun, pl* **-gers**

1 a [*noncount*] **:** the possibility that you will be hurt or killed ▪ I was unaware of the *danger* that lay ahead. ▪ She was fearless in the face of *danger.* ▪ None of us had any real sense of *danger.* [=we did not think that we might be hurt or killed] ▪ It was a journey fraught with *danger.* [=a very dangerous journey] ▪ Patients need to be informed about the *danger* posed by the drug. [=about the ways the drug could possibly hurt them] ▪ The sign on the door read "*Danger.* Keep out." ▪ Their lives are ***in*** (grave/great/serious) ***danger.*** ▪ We're not ***out of danger*** yet. [=there is still a chance that we could be hurt or killed] **b :** the possibility that something unpleasant or bad will happen [*noncount*] There's less *danger* that you'll lose your money if you have a wide variety of investments. ▪ We're all ***in danger*** of losing our jobs. [=we may all lose our jobs] ▪ These animals are *in danger* of becoming extinct. = They are *in danger* of extinction. ▪ (*humorous*) Don't worry about being ready for us by noon. There's no *danger* [=no chance] that we'll actually be there on time. [*singular*] There's a *danger* that your apology will be taken as a sign of weakness. ▪ The *danger* is that we'll become careless as the process becomes more familiar. ✧ A ***danger zone*** is a place or situation in which you may be hurt or killed or in which something unpleasant or bad may happen. ▪ The doctor warned that too much exertion could push my heart rate into the *danger zone.* ▪ The houses are in a *danger zone* for wildfires. [=an area in which wildfires sometimes happen]
2 [*count*] **:** a person or thing that is likely to cause injury, pain, harm, or loss ▪ It's important to teach your children about the *dangers* of smoking. ▪ Here is a list of possible *dangers* associated with the procedure. ▪ We believe it poses a serious *danger* to our national security. ▪ He is a *danger* to himself and others. [=he might hurt himself and other people]

danger money *noun* [*noncount*] *Brit* **:** HAZARD PAY

dan·ger·ous /ˈdeɪnʤərəs/ *adj* [*more* ~; *most* ~]

1 : involving possible injury, harm, or death **:** characterized by danger ▪ Mining is *dangerous* [=*hazardous*] work. ▪ They complained to their boss about the *dangerous* [=*unsafe*] working conditions. ▪ She got into a car accident while driving through a *dangerous* intersection. ▪ He often drives at *dangerous* speeds. ▪ The city can be a *dangerous* place to live. ▪ *dangerous* neighborhoods — often + *to* ▪ Smoking is *dangerous* [=*hazardous*] *to* your health.
2 : able or likely to cause injury, pain, harm, etc. ▪ The storms may cause *dangerous* flooding. ▪ He is wanted for assault with a *dangerous* weapon. ▪ *dangerous* animals ▪ the most *dangerous* of drugs ▪ a *dangerous* enemy ▪ The police say that the man is ***armed and dangerous.*** [=he has a gun and he might try to shoot someone]
dangerous ground/territory **:** a situation in which you may do or say something that will have a bad result, make people angry, etc. ▪ As the conversation turned to politics, I knew we were heading into *dangerous territory.* ▪ You know you're treading on *dangerous ground,* don't you?
– dan·ger·ous·ly *adv* ▪ She suddenly became *dangerously* ill. ▪ *dangerously* high levels of pollution ▪ They came *dangerously* close to being caught. ▪ He has always enjoyed living *dangerously.* **– dan·ger·ous·ness** *noun* [*noncount*]

danger pay *noun* [*noncount*] *US* **:** HAZARD PAY

dan·gle /ˈdæŋgəl/ *verb* **dan·gles; dan·gled; dan·gling**
1 : to hang down loosely especially in a way that makes it possible to swing freely [*no obj*] Let your arms *dangle* at your sides. ▪ *dangling* earrings — often + *from* ▪ Diamonds and pearls *dangled from* her ears. ▪ Wires were *dangling* dangerously *from* the ceiling. ▪ A cigarette *dangled from* his lips. [+ *obj*] She sat on the edge of the pool, *dangling* her feet in the water. ▪ He *dangled* a piece of string in front of the cat.
2 [+ *obj*] *informal* **:** to offer (something) in order to persuade someone to do something ▪ The money she ***dangled in front of him*** wasn't enough to convince him to sell. ▪ They refused to accept the money that was ***dangled before their eyes***.
leave someone dangling *also* ***keep someone dangling*** *informal* **:** to force someone to be in an uncertain position or to wait for a decision ▪ We were *kept dangling* for weeks while the bank reviewed our loan application.

[1]**Dan·ish** /ˈdeɪnɪʃ/ *adj* **:** of or relating to Denmark, its people, or their language ▪ the *Danish* countryside ▪ *Danish* customs ▪ She knows a few *Danish* phrases.

[2]**Danish** *noun, pl* **Danish** *also* **Dan·ish·es**
1 [*noncount*] **:** the language of the Danes
2 *US* **:** DANISH PASTRY [*noncount*] We had cheese *Danish* for breakfast. [*count*] two raspberry *Danish/Danishes*

Danish pastry *noun, pl* **~ -tries** [*count, noncount*] **:** a sweet pastry that often has fruit, icing, etc., on top — see picture at BAKING

dank /ˈdæŋk/ *adj* **dank·er; -est :** wet and cold in a way that is unpleasant ▪ a dark *dank* cave ***synonyms*** see MOIST

dap·per /ˈdæpɚ/ *adj* [*more ~; most ~*] *somewhat old-fashioned*
1 : having a neat appearance **:** dressed in attractive clothes ▪ The students all looked very *dapper* in their uniforms. ▪ a *dapper* old gentleman
2 *of clothing* **:** attractive and of high quality ▪ a *dapper* [=*smart*] suit

dap·pled /ˈdæpəld/ *also* **dap·ple** /ˈdæpəl/ *adj* [*more ~; most ~*] **:** marked with many spots of color or light ▪ a *dappled* gray horse ▪ *dappled* shade

[1]**dare** /ˈdeɚ/ *verb* **dares; dared; dar·ing**
1 [*no obj*] **:** to have enough courage or confidence to do something **:** to not be too afraid to do something ▪ Try it if you *dare*. ▪ We wanted to laugh but didn't *dare*. — often followed by *to + verb* ▪ We didn't *dare to stop*. ▪ No one *dared to say* anything. ▪ It was more than I had *dared to hope* for. ▪ She won their respect by *daring to ask* questions. — often followed by an infinitive verb without *to* ▪ We didn't *dare stop*. = We *dared* not *stop*. ▪ No one *dared say* anything. ▪ It was more than I had *dared hope* for. ▪ I need to know, but I don't *dare ask*. ▪ I wouldn't *dare do* it alone. = (*formal*) I *dare not* do it alone. ▪ Do we *dare* ask why? = *Dare* we ask why?
2 [+ *obj*] **:** to do (something that is difficult or that people are usually afraid to do) ▪ The actress *dared* a new interpretation of the classic role.
3 [+ *obj*] **:** to tell (someone) to do something especially as a way of showing courage ▪ She *dared* him to dive off the bridge. ▪ She *dared* me to ask him out on a date. I did, and he said yes.
don't you dare — used in speech to forcefully tell someone not to do something ▪ *Don't you dare* do that again, or you'll be sorry! ▪ "I'm going to tell mom that you got an 'F' on your test." "*Don't you dare!*"
how dare you — used in speech to show that you are angry about what someone has done or said ▪ *How dare you* touch me! ▪ *How dare he* speak to you like that!
I dare say *or chiefly Brit* ***I daresay*** *somewhat formal + old-fashioned* — used when you are stating your opinion about something ▪ *I dare say* he's right. ▪ This is, *I dare say*, one of the most beautiful places in the world.

[2]**dare** *noun, pl* **dares** [*count*] **:** the act of telling someone to do something as a way of showing courage — usually singular ▪ He dared her to go, but she refused to take/accept the *dare*. ▪ (*US*) He jumped from the bridge ***on a dare***. = (*Brit*) He jumped from the bridge ***for a dare***. [=someone dared him to jump from the bridge]

dare·dev·il /ˈdeɚˌdɛvl/ *noun, pl* **-ils** [*count*] **:** a person who does dangerous things especially in order to get attention ▪ He has always been a bit of a *daredevil*.
– daredevil *adj, always used before a noun* ▪ a *daredevil* driver/pilot

daren't /ˈderənt/ *chiefly Brit* — used as a contraction of *dare not* or *dared not* ▪ I *daren't* tell her what really happened.

dare·say /ˌdeɚˈseɪ/ *verb*
I daresay see [1]DARE

[1]**daring** *adj* [*more ~; most ~*]
1 : willing to do dangerous or difficult things ▪ a *daring* reporter who has covered several wars ▪ She's a *daring* innovator in the field of biotechnology.
2 : showing a lack of fear ▪ Emergency crews quickly planned a *daring* [=*bold*] rescue to get the people out of the burning building. ▪ a *daring* plan to steal the famous painting ▪ She decided to wear a *daring* dress to the party. ▪ ideas that are new and *daring* ▪ the artist's *daring* use of color
– dar·ing·ly /ˈderɪŋli/ *adv* ▪ a *daringly* original idea

[2]**daring** *noun* [*noncount*] **:** the quality of being willing to do dangerous or difficult things **:** courage or fearlessness ▪ Skydiving requires both skill and *daring*. ▪ He performs the trick with the *daring* of a stuntman.

[1]**dark** /ˈdɑɚk/ *adj* **dark·er; -est** [*also more ~; most ~*]
1 : having very little or no light ▪ She sat in the *dark* room alone. ▪ It gets *dark* early in winter. [=the sun sets early; night comes sooner] ▪ It's getting *darker* outside. ▪ Soon it will be *dark* enough to see the stars. ▪ It was a *dark* and stormy night. ▪ Suddenly the room ***went dark***. [=suddenly there was no light in the room] — opposite LIGHT
2 : not light in color **:** of a color that is closer to black than white ▪ *Dark* clouds of smoke were coming from the windows. ▪ She's wearing a *dark* suit to the interview. ▪ a man wearing *dark* clothing ▪ You've got *dark* circles under your eyes this morning. ▪ *dark* spots/lines on the skin
3 *of a color* **:** having more black than white **:** not light ▪ *dark* blue ▪ a *dark* green shirt — opposite LIGHT
4 *of a person's hair, eyes, skin, etc.* **:** black or brown in color ▪ a person with a *dark* complexion = a *dark*-skinned person ▪ He is tall, *dark*, and handsome. [=he is a tall, handsome man with dark hair and eyes] — opposite FAIR
5 : less light in color than other things of the same kind ▪ *dark* rum ▪ *dark* roasted coffee beans — see also DARK CHOCOLATE, DARK MEAT
6 : lacking hope or happiness ▪ She had a rather *dark* [=*gloomy, dismal*] view of the future. ▪ I met her during a very *dark* time in my life. ▪ These are *dark* days for many companies.
7 : bad or evil ▪ The movie follows three heroes who fight the *dark* forces/powers that threaten the world. ▪ his *darker* side = the *darker* side of his personality ▪ He told no one his deep, *dark* secret. ▪ Drowning is his *darkest* [=*worst*] fear.
8 : dealing with unpleasant subjects such as crime, war, unhappy relationships, etc. ▪ a *dark* [=*black*] comedy about drug abuse ▪ *dark* humor ▪ It's a good movie, but it's really *dark*.
9 : full of mystery ▪ the government's *dark* secrets — see also DARK HORSE
10 *of a place* **:** not known or explored because it is far from where most people live ▪ the *darkest* regions of the continent
11 *of a voice* **:** low and full in sound ▪ his deep, *dark* voice
cast a dark cloud see [1]CLOUD
darkest hour see HOUR
– dark·ish /ˈdɑɚkɪʃ/ *adj* [*more ~; most ~*] ▪ Her hair was a *darkish* red color.

[2]**dark** *noun, pl* **darks**
1 ***the dark*** **a :** a state in which no light can be seen ▪ She stumbled around in *the dark* [=*darkness*] until she finally found the light switch. ▪ He's 12 years old and still afraid of *the dark*. **b :** a place where little or no light can be seen ▪ The burglars hid in *the dark* between the two buildings. ▪ He bought the kids special rings that glow in *the dark*.
2 [*noncount*] **:** the time of day when night begins **:** the time when the sky becomes dark for the night ▪ We'd better get home before *dark*. ▪ They waited until ***after dark*** to begin their escape.
3 ***darks*** [*plural*] **a :** dark colors **:** colors that are more black than white ▪ He uses lots of *darks* in his decorating. **b :** dark clothes **:** clothes that are black, dark brown, etc. ▪ Wash the lights and the *darks* separately.
in the dark **1 :** in a state in which something is hidden or kept secret ▪ Most of their deals were made *in the dark*. **2 :** in a state of not knowing about something ▪ The public was ***kept in the dark*** about the agreement. ▪ They *kept* us all *in the dark*. — see also *leap in the dark* at [2]LEAP, *shot in the dark* at [1]SHOT, *whistle in the dark* at [2]WHISTLE

Dark Ages *noun*
1 ***the Dark Ages*** **:** the period of European history from about A.D. 500 to 1000 **:** the first 500 years of the Middle Ages

D

2 ***the Dark Ages or the dark ages*** *often humorous* **:** the period of time before things developed into their modern form ▪ In *the dark ages* before computers, we often wrote our letters by hand. ▪ Her father's ideas about women are from *the Dark Ages*.

dark chocolate *noun, pl* ~ **-lates** [*count, noncount*] *US* **:** a kind of chocolate that is a very dark brown color and that is made without milk — called also (*Brit*) *plain chocolate*; compare MILK CHOCOLATE, WHITE CHOCOLATE

dark·en /ˈdɑɚkən/ *verb* **-ens; -ened; -en·ing**

1 : to make (something) dark or to become dark or darker in color [+ *obj*] Clouds *darkened* the sky. ▪ The hours I spent in the sun *darkened* [=*tanned*] my skin. [*no obj*] The sky *darkened* and it started to rain. ▪ Her face *darkens* to a deep red when she gets angry. ▪ The wood will *darken* as it ages.

2 : to make (something) less happy or to become less happy [+ *obj*] The bad news *darkened* his mood. ▪ The last days of her life were *darkened* by illness. [*no obj*] His mood *darkened* after he heard the bad news.

darken someone's door/doors **:** to go to or appear at a place where you are not welcome anymore ▪ She told him to leave and to never *darken her door* again. [=to never go to her house/apartment again]

– darkened *adj* ▪ He was sitting in a *darkened* [=*dark*] corner of the room. ▪ a car with *darkened* [=*dark*] windows

dark glasses *noun* [*plural*] **:** SUNGLASSES

dark horse *noun, pl* ~ **-es** [*count*]

1 : a person (such as a politician), animal, or thing that competes in a race or other contest and is not expected to win ▪ The Democrat from Utah has gone from being a *dark horse* to the front-runner in the campaign for President. ▪ The movie is a *dark horse* for the award.

2 *Brit* **:** a person who has interesting qualities or abilities that most people do not know about ▪ He is a *dark horse*, but I did find out that he once played football professionally.

dark·ly /ˈdɑɚkli/ *adv* [*more* ~; *most* ~]

1 : in dark colors ▪ They were both *darkly* dressed in business suits. [=they were wearing dark suits] ▪ *darkly* colored clothing/fabric

2 : having black or brown eyes, hair, or skin ▪ a *darkly* handsome man

3 : in a way that shows a lack of hope or happiness ▪ He spoke *darkly* of the coming war. ▪ "We're heading for trouble," she warned *darkly*.

4 : in a way that is threatening ▪ She hinted *darkly* that they might regret not helping her.

5 : in a way that relates to unpleasant subjects (such as crime, war, unhappy relationships, etc.) ▪ His movie is a *darkly* comic portrayal of a troubled family. ▪ a *darkly* humorous/amusing story

6 : without being able to see clearly ▪ "For now we see through a glass, *darkly* . . . " —1 Corinthians 13:12 (KJV)

dark meat *noun* [*noncount*] **:** the meat that comes from the legs and thighs of chickens, turkeys, ducks, etc. ▪ Would you like white meat or *dark meat*? — compare WHITE MEAT

dark·ness /ˈdɑɚknəs/ *noun* [*noncount*]

1 : a state in which little or no light can be seen **:** a dark state or condition ▪ We tried to find our way through the *darkness*. [=*dark*] ▪ the *darkness* of the movie theater ▪ He escaped under cover of *darkness*. [=while it was dark outside; at night] ▪ in the early morning *darkness* = in the *darkness* of early morning ▪ We watched the mountains fade into the *darkness*. ▪ 12 hours of *darkness* ▪ Although the picture was taken in near *darkness*, you can still see her white dress. ▪ absolute/complete/total *darkness* — opposite LIGHT

2 : the state of having a color or shade that is closer to black than white ▪ The *darkness* of the clouds warned us that rain was coming. ▪ the rich *darkness* of his skin

3 : a state in which information is hidden from most people ▪ The family's secret remained hidden/shrouded in *darkness* [=*secrecy*] and mystery.

4 *literary* **a :** evil or wickedness ▪ They set off to fight the forces/powers of *darkness*. **b :** a lack of knowledge, understanding, or education **:** a state in which little is known or understood ▪ people living in *darkness* [=*ignorance*] and sin

dark·room /ˈdɑɚkˌruːm/ *noun, pl* **-rooms** [*count*] **:** a room that is used for making photographs and that is lit with a special kind of red light

¹dar·ling /ˈdɑɚlɪŋ/ *noun, pl* **-lings** [*count*]

1 a : a person you love very much ▪ She was mother's little *darling*. — often used to address someone you love ▪ How was your day, *darling*? [=*sweetheart, dear*] ▪ *Darling*, what's the matter? **b :** a kind and helpful person ▪ Be a *darling* [=*dear, sweetie*] and carry this inside for me.

2 : someone who is liked very much by a person or group ▪ a media *darling* — often + *of* ▪ They are the newest *darlings of* the pop rock world. ▪ an actress who is the *darling of* critics

²darling *adj* [*more* ~; *most* ~]

1 *always used before a noun* **:** greatly loved ▪ This is my *darling* daughter, Sara.

2 *informal* **:** very pleasing or attractive ▪ What a *darling* [=*cute, adorable*] dress! ▪ He told the children a *darling* [=*charming*] story after dinner. ▪ That dress is just *darling*.

¹darn /ˈdɑɚn/ *verb* **darns; darned; darn·ing** [+ *obj*] **:** to fix (a piece of clothing, a hole, etc.) by sewing ▪ Would you *darn* these socks, please? ▪ She is *darning* a tear in the dress. — compare ⁴DARN

²darn *noun, pl* **darns** [*count*] **:** a hole or tear that has been fixed by sewing ▪ The old sweater is full of *darns*. — compare ⁵DARN

³darn *interj, US, informal* — used as a more polite form of *damn* ▪ *Darn*! That hurt! ▪ *Darn*! We missed meeting them.

⁴darn *verb, chiefly US, informal* — used as a more polite form of *damn* ▪ *Darn* him! Why won't he call? ▪ *Darn* this car. It never starts right anymore. ▪ ***Darn it***! I forgot to call them! ▪ ***Darn it all***! ▪ Be quiet, ***gosh darn it***! I can't hear myself think! ▪ Well ***I'll be darned***! You actually showed up! [=I am very surprised that you showed up] ▪ ***I'll be darned if*** the train didn't leave until an hour later. ▪ I offered to help, but ***darned if*** she didn't do the whole thing herself. [=I was very surprised that she did the whole thing herself] — see also DARNEDEST — compare ¹DARN

⁵darn *noun, chiefly US, informal* — used as a more polite form of *damn* ▪ His opinion isn't ***worth a darn***. [=it has no value; it is worthless] ▪ I don't ***give a darn*** [=I do not care at all] what people say about me. ▪ Nobody ***cares a darn*** [=cares at all] about them. — compare ²DARN

⁶darn *or* **darned** *adj, chiefly US, informal* — used as a more polite form of *damn* ▪ Shut your *darn* mouth and pay attention! ▪ This ***gosh darn*** computer isn't working right. ▪ I didn't learn a *darn* thing in class today. ▪ This *darned* window won't open! ▪ It's a *darn* shame that they couldn't stay longer. [=it is a complete shame; it is very unfortunate] ▪ If he believes that, he's a *darn* fool! [=he is very foolish to believe that] ▪ There's not a *darn* thing anyone can say to make her do it. ▪ That was the best *darn* pie I ever ate. — see also DARNEDEST

– darn /ˈdɑɚn/ *or* **darned** *adv* ▪ That was a *darn* good meal. ▪ I spent the summer learning how to play chess and got pretty *darn* good at it. ▪ He's too *darned* nice. ▪ We ***darn near*** [=very nearly] didn't get there in time. ▪ You ***darn well*** know what happened. [=you know exactly what happened] ▪ I'll do whatever I *darn well* please. [=I will do whatever I want to do]

darned·est /ˈdɑɚndəst/ *adj, chiefly US, informal* — used as a more polite form of *damnedest* ▪ It was the *darnedest* thing I ever saw. ▪ Kids do and say the *darnedest* things.

– darnedest *noun* [*noncount*] ▪ He was ***doing/trying his darnedest*** to please everyone.

¹dart /ˈdɑɚt/ *noun, pl* **darts**

1 [*count*] **:** a small object that has a sharp point at one end and that is thrown in the game of darts or used as a weapon ▪ throwing *darts* ▪ He was hit with a poisoned *dart*. — often used figuratively ▪ She frequently uses her editorials to hurl/throw *darts* at the White House. [=to sharply criticize the White House] ▪ He'd been sending *darts of* sarcasm in her direction all evening.

2 ***darts*** [*noncount*] **:** a game in which darts are thrown at a board that is marked with circles ▪ Her favorite game is *darts*. ▪ Let's play *darts*. — see also DARTBOARD

3 [*singular*] **:** a quick movement ▪ a quick *dart* to the left ▪ (*chiefly Brit*) The cat ***made a dart for*** the door.

4 [*count*] **:** a sudden, sharp pain ▪ A *dart* of pain ran through his back.

5 [*count*] **:** a small fold that is sewn into a piece of clothing ▪ She sewed a couple of *darts* in the skirt to make it fit better.

²dart *verb, always followed by an adverb or preposition* **darts; dart·ed; dart·ing :** to run or move quickly or suddenly in a particular direction or to a particular place [*no obj*] We saw a deer *dart across* the road. ▪ I *darted* [=*dashed*] *inside* to get some ice. ▪ Her eyes *darted from* the door to the window. [=she looked suddenly and briefly at the door and then at the window] [+ *obj*] The frog *darted* its tongue at a fly.

dart a glance/look at **:** to look suddenly and briefly at (something or someone) ▪ She *darted a* suspicious *glance at* her sister.

dart·board /ˈdɑɚtˌboɚd/ *noun, pl* **-boards** [*count*] : a round board that is marked with circles, lines, and numbers and that is used as a target in the game of darts

dartboard

Dar·win·ian /dɑɚˈwɪnijən/ *adj*
1 : of or relating to Charles Darwin or to the ideas and theories of Charles Darwin ▪ a *Darwinian* theory/principle ▪ a *Darwinian* approach to evolution
2 : of or relating to a situation in which only people, businesses, etc., with the strongest skills or abilities are successful ▪ The competition among manufacturers is very *Darwinian.* ▪ the *Darwinian* world of professional sports
– Darwinian *noun, pl* **-ians** [*count*] ▪ The scientist considers himself a *Darwinian.* [=a person who agrees with the ideas of Charles Darwin]

Dar·win·ism /ˈdɑɚwəˌnɪzəm/ *noun* [*noncount*] : the theory of Charles Darwin about how plant and animal species develop : EVOLUTION
– Dar·win·ist /ˈdɑɚwənɪst/ *adj* **– Darwinist** *noun, pl* **-ists** [*count*]

[1]**dash** /ˈdæʃ/ *verb* **dash·es; dashed; dash·ing**
1 [*no obj*] : to run or move quickly or suddenly ▪ I'm sorry, but I must *dash.* I'm late. ▪ She *dashed* down the hallway to the bathroom. ▪ People were *dashing* inside to get out of the rain. ▪ The dog *dashed* [=*darted*] across the busy street. — often + *off* ▪ She *dashed off* [=left suddenly and quickly] without finishing her breakfast.
2 *always followed by an adverb or preposition* **a** [*no obj*] : to hit something in a violent and forceful way ▪ The waves *dashed* [=*smashed*] against the rocks. **b** [+ *obj*] : to break or destroy (something) by throwing or hitting it against something ▪ The waves *dashed* the boat against the rocks. ▪ In her anger, she *dashed* [=*smashed*] the plate to pieces on the floor.
3 [+ *obj*] : to destroy or ruin (something, such as a hope or an expectation) ▪ Her hopes of winning a medal were *dashed* after she broke her leg. ▪ our *dashed* expectations/dreams
dash it (all) *Brit, informal + old-fashioned* — used in speech to express anger, frustration, etc. ▪ *Dash it all!* I've forgotten my keys!
dash off [*phrasal verb*] ***dash off (something)*** *or* ***dash (something) off*** : to write (something) in a very quick and hurried way ▪ I have just enough time to *dash off* a letter. — see also [1]DASH 1 (above)

[2]**dash** *noun, pl* **dashes**
1 [*count*] : a punctuation mark — that is used especially to show a break in thought or in the structure of a sentence (as in "We don't know where—or how—the problem began.")
2 [*count*] : a small amount of something that is added to something else — usually singular ▪ Add some salt, but just a *dash.* — usually + *of* ▪ The soup needs a *dash of* salt. ▪ Add a couple *dashes* [=*splashes*] *of* wine or lemon juice. ▪ Red roses can bring a *dash* [=*touch*] *of* romance to your evening. ▪ The essay has a *dash of* humor.
3 [*singular*] : the act of running or moving quickly or suddenly in a particular direction or to a particular place ▪ We ***made a dash*** for the exit. ▪ In his ***mad dash*** [=*mad rush*] to the store, he forgot his wallet.
4 [*count*] : a short, fast race ▪ She ran in the 50-meter *dash.*
5 [*noncount*] *old-fashioned* : a way of behaving that is full of energy and spirit ▪ She was a leader with *dash* and confidence. ▪ He had daring and *dash.*
6 [*count*] *informal* : DASHBOARD ▪ The map is on the *dash.*
7 [*count*] : a long signal (such as a sound or a flash of light) that represents a letter or part of a letter in Morse code ▪ The Morse code for the letter *u* is two dots and a *dash.* — compare [1]DOT 3
cut a dash *Brit, informal + old-fashioned* : to look attractive in the clothes you are wearing ▪ He really *cuts a dash* in his new suit.

dash·board /ˈdæʃˌboɚd/ *noun, pl* **-boards** [*count*] : the part of the inside of a car, truck, etc., that is below the windshield and that has the controls on it — called also (*Brit*) *fascia*; see picture at CAR; compare INSTRUMENT PANEL

dashed /ˈdæʃt/ *adj* : made up of a set of dashes (sense 1) ▪ a *dashed* line

dashing *adj* [*more ~; most ~*] *of a man or a man's appearance* : attractive and impressive in a way that shows confidence ▪ She married a *dashing* young lawyer from the city. ▪ a brave and *dashing* soldier ▪ his *dashing* good looks ▪ The actor ***cuts a dashing figure*** as a young Jack Kennedy.
– dash·ing·ly /ˈdæʃɪŋli/ *adv* ▪ He is *dashingly* handsome.

das·tard·ly /ˈdæstɚdli/ *adj* [*more ~; most ~*] *old-fashioned* : very cruel : using tricks to hurt people ▪ a *dastardly* villain ▪ *dastardly* deeds ▪ a *dastardly* attack on innocent civilians

da·ta /ˈdeɪtə, ˈdætə/ *noun*
1 [*plural*] : facts or information used usually to calculate, analyze, or plan something ▪ She spent hours reviewing the *data* from the experiment. ▪ They made their decisions based on the survey *data.* ▪ Much of the *data* is inconclusive. ▪ The company has access to your personal *data.*

> ***usage*** *Data* is plural in form but is used with both plural and singular verbs. ▪ Is this *data* accurate? ▪ Are these *data* reliable? When used with plural verbs, *data* is thought of as the plural form of the noun *datum.* It is usually used with plural verbs only in formal or technical writing. ▪ Many of these *data* are incorrect.

2 [*noncount*] : information that is produced or stored by a computer ▪ She works as a *data* entry clerk. ▪ There was too much *data* for the computer to process. ▪ He is an expert in *data* retrieval. [=finding information stored on a computer]

da·ta·base /ˈdeɪtəˌbeɪs, ˈdætəˌbeɪs/ *noun, pl* **-bas·es** [*count*] : a collection of pieces of information that is organized and used on a computer ▪ All of our customers' information was kept in/on a *database.* ▪ an online *database* — called also *data bank*

data processing *noun* [*noncount*] : the process of putting information into a computer so that the computer can organize it, change its form, etc. — often used before another noun ▪ *data-processing* software

[1]**date** /ˈdeɪt/ *noun, pl* **dates** [*count*]
1 a : a particular day of a month or year ▪ The *date* of the party is March 1. ▪ What's today's *date*? ▪ They announced June 10th as their wedding *date.* [=they announced that they would get married on June 10th] ▪ They have not yet ***set a date*** for the trial. [=they have not decided what day the trial will start on] ▪ The decision will be made ***at a later/future date.*** [=at some time in the future] ▪ your ***date of birth*** = your ***birth date*** [=the day you were born] — see also DUE DATE, OUT-OF-DATE, UP-TO-DATE **b** : writing that shows when something was done or made ▪ The *date* on the letter was the 26th of April. ▪ a coin with a *date* of 1902
2 : an agreement to meet someone at a particular time or on a particular day ▪ He set up a *date* [=(more commonly) *appointment*] to meet with his professor. ▪ "So we'll meet for coffee next Tuesday?" "Yes. It's a *date.*" [=I agree to meet you then]
3 a : an occasion when two people who have or might have a romantic relationship do an activity together ▪ We went (out) on a few *dates* last year. ▪ She asked him (out) on a *date.* ▪ They went to an Italian restaurant on their first *date.* ▪ I'm ***going (out) on a date*** with him tomorrow night. = I ***have a date*** with him tomorrow night. — see also BLIND DATE, DOUBLE DATE **b** *chiefly US* : a person you have a date with ▪ I have to pick up my *date* at seven o'clock. ▪ Are you bringing a *date* to the dance? ▪ He has a different *date* every night. [=he dates a different person every night]
to date : up to now : until the present time ▪ We've received no complaints *to date.* [=*yet*] ▪ This is their greatest success *to date.* ▪ *To date,* most of their work has been preparatory.
up to date **1** — used to say that something or someone has or does not have the newest information ▪ These textbooks are not *up to date.* — usually used with *bring* or *keep* ▪ They needed to *bring* the first edition of the textbook *up to date.* ▪ It's hard to *keep* all our records *up to date.* ▪ This memo should *bring* everyone *up to date* on the latest changes. [=give everyone the newest information about the most recent changes] ▪ She reads the magazines to *keep up to date* on the latest fashions. [=to know what is fashionable] **2** — used to say that something is or is not modern or new ▪ The styles are not *up to date.* — usually used with *bring* or *keep* ▪ The book *brings* the familiar fable *up to date* by setting it in the present day. — see also UP-TO-DATE
– compare [3]DATE
– date·less /ˈdeɪtləs/ *adj* ▪ a *dateless* letter/photo ▪ another *dateless* Friday night

[2]date *verb* **dates; dat·ed; dat·ing**

1 *chiefly US* **:** to do an activity with someone you have might have a romantic relationship with **:** to go on a date or several dates with (someone) [+ *obj*] She *dated* a couple guys during college. • He only *dates* younger women. [*no obj*] They *dated* a couple of times. [=they went on a couple of dates] • They've been *dating* for six months. • I haven't *dated* [=gone on a date] in 20 years. — see also DOUBLE-DATE

2 [+ *obj*] **:** to write the date on (something) • Don't forget to sign and *date* the application. • The letter was not *dated*. • a memo *dated* July 12th, 2003 • a coin *dated* 1902 — see also ANTEDATE, BACKDATE, POSTDATE, PREDATE

3 [+ *obj*] **:** to show or find out when (something) was made or produced • Historians *date* the document to the early 1700s. • The ancient building was *dated* by a coin found in one of the rooms. • Scientists use various techniques to *date* fossils. — see also CARBON DATING, RADIOCARBON DATING

4 [+ *obj*] **:** to show or prove that (someone or something) is old or from a long time ago **:** to make (someone or something) seem old-fashioned or out-of-date • The decor really *dates* the house. • I'm *dating* myself in saying this, but I remember when cell phones were rare.

5 [*no obj*] **:** to begin to exist **:** to appear for the first time • This bowl ***dates from*** the sixth century. [=this bowl was made in the sixth century] • a custom that ***dates back*** [=*goes back*] 400 years [=a custom that began 400 years ago] • They found jewelry ***dating back to*** [=that was made in] the 1700s. • a set of rules *dating* as far *back* as the Middle Ages

– dat·able *also* **date·able** /ˈdeɪtəbəl/ *adj* • All the furniture is *datable* to the 1800s.

[3]date *noun, pl* **dates** [*count*] **:** a small, sweet, brown fruit from a kind of palm tree — compare [1]DATE

date·book /ˈdeɪtˌbʊk/ *noun, pl* **-books** [*count*] **:** a small book or calendar in which people write dates, appointments, etc., that they have planned or scheduled — called also (*Brit*) *diary*

dated *adj* [*more* ~; *most* ~] **:** coming from or belonging to a time in the past **:** old-fashioned or out-of-date • the restaurant's *dated* decor • The band's music sounds *dated* now. • The information was quite *dated* and no longer useful.

date line *noun* [*singular*] **:** INTERNATIONAL DATE LINE

date rape *noun* [*noncount*] **:** the crime of forcing someone you know to have sex with you especially while on a date • He was accused of *date rape*.

– date rapist *noun, pl* **~ -ists** [*count*]

dating service *noun, pl* **~ -vices** [*count*] **:** a business that introduces people to each other so that they can decide if they want to date each other • online *dating services* — called also (*Brit*) *dating agency*

da·tive /ˈdeɪtɪv/ *noun* [*noncount*] *grammar* **:** the form of a noun or pronoun when it is the indirect object of a verb • a noun in the *dative*

– dative *adj* • words in the *dative case* • a *dative* ending

da·tum /ˈdeɪtəm, ˈdætəm/ *noun, pl* **da·ta** /ˈdeɪtə, ˈdætə/ *or* **da·tums** [*count*] *formal + technical* **:** a single piece of information • an important historical *datum* [=*fact*] ***usage*** see DATA

[1]daub /ˈdɑːb/ *verb* **daubs; daubed; daub·ing**

1 [+ *obj*] **a :** to put something on something with quick, small motions **:** DAB • He *daubed* some cologne on his neck. • *Daub* the potatoes with a little butter. **b :** to write (something) on a surface • Various political slogans had been *daubed* on the walls.

2 : to lightly touch (something) usually with quick, small motions **:** DAB [+ *obj*] He sighed deeply and *daubed* his eyes with a tissue. [*no obj*] — usually + *at* • She *daubed at* the wound with a wet cloth.

[2]daub *noun, pl* **daubs** [*count*] **:** a small amount of something **:** DAB • She added a few *daubs* of color to the painting.

daugh·ter /ˈdɑːtɚ/ *noun, pl* **-ters** [*count*] **:** a female child • We have a *daughter* and two sons. • my 20-year-old *daughter* • an adopted *daughter* — see also GODDAUGHTER, GRANDDAUGHTER, STEPDAUGHTER

– daugh·ter·ly /ˈdɑːtɚli/ *adj* • *daughterly* love

daugh·ter–in–law /ˈdɑːtərɪnˌlɑː/ *noun, pl* **-ters–in–law** /-tɚzɪnˌlɑː/ [*count*] **:** the wife of your son — see also IN-LAW

daunt /ˈdɑːnt/ *verb* **daunts; daunt·ed; daunt·ing** [+ *obj*] *somewhat formal* **:** to make (someone) afraid or less confident • The project doesn't seem to *daunt* [=*intimidate*] them. [=they seem to be undaunted by the project] — often used as (*be*) *daunted* • She *was* not *daunted* by the difficult task.

nothing daunted *Brit, old-fashioned* — used to say that someone is not afraid at all • It was a difficult situation, but *nothing daunted*, she refused to quit.

daunting *adj* [*more* ~; *most* ~] *somewhat formal* **:** tending to make people afraid or less confident **:** very difficult to do or deal with • a *daunting* [=*intimidating, overwhelming*] task • Few things are more *daunting* than having to speak in front of a large crowd. • Shakespeare's plays can be *daunting* for a young reader.

– daunt·ing·ly *adv* • The system is *dauntingly* complex.

daunt·less /ˈdɑːntləs/ *adj* [*more* ~; *most* ~] *formal + literary* **:** very brave • *dauntless* [=*fearless*] heroes

– daunt·less·ly *adv* **– daunt·less·ness** *noun* [*noncount*]

daw·dle /ˈdɑːdl/ *verb* **daw·dles; daw·dled; daw·dling** [*no obj*] **:** to move or act too slowly • Hurry up! There's no time to *dawdle*. • Come home immediately after school, and don't *dawdle*. • She *dawdled* [=*lingered*] over her breakfast.

– daw·dler *noun, pl* **daw·dlers** [*count*]

[1]dawn /ˈdɑːn/ *noun, pl* **dawns**

1 : the time of day when sunlight first begins to appear [*noncount*] We arrived at/before/after *dawn*. [=*sunrise, daybreak*] • We danced till *dawn*. • the *dawn's* clear light • as ***dawn breaks*** over the city • He woke up ***at the crack of dawn***. [=very early in the morning] • She drove ***from dawn to/until dusk*** [=from early morning until early evening] [*count*] Winter brings late *dawns* and early sunsets. — compare DUSK

2 [*count*] **:** the beginning of something — usually singular; usually + *of* • People have fought with each other since the *dawn of* history/time/civilization. • the *dawn of* a new era/age • at the *dawn of* the 21st century

[2]dawn *verb* **dawns; dawned; dawn·ing** [*no obj*]

1 : to begin to become light as the sun rises • They waited for the day to *dawn*.

2 : to start or begin • A new age/era is *dawning*.

3 : to begin to be understood • Suddenly, the truth *dawns*. — see also *light dawns* at [1]LIGHT

dawn on [*phrasal verb*] ***dawn on (someone)*** **:** to begin to be understood or realized by (someone) for the first time • The solution finally *dawned on* him. [=he finally saw the solution] • It suddenly *dawned on* me that I hadn't eaten all day. • It began to *dawn on* her that she was lost.

– dawn·ing *noun* [*noncount*] • the *dawning* [=*beginning*] of a new day/age/era

day /ˈdeɪ/ *noun, pl* **days**

1 [*count*] **:** a period of 24 hours beginning at midnight **:** one of the seven time periods that make up a week • We're open seven *days* a week, 365 *days* a year. • Payment is due on the first *day* of every month. • "What *day* is (it) today?" "Tuesday." • "What *day* [=*date*] is Friday?" "It's the 28th." • "What *day* of the week is the 28th?" "It's a Friday." • He spent five *days* in the hospital. • She left on Thursday and came back four *days* later. • The baby is due (to be born) in three *days*. • That was the happiest *day* of my life. • Parenthood gets better every *day*. • We'll be finished in a *day* or two. = We'll be finished in a couple of *days*. • It rained for a *day* and a half. [=it rained for about 36 hours] • The office is closed for the *day*. • I call him every (single) *day*. • Tomorrow is another *day*. [=there will be more opportunities to do things tomorrow] • a *day* of celebration/mourning [=a day for people to celebrate/mourn] • Take one pill two times ***a day***. [=each day] • She works eight hours *a day*. • It costs 10 dollars *a day* to park there. • The party is ***the day after tomorrow***. = The party is in two *days*. • It happened ***the day before yesterday***. = It happened two *days* ago. • Sometimes they didn't speak to each other for ***days on end***. [=several days] • ***From that day forth/forward*** [=(less formally) *from then on*], I was determined to do better. ✧ If you ***do not look a day over*** a particular age, you appear to be that age. • "Today's my 50th birthday." "Really? I'm surprised. You *don't look a day over* 40." [=you don't look any older than 40 years old] ✧ If you say that someone is a particular age ***if he/she is a day***, you mean that the person is that age or older. • The man she's dating is 60 *if he's a day*. [=he is at least sixty years old]

2 : the time of light between one night and the next **:** the part of the day when light from the sun can be seen [*count*] What a beautiful summer *day*! • a cold/wet/rainy *day* • The shortest *day* of the year is usually December 22, and June 22 is usually the longest. [*noncount*] He sleeps during the *day* [=*daytime*] and works at night. • You can call me any time, *day* or night. • These animals are mostly active during the *day*. • I work during the *day*. [=I work days] • She's a student ***by day*** [=during the day] and a waitress by night. • I woke at (the) ***break of day***. [=(more commonly) *dawn, daybreak, sun-*

rise] ▪ ***day workers*** [=people who work during the day] — opposite NIGHT

3 : the part of the day when people are usually most active and when most businesses are open [*singular*] I like to start my *day* with a cup of coffee. [=I like to drink a cup of coffee as soon as I wake up] ▪ We decided to rent a car for the *day*. ▪ How was your *day*? ▪ By the end of the *day*, we were all exhausted. ▪ Our neighbors play their loud music ***at all hours of the day***. [=throughout the day] ▪ Let's go to bed. We have an ***early day*** [=we will get out of bed early] tomorrow. ▪ I needed to relax after a ***long day*** at work/school. [=after working/being at school for a long time] ▪ "Thank you, ma'am. ***Have a nice day***!" [*noncount*] I'll be gone ***all day***. ▪ It rained ***all day long***. ✧ People sometimes say that they ***can't wait all day*** or ***don't have all day*** when they are in a hurry and need someone to move or act more quickly. These phrases are usually used in a rude way. ▪ Hurry up! I *can't wait all day*! = I *don't have all day*. = I *haven't got all day*.

4 [*count*] **:** the hours during a day when a person works or goes to school or when a company does business ▪ I put in four twelve-hour *days* [=*workdays*] this week. ▪ She makes about 50 dollars a/per *day*. ▪ He was late for his first *day* on the job. ▪ They collected a full *day*'s pay for half a *day*'s work. ▪ We had a busy couple of *days* at the store. ▪ We have a short *day* tomorrow. [=we have to work fewer hours tomorrow than usual] ▪ The school committee is pushing for a longer school *day*. ▪ Tomorrow's our last *day* of school (for the school year). ▪ Please allow 14 ***business days*** [=days when most businesses are open; weekdays that are not holidays] for delivery. ✧ If something is ***all in a day's work*** for someone, it is part of a person's typical work. ▪ Solving violent crimes is *all in a day's work* for these police detectives. ✧ To ***take a/the day off*** is to decide not to work on a particular day. ▪ He *took the day off* to go fishing.

5 [*count*] **:** the day on which something specified happens or is expected to happen ▪ It rained on their wedding *day*. ▪ the *day* of his birth ▪ This Sunday is ***family day*** [=a day for families especially with young children] at the amusement park. ▪ If you've been waiting for the perfect skiing conditions, ***today's the day***. [=the conditions are perfect today] ▪ So, when's ***the big day***? When are you getting married? ▪ Did you ever think you'd ***see the day*** when he would apologize? [=did you believe he would ever apologize?] ▪ I never thought I would ***live to see the day*** when you would graduate from college. [=I did not think I would live long enough to see you graduate] ▪ Let her have her ***day in court*** [=let her defend herself in a court of law] before you pass judgment on her. ▪ This is ***your lucky day***. [=a day when something good happens to you] ✧ If a day ***is your day***, something good will happen to you on that day. ▪ You never know. Maybe today will *be my day*. [=maybe I will succeed, win, etc., today] ▪ I'm sorry you lost. I guess it just *wasn't your day*. ✧ People sometimes use the phrase ***that'll be the day*** to say that they think something will not happen. ▪ "Do you think he'll ever admit he made a mistake?" "*That'll be the day*!"

6 [*count*] **:** a particular period of time ▪ She was the most talented actress of her *day*. [=during the time when she lived and worked as an actress] ▪ ***In my day*** [=when I was young], boys asked girls out on dates, not the other way around. ▪ Life was simpler *in my grandmother's day*, but it wasn't easier. ▪ We sell books dating from 1875 to ***the present day***. [=*today*] — often plural ▪ He often spoke about his *days* as a soldier. ▪ I was quite an athlete in my younger *days*. [=when I was young] ▪ The practice dates back to the *days* of ancient Rome. ▪ the olden *days* ▪ my college *days* [=when I was in college] ▪ the *days* of stagecoaches [=when stagecoaches were used] ▪ In those *days* many factory workers were children. ✧ The saying ***those were the days*** is sometimes used to say that a period of time in the past was pleasant and often better than the present time. ▪ When I was a kid, we spent our summers at the beach. *Those were the days*! ▪ In the 1960s, everything seemed possible. Those were ***the good old days***.

(all) the livelong day see LIVELONG

***any day now* :** within the next few days **:** SOON ▪ We're expecting a phone call from him *any day now*. [=in the near future] ▪ *Any day now*, the decision could be made.

at the end of the day see [1]END

call it a day see [1]CALL

***carry/win the day* :** to win or be successful ▪ The "no" vote *carried the day*. [=*prevailed*] ▪ We believe that truth and justice will *carry/win the day*.

***day after day* :** for several days without stopping or changing ▪ She wore the same pants *day after day*. ▪ *Day after day*, we hear the same complaints from our customers.

day and night or ***night and day*** **1 :** all the time **:** without stopping ▪ We've been working on it *day and night*. = We've been working on it *night and day*. **2 :** complete or total ▪ The difference between them is *day and night*. = The difference between them is *night and day*. [=they are completely different]

day by day* :** in small amounts every day ▪ *Day by day*, the situation is becoming more complex. ▪ She felt herself growing stronger *day by day*. [=every day] ✧ If you ***take it/things day by day, you make progress in a slow and careful way by dealing with each day as it comes. ▪ He hopes to make a full recovery after his surgery, but right now he's just *taking it day by day*. [=*taking it one day at a time, taking each day as it comes*] ▪ I don't know if our relationship is going to work out. I'm *taking things day by day* at this point.

day in, day out or ***day in and day out* :** every day for many days **:** for a long time without stopping or changing ▪ She does the same thing at her job *day in, day out*. ▪ It can be difficult to spend all of your time with one person *day in and day out*.

days are numbered see [2]NUMBER

early days (yet) see [2]EARLY

every dog has its day see [1]DOG

for a rainy day see RAINY

***from day to day* :** every day ▪ His opinions seem to change *from day to day*. [=*from one day to the next*] — see also DAY-TO-DAY

***from one day to the next* :** every day ▪ She changes her mind *from one day to the next*. [=*from day to day*]; as one day becomes another day ▪ You never know *from one day to the next* what's going to happen to you.

give (someone) the time of day *chiefly US, informal* **:** to pay attention to someone — usually used in negative statements ▪ No one would *give us the time of day*. ▪ I needed their help, but they wouldn't *give me the time of day*.

glory days see [1]GLORY

have seen/known better days see [1]BETTER

in all your born days see BORN

in the cold light of day see [1]COLD

***in this day and age* :** at the present time in history ▪ Computers are essential to getting work done *in this day and age*. [=*nowadays*] ▪ It's unbelievable that *in this day and age* people are still dying from hunger.

it is not every day — used to say that something happens very rarely ▪ *It's not every day* that I get to meet the President. ▪ Go ahead and spend the extra money. *It's not every day* that you get married.

late in the day see [1]LATE

***make someone's day* :** to cause someone's day to be pleasant or happy ▪ Thanks for the compliment. You've really *made my day*! ▪ It *made my day* to see his smiling face.

of the day **1 :** served in a restaurant as a special item on a particular day ▪ What's the fish/vegetable *of the day*? ▪ Our soup *of the day* [=*du jour*] is vegetable beef. **2 :** of a particular period of time ▪ What were some of the popular movies *of the day*? [=that were popular during that time] ▪ the important issues *of the day*

one day **1 :** at some time in the future ▪ *One day*, it'll happen. You'll see. ▪ People may *one day* [=*someday*] be able to take vacations to the moon. **2 :** on a day in the past ▪ I went to her house *one day* and had lunch with her. ▪ *One day*, we had a terrible argument.

on the day *Brit* **:** on the day that an event happens ▪ I know we seem a bit disorganized now, but we'll be all right *on the day*. ▪ Whether we win or not depends on which players are healthy *on the day*.

save the day see [1]SAVE

see the light of day see [1]LIGHT

***some day* :** at some time in the future **:** SOMEDAY ▪ *Some day* I may be rich enough to own two houses. ▪ I'd like to return there *some day*.

take each day as it comes or ***take one day at a time*** or ***take it/things one day at a time* :** to deal with each day's problems as they come instead of worrying about the future ▪ There's no way to know what the future will bring, so just *take each day as it comes* and hope for the best. ▪ *Take one day at a time* and don't expect things to change overnight. ▪ It's important to *take things one day at a time* so you don't feel too overwhelmed.

the other day see [1]OTHER

these days* :** at the present time ▪ It seems that everyone has a cell phone *these days.* [=*nowadays*] ▪ What kind of music are you listening to *these days?* ▪ *These days,* she has a very busy social life. ✧ The phrase ***one of these days means at some time in the future. ▪ *One of these days,* [=*one day*] I'm going to buy myself a boat.

those days : a period of time in the past ▪ Remember when we were kids and life was easy? Well, *those days* are gone. ▪ ***In those days,*** women weren't allowed to own property. ▪ No one knew *in those days* what caused the disease. ✧ If it is ***(just) one of those days,*** it is a day in which many bad or unpleasant things happen. ▪ It's *just one of those days* when everything seems to go wrong. ▪ I missed the bus and sprained my ankle; it was *one of those days* when nothing was going right.

to the day : to exactly a specified number of years ▪ It's been 100 years *to the day* since their great discovery. ▪ Soon after their wedding, almost a year *to the day,* they got divorced.

to this day : up to now : continuing until today ▪ *To this day,* I still don't know what happened. ▪ The belief persists *to this day.*

day·bed /ˈdeɪˌbɛd/ *noun, pl* **-beds** [*count*] : a bed that is made to be used also as a seat or couch

day·break /ˈdeɪˌbreɪk/ *noun* [*noncount*] : the time of day when sunlight first begins to appear ▪ She left at *daybreak* [=*dawn, the break of day*]

day care *noun* [*noncount*] : a place, program, or organization that takes care of children or sick adults during the day usually while their family members are at work ▪ She left work early to pick up her son from *day care.* — often used before another noun ▪ He works for/at a *day care* center.

[1]day·dream /ˈdeɪˌdriːm/ *noun, pl* **-dreams** [*count*] : pleasant thoughts about your life or future that you have while you are awake ▪ I drifted off in a *daydream* during the class.

[2]daydream *verb* **-dreams; -dreamed; -dream·ing** [*no obj*] : to think pleasant thoughts about your life or future while you are awake ▪ Instead of studying, he spent the afternoon *daydreaming* about his vacation.

– day·dream·er *noun, pl* **-ers** [*count*]

Day–Glo /ˈdeɪˌgloʊ/ *trademark* — used for materials or colors that are very bright

day laborer *noun, pl* **~ -ers** [*count*] : a person who is hired for a day or more to do work that usually does not require special skills ▪ They hire *day laborers* to pick the apples.

day·light /ˈdeɪˌlaɪt/ *noun, pl* **-lights**

1 [*noncount*] : the light of the sun and sky during the day : the natural light of day ▪ Open up the curtains and let some *daylight* into the room. ▪ As *daylight* fades into darkness, everyone returns to their homes. ▪ For pictures taken in *daylight,* use a different film. ▪ We could see *daylight* through the cracks in the wall. ▪ They stole my car ***in broad daylight*** [=during the day; without darkness to hide them] ▪ Some of the stuff in that closet hasn't ***seen daylight*** [=*seen the light of day*] since the 1970s.

2 [*noncount*] **a** : the time of day when the sky is light ▪ It's almost *daylight.* [=*daytime*] ▪ during the hours of *daylight* = during ***daylight hours*** **b** : the time of day when sunlight first begins to appear ▪ I arrived before *daylight.* [=*dawn, daybreak*] ▪ The accident happened just after *daylight.*

3 [*noncount*] *informal* : distance or difference *between* people or things ▪ They said there was no *daylight between* the two governments' positions. ▪ The team has won five straight games to ***put some daylight between*** themselves and their nearest rivals. [=to gain a larger lead over their nearest rivals]

4 ***daylights*** [*plural*] *informal* ✧ To ***scare/frighten the (living) daylights out of*** someone is to frighten someone very much. ▪ You scared *the daylights out of* me! ✧ To ***beat/kick/knock the (living) daylights out of*** someone is to hit or kick someone very badly. ▪ They beat *the daylights out of* that guy.

daylight saving time *noun* [*noncount*] *US* : a period of the year between spring and fall when clocks in the U.S. are set one hour ahead of standard time — called also *daylight savings time;* compare BRITISH SUMMER TIME

day·lily /ˈdeɪˌlɪli/ *noun, pl* **-lilies** [*count*] : a kind of plant that has long thin leaves and usually yellow or orange flowers that bloom for a short time

day·long /ˈdeɪˌlɑːŋ/ *adj* : lasting an entire day ▪ a *daylong* tour of the city

day one *or* **Day One** *noun* [*singular*] : the first day or very beginning of something ▪ We've known this about the project since/from *Day One.* ▪ The new governor will start implementing these changes on *day one.* [=the first day of the governor's term]

day·pack /ˈdeɪˌpæk/ *noun, pl* **-packs** [*count*] : a bag for carrying things that has two shoulder straps and is carried on the back : a usually small backpack — see picture at CAMPING

day·room /ˈdeɪˌruːm/ *noun, pl* **-rooms** [*count*] : a room in a hospital, prison, etc., where people can watch television, talk, etc.

days /ˈdeɪz/ *adv, chiefly US* : during the day : in the daytime ▪ She works *days* and goes to school nights. — compare NIGHTS

day·time /ˈdeɪˌtaɪm/ *noun* [*noncount*]

1 : the time of day when the sky is light ▪ These animals are active during the *daytime.* ▪ *daytime* [=*daylight*] hours

2 : television that is shown during the day ▪ It's the best new show on *daytime.* — usually used before another noun ▪ *daytime* talk shows ▪ *daytime* TV

day–to–day /ˈdeɪtəˌdeɪ/ *adj, always used before a noun*

1 : done or happening every day ▪ She is in charge of the company's *day-to-day* operations. ▪ *day-to-day* activities ▪ Little is known about his *day-to-day* [=*everyday*] life. ▪ our *day-to-day* problems/concerns/worries ▪ people who use computers ***on a day-to-day basis*** [=every day]

2 : preparing for one day at a time without thinking about the future ▪ He had been living a *day-to-day* existence.

day trader *noun, pl* **~ -ers** [*count*] : a person who tries to earn money by buying stocks and then selling them very quickly after they increase slightly in value

– day trading *noun* [*noncount*]

daze /ˈdeɪz/ *noun* [*singular*] : a state in which someone (such as a person who has been surprised or injured) is not able to think or act normally — used in the phrase ***in a daze*** ▪ After the test, I spent the rest of the day *in a daze.* ▪ lost *in a daze*

dazed /ˈdeɪzd/ *adj* [*more ~; most ~*] : not able to think or act normally because you have been surprised, injured, etc. ▪ She was *dazed* and confused after being hit on the head with a golf ball. ▪ He had a *dazed* [=*stunned*] look on his face.

daz·zle /ˈdæzəl/ *verb* **daz·zles; daz·zled; daz·zling**

1 [+ *obj*] *of a bright light* : to cause (someone) to be unable to see for a short time ▪ He was *dazzled* [=*blinded*] by the camera flash.

2 : to greatly impress or surprise (someone) by being very attractive or exciting [+ *obj*] Elvis always *dazzled* his audiences. ▪ Visitors were *dazzled* by the mansion's ornate rooms. — often + *with* ▪ She *dazzled* us *with* her wit. [*no obj*] She truly *dazzles* in her live concerts. — see also RAZZLE-DAZZLE

– dazzle *noun* [*noncount*] ▪ the *dazzle* [=*sparkle*] of the diamonds **– daz·zler** *noun, pl* **daz·zlers** [*count*] ▪ He's a real *dazzler.* **– dazzling** *adj* [*more ~; most ~*] ▪ a *dazzling* array/variety of jewelry ▪ the most *dazzling* display of color ▪ her *dazzling* smile **– daz·zling·ly** *adv* [*more ~; most ~*] ▪ Her teeth were *dazzlingly* white.

dB *abbr* decibel

DC *abbr* **1** direct current **2** *or* **D.C.** District of Columbia

D–day *noun* [*singular*] : a day on which something important is planned or expected to happen ▪ The day after Thanksgiving is *D-day* for many retail stores. ✧ *D-day* is most commonly used to refer to the specific date of June 6, 1944, when Allied forces began the invasion of France in World War II.

DDS *abbr* doctor of dental surgery

DDT /ˌdiːˌdiːˈtiː/ *noun* [*noncount*] : a poisonous chemical that was used especially in the past to protect plants from insects and that is now banned in the U.S.

DE *abbr* Delaware

de- *prefix*

1 : do the opposite of ▪ *de*code ▪ *de*activate

2 a : remove (a specified thing) from something ▪ *de*claw a cat ▪ *de*frost a windshield **b** : remove someone or something from something ▪ The king was *de*throned. **c** : leave or get off something ▪ *de*rail ▪ *de*plane

3 : reduce ▪ *de*value currency

dea·con /ˈdiːkən/ *noun, pl* **-cons** [*count*]

1 : an official in some Christian churches whose rank is just below a priest

2 : a member of some Christian churches who has special duties

dea·con·ess /ˈdiːkənəs/ *noun, pl* **-ess·es** [*count*] : a woman in some Christian churches who has special duties : a female deacon

de·ac·ti·vate /diˈæktəˌveɪt/ *verb* **-vates; -vat·ed; -vat·ing** [+ *obj*] : to make (something) no longer active or effective ▪ They were able to *deactivate* [=(more commonly) *dis-*

arm] the bomb. • *deactivate* an alarm

[1]dead /ˈdɛd/ *adj*
1 : no longer alive or living **:** no longer having life • Her husband is *dead.* He died last year. • She's been *dead* for over 10 years now. [=she died more than 10 years ago] • a *dead* insect/bird/dog • *dead* trees/leaves/skin • the *dead* [=*lifeless*] bodies of the soldiers • He was found *dead* in his apartment yesterday. • He lay *dead* on the floor. • The lost mountain climbers were believed/presumed *dead.* • She shot him *dead.* [=she killed him by shooting him] • When we found her, she was ***more dead than alive.*** [=almost dead; very close to death] • The poster said that the robbers were wanted ***dead or alive.*** • He was ***as good as dead.*** [=he was almost dead] • She taught her dog to ***play dead.*** [=to lie on its back and pretend to be dead] ***usage*** see DECEASED ✧ To ***leave (someone or something) for dead*** is to leave a person or animal that you know will probably die instead of trying to help. • They hit the dog with their car and *left it for dead* on the side of the road. • He had been badly beaten and *left for dead.*
2 a dead·er; -est [*or more* ~; *most* ~] **:** not able to feel or move • My hand was *dead* [=*numb*] after holding the bag for so long. **b :** very tired • Our legs were completely *dead* after hiking all day. • I arrived home from work ***half dead.*** [=*exhausted*] • By the end of the day the workers were ***dead on their feet.*** [=very tired but still standing, working, etc.] **c :** feeling no emotions • After the war, I was emotionally *dead.* [=I was no longer able to feel happiness, sadness, etc.]
3 *informal* **:** certain to be punished or hurt • I'm *dead* if I come in late for work again. • If I ever get my hands on you, you're *dead!*
4 *of a machine or device* **:** no longer working especially because of not having electricity • The car's battery is *dead.* • *dead* electrical outlets • a *dead* telephone line • The phones ***went dead*** during the storm.
5 : no longer active or operating • a *dead* [=*extinct*] volcano • *dead* companies • That plan is *dead* for now. We've started developing a new one. • a *dead* deal
6 : naturally not living • rocks and other *dead* [=*inanimate*] matter
7 deader; -est [*or more* ~; *most* ~] **:** lacking in activity or excitement • The store's been *dead* [=*quiet*] all day. • This party's completely *dead.* [=it is not lively] • The audience was kind of *dead* tonight.
8 — used to describe a time when nothing is being said or done • We played cards to fill in the *dead* time between the two performances.
9 : no longer performed or enjoyed • He says that disco is *dead.* • a *dead* art form
10 *of a language* **:** no longer spoken • Latin is a *dead* language.
11 *sports* **—** used to describe a situation in which play stops during a game • In American football, the ball is *dead* [=*out of play*] after an incomplete forward pass. • The ball is *dead* if it goes beyond the white line.
12 a : complete, total, or absolute • There was *dead* silence in the room. • She spoke with *dead* certainty. • I chased them at a *dead* run for three miles. • The camera is a ***dead giveaway*** [=clearly shows] that you're a tourist. • She fell to the floor in a ***dead faint.*** • The evening wasn't all I had hoped for, but is wasn't a ***dead loss.*** [=it wasn't completely bad] • He's ***a dead ringer for*** [=he looks exactly like] his father. • (*Brit, informal*) They're ***a dead cert*** [=*a sure thing, a sure bet*] to win. [=they are certain to win] **b :** sudden and complete • The bus came to a *dead* [=*abrupt*] stop.
13 : perfect or exact • Her arrow hit the *dead* [=*very*] center of the target.
(as) dead as a doornail (*chiefly US*) *or chiefly Brit* ***(as) dead as a dodo*** *informal* **—** used to stress that someone or something is dead • The old captain was *dead as a doornail.* **—** often used figuratively • The negotiations are *as dead as a doornail.* • The deal is *dead as a doornail.*
beat a dead horse *or* ***flog a dead horse*** see [1]HORSE
catch/see (someone) dead *informal* ✧ If you say that people ***wouldn't/won't catch/see you dead*** or that you ***wouldn't/won't be caught/seen dead*** doing something, you refuse to let others see you doing it because it would cause you to be embarrassed. • I *wouldn't be caught/seen dead* wearing that hideous outfit. • She *won't be caught dead* going to the movies with her obnoxious brother.
dead and buried *or* ***dead and gone*** **1 :** no longer living **:** DEAD • He's been *dead and buried* for 50 years. • relatives long *dead and gone* **2 :** no longer used or accepted • Those old family traditions are *dead and buried.* • That idea is *dead and buried.* • The days of our childhood are *dead and gone.*
dead from the neck up *informal* **:** very stupid or foolish • Most of his friends are *dead from the neck up.*
dead in the water *informal* **:** not making any progress **:** not having any chance of success • The peace talks were *dead in the water.* • His election campaign is *dead in the water.*
dead men tell no tales see TALE
dead on arrival **:** having died before getting to a hospital, emergency room, etc. • The victim was *dead on arrival* at the hospital. **—** often used figuratively • Some are saying that any new tax proposal would be *dead on arrival.* [=would have no chances of being approved]
dead to rights see [3]RIGHT
dead to the world *informal* **:** sleeping very deeply • You can't wake him up. He's *dead to the world.*
drop dead *informal* **1 :** to fall to the ground and die very suddenly • She *dropped dead* while playing basketball. **2 —** used as a rude way to tell someone to leave you alone • "He asked you for help after being such a jerk? You should have told him to *drop dead!*" **—** see also DROP-DEAD
knock dead see [1]KNOCK
over my dead body see BODY
– dead·ness *noun* [*noncount*]

[2]dead *noun, pl* **dead**
1 [*plural*] **:** people who have died • By the end of the war, there were over two million *dead.* **—** usually used with *the* • the living and *the dead* • His mother and brother were among *the dead.* • the souls/spirits of *the dead*
2 ***the dead*** **:** the state of being dead **—** usually used in the phrases ***rise from the dead*** or ***come back from the dead*** or ***return from the dead*** to mean to become alive again after dying • For a moment, I thought that my grandfather had *come back from the dead.* • They believe that Jesus Christ *rose from the dead.*
3 [*noncount*] **:** the time in the middle of the night or winter • She left ***in the dead of the night.*** = She left ***at dead of night.*** [=she left very late at night] • He began his journey ***in the dead of winter.***

[3]dead *adv*
1 : completely or totally • I think you're *dead* [=*absolutely, utterly*] wrong. • She's *dead* certain that she can finish the job. • We were *dead* tired by the end of the day. • He's not joking. In fact, he's *dead* serious. • They were both *dead* drunk and passed out on the floor. • She finished the race ***dead last.*** • The mayor was ***dead set against*** [=strongly opposed to] the plan. • She was ***dead set on*** going to college. [=she was completely certain she wanted to go to college]
2 : in a sudden and complete way • He ***stopped dead in his tracks.*** [=stopped suddenly]
3 : directly or exactly • The island is ***dead ahead*** of us. [=the island is right in front of us] • She hung the picture ***dead center*** on the wall. [=she hung the picture in the exact center of the wall]

dead air *noun* [*noncount*] **:** a period of silence especially during a radio broadcast • After the commercial, there were a few seconds of *dead air* before the show continued.

dead·beat /ˈdɛdˌbiːt/ *noun, pl* **-beats** [*count*] *disapproving*
1 : a lazy person **:** a person who does not work • His friends are just a bunch of *deadbeats.*
2 *chiefly US* **:** a person who does not pay money that is owed • He was accused of being a *deadbeat.* **—** often used before another noun • a ***deadbeat dad*** [=a father who owes money to his former wife to help raise their children but does not pay it]

dead bolt *noun, pl* **~ bolts** [*count*] *chiefly US* **:** a lock with a heavy sliding bar that is moved by turning a knob or key **—** called also (*Brit*) *deadlock, mortise lock*

dead duck *noun, pl* **~ ducks** [*count*] *informal + humorous* **:** a person or thing that is certain to fail, suffer, or be punished • If they find out what I did, I'm a *dead duck!*

dead·en /ˈdɛdn̩/ *verb* **-ens; -ened; -en·ing** [+ *obj*] **:** to make (something) weaker or less noticeable • All the different perfumes *deadened* [=*dulled*] her sense of smell. • He took aspirin to *deaden* the pain. • The new insulation will help to *deaden* the noise from the street outside.
– deadening *adj* [*more* ~; *most* ~] • All the different perfumes had a *deadening* effect on her sense of smell.

dead end *noun, pl* **~ ends** [*count*]
1 : a street that ends instead of joining with another street so that there is only one way in and out of it • We came to a *dead end* and had to turn around.

D

D

2 : a situation, plan, or way of doing something that leads to nothing further • My career has hit a *dead end.* • political *dead ends*
– dead–end /ˈdɛdˌɛnd/ *adj, always used before a noun* • *dead-end* streets/roads • He's stuck in a *dead-end* job. [=a job that does not pay you very much and does not give you a chance to get a better job] • a *dead-end* relationship

dead•head /ˈdɛdˌhɛd/ *verb* **-heads; -head•ed; -head•ing** [+ *obj*] **:** to remove dead flowers from (a plant) • She's out in the garden *deadheading* the rosebushes.

dead heat *noun, pl* **~ heats** [*count*] **:** a contest in which two or more competitors earn the same score or finish at the same time — usually singular • The two horses finished in a *dead heat.* • The election poll showed a statistical *dead heat.* [=showed that the two candidates were equally popular]

dead letter *noun, pl* **~ -ters** [*count*]
1 : a letter that cannot be delivered or returned by the post office because of an incorrect address or other problem
2 : a law or agreement that has lost its force or authority — usually singular • Unfortunately, the treaty is now a *dead letter* in this country.

dead•line /ˈdɛdˌlaɪn/ *noun, pl* **-lines :** a date or time when something must be finished **:** the last day, hour, or minute that something will be accepted [*count*] She worked on her composition right up until the *deadline.* • We had to hurry to meet/make the *deadline.* • We missed the *deadline.* • The project was completed a week past its *deadline.* • The *deadline* for submitting college applications is April 19th. • They're working under/with a *deadline.* [*noncount*] They're working ***under deadline.***

[1]**dead•lock** /ˈdɛdˌlɑːk/ *noun, pl* **-locks** [*count*]
1 : a situation in which an agreement cannot be made **:** a situation in which ending a disagreement is impossible because neither side will give up something that it wants • The jury was unable to break/end the *deadlock.* [=unable to agree on a verdict] • City councilors reached a *deadlock* over the law.
2 *US* **:** a situation in which players, teams, etc., have the same score **:** TIE • His goal broke a 3–3 *deadlock.*
3 *Brit* **:** DEAD BOLT

[2]**deadlock** *verb* **-locks; -locked; -lock•ing**
1 [*no obj*] **:** to be unable to end a disagreement • The jury *deadlocked* [=failed to agree on a verdict] after three days of deliberations.
2 *US* **:** to have the same number of points, votes, etc., as your opponent [*no obj*] The two teams *deadlocked* [=*tied*] in a scoreless match. [+ *obj*] Her home run *deadlocked* [=*tied*] the game at 3–3.
– deadlocked *adj* • City councilors are *deadlocked* over the budget. • a *deadlocked* jury • a *deadlocked* game

[1]**dead•ly** /ˈdɛdli/ *adj* **dead•li•er; -est** [*or more ~; most ~*]
1 : causing or able to cause death • *deadly* weapons • the world's most *deadly* snake • a more *deadly* form of the disease • They launched a *deadly* attack. • Officers are allowed to use ***deadly force*** if necessary. — compare DEATHLY
2 : extremely accurate and effective • She shoots with *deadly* accuracy. • a basketball player with *deadly* aim
3 *always used before a noun* **:** extreme or complete • A *deadly* silence followed his question. • The two gang leaders are *deadly* enemies. • He spoke with *deadly* seriousness.
4 *informal* **:** very boring • The lecture was pretty *deadly.*
– dead•li•ness *noun* [*noncount*] • the *deadliness* of the disease

synonyms DEADLY, MORTAL, FATAL, and LETHAL mean causing or able to cause death. DEADLY describes something that is very dangerous and likely or able to cause death. • *deadly* diseases • *deadly* weapons MORTAL describes a wound or injury that has already caused death or will soon cause death. • She received a *mortal* wound and died the next day. FATAL describes something that has actually caused a person's death. • The disease is sometimes *fatal.* • The wounds later proved to be *fatal.* LETHAL usually describes something like a poison that is used for the purpose of destroying life. • a *lethal* gas

[2]**deadly** *adv* **deadlier; -est** [*or more ~; most ~*] **:** extremely or completely • He's *deadly* [=*dead*] serious about finding another job. • a *deadly* boring/dull meeting

deadly night•shade /-ˈnaɪtˌʃeɪd/ *noun, pl* **~ -shades** [*count*] **:** BELLADONNA

deadly sin *noun, pl* **~ sins** [*count*] **:** one of seven sins that in the Christian religion are considered to be very serious and are believed to cause other sins ✧ The seven deadly sins are usually considered to be pride, envy, lust, gluttony, greed, anger, and sloth.

dead meat *noun* [*noncount*] *informal + humorous* **:** a person or thing that is certain to fail, suffer, or be punished • Politically, she's *dead meat.* [=her political career is ruined] • If they find out what you did, you're *dead meat!*

dead–on /ˈdɛdˈɑːn/ *adj, somewhat informal* **:** exactly correct or accurate • His impersonation of the President was *dead-on.* • She was *dead-on* about what was going to happen. • a *dead-on* analysis

[1]**dead•pan** /ˈdɛdˌpæn/ *adj* [*more ~; most ~*] **:** showing no feeling or emotion — used to describe humor that is done or said in a serious way • *deadpan* humor • a *deadpan* comedian • the *deadpan* delivery of his jokes
– deadpan *adv* • "We're not interested," she said *deadpan.*

[2]**deadpan** *noun* [*noncount*] **:** a way of saying funny things without showing any feeling or emotion • He tells the joke in his best *deadpan.* • She's a master of *deadpan.* • the art of *deadpan*

[3]**deadpan** *verb* **-pans; -pan•ned; -pan•ning** [+ *obj*] **:** to say (something funny) in a way that shows no feeling or emotion • "I went back to doing push-ups again, and this time I almost completed one," he *deadpanned.*

dead presidents *noun* [*plural*] *US slang* **:** U.S. money in the form of paper bills • a briefcase full of *dead presidents*

dead weight *noun, pl* **~ weights**
1 : something heavy that is being carried [*count*] The injured child was a *dead weight* in her arms. [*noncount*] carrying 150 pounds of *dead weight*
2 : someone or something that makes success more difficult [*count*] He was a *dead weight* on the team this year. [*noncount*] The company has a lot of *dead weight* [=*deadwood*] it needs to get rid of.

dead•wood /ˈdɛdˌwʊd/ *noun* [*noncount*]
1 : people or things that are not useful or helpful in achieving a goal • She's determined to get the *deadwood* out of the company. • the government's bureaucratic *deadwood*
2 : dead wood on a tree • a healthy tree with no *deadwood*

deaf /ˈdɛf/ *adj* [*more ~; most ~*]
1 : not able to hear • He has been *deaf* since birth. • a *deaf* child • She's completely/partially *deaf* in her right ear. • a disease that caused her to ***go deaf*** [=become unable to hear] • He's *going* a little *deaf* so you'll have to speak up. • (*informal*) My grandmother's a sweet old lady, but she's ***as deaf as a post.*** [=she's very deaf] — see also TONE-DEAF
2 : not willing to listen to or consider something — usually + *to* • They were *deaf to* all of our suggestions. • *deaf to* reason
fall on deaf ears see [1]EAR
***the deaf* :** deaf people **:** people who are not able to hear • She goes to a school for *the deaf.*
turn a deaf ear see [1]EAR
– deaf•ness *noun* [*noncount*] • The disease can cause blindness and *deafness.*

deaf•en /ˈdɛfən/ *verb* **-ens; -ened; -en•ing** [+ *obj*] **:** to make (someone) unable to hear • We were *deafened* by the explosion.

deafening *adj* [*more ~; most ~*] **:** extremely loud • The sign fell with a *deafening* [=*earsplitting*] crash. • the *deafening* roar of the planes • The music was *deafening.* ✧ If there is a ***deafening silence*** or the ***silence is deafening,*** there is a lack of sound or speech that is very noticeable. • The *silence was deafening* as they both sat there stubbornly refusing to apologize. • As the controversy rages on, the *deafening silence* from the White House is drawing increasing criticism.
– deaf•en•ing•ly *adv* • *deafeningly* loud music

deaf–mute /ˈdɛfˈmjuːt/ *noun, pl* **-mutes** [*count*] *old-fashioned + often offensive* **:** a deaf person who cannot speak

[1]**deal** /ˈdiːl/ *verb* **deals; dealt** /ˈdɛlt/; **deal•ing**
1 : to give cards to the players in a card game [*no obj*] It's your turn to *deal.* [+ *obj*] Each player is *dealt* five cards. • She was *dealt* a full house. • *dealing* out the cards for a game of poker — often used figuratively • She was *dealt* a bad/cruel/terrible hand in life. [=many bad things happened to her throughout her life] • You have to play the hand you're *dealt.* [=you must accept and deal with the things that happen to you in your life]
2 [+ *obj*] **:** to give (something or an amount of something) to someone • The offending players were *dealt* harsh penalties. • The team was *dealt* another loss last night. [=the team lost another game] — usually + *out* • The teacher *dealt* [=*handed*] *out* three books to each of us. • The author *deals* [=*doles*] *out* advice on all kinds of subjects.

3 : to buy and sell (drugs, art, etc.) as a business [+ *obj*] She got caught *dealing* drugs in school. [*no obj*] (*informal*) How long has he been *dealing*? [=dealing drugs] — see also *wheel and deal* at ²WHEEL

deal a blow ✧ To *deal a blow* to someone means to hit someone. ▪ (*formal*) He *dealt* his enemy *a* mighty *blow.* [=he hit his enemy hard] — usually used figuratively ▪ The factory closing will *deal a* serious/severe/devastating/crushing *blow* to the town's economy. ▪ Her career as an ice skater was ***dealt a fatal blow*** [=her career was ruined] when she broke her leg.

deal in [*phrasal verb*] **1** ***deal in (something)*** **a :** to buy and sell (something) as a business ▪ He *deals in* rare books. **b :** to use or be involved in (something) ▪ tales *dealing in* myth and mystery ▪ We don't *deal in* rumor or gossip. **2** ***deal (someone) in*** **:** to include someone in a card game ▪ "Do you want to play cards with us?" "Sure, *deal me in.*"

deal with [*phrasal verb*] ***deal with (someone or something)*** **1 :** to be about (something) **:** to have (something) as a subject ▪ The book *deals with* World War II. ▪ Her speech *dealt with* health care and the nation's economy. ▪ The film *deals with* some serious issues. **2 :** to make business agreements with (someone) ▪ He *deals* fairly *with* all his customers. ▪ Their salespeople are very easy to *deal with.* **3 :** to do something about (a person or thing that causes a problem or difficult situation) ▪ The government *dealt* harshly *with* the rebels. ▪ I'll *deal with* you later. ▪ Who's going to *deal with* this mess? ▪ I *dealt with* the problem myself. ▪ Can you suggest some ways of *dealing with* a difficult child? ▪ We weren't able/equipped/prepared to *deal with* such a large crowd of people. ▪ He needs to learn how to *deal with* his anger. **4 :** to accept or try to accept (something that is true and cannot be changed) **:** to control your feelings about (something) ▪ She's still trying to *deal with* his death. ▪ I'm still *dealing with* the fact that we lost the game. ▪ The weather is bad, but we'll just have to *deal with it.*

– deal·er *noun, pl* **-ers** [*count*] ▪ a used car *dealer* ▪ drug *dealers*

²deal *noun, pl* **deals**

1 [*singular*] **:** a large number or amount **:** a lot — used in the phrases ***a good deal*** or ***a great deal*** ▪ It doesn't cost *a great deal* of money. [=doesn't cost much money] ▪ I spent *a good deal* of time [=a lot of time] thinking about it. ▪ It would mean *a great deal* to us if you would come. ▪ I learned *a great deal* from my mistakes. ▪ It's *a good deal* [=*much*] faster to go by bus. ▪ I felt *a great deal* better after the surgery. ▪ The town hasn't changed *a great deal* since we left.

2 [*count*] **:** the act of giving cards to each player in a card game — usually singular ▪ It's your *deal.* [=it's your turn to deal] ▪ I have time for one more *deal.* [=*hand, round*]

– compare ³DEAL

³deal *noun, pl* **deals**

1 [*count*] **:** an agreement between two or more people or groups that helps each in some way ▪ business *deals* ▪ I'll make you a *deal.* If you help me fix my flat tire, I'll buy you dinner. ▪ The company made/negotiated a new 10-million-dollar *deal* with the government. ▪ We were about to ***close/seal the deal*** [=make the agreement official] when we realized that there was a mistake in the contract. ▪ The two sides finally ***struck a deal*** [=came to an agreement] after weeks of negotiations. ▪ an ***arms deal*** [=an agreement to buy or sell weapons] between two countries ▪ The band got/landed/signed a ***record deal.*** = The band ***cut a deal*** with the record company. ▪ She got a ***book deal*** with a major publisher. ▪ We were offered a ***package deal*** [=a single price for a set of items or services] that included plane tickets, hotel accommodations, and tickets to shows in the area. ▪ We think it's a ***fair/square deal.*** [=a fair agreement] — see also DONE DEAL, SWEETHEART DEAL

2 [*singular*] **:** a way of treating someone ▪ He was going to take the promotion here but another company offered him a better *deal.* [=offered him more money, benefits, prestige, etc.] — see also BIG DEAL, RAW DEAL

3 [*count*] **:** a price that is fair or lower than the usual price ▪ We got a (good) *deal* on a new car. ▪ I think we can get a better *deal* somewhere else. ▪ Now that's a great *deal*!

4 ***the deal*** *informal* **:** basic information about a person, thing, or situation ▪ What's *the deal* [=*story, situation*] with that guy? ▪ Here's *the deal.* You're going to stay here while I go find help. ▪ What's *the deal* with those shoes you're wearing? [=Why are you wearing those shoes?]

one-shot deal **:** something that happens only one time ▪ This offer is a *one-shot-deal.* ▪ We don't want this to be a *one-shot deal.* We hope to have the festival every year.

the real deal *informal* **:** something or someone that is real or genuine **:** a thing or person that is not a copy or imitation ▪ These diamonds aren't fake. They're *the real deal.* ▪ That guy looked so much like Elvis, I almost thought he was *the real deal.* [=I almost thought he was Elvis]

– compare ²DEAL

deal·er·ship /ˈdiːlɚˌʃɪp/ *noun, pl* **-ships** [*count*] **:** a business that sells a specified kind of product ▪ a car *dealership*

dealing *noun, pl* **-ings**

1 ***deal·ings*** [*plural*] **:** the actions that are a main part of the relationship between people, groups, organizations, etc. **:** social or business interactions ▪ There were reports of shady *dealings* between the two sides. — often + *with* ▪ They were honest in their *dealings with* other nations. ▪ her financial *dealings with* the company

2 [*noncount*] **:** a way of behaving or of doing business ▪ He has a reputation for fair *dealing.*

dealt *past tense and past participle of* ¹DEAL

dean /ˈdiːn/ *noun, pl* **deans** [*count*]

1 : a person who is in charge of one of the parts of a university (such as a college or school) ▪ She's the *dean* of the university's business school. ▪ the *dean* of liberal arts

2 : a person whose job is to give advice to the students in a college or high school and to make sure that they obey the school's rules ▪ the *dean* of students

3 *US* **:** a person who has more experience in or knowledge about a particular profession, subject, etc., than anyone or almost anyone ▪ She's considered the *dean* [=*doyen*] of American architecture.

4 : a Christian priest who is in charge of several other priests or churches

– dean·ship /ˈdiːnˌʃɪp/ *noun, pl* **-ships** [*count*] ▪ She recently resigned her *deanship.*

dean's list *noun, pl* **~ lists** [*count*] *US* **:** a list of students at a college or university who have earned high grades — compare HONOR ROLL

¹dear /ˈdiɚ/ *adj* **dear·er; -est** [*also more ~; most ~*]

1 : loved or valued very much ▪ He's a *dear* [=*precious*] friend of mine. ▪ my *dearest* friend ▪ Our neighbor is a *dear* old lady. — often + *to* ▪ My grandmother was very *dear to* me. ▪ The book is *dear to* the hearts of many young readers.

2 — used in writing to address someone ▪ *Dear* Sir or Madam ▪ *Dear* Jane

3 *chiefly Brit* **:** having a high price **:** EXPENSIVE ▪ Peaches are *dear* this time of year.

for dear life see ¹LIFE

²dear *adv* **:** with love and respect — used in the phrase ***hold dear*** ▪ She lost her family, her home—everything that she *held dear.* [=loved and valued most] ▪ the way of life they *hold dear* — see also *cost you dear* at ²COST

³dear *noun, pl* **dears** [*count*]

1 — used to address someone you love ▪ Hello, *dear.* [=*darling, sweetheart*] ▪ Yes, my *dear*? ▪ John, *dear*, what time will you be home?

2 : a kind and helpful person ▪ Be a *dear* and take this for me.

⁴dear *interj* — used especially to express surprise, fear, or disappointment ▪ Oh *dear*! What a mess! ▪ Oh, *dear* me! ▪ *Dear* God! What are we going to do?

dear·ly /ˈdiɚli/ *adv* [*more ~; most ~*]

1 : very much ▪ She loved him *dearly.* ▪ I would *dearly* love to see them again. ▪ He *dearly* wanted to believe that it was true. ▪ her *dearly* beloved husband [=her husband, whom she loved very much] — see also *dearly beloved* at BELOVED

2 : in a way that is difficult or severe ▪ The men paid *dearly* for their crimes. [=they were punished severely] — see also *cost you dearly* at ²COST

dearth /ˈdɚθ/ *noun* [*singular*] *formal* **:** the state or condition of not having enough of something **:** LACK — + *of* ▪ The *dearth* [=*scarcity*] *of* jobs in the city forced many families to leave the area. ▪ a *dearth of* evidence

death /ˈdɛθ/ *noun, pl* **deaths**

1 a [*noncount*] **:** the end of life **:** the time when someone or something dies ▪ birth, life, and eventual *death* ▪ fear of *death* ▪ She is close to *death.* [=she will die soon] ▪ *death* threats ▪ The hostage managed to ***escape death.*** [=avoid being killed] ▪ The newspaper did not report the ***cause of death.*** ▪ She was convicted of murder and ***sentenced/condemned to death.*** [=told that she would be killed as punishment] — see also BRAIN DEATH, *death knell* at KNELL **b** [*count*] **:** the ending of a particular person's life ▪ People around the world mourned his *death*. ▪ She worked at the newspaper until her *death* at (age) 74. ▪ The accident resulted in two *deaths*. ▪ The number of *deaths* from cancer is rising. ▪ He died a violent/tragic *death*. ▪ There has been ***a death in the family***. ▪ She survived the plane crash and many years later died ***a natural death***. [=from natural causes; because she was old] ▪ The general ***met his death*** on the battlefield.

2 [*count*] **:** the permanent end of something that is not alive **:** the ruin or destruction of something ▪ the *death* of innocence ▪ the *death* of vaudeville ▪ the *death* of a marriage

3 ***Death*** [*noncount*] *literary* **:** the force that ends life and is often shown in art or literature as a skeleton ▪ *Death* could be seen lurking in the corner of the painting. ▪ when *Death* comes to take me away

a matter of life and death see [1]LIFE

at death's door **:** about to die **:** very sick and in danger of dying ▪ He is sick, but he's not *at death's door*.

be the death of **:** to cause (someone) to die ▪ I worry that his drug addiction will *be the death of* him. — often used figuratively ▪ Those kids ***will be the death of*** me! [=they worry and upset me very much]

catch your death (of cold) see [1]CATCH

like death warmed over (*US*) *or Brit* ***like death warmed up*** *informal* **:** very tired or sick ▪ We worked through the night, and by morning we looked *like death warmed over*.

put to death ✧ A person or animal that is *put to death* is killed at a scheduled time by someone who is legally allowed to do so. ▪ a serial killer who was *put to death* [=*executed*] for the murder of 28 people ▪ The dog that attacked the children was later *put to death*.

to death **1** — used to say how someone died or was killed ▪ He was shot/stabbed *to death*. ▪ They froze/starved *to death*. ▪ She drank herself *to death*. [=drank a lot of alcohol until it made her so sick that she died] **2 :** very much **:** to a great degree ▪ We were bored/scared *to death*. [=extremely bored/scared] ▪ That teacher works her students *to death*. [=she makes them work too hard] ▪ He's wonderful! I just love him *to death*! ▪ I'm ***sick to death*** of hearing about the scandal. [=I don't want to hear anything more about the scandal; I've heard too much about it] ▪ That song has been ***done to death***. [=many musicians have performed that song]

to the death **1 :** until someone is dead ▪ The warriors would fight *to the death*. ▪ a battle *to the death* **2 :** with all of your energy and effort ▪ Some parents do not want the school to be closed, and say they'll fight *to the death* for it.

— see also BLACK DEATH, KISS OF DEATH, SUDDEN DEATH

— **death·like** /ˈdɛθˌlaɪk/ *adj* ▪ a *deathlike* state

death·bed /ˈdɛθˌbɛd/ *noun, pl* **-beds**

on your deathbed **:** in the bed that you will soon die in ▪ She made a startling confession *on her deathbed*. [=just before she died] — often used figuratively to say that someone is very close to dying or very sick ▪ She's convinced that the old man is *on his deathbed*, but he looks healthy enough to me. ▪ I was so sick with the flu—practically *on my deathbed*.

— **deathbed** *adj, always used before a noun* ▪ a *deathbed* confession [=a confession made just before someone dies]

death benefit *noun, pl* ~ **-fits** [*count*] **:** money that an insurance company pays to the family of someone who has died because that person had life insurance

death blow *noun, pl* ~ **blows** [*count*]

1 : an act that kills a person or animal ▪ The general received his *death blow* in battle.

2 : an act or event that causes the end of something ▪ Recent declines in the economy have dealt the ailing company its final *death blow*.

death camp *noun, pl* ~ **camps** [*count*] **:** a place where large numbers of prisoners are taken to be killed during a war **:** a concentration camp where many people are killed ▪ Nazi *death camps*

death certificate *noun, pl* ~ **-cates** [*count*] **:** an official document that gives information about a person's death (such as when and how the death happened)

death–defying *adj* **:** very dangerous ▪ *death-defying* stunts

death duty *noun, pl* ~ **duties** [*count*] *Brit* **:** ESTATE TAX

death grip *noun* [*singular*] **:** a very tight hold on something ▪ He drove straight through the storm, never loosening his *death grip* on the steering wheel. — often used figuratively to suggest that something has a powerful and harmful effect on something else ▪ The group is trying to release the *death grip* [=*hold*] that drugs have on their neighborhood.

death·less /ˈdɛθləs/ *adj* — used to describe something that will never end or be forgotten ▪ *deathless* [=*immortal*] fame — often used in a joking or ironic way to describe writing that is very bad ▪ The band's *deathless* lyrics still haunt the airwaves. ▪ *deathless* prose

[1]**death·ly** /ˈdɛθli/ *adj* **:** relating to or seeming like death **:** causing you to think of death ▪ a *deathly* fear ▪ A *deathly* silence filled the room. — compare [1]DEADLY

[2]**deathly** *adv*

1 : in a way that is close to death or dying ▪ He became *deathly* ill.

2 : in a way that makes you think of death ▪ The room was *deathly* [=*utterly*] quiet. ▪ She's *deathly* afraid of snakes.

death mask *noun, pl* ~ **masks** [*count*] **:** a mask of a person's face that is created just after the person has died by pressing a substance over the face and leaving it there until it becomes hard

death penalty *noun*

the death penalty **:** death as a punishment given by a court of law for very serious crimes ▪ If convicted, he could face *the death penalty*. [=his punishment may be that he will be killed] ▪ She opposes *the death penalty*. [=*capital punishment*]

death rate *noun, pl* ~ **rates** [*count*]

1 : a number that shows how many people died in a particular place or during a particular time ▪ There was a decline in the country's *death rate* after its health care improved. — compare BIRTHRATE

2 : the number of deaths from a specific cause in a particular area during a particular time period ▪ Lung cancer *death rates* are up. ▪ The *death rate* from accidents is rising.

death rattle *noun, pl* ~ **rattles** [*count*] **:** a sound that is sometimes heard coming from a dying person's throat or chest — often used figuratively ▪ the *death rattle* of a dying industry

death ray *noun, pl* ~ **rays** [*count*] *in stories* **:** a weapon that sends out a very strong beam of energy that usually looks like light and that is able to destroy almost anything

death row *noun* [*noncount*] **:** the part of a prison where prisoners who will be killed as punishment for their crimes live until they are killed ▪ *death row* inmates — often used after *on* ▪ He was *on death row* for 12 years before he was executed.

death sentence *noun, pl* ~ **-tences** [*count*]

1 : the decision by a court of law that the punishment for someone's crime will be death ▪ She received a *death sentence* for the murders.

2 a : something (such as a disease) that is sure to cause death — usually singular ▪ With the new medicines available, AIDS is no longer an automatic *death sentence*. **b :** an act or event that ends something permanently — usually singular ▪ The cut in funding was a *death sentence* for the school's music program.

death's–head /ˈdɛθsˌhɛd/ *noun, pl* **-heads** [*count*] **:** a picture of the bones of a human head **:** a human skull used as a symbol for death ▪ a black shirt with a white *death's-head* on the back

death squad *noun, pl* ~ **squads** [*count*] **:** a group of people who kill people who oppose a particular ruler or political group

death tax *noun, pl* ~ **taxes** [*count*] *chiefly US* **:** ESTATE TAX

death throes *noun* [*plural*] **:** the violent movements and noises that are sometimes made by a person who is about to die ▪ The opera ends with the hero ***in his death throes***. — often used figuratively ▪ the *death throes* of a failing industry ▪ a sinking ship *in its death throes*

death toll *noun, pl* ~ **tolls** [*count*] **:** the number of people who die in an accident, disaster, war, etc. — usually singular ▪ Three people who were injured in the accident have died, pushing the *death toll* up to 116. ▪ The virus's *death toll* is expected to rise.

death trap *noun, pl* ~ **traps** [*count*] *informal* **:** a building, vehicle, etc., that is very dangerous and could cause someone's death ▪ That old elevator is a *death trap*. ▪ The factory was a *death trap* with too few exits for the workers to use in case of a fire.

death warrant *noun, pl* ~ **-rants** [*count*] **:** an official document ordering a person to be killed as a punishment — often used figuratively ▪ The law suit was the company's *death warrant*. ▪ If you share needles with other drug users, you're ***signing your own death warrant***. [=you are doing something that will cause your own death]

death·watch /ˈdɛθˌwɑːʧ/ *noun, pl* **-watch·es** [*count*] : a situation in which people stay with someone who is dying while waiting for death to occur — usually singular ▪ Her family gathered for the *deathwatch*.— sometimes used figuratively ▪ It looked like his acting career was over, but this new movie suggests that it is time to call off the *deathwatch*. [=the actor may become successful again]

death wish *noun* [*singular*] : a desire to die ▪ Have you seen the way she drives? She must have a *death wish*.

deb /ˈdɛb/ *noun, pl* **debs** [*count*] *informal* : DEBUTANTE

de·ba·cle /diˈbɑːkəl, *Brit* deɪˈbɑːkəl/ *noun, pl* **de·ba·cles** [*count*] : a great disaster or complete failure ▪ After the *debacle* of his first novel, he had trouble getting a publisher for his next book. ▪ a military *debacle* ▪ an economic *debacle*

de·bar /dɪˈbɑɚ/ *verb* **-bars; -barred; -bar·ring** [+ *obj*] *formal* : to officially prevent (someone) from having or doing something — usually + *from* ▪ The law *debars* him *from* running for reelection.— often used as *(be) debarred* ▪ She *was debarred from* receiving the scholarship when her criminal record came to light.

– **de·bar·ment** /dɪˈbɑɚmənt/ *noun* [*noncount*]

de·bark /dɪˈbɑɚk/ *verb* **-barks; -barked; -bark·ing** [*no obj*] : to leave a ship or plane ▪ The passengers *debarked* [=(more commonly) *disembarked*] in Miami. — opposite EMBARK

de·base /dɪˈbeɪs/ *verb* **-bas·es; -based; -bas·ing** [+ *obj*] : to lower the value or reputation of (someone or something) : to make (someone or something) less respected ▪ The governor *debased* himself by lying to the public. ▪ The holiday has been *debased* by commercialism.

– **debased** *adj* [*more* ~; *most* ~] ▪ a *debased* form of entertainment ▪ a *debased* coin/currency – **de·base·ment** /dɪˈbeɪsmənt/ *noun* [*noncount*] ▪ the *debasement* of women – **debasing** *adj* [*more* ~; *most* ~] ▪ Those ads are *debasing* [=*insulting*] to women. ▪ a *debasing* comment

de·bat·able /dɪˈbeɪtəbəl/ *adj* [*more* ~; *most* ~] — used to say that something may or may not be true or real ▪ The benefit of the tax cuts is highly *debatable*. ▪ The vaccine is of *debatable* [=*questionable*] value—it has been known to make some people quite sick. ▪ Whether the report is entirely accurate is *debatable*.

[1]**de·bate** /dɪˈbeɪt/ *noun, pl* **-bates** : a discussion between people in which they express different opinions about something ✧ A debate can be an organized event, an informal discussion between two or more people, or a general discussion that involves many people. [*count*] The candidates participated in several *debates* before the election was held. ▪ Our polite chat about politics slowly turned into a heated *debate*. [=*argument*] ▪ At the center/core/heart of the *debate* [=*controversy*] is the question of responsibility. — often + *on, about*, or *over* ▪ The university is hosting a *debate on* gun control. ▪ current *debates on/about* the value of public schools ▪ The town held a *debate over* what to do about the recent traffic problems. ▪ The court decision sparked a raging/furious *debate over* property rights. [*noncount*] The meaning of the text has been the subject of considerable/intense/lively *debate* among scholars for many years. ▪ What topics will be ***under debate***? [=*debated*] — often + *on, about*, or *over* ▪ There was much *debate on/about/over* whether the new program was worth the cost. ▪ There's little *debate* [=*controversy*] *about* the health benefits of moderate exercise. ▪ The book traces centuries of *debate over* the origins of language. ✧ If something is ***a matter of debate*** or ***open to debate***, people have different ideas and opinions about it. ▪ Whether or not the tax cuts benefit the poor is still *a matter of debate*. [=*debatable*] ▪ The accuracy of the report is *open to debate*.

[2]**debate** *verb* **-bates; -bat·ed; -bat·ing**

1 [+ *obj*] : to discuss (something) with people whose opinions are different from your own ▪ Scholars have been *debating* the meaning of the text for years. ▪ Whether or not the tax cuts benefit the lower classes is still hotly *debated* among economists. ▪ The energy bill is currently *being debated* in Congress.

2 : to compete against (someone) in a debate : to argue against another person's opinions as part of an organized event [+ *obj*] The President *debated* his challenger in front of a live audience on Tuesday. [*no obj*] The students *debated* for an hour. ▪ She was on the ***debating team*** [=a group that competes against other teams in formal debates] at school.

3 [+ *obj*] : to think about (something) in order to decide what to do ▪ I *debated* [=*considered*] moving to the city, but eventually decided against it.— often + *whether, what*, etc. ▪ I am still *debating* (with myself) *whether* to attend the wedding or not. ▪ She is still *debating what* to do.

– **de·bat·er** *noun, pl* **-ers** [*count*] ▪ He is one of the best *debaters* in on our school's team.

de·bauched /dɪˈbɑːʧt/ *adj* [*more* ~; *most* ~] *formal* : behaving in an immoral way that involves drinking too much alcohol, taking drugs, having sex with many people, etc. ▪ a *debauched* poet ▪ a *debauched* society

de·bauch·ery /dɪˈbɑːʧəri/ *noun, pl* **-er·ies** *formal* : bad or immoral behavior that involves sex, drugs, alcohol, etc. [*noncount*] He later regretted the *debauchery* of his youth. ▪ drunken *debauchery* [*count*] He recalled the evening's *debaucheries* with regret.

de·bil·i·tate /dɪˈbɪləˌteɪt/ *verb* **-tates; -tat·ed; -tat·ing** [+ *obj*] *formal* + *technical* : to make (someone or something) weak : to reduce the strength of (someone or something) ▪ The virus *debilitates* the body's immune system.— usually used as *(be) debilitated* ▪ His body *was debilitated* [=*weakened*] by the disease. ▪ The country's economy *has been debilitated* by years of civil war.

– **debilitating** *adj* [*more* ~; *most* ~] ▪ a *debilitating* condition/disease/illness ▪ The symptoms can be *debilitating*.
– **de·bil·i·ta·tion** /dɪˌbɪləˈteɪʃən/ *noun* [*noncount*] ▪ physical *debilitation*

de·bil·i·ty /dɪˈbɪləti/ *noun, pl* **-ties** *formal* : physical weakness caused by illness or old age [*noncount*] The disease leads to *debility* but rarely kills. [*count*] the *debilities* of elderly people

[1]**deb·it** /ˈdɛbət/ *noun, pl* **-its** [*count*] : an amount of money that is taken from an account ▪ I forgot to enter some of the *debits* in my bank account register. ▪ The account's credits were added and the *debits* subtracted. ▪ a $30 *debit* for groceries— opposite CREDIT; see also DIRECT DEBIT

***on the debit side* 1** *chiefly Brit* : in the section of a financial record where debits are written ▪ Enter these amounts *on the debit side*. **2** — used when mentioning the things that you do not like about something ▪ *On the debit side*, there have been a number of complaints about noise from the restaurant.

[2]**debit** *verb* **-its; -it·ed; -it·ing** [+ *obj*] : to take money from (an account) ▪ The bank mistakenly *debited* my account $200! ▪ Your account will automatically be *debited* for the amount of your insurance bill every month. — opposite CREDIT

debit card *noun, pl* ~ **cards** [*count*] : a small plastic card that is used to buy things by having the money to pay for them taken directly from your bank account — compare BANK CARD, CASH CARD, CREDIT CARD

deb·o·nair /ˌdɛbəˈneɚ/ *adj* [*more* ~; *most* ~] *somewhat old-fashioned, of a man* : dressing and acting in an appealing and sophisticated way : fashionable, attractive, and confident ▪ a *debonair* man in a suit and top hat ▪ His handsome face and *debonair* [=*suave, urbane*] manner made him very popular with the ladies.

de·bone /diˈboun/ *verb* **-bones; -boned; -bon·ing** [+ *obj*] : to remove the bones from (something) : BONE ▪ Have the butcher *debone* the lamb for you. ▪ a *deboned* chicken breast

de·brief /diˈbriːf/ *verb* **-briefs; -briefed; -brief·ing** [+ *obj*] *formal* : to officially question (someone) about a job that has been done or about an experience ▪ Police *debriefed* the hostages upon their return. ▪ The pilot was *debriefed* after his flight.— compare [3]BRIEF

– **debriefing** *noun* [*count*] the *debriefings* of hostages ▪ a full *debriefing* [*noncount*] The crew met for *debriefing*.

de·bris /dəˈbriː, *Brit* ˈdɛˌbriː/ *noun* [*noncount*]

1 : the pieces that are left after something has been destroyed ▪ After the earthquake, rescuers began digging through the *debris* in search of survivors. ▪ Everything was covered by dust and *debris*.— sometimes used figuratively ▪ She sifted through the *debris* of her broken marriage.

2 : things (such as broken pieces and old objects) that are lying where they fell or that have been left somewhere because they are not wanted ▪ The crew cleaned up cigarette butts and other *debris*. [=*trash, rubbish*]

debt /ˈdɛt/ *noun, pl* **debts**

1 [*count*] : an amount of money that you owe to a person, bank, company, etc. ▪ He is trying to pay off gambling *debts*. ▪ The company has run up huge *debts*. ▪ Their *debts* are piling up. ▪ She's finally paid off her mortgage *debt*. [=the money that she owed the bank to pay for her house] ▪ the nation's growing ***foreign debt*** [=the amount of money that a country owes other countries] ▪ Most of his debts are ***consumer***

D

debts [=most of his debts are from buying things at stores] — see also NATIONAL DEBT
2 [*noncount*] **:** the state of owing money to someone or something • He is drowning in a sea of *debt.* [=he owes a very large amount of money] • a mountain of *debt* • He's been working three jobs in an attempt to get ***out of debt*** • The company was ***in debt*** but is now turning a profit. • I am deep/heavily *in debt.* • I'm thousands of dollars *in debt.* • She went ***into debt*** to pay for college. • I'm worried that we will fall *into debt.* • banks with millions of dollars of ***bad debt*** [=banks that have loaned millions of dollars that will not be repaid] • a ***debt-ridden*** country [=a country with more debt than it can pay]
3 [*count*] **:** the fact that you have been influenced or helped by someone or something — usually singular • The photographer has acknowledged a/his *debt* to Andy Warhol. [=the photographer has said that his work was influenced by the photographs made by Andy Warhol]
debt to society — used in phrases like ***pay your debt to society*** to refer to being punished for committing a crime • after 10 years in prison, he has *paid his debt to society* and is a free man.
in someone's debt ✧ If you are *in someone's debt,* you are very thankful for something that someone has done for you. • I am *in your debt* for your help and support.
owe a debt of gratitude/thanks to **:** to have a good reason to be very grateful to (someone) • The whole town *owes a debt of gratitude to* the people who organized the parade.

debt·or /ˈdɛtɚ/ *noun, pl* **-ors** [*count*] **:** a person, organization, government, etc., that owes money • The *debtor* agrees to pay the debt over a three-year period. — opposite CREDITOR

de·bug /diˈbʌg/ *verb* **-bugs; -bugged; -bug·ging** [+ *obj*] *technical* **:** to remove the mistakes from (something, such as a computer program) • She's been hired to write and *debug* computer programs.

de·bunk /diˈbʌŋk/ *verb* **-bunks; -bunked; -bunk·ing** [+ *obj*] **:** to show that something (such as a belief or theory) is not true **:** to show the falseness of (a story, idea, statement, etc.) • The article *debunks* the notion that life exists on Mars. • The results of the study *debunk* his theory.
— de·bunk·er *noun, pl* **-ers** [*count*] • *debunkers* of the myth

¹de·but /ˈdeɪˌbjuː/ *noun, pl* **-buts** [*count*] **:** the first time an actor, musician, athlete, etc., does something in public or for the public • my *debut* as a pianist • He made his singing *debut* at a very young age. • She is making her television/film *debut.* — sometimes used to refer to the first appearance of a product, sport, event, etc. • the *debut* of a new car • The sport's Olympic *debut* took place in 1980. — often used before another noun • her *debut* album/film/novel

²debut *verb* **de·buts; de·buted; de·but·ing**
1 [*no obj*] **:** to appear in public for the first time **:** to make a debut • The singer *debuted* 10 years ago, at the age of 15. • The car *debuted* 30 years ago. • The computer will soon be *debuting* in stores across the country.
2 [+ *obj*] **:** to show or provide (something, such as a product, television show, etc.) to the public for the first time • The network *debuts* a new sitcom tonight.

deb·u·tante /ˈdɛbjʊˌtɑːnt/ *noun, pl* **-tantes** [*count*] **:** a young upper-class woman who has begun going to special parties where she will meet and be seen by other people from the upper class

Dec. *abbr* December • *Dec.* 1, 2004

de·cade /ˈdɛˌkeɪd/ *noun, pl* **-cades** [*count*] **:** a period of 10 years • The war lasted nearly a *decade.* • a *decade* of drought [=a drought that lasted 10 years] • The bridge was built a *decade* ago.; *especially* **:** a 10-year period beginning with a year ending in 0 • The *decade* of the 1920s runs from January 1, 1920 to December 31, 1929. • the first *decade* of the 21st century • There have been a lot of changes during/in/over the past two *decades.*

dec·a·dence /ˈdɛkədəns/ *noun* [*noncount*] *disapproving* **:** behavior that shows low morals and a great love of pleasure, money, fame, etc. • The book condemns the *decadence* of modern society. • Western *decadence*

dec·a·dent /ˈdɛkədənt/ *adj* [*more ~; most ~*]
1 *disapproving* **a :** having low morals and a great love of pleasure, money, fame, etc. • The book condemns some of society's wealthiest members as *decadent* fools. **b :** attractive to people of low morals who are only interested in pleasure • the city's *decadent* nightclubs
2 : extremely pleasing • a wealthy and *decadent* lifestyle • the restaurant's *decadent* desserts • rich, *decadent* pastries • a *decadent* hotel room, complete with a hot tub • We relaxed in *decadent* luxury.
— dec·a·dent·ly *adv* • *decadently* rich pastries

de·caf /ˈdiːˌkæf/ *noun, pl* **-cafs :** coffee that does not contain caffeine **:** decaffeinated coffee [*noncount*] Would you like regular coffee or *decaf?* [*count*] Can I have a *decaf,* please? • They ordered two *decafs* and a regular (coffee).

de·caf·fein·at·ed /diˈkæfəˌneɪtəd/ *adj* **:** not containing caffeine **:** having the caffeine removed • *decaffeinated* coffee/tea • *decaffeinated* cola

de·cal /ˈdiːˌkæl/ *noun, pl* **-cals** [*count*] *US* **:** a picture, design, or label that will stick to the surface on which it is placed after the paper on the back of it is removed • She put some new *decals* [=*stickers,* (*Brit*) *transfers*] on her car window.

de·camp /dɪˈkæmp/ *verb* **-camps; -camped; -camp·ing** [*no obj*] **:** to leave a place suddenly and secretly • She took the papers and *decamped.* • He *decamped* to/for Europe soon after news of the scandal broke.

de·cant /dɪˈkænt/ *verb* **-cants; -cant·ed; -cant·ing** [+ *obj*] *formal* **:** to pour (a liquid, especially wine) from one container into another • The bottles were uncorked and the wine was *decanted* an hour before the meal.

de·cant·er /dɪˈkæntɚ/ *noun, pl* **-ers** [*count*] **:** a special glass bottle into which wine, whiskey, etc., is poured from its original bottle and from which it is served • The waiter served us wine from an elegant *decanter.* • a *decanter* of port

de·cap·i·tate /dɪˈkæpəˌteɪt/ *verb* **-tates; -tat·ed; -tat·ing** [+ *obj*] **:** to cut off the head of (a person or animal) • Hundreds were *decapitated* [=*beheaded*] by the guillotine. • the monster's *decapitated* body
— de·cap·i·ta·tion /dɪˌkæpəˈteɪʃən/ *noun, pl* **-tions** [*noncount*] death by *decapitation* [*count*] gruesome *decapitations*

de·cath·lon /dɪˈkæθlən/ *noun, pl* **-lons** [*count*] **:** a sports contest for men that consists of 10 different events • the Olympic *decathlon*
— de·cath·lete /dɪˈkæθˌliːt/ *noun, pl* **-letes** [*count*]

¹de·cay /dɪˈkeɪ/ *verb* **-cays; -cayed; -cay·ing**
1 : to be slowly destroyed by natural processes **:** to be slowly broken down by the natural processes that destroy a dead plant or body [*no obj*] Tomatoes that fall off the vine will *decay* [=*rot*] on the ground. • a dead fish *decaying* [=*decomposing*] on the beach • the smell of *decaying/decayed* rubbish [+ *obj*] dead plants and leaves *decayed* by bacteria
2 [*no obj*] **:** to slowly lose strength, health, etc. • She believes that the moral fiber of our society is *decaying.* • our *decaying* public school system • His mind/health is beginning to *decay.* [=*decline*]
3 [*no obj*] *of a building, area, etc.* **:** to go slowly from a bad condition to a worse condition **:** to slowly enter a state of ruin • The city's neighborhoods are *decaying.*

> ***synonyms*** DECAY, DECOMPOSE, ROT, PUTREFY, and SPOIL mean to slowly fall apart and become destroyed by natural processes. DECAY is the most general of these terms. It often suggests a slow change from a state of strength or perfection. • a *decaying* mansion DECOMPOSE stresses that bacteria, worms, insects, etc., are destroying and breaking apart something that is dead. • the animal's *decomposing* flesh • Eventually the vegetation *decomposes* and is mixed with dirt and used in the garden. ROT is a close synonym of DECOMPOSE but also suggests a bad smell. • Flies swarmed around the *rotting* fruit. PUTREFY is very similar to DECOMPOSE and ROT but is used to refer to dead people or animals and not to plants. It suggests that something is extremely unpleasant to see or smell. • corpses *putrefying* on the battlefield SPOIL is used when talking about food that is no longer safe to eat. • The meat will *spoil* if it is not kept cold.

²decay *noun* [*noncount*] **:** the process or result of decaying: such as **a :** the process or result of being slowly destroyed by natural processes • the *decay* of dead plants and leaves • tooth *decay* **b :** the slow loss of strength, health, etc. • She writes about the moral *decay* of our society. • We're concerned about the *decay* [=*deterioration*] of our public school system. • the patient's physical and mental *decay* **c** *of a building, area, etc.* **:** the process or result of going slowly from a bad condition to a worse condition • The city's neighborhoods are in slow *decay.* • She wants to restore an old theater that is ***falling into decay.*** [=falling into ruin]

de·cease /dɪˈsiːs/ *noun* [*noncount*] *formal* **:** the death of a person ▪ He had many debts at the time of his *decease*.

de·ceased *adj* : no longer living ▪ Both his parents are *deceased*. [=*dead*] ▪ his *deceased* aunt

> ***usage*** *Dead* and *deceased* both mean "no longer living," but *deceased* is a gentler term, and people often use it when the person who died was close to them or when they are talking to someone who knew the person who died. ▪ My mother is *deceased*. ▪ Is your grandfather alive or *deceased*?

the deceased *formal* : a dead person or dead people ▪ a relative of *the deceased* ▪ Three of *the deceased* are being buried today.

de·ce·dent /dɪˈsiːdn̩t/ *noun, pl* **-dents** [*count*] *US, law* : a dead person ▪ a tax on the estate of the *decedent*

de·ceit /dɪˈsiːt/ *noun, pl* **-ceits** : dishonest behavior : behavior that is meant to fool or trick someone [*noncount*] He achieved his goals through lies and (a web of) *deceit*. [=*deception*] ▪ I began to suspect them of *deceit*. [=*deceitfulness*] [*count*] We were angry when we discovered that her excuse was really a *deceit*. [=*lie*]

de·ceit·ful /dɪˈsiːtfəl/ *adj* [*more* ~; *most* ~] : not honest : making or trying to make someone believe something that is not true ▪ a scheming, *deceitful* [=*dishonest*] person ▪ a *deceitful* answer ▪ *deceitful* [=*deceiving*] advertisements

– de·ceit·ful·ly *adv* ▪ He acted *deceitfully*. **– de·ceit·ful·ness** *noun* [*noncount*] ▪ He was surprised by the child's *deceitfulness*.

de·ceive /dɪˈsiːv/ *verb* **-ceives; -ceived; -ceiv·ing** : to make (someone) believe something that is not true [+ *obj*] Her parents punished her for trying to *deceive* them. ▪ The wall doesn't look real—it wouldn't *deceive* [=*fool*] a child. ▪ He was accused of *deceiving* the customer about the condition of the car. ▪ People who think they can eat whatever they want without harming their health are *deceiving* themselves. ▪ Unless my eyes *deceive* me [=unless I am mistaken about what I am seeing], there are no children in the room. ▪ It's no use ***deceiving ourselves into thinking*** [=it will not be helpful if we pretend] that everything will be fine. [*no obj*] Remember that appearances can *deceive*—just because something looks good doesn't mean it is good.

– de·ceiv·er *noun, pl* **-ers** [*count*] **– de·ceiv·ing** *adj* [*more* ~; *most* ~] ▪ Appearances can be very *deceiving*. [=*deceptive*] **– de·ceiv·ing·ly** /dɪˈsiːvɪŋli/ *adv* ▪ The game is *deceivingly* [=*deceptively*] easy.

de·cel·er·ate /diˈsɛləˌreɪt/ *verb* **-ates; -at·ed; -at·ing**

1 : to move slower : to lose speed [*no obj*] He *decelerated* [=*slowed down*] as he neared the exit on the highway. ▪ The car slowly *decelerated*. [+ *obj*] *decelerate* an airplane/automobile — opposite ACCELERATE

2 : to cause (something) to happen more slowly [+ *obj*] *decelerate* soil erosion ▪ *decelerate* economic growth [*no obj*] Economic growth is *decelerating*. [=happening more slowly]

– de·cel·er·a·tion /diˌsɛləˈreɪʃən/ *noun* [*noncount*] ▪ the airplane's *deceleration* ▪ the *deceleration* of soil erosion

De·cem·ber /dɪˈsɛmbɚ/ *noun, pl* **-bers** : the 12th and last month of the year [*noncount*] Her birthday is in late *December*. ▪ The first snow of that winter came in (early/mid-/late) *December*. ▪ The party is on the 10th of *December*. = (*US*) The party is on *December* 10th. = The party is on *December* the 10th. [*count*] This *December* was not as cold as the past few *Decembers* have been. — abbr. *Dec.*

de·cen·cy /ˈdiːsn̩si/ *noun, pl* **-cies**

1 [*noncount*] : polite, moral, and honest behavior and attitudes that show respect for other people ▪ *Decency*, not fear of punishment, caused them to do the right thing. ▪ Their behavior goes beyond the bounds of *decency*. [=it is not decent or acceptable] ▪ Sending aid to the victims was simply a matter of ***common decency***. ▪ If you're going to be late, please ***have the decency to*** call and let me know. ▪ Have you no ***sense of decency***?

2 ***decencies*** [*plural*] *formal* : the behaviors that people in a society consider to be proper or acceptable ▪ He had been taught to observe the ordinary *decencies*.

de·cent /ˈdiːsn̩t/ *adj* [*more* ~; *most* ~]

1 a : polite, moral, and honest ▪ I don't understand how so *decent* a person could be involved with this kind of crime. ▪ *decent*, hardworking people ▪ He is a *decent* guy who would help anyone in need. ▪ You need to do the *decent* thing and tell her what happened. **b** *somewhat informal* : showing kindness : seeming to care about the feelings or problems of other people ▪ It's really *decent* [=*nice, thoughtful*] of them to help us like this. ▪ I apologized for the damage to his car, and he was pretty *decent* [=*understanding*] about it.

2 : good enough but not the best : adequate or acceptable ▪ She's a *decent* [=*fairly good*] tennis player. ▪ They can't afford *decent* [=*adequate*] housing. ▪ Are there any *decent* schools in that area? ▪ They served us a *decent* (enough) meal. ▪ I've got to get some *decent* clothes. ▪ He makes a *decent* living. = He has a job making/earning *decent* money. ▪ a ***halfway decent*** [=*pretty good*] movie

3 : appropriate or suitable ▪ I know you've got a lot to do, but try to get to bed at a *decent* hour. [=at a time that is not too late at night] ▪ We were asked to wait a *decent* interval [=wait for an appropriate amount of time] before making the announcement. — opposite INDECENT

4 : not using language that offends people : not including behavior or ideas that people commonly find offensive ▪ Please keep your jokes *decent*—there are children in the room. — opposite INDECENT

5 *informal* : wearing enough clothes : wearing clothes that cover enough of your body so that you are not embarrassed if someone sees you ▪ I can't come to the door right now—I'm not *decent*. Wait a minute, OK? ▪ Can I come in? Are you *decent*?

– de·cent·ly *adv* ▪ He's fair and always treats everyone *decently*. ▪ The book is selling *decently* [=*fairly well; well enough*] but we were expecting it to sell better. ▪ *decently* dressed

de·cen·tral·ize *also Brit* **de·cen·tral·ise** /diˈsɛntrəˌlaɪz/ *verb* **-iz·es; -ized; -iz·ing** : to change (something) by taking control, power, etc., from one person or group and giving it to many people or groups throughout an area [+ *obj*] The plan is to *decentralize* the school system and give each district control over its own policies. ▪ a highly *decentralized* organization [=an organization in which many people have power] [*no obj*] The organization has decided to *decentralize*.

– de·cen·tral·i·za·tion *also Brit* **de·cen·tral·i·sa·tion** /diˌsɛntrələˈzeɪʃən, *Brit* diˌsɛntrəˌlaɪˈzeɪʃən/ *noun* [*singular*] a *decentralization* of power [*noncount*] government *decentralization*

de·cep·tion /dɪˈsɛpʃən/ *noun, pl* **-tions**

1 [*noncount*] : the act of making someone believe something that is not true : the act of deceiving someone ▪ She accuses the company of willful *deception* in its advertising. ▪ The article describes the government's use of *deception* [=*deceit*] to gain public support for the program. ▪ She ***practiced deception*** on her unsuspecting clients. [=she deceived them]

2 [*count*] : an act or statement intended to make people believe something that is not true ▪ His many *deceptions* did not become known until years after he died. ▪ It was a misunderstanding on her part, not a deliberate *deception* on his (part). [=he didn't try to deceive her or lie to her] ▪ a clever *deception* [=*trick*] — see also SELF-DECEPTION

de·cep·tive /dɪˈsɛptɪv/ *adj* [*more* ~; *most* ~]

1 : intended to make someone believe something that is not true ▪ The article accuses the company of *deceptive* [=*misleading*] advertising. ▪ The low price is *deceptive*. [=*deceiving, misleading*] Many fees are added to it before the purchase is complete.

2 : likely to make someone believe something that is not true ▪ the *deceptive* simplicity of the lyrics [=the lyrics are not as simple as they seem] ▪ Don't buy the car without driving it first—appearances can be *deceptive*. [=something can look much better than it actually is]

– de·cep·tive·ly *adv* ▪ *deceptively* simple lyrics ▪ *deceptively* low prices

deci·bel /ˈdɛsəˌbɛl/ *noun, pl* **-bels** [*count*] *technical* : a unit for measuring how loud a sound is ▪ a rock concert blasting music at 110 *decibels* ▪ suffered hearing loss from repeated exposure to high *decibels* [=to loud sounds] — abbr. *dB*

de·cide /dɪˈsaɪd/ *verb* **-cides; -cid·ed; -cid·ing**

1 a : to make a choice about (something) : to choose (something) after thinking about it [+ *obj*] He *decided* that dinner would be at 7 o'clock, and asked guests to arrive at 6. — often followed by *to* + *verb* ▪ She *decided to go* along with us. ▪ They have *decided* not *to leave*. — often + *what, where, whether, if*, etc. ▪ Have you *decided what* you'd like for breakfast? ▪ He is having trouble *deciding which* school to go to. ▪ She says she'll *decide* by January *whether* (or not) to run for office. ▪ We are *deciding if* we should stay. [*no obj*] She is having difficulty *deciding* about the offer. ▪ I *decided* in favor of the other candidate. [=I chose the other candidate] ▪ Vot-

D

ers must ***decide between*** the two candidates. [=voters must choose one or the other candidate] • You have to ***decide for yourself***. [=you are the only one who can decide] • I ***decided against*** telling her. [=I decided not to tell her] **b** : to choose whether or not to believe (something) after thinking about it : to reach a conclusion about (something) because of evidence [+ *obj*] They *decided* that he was right. • I am trying to *decide* if it's warm enough for swimming. [*no obj*] "Do you think she is telling the truth?" "I'm not sure. I'm still trying to *decide*."

2 : to cause (something) to end in a particular way : to determine what the result of (something) will be [+ *obj*] A few hundred votes could *decide* the election. • One blow *decided* the fight. • This battle could very well *decide* the war. [*no obj*] Will the business be successful? Let the public *decide*. — often used as *deciding* • the *deciding* game in the series [=the game that determines who wins the series] • The vice president will cast the *deciding* vote.

3 *law* : to end (a court case) in a particular way : to make a judgment in a court of law [+ *obj*] The case will be *decided* by the Supreme Court. [*no obj*] The court ***decided against*** the defendant. [=the defendant was found guilty] • The court *decided* in favor of the plaintiff. = (less commonly) The court ***decided for*** the plaintiff. [=the plaintiff won the case]

decide on/upon [*phrasal verb*] ***decide on/upon (something)*** : to choose (something) after thinking about the possible choices • He *decided on* blue rather than green. • We looked at all the cats in the pet store and finally *decided on* a little black-and-white one. • I am having trouble *deciding on* a gift for them.

deciding factor **1** : something that causes you to make a particular decision • The *deciding factor* was cost. [=the decision was based on cost; the least expensive option was chosen] • His lack of experience was the *deciding factor* in my decision not to hire him. **2** : something that causes something to end a particular way • His home run was the *deciding factor* in the game. [=his home run won the game]

decided *adj, always used before a noun* : clear and definite : easy to notice • The team has a *decided* [=*clear, obvious*] advantage in this competition. • The new paint on the house is a *decided* [=*definite*] improvement.

de·cid·ed·ly /dɪˈsaɪdədli/ *adv*
1 : clearly and definitely : in a way that is easy to notice • The phrases have *decidedly* different meanings. • The movie received *decidedly* mixed reviews. [=received very good reviews and very bad reviews]
2 *chiefly Brit* : in a way that shows that you are certain : in a way that shows that you have no doubt • She answered the question *decidedly*: "No, I will not lie for him."

de·cid·er /dɪˈsaɪdɚ/ *noun, pl* **-ers** [*count*] : the last part of a game or competition that will decide a winner — usually singular • The series is tied 3–3, and the *decider* [=the last game of the series; the deciding game] will be played tonight.

de·cid·u·ous /dɪˈsɪʤəwəs/ *adj, of a tree, bush, etc.* : having leaves that fall off every year • the bare branches of a *deciduous* tree in winter • the region's *deciduous* forests [=forests that are made up of deciduous trees] • *deciduous* and coniferous trees/forests

[1]**dec·i·mal** /ˈdɛsəməl/ *adj, mathematics* : based on the number 10 • the *decimal* system • a number with three ***decimal places*** [=a number with three digits that follow the decimal point; a number like 1.234 or .567] • In the number 8.901, the 9 is in the first *decimal place*.

[2]**decimal** *noun, pl* **-mals** [*count*] *mathematics* : a number that is written with a dot between the part of the number that is equal to 1 or more and the part of the number that is less than 1 • The number 67.398 is a *decimal*. It is equal to the whole number 67 plus the *decimal* .398. • Seven-tenths written as a *decimal* is .7. Seven-tenths written as a fraction is 7⁄10. • The *decimal* .2 is equal to the fraction 2⁄10. — called also *decimal fraction*

decimal point *noun, pl* **~ points** [*count*] *mathematics* : the dot (as in .678 or 3.678) that separates a whole number from tenths, hundredths, etc.

dec·i·mate /ˈdɛsəˌmeɪt/ *verb* **-mates; -mat·ed; -mat·ing** [+ *obj*]
1 : to destroy a large number of (plants, animals, people, etc.) • This kind of moth is responsible for *decimating* thousands of trees in our town. — usually used as *(be) decimated* • The bay's lobsters *have been decimated* by disease. • The village/population *was decimated* by plague.
2 : to severely damage or destroy a large part of (something) • Budget cuts have *decimated* public services in small towns. — usually used as *(be) decimated* • The landscape *is decimated* by pollution. • the company's *decimated* stock prices
– dec·i·ma·tion /ˌdɛsəˈmeɪʃən/ *noun* [*noncount*]

de·ci·pher /dɪˈsaɪfɚ/ *verb* **-phers; -phered; -pher·ing** [+ *obj*] : to find the meaning of (something that is difficult to read or understand) • *decipher* [=*decode*] a secret message • The ancient scrolls were recently *deciphered*. [=*translated*] • We spent hours trying to *decipher* [=*figure out*] the lyrics to the song. • I couldn't *decipher* his sloppy handwriting.
– de·ci·pher·able /dɪˈsaɪfərəbəl/ *adj* [*more ~; most ~*] • barely *decipherable* handwriting **– de·ci·pher·ment** /dɪˈsaɪfɚmənt/ *noun* [*noncount*] • the *decipherment* of the ancient scrolls

de·ci·sion /dɪˈsɪʒən/ *noun, pl* **-sions**
1 [*count*] : a choice that you make about something after thinking about it : the result of deciding • She announced her *decision* to go to medical school. • a big/controversial/final *decision* • Have you ***made/reached a decision***? • After weeks of deliberation, he finally ***came to a decision***. = After weeks of deliberation, he finally ***arrived at a decision***. • He ***based his decision on*** facts, not emotions. • She made a ***conscious decision*** to leave the painting unfinished. • (*Brit*) The government has ***taken a decision*** to withdraw all troops. [=the government has made an important and official decision to withdraw all troops] • an ***informed decision*** [=a decision based on facts or information] • a ***split-second decision*** [=a decision that must be made in an instant] ✧ In informal spoken English, someone who says "***Decisions, decisions***" is having difficulty making a decision, usually about an unimportant matter. • "*Decisions, decisions*. I can't decide which flavor of ice cream to get."
2 [*noncount*] *formal* : the ability to make choices quickly and confidently • a leader of courage and *decision* [=*decisiveness*] • We need someone who will act with *decision* even under pressure. — opposite INDECISION
3 [*count*] **a** : the particular end of a legal or official argument : a legal or official judgment • The U.S. Supreme Court's 1954 *decision* brought an end to racial segregation in public schools. • The Supreme Court ***handed down a 5–4 decision***. [=five members of the court voted one way, and the other four members voted the opposite way, and the side with the five votes won] • The appeals court ***upheld the decision***. [=the appeals court agreed with the decision made earlier by a lower court] • The appeals court ***overturned the decision***. [=the appeals court disagreed with the decision made earlier by a lower court] **b** : a report explaining why a legal or official judgment was made in a particular way • the court's ten-page *decision*
4 [*noncount*] : the act of deciding something • The moment of *decision* has come. You must decide. • The judge has the power of *decision*. [=the judge has the power to make the decision]

decision–making *noun* [*noncount*] : the act or process of deciding something especially with a group of people • The project will require some difficult *decision-making*. • All members of the organization have a role in *decision-making*. — often used before another noun • the company's *decision-making* process

de·ci·sive /dɪˈsaɪsɪv/ *adj* [*more ~; most ~*]
1 : able to make choices quickly and confidently • You must be *decisive* and persistent to succeed in this competitive field. • I stood there wondering what to do, but my sister was more *decisive* and immediately went to the phone. • a *decisive* leader • In emergency situations, one must be able to take ***decisive action***. [=to act quickly and with confidence] — opposite INDECISIVE
2 : causing something to end in a particular way : determining what the result of something will be • She cast the *decisive* [=*deciding*] vote. • The fight ended with a *decisive* blow. • the *decisive* battle of the war • The poverty of his childhood played a *decisive* role in his adult life. • The meeting is seen as a ***decisive step*** toward a peace treaty. ✧ A ***decisive factor*** is a reason to make a particular choice or decision. • The *decisive factor* [=*deciding factor*] was cost. • His lack of experience was the *decisive factor* in my decision not to hire him.
3 : very clear and obvious • a *decisive* victory/win/advantage
– de·ci·sive·ly *adv* • You must be able to act *decisively* to succeed in this competitive field. • She *decisively* rejected their proposal. **– de·ci·sive·ness** *noun* [*noncount*] • The job requires *decisiveness* [=*decision*] and persistence.

[1]**deck** /ˈdɛk/ *noun, pl* **decks**

1 : a flat surface that forms the main outside floor of a boat or ship [*count*] We stood on the *deck* and watched dolphins swim near the ship. [*noncount*] A number of passengers had come ***on deck***. ✧ When you are ***below deck*** or ***below decks***, you are in the section of a boat or ship that is under the deck. • We went *below deck* to our cabin. • I stowed my gear *below decks*. ✧ The phrase ***all hands on deck*** is used to call all people on a boat or ship to the deck to do work that must be done. • We heard the captain shout "*All hands on deck*!" as waves crashed over the boat's bow.
2 [*count*] **a** : one of the levels on a bus, ship, etc. • the lower/middle/upper *deck* • a seat on the streetcar's top *deck* • a cabin on B *deck* **b** : one of the seating levels in a sports stadium • We sat in the lower/upper *deck*.
3 [*count*] *chiefly US* : a wood structure that has a floor but no walls or roof, is attached to a house or other building, and is used for sitting and relaxing • We ate out on the *deck*. • You can see into three different states from the mountaintop restaurant's ***observation deck***. [=a platform built so that people can see or watch something] — see picture at HOUSE
4 [*count*] *chiefly US* : a complete set of playing cards : a group of 52 playing cards • The dealer shuffled the *deck* (of cards). — called also *pack* ✧ In informal U.S. English, someone who is ***not playing with a full deck*** is not able to think or act in a normal way. • "He seemed a little weird." "Yeah, he's *not playing with a full deck*."
5 [*count*] : TAPE DECK
clear the decks *also* ***clear the deck*** : to get ready for action or for something new : to get rid of something to make room for something else • He wants to *clear the decks* before the election campaign starts. • Firing the CEO will *clear the decks* for change within the company.
hit the deck see [1]HIT
on deck *US* **1** *baseball* : waiting to bat next • Smith is batting and Jones is *on deck*. **2** *informal* : next in a series • The band's new song is *on deck* [=*next*] after this commercial break. — see also [1]DECK 1 (above)

[2]**deck** *verb* **decks; decked; deck·ing** [+ *obj*]
1 : to decorate (something) • We spent hours *decking* the chapel with flowers before the wedding. — see also DECKED OUT 2 (below)
2 *informal* : to knock (someone) down by hitting very hard • He *decked* him with one punch.
decked out **1** : dressed in a very fancy way • We got ***all decked out*** for the occasion. — often + *in* • She was *decked out in* furs. • guys *decked out in* fancy tuxedos • She was *all decked out in* a new dress. **2** : decorated in a fancy way — often + *with* • a room *decked out with* hundreds of little lights

deck chair *noun, pl* ~ **chairs** [*count*] : a chair that can be folded up and that is used for sitting outside on the deck of a ship, on a beach, etc.

deck·hand /ˈdɛkˌhænd/ *noun, pl* **-hands** [*count*] : a worker on a ship who does work that does not require special training

deck·ing /ˈdɛkɪŋ/ *noun* [*noncount*] : material that is used to build a deck (sense 3) • wooden *decking*

deck shoe *noun, pl* ~ **shoes** [*count*] : a flat shoe that is usually made of thick cloth and has a rubber bottom

de·claim /dɪˈkleɪm/ *verb* **-claims; -claimed; -claim·ing** *formal* : to say (something) in usually a loud and formal way [+ *obj*] The actress *declaimed* her lines with passion. [*no obj*] The speakers *declaimed* on a variety of issues.
– dec·la·ma·tion /ˌdɛkləˈmeɪʃən/ *noun, pl* **-tions** [*count, noncount*]

de·clam·a·to·ry /dɪˈklæməˌtori, *Brit* dɪˈklæmətri/ *adj* [*more* ~; *most* ~] *formal* : expressing feelings or opinions in a way that is loud and forceful • *declamatory* speeches/statements

dec·la·ra·tion /ˌdɛkləˈreɪʃən/ *noun, pl* **-tions**
1 : the act of making an official statement about something : the act of declaring something • The government has made/issued a *declaration* of war on/against its enemies. [*noncount*] We awaited the *declaration* [=*announcement*] of the results. • The case was ended by *declaration* of a mistrial.
2 [*count*] : something that is stated or made known in an official or public way • a *declaration* of love • You will need to make a *declaration* of your income.
3 [*count*] : a document that contains an official statement : a document that makes a declaration — usually singular • The museum has a copy of the country's *declaration* of independence/sovereignty. • the American *Declaration* of Independence • Every 4th of July, we read a copy of the *Declaration*. [=the U.S. Declaration of Independence]

de·clar·a·tive /dɪˈklerətɪv/ *adj, grammar* : having the form of a statement rather than a question or a command • "They went to school" is a *declarative* sentence. — compare IMPERATIVE, INTERROGATIVE
the declarative *grammar* : the form that a phrase or sentence has when it is stating something • "They went to school" is in *the declarative*.

de·clare /dɪˈkleə/ *verb* **-clares; -clared; -clar·ing** [+ *obj*]
1 : to say or state (something) in an official or public way • She publicly *declared* [=*announced*] her opposition to the plan. • The government has just *declared* a state of emergency. • The company was forced to ***declare bankruptcy***. [=to formally say in a legal document that it was bankrupt] • He *declared* himself the winner. = He *declared* that he was the winner. = He ***declared victory***.
2 : to say (something) in a strong and confident way • He still *declares* [=*affirms, asserts*] his innocence. • She *declared* [=*announced*] that she would not attend the party under any circumstances. • He openly *declared* his love for her.
synonyms see ASSERT
3 **a** : to tell the government about (money you have earned or received) in order to pay taxes • They failed to *declare* all of their earnings on their tax return. **b** : to list and show the cost of (something bought in a different country) so that you can pay taxes on it • Large purchases must be *declared* at customs. • Do you have anything to *declare*?
declare against [*phrasal verb*] ***declare against (someone or something)*** *Brit, formal* : to officially say that you oppose (someone or something) • She *declared against* the government's policies.
declare for [*phrasal verb*] **1** ***declare for (something)*** *US* : to officially say that you will take part in (something) • a college basketball player who *declared for* the NBA draft after his junior year **2** ***declare for (someone or something)*** *Brit, formal* : to officially say that you support (someone or something) • He *declared for* the plan.
declare war : to officially decide to fight or go to war • Congress has the power to *declare war* on/against other countries. — often used figuratively • The state has *declared war on* illiteracy.
– declared *adj* • His *declared* [=publicly stated] aim/goal/intention is to improve the city's downtown area.

de·clas·si·fy /diˈklæsəˌfaɪ/ *verb* **-fies; -fied; -fy·ing** [+ *obj*] : to allow the public to see or learn about (something that has been a secret) • The government has not yet *declassified* that information.
– de·clas·si·fi·ca·tion /diˌklæsəfəˈkeɪʃən/ *noun* [*noncount*] • the *declassification* of a secret document
– declassified *adj* • a *declassified* document

de·claw /diˈklɑː/ *verb* **-claws; -clawed; -claw·ing** [+ *obj*] : to permanently remove the claws of (a cat) • We had our cats *declawed*.

[1]**de·cline** /dɪˈklaɪn/ *verb* **-clines; -clined; -clin·ing**
1 [*no obj*] : to become lower in amount or less in number • Oil prices continue to *decline*. [=*decrease, fall*] • The construction of new houses *declined* five percent this year. • The animal's numbers are *declining* rapidly.
2 [*no obj*] : to become worse in condition or quality • The patient's condition has *declined*. [=*worsened, deteriorated*] • My grandmother's health has been *declining* since she broke her hip. • The civilization began to *decline* around 1000 B.C.
3 *somewhat formal* **a** [+ *obj*] : to say that you will not or cannot do something • The company *declined* comment on the scandal. — usually followed by *to + verb* • The company *declined to comment* on the scandal. • She *declined to run* for a second term as governor. **b** : to say no to something in a polite way [+ *obj*] Regretfully, we have to *decline* [=*turn down*] the invitation to your wedding. • He changed his mind and *declined* the company's offer. [*no obj*] I invited him, but he *declined*. — opposite ACCEPT
4 [+ *obj*] *grammar* : to list the different forms of (a noun, pronoun, or adjective) • We had to *decline* the Latin adjective "brevis" on our test.
– de·clin·er /dɪˈklaɪnə/ *noun, pl* **-ers** [*count*] • There were more advancers than *decliners* [=stocks that decreased in value] in the stock market today. **– de·clin·ing** /dɪˈklaɪnɪŋ/ *adj* • *declining* health • in her *declining* years [=in the last years of her life]

[2]**decline** *noun, pl* **-clines**
1 : the process of becoming worse in condition or quality

D

[*noncount*] a period of economic *decline* • He says that American industry is in a state of *decline*. • There was a general feeling that the country was ***in decline*** [=was becoming less powerful, wealthy, etc.] • The town ***fell/went into decline*** after the factory closed down. [*count*] — usually singular • He has experienced a *decline* in health. • the *decline* and fall of the Roman empire • The company's products suffered a *decline* in quality. • a gradual physical/mental *decline*
2 : a change to a lower number or amount [*count*] The economy experienced a *decline* of two million jobs. • We saw a sharp/steep *decline* in sales this month. • *Declines* led advances at the end of the trading day. [*noncount*] There was some *decline* in stock prices at the end of the trading session.
on the decline **:** becoming worse in condition or less in size, amount, number, etc. **:** declining • His health is *on the decline*. • Sales are *on the decline*.

de·code /diˈkoʊd/ *verb* **-codes; -cod·ed; -cod·ing** [+ *obj*]
1 : to change (secret messages, documents, etc.) from a set of letters, numbers, symbols, etc., you cannot understand into words you can understand • The government agents finally *decoded* [=*deciphered*] the message. — compare CODE, ENCODE
2 : to find or understand the true or hidden meaning of (something) • Readers can easily *decode* the novel's imagery. • I'm trying to *decode* the expression on her face.
3 *technical* **:** to change signals for a radio, television, etc., to a form that can be heard or seen correctly • The box *decodes* the digital signal for your CD player.

de·cod·er /diˈkoʊdɚ/ *noun, pl* **-ers** [*count*] *technical* **:** an electronic device that changes signals for a radio, television, etc., to a form that can be heard or seen correctly

dé·col·le·tage /deɪˌkɑːləˈtɑːʒ/ *noun* [*noncount*] **:** the top of a woman's dress, blouse, etc., that is cut very low so the top of the woman's breasts can be seen
– dé·col·le·té /deɪˌkɑːlˈteɪ/ *adj* • a *décolleté* dress

de·col·o·ni·za·tion *also Brit* **de·col·o·ni·sa·tion** /diˌkɑːlənəˈzeɪʃən, *Brit* diˌkɒləˌnaɪˈzeɪʃən/ *noun* [*noncount*] **:** the process of making a colony or a group of colonies independent • the British *decolonization* of India

de·com·mis·sion /ˌdiːkəˈmɪʃən/ *verb* **-sions; -sioned; -sion·ing** [+ *obj*] **:** to officially stop using (a ship, weapon, dam, etc.) **:** to remove (something) from service • Several military bases are scheduled to be *decommissioned*. • The government is *decommissioning* the nuclear power plant.

de·com·pose /ˌdiːkəmˈpoʊz/ *verb* **-pos·es; -posed; -pos·ing**
1 : to cause something (such as dead plants and the bodies of dead animals) to be slowly destroyed and broken down by natural processes, chemicals, etc. [+ *obj*] Bacteria and fungi help *decompose* organic matter. • partially *decomposed* bodies [*no obj*] The wood on our deck is beginning to *decompose*. [=(less formally) *rot*] • the smell of *decomposing* leaves
synonyms see [1]DECAY
2 *technical* **:** to cause something (such as a chemical) to be separated into smaller or simpler parts [+ *obj*] *decompose* a chemical compound [*no obj*] The compound will *decompose* in the presence of light.
– de·com·po·si·tion /diˌkɑːmpəˈzɪʃən/ *noun* [*noncount*] • The wood is already showing signs of *decomposition*. • the *decomposition* of organic matter

de·com·press /ˌdiːkəmˈprɛs/ *verb* **-press·es; -pressed; -press·ing**
1 : to release or reduce the physical pressure on something [+ *obj*] Surgery *decompressed* the vertebrae. [*no obj*] Once pressure was released, the vertebrae *decompressed*.
2 [+ *obj*] *computers* **:** to change (a computer file that has been made smaller) back to its original size by using special software • The file must be *decompressed* before it can be read.
3 [*no obj*] *US, informal* **:** to rest and relax • After their busy week, they needed some time to *decompress*. [=*unwind*]
– de·com·pres·sion /ˌdiːkəmˈprɛʃən/ *noun* [*noncount*] • The divers underwent *decompression*. [=a process in which air pressure is slowly decreased to allow a person who has been deep underwater to adapt safely to the pressure at the surface] • data/file *decompression*

decompression chamber *noun, pl* ~ **-bers** [*count*] **:** a small room that allows a person (such as an ocean diver) to slowly experience lower amounts of air pressure until normal air pressure is reached

decompression sickness *noun* [*noncount*] *medical* see *the bends* at [2]BEND 3

de·con·ges·tant /ˌdiːkənˈʤɛstənt/ *noun, pl* **-tants** [*count, noncount*] **:** a medicine that helps stop thick fluid from building up in your nose, throat, or chest when you have a cold or similar illness

de·con·struc·tion /ˌdiːkənˈstrʌkʃən/ *noun* [*noncount*] *technical* **:** a theory used in the study of literature or philosophy which says that a piece of writing does not have just one meaning and that the meaning depends on the reader
– de·con·struct /ˌdiːkənˈstrʌkt/ *verb* **-structs; -struct·ed; -struct·ing** [+ *obj*] • *deconstruct* a literary passage

de·con·tam·i·nate /ˌdiːkənˈtæməˌneɪt/ *verb* **-nates; -nat·ed; -nat·ing** [+ *obj*] **:** to remove dirty or dangerous substances (such as radioactive material) from (a person, thing, place, etc.) • Special workers were called in to *decontaminate* the area after the oil spill.
– de·con·tam·i·na·tion /ˌdiːkənˌtæməˈneɪʃən/ *noun* [*noncount*] • the *decontamination* of drinking water

de·cor *or* **dé·cor** /deɪˈkoɚ, ˈdeɪˌkoɚ/ *noun, pl* **-cors :** the way that a room or the inside of a building is decorated [*count*] — usually singular • We loved the *decor* of the restaurant. • It had a very elegant *décor*. [*noncount*] The store offers a lot in home *decor*.

dec·o·rate /ˈdɛkəˌreɪt/ *verb* **-rates; -rat·ed; -rat·ing**
1 : to make (something) more attractive usually by putting something on it [+ *obj*] Several expensive paintings *decorate* [=*adorn*] the walls. • I always enjoy *decorating* the Christmas tree. • I *decorated* my apartment in dark colors. • a beautifully *decorated* box — often + *with* • We're going to *decorate* the room *with* balloons and flowers for her birthday party. • The gift was beautifully *decorated with* lace and ribbons. [*no obj*] I love *decorating* [=putting up decorations] for the holidays.
2 [+ *obj*] **:** to give a medal or award to (someone, such as a soldier) — usually used as *(be) decorated* • He *was decorated* for courage during the war. • a *decorated* war veteran

dec·o·ra·tion /ˌdɛkəˈreɪʃən/ *noun, pl* **-tions**
1 : something that is added to something else to make it more attractive [*count*] The vase has a fancy *decoration* on one side. • a box of Christmas *decorations* [=*ornaments*] [*noncount*] a plain sweater knit without *decoration* • The handles are not just ***for decoration*** [=are not just decorative], they serve a practical purpose.
2 [*noncount*] **:** the act of decorating something (such as a room) • He's a genius at home *decoration*. • a unique style of *decoration* • She is certified to do ***interior decoration***. [=*interior design*]
3 [*count*] **:** a medal or award that is given to someone for doing something brave or honorable (such as fighting bravely in a war) • He received a *decoration* from the President.

dec·o·ra·tive /ˈdɛkrətɪv/ *adj* [*more* ~; *most* ~] **:** used to make something more attractive **:** used for decoration • We added some *decorative* details/elements/touches to the room. • *decorative* [=*ornamental*] shrubs • The handles are *decorative* and practical.
– dec·o·ra·tive·ly *adv* • Arrange the fruit *decoratively* in the bowl.

dec·o·ra·tor /ˈdɛkəˌreɪtɚ/ *noun, pl* **-tors** [*count*] **:** a person who decorates something especially as a job • a cake *decorator* • They hired a *decorator* to redesign their dining room. • She became an ***interior decorator***. [=*interior designer*]

dec·o·rous /ˈdɛkərəs/ *adj* [*more* ~; *most* ~] *formal* **:** correct and polite in a particular situation • We expect *decorous* [=*proper*] behavior/conduct from our students. • a *decorous* [=*civilized, respectable*] young woman
– dec·o·rous·ly *adv*

de·co·rum /dɪˈkorəm/ *noun* [*noncount*] *formal* **:** correct or proper behavior that shows respect and good manners • He has no sense of *decorum*. • Court *decorum* [=proper behavior in a courtroom] requires that all parties address the judge as "Your Honor."

de·coy /ˈdiːˌkoɪ/ *noun, pl* **-coys** [*count*]
1 : a wooden or plastic bird (such as a duck) that is used by hunters to attract live birds
2 : a person or thing that attracts people's attention so they will not notice someone or something else • He had a *decoy* distract the guard while he jumped over the fence.
– de·coy /dɪˈkʰoɪ/ *verb* **-coys; -coyed; -coy·ing** [+ *obj*] • Hunters *decoyed* the ducks to the pond.

[1]**de·crease** /dɪˈkriːs/ *verb* **-creas·es; -creased; -creas·ing**
1 [*no obj*] **:** to become smaller in size, amount, number, etc. • Sales *decreased* by five percent this year. • The population is *decreasing* steadily. = The population is steadily *decreasing* in size.

2 [+ *obj*] : to make (something) smaller in size, amount, number, etc. • By exercising often, you can *decrease* [=*reduce, lower*] your chance of developing heart disease. • The driver *decreased* her speed as she approached the curve. • These changes will *decrease* our expenses. — opposite INCREASE

– decreased *adj* • The patient has a *decreased* appetite. • a *decreased* risk of heart disease **– decreasingly** *adv* • The medication has been *decreasingly* effective. [=has gradually been becoming less effective]

²de·crease /ˈdiːˌkriːs/ *noun, pl* **-creas·es**

1 : the act of becoming smaller or of making something smaller in size, amount, number, etc. [*count*] Studies report a recent *decrease* in traffic accidents. • We've had a *decrease* [=*reduction*] in the number of students enrolling in the school. • significant *decreases* in activity [*noncount*] Because of the injury, some *decrease* in mobility is to be expected.

2 [*count*] : the amount by which something is made smaller • The report showed *decreases* [=*reductions*] of between 20 and 30 percent. • a *decrease* of three dollars — opposite INCREASE

on the decrease : becoming less in size, amount, number, etc. : decreasing • The number of college applications is *on the decrease*. [=*on the decline*]

¹de·cree /dɪˈkriː/ *noun, pl* **-crees**

1 : an official order given by a person with power or by a government [*count*] The President issued a *decree* making the day a national holiday. • The soldiers read the people a ***royal decree***. [=an order given by a king or queen] • a ***papal decree*** [=a decree from a Pope] [*noncount*] He took his position ***by decree*** [=because of a decree] of the national government. • *by* royal *decree*

2 : an official decision made by a court of law [*count*] She tried to have the court's *decree* [=*judgment, ruling*] reversed. • a divorce *decree* [*noncount*] Their marriage was annulled by judicial *decree*.

²decree *verb* **-crees; -creed; -cree·ing** : to order or decide (something) in an official way [+ *obj*] The government *decreed* a national holiday. • The change was *decreed* by the President. • The City Council has *decreed* that all dogs must be kept on a leash. [*no obj*] He was favored to win, but fate *decreed* otherwise. [=it was not his fate to win; he did not win]

de·crep·it /dɪˈkrɛpət/ *adj* [*more ~; most ~*] : old and in bad condition or poor health • The *decrepit* [=*run-down, dilapidated*] building was badly in need of repair. • My *decrepit* car barely starts. • a *decrepit* old man

de·crep·i·tude /dɪˈkrɛpəˌtuːd, *Brit* dɪˈkrɛpəˌtjuːd/ *noun* [*noncount*] *formal* : the state of being old and in bad condition or poor health • The house has fallen into *decrepitude*.

de·crim·i·nal·ize *also Brit* **de·crim·i·nal·ise** /diˈkrɪmənəˌlaɪz/ *verb* **-iz·es; -ized; -iz·ing** [+ *obj*] : to make (something that is illegal) legal by changing the law • He believes that the government should *decriminalize* [=*legalize*] the use of marijuana.

– de·crim·i·nal·i·za·tion *also Brit* **de·crim·i·nal·i·sa·tion** /diˌkrɪmənələˈzeɪʃən, *Brit* diˌkrɪmənəˌlaɪˈzeɪʃən/ *noun* [*noncount*] • the *decriminalization* of marijuana

de·cry /dɪˈkraɪ/ *verb* **-cries; -cried; -cry·ing** [+ *obj*] *formal* : to say publicly and forcefully that you regard (something) as bad, wrong, etc. • In her article, she *decries* the pollution of the environment by manufacturers. • Parents *decried* [=*condemned*] the movie's emphasis on sex. • Violence on television is generally *decried* as harmful to children.

ded·i·cate /ˈdɛdɪˌkeɪt/ *verb* **-cates; -cat·ed; -cat·ing** [+ *obj*] : to officially make (something) a place for honoring or remembering a person, event, etc. • The new park was *dedicated* today. — often + *to* • The memorial is *dedicated to* all the soldiers who died in the war.

dedicate to [*phrasal verb*] **1** ***dedicate (something) to (something)*** : to decide that (something) will be used for (a special purpose) : to use (time, money, energy, attention, etc.) for (something) • She *dedicates* 10 percent of each paycheck *to* her savings. • He *dedicated* [=*devoted*] his life/time *to* helping the poor. = He ***dedicated himself to*** helping the poor. [=he used his time, energy, etc., to help the poor] • After graduating from college, he *dedicated himself to* his career. **2** ***dedicate (something) to (someone)*** : to say that (a book, song, etc.) was written or is being performed to honor or express affection for (someone) • She *dedicated* her first novel *to* her father. • I would like to *dedicate* this next song *to* my mother.

dedicated *adj*

1 [*more ~; most ~*] : having very strong support for or loyalty to a person, group, cause, etc. • the band's most *dedicated* [=*devoted*] fans • They are a group of highly *dedicated* [=*committed, enthusiastic*] individuals. • He is a *dedicated* teacher. = He is *dedicated* to the teaching profession.

2 *always used before a noun, technical* : used only for one particular purpose • We have a *dedicated* phone line for our computer. [=a phone line that we use only for our computer]

ded·i·ca·tion /ˌdɛdɪˈkeɪʃən/ *noun, pl* **-tions**

1 [*noncount*] : a feeling of very strong support for or loyalty to someone or something : the quality or state of being dedicated to a person, group, cause, etc. • It took a lot of hard work and *dedication*, but we managed to finish the project on time. — often + *to* • We admire her *dedication to* helping the poor. • his tireless/unwavering *dedication to* the cause

2 [*count*] : a message at the beginning of a book, song, etc., saying that it was written or is being performed in order to honor or express affection for someone — often + *to* • His novel includes a brief *dedication to* his family.

3 [*count*] : the act of officially saying that something (such as a new building) was created for a particular purpose (such as worship) or to remember or honor a particular person • the *dedication* of the temple • They celebrated the *dedication* of the new building with a ribbon-cutting ceremony. — sometimes used before another noun • *dedication* ceremonies

de·duce /dɪˈduːs, *Brit* dɪˈdjuːs/ *verb* **-duc·es; -duced; -duc·ing** [+ *obj*] *formal* : to use logic or reason to form (a conclusion or opinion about something) : to decide (something) after thinking about the known facts • Scientists use several methods to *deduce* [=*determine*] the age of ancient objects. • They *deduced* [=*concluded*] that he was present at the scene of the crime. — often + *from* • A word's meaning can often be *deduced from* its context.

de·duct /dɪˈdʌkt/ *verb* **-ducts; -duct·ed; -duct·ing** [+ *obj*] : to take away (something, especially an amount of money) from a total • When paying our taxes, can we *deduct* [=*subtract*] the cost of our child's education? • You can *deduct* up to $500 for money given to charity. — often + *from* • *Deduct* the points *from* the total score. • Payments are directly *deducted from* [=taken out of] your bank account. — opposite CREDIT

¹de·duct·ible /dɪˈdʌktəbəl/ *adj* : able to be subtracted from an amount of money • The trip was *deductible* as a business expense. • All donations to charities are *deductible*. [=taxes do not have to be paid on money given to charities] • tax-*deductible* expenses/donations

²deductible *noun, pl* **-ibles** [*count*] *US* : an amount of money that you have to pay for something (such as having your car fixed after an accident) before an insurance company pays for the remainder of the cost • I have an insurance policy with a $1,000 *deductible*.

de·duc·tion /dɪˈdʌkʃən/ *noun, pl* **-tions**

1 a [*noncount*] : the act of taking away something (such as an amount of money) from a total • He pays for his insurance by automatic payroll *deduction*. [=the money for his insurance is automatically taken out of his paycheck] **b** [*count*] : something (such as an amount of money) that is or can be subtracted from a total • The government is offering new tax *deductions* for small businesses. • What is your pay after the *deductions* have been taken out?

2 a [*noncount*] : the act or process of using logic or reason to form a conclusion or opinion about something : the act or process of deducing something • His guess was based on intuition rather than *deduction*. **b** [*count*] : a conclusion or opinion that is based on logic or reason • Our *deduction* was based on the information given to us at the time. • It was a logical *deduction*.

de·duc·tive /dɪˈdʌktɪv/ *adj* : using logic or reason to form a conclusion or opinion about something • a conclusion based on *deductive* reasoning/logic

¹deed /ˈdiːd/ *noun, pl* **deeds**

1 : something that is done : an act or action [*count*] They taught their children to be kind and to do good *deeds*. • evil/dirty *deeds* • We are judged by our *deeds*. [=we are judged by what we do] • News of their heroic *deeds* spread far and wide. • It's too late now. The *deed* is done. [*noncount*] He is honest in word and in *deed*. [=he says things that are true and does the things he says he will]

2 : a legal document that shows who owns a building or piece of land [*noncount*] The land was transferred by *deed*. [*count*] He gave them the *deed* to the property. — often plu-

D

ral in British English ▪ The bank holds the *deeds* to your property.

[2]**deed** *verb* **deeds; deed·ed; deed·ing** [+ *obj*] *US* : to give someone ownership of (a building or piece of land) by means of a deed ▪ She *deeded* the house to her children.

[1]**dee·jay** /ˈdiːˌʤeɪ/ *noun, pl* **-jays** [*count*] *informal* : DISC JOCKEY

[2]**deejay** *verb* **-jays; -jayed; -jay·ing** *informal* : to play popular recorded music on the radio or at a party, nightclub, etc., especially as a job : to work as a disc jockey [*no obj*] He has *deejayed* at the radio station for over 20 years. [+ *obj*] Who is *deejaying* your wedding?

D

deem /ˈdiːm/ *verb* **deems; deemed; deem·ing** [+ *obj*] *formal* : to think of (someone or something) in a particular way ▪ The building was *deemed* [=*considered, judged*] unsafe after the fire. ▪ We *deemed* [=*believed, thought*] it wise to wait. ▪ Do whatever you *deem* (to be) necessary. ▪ The principal will take whatever action she *deems* appropriate in this case.

[1]**deep** /ˈdiːp/ *adj* **deep·er; -est**

1 a : having a large distance to the bottom from the surface or highest point ▪ We walked in the *deep* snow. ▪ a *deep* well/pool/hole ▪ a *deep* valley between the mountains ▪ The water is *deepest* in the middle of the lake. ▪ She's afraid of swimming in *deep* water. ▪ a plant with *deep* roots — often used figuratively ▪ The tradition has *deep* roots in our culture. — opposite SHALLOW **b :** going far inward from the outside or the front edge of something ▪ The house has lots of *deep* closets. ▪ *deep* shelves ▪ She has a small but *deep* wound on her arm. — opposite SHALLOW **c :** located far inside something — usually + *in* or *within* ▪ The animals live *deep in/within* the forest/jungle/mountains, far from any people. ▪ His hands were *deep in* his pockets. ▪ The sound came from *deep within* his throat. — often used figuratively ▪ The memories were hidden *deep in* his mind. [=he had not thought about the memories in a long time] ▪ I knew *deep in* my heart [=I believed very strongly] that we would succeed.

2 *not used before a noun* **:** having a specified measurement downward, inward, or backward ▪ This enormous canyon is over a mile *deep*. ▪ The shelves are 10 inches *deep*. ▪ We walked through knee-*deep* snow [=snow as high as our knees] to get to school. ▪ The basement was waist-*deep* in water. [=the top of the water that filled the basement was as high as a person's waist] ▪ He stepped into an ankle-*deep* puddle of mud. — see also SKIN-DEEP

3 a : located near the outside edges of an area ▪ (*baseball*) He hit a fly ball to *deep* right field. **b :** hit, thrown, or kicked a long distance ▪ The quarterback threw a *deep* [=*long*] pass into the end zone.

4 : done by taking in or breathing out a large amount of air ▪ Take a *deep* breath and try to relax. ▪ a *deep* sigh

5 : low in sound or musical pitch ▪ I could hear my father's *deep* voice from down the street. ▪ a *deep* bass line — opposite HIGH

6 : having a dark, strong color ▪ She painted white clouds in a *deep* blue sky. ▪ The walls were a *deep* red. ▪ *deep* rich colors — opposite LIGHT, PALE

7 : very intelligent and serious but complex or difficult to understand ▪ She's always been a *deep* [=*profound*] thinker. = She's very *deep*. ▪ This book is far too *deep* for me. ▪ He has some very *deep* thoughts on the issue. ▪ a *deep* discussion on the meaning of life

8 : full of mystery ▪ The main character has a *deep*, dark secret that is revealed at the end of the movie.

9 a : completely involved in an activity : concentrating and giving all of your attention to something — + *in* ▪ He was so *deep in* thought that he didn't hear us come in. ▪ We spent the next few hours *deep in* conversation. **b :** affected by something in a very serious way — + *in* ▪ They found themselves ***deep in debt***. [=they had a lot of debt; they owed a large amount of money]

10 : very bad, serious, or severe ▪ The country's economy fell into a *deep* depression/recession. ▪ There are still *deep* divisions within the group. [=people in the group have very different opinions and can't agree] ▪ Many people here live in *deep* poverty. [=many people are very poor] ▪ The entire family was in *deep* shock after hearing about the accident. ▪ I got in *deep* trouble with my parents for staying out too late.

11 : very strongly felt ▪ I offered them my *deepest* sympathy. ▪ They shared a *deep* [=*profound*] concern for the environment. ▪ She felt a *deep* [=*heartfelt*] connection with the culture. ▪ a *deep* sense of happiness and well-being ▪ the *deep* emotional bond between parent and child ▪ *deep* feelings of loss ▪ The book made a *deep* impression on his young mind.

12 : full, complete, or thorough ▪ She has a *deep* understanding of the company's needs. ✧ If you are in a ***deep sleep***, you are thoroughly asleep and it is hard to wake you up. ▪ He fell into a *deep sleep* and didn't wake up until the afternoon.

13 *US* **:** going down to a very low price, level, etc. ▪ a *deep* reduction in price ▪ The store offered *deep* discounts during the grand opening sale.

14 *US, sports* **:** having many good players ▪ The team is very *deep* this year. ▪ The baseball team has a *deep* bullpen.

in deep water : in a difficult situation : in trouble ▪ I thought I could handle the work, but I soon found myself *in deep water*.

the deep end *informal* **1** — used in phrases like ***throw in (at) the deep end*** and ***jump in (at) the deep end*** to describe starting a new and difficult activity when you are not fully prepared or ready to do it ▪ After graduating, he was not afraid to *jump in at the deep end* and start his new business alone. ▪ Teachers are *thrown in the deep end* when they first start teaching. **2** ✧ To ***go off the deep end*** is to go crazy, such as by behaving foolishly or by becoming very angry or upset. ▪ Her friends thought she had *gone off the deep end* when she suddenly decided to quit her job. ▪ After his wife died, he started *going off the deep end*. ▪ I understand that you're angry, but there's no reason to *go off the deep end*.

— **deep·ness** *noun* [*noncount*] ▪ the *deepness* [=*depth*] of the water

[2]**deep** *adv* **deeper; -est**

1 a : far into or below the surface of something ▪ The ship now lies *deep* below/beneath the water's surface. ▪ Our feet sank *deeper* into the mud. ▪ The treasure was buried *deep* within the ground. ▪ Their secret offices were located *deep* underground. — often used figuratively ▪ Her angry words hurt/cut him *deep*. [=*deeply*] ▪ He stared *deep* into her eyes. ▪ The detective dug *deeper* into the murder case. **b :** far into or inside something ▪ We walked *deep* into the forest. ▪ The soldiers are operating *deep* within enemy territory.

2 *not used before a noun* **:** at a specified measurement downward, inward, or backward ▪ I stood three feet *deep* in the water. ▪ They parked the cars three *deep* [=three cars in a row], and our car was stuck in the middle. ▪ We walked knee-*deep* in the snow. [=we walked in snow that was deep enough to reach our knees] ▪ He stepped ankle-*deep* into a puddle of mud.

3 : to a late time ▪ They danced *deep* [=*late, well, far*] into the night. [=they danced until it was very late at night]

4 *sports* **a :** near the outside edges of a playing area ▪ The outfielder was playing *deep*. **b :** for a long distance ▪ He hit/threw/kicked the ball *deep* down the field.

5 ✧ If you ***breathe deep***, you take a large amount of air into your lungs. ▪ The doctor told her to *breathe deep*. [=breathe deeply]

deep down (inside) ✧ If you feel or believe something *deep down* or *deep down inside*, you feel or believe it completely even if you do not say it or show it to other people. ▪ He knew *deep down inside* that she was right. ▪ I believed *deep down* that we were going to win. ▪ *Deep down*, I think we all felt the same way. ▪ He might look like a mean old man, but *deep down inside* he is a very kind person.

in (too) deep *informal* : in a difficult situation that you cannot get out of ▪ He wanted to get out of the deal, but he was *in too deep*.

run deep : to be felt very strongly ▪ Fear *runs deep* in this small town. ▪ Her love for her family *runs deep*. — see also *still waters run deep* at [2]STILL

[3]**deep** *noun*

the deep **1** *literary + formal* : the ocean ▪ *the* briny *deep* ▪ creatures of *the deep* **2** *literary* : the middle part of something ▪ He left home in ***the deep of the night***. [=*the dead of the night*]

the deeps *literary + formal* : the deep parts of the ocean ▪ *the* ocean *deeps*

deep–dish /ˈdiːpˌdɪʃ/ *adj, always used before a noun, US* : baked in a dish that has high sides ▪ *deep-dish* pizza ▪ a *deep-dish* apple pie

deep·en /ˈdiːpən/ *verb* **-ens; -ened; -en·ing**

1 : to become or to cause (something) to become deep or deeper [+ *obj*] They *deepened* the river so that larger boats could sail through. ▪ Age had *deepened* the lines in his face. [*no obj*] The water *deepens* toward the center of the river.

2 : to become or to cause (something, such as a feeling or emotion) to become stronger or more powerful [+ *obj*] The

experience *deepened* [=*strengthened*] his love for acting. • Her powerful words *deepened* our commitment to the cause. • The vacation together *deepened* their relationship with each other. • The mystery was *deepened* by her silence. [*no obj*] Their friendship *deepened* [=grew deeper] with time.
3 [+ *obj*] **:** to make (your knowledge, understanding, etc.) fuller or more complete • This class will *deepen* your understanding of economics. • Living in the country's capital had *deepened* her knowledge of politics.
4 : to become or to cause (something) to become worse or more severe [+ *obj*] The government's policies have *deepened* the country's economic recession. • The situation is *deepening* the divisions between the two groups. [*no obj*] These divisions have *deepened* over the years.
5 : to become or to cause (something, such as a person's voice) to become lower in sound [*no obj*] His voice has *deepened* over the years. [+ *obj*] Time has *deepened* his voice.
6 [*no obj*] **:** to become darker or stronger in color • The sunset *deepened* from a pale yellow to a bright orange. • Rather than fading, the colors *deepened* in tone. • The sky *deepened* to a dark blue.
7 ✧ To ***deepen your breathing*** is to take more air into your lungs when you breathe.
– deep·en·ing /ˈdiːpəˌnɪŋ/ *adj* • It confirmed our *deepening* suspicions that she was planning to leave. • A *deepening* [=*worsening*] financial crisis threatened the economy. • the country's *deepening* poverty • *deepening* shadows [=shadows that are becoming darker]

deep fat *noun* [*noncount*] **:** a deep layer of oil or fat that is heated in a pan or machine and used to fry food • a *deep-fat* fryer [=a machine used to fry food in deep fat]

deep freeze *noun, pl* **~ freezes**
1 : a state of extreme cold [*count*] This part of the world experienced a *deep freeze* for several thousand years. [*noncount*] a period of *deep freeze* — sometimes used figuratively • Their relationship went into a *deep freeze* when she left for school.
2 [*count*] *Brit* **:** FREEZER

deep–fry /ˈdiːpˈfraɪ/ *verb* **-fries; -fried; -fry·ing** [+ *obj*] **:** to cook (food) in a deep layer of oil or fat • *Deep-fry* the chicken in two inches of oil.
– deep–fried *adj* • *deep-fried* chicken/potatoes

deep·ly /ˈdiːpli/ *adv* [*more ~; most ~*]
1 : in a way that is very complete, extreme, strongly felt, etc. **:** in a deep way • They fell *deeply* in love. • The car expenses sent him even more *deeply* into debt. • He asked us to think *deeply* [=to think seriously and for a long time] about the issue, because he felt it was very important. • I'm *deeply* [=*very, extremely*] sorry. • He came from a *deeply* religious family. • They're *deeply* [=*sharply*] divided on the issues. • I thought the movie was *deeply* moving/disturbing. = I was *deeply* moved/disturbed by the movie. • a *deeply* flawed design • The senator gave a *deeply* personal speech last night. • We are all *deeply* committed to peace. • The beliefs are *deeply* ingrained/embedded/entrenched in American culture. • *deeply* held beliefs/values • *deeply* felt emotions • She cares very *deeply* about/for him. • These traditions are *deeply* rooted in the past. = They are rooted *deeply* in the past.
2 : far into or below the surface of something • The designs are carved/cut *deeply* into the wooden chairs. • *deeply* buried beneath the snow — often used figuratively • You'll have to dig/delve *deeply* into the library to find that information.
3 ✧ If you ***breathe deeply*** or ***sigh deeply***, you take a large amount of air into your lungs when you breathe or sigh.
4 ✧ If you are ***sleeping deeply***, you are thoroughly asleep and it is hard to wake you up.

deep pockets *noun* [*plural*] *somewhat informal* **:** large amounts of money that can be used **:** great financial resources • a company with *deep pockets*
– deep–pock·et·ed /ˈdiːpˈpɑːkətəd/ *adj* • *deep-pocketed* companies

deep–root·ed /ˈdiːpˈruːtəd/ *adj* [*more ~; most ~*] **:** existing for a long time and very difficult to change **:** firmly established • The country's economic troubles are *deep-rooted*. [=*deep-seated*] • *deep-rooted* beliefs

deep–sea /ˈdiːpˈsiː/ *adj, always used before a noun* **:** living in, relating to, or done in the deep parts of the ocean • *deep-sea* creatures • We went *deep-sea* fishing/diving.

deep–seat·ed /ˈdiːpˈsiːtəd/ *adj* [*more ~; most ~*] **:** existing for a long time and very difficult to change **:** firmly established • She has a *deep-seated* fear of flying. • The problems are far more *deep-seated* [=*deep-rooted*] than we thought.

deep–six /ˈdiːpˈsɪks/ *verb* **-six·es; -sixed; -six·ing** [+ *obj*] *US, informal* **:** to get rid of (something) **:** to no longer use or consider (something) • The government plans to *deep-six* [=*eliminate*] the program next year. • The committee *deep-sixed* the plan.

Deep South *noun*
the Deep South **:** the states in the most southern and eastern part of the U.S. and especially Georgia, Alabama, South Carolina, Louisiana, and Mississippi

deer /ˈdiɚ/ *noun, pl* **deer** [*count*] **:** a large wild animal that has four long thin legs, brown fur, and antlers if male

deer tick *noun, pl* **~ ticks** [*count*] *US* **:** a very small insect found in the eastern U.S. and in Canada that usually feeds on deer and that can give the person or animal it bites various diseases (such as Lyme disease)

DEET /ˈdiːt/ *noun* [*noncount*] *chiefly US* **:** a chemical that is used to keep insects away from people and animals

de·face /dɪˈfeɪs/ *verb* **-fac·es; -faced; -fac·ing** [+ *obj*] **:** to ruin the surface of (something) especially with writing or pictures • The building was *defaced* with graffiti. • He was fined for *defacing* public property.
– de·face·ment /dɪˈfeɪsmənt/ *noun* [*noncount*]

de fac·to /dɪˈfæktoʊ, *Brit* ˌdeɪˈfæktoʊ/ *adj, always used before a noun, formal* — used to describe something that exists but that is not officially accepted or recognized • She became the *de facto* leader of the group. [=she was the unofficial leader] • a *de facto* state of war • *de facto* government policies — compare DE JURE
– de facto *adv* • She became the leader *de facto*.

def·a·ma·tion /ˌdɛfəˈmeɪʃən/ *noun, pl* **-tions** *formal* **:** the act of saying false things in order to make people have a bad opinion of someone or something **:** the act of defaming someone or something [*noncount*] He sued the newspaper for *defamation* (of character). [*count*] The article was full of lies and *defamations*.

de·fam·a·to·ry /dɪˈfæməˌtori, *Brit* dɪˈfæmətri/ *adj* [*more ~; most ~*] *formal* **:** meant to hurt the reputation of someone or something • *defamatory* statements [=statements that defame someone]

deer

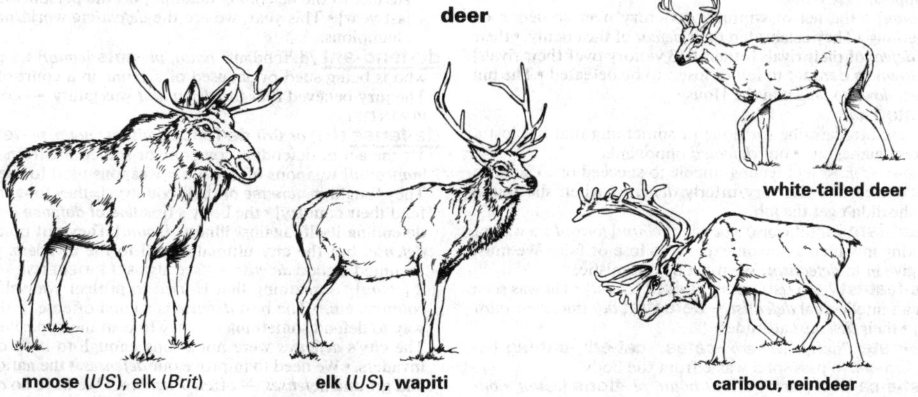

de·fame /dɪˈfeɪm/ *verb* **-fames; -famed; -fam·ing** [+ *obj*] *formal* : to hurt the reputation of (someone or something) especially by saying things that are false or unfair • He says he was *defamed* by reports that falsely identified him as a former gangster.

[1]**de·fault** /dɪˈfɑːlt/ *noun, pl* **-faults**

1 [*noncount*] — used to describe something that happens or is done when nothing else has been done or can be done; usually used in the phrase ***by default*** • No one else wanted the job, so he became the club's president *by default.* • Their decision was made *by default.* All of the other options were no longer possible. • We won the game *by default* when the other team failed to show up. — sometimes used before another noun • the *default* winner

2 a : a failure to make a payment (such as a payment on a loan) [*noncount*] She's ***in default*** on her loan. [=she missed a payment on her loan] [*count*] mortgage *defaults* **b** [*noncount*] *law* : failure to appear in court • The defendant has made no appearance in the case and is ***in default.***

3 [*count*] *computers* : a setting, option, etc., that a computer uses if you do not choose a different one • You can enter your own settings or use the *defaults.* • Which font is the *default* in that computer program? — often used before another noun • the computer's *default* settings

in default of *formal* : in the absence of (something) : without (something) • *In default of* evidence, there can be no trial.

[2]**default** *verb* **-faults; -fault·ed; -fault·ing** [*no obj*]

1 : to fail to do something that legally must be done; *especially* : to fail to make the payments you must make on a loan, mortgage, etc. • He *defaulted* on his loan (payments). • If the borrower *defaults,* the bank can take the house.

2 *of a computer* : to automatically use a particular setting, option, etc., unless you choose a different one • The program *defaults* to a standard font.

– de·fault·er *noun, pl* **-ers** [*count*] • loan *defaulters*

[1]**de·feat** /dɪˈfiːt/ *verb* **-feats; -feat·ed; -feat·ing** [+ *obj*]

1 : to win a victory over (someone or something) in a war, contest, game, etc. • We lost to their team last year, but this year we're going to *defeat* [=*beat*] them. • We must be ready to *defeat* our enemies in battle. • Our candidate *defeated* him in the last election. • He *defeated* his opponent.

2 a : to cause (someone or something) to fail • She finally found a solution to a problem that had *defeated* many other researchers. • The bill was *defeated* in the state senate. • It would ***defeat the purpose*** of having a nice car if you never got to drive it. [=there would be no reason to have a nice car if you did not drive it] **b :** to control or overcome (something) • Scientists from around the world are working to *defeat* the disease. — see also DEFEATED

[2]**defeat** *noun, pl* **-feats**

1 : failure to succeed or to win [*noncount*] We weren't prepared for *defeat.* • One small error could make the difference between success and *defeat.* • After several tries we were forced to accept/admit/concede *defeat.* • The bill suffered *defeat* [=the bill was defeated] in the state senate. • Even ***in defeat*** [=even when he didn't win], he was a hero to those who loved the sport. [*count*] — usually singular • The passage of the law represented a *defeat* for their cause. • Her basketball team suffered a bitter/crushing/devastating *defeat.* [=*loss*] • That was his first *defeat* as a professional boxer. — opposite VICTORY

2 [*count*] : the act of winning a victory over someone or something • They celebrated their *defeat* of the enemy. • their 6–3 *defeat* of their rivals [=their 6–3 victory over their rivals]

go down to defeat : to fail or lose : to be defeated • The bill *went down to defeat* in the House.

defeated *adj*

1 — used to describe someone or something that has lost a contest, game, etc. • our *defeated* opponents

2 [*more ~; most ~*] : feeling unable to succeed or to achieve something • She felt very/utterly *defeated* when she found out she didn't get the job.

de·feat·ism /dɪˈfiːtˌɪzəm/ *noun* [*noncount*] *formal* : a way of thinking in which a person expects to lose or fail • We must not give in to *defeatism.* We must be optimistic.

– de·feat·ist /dɪˈfiːtɪst/ *noun, pl* **-ists** [*count*] • He was seen as an intellectual *defeatist.* **– defeatist** *adj* [*more ~; most ~*] • their *defeatist* attitudes

def·e·cate /ˈdɛfɪˌkeɪt/ *verb* **-cates; -cat·ed; -cat·ing** [*no obj*] *formal* : to pass solid waste from the body

– def·e·ca·tion /ˌdɛfɪˈkeɪʃən/ *noun, pl* **-tions** [*count, noncount*]

[1]**de·fect** /ˈdiːˌfɛkt/ *noun, pl* **-fects** [*count*] : a problem or fault that makes someone or something not perfect: such as **a :** a physical problem that causes something to be less valuable, effective, healthy, etc. • This small *defect* [=*flaw*] greatly reduces the diamond's value. • They examine their products for *defects.* • a minor/major *defect* • She was born with a heart *defect.* • a ***birth defect*** [=a physical problem that someone is born with] **b :** something that causes weakness or failure • We had to point out the *defect* [=*flaw*] in their logic. • Vanity and pride were his two worst character *defects.*

[2]**de·fect** /dɪˈfɛkt/ *verb* **-fects; -fect·ed; -fect·ing** [*no obj*] *formal* : to leave a country, political party, organization, etc., and go to a different one that is a competitor or an enemy • The Russian scholar *defected* in 1979. • She *defected* from the conservative party. • He *defected* to the West before the war began. • The reporter *defected* to another TV network.

– de·fec·tion /dɪˈfɛkʃən/ *noun, pl* **-tions** [*count, noncount*] **– de·fec·tor** /dɪˈfɛktɚ/ *noun, pl* **-tors** [*count*] • the party's *defectors*

de·fec·tive /dɪˈfɛktɪv/ *adj* [*more ~; most ~*] : having a problem or fault that prevents something from working correctly : having a defect or flaw • Our car had *defective* [=*faulty*] brakes, so we had them replaced. • This computer is *defective.* I want my money back. • *defective* products/merchandise • The disease is caused by a *defective* gene.

de·fend /dɪˈfɛnd/ *verb* **-fends; -fend·ed; -fend·ing**

1 : to fight in order to keep (someone or something) safe : to not allow a person or thing to hurt, damage, or destroy (someone or something) [+ *obj*] We are prepared to *defend* [=*protect, guard*] our country. — often + *from* or *against* • They have every right to *defend* themselves *from* those who would hurt them. • The army *defended* the territory *against* invaders. • Her body was no longer able to *defend* itself *against* disease. [*no obj*] — usually + *against* • These new weapons will make us better able to *defend against* attack. • The body's immune system *defends against* illness.

2 [+ *obj*] : to fight or work hard in order to keep (something, such as a right, interest, cause, etc.) from being taken away • The group *defends* [=*protects*] the rights of the poor. • The company must *defend* its own interests.

3 [+ *obj*] : to speak or write in support of (someone or something that is being challenged or criticized) • As a U.S. senator, it is my responsibility to *defend* [=*uphold*] the Constitution. • We believed it was a cause worth *defending.* • She *defended* her friend's behavior. • Stop *defending* him. What he did was wrong.

4 *sports* : to try to stop opponents from scoring [+ *obj*] Your job is to *defend* the goal. • Focus on *defending* the basket. [*no obj*] He *defended* well throughout the game. — often + *against* • She tried to *defend against* the jump shot.

5 [+ *obj*] : to compete in order to try to keep (a title, championship, etc.) • The team is looking to *defend* its national title. [=to win the national title again] • She successfully *defended* her championship. [=she won the championship again]

6 [+ *obj*] : to work as a lawyer for (someone who is being sued or accused of a crime) • They hired a famous lawyer to *defend* their son. • She *defended* herself during her trial.

– de·fend·er *noun, pl* **-ers** [*count*] • The player got past two *defenders.* • She's a staunch/tireless *defender* of human rights. — see also PUBLIC DEFENDER **– defending** *adj* • He lost to the *defending* champ. [=to the person who won last year] • This year, we are the *defending* world/national champions.

de·fend·ant /dɪˈfɛndənt/ *noun, pl* **-ants** [*count*] : a person who is being sued or accused of a crime in a court of law • The jury believed that the *defendant* was guilty. — compare PLAINTIFF

de·fense (*US*) *or Brit* **de·fence** /dɪˈfɛns/ *noun, pl* **-fens·es**

1 : the act of defending someone or something from attack [*noncount*] weapons of *defense* = weapons used for *defense* • They fought ***in defense of*** their country. [=they fought to defend their country] • the body's first ***line of defense*** [=way of defending itself] against illness [*count*] They put up a good *defense,* but the city ultimately fell to the invaders. • They mounted a good *defense.* — see also SELF-DEFENSE

2 [*count*] : something that is used to protect yourself, your country, etc. • The best *defense* is a good offense. [=the best way to defend something is to try to beat the opposite side] • The city's *defenses* were not strong enough to keep out the invaders. • We need to improve our *defenses.* • the nation's air and ground *defenses* — often + *against* • We have no *defense*

against such powerful weapons. [=we have no way to defend ourselves against such powerful weapons] • the body's natural *defenses against* disease and infection
3 : the act of speaking or writing in support of someone or something that is being attacked or criticized [*noncount*] His friends quickly ***came/jumped to his defense.*** [=his friends began saying that he was right or good] — often used in the phrase ***in defense*** • She spoke out *in defense* of justice. [=she defended justice] • Let me say, *in her defense*, that I would have done the same thing that she did. • He spoke up *in his own defense*. [=he defended himself] [*count*] — usually singular • She offered no *defense* [=*justification*] for her actions. • We listened to a passionate/spirited *defense* of the governor's decision.
4 [*noncount*] : the things that are done by a country to protect itself from enemies • In my view, the most important issue facing our country today is national *defense*. • The candidates accused each other of being soft/weak on *defense*. • The President wants to increase spending on *defense*. • He was the Secretary of *Defense* under the last President. — often used before another noun • He proposed an increase in *defense* spending. • the *defense* secretary/minister/department • They signed a billion-dollar *defense* contract with the company. • cuts in the *defense* budget
5 a [*singular*] : the side of a legal case which argues that a person who is being sued or accused of a crime is innocent : the lawyer or lawyers who represent the defendant in a court case • His friends are raising money (to pay) for his *defense*. • ***The defense*** rests, Your Honor. • *The defense* told the jury that the prosecution had not proved its case. — often used before another noun • *defense* attorneys/lawyers • a *defense* witness [=a person who speaks to support the defense's case] • He had three lawyers on his *defense* team. — compare PROSECUTION **b** [*count*] : the method that is used in a court case to prove that someone is innocent • Her lawyers plan to use an insanity *defense*. [=they will say that she was not sane when she committed the crime] • It's a valid *defense*, and I think we should be able to win the case.
6 /ˈdiːˌfɛns/ **a** : the group of players on a team who try to stop an opponent from scoring [*count*] He ran through the *defense* and scored a touchdown. • Our team has the best *defense* in the league. • a talented *defense* [*noncount*] She began the season ***on defense*** [=playing on the part of the team that defends the goal], but her coach later put her on offense. **b** [*noncount*] : the way that players on a team try to stop an opponent from scoring • The team needs some work on its *defense*. • These guys play good/strong/tough *defense*. — compare OFFENSE 4

de·fense·less (*US*) *or Brit* **de·fence·less** /dɪˈfɛnsləs/ *adj* [*more ~; most ~*] : not able to defend yourself, your country, etc. • Without weapons of any kind, the people of the town were completely *defenseless*. • Don't hurt them. They're just poor, *defenseless* [=*helpless*] animals. — often + *against* • The disease leaves the body *defenseless against* infection.

de·fense·man (*US*) *or Brit* **de·fence·man** /dɪˈfɛnsmən/ *noun, pl* **-men** /-mən/ [*count*] : a player in a sport (such as hockey) who tries to stop the other team from scoring

defense mechanism (*US*) *or Brit* **defence mechanism** *noun, pl* **~ -nisms** [*count*] *technical*
1 : a process in the brain that makes you forget or ignore painful or disturbing thoughts, situations, etc. • She is projecting her anger on you as a *defense mechanism*.
2 : a reaction in your body that protects against disease or danger • the cell's normal *defense mechanisms* against infection

de·fen·si·ble /dɪˈfɛnsəbəl/ *adj* [*more ~; most ~*] *formal*
1 : able to be thought of as good or acceptable • Both candidates hold *defensible* positions on the issue. • Under those circumstances, her actions were completely *defensible*. • Slavery is not morally *defensible*.
2 : able to be defended or protected : able to be kept safe from damage or harm • The city has a *defensible* location. • a *defensible* bridge

¹de·fen·sive /dɪˈfɛnsɪv/ *adj*
1 *always used before a noun* : defending or protecting someone or something from attack : helping to keep a person or thing safe • The city began building a *defensive* wall around its borders. • The government decided to join a *defensive* alliance with several other nations. • *Defensive* driving classes [=classes that teach you how to be a safe driver] can help you avoid accidents. • We have taken many *defensive* measures [=we have done things to protect ourselves] against terrorist attacks. • *defensive* actions — compare ¹OFFENSIVE 4
2 [*more ~; most ~*] : behaving in a way that shows that you feel people are criticizing you • I was surprised by his *defensive* reaction to my suggestion. • *defensive* behaviors/attitudes • There's no need to get so *defensive*. I was only making a suggestion. • When we asked her about the mistakes, she became *defensive*. — often + *about* • He can be a bit *defensive about* his work as an artist.
3 *always used before a noun, sports* : of or relating to the way that players try to stop an opponent from scoring in a game or contest • The coach has a strong *defensive* strategy. • a *defensive* player/lineman — compare ¹OFFENSIVE 3
– de·fen·sive·ly *adv* • "It wasn't my fault," she said *defensively*. • The team needs to improve its game *defensively*. [=it needs to make its defense better] **– de·fen·sive·ness** *noun* [*noncount*] • There was a bit of *defensiveness* in his answer.

²defensive *noun*
on/onto the defensive **1** : in or into a situation in which you are forced to defend or protect someone or something • We won after keeping the other team *on the defensive* for most of the game. • Their soldiers appear to be *on the defensive*. • The company was pushed/forced *onto the defensive* in the lawsuit. **2** : in or into a position in which you have to argue that something (such as one of your actions or beliefs) is good or correct when others say that it is bad or wrong • The reporter often asks questions that put/place people *on the defensive*. • He found himself *on the defensive* when the subject of the environment was discussed. • The company is now *on the defensive* for its illegal business dealings.

de·fer /dɪˈfɚ/ *verb* **-fers; -ferred; -fer·ring** [+ *obj*] : to choose to do (something) at a later time • She *deferred* work on her book. • The accountant advised us not to *defer* our taxes. [=not to pay our taxes later] • She'll *defer* her decision. — see also TAX-DEFERRED
defer to [*phrasal verb*] **1** ***defer to (someone)*** : to allow (someone else) to decide or choose something • You have more experience with this, so I'm going to *defer to* you. • *deferring to* the experts **2** ***defer to (something)*** : to agree to follow (someone else's decision, a tradition, etc.) • The court *defers to* precedent in cases like these. • He *deferred to* his parents' wishes.

def·er·ence /ˈdɛfərəns/ *noun* [*noncount*] *formal* : a way of behaving that shows respect for someone or something • Her relatives treat one another with *deference*. • He is shown much *deference* by his colleagues. — often + *to* • The children were taught to show proper *deference to* their elders.
in deference to *or* ***out of deference to*** : in order to show respect for the opinions or influence of (someone or something) : out of respect for (someone or something) • He decided not to get a tattoo *in deference to* his mother. • The police have not yet revealed the victim's name *out of deference to* his family. • customs used *in deference to* tradition
– def·er·en·tial /ˌdɛfəˈrɛnʃəl/ *adj* [*more ~; most ~*] • The class listened with *deferential* [=*respectful*] attention. • *deferential* to tradition **– def·er·en·tial·ly** *adv* • She bowed *deferentially*.

de·fer·ment /dɪˈfɚmənt/ *noun, pl* **-ments** : the act of allowing something to be delayed or deferred: such as **a** : official permission to pay for something at a later time [*count*] She requested a six-month *deferment* on her loan. [*noncount*] She requested *deferment* of her loan. **b** : official permission to do required military service at a later time [*count*] a draft *deferment* • He received a ***college/student deferment*** [=permission to finish school before entering the military] [*noncount*] the policies of military *deferment*

de·fer·ral /dɪˈfərəl/ *noun, pl* **-rals** : the act of delaying or deferring something [*count*] a tax *deferral* [*noncount*] He applied for *deferral*.

de·fi·ance /dɪˈfajəns/ *noun* [*noncount*] : a refusal to obey something or someone : the act of defying someone or something • acts of *defiance* — often + *of* • He was jailed for his *defiance of* the law.
in defiance of : against or despite the wishes, rules, or laws of (someone or something) • The group is acting *in defiance of* a government order. • She married him *in defiance of* her parents. • The dancers leap *in* seeming *defiance of* the laws of gravity.

de·fi·ant /dɪˈfajənt/ *adj* [*more ~; most ~*] : refusing to obey something or someone : full of defiance • *defiant* rebels • a *defiant* act • He's taken a *defiant* stand/stance on the issue.

– **de·fi·ant·ly** *adv* ▪ He's spoken out *defiantly* against the new law.

de·fi·bril·la·tor /dɪˈfɪbrəˌleɪtɚ/ *noun, pl* **-tors** [*count*] *medical* : a device that gives an electric shock to a person's heart in order to make it beat normally again especially after a heart attack

de·fi·cien·cy /dɪˈfɪʃənsi/ *noun, pl* **-cies**
1 : a lack of something that is needed : the state of not having enough of something necessary [*count*] The disease may be caused by nutritional *deficiencies*. ▪ The book's major *deficiency* is its poor plot. ▪ a *deficiency* of vitamin C [*noncount*] vitamin *deficiency*
2 [*count*] : a problem in the way something is made or formed ▪ There are several *deficiencies* in his plan. ▪ The accident was caused by *deficiencies* in the engine.

de·fi·cient /dɪˈfɪʃənt/ *adj* [*more ~; most ~*]
1 : not having enough of something that is important or necessary ▪ a nutritionally *deficient* diet — usually + *in* ▪ a diet *deficient in* certain vitamins ▪ a man who is *deficient in* judgment [=a man whose judgment is poor] ▪ students who are *deficient* [=*lacking*] in their knowledge of history
2 : not good enough : not as good as others ▪ mentally *deficient* ▪ Several bridges in the city are structurally *deficient*.

def·i·cit /ˈdɛfəsət/ *noun, pl* **-cits** [*count*]
1 : an amount (such as an amount of money) that is less than the amount that is needed ▪ The government is facing a *deficit* of $3 billion. ▪ We will reduce the federal budget *deficit*. ▪ Some economists advocate ***deficit spending*** [=spending borrowed money] to boost a slumping economy. — opposite SURPLUS; see also TRADE DEFICIT
2 : the amount by which a person or team is behind in a game or contest ▪ The team overcame a four-point *deficit* to win the game.
3 *chiefly US* : a problem that causes a decrease in some ability ▪ She has a slight hearing *deficit* in her left ear. — see also ATTENTION DEFICIT DISORDER

[1]**de·file** /dɪˈfajəl/ *verb* **-files; -filed; -fil·ing** [*+ obj*] *formal*
1 : to make (something) dirty ▪ The lake has been *defiled* by polluters.
2 : to take away or ruin the purity, honor, or goodness of (something or someone important) ▪ She thinks slang *defiles* the language. ▪ *defiling* the country's flag ▪ Vandals *defiled* the holy shrine.
– **de·file·ment** /dɪˈfajəlmənt/ *noun* [*noncount*] ▪ the *defilement* of the shrine

[2]**defile** *noun, pl* **-files** [*count*] *formal* : a narrow passage through mountains : GORGE

de·fine /dɪˈfaɪn/ *verb* **-fines; -fined; -fin·ing** [*+ obj*]
1 : to explain the meaning of (a word, phrase, etc.) ▪ How would you *define* (the word) "grotesque"? ▪ a term that is difficult to *define*
2 : to show or describe (someone or something) clearly and completely ▪ The government study seeks to *define* urban poverty. ▪ Her book aims to *define* acceptable social behavior. ▪ He was *defined* by his passions. [=his passions showed what kind of person he was] ▪ She believes that success should be ***defined in terms of*** health and happiness. ▪ Tigers are ***broadly/loosely defined*** [=described very generally] as large cats. ▪ He ***narrowly defines*** [=describes very specifically] a hero as someone who has earned a medal in battle.
3 : to show the shape, outline, or edge of (something) very clearly ▪ That fence *defines* the far edge of the property.
– **de·fin·able** /dɪˈfaɪnəbəl/ *adj* [*more ~; most ~*] ▪ an easily *definable* word ▪ *definable* risk factors – **defined** *adj* [*more ~; most ~*] ▪ a clearly *defined* neighborhood ▪ Her cheekbones are well-*defined*. – **defining** *adj, always used before a noun* ▪ That was the campaign's ***defining moment***. [=the moment that showed very clearly what kind of campaign it was]

def·i·nite /ˈdɛfənɪt/ *adj* [*more ~; most ~*]
1 : said or done in a such way that others know exactly what you mean ▪ We'll need a *definite* answer by Tuesday. ▪ The answer is a *definite* no.
2 : not likely to change : already set or decided ▪ Are her plans *definite*? ▪ I don't know anything *definite* yet. ▪ The teacher sets *definite* standards for her students.
3 *not used before a noun* : confident or certain about doing something or that something will happen ▪ She seems to be pretty *definite* about leaving. ▪ I am *definite* that we will win.

definite article *noun, pl* **~ articles** [*count*] *grammar* : the word *the* used in English to refer to a person or thing that is identified or specified; *also* : a word that is used in a similar way in another language — compare INDEFINITE ARTICLE

def·i·nite·ly /ˈdɛfənɪtli/ *adv* [*more ~; most ~*] : without doubt : in a way that is certain or clear ▪ The new model is *definitely* an improvement. ▪ The party will *definitely* be next week. ▪ The room is *definitely* not ready. ▪ "Will you come over on Saturday?" "*Definitely*!" [=*yes*]

def·i·ni·tion /ˌdɛfəˈnɪʃən/ *noun, pl* **-tions**
1 [*count*] **a** : an explanation of the meaning of a word, phrase, etc. : a statement that defines a word, phrase, etc. ▪ dictionary *definitions* **b** : a statement that describes what something is ▪ What is the legal *definition* of a corporation? ▪ a *definition* of happiness
2 [*singular*] : a clear or perfect example of a person or thing ▪ He was the very *definition* of a gentleman. [=he was a perfect gentleman] ▪ A week of fishing is my *definition* of a vacation.
3 [*noncount*] : the quality that makes it possible to see the shape, outline, and details of something clearly ▪ muscle *definition* ▪ The picture lacks *definition*. [=the picture is not sharp/clear] ▪ a monitor with good *definition* and vibrant colors — see also HIGH-DEFINITION
by definition : because of what something or someone is : according to the definition of a word that is being used to describe someone or something ▪ A volunteer *by definition* is not paid. ▪ A glider is *by definition* an aircraft with no engine.

de·fin·i·tive /dɪˈfɪnətɪv/ *adj* [*more ~; most ~*]
1 : not able to be argued about or changed : final and settled ▪ We need a *definitive* answer to this question. ▪ The court has issued a *definitive* ruling.
2 : complete, accurate, and considered to be the best of its kind ▪ a *definitive* biography ▪ a *definitive* collection of the band's albums
– **de·fin·i·tive·ly** *adv* ▪ a virus *definitively* linked to some stomach diseases

de·flate /dɪˈfleɪt/ *verb* **-flates; -flat·ed; -flat·ing**
1 a [*+ obj*] : to release air or gas from (something, such as a tire or balloon) and make it smaller ▪ *deflate* the tires ▪ a *deflated* football **b** [*no obj*] : to lose air or gas from inside ▪ The birthday balloons *deflated* after a few days. — opposite INFLATE
2 [*+ obj*] **a** : to make (someone) lose confidence or pride ▪ The harsh criticism left him utterly *deflated*. ▪ an insult that would *deflate* their egos **b** : to show that (something) is not important or true ▪ *deflate* [=*defuse*] an argument ▪ He has worked to *deflate* popular myths about investing.
3 [*+ obj*] : to cause (prices, costs, etc.) to decrease : to cause (something, such as money or real estate) to lose value ▪ economic polices that could *deflate* (the value of) the dollar ▪ *Deflated* prices mean that farmers are getting less for their products.

de·fla·tion /dɪˈfleɪʃən/ *noun* [*noncount*]
1 : a decrease in the amount of available money or credit in an economy that causes prices to go down ▪ Economists worry that *deflation* will bring the country into recession. — compare INFLATION
2 : the act or process of letting air or gas out of (something) ▪ *deflation* of a balloon
– **de·fla·tion·ary** /dɪˈfleɪʃəˌneri, *Brit* dɪˈfleɪʃənri/ *adj* [*more ~; most ~*] ▪ a *deflationary* period in the economy

de·flect /dɪˈflɛkt/ *verb* **-flects; -flect·ed; -flect·ing**
1 a [*+ obj*] : to cause (something that is moving) to change direction ▪ armor that can *deflect* bullets ▪ The goalie *deflected* the ball with his hands. **b** [*no obj*] : to hit something and suddenly change direction ▪ The ball *deflected* off the goalie's shoulder.
2 [*+ obj*] : to keep (something, such as a question) from affecting or being directed at a person or thing ▪ She's skilled at *deflecting* [=*avoiding*] questions/criticism. ▪ They are trying to *deflect* attention from the troubled economy. ▪ The blame was *deflected* from the chairman.
– **de·flec·tor** /dɪˈflɛktɚ/ *noun, pl* **-tors** [*count*] ▪ a wind *deflector*

de·flec·tion /dɪˈflɛkʃən/ *noun, pl* **-tions** : the act of changing or causing something to change direction [*noncount*] measuring the angle of *deflection* [*count*] He scored with a *deflection* off another player's stick.

de·flow·er /diˈflawɚ/ *verb* **-ers; -ered; -er·ing** [*+ obj*] *literary* : to have sex with (someone who has not had sex before)

de·fog /diˈfɑːg/ *verb* **-fogs; -fogged; -fog·ging** [*+ obj*] *US* : to remove mist from (a window, mirror, etc.) by using dry heat ▪ *defog* [=(*Brit*) *demist*] the windshield — compare DEFROST, DEICE

– **de·fog·ger** *noun, pl* **-gers** [*count*] • a window *defogger*

de·fo·li·ant /diˈfoʊlijənt/ *noun, pl* **-ants** [*count*] *technical* : a chemical that is sprayed on plants to make their leaves fall off

de·fo·li·ate /diˈfoʊliˌeɪt/ *verb* **-ates; -at·ed; -at·ing** [+ *obj*] *technical* : to cause the leaves of (a plant) to fall off • a chemical used to *defoliate* trees • Insects are *defoliating* the trees.
– **de·fo·li·a·tion** /diˌfoʊliˈeɪʃən/ *noun* [*noncount*]

de·for·es·ta·tion /diˌforəˈsteɪʃən/ *noun* [*noncount*] : the act or result of cutting down or burning all the trees in an area • the *deforestation* of the island • mudslides caused by *deforestation* — compare REFORESTATION
– **de·for·est** /diˈforəst/ *verb* **-ests; -est·ed; -est·ing** [+ *obj*] — usually used as *(be) deforested* • regions that have *been deforested* • *deforested* areas

de·form /dɪˈfoɚm/ *verb* **-forms; -formed; -form·ing** : to change something so that it no longer has its normal or original shape [+ *obj*] The disease eventually *deforms* the bones. • a face *deformed* [=*distorted, contorted*] by hatred [*no obj*] The disease eventually causes the bones to *deform*.
– **de·for·ma·tion** /ˌdiːˌfoɚˈmeɪʃən/ *noun, pl* **-tions** [*count*] skeletal *deformations* [=(more commonly) *deformities*] [*noncount*] the *deformation* of steel

deformed *adj* [*more ~; most ~*] : not having the normal or expected shape especially because of a problem in the way something has developed or grown • *deformed* frogs • a *deformed* [=*misshapen*] hand

de·for·mi·ty /dɪˈfoɚməti/ *noun, pl* **-ties** : a condition in which part of the body does not have the normal or expected shape [*count*] facial *deformities* [*noncount*] a disease causing *deformity* of the spine

de·frag /diˈfræg/ *verb* **-frags; -fragged; -frag·ging** [+ *obj*] *chiefly US, computers, informal* : DEFRAGMENT

de·frag·ment /diˈfrægmənt/ *verb* **-ments; -ment·ed; -ment·ing** [+ *obj*] *chiefly US, computers* : to use a special program to move data on (a computer disk) so that related information is stored together • I *defragmented* my hard drive.

de·fraud /dɪˈfrɑːd/ *verb* **-frauds; -fraud·ed; -fraud·ing** : to trick or cheat someone or something in order to get money : to use fraud in order to get money from a person, an organization, etc. [+ *obj*] They were accused of trying to *defraud* the public. • They conspired to *defraud* the government. [*no obj*] She was convicted of writing bad checks ***with intent to defraud.***

de·fray /dɪˈfreɪ/ *verb* **-frays; -frayed; -fray·ing** [+ *obj*] *somewhat formal* : to pay for (something) • This will *defray* the costs/expenses.

de·frock /diˈfrɑːk/ *verb* **-frocks; -frocked; -frock·ing** [+ *obj*] : to officially remove (a priest) from his or her job as punishment for doing something wrong — usually used as *(be) defrocked* • He *was defrocked* last year. • a *defrocked* priest

de·frost /dɪˈfrɑːst/ *verb* **-frosts; -frost·ed; -frost·ing**
1 : to warm something that is frozen until it is no longer frozen [+ *obj*] You can *defrost* the soup in the microwave. [*no obj*] He took some fish out of the freezer to *defrost* [=*thaw*] in the fridge. — sometimes used figuratively • It took a while for her to *defrost* [=to stop being unfriendly] and open up to us.
2 : to melt ice that has built up on the inside of a freezer or refrigerator [+ *obj*] *defrost* the freezer [*no obj*] Has the refrigerator *defrosted* yet?
3 [+ *obj*] : to melt ice on a car's windows by using heat • *defrost* the windshield — compare DEFOG, DEICE

de·frost·er /dɪˈfrɑːstɚ/ *noun, pl* **-ers** [*count*] *US* : a device that uses heat or hot air to melt ice on or remove moisture from a surface • the car's rear *defroster* • a freezer with a built-in *defroster*

deft /ˈdɛft/ *adj* **deft·er; deft·est** [*or more ~; most ~*]
1 : skillful and clever • a *deft* politician • The photographer is known for her *deft* use of lighting.
2 : able to do something quickly and accurately • the trumpeter's *deft* fingers
– **deft·ly** *adv* • a *deftly* played symphony – **deft·ness** /ˈdɛftnəs/ *noun* [*noncount*] • political *deftness* • the *deftness* of the surgeon

de·funct /dɪˈfʌŋkt/ *adj* [*more ~; most ~*] *formal* : no longer existing or being used • a *defunct* steel company • She wrote for the now-*defunct* newspaper.

de·fuse /diˈfjuːz/ *verb* **-fus·es; -fused; -fus·ing** [+ *obj*]
1 : to make (something) less serious, difficult, or tense • Skilled negotiators helped *defuse* the crisis/situation. • Her joke *diffused* the tension in the room.
2 : to remove the part of (an explosive) that makes it explode : to remove the fuse from (an explosive) • *defuse* a bomb

de·fy /dɪˈfaɪ/ *verb* **-fies; -fied; -fy·ing** [+ *obj*]
1 : to refuse to obey (something or someone) • She *defied* her parents and dropped out of school.
2 : to make (something) very difficult or impossible • The article *defies* a simple summary. [=the article cannot be explained by a simple summary] • views of nature that *defy* belief/description [=that are hard to believe/describe]
3 : to resist or fight (something) • The group has continued to *defy* all efforts to stop them.
4 : to go against (something) • The team *defied* the odds [=did something that was very unlikely] and won the championship. • an explanation that *defies* all logic [=an explanation that does not make any sense]
5 : to tell (someone) to do something that you think cannot be done • I *defy* you to prove that I lied. • I *defy* anyone to name a better film. [=I do not think that anyone can name a better film; I do not think that there is a better film]

deg. *abbr* degree

¹de·gen·er·ate /dɪˈʤɛnəˌreɪt/ *verb* **-ates; -at·ed; -at·ing** [*no obj*] : to change to a worse state or condition : to become worse, weaker, less useful, etc. • As the disease progresses, the patient's health will *degenerate* [=*deteriorate*] rapidly. — often + *into* • Experts fear that the country is *degenerating into* chaos. • The meeting *degenerated into* a shouting match.
– **de·gen·er·a·tion** /dɪˌʤɛnəˈreɪʃən/ *noun* [*noncount*] • muscle tissue *degeneration* • Experts fear the *degeneration* of the country into chaos.

²de·gen·er·ate /dɪˈʤɛnərət/ *adj* [*more ~; most ~*] : having low moral standards : not honest, proper, or good • He criticizes what he believes is a *degenerate* society.
– **de·gen·er·a·cy** /dɪˈʤɛnərəsi/ *noun* [*noncount*] • moral *degeneracy*

³de·gen·er·ate /dɪˈʤɛnərət/ *noun, pl* **-ates** [*count*] *disapproving* : a person whose behavior is not morally right or socially acceptable • a couple of *degenerates* on a crime spree

de·gen·er·a·tive /dɪˈʤɛnərətɪv/ *adj* [*more ~; most ~*] *medical* : causing the body or part of the body to become weaker or less able to function as time passes • a *degenerative* disease/disorder

de·grad·able /dɪˈgreɪdəbəl/ *adj* [*more ~; most ~*] *technical* : capable of being slowly broken down into simple parts • plastic that is not *degradable* — compare BIODEGRADABLE

deg·ra·da·tion /ˌdɛgrəˈdeɪʃən/ *noun, pl* **-tions** *somewhat formal*
1 : the act or process of damaging or ruining something [*noncount*] *degradation* of the environment [*count*] There has been a slight *degradation* [=*decline*] in the car's performance.
2 : the act of treating someone or something poorly and without respect [*noncount*] the *degradation* of women • He was forced to live a life of *degradation*. [=a life in which he suffered and was treated very poorly] [*count*] He was forced to suffer the *degradations* [=*indignities*] of poverty and abuse.

de·grade /dɪˈgreɪd/ *verb* **-grades; -grad·ed; -grad·ing**
1 [+ *obj*] : to treat (someone or something) poorly and without respect • The group accuses the company of *degrading* women in its ads. • I am not going to *degrade* [=*lower*] myself by responding to these baseless accusations. • He felt *degraded* by their remarks.
2 [+ *obj*] : to make the quality of (something) worse • Scratches on a camera lens will *degrade* the image. • Pollution has *degraded* air quality.
3 *technical* : to cause (something complex) to break down into simple substances or parts [+ *obj*] enzymes that *degrade* proteins [*no obj*] plastics that don't *degrade* [=*decompose*] easily
– **degrading** *adj* [*more ~; most ~*] • a *degrading* job • He made a *degrading* remark about my weight.

de·gree /dɪˈgriː/ *noun, pl* **-grees**
1 [*count*] : a unit for measuring temperature • Bake the bread at 350 *degrees* (Fahrenheit) for 35 minutes. • 20 *degrees* Fahrenheit/Celsius [=20° F/C] — abbr. *deg.*
2 [*count*] : a unit for measuring the size of an angle • There are 360 *degrees* in a circle. • 47 *degrees* latitude/longitude • a 15 *degree* angle [=a 15° angle] — abbr. *deg.*
3 : an amount or level that can be measured or compared to another amount or level [*noncount*] These trees will thrive,

to a greater or lesser *degree*, in a number of climates. ▪ ***To what degree*** [=how much] is she interested in finance? ▪ We don't yet know ***the degree to which*** [=how much] the roof is damaged. [*count*] — usually + *of* ▪ a high *degree of* difficulty/skill ▪ They have had varying *degrees of* success. ▪ We can now predict the weather with a greater *degree of* accuracy. [=with more accuracy]
4 [*noncount*] : a measure of how severe or serious something is ▪ He was accused of murder in the first *degree*. = He was accused of first-*degree* murder. [=the most serious kind of murder] ▪ a second-*degree* burn — see also FIRST-DEGREE, SECOND-DEGREE, THIRD-DEGREE
5 [*count*] : an official document and title that is given to someone who has successfully completed a series of classes at a college or university ▪ She has a *degree* in engineering. ▪ a four-year *degree* [=a degree that is given to someone who has completed four years of study] ▪ a ***bachelor's/master's degree*** ▪ She received an ***honorary degree***. [=a degree given by a college or university to someone who is not a student but who has done something important]
by degrees : very slowly : by a series of small changes ▪ The tomatoes changed *by degrees* from green to red.
to some degree *also* ***to a (certain) degree*** : not completely but partly ▪ *To some degree*, they're right. ▪ We simplified the process *to a certain degree*. [=somewhat]
to the nth degree see NTH

de•hu•man•ize *also Brit* **de•hu•man•ise** /diˈhjuːməˌnaɪz/ *verb* **-iz•es**; **-ized**; **-iz•ing** [+ *obj*] : to treat (someone) as though he or she is not a human being ▪ Inspectors have observed terrible factory conditions that *dehumanize* workers. ▪ The government's propaganda is meant to *dehumanize* the enemy. [=to make the enemy seem less human] ▪ the *dehumanizing* nature of torture
— **de•hu•man•iz•a•tion** *also Brit* **de•hu•man•is•a•tion** /diˌhjuːmənəˈzeɪʃən, *Brit* diˌhjuːməˌnaɪˈzeɪʃən/ *noun* [*noncount*]

de•hu•mid•i•fi•er /ˌdiːhjuˈmɪdəˌfajɚ/ *noun, pl* **-ers** [*count*] : a machine that takes moisture out of the air — compare HUMIDIFIER

de•hy•drate /diˈhaɪˌdreɪt/ *verb* **-drates**; **-drat•ed**; **-drat•ing** *somewhat technical*
1 [+ *obj*] : to remove water or moisture from (something, such as food) ▪ Salt *dehydrates* the meat and keeps it from spoiling.
2 : to lose too much water [*no obj*] Athletes drink lots of water so they don't *dehydrate*. [+ *obj*] Exercising in this heat will *dehydrate* you.
— **dehydrated** *adj* [*more* ~; *most* ~] ▪ *dehydrated* fruit ▪ *dehydrated* athletes — **de•hy•dra•tion** /ˌdiːˌhaɪˈdreɪʃən/ *noun* [*noncount*] ▪ Athletes drink lots of water to prevent *dehydration*.

de•ice /diˈaɪs/ *verb* **-ic•es**; **-iced**; **-ic•ing** [+ *obj*] : to remove ice from (something) ▪ We watched while they *deiced* the plane before takeoff. — compare DEFOG, DEFROST

de•i•fy /ˈdijəˌfaɪ, ˈdejəˌfaɪ/ *verb* **-fies**; **-fied**; **-fy•ing** [+ *obj*] : to treat (someone or something) like a god or goddess ▪ The people *deified* the emperor. ▪ Our society *deifies* [=*worships*] money.
— **de•i•fi•ca•tion** /ˌdijəfəˈkeɪʃən, ˌdejəfəˈkeɪʃən/ *noun* [*noncount*] ▪ the *deification* of celebrities

deign /ˈdeɪn/ *verb* **deigns**; **deigned**; **deign•ing** [*no obj*] *formal + disapproving* : to do something that you think you should not have to do because you are too important — usually followed by *to + verb* ▪ She finally *deigned to speak* to me. ▪ The actor walked by, not even *deigning* [=*stooping, condescending*] *to acknowledge* his fans.

de•i•ty /ˈdiːjəti, ˈdejəti/ *noun, pl* **-ties** [*count*] : a god or goddess ▪ ancient Greek *deities* ▪ a reference to ***the Deity*** [=*God*]

dé•jà vu /ˌdeɪˌʒɑːˈvuː/ *noun* [*noncount*]
1 : the feeling that you have already experienced something that is actually happening for the first time ▪ I entered the room and immediately felt a sense of *déjà vu*.
2 *chiefly US, informal* : something that has happened many times before : something that is very familiar ▪ When the car broke down again, it was *déjà vu*. ▪ The rise in housing costs is ***déjà vu all over again***.

de•ject•ed /dɪˈʤɛktəd/ *adj* [*more* ~; *most* ~] : sad because of failure, loss, etc. ▪ The *dejected* players left the field. ▪ She's been so *dejected* [=*depressed, unhappy*] since her sister moved away.
— **de•ject•ed•ly** *adv* ▪ The players *dejectedly* walked off the field.

de•jec•tion /dɪˈʤɛkʃən/ *noun* [*noncount*] : sadness that is caused by failure, loss, etc. ▪ You could see the *dejection* [=*unhappiness*] on her face.

de ju•re /diˈʤuri/ *adj, always used before a noun, law* : based on or according to the law ▪ the end of *de jure* segregation ▪ *de jure* authority — compare DE FACTO
— **de jure** *adv* ▪ The UN has recognized the country *de jure*.

Del. *abbr, US* Delaware

¹de•lay /dɪˈleɪ/ *noun, pl* **-lays**
1 : a situation in which something happens later than it should [*count*] Do you know what's causing the *delay*? ▪ The nurse apologized for the *delay* [=*wait*] and said that the doctor would be in shortly. ▪ a number of flight *delays* [*noncount*] After months of *delay*, construction on the new school began. ▪ The roof must be repaired ***without delay***. [=*immediately*]
2 [*count*] : the amount of time that you must wait for something that is late ▪ Airline travelers are experiencing *delays* of up to three hours.

²delay *verb* **-lays**; **-layed**; **-lay•ing**
1 : to wait until later to do something : to make something happen later [+ *obj*] The doctor wants to *delay* surgery for a few weeks. ▪ They *delayed* [=*put off*] having children until their late 30s. ▪ She's planning to *delay* her retirement. [*no obj*] He *delayed* too long, and now it's too late. ▪ "Don't *delay*! Sale ends Saturday."
2 [+ *obj*] : to make (something or someone) late : to make (something or someone) take longer than expected or planned ▪ Production problems *delayed* the introduction of the new model by several months. — often used as *(be) delayed* ▪ We *were delayed* by traffic. ▪ Many flights *were delayed*.
— **delayed** *adj* [*more* ~; *most* ~] ▪ He had a very *delayed* reaction to the medication. [=a reaction that did not happen immediately]

delaying tactic *noun* [*count*] : something that is done in order to delay a decision, an occurrence, etc. — called also (*chiefly US*) *delay tactic*

de•lec•ta•ble /dɪˈlɛktəbəl/ *adj* [*more* ~; *most* ~] *somewhat formal*
1 : very pleasant to taste or smell : DELICIOUS ▪ the restaurant's *delectable* food ▪ The meals he prepares are always *delectable*.
2 *humorous* : very attractive ▪ one of the most *delectable* men she's ever met
— **de•lec•ta•bly** /dɪˈlɛktəbli/ *adv* ▪ a *delectably* seasoned steak

de•lec•ta•tion /ˌdiːˌlɛkˈteɪʃən/ *noun* [*noncount*] *formal* : pleasure or enjoyment ▪ Here is some chocolate for your *delectation*.

¹del•e•gate /ˈdɛlɪgət/ *noun, pl* **-gates** [*count*] : a person who is chosen or elected to vote or act for others : REPRESENTATIVE ▪ the U.N. *delegates* from African countries ▪ He's been chosen as a *delegate* to the convention.

²del•e•gate /ˈdɛlɪˌgeɪt/ *verb* **-gates**; **-gat•ed**; **-gat•ing**
1 : to give (control, responsibility, authority, etc.) to someone : to trust someone with (a job, duty, etc.) [+ *obj*] A manager should *delegate* authority to the best employees. ▪ Those chores can be *delegated* to someone else. [*no obj*] He doesn't *delegate* very well.
2 [+ *obj*] : to choose (someone) to do something — often used as *(be) delegated* ▪ He *was delegated* by the town to take care of the monument.

del•e•ga•tion /ˌdɛlɪˈgeɪʃən/ *noun, pl* **-tions**
1 [*count*] : a group of people who are chosen to vote or act for someone else ▪ a *delegation* of diplomats ▪ He's been chosen to lead the *delegation* to the conference. ▪ the state's ***congressional delegation*** [=the group of officials elected to the U.S. Congress from a particular state]
2 [*noncount*] *formal* : the act of giving control, authority, a job, a duty, etc., to another person — usually + *of* ▪ the *delegation of* responsibilities

de•lete /dɪˈliːt/ *verb* **-letes**; **-let•ed**; **de•let•ing** [+ *obj*] : to remove (something, such as words, pictures, or computer files) from a document, recording, computer, etc. ▪ *Delete* this name from the list. ▪ When the movie was shown on TV all the swearwords had been *deleted*. ▪ She accidentally *deleted* [=*erased*] the file/e-mail.
— **de•le•tion** /dɪˈliːʃən/ *noun, pl* **-tions** [*count*] The *deletions* shouldn't affect the meaning of the letter. [*noncount*] The *deletion* of that paragraph makes your letter read better.

del·e·te·ri·ous /ˌdɛləˈtirijəs/ *adj* [*more* ~; *most* ~] *formal* : damaging or harmful • The chemical is *deleterious* to the environment. • The drug has no *deleterious* effects on patients.

deli /ˈdɛli/ *noun, pl* **del·is** [*count*] : a store where you can buy foods (such as meats, cheese, salads, and sandwiches) that are already cooked or prepared • We bought sandwiches and drinks at the *deli.* — called also *delicatessen*

[1]**de·lib·er·ate** /dɪˈlɪbərət/ *adj* [*more* ~; *most* ~]
1 : done or said in a way that is planned or intended : done or said on purpose • I don't think that was a mistake; I think it was *deliberate.* [=*intentional*] • a *deliberate* [=*planned*] attempt to trick people
2 : done or decided after careful thought • a *deliberate* choice/decision
3 : slow and careful • She spoke in a clear, *deliberate* manner/way. • He advocates a slow and *deliberate* approach to the problem.

[2]**de·lib·er·ate** /dɪˈlɪbəˌreɪt/ *verb* **-ates; -at·ed; -at·ing** : to think about or discuss something very carefully in order to make a decision [*no obj*] The jury *deliberated* for two days before reaching a verdict. [+ *obj*] They will *deliberate* the question. — often + *whether, what,* etc. • I've been *deliberating* [=*debating*] *whether* or not to accept the job offer.

de·lib·er·ate·ly /dɪˈlɪbərətli/ *adv* [*more* ~; *most* ~]
1 : in a way that is meant, intended, or planned • He *deliberately* tricked them.
2 : slowly and carefully : in a way that is not hurried • She spoke clearly and *deliberately* to the audience.

de·lib·er·a·tion /dɪˌlɪbəˈreɪʃən/ *noun, pl* **-tions**
1 : careful thought or discussion done in order to make a decision [*noncount*] After hours of *deliberation,* the council came to a decision. [*count*] Jury *deliberations* lasted two days.
2 [*noncount*] : the quality of being slow and careful • She spoke to the audience with clarity and *deliberation.*

de·lib·er·a·tive /dɪˈlɪbəˌreɪtɪv, dɪˈlɪbərətɪv/ *adj* [*more* ~; *most* ~] *formal* : created or done in order to discuss and consider facts and reasons carefully • Congress is a *deliberative* body. • a *deliberative* process

del·i·ca·cy /ˈdɛlɪkəsi/ *noun, pl* **-cies**
1 [*count*] : a food that people like to eat because it is special or rare • The restaurant serves delicious sausages and other regional *delicacies.*
2 [*noncount*] : the quality of being delicate: such as **a** : the quality of being easily broken or damaged • the *delicacy* of the glassware **b** : the quality of being easily injured, hurt, or made sick • the *delicacy* [=*frailty*] of his health **c** : the attractive quality of something that is formed from many small or fine parts • The curtains were made from fine lace of great *delicacy.* • a musician known for the *delicacy* of her compositions • the *delicacy* of the young boy's features **d** : the appealing quality of something that is not too strong • the *delicacy* of the perfume • the *delicacy* of the wine's flavor
3 [*noncount*] **a** : special care or skill that is needed to prevent people from becoming upset or angry • This is a difficult situation that should be handled with *delicacy.* [=*tact*] **b** : the quality of requiring special care or skill • Because of the *delicacy* of the situation, we needed to speak privately.

del·i·cate /ˈdɛlɪkət/ *adj* [*more* ~; *most* ~]
1 a : easily broken or damaged • The cup is very *delicate* [=*fragile*], so please handle it carefully. • *delicate* flowers **b** : easily injured, hurt, or made sick • Her health is very *delicate.* [=*frail*] • He has a *delicate* stomach and often gets sick when traveling.
2 a : attractive and made up of small or fine parts • The fabric has a *delicate* floral print. • a small boy with *delicate* (facial) features • She has *delicate* hands. [=small and attractive hands] **b** : very carefully and beautifully made • We hung *delicate* lace curtains in the windows. • The tomb was adorned with *delicate* carvings.
3 : attractive because of being soft, gentle, light, etc. : pleasant or attractive in a way that is not too strong • the *delicate* flavor of the wine • a *delicate* perfume/sauce • a *delicate* color
4 : easily disturbed or upset • Many people struggle to maintain the *delicate* balance between work and family. • The violence in the film offended her *delicate* sensibilities. • The movie is not for *delicate* [=*squeamish*] people.
5 : requiring special care or skill : difficult to manage or do well • The doctor performed the *delicate* operation. • This is a *delicate* situation that needs to be handled carefully. • The situation calls for a very *delicate* approach.
— **del·i·cate·ly** *adv* • a *delicately* carved tomb • a *delicately* flavored ginger sauce • This situation must be handled *delicately.*

del·i·cates /ˈdɛlɪkəts/ *noun* [*plural*] : clothes made of delicate material that must be washed carefully

del·i·ca·tes·sen /ˌdɛlɪkəˈtɛsn̩/ *noun, pl* **-sens** [*count*] : DELI

de·li·cious /dɪˈlɪʃəs/ *adj* [*more* ~; *most* ~]
1 a : very pleasant to taste • Dinner was *delicious.* • This is the most *delicious* ice cream I have ever eaten. **b** : having a smell that suggests a very pleasant taste • The bread smells *delicious.* • *Delicious* aromas were floating from the kitchen.
2 *literary* : very pleasing or enjoyable • a *delicious* [=*delightful*] comedy about parenthood • a *delicious* bit of gossip
— **de·li·cious·ly** *adv* • They served a *deliciously* fruity dessert. • a *deliciously* witty writer — **de·li·cious·ness** *noun* [*noncount*]

[1]**de·light** /dɪˈlaɪt/ *noun, pl* **-lights**
1 [*noncount*] : a strong feeling of happiness : great pleasure or satisfaction • His expression when he saw the baby was one of pure *delight.* [=*joy*] • We watched the fireworks with *delight.* • The kids screamed ***in delight*** as they chased one another around the park. • ***To our delight,*** our guests decided to stay another night. [=we were very happy that our guests decided to stay another night] • ***To the delight of*** the children, there were enough cookies for everyone to have two. • She ***takes delight in*** [=very much enjoys] her new job. • Some people seem to *take* great *delight in* hearing about the misfortunes of others.
2 [*count*] : something that makes you very happy : something that gives you great pleasure or satisfaction • The trip was a *delight.* • a garden full of tasty *delights* • The magazine is a cook's *delight.* • The stories are a *delight* to read.
— see also TURKISH DELIGHT

[2]**delight** *verb* **-lights; -light·ed; -light·ing** [+ *obj*] : to make (someone) very happy : to give (someone) great pleasure or satisfaction • The toy *delighted* the children. • The stories will *delight* readers of all ages.
delight in [*phrasal verb*] ***delight in (something)*** : to be very happy because of (something) : to enjoy (something) very much • I walked slowly, *delighting in* the crisp autumn air. • He *delights in* meeting new people.

delighted *adj* [*more* ~; *most* ~] : made very happy : full of great pleasure or satisfaction • I am *delighted* [=*very pleased*] to meet you. • the *delighted* [=*joyful*] expression on his face • The children were especially *delighted* that there were enough cookies for each of them to have two. • She's *delighted* with her new job. [=she likes her new job very much] • We were *delighted* by the performance. • They are *delighted* at the prospect of a visit from their grandchildren.
— **de·light·ed·ly** *adv* • He laughed *delightedly.*

de·light·ful /dɪˈlaɪtfəl/ *adj* [*more* ~; *most* ~] : very pleasant : giving or causing delight • It has been *delightful* meeting you. • It is *delightful* [=*wonderful, great*] to be here. • That was a *delightful* party. • She's a *delightful* person.
— **de·light·ful·ly** *adv* • a *delightfully* sunny day

de·lim·it /dɪˈlɪmət/ *verb* **-its; -it·ed; -it·ing** [+ *obj*] *formal* : to officially set or state the limits of (something) • Strict guidelines *delimit* his responsibilities.

de·lin·eate /dɪˈlɪniˌeɪt/ *verb* **-eates; -eat·ed; -eat·ing** [+ *obj*] *formal* : to clearly show or describe (something) • The report clearly *delineates* the steps that must be taken. • The characters in the story were carefully *delineated.*
— **de·lin·ea·tion** /dɪˌlɪniˈeɪʃən/ *noun* [*noncount*]

de·lin·quen·cy /dɪˈlɪŋkwənsi/ *noun, pl* **-cies**
1 : crimes or other morally wrong acts : illegal or immoral behavior especially by young people [*noncount*] They tried to steer him away from *delinquency* by giving him a job in their store. • She's been charged with contributing to the *delinquency* of a minor. [*count*] a series of minor *delinquencies* — see also JUVENILE DELINQUENCY
2 *US* : the condition of someone who owes money and is not making payments at the required or expected time [*count*] Loan *delinquencies* are on the rise. [=an increasing number of people are failing to make their loan payments on time] [*noncount*] a high rate of *delinquency* • *Delinquency* rates are soaring.

[1]**de·lin·quent** /dɪˈlɪŋkwənt/ *noun, pl* **-quents** [*count*] : a young person who regularly does illegal or immoral things : JUVENILE DELINQUENT • a group of violent *delinquents*

[2]**delinquent** *adj*

1 : doing things that are illegal or immoral • a school for *delinquent* children • His *delinquent* behavior could lead to more serious problems.
2 *US* **a :** not paid at the required or expected time • Her credit card account was *delinquent.* [=she had not made the payments that were due on her credit card account] • The town is trying to collect *delinquent* taxes. **b :** failing to pay an amount of money that is owed • people who are *delinquent* in their loan payments [=people who have not been paying back their loans when they said they would] • *delinquent* borrowers

D

de·lir·i·ous /dɪˈlirijəs/ *adj* [*more* ~; *most* ~]
1 : not able to think or speak clearly especially because of fever or other illness • As the child's temperature went up, he became *delirious* and didn't know where he was. • He was *delirious* with fever.
2 : very excited • a group of *delirious* fans celebrating the team's victory — often + *with* • We were *delirious with* happiness when we heard the news.
– de·lir·i·ous·ly *adv* • *deliriously* happy • *deliriously* in love • He spoke *deliriously.*

de·lir·i·um /dɪˈlirijəm/ *noun, pl* **-iums**
1 : a mental state in which you are confused and not able to think or speak clearly usually because of fever or some other illness [*noncount*] In her *delirium,* nothing she said made any sense. • a period of *delirium* [*count*] drug *deliriums*
2 [*noncount*] **:** a state of wild excitement and great happiness • The team's victory sent fans into (a state of) *delirium.*

delirium tre·mens /-ˈtri:mənz/ *noun* [*noncount*] *medical* **:** D.T.'S

de·lish /dɪˈlɪʃ/ *adj* [*more* ~; *most* ~] *US, informal* **:** DELICIOUS • The whole meal was *delish.*

de·list /diˈlɪst/ *verb* **-lists; -list·ed; -list·ing** [+ *obj*] *formal* **:** to remove (something) from a list • The company has been *delisted* from the stock exchange. [=the company is no longer one of the companies listed on the stock exchange]

de·liv·er /dɪˈlɪvɚ/ *verb* **-ers; -ered; -er·ing**
1 : to take (something) to a person or place [+ *obj*] The package was *delivered* to the office this morning. • She *delivers* the mail on my street. • They are having the furniture *delivered* next week. • The supermarket *delivers* groceries for free within 30 miles of the store. [*no obj*] "Does the restaurant *deliver*?" "No, you have to pick up the food yourself."
2 [+ *obj*] **:** to say (something) officially or publicly **:** to present (a speech, statement, etc.) to a group of people • He will *deliver* the speech at noon. • The actors *delivered* their lines with passion. • The jury is expected to *deliver* a verdict later today. • The judge *delivered* a warning to the protesters.
3 a [*no obj*] **:** to do what you say you will do or what people expect you to do **:** to produce the promised, wanted, or expected results • We gave her the job because we know she'll *deliver.* [=*come through*] • He failed to ***deliver on*** his promise. [=he failed to do what he promised to do] **b** [+ *obj*] **:** to provide or produce (something) • The novel *delivers* an inspiring look into the life and ideas of Gandhi. • The company charges too much for what it *delivers.* • The car *delivers* excellent/poor gas mileage. — see also *deliver the goods* at [2]GOOD
4 [+ *obj*] **a :** to give birth to (a baby) • She *delivered* healthy twin girls early this morning. • (*technical*) The patient ***was delivered of*** [=gave birth to] healthy twin girls this morning. **b :** to help someone give birth to (a baby) • The doctor is *delivering* a baby right now.
5 [+ *obj*] **:** to give control of (someone or something) to another person or group — + *to* or *into* • He argues that by letting children watch too much television, we are *delivering* them *into* the hands of advertisers. • A group of soldiers were ***delivered up to*** [=*handed over to*] the enemy at the border. • The agreement ***delivered over*** [=*transferred*] the documents ***into*** the possession of the museum.
6 [+ *obj*] **:** to cause (something, such as a punch, a thrown ball, etc.) to hit or go to a person or place • The boxer *delivered* a crushing blow to his opponent's head. • He *delivered* [=*threw*] a fastball right over the plate. • The country is believed to have the ability to *deliver* nuclear warheads. [=to attack other countries with nuclear warheads]
7 [+ *obj*] *chiefly US* **:** to get (votes) for a particular person or issue in an election • She is doing her best to *deliver* the college student vote. [=to convince college students to vote a particular way]
8 [+ *obj*] *formal* + *literary* **:** to free (someone) *from* something • all those who long to be *delivered from* slavery/tyranny • "... *deliver* [=*save*] us *from* evil." —Matthew 6:13 (KJV)
deliver yourself of *formal* **:** to make, create, or produce (something) • She has finally *delivered herself of* her long-awaited third novel.
– de·liv·er·able /dɪˈlɪvərəbəl/ *adj* • a *deliverable* product **– deliverable** *noun, pl* **-ables** [*count*] — usually plural • computer software *deliverables* [=products that can be delivered to customers] **– de·liv·er·er** /dɪˈlɪvərɚ/ *noun, pl* **-ers** [*count*] • When are the *deliverers* bringing the sofa?

de·liv·er·ance /dɪˈlɪvərəns/ *noun* [*noncount*] *formal* **:** the state of being saved from something dangerous or unpleasant • She prayed for *deliverance* as the famine got worse. — often + *from* • He knew that his retirement would bring *deliverance from* the worries and stresses of his job.

de·liv·ery /dɪˈlɪvəri/ *noun, pl* **-er·ies**
1 a : the act of taking something to a person or place [*count*] The *delivery* is scheduled for this morning. • The supermarket ***makes deliveries*** [=takes goods to customers] for free within 30 miles of the store. • The restaurant doesn't ***do deliveries.*** [=does not take food to customers] [*noncount*] The company offers free *delivery* with orders over $100. • She does the mail *delivery* [=she delivers the mail] on my street. • a *delivery* truck/service [=a truck/service that delivers something] • Someone has to be home to accept/receive *delivery* of the package. • Payment is due ***on delivery*** of the goods. [=when you receive the goods] • Allow six weeks ***for delivery.*** — see also SPECIAL DELIVERY **b** [*count*] **:** something that is taken to a person or place **:** something that is delivered • The store got a *delivery* [=*shipment*] of shirts yesterday.
2 : the act or process of giving birth [*noncount*] The baby weighed almost seven pounds at the time of *delivery.* • the ***delivery room*** [=a special room in a hospital where women give birth to babies] [*count*] The doctor expects it to be a routine *delivery.* • The doctor has had three *deliveries* today.
3 [*singular*] **:** the way someone says something officially or publicly **:** the way someone delivers a speech, statement, etc., to a group of people • The joke was funny, but his *delivery* was terrible. • I need to work on my *delivery* before I give the speech.
4 [*count*] *sports* **:** the way a ball is thrown in baseball or cricket • The pitchers have similar *deliveries.* • a high *delivery*
take delivery of *formal* **:** to receive (something that is being delivered to you) • The city will *take delivery of* the vehicles tomorrow.

delivery boy *noun, pl* ~ **boys** [*count*] *somewhat old-fashioned* **:** a boy or young man who delivers goods to customers from a store or restaurant

de·liv·ery·man /dɪˈlɪvərimən/ *noun, pl* **-men** /-mən/ [*count*] **:** a man who delivers goods to customers

dell /ˈdɛl/ *noun, pl* **dells** [*count*] *formal* + *literary* **:** a small valley with trees and grass growing in it

de·louse /diˈlaʊs/ *verb* **-lous·es; -loused; -lous·ing** [+ *obj*] **:** to remove lice from (someone or something) • *delouse* clothing

del·ta /ˈdɛltə/ *noun, pl* **-tas**
1 [*count*] **:** the fourth letter of the Greek alphabet — Δ or δ
2 [*count*] **:** a piece of land shaped like a triangle that is formed when a river splits into smaller rivers before it flows into an ocean • a river *delta* • the Ganges/Nile *Delta*
3 *or* **Delta** [*singular*] *US* **:** an area of low land along the Mississippi River that is mainly in the state of Mississippi • the Mississippi *Delta* • *delta* blues [=blues music that comes from the Mississippi delta]

del·toid /ˈdɛlˌtoɪd/ *noun, pl* **-toids** [*count*] **:** a large muscle of the shoulder • well-developed *deltoids* • the *deltoid* muscles

de·lude /dɪˈlu:d/ *verb* **-ludes; -lud·ed; -lud·ing** [+ *obj*] **:** to cause (someone) to believe something that is not true • If she thinks I care, she's *deluding* [=*fooling*] herself. • He was *deluded* [=*deceived*] by their lies. — often + *into* • They *deluded* themselves *into* believing their team would win.
– deluded *adj* [*more* ~; *most* ~] • His *deluded* family believed everything he said. • a very *deluded* way of thinking

[1]**del·uge** /ˈdɛlˌju:ʤ/ *noun, pl* **-ug·es** [*count*]
1 a : a large amount of rain that suddenly falls in an area • The *deluge* caused severe mudslides. **b :** a situation in which a large area of land becomes completely covered with water **:** FLOOD • the biblical *deluge*
2 : a large amount of things that come at the same time • an advertising *deluge* [=many advertisements] — often + *of* • The office receives a *deluge of* mail every day. • a *deluge of* phone calls

[2]**deluge** *verb* **-uges; -uged; -ug·ing** [+ *obj*]
1 : to give or send (someone) a large amount of things at the

same time — usually used as *(be) deluged* • The family *was deluged* [=*inundated, swamped*] with calls about the free puppies. • The office *is deluged* with mail every day.
2 : to flood (a place) with water • Heavy rains *deluged* the region.

de•lu•sion /dɪˈluːʒən/ *noun, pl* **-sions** [*count*]
1 : a belief that is not true : a false idea • He has *delusions* about how much money he can make at that job. • He is living/laboring ***under the delusion*** that he is incapable of making mistakes. • She is *under the delusion* that we will finish on time.
2 : a false idea or belief that is caused by mental illness • As the illness progressed, his *delusions* took over and he had violent outbursts. ✧ If you have ***delusions of grandeur***, you believe that you are much more important than you really are. • The patient is suffering from hallucinations and *delusions of grandeur*. • a young actress with *delusions of grandeur*
– **de•lu•sion•al** /dɪˈluːʒənl/ *adj* [*more* ~; *most* ~] • He showed signs of *delusional* thinking near the end of his life. • If you think we can afford a new car, you are *delusional*.

de•luxe /dɪˈlʌks/ *adj* [*more* ~; *most* ~] : of better quality and usually more expensive than the usual ones of its kind : very luxurious • We stayed at a *deluxe* [=*fancy*] hotel. • the *deluxe* model of the car • The *deluxe* edition of the book includes many more illustrations.

delve /ˈdɛlv/ *verb* **delves; delved; delv•ing** [*no obj*]
1 : to search for information about something • He tried to *delve* inside his memory for clues about what had happened. — usually + *into* • Before the trip, I *delved into* the history of the city. • Now is not the time to *delve into* the past. • He *delved* deeply/further *into* his research.
2 *chiefly Brit* : to reach into a bag, container, etc., in order to find something — usually + *in* or *into* • He *delved in* the drawer for a torch. • She *delved into* her handbag in search of a pen.

Dem. *abbr, US* Democrat

dem•a•gogue /ˈdɛməˌgɑːg/ *noun, pl* **-gogues** [*count*] *disapproving* : a political leader who tries to get support by making false claims and promises and using arguments based on emotion rather than reason • His opponent called him a bigoted *demagogue*.
– **dem•a•gog•ic** /ˌdɛməˈgɑːgɪk/ *adj* [*more* ~; *most* ~] • a *demagogic* politician – **dem•a•gogu•ery** /ˈdɛməˌgɑːgəri/ *also* **dem•a•gogy** /ˈdɛməˌgɑːgi/ *noun* [*noncount*] • political *demagoguery*

[1]**de•mand** /dɪˈmænd, *Brit* dɪˈmɑːnd/ *noun, pl* **-mands**
1 [*count*] : a forceful statement in which you say that something must be done or given to you • The committee is considering her *demand* that she be given more time to complete the study. • The workers said they would not end the strike until their *demands* were met/satisfied. — often + *for* • The store refused to meet the customer's *demand for* a refund. • Parents made *demands for* the teacher's resignation.
2 [*singular*] : a strong need *for* something • The *demand for* low-income housing is increasing as the economy gets worse. • We are seeing an increased *demand for* hospital beds.
3 : the ability and need or desire to buy goods and services [*noncount*] The company increased production to meet *demand*. — often + *for* • *Demand for* fresh milk has surpassed supply in the region. [=people want to buy more milk than is available] [*singular*] — often + *for* • Local farmers say they will increase the number of peach trees they grow in order to meet a rising *demand for* peaches. [=in order to have as many peaches as customers want to buy] — see also SUPPLY AND DEMAND
4 ***demands*** [*plural*] **a** : difficult things you have to do because someone requires you to do them or because they are part of a job, activity, etc. — often + *of* • He wasn't sure he could handle the physical *demands of* the work. • The *demands of* the job became too much for him. • New parents are sometimes overwhelmed by the *demands of* parenthood. **b** — used to describe something that requires a large amount of energy, time, etc. • Record high temperatures have ***placed heavy demands on*** the nation's energy supplies. [=because of the high temperatures, a lot of the nation's energy is being used] • A full-time job in addition to school ***puts great demands on*** her time. [=most of her time is spent working and going to school] • His novels ***make many demands on*** the reader. [=his novels are difficult for people to read and understand]
in demand : needed or wanted by many people • Tickets for her concerts are always *in* great *demand*. • Good plumbers are *in demand* in our town.
on demand : when needed or wanted • Help is available 24 hours a day *on demand*. • The debt is payable *on demand*. [=it must be paid whenever the person who is owed the money wants it] — see also ON-DEMAND
popular demand : a request made by or a desire shared by many people • Because of *popular demand*, the restaurant has published a cookbook of favorite recipes. • The show will continue for another week due to *popular demand*. • The circus will be back *by popular demand* [=because many people want it to come back] later this summer.

[2]**demand** *verb* **-mands; -mand•ed; -mand•ing** [+ *obj*]
1 : to say in a forceful way that something must be done or given to you : to say that you have a right to (something) • The customer *demanded* a refund. • He *demanded* an apology. • Parents have *demanded* that the teacher resign. • The reporter *demanded* to see the documents. • I *demand* to know what is going on here!
2 : to say or ask (something) in a very forceful way • "Come here at once!" he *demanded*. • "Why won't you answer me?" she *demanded*.
3 : to require (something) • He is very sick and *demands* constant care. [=he has to be given constant care] • The situation *demands* immediate action. • A certain standard of dress is *demanded* by some professions. [=some people have to dress a certain way because of their jobs] • The job *demands* too much of him. [=the job requires him to do too much] • The group *demands* [=*insists on*] total honesty from its members.

demanding *adj* [*more* ~; *most* ~]
1 : requiring much time, attention, or effort • She had a *demanding* schedule with little free time. • Factory work can be physically *demanding*. • I have heard it is one of the most *demanding* courses at the university.
2 : expecting much time, attention, effort, etc., from other people : hard to satisfy • Their boss was really *demanding*, often expecting them to work long into the night. — opposite UNDEMANDING

de•mar•cate /dɪˈmɑɚˌkeɪt, ˈdiːˌmɑɚˌkeɪt/ *verb* **-cates; -cat•ed; -cat•ing** [+ *obj*] *formal* : to show the limits or edges of (something) • The plot of land is *demarcated* by a low brick wall. • The bounardy between the countries must be clearly *demarcated*.
– **de•mar•ca•tion** /ˌdiːˌmɑɚˈkeɪʃən/ *noun, pl* **-tions** [*noncount*] the *demarcation* of the boundary • Troops are positioned on either side of the line of *demarcation*. = Troops are positioned on either side of the *demarcation* line. [*count*] The media has blurred the *demarcations* [=*lines, boundaries*] between news and entertainment.

de•mean /dɪˈmiːn/ *verb* **-means; -meaned; -mean•ing** [+ *obj*] : to cause (someone or something) to seem less important or less worthy of respect • He was careful not to *demean* [=*debase, put down*] his opponent, choosing instead to show him respect. • Her statement *demeans* the hard work the group has done. • Their casual reaction *demeans* the seriousness of the problem. [=fails to treat the problem in an appropriately serious way] • I refuse to ***demean myself*** by replying to these unjust accusations.
– **demeaning** *adj* [*more* ~; *most* ~] • Our petty arguments are *demeaning* to us both. • His comment is *demeaning* to women. • He found the work *demeaning*. [=*degrading*] • *demeaning* stereotypes

de•mean•or (*US*) *or Brit* **de•mean•our** /dɪˈmiːnɚ/ *noun, pl* **-ors** [*count*] : a person's appearance and behavior : the way someone seems to be to other people — usually singular • She has a shy/friendly/warm *demeanor*. • His quiet *demeanor* [=*manner, bearing*] had a calming effect on us. • They maintained a solemn *demeanor* as they told us the bad news.

de•ment•ed /dɪˈmɛntəd/ *adj* [*more* ~; *most* ~] : not able to think clearly or to understand what is real and what is not real : crazy or insane • Many of the patients there were *demented*. • In the movie, he plays a *demented* man trying to survive on the streets of Los Angeles. • Her *demented* ramblings are a symptom of her illness. • He gave me a *demented* little smile. • parents who are almost *demented* with worry

de•men•tia /dɪˈmɛnʃə/ *noun, pl* **-tias** *medical* : a mental illness that causes someone to be unable to think clearly or to understand what is real and what is not real [*noncount*] This patient suffers from *dementia*. [*count*] a new study on age-related *dementias* — see also SENILE DEMENTIA

dem•e•rara sugar /ˌdɛməˈrɑrə-, ˌdɛməˈrerə-/ *noun* [*noncount*] *Brit* : a kind of light brown sugar

de·mer·it /dɪˈmerət/ *noun, pl* **-its** [*count*]
1 *US* : a mark that is made on the school record of a student who has done something wrong • Students are given *demerits* if they arrive late for classes.
2 *formal* : a bad quality in something or someone : a feature or part of something or someone that is unpleasant — usually plural • The *demerits* of that job outweigh the benefits. • We considered both the ***merits and demerits*** of the plan.

demi- /ˈdɛmi/ *prefix* : half or partly • *demigod*

demi·god /ˈdɛmi,gɑ:d/ *noun, pl* **-gods** [*count*]
1 : an extremely impressive or important person : a person who seems like a god in some way • the *demigods* of jazz
2 : a person in mythology who has some of the powers of a god : a being in mythology who is part god and part human • the Greek *demigod* Triton

de·mil·i·ta·rize *also Brit* **de·mil·i·ta·rise** /dɪˈmɪlətə,raɪz/ *verb* **-riz·es; -rized; -riz·ing** [+ *obj*] : to remove weapons and military forces from (an area) — usually used as *(be) demilitarized* • Analysts predict that the area will not *be* fully *demilitarized* this year. • the ***demilitarized zone*** [=*DMZ*] between North and South Korea — opposite MILITARIZE
– de·mil·i·ta·ri·za·tion *also Brit* **de·mil·i·ta·ri·sa·tion** /dɪ,mɪlətərəˈzeɪʃən, *Brit* ,dɪ,mɪlətə,raɪˈzeɪʃən/ *noun* [*noncount*]

de·mise /dɪˈmaɪz/ *noun* [*singular*] *formal*
1 : an end of life : DEATH • She had/owned no property at the time of her *demise*. • The musician met an untimely *demise*. • There are several theories about what caused the *demise* [=*extinction*] of the dinosaurs.
2 : the end of something that is thought of as being like a death • We have not had truly local news coverage since the town newspaper's *demise* three years ago. • the company's imminent *demise* • Losing this game will mean/spell the team's *demise*.

de·mist /diˈmɪst/ *verb* **-mists; -mist·ed; -mist·ing** [+ *obj*] *Brit* : DEFOG

demi·tasse /ˈdɛmɪ,tæs/ *noun, pl* **-tass·es** [*count*] *chiefly US* : a small amount of black coffee that is served in a small cup; *also* : the cup used to serve it

demo /ˈdɛmoʊ/ *noun, pl* **dem·os** [*count*]
1 : an example of a product that is not yet ready to be sold • She will be showing a *demo* of the company's new alarm system. • a *demo* version of the software
2 : an act of showing someone how something is used or done : DEMONSTRATION • I saw a *demo* on how to use the computer program. • The salesman ***gave us a demo*** of the vacuum cleaner, and it seemed to work very well.
3 : a recording that musicians make in order to show what their music is like • They sent the *demo* to several record companies. • She cut/made a *demo* last week.
4 *Brit, informal* : DEMONSTRATION 2 • an antiwar *demo*

de·mob /diˈmɑb/ *verb* **-mobs; -mobbed; -mob·bing** [+ *obj*] *chiefly Brit* : DEMOBILIZE

de·mo·bi·lize *also Brit* **de·mo·bi·lise** /dɪˈmoʊbə,laɪz/ *verb* **-liz·es; -lized; -liz·ing** [+ *obj*] : to release (someone or something) from military service • Both leaders agreed to *demobilize* their armies and sign the peace treaty. • Ships returned to port to be *demobilized*. [=to be changed so that they were no longer ready for war]
– de·mo·bi·li·za·tion *also Brit* **de·mo·bi·li·sa·tion** /dɪ,moʊbələˈzeɪʃən, *Brit* dɪ,moʊbə,laɪˈzeɪʃən/ *noun* [*noncount*]

de·moc·ra·cy /dɪˈmɑ:krəsi/ *noun, pl* **-cies**
1 a [*noncount*] : a form of government in which people choose leaders by voting • The nation has chosen *democracy* over monarchy. • the principles of *democracy* **b** [*count*] : a country ruled by democracy • In a *democracy*, every citizen should have the right to vote. • Western *democracies*
2 : an organization or situation in which everyone is treated equally and has equal rights [*count*] The company is not a *democracy*; decisions are made by a board of directors, not the workers. [*noncount*] There is *democracy* within the company. — see also SOCIAL DEMOCRACY

dem·o·crat /ˈdɛmə,kræt/ *noun, pl* **-crats** [*count*]
1 : a person who believes in or supports democracy
2 ***Democrat*** : a member of the Democratic Party of the U.S. • a lifelong *Democrat* — compare REPUBLICAN

dem·o·crat·ic /,dɛməˈkrætɪk/ *adj*
1 : based on a form of government in which the people choose leaders by voting : of or relating to democracy • The dictatorship gave way to a *democratic* (form of) government. • *Democratic* elections were held there today for the first time. • the country's new *democratic* constitution • Debates are an important part of the *democratic* process.
2 ***Democratic*** : of or relating to one of the two major political parties in the U.S. • The *Democratic* candidate for governor won the debate. • Most of these policies appeal to *Democratic* voters. • an interview with a leader of the ***Democratic Party*** — compare REPUBLICAN
3 [*more* ~; *most* ~] : relating to the idea that all people should be treated equally • *democratic* principles • The organization works to promote *democratic* reforms/changes around the world. • a more *democratic* society
4 [*more* ~; *most* ~] *formal* : designed for or liked by most people • *democratic* art • Her article extols the benefits of *democratic* education.
– dem·o·crat·i·cal·ly /,dɛməˈkrætɪkli/ *adv* • a *democratically* elected leader • Decisions in the company are made *democratically*.

de·moc·ra·tize *also Brit* **de·moc·ra·tise** /dɪˈmɑ:krə,taɪz/ *verb* **-tiz·es; -tized; -tiz·ing**
1 : to make (a country or organization) more democratic [+ *obj*] Community leaders have had some success in *democratizing* the organization. [*no obj*] There is internal pressure on the government to *democratize*.
2 [+ *obj*] *formal* : to make (something) available to all people : to make it possible for all people to understand (something) • The magazine's goal is to *democratize* art. • an effort to *democratize* politics
– de·moc·ra·ti·za·tion *also Brit* **de·moc·ra·ti·sa·tion** /dɪ,mɑ:krətəˈzeɪʃən, *Brit* dɪ,mɒkrə,taɪˈzeɪʃən/ *noun* [*noncount*]

¹de·mo·graph·ic /,dɛməˈgræfɪk/ *noun, pl* **-ics**
1 ***demographics*** [*plural*] : the qualities (such as age, sex, and income) of a specific group of people • The town's *demographics* suggest that the restaurant will do well there. • The newspaper will be making some changes in order to adapt to the region's shifting *demographics*. • The *demographics of* the disease are changing, and we are seeing much younger people being affected by it.
2 [*count*] : a group of people that has a particular set of qualities — usually singular • The magazine is trying to reach a younger/older *demographic*.

²demographic *adj* : of or relating to the study of changes that occur in large groups of people over a period of time : of or relating to demography • The *demographic* information shows that the population increased but the average income went down. • *demographic* trends/changes

de·mog·ra·phy /dɪˈmɑ:grəfi/ *noun* [*noncount*] : the study of changes (such as the number of births, deaths, marriages, and illnesses) that occur over a period of time in human populations; *also* : a set of such changes • the shifting *demography* of Europe
– de·mog·ra·pher /dɪˈmɑ:grəfɚ/ *noun, pl* **-phers** [*count*]

de·mol·ish /dɪˈmɑ:lɪʃ/ *verb* **-ish·es; -ished; -ish·ing** [+ *obj*]
1 a : to destroy (a building, bridge, etc.) : to forcefully tear down or take apart (a structure) • The old factory was *demolished* to make way for a new parking lot. • Tons of explosives were used to *demolish* the building. • The town hopes to restore the old theater rather than have it *demolished*. **b** : to damage (something) so that it cannot be repaired • The car was *demolished* in the accident. — often used figuratively • His professional reputation was *demolished* [=*ruined*] by the scandal. • The research *demolished* several myths about the disease. • Her study *demolished* a theory that had gone unquestioned for years.
2 *informal* : to eat all of (something) quickly • We *demolished* [=*devoured*] the pie in only a few minutes.
3 *informal* : to defeat (a person or team) easily or completely • They *demolished* the other team 51–7.

de·mo·li·tion /,dɛməˈlɪʃən/ *noun, pl* **-tions** : deliberate destruction of a building or other structure [*noncount*] The old factory is scheduled for *demolition* next week. [*count*] The *demolitions* should be complete by the end of the year. — often used before another noun • He is part of the *demolition* crew/team. • a *demolition* project • a *demolitions* expert — sometimes used figuratively • the *demolition* of several myths about the disease

demolition derby *noun, pl* **~ -bies** [*count*] *chiefly US* : a contest in which drivers in old cars crash into each other until only one car is still running

de·mon /ˈdi:mən/ *noun, pl* **-mons** [*count*]
1 : an evil spirit • angels and *demons* [=*devils*]

2 *informal* **:** a person who has a lot of energy or enthusiasm ▪ She is a *demon* for work. = She works ***like a demon.*** [=she works very hard] — see also SPEED DEMON
3 : something that causes a person to have a lot of trouble or unhappiness — usually plural ▪ She spent her whole life battling the *demons* of drug and alcohol addiction. ▪ He finally was able to face the *demons* from his unhappy childhood. ▪ his ***inner demons***

demon drink *noun*
the demon drink *Brit, usually humorous* **:** alcoholic drink ▪ slave to *the demon drink* [=unable to resist drinking alcohol]

de·mo·ni·ac /dɪˈmouniˌæk/ *also* **de·mo·ni·a·cal** /ˌdiːməˈnajəkəl/ *adj* [*more* ~; *most* ~] **:** DEMONIC ▪ *demoniac* possession ▪ *demoniac* fury/energy

de·mon·ic /dɪˈmɑːnɪk/ *adj* [*more* ~; *most* ~] **:** caused or done by a demon ▪ *demonic* possession **:** of, relating to, or like a demon ▪ *demonic* cruelty/laughter/energy

de·mon·stra·ble /dɪˈmɑːnstrəbəl/ *adj* [*more* ~; *most* ~] *formal* **:** able to be proven or shown **:** possible to demonstrate ▪ There is no *demonstrable* evidence that the treatment is effective. ▪ a clearly *demonstrable* improvement
– de·mon·stra·bly /dɪˈmɑːnstrəbli/ *adv* ▪ The statements are *demonstrably* untrue/false.

dem·on·strate /ˈdɛmənˌstreɪt/ *verb* **-strates; -strat·ed; -strat·ing**
1 [+ *obj*] **a :** to prove (something) by showing examples of it **:** to show evidence of (something) ▪ Each student must *demonstrate* mastery of the subject matter in order to pass the class. ▪ Employees must *demonstrate* competence in certain skills before they can work independently. ▪ The medication will not be marketed until it is *demonstrated* to be safe. **b :** to prove (something) by being an example of it **:** to be evidence of (something) ▪ The town's crowded classrooms *demonstrate* [=*point to*] the need for more schools in the area. ▪ The latest test results clearly *demonstrate* that the vaccine works. ▪ The group's failed efforts *demonstrate* how difficult it is to convince people to change their habits.
2 [+ *obj*] **:** to show (a quality, feeling, etc.) clearly to other people ▪ They have *demonstrated* a willingness to negotiate.
3 [+ *obj*] **:** to show or explain how something is used or done **:** to show or explain the function or use of (something) ▪ Several people will be *demonstrating* traditional farming techniques. ▪ The instructor *demonstrated* the correct procedure for pruning a tree. ▪ Would you mind *demonstrating* how the machine works?
4 [*no obj*] **:** to take part in an event in which people gather together in order to show that they support or oppose something or someone ▪ A large crowd was *demonstrating* [=*protesting*] downtown. ▪ Protesters *demonstrated* against the war.

dem·on·stra·tion /ˌdɛmənˈstreɪʃən/ *noun, pl* **-tions**
1 : an act of showing someone how something is used or done [*count*] I went to a sculpture *demonstration* last weekend. ▪ One of the instructors gave/did a *demonstration* of how to prune a tree. ▪ Would you mind giving us *a demonstration* so that we can see how the machine works? [*noncount*] He brought along a copy of the software for *demonstration.* — sometimes used before another noun ▪ We saw a *demonstration* [=*demo*] version of the new software.
2 : an event in which people gather together in order to show that they support or oppose something or someone [*count*] Students took part in several nonviolent/peaceful *demonstrations* against the government. ▪ *demonstrations* against the war = antiwar *demonstrations* ▪ *demonstrations* for women's rights [*noncount*] Protesters marched in *demonstration.*
3 : an act of showing or proving something [*count*] The latest tests are a clear *demonstration* that the vaccine works. — often + *of* ▪ a *demonstration of* their power/loyalty/skill ▪ a *demonstration of* grief/bravery ▪ They brought some bread to share as a *demonstration* [=*token*] *of* goodwill. [*noncount*] Many people sent cards and flowers in *demonstration of* their sympathy.
– dem·on·stra·tion·al /ˌdɛmənˈstreɪʃənl/ *adj* ▪ a *demonstrational* video

[1]**de·mon·stra·tive** /dɪˈmɑːnstrətɪv/ *adj*
1 [*more* ~; *most* ~] *formal* **:** freely and openly showing emotion or feelings ▪ She is more *demonstrative* (about her feelings) than I am. [=she shows her feelings more openly than I do]
2 *grammar* **:** showing who or what is being referred to ▪ In the phrase "this is my hat," the word "this" is a ***demonstrative pronoun.*** ▪ In the phrase "give me that book," the word "that" is a ***demonstrative adjective.***

[2]**demonstrative** *noun, pl* **-tives** [*count*] **:** a word (such as "this," "that," "these," or "those") that tells who or what is being referred to

dem·on·stra·tor /ˈdɛmənˌstreɪtə/ *noun, pl* **-tors** [*count*]
1 : a person who is part of an event in which people gather together in order to show that they support or oppose something or someone **:** a person who participates in a demonstration ▪ Thousands of *demonstrators* marched through the streets. ▪ antiwar *demonstrators*
2 : a person who shows other people how something is used or done ▪ a product *demonstrator*

de·mor·al·ize *also Brit* **de·mor·al·ise** /dɪˈmorəˌlaɪz/ *verb* **-iz·es; -ized; -iz·ing** [+ *obj*] **:** to cause (someone) to lose hope, courage, or confidence **:** to weaken the morale of (a person or group) ▪ They *demoralized* [=*discouraged, disheartened*] the other team by scoring three goals in a row.
– de·mor·al·i·za·tion /dɪˌmorələˈzeɪʃən, *Brit* dɪˌmɒrəˌlaɪˈzeɪʃən/ *noun* [*noncount*] **– demoralized** *adj* [*more* ~; *most* ~] ▪ The troops were completely *demoralized.* **– demoralizing** *adj* [*more* ~; *most* ~] ▪ They suffered a series of *demoralizing* defeats.

de·mote /dɪˈmout/ *verb* **-motes; -mot·ed; -mot·ing** [+ *obj*] **:** to change the rank or position of (someone) to a lower or less important one ▪ Teachers can choose to *demote* a student to a lower grade. ▪ The army major was *demoted* to captain. — opposite PROMOTE
– de·mo·tion /dɪˈmouʃən/ *noun, pl* **-tions** [*count, noncount*]

de·mot·ic /dɪˈmɑːtɪk/ *adj* [*more* ~; *most* ~] *formal* **:** popular or common ▪ a more *demotic* way of speaking ▪ *demotic* culture

[1]**de·mur** /dɪˈmə/ *verb* **-murs; -murred; -mur·ring** [*no obj*] *formal*
1 : to disagree politely with another person's statement or suggestion ▪ She suggested that he would win easily, but he *demurred,* saying he expected the election to be close.
2 : to politely refuse to accept a request or suggestion ▪ A number of people wanted her to run for governor, but she *demurred.* [=*declined*]

[2]**demur** *noun* [*count*] *chiefly Brit, formal* **:** an act of disagreeing about something — usually used in the phrase ***without demur*** ▪ She accepted the group's decision *without demur.* [=(more commonly) *without protest*]

de·mure /dɪˈmjuə/ *adj* [*more* ~; *most* ~]
1 : quiet and polite — usually used to describe a woman or girl ▪ a *demure* young lady
2 : not attracting or demanding a lot of attention **:** not showy or flashy ▪ She was wearing a *demure* gray suit. ▪ the *demure* charm of the cottage ▪ a *demure* personality
– de·mure·ly *adv* ▪ a *demurely* dressed young woman ▪ She smiled *demurely.* **– de·mure·ness** *noun* [*noncount*]

de·mur·ral /dɪˈmərəl/ *noun, pl* **-als** [*count*] *formal* **:** an act of disagreeing politely about something **:** an act of demurring ▪ Suggestions that she run for president have been met with repeated *demurrals.*

de·mys·ti·fy /diˈmɪstəˌfaɪ/ *verb* **-fies; -fied; -fy·ing** [+ *obj*] **:** to make (something) clear and easy to understand **:** to explain (something) so that it no longer confuses or mystifies someone ▪ The class is intended to *demystify* the process of using a computer.
– de·mys·ti·fi·ca·tion /diˌmɪstəfəˈkeɪʃən/ *noun* [*noncount*]

den /ˈdɛn/ *noun, pl* **dens** [*count*]
1 : the home of some kinds of wild animals ▪ a fox's *den* [=*lair*] ▪ The bears will spend most of the winter in their *den.* — see also LION'S DEN
2 a *US* **:** an informal and comfortable room in a house ▪ The TV is in the *den.* **b** *chiefly Brit, informal + old-fashioned* **:** a small and quiet room in a house where someone goes to read, work, etc. ▪ He spent most evenings in the *den* reading and smoking his pipe.
3 : a secret place where people meet especially to do things that are illegal or immoral ▪ a *den* of thieves ▪ a gambling *den* ▪ an opium *den* ▪ the club's reputation as a ***den of iniquity*** [=a place where immoral or illegal things are done]
4 *Brit* **:** a small often secret structure that children play in ▪ The children had built themselves a *den* in the woods.
5 *US* **:** a group of Cub Scouts — see also DEN MOTHER

de·na·tion·al·ize *also* **de·na·tion·al·ise** /diˈnæʃənəˌlaɪz/ *verb* **-iz·es; -ized; -iz·ing** [+ *obj*] *Brit* **:** PRIVATIZE

de·ni·able /dɪˈnajəbəl/ *adj* **:** possible to deny ▪ The failure of

D

the policy is no longer *deniable.* [=it is no longer reasonable to say that the policy is not failing] — opposite UNDENIABLE

de·ni·al /dɪˈnajəl/ *noun, pl* **-als**

1 [*count*] **:** a statement saying that something is not true or real **:** a statement in which someone denies something • She issued a flat/absolute/outright *denial* of the charges made against her. • The accusations have met with angry *denials* from school officials. • The city government has been heavily criticized for its *denial* of the seriousness of the situation. • her *denial* of responsibility

2 [*noncount*] *psychology* **:** a condition in which someone will not admit that something sad, painful, etc., is true or real • I think she's still in ***a state of denial*** about her husband's death. [=she still has not fully accepted that her husband is dead] — often used in the phrase ***in denial*** • He's *in denial* about his drinking problem. [=he will not admit that he drinks too much alcohol]

3 : the act of not allowing someone to have something [*noncount*] The hardest part of the punishment was the *denial* of his right to see his children. • The group is protesting the *denial* of voting rights to convicted felons. • The lawyers were disappointed by the court's *denial* of their motion to dismiss the case. [*count*] — usually singular • Making false statements on a job application will result in a *denial* of employment. • The court has issued a *denial* of their motion. — see also SELF-DENIAL

den·i·grate /ˈdɛnɪˌgreɪt/ *verb* **-grates; -grat·ed; -grat·ing** [+ *obj*] *formal*

1 : to say very critical and often unfair things about (someone) • Various groups *denigrated* [=*slandered, maligned*] both candidates throughout the presidential campaign. • Her story *denigrates* him as a person and as a teacher.

2 : to make (something) seem less important or valuable • Such behavior *denigrates* [=*belittles*] the value of honesty in the workplace. • No one is trying to *denigrate* the importance of a good education. We all know that it is crucial for success. • *denigrating* the talents and achievements of women

– den·i·gra·tion /ˌdɛnɪˈgreɪʃən/ *noun* [*noncount*]

den·im /ˈdɛnəm/ *noun, pl* **-ims**

1 [*noncount*] **:** a strong usually blue cotton cloth that is used especially to make jeans — often used before another noun • *denim* jeans • a *denim* skirt/jacket

2 denims [*plural*] **:** pants that are made of denim • He's wearing faded *denims* and cowboy boots.

den·i·zen /ˈdɛnəzən/ *noun, pl* **-zens** [*count*] **:** a person, animal, or plant that lives in or often is found in a particular place or region • the city's nightclub *denizens* [=people who often go to nightclubs] — usually + *of* • the *denizens of* the forest • He was well known among the *denizens of* the city's criminal underworld. • *denizens of* the deep [=plants and animals that live in the deepest parts of the ocean]

den mother *noun, pl* **~ -ers** [*count*] *US* **:** a woman who is the leader of a group of Cub Scouts

de·nom·i·na·tion /dɪˌnɑːməˈneɪʃən/ *noun, pl* **-tions** [*count*]

1 : a religious group • People from several different religious *denominations* participated in the event. • Methodists, Baptists, and other Christian *denominations* • It's one of the more conservative *denominations.*

2 a : the value that a particular coin or bill has • coins of different *denominations* [=pennies, nickels, dimes, etc.] • The kidnappers asked for bills in small *denominations.* **b :** an amount of money that something is worth • The gift certificates are available in $5 and $10 *denominations.*

3 *formal* **:** a general name for a group or kind • She spoke with people of many different political *denominations.*

– de·nom·i·na·tion·al /dɪˌnɑːməˈneɪʃənl/ *adj* • *denominational* differences

de·nom·i·na·tor /dɪˈnɑːməˌneɪtɚ/ *noun, pl* **-tors** [*count*] *mathematics* **:** the number in a fraction that is below the line and that divides the number above the line • In the fraction ⅔, the numerator is 2 and the *denominator* is 3. — compare NUMERATOR; see also COMMON DENOMINATOR

de·no·ta·tion /ˌdiːnoʊˈteɪʃən/ *noun, pl* **-tions** [*count*] **:** the meaning of a word or phrase • The word has one literal *denotation* but several different connotations. • The definition provides the word's *denotation.* — compare CONNOTATION

de·note /dɪˈnoʊt/ *verb* **-notes; -not·ed; -not·ing** [+ *obj*] *formal*

1 *of a word* **:** to have (something) as a meaning **:** to mean (something) • The word "derby" can *denote* a horse race or a kind of hat. — compare CONNOTE

2 : to show, mark, or be a sign of (something) • The symbol * next to a name *denotes* [=*indicates*] a contest finalist. • Her death *denoted* the end of an era.

de·noue·ment *also* **dé·noue·ment** /ˌdeɪˌnuːˈmɑːn/ *noun, pl* **-ments** [*count*] *formal* **:** the final part of something (such as a book, a play, or a series of events) • In the play's *denouement,* the two lovers kill themselves. • the competition's exciting *denouement*

de·nounce /dɪˈnaʊns/ *verb* **-nounc·es; -nounced; -nounc·ing** [+ *obj*]

1 : to publicly state that someone or something is bad or wrong **:** to criticize (someone or something) harshly and publicly • The government called on the group to *denounce* the use of violence. • *denouncing* their political enemies • The film was *denounced* for the way it portrayed its female characters. — often + *as* • The film was *denounced* [=*condemned*] *as* sexist. • His former followers now *denounce* him *as* a traitor. • The plan was *denounced as* risky and dangerous.

2 : to report (someone) *to* the police or other authorities for illegal or immoral acts — often + *as* • She had to flee the country after being *denounced as* a spy *to* government authorities.

dense /ˈdɛns/ *adj* **dens·er; -est** [*or more ~; most ~*]

1 : having parts that are close together • They cut a path through the *dense* jungle. • *dense* undergrowth • The book's pages were *dense* [=*packed, filled*] with helpful ideas. • the cat's *dense* [=*thick*] coat of fur • a *dense* tangle of wires • heavy, *dense* bread • a *dense* cluster of stars

2 : crowded with people • That part of the city has a *dense* population of immigrants. • A *dense* mass of spectators filled the courtroom.

3 *informal* **:** not smart **:** not able to understand things easily • I'm sorry to be so *dense* [=*slow-witted, stupid, dumb*] this morning. • In the movie, she plays his kind but somewhat *dense* aunt.

4 : difficult to see through • We drove though *dense* [=*thick*] fog/smoke.

5 : difficult to understand; *especially* **:** hard to read • The book's technical subject and *dense* prose will discourage many readers.

6 *technical* **:** heavier than most things of the same size • a *dense* substance like lead or mercury • a disease that causes bones to become less *dense* [=to become less solid and heavy]

– dense·ly *adv* • a *densely* populated area [=an area in which many people live] • *densely* forested mountains • a *densely* packed sports arena **– dense·ness** *noun* [*noncount*]

den·si·ty /ˈdɛnsəti/ *noun, pl* **-ties**

1 [*noncount*] **:** the quality or state of being dense: such as **a :** the quality of having parts that are close together • the jungle's *density* **b :** the quality of being difficult to see through • We were surprised by the fog's *density.* **c :** the quality of being difficult to understand • the *density* of her writing style

2 : the amount of something in a particular space or area [*count*] This part of the country has a high ***population density.*** [=many people live in this part of the country] [*noncount*] There has been an increase in (population) *density* in this area.

3 *technical* **:** the amount of matter in something that is shown by the relationship between its weight and size [*count*] metals with different *densities* • These instruments are used for measuring the *density* of the atmosphere. [*noncount*] older women who have lost bone *density* [=whose bones are less solid and heavy]

¹dent /ˈdɛnt/ *noun, pl* **dents** [*count*] **:** an area on a surface that is lower than the rest of the surface especially because of being hit or pushed in • The accident left/made a small *dent* in the car's fender. • a few small *dents* in the wall

make/put a dent ✧ In figurative use, to ***make a dent (in something)*** or to ***put a dent in something*** is to decrease something slightly or to make it somewhat weaker. • We tried our best to fix the problem, but nothing we did seems to have *made a dent.* [=nothing we did has had any effect] • It's going to take more than a new law to *make a dent in* the city's drug crime. [=a new law is not enough to decrease the city's drug crime] • The $10,000 payment hardly *makes a dent in* the amount the company owes. • a vacation that won't *put* too big *a dent in* your wallet [=a vacation that will not cost a lot of money]

²dent *verb* **dents; dent·ed; dent·ing**

1 : to make a dent in (something) [+ *obj*] I'm afraid I *dented* the wall pretty badly when I was hammering in that nail. • He

dented his (car's) fender in the accident. • Many of the cans were badly *dented*. [*no obj*] Some types of metal *dent* more easily than others.
2 [+ *obj*] : to decrease (something) : to make (something) weaker • The team's confidence has been *dented* by a recent series of losses.

den·tal /ˈdɛntl̩/ *adj* : of or relating to teeth or to the work dentists do • *dental* decay • your ***dental records*** [=the information about your teeth that your dentist has] • She decided to go to ***dental school***. [=a school where you are trained to be a dentist]

dental floss *noun* [*noncount*] : a special thread that is used to clean between your teeth — see picture at GROOMING

dental hygienist *noun, pl* **~ -ists** [*count*] : a person who works with a dentist and whose job includes cleaning people's teeth

dente see AL DENTE

den·tist /ˈdɛntəst/ *noun, pl* **-tists** [*count*]
1 : a person whose job is to care for people's teeth • I have an appointment with my *dentist* today. = I have a *dentist* appointment today.
2 ***the dentist*** *or* ***the dentist's*** : the place where a dentist works • I saw her at *the dentist* last week. • He goes to *the dentist's* for a check-up every six months.

den·tist·ry /ˈdɛntəstri/ *noun* [*noncount*] : the work that a dentist does • a career in *dentistry*

den·ture /ˈdɛntʃɚ/ *noun, pl* **-tures** [*count*] : a set of artificial teeth — usually plural • She takes out her *dentures* before going to bed. • a new pair of *dentures* [=*false teeth*] • partial *dentures* [=a partial set of artificial teeth]

de·nude /dɪˈnuːd, *Brit* dɪˈnjuːd/ *verb* **-nudes; -nud·ed; -nud·ing** [+ *obj*] : to remove all the trees from (an area) or all the leaves from (a tree) • Excessive logging has *denuded* the hillside of trees. — usually used as *(be) denuded* • a countryside *denuded* by wildfires • a landscape of *denuded* trees — sometimes used figuratively • people *denuded* of hope [=people who have lost all hope]

de·nun·ci·a·tion /dɪˌnʌnsiˈeɪʃən/ *noun, pl* **-tions** : a public statement that strongly criticizes someone or something as being bad or wrong : a statement that denounces something or someone [*count*] The attack drew strong *denunciations* from leaders around the world. • a *denunciation* of violence [*noncount*] a letter of *denunciation*

Den·ver boot /ˈdɛnvɚ-/ *noun, pl* **~ boots** [*count*] *US* : an object that the police lock onto one of the wheels of a car so that the car cannot be moved ✧ A Denver boot is usually placed on a car in order to force the car's owner to pay money that is owed for parking illegally. — called also *(US) boot, (Brit) clamp, (Brit) wheel clamp*

de·ny /dɪˈnaɪ/ *verb* **-nies; -nied; -ny·ing** [+ *obj*]
1 a : to say that something is not true • He *denied* the report that he would be quitting his job. • She *denies* all the charges that have been made against her. • I don't *deny* that I have made some mistakes. [=I admit that I have made some mistakes] • They are still *denying* (that) the problem exists. • The police *deny* that racism is a problem in the department. • Yes, I was there. I don't *deny* it. • ***There's no denying*** [=it is clearly true] that he knows how to run a successful company. **b** : to refuse to accept or admit (something) • You can't *deny* her beauty. = You can't *deny* that she is beautiful. • She *denied* responsibility [=she said that she was not responsible] for the error.
2 : to refuse to give (something) to someone : to prevent someone from having or receiving (something) • The banks *denied* [=*refused*] them credit. • The judge *denied* their request. • I don't want to *deny* them this pleasure. = I don't want to *deny* this pleasure to them. • a government that *denies* its citizens basic freedoms — see also *denied bail* at ¹BAIL
deny yourself : to not allow yourself to enjoy things or to have the things that you want • On this diet, I don't feel like I'm *denying myself*. • I'm not *denying myself* the foods that I love, I'm just eating smaller amounts. • He's always *denied himself* the simple pleasures in life.

de·odor·ant /diˈoʊdərənt/ *noun, pl* **-ants** [*count, noncount*] : a substance that you put on your body and especially under your arms to prevent, remove, or hide unpleasant smells — see picture at GROOMING; compare ANTIPERSPIRANT
– deodorant *adj, always used before a noun* • *deodorant* soap

de·odor·ize *also Brit* **de·odor·ise** /diˈoʊdəˌraɪz/ *verb* **-iz·es; -ized; -iz·ing** [+ *obj*] : to remove an unpleasant smell from (something) • We had the carpet cleaned and *deodorized*.
– de·odor·iz·er *also Brit* **de·odor·is·er** *noun, pl* **-ers** [*count*] • room *deodorizers*

de·oxy·ri·bo·nu·cle·ic acid /diˈɑːksiˌraɪboʊnuˈkliːjɪk-/ *noun* [*noncount*] *technical* : DNA

dep. *abbr* depart; departure • flight 348 *dep.* 8:30 a.m.

de·part /dɪˈpɑɚt/ *verb* **-parts; -part·ed; -part·ing**
1 *somewhat formal* **a** : to leave a place especially to start a journey [*no obj*] The group is scheduled to *depart* tomorrow at 8:00 a.m. • Our flight *departs* at 6:15 a.m. • The train *departed* (from the station) on time. [+ *obj*] (*US*) • The train *departed* the station on time. **b** [*no obj*] : to leave a job or position • He is *departing* after 20 years with the company. • She is replacing the *departing* manager. [=the manager who is leaving that job]
2 [*no obj*] : to change something or do something in a different way — usually + *from* • The river *departs* [=*turns, deviates*] *from* its original course a few miles downstream. • The actors were not allowed to *depart from* the script. [=they were not allowed to say anything that was not in the script] • The company's managers don't want to *depart from* an approach that has worked well in the past. [=they do not want to change their approach]
depart this life *formal* : to die • My aunt *departed this life* at the age of 92.

departed *adj*
1 *somewhat formal* : no longer living — used as a polite way to say that someone is dead • We have come to say goodbye to our dear *departed* friend. • his recently *departed* father
2 *literary* : existing in the past • These clothes recall the elegance of a *departed* [=*bygone*] era.
the departed : people who have died • They left flowers at the graves of *the departed*. • the spirits of *the departed*

de·part·ment /dɪˈpɑɚtmənt/ *noun, pl* **-ments** [*count*]
1 : one of the major parts of a company, organization, government, or school • Your letter has been forwarded to our sales *department*. • When you get to the hospital, go directly to the X-ray *department*. • the country's energy *department* • the *Department* of Defense = the Defense *Department* • the county sheriff's *department* • the university's math and science *departments* • the *department* of modern languages • the college's athletic *department* • She joined the town's ***police department***. — abbr. *dept.*; see also FIRE DEPARTMENT
2 : an area in a store where a particular kind of product is sold • the toy *department* • "Which *department* should we go to first?" "I'd like to start in the men's *department*." [=the part of the store that sells clothing for men]
3 *informal* **a** : a subject or activity that a person is interested in or responsible for • Taking care of the cat is not my *department*. [=*responsibility*] **b** *often humorous* — used to say that someone or something has or does not have a particular quality • She's sweet, but she's somewhat lacking in the intelligence *department*. [=she is not very intelligent] • He does pretty well in the looks *department*. [=he is attractive] • Both cars do well in the safety *department*. [=both cars are safe to drive]
– de·part·men·tal /dɪˌpɑɚtˈmɛntl̩/ *adj* • *departmental* responsibilities • the *departmental* budget

de·part·men·tal·ize *also Brit* **de·part·men·tal·ise** /dɪˌpɑɚtˈmɛntəˌlaɪz/ *verb* **-iz·es; -ized; -iz·ing** [+ *obj*] : to divide (something, such as a company) into departments • The organization is highly *departmentalized*.

department store *noun, pl* **~ stores** [*count*] : a large store that has separate areas in which different kinds of products are sold

de·par·ture /dɪˈpɑɚtʃɚ/ *noun, pl* **-tures**
1 : the act of departing: such as **a** : the act of leaving a place especially to start a journey [*noncount*] What is your time of *departure*? • Our *departure* is scheduled for 5 p.m. = Our *departure* time is 5 p.m. • They had to postpone (their) *departure* because of bad weather. • You should plan to arrive at the airport an hour before *departure*. • the ferry's *departure* point [*count*] a schedule of arrivals and *departures* **b** [*count*] : the act of leaving a job, an organization, etc. • The *departures* of several key employees have caused problems for the company. • her sudden *departure* from the company • The team has struggled since the *departure* of its head coach.
2 [*count*] : a new or different way of doing something • His previous movies have all been comedies, so this dramatic role is a real *departure* for him. — often + *from* • These new techniques are major/dramatic/radical *departures* from stan-

dard practices. ▪ a *departure from* tradition — see also POINT OF DEPARTURE

de·pend /dɪˈpɛnd/ *verb* **-pends; -pend·ed; -pend·ing** [*no obj*] *informal* — used in speech in phrases like ***it depends*** and ***that depends*** to say that the answer to a question will be different in different situations ▪ "Are you going to the party?" "I might. *It depends.*" [=I do not know yet; there may be something that prevents me from being able to go or from wanting to go] ▪ "Do you think you'll go back to college?" "*It all depends.* I will if I can afford it." ▪ "Which team do you think will win?" "*That depends.* If all of our players are healthy, I think we'll win." ▪ (*very informal*) "How long does it take to get to the airport?" "*Depends.* If you're going during rush hour it'll take at least an hour. If not, you can probably be there in 20 minutes."

depend on/upon [*phrasal verb*] ***depend on/upon (someone or something)*** **1 :** to be determined or decided by (something) ▪ We're not sure if we'll have the picnic. It *depends on* the weather. [=if the weather is good we will have the picnic] ▪ "Will you go back to college?" "I don't know. It *depends on* whether or not I can afford it." ▪ The stamp's value *depends on* how rare it is. ▪ *Depending upon* your child's weight and height, she or he may have to sit in the back seat of the car. ▪ It's not clear how many people were at the rally. Reports vary between 10,000 and 20,000, *depending on* who's counting. [=some people report that there were 10,000 people at the rally, others report that there were 20,000] — sometimes used informally without *on* or *upon* ▪ "Are you happy?" "It *depends* what you mean by 'happy.'" — see also *life depends on* at [1]LIFE **2 :** to need (someone or something) for support, help, etc. ▪ He no longer *depends on* [=*relies on*] his parents for money. ▪ They *depend* heavily/largely/solely/entirely *on* her income to pay the bills. [=without her income they would not be able to pay their bills] **3 :** to be sure about (someone or something) : to trust (someone or something) ▪ She's someone you can always *depend on.* [=*count on*] ▪ She will be remembered as a woman *upon* whom people could *depend.* ▪ The manufacturer promises quality you can *depend on.* — sometimes used humorously ▪ You could always *depend on* him to disagree. [=you could always be sure that he would disagree] ▪ I can always *depend on* it to rain on days when I forget my umbrella.

de·pend·able /dɪˈpɛndəbəl/ *adj* [*more* ~; *most* ~] **:** able to be trusted to do or provide what is needed : able to be depended on ▪ The old well is a *dependable* source of water. [=there is always water in the old well] ▪ a *dependable* [=*reliable*] old car ▪ He's the team's most *dependable* [=*consistent*] player.

— **de·pend·abil·i·ty** /dɪˌpɛndəˈbɪləti/ *noun* [*noncount*] ▪ the car's proven *dependability* [=*reliability*] — **de·pend·ably** /dɪˈpɛndəbli/ *adv* ▪ a plant that will bloom *dependably* [=*reliably*], year after year

de·pen·dence /dɪˈpɛndəns/ *noun* **:** the state of being dependent: such as **a :** the state of needing something or someone else for support, help, etc. — + *on* or *upon* [*noncount*] The company was hurt by its *dependence on* government loans. ▪ Our *dependence upon* foreign oil makes our economy vulnerable. [*singular*] a harmful *dependence* on foreign oil **b :** the state of being addicted to alcohol or a drug [*noncount*] drug and alcohol *dependence* [=*addiction, dependency*] [*singular*] — usually + *on* ▪ She eventually developed a *dependence on* the painkillers she was taking.

de·pen·den·cy /dɪˈpɛndənsi/ *noun, pl* **-cies**

1 : the quality of being dependent : DEPENDENCE [*noncount*] the country's *dependency* on foreign oil ▪ drug/chemical *dependency* [=*addiction*] [*singular*] a *dependency* on foreign oil

2 [*count*] **:** an area that is controlled by a country but that is not formally a part of it

[1]**de·pen·dent** /dɪˈpɛndənt/ *adj* [*more* ~; *most* ~]

1 : decided or controlled by something else — + *on* or *upon* ▪ The stamp's value is *dependent on* how rare it is. ▪ She believes that success is *dependent upon* hard work. ▪ Whether or not we go is entirely *dependent on* the weather.

2 : needing someone or something else for support, help, etc. ▪ soldiers with *dependent* children [=soldiers who have children whose food, clothing, etc., they are responsible for providing] — usually + *on* or *upon* ▪ The region's economy is heavily/highly/largely *dependent on* tourism. ▪ They're entirely *dependent on* her income to pay the bills. ▪ He remained financially *dependent on* his parents even as an adult. ▪ children who are emotionally *dependent on* their mothers ▪ The theater is *dependent upon* the generosity of its patrons to pay for basic operating expenses.

3 : addicted to alcohol or a drug ▪ He has been alcohol *dependent* for several years. ▪ ***chemically dependent*** patients [=patients who are addicted to a drug]

[2]**dependent** *also Brit* **de·pen·dant** /dɪˈpɛndənt/ *noun, pl* **-ents** [*count*] **:** a person (such as a child) whose food, clothing, etc., you are responsible for providing ▪ The insurance provides coverage for workers and their *dependents.* ▪ a person's spouse and *dependents* ▪ Do you have any *dependents*?

dependent clause *noun, pl* **~ clauses** [*count*] *grammar* **:** SUBORDINATE CLAUSE

de·pict /dɪˈpɪkt/ *verb* **-picts; -pict·ed; -pict·ing** [+ *obj*]

1 : to show (someone or something) in a picture, painting, photograph, etc. ▪ The wall was painted with a large mural *depicting* famous scenes from American history. ▪ Several of the architect's most famous buildings will soon be *depicted* on postage stamps. ▪ The photograph *depicts* the two brothers standing in front of a store. ▪ Angels are usually *depicted* with wings. ▪ In the drawing, the magic cap was *depicted* as a soft, black hat.

2 : to describe (someone or something) using words, a story, etc. ▪ The movie *depicts* the life of early settlers. ▪ I like the way she *depicts* the characters in her novels. ▪ His enemies *depict* [=*portray*] him as a cruel and dangerous leader.

— **de·pic·tion** /dɪˈpɪkʃən/ *noun, pl* **-tions** [*count*] an honest *depiction* of life in the city [*noncount*] The book is fascinating in its *depiction* of the country's early history.

de·pil·a·to·ry /dɪˈpɪləˌtori, *Brit* dɪˈpɪlətri/ *noun, pl* **-ries** [*count*] **:** a substance that removes body hair you do not want

— **depilatory** *adj, always used before a noun* ▪ a *depilatory* cream

de·plane /diˈpleɪn/ *verb* **-planes; -planed; -plan·ing** [*no obj*] *chiefly US* **:** to get out of an airplane after it arrives at an airport ▪ We were the last passengers to *deplane.* [=get off the plane]

de·plete /dɪˈpliːt/ *verb* **-pletes; -plet·ed; -plet·ing** [+ *obj*] **:** to use most or all of (something important) : to greatly reduce the amount of (something) ▪ Activities such as logging and mining *deplete* our natural resources. ▪ We completely *depleted* our life savings when we bought our new house. — often used as *(be) depleted* ▪ The soil has *been depleted* by years of drought. ▪ lakes and rivers that *are depleted* of fish ▪ *depleted* soil ▪ the country's badly *depleted* resources

— **de·ple·tion** /dɪˈpliːʃən/ *noun, pl* **-tions** [*count*] a *depletion* of the water supply [*noncount*] the *depletion* of the ozone layer = ozone *depletion*

de·plor·able /dɪˈplorəbəl/ *adj* [*more* ~; *most* ~] **:** very bad in a way that causes shock, fear, or disgust : deserving to be deplored ▪ The company has shown a *deplorable* [=*appalling, unconscionable*] lack of concern for the environment. ▪ children living in *deplorable* [=*horrible, disgusting, terrible*] conditions ▪ *deplorable* ignorance

— **de·plor·ably** /dɪˈplorəbli/ *adv* ▪ *deplorably* cruel

de·plore /dɪˈploɚ/ *verb* **-plores; -plored; -plor·ing** [+ *obj*] **:** to hate or dislike (something) very much : to strongly disapprove of (something) ▪ We *deplore* the development of nuclear weapons. ▪ Many people *deplored* the change. ▪ Although *deplored* by many, her decisions have greatly benefited the company.

de·ploy /dɪˈploɪ/ *verb* **-ploys; -ployed; -ploy·ing**

1 [+ *obj*] **:** to organize and send out (people or things) to be used for a particular purpose ▪ The troops were *deployed* for battle. ▪ They plan to *deploy* more American soldiers over the next six months. ▪ Two scientists were *deployed* to study the problem. ▪ Both campaigns are *deploying* volunteers to the cities to encourage people to vote. ▪ Equipment and supplies have been *deployed* across the country. ▪ He *deploys* several arguments to prove his point.

2 : to open up and spread out the parts of (something, such as a parachute) [+ *obj*] Wait several seconds before *deploying* the parachute. ▪ The boat's sails were not fully *deployed.* [*no obj*] The parachute failed to *deploy* properly.

— **de·ploy·ment** /dɪˈploɪmənt/ *noun, pl* **-ments** [*count*] additional troop *deployments* ▪ a monthlong *deployment* [*noncount*] the *deployment* of ground troops

de·po·lit·i·cize *also Brit* **de·po·lit·i·cise** /ˌdiːpəˈlɪtəˌsaɪz/ *verb* **-ciz·es; -cized; -ciz·ing** [+ *obj*] **:** to change (something) so that it is no longer influenced or controlled by politics ▪ She says we need to *depoliticize* the process by which judges are chosen. • The humanitarian aid groups want to see foreign aid *depoliticized*. — opposite POLITICIZE

– de·po·lit·i·ci·za·tion *also Brit* **de·po·lit·i·ci·sa·tion** /ˌdiːpəˌlɪtəsəˈzeɪʃən, *Brit* ˌdiːpəˌlɪtəˌsaɪˈzeɪʃən/ *noun* [*noncount*]

de·pop·u·late /diˈpɑːpjəˌleɪt/ *verb* **-lates; -lat·ed; -lat·ing** [+ *obj*] **:** to greatly reduce the number of people living in (a city, region, etc.) • Large areas of the country had been *depopulated* by disease. • an empty, *depopulated* landscape

– de·pop·u·la·tion /diˌpɑːpjəˈleɪʃən/ *noun* [*noncount*]

de·port /dɪˈpoət/ *verb* **-ports; -port·ed; -port·ing** [+ *obj*] **:** to force (a person who is not a citizen) to leave a country • Thousands of immigrants had been illegally *deported*.

– de·por·ta·tion /ˌdiːˌpoəˈteɪʃən/ *noun, pl* **-tions** [*noncount*] She is now facing *deportation*. [=she may be forced to leave the country] • a *deportation* hearing [*count*] The government has ordered thousands of *deportations*. **– de·por·tee** /diˌpoəˈtiː/ *noun, pl* **-tees** [*count*] • thousands of *deportees* [=people who have been deported]

de·port·ment /dɪˈpoətmənt/ *noun* [*noncount*] *formal* **:** the way that a person behaves, stands, and moves especially in a formal situation • The new students were instructed in proper dress and *deportment*. • His stiff *deportment* matched his strict demeanor.

de·pose /dɪˈpouz/ *verb* **-pos·es; -posed; -pos·ing** [+ *obj*] **:** to remove (someone) from a powerful position • The group is plotting to *depose* [=*overthrow*] the king. • a *deposed* military leader

[1]**de·pos·it** /dɪˈpɑːzət/ *verb* **-its; -it·ed; -it·ing** [+ *obj*]

1 : to put (money) in a bank account • Your paycheck will be automatically *deposited* into your account. • I *deposited* over $3,000 this afternoon.

2 *somewhat formal* **:** to put or leave (someone or something) in a particular place • He carefully *deposited* [=(more commonly) *put, placed*] the tools in the trunk of his car. • Please *deposit* your things in your room and return to the hotel lobby. • The taxi *deposited* us at the train station.

3 : to leave an amount of (something, such as sand, snow, or mud) on a surface or area especially over a period of time • layers of mud *deposited* by flood waters • The storm may *deposit* [=*leave*] up to three feet of snow in some areas.

– de·pos·i·tor /dɪˈpɑːzətə/ *noun, pl* **-tors** [*count*] • bank *depositors* [=people who put money in a bank account]

[2]**deposit** *noun, pl* **-its** [*count*]

1 : an amount of money that is put in a bank account • a bank *deposit* • a *deposit* of $3,000 • savings *deposits* [=money put into savings accounts] • I need to ***make a deposit*** [=put some money in a bank account] this afternoon. • Our records show that she *made* a large *deposit* to her account earlier in the month. — opposite WITHDRAWAL; see also DIRECT DEPOSIT, SAFE-DEPOSIT BOX

2 a : money that you give someone when you agree to buy something (such as a house or car) ✧ A *deposit* shows that there is an agreement between a buyer and seller. When the sale is made final, the seller keeps the deposit as the first payment. • He just put a *deposit* on a new house. • The company will refund your *deposit* since they are unable to do the project for you. **b :** money that you pay when you buy or rent something and that you can get back if you return the thing or leave it in good condition • If you return that empty soda can, you'll get back the five-cent *deposit* you paid when you bought the soda. • The rental car company requires a *deposit* for drivers under the age of 25. — see also SECURITY DEPOSIT

3 a : an amount of something (such as sand, snow, or mud) that has formed or been left on a surface or area over a period of time • a *deposit* of mud left by the flood • He had surgery to remove calcium *deposits* from his knee. • the buildup of fat/fatty *deposits* in the arteries **b :** an amount of a substance (such as oil or coal) that exists naturally in the ground • Their company has discovered new oil *deposits* below the ocean floor. • mineral *deposits*

on deposit ✧ Money that has been put in a bank is *on deposit*. • The company has millions of dollars *on deposit* with several foreign banks. • money/funds *on deposit* in/at the bank

deposit account *noun, pl* **~ -counts** [*count*] *chiefly Brit* **:** SAVINGS ACCOUNT

de·po·si·tion /ˌdɛpəˈzɪʃən/ *noun, pl* **-tions**

1 [*count*] *law* **:** a formal statement that someone who has promised to tell the truth makes so that the statement can be used in court; *especially* **:** a formal statement that is made before a trial by a witness who will not be present at the trial • She gave a videotaped *deposition* about what she saw that night. • His attorneys took *depositions* from the witnesses.

2 [*noncount*] *technical* **:** the action of depositing something (such as sand, snow, or mud) on a surface or area especially over a period of time • the *deposition* of sand and gravel on the river bed

3 [*count, noncount*] *formal* **:** the act removing someone from a powerful position **:** the act of deposing someone • *deposition* of the king

de·pos·i·to·ry /dɪˈpɑːzəˌtori, *Brit* dɪˈpɒzətri/ *noun, pl* **-ries** [*count*] **:** a place where something is put so that is can be kept safe • a book/food *depository* • The bank is used as a *depository* for government funds.

deposit slip *noun, pl* **~ slips** [*count*] *US* **:** a piece of paper that you give with a bank deposit to show how much money you are putting in an account — called also (*Brit*) *paying-in slip*

de·pot /ˈdɛpou, ˈdiːpou/ *noun, pl* **depots** [*count*]

1 *US* **:** a train or bus station • the train/bus *depot*

2 : a place where military supplies are kept or where soldiers are trained • supply/weapons *depots*

3 : a place where goods are stored **:** STOREHOUSE • a storage *depot*

de·praved /dɪˈpreɪvd/ *adj* [*more ~; most ~*] **:** very evil **:** having or showing an evil and immoral character • a *depraved* criminal • the work of *depraved* minds • He acted with *depraved* indifference to human suffering.

de·prav·i·ty /dɪˈprævəti/ *noun, pl* **-ties**

1 [*noncount*] **:** a very evil quality or way of behaving • He was sinking into a life of utter *depravity*. • moral/sexual *depravity* • People were shocked by the *depravity* of her actions.

2 [*count*] **:** an evil or immoral act • the *depravities* of war

dep·re·cate /ˈdɛprɪˌkeɪt/ *verb* **-cates; -cat·ed; -cat·ing** [+ *obj*] *formal* **:** to criticize or express disapproval of (someone or something) • I don't mean to *deprecate* [=*belittle, minimize*] his accomplishments.

– deprecating *adj* [*more ~; most ~*] • Her office issued an apology after she made some *deprecating* remarks about her opponent. — see also SELF-DEPRECATING **– dep·re·ca·tion** /ˌdɛprɪˈkeɪʃən/ *noun* [*noncount*] • the *deprecation* of old methods **– dep·re·ca·to·ry** /ˈdɛprɪˌkeɪtəri, ˈdɛprɪkəˌtori, *Brit* ˈdɛprɪkeɪtri/ *adj* [*more ~; most ~*] • She had made some *deprecatory* remarks about her opponent.

de·pre·ci·ate /dɪˈpriːʃiˌeɪt/ *verb* **-ates; -at·ed; -at·ing**

1 a [+ *obj*] **:** to cause (something) to have a lower price or value • These changes have greatly *depreciated* the value of the house. **b** [*no obj*] **:** to decrease in value • New cars *depreciate* rapidly. • The value of the house has *depreciated* greatly. — opposite APPRECIATE

2 [+ *obj*] *formal* **:** to describe (something) as having little value • He often *depreciates* [=*disparages, belittles*] the importance of his work.

de·pre·ci·a·tion /dɪˌpriːʃiˈeɪʃən/ *noun* [*noncount*]

1 : a decrease in the value of something • You'll need to estimate the car's *depreciation*. • currency *depreciation* — opposite APPRECIATION

2 *formal* **:** the act of making a person or a thing seem less valuable • the *depreciation* of the role of art in our schools

dep·re·da·tion /ˌdɛprəˈdeɪʃən/ *noun, pl* **-tions** *formal* **:** a usually violent act in which something is damaged or destroyed or in which a person or animal is killed [*count*] — usually plural • The town had somehow escaped the *depredations* of enemy soldiers. [*noncount*] a brutal act of *depredation* • trying to prevent livestock *depredation* by wolves

de·press /dɪˈprɛs/ *verb* **-press·es; -pressed; -press·ing** [+ *obj*]

1 : to make (someone) feel sad **:** to make (someone) depressed • The news seemed to *depress* him a little. • I don't mean to *depress* you, but there's no way we can win. • We were all *depressed* by the loss. • You shouldn't let this kind of problem *depress* you.

2 : to decrease the activity or strength of (something) • This medicine may *depress* [=*decrease*] your appetite. [=it may make you less hungry] • These changes could *depress* the economy. • Market conditions are likely to *depress* earnings in the next quarter. • *depressing* the price of a stock

3 *formal* **:** to press (something) down • Slowly *depress* the car's brake pedal. • *Depress* the "shift" key on your keyboard. • The doctor will *depress* your tongue and look at your throat.

de·pres·sant /dɪˈprɛsnt/ *noun, pl* **-sants** [*count*] **:** a chem-

ical substance (such as a drug) that makes a body's systems less active • alcohol and other *depressants* — see also ANTIDEPRESSANT
– depressant *adj* • the *depressant* effects of alcohol

de·pressed /dɪˈprɛst/ *adj* [*more ~; most ~*]
1 a : feeling sad • I've been feeling a little *depressed* [=(informally) *down, blue*] lately. • The rainy weather had her feeling lonely and *depressed*. • He was *depressed* about having to return to school. • in a *depressed* mood **b :** having a serious medical condition that causes a person to feel very sad, hopeless, and unimportant : suffering from mental depression • The new drug is being tested on a group of severely *depressed* patients.
2 : having little economic activity and few jobs : suffering from economic depression • living in a *depressed* area • a *depressed* economy
3 : less strong, active, high, etc., than usual • The patient has a somewhat *depressed* appetite. • Prices have remained at a *depressed* level.

depressing *adj* [*more ~; most ~*] **:** causing someone to feel sad or without hope : causing depression • This rainy weather is *depressing*. • He paints a *depressing* picture of modern life. • a very/deeply *depressing* movie
– de·press·ing·ly *adv* • *depressingly* bad weather • a *depressingly* familiar situation

de·pres·sion /dɪˈprɛʃən/ *noun, pl* **-sions**
1 [*noncount*] **a :** a state of feeling sad • anger, anxiety, and *depression* **b :** a serious medical condition in which a person feels very sad, hopeless, and unimportant and often is unable to live in a normal way • She has been undergoing treatment for severe/deep *depression*. • Many people suffer from clinical *depression* for years before being diagnosed. • bouts/periods of *depression* — see also MANIC DEPRESSION
2 : a period of time in which there is little economic activity and many people do not have jobs [*count*] After several years of an economic boom, it looks as though we may be heading toward a *depression*. • He grew up during ***the (Great) Depression***. [=the 1930s, when the U.S. and many other countries were in a very bad depression] [*noncount*] periods of economic *depression*
3 [*count*] **:** an area on a surface that is lower than other parts : a low spot • The photographs show *depressions* in the moon's surface.
4 [*count*] *weather* **:** a large area where there is low pressure in the atmosphere with usually clouds and rain • a tropical *depression*

de·pres·sive /dɪˈprɛsɪv/ *adj, medical* **:** of or relating to the medical condition of depression • a *depressive* disorder/illness — see also MANIC-DEPRESSIVE
– depressive *noun, pl* **-sives** [*count*] • treatment of *depressives* [=people who suffer from depression]

dep·ri·va·tion /ˌdɛprəˈveɪʃən/ *noun, pl* **-tions :** the state of not having something that people need : the state of being deprived of something [*noncount*] She is studying the effects of sleep *deprivation*. • social/emotional *deprivation* [*count*] She eventually overcame the *deprivations* of her childhood.

de·prive /dɪˈpraɪv/ *verb* **-prives; -prived; -priv·ing**
deprive of [*phrasal verb*] ***deprive (someone or something) of (something)* :** to take something away from someone or something : to not allow (someone or something) to have or keep (something) • The change in her status *deprived* her *of* access to classified information. • The new environmental law will *deprive* some fishermen *of* their livelihood. • They're *depriving* him *of* a chance to succeed. • I don't want to *deprive* you *of* this opportunity to meet new people. — often used as *(be) deprived of* • The children are *being deprived of* a good education. • The study is examining what happens to people when they *are deprived of* sleep.

deprived *adj* [*more ~; most ~*] **:** not having the things that are needed for a good or healthy life • emotionally *deprived* children • The diet allows you to eat small amounts of your favorite foods, so you won't feel *deprived*. • people who are ***sleep-deprived*** [=people who do not get enough sleep]

dept. *abbr* department

depth /ˈdɛpθ/ *noun, pl* **depths**
1 a : a distance below a surface [*count*] These fish typically live at *depths* of 500 feet or more. • Students will test the temperature of the water at different/varying/various *depths*. • shallow/great *depths* • The boat sank to a *depth* of several hundred feet. • measuring the *depth* of the water/river/sea • the *depth* of a hole • The pool has a *depth* of 12 feet. [*noncount*] The pool is 12 feet ***in depth***. [=12 feet deep] **b** [*count*] **:** the distance from the front of something to the back — usually singular • Measure the height, width, and *depth* of the cabinet. • The bench's *depth* is 22 inches.
2 [*count*] **:** an area that exists far below a surface or far inside something : a deep place or area — usually plural • They disappeared into the *depths* of the forest. • Scientists have begun using the machine to explore the ocean *depths*. • the black *depths* of outer space — often used figuratively • The actress must examine her own emotional *depths* to perform the role successfully. • Around midnight, a loud noise woke us from the *depths* of sleep. • I knew in ***the depths of my heart/soul/being*** [=I believed very strongly] that we would survive. • The memory lies hidden in ***the depths of her mind***. [=she has not thought about the memory in a long time] • in ***the depths of winter*** [=in the middle of winter; in the coldest part of winter]
3 [*count*] **a :** a very low or bad state or condition — usually plural • After losing his job, he sank into the *depths* of misery/despair/depression. • The film portrays a family's difficult climb from the *depths* of poverty. • I can't believe he lied. He's really ***sunk to new depths***. • The team is ***reaching/plumbing new depths*** this season. [=the team is playing worse than it ever has before] **b :** the worst part of something • I began working at the factory during the *depth/depths* of the Depression.
4 [*noncount*] **:** the quality of being deep: such as **a :** the quality of being strongly felt • We were surprised by the *depth* of her anger/pain/shame. • He wanted to express the *depth* of his love for her. • No one doubted the *depth* of his faith. [=they all knew that his faith was strong] • the *depth* of her commitment to the project • The dancers expressed great *depth* of feeling/emotion. **b :** the quality of being very bad or serious • I was shocked when I realized the *depth* of the problem. **c :** the quality of being complete or thorough • We were impressed by the *depth* [=*extent*] of her experience/knowledge. • Your essay lacks *depth*. [=it does not cover its topic in a complete way] **d :** the quality of being strong in color, taste, etc. • the *depth* of a color • The wine has great *depth* of flavor. **e :** the quality of being low in sound • the *depth* of his voice **f** *US, sports* **:** the quality of having many good players on a team • The team lacks *depth* this year.
***in depth* :** in a thorough or complete way • The problem has yet to be examined/explored/studied *in depth*. [=*thoroughly*] • These topics need to be discussed *in* (more/greater) *depth*. — see also IN-DEPTH
out of your depth *also* ***beyond your depth*** **1 :** dealing with a situation or subject that is too difficult for you • When the debate turned to physics, I knew that I was *out of my depth*. [=*in over my head*] **2** *chiefly Brit* **:** in water that is deeper than your height • He is just getting used to swimming in water that is *out of his depth*. [=*over his head*]

depth charge *noun, pl* **~ charges** [*count*] **:** a bomb that is made to explode under water at a particular depth in order to destroy submarines

depth perception *noun* [*noncount*] **:** the ability to see how far away something is or how much space is between things

dep·u·ta·tion /ˌdɛpjəˈteɪʃən/ *noun, pl* **-tions** [*count*] *formal* **:** a group of people who are sent to a place to represent other people • Many countries will be sending *deputations* to the peace conference.

de·pute /dɪˈpjuːt/ *verb* **-putes; -put·ed; -put·ing** [*+ obj*] *chiefly Brit, formal* **:** to give (someone) a job or responsibility • Several officers were *deputed* to guard the building. • I've been *deputed* to meet them at the airport.

dep·u·tize *also Brit* **dep·u·tise** /ˈdɛpjəˌtaɪz/ *verb* **-tiz·es; -tized; -tiz·ing**
1 [*+ obj*] *chiefly US* **:** to give (someone) the power to do something in place of another person : to make (someone) a deputy — often followed by *to + verb* • The new system *deputizes* the nurses *to perform* some of the doctors' duties.
2 [*no obj*] *Brit* **:** to act in place of another person : to act *for* someone as a deputy • I *deputize for* the newspaper's editor on the weekends.

dep·u·ty /ˈdɛpjəti/ *noun, pl* **-ties** [*count*]
1 : an important assistant who helps the person who the leader of a government, organization, etc. • (*US*) a sheriff's *deputy* [=an assistant who helps a sheriff enforce the law] — often used before another noun • a *deputy* sheriff • She's now the department's *deputy* director. • a *deputy* mayor
2 : a member of Parliament in some countries

de·rail /dɪˈreɪl/ *verb* **-rails; -railed; -rail·ing**

1 [*no obj*] *of a train* : to leave its tracks ▪ The train *derailed* in heavy snow.
2 [+ *obj*] : to cause (a train) to leave its tracks ▪ The train was *derailed* by heavy snow. — often used figuratively ▪ His plans for becoming a professional football player were *derailed* [=*ruined*] by several injuries in college. ▪ The incident threatened to *derail* her career.
– de•rail•ment /dɪˈreɪlmənt/ *noun, pl* **-ments** [*count*] train *derailments* [*noncount*] the threat of *derailment* ▪ *derailment* of the peace process

derailleur *noun, pl* **-leurs** [*count*] : a part on a bicycle that is used to change gears by moving the chain from one gear to another one — see picture at BICYCLE

de•ranged /dɪˈreɪnʤd/ *adj* [*more* ~; *most* ~] : unable to think or act in a normal or logical way especially because of severe mental illness : crazy or insane ▪ The actor was being followed by a (mentally) *deranged* fan. ▪ *deranged* criminals ▪ a *deranged* mind
– de•range•ment /dɪˈreɪnʤmənt/ *noun* [*noncount*] ▪ mental *derangement*

der•by /ˈdɚbi, *Brit* ˈdɑːbi/ *noun, pl* **-bies** [*count*]
1 : a type of horse race that takes place every year — used especially in proper names ▪ the Kentucky *Derby*
2 : a race or contest ▪ a fishing *derby* — see also DEMOLITION DERBY, ROLLER DERBY
3 *Brit* : a game between local sports teams ▪ a *derby* between Manchester United and Manchester City
4 *US* : a hard usually black cloth hat that has a round top and that was worn by men especially in the 1800s — called also (*US*) *derby hat,* (*chiefly Brit*) *bowler*

de•reg•u•late /diˈrɛgjəˌleɪt/ *verb* **-lates; -lat•ed; lat•ing** [+ *obj*] : to give up control of (something, such as an industry) by removing laws : to remove regulations or restrictions from (something) ▪ The government plans to further *deregulate* the oil industry.
– de•reg•u•la•tion /diˌrɛgjəˈleɪʃən/ *noun* [*noncount*]

[1]**der•e•lict** /ˈderəˌlɪkt/ *adj, formal*
1 : no longer cared for or used by anyone ▪ a *derelict* house/ship/place ▪ a slum filled with *derelict* [=*run-down, dilapidated*] warehouses
2 [*more* ~; *most* ~] *US, formal* : failing to do what should be done : NEGLIGENT ▪ The officer was charged with being ***derelict in*** his duty.

[2]**derelict** *noun, pl* **-licts** [*count*] *formal + disapproving* : a person who has no money, job, home, etc. ▪ a drunken *derelict* [=*vagrant, bum*] ▪ It was a run-down neighborhood filled with drugs addicts and *derelicts*.

der•e•lic•tion /ˌderəˈlɪkʃən/ *noun, formal*
1 [*noncount*] **a** : the act of no longer caring for, using, or doing something : the act of abandoning something ▪ the *dereliction* of a cause by its leaders **b** : the condition of being no longer cared for ▪ The building is in a state of *dereliction*. [=is in poor condition from being abandoned]
2 [*singular*] *law* : failure to do your job or duty : failure to do what you should do ▪ The officer was formally charged with ***dereliction of duty***. ▪ a serious *dereliction of duty* ✧ *Dereliction* is usually used to refer to the crime that is committed when a military officer or police officer fails to do an important part of his or her job.

de•ride /dɪˈraɪd/ *verb* **-rides; -rid•ed; -rid•ing** [+ *obj*] *formal* : to talk or write about (someone or something) in a very critical or insulting way : to say that (someone or something) is ridiculous or has no value ▪ politicians attempting to win votes by *deriding* [=*belittling*] their opponents — often + *as* ▪ One critic *derides* the book *as* dull and predictable. — often used as *(be) derided* ▪ For years women *were derided as* the weaker sex.

de ri•gueur /dəˌriˈgɚ/ *adj, formal* : necessary if you want to be fashionable, popular, socially acceptable, etc. ▪ Dark sunglasses are *de rigueur* these days. ✧ The phrase *de rigueur* comes from French.

de•ri•sion /dɪˈrɪʒən/ *noun* [*noncount*] *formal* : the feeling that people express when they criticize and laugh at someone or something in an insulting way ▪ yells of *derision* ▪ The governor's plan was greeted with *derision* [=*ridicule*] by most journalists and pundits. ▪ One of the students laughed/snorted in *derision* at my error. ▪ The team's awful record has made it an ***object of derision*** in the league. ▪ "Nerd" is a ***term of derision***.
– de•ri•sive /dɪˈraɪsɪv/ *adj* [*more* ~; *most* ~] ▪ *derisive* [=*scornful*] laughter ▪ a *derisive* [=*derogatory*] term **– de•ri•sive•ly** *adv* ▪ laughing *derisively* [=*scornfully*]

de•ri•so•ry /dɪˈraɪsəri/ *adj* [*more* ~; *most* ~] *formal*
1 : of too little value to be considered seriously : ridiculously small ▪ He offered to buy the car for some *derisory* [=*paltry, measly*] sum/amount, but I turned him down.
2 : expressing a belief that something or someone is ridiculous or without value : expressing derision ▪ The presentation was so bad that it received only a few *derisory* [=(more commonly) *derisive*] comments.

der•i•va•tion /ˌderəˈveɪʃən/ *noun, pl* **-tions**
1 a : the origin of a word [*count*] It is a word for which several *derivations* [=*etymologies*] have been suggested. ▪ He is doing research into the *derivation* of "Yankee." [*noncount*] words of Latin *derivation* **b** [*noncount*] : the act of forming a word *from* another word ▪ "Childish" was formed by *derivation from* "child."
2 a [*noncount*] : the source or origin of something ▪ foods of Indian *derivation* [=foods originally from India] **b** [*count*] : an act or process by which one thing is formed or created *from* another ▪ Scientists are debating the possible *derivation* of birds *from* dinosaurs.

[1]**de•riv•a•tive** /dɪˈrɪvətɪv/ *noun, pl* **-tives** [*count*]
1 : a word formed from another word ▪ The word "childish" is a *derivative* of "child."
2 : something that comes from something else : a substance that is made from another substance ▪ Tofu is one of many soybean *derivatives*. ▪ Petroleum is a *derivative* of coal tar.

[2]**derivative** /dɪˈrɪvətɪv/ *adj*
1 [*more* ~; *most* ~] *usually disapproving* : made up of parts from something else : not new or original ▪ *derivative* poetry ▪ A number of critics found the film *derivative* and predictable. ▪ His style seems too *derivative* of Hemingway.
2 : formed from another word ▪ a *derivative* term

de•rive /dɪˈraɪv/ *verb* **-rives; -rived; -riv•ing**
1 [+ *obj*] : to take or get (something) *from* (something else) ▪ The river *derives* its name *from* a Native American tribe. ▪ She *derived* [=*received, took*] great satisfaction *from* their friendship. — often used as *(be) derived* ▪ Many English words *are derived from* French. ▪ Petroleum *is derived from* coal tar and used to make gasoline.
2 [*no obj*] : to have something as a source : to come *from* something ▪ Much of the book's appeal *derives from* the personality of its central character.
– de•riv•able /dɪˈraɪvəbəl/ *adj* ▪ a substance *derivable* from coal tar

der•ma•ti•tis /ˌdɚməˈtaɪtəs/ *noun* [*noncount*] *medical* : a disease in which the skin becomes red, swollen, and sore

der•ma•tol•o•gy /ˌdɚməˈtɑːləʤi/ *noun* [*noncount*] *medical* : the scientific study of the skin and its diseases ▪ One of the doctors at the clinic specializes in *dermatology*.
– der•ma•tol•o•gist /ˌdɚməˈtɑːləʤɪst/ *noun, pl* **-gists** [*count*] ▪ The *dermatologist* said that the baby's rash was nothing to worry about.

der•o•gate /ˈderəˌgeɪt/ *verb* **-gates; -gat•ed; -gat•ing** [+ *obj*] *formal* : to insult (someone or something) : to say or suggest that (something or someone) is not important or worthy of respect ▪ The title of the book *derogates* the people it is about. ▪ Her parents are constantly *derogating* her achievements.
derogate from [*phrasal verb*] ***derogate from (something or someone)*** *formal* : to lessen the importance or value of (something or someone) ▪ These criticisms are not meant to *derogate from* [=*detract from*] the excellent work they have done.
– de•rog•a•tion /ˌderəˈgeɪʃən/ *noun, pl* **-tions** [*count, noncount*]

de•rog•a•to•ry /dɪˈrɑːgəˌtori, *Brit* dɪˈrɒgətri/ *adj* [*more* ~; *most* ~] : expressing a low opinion of someone or something : showing a lack of respect for someone or something ▪ He was accused of making *derogatory* [=*insulting, disrespectful*] remarks about her. ▪ a *derogatory* [=*disparaging*] term/word

der•rick /ˈderɪk/ *noun, pl* **-ricks** [*count*]
1 : a tall machine with a long part like an arm that is used to move or lift heavy things especially on ships
2 : a tall tower that is built over an oil well and used to support and guide the tool that is used to dig the hole and get oil out of the ground

der•ri•ere *or* **der•ri•ère** /ˌderiˈeə/ *noun, pl* **-eres** *or* **-ères** [*count*] *humorous* : the part of the body you sit on : BUTTOCKS ▪ I slipped on the ice and fell on my *derriere*.

der•ring–do /ˌderɪŋˈduː/ *noun* [*noncount*] *old-fashioned + humorous* : brave acts : behavior that requires courage ▪ She is known for her spectacular feats of *derring-do*. [=*bravery*] ✧

Derring-do suggests the brave acts of characters in movies and stories about adventure.

der·vish /ˈdɚvɪʃ/ *noun, pl* **-vish·es** [*count*] **:** a member of a Muslim religious group that is known for its customs including a fast spinning dance that is done as part of worship ✧ In U.S. English, *dervish* is most common in figurative uses where it describes someone or something that is spinning or moving very fast. ▪ The actor whirled like a *dervish* on stage.

de·sa·li·nate /diˈsæləˌneɪt/ *verb* **-nates; -nat·ed; -nat·ing** [+ *obj*] *technical* **:** to remove salt from (something, such as water) ▪ The company is building a plant that will *desalinate* seawater.
— **de·sa·li·na·tion** /diˌsæləˈneɪʃən/ *noun* [*noncount*]

de·scale /diˈskeɪl/ *verb* **-scales; -scaled; -scal·ing** [+ *obj*] *Brit, technical* **:** to remove the hard white substance that forms on the inside of something (such as pipes or a boiler) that heats water

des·cant /ˈdɛsˌkænt/ *noun, pl* **-cants** [*count*] *music* **:** a high melody that is sung or played along with the main melody of a song

de·scend /dɪˈsɛnd/ *verb* **-scends; -scend·ed; -scend·ing** *formal*

1 : to go down **:** to go or move from a higher to a lower place or level [*no obj*] Wait for the elevator to *descend*. ▪ The workers *descended* into the hole. ▪ The submarine was *descending*. ▪ They *descended* from [=got down from] the platform. ▪ A herd of goats *descended* into the valley. ▪ The airplane will *descend* to a lower altitude soon. [+ *obj*] *Descending* the mountain was even more dangerous than climbing/ascending it. ▪ The children *descended* the staircase silently. ▪ *descend* a ladder — opposite ASCEND

2 [*no obj*] **:** to slope or lead downward ▪ The path *descends* to the river. ▪ The stairs *descended* into the tunnel. — opposite ASCEND

3 [*no obj*] **:** to go or change to a worse state or condition — + *into* ▪ After his wife died, he *descended* [=*sank*] *into* a deep depression. ▪ The classroom *descended into* chaos after the teacher left.

4 [*no obj*] **:** to appear or happen like something that comes down from the sky ▪ As night *descended*, the campers built a fire. — usually + *on* or *upon* ▪ The invaders *descended on* the village without warning. [=the invaders attacked without warning] ▪ In autumn/fall, thousands of students *descend on/upon* [=*visit*] our town. ▪ Silence *descended upon* the crowd. [=the crowd became silent]

descend from [*phrasal verb*] ***descend from (something or someone)*** **:** to have (something or someone in the past) as an origin or source ▪ Recent evidence supports the theory that birds *descended from* dinosaurs. ▪ The plants *descend from* a common ancestor. ▪ The tradition *descends from* [=*comes from*] an ancient custom. ▪ They claim to ***be descended from*** a noble British family.

descend to [*phrasal verb*] **1** ***descend to (someone)*** *formal* **:** to become owned by (someone) when the former owner has died ▪ The estate *descended to* her from her grandparents. [=she inherited the estate from her grandparents] **2** ***descend to (something)*** **:** to lower yourself by doing (something) ▪ She was desperate for money, but she would not *descend to* [=(more commonly) *stoop to*] asking her friends for help. — see also *descend to someone's level* at ¹LEVEL

in descending order ✧ If people or things are ***in descending order***, they are are arranged in a series that begins with the greatest or largest and ends with the least or smallest. ▪ The states are listed *in descending order* of population size. ▪ The sale items are arranged *in descending order* according to price.

de·scen·dant /dɪˈsɛndənt/ *noun, pl* **-dants** [*count*]

1 : someone who is related to a person or group of people who lived in the past ▪ One of the famous inventor's *descendants* is also an inventor. ▪ Many people in this area are *descendants* of German immigrants.

2 : a plant or animal that is related to a particular plant or animal that lived long ago ▪ Recent evidence supports the theory that birds are the modern *descendants* of dinosaurs.

3 : something that developed from another thing that was made or existed earlier ▪ The Italian language is one of Latin's *descendants*.

de·scent /dɪˈsɛnt/ *noun, pl* **-scents** *formal*

1 [*count*] **:** the act or process of descending: such as **a :** the act or process of going from a higher to a lower place or level — usually singular ▪ The climbers were faced with a dangerous *descent* in bad weather. ▪ the submarine's *descent* ▪ After only an hour of flight, the pilot announced our *descent*. — opposite ASCENT **b :** the act or process or changing to a worse state or condition ▪ The book describes his *descent* into a deep depression after the death of his wife. ▪ her slow *descent* to a life of addiction

2 [*count*] **:** a way of going down something **:** a downward slope, path, etc. ▪ The only path that goes down to the river is a rather steep *descent*, so be careful.

3 [*noncount*] **:** the people in your family who lived before you were born **:** your ancestors ▪ Many people in this area are of German *descent*. [=*ancestry*] ▪ They claim to be ***of royal descent***. [=they say that their ancestors were kings, queens, etc.]

de·scribe /dɪˈskraɪb/ *verb* **-scribes; -scribed; -scrib·ing** [+ *obj*]

1 : to tell someone the appearance, sound, smell, events, etc., of (something or someone) **:** to say what something or someone is like ▪ The witness wasn't able to *describe* the robber. ▪ He *described* the house in perfect detail. ▪ The article *describes* how the experiment was done. ▪ She *described* watching dolphins play beside the ship. ▪ Please *describe* what happened next. ▪ Can you *describe* the lost dog to me? — often + *as* ▪ He was *described* by his friends *as* generous and loyal. ▪ Reporters *described* the scene *as* a disaster area.

2 *formal* **:** to make a motion or draw a line that shows the shape of (something) ▪ She used a stick to *describe* a circle on the ground.

— **de·scrib·able** /dɪˈskraɪbəbəl/ *adj* ▪ The process is not easily *describable*.

de·scrip·tion /dɪˈskrɪpʃən/ *noun, pl* **-tions**

1 : a statement that tells you how something or someone looks, sounds, etc. **:** words that describe something or someone [*count*] Reporters called the scene "a disaster area," and I think that was an accurate *description*. ▪ I applied for the position after reading the job *description*. ▪ We are looking for someone with experience and a sense of humor. Do you know anyone who fits/matches that *description*? [=anyone who has those qualities] — often + *of* ▪ a brief/general *description of* the process ▪ The witness was unable to give/provide a *description of* the robber. [=was unable to describe the robber] ▪ Someone fitting/answering/matching the witness' *description of* the burglar has been arrested. [*noncount*] a writer with a gift of/for *description* ▪ The landscape is beautiful ***beyond description***. [=is extremely beautiful]

2 [*count*] **:** type or kind — used after *of* ▪ We saw people *of* every *description*. [=*sort*] ▪ The museum features toys *of* all *descriptions*. [=*kinds*] ▪ The store sells hats, gloves, and things *of* that *description*. [=*nature, ilk*]

de·scrip·tive /dɪˈskrɪptɪv/ *adj*

1 [*more* ~; *most* ~] **:** giving information about how something or someone looks, sounds, etc. **:** using words to describe what something or someone is like ▪ She gave a *descriptive* account of the journey. ▪ a talent for *descriptive* writing ▪ a poem full of *descriptive* detail ▪ The black cat was given the *descriptive* name "Midnight." — often + *of* ▪ They chose a name *descriptive of* the company's philosophy.

2 *technical* **:** providing facts about how a language is actually used rather than rules that tell people how it should be used ▪ The book is a *descriptive* grammar. ▪ *descriptive* dictionaries — opposite PRESCRIPTIVE

— **de·scrip·tive·ly** *adv* [*more* ~; *most* ~]

des·e·crate /ˈdɛsɪˌkreɪt/ *verb* **-crates; -crat·ed; -crat·ing** [+ *obj*] **:** to damage (a holy place or object) **:** to treat (a holy place or object) with disrespect ▪ The vandals were accused of *desecrating* graves. ▪ a *desecrated* church

— **des·e·cra·tion** /ˌdɛsɪˈkreɪʃən/ *noun* [*noncount*] ▪ The law forbids *desecration* of the flag.

de·seg·re·gate /diˈsɛgrəˌgeɪt/ *verb* **-gates; -gat·ed; -gat·ing :** to end a policy that keeps people of different races apart **:** to end a policy of segregation [+ *obj*] efforts to *desegregate* the town's buses — usually used as *(be) desegregated* ▪ The city's schools *were* finally *desegregated* in the 1960s. [*no obj*] Eventually the city's schools *desegregated*.

— **de·seg·re·ga·tion** /diˌsɛgrɪˈgeɪʃən/ *noun* [*noncount*]

de·se·lect /ˌdiːsəˈlɛkt/ *verb* **-lects; -lect·ed; -lect·ing** [+ *obj*]

1 *computers* **:** to remove (something) from a list of choices especially by clicking with a computer mouse ▪ If you don't want the computer program to automatically correct your spelling, you will have to *deselect* that option.

2 *Brit, politics* **:** to choose not to have (a current member of

Parliament) as a candidate again at the next election
– de·se·lec·tion *noun [noncount]*

de·sen·si·tize *also Brit* **de·sen·si·tise** /diˈsɛnsəˌtaɪz/ *verb* **-tiz·es; -tized; -tiz·ing** [+ *obj*] **:** to cause (someone or something) to react less to or be less affected by something **:** to cause (someone or something) to be less sensitive • The shot will help to *desensitize* the nerve. — usually + *to*; often used as *(be/become) desensitized* • People can *become desensitized to* violence by endless images of war. • Her body has *become desensitized to* the medication.
– de·sen·si·ti·za·tion *also Brit* **de·sen·si·ti·sa·tion** /diˌsɛnsətəˈzeɪʃən, *Brit* diˌsɛnsəˌtaɪˈzeɪʃən/ *noun [noncount]*

¹des·ert /ˈdɛzət/ *noun, pl* **-erts**
1 : an area of very dry land that is usually covered with sand and is very hot [*count*] Many settlers died while trying to cross the *desert*. • the Arabian and African *deserts* [*noncount*] The region is mostly *desert*. — often used before another noun • the shifting *desert* sands • a study of *desert* plants • stranded on a ***desert island*** [=an island where no people live] — see color picture on page C7
2 [*count*] **:** a place or area that does not have something interesting or important • For many years, the city was a cultural *desert*, but now there are several museums and also a concert hall. — see also DESERTS

Do not confuse *desert* with *dessert*.

²de·sert /dɪˈzət/ *verb* **-serts; -sert·ed; -sert·ing**
1 [+ *obj*] **:** to go away from (a place) **:** to leave (a place) • The inhabitants had *deserted* the town. • If the nest is disturbed, the bird may *desert* [=*abandon*] it.
2 [+ *obj*] **:** to leave and stop helping or supporting (someone or something) • She had been married for just over a year when her husband *deserted* her. • He was *deserted* by his friends and family. • He vowed that he would never *desert* [=*abandon*] a friend in trouble. • He urged people not to *desert* the cause. [=not to stop supporting the cause]
3 [+ *obj*] *of a useful quality or ability* **:** to no longer be with (someone) in a time of need • The soldiers prayed that their courage would not *desert* them. [=that they would not lose their courage] • She was a respected academic until late in life when her memory *deserted* her. [=she lost her ability to remember things]
4 [*no obj*] *of a soldier* **:** to leave the military without permission and without intending to return • Many soldiers *deserted* during the first weeks of the war.
– deserted *adj* • The town was *deserted*. [=there were no people in the town] • We came upon a *deserted* [=*abandoned*] old hotel. • a *deserted* street/road • *deserted* wives/husbands/children **– de·ser·tion** /dɪˈzəʃən/ *noun, pl* **-tions** [*noncount*] the mysterious *desertion* of the town by its inhabitants • He was guilty of *desertion* during wartime. [*count*] The military has reported 350 *desertions*.

de·sert·er /dɪˈzətə/ *noun, pl* **-ers** [*count*] **:** a soldier who leaves without permission **:** a military person who deserts

de·sert·i·fi·ca·tion /dɪˌzətəfəˈkeɪʃən/ *noun [noncount] technical* **:** the process by which an area becomes a desert • The organization was awarded for its efforts to prevent further *desertification* in Africa.

de·serts /dɪˈzəts/ *noun [plural]* **:** punishment that someone deserves • We all want to see this criminal ***get/receive his just deserts***.

de·serve /dɪˈzəv/ *verb* **-serves; -served; -serv·ing** [+ *obj*] — used to say that someone or something should or should not have or be given something • She *deserves* another chance. • He doesn't *deserve* the award. • Every defendant *deserves* a fair trial. • The newspaper *deserves* a lot of credit for calling attention to the problem. • I think the idea *deserves* [=*merits*] consideration. • The story *deserves* telling. [=the story should be told; the story is important enough to tell] • What did I do to *deserve* this kind of harsh treatment? [=you should not treat me this way] • She believes that people eventually get what they *deserve*. • He ***deserves a medal*** for coming up with a solution so quickly. [=he did something very good and impressive by coming up with a solution so quickly] — often followed by *to* + *verb* • Anyone who will not use a map *deserves to get* lost. • They *deserve to be* punished. • He *deserves to win*.
– deserved /dɪˈzəvd/ *adj* • a well-*deserved* vacation/break • a *deserved* win/victory/reputation • The award/criticism was not *deserved*. **– de·serv·ed·ly** /dɪˈzəvədli/ *adv* • She was *deservedly* praised for her generosity. • He has been accused of being selfish, and ***deservedly so***. [=he deserves to be called selfish; it is reasonable to call him selfish because of his behavior]

deserving *adj [more ~; most ~]*
1 *always used before a noun* **:** having good qualities that deserve praise, support, etc. • He's a very *deserving* young man. • The church provides aid to *deserving* families.
2 *not used before a noun* — used to say that someone or something should have or be given something; + *of* • She was *deserving of* praise. [=she deserved praise] • criminals *deserving of* harsh punishment • an idea that is *deserving of* attention

des·ic·cat·ed /ˈdɛsɪˌkeɪtəd/ *adj*
1 *technical* **:** having had the water removed • *desiccated* [=(more commonly) *dried, dehydrated*] coconut
2 *formal* **:** very dry • *desiccated* land

des·ic·ca·tion /ˌdɛsɪˈkeɪʃən/ *noun [noncount] technical* **:** the process by which something becomes completely dry • *desiccation* of soil

de·sid·er·a·tum /dɪˌsɪdəˈrɑːtəm/ *noun, pl* **-ta** /-tə/ [*count*] *formal* **:** something that is needed or wanted • a list of political *desiderata*

¹de·sign /dɪˈzaɪn/ *verb* **-signs; -signed; -sign·ing** [+ *obj*]
1 : to plan and make decisions about (something that is being built or created) **:** to create the plans, drawings, etc., that show how (something) will be made • A team of engineers *designed* the new engine. • a badly *designed* building • She *designs* clothes. • Who *designed* the book's cover?
2 : to plan and make (something) for a specific use or purpose • He *designed* the chair to adjust automatically. — usually used as *(be) designed* • The course *is designed* to teach beginners. [=the purpose of the course is to teach beginners] • The book *is designed* as a college textbook. • The shoes *are designed* to keep your feet warm and dry. • The book *is* specially *designed* for learners. • The new models have *been designed* for easier use.
3 : to think of (something, such as a plan) **:** to plan (something) in your mind • They thought they could *design* the perfect crime. • *design* a strategy for battle

²design *noun, pl* **-signs**
1 : the way something has been made **:** the way the parts of something (such as a building, machine, book, etc.) are formed and arranged for a particular use, effect, etc. [*noncount*] There are problems with the *design* of the airplane's landing gear. • I like the *design* of the textbook. • I love the sculpture's *design*. [*count*] The machine had a flawed *design*.
2 [*noncount*] **:** the process of planning how something will look, happen, be made, etc. **:** the process of designing something • She is studying furniture/Web *design*. [=how to design furniture/Web sites] • the *design* and development of new products • The new model is still in the *design* stage. [=is still being designed] • Correcting mistakes is part of the *design* process. • a number of *design* concepts/ideas — see also INTERIOR DESIGN
3 [*count*] **:** a drawing of something that is being planned or created — often + *for* • We reviewed the preliminary *design for* the new stadium. • Can I see the *designs* [=*plans*] *for* both bridges?
4 [*count*] **:** a decorative pattern that covers something **:** a repeating picture, shape, etc., on something • The wallpaper in the bedroom has a floral *design*. • a skirt with a paisley *design* • fabric sold in a variety of colors and *designs*
5 : something that you plan to do **:** INTENTION [*count*] My *design* [=(more commonly) *purpose*] in writing to you is to ask for your support. [*noncount*] The motor is loud ***by design***. [=because it was intended to be loud] • The meeting happened by accident, not *by design*. [=*on purpose*]
have designs on **1 :** to have a secret desire and plan to get (something) • She *had designs on* my job. **2** *formal* + *humorous* **:** to want to date or have a sexual relationship with (someone) • You can deny it all you want, but I think it's pretty obvious that you *have designs on* her.

¹des·ig·nate /ˈdɛzɪgˌneɪt/ *verb* **-nates; -nat·ed; -nat·ing** [+ *obj*]
1 : to officially choose (someone or something) to do or be something **:** to officially give (someone or something) a particular role or purpose • It might be difficult to *designate* [=*select*] an appropriate place for the event. • We need to *designate* [=*appoint*] a new leader. — often used as *(be) designated* • money *designated* [=*set aside*] for the scholarship fund • He *was designated* team captain. = He ***was designated as*** team captain. [=he was made team captain] • The park has *been designated as* a wildlife refuge. — often followed by *to* +

verb • He *was designated to be* team captain.
2 a : to call (something or someone) by a particular name or title • We *designated* [=*named*] the first one "alpha." — often used as *(be) designated* • The four parts *were designated A, B, C,* and *D* in the diagram. **b :** to be used as a name for (something or someone) • The word eventually came to *designate* [=*refer to*] any kind of mistake.
3 : to mark, show, or represent (something) • The wooden stakes *designate* the edge of the building site. — usually used as *(be) designated* • Free items *are designated* by blue stickers. • The state capital *is designated* [=*indicated*] by a star.
– **designated** *adj* • We all agreed to meet at a *designated* time. [=a specific time that we agreed on] • 18 years old is the *designated* age to vote. — see also DESIGNATED DRIVER, DESIGNATED HITTER – **des·ig·na·tor** /ˈdɛzɪgˌneɪtɚ/ *noun, pl* **-tors** [*count*]

[2]**designate** *adj, not used before a noun, formal* **:** chosen for a particular job but not officially doing that job yet • the governor *designate* [=the governor elect]

designated driver *noun, pl* ~ **-ers** [*count*] **:** a person who agrees not to drink alcohol on a particular occasion so that he or she will be able to safely drive around other people who will be drinking alcohol

designated hitter *noun, pl* ~ **-ters** [*count*] *baseball* **:** a player who is chosen at the beginning of a game to bat in the place of the pitcher and who does not play a position in the field — called also *DH*

des·ig·na·tion /ˌdɛzɪgˈneɪʃən/ *noun, pl* **-tions** *formal*
1 [*noncount*] **:** the act of officially choosing someone or something to do or be something — + *as* • Everyone supported the park's *designation as* a wildlife refuge. • The committee favors *designation* of the house *as* an historic building.
2 [*count*] **:** a name or title that identifies someone or something • Though many people call her a liberal, it is not a *designation* she uses herself.

des·ig·nee /ˌdɛzɪgˈniː/ *noun, pl* **-nees** [*count*] *chiefly US, formal* **:** a person who has been officially chosen to do or be something **:** a person who has been designated • the President's *designees* for Cabinet positions

[1]**de·sign·er** /dɪˈzaɪnɚ/ *noun, pl* **-ers** [*count*] **:** a person who plans how something new will look and be made **:** a person who creates and often produces a new product, style, etc. • She is one of the leading *designers* in the fashion world. • He is a *designer* and engineer for a car company. • She was the *designer* of the book's jacket. • a boat/clothing/computer/costume *designer* • a Web (site) *designer* — see also INTERIOR DESIGNER

[2]**designer** *adj, always used before a noun*
1 : created by a famous designer • *designer* jeans/fashions • *designer* wallpaper
2 : very fashionable and popular • *designer* coffee drinks • *designer* perfumes
3 *technical* **:** scientifically changed from the usual or natural form • *designer* foods • *designer* estrogen

designer drug *noun, pl* ~ **drugs** [*count*]
1 : a drug that is created to be only slightly different from an illegal drug so that it will not be considered illegal
2 : an artificially made drug that is used for pleasure • Ecstasy is a *designer drug.*

de·sign·ing /dɪˈzaɪnɪŋ/ *adj* [*more* ~; *most* ~] *old-fashioned* **:** having plans to get something in a way that is not honest or fair • a plot by a group of wicked and *designing* [=*crafty, scheming*] men

de·sir·able /dɪˈzaɪrəbəl/ *adj* [*more* ~; *most* ~]
1 : having good or pleasing qualities **:** worth having or getting • The house is in a highly *desirable* location/neighborhood. • *desirable* jobs • The new stove has many *desirable* features/characteristics. • the qualities that make a *desirable* business partner • The experiment did not achieve a *desirable* result. • It is *desirable* [=(more commonly) *advisable, smart*] to talk with a lawyer before signing any contract. — opposite UNDESIRABLE
2 : sexually attractive • a beautiful and *desirable* woman
– **de·sir·abil·i·ty** /dɪˌzaɪrəˈbɪləti/ *noun* [*noncount*] • Housing prices vary according to the *desirability* of the location. – **de·sir·ably** /dɪˈzaɪrəbli/ *adv* [*more* ~; *most* ~] • a *desirably* located apartment

[1]**de·sire** /dɪˈzajɚ/ *verb, not used in progressive tenses* **-sires; -sired; -sir·ing** [+ *obj*]
1 *somewhat formal* **:** to want or wish for (something) **:** to feel desire for (something) • Many people *desire* wealth. • He *desired* her approval more than anything. • The apartment has modern amenities, a great location—everything you could *desire.* • Those *desiring* [=*looking for*] a more relaxed atmosphere will prefer the pub in the restaurant's lower level. — sometimes followed by *to* + *verb* • I have always *desired* [=*wanted*] *to go* to France.
2 : to want to have sex with (someone) • She knew that men still *desired* her.
3 *formal* **:** to express a wish for (something) • The committee *desires* [=*requests*] an immediate answer.
leave much to be desired *or* ***leave a lot to be desired*** *or* ***leave a great deal to be desired*** — used to say that something is not very good at all or is not close to being good enough • Your work *leaves much to be desired.* • Although her education *left much to be desired,* she was an extremely intelligent person. • The working conditions here *leave a lot to be desired.*
– **desired** *adj* • an artist mixing paints to get a *desired* color • a *desired* effect/result

[2]**desire** *noun, pl* **-sires**
1 a [*noncount*] **:** the feeling of wanting something • *Desire* is a common theme is music and literature. • an ***object of desire*** [=something that people want to have] **b** [*count*] **:** a strong wish • It is our *desire* that all of you be treated fairly. [=we want all of you to be treated fairly] • The magazine tries to attend to the needs and *desires* of its readers. **:** a wish *for* something or *to do* something • Both sides feel a real *desire for* peace. • His decisions are guided by his *desire for* land/money/power/change. • They expressed a *desire to go* with us. • They have a *desire to have* children. • a strong/burning/aching *desire to travel* around the world
2 : a feeling of wanting to have sex with someone [*count*] He had/felt a strong (sexual) *desire* for her. [*noncount*] He was overcome with *desire* for her.
3 [*count*] **:** someone or something that you want or wish for — usually singular • He worried that he might never achieve his *desire.* [=might never do the thing that he wanted to do] • A good education had always been her ***heart's desire.*** [=something she wanted very much] • "You are my *heart's desire,*" he told her.

de·sir·ous /dɪˈzaɪrəs/ *adj, not used before a noun* [*more* ~; *most* ~] *somewhat formal* **:** wanting or wishing for something very much **:** feeling desire for something — usually + *of* • parents *desirous of* a better way to educate their children [=parents who want a better way to educate their children] • consumers *desirous of* saving money [=consumers who want to save money]

de·sist /dɪˈsɪst/ *verb* **-sists; -sist·ed; -sist·ing** [*no obj*] *formal* **:** to stop doing something • Despite orders from the police, the protesters would not *desist.* — often + *from* • They were ordered to *desist from* using the symbol as a logo. • The court ordered the company to ***cease and desist from*** selling the photographs. [=to immediately stop selling the photographs] — see also CEASE AND DESIST ORDER

desk /ˈdɛsk/ *noun, pl* **desks** [*count*]
1 : a piece of furniture that is like a table and often has drawers ✧ People often sit at desks when they are writing or using a computer. • a cluttered *desk* • a classroom with *desks* arranged in rows ✧ Often *desk* refers specifically to the desk a person uses to do his or her job. • I'm sorry I missed your call. I've been away from my *desk.* — often used before another noun • a *desk* lamp/calendar/chair • She left her ***desk job*** [=the job that she did while sitting at a desk] to become a farmer. — see picture at OFFICE
2 : a place where people can get information or be served at an office, a hotel, etc. • an information *desk* at an airport • We will ask for directions to the restaurant at the ***front desk.*** • We went to the ***reception desk*** to check into our room.
3 : the part of a company or organization that deals with a particular subject • the television network's financial/foreign *desk* [=*department*] • the newspaper's sports *desk* • the ***news desk*** [=the office where news is gathered to be reported in a newspaper, on television, etc.] — see also CITY DESK

desk·bound /ˈdɛksˌbaʊnd/ *adj* **:** having a job that requires you to be at a desk • *deskbound* office workers

[1]**desk·top** /ˈdɛskˌtɑːp/ *noun, pl* **-tops** [*count*]
1 : the top surface of a desk • The *desktop* was covered with books and stacks of papers.
2 a : a computer that is designed to be used on a desk or table **:** a desktop computer — compare LAPTOP, NOTEBOOK **b :** an area or window on a computer screen in which small pictures (called icons) are arranged like objects on top of a desk • He created a new folder on his *desktop.*

²desktop *adj, always used before a noun*
1 : of a size that is suitable to be used on a desk or table • a *desktop* computer
2 : done using a personal computer • She is working on a *desktop* video project. • Do you have any experience in ***desktop publishing***? [=the use of a computer to design and produce magazines, books, etc.]

¹des•o•late /ˈdɛsələt/ *adj [more ~; most ~]*
1 : lacking the people, plants, animals, etc., that make people feel welcome in a place • a landscape as *desolate* [=*barren, lifeless*] as the moon • We drove for hours along a *desolate* [=*deserted*] stretch of road.
2 : very sad and lonely especially because someone you love has died or left • *desolate* [=*grief-stricken*] parents grieving over the death of their son • *desolate* thoughts and memories

²des•o•late /ˈdɛsəˌleɪt/ *verb* **-lates; -lat•ed; -lat•ing** [+ *obj*] *formal + literary*
1 : to make (someone) feel very sad and lonely for a long time — usually used as *(be) desolated* • They *were desolated* [=(more commonly) *devastated*] by the death of their son.
2 : to damage (a place) in such a way that it is no longer suitable for people to live in • The constant bombings had *desolated* [=(more commonly) *destroyed, devastated*] the town.
– desolated *adj* • a *desolated* village

des•o•la•tion /ˌdɛsəˈleɪʃən/ *noun [noncount]*
1 : extreme sadness caused by loss or loneliness • She sank into a state of *desolation* and despair.
2 : the condition of a place or thing that has been damaged in such a way that it is no longer suitable for people to live in : the state or condition of being desolate • photos that show the *desolation* of war • It was a scene of utter *desolation*. [=*ruin, devastation*]

¹de•spair /dɪˈspeɚ/ *noun [noncount]*
1 : the feeling of no longer having any hope • His *despair* nearly drove him mad. • She let out a cry of *despair*. [=*desperation*] • I was overcome by *despair* at being unable to find them. • She finally gave up ***in despair***. • The people were ***driven to despair*** by the horrors of war. • This latest setback has brought/carried/driven her ***to the depths of despair***.
2 : someone or something that causes extreme sadness or worry — + *of* • He ***was the despair of*** his parents.

²despair *verb* **-spairs; -spaired; -spair•ing** [*no obj*] : to no longer have any hope or belief that a situation will improve or change • Things look bad now, but don't *despair*. — often + *of* • We had begun to *despair of* ever finding a house we could afford.

despairing *adj [more ~; most ~]* : feeling very sad and without hope : showing or feeling despair • He plays the role of a lonely and *despairing* [=*despondent*] widower. • a *despairing* cry/look
– de•spair•ing•ly *adv* • They cried out *despairingly*.

despatch *Brit spelling of* DISPATCH

des•per•a•do /ˌdɛspəˈrɑːdoʊ/ *noun, pl* **-dos** *or* **-does** [*count*] *old-fashioned* : a violent criminal who is not afraid of getting hurt or caught • the notorious *desperados* of the Wild West

des•per•ate /ˈdɛsprət/ *adj [more ~; most ~]*
1 : very sad and upset because of having little or no hope : feeling or showing despair • The collapse of her business had made her *desperate*. • As the supply of food ran out, people became *desperate*. • We could hear their *desperate* cries for help. • a *desperate* phone call
2 : very bad or difficult to deal with • The building is in *desperate* [=*terrible, awful*] shape and may have to be demolished. • *desperate* [=*hopeless*] situations • The outlook was *desperate*.
3 : done with all of your strength or energy and with little hope of succeeding • a *desperate* struggle to defeat the enemy • He made a *desperate* bid/attempt to save his job. • They made one last *desperate* attempt to fight their way out.
4 : having a strong need or desire *for* something or *to do* something • He is *desperate for* money/attention/work. • After traveling all night, they were *desperate for* sleep. • She was *desperate to prove* that she was right.
5 : very severe or strong • The animals were in *desperate* need of food and water when they were found. • a *desperate* shortage of medical supplies • The situation called for *desperate* measures.
– des•per•ate•ly /ˈdɛsprətli/ *adv* • We are trying *desperately* to find a solution. • They *desperately* struggled to defeat the enemy. • They were *desperately* [=*extremely, terribly*] unhappy/poor. • *desperately* ill patients • We were *desperately* in need of food and water.

des•per•a•tion /ˌdɛspəˈreɪʃən/ *noun [noncount]* : a strong feeling of sadness, fear, and loss of hope • She felt overcome by *desperation*. • a life of *desperation* • the *desperation* of severe poverty • The robbery was an act of *desperation*. [=a desperate act] • They hired me ***out of desperation***, because they couldn't get anyone else. • Finally, ***in desperation***, he tried to flee the country.

de•spi•ca•ble /dɪˈspɪkəbəl/ *adj [more ~; most ~] somewhat formal* : very bad or unpleasant : deserving to be despised • She is a *despicable* traitor. • It was a *despicable* [=*contemptible*] act of racism.
– de•spi•ca•bly /dɪˈspɪkəbli/ *adv* • He behaved *despicably*.

de•spise /dɪˈspaɪz/ *verb* **-spis•es; -spised; -spis•ing** [+ *obj*] : to dislike (something or someone) very much • He *despises* [=*hates, loathes*] pop music. • Although *despised* [=*scorned, disdained*] by critics, the movie attracted a wide audience. • She was *despised* as a hypocrite.

de•spite /dɪˈspaɪt/ *prep* : without being prevented by (something) — used to say that something happens or is true even though there is something that might prevent it from happening or being true • *Despite* [=*in spite of*] our objections, he insisted on driving. • She ran the race *despite* an injury. • *Despite* our best efforts to save him, the patient died during the night. • They are not getting married, *despite* rumors to the contrary. [=even though there have been rumors saying they are getting married] • *Despite* its small size, the device is able to store thousands of hours of music. • The law has yet to be passed, ***despite the fact that*** most people are in favor of it.
despite yourself : even though you do not want to • She stared at the couple *despite herself*. • *Despite myself*, I began to enjoy the movie. • They grew to love each other, almost *despite themselves*.

de•spoil /dɪˈspojəl/ *verb* **-spoils; -spoiled; -spoil•ing** [+ *obj*] *literary*
1 : to severely damage or ruin (a place) • The landscape has been *despoiled* by industrial development.
2 : to forcefully take what is valuable from (a place) • The invaders *despoiled* [=*plundered*] the village.
– de•spoil•er *noun, pl* **-ers** [*count*] • He sees human beings as *despoilers* of nature.

de•spond•ent /dɪˈspɑːndənt/ *adj [more ~; most ~] formal* : very sad and without hope • I had never seen them looking so *despondent*. • a group of *despondent* fans — often + *over* or *about* • She is *despondent over* losing her job. • He grew increasingly *despondent about* her illness.
– de•spond•en•cy /dɪˈspɑːndənsi/ *also* **de•spon•dence** /dɪˈspɑːndəns/ *noun [noncount]* • He went through a period of deep *despondency* after his divorce.

des•pot /ˈdɛspət/ *noun, pl* **-pots** [*count*]
1 : a ruler who has total power and who often uses that power in cruel and unfair ways • medieval *despots* [=*tyrants*]
2 *formal* : a person who has a lot of power over other people • He was a successful basketball coach, but many people regarded him as a petty *despot*. • The company is run by a benevolent *despot*.
– des•pot•ic /dɛˈspɑːtɪk/ *adj [more ~; most ~]* • a *despotic* government

des•po•tism /ˈdɛspəˌtɪzəm/ *noun [noncount]* : rule by a despot • The people have had to endure many years of *despotism*. [=(more commonly) *tyranny*]

des•sert /dɪˈzɚt/ *noun, pl* **-serts** : sweet food eaten after the main part of a meal [*count*] She doesn't care for rich *desserts*. • a chocolate *dessert* [*noncount*] Coffee and tea will be served with *dessert*. • We had ice cream and apple pie ***for dessert***. — sometimes used before another noun • They asked to look at the *dessert* menu. • *dessert* plates

Do not confuse *dessert* with *desert*.

des•sert•spoon /dɪˈzɚtˌspuːn/ *noun, pl* **-spoons** [*count*] *Brit*
1 : a spoon of medium size that is used to eat desserts and other foods
2 : the amount that a dessertspoon will hold • a *dessertspoon* of sugar

des•sert•spoon•ful /dɪˈzɚtˌspuːnˌfʊl/ *noun, pl* **-fuls** [*count*] *Brit* : DESSERTSPOON 2

dessert wine *noun, pl* **~ wines** [*count, noncount*] : a sweet wine that people drink with dessert or after dessert

de•sta•bi•lize *also Brit* **de•sta•bi•lise** /diˈsteɪbəˌlaɪz/ *verb* **-liz•es; -lized; -liz•ing** [+ *obj*] : to cause (something, such

D

as a government) to be unable to continue existing or working in the usual or desired way : to make (something) unstable • The group hoped the assassination of the new President would *destabilize* the government. • Economists warn that the crisis could *destabilize* the nation's currency.
– de·sta·bi·li·za·tion *also Brit* **de·sta·bi·li·sa·tion** /dɪˌsteɪbələˈzeɪʃən, *Brit* dɪˌsteɪbəˌlaɪˈzeɪʃən/ *noun* [*noncount*] **– destabilizing** *also Brit* **destabilising** *adj* • a *destabilizing* influence/force/factor

des·ti·na·tion /ˌdɛstəˈneɪʃən/ *noun, pl* **-tions** [*count*] : a place to which a person is going or something is being sent • After stopping for lunch, we continued on toward/to our *destination*. • The package reached its *destination* two days later. • He enjoys traveling to remote and exotic *destinations*. • a popular tourist *destination* • We traveled through three states before reaching our final *destination*. • a *destination* restaurant/resort [=a restaurant/resort that people are willing to travel a long distance to go to]

des·tined /ˈdɛstənd/ *adj, not used before a noun*
1 a : certain *to do* or *to be* something • Without the support of the unions, the plan seems *destined to fail*. • He is *destined to be* famous. • She felt that she was *destined* [=*fated, meant*] *to become* a writer. **b :** certain to achieve or experience something : certain to have a particular job, status, etc. — *+ for* • a nation *destined for* greatness • They believed that their son was *destined for* the priesthood. • a technology that is *destined for* a short life
2 : going or traveling to a particular place — *+ for* • The ship was *destined* [=*headed, heading, bound*] *for* New York. • The shipment is *destined for* Bombay.

des·ti·ny /ˈdɛstəni/ *noun, pl* **-nies**
1 [*count*] : what happens in the future : the things that someone or something will experience in the future • They believed it was their *destiny* to be together. • His parents believed that the priesthood was his *destiny*. [=that he would or should become a priest because fate or God intended it] • The factory's closing shaped the *destiny* [=*fate*] of the entire town. • She believes that people can choose/control their own *destinies*. [=that people can control what will happen to them]
2 [*noncount*] : a power that is believed to control what happens in the future • She felt that *destiny* [=*fate*] had decided that she would one day be President. • motivated by a sense of *destiny* — see also MANIFEST DESTINY

> ***synonyms*** DESTINY, FATE, and LOT mean a future that someone or something will have. DESTINY and FATE both suggest that the future has been decided or planned by God or by some godlike power. DESTINY often suggests a future that includes something great and important. • He was a great leader whose *destiny* was to free the people of his country. FATE often suggests a future that cannot be avoided and that is usually sad or unpleasant. • It was the explorer's *fate* to die lost and alone. LOT suggests that someone's future has been decided by luck. • It was not their *lot* in life to have children.

des·ti·tute /ˈdɛstəˌtuːt, *Brit* ˈdɛstəˌtjuːt/ *adj* [*more ~; most ~*]
1 : extremely poor • His business failures left him *destitute*.
2 *formal + literary* **:** without something that is needed or wanted — *+ of* • a lake *destitute of* fish • a man *destitute of* wisdom
the destitute : people who are extremely poor : destitute people • The charity provides food and clothing for *the destitute*. [=*the needy*]
– des·ti·tu·tion /ˌdɛstəˈtuːʃən, *Brit* ˌdɛstəˈtjuːʃən/ *noun* [*noncount*] • lives of *destitution* [=*poverty*]

de–stress /ˈdiːˈstrɛs/ *verb* **-stress·es; -stressed; -stress·ing** [*no obj*] : to relax your body or mind : to stop feeling the effects of stress • Taking a hot bath is a good way to *de-stress* [=*unwind*] after a busy day.

de·stroy /dɪˈstrɔɪ/ *verb* **-stroys; -stroyed; -stroy·ing** [*+ obj*]
1 : to cause (something) to end or no longer exist : to cause the destruction of (something) • Eventually our problems with money *destroyed* our marriage. • All the files were deliberately *destroyed*. • The disease *destroys* the body's ability to fight off illness. : to damage (something) so badly that it cannot be repaired • The bomb blast *destroyed* the village. • The scandal *destroyed* [=*ruined*] his reputation. • The building was partially *destroyed* [=*demolished*] by fire.
2 : to kill (an animal) especially because it is sick, injured, or dangerous • The dog had to be *destroyed* since its owner could not prevent it from attacking people.
3 *informal* **:** to defeat (someone or something) easily or completely • They *destroyed* [=*demolished*] the other team 51–7.

de·stroy·er /dɪˈstrɔjɚ/ *noun, pl* **-ers** [*count*]
1 : a small and fast military ship that protects bigger ships
2 : something that causes the destruction of something • The pamphlet describes alcohol as a *destroyer* of families.

de·struc·tion /dɪˈstrʌkʃən/ *noun* [*noncount*] **:** the act or process of damaging something so badly that it no longer exists or cannot be repaired : the act or process of destroying something • a scene of *destruction* • War results in death and widespread *destruction*. • We are trying to save the building from *destruction*. • ***weapons of mass destruction*** [=weapons that can destroy entire buildings, cities, etc.] • His phenomenal success carried within it the ***seeds of its own destruction***. [=the thing that made him successful eventually caused him to fail] — often *+ of* • the *destruction of* documents/evidence • The storm caused the *destruction of* many homes. — see also SELF-DESTRUCTION

de·struc·tive /dɪˈstrʌktɪv/ *adj* [*more ~; most ~*] **:** causing a very large amount of damage : causing destruction or harm • It was one of the most *destructive* storms in recent memory. • She argued that the law was *destructive* of personal liberties. • The school is concerned about the *destructive* behavior of a few students. • These kinds of budget cuts can be *destructive* to morale. [=can damage morale] • *destructive* criticism [=harsh criticism that hurts someone] — compare CONSTRUCTIVE; see also SELF-DESTRUCTIVE
– de·struc·tive·ly *adv* • The dog behaves *destructively*. **– de·struc·tive·ness** *noun* [*noncount*] • the *destructiveness* of the storm

des·ul·to·ry /ˈdɛsəlˌtori, *Brit* ˈdɛsəltri/ *adj* [*more ~; most ~*] *formal*
1 : not having a plan or purpose • *desultory* [=*aimless*] conversation.
2 : done without serious effort • He made a *desultory* [=*half-hearted*] attempt to study.
– des·ul·to·ri·ly /ˌdɛsəlˈtorəli, *Brit* ˈdɛsəltrəli/ *adv* • Talk drifted *desultorily* from one topic to another.

de·tach /dɪˈtætʃ/ *verb* **-tach·es; -tached; -tach·ing**
1 : to separate (something) from something larger [*+ obj*] *Detach* the upper part of the form and return it with your payment. • During the accident the trailer was *detached* from the car. [*no obj*] The brush *detaches* from the vacuum cleaner for easy cleaning. — opposite ATTACH
2 [*+ obj*] : to separate (yourself) *from* someone or something • It can be difficult to *detach* yourself *from* the chaos of the situation. • She has been trying to *detach* herself *from* an abusive relationship.
– de·tach·able /dɪˈtætʃəbəl/ *adj* • The stereo is equipped with *detachable* speakers.

detached *adj*
1 [*more ~; most ~*] **:** not emotional : not influenced by emotions or personal interest • They wanted the opinion of a *detached* [=*impartial, unbiased*] observer. • The article takes a *detached* [=*objective*] view of the issue. • He watched them work with a *detached* [=*indifferent*] amusement.
2 : not joined or connected : separate from another part or thing • The house has a *detached* garage. • a *detached* house [=a house that is not connected to any other house or building] — see also SEMIDETACHED

de·tach·ment /dɪˈtætʃmənt/ *noun, pl* **-ments**
1 [*noncount*] : lack of emotion or of personal interest • I wish the article had approached the issue with a bit more *detachment*. • In her films she views the modern world with an air/sense of *detachment*. [=*aloofness*] • He was able to discuss their concerns with cool *detachment*. [=*impartiality*]
2 [*noncount*] **a :** the act or process of separating something from a larger thing • The form is perforated to make *detachment* of the bottom section easier. **b :** a condition in which something has become separated from something else • a patient diagnosed with ***retinal detachment*** [=a condition in which the retina of the eye is no longer connected to the eye as it should be]
3 [*count*] : a group of soldiers who have a special job or function • A *detachment* of soldiers was called to assist the police. • helicopter *detachments* [=groups of soldiers traveling in helicopters]

[1]**de·tail** /dɪˈteɪl, ˈdiːˌteɪl/ *noun, pl* **-tails**
1 [*count*] **a :** a small part of something • Every/each *detail* of the wedding was carefully planned. • They designed every *detail* of the house. • He planned the party ***down to the small-***

est/last/tiniest detail. [=he planned everything about the party] • Don't ***sweat the details.*** [=don't worry about minor things] **b** [*noncount*] : the small parts of something • the wooden box's fine carved *detail* • We admired the *detail* of the artist's work. • Use a small paintbrush for the ***detail work.*** [=decorative work or work done using small pieces] • The job requires ***attention to detail.*** ♦ If you have ***an eye for detail*** or ***a fine/good/keen eye for detail,*** you are good at noticing small but important things that other people might not notice. • It is helpful to have *a good eye for detail* when you are building a house. • a filmmaker with *an eye for detail*
2 a [*count*] : a particular fact or piece of information about something or someone • The article provides further *details.* • You left out an important *detail* about their new baby: is it a girl or boy? • The novel is full of historical *details.* **b** [*noncount*] : information about something or someone that is often specific or precise • The book includes a wealth of *detail* on living conditions aboard ships at that time. • The novel is full of historical *detail.* • The book covers the topic of grammar at a ***level of detail*** that most people would find boring.
3 [*count*] : a special job that is given to a soldier or group of soldiers — usually singular • They were assigned to security/maintenance/kitchen *detail.*
go into detail : to discuss or describe everything about something including the small or unimportant parts • The newspaper reports *went into (great) detail* about his political background. • I will try to tell the story without *going into* too much *detail.*
in detail : including a lot of information about something : without leaving out any important parts • She explained *in detail* how they met. • We will discuss/examine/explore the plan *in detail.* • Please describe the scene *in* as much *detail* as you can. [=in a way that includes as much information as possible] • We will talk about this issue *in* more/further/greater *detail* tomorrow.

²detail *verb* **-tails; -tailed; -tail·ing** [+ *obj*]
1 : to state particular facts or information about (something) : to describe or discuss the details of (something) • The book *details* the series of events that led to the tragedy. • She wrote a letter *detailing* her complaints.
2 *US* : to thoroughly clean (a car) in an attempt to make it look new • I am going to have the car *detailed* [=(*Brit*) *valeted*] before I try to sell it.
3 *formal* : to choose (a person or group of people) to do a special job • The Army has *detailed* him to investigate the complaints. — often used as *(be) detailed* • The infantry officer *was detailed* to another unit during maneuvers.

detailed *adj* [*more* ~; *most* ~] : including many details : including a lot information • a *detailed* report/analysis • We need a more *detailed* comparison of the available options. • a *detailed* account/description • He gave us very *detailed* instructions. • *detailed* maps/pictures

detailing *noun* [*noncount*]
1 : small decorative parts : details added to a building, piece of clothing, etc. • the building's fine architectural *detailing* • a bowl with gold *detailing*
2 *US* : the act or process of thoroughly cleaning a car in an attempt to make it look new — called also (*Brit*) *valeting*

de·tain /dɪˈteɪn/ *verb* **-tains; -tained; -tain·ing** [+ *obj*]
1 : to officially prevent (someone) from leaving a place : to hold or keep (someone) in a prison or some other place • They were *detained* by the police for questioning. • He claimed he had been illegally *detained.*
2 *formal* : to keep or prevent (someone) from leaving or arriving at the expected time • We were *detained* [=*delayed*] for 15 minutes by a flat tire. • Unexpected business had *detained* her.
– de·tain·ment /dɪˈteɪnmənt/ *noun, pl* **-ments** [*noncount*] He demanded to be released after two hours of *detainment.* [*count*] He ordered the *detainments* of two suspects.

de·tain·ee /dɪˌteɪˈniː/ *noun, pl* **-ees** [*count*] : a person who is being kept in a prison especially for political reasons : a person who is being detained

de·tect /dɪˈtɛkt/ *verb* **-tects; -tect·ed; -tect·ing** [+ *obj*] : to discover or notice the presence of (something that is hidden or hard to see, hear, taste, etc.) • The test is used to *detect* the presence of alcohol in the blood. • This type of cancer is difficult to *detect* in its early stages. • He thought he *detected* [=*sensed*] a note of irony in her comments.
– de·tect·able /dɪˈtɛktəbəl/ *adj* • a dim star that is only *detectable* with a powerful telescope • sounds barely *detectable* by the human ear

de·tec·tion /dɪˈtɛkʃən/ *noun* [*noncount*] : the act or process of discovering, finding, or noticing something • I don't know how the errors managed to avoid/escape *detection* for so long. • methods of crime *detection* — sometimes used before another noun • a *detection* system/device

¹de·tec·tive /dɪˈtɛktɪv/ *noun, pl* **-tives** [*count*]
1 : a police officer whose job is to find information about crimes that have occurred and to catch criminals • She is a *detective* on the police force. • *Detective* Sgt. Lee is working on the case. • a homicide *detective*
2 : a person whose job is to find information about something or someone : PRIVATE INVESTIGATOR • She hired a *detective* to follow her husband.

²detective *adj, always used before a noun*
1 : done in order to find out hidden or unknown information • We had to do some *detective* work to find out who used to own the property.
2 : of or relating to crimes and detectives • a *detective* story • He enjoys reading *detective* novels.

de·tec·tor /dɪˈtɛktɚ/ *noun, pl* **-tors** [*count*] : a device that can tell if a substance or object is present : a device that detects the presence of something • a smoke/radar *detector* • using metal *detectors* to improve safety at airports — see also LIE DETECTOR

dé·tente *or* **de·tente** /deɪˈtɑːnt/ *noun, formal* : an ending of unfriendly or hostile relations between countries [*noncount*] as the countries move toward *détente* • a period of *détente* [*count*] the start of a *détente*

de·ten·tion /dɪˈtɛnʃən/ *noun, pl* **-tions**
1 a : the act of keeping someone in a prison or similar place [*noncount*] the *detention* of suspected terrorists • *detention* camps/facilities [*count*] The jail is only used for brief *detentions.* **b** [*noncount*] : the state of being kept in a prison or similar place • Dozens of protesters were held/kept ***in detention*** for six hours. [=were detained for six hours]
2 : a punishment in which a student is required to stay at school after the rest of the students have left [*count*] They both got/received three *detentions* this year. [*noncount*] He got *detention* for being late to class.

detention center (*US*) *or Brit* **detention centre** *noun, pl* **~ -ters** [*count*]
1 : a place where people who have entered a country illegally are kept for a period of time
2 : a place where people who have committed crimes are kept as punishment • She spent several months in a *detention center* for women. • a juvenile *detention center*

de·ter /dɪˈtɚ/ *verb* **-ters; -terred; -ter·ring** [+ *obj*]
1 : to cause (someone) to decide not to do something • Some potential buyers will be *deterred* by the price. — often + *from* • They hoped that the new law would *deter* advertisers *from* making false claims. • The heavy fines should *deter* [=*discourage*] people *from* dumping garbage here.
2 : to prevent (something) from happening • He played an important role in international efforts to *deter* [=*prevent*] nuclear war. • Painting the metal will *deter* rust.

de·ter·gent /dɪˈtɚʤənt/ *noun, pl* **-gents** : a powder or liquid that is used to clean clothes, dishes, etc. : a chemical substance that is like soap [*count*] We have tried different laundry *detergents.* [*noncount*] a box of *detergent* — see picture at KITCHEN

de·te·ri·o·rate /dɪˈtirijəˌreɪt/ *verb* **-rates; -rat·ed; -rat·ing**
1 [*no obj*] : to become worse as time passes • The weather gradually *deteriorated* [=*worsened*] as the day went on. • Her health continues to *deteriorate.* [=*decline*] • efforts to save a *deteriorating* rain forest • The disagreement ***deteriorated into*** a fight. [=the disagreement got worse and eventually became a fight]
2 [+ *obj*] : to make (something) worse • Exposure to rain and sun will gradually *deteriorate* the paint.
– deteriorated *adj* • a *deteriorated* [=*run-down, dilapidated*] building • a badly *deteriorated* part of the city

de·te·ri·o·ra·tion /dɪˌtirijəˈreɪʃən/ *noun* [*singular*] : the act or process of becoming worse • economic *deterioration* • the gradual *deterioration* of the weather • a *deterioration* of academic standards • a *deterioration* in quality

de·ter·min·able /dɪˈtɚmənəbəl/ *adj, formal* : possible to know or calculate : able to be determined • a *determinable* amount/value • The cause of the accident is not *determinable* at this time.

de·ter·mi·nant /dɪˈtɚmənənt/ *noun, pl* **-nants** [*count*] *formal* : a thing that controls or influences what happens — often + *of* ▪ Level of education is often a *determinant of* income.

de·ter·mi·nate /dɪˈtɚmənət/ *adj, formal* : definitely known or decided ▪ a *determinate* period of time — opposite INDETERMINATE

de·ter·mi·na·tion /dɪˌtɚməˈneɪʃən/ *noun, pl* **-tions**

1 [*noncount*] : a quality that makes you continue trying to do or achieve something that is difficult ▪ What he lacked in talent he made up for in *determination.* ▪ dogged/fierce/steely/stubborn *determination* — often followed by *to + verb* ▪ We all respected her fierce *determination to succeed.* — see also SELF-DETERMINATION

2 *formal* : the act of finding out or calculating something [*count*] age *determinations* — often + *of* ▪ They were unable to make an accurate *determination of* the ship's position. [*noncount*] The new instruments allow for more precise *determination of* the size of the tumor.

3 *formal* : the act of officially deciding something [*noncount*] The document will be used for *determination* of ownership. [*count*] judicial *determinations* ▪ The inspectors made the *determination* that the building was unsafe. [=they determined/decided that the building was unsafe]

de·ter·mine /dɪˈtɚmən/ *verb* **-mines; -mined; -min·ing** [+ *obj*]

1 a : to officially decide (something) especially because of evidence or facts : to establish (something) exactly or with authority ▪ The town has finally *determined* ownership of the land. = The town has finally *determined* who owns the land. ▪ The new policy will be *determined* by a special committee. **b** : to be the cause of or reason for (something) ▪ The demand for a product *determines* its price. ▪ He believes that one's personality is *determined* mostly by genetics. ✧ A ***determining factor*** is a reason to make a particular choice or decision. ▪ Price was the *determining factor* in their decision.

2 : to learn or find out (something) by getting information ▪ An autopsy will be performed to *determine* the cause of death. ▪ They are unable to accurately *determine* the ship's position at this time. ▪ Scholars have *determined* that the book was written in the late 16th century. ▪ I am trying to *determine* what happened and when.

3 *formal* : to make a decision : DECIDE ▪ They are *determining* if/whether they should stay. ▪ They *determined* to leave immediately. ▪ He *determined* [=*resolved*] that he would learn a foreign language.

determined *adj* [*more* ~; *most* ~]

1 *not used before a noun* : having a strong feeling that you are going to do something and that you will not allow anyone or anything to stop you — often followed by *to + verb* ▪ They are *determined to find out* the cause of the accident. ▪ Her early failures made her even more *determined to succeed.* ▪ We are *determined* not *to let* it happen again. ▪ We were ***bound and determined*** [=very determined] *to finish* the project on time. — often + *that* ▪ We are *determined that* it will never happen again.

2 : not weak or uncertain : having or showing determination to do something ▪ He is a very *determined* [=*resolute*] opponent. ▪ We are making a *determined* effort to correct our mistakes. ▪ a *determined* smile

– **de·ter·mined·ly** *adv* ▪ They fought *determinedly* for a new trial. ▪ She is a *determinedly* cheerful hostess.

de·ter·mi·ner /dɪˈtɚmənɚ/ *noun, pl* **-ers** [*count*] *grammar* : a word (such as "a," "the," "some," "any," "my," or "your") that comes before a noun and is used to show which thing is being referred to

de·ter·min·ism /dɪˈtɚməˌnɪzəm/ *noun* [*noncount*] *philosophy* : the belief that all events are caused by things that happened before them and that people have no real ability to make choices or control what happens

– **de·ter·min·ist** /dɪˈtɚmənəst/ *noun, pl* **-ists** [*count*] – **de·ter·min·is·tic** /dɪˌtʰɚməˈnɪstɪk/ *or* **determinist** *adj* ▪ a *deterministic* view of life ▪ *determinist* philosophers

de·ter·rence /dɪˈtɚrəns/ *noun* [*noncount*] *formal*

1 : the act of making someone decide not to do something : the act of preventing a particular act or behavior from happening ▪ the *deterrence* of crime

2 *politics* : the policy of developing a lot of military power so that other countries will not attack your country ▪ The author argues that *deterrence* is no longer the best way to prevent war. ▪ nuclear *deterrence*

de·ter·rent /dɪˈtɚrənt/ *noun, pl* **-rents** [*count*] : something that makes someone decide not to do something ▪ We would like to go, but cost is a major *deterrent.* ▪ The security alarm is a theft *deterrent.* ▪ a crime *deterrent* — often + *to* or *against* ▪ They argued over whether the death penalty is an effective *deterrent to* murder. ▪ They hope that the new law will be a *deterrent against* false advertising.

– **deterrent** /dɪˈtɚrənt/ *adj* [*more* ~; *most* ~] ▪ They hope that the new law will have a *deterrent* effect.

de·test /dɪˈtɛst/ *verb* **-tests; -test·ed; -test·ing** [+ *obj*] *formal* : to dislike (someone or something) very strongly ▪ Those two really seem to *detest* [=*hate, despise*] each other. ▪ She *detested* [=*loathed*] living in the city.

de·test·able /dɪˈtɛstəbəl/ *adj* [*more* ~; *most* ~] *formal* : causing or deserving strong dislike : deserving to be detested ▪ He found her selfish attitude *detestable.* [=*contemptible, despicable*] ▪ He is a *detestable* villain.

– **de·test·ably** /dɪˈtɛstəbli/ *adv* ▪ a *detestably* cruel act

de·throne /dɪˈθroʊn/ *verb* **-thrones; -throned; -thron·ing** [+ *obj*] : to take away the power and authority of (a king or queen) : to remove (a king or queen) from power — now usually used figuratively ▪ Last year's champion was *dethroned* in the first round of the play-offs.

– **de·throne·ment** /dɪˈθroʊnmənt/ *noun* [*noncount*] ▪ the *dethronement* of the queen/champion

det·o·nate /ˈdɛtn̩ˌeɪt/ *verb* **-nates; -nat·ed; -nat·ing** : to explode or to cause (something, such as a bomb) to explode [*no obj*] They knew that the bomb could *detonate* [=*blow up*] at any time. [+ *obj*] The first atomic bomb was *detonated* in 1945.

– **det·o·na·tion** /ˌdɛtn̩ˈeɪʃən/ *noun, pl* **-tions** [*count, noncount*]

det·o·na·tor /ˈdɛtn̩ˌeɪtɚ/ *noun, pl* **-tors** [*count*] : a device that is used to make a bomb explode

¹de·tour /ˈdiːˌtuɚ/ *noun, pl* **-tours** [*count*]

1 : the act of going or traveling to a place along a way that is different from the usual or planned way ▪ After a number of unexpected *detours,* we finally arrived at our destination. ▪ The little restaurant is worth a *detour.* ▪ We had to ***make a detour*** around the heaviest traffic. ▪ We ***took a detour*** from the main streets. — often used figuratively ▪ After teaching for many years, he *made a brief detour* into professional cooking. [=he worked as a cook for a short period of time] ▪ The conversation *took a detour* onto another topic.

2 *US* : a road, highway, etc., that you travel on when the the usual way of traveling cannot be used ▪ The road is closed ahead, so traffic will have to follow the *detour.* ▪ a *detour* sign/route — called also (*Brit*) *diversion*

²detour *verb* **-tours; -toured; -tour·ing** *US*

1 *always followed by an adverb or preposition* [*no obj*] : to go along a way that is different from and usually longer than the usual or planned way ▪ We *detoured around* the heaviest traffic. — often used figuratively ▪ After teaching for many years, he briefly *detoured into* professional cooking.

2 [+ *obj*] **a** : to make (someone or something) go in a direction that is not planned or expected ▪ A police officer was *detouring* traffic around the scene of the accident. ▪ Traffic will be *detoured* to 72nd Street. — often used figuratively ▪ Her athletic career was *detoured* by a series of injuries. **b** : to avoid (something) by going around it ▪ Commuters are being advised to *detour* [=*bypass*] this section of the road. — often used figuratively ▪ You can *detour* the whole process by applying online.

de·tox /ˈdiːˌtɑːks/ *noun, pl* **-tox·es** *informal* : special treatment that helps a person to stop using drugs or alcohol [*noncount*] He spent one week in *detox.* ▪ The famous writer recently went into *detox.* [*count*] She has been through two *detoxes* in the past year. — often used before another noun ▪ a *detox* center/clinic/program

de·tox·i·fy /diˈtɑːksəˌfaɪ/ *verb* **-fies; -fied; -fy·ing** [+ *obj*]

1 : to remove a poisonous or harmful substance from (something) ▪ a special tea that is supposed to *detoxify* the body

2 : to cause (someone) to stop using drugs or alcohol by providing special help and treatment ▪ a drug addict who is being *detoxified*

– **de·tox·i·fi·ca·tion** /diˌtɑːksəfəˈkeɪʃən/ *noun* [*noncount*] ▪ the *detoxification* of drug addicts — often used before another noun ▪ a *detoxification* [=*detox*] process/program

de·tract /dɪˈtrækt/ *verb* **-tracts; -tract·ed; -tract·ing**

detract from [*phrasal verb*] ***detract from (something)*** *formal* : to reduce the strength, value, or importance of (something) ▪ They worried that the scandal would seriously *detract from* [=*diminish, hurt*] her chances for reelection. ▪ The overcooked vegetables *detracted* somewhat *from* an otherwise fine meal.

de·trac·tor /dɪˈtræktɚ/ *noun, pl* **-tors** [*count*] *formal* : a person who criticizes something or someone ▪ Despite his popularity, his many *detractors* [=*critics*] still think his work is overrated. ▪ Even her *detractors* had to admit that she had made the company successful.

de·train /diˈtreɪn/ *verb* **-trains; -trained; -train·ing** [*no obj*] : to get off a train ▪ They were the first passengers to *detrain.*

det·ri·ment /ˈdɛtrəmənt/ *noun, formal*
1 [*count*] : something that will cause damage or injury to something or someone — usually singular; often + *to* ▪ He saw the new regulations as a *detriment to* progress.
2 [*noncount*] : the act of causing damage or injury to something or someone ▪ He puts all his time into his career, ***to the detriment of*** [=in a way that is harmful to] his personal life. ▪ relying on bad advice, much ***to your detriment*** [=in a way that is harmful to you] — often + *to* ▪ She was able to work long hours ***without detriment to*** her health. [=without harming her health]

det·ri·men·tal /ˌdɛtrəˈmɛntl/ *adj* [*more ~; most ~*] *formal* : causing damage or injury ▪ The *detrimental* [=*harmful*] effects of overeating are well known. — often + *to* ▪ She argues that watching too much TV is *detrimental to* a child's intellectual and social development.
– det·ri·men·tal·ly *adv*

de·tri·tus /dɪˈtraɪtəs/ *noun* [*noncount*] *formal* : the pieces that are left when something breaks, falls apart, is destroyed, etc. ▪ the *detritus* of ancient civilizations ▪ As he packed, he sifted through the *detritus of* a failed relationship.

deuce /ˈduːs, *Brit* ˈdjuːs/ *noun, pl* **deuc·es**
1 [*count*] *chiefly US, informal* : a playing card that has the number two on it or two symbols on it ▪ a pair of *deuces* [=*twos*]
2 *tennis* : a situation in which each side has a score of 40 [*count*] She beat her opponent after eight *deuces.* [*noncount*] The score is *deuce.*
3 [*singular*] *old-fashioned + informal* — used to make a question or statement more forceful ▪ Who the *deuce* [=*devil, hell*] was that? ▪ We've had ***a deuce of a*** time finding a good doctor. [=it has been very difficult to find a good doctor]

de·us ex ma·chi·na /ˈdejəsˌɛksˈmɑːkɪnə/ *noun* [*singular*] : a character or thing that suddenly enters the story in a novel, play, movie, etc., and solves a problem that had previously seemed impossible to solve

deutsche mark *or* **deutsch·mark** /ˈdɔɪtʃˌmɑɚk/ *noun, pl* **~ marks** [*count*] : a basic unit of money that was formerly used in Germany; *also* : a coin or bill representing one deutsche mark — called also *mark, German mark*

de·val·ue /diˈvælju/ *verb* **-ues; -ued; -u·ing**
1 *finance* : to lower the value of a country's money so that it is worth less when it is traded with another country's money [+ *obj*] The government has decided to *devalue* its currency. [*no obj*] Economic woes forced the government to *devalue.*
2 [+ *obj*] : to cause (something or someone) to seem or to be less valuable or important ▪ He argues that placing too many requirements on schools *devalues* the education they provide. ▪ Domestic work is often *devalued.* [=*undervalued*]
– de·val·u·a·tion /diˌvæljəˈweɪʃən/ *noun, pl* **-tions** [*noncount*] attempts to avoid *devaluation* [*count*] currency *devaluations*

dev·as·tate /ˈdɛvəˌsteɪt/ *verb* **-tates; -tat·ed; -tat·ing** [+ *obj*]
1 : to destroy much or most of (something) : to cause great damage or harm to (something) ▪ The flood *devastated* the town. ▪ The disease has *devastated* the area's oak tree population. ▪ The hurricane left the island completely *devastated.* ▪ The town was *devastated* [=*ruined*] when the factory closed.
2 : to cause (someone) to feel extreme emotional pain — usually used as *(be) devastated* ▪ She was *devastated* by the breakup of her marriage.
– dev·as·ta·tion /ˌdɛvəˈsteɪʃən/ *noun* [*noncount*] ▪ economic *devastation* ▪ the *devastation* of war [=the damage and destruction caused by war]

devastating *adj* [*more ~; most ~*]
1 : causing great damage or harm ▪ It was a *devastating* flood. ▪ a rare but *devastating* disease ▪ *devastating* consequences — often + *to* ▪ The fall in prices dealt a *devastating* blow *to* the company.
2 : causing extreme emotional pain ▪ The news was *devastating.* ▪ They suffered a *devastating* loss.
3 : extremely effective or powerful ▪ The movie is a *devastating* satire of the current political scene. ▪ a writer known for his *devastating* wit
– dev·as·tat·ing·ly *adv* ▪ a *devastatingly* accurate portrayal

de·vel·op /dɪˈvɛləp/ *verb* **-ops; -oped; -op·ing**
1 a [+ *obj*] : to cause (something) to grow or become bigger or more advanced ▪ She has been exercising regularly to *develop* her back muscles. ▪ The story was later *developed* into a novel. ▪ The island has *developed* its economy around tourism. ▪ The course is designed to *develop* your writing skills. **b** [*no obj*] : to grow or become bigger or more advanced ▪ A blossom *develops* from a bud. ▪ The doctor says that the child is *developing* normally. ▪ In this class, we will be learning about how languages *develop.* — often + *into* ▪ In a short time, the town *developed into* a city.
2 [+ *obj*] : to create (something) over a period of time ▪ Scientists are *developing* a treatment for the disease. ▪ The company has *developed* a new method for recycling old tires.
3 [+ *obj*] : to make (an idea, argument, theory, etc.) easier to understand by giving more information ▪ He *develops* the concept/theory more fully in his book. ▪ You need to *develop* your argument more.
4 [*no obj*] : to gradually begin to exist ▪ A dangerous situation is *developing.* ▪ Romantic relationships often *develop* between coworkers. ▪ Towns *developed* along this trade route hundreds of years ago.
5 [+ *obj*] : to gradually begin to have (something) ▪ As he grew older he *developed* [=*acquired*] a taste for expensive wines. ▪ She *developed* an interest in music when she was just a child. ▪ He *developed* a close relationship with her.
6 [+ *obj*] : to begin to suffer from or be affected by (an illness, problem, etc.) ▪ people who *develop* cancer late in life ▪ The patient later *developed* a cough. ▪ At some point the pipe *developed* a leak.
7 [*no obj*] *chiefly US* : to become known or understood ▪ The facts of what had happened slowly *developed* over the next several days. ▪ It eventually *developed* [=*turned out*] that he had forgotten to mail the package.
8 [+ *obj*] **a** : to build houses or other buildings on (land) ▪ A builder wants to *develop* a large piece of land along the river. **b** : to make (something) available for use ▪ The government plans to *develop* the natural resources of this region.
9 [+ *obj*] : to make a photograph from (film) by using special chemicals and a special process ▪ Our vacation pictures should be *developed* by tomorrow. ▪ Did you get the film *developed* yet?
– de·vel·op·able /dɪˈvɛləpəbəl/ *adj* ▪ *developable* land

developed *adj* [*more ~; most ~*]
1 *of a country, society, etc.* : having many industries and relatively few poor people who are unable to buy the things they need ▪ The disease is almost unheard of in *developed* countries. — opposite DEVELOPING, UNDERDEVELOPED
2 : larger or more advanced ▪ Many dogs have a highly *developed* sense of smell. [=a very strong sense of smell] ▪ The younger plant has a less *developed* root system.

de·vel·op·er /dɪˈvɛləpɚ/ *noun, pl* **-ers** : a person or thing that develops something: such as **a** [*count*] : a person or company that builds and sells houses or other buildings on a piece of land ▪ a real estate *developer* **b** [*count*] : a person or company that creates computer software ▪ a software *developer* **c** [*noncount*] : a chemical that is used to develop photographs

developing *adj, always used before a noun*
1 : having few industries and many poor people who are unable to buy the things they need ▪ international programs to assist *developing* [=*underdeveloped*] nations — opposite DEVELOPED
2 : growing larger or more advanced ▪ a *developing* embryo ▪ the *developing* crisis

de·vel·op·ment /dɪˈvɛləpmənt/ *noun, pl* **-ments**
1 [*noncount*] : the act or process of growing or causing something to grow or become larger or more advanced ▪ Good nutrition is important for proper muscle *development.* ▪ efforts to promote economic *development* [=*growth*] ▪ experts in child *development* ▪ The company offers many opportunities for professional/personal/career *development.* — often + *of* ▪ the *development of* the English language ▪ The vitamin may help prevent the *development of* cancer.
2 [*noncount*] **a** : the act or process of creating something over a period of time ▪ The software is still in the early stages of *development.* — often + *of* ▪ The company is working on (the) *development of* a new method for recycling old tires. — see also RESEARCH AND DEVELOPMENT **b** : the state of

being created or made more advanced • The new system is still ***under development***. [=being developed] • She has a number of projects ***in development***. [=(*informal*) *in the works*]

3 [*count*] **:** something that has happened or has become known • I try to keep up with the latest *developments* in computer technology. • Have there been any new *developments* in the case?

4 a [*count*] **:** an area of land with buildings that were all built at around the same time • a condominium *development* • new commercial and industrial *developments* — see also HOUSING DEVELOPMENT **b** [*noncount*] **:** the process of building a group of houses or other buildings on an area of land • A large piece of land along the river was sold for *development*.

5 [*noncount*] **:** the chemical process by which photographic film is used to make a photograph • chemicals used for the *development* of film

de·vel·op·men·tal /dɪˌvɛləpˈmɛntl̩/ *adj*

1 : of or relating to the growth or development of someone or something • A drop in temperature can slow the plant's *developmental* process. • *developmental* biology/psychology • a child with *developmental* abnormalities/defects/disabilities/problems • My theory is still in its *developmental* stage.

2 : designed to help a child grow or learn • *developmental* toys

– de·vel·op·men·tal·ly *adv* • a ***developmentally disabled*** child [=a child who is not able to develop in the normal way because of a physical or mental problem]

[1]de·vi·ant /ˈdiːvijənt/ *adj* [*more* ~; *most* ~] **:** different from what is considered to be normal or morally correct • a *deviant* lifestyle • a study of *deviant* behavior among criminals

– de·vi·ance /ˈdiːvijəns/ *also* **de·vi·an·cy** /ˈdiːvijənsi/ *noun* [*noncount*] • sexual *deviance/deviancy*

[2]deviant *noun, pl* **-ants** [*count*] **:** a person who behaves in a way that most people consider to be not normal or morally correct • a sexual *deviant*

de·vi·ate /ˈdiːviˌeɪt/ *verb* **-ates; -at·ed; -at·ing** [*no obj*] **:** to do something that is different or to be different from what is usual or expected — usually + *from* • He almost never *deviates from* his usual routine. • The investigation showed that the airplane had *deviated* [=*strayed*] *from* its scheduled route. • This pattern of behavior *deviates* slightly *from* the norm.

de·vi·a·tion /ˌdiːviˈeɪʃən/ *noun, pl* **-tions**

1 : an action, behavior, or condition that is different from what is usual or expected [*count*] There have been slight *deviations* in the satellite's orbit. • Having juice instead of coffee was a *deviation* from his usual routine. [*noncount*] The pattern's *deviation* from the norm is significant. • The book discusses sexual *deviation* [=*deviance*] in serial killers.

2 [*count*] *technical* **:** the difference between the average of a group of numbers and a particular number in that group

de·vice /dɪˈvaɪs/ *noun, pl* **-vic·es** [*count*]

1 : an object, machine, or piece of equipment that has been made for some special purpose • mechanical *devices* • The store sells TVs, VCRs, and other electronic *devices*. • a hidden recording *device*

2 : a weapon that explodes • an explosive *device* [=a bomb] • agreeing to dismantle all nuclear *devices*

3 : something that is done in order to achieve a particular effect • a marketing *device* • a useful mnemonic *device* for remembering the names of the planets • The company's method of tracking expenses is just a *device* to make it seem more profitable.

4 : something in a book, play, poem, movie, etc., that is used to achieve a particular effect • He is known for his use of irony and other literary *devices*. • a contrived plot *device* • the play's use of traditional comic *devices* such as slapstick

leave you to your own devices ◇ If someone ***leaves you to your own devices*** or you are ***left to your own devices***, you are allowed to do what you want or what you are able to do without being controlled or helped by anyone else. • The students were *left to their own devices* when the teacher failed to appear on time. • *Left to its own devices*, the school would accept only the most advanced students.

dev·il /ˈdɛvl̩/ *noun, pl* **-ils**

1 a ***the Devil*** **:** the most powerful spirit of evil in Christianity, Judaism, and Islam who is often represented as the ruler of hell • He went to the Halloween party dressed up as *the Devil*. [=*Satan*] **b** [*count*] **:** an evil spirit • an imaginary world haunted by ghosts and *devils* [=*demons*]

2 [*count*] *informal* **a :** a person who does bad things or causes trouble usually in a way that is not too serious • She is a tricky *devil*, so be careful. • Those kids can be little *devils* sometimes. **b :** a person (especially a man) who is lucky, unlucky, etc. • The ***poor devil*** [=*poor guy*] broke his leg on the first day of his skiing vacation. • He's such a ***lucky devil*** that he'll probably win the lottery someday.

3 ***the devil*** *informal* — used to make a statement or question more forceful • What *the devil* are you talking about? • Where *the devil* have you been?

4 [*singular*] *informal* **:** something that is very difficult or that causes a lot of trouble • The shoes look great, but they're ***the devil*** to walk in. [=they are very difficult to walk in] — usually used in the phrase ***a devil of*** • The new regulations have created *a devil of* a problem [=a very difficult problem] for many small businesses. • He had ***a devil of a time*** getting another job. [=he found it very difficult to get another job] — see also *the devil to pay* at [1]PAY

be a devil *Brit, informal* — used to tell someone who is not sure about doing something to go ahead and do it • "I don't know if I should eat anything else." "Oh, go on, *be a devil*, order dessert!"

better the devil you know than the devil you don't — used to say that it is better to deal with a difficult person or situation you know than with a new person or situation that could be worse

between the devil and the deep blue sea *old-fashioned* **:** in a situation that is difficult because you must choose between two unpleasant things • She felt caught *between the devil and the deep blue sea*. [=in a very bad situation]

go to the devil *informal* — used to forcefully and rudely tell someone to go away and leave you alone • She angrily told him to *go to the devil*. [=(more commonly) *go to hell*]

like the devil *informal* **1 :** very much • I'm sorry to hear about your injury. It must hurt *like the devil*. **2 :** with a lot of energy and speed • He ran *like the devil*. [=he ran very fast]

speak/talk of the devil *informal* — used in speech to say that someone you have been talking about has unexpectedly appeared • "Well, *speak of the devil*! We were just talking about you!"

dev·iled (*US*) *or Brit* **dev·illed** /ˈdɛvl̩d/ *adj, always used before a noun* **:** spicy or highly seasoned • *deviled* eggs/ham

dev·il·ish /ˈdɛvl̩ɪʃ/ *adj* [*more* ~; *most* ~]

1 : evil and cruel • a *devilish* [=*sinister*] villain • *devilish* [=*diabolical*] tricks

2 : showing a desire to cause trouble but in a way that is not serious • She was attracted by his *devilish* charm. • There was a *devilish* look of mischief in her eyes. • a *devilish* [=*mischievous*] grin

have a devilish time *informal + somewhat old-fashioned* **:** to have a difficult time doing something • We *had a devilish time* finding a parking space.

– dev·il·ish·ly /ˈdɛvl̩ɪʃli/ *adv* • a *devilishly* cruel villain • a *devilishly* attractive man • a *devilishly* [=very] hard/difficult problem

dev·il–may–care /ˌdɛvl̩ˌmeɪˈkeə/ *adj* [*more* ~; *most* ~] **:** relaxed and without worry • He has a *devil-may-care* attitude about life.

dev·il·ment /ˈdɛvl̩mənt/ *noun* [*noncount*] *chiefly Brit, formal* **:** behavior that causes trouble • engaging in all kinds of *devilment* [=*mischief*] **:** a desire to cause trouble • Ruffians were breaking windows out of sheer *devilment*.

devil's advocate *noun, pl* ~ **-cates** [*count*] **:** a person who expresses an opinion that disagrees with others so that there will be an interesting discussion about some issue • Teachers often ***play devil's advocate*** to provoke discussion in the classroom.

devil's food cake *noun, pl* ~ **cakes** [*count, noncount*] *US* **:** a sweet chocolate cake — compare ANGEL FOOD CAKE

de·vi·ous /ˈdiːvijəs/ *adj* [*more* ~; *most* ~]

1 : willing to lie and trick people in order to get what is wanted • a dishonest and *devious* politician • The company was accused of using *devious* [=*dishonest, deceptive*] methods/ways to get the contract.

2 *formal* **:** not straight or direct **:** having many twists and turns • He took us by a *devious* route to the center of the city.

– de·vi·ous·ly *adv* **– de·vi·ous·ness** *noun* [*noncount*]

de·vise /dɪˈvaɪz/ *verb* **-vis·es; -vised; -vis·ing** [+ *obj*] **:** to invent or plan (something that is difficult or complicated) • They have *devised* a new method for converting sunlight into electricity. • She is accused of *devising* [=*hatching*] a plot to overthrow the government.

de·void /dɪˈvoɪd/ *adj*

devoid of **:** not having (something usual or expected) **:** completely without (something) ▪ He is *devoid of* (any) ambition. [=he has no ambition] ▪ The landscape seems to be completely *devoid of* life.

de·vo·lu·tion /ˌdɛvəˈluːʃən/ *noun* [*noncount*] : the act or process by which a central government gives power, property, etc., to local groups or governments ▪ *devolution* of power

de·volve /dɪˈvɑːlv/ *verb* **-volves; -volved; -volv·ing** *formal*

1 [*no obj*] *chiefly US* : to gradually go from an advanced state to a less advanced state ▪ She cynically asserts that our species is *devolving*. ▪ Somehow the debate *devolved* into a petty competition to see who could get more applause. — opposite EVOLVE

2 : to pass (responsibility, power, etc.) from one person or group to another person or group at a lower level of authority — + *to, on,* or *upon* [+ *obj*] Community leaders hope that the new government will *devolve* more power *to/on/upon* the community itself. [*no obj*] Responsibility has *devolved to/upon* the individual teachers.

3 [*no obj*] : to be given to someone after the owner has died — + *to, on,* or *upon* ▪ Upon his death, the estate *devolved to/on/upon* a distant cousin. [=a distant cousin inherited the estate]

de·vote /dɪˈvoʊt/ *verb* **-votes; -vot·ed; -vot·ing**

devote to [*phrasal verb*] ***devote (something) to (something or someone)*** : to decide that (something) will be used for (a special purpose) : to use (time, money, energy, attention, etc.) for (something) ▪ They *devote* [=*dedicate*] an hour every day *to* worship. ▪ She plans to *devote* part of her vacation *to* reading. ▪ Some of the money they raise will be *devoted to* repairing the church's roof. ▪ Part of the class was *devoted to* questions from last week's reading. ▪ The magazine will *devote* an entire issue *to* this year's winner of the Nobel Peace Prize. ▪ He *devoted* [=*dedicated*] his life/time *to* helping the poor. = He ***devoted himself to*** helping the poor. [=he used his time, energy, etc., to help the poor] ▪ She *devoted herself to* her family.

devoted *adj* [*more* ~; *most* ~] : having strong love or loyalty for something or someone ▪ a rock star's most *devoted* fans ▪ The author's *devoted* [=*loyal, faithful*] readers have been eagerly waiting for the new book. ▪ The TV show has a *devoted* following. — often + *to* ▪ He remains *devoted to* his wife. ▪ Her grandchildren are *devoted to* her.

— **de·vot·ed·ly** *adv* ▪ They worked *devotedly* [=*faithfully*] to help him win reelection.

dev·o·tee /ˌdɛˌvoʊˈtiː/ *noun, pl* **-tees** [*count*]

1 : a person who enjoys or is interested in something very much ▪ The nightclub is popular among jazz *devotees*. — often + *of* ▪ She is a *devotee of* Italian cooking. ▪ a *devotee of* the arts

2 : a person who has very strong loyalty to a particular religion or religious figure ▪ a group of religious *devotees*

de·vo·tion /dɪˈvoʊʃən/ *noun, pl* **-tions**

1 [*singular*] : a feeling of strong love or loyalty : the quality of being devoted ▪ acts of *devotion* ▪ She has cared for the poor with selfless *devotion*. ▪ The *devotion* they felt for each other was obvious. — often + *to* ▪ I admire his *devotion to* his wife. ▪ She has a strong *devotion to* the cause.

2 [*noncount*] : the use of time, money, energy, etc., for a particular purpose ▪ The project will require the *devotion* of a great deal of time and money.

3 ***devotions*** [*plural*] : prayer, worship, or other religious activities that are done in private rather than in a religious service ▪ They spend an hour each morning at their *devotions*.

de·vo·tion·al /dɪˈvoʊʃənl/ *adj* : relating to or used in religious services ▪ *devotional* music/literature

de·vour /dɪˈvawɚ/ *verb* **-vours; -voured; -vour·ing** [+ *obj*]

1 : to quickly eat all of (something) especially in a way that shows that you are very hungry ▪ He *devoured* everything on his plate. ▪ The lions *devoured* their prey. ***synonyms*** see EAT

2 : to enjoy (something) in a way that shows you are excited about it: such as **a** : to read (something) quickly and with much enthusiasm ▪ She *devoured* every golf magazine she could find. **b** : to look at (something) with much enjoyment or enthusiasm ▪ He watched intently, *devouring* the scene before him with his eyes.

3 : to destroy (something) completely ▪ The forest was *devoured* [=*consumed*] by fire.

4 *of an emotion* : to greatly affect or control (someone) ▪ Jealousy *devoured* [=*consumed*] him. — usually used as *(be) devoured* ▪ She *was devoured* by guilt/remorse.

de·vout /dɪˈvaʊt/ *adj* [*more* ~; *most* ~]

1 : deeply religious : devoted to a particular religion ▪ They are *devout* Catholics.

2 a : loyal to something : devoted to a particular belief, organization, person, etc. ▪ His parents are *devout* [=*staunch*] believers in the value of a good education. **b** : serious and sincere ▪ It is his *devout* wish to help people in need.

— **de·vout·ly** *adv* ▪ a *devoutly* religious family ▪ It is ***a thing devoutly to be wished***. [=a thing worth wishing for; a thing you want very much to happen]

dew /ˈduː, *Brit* ˈdjuː/ *noun* [*noncount*] : drops of water that form outside at night on grass, trees, etc. ▪ The grass was wet with the morning *dew*.

dew·drop /ˈduːˌdrɑːp, *Brit* ˈdjuːˌdrɒp/ *noun, pl* **-drops** [*count*] : a drop of dew

dew point *noun* [*count*] *technical* : the temperature at which the moisture in the air forms visible drops of water : the temperature at which dew forms ▪ It's 78° outside and the *dew point* is 63°.

dewy /ˈduːwi, *Brit* ˈdjuːwi/ *adj* : wet with dew or with something like dew ▪ a *dewy* meadow ▪ *dewy* eyes

dewy–eyed /ˈduːwiˌaɪd, *Brit* ˈdjuːwiˌaɪd/ *adj, usually disapproving*

1 : showing too much emotion ▪ the author's *dewy-eyed* [=*sentimental*] nostalgia ▪ He gets annoyed by people who get all *dewy-eyed* [=*teary-eyed*] at weddings.

2 : young and innocent ▪ a *dewy-eyed* adolescent

dex·ter·i·ty /dɛkˈstɛrəti/ *noun* [*noncount*]

1 a : the ability to use your hands skillfully ▪ The job requires manual *dexterity*. ▪ He has the *dexterity* needed to deal cards quickly. **b** : the ability to easily move in a way that is graceful ▪ The amazing *dexterity* of the acrobat.

2 *formal* : clever skill : the ability to think and act quickly and cleverly ▪ He's a teacher known for his imagination and verbal *dexterity*. ▪ political *dexterity* [=*adroitness*]

dex·ter·ous *also* **dex·trous** /ˈdɛkstrəs/ *adj* [*more* ~; *most* ~] *formal* : having or showing great skill or cleverness : showing dexterity ▪ They praised her *dexterous* handling of the crisis. ▪ The movie is a *dexterous* retelling of a classic love story. ▪ a *dexterous* maneuver ▪ a *dexterous* carpenter

— **dex·ter·ous·ly** *also* **dex·trous·ly** *adv* ▪ The various elements of the book have been *dexterously* combined.

dex·trose /ˈdɛkˌstroʊs/ *noun* [*noncount*] *technical* : a kind of sugar found in fruits, plants, etc. : a form of glucose

DH /ˌdiˈeɪtʃ/ *noun, pl* **DHs** [*count*] *baseball* : DESIGNATED HITTER

dhow /ˈdaʊ/ *noun, pl* **dhows** [*count*] : an Arab boat that is low in the front, high in the back, and that usually has one or two sails that are shaped like triangles

di- *prefix, chemistry* : containing two atoms or groups of a specified kind ▪ carbon *dioxide*

di·a·be·tes /ˌdajəˈbiːtiz/ *noun* [*noncount*] *medical* : a serious disease in which the body cannot properly control the amount of sugar in your blood because it does not have enough insulin

[1]di·a·bet·ic /ˌdajəˈbɛtɪk/ *adj*

1 : affected with diabetes ▪ new drugs for treating *diabetic* patients ▪ He became *diabetic* [=he developed diabetes] in his old age.

2 : caused by diabetes ▪ a *diabetic* coma

3 : suitable for people with diabetes ▪ a *diabetic* diet

[2]diabetic *noun, pl* **-ics** [*count*] : a person who has diabetes

di·a·bol·i·cal /ˌdajəˈbɑːlɪkəl/ *adj* [*more* ~; *most* ~]

1 *also* ***di·a·bol·ic*** /ˌdajəˈbɑːlɪk/ : extremely evil ▪ a *diabolical* [=*fiendish, devilish*] enemy ✧ *Diabolical* often describes a plot, scheme, etc., that is very clever and that is intended for an evil purpose. ▪ a *diabolical* plot to overthrow the government

2 *Brit, informal* : very unpleasant, bad, or annoying ▪ The party was awful: the guests were boring and the food was *diabolical*. [=*awful, terrible*]

— **di·a·bol·i·cal·ly** /ˌdajəˈbɑːlɪkli/ *adv* ▪ a *diabolically* clever plan

di·a·crit·ic /ˌdajəˈkrɪtɪk/ *noun, pl* **-ics** [*count*] *technical* : a mark that is placed over, under, or through a letter in some languages to show that the letter should be pronounced in a particular way ▪ Two *diacritics* appear in the word "déjà vu."

di·a·dem /ˈdajəˌdɛm/ *noun, pl* **-dems** [*count*] *literary* : a crown that is worn especially by a king or queen as a symbol of royalty

di·ag·nose /ˈdajəgˌnoʊs/ *verb* **-nos·es; -nosed; -nos·ing** [+ *obj*]

1 a : to recognize (a disease, illness, etc.) by examining someone ▪ The test is used to help in *diagnosing* heart disease. ▪ Thousands of new cases have been *diagnosed* in the past year. ▪ The doctor was unable to *diagnose* the skin condition. — often + *as* ▪ The tumor was *diagnosed as* benign. ▪ Her illness was incorrectly *diagnosed as* a bacterial infection. **b :** to recognize a disease, illness, etc., in (someone) ▪ a new doctor with little experience *diagnosing* patients ▪ She was *diagnosed as* having cancer. = She was ***diagnosed with*** cancer. **2 :** to find the cause of (a problem) ▪ The mechanic was unable to *diagnose* the problem. — often + *as* ▪ The mechanic *diagnosed* the problem *as* a faulty spark plug.

D

di·ag·no·sis /ˌdajəgˈnousəs/ *noun, pl* **-no·ses** /ˌdajəgˈnouˌsiːz/

1 [*noncount*] **:** the act of identifying a disease, illness, or problem by examining someone or something ▪ The unusual combination of symptoms made accurate *diagnosis* difficult. ▪ She is an expert in the *diagnosis* and treatment of eye diseases.

2 [*count*] **:** a statement or conclusion that describes the reason for a disease, illness, or problem ▪ The *diagnosis* was a mild concussion. ▪ His doctor made an initial *diagnosis* of pneumonia. ▪ The committee published its *diagnosis* of the problems affecting urban schools. — compare PROGNOSIS

di·ag·nos·tic /ˌdajəgˈnɑːstɪk/ *adj, technical* **:** of, relating to, or used in diagnosis **:** used to help identify a disease, illness, or problem ▪ *diagnostic* tests for cancer ▪ Ultrasound is now widely used as a *diagnostic* tool. ▪ One important *diagnostic* feature of this condition is a mild rash.

di·ag·nos·tics /ˌdajəgˈnɑːstɪks/ *noun* [*plural*] *technical* **:** the skill or practice of identifying illnesses or problems **:** methods used for diagnosis ▪ This technology could revolutionize medical *diagnostics.* ▪ automotive *diagnostics*

[1]**di·ag·o·nal** /daɪˈægənl/ *adj*

1 *of a straight line* **:** joining two opposite corners of a shape (such as a square or rectangle) especially by crossing the center point of the shape ▪ Draw a *diagonal* line. — compare HORIZONTAL, VERTICAL

2 : not going straight across or up and down ▪ The blanket is covered with *diagonal* stripes. ▪ a *diagonal* pattern

– di·ag·o·nal·ly *adv* ▪ *diagonally* striped ▪ The stone wall runs *diagonally* across the field.

[2]**diagonal** *noun, pl* **-nals** [*count*] **:** a diagonal line, direction, or pattern ▪ a design with strong *diagonals* ▪ The stone wall cuts across the field ***on a diagonal*** [=*diagonally*] ▪ Slice the vegetables ***on the diagonal*** [=*diagonally*]

[1]**di·a·gram** /ˈdajəˌgræm/ *noun, pl* **-grams** [*count*] **:** a drawing that explains or shows the parts of something ▪ a *diagram* of the nervous system ▪ This *diagram* shows how the clock operates.

– di·a·gram·mat·ic /ˌdajəgrəˈmætɪk/ *adj* ▪ a *diagrammatic* representation of the nervous system **– di·a·gram·mat·i·cal·ly** /ˌdajəgrəˈmætɪkli/ *adv*

[2]**diagram** *verb* **-grams; -grammed** *or* **-gramed; -gramming** *or* **-gram·ing** [+ *obj*] *US* **:** to show or explain (something) in a diagram ▪ The coach *diagrammed* the new play on the blackboard. ▪ The students were required to *diagram* a sentence.

[1]**di·al** /ˈdajəl/ *noun, pl* **di·als** [*count*]

1 a : the part of a clock or watch that has the numbers on it ▪ a clock with a shiny silver *dial* [=*face*] — see also SUNDIAL **b :** the part of a piece of equipment that shows the measurement of something with a moving piece (such as a needle) that points to a number ▪ the *dial* of a pressure gauge

2 : a round part on a piece of equipment that you turn to operate something: such as **a :** a round control on a radio or television that you use to select a station or channel or to make the volume louder or quieter ▪ I had to keep adjusting the radio *dial* to make the station come in clearly. ▪ We'll be back right after this commercial, so ***don't touch that dial*** [=don't change the channel/station] **b :** a round part of some telephones that you move to select numbers

[2]**dial** *verb* **di·als;** *US* **di·aled** *or Brit* **di·alled;** *US* **di·al·ing** *or Brit* **di·al·ling** [+ *obj*]

1 : to select (a series of numbers) on a telephone by turning a dial or pushing buttons ▪ In an emergency you should *dial* [=*call*] 911. ▪ I'm sorry. I must have *dialed* the wrong number.

2 : to make a telephone call to (a person, business, etc.) ▪ She *dialed* [=(more commonly) *called*] her office as soon as she got home. ▪ He *dialed* (up) a friend to say he was in town.

di·a·lect /ˈdajəˌlɛkt/ *noun, pl* **-lects :** a form of a language that is spoken in a particular area and that uses some of its own words, grammar, and pronunciations [*count*] They speak a southern *dialect* of French. ▪ peasant/regional/local *dialects* [*noncount*] The author uses *dialect* in his writing. ▪ The play was hard to understand when the characters spoke ***in dialect***

– di·a·lec·tal /ˌdajəˈlɛktl/ *adj* ▪ the many *dialectal* forms of English

di·a·lec·tic /ˌdajəˈlɛktɪk/ *also* **di·a·lec·tics** /ˌdajəˈlɛktɪks/ *noun* [*noncount*] *philosophy* **:** a method of examining and discussing opposing ideas in order to find the truth

– di·a·lec·ti·cal /ˌdajəˈlɛktɪkəl/ *adj* ▪ a *dialectical* method/philosophy

dialling code *noun, pl* **~ codes** [*count*] *Brit* **:** AREA CODE

dialling tone *noun, pl* **~ tones** [*count*] *Brit* **:** DIAL TONE

dialog box *noun, pl* **~ boxes** [*count*] *computers* **:** a box that appears on a computer screen with a question inside asking the user to make a choice or give information

di·a·logue *also US* **di·a·log** /ˈdajəˌlɑːg/ *noun, pl* **-logues** *also* **-logs**

1 : the things that are said by the characters in a story, movie, play, etc. [*noncount*] He is an expert at writing *dialogue.* ▪ There's very little *dialogue* in the film. ▪ The best part of the book is the clever *dialogue.* [*count*] Students were asked to read *dialogues* from the play.

2 *formal* **a :** a discussion or series of discussions that two groups or countries have in order to end a disagreement [*count*] The two sides involved in the labor dispute are trying to establish a *dialogue.* [*noncount*] The two parties have been in constant *dialogue* with each other. **b** [*count*] **:** a conversation between two or more people ▪ They had a lengthy *dialogue* [=(more commonly) *talk*] about her plans for college.

dial tone *noun, pl* **~ tones** [*count*] *US* **:** the sound that comes from a telephone when it is ready for a call to be made — called also (*Brit*) *dialling tone*

dial–up /ˈdajəlˌʌp/ *adj, always used before a noun, computers* **:** done using an ordinary telephone line ▪ *dial-up* Internet access ▪ a *dial-up* connection

di·al·y·sis /daɪˈæləsəs/ *noun* [*noncount*] *medical* **:** the process of removing some of a person's blood, cleaning it, and then returning it to the person's body ▪ patients undergoing/receiving *dialysis* ▪ a *dialysis* machine ✧ People usually receive dialysis when they have damaged kidneys.

di·am·e·ter /daɪˈæmətɚ/ *noun, pl* **-ters**

1 [*count*] **:** a straight line from one side of something (such as a circle) to the other side that passes through the center point ▪ The dotted line indicates the *diameter* of the circle. — see picture at GEOMETRY

2 : the distance through the center of something from one side to the other [*count*] What is the *diameter* of the tree trunk? ▪ a pipe with a *diameter* of two inches = a pipe with a two-inch *diameter* [*noncount*] Dig a hole that's two feet deep and three feet ***in diameter.*** — compare RADIUS

di·a·met·ri·cal·ly /ˌdajəˈmɛtrɪkli/ *adv* **:** completely or entirely ▪ His position on the issue is ***diametrically opposed to*** that of his partner. [=his position is the exact opposite of his partner's position] ▪ They grew up in ***diametrically opposite*** [=completely different] environments.

[1]**di·a·mond** /ˈdaɪmənd/ *noun, pl* **-monds**

1 : a very hard usually colorless stone that is a form of carbon and is used especially in jewelry [*count*] a necklace studded with *diamonds* and rubies ▪ Her husband gave her a *diamond* [=a diamond ring] for her birthday. [*noncount*] The ruby was surrounded by a ring of *diamond.* — often used before another noun ▪ a *diamond* mine/ring — see color picture on page C11

diamond

2 [*count*] **:** a shape that is formed by four equal straight lines and that has two opposite angles that are smaller than a right angle and two opposite angles that are larger than a right angle ▪ The children cut the fabric into *diamonds.* — compare SQUARE

3 a [*count*] **:** a playing card that is marked with a red diamond shape ▪ one heart, two *diamonds,* and two clubs — see picture at PLAYING CARD **b** ***diamonds*** [*plural*] **:** the suit in a deck of playing cards that is marked by red diamond shapes ▪ He played the queen of *diamonds.* — compare CLUB, HEART, SPADE

4 [*count*] **a :** the part of a baseball field that includes the area within and around the three bases and home plate **:** IN-

FIELD • The infielders warmed up by throwing the ball around the *diamond*. **b** : the entire playing field in baseball • It's sad to see the town's old baseball *diamond* deserted.

²diamond *adj, always used before a noun* : of or relating to the 60th or 75th anniversary of an important event (such as a marriage) • The couple celebrated their ***diamond (wedding) anniversary*** a few months ago. = *(Brit)* They celebrated their ***diamond wedding***. • the celebration of Queen Victoria's ***diamond jubilee*** in 1897 ✧ It is more common for *diamond* to refer to the 60th anniversary of something. — compare GOLDEN, SILVER

diamond in the rough *noun, pl* **diamonds in the rough** *[count] US*
1 : a person who has talent or other good qualities but who is not polite, educated, socially skilled, etc. — called also *(Brit) rough diamond*
2 : something that is in poor condition but that is likely to become valuable with appropriate care or attention • The house is a *diamond in the rough*, and with some hard work it will be really beautiful.

¹di·a·per /ˈdaɪpɚ/ *noun, pl* **-pers** *[count] US* : a piece of cloth or other material that is placed between a baby's legs and fastened around the waist to hold body waste • disposable *diapers* • changing a baby's *diaper* — called also *(Brit) nappy*

²diaper *verb* **-pers; -pered; -per·ing** *[+ obj] US* : to put a diaper on (someone) • *diaper* a baby

diaper rash *noun [noncount] US* : sore red spots that sometimes form on the area of a baby's skin that a diaper covers — called also *(Brit) nappy rash*

di·aph·a·nous /daɪˈæfənəs/ *adj, formal* — used to describe cloth that is very thin and light • a *diaphanous* scarf • *diaphanous* fabrics

di·a·phragm /ˈdajəˌfræm/ *noun, pl* **-phragms** *[count]*
1 *medical* : a large flat muscle that separates the lungs from the stomach area and that is used in breathing — see picture at HUMAN
2 *technical* : a device that controls the amount of light passing through the lens of a camera
3 : a device shaped like a cup that is placed in the vagina to prevent pregnancy — called also *(Brit) cap*
4 *technical* : a thin disk that is used in microphones, telephones, speakers, etc., to help reproduce sound or make sounds louder

di·a·rist /ˈdajərəst/ *noun, pl* **-rists** *[count]* : a person who writes a diary

di·ar·rhea *(US) or chiefly Brit* **di·ar·rhoea** /ˌdajəˈriːjə/ *noun [noncount] medical* : an illness that causes you to pass waste from your body very frequently and in liquid rather than solid form • The symptoms of the disease include fever, nausea, and *diarrhea*.

di·a·ry /ˈdajəri/ *noun, pl* **-ries** *[count]*
1 : a book in which you write down your personal experiences and thoughts each day • His *diaries* [=*journals*] were published after his death. • She ***kept a diary*** [=wrote regularly in her diary] while she was traveling in Europe.
2 *Brit* : DATEBOOK

di·as·po·ra *or* **Di·as·po·ra** /daɪˈæspərə/ *noun, pl* **-ras** *[count] formal* : a group of people who live outside the area in which they had lived for a long time or in which their ancestors lived — usually singular • the art of the African/Chinese *diaspora* • members of ***the Diaspora*** [=Jewish people throughout the world who do not live in Israel]

dia·ton·ic /ˌdajəˈtɑːnɪk/ *adj, music* : of or relating to a musical scale that has five whole steps and two semitones • *diatonic* harmonies/notes • the *diatonic* scale — compare CHROMATIC

di·a·tribe /ˈdajəˌtraɪb/ *noun, pl* **-tribes** *[count] formal* : an angry and usually long speech or piece of writing that strongly criticizes someone or something • The article is a *diatribe* against mainstream media. • a bitter *diatribe* about/on how unfair the tax system is

dibs /ˈdɪbz/ *noun [plural] US, informal* : the right to have or choose something — usually + *on* • We stood in line for hours to ***get/have dibs on*** the best seats in the theater. • The farm always ***gives first dibs on*** its vegetables to local families. [=the farm sells its vegetables to local families before anyone else] • "***Dibs on*** the front seat!" [=I am claiming the front seat for myself]

¹dice /ˈdaɪs/ *noun, pl* **dice**
1 *[count]* : a small cube that is made of plastic, wood, etc., that has one to six dots on each side, and that is used usually in pairs in various games • a pair of *dice* • Throw the *dice*. • In this game, each player rolls the *dice* to see who plays first. • He was caught using a pair of ***loaded dice***. [=dice used for cheating]

dice

2 *[noncount]* : a gambling game played with dice • They were ***shooting dice*** in one of the bar's back rooms.
3 *[count]* : a small cube • Chop the onions into ¼-inch *dice*.

a roll of the dice *informal* — used to say that something could have either a good result or a bad result • Opening a new restaurant is always *a roll of the dice*. • It's *a roll of the dice* whether we succeed or fail.

load the dice *informal* : to unfairly make one possible result more likely than another • We received information that would *load the dice* in favor of our arguments. • The *dice were loaded* against them but they still managed to win.

no dice *US, informal* — used to say that something hoped for or wanted was not possible to do or to get • We hoped that tickets would still be available, but *no dice*, they were all sold. • I've proposed several different deals, but their response continues to be *no dice*. [=their response continues to be no]

roll the dice *informal* : to do something that may have a good result or a bad result : to take a chance • They decided to *roll the dice* and start their own business.

²dice *verb* **dic·es; diced; dic·ing** *[+ obj]* : to cut (food) into small cubes • *Dice* the potatoes and add them to the soup.

slice and dice see ²SLICE

– diced *adj* • *diced* carrots **– dic·er** *noun, pl* **-ers** *[count]*

dic·ey /ˈdaɪsi/ *adj* **dic·i·er; -est** *informal* : involving a chance that something bad or unpleasant could happen : RISKY • Starting a business can be quite a *dicey* proposition. • The weather looks a little *dicey* this morning. I hope it doesn't rain.

di·chot·o·my /daɪˈkɑːtəmi/ *noun, pl* **-mies** *[count] formal* : a difference between two opposite things : a division into two opposite groups • Her essay discusses the *dichotomy* between good and evil in the author's novels.

dick /ˈdɪk/ *noun, pl* **dicks** *[count]*
1 *informal + offensive* : PENIS
2 *informal + offensive* : a mean, stupid, or annoying man
3 *US, informal + old-fashioned* : DETECTIVE • a private *dick* — see also CLEVER DICK

dick·ens /ˈdɪkənz/ *noun*

the dickens *informal + old-fashioned* — used to make a statement or question more forceful • What *the dickens* [=*the devil*] do you mean? • We'll have to work ***like the dickens*** [=very hard] to finish this project. • *(US)* It ***scared/frightened the dickens*** out of people. [=scared people very badly] • *(US)* She's as ***cute as the dickens***. [=she's very cute]

dick·er /ˈdɪkɚ/ *verb* **-ers; -ered; -er·ing** *[no obj] chiefly US* : to talk or argue with someone about the conditions of a purchase, agreement, or contract • I tried to *dicker* for a discounted price. — often + *with* or *over* • I don't have time to *dicker with* you. • They spent hours *dickering* [=*haggling*] *over* the car's price.

dick·head /ˈdɪkˌhɛd/ *noun, pl* **-heads** *[count] informal + offensive* : a mean, stupid, or annoying man

dicta *plural of* DICTUM

Dic·ta·phone /ˈdɪktəˌfoʊn/ *trademark* — used for a machine that records a person's spoken words so that the words can be written down later

¹dic·tate /ˈdɪkˌteɪt/ *verb* **-tates; -tat·ed; -tat·ing** *[+ obj]*
1 : to speak or read (something) to a person who writes it down or to a machine that records it • She's *dictating* a letter to her secretary.
2 : to say or state (something) with authority or power • They insisted on being able to *dictate* the terms of surrender.
3 : to make (something) necessary • Our choice of activities will likely be *dictated* [=*determined, controlled*] by the weather. • His health *dictates* [=*requires*] that he work at home. • Tradition *dictates* that the youngest member should go first. • The basket's function *dictates* its size and shape.

dictate to *[phrasal verb]* ***dictate to (someone)*** : to give orders to (someone) — usually used as *(be) dictated to* • I resent *being dictated to* by someone with half my experience.

²dictate *noun, pl* **-tates** *[count] formal*
1 : an order or direction given with authority — usually plural • They don't allow any disagreement with the *dictates* of the party.
2 : a rule or principle that guides something (such as an ac-

tivity or a person's behavior) — usually plural • She tried to live her life according to the *dictates* of her conscience. • We pay no attention to the *dictates* of fashion. • the *dictates* of common sense

dic·ta·tion /dɪkˈteɪʃən/ *noun* [*noncount*] : the act of speaking words that someone writes down or that a machine records : the act of dictating words • He used a tape recorder for *dictation*. • writing from *dictation*

take dictation : to write down the words that someone says so that they can be used in a letter, report, etc. • Her secretary's very good at *taking dictation*.

D

dic·ta·tor /ˈdɪkˌteɪtɚ/ *noun, pl* **-tors** [*count*] : a person who rules a country with total authority and often in a cruel or brutal way • The country was ruled by a military *dictator*. • fascist *dictators*

dic·ta·to·ri·al /ˌdɪktəˈtorijəl/ *adj*

1 : of, relating to, or ruled by a dictator • a *dictatorial* ruler [=a ruler who is a dictator] • He was given *dictatorial* powers. • a *dictatorial* government • *dictatorial* regimes

2 [*more* ~; *most* ~] *disapproving* — used to describe a person who tries to control other people in a forceful and unfair way • a *dictatorial* boss [=a boss who acts like a dictator] • All his students resented his harsh, *dictatorial* manner.

– dic·ta·to·ri·al·ly *adv* • behaving *dictatorially*

dic·ta·tor·ship /dɪkˈteɪtɚˌʃɪp/ *noun, pl* **-ships**

1 [*noncount*] : rule by a dictator : rule, control, or leadership by one person with total power • The country suffered for many years under his *dictatorship*.

2 [*count*] : a government or country in which total power is held by a dictator or a small group • His enemies accused him of establishing a *dictatorship*. • a military *dictatorship*

dic·tion /ˈdɪkʃən/ *noun* [*noncount*]

1 : the clearness of a person's speech • The actor's *diction* was so poor I could hardly understand what he was saying.

2 : the way in which words are used in speech or writing • The student's essay was full of careless *diction*.

dic·tio·nary /ˈdɪkʃəˌneri, *Brit* ˈdɪkʃənri/ *noun, pl* **-nar·ies** [*count*]

1 : a reference book that contains words listed in alphabetical order and that gives information about the words' meanings, forms, pronunciations, etc. • an English *dictionary* • Look it up in the *dictionary*.

2 : a reference book that lists in alphabetical order the words of one language and shows their meanings or translations in a different language • an English-French *dictionary*

3 : a reference book that lists in alphabetical order words that relate to a particular subject along with their definitions and uses • a law *dictionary* • a *dictionary* of medicine

dic·tum /ˈdɪktəm/ *noun, pl* **dic·ta** /ˈdɪktə/ *also* **dic·tums** [*count*] *formal* : a statement or well-known remark that expresses an important idea or rule • A doctor must follow the *dictum* of "First, do no harm."

did *past tense of* DO

di·dac·tic /daɪˈdæktɪk/ *adj* [*more* ~; *most* ~] *formal*

1 : designed or intended to teach people something • *didactic* poetry

2 *usually disapproving* — used to describe someone or something that tries to teach something (such as proper or moral behavior) in a way that is annoying or unwanted • Audiences were turned off by the movie's *didactic* quality.

– di·dac·ti·cal·ly /daɪˈdæktɪkli/ *adv*

did·dle /ˈdɪdl/ *verb* **did·dles**; **did·dled**; **did·dling** *informal*

1 [*no obj*] *US* : to spend time doing something or handling something in an aimless way • He spent hours *diddling* [=*fiddling*] *with* the car's engine.

2 [+ *obj*] *Brit* : to steal money from (someone) by cheating • He had tried to *diddle* his insurance agency. • She felt she had been *diddled* out of her inheritance.

did·dly /ˈdɪdli/ *noun* [*noncount*] *US slang* : DIDDLY-SQUAT • Her contributions don't amount to *diddly*. [=*anything*] • He helped us a lot, but she didn't do *diddly*.

did·dly–squat /ˈdɪdliˌskwɑːt/ *noun* [*noncount*] *US slang* : the least amount : anything at all • You don't know *diddly-squat* about sports. • He loved his job even though it didn't pay *diddly-squat*.

didn't /ˈdɪdn̩t/ — used as a contraction of *did not* • I *didn't* know you were coming.

[1]die /ˈdaɪ/ *verb* **dies**; **died**; **dy·ing** /ˈdajɪŋ/

1 a [*no obj*] : to stop living • She claims she's not afraid to *die*. • More than a hundred people *died* [=were killed] in the crash. • He *died* in 1892 at the age of 37. • His mother *died* [=*passed away*, *passed on*] on April 15. • People in the town began *dying* suddenly/unexpectedly. • He ***died in his sleep***. [=he died while he was sleeping] • She ***died in childbirth***. [=she *died* while giving birth to a baby] **b** [*no obj*] : to end life in a specified state or condition — followed by an adjective, noun, or noun phrase • He *died* happy. • They both *died* young. • She *died* a hero. • One day, you're going to *die* a lonely and bitter old man. **c** [+ *obj*] : to have or suffer (a specified kind of death) • He *died* a violent and painful death. • *dying* a natural death

2 [*no obj*] : to wish strongly or desperately *for* something or *to do* something — used as *(be) dying* • *I'm dying for* a cold drink. • They *were dying to leave*. • We've *been dying to see* that movie.

3 [*no obj*] **a** : to pass out of existence : to come to an end • Her secret *died* with her. • He's the last of a *dying* breed. **b** : to disappear gradually or become less strong • The wind gradually *died*. [=*died away, died down*]

4 [*no obj*] **a** : to stop working or running • The motor *died*. **b** : to end in failure • The bill ***died in committee***. [=the bill was considered and rejected by a committee]

die away [*phrasal verb*] : to disappear gradually or become less strong • The echo slowly *died away*.

die back [*phrasal verb*] *of a plant* : to die in the parts that are above the ground but to remain alive in the roots • The plant *dies back* every winter and sends up new shoots each spring.

die down [*phrasal verb*] : to gradually become less strong • The wind will *die down* in the evening. • She waited for the noise to *die down* before she started singing.

die hard : to take a long time to die or end : to continue for a long time • Such rumors *die hard*. • That kind of determination *dies hard*. — see also DIE-HARD

die in bed *or* ***die in your bed*** : to die of disease or old age • After a long and adventurous life, he ended up *dying in his bed*.

die laughing *informal* : to laugh for a long time in an uncontrollable way : to laugh very hard • If the guys hear about this, they're going to *die laughing*.

die of [*phrasal verb*] ***die of (something)*** : to die because of (something) • My uncle *died of* cancer. • She *died of* old age. • They say that he *died of* a broken heart. • I almost *died of* embarrassment. [=I was extremely embarrassed] ✧ People often say that they are ***dying of*** something that causes a lot of discomfort, distress, etc. • Would you like some water? You must be *dying of* thirst. [=you must be very thirsty] • We're all *dying of* the heat. [=we're all very hot and uncomfortable]

die off [*phrasal verb*] : to die one after another so that fewer and fewer are left • The remaining members of her family gradually *died off*. • The animals *died off* one by one.

die on the vine *informal* : to fail at an early stage because of a lack of support or enthusiasm • Her plan to run for public office *died on the vine*.

die out [*phrasal verb*] : to disappear gradually • Like most fads, this one eventually *died out*. • The disease gradually *died out* over the last two generations. • Many more species are expected to *die out* completely [=to become extinct] unless we do something to help.

never say die — used to encourage someone to continue something or to remain hopeful • It doesn't look good for the team, but *never say die*. [=but don't give up hope] They could pull off a miracle.

to die for *informal* : worth dying for : extremely desirable or appealing • Dinner was nothing special, but the dessert was *to die for*. • The apartment has a view *to die for*. [=has a great view]

[2]die /ˈdaɪ/ *noun* [*count*]

1 *pl* **dice** /ˈdaɪs/ : [1]DICE 1 • Each player throws/rolls one *die*.

2 *pl* **dies** /ˈdaɪz/ : a tool that is used for cutting, shaping, or stamping a material or an object

the die is cast — used to say that a process or course of action has been started and that it cannot be stopped or changed • Once we signed the contract, *the die was cast*, and there was no turning back.

die–hard /ˈdaɪˌhɑɚd/ *adj* [*more* ~; *most* ~] : very determined or loyal • *die-hard* fans; *especially* : very loyal to a set of beliefs and not willing to change those beliefs • a *die-hard* conservative — see also *die hard* at [1]DIE

– die·hard *noun, pl* **-hards** [*count*] • a bunch of conservative *diehards*

diem see PER DIEM

die·sel /ˈdiːzəl/ *noun, pl* **-sels**

1 [*count*] : a vehicle (such as a truck or bus) that has a diesel engine ▪ His truck's a *diesel.*
2 [*noncount*] : DIESEL FUEL ▪ Does your car take *diesel* or gasoline?

diesel engine *noun, pl* ~ **-gines** [*count*] : a type of engine that uses diesel fuel rather than gasoline and that is used especially in large vehicles (such as trucks and buses)

diesel fuel *noun* [*noncount*] : a type of fuel that is used in vehicles with diesel engines

¹di·et /ˈdajət/ *noun, pl* **-ets**
1 : the food that a person or animal usually eats [*count*] *Diets* that are rich in fruits and vegetables have been shown to help prevent disease. ▪ a balanced *diet* — often + *of* ▪ Many birds live on a *diet of* insects. [*noncount*] studying the association between *diet* and disease
2 : the kind and amount of food that a person eats for a certain reason (such as to improve health or to lose weight) [*noncount*] She lost a lot of weight through *diet* and exercise. [*count*] a low-fat *diet* ▪ a liquid *diet* ▪ He's ***on a diet.*** [=he is eating less food or only particular kinds of food in order to lose weight] ▪ He ***went on a diet*** and lost 30 pounds in six months.
3 [*singular*] : something that is provided or experienced repeatedly — + *of* ▪ We've been given a steady *diet of* political scandals in recent months.

²diet *verb* **-ets; -et·ed; -et·ing** [*no obj*] : to eat less food or to eat only particular kinds of food in order to lose weight : to be on a diet ▪ I've been *dieting* for two months.

³diet *adj, always used before a noun*
1 : having a smaller number of calories than usual ▪ a *diet* soda
2 : intended to help people lose weight ▪ *diet* pills

di·e·tary /ˈdajəˌteri, *Brit* ˈdajətri/ *adj, always used before a noun* : of or relating to a diet ▪ Many of our patients have special *dietary* needs. ▪ *dietary* deficiencies

di·et·er /ˈdajətɚ/ *noun, pl* **-ers** [*count*] : a person who is trying to lose weight : a person who is dieting ▪ I've been an unsuccessful *dieter* for years. ▪ chronic *dieters* — called also (*Brit*) *slimmer*

di·eti·tian *or* **di·eti·cian** /ˌdajəˈtɪʃən/ *noun, pl* **-tians** *or* **-cians** [*count*] : a person whose job is to give people advice about what to eat in order to be healthy

dif·fer /ˈdɪfɚ/ *verb* **-fers; -fered; -fer·ing** [*no obj*]
1 : to be different ▪ Their styles *differ.* ▪ The two schools *differ* in their approach to discipline. — often + *from* ▪ The new version *differs* significantly *from* the old one.
2 : to have opinions that don't agree ▪ We *differ* [=*disagree*] on/about/over how best to raise the money. — often + *with* ▪ They *differed with* each other on religious matters.
agree to differ see AGREE
beg to differ see BEG
– differing *adj* [*more* ~; *most* ~] ▪ The students had widely *differing* [=*different*] interpretations of the poem. ▪ *differing* views

dif·fer·ence /ˈdɪfrəns/ *noun, pl* **-enc·es**
1 : the quality that makes one person or thing unlike another [*noncount*] She knows the *difference* between right and wrong. ▪ There's no *difference* between the two houses. They look exactly the same. [*singular*] There's a striking *difference* in the sisters' looks. [=they look very different from each other] ◊ To ***tell the difference*** between two people or things is to see how they are unlike each other. ▪ It's hard to *tell the difference* [=*distinguish*] between one action movie and another. ▪ The new version is supposed to be much better than the old one, but I can't *tell the difference* (between them).
2 [*count*] : something that people do not agree about : a disagreement in opinion ▪ They've always ***had their differences.*** [=they have always disagreed about some things] ▪ The debate gave them a chance to ***air their differences.*** [=to discuss the things that they disagree about] ▪ We need to find a way to ***resolve/settle our differences.*** [=to stop disagreeing, arguing, etc.] ▪ There seems to be ***a difference of opinion*** [=people disagree] about what we should do next. ▪ They divorced because of ***irreconcilable differences.*** [=serious disagreements that they were not able to settle]
3 [*count*] : the degree or amount by which things differ ▪ There's a big *difference* in price. ▪ There's a 15-year ***age difference*** between her oldest and youngest children. [=her oldest child is fifteen years older than her youngest child]
make a difference **1** : to cause a change : to be important in some way ▪ Cost can *make a difference* in deciding on a college. ▪ "When would you like to leave?" "It ***makes no difference*** (to me)." [=it doesn't matter to me; I don't care] ▪ The weather ***didn't make any difference*** in our plans. [=didn't change our plans] ▪ It would ***make a lot of difference*** if you came. ▪ Your help ***made a big difference.*** ▪ ***It makes very little difference.*** [=it matters very little] ▪ The size of the engine can ***make all the difference.*** [=can be very important; can matter most] ▪ It may not matter to you, but it ***makes all the difference in the world*** to me. = It ***makes a world of difference*** to me. [=it matters very much to me] **2** : to do something that is important : to do something that helps people or makes the world a better place ▪ She says that she got into politics because she wanted to *make a difference.*
same difference *chiefly US, informal* — used to say that two things are not really different in any important way ▪ "They lost 100 games last year." "Actually, they only lost 96 games." "*Same difference.* The point is, they were awful."
split the difference see ¹SPLIT
what's the difference? **1** — used to ask how one thing is different from another ▪ "I like this one a lot more than that one." "Why? *What's the difference* (between them)?"
2 *or* ***what difference does it/that make?*** — used to ask why something is important or to suggest that something is not important ▪ *What's the difference* whether I go or not? ▪ *What difference does it make* [=what does it matter] if I go with you?

dif·fer·ent /ˈdɪfrənt/ *adj*
1 [*more* ~; *most* ~] : not of the same kind : partly or totally unlike ▪ The two brothers could not have been more *different.* ▪ The students come from (very) *different* backgrounds. ▪ We need to try an entirely *different* approach. — often + *from, than,* or *to* ▪ Our house is *different from* the others on our street. ▪ (*US*) The movie was *different than* I expected. ▪ (*Brit*) Her dress is *different to* mine.

> ***usage*** In both U.S. English and British English, one person or thing is said to be *different from* another. *Different* is also often followed by *than* in U.S. English. Some people believe that *different than* is incorrect, but it is very common. In British English, *different* can be followed by *to. Different to* is not used in U.S. English. ▪ The old house looks *different from* what I remember. = (*Brit*) The old house looks *different to* what I remember. = (*US*) The old house looks *different than* I remember.

2 *always used before a noun* : not the same ▪ They met with each other on several *different* occasions.
3 [*more* ~; *most* ~] : not ordinary or common : UNUSUAL ▪ advertising that tries to be *different* ▪ That movie certainly was *different.* ▪ He has a very *different* style of dressing.
a horse of a different color see ¹HORSE
different drummer see DRUMMER
put a different complexion on see COMPLEXION
– dif·fer·ent·ly *adv* ▪ She sees the situation a little *differently.* ▪ He dresses *differently* now that he's out of college.

¹dif·fer·en·tial /ˌdɪfəˈrɛnʃəl/ *adj, always used before a noun* [*more* ~; *most* ~] *formal* : relating to or based on a difference : treating some people or groups differently from others ▪ The law is intended to prevent *differential* [=*discriminatory*] treatment of women in the workplace.
– dif·fer·en·tial·ly *adv*

²differential *noun, pl* **-tials** [*count*]
1 : a difference between people or things ▪ Although there is a small price *differential* [=a small difference in price], we believe it's worth buying the computer with a faster processor.
2 *technical* : a gear or an arrangement of gears in a vehicle that allows one wheel to turn faster than another when the vehicle is going around a curve — called also *differential gear*; see picture at CAR

dif·fer·en·ti·ate /ˌdɪfəˈrɛnʃiˌeɪt/ *verb* **-ates; -at·ed; -at·ing**
1 [+ *obj*] : to make (someone or something) different in some way ▪ The only thing that *differentiates* the twins is the color of their eyes. — often + *from* ▪ Our excellent customer service *differentiates* us *from* our competitors.
2 : to see or state the difference or differences between two or more things [*no obj*] — often + *between* ▪ We've been learning how to *differentiate between* different types of plants. [+ *obj*] — often + *from* ▪ It's sometimes hard to *differentiate* one action movie *from* all the others.
– dif·fer·en·ti·a·tion /ˌdɪfəˌrɛnʃiˈeɪʃən/ *noun* [*noncount*]

dif·fi·cult /ˈdɪfɪkəlt/ *adj* [*more* ~; *most* ~]
1 : not easy : requiring much work or skill to do or make ▪

Our last test was extremely *difficult*. [=*hard, tough*] • We were asked lots of *difficult* questions. • I had to make a very *difficult* decision/choice. • We'll be hiking over *difficult* terrain. • It's more *difficult* than it sounds. — often followed by *to* + *verb* • It's *difficult to imagine* why she would do that. — often + *for* • It is *difficult for* me *to say* this, but you have to leave. • She has a cold, which ***makes it difficult*** *for* her *to breathe*.
2 : not easy to deal with or manage • He gave a good performance under *difficult* [=*trying*] circumstances. • I found myself in a *difficult* position/situation. • Some *difficult* days lie ahead of us. • He's been having a *difficult* time coping [=he has not been dealing well] with his father's death. • These changes will ***make life/things difficult*** for everyone involved.
3 : not willing to help others by changing your behavior : stubborn or unreasonable • My parents tell me that I was a *difficult* child. [=I did not obey my parents] • Why do you have to be so *difficult*? [=*uncooperative*]

dif·fi·cul·ty /ˈdɪfɪkəlti/ *noun, pl* **-ties**
1 [*noncount*] : the quality of something that makes it hard to do : the difficult nature of something • He has *difficulty* [=*trouble*] reading without his glasses. [=it is difficult for him to read without his glasses] • She underestimated the *difficulty* of saving so much money. • They had some *difficulty* (in) explaining their behavior. ✧ If something can be done ***with difficulty***, it is difficult to do. • It was only *with* (great/considerable) *difficulty* that we were able to continue. ✧ To do something ***without difficulty*** is to do it easily or without problems. • I couldn't breathe *without difficulty*.
2 [*count*] : something that is not easy to do or to deal with : a difficult situation — usually plural • He had to overcome many *difficulties*. [=*hardships*] • Since the election, the country has been facing serious economic/financial *difficulties*. • This television station is currently experiencing ***technical difficulties***. [=having technical problems]
3 [*count*] : a disagreement in opinion — usually plural • The partners have been unable to iron out their *difficulties*. = They haven't been able to resolve their *difficulties*.

dif·fi·dent /ˈdɪfɪdənt/ *adj* [*more* ~; *most* ~]
1 : lacking confidence : not feeling comfortable around people • He becomes *diffident* [=*shy, timid*] around girls.
2 : very careful about acting or speaking • She has a *diffident* [=*reserved*] manner. • She was *diffident* about stating her opinion.
— **dif·fi·dence** /ˈdɪfədəns/ *noun* [*noncount*] — **dif·fi·dent·ly** *adv* • He asked *diffidently* about her family.

dif·fract /dɪˈfrækt/ *verb* **-fracts; -fract·ed; -fract·ing** [+ *obj*] *technical* : to cause (a beam of light) to bend or spread • Light is *diffracted* when it passes through a prism.
— **dif·frac·tion** /dɪˈfrækʃən/ *noun* [*noncount*] • a light undergoing *diffraction*

[1]**dif·fuse** /dɪˈfjuːs/ *adj* [*more* ~; *most* ~] : spread out over a large space : not concentrated in one area • The forest was filled with a soft, *diffuse* light. • *diffuse* pain
— **dif·fuse·ly** *adv* • The pain spread *diffusely* through his legs. — **dif·fuse·ness** *noun* [*noncount*]

[2]**dif·fuse** /dɪˈfjuːz/ *verb* **-fus·es; -fused; -fus·ing**
1 a : to spread out : to move freely throughout a large area [*no obj*] The heat from the radiator *diffuses* throughout the room. [+ *obj*] The heat was *diffused* throughout the room. **b :** to exist or be known throughout an area [*no obj*] Their culture gradually *diffused* [=*spread*] westward. [+ *obj*] *diffusing* their ideas
2 [+ *obj*] : to cause (light) to be soft and spread out • The photographer uses a screen to *diffuse* the light. • an area of *diffused* light
— **dif·fu·sion** /dɪˈfjuːʒən/ *noun* [*noncount*]

[1]**dig** /ˈdɪg/ *verb* **digs; dug** /ˈdʌg/; **dig·ging**
1 a [*no obj*] : to move soil, sand, snow, etc., in order to create a hole • Some animal has been *digging* in the garden. • They *dug* into the sand with their hands. • He ***dug down*** about 10 feet before he hit water. **b** [+ *obj*] : to form (a hole, tunnel, etc.) by removing soil, sand, snow, etc. • *Dig* a hole three feet deep. • The first step in building a house is to *dig* the foundation. • The prisoners escaped by *digging* a tunnel under the fence.
2 [+ *obj*] : to uncover (something that is underground) by moving earth, soil, sand, etc. • *digging* potatoes • *digging* clams on the beach — see also DIG FOR (below)
3 [*no obj*] : to look for information about something • These detectives won't stop *digging* until they find out what happened.
4 *slang* **a** [+ *obj*] : to like or admire (someone or something) • I really *dig* this music. **b :** to understand or appreciate (someone or something) [+ *obj*] You *dig* me? [*no obj*] We don't want you here. You *dig*? **c** [+ *obj*] : to pay attention to or look at (someone or something) • Hey, *dig* that hat. ✧ Senses 4b and 4c have an old-fashioned quality. They are still used, but they are often intended to suggest the language of the 1950s and '60s. Sense 4a is somewhat more common.
5 : to reach for something [*no obj*] She *dug* (around) in her purse for her keys. : to put (your hand) into something [+ *obj*] He *dug* his hands into his pockets.

dig for [*phrasal verb*] ***dig for (something)*** : to search for (something) by digging • miners *digging for* coal — often used figuratively • The police have been *digging for* clues to help solve this murder.
dig in [*phrasal verb*] **1** ***dig (something) in or dig in (something)*** : to mix (something) into the soil in the ground by digging • *dig* the compost *in* **2** ***dig in or dig (yourself) in*** : to dig a trench and take position inside it • The soldiers *dug in* and waited for the enemy to approach. • The soldiers *dug themselves in*. — often used figuratively • We just have to *dig in* and prepare ourselves for the tough times ahead. **3** *informal* : to begin eating • Just grab a plate and *dig in*. **4** ***dig in your heels or dig your heels in*** : to behave in a stubborn way : to refuse to change • The salesman *dug in his heels* and refused to lower the price any further.
dig into [*phrasal verb*] **1** ***dig (something) into (something)*** : to mix (something) into (soil) by digging • *dig* the compost *into* the soil **2** ***dig into (something)*** **a** *informal* : to begin eating (something) • The family was *digging into* a delicious meal. • They *dug into* their steaks. **b** *somewhat informal* : to try to learn or uncover information by studying (something) • The detectives *dug into* his past and learned that he had once lived in another country. **3** ***dig (something) into (something) or dig into (something)*** : to push against (a body part) in a sharp and painful way • The bed's springs are *digging into* my back. • Her fingernails *dug into* my hand. = She *dug* her fingernails *into* my hand. • He *dug* his elbow *into* my ribs.
dig out [*phrasal verb*] ***dig (something) out or dig out (something)*** **1 :** to get (something) by searching • I *dug* some old books *out* of the attic. • She *dug out* some change from her purse. **2 :** to get (something) out of soil, sand, snow, etc., by digging • We had to *dig* the car *out* of the snow after the storm. • We spent the afternoon *digging out* [=shoveling snow] after the blizzard.
dig up [*phrasal verb*] ***dig up (something) or dig (something) up*** **1 :** to uncover or find (something) by digging • They *dug up* [=*unearthed*] buried treasure. • *digging up* large rocks • I want to move this bush. Will you help me *dig* it *up*? **2** *informal* : to discover (information) • The investigators did a lot of research to *dig up* the facts.
dig up (the) dirt see DIRT
dig your own grave : to behave in a way that will cause you to lose or fail • The coach *dug his own grave* when he publicly insulted the team's owner.

[2]**dig** *noun, pl* **digs**
1 [*count*] : a push with a body part (such as your elbow) : a poke or thrust • She gave me a *dig* in the ribs to get my attention.
2 [*count*] : a criticism or insult that is directed toward a particular person or group • a personal *dig* — often + *at* • Her comments have been interpreted as a sly *dig at* her former husband.
3 [*count*] : a place where scientists try to find buried objects by digging • archaeological *digs*; *also* : the act of digging for buried objects • She participated in a *dig* last summer.
4 ***digs*** [*plural*] *informal* **a** *US* : the place where someone lives • She's buying furniture for her new *digs* in the city. **b** *Brit, old-fashioned* : a room rented in another person's home • He still lives ***in digs*** [=in a rented room] just outside the city.

[1]**di·gest** /daɪˈʤɛst/ *verb* **-gests; -gest·ed; -gest·ing**
1 : to change (food that you have eaten) by a biological process into simpler forms that can be used by the body [+ *obj*] He has trouble *digesting* certain foods. • an easily *digested* protein [*no obj*] Soft-boiled eggs *digest* easily.
2 [+ *obj*] : to think over and try to understand (news, information, etc.) • It will take me a while to *digest* this news.
— **di·gest·ible** /daɪˈʤɛstəbəl/ *adj* [*more* ~; *most* ~] • easily *digestible* foods — **di·gest·ibil·i·ty** /daɪˌʤɛstəˈbɪləti/ *noun* [*noncount*]

[2]**di·gest** /ˈdaɪˌʤɛst/ *noun, pl* **-gests** [*count*] : information or a piece of writing that has been made shorter • a *digest* of the

laws ✧ *Digest* is often used in the names of magazines, such as "Reader's Digest" and "Architectural Digest."

di·ges·tion /daɪˈʤɛsʧən/ *noun* [*noncount*] **:** the process by which food is changed to a simpler form after it is eaten • an enzyme that aids in the *digestion* of protein • She began to suffer from poor *digestion* as she grew older.

di·ges·tive /daɪˈʤɛstɪv/ *adj, always used before a noun*
1 **:** of or relating to digestion • the *digestive* system of the body
2 **:** having the power to cause or help digestion • *digestive* enzymes

dig·ger /ˈdɪgɚ/ *noun, pl* **-gers** [*count*] **:** a large machine that digs and moves dirt, rocks, etc. — see also GOLD DIGGER

dig·it /ˈdɪʤət/ *noun, pl* **-its** [*count*]
1 **:** a written symbol for any of the numbers 0 to 9 • a three-*digit* number like 507 • a five-*digit* zip code
2 **:** a finger or toe • She suffered several broken *digits.*

dig·i·tal /ˈdɪʤətl/ *adj*
1 **:** showing the time with numbers instead of with hour and minute hands • a *digital* watch • *digital* clocks — compare ANALOG
2 **:** of or relating to information that is stored in the form of the numbers 0 and 1 • You can transfer *digital* images/pictures from your camera to your computer. • a *digital* radio broadcast • a *digital* recording of a sound
3 **:** using or characterized by computer technology • laptop computers and other *digital* [=*electronic*] devices • In this new *digital* age, computers and the Internet are part of our everyday lives.
4 **:** of or relating to the fingers or toes • *digital* dexterity
– dig·i·tal·ly *adv* • *digitally* recorded music

digital camera *noun, pl* **~ -eras** [*count*] **:** a camera that takes pictures without using film **:** a camera that records images as digital data

digital computer *noun, pl* **~ -ers** [*count*] **:** a computer that works with numbers that are represented by the digits 0 and 1

dig·i·tize *also Brit* **dig·i·tise** /ˈdɪʤəˌtaɪz/ *verb* **-tiz·es; -tized; -tiz·ing** [+ *obj*] **:** to change (information or pictures) to digital form • The record company *digitized* the songs and made them available on the Internet.

dig·ni·fied /ˈdɪgnəˌfaɪd/ *adj* [*more ~; most ~*] **:** serious and somewhat formal **:** having or showing dignity • She has a kind but *dignified* manner. • He looked very *dignified* in his new suit. • The hotel's lobby is *dignified* but inviting.

dig·ni·fy /ˈdɪgnəˌfaɪ/ *verb* **-fies; -fied; -fy·ing** [+ *obj*]
1 **:** to cause (something) to have more serious and important quality **:** to give dignity or importance to (something) • She felt that formal clothing would help *dignify* the occasion.
2 **:** to treat (something or someone) with respect or seriousness that is not deserved • He said he wouldn't *dignify* his opponents' accusations by responding to them.

dig·ni·tary /ˈdɪgnəˌteri, *Brit* ˈdɪgnətri/ *noun, pl* **-tar·ies** [*count*] **:** a person who has a high rank or an important position • The dinner was attended by many foreign *dignitaries.* • *dignitaries* of the church

dig·ni·ty /ˈdɪgnəti/ *noun* [*noncount*]
1 **:** a way of appearing or behaving that suggests seriousness and self-control • She showed *dignity* in defeat. • The ceremony was conducted with great *dignity.*
2 **:** the quality of being worthy of honor or respect • Theirs is a country that cherishes freedom and human *dignity.*
beneath your dignity **:** suitable for someone who is less important than you • He thought washing dishes was *beneath his dignity.* [=he thought that he was too good or important to wash dishes]

di·gress /daɪˈgrɛs/ *verb* **-gress·es; -gressed; -gress·ing** [*no obj*] **:** to speak or write about something that is different from the main subject being discussed • He *digressed* so often that it was hard to follow what he was saying. • If I can *digress* for a moment, I'd like to briefly mention her earlier films.
– di·gres·sion /daɪˈgrɛʃən/ *noun, pl* **-sions** [*count*] • The story is filled with humorous *digressions.*

dike (*chiefly US*) *or chiefly Brit* **dyke** /ˈdaɪk/ *noun, pl* **dikes** [*count*]
1 **:** a long narrow hole that is dug in the ground to carry water **:** a ditch or trench
2 **:** a bank or mound of earth that is built to control water and especially to protect an area from flooding **:** LEVEE

dik·tat /dɪkˈtɑːt/ *noun, pl* **-tats** [*count*] *disapproving* **:** an order that must be followed • The company president issued a *diktat* that employees may not wear jeans to work.

di·lap·i·dat·ed /dəˈlæpəˌdeɪtəd/ *adj* [*more ~; most ~*] **:** in very bad condition because of age or lack of care • She was living in a *dilapidated* [=*run-down*] old apartment building. • a *dilapidated* neighborhood

di·lap·i·da·tion /dəˌlæpəˈdeɪʃən/ *noun* [*noncount*] **:** a bad condition caused by age or lack of care **:** a dilapidated condition • The old houses were in various stages of *dilapidation.*

di·late /ˈdaɪˌleɪt/ *verb* **-lates; -lat·ed; -lat·ing :** to become larger or wider [*no obj*] The drug causes the blood vessels to *dilate.* • During labor, a woman's cervix will *dilate* to about 10 centimeters. [+ *obj*] The drug *dilates* the blood vessels.
dilate on/upon [*phrasal verb*] ***dilate on/upon (something)*** *formal* **:** to talk about (a subject) for a long time • We spent a long evening listening to him *dilate on* the need for tax relief.
– dilated *adj* [*more ~; most ~*] • *dilated* pupils **– di·la·tion** /daɪˈleɪʃən/ *noun* [*noncount*] • *dilation* of the arteries

dil·a·to·ry /ˈdɪləˌtori, *Brit* ˈdɪlətri/ *adj, formal*
1 **:** causing a delay • The committee's *dilatory* [=*delaying*] actions caused the loss of hundreds of jobs.
2 [*more ~; most ~*] **:** tending to be late **:** slow to do something • She tends to be *dilatory* [=*slow*] about answering letters.
– dil·a·to·ri·ness *noun* [*noncount*]

dil·do /ˈdɪldoʊ/ *noun, pl* **-dos** [*count*] **:** an artificial penis that is used to give sexual pleasure

di·lem·ma /dəˈlɛmə/ *noun, pl* **-mas** [*count*] **:** a situation in which you have to make a difficult choice • The country's decision to go to war has caused a major *dilemma* for its allies. • We're facing a terrible *dilemma.* • I don't know what to do; it's a real *dilemma.* • a moral *dilemma*
on the horns of a dilemma see [1]HORN

dil·et·tante /ˈdɪləˌtɑːnt, *Brit* ˌdɪləˈtænti/ *noun, pl* **-tantes** *also* **-tan·ti** /ˌdɪləˈtɑːnti, *Brit* ˌdɪləˈtænti/ [*count*] **:** a person whose interest in an art or in an area of knowledge is not very deep or serious • You can always tell a true expert from a *dilettante.*
– dil·et·tant·ish /ˈdɪləˌtɑːntɪʃ/ *adj* [*more ~; most ~*] • a *dilettantish* interest in the arts **– dil·et·tan·tism** /ˈdɪləˌtɑːnˌtɪzəm, *Brit* ˌdɪləˈtæntɪzəm/ *noun* [*noncount*]

dil·i·gence /ˈdɪləʤəns/ *noun* [*noncount*] **:** careful hard work **:** continued effort • The reporter showed great *diligence* in tracking down the story. • The company's success reflects the *diligence* of its employees.
– dil·i·gent /ˈdɪləʤənt/ *adj* [*more ~; most ~*] • Many hours of *diligent* [=*painstaking, careful*] research were required. • a *diligent* worker **– dil·i·gent·ly** *adv*

dill /ˈdɪl/ *noun* [*noncount*] **:** an herb with leaves that are used in cooking and with seeds that are used in flavoring foods such as pickles — called also (*US*) *dill weed*; see color picture on page C6

dill pickle *noun, pl* **~ pickles** [*count*] **:** a pickle that is flavored with dill

dil·ly·dal·ly /ˈdɪliˌdæli/ *verb* **-dal·lies; -dal·lied; -dal·ly·ing** [*no obj*] *informal* **:** to move or act too slowly **:** to waste time • We need to stop *dillydallying* [=*dawdling, fooling around*] and get to work.

[1]**di·lute** /daɪˈluːt/ *verb* **-lutes; -lut·ed; -lut·ing** [+ *obj*]
1 **:** to make (a liquid) thinner or less strong by adding water or another liquid • You can *dilute* the medicine with water.
2 **:** to lessen the strength of (something) • The hiring of the new CEO *diluted* the power of the company's president. • *diluting* the quality of our products
– diluted *adj* • *diluted* wine **– di·lu·tion** /daɪˈluːʃən/ *noun, pl* **-tions** [*count*] lower *dilutions* of the medicine [*noncount*] There's been some *dilution* in the stock's value.

[2]**dilute** *adj* [*more ~; most ~*] *technical* **:** reduced in strength as a result of containing an added liquid • a *dilute* solution of acid

[1]**dim** /ˈdɪm/ *adj* **dim·mer; dim·mest**
1 **:** not bright or clear • I found her sitting in a *dim* [=*dark*] corner of the restaurant. • a *dim* [=*obscure, faint*] light • *dim* stars **:** not seen clearly • Just the *dim* outline of the building could be seen through the fog.
2 **:** not understood or remembered in a clear way • We had only a *dim* [=*faint, vague*] notion of what was going on. • I have a *dim* memory of your last visit. — see also *the dim and distant past* at DISTANT
3 **:** not likely to to be good or successful • Prospects for a quick settlement of the strike appear *dim.* [=*unlikely*] • (*US*) The industry faces a *dim* [=*grim*] future.

4 : not good or favorable — used in the phrase *dim view* • The author's *dim view* [=bad opinion] of politicians is apparent throughout the book. • She ***takes a dim view of*** human nature. [=she believes that people are naturally bad] • Many fans *take a dim view of* [=many fans are unhappy about] recent changes in the team.
5 *informal* : not intelligent : stupid or dim-witted • She found him pretty *dim* at times.
– dim·ly *adv* • The lights were shining *dimly*. • a *dimly* lit room • I *dimly* remember him. **– dim·ness** *noun* [*noncount*] • the gray *dimness* of dawn

D

²dim *verb* **dims; dimmed; dim·ming**
1 : to make (a light) less bright or to become less bright [+ *obj*] *Dim* the lights. • The car's headlights were *dimmed*. [=(*Brit*) *dipped*] [*no obj*] The lights *dimmed*.
2 : to make (something) less strong or clear or to become less strong or clear [+ *obj*] The latest setback has *dimmed* hopes of an early settlement. [*no obj*] Hopes of an early settlement have *dimmed*. • Her beauty *dimmed* rapidly.

dim bulb *noun, pl* **~ bulbs** [*count*] *US, informal* : a person who is not very smart • He was considered something of a *dim bulb* by his coworkers.

dime /ˈdaɪm/ *noun, pl* **dimes** [*count*] : a U.S. or Canadian coin that is worth 10 cents
a dime a dozen *US, informal* : too common to be valuable or interesting • Beautiful actresses are a *dime a dozen*.
on a dime *informal* **1** : very quickly • My new car can stop *on a dime*. **2** : in a very small space • turn *on a dime*
— see also FIVE-AND-DIME, NICKEL-AND-DIME

di·men·sion /dəˈmenʃən/ *noun, pl* **-sions** [*count*]
1 : the length, width, height, or depth of something : a measurement in one direction (such as the distance from the ceiling to the floor in a room) • She carefully measured each *dimension* of the room. • The room's *dimensions* [=its length, width, and height] were surprisingly small.
2 : the amount or number of things that something affects or influences — usually plural • We underestimated the *dimensions* [=*extent, range*] of this problem. • the vast *dimensions* [=*magnitude, scope*] of the disaster
3 : a part of something • There are many *dimensions* [=*aspects*] to the problem. • The social/political/religious *dimensions* of the problem must also be taken into account. • The more powerful engine gives this car a (whole) new *dimension*. [=makes the car very different]
– di·men·sion·al /dəˈmenʃənl/ *adj* — usually used in combination • a multi-*dimensional* problem — see also ONE-DIMENSIONAL, TWO-DIMENSIONAL, THREE-DIMENSIONAL

dime store *noun, pl* **~ stores** [*count*] *US, old-fashioned* : a store that sells inexpensive goods : FIVE-AND-DIME

dime–store /ˈdaɪmˌstoɚ/ *adj, always used before a noun, informal* : poor or inferior in quality • *dime-store* [=*cheap*] perfume • They regarded him as just another *dime-store* [=*second-rate*] philosopher.

di·min·ish /dəˈmɪnɪʃ/ *verb* **-ish·es; -ished; -ish·ing**
1 : to become or to cause (something) to become less in size, importance, etc. [+ *obj*] The passing years did nothing to *diminish* [=*decrease, lessen*] their friendship. • The strength of the army was greatly *diminished* by outbreaks of disease. [*no obj*] My interest in the subject has steadily *diminished*. [=*dwindled*] • The drug's side effects should *diminish* over time.
2 [+ *obj*] : to lessen the authority or reputation of (someone or something) • Nothing could *diminish* the importance of his contributions. : to describe (something) as having little value or importance • I don't mean to *diminish* [=*belittle, disparage*] her accomplishments.
– di·min·ish·ment /dəˈmɪnɪʃmənt/ *noun* [*noncount*] • the *diminishment* of her reputation

di·min·u·en·do /dəˌmɪnjuˈɛndoʊ/ *noun, pl* **-dos** [*count*] *music* : a gradual decrease in the loudness of a section of music

dim·i·nu·tion /ˌdɪməˈnuːʃən/ *noun, pl* **-tions** *formal* : the act or process of becoming less [*singular*] a *diminution* [=(more commonly) *decrease*] of power [*noncount*] the *diminution* of wealth

¹di·min·u·tive /dəˈmɪnjətɪv/ *adj*
1 [*more ~; most ~*] : very small • a *diminutive* actor • a radio with a *diminutive* set of speakers
2 *linguistics* : indicating small size • the *diminutive* suffixes "-ette" and "-ling" • the *diminutive* noun "duckling" ✧ A *diminutive* word or suffix is usually used in describing something small, often with the added suggestion that it is appealing or lovable in some way.
– di·min·u·tive·ness *noun* [*noncount*]

²diminutive *noun, pl* **-tives** [*count*]
1 : a word or suffix that indicates that something is small • the *diminutives* "-ette" and "kitchenette"
2 : an informal form of a name ✧ *Diminutives* can be a shortened form of a name (such as "Jen" for "Jennifer" and "Dick" for "Richard") or a name with a diminutive suffix added to it (such as "Bobby" for "Bob").

dim·mer /ˈdɪmɚ/ *noun, pl* **-mers** [*count*] : a device that allows you to control the brightness of a light • All the lights in the room are on *dimmers*. [=all the lights can be made brighter or dimmer because they have special switches] • a *dimmer* switch

dim·ple /ˈdɪmpəl/ *noun, pl* **dim·ples** [*count*]
1 : a small area on a part of a person's body (such as the cheek or chin) that naturally curves in • She noticed his *dimples* when he smiled.
2 : a small area on a surface that curves in • the *dimples* on a golf ball

dim·pled /ˈdɪmpəld/ *adj* [*more ~; most ~*] : having dimples • her *dimpled* face/smile • a *dimpled* chin • the baby's chubby, *dimpled* hands

dim·wit /ˈdɪmˌwɪt/ *noun, pl* **-wits** [*count*] *informal* : a stupid person • a harmless *dimwit*

dim–wit·ted /ˈdɪmˈwɪtəd/ *adj* [*more ~; most ~*] *informal* : not intelligent • In the comedy, he plays the part of a bumbling, *dim-witted* salesman.

din /ˈdɪn/ *noun* [*singular*] : a loud, confusing mixture of noises that lasts for a long time • It was hard to hear anything above/over the *din* in the restaurant.

dine /ˈdaɪn/ *verb* **dines; dined; din·ing** [*no obj*] *somewhat formal* : to eat dinner : to have the main meal of the day • We'll be *dining* at six o'clock. • She likes to *dine* at/in expensive restaurants. • I will be *dining* alone tonight. • We hope you have an enjoyable *dining* experience.
dine in [*phrasal verb*] : to have dinner at home • I'm tired of *dining in*. [=*eating in*] Let's go out to eat tonight.
dine on [*phrasal verb*] ***dine on (something)*** : to eat (something) for dinner • We *dined on* pasta and fresh vegetables. • They *dined on* chicken every day for a month. • animals *dining on* fruits, leaves, and insects
dine out [*phrasal verb*] : to have dinner at a restaurant • We always *dine out* [=*eat out*] on Fridays.
wine and dine see ²WINE

din·er /ˈdaɪnɚ/ *noun, pl* **-ers** [*count*]
1 : a person who is eating dinner in a restaurant • wealthy *diners*
2 *chiefly US* : a small, informal, and inexpensive restaurant that looks like a railroad car • a roadside *diner*

di·nette /daɪˈnɛt/ *noun, pl* **-nettes** [*count*] : a small room or an area near a kitchen that is used for dining • The apartment includes a *dinette*. • a cheap ***dinette set*** [=a small dining table and chairs]

ding·bat /ˈdɪŋˌbæt/ *noun, pl* **-bats** [*count*] *US, informal* : a stupid or crazy person • I told you it wouldn't work, you *dingbat*!

ding–dong /ˈdɪŋˌdɑːŋ/ *noun, pl* **-dongs** [*count*]
1 : the sound of a bell ringing • We were startled by the *ding-dong* of the doorbell.
2 *Brit, informal* : a noisy argument • They were having another *ding-dong* about money.

din·ghy /ˈdɪŋi/ *noun, pl* **-ghies** [*count*]
1 : a small boat that is often carried on or towed behind a larger boat
2 : a small rubber boat that is used by people escaping from a sinking boat

din·go /ˈdɪŋgoʊ/ *noun, pl* **-goes** [*count*] : a wild dog of Australia

dingo

din·gy /ˈdɪnʤi/ *adj* **din·gi·er; -est** [*also more ~; most ~*] : dark and dirty : not fresh or clean • He's been staying in a *dingy* motel. • a *dingy* room • *dingy* colors
– din·gi·ness *noun* [*noncount*]

dining car *noun, pl* **~ cars** [*count*] : a railroad car in which meals are served — called also (*Brit*) *buffet car*

dining hall *noun, pl* ~ **halls** [*count*] : a large room where meals are served at a school, college, etc.

dining room *noun, pl* ~ **rooms** [*count*] : a room that is used for eating meals

din·ky /ˈdɪŋki/ *adj* **din·ki·er; -est** *informal*
1 *US* : very small and not appealing • a *dinky* apartment • I used to drive a *dinky* little car.
2 *Brit* : small and appealing • wearing nice shoes and *dinky* [=*cute*] accessories

din·ner /ˈdɪnɚ/ *noun, pl* **-ners**
1 : the main meal of the day [*count*] We had many pleasant *dinners* together. • a steak/lobster *dinner* [*noncount*] What's for *dinner*? • They had *dinner* early. • We're planning to ask them to *dinner* soon. • *Dinner* is served. [=dinner is ready; it's time to come to the table for dinner] — often used before another noun • *dinner* guests • *dinner* rolls • an enjoyable *dinner* companion • My new boyfriend and I had a ***dinner date*** [=a date to eat dinner together] last night. • She hosted a ***dinner party*** [=a party at which dinner is served] at her apartment. • the ***dinner table*** [=the table where people eat dinner] ✧ To go ***out to dinner*** is to have dinner at a restaurant. • We haven't gone *out to dinner* in weeks. • He took her *out to dinner* several times.

> ***usage*** Most Americans have dinner in the evening, although if the main meal of the day is served in the afternoon it is also referred to as dinner. When referring to the evening meal, *dinner* and *supper* are basically synonyms in U.S. English. *Dinner* is a somewhat more formal word than *supper* and it tends to describe a somewhat more formal meal.

2 [*count*] : a usually large formal event at which dinner is eaten • Two hundred people attended his retirement *dinner*. • the club's annual *dinner* [=*banquet*] • an awards *dinner* [=a dinner at which awards are given]
3 [*count*] : a cooked and packaged meal that usually only needs to be heated before it is eaten • a frozen *dinner* — see also TV DINNER

dinner jacket *noun, pl* ~ **-ets** [*count*] : a jacket that is worn by men on formal occasions : the jacket of a tuxedo

dinner suit *noun, pl* ~ **suits** [*count*] *Brit* : TUXEDO

dinner theater *noun, pl* ~ **-aters** [*count*] *US* : a restaurant in which a play is presented after the meal is over

din·ner·time /ˈdɪnɚˌtaɪm/ *noun* [*noncount*] : the usual time for dinner • I hate getting phone calls at *dinnertime*.

din·ner·ware /ˈdɪnɚˌweɚ/ *noun* [*noncount*] *chiefly US* : plates, bowls, glasses, etc., that are used for serving and eating dinner

di·no·saur /ˈdaɪnəˌsoɚ/ *noun, pl* **-saurs** [*count*]
1 : one of many reptiles that lived on Earth millions of years ago
2 : someone or something that is no longer useful or current : an obsolete or out-of-date person or thing • The old factory is now a rusting *dinosaur*. • The character she plays is a *dinosaur*—a former beauty queen who is living in the past.

dint /ˈdɪnt/ *noun*
by dint of *formal* : because of (something) : by means of (something) • They succeeded *by dint of* hard work.

di·o·cese /ˈdajəsəs/ *noun, pl* **-ces·es** /ˈdajəsəsəz/ [*count*] : the area that is controlled by a bishop in a Christian church • a Catholic *diocese*
— **di·oc·e·san** /daɪˈɑːsəsən/ *adj* • *diocesan* priests

di·ode /ˈdaɪˌoud/ *noun, pl* **-odes** [*count*] *technical* : an electronic device that allows an electric current to flow in one direction only

di·ox·ide /daɪˈɑːkˌsaɪd/ *noun, pl* **-ides** [*count*] *chemistry* : a molecule that has two atoms of oxygen and one atom of another element (such as carbon) — see also CARBON DIOXIDE, SULFUR DIOXIDE

di·ox·in /daɪˈɑːksən/ *noun, pl* **-ins** [*count*] : a poisonous chemical that is sometimes used in farming and industry

[1]**dip** /ˈdɪp/ *verb* **dips; dipped; dip·ping**
1 [+ *obj*] **a** : to put (something) into a liquid and pull it out again quickly — usually + *in* or *into* • Lightly *dip* the paintbrush *into* the paint. • We *dipped* our toes *into* the water to see how cold it was. • The shrimp are *dipped in* batter and then fried. • a *dipping* sauce [=a sauce that food is dipped into] **b** : to move (something) into and out of something — + *in* or *into* • He *dipped* his hand *into* his pocket and pulled out a key.
2 [+ *obj*] : to lift (liquid) out from a container • Use a ladle to *dip* some water out of the pot. • *dipping* water from a well
3 : to move downward [*no obj*] The sun *dipped* below the horizon. • The road *dips* over the hill. • I saw his head *dip* below the surface of the water. [+ *obj*] He *dipped* his head.
4 [*no obj*] : to decrease somewhat usually for a short time • Gasoline prices have *dipped* again. • The temperature could *dip* below freezing tonight.
5 [+ *obj*] *Brit* : to reduce the amount of light coming from (headlights) • *Dip* [=(*US*) *dim*] the car's headlights.
6 [+ *obj*] : to put (an animal) into a liquid containing a chemical that kills insects • *dipping* sheep
dip into [*phrasal verb*] ***dip into (something)*** **1 a** : to take out an amount of money from (something) • They had to *dip into* their savings to pay for the repairs. • Consumers are *dipping into* their pocketbooks [=they are spending money] this season. **b** : to use part of (something) • He *dipped into* his knowledge of history to reconsider the present political situation. • a company *dipping into* its pool of job applicants **2** : to read parts of (something) in a casual or brief way • *dip into* a book of poetry — see also [1]DIP 1 (above)

[2]**dip** *noun, pl* **dips**
1 [*count*] : a brief swim • They went for a quick *dip* in the pool.
2 [*count*] : a low place in a surface • There's a *dip* in the road just beyond the curve.
3 [*count*] : a decrease that continues usually for a short time • There's been a slight *dip* [=*drop*] in the unemployment rate. • a *dip* in prices
4 [*count*] : an amount of something (such as food) that is taken by dipping into a container • a *dip* [=*scoop*] of ice cream
5 : a sauce or soft mixture into which food (such as raw vegetables) may be dipped [*noncount*] All they had to eat were crackers and cheese *dip*. • potato chips and onion *dip* [*count*] a delicious bean *dip*
6 [*count, noncount*] : a liquid into which an animal is dipped in order to kill insects • sheep *dip*
7 [*count*] *US slang* : a stupid person • That guy's a complete *dip*.

diph·the·ria /dɪfˈθirijə/ *noun* [*noncount*] *medical* : a serious disease that makes breathing very difficult

diph·thong /ˈdɪfˌθɑːŋ/ *noun, pl* **-thongs** [*count*] *linguistics* : two vowel sounds joined in one syllable to form one speech sound • The sounds of "ou" in "out" and of "oy" in "boy" are *diphthongs*.

di·plo·ma /dəˈploumə/ *noun, pl* **-mas** [*count*] : a document which shows that a person has finished a course of study or has graduated from a school • He earned his high school *diploma* by attending classes at night.

di·plo·ma·cy /dəˈplouməsi/ *noun* [*noncount*]
1 : the work of maintaining good relations between the governments of different countries • She has had a long and distinguished career in *diplomacy*. • The government avoided a war by successfully resolving the issues through *diplomacy*. • international *diplomacy* — see also *gunboat diplomacy* at GUNBOAT
2 : skill in dealing with others without causing bad feelings • This is a situation that calls for tactful *diplomacy*.

dip·lo·mat /ˈdɪpləˌmæt/ *noun, pl* **-mats** [*count*]
1 : a person who represents his or her country's government in a foreign country : someone whose work is diplomacy • The President will be meeting with foreign *diplomats*.
2 : a person who has skill in dealing with other people • He's a talented architect but a poor *diplomat*.

dip·lo·mat·ic /ˌdɪpləˈmætɪk/ *adj*
1 : involving the work of maintaining good relations between the governments of different countries : of or relating to diplomats or their work • Negotiators are working to restore full *diplomatic* relations. • *diplomatic* credentials • a *diplomatic* career
2 [*more* ~; *most* ~] : not causing bad feelings : having or showing an ability to deal with people politely • We need to find a *diplomatic* [=*tactful*] way to say no.
— **dip·lo·mat·i·cal·ly** /ˌdɪpləˈmætɪkli/ *adv* • The situation was resolved *diplomatically*. • One critic *diplomatically* described the show as "interesting."

diplomatic corps *noun, pl* **diplomatic corps** [*count*] : all of the foreign diplomats in a country • She is an important member of the *diplomatic corps*.

diplomatic immunity *noun* [*noncount*] : an international law that gives foreign diplomats special rights in the country where they are working ✧ Under *diplomatic immunity*, diplomats cannot be arrested and do not have to pay taxes while working in other countries.

dip·per /ˈdɪpɚ/ *noun, pl* **-pers** [*count*] : a large spoon with a long handle that is used for dipping liquids : LADLE — see also BIG DIPPER, LITTLE DIPPER

dip·py /ˈdɪpi/ *adj* **dip·pi·er**; **-est** *informal* : silly or foolish in usually an appealing way • a *dippy* comedy • a movie about a slightly *dippy* young musician

dip·so /ˈdɪpsoʊ/ *noun, pl* **-sos** [*count*] *informal + old-fashioned* : DIPSOMANIAC

dip·so·ma·ni·ac /ˌdɪpsəˈmeɪnijæk/ *noun, pl* **-acs** [*count*] : a person who has an extreme and uncontrollable desire for alcohol : ALCOHOLIC

dip·stick /ˈdɪpˌstɪk/ *noun, pl* **-sticks** [*count*]
1 : a long thin piece of metal with marks that are used to show how much of a fluid (such as motor oil) is in a container or an engine
2 *informal* : a stupid person • Some *dipstick* cut in front of me on the highway.

dip switch *noun, pl* **~ switches** [*count*] *Brit* : a switch for dimming or lowering the headlights of an automobile

dire /ˈdajɚ/ *adj* **dir·er**; **dir·est** [*or more ~; most ~*]
1 : very bad : causing great fear or worry • Even the smallest mistake could have *dire* [=*terrible, dreadful*] consequences. • a *dire* emergency • The circumstances are now more *dire* than ever. • With its best player out of the game, the team found itself ***in dire straits*** [=in a very bad or difficult situation] • The company now finds itself *in dire* financial *straits*. [=the company is having bad financial problems]
2 : warning of disaster : showing a very bad future • Some analysts are issuing *dire* economic forecasts. • a *dire* prediction/warning
3 a : requiring immediate action : very urgent • The government is in *dire* [=*desperate*] need of reform. • *dire* necessity **b** : very serious or extreme • They live in *dire* poverty.

[1]**di·rect** /dəˈrɛkt/ *verb* **-rects**; **-rect·ed**; **-rect·ing**
1 [+ *obj*] : to cause (someone or something) to turn, move, or point in a particular way • Lights were *directed* [=*aimed*] toward the paintings on the wall. • Be sure that the water nozzle is *directed* downward. • The sloping ground helps *direct* water away from the home.
2 [+ *obj*] **a** : to cause (someone's attention, thoughts, emotions, etc.) to relate to a particular person, thing, goal, etc. • Let me *direct* your attention to the book's second chapter. • We were asked to *direct* our thoughts and prayers to the people who survived the disaster. • The students *directed* their efforts/energies/talents toward improving their community. • He *directed* [=*aimed*] much of his anger at his coworkers. • A lot of the criticism has been *directed* toward the concert's organizers. **b** : to say (something) to a particular person or group • I'd like to *direct* [=*address*] my opening comments to the younger members of the audience.
3 [+ *obj*] : to guide, control, or manage (someone or something) • She's been chosen to *direct* [=*handle*] the project. • He is responsible for *directing* the activities of the sales team. • In my current position, I *direct* a staff of over 200 employees. • We need someone to *direct* traffic.
4 : to lead a group of people in performing or filming (a movie, play, etc.) [+ *obj*] They're still looking for someone to *direct* the show. • She has *directed* over 20 films in her career. • The play was poorly *directed*. [*no obj*] She enjoys both acting and *directing*. • I think I'd like to *direct* some day.
5 [+ *obj*] : to show or tell (someone) how to go to a place : to give (someone) directions • The signs *directed* [=*guided*] us to the museum. • Could you please *direct* me to the office? [=please tell me where the office is]
6 [+ *obj*] *somewhat formal* **a** : to ask or tell (a person or group) *to do* something • He *directed* [=*instructed, ordered*] the workers *to stop* what they were doing. • The judge *directed* the jury *to disregard* several of the attorney's comments. • The resolution *directed* the commission *to prepare* proposals. **b** : to order (something) to be done — *+ that* • His will *directed that* the money be used to support local schools.
7 [+ *obj*] : to send (a letter, note, etc.) to a specified person or place • Please *direct* [=*address, send*] your letters to my office. • The letter was *directed* to the company's president.

[2]**direct** *adj*
1 [*more ~; most ~*] : going the shortest distance from one place to another : going straight without turning or stopping • I found a more *direct* route to the city. • We'll be taking a *direct* [=*nonstop*] flight from New York to Los Angeles. • That way is more *direct*. — opposite INDIRECT
2 *always used before a noun* [*more ~; most ~*] : coming straight from a source • Keep these plants out of *direct* sunlight. • The coastline was exposed to the *direct* force of the hurricane. — opposite INDIRECT
3 *always used before a noun* [*more ~; most ~*] : coming straight from a cause or reason : connected or related to something in a clear way • These problems are a *direct* result of poor planning. [=poor planning was the cause of these problems] • The weather had a *direct* effect/impact on our plans. • There's a *direct* connection between the two events. • The investigation began in *direct* response to the newspaper story. — opposite INDIRECT
4 *always used before a noun* [*more ~; most ~*] : having no people or things in between that could have an effect • His position gives him *direct* access to the president. [=he can talk to the president face-to-face] • This is a *direct* order from the General. • The board of directors has *direct* control of the company's future. • Her theory was based on *direct* observation. • There's no *direct* evidence to support his claims. • *direct* knowledge/experience — opposite INDIRECT
5 *always used before a noun* : related in a line from your parent, grandparent, great-grandparent, etc. • She's my *direct* ancestor. • He claims to be a *direct* descendant of George Washington.
6 *always used before a noun* : perfect or exact • The word has no *direct* translation in English. • The building took a ***direct hit*** from an enemy plane.
7 [*more ~; most ~*] **a** : said or done in a clear and honest way : sincere and straightforward • We need a *direct* answer. Are you coming or not? • The candidate made a *direct* appeal to the voters. **b** : speaking in a clear and honest way • I wish you would be more *direct*. • She has a very *direct* way of dealing with customers. — opposite INDIRECT
8 *always used before a noun, grammar* : consisting of the exact words of a speaker or writer • She used several *direct* quotations from the artist in her article. — opposite INDIRECT

[3]**direct** *adv* : in a direct way: such as **a** : in a straight line without turning or stopping • We flew *direct* [=*straight, nonstop*] from Chicago to Paris. **b** : straight from a source with nothing and nobody in between • The company sells its product *direct* [=*directly*] to customers on the streets. • It costs less if you buy it *direct* from the manufacturer.

direct current *noun* [*noncount*] : an electric current that is flowing in one direction only — abbr. *DC*; compare ALTERNATING CURRENT

direct debit *noun, pl* **~ -its** [*count, noncount*] *chiefly Brit* : a way of paying bills by allowing people or companies to take money directly from your bank account on a particular day • paying your bills by *direct debit*

direct deposit *noun* [*noncount*] *US* : a way of paying someone so that the money is sent directly into the person's bank account without the use of checks or cash • Our employees are paid by *direct deposit*.

di·rec·tion /dəˈrɛkʃən/ *noun, pl* **-tions**
1 [*count*] : the course or path on which something is moving or pointing • The army attacked from three different *directions*. • Down the road, he could see a bus coming from the opposite *direction*. • The wind ***changed direction*** and started blowing in our faces. • I've got a bad ***sense of direction***. [=I become lost frequently; I often don't know which way to go] — often used after *in* • She and I were walking *in* the same *direction*. • You're headed *in* the wrong *direction*. • The top of the hill provides a view *in* all *directions*. • The car was last seen headed ***in the direction of*** [=*towards*] the stadium. • She started walking ***in my direction***. [=toward me]
2 ***directions*** [*plural*] **a** : a statement that tells a person what to do and how to do it : an order or instruction • Carefully read the *directions* before you begin the test. • *Directions* appear on the package. • You have to learn to ***follow directions***. [=do what you are told or are instructed to do] **b** : instructions that tell you how to go to a place • We had to stop to ask for *directions* to the beach. • Excuse me. Could you please give me *directions* to the movie theater?
3 [*noncount*] **a** : control or management of someone or something • He was put in charge and given overall *direction* of the program. • Twenty-three employees work ***under her direction***. • Several nurses working ***under the direction of*** this doctor have made complaints. **b** : the act or process of directing a play, movie, television show, or musical performance • The play's unusual *direction* demanded much from the actors.

4 a [*count*] : the way that something is progressing or developing ▪ These discoveries have given a new *direction* to their research. ▪ Our business is expanding in all *directions*. ▪ He hasn't yet decided what *direction* he should take as a writer. [=hasn't decided exactly what he should try to do as a writer] **b** [*noncount*] : a goal or purpose that guides your actions or decisions ▪ Her life seemed to lack *direction* after she left school.

– **di·rec·tion·less** *adj* ▪ a talented but *directionless* musician – **di·rect·ness** /dəˈrɛktnəs/ *noun* [*noncount*] ▪ the *directness* of the route/connection ▪ He answered their questions with honesty and *directness*.

di·rec·tion·al /dəˈrɛkʃənl/ *adj*

1 : relating to or showing direction ▪ We work with maps to improve the students' *directional* skills. ▪ *directional* stability ▪ the *directional* signal lights on an automobile

2 *technical* : used for receiving sounds, radio signals, etc., that are coming from a particular direction ▪ a *directional* microphone ▪ The radio has a *directional* antenna.

di·rec·tive /dəˈrɛktɪv/ *noun, pl* **-tives** [*count*] *formal* : an official order or instruction ▪ They received a written *directive* instructing them to develop new security measures. ▪ a presidential *directive*

¹di·rect·ly /dəˈrɛktli/ *adv*

1 [*more ~; most ~*] : in a direct way ▪ He refused to answer the question *directly*. ▪ She said that she wanted to speak to you *directly*. ▪ The package will be sent *directly* to your home. ▪ The two accidents are *directly* related. ▪ Thousands of people were *directly* affected by the disaster. ▪ Antonyms are words that are *directly* opposite in meaning.

2 : in a straight or direct line from a particular position ▪ We parked *directly* behind the store. ▪ He sat *directly* across from me at the dinner table. ▪ Their house is *directly* ahead. = It's *directly* in front of us.

3 : without delay ▪ The second game followed *directly* [=*immediately*] after the first.

4 *somewhat old-fashioned* : in a little while ▪ We'll be leaving *directly*. [=*soon, shortly*]

²directly *conj, Brit* : immediately after : as soon as ▪ I came *directly* I received your message.

directly proportional *adj* : related so that one becomes larger or smaller when the other becomes larger or smaller ▪ His earnings are *directly proportional* to the number of units he sells. — compare INVERSELY PROPORTIONAL

direct mail *noun* [*noncount*] : papers containing advertisements that are mailed directly to people's homes

direct marketing *noun* [*noncount*] : a way of selling things by calling people on the telephone or mailing them advertisements or catalogs

direct object *noun, pl* ~ **-jects** [*count*] *grammar* : a noun, pronoun, or noun phrase which indicates the person or thing that receives the action of a verb ▪ "Me" in "He likes me" is a *direct object*. ▪ In the sentence "They built a house for her," the *direct object* is "house" and the indirect object is "her." — compare INDIRECT OBJECT

di·rec·tor /dəˈrɛktɚ/ *noun, pl* **-tors** [*count*]

1 : a person who manages an organized group of people or a part of an organization (such as a school or business) ▪ the choir *director* ▪ The company will hire a new *director* of marketing. ▪ She's the *director* of graduate studies at the university. ▪ the school's athletic *director* — see also FUNERAL DIRECTOR

2 : one of a group of managers who control a company or corporation ▪ executive/deputy/associate *directors* ▪ She's on the ***board of directors*** [=a group of people who make decisions] for a large corporation. — see also MANAGING DIRECTOR

3 : a person who directs a play, movie, etc. ▪ She's considered one of the best young *directors* in Hollywood. ▪ a movie/film/theater *director*

di·rec·tor·ate /dəˈrɛktərət/ *noun, pl* **-ates** [*count*]

1 : a group of managers who control a company or corporation : a board of directors ▪ the corporation's eight-member *directorate*

2 : a group of people who are in charge of a program or department ▪ the government's agricultural *directorate*

di·rec·to·ri·al /dəˌrɛkˈtorijəl/ *adj* : of or relating to a director and especially to the director of a play, movie, etc. ▪ her *directorial* style ✧ A movie director's first film is often called a ***directorial debut***. ▪ He made his *directorial debut* with a film that he also wrote and produced.

di·rec·tor·ship /dəˈrɛktɚˌʃɪp/ *noun, pl* **-ships**

1 [*count*] : a position as a director of a company or corporation ▪ He holds *directorships* at several banks.

2 [*noncount*] : the time when a person holds the position of director ▪ The museum has flourished under her *directorship*.

di·rec·to·ry /dəˈrɛktəri/ *noun, pl* **-ries** [*count*] : a book that contains an alphabetical list of names of people, businesses, etc.; *especially* : PHONE BOOK

directory assistance *noun* [*noncount*] *US* : a service that people can call to get the telephone number for a person or organization : INFORMATION — called also (*Brit*) *directory enquiries*

dirge /ˈdɚʤ/ *noun, pl* **dirg·es** [*count*] : a slow song that expresses sadness or sorrow ▪ a funeral *dirge*

dirt /ˈdɚt/ *noun* [*noncount*]

1 : loose earth or soil ▪ Pack *dirt* loosely around the base of the plant. ▪ mounds/piles of *dirt*

2 : a substance (such as mud or dust) that makes things unclean ▪ You've got some *dirt* on your face. ▪ Their shoes were covered with *dirt*. ▪ No amount of cleaning will get rid of all this *dirt*.

3 *informal* : a person or thing that has no value ▪ He ***treated me like dirt***. [=he treated me very badly]

4 *informal* : information about someone that could harm the person's reputation ▪ She's been spreading *dirt* [=*gossip*] about her ex-husband. ✧ To ***dig up (the) dirt*** on someone is to find out information that is harmful to that person's reputation. ▪ He's been *digging up dirt* on his political rivals. ✧ To ***dish (the) dirt*** is to spread harmful gossip or information. ▪ He seems to have written his memoirs mainly so that he can *dish the dirt* on all his former lovers.

hit the dirt see ¹HIT

in the dirt ✧ In baseball, a pitch is *in the dirt* when it hits the ground near home plate before reaching the catcher. ▪ He swung and missed at a curveball *in the dirt*.

– see also PAY DIRT

dirt·bag /ˈdɚtˌbæg/ *noun, pl* **-bags** [*count*] *chiefly US, informal* : a very bad and unpleasant person ▪ a sleazy *dirtbag*

dirt bike *noun, pl* ~ **bikes** [*count*] : a small motorcycle that is designed to be used on rough surfaces

dirt cheap *adj, informal* : very cheap or inexpensive ▪ The tickets were *dirt cheap*. ▪ *dirt cheap* prices

– **dirt cheap** *adv* ▪ I can get you a stereo system *dirt cheap*.

dirt farmer *noun, pl* ~ **-ers** [*count*] *US, informal* : a poor farmer who lives by farming the land usually without the help of paid workers

dirt floor *noun, pl* ~ **floors** [*count*] : a floor with a hard dirt surface

dirt–poor /ˈdɚtˈpuɚ/ *adj, informal* : very poor : suffering extreme poverty ▪ When I was growing up, my family was *dirt-poor*.

dirt road *noun, pl* ~ **roads** [*count*] : a road with a hard dirt surface : an unpaved road

¹dirty /ˈdɚti/ *adj* **dirt·i·er; -est**

1 : not clean ▪ All my socks are *dirty*. ▪ Try not to get your clothes *dirty*. ▪ *dirty* dishes ▪ I can't breathe this *dirty* city air. ▪ The baby has a *dirty* diaper.

2 a : indecent and offensive ▪ *dirty* language — see also DIRTY WORD **b** : relating to sex in an indecent or offensive way ▪ *dirty* [=*pornographic*] movies/magazines/pictures ▪ I hate listening to his *dirty* jokes. ▪ He has a ***dirty mind***. [=he often thinks about sex] — see also DIRTY OLD MAN

3 : not fair or honest ▪ He has a reputation as a *dirty* player. [=he cheats; he tries to hurt his opponents] ▪ a criminal's ***dirty money*** [=money earned in an illegal activity] ▪ That was a ***dirty trick***! [=an unkind thing to do]

4 a : very bad : deserving to be hated or regretted ▪ War is a *dirty* business. ▪ It's a *dirty* shame that nobody tried to help him. ▪ That's a *dirty* lie! ▪ He's a *dirty* liar! **b** : likely to cause shame or disgrace ▪ That's the *dirty* [=*shameful*] little secret that the industry doesn't want you to know.

5 : difficult or unpleasant ▪ Why do I always get stuck doing the *dirty* work? ▪ It's a *dirty* job, but somebody's got to do it. ✧ To ***get your hands dirty*** is to do difficult and often unpleasant work. ▪ Our boss isn't afraid to *get her hands dirty* and help us finish the work on time.

6 : showing dislike or anger ▪ She gave me a ***dirty look***.

7 : not clear or bright in color ▪ a *dirty* [=*dull*] red — see also *dirty blond* at ¹BLOND

– **dirt·i·ness** *noun* [*noncount*] ▪ the *dirtiness* of the house

²dirty *verb* **dirt·ies; dirt·ied; dirty·ing** [+ *obj*] : to make (something) dirty ▪ Take off your shoes to keep from *dirtying* the floor. ▪ Her fingers were *dirtied* with ink. ▪ The baby just

D

dirtied [=*soiled*] her diaper. • The river was *dirtied* [=*polluted*] with industrial waste.

[3]**dirty** *adv*

1 : in an unfair or dishonest way • Watch out for her. She plays *dirty*. • He usually wins because he fights *dirty*.

2 : in an indecent or offensive way • talking *dirty*

dirty bomb *noun, pl* **~ bombs** [*count*] **:** a bomb that is designed to spread a large amount of radioactive material

dirty laundry *noun* [*noncount*] **:** private information that causes shame and embarrassment when it is made public • The company is trying to keep its *dirty laundry* from being aired/washed in public. • Let's not ***air our dirty laundry*** [=discuss our problems, make our problems known] in public. — called also *dirty linen*

D

dirty old man *noun, pl* **~ men** [*count*] *disapproving* **:** an old man who is too interested in sex

dirty tricks *noun* [*plural*] **:** secret and dishonest activities that are done to ruin someone's or something's chance of success • political *dirty tricks*

dirty word *noun, pl* **~ words**

1 [*count*] **:** an offensive word • The movie is just a lot of sex, violence, and *dirty words*.

2 [*singular*] **:** a word, subject, or idea that is disliked by some people • They regard "taxes" as a *dirty word*. • Politics is a *dirty word* [=they don't talk about politics] in their home. • The way he acts, you'd think compassion was a *dirty word*.

dis *also* **diss** /ˈdɪs/ *verb* **dis·ses; dissed; dis·sing** [+ *obj*] *US slang*

1 : to treat (someone) with disrespect **:** to be rude to (someone) • He got *dissed* [=*insulted*] by the other guys on the team.

2 : to criticize (something) in a way that shows disrespect • Don't *dis* my car.

– dis *also* **diss** *noun, pl* **disses** [*count*] • It's not a *dis*. [=not an insult]

dis- *prefix*

1 *in verbs* **:** to do the opposite of • *disagree* • *disappear* • *disapprove*

2 *in nouns* **:** opposite or absence of • *dis*belief • *dis*comfort • *dis*honor

3 *in adjectives* **:** not • *dis*agreeable • *dis*connected • *dis*interested

dis·abil·i·ty /ˌdɪsəˈbɪləti/ *noun, pl* **-ties**

1 [*count*] **:** a condition (such as an illness or an injury) that damages or limits a person's physical or mental abilities • She has learned to keep a positive attitude about her *disability*. • *disabilities* such as blindness and deafness • a program for children with *disabilities* — see also LEARNING DISABILITY

2 [*noncount*] **:** the condition of being unable to do things in the normal way **:** the condition of being disabled • It's a serious disease that can cause *disability* or death.

3 [*noncount*] *US* **:** a program that provides financial support to a disabled person • After he injured his back he had to quit his job and go ***on disability***.

dis·able /dɪsˈeɪbəl/ *verb* **-ables; -abled; -abling** [+ *obj*]

1 : to cause (something) to be unable to work in the normal way • *disable* a bomb • *disable* an alarm • *disable* a computer program

2 : to make (someone) unable to do something (such as use part of the body) in the usual way — often used as *(be) disabled* • He *was disabled* by the accident.

– dis·able·ment /dɪsˈeɪbəlmənt/ *noun* [*noncount*]

– disabling *adj* • He suffered a *disabling* illness when he was in college. • a *disabling* injury/condition • The patient was experiencing severe, *disabling* pain.

disabled *adj* [*more ~; most ~*] **:** having a physical or mental disability **:** unable to perform one or more natural activities (such as walking or seeing) because of illness, injury, etc. • The organization is working to protect the rights of *disabled* veterans. • special classes for ***learning disabled*** children [=for children who have a learning disability]

the disabled **:** people who are disabled **:** people who have a disability • She's always been an effective spokesperson for *the disabled*.

disabled list *noun*

the disabled list *US, sports* **:** a list of players on a team (such as a baseball team) who are unable to play because of injury or illness • The team has had to place several key players on *the disabled list*. — abbr. *DL*

dis·abuse /ˌdɪsəˈbjuːz/ *verb* **-abus·es; -abused; -abus·ing** [+ *obj*] *formal* **:** to show or convince (someone) that a belief is incorrect — + *of* • He offered to *disabuse* us *of* what he called our "cherished myths." • Anyone expecting a romantic story will be quickly *disabused of* that notion by the opening chapter.

dis·ad·van·tage /ˌdɪsədˈvæntɪʤ/ *noun, pl* **-tag·es**

1 [*count*] **a :** something that causes difficulty **:** something that makes someone or something worse or less likely to succeed than others • This program has the *disadvantage* [=*shortcoming*] of being more expensive than the others. • She had the *disadvantage* of growing up in a poor community. • He felt that his lack of formal education ***put/placed him at a disadvantage*** [=made it harder for him to succeed] in the business world. • They argued that the new regulations would *place* their company *at a competitive disadvantage* in the marketplace. **b :** a bad or undesirable quality or feature • There are advantages and *disadvantages* to the new system.

2 [*noncount*] **:** loss, damage, or harm • The deal worked ***to our disadvantage***. [=the deal was harmful to us in some way] — opposite ADVANTAGE

dis·ad·van·taged /ˌdɪsədˈvæntɪʤd/ *adj* [*more ~; most ~*] **:** lacking the things (such as money and education) that are considered necessary for an equal position in society • The program provides aid for economically *disadvantaged* groups/communities. • *disadvantaged* [=*underprivileged*] children

the disadvantaged **:** disadvantaged people • protecting the rights of *the disadvantaged*

dis·ad·van·ta·geous /dɪsˌædˌvænˈteɪʤəs/ *adj* [*more ~; most ~*] *formal* **:** making it harder for a person to succeed or to do something **:** causing someone to have a disadvantage • They might have to resell the property at a *disadvantageous* time. • Minority groups find themselves in a *disadvantageous* position. • The current system is *disadvantageous* to women. — opposite ADVANTAGEOUS

– dis·ad·van·ta·geous·ly *adv* [*more ~; most ~*]

dis·af·fect·ed /ˌdɪsəˈfɛktəd/ *adj* [*more ~; most ~*] *formal* **:** no longer happy and willing to support a leader, government, etc. • bored and *disaffected* youth • The troops had become *disaffected*. • Both political parties are looking for ways to regain the trust of *disaffected* voters.

– dis·af·fec·tion /ˌdɪsəˈfɛkʃən/ *noun* [*noncount*] • There was widespread *disaffection* among the troops.

dis·agree /ˌdɪsəˈgriː/ *verb* **-agrees; -agreed; -agree·ing** [*no obj*]

1 : to have a different opinion **:** to fail to agree • I think that I should sell my car, but he *disagrees*. — often + *with* • I strongly *disagree with* that statement. • She *disagrees with* him on almost every subject. — often + *on, about,* or *over* • They *disagreed about* the price. • We *disagree on* the best way to raise the money. • We found ourselves *disagreeing over* the meaning of the poem.

2 : to be different • The two descriptions *disagree*. [=they do not match] — often + *with* • Her story *disagrees with* the facts of the case.

3 : to not be suitable for or pleasing to someone — + *with* • Fried foods *disagree with* me. [=make me feel unwell]

agree to disagree see AGREE

dis·agree·able /ˌdɪsəˈgriːjəbəl/ *adj* [*more ~; most ~*]

1 : not pleasing **:** unpleasant or offensive • The medicine had a *disagreeable* taste. • the *disagreeable* odor of the garbage • Some of her duties are very *disagreeable* (to her).

2 *of a person* **:** difficult to deal with **:** easily angered or annoyed • His health problems made him surly and *disagreeable*. [=*irritable, querulous*] • I've never known her to be so *disagreeable*. — opposite AGREEABLE

– dis·agree·ably /ˌdɪsəˈgriːjəbli/ *adv* • a *disagreeably* bitter taste

dis·agree·ment /ˌdɪsəˈgriːmənt/ *noun, pl* **-ments**

1 a [*noncount*] **:** failure to agree • There's been a lot of *disagreement* about/on/over how best to spend the money. • He has expressed *disagreement* [=he has said that he disagrees] with some aspects of the proposal. **b** [*count*] **:** a difference of opinion **:** an argument caused by people having different opinions about something • We've had a number of serious *disagreements* [=*disputes, arguments*] over the years. • Several *disagreements* have yet to be resolved.

2 [*noncount*] **:** the state of being different or unalike • There's considerable *disagreement* between the descriptions given by the two witnesses. [=the two descriptions do not agree/match]

dis·al·low /ˌdɪsəˈlaʊ/ *verb* **-lows; -lowed; -low·ing** [+ *obj*] **:** to refuse to allow (something) **:** to officially decide that (something) is not acceptable or valid • The court *disallowed*

[=*rejected*] their claim. • The touchdown was *disallowed* because of a penalty.
– **dis·al·low·ance** /ˌdɪsəˈlawəns/ *noun* [*noncount*] • *disallowance* [=*rejection*] of the tax deductions

dis·ap·pear /ˌdɪsəˈpiɚ/ *verb* **-pears; -peared; -pear·ing** [*no obj*]
1 : to stop being visible : to pass out of sight • The moon *disappeared* [=*vanished*] behind a cloud. • The two men *disappeared* around the corner.
2 a : to stop existing : to die or go away completely • The dinosaurs *disappeared* millions of years ago. • Their original enthusiasm has all but *disappeared*. [=*vanished*] • These problems won't just *disappear* by themselves. **b** : to become lost : to go to a place that is not known • My car keys have *disappeared* again. [=I can't find them] • He *disappeared* without a trace two years ago. • The speaker suddenly *disappeared* just before the beginning of the ceremony.
– **dis·ap·pear·ance** /ˌdɪsəˈpirəns/ *noun, pl* **-anc·es** [*noncount*] We're witnessing the gradual *disappearance* of an old way of life. [*count*] Police are investigating several mysterious *disappearances*.

dis·ap·point /ˌdɪsəˈpoɪnt/ *verb* **-points; -point·ed; -point·ing** : to make (someone) unhappy by not being as good as expected or by not doing something that was hoped for or expected [+ *obj*] The team *disappointed* its fans. • The show may *disappoint* some viewers. [*no obj*] The novel *disappoints* by being predictable and overly long.
– **dis·ap·point·ing** /ˌdɪsəˈpoɪntɪŋ/ *adj* [*more* ~; *most* ~] • Dinner was *disappointing*. • The team had a very *disappointing* season. – **dis·ap·point·ing·ly** /ˌdɪsəˈpoɪntɪŋli/ *adv* • a *disappointingly* poor performance

dis·ap·point·ed /ˌdɪsəˈpoɪntəd/ *adj* [*more* ~; *most* ~]
1 : feeling sad, unhappy, or displeased because something was not as good as expected or because something you hoped for or expected did not happen • We were *disappointed* that they couldn't go. • *Disappointed* fans slowly left the ballpark. • I was *disappointed* to see that my suggestions had been ignored. • They were deeply *disappointed* by her lack of interest. • Don't be too *disappointed* if everything doesn't go as planned.
2 : unhappy because someone has behaved badly • Your father and I are very *disappointed* in/with you.

dis·ap·point·ment /ˌdɪsəˈpoɪntmənt/ *noun, pl* **-ments**
1 [*noncount*] : the state or feeling of being disappointed • She couldn't hide her *disappointment*. • ***To our disappointment***, the game was rained out. [=we were disappointed that the game was rained out]
2 [*count*] : someone or something that disappoints people : a disappointing person or thing • The play was a (big) *disappointment*. [=it was very disappointing] • He's a *disappointment* to his parents.

dis·ap·pro·ba·tion /dɪsˌæprəˈbeɪʃən/ *noun* [*noncount*] *formal* : DISAPPROVAL • the constant *disapprobation* of critics

dis·ap·prov·al /ˌdɪsəˈpruːvəl/ *noun* [*noncount*] : lack of approval : the belief that someone or something is bad or wrong • The plan met with *disapproval*. [=*opposition*] • I could sense her *disapproval*. • They made their *disapproval* of our behavior very clear. — opposite APPROVAL

dis·ap·prove /ˌdɪsəˈpruːv/ *verb* **-proves; -proved; -prov·ing**
1 : to believe that someone or something is bad or wrong : to not approve of someone or something [*no obj*] She married him even though her parents *disapproved*. — often + *of* • She *disapproves of* smoking. • Some people may *disapprove of* the government's actions. • I *disapproved of* [=I disagreed with] their decision, but I said nothing against it. [+ *obj*] The word "ain't" is *disapproved* [=*criticized*] by most teachers.
2 [+ *obj*] : to officially refuse to approve or accept (something) • They *disapproved* [=*rejected*] the architect's plans. • The treaty was *disapproved* by the Senate. — opposite APPROVE
– **dis·ap·prov·ing** *adj* [*more* ~; *most* ~] • She gave him a *disapproving* look. • a *disapproving* frown • He felt uncomfortable in the presence of his *disapproving* parents. – **dis·ap·prov·ing·ly** *adv* • She shook her head *disapprovingly*.

dis·arm /dɪsˈɑɚm/ *verb* **-arms; -armed; -arm·ing**
1 a [+ *obj*] : to take weapons from (someone or something) • *disarm* a prisoner • The government has been unsuccessful at *disarming* the rebels. **b** [*no obj*] : to give up weapons • The terrorists have refused to *disarm*. — opposite ARM
2 [+ *obj*] : to make (a bomb, mine, etc.) harmless • It took more than an hour to *disarm* the bomb. — opposite ARM
3 [+ *obj*] : to make (someone) friendly or less suspicious • He has a way of *disarming* [=*winning over*] his critics by flattering them. • We were *disarmed* [=*charmed, captivated*] by her sense of humor.

dis·ar·ma·ment /dɪsˈɑɚməmənt/ *noun* [*noncount*] : the process of reducing the number of weapons controlled by a country's military • nuclear *disarmament* — opposite ARMAMENT

disarming *adj* [*more* ~; *most* ~] : tending to remove any feelings of unfriendliness or distrust • We were all charmed by his *disarming* openness and modesty. • a *disarming* smile
– **dis·arm·ing·ly** *adv* • Her answers were *disarmingly* [=*surprisingly*] honest.

dis·ar·range /ˌdɪsəˈreɪnʤ/ *verb* **-rang·es; -ranged; -rang·ing** [+ *obj*] *formal* : to make (something) messy or untidy • The wind *disarranged* my hair. • His bed was *disarranged* and clothes were strewn on the floor.

dis·ar·ray /ˌdɪsəˈreɪ/ *noun* [*noncount*] : a lack of order : a confused or messy condition • The room was in *disarray*. • The company has fallen into complete/total *disarray*.

dis·as·sem·ble /ˌdɪsəˈsɛmbəl/ *verb* **-sem·bles; -sem·bled; -sem·bling**
1 [+ *obj*] : to disconnect the pieces of (something) • *disassemble* [=*take apart*] an engine
2 [*no obj*] : to come apart into smaller pieces • The bookshelf *disassembles* for easy storage.
– **dis·as·sem·bly** /ˌdɪsəˈsɛmbli/ *noun* [*noncount*]

dis·as·so·ci·ate /ˌdɪsəˈsousiˌeɪt/ *verb* **-ates; -at·ed; -at·ing** [+ *obj*] : DISSOCIATE

di·sas·ter /dɪˈzæstɚ, *Brit* dɪˈzɑːstə/ *noun, pl* **-ters**
1 [*count*] : something (such as a flood, tornado, fire, plane crash, etc.) that happens suddenly and causes much suffering or loss to many people • The program examined several bridge failures and other engineering *disasters*. • a nuclear *disaster* • The earthquake was one of the worst ***natural disasters*** [=a disaster caused by natural forces] of this century. • The state is asking for federal ***disaster relief***. [=money to help rebuild an area after a disaster]
2 a : something that has a very bad effect or result [*count*] The new regulations could be a *disaster* for smaller businesses. • Opponents say the government's policy is ***a disaster waiting to happen***. [=something that will probably have a very bad or tragic result] [*noncount*] They're trying to find a way to avoid *disaster*. • They narrowly escaped *disaster*. • The new regulations could ***spell disaster*** [=result in serious problems] for smaller businesses. • The government's policy is ***a recipe for disaster***. = The government is ***flirting with disaster*** by pursuing this policy. • When ***disaster strikes***, [=when something very bad happens] we will be prepared. **b** [*count*] : a complete or terrible failure • economic/financial *disasters* • The dinner party was a complete *disaster*.

disaster area *noun, pl* **~ areas** [*count*]
1 : an area where there has been a major disaster (such as a flood, tornado, or earthquake) and where people can receive special help from the government (such as money to rebuild homes or emergency supplies) • After the hurricane, the state was declared a *disaster area*.
2 *informal* : a place that is very messy or dirty • His office is a *disaster area*. How can he find anything in all this clutter?

di·sas·trous /dɪˈzæstrəs, *Brit* dɪˈzɑːstrəs/ *adj* [*more* ~; *most* ~]
1 : causing great suffering or loss • Half the city was destroyed by a *disastrous* fire.
2 : very bad or unfortunate • The bad weather could have a *disastrous* effect on the area's tourism industry. • His failure to back up the computer files had *disastrous* consequences. • The strike was economically *disastrous*.
– **di·sas·trous·ly** *adv* • a *disastrously* bad choice/idea

dis·avow /ˌdɪsəˈvau/ *verb* **-avows; -avowed; -avow·ing** [+ *obj*] *formal* : to say that you are not responsible for (something) : to deny that you know about or are involved in (something) • He *disavowed* the actions of his subordinates. • She now seems to be trying to *disavow* her earlier statements.
– **dis·avow·al** /ˌdɪsəˈvawəl/ *noun, pl* **-als** [*count, noncount*]

dis·band /dɪsˈbænd/ *verb* **-bands; -band·ed; -band·ing** : to end an organization or group (such as a club) [+ *obj*] They've decided to *disband* the club. [*no obj*] The members of the organization have decided to *disband*.
– **dis·band·ment** /dɪsˈbændmənt/ *noun* [*noncount*]

dis·bar /dɪsˈbɑɚ/ *verb* **-bars; -barred; -bar·ring** [+ *obj*] : to take away the right of (a lawyer) to work in the legal profession — often used as *(be) disbarred* ▪ She *was disbarred* for unethical practices.

– **dis·bar·ment** /dɪsˈbɑɚmənt/ *noun* [*noncount*] ▪ The charges could lead to his *disbarment*.

dis·be·lief /ˌdɪsbəˈliːf/ *noun* [*noncount*] **:** a feeling that you do not or cannot believe or accept that something is true or real ▪ The initial reports were met with widespread *disbelief*. [=many people did not believe the reports] ▪ She stared at him in utter *disbelief*. ▪ If you want to enjoy this story, you have to ***suspend your disbelief***. [=allow yourself to believe things that cannot be true] — compare UNBELIEF

dis·be·lieve /ˌdɪsbəˈliːv/ *verb* **-lieves; -lieved; -liev·ing** *formal* **:** to not believe (someone or something) [+ *obj*] Several jurors *disbelieved* the witness's testimony. [*no obj*] — + *in* ▪ She *disbelieves in* the value of exercise.

– **disbelieving** *adj* ▪ The announcement was met with shocked and *disbelieving* silence. – **dis·be·liev·er** *noun, pl* **-ers** [*count*]

dis·burse /dɪsˈbɚs/ *verb* **-burse; -bursed; -burs·ing** [+ *obj*] *formal* **:** to pay out (money) from a fund that has been created for a special purpose ▪ The money will be *disbursed* on the basis of need. ▪ The government has *disbursed* millions of dollars in foreign aid.

– **dis·burse·ment** /dɪsˈbɚsmənt/ *noun, pl* **-ments** [*noncount*] *disbursement* of government funds [*count*] The company has made large *disbursements* for research.

disc *or* **disk** /ˈdɪsk/ *noun, pl* **discs** *or* **disks** [*count*]

1 : a flat, thin, round object ▪ a plastic *disc* ▪ a cracker topped with a thin *disk* of sausage

2 ***disk*** **:** a flat, thin, round object that is used to store large amounts of information (such as computer data) ▪ Insert the *disk* into the CD drive. ▪ There isn't much ***disk space*** [=room for storage on a computer disk] left. — see also DISK DRIVE, FLOPPY DISK, HARD DISK, OPTICAL DISK

3 ***disc*** **a :** CD ▪ I don't have that recording on vinyl, but I have it ***on disc***. **b** *old-fashioned* **:** [1]RECORD 4 — see also DISC JOCKEY

4 *medical* **:** one of the flat, rubbery pieces that separate the bones of the backbone — called also *intervertebral disc*; see also SLIPPED DISC

[1]**dis·card** /dɪˈskɑɚd/ *verb* **-cards; -card·ed; -card·ing** [+ *obj*]

1 : to throw (something) away because it is useless or unwanted ▪ Remove and *discard* the stems. ▪ a pile of *discarded* tires — often used figuratively ▪ Many of his original theories have been *discarded* [=*rejected*] in recent years.

2 : to remove (a playing card) from your hand in a card game ▪ She *discarded* the six of hearts.

[2]**dis·card** /ˈdɪsˌkɑɚd/ *noun, pl* **-cards** [*count*] **:** something (such as a playing card) that has been discarded

disc brake *noun, pl* **~ brakes** [*count*] **:** a brake that works by two plates pressing against the sides of a disc that is connected to the center of a wheel

dis·cern /dɪˈsɚn/ *verb* **-cerns; -cerned; -cern·ing** [+ *obj*]

1 : to see, hear, or notice (something) with difficulty or effort ▪ We could just *discern* [=*distinguish, make out*] the ship through the fog.

2 : to come to know, recognize, or understand (something) ▪ The reasons behind this sudden change are difficult to *discern*. ▪ The purpose of the study is to *discern* [=*identify*] patterns of criminal behavior. ▪ unable to *discern* [=*distinguish*] right from wrong

– **dis·cern·ible** /dɪˈsɚnəbəl/ *adj* [*more ~; most ~*] ▪ There is no *discernible* difference between the original and the copy. – **dis·cern·ibly** /dɪˈsɚnəbli/ *adv* [*more ~; most ~*] ▪ The original and copy aren't *discernibly* different.

discerning *adj* [*more ~; most ~*] **:** able to see and understand people, things, or situations clearly and intelligently ▪ a *discerning* critic ▪ She has a *discerning* eye for good art.

– **dis·cern·ing·ly** *adv*

dis·cern·ment /dɪˈsɚnmənt/ *noun* [*noncount*] **:** the ability to see and understand people, things, or stituations clearly and intelligently ▪ His lack of *discernment* led to his disastrous choice of business partners.

[1]**dis·charge** /dɪsˈʧɑɚʤ/ *verb* **-charg·es; -charged; -charg·ing**

1 [+ *obj*] **:** to allow (someone) to leave a hospital, prison, etc. ▪ She's due to be *discharged* from the hospital on Wednesday. ▪ *Discharge* the prisoners.

2 [+ *obj*] **a :** to take away the job of (someone) **:** to end the employment of (someone) ▪ The company illegally *discharged* [=*fired*] several union organizers. ▪ We had to *discharge* several employees last week. **b :** to end the service of (someone) in a formal or official way ▪ Thousands of soldiers were *discharged* after the war. **:** to release (someone) from duty ▪ The judge *discharged* the jury.

3 : to shoot or fire (a weapon) [+ *obj*] The ship *discharged* missiles against enemy targets. ▪ *discharging* a firearm [*no obj*] The gun failed to *discharge*.

4 [+ *obj*] **:** to allow (someone) to get out of a vehicle ▪ The bus had stopped to *discharge* [=*let off*] passengers.

5 a : to send out (a liquid, gas, or waste material) [+ *obj*] Smokestacks from the factory *discharge* [=*emit*] chemicals into the air. ▪ *discharging* pollution into a lake ▪ The wound began to *discharge* pus. [*no obj*] a river that *discharges* [=*flows*] into the ocean **b :** to send out (electricity) [+ *obj*] *discharge* electricity from a battery [*no obj*] allowing the electricity to *discharge* safely

6 [+ *obj*] *formal* **a :** to do what is required by (something) ▪ He vowed to faithfully *discharge* [=*fulfill*] the duties/responsibilities of his office. ▪ *discharging* an obligation **b :** to pay (a debt) ▪ They have failed to *discharge* their debts.

[2]**dis·charge** /ˈdɪsˌʧɑɚʤ/ *noun, pl* **-charg·es**

1 : the release of someone from a hospital, prison, etc. [*noncount*] The doctors approved her *discharge* from the hospital. [*count*] early hospital *discharges*

2 a : the act of firing or dismissing someone from a job [*noncount*] Several former employees are suing the company for wrongful *discharge*. [*count*] a *discharge* from employment **b** [*count*] **:** the act of ending a person's service to the military ▪ After his *discharge* from the military, he went to college to become a teacher. ✧ A ***dishonorable discharge*** is given to a soldier who has done something wrong and is forced to leave the military. ▪ He was court-martialed for improper conduct and left the navy with a *dishonorable discharge*. ✧ An ***honorable discharge*** is given to a soldier who has not done anything wrong and is not being forced to leave. ▪ He went to college after receiving an *honorable discharge* from the army.

3 : the act of firing a weapon [*noncount*] The damage was caused by accidental *discharge* of a hunting rifle. [*count*] a rapid *discharge* from a gun

4 a [*count*] **:** a liquid or gas that flows out of something ▪ a clear *discharge* from the nose and eyes ▪ nasal *discharges* **b** [*noncount*] **:** the movement of a liquid or gas from something ▪ The factory was charged with the illegal *discharge* of pollution into a stream. ▪ the *discharge* of pus from a wound

5 [*count*] **:** a flow of electricity ▪ an electrical *discharge*

6 *formal* **:** the act of doing what is required or of paying a debt [*noncount*] the *discharge* of debts/obligations [*count*] a *discharge* of debt

dis·ci·ple /dɪˈsaɪpəl/ *noun, pl* **-ci·ples** [*count*]

1 : someone who accepts and helps to spread the teachings of a famous person ▪ a *disciple* of Sigmund Freud

2 : one of a group of 12 men who were sent out to spread the teachings of Jesus Christ **:** APOSTLE

– **dis·ci·ple·ship** /dɪˈsaɪpəlˌʃɪp/ *noun* [*noncount*]

dis·ci·pli·nar·i·an /ˌdɪsəpləˈnerijən/ *noun, pl* **-ans** [*count*] **:** a person who is very strict about punishing bad behavior **:** a person who uses discipline as a way of making sure that rules or orders are obeyed ▪ The school's principal is a strict/rigid *disciplinarian*.

dis·ci·plin·ary /ˈdɪsəpləˌneri, *Brit* ˈdɪsəplənri/ *adj* **:** intended to correct or punish bad behavior **:** of or relating to discipline ▪ a *disciplinary* hearing ▪ taking *disciplinary* action ▪ The committee is considering *disciplinary* measures against him.

[1]**dis·ci·pline** /ˈdɪsəplən/ *noun, pl* **-plines**

1 [*noncount*] **a :** control that is gained by requiring that rules or orders be obeyed and punishing bad behavior ▪ The teacher has a hard time maintaining *discipline* in the classroom. **b :** a way of behaving that shows a willingness to obey rules or orders ▪ The troops were praised for their dedication and *discipline*. **c :** behavior that is judged by how well it follows a set of rules or orders ▪ poor *discipline* ▪ maintaining good *discipline* **d :** punishment for bad behavior ▪ Some parents feel that the school's principal has been too harsh in meting out *discipline*.

2 [*noncount*] **:** the ability to keep working at something that is difficult ▪ I tried learning the piano, but I lacked the *discipline* [=*self-discipline*] to stick with it. ▪ He doesn't have the *discipline* [=*self-control*] to stay on his diet.

3 [*count*] **:** an activity that is done regularly as a way of training yourself to do something or to improve your behavior ▪ Keeping a journal is a good *discipline* for a writer.

4 [*count*] : a field of study : a subject that is taught ▪ She has received training in several academic *disciplines*.

[2]**discipline** *verb* **-plines; -plined; -plin·ing** [+ *obj*]
1 : to punish (someone) as a way of making sure that rules or orders are obeyed ▪ She was *disciplined* for misbehaving in class. ▪ He seems unwilling or unable to *discipline* his children. ▪ *disciplining* the troops
2 : to train (yourself) to do something by controlling your behavior ▪ I'm trying to *discipline* myself to eat less.
– **disciplined** *adj* [*more* ~; *most* ~] ▪ I'm not *disciplined* enough to exercise everyday. ▪ We need a more *disciplined* approach if the program is to be successfully implemented. ▪ an orderly and *disciplined* mind

disc jockey *noun, pl* ~ **-eys** [*count*] : a person who plays popular recorded music on the radio or at a party or nightclub — called also *DJ*, (*informal*) *deejay*

dis·claim /dɪsˈkleɪm/ *verb* **-claims; -claimed; -claim·ing** [+ *obj*] *formal* : to say that you do not have (something, such as knowledge, responsibility, etc.) ▪ The government *disclaimed* [=*disavowed*] any knowledge of his activities. ▪ She *disclaimed* [=(less formally) *denied*] all responsibility for the accident.

dis·claim·er /dɪsˈkleɪmɚ/ *noun, pl* **-ers** [*count*] : a statement that is meant to prevent an incorrect understanding of something (such as a book, a movie, or an advertisement) ▪ The documentary opens with a *disclaimer* that many of its scenes are "fictional re-creations" of real events.

dis·close /dɪsˈkloʊz/ *verb* **-clos·es; -closed; -clos·ing** [+ *obj*] : to make (something) known to the public ▪ He refused to *disclose* the source of his information. ▪ The company has *disclosed* that it will be laying off thousands of workers later this year. ▪ The identity of the victim has not yet been *disclosed*.
– **dis·clos·er** *noun, pl* **-ers** [*count*]

dis·clo·sure /dɪsˈkloʊʒɚ/ *noun, pl* **-sures**
1 [*noncount*] : the act of making something known : the act of disclosing something ▪ We demand full *disclosure* of the facts.
2 [*count*] : something (such as information) that is made known or revealed : something that is disclosed ▪ This is just the latest in a series of shocking *disclosures* [=*revelations*] about his criminal past.

dis·co /ˈdɪskoʊ/ *noun, pl* **-cos**
1 [*count*] : a nightclub where people dance to recorded popular music
2 [*noncount*] : a type of popular dance music

dis·col·or (*US*) *or Brit* **dis·col·our** /dɪsˈkʌlɚ/ *verb* **-ors; -ored; -or·ing** : to change in color especially in a bad way [*no obj*] The fabric is guaranteed not to *discolor*. [+ *obj*] The wine stain *discolored* the rug.
– **discolored** *adj* [*more* ~; *most* ~] ▪ badly *discolored* teeth

dis·col·or·a·tion /dɪsˌkʌləˈreɪʃən/ *noun, pl* **-tions**
1 [*noncount*] : the act of changing color in a bad way ▪ The medicine may cause *discoloration* [=*staining*] of the teeth.
2 [*count*] : a discolored spot or area ▪ His shirt has a small *discoloration* [=*stain*] on the sleeve.

dis·com·fit /dɪsˈkʌmfət/ *verb* **-fits; -fit·ed; -fit·ing** [+ *obj*] *formal* : to make (someone) confused or upset — often used as (*be*) *discomfited* ▪ The governor *was* clearly *discomfited* [=*disconcerted*] by the question.
– **discomfiting** *adj* [*more* ~; *most* ~] ▪ She bears a *discomfiting* resemblance to one of my old teachers. – **dis·com·fi·ture** /dɪsˈkʌmfəʧɚ/ *noun* [*noncount*] ▪ His *discomfiture* was obvious.

[1]**dis·com·fort** /dɪsˈkʌmfɚt/ *noun, pl* **-forts**
1 : an uncomfortable or painful feeling in the body [*noncount*] The patient is still experiencing some *discomfort*. [*count*] the *discomforts* of pregnancy
2 [*noncount*] : a feeling of being somewhat worried, unhappy, etc. ▪ These new developments are being watched with *discomfort* by many of our allies.

[2]**discomfort** *verb* **-forts; -fort·ed; -fort·ing** [+ *obj*] *formal* : to make (someone) uncomfortable, worried, etc. — often used as (*be*) *discomforted* ▪ Some audience members *were discomforted* by the graphic violence.
– **discomforting** *adj* [*more* ~; *most* ~] ▪ *discomforting* questions/thoughts

dis·con·cert /ˌdɪskənˈsɚt/ *verb* **-certs; -cert·ed; -cert·ing** [+ *obj*] *somewhat formal* : to make (someone) upset or embarrassed ▪ News of his criminal past has *disconcerted* even his admirers. — often used as (*be*) *disconcerted* ▪ I *was disconcerted* by her tone of voice.
– **disconcerted** /ˌdɪskənˈsɚtəd/ *adj* [*more* ~; *most* ~] ▪ We were very *disconcerted* to learn that our flight had been canceled. – **disconcerting** /ˌdɪskənˈsɚtɪŋ/ *adj* [*more* ~; *most* ~] ▪ I found it *disconcerting* to be left alone in her office. ▪ He has a *disconcerting* habit of answering a question with another question. – **dis·con·cert·ing·ly** *adv*

dis·con·nect /ˌdɪskəˈnɛkt/ *verb* **-nects; -nect·ed; -nect·ing** [+ *obj*]
1 : to separate (something) from something else : to break a connection between two or more things ▪ *disconnect* a hose ▪ The hose and faucet had been *disconnected*. — often + *from* ▪ *Disconnect* the hose *from* the faucet.
2 **a** : to stop or end the supply of electricity, water, gas, etc., to (something, such as a piece of electronic equipment) ▪ *Disconnect* the old printer and connect the new one. ▪ The alarm system had been *disconnected*. **b** : to stop or end the supply of (electricity, water, gas, etc.) ▪ Before starting, be sure to *disconnect* the power supply. ▪ Our landlord threatened to *disconnect* our electricity.
3 : to end the connection to a system, network, etc., through a telephone, computer, or other device ▪ We were talking on the phone but suddenly we got *disconnected*. ▪ I got *disconnected* when I was surfing the Internet. [=I lost my Internet connection] — opposite CONNECT
– **dis·con·nec·tion** /ˌdɪskəˈnɛkʃən/ *noun, pl* **-tions** [*count*] telephone *disconnections* [*noncount*] *disconnection* from a power source

disconnected *adj*
1 : not connected to something (such as a power source) ▪ The phone lines are all *disconnected*. ▪ a *disconnected* television set
2 [*more* ~; *most* ~] : not having parts joined together in a logical way ▪ Her biography reads like a series of *disconnected* stories. ▪ a *disconnected* [=*incoherent*] speech
– **dis·con·nect·ed·ness** *noun* [*noncount*]

dis·con·so·late /dɪsˈkɑːnsələt/ *adj* [*more* ~; *most* ~] *formal* : very unhappy or sad ▪ Campaign workers grew increasingly *disconsolate* as the results came in.
– **dis·con·so·late·ly** *adv*

[1]**dis·con·tent** /ˌdɪskənˈtɛnt/ *noun* [*noncount*] : a feeling of unhappiness or disapproval : a lack of contentment ▪ The survey indicates public *discontent* [=*dissatisfaction*] with the current administration. ▪ There was widespread *discontent* [=(less commonly) *discontentment*] over the court's ruling. — opposite CONTENTMENT

[2]**discontent** *adj* [*more* ~; *most* ~] : not pleased or satisfied : DISCONTENTED ▪ Polls show that voters are growing increasingly *discontent*.
– **dis·con·tent·ment** /ˌdɪskənˈtɛntmənt/ *noun* [*noncount*]

dis·con·tent·ed /ˌdɪskənˈtɛntəd/ *adj* [*more* ~; *most* ~] : not happy with your situation, position, etc. : not contented ▪ *discontented* employees — often + *with* ▪ She's been feeling *discontented with* life in general.
– **dis·con·tent·ed·ly** *adv*

dis·con·tin·ue /ˌdɪskənˈtɪnju/ *verb* **-tin·ues; -tin·ued; -tin·u·ing** [+ *obj*]
1 : to end (something) : STOP ▪ He *discontinued* his visits to the psychiatrist. ▪ She chose to *discontinue* her studies. — often used as (*be*) *discontinued* ▪ The treatment has *been discontinued*.
2 : to stop making or offering (a product, service, etc.) ▪ The company has announced that the current model will be *discontinued* next year. ▪ They are planning to *discontinue* bus service between the two towns.
– **discontinued** *adj* ▪ They're having a sale on *discontinued* models. ▪ a *discontinued* line of products – **dis·con·tin·u·a·tion** /ˌdɪskənˌtɪnjuˈeɪʃən/ *noun* [*noncount*] ▪ the *discontinuation* of services

dis·con·ti·nu·i·ty /dɪsˌkɑːntəˈnuːwəti, *Brit* dɪsˌkɒntəˈnjuːwəti/ *noun, pl* **-ties**
1 [*noncount*] : the quality or state of not being continuous : lack of continuity ▪ There is a sense of *discontinuity* between the book's chapters.
2 [*count*] : a change or break in a process ▪ Some patients have experienced delays or *discontinuities* [=*gaps*] in their care.

dis·con·tin·u·ous /ˌdɪskənˈtɪnjəwəs/ *adj* [*more* ~; *most* ~] : not continuous : having interruptions or gaps ▪ *discontinuous* sleep ▪ a *discontinuous* series of events

dis·cord /ˈdɪsˌkoɚd/ *noun, pl* **-cords** *formal*
1 [*noncount*] : lack of agreement between people, ideas, etc. ▪ marital *discord* [=*conflict*] ▪ *discord* between political parties ▪

The city has long been known as a scene of racial intolerance and *discord*.

2 : an unpleasant combination of musical notes [*count*] The song ends on a *discord*. [*noncount*] musical *discord*

dis·cord·ant /dɪsˈkoɚdn̩t/ *adj* [*more ~; most ~*]

1 : harsh or unpleasant in sound • *discordant* music

2 : not agreeing : not in harmony • She has the difficult task of bringing together a number of *discordant* elements. • *discordant* opinions ◊ To ***strike/sound a discordant note*** means to express an opinion that disagrees with what other people are saying. • Most reviewers loved the show, but one critic *struck a discordant note*, finding it "trite and predictable."

dis·co·theque /ˌdɪskəˈtɛk/ *noun, pl* **-theques** [*count*] : DISCO 1

[1]dis·count /ˈdɪsˌkaʊnt/ *noun, pl* **-counts** [*count*] : an amount taken off a regular price : a price reduction • The store offers a two percent *discount* when customers pay in cash. • We were able to buy our tickets ***at a discount*** [=for less than the usual price]

[2]discount *adj, always used before a noun*

1 : selling goods or services at reduced prices • a *discount* store/chain/retailer • *discount* airlines

2 : offered or sold at a reduced price • *discount* tickets

3 : cheaper than usual • *discount* prices/rates

[3]discount *verb* **-counts; -count·ed; -count·ing** [+ *obj*]

1 a : to lower the amount of (a bill, price, etc.) • The vacation plan included a *discounted* price/rate on our hotel room. **b :** to lower the price of (a product) • Car dealers are heavily *discounting* last year's unsold models.

2 a : to think of (something) as having little importance or value • You shouldn't *discount* [=*minimize*] the importance of studying. **b :** to believe that (something, such as information, a rumor, etc.) is not worth serious attention • We can't *discount* [=*dismiss, disregard*] the possibility that the economy will worsen in the near future. • These threats cannot be entirely *discounted*.

dis·cour·age /dɪˈskɚrɪʤ/ *verb* **-ag·es; -aged; -ag·ing** [+ *obj*]

1 : to make (someone) less determined, hopeful, or confident • Try not to let losing *discourage* you. — often used (*be/get*) *discouraged* • We *were discouraged* by their lack of enthusiasm. • Students may *get discouraged* by activities that are too advanced.

2 a : to make (something) less likely to happen • The area's dry climate *discourages* agriculture. • He claims the new regulations will *discourage* investment. **b :** to try to make people not want to do (something) • The purpose of the law is to *discourage* [=*deter*] speeding. • That type of behavior ought to be *discouraged*. ◊ To ***discourage (someone) from doing*** (something) is to tell or advise someone not to do something. • His parents *discouraged him from watching* too much television. [=told him he should not watch too much television] • They *discouraged her from going*. [=they told her why she should not go] — opposite ENCOURAGE

– discouraged *adj* [*more ~; most ~*] • The team's losing streak has left many fans feeling hopeless and *discouraged*. [=*downhearted, disheartened*]

dis·cour·age·ment /dɪˈskɚrɪʤmənt/ *noun, pl* **-ments**

1 [*noncount*] : the act of making something less likely to happen or of making people less likely to do something • the *discouragement* of drug use among teenagers • He joined the army despite *discouragement* from his parents. [=despite being discouraged from joining by his parents]

2 [*noncount*] : a feeling of having lost hope or confidence • She expressed *discouragement* over the difficulty of finding a good job. • The team's losses have left fans with a feeling of *discouragement*.

3 [*count*] : something (such as a failure or difficulty) that discourages someone • He says that the tax is a *discouragement* to doing business in this state. • Despite the *discouragements* of the past week, we need to continue moving forward.

discouraging *adj* [*more ~; most ~*] : causing loss of hope or confidence • The team suffered another *discouraging* loss. • The latest test results were very *discouraging*. — opposite ENCOURAGING

– dis·cour·ag·ing·ly *adv* • *discouragingly* expensive

[1]dis·course /ˈdɪsˌkoɚs/ *noun, pl* **-cours·es** *formal*

1 [*noncount*] : the use of words to exchange thoughts and ideas • It's a word that doesn't have much use in ordinary *discourse*. [=*conversation*] • He likes to engage in lively *discourse* with his visitors. • public/political *discourse*

2 [*count*] : a long talk or piece of writing about a subject • She delivered an entertaining *discourse* on the current state of the film industry.

[2]dis·course /dɪˈskoɚs/ *verb* **-cours·es; -coursed; -cours·ing** [*no obj*] *formal* : to talk about something especially for a long time • She could *discourse* for hours on/about almost any subject.

dis·cour·te·ous /dɪsˈkɚtijəs/ *adj* [*more ~; most ~*] *formal* : rude or impolite : not showing good manners • The waiter was *discourteous* to me. • It was thoughtless and *discourteous* to leave us waiting so long. — opposite COURTEOUS

– dis·cour·te·ous·ly *adv* • They treated us *discourteously*.

– dis·cour·te·ous·ness *noun* [*noncount*]

dis·cour·te·sy /dɪsˈkɚtəsi/ *noun, pl* **-sies** *formal*

1 [*noncount*] : rude or impolite behavior • They've received many complaints about customers being treated with disrespect and *discourtesy*. [=*rudeness*]

2 [*count*] : a rude act • His tardiness was just another in a series of small *discourtesies*.

dis·cov·er /dɪˈskʌvɚ/ *verb* **-ers; -ered; -er·ing** [+ *obj*]

1 : to see, find, or become aware of (something) for the first time • Christopher Columbus *discovered* the New World in 1492. • Several new species of plants have recently been *discovered*. • Scientists claim to have *discovered* [=*found*] a new way of controlling high blood pressure. • It took her several weeks to *discover* the solution. • His life was never the same after he *discovered* sailing. [=after he first went sailing; after he found how much he enjoyed sailing]

2 : to show the presence of (something hidden or difficult to see) : to make (something) known • The autopsy *discovered* [=*revealed, uncovered*] traces of poison in the victim's blood. • The tests have *discovered* problems in the current design.

3 : to learn or find out (something surprising or unexpected) • I was surprised to *discover* [=*realize*] that I had lost my keys. • She soon *discovered* what had been going on.

4 : to find out about and help (a talented new performer, writer, etc.) • During her career she was responsible for *discovering* many now famous musicians.

– dis·cov·er·er *noun, pl* **-ers** [*count*] • The species is named for its *discoverer*.

dis·cov·ery /dɪˈskʌvəri/ *noun, pl* **-er·ies**

1 : the act of finding or learning something for the first time : the act of discovering something [*count*] Scientists announced the *discovery* of a new species of plant. • Her research led to a number of important *discoveries* about the disease. • Reporters made the shocking *discovery* that the governor had been unfaithful to his wife. • the *discovery* of pollution in the river • the *discovery* of a talented musician [*noncount*] voyages of *discovery* [=voyages that are done to discover and learn about new places, people, etc.] • sailors during the age of *discovery*

2 [*count*] : something seen or learned for the first time : something discovered • recent archaeological *discoveries* • It was one of the most important *discoveries* in the history of medicine.

[1]dis·cred·it /dɪsˈkrɛdət/ *verb* **-its; -it·ed; -it·ing** [+ *obj*]

1 : to cause (someone or something) to seem dishonest or untrue • The prosecution *discredited* the witness by showing that she had lied in the past. • Many of his theories have been thoroughly *discredited*.

2 : to damage the reputation of (someone) • an attempt to *discredit* the governor

– dis·cred·it·able /dɪsˈkrɛdətəbəl/ *adj* [*more ~; most ~*] • *discreditable* conduct **– dis·cred·it·ably** /dɪsˈkrɛdətəbli/ *adv*

[2]discredit *noun* [*noncount*] : loss of reputation or respect — often used with *bring* • His criminal activities *brought discredit* on/upon/to his family. • This scandal has *brought* the whole enterprise into lasting *discredit*. ◊ Something that is ***to your discredit*** causes people to have a less favorable opinion of you. • *To our discredit*, we failed to offer help when it was most needed.

dis·creet /dɪˈskriːt/ *adj* [*more ~; most ~*]

1 — used to suggest that someone is being careful about not allowing something from being known or noticed by many people • a *discreet* way to handle the problem • She was always very *discreet* about her personal life. • He made *discreet* inquiries about the job. • He maintained a *discreet* silence. — opposite INDISCREET

2 : not likely to be seen or noticed by many people • A photographer followed the bride and groom at a *discreet* [=*unobtrusive*] distance.

Do not confuse *discreet* with *discrete*.

– dis·creet·ly *adv* ▪ a letter *discreetly* hidden in the pages of an old book

dis·crep·an·cy /dɪˈskrɛpənsi/ *noun, pl* **-cies :** a difference especially between things that should be the same [*count*] *Discrepancies* in the firm's financial statements led to an investigation. ▪ There were *discrepancies* between their accounts of the accident. [*noncount*] There is some *discrepancy* [=*disagreement*] between the results of the two studies.

dis·crete /dɪˈskriːt/ *adj, formal* **:** separate and different from each other ▪ The process can be broken down into a number of *discrete* [=*separate, individual*] steps.

Do not confuse *discrete* with *discreet*.

– dis·crete·ly *adv*

dis·cre·tion /dɪˈskrɛʃən/ *noun* [*noncount*]

1 : the right to choose what should be done in a particular situation ▪ Each artist in the gallery has *discretion* over the price that will be charged for his or her work. ▪ The coach ***used/exercised his own discretion*** to let the injured quarterback play. ▪ The amount each person contributes will be ***left to the discretion of*** the individual. [=each person will decide how much he or she will contribute] ▪ Because of the violence in the movie, ***parental discretion*** is advised. [=parents are advised to think about whether or not they want their children to see the movie] ✧ Something that is done ***at your discretion*** is done if, how, when, etc., you choose to do it. ▪ You can cancel the service *at your (own) discretion.* [=you can cancel the service whenever you choose] ▪ Exactly how much to tip a server is ***at the discretion of*** the customer.

2 : the quality of being careful about what you do and say so that people will not be embarrassed or offended **:** the quality of being discreet ▪ He always uses care and *discretion* when dealing with others. ▪ She handled the awkward situation with great *discretion.* ▪ She is ***the soul of discretion***. [=she is very discreet] — opposite INDISCRETION

discretion is the better part of valor — used to say that it is better to be careful than to do something that is dangerous and unnecessary

dis·cre·tion·ary /dɪˈskrɛʃəˌneri, *Brit* dɪˈskrɛʃənri/ *adj*

1 : available to be used when and how you decide ▪ She has enough ***discretionary income*** [=income that is left after paying for things that are essential, such as food and housing] to pay for a nice vacation each year.

2 : done or used when necessary ▪ the governor's *discretionary* power

dis·crim·i·nate /dɪˈskrɪməˌneɪt/ *verb* **-nates; -nat·ed; -nat·ing**

1 [*no obj*] **:** to unfairly treat a person or group of people differently from other people or groups ▪ The school is not allowed to *discriminate.* ▪ It is illegal to *discriminate* on the grounds/basis of race/sex. [=it is illegal to treat someone differently because of his or her race/sex] — often + *against* ▪ The firm *discriminated against* him because of his race.

2 *somewhat formal* **:** to notice and understand that one thing is different from another thing **:** to recognize a difference between things [+ *obj*] He is old enough to *discriminate* [=*distinguish, tell*] right from wrong. ▪ I can *discriminate* [=*differentiate*] the individual voices in the choir. [*no obj*] — often + *among* or *between* ▪ He could *discriminate among* the birds by their calls. ▪ She can *discriminate between* ripe and unripe fruit by smell alone.

discriminating *adj* [*more* ~; *most* ~] *approving* **:** liking only things that are of good quality **:** able to recognize the difference between things that are of good quality and those that are not ▪ a *discriminating* audience ▪ Those with more *discriminating* [=*discerning*] tastes are likely to find the movie dull and clichéd.

dis·crim·i·na·tion /dɪˌskrɪməˈneɪʃən/ *noun, pl* **-tions**

1 [*noncount*] **:** the practice of unfairly treating a person or group of people differently from other people or groups of people ▪ racial/sexual/religious *discrimination* = *discrimination* based on race/sex/religion = *discrimination* on the basis of race/sex/religion ▪ The law prohibits *discrimination* in hiring. ▪ He sued the company for age *discrimination.* ▪ blatant forms of *discrimination* — often + *against* ▪ Company policy does not allow *discrimination against* women.

2 [*noncount*] *formal* **a :** the ability to recognize the difference between things that are of good quality and those that are not ▪ Those with more *discrimination* [=*discernment*] are likely to find the movie dull and clichéd. **b :** the ability to understand that one thing is different from another thing ▪ the animal's impressive scent/visual *discrimination*

3 [*count*] **:** a difference that is understood or recognized ▪ He was able to ***make discriminations*** among/between the birds by their calls. [=able to distinguish the birds by their calls]

dis·crim·i·na·to·ry /dɪˈskrɪmənəˌtori, *Brit* dɪˈskrɪmənətri/ *adj* [*more* ~; *most* ~] **:** not fair **:** unfairly treating a person or group of people differently from other people or groups of people ▪ The law prohibits *discriminatory* hiring practices. ▪ *discriminatory* treatment of minorities

dis·cur·sive /dɪˈskɚsɪv/ *adj* [*more* ~; *most* ~] *formal* **:** talking or writing about many different things in a way that is not highly organized ▪ The instructor gave a *discursive* [=*rambling*] lecture that wandered from one topic to another. ▪ *discursive* prose

– dis·cur·sive·ly *adv* ▪ He writes *discursively.*

dis·cus /ˈdɪskəs/ *noun, pl* **-cus·es**

1 [*count*] **:** a heavy flat round object that people throw as far as they can as a sport ▪ a *discus* thrower

2 ***the discus*** **:** an athletic event in which people compete by trying to throw a discus farther than everyone else ▪ winner of *the discus*

discus

dis·cuss /dɪˈskʌs/ *verb* **-cuss·es; -cussed; -cus·sing** [+ *obj*]

1 : to talk about (something) with another person or group ▪ She *discussed* the plan with several colleagues. ▪ They held a meeting to *discuss* the future of the company. ▪ We'll *discuss* where to meet later. ▪ Have you *discussed* the matter with your family?

2 : to give information, ideas, opinions, etc., about (something) in writing or speech ▪ In the first chapter, the author *discusses* childcare issues. ▪ The article *discusses* the theory in depth.

dis·cus·sion /dɪˈskʌʃən/ *noun, pl* **-sions**

1 : the act of talking about something with another person or a group of people **:** a conversation about something [*count*] The class was involved in a heated *discussion* about politics. ▪ I hope to ***have a discussion*** with them about the matter soon. [*noncount*] After much *discussion* of the plan, the idea was rejected entirely. ▪ She usually has an opinion about whatever subject/topic/issue is ***under discussion***. [=being talked about] ▪ During the period *under discussion,* the town grew in size. ▪ The smoking ban is a major ***topic of discussion*** these days. ▪ The proposal is ***up for discussion*** [=the proposal will be talked about] at today's meeting.

2 [*count*] **:** a speech or piece of writing that gives information, ideas, opinions, etc., about something ▪ The article is an in-depth *discussion* of his theories. ▪ The first chapter includes a *discussion* of childcare issues.

[1]dis·dain /dɪsˈdeɪn/ *noun* [*singular*] **:** a feeling of strong dislike or disapproval of someone or something you think does not deserve respect ▪ He glared at the waiter with a look of *disdain* [=*contempt, scorn*] on his face. ▪ He regarded their proposal with *disdain.* ▪ I have a healthy *disdain* for companies that mistreat their workers.

[2]disdain *verb* **-dains; -dained; -dain·ing** [+ *obj*] *formal*

1 : to strongly dislike or disapprove of (someone or something) ▪ They *disdained* him for being weak. ▪ teenagers who *disdain* [=*loathe, detest*] authority ▪ a critic who *disdains* [=*abhors, hates*] all modern art ▪ She *disdains* gambling.

2 : to refuse *to do* (something) because of feelings of dislike or disapproval ▪ She *disdained to answer* their questions.

dis·dain·ful /dɪsˈdeɪnfəl/ *adj* [*more* ~; *most* ~] *somewhat formal* **:** felling strong dislike or disapproval for something or someone you think does not deserve respect **:** feeling or showing disdain ▪ He looked at the waiter with a *disdainful* glare. ▪ a *disdainful* attitude toward authority — often + *of* ▪ a critic who is *disdainful of* all modern art

– dis·dain·ful·ly *adv* ▪ He glared *disdainfully* at the waiter.

dis·ease /dɪˈziːz/ *noun, pl* **-eas·es**

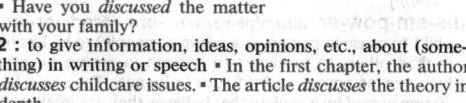

1 : an illness that affects a person, animal, or plant **:** a condition that prevents the body or mind from working normally [*count*] infectious/contagious *diseases* ▪ He suffers from a rare genetic *disease.* ▪ a deadly/debilitating *disease* ▪ a *disease* of the mind/kidneys ▪ *diseases* of poultry [*noncount*] Thousands die of heart *disease* each year. ▪ They are working to

stop the spread of *disease* in rural areas. ▪ gum/liver *disease*
2 [*count*] : a problem that a person, group, organization, or society has and cannot stop ▪ The article cites intolerance as one of the most dangerous of society's *diseases.* ▪ He sees crime as a *disease* that too often plagues the poor and disadvantaged.
— **dis·eased** /dɪˈziːzd/ *adj* [*more* ~; *most* ~] ▪ She removed the *diseased* tree limbs. ▪ *diseased* cells/lungs/plants ▪ a *diseased* mind

dis·em·bark /ˌdɪsəmˈbɑɚk/ *verb* **-barks; -barked; -bark·ing**
1 [*no obj*] : to leave a ship or airplane ▪ The plane's crew members were the last ones to *disembark.* ▪ Passengers *disembarked* [=*debarked*] from the ship. — opposite EMBARK
2 [+ *obj*] : to remove (something or someone) from a ship or airplane ▪ They *disembarked* [=(more commonly) *unloaded*] the cargo at the dock.
— **dis·em·bar·ka·tion** /dɪsˌɛmˌbɑɚˈkeɪʃən/ *noun* [*noncount*]

dis·em·bod·ied /ˌdɪsəmˈbɑːdid/ *adj*
1 : not having a body ▪ *disembodied* spirits : not attached to a body ▪ a *disembodied* head
2 : coming from a person who cannot be seen ▪ We heard *disembodied* voices coming over the speakers.

dis·em·bow·el /ˌdɪsəmˈbawəl/ *verb* **-els;** *US* **-eled** *or Brit* **-elled;** *US* **-el·ing** *or Brit* **-el·ling** [+ *obj*] : to take the stomach, intestines, etc., out of (an animal or person) : to remove the bowels of (an animal or person) ▪ The fierce cat uses its claws to *disembowel* its prey. — sometimes used figuratively ▪ Critics say that the spending cuts will *disembowel* the program.
— **dis·em·bow·el·ment** /ˌdɪsəmˈbawəlmənt/ *noun* [*noncount*]

dis·em·pow·er /ˌdɪsɪmˈpawɚ/ *verb* **-ers; -ered; -er·ing** [+ *obj*] : to cause (a person or a group of people) to be less likely than others to succeed : to prevent (a person or group) from having power, authority, or influence ▪ They have been *disempowered* by a society that believes they are intellectually inferior. ▪ *disempowered* minorities — opposite EMPOWER
— **dis·em·pow·er·ment** /ˌdɪsɪmˈpawɚmənt/ *noun* [*noncount*] ▪ the *disempowerment* of minorities

dis·en·chant·ed /ˌdɪsɪnˈʧæntəd, *Brit* ˌdɪsɪnˈʧɑːntəd/ *adj* [*more* ~; *most* ~] : no longer happy or satisfied with something ▪ *disenchanted* voters — often + *with* ▪ He became more *disenchanted* [=*dissatisfied*] *with* his job every day.
— **dis·en·chant·ment** /ˌdɪsɪnˈʧæntmənt, *Brit* ˌdɪsɪnˈʧɑːntmənt/ *noun* [*noncount*] ▪ voter *disenchantment* ▪ He talked about his growing *disenchantment* with his job.

dis·en·fran·chise /ˌdɪsɪnˈfrænˌʧaɪz/ *verb* **-chis·es; -chised; -chis·ing** [+ *obj*] : to prevent (a person or group of people) from having the right to vote ▪ They *disenfranchised* poor people by making property ownership a requirement for registering to vote. ▪ *disenfranchised* minorities — opposite ENFRANCHISE
— **dis·en·fran·chise·ment** /ˌdɪsɪnˈfrænˌʧaɪzmənt/ *noun* [*noncount*] ▪ the *disenfranchisement* of minorities

dis·en·gage /ˌdɪsn̩ˈgeɪʤ/ *verb* **-gag·es; -gaged; -gag·ing**
1 : to separate from someone or something [*no obj*] The two dancers moved together in a series of quick movements before *disengaging* and leaping apart. [+ *obj*] — usually + *from* ▪ I was trying to *disengage* [=*free*] myself *from* the safety harness.
2 [*no obj*] : to stop being involved with a person or group : to stop taking part in something — usually + *from* ▪ He began to *disengage* [=(more commonly) *withdraw*] *from* the family when he was 15 or so.
3 : to move (a mechanism or part of a machine) so that it no longer fits into another part [+ *obj*] Put the car in gear, and then slowly *disengage* the clutch while pressing on the gas pedal. [*no obj*] If there is a malfunction, the gears will automatically *disengage.* — opposite ENGAGE
4 *military* : to order (a group of soldiers) to stop fighting and move away from an area [+ *obj*] The government says it will gradually *disengage* [=*withdraw*] soldiers from the region. [*no obj*] Troops in the area have begun to *disengage.* [=*withdraw*]
— **dis·en·gaged** /ˌdɪsn̩ˈgeɪʤd/ *adj* [*more* ~; *most* ~] ▪ She became more and more *disengaged* [=*withdrawn*] as her depression worsened. — **dis·en·gage·ment** /ˌdɪsn̩ˈgeɪʤmənt/ *noun* [*noncount*] ▪ emotional *disengagement* [=*withdrawal*] ▪ *disengagement* of the clutch ▪ the *disengagement* of troops from the region

dis·en·tan·gle /ˌdɪsɪnˈtæŋgəl/ *verb* **-tan·gles; -tan·gled; -tan·gling** [+ *obj*]
1 : to separate (things that are twisted together or caught on one another) ▪ I can't *disentangle* [=*untangle*] the wires/hangers. — often + *from* ▪ She was trying to *disentangle* her hair *from* her necklace. — often used figuratively ▪ She finally *disentangled* herself *from* a bad relationship.
2 : to remove the twists or knots in (something) ▪ *disentangle* [=*untangle*] a knotted string/rope
— **dis·en·tan·gle·ment** /ˌdɪsɪnˈtæŋgəlmənt/ *noun* [*noncount*]

dis·equi·lib·ri·um /dɪsˌiːkwəˈlɪbrijəm/ *noun* [*singular*] *formal + technical* : a loss or lack of balance ▪ The condition is caused by a *disequilibrium* in the brain's chemistry. ▪ the *disequilibrium* of power

dis·es·tab·lish /ˌdɪsəˈstæblɪʃ/ *verb* **-lish·es; -lished; -lish·ing** [+ *obj*] *formal* : to take away a particular church's status as the official church of a nation or state ▪ efforts to *disestablish* the Church of England
— **dis·es·tab·lish·ment** /ˌdɪsəˈstæblɪʃmənt/ *noun* [*noncount*]

[1]**dis·fa·vor** (*US*) *or Brit* **dis·fa·vour** /dɪsˈfeɪvɚ/ *noun* [*noncount*] *formal*
1 : a feeling of disapproval or dislike ▪ He regarded their proposal with *disfavor.* ▪ They looked with *disfavor* upon her.
2 : the condition of being disapproved of or disliked ▪ The theory has long been ***in disfavor.*** [=the theory has been unpopular for a long time] ▪ The style ***fell into disfavor*** [=became unpopular] a decade ago.

[2]**disfavor** (*US*) *or Brit* **disfavour** *verb* **-vors; -vored; -vor·ing** [+ *obj*] *formal*
1 : to disapprove of or dislike (someone or something) ▪ Some bar owners *disfavor* [=(more commonly) *are against*] the ban on smoking.
2 : to make it more difficult for (a person, organization, etc.) to succeed or achieve something than it is for another person, organization, etc. ▪ The current laws favor large businesses and *disfavor* smaller businesses.

dis·fig·ure /dɪsˈfɪgjɚ, *Brit* dɪsˈfɪgə/ *verb* **-ures; -ured; -ur·ing** [+ *obj*] : to spoil or damage the appearance of (something or someone) ▪ His face was *disfigured* by a scar. ▪ Vandals *disfigured* [=(more commonly) *defaced*] the wall with graffiti.
— **disfigured** *adj* [*more* ~; *most* ~] ▪ The fire left her horribly *disfigured.* — **dis·fig·ure·ment** /dɪsˈfɪgjɚmənt/ *noun, pl* **-ments** [*count*] His *disfigurements* were caused by an accident. [*noncount*] The lifesaving operation will cause some *disfigurement.* — **disfiguring** *adj* ▪ *disfiguring* surgery

dis·gorge /dɪsˈgoɚʤ/ *verb* **-gorg·es; -gorged; -gor·ging**
1 [+ *obj*] *somewhat formal* : to empty whatever is in the stomach through the mouth ▪ The cat coughed and then *disgorged* [=(more commonly) *vomited, threw up*] a wad of hair.
2 a [+ *obj*] : to let out or release (something) ▪ We watched the airplane *disgorging* its passengers at the gate. ▪ The damaged ship *disgorged* thousands of gallons of oil into the bay. **b** [*no obj*] : to flow out ▪ The river *disgorges* into the ocean just south of the city.

[1]**dis·grace** /dɪˈskreɪs/ *verb* **-grac·es; -graced; -grac·ing** [+ *obj*]
1 : to cause (someone) to feel ashamed ▪ Her behavior *disgraced* [=*shamed*] the whole family.
2 : to cause (someone or something) to lose or become unworthy of respect or approval ▪ Many feel that the mayor has *disgraced* the town government by accepting personal favors from local businesspeople. ▪ He felt he had *disgraced* himself by failing at school. — often used as *(be) disgraced* ▪ The administration *was disgraced* by the scandal.

[2]**disgrace** *noun*
1 [*noncount*] : the condition of feeling ashamed or of losing or becoming unworthy of respect or approval ▪ The secret was protected out of a fear of political *disgrace.* ▪ The family is enduring the *disgrace* [=*dishonor, shame*] of scandal/suicide. ▪ Many feel that the mayor has ***brought disgrace upon/on*** the town. ▪ She was forced to leave ***in disgrace.***
2 [*singular*] : something that you are or should be ashamed of ▪ His table manners are a *disgrace.* ▪ It is an absolute/utter *disgrace* [=*shame*] that the city has ignored the problem for so long. ▪ The health-care system is a national *disgrace.* ▪ ***It is no disgrace*** to be poor. [=you should not feel ashamed be-

cause you are poor] — often + *to* • The politicians responsible for this scandal are a *disgrace to* their country.
– **dis·grace·ful** /dɪˈskreɪsfəl/ *adj* [*more* ~; *most* ~] • her *disgraceful* behavior • His table manners are *disgraceful.* • It's *disgraceful* that the city has ignored the problem for so long. – **dis·grace·ful·ly** *adv* • He behaved *disgracefully.* • *disgracefully* selfish

dis·grun·tled /dɪsˈgrʌntl̩d/ *adj* [*more* ~; *most* ~] : unhappy and annoyed • She has to deal with *disgruntled* customers all day. • *disgruntled* employees • He was *disgruntled* over the lack of recognition he received.

[1]**dis·guise** /dəˈskaɪz/ *verb* **-guis·es; -guised; -guis·ing** [+ *obj*]
1 : to change the usual appearance, sound, taste, etc., of (someone or something) so that people will not recognize that person or thing • He tried to *disguise* his voice on the phone but I could tell it was him. • She *disguised* herself in a wig and glasses. — often + *as* • The journalist traveled the city *disguised as* [=dressed like; pretending to be] a beggar. • She *disguised* herself *as* a musician to get into the concert hall early.
2 : to hide (something) so that it will not be seen or noticed • I could not *disguise* [=*hide*] my surprise. • They *disguised* [=*masked*] their true feelings. • We *disguised* the fact that we were disappointed. • I was aware of her ***thinly disguised*** [=poorly hidden] hostility.

[2]**disguise** *noun, pl* **-guis·es**
1 [*count*] **:** clothes or other things that you wear so that people will not recognize you • He wore a *disguise* of glasses, a fake mustache, and a cap.
2 [*noncount*] **:** the act of changing your appearance so that people will not recognize you • The famous thief is known to be a ***master of disguise.***
a blessing in disguise see BLESSING
in disguise **1 :** wearing a disguise • I've heard that she sometimes travels around the country *in disguise.* **2 :** made to look like something else : presented as another thing • He says that the new fee is really just a tax increase *in disguise.*

[1]**dis·gust** /dɪˈskʌst/ *noun* [*noncount*]
1 : a strong feeling of dislike for something that has a very unpleasant appearance, taste, smell, etc. • He eyed the greasy food ***with disgust.*** • As the smell of garbage drifted through the air, she wrinkled her nose ***in disgust.***
2 : annoyance and anger that you feel toward something because it is not good, fair, appropriate, etc. • He talked about his *disgust* with/at the way the news media focuses on celebrities. • ***Much to the disgust of*** some listeners, the speech was interrupted several times by a few people in the audience. • She shook her head ***in disgust*** when I described the scene.

[2]**disgust** *verb* **-gusts; -gust·ed; -gust·ing** [+ *obj*]
1 : to cause (someone) to have a strong feeling of dislike for something especially because it has a very unpleasant appearance, taste, smell, etc. • The greasy food they were serving *disgusted* [=*repulsed*] him. • She's a vegetarian because the idea of eating meat totally *disgusts* her.
2 *of something bad, unfair, improper, etc.* **:** to cause (someone) to feel very annoyed and angry • The way the news media focuses on celebrities *disgusts* [=*revolts*] me. • The photographs *disgust* some people.

disgusted *adj* [*more* ~; *most* ~] : very annoyed or angry about something : feeling or showing disgust • He's *disgusted* by all the attention people give to celebrities. • He had a *disgusted* expression on his face. • She was *disgusted* with herself for not knowing the answer.
– **dis·gust·ed·ly** *adv* • He turned away *disgustedly* and walked out the door.

disgusting *adj* [*more* ~; *most* ~]
1 : so unpleasant to see, smell, taste, consider, etc., that you feel slightly sick • The food was *disgusting.* [=(informally) *gross*] • She finds the idea of eating meat totally *disgusting.* [=*repulsive*] • a *disgusting* [=*repugnant*] photograph
2 : so bad, unfair, inappropriate, etc., that you feel annoyed and angry • I think the way the news media focuses on celebrities is *disgusting.* [=*repugnant*] • What a *disgusting* way to treat people.
– **dis·gust·ing·ly** /dɪˈskʌstɪŋli/ *adv* • *disgustingly* greasy food • *disgustingly* filthy • (*informal* + *humorous*) a *disgustingly* good player [=an extremely good player]

[1]**dish** /ˈdɪʃ/ *noun, pl* **dish·es**
1 [*count*] **a :** a shallow container that you cook or serve food in • a baking/serving *dish* [=a container used to bake/serve food] • a casserole/pie *dish* [=a container used to bake a casserole/pie]; *specifically* : a shallow bowl • a candy *dish* [=a container used to serve candy] • the cat's food/water *dish* **b :** the food served in a dish • a *dish* of strawberries • a small *dish* of ice cream
2 [*count*] **:** food that is prepared in a particular way • Each person made a *dish* for the potluck supper. • The restaurant serves some of my favorite *dishes.* • a fish/pasta/potato *dish* [=food that has fish/pasta/potatoes as a main ingredient] • The ***main dish*** [=the biggest dish of a meal] was poached salmon, and it was served with a ***side dish*** [=a food that is served at the same time as the main dish] of spinach.
3 ***dishes*** [*plural*] **:** all the things (such as plates, forks, glasses, pans, cooking utensils, etc.) that are used to prepare, serve, and eat a meal • We piled all the *dishes* in the sink after dinner. • Will you wash the breakfast *dishes,* please? • a sink full of dirty *dishes* • It's your turn to ***do the dishes.*** [=wash the dishes]
4 [*count*] **a :** a shallow container that holds something other than food • a soap *dish* **b :** something that is shaped like a shallow bowl • Do you have cable TV or a *dish*? [=an antenna shaped like a dish that receives television signals from a satellite] • a *dish* antenna — see also PETRI DISH, SATELLITE DISH
5 [*singular*] *informal* + *old-fashioned* **:** a sexually attractive person • I hear your cousin is a *dish.* [=*hottie*]

[2]**dish** *verb* **dishes; dished; dish·ing** [*no obj*] *slang* : to talk about the personal life of someone else : GOSSIP • The two of them are always *dishing* about their coworkers.
dish out [*phrasal verb*] ***dish out (something)*** *also* ***dish (something) out*** *informal* **1 :** to serve (food) • The restaurant *dishes out* more than 500 meals every night. **2 :** to give (something) freely or in large amounts • She *dishes out* advice to anyone who'll listen. • He's always *dishing out* money and gifts to his grandchildren. **3** ***dish it out*** **:** to criticize other people • He can *dish it out,* but he can't take it. [=he likes to criticize other people, but he doesn't like being criticized]
dish (the) dirt see DIRT
dish up [*phrasal verb*] ***dish up (something)*** *also* ***dish (something) up*** *informal* **:** to put (food) into a dish or dishes for serving or eating • *dish up* some soup — sometimes used figuratively • The movie *dishes up* [=*serves up*] a wild mix of sex and violence.

dis·har·mo·ny /dɪsˈhɑɚməni/ *noun* [*noncount*] *somewhat formal* : lack of agreement that often causes unhappiness or trouble • a period of *disharmony* [=*discord*] between the two groups • Money problems are often a source of marital *disharmony.* [=*strife*]
– **dis·har·mo·ni·ous** /ˌdɪsˌhɑɚˈmounijəs/ *adj* • a *disharmonious* relationship

dish·cloth /ˈdɪʃˌklɑːθ/ *noun, pl* **-cloths** [*count*] : a cloth that is used for washing dishes — called also (*US*) *dish rag*

dish detergent *noun, pl* ~ **-gents** [*count, noncount*] *US* : liquid soap that is used for washing dishes — called also (*US*) *dishwashing detergent,* (*US*) *dishwashing liquid,* (*Brit*) *washing-up liquid*

dis·heart·en /dɪsˈhɑɚtn̩/ *verb* **-ens; -ened; -en·ing** [+ *obj*] : to cause (a person or group of people) to lose hope, enthusiasm, or courage : to discourage (someone) • The conflict between their families *disheartened* them. — often used as *(be) disheartened* • I *was disheartened* by the news.
– **disheartened** *adj* [*more* ~; *most* ~] • I felt very *disheartened.* – **disheartening** *adj* [*more* ~; *most* ~] • a *disheartening* failure • It was *disheartening* to hear the news. – **dis·heart·en·ing·ly** *adv*

di·shev·eled (*US*) *also Brit* **di·shev·elled** /dɪˈʃɛvəld/ *adj* [*more* ~; *most* ~] : not neat or tidy • His wrinkled suit gave him a *disheveled* appearance. • *disheveled* hair • They looked dirty and *disheveled.*

dis·hon·est /dɪsˈɑːnəst/ *adj* [*more* ~; *most* ~] : not honest: such as **a :** saying or likely to say things that are untrue • I think he is being *dishonest* [=*untruthful*] about what he knows. • a *dishonest* car dealer **b :** containing information that is untrue • *dishonest* advertising • She gave *dishonest* answers to our questions. **c :** used to deceive someone • *dishonest* [=*deceitful*] business practices
– **dis·hon·est·ly** *adv* • I think she answered our questions *dishonestly.* • They have been running their business *dishonestly.*

dis·hon·es·ty /dɪsˈɑːnəsti/ *noun* [*noncount*] : lack of honesty : the quality of being untruthful or deceitful • *dishonesty*

D

in advertising • Are you accusing him of *dishonesty*? • her *dishonesty* about what happened

[1]**dis•hon•or** (US) *or Brit* **dis•hon•our** /dɪsˈɑːnɚ/ *noun* [*noncount*] *somewhat formal* : loss or lack of honor : damage to your reputation and loss of respect from other people • warriors who choose death before *dishonor* • She found it difficult to endure the *dishonor* [=*disgrace*] of being involved in a scandal. • He is afraid that his confession will ***bring dishonor on/upon*** the family. • ***There's no dishonor in*** doing manual labor. [=doing manual labor does not make you unworthy of respect]

D

[2]**dishonor** (US) *or Brit* **dishonour** *verb* **-ors; -ored; -oring** [+ *obj*] *somewhat formal*

1 : to cause (someone or something) to lose honor : to cause (someone or something) to no longer be respected • His actions *dishonored* [=brought dishonor on] the family. • Quitting now would *dishonor* [=*disgrace*] the memory of our predecessors.

2 : to fail to do what is required by (a promise, contract, etc.) : to fail to honor (something) • She *dishonored* her oath of office.

3 *of a bank* : to refuse to give out the money promised by (a check) • The bank *dishonored* my check. • a *dishonored* check

dis•hon•or•able (US) *or Brit* **dis•hon•our•able** /dɪsˈɑːnərəbəl/ *adj* [*more* ~; *most* ~] : not deserving honor or respect : not morally or socially acceptable • His *dishonorable* behavior has shamed the family. • *dishonorable* [=*shameful*] conduct • Her military career ended with a ***dishonorable discharge***. [=she was forced to leave the military because of unacceptable behavior] — opposite HONORABLE

– **dis•hon•or•ably** (US) *or Brit* **dis•hon•our•ably** /dɪsˈɑːnərəbli/ *adv* • He behaved *dishonorably*.

dish•pan /ˈdɪʃˌpæn/ *noun, pl* **-pans** [*count*] *US* : a large usually plastic container with a flat bottom that holds water to wash dishes in

dishpan hands *noun* [*plural*] *chiefly US* : hands that are red, rough, and sore because of washing a lot of dishes

dish rack *noun, pl* ~ **racks** [*count*] *US* : a rack that you place dishes on so they can dry — see picture at KITCHEN

dish•rag /ˈdɪʃˌræg/ *noun, pl* **-rags** [*count*] *US* : DISHCLOTH

dish towel *noun, pl* ~ **-els** [*count*] *US* : a cloth that is used for drying dishes — called also (*Brit*) *tea cloth*, (*chiefly Brit*) *tea towel*; see picture at KITCHEN

dish•ware /ˈdɪʃˌweɚ/ *noun* [*noncount*] *chiefly US* : plates, bowls, cups, etc., that are usually part of a set

dish•wash•er /ˈdɪʃˌwɑːʃɚ/ *noun, pl* **-ers** [*count*]

1 : a person whose job is to wash dishes in a restaurant

2 : a machine that is used to wash dishes — see picture at KITCHEN

– **dish•wash•ing** /ˈdɪʃˌwɑːʃɪŋ/ *adj* • *dishwashing* soap

dishwashing detergent *noun, pl* ~ **-gents** [*count, noncount*] *US* : DISH DETERGENT

dishwashing liquid *noun, pl* ~ **-quids** [*count, noncount*] *US* : DISH DETERGENT

dish•wa•ter /ˈdɪʃˌwɑːtɚ/ *noun* [*noncount*] : water in which dishes have been or are going to be washed

(as) dull as dishwater *US, informal* : very boring or dull • The conversation was *as dull as dishwater*. [=(*Brit*) *as dull as ditchwater*]

like dishwater *informal* : having very little flavor — used to describe soups or drinks • This coffee is *like dishwater*!

dishy /ˈdɪʃi/ *adj* **dish•i•er; -est** *informal*

1 : sexually attractive • a *dishy* actor

2 *US* : containing gossip or information about a usually famous person's private life • a *dishy* new biography

dis•il•lu•sion /ˌdɪsəˈluːʒən/ *verb* **-sions; -sioned; -sioning** [+ *obj*] : to cause (someone) to stop believing that something is good, valuable, true, etc. • Working at that store for six months was enough to *disillusion* me about retail work.

– **disillusion** *noun* [*noncount*] • His *disillusion* [=*disillusionment*] with the job was obvious. – **disillusioning** *adj* [*more* ~; *most* ~] • a very *disillusioning* experience – **dis•il•lu•sion•ment** /ˌdɪsəˈluːʒənmənt/ *noun* [*noncount*] • *Disillusionment* with the city government grew as conditions worsened.

disillusioned *adj* [*more* ~; *most* ~] : having lost faith or trust in something : disappointed that something is not as good, valuable, true, etc., as it had seemed • a *disillusioned* journalist — often + *with* • She became more and more *disillusioned with* politics.

dis•in•cen•tive /ˌdɪsɪnˈsɛntɪv/ *noun, pl* **-tives** [*count*] : something that causes or that could cause a person to decide not to do something • We considered volunteering, but the complicated application process was a *disincentive*. • The complicated application process was a *disincentive* to volunteering our time. — opposite INCENTIVE

dis•in•cli•na•tion /dɪsˌɪnkləˈneɪʃən/ *noun* [*singular*] *formal* : a feeling of not wanting to do something : a tendency to avoid a particular activity — usually followed by *to* + *verb* • Her *disinclination* [=*reluctance*] *to talk* about her past made them all the more curious. — sometimes + *for* • a *disinclination for* [=*dislike of*] outdoor work

dis•in•clined /ˌdɪsɪnˈklaɪnd/ *adj* [*more* ~; *most* ~] *formal* : not wanting to do something : not inclined to do something — usually followed by *to* + *verb* • I'm *disinclined* [=*reluctant*] *to accept* her explanation. • He seemed *disinclined* [=*hesitant*] *to take part* in the discussion.

dis•in•fect /ˌdɪsɪnˈfɛkt/ *verb* **-fects; -fect•ed; -fect•ing** [+ *obj*]

1 : to clean (something) especially by using a chemical substance that kills all germs and bacteria • Chemicals were added to *disinfect* the water. • The wound needs to be *disinfected*. • a clean, *disinfected* knife

2 *computers* : to remove a virus from (a computer) by using a special program

– **dis•in•fec•tion** /ˌdɪsɪnˈfɛkʃən/ *noun* [*noncount*] • methods of water *disinfection*

dis•in•fect•ant /ˌdɪsɪnˈfɛktənt/ *noun, pl* **-ants** : a chemical substance that is used to kill harmful germs and bacteria : a substance that disinfects something [*count*] They use a strong *disinfectant* on the medical equipment. [*noncount*] a bottle of *disinfectant* • Clean the area with *disinfectant*.

dis•in•for•ma•tion /dɪsˌɪnfɚˈmeɪʃən/ *noun* [*noncount*] : false information that is given to people in order to make them believe something or to hide the truth • The government used *disinformation* to gain support for the policy. • a campaign of *disinformation* = a *disinformation* campaign — compare MISINFORMATION

dis•in•gen•u•ous /ˌdɪsɪnˈʤɛnjəwəs/ *adj* [*more* ~; *most* ~] *formal* : not truly honest or sincere : giving the false appearance of being honest or sincere • Her recent expressions of concern are self-serving and *disingenuous*. • a *disingenuous* response — compare INGENUOUS

– **dis•in•gen•u•ous•ly** *adv* • He claims *disingenuously* to have supported the plan from the beginning. – **dis•in•gen•u•ous•ness** *noun* [*noncount*]

dis•in•her•it /ˌdɪsɪnˈherət/ *verb* **-its; -it•ed; -it•ing** [+ *obj*] : to prevent (someone, such as your daughter or son) from having the legal right to receive your money or property after you die • She threatened to *disinherit* her son and leave him penniless.

dis•in•te•grate /dɪsˈɪntəˌgreɪt/ *verb* **-grates; -grat•ed; -grat•ing** : to break apart into many small parts or pieces [*no obj*] The old iron hinge rusted and eventually *disintegrated* [=*crumbled*] into dust. • The paper will *disintegrate* if it gets wet. — often used figuratively • Their relationship gradually *disintegrated*. • With the rise of nationalism, the colonial empires began to *disintegrate*. [+ *obj*] The laser can *disintegrate* most kinds of rock.

– **dis•in•te•gra•tion** /dɪsˌɪntəˈgreɪʃən/ *noun* [*noncount*]

dis•in•ter /ˌdɪsɪnˈtɚ/ *verb* **-ters; -terred; -ter•ring** [+ *obj*] *formal* : to take (a body) out of a grave or tomb : to dig up (a body) • The body was *disinterred* for further study. — sometimes used figuratively • *disinter* an old manuscript

dis•in•ter•est /dɪsˈɪntrəst/ *noun* [*noncount*]

1 : lack of interest • His proposal was met with complete *disinterest*. — often + *in* • Their *disinterest in* politics is obvious.

2 : the quality or state of not being influenced by personal feelings, opinions, or concerns • The jurors must look at the facts of the case with complete *disinterest*. [=*objectivity, impartiality*]

dis•in•ter•est•ed /dɪsˈɪntrəstəd/ *adj* [*more* ~; *most* ~]

1 : not influenced by personal feelings, opinions, or concerns • A *disinterested* [=*unbiased, impartial*] third party mediated the dispute. • the *disinterested* pursuit of truth

2 : having no desire to know about a particular thing : not interested — often + *in* • They are obviously *disinterested* [=*uninterested*] *in* politics. ✧ This sense is commonly used but some people consider it to be incorrect and say that "uninterested" should be used instead.

– **dis•in•ter•est•ed•ly** *adv* • observing *disinterestedly*

– **dis·in·ter·est·ed·ness** *noun* [*noncount*] ▪ the *disinterestedness* of judges

dis·in·vest /ˌdɪsɪnˈvɛst/ *verb* **-vests; -vest·ed; -vest·ing** [*no obj*] *finance* : to take your money out of an area, industry, company, etc., by selling property, shares, or stock ▪ Several companies have *disinvested* from the country to protest its human rights policies. ▪ *disinvesting* in real estate
– **dis·in·vest·ment** /ˌdɪsɪnˈvɛstmənt/ *noun* [*noncount*] ▪ *disinvestment* in real estate

dis·joint·ed /dɪsˈʤoɪntəd/ *adj* [*more* ~; *most* ~] : lacking order and organization ▪ She could hardly follow their *disjointed* [=*incoherent, disconnected*] conversation. ▪ a *disjointed* narrative/book

dis·junc·tion /dɪsˈʤʌŋkʃən/ *noun, pl* **-tions** [*count*] *formal* : a lack of connection between things that are related or should be connected — often + *between* ▪ It is difficult to reconcile the *disjunction between* what he says and what he does.

dis·junc·tive /dɪsˈʤʌŋktɪv/ *adj, grammar* : showing choice or opposition ▪ "Or" and "but" are *disjunctive* conjunctions.
– **disjunctive** *noun, pl* **-tives** [*count*] ▪ "Or" and "but" are *disjunctives*.

dis·junc·ture /dɪsˈʤʌŋkʧɚ/ *noun, pl* **-tures** [*count*] *formal* : DISJUNCTION

disk *variant spelling of* DISC

disk drive *noun, pl* ~ **drives** [*count*] : a computer part that holds a computer disk or set of disks and that reads data from and copies data to disks

dis·kette /ˌdɪˈskɛt/ *noun, pl* **-kettes** [*count*] *computers* : FLOPPY DISK

[1]**dis·like** /dɪsˈlaɪk/ *verb* **-likes; -liked; -lik·ing** [+ *obj*] : to not like (something or someone) : to feel dislike for (something or someone) ▪ I *dislike* basketball, but I enjoy baseball. ▪ She *dislikes* [=she does not like] the cold weather. ▪ He *dislikes* being interviewed. ▪ Most people *dislike* it when they are told what to do.

[2]**dislike** *noun, pl* **-likes**
1 [*singular*] : a feeling of not liking or approving of something or someone — often + *of* or *for* ▪ His *dislike of* cats was obvious. ▪ She developed a general *dislike for* journalists. ✧ If you ***take a dislike to*** someone or something, you begin to not like that person or thing. ▪ They *took an instant dislike to* the new neighbors.
2 [*count*] : something that you do not like, approve of, or enjoy — usually plural ▪ among his *dislikes* ▪ He soon knew all of her ***likes and dislikes***.

dis·lo·cate /ˈdɪsloʊˌkeɪt/ *verb* **-cates; -cat·ed; -cat·ing** [+ *obj*]
1 *medical* : to move (a bone) out of its normal location or position in a joint ▪ She fell and *dislocated* her shoulder.
2 *chiefly US, formal* : to force (someone or something) to move from a place or position ▪ The new hotel will *dislocate* several businesses. ▪ Thousands of workers have been *dislocated* by the latest economic crisis.
3 *formal* : to cause (a business, system, etc.) to change in some major way : to stop (something) from functioning as it used to function ▪ economies *dislocated* [=*disrupted*] by war
– **dislocated** *adj* ▪ a *dislocated* shoulder/finger/hip/wrist ▪ (*US*) thousands of *dislocated* workers – **dis·lo·ca·tion** /ˌdɪsloʊˈkeɪʃən/ *noun, pl* **-tions** [*count*] patients with fractures and *dislocations* ▪ the *dislocations* of war [*noncount*] The brace will prevent recurring hip *dislocation*. ▪ social and economic *dislocation*

dis·lodge /dɪsˈlɑːʤ/ *verb* **-lodg·es; -lodged; -lodg·ing** [+ *obj*] : to forcefully remove (something or someone) from a place or position ▪ The earthquake *dislodged* several boulders from the cliff. ▪ He kicked at the stone to *dislodge* it. ▪ The army has *dislodged* enemy forces from their stronghold.

dis·loy·al /dɪsˈlojəl/ *adj* [*more* ~; *most* ~] : failing to support or be true to someone or something : not loyal or faithful to your friends, family, country, etc. ▪ It would be *disloyal* to abandon them. ▪ *disloyal* employees — often + *to* ▪ a traitor *disloyal to* his country
– **dis·loy·al·ty** /dɪsˈlojəlti/ *noun* [*noncount*] ▪ His *disloyalty* to the company led to his dismissal.

dis·mal /ˈdɪzməl/ *adj* [*more* ~; *most* ~]
1 : showing or causing unhappiness or sad feelings : not warm, cheerful, etc. ▪ a dark, *dismal* room ▪ *dismal* [=*gloomy, dreary*] weather ▪ The barren landscape looks *dismal* [=*bleak, desolate*] in winter.
2 : very bad or poor ▪ The show was a *dismal* failure. ▪ a *dismal* performance ▪ The team's record is *dismal*.
– **dis·mal·ly** *adv* ▪ The show failed *dismally*.

dis·man·tle /dɪsˈmæntl/ *verb* **-man·tles; -man·tled; -man·tling** [+ *obj*]
1 : to take (something, such as a machine or structure) apart so that it is in separate pieces ▪ The mechanic *dismantled* the engine to repair it. ▪ When will they *dismantle* the old bridge? ▪ a *dismantled* power plant
2 : to destroy (something) in an orderly way : to gradually cause (something) to come to an end ▪ The after-school program was *dismantled* due to lack of funding. ▪ He accuses them of trying to *dismantle* the country's legal system.
– **dis·man·tle·ment** /dɪsˈmæntḷmənt/ *noun* [*noncount*] ▪ the *dismantlement* of the power plant – **dismantling** *noun* [*noncount*] ▪ the *dismantling* of old factories ▪ the *dismantling* of government programs

D

[1]**dis·may** /dɪsˈmeɪ/ *verb* **-mays; -mayed; -may·ing** [+ *obj*] : to cause (someone) to feel very worried, disappointed, or upset ▪ Her choice of career *dismays* her parents. ▪ What especially *dismayed* [=*upset, bothered*] me was that no one else protested.
– **dismayed** *adj* [*more* ~; *most* ~] ▪ She was very *dismayed* to learn/discover that he was so ill. ▪ I was *dismayed* by/at his indifference. – **dismaying** *adj* [*more* ~; *most* ~] ▪ her *dismaying* indifference – **dis·may·ing·ly** /dɪsˈmejɪŋli/ *adv* ▪ *dismayingly* indifferent

[2]**dismay** *noun* [*noncount*] : a strong feeling of being worried, disappointed, or upset ▪ His comments were met with cries of *dismay*. ▪ They watched ***in dismay*** as the house burned. ▪ Much ***to the dismay of*** her fans, she announced her retirement immediately after the book's release. ▪ ***To my dismay***, I did not get chosen for the job. ▪ We listened ***with dismay*** to the news of the accident.

dis·mem·ber /dɪsˈmɛmbɚ/ *verb* **-bers; -bered; -ber·ing** [+ *obj*]
1 : to cut or tear (a body) into pieces ▪ The victims' bodies had been *dismembered* and buried in the basement. ▪ a *dismembered* corpse
2 *formal* : to separate (something) into smaller parts ▪ *dismembering* a corporate empire
– **dis·mem·ber·ment** /dɪsˈmɛmbɚmənt/ *noun, pl* **-ments** [*count, noncount*]

dis·miss /dɪsˈmɪs/ *verb* **-miss·es; -missed; -mis·sing** [+ *obj*]
1 : to decide not to think about or consider (something or someone) ▪ We *dismissed* his accusations. ▪ We can't completely *dismiss* [=*discount*] the possibility that she's right. ▪ I don't think we should *dismiss* the matter lightly. — often + *as* ▪ His idea was *dismissed as* impractical. ▪ For a long time they *dismissed* her *as* a silly old woman.
2 : to send (someone) away : to cause or allow (someone) to leave ▪ The students were *dismissed* early because of the snowstorm. ▪ Class is *dismissed*. [=the class is over and students are free to leave]
3 : to officially make (someone) leave a job : to end the employment or service of (someone) ▪ He was *dismissed* [=*fired*] from his job. ▪ Several employees were recently *dismissed*.
4 *law* : to officially end or stop (something, such as a legal case) ▪ The judge *dismissed* the case/suit. ▪ All charges were *dismissed*. [=*dropped*]
– **dis·miss·al** /dɪsˈmɪsəl/ *noun, pl* **-als** [*count*] I was surprised by his *dismissal* of the idea. ▪ A small group is protesting the *dismissals* of several employees. ▪ the *dismissal* of the lawsuit [*noncount*] He still hopes to win his claim for unfair *dismissal*.

dis·miss·ive /dɪsˈmɪsɪv/ *adj*
1 : refusing to think about or consider something or someone — usually + *of* ▪ He was *dismissive of* my idea.
2 : showing that you do not think something or someone is worth thinking about or considering ▪ a *dismissive* remark ▪ a *dismissive* wave of the hand
– **dis·miss·ive·ly** *adv* ▪ He spoke *dismissively* about the accident. ▪ She laughed *dismissively* [=*scornfully*] when I expressed admiration for the book.

dis·mount /dɪsˈmaʊnt/ *verb* **-mounts; -mount·ed; -mount·ing** [*no obj*] : to get down from something (such as a horse or bicycle) ▪ The cyclist *dismounted* and walked her bike across the street. ▪ The gymnast *dismounted* from the parallel bars. — opposite MOUNT
– **dismount** *noun, pl* **-mounts** [*count*] ▪ the gymnast's perfect *dismount*

dis·obe·di·ence /ˌdɪsəˈbiːdijəns/ *noun* [*noncount*] : refusal or failure to obey rules, laws, etc. : a lack of obedience ▪ The student's *disobedience* shocked the teacher. ▪ The dog was punished for its *disobedience*. — see also CIVIL DISOBEDIENCE

dis·obe·di·ent /ˌdɪsəˈbiːdijənt/ *adj* [*more ~; most ~*] **:** not doing what someone or something with authority tells you to do **:** refusing or failing to obey rules, laws, etc. ▪ The *disobedient* soldier was given cleanup duty. ▪ The dog was being *disobedient*. — opposite OBEDIENT
– **dis·obe·di·ent·ly** *adv*

dis·obey /ˌdɪsəˈbeɪ/ *verb* **-obeys; -obeyed; -obey·ing** **:** to not do what someone or something with authority tells you to do **:** to refuse or fail to obey rules, laws, etc. [*no obj*] If you *disobey*, you will be severely punished. [*+ obj*] The soldier *disobeyed* the general's orders. ▪ He was afraid to *disobey* his father. ▪ The driver had *disobeyed* the law.

dis·or·der /dɪsˈoədɚ/ *noun, pl* **-ders**
1 [*noncount*] **:** a confused or messy state **:** a lack of order or organization ▪ People who witnessed the tragedy describe a scene of *disorder* [=*chaos*] as rescuers tried to find survivors. ▪ The filing system was ***thrown into disorder*** [=was disrupted or upset] when the computer program malfunctioned. — often used with *in* ▪ His finances were *in* complete *disorder*. [=his finances were not organized] ▪ The clothes/papers were *in* (a state of) *disorder*. — opposite ORDER
2 [*noncount*] **:** a state or situation in which there is a lot of noise, crime, violent behavior, etc. ▪ The mayor is concerned that a rally could create/cause public *disorder*. ▪ problems of crime and social *disorder* — opposite ORDER
3 *medical* **:** a physical or mental condition that is not normal or healthy [*count*] A dermatologist treats *disorders* [=*diseases*] of the skin. ▪ an eating *disorder* ▪ a *disorder* of the blood = a blood *disorder* [*noncount*] Millions of people suffer from some form of personality/mental *disorder*.

dis·or·dered /dɪsˈoədəd/ *adj*
1 [*more ~; most ~*] **:** in a confused or messy state **:** having a lack of order or organization ▪ The project was in a *disordered* state. ▪ The file was completely *disordered*. — opposite ORDERED
2 *medical* **:** not working in a normal, healthy way ▪ a *disordered* mind ▪ The child is emotionally *disordered*. [=(more commonly) *disturbed*]

dis·or·der·ly /dɪsˈoədəli/ *adj* [*more ~; most ~*]
1 : causing a problem especially in a public place by making a lot of noise, behaving violently, etc. ▪ Two *disorderly* [=*unruly*] persons were arrested. ▪ She was charged with being drunk and *disorderly*. ▪ He was found guilty of ***disorderly conduct***.
2 : not neat or orderly ▪ A *disorderly* [=*disordered*] pile of papers covered most of her desk.

dis·or·ga·nized *also Brit* **dis·or·ga·nised** /dɪsˈoəgəˌnaɪzd/ *adj* [*more ~; most ~*] **:** not organized: such as **a :** not arranged or planned in a particular way ▪ The meeting was very *disorganized*. **b :** not having parts arranged in a neat and effective way ▪ a *disorganized* essay ▪ a *disorganized* desk **c :** not able to keep things arranged in a neat or effective way ▪ He is very *disorganized*. ▪ *disorganized* students
– **dis·or·ga·ni·za·tion** *also Brit* **dis·or·ga·ni·sa·tion** /dɪsˌoəgənəˈzeɪʃən, *Brit* dɪsˌɔːgəˌnaɪˈzeɪʃən/ *noun* [*noncount*]

dis·ori·ent /dɪsˈorijənt/ *verb* **-ents; -ent·ed; -ent·ing** [*+ obj*] **:** to make (someone) lost or confused ▪ Thick fog can *disorient* even an experienced hiker. — compare ORIENT
– **dis·ori·en·ta·tion** /dɪsˌorijənˈteɪʃən/ *noun* [*noncount*] ▪ The medication may cause drowsiness and *disorientation*.
– **disoriented** *adj* [*more ~; most ~*] ▪ The patient became increasingly *disoriented* as the illness progressed. ▪ a *disoriented* hiker – **disorienting** *adj* [*more ~; most ~*] ▪ It's *disorienting* to wake up in total darkness.

dis·ori·en·tate /dɪsˈorijənˌteɪt/ *verb* **-tates; -tat·ed; -tat·ing** [*+ obj*] *chiefly Brit* **:** DISORIENT

dis·own /dɪsˈoun/ *verb* **-owns; -owned; -own·ing** [*+ obj*] **:** to say or decide that you will no longer be connected with, associated with, or responsible for (someone or something) ▪ Her parents threatened to *disown* her if she didn't go back to school. ▪ He was *disowned* for bringing shame to the family.

dis·par·age /dɪˈsperɪʤ/ *verb* **-ag·es; -aged; -ag·ing** [*+ obj*] *formal* **:** to describe (someone or something) as unimportant, weak, bad, etc. ▪ Voters don't like political advertisements in which opponents *disparage* one another. ▪ It's a mistake to *disparage* their achievements. ▪ The article *disparaged* polo as a game for the wealthy.
– **dis·par·age·ment** /dɪˈsperɪʤmənt/ *noun* [*noncount*] ▪ a term of *disparagement* ▪ the author's relentless *disparagement* of politicians – **disparaging** *adj* [*more ~; most ~*] ▪ I heard her making *disparaging* remarks about her coworkers. – **dis·par·ag·ing·ly** *adv* ▪ He referred *disparagingly* to his car as "an old clunker."

dis·par·ate /ˈdɪspərət/ *adj* [*more ~; most ~*] *formal* **:** different from each other ▪ The conversation covered topics as *disparate* [=*diverse*] as fashion and biology. ▪ *disparate* cultures ▪ music that combines/blends *disparate* [=*dissimilar*] elements

dis·par·i·ty /dɪˈsperəti/ *noun, pl* **-ties** *formal* **:** a noticeable and often unfair difference between people or things [*count*] problems that exist when there is a *disparity* of power [=when one person, group, etc., has much more power than another] ▪ There is a great *disparity* between (the) rich and (the) poor in this country. ▪ The age *disparity* between the players is obvious. [*noncount*] the region's increasing income *disparity*

dis·pas·sion·ate /dɪsˈpæʃənət/ *adj* [*more ~; most ~*] **:** not influenced or affected by emotions ▪ Journalists aim to be *dispassionate* observers. ▪ He spoke in a *dispassionate* tone about the accident.
– **dis·pas·sion·ate·ly** *adv* [*more ~; most ~*]

[1]**dis·patch** *also Brit* **des·patch** /dɪˈspæʧ/ *verb* **-patch·es; -patched; -patch·ing** [*+ obj*]
1 : to send (someone or something) quickly to a particular place for a particular purpose ▪ Rescue workers were immediately *dispatched* to the area. ▪ The hotel *dispatched* a limo to pick us up from the airport. ▪ (*formal*) The message was *dispatched* to the general.
2 : to defeat (a person or team) in a game, contest, etc. ▪ She easily *dispatched* [=(more commonly) *beat*] her opponent.
3 *old-fashioned* **:** to kill (a person or animal) quickly ▪ He *dispatched* the guard with one bullet.

[2]**dispatch** *also Brit* **despatch** *noun, pl* **-patches**
1 [*count*] **:** an important official message ▪ The general sent a *dispatch* to headquarters. ✧ In British English, a soldier who is ***mentioned in dispatches*** is noted for bravery.
2 [*noncount*] *somewhat formal* **:** the act of sending someone or something to a particular place for a particular purpose ▪ He requested the immediate *dispatch* of supplies/troops.
3 [*count*] **:** a news story that a reporter sends to a newspaper usually from a foreign country ▪ The reporter sent many *dispatches* from the war zone.
with dispatch *formal* **:** in a quick and efficient way ▪ The problem was handled *with dispatch*.

dispatch box *also* **despatch box** *noun, pl* **~ boxes** *Brit*
1 *the Dispatch Box* : a box on a table in the House of Commons that important government officials stand behind when speaking
2 [*count*] **:** a container for holding important documents

dis·patch·er /dɪˈspæʧɚ/ *noun, pl* **-ers** [*count*] *US*
1 : someone whose job is to talk by radio with people in vehicles (such as police cars, ambulances, or taxis) in order to send them to a particular place
2 : someone who is in charge of the departure of trains, airplanes, buses, trucks, etc.

dispatch rider *also Brit* **despatch rider** *noun, pl* **~ -ers** [*count*] *chiefly Brit* **:** someone who delivers messages or packages especially by traveling on a motorcycle

dis·pel /dɪˈspɛl/ *verb* **-pels; -pelled; -pel·ling** [*+ obj*] **:** to make (something, such as a belief, feeling, or idea) go away or end ▪ This report should *dispel* any doubts you have about the plan. ▪ She made an official statement to *dispel* any rumors about her retirement. ▪ The experience *dispelled* some of our fears about the process.

dis·pens·able /dɪˈspɛnsəbəl/ *adj* [*more ~; most ~*] **:** not necessary or required ▪ Computers have made typewriters *dispensable*. ▪ Do you consider any of the staff to be *dispensable*? ▪ *dispensable* luxuries — opposite INDISPENSABLE

dis·pen·sa·ry /dɪˈspɛnsəri/ *noun, pl* **-ries** [*count*] **:** a place where medicine or minor medical treatment is given ▪ a hospital *dispensary*

dis·pen·sa·tion /ˌdɪspənˈseɪʃən/ *noun, pl* **-tions** *formal*
1 : permission to break a law or an official promise you have made **:** release from a rule, vow, or oath [*noncount*] The priest asked for *dispensation* from his vows. [*count*] The state gave the town a special *dispensation*, allowing it to ignore the law in this case.
2 [*singular*] **:** an act of providing something to people ▪ The ship's doctor handled the *dispensation* [=*distribution*] of medicine. ▪ a speedy *dispensation* [=*administration*] of justice

dis·pense /dɪˈspɛns/ *verb* **-pens·es; -pensed; -pens·ing** [+ *obj*]
1 : to give or provide (something) ▪ The ATM only *dispenses* $20 bills. ▪ A judge's job is to *dispense* [=*administer*] justice. ▪ a newspaper columnist who *dispenses* advice to millions of readers each week
2 : to prepare and give (medicine) ▪ Pharmacists are certified to *dispense* medication.
dispense with [*phrasal verb*] ***dispense with (something)*** *formal* **:** to no longer use or require (something) **:** to get rid of (something) ▪ Let's *dispense with* the usual introductions and get down to business. ▪ The new cleaning process will *dispense with* the need for ventilation.

dis·pens·er /dɪˈspɛnsɚ/ *noun, pl* **-ers** [*count*]
1 : a machine or container that lets you take small amounts of something ▪ a paper towel *dispenser* ▪ a soap/tape *dispenser*
2 : a person or organization that gives or provides something to people ▪ hospitals and other health-care *dispensers* — often + *of* ▪ A teacher should be more than a *dispenser of* knowledge.

dis·perse /dɪˈspɚs/ *verb* **-pers·es; -persed; -pers·ing :** to go or move in different directions **:** to spread apart [*no obj*] Police ordered the crowd to *disperse*. ▪ The clouds *dispersed* [=*broke*], revealing blue sky above. ▪ The fog gradually *dispersed* [=*dissipated, vanished*] as the day grew warmer. [+ *obj*] Police *dispersed* the protesters.
— **dis·per·sal** /dɪˈspɚsəl/ *noun* [*noncount*] ▪ The police are trained in crowd *dispersal*. — **dis·per·sion** /dɪˈspɚʒən/ *noun* [*noncount*] *technical* ▪ Laws were established to limit the *dispersion* of pollutants.

dis·pir·it·ed /dɪˈspirətəd/ *adj* [*more* ~; *most* ~] **:** feeling unhappy and without hope or enthusiasm ▪ The loss left the team *dispirited*. [=*disheartened, discouraged*] ▪ *dispirited* supporters — opposite SPIRITED
— **dis·pir·it·ed·ly** *adv* ▪ The team sat *dispiritedly* on the bench.

dis·pir·it·ing /dɪˈspirətɪŋ/ *adj* [*more* ~; *most* ~] **:** causing a loss of hope or enthusiasm ▪ It was very *dispiriting* [=*discouraging, disheartening*] to lose yet another game. ▪ a *dispiriting* failure

dis·place /dɪˈspleɪs/ *verb* **-plac·es; -placed; -plac·ing** [+ *obj*]
1 : to take the job or position of (someone or something) ▪ Many of the company's workers were *displaced* [=*replaced*] by machines. ▪ Some say football has *displaced* [=*replaced, supplanted*] baseball as America's national pastime.
2 a : to force (people or animals) to leave the area where they live ▪ The war has *displaced* thousands of people. ▪ The hurricane *displaced* most of the town's residents. ▪ animals *displaced* by wildfire **b** *chiefly US* **:** to remove (someone) from a job or position ▪ The closing of the factory has *displaced* many workers.
3 : to move (something) so that it is no longer in its original or regular location or position ▪ farming practices that *displace* large amounts of soil ▪ (*technical*) The ship *displaces* 20,000 tons (of water).
— **displaced** *adj* ▪ a crisis involving thousands of *displaced* persons/people [=people who have been forced to leave the area/country where they live]

dis·place·ment /dɪˈspleɪsmənt/ *noun, pl* **-ments**
1 : the act of displacing something: such as **a :** the act of forcing people or animals to leave the area where they live [*noncount*] The war has caused the *displacement* of thousands of people. [*count*] population *displacements* **b :** the movement of something from its original or regular position [*count*] *displacements* in the Earth's crust [*noncount*] soil *displacement* caused by farming
2 [*count*] *technical* **:** the amount of water that is moved by an object when it is placed in water — usually singular ▪ The ship has a very large *displacement*.

[1]**dis·play** /dɪˈspleɪ/ *verb* **-plays; -played; -play·ing** [+ *obj*]
1 : to put (something) where people can see it ▪ Students *displayed* their projects at the science fair. ▪ The results are *displayed* [=*shown*] on the computer screen. ▪ Toys were *displayed* in the store window. ▪ Her awards are prominently/proudly *displayed* on the mantel. ▪ The museum *displays* relics found during the excavation of the site. — sometimes used figuratively ▪ The tree *displays* pretty pink flowers in the spring.
2 : to show that you have (an emotion, quality, skill, etc.) ▪ He *displayed* no emotion when I told him the news. ▪ I was impressed by the care she *displayed* in making the flower arrangements. ▪ The children *displayed* [=*exhibited*] no interest in learning how to play the piano. ▪ The rookie player *displayed* great skill. ▪ The company has *displayed* exceptional dedication to this community.

[2]**display** *noun, pl* **-plays** [*count*]
1 : an arrangement of objects intended to decorate, advertise, entertain, or inform people about something ▪ Each table had a beautiful *display* of flowers. = Each table had a beautiful flower *display*. ▪ the bookstore's *display* of dictionaries = the bookstore's dictionary *display* ▪ The library's current *display* features locally made crafts. ▪ There is a *display* [=*exhibit, exhibition*] of his early paintings at the museum. ▪ Her trophies are in a *display* case/cabinet. ▪ a store's ***window display*** [=a display of products shown in a store's window]
2 : an event at which something is done or shown to impress or entertain people ▪ The celebration ended with a spectacular fireworks *display*.
3 : an action, performance, etc., which shows very clearly that you have some ability, feeling, quality, etc. — usually + *of* ▪ a *display of* anger ▪ In a remarkable *display of* generosity, the students gave the money they had raised for the class trip to their sick classmate. ▪ the soccer player's impressive *display of* footwork ▪ shocking *displays of* wealth in a country of extreme poverty ▪ He disapproved of their public *displays of* affection. [=hugging, kissing, etc., in public]
4 : an electronic device (such as a computer monitor) that shows information ▪ The computer comes with a high-resolution color *display*. ▪ The *display* showed an error message. ▪ a calculator's *display* screen
5 *biology* **:** a way of behaving that a bird or animal uses to show another bird or animal that it wants to mate, fight, etc. ▪ courtship/threat *displays*
on display **:** put somewhere for people to see **:** in a display ▪ Autographed baseballs are *on display* at the show. ▪ Only a few of the artifacts will be ***put on display***. = Only a few of the artifacts will ***go on display***.

dis·please /dɪsˈpliːz/ *verb* **-pleas·es; -pleased; -pleas·ing** [+ *obj*] **:** to make (someone) feel unhappy or annoyed ▪ What I said obviously *displeased* her. = She was obviously *displeased* by what I said. — opposite PLEASE
— **displeased** *adj* [*more* ~; *most* ~] ▪ She looked *displeased* when I told her about it. ▪ We're very *displeased* with the delays. — **displeasing** *adj* [*more* ~; *most* ~] ▪ visually *displeasing* buildings

dis·plea·sure /dɪsˈplɛʒɚ/ *noun* [*noncount*] **:** a feeling of unhappiness or annoyance ▪ The meeting will give people who object to the policy a chance to voice/express their *displeasure*. ▪ Fans showed their *displeasure* at the umpire's call by booing loudly.

[1]**dis·pos·able** /dɪˈspoʊzəbəl/ *adj*
1 : made to be used once or only a few times **:** made to be thrown away after one use or several uses ▪ *disposable* diapers/razors
2 *somewhat formal* **:** available to be used ▪ *disposable* resources/assets ▪ I don't have enough ***disposable income*** [=income that is left after paying taxes and for things that are essential, such as food and housing] to buy such luxuries.

[2]**disposable** *noun, pl* **-ables** [*count*] **:** something that is made to be thrown away after it is used once — usually plural ▪ Do you use cloth diapers or *disposables*? [=disposable diapers]

dis·pos·al /dɪˈspoʊzəl/ *noun, pl* **-als**
1 [*noncount*] **:** the act of disposing of something: such as **a :** the act of throwing something away ▪ trash *disposal* ▪ the *disposal* of nuclear waste **b** *law* **:** the act of giving control or ownership of land, possessions, etc., to someone ▪ the *disposal* of property
2 [*count*] *US* **:** GARBAGE DISPOSAL
at someone's disposal **:** available for someone to use ▪ We had plenty of money *at our disposal*. ▪ I'm *at your disposal*. [=I'm ready to do whatever you would like me to do] ▪ They are using every legal tool *at their disposal* to prevent the bridge from being built.

dis·pose /dɪˈspoʊz/ *verb* **-pos·es; -posed; -pos·ing** [+ *obj*] *formal*
1 : to cause (someone) to be likely to do or have something — + *to* or *toward* ▪ His upbringing *disposes* him *to* question authority. ▪ people whose genes *dispose* them *toward* a particular disease
2 *always followed by an adverb or preposition* **:** to put (someone or something) in a particular position or place ▪ The

troops/cottages were *disposed* [=(more commonly) *arranged*] along either side of the river.

dispose of [*phrasal verb*] **1** ***dispose of (something)*** **a** : to throw (something) away : to get rid of (something) • The waste was not properly *disposed of*. • Please *dispose of* your cigarette butts in one of the ashtrays available. **b** *formal* : to deal with and finish (something) • I have some business to *dispose of* [=(less formally) *wrap up, take care of*] before we meet. **c** *law* : to give control or ownership of (land, possessions, etc.) to someone • A will is a legal document that is used to *dispose of* property. **2** ***dispose of (someone or something)*** **a** : to defeat (a person or team) in a game, contest, etc. • She easily *disposed of* her opponent. **b** : to kill (a person or animal) • The article includes a list of the weapons the soldiers used to *dispose of* their enemies.

disposed *adj, not used before a noun, formal*
1 : wanting to do something or likely to do something • Join us for dinner if you feel ***so disposed*** [=if you want to] • dogs that are naturally *disposed* toward fighting — usually followed by *to + verb* • He disagreed but was not *disposed* [=*inclined*] *to argue*. • Many people seem *disposed to distrust* salespeople.
2 : feeling or thinking in a specified way about something — usually + *to* or *toward* • They were favorably/unfavorably *disposed to/toward* the idea. [=they liked/disliked the idea] — see also ILL-DISPOSED, WELL-DISPOSED

dis·po·si·tion /ˌdɪspəˈzɪʃən/ *noun, pl* **-tions**
1 [*count*] : the usual attitude or mood of a person or animal • He always had a cheerful/nervous *disposition*. [=*temperament, personality*] • It's nice to work with someone who has such a sunny *disposition*. [=who is usually cheerful] • a dog with an excellent *disposition*
2 *formal* **a** [*singular*] : a tendency to act or think in a particular way • Her *disposition* was to always think negatively. • He has a *disposition* toward criminal behavior. **b** [*count*] : a tendency to develop a disease, condition, etc. • people with a genetic *disposition* toward a particular disease
3 *formal* : the act or power of officially or legally giving land, possessions, etc., to someone [*count*] the philanthropist's charitable *dispositions* [=(less formally) *donations*] [*noncount*] A will is a legal document that is used in the *disposition* of property.
4 [*count*] *formal* : the way things are placed or arranged — usually singular; often + *of* • The map showed the *disposition of* troops on the border.

dis·pos·sess /ˌdɪspəˈzɛs/ *verb* **-sess·es; -sessed; -sess·ing** [+ *obj*] *formal* : to take land, possessions, etc., from (someone) • The land was settled by *dispossessing* the native people who lived here. — often + *of* • The new regime *dispossessed* many people *of* their land.
– dis·pos·ses·sion /ˌdɪspəˈzɛʃən/ *noun* [*noncount*]

dispossessed *adj, always used before a noun, formal* : having had your land, possessions, etc., taken away from you • The organization helps *dispossessed* people rebuild their lives.

the dispossessed : people whose land, possessions, etc., have been taken away from them • helping the poor and *the dispossessed*

dis·pro·por·tion /ˌdɪsprəˈpoɚʃən/ *noun, pl* **-tions** *formal* : a difference that is not fair, reasonable, or expected [*count*] The author does not explain the *disproportion* [=(more commonly) *disparity*] between the value of the stones. [*noncount*] His salary is ***in disproportion to*** what people who have similar jobs earn.
– dis·pro·por·tion·al /ˌdɪsprəˈpoɚʃənl/ *adj* [*more* ~; *most* ~] • The punishment was *disproportional* [=(more commonly) *disproportionate*] to the crime. **– dis·pro·por·tion·al·ly** *adv* [*more* ~; *most* ~]

dis·pro·por·tion·ate /ˌdɪsprəˈpoɚʃənət/ *adj* [*more* ~; *most* ~] : having or showing a difference that is not fair, reasonable, or expected : too large or too small in relation to something • He believes that middle-class people bear a *disproportionate* share of the tax burden. • A *disproportionate* number of the students are poor. — often + *to* • The organization's political influence is *disproportionate to* its size.
– dis·pro·por·tion·ate·ly *adv* [*more* ~; *most* ~] • A *disproportionately* high number of the students are poor.

dis·prove /dɪsˈpruːv/ *verb* **-proves; -proved** *or chiefly US* **-prov·en** /dɪsˈpruːvən/; **-prov·ing** [+ *obj*] : to show that (something) is false or wrong • *disprove* [=*refute*] an argument/claim — often used as *(be) disproved* • The theory *has been disproved*. — opposite PROVE

dis·put·able /dɪˈspjuːtəbəl/ *adj* [*more* ~; *most* ~] : not yet proved or shown to be true : likely to be questioned or doubted • The source of the text is *disputable*. [=*debatable*] • a *disputable* claim • The conclusion was based on *disputable* [=*questionable*] evidence. — opposite INDISPUTABLE
– dis·put·ably /dɪˈspjuːtəbli/ *adv* • It's been proved *indisputably*.

dis·pu·tant /dɪˈspjuːtn̩t, *Brit* ˈdɪspjətənt/ *noun, pl* **-tants** [*count*] *formal* : a person who is involved in a dispute and especially in a legal dispute

dis·pu·ta·tion /ˌdɪspjəˈteɪʃən/ *noun, pl* **-tions** *formal* : a disagreement or argument [*count*] legal *disputations* [*noncount*] years of debate and *disputation*
– dis·pu·ta·tious /ˌdɪspjəˈteɪʃəs/ *adj* [*more* ~; *most* ~] • a *disputatious* person [=a person who often disagrees and argues with other people]

[1]dis·pute /dɪˈspjuːt/ *noun, pl* **-putes** : a disagreement or argument [*count*] They could not settle their *dispute*. • legal *disputes* • There is a labor *dispute* between workers and management. • The two farmers are involved in a land *dispute*. • a domestic *dispute* [=an argument between people who live together] — often + *over* or *about* • There was a *dispute* [=*disagreement*] *over/about* what to do with the extra money. [*noncount*] There is *dispute* [=*debate*] among scholars as to the source of the text. = The source of the text is a matter/subject of *dispute* among scholars. • The matter/issue is still ***in dispute***. [=people still disagree about it] • The drug's effectiveness is ***beyond dispute***. [=it is certain that the drug is effective] • How it happened is ***open to dispute***. [=people disagree about how it happened]

[2]dispute *verb* **-putes; -put·ed; -put·ing**
1 [+ *obj*] : to say or show that (something) may not be true, correct, or legal • The lawyer *disputed* [=*challenged*] the witness's statement. • You can *dispute* your bill if you believe it is inaccurate. • She *disputed* the claim. • These estimates are hotly/much *disputed* by scientists. • No one ever *disputed* that it was the right decision. • There is ***no disputing*** the drug's effectiveness. [=it is certain that the drug is effective]
2 : to argue about (something) [+ *obj*] The source of the text has been *disputed* for centuries. • We were *disputing* [=*debating*] whether we should call the police or look for the thief ourselves. [*no obj*] It's no use *disputing* [=(more commonly) *arguing*] with them.
3 [+ *obj*] *formal* : to fight in order to take control of (something) • a part of the city where two drug gangs are *disputing* territory
– disputed *adj* • a *disputed* phone bill • various *disputed* claims/questions • the *disputed* territory/area/land

dis·qual·i·fy /dɪsˈkwɑːləˌfaɪ/ *verb* **-fies; -fied; -fy·ing** [+ *obj*] : to stop or prevent (someone) *from* doing, having, or being a part of something • His poor eyesight *disqualified* him *from* becoming a pilot. • The judge might *disqualify* [=*bar*] her *from* serving on the jury. — usually used as *(be) disqualified* • The winner *was* later *disqualified* for cheating. • (*Brit*) He *was disqualified from* driving for three months. [=he was not allowed to drive for three months]
– dis·qual·i·fi·ca·tion /dɪsˌkwɑːləfəˈkeɪʃən/ *noun, pl* **-tions** [*noncount*] A positive drug test is grounds/reason for *disqualification*. [*count*] What are the *disqualifications* for military service?

[1]dis·qui·et /dɪsˈkwajət/ *verb* **-ets; -et·ed; -et·ing** [+ *obj*] *formal* : to make (someone) worried or nervous — usually used as *(be) disquieted* • We *were disquieted* by the news.
– disquieting *adj* [*more* ~; *most* ~] • We found the news *disquieting*. • The letter gave *disquieting* news of the war.

[2]disquiet *noun* [*noncount*] *formal* : a feeling of worry or nervousness • There is increasing public *disquiet* about/over the number of violent crimes in the city. • The falling stock prices have caused great *disquiet* [=*concern*] among shareholders.

dis·qui·si·tion /ˌdɪskwəˈzɪʃən/ *noun, pl* **-tions** [*count*] *formal* : a long speech or written report on a subject • a lengthy *disquisition* on foreign policy

[1]dis·re·gard /ˌdɪsrɪˈgaɚd/ *verb* **-gards; -gard·ed; -gard·ing** [+ *obj*] : to ignore (something) or treat (something) as unimportant • Please *disregard* what I said before. • He *disregarded* his father's advice and left school. • Some students completely *disregard* the rules of the school.

[2]disregard *noun* : the act of ignoring something or treating something as unimportant [*noncount*] They treated the rules with complete/total *disregard*. — usually + *for* or *of* • the government's casual *disregard for* the rights of its citizens • The terrorists acted in complete/total *disregard of* human life. • The judge found that the statements were made with ***reckless disregard for/of*** the truth. [*singular*] — usually + *for* or *of* • Some students show a complete *disregard for* the rules of the school. • a *disregard of* the evidence

dis•re•pair /ˌdɪsrɪˈpeɚ/ *noun* [*noncount*] : the state of needing to be repaired : bad condition • The lighthouse was ***in disrepair*** until the volunteers cleaned it up. • A number of major bridges are *in* (states of) *disrepair*. • After years of neglect, the house ***fell into disrepair***.

dis•rep•u•ta•ble /dɪsˈrɛpjətəbəl/ *adj* [*more* ~; *most* ~] *formal* : not respected or trusted by most people : having a bad reputation • *disreputable* people • The company was using *disreputable* [=*dishonest*] hiring practices. — opposite REPUTABLE

dis•re•pute /ˌdɪsrɪˈpjuːt/ *noun* [*noncount*] *formal* : a state of not being respected or trusted by most people : a state of having a bad reputation • The theory has been ***in disrepute*** for years. • The star player's drug use will ***bring*** the game ***into disrepute***. [=give the game a bad reputation; make people not respect the game] • The technique has ***fallen into disrepute***. [=it is no longer respected or trusted]

[1]**dis•re•spect** /ˌdɪsrɪˈspɛkt/ *noun* : speech or behavior which shows that you do not think someone or something is valuable, important, etc. : lack of respect [*noncount*] The student treated the teacher with *disrespect*. • With no *disrespect* to the other players [=I do not mean to say that other players are not good], he is clearly the star of the team. • I'm sorry. I meant no *disrespect*. [*singular*] He showed a shocking *disrespect* for authority.

— **dis•re•spect•ful** /ˌdɪsrɪˈspɛktfəl/ *adj* [*more* ~; *most* ~] • She was very *disrespectful* to the teacher. • *disrespectful* behavior — **dis•re•spect•ful•ly** *adv*

[2]**disrespect** *verb* **-spects; -spect•ed; -spect•ing** [+ *obj*] : to say or do something that shows a lack of respect for (someone or something) • He *disrespected* [=*insulted*] the police officer. • He was angry because he felt he had been *disrespected*. [=treated with disrespect]

dis•robe /dɪsˈroʊb/ *verb* **-robes; -robed; -rob•ing** *formal*
1 [*no obj*] : to remove your clothes : UNDRESS • She *disrobed* and stepped into the bathtub.
2 [+ *obj*] : to remove the clothes of (someone) : UNDRESS • She *disrobed* herself.

dis•rupt /dɪsˈrʌpt/ *verb* **-rupts; -rupt•ed; -rupt•ing** [+ *obj*] : to cause (something) to be unable to continue in the normal way : to interrupt the normal progress or activity of (something) • Protesters *disrupted* the conference. • The barking dogs *disrupted* my sleep. • The weather *disrupted* our travel plans. • a chemical that *disrupts* cell function

— **dis•rup•tion** /dɪsˈrʌpʃən/ *noun, pl* **-tions** [*count*] The construction caused *disruptions* in bus service. • The chemical causes a *disruption* of cell function. [*noncount*] The change will be made with minimal *disruption* of service.

— **dis•rup•tive** /dɪsˈrʌptɪv/ *adj* [*more* ~; *most* ~] • *disruptive* behavior • She has a *disruptive* influence on the other students. — **dis•rup•tive•ly** *adv*

diss *variant spelling of* DIS

dis•sat•is•fac•tion /dɪsˌsætəsˈfækʃən/ *noun, pl* **-tions** : a feeling of unhappiness or disapproval [*count*] — usually singular • We're aware of a growing *dissatisfaction* among group members. • She expressed her *dissatisfaction* with the restaurant's service. [*noncount*] There was widespread *dissatisfaction* with the President and his administration. • a source of *dissatisfaction* — opposite SATISFACTION

dis•sat•is•fied /dɪsˈsætəsˌfaɪd/ *adj* [*more* ~; *most* ~] : not happy or pleased • *dissatisfied* customers — often + *with* • He was *dissatisfied with* his job. — opposite SATISFIED; compare UNSATISFIED

dis•sat•is•fy /dɪsˈsætəsˌfaɪ/ *verb* **-fies; -fied; -fy•ing** [+ *obj*] : to fail to make (someone) happy or pleased • Their final decision *dissatisfied* [=*displeased*] everyone. • She was *dissatisfied* by the poor service. — opposite SATISFY

— **dissatisfying** *adj* [*more* ~; *most* ~] • a *dissatisfying* experience • The movie was *dissatisfying*.

dis•sect /daɪˈsɛkt, dɪˈsɛkt/ *verb* **-sects; -sect•ed; -sect•ing** [+ *obj*]
1 : to cut (a plant or dead animal) into separate parts in order to study it • We *dissected* a frog in science class.
2 : to study or examine (something) closely and carefully : ANALYZE • She *dissected* each point of his argument. • We *dissected* the poem in class.
3 : to divide (something) into parts • Streams *dissect* the land. • The city is *dissected* by a network of highways.

— **dis•sec•tion** /daɪˈsɛkʃən, dɪˈsɛkʃən/ *noun, pl* **-tions** [*count*] The students performed a *dissection*. • Her essay includes an excellent *dissection* of the poem. [*noncount*] a process of careful *dissection*

dis•sem•ble /dɪˈsɛmbəl/ *verb* **-sem•bles; -sem•bled; -sem•bling** [*no obj*] *formal + literary* : to hide your true feelings, opinions, etc. • It's now clear that he *dissembled* about the risks involved. [=he did not tell the truth about the risks involved]

— **dissembling** *noun* [*noncount*] • Such *dissembling* from a politician is nothing new.

dis•sem•i•nate /dɪˈsɛməˌneɪt/ *verb* **-nates; -nat•ed; -nat•ing** [+ *obj*] *formal* : to cause (something, such as information) to go to many people • The Internet allows us to *disseminate* information/news/ideas faster. • The findings were widely *disseminated*.

— **dis•sem•i•na•tion** /dɪˌsɛməˈneɪʃən/ *noun* [*noncount*] • the *dissemination* of information — **dis•sem•i•na•tor** /dɪˈsɛməˌneɪtɚ/ *noun, pl* **-tors** [*count*] • *disseminators* of information

dis•sen•sion /dɪˈsɛnʃən/ *noun* [*noncount*] *formal* : disagreement that causes the people in a group to argue about something that is important to them • The incident has caused a lot of *dissension* within/in the police department. • Religious *dissension* threatened to split the colony.

[1]**dis•sent** /dɪˈsɛnt/ *verb* **-sents; -sent•ed; -sent•ing** [*no obj*] *formal* : to publicly disagree with an official opinion, decision, or set of beliefs • The Supreme Court, with two justices *dissenting*, ruled that the law was constitutional. — often + *from* • Several scientists *dissented from* the decision.

— **dis•sent•er** /dɪˈsɛntɚ/ *noun, pl* **-ers** [*count*]
— **dissenting** *adj* • *dissenting* opinions/views • There are few *dissenting* voices within the party.

[2]**dissent** *noun, pl* **-sents**
1 *formal* : public disagreement with an official opinion, decision, or set of beliefs [*noncount*] Church leaders permitted no *dissent* from church teachings. • He did everything in his power to suppress political *dissent*. [*count*] These *dissents* come from prominent scientists and should not be ignored.
2 [*count*] *US, law* : a statement by a judge giving reasons why the judge does not agree with the decision made by the other judges in a court case • She argued in her *dissent* that Congress had exceeded its authority.

dis•ser•ta•tion /ˌdɪsɚˈteɪʃən/ *noun, pl* **-tions** [*count*] : a long piece of writing about a particular subject that is done to earn an advanced degree at a university • He wrote his *dissertation* on an obscure 16th-century poet.

dis•ser•vice /dɪsˈsɚvɪs/ *noun* [*singular*] : something that harms or damages someone or something • Her comments were a *disservice* to those volunteers. — usually used in the phrase ***do a disservice*** • He *did a disservice* to readers by providing wrong information. • Her behavior has *done* the sport *a great disservice*. [=her behavior has hurt the sport]

dis•si•dent /ˈdɪsədənt/ *noun, pl* **-dents** [*count*] : someone who strongly and publicly disagrees with and criticizes the government • Many political *dissidents* were arrested.

— **dis•si•dence** /ˈdɪsədəns/ *noun* [*noncount*] • political/religious *dissidence* [=*dissent*] — **dissident** *adj, always used before a noun* • *dissident* scholars/students • the *dissident* movement

dis•sim•i•lar /dɪsˈsɪmələ/ *adj* [*more* ~; *most* ~] : not the same : different or unalike • The two movies are very *dissimilar*. • The writers have *dissimilar* backgrounds. • A ***not dissimilar*** [=*similar*] situation has occurred overseas. • The question is *not dissimilar* to one asked earlier. — opposite SIMILAR

— **dis•sim•i•lar•i•ty** /dɪsˌsɪməˈlerəti/ *noun, pl* **-ties** [*count*] *dissimilarities* in the writers' backgrounds [*noncount*] I could see no *dissimilarity* between the twins.

dis•si•pate /ˈdɪsəˌpeɪt/ *verb* **-pates; -pat•ed; -pat•ing** *formal*
1 a [+ *obj*] : to cause (something) to spread out and disappear • The morning sun *dissipated* the fog. **b** [*no obj*] : to separate into parts and disappear or go away • The fog should *dissipate* soon. • By noon the crowd had *dissipated*. [=(more commonly) *dispersed*] — often used figuratively • Her anger began to *dissipate* after a while.
2 [+ *obj*] : to use all or a lot of (something, such as money or time) in a foolish way • He had *dissipated* [=*squandered*] his family's fortune in only a few years.

dis•si•pa•tion /ˌdɪsəˈpeɪʃən/ *noun, pl* **-tions** *formal*
1 [*noncount*] : the process of slowly disappearing or becom-

ing less • Insulation helps prevent the *dissipation* of heat from houses in the winter.

2 [*noncount*] : the act of using all or a lot of money, time, etc., in a foolish way • a movie about the *dissipation* of a famous heir's fortune • the *dissipation* of resources

3 *disapproving* : behavior that shows you are interested only in pleasure, money, etc. [*noncount*] He lived a life of *dissipation*. [*count*] her gambling and *dissipations*

dis·so·ci·ate /dɪˈsoʊʃiˌeɪt/ *verb* **-ates; -at·ed; -at·ing** [+ *obj*] : to end your relationship with or connection to someone or something : to separate (yourself) *from* someone or something • She became famous and *dissociated* [=*disassociated*] herself *from* her past. • The director has tried to *dissociate* himself *from* his earlier films. • Why is the organization choosing to *dissociate* itself *from* its founder?

– dis·so·ci·a·tion /dɪˌsoʊʃiˈeɪʃən/ *noun* [*noncount*]

dis·so·lute /ˈdɪsəˌluːt/ *adj* [*more* ~; *most* ~] *formal* + *disapproving* — used to describe someone (such as a person who often gets drunk) whose way of living is considered morally wrong • a *dissolute* drunk • She has led a *dissolute* life.

dis·so·lu·tion /ˌdɪsəˈluːʃən/ *noun* [*noncount*] *formal*

1 : the act of officially ending a marriage, organization, agreement, etc. • the *dissolution* of the marriage/business/contract

2 : the process of making something slowly end or disappear • the *dissolution* of old beliefs • The treatment is used for the *dissolution* of kidney stones.

dis·solve /dɪˈzɑːlv/ *verb* **-solves; -solved; -solv·ing**

1 *of something solid* : to mix with a liquid and become part of the liquid [*no obj*] Sugar/salt *dissolves* in water. [+ *obj*] *Dissolve* the tablet in water.

2 [+ *obj*] *formal* : to officially end (something, such as a marriage, organization, or agreement) • She *dissolved* [=*terminated*] their partnership. — often used as *(be) dissolved* • The marriage/business/government *was dissolved*. • The company *has been dissolved*.

3 *somewhat formal* : to end or disappear or cause (something) to end or disappear [*no obj*] His smile *dissolved* [=*disappeared*] when I told him the news. • Hopes for peace *dissolved* in renewed violence. [+ *obj*] His kind words *dissolved* her sadness. • The treatment is used to *dissolve* kidney stones.

✧ If you ***dissolve in/into tears/laughter, etc.***, you start to cry, laugh, etc., in an uncontrolled way. • The audience *dissolved into* tears during the play's final scene. • The children *dissolved into* laughter/giggles.

– dis·solv·able /dɪˈzɑːlvəbəl/ *adj* • The doctor used *dissolvable* stitches to close the wound.

dis·so·nant /ˈdɪsənənt/ *adj* [*more* ~; *most* ~]

1 *formal* : not in agreement with something : DISCORDANT • *dissonant* views

2 *music* : not in harmony : DISCORDANT • *dissonant* chords — opposite CONSONANT

– dis·so·nance /ˈdɪsənəns/ *noun, pl* **-nanc·es** [*noncount*] The *dissonance* [=*conflict*] between the truth and what people want to believe. • When played together, the chords create *dissonance*. [*count*] The composer uses *dissonances* freely.

dis·suade /dɪˈsweɪd/ *verb* **-suades; -suad·ed; -suad·ing** [+ *obj*] : to convince (someone) not to do something • Our warnings did not *dissuade* them. — often + *from* • He tried to *dissuade* them *from* going. — compare PERSUADE

dis·taff /ˈdɪˌstæf, *Brit* ˈdɪˌstɑːf/ *adj, always used before a noun, formal* : of, relating to, or being a woman : FEMALE • the *distaff* [=*maternal*] side of the family • *distaff* executives

[1]**dis·tance** /ˈdɪstəns/ *noun, pl* **-tanc·es**

1 : the amount of space between two places or things [*count*] What is the *distance* between the Earth and the Sun? • The gas station is a short *distance* away. • He spotted the group ***at a distance of*** one mile. [=he saw the group when they were one mile away from him] [*noncount*] Speed is measured in time and *distance*. • The nearest gas station is ***some distance*** away. [=it is not nearby] • Her house is within ***walking/striking distance*** of the school. [=she lives very close to the school] — see also LONG DISTANCE, MIDDLE DISTANCE

2 [*singular*] : a point or place that is far away from another point or place • She kept the children a safe *distance* from the road. • The sign was hard to read ***from a distance***. • We followed them ***at a distance***. • He saw a light ***in the distance***. [=he saw a light that was far away] — often used figuratively • After observing politics *from a distance* for years, I've decided to run for office. • (*Brit*) The book is better than the movie ***by some distance***. [=the book is much better than the movie]

3 : a state in which people are not involved with or friendly toward each other [*singular*] She feels a *distance* from her brother that wasn't there before. • He heard the *distance* [=*unfriendliness*] in her voice. [*noncount*] Although they were once good friends, there was now considerable *distance* between them. • He wants to put *distance* between himself and his former boss.

go the distance also ***last the distance*** : to complete something you have started • Even with an injured elbow, he *went/lasted the distance* and pitched the rest of the game. • Don't volunteer for the job if you can't *go the distance*.

keep (someone) at a distance : to be unfriendly toward (someone) • She always *kept her coworkers at a distance*.

keep your distance **1** : to stay far enough away from someone or something to be safe • Visitors are told to *keep their distance* from the monkeys. **2** : to avoid getting involved in something or becoming friendly with someone • He tried to *keep his distance* from the scandal. • After their break-up, she thought it was wise to *keep her distance*.

[2]**distance** *verb* **-tances; -tanced; -tanc·ing** [+ *obj*] : to show that you are not involved with someone or something : to end a connection to or relationship with someone or something — usually + *from* • She has tried to *distance* herself *from* her family. • They all want to *distance* themselves *from* the scandal.

distance learning *noun* [*noncount*] : a method of study where teachers and students do not meet in a classroom but use the Internet, e-mail, mail, etc., to have classes — called also *distance education*

dis·tant /ˈdɪstənt/ *adj*

1 [*more* ~; *most* ~] : existing or happening far away in space : separated by space • astronomers studying *distant* galaxies • They visited all sorts of *distant* [=*far-off*] places. • He finished the race a *distant* second. [=he was the second person to finish the race but he was far behind the winner] • The town is about 30 miles *distant*. [=(more commonly) *away*]

2 *always used before a noun* [*more* ~; *most* ~] : far away in time : happening far in the past or far into the future • In the *distant* past, dinosaurs roamed the earth. • The day I left home is now a *distant* memory. • the *distant* future • We're expecting major changes ***in the not too distant future***. [=*soon*]

3 *always used before a noun* [*more* ~; *most* ~] — used to describe a relative who is not closely related to you • She's a *distant* cousin of mine. • Some of my more *distant* relatives still live there. — opposite CLOSE; compare IMMEDIATE

4 : having to do with something that is not related to what is happening where you are or at the present time • His mind drifted to *distant* thoughts. • I remember when the restaurant's opening was nothing more than a *distant* possibility. • She has a ***distant look in her eye***. [=the look on her face shows that she is thinking about something that is not related to what is happening now]

5 [*more* ~; *most* ~] *somewhat formal* : not friendly or showing emotion • People did not like her *distant* manner. • He was cold and *distant*.

6 [*more* ~; *most* ~] : not like someone or something else — usually + *from* • The values of that time seem very *distant* [=*different*] *from* our own.

the dim and distant past *chiefly Brit* : a time that is so far in the past it is difficult to remember • I remember *the dim and distant past* when the town was much smaller.

– dis·tant·ly *adv* • We are *distantly* related to each other. • She stared *distantly* out the window.

dis·taste /dɪsˈteɪst/ *noun, pl* **-tastes** : a strong feeling of not liking someone or something [*count*] — usually singular • I've developed a real *distaste* [=*dislike*] for paperwork. [*noncount*] "I see you still smoke," she said with *distaste*.

dis·taste·ful /dɪsˈteɪstfəl/ *adj* [*more* ~; *most* ~]

1 : not pleasant or enjoyable • The work was *distasteful*, but it was the best I could find at the time. • It was a *distasteful* subject to him.

2 : morally offensive • *distasteful* jokes/behavior

– dis·taste·ful·ly *adv*

dis·tem·per /dɪsˈtɛmpɚ/ *noun* [*noncount*] *medical* : a serious disease of animals (such as dogs and cats) that is easily passed to other animals

dis·tend /dɪˈstɛnd/ *verb* **-tends; -tend·ed; -tend·ing** *medical* + *formal* : to become larger and rounder because of pressure from inside [*no obj*] The illness can cause the stomach to *distend*. [=*swell*] [+ *obj*] an abdomen *distended* by disease • a *distended* abdomen/stomach

– **dis·ten·sion** *or US* **dis·ten·tion** /dɪˈstɛnʃən/ *noun* [*noncount*] • abdominal *distension* [=*swelling*]

dis·till (*US*) *or chiefly Brit* **dis·til** /dɪˈstɪl/ *verb* **-tills**; **-tilled**; **-till·ing** [+ *obj*]

1 a : to make (a liquid) pure by heating it until it becomes a gas and then cooling it until it is a liquid again **:** to purify (a liquid) by distillation • *distilled* water **b :** to make (a strong alcoholic drink) by using this process • They *distill* the whiskey from malted barley.

2 : to take the most important parts of something and put them in a different and usually improved form • He has perfectly *distilled* the meaning of the holiday into a poem. • Her wisdom is *distilled* from [=her wisdom comes from] many years of experience.

– **dis·til·la·tion** /ˌdɪstəˈleɪʃən/ *noun, pl* **-tions** [*noncount*] the *distillation* of brandy from wine • the *distillation* of experience [*count*] The poem is a perfect *distillation* of the meaning of the holiday.

dis·till·er /dɪˈstɪlɚ/ *noun, pl* **-ers** [*count*] **:** a person or company that produces strong alcoholic drinks (such as whiskey) by distilling them

dis·till·ery /dɪˈstɪləri/ *noun, pl* **-er·ies** [*count*] **:** a place where alcoholic drinks (such as whiskey) are produced

dis·tinct /dɪˈstɪŋkt/ *adj* [*more* ~; *most* ~]

1 : different in a way that you can see, hear, smell, feel, etc. **:** noticeably different • There are three *distinct* categories/classes/groups/types. • The two plants are quite *distinct* (from one another). • Each herb has its own *distinct* flavor. • The phrase has three *distinct* meanings. • The class focuses on U.S. English, ***as distinct from*** British English. [=the class focuses on U.S. English and not on British English]

2 : easy to see, hear, smell, feel, etc. • He speaks with a *distinct* [=*noticeable*] Southern accent. • There was the *distinct* smell of something burning. • The outline became less and less *distinct* as the light faded.

3 : strong and definite • A flight cancellation is a *distinct* [=*real*] possibility. • We had the *distinct* impression that they were lying.

– **dis·tinct·ly** *adv* • Each island has a *distinctly* different character. • I *distinctly* told you not to call me. • a *distinctly* American phenomenon [=something that happens only in America] – **dis·tinct·ness** *noun* [*noncount*] • *distinctness* of form

dis·tinc·tion /dɪˈstɪŋkʃən/ *noun, pl* **-tions**

1 [*count*] **:** a difference that you can see, hear, smell, feel, etc. **:** a noticeable difference between things or people • These dogs are different breeds, but this *distinction* is lost on most people. [=most people do not see a difference between these dogs] • There are no obvious *distinctions between* the two designs. • *distinctions between* social classes • She ***made/drew a distinction between*** the words "less" and "fewer."

2 [*noncount*] **:** the separation of people or things into different groups • The law should be enforced without *distinction* as to race, sex, or religion. [=the law should not treat people of different races, sexes, or religions differently]

3 [*noncount*] **:** importance, excellence, or achievement • He was raised in a small town of no great *distinction*. • Her talents gave *distinction* to the work. • She was a politician of some *distinction*. [=she was a distinguished politician]

4 : a special honor, recognition, or award [*count*] She's won many *distinctions*. • (*Brit*) She was awarded a *distinction* for her dissertation. [*noncount*] They should give him the *distinction* he deserves. • He graduated ***with distinction***. [=with special awards or recognition]

5 [*noncount*] **:** the quality that makes a person or thing special or different — + *of* • It had the *distinction of* being the oldest house in the city. • The city bears the ***dubious distinction of*** being the most polluted in the nation.

dis·tinc·tive /dɪˈstɪŋktɪv/ *adj* [*more* ~; *most* ~]

1 : having a quality or characteristic that makes a person or thing different from others **:** different in a way that is easy to notice • He had a very *distinctive* walk. • This wine has a more *distinctive* flavor than that one. • a cooking style that is *distinctive* [=*characteristic*] of this region

2 : appealing or interesting because of an unusual quality or characteristic • The store sells only the most *distinctive* chocolates.

– **dis·tinc·tive·ly** *adv* • a *distinctively* regional cooking style – **dis·tinc·tive·ness** *noun* [*noncount*] • the *distinctiveness* of the store's chocolates

dis·tin·guish /dɪˈstɪŋgwɪʃ/ *verb* **-guish·es**; **-guished**; **-guish·ing**

1 : to notice or recognize a difference between people or things [*no obj*] You're old enough to *distinguish* between fact and fantasy. • I have trouble *distinguishing* between the two of them. [+ *obj*] Their voices are hard to *distinguish*. [=*tell apart*] • I have trouble *distinguishing* the difference between the two of them. • You should be able to *distinguish* fact from fantasy.

2 *not used in progressive tenses* [+ *obj*] **:** to make (someone or something) different or special in some way • The only thing that *distinguishes* the dogs is their bark. • The recipe is *distinguished* by its simplicity. [=the unusual or interesting thing about the recipe is its simplicity] • The singer's voice is what *distinguishes* the band. — often + *from* • Our excellent customer service *distinguishes* us *from* our competitors. • The law affects private property ***as distinguished from*** public property. [=the law affects private property and not public property]

3 *not used in progressive tenses* [+ *obj*] **:** to see or hear (someone or something) clearly • You can't *distinguish* the detail from this distance.

distinguish yourself **:** to do something very well or in a way that deserves special recognition • She has *distinguished herself* as a leader in the community. • He *distinguished himself* in the war.

– **dis·tin·guish·able** /dɪˈstɪŋgwɪʃəbəl/ *adj* [*more* ~; *most* ~] • The plant is *distinguishable* by its oddly shaped leaves. • There are four *distinguishable* types. • The copy is clearly/barely *distinguishable* from the original. – **distinguishing** *adj* [*more* ~; *most* ~] • The plant has several *distinguishing* characteristics/features.

dis·tin·guished /dɪˈstɪŋgwɪʃt/ *adj* [*more* ~; *most* ~]

1 : known by many people because of some quality or achievement • a *distinguished* scientist/career • She is *distinguished* for her achievements in genetic research.

2 : making someone seem important and worth respect • the professor's *distinguished* appearance • He's a *distinguished*-looking gentleman.

dis·tort /dɪˈstoɚt/ *verb* **-torts**; **-tort·ed**; **-tort·ing**

1 : to change the natural, normal, or original shape, appearance, or sound of (something) in a way that is usually not attractive or pleasing [+ *obj*] Her face was *distorted* by pain. • The odd camera angle *distorted* her figure in the photograph. • The sound of the guitar was *distorted*. [*no obj*] Heat caused the plastic to *distort*.

2 [+ *obj*] **:** to change (something) so that it is no longer true or accurate • She felt he was *distorting* the facts. • The story was *distorted* by the press. • The loss of both her parents at an early age *distorted* her outlook on life.

– **distorted** *adj* [*more* ~; *most* ~] • a *distorted* face/image • He had a *distorted* view of the situation. • His voice sounded *distorted* over the phone. – **dis·tor·tion** /dɪˈstoɚʃən/ *noun, pl* **-tions** [*count*] The statement was an intentional *distortion* of the facts. • Curved mirrors cause image *distortions*. [*noncount*] an image/sound that is free of *distortion*

dis·tract /dɪˈstrækt/ *verb* **-tracts**; **-tract·ed**; **-tract·ing** [+ *obj*]

1 : to cause (someone) to stop thinking about or paying attention to someone or something and to think about or pay attention to someone or something else instead • You sneak into his room while I *distract* him. • He was *distracted* from his studies. • The students are easily *distracted*, especially when they're tired. • I was *distracted* by a loud noise.

2 : to take (attention) away from someone or something • The local story ***distracted attention from*** news of the war overseas.

– **distracting** *adj* [*more* ~; *most* ~] • The music was very *distracting*. • a *distracting* noise

distracted /dɪˈstræktəd/ *adj* [*more* ~; *most* ~] **:** unable to think about or pay attention to something **:** unable to concentrate • If you're feeling *distracted*, take a break.

– **dis·tract·ed·ly** *adv* • "I wonder if it's going to snow," she said *distractedly*. [=*absentmindedly*]

dis·trac·tion /dɪˈstrækʃən/ *noun, pl* **-tions**

1 : something that makes it difficult to think or pay attention [*count*] It was hard to work with so many *distractions*. • One of them created a *distraction* while the other grabbed the money. [*noncount*] He worked without *distraction*.

2 [*count*] **:** something that amuses or entertains you so that you do not think about problems, work, etc. • He found reading to be a good *distraction*. [=*diversion*] • A weekend at

the beach was a good *distraction* from her troubles.
3 [*noncount*] : a state in which you are very annoyed or upset • Their endless chatter ***drove her to distraction.***

dis·traught /dɪˈstrɑːt/ *adj* [*more* ~; *most* ~] : very upset : so upset that you are not able to think clearly or behave normally • *Distraught* relatives are waiting for news of the missing children. • She was *distraught* over the death of her partner.

[1]**dis·tress** /dɪˈstrɛs/ *noun* [*noncount*]
1 : unhappiness or pain : suffering that affects the mind or body • Citizens voiced their *distress* over delays in fixing the problem. • The patient showed no obvious signs of *distress.* • He suffered severe emotional *distress* as a result of the accident. • The new drug can cause abdominal/gastric *distress.* [=stomach pain] • a cry of *distress* • He was clearly ***in distress*** [=very upset] upon hearing the news.
2 : a very difficult situation in which you do not have enough money, food, etc. • She's chosen to devote her life to helping those ***in distress.*** [=*in trouble, in need*] • Donations were given to families *in* (financial) *distress.*
3 *of a boat, airplane, etc.* : a state of danger or desperate need • The ship was ***in distress.*** [=the ship was possibly going to sink] • The Coast Guard responded to the ship's ***distress signal/call.*** [=signal or call for help]
damsel in distress see DAMSEL

[2]**distress** *verb* **-tress·es; -tressed; -tress·ing** [+ *obj*] : to worry or upset (someone) • The news *distressed* [=*disturbed*] her. — usually used as *(be) distressed* • I *was distressed* to learn that the hospital had closed.
– distressing *adj* [*more* ~; *most* ~] • I heard some *distressing* news. • It was *distressing* to learn that the hospital had closed. **– dis·tress·ing·ly** *adv*

distressed *adj*
1 [*more* ~; *most* ~] : feeling or showing extreme unhappiness or pain • He was very *distressed* [=*upset*] about the accident. • She felt emotionally and physically *distressed.*
2 [*more* ~; *most* ~] *somewhat formal* : not having enough money : experiencing financial trouble • The government provided funds to the economically *distressed* city. • Donations were given to financially *distressed* families.
3 — used to describe something (such as a piece of clothing or furniture) that has been made to look old or to look like something that has been used a lot • a *distressed* pair of jeans • *distressed* leather • a *distressed* oak table

dis·trib·ute /dɪˈstrɪbjuːt/ *verb* **-utes; -ut·ed; -ut·ing** [+ *obj*]
1 a : to give or deliver (something) to people • She *distributes* [=*hands out*] the paychecks every week. — usually + *to* • He'd been hired to *distribute* leaflets *to* people who passed by. • The organization *distributes* food and clothing *to* needy families. **b** : to deliver (something) to a store or business — usually + *to* • The trucking company *distributes* goods *to* stores throughout the state. • One million copies of the CD were *distributed to* stores.
2 : to divide (something) among the members of a group — usually + *between* or *among*; often used as *(be/get) distributed* • The profits *are* evenly *distributed between* them. • The work for the project *gets distributed among* the editors.
3 : to spread or place (something) over an area • The machine *distributes* [=*scatters*] the seeds evenly on the ground. — often used as *(be/get) distributed* • Make sure the paint *is distributed* evenly over the surface area. — often used figuratively • The player's 200 pounds ***are evenly distributed*** over his six-foot frame. • The plant ***is widely distributed*** throughout the world. [=the plant grows throughout the world]

dis·tri·bu·tion /ˌdɪstrəˈbjuːʃən/ *noun, pl* **-tions**
1 [*noncount*] **a** : the act of giving or delivering something to people • The group collects food and clothing for *distribution* to needy families. • The *distribution* of paychecks will happen every other Friday. • The university does not permit *distribution* of leaflets on campus. **b** : the act of delivering something to a store or business • She was responsible for product *distribution.* • The company handles the *distribution* of goods to stores nationwide. — often used before another noun • The company acquired U.S. *distribution* rights. • *distribution* costs • a *distribution* company/center
2 : the way that something is divided or spread out [*count*] He complained that the *distribution* of work was unfair. • He studies the *distributions* of wildcats in North America. [*noncount*] The new design provides better weight *distribution.*

dis·trib·u·tor /dɪˈstrɪbjətɚ/ *noun, pl* **-tors** [*count*]
1 : a person or company that supplies stores or businesses with goods • a software *distributor*
2 *technical* : a device that sends electricity to the spark plugs of an engine — see picture at ENGINE

dis·trict /ˈdɪstrɪkt/ *noun, pl* **-tricts** [*count*] : an area or section of a country, city, or town: such as **a** : an area established by a government for official government business • postal/election *districts* • Six police officers are in charge of the *district.* • She represents the eighth congressional *district.* — see also SCHOOL DISTRICT **b** : an area or section that has some special characteristic or purpose • a church/sales *district* • the city's entertainment/shopping *district* • He was promoted to *district* manager. [=he was put in charge of that company's activities in a particular district]

district attorney *noun, pl* ~ **-neys** [*count*] : a lawyer who works for the U.S. government in a state, county, etc., and who is responsible for starting a criminal case against someone — abbr. *DA*

district court *noun, pl* ~ **courts** [*count*] *law* : a court in the U.S. in which cases in a particular area are brought to trial; *especially* : one of the trial courts for cases involving federal law

[1]**dis·trust** /dɪsˈtrʌst/ *verb* **-trusts; -trust·ed; -trust·ing** [+ *obj*] : to have no trust or confidence in (someone or something) : MISTRUST • He generally *distrusts* doctors. • She's always *distrusted* their promises.

[2]**distrust** *noun* : lack of trust or confidence : a feeling that someone or something is not honest and cannot be trusted [*noncount*] He regards doctors with *distrust.* [=*mistrust*] [*singular*] He has a *distrust* of doctors.
– dis·trust·ful /dɪsˈtrʌstfəl/ *adj* [*more* ~; *most* ~] • He is generally *distrustful* [=*mistrustful*] of doctors. **– dis·trust·ful·ly** *adv* • He looked *distrustfully* at them.

dis·turb /dɪˈstɚb/ *verb* **-turbs; -turbed; -turb·ing** [+ *obj*]
1 : to stop (someone) from working, sleeping, etc. : to interrupt or bother (someone or something) • I'm sorry to *disturb* you at such a late hour. • She doesn't want to be *disturbed* while she's working. • Don't *disturb* the baby when he's sleeping. • The noise *disturbed* my concentration. • They were arrested for ***disturbing the peace.*** [=behaving in a violent or noisy manner in public]
2 : to worry or upset (someone) • The news *disturbed* [=*distressed*] him. • His behavior *disturbs* me. — often used as *(be) disturbed* • I *am disturbed* at/by his behavior. • She *was disturbed* to learn that her son was failing one of his classes.
3 : to change the position, arrangement, or order of (something) • The police ordered that nothing be *disturbed* in the room. [=that nothing be touched or moved] • His visit *disturbed* [=*disrupted*] our morning routine.
– disturbing *adj* [*more* ~; *most* ~] • It was a deeply *disturbing* sight. • I thought the movie was very *disturbing.* **– dis·turb·ing·ly** *adv* • There was a *disturbingly* high number of crimes last year. • *Disturbingly,* the story is true.

dis·turb·ance /dɪˈstɚbəns/ *noun, pl* **-anc·es**
1 a : something that stops you from working, sleeping, etc. : the act of disturbing someone or something [*count*] She doesn't want any more *disturbances* while she is studying. • She suffered from frequent sleep *disturbances.* [=*disruptions*] [*noncount*] He reacts badly to *disturbance* of his daily routine. **b** : a change in the position, arrangement, or order of something [*count*] Fish are able to detect even slight *disturbances* in the water. [*noncount*] *Disturbance* of the river's sediment causes cloudy water.
2 : violent or noisy behavior especially in public [*count*] Neighbors called the police to report a *disturbance.* • They were arrested for ***creating/causing a disturbance.*** [*noncount*] He was arrested for ***disturbance of the peace.*** [=behaving in a violent or noisy way in public]
3 : an unhealthy physical or mental condition in which something is not normal [*count*] heart rhythm *disturbances* • visual/emotional/mental *disturbances* [*noncount*] The violence that soldiers experience in war can lead to emotional *disturbance* in later years.

disturbed *adj* [*more* ~; *most* ~]
1 : having or showing evidence of a mental or emotional illness • mentally/emotionally *disturbed* children
2 : worried and unhappy • He seems very *disturbed* about his work lately.
3 *of sleep* : affected by a disturbance • She'd been experiencing *disturbed* sleep. [=sleep that is interrupted]

dis·unit·ed /ˌdɪsjuˈnaɪtəd/ *adj, chiefly Brit* : not able to work or agree with other people within the same group, organization, etc. • The rebels seem to be increasingly *disunited.* • a *disunited* political party

dis·uni·ty /dɪsˈjuːnəti/ *noun [noncount]* : the state of not being able to agree about important things : lack of unity ▪ They are concerned about *disunity* [=*dissension, disagreement*] within the party.

dis·use /dɪsˈjuːs/ *noun [noncount]* : the state of not being used : lack of use ▪ The room was dusty from/with *disuse.* ▪ The word ***fell into disuse*** [=people stopped using it] many years ago.

dis·used /dɪsˈjuːzd/ *adj, always used before a noun* : no longer used ▪ *disused* buildings/mines ▪ a *disused* word

¹ditch /ˈdɪʧ/ *noun, pl* **ditch·es** *[count]* : a long narrow hole that is dug along a road, field, etc., and used to hold or move water ▪ irrigation *ditches* ▪ He drove the car into the *ditch.* — see also LAST-DITCH

²ditch *verb* **ditches; ditched; ditch·ing**
1 *[+ obj] informal* : to stop having or using (something you no longer want or need) : to get rid of (something) ▪ The thief *ditched* the purse in an alley. ▪ They *ditched* the car in a vacant lot. ▪ We've *ditched* [=*abandoned*] plans to open a café together.
2 *[+ obj] informal* : to end a relationship with (someone) ▪ His girlfriend *ditched* him. = He ***got ditched*** by his girlfriend. ▪ The team's owner *ditched* [=*fired, dismissed*] the head coach.
3 *[+ obj] US, informal* : to get away from (someone you do not want to be with) without saying that you are leaving ▪ They *ditched* me at the concert.
4 *[+ obj] US, informal* : to not go to (something, such as school, work, etc.) ▪ Let's *ditch* [=*skip*] school today. ▪ He *ditched* [=*left, quit*] school to join the army.
5 : to land an aircraft on water because of an emergency : to crash-land on water *[no obj]* Engine trouble forced the pilot to *ditch.* *[+ obj]* He had to *ditch* the helicopter.

ditch·wa·ter /ˈdɪʧˌwɑːtɚ/ *noun*
(as) dull as ditchwater *Brit, informal* : very boring ▪ The book is *as dull as ditchwater.* [=(*US*) *(as) dull as dishwater*]

¹dith·er /ˈdɪðɚ/ *noun [singular] informal* : a very nervous, confused, or excited state — usually used in the phrase ***in a dither*** ▪ They're *in a dither* over what to do next. ▪ The news of his arrival had us (all) *in a dither.*

²dither *verb* **-ers; -ered; -er·ing** *[no obj] informal* : to delay taking action because you are not sure about what to do ▪ We don't have time to *dither.* ▪ She did not *dither* about/over what to do next.
– dith·er·er *noun, pl* **-ers** *[count]*

¹dit·to /ˈdɪtoʊ/ *adv, informal*
1 — used to say that whatever you have said about one person or thing is also true of another person or thing ▪ Boston is getting a lot of rain. *Ditto* New York. [=New York is also getting a lot of rain] ▪ He is good at baseball, *ditto* at golf.
2 — used in speech to show you agree with what someone has just said or have the same opinion ▪ "I don't like spinach." "*Ditto.*" [=I don't like spinach either]

²ditto *noun, pl* **-tos** *[count]* : a pair of marks " used underneath a word to save space and show that the word is repeated where the marks are — called also *ditto marks*

dit·ty /ˈdɪti/ *noun, pl* **-ties** *[count] sometimes humorous* : a short and simple song ▪ Play us a little *ditty.*

ditz /ˈdɪts/ *noun, pl* **ditz·es** *[count] chiefly US, informal + sometimes disapproving* : a silly person who often forgets things ▪ His girlfriend is nice but she's a bit of a *ditz.* [=his girlfriend is somewhat ditzy]

dit·zy *or* **dit·sy** /ˈdɪtsi/ *adj* **ditz·i·er** *or* **dits·i·er; -est** *[or more ~; most ~] chiefly US, informal* : silly and tending to forget things : DIZZY — used especially of a woman ▪ a *ditzy* blonde

di·uret·ic /ˌdajəˈrɛtɪk/ *noun, pl* **-ics** *[count] medical* : a substance that increases the amount of urine you pass from your body ▪ The drug is a *diuretic.*
– diuretic *adj* ▪ a *diuretic* drug/effect

di·ur·nal /daɪˈɚnl/ *adj, technical*
1 : active mainly during the day ▪ *diurnal* animals — opposite NOCTURNAL
2 : happening every day ▪ *diurnal* tides

div. *also* **div** *abbr* division

di·va /ˈdiːvə/ *noun, pl* **-vas** *[count]*
1 : the main female singer in an opera company
2 : a famous and successful woman who is very attractive and fashionable; *especially* : an attractive and successful female performer or celebrity ▪ pop *divas* ▪ a fashion *diva*

di·van /dɪˈvæn/ *noun, pl* **-vans** *[count]*
1 : a long, low seat that has no back or arms or only part of a back and one arm
2 *Brit* : a bed that has a thick base and usually no footboard

¹dive /ˈdaɪv/ *verb* **dives; dived** /ˈdaɪvd/ *or chiefly US* **dove** /ˈdoʊv/; **div·ing** *[no obj]*
1 : to jump into water with your arms and head going in first ▪ She *dove* into the swimming pool. ▪ The children like to *dive* off the boat. ▪ The competitors will be *diving* from the highest platform.
2 : to swim underwater usually while using special equipment to help you breathe ▪ Many people enjoy *diving* on the island's coral reefs. ▪ You can't *dive* in this water without a wet suit. ▪ He *dives* for pearls. [=he dives in order to find pearls] — see also SCUBA DIVE, SKIN-DIVE
3 : to go underwater or down to a deeper level underwater ▪ The submarine can *dive* to 3,000 feet. ▪ The whale *dove* down to deeper water.
4 : to move down through the air at a steep angle ▪ We watched the hawk *dive* for its prey. ▪ The plane suddenly *dove.* — see also DIVE-BOMB, NOSE-DIVE, SKYDIVE
5 : to fall suddenly and quickly in amount, value, etc. ▪ The temperature *dived* [=(more commonly) *plunged, dropped*] down below zero. ▪ The stock's value *dove* to an all-time low.
6 : to suddenly jump toward something that is on or near the ground ▪ The goalie *dove* in front of the goal. — often + *for* ▪ He *dove for* the ball. ▪ He ***dove for cover.*** [=he suddenly jumped to a place where he would be safe or protected] — sometimes used figuratively ▪ Her books always have me *diving for* my dictionary. [=I often need a dictionary to understand the words she uses in her books]
7 *informal* : to start doing something with enthusiasm — usually + *into* or *in* ▪ They *dove into* their work. ▪ I'm just not ready to *dive* (right) *into* another romantic relationship. ▪ They sat down at the dinner table and ***dove (right) in.*** [=started eating immediately] ▪ We have a lot of things to discuss, so let's *dive right in.* [=let's get started immediately]
8 *informal* : to quickly reach *into* (a bag, pocket, etc.) ▪ She *dove into* her purse to find some change.

²dive *noun, pl* **dives** *[count]*
1 : a jump into water with your arms and head going in first ▪ She practiced her *dives* for the competition. ▪ a perfect *dive*
2 : an act of swimming underwater usually while using special equipment (such as a snorkel or air tank) to help you breathe ▪ This will be my first *dive* on a coral reef. ▪ She has done *dives* all around the world.
3 : a usually steep downward movement of a submarine, airplane, bird, etc. ▪ The crew of the submarine prepared for a *dive.* ▪ The jet rolled into a *dive.*
4 : a sudden quick fall in amount, value, etc. ▪ Temperatures across the region will ***take a dive*** tonight. ▪ The stock market *took a dive.*
5 *informal* : a bar, nightclub, etc., that is cheap and dirty ▪ That bar is a real *dive.*
6 : a sudden jump or movement toward something that is on or near the ground ▪ He ***made a dive for*** the ditch/ball/gun. ▪ He ***made a dive for cover.*** [=he suddenly jumped to a place where he would be safe or protected]

dive–bomb /ˈdaɪvˌbɑːm/ *verb* **-bombs; -bombed; -bomb·ing** *[+ obj]*
1 : to drop a bomb from an airplane on (something) after approaching it at a sharp or steep angle ▪ The pilots/planes *dive-bombed* the enemy ships.
2 : to attack (someone or something) from the air at a sharp or steep angle ▪ We were *dive-bombed* by seagulls at the beach.

div·er /ˈdaɪvɚ/ *noun, pl* **-ers** *[count]*
1 : a person who dives into water ▪ competitive *divers*
2 : a person who swims underwater usually while using special equipment to breathe ▪ pearl *divers* ▪ a deep-sea *diver* — see also SCUBA DIVER, SKIN DIVER, SKYDIVER

di·verge /dəˈvɚʤ/ *verb* **-verg·es; -verged; -verg·ing** *[no obj] formal*
1 : to split and move out in different directions from a single point ▪ A prism causes rays of light to *diverge.* ▪ "Two roads *diverged* in a yellow wood . . ." —Robert Frost, "The Road Not Taken" (1916) — opposite CONVERGE
2 : to be or become different ▪ They were close friends in college, but after graduation, their lives *diverged.* ▪ When it comes to politics, their opinions/views *diverge.* [=they have different opinions/views]
– di·ver·gence /dəˈvɚʤəns/ *noun, pl* **-genc·es** *[count]* *divergences* between dialects ▪ There is a wide *divergence* of opinion between the parties. *[noncount]* He is studying the

D

levels of *divergence* between the species. **– di·ver·gent** /dəˈvɚʤənt/ *adj* [*more* ~; *most* ~] ▪ *divergent* lines/opinions/cultures ▪ Their views are widely *divergent*.

di·verse /daɪˈvɚs/ *adj* [*more* ~; *most* ~]
1 : different from each other ▪ The magazine covers topics as *diverse* [=*varied*] as chemistry and sculpture. ▪ people with *diverse* interests
2 : made up of people or things that are different from each other ▪ His message appealed to a *diverse* audience. ▪ The group of students is very *diverse*. [=the students are different ages, races, etc.] ▪ a *diverse* group of subjects
– di·verse·ly *adv* **– di·verse·ness** *noun* [*noncount*]

D

di·ver·si·fy /dəˈvɚsəˌfaɪ/ *verb* **-fies; -fied; -fy·ing**
1 : to change (something) so that it has more different kinds of people or things [*+ obj*] The country is *diversifying* its energy sources. ▪ farmers who want to *diversify* their crops ▪ You should *diversify* your investments. = Your investments should be *diversified*. [=you should invest your money in several different ways instead of investing it all in one thing] [*no obj*] Investors should *diversify*.
2 : to produce or sell more kinds of products **:** to increase the variety of goods or services produced or offered by (someone or something) [*+ obj*] The new CEO's chief aim is to *diversify* the company. [*no obj*] The company needs to *diversify*. ▪ Many publishing companies have ***diversified into*** online services.
– di·ver·si·fi·ca·tion /dəˌvɚsəfəˈkeɪʃən/ *noun* [*noncount*] ▪ The company's efforts at *diversification* have been successful. **– di·ver·si·fied** *adj* [*more* ~; *most* ~] ▪ a *diversified* company ▪ a *diversified* economy [=an economy that has a variety of industries]

di·ver·sion /dəˈvɚʒən/ *noun, pl* **-sions**
1 *formal* **:** the act of changing the direction or use of something **:** the act of diverting something [*count*] The bad weather forced the *diversion* of several flights. [=several flights had to land somewhere else because of bad weather] ▪ small *diversions of* river water for irrigation [*noncount*] The officials were charged with illegal *diversion* of public funds. [=they were charged with using public money illegally for some improper purpose]
2 *formal* **:** something that people do because it is enjoyable, entertaining, or pleasant [*count*] Hiking is one of my favorite *diversions*. ▪ Our town offers few *diversions*. ▪ Sports provide him with a welcome *diversion* from the pressures of his job. [*noncount*] We're in need of some *diversion*. [=*amusement, entertainment*]
3 [*count*] **:** something that takes attention away from what is happening ▪ He ***created a diversion*** while his partner stole her pocketbook.
4 [*count*] *Brit* **:** [1]DETOUR 2 ▪ The road is closed—please follow the *diversion*.

di·ver·sion·ary /dəˈvɚʒəˌneri, *Brit* dəˈvɜːʒənri/ *adj, formal* **:** tending or intended to take attention away from someone or something important ▪ This is nothing more than a ***diversionary tactic*** to distract attention from the issues.

di·ver·si·ty /dəˈvɚsəti/ *noun, pl* **-ties**
1 : the quality or state of having many different forms, types, ideas, etc. [*noncount*] The island has more *diversity* in plant life than other islands nearby. ▪ biological/genetic/linguistic *diversity* ▪ There was some *diversity* of opinion about what should be done. [=people had different opinions about what should be done] [*count*] — usually singular ▪ The area has a great *diversity* [=*variety*] of birds. ▪ She has a wide *diversity* of interests. [=she has many different interests]
2 : the state of having people who are different races or who have different cultures in a group or organization [*noncount*] The city is known for its cultural/ethnic *diversity*. ▪ The school aims for *diversity* in its student population. [*count*] — usually singular ▪ There is a greater *diversity* in the city's population now.

di·vert /dəˈvɚt/ *verb* **-verts; -vert·ed; -vert·ing** [*+ obj*]
1 : to change the direction or use of (something) ▪ Police *diverted* traffic to a side street. ▪ The stream was *diverted* toward the farmland. ▪ They were charged with illegally *diverting* public funds for private use.
2 a : to take (attention) away *from* someone or something ▪ He lied to ***divert attention from*** the real situation. ▪ They're only proposing the law to *divert attention from* important issues. **b :** to take the attention of (someone) away from something or someone ▪ Nothing can *divert* [=*distract*] me from my goal.
3 *formal* **:** to entertain (someone) ▪ The children *diverted* [=(more commonly) *amused*] themselves with games.
– diverting *adj* [*more* ~; *most* ~] ▪ some fairly/mildy *diverting* [=(more commonly) *amusing, entertaining*] books/movies/evenings

di·vest /daɪˈvɛst/ *verb* **-vests; -vest·ed; -vest·ing** [*+ obj*] *finance* **:** to sell (something valuable, such as property or stocks) ▪ The company is *divesting* 8 of its 20 stores. ▪ We may have to *divest* assets to raise capital/money.
divest of [*phrasal verb*] *formal* **1** ***divest (someone or something) of (something)*** **:** to take (something) away from (someone or something else) **:** to cause (someone or something) to lose or give up (something) ▪ The document does not *divest* her *of* her right to use the property. — often used as *(be) divested* ▪ He *was divested of* his title/power/dignity. **2** ***divest (yourself) of (something)*** **a :** to sell or give away (possessions, money, etc.) ▪ She *divested herself of* most of her possessions. **b** *old-fashioned* **:** to remove (clothing, equipment, etc.) from your body ▪ He *divested himself of* his coat.
– di·vest·ment /daɪˈvɛstmənt/ *noun, pl* **-ments** [*count*] asset *divestments* [*noncount*] the *divestment* of assets

di·ves·ti·ture /daɪˈvɛstəˌʧuɚ/ *noun, pl* **-tures** *finance* **:** the act of selling stock, property, etc., because of a government order [*count*] *Divestitures* are used to break up monopolies. [*noncount*] Before *divestiture*, the telephone company monopolized the state.

[1]di·vide /dəˈvaɪd/ *verb* **-vides; -vid·ed; -vid·ing**
1 a : to separate (something) into two or more parts or pieces [*+ obj*] He *divided* [=*split*] the loaf in half. ▪ The river *divides* the town. [=parts of the town are on both sides of the river] ▪ She *divided* the pie into eight pieces. ▪ The equator *divides* the Earth into two hemispheres. ▪ The teacher *divided* the class (up) into four groups. = The teacher *divided* (up) the class *into* four groups. — often used as *(be) divided* ▪ The class *was divided* (up) into four groups. ▪ The book *is divided* into three sections. [*no obj*] The cells *divide* rapidly. ▪ The river *divides* after the bridge. **b** [*+ obj*] **:** to separate (something) into classes or categories ▪ We *divided* (up) the beads according to size and color. ▪ The author *divides* literature into three categories. [=the author says that there are three categories of literature] — often used as *(be) divided* ▪ Animals can *be divided* into several major types.
2 [*+ obj*] **a :** to give (something) out in usually equal amounts ▪ They *divided* [=*distributed*] the profits between/among themselves. ▪ We *divided* the work (up) equally. ▪ They *divided* (up) [=*shared*] the remaining food. **b :** to use (your time, energy, etc.) for two or more purposes or activities — usually + *between* ▪ He *divides* his energy *between* sports and school. ▪ Her time is *divided between* home, work, and school.
3 [*+ obj*] **:** to cause (something) to be separate or apart from something else ▪ A tall fence *divides* the two yards. — often + *from* ▪ Her cubicle is *divided from* his by a low wall. ▪ A screen *divides* (off) the dining area *from* the living room.
4 [*+ obj*] **a :** to separate (people) into groups that disagree ▪ The war *divided* the nation. ▪ The divorce *divided* the family. — often used as *(be) divided* ▪ The nation *was divided* by war. = We were a nation *divided* by war. **b :** to cause (opinions, views, etc.) to not agree — usually used as *(be) divided* ▪ Opinions on the issue *are divided*. [=people do not agree about the issue]
5 *mathematics* **:** to calculate how many times one number contains another number [*+ obj*] *Divide* 8 by 2. ▪ Eight *divided* by two is four. [=$8 \div 2 = 4$; $8/2 = 4$] [*no obj*] The teacher taught the children how to *divide*. ▪ Two ***divides evenly into*** eight. [=eight can be divided into two an exact number of times with nothing left over] — compare MULTIPLY
divide and conquer *or* ***divide and rule*** **:** to make a group of people disagree and fight with one another so that they will not join together against you ▪ His military strategy is to *divide and conquer*.

[2]divide *noun, pl* **-vides** [*count*]
1 *chiefly US* **:** a line of hills or mountains from which rivers drain **:** a ridge between two rivers **:** WATERSHED
2 : a separation of people into two or more groups that is caused by different opinions or beliefs or by a disagreement — usually singular ▪ The argument created a *divide* within the group. — usually + *among* or *between* ▪ We must bridge the *divide among* races. ▪ the *divide between* generations

divided *adj*
1 [*more* ~; *most* ~] **:** separated by different opinions **:** in a state of disagreement ▪ Experts are sharply *divided* on/over

the issue. ▪ The issue has created a deeply *divided* nation.
2 : given to two or more people or things rather than to just one person or thing ▪ She feels like she only gets her mother's *divided* attention. ▪ He has ***divided loyalties***. [=he is trying to be loyal to opposing groups, ideals, etc.]

divided highway *noun, pl* ~ **-ways** [*count*] *US* : a major road that has something (such as a guardrail or an area with grass and trees) that separates lanes of traffic moving in opposite directions — called also (*Brit*) *dual carriageway*

div·i·dend /ˈdɪvəˌdɛnd/ *noun, pl* **-dends** [*count*]
1 *finance* : an amount of a company's profits that the company pays to people who own stock in the company ▪ Profits are distributed to shareholders/stockholders as *dividends*.
2 : an advantage or benefit that you get because of something you have done — usually plural ▪ Eating healthy and exercising yields big *dividends*. ▪ Our efforts are finally ***paying dividends***. [=we are finally benefiting from our efforts]
3 *mathematics* : a number that is being divided by another number ▪ In the equation 8 ÷ 2 = 4, eight is the *dividend*. — compare DIVISOR

di·vid·er /dəˈvaɪdɚ/ *noun, pl* **-ers**
1 [*count*] **a** : a thing that keeps two spaces or areas separate ▪ Concrete barriers are used as highway *dividers*. **b** : someone or something that causes people to disagree with one another ▪ She has proven to be a *divider* of people. ▪ He says that he's a uniter, not a *divider*.
2 dividers [*plural*] : a tool that consists of two pointed sticks joined at the top and that is used for measuring or marking lines and angles ▪ a pair of *dividers*

dividing line *noun, pl* ~ **lines** [*count*] : a line or object that separates two areas ▪ The *dividing lines* on the street were newly painted. ▪ A fence marked the *dividing line* between the two properties. — often used figuratively ▪ the *dividing line* between right and wrong

div·i·na·tion /ˌdɪvəˈneɪʃən/ *noun* [*noncount*] : the practice of using signs (such as an arrangement of tea leaves or cards) or special powers to predict the future ▪ the art of reading tea leaves and other forms of *divination*

[1]**di·vine** /dəˈvaɪn/ *adj*
1 : relating to or coming from God or a god ▪ *divine* will/law/love/inspiration ▪ They prayed for *divine* intervention/help. ▪ The pharaohs of ancient Egypt were considered *divine*. [=were considered to be gods] ▪ a *divine* ruler [=a ruler who is believed to be a god] ▪ *divine* beings
2 [*more* ~; *most* ~] *informal* + *somewhat old-fashioned* : very good ▪ This pie is *divine*. [=*heavenly*] ▪ You look *divine*.
— **di·vine·ly** *adv* ▪ a *divinely* inspired prophet ▪ *divinely* [=*wonderfully*] clever

[2]**divine** *verb* **-vines; -vined; -vin·ing** [+ *obj*] *formal* + *literary* : to discover or understand (something) without having direct evidence ▪ He *divined* [=(more commonly) *sensed*] her unhappiness before she said a word. ▪ *divine* the answer to a question

di·vin·er *noun, pl* **-ers** [*count*]
1 *formal* + *literary* : a person who uses special powers to predict future events ▪ *Diviners* foretold of the event.
2 : a person who searches for water under the ground by using a special stick (called a divining rod) ▪ a water *diviner*

divine right *noun* [*singular*]
1 : the right that is supposedly given to a king or queen by God to rule a country ▪ He ruled by *divine right*.
2 *informal* : the right to do or have something without having to ask permission ▪ My boss seems to think he has a *divine right* to order people around.

diving *noun* [*noncount*]
1 : a sport or activity in which people dive into water from a diving board or a platform ▪ He won a gold medal in *diving*.
2 : a sport or activity in which people swim underwater while using special equipment to breathe ▪ He likes deep-sea *diving*. ▪ We ***went diving*** on the coral reef. — often used before another noun ▪ *diving* equipment ▪ *diving* lessons — see also SCUBA DIVING

diving bell *noun, pl* ~ **bells** [*count*] : a large container that is open at the bottom, filled with air, and lowered into deep water to provide a dry place for underwater workers

diving board *noun, pl* ~ **boards** [*count*] : a board above a swimming pool, lake, etc., that people can jump off of to dive into the water

divining rod *noun, pl* ~ **rods** [*count*] : a stick that is usually shaped like a Y and is used by some people to search for an underground source of water — called also *dowsing rod*

di·vin·i·ty /dəˈvɪnəti/ *noun, pl* **-ties**
1 [*noncount*] : the state of being a god : the state of being divine ▪ Christians believe in the *divinity* of Jesus Christ.
2 [*count*] : a god or goddess ▪ Hindu *divinities* ▪ the *divinities* of ancient Greece

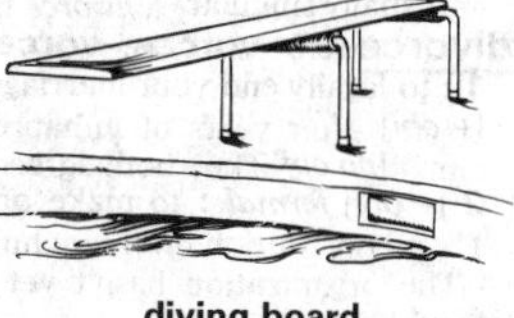
diving board

3 [*noncount*] : the formal study of religion, religious practices, and religious beliefs ▪ a doctor of *divinity* ▪ a *divinity* student ▪ She attends the ***divinity school***. [=a professional school that teaches religious subjects and trains people for religious jobs]

di·vis·i·ble /dəˈvɪzəbəl/ *adj, not used before a noun* : able to be divided ▪ 9 is *divisible* by 3 ▪ (*formal*) The piece of land is *divisible* into three small lots.

di·vi·sion /dəˈvɪʒən/ *noun, pl* **-sions**
1 : the act or process of dividing something into parts : the way that something is divided [*noncount*] the process of cell *division* [*singular*] a *division* of profits into equal shares ▪ Their society has a clear *division* of labor between men and women. [=in their society, the men do one kind of work and the women do another kind of work]
2 [*count*] : something that physically divides or separates something else — often + *between* ▪ A line of trees served as a *division between* our property and theirs.
3 [*noncount*] *mathematics* : the process of finding out how many times one number is contained in another ▪ After learning multiplication, the students were taught *division*. — see also LONG DIVISION
4 [*count*] : a group of people who do a particular job within a larger organization (such as a government, business, or school) ▪ She was transferred to a different *division* within the company. ▪ He worked for many years in the news *division* [=*department*] of a major television network.
5 [*count*] : a large military group ▪ The infantry *division* is made up of five brigades.
6 [*count*] **a** : a group of teams that form one section of a sports league ▪ There are five teams in the league's western *division*. ▪ Both *divisions* in the league have agreed to the new rules. ▪ teams that are in the first/second *division* **b** : a group of people who are similar in age, size, etc., and who compete against each other — usually singular ▪ She finished third in her *division* at the national championships. ▪ boxers competing in the heavyweight *division*
7 : a situation in which different groups, countries, etc., have different opinions, beliefs, or ways of life that separate them from each other [*count*] We're attempting to resolve the *divisions* [=*disagreements*] between our two countries. ▪ There were serious *divisions* within the party on a number of issues. ▪ The book explores the racial and economic *divisions* in/of our society. [*noncount*] The issue caused *division* within the group.
8 [*count*] : any one of the parts or groups that form something : SECTION ▪ a major *division* of the earth's surface

di·vi·sion·al /dəˈvɪʒənl/ *adj, always used before a noun*
1 : of or relating to a large division of a business or a branch of the military ▪ the *divisional* manager/commander
2 : of or relating to a group of teams that make up one part of a sports league ▪ the *divisional* champion/play-offs

division sign *noun, pl* ~ **signs** [*count*] *mathematics* : the symbol ÷ that is used to show that two numbers are to be divided into each other — usually singular

di·vi·sive /dəˈvaɪsɪv/ *adj* [*more* ~; *most* ~] *formal* : causing a lot of disagreement between people and causing them to separate into different groups ▪ *divisive* issues like abortion
— **di·vi·sive·ness** *noun* [*noncount*]

di·vi·sor /dəˈvaɪzɚ/ *noun, pl* **-sors** [*count*] *mathematics* : the number by which another number is being divided — usually singular ▪ In the equation 8 ÷ 2 = 4, two is the *divisor*. — compare DIVIDEND

[1]**di·vorce** /dəˈvoɚs/ *noun, pl* **-vorc·es**
1 : the ending of a marriage by a legal process [*count*] Since getting a *divorce*, she has been raising her children alone. ▪ They went through a lengthy/messy *divorce*. [*noncount*] Their marriage ended in *divorce*. ▪ They are filing for *divorce*. [=they are filing a paper with the courts asking that their marriage be legally ended] ▪ Financial problems are a leading cause of *divorce*. — often used before another noun ▪ a *divorce* lawyer/court ▪ a high *divorce* rate ▪ *divorce* proceedings
2 [*count*] *formal* : a complete separation between two things

— usually singular • a *divorce* between theory and practice

²divorce *verb* **-vorces; -vorced; -vorc·ing**

1 : to legally end your marriage with (your husband or wife) [+ *obj*] After years of unhappiness, she decided to *divorce* him. [*no obj*] They both agreed it was best to *divorce*.

2 [+ *obj*] *formal* **:** to make or keep (something) separate • Their constitution *divorces* church and state. — often + *from* • The organization hasn't yet fully *divorced* itself *from* its troubled past.

– divorced *adj* • They're getting *divorced*. • He's been *divorced* since 2003. • a *divorced* man = a man who is *divorced* • a theory that is completely ***divorced from reality*** [=a wrong theory that shows no connection to reality]

D

di·vor·cé /də͵voɚˈseɪ/ *noun, pl* **-cés** [*count*] *chiefly US* **:** a man who is divorced

di·vor·cée /də͵voɚˈseɪ/ *noun, pl* **-cées** [*count*] **:** a divorced person; *especially* **:** a woman who is divorced

div·ot /ˈdɪvət/ *noun, pl* **-ots** [*count*] **:** a loose piece of grass and dirt that is dug out of the ground when the ground is struck by something (such as a golf club)

di·vulge /dəˈvʌlʤ/ *verb* **-vulg·es; -vulged; -vulg·ing** [+ *obj*] *formal* **:** to make (information) known **:** to give (information) to someone • She refused to *divulge* [=*reveal, tell*] the name of her informant. • The company will not *divulge* its sales figures.

div·vy /ˈdɪvi/ *verb* **-vies; -vied; -vy·ing**

divvy up [*phrasal verb*] ***divvy (something) up*** *or* ***divvy up (something)*** *informal* **:** to divide or share (something) • We *divvied up* the money.

Dix·ie·land /ˈdɪksi͵lænd/ *noun* [*noncount*] **:** a type of traditional American jazz music that was popular in the 1920s

DIY /͵di:͵aɪˈwaɪ/ *adj, always used before a noun* **:** DO-IT-YOURSELF • a *DIY* home improvement project • *DIY* home repair

diz·zy /ˈdɪzi/ *adj* **diz·zi·er; -est**

1 : feeling that you are turning around in circles and are going to fall even though you are standing still • The children were *dizzy* after spinning in circles. • I'm feeling a bit weak and *dizzy*. I think I'm having a ***dizzy spell***.

2 : mentally or emotionally upset or confused • Complex math problems make me *dizzy*. • *dizzy* with anger/relief

3 *always used before a noun* **:** causing you to feel dizzy: such as **a :** very high • looking down from *dizzy* heights — sometimes used figuratively • She has reached the *dizzy* heights of vice president. **b :** very fast • Prices rose at a *dizzy* rate. • the *dizzy* pace of our lives

4 *informal* **:** very silly and tending to forget things — used especially of a woman • an actress who is known for playing *dizzy* [=*ditzy*] blondes

– diz·zi·ly /ˈdɪzəli/ *adv* • He staggered *dizzily* toward the couch. **– diz·zi·ness** /ˈdɪzinəs/ *noun* [*noncount*] • This medicine may cause *dizziness* and nausea.

diz·zy·ing /ˈdɪzijɪŋ/ *adj, always used before a noun* **:** causing or likely to cause dizziness • The cars move at *dizzying* speeds around the track. • a *dizzying* array of choices • the skyscraper's *dizzying* heights

DJ /ˈdi:͵ʤeɪ/ *noun, pl* **DJs** [*count*] **:** DISC JOCKEY

djinn /ˈʤɪn/ *variant spelling of* JINNI

DL *abbr* disabled list • He was put on the *DL* for the remainder of the season.

DMV *abbr, US* Department of Motor Vehicles • I'm going to the *DMV* this afternoon to get my driver's license renewed.

DMZ *abbr* demilitarized zone • Forces were not allowed in the *DMZ*.

DNA /͵di:͵ɛnˈeɪ/ *noun* [*noncount*] **:** a substance that carries genetic information in the cells of plants and animals — often used before another noun • *DNA* analysis • *DNA* testing • a ***DNA fingerprint*** [=a sample of a person's DNA that can be used to identify someone, such as a criminal] • ***DNA fingerprinting*** ✧ *DNA* is an abbreviation of "deoxyribonucleic acid." — compare NUCLEIC ACID, RNA

¹do /ˈdu:/ *verb* **does** /ˈdʌz/; **did** /ˈdɪd/; **done** /ˈdʌn/; **do·ing** /ˈdu:wɪŋ/

1 a : to perform (an action or activity) [+ *obj*] We should *do* something special to celebrate your birthday. • This crime was *done* deliberately. • I have to *do* some chores this afternoon. • Tell me what to *do* and I'll *do* it. • I'm obliged to *do* my duty. • He *does* his work without complaining. • I *do* the ironing on Wednesdays and the cooking on Thursdays. [=I iron on Wednesdays and cook on Thursdays] • I *did* a favor for him. = I *did* him a favor. • "What do you *do* with this lever? = What does this lever *do*?" "It operates the pump." • He *did* a lot for us. • What can I *do* to help you? = What can I ***do for*** you? [=how can/may I help you?] • What have I ***done to*** you to make you so angry? • Have you ***done something to/with*** this room? [=have you changed this room in some way?] It looks different. • My knee is sore. I must have ***done something to*** it [=I must have hurt it] when I fell. • Don't just stand there: ***do something***. [=take some sort of action to stop what is happening] • We need to ***do something about*** this problem. [=we need to take some action to correct this problem] • ***All we can do*** is hope for the best. [=there is no other action we can take except to hope for the best] • I didn't *do* it! = I didn't ***do anything***. [=I didn't do what you said I did] • Are you ***doing anything*** right now? [=are you busy right now?] • If you're ***not doing anything*** this evening [=if you're not busy this evening], why not come over for dinner? • "What are you *doing* this weekend?" "I'm just relaxing at home." • What is the stock market *doing* now: rising or falling? • ***What have I done with*** my keys? [=where did I put my keys?] • My hair is a mess. I ***can't do anything with*** it. • There's ***nothing to do*** in this town on a Saturday night! [*no obj*] *Do* as I say, not as I *do*. [=do the things that I say you should do, not the things that I do myself] • Shut up and ***do as you're told***. [=do what I tell you to do] **b** [+ *obj*] — used with *what* to ask or talk about a person's job • "What does your husband *do*?" "He's a writer." • She's a lawyer. I'm not sure what her husband *does*. • What does she ***do for a living***? [=what is her job?]

2 [+ *obj*] **:** to finish working on (something) • His mother won't let him watch television until he has *done* his homework. • I've only *done* three of the walls so far—I'll paint the last one tomorrow. — compare ²DONE 1

3 [*no obj*] — used to describe the success or progress of someone or something • "How is she *doing* in school?" "She *did* badly/poorly at first, but now she's *doing* much better." • She *does* well in math but badly in history. • The company is *doing* well. • How is the stock market *doing* these days? • He started out poor, worked hard, *did* very well (for himself) in business [=was very successful in business], and died rich. ✧ ***How are you doing?*** or (very informally) ***How you doing?*** is used as a greeting. • "Hi, Dave. *How are you doing*?" "I'm fine, thanks. How are you?"

4 [+ *obj*] — used to describe the effect that something has • You've been working too hard. A few days off will ***do you (some) good***. [=a few days off will be good for you] • We didn't mean to ***do him (any) harm***. [=to harm him] • Criticism can *do* people a lot of harm/damage; praise can *do* people a lot of good. • The new design ***doesn't do much for*** me. [=I don't like the new design very much] • That hat ***does nothing for you***. [=that hat does not look good on you]

5 — used to describe the amount of effort someone makes [+ *obj*] She *did* nothing to help us. [=she did not try to help us at all] • I ***did my best***. = I ***did my utmost***. = I ***did all that I could***. = I ***did everything I could***. [*no obj*] I *did* as well as I could.

6 [+ *obj*] **a :** to create or produce (something) • a writer who is *doing* a new biography on Abraham Lincoln • a painter who has *done* some beautiful landscapes **b :** to perform in or be the producer or director of (a movie, play, etc.) • an actress who has *done* several hit movies • a director who is *doing* a play on Broadway

7 [+ *obj*] **a :** to play (a role or character) • an actor who *did* Hamlet on Broadway **b :** to pretend to be (someone, such as a famous person) **:** to copy the speech and appearance of (someone) • a comedian who *does* a great George Bush [=a comedian who does a very good and entertaining imitation of George Bush] **c** *informal* **:** to behave like (someone) • I wish he'd *do* a Houdini and disappear. [=I wish he'd go away]

8 [+ *obj*] **a :** to wash or clean (something) • It's your turn to *do* [=*wash*] the laundry. • The woman we hired to clean our house doesn't *do* windows. **b :** to decorate (a place) • They *did* the bedroom in blue and the living room in green. — see also DO OVER 2 (below) **c :** to make (someone's face, hair, etc.) more attractive by putting on makeup, etc. • She wanted to *do* her face before the party. • She had her hair *done* [=*styled*] at the beauty parlor. • She was *doing* her fingernails/nails. **d :** to put on (makeup) • It took her a few minutes to *do* her makeup.

9 [+ *obj*] **:** to cook or prepare (food) • I like my steak *done* rare. • I'll *do* the salad while you *do* the pasta. — compare ²DONE 2

10 [+ *obj*] **:** to make or sell (a product) • This is the company's most popular computer, but they also *do* a less expensive model.

11 [+ *obj*] *chiefly US, informal* : to participate in (an activity) with other people ▪ We should ***do dinner*** some time. [=we should have dinner together some time] ▪ *do* a meeting [=have a meeting] ▪ We should *do* a movie [=go to a movie] this weekend. — see also *do lunch* at [1]LUNCH
12 [+ *obj*] : to go to (a place) when traveling ▪ a group of tourists who are *doing* [=*visiting*] 12 countries in 30 days
13 [+ *obj*] **a** : to move or travel (a distance) ▪ We *did* [=*traveled*] 500 miles yesterday. **b** : to move at (a speed) ▪ They were *doing* [=*going, driving*] 85 on the turnpike. ▪ That plane can *do* [=*go*] 1,400 mph!
14 [+ *obj*] : to be in a place for (a period of time) ▪ He *did* [=*spent*] two years in college before he dropped out.; *especially* : to be in a prison for (a period of time) ▪ He *did* [=*served*] five years (in prison) for robbery. ▪ He has been ***doing time*** in a federal penitentiary. — sometimes used figuratively ▪ I've ***done my time*** at that terrible job, and now it's time to move on.
15 a : to be enough : to be adequate [*no obj*] I don't need any more cake, thank you. One piece ***will do***. [=one piece is enough] ▪ I'd prefer to use glue, but tape ***will/would do***. [+ *obj*] (*informal*) One piece of cake *will do* me. [=one piece of cake is enough for me] **b** ✧ Phrases like ***that will do (it)*** and ***that should do (it)*** are used in informal speech to tell someone that you do not want or need anything more. ▪ "Would you like anything else?" "No, *that'll do it*." = "No, *that should do it*." *That will do it* and *that should do it* are also used to say that you have finished doing something or are about to finish doing something. ▪ I just have one more letter to sign and *that should do it*. [=and then I'll be finished] *That will do* is also sometimes used to tell someone (such as a child) to stop doing or saying something that is bothering you or making you angry. ▪ *That will do* [=*that's enough*], young man: one more word out of you and you're grounded! **c** ✧ The phrase ***that does it*** is used to say that you have finished doing something. ▪ I just need to sign one more letter . . . There, *that does it*. *That does it* is also used in angry speech to say that you will not accept or allow something anymore. ▪ "They say we'll have to wait another hour." "*That does it*! We're leaving right now!"
16 [*no obj*] : to be proper — used in negative statements ▪ It ***doesn't do*** for a doctor to become too friendly with his patients. = It ***won't/wouldn't do*** for a doctor to become too friendly with his patients. [=a doctor should not become too friendly with his patients] ▪ Such behavior will never *do*! [=such behavior should not be allowed] ▪ We should leave soon. It won't *do* to be late. ▪ This is a formal occasion, so jeans simply won't *do*. [=jeans are not appropriate] ✧ In U.S. English, this sense of *do* has a somewhat formal or old-fashioned quality. — compare [2]DONE 3
17 [+ *obj*] *informal* : to use (illegal drugs) ▪ He says that he doesn't *do* drugs anymore.
18 [*no obj*] *informal* **a** : to happen ▪ Is there anything *doing* tomorrow? ▪ There is nothing *doing* around here. ▪ Let's find out ***what's doing*** downtown. **b** ✧ People ask ***what is something/someone doing . . . ?*** when they are surprised or upset about where someone or something is. ▪ *What are all my clothes doing* (lying/scattered) on the floor? [=why are all my clothes on the floor?] ▪ *What were you doing* (standing) outside in the rain? [=why were you outside in the rain?] People ask ***what is someone doing with (something)?*** when they are surprised or upset because someone has something. ▪ *What are you doing with* my notebook? = ***What do you think you're doing with*** my notebook? [=why do you have my notebook?]
19 [+ *obj*] *informal + offensive* : to have sex with (someone)
be to do with see HAVE TO DO WITH (below)
do a number on see [1]NUMBER
do away with [*phrasal verb*] **1** ***do away with (someone)*** : to kill (someone) ▪ She's accused of hiring a hit man to *do away with* [=*murder, do in*] her husband. **2** ***do away with (something)*** : to cause the end of (something) : to get rid of (something) ▪ The struggling company had to *do away with* a number of jobs.
do battle see [1]BATTLE
do by [*phrasal verb*] ***do by (someone)*** : to deal with or treat (someone) well or badly ▪ She feels that they *did* poorly/badly *by* her. [=that they treated her poorly/badly] ▪ They ***did pretty well by*** me when I retired. [=they treated me pretty well when I retired] — see also *hard done by* at [2]HARD
do down [*phrasal verb*] ***do (someone) down*** *Brit, informal* : to talk about (someone) in an insulting or critical way ▪ She thinks that if she *does* everybody else *down*, people will think more highly of her. ▪ Stop *doing* yourself *down*: you've got a lot to offer!
do for [*phrasal verb*] ***do for (someone)*** *Brit, informal* **1** : to cause the death or ruin of (someone) ▪ All that hard work nearly *did for* him. [=nearly killed him] — see also *done for* at [2]DONE **2** : to do the cleaning and cooking for (someone) ▪ Mrs. Jones *does for* the vicar now his wife's passed on.
do good see [2]GOOD
do in [*phrasal verb*] ***do (someone) in*** *informal* **1 a** : to kill (someone) ▪ They threatened to *do* him *in* if he didn't pay the money he owed them. ▪ He's been so depressed lately that his friends are afraid he might ***do himself in***. [=he might kill himself] : to cause the death of (someone) ▪ He struggled with lung disease for many years, but it was a heart attack that finally *did* him *in*. **b** : to cause the failure of (someone) ▪ His inability to attract Southern voters is what finally *did* him *in* as a presidential candidate. [=he failed because he was unable to attract Southern voters] ▪ a businessman who was *done in* by greed **2** : to make (someone) very tired ▪ Working in the garden all day really *did* me *in*. = After working in the garden all day, I was/felt *done in*. [=*exhausted*] — see also *done in* at [2]DONE
do it *informal* : to have sex ▪ They've kissed—but have they actually *done it*?
do justice see JUSTICE
do out of [*phrasal verb*] ***do (someone) out of (something)*** *informal* : to unfairly prevent (someone) from getting or having (something) ▪ I've been *done out of* what was rightfully mine! ▪ They *did* [=*cheated*] him *out of* his inheritance.
do over [*phrasal verb*] **1** ***do (something) over*** *US* : to do (something) again ▪ I made a mistake when I measured the window and I had to *do it over* (again). ▪ If I had to *do* it (all) *over* again, I would have stayed in college. **2** ***do (something) over or do over (something)*** : to decorate or change a room, house, etc., so that it looks very different ▪ We're planning to *do over* the kitchen next year. **3** ***do (someone) over or do over (someone)*** *Brit, informal* : to attack and beat (someone) ▪ He got *done over* by a gang of teenagers.
do someone proud see PROUD
do the trick see [1]TRICK
do up [*phrasal verb*] **1** ***do up (something) or do (something) up*** **a** : to decorate (something) ▪ They *did up* the room in bright colors for the party. = The room was all *done up* in bright colors for the party. **b** : to adjust (something, such as your hair) in a particular way ▪ She *did up* her hair in a ponytail. **c** *chiefly Brit* : to wrap (something) ▪ packages *done up* [=*wrapped up*] in paper and ribbon **d** *chiefly Brit* : to repair (something) ▪ *do up* [=*fix up*] old furniture ▪ *do up* an old house **2** ***do (someone) up*** : to dress (someone) up : to put attractive clothes, makeup, etc., on (someone) ▪ She really ***did herself up*** for the party. = She was all *done up* for the party. **3** ***do up or do (something) up or do up (something) of clothing*** : to be fastened or to fasten (something) with buttons, a zipper, etc. ▪ a dress that *does up* at the back = a dress that is *done up* at the back ▪ She *did up* her dress. ▪ buttons that *do up* easily = buttons that you can *do up* easily [=buttons that can be easily buttoned]
do well ✧ If you ***would do well*** to do something, you should do it. ▪ You *would do well* to avoid him right now. [=you should avoid him right now] If you ***did well*** to do something, you were correct to do it. ▪ You *did well to avoid* him when he was in a bad mood. If you ***did well to escape, survive***, etc., you were lucky to escape, survive, etc. ▪ When the tornado hit, they *did well to escape* uninjured.
do with [*phrasal verb*] ***do with (something)*** : to be helped by having (something) ▪ I ***could (really) do with*** a cup of hot coffee right now! [=I could use a cup of coffee; I would like/appreciate a cup of coffee] ▪ I *could do with* a little less criticism right now, if you don't mind!
do without [*phrasal verb*] ***do without or do without (something or someone)*** : to not have (something) : to live, work, etc., without having (something) ▪ If you can't afford a new car, you'll just have to *do without* (one). ▪ I don't know how we ever *did without* computers. ▪ I'd like to get a new car, but I can *do without* it for now. ✧ The phrase ***can/could do without*** is often used to say that you do not like or approve of something. ▪ I enjoy traveling, but I *can do without* having to wait around in crowded airports. [=I don't like having to wait around] ▪ He was late again. That's the kind of selfish behavior I *could do without*.
do your bit see [1]BIT

D

D

easy does it see [2]EASY

have to do with **1** *or chiefly Brit* **be to do with** **a :** to relate to (something) : to be about (something) • The problem *has to do with* fishing rights. = (*chiefly Brit*) The problem *is to do with* fishing rights. • "What does her husband do?" "I think ***it has something to do with*** computers." = "I think ***it's got something to do with*** computers." [=it involves computers in some way] **b :** to relate to or involve (someone) • That's your problem: ***it has nothing to do with*** me! = (*chiefly Brit*) *It's nothing to do with* me! [=it doesn't involve me in any way; it's not my problem] • You're wrong. ***It's got everything to do with*** you: you're legally responsible for what went wrong. **2 :** to be involved in or in some way responsible for (something) • He claims that he ***had nothing to do with*** the accident. = He claims that he ***didn't have anything to do with*** the accident. [=that he was not involved in the accident] • He claims he wasn't involved, but I know he ***had something to do with*** it. **3** ✧ If you do not want to ***have anything to do with*** someone or if you ***want nothing to do with*** someone, you do not want to be involved with that person in any way. • She thinks he's a liar and she refuses to *have anything to do with* him. [=she refuses to talk to him, to see him, etc.] • After the way he's treated me, I *want nothing (further) to do* with him. = I *don't want (to have) anything (further) to do* with him.

how do you do? see [1]HOW

make do see [1]MAKE

nothing doing see [1]NOTHING

– compare [2]DO

[2]**do** *verb* **does; did; doing;** *negative forms* **do not** *or* **don't; did not** *or* **didn't; does not** *or* **doesn't** [*auxiliary verb*]

1 a — used before the subject in a question • *Do* you play the piano? • How well *do* you play the piano? • What *did* he say? • What *does* her husband do for a living? • When *does* the train leave? **b** — used to form brief questions (called tag questions) that come at the end of a statement • You play the piano, *don't* you? • So you play the piano, *do* you? • Her husband works with computers, *doesn't* he?

2 a — used with ***not*** to form negative statements • I *do not* know. = I *don't* know. • I *don't* believe anything he says. **b** — used with ***not*** to form commands • *Do not* lie to me! = (more commonly) *Don't* lie to me! • *Don't* touch the stove. • *Don't* be afraid. Everything will be all right. **c** *somewhat formal* — used before the subject in a statement after words like *never, seldom,* and *rarely* • *Never did* he see his native land again. [=he never saw his native land again] • *Seldom do* we experience such joy! [=we seldom experience such joy]

3 — used to replace another verb or verb phrase • "May I come in?" "Yes, (please) *do.*" • You work harder than I *do.* • "Do you play the piano?" "No, I *don't,* but my sister *does.*" • He works hard and I *do,* too. = He works hard and so *do* I. • Don't touch the stove: if you *do,* you'll burn yourself! • She asked me to open the window, which I *did.* = What I *did* was (to) open the window when she asked me to. • (*informal*) "Can you finish it by tomorrow?" "Sure, boss, ***will do***!" [=I will finish it by tomorrow] • (*informal*) "Can you finish it by tomorrow?" "Sorry, boss, ***no can do***!" [=I can't finish it by tomorrow] • (*Brit*) "Are you going to the party?" "I might *do.*" [=I might] • (*Brit*) He can work hard and I can *do* too. [=I can too] • (*Brit*) Would you mind feeding the dog if nobody else already has *done*? [=if nobody else already has]

4 a — used to make a statement stronger • You really *do* look lovely today! • "It hurts!" "Well, I *did* warn you it would sting a little!" • I never *did* like him much. • Oh, *do* be quiet! **b** *somewhat formal* — used as a polite way to tell or urge someone to do something • *Do* come in and have a seat. • *Do* come and see us again soon. • *Do* be careful.

– compare [1]DO

[3]**do** *noun, pl* **dos** [*count*] *informal*

1 : something that a person should do — usually used in the phrase ***dos and don'ts*** • She told her daughter about the *dos and don'ts* of dating. [=about the things that she should and should not do when dating someone]

2 *US* **:** a way of cutting and arranging a person's hair : HAIRDO • She was worried that the wind might mess up her *do.*

3 : a party or social gathering • We threw a big *do* for her after graduation.

– compare [4]DO

[4]**do** /ˈdoʊ/ *or chiefly Brit* **doh** *noun* [*noncount*] **:** the first note of a musical scale • *do,* re, mi, fa, sol, la, ti — compare [3]DO

DOA *abbr* dead on arrival ✧ In U.S. English, people who are dead when brought to a hospital are said to be *DOA.* • The patient was *DOA.* — sometimes used figuratively • Because of budget cuts, the proposed park is *DOA.*

do·able /ˈduːwəbəl/ *adj* [*more* ~; *most* ~] **:** able to be done • It will be difficult, but it's still *doable.*

DOB *abbr* date of birth

Do·ber·man pin·scher /ˌdoʊbəmənˈpɪnʃɚ/ *noun, pl* **~ -schers** [*count*] **:** a type of tall, thin, muscular dog with short hair that is usually black and tan — called also *Doberman*

doc /ˈdɑːk/ *noun, pl* **docs** [*count*] *informal* **:** DOCTOR • Am I going to be OK, *doc*?

doc. *abbr* document

doc·ile /ˈdɑːsəl, *Brit* ˈdəʊˌsaɪl/ *adj* [*more* ~; *most* ~] **:** easily taught, led, or controlled • His students were *docile* and eager to learn. • a *docile,* well-behaved pet

– **doc·ile·ly** *adv* • The horses behaved *docilely.* – **do·cil·i·ty** /dɑˈsɪləti, *Brit* dəʊˈsɪləti/ *noun* [*noncount*] • This breed is known for its gentleness and *docility.*

[1]**dock** /ˈdɑːk/ *noun, pl* **docks**

1 a : an area of water in a port where ships are loaded, unloaded, or repaired [*count*] A crowd was waiting at the *dock* to greet them. [*noncount*] The ship is ***in dock*** for repairs. — see also DRY DOCK **b *the docks* :** the area in a town or city that has rows of docks, offices, and other buildings • We went down to *the docks* to watch the ships come in.

2 [*count*] *US* **:** a long structure that is built out into water and used as a place to get on, get off, or tie up a boat • Tie the boat to the *dock.*

3 [*count*] *US* **:** a place for loading materials onto ships, trucks, trains, etc. • a ***loading dock***

4 [*count*] **:** the place in a court of law where a person who is accused of a crime stands or sits during a trial

***in the dock* :** on trial for committing a crime • He was arrested and is *in the dock* on charges of assault and battery.

[2]**dock** *verb* **docks; docked; dock·ing**

1 : to bring a ship or boat into a dock [*no obj*] We spent two days at sea before *docking* in Miami, Florida. [*+ obj*] The captain was forced to *dock* the ship.

2 : to join together (two spacecraft) while in space [*no obj*] The shuttle was scheduled to *dock* with the space station. [*+ obj*] They *docked* the spaceship with the satellite.

3 [*+ obj*] **:** to connect an electronic device (such as a computer or a digital camera) to another device • You can *dock* the camera directly to the printer and download the pictures. • The handheld PC can be *docked* into/with your desktop computer. • a *docking* station

– compare [3]DOCK

[3]**dock** *verb* **docks; docked; dock·ing** [*+ obj*]

1 : to take away part of (the money that is paid to someone) • Her boss *docked* her pay/wages for coming in late.

2 : to cut off the end of (an animal's tail) • The puppy's tail was *docked.*

– compare [2]DOCK

dock·er /ˈdɑːkɚ/ *noun, pl* **-ers** [*count*] *Brit* **:** DOCKWORKER

dock·et /ˈdɑːkət/ *noun, pl* **-ets** [*count*] *US*

1 : a list of the legal cases that will be tried in a court of law • The judge had to postpone some of the cases ***on the docket.***

2 : a list of things to do or discuss • The new library will be the first item ***on the committee's docket.*** [=on the committee's agenda]

dock·land /ˈdɑkˌlænd/ *noun, pl* **-lands** *Brit* **:** the part of a port where there are docks [*noncount*] an area of *dockland* [*count*] an old *dockland* — called also *docklands*

dock·side /ˈdɑːkˌsaɪd/ *noun* [*singular*] **:** the area along a shore next to a dock • The fish are unloaded at *dockside* and taken right to the market. — often used before another noun • *dockside* warehouses/restaurants

dock·work·er /ˈdɑːkˌwɚkɚ/ *noun, pl* **-ers** [*count*] *US* **:** a person who loads and unloads ships at a port : LONGSHOREMAN

dock·yard /ˈdɑːkˌjaɚd/ *noun, pl* **-yards** [*count*] **:** a place where ships are built and repaired : SHIPYARD

[1]**doc·tor** /ˈdɑːktɚ/ *noun, pl* **-tors** [*count*] ✧ The abbreviation *Dr.* is usually used in writing when *doctor* is being used as a title for a specific person. • I have an appointment with *Dr.* Brown.

1 a : a person who is skilled in the science of medicine : a person who is trained and licensed to treat sick and injured people • I think you should see a *doctor.* [=*physician*] • He needed medicine but refused to go to a *doctor.* • a visit to the *doctor's* office = a *doctor's* visit • She was under *doctor's* orders not to return to work. • Most of her money goes to paying ***doctors' bills.*** [=bills for visits to doctors and medical

treatment] **b** ***the doctor*** *or* ***the doctor's*** **:** the place where a doctor works • I saw her at *the doctor's* last week. • How long will you be at *the doctor*?
2 *US* **a :** a dentist — used chiefly as a title or as a form of address • My dentist is *Dr.* Smith. **b :** a person who is trained to treat sick and injured animals **:** VETERINARIAN • an animal *doctor* — used chiefly as a title or as a form of address • We took our dog to *Dr.* Jones.
3 : a person who has the highest degree (such as a PhD) given by a university • Most of the faculty members at this college are *doctors* in their fields. • a *Doctor* of Philosophy • *Dr.* Smith, can you explain the exam requirements again?
just what the doctor ordered *informal* **:** exactly what is wanted or needed • A day at the beach was *just what the doctor ordered.* — see also SPIN DOCTOR, WITCH DOCTOR

²doctor *verb* **-tors; -tored; -tor·ing** [+ *obj*]
1 : to change (something) especially in order to trick or deceive people • They were accused of *doctoring* the company's financial records. • a *doctored* photo of the actress
2 : to add something (such as alcohol or drugs) to (a food or drink) • I think somebody *doctored* the punch.
3 : to give medical treatment to (an injury, a person, etc.) • He had time to *doctor* his wounds. • She *doctored* the sick child until the physician arrived.

doc·tor·al /ˈdɑːktərəl/ *adj, always used before a noun* **:** of or relating to the highest degree that is given by a university • a *doctoral* degree • He wrote his *doctoral* dissertation/thesis on William Shakespeare. • *doctoral* candidates [=students trying to earn their doctorates] — see also POSTDOCTORAL

doc·tor·ate /ˈdɑːktərət/ *noun, pl* **-ates** [*count*] **:** the highest degree that is given by a university • She got a job teaching at the university after earning her *doctorate.* [=*PhD*]

doc·tri·naire /ˌdɑːktrəˈneɚ/ *adj* [*more* ~; *most* ~] *formal* + *disapproving* — used to describe a person who has very strong beliefs about what should be done and will not change them or accept other people's opinions • The senator is less *doctrinaire* than generally believed. • a *doctrinaire* conservative/socialist

doc·trine /ˈdɑːktrən/ *noun, pl* **-trines**
1 : a set of ideas or beliefs that are taught or believed to be true [*count*] The government was founded on a *doctrine* of equality for all people. • Many psychologists now question the *doctrines* of Sigmund Freud. [*noncount*] teaching religious *doctrine* to young people
2 [*count*] *US* **:** a statement of government policy especially in international relations • the Truman/Monroe *doctrine*
– doc·tri·nal /ˈdɑːktrənl, *Brit* dɒkˈtraɪnl/ *adj* • The group split into two parties as a result of *doctrinal* differences.
– doc·tri·nal·ly *adv*

do·cu·dra·ma /ˈdɑːkjəˌdrɑːmə/ *noun, pl* **-mas** [*count*] **:** a movie that is usually made for television and that tells a story about real events that have happened recently • They are making a *docudrama* about the controversial court case.

¹doc·u·ment /ˈdɑːkjəmənt/ *noun, pl* **-ments** [*count*]
1 : an official paper that gives information about something or that is used as proof of something • It is important to keep all of your financial *documents* in a safe place. • legal/official/historical *documents* • An important classified *document* has been leaked to the media.
2 : a computer file that contains text that you have written • creating a new *document* on your computer • I lost the *document* when the hard drive crashed.

²doc·u·ment /ˈdɑːkjəˌmɛnt/ *verb* **-ments; -ment·ed; -ment·ing** [+ *obj*]
1 : to create a record of (something) through writing, film, photography, etc. • Her study was the first to *document* this type of behavior in gorillas. • He wrote a book *documenting* their struggle.
2 : to prove (something) by using usually written evidence • Can you *document* the claims you're making? • The charges are well/fully *documented.*
– doc·u·ment·able /ˈdɑːkjəˌmɛntəbəl/ *adj* • *documentable* evidence

¹doc·u·men·ta·ry /ˌdɑːkjəˈmɛntri/ *noun, pl* **-ries** [*count*] **:** a movie or television program that tells the facts about actual people and events • We watched a *documentary* on the early history of jazz. — often used before another noun • a *documentary* filmmaker • She has produced several award-winning *documentary* films.

²documentary *adj, always used before a noun* **:** consisting of documents **:** written down • You must present *documentary* proof of your residence. • *documentary* evidence

doc·u·men·ta·tion /ˌdɑːkjəmənˈteɪʃən/ *noun* [*noncount*]
1 : the documents, records, etc., that are used to prove something or make something official • You cannot visit the country unless you have the proper *documentation.* • Keep your receipts as *documentation* of your purchases. • written *documentation* • Can you provide *documentation* of the claims you're making?
2 : written instructions for using a computer or computer program • The program's *documentation* is poorly written.

DOD *abbr, US* Department of Defense

dod·der·ing /ˈdɑːdərɪŋ/ *adj* **:** walking and moving in a slow and unsteady way because of old age • a *doddering* old man

dod·dle /ˈdɑːdl̩/ *noun* [*singular*] *Brit, informal* **:** something that is very easy to do • This machine makes cleaning your home a *doddle.* [=*cinch*]

¹dodge /ˈdɑːʤ/ *verb* **dodg·es; dodged; dodg·ing**
1 a [+ *obj*] **:** to move quickly to one side in order to avoid being hit by (someone or something) • He *dodged* the first punch but was hit by the second. • *dodging* traffic **b** ***always followed by an adverb or preposition*** [*no obj*] **:** to move quickly in order to avoid being hit, seen, stopped, etc. • She *dodged* through the crowds as she hurried home. • He *dodged* [=*ducked*] behind the bushes. • We *dodged* between the cars as we raced across the street.
2 [+ *obj*] **:** to get away from or avoid (someone or something) in a skillful or dishonest way • She *dodged* [=*evaded*] the question by changing the subject. • They managed to *dodge* the reporters by leaving through the back exit. • She accused him of *dodging* his responsibilities as a parent. • Many young men tried to ***dodge the draft*** [=to avoid being drafted into the military] by leaving the country.
dodge a/the bullet *chiefly US, informal* **:** to barely avoid being hit or affected by something harmful • The island *dodged a bullet* when the hurricane turned south.

²dodge *noun, pl* **dodges** [*count*] **:** a clever or dishonest trick done in order to avoid something • It was just another *dodge* to get out of working. • a tax *dodge*

dodge·ball /ˈdɑːʤˌbɑːl/ *noun* [*noncount*] **:** a game in which players try to hit their opponents with an inflated ball in order to get them removed from the game

dodg·em car /ˈdɑːʤəm-/ *noun, pl* ~ **cars** [*count*] *Brit* **:** BUMPER CAR

dodg·er /ˈdɑːʤɚ/ *noun, pl* **-ers** [*count*] **:** a person who avoids doing something by being dishonest • tax *dodgers* [=*evaders*] • a ***draft dodger*** [=a person who illegally avoids being drafted into the military]

dodgy /ˈdɑːʤi/ *adj* **dodgier; -est** [*also more* ~; *most* ~] *chiefly Brit, informal*
1 a : false or dishonest • *dodgy* business deals • a *dodgy* insurance claim **b :** causing a lack of trust or confidence • I heard he has a pretty *dodgy* [=*questionable*] reputation.
2 : in bad condition • The car's got a *dodgy* engine. • my *dodgy* knees
3 : difficult or risky • They got into a *dodgy* situation.

do·do /ˈdoʊˌdoʊ/ *noun, pl* **-does** *or* **-dos** [*count*]
1 : a type of bird that lived in the past and that was large, heavy, and unable to fly
2 *US, informal* + *humorous* **:** a stupid or silly person • That *dodo* can't do anything right. • I feel like a complete *dodo.*
(as) dead as a dodo see ¹DEAD

doe /ˈdoʊ/ *noun, pl* **does** *or* **doe** [*count*] **:** a female animal (such as a deer, rabbit, or kangaroo) — compare BUCK; see also JANE DOE, JOHN DOE

doe–eyed /ˈdoʊˌaɪd/ *adj* **:** having large eyes that make you look innocent • a *doe-eyed* little boy

do·er /ˈduːwɚ/ *noun, pl* **-ers** [*count*] **:** a person who actively does things instead of just thinking or talking about them • I'm more of a thinker than a *doer.*

does see DO

doesn't /ˈdʌzn̩t/ — used as a contraction of *does not* • She *doesn't* like cake. • This shirt *doesn't* fit.

doff /ˈdɑːf/ *verb* **doffs; doffed; doff·ing** [+ *obj*] *old-fashioned* **:** to take off or remove (a hat or a piece of clothing) • He *doffed* his cap as he introduced himself. • They *doffed* their coats when they came inside.

¹dog /ˈdɑːg/ *noun, pl* **dogs**
1 [*count*] **a :** a type of animal that is often kept as a pet or trained to work for people by guarding buildings, hunting, etc. • That *dog* barks all day long. • children playing with the family *dog* • a guard *dog* • a hunting *dog* • wild *dogs* such as the Australian dingo — often used before another noun • a

dog collar • *dog* food/shows • I'm not really a *dog* person. [=I don't particularly like dogs] **b** : a male dog
2 [*count*] *informal* **a** : a person who is regarded as lucky, unlucky, etc. • You lucky *dog*! — see also TOP DOG **b** : a person who is lazy or who is not liked • He's a lazy *dog*. • He's a worthless *dog*. [=*bum*] **c** *offensive* : an unattractive girl or woman • They say she's a real *dog*.
3 [*count*] *US, informal* : something that is poor in quality • Her latest book turned out to be a real *dog*. • That was a *dog* of a movie.
4 [*count*] *US, informal* : HOT DOG • Would you like another *dog*? — see also CHILI DOG, CORN DOG
5 dogs [*plural*] *US, informal + old-fashioned* : FEET • My *dogs* were tired from standing all day.

a dog's breakfast *Brit, informal* : something that is messy or poorly done • It was *a dog's breakfast* of a match, and our coach was understandably upset.

a dog's life : a difficult, boring, and unhappy life • Everyone knows it's *a dog's life* in this business.

(as) sick as a dog *informal* : very sick • I'm *sick as a dog*.

dog and pony show *US, usually disapproving* : a very fancy and elaborate event that is done to sell something, to impress people, etc. • The sales presentation was a real *dog and pony show*.

every dog has his/its day *informal* — used to say that every person has a successful moment in life

go to the dogs *informal* : to become ruined : to change to a much worse condition • Our favorite restaurant has *gone to the dogs* lately. • The economy is *going to the dogs*.

hair of the dog (that bit you) see HAIR

in a dog's age see [1]AGE

let sleeping dogs lie : to ignore a problem because trying to deal with it could cause an even more difficult situation • I thought about bringing up my concerns but decided instead to *let sleeping dogs lie*.

put on the dog *US, informal + old-fashioned* : to pretend that you are very stylish or rich • They really *put on the dog* for their daughter's wedding.

rain cats and dogs see [2]RAIN

the tail wagging the dog see [1]TAIL

you can't teach an old dog new tricks — used to say that a person who is old or is used to doing things in a certain way cannot learn or does not want to learn a new way • I tried to get my mother to start using a computer, but she says *you can't teach an old dog new tricks*.

[2]**dog** *verb* **dogs; dogged; dog·ging** [+ *obj*]
1 : to follow (someone) very closely • He *dogged* her every move.
2 : to ask (someone) about something or for something constantly or frequently • Creditors *dogged* him until he finally paid his bills. • Reporters kept *dogging* [=*pestering*] her for information.
3 : to cause problems for (someone) for a long time — often used as *(be) dogged* • His career *has been dogged* [=*plagued*] by controversy. • an athlete *dogged* by injuries [=an athlete who has had many injuries]

dog biscuit *noun, pl* ~ **-cuits** [*count*] : a hard, dry cracker for dogs

dog·catch·er /ˈdɑːgˌkɛʧɚ/ *noun, pl* **-ers** [*count*] *US* : a public official who is responsible for catching dogs that do not have homes — called also (*Brit*) *dog warden*

dog days *noun* [*plural*] : the hottest time of the year • The kids used to go swimming every afternoon during the *dog days* of summer.

dog–eared /ˈdɑːgˌiɚd/ *adj* [*more* ~; *most* ~] : having some pages with the top corners folded down • All I had was a few old *dog-eared* copies of my favorite books. • a *dog-eared* magazine — sometimes used figuratively • *dog-eared* jokes [=old jokes that have been told many times]

dog–eat–dog /ˌdɑːgˌiːtˈdɑːg/ *adj* — used to describe a situ-

dog

ation in which people compete with each other for success in a cruel and selfish way • It's a *dog-eat-dog* business we're in. • *dog-eat-dog* competitions

dog·fight /ˈdɑːgˌfaɪt/ *noun, pl* **-fights** [*count*]
1 : a fight between dogs
2 : a fight between fighter planes that are flying close to each other • He was shot down in a *dogfight* over enemy territory.
3 : a fierce fight or struggle between people or groups • The election has turned into a real *dogfight*.

dog·ged /ˈdɑːgəd/ *adj* [*more* ~; *most* ~] **:** having or showing the attitude of a person who wants to do or get something and will not stop trying **:** stubborn and determined • Her *dogged* efforts eventually paid off. • a *dogged* pursuit of power
– dog·ged·ly *adv* • He worked *doggedly* to maintain his lead. • The press *doggedly* pursues him wherever he goes.
– dog·ged·ness *noun* [*noncount*]

dog·ger·el /ˈdɑːgərəl/ *noun* [*noncount*] **:** poetry that is poorly written and that often is not meant to be taken seriously • a few lines of *doggerel*

doggie bag *also* **doggy bag** *noun, pl* ~ **bags** [*count*] **:** a bag that is used for carrying home food that is left over from a meal eaten at a restaurant

[1]**dog·gone** /ˈdɑːgˈgɑːn/ *interj, US, informal + somewhat old-fashioned* — used as a more polite form of *damn* • *Doggone*! That hurt!

[2]**doggone** *verb, US, informal + somewhat old-fashioned* [+ *obj*] — used as a more polite form of *damn* • ***Doggone it***! I forgot my keys! • Listen to me, *doggone* it! • (I'll be) ***Doggoned if*** he didn't leave early. [=I'm surprised that he left early]

[3]**doggone** *or* **doggoned** /ˈdɑːgˈgɑːnd/ *adj, US, informal + somewhat old-fashioned* — used as a more polite form of *damn* • Those *doggone* kids stepped on our flowers! • He didn't do a *doggone* thing today. • It's a *doggone* shame that you missed it. • If you believe that, you're a *doggoned* fool!
– doggone /ˈdɑːgˈgɑːn/ *or* **doggoned** /ˈdɑːgˈgɑːnd/ *adv* • What's so *doggone* funny? • She's too *doggoned* skinny.

dog·gy *or* **dog·gie** /ˈdɑːgi/ *noun, pl* **-gies** [*count*] *informal* **:** a dog ✧ *Doggy* is used especially by children or when talking to children. • Oh, what a cute little *doggy*!
– doggy *adj* [*more* ~; *most* ~] • a *doggy* smell

dog·house /ˈdɑːgˌhaʊs/ *noun, pl* **-hous·es** [*count*] *US* **:** an outdoor shelter with a roof for a dog
in the doghouse *informal* **:** in a bad situation because someone is angry at you **:** in trouble • He's *in the doghouse* with his wife [=his wife is angry at him] for being late.

dog·leg /ˈdɑːgˌlɛg/ *noun, pl* **-legs** [*count*] **:** a place where a road, golf course, etc., bends or turns sharply • a sharp *dogleg* to the left
– dogleg *adj, always used before a noun* • *dogleg* fairways
– dogleg *verb* **-legs; -legged; -leg·ging** [*no obj*] • a fairway that *doglegs* to the left

dog·ma /ˈdɑːgmə/ *noun, pl* **-mas** [*count, noncount*] *formal*
1 *usually disapproving* **:** a belief or set of beliefs that is accepted by the members of a group without being questioned or doubted • These new findings challenge the current *dogma* in the field. • political *dogma*
2 : a belief or set of beliefs that is taught by a religious organization

dog·mat·ic /dɑgˈmætɪk/ *adj* [*more* ~; *most* ~] *disapproving* **:** expressing personal opinions or beliefs as if they are certainly correct and cannot be doubted • She's become so *dogmatic* lately that arguing with her is pointless. • *dogmatic* critics • *dogmatic* statements
– dog·mat·i·cal·ly /dɑgˈmætɪkli/ *adv* [*more* ~; *most* ~]
– dog·ma·tism /ˈdɑːgməˌtɪzəm/ *noun* [*noncount*] • moral/religious/political *dogmatism* **– dog·ma·tist** /ˈdɑːgmətɪst/ *noun, pl* **-tists** [*count*] • a political *dogmatist* [=a person with dogmatic political opinions]

do–good·er /ˈduːˌgʊdɚ/ *noun, pl* **-ers** [*count*] *disapproving* **:** someone whose desire and effort to help people (such as poor people) is regarded as wrong, annoying, useless, etc. • He dismisses his critics as a bunch of politically correct *do-gooders*.

dog–paddle *also* **doggy–paddle** *verb* **-pad·dles; -pad·dled; -pad·dling** [*no obj*] **:** to swim like a dog with your head above water and your arms and legs paddling under the water • When she first learned to swim, all she could do was *dog-paddle*.
– dog paddle *also* **doggy paddle** *noun* [*singular*] • doing a/the *dog paddle*

dog·sled /ˈdɑːgˌslɛd/ *noun, pl* **-sleds** [*count*] *chiefly US* **:** a type of sled that is pulled by dogs
– dogsled *verb* **-sleds; -sled·ded; -sled·ding** [*no obj*] He *dogsledded* across the tundra. [+ *obj*] They *dogsledded* supplies to the fort. **– dogsledding** *noun* [*noncount*] • She likes to ***go dogsledding*** in the winter.

dog tag *noun, pl* ~ **tags** [*count*] **:** a small, thin piece of metal that is worn around the neck of an American soldier and that lists the soldier's name, service number, and other information

dog–tired *adj* [*more* ~; *most* ~] *informal* **:** very tired **:** EXHAUSTED • I was *dog-tired* and ready for bed.

dog warden *noun, pl* ~ **-dens** [*count*] *Brit* **:** DOGCATCHER

dog·wood /ˈdɑːgˌwʊd/ *noun, pl* **-woods**
1 [*count*] **:** a type of bush or small tree with groups of small flowers • We planted two *dogwoods*. • a *dogwood* tree
2 [*noncount*] **:** the hard wood of a dogwood • The furniture is made of *dogwood*.

doh *chiefly Brit spelling of* [4]DO

DoH *abbr, Brit* Department of Health

d'oh /ˈdoʊ/ *interj, informal + humorous* — used when you realize that you have just said or done something stupid or foolish

doi·ly /ˈdoɪli/ *noun, pl* **-lies** [*count*] **:** a usually round cloth or paper that has a decorative pattern made of many small holes ✧ Doilies are typically placed on top of something (such as a piece of furniture) to protect it or for decoration. • She placed a lace *doily* under the vase.

do·ing /ˈduːwɪŋ/ *noun, pl* **-ings**
1 [*noncount*] **:** the act of making something happen through your own action • It's the *doing* of the good deed that is important, not the thanks you receive. ✧ Informal phrases like ***take a bit of doing, take some doing,*** and ***take a lot of doing*** are used to say that something is difficult to do and requires a lot of effort or work. • Finishing the work on time may *take a bit of doing*. • It will *take some doing* to win the game. • Getting the project done on time will *take a lot of doing*. ✧ If something is ***your doing***, you did it. • Is this mix-up *your doing*? [=did you cause the mix-up?] • The surprise party was not all *our doing*; we had lots of help.
2 *doings* [*plural*] **:** things that someone does • I've been reading about the governor's latest *doings*. [=*activities*] **:** things that happen • There have been some strange *doings* [=*goings-on, occurrences*] lately.

do–it–yourself *adj, always used before a noun* **:** of or relating to work (such as fixing or building something) that you do yourself instead of hiring someone to do it • a *do-it-yourself* [=*DIY*] home improvement project • *do-it-yourself* home repair • *do-it-yourself* stores [=stores where you buy materials to fix or build things]
– do–it–your·self·er *noun, pl* **-ers** [*count*] • a how-to guide for *do-it-yourselfers*

do·jo /ˈdoʊʤoʊ/ *noun, pl* **-jos** [*count*] **:** a school for teaching people karate, judo, etc.

Dol·by /ˈdɑːlbi, ˈdoʊlbi/ *trademark* — used for an electronic device that removes unwanted noise from recorded or broadcast sound

dol·drums /ˈdoʊldrəmz/ *noun* [*plural*]
1 : a state or period of sadness or depression • We watched movies to fight off the winter *doldrums*. — often used in the phrase ***in the doldrums*** • She has been *in the doldrums* since her best friend moved away.
2 : a state or period in which there is no activity or improvement • The company is slowly climbing out of its economic *doldrums*. — often used in the phrase ***in the doldrums*** • The market is *in the doldrums*.

[1]**dole** /ˈdoʊl/ *noun* [*noncount*] **:** money that a government (especially the British government) gives to people who do not have jobs or who are very poor • *dole* money — usually used as ***the dole*** • The government is changing the rules for receiving *the dole*. [=(*US*) *welfare*] • They've been ***on/off the dole*** for a year. • They're going *on/off the dole*.

[2]**dole** *verb* **doles; doled; dol·ing**
dole out [*phrasal verb*] ***dole out (something)*** *also* ***dole (something) out*** **:** to give (something) to people • She is always *doling out* advice on relationships. • The organization has *doled out* millions of dollars in grants. • The nurse *doles* the pills *out* carefully. • The agency *doles out* [=*hands out, distributes*] food to thousands of needy families each year.

dole·ful /ˈdoʊlfəl/ *adj* [*more* ~; *most* ~] **:** very sad • The girl had a *doleful* look/expression on her face. • You sounded so *doleful* about your future that night.

D

– **dole·ful·ly** *adv*

[1]**doll** /ˈdɑːl/ *noun, pl* **dolls** [*count*]
1 : a child's toy in the form of a baby or small person ▪ The child was busy playing with her (baby) *dolls.* ▪ My aunt collects porcelain *dolls.* — see also RAG DOLL
2 *chiefly US, informal* **:** a kind and helpful person — usually singular ▪ Thanks for the help. You're a *doll.* [=*dear*]
3 *informal + old-fashioned* **:** a woman; *especially* **:** an attractive woman ✧ This sense of *doll* is now often considered offensive especially when it is used as a way to address a woman.

D

[2]**doll** *verb* **dolls; dolled; doll·ing**
doll up [*phrasal verb*] ***doll (yourself) up informal*** **:** to make (yourself) attractive with makeup and fancy or stylish clothes ▪ She *dolled herself up* for the party. = She ***got (all) dolled up*** for the party.

dol·lar /ˈdɑːlɚ/ *noun, pl* **-lars**
1 [*count*] **a :** a basic unit of money in the U.S., Canada, Australia, and other countries that is equal to 100 cents ▪ The shirt costs 20 *dollars.* [=$20] ▪ She had to pay hundreds of *dollars* in auto repairs. ▪ The property is worth a million *dollars.* = It's a million-*dollar* property. ▪ Do you have a 20-*dollar bill*? [=a twenty] ▪ It costs 500 pesos. How much is that ***in dollars***? [=how many dollars equals 500 pesos?] **b :** a bill or coin that is worth one dollar ▪ I found a *dollar* on the sidewalk. = I found a ***dollar bill*** on the sidewalk. ▪ She put a wrinkled *dollar* down on the counter. — see also HALF-DOLLAR, TOP DOLLAR
2 ***the dollar*** *technical* **:** the value of a dollar when it is compared to another unit of money ▪ *The dollar* dropped sharply against the pound. ▪ the strength/weakness of *the dollar* ▪ *The dollar* is worth more in Mexico.
3 [*count*] **:** money that is from a specified source or used for a specified purpose ▪ You want to know how the state spends every federal *dollar* [=money from the federal government] it receives? — usually plural ▪ Should a program like this be paid for with tax/taxpayer *dollars*? [=with money the government collects through taxes] ▪ tourist/tourism *dollars* [=money that an economy gets because of the money tourists spend there] ▪ The company needs to invest its advertising *dollars* wisely.
bet your bottom dollar see [2]BET
look/feel like a million dollars see MILLION
– see also SAND DOLLAR

dollar sign *noun, pl* **~ signs** [*count*] **:** a symbol $ placed before a number to show that it represents an amount of dollars — often used figuratively ▪ Where other people saw junk, she ***saw dollar signs.*** [=she saw a way to earn money] ▪ investors with ***dollar signs in their eyes*** [=investors who want very much to earn money]

doll·house /ˈdɑːlˌhaʊs/ *noun, pl* **-hous·es** [*count*] *US* **:** a small toy house that is used by children for playing with dolls — called also (*Brit*) *doll's house*

dol·lop /ˈdɑːləp/ *noun, pl* **-lops** [*count*]
1 : a small amount of soft food ▪ My piece of pie was served with a *dollop* of whipped cream. ▪ a *dollop* of ketchup
2 : a usually small amount of something ▪ A *dollop* of milk was left in the container. ▪ large *dollops* of wit and humor

doll's house *noun, pl* **dolls' houses** [*count*] *Brit* **:** DOLLHOUSE

dol·ly /ˈdɑːli/ *noun, pl* **-lies** [*count*]
1 : a child's toy doll ✧ *Dolly* is usually used by children or by adults speaking to children.
2 : a piece of equipment that has wheels and that is used for moving heavy objects ▪ We'll need a *dolly* to move the refrigerator.

dol·men /ˈdoʊlmən, ˈdɑːlmən/ *noun, pl* **-mens** [*count*] *technical* **:** an ancient structure made of two or more upright stones and a single stone lying across them ✧ Dolmens are believed to be tombs.

dol·phin /ˈdɑːlfən/ *noun, pl* **-phins** [*count*] **:** a small usually gray whale that has a pointed nose — compare PORPOISE

dolt /ˈdoʊlt/ *noun, pl* **dolts** [*count*] *informal* **:** a stupid person ▪ What a *dolt* I've been!
– **dolt·ish** /ˈdoʊltɪʃ/ *adj* [*more ~; most ~*] ▪ a *doltish* person ▪ *doltish* behavior

-dom /dəm/ *noun suffix*
1 : the state of being (something) ▪ free*dom*
2 : the rank of ▪ duke*dom*
3 : the area ruled by ▪ king*dom*
4 : the group having a specified job, position, interest, or character ▪ official*dom*

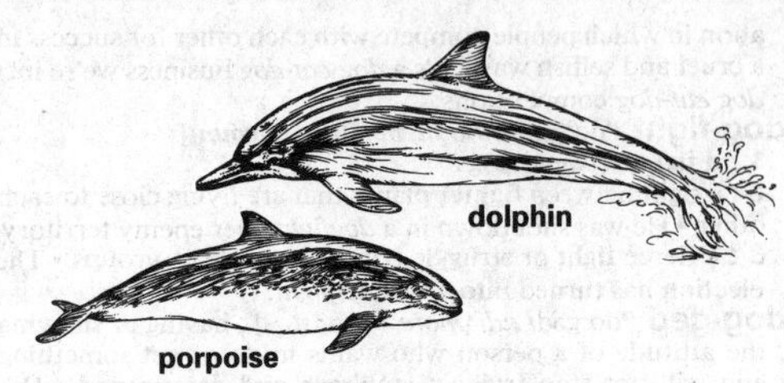

do·main /doʊˈmeɪn/ *noun, pl* **-mains** [*count*]
1 : the land that a ruler or a government controls **:** TERRITORY ▪ The forest is part of the king's *domain.* ▪ the British/Ottoman imperial *domain* — see also EMINENT DOMAIN, PUBLIC DOMAIN
2 : an area of knowledge or activity ▪ My sister is the math expert in the family, but literature is my *domain.* ▪ Childcare is no longer solely a female *domain.* — often + *of* ▪ Federal crimes are outside the *domain of* city police.
3 *computers* **a :** a section of the Internet that is made up of computers or sites that are related in some way (such as by use or source) ✧ An abbreviation of an Internet site's domain (such as .gov, .org, and .com) is included in its address: www.Merriam-Webster.com. **b :** DOMAIN NAME

domain name *noun, pl* **~ names** [*count*] *computers* **:** the characters (such as Merriam-Webster.com or Whitehouse.gov) that form the main part of an Internet address

dome /ˈdoʊm/ *noun, pl* **domes** [*count*]
1 : a large rounded roof or ceiling that is shaped like half of a ball ▪ the *dome* of the Capitol building ▪ the church's high *dome*
2 : a structure that looks like the dome of a building ▪ a *dome* of ice
3 : a stadium that is covered by a roof ▪ The team's new stadium is a *dome.*
4 *informal* **:** a person's head ▪ He wears a hat to protect his bald *dome* from the summer sun.

domed /ˈdoʊmd/ *adj* **:** shaped like or covered with a dome ▪ The dog's skull is slightly *domed.* ▪ a *domed* ceiling/church/stadium

[1]**do·mes·tic** /dəˈmɛstɪk/ *adj*
1 : of, relating to, or made in your own country ▪ the *domestic* economy/market ▪ foreign and *domestic* affairs/policy ▪ international and *domestic* politics ▪ The company hopes to attract both foreign and *domestic* investors. ▪ The wine is *domestic.* ▪ *domestic* and imported cheeses ▪ The airline only offers *domestic* flights. [=flights to and from places within the country] — opposite FOREIGN
2 *always used before a noun* **:** relating to or involving someone's home or family ▪ *domestic* happiness ▪ His *domestic* [=*home*] life was not very happy. ▪ *domestic* abuse/violence [=physical harm done to a member of a family or household by another member of the same family or household]
3 a *always used before a noun* **:** relating to the work (such as cooking and cleaning) that is done in a person's home ▪ *domestic* chores/duties/work/services/help ▪ a *domestic* worker/servant [=a worker/servant who is hired to work in someone's home] **b** [*more ~; most ~*] — used to describe a person who enjoys work and activities that are done at home ▪ I'm not a *domestic* person. ▪ She is not very *domestic.* **c** *always used before a noun* **:** used in the home ▪ *domestic* furniture/appliances
4 *of an animal* **:** living with people **:** bred or trained to need and accept the care of human beings **:** DOMESTICATED ▪ The wolf is related to the *domestic* dog. ▪ wild and *domestic* cats ▪ *domestic* animals/cattle
– **do·mes·ti·cal·ly** /dəˈmɛstɪkli/ *adv* ▪ It is a *domestically* produced wine. ▪ *Domestically,* the economy is not doing well.

[2]**domestic** *noun, pl* **-tics** [*count*]
1 *old-fashioned* **:** a servant who is hired to work in someone's home **:** a domestic servant
2 *Brit, informal* **:** a fight between members of a family or household ▪ She got in a *domestic* with her husband.

do·mes·ti·cate /dəˈmɛstəˌkeɪt/ *verb* **-cates; -cat·ed; -cat·ing** [*+ obj*]
1 a : to breed or train (an animal) to need and accept the care of human beings **:** to tame (an animal) ▪ Humans have *domesticated* dogs/cattle/chickens. ▪ Horses and oxen have

been *domesticated* to work on farms. **b** : to grow (a plant) for human use • Native Americans *domesticated* corn.
2 *humorous* : to train (someone) to behave in an appropriate way at home (such as by using good manners, being polite, being helpful, etc.) • She jokes that dogs are easier to *domesticate* than men.
– **domesticated** *adj* [*more* ~; *most* ~] • *domesticated* animals – **do·mes·ti·ca·tion** /dəˌmɛstəˈkeɪʃən/ *noun* [*noncount*] • the *domestication* of animals

do·mes·tic·i·ty /ˌdoʊˌmɛˈstɪsəti/ *noun* [*noncount*] *formal* : life inside a home : the activities of a family or of the people who share a home • We got married and settled into a life of comfortable *domesticity*.

domestic partner *noun, pl* ~ **-ners** [*count*] *US, formal* : a person you live with and have a sexual relationship with but are not married to ✧ *Domestic partner* is usually used in legal situations. • The organization is trying to get tax and insurance benefits for *domestic partners*.
– **domestic partnership** *noun, pl* ~ **-ships** [*count*] • People in *domestic partnerships* qualify for insurance benefits.

domestic science *noun* [*noncount*] *old-fashioned* : HOME ECONOMICS

dom·i·cile /ˈdɑːməˌsajəl/ *noun, pl* **-ciles** *law* : the place where you live : your home [*noncount*] You will need to report your change of *domicile* to your insurance company. [*count*] Students must establish a *domicile* in the state to be eligible for reduced tuition.

dom·i·ciled *adj, not used before a noun, law* : living or established in a particular place • The defendant/corporation is *domiciled* in Texas. • students *domiciled* outside the state

dom·i·nant /ˈdɑːmənənt/ *adj*
1 [*more* ~; *most* ~] : more important, powerful, or successful than most or all others • The university has/plays a *dominant* [=*major*] role in the local economy. • Money is the *dominant* [=*main*] force in consumer societies. • The company is now *dominant* in its market. • What is the *dominant* [=*major, predominant*] theme of the play? • It is the *dominant* culture/tribe in the region. • She has a very *dominant* [=*domineering*] personality. • the *dominant* female/male of the pack
2 : most common • the *dominant* [=*prevailing*] language/religion of the country
3 *biology* : causing or relating to a characteristic or condition that a child will have if one of the child's parents has it • *dominant* genes • Brown hair is a *dominant* trait. = Brown hair is *dominant*. — opposite RECESSIVE
– **dom·i·nance** /ˈdɑːmənəns/ *noun* [*noncount*] The companies are competing for *dominance* in the market. = The companies are competing for market *dominance*. • military/political *dominance* [=*predominance*] • male *dominance* [=the state of men or male animals having more power than women or female animals] • the French language's *dominance* in the region = the regional *dominance* of the French language [*singular*] The company has established a *dominance* in the market. • the team's *dominance* over its rivals • a neighborhood with a *dominance* [=*predominance*] of older homes – **dom·i·nant·ly** *adv* • The population is *dominantly* [=(more commonly) *predominantly*] Catholic. • a *dominantly* inherited disease

dom·i·nate /ˈdɑːməˌneɪt/ *verb* **-nates**; **-nat·ed**; **-nat·ing**
1 [+ *obj*] : to have control of or power over (someone or something) • The king dreamed of *dominating* [=*ruling*] the world. • One company has *dominated* the market for years. • Men *dominate* the field. = It's a male-*dominated* field. • He *dominated* her life for many years.
2 [+ *obj*] : to be the most important part of (something) • His work *dominated* the art scene last year. • The business *dominated* her life. [=most of her life/time was devoted to the business] • The topic of her arrest *dominated* the conversation. [=most of the conversation was about her arrest]
3 : to be much more powerful or successful than others in a game, competition, etc. [*no obj*] Our team *dominated* throughout the game. [+ *obj*] Our team *dominated* play throughout the game. • She *dominated* the match.
4 [*no obj*] : to be most common • Pine trees *dominate* in the eastern part of the forest. • French *dominates* throughout the region, but German is also spoken.
5 [+ *obj*] : to be the largest or most noticeable object in (a place) • The statue *dominates* the town's square. • The room was *dominated* by a large table.
– **dominating** *adj* [*more* ~; *most* ~] • He has had a *dominating* influence in her life. • a very *dominating* team – **dom·i·na·tion** /ˌdɑːməˈneɪʃən/ *noun* [*noncount*] • The king had dreams of world *domination*. • market *domination* – **dom·i·na·tor** /ˈdɑːməˌneɪtɚ/ *noun, pl* **-tors** [*count*] • The company is a market *dominator*.

do·mi·na·trix /ˌdɑːmɪˈneɪtrɪks/ *noun, pl* **-tri·ces** /-trəˌsiːz/ *also* **-trix·es** [*count*] : a woman who controls and hurts her partner during sexual activity in order to give her partner sexual pleasure

dom·i·neer·ing /ˌdɑːməˈnirɪŋ/ *adj* [*more* ~; *most* ~] : tending too often to tell people what to do : often trying to control the behavior of others • a *domineering* [=*controlling*] parent • Their manager is much too *domineering*. [=(*informal*) *bossy*]

Do·min·i·can /dəˈmɪnɪkən/ *noun, pl* **-cans** [*count*] : a member of a Roman Catholic group of friars founded in 1215 by St. Dominic
– **Dominican** *adj* • the *Dominican* order • *Dominican* friars

do·min·ion /dəˈmɪnjən/ *noun, pl* **-ions** *formal*
1 [*noncount*] : the power to rule : control of a country, region, etc. • The U.S. has/holds *dominion* over the island. • The countries fought for *dominion* of the territory.
synonyms see [1]POWER
2 [*count*] : the land that a ruler or government controls • The whole island is the king's *dominion*. [=*domain*] • the *dominions* of the empire
3 ***Dominion*** [*count*] : a country that was part of the British Empire but had its own government ✧ Countries that were formerly Dominions are now members of the Commonwealth.

dom·i·no /ˈdɑːməˌnoʊ/ *noun, pl* **-noes** *or* **-nos**
1 [*count*] : a small flat rectangular block made of wood or plastic that has one or more dots on one side and that is used in playing games
2 ***dominoes*** [*noncount*] : a game played with dominoes • *Dominoes* is one of my favorite games.

domino effect *noun* [*singular*] : a situation in which one event causes a series of similar events to happen one after another • The delay created a *domino effect* [=*ripple effect*], disrupting deliveries around the country.

[1]**don** /ˈdɑːn/ *noun, pl* **dons** [*count*]
1 *Brit* : a teacher in a college or university; *especially* : a teacher at Oxford or Cambridge University
2 *informal* : a powerful Mafia leader

[2]**don** *verb* **dons**; **donned**; **don·ning** [+ *obj*] *formal* + *old-fashioned* : to put on (a piece of clothing) • He *donned* his gloves and hat. • She *donned* her jacket.

do·nate /ˈdoʊˌneɪt, doʊˈneɪt/ *verb* **-nates**; **-nat·ed**; **-nat·ing**
1 : to give (money, food, clothes, etc.) in order to help a person or organization [+ *obj*] The computers were *donated* by local companies. • We *donated* our old clothes to charity. • people who *donate* money to political candidates • He *donates* some of his free time to volunteer work. [*no obj*] Everyone is encouraged to *donate*.
2 : to give (blood, a body organ, etc.) to a hospital or other medical organization so that it can be given to someone who needs it [+ *obj*] People are encouraged to *donate* blood. • Please sign this form if you would like to *donate* your organs when you die. [*no obj*] You can *donate* at the blood bank every eight weeks.
– **do·na·tor** /ˈdoʊˌneɪtɚ, doʊˈneɪtɚ/ *noun, pl* **-ors** [*count*] • The *donators* [=(more commonly) *donors*] of the money did not give their names.

do·na·tion /doʊˈneɪʃən/ *noun, pl* **-tions**
1 : something (such as money, food, clothes, etc.) that you give in order to help a person or organization [*count*] All *donations* are appreciated. • They thanked her for the generous *donation*. [=*gift*] • The organization is funded by private *donations*. • Would you like to ***make a donation***? [=make a contribution; give money] [*noncount*] We are grateful for the *donation* of whatever you can afford to give.
2 : something (such as blood or a body organ) that you give to a hospital or clinic so that it can be given to someone who needs it [*count*] blood/organ *donations* [*noncount*] trying to encourage the *donation* of blood/organs

[1]**done** *past participle of* [1]DO

[2]**done** *adj, not used before a noun*
1 — used to say that an activity, job, etc., has ended • One more question and we're *done*. • He'll travel many miles before he's *done*. [=*through*] • My work is never *done*. [=*finished, completed*] • I'm (almost) *done* reading this book. • Turn out the light when you're *done*. • Are you *done* with the scissors? • When will you ***be done with*** [=*finish, complete*] the

project? = (*Brit*) When will you ***have done with*** the project? • Just call her and ***be done with it***. [=*get it over with*] = (*Brit*) Just call her and ***have done with it***. — compare [1]DO 2

2 : cooked completely or enough • The cake is *done*. • Check to see if the meat is *done*. — see also OVERDONE, UNDERDONE, WELL-DONE

3 : socially acceptable or fashionable • Getting a divorce just wasn't *done* at the time.

consider it done see CONSIDER

done for *informal* **1 :** in a very bad situation : certain to fail, lose, be punished, etc. • If she finds out we cheated, we're *done for*. [=*in trouble*] • We'll never catch up now. We're *done for*. **2 :** certain to die or be killed • When we saw the explosion, we thought she was *done for*. — see also *do for* 1 at [1]DO

done in *informal* **:** very tired • After working in the garden all day, I was/felt completely *done in*. [=*exhausted*] — see also *do in* 2 at [1]DO

hard done by see [2]HARD

no harm done see [1]HARM

over and done with see [1]OVER

when all is said and done see [3]ALL

[3]**done** *interj* — used to say that you agree with the conditions of a deal or accept an offer • "I'll offer you $5,000 for the car." "*Done*."

done deal *noun* [*singular*] *informal* **:** something that has been done and that cannot be changed • It's a *done deal*. • The sale is far from a *done deal*. [=it is very possible that it will not happen]

done·ness /ˈdʌnnəs/ *noun* [*noncount*] **:** the state of being cooked completely or enough • Cover the pan and cook to (the) desired *doneness*.

Don Juan /ˌdɑːnˈwɑːn/ *noun, pl* **~ Juans** [*count*] **:** a man who has sexual relationships with many women • She was wined and dined by the local *Don Juan*. [=*Casanova*]

don·key /ˈdɑːŋki/ *noun, pl* **-keys** [*count*] **:** an animal that is like a small horse with large ears

donkey work *noun* [*noncount*] *chiefly Brit, informal* **:** hard work that is not interesting • I had to do the *donkey work*.

donkey's years *noun* [*plural*] *chiefly Brit, informal* **:** a very long time • It's been *donkey's years* [=*ages*] since I saw her.

don·nish /ˈdɑːnɪʃ/ *adj* [*more ~; most ~*] *chiefly Brit* **:** like a typical don (sense 1) • a *donnish* [=*bookish*] manner • a *donnish* old professor

don·ny·brook /ˈdɑːniˌbrʊk/ *noun, pl* **-brooks** [*count*]

1 : a public argument • a political *donnybrook* [=*dispute*] • A *donnybrook* has erupted over the court's decision.

2 : an uncontrolled fight • A *donnybrook* [=*brawl, free-for-all*] broke out at the end of the game.

do·nor /ˈdounɚ/ *noun, pl* **-nors** [*count*]

1 : a person or group that gives something (such as money, food, or clothes) in order to help a person or organization • The money was raised from individual *donors*. • She is one of the charity's/cause's major *donors*.

2 : a person who gives something (such as blood or a body organ) so that it can be given to someone who needs it • blood/organ *donors* • a kidney *donor* • a *donor* organ • a ***donor card*** [=a card that says that you want to donate your organs when you die]

[1]**do–noth·ing** /ˈduːˌnʌθɪŋ/ *adj, always used before a noun*

1 : not willing to work, help, etc. **:** LAZY • a *do-nothing* husband

2 : failing to achieve or do anything important • a *do-nothing* policy/government/politician

[2]**do–nothing** *noun, pl* **-ings** [*count*] *informal* **:** someone who is lazy • He's a no-good *do-nothing*.

[1]**don't** /ˈdount/ — used as a contraction of *do not* • I *don't* like it. • The shoes *don't* fit.

> ***usage*** *Don't* is also sometimes used as a contraction of "does not." • She *don't* like it. This use is usually regarded as an error, but it is common in the very informal speech of some people. It is often used in stories in the speech of characters who do not have much education.

[2]**don't** *noun, pl* **don'ts** [*count*] *informal* **:** something that a person should not do — usually used in the phrase ***dos and don'ts*** • We each got a long list of *dos and don'ts*. [=things we should and should not do]

donut *chiefly US spelling of* DOUGHNUT

doo·bie /ˈduːbi/ *noun, pl* **-bies** [*count*] *US slang* **:** a marijuana cigarette • He lit up a *doobie*. [=*joint*]

doo·dad /ˈduːˌdæd/ *noun, pl* **-dads** [*count*] *US, informal*

1 : a usually small object that is used as a decoration — usually plural • a shelf cluttered with *doodads* [=*knickknacks*]

2 : a small useful device **:** GADGET — usually plural • The shop sells all kinds of nifty *doodads*.

doo·dah /ˈduːˌdɑː/ *noun, pl* **-dahs** [*count*] *Brit, informal* **:** DOODAD 2

doo·dle /ˈduːdl/ *verb* **doo·dles; doo·dled; doo·dling** [*no obj*] **:** to draw something without thinking about what you are doing • She *doodled* in her notebook instead of taking notes.

– doodle *noun, pl* **doodles** [*count*] • Her notebook was full of *doodles*.

doo–doo /ˈduːˌduː/ *noun* [*noncount*] *informal* **:** solid waste discharged from the body • I stepped in dog *doo-doo*. [=*poop*]

in deep doo-doo *informal* **:** in a very bad situation • If the car won't start, we're *in deep doo-doo*. [=*in deep trouble*]

doo·fus /ˈduːfəs/ *noun, pl* **-fus·es** [*count*] *US slang* **:** a stupid or foolish person • Don't be such a *doofus*.

doo·hick·ey /ˈduːˌhɪki/ *noun, pl* **-eys** [*count*] *US, informal* **:** an object or device whose name you do not know or have forgotten • I need one of those *doohickeys* [=*thingamajigs, whatchamacallits*] with the long handles.

[1]**doom** /ˈduːm/ *noun* [*noncount*]

1 : very bad events or situations that cannot be avoided • The sailors had a sense/feeling of (impending) *doom* as the storm approached. [=they sensed or felt that something very bad was going to happen] • The ***prophets of doom*** [=people who predict that bad things will happen] say that the Internet will kill off print newspapers. • The papers are filled with stories of ***gloom and doom***.

2 : death or ruin • the story of a mysterious creature who lures travelers to their *doom* • Prepare to ***meet your doom***. [=*die*] • The poor economy ***spelled doom*** for many small businesses. [=many small businesses would fail because of the poor economy]

[2]**doom** *verb* **dooms; doomed; doom·ing** [+ *obj*] **:** to make (someone or something) certain to fail, suffer, die, etc. • A criminal record will *doom* your chances of becoming a politician. — usually used as *(be) doomed* • The plan *was doomed* from the start. • The treaty *is doomed* [=*destined*] to failure/fail. • If no one rescues us, we *are doomed*. • a project *doomed* by the poor/weak economy • The species *is doomed* to extinction.

– doomed *adj* • a *doomed* plan/mission/ship

doom·say·er /ˈduːmˌsejɚ/ *noun, pl* **-ers** [*count*] **:** someone who predicts that bad things will happen • Don't listen to the *doomsayers*.

dooms·day /ˈduːmzˌdeɪ/ *noun* [*singular*] **:** the day the world ends or is destroyed • a warning that *doomsday* is near • *doomsday* predictions • The book explores a ***doomsday scenario*** in which an asteroid hits the Earth. • a ***doomsday machine*** [=a machine that will destroy the world] • It'll be like that ***from now until doomsday***. [=for a very long time; forever]

doom·ster /ˈduːmstɚ/ *noun, pl* **-sters** [*count*] *Brit, informal* **:** DOOMSAYER

door /ˈdoɚ/ *noun, pl* **doors** [*count*]

1 a : a movable piece of wood, glass, or metal that swings or slides open and shut so that people can enter or leave a room, building, vehicle, etc. • open/shut/slam/lock/bolt the *door* • I heard a knock on/at the *door*. • the bedroom/bathroom/cellar *door* • The car has four *doors*. = It's a four-*door* car. • Leave the package at the front/back/side *door*. [=the door at the front/back/side of the house, building, etc.] • Can you ***answer the door***? [=open the door to see who is knocking on the door or ringing the doorbell] • Is somebody ***at the door***? [=knocking on the door or ringing the doorbell] • Let me open the *door* for you. = (*US*) Let me ***get the door*** for you. • (*US*) Can you *get the door*? [=can you open or close the door for me?] My hands are full. • an ***exterior/outside door*** [=a door that can be used to enter or leave a building] • an ***interior door*** [=a door inside a building; a door that connects rooms] • a ***garage door*** [=a large door that covers the opening through which a car enters and leaves a garage] • turn/pull the ***door handle*** • a large brass ***door knocker*** [=*knocker*] — see also BACK DOOR, DUTCH DOOR, FRENCH DOOR, REVOLVING DOOR, STORM DOOR, TRAPDOOR **b :** a part of an object (such as piece of furniture or an appliance) that swings or slides open and shut • the cupboard/closet/refrigerator/oven *door*

2 : the opening for a door **:** the entrance to a room or building **:** DOORWAY • Please don't block the *door*. • I peeked

through the open *door*. ▪ He stood at/before the *door*. ▪ He greeted his guests as they ***came in/through the door***. = He greeted his guests ***at the door***. ▪ She ***walked out the door*** [=*left*] without saying goodbye. ▪ standing (just/right) ***inside/outside the door*** [=inside/outside the room, building, etc., near the door]
3 : a house, building, apartment, office, etc. — used with an adverb to indicate where something is in relation to something else ▪ She lives in a house two ***doors down/up*** from me. [=there is one house between our houses] ▪ The library is a ***few doors down*** from the bank. [=there are several buildings between the library and the bank] ▪ We grew up ***two doors apart***. [=with one house/apartment between our houses/apartments] ✧ If you do something ***(from) door to door***, you do it at each of the houses, apartments, or buildings in an area. ▪ Girl Scouts are selling cookies *door to door*. = Girl Scouts are ***going door to door*** selling cookies. ▪ She *went (from) door to door* looking for her cat. — see also DOOR-TO-DOOR, NEXT DOOR
4 — used especially with *open* or *unlock* to describe an opportunity or possibility ▪ The grant will *open* new *doors* for our town. [=will give our town new opportunities] ▪ The discovery may *unlock* the *door* to a cure for the disease. ▪ The *door* is *open* (to you) if you want a better job. ▪ A good education can *open/unlock* the *door* of success. [=can make success possible] ▪ The patent on the product has expired, which ***leaves the door open for*** [=makes it possible for] other companies to make it. — see also OUT OF DOORS
at death's door see DEATH
behind closed doors see CLOSED
***close the door on* :** to no longer think about, consider, or accept (something) ▪ I'd like to *close the door on* that chapter in my life. ▪ The former senator says she hasn't *closed the door on* politics. ▪ Don't *close the door on* your options.
***close your doors* 1 :** to not allow someone to enter ▪ The country has *closed its doors* to immigrants. **2** *of a business or organization* **:** to close permanently : to stop operating ▪ The museum may be forced to *close its doors*. ▪ The store *closed its doors* (for the last time) last fall.
darken someone's door/doors see DARKEN
get your foot in the door see [1]FOOT
keep the wolf from the door see [1]WOLF
***lay the blame for (something) at someone's door* :** to blame someone for (something) ▪ They *laid the blame for* the book's failure *at my door*.
open doors for see [2]OPEN
open the door see [2]OPEN
***open your doors* 1 :** to allow someone to enter ▪ The country has *opened its doors* to immigrants. ▪ local churches that *open their doors* to the homeless in the winter months [=that let homeless people stay there] **2** *of a business or organization* **:** to open for business : to begin operating ▪ The new store will be *opening its doors* next month.
***show (someone) the door* :** to tell or force (someone) to leave ▪ We don't tolerate bad behavior. If you cause trouble, we'll *show you the door*. ▪ If the coach doesn't win this year, they'll *show him the door*. [=they'll fire him]
***show/see (someone) to the door* :** to go to the door with (someone who is leaving) ▪ My secretary will *show you to the door*. [=*show you out*]
– doorless *adj* ▪ a *doorless* cubicle

door·bell /ˈdoɚˌbɛl/ *noun, pl* **-bells** [*count*] **:** a bell inside a house or building that is rung usually by pushing a button beside an outside door ▪ We ***rang the doorbell*** until someone came to let us in.

do–or–die /ˈduːwɚˈdaɪ/ *adj*
1 *always used before a noun* **:** very determined ▪ Her *do-or-die* attitude is inspiring.
2 — used to describe a situation in which you have to do something or you will fail, lose, etc. ▪ With only 10 seconds left, this is a *do-or-die* situation for the team. If they don't score, the game is over. ▪ It is *do-or-die* for the team.

door·frame /ˈdoɚˌfreɪm/ *noun, pl* **-frames** [*count*] **:** a door's frame : the structure around the opening of a door

door·jamb /ˈdoɚˌʤæm/ *noun, pl* **-jambs** [*count*] **:** an upright piece that forms the side of a door's frame

door·keep·er /ˈdoɚˌkiːpɚ/ *noun, pl* **-ers** [*count*] **:** someone who guards a door and checks people to see if they are allowed to enter the building

door·knob /ˈdoɚˌnɑːb/ *noun, pl* **-knobs** [*count*] **:** a round handle that you turn to open a door — see pictures at DOOR, KNOB

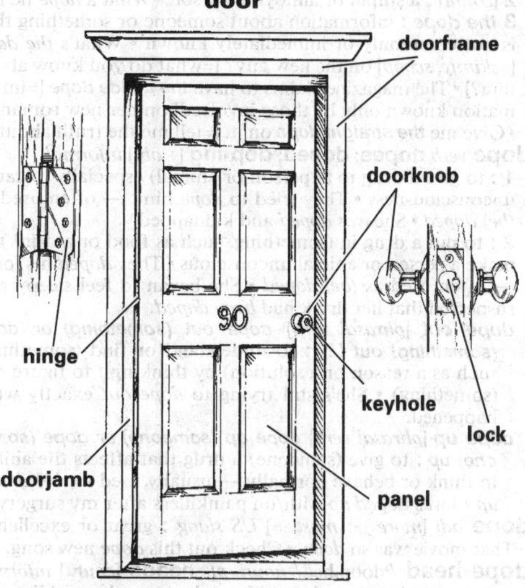

door·man /ˈdoɚˌmæn/ *noun, pl* **-men** /-ˌmɛn/ [*count*] **:** a person (especially a man) whose job is to stand next to the main door of a building (such as a hotel or apartment building) and help people by opening the door, calling taxis, etc.

door·mat /ˈdoɚˌmæt/ *noun, pl* **-mats** [*count*]
1 : a mat that you put on the floor or ground on one side of a door so that people can wipe the bottoms of their shoes on it
2 *informal* **:** someone who is treated badly by other people and does not complain ▪ She was tired of being a *doormat* and decided it was time to stand up for herself.

door·nail /ˈdoɚˌneɪl/ *noun*
(as) dead as a doornail see [1]DEAD

door·post /ˈdoɚˌpoʊst/ *noun, pl* **-posts** [*count*] **:** DOORJAMB

door prize *noun, pl* **~ prizes** [*count*] *US* **:** a prize that you get at a social event if you were given the winning ticket when you arrived

door·step /ˈdoɚˌstɛp/ *noun, pl* **-steps** [*count*] **:** a step or series of steps leading up to one of the doors that is used to enter or leave a building ▪ We sat on the *doorstep*. ▪ The police were at my *doorstep*. — often used figuratively ▪ The beach is right at your *doorstep*. [=the beach is very close] ▪ Bars and restaurants are on the *doorstep* of the hotel. [=bars and restaurants are very close to the hotel] — see picture at HOUSE

door·stop /ˈdoɚˌstɑːp/ *noun, pl* **-stops** [*count*]
1 : an object that is attached to a wall or the floor to prevent a door from hitting and damaging the wall
2 : something (such as a wedge or weight) that is used to hold a door open

door–to–door /ˌdoɚtəˈdoɚ/ *adj, always used before a noun* **:** going or made by going to each house, apartment, or building in an area ▪ a *door-to-door* salesman ▪ a *door-to-door* survey — see also *(from) door to door* at DOOR

door·way /ˈdoɚˌweɪ/ *noun, pl* **-ways** [*count*]
1 : the opening where a door is ▪ Please don't block the *doorway*. ▪ She stepped through the *doorway*. ▪ the castle's arched *doorways* — sometimes used figuratively ▪ We hope that these talks will be a *doorway* to peace. [=will lead to peace]
2 : the space in front of a door ▪ He stood in the *doorway*, wondering if he should go in. ▪ Homeless people sleep in the *doorways* of the shops.

door·yard /ˈdoɚˌjɑɚd/ *noun, pl* **-yards** [*count*] *US* **:** a yard next to the door of a house ▪ flowers blooming in the *dooryard* ▪ *dooryard* gardens

doo–wop /ˈduːˌwɑːp/ *noun* [*noncount*] **:** a style of popular music that involves singing nonsense syllables

doo·zy *or* **doo·zie** /ˈduːzi/ *noun, pl* **-zies** [*count*] *US, informal* **:** something that is unusually good, bad, big, severe, etc. ▪ They say the snowstorm tonight is going to be a *doozy*. ▪ Watch out for that first step. It's a *doozy*. ▪ Some of her comments have been real *doozies*. ▪ a *doozy* of a year

[1]**dope** /ˈdoʊp/ *noun, pl* **dopes** *informal*
1 [*noncount*] **:** an illegal drug (such as marijuana or heroin) ▪ They were caught smoking *dope*. ▪ a *dope* addict/dealer

2 [*count*] : a stupid or annoying person ▪ What a *dope* he is.
3 ***the dope*** : information about someone or something that is not commonly or immediately known ▪ What's *the dope* [=*skinny, scoop*] on the new guy? [=what do you know about him?] ▪ The magazine claims to have ***the inside dope*** [=information known only by those involved] on her new romance. ▪ Give me ***the straight dope*** on it. [=tell me the truth about it]

²**dope** *verb* **dopes; doped; dop·ing** [+ *obj*] *informal*
1 : to give a drug to (a person or animal) especially to cause unconsciousness ▪ They tried to *dope* him. — often used as *(be) doped* ▪ She *was doped* and kidnapped.
2 : to put a drug in (something, such as food or a drink) to make a person or animal unconscious ▪ They *doped* his food. — often used as *(be) doped* ▪ She began to feel sleepy and suspected that her drink had *been doped*.
dope out [*phrasal verb*] ***dope out (something) or dope (something) out US*** : to understand or find (something, such as a reason or a solution) by thinking : to figure out (something) ▪ She's still trying to *dope out* exactly what happened.
dope up [*phrasal verb*] ***dope up (someone) or dope (someone) up*** : to give (someone) a drug that affects the ability to think or behave normally — usually used as *(be) doped up* ▪ I *was doped up* with/on painkillers after my surgery.

³**dope** *adj* [*more ~; most ~*] *US slang* : great or excellent ▪ That movie was so *dope*. ▪ Check out this *dope* new song.

dope·head /ˈdoʊpˌhɛd/ *noun, pl* **-heads** [*count*] *informal* : a person who uses a lot of illegal drugs : a drug addict

dop·ey /ˈdoʊpi/ *adj* **dop·i·er; -est** [*also more ~; most ~*] *informal*
1 a : feeling the effects of a drug ▪ I'm still a little *dopey* from the painkillers. b : slow because you are tired ▪ After being up all night I was pretty *dopey* at work.
2 : foolish or stupid ▪ a *dopey* movie ▪ He's a little *dopey*.

doping *noun* [*noncount*] : the illegal use of a drug (such as a steroid) to improve an athlete's performance ▪ increased efforts to detect *doping* at the Olympic Games ▪ *doping* tests/scandals — see also BLOOD DOPING

dop·pel·gäng·er *or* **dop·pel·gang·er** /ˈdɑːpəlˌgæŋɚ/ *noun, pl* **-ers** [*count*]
1 : someone who looks like someone else ▪ I saw your *doppelgänger* [=(more commonly) *double*] yesterday.
2 *literary* : a ghost that looks like a living person ▪ In the story, the character is haunted by a *doppelgänger*.

Dopp·ler radar /ˈdɑːplɚ-/ *noun* [*noncount*] : a radar system that is used especially for predicting the weather

do–rag /ˈduːˌræg/ *noun, pl* **-rags** [*count*] *US, informal* : a piece of cloth that is worn on the head to cover the hair

dork /ˈdoɚk/ *noun, pl* **dorks** [*count*] *informal* : a person who behaves awkwardly around other people and usually has unstylish clothes, hair, etc. ▪ Back in high school, all the kids thought he was a *dork*. [=*nerd, loser*] ▪ I look like a complete *dork* in these clothes.
– dorky /ˈdoɚki/ *adj* **dork·i·er; -est** ▪ He's that tall, *dorky* [=*nerdy*] guy with the glasses.

dorm /ˈdoɚm/ *noun, pl* **dorms** [*count*] *informal* : DORMITORY ▪ We all lived in the same *dorm* during our sophomore year. ▪ my old *dorm* room

dor·mant /ˈdoɚmənt/ *adj* [*more ~; most ~*] : not doing anything at this time : not active but able to become active ▪ a *dormant* volcano ▪ The seeds will ***remain/lie dormant*** until the spring. ▪ Her emotions have *lain dormant* for many years.
– dor·man·cy /ˈdoɚmənsi/ *noun* [*noncount*] ▪ The volcano has been in a state of *dormancy* for many years. ▪ a period of *dormancy*

dor·mer /ˈdoɚmɚ/ *noun, pl* **-mers** [*count*]
1 : a window that is in a part of a building that sticks out from a slanted roof — called also *dormer window*; see picture at HOUSE
2 : the part of a building that contains a dormer
– dor·mered /ˈdoɚmɚd/ *adj* ▪ *dormered* windows

¹**dor·mi·to·ry** /ˈdoɚməˌtori, *Brit* ˈdɔːmətri/ *noun, pl* **-ries** [*count*]
1 *US* : a building on a school campus that has rooms where students can live ▪ a college *dormitory* [=*dorm, residence hall*]
2 : a large room with many beds where people can sleep ▪ Guests at the camp can stay in private cabins or for a smaller fee in the *dormitories*.

²**dormitory** *adj, always used before a noun, Brit* : lived in by people who go to another town or city to work ▪ a ***dormitory town*** [=(*US*) *bedroom community*]

dor·mouse /ˈdoɚˌmaʊs/ *noun, pl* **-mice** /-ˌmaɪs/ [*count*] : a European animal that looks like a small squirrel

dor·sal fin /ˈdoɚsəl-/ *noun, pl* **~ fins** [*count*] : a flat thin part on the back of some fish (such as sharks)

do·ry /ˈdori/ *noun, pl* **-ries** [*count*] : a boat that has a flat bottom and high sides and that is used especially for fishing

dos·age /ˈdoʊsɪʤ/ *noun, pl* **-ag·es** [*count*] : the amount of a medicine, drug, or vitamin that should be taken at one time or regularly during a period of time — usually singular ▪ Each pill/tablet has the *dosage* necessary to reduce pain and swelling. ▪ Some patients may benefit from a larger *dosage* of this medication. ▪ Do not exceed the recommended *dosage*. [=do not take more than doctors recommend]

¹**dose** /ˈdoʊs/ *noun, pl* **dos·es** [*count*]
1 : the amount of a medicine, drug, or vitamin that is taken at one time ▪ I've been taking the same *dose* for five years. ▪ a large *dose* of vitamin C
2 : an amount of a substance ▪ The drug is lethal even in small *doses*. ▪ a large *dose* of sugar ▪ a high *dose* of radiation
3 : an amount of something that a person experiences ▪ Her parents hoped a daily *dose* of hard work would keep her out of trouble. ▪ He needs a good *dose* of reality.
a dose of your own medicine see MEDICINE

²**dose** *verb* **doses; dosed; dos·ing** [+ *obj*]
1 : to give a dose of medicine to (someone or something) ▪ Most patients are *dosed* at 50 milligrams per day. — often + *with* ▪ She *dosed* herself daily *with* aspirin.
2 : to give an amount of a substance to (someone or something) — usually + *with* ▪ The victims were *dosed with* poison.
3 *US* : to add something to (something) — usually + *with* ▪ The pasta sauce was heavily *dosed with* garlic. [=there was a lot of garlic in the pasta sauce]

dosh /ˈdɑːʃ/ *noun* [*noncount*] *Brit, informal* : MONEY ▪ earning lots of *dosh*

doss /ˈdɑːs/ *verb* **doss·es; dossed; doss·ing** [*no obj*] *Brit, informal* : to sleep in a usually uncomfortable place that does not have a bed — usually + *down* ▪ We'll have to *doss down* [=*bed down*] in the car for the night.

doss·er /ˈdɑːsɚ/ *noun, pl* **-ers** [*count*] *Brit, informal* : a person who does not have a home to sleep in : a homeless person

doss–house /ˈdɑːsˌhaʊs/ *noun, pl* **-hous·es** [*count*] *chiefly Brit, informal* : FLOPHOUSE

dos·sier /ˈdɑːsˌjeɪ/ *noun, pl* **-siers** [*count*] : a group of papers that contain detailed information about someone or something ▪ the patient's medical *dossier* [=(more commonly) *file*] — often + *on* ▪ Investigators began compiling a *dossier on* him after he was suspected of stealing.

¹**dot** /ˈdɑːt/ *noun, pl* **dots** [*count*]
1 : a small round mark ▪ Put a *dot* over the *i*. ▪ The *dots* on the map represent cities. ▪ She said, "Go to Learners Dictionary dot com [=the Web site www.learnersdictionary.com] for more information." — see also POLKA DOT
2 : a small spot : a small area that is different in color from the main part ▪ You have a *dot* of ketchup on your shirt. ▪ As we drove away, the house became just a *dot* on the horizon.
3 : a short signal (such as a sound or a flash of light) that represents a letter or a part of a letter in Morse code ▪ The Morse code for the letter *v* is three *dots* and a dash. — compare ²DASH 7
connect the dots see CONNECT
on the dot *informal* : exactly at a particular time ▪ She arrived at 3 o'clock *on the dot*. = She arrived *on the dot of* 3. [=she arrived exactly at 3 o'clock]
since the year dot see YEAR

²**dot** *verb* **dots; dot·ted; dot·ting** [+ *obj*]
1 : to mark (something) with a dot ▪ Don't forget to *dot* the *i*. ✧ If you ***dot the/your i's and cross the/your t's***, you make sure that all of the small details in something have been completed. ▪ We need some extra time to *dot the i's and cross the t's* on the report.
2 : to appear at many different places on the surface of (something) ▪ Quaint cottages *dot* the countryside. ▪ The fields were *dotted* with wildflowers.
3 : to put a small amount of something on different parts of (a surface) ▪ *Dot* the cream all over your face.

dot·age /ˈdoʊtɪʤ/ *noun* [*noncount*] : the period of old age : the time when a person is old and often less able to remember or do things — often used after *in* or *into* ▪ He has become friendlier *in his dotage*. ▪ The actress continued to work well *into her dotage*.

dot–com /ˈdɑːtˌkɑːm/ *noun, pl* **-coms** [*count*] : a company that sells its products or services only on the Internet ▪ a successful *dot-com* — often used before another noun ▪ She owned thousands of dollars in *dot-com* stock. ▪ the *dot-com* boom of the 1990s

dote /ˈdoʊt/ *verb* **dotes; dot·ed; dot·ing**
dote on/upon [*phrasal verb*] ***dote on/upon (someone or something)*** : to give a lot of love or attention to (someone or something) ▪ She *doted on* her new grandchild.

doting *adj, always used before a noun* : showing a lot of love or attention ▪ the child's *doting* grandmother
– **dot·ing·ly** *adv* ▪ She smiled *dotingly* at the baby.

dot matrix *noun, pl* **~ matrices** *or* **~ matrixes** [*count*] : a pattern of dots that form letters, numbers, etc., on a computer screen or on something printed from a computer — often used before another noun ▪ *Dot matrix* printers have been largely replaced with laser printers.

dotted *adj* : covered with dots ▪ the plant's *dotted* green and white leaves [=leaves covered with green and white dots] ▪ He drew a ***dotted line***. [=a line that is made up of a series of dots] ✧ *Dotted line* is often used to refer to the place at the bottom of a document where a person signs and agrees to the terms in the document. ▪ Just sign on the *dotted line* and we'll have a deal.

dot·ty /ˈdɑːti/ *adj* **dot·ti·er; -est** *old-fashioned + informal* : somewhat crazy ▪ my *dotty* old grandparents

[1]**dou·ble** /ˈdʌbəl/ *adj*
1 : made of two parts that are similar or exactly the same ▪ One of the eggs had a *double* yolk. ▪ The truck crossed the *double* yellow line and entered the other lane. ▪ My name is "Allison," with a *double* "l." ▪ The band is releasing a ***double album*** [=a set of two records, CDs, etc.] later this year. ▪ Go through those ***double doors*** and walk to the end of the hall. ▪ He was convicted of a ***double murder***. [=of killing two people at the same time]
2 : having two very different parts or qualities ▪ He served a *double* [=*dual*] role as both king and servant to his people. ▪ His statement has a *double* meaning. [=it means two different things] ▪ In this film, he does ***double duty*** [=performs two roles] as both actor and director. ✧ If you are ***leading/living a double life***, you have something secret that you do as an important part of your life in addition to the regular parts of your life that other people know about. ▪ She was a newspaper reporter who *led/lived a double life* as a spy.
3 a : of a size that is twice as big as usual : of an amount that is twice as much as usual ▪ I'll have a *double* espresso, please. ▪ two *double* martinis ▪ a *double* dose of medicine ▪ Line the pan with a *double* thickness [=two layers] of foil. ▪ a *double* order of fries **b** : coming from two different places or sources ▪ families with a *double* income [=two incomes]
4 : two times as great or as many as the number, amount, size, etc., of something else ▪ The college had *double* [=*twice*] the number of expected applicants. ▪ Our new car was *double* the price of our last one. ▪ The CEO's salary is nearly *double* that of the president.
5 : made for two people to use ▪ We'll need a *double* room. ▪ a room with a ***double bed***
6 *of a flower* : having more than the usual number of petals ▪ *double* flowers/blooms

[2]**double** *verb* **dou·bles; dou·bled; dou·bling**
1 a [*+ obj*] : to cause (something) to become two times as great or as many ▪ They *doubled* their winnings. **b** [*no obj*] : to become two times as great or as many ▪ The price of the house had *doubled*. = The house had *doubled* in price.
2 [*no obj*] : to have a second job or use — *+ as* ▪ Our couch often *doubles as* a bed. [=is often used as a bed] ▪ Their living room *doubles as* a home office.
3 a [*+ obj*] : to bend or fold (something, such as a piece of paper) usually in the middle — usually *+ over* or *up* ▪ I *doubled over* the paper and put it in my notebook. **b** : to bend forward at the waist — usually *+ over* or *up* [*no obj*] We all *doubled over* laughing. ▪ He *doubled up* in pain. [*+ obj*] The pain *doubled* him *over*. = He was *doubled over* with pain.
4 [*no obj*] *baseball* : to hit a double : to hit the ball so that you can reach second base ▪ He *doubled* to left field.
double back [*phrasal verb*] : to turn around and return on the same path ▪ I'm going to *double back* to see if I dropped the ring on the way here.
double up [*phrasal verb*] : to share a place to live or sleep that is made for one person or one family ▪ Some families have to *double up* [=live with another family] in crowded apartments. ▪ There was only one bed, so we had to *double up*. — see also [2]DOUBLE 3b (above)
double up on [*phrasal verb*] ***double up on (something)*** : to use or do two times as many of (something) ▪ I'm going to have to *double up on* [=take twice as many] classes this semester if I want to graduate this year.

[3]**double** *noun, pl* **doubles**
1 [*singular*] : something that is two times the usual size, strength, or amount ▪ I'll have one more glass of vodka. Make it a *double*, please.
2 [*count*] **a** : someone who looks very much like another person ▪ People often tell me that I'm his *double*. **b** : a person who looks like an actor and takes the actor's place in some scenes in a movie or TV show ▪ The actress's *double* did all of the dangerous scenes. ▪ Can you tell if it's the actor or his *double* in that shot? — see also BODY DOUBLE, STUNT DOUBLE
3 [*count*] *baseball* : a hit in baseball that allows a batter to reach second base ▪ He hit a *double* in the eighth inning. — compare HOME RUN, SINGLE, TRIPLE
4 ***doubles*** [*plural*] : a game of tennis or a similar sport that is played between two pairs of players ▪ We play *doubles* with another couple on the weekends. ▪ He's my *doubles* partner.
5 [*count*] : a room in a hotel, inn, etc., for two people ▪ We'll need a *double* for the night. — compare SINGLE
double or nothing (*US*) *or Brit* ***double or quits*** : a gambling bet in which you could win two times as much money as you have already won or you could lose all of the money ▪ I won $20 on the first game but lost it on the second game going *double or nothing*.
on the double (*US*) *or Brit* ***at the double*** *informal* : very quickly : as soon as possible ▪ I need you back here *on the double*. [=*immediately*]

[4]**double** *adv*
1 : two times as many or as much ▪ The last question on the exam counts *double*. [=is worth twice as many points] ▪ I was charged/billed *double*. [=twice the usual amount]
2 : two times — usually used in combination ▪ I was ***double-charged/billed***. [=I was charged/billed twice for the same product or service]
bend double : to fold in the middle. ▪ I held on tight as my fishing rod *bent double*. ▪ He *bent double* [=*doubled over*] in pain. ✧ *Bend double* is used more frequently in British English than in U.S. English.
see double : to see two things when only one thing is present ▪ As her eyesight got worse, she began *seeing double*.
that goes double for *informal* — used to say that something you have just said about one person or thing relates even more strongly to another ▪ You're in trouble, Steven. And *that goes double for* you, John. [=you, John, are in even more trouble than Steven]

double agent *noun, pl* **~ agents** [*count*] : a spy who pretends to spy for one government while actually spying for another ▪ He was secretly working as a *double agent* for the Americans during the war.

dou·ble–bar·reled (*US*) *or Brit* **dou·ble–bar·relled** /ˌdʌbəlˈberəld/ *adj*
1 *of a gun* : having two tubes (called barrels) that bullets or pellets are shot through ▪ a *double-barreled* shotgun
2 *US* : having two parts or purposes ▪ She made a *double-barreled* announcement that she was both leaving the company and getting married. ▪ a *double-barreled* question

double bass *noun, pl* **~ basses** [*count*] : a very large musical instrument that is shaped like a violin — called also *contrabass*; see picture at STRINGED INSTRUMENT

double bill *noun, pl* **~ bills** [*count*] : two movies, plays, concerts, etc., that are seen one after the other — compare DOUBLE FEATURE

double bind *noun, pl* **~ binds** [*count*] : a very difficult situation that has no good solution — usually singular ▪ He finds himself caught in a *double bind*: By doing his job, he could end up hurting his family.

dou·ble–blind /ˌdʌbəlˈblaɪnd/ *adj, technical* — used to describe an experiment that is done so that neither the people who are doing the experiment nor the people who are the subjects of the experiments know which of the groups being studied is the control group and which is the test group ▪ a *double-blind* drug trial

double bogey *noun, pl* **~ -geys** [*count*] *golf* : a score that is two more than the official standard score for a particular hole : a score of two strokes over par on a hole ▪ He made/scored a *double bogey* on the fourth hole.
– **double bogey** *verb* **~ -geys; ~ -geyed; ~ -geying** [*+ obj*] ▪ He *double bogeyed* the fourth hole.

double boiler *noun, pl* ~ **-ers** [*count*] : a pair of deep cooking pans that fit together so that the contents of the top pan can be cooked or heated by boiling water in the bottom pan ▪ Melt the chocolate in a *double boiler.* — see picture at KITCHEN

double bond *noun, pl* ~ **bonds** [*count*] *technical* : a chemical bond in which two atoms in a molecule share two pairs of electrons — compare SINGLE BOND, TRIPLE BOND

double–book *verb* **-books; -booked; -book·ing** [+ *obj*]
1 : to make plans for (someone or something) to be in two different places at the same time ▪ My husband and I are *double-booked* for/on Friday night. [=we are scheduled to go to two different places at the same time on Friday night]
2 : to promise a room, seat, table, etc., to two different people or groups at the same time ▪ The airline *double-booked* my seat. = The airline *double-booked* me. — compare OVERBOOK

D

dou·ble–breast·ed /ˌdʌbəlˈbrɛstəd/ *adj, of a coat or jacket* : having two rows of buttons ▪ He is wearing a tan *double-breasted* jacket. — compare SINGLE-BREASTED

dou·ble–check /ˌdʌbəlˈʧɛk/ *verb* **-checks; -checked; -check·ing** : to check (something) again in order to be certain [+ *obj*] Be sure to *double-check* your answers before handing in your test. [*no obj*] I thought I mailed the letter already, but let me *double-check.*
– double check *noun, pl* ~ **checks** [*count*] ▪ Did you do a *double check* of the list?

double chin *noun, pl* ~ **chins** [*count*] : a fold of fat that some people have under their chin and that looks like a second chin

double–click *verb* **-clicks; -clicked; -click·ing** : to choose something on a computer screen by quickly pressing a button on a computer mouse or other device two times [+ *obj*] *Double-click* the icon to start the program. [*no obj*] — often + *on* ▪ *Double-click on* the icon.
– double click *noun, pl* ~ **clicks** [*count*] ▪ A *double click* with the mouse will start the program.

double cream *noun* [*noncount*] *Brit* : HEAVY CREAM

dou·ble–cross /ˌdʌbəlˈkrɑːs/ *verb* **-cross·es; -crossed; -cross·ing** [+ *obj*] : to cheat or deceive (someone) especially by doing something that is different from what you said you would do ▪ I thought I could trust her, but she *double-crossed* me.
– double cross *noun, pl* ~ **crosses** [*count*] ▪ He accused his manager of a dirty *double cross.* ▪ lies and *double crosses*
– dou·ble–cross·er *noun, pl* **-ers** [*count*] ▪ They're a couple of dirty *double-crossers.*

double date *noun, pl* ~ **dates** [*count*] : an activity (such as going to the movies or going out to eat) that two couples do together ▪ Would you two ladies like to go on a *double date* with me and my friend?
– double–date *verb* **-dates; -dated; -dat·ing** [*no obj*] ▪ My boyfriend and I often *double-date* with a couple that we met in college.

dou·ble–deal·ing /ˌdʌbəlˈdiːlɪŋ/ *noun* [*noncount*] : the practice of pretending to do or think one thing while really doing or thinking something different : dishonest or deceptive behavior ▪ His *double-dealing* [=*duplicity, deceitfulness*] has caused many of his former friends to distrust him.
– dou·ble–deal·er /ˌdʌbəlˈdiːlɚ/ *noun, pl* **-ers** [*count*]
– double–dealing *adj* ▪ He could no longer trust his *double-dealing* friend.

dou·ble–deck·er /ˌdʌbəlˈdɛkɚ/ *noun, pl* **-ers** [*count*] : something that has two levels or layers ▪ The bus we rode on was a *double-decker.* — usually used before another noun ▪ We took a tour of London on a *double-decker* bus. ▪ *double-decker* trains ▪ a *double-decker* sandwich — compare SINGLE-DECKER, TRIPLE-DECKER

double digits *noun* [*plural*] *chiefly US* : a number or percentage that is 10 or greater ▪ They won the game by *double digits.* [=by 10 or more] ▪ The state's unemployment rate remains in the *double digits.* — called also *double figures*
– dou·ble–dig·it /ˌdʌbəlˈdɪʤɪt/ *adj, always used before a noun* ▪ the state's *double-digit* unemployment rate ▪ *double-digit* price increases

double dribble *noun, pl* ~ **dribbles** [*count*] *basketball* : an illegal action that happens when a player dribbles the ball with two hands at the same time or starts to dribble again after stopping

double Dutch *noun* [*noncount*]
1 *US* : the activity of jumping over two jump ropes that two people are swinging in circles in opposite directions ▪ The girls were playing *double Dutch* on the sidewalk.
2 *chiefly Brit, informal* : language that cannot be understood ▪ It was all *double Dutch* [=*nonsense, gibberish*] to me.

dou·ble–edged /ˌdʌbəlˈɛʤd/ *adj*
1 : having two sharp edges ▪ a *double-edged* knife
2 : having two different and opposite parts ▪ a *double-edged* problem/strategy
3 : able to be understood in two different ways ▪ *double-edged* remarks ▪ a *double-edged* description

double–edged sword *noun, pl* ~ **swords** [*count*]
1 : a sword that has two sharp edges
2 : something that has both good and bad parts or results ▪ Freedom of expression can be a *double-edged sword.*

dou·ble en·ten·dre /ˈdʌbəlɑnˈtɑːndrə/ *noun, pl* ~ **-dres** [*count*] : a word or expression that can be understood in two different ways with one way usually referring to sex ▪ The song's title is a *double entendre.*

double fault *noun, pl* ~ **faults** [*count*] *tennis* : two bad serves that result in the loss of a point

double feature *noun, pl* ~ **-tures** [*count*] *US* : two movies that are shown one after the other — compare DOUBLE BILL

double figures *noun* [*plural*] : DOUBLE DIGITS

double glazing *noun* [*noncount*] *technical* : two layers of glass that are set in a window to keep heat inside and reduce noise
– double–glazed *adj* ▪ *double-glazed* windows

dou·ble·head·er /ˌdʌbəlˈhɛdɚ/ *noun, pl* **-ers** [*count*] *chiefly US* : two games (especially baseball games) that are played one after the other on the same day ▪ The two teams will meet in a *doubleheader* this Saturday.

double helix *noun, pl* ~ **helices** *also* ~ **helixes** [*count*] *technical* : the shape formed by two parallel lines that twist around each other ✧ The strands of DNA are arranged in a double helix.

double–hung window *noun, pl* ~ **-dows** [*count*] *US* : a window that can be opened either by sliding the bottom half up or by sliding the top half down — called also (*Brit*) *sash window*; see picture at WINDOW

double jeopardy *noun* [*noncount*] *US, law* : the act of causing a person to be put on trial two times for the same crime ▪ constitutional protections against *double jeopardy*

dou·ble–joint·ed /ˌdʌbəlˈʤoɪntəd/ *adj* : having a joint that allows body parts to move in ways that are not typical ▪ His right shoulder is *double-jointed.* ▪ *double-jointed* fingers

double knit *noun, pl* ~ **knits**
1 [*noncount*] : a type of cloth that is made with two sets of needles and has two connected layers
2 [*count*] *US* : a piece of clothing that is made of double knit ▪ 1960s-style *double knits*
– dou·ble–knit *adj* ▪ a pair of polyester *double-knit* pants

double negative *noun, pl* ~ **-tives** [*count*] *grammar* : a clause that has two negative words (such as "nothing" and "don't") when only one is necessary ✧ *Double negatives* are usually considered incorrect in English. ▪ "I didn't do nothing" is a *double negative.* If you want to be correct, you should say "I didn't do anything."

dou·ble–park /ˌdʌbəlˈpɑɚk/ *verb* **-parks; -parked; -park·ing** : to park (a car or other vehicle) beside a row of vehicles that are already parked on the side of the street [+ *obj*] — usually used as *(be) double-parked* ▪ My truck *is double-parked* outside. [*no obj*] If you *double-park,* you will get a ticket.

double play *noun, pl* ~ **plays** [*count*] *baseball* : a play in which the team in the field causes two runners to be put out ▪ The batter hit into a *double play.* ▪ They ***turned a double play*** to end the inning. — compare TRIPLE PLAY

dou·ble–quick /ˈdʌbəlˌkwɪk/ *adj, always used before a noun, chiefly Brit, informal* : extra fast or quick ▪ They've been working in *double-quick* time [=they've been working very quickly] to finish the project.
– double–quick *adv* ▪ We have to get this done *double-quick.*

double–sided *adj* : having two sides that can be used ▪ Fill out this *double-sided* form. ▪ *double-sided* adhesive tape

dou·ble–space /ˌdʌbəlˈspeɪs/ *verb* **-spac·es; -spaced; -spac·ing** : to write or type (a paper, letter, etc.) so that each line of words is followed by a line without words [+ *obj*] — often used as *(be) double-spaced* ▪ All essays must *be* typed and *double-spaced.* [*no obj*] Be sure to *double-space.* It makes reading much easier.

dou·ble·speak /ˈdʌbəlˌspiːk/ *noun* [*noncount*] *disapproving*

: language that can be understood in more than one way and that is used to trick or deceive people • political *doublespeak*

double standard *noun, pl* ~ **-dards** [*count*] : a situation in which two people, groups, etc., are treated very differently from each other in a way that is unfair to one of them • She argued that society applies a *double standard* in dealing with women who commit adultery.

double take *noun, pl* ~ **takes** [*count*] : an act of quickly looking at something that is surprising or unusual a second time after looking at it a moment earlier • His parents ***did a double take*** when he came home with a tattoo.

dou·ble–talk /ˈdʌbəlˌtɑːk/ *noun* [*noncount*] *disapproving* : language that uses many words but has very little meaning • We asked for a clear and honest answer, but all we got was a bunch of meaningless *double-talk*.

double–team /ˈdʌbəlˌtiːm/ *verb* **-teams; -teamed; -team·ing** [+ *obj*] *US, sports* : to block or guard (an opponent) with two players at one time • He was *double-teamed* [=two players guarded him] in the first half of the game.

double time *noun* [*noncount*] : payment of a worker at two times the usual rate • She was paid *double time* [=she was paid twice as much as usual] for working on Thanksgiving. — compare TIME AND A HALF

double vision *noun* [*noncount*] : a problem with the eyes that causes a person to see two objects when only one is present • He wore special glasses to correct his *double vision*.

double wham·my /-ˈwæmi/ *noun, pl* ~ **-mies** [*count*] *informal* : a situation that is bad in two different ways : a situation in which two bad conditions exist at the same time or two bad things happen one after the other • With the cold weather and the high cost of heating fuel, homeowners were hit with a *double whammy* this winter.

dou·ble–wide /ˌdʌbəlˈwaɪd/ *noun, pl* **-wides** [*count*] *US* : a mobile home that is made of two units that have been connected together side by side — called also *double-wide trailer*

dou·bly /ˈdʌbli/ *adv, always used before an adjective*
1 : much more than usual or previously : to a much higher degree than usual • We did the test again because we wanted to be *doubly* [=*extra, especially, very*] sure the results were accurate. • I had to work *doubly* [=*twice as*] hard after my partner left the competition.
2 : in two ways : for two reasons • Her grades and musical talent make her parents *doubly* proud of her.

[1]**doubt** /ˈdaʊt/ *verb* **doubts; doubt·ed; doubt·ing** [+ *obj*]
1 : to be uncertain about (something) : to believe that (something) may not be true or is unlikely • She began to *doubt* [=*question*] everything he said. • I have always *doubted* the existence of life on other planets. • No one *doubts* that the mission will be a success. • I seriously *doubt* my parents will let me go. • "Do you think you can come tonight?" "I *doubt* it."
2 : to have no confidence in (someone or something) • I began to *doubt* [=*question*] my own judgment. • She *doubted* his ability to succeed. • He said he could do it, but I couldn't help *doubting* him.
– doubt·er *noun, pl* **-ters** [*count*] • He did everything he could to reassure the *doubters*.

[2]**doubt** *noun, pl* **doubts** : a feeling of being uncertain or unsure about something [*noncount*] I still have moments of *doubt*. • There can be little *doubt* that smoking is bad for your health. • There is no *doubt* [=*question*] in my mind that he is best candidate. • These mistakes ***cast/throw doubt on*** her ability. = They ***cast/throw into doubt*** her ability. [=they make people question or lose confidence in her ability] • (*US*) The results of the study have been ***called into doubt***. [=people are expressing doubts about the results] — often + *about* • She was filled with *doubt* [=*uncertainty*] *about* the future. • The evidence against her leaves little room for *doubt about* her guilt. [=the evidence shows that she is guilty] [*count*] I had a nagging *doubt* in the back of my mind. — often + *about* • He still has *doubts about* his chances of success. • I've always had my *doubts about* him. • Two separate studies have ***raised doubts about*** the car's safety.
beyond doubt ◊ If something is *beyond doubt*, it is definitely true. • The test results proved *beyond* (all/any) *doubt* that he was not the child's father. • If she is to be found guilty, the charges against her must be proved ***beyond a reasonable doubt***. • I knew, ***beyond a shadow of a doubt***, that everything was going to be okay.
in doubt : in a state of being uncertain or unsure • The outcome was *in doubt* [=not known with certainty] until the final seconds of the game. • The future of the company remains very much *in doubt*. • When/if *in doubt*, please contact us with your questions.
no doubt : without doubt or with very little doubt — used when you are making a statement that you think is certainly or almost certainly true • She was *no doubt* [=*certainly, doubtless, unquestionably*] the smartest person in her class. • *No doubt* many readers will find the book too long. • By now, you have *no doubt* heard the news. • "He'll probably blame someone else." "*No doubt*." [=I agree that he'll blame someone else]
no doubt about it — used to stress that something is true • *No doubt about it*, the fans are disappointed in the team.
the benefit of the doubt see [1]BENEFIT
without (a) doubt — used to stress that something is true • They are, *without doubt*, the nicest people I've ever met.

doubt·ful /ˈdaʊtfəl/ *adj* [*more* ~; *most* ~]
1 : uncertain or unsure about something • I tried to reassure them, but they remained *doubtful*. • She gave him a *doubtful* look. [=a look that shows doubt] — often + *about* or *of* • They were *doubtful about* the benefits of the new system. = They were *doubtful of* its benefits.
2 : not likely to be true : not probable • He made the *doubtful* [=*dubious*] claim that he had never been sick a day in his life. • The truth of the statements was *doubtful*. — often + *that, if*, or *whether* • It's highly *doubtful* [=*unlikely, improbable*] *that* anyone will notice. • It is *doubtful if* she really meant what she said. • The situation is bad and it's *doubtful whether* it will get better soon.
3 : likely to be bad : not worthy of trust • The water available in the village is of *doubtful* [=*questionable*] quality. • Their decisions were based on data of *doubtful* accuracy.
4 : not certain : unknown or undecided • The outcome of the election remains *doubtful*. • The company is facing a *doubtful* future.
– doubt·ful·ly *adv* • She looked at him *doubtfully*.

doubting Thom·as /-ˈtɑːməs/ *noun, pl* ~ **-as·es** [*count*] *somewhat old-fashioned* : someone who rarely trusts or believes things before having proof : a doubtful or skeptical person • She kept trying, hoping to prove all those *doubting Thomases* wrong.

doubt·less /ˈdaʊtləs/ *adv* [*more* ~; *most* ~] : without doubt or with very little doubt — used when you are making a statement that you think is certainly or almost certainly true • She was *doubtless* [=*unquestionably, no doubt*] the smartest person in her class. • There will *doubtless* be many more issues to deal with before this is over. • The car accident will *doubtless* result in a lawsuit.

douche /ˈduːʃ/ *noun, pl* **douch·es** [*count*] : a liquid that a woman squirts into her vagina to wash it; *also* : an object used to squirt such a liquid into the vagina
– douche *verb* **douches; douched; douch·ing** [*no obj*] • She advises her patients not to *douche* because doing so can lead to infections.

dough /ˈdoʊ/ *noun, pl* **doughs**
1 [*count, noncount*] : a mixture of flour, water, and other ingredients that is baked to make bread, cookies, etc.
2 [*noncount*] *informal* : MONEY • I don't have much *dough*.

dough·nut *or chiefly US* **do·nut** /ˈdoʊˌnʌt/ *noun, pl* **-nuts** [*count*]
1 : a piece of sweet fried dough that is often shaped like a ring • powdered *doughnuts* • a jelly *donut*
2 : something that has a round shape like a doughnut • drawing *doughnuts* in the sand • a foam *doughnut*

dough·ty /ˈdaʊti/ *adj, always used before a noun* **dough·ti·er; -est** [*also more* ~; *most* ~] *old-fashioned* : brave, strong, and determined • a *doughty* fighter

doughy /ˈdowi/ *adj* [*more* ~; *most* ~] : resembling dough: such as **a** : not completely baked • High humidity can make your loaves turn out *doughy*. **b** : not hard or firm • a *doughy* consistency **c** : pale in color and unhealthy • her *doughy* [=*pasty*] white skin

Doug·las fir /ˌdʌgləs-/ *noun, pl* ~ **firs** [*count*] : a very tall evergreen tree that grows in the western U.S.

dou·la /ˈduːlə/ *noun, pl* **-las** [*count*] *medical* : a woman whose job is to give advice and comfort to a woman who is giving birth

dour /ˈduɚ, ˈdawɚ/ *adj* **dour·er; -est** [*also more* ~; *most* ~] *formal* : serious and unfriendly • a *dour* politician • a *dour* manner • She had a *dour* expression on her face. : silent and gloomy • the *dour* mood of the crowd

– **dour·ly** *adv* [*more* ~; *most* ~] – **dour·ness** *noun* [*noncount*]

douse /ˈdaʊs/ *verb* **dous·es; doused; dous·ing** [+ *obj*]
1 a : to cause (a fire) to stop burning by pouring or spraying water on it : to extinguish (a fire) with water • It took firefighters 15 minutes to *douse* the blaze. • She managed to *douse* the flames with water. **b :** to turn off (a light) • Don't forget to *douse* the lights before coming to bed.
2 : to cover (someone or something) with a liquid — usually + *in* or *with* • The books were *doused in* gasoline and set on fire. • She *doused* herself *with* perfume.

D

[1]**dove** /ˈdʌv/ *noun, pl* **doves** [*count*]
1 : a small wild bird that is related to pigeons ✧ Doves are often used as a symbol of peace.
2 : a person who does not want war and does want peace • The President sided with the *doves* and worked to avoid war. — compare HAWK
– **dov·ish** /ˈdʌvɪʃ/ *adj* [*more* ~; *most* ~] • a *dovish* politician

[2]**dove** *past tense and past participle of* [1]DIVE

dove·cote /ˈdʌvˌkoʊt/ *also* **dove·cot** /ˈdʌvˌkɑːt/ *noun, pl* **-cotes** *also* **-cots** [*count*] : a small house or box for pigeons to live in

[1]**dove·tail** /ˈdʌvˌteɪl/ *noun, pl* **-tails** [*count*] : a type of joint that is used to connect two pieces of wood together — called also *dovetail joint*

[2]**dovetail** *verb* **-tails; -tailed; -tail·ing**
1 [+ *obj*] **:** to join (two pieces of wood) with dovetail joints • The carpenter *dovetailed* (together) the corners (of the boards) for extra strength.
2 [*no obj*] *formal* **:** to fit together in a pleasing or satisfying way • She found that the positions of the party and her own opinions *dovetailed* [=*agreed, corresponded*] nicely. — often + *with* • His research *dovetails with* other similar studies.

Dow /ˈdaʊ/ *noun*
the Dow *US* **:** DOW JONES INDUSTRIAL AVERAGE

dow·a·ger /ˈdawɪʤɚ/ *noun, pl* **-gers** [*count*]
1 : a woman who has inherited property or a title from her dead husband — often used before another noun • the *dowager* Duchess
2 : an old woman who is very formal or serious • The estate is owned by a wealthy *dowager*.

dowdy /ˈdaudi/ *adj* **dowd·i·er; -est** [*or more* ~; *most* ~] **:** having a dull or uninteresting appearance : not attractive or stylish • She played a *dowdy* old woman in the film. • a *dowdy* [=*frumpy, drab*] gray dress

dow·el /ˈdawəl/ *noun, pl* **-els** [*count*] **:** a pin or peg that is used for joining together two pieces of wood, metal, plastic, etc. • wooden/steel *dowels*

Dow Jones Industrial Average /ˌdaʊˌʤoʊnz-/ *noun*
the Dow Jones Industrial Average **:** the daily average of the stock prices of a group of large American companies

[1]**down** /ˈdaʊn/ *adv*
1 a : from a higher to a lower place or position • The land slopes *down* to the sea. • Please pull *down* the window shade. = Please pull the window shade *down*. • I'll come *down* [=*downstairs*] in a minute. • She called *down* to her friends in the street below. • They set/put the cake *down* on the table. • Lay *down* your book for a minute. • We watched the sun go *down*. **b :** in a low position or place • Keep your head *down*. • We keep our wine collection *down* in the basement. • What's going on *down* there?
2 : to or toward the ground or floor • He fell *down* and hurt his knee. • Climb *down* out of that tree! • He knocked him *down* with one punch. • Don't look *down*! • Brightly colored flags hang *down* from the ceiling.
3 : to a lying or sitting position • Please, sit *down*. • Lie *down* and go to sleep.
4 a : to or toward the south • They went *down* to Florida for two weeks. • We drove *down* from New York. • The weather's much warmer ***down south***. **b** *informal* **:** to or toward a place that is thought of as below or away from another place • She drove *down* to our house. • Come on *down* and see us sometime. **c :** to or toward a place that is away from the speaker • He is heading *down* to the store. • Would you mind moving (further) *down* so that we can sit here, too?
5 : on a piece of paper • Write *down* everything he says. • Take *down* this number. • Did you get that *down*?
6 : at a lower or lesser important position in a list or series • Supporting public education seems to be ***far down*** [=*low*] on the government's agenda. • Cleaning my house ranks pretty *far down* on my list. [=there are many other things I'd rather do] — **opposite** UP
7 : to a lower or lesser degree, level, or rate • Slow *down*. • Could you turn the volume *down*, please? • We should give them some time to cool *down*. • We should wait for the winds to calm *down* before we set sail. • The company's stock went *down* last week. • The team was 10 points *down* [=it had 10 fewer points than the other team] in the third quarter. • The price of gasoline is starting to go *down* again. — **opposite** UP
8 : to a smaller or weaker state • We have scaled *down* our plans for the new building. • Some people want to use the budget surplus to pay *down* the national debt. [=to make payments that will reduce the a national debt] • They have cut/whittled *down* the number of candidates. — **often** + *to* • He finally got his report *down to* three pages.
9 : to a state of failure or defeat • The school board voted the budget *down* 55 to 15. [=it voted not to pass the budget]
10 : in a way that causes someone or something to be less able to move • Remember to tie *down* the load. • They had to strap the patient *down* to his bed.
11 : in a thorough or complete way • The car needs to be washed *down*. • Hose the dog *down* outside.
12 : to the place where a person or thing is or came from • They use dogs to hunt *down* escaped prisoners. • He chased the ball *down* and threw it to third base. • Every attempt to pin *down* the cause of the disease has proved unsuccessful. • I haven't been able to track *down* that quotation.
13 : from a past time • This vase has been handed *down* in our family for several generations. • Most of these stories were passed *down* by word of mouth.
14 : as a first payment : as a down payment • We put 10 percent *down* [=we made a 10 percent down payment] on the house. • Buy a car now with no money *down*. [=without making a down payment]
15 : in the stomach • The baby is having trouble keeping food *down*.
16 *Brit* **:** away from a school or university • He was sent *down* for misconduct and never earned his degree.
down in the mouth see [1]MOUTH
down to **1 :** in a way that includes even (the smallest or least important part) • Our work must be accurate *down to* the last detail. • They knew everything about him *down to* the cologne he wore. **2 :** to the last person or thing that can be used • It looks like it's *down to* you and me. [=we are the last two people that are available] • I'm *down to* my last dollar. [=I have only one dollar left]
down with — used to say that you do not like something and want it to stop or fail • *Down with* racism! • *Down with* the government!
keep your head down see [1]HEAD
let your hair down see HAIR
put your foot down see [1]FOOT
up and down see [1]UP
with your pants down see PANTS

[2]**down** *adj*
1 : in a low place or position • The window shades were *down*. • The candy is *down* on the bottom shelf. **:** on the ground or floor • There was a pile of dirty clothes *down* on the floor.
2 : going downward • She took the *down* escalator.
3 : lower in price or value • These changes should help keep prices *down*. • Stocks are *down* again today.
4 : less than an earlier or normal level • Attendance has been *down* lately. • New construction is *down* sharply this month.
5 : having a lower level of activity • Our business is having a *down* year. • a *down* market/economy
6 : having fewer points than an opponent • His team was *down* by 10 points [=trailed by 10 points] in the third quarter. • We're *down* two runs.
7 : not operating properly : not able to function • We can't get any work done while the network/system is *down*.
8 [*more* ~; *most* ~] **:** sad or unhappy • You look pretty *down*. What's the matter? • She was feeling *down*.
9 : finished or completed • I've got eight *down* and only two more to go. [=I've finished eight and have two more to do]
10 : learned in a complete way • Do you all have your lines *down*? [=*memorized*] • We have our routine ***down pat*** [=we have mastered our routine; we can do it easily]
11 : having something written or recorded in an official way • You are *down* for two tickets. [=you are signed up to get two tickets]
12 *US slang* — used to say that you understand or approve of something; usually + *with* • I told them I wasn't *down with* lying to people. [=I don't think that lying to people is right] • Yeah, I'm *down with* that.

13 *baseball* — used to say how many outs have been made in the inning by the team that is batting ▪ There are now two (men) *down* in the top of the third inning.
14 *American football* — used to say that the ball or the player who has the ball is on the ground and the play has ended ▪ The runner was *down* on the fify-yard line. ▪ The ball was *down*.
down for the count see [2]COUNT
down on *informal* : having a bad opinion of someone or something ▪ My coach has been *down on* me lately.
down on your luck see [1]LUCK
down with : affected by (an illness) ▪ She has been *down with* the flu for a week.
when the chips are down see [1]CHIP

[3]down *prep*
1 : from a higher to a lower part of (something) ▪ Sweat dripped *down* her neck. ▪ The children ran *down* the hill. ▪ She fell *down* the stairs. ▪ He climbed *down* the ladder. ▪ He spilled mustard *down* the front of his shirt. ▪ Her hair hung loosely *down* her back.
2 : along the course or path of (something) ▪ Go *down* the road/street and turn left. ▪ We grew up *down* the block from each other. ▪ There's a bridge three miles *down* the river. [=three miles in the same direction that the water is going in the river] ▪ ships sailing *down* the coast [=along the coast usually toward the south] ▪ The bathroom is halfway *down* the hall on the right. ▪ His pitches were right *down* the middle of the plate. ▪ I usually part my hair *down* the center. ▪ He is still pacing ***up and down*** [=back and forth in] the room.

[4]down *noun, pl* **downs**
1 [*count*] : a period or state of failure, trouble, etc. — usually plural ▪ The company has had more *downs* than ups this year. ▪ We have had our ***ups and downs***.
2 *American football* : one of a series of four chances that a team has to move the ball forward 10 yards in order to keep the ball and begin a new series [*noncount*] He caught the ball on second/third *down*. [*count*] a series of *downs* — see also FIRST DOWN
— compare [5]DOWN, DOWNS

[5]down *noun* [*noncount*]
1 : small and very soft feathers ▪ goose *down* ▪ a pillow filled with *down* — often used before another noun ▪ a *down* pillow/comforter/jacket
2 : small soft hairs ▪ The young man had just a light trace of *down* on his cheeks. ▪ the *down* of a peach
— compare [4]DOWN, DOWNS

[6]down *verb* **downs; downed; down·ing** [+ *obj*]
1 : to cause (something) to fall to the ground ▪ He *downed* [=*shot down*] four enemy planes. ▪ The storm *downed* power lines throughout the city. ▪ a *downed* bird/plane ▪ a large number of *downed* power lines
2 *informal* : to eat or drink (something) especially quickly ▪ She quickly *downed* [=*took, swallowed*] the pills I gave her. ▪ They were *downing* beers and watching the game on TV.
3 *American football* : to cause (a football) to be out of play ▪ The quarterback *downed* the ball to stop the clock.
4 *informal* : DEFEAT ▪ Smith *downed* Jones in the first round of the tournament. ▪ The Cardinals *downed* the Braves by a score of 5–2.

down–and–dirty *adj* [*more* ~; *most* ~] *chiefly US, informal*
1 : involving methods that are regarded as harsh, unfair, etc. ▪ *down-and-dirty* business practices ▪ *down-and-dirty* competition
2 : dirty and in poor condition ▪ The story takes place on the *down-and-dirty* [=*seedy, decrepit*] streets of the city.
3 : relating to harsh and unpleasant subjects in an honest and often shocking way ▪ I told them the *down-and-dirty* truth. ▪ a *down-and-dirty* interview
4 : basic and practical ▪ We have to get down to the *down-and-dirty* [=*nitty-gritty*] details.
get down and dirty : to do or say harsh and unpleasant things ▪ Sometimes you have to *get down and dirty* with your competitors.

down–and–out *adj* [*more* ~; *most* ~] *informal* : very poor and without hope : having no money, job, etc. ▪ No one would help him when he was *down-and-out*. ▪ a movie about a *down-and-out* musician living on the streets

down–at–the–heels (*chiefly US*) *or chiefly Brit* **down–at–heel** *adj* : looking or seeming cheap or poor and dirty or worn ▪ We got a room at a *down-at-the-heels* [=*dingy, seedy*] motel. ▪ a *down-at-heel* traveler

[1]down·beat /ˈdaʊnˌbiːt/ *noun, pl* **-beats** [*count*] *music*
1 : the downward movement that a conductor makes to show which note is played with the greatest stress or force
2 : the first beat of a measure of music

[2]downbeat *adj* [*more* ~; *most* ~] : sad or depressing : not happy or hopeful ▪ Many will be surprised by the movie's unusually *downbeat* [=*pessimistic, gloomy*] ending. — opposite UPBEAT

down·cast /ˈdaʊnˌkæst, *Brit* ˈdaʊnˌkɑːst/ *adj*
1 [*more* ~; *most* ~] : not happy, confident, or hopeful ▪ I've never seen her looking so *downcast*. [=*depressed, unhappy, sad*] ▪ There were a lot of *downcast* faces in the crowd.
2 *of eyes* : looking downward ▪ *downcast* eyes

down·court /ˈdaʊnˈkoɚt/ *adv* : into or toward the opposite end of a basketball court ▪ He passed the ball *downcourt*. ▪ running *downcourt*

down·draft /ˈdaʊnˌdræft, *Brit* ˈdaʊnˌdrɑːft/ *noun, pl* **-drafts** [*count*] *technical* : a downward flow of air ▪ a strong *downdraft* from the thunderstorm

down·er /ˈdaʊnɚ/ *noun, pl* **-ers** [*count*] *informal*
1 : a drug that makes the body relax; *especially* : BARBITURATE ▪ I took some *downers* to help me sleep. — compare UPPER
2 : something that is unpleasant or depressing ▪ "His cat just died." "Oh, that's a real *downer*." ▪ Our conversation about death was a bit of a *downer*.

down·fall /ˈdaʊnˌfɑːl/ *noun, pl* **-falls** [*count*]
1 : a sudden loss of power, happiness, success, etc. ▪ She was blamed for the company's *downfall*. [=*decline, ruin*] ▪ Their *downfall* was the result of several bad decisions.
2 : something that causes failure ▪ In the end, gambling proved to be his *downfall*. [=*ruin, undoing*] ▪ Bad decision-making was their *downfall*.

down·field /ˈdaʊnˈfiːld/ *adv, sports* : into or toward the part of the field toward which a team is headed ▪ He threw/kicked the ball *downfield*.
— **downfield** *adj* ▪ a *downfield* pass

[1]down·grade /ˈdaʊnˌgreɪd/ *verb* **-grades; -grad·ed; -grad·ing** [+ *obj*]
1 : to give (someone or something) a lower rank or grade ▪ If you confess to the crime, we may be able to *downgrade* [=*reduce*] the charge. ▪ The restaurant was *downgraded* from three to two stars. ▪ a soldier *downgraded* [=*demoted*] in rank for misconduct — opposite UPGRADE
2 : to cause (someone or something) to be thought of as less valuable, important, etc. ▪ She didn't intend to *downgrade* the importance of her colleague's work.

[2]downgrade *noun, pl* **-grades** [*count*] *chiefly US*
1 : an area or surface that goes downward : a downward slope ▪ a steep *downgrade*
2 : an occurrence in which something becomes worse, less valuable, etc. ▪ a *downgrade* in the company's stock prices ▪ slight *downgrades* in quality

down·heart·ed /ˈdaʊnˈhɑɚtəd/ *adj* [*more* ~; *most* ~] : not happy, confident, or hopeful ▪ Everyone was *downhearted* [=*sad, depressed*] about the decision to close the factory.

[1]down·hill /ˌdaʊnˈhɪl/ *adv*
1 : toward the bottom of a hill or mountain ▪ It is easier to ride a bike *downhill* than uphill.
2 : toward a worse state ▪ Her career/health is heading *downhill*. ▪ After his divorce, he ***went downhill*** fast. ▪ The service has *gone downhill* under the new owner.

[2]down·hill /ˈdaʊnˌhɪl/ *adj*
1 : going or sloping down toward the bottom of a hill or mountain ▪ The second half of the hike is mostly *downhill*. ▪ a *downhill* path/slope
2 *not used before a noun* **a** : not difficult : easy to do, deal with, etc. ▪ The worst part is over. It's all *downhill* from here. **b** : becoming worse or less successful ▪ The first part of the movie was pretty good, but after that it was all *downhill*. ▪ His career has been all *downhill* in recent years.
3 *always used before a noun* : relating to or used in a kind of skiing that is done down a mountain or hill instead of over the countryside ▪ I enjoy *downhill* skiing. ▪ a *downhill* skier/competition ▪ *downhill* skis — compare [1]CROSS-COUNTRY 3

[3]down·hill /ˈdaʊnˌhɪl/ *noun, pl* **-hills** [*count*] : a downhill skiing race — usually singular ▪ He finished first in the *downhill*.

down–home /ˈdaʊnˌhoʊm/ *adj* [*more* ~; *most* ~] *US* : simple and informal in a way that reminds people of life in a small town or in the country especially in the southern U.S. ▪ She's very famous but there is something quiet and *down-home* about her. ▪ *down-home* cooking

D

Dow·ning Street /ˈdaʊnɪŋ-/ *noun* [*singular*] : the British Prime Minister or the British government • *Downing Street* and the White House are currently discussing the issue. ✧ The term *Downing Street* comes from the address of the official home of the British Prime Minister at Number 10 Downing Street in London.

[1]**down·load** /ˈdaʊnˌloʊd/ *verb* **-loads; -load·ed; -load·ing** *computers* : to move or copy (a file, program, etc.) from a usually larger computer system to another computer or device [+ *obj*] He *downloaded* the files onto his computer. • She *downloads* songs from/off the Internet. [*no obj*] The software *downloads* quickly. • The new program makes *downloading* faster. — compare UPLOAD
– **down·load·able** /ˈdaʊnˌloʊdəbəl/ *adj* • *downloadable* files

[2]**download** *noun, pl* **-loads** *computers*
1 : an act of moving or copying a file, program, etc., from a usually larger computer system to another computer or device [*count*] The modem is capable of high-speed *downloads*. • The *download* will take about three minutes. [*noncount*] The program is available for *download* at the company's Web site.
2 [*count*] : a file, program, etc., that is downloaded • The *downloads* are all in this folder.

down–mar·ket /ˈdaʊnˌmɑɚkət/ *adj* [*more* ~; *most* ~] *chiefly Brit* : made for or appealing to people who do not have much money • a *down-market* [=(*US*) *downscale*] store/hotel; *also* : of low quality • *down-market* tabloids/products
– **down–market** *adv* • The store is ***going/moving down-market***. [=starting to sell products for people with less money]

down payment *noun, pl* ~ **-ments** [*count*] : a first payment that you make when you buy something with an agreement to pay the rest later • She made a 10 percent *down payment* on the car. • We put/made a *down payment* on the house.

downpipe *noun, pl* **-pipes** [*count*] *Brit* : DOWNSPOUT

down·play /ˈdaʊnˌpleɪ/ *verb* **-plays; -played; -play·ing** [+ *obj*] : to make (something) seem smaller or less important • She *downplayed* [=*played down*] her role in the research. • Athletes often *downplay* their injuries.

down·pour /ˈdaʊnˌpoɚ/ *noun, pl* **-pours** [*count*] : a sudden heavy rain — usually singular • We got caught in a torrential *downpour*.

down·right /ˈdaʊnˌraɪt/ *adv* : to the fullest degree : completely or totally • The movie was *downright* stupid/bad/scary. • It's very difficult, if not *downright* impossible. • They were *downright* overjoyed.
– **downright** *adj, always used before a noun* • a *downright* [=*absolute, outright*] lie • I was met with *downright* hostility.

down·riv·er /ˈdaʊnˈrɪvɚ/ *adv* : in the direction in which a river flows : DOWNSTREAM • The raft drifted *downriver*.

downs /ˈdaʊnz/ *noun* [*plural*] : a high area of land that has low hills and no trees • Sheep graze on the grassy *downs*. • the South *Downs* of Southern England ✧ *Downs* often appears in the names of racetracks that are used for horseracing. • His horse won the Kentucky Derby at Churchill *Downs*.

Down's /ˈdaʊnz/ *noun* [*noncount*] *medical* : DOWN SYNDROME • He has *Down's*. • (*informal*) a *Down's* baby

[1]**down·scale** /ˈdaʊnˌskeɪl/ *verb* **-scales; -scaled; -scal·ing** [+ *obj*] *US* : to make (something) smaller • The company has *downscaled* production. [=the company is making fewer products] • The festival will have to be *downscaled* this year.

[2]**downscale** *adj* [*more* ~; *most* ~] *US* : relating or appealing to people who do not have much money • an apartment in a *downscale* neighborhood • The company aims to reach a more *downscale* market with its new stores; *also* : of low quality • *downscale* [=(*chiefly Brit*) *down-market*] products

down·shift /ˈdaʊnˌʃɪft/ *verb* **-shifts; -shift·ed; -shift·ing** [*no obj*]
1 : to put the engine of a vehicle into a lower gear • You can *downshift* to slow the car down. — opposite UPSHIFT
2 : to begin to work or happen at a level that is slower, easier, or more relaxed • Several employees will be *downshifting* from full-time to part-time. [=will start working less than the regular number of hours] • Expect the real estate market to *downshift* in the next few months. [=expect that fewer people will be buying and selling houses, buildings, etc.]
– **downshift** *noun, pl* **-shifts** [*count*] • a *downshift* into first gear • *downshifts* in economic growth

down·side /ˈdaʊnˌsaɪd/ *noun, pl* **-sides** [*count*] : a part of something that you do not want or like : a drawback or disadvantage • He could find no *downside* to the car. • ***On the downside*** [=when you consider the disadvantages], the car does not have much trunk space. — often + *of* • The *downside of* the camera is that the batteries have to be replaced often. — opposite UPSIDE

down·size /ˈdaʊnˌsaɪz/ *verb* **-siz·es; -sized; -siz·ing**
1 : to make (something) smaller [+ *obj*] They have *downsized* the car's engine in the new model. [*no obj*] We *downsized* to a smaller apartment last year. [=we moved to a smaller apartment]
2 : to make a company smaller and more efficient by reducing the number of workers [*no obj*] The company is planning to *downsize* next year. [+ *obj*] The company will be *downsized* next year. • The company has *downsized* [=*reduced*] its staff. • She was *downsized* [=she was dismissed from her job] after 15 years with the company.
– **downsizing** *noun, pl* **-ings** [*count*] He lost his job in a recent *downsizing* at the company. • corporate *downsizings* [*noncount*] problems caused by corporate *downsizing*

down·slide /ˈdaʊnˌslaɪd/ *noun, pl* **-slides** [*count*] *US* : a situation in which something decreases or becomes worse — usually singular • an economic *downslide* [=(more commonly) *downturn*] • Her career has been on a/the *downslide*.

down·slope /ˈdaʊnˌsloʊp/ *adv, US* : toward the bottom of a hill or mountain : down a slope • We slowly walked *downslope*. [=(more commonly) *downhill*] — opposite UPSLOPE
– **downslope** *adj* • *downslope* winds – **downslope** *noun, pl* **-slopes** [*count*] • We'll stop to rest on the *downslope*.

down·spout /ˈdaʊnˌspaʊt/ *noun, pl* **-spouts** [*count*] *US* : a pipe that carries rainwater from the roof of a building to the ground — called also *drainpipe*, (*Brit*) *downpipe*; see picture at HOUSE

Down's syndrome *noun* [*noncount*] *medical* : DOWN SYNDROME

down·stage /ˈdaʊnˈsteɪʤ/ *adv* : toward the front part of a stage • The actress walked *downstage* to address the audience.

[1]**down·stairs** /ˈdaʊnˈsteɚz/ *adv* : on or to a lower floor of a building • He ran *downstairs* to answer the door. • He lives *downstairs* from us. • "Where are the kids?" "They're *downstairs*."

[2]**down·stairs** /ˈdaʊnˌsteɚz/ *adj, always used before a noun* : located on a lower, main, or first floor of a building • the *downstairs* bathroom • There are five *downstairs* rooms.

[3]**down·stairs** /ˈdaʊnˈsteɚz/ *noun*
the downstairs : the lower and usually main floor of a building • *The downstairs* needs to be cleaned. • We painted *the downstairs*.

down·state /ˈdaʊnˌsteɪt/ *noun* [*noncount*] *US* : the southern part of a state • He is from *downstate*.
– **downstate** *adj* • *downstate* New York – **down·state** /ˈdaʊnˈsteɪt/ *adv* • She moved *downstate* last year. • He lives *downstate*.

down·stream /ˈdaʊnˈstriːm/ *adv* : in the direction in which a stream, river, etc., flows • The next town is six miles *downstream*. • float *downstream*

down·swing /ˈdaʊnˌswɪŋ/ *noun, pl* **-swings** [*count*]
1 : a situation in which something decreases or becomes worse • The company is experiencing a financial *downswing*. [=(more commonly) *downturn*] • The company's sales are ***on a/the downswing***. [=are decreasing]
2 *golf* : a forward and downward movement of a club as a golfer hits a shot

Down syndrome /ˈdaʊn-/ *noun* [*noncount*] *medical* : a condition that someone is born with and that causes below average mental abilities and problems in physical development. — called also *Down's*, *Down's syndrome*

down·time /ˈdaʊnˌtaɪm/ *noun* [*noncount*]
1 *US* : time when you are not working or busy • After a busy day at work, I look forward to some *downtime* at home. • The kids napped during their *downtime*.
2 : time during which a computer or machine is not working • We need to minimize network *downtime*.

down–to–earth *adj* [*more* ~; *most* ~]
1 : informal and easy to talk to • a *down-to-earth* person • He's very *down-to-earth* despite his fame.
2 : practical and sensible • *down-to-earth* advice • Students liked the teacher's *down-to-earth* approach.

[1]**down·town** /ˈdaʊnˌtaʊn/ *noun, pl* **-towns** [*count*] *chiefly US* : the main or central part of a city or town : the part of a city or town where there are tall buildings, stores, offices, etc. — usually singular • I live close to *downtown*. • The city's

downtown is thriving. — compare UPTOWN

[2]**downtown** /ˌdaʊnˈtaʊn/ *adv, chiefly US* : to, toward, or in the main or central part of a city or town • Does this bus go *downtown*? • We went shopping *downtown*.

– **downtown** *adj, always used before a noun* • *downtown* stores/restaurants • *downtown* Boston

down·trod·den /ˈdaʊnˈtrɑːdn/ *adj, somewhat formal* : without hope because of being treated badly by powerful people, governments, etc. • *downtrodden* people • They were poor and *downtrodden*.

the downtrodden : downtrodden people • He showed compassion for *the downtrodden*.

down·turn /ˈdaʊnˌtən/ *noun, pl* **-turns** [*count*] : a situation in which something (such as business or economic activity) decreases or becomes worse — usually singular • an economic *downturn* = a *downturn* in the economy • There's been a *downturn* in the housing market.

[1]**down·ward** (*chiefly US*) /ˈdaʊnwəd/ *or chiefly Brit* **downwards** /ˈdaʊnwədz/ *adv*

1 : from a higher place or level to a lower place or level • The mountain streams flow *downward* to the lake. • Heating costs rise as the temperature heads *downward*. [=as the weather becomes colder]

2 : toward the ground, floor, etc. : not up • The hawk flew *downward*. • The arrow pointed *downward*. • Mud covered his pants from the knees *downward*.

3 : toward people with less power, money, etc. • Everyone in the company, from the president *downward*, has been involved in these decisions. [=the president and all the employees with less authority, power, etc., have been involved]

4 : to a smaller amount : to a lower number • We received an estimate, but the number has since been revised *downward*.

[2]**downward** *adj, always used before a noun*

1 : moving or going from a higher place or level to a lower place or level • a *downward* slope • Sales continued their *downward* trend. • Her life was in a ***downward spiral*** [=a process of constantly getting worse] as she battled depression and addiction.

2 : moving or going toward the ground, floor, etc. • the hawk's *downward* flight

3 : changing to a smaller amount or lower number • the *downward* revision of an estimate

down·wind /ˈdaʊnˈwɪnd/ *adv* : in the direction that the wind is moving • We sailed *downwind*. — often + *of* or *from* • His clothes smelled like smoke after standing *downwind of* the campfire. • Pollution from the factory affects those who live *downwind from* it.

– **downwind** *adj* • the *downwind* side of a campfire

downy /ˈdaʊni/ *adj* **down·i·er; -est**

1 — used to describe small, soft feathers or something that resembles such feathers • the down feathers of a baby bird • her soft *downy* hair

2 : covered or filled with small, soft feathers or something like them • *downy* chicks/leaves/pillows

dow·ry /ˈdaʊri/ *noun, pl* **-ries** [*count*] : money or property that a wife or wife's family gives to her husband when the wife and husband marry in some cultures

dowse /ˈdaʊz/ *verb* **dows·es; dowsed; dows·ing** [*no obj*] : to search for an underground supply of water by using a special stick that leads you to it — usually + *for* • *dowse for* water

– **dows·er** *noun, pl* **-ers** [*count*]

dowsing rod *noun, pl* ~ **rods** [*count*] : DIVINING ROD

doy·en /ˈdojən/ *noun, pl* **-ens** [*count*] *formal* : a person who has a lot of experience in or knowledge about a particular profession, subject, etc. • a fashion *doyen* • He is considered the *doyen* of political journalists/journalism.

doy·enne /dɔɪˈɛn/ *noun, pl* **-ennes** [*count*] : a woman who has a lot of experience in or knowledge about a particular profession, subject, etc. • the *doyenne* of the fashion industry

doz. *abbr* dozen

doze /ˈdoʊz/ *verb* **doz·es; dozed; doz·ing** [*no obj*] : to sleep lightly especially for a short period of time • He was *dozing* [=*napping*] on the sofa when I got home.

doze off [*phrasal verb*] : to fall asleep especially for a short period of time • A few students *dozed off* [=*nodded off, dropped off*] during the movie.

– **doze** *noun* [*singular*] • He drifted into a light *doze*.

doz·en /ˈdʌzn/ *noun, pl* **doz·ens** *or* **dozen**

1 *pl* ***dozen*** [*count*] : a group of 12 people or things • a *dozen* eggs [=12 eggs] • half a *dozen* eggs = a half-*dozen* eggs [=six eggs] • two *dozen* roses [=24 roses] • We'll need a couple *dozen* hot dogs for the party. [=we will need about 24 hot dogs] • A few *dozen* people were at the party. [=about 36 people were at the party] • She has published ***several dozen*** [=many, probably more than 36] poems. — see also BAKER'S DOZEN

2 ***dozens*** [*plural*] : large numbers of people or things • People entered the park ***by/in the dozens*** [=large groups of people entered the park] — often + *of* • *Dozens of* [=*many*] people were at the park. • The shop sells ***dozens and dozens of*** [=very many] kinds of tea.

a dime a dozen see DIME

six of one, half a dozen of the other see SIX

dozy /ˈdoʊzi/ *adj* **doz·i·er; -est** [*also more* ~; *most* ~] *informal*

1 : tired or sleepy • I feel *dozy*.

2 *Brit* : stupid or silly • He's a *dozy* old chap. • He's a little *dozy*.

dpi *abbr* dots per inch • an image with 72 *dpi* [=an image that is made of 72 dots of ink in each inch]

Dr. (*US*) *or Brit* **Dr** *abbr* **1** doctor • *Dr.* Jones **2** drive • The reception will be held at 27 Chestnut *Dr.*

drab /ˈdræb/ *adj* **drab·ber; drab·best** [*also more* ~; *most* ~] : not bright or colorful : too plain or dull to be interesting • *drab* buildings/clothes/offices/rooms • He lives a *drab* life. — see also OLIVE DRAB

– **drab·ly** *adv* • a *drably* dressed woman – **drab·ness** *noun* [*noncount*] • the *drabness* of the buildings

drabs /ˈdræbz/ *noun*

dribs and drabs see DRIBS

dra·co·ni·an /dreɪˈkoʊnijən/ *adj* [*more* ~; *most* ~] *formal* + *disapproving* : very severe or cruel • The editorial criticizes the *draconian* measures being taken to control the spread of the disease. • *draconian* punishments

[1]**draft** /ˈdræft, *Brit* ˈdrɑːft/ *noun, pl* **drafts**

1 [*count*] : a version of something (such as a document) that you make before you make the final version • The published poem differs quite a bit from earlier *drafts*. • I just completed a ***rough draft*** [=a first version that needs a lot of editing and rewriting] of my speech. • The ***final draft*** [=the final version] is due tomorrow.

2 *US* **draft** *or Brit* **draught** [*count*] : cool air moving in a closed space (such as a room) • You may want to seal the windows with plastic to stop *drafts*.

3 [*count*] *US* **a** : a system in which young people are required to join the armed forces of a country for a period of service — usually singular • There is debate about whether the country needs a *draft*. • Congress reinstated ***the draft*** — often used before another noun • He burned his *draft* card. • He's a ***draft dodger***. [=a person who illegally avoids joining the armed forces] **b** : a system by which professional sports teams choose players from college or high school teams — usually singular • He was chosen in the first round of the *draft*. — often used before another noun • *draft* day • He was a first-round *draft* pick.

4 *US* **draft** *or Brit* **draught** [*count*] *formal* + *literary* : an act of drinking something; *also* : the amount swallowed at one time • He took a big *draft* of beer.

5 *US* **draft** *or Brit* **draught** [*count*] : a beer that is stored in and poured from a large container • The bar has 15 different *drafts* on tap.

6 : an order for the payment of money from a person or bank to another person or bank [*count*] The bank issued a *draft*. [*noncount*] Payment must be made by ***bank draft***

7 *US* **draft** *or Brit* **draught** *technical* **a** : the depth of water that a boat needs in order to be able to float [*count*] — usually singular • a boat with a deep/shallow *draft* [*noncount*] a ship with 45 feet of *draft* **b** [*noncount*] : the depth of the water in a river, channel, etc. • a canal/channel that provides 60 feet of *draft*

8 ***draught*** [*count*] *Brit* : [2]CHECKER

on draft (*US*) *or Brit* ***on draught*** *of beer* : stored in and poured from a large container instead of in individual bottles or cans • The bar has beer *on draft*. [=*on tap*]

[2]**draft** *adj, always used before a noun*

1 *US* **draft** *or Brit* **draught** *of an animal* : used for pulling heavy loads • *draft* animals/horses

2 *US* **draft** *or Brit* **draught** *of beer* : stored in and poured from a large container • *draft* beer

3 : not yet in the final form • a *draft* law/constitution/treaty

[3]**draft** *verb* **drafts; draft·ed; draft·ing** [+ *obj*]

1 : to make a version of (something, such as a document or plan) that will need more work in order to be finished • He *drafted* a speech. • The two countries are *drafting* a treaty.

2 a : to choose (someone) for a special purpose • The drama club *drafted* three teenagers to be in the parade. — often used as *(be/get) drafted* • A few of us *were drafted* to help distribute flyers. • He *got drafted* for the fall play. **b** *US* **:** to officially order (someone) to join the armed forces • The legislature debated *drafting* more soldiers. — often used as *(be/get) drafted* • He *was drafted* for the war. • He *got drafted* into the army. **c** *US* **:** to choose (someone) to play on a professional sports team • The new rule prohibits teams from *drafting* players under 18. — often used as *(be/get) drafted* • He *was drafted* in the first round. • He *got drafted* by the Jets.

draft·ee /ˌdræfˈtiː, *Brit* ˌdrɑːfˈtiː/ *noun, pl* **-ees** [*count*] *US*
1 : someone who is officially ordered to join the armed forces
2 : someone who is chosen to play on a professional sports team

draft·er /ˈdræftɚ, *Brit* ˈdrɑːftə/ *noun, pl* **-ers** [*count*]
1 : someone who writes an official or legal document (such as a law) based on the ideas that have been officially discussed • the *drafters* of the amendment/constitution
2 : a person whose job is to make drawings that will be used to make machines, buildings, etc. **:** DRAFTSMAN
3 : someone who makes a version of something (such as a document or plan) that will need more work in order to be finished • She spoke to the *drafter* of the report.

drafts·man /ˈdræftsmən, *Brit* ˈdrɑːftsmən/ *noun, pl* **drafts·men** /ˈdræftsmən, *Brit* ˈdrɑːftsmən/ [*count*]
1 *US* ***draftsman*** *or Brit* ***draughtsman*** **:** a person whose job is to make drawings that will be used to make machines, buildings, etc.
2 : someone who writes an official or legal document (such as a law) based on the ideas that have been officially discussed • the *draftsmen* [=(more commonly) *drafters*] of the U.S. Constitution
3 *US* ***draftsman*** *or Brit* ***draughtsman*** **:** an artist who draws well • Her use of color is not outstanding, but she is a first-rate *draftsman*.
– drafts·man·ship (*US*) *or Brit* **draughts·man·ship** /ˈdræftsmənˌʃɪp, *Brit* ˈdrɑːftsmənˌʃɪp/ *noun* [*noncount*] • Her work shows sophisticated *draftsmanship*.

drafts·per·son (*US*) *or Brit* **draughts·per·son** /ˈdræftsˌpɚsn̩, *Brit* ˈdrɑːftsˌpəːsn/ *noun, pl* **drafts·peo·ple** /ˈdræftsˌpiːpəl, *Brit* ˈdrɑːftsˌpiːpəl/ [*count*] **:** DRAFTSMAN • She was one of the bill's *draftspeople*.

drafty (*US*) *or Brit* **draughty** /ˈdræfti, *Brit* ˈdrɑːfti/ *adj* **draft·i·er; -est :** having cold air moving through in a way that is unpleasant or uncomfortable • a *drafty* room • The house is very *drafty*.
– draft·i·ness (*US*) *or Brit* **draught·i·ness** /ˈdræftinəs, *Brit* ˈdrɑːftinəs/ *noun* [*noncount*]

[1]drag /ˈdræg/ *verb* **drags; dragged; drag·ging**
1 [+ *obj*] **:** to pull (someone or something that is heavy or difficult to move) • She *dragged* one of the other tables over to ours. • Firefighters *dragged* the man to safety. • One of the parents eventually *dragged* the screaming toddler out of the store. — often used figuratively • She practically had to *drag* her husband to the opera. • You *drag* me all the way out here only to tell me that the store is closed!? • She was ***dragged kicking and screaming*** into the family business. [=she was forced to join the family business]
2 a [*no obj*] **:** to move along the ground, floor, etc., while being pulled • Your scarf is *dragging*. • The broken muffler *dragged* behind the car. • The dog's leash was *dragging* along the ground. **b** [+ *obj*] **:** to cause (something) to move along the ground, floor, etc., by pulling it • The child is always *dragging* his blanket. • The puppy ran up to us, *dragging* her leash behind her.
3 a *always followed by an adverb or preposition* [+ *obj*] **:** to force (yourself) to move or to go to a place when you are tired, busy, etc. • He *dragged* himself up the stairs and climbed into bed. • Can you *drag* yourself away from that computer? • I could barely *drag* myself out of bed. [=I had a hard time waking up] **b** [*no obj*] **:** to go or move more slowly than others • Quit *dragging*—walk faster. • The nation's economy is *dragging* [=(more commonly) *lagging*] behind the rest of the world.
4 [+ *obj*] **:** to bring (an unpleasant or complicated subject, fact, etc.) into a discussion or argument — + *up* or *into* • Do you always have to *drag* [=*dredge*] *up* the past? • They can't seem to avoid *dragging* religion *into* politics. [=mentioning religion in a discussion about politics]
5 [*no obj*] **:** to go on for a long time in a way that seems slow and boring • The movie was good, but I thought it *dragged* at the end. • The hours seemed to *drag* (by) as the day went on.
6 [+ *obj*] **:** to pull a net or set of hooks through (a river, lake, pond, etc.) in order to search for or collect something • Searchers used three boats to *drag* the river. • They *dragged* [=*trawled*] the waters for fish.
7 [+ *obj*] *computers* **:** to move (items on a computer screen) by using a computer mouse • *Drag* the file/picture to this folder.

drag down [*phrasal verb*] **1** ***drag (someone) down*** *or* ***drag down (someone)*** **:** to force (someone) into a bad situation or condition • We cannot let our enemies *drag* us *down* to their level. [=we should not let their bad behavior convince us to behave badly] **2** ***drag (someone) down*** **:** to make (someone) unhappy • You can't let her bad moods *drag* you *down*. **3** ***drag down (something)*** *or* ***drag (something) down*** **:** to make (something) lower in amount or quality • High energy costs are *dragging down* profits.

drag into [*phrasal verb*] ***drag (someone) into (something)*** **:** to involve (a person, group, etc.) in (a difficult or complicated situation) • I'm sorry for *dragging* you *into* this. • Don't *drag* the children *into* this. • We will not let the country be *dragged into* another war. — see also [1]DRAG 4 (above)

drag on [*phrasal verb*] *disapproving* **:** to go on for a long time **:** to progress slowly • The meeting *dragged on* until almost midnight. • The lawsuit *dragged on* for years.

drag out [*phrasal verb*] **1** ***drag out (something)*** *or* ***drag (something) out*** **:** to cause (something) to take more time than necessary • He *dragged out* the speech much too long. • Stop *dragging* the story *out* and get to the point. **2** ***drag (something) out of (someone)*** **:** to force (something, such as a confession) from (someone) **:** to make (someone) tell you (something) • The teacher eventually *dragged* a confession *out of* one of the students. • Doctors sometimes have to *drag* information *out of* their patients.

drag someone's name through the mud **:** to publicly say false or bad things that harm someone's reputation • My opponent has *dragged my name through the mud*.

drag your feet *also* ***drag your heels*** **:** to avoid doing something for a long time because you do not want to do it • Quit *dragging your feet* and make a decision! • After months of *dragging its heels*, Congress voted on the bill.

like something the cat dragged in see CAT

Look what the cat dragged in! see CAT

[2]drag *noun, pl* **drags**
1 [*singular*] *informal* **:** someone or something that is boring, annoying, or disappointing • My parents can be such a *drag*. They won't let me do anything. • These meetings are a total *drag*.
2 [*singular*] *informal* **:** someone or something that makes action or progress slower or more difficult — usually + *on* • High taxes have been a *drag on* the economy. • The senator should resign before she becomes a *drag on* the party. [=before she causes people to vote for candidates in another political party]
3 [*count*] *informal* **:** the act of breathing in smoke from a cigarette, cigar, pipe, etc. • Let me have a *drag* from your cigarette. • He ***took a long drag on*** the cigarette.
4 [*noncount*] *physics* **:** the force of air that pushes against an airplane, a car, etc., as it moves forward • The jet's sleek design reduces *drag*.

in drag **:** wearing clothes that are usually worn by the opposite sex • They went to the party (dressed) *in drag*. • She's *in drag*. [=dressed as a man]

— see also MAIN DRAG

drag·net /ˈdrægˌnɛt/ *noun, pl* **-nets** [*count*]
1 : a series of actions that are done by the police in order to catch criminals • Nine suspects were caught in the police *dragnet*.
2 : a net that is pulled along the bottom of a river, lake, pond, etc., to search for or collect something

drag·on /ˈdrægən/ *noun, pl* **-ons** [*count*] **:** an imaginary animal that can breathe out fire and looks like a very large lizard with wings, a long tail, and large claws

drag·on·fly /ˈdrægənˌflaɪ/ *noun, pl* **-flies** [*count*] **:** a large insect that has a long thin body and four wings and that is often seen near water — see color picture on page C10

dragon lady *noun, pl* **~ ladies** [*count*] *chiefly US, informal + disapproving* **:** a woman who is often angry or cruel especially when people do not do what she wants • The new boss is a real *dragon lady*.

[1]dra·goon /drəˈguːn/ *noun, pl* **-goons** [*count*] *chiefly Brit* : a soldier especially in the past who rode a horse and carried a gun

[2]dragoon *verb* **-goons; -gooned; -goon·ing**
dragoon into [*phrasal verb*] ***dragoon (someone) into (something)*** : to force or convince (someone) to do (something) • Somehow I was *dragooned into* working overtime.

drag queen *noun, pl* **~ queens** [*count*] *informal* : a homosexual man who dresses as a woman especially to entertain people

drag race *noun, pl* **~ races** [*count*] : a contest in which people race cars at very high speeds over a short distance
– **drag racer** *noun, pl* **~ -ers** [*count*] • He is one of the best *drag racers* in the country. – **drag racing** *noun* [*noncount*] • He likes *drag racing.*

drag·ster /ˈdrægstɚ/ *noun, pl* **-sters** [*count*] : a car that is made for drag racing

drag strip *noun, pl* **~ strips** [*count*] : a place where drag races happen

[1]drain /ˈdreɪn/ *verb* **drains; drained; drain·ing**
1 a [+ *obj*] : to remove (liquid) from something by letting it flow away or out • *Drain* the canned tomatoes before adding them to the pot. • The swamp has been *drained.* — often + *from* • *Drain* the fat/grease *from* the pan. • We have to *drain* some water *from* the pool. **b** [*no obj*] *of a container* : to become empty of a liquid I was waiting for the bathtub to *drain.* • The sink won't *drain.* **c** [*no obj*] *of a liquid* : to flow into, away from, or out of something • The river *drains* into a lake. • The ***blood/color drained from her face***. [=she got pale]
2 a [+ *obj*] : to cause (something) to lose something important — + *of* • Years of civil war have *drained* the country *of* its resources. [=have used up the country's resources] • Overuse has *drained* the phrase *of* all meaning. **b** : to slowly be used up or to cause (something) to slowly be used up [+ *obj*] Years of civil war have *drained* the country's resources. • The city's emergency fund has been *drained.* [*no obj*] — usually + *away* • She felt her anger *drain away.*
3 [+ *obj*] : to make (someone) very physically or mentally tired • The work *drained* [=*exhausted*] me. • I feel totally *drained* of energy this evening. • Her work is very *draining.* [=*tiring*]
4 [+ *obj*] : to drink all of the liquid in (something) • He *drained* the mug and left.
5 [+ *obj*] *US, sports, informal* : to make (a successful shot) in a very skillful and impressive way • (*basketball*) She took a long jump shot and *drained* it. • (*golf*) He *drained* the putt for a birdie.
drain off [*phrasal verb*] ***drain off (something) or drain (something) off*** **a** : to cause (a liquid) to flow away from something or to leave the surface of something • When the beans have cooked long enough to be tender, *drain off* the water and set them aside. **b** : to take (something important or valuable) from something • An independent candidate could *drain off* [=*siphon off*] votes from either party.

[2]drain *noun, pl* **drains** [*count*]
1 : something (such as a pipe) that is used for removing a liquid from a place or container • He poured the spoiled milk down/into the *drain.* [=(*Brit*) *plughole*] • The *drain* in the bathtub/sink is blocked/clogged. • (*chiefly Brit*) They are repairing the *drains.* [=sewer system]
2 : something that uses a lot of time, money, etc. — usually singular; usually + *on* • Tuition costs are a *drain on* the family income. • The war has been a big *drain on* the country's resources. — see also BRAIN DRAIN
down the drain *informal* **1** — used to describe something that is being wasted or lost • All my hard work ***went down the drain***. • You're ***pouring your money down the drain***. [=you're wasting your money] **2** — used to describe something that is getting much worse • The public schools are ***going down the drain***.

drain·age /ˈdreɪnɪʤ/ *noun* [*noncount*] : the act or process of draining something : the act or process of removing water or liquid from a place or thing • the *drainage* of swamps • The soil has good *drainage.* [=extra water does not stay in the soil] • The holes in the bottom of the flower pot are for *drainage.* [=are for the extra water to flow out] — often used before another noun • a *drainage* system/basin/ditch/channel

drain·board /ˈdreɪnˌboɚd/ *noun, pl* **-boards** [*count*] *US* : a sloping area near a kitchen sink used for drying dishes — called also (*Brit*) *draining board*

drained /ˈdreɪnd/ *adj*
1 : with the water or liquid removed • a *drained* swamp • Add one cup tomatoes, *drained.* • well-*drained* soil
2 *not used before a noun* [*more ~; most ~*] : very tired : EXHAUSTED • I feel totally *drained.*

drain·pipe /ˈdreɪnˌpaɪp/ *noun, pl* **-pipes** [*count*]
1 : a pipe that carries rainwater from the roof of a building to the ground : DOWNSPOUT
2 *US* : a pipe that carries liquid waste and water away from buildings — see picture at PLUMBING

drake /ˈdreɪk/ *noun, pl* **drakes** [*count*] : a male duck

dram /ˈdræm/ *noun, pl* **drams** [*count*] : a small amount of an alcoholic drink • a *dram* of whiskey

dra·ma /ˈdrɑːmə/ *noun, pl* **-mas**
1 a [*count*] : a piece of writing that tells a story and is performed on a stage • He is reading an ancient Greek *drama.* **b** : a play, movie, television show, or radio show that is about a serious subject and is not meant to make the audience laugh [*count*] a television/radio *drama* • a police *drama* [=a serious show about police work] [*noncount*] I prefer *drama* to comedy.
2 [*noncount*] : the art or activity of performing a role in a play, show, etc. : ACTING • His interest in *drama* began at a very young age. • She studied *drama* in college. • *drama* school • a *drama* teacher/student
3 : a situation or series of events that is exciting and that affects people's emotions [*count*] the *dramas* of teenage life • She watched the *drama* unfold as they began screaming at each other. [*noncount*] a competition full of *drama* • the *drama* of the courtroom proceedings • a moment of ***high drama*** [=a very exciting and dramatic moment]

Dram·a·mine /ˈdræməˌmiːn/ *trademark* — used for a drug that people take to prevent nausea

drama queen *noun, pl* **~ queens** [*count*] *disapproving* : a person (especially a woman) who acts as though things are much worse than they really are

dra·mat·ic /drəˈmætɪk/ *adj*
1 [*more ~; most ~*] **a** : sudden and extreme • His parents noticed a *dramatic* change/improvement/difference in his behavior. • There was a *dramatic* increase/decrease/rise/fall in prices. **b** : greatly affecting people's emotions • the team's *dramatic* [=*exciting*] overtime victory • The book tells the *dramatic* story of her battle with cancer. **c** : attracting attention : causing people to carefully listen, look, etc. • She made a *dramatic* entrance wearing a bright red dress. • There was a *dramatic* pause before his big announcement. • The painter used *dramatic* colors/accents. **d** : often showing a lot of emotion : tending to behave and react in an exaggerated way • Oh, you're fine—don't be so *dramatic.* [=*melodramatic*]
2 *always used before a noun* : of or relating to plays and the performance of plays • They are members of the local *dramatic* society.
– **dra·mat·i·cal·ly** /drəˈmætɪkli/ *adv* [*more ~; most ~*] • His behavior has improved *dramatically.* [=very much] • They called to us from shore, waving their arms *dramatically.* [=using large motions]

dra·mat·ics /drəˈmætɪks/ *noun*
1 [*plural*] : behavior that is very emotional in a way that does not seem sincere : exaggerated behavior • a child prone to *dramatics*
2 [*noncount*] : the study or practice of acting in or producing plays • She is studying/learning *dramatics* in school. — see also AMATEUR DRAMATICS

dra·ma·tis per·so·nae /ˌdræmətəspɚˈsouni/ *noun* [*plural*] *formal* : the characters or actors in a play, movie, etc.

dram·a·tist /ˈdræmətɪst/ *noun, pl* **-tists** [*count*]
1 : someone who writes plays : PLAYWRIGHT • the American *dramatist* Arthur Miller
2 : someone who writes dramas (sense 1b) • a radio/television *dramatist*

dram·a·tize *also Brit* **dram·a·tise** /ˈdræməˌtaɪz/ *verb* **-tizes; -tized; -tiz·ing** [+ *obj*]
1 : to make (a book, an event, etc.) into a play, movie, television show, etc. • The movie *dramatizes* her early life. • The book is *dramatized* in a new play.
2 : to make a situation seem more important or serious than it really is • I know I tend to *dramatize* things but it really was awful.
3 : to show (something that might not be noticed) in a clear and effective way • She cited a series of statistics to *dramatize* the seriousness of the problem. • This tragedy *dramatizes* the need for improvements in highway safety.
– **dram·a·ti·za·tion** *also Brit* **dram·a·ti·sa·tion**

/ˌdræmətəˈzeɪʃən, *Brit* ˌdræməˌtaɪˈzeɪʃən/ *noun, pl* **-tions** [*count*] — often + *of* ▪ a radio *dramatization of* the novel ▪ The TV show included many *dramatizations of* actual events. [*noncount*] The novel is not fit for *dramatization*.

drank *past tense of* [1]DRINK

drape /ˈdreɪp/ *verb* **drapes; draped; drap·ing**
1 a [+ *obj*] **:** to loosely place or hang (something) ▪ We'll *drape* strings of lights between the trees for the party. — often + *over* or *around* ▪ He had one leg *draped over* the arm of the sofa. ▪ She *draped* the coat *around* my shoulders. ▪ He had a scarf *draped around* his neck. **b** [*no obj*] *of cloth* **:** to hang in a pleasing way ▪ This silk *drapes* beautifully.
2 [+ *obj*] **:** to cover (someone or something) with a cloth — usually + *with* or *in* ▪ The police *draped* the body *with* a blanket. ▪ The tables were *draped in* linen. — sometimes used figuratively ▪ She was *draped in* gold chains. [=she was wearing many gold chains]

drap·ery /ˈdreɪpəri/ *noun, pl* **-er·ies**
1 *US* **:** long heavy curtains [*plural*] We bought new *draperies* [=(more commonly) *drapes*] for the room. [*noncount*] (*somewhat formal*) I'd like to replace the *drapery* in the living room.
2 [*noncount*] **:** a decorative cloth that is arranged or hung in loose folds ▪ The painter arranged several items among *drapery* and began to work.

drapes /ˈdreɪps/ *noun* [*plural*] *chiefly US* **:** long heavy curtains ▪ This room needs new *drapes*.

dras·tic /ˈdræstɪk/ *adj* [*more* ~; *most* ~] **:** extreme in effect or action **:** severe or serious ▪ The situation calls for *drastic* measures/action. ▪ *drastic* cuts/reductions in spending ▪ Maybe we should try something less *drastic* first.
— **dras·ti·cal·ly** /ˈdræstɪkli/ *adv* ▪ In recent years, the town's population has declined *drastically*. [=(more commonly) *dramatically*] ▪ The neighborhood has *drastically* changed.

drat /ˈdræt/ *interj, informal + old-fashioned* — used to show that you are annoyed or disappointed ▪ *Drat!* I forgot the tickets.

drat·ted /ˈdrætəd/ *adj, always used before a noun, informal + old-fashioned* **:** annoying or disappointing ▪ That *dratted* [=*darn, darned*] dog is back again.

[1]**draught** *Brit spelling of* DRAFT

[2]**draught** /ˈdræft, *Brit* ˈdrɑːft/ *noun, pl* **draughts** [*count*] *Brit* **:** [2]CHECKER

draught·board /ˈdræftˌboəd, *Brit* ˈdrɑːftˌbɔːd/ *noun, pl* **-boards** [*count*] *Brit* **:** CHECKERBOARD

draughts /ˈdræfts, *Brit* ˈdrɑːfts/ *noun* [*noncount*] *Brit* **:** CHECKERS

draughtsman, draughtsperson, draughty *Brit spellings of* DRAFTSMAN, DRAFTSPERSON, DRAFTY

[1]**draw** /ˈdrɑː/ *verb* **draws; drew** /ˈdruː/; **drawn** /ˈdrɑːn/; **draw·ing**
1 : to make (a picture, image, etc.) by making lines on a surface especially with a pencil, pen, marker, chalk, etc., but not usually with paint [+ *obj*] He *drew* me a picture of the bike. = He *drew* a picture of the bike for me. ▪ The computer can *draw* the graph for you. ▪ Students *drew* maps of the states and labeled them. [*no obj*] You *draw* very well. ▪ She sat down and began to *draw*. — compare PAINT
2 [+ *obj*] **:** to cause (attention) to be given *to* someone or something ▪ The case has *drawn* attention *to* the fact that many athletes never graduate. ▪ I would like to *draw* your attention *to* the third line. ▪ He didn't want to *draw* attention *to* himself. [=he did not want to cause people to notice him]
3 [+ *obj*] **a :** to cause (someone or something) to come **:** to attract (someone or something) ▪ The band always *draws* a large crowd. ▪ She felt *drawn* [=*attracted*] to the young man. ▪ The college *draws* students from around the world. ▪ The animals were *drawn* to the campsite by the smell of food. ▪ We hope the display in the window will *draw* customers in from the street. ▪ The lure of city life has *drawn* away many of the town's young people. ▪ My eye was *drawn* to the painting. [=some characteristic of the painting made me want to look at it] **b :** to cause (someone) to become involved or interested in something or someone — + *in, into*, or *to* ▪ What first *drew* you *to* teaching? ▪ A good writer knows how to *draw* readers *in*. [=how to make readers interested; how to make people want to read something] — often used as *(be/get) drawn* ▪ She *was drawn in* by his friendly manner. [=she wanted to know and talk to him because he was friendly] ▪ She *got drawn into* the conversation.
4 [+ *obj*] **:** to get or receive (something) ▪ a television show that has *drawn* consistently high ratings ▪ The player *drew* a foul. **:** to get (a particular response or reaction) ▪ His speech *drew* cheers from the crowd. ▪ The movie has *drawn* much criticism/praise from critics. ▪ He is a talented high school athlete who has *drawn* the interest of several major colleges. ▪ The principal's remarks have ***drawn fire*** [=attracted angry criticism] from both parents and teachers.
5 a *always followed by an adverb or preposition* [*no obj*] **:** to move in a specified direction ▪ She *drew* away from the spider. ▪ He opened the door and *drew* back in horror/shock/fear. ▪ The car *drew* (up) alongside us. ▪ The train *drew* [=pulled] into the station. ▪ She *drew* her eyebrows together in a frown of concentration. — sometimes used figuratively ▪ He *drew* away [=(more commonly) *withdrew*] from his family. **b** [+ *obj*] **:** to move (something) by pulling ▪ a carriage *drawn* by horses = a horse-*drawn* carriage ▪ *Draw* the curtains/blinds/shades. [=open or close the curtains/blinds/shades] ▪ a special fabric that *draws* moisture away from the skin ▪ She *drew* the blanket over her head. ▪ *Draw* up a chair and join us. [=bring a chair to where we are and sit down with us] ▪ She sat down in the chair and ***drew up her knees/legs***. [=she bent her legs and moved her knees toward her chest] — sometimes used figuratively ▪ The tragedy *drew* us closer together. [=made us emotionally closer]
6 [*no obj*] **:** to move gradually or steadily in time or space ▪ The lion *drew* closer to its prey. ▪ The sun is setting and the day is ***drawing to a close***. [=*ending*] ▪ Spring is ***drawing near/nigh***. [=*approaching*] ▪ The car ***drew to a halt/stop***. [=the car slowed down and stopped]
7 [+ *obj*] **a :** to form (something, such as an idea or conclusion) after thinking carefully about information you have ▪ You can *draw* your own conclusions. — often + *from* ▪ a writer who *draws* ideas *from* newspaper stories ▪ We can ***draw lessons from*** past mistakes. [=we can learn from past mistakes] **b :** to describe how two or more things are similar or different **:** to make (a comparison, distinction, etc.) *between* two or more things ▪ Many people have been *drawing* comparisons *between* the two movies. [=have been saying that the movies are similar] ▪ She *drew* important distinctions *between* the two methods. [=described important ways that the two methods are different]
8 a [+ *obj*] **:** to take (something) out of a container, pocket, etc. ▪ They were arguing, and then one of them *drew* [=*pulled*] a gun. ▪ One of the thieves *drew* a knife on her. [=one of the thieves took a knife out of a pocket, container, etc., and pointed it at her] ▪ She *drew* water from the well. — see also *at daggers drawn* at DAGGER **b** [+ *obj*] **:** to cause (something) to come out of a source ▪ He *drew* [=*ran*] water for a bath. **c** [+ *obj*] **:** to get (something) *from* a source ▪ The car also *draws* power *from* a battery. ▪ She *draws* strength/inspiration *from* her loving family. **d :** to take (a card) from a group of cards [+ *obj*] *Draw* four cards. [*no obj*] You haven't *drawn* yet.
9 a [+ *obj*] **:** to choose (a thing) from a group without knowing which one you are choosing ▪ She *drew* the winning number/ticket. ▪ We *drew* names from a hat to decide who would go on the trip. ▪ (*Brit*) The U.S. team have been ***drawn against*** [=chosen to play against] Greece in the first round. — see also *draw lots* at LOT **b** [*no obj*] **:** to decide something by choosing something from a group ▪ We'll *draw* to see who will drive. — see also DRAW STRAWS (below)
10 [+ *obj*] **:** to make (something, such as a legal document) in a proper or legal form ▪ We hired a lawyer to *draw* a will. — often + *up* ▪ They *drew up* a contract/proposal/plan/list.
11 a [+ *obj*] **:** to take (something, such as air or smoke) into your lungs by breathing ▪ She *drew* a deep breath before responding. — often + *in* ▪ He *drew* the fresh air *in*. = He *drew in* the fresh air. **b** [*no obj*] **:** to let air flow through ▪ Make sure the chimney is *drawing* properly. ▪ The pipe *draws* well.
12 [+ *obj*] **a :** to take (money) from a bank account **:** WITHDRAW — usually + *from* or *out* ▪ He *drew* $100 *from* the bank. ▪ She *drew out* the money. **b :** to receive (money) regularly from an employer, government, bank, etc. ▪ He *draws* a salary of about $100,000. ▪ He *draws* unemployment benefits. ▪ She has started to *draw* her pension. **c :** to write (a check) and have money taken from a bank account ▪ You are now authorized to *draw* checks from the corporate account.
13 *Brit* **:** to finish a game, contest, etc., without having a winner **:** TIE [+ *obj*] We *drew* [=(*US*) *tied*] the game 3–3. [*no obj*] The teams *drew* [=(*US*) *tied*] 3–3. [=each team scored three points] — often + *against* ▪ The teams have *drawn against* each other.
14 [+ *obj*] *archery* **:** to bend (a bow) by pulling back the string ▪ He *drew* his bow and aimed at the target.

15 [+ *obj*] *Brit* : to cause (someone) to say more about something especially by questioning — often used as *(be) drawn*; usually + *on* ▪ She refused to *be drawn on* whether the company is considering a merger.
16 [+ *obj*] *technical, of a boat* : to need (a particular depth of water) in order to float ▪ The ship *draws* 45 feet of water.
draw a bead on see BEAD
draw a blank see [2]BLANK
draw a/the line see [1]LINE
draw blood see BLOOD
draw in your horns see [1]HORN
draw off [*phrasal verb*] ***draw off (something)*** *or* ***draw (something) off*** : to take or remove (something) from a source or supply ▪ They illegally *drew off* thousands of dollars that had been donated to the charity.
draw on/upon [*phrasal verb*] **1** ***draw on*** *literary* : to come closer in time ▪ It became colder as night *drew on.* [=*approached*] **2** ***draw on/upon (something)*** **a** : to use (something) as a source or supply ▪ The family is *drawing on/upon* the community for support. **b** : to use (information, experience, knowledge, etc.) to make something ▪ Her new book *draws on* her personal experience as a firefighter. ▪ The report *draws upon* several recent studies. **3** ***draw on (something)*** : to breathe in smoke from (a cigarette, cigar, pipe, etc.) ▪ He *drew on* his cigarette.
draw out [*phrasal verb*] **1** ***draw (something) out*** *or* ***draw out (something)*** : to cause (something) to leave a source or supply ▪ Trees *draw* water *out* of the soil. ▪ Salt will *draw out* moisture from vegetables. **2** ***draw (something) out*** *or* ***draw out (something)*** : to cause (something) to last longer than the usual or expected amount of time ▪ Questions *drew* the meeting *out* for another hour. ▪ The movie's love scene was *drawn out.* — see also DRAWN-OUT, LONG-DRAWN-OUT **3** ***draw (someone) out*** *or* ***draw out (someone)*** : to cause (someone) to talk freely ▪ She tried to *draw* the frightened child *out* by asking him questions about his toys. ▪ The reporter had an ability to *draw out* people.
draw straws ✧ If you *draw straws*, you choose a stick from a group of sticks that are different sizes but that are being held in such a way that they look like they are all the same size. Usually, whoever chooses the shortest stick or ***gets/draws the short straw*** will have to do a particular thing. ▪ Let's *draw straws* to see who will drive. ▪ He *drew the short straw* so he has to drive.
draw the blinds/curtain/shades on : to end (something that has been continuing for a long time) ▪ Let's *draw the curtain on* this investigation. — see also [1]DRAW 5b (above)
draw up [*phrasal verb*] **1** *of a vehicle* : to approach and stop at a place ▪ A car *drew up* [=*pulled up*] in front of the house. **2** ***draw (yourself) up*** : to stand as straight and tall as you can ▪ He *drew himself up* to (his) full height. — see also [1]DRAW 10 (above)

[2]**draw** *noun, pl* **draws** [*count*]
1 : someone or something that causes a lot of people to come to a place : ATTRACTION ▪ Their band is the main *draw* at the festival. ▪ The festival is always a big *draw*.
2 : the final result of a game, contest, etc., that does not have a winner : TIE ▪ The game ended in a *draw*. = The game was a *draw*. [=both teams/players had the same score] ▪ They played to a 3–3 *draw*. [=each team/player had 3 points when the game ended]
3 *chiefly Brit* : DRAWING ▪ Who won the (prize) *draw*? — often + *for* ▪ The *draw for* the raffle will take place in one hour.
4 : an act of breathing in smoke from a cigarette, cigar, pipe, etc. : DRAG — often + *on* or *from* ▪ He ***took a long draw on/from*** his cigarette.
be quick on the draw : to be quick about removing a gun from where it is kept : to quickly draw a gun and be ready to shoot it — often used figuratively ▪ When the huge crowd suddenly became unruly, security *was quick on the draw*. [=security reacted very quickly] ▪ Critics may have *been* a little too *quick on the draw.*
the luck of the draw see [1]LUCK

draw·back /ˈdrɑːˌbæk/ *noun, pl* **-backs** [*count*] : something that causes problems : DISADVANTAGE ▪ The only *drawback* [=*downside*] to the plan is that we don't have the time it requires. ▪ The trip sounds great, but cost is a major *drawback.*

draw·bridge /ˈdrɑːˌbrɪʤ/ *noun, pl* **-bridg·es** [*count*] : a bridge that can be raised up so that people cannot cross it or so that boats can pass under it ▪ raise/lower the *drawbridge*

draw·er /ˈdrɑːɚ/ *noun, pl* **-ers**
1 [*count*] : a box that slides into and out of a piece of furniture (such as a desk) and that is used to store things ▪ the top/middle/bottom *drawer* of the desk/dresser ▪ There are some pens in my desk *drawer*. ▪ a sock/cash *drawer* [=a drawer for storing socks/cash] — see picture at OFFICE; see also CHEST OF DRAWERS
2 ***drawers*** [*plural*] *old-fashioned + humorous* : underwear for the lower part of the body ▪ He stood there in only his *drawers*. — often used informally in the phrase ***drop your drawers*** ▪ At least the doctor didn't make me *drop my drawers*. [=pull down my underpants]

draw·ing /ˈdrɑːɪŋ/ *noun, pl* **-ings**
1 a [*count*] : a picture, image, etc., that is made by making lines on a surface with a pencil, pen, marker, chalk, etc., but usually not with paint ▪ She made a *drawing* of my house. ▪ pencil *drawings* of flowers — see also LINE DRAWING **b** [*noncount*] : the act or art of making a picture, image, etc., with a pencil, pen, marker, chalk, etc., but usually not with paint ▪ I've always loved *drawing*. — see also MECHANICAL DRAWING
2 [*count*] *US* : an act of choosing something (such as a winning ticket) from a group without knowing which one you are choosing ▪ Who won the (prize) *drawing*? — often + *for* ▪ The *drawing for* the raffle will take place in one hour. — called also (*chiefly Brit*) *draw*

drawing board *noun, pl* **~ boards**
1 [*count*] : a large flat board that is used for holding paper for drawing; *also* : DRAWING TABLE
2 [*noncount*] : the time during which something is being planned : the planning stage of something ▪ Plans for the new stadium are ***on the drawing board.*** [=are being created] ▪ The project will never get ***off the drawing board.*** [=will never go beyond the planning stage] ▪ The company went ***back to the drawing board*** [=started over] to make a better product.

drawing pin *noun, pl* **~ pins** [*count*] *Brit* : THUMBTACK

drawing power *noun* [*noncount*] : the ability to attract a lot of people to a performance, event, etc. ▪ The team has a lot of *drawing power*. — called also (*chiefly Brit*) *pulling power*

drawing room *noun, pl* **~ rooms** [*count*] *formal + old-fashioned* : a formal room that is used for spending time with guests or relaxing

drawing table *noun, pl* **~ -bles** [*count*] : a table that has a surface that can be raised up or down or turned to different angles and that is used for drawing

drawl /ˈdrɑːl/ *verb* **drawls; drawled; drawl·ing** : to speak slowly with vowel sounds that are longer than usual [+ *obj*] "Well, hello there," she *drawled*. ▪ He *drawled* his name in a Southern accent. [*no obj*] a *drawling* voice
– **drawl** *noun, pl* **drawls** [*count*] — usually singular ▪ He had a charming Southern *drawl*. ▪ She spoke with a *drawl*.

[1]**drawn** *past participle of* [1]DRAW

[2]**drawn** /ˈdrɑːn/ *adj* [*more ~; most ~*] : looking very thin and tired especially from worry, pain, or illness ▪ His illness left him looking very pale and *drawn*. ▪ She had a *drawn* face.

drawn–out *adj* [*more ~; most ~*] : continuing for or taking a long time ▪ We're trying to avoid a *drawn-out* process. — compare LONG-DRAWN-OUT

draw·string /ˈdrɑːˌstrɪŋ/ *noun, pl* **-strings** [*count*] : a string that can be pulled to close or tighten something (such as a bag or a piece of clothing) ▪ a *drawstring* bag ▪ *drawstring* pants [=pants that have a drawstring at the waist]

[1]**dread** /ˈdrɛd/ *verb* **dreads; dread·ed; dread·ing** [+ *obj*] : to fear something that will or might happen ▪ He can't swim and *dreads* going in the water. ▪ She *dreaded* making speeches in front of large audiences. ▪ I *dread* the day I will have to leave my friends. ▪ I *dread* the thought of moving next week. ▪ I ***dread to think*** about what they might do next.
– **dreaded** *adj* [*more ~; most ~*] ▪ The *dreaded* moment had arrived. ▪ a *dreaded* disease ▪ the *dreaded* word "cancer"

[2]**dread** *noun, pl* **dreads**
1 : a strong feeling of fear about something that will or might happen [*singular*] She has a *dread* of failure. ▪ He ***lives with the/a constant dread*** of rejection. [*noncount*] She awaited her punishment with *dread*. ▪ The news about the war ***fills me with dread.*** ▪ They live ***in constant dread*** of another attack. ***synonyms*** see [1]FEAR
2 [*count*] : a person or thing that causes fear — usually singular ▪ They lived in tight rows of wooden houses, and fire was a constant *dread*.
3 ***dreads*** [*plural*] *informal* : DREADLOCKS

[3]**dread** *adj, always used before a noun, formal* : causing great fear ▪ a *dread* [=*dreaded*] disease

dread·ful /ˈdrɛdfəl/ *adj* [*more* ~; *most* ~] **:** very bad or unpleasant • Her performance was absolutely/simply *dreadful.* • She has a *dreadful* [=*awful, terrible*] cold. • Those children have such *dreadful* manners. • What *dreadful* weather! • a *dreadful* mistake/accident • a *dreadful* storm/scream
– **dread·ful·ly** /ˈdrɛdfəli/ *adv* • a *dreadfully* bad performance • *dreadfully* [=*extremely*] dull • He was *dreadfully* lonely. • I miss you *dreadfully.* [=very much]

dread·locks /ˈdrɛd,lɑ:ks/ *noun* [*plural*] **:** hair that is twisted together into long pieces that hang down around your shoulders ✧ *Dreadlocks* are often worn by people who are Rastafarians. — called also *dreads*; see picture at HAIR

D

[1]**dream** /ˈdri:m/ *noun, pl* **dreams**
1 [*count*] **:** a series of thoughts, visions, or feelings that happen during sleep • He had a *dream* about climbing a mountain. • You were in my *dream* last night. • Scary movies always give me ***bad dreams.*** [=*nightmares*] • "Good night, my love. ***Sweet dreams.***" [=I hope you will sleep well and have pleasant dreams] — see also WET DREAM
2 [*count*] **:** an idea or vision that is created in your imagination and that is not real • She indulged in *dreams* [=*fantasies*] of living in a palace. • I've found ***the man/woman of my dreams.*** • They succeeded ***beyond their wildest dreams.*** • ***Never in my wildest dreams*** did I imagine it would be so much fun. • If you think the work will be easy, you're ***living in a dream world.***
3 a [*count*] **:** something that you have wanted very much to do, be, or have for a long time • He has had a lifelong *dream* of becoming an actor. • It's a *dream* of mine to own a house in the country. • Tell me your hopes and *dreams.* • She followed/fulfilled her *dreams.* • Making it to the Olympics was a ***dream come true.*** • Many believe that worldwide peace is an ***impossible dream.*** — see also AMERICAN DREAM, PIPE DREAM **b** [*singular*] **:** someone or something that has the qualities that a person wants most • The meal was a garlic lover's *dream.* • He's every woman's *dream.* — usually used before another noun • She's still trying to find her *dream* husband. • Managing a professional baseball team is his ***dream job.*** • They just moved into their ***dream home.*** — see also DREAM TEAM
4 [*singular*] *informal* **:** something that is beautiful, excellent, or pleasing • It's a *dream* of a house. • The new car is a *dream* to drive. = The new car drives ***like a dream.*** • My new computer works *like a dream.* [=works very well]
5 [*singular*] **:** a state or condition in which you are not thinking about or aware of the real things that are around you • He was walking around ***in a dream.***
in your dreams *informal* — used to say that you do not think something that another person wants or expects will ever happen • "Maybe my parents will lend me the car tonight." "*In your dreams.*"

[2]**dream** *verb* **dreams; dreamed** /ˈdrɛmt, ˈdri:md/ *or* **dreamt** /ˈdrɛmt/; **dream·ing**
1 : to have visions and thoughts in your sleep **:** to have a dream while you are sleeping [*no obj*] — often + *of* or *about* • He *dreamed of* drowning and woke up trembling. • I have trouble remembering the things I *dream about.* [+ *obj*] Last night I *dreamed* (that) you were here talking to me. • Did it really happen or did I just *dream* it?
2 : to think about something that you wish would happen or something that you want to do or be [*no obj*] He tends to *dream* big but he never really does the things he dreams of doing. • She stared out the window *dreaming.* [=*daydreaming*] • ***You're dreaming*** [=you're completely wrong] if you think being a parent is going to be easy. — often + *of* • She spent hours reading love stories and *dreaming of* romance. • They *dreamed of* success. • He *dreamed of* becoming a teacher. [+ *obj*] As a child, I always *dreamed* (that) I would be an astronaut when I grew up. • I sat on the porch and ***dreamed away*** the day. [=I spent the whole day thinking and dreaming] • I ***never dreamt*** that it would be so difficult. [=it was much more difficult than I expected it to be]
dream on *informal* — used to say that you do not think something that another person wants or expects will ever happen • "I think my band will be famous one day." "*Dream on.*"
dream up [*phrasal verb*] ***dream up (something)*** *also* ***dream (something) up*** **:** to think of or invent (something) in your mind • He *dreams up* all sorts of fantastic adventures. • She tries a lot of new recipes that she *dreams up* herself. • They *dreamed up* a plan to get the information.
never/not dream of — used to say that you would never do something or think of doing something • I ***would never dream of*** asking for more money. • "Did you ever do anything to hurt her?" "I ***wouldn't dream of it!***"

dream·boat /ˈdri:m,boʊt/ *noun, pl* **-boats** [*count*] *informal + old-fashioned* **:** a very attractive person — usually used of a man • an actor who's a real *dreamboat*

dream·er *noun, pl* **-ers** [*count*]
1 *disapproving* **:** a person whose ideas and plans are not practical or based in reality • I am a realist, but my sister is a *dreamer.*
2 : a person who dreams while sleeping • Some *dreamers* talk in their sleep to the people in their dreams.

dream·land /ˈdri:m,lænd/ *noun, informal* **:** a pleasant place or situation that exists only in the mind [*noncount*] Bored with the classroom lecture, she drifted off to *dreamland.* [=she started daydreaming] • (*disapproving*) He's in *dreamland* [=he's dreaming] if he thinks he can get by without a full-time job. [*singular*] He's living in a *dreamland.*

dream·less /ˈdri:mləs/ *adj, of sleep* **:** without dreams **:** deep and peaceful • She fell into a *dreamless* sleep.

dream·like /ˈdri:m,laɪk/ *adj* **:** seeming to exist in a dream **:** like a dream • Her photographs have a *dreamlike* quality.

dreamt *past tense and past participle of* [2]DREAM

dream team *noun, pl* **~ teams** [*count*] **:** a group of people who work or play a sport together and who are the best at what they do — usually singular • She got a legal *dream team* to work on the case.

dreamy /ˈdri:mi/ *adj* **dream·i·er; -est** [*also more* ~; *most* ~]
1 : tending to dream instead of thinking about what is real or practical • She was a *dreamy* young woman who never gave much serious thought to her future.
2 : having a quality which shows or suggests that you are not noticing or thinking about what is happening around you • He gazed at me with a *dreamy* look in his eyes.
3 : pleasant, peaceful, and relaxing • *dreamy* music
4 *informal + old-fashioned* **:** very attractive • Her boyfriend is so *dreamy.*
– **dream·i·ly** /ˈdri:məli/ *adv* • She spoke *dreamily* of traveling around the world. • They stared *dreamily* into each other's eyes. – **dream·i·ness** /ˈdri:minəs/ *noun* [*noncount*]

drea·ry /ˈdriri/ *adj* **drea·ri·er; -ri·est** [*or more* ~; *most* ~] **:** causing unhappiness or sad feelings **:** not warm, cheerful, etc. • It was a gray, *dreary* morning. • She longed to leave her *dreary* [=*gloomy, dismal*] hometown. • The family struggled through *dreary* economic times.
– **drea·ri·ly** /ˈdrirəli/ *adv* [*more* ~; *most* ~] • He spoke *drearily* of his meager job prospects. – **drea·ri·ness** *noun* [*noncount*]

dreck /ˈdrɛk/ *noun* [*noncount*] *US, informal* **:** something that is of very bad quality **:** trash or rubbish • The movie was pure *dreck.*

[1]**dredge** /ˈdrɛʤ/ *verb* **dredg·es; dredged; dredg·ing**
1 : to remove mud from the bottom of (a lake, river, etc.) in order to deepen it or to search for something [+ *obj*] They *dredged* the river. [*no obj*] They are *dredging* for oysters.
2 [+ *obj*] **:** to dig (something) out of the bottom of a lake, river, etc. • They *dredged* sand from the river to add to the eroding beach. • They *dredge* oysters in the bay. — often + *up* • They are *dredging up* silt from the canal bottom.
dredge up [*phrasal verb*] ***dredge up (something)*** *or* ***dredge (something) up*** **:** to start talking or thinking again about (something unpleasant that happened a long time ago) • Reporters *dredged up* the fact that the senator avoided the military draft. • She didn't like to *dredge up* bad memories.
– compare [3]DREDGE

[2]**dredge** *noun, pl* **dredges** [*count*] **:** a machine or boat that removes mud, sand, etc., from the bottom or a lake, river, etc. — called also *dredger*

[3]**dredge** *verb* **dredges; dredged; dredg·ing** [+ *obj*] **:** to lightly cover (food) with a dry substance (such as sugar or flour) — often + *with* or *in* • *Dredge* the fish *in* flour before frying it. • The cookies had been *dredged with* powdered sugar. — compare [1]DREDGE

dredg·er /ˈdrɛʤɚ/ *noun, pl* **-ers** [*count*] **:** [2]DREDGE

dregs /ˈdrɛgz/ *noun* [*plural*]
1 : solid materials that fall to the bottom of a container full of a liquid • the *dregs* in a bottle of wine • He discarded the *dregs* of his coffee.
2 : the worst or most useless part of something • people who were regarded as the ***dregs of society***

drench /ˈdrɛnʧ/ *verb* **drench·es; drenched; drench·ing** [+ *obj*] **:** to make (someone or something) completely wet —

often + *with* or *in* ▪ She *drenched* him *with* a bucket of cold water. — often used as *(be) drenched* ▪ The players *were drenched in* sweat after the game. ▪ pancakes *drenched in* syrup ▪ She was *drenched in* perfume. [=she was wearing a lot of perfume] — sometimes used figuratively ▪ a beach *drenched in* sunlight ▪ Her novels are *drenched in* history. — see also SUN-DRENCHED

¹dress /ˈdrɛs/ *verb* **dress·es; dressed; dress·ing**
1 a [+ *obj*] : to put clothes on (yourself or someone else) ▪ They *dressed* themselves in a hurry. ▪ He *dressed* the child in a snowsuit. — opposite UNDRESS **b** [*no obj*] : to put clothes on yourself ▪ She showered, *dressed*, and ate breakfast. — opposite UNDRESS
2 [*no obj*] **a** : to put on or wear a particular type or style of clothes ▪ She *dressed* warmly for skiing. ▪ He *dresses* fashionably/well. ▪ She always *dresses* in black (clothes). **b** : to put on or wear formal clothes ▪ She is *dressing* for the opera. ▪ They always *dress* for dinner.
3 [+ *obj*] : to clean, put medicine on, and cover (a wound) ▪ The nurse *dressed* the cut on my knee.
4 [+ *obj*] : to prepare (food) for cooking or eating ▪ *dress* the chicken/salad
5 [+ *obj*] : to decorate (something, especially a window) for display ▪ His job is to *dress* the store window for the holiday.
6 [+ *obj*] *technical* : to prepare (wood, stone, leather, etc.) for use
dress down [*phrasal verb*] **1** : to wear informal clothes ▪ Most of the students *dress down* for class, usually wearing jeans and T-shirts. ▪ On Fridays everyone in the office *dresses down*. — see also DRESS-DOWN **2** ***dress (someone) down or dress down (someone)*** : to speak angrily to (someone) for doing something wrong ▪ He was/got *dressed down* for failing to follow orders. — see also DRESSING-DOWN
dress up [*phrasal verb*] **1 a** : to put on or wear formal clothes ▪ We *dressed up* for the awards banquet. ▪ Do I need to *dress up* for the party? **b** ***dress (someone) up or dress up (someone)*** : to put formal or fancy clothes on (someone) ▪ She *dressed up* the children for the wedding. **2 a** : to put on a costume ▪ We *dressed up* like/as ghosts for Halloween. **b** ***dress (someone) up or dress up (someone)*** : to put a costume on (someone) ▪ We *dressed* the baby *up* as a lion. **3** ***dress up (something) or dress (something) up*** : to make (something) more attractive, impressive, or fancy ▪ *dress up* a plain dessert with a rich chocolate sauce

²dress *noun, pl* **dresses**
1 [*count*] : a piece of clothing for a woman or a girl that has a top part that covers the upper body and a skirt that hangs down to cover the legs ▪ She wore *dresses* only on special occasions. ▪ She wore a short/long black *dress* to the party. ▪ Her ***wedding dress*** was decorated with lace. — see color picture on page C15; see also HOUSEDRESS, SUNDRESS
2 [*noncount*] : a particular type of clothing ▪ The guests were clothed in traditional Indian *dress*. ▪ It is wise to wear conservative *dress* to an interview.

³dress *adj, always used before a noun* : suitable or required for a formal event ▪ I wore *dress* pants and a nice sweater. ▪ uncomfortable *dress* shoes

dres·sage /drəˈsɑːʒ, *Brit* ˈdrɛˌsɑːʒ/ *noun* [*noncount*] : a competition in which horses perform special movements in response to signals from their riders ▪ a *dressage* horse

dress circle *noun, pl* **~ circles** [*count*] *chiefly Brit* : the lowest section of seats above the main floor in a theater or opera house ▪ sitting in the *dress circle*

dress code *noun, pl* **~ codes** [*count*] : a set of rules about what clothing may and may not be worn at a school, office, restaurant, etc. ▪ The school imposed a new *dress code* that forbids students from wearing jeans. ▪ a casual *dress code*

dress–down *adj, always used before a noun* — used to describe a day during which people are allowed to wear informal clothes at work or school ▪ Friday is *dress-down* day at the office. ▪ *dress-down* Friday — see also *dress down* at ¹DRESS

dressed *adj* : wearing clothes ▪ Don't come in. I'm not *dressed* yet. ▪ It's time to get out of bed and ***get dressed***. [=put on clothes] : wearing clothes of a particular type ▪ She wasn't *dressed* for such a fancy restaurant. ▪ He is usually *dressed* in black. ▪ She was *dressed* (up) as a ladybug. ▪ a ***well-dressed*** young man
dressed to kill *informal* : wearing very fancy or attractive clothes ▪ We attended the party *dressed to kill*.

dress·er /ˈdrɛsɚ/ *noun, pl* **-ers** [*count*]
1 : a person who dresses in a particular way ▪ She is a stylish/sloppy *dresser*.
2 *US* : a piece of furniture that has drawers for storing clothes : CHEST OF DRAWERS
3 *Brit* : HUTCH 1
– see also HAIRDRESSER, WINDOW DRESSER

dress·ing /ˈdrɛsɪŋ/ *noun, pl* **-ings**
1 [*count, noncount*] : a usually seasoned mixture of liquids that is added to a salad — called also *salad dressing*; see also FRENCH DRESSING, ITALIAN DRESSING, RANCH DRESSING, RUSSIAN DRESSING, THOUSAND ISLAND DRESSING
2 *US* : STUFFING 2 [*noncount*] We had turkey with *dressing* and potatoes for dinner. [*count*] bread *dressings*
3 [*count*] : special material that is used to cover a wound ▪ The nurse cleaned the cut and applied a *dressing*.
4 [*noncount*] : the act or process of putting on clothes ▪ After breakfast, there will still be enough time for bathing and *dressing*. — see also CROSS-DRESSING, WINDOW DRESSING

dres·sing–down /ˌdrɛsɪŋˈdaʊn/ *noun* [*singular*] : the act of speaking angrily to someone about something done wrong ▪ He received a furious *dressing-down* from his boss in front of his colleagues. — see also *dress down* at ¹DRESS

dressing gown *noun, pl* **~ gowns** [*count*] : a loose piece of clothing that is worn indoors while relaxing, getting ready for bed, etc. ✧ *Dressing gown* is more common in British English than in U.S. English. In U.S. English, *robe* and *bathrobe* are more commonly used.

dressing room *noun, pl* **~ rooms** [*count*]
1 : a room where performers, actors, etc., can change their clothes ▪ He waited in his *dressing room* until it was time for him to appear on stage.
2 *US* : FITTING ROOM

dressing table *noun, pl* **~ tables** [*count*] : a table often with drawers and a mirror in front of which you sit while dressing, putting on makeup, etc.

dress·mak·er /ˈdrɛsˌmeɪkɚ/ *noun, pl* **-ers** [*count*] : a person who makes dresses and other clothes as a job
– dress·mak·ing /ˈdrɛsˌmeɪkɪŋ/ *noun* [*noncount*]

dress rehearsal *noun, pl* **~ -als** [*count*] : the final practice of a play that is done with all the costumes, scenery, etc., that will be used in the first real performance before an audience — often used figuratively ▪ The local election is a *dress rehearsal* for the national election that will take place later this year.

dress shirt *noun, pl* **~ shirts** [*count*]
1 *US* : a man's shirt that is usually worn with a necktie — see color picture on page C14
2 : a man's formal white shirt that is worn with a bow tie

dress uniform *noun, pl* **~ -forms** [*count*] : a military uniform that is worn at formal events

dressy /ˈdrɛsi/ *adj* **dress·i·er; -est**
1 : suitable for formal events ▪ Those shoes are so *dressy*, I rarely wear them. ▪ She wore an outfit that was much too *dressy* for the occasion.
2 : requiring fancy or formal clothes ▪ a *dressy* affair/restaurant
3 : liking to wear fancy or formal clothes ▪ a *dressy* chap

drew *past tense of* ¹DRAW

¹drib·ble /ˈdrɪbəl/ *verb* **drib·bles; drib·bled; drib·bling**
1 *always followed by an adverb or preposition* **a** [*no obj*] : to fall or flow in small drops ▪ Coffee *dribbled* [=*trickled*] down the side of the mug. ▪ Juice *dribbled* down his chin. **b** [+ *obj*] : to let (a liquid) fall in small drops ▪ She accidentally *dribbled* wine onto the rug. ▪ *Dribble* olive oil over the warm bread before serving.
2 [*no obj*] : to let saliva or another liquid drip or trickle from your mouth ▪ The baby *dribbled* [=*drooled*] down the back of her dad's shirt.
3 : to move a ball or puck forward by tapping, bouncing, or kicking it [*no obj*] She *dribbled* across the basketball court. [+ *obj*] He skillfully *dribbled* the soccer ball towards the goal.

²dribble *noun, pl* **dribbles** [*count*]
1 : a small flow of liquid ▪ He wiped a *dribble of* juice from the corner of the baby's mouth. ▪ *dribbles* of blood
2 : an act of moving a ball or puck forward by tapping, bouncing, or kicking it ▪ She gave the ball a *dribble* before passing it. — see also DOUBLE DRIBBLE

dribs /ˈdrɪbz/ *noun*
dribs and drabs *informal* : small amounts that come or happen over a period of time ▪ They received donations ***in dribs and drabs***.

dried *adj* — used to describe foods and plants that have had all their liquid removed so that they will last for a long time • *dried* beans/mushrooms/pasta • *dried* milk/fish • a mixture of nuts and *dried* fruit • an arrangement of *dried* flowers • sun-*dried* tomatoes

drier *variant spelling of* DRYER

[1]drift /ˈdrɪft/ *noun, pl* **drifts**

1 [*singular*] **:** a slow and gradual movement or change from one place, condition, etc., to another • the slow *drift* of the clouds • As she got older, you could observe a *drift* in her writing towards more serious subjects. • the government's *drift* towards a centralization of power • a ***population drift*** [=a gradual movement of people that lowers the population in one area and increases it in another] — see also CONTINENTAL DRIFT

2 [*count*] **:** a large pile of snow or sand that has been blown by the wind • We sped over the *drifts* [=*snowdrifts*] on our skis.

3 [*singular*] *informal* **:** the general or basic meaning of something said or written • I don't ***get your drift.*** [=I don't understand what you're saying] • I won't tell you his name, but he's someone you know very well, if you ***catch my drift.*** [=if you understand what I'm suggesting]

4 [*noncount*] **:** movement of an airplane or a ship in a direction different from the one desired because of air or water currents

[2]drift *verb* **drifts; drift·ed; drift·ing** [*no obj*]

1 : to move slowly on water, wind, etc. • The boat slowly *drifted* out to sea. • The clouds *drifted* across the sky.

2 *of snow or sand* **:** to form a pile by being blown by the wind **:** to form a drift • The snow *drifted* against the side of the house. • *Drifting* snow covered most of the car.

3 a : to move smoothly or easily in a way that is not planned or guided • The party guests *drifted* from room to room, eating and mingling. • Her eyes *drifted* across the crowd. • The conversation *drifted* from topic to topic. • My thoughts *drifted* back to the time when we first met. **b :** to behave or live in a way that is not guided by a definite purpose or plan • After he left the army he just *drifted* for a few years. • She *drifted* from job to job. • He has always ***drifted through life*** without a care. — see also DRIFTER

4 : to change slowly from one state or condition to another • The patient *drifted* in and out of consciousness all day.

drift apart [*phrasal verb*] **:** to stop having a close relationship • They used to be great friends, but they've gradually *drifted apart* over the years.

drift off [*phrasal verb*] *informal* **:** to fall asleep • She *drifted off* while I was still talking. • He gradually ***drifted off to sleep.***

drift·er /ˈdrɪftɚ/ *noun, pl* **-ers** [*count*] **:** a person who moves from one place or job to another without a purpose or plan • He was a *drifter* who hitchhiked from state to state.

drift net *noun, pl* ~ **nets** [*count*] **:** a large fishing net that floats in the water or is pulled behind a boat

drift·wood /ˈdrɪftˌwʊd/ *noun* [*noncount*] **:** wood that is floating in water or carried to the shore by water

[1]drill /ˈdrɪl/ *noun, pl* **drills**

1 [*count*] **:** a tool used for making holes in hard substances • an electric/power *drill* • the dentist's *drill* — see picture at CARPENTRY; see also PNEUMATIC DRILL

2 a : an exercise done to practice military skills or procedures [*count*] During basic training, the recruits spent hours a day doing *drills.* • a ***drill sergeant*** [=a sergeant who trains new soldiers] [*noncount*] (*chiefly Brit*) • soldiers doing *drill* **b :** a physical or mental activity that is done repeatedly in order to learn something, become more skillful, etc. [*count*] The students do vocabulary/multiplication *drills* every Monday. • The players are doing their *drills.* [*noncount*] The students were taught by *drill.* — see also FIRE DRILL

know the drill *informal* **:** to know how something is done **:** to be familiar with a regular process, procedure, etc. • You don't have to tell us what to do. We all *know the drill* by now.

– compare [3]DRILL, [5]DRILL

[2]drill *verb* **drills; drilled; drill·ing**

1 : to make a hole in something with a drill [+ *obj*] He *drilled* a hole in the back of the cabinet. • The dentist *drilled* the tooth. [*no obj*] They are planning to *drill* for oil here.

2 [+ *obj*] **a :** to teach or train (someone) by repeating a lesson or exercise again and again • We *drilled* the children on their multiplication tables. • The players were *drilled* in practice. **b :** to train (soldiers) by making them practice military procedures and exercises • The commander *drilled* the troops.

3 [+ *obj*] *US, sports, informal* **:** to hit (someone or something) very hard • He *drilled* a single to right field. • The quarterback got *drilled.*

drill into [*phrasal verb*] ***drill (something) into (someone)*** **:** to force (something) to be learned very well by (someone) by repeating it again and again • Our teacher *drilled* the lesson *into* our heads. • The importance of saying "please" and "thank you" was *drilled into* us as children.

– compare [4]DRILL

– drill·er *noun, pl* **-ers** [*count*] • an oil *driller*

[3]drill *noun, pl* **drills** [*count*]

1 : a row of seeds planted by a special machine

2 : a special machine that plants seeds in rows

– compare [1]DRILL, [5]DRILL

[4]drill *verb* **drills; drilled; drilling** [+ *obj*] **:** to plant (seeds) in a row with a special machine — compare [2]DRILL

[5]drill *noun* [*noncount*] **:** a type of strong cotton cloth — compare [1]DRILL, [3]DRILL

drily *variant spelling of* DRYLY

[1]drink /ˈdrɪŋk/ *verb* **drinks; drank** /ˈdræŋk/; **drunk** /ˈdrʌŋk/; **drink·ing**

1 : to take a liquid into your mouth and swallow it [*no obj*] The baby still *drinks* from a bottle. • What would you like to *drink*? [+ *obj*] We *drank* orange juice with breakfast. • I *drink* lots of water when I'm hiking.

2 a [*no obj*] **:** to drink alcohol • She *drank* too much last night and woke up sick this morning. • I don't *drink.* [=I never drink alcohol] • It's not safe to ***drink and drive.*** ✧ Someone who ***drinks like a fish*** regularly drinks too much alcohol. • When he was younger he used to *drink like a fish.* **b** [+ *obj*] **:** to put (yourself) into a specified state by drinking alcohol • She *drank* herself into a stupor. • He nearly *drank* himself to death. — see also *drink someone under the table* at [1]TABLE

drink in [*phrasal verb*] ***drink in (something) or drink (something) in*** **:** to stop and look at or listen to something in order to enjoy it fully • The view is so beautiful. Let's just take a minute to *drink* it all *in.*

drink to [*phrasal verb*] ***drink to (someone or something)*** **:** to speak words that honor or express good wishes for (someone or something) and then take a drink **:** to make a toast to (someone) • We *drank to* their 30th anniversary. = We ***drank a toast to*** their 30th anniversary. • We ***drank to their health.*** ✧ ***I'll drink to that!*** means that you agree completely with something that someone has said. • "It will be the best vacation of our lives." "*I'll drink to that!*"

drink up [*phrasal verb*] ***drink up or drink up (something) or drink (something) up*** **:** to drink all of (something) • They *drank up* (all) the orange juice. • Here's a glass of the vineyard's latest wine. *Drink up!*

– drinking *noun* [*noncount*] • *Drinking* is not allowed in the park. [=you are not allowed to drink alcohol in the park] • a night of heavy *drinking* — often used before another noun • a *drinking* buddy/partner • (*US*) She has a ***drinking problem.*** [=(*Brit*) *drink problem*; she regularly drinks too much alcohol] • The ***drinking age*** [=the age at which a person can legally buy and drink alcohol] in the U.S. is 21.

[2]drink *noun, pl* **drinks**

1 : a liquid that you can drink **:** BEVERAGE [*count*] We serve coffee, tea, and other hot *drinks.* [*noncount*] Food and *drink* will be provided. — see also SOFT DRINK

2 a [*count*] **:** an alcoholic beverage • They went to the bar for a few *drinks.* • Can I get you another *drink*? • He poured himself a ***stiff drink.*** [=a strong alcoholic drink] **b** [*noncount*] **:** the habit or practice of drinking a lot of alcohol • It was during this period that she ***took to drink.*** [=began drinking lots of alcohol] • The stress of the job ***drove him to drink.*** [=caused him to drink lots of alcohol] • (*Brit*) She has a ***drink problem.*** [=(*US*) *drinking problem*; she regularly drinks too much alcohol] — see also DEMON DRINK, MIXED DRINK

3 [*singular*] **:** an act of drinking • He took a long *drink* from his glass.

4 [*count*] **:** an amount of liquid for drinking • Give the dog a *drink* of water.

the drink *old-fashioned* **:** an area of water (such as a lake or pond) • The ball rolled down the hill and into *the drink.*

drink·able /ˈdrɪŋkəbəl/ *adj*

1 : able to be drunk • They boiled the water to make it *drinkable.* [=safe for drinking] • This coffee is so hot it's not *drinkable.*

2 [*more* ~; *most* ~] **:** having a pleasant taste • a very *drinkable* wine

drink–driver *noun, pl* **-ers** [*count*] *Brit* **:** DRUNK DRIVER

drink–driv·ing /ˈdrɪŋkˈdraɪvɪŋ/ *noun* [*noncount*] *Brit* : DRUNK DRIVING

drink·er /ˈdrɪŋkɚ/ *noun, pl* **-ers** [*count*]
1 : a person who drinks alcohol especially in large amounts • He's a heavy/moderate *drinker.* • I'm not much of a *drinker.* • Most of his friends are *drinkers.*
2 : a person who drinks a particular beverage • She's a big beer/wine/coffee *drinker.* [=she drinks a lot of beer/wine/coffee]

drinking fountain *noun, pl* ∼ **-tains** [*count*] : a device in a public place that produces a stream of water for people to drink from — called also (*chiefly US*) *water fountain*

drinking water *noun* [*noncount*] : water that is clean enough for people to drink • Pollution is seeping into our *drinking water.*

drinks party *noun, pl* ∼ **ties** [*count*] *Brit* : COCKTAIL PARTY

[1]**drip** /ˈdrɪp/ *verb* **drips; dripped; drip·ping**
1 [*no obj*] : to fall in drops • Water *dripped* from a leak in the ceiling. • Blood *dripped* down his leg from the cut. • Hot wax *dripped* onto my fingers.
2 : to let drops of (a liquid) fall [+ *obj*] The pine trees *dripped* sap onto the cars. • The kids *dripped* water all over the house. [*no obj*] The faucet is *dripping.* [=water is dripping from the faucet] • a *dripping* faucet — often + *with* • His face was *dripping with* sweat. [=sweat was dripping from his face] • The toast was *dripping with* butter. ✧ If you are ***dripping wet*** you are so wet that drops of water are falling off you. • The kids were *dripping wet.*
3 [*no obj*] : to have or show a large amount of something — usually + *with* • Her voice *dripped with* contempt/charm. • She was *dripping with* diamonds. [=she was wearing a lot of diamonds]

[2]**drip** *noun, pl* **drips**
1 a [*count*] : a drop of liquid that falls from something • *Drips* of water fell from a leak in the ceiling. **b** [*singular*] : the sound of liquid falling in drops • We heard the *drip* of the rain. • the steady *drip, drip, drip* of the faucet **c** [*singular*] : the act or action of falling in drops • Water fell from the ceiling in a steady/slow *drip.*
2 [*count*] *medical* : a device used in hospitals to pass fluid slowly through a tube into a patient's blood • The doctor put the patient on a morphine *drip* to manage the pain.
3 [*count*] *informal + old-fashioned* : a dull and often weak person • Don't invite that *drip* to your party!

[1]**drip–dry** /ˈdrɪpˌdraɪ/ *verb* **-dries; -dried; -dry·ing** : to dry wet clothing by hanging it so that water drips from it [*no obj*] I washed the shirt and hung it on the line to *drip-dry.* [+ *obj*] I *drip-dried* the shirt.

[2]**drip–dry** *adj* : able to dry with few or no wrinkles when hung up while wet • a *drip-dry* shirt

drip·ping /ˈdrɪpɪŋ/ *noun, pl* **-pings** : the fat and juices that come out of meat during cooking [*plural*] (*US*) • He cooked a turkey and made gravy from the *drippings.* [*noncount*] (*Brit*) • Pour the *dripping* from the pan.

[1]**drive** /ˈdraɪv/ *verb* **drives; drove** /ˈdroʊv/; **driv·en** /ˈdrɪvən/; **driv·ing**
1 a : to direct the movement of (a car, truck, bus, etc.) [+ *obj*] He *drove* the car down a bumpy road. • She *drives* a taxi. [=her job is driving a taxi] [*no obj*] Do you want to *drive* or should I? • He is learning to *drive.* **b** *always followed by an adverb or preposition* [*no obj*] *of a car, truck, etc.* : to move in a specified manner or direction • The car stopped and then *drove* off. • A car *drove* by us slowly. • The bus slowly *drove* away. **c** : to travel in a car [*no obj*] We *drove* all night and arrived at dawn. • Are you *driving* or flying to Canada? [=will you travel to Canada by car or airplane?] • We *drove* (for) eight hours yesterday. • We *drove* 160 miles to get here. • I *drive* on/along this route every day. [+ *obj*] I *drive* this route every day. **d** [+ *obj*] : to take (someone or something) to a place in a car, truck, etc. • I *drove* her to the train station this morning. • I had to *drive* myself to the hospital. • Her mom *drove* us home. **e** [+ *obj*] : to own and use (a vehicle of a specified kind) • He *drives* a pickup/motorcycle. • She *drives* a Ford.
2 [+ *obj*] : to move (people or animals) to or from a place by using force • Cowboys *drove* the herds across the prairie. • They *drove* the invaders back across the border. • Thousands of people have been *driven* from their homes. [=have been forced to leave their homes]
3 [+ *obj*] : to push (something) with force • *drive* a nail with a hammer — often + *into* • He *drove* a nail *into* the wall. • She *drove* the sword *into* her enemy's side.
4 [+ *obj*] : to make (a machine or vehicle) work or move : to provide power for (something) • Electricity *drives* the machinery. • a steam-*driven* turbine [=a turbine that gets its power from steam] — often used figuratively • What *drives* the economy? • a market-*driven* industry
5 [+ *obj*] **a** : to cause (someone) to behave in a particular way • They were *driven* [=*motivated*] by hunger to steal. • Poverty *drove* them to a life of crime. • Ambition *drove* her to succeed. **b** : to force (someone) to work very hard • The sergeant *drove* the recruits. • The team was ***driven hard*** by the coach. • He's been ***driving himself*** too hard. [=he's been working too hard]
6 [+ *obj*] : to bring (someone) into a particular condition • That noise is *driving* me insane/crazy. • The new store *drove* him out of business. [=caused him to go out of business] • Her perfume ***drives me wild*** [=gets me sexually excited]
7 [+ *obj*] : to cause (a price, number, etc.) to increase or decrease — + *up* or *down* • The government report *drove* stock prices *up.* • An increase in investments is *driving down* interest rates.
8 [*no obj*] *sports* : to move toward or through something with a lot of force or speed • He took a pass and *drove* to/toward the basket/net. • The running back *drove* through the line of scrimmage.
9 [+ *obj*] *sports* : to hit or kick (a ball or puck) with a lot of force or speed • She *drove* the (golf) ball down the fairway. • He *drove* the puck into the net. — see also DRIVING RANGE
10 [*no obj*] *of rain, wind, etc.* : to fall or blow with great force • The rain *drove* against the windows. — see also DRIVING

drive a hard bargain see [1]BARGAIN

drive at [*phrasal verb*] ***drive at (something)*** : to attempt to say or do (something) — usually used as *(be) driving at* • I have no idea what he *was driving at.* • I think I see what you*'re driving at.*

drive away [*phrasal verb*] ***drive (someone) away*** *or* ***drive away (someone)*** : to cause or force (someone) to leave especially by making a situation unpleasant or unattractive • The store's high prices are *driving away* customers.

drive a wedge between see [1]WEDGE

drive in [*phrasal verb*] ***drive (someone or something) in*** *or* ***drive in (someone or something)*** ***baseball*** : to cause (a run or runner) to score • He *drove in* another run. • The hit *drove* him *in* for a 5–4 lead.

drive off [*phrasal verb*] ***drive (someone or something) off*** *or* ***drive off (someone or something)*** : to cause or force (someone or something) to leave • They *drove off* the invaders.

drive out [*phrasal verb*] ***drive (someone or something) out*** *or* ***drive out (someone or something)*** : to cause or force (someone or something) to leave • They *drove out* the invaders. • The family was *driven out* of the neighborhood by rising real estate prices.

drive (someone) up a/the wall see [1]WALL

drive your point home see [2]HOME

[2]**drive** *noun, pl* **drives**
1 [*count*] : a journey in a car • It's a two-hour *drive* to the beach. • Her house is an hour's *drive* east of Los Angeles. • We took a pleasant *drive* in the country. • Would you like to ***go for a drive?*** — see also TEST DRIVE
2 [*count*] : a hard area or small road outside of a house where cars can be parked : DRIVEWAY • A white car was parked in the *drive.*
3 — used in the name of some public roads • Morningside *Drive* • They live at 156 Woodland *Drive.* — abbr. *Dr.*
4 [*count*] : an effort made by a group of people to achieve a goal, to collect money, etc. • a fund-raising *drive* • The school holds a canned food *drive* every winter. • a membership *drive* [=an effort to get more people to join a group, club, etc.]
5 : a strong natural need or desire [*count*] The need for food and water are basic *drives* for all living things. [*noncount*] ***Sex drive*** [=the desire to have sex] generally decreases as you get older.
6 [*noncount*] : a strong desire for success • She is an ambitious young woman, full of *drive* and determination. — see also DRIVEN
7 [*count*] : a device in a computer that can read information off and copy information onto disks or tape • Insert the disk into the floppy *drive.* • a CD-ROM *drive* — see also DISK DRIVE, HARD DRIVE
8 [*noncount*] **a** : the way power from an engine controls and directs the movement of a vehicle • The car has front-wheel/rear-wheel *drive.* — see also FOUR-WHEEL DRIVE **b**

chiefly US : a condition in which the gears of a vehicle are working in a way that allows the vehicle to move forward • He ***put the car in/into drive*** and pulled onto the street.

9 [*count*] **a** *sports* : a ball, puck, etc., that is hit very hard • He hit a hard/long *drive* down the left-field line. — see also LINE DRIVE **b** *golf* : a long shot that is hit from a tee • She hit her *drive* into the rough.

10 [*count*] : a long or forceful military attack on an enemy • an armored *drive* into enemy territory

11 [*count*] *American football* : a series of plays that move the ball down the field toward the opponent's end zone • They scored a touchdown following a ten-play *drive*.

12 [*count*] : an act of leading cattle or sheep over land and keeping them in a group • a cattle *drive*

D

drive–by /ˈdraɪvˈbaɪ/ *adj, always used before a noun* : done from a moving vehicle • a ***drive-by shooting/killing***

– **drive–by** /ˈdraɪvˌbaɪ/ *noun, pl* **-bys** [*count*] • They were both shot in a *drive-by*. [=a drive-by shooting]

drive–in /ˈdraɪvˌɪn/ *noun, pl* **-ins** [*count*]

1 : a place where people can watch movies outdoors while sitting in their cars — called also *drive-in theater*

2 : a restaurant at which people are served in their cars — called also *drive-in restaurant*

[1]driv•el /ˈdrɪvəl/ *noun* [*noncount*] : foolish writing or speech • I'm not going to waste my time reading this *drivel*. [=*nonsense*]

[2]drivel *verb* **-els**; *US* **-eled** *or Brit* **-elled**; *US* **-el•ing** *or Brit* **-el•ling** [*no obj*] *informal* : to talk in a very foolish or silly way • What is he *driveling* about now?

– **driveling** (*US*) *or Brit* **drivelling** *adj* • a *driveling* idiot

[1]driven *past participle of* [1]DRIVE

[2]driven *adj* : very determined to succeed • They are *driven*, successful people.

driv•er /ˈdraɪvɚ/ *noun, pl* **-ers** [*count*]

1 a : a person who drives a car, truck, etc. • Who was the *driver* at the time of the accident? • He's a good/careful/fast/bad *driver*. • The front door on the ***driver's side*** [=the side of the car where the driver sits] is scratched. — see also BACK-SEAT DRIVER **b** : a person whose job is to drive a vehicle (such as a taxi, truck, or bus) • We told the taxi *driver* to take us to the library. • He likes to sit at the front of the bus, near the *driver*. • an ambulance/truck *driver*

2 *technical* : a piece of computer software that controls a device (such as a mouse or printer) that is attached to the computer • There's a problem with the printer's *driver*.

3 *golf* : a club that is used for hitting long shots off a tee

in the driver's seat : in a position in which you are able to control what happens • When his boss went on vacation, he suddenly found himself *in the driver's seat*.

– see also PILE DRIVER

driver's license *noun, pl* ~ **-censes** [*count*] *US* : an official document or card which shows that you have the legal right to drive a vehicle — called also (*Brit*) *driving licence*

drive•shaft /ˈdraɪvˌʃæft, *Brit* ˈdraɪvˌʃɑːft/ *noun, pl* **-shafts** [*count*] *technical* : a part of a vehicle that carries power from the gears to the wheels

drive–through *also* **drive–thru** /ˈdraɪvˌθruː/ *noun, pl* **-throughs** *also* **-thrus** [*count*] : a business (such as a bank or restaurant) that is designed so that customers can be served while remaining in their cars; *also, US* : the window from which people are served • I ordered a salad and fries at the *drive-through*.

– **drive–through** *also* **drive–thru** /ˈdraɪvˌθruː/ *adj, always used before a noun* • a *drive-through* restaurant • (*US*) the *drive-through* window

drive time *noun* [*noncount*] *chiefly US* : the time when people are driving to or from work and are listening to the radio in their cars • Her show airs during the morning *drive time*. • a *drive-time* radio show

drive–up /ˈdraɪvˌʌp/ *adj, always used before a noun, US* : designed to allow people to remain in their cars while being served • a bank with a ***drive-up window***

drive•way /ˈdraɪvˌweɪ/ *noun, pl* **-ways** [*count*] : a short private road from a street to a house or other building where cars can usually be parked • A long *driveway* led to the mansion. • We shoveled the *driveway* [=*drive*] after the snowstorm. — see picture at HOUSE

[1]driving *adj, always used before a noun*

1 : falling or blowing with great force and speed • a hard *driving* rain/wind

2 — used in the phrase ***driving force*** to describe the person or thing that causes or controls something • He has been the *driving force* behind these changes. [=he has been the person who has caused these changes to happen] • She believes that greed is the *driving force* behind our economy.

– see also HARD-DRIVING

[2]driving *noun* [*noncount*]

1 : the act of operating a vehicle • I enjoy *driving* in good weather. • She doesn't like ***night driving***. [=driving at night] • (*US*) He was arrested for ***driving under the influence***. = He was arrested for ***driving while intoxicated***. [=for driving when he was drunk] — often used before another noun • a *driving* school • He failed his *driving* test.

2 : the way someone operates a vehicle • I don't trust her *driving* and would rather take my own car. • He got pulled over for ***reckless driving***. — see also DRUNK DRIVING, *driving to endanger* at ENDANGER

driving licence *noun, pl* ~ **-cences** [*count*] *Brit* : DRIVER'S LICENSE

driving range *noun, pl* ~ **ranges** [*count*] : a place where people can practice hitting golf balls

[1]driz•zle /ˈdrɪzəl/ *verb* **driz•zles**; **driz•zled**; **driz•zling**

1 [*no obj*] : to rain in very small drops • It was beginning to *drizzle*, so she pulled on her hood.

2 [+ *obj*] : to pour a small amount of liquid onto or over something • She *drizzled* syrup on her pancakes. = She *drizzled* her pancakes with syrup. • The vegetables were *drizzled* with olive oil.

[2]drizzle *noun* [*singular*] : rain that falls lightly in very small drops • Yes, it's raining, but it's only a *drizzle*.

– **driz•zly** /ˈdrɪzəli/ *adj* **driz•li•er**; **-est** • It was a *drizzly*, gray weekend.

droll /ˈdroʊl/ *adj* **droll•er**; **-est** : having an odd and amusing quality • a *droll* little man with a peculiar sense of humor • a book of *droll* stories

drom•e•dary /ˈdrɑːməˌderi, *Brit* ˈdrɒmədri/ *noun, pl* **-daries** [*count*] : a camel of western Asia and northern Africa that has one hump on its back

[1]drone /ˈdroʊn/ *noun, pl* **drones** [*count*] : a deep continuous sound : HUM — usually singular • the endless *drone* of washing machines at the laundry • the *drone* of passing traffic — compare [3]DRONE

[2]drone *verb* **drones**; **droned**; **dron•ing** [*no obj*] : to make a continuous low humming sound • A plane *droned* overhead. • We could hear wasps *droning* in the garden.

drone on [*phrasal verb*] *informal* : to speak for a long time in a dull voice without saying anything interesting • She had trouble keeping awake as he *droned on* about himself.

[3]drone *noun, pl* **drones** [*count*]

1 : a type of male bee that does not gather honey

2 *chiefly US, informal* : a person who does work that is boring and not very important • one of many office *drones*

– compare [1]DRONE

[1]drool /ˈdruːl/ *verb* **drools**; **drooled**; **drool•ing** [*no obj*]

1 : to let saliva flow out from the mouth • a *drooling* baby

2 : to show admiration or desire for something in an exaggerated way — usually + *over* • Everyone was *drooling over* his new car.

[2]drool *noun* [*noncount*] *chiefly US* : saliva that drips from the mouth • He wiped the *drool* from the baby's face.

droop /ˈdruːp/ *verb* **droops**; **drooped**; **droop•ing** [*no obj*]

1 : to sink, bend, or hang down • The flowers were *drooping* in the hot sun. • Her eyelids *drooped* as she grew tired. • The tree's branches *drooped* under the weight of the snow.

2 : to become sad or weak • His spirits *drooped* when he didn't get the job.

– **droop** *noun* [*singular*] • the sad *droop* of the dog's tail

– **droopy** /ˈdruːpi/ *adj* **droop•i•er**; **-est** • a *droopy* mustache

[1]drop /ˈdrɑːp/ *noun, pl* **drops**

1 [*count*] : a very small amount of liquid that falls in a rounded shape • He squeezed the bottle until a few *drops* came out. • She knew rain was coming when she felt a *drop* [=*raindrop*] land on her arm. — often + *of* • *Drops of* water fell from the leaky faucet. • a *drop of* blood — see also DEWDROP, RAINDROP, TEARDROP

2 [*count*] *informal* : a small amount of a drink — usually singular • I didn't have a *drop* of your orange juice. • I'd just like a *drop* of brandy, please. • He used to have a drinking problem but he ***hasn't touched a drop*** [=hasn't drunk any alcohol] in years.

3 [*singular*] : a small amount of something (such as a quality) • She doesn't have a single *drop* of selfishness in her. • The poet wrings the last *drop* of meaning from every word.

4 drops [*plural*] **:** liquid medicine that is measured in drops and put into your eyes, ears, or nose ▪ The doctor prescribed daily *drops* for the child's ears. ▪ ***eye/ear drops***
5 [*count*] **:** a usually small, round piece of candy with a particular flavor ▪ We sucked on lemon *drops*. — see also COUGH DROP, GUMDROP
6 [*count*] **a :** the distance from a higher to a lower level — usually singular ▪ It is a 50-foot *drop* from the cliff to the ground below. **b :** an area that goes downward suddenly ▪ A steep *drop* in the river forms a waterfall.
7 [*count*] **:** a decrease in amount or quality — usually singular ▪ His income took a sudden *drop*. — often + *in* ▪ He had a sudden *drop in* income. ▪ The patient experienced a sharp *drop in* blood pressure. ▪ a *drop* [=*decline*] *in* prices/sales ▪ a four percent *drop in* body weight
8 [*count*] *informal* **a :** the act of taking something (such as something secret or illegal) to a place and leaving it there ▪ He made the *drop*. **b :** a place where something is taken to and left to be picked up ▪ I left the package at the *drop*. — see also AIRDROP, MAIL DROP
9 [*count*] *American football* **:** a move back from the line of scrimmage — usually singular ▪ The quarterback made a quick three-step *drop*.
a drop in the bucket (*US*) *or Brit* ***a drop in the ocean*** *informal* **:** an amount that is so small that it does not make an important difference or have much effect ▪ They need to raise thousands of dollars for this project, so our 20-dollar donation is just *a drop in the bucket*.
at the drop of a hat **:** very quickly and immediately ▪ He says he's ready to help us *at the drop of a hat*. ▪ She loses her temper *at the drop of a hat*.

²drop *verb* **drops; dropped; drop·ping**
1 a [+ *obj*] **:** to let (something) fall ▪ Be careful not to *drop* the chair on your foot. ▪ She *dropped* the apple core into the trash can. ▪ They *dropped* bombs on the city. ▪ He *dropped* the vase and it shattered into pieces. ▪ The player *dropped* the ball. ▪ The trees *drop* their needles in the winter. [=the needles fall off the trees in the winter] **b** [*no obj*] **:** to fall ▪ The pen rolled to the edge of the table and *dropped* to the floor. ▪ The book *dropped* from my hand. ▪ The ball *dropped* between the right and center fielders.
2 [*no obj*] **a :** to lie down or fall down suddenly ▪ He *dropped* (down) to the floor and hid under the bed. **b :** to lie down or become unconscious because you are sick or exhausted **:** COLLAPSE ▪ She was so tired she felt she would *drop*. ▪ He worked until he *dropped*. ▪ (*informal*) We're going to the mall to ***shop till we drop***.
3 [*no obj*] **:** to go down suddenly and form a steep slope ▪ The road *drops* into the valley. ▪ The cliff *drops* almost vertically.
4 a [*no obj*] **:** to change to a lower level, amount, position, etc. ▪ The temperature *dropped* (to 50 degrees). ▪ His voice *dropped* [=became quieter] as he told us the secret. ▪ Increased competition has caused prices to *drop*. [=*decline, go down*] ▪ Production has *dropped*. [=*decreased*] ▪ The team has *dropped* [=*fallen*] to third place. ▪ He *dropped* [=*fell*] behind the other runners when he hurt his ankle. **b** [+ *obj*] **:** to cause (something) to lessen or decrease in level or amount ▪ He *dropped* [=*lowered*] his voice. ▪ She *dropped* [=*reduced*] her speed when she saw the patrol car.
5 [+ *obj*] **:** to send (someone) a letter, note, etc. ▪ I'll *drop* you an e-mail when I know my schedule. ▪ ***Drop me a line*** [=write me a letter] sometime.
6 a [+ *obj*] **:** to stop talking or thinking about (something) ▪ You can *drop* that idea right now. ▪ Let's just ***drop the subject***. ▪ Just ***drop it***. I don't want to talk about it any more. **b** [*no obj*] **:** to stop being talked about ▪ Please let the matter *drop*. ▪ Once he starts talking about a subject he just won't ***let it drop***.
7 [+ *obj*] **:** to stop doing or continuing with (something) ▪ I'm going to *drop* my calculus class and take a biology course instead. ▪ New evidence was found and the case was *dropped*. ▪ The prosecutors ***dropped the charges*** against her. ▪ I ***dropped everything*** [=stopped what I was doing] and ran to the window to see what was going on.
8 [+ *obj*] **:** to not include (someone or something) ▪ You should *drop* [=*cut, omit*] this sentence from your essay. ▪ The newspaper decided to *drop* the story. ▪ He was *dropped* from the team.
9 [+ *obj*] **:** to suddenly end a relationship or connection with (someone) ▪ They dated for a while, but then she suddenly *dropped* him. ▪ She moved away and *dropped* her old friends.
10 [+ *obj*] **:** to take (someone or something) to a place and then leave ▪ She *dropped* him in front of the library. ▪ He *dropped* the package at the post office this morning. — often + *off* ▪ I *drop* the kids *off* at school in the morning. ▪ I'll *drop off* the paperwork as soon as it's all filled out.
11 *always followed by an adverb or preposition* [*no obj*] **:** to make a brief social visit — usually + *by* or *in* or *over* ▪ His sister *dropped by* unexpectedly. ▪ They *dropped in* for a chat. ▪ *Drop over* sometime! ▪ We were in the neighborhood and thought we would ***drop in on*** you. — see also DROP-IN
12 [+ *obj*] **:** to say (something) in an informal or casual way ▪ He casually *dropped* the news that they are getting married. ▪ She's always ***dropping names***. [=saying the names of famous people she knows to try to impress others] ▪ She has been ***dropping hints*** that she is looking for another job.
13 [+ *obj*] *informal* **:** to lose (a game) ▪ They *dropped* the first game but won the next two.
14 [+ *obj*] *informal* **:** to spend (an amount of money) — usually + *on* ▪ She *dropped* $300 *on* a new suit.
15 [+ *obj*] *informal* **:** to lose (an amount of weight) ▪ Through diet and exercise, I managed to *drop* 20 pounds in a year.
16 : to move down [+ *obj*] When the teacher became angry at her, she ***dropped her eyes/head***. [=she looked down] [*no obj*] His gaze *dropped* to the floor in embarrassment.
17 [+ *obj*] *knitting* **:** to let (a loop of yarn) fall off a knitting needle ▪ Count the stitches on the needle to make sure you didn't *drop* one. ▪ Be careful you don't ***drop a stitch***.
18 [+ *obj*] **:** to not pronounce (a letter) when you speak ▪ When she spoke quickly, she *dropped* the "g" in "running."
19 [+ *obj*] *informal* **:** to take (a drug) by swallowing it ▪ They ***dropped acid***. [=they took LSD]
drop a brick *or* ***drop a clanger*** *Brit, informal* **:** to make a very bad or embarrassing mistake
drop back [*phrasal verb*] *American football* **:** to move straight back from the line of scrimmage ▪ The quarterback *dropped back* and threw a long pass down the field.
drop dead see ¹DEAD
drop in/into/on your lap see ¹LAP
drop off [*phrasal verb*] **1 :** to decrease in amount ▪ After the holidays, business usually *drops off*. **2 :** to fall asleep ▪ The baby tends to *drop off* after he eats. ▪ She lay down and ***dropped off to sleep***. — see also ²DROP 10 (above)
drop out [*phrasal verb*] **1 :** to stop attending a school or university before you have completed your studies ▪ He *dropped out* after 10th grade. — often + *of* ▪ He *dropped out of* [=*quit*] college/school and began working full-time. **2 :** to stop being part of a group — usually + *of* ▪ She was the first to *drop out of* the band. **3 :** to stop being involved in regular society because you do not agree with or support its rules, customs, and values ▪ Back in the sixties he *dropped out* and lived as a hippie for several years. — see also DROPOUT
drop out of sight **:** to stop being seen ▪ The house *dropped out of sight* as we drove over the hill. ▪ a famous and successful actor who suddenly *dropped out of sight*
drop the ball see ¹BALL
jaw drops see ¹JAW
the bottom drop out see ¹BOTTOM
the penny drops see PENNY
you could hear a pin drop see ¹PIN

drop cloth *noun, pl* **~ cloths** [*count*] *US* **:** a sheet of cloth or plastic that is used to cover the floor and furniture while you are painting a room — compare DUST SHEET

drop–dead /ˈdrɑːpˈdɛd/ *adj, informal* **:** very attractive or impressive ▪ a *drop-dead* evening gown
– drop–dead *adv* ▪ an actress who is *drop-dead* gorgeous

drop–dead date *noun, pl* **~ dates** [*count*] *US* **:** a date by which something must be done or finished **:** a deadline that must be met ▪ They were given a *drop-dead date* of June 30 to accept or reject the contract.

drop–down menu *noun, pl* **~ menus** [*count*] *computers* **:** a list of choices that appears on a computer screen when a person clicks on the menu's title ▪ To print the document, click on "print" in the "file" *drop-down menu*. — called also *drop-down list, pull-down menu*

drop goal *noun, pl* **~ goals** [*count*] *rugby* **:** a goal that is made by a dropkick

drop–in /ˈdrɑːpˌɪn/ *adj, always used before a noun*
1 *of a place* **:** able to be visited without an appointment ▪ a *drop-in* clinic/lab/restaurant ▪ a *drop-in* medical center
2 *of a person* **:** visiting a place without an appointment ▪ *drop-in* customers/clients

drop·kick /ˈdrɑːpˌkɪk/ *noun, pl* **-kicks** [*count*] **:** a kick that

is made by dropping a ball to the ground and kicking it as it begins to bounce back up
– drop–kick /ˈdrɑːpˌkɪk/ *verb* **-kicks**; **-kicked**; **-kick•ing** [+ *obj*] ▪ He *drop-kicked* the ball.

drop•let /ˈdrɑːplət/ *noun, pl* **-lets** [*count*] **:** a very small drop of liquid ▪ *Droplets* of water collected on the windows.

drop–off /ˈdrɑːpˌɑːf/ *noun, pl* **-offs** [*count*]
1 : a very steep downward slope ▪ The *drop-off* along the trail is very steep.
2 : a very large decrease in level or amount ▪ There has been a *drop-off* in attendance this year. — see also *drop off* at ²DROP
3 : the act of taking someone or something to a place and then leaving **:** the act of dropping someone or something off ▪ This area is for student *drop-offs*.

drop•out /ˈdrɑːpˌaʊt/ *noun, pl* **-outs** [*count*]
1 : a person who stops going to a school, college, etc., before finishing **:** a person who drops out of school ▪ The program is designed for *dropouts* who wish to get high school equivalency certificates. ▪ a high school *dropout*
2 : a person who stops being involved in society because he or she does not believe in its rules, customs, and values — see also *drop out* at ²DROP

drop pass *noun, pl* **~ passes** [*count*] *ice hockey* **:** a pass in which a player stops the puck and skates past it in order to leave it for another player who is close behind

dropped *adj, always used before a noun, of clothing* **:** made to be in a lower position on the body than is usual ▪ a dress with a *dropped* waist ▪ *dropped* shoulders

drop•per /ˈdrɑːpɚ/ *noun, pl* **-pers** [*count*] **:** a glass or plastic tube that is used to measure out liquids by drops ▪ He put drops in his eyes with a *dropper*. — called also *eyedropper, medicine dropper*

drop•ping /ˈdrɑːpɪŋ/ *noun, pl* **-pings** [*count*] **:** a piece of solid waste from an animal or bird — usually plural ▪ bird *droppings*

drop shot *noun, pl* **~ shots** [*count*] **:** a softly hit shot in tennis or a similar game that falls quickly after passing over the net

dross /ˈdrɑːs/ *noun* [*noncount*]
1 *technical* **:** unwanted material that is removed from a mineral (such as gold) to make it better
2 : something of low value or quality ▪ There is quite a lot of *dross* on TV these days. ▪ His editor has a talent for turning literary *dross* into gold.

drought /ˈdraʊt/ *noun, pl* **droughts :** a long period of time during which there is very little or no rain [*count*] The *drought* caused serious damage to crops. [*noncount*] a period of *drought* that lasted several years

¹drove /ˈdroʊv/ *noun, pl* **droves** [*count*] **:** a large group of people or animals that move or act together ▪ a *drove* of cattle — usually plural ▪ *droves* of students ▪ People came ***in droves*** [=many people came] to hear her sing.

²drove *past tense of* ¹DRIVE

drov•er /ˈdroʊvɚ/ *noun, pl* **-ers** [*count*] *chiefly Brit* **:** a person who moves groups of animals (such as cattle or sheep) from one place to another

drown /ˈdraʊn/ *verb* **drowns; drowned; drown•ing**
1 a [*no obj*] **:** to die by being underwater too long and unable to breathe ▪ Four people *drowned* in the flood. ▪ She fell in the river and *drowned*. **b** [+ *obj*] **:** to hold (a person or animal) underwater until death occurs ▪ She claims that he tried to *drown* her. ▪ He tried to *drown* himself.
2 [+ *obj*] **:** to cover (something) completely with a liquid ▪ The river overflowed, *drowning* whole villages. ▪ The food was *drowned* in sauce.
3 [+ *obj*] **:** to cause (something or someone) not to be heard by making a loud noise ▪ The loud music *drowned* the sound of their conversation. — usually + *out* ▪ Noise from the passing airplane *drowned out* our conversation. ▪ He talked loudly to try to *drown* her *out*.
4 : to experience or be affected by too much of something **:** to be overwhelmed by something — usually + *in* [*no obj*] Many young people today are *drowning in* credit card debt. ▪ She was *drowning in* sadness. [+ *obj*] I'm being *drowned in* paperwork. [=I'm being overwhelmed by paperwork]
5 [+ *obj*] **:** to forget about (unpleasant feelings or thoughts) by getting drunk ▪ He went to the bar to ***drown his sorrows***. ▪ He was trying to ***drown his fears***. [=to get drunk so that he wouldn't be afraid]
– drowning *noun, pl* **-ings** [*count, noncount*]

drowse /ˈdraʊz/ *verb* **drows•es; drowsed; drows•ing** [*no obj*] **:** to sleep lightly or to almost be asleep ▪ She drove while I *drowsed* [=(more commonly) *dozed*] in the back seat.

drowsy /ˈdraʊzi/ *adj* **drows•i•er; -est** [*also more ~; most ~*]
1 : tired and ready to fall asleep ▪ I started feeling *drowsy* [=*sleepy*] and decided to take a nap.
2 : causing you to feel relaxed and ready to sleep ▪ We spent a *drowsy* afternoon by the pool.
– drows•i•ly /ˈdraʊzəli/ *adv* **– drows•i•ness** *noun* [*noncount*] ▪ These medications may cause *drowsiness*.

drub•bing /ˈdrʌbɪŋ/ *noun, pl* **-bings** [*count*] *informal* **:** an occurrence in which one person or team easily beats another person or team ▪ She withdrew after her *drubbing* [=after she was badly beaten] in the New Hampshire primary. ▪ Our team ***took a drubbing***. = They ***gave us a drubbing***. [=they beat us very easily]

drudge /ˈdrʌʤ/ *noun, pl* **drudg•es** [*count*] **:** a person who does boring, difficult, or unpleasant work ▪ She was tired of working as an office *drudge*. — often used before another noun ▪ *drudge* work ▪ a *drudge* job

drudg•ery /ˈdrʌʤəri/ *noun* [*noncount*] **:** boring, difficult, or unpleasant work ▪ He hated the *drudgery* of his job.

¹drug /ˈdrʌg/ *noun, pl* **drugs** [*count*]
1 : a substance that is used as a medicine ▪ a new *drug* used to treat people with high blood pressure ▪ an experimental *drug* for the treatment of AIDS ▪ ***prescription drugs*** [=drugs that people are allowed to use only if they have a note from a doctor] ▪ a ***miracle/wonder drug*** [=a drug that is very effective] — often used before another noun ▪ *drug* treatment/therapy ▪ *drug* companies
2 : an illegal and often harmful substance (such as heroin, cocaine, LSD, or marijuana) that people take for pleasure ▪ Have you ever taken/used any illegal *drugs*? ▪ He got ***hooked on drugs*** [=he became addicted to drugs] at an early age. ▪ I don't smoke, drink, or ***do drugs***. ▪ She looks like she's ***on drugs***. [=like she uses drugs or is high on a drug] — often used before another noun ▪ intravenous *drug* users [=people who inject drugs into their veins] ▪ She died of a *drug* overdose. ▪ *drug*-treatment programs ▪ *drug* addiction/addicts/abuse — see also DESIGNER DRUG, GATEWAY DRUG

²drug *verb* **drugs; drugged; drug•ging** [+ *obj*]
1 : to give a drug to (a person or animal) in order to make that person or animal very sleepy or unconscious ▪ He looks like he's been *drugged*.
2 : to add a drug to (a food or drink) in order to make someone sleepy or unconscious ▪ Someone could have *drugged* your drink.

drug dealer *noun, pl* **~ -ers** [*count*] **:** a person who sells illegal drugs

drug•gie /ˈdrʌgi/ *noun, pl* **-gies** [*count*] *informal* **:** a person who often uses illegal drugs

drugging *noun* [*noncount*] *chiefly US, informal* **:** use of illegal drugs ▪ His drinking and *drugging* will kill him one day.

drug•gist /ˈdrʌgɪst/ *noun, pl* **-gists** [*count*] *US, somewhat old-fashioned* **:** a person who prepares and sells medicines **:** PHARMACIST ▪ Your local *druggist* can fill the prescription.

drug•store /ˈdrʌgˌstoɚ/ *noun, pl* **-stores** [*count*] *US* **:** a store that sells medicines and various other products (such as newspapers, candy, soap, etc.)

dru•id *or* **Druid** /ˈdruːwɪd/ *noun, pl* **-ids** [*count*] **:** a member of a group of priests in an ancient British religion

¹drum /ˈdrʌm/ *noun, pl* **drums**
1 [*count*] **:** a musical instrument that is made with a thin layer of skin or plastic stretched over the end of a round frame and that is played by hitting the skin or plastic with sticks or with your hands ▪ a child beating on a *drum* ▪ We heard the rhythmic beating of *drums*. ▪ She plays the *drums*. ▪ That was Miles Davis on trumpet and Max Roach ***on drums***. [=playing the drums] — see also KETTLEDRUM, SNARE DRUM, STEEL DRUM
2 [*noncount*] **:** the sound that is made when something hits a surface over and over again ▪ He lay listening to the steady *drum* of the rain on the roof.
3 [*count*] **a :** a large usually metal container for liquids ▪ oil *drums* ▪ a 55-gallon *drum* **b :** a machine or part of a machine that is shaped like a cylinder ▪ the *drum* of a clothes dryer
beat/bang the drum for **:** to say or write things that strongly support (someone or something) ▪ They joined together to *beat the drum for* their candidate. ▪ *banging the drum for* human rights

²drum *verb* **drums; drummed; drum•ming**

1 [*no obj*] **:** to beat or play a drum or set of drums • She *drummed* while he played the guitar.

2 : to make a sound by hitting a surface over and over again [*no obj*] Rain *drummed* [=*beat*] on the roof. • Her fingers *drummed* nervously on the table. [+ *obj*] He was nervously *drumming* a pencil on the desk. • She was ***drumming her fingers*** [=rapidly tapping her fingertips] on the table.

drum into [*phrasal verb*] ***drum (something) into (someone)*** **:** to force (something) to be learned by (someone) by repeating it over and over again • Our teacher *drummed* the lesson *into* our heads. • The importance of saying "please" and "thank you" was *drummed into* us as children.

drum out of [*phrasal verb*] ***drum (someone) out of (something)*** **:** to force (someone) to leave (a place or organization) • They *drummed* her *out of* the club. • He got *drummed out* of the military.

drum up [*phrasal verb*] ***drum up (something)*** *also* ***drum (something) up*** **:** to get or create (support, business, etc.) through hard work and a lot of effort • They sent out flyers to *drum up* support for their candidate. • Somehow, we need to *drum up* some new business. • The company is trying to *drum up* demand for a new product.

drum•beat /ˈdrʌmˌbiːt/ *noun, pl* **-beats** [*count*] **:** the sound made by beating a drum • I could hear the *drumbeat* of a parade down the street. • hard and fast *drumbeats* • a rock-and-roll *drumbeat* — often used figuratively • The constant *drumbeat* for better working conditions [=the constant effort and complaints from people who demanded better working conditions] finally made a difference. • The *drumbeat* of opposition has increased in recent months. • We have been subjected to a steady *drumbeat* [=*barrage*] of bad news.

drum kit *noun, pl* **~ kits** [*count*] **:** a set of drums and cymbals

drum machine *noun, pl* **~ -chines** [*count*] **:** an electronic device that makes sounds like the sounds of a drum

drum major *noun, pl* **~ -jors** [*count*] **:** the leader of a marching band

drum majorette *noun, pl* **~ -ettes** [*count*] **:** MAJORETTE

drum•mer /ˈdrʌmɚ/ *noun, pl* **-mers** [*count*] **:** a person who plays a drum or a set of drums • The band got a new *drummer*.

different drummer *US* — used in phrases like ***march to the beat of a different drummer*** to describe a person who thinks, lives, or behaves in an unusual way • His strange behavior was no surprise—he had always *marched to (the beat of) a different drummer*. [=done things differently from other people] • Her friends went to college, but she ***heard a different drummer*** and moved to the city to be an actor.

drum roll *noun, pl* **~ rolls** [*count*] **:** a continuous sound made by a series of very quick hits on a drum especially in order to introduce an exciting public announcement, act, etc.

drum•stick /ˈdrʌmˌstɪk/ *noun, pl* **-sticks** [*count*]

1 : the lower part of the leg of a bird (such as a chicken or turkey) that is eaten as food

2 : a stick used for playing a drum

[1]**drunk** *past participle of* [1]DRINK

[2]**drunk** /ˈdrʌŋk/ *adj* **drunk•er; -est** [*also more ~; most ~*]

1 : having drunk so much alcohol that normal actions (such as talking, thinking, and moving) become difficult to do • I don't like being around *drunk* people. • She was so *drunk* that she could barely walk. • I was *drunk* and couldn't think straight. • We ***got drunk*** on wine. • He was ***blind drunk***. = He was ***roaring drunk***. = (*chiefly US*) He was ***stinking drunk***. [=he was extremely drunk] • (*US*) He was ***(as) drunk as a skunk***. = (*Brit*) He was ***(as) drunk as a lord***. [=he was extremely drunk]

2 : behaving in an unusual or improper way because of excitement, anger, etc. — usually + *with* • He was *drunk with* power/anger/excitement. — see also PUNCH-DRUNK

[3]**drunk** *noun, pl* **drunks** [*count*]

1 *disapproving* **:** a person who is drunk or who often gets drunk • the town *drunk*

2 *informal* **:** a period of time when someone drinks too much alcohol • They went on a two-day *drunk*. [=*bender, binge*]

drunk•ard /ˈdrʌŋkɚd/ *noun, pl* **-ards** [*count*] *disapproving* **:** a person who is drunk or who often gets drunk • Her father was a *drunkard*.

drunk driver *noun, pl* **~ -ers** [*count*] *chiefly US* **:** a person who drives a vehicle while drunk • He was killed by a *drunk driver*. — called also *drunken driver, (Brit) drink-driver*

drunk driving *noun* [*noncount*] *chiefly US* **:** the act of driving a vehicle while drunk • He was arrested for *drunk driving*. — called also *drunken driving, (Brit) drink-driving*

drunk•en /ˈdrʌŋkən/ *adj, always used before a noun*

1 : drunk or often becoming drunk • The streets were filled with *drunken* revelers on New Year's Eve. • He lives in an apartment with his *drunken* mother.

2 : caused by drinking too much alcohol • He fell into a *drunken* stupor.

3 : involving people who are drunk • A *drunken* brawl broke out at the bar.

– drunk•en•ly *adv* • She staggered *drunkenly* to a chair. **– drunk•en•ness** /ˈdrʌŋkənnəs/ *noun* [*noncount*]

drunk tank *noun, pl* **~ tanks** [*count*] *US, informal* **:** a large jail cell where drunk people who have been arrested are kept

druth•ers /ˈdrʌðɚz/ *noun* [*plural*] *US, informal* **:** the power or opportunity to choose • ***If I had my druthers***, [=if I could choose what to do] I would travel all the time. • ***Given her druthers***, she would play tennis every day.

D

[1]**dry** /ˈdraɪ/ *adj* **dri•er; -est** [*also more ~; most ~*]

1 a : having no or very little water or liquid • a *dry* riverbed • Mix the *dry* ingredients first, then add the milk and eggs. • a cool, *dry* place • Wipe the surface *dry*. [=wipe the surface until it is dry] • The air is usually *dry* during the winter. [=there is very little moisture in the air] • the *dry* heat of the desert • We tried to ***stay/keep dry*** in the rain by standing under a tree. • The stream is usually ***(as) dry as a bone*** [=completely dry] this time of year. • The stream is ***bone dry***. **b :** no longer wet • Are the clothes *dry* yet? • The paint should be *dry* in a few hours.

2 : having no rain or little rain • This has been an unusually *dry* summer. [=there has been little rain this summer] • a stretch of *dry* weather • a *dry* spell/season • a country with a very *dry* climate • This plant does well in *dry* conditions.

3 a : not having the usual or desired amount of moisture • My throat is *dry*. • My lips are *dry*. • *dry*, itchy skin • *dry* hair • The medication can cause ***dry mouth***. [=a condition in which the inside of your mouth become very dry] **b :** having the moisture removed by cooking or some other process • The chicken was *dry* and tasteless. • *dry* [=*powdered*] milk

4 : not producing a wet substance • a *dry* cough [=a cough that does not produce any phlegm] • The baby stayed *dry* all night. [=the baby did not urinate all night] • His eyes were *dry*. [=there were no tears in his eyes] ✧ If there is ***not a dry eye in the house/room (etc.)***, everyone in a place is emotional or is affected deeply by something. • When the hero proclaimed his love for the heroine at the end of the play, there *wasn't a dry eye in the house*.

5 : no longer producing water, oil, etc. • a *dry* well • a *dry* oil well • The well ***went/ran dry***. • (*chiefly US*) They drilled for oil but the well ***came up dry***. — often used figuratively • The author went through a *dry* [=*unproductive*] period and couldn't write anything. • The group stayed together despite several *dry* [=*unsuccessful*] years. • They went searching for clues but *came up dry*. [=*came up empty*]

6 : served or eaten without butter, jam, etc. • a breakfast of *dry* toast and coffee

7 *of wine, sherry, etc.* **:** not sweet • a very *dry* red wine • *dry* sherry

8 : not interesting, exciting, or emotional • The novel included several long, *dry* [=*boring*] passages. • His lectures were usually very *dry*.

9 : funny or clever but expressed in a quiet or serious way • He has a very *dry* sense of humor. • a *dry* wit

10 a : not having or offering alcoholic beverages • a *dry* party **b :** not allowing alcoholic beverages • The college campus has been *dry* for 10 years. • a *dry* state/county [=a state/county where alcoholic beverages cannot be sold] **c :** not drinking alcoholic beverages • He's been *dry* [=*sober*] for several years now.

high and dry see [2]HIGH

home and dry see [2]HOME

keep your powder dry see [1]POWDER

milk/bleed/suck (someone or something) dry *informal* **:** to take or use up everything from (someone or something) • He married her for her money and then *bled* her *dry*. • She *milked* the system *dry*.

– dry•ness *noun* [*noncount*]

[2]**dry** *verb* **dries; dried; dry•ing**

1 a [+ *obj*] **:** to remove water or moisture from (something or someone) **:** to make (something or someone) dry • I'll wash the dishes if you *dry* them. • Make sure you *dry* your hands. • He *dried* himself with the towel. • Stop crying and *dry* your

eyes. **b** [*no obj*] **:** to make plates, dishes, pots, etc., dry by rubbing them with a towel • I'll wash and you *dry*, okay?
2 [*no obj*] **:** to become dry • Your shirt is *drying* on the clothesline. • The paint *dried* overnight. — see also AIR-DRY, DRIP-DRY, FREEZE-DRY

dry off [*phrasal verb*] **1 a :** to become dry • My umbrella's *drying off* in the hall. **b :** to make your body dry • We got out of the pool and *dried off*. **2 *dry off (someone or something) or dry (someone or something) off* :** to make (someone or something) dry • He *dried off* the bench and sat down. • *Dry* yourself *off* and get dressed.

dry out [*phrasal verb*] **1 :** to become dry • Water the plant every week; don't allow the soil to *dry out* completely. **2 *dry out (something) or dry (something) out* :** to make (something) dry • The wind *dries out* my eyes. • Baking at a high temperature will *dry* the meat *out*. • We *dried out* our shoes near the fire. **3 *informal* :** to stop using drugs or alcohol for a period of time especially by going to a special kind of hospital • After years of alcoholism, he went to a clinic to *dry out*.

dry up [*phrasal verb*] **1 :** to become completely dry • The river/well is *drying up*. • The stream *dries up* every summer. **2 *dry up (something) or dry (something) up* :** to make (something) dry • The sun had *dried up* the roads an hour after it stopped raining. **3 *informal* :** to go away or disappear completely • Interest in the project *dried up* when he withdrew his support. • After several months, new leads in the murder investigation *dried up*. **4 *dry up (something) or dry (something) up* :** to cause the supply of (something) to go away or disappear • Closing the factory *dried up* local job opportunities. **5 *informal + impolite*** — used as a command to tell someone to stop talking • Oh, *dry up*! [=*shut up*] I'm sick of hearing what you have to say. • He told her to *dry up*.

hang (someone or something) out to dry see *hang out* at [1]HANG

dry cell *noun, pl* **~ cells** [*count*] **:** a sealed container that holds chemicals which are used for producing electricity — called also *dry battery*

dry–clean /ˈdraɪˌkliːn/ *verb* **-cleans; -cleaned; -cleaning** [+ *obj*] **:** to clean (clothing, curtains, etc.) by using special chemicals instead of water • His suit was *dry-cleaned*.

dry cleaner *noun, pl* **~ -ers** [*count*] **:** a shop where clothes and other cloth items are dry-cleaned • I take my clothes to a local *dry cleaner*. • My wool coat is still at ***the dry cleaner's/cleaners***.

dry cleaning *noun* [*noncount*]
1 : the process of cleaning cloth with special chemicals instead of water • *Dry cleaning* is recommended. • a *dry-cleaning* shop [=a shop that does dry cleaning]
2 : clothing or cloth items that have been dry-cleaned • I can pick up the *dry cleaning* on my way home.

dry dock *noun, pl* **~ docks :** a dock that can be kept dry and that is used for building or repairing boats or ships [*count*] The *dry dock* is full. [*noncount*] The ship is in *dry dock*.

dry•er *also* **dri•er** /ˈdrajɚ/ *noun, pl* **-ers** [*count*] **:** a device that is used for drying something (such as clothes or hair) by using heat or air • He threw his wet clothes in the *dryer*. • Her hair *dryer* broke. — see also BLOW-DRYER

dry–eyed /ˈdraɪˌaɪd/ *adj* **:** not crying • She was *dry-eyed* during the funeral but cried all the way home afterwards.

dry goods *noun* [*plural*]
1 : items (such as tobacco, tea, and coffee) that do not contain liquid
2 *US, old-fashioned* **:** items made of cloth (such as fabrics, lace, and ribbon)

dry heaves *noun* [*plural*] *US* **:** a condition in which someone is vomiting but nothing is coming up from the stomach • He had a case of (the) *dry heaves*.

dry ice *noun* [*noncount*] **:** solid carbon dioxide that is used mainly to keep food and other things cold and to create the appearance of smoke and fog in plays, movies, etc.

dry land *noun* [*noncount*] **:** land that is not covered with water **:** land as opposed to the ocean, a lake, etc. • The sea was rough and we couldn't wait to get back to *dry land*.

dry•ly *also* **dri•ly** /ˈdraɪli/ *adv* [*more ~; most ~*]
1 : in a funny but quiet or serious way • "I love this store!" "I couldn't tell," she said *dryly*.
2 : without excitement or emotion • "If that's the way it must be," he remarked *dryly*, "that's the way it will be."

dry rot *noun* [*noncount*] **:** a condition in which wood is destroyed by a type of fungus • The windowsill was badly damaged by *dry rot*. • *Dry rot* had eaten away part of the beam.

dry run *noun, pl* **~ runs** [*count*] **:** a practice event that is done to prepare for the actual event that will happen in the future • We did a *dry run* of the experiment. • After several *dry runs*, she was ready to give the speech. — called also (*Brit*) *dummy run*

dry•stone wall /ˈdraɪˌstoʊn-/ *noun, pl* **~ walls** [*count*] *Brit* **:** a stone wall that is made without mortar to hold the stones together

dry•wall /ˈdraɪˌwɑːl/ *noun* [*noncount*] *US* **:** building material that is used for making walls and ceilings and that is made of large sheets of plaster covered with thick paper **:** PLASTERBOARD

DSL *abbr* digital subscriber line • high-speed *DSL* Internet access ✧ *DSL* refers to a system that uses telephone lines to allow you to connect to the Internet at high speeds.

DSS *abbr* Department of Social Services ✧ In the U.S., a state's Department of Social Services is usually responsible for protecting children from harmful treatment, helping people to adopt children, and providing advice and support to families and children who need it.

DTP *abbr* **1** desktop publishing **2** *or* ***DTaP*** diphtheria, tetanus, and pertussis • You need to have the *DTaP* vaccine before you can enroll in school.

D.T.'s /ˌdiːˈtiːz/ *noun* [*plural*] **:** a condition that is caused by drinking too much alcohol for a very long time and that causes a person to shake and see things that are not real — usually used with *the* • an alcoholic who has *the D.T.'s* — called also *delirium tremens*

du•al /ˈduːwəl, *Brit* ˈdjuːwəl/ *adj, always used before a noun*
1 : having two different parts, uses, etc. • the *dual* purpose of the study • The song's lyrics have a *dual* [=(more commonly) *double*] meaning. • a *dual* function • She held ***dual citizenship*** in France and the United States. [=she was a citizen of both countries]
2 : having two of something • Our car has *dual* air bags. [=has two air bags] • She pursued *dual* careers in music and acting. • families with *dual* incomes
– du•al•ly *adv* • He is *dually* certified to teach math and science.

dual car•riage•way /-ˈkerɪʤˌweɪ/ *noun, pl* **~ -ways** [*count*] *Brit* **:** DIVIDED HIGHWAY

du•al•ism /ˈduːwəˌlɪzəm, *Brit* ˈdjuːwəˌlɪzəm/ *noun* [*noncount*]
1 *philosophy* **:** the idea or belief that everything has two opposite parts or principles
2 *formal* **:** the quality or state of having two different or opposite parts or elements • the *dualism* of human nature • the *dualism* of good and evil
– du•al•ist /ˈduːwəlɪst, *Brit* ˈdjuːwəlɪst/ *noun, pl* **-ists** [*count*] **– du•al•is•tic** /ˌduːwəˈlɪstɪk, *Brit* ˌdjuːwəˈlɪstɪk/ *adj* • a *dualistic* view/approach

du•al•i•ty /duˈæləti, *Brit* djuˈæləti/ *noun, pl* **-ties** *formal* **:** the quality or state of having two parts [*noncount*] the *duality* of human nature [*count*] They discussed the *dualities* of the novel's characters.

[1]**dub** /ˈdʌb/ *verb* **dubs; dubbed; dub•bing** [+ *obj*]
1 : to give (someone or something) a name or title • The actress was *dubbed* "America's sweetheart." • Critics *dubbed* him the new king of rock 'n' roll.
2 : to give (someone) the title of a knight • The queen *dubbed* him Sir Philip.
– compare [2]DUB

[2]**dub** *verb* **dubs; dubbed; dub•bing** [+ *obj*]
1 : to replace the original recorded speech in a movie or television show with speech recorded in another language • He was hired to *dub* the dialogue for a foreign film. — often used as *(be) dubbed* • The film *was dubbed* in/into French and Spanish.
2 : to add (speech or other sounds) to a movie or television show — usually + *in* • They *dubbed in* the music. = They *dubbed* the music *in*.
3 : to make a copy of (a movie, piece of music, etc.) that has already been recorded • *dub* a CD
– compare [1]DUB

du•bi•ous /ˈduːbijəs, *Brit* ˈdjuːbijəs/ *adj* [*more ~; most ~*]
1 *not used before a noun* **:** unsure or uncertain **:** feeling doubt about something — usually + *about* • I was *dubious* [=*doubtful*] *about* our chances for success.
2 : causing doubt, uncertainty, or suspicion **:** likely to be bad or wrong • Her conclusions are pretty *dubious*, if you

ask me. [=her conclusions are probably wrong] ▪ He made the highly *dubious* claim that Elvis is still alive and living in Hawaii. ▪ She was a *dubious* choice for the job. [=she was not a good choice for the job] ▪ They got their money through *dubious* means/methods. [=methods that were probably dishonest or illegal] ▪ a man of *dubious* character

3 — used ironically in phrases like ***dubious honor*** and ***dubious distinction*** to describe something bad or undesirable as if it were an honor or achievement ▪ He is the lawyer with the *dubious honor* of having lost the most cases in the firm. ▪ We had the *dubious distinction* of losing 12 games in a row.

– **du·bi·ous·ly** *adv* ▪ He looked at me *dubiously* when I explained why I was late. – **du·bi·ous·ness** *noun* [*noncount*]

du·cal /ˈduːkəl, *Brit* ˈdjuːkəl/ *adj, always used before a noun* : of or relating to a duke ▪ the *ducal* palace ▪ a *ducal* title

duch·ess /ˈdʌʧəs/ *noun, pl* **-ess·es** [*count*]

1 : the wife or widow of a duke

2 : a woman who has the same rank as a duke

duchy /ˈdʌʧi/ *noun, pl* **duch·ies** [*count*] : an area of land that is controlled by a duke or duchess

[1]**duck** /ˈdʌk/ *noun, pl* **ducks**

1 [*count*] : any one of many different kinds of birds that swim and have a flat beak, a short neck, a heavy body, short legs, and webbed feet — often used before another noun ▪ *duck* eggs/feathers ▪ a *duck* pond ▪ *duck* hunting — see color picture on page C9

2 [*count*] : a female duck — compare DRAKE

3 [*noncount*] : the meat of a duck used as food ▪ crispy roast *duck*

4 [*count*] *informal* : a person who you think is lucky, unusual, etc. ▪ He's an ***odd duck*** [=a strange person] ▪ You ***lucky duck***!

5 *or* ***ducks*** *Brit, informal* — used to address someone you love ▪ How was your day, *ducks*? [=*sweetheart, darling*]

like a duck to water *informal* : very quickly or easily ▪ She ***took to dancing like a duck (takes) to water.*** [=she learned to dance very quickly and easily] ▪ He *took to her like a duck to water.* [=he liked her immediately]

water off a duck's back see [1]WATER

– see also DEAD DUCK, LAME DUCK, SITTING DUCK

[2]**duck** *verb* **ducks; ducked; duck·ing**

1 a [*no obj*] : to lower your head or body suddenly to avoid being seen or hit ▪ The ceiling was so low I had to *duck*. — often + *down* ▪ Quick, *duck down* before they see us! **b** [+ *obj*] : to lower (your head) suddenly ▪ The ceiling was so low I had to *duck* my head. ▪ He *ducked* his head so they wouldn't see him. **c** [+ *obj*] : to avoid (something, such as a punch) by lowering your head or body suddenly ▪ He *ducked* the punch.

2 [+ *obj*] : to avoid (something or someone you do not want to see or deal with) ▪ We can't afford to *duck* the issue any longer. ▪ He managed to *duck* [=*evade*] the question. ▪ They've been *ducking* each other for months.

3 *always followed by an adverb or preposition* [*no obj*] : to move quickly ▪ She *ducked* into a store when it started to rain. ▪ He *ducked* around a corner.

4 [+ *obj*] *Brit* : to push (someone or something) underwater : DUNK ▪ The children were *ducking* each other in the pool.

duck out [*phrasal verb*] *informal* : to leave suddenly and usually without telling anyone that you are leaving ▪ We *ducked out* after the first act of the play. — often + *on* or *of* ▪ They *ducked out on* us without even saying goodbye. ▪ I had to *duck out of* the meeting to take a phone call. — often used figuratively ▪ He wants to *duck out of* the contract. [=to get out of the contract] ▪ She *ducked out on* paying the bill for the meal. [=she avoided paying the bill in a sneaky or improper way]

duck–billed platypus *noun, pl* ~ **-puses** [*count*] : PLATYPUS

duck·ling /ˈdʌklɪŋ/ *noun, pl* **-lings** [*count*]

1 : a young duck — see also UGLY DUCKLING

2 : the meat of a young duck that is used as food ▪ roast *duckling*

duck sauce *noun* [*noncount*] *US* : a sweet, thick sauce that is used in Chinese cooking

duck soup *noun* [*noncount*] *US, informal + old-fashioned* : something that is very easy to do ▪ The trip was *duck soup* for experienced travelers.

[1]**ducky** /ˈdʌki/ *adj* **duck·i·er; -est** [*also more* ~; *most* ~] *US, informal + somewhat old-fashioned* : very pleasing, delightful, or attractive ▪ Everything is just *ducky*. [=*satisfactory, fine*] — often used ironically to describe something that is bad or unpleasant ▪ "Our flight is delayed." "Well, isn't that just *ducky*!"

[2]**ducky** *noun, pl* **duck·ies** [*count*] *chiefly US, informal*

1 : a duck ✧ *Ducky* is used especially by children or when talking to children. ▪ Look at the cute little *ducky*!

2 : a toy duck ▪ a rubber *ducky* [=a rubber toy that looks like a duck]

duct /ˈdʌkt/ *noun, pl* **ducts** [*count*]

1 : a pipe or tube for air, water, electric power lines, etc., to pass through ▪ a building's air/heating/ventilation *ducts*

2 : a tube in the body that carries a particular liquid ▪ tear *ducts* ▪ the bile *duct*

duc·tile /ˈdʌktl, ˈdʌkˌtʰajəl/ *adj, technical, of a metal* : capable of being bent or pulled into different shapes ▪ *ductile* iron

duct·ing /ˈdʌktɪŋ/ *noun* [*noncount*] *technical*

1 : the material used to make ducts ▪ a piece of *ducting*

2 *chiefly Brit* : DUCTWORK

duct tape *noun* [*noncount*] : a wide, sticky, and usually silver tape that is made of cloth and that is used especially to repair things

duct·work /ˈdʌktˌwək/ *noun* [*noncount*] *chiefly US* : a system of ducts

[1]**dud** /ˈdʌd/ *noun, pl* **duds**

1 [*count*] : something that does not do what it is supposed to do : something that is a complete failure ▪ The movie was a box office *dud*. [=few people went to see the movie] ▪ The seeds must have been *duds* because the plants never grew. ▪ The firework was a *dud*. [=the firework did not explode]

2 ***duds*** [*plural*] *informal* : clothes ▪ She put on her new *duds* for the party.

[2]**dud** *adj, always used before a noun* — used to describe something that fails completely or does not work properly ▪ a *dud* grenade [=a grenade that does not explode] ▪ a *dud* movie [=a movie that fails] ▪ (*Brit*) a *dud* cheque [=a bad check, a check that cannot be cashed]

dude /ˈduːd, *Brit* ˈdjuːd/ *noun, pl* **dudes** [*count*] *chiefly US slang* : a man — used especially by young people ▪ He's a cool *dude*. [=*guy*] ▪ Ask that *dude* over there. ▪ a surfer *dude* ▪ Hey, *dude*, what's up?

dude ranch *noun, pl* ~ **ranches** [*count*] : a large farm especially in the western U.S. where people on vacation can ride horses and do other activities that cowboys typically do

dud·geon /ˈdʌʤən/ *noun*

in high dudgeon *formal* : feeling and usually showing that you are angry or offended ▪ She walked out of the meeting *in high dudgeon*.

[1]**due** /ˈduː, *Brit* ˈdjuː/ *adj*

1 *not used before a noun* : required or expected to happen : expected to be in a particular place at a particular time ▪ When is the assignment *due*? [=when are you supposed to give the completed assignment to your teacher?] ▪ Your books are *due* back to the library (by/on) May 15. [=you must return your books to the library by May 15] ▪ The movie is *due* out this summer. [=the movie is supposed to be released in theaters this summer] — often followed by *to + verb* ▪ They are *due to arrive* any minute now.

2 *not used before a noun* **a** : expected to be born ▪ The baby is *due* [=the baby will probably be born] in three weeks. **b** : expected to give birth ▪ When is she *due*? ▪ My wife is *due* in three weeks.

3 *not used before a noun* : having reached the date by which payment is required ▪ The bill is *due* at the end of the month. ▪ The balance is now *due*. ▪ The amount *due* is 45 dollars. ▪ The bill is ***past due***. [=it is late; it should have been paid before now]

4 *not used before a noun* — used to say that someone should be given something or has earned something ▪ He is *due* a full day's pay. ▪ Teachers are not always accorded the respect *due* (to) them. = They are not always given the respect they are *due*. ▪ He finally got the recognition he was *due*. ▪ I will ***give credit where credit is due.***

5 *always used before a noun* : appropriate or proper ▪ She accepted the compliment with *due* modesty. ▪ The issue demands *due* consideration. ▪ I will answer all of your questions ***in due time***. [=eventually at an appropriate time] ▪ The court agreed that he failed to exercise ***due care/caution/diligence*** in trying to prevent the accident. [=he should have done more to prevent the accident from happening]

due for : needing, requiring, or expecting something to happen ▪ I'm *due for* a dentist's appointment. [=I need to go to the dentist soon] ▪ He will be *due for* another raise in June.

D

due to : because of (something) • The accident was primarily *due to* her carelessness. • *Due to* the bad weather, the game was canceled. • Their success is *due to* a lot of hard work. = They are successful *due to* the fact that they work hard. • Traffic was slow *due to* roadwork. • The pool is closed *due to* the approaching storm.

in due course see [1]COURSE

with (all) due respect see [1]RESPECT

[2]**due** *noun, pl* **dues**

1 ***dues*** [*plural*] : a regular payment that you make to be a member of an organization • Membership *dues* are $45. • *Dues* are increasing this year. • Workers are required to join the union and pay *dues*.

2 [*noncount*] : something that someone should be given : something that a person has earned • He deserves to be given his *due*. • She has yet to receive her *due*. = She is still being denied her *due*. ✧ People use the phrase ***to give someone his/her due*** when they are going to say something good about someone they have criticized. • I can't say that I like him, but *to give him his due* [=to be fair to him], I trust him completely.

pay your dues : to work hard and have difficult experiences in order to become successful • I've *paid my dues*. It's time that I began reaping some benefits.

[3]**due** *adv* : directly or exactly — followed by *north, south, east,* or *west* • The lake is *due north* of the city. • The road runs *due south*.

due date *noun, pl* **~ dates** [*count*] : the day when someone or something is due: such as **a** : the day by which something must be done, paid, etc. • The *due date* for the assignment is Friday. • Tomorrow's the *due date* for our electricity bill. [=the bill must be paid by tomorrow] **b** : the day when a woman is expected to give birth • She started having contractions two weeks before her *due date*.

[1]**du·el** /ˈduːwəl, *Brit* ˈdjuːwəl/ *noun, pl* **-els** [*count*]

1 : a fight between two people that includes the use of weapons (such as guns or swords) and that usually happens while other people watch ✧ Duels were used in the past to settle arguments or protect someone's honor. • I challenge you to a *duel*.

2 : a situation in which two people or groups argue or compete with each other • They engaged in a *duel* of wits. • The baseball game turned into a *duel* between the teams' pitchers. = The game turned into a pitching *duel*.

[2]**duel** *verb* **duels**; *US* **du·eled** *or Brit* **du·elled**; *US* **du·el·ing** *or Brit* **du·el·ling** [*no obj*] : to fight a duel: such as **a** : to fight with someone using weapons (such as guns or swords) while other people watch • He accepted the challenge to *duel*. **b** : to compete or argue with someone • Legislators *dueled* over the tax increases. • The two runners *dueled* for the lead.

due process *noun* [*noncount*] *US, law* : the official and proper way of doing things in a legal case : the rule that a legal case must be done in a way that protects the rights of all the people involved • *Due process* requires that evidence not be admitted when it is obtained through illegal methods.

du·et /duˈɛt, *Brit* djuˈɛt/ *noun, pl* **-ets** [*count*] : a piece of music that is performed by two singers or musicians • They sang the *duet* beautifully. • a piano and flute *duet*

duff /ˈdʌf/ *noun, pl* **duffs** [*count*] *US, informal* : the part of the body you sit on : BUTTOCKS • Get off your *duff* [=*butt, rear*] and help me!

duf·fel bag *or* **duf·fle bag** /ˈdʌfəl-/ *noun, pl* **~ bags** [*count*] : a large cloth bag that is held by a strap or handles and is used to carry personal belongings — see picture at BAG

duf·fer /ˈdʌfɚ/ *noun, pl* **-fers** [*count*] *informal*

1 *chiefly US* : a person who plays golf without much skill • We joined the other *duffers* at the course. • a weekend *duffer*

2 *Brit* : a clumsy or awkward person • He's a lovable old *duffer*.

dug *past tense and past participle of* [1]DIG

dug·out /ˈdʌgˌaʊt/ *noun, pl* **-outs** [*count*]

1 : a low shelter that faces a baseball field and contains the bench where the players and coaches of a team sit

2 : a shelter that is made by digging a hole in the ground or into the side of a hill

3 : a small boat that is made by cutting out the center of a large tree trunk — called also *dugout canoe*

duh /ˈdʌ, *usually with a prolonged vowel*/ *interj, US, informal*

1 — used in an angry or annoyed way to show that something just said is already known or is obvious • "It sure is dark out." "*Duh*, it's the middle of the night." • "You have to turn the key to start the car." "Well, *duh*." [=I know that]

2 — used to show or pretend that you do not know something • "Why didn't you leave earlier?" "*Duh*, I don't know."

DUI /ˌdiːˌjuːˈaɪ/ *noun, pl* **DUIs** *US* : the crime of driving a vehicle while drunk [*noncount*] He was arrested for *DUI*. [*count*] She was in jail on a *DUI*. — often used before another noun • a *DUI* arrest/conviction; *also* [*count*] : a person who is arrested for driving a vehicle while drunk • He is a convicted *DUI*. — called also *DWI* ✧ *DUI* is an abbreviation of "driving under the influence."

du jour /duˈʒɚ/ *adj, not used before a noun*

1 : served in a restaurant as a special item on a particular day • Our soup *du jour* is chicken noodle. • the vegetable/dessert *du jour*

2 *formal* : happening or popular at a particular time • Long hair was the style *du jour*. • the crisis *du jour* ✧ *Du jour* is a French phrase that means "of the day."

[1]**duke** /ˈduːk, *Brit* ˈdjuːk/ *noun, pl* **dukes**

1 [*count*] : a man of very high rank in the British nobility

2 [*count*] : the ruler of an independent area of land especially in some parts of Europe in the past — compare DUCHESS; see also ARCHDUKE

3 ***dukes*** [*plural*] *US slang, old-fashioned* : fists or hands • ***Put up your dukes*** and fight, you coward!

[2]**duke** *verb* **dukes**; **duked**; **duk·ing**

duke it out *US, informal* : to fight with your fists • A couple of drunks were *duking it out*. — often used figuratively • Scientists *duked it out* [=*argued*] over the causes of global warming. • Airlines are *duking it out* [=*competing*] for customers by lowering airfares.

duke·dom /ˈduːkdəm, *Brit* ˈdjuːkdəm/ *noun, pl* **-doms** [*count*]

1 : an area of land that is controlled by a duke or duchess : DUCHY

2 : the rank of a duke

dul·cet /ˈdʌlsət/ *adj* [*more ~; most ~*] *formal* : pleasant to hear • the *dulcet* [=*melodious*] sounds of the piano • her *dulcet* [=*sweet*] voice • the ***dulcet tones*** of her voice

dul·ci·mer /ˈdʌlsəmɚ/ *noun, pl* **-mers** [*count*]

1 : a flat musical instrument that has strings stretched across it and is played with two light hammers

2 : an instrument used in American folk music that has three or four strings, is held on the lap, and is played with the fingers, a pick, or a small stick

[1]**dull** /ˈdʌl/ *adj* **dull·er**; **-est**

1 : not exciting or interesting : BORING • a *dull* lecture/speaker • There's ***never a dull moment*** in our house. [=our house is always very busy or exciting]

2 : having an edge or point that is not sharp • a *dull* [=*blunt*] knife • a *dull* pencil

3 *of a sound* : not clear and loud • the *dull* roar of the crowd • He heard a *dull* [=*muffled*] thud.

4 *of pain* : constant but not sharp or severe • She complained of a *dull* ache/pain in her knee.

5 : not shiny • The paint has a *dull* finish. • The dog had no appetite and its eyes were *dull*.

6 : not sunny : having a lot of clouds • a *dull* winter sky

7 : slightly grayish or dark : not bright • a *dull* light • The sky was a *dull* blue.

8 *old-fashioned* : stupid or slow in understanding something • a *dull* student

9 : not having a lot of business or financial activity • a *dull* [=*slow, sluggish*] market

(as) dull as dishwater see DISHWATER

(as) dull as ditchwater see DITCHWATER

– dull·ness *noun* [*noncount*] • I couldn't get past the *dullness* of the book's topic. **– dul·ly** *adv* • He sat staring *dully* into the distance.

[2]**dull** *verb* **dulls**; **dulled**; **dull·ing** : to become dull or to make (something) dull: such as **a** : to become or cause (something) to become less clear, distinct, bright, or shiny [+ *obj*] Fog *dulled* the morning sunlight. • Special earplugs *dulled* the sound of the chain saw. [*no obj*] His hair *dulled* as he aged. • The dog's eyes *dulled* as he got sick. **b** [+ *obj*] : to make (something, such as a feeling) less sharp, strong, or severe • She takes medicine to *dull* the pain. • Fear *dulled* his need for adventure. • (*formal*) Her mind was *dulled* by the medication. **c** : to become or cause (something, such as a knife or blade) to become less sharp [+ *obj*] The knife was *dulled* from use. [*no obj*] The blade should be replaced as soon as it *dulls*.

dull·ard /ˈdʌlɚd/ *noun, pl* **-ards** [*count*] *old-fashioned* **:** a stupid and uninteresting person ▪ The company is run by a bunch of *dullards*.

du·ly /ˈdu:li, *Brit* ˈdju:li/ *adv, formal*
1 : in the proper or expected way ▪ They were *duly* impressed by her speech. ▪ The objections were ***duly noted***.
2 : at the correct or expected time ▪ The singer *duly* appeared back on stage for an encore.

[1]**dumb** /ˈdʌm/ *adj* **dumb·er; -est**
1 *informal* **a :** not showing or having good judgment or intelligence **:** stupid or foolish ▪ I'm not *dumb* enough to believe that. ▪ It was a *dumb* idea in the first place. ▪ He just stood there with a *dumb* grin on his face. ▪ This is one of the *dumbest* TV shows I've ever seen. ▪ She ***played/acted dumb*** [=pretended to know or understand less than she really did] so we would assign her the easier tasks. **b :** not requiring or resulting from intelligence ▪ It was ***dumb luck*** that we found this place at all. ▪ His success is just a matter of *dumb luck*.
2 a : not able to speak especially after being shocked or surprised ▪ I was ***struck dumb*** [=made speechless] by the surprise. — see also DUMBSTRUCK **b** *old-fashioned + often offensive* **:** not having the ability to speak ▪ He was born deaf and *dumb*.
– dumb·ly *adv* ▪ He stared *dumbly* at the test. **– dumb·ness** *noun* [*noncount*] *informal* ▪ The movie's *dumbness* [=*stupidity*] is actually pretty funny.

[2]**dumb** *verb* **dumbs; dumbed; dumb·ing**
dumb down [*phrasal verb*] ***dumb down (something) or dumb (something) down*** *usually disapproving* **1 :** to make (something) easier to understand ▪ She refused to *dumb down* the language in her report. ▪ The movie was a *dumbed down* version of the play. **2 :** to make (a group of people) less intelligent or educated ▪ Cutting training programs will *dumb down* the American workforce.
– dumbing down *noun* [*noncount*] ▪ She thinks television is contributing to the *dumbing down* of America.

dumb·bell /ˈdʌm,bɛl/ *noun, pl* **-bells** [*count*]
1 : a short bar with weights at the ends that is used to make muscles stronger — see picture at GYM
2 *US, informal* **:** a stupid or foolish person ▪ I feel like a *dumbbell* for making such a stupid mistake.

dumb·found·ed /ˌdʌmˈfaʊndəd/ *adj* [*more* ~; *most* ~] **:** very shocked or surprised ▪ We were *dumbfounded* at what we saw. ▪ I was *dumbfounded* to hear that she resigned.
– dumb·found /ˌdʌmˈfaʊnd/ *verb* **-founds; -found·ed; -found·ing** [+ *obj*] ▪ It *dumbfounded* me to hear that she had resigned.

dumb·struck /ˈdʌm,strʌk/ *adj* **:** so shocked or surprised that you cannot speak ▪ The people in the courtroom were *dumbstruck* by his confession.

dumb·wait·er /ˈdʌm,weɪtɚ/ *noun, pl* **-ers** [*count*] **:** a small elevator for carrying food or goods from one floor of a building to another

dum·dum /ˈdʌm,dʌm/ *noun, pl* **-dums** [*count*] **:** a bullet that expands or explodes when it hits an object in order to cause greater damage — called also *dumdum bullet*

[1]**dum·my** /ˈdʌmi/ *noun, pl* **dum·mies**
1 [*count*] *chiefly US, informal* **:** a stupid person ▪ He's no *dummy*. [=*fool*] ▪ She loves you, you *dummy*.
2 [*count*] **:** a doll that is shaped like and is as large as a person ▪ a tailor's/dressmaker's *dummy* ▪ They practiced CPR on a *dummy*. ▪ a ***crash test dummy*** [=a life-size model of a person used in tests to see what happens to people when a car gets in an accident]
3 [*count*] **:** a copy of a finished object that is used during practice or training ▪ The bomb was just a *dummy*.
4 [*count*] **:** a large doll with a movable mouth that is used by a performer ▪ a ventriloquist's *dummy*
5 [*noncount*] **:** the set of cards in a game of bridge that are played faceup so everyone can see them
6 [*count*] *Brit* **:** PACIFIER

[2]**dummy** *adj, always used before a noun* **:** looking real but not functioning or able to be used ▪ They took apart a *dummy* bomb. ▪ a *dummy* corporation [=a corporation that is not real] ▪ a ***dummy pill*** [=*placebo*]

dummy run *noun, pl* ~ **runs** [*count*] *Brit* **:** DRY RUN

[1]**dump** /ˈdʌmp/ *verb* **dumps; dumped; dump·ing** [+ *obj*]
1 : to put (something) somewhere in a quick and careless way ▪ You can *dump* the coats on the bed. ▪ I *dumped* the coffee down the drain. ▪ The murderer *dumped* the body in the river. — sometimes used figuratively ▪ The blizzard *dumped* three feet of snow in one night.
2 : to leave or get rid of (something or someone) quickly or without concern ▪ They *dumped* [=*left*] their friends at the party and went home. ▪ The team's coach was *dumped* [=*fired*] after a season of losses. ▪ They had to *dump* [=quickly sell] most of their stock to pay off their debts.
3 *informal* **:** to end a romantic relationship with (someone) ▪ My girlfriend *dumped* me. ▪ I got *dumped* yesterday.
4 : to get rid of (waste or garbage) especially in a secret and illegal way ▪ The factory has been *dumping* waste into the river.
5 : to sell (goods) in foreign countries for less than what they would sell for in your own country ▪ The company *dumped* its unsold parts on the U.S. market.
6 *computers* **:** to copy or move (data) from a computer's memory to a disk, another computer, etc. ▪ *Dump* the file to a disk.
dump in your lap see [1]LAP
dump on [*phrasal verb*] *informal* **1 *dump on (someone)*** *US* **:** to criticize (someone) severely ▪ I'm tired of getting *dumped on* every time I make a little mistake. **2 *dump (something) on (someone)* :** to give (something) to (someone else) to do, deal with, or think about because you do not want to ▪ She *dumped* her chores *on* her little brother. ▪ I can't stand it when he *dumps* all his problems *on* me. ▪ I hate to *dump* this *on* you.

[2]**dump** *noun, pl* **dumps** [*count*]
1 : a place where waste (such as trash) is taken and left ▪ We bring our trash to the town *dump* on Saturdays. ▪ (*US*) a ***garbage dump*** ▪ The site has become a ***toxic (waste) dump***. [=a place where dangerous waste is left usually illegally]
2 : a place where military supplies are stored ▪ an ammunition *dump*
3 *informal* **:** a messy, dirty, and unpleasant place ▪ I can't believe you live in this *dump*. [=*pigsty*] ▪ What a *dump*!
4 *computers* **:** an act of sending data stored in a computer to another place ▪ a screen *dump* to the printer
down in the dumps *informal* **:** feeling very sad ▪ I guess I'm just *down in the dumps*.
take a dump *informal + impolite* **:** to pass solid waste from the body

dump·er /ˈdʌmpɚ/ *noun, pl* **-ers** *chiefly US*
1 [*count*] **:** a person who leaves waste where it is not supposed to be left ▪ The cops caught the illegal *dumpers*.
2 *the dumper* *informal* **:** a state of failure ▪ The economy is ***in the dumper***. ▪ His career has ***gone down the dumper***. [=his career has been ruined]

dumper truck *noun, pl* ~ **trucks** [*count*] *Brit* **:** DUMP TRUCK

dump·ing /ˈdʌmpɪŋ/ *noun* [*noncount*] **:** the act of getting rid of waste or garbage especially in an illegal way ▪ No *dumping* allowed. ▪ laws that prohibit the *dumping* of toxic materials

dumping ground *noun, pl* ~ **grounds** [*count*] **:** a place where people or things that are not wanted are sent — often + *for* ▪ The class became a *dumping ground for* students with behavioral problems.

dump·ling /ˈdʌmplɪŋ/ *noun, pl* **-lings** [*count*]
1 : a small lump of dough that is boiled or steamed ▪ chicken and *dumplings*
2 : a piece of food that is wrapped in dough and cooked ▪ We had vegetarian/pork *dumplings* as an appetizer. ▪ an apple *dumpling*

Dump·ster /ˈdʌmpstɚ/ *trademark* — used for a large trash container

dump truck *noun, pl* ~ **trucks** [*count*] *US* **:** a large truck usually with a container on the back of it that is used for carrying and unloading loose material — called also (*Brit*) *dumper truck*; see picture at TRUCK

dumpy /ˈdʌmpi/ *adj* **dump·i·er; -est** *informal*
1 : short and fat ▪ a *dumpy* guy in his forties
2 *US* **:** dirty and in bad condition ▪ *dumpy* hotel rooms

dunce /ˈdʌns/ *noun, pl* **dunc·es** [*count*] *old-fashioned* **:** someone who is stupid or slow at learning things ▪ Don't be a *dunce*. ▪ a ***dunce/dunce's cap*** [=a tall pointy hat worn in the past by students as a punishment for failing to learn their lessons]

dune /ˈdu:n, *Brit* ˈdju:n/ *noun, pl* **dunes** [*count*] **:** a hill of sand near an ocean or in a desert that is formed by the wind ▪ We wandered over the *dunes*. — called also *sand dune*; see color picture on page C7

dune buggy *noun, pl* ~ **-gies** [*count*] **:** a small vehicle with very large tires for driving on sand — called also *beach buggy*

dung /ˈdʌŋ/ *noun* [*noncount*] : solid waste from an animal • cow/cattle *dung*

dun·ga·rees /ˌdʌŋgəˈriːz/ *noun* [*plural*]
1 *US, old-fashioned* : pants or work clothes made of usually blue denim • a new pair of *dungarees* [=(more commonly) *jeans*]
2 *Brit* : OVERALLS

dun·geon /ˈdʌnʤən/ *noun, pl* **-geons** [*count*] : a dark underground prison in a castle • The king threw them in/into the *dungeon*.

D

¹dunk /ˈdʌŋk/ *verb* **dunks; dunked; dunk·ing**
1 [+ *obj*] **a** : to dip (food) quickly into a liquid (such as coffee or milk) while eating • I like to *dunk* my doughnut in my coffee. **b** *chiefly US* : to push (someone or something) under water or other liquid for a short amount of time • She *dunked* him while they were swimming. • He *dunked* the ladle into the soup.
2 *basketball* : to jump high in the air and push (the ball) down through the basket [+ *obj*] He *dunked* the ball. [*no obj*] He could *dunk* when he was 16.

²dunk *noun, pl* **dunks** [*count*] *basketball* : a shot that is made by jumping high in the air and pushing the ball down through the basket • The pass led to a *dunk*. — called also *dunk shot, slam dunk*

dun·no /dəˈnoʊ/ — used in writing to represent the sound of the phrase *don't know* or *I don't know* when it is spoken quickly • "What do you want to do today?" "I *dunno*." • "Where did he go?" "*Dunno*." ✧ The pronunciation represented by *dunno* is common in informal speech. The written form should be avoided except when you are trying to represent or record such speech.

duo /ˈduːwoʊ, *Brit* ˈdjuːwəʊ/ *noun, pl* **du·os** [*count*]
1 : two people who perform together, are usually seen together, or are associated with each other • The comedy *duo* will perform tonight. • The author-illustrator *duo* will be signing their books tomorrow. • He and his partner make/form quite a *duo*.
2 : a piece of music that is performed by two musicians • They sang a *duo*. [=(more commonly) *duet*]

du·o·de·num /ˌduːwəˈdiːnəm, *Brit* ˌdjuːwəˈdiːnəm/ *noun, pl* **-de·na** /-ˈdiːnə/ *or* **-de·nums** [*count*] *medical* : the part of the small intestine that is right below your stomach
– **du·o·de·nal** /ˌduːwəˈdiːnl̩, *Brit* ˌdjuːwəˈdiːnl̩/ *adj* • *duodenal* ulcers

¹dupe /ˈduːp, *Brit* ˈdjuːp/ *verb* **dupes; duped; dup·ing** [+ *obj*] : to deceive or trick (someone) into believing or doing something • They *duped* her out of $300. — usually used as *(be) duped* • He *was duped* into buying a phony watch. • We *were duped* by the con artist.

²dupe *noun, pl* **dupes** [*count*] : a person who is easily deceived or tricked • He was an unwitting *dupe* in the scheme.

du·plex /ˈduːˌplɛks, *Brit* ˈdjuːˌplɛks/ *noun, pl* **-plex·es** [*count*] *US*
1 : a building that is divided into two separate homes • We live in the brick *duplex*.
2 : an apartment with two floors • a *duplex* penthouse

¹du·pli·cate /ˈduːplɪkət, *Brit* ˈdjuːplɪkət/ *adj, always used before a noun* : exactly the same as something else • I began receiving *duplicate* copies of the magazine every month. : made as an exact copy of something else • I had a *duplicate* key made. — compare TRIPLICATE

²du·pli·cate /ˈduːplɪˌkeɪt, *Brit* ˈdjuːplɪˌkeɪt/ *verb* **-cates; -cat·ed; -cat·ing** [+ *obj*]
1 : to make an exact copy of (something) • She *duplicated* the video to give to family and friends. • Unfortunately, the results of the first study could not be *duplicated*.
2 : to produce (something) in another form • They tried to *duplicate* [=*repeat*] last year's performance. • If we both do the project, we'll just be *duplicating* the work. [=doing the same work twice; doing more work than we need to]

³du·pli·cate /ˈduːplɪkət, *Brit* ˈdjuːplɪkət/ *noun, pl* **-cates** [*count*] : something that is exactly the same as something else : an exact copy of something else • In case you lose your keys, keep a set of *duplicates* somewhere safe. — often + *of* • He made *duplicates of* the forms before mailing them. • an exact *duplicate of* the original
in duplicate 1 : two times so that there are two copies • We were required to fill out the paperwork *in duplicate*. 2 : with an exact copy • Please send the contract *in duplicate*.

du·pli·ca·tion /ˌduːplɪˈkeɪʃən, *Brit* ˌdjuːplɪˈkeɪʃən/ *noun*
1 [*noncount*] : the act or process of copying something • He sent the manuscript out for *duplication*.
2 : the state of containing copies of something or being a copy of something [*noncount*] Please eliminate *duplication* when combining the lists. [*count*] It was a needless *duplication* of work. [=they did the work twice though they did not need to]

du·plic·i·ty /dʊˈplɪsəti, *Brit* djuˈplɪsəti/ *noun* [*noncount*] *formal* : dishonest behavior that is meant to trick someone • He exposed the spy's *duplicity*.
– **du·plic·i·tous** /dʊˈplɪsətəs, *Brit* djuˈplɪsətəs/ *adj* • *duplicitous* [=*deceptive*] tactics

du·ra·ble /ˈdurəbəl, *Brit* ˈdjʊrəbəl/ *adj* [*more* ~; *most* ~] : staying strong and in good condition over a long period of time • *durable* fabric — often used figuratively • She is one of Hollywood's most *durable* stars. • a *durable* athlete • *durable* myths
– **du·ra·bil·i·ty** /ˌdurəˈbɪləti, *Brit* ˌdjʊrəˈbɪləti/ *noun* [*noncount*] • cars known for their *durability* – **du·ra·bly** /ˈdurəbli, *Brit* ˈdjʊrəbli/ *adv* • *durably* built homes

durable goods *noun* [*plural*] *US* : products (such as cars and stoves) that that usually last a very long time — called also *(Brit) consumer durables*

du·ra·tion /dʊˈreɪʃən, *Brit* djuˈreɪʃən/ *noun* [*noncount*] : the length of time that something exists or lasts • You should gradually increase the *duration* of your workout.
for the duration : until the end of something • He was living in England when the war began and remained there *for the duration*. — often + *of* • The camera remained on the President *for the duration of* his speech.

du·ress /dʊˈrɛs, *Brit* djuˈrɛs/ *noun* [*noncount*] *formal* : force or threats meant to make someone do something • He gave the information ***under duress***.

dur·ing /ˈdurɪŋ, *Brit* ˈdjʊrɪŋ/ *prep*
1 : throughout the entire time of (an event, period, occurrence, etc.) • She swims every day *during* the summer. • We got along well *during* the trip. • He worked in the field *during* most of the day.
2 : at some time in the course of (something) • You can call me *during* the day. [=at some time in the day] • *During* the interview, they asked about my previous jobs. • The fire alarm went off *during* the ceremony.

dusk /ˈdʌsk/ *noun* [*noncount*] : the time when day changes into night and the sky begins to get darker • The park closes ***at dusk*** — compare ¹DAWN

dusky /ˈdʌski/ *adj* **dusk·i·er; -est** : somewhat dark • a *dusky* brown • in the *dusky* firelight

¹dust /ˈdʌst/ *noun* [*noncount*]
1 : fine dry powder that builds up inside buildings on surfaces that have not recently been cleaned • The floor was covered with *dust*. • You can see the ***dust particles*** floating through the air. • There is not a ***speck of dust*** in that house. ✧ Something that is ***collecting/gathering dust*** is not being used. • The book just sat on the shelf *gathering dust*.
2 : fine powder made up of very small pieces of earth or sand • As the car sped down the dirt road, it left a cloud of *dust* behind. • The wind ***kicked up dust*** [=blew dust into the air]
3 : fine powder made from a particular substance • coal/gold *dust* • He wiped the chalk *dust* off his hands. — see also SAWDUST
bite the dust see ¹BITE
eat dust *US, informal* : to breathe the dust that has been raised into the air by the vehicle that is moving in front of you • He said, "***Eat my dust!***" as he jumped in his car and drove away. — often used figuratively • They've left other companies *eating their dust*. [=they have gone far ahead of other companies]
leave (someone) in the dust *US, informal* : to go far ahead of (someone) : to be much more advanced than (someone) • The company has *left* its competitors *in the dust*.
the dust settles — used to talk about what happens when things become clear or calm after a period of change or confusion • I'll call you ***as soon as the dust settles*** from the move. [=as soon as I am not busy with moving] • ***When the dust settled*** [=when the situation became less confusing] and the votes were recounted, she had won the election. • You should ***let the dust settle*** before you make any big decisions.

²dust *verb* **dusts; dust·ed; dust·ing**
1 : to make (something) clean by brushing or wiping dirt and dust from the surface [+ *obj*] He *dusted* the furniture. — often + *off* or *down* • She *dusted* the sand *off* her leg. • (*US*) He stood up and ***dusted himself off***. = (*Brit*) He stood up and

dusted himself down. [=he brushed the dirt/dust off his clothes] [*no obj*] I *dust* at least once a week.
2 [+ *obj*] : to cover (something) with a fine powder • *Dust* the pan with flour. • The police *dusted* the table for fingerprints. [=they put a fine powder on the table so that any fingerprints could be seen] • The crops will be *dusted* with pesticide.
dust off [*phrasal verb*] ***dust (something) off*** or ***dust off (something)*** : to use (something) again after not using it for a long time • For his comeback tour, the comedian *dusted off* some of his old jokes. — see also [2]DUST 1 (above)

dust·bin /ˈdʌstˌbɪn/ *noun, pl* **-bins** [*count*] *Brit* : a can for trash or garbage : a garbage can or trash can

dust bowl *noun, pl* ~ **bowls** [*count*] : an area of land that was once used for farming but that has become a desert because of a lack of rain • They left the *dust bowl* and moved west.

dust bunny *noun, pl* ~ **-nies** [*count*] *US, informal* : a ball of dust that forms in places that are not swept or dusted often • I swept the *dust bunnies* from under the bed.

dust·cart /ˈdʌstˌkaət/ *noun, pl* **-carts** [*count*] *Brit* : GARBAGE TRUCK

dust cover *noun, pl* ~ **-ers** [*count*]
1 : DUST JACKET
2 : a piece of cloth, plastic, etc., that covers and protects something from dust

dust devil *noun, pl* ~ **-ils** [*count*] *chiefly US* : a small area of rapidly spinning wind that contains sand or dust

dust·er /ˈdʌstɚ/ *noun, pl* **-ers** [*count*]
1 : something that removes dust • a ***feather duster*** [=a tool with feathers at one end used to remove dust]
2 *US* : a device that is used by farmers to spray chemicals (such as pesticides) over a large area • a crop *duster*
3 *US, somewhat old-fashioned* : a long light coat • He wore a tan *duster*.

dusting *noun* [*singular*]
1 : the act of making something clean by brushing or wiping away dirt and dust from the surface • The table needs *dusting*. • The shelves need a good *dusting*.
2 : a small amount of something that falls over a surface • There was a light *dusting* of snow on the ground.

dust jacket *noun, pl* ~ **-ets** [*count*] : a paper cover that protects a book and can be removed • The *dust jacket* was torn. — called also *dust cover, jacket*

dust·man /ˈdʌstmən/ *noun, pl* **-men** /-mən/ [*count*] *Brit* : GARBAGEMAN

dust mite *noun, pl* ~ **mites** [*count*] : a very small creature that lives in the dust in your house and that can cause an allergic reaction

dust·pan /ˈdʌstˌpæn/ *noun, pl* **-pans** [*count*] : a flat pan that is open on one side and into which dirt from the floor is swept • Here's a broom and *dustpan*. Go sweep the kitchen.

dustpan

dust sheet *noun, pl* ~ **sheets** [*count*] *Brit* : a large piece of cloth that is used to protect furniture from dust, paint, etc. — compare DROP CLOTH

dust storm *noun, pl* ~ **storms** [*count*] : a very strong wind that carries clouds of dust across a large area

dust·up /ˈdʌstˌʌp/ *noun, pl* **-ups** [*count*] *informal* : a fight or loud argument • He had a *dustup* with a guy in the bar.

dusty /ˈdʌsti/ *adj* **dust·i·er; -est** [*also more* ~; *most* ~]
1 : filled or covered with dust • He pulled *dusty* candlesticks from the shelf. • a *dusty* basement • a *dusty* road/town
2 : slightly gray : somewhat dark or dull in color • His new tie is a *dusty* blue.

[1]**Dutch** /ˈdʌtʃ/ *adj* : of or relating to the Netherlands • *Dutch* history • Her family is *Dutch*. • a *Dutch* woman

[2]**Dutch** *noun*
1 [*noncount*] : the language of the Netherlands • He speaks *Dutch* fluently.
2 ***the Dutch*** : the people of the Netherlands • He loves learning about *the Dutch*.

[3]**Dutch** *adv*
go Dutch : to go to a movie, restaurant, etc., as a group with each person paying for his or her own ticket, food, etc. • We *went Dutch* on dinner. • I'll *go Dutch* with you on the movie if you want.

Dutch courage *noun* [*noncount*] *chiefly Brit, informal* : courage or confidence that a person gets from drinking alcohol

Dutch door *noun, pl* ~ **doors** [*count*] *US* : a door that is divided into a top and bottom half that open and close separately

Dutch elm disease *noun* [*noncount*] : a disease that kills elm trees and that is caused by a fungus

Dutch·man /ˈdʌtʃmən/ *noun, pl* **-men** /-mən/ [*count*] : a Dutch man

Dutch oven *noun, pl* ~ **-ens** [*count*] *US* : a large covered pot

Dutch treat *noun* [*noncount*] *chiefly US* : something (such as a dinner or movie) for which each person pays his or her own share of the cost • It was *Dutch treat*—we each bought our own ticket. • a *Dutch treat* luncheon

du·ti·ful /ˈduːtɪfəl, *Brit* ˈdjuːtɪfəl/ *adj* [*more* ~; *most* ~] : doing what is expected of you • a *dutiful* servant/daughter/father • the *dutiful* way he took care of his sick mother
— **du·ti·ful·ly** /ˈduːtɪfli, *Brit* ˈdjuːtɪfli/ *adv* • He *dutifully* answered my questions.

du·ty /ˈduːti, *Brit* ˈdjuːti/ *noun, pl* **-ties**
1 : something that is done as part of a job [*count*] His primary/main *duty* at the event is to take attendance. • If new employees are unable to carry out their *duties*, they may be fired. • She has a variety of adminsitrative *duties*. [*noncount*] Please ***report for duty*** [=show up for work] at 7 a.m. • This year no firefighters/police were killed ***in the line of duty***. [=while they were doing their jobs] • In helping them, he went ***beyond the call of duty***. [=did more than he was required or expected to do] ***synonyms*** see [1]TASK
2 : something that you must do because it is morally right or because the law requires it [*count*] We felt it was our *duty* to help. • He has a *duty* to support his family. [*noncount*] They helped her out of a sense of *duty*. • I'll be ready when ***duty calls***. • He was selected for ***jury duty***. [=to serve on a jury]
3 [*noncount*] : active military service • Her brother returned from *duty* overseas. • a twelve-month ***tour of duty*** • Many reserve troops were called into ***active duty***.
4 : a tax on goods that are being brought into a country [*count*] All goods had a 15 percent (import) *duty*. • ***customs duties*** [*noncount*] We had to pay *duty* on our souvenirs.
do duty as 1 : to do the work of (someone or something) • He *did (double) duty as* the star and director of the film. 2 : to be used as (something) • The backpack she uses at school also *does duty as* an overnight bag.
off duty : not working at a particular time • I go *off duty* in two hours.
on duty : working at a particular time • I can't take any personal calls while I'm *on duty*.
– see also HEAVY DUTY

duty–free /ˌduːtiˈfriː, *Brit* ˌdjuːtiˈfriː/ *adj*
1 : not taxed when taken into another country • *duty-free* goods
2 : selling goods that will not be taxed when taken into another country • I bought chocolate at the ***duty-free shop*** at the airport.
– **duty–free** *adv* • A certain amount of liquor can be imported *duty-free*.

du·vet /duˈveɪ, ˈduːˌveɪ/ *noun, pl* **-vets** [*count*] *chiefly Brit* : COMFORTER

DVD /ˌdiːˌviːˈdiː/ *noun, pl* **DVDs** [*count*] : a computer disk that contains a large amount of information (such as a movie) • a *DVD* player • The movie just came out ***on DVD***.; *also* : a movie that is recorded on a DVD • Do you want to pick up a few *DVDs* for the weekend? ✧ *DVD* is an abbreviation of "digital video disc" or "digital versatile disc."

DVR /ˌdiːˌviːˈaɚ/ *noun, pl* **DVRs** [*count*] : a machine that is used to make and watch recordings of television programs ✧ DVR is an abbreviation of "digital video recorder."

[1]**dwarf** /ˈdwoɚf/ *noun, pl* **dwarfs** /ˈdwoɚfs/ *also* **dwarves** /ˈdwoɚvz/ [*count*]
1 *in stories* : a creature that looks like a small man and that often lives underground and has magical powers
2 *sometimes offensive* : a person who is much smaller than most people because of a medical condition
– see also WHITE DWARF
– **dwarf·ish** /ˈdwoɚfɪʃ/ *adj*

[2]**dwarf** *verb* **dwarfs; dwarfed; dwarf·ing** [+ *obj*] : to make (something) look very small or unimportant when compared

with something else — usually used as *(be) dwarfed* • The bike *was dwarfed* by the truck next to it. [=the bike looked very small compared to the truck]

[3]**dwarf** *adj, always used before a noun, of a plant or animal* : smaller than normal size • *dwarf* evergreens • a *dwarf* porcupine

dwarf·ism /ˈdwoɚˌfɪzəm/ *noun [noncount] medical* : a condition that causes a person to stop growing before reaching normal adult size

dweeb /ˈdwi:b/ *noun, pl* **dweebs** *[count] US, informal* : a person who behaves awkwardly around other people and usually has unstylish hair, clothes, etc. • She's such a *dweeb*.
– **dweeby** /ˈdwi:bi/ *adj* • I was a *dweeby* kid.

dwell /ˈdwɛl/ *verb* **dwells; dwelled** /ˈdwɛld, ˈdwɛlt/ *or* **dwelt** /ˈdwɛlt/; **dwell·ing** *[no obj] literary + formal* : to live in a particular place • a cave where bats *dwell* • He *dwelled* [=*lived*] in the same town for years. • In ancient Greek mythology, Mount Olympus was the ***dwelling place*** of the gods. [=the place where the gods lived]

dwell on/upon *[phrasal verb]* ***dwell on/upon (something)*** : to think or talk about (something) for a long time • There is no need to *dwell on* the past. • Don't *dwell upon* your mistakes.

dwell·er /ˈdwɛlɚ/ *noun, pl* **-ers** *[count]* : a person or animal that lives in a particular place • a city *dweller* • cave *dwellers*

dwelling *noun, pl* **-ings** *[count] formal* : a place where a person lives • cave *dwellings* • Sales of single-family *dwellings* [=*houses*] are improving.

DWI /ˌdi:ˌdʌbəljuˈaɪ/ *noun, pl* **DWIs** *[count, noncount] US* : DUI ✧ *DWI* is an abbreviation of "driving while intoxicated."

dwin·dle /ˈdwɪndl̩/ *verb* **dwin·dles; dwin·dled; dwin·dling** *[no obj]* : to gradually become smaller • Our energy *dwindled* as the meeting dragged on. • The town's population is *dwindling* away. • *dwindling* resources/numbers

[1]**dye** /ˈdaɪ/ *noun, pl* **dyes** *[count, noncount]* : a substance used for changing the color of something (such as hair or cloth) usually permanently • purple *dye* • hair *dye*

[2]**dye** *verb* **dyes; dyed; dye·ing** *[+ obj]* : to change the color of (something, such as hair or cloth) by using a dye • She had been *dyeing* her hair for years. • The fabric is bleached, *dyed*, and then washed. • *dyed* hair — see also TIE-DYEING

dyed–in–the–wool /ˌdaɪdn̩ðəˈwʊl/ *adj, always used before a noun, often disapproving* : having very strong beliefs, opinions, etc., that you are not willing to change • He is known as a *dyed-in-the-wool* conservative.

[1]**dying** *present participle of* [1]DIE

[2]**dy·ing** /ˈdajɪŋ/ *adj, always used before a noun* : happening as someone dies : relating to someone's death • It was her ***dying wish*** [=her last wish] to see them married. • I will remember his words ***until my dying day***. [=until I die]

[1]**dyke** *chiefly Brit spelling of* DIKE

[2]**dyke** /ˈdaɪk/ *noun, pl* **dykes** *[count] informal + offensive* : LESBIAN

[1]**dy·nam·ic** /daɪˈnæmɪk/ *adj*
1 *[more ~; most ~]* **a** : always active or changing • a *dynamic* city • a *dynamic* relationship **b** : having or showing a lot of energy • a *dynamic* [=*enthusiastic*] speaker • an exciting and *dynamic* performance
2 *technical* : of or relating to energy, motion, or physical force • the *dynamic* theory of heat • *dynamic* and potential energy
– **dy·nam·i·cal·ly** /daɪˈnæmɪkli/ *adv* • The camera moves *dynamically* around the actors.

[2]**dynamic** *noun, pl* **-ics**
1 : the way that two or more people behave with each other because of a particular situation *[singular]* the *dynamic* between a doctor and a patient • the teacher-student *dynamic* *[plural]* Group *dynamics* are important to consider. • The *dynamics* of this class are different from those of other classes.
2 *[count]* : something that causes change or growth in something else • Disease was a central *dynamic* in the decrease in population. • a study on famine and population *dynamics*
3 **dynamics** *[noncount] technical* : the science that studies motion and the forces that cause or stop motion • molecular/fluid *dynamics*
4 **dynamics** *[plural] music* : changes in how loudly a piece of music is played or sung • *Dynamics* greatly affect the impact of the music.

dy·na·mism /ˈdaɪnəˌmɪzəm/ *noun [noncount] somewhat formal* : energy and a strong desire to make something happen • He has the *dynamism* of a natural leader.

[1]**dy·na·mite** /ˈdaɪnəˌmaɪt/ *noun [noncount]*
1 : a powerful explosive that is often used in the form of a stick • a stick of *dynamite*
2 : someone or something that may cause arguments or trouble • The death penalty is political *dynamite*.

[2]**dynamite** *verb* **-mites; -mit·ed; -mit·ing** *[+ obj]* : to blow up (something) using dynamite • They plan to *dynamite* the old building.

[3]**dynamite** *adj, informal* : exciting and very impressive or pleasing • Her new album is *dynamite*! [=*terrific, wonderful*] • They put on a *dynamite* performance.

dy·na·mo /ˈdaɪnəˌmoʊ/ *noun, pl* **-mos** *[count]*
1 : a machine that produces electricity : GENERATOR
2 *informal* : someone who has a lot of energy • He's a *dynamo* on-screen. • a human *dynamo*

dy·nas·ty /ˈdaɪnəsti, *Brit* ˈdɪnəsti/ *noun, pl* **-ties** *[count]*
1 : a family of rulers who rule over a country for a long period of time • a *dynasty* that ruled China for nearly 300 years; *also* : the period of time when a particular dynasty is in power • There was a civil war during the *dynasty*.
2 : a family, team, etc., that is very powerful or successful for a long period of time • She was born into a powerful political *dynasty*. • a baseball *dynasty*
– **dy·nas·tic** /daɪˈnæstɪk, *Brit* dɪˈnæstɪk/ *adj, always used before a noun* • *dynastic* succession

dys·en·tery /ˈdɪsn̩ˌteri, *Brit* ˈdɪsn̩tri/ *noun [noncount] medical* : a serious disease that causes severe diarrhea and a loss of blood

dys·func·tion /dɪsˈfʌŋkʃən/ *noun, pl* **-tions**
1 *[noncount]* : the condition of having poor and unhealthy behaviors and attitudes within a group of people • family *dysfunction*
2 *medical* : the state of being unable to function in a normal way *[noncount]* treatment for erectile/sexual *dysfunction* *[count]* The disease causes gastrointestinal *dysfunctions*.
– **dys·func·tion·al** /dɪsˈfʌŋkʃənl/ *adj [more ~; most ~]* • He hated spending holidays with his girlfriend's *dysfunctional* family. • a *dysfunctional* kidney

dys·lex·ia /dɪsˈlɛksijə/ *noun [noncount] medical* : a condition in the brain that makes it hard for a person to read, write, and spell
– **dys·lex·ic** /dɪsˈlɛksɪk/ *adj* • a *dyslexic* child – **dyslexic** *noun, pl* **-ics** *[count]* • a *dyslexic* [=a person with dyslexia] who overcame early problems with reading

dys·pep·sia /dɪsˈpɛpʃə, dɪsˈpɛpsijə/ *noun [noncount] medical* : pain in the area of your stomach caused by a difficulty in digesting food : INDIGESTION • He is suffering from *dyspepsia*.

dys·pep·tic /dɪsˈpɛptɪk/ *adj*
1 : suffering from pain caused by digestive problems • *dyspeptic* patients
2 *formal + old-fashioned* : having a bad temper • a *dyspeptic* old man

dys·to·pia /dɪsˈtoʊpijə/ *noun, pl* **-pias** *[count]* : an imaginary place where people are unhappy and usually afraid because they are not treated fairly — compare UTOPIA
– **dys·to·pi·an** /dɪsˈtoʊpijən/ *adj* • a *dystopian* society

dystrophy see MUSCULAR DYSTROPHY

E

e *or* **E** /ˈiː/ *noun, pl* **e's** *or* **es** *or* **E's** *or* **Es**
1 : the fifth letter of the English alphabet [*count*] a word that begins with an *e* [*noncount*] a word that begins with *e*
2 : the musical note or key referred to by the letter E **:** the third tone of a C-major scale [*count*] play/sing an *E* [*noncount*] a song in the key of *E*
an E for effort see EFFORT

E *abbr* east, eastern

e- *combining form* **:** electronic **:** Internet **:** online • *e*-mail • *e*-commerce [=commerce on the Internet] • *e*-retailing

[1]**each** /ˈiːʧ/ *adj* **:** every one of two or more people or things considered separately • A rope was tied to *each* end of the boat. • *Each* student had a different explanation. • *Each* student has done his best. = *Each* student has done his or her best. = (*informal*) *Each* student has done their best. • *Each* one of them has done his/her best. = (*informal*) *Each* one of them has done their best. • *Each* one of us took a turn. [=we each took a turn] • *Each* one of them costs 50 cents. [=they each cost 50 cents]
each and every — used as a more forceful way of saying *each* • I want to thank *each and every* person who has contributed to this project.

[2]**each** *pronoun* **:** each one • *Each* of us took a turn. = We *each* took a turn. • *Each* (of them) costs 50 cents. • They *each* have done their best. = They have *each* done their best. • He took shot after shot, *each* missing by inches.
to each his own *or* ***each to his own*** — used to say that other people are free to like different things than you do • I don't care for football, but *to each his own*.

[3]**each** *adv* **:** to or for each **:** APIECE • They cost 50 cents *each*. • We were allowed two tries *each*.

each other *pronoun* **:** each of two or more people, animals, etc., who are doing something together or in relationship to the other or others in the group • My brother and I looked at *each other*. [=we looked at one another; he looked at me and I looked at him] • The twins can wear *each other's* clothes. [=each one can wear the other's clothes]
made for each other see [2]MADE

ea·ger /ˈiːgɚ/ *adj* [*more* ~; *most* ~] **:** very excited and interested • an *eager* student • *eager* enthusiasm/anticipation **:** feeling a strong and impatient desire *to do* something or *for* something • She was *eager to get* started. • They were *eager to hear* the latest news. = They were *eager for* the latest news. • The crowd was *eager for* more.
– ea·ger·ly *adv* • The news was *eagerly* awaited. • His offer was *eagerly* [=*enthusiastically*] accepted. **– ea·ger·ness** *noun* [*noncount*] • In their *eagerness* to leave they forgot to lock the door.

eager beaver *noun, pl* ~ **-vers** [*count*] *informal* **:** a person who is very enthusiastic about doing something **:** a hardworking and eager person • When she first started working she was a real *eager beaver*.

[1]**ea·gle** /ˈiːgəl/ *noun, pl* **ea·gles**
1 [*count*] **:** a large bird that has very good eyesight and that kills other birds and animals for food — see color picture on page C9
2 *golf* **:** a golf score of two strokes less than par on a hole [*count*] She made/scored an *eagle* on the fourth hole. [*noncount*] She made *eagle* on the fourth hole. — compare BIRDIE, BOGEY

[2]**eagle** *verb* **eagles; ea·gled; ea·gling** [+ *obj*] **:** to score an eagle on (a hole in golf) • She *eagled* the fourth hole.

eagle eye *noun*
1 ***eagle eyes*** [*plural*] **:** eyes that watch or look carefully and see or notice many things • watching with *eagle eyes* • students working under the *eagle eyes* of the teacher
2 [*count*] **:** an unusually good ability to see or notice things • an editor with an *eagle eye* • an editor with *eagle eyes*
3 [*singular*] **:** close watch • The guard ***kept an eagle eye on*** the prisoner. [=the guard watched the prisoner very closely]
– ea·gle–eyed /ˈiːgəlˌaɪd/ *adj* [*more* ~; *most* ~] • an *eagle-eyed* [=*sharp-eyed*] proofreader

Eagle Scout *noun, pl* ~ **Scouts** [*count*] **:** a Boy Scout who has reached the highest level of achievement in scouting

ea·glet /ˈiːglət/ *noun, pl* **-glets** [*count*] **:** a young eagle

-ean see [1]-AN

[1]**ear** /ˈiɚ/ *noun, pl* **ears**
1 [*count*] **:** the part of the body that you hear with • He was whispering something in her *ear*. • a dog with floppy *ears* • ***pierced ears*** [=ears with earlobes that have been pierced for wearing earrings] — see picture at FACE
2 [*singular*] **a :** an ability to understand and appreciate something heard • He has a good *ear* for music/languages. **b** — used to describe the way something sounds to you • It sounds a little old-fashioned to my *ear*. [=it sounds old-fashioned to me]
3 [*count*] **:** attention that is shown or given by listening to what someone says • Thanks for your *ear*. [=thanks for listening] • When I told my story, my brother ***listened with only half an ear.*** [=did not listen closely] ✧ To ***lend an ear*** or, in literary language, to ***lend someone your ears*** is to listen to what someone has to say. • She's always willing to *lend a* sympathetic *ear*. • "Friends, Romans, countrymen, *lend me your ears*." —Shakespeare, *Julius Caesar* (1599)
all ears informal — used to say that someone is listening very closely • As I told the story, my daughter was *all ears*.
a word in someone's ear see [1]WORD
bend someone's ear see [1]BEND
box someone's ears see [3]BOX
can't believe your ears see BELIEVE
cock an/your ear see [2]COCK
ears are burning ✧ If ***your ears are burning*** or you ***feel your ears burning,*** you have the feeling that other people are talking about you. • (*humorous*) "We were talking about you last night." "That explains why I *felt my ears burning*."
ears pop see [1]POP
fall on deaf ears **:** to fail to be heard **:** to be ignored • Her pleas for mercy *fell on deaf ears*.
grin/smile from ear to ear **:** to smile widely **:** to have a big smile on your face • He was *grinning from ear to ear*.
have someone's ear ✧ If you *have someone's ear* you can talk and give advice to that person because you are trusted. • an adviser who *has the President's ear*
in one ear and out the other **:** through someone's mind without being remembered or noticed • Everything you say to him goes *in one ear and out the other*. [=he doesn't listen to or remember what you say]
out on your ear informal **:** forced out **:** thrown out • If you're late to work again, you'll be *out on your ear*! [=you'll be fired]
play by ear **1** ✧ To play a song or a piece of music *by ear* is to play it after hearing it without looking at written music. • He could play any tune *by ear* after hearing it only once. **2** ✧ To ***play it by ear*** is to do something without special preparation. • I don't know how they'll react to our proposal, so we'll just have to *play it by ear* [=*improvise*, (*informal*) *wing it*] and hope for the best.
set (something) on its ear informal **:** to cause something to be in a state of great excitement or shock • She *set* the racing world *on its ear* [=she surprised and shocked the racing world] by winning several major races. • His early recordings *set* the jazz world *on its ear*. [=his recordings caused a sensation in the jazz world]
talk someone's ear off see [1]TALK
turn a deaf ear **:** to refuse to listen to what someone says • The company president *turned a deaf ear* to my proposals.
up to your ears **:** deeply involved in something • They are *up to their ears* in debt. [=they are deeply in debt] • We're *up to our ears* in work. [=we are very busy]
wet behind the ears see [1]WET
– compare [2]EAR
– eared /ˈiɚd/ *adj* • a long-*eared* dog **– ear·less** /ˈiɚləs/ *adj*

[2]**ear** *noun, pl* **ears** [*count*] **:** the part of a corn plant on which the seeds grow • an *ear* of corn — compare [1]EAR

ear·ache /ˈiɚˌeɪk/ *noun, pl* **-aches :** an ache or pain in the ear [*count*] He has/gets frequent *earaches*. [*noncount*] (*chiefly Brit*) • He has/gets frequent *earache*.

ear canal *noun, pl* ~ **-nals** [*count*] **:** the tube that leads into the ear

ear candy *noun* [*noncount*] *US, informal* **:** music that is

E

pleasing to listen to but is not serious or interesting

ear·drum /ˈiɚˌdrʌm/ *noun, pl* **-drums** [*count*] : a thin, tightly stretched piece of tissue in the ear that vibrates when sound waves hit it

ear·ful /ˈiɚˌfʊl/ *noun* [*singular*] *informal* : a lot of angry talk • I got an *earful* about what a bad job I had done. • He gave me an *earful.*

earl /ˈɚl/ *noun, pl* **earls** [*count*] : a high-ranking member of the British nobility

earliest *noun*

at the earliest — used to indicate the earliest possible time when something will happen or be done • The job will not be finished until next year *at the* (very) *earliest.* [=it will not be finished before next year] — compare LATEST

ear·lobe /ˈiɚˌloʊb/ *noun, pl* **-lobes** [*count*] : the soft part of the ear that hangs down from the bottom — see picture at FACE

[1]**ear·ly** /ˈɚli/ *adv* **ear·li·er; -est**

1 : at or near the beginning of a period of time or a process, activity, series, etc. • *Early* in his career he moved to the city. • a word first recorded *early* in the 17th century • They were trailing by a touchdown *early* in the fourth quarter. • We learned *early* [=*early on*] not to question his decisions. • The package should be arriving *early* next week. — opposite LATE

2 : before the usual or expected time • She arrived *early* to help with the preparations. • I got up *early* to finish packing. • I got up ***bright and early.*** [=very early] — opposite LATE

early on : at or during an early point or stage • The reasons were obvious *early on* [=*early*] in the experiment. ✧ *Early on* originated in British English. Some American writers have objected to it, but it is now very common in the U.S. Note that unlike *early, early on* can appear at the beginning of a sentence. • *Early on,* the project was in trouble.

[2]**early** *adj* **earlier; -est**

1 a : existing or happening near the beginning of a period of time • *early* morning • the *early* 20th century • He is in his *early* thirties. [=he is about 31 or 32 years old] • She works the *early* shift. [=the shift that is in the early part of the day] • It was still *early* (in the morning) when she got out of bed. — opposite LATE **b** *always used before a noun* : happening near the beginning of a process, activity, series, etc. • the *early* symptoms of the disease • the composer's *early* works [=works created at the beginning of the composer's career] • The *early* part of the book is better than the later part.

2 a : coming or happening before the usual or expected time • We had an *early* spring this year. • an *early* bedtime • We're *early.* The show doesn't start for half an hour. — opposite LATE **b :** doing something before the usual time or before others usually do • I've always been an *early* riser. • My daughter was an *early* reader. [=she learned to read at a young age] ✧ The expression ***the early bird catches/gets the worm*** means that people who start or arrive before others are more likely to succeed. — opposite LATE

early days (yet) *Brit* — used to say that it is too soon to know how something will turn out • Things haven't gone well so far, but it's *early days yet.*

early hours see HOUR

get/make an early start : to get started on a journey, activity, etc., early in the day • We want to *make an early start* tomorrow.

make an early night of it : to go home or go to bed early • They decided to *make an early night of it.*

[1]**ear·mark** /ˈiɚˌmaɚk/ *noun, pl* **-marks** [*count*] : a mark or quality that shows what something is or what it could be • The business plan ***had (all) the earmarks*** of success. [=it seemed likely to succeed] — compare HALLMARK

[2]**earmark** *verb* **-marks; -marked; -mark·ing** [+ *obj*]

1 : to say that something will be used or treated in a specified way — often used as *(be) earmarked* • The old building has *been earmarked* for demolition.

2 : to put (money) aside for a special purpose • The project uses funds that had been *earmarked* for education.

ear·muff /ˈiɚˌmʌf/ *noun, pl* **-muffs** [*count*] : either one of a pair of pads that cover the ears to keep them warm and that are connected by a flexible band • wearing a pair of *earmuffs*

earn /ˈɚn/ *verb* **earns; earned; earn·ing** [+ *obj*]

1 : to get (money, a salary, etc.) for work that you have done • She *earns* a good salary. • I need to *earn* some money. • He will do anything to ***earn his keep.*** [=to earn what is needed to support himself] • She's just trying to ***earn a living.*** [=to earn the money needed for food, clothing, etc.]

2 a : to deserve or get (something) because of something you have done • He *earned* a promotion through hard work. • The team has *earned* [=*gained*] a reputation for poor sportsmanship. • She needs to *earn* [=*gain, win*] their trust/respect. **b :** to make (someone) worthy or deserving of (something) • His hard work *earned* [=*gained*] him a promotion. • Her honesty *earned* [=*gained, won*] her their trust/respect.

earn a/your crust see CRUST

earn your spurs see [1]SPUR

earn your stripes see [1]STRIPE

– earn·er *noun, pl* **-ers** [*count*] • high *earners* on Wall Street

[1]**ear·nest** /ˈɚnəst/ *adj* [*more ~; most ~*] : serious and sincere : not lighthearted or playful • an *earnest* plea for help • an *earnest* young journalist

– ear·nest·ly *adv* • speaking *earnestly* **– ear·nest·ness** /ˈɚnəstnəs/ *noun* [*noncount*]

[2]**earnest** *noun*

in earnest **1 :** in an earnest or serious way • The search began *in earnest* when the police arrived. • It began to rain *in earnest* [=*heavily*] in the evening. • It's hard to tell if he's making this proposal *in earnest.* **2 :** not fooling : serious and sincere • We thought he was joking at first, but then we realized that he was *in earnest.* [=he was being serious] — compare *for real* at [1]REAL

earn·ings /ˈɚnɪŋz/ *noun* [*plural*] : money received as wages or gained as profit • corporate *earnings*

ear·phone /ˈiɚˌfoʊn/ *noun, pl* **-phones** [*count*] : a device that is worn over or inserted into the ear and is used for listening to something (such as music or a radio) without having other people hear it

ear·piece /ˈiɚˌpiːs/ *noun, pl* **-piec·es** [*count*]

1 : a part of a device that is placed in the ear for listening to something • the *earpiece* of a stethoscope

2 : either one of the two pieces that support eyeglasses by resting on the ears

ear·plug /ˈiɚˌplʌg/ *noun, pl* **-plugs** [*count*] : a piece of soft material that you put in your ear to keep out water, noise, etc.

ear·ring /ˈirɪŋ/ *noun, pl* **-rings** [*count*] : a piece of jewelry that is worn on the ear and especially on the earlobe — see color picture on page C11

ear·shot /ˈiɚˌʃɑːt/ *noun* [*noncount*] : the distance within which someone's voice can be heard • They were ***within earshot*** of each other. • We waited until he was ***out of earshot*** [=until he could no longer hear us] before speaking again.

ear·split·ting /ˈiɚˌsplɪtɪŋ/ *adj* [*more ~; most ~*] *of a sound* : extremely loud or harsh • The train's whistle made an *earsplitting* noise.

[1]**earth** /ˈɚθ/ *noun*

1 *or* **Earth** [*singular*] : the planet on which we live • (The) *Earth* is the third planet from the sun. • life on *earth* • the planet *Earth* • Many species are in danger of vanishing from (the face of) the *earth.*

2 [*noncount*] : land as opposed to the sea, the air, etc. • The moisture will eventually fall to *earth* in the form of rain or snow. • We could feel the *earth* shake.

3 [*noncount*] : the material in which plants grow : SOIL • a mound of *earth*

4 [*count*] *Brit* : [1]GROUND 10

5 [*singular*] *chiefly Brit, informal* : a large amount of money • furniture that looks good and that doesn't cost the *earth* • pay the *earth*

(a) heaven on earth see HEAVEN

move heaven and earth see [1]MOVE

on earth **1 :** in the world • It's the tallest building *on earth.* • She said she wouldn't marry him if he were the last man *on earth.* • He says that ***nothing on earth*** will change his mind. **2** — used to make a question more forceful • Why *on earth* [=*in the world, ever*] did you do that? • What *on earth* is he talking about? • Where *on earth* are my keys?

promise someone the earth see [2]PROMISE

the ends of the earth see [1]END

the salt of the earth see [1]SALT

[2]**earth** *verb* **earths; earthed; earth·ing** [+ *obj*] *Brit* : [2]GROUND 5 • The appliance is dangerous unless properly *earthed.* [=(*US*) *grounded*]

earth·bound /ˈɚθˌbaʊnd/ *adj*

1 : located on the surface of the earth : not able to fly or to go to outer space • *earthbound* astronomers

2 : not having or showing imagination • a dull and *earthbound* mind

earth·en /ˈɚθən/ *adj, always used before a noun* **:** made of earth or of baked clay ▪ an *earthen* dam ▪ *earthen* [=*earthenware*] dishes

earth·en·ware /ˈɚθənˌweɚ/ *noun* [*noncount*] **:** a heavy substance that is made by baking clay and that is usually covered with another substance (called a glaze) before it is baked so that it will not absorb water ▪ The dish is made of/from *earthenware*. ▪ *earthenware* pottery

earth·ling /ˈɚθlɪŋ/ *noun, pl* **-lings** [*count*] **:** a human being living on Earth ✧ *Earthling* is usually used in stories and movies that involve creatures from outer space.

earth·ly /ˈɚθli/ *adj, always used before a noun*
1 : having to do with life on the Earth ▪ *earthly* joys/delights/pleasures ▪ our *earthly* existence — compare EARTHY
2 : imaginable or possible — used to make a question or a negative statement more forceful ▪ What *earthly* [=*possible, conceivable*] good could it do him? ▪ There is no *earthly* reason [=there is no reason on earth; there is no reason at all] for feeling that way.

earth mother *noun, pl* **~ -thers** [*count*] **:** a woman who takes care of other people and has qualities that are associated with being a mother in a traditional culture where people live in a simple and natural way

earth·quake /ˈɚθˌkweɪk/ *noun, pl* **-quakes :** a shaking of a part of the earth's surface that often causes great damage [*count*] a devastating *earthquake* [*noncount*] a building destroyed by *earthquake* — called also *quake*

earth·shak·ing /ˈɚθˌʃeɪkɪŋ/ *adj* [*more ~; most ~*] **:** very important ▪ an *earthshaking* [=*momentous*] decision/event

earth·shat·ter·ing /ˈɚθˈʃætərɪŋ/ *adj* [*more ~; most ~*] **:** very important **:** EARTHSHAKING ▪ There haven't been any *earthshattering* developments lately.

earth tone *noun, pl* **~ tones** [*count*] *chiefly US* **:** a color that contains some brown ▪ She wears a lot of *earth tones*.
– **earth–toned** *adj*

earth·work /ˈɚθˌwɚk/ *noun, pl* **-works** [*count*] **:** a raised bank or wall made of soil — usually plural ▪ prehistoric *earthworks*

earth·worm /ˈɚθˌwɚm/ *noun, pl* **-worms** [*count*] **:** a long worm that lives in damp soil

earthy /ˈɚθi/ *adj* **earth·i·er; -est**
1 : suggesting earth or soil in texture, odor, color, etc. ▪ *earthy* aromas ▪ a blend of *earthy* colors ▪ The wine had an *earthy* flavor. — compare EARTHLY
2 [*more ~; most ~*] **a :** practical and straightforward **:** open and direct ▪ Critics were impressed by the movie's *earthy* realism. ▪ an *earthy* [=*down-to-earth*] person **b** *chiefly US* **:** plain and simple in style ▪ food made with simple, *earthy* ingredients **c :** not polite **:** somewhat rude or crude ▪ *earthy* humor
– **earth·i·ness** *noun* [*noncount*] ▪ the *earthiness* of the ingredients/humor

ear·wax /ˈiɚˌwæks/ *noun* [*noncount*] **:** a waxlike substance produced inside the ear

ear·wig /ˈiɚˌwɪg/ *noun, pl* **-wigs** [*count*] **:** an insect that has long, thin feelers and two curved, pointed parts at the end of the body — see color picture on page C10

¹ease /ˈiːz/ *noun* [*noncount*]
1 : freedom from pain or trouble **:** comfort of body or mind ▪ a life of *ease*
2 : lack of difficulty ▪ The program is known for its *ease* of use. [=it is easy to use] ▪ I was able to do it ***with*** (surprising) ***ease***. [=easily] ▪ These features can be modified ***with the greatest of ease***. [=very easily]
3 : a relaxed and informal way of behaving ▪ He delighted people with his charm and *ease* of manner. [=his relaxed and easy manner]
at ease **1** *also* ***at your ease* :** in a relaxed and comfortable state ▪ Her relaxed manner at the meeting put/set everyone *at* (*their*) *ease*. ▪ They no longer felt *at ease* [=*comfortable*] with each other. ▪ You can ***set/put your mind at ease***. [=you can relax and stop worrying] — see also ILL AT EASE **2 :** standing silently with the feet apart and one or both hands behind the body ▪ The troops ***stood at ease***. — often used as a military command ▪ *At ease*! compare *at attention* at ATTENTION
***take your ease* :** to rest or relax ▪ I found him *taking his ease* on the front porch.

²ease *verb* **eas·es; eased; eas·ing**
1 [*+ obj*] **:** to free (someone or something) from trouble or worry ▪ trying to *ease* my troubled mind
2 [*+ obj*] **:** to make (something) less painful ▪ We were unable to *ease* [=*alleviate*] their suffering.
3 a [*+ obj*] **:** to make (tension, a problem, etc.) less severe or troubling ▪ The diplomats failed to *ease* tensions between the two nations. ▪ Authorities are looking for ways to *ease* prison overcrowding. ▪ The government is expected to *ease* travel restrictions. **b** [*no obj*] **:** to become less severe or troubling ▪ Tensions have *eased* [=*moderated*] in recent weeks.
4 *always followed by an adverb or preposition* **a** [*+ obj*] **:** to move (someone or something) gently or carefully ▪ He *eased* the car into the parking space. ▪ She *eased* herself into the driver's seat. ▪ They *eased* the heavy block into position. **b** [*no obj*] **:** to move or pass slowly or easily ▪ The car *eased* out into traffic. ▪ She wants to *ease* into her new job slowly.
ease off or ease up [*phrasal verb*] **:** to become less severe ▪ The slope gradually *eased off*. ▪ The pressure should *ease up* soon.
ease up on [*phrasal verb*] **1 a *ease up on (someone)* :** to treat (someone) in a less harsh or demanding way ▪ The students might respond better if the teacher *eased up on* them a little. **b *ease up on (something)* :** to apply less pressure to (something) ▪ *ease up on* the accelerator **2 *ease up on (something)* :** to do or use less of (something) ▪ My doctor told me I should *ease up on* fatty foods.

ea·sel /ˈiːzəl/ *noun, pl* **-sels** [*count*] **:** a frame for supporting an artist's painting

easel

eas·i·ly /ˈiːzəli/ *adv*
1 [*more ~; most ~*] **:** in an easy manner **:** without difficulty ▪ We won the game *easily*. [=*with ease*] ▪ These ingredients are *easily* obtained. ▪ I'm too heavy to be carried *easily*.
2 : by a great extent or degree **:** by far ▪ She's *easily* the best player on the team. [=she is much better than the other players]
breathe easily see BREATHE

¹east /ˈiːst/ *noun*
1 [*noncount*] **:** the direction where the sun rises **:** the direction that is the opposite of west ▪ The city is framed by mountain ranges to the *east* and west. ▪ The wind blew from the *east*. ▪ Which way is *east*?
2 *the east or the East* : regions or countries east of a certain point: such as **a :** the eastern part of the U.S. ▪ This summer has been unusually hot in *the East*. **b :** the countries of Asia (such as Japan, China, and Korea) — see also FAR EAST, MIDDLE EAST

²east *adj, always used before a noun*
1 : lying toward or at the east ▪ the *east* side of town
2 : coming from the east ▪ an *east* wind

³east *adv* **:** to or toward the east ▪ The ships sailed *east*. [=*easterly, eastward*]
back East or back east *US, informal* **:** in or toward the eastern part of a country or region ▪ She attended college *back East*.

east·bound /ˈiːstˌbaʊnd/ *adj* **:** going toward the east ▪ an *eastbound* train

Eas·ter /ˈiːstɚ/ *noun, pl* **-ters** [*count, noncount*] **:** a Christian church festival that celebrates the return of Jesus Christ to life following his death; *also* **:** the Sunday in early spring on which this festival is observed — often used before another noun ▪ *Easter* Sunday ▪ an ***Easter egg*** [=an egg that is specially decorated at Easter] ▪ an ***Easter basket*** [=a basket of candy, toys, etc., that is given to children at Easter]

Easter lily *noun, pl* **~ lilies** [*count*] **:** a white garden flower that blooms in spring

east·er·ly /ˈiːstɚli/ *adj* [*more ~; most ~*]
1 : located or moving toward the east ▪ They sailed in an *easterly* direction.
2 : blowing from the east ▪ an *easterly* wind

east·ern /ˈiːstɚn/ *adj*
1 [*more ~; most ~*] **:** located toward the east ▪ They live in the *eastern* part of the state. ▪ the *eastern* shore of the river ▪ *Eastern* Europe
2 *Eastern* : of or relating to the countries of Asia **:** ASIAN ▪ *Eastern* philosophy
– **east·ern·most** /ˈiːstɚnˌmoʊst/ *adj*

East·ern·er /ˈiːstɚnɚ/ *noun, pl* **-ers** [*count*] **:** a person born or living in the East; *especially* **:** a person born or living in the eastern U.S. — compare WESTERNER

east·ward /ˈiːstwɚd/ *also chiefly Brit* **east·wards** /ˈiːstwɚdz/ *adv* [*more ~; most ~*] **:** toward the east ▪ We sailed *eastward*. [=*east*]

– **eastward** *adj* • an *eastward* course

[1]easy /ˈiːzi/ *adj* **eas·i·er; -est**

1 : not hard to do : not difficult • an *easy* lesson • It's surprisingly *easy* to use. • It was an *easy* decision to make. • They scored an *easy* goal late in the game. • It wasn't *easy* for her to leave home. • He's an *easy* person (for other people) to like. = It's *easy* (for other people) to like him. • There are no *easy* solutions to this problem. • He likes to keep a dictionary ***within easy reach*** [=*nearby*] when he's writing.

2 a : free from pain, trouble, or worry • He's had an *easy* life. • This new schedule should make our lives *easier*. • I hope this will make things *easier* for you. • I won't feel *easy* until I know that she arrived safely. • an *easy* mind **b :** not hurried • We proceeded at an *easy* [=*leisurely*] pace. **c :** not requiring much strength or energy • *easy*, gentle movements

3 a : not harsh or severe in punishing or criticizing someone • I think they're being too ***easy on*** him. [=they're not criticizing/punishing him harshly enough] **b :** not hard to please • an *easy* [=*lenient*] teacher ✧ The informal phrase ***I'm easy*** is used as a way of saying that you are easy to please and will accept what someone else decides. • "Should we stay at home or go out?" "Whatever you like: *I'm easy*."

4 : not steep • *easy* slopes

5 *informal* **:** not hard to get • *easy* money • ***easy pickings*** [=things that are easy to get]

6 : relaxed and informal • He has an *easy* [=*easygoing*] manner. • an *easy* smile — see also *free and easy* at [1]FREE

7 — used to describe someone or something that is easy to attack, trick, criticize, etc. • His lack of experience makes him an ***easy target*** for his political enemies. • insects that are ***easy prey*** for many birds • (*US*) He's an ***easy mark*** for anyone needing a loan.

8 *informal* **:** lightly pleasant and enjoyable • music for *easy* listening

9 *informal + old-fashioned* **:** not sexually respectable • an *easy* woman [=a woman who has sex with many men] • *easy* morals • a woman ***of easy virtue***

(as) easy as ABC *or* ***(as) easy as pie*** *or* ***(as) easy as falling off a log*** *informal* **:** very easy • Getting the permit turned out to be *as easy as pie*.

easy on the eye *or US* ***easy on the eyes*** *informal* **:** easy or pleasant to look at • The monitor's display is *easy on the eyes*. • She's very *easy on the eyes*. [=*pretty, good-looking*]

over easy see [3]OVER

– **eas·i·ness** *noun* [*noncount*]

[2]easy *adv* **easier; -est :** without difficulty or stress • He just wants to take life *easy* now. • The repairs will cost $100, *easy*. [=the repairs will cost at least $100] • "We just need to raise the money." "That's ***easier said than done***" [=that will not be easy to do] • Success hasn't ***come easy*** for her. [=success has not been easy to achieve]

breathe easy see BREATHE

easy come, easy go *informal* — used to say that you are not bothered about losing something • His attitude toward money has always been, *easy come, easy go*.

easy does it *informal* — used to tell someone to move slowly and carefully • *Easy does it*! We don't want anyone to get hurt.

go easy *informal* **1** ***go easy on (someone)*** **:** to treat (someone) in a way that is not harsh or demanding • The students might respond better if the teacher *went* (a little) *easy on* them. **2** ***go easy on/with (something)*** **:** to use less of (something) • My doctor said to *go easy on* fatty foods.

nice and easy see NICE

rest easy see [3]REST

take it easy *informal* **1 :** to relax and avoid hard work or strain • The doctor told her she should *take it easy* for a while. **2 :** to stay or become calm and unexcited — usually used as a command • *Take it easy*, Joe. Everything is going to be just fine.

easy chair *noun, pl* **~ chairs** [*count*] **:** a chair that is large, soft, and very comfortable

easy·go·ing /ˌiːziˈgowɪŋ/ *adj* [*more ~; most ~*] **:** relaxed and informal • an *easygoing* boss • a boss with an *easygoing* [=*easy*] manner

easy street *noun* [*singular*] **:** a situation with no worries : a situation of wealth and ease • If I'd been smarter about investing my money, I could be ***on easy street*** now. [=I could be rich now]

eat /ˈiːt/ *verb* **eats; ate** /ˈeɪt, *Brit* ˈɛt, ˈeɪt/; **eat·en** /ˈiːtn/; **eat·ing**

1 : to take food into your mouth and swallow it [+ *obj*] You'll feel better if you *eat* something. • I *ate* a big breakfast so I'm not very hungry. • Let's grab a bite to *eat*. = Let's get something to *eat*. • I've been trying ***to watch what I eat*** [=to be more careful about eating healthy foods and not eating too much] [*no obj*] I'm hungry. Let's *eat*. • They like to *eat* at home. • It's important to ***eat right*** [=to eat healthy foods] ✧ To ***eat out*** is to dine at a restaurant rather than at home. • We like to *eat out* on Fridays. ✧ To ***eat in*** is to dine at home. • Let's *eat in* tonight.

2 : to gradually destroy, use, or take away something : to wear something away [+ *obj*] — usually + *away* • The rocks were *eaten away* by erosion. [*no obj*] — usually + *into, away at*, or *at* • Marketing costs *ate into* their profits. • The acids were *eating away at* the metal finish. • The failure of his business has *eaten away at* his confidence.

3 [+ *obj*] *informal* **:** to bother or annoy (someone) • What's *eating* you?

be eating out of someone's hand **:** to be completely controlled by someone • He had them *eating out of his hand*. [=he controlled them completely]

eat a horse see [1]HORSE

eat crow *(US) or* ***eat humble pie*** *informal* **:** to admit that you were wrong or accept that you have been defeated • He was forced to *eat crow* when the company fired him. • They had to *eat humble pie* when the rumors they were spreading were proved false.

eat light see [5]LIGHT

eat (someone or something) alive **1** *of insects* **:** to bite (someone or something) many times • The mosquitoes were *eating us alive*. [=we were being bitten frequently by many mosquitoes] **2 :** to badly defeat or harm someone or something • Their competitors are going to *eat them alive* if they don't cut their prices. • If this story gets out, the press will *eat him alive*.

eat someone's or something's lunch see [1]LUNCH

eat up [*phrasal verb*] **1** — used to tell someone to start or continue eating • *Eat up*! Your dinner is getting cold. **2** ***eat up (something) or eat (something) up*** **a :** to eat all of (something) • *Eat* your dinner *up* before it gets cold. **b :** to use up (time, resources, etc.) • This project has been *eating up* a large part of the budget. • Your savings may be *eaten up* by inflation. **3** ✧ A person who is ***eaten up*** with or by jealousy, bitterness, etc., cannot escape that feeling and is made unhappy by it. • He was *eaten up* with envy of his brother's success. **4** ***eat (something) up*** *informal* **:** to enjoy (something) greatly • I thought the speech was stupid, but the audience *ate it up*.

eat up the clock see [1]CLOCK

eat your fill see [2]FILL

eat your heart out **:** to be jealous • "*Eat your heart out*," he jokingly told his friend before getting on his new boat.

eat your words **:** to take back what you have said : to admit that you were wrong about something • She said she would *eat her words* if the wedding was called off. • They promised success, but if things don't get better soon, they may have to *eat their words*.

have your cake and eat it too *or* ***have your cake and eat it*** see [1]CAKE

I'll eat my hat *informal + old-fashioned* — used to say that something will not happen or cannot be true • If he wins the election, *I'll eat my hat*! [=I don't believe he has any chance to win the election]

the proof of the pudding is in the eating see PUDDING

– **eat·able** /ˈiːtəbəl/ *adj* • an *eatable* [=(more commonly) *edible*] plant – **eat·er** *noun, pl* **-ers** [*count*] • a picky *eater* [=someone who dislikes many kinds of food] • a big *eater* [=someone who eats a lot]

> ***synonyms*** EAT, CONSUME, and DEVOUR mean to chew and swallow food. EAT is a general word that can apply to any manner of taking in food. • *Eat* your dinner. CONSUME suggests completely eating something up so that none is left. • By noon they had *consumed* all of their food supplies. DEVOUR suggests eating quickly and greedily. • The hungry children *devoured* the grapes.

eat·ery /ˈiːtəri/ *noun, pl* **-er·ies** [*count*] *chiefly US, informal* **:** a usually small and informal restaurant

eats /ˈiːts/ *noun* [*plural*] *informal* **:** FOOD • cheap *eats* • good *eats*

eau de co·logne /ˌoudəkəˈloun/ *noun, pl* **eaux de cologne** *or* **eau de colognes** [*count, noncount*] **:** COLOGNE

eaves /ˈiːvz/ *noun* [*plural*] **:** the lower edge of a roof that sticks out past the wall — see picture at HOUSE

eaves·drop /ˈiːvz͵drɑːp/ *verb* **-drops; -dropped; -drop·ping** [*no obj*] **:** to listen secretly to what other people are saying — usually + *on* ▪ He was *eavesdropping* [=*listening in*] *on* his sister and her friends in the next room. ▪ She was accused of *eavesdropping on* private telephone conversations.
– **eaves·drop·per** *noun, pl* **-pers** [*count*] – **eaves·dropping** *noun* [*noncount*] ▪ electronic *eavesdropping*

¹ebb /ˈɛb/ *noun, pl* **ebbs** [*count*]
1 : the time when the tide flows out from the land
2 : a low point or condition **:** a condition of weakness, failure, etc. ▪ Morale seems to have reached its lowest *ebb*. — often used after *at* ▪ Our spirits were *at* a low *ebb*. [=were very low] ▪ His fortunes were *at* their lowest *ebb*.
ebb and flow — used to describe something that changes in a regular and repeated way ▪ the *ebb and flow* of fashion ▪ the *ebb and flow* of human history

²ebb *verb* **ebbs; ebbed; ebb·ing** [*no obj*]
1 *of a tide* **:** to flow outward from the land ▪ waiting for the tide to *ebb*
2 : to get worse ▪ Their fortunes had already begun to *ebb*. [=*decline*]

ebb tide *noun, pl* **~ tides** [*count*]
1 : the tide while it is flowing outward from the land
2 : a low point or condition ▪ the empire's *ebb tide*

¹eb·o·ny /ˈɛbəni/ *noun* [*noncount*] **:** a hard, heavy wood that comes from tropical trees

²ebony *adj*
1 : made of or resembling ebony
2 : very dark or black ▪ *ebony* skin

e–book /ˈiː͵bʊk/ *noun, pl* **-books** [*count*] **:** a book that is read on a computer or other electronic device

ebul·lient /ɪˈbʊljənt/ *adj* [*more ~; most ~*] **:** lively and enthusiastic ▪ her *ebullient* charm ▪ an *ebullient* entertainer
– **ebul·lience** /ɪˈbʊljəns/ *noun* [*noncount*] ▪ her delightful *ebullience* – **ebul·lient·ly** *adv* ▪ speaking *ebulliently*

¹ec·cen·tric /ɪkˈsɛntrɪk/ *adj* [*more ~; most ~*]
1 a : tending to act in strange or unusual ways ▪ He was a kind but *eccentric* man. ▪ an *eccentric* inventor ▪ She's become more *eccentric* over the years. **b :** strange or unusual ▪ *eccentric* behavior/ideas ▪ *eccentric* clothes
2 *technical* **:** not following a perfectly circular path ▪ an *eccentric* orbit
– **ec·cen·tri·cal·ly** /ɪkˈsɛntrɪkəli/ *adv* ▪ behaving *eccentrically*

²eccentric *noun, pl* **-trics** [*count*] **:** a person who acts in strange or unusual ways **:** an eccentric person ▪ a wealthy *eccentric*

ec·cen·tric·i·ty /͵ɛksənˈtrɪsəti/ *noun, pl* **-ties**
1 [*noncount*] **:** the quality of being strange or unusual in behavior ▪ Some people weren't very tolerant of his *eccentricity*.
2 [*count*] **:** an act or habit that is strange or unusual ▪ Talking to her plants is one of her many *eccentricities*.

ec·cle·si·as·tic /ɪ͵kliːziˈæstɪk/ *noun, pl* **-tics** [*count*] *formal* **:** a Christian priest or minister

ec·cle·si·as·ti·cal /ɪ͵kliːziˈæstɪkəl/ *also* **ecclesiastic** *adj* **:** of or relating to the Christian church or clergy ▪ *ecclesiastical* history ▪ civil or *ecclesiastical* authorities

ECG /͵iː͵siːˈʤiː/ *noun, pl* **ECGs** [*count*] **:** EKG

ech·e·lon /ˈɛʃə͵lɑːn/ *noun, pl* **-lons** [*count*] **:** a level in an organization **:** a level of authority or responsibility ▪ the lower *echelons* of the bureaucracy ▪ the industry's top *echelon* ▪ We heard stories of corruption in the upper/higher *echelons* of the firm.

¹echo /ˈɛkoʊ/ *noun, pl* **ech·oes** [*count*]
1 : a sound that is a copy of another sound and that is produced when sound waves bounce off a surface (such as a wall) ▪ We shouted into the canyon and listened to the *echo* of our voices. ▪ the *echo* of footsteps in the hall ▪ faint *echoes*
2 a : something (such as a feature or quality) that repeats or resembles something else ▪ His work contains *echoes* of older and greater poets. ▪ The book's title is an *echo* of a line from an old folk song. **b :** something that is similar to something that happened or existed before ▪ The crime is a chilling *echo* of the murders that shocked the city two years ago.

²echo *verb* **echoes; ech·oed; echo·ing**
1 [*no obj*] **a :** to be filled with sounds and especially with echoes ▪ The stadium *echoed* [=*resounded*] with cheers. **b :** to fill a space, area, etc., with sounds and especially with echoes ▪ The music *echoed* through the church. ▪ Laughter *echoed* across the lake. ▪ Their voices *echoed* in/along the hall. — sometimes used figuratively ▪ His words *echoed* in my head/ears. [=I kept thinking about what he had said]
2 [+ *obj*] **:** to repeat (what someone else has said or written) ▪ His warnings are *echoed* by many other experts in the field. ▪ "It's in Rome." "In Rome?" she *echoed*. ▪ Others have *echoed* her criticisms.
3 [+ *obj*] **a :** to have a feature or quality that repeats or resembles (something else) ▪ The book's title *echoes* a line from an old folk song. ▪ The color of the sofa is *echoed* in the painting above it. = The painting *echoes* the color of the sofa. [=the color of the painting is like the color of the sofa] **b :** to be similar to something that happened or existed before ▪ The crime *echoes* last year's shocking murders.

éclair /ɪˈkleɚ/ *noun, pl* **éclairs** [*count*] **:** a type of long pastry that is filled with whipped cream or a sweet cream filling and usually topped with chocolate

eclec·tic /ɪˈklɛktɪk/ *adj* [*more ~; most ~*] **:** including things taken from many different sources ▪ The collection includes an *eclectic* mix of historical artifacts. ▪ a person with *eclectic* tastes [=a person who likes many different kinds of things]
– **eclec·ti·cal·ly** /ɪˈklɛktɪkli/ *adv* ▪ an *eclectically* decorated room – **eclec·ti·cism** /ɪˈklɛktə͵sɪzəm/ *noun* [*noncount*] ▪ the *eclecticism* of her tastes

¹eclipse /ɪˈklɪps/ *noun, pl* **eclips·es**
1 [*count*] **a :** an occasion when the sun looks like it is completely or partially covered with a dark circle because the moon is between the sun and the Earth ▪ a total/partial solar *eclipse* ▪ an *eclipse* of the sun **b :** an occasion when the moon looks like it is completely or partially covered with a dark circle because the Earth's shadow is on it ▪ a total/partial lunar *eclipse*
2 : a loss of power, success, popularity, etc. [*singular*] the civilization's sudden/eventual *eclipse* ▪ The popularity of television led to the *eclipse* of the radio drama. [*noncount*] an author who has fallen/gone ***into eclipse*** [=who has become much less popular] ▪ an artist whose reputation/career has long been ***in eclipse***

²eclipse *verb* **eclipses; eclipsed; eclips·ing** [+ *obj*]
1 : to cause an eclipse of (the sun or moon) ▪ The sun was partially *eclipsed* by the moon.
2 a : to make (something) less important or popular ▪ Train travel was *eclipsed* by the growth of commercial airlines. **b :** to do or be much better than (someone or something) ▪ Her sister's accomplishments always seemed to *eclipse* [=*outshine*] her own. ▪ The new runner's time *eclipsed* [=*surpassed*] the old record.

eco- *combining form* **:** ecology **:** ecological ▪ *eco*-friendly technologies [=technologies that do not harm the environment] ▪ *eco*-politics [=politics that relate to ecology]

E. coli /͵iːˈkoʊ͵laɪ/ *noun* [*noncount*] **:** a kind of bacteria that is sometimes in food and water and that can make people sick

ecol·o·gy /ɪˈkɑːləʤi/ *noun, pl* **-gies**
1 [*noncount*] **:** a science that deals with the relationships between groups of living things and their environments ▪ She studies plant/marine *ecology*.
2 [*count*] **:** the relationships between a group of living things and their environment — usually singular ▪ the behavior and *ecology* of the great white shark ▪ the fragile *ecology* of the desert = the fragile desert *ecology*
– **eco·log·i·cal** /͵iːkəˈlɑːʤɪkəl/ *adj* ▪ the *ecological* consequences of water pollution ▪ The organization promotes *ecological* awareness. – **eco·log·i·cal·ly** /͵iːkəˈlɑːʤɪkli/ *adv* ▪ *ecologically* sound technologies ▪ an *ecologically* stable environment – **ecol·o·gist** /ɪˈkɑːləʤɪst/ *noun, pl* **-gists** [*count*]

e–com·merce /ˈiː͵kɑːmɚs/ *noun* [*noncount*] **:** activities that relate to the buying and selling of goods and services over the Internet

ec·o·nom·ic /͵ɛkəˈnɑːmɪk/ *adj*
1 a : relating to an economy **:** relating to the process or system by which goods and services are produced, sold, and bought ▪ a program to prevent inflation and *economic* collapse ▪ the country's *economic* growth ▪ the President's chief *economic* adviser **b :** relating to the science of economics ▪ controversial *economic* theories
2 [*more ~; most ~*] **:** ECONOMICAL 1 ▪ We're looking for a more *economic* way of doing business.

ec·o·nom·i·cal /͵ɛkəˈnɑːmɪkəl/ *adj* [*more ~; most ~*]
1 : using money, resources, etc., carefully ▪ an *economical* way to heat your house ▪ a practical and *economical* solution to the problem ▪ an *economical* cook [=a cook who does not waste food] ▪ The author is often praised for her simple, *economical* writing style. [=a way of writing that uses only the

words that are most necessary] ▪ We offer quality products at ***economical prices*** [=prices that many people can afford]
2 — used to describe a product that is not expensive to own and use ▪ The company is making smaller, more *economical* cars. [=cars that do not use a lot of fuel]

ec·o·nom·i·cal·ly /ˌɛkəˈnɑːmɪkli/ *adv*
1 : in a way that relates to an economy ▪ An increase in tourism will help the city *economically*. [=will help the city's economy] ▪ an *economically* depressed area ▪ *economically* disadvantaged people [=poor people]
2 : in an economical way ▪ a way to *economically* heat your house ▪ She writes simply and *economically*.

ec·o·nom·ics /ˌɛkəˈnɑːmɪks/ *noun*
1 [*noncount*] **:** a science concerned with the process or system by which goods and services are produced, sold, and bought ▪ She studied *economics* before becoming a banker. ▪ a professor of *economics* ▪ *Economics* is my least favorite subject.
2 [*plural*] **:** the part of something that relates to money ▪ the *economics* of buying a house [=the financial aspects of buying a house] ▪ The *economics* of this agreement are complicated.
— see also HOME ECONOMICS

econ·o·mist /ɪˈkɑːnəmɪst/ *noun, pl* **-mists** [*count*] **:** a person who studies or specializes in economics (sense 1) ▪ *Economists* are predicting rapid inflation.

econ·o·mize *also Brit* **econ·o·mise** /ɪˈkɑːnəˌmaɪz/ *verb* **-miz·es; -mized; -miz·ing :** to use money, resources, etc., carefully [*no obj*] He was born into a wealthy family and never learned to *economize*. — often + *on* ▪ We're finding new ways to *economize* [=*save*] *on* fuel. [+ *obj*] (*chiefly US*) ▪ efforts to *economize* [=*save*] fuel/time

[1]**econ·o·my** /ɪˈkɑːnəmi/ *noun, pl* **-mies**
1 [*count*] **:** the process or system by which goods and services are produced, sold, and bought in a country or region ▪ The war altered the country's *economy*. ▪ An increase in tourism will help the city's *economy*. ▪ We currently have a strong/weak *economy*. [=many/few goods and services are being produced, sold, and bought] ▪ the Mexican *economy* = Mexico's *economy* ▪ the world/global *economy* ▪ the region's fishing/information/retail *economy* ▪ People are worried about (the state of) ***the economy***. [=their country's economy] ▪ changes in *the economy*
2 [*noncount*] **:** careful use of money, resources, etc. ▪ We must learn to practice *economy*. ▪ a writer known for her *economy* of language [=her careful use of language; her use of only the words that are most necessary] ▪ cars with better ***fuel economy*** [=cars that use less fuel]
3 : something that makes it possible for you to spend less money [*count*] We'll also benefit from the *economies* provided by more efficient energy sources. ▪ Mass production creates ***economies of scale*** [=situations in which it costs less to produce something because you are producing a lot at one time] ▪ Using cheap materials proved to be a ***false economy***. [=it cost less at first but resulted in more money being spent later] [*noncount*] It would be *false economy* to repair the leak without replacing the pipe.

[2]**economy** *adj, always used before a noun* **:** designed to cost less money ▪ an *economy* car [=a car that costs less to buy, drive, maintain, etc.] ▪ an *economy* class ticket [=the least expensive kind of airline ticket] — often used in combination ▪ an *economy*-size bottle/bag/box [=a large bottle/bag/box that you buy for less money than it would cost to get the same amount in several smaller containers]

eco·sys·tem /ˈiːkoʊˌsɪstəm/ *noun, pl* **-tems** [*count*] **:** everything that exists in a particular environment ✧ An ecosystem includes living things, such as plants and animals, and things that are not living, such as rocks, soil, sunlight, and water. ▪ the forest's *ecosystem*

eco·tour·ism /ˌiːkoʊˈtuəˌrɪzəm/ *noun* [*noncount*] **:** the practice of traveling to beautiful natural places for pleasure in a way that does not damage the environment there

ecru /ˈɛkru/ *noun, pl* **ecrus** [*count, noncount*] **:** a pale color that is slightly yellow or brown
— **ecru** *adj*

ec·sta·sy /ˈɛkstəsi/ *noun, pl* **-sies**
1 : a state of very great happiness **:** extreme delight [*noncount*] shouts of pure/sheer *ecstasy* ▪ shrieking with/in *ecstasy* [*count*] His performance sent the audience into *ecstasies*.
2 *or* ***Ecstasy*** [*noncount*] **:** an illegal drug that is used to produce a feeling of excitement and pleasure

ec·stat·ic /ɛkˈstætɪk/ *adj* [*more* ~; *most* ~] **:** very happy or excited **:** feeling or showing ecstasy ▪ He was *ecstatic* when he heard that he was going to be a father. ▪ *ecstatic* applause
— **ec·stat·i·cal·ly** /ɛkˈstætɪkli/ *adv* ▪ She was *ecstatically* happy.

ECT /ˌiːˌsiːˈtiː/ *noun* [*noncount*] *medical* **:** SHOCK THERAPY

ec·u·men·i·cal /ˌɛkjəˈmɛnɪkəl/ *adj* **:** involving people from different kinds of Christian churches ▪ an *ecumenical* council/service
— **ec·u·men·i·cal·ly** /ˌɛkjəˈmɛnɪkli/ *adv*

ec·ze·ma /ˈɛgzəmə/ *noun* [*noncount*] *medical* **:** a skin disease that causes areas of the skin to become red, rough, and itchy

ed /ˈɛd/ *noun* [*noncount*] *informal* **:** education ▪ driver's *ed* [=classes or lessons that teach students to drive]

ed. *abbr* edited, edition, editor

-ed /əd, ɪd *after* t *or* d; t *after* p, k, ʧ, f, θ, s, *or* ʃ; d *elsewhere; exceptions are pronounced at their entries*/ *verb suffix or adj suffix*
1 — used to form the past tense and past participle of regular verbs ▪ It end*ed*. ▪ It has end*ed*. ▪ clapp*ed* ▪ tri*ed* ▪ patt*ed*
2 : having **:** characterized by ▪ dom*ed* ▪ cultur*ed* ▪ two-legg*ed* ▪ blue-ey*ed*

[1]**ed·dy** /ˈɛdi/ *noun, pl* **ed·dies** [*count*] **:** a circular movement of air or water ▪ The boat was caught in a powerful *eddy*.

[2]**eddy** *verb* **ed·dies; ed·died; ed·dy·ing** [*no obj*] **:** to move in a circle **:** to form an eddy ▪ The wind gusted and *eddied* around us. ▪ The waves swirled and *eddied* against the pier.

Eden /ˈiːdn̩/ *noun, pl* **Edens**
1 [*singular*] *in the Bible* **:** the garden where Adam and Eve first lived — called also *Garden of Eden*
2 a [*count*] **:** a very beautiful natural place ▪ a tropical *Eden* **b** [*singular*] **:** a place that is perfect for a particular activity or for a person who enjoys that activity **:** PARADISE ▪ The new store is an *Eden* for book lovers.

[1]**edge** /ˈɛʤ/ *noun, pl* **edg·es** [*count*]
1 : the line or part where an object or area begins or ends ▪ They peered over the *edge* of the roof. ▪ The fabric was frayed at the *edge*. ▪ He made us all nervous by standing so close to the *edge* of the cliff. ▪ We sat at the water's *edge*. [=where the water touched the land] ▪ She sat on the *edge* of the counter, swinging her legs.
2 a : the part of a blade that cuts ▪ the *edge* of an ax ▪ a razor's *edge* **b :** the sharpness of a blade ▪ This knife has no *edge*. [=this knife is not sharp]
3 a : a harsh or unkind quality ▪ His voice/comments had a sarcastic/sardonic *edge*. **b :** force or effectiveness ▪ Her writing seem to have lost its *edge*. ▪ These amendments will blunt the *edge* of the legislation.
4 : an advantage over others ▪ Our experience gave us an/the *edge*. ▪ You need to get/gain an *edge* on your competition. ▪ The company still has/holds an *edge* over its competitors. ▪ a competitive *edge* — see also CUTTING EDGE, LEADING EDGE

close to the edge *or* ***on the edge*** ✧ Someone who ***lives (life) on the edge*** or ***lives close to the edge*** often deals with dangerous situations and takes many risks. ▪ He likes to *live on the edge*.

on edge **:** feeling nervous **:** not calm or relaxed ▪ She was *on edge* [=*edgy*] before her exam. = Her nerves were *on edge* before her exam.

on the edge of **:** very close to (something) ▪ a species *on the edge of* extinction ▪ The company was teetering *on the edge of* disaster/bankruptcy. ▪ They were poised *on the edge of* success. ▪ He was *on the edge of* saying something when the phone rang.

on the edge of your seat ✧ If you are *on the edge of your seat*, you are watching or listening to something with great interest especially because you do not know what is going to happen. ▪ It's a thrilling movie that keeps audiences *on the edge of their seats*.

on the ragged edge see RAGGED

over the edge **:** into a mental or emotional state that makes someone completely lose control ▪ His friends worried that the news might send/drive/push him *over the edge*.

razor/razor's edge see RAZOR

set your teeth on edge see TOOTH

take the edge off **:** to make (something) weaker or less severe ▪ a medication that *takes the edge off* the pain ▪ A glass of milk will *take the edge off* your hunger/appetite. [=will make you feel less hungry]

— **edged** /ˈɛʤd/ *adj* ▪ an *edged* weapon [=a weapon with a sharp edge, such as a sword or knife] — see also TWO-EDGED

²edge *verb* **edg·es; edged; edg·ing**

1 [+ *obj*] **a :** to give an edge to (something) • *Edge* the sleeve with lace. — usually used as *(be) edged* • The sleeve *was edged* with/in lace. [=it had a lace edge] **b :** to be on the edge of (something) • Trees *edge* the lake. — usually used as *(be) edged* • The garden *is edged* [=*fringed, bordered*] with/in/by flowers.

2 *always followed by an adverb or preposition* **:** to move slowly or with small movements in a specified direction [*no obj*] She *edged* away from him. • Gasoline prices have been *edging* upward. [+ *obj*] I *edged* my chair closer to the table.

3 [+ *obj*] **:** to defeat (someone) by a small amount • (*chiefly US*) He was *edged* in the semifinals by the defending champion. — usually + *out* • He was *edged out* in the semifinals. • She barely/narrowly *edged out* her opponent.

edge out [*phrasal verb*] ***edge (someone or something) out*** or ***edge out (someone or something)* :** to slowly become more successful, popular, etc., than (someone or something) • The company is gradually *edging out* the competition. • Efficiency has *edged out* price as the top reason people give for buying the car. — see also ²EDGE 3 (above)

edge·wise (*US*) /ˈɛʤˌwaɪz/ *or chiefly Brit* **edge·ways** /ˈɛʤˌweɪz/ *adv* **:** SIDEWAYS ✧ If you can't ***get a word in edgewise*** it means that someone else is talking so much that you are not able to say anything. • I wanted to explain what had happened but I couldn't *get a word in edgewise*.

edg·ing /ˈɛʤɪŋ/ *noun, pl* **-ings :** something that forms an edge or border [*count*] sleeves with lace *edgings* [*noncount*] sleeves with lace *edging*

edgy /ˈɛʤi/ *adj* **edg·i·er; -est** [*also more ~; most ~*]

1 : nervous and tense • Too much coffee makes me *edgy*. • Why are you so *edgy*? • People are starting to get *edgy* [=*on edge*] about rising prices.

2 : having or showing a harsh or unkind quality • *edgy* humor • an *edgy* scene/situation • Their relationship has always been *edgy*.

3 : new and unusual in a way that is likely to make some people uncomfortable • one of the director's *edgier* films • an *edgy* artist

– edg·i·ly /ˈɛʤəli/ *adv* • *edgily* funny **– edg·i·ness** /ˈɛʤinəs/ *noun* [*noncount*] the excitement and *edginess* in the artist's work [*singular*] There was an *edginess* [=a harsh quality] in her voice.

ed·i·ble /ˈɛdəbəl/ *adj* **:** suitable or safe to eat • *edible* fruit • a plant with *edible* leaves • All of the decorations on the gingerbread house were *edible*. — opposite INEDIBLE

– ed·i·bil·i·ty /ˌɛdəˈbɪləti/ *noun* [*noncount*] **– edibles** *noun* [*plural*] *informal* • cheese, crackers, and other *edibles*

edict /ˈiːˌdɪkt/ *noun, pl* **edicts** [*count*] **:** an official order given by a person with power or by a government **:** DECREE • The government issued an *edict* banning public demonstrations. • a royal/religious *edict*

ed·i·fice /ˈɛdəfəs/ *noun, pl* **-fic·es** [*count*] **:** a large and usually impressive building (such as a church or government building) • a magnificent *edifice* with a domed ceiling

ed·i·fy /ˈɛdəˌfaɪ/ *verb* **-fies; -fied; -fy·ing** [+ *obj*] **:** to teach (someone) in a way that improves the mind or character • These books will both entertain and *edify* readers.

– ed·i·fi·ca·tion /ˌɛdəfəˈkeɪʃən/ *noun* [*noncount*] • books that provide both entertainment and *edification* **– edifying** *adj* [*more ~; most ~*] • an *edifying* sermon/experience • The books are both entertaining and *edifying*.

ed·it /ˈɛdət/ *verb* **ed·its; ed·it·ed; ed·it·ing** [+ *obj*]

1 a : to prepare (something written) to be published or used **:** to make changes, correct mistakes, etc., in (something written) • *edit* a poem • This chapter needs to be *edited*. • The book was poorly *edited*. • The stories have been *edited* for a younger audience. • Students learn to *edit* their essays for grammar and punctuation. **b :** to prepare (a film, recording, photo, etc.) to be seen or heard **:** to change, move, or remove parts of (a film, recording, photo, etc.) • The software allows you to *edit* videos on your computer. • This film has been *edited* for television.

2 : to be in charge of the publication of (something) • *edit* a magazine/daily newspaper • an anthology of ancient poetry *edited* by a local professor

edit out [*phrasal verb*] ***edit out (something)*** or ***edit (something) out* :** to remove (something, such as an unwanted word or scene) while preparing something to be seen, used, published, etc. • They *edited out* the scene. • Write freely. You can always *edit* things *out* later.

***edit yourself* :** to change what you were going to say or would normally say • I feel like I have to *edit myself* when I talk to them. • "I never saw it," she said before quickly *editing herself*, "or at least I don't remember seeing it."

– editing *noun* [*noncount*] • The *editing* was done poorly. • *editing* techniques

edi·tion /ɪˈdɪʃən/ *noun, pl* **edi·tions** [*count*]

1 a : a particular version of a book • an illustrated *edition* [=a version that has pictures] • a hardcover/paperback *edition* **b :** a particular version of a product • the latest *edition* of the software

2 : all the copies of a book that are printed or published at one time • The errors were corrected in the book's second *edition*. — see also FIRST EDITION, LIMITED EDITION

3 : one of the several versions of a newspaper that are printed for a single day • the late *edition* • the city *edition*

4 : something that is presented as one of a series • the most recent *edition* of the city's film festival • tonight's *edition* [=*episode*] of the show

ed·i·tor /ˈɛdətɚ/ *noun, pl* **-tors** [*count*]

1 : a person whose job is to edit something • the *editor* of the city paper • working as a film *editor* • the fiction *editor* of a magazine [=the person who decides what fiction pieces get published]

2 : a computer program that is used to create and make changes to data (such as words or pictures) • a text *editor*

– ed·i·tor·ship /ˈɛdətɚˌʃɪp/ *noun* [*noncount*] • The magazine has done well under her *editorship*.

¹ed·i·to·ri·al /ˌɛdəˈtorijəl/ *adj* **:** of or relating to an editor • *editorial* offices • He got an *editorial* job at the newspaper.

– ed·i·to·ri·al·ly *adv*

²editorial *noun, pl* **-als** [*count*] **:** an essay in a newspaper or magazine that gives the opinions of its editors or publishers • The paper published an *editorial* strongly criticizing the mayor's actions. — called also *(Brit) leader, (Brit) leading article*

editor in chief *noun, pl* **editors in chief** [*count*] **:** a person whose job is to be in charge of a group of editors • the magazine's *editor in chief* = the *editor in chief* of the magazine

ed·u·cate /ˈɛʤəˌkeɪt/ *verb* **-cates; -cat·ed; -cat·ing**

1 : to teach (someone) especially in a school, college, or university [+ *obj*] Parents trust schools to *educate* their children. — often used as *(be) educated* • She *was educated* at private schools. [*no obj*] The job of our public schools is to *educate*.

2 [+ *obj*] **:** to give (someone) information about something **:** to train (someone) to do something • It takes time to *educate* [=*train*] new workers on how to use the machines. • We need to *educate* [=*inform*] the public about this dangerous disease. — sometimes followed by *to + verb* • *educating* consumers *to use* these products more effectively

educated *adj* [*more ~; most ~*]

1 a : having an education and especially a good education • These companies want an *educated* work force. • an *educated* woman with an impressive career — opposite UNEDUCATED **b :** having a particular kind of education • He is poorly/well *educated*. — sometimes used in combination • college-*educated* people • a Harvard-*educated* economist — see also SELF-EDUCATED

2 : showing education (sense 1b) • *educated* speech/tastes — opposite UNEDUCATED; see also *educated guess* at ²GUESS

ed·u·ca·tion /ˌɛʤəˈkeɪʃən/ *noun, pl* **-tions**

1 a [*noncount*] **:** the action or process of teaching someone especially in a school, college, or university • The school is devoted to the *education* of children with reading difficulties. — see also ADULT EDUCATION, HIGHER EDUCATION, PHYSICAL EDUCATION **b :** the knowledge, skill, and understanding that you get from attending a school, college, or university [*count*] a college *education* • She received her *education* at private schools. • The applicants had comparable *educations*. [*noncount*] He had little formal *education*. [=*schooling*]

2 [*noncount*] **:** a field of study that deals with the methods and problems of teaching • She earned her master's degree in *education*. • a school of *education*

ed·u·ca·tion·al /ˌɛʤəˈkeɪʃənl/ *adj*

1 : having to do with education • *educational* theorists • a leading *educational* institution

2 [*more ~; most ~*] **:** teaching something • an *educational* film • *educational* television • Our vacation turned out to be a very *educational* experience.

E

ed·u·ca·tion·ist /ˌɛʤəˈkeɪʃənɪst/ *or* **ed·u·ca·tion·al·ist** /ˌɛʤəˈkeɪʃənlɪst/ *noun, pl* **-ists** [*count*] *Brit* : EDUCATOR

ed·u·ca·tor /ˈɛʤəˌkeɪtɚ/ *noun, pl* **-tors** [*count*] *chiefly US* : a person (such as a teacher or a school administrator) who has a job in the field of education ▪ The conference will attract many leading scholars and *educators*.

ed·u·tain·ment /ˌɛʤəˈteɪnmənt/ *noun* [*noncount*] : entertainment (such as through games, films, or shows) that is designed to teach something

-ee /i/ *noun suffix*
1 : a person who gets or is affected by a specified action or thing ▪ appoint*ee* ▪ train*ee*
2 : a person who does a specified action ▪ escap*ee* ▪ stand*ee*

EEG /ˌiːˌiːˈʤiː/ *noun, pl* **EEGs** [*count*] *medical*
1 : a printed recording of the brain's electrical activity made by a special machine — called also *electroencephalogram*
2 : a machine that detects and records the electrical activity of the brain — called also *electroencephalograph*

eek /ˈiːk/ *interj* — used to express surprise and fear ▪ *Eek*! There's a mouse in the cupboard!

eel /ˈiːl/ *noun, pl* **eels** [*count*] : a long fish that looks like a snake and has smooth slippery skin — see color picture on page C8
– **eel·like** /ˈiːlˌlaɪk/ *adj*

-eer /iɚ/ *noun suffix* : a person who is connected with or who operates or produces something ▪ auction*eer* ▪ puppet*eer*

ee·rie /ˈiri/ *adj* **ee·ri·er**; **-est** [*or more* ~; *most* ~] : strange and mysterious ▪ a coyote's *eerie* howl ▪ The flames cast an *eerie* glow. ▪ a land of *eerie* beauty ▪ an *eerie* coincidence
– **ee·ri·ly** /ˈirəli/ *adv* ▪ The two towns are *eerily* similar.
– **ee·ri·ness** /ˈirinəs/ *noun* [*noncount*] the *eeriness* of the coyote's howl [*singular*] There is an *eeriness* about that coincidence.

ef·face /ɪˈfeɪs/ *verb* **-fac·es**; **-faced**; **-fac·ing** [+ *obj*] *formal* : to cause (something) to fade or disappear ▪ coins with dates *effaced* by wear ▪ a memory *effaced* by time — see also SELF-EFFACING
– **ef·face·ment** /ɪˈfeɪsmənt/ *noun* [*noncount*]

[1]**ef·fect** /ɪˈfɛkt/ *noun, pl* **-fects**
1 : a change that results when something is done or happens : an event, condition, or state of affairs that is produced by a cause [*count*] The defeat had a terrible *effect* [=*impact*] on the team's spirits. ▪ He now needs more of the drug to achieve/get/produce the same *effect*. ▪ The experience has had a bad/adverse/negative *effect* on him. ▪ a good/beneficial/positive *effect* ▪ Computers have had a profound/significant *effect* on our lives. ▪ The *effects* of the drug soon wore off. ▪ He was able to stop taking the drug with no ***ill effects***. [=with nothing bad happening] ▪ This treatment causes fewer *ill effects*. [*noncount*] The change in policy had little *effect* on most people. ▪ the *effect* [=*influence*] of climate on growth ▪ He was able to stop taking the drug without ***ill effect***. ✧ If something ***has an effect on*** something or someone, it changes or influences that thing or person in some way. ▪ The new regulations may *have an effect on* small businesses. ▪ It could *have effects on* other businesses as well. — see also DOMINO EFFECT, GREENHOUSE EFFECT, RIPPLE EFFECT, SIDE EFFECT, SNOWBALL EFFECT, *placebo effect* at PLACEBO
2 [*count*] **:** a particular feeling or mood created by something ▪ The total *effect* of the painting was one of gloom. ▪ The color gives the *effect* of being warm. ▪ He achieves/gets amazing *effects* with wood. ✧ Something that is done ***for effect*** is done in a deliberate way to produce a particular feeling or reaction. ▪ Her tears were only *for effect*. [=she was crying or pretending to cry to make people feel sympathy for her] ▪ The movie exaggerates his odd habits *for* comic/humorous *effect*. ▪ Before making the announcement, he paused *for* dramatic *effect*. [=he paused to make the announcement more dramatic]
3 [*count*] **:** an image or a sound that is created in television, radio, or movies to imitate something real : SPECIAL EFFECT — usually plural ▪ Computers are essential now in creating *effects* for the movies. ▪ sound *effects* ▪ visual *effects*
4 [*noncount*] **:** the state of something that is actually working or operating ▪ The policy will be in *effect* next year. ✧ If a law or something like a law ***takes effect***, ***comes into effect***, or ***goes into effect***, it begins to work or to be enforced. ▪ The law *went/came into effect* today. ▪ The new regulations will *take effect* next year. ✧ If a drug or something like a drug ***takes effect***, it begins to produce the results it is meant to produce. ▪ The medication should *take effect* half an hour after you take the pills. ✧ To ***give effect to something*** or to ***carry/bring/put something into effect*** is to make it begin doing what it was intended to do. ▪ The court refused to *give effect to* that part of the document. ▪ The company has not yet *carried these plans into effect*. [=the company has not yet acted on these plans] ▪ The new regulations will be *put into effect* next year.
5 ***effects*** [*plural*] **:** personal property or possessions ▪ household *effects* ▪ Pick up your (personal) *effects* before you leave.

in effect — used to say that one thing has the same effect or result as something else ▪ The suggestion was *in effect* an order.

to good effect ✧ If you use something ***to good/great/fine/outstanding (etc.) effect***, you use it in a way that produces good results. ▪ The city has used these resources *to good effect*. ▪ These changes have been implemented *to great effect*.

to little/no effect ✧ If something is done *to little effect* or *to no effect*, it produces little or no change. ▪ His doctors have repeatedly adjusted his medication *to little effect*.

to that effect *or* ***to the effect that*** — used to indicate that the meaning of words is roughly correct even if the words themselves are not completely accurate ▪ He said more time was needed to reach a decision, or words *to that effect*. = He said something *to the effect that* more time was needed to reach a decision.

[2]**effect** *verb* **-fects**; **-fect·ed**; **-fect·ing** [+ *obj*] *formal*
1 : to cause (something) : to make (something) happen ▪ The president could not *effect* [=*bring about*] a change in policy. ▪ They are trying to *effect* a settlement of the dispute.
2 : to cause (something) to produce the desired result ▪ The duty of the legislature is to *effect* the will of the people.
usage see AFFECT

ef·fec·tive /ɪˈfɛktɪv/ *adj*
1 [*more* ~; *most* ~] **:** producing a result that is wanted : having an intended effect ▪ drugs *effective* in the treatment of a disease = drugs *effective* in treating a disease = drugs *effective* against a disease ▪ It's a simple but *effective* technique. ▪ He gave an *effective* speech. — opposite INEFFECTIVE
2 *of a law, rule, etc.* **:** in use : ACTIVE ▪ The law becomes *effective* [=the law takes effect; the law will start to be used] next year. ▪ the ***effective date*** of the law [=the day when the law starts to be used]
3 : starting at a particular time — used to introduce a clause ▪ *Effective* [=*starting, as of*] tomorrow, the store will be open until 8:00 p.m. every day. ▪ *Effective* next month, the landfill will no longer accept old televisions.
4 *always used before a noun* — used to describe something that exists or has an effect but that is not officially stated or recognized ▪ the *effective* tax rate ▪ The army has taken *effective* control of the city.
– **ef·fec·tive·ness** *noun* [*noncount*] ▪ The *effectiveness* of the drug was questioned.

ef·fec·tive·ly /ɪˈfɛktɪvli/ *adv* [*more* ~; *most* ~]
1 : in a way that produces a desired result : in an effective manner ▪ Try to communicate your ideas more *effectively*.
2 : in an indirect way — used to say that one thing has the same effect or result as something else ▪ By turning down the permit they *effectively* [=*in effect, for all practical purposes*] ended the housing plans.

ef·fec·tu·al /ɪˈfɛkʧəwəl/ *adj* [*more* ~; *most* ~] *formal* : producing a desired result or effect ▪ an *effectual* [=*effective*] remedy — opposite INEFFECTUAL
– **ef·fec·tu·al·ly** /ɪˈfɛkʧəwəli/ *adv* ▪ The law would *effectually* bar new development in the neighborhood.

ef·fem·i·nate /ɪˈfɛmənət/ *adj* [*more* ~; *most* ~] : having or showing qualities that are considered more suited to women than to men : not manly ▪ an *effeminate* manner ▪ He had a high and somewhat *effeminate* voice.
– **ef·fem·i·na·cy** /ɪˈfɛmənəsi/ *noun* [*noncount*] – **ef·fem·i·nate·ly** *adv* ▪ dressed *effeminately*

ef·fer·ves·cence /ˌɛfɚˈvɛsn̩s/ *noun* [*noncount*]
1 : an exciting or lively quality ▪ The actress's *effervescence* was charming. ▪ the *effervescence* of his writing style
2 : bubbles that form and rise in a liquid
– **ef·fer·ves·cent** /ˌɛfɚˈvɛsn̩t/ *adj* [*more* ~; *most* ~] ▪ her *effervescent* [=*bubbly*] personality ▪ an *effervescent* drink
– **ef·fer·ves·cent·ly** *adv*

ef·fete /ɪˈfiːt/ *adj* [*more* ~; *most* ~] *disapproving*
1 : lacking strength, courage, or spirit ▪ *effete* intellectuals ▪ *effete* members of the aristocracy
2 : resembling a woman : EFFEMINATE ▪ an *effete* young man

ef·fi·ca·cious /ˌɛfəˈkeɪʃəs/ *adj* [*more* ~; *most* ~] *formal*

: having the power to produce a desired result or effect : EFFECTIVE ▪ an *efficacious* remedy
– **ef·fi·ca·cious·ly** *adv* – **ef·fi·ca·cious·ness** *noun* [*noncount*]

ef·fi·ca·cy /ˈɛfɪkəsi/ *noun* [*noncount*] *formal* : the power to produce a desired result or effect ▪ The *efficacy* [=*effectiveness*] of this treatment has not yet been proved.

ef·fi·cien·cy /ɪˈfɪʃənsi/ *noun, pl* **-cies**
1 : the ability to do something or produce something without wasting materials, time, or energy : the quality or degree of being efficient [*noncount*] Because of her *efficiency*, we got all the work done in a few hours. ▪ The factory was operating at peak *efficiency*. ▪ a car with greater fuel *efficiency* [=a car that uses fuel more efficiently] ▪ A furnace with 80 percent fuel *efficiency* wastes 20 percent of its fuel. [*plural*] (*technical*) ▪ The company is trying to lower costs and improve *efficiencies*.
2 [*count*] *US* : EFFICIENCY APARTMENT

efficiency apartment *noun, pl* **~ -ments** [*count*] *US* : a small apartment that usually includes furniture and has a small and simple kitchen area

ef·fi·cient /ɪˈfɪʃənt/ *adj* [*more ~; most ~*] : capable of producing desired results without wasting materials, time, or energy ▪ an *efficient* worker ▪ *efficient* machinery
– **ef·fi·cient·ly** *adv* ▪ learning to work more *efficiently*

ef·fi·gy /ˈɛfəʤi/ *noun, pl* **-gies** [*count*] : an image of a person ✧ An *effigy* is often a large doll made to look like someone who is disliked or hated. ▪ The governor was ***hanged/burned in effigy*** by a mob of protesters. [=a large doll that looked like the governor was hanged or burned by the mob]

ef·flu·ent /ˈɛˌfluːwənt/ *noun, pl* **-ents** *formal* : liquid (such as sewage or industrial chemicals) that is released as waste [*noncount*] The factory has been accused of discharging *effluent* into the river. [*count*] industrial *effluents*

ef·fort /ˈɛfət/ *noun, pl* **-forts**
1 : work done by the mind or body : energy used to do something [*noncount*] He put a lot of *effort* into finishing the project on time. ▪ It wasn't easy, but it was worth the *effort*. ▪ We need to expend more/extra *effort*. ▪ The job will require/take a great deal of time and *effort*. ▪ a lack of *effort* ▪ She seems to do everything ***without effort*** [=*effortlessly*; very easily] [*count*] Our success is due to the combined/concerted *efforts* of many people. ▪ Her *efforts* were rewarded with a new contract. ▪ He lost the campaign despite the best *efforts* of his supporters. ✧ If you get ***an A for effort*** or ***an E for effort*** or (*Brit*) ***full marks for effort***, you are given credit for working hard to do something, even though the result of the work was not successful. ▪ His novel's surprise ending is not really convincing, but we'll give him *an A for effort*.
2 [*count*] : a serious attempt to do something ▪ Even though they didn't win, the team made a good/valiant *effort*. ▪ a determined/desperate *effort* ▪ a last-ditch *effort* ▪ Her early *efforts* at writing a novel were awkward. ▪ The project is a ***team effort*** [=is being done by a group of people] ▪ Despite my ***best efforts***, I never found out who she was. — often followed by *to* + *verb* ▪ He made no *effort to hide* his feelings. [=he showed his feelings openly] ▪ In an *effort to avoid* further delays, the delivery process has been simplified. ▪ I had to make a conscious/deliberate *effort* not *to laugh*. ▪ The school ***makes every effort*** [=the school does all that it can] *to help* new students become adjusted to college life.
3 [*count*] : something produced by work ▪ This painting was one of my best *efforts*. ▪ It wasn't bad for a first *effort*.
4 [*singular*] : something that is hard to do ▪ I was so tired this morning that is was an *effort* (for me) to get out of bed.
5 [*noncount*] : all that is being done to achieve a particular goal ▪ He wanted to contribute in some way to the ***war effort*** [=to the effort to win the war]

ef·fort·less /ˈɛfətləs/ *adj* [*more ~; most ~*] : showing or needing little or no effort : appearing very easy ▪ She walked with *effortless* grace. ▪ His writing is known for its seemingly *effortless* style. ✧ *Effortless* usually describes something that appears to be easy because of the skill of the person who is doing it. ▪ The skier made a series of *effortless* turns.
– **ef·fort·less·ly** *adv* ▪ gliding *effortlessly* across the ice
– **ef·fort·less·ness** *noun* [*noncount*]

ef·fron·tery /ɪˈfrʌntəri/ *noun* [*noncount*] *formal* : a very confident attitude or way of behaving that is shocking or rude : NERVE ✧ *Effrontery* describes the attitude of a person who does something very boldly and without shame even though it is wrong or offensive in some way. ▪ He had the *effrontery* to deny doing something that we saw him do.

ef·fu·sion /ɪˈfjuːʒən/ *noun, pl* **-sions**
1 [*count*] *formal* : something that is said or expressed too much or with a lot of emotion ▪ Her poetic *effusions* became tiresome.
2 [*count, noncount*] *technical* : a flow of liquid or gas

ef·fu·sive /ɪˈfjuːsɪv/ *adj* [*more ~; most ~*] : expressing a lot of emotion ▪ They offered *effusive* thanks for our help. ▪ He was *effusive* in praising their work. = He gave their work *effusive* praise. ▪ an *effusive* welcome
– **ef·fu·sive·ly** *adv* ▪ praising their work *effusively* – **ef·fu·sive·ness** *noun* [*noncount*]

EFL /ˌiːˌɛfˈɛl/ *noun* [*noncount*] : the teaching of English as a foreign language

e.g. *abbr* for example ▪ products imported from many countries, *e.g.*, France, Germany, and Japan ✧ The abbreviation *e.g.* comes from the Latin phrase "exempli gratia," which means "for example."

egal·i·tar·i·an /ɪˌgæləˈterijən/ *adj* [*more ~; most ~*] *formal* : aiming for equal wealth, status, etc., for all people ▪ *egalitarian* policies for the redistribution of wealth
– **egalitarian** *noun, pl* **-ans** [*count*] ▪ He is a committed *egalitarian*. – **egal·i·tar·i·an·ism** /ɪˌgæləˈterijəˌnɪzəm/ *noun* [*noncount*]

[1]egg /ˈɛg/ *noun, pl* **eggs**
1 [*count*] : a hard-shelled oval thing from which a young bird is born ▪ The *egg* will hatch about 10 days after it is laid.; *also* : an oval or round thing from which a snake, frog, insect, etc., is born
2 : the egg of a bird (especially a chicken) eaten as food [*count*] poached/fried/boiled *eggs* ▪ hard-boiled/soft-boiled *eggs* ▪ the smell of rotten *eggs* ▪ (*US*) scrambled *eggs* ▪ I bought a carton of *eggs*. ▪ (*US*) They served us ***bacon and eggs*** for breakfast. = (*Brit*) They served us ***eggs and bacon*** for breakfast. ▪ an ***Easter egg*** [=an egg that is specially decorated at Easter] [*noncount*] (*Brit*) scrambled *egg* ▪ a batter made from flour and *egg* ▪ *egg* white(s)/yolk
3 [*count*] *biology* : a cell that is produced by the female sexual organs and that combines with the male's sperm in reproduction ▪ The *egg* is fertilized by the sperm. — called also *ovum*
4 [*count*] : something that is shaped like a bird's egg ▪ a chocolate *egg*
bad egg *informal + somewhat old-fashioned* : someone who does bad things ▪ He was dishonest, but he was the only *bad egg* in the group.
curate's egg see CURATE
egg on your face ✧ If you have *egg on your face* you appear foolish, usually because something that you said would happen has not happened. ▪ The unexpected election result left a lot of journalists with *egg on their faces*.
good egg *informal + somewhat old-fashioned* : a likeable person ▪ I've known Jim for years. He's a *good egg*.
lay an egg *US, informal* : to fail completely : to fail in a very obvious or embarrassing way ▪ He used to be a very popular star, but his last two movies have *laid an egg*.
put all your eggs in one basket ✧ If you *put all your eggs in one basket*, you risk all you have on the success or failure of one thing (such as an investment), so that if something goes wrong you could lose everything. ▪ Investors should diversify their investments instead of *putting all their eggs in one basket*. [=instead of investing all their money in one company or one kind of company]
the goose that lays the golden egg see [1]GOOSE
walk on eggs see [1]WALK
– see also NEST EGG

[2]egg *verb* **eggs; egged; egg·ing**
egg on [*phrasal verb*] ***egg (someone) on*** : to urge or encourage (someone) to do something that is usually foolish or dangerous ▪ He continued to take off his clothes while the crowd *egged* him *on*.

eggbeater *noun, pl* **-ers** [*count*] : a tool that is used by cooks to mix eggs very thoroughly

egg·cup /ˈɛgˌkʌp/ *noun, pl* **-cups** [*count*] : a cup-shaped device which holds an egg that is being eaten

egg·head /ˈɛgˌhɛd/ *noun, pl* **-heads** [*count*] *informal + usually disapproving* : a highly educated person who may not know much about real life ▪ He dismissed all scientists as a bunch of *eggheads*.
– **egg·head·ed** /ˈɛgˌhɛdəd/ *adj* [*more ~; most ~*] *informal* ▪ *eggheaded* scientists

egg·nog /ˈɛgˌnɑːg/ *noun, pl* **-nogs** [*count, noncount*] : a drink made of eggs beaten with sugar, milk or cream, and of-

E

ten alcoholic liquor ✧ Eggnog is a traditional drink at Christmastime.

egg·plant /ˈɛg,plænt/ *noun, pl* **-plants** [*count, noncount*] *chiefly US* : a somewhat egg-shaped vegetable with usually purple skin — called also (*Brit*) *aubergine*; see color picture on page C4

egg roll *noun, pl* ~ **rolls** [*count*] *US* : a very thin flat piece of dough that is wrapped around a mixture of chopped vegetables and often meat and then usually fried — called also *spring roll* ✧ Egg rolls are served in Chinese restaurants.

egg·shell /ˈɛg,ʃɛl/ *noun, pl* **-shells** [*count*] : the hard outside part of an egg : the shell of an egg
walk on eggshells see [1]WALK

ego /ˈi:goʊ/ *noun, pl* **egos** [*count*]
1 : the opinion that you have about yourself • Winning was good for our *egos*. = Winning boosted our *egos*. [=winning made us proud of ourselves] • He has a big/inflated/enormous *ego*. [=he has an overly high opinion of himself] • She has a fragile *ego*. [=she lacks confidence in herself] • a bruised *ego* [=a feeling that you are not as important as you thought you were] • a healthy/strong *ego*
2 *psychology* : a part of the mind that senses and adapts to the real world — compare ID, SUPEREGO
massage your ego see [2]MASSAGE
– see also ALTER EGO

ego·cen·tric /,i:goʊˈsɛntrɪk/ *adj* [*more* ~; *most* ~] : caring too much about yourself and not about other people : SELF-CENTERED • an *egocentric* movie actor

ego·ism /ˈi:gə,wɪzəm/ *noun* [*noncount*] : EGOTISM
– **ego·ist** /ˈi:gə,wɪst/ *noun, pl* **-ists** [*count*] – **ego·is·tic** /,i:gəˈwɪstɪk/ *adj* [*more* ~; *most* ~]

ego·ma·ni·ac /,i:goʊˈmeɪni,æk/ *noun, pl* **-acs** [*count*] : someone who does not care about other people and thinks that their problems and concerns are not important : a very egotistical person • an insufferable *egomaniac*
– **ego·ma·nia** *noun* [*noncount*]

ego·tism /ˈi:gə,tɪzəm/ *noun* [*noncount*] : the feeling or belief that you are better, more important, more talented, etc., than other people : CONCEIT • In his *egotism* he thought everyone was coming just to see him.
– **ego·tist** /ˈi:gə,tɪst/ *noun, pl* **ego·tists** [*count*] • a selfish *egotist* – **ego·tis·tic** /,i:gəˈtɪstɪk/ *or* **ego·tis·ti·cal** /,i:gəˈtɪstɪkəl/ *adj* [*more* ~; *most* ~] • an *egotistical* person • She had an *egotistic* obsession with her looks. – **ego·tis·ti·cal·ly** /,i:gəˈtɪstɪkəli/ *adv*

ego trip *noun, pl* ~ **trips** [*count*] *informal* : something that someone does to feel more important or better than other people • He's on a self-indulgent *ego trip* with his latest movie, which he wrote, directed, and starred in himself.

egre·gious /ɪˈgri:ʤəs/ *adj* [*more* ~; *most* ~] *formal* : very bad and easily noticed • The article contains a number of *egregious* [=*glaring, obvious*] errors. • an *egregious* example of political bias • *egregious* misconduct
– **egre·gious·ly** *adv* – **egre·gious·ness** *noun* [*noncount*]

egress /ˈi:,grɛs/ *noun* [*noncount*] *formal* : a way to get out of a place or the act of leaving a place : EXIT • The auditorium is designed to provide easy *egress* in an emergency. — compare INGRESS

egret /ˈi:grət/ *noun, pl* **egrets** [*count*] : a large, long-legged bird that has a long neck and bill and usually white feathers

Egyp·tian /ɪˈʤɪpʃən/ *noun, pl* **-tians**
1 [*count*] : a person born or living in Egypt
2 [*noncount*] : the language spoken by ancient Egyptians
– **Egyptian** *adj* • *Egyptian* culture

eh /ˈeɪ/ *interj*
1 — used to ask someone to repeat something • "He's only three feet tall!" "*Eh*? How's that again?" [=please repeat what you said because it seems wrong]
2 — used to urge someone to agree • Let's have another drink, *eh*? ✧ This use of *eh* occurs especially in British and Canadian English.

ei·der·down /ˈaɪdɚ,daʊn/ *noun, pl* **-downs**
1 [*noncount*] : soft feathers that come from ducks and that are used in warm clothing and bed covers
2 [*count*] : a bed cover made with eiderdown

eight /ˈeɪt/ *noun, pl* **eights**
1 [*count*] : the number 8
2 [*count*] : the eighth in a set or series • the *eight* of hearts
3 [*noncount*] : eight o'clock • Dinner is at *eight*. • He's working until *eight*.
– **eight** *adj* • *eight* cars – **eight** *pronoun* • *Eight* (of them) passed the test.

eight ball *noun, pl* ~ **balls** [*count*] : a black ball that is numbered 8 in the game of pool
behind the eight ball informal : in a bad position • The loss of this contract puts the company *behind the eight ball*.

eigh·teen /,eɪtˈti:n/ *noun, pl* **-teens** [*count*] : the number 18
– **eighteen** *adj* • *eighteen* years – **eighteen** *pronoun* • *Eighteen* (of them) were present. – **eigh·teenth** /,eɪtˈti:nθ/ *noun, pl* **-teenths** [*count*] • one *eighteenth* of the total – **eighteenth** *adj* • the *eighteenth* day – **eighteenth** *adv* • He finished *eighteenth* in the race.

eight·fold /ˈeɪt,foʊld/ *adj* : eight times as great or as many • There has been an *eightfold* increase in membership in the past year.
– **eight·fold** /ˈeɪtˈfoʊld/ *adv* • Membership has increased *eightfold*.

[1]**eighth** /ˈeɪtθ/ *noun, pl* **eighths**
1 [*singular*] : number eight in a series • My appointment is on the *eighth* (of the month).
2 [*count*] : one of eight equal parts of something • one *eighth* of the pie • An *eighth* of a pound is two ounces.

[2]**eighth** *adj* : occupying the number eight position in a series • the *eighth* car in line • the *eighth* edition • Her son is in (the) *eighth* grade.
– **eighth** *adv* • She finished *eighth* (in the race).

eighth note *noun, pl* ~ **notes** [*count*] *music* : a musical note that lasts to ⅛ of the length of a whole note — called also (*Brit*) *quaver*

800 number /,eɪtˈhʌndrəd-/ *noun, pl* ~ **-bers** [*count*] *US* : a telephone number that people can use to call a distant place (such as a business) for free ✧ In the U.S. 800 numbers usually have 800 as an area code. • Call our *800 number* to place an order or ask questions.

eighty /ˈeɪti/ *noun, pl* **eight·ies**
1 [*count*] : the number 80
2 ***eighties*** [*plural*] **a** : the numbers ranging from 80 to 89 • The temperature rose to the high *eighties*. **b** : a set of years ending in digits ranging from 80 to 89 • She is in her mid-*eighties*. • a television show from the (nineteen) *eighties* [=from 1980–1989]
– **eight·i·eth** /ˈeɪtijəθ/ *noun, pl* **-eths** [*count*] • one *eightieth* of the total – **eightieth** *adj* • the *eightieth* day – **eighty** *adj* • *eighty* days – **eighty** *pronoun* • *Eighty* (of them) were rejected.

[1]**ei·ther** /ˈi:ðɚ, *Brit* ˈaɪðə/ *adj*
1 : one and the other of two • Flowers bloomed on *either* side [=on both sides] of the walk. • *Either* [=*each*] answer is correct. [=both answers are correct] • I don't like *either* book. [=I like neither book] • French and English are closer to each other than *either* language is to Chinese. • I haven't written to *either* parent. [=I haven't written to the mother or the father]
2 : one or the other of two • You may take *either* road. • You may choose *either* answer. • *Either* way/option is all right with me. • It's all right with me ***either way***. = I don't mind *either way*. = *Either way*, I don't mind. [=both possibilities are okay to me]

[2]**either** *pronoun* : the one or the other • *Either* (of the two answers) is correct. [=both answers are correct] • I don't think that *either* of the two answers is correct. = Of the two answers, I don't think that *either* is correct. • I don't like *either* of the answers. [=I like neither of the answers] • I haven't written to *either* of my parents. • French and English are closer to each other than *either* (of the two languages) is to Chinese.

> ***usage*** According to the rules of grammar, the pronoun *either* is singular and requires a singular verb. • *Either* is correct. However, in informal writing and speech, a plural verb is common when *either* is followed by *of*. • *Either of* the answers is/are correct. • This was not something that *either of* them was/were happy about.

[3]**either** *conj* — used with *or* to indicate choices or possibilities • You can *either* go *or* stay. • I can't remember her name. It's *either* Marie *or* Mary. • He will give the money *either* to his son *or* his daughter. = He will give the money to *either* his son *or* his daughter. • A statement is *either* true *or* false. [=no statement is both true and false] • They can *either* be black, brown, *or* blue. = They can be *either* black, brown, *or* blue. ✧ When *either* and *or* are used to join two subjects in a sentence, the verb should agree with the subject that is closer to it. • *Either* the professor *or* the students are wrong. • *Either* you *or* I am wrong.

[4]either *adv* : in addition — used after a negative statement • The cars are reliable and are not expensive *either*. • He is not wise or handsome *either*. [=he is neither wise nor handsome] ✧ The phrase ***me either*** is used in informal U.S. speech to say that you agree with a negative statement that someone has made. • "I didn't like the movie." "*Me either*." [=I also didn't like the movie] The phrase ***me neither*** is used in the same way. • "I don't like that guy." "*Me neither*."

ejac•u•late /ɪˈʤækjəˌleɪt/ *verb* **-lates; -lat•ed; -lat•ing**
1 *medical* : to release semen from the penis [+ *obj*] *ejaculate* semen [*no obj*] He was unable to *ejaculate*.
2 [+ *obj*] *old-fashioned* : to say (something) suddenly and forcefully • "Good God!" he *ejaculated*.
– **ejac•u•la•to•ry** /ɪˈʤækjələˌtori/ *adj, medical* • *ejaculatory* ducts

ejac•u•la•tion /ɪˌʤækjəˈleɪʃən/ *noun, pl* **-tions**
1 [*count, noncount*] *medical* : the release of semen from the penis • premature *ejaculation*
2 [*count*] *old-fashioned* : a short and sudden expression of emotion • He was greeted with *ejaculations* of surprise.

eject /ɪˈʤɛkt/ *verb* **ejects; eject•ed; eject•ing**
1 [+ *obj*] : to force (someone) to leave — often + *from* • They *ejected* him *from* the game for hitting another player. • She was *ejected from* the restaurant. ✧ When someone is *ejected from* a place, it often means that physical force was used to make that person leave. • Several drunks had to be physically *ejected from* the bar.
2 [+ *obj*] : to push (something) out • The machine automatically *ejected* the CD.
3 [*no obj*] : to use a special device that throws you out and away from an airplane in an emergency : to use an ejection seat • The pilot *ejected* when his plane caught fire.
– **ejec•tion** /ɪˈʤɛkʃən/ *noun, pl* **-tions** [*count*] protesting their *ejections* from the game • the foul meant an automatic *ejection* [*noncount*] automatic *ejection* of the CD

ejection seat (*US*) *or* **ejec•tor seat** /ɪˈʤɛktɚ-/ *noun, pl* ~ **seats** [*count*] : a special seat in an airplane that is used to throw you out and away from the plane when the plane is going to crash

eke /ˈiːk/ *verb* **ekes; eked; ek•ing**
eke out [*phrasal verb*] ***eke out (something)*** *also* ***eke (something) out*** **1** : to get or achieve (a living, a victory, etc.) with great difficulty • They *eked out* a living from the poor soil of the family's farm. [=they could grow only enough food to survive] • It looks like he has narrowly *eked out* a win in the election. • The company *eked out* a tiny profit last year. **2** : to increase (something) by a small amount • He *eked out* [=(more commonly) *supplemented*] his small income by working for neighbors. **3** : to make (a limited amount of something) last by using it carefully in small amounts • *eke out* food supplies

EKG /ˌiːˌkeɪˈʤiː/ *noun, pl* **EKGs** [*count*] *medical*
1 : a printed recording of the heart's electrical activity made by a special machine — called also *ECG, electrocardiogram*
2 : a machine that detects and records the electrical activity of the heart — called also *ECG, electrocardiograph*

[1]elab•o•rate /ɪˈlæbərət/ *adj* [*more* ~; *most* ~] : made or done with great care or with much detail : having many parts that are carefully arranged or planned • They made *elaborate* preparations for his visit. • I see now that her behavior was all part of an *elaborate* plan/plot/scheme. • The dancers were wearing *elaborate* costumes. • He told the story in *elaborate* detail. • an *elaborate* meal
– **elab•o•rate•ly** *adv* • The room was *elaborately* decorated.
– **elab•o•rate•ness** *noun* [*noncount*]

[2]elab•o•rate /ɪˈlæbəˌreɪt/ *verb* **-rates; -rat•ed; -rat•ing**
1 [*no obj*] : to give more details about something : to discuss something more fully • I'll be glad to *elaborate* if you want to hear more. • She was asked to say more about her earlier statements, but she declined/refused to *elaborate*.— often + *on* • She refused to *elaborate on* her earlier statements.
2 [+ *obj*] : to bring (something, such as an idea or a plan) to a more advanced or developed state • The philosopher spent years *elaborating* [=*developing*] his ideas.
– **elab•o•ra•tion** /ɪˌlæbəˈreɪʃən/ *noun, pl* **-tions** [*noncount*] The design requires further *elaboration*. [*count*] his *elaborations* of the basic design

élan /eɪˈlɑːn/ *noun* [*noncount*] *literary* : energy and enthusiasm • The dancer performed with great *élan*.

elapse /ɪˈlæps/ *verb* **elaps•es; elapsed; elaps•ing** [*no obj*] *of time* : to pass by • Weeks *elapsed* [=*passed*] before he returned home.

[1]elas•tic /ɪˈlæstɪk/ *adj* [*more* ~; *most* ~]
1 : able to return to an original shape or size after being stretched, squeezed, etc. • *elastic* fibers • an *elastic* bandage • pants with an *elastic* [=*stretchable*] waist
2 : able to be changed • an *elastic* [=*flexible*] plan • an *elastic* concept
– **elas•tic•i•ty** /ɪˌlæsˈtɪsəti/ *noun* [*noncount*] • the *elasticity* of the fibers

[2]elastic *noun, pl* **-tics**
1 [*noncount*] : material that can be stretched : elastic fabric • the *elastic* in socks
2 [*count*] *US* : RUBBER BAND • She wrapped an *elastic* around the cards.

elas•ti•cat•ed /ɪˈlæstəˌkeɪtəd/ *adj, Brit* : ELASTICIZED

elastic band *noun, pl* ~ **bands** [*count*] *Brit* : RUBBER BAND

elas•ti•cized /ɪˈlæstəˌsaɪzd/ *adj, US* : containing something that returns to an original shape or size after being stretched : made with an elastic material inside • an *elasticized* waistband

elate /ɪˈleɪt/ *verb* **elates; elat•ed; elat•ing** [+ *obj*] : to make (someone) very happy and excited • The discovery has *elated* researchers.
– **ela•tion** /ɪˈleɪʃən/ *noun* [*noncount*] • her feelings of *elation* at being chosen for the job

elat•ed /ɪˈleɪtəd/ *adj* [*more* ~; *most* ~] : very happy and excited • She was *elated* at/about/over the news. • She was *elated* to be chosen for the job. = She was *elated* that she was chosen for the job.

[1]el•bow /ˈɛlˌboʊ/ *noun, pl* **-bows** [*count*]
1 a : the joint where your arm bends — see picture at HUMAN **b** : the part of a piece of clothing that covers the elbow • He wore a tattered coat with holes in the *elbows*.
2 : something (such as a pipe or a piece of food) that is bent like an elbow • *elbow* macaroni— see picture at PLUMBING
at someone's elbow : next to someone : at someone's side • His assistant is always *at his elbow*. • The drink *at her elbow* was untouched.
give (someone) the elbow *Brit, informal* : to end a relationship with someone : to tell someone to go away • She *gave her boyfriend the elbow* after he lied to her.
rub elbows see [1]RUB

[2]elbow *verb* **elbows; el•bowed; el•bow•ing** : to push or shove (someone) with your elbow [+ *obj*] The actor's bodyguards rudely *elbowed* everyone out of the way. • I quietly *elbowed* [=*nudged*] my friend to get his attention. — sometimes used figuratively • Some of the older workers are being *elbowed* [=*pushed*] aside as the company tries to attract young employees. [*no obj*] Everyone was shoving and *elbowing* to get a good position. ✧ If you ***elbow your way*** through a crowd, you move ahead by pushing and forcing people to move out of the way. • He *elbowed his way* through the crowd to get closer to the stage.

elbow grease *noun* [*noncount*] *informal* : physical effort : hard work • It's going to take some *elbow grease* to get this counter clean. ✧ *Elbow grease* usually refers to the effort needed to clean or polish something.

elbow room *noun* [*noncount*] : room or space to move or work freely • It's a small kitchen with very little *elbow room*. — often used figuratively • The company provides its workers with *elbow room* to try new ideas.

[1]elder /ˈɛldɚ/ *adj, always used before a noun* : of greater age : OLDER ✧ *Elder* is usually used to describe people who are members of the same family. • my *elder* brother/sister [=my brother/sister who is older than I am] • my *elder* son/daughter [=the older one of my two sons/daughters]
the elder **1** — used in comparing the ages of two people who are members of the same family • He's *the elder* of her two brothers. **2** — used to refer to the older of two people (such as a father and son) who have the same name • Pliny *the Elder* and his nephew Pliny the Younger

[2]elder *noun, pl* **el•ders**
1 [*count*] : a person who is older — usually plural • He was told to respect his *elders*. [=people who were older than he was] • She learned from her *elders*. • (*formal*) He was my *elder* by 11 months. [=he was 11 months older than I was] • (*chiefly Brit*) You should respect ***your elders and betters***. [=people who are older and more important than you]
2 [*count*] : a person who has authority because of age and experience • a village *elder* • Traditions passed down by *elders* in the tribe.

3 ***elders*** [*plural*] : old people ▪ day care for *elders* [=*the elderly*]
4 [*count*] : an official in some Christian churches
— compare ³ELDER

³**elder** *noun, pl* **elders** [*count*] : ELDERBERRY 2 — compare ²ELDER

el·der·ber·ry /ˈɛldəˌberi/ *noun, pl* **-ries** [*count*]
1 : a black or red berry that comes from a type of bush or tree with bunches of white or pink flowers
2 : a tree or bush that produces elderberries

elder care *noun* [*noncount*] *US* : the care of old people ▪ an *elder care* facility [=a place that provides care for elderly people] : the care of elderly parents by their children ▪ resources for childcare and *elder care*

el·der·ly /ˈɛldəli/ *adj* [*more* ~; *most* ~] : old or rather old : past middle age ▪ The program is intended to provide medical care for *elderly* people. ▪ an *elderly* couple
the elderly : elderly people ▪ providing care for *the elderly*

elder statesman *noun, pl* ~ **-men** [*count*]
1 : a retired government leader who gives advice to current leaders
2 : a respected man who has been a member of a group or organization for a long time ▪ an *elder statesman* of baseball coaches

el·dest /ˈɛldəst/ *adj, always used before a noun* : of the greatest age : OLDEST ✧ *Eldest* is usually used to describe people who are members of the same family. ▪ my *eldest* brother/sister/son/daughter/child
the eldest — used in comparing the ages of people who are members of the same family ▪ He's *the eldest* of her three brothers.

¹**elect** /ɪˈlɛkt/ *verb* **elects; elect·ed; elect·ing** [+ *obj*]
1 : to select (someone) for a position, job, etc., by voting ▪ She was *elected* (as) senator. = She was *elected* to the Senate. ▪ He hopes to be *elected* to the committee. ▪ an *elected* official
2 *somewhat formal* : to choose to do (something) — followed by *to* + *verb* ▪ We *elected* [=*decided*] *to stay* home.

²**elect** *noun* [*plural*] : people who belong to a special group and have privileges that other people do not have ▪ His new status earned him a place among the city's *elect*. [=(more commonly) *elite*]

³**elect** *adj, always used after a noun* : having been elected : chosen for a public office but not yet holding that office ▪ the governor *elect* — often hyphenated ▪ the president-*elect*

elec·tion /ɪˈlɛkʃən/ *noun, pl* **-tions** [*count*]
1 : the act or process of choosing someone for a public office by voting ▪ a presidential/gubernatorial *election* ▪ He's favored to win the *election*. — often used before another noun ▪ The *election* results are in. ▪ (*US*) Today is ***election day***. [=(*Brit*) *polling day*] — see also GENERAL ELECTION
2 : the fact of being elected ▪ The scandal may affect his chances for *election*. ▪ Her *election* to the Senate was a surprise to many.

elec·tion·eer·ing /ɪˌlɛkʃəˈnirɪŋ/ *noun* [*noncount*] : the things that are done and said to help a political candidate or party to win an election ▪ Her tireless *electioneering* won her the election.

¹**elec·tive** /ɪˈlɛktɪv/ *adj*
1 : held by a person who is elected ▪ He's never held an *elective* office.
2 : done or taken by choice: such as **a** : not medically necessary ▪ Plastic surgery is *elective* surgery. **b** *chiefly US* : not required in a particular course of study ▪ She took three *elective* courses last term.

²**elective** *noun, pl* **-tives** [*count*] *US* : a class that is not required in a particular course of study ▪ She's taking several *electives* this year. — called also (*Brit*) *option*

elec·tor /ɪˈlɛktər/ *noun, pl* **-tors** [*count*]
1 : a member of the Electoral College in the U.S.
2 *formal* : someone who can vote in an election : VOTER

elec·tor·al /ɪˈlɛktərəl, ˌiːlɛkˈtorəl/ *adj, always used before a noun* : of or relating to an election or to the process by which people are elected ▪ *electoral* politics ▪ an *electoral* district ▪ an *electoral* system

Electoral College *noun*
the Electoral College : a group of people chosen from each U.S. state who meet to elect the President and Vice President of the U.S. based on the votes of all the people in each state

elec·tor·ate /ɪˈlɛktərət/ *noun, pl* **-ates** [*count*] : the people who can vote in an election — usually singular ▪ The candidates try hard to appeal to the *electorate*. [=*voters*]

electr- *or* **electro-** *combining form*
1 : electricity ▪ *electro*magnet
2 : electric ▪ *electro*de : electric and ▪ *electro*chemical

elec·tric /ɪˈlɛktrɪk/ *adj*
1 *or* ***elec·tri·cal*** /ɪˈlɛktrɪkəl/ **a** : of or relating to electricity ▪ an *electric/electrical* current ▪ The device administers a mild *electric* shock. **b** : operated by electricity ▪ an *electric* motor/heater/blanket/razor/appliance ▪ The pasture was surrounded by an ***electric fence*** [=a fence that has an electrical current passing through it] **c** : providing electricity ▪ It plugs into any *electric* socket. ▪ The *electrical* cord is damaged. ▪ There's a problem with the building's *electrical* wiring. — compare ELECTRONIC
2 : producing sound by using electricity ▪ an *electric* piano ▪ *electric* guitars
3 [*more* ~; *most* ~] : very exciting or thrilling ▪ The pianist gave an *electric* performance. ; *also* : filled with tension or excitement ▪ The atmosphere in the room was *electric*.
— **elec·tri·cal·ly** /ɪˈlɛktrɪkli/ *adv* ▪ an *electrically* operated switch

electrical engineering *noun* [*noncount*] : a type of engineering that deals with the uses of electricity
— **electrical engineer** *noun, pl* ~ **-neers** [*count*]

electrical storm *noun, pl* ~ **storms** [*count*] : a storm that has a lot of lightning — called also *electric storm*

electric chair *noun* [*singular*] : a special chair in which a criminal who has been sentenced to death is killed by using a strong electric current

electric eel *noun, pl* ~ **eels** [*count*] : a long, thin South American fish that is able to give a severe electric shock

elec·tri·cian /ɪˌlɛkˈtrɪʃən/ *noun, pl* **-cians** [*count*] : a person who works on and repairs electrical equipment

elec·tric·i·ty /ɪˌlɛkˈtrɪsəti/ *noun* [*noncount*]
1 : a form of energy that is carried through wires and is used to operate machines, lights, etc. ▪ *Electricity* can be dangerous. — see also STATIC ELECTRICITY
2 : electric current or power ▪ The *electricity* went off during the storm. ▪ an old building with no plumbing or *electricity*
3 : a feeling of excitement or tension ▪ You could feel the *electricity* in the room.

elec·trics /ɪˈlɛktrɪks/ *noun* [*plural*] *Brit* : the electrical parts of something (such as a machine or a house)

electric storm *noun, pl* ~ **storms** [*count*] : ELECTRICAL STORM

elec·tri·fy /ɪˈlɛktrəˌfaɪ/ *verb* **-fies; -fied; -fy·ing** [+ *obj*]
1 **a** : to pass electricity through (something) ▪ an ***electrified fence*** [=a fence that has electricity running through it] **b** : to supply (an area, building, etc.) with electric power ▪ Many of the rural areas still aren't *electrified*.
2 : to cause (someone) to feel great excitement ▪ The news *electrified* the nation.
— **elec·tri·fi·ca·tion** /ɪˌlɛktrəfəˈkeɪʃən/ *noun* [*noncount*] ▪ rural *electrification* programs [=programs for supplying electricity to rural areas] — **electrifying** *adj* [*more* ~; *most* ~] ▪ His performance was *electrifying*. [=very exciting] ▪ *electrifying* news

electro- see ELECTR-

elec·tro·car·dio·gram /ɪˌlɛktroʊˈkɑədijəˌgræm/ *noun, pl* **-grams** [*count*] *medical* : EKG

elec·tro·car·dio·graph /ɪˌlɛktroʊˈkɑədijəˌgræf, *Brit* ɪˌlɛktrəʊˈkɑːdiəˌgrɑːf/ *noun, pl* **-graphs** [*count*] *medical* : EKG

elec·tro·con·vul·sive therapy /ɪˌlɛktroʊkənˈvʌlsɪv-/ *noun* [*noncount*] *medical* : SHOCK THERAPY

elec·tro·cute /ɪˈlɛktrəˌkjuːt/ *verb* **-cutes; -cut·ed; -cut·ing** [+ *obj*] : to kill (a person or animal) by electric shock — usually used as (*be/get*) *electrocuted* ▪ He stepped on the power line and *was* nearly *electrocuted*.
— **elec·tro·cu·tion** /ɪˌlɛktrəˈkjuːʃən/ *noun, pl* **-tions** [*noncount*] There is a risk of *electrocution*. [*count*] There have been two *electrocutions* this year.

elec·trode /ɪˈlɛkˌtroud/ *noun, pl* **-trodes** [*count*] : one of the two points through which electricity flows into or out of a battery or other device

elec·tro·en·ceph·a·lo·gram /ɪˌlɛktrowɪnˈsɛfələˌgræm/ *noun, pl* **-grams** [*count*] *medical* : EEG

elec·tro·en·ceph·a·lo·graph /ɪˌlɛktrowɪnˈsɛfələˌgræf, *Brit* ɪˌlɛktrəwɪnˈsɛfələˌgrɑːf/ *noun, pl* **-graphs** [*count*] *medical* : EEG

elec·trol·y·sis /ɪˌlɛkˈtrɑːləsəs/ *noun* [*noncount*]

1 : the process of removing unwanted hair by killing the hair root with an electric current ▪ She had *electrolysis* done on her upper lip.
2 *chemistry* **:** the process of separating a liquid into its different chemical parts by passing an electric current through it

elec·tro·lyte /ɪˈlɛktrəˌlaɪt/ *noun, pl* **-lytes** [*count*]
1 *chemistry* **:** a liquid (such as the liquid in a battery) through which electricity can pass
2 *technical* **:** any one of various substances in the fluid of your body that control how your body processes waste and absorbs vitamins, minerals, etc. ▪ The drink will replenish your *electrolytes*.
– elec·tro·lyt·ic /ɪˌlɛktrəˈlɪtɪk/ *adj, technical* ▪ *electrolytic* processes

elec·tro·mag·net /ɪˌlɛktroʊˈmægnət/ *noun, pl* **-nets** [*count*] **:** a piece of metal that becomes magnetic when an electric current is passed through or near it

elec·tro·mag·ne·tism /ɪˌlɛktroʊˈmægnəˌtɪzəm/ *noun* [*noncount*] *technical* **:** a magnetic field that is produced by a current of electricity
– elec·tro·mag·net·ic /ɪˌlɛktroʊmægˈnɛtɪk/ *adj* ▪ the *electromagnetic* spectrum ▪ *electromagnetic* waves

elec·tron /ɪˈlɛkˌtrɑːn/ *noun, pl* **-trons** [*count*] *physics* **:** a very small particle of matter that has a negative charge of electricity and that travels around the nucleus of an atom

elec·tron·ic /ɪˌlɛkˈtrɑːnɪk/ *adj*
1 : operating through the use of many small electrical parts (such as microchips and transistors) ▪ *electronic* devices such as televisions and computers ▪ an *electronic* circuit — compare ELECTRIC
2 : produced by the use of electronic equipment ▪ *electronic* music
3 a : operating by means of a computer **:** involving a computer or a computer system ▪ an *electronic* dictionary ▪ We did an ***electronic funds transfer***. [=moved money from one bank to another using their computer systems] **b :** done over the Internet ▪ Sign up for *electronic* banking. ▪ *electronic* messaging services
– elec·tron·i·cal·ly /ɪˌlɛkˈtrɑːnɪkli/ *adv* ▪ We transferred the money *electronically* from one bank to another.

elec·tron·i·ca /ɪˌlɛkˈtrɑːnɪkə/ *noun* [*noncount*] **:** a kind of popular dance music that is produced using electronic equipment (such as synthesizers)

electronic mail *noun* [*noncount*] **:** E-MAIL ▪ They communicate frequently by *electronic mail*.

elec·tron·ics /ɪˌlɛkˈtrɑːnɪks/ *noun*
1 [*plural*] **a** *US* **:** devices (such as televisions, radios, and computers) that operate using many small electrical parts ▪ Sales of consumer *electronics* are up. **b :** electronic parts ▪ There are problems with the system's *electronics*.
2 [*noncount*] *technical* **:** a science that deals with the uses and effects of electrons

electron microscope *noun, pl* **~ -scopes** [*count*] *technical* **:** a very powerful microscope that uses a beam of electrons to produce a large image of a very small object

elec·tro·plate /ɪˈlɛktrəˌpleɪt/ *verb* **-plates; -plat·ed; -plat·ing** [+ *obj*] **:** to coat (something) with a thin layer of metal (such as silver) by using electrolysis (sense 2) — usually used as *(be) electroplated* ▪ The platter has an *electroplated* finish.

el·e·gant /ˈɛlɪgənt/ *adj* [*more ~; most ~*]
1 : showing good taste **:** graceful and attractive ▪ *elegant* clothes ▪ *elegant* prose ▪ an *elegant* dinner
2 : simple and clever ▪ an *elegant* solution to the problem
– el·e·gance /ˈɛlɪgəns/ *noun* [*noncount*] ▪ She's known for her *elegance*. ▪ the *elegance* of the solution **– el·e·gant·ly** *adv* ▪ *elegantly* dressed ▪ an *elegantly* simple solution

el·e·gy /ˈɛləʤi/ *noun, pl* **-gies** [*count*] *literary* **:** a sad poem or song **:** a poem or song that expresses sorrow for someone who is dead — compare EULOGY
– el·e·gi·ac /ˌɛləˈʤajək/ *adj* [*more ~; most ~*] ▪ *elegiac* poetry ▪ The passage has an *elegiac* tone.

el·e·ment /ˈɛləmənt/ *noun, pl* **-ments**
1 [*count*] *chemistry* **:** one of the basic substances that are made of atoms of only one kind and that cannot be separated by ordinary chemical means into simpler substances ▪ chemical *elements* ▪ Water is composed of the *elements* hydrogen and oxygen.
2 [*count*] **:** a particular part of something (such as a situation or activity) ▪ Self-confidence was a key/vital *element* [=*factor*] in her success. ▪ There's always an *element* of risk [=there's always some risk] in starting a new business. ▪ There's a large *element* of truth [=there's a great deal of truth] in what she says. ▪ The attackers were relying on the ***element of surprise***. [=they were relying on their attack being a surprise]
3 [*count*] **:** a part of an electrical device that produces heat ▪ the (heating) *element* of an electric iron
4 elements [*plural*] **:** the most basic parts of a subject of study ▪ the *elements* [=*rudiments*] of grammar
5 [*count*] **:** a group of people that form part of a larger group ▪ the different *elements* of society ▪ the criminal *element*
6 elements [*plural*] **:** the weather and especially stormy or cold weather ▪ The deck's bare wood was exposed to the *elements*. ▪ The climbers battled/braved the *elements* to reach the summit.
7 [*singular*] **:** the state or place that is normal or suited to a person or thing ▪ At school she was (really) ***in her element***. [=in a place where she was comortable and did well] ▪ I tried living in the city, but I was/felt ***out of my element*** there. [=living in the city did not suit me]
8 [*count*] **:** one of the four substances (air, water, fire, and earth) that were believed in the past to make up every physical thing in the universe

el·e·men·tal /ˌɛləˈmɛntl/ *adj*
1 [*more ~; most ~*] *somewhat formal* **:** basic and important **:** FUNDAMENTAL ▪ *elemental* human needs ▪ an *elemental* difference between the two — compare ELEMENTARY
2 [*more ~; most ~*] *literary* **:** having the power of a force of nature ▪ Their *elemental* passion led to tragedy. ▪ the *elemental* power/violence/fury of the storm
3 *technical* **:** of or relating to a chemical element ▪ *elemental* components ▪ an *elemental* analysis of the solution
– el·e·men·tal·ly *adv* ▪ an *elementally* [=*fundamentally*] simple notion

el·e·men·ta·ry /ˌɛləˈmɛntri/ *adj*
1 [*more ~; most ~*] **:** basic and simple ▪ an *elementary* principle ▪ He is lacking even the most *elementary* notions of fairness. ▪ The researchers made an *elementary* error.**:** involving the simplest parts of a subject ▪ He has an *elementary* understanding of calculus. ▪ *elementary* arithmetic — compare ELEMENTAL
2 *always used before a noun, chiefly US* **:** of or relating to elementary school ▪ *elementary* [=*grade-school*] students ▪ *elementary* education

elementary particle *noun, pl* **~ -cles** [*count*] *physics* **:** a particle (such as an electron or proton) that is smaller than an atom and does not appear to be made up of a combination of more basic things

elementary school *noun, pl* **~ schools** [*count, noncount*] **:** a school in the U.S. for young children ✧ Children in the U.S. attend elementary school for their first four to eight years of schooling. — called also *grade school, grammar school, primary school*

el·e·phant /ˈɛləfənt/ *noun, pl* **-phants** [*count*] **:** a very large gray animal that has a long, flexible nose and two long tusks — see also WHITE ELEPHANT

elephant

el·e·phan·tine /ˌɛləˈfænˌtiːn, *Brit* ɛləˈfænˌtaɪn/ *adj* [*more ~; most ~*]
1 : very large like an elephant ▪ a problem of *elephantine* [=*massive*] proportions ▪ He has an *elephantine* ego.
2 : not graceful **:** awkward or clumsy ▪ *elephantine* movements

el·e·vate /ˈɛləˌveɪt/ *verb* **-vates; -vat·ed; -vat·ing** [+ *obj*]
1 : to lift (something) up ▪ The doctor told her to *elevate* [=*raise*] her leg.
2 : to increase the level of (something) **:** to make (something) higher ▪ exercises that *elevate* the heart rate
3 : to raise (someone) to a higher rank or level ▪ He was *elevated* to (the position of) chairman. = He was *elevated* to the chairmanship.
4 *somewhat formal* **:** to improve the mind or mood of (someone) ▪ A great book can both *elevate* and entertain its readers. ▪ A great book can *elevate* the human spirit. ▪ It was an *elevating* [=*uplifting*] experience.
elevate something to an art (form) see ART

el·e·vat·ed /ˈɛləˌveɪtəd/ *adj* [*more ~; most ~*]

1 : raised above the ground • an *elevated* highway
2 : higher than normal • *elevated* blood pressure
3 : having an intelligent and usually formal tone or quality • an *elevated* mind • *elevated* discourse • Her poetry is known for its *elevated* style/tone.

el·e·va·tion /ˌɛləˈveɪʃən/ *noun, pl* **-tions** [*count*]
1 : the height of a place • a plant species found only at higher/lower *elevations* • an *elevation* [=*altitude*] of 4,000 feet (above sea level)
2 : an act or result of lifting or raising someone or something • We charted the *elevations* in her temperature. • His *elevation* to (the position of) chairman was a surprise to many.
3 : a place (such as a hill) that is higher than the area around it

el·e·va·tor /ˈɛləˌveɪtɚ/ *noun, pl* **-tors** [*count*] *US*
1 : a machine used for carrying people and things to different levels in a building • We took/rode the *elevator* to the 10th floor. — called also (*Brit*) *lift*
2 : a tall building for storing grain — called also *grain elevator*

elevator music *noun* [*noncount*] *US* **:** instrumental versions of popular songs that are often played in elevators, offices, etc.

elev·en /ɪˈlɛvən/ *noun, pl* **-ens**
1 [*count*] **:** the number 11
2 [*count*] **:** the eleventh in a set or series • page *eleven* • item/question number *eleven*
3 [*noncount*] **:** eleven o'clock • I got home last night at *eleven*.
– eleven *adj* • *eleven* turtles **– eleven** *pronoun* • *Eleven* (of them) were absent from the ceremony. **– elev·enth** /ɪˈlɛvənθ/ *noun, pl* **-enths** [*count*] • one *eleventh* of the total **– eleventh** *adj* • the *eleventh* person in line **– eleventh** *adv* • He finished *eleventh* in the race.

eleventh hour *noun* [*singular*] **:** the latest possible time — usually used in the phrase ***at the eleventh hour*** • The killer's life was spared *at the eleventh hour*. [=at the last minute]

elf /ˈɛlf/ *noun, pl* **elves** /ˈɛlvz/ [*count*] **:** a small creature in stories usually with pointed ears and magical powers • a mischievous *elf*
– elf·ish /ˈɛlfɪʃ/ *adj* [*more* ~; *most* ~] • an *elfish* face

elf·in /ˈɛlfən/ *adj* [*more* ~; *most* ~] **:** having to do with elves **:** looking like an elf • They were delighted with the child's *elfin* charm. • a cute, *elfin* face

elic·it /ɪˈlɪsət/ *verb* **elic·its; elicit·ed; elicit·ing** [+ *obj*] *formal* **:** to get (a response, information, etc.) from someone • She's been trying to *elicit* the support of other committee members. • My question *elicited* no response. • She's been unable to *elicit* much sympathy from the public.

el·i·gi·ble /ˈɛləʤəbəl/ *adj*
1 : able to be chosen for something **:** able to do or receive something • I'd like to join but I'm not *eligible* yet. • *eligible* voters — often followed by *to* + *verb* • She is *eligible to be* (elected) president. • He won't be *eligible to retire* until next year. — often + *for* • He's *eligible for* health insurance through his employer. • *eligible for* a loan
2 [*more* ~; *most* ~] **:** suitable and desirable for marriage • He's an ***eligible bachelor*** [=an unmarried man who would make a good husband]
– el·i·gi·bil·i·ty /ˌɛləʤəˈbɪləti/ *noun* [*noncount*] • *eligibility* for a loan

elim·i·nate /ɪˈlɪməˌneɪt/ *verb* **-nates; -nat·ed; -nat·ing** [+ *obj*]
1 : to remove (something that is not wanted or needed) **:** to get rid of (something) • Doctors seek to *eliminate* the causes of the epidemic. • The body naturally *eliminates* waste products. • The company plans to *eliminate* more than 2,000 jobs in the coming year. • The regime has ruthlessly *eliminated* [=*killed*] the leaders of the opposition. • She's trying to *eliminate* fatty foods from her diet.
2 : to defeat and remove (a team, player, etc.) from a competition — often used as *(be/get) eliminated* • The team *was eliminated* in the first round of the play-offs.

elim·i·na·tion /ɪˌlɪməˈneɪʃən/ *noun* [*noncount*] **:** the act or process of removing something or someone • the *elimination* of waste products from the body • They arrived at their decision by a ***process of elimination*** [=by considering and rejecting each possible choice until only one was left]

elite /ɪˈliːt/ *noun, pl* **elites** [*count*]
1 : the people who have the most wealth and status in a society **:** the most successful or powerful group of people — usually singular • a store that caters to the (social) *elite* • the intellectual/political/academic *elite* ✧ *Elite* can be used with either a singular or, more commonly, a plural verb. • The country's *elite* is/are opposed to the new ruler.
2 *US* **:** a person who is a member of an elite **:** a successful and powerful person — usually plural • Many business *elites* oppose the new policy.
– elite *adj, always used before a noun* [*more* ~; *most* ~] • *elite* members of the division • an *elite* corps/club/university

elit·ist /ɪˈliːtɪst/ *adj* [*more* ~; *most* ~] *disapproving*
1 : giving special treatment and advantages to wealthy and powerful people • *elitist* colleges • The country club is very *elitist*.
2 : regarding other people as inferior because they lack power, wealth, etc. • She's an *elitist* snob.
– elit·ism /ɪˈliːˌtɪzəm/ *noun* [*noncount*] • the *elitism* of top colleges **– elitist** *noun, pl* **-ists** [*count*] • a country club full of *elitists*

elix·ir /ɪˈlɪksɚ/ *noun, pl* **-irs** [*count*] **:** a magical liquid that can cure illness or extend life • the *elixir* of life

Eliz·a·be·than /ɪˌlɪzəˈbiːθən/ *adj* **:** relating to Queen Elizabeth I of England or the time when she ruled (1558 to 1603) • *Elizabethan* poetry
– Elizabethan *noun, pl* **-thans** [*count*] • Shakespeare and other great *Elizabethans*

elk /ˈɛlk/ *noun, pl* **elk** *or* **elks** [*count*]
1 *US* **:** a large kind of North American deer with big antlers — see picture at DEER; compare RED DEER
2 *Brit* **:** a European or Asian moose

el·lipse /ɪˈlɪps/ *noun, pl* **-lips·es** [*count*] **:** a shape that resembles a flattened circle **:** OVAL

el·lip·sis /ɪˈlɪpsəs/ *noun, pl* **-lip·ses** /ɪˈlɪpˌsiːz/
1 [*noncount*] **:** the act of leaving out one or more words that are not necessary for a phrase to be understood • "Begin when ready" for "Begin when you are ready" is an example of *ellipsis*.
2 [*count*] **:** a sign (such as . . .) used in printed text to show that words have been left out

el·lip·ti·cal /ɪˈlɪptɪkəl/ *or* **el·lip·tic** /ɪˈlɪptɪk/ *adj* [*more* ~; *most* ~]
1 : shaped like a flattened circle **:** OVAL • The moon follows an *elliptical* path around the Earth.
2 : using few words and therefore hard to understand • a writer with an *elliptical* style
– el·lip·ti·cal·ly /ɪˈlɪptɪkli/ *adv*

elm /ˈɛlm/ *noun, pl* **elms**
1 [*count, noncount*] **:** a tall shade tree with spreading branches
2 [*noncount*] **:** the wood of an elm

El Ni·ño /ɛlˈniːnyoʊ/ *noun, pl* **~ Ni·ños** [*count*] **:** a flow of unusually warm water along the western coast of South America that causes many changes in weather in other places (such as a lot of rain in areas that are usually dry)

el·o·cu·tion /ˌɛləˈkjuːʃən/ *noun* [*noncount*] *formal* **:** the study of how to speak clearly and in a way that is effective and socially acceptable • He took lessons in *elocution*.
– el·o·cu·tion·ary /ˌɛləˈkjuːʃəˌneri/ *adj* • her *elocutionary* skill **– el·o·cu·tion·ist** /ˌɛləˈkjuːʃənɪst/ *noun, pl* **-ists** [*count*] • He took lessons from an *elocutionist*.

elon·gate /ɪˈlɑːŋˌgeɪt, *Brit* ˈiːlɒŋgeɪt/ *verb* **-gates; -gat·ed; -gat·ing :** to make (something) longer or to grow longer **:** LENGTHEN [+ *obj*] These stretching exercises can help *elongate* your leg muscles. • New medical procedures have *elongated* the careers of many athletes. [*no obj*] an *elongating* cell
– elon·gat·ed /ɪˈlɑːŋˌgeɪtəd, *Brit* ˈiːlɒŋgeɪtəd/ *adj* [*more* ~; *most* ~] • an *elongated* pause • an *elongated* [=long and thin] figure **– elon·ga·tion** /iːˌlɑːŋˈgeɪʃən/ *noun* [*noncount*] • muscular *elongation*

elope /ɪˈloʊp/ *verb* **elopes; eloped; elop·ing** [*no obj*] **:** to run away secretly to get married • The couple *eloped* in the middle of the night.
– elope·ment /ɪˈloʊpmənt/ *noun, pl* **-ments** [*count, noncount*]

el·o·quence /ˈɛləkwəns/ *noun* [*noncount*] **:** the ability to speak or write well and in an effective way • The senator's *eloquence* is well known. • She spoke with *eloquence* on the need for better schools. • We were moved by her *eloquence*. = We were moved by the *eloquence* of her words.

el·o·quent /ˈɛləkwənt/ *adj* [*more* ~; *most* ~]
1 : having or showing the ability to use language clearly and effectively • an *eloquent* speech/speaker • an *eloquent* essay • He ***waxed eloquent*** [=he said many things] on/about the pleasures of gardening.

2 : clearly showing feeling or meaning ▪ His success serves as an *eloquent* reminder of the value of hard work.

– el·o·quent·ly *adv* [*more* ~; *most* ~] ▪ She spoke *eloquently* about the need for better schools.

[1]else /ˈɛls/ *adv* **:** in a different or additional manner or place ▪ How *else* could it be done? [=in what other way could it be done?] ▪ Where *else* can we meet? [=at what other place can we meet?] ▪ "Where did you meet that actor?" "In Hollywood—where *else*?" [=at what other place would I be likely to meet an actor?] ▪ We decided to go someplace *else* for dinner. **:** at a different or additional time ▪ I don't know when *else* we could go. [=don't know another time when we could go]

or else **1** — used to say what will happen if something is not done ▪ You have to leave *or else* you will be arrested for trespassing. **2** — used to say what another possibility is ▪ He either thinks he can't do it *or else* he just isn't interested. **3** *informal* — used in angry speech to express a threat without saying exactly what the threat is ▪ Do what I say *or else*!

[2]else *adj* — used to refer to a different or additional person or thing ▪ He values friendship more than anything *else*. = He values friendship above all *else*. ▪ That's somebody *else's* [=some other person's] problem. ▪ If all *else* fails, surgery is an option. ▪ Someone *else* in addition to him will have to do it. ▪ What *else* did he say? ▪ There was nothing *else* to be done. ▪ Who *else* is coming to the party? ▪ Would you like anything/something *else*? ▪ There isn't much *else* [=*more*] going on. ▪ The food was cheap, ***if nothing else***. [=the food was not very good, but at least it was cheap]

nothing else for it see [1]NOTHING

something else see [1]SOMETHING

what else is new? *informal* — used to say that you are not surprised by something you have been told ▪ "They lost again." "So *what else is new*?"

else·where /ˈɛlsˌweɚ/ *adv* **:** in or to another place ▪ The angry customer said he would take his business *elsewhere*. ▪ *Elsewhere* in the same book she gives another date. ▪ The parts are produced *elsewhere*.

elu·ci·date /ɪˈluːsəˌdeɪt/ *verb* **-dates; -dat·ed; -dat·ing** *formal* **:** to make (something that is hard to understand) clear or easy to understand [+ *obj*] The spokesman was asked to *elucidate* [=*clarify*, *explain*] the government's policies (to/for us). [*no obj*] When asked for details, he declined to *elucidate* further.

– elu·ci·da·tion /ɪˌluːsəˈdeɪʃən/ *noun, pl* **-tions** [*noncount*] notes providing *elucidation* of the text ▪ reporters seeking *elucidation* of the government's policy [*count*] reporters seeking *elucidations* of the government's policy

elude /iˈluːd/ *verb* **eludes; elud·ed; elud·ing** [+ *obj*]

1 : to avoid or escape (someone or something) by being quick, skillful, or clever ▪ The killer was able to *elude* the police. ▪ The killer has *eluded* capture. ▪ (*American football*) The running back *eluded* five tacklers.

2 a : to fail to be understood or remembered by (someone) ▪ The cause of the disease continues to *elude* researchers. ▪ The name of the author *eludes* me for the moment. [=I don't remember the name of the author] **b :** to fail to be achieved by (someone) ▪ Victory has *eluded* us. [=we have been unable to achieve victory] **c** ◊ When something ***eludes detection/discovery***, people try to find it but are unable to. ▪ The cause of the disease has *eluded detection/discovery*.

> Do not confuse *elude* with *allude*.

elu·sive /iˈluːsɪv/ *adj* [*more* ~; *most* ~]

1 : hard to find or capture ▪ *elusive* creatures ▪ The solution remains *elusive*. ▪ The truth may prove *elusive*.

2 : hard to understand, define, or remember ▪ an *elusive* concept/idea/name

– elu·sive·ly *adv* **– elu·sive·ness** *noun* [*noncount*] ▪ the *elusiveness* of truth

elves *plural of* ELF

em- see EN-

'em /əm/ *pronoun, informal* **:** THEM — used to represent an informal pronunciation of "them" ▪ He said, "Let *'em* think what they want."

ema·ci·at·ed /ɪˈmeɪʃiˌeɪtəd/ *adj* [*more* ~; *most* ~] **:** very thin because of hunger or disease ▪ The illness left her in an *emaciated* condition. = The illness left her *emaciated*.

– ema·ci·a·tion /ɪˌmeɪʃiˈeɪʃən/ *noun* [*noncount*]

[1]e–mail /ˈiːˌmeɪl/ *noun, pl* **-mails**

1 [*noncount*] **:** a system for sending messages from one computer to another computer ▪ They communicate with each other by *e-mail*. ▪ an *e-mail* message

2 a [*noncount*] **:** messages that are sent electronically from one computer to another ▪ I seem to spend most of my time these days reading *e-mail*. **b** [*count*] **:** an e-mail message ▪ She sent me an *e-mail*.

[2]e–mail *verb* **-mails; -mailed; -mail·ing** [+ *obj*] **:** to send e-mail to (someone) ▪ I'll *e-mail* you tomorrow. **:** to send (a message) to someone by e-mail ▪ I'll *e-mail* my response to you tomorrow. = I'll *e-mail* you my response tomorrow.

em·a·nate /ˈɛməˌneɪt/ *verb* **-nates -nat·ed; -nat·ing**

1 [*no obj*] **:** to come out *from* a source ▪ Good smells *emanated from* the kitchen. ▪ Constant criticism has *emanated from* her opponents. ▪ Happiness seems to *emanate from* her.

2 [+ *obj*] **:** to send (something) out **:** to give out (something) ▪ Some radioactive substances can *emanate* [=(more commonly) *emit*] radiation for many years. ▪ She seems to *emanate* happiness.

– em·a·na·tion /ˌɛməˈneɪʃən/ *noun, pl* **-tions** [*count*] radioactive *emanations* [*noncount*] the continuous *emanation* of new ideas

eman·ci·pate /ɪˈmænsəˌpeɪt/ *verb* **-pates; -pat·ed; -pat·ing** [+ *obj*] *formal* **:** to free (someone) from someone else's control or power ▪ *emancipate* a slave ▪ He felt the only way to *emancipate* himself from his parents was to move away.

– emancipated *adj* ▪ an *emancipated* slave ▪ She considers herself an ***emancipated woman***. [=a woman who is free from old social limitations and customs] **– eman·ci·pa·tion** /ɪˌmænsəˈpeɪʃən/ *noun* [*noncount*] ▪ the *emancipation* of the slaves **– eman·ci·pa·tor** /ɪˈmænsəˌpeɪtɚ/ *noun, pl* **-tors** [*count*] *chiefly US* ▪ an *emancipator* of slaves ▪ Abraham Lincoln is sometimes called the Great *Emancipator*.

emas·cu·late /ɪˈmæskjəˌleɪt/ *verb* **-lates; -lat·ed; -lat·ing** [+ *obj*]

1 : to make (a man) feel less masculine **:** to deprive (a man) of his male strength, role, etc. ▪ He plays the role of a meek husband who has been *emasculated* by his domineering wife.

2 : to make (something) weaker or less effective ▪ Critics charged that this change would *emasculate* the law.

– emas·cu·la·tion /ɪˌmæskjəˈleɪʃən/ *noun* [*noncount*]

em·balm /ɪmˈbɑːm/ *verb* **-balms; -balmed; -balm·ing** [+ *obj*] **:** to treat (a dead body) with special chemicals to keep it from decaying

– em·balm·er *noun, pl* **-ers** [*count*]

em·bank·ment /ɪmˈbæŋkmənt/ *noun, pl* **-ments** [*count*] **:** a raised bank or wall that is built to carry a roadway or hold back water

em·bar·go /ɪmˈbɑɚgoʊ/ *noun, pl* **-goes** [*count*] **:** a government order that limits trade in some way — often + *on* ▪ The government has placed/put an *embargo on* arms shipments. ▪ The *embargo on* oil will be lifted. ▪ an *embargo on* oil/arms = an oil/arms *embargo*

– embargo *verb* **-goes; -goed; -go·ing** [+ *obj*] ▪ The government has *embargoed* all arms shipments.

em·bark /ɪmˈbɑɚk/ *verb* **-barks; -barked; -bark·ing** [*no obj*] **:** to begin a journey especially on a ship or airplane ▪ The troops are waiting to *embark*. ▪ Millions of Europeans *embarked* for America in the late 19th century. — opposite DEBARK, DISEMBARK

embark on *also* ***embark upon*** [*phrasal verb*] ***embark on/upon (something)*** **1 :** to begin (a journey) ▪ They *embarked on* their trip to America with high hopes. **2 :** to begin (something that will take a long time or happen for a long time) ▪ She's *embarking on* a new career. ▪ The company has *embarked upon* a risky new project.

– em·bar·ka·tion /ˌɛmˌbɑɚˈkeɪʃən/ *noun* [*noncount*] ▪ a port of *embarkation*

em·bar·rass /ɪmˈberəs/ *verb* **-rass·es; -rassed; -rass·ing**

1 : to make (someone) feel confused and foolish in front of other people [+ *obj*] Unexpected laughter *embarrassed* the speaker. ▪ She's worried about *embarrassing* herself in front of such a large audience. [*no obj*] She doesn't *embarrass* easily. [=she is not easily embarrassed]

2 [+ *obj*] **:** to make (a person, group, government, etc.) look foolish in public ▪ I would never do anything to *embarrass* my family. ▪ The protest was staged as a deliberate attempt to *embarrass* the government.

– embarrassed *adj* [*more* ~; *most* ~] ▪ I've never been more *embarrassed* in my life. ▪ I'm *embarrassed* (to admit) that I've never actually read the book. **– embarrassing** *adj* [*more* ~; *most* ~] ▪ It was one of my most *embarrassing* moments. • a very *embarrassing* scandal for the government – **em·bar·rass·ing·ly** /ɪmˈberəsɪŋli/ *adv* • He was *embarrassingly* unprepared for the job interview.

em·bar·rass·ment /ɪmˈberəsmənt/ *noun, pl* **-ments**
1 [*noncount*] **:** the state of feeling foolish in front of others • She couldn't hide her *embarrassment.* • Much to my *embarrassment,* I realized that I had forgotten his name. [=I was very embarrassed when I realized that I had forgotten his name]
2 [*count*] **:** something or someone that causes a person or group to look or feel foolish • The scandal was a major *embarrassment* for the government. • He's an *embarrassment* to his family.
3 [*count*] **:** a very large number of things from which to choose — usually singular; *+ of* • We have an *embarrassment of* choices/options. [=we have a very large number of choices/options] • With so many fine restaurants in the city, diners are faced with an ***embarrassment of riches***. [=there are so many fine restaurants that it is difficult to choose one]

E

em·bas·sy /ˈɛmbəsi/ *noun, pl* **-sies** [*count*]
1 : a group of people who work under an ambassador and represent their country in a foreign country • *embassy* officials
2 : the building where an ambassador lives and works • Protesters marched outside the American *embassy.*

em·bat·tled /ɪmˈbætl̩d/ *adj*
1 : engaged in battle or conflict **:** surrounded by enemies • an *embattled* city
2 [*more ~; most ~*] **:** constantly criticized or attacked • the *embattled* coach of a losing team • the company's *embattled* president

em·bed *also* **im·bed** /ɪmˈbɛd/ *verb* **-beds; -bed·ded; -bed·ding** [*+ obj*] **:** to place or set (something) firmly in something else • *embed* a post in concrete — often used figuratively • deeply *embedded* dislikes [=dislikes that have been felt for a long time and that are very deep] • values and beliefs that are *embedded* in our culture [=that are established as part of our culture]

em·bel·lish /ɪmˈbɛlɪʃ/ *verb* **-lish·es; -lished; -lish·ing** [*+ obj*] **:** to decorate (something) by adding special details and features **:** to make (something) more appealing or attractive • a book *embellished* with colorful illustrations • He *embellished* his speech with a few quotations. • (*humorous*) I didn't lie, I just *embellished* the story a little bit.
– em·bel·lish·ment /ɪmˈbɛlɪʃmənt/ *noun, pl* **-ments** [*noncount*] a story that doesn't require *embellishment* [*count*] architectural *embellishments*

em·ber /ˈɛmbɚ/ *noun, pl* **-bers** [*count*] **:** a glowing piece of coal or wood from a fire — usually plural • He sat staring at the *embers* in the fireplace.

em·bez·zle /ɪmˈbɛzəl/ *verb* **-bez·zles; -bez·zled; -bez·zling :** to steal money that you have been trusted with [*+ obj*] He was caught *embezzling* money/funds from his clients. [*no obj*] He was convicted of *embezzling.*
– em·bez·zle·ment /ɪmˈbɛzəlmənt/ *noun* [*noncount*] • the *embezzlement* of funds **– em·bez·zler** /ɪmˈbɛzəlɚ/ *noun, pl* **-zlers** [*count*] • a convicted *embezzler*

em·bit·ter /ɪmˈbɪtɚ/ *verb* **-ters; -tered; -ter·ing** [*+ obj*] **:** to cause bitter feelings in (someone) • The soldier was *embittered* by the war.
– embittered *adj* [*more ~; most ~*] • The war left him angry and *embittered.*

em·bla·zon /ɪmˈbleɪzn̩/ *verb* **-zons; -zoned; -zon·ing** [*+ obj*]
1 : to write or draw (a name, picture, etc.) *on* a surface so that it can be seen very clearly — usually used as *(be) emblazoned* • The team's name *was emblazoned on* their helmets. • slogans and portraits *emblazoned on* banners
2 : to decorate (a surface) *with* something (such as a name or a picture) — usually used as *(be) emblazoned* • The helmets *were emblazoned with* the team's name. • banners *emblazoned with* slogans and portraits

em·blem /ˈɛmbləm/ *noun, pl* **-blems** [*count*]
1 : an object or picture used to suggest a thing that cannot be shown • The flag is the *emblem* of our nation. • our national *emblem*
2 : a person or thing that represents an idea • He has come to be regarded as an *emblem* of conservatism.

em·blem·at·ic /ˌɛmbləˈmætɪk/ *adj* [*more ~; most ~*] **:** representing something (such as an idea, state, or emotion) that cannot be seen by itself • an *emblematic* image — usually *+ of* • The crown is *emblematic of* royalty. • The project's failure is now seen as *emblematic of* poor corporate judgment.

em·bod·i·ment /ɪmˈbɑːdɪmənt/ *noun, pl* **-ments** [*count*] *somewhat formal* **:** someone or something that is a perfect representative or example of a quality, idea, etc. • She's the *embodiment* of all our hopes. • Some consider him the (very) *embodiment* of evil.

em·body /ɪmˈbɑːdi/ *verb* **-bod·ies; -bod·ied; -body·ing** [*+ obj*]
1 : to represent (something) in a clear and obvious way **:** to be a symbol or example of (something) • He is a leader who *embodies* courage. [=he is a very courageous leader]
2 *formal* **:** to include (something) as a part or feature • The legislature *embodied* a revenue provision in the new law. • The new law *embodies* a revenue provision. = A revenue provision is *embodied* in the new law.

em·bold·en /ɪmˈbouldən/ *verb* **-ens; -ened; -en·ing** [*+ obj*] **:** to make (someone) more confident — usually used as *(be) emboldened* • He *was emboldened* by the success of his speech.

em·boss /ɪmˈbɑːs/ *verb* **-boss·es; -bossed; -boss·ing** [*+ obj*] **:** to decorate a surface with a raised pattern or design — usually used as *(be) embossed* • His stationery *was embossed* with his initials. • His initials *were embossed* on his stationery.
– embossed *adj* • *embossed* stationery/paper/leather • an *embossed* pattern/image

[1]**em·brace** /ɪmˈbreɪs/ *verb* **-brac·es; -braced; -brac·ing**
1 : to hold someone in your arms as a way of expressing love or friendship [*+ obj*] He *embraced* her warmly/lovingly/tenderly. • two old friends (warmly) *embracing* [=*hugging*] each other [*no obj*] They *embraced* one last time before going their separate ways. ✧ Although *embrace* and *hug* each describe holding another person in your arms, *embrace* usually suggests deeper or stronger feelings than *hug* does.
2 [*+ obj*] **a :** to accept (something or someone) readily or gladly • a politician who has been *embraced* by conservatives • *embrace* [=*adopt*] a cause/religion • These ideas have been (widely) *embraced* by a the scientific community. **b :** to use (an opportunity) eagerly • She gladly/eagerly *embraced* [=*welcomed*] the opportunity/chance to study abroad.
3 [*+ obj*] *formal* **:** to contain or include (something) as a part of something larger • Charity *embraces* all acts of generous giving. • It's a subject that *embraces* many areas of learning.
4 [*+ obj*] *literary* **:** to enclose (something) on all sides — usually used as *(be) embraced* • a town *embraced* [=*surrounded*] by low hills
– em·brace·able /ɪmˈbreɪsəbəl/ *adj* [*more ~; most ~*]
– em·brac·er *noun, pl* **-ers** [*count*] • an *embracer* of new technology

[2]**embrace** *noun, pl* **embraces** [*count*] **:** the act of holding someone in your arms **:** the act of embracing someone • He held her in a warm/loving/tender *embrace.*

em·broi·der /ɪmˈbroɪdɚ/ *verb* **-ders; -dered; -der·ing** [*+ obj*]
1 : to sew a design on a piece of cloth • She *embroidered* tiny flowers on the baby's scarf. • a scarf *embroidered* with tiny flowers • an *embroidered* scarf
2 : to make (a story, the truth, etc.) more interesting by adding details that are not true or accurate • He is known to *embroider* the truth about his service in the army.
– em·broi·der·er /ɪmˈbroɪdərɚ/ *noun, pl* **-ers** [*count*] • a skillful *embroiderer*

em·broi·dery /ɪmˈbroɪdəri/ *noun, pl* **-der·ies**
1 [*noncount*] **:** the process or art of sewing a design on cloth • She learned *embroidery* from her grandmother.
2 : cloth decorated by sewing **:** embroidered material [*count*] a beautiful *embroidery* [*noncount*] her collection of *embroidery*
3 [*noncount*] **:** extra details that are added to make a story more interesting and that are not true or accurate • His stories about his travels include a good deal of *embroidery.*

em·broil /ɪmˈbrojəl/ *verb* **-broils; -broiled; -broil·ing** [*+ obj*] **:** to involve (someone or something) *in* conflict or difficulties • His stand on this issue has *embroiled* him *in* controversy. • The new drug has been *embroiled in* controversy. • They were *embroiled in* a complicated lawsuit.
– em·broil·ment /ɪmˈbrojəlmənt/ *noun* [*noncount*]

em·bryo /ˈɛmbriˌoʊ/ *noun, pl* **-bry·os** [*count*] **:** a human or animal in the early stages of development before it is born, hatched, etc. — compare FETUS
in embryo *formal* **:** in an early or undeveloped stage • The ideas he explored fully in his later work can be seen *in embryo* in his early books.

em·bry·on·ic /ˌɛmbriˈɑːnɪk/ *adj*
1 : of or relating to an embryo ▪ human *embryonic* development ▪ *embryonic* tissue/cells
2 : in an early or undeveloped stage ▪ an *embryonic* plan ▪ The tourism industry there is still in/at an *embryonic* stage.

¹em·cee /ˌɛmˈsiː/ *noun, pl* **-cees** [*count*] *US* : MASTER OF CEREMONIES ▪ It was his third appearance as *emcee* [=*host*] of the awards dinner.

²emcee *verb* **-cees; -ceed; -cee·ing** *US* : to be the master of ceremonies for something [+ *obj*] She agreed to *emcee* [=*host*] an awards dinner. [*no obj*] She agreed to *emcee* at an awards dinner.

emend /iˈmɛnd/ *verb* **emends; emend·ed; emend·ing** [+ *obj*] : to correct errors in (something written) ▪ *emend* a text — compare AMEND
– **emen·da·tion** /ˌiːˌmɛnˈdeɪʃən/ *noun, pl* **-tions** [*count, noncount*]

em·er·ald /ˈɛmərəld/ *noun, pl* **-alds**
1 [*count*] : a bright green stone that is used in jewelry — see color picture on page C11
2 [*noncount*] : a bright or rich green color — called also *emerald green*; see color picture on page C2
– **emerald** /ˈɛmərəld/ *adj* ▪ *emerald* [=bright green] eyes

emerge /ɪˈmədʒ/ *verb* **emerg·es; emerged; emerg·ing** [*no obj*]
1 **a** : to become known or apparent ▪ The facts *emerged* after a lengthy investigation. ▪ A simple pattern has *emerged*. [=become clear] ▪ Several possible candidates have *emerged*. **b** : to become known or regarded *as* something ▪ She has *emerged as* a leading contender in the field. ▪ His war record has *emerged as* a key issue in the election. ▪ The movie has (suddenly/quickly/rapidly) *emerged as* one of the year's most surprising hits.
2 : to rise or appear *from* a hidden or unknown place or condition : to come out into view ▪ when land first *emerged from* the sea ▪ The cat *emerged from* its hiding place behind the couch. ▪ animals *emerging from* a long period of inactivity
3 — used to indicate the usually good state or condition of someone or something at the end of an event, process, etc. ▪ Both sides in the election remain confident that they will *emerge* victorious/triumphant. [=that they will win] ▪ He *emerged* unharmed from the accident. [=he was not harmed in the accident]

emer·gence /ɪˈmədʒəns/ *noun* [*noncount*] : the act of becoming known or coming into view : the act of emerging ▪ his surprising *emergence* [=*arrival, appearance*] as a leader ▪ the *emergence* of the Internet as an important means of communication ▪ the economy's *emergence* from a recession

emer·gen·cy /ɪˈmədʒənsi/ *noun, pl* **-cies** [*count*] : an unexpected and usually dangerous situation that calls for immediate action ▪ Her quick thinking in an *emergency* saved the baby's life. ▪ Here's a phone number where I can be reached in (the event of) an *emergency*. — often used before another noun ▪ *emergency* vehicles/procedures/exits ▪ The pilot was forced to make an *emergency* landing when one of the engines failed. ✧ A ***state of emergency*** is declared to give the government special powers to deal with an emergency. ▪ The government declared a *state of emergency* to deal with all damage caused by the hurricane.

emergency brake *noun, pl* ~ **brakes** [*count*] *chiefly US* : a special brake (such as a parking brake in an automobile) that can be used for stopping when the main brakes fail

emergency medical technician *noun, pl* ~ **-cians** [*count*] *US* : EMT

emergency room *noun, pl* ~ **rooms** [*count*] *US* : a hospital room or area that is used for treating people who need immediate medical care — abbr. *ER* — called also (*Brit*) *casualty*

emer·gent /ɪˈmədʒənt/ *adj, always used before a noun* : EMERGING ▪ newly *emergent* nations

emerging *adj, always used before a noun* : newly created or noticed and growing in strength or popularity : becoming widely known or established ▪ an *emerging* breed/group of new filmmakers [=a group of filmmakers who are becoming well known] ▪ There is an *emerging* consensus that the war will end soon. ▪ newly *emerging* countries/markets

emer·i·tus /ɪˈmerətəs/ *adj* : retired with an honorary title from an office or position especially in a university ▪ a professor *emeritus* of American history = an *emeritus* professor of American history

em·ery board /ˈɛməri-/ *noun, pl* ~ **boards** [*count*] : a piece of cardboard that is covered with a rough material and that is used for smoothing and shaping fingernails

em·i·grant /ˈɛmɪgrənt/ *noun, pl* **-grants** [*count*] : a person who leaves a country or region to live in another one : a person who emigrates ▪ Millions of European *emigrants* came to America in the 19th century. ▪ *emigrants* from Europe ▪ *emigrants* to America — compare IMMIGRANT, MIGRANT

em·i·grate /ˈɛməˌgreɪt/ *verb* **-grates; -grat·ed; -grat·ing** [*no obj*] : to leave a country or region to live elsewhere — often + *from* ▪ My grandparents *emigrated from* Hungary. — sometimes + *to* ▪ My grandparents *emigrated to* America. — compare IMMIGRATE, MIGRATE
– **em·i·gra·tion** /ˌɛməˈgreɪʃən/ *noun* [*noncount*] ▪ Political unrest caused mass *emigration* following the war.

émi·gré *also US* **emi·gré** /ˈɛmɪˌgreɪ/ *noun, pl* **-grés** [*count*] : EMIGRANT; *especially* : a person who is forced to leave a country for political reasons ▪ He was one of a group of Soviet *émigrés* living in New York.

em·i·nence /ˈɛmɪnəns/ *noun, pl* **-nenc·es**
1 [*noncount*] : a condition of being well-known and successful ▪ literary/social *eminence* [=*prestige*] ▪ Many of his students have achieved *eminence* [=*distinction*] in their fields.
2 [*count*] *formal* : a person of high rank or achievements ▪ a literary *eminence* — used as a title for a cardinal in the Roman Catholic church ▪ His *Eminence*, Cardinal Cushing ▪ Will Your *Eminence* please step this way.
3 [*count*] *formal* : an area of high ground ▪ He built his home on an *eminence* [=*height, hill*] overlooking the city.

em·i·nent /ˈɛmɪnənt/ *adj* [*more* ~; *most* ~] : successful, well-known and respected ▪ an *eminent* physician

> Do not confuse *eminent* with *imminent*.

eminent domain *noun* [*noncount*] *law* : a right of a government to take private property for public use ▪ The state took the homes by *eminent domain* to build the new road.

em·i·nent·ly /ˈɛmɪnəntli/ *adv* [*more* ~; *most* ~] *somewhat formal* : to a high degree ▪ It was an *eminently* [=*extremely, very*] enjoyable evening. ▪ an *eminently* sensible plan

emir /əˈmiə/ *noun, pl* **emirs** [*count*] : a ruler, chief, or commander in an Islamic country

emir·ate /ˈɛmərət/ *noun, pl* **-ates** [*count*] : the country or position of an emir

em·is·sary /ˈɛməˌseri, *Brit* ˈɛməsri/ *noun, pl* **-sar·ies** [*count*] : a person who is sent on a mission to represent another person or organization ▪ government *emissaries* [=*envoys*] trying to negotiate a settlement ▪ She acted as the president's personal *emissary* to the union leaders.

emis·sion /iˈmɪʃən/ *noun, pl* **-sions**
1 [*noncount*] : the act of producing or sending out something (such as energy or gas) from a source ▪ *emission* of light ▪ trying to reduce the *emission* of greenhouse gases
2 [*count*] : something sent out or given off ▪ The new regulations are intended to reduce auto *emissions*. [=harmful substances released into the air by automobiles]

emit /iˈmɪt/ *verb* **emits; emit·ted; emit·ting** [+ *obj*]
1 : to send (light, energy, etc.) out from a source ▪ The telescope can detect light *emitted* by distant galaxies. ▪ chimneys *emitting* thick, black smoke ▪ The flowers of this plant *emit* [=*give off*] a powerful odor.
2 : to make (a certain sound) ▪ The brakes *emitted* a loud squeal. ▪ The students *emitted* [=*let out*] a (collective) groan as the test results were announced.

Em·my /ˈɛmi/ *noun, pl* **-mys** [*count*] : a small statue that is awarded each year to the best actors, programs, etc., in American television ▪ She won an *Emmy* for that role.

emote /ɪˈmoʊt/ *verb* **emotes; emot·ed; emot·ing** [*no obj*] : to express emotion in a very dramatic or obvious way ▪ He stood on the stage, *emoting* and gesturing wildly.

emo·ti·con /ɪˈmoʊtɪˌkɑːn/ *noun, pl* **-cons** [*count*] : a group of keyboard characters that are used to represent a facial expression (such as a smile or frown) ✧ Emoticons are used by people writing on computers to indicate the tone or attitude of what is written. People often use a smiling emoticon like :-) to show that their comments are meant in a friendly or joking way.

emo·tion /ɪˈmoʊʃən/ *noun, pl* **-tions** : a strong feeling (such as love, anger, joy, hate, or fear) [*count*] He's always found it hard to express (his) *emotions*. [=to show his feelings] ▪ strong/deep *emotions* ▪ negative/positive *emotions* ▪ I have ***mixed emotions*** [=*mixed feelings*] about doing this. [=I'm not sure if I want to do this or not] [*noncount*] He spoke with great *emotion*. [=*passion*] ▪ a display of raw *emotion* ▪ The defendant showed/displayed no *emotion* when the verdict was read. ▪ She was overcome with/by *emotion* at the news of her friend's death.

emo·tion·al /ɪˈmoʊʃənl/ *adj*
1 : relating to emotions ▪ an *emotional* disorder
2 [*more ~; most ~*] **a :** likely to show or express emotion **:** easily upset, excited, etc. ▪ He's a very *emotional* person. **b :** showing emotion — used especially to describe someone who is crying because of strong emotion ▪ He tends to get *emotional* at weddings.
3 [*more ~; most ~*] **:** causing a person to feel emotion ▪ He gave an *emotional* [=*moving*] speech. ▪ an *emotional* experience ▪ Abortion is an *emotional* issue. [=an issue that causes people to feel strong emotions]
– emo·tion·al·ly /ɪˈmoʊʃənəli/ *adv* [*more ~; most ~*] ▪ He wasn't *emotionally* ready to become a father. ▪ an *emotionally* disturbed person

emo·tion·less /ɪˈmoʊʃənləs/ *adj* [*more ~; most ~*] **:** showing, having, or expressing no emotion ▪ She did her job with *emotionless* efficiency. ▪ *emotionless* eyes

emo·tive /ɪˈmoʊtɪv/ *adj* [*more ~; most ~*]
1 : of or relating to emotions ▪ *emotive* language
2 *Brit* **:** causing strong emotions for or against something ▪ Abortion is a very *emotive* [=(*US*) *emotional*] issue.

empanel *variant spelling of* IMPANEL

em·pa·thize *also Brit* **em·pa·thise** /ˈɛmpəˌθaɪz/ *verb* **-thiz·es; -thized; -thiz·ing** [*no obj*] **:** to have the same feelings as another person **:** to feel empathy for someone — often + *with* ▪ He learned to *empathize with* the poor. — compare SYMPATHIZE

em·pa·thy /ˈɛmpəθi/ *noun* [*noncount*] **:** the feeling that you understand and share another person's experiences and emotions ▪ He felt great *empathy* with/for/toward the poor. **:** the ability to share someone else's feelings ▪ His months spent researching prison life gave him greater *empathy* towards/for convicts. — compare SYMPATHY

em·per·or /ˈɛmpərɚ/ *noun, pl* **-ors** [*count*] **:** a man who rules an empire ▪ Roman *emperors* — compare EMPRESS

em·pha·sis /ˈɛmfəsəs/ *noun, pl* **-pha·ses** /-fəˌsiːz/
1 [*noncount*] **:** a forceful quality in the way something is said or written ▪ You need to state your arguments with greater *emphasis*. [=state your arguments more forcefully]
2 [*noncount*] **:** added force that is given to a word or syllable when speaking ▪ The *emphasis* [=*stress*] in the word "happiness" is on the first syllable.
3 : special importance or attention given to something [*noncount*] — usually + *on* ▪ The *emphasis* in this drill is *on* using proper technique. ▪ She puts/places/lays (particular/special/great) *emphasis on* developing good study habits. [*count*] Our candidate's plan has a different *emphasis*.

em·pha·size *also Brit* **em·pha·sise** /ˈɛmfəˌsaɪz/ *verb* **-siz·es; -sized; -siz·ing** [+ *obj*] **:** to give special attention to (something) **:** to place emphasis on (something) ▪ Their father always *emphasized* [=*stressed*] the importance of discipline. [=always said that discipline was important] ▪ He wanted to *emphasize* (to us) that he hadn't meant to offend anyone.

em·phat·ic /ɪmˈfætɪk/ *adj* [*more ~; most ~*]
1 : said or done in a forceful or definite way ▪ Her answer was an *emphatic* [=*resounding*] "Yes!" ▪ a man with *emphatic* [=*strong, definite*] opinions ▪ an *emphatic* victory
2 : speaking or acting in a forceful way ▪ They were *emphatic* about their political differences.
– em·phat·i·cal·ly /ɪmˈfætɪkli/ *adv* ▪ He declared *emphatically* [=*forcefully*] that he did not believe them. ▪ This is *emphatically* [=*definitely*] not the right thing to do.

em·phy·se·ma /ˌɛmfəˈziːmə, *Brit* ˌɛmfəˈsiːmə/ *noun* [*noncount*] *medical* **:** a disease in which the lungs become stretched and breathing becomes difficult

em·pire /ˈɛmˌpajɚ/ *noun, pl* **-pires** [*count*]
1 : a group of countries or regions that are controlled by one ruler or one goverment; *especially* **:** a group of countries ruled by an emperor or empress ▪ the Roman *Empire*
2 : a very large business or group of businesses under the control of one person or company ▪ She built a tiny business into a worldwide *empire*. ▪ He controlled a cattle *empire* in the heart of Texas. ▪ a media *empire*

em·pir·i·cal /ɪmˈpirɪkəl/ *also* **em·pir·ic** /ɪmˈpirɪk/ *adj* **:** based on testing or experience ▪ They collected plenty of *empirical* data/evidence from their experiments. ▪ *empirical* laws
– em·pir·i·cal·ly /ɪmˈpirɪkli/ *adv* ▪ Her theory had not yet been tested *empirically*.

em·pir·i·cism /ɪmˈpirəˌsɪzəm/ *noun* [*noncount*] **:** the practice of basing ideas and theories on testing and experience
– em·pir·i·cist /ɪmˈpirəsɪst/ *noun, pl* **-cists** [*count*]

em·place·ment /ɪmˈpleɪsmənt/ *noun, pl* **-ments**
1 [*count*] **:** a position that is specially prepared for a weapon ▪ machine-gun *emplacements*
2 [*noncount*] **:** the act of putting something (such as a weapon) into position ▪ secret *emplacement* of missiles on the island

[1]em·ploy /ɪmˈplɔɪ/ *verb* **-ploys; -ployed; -ploy·ing** [+ *obj*]
1 *somewhat formal* **a :** to use (something) *for* a particular purpose or *to do* something ▪ She *employed* [=*used*] a pen *for* sketching wildlife. ▪ a method (widely/commonly/frequently) *employed to improve* garden soil ▪ The company is accused of *employing* questionable methods *to obtain* the contract. **b :** to use or direct (something, such as your time or effort) in order to achieve a particular goal ▪ You should find better ways to *employ* your time. ▪ Your time could be better *employed* [=*spent*] in learning a new skill.
2 a : to use or get the services of (someone) to do a particular job ▪ I had to *employ* a lawyer to review the contract. **b :** to provide (someone) with a job that pays wages or a salary ▪ It's a small company, *employing* a staff of only 20. ▪ He's *employed* by the local drugstore. [=he has a job at the local drugstore] ▪ She hasn't been ***gainfully employed*** [=hasn't had a job that pays wages or a salary] for a few years. — often + *as* ▪ She's been *employed as* a gardener for many years.
– em·ploy·able /ɪmˈplɔjəbəl/ *adj* [*more ~; most ~*] ▪ He lacks the skills needed to be *employable*.

[2]employ *noun*
in someone's employ *formal* **:** employed by someone for wages or a salary ▪ The company has been generous to people *in their employ*. [=generous to their employees] ▪ The defendant was at that time *in the employ of* [=*employed by*] a trucking company.

em·ploy·ee /ɪmˌplɔɪˈiː, ɪmˈplɔɪˌiː/ *noun, pl* **-ees** [*count*] **:** a person who works for another person or for a company for wages or a salary ▪ A good boss listens to his *employees*. ▪ The company has more than 2,000 *employees* worldwide. ▪ *employee* benefits

em·ploy·er /ɪmˈplɔjɚ/ *noun, pl* **-ers** [*count*] **:** a person or company that has people who do work for wages or a salary **:** a person or company that has employees ▪ It was the *employer's* responsibility to improve workplace safety. ▪ Your travel expenses should be paid for by your *employer*.

em·ploy·ment /ɪmˈplɔɪmənt/ *noun* [*noncount*]
1 : the act of employing someone or something: such as **a :** the act of using something ▪ We object to the company's *employment* [=*use, utilization*] of pesticides. **b :** the act of paying someone to do a job ▪ laws that have encouraged the *employment* of women
2 a : work that a person is paid to do ▪ I've been looking for *employment* in the machine trade. ▪ The new factory should provide *employment* for hundreds of workers. ▪ unskilled workers trying to find paid/gainful *employment* ▪ full-time/part-time *employment* ▪ She hopes to find *employment* as a teacher. — often used before another noun ▪ an *employment* contract ▪ my *employment* history **b :** the state of being employed **:** the state of being paid to do a job ▪ The magazine did well during the course of her *employment* as editor. **c :** the number of people who have jobs in a particular place or area ▪ *Employment* is at an all-time high in this part of the state. **d :** jobs that are available for workers ▪ The city is faced with inadequate housing and a lack of *employment*.

employment agency *noun, pl* **~ -cies** [*count*] **:** a company whose business is to find jobs for people ▪ He found work as a mechanic through an *employment agency*.

em·po·ri·um /ɪmˈporijəm/ *noun, pl* **-po·ri·ums** *also* **-po·ria** /-ˈporijə/ [*count*] *old-fashioned* **:** a store or shop ▪ a furniture *emporium* ▪ a men's clothing *emporium*

em·pow·er /ɪmˈpawɚ/ *verb* **-ers; -ered; -er·ing** [+ *obj*]
1 : to give power to (someone) ▪ seeking changes in the workplace that will *empower* women
2 : to give official authority or legal power to (someone) — followed by *to* + *verb* ▪ Congress has *empowered* state legislatures *to set* educational standards. — often used as *(be) empowered* ▪ His attorney *was empowered to act* on his behalf. — opposite DISEMPOWER
– em·pow·er·ment /ɪmˈpawɚmənt/ *noun* [*noncount*] ▪ *empowerment* of women

em·press /ˈɛmprəs/ *noun, pl* **-press·es** [*count*]

1 : the wife or widow of an emperor ▪ the Emperor and *Empress* of Japan
2 : a woman who rules an empire ▪ Catherine the Great was *Empress* of Russia. — compare EMPEROR

emptor see CAVEAT EMPTOR

[1]**emp·ty** /ˈɛmpti/ *adj* **emp·ti·er; -est**
1 : containing nothing ▪ The box was *empty*. ▪ an *empty* beer can ▪ vast *empty* spaces ▪ *empty* shelves ▪ This medication should not be taken ***on an empty stomach***. [=you should eat something before taking this medication]
2 : not having any people : not occupied ▪ an *empty* house ▪ an *empty* beach/street ▪ *empty* beds/seats ▪ an *empty* factory ▪ The arena was completely *empty*.
3 : having no real purpose or value ▪ She felt trapped in an *empty* marriage. ▪ unhappy people leading *empty* lives
4 : having no effect : not sincere or meaningful ▪ an *empty* [=*hollow, idle*] threat ▪ an *empty* promise ▪ Her apology was just an *empty* gesture. ▪ Their promises are just a lot of *empty* talk/words.
5 : not showing emotion or life ▪ She looked at me with *empty* eyes. ▪ a crowd of *empty* faces
come up empty see [1]COME
empty of **:** completely without (something) ▪ The arena was *empty of* spectators. ▪ The streets are now *empty of* traffic.
– emp·ti·ly /ˈɛmptəli/ *adv* ▪ He stared *emptily* out the window. **– emp·ti·ness** /ˈɛmptinəs/ *noun* [*noncount*] ▪ the vast *emptiness* of outer space

[2]**empty** *verb* **emp·ties; emp·tied; emp·ty·ing**
1 [+ *obj*] **:** to remove the contents of (something) : to make (something) empty ▪ *empty* (out) a bag ▪ She *emptied* her purse (out) onto the table. ▪ The bomb threat *emptied* the crowded theater. [=caused everyone to leave the theater] ▪ He *emptied* his glass. [=he drank everything that was in his glass] ▪ She tried to *empty* her mind (of thoughts). ▪ He *emptied* his gun. [=he shot all the bullets in his gun]
2 [+ *obj*] **:** to remove all of (something) from a container ▪ She *emptied* the contents of her purse onto the table. ▪ It's your turn to *empty* the trash.
3 [*no obj*] **:** to become empty ▪ The theater *emptied* (out) quickly after the show.
empty into [*phrasal verb*] ***empty into (something) of a river, stream, etc.*** **:** to flow into (something) ▪ The river *empties into* the Indian Ocean.

[3]**empty** *noun, pl* **empties** [*count*] **:** an empty bottle or can — usually plural ▪ Return your *empties* here.

emp·ty–hand·ed /ˌɛmptiˈhændəd/ *adj* **:** without having, carrying, or bringing anything ▪ I don't want to show up (at the party) *empty-handed*. ▪ She came back (from the conference) *empty-handed*.

emp·ty–head·ed /ˌɛmptiˈhɛdəd/ *adj* [*more* ~; *most* ~] **:** not intelligent : STUPID ▪ He thinks all athletes are just *empty-headed* jocks.
– emp·ty–head·ed·ness /ˌɛmptiˈhɛdədnəs/ *noun* [*noncount*]

empty nester *noun, pl* ~ **-ers** [*count*] **:** a parent whose children have grown up and moved away from home

EMT /ˌiːˌɛmˈtiː/ *noun, pl* **EMTs** *or* **EMT's** [*count*] **:** a person who is trained to provide emergency medical services to patients who are being taken to a hospital — called also *emergency medical technician*

emu /ˈiːmju, ˈiːmu/ *noun, pl* **emus** [*count*] **:** an Australian bird that does not fly but is a very fast runner

em·u·late /ˈɛmjəˌleɪt/ *verb* **-lates; -lat·ed; -lat·ing** [+ *obj*] **:** to try to be like (someone or something you admire) ▪ She grew up *emulating* her sports heroes. ▪ artists *emulating* the style of their teachers
– em·u·la·tion /ˌɛmjəˈleɪʃən/ *noun* [*noncount*]

em·u·la·tor /ˈɛmjəˌleɪtɚ/ *noun, pl* **-tors** [*count*]
1 : a person who tries to be like someone else ▪ great artists and their *emulators* [=*imitators*]
2 *computers* **:** a program or device that permits programs written for one kind of computer to be used on another kind of computer

emul·si·fy /ɪˈmʌlsəˌfaɪ/ *verb* **-fies; -fied; -fy·ing** *technical* **:** to mix liquids together to form an emulsion [+ *obj*] *emulsify* oil and vinegar [*no obj*] mix the oil and vinegar until they *emulsify*
– emul·si·fi·ca·tion /ɪˌmʌlsəfəˈkeɪʃən/ *noun* [*noncount*]
– emul·si·fi·er /ɪˈmʌlsəˌfajɚ/ *noun, pl* **-ers** [*count, noncount*]

emul·sion /ɪˈmʌlʃən/ *noun, pl* **-sions** [*count*] *technical*
1 : a mixture of liquids ✧ In an emulsion, small drops of one liquid are mixed throughout another liquid. ▪ an *emulsion* of oil in water
2 : a thin coating on photographic film or paper that contains chemicals which are sensitive to light

en- /ɪn/ *also* **em-** /ɪm/ *prefix* ✧ In all senses *em-* is usually used before words starting with *b, m,* or *p*.
1 : to put into or onto ▪ *en*code ▪ *en*danger ▪ *en*throne ▪ *em*bed
2 : to cause to be ▪ *en*rich ▪ *en*slave
3 : to provide with ▪ *em*power ▪ *em*body
4 : to cover with ▪ *en*shroud
5 : thoroughly ▪ *en*snare ▪ *en*tangle

[1]**-en** /ən/ *adj suffix* **:** made of : consisting of ▪ earth*en* ▪ wool*en*

[2]**-en** *verb suffix*
1 : to become or cause to be ▪ sharp*en* ▪ whit*en* ▪ sadd*en* ▪ broad*en*
2 : to cause or come to have ▪ length*en* ▪ strength*en*

en·able /ɪˈneɪbəl/ *verb* **-ables; -abled; -abling** [+ *obj*]
1 a : to make (someone or something) able *to do* or *to be* something ▪ The machine *enables* us *to create* copies without losing quality. ▪ The system *enables* students *to access* class materials online. ▪ These choices are part of what *enabled* the company *to be* successful. **b :** to make (something) possible, practical, or easy ▪ a filing system that *enables* easy access to information ▪ The proposed tax will *enable* [=*facilitate*] the hiring of more police officers.
2 *technical* **:** to cause (a feature or capability of a computer) to be active or available for use ▪ Be sure to *enable* your computer's firewall. — often used in combination ▪ a wireless-*enabled* laptop [=a laptop that is able to send and receive wireless signals]

en·act /ɪˈnækt/ *verb* **-acts; -act·ed; -act·ing** [+ *obj*]
1 *somewhat formal* **:** to perform (something, such as a scene in a play) ▪ We will *enact* [=*act out*] parts of three plays.
2 : to make (a bill or other legislation) officially become part of the law ▪ Congress will *enact* legislation related to that issue. ▪ The law was finally *enacted* today.
– en·act·ment /ɪˈnæktmənt/ *noun, pl* **-ments** [*noncount*] The *enactment* [=*passage*] of this law will save lives. [*count*] legislative *enactments*

enam·el /ɪˈnæməl/ *noun, pl* **-els**
1 a : a material like colored glass that is heated until it is liquid and then used to decorate the surface of metal, glass, or pottery [*noncount*] The tea set is decorated with *enamel*. [*count*] an artist who works with *enamels* **b** [*count*] **:** something decorated with enamel ▪ The museum has a fine collection of *enamels*.
2 [*noncount*] **:** the very hard outer layer of a tooth
3 : a kind of paint that is shiny and very hard when it dries [*noncount*] We painted the doors with *enamel* (paint). [*count*] *enamels* and acrylics
– enam·eled (*US*) *or Brit* **enam·elled** /ɪˈnæməld/ *adj* ▪ colorful *enameled* jewelry [=jewelry that is decorated with enamel] ▪ an *enameled* pot

enam·e·ling (*US*) *or Brit* **enam·el·ling** /ɪˈnæməlɪŋ/ *noun* [*noncount*]
1 : decoration done with enamel ▪ The box was covered with elaborate *enameling*. ▪ The *enameling* on the teapot is beautiful.
2 : the act or technique of decorating things with enamel ▪ He studied *enameling* with a master craftsman.

en·am·or (*US*) *or Brit* **en·am·our** /ɪˈnæmɚ/ *verb* **-ors; -ored; -or·ing** [+ *obj*] **:** to cause (someone) to be loved or admired — usually used in negative statements; usually + *to* ▪ His bad temper did not *enamor* [=*endear*] him *to* his employees. [=his bad temper made his employees dislike him]

enamored (*US*) *or Brit* **enamoured** *adj* [*more* ~; *most* ~] **:** in a state in which you love, admire, or are very interested in something or someone ▪ the movie star's *enamored* fans — usually + *of* or *with* ▪ I became completely *enamored of* [=*fascinated with*] the island and its people. ▪ He was *enamored with* her [=in love with her] from the day they met. ▪ She is less than *enamored with* her new job. [=she does not like it]

en bloc /ɑnˈblɑːk/ *adv, chiefly Brit* **:** as or in a united group : all together ▪ The amendments were accepted *en bloc*.

enc. *abbr* enclosure

en·camp /ɪnˈkæmp/ *verb* **-camps; -camped; -camp·ing** *formal* **:** to set up and use a camp [*no obj*] Napoleon's troops *encamped* there. [+ *obj*] — usually used as *(be) encamped* ▪ the location where Napoleon's troops *were encamped* ▪ Refugees *are encamped* along the border. — sometimes used figuratively ▪ Reporters *were encamped* [=(more commonly)

E

camped out] in front of the courthouse.
— **en·camp·ment** /ɪnˈkæmpmənt/ *noun, pl* **-ments** [*count*] ▪ a military *encampment*

en·cap·su·late /ɪnˈkæpsəˌleɪt/ *verb* **-lates; -lat·ed; -lat·ing** [+ *obj*]
1 : to show or express the main idea or quality of (something) in a brief way ▪ a phrase that perfectly *encapsulates* [=*sums up*] my feelings about the day ▪ The first song *encapsulates* [=*captures*] the mood of the whole album.
2 : to completely cover (something) especially so that it will not touch anything else ▪ The contaminated material should be *encapsulated* and removed.
— **en·cap·su·la·tion** /ɪnˌkæpsəˈleɪʃən/ *noun, pl* **-tions** [*count*] The book is an *encapsulation* of the history of marathons. [*noncount*] a complex subject that resists *encapsulation*

E

en·case /ɪnˈkeɪs/ *verb* **-cas·es; -cased; -cas·ing** [+ *obj*] **:** to completely cover (something) ▪ Ice *encased* the trees and power lines after the storm. — often used as *(be) encased* ▪ The package *is encased* in plastic. ▪ His feet *were encased* in heavy boots.

-ence /əns/ *noun suffix*
1 : the state of having a particular quality ▪ confid*ence* ▪ depend*ence* ▪ despond*ence*
2 : the action or process of doing something ▪ emerg*ence* ▪ refer*ence* ▪ reminisc*ence*

en·chant /ɪnˈʧænt, *Brit* ɪnˈʧɑːnt/ *verb* **-chants; -chant·ed; -chant·ing**
1 : to attract and hold the attention of (someone) by being interesting, pretty, etc. [+ *obj*] The book has *enchanted* children for almost a century. — often used as *(be) enchanted* ▪ Visitors will *be enchanted* [=*captivated, charmed*] by the beauty of the place. [*no obj*] The beauty of the place *enchants.*
2 [+ *obj*] **:** to put a magic spell on (someone or something) ▪ a tale about a wizard who *enchants* [=*bewitches*] a princess
— **enchanted** *adj* ▪ It's a beautiful, *enchanted* [=*enchanting, captivating*] place. ▪ The story takes place in an *enchanted* forest. — **enchanting** *adj* [*more* ~; *most* ~] ▪ an *enchanting* book ▪ the *enchanting* beauty of the place — **en·chant·ing·ly** *adv* ▪ an *enchantingly* beautiful place

en·chant·er /ɪnˈʧæntɚ, *Brit* ɪnˈʧɑːntə/ *noun, pl* **-ers** [*count*] **:** a person who uses spells or magic **:** a sorcerer or wizard

en·chant·ment /ɪnˈʧæntmənt, *Brit* ɪnˈʧɑːntmənt/ *noun, pl* **-ments**
1 [*noncount*] **:** a feeling of being attracted by something interesting, pretty, etc. **:** the state of being enchanted ▪ Our *enchantment* faded when we found that the house needed even more repairs. — often + *with* ▪ My *enchantment* [=*fascination*] *with* the place continues to grow. — compare DISENCHANTMENT
2 : a quality that attracts and holds your attention by being interesting, pretty, etc. [*noncount*] the *enchantment* of a snowy field bathed in moonlight [*count*] He writes about the dangers as well as the *enchantments* of sailing.
3 [*count*] **:** a magic spell ▪ stories about wizards and *enchantments*

en·chant·ress /ɪnˈʧæntrəs, *Brit* ɪnˈʧɑːntrəs/ *noun, pl* **-ress·es** [*count*]
1 : a woman who uses spells or magic **:** a sorceress or witch
2 : a very interesting or beautiful woman

en·chi·la·da /ˌɛnʧəˈlɑːdə/ *noun, pl* **-das** [*count*] **:** a Mexican food that consists of a flat piece of bread (called a tortilla) that is rolled around a meat, bean, or cheese filling and covered with a sauce
the big enchilada *US, informal* **:** the most important issue, person, etc. ▪ She's won many awards for her writing in the past, but this one is *the big enchilada.*
the whole enchilada *US, informal* **:** the entire thing **:** EVERYTHING ▪ The celebration included music, food, fireworks—*the whole enchilada.* ▪ The team may win *the whole enchilada* [=the championship] this year.

en·cir·cle /ɪnˈsɚkəl/ *verb* **-cir·cles; -cir·cled; -cir·cling** [+ *obj*] **:** to form a circle around (someone or something) ▪ A fence *encircles* the field. = The field is *encircled* by a fence. **:** to surround (someone or something) ▪ A crowd of reporters *encircled* the mayor.

encl. *abbr* enclosure

en·clave /ˈɛnˌkleɪv, ˈɑːnˌkleɪv/ *noun, pl* **-claves** [*count*] **:** an area with people who are different in some way from the people in the areas around it ▪ The city has a large Chinese *enclave.* [=an area where many Chinese people live] ▪ one of the city's wealthy *enclaves* [=one of the areas in the city where only wealthy people can afford to live]

en·close /ɪnˈkloʊz/ *verb* **-clos·es; -closed; -clos·ing** [+ *obj*]
1 a : to surround (something) ▪ High walls *enclose* the courtyard. = The courtyard is *enclosed* by high walls. ▪ The pie's flaky crust *encloses* a fruit filling. **b :** to put something around (something) ▪ We want to *enclose* the porch [=build walls around the porch] and use it as a dining room. ▪ *Enclose* the fish in foil and bake.
2 : to include (something) with a letter or in a package ▪ She *enclosed* a photo with the card. ▪ Please *enclose* a check with your application. ▪ *Enclosed* with this letter are the tickets you ordered.
— **enclosed** *adj* ▪ an *enclosed* porch/courtyard ▪ The *enclosed* tickets are for you.

en·clo·sure /ɪnˈkloʊʒɚ/ *noun, pl* **-sures**
1 [*count*] **:** an area that is surrounded by a wall, fence, etc. **:** an enclosed space ▪ During the day the horses are kept in an *enclosure.* ▪ a garden *enclosure*
2 [*count*] **:** something that is included with a letter or in a package ▪ a letter with two *enclosures* ▪ One of the *enclosures* was a photograph. — abbr. *enc.* or *encl.*
3 [*noncount*] **:** the act of enclosing something ▪ the *enclosure* of a photograph with a letter ▪ the *enclosure* of the garden

en·code /ɪnˈkoʊd/ *verb* **-codes; -cod·ed; -cod·ing** [+ *obj*]
1 : to put (a message) into the form of a code so that it can kept secret **:** CODE ▪ an *encoded* message — compare DECODE
2 : to put information in the form of a code on (something) ▪ Credit cards are *encoded* with cardholder information.
3 : to change (information) into a set of letters, numbers, or symbols that can be read by a computer ▪ a technology that *encodes* images/files
— **en·cod·er** *noun, pl* **-ers** [*count*]

en·com·pass /ɪnˈkʌmpəs/ *verb* **-pass·es; -passed; -pass·ing** [+ *obj*]
1 : to include (something) as a part ▪ My interests *encompass* [=*cover, include*] a broad range of topics. ▪ The district *encompasses* most of the downtown area. — see also ALL-ENCOMPASSING
2 : to cover or surround (an area) ▪ A thick fog *encompassed* [=*enveloped*] the city. ▪ a neighborhood *encompassed* by a highway

[1]encore /ˈɑːnˌkoɚ/ *interj* — used by an audience to call for another song, dance, etc., when a performance has ended ▪ The audience shouted "*Encore!*" as the singer left the stage.

[2]encore *noun, pl* **en·cores** [*count*]
1 : an extra piece of music performed in response to a request from the audience ▪ He sang a folk song as/for an *encore.*
2 : something that follows a success ▪ Her first novel was a best seller—but what is she going to do for an *encore?*

[1]en·coun·ter /ɪnˈkaʊntɚ/ *verb* **-ters; -tered; -ter·ing** [+ *obj*]
1 : to have or experience (problems, difficulties, etc.) ▪ We *encountered* problems early in the project. ▪ The pilot told us that we might *encounter* turbulence during the flight. ▪ Her suggestion has *encountered* a lot of opposition.
2 *formal* **:** to meet (someone) without expecting or intending to ▪ I *encountered* [=*ran into*] an old friend on a recent business trip.

[2]encounter *noun, pl* **-ters** [*count*]
1 a : a meeting that is not planned or expected ▪ an accidental *encounter* ▪ a chance *encounter* with a famous writer **b :** a usually brief experience with another person ▪ a brief/painful *encounter* ▪ He's accused of having had sexual *encounters* with several young women. ▪ They had a ***romantic encounter*** [=a brief romantic relationship] several years ago. **c :** a violent or very unfriendly meeting ▪ Two protesters were arrested during an *encounter* [=*clash*] with police. ▪ There was a violent *encounter* between fans of the opposing teams.
2 : an occasion when you deal with or experience something ▪ It was her first *encounter* with cigarettes. ✧ To have a ***close encounter*** with something is to come very close to being hurt or damaged by it. ▪ The island has had several *close encounters* with major hurricanes in recent years.

en·cour·age /ɪnˈkɚrɪʤ/ *verb* **-ag·es; -aged; -ag·ing** [+ *obj*]
1 : to make (someone) more determined, hopeful, or confident ▪ They *encouraged* us in our work. ▪ *Encourage* each

other with kind words. — often used as *(be) encouraged* • We *were encouraged* by their enthusiasm. • Researchers *are encouraged* by the findings. • I *am encouraged* that the project seems to be moving ahead. — sometimes followed by *to* + *verb* • We *were encouraged to learn* of their enthusiasm. — opposite DISCOURAGE

2 a : to make (something) more appealing or more likely to happen • The program is meant to *encourage* savings. • Warm weather *encourages* plant growth. • He claims the new regulations will *encourage* investment. **b :** to make (someone) more likely *to do* something • He claims the new regulations will *encourage* people *to invest*. • We want to *encourage* students *to read* more.: to tell or advise (someone) *to do* something • My parents *encouraged* me *to go* back to college. • They *encouraged* her *to go*. — opposite DISCOURAGE

– encouraged *adj [more ~; most ~]* • Our early success left us feeling hopeful and *encouraged*.

en·cour·age·ment /ɪnˈkərɪʤmənt/ *noun, pl* **-ments**

1 *[noncount]* **:** the act of making something more appealing or more likely to happen • Our aim is the *encouragement* of investment. • the *encouragement* of plant growth

2 a : something that makes someone more determined, hopeful, or confident *[noncount]* teachers who give their students a lot of *encouragement* • words of *encouragement* • With support and *encouragement* from their parents, the students organized a fundraiser. *[count]* kind words and *encouragements* **b** *[count]* **:** something that makes someone more likely to do something • They offered him gifts of money and other *encouragements*.

en·cour·ag·ing /ɪnˈkərɪʤɪŋ/ *adj [more ~; most ~]* **:** causing a hopeful feeling • We've just heard some *encouraging* news. • an *encouraging* smile — opposite DISCOURAGING

– en·cour·ag·ing·ly *adv* • She smiled *encouragingly* at the new student.

en·croach /ɪnˈkroʊʧ/ *verb* **-croach·es; -croached; -croach·ing** *[no obj]*

1 : to gradually move or go into an area that is beyond the usual or desired limits • The suburbs *encroach* further into the rural areas each year. — usually + *on* or *upon* • People are *encroaching on* the animal's habitat. • The ocean is slowly *encroaching upon* the shoreline.

2 : to gradually take or begin to use or affect something that belongs to someone else or that someone else is using — usually + *on* or *upon* • He argues that the law would *encroach on/upon* states' authority. • The new company is *encroaching on* their traditional market.

– en·croach·ment /ɪnˈkroʊʧmənt/ *noun, pl* **-ments** *[noncount]* the gradual *encroachment* of the ocean *[count]* the *encroachments* of neighboring countries

en·crust·ed /ɪnˈkrʌstəd/ *adj* **:** coated or covered with something • The crown is *encrusted* with jewels. • mud-*encrusted* shoes

en·crypt /ɪnˈkrɪpt/ *verb* **-crypts; -crypt·ed; -crypt·ing** *[+ obj]* **:** to change (information) from one form to another especially to hide its meaning • The software will *encrypt* the message before it is sent. • The passwords are *encrypted*.

en·cum·ber /ɪnˈkʌmbɚ/ *verb* **-bers; -bered; -ber·ing** *[+ obj] somewhat formal*

1 : to make (someone or something) hold or carry something heavy — usually used as *(be) encumbered* • We *were encumbered* by our heavy coats and boots. • *encumbered* [=*burdened*] by equipment and supplies — often used figuratively • The company *is encumbered* with debt.

2 : to cause problems or difficulties for (someone or something) • These rules will only *encumber* the people we're trying to help. • Lack of funding has *encumbered* the project. — usually used as *(be) encumbered* • Peace talks have *been encumbered* by a mutual lack of trust.

– en·cum·brance /ɪnˈkʌmbrəns/ *noun, pl* **-branc·es** *[count]* • the *encumbrances* of equipment and supplies • These rules will only be an *encumbrance*.

-en·cy /ənsi/ *noun suffix* **:** the quality or state of being (something) — used to form nouns from adjectives that end in *-ent* • dependen*cy* • efficien*cy* • frequen*cy*

en·cyc·li·cal /ɪnˈsɪklɪkəl/ *noun, pl* **-cals** *[count]* **:** an official letter from the Pope to the Roman Catholic bishops

en·cy·clo·pe·dia *also* **en·cy·clo·pae·dia** /ɪnˌsaɪkləˈpiːdijə/ *noun, pl* **-pe·dias** *also* **-pae·dias** *[count]* **:** a reference work (such as a book, series of books, Web site, or CD-ROM) that contains information about many different subjects or a lot of information about a particular subject • a general *encyclopedia* • an *encyclopedia* of literature

en·cy·clo·pe·dic *also* **en·cy·clo·pae·dic** /ɪnˌsaɪkləˈpiːdɪk/ *adj [more ~; most ~]* **:** dealing with or knowing a subject thoroughly or completely • She published an *encyclopedic* study of ancient Egypt. • The event was described in *encyclopedic* detail. • his almost *encyclopedic* knowledge of movies

[1]**end** /ˈɛnd/ *noun, pl* **ends**

1 *[singular]* **a :** a point that marks the limit of something **:** the point at which something no longer continues to happen or exist • The report is due at/by the *end* of the month. • She interviewed several players at the *end* of the game. • There is no *end* [=*limit*] to their generosity. [=they are extremely generous] • I'm ***at the end of*** my patience. = I've ***reached the end of*** my patience. [=I can no longer be patient; I have run out of patience] **b :** the last part of a story, movie, song, etc. • I liked most of the book, but I didn't like the *end*. [=*ending*] • He read the book from beginning to *end* [=he read the entire book] in one day.

2 *[count]* **a :** the part at the edge or limit of an area • The restaurant is in the north *end* of the city. • We biked from one *end* of the island to the other. • The house is at the *end* of the road. • They live at opposite *ends* of town. • He left the car at the far *end* [=most distant part] of the parking lot. • the deep/shallow *end* of a swimming pool — see also DEAD END, REAR END **b :** the first or last part or section of something that is long • She drove the *end* of the stake into the ground. • The car's front/rear/back *end* was damaged. • One *end* of the rope was tangled. • Smoke curled off the *end* of the cigarette. • The hose is leaking at both *ends*. • the pointed *end* of the knife **c :** either limit of a scale or range • The car was in the high/low *end* of the price range. • The candidates represent opposite *ends* of the political spectrum. • The resort attracts tourists from the upper *end* of the social scale.

3 *[count]* **:** the stopping of a condition, activity, or course of action • The agency's goal is the *end* of world hunger. • The treaty marked the *end* of the war. • His death marks the *end* of an era. ✧ When something is ***at an end*** it is finished or completed. • The battle was *at an end*. [=*over*] • We would like to see this matter *at an end*. ✧ If you ***bring something to an end*** or ***bring an end to something***, you stop, finish, or complete it. • She *brought* the concert *to an end* with a piano solo. • Negotiations *brought an end to* the conflict. ✧ If you ***put an end to something***, you cause it to stop or prevent it from continuing. • They promise to *put an end to* unfair policies. • The new mayor vowed to *put an end to* the violence. ✧ Something ***comes to an end*** when it stops or finishes. • After three weeks the strike finally *came to an end*. • Summer always seems to *come to an end* much too quickly. • The curtain fell as the play *came to an end*. ✧ If there is ***no end in sight***, the point at which something will be finished is not known. • There is *no end in sight* to this heat wave. • Prices continue to go up with *no end in sight*.

4 *[count]* **:** the point at which someone is no longer living **:** DEATH • He came to a tragic *end* [=he died] in a freak accident. • The doctors told her that the *end* was near. [=that she would die soon] — sometimes used with *meet* • He *met* his *end* [=he died] in the icy water. • She *met* an untimely *end*.

5 *[count]* **:** a goal or purpose • Our ultimate *end* [=*aim*] in sponsoring the event is to raise money for charity. • corrupt leaders who use their power for their own *ends* • There are several ways to achieve/accomplish the same *end*. ✧ If something is ***an end in itself***, it is something that you do because you want to and not because it will help you achieve or accomplish something else. • She started exercising for her health, but she enjoyed it so much that exercising became *an end in itself*. • For him, taking classes was *an end in itself*. ✧ If ***the end justifies the means***, a desired result is so good or important that any method, even a morally bad one, may be used to achieve it. • They believe that *the end justifies the means* and will do anything to get their candidate elected.

6 *[count] American football* **:** a player whose position is at the end of the line of scrimmage — see also END RUN, SPLIT ENDS, TIGHT END

7 *[count]* **:** a specific part of a project, activity, etc. • She is in the creative *end* of the business. • It's important to know what's going on in all *ends* of a business; *especially* **:** the part of a project, activity, etc., that you are responsible for • Let me know if you have any problems at your *end*. — usually used with *keep up* or *hold up* • He promised to *keep up* his *end* of the agreement. [=he promised to do what he had agreed to do] • You can count on her to *hold up* her *end*. [=to do what she is supposed to do]

8 *[count]* **:** any one of the places connected by a telephone

call • She picked up the phone and heard an unfamiliar voice at the other *end*. • I can't hear you very well—there is a lot of noise at this *end*.
9 ends [*plural*] : parts of something that are left after the main part has been used • a quilt made from bits and *ends* of fabric — see also LOOSE END, ODDS AND ENDS
a light at the end of the tunnel see [1]LIGHT
at the end of the day *informal* : when all things are considered : in the end • It was a difficult decision, but *at the end of the day*, we knew we made the right choice.
at (your) wits'/wit's end see WIT
burn the candle at both ends see [1]BURN
come to a bad end **1** : to end up in a bad situation because of your actions • If he keeps living this way he's sure to *come to a bad end*. **2** : to die in an unpleasant way • According to legend, more than one person *came to a bad end* because of her.
end to end : with ends touching each other • Put the two small tables *end to end*. • railroad cars lined up *end to end*
go off the deep end see [1]DEEP
in the end **1** : finally or after a long time • We worked hard, and *in the end* [=*ultimately*], we achieved our goal. **2** : when all things are considered • He thought about moving to the city, but *in the end*, decided to stay where he was. • *In the end*, what really matters in a relationship is trust.
make ends meet : to pay for the things that you need to live when you have little money • We had a hard time *making ends meet*.
make your hair stand on end see HAIR
never/not hear the end of it see HEAR
not the end of the world *informal* ✧ If something is *not the end of the world*, it is not as terrible or unpleasant as it seems to be. • It *won't be the end of the world* if it rains on the day of the wedding. • Losing your job does *not* have *to be the end of the world*.
on end **1** : without interruption • For days *on end* [=for many days] she didn't answer the phone. **2** : in an upright position : not lying flat • We set the bricks *on end* around the garden. • His skis stood *on end* in the corner.
on/at the receiving end see RECEIVE
the end of the line *or* ***the end of the road*** *informal* : the point or time when someone or something stops or cannot continue : the end • A loss in the primary elections will mean *the end of the road* for his campaign. • It will be *the end of the line* for me unless there are some changes around here. • They reached *the end of the road* as a couple [=their relationship was over] a long time ago.
the end of time : FOREVER, ALWAYS — used figuratively after *to, till*, or *until* • He promised to love her *to the end of time*. • Their heroism will be remembered *until the end of time*.
the end of your rope *or chiefly Brit* ***the end of your tether*** *informal* : a state in which you are not able to deal with a problem, difficult situation, etc., any longer • It was clear from her outburst that she was at *the end of her rope*. • I've been dealing with their lies for too long. I'm at the *end of my rope*.
the ends of the earth : places in the world that are very far away from cities, large groups of people, etc. : the most remote places in the world — used figuratively • He would go to *the ends of the earth* [=he would do anything] to please her. • We will search *the ends of the earth* [=*everywhere; for a long time*] if we have to.
the short end of the stick see [1]STICK
the wrong end of the stick see [1]STICK
(to) no end : a lot : a great deal • It pleases me *to no end* [=*very much*] to see you so happy. • We've had *no end* of trouble finding somewhere to live.
to that/this end *formal* : as a way of dealing with or doing something • We want to save the building. *To this end*, we have hired someone to assess its current state.
to/till/until the bitter end see [1]BITTER

[2]**end** *verb* **ends; end•ed; end•ing**
1 a [*no obj*] : to stop or finish : to no longer continue to happen or exist • The meeting *ended* [=*concluded*] at noon. • The line of people *ended* around the corner. • The road *ends* at the top of the hill. • As soon as school *ends* [=(*Brit*) *breaks up*] she'll start her summer job. • The demonstration *ended* peacefully. • The meeting *ended* on a positive note. • She started out poor but *ended* (up) a rich woman. **b** [+ *obj*] : to stop or finish (something) : to cause (something) to no longer continue to happen or exist • They *ended* [=*concluded*] the meeting at noon. • The allegations could *end* his career. • Her speech *ended* the convention. • The argument *ended* their friendship. • The company claims that its new product will be a/the computer ***to end all*** computers. [=a computer that is the ultimate or perfect computer] • World War I was supposed to be the war *to end all* wars. **:** to come to the end of (something) • She *ended* her career (as) a rich woman. [=she was rich at the end of her career] • He *ended* his life/days (living) in a nursing home. [=he spent the last part of his life in a nursing home]
2 [+ *obj*] : to be the final part of (something) • The letters "ing" *end* the word "going." • A wedding scene *ends* the film. • A marching band will *end* the parade. • Her speech will *end* the convention.
end in [*phrasal verb*] ***end in (something)*** : to have (something) at the end • The word *ends in* a suffix. [=the last part of the word is a suffix] • The knife *ends in* a sharp point. • Their marriage *ended in* divorce. • The race *ended in* a tie. • The demonstration *ended in* chaos.
end up [*phrasal verb*] ***end up*** *or* ***end up (something)*** *or* ***end up (doing something)*** : to reach or come to a place, condition, or situation that was not planned or expected • The book *ended up* in the trash. • He didn't want to *end up* [=*wind up*] like his father. • She *ended up* rich. = She *ended up* a rich woman. • He *ended up* (living) in a nursing home. • The movie we wanted to see was sold out so we *ended up* seeing a different one.
end with [*phrasal verb*] **1** ***end with (something)*** : to have (something) at the end • The film *ends with* a wedding scene. [=the last part of the film is a wedding scene] • The convention will *end with* her speech. • The parade will *end with* a marching band. **2** ***end (something) with (something)*** : to cause (something) to have (something) at the end • She will *end* the convention *with* her speech. [=the convention will be over after her speech] • He *ended* the concert *with* one of his new songs.
end your life *or* ***end it all*** : to kill yourself : to commit suicide • He tried to *end his life* by taking an overdose of pills. • She thought about *ending it all* after her baby died.

[3]**end** *adj, always used before a noun* : [1]FINAL • the *end* product/result of a process • the *end* point/stage of the operation — see also END USER

en•dan•ger /ɪnˈdeɪnʤɚ/ *verb* **-gers; -gered; -ger•ing** /ɪnˈdeɪnʤrɪŋ/ [+ *obj*] : to cause (someone or something) to be in a dangerous place or situation • Parents feared that the dog could *endanger* their children. • The severe drought has *endangered* crops throughout the area. • The controversy *endangered* [=*threatened*] his chances for reelection. ✧ In the U.S., if you drive in a way that is not safe the police may officially accuse you of ***driving to endanger.***

endangered *adj* [*more* ~; *most* ~] — used to describe a type of animal or plant that has become very rare and that could die out completely • *endangered* plants • Two more species have been added to the ***endangered list*** [=a list of plant and animal species that are protected by law because there are very few of them] • The bald eagle is no longer considered an ***endangered species*** [=a species that is in danger of becoming extinct] — sometimes used figuratively • She claims that honest politicians are an *endangered species*.

en•dear /ɪnˈdiɚ/ *verb* **-dears; -deared; -dear•ing**
endear to [*phrasal verb*] ***endear (someone) to (someone or something)*** : to cause (someone) to be loved or admired by (someone or something) • They *endeared* themselves *to* the whole town. • His generosity has *endeared* him *to* the public. [=the people in his country, city, etc., love and admire him because he is generous] • Her bad temper did not *endear* her *to* her coworkers. [=her bad temper made it difficult for people to like her]
– endearing *adj* [*more* ~; *most* ~] • Good humor is one of your most *endearing* traits. **– en•dear•ing•ly** *adv* [*more* ~; *most* ~] • an *endearingly* good-humored person

en•dear•ment /ɪnˈdiɚmənt/ *noun, pl* **-ments** [*count*] : a word or phrase that shows love or affection • two lovers whispering *endearments* to each other ✧ A special word or name that friends or lovers use when they speak to each other is sometimes called a ***term of endearment.*** • "honey," "sweetie," and other *terms of endearment*

[1]**en•deav•or** (*US*) *or Brit* **en•deav•our** /ɪnˈdɛvɚ/ *verb* **-ors; -ored; -or•ing** [+ *obj*] *formal* : to seriously or continually try *to do* (something) • The school *endeavors to teach* students to be good citizens. • They *endeavored to create* a government that truly serves its people. ***synonyms*** see [1]ATTEMPT

[2]**endeavor** (*US*) *or Brit* **endeavour** *noun, pl* **-ors** *formal* : a

serious effort or attempt [*count*] His *endeavors* have gone unrewarded. • He failed despite his best *endeavors*. [=*efforts*] • She is involved in several artistic *endeavors*. [*noncount*] Technology is the fastest-changing area/field of human *endeavor*.

en·dem·ic /ɛnˈdɛmɪk/ *adj*
1 : growing or existing in a certain place or region • *endemic* diseases • *endemic* wildlife — often + *to* or *in* • A wide variety of animal and plant species are *endemic to* this area. • The disease is *endemic in* parts of northern Europe.
2 : common in a particular area or field — often + *to* or *in* • A distrust of strangers is *endemic in/to* this community. • Sentimentality is *endemic to* that style of writing.

end·ing /ˈɛndɪŋ/ *noun, pl* **-ings** [*count*]
1 : the final part of something • The movie has a happy *ending*. [=*end, conclusion*] • I didn't like the book's *ending*.
2 : a letter or group of letters added to the end of a word **:** SUFFIX • Common verb *endings* in English are "-s," "-ed," and "-ing." • You can often recognize an English adverb by its "-ly" *ending*.

en·dive /ˈɛn,daɪv, ˌɑːnˈdiːv/ *noun, pl* **-dives** [*count, noncount*]
1 : a plant with curly green leaves that are eaten raw
2 *US* **:** BELGIAN ENDIVE

end·less /ˈɛndləs/ *adj* **:** having no end **:** seeming to have no end **:** lasting or taking a long time • We endured *endless* meetings. • The flight seemed *endless*. • There was an *endless* line at the bank. • There is *endless* work to do on the house.
– end·less·ly *adv* • She talks about it *endlessly*. **– end·less·ness** *noun* [*noncount*]

en·dorse *also* **in·dorse** /ɪnˈdoɚs/ *verb* **-dors·es; -dorsed; -dors·ing** [+ *obj*]
1 : to publicly or officially say that you support or approve of (someone or something) • The newspaper has *endorsed* the conservative candidate for mayor. • The committee must *endorse* [=*approve*] the decision. • We do not *endorse* their position.
2 : to publicly say that you like or use (a product or service) in exchange for money • She *endorses* a line of clothing. • That brand of sneaker is *endorsed* by several basketball stars.
3 : to write your name on the back of (a check) • You must *endorse* the check before you deposit it in the bank.
4 *Brit* **:** to put information about a driving offense on (a person's driver's license) — usually used as *(be) endorsed* • His driving license *was endorsed* for speeding.
– en·dors·er *noun, pl* **-ers** [*count*]

en·dorse·ment *also* **in·dorse·ment** /ɪnˈdoɚsmənt/ *noun, pl* **-ments :** the act or result of endorsing someone or something: such as **a :** a public or official statement of support or approval [*count*] The newspaper has announced its political *endorsements*. • We're pleased that the project has received your *endorsement*. [*noncount*] Without official *endorsement*, the project cannot proceed. **b** [*count*] **:** the act of publicly saying that you like or use a product or service in exchange for money • Many retired athletes are able to make a lot of money by doing product *endorsements*. **c** [*count*] **:** the act or result of writing your name on the back of a check • The bank requires that someone witness the *endorsement* of the check. • We need your *endorsement* before we can cash this check. **d** *Brit* **:** the act or result of putting information about a driving offense on a person's driver's license [*noncount*] the *endorsement* of a license [*count*] receive/get an *endorsement* for speeding

en·dow /ɪnˈdaʊ/ *verb* **-dows; -dowed; -dow·ing** [+ *obj*]
1 : to give a large amount of money to a school, hospital, etc., in order to pay for the creation or continuing support of (something) • The wealthy couple *endowed* a new wing of the hospital. • She plans to *endow* a faculty position at the university. • The money will be used to *endow* the museum and research facility.
2 : to freely or naturally provide (someone or something) *with* something — usually used as *(be) endowed* • Human beings *are endowed with* reason. [=they naturally have reason; they are naturally able to think in a logical way] • The country *is* richly *endowed with* mineral deposits. • ". . . all men . . . *are endowed* by their Creator *with* certain unalienable rights . . . " —*U.S. Declaration of Independence* (1776) — see also WELL-ENDOWED

en·dow·ment /ɪnˈdaʊmənt/ *noun, pl* **-ments**
1 a [*count*] **:** a large amount of money that has been given to a school, hospital, etc., and that is used to pay for its creation and continuing support • The hospital's *endowment* was established by a local family. • The college has a large *endowment*. • an *endowment* fund **b :** the act of providing money to create or support a school, organization, etc. [*noncount*] the *endowment* of a hospital wing [*count*] generous *endowments*
2 [*count*] **:** a person's natural ability or talent • an athlete's physical *endowments*

end run *noun, pl* ~ **runs** [*count*] *American football* **:** a play in which the player carrying the ball tries to run around the line of defensive players — often used figuratively in U.S. English to describe a secret or dishonest attempt to avoid a rule, problem, etc. • They tried to ***make/do an end run around*** the law but they failed.

end table *noun, pl* ~ **tables** [*count*] *US* **:** a small table next to a sofa or chair — see picture at LIVING ROOM

en·dur·ance /ɪnˈdərəns, *Brit* ɪnˈdjʊərəns/ *noun* [*noncount*]
1 a : the ability to do something difficult for a long time • The exercise program is designed to increase both strength and *endurance*. • a test of *endurance* = an *endurance* test [=a task that tests your ability to do something difficult for a long time] • *endurance* training **b :** the ability to deal with pain or suffering that continues for a long time • The overseas flight tested our (powers of) *endurance*. • children who are teased ***beyond endurance*** [=for such a long time or to such a great degree that they can no longer deal with it]
2 : the quality of continuing for a long time • We need to assure the *endurance* [=*survival*] of this tradition.

en·dure /ɪnˈdɚ, *Brit* ɪnˈdjʊə/ *verb* **-dures; -dured; -dur·ing**
1 [*no obj*] **:** to continue to exist in the same state or condition • This tradition has *endured* [=*lasted*] for centuries. • She wants to make sure her legacy will *endure*.
2 [+ *obj*] **a :** to experience (pain or suffering) for a long time • The refugees have *endured* [=*suffered*] more hardship than most people can imagine. • He *endured* five years as a prisoner of war. **b :** to deal with or accept (something unpleasant) • We *endured* the lecture for as long as we could. — often used in negative statements • I cannot *endure* [=(more commonly) *stand*] the sound of her voice. • I refuse to *endure* [=(more commonly) *put up with, stand for*] such behavior any longer.
– en·dur·able /ɪnˈdərəbəl, *Brit* ɪnˈdjʊərəbəl/ *adj* • Such behavior is no longer *endurable*. [=it is unendurable] **– enduring** *adj* • *enduring* [=*lasting*] friendships • an *enduring* tradition/legacy **– en·dur·ing·ly** *adv* • an *enduringly* popular tradition

end user *noun, pl* ~ **users** [*count*] **:** the person who will eventually use a product • Programmers should always keep the *end user* in mind when designing a new piece of software.

end zone *noun, pl* ~ **zones** [*count*] **:** the area beyond the goal line at each end of the field in American football

en·e·ma /ˈɛnəmə/ *noun, pl* **-mas** [*count*] *medical* **:** a procedure in which liquid is forced into the intestines through the anus in order to make solid waste pass from the body • The nurse gave the patient an *enema*.; *also* **:** the liquid that is used for an enema

en·e·my /ˈɛnəmi/ *noun, pl* **-mies** [*count*]
1 : someone who hates another **:** someone who attacks or tries to harm another • They are sworn/bitter *enemies*. • He made a lot of *enemies* during the course of his career. ✧ If you are ***your own worst enemy*** you act in a way that causes harm to yourself or to the people or things that you care about.
2 : something that harms or threatens someone or something • Tradition is the *enemy* of progress. • In many countries today, drug abuse is ***public enemy number one***. [=the most dangerous threat to society]
3 a : a group of people (such as a nation) against whom another group is fighting a war — usually singular • Some of the soldiers went over to the *enemy*. • He found himself behind *enemy* lines. • The plane was shot down by *enemy* fire. **b :** a military force, a ship, or a person belonging to the other side in a war — usually singular • They targeted the *enemy* at close range.

en·er·get·ic /ˌɛnɚˈʤɛtɪk/ *adj* [*more* ~; *most* ~]
1 : having or showing a lot of energy • She has an *energetic* personality. • The children are *energetic* workers.
2 : involving a lot of effort • They mounted an *energetic* campaign.
– en·er·get·i·cal·ly /ˌɛnɚˈʤɛtɪkli/ *adv* [*more* ~; *most* ~] • They were working *energetically*.

en·er·gize *also Brit* **en·er·gise** /ˈɛnɚˌʤaɪz/ *verb* **-giz·es;**

-**gized**; -**giz·ing** [+ *obj*] **:** to give energy or excitement to (someone or something) ▪ His rousing speech *energized* the crowd. ▪ You'll feel more *energized* after a bit of exercise.
– **en·er·giz·er** *also Brit* **en·er·gis·er** *noun, pl* -**ers** [*count*]
– **energizing** *also Brit* **energising** *adj* [*more* ~; *most* ~] ▪ Our vacation was a very *energizing* experience.

en·er·gy /ˈɛnɚʤi/ *noun, pl* -**gies**
1 : ability to be active **:** the physical or mental strength that allows you to do things [*noncount*] The kids are always so full of *energy*. ▪ They devoted all their *energy* to the completion of the project. ▪ I have a lot of ***nervous energy***. [=energy that comes from being nervous] [*plural*] They devoted all their *energies* to the completion of the project.
2 [*noncount*] **:** natural enthusiasm and effort ▪ She puts a lot of *energy* into her work.
3 [*noncount*] **:** usable power that comes from heat, electricity, etc. ▪ The newer appliances conserve more *energy*. ▪ an *energy* crisis ▪ renewable *energy* — see also NUCLEAR ENERGY
4 *technical* **:** the ability of something (such as heat, light, or running water) to be active or do work [*noncount*] kinetic *energy* [*plural*] particles with high kinetic *energies*
5 [*noncount*] *informal* **:** a type of power that some people believe a person or place produces ▪ I sense a lot of ***negative/bad energy*** coming from her right now. ▪ There's ***good/positive energy*** in this room.

en·er·vate /ˈɛnɚˌveɪt/ *verb* -**vates**; -**vat·ed**; -**vat·ing** [+ *obj*] *formal* **:** to make (someone or something) very weak or tired — usually used as *(be) enervated* ▪ The government *was enervated* by corruption.
– **enervating** *adj* [*more* ~; *most* ~] ▪ The heat was *enervating*. – **en·er·va·tion** /ˌɛnɚˈveɪʃən/ *noun* [*noncount*]

en·fant ter·ri·ble /ˌɑːnˌfɑːntɛˈriːblə/ *noun, pl* **en·fants ter·ri·bles** /ˌɑːnˌfɑːntɛˈriːblə/ [*count*] *formal* **:** a young and successful person who is sometimes shocking and does things in a way that is very different from normal ▪ He is the *enfant terrible* [=*bad boy*] of daytime television.

en·fee·bled /ɪnˈfiːbəld/ *adj* [*more* ~; *most* ~] *formal* **:** made very weak or tired ▪ They took measures to stabilize the *enfeebled* economy. ▪ a patient *enfeebled* by illness
– **en·fee·ble·ment** /ɪnˈfiːbəlmənt/ *noun* [*noncount*]

en·fold /ɪnˈfoʊld/ *verb* -**folds**; -**fold·ed**; -**fold·ing** [+ *obj*] *formal*
1 : to cover (someone or something) completely ▪ The dish is made of vegetables *enfolded* in a pastry crust. ▪ We watched as darkness *enfolded* the city.
2 : to hold (someone or something) *in* your arms ▪ He *enfolded* the child *in* his arms. [=he hugged the child]

en·force /ɪnˈfoɚs/ *verb* -**forc·es**; -**forced**; -**forc·ing** [+ *obj*]
1 : to make (a law, rule, etc.) active or effective **:** to make sure that people do what is required by (a law, rule, etc.) ▪ Police will be *enforcing* the parking ban. ▪ *enforce* a contract
2 : to make (something) happen **:** to force or cause (something) ▪ trying to *enforce* obedience/cooperation
– **en·force·able** /ɪnˈfoɚsəbəl/ *adj* [*more* ~; *most* ~] ▪ This is not an *enforceable* contract. – **en·force·ment** /ɪnˈfoɚsmənt/ *noun* [*noncount*] ▪ the *enforcement* of the treaty ▪ She works in ***law enforcement***. [=she works for the police]
– **en·forc·er** /ɪnˈfoɚsɚ/ *noun, pl* -**ers** [*count*] ▪ law *enforcers* [=police officers]

en·fran·chise /ɪnˈfrænˌʧaɪz/ *verb* -**chis·es**; -**chised**; -**chis·ing** [+ *obj*] *formal* **:** to give (someone) the legal right to vote ▪ newly *enfranchised* voters — opposite DISENFRANCHISE
– **en·fran·chise·ment** /ɪnˈfrænˌʧaɪzmənt/ *noun* [*noncount*] ▪ She was a leader in the movement for the *enfranchisement* of women in the early 20th century.

Eng. *abbr* English

en·gage /ɪnˈgeɪʤ/ *verb* -**gag·es**; -**gaged**; -**gag·ing**
1 [+ *obj*] *formal* **:** to hire (someone) to perform a particular service ▪ He was *engaged* as a tutor. **:** to pay for (help, services, etc.) ▪ I suggest you *engage* the services of a lawyer. [=I suggest you hire a lawyer]
2 [+ *obj*] **:** to get and keep (someone's attention, interest, etc.) ▪ He sure can *engage* an audience. ▪ The story *engaged* my interest.
3 : to start fighting against (an opponent) [+ *obj*] The troops prepared to *engage* the enemy. [*no obj*] (*formal*) ▪ The troops prepared to *engage* with the enemy. — opposite DISENGAGE
4 : to move (a mechanism or part of a machine) so that it fits into another part [+ *obj*] He *engaged* the clutch and drove away. [*no obj*] As I released the clutch, the gears *engaged*. — opposite DISENGAGE

engage in [*phrasal verb*] **1** ***engage in (something)*** **:** to do (something) ▪ At college she *engaged in* various sports. ▪ We don't *engage in* that sort of behavior. **2** ***engage (someone) in (something)*** **:** to cause (someone) to take part in (something) ▪ She *engaged* him *in* conversation. [=she started a conversation with him]

engage with [*phrasal verb*] ***engage with (someone or something)*** *formal* **:** to give serious attention to (someone or something) ▪ The book fails to *engage with* the problems of our time. **:** to become involved with (someone or something) ▪ a teacher who will not *engage with* the students

en·gaged /ɪnˈgeɪʤd/ *adj*
1 : promised to be married ▪ They recently got *engaged* (to be married). ▪ She's *engaged* to him. ▪ an *engaged* couple
2 : busy with some activity ▪ (*US*) He is *engaged* in research. = (*Brit*) He is *engaged* on research. ▪ He won't be able to attend because he's ***otherwise engaged***. [=he is busy doing something else]
3 a *chiefly Brit, of a telephone or telephone line* **:** being used ▪ The line is still *engaged*. [=(*US*) *busy*] ▪ I keep getting the ***engaged tone***. [=(*US*) *busy signal*] **b** *Brit, of a public toilet* **:** being used ▪ Is the bathroom *engaged*? [=(*US*) *occupied*]

en·gage·ment /ɪnˈgeɪʤmənt/ *noun, pl* -**ments**
1 [*count*] **:** an agreement to be married **:** the act of becoming engaged or the state of being engaged to be married ▪ The couple recently announced their *engagement*. ▪ She surprised everyone by breaking off her yearlong *engagement*. — often used before another noun ▪ We're invited to their *engagement* party. ▪ an *engagement* ring
2 [*count*] **a :** a promise to meet or be present at a particular place and time ▪ He was forced to decline due to a previous *engagement*. [=*commitment, appointment*] ▪ We have a dinner *engagement* this weekend. **b :** a job as a performer ▪ She's been offered several speaking *engagements*.
3 : the act or state of being involved with something **:** INVOLVEMENT [*singular*] his lifelong *engagement* with politics [*noncount*] a lack of emotional *engagement*
4 : a fight between military forces [*count*] a naval *engagement* [*noncount*] the rules of *engagement*
5 [*noncount*] *formal* **:** the act of hiring someone to do work or to perform a service ▪ *engagement* of a lawyer
6 [*noncount*] **:** the act or result of moving a mechanism or part of a machine so that it fits into another part ▪ *engagement* of the gears/clutch

engaging *adj* [*more* ~; *most* ~] **:** very attractive or pleasing in a way that holds your attention ▪ an *engaging* smile ▪ a very *engaging* story
– **en·gag·ing·ly** *adv* ▪ an *engagingly* sweet song

en·gen·der /ɪnˈʤɛndɚ/ *verb* -**ders**; -**dered**; -**der·ing** [+ *obj*] *formal* **:** to be the source or cause of (something) ▪ The issue has *engendered* a considerable amount of debate.

en·gine /ˈɛnʤən/ *noun, pl* -**gines** [*count*]
1 : a machine that changes energy (such as heat from burning fuel) into mechanical motion ▪ The car has a four-cylinder *engine*. ▪ jet/diesel *engines*
2 : the vehicle that pulls a train **:** LOCOMOTIVE
3 *formal + literary* **a :** something that is used for a particular purpose ▪ tanks, planes, and other *engines* of war/destruction **b :** something that produces a particular and usually desirable result ▪ The tax cut could be an *engine* of economic growth.
— see also FIRE ENGINE, SEARCH ENGINE

¹en·gi·neer /ˌɛnʤəˈniɚ/ *noun, pl* -**neers** [*count*]
1 : a person who has scientific training and who designs and builds complicated products, machines, systems, or structures **:** a person who specializes in a branch of engineering ▪ Design *engineers* are working on ways to make the cars run more efficiently. ▪ a mechanical/civil/electrical *engineer* ▪ a software *engineer*
2 a : a person who runs or is in charge of an engine in an airplane, a ship, etc. ▪ a flight *engineer* **b** *US* **:** a person who runs a train ▪ The *engineer* stopped the train. **c** *Brit* **:** a person who is trained to repair electrical or mechanical equipment ▪ The telephone *engineer* [=(*US*) *repairman*] soon got my phone working again.
3 : a soldier who builds roads, bridges, etc. ▪ Army *engineers* were called in to construct the canal.

²engineer *verb* -**neers**; -**neered**; -**neer·ing** [+ *obj*]
1 : to plan, build, or manage (something) by using scientific methods — usually used as *(be) engineered* ▪ The system *is engineered* [=*designed*] for maximum efficiency. ▪ a well-*engineered* highway ▪ *engineered* materials

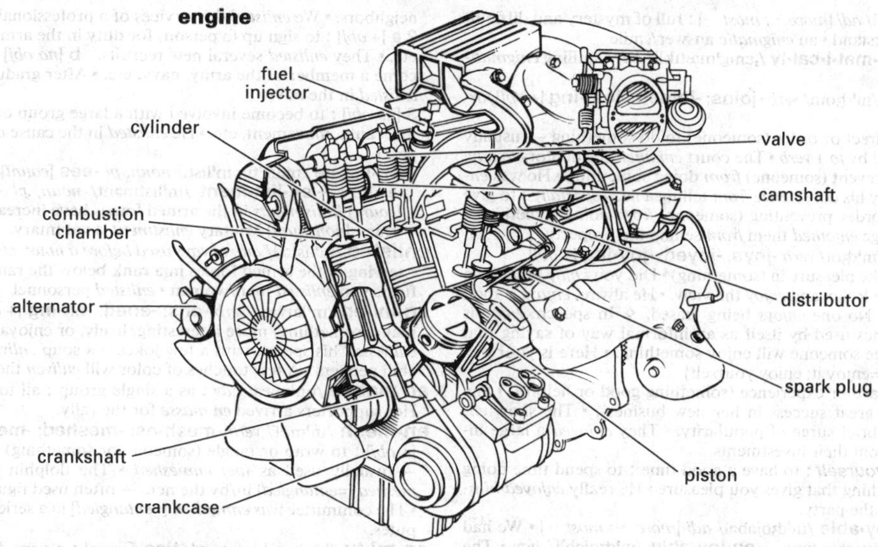

2 : to produce or plan (something) especially in a clever and skillful way • a brilliantly *engineered* [=*crafted*] plan • She managed to *engineer* [=*finagle*] a deal. • The rebels *engineered* a successful attack.
3 *technical* : to change the genetic structure of (a plant or animal) — usually used as *(be) engineered* • These soybeans *were engineered* for greater yield. • genetically *engineered* crops

engineering /ˌɛnʤəˈnirɪŋ/ *noun [noncount]*
1 : the work of designing and creating large structures (such as roads and bridges) or new products or systems by using scientific methods • She studied mechanical/civil/chemical *engineering*. • software *engineering* • This control panel is a good example of smart *engineering*.
2 : the control or direction of something (such as behavior) • social *engineering* — see also GENETIC ENGINEERING

[1]En·glish /ˈɪŋglɪʃ/ *adj*
1 : of or relating to England or its people • an *English* town/poet/garden • *English* customs
2 : of or relating to the chief language of Great Britain, the U.S., etc. • They're studying *English* grammar. • the *English* language • an *English* dictionary

[2]English *noun*
1 *[noncount]* **a** : the chief language of Great Britain, the U.S., and many areas now or formerly under British control • Do you speak *English*? • the grammar of *English* **b** : a particular type of English • American/British/Indian/Irish *English* **c** : English language, literature, or writing as a subject of study • I teach high-school *English*.
2 ***the English*** : the people of England • *The English* traditionally have afternoon tea.
3 *[noncount]* : normal English that is not difficult to understand • I asked the doctor to give me my diagnosis in *English*, not medical jargon. — often used in the phrase ***in plain English*** • She's good at explaining difficult scientific concepts *in plain English*. • The contract is written *in plain English*.

English breakfast *noun, pl* **~ -fasts** *[count] chiefly Brit* : a large breakfast that usually includes eggs, meat, toast, and coffee or tea — compare CONTINENTAL BREAKFAST

English horn *noun, pl* **~ horns** *[count] chiefly US* : a musical instrument that is similar to the oboe but lower in pitch — called also *(Brit) cor anglais*

English ivy *noun, pl* **~ ivies** *[count, noncount] US* : IVY

En·glish·man /ˈɪŋglɪʃmən/ *noun, pl* **-men** /-mən/ *[count]* : an English man

English muffin *noun, pl* **~ -fins** *[count] US* : a type of flat, round bread that is split and toasted just before it is eaten • We had coffee and *English muffins* for breakfast. — see picture at BAKING

En·glish·wom·an /ˈɪŋglɪʃˌwʊmən/ *noun, pl* **-wom·en** /-ˌwɪmən/ *[count]* : an English woman

en·gorged /ɪnˈgoɚʤd/ *adj [more ~; most ~]* : swollen and filled completely with a liquid (such as blood) • *engorged* tissue
— en·gorge·ment /ɪnˈgoɚʤmənt/ *noun [noncount]*

en·grave /ɪnˈgreɪv/ *verb* **-graves; -graved; -grav·ing** *[+ obj]* : to cut or carve lines, letters, designs, etc., onto or into a hard surface • They will *engrave* your initials on the ring for free. • She had the ring *engraved* with her initials. • The image was *engraved* on the plaque. — often used figuratively • That incident was *engraved* in my memory. = That incident *engraved* itself on my memory. [=I will never forget that incident]
— engraved *adj* • *engraved* wedding invitations [=wedding invitations that are printed from a surface that has letters, designs, etc., engraved into it] **— en·grav·er** *noun, pl* **-ers** *[count]* • He is a skillful *engraver*.

engraving *noun, pl* **-ings**
1 *[noncount]* : the art of cutting something into the surface of wood, stone, or metal • She studied *engraving* in an art class.
2 *[count]* : a picture made from an engraved surface • a wood *engraving*

en·gross /ɪnˈgrous/ *verb* **-gross·es; -grossed; -gross·ing** *[+ obj]* : to hold the complete interest or attention of (someone) — usually used as *(be/get) engrossed* • She *gets* completely *engrossed* in her work. • They *were engrossed* in conversation.
— engrossing *adj [more ~; most ~]* • The book explains the sequence of events in *engrossing* detail. • an *engrossing* story/account/study

en·gulf /ɪnˈgʌlf/ *verb* **-gulfs; -gulfed; -gulf·ing** *[+ obj]* : to flow over and cover (someone or something) • The valley was *engulfed* in a thick fog. • Flames *engulfed* the building. — often used figuratively • The city threatens to *engulf* the nearby suburbs. • The entire country has been *engulfed* by chaos/crisis/violence. • He found himself *engulfed* by fear.

en·hance /ɪnˈhæns, *Brit* ɪnˈhɑːns/ *verb* **-hanc·es; -hanced; -hanc·ing** *[+ obj]* : to increase or improve (something) • You can *enhance* the flavor of the dish by using fresh herbs. • The image has been digitally *enhanced* to show more detail. • The company is looking to *enhance* its earnings potential. • drugs that *enhance* [=*improve*] performance = performance-*enhancing* drugs
— enhanced *adj* • The new version includes many *enhanced* features. • She approached the meeting with an *enhanced* understanding of the issues. **— en·hance·ment** /ɪnˈhænsmənt, *Brit* ɪnˈhɑːnsmənt/ *noun, pl* **-ments** *[noncount]* techniques for color *enhancement* *[count]* software *enhancements* **— en·hanc·er** *noun, pl* **-ers** *[count]* • flavor *enhancers*

enig·ma /ɪˈnɪgmə/ *noun, pl* **-mas** *[count]* : someone or something that is difficult to understand or explain • To his friends, he was always something of an *enigma*. • one of the great *enigmas* of our time

en·ig·mat·ic /ˌɛnɪgˈmætɪk/ *also* **en·ig·mat·i·cal** /ˌɛnɪg-

ˈmætɪkəl/ *adj [more ~; most ~]* **: full of mystery and difficult to understand** ▪ an *enigmatic* answer/smile
— **en·ig·mat·i·cal·ly** /ˌɛnɪgˈmætɪkli/ *adv* ▪ smiling *enigmatically*

en·join /ɪnˈʤoɪn/ *verb* **-joins; -joined; -join·ing** *[+ obj] formal*
1 : to direct or order (someone) to do something — usually followed by *to + verb* ▪ The court *enjoined* the debtors *to pay.*
2 : to prevent (someone) *from* **doing something** ▪ He was *enjoined* by his conscience *from* telling a lie.; *especially* **: to give a legal order preventing (someone)** *from* **doing something** ▪ The judge *enjoined* them *from* selling the property.

en·joy /ɪnˈʤoɪ/ *verb* **-joys; -joyed; -joy·ing** *[+ obj]*
1 : to take pleasure in (something) ▪ Did you *enjoy* [=*like*] the movie? ▪ Relax and *enjoy* the view. ▪ He always *enjoys* a good laugh. ▪ No one *enjoys* being teased. ✧ **In speech,** ***enjoy*** **is sometimes used by itself as an informal way of saying that you hope someone will enjoy something.** ▪ Here is your pie. *Enjoy*! [=enjoy it; enjoy yourself]
2 : to have or experience (something good or helpful) ▪ She *enjoyed* great success in her new business. ▪ The show *enjoyed* a brief surge of popularity. ▪ They *enjoyed* a large income from their investments.
enjoy yourself **: to have a good time : to spend time doing something that gives you pleasure** ▪ He really *enjoyed himself* at the party.
— **en·joy·able** /ɪnˈʤojəbəl/ *adj [more ~; most ~]* ▪ We had an *enjoyable* time. — **en·joy·ably** /ɪnˈʤojəbli/ *adv* ▪ The book is *enjoyably* silly.

en·joy·ment /ɪnˈʤoɪmənt/ *noun*
1 *[noncount]* **: a feeling of pleasure caused by doing or experiencing something you like** ▪ She always found sports to be a source of great *enjoyment.* ▪ I read the book strictly for my own *enjoyment.*
2 *[noncount]* **: the condition of having and using something that is good, pleasant, etc.** ▪ the *enjoyment* of good health ▪ This is land set aside for the public's *enjoyment.*
3 ***enjoyments*** *[plural]* **: things that give you pleasure** ▪ life's simple *enjoyments* [=(more commonly) *pleasures*]

en·large /ɪnˈlɑɚʤ/ *verb* **-larg·es; -larged; -larg·ing : to make (something) larger or to become larger** *[+ obj]* We had the photograph *enlarged.* ▪ The company is in the process of *enlarging* [=*expanding*] its offices. *[no obj]* The glands *enlarge* [=*swell*] when you have an infection.
enlarge on/upon *[phrasal verb]* ***enlarge on/upon (something) formal*** **: to give more information about (something)** ▪ Would you kindly *enlarge* [=*elaborate*] *on* that point?
— **en·larg·er** *noun, pl* **-ers** *[count]* ▪ a photo *enlarger*

en·large·ment /ɪnˈlɑɚʤmənt/ *noun, pl* **-ments**
1 : the act of making something larger or of becoming larger *[noncount]* Symptoms include *enlargement* of the lymph nodes. *[count]* The plans call for an *enlargement* of the company's offices.
2 *[count]* **: a larger copy of a photograph** ▪ I ordered several *enlargements.*

en·light·en /ɪnˈlaɪtn̩/ *verb* **-ens; -ened; -en·ing** *[+ obj]* **: to give knowledge or understanding to (someone) : to explain something to (someone)** ▪ I don't understand what's going on; can someone please *enlighten* me?
— **enlightening** *adj [more ~; most ~]* ▪ We found the talk very *enlightening.* [=*informative*]

enlightened *adj [more ~; most ~]* **: having or showing a good understanding of how people should be treated : not ignorant or narrow in thinking** ▪ an *enlightened* people/attitude/society ▪ an *enlightened* approach to prison reform

en·light·en·ment /ɪnˈlaɪtn̩mənt/ *noun [noncount]*
1 : the state of having knowledge or understanding ▪ the search for spiritual *enlightenment* ▪ His comments failed to provide *enlightenment.* **: the act of giving someone knowledge or understanding** ▪ the *enlightenment* of the public through education
2 ***the Enlightenment*** **: a movement of the 18th century that stressed the belief that science and logic give people more knowledge and understanding than tradition and religion**
3 *Buddhism* **: a final spiritual state marked by the absence of desire or suffering**

en·list /ɪnˈlɪst/ *verb* **-lists; -list·ed; -list·ing**
1 *[+ obj]* **a : to get the support and help of (someone or something)** ▪ They're *enlisting* volunteers for an experiment. ▪ We *enlisted* all available resources. **b : to get (help, support, sympathy, etc.) from someone** ▪ I *enlisted* the help of our neighbors. ▪ We *enlisted* the services of a professional.
2 a *[+ obj]* **: to sign up (a person) for duty in the army, navy, etc.** ▪ They *enlisted* several new recruits. **b** *[no obj]* **: to become a member of the army, navy, etc.** ▪ After graduating, I *enlisted* in the navy.
3 *[no obj]* **: to become involved with a large group of people in a cause, movement, etc.** ▪ He *enlisted* in the cause of world peace.
— **en·list·ee** /ɪnˌlɪsˈtiː, ɪnˈlɪsti/ *noun, pl* **-ees** *[count]* ▪ Army *enlistees* — **en·list·ment** /ɪnˈlɪstmənt/ *noun, pl* **-ments** *[count] Enlistments* in the armed forces have increased this year. *[noncount]* Military *enlistment* is voluntary.

enlisted /ɪnˈlɪstəd/ *adj, always used before a noun, chiefly US* **: serving in the armed forces in a rank below the rank of officers** ▪ an *enlisted* man/woman ▪ *enlisted* personnel

en·liv·en /ɪnˈlaɪvən/ *verb* **-ens; -ened; -en·ing** *[+ obj]* **: to make (something) more interesting, lively, or enjoyable** ▪ He *enlivened* his speech with a few jokes. ▪ a soup *enlivened* by chili peppers ▪ A few touches of color will *enliven* the room.

en masse /ɑnˈmæs/ *adv* **: as a single group : all together** ▪ Her supporters arrived *en masse* for the rally.

en·mesh /ɪnˈmɛʃ/ *verb* **-mesh·es; -meshed; -mesh·ing** *[+ obj]* **: to wrap or tangle (someone or something) in a net — usually used as** *(be) enmeshed* ▪ The dolphin *was enmeshed* [=*entangled*] in/by the net. **— often used figuratively** ▪ The committee *was enmeshed* [=*entangled*] in a series of disputes.

en·mi·ty /ˈɛnməti/ *noun, pl* **-ties** *formal* **: a very deep unfriendly feeling** *[noncount]* There's a long history of *enmity* between them. ▪ His comments earned him the *enmity* of his coworkers. *[count]* We need to put aside old *enmities* for the sake of peace.

en·no·ble /ɪˈnoʊbəl/ *verb* **-no·bles; -no·bled; -no·bling** *[+ obj] formal*
1 : to make (someone or something) better or more worthy of admiration ▪ a life *ennobled* by suffering ▪ Her skill and talent *ennoble* her profession.
2 : to make (someone) a member of the nobility ▪ He was *ennobled* by the queen.
— **en·no·ble·ment** /ɪˈnoʊbəlmənt/ *noun [noncount]*
— **ennobling** *adj [more ~; most ~]* ▪ Volunteering is an *ennobling* experience.

en·nui /ˌɑːnˈwiː/ *noun [noncount]* **: a lack of spirit, enthusiasm, or interest** ▪ He suffered from a general sense of *ennui.* [=*boredom*]

enor·mi·ty /ɪˈnoɚməti/ *noun, pl* **-ties**
1 *[count] formal* **: a shocking, evil, or immoral act — usually plural** ▪ the *enormities* of war
2 *[noncount]* **: great evil or wickedness** ▪ We were shocked at the *enormity* of the crime.
3 *[noncount]* **a : great size** ▪ I was overwhelmed by the *enormity* [=*immensity*] of the task at hand. **b : great importance** ▪ They didn't fully grasp the *enormity* of their decision. ✧ **Although senses 3a and b are sometimes criticized, they are commonly used.**

enor·mous /ɪˈnoɚməs/ *adj [more ~; most ~]* **: very great in size or amount** ▪ They live in an *enormous* house. ▪ We chose not to undertake the project because of the *enormous* costs involved. ▪ He enjoys *enormous* popularity.
— **enor·mous·ly** *adv* ▪ Their new album is *enormously* popular. ▪ He enjoyed himself *enormously.* [=very much]
— **enor·mous·ness** *noun [noncount]* ▪ the *enormousness* of the house

¹enough /ɪˈnʌf/ *adj* **: equal to what is needed** ▪ Have you got *enough* money? ▪ That's *enough* talk for now; let's get started. ▪ There's *enough* food for everyone. ▪ There's *enough* room for five people. = There's room *enough* for five people.

²enough *adv, always used after an adjective, adverb, or verb*
1 : in the amount needed : to the necessary degree ▪ I couldn't run fast *enough* to catch up with her. ▪ She's old *enough* to know better. ▪ Are you rich *enough* to retire? ▪ That's good *enough* for me. ▪ Oddly/curiously/strangely/amazingly/surprisingly *enough*, they've never actually met. ▪ As if the crowds aren't bad *enough*, the parking situation is terrible. ▪ You're always ready *enough* [=always very or too ready] to blame someone else for your mistakes. ▪ I was happy/willing *enough* [=I was happy/willing] to go along with his plan. ▪ We can do it if they help *enough.*
2 : to a degree that is not very high or very low : to a reasonable extent ▪ He sings well *enough.* [=he sings fairly well] ▪ The solution seems simple *enough.* [=the solution seems fairly simple]

fair enough see [1]FAIR
sure enough see [2]SURE

[3]**enough** *pronoun* [*noncount*] : an amount that provides what is needed or wanted : an amount that is enough • There's *enough* for everyone. • Have you had *enough* to eat? • He hasn't had much Spanish, but he knows *enough* to get by. • The crowds are *enough* of a problem as it is, without having to worry about parking as well! • It's *enough* to drive you crazy! • I've had (more than) *enough* of their foolishness. [=I'm sick of their foolishness] • That's *enough*, young lady! [=stop behaving or talking in that way]

enough is enough — used to say that you want something to stop because you can no longer accept or deal with it • I don't mind loaning her a bit of money now and then, but *enough is enough*!

enough said *informal* — used in speech to say that you understand what someone is telling you and no further information is needed • "Is he in good condition?" "Well, he ran in the Boston Marathon last month." "*Enough said*."

enquire, enquiring, enquiry *chiefly Brit spellings of* INQUIRE, INQUIRING, INQUIRY

en•rage /ɪnˈreɪʤ/ *verb* **-rag•es; -raged; -rag•ing** [+ *obj*] : to make (someone) very angry : to fill (someone) with rage • His thoughtless behavior *enraged* us. • People were *enraged* by/at/over the decision.

en•rap•ture /ɪnˈræpʧɚ/ *verb* **-tures; -tured; -tur•ing** [+ *obj*] *formal* : to fill (someone) with delight • Her melodious voice *enraptured* the audience. — usually used as *(be) enraptured* • The children *were enraptured* by his stories.

en•rich /ɪnˈrɪʧ/ *verb* **-rich•es; -riched; -rich•ing** [+ *obj*]
1 : to make (someone) rich or richer • They tried to *enrich* themselves at the expense of the poor.
2 : to improve the quality of (something) : to make (something) better • Their lives were *enriched* by the experience. = It was a life-*enriching* experience for them. • Their research has *enriched* [=*improved*] our understanding of the problem. • How can I *enrich* my vocabulary?
3 : to improve the usefulness or quality of (something) by adding something to it • He used manure to *enrich* the soil. • The drink is *enriched* with vitamin C. • *enriched* flour
– en•rich•ment /ɪnˈrɪʧmənt/ *noun* [*noncount*] • after-school *enrichment* programs • uranium *enrichment*

en•roll *(US) or chiefly Brit* **en•rol** /ɪnˈroʊl/ *verb* **-rolls; -rolled; -roll•ing**
1 [+ *obj*] **:** to enter (someone) as a member of or participant in something — usually + *in* • They *enrolled* their children *in* a private school. • He *enrolled* himself *in* a weight-loss program. [=he joined a weight-loss program]
2 a [+ *obj*] **:** to take (someone) as a member or participant • The college *enrolls* about 25,000 students. • They *enrolled* several volunteers for the study. **b** [*no obj*] **:** to become a member or participant — usually + *in* • After graduating from high school he *enrolled in* the army. • We *enrolled in* the history course.
– en•roll•ment *(US) or chiefly Brit* **en•rol•ment** /ɪnˈroʊlmənt/ *noun, pl* **-ments** [*noncount*] the *enrollment* of volunteers • School *enrollment* is up this year. [*count*] School *enrollments* are up this year.

en route /ɑnˈruːt/ *adv* **:** on or along the way when you are going to a place • We stopped to eat *en route* to the museum.
– en route *adj* • They arrived early despite several *en route* delays.

en•sconce /ɪnˈskɑːns/ *verb* **-sconc•es; -sconced; -sconc•ing** [+ *obj*] **:** to firmly place or hide (someone or something) • The sculpture is safely *ensconced* behind glass. • He *ensconced* himself in front of the television. • She's already *ensconced* in her new job. [=she is comfortably settled into her new job]

en•sem•ble /ɑnˈsɑːmbəl/ *noun, pl* **-sem•bles** [*count*] **:** a group of people or things that make up a complete unit (such as a musical group, a group of actors or dancers, or a set of clothes) • We went to listen to a new jazz *ensemble*. • She wore an elegant three-piece *ensemble*. • The actor performed an *ensemble* piece.

en•shrine /ɪnˈʃraɪn/ *verb* **-shrines; -shrined; -shrin•ing** [+ *obj*] *formal* **:** to remember and protect (someone or something that is valuable, admired, etc.) — usually used as *(be) enshrined* • The artifacts *are* now safely *enshrined* in a museum. • great players *enshrined* in the Hall of Fame • These rights *are enshrined* in the U.S. Constitution.

en•shroud /ɪnˈʃraʊd/ *verb* **-shrouds; -shroud•ed; -shroud•ing** [+ *obj*] *formal* **:** to cover (something or someone) in a way that makes seeing or understanding difficult • The details of his life are *enshrouded* [=(more commonly) *shrouded*] in mystery. • Darkness *enshrouded* the earth.

en•sign /ˈɛnsən, ˈɛnˌsaɪn/ *noun, pl* **-signs** [*count*]
1 : an officer of the lowest rank in the U.S. Navy
2 : a flag that is flown on a ship to show what country the ship belongs to

en•slave /ɪnˈsleɪv/ *verb* **-slaves; -slaved; -slav•ing** [+ *obj*] **:** to make (someone) a slave — usually used as *(be) enslaved* • Her ancestors *were enslaved* during the war. — sometimes used figuratively • She felt like she *was enslaved* in a loveless marriage.
– en•slave•ment /ɪnˈsleɪvmənt/ *noun* [*noncount*] **– en•slav•er** *noun, pl* **-ers** [*count*]

en•snare /ɪnˈsneɚ/ *verb* **-snares; -snared; -snar•ing** [+ *obj*] **:** to catch (an animal or person) in a trap or in a place from which there is no escape • The animals got *ensnared* in the net. • The police successfully *ensnared* the burglar. — often used figuratively • He was *ensnared* [=*trapped, caught*] in/by his own web of lies. • The project became hopelessly *ensnared* [=*entangled*] in red tape.

en•sue /ɪnˈsuː, *Brit* ɪnˈsjuː/ *verb* **-sues; -sued; -su•ing** [*no obj*] **:** to come at a later time : to happen as a result • When the news broke, a long period of chaos *ensued*. [=*followed*]
– ensuing *adj* • In the *ensuing* weeks, [=in the weeks afterward] her health gradually improved.

en suite /ɑnˈswiːt/ *adj or adv* — used to describe a bedroom to which a bathroom is directly connected or a bathroom that is directly connected to a bedroom • an *en suite* bedroom/bathroom • The bathroom is *en suite*.

en•sure /ɪnˈʃuɚ/ *verb* **-sures; -sured; -sur•ing** [+ *obj*] **:** to make (something) sure, certain, or safe • They took steps to *ensure* the safety of the passengers. • We want to *ensure* [=make certain/sure] that it doesn't happen again.

en•tail /ɪnˈteɪl/ *verb* **-tails; -tailed; -tail•ing** [+ *obj*] **:** to have (something) as a part, step, or result • I'll need to know a little more about what the job *entails*. [=*involves*] • The procedure does *entail* [=*carry*] certain risks. • He accepted the responsibility, with all that it *entails*.

en•tan•gle /ɪnˈtæŋgəl/ *verb* **-tan•gles; -tan•gled; -tan•gling** [+ *obj*]
1 : to cause (something) to get caught *in* or twisted *with* something else : TANGLE — usually used as *(be/get) entangled* • The kite *got entangled in* the tree. • She tried to get up, but her foot *was entangled in* the strap. • The birds fly into the net and become *entangled*.
2 : to get (someone) involved in a confusing or difficult situation — usually used as *(be/get) entangled* • They *were entangled* in a messy lawsuit. • He *was/got* romantically *entangled* with the girl next door.
– en•tan•gle•ment /ɪnˈtæŋgəlmənt/ *noun, pl* **-ments** [*count*] romantic/legal *entanglements* [*noncount*] the *entanglement* of his kite in the tree

en•ter /ˈɛntɚ/ *verb* **-ters; -tered; -ter•ing**
1 : to go or come into (something) [+ *obj*] Knock on the door before you *enter* the room. • The medication will quickly *enter* the blood stream. • The river *enters* the sea near here. [*no obj*] Knock before you *enter*. = Knock before *entering*. [=knock on the door before you open it to go into the room] • You may *enter* now. — opposite EXIT
2 [+ *obj*] **a :** to begin to be in (an organization, school, etc.) • Our son will be *entering* college next year. **b :** to cause (someone) to be in an organization, school, etc. • *enter* a child in kindergarten • *(Brit)* We *entered* him *for* a good school.
3 [+ *obj*] **a :** to start to do something • He was a teacher before he *entered* politics. [=before he began his political career] • He's been faced with many scandals since he ***entered office***. [=since he began his term in office] • The new battleship is scheduled to ***enter service*** next spring. **b :** to begin to be in (a particular situation, period of time, etc.) • *enter* middle age • an actor who's just now *entering* his prime • The strike has now *entered* its second week. • We've *entered* a new phase in our relationship. • The country is *entering* a period of prosperity. • *Entering* [=*at the start of*] the season, he was expected to be an important part of the team. • The word has ***entered common usage*** [=become commonly used] in recent decades. **c :** to appear for the first time in (something) • He *entered* the game in the fifth inning. • The company has several new products now *entering* the marketplace.
4 a : to officially say that you will be in a race, competition,

etc. [+ *obj*] She *entered* every race. • Several leading players have *entered* the tournament. [*no obj*] She won the race last year, but this year she decided not to *enter*. • (*Brit*) He *entered for* the tournament. **b** [+ *obj*] **:** to officially say that (someone) will be in a race, competition, etc. • Her coach *entered* her in every race. ✧ If you ***are entered*** in a race, competition, etc., you are one of the people who are competing in it. • She *was entered* in every race.

5 [+ *obj*] **a :** to include (something) in a book, list, etc. • The teacher *entered* my name on the roster. • *enter* an item in a journal • These words are not yet *entered* in the dictionary. [=they do not yet appear in the dictionary] **b :** to type in (words, data, etc.) on a computer • You need to *enter* your password in order to log on. • Please *enter* the new data in the spreadsheet.

6 [+ *obj*] **:** to make or state (something) in a formal and official way • *enter* a complaint • The defendant *entered* a guilty plea to a lesser charge of manslaughter.

enter into [*phrasal verb*] ***enter into (something)*** **1 :** to begin to be in or to take part in (something) • *enter into* a discussion • *enter into* an agreement • The two companies finally *entered into* a partnership. **2 :** to be a part of or to influence (something, such as a choice or decision) • You shouldn't allow your prejudices to *enter into* your decision. **3 :** to share or become involved in (something) • You need to ***enter into the spirit*** of the occasion.

enter on/upon [*phrasal verb*] ***enter on/upon (something)*** **:** to begin to be in or to take part in (something) • She will soon be *entering on* [=*starting*] a new career. • The country is *entering upon* a period of prosperity.

enter the picture/scene **1 :** to become involved in something • The company went through many drastic changes after its new owner *entered the scene*. **2** *or* ***enter (into) the equation*** **:** to become something that must be considered or dealt with • Once politics *enters the picture*, chances for a quick settlement are greatly reduced. • Money didn't *enter the equation* when he offered to help. [=he didn't expect to be paid for helping]

enter your mind/head **:** to occur in your thoughts • The idea of quitting never *entered my mind*. [=I never thought of quitting]

en·ter·prise /ˈɛntɚˌpraɪz/ *noun, pl* **-pris·es**

1 [*count*] **:** a project or activity that involves many people and that is often difficult • Moving the drilling rig offshore was a costly *enterprise*. • a criminal *enterprise* • Agriculture is the main economic *enterprise* among these people.

2 [*count*] **:** a business organization • When he purchased the company it was a thriving commercial *enterprise*. • The new regulations are intended to encourage the growth of small, independent *enterprises*. [=*companies*]

3 [*noncount*] **:** the ability or desire to do dangerous or difficult things or to solve problems in new ways • She showed great *enterprise* [=*initiative*] as a young reporter. • He was criticized for his lack of *enterprise* in dealing with the crisis. — see also FREE ENTERPRISE, PRIVATE ENTERPRISE

en·ter·pris·ing /ˈɛntɚˌpraɪzɪŋ/ *adj* [*more* ~; *most* ~] **:** having or showing the ability or desire to do new and difficult things • As an *enterprising* young reporter, she covered many important stories.

en·ter·tain /ˌɛntɚˈteɪn/ *verb* **-tains; -tained; -tain·ing**

1 : to have people as guests in your home or in a public place (such as a restaurant) [+ *obj*] They like to *entertain* their friends at their summer home. • Much of his job as a salesman involves *entertaining* clients. [*no obj*] They enjoy cooking and *entertaining*. [=hosting dinner parties and other social occasions]

2 a [+ *obj*] **:** to perform for (an audience) **:** to provide amusement for (someone) by singing, acting, etc. • Jugglers were on hand to *entertain* the crowd. • Our father *entertained* us with stories. **b :** to provide or be entertainment for (someone) [+ *obj*] Our father's stories *entertained* us. [*no obj*] Our father's stories never failed to *entertain*. [=his stories were always enjoyable]

3 [+ *obj*] **:** to have (a thought, idea, etc.) in your mind • She was so unhappy with her job that she *entertained* thoughts of quitting. [=she thought about quitting] • It now seems possible to *entertain* hopes [=to hope] that the strike will be settled soon.

en·ter·tain·er /ˌɛntɚˈteɪnɚ/ *noun, pl* **-ers** [*count*] **:** a person (such as a singer, an actor, or a comedian) who entertains other people **:** a professional performer • a singer regarded as one of the great *entertainers* of our time

entertaining /ˌɛntɚˈteɪnɪŋ/ *adj* [*more* ~; *most* ~] **:** amusing and enjoyable **:** providing entertainment • an *entertaining* book • an *entertaining* speaker

— **en·ter·tain·ing·ly** *adv* • She wrote an *entertainingly* honest account of her childhood.

en·ter·tain·ment /ˌɛntɚˈteɪnmənt/ *noun, pl* **-ments**

1 : amusement or pleasure that comes from watching a performer, playing a game, etc. [*noncount*] *Entertainment* was provided by jugglers. • plays, movies, and other forms of *entertainment* • They played games in the evening for *entertainment*. [*count*] plays, movies, and other *entertainments*

2 [*noncount*] **:** the act of amusing or entertaining people • They hired a band for the *entertainment* of the guests. [=to entertain the guests]

en·thrall (*chiefly US*) *or Brit* **en·thral** /ɪnˈθrɑːl/ *verb* **-thralls; -thralled; -thrall·ing** [+ *obj*] **:** to hold the attention of (someone) by being very exciting, interesting, or beautiful • The movie has *enthralled* [=*charmed, captivated*] audiences across the country. — often used as *(be) enthralled* • I *was enthralled* by/with the beauty of the landscape.

— **enthralling** *adj* [*more* ~; *most* ~] • The movie is an *enthralling* adventure story.

en·throne /ɪnˈθroʊn/ *verb* **-thrones; -throned; -thron·ing** [+ *obj*] **:** to make (someone) a king, queen, bishop, etc., in a formal ceremony — usually used as *(be) enthroned* • The archbishop *was enthroned* last year.

— **en·throne·ment** /ɪnˈθroʊnmənt/ *noun, pl* **-ments** [*count, noncount*]

en·thuse /ɪnˈθuːz, *Brit* ɪnˈθjuːz/ *verb* **-thus·es; -thused; -thus·ing**

1 a [+ *obj*] **:** to say (something) with enthusiasm • "This dinner is wonderful!" he *enthused*. **b** [*no obj*] **:** to show enthusiasm **:** to talk about something with enthusiasm — usually + *over* or *about* • She *enthused over/about* the variety of flowers in the garden.

2 [+ *obj*] **:** to make (someone) enthusiastic • His presentation failed to *enthuse* the committee.

— **enthused** *adj* [*more* ~; *most* ~] • The committee members are not *enthused* [=*enthusiastic*] about the project.

en·thu·si·asm /ɪnˈθuːziˌæzəm, *Brit* ɪnˈθjuːziˌæzəm/ *noun, pl* **-asms**

1 [*noncount*] **:** strong excitement about something **:** a strong feeling of active interest in something that you like or enjoy • The party supported its candidate with *enthusiasm*. • He seems to lack *enthusiasm* for the work he's doing.

2 [*count*] **:** something causing a feeling of excitement and active interest **:** a hobby that someone feels enthusiastic about • Among his latest *enthusiasms* are sailing and fishing.

en·thu·si·ast /ɪnˈθuːziˌæst, *Brit* ɪnˈθjuːziˌæst/ *noun, pl* **-asts** [*count*] **:** a person who feels enthusiasm for something **:** a person who enjoys something very much • a golf *enthusiast*

en·thu·si·as·tic /ɪnˌθuːziˈæstɪk, *Brit* ɪnˌθjuːziˈæstɪk/ *adj* [*more* ~; *most* ~] **:** feeling or showing strong excitement about something **:** filled with or marked by enthusiasm • They were *enthusiastic* supporters of the president. • I'm not wildly *enthusiastic* about your latest idea. • They were less than *enthusiastic*. = They were far from *enthusiastic*. • She received an *enthusiastic* welcome.

— **en·thu·si·as·ti·cal·ly** /ɪnˌθuːziˈæstɪkli, *Brit* ɪnˌθjuːziˈæstɪkli/ *adv* • They welcomed her *enthusiastically*.

en·tice /ɪnˈtaɪs/ *verb* **-tic·es; -ticed; -tic·ing** [+ *obj*] **:** to attract (someone) especially by offering or showing something that is appealing, interesting, etc. • The store hopes to *entice* [=*tempt, lure*] shoppers with attractive window displays.

— **en·tice·ment** /ɪnˈtaɪsmənt/ *noun, pl* **-ments** [*count*] The city offered the company tax breaks as an *enticement* [=*inducement*] to build a factory there. [*noncount*] using attractive displays for the *enticement* of customers

— **enticing** *adj* [*more* ~; *most* ~] • an *enticing* display of merchandise — **en·tic·ing·ly** /ɪnˈtaɪsɪŋli/ *adv* [*more* ~; *most* ~]

en·tire /ɪnˈtajɚ/ *adj* **:** complete or full **:** not lacking or leaving out any part • We spent the *entire* [=*whole*] day at the beach. • He had *entire* [=*complete, total*] control of the project. • The war affected an *entire* generation of young Americans. • the *entire* community • The fence runs along the *entire* length of the building. • She has dedicated her *entire* life to helping others. • He was listening the *entire* time. [=the whole time, all the time]

— **en·tire·ly** *adv* • The decision is *entirely* yours. • That's an *entirely* different question. = That's a different question *entirely*.

en·tire·ty /ɪnˈtajəti/ *noun* [*noncount*] **:** the whole or total amount of something • the *entirety* of an estate

in its/their entirety **:** with nothing left out • He played the song *in its entirety*. [=he played the entire song] • His comments will be broadcast *in their entirety*. [=all of his comments will be broadcast]

en·ti·tle /ɪnˈtaɪtl̩/ *verb* **-ti·tles; -ti·tled; -ti·tling** [+ *obj*]

1 : to give a title to (something, such as a book) **:** TITLE • He *entitled* his book "My Life on Mars."

2 : to give a right to (someone) — *+ to* • The card *entitles* us *to* a discount. [=we can get a discount because we have this card] — often used as *(be) entitled* • I'*m entitled to* a refund. [=I should be given a refund] • You'*re entitled to* your opinion. [=I don't agree with you, but you are free to think what you want]

en·ti·tle·ment /ɪnˈtaɪtl̩mənt/ *noun, pl* **-ments**

1 [*noncount*] **a :** the condition of having a right to have, do, or get something • my *entitlement* to a refund **b :** the feeling or belief that you deserve to be given something (such as special privileges) • celebrities who have an arrogant sense of *entitlement*

2 [*count*] *US* **:** a type of financial help provided by the government for members of a particular group • *entitlements* such as medical aid for the elderly and poor

en·ti·ty /ˈɛntəti/ *noun, pl* **-ties** [*count*] *formal* **:** something that exists by itself **:** something that is separate from other things • One division of the company was broken off as a separate *entity*. • a business/commercial/corporate *entity* • governmental/political/legal *entities* • distinct/independent *entities*

en·tomb /ɪnˈtuːm/ *verb* **-tombs; -tombed; -tomb·ing** [+ *obj*] **:** to place (someone or something) in a tomb — often used as *(be) entombed* • The remains of former kings *are entombed* there. — sometimes used figuratively • fossils *entombed* in sediment

– en·tomb·ment /ɪnˈtuːmmənt/ *noun, pl* **-ments** [*count, noncount*]

en·to·mol·o·gy /ˌɛntəˈmɑːləʤi/ *noun* [*noncount*] **:** a branch of science that deals with the study of insects

– en·to·mo·log·i·cal /ˌɛntəməˈlɑːʤɪkəl/ *adj* • *entomological* studies **– en·to·mol·o·gist** /ˌɛntəˈmɑːləʤɪst/ *noun, pl* **-gists** [*count*]

en·tou·rage /ˌɑːntʊˈrɑːʒ/ *noun, pl* **-rag·es** [*count*] **:** a group of people who go with and assist an important person • the President and his *entourage*

en·trails /ˈɛnˌtreɪlz/ *noun* [*plural*] **:** the internal organs of an animal • sheep *entrails* — sometimes used figuratively • examining the *entrails* of a computer

[1]**en·trance** /ˈɛntrəns/ *noun, pl* **-tranc·es**

1 [*count*] **:** the act of entering something • the *entrance* of the army into the city • the country's *entrance* into war • The book describes his *entrance* into politics. • The thieves gained *entrance* to/into our house by breaking a window. • She always knew how to make a grand *entrance*. • Everyone noticed when she ***made her entrance***. [=when she entered]

2 [*count*] **:** something (such as a door) that is used for entering something • The main *entrance* is on the left side. • There are two *entrances* to the park. • The ship passed through the narrow *entrance* to the bay. • a building's front/back/side/main *entrance* • a large ***entrance hall*** [=a hall located near an entrance to a building] — compare [1]EXIT 1

3 [*noncount*] **:** the right to enter something • We gained *entrance* [=*entry, admission*] to the club. • He was denied *entrance* into the country. • She applied for *entrance* at/to several colleges. — often used before another noun • a college *entrance* exam • an *entrance* fee

[2]**en·trance** /ɪnˈtræns, *Brit* ɪnˈtrɑːns/ *verb* **-tranc·es; -tranced; -tranc·ing** [+ *obj*] **:** to fill (someone) with delight and wonder — usually used as *(be) entranced* • We *were entranced* by/with the magnificent view.

– en·trance·ment /ɪnˈtrænsmənt, *Brit* ɪnˈtrɑːnsmənt/ *noun* [*noncount*] **– entrancing** *adj* [*more* ~; *most* ~] • an *entrancing* view

en·trant /ˈɛntrənt/ *noun, pl* **-trants** [*count*] **:** a person who enters something (such as a competition) • Each *entrant* had to agree to the contest rules. • new *entrants* into a highly competitive field

en·trap /ɪnˈtræp/ *verb* **-traps; -trapped; -trap·ping** [+ *obj*] *formal* **:** to catch (someone or something) in a trap or in something like a trap **:** TRAP • We used the net to *entrap* a school of fish. • The air bubbles were *entrapped* in ice. • She felt that she was *entrapped* in an unhappy marriage.

en·trap·ment /ɪnˈtræpmənt/ *noun* [*noncount*]

1 : the act of entrapping someone or something or the condition of being entrapped • her *entrapment* in an unhappy marriage

2 : the illegal act of tricking someone into committing a crime so that the person you have tricked can be arrested • His lawyer argued that he was a victim of police *entrapment*.

en·treat /ɪnˈtriːt/ *verb* **-treats; -treat·ed; -treat·ing** [+ *obj*] *formal* **:** to ask (someone) in a serious and emotional way • I *entreat* you to help me. • His parents *entreated* [=*implored, begged*] him to return to school.

en·treaty /ɪnˈtriːti/ *noun, pl* **-treat·ies** [*count*] *formal* **:** a serious request for something • The senator has resisted repeated *entreaties* [=*appeals*] to run for president. • He finally succumbed to their *entreaties*. [=he did what they asked]

en·trée *or* **en·tree** /ˈɑːnˌtreɪ/ *noun, pl* **-trées** *or* **-trees**

1 [*count*] **:** the main dish of a meal especially in a restaurant • We had steak as an *entrée*.

2 *formal* **a** [*count*] **:** the act or manner of entering something • She made a graceful *entrée* [=*entrance*] into the ballroom. • His *entrée* [=*entry*] into the restaurant business was unexpected. **b** [*noncount*] **:** the right to enter something • His family connections have given him *entrée* [=*entry*] into the most exclusive clubs in the city.

en·trench /ɪnˈtrɛntʃ/ *verb* **-trench·es; -trenched; -trench·ing** [+ *obj*] **:** to place (someone or something) in a very strong position that cannot easily be changed • officials who have tried to *entrench* themselves in office

– entrenched *adj* [*more* ~; *most* ~] • These attitudes are (deeply/firmly) *entrenched* in our culture. • Computers are now an *entrenched* part of modern life. **– en·trench·ment** /ɪnˈtrɛntʃmənt/ *noun* [*noncount*] • the *entrenchment* of certain attitudes

en·tre·pre·neur /ˌɑːntrəprəˈnɚ/ *noun, pl* **-neurs** [*count*] **:** a person who starts a business and is willing to risk loss in order to make money

– en·tre·pre·neur·ial /ˌɑːntrəprəˈnərijəl/ *adj* • *entrepreneurial* skills **– en·tre·pre·neur·ship** /ˌɑːntrəprəˈnɚˌʃɪp/ *noun* [*noncount*] • admired for her *entrepreneurship*

en·trust /ɪnˈtrʌst/ *verb* **-trusts; -trust·ed; -trust·ing** [+ *obj*] **:** to give someone the responsibility of doing something or of caring for someone or something • She was *entrusted* with the job of organizing the reception. • *entrust* your car to a friend = *entrust* a friend with your car

en·try /ˈɛntri/ *noun, pl* **-tries**

1 [*noncount*] **:** the act of entering something • His parents tried to make his *entry* into school life as smooth as possible. • His friends were surprised by his *entry* into politics. • The thieves gained *entry* [=they entered] through a back window.

2 [*noncount*] **:** the right to enter something • He was able to gain *entry* [=*entrance, admission*] to an exclusive club. • She was denied *entry* into the courtroom. • students competing for *entry* into the college • The sign read "No *Entry*." [="do not enter"] — often used before another noun • an *entry* fee/form

3 [*count*] **:** a place for entering something • He hung up his hat in the *entry*. [=*entryway*] • the south *entry* [=*entrance*] of the church — see also PORT OF ENTRY

4 a [*noncount*] **:** the act of entering something in a book, list, etc. • The word is not common enough for *entry* in the dictionary. • She was hired to do data *entry*. [=to enter data on a computer] **b** [*count*] **:** something that is entered in a book, list, etc. • dictionary *entries* • a diary *entry* • a database *entry*

5 [*count*] **a :** a person or thing that is entered in a contest • Her pie was the winning *entry* in the baking competition. • The race has attracted a record number of *entries*. **b** *chiefly Brit* **:** the number of people or things entered in a contest • The race has attracted a record *entry*.

entry–level *adj* **:** at the lowest level **:** at the level of someone who is just starting a job or career • The company is looking to fill several *entry-level* positions.

en·try·way /ˈɛntriˌweɪ/ *noun, pl* **-ways** [*count*] **:** a place for entering something • A truck was blocking the *entryway*. [=*entry, entrance*]

en·twine /ɪnˈtwaɪn/ *verb* **-twines; -twined; -twin·ing :** to twist together or around [+ *obj*] The snake *entwined* itself around the branch. — often used as *(be) entwined* • The roses *were entwined* in an iron fence. — often used figuratively • Their lives *were* tragically *entwined*. [=*intertwined*] • The themes in the novel are closely *entwined*. [*no obj*] Their lives *entwined* tragically.

enu·mer·ate /ɪˈnuːməˌreɪt, *Brit* ɪˈnjuːməˌreɪt/ *verb* **-ates; -at·ed; -at·ing** [+ *obj*] : to name (things) one after another in a list ▪ Let me *enumerate* my reasons for doing this.
– **enu·mer·a·tion** /ɪˌnuːməˈreɪʃən, *Brit* ɪˌnjuːməˈreɪʃən/ *noun, pl* **-tions** [*count, noncount*]

enun·ci·ate /ɪˈnʌnsiˌeɪt/ *verb* **-ates; -at·ed; -at·ing**
1 [+ *obj*] *formal* : to make a clear statement of (ideas, beliefs, etc.) ▪ He set out to *enunciate* the basic principles of his system. ▪ *enunciate* a basic set of beliefs
2 : to pronounce words or parts of words clearly [+ *obj*] Be sure to *enunciate* [=*articulate*] every syllable. [*no obj*] Children should be taught to *enunciate* clearly.
– **enun·ci·a·tion** /ɪˌnʌnsiˈeɪʃən/ *noun* [*noncount*] ▪ the *enunciation* of principles ▪ precise *enunciation* – **enun·ci·a·tor** /ɪˈnʌnsiˌeɪtə/ *noun, pl* **-tors** [*count*] ▪ a careful *enunciator*

E

en·vel·op /ɪnˈvɛləp/ *verb* **-ops; -oped; -op·ing** [+ *obj*] : to completely cover (someone or something) : to completely enclose or surround (someone or something) ▪ She *enveloped* [=*wrapped*] the baby in a large towel. ▪ Mist *enveloped* the mountains. = The mountains were *enveloped* by/in mist.
– **en·vel·op·ment** /ɪnˈvɛləpmənt/ *noun* [*noncount*]

en·ve·lope /ˈɛnvəˌloʊp, ˈɑːnvəˌloʊp/ *noun, pl* **-lopes** [*count*] : an enclosing cover for a letter, card, etc. — see picture at MAIL
push the envelope : to go beyond the usual or normal limits by doing something new, dangerous, etc. ▪ a director who has *pushed the envelope* in his recent films ▪ a new airplane design that *pushes the envelope*

en·vi·able /ˈɛnvijəbəl/ *adj* [*more* ~; *most* ~] : causing envy : very desirable ▪ The company is in the *enviable* position of having no real competitors. ▪ an *enviable* task ▪ She has an *enviable* reputation for honesty. — compare UNENVIABLE
– **en·vi·ably** /ˈɛnvijəbli/ *adv* ▪ The company has had *enviably* high profits.

en·vi·ous /ˈɛnvijəs/ *adj* [*more* ~; *most* ~] : feeling or showing a desire to have what someone else has : feeling or showing envy ▪ *envious* neighbors ▪ an *envious* look — often + *of* ▪ His neighbors were *envious* [=*jealous*] *of* his success.
– **en·vi·ous·ly** *adv* ▪ We looked *enviously* at his new car.

en·vi·ron·ment /ɪnˈvaɪrənmənt/ *noun, pl* **-ments**
1 : the conditions that surround someone or something : the conditions and influences that affect the growth, health, progress, etc., of someone or something [*count*] He grew up in a loving *environment*. ▪ an informal office *environment* ▪ We're trying to create a better business/learning *environment*. ▪ These animals were raised in a controlled *environment*. ▪ Many plants are unable to survive in such a harsh/hostile *environment*. [*noncount*] Heredity and *environment* are both important.
2 ***the environment*** : the natural world ▪ Pollution is bad for *the environment*. ▪ protecting *the* (natural) *environment*
– **en·vi·ron·men·tal** /ɪnˌvaɪrənˈmɛntl/ *adj* ▪ The chemical refinery explosion was an *environmental* disaster. ▪ *environmental* laws ▪ *environmental* protection – **en·vi·ron·men·tal·ly** /ɪnˌvaɪrənˈmɛntḷi/ *adv* ▪ *environmentally* safe methods of waste disposal

en·vi·ron·men·tal·ist /ɪnˌvaɪrənˈmɛntəlɪst/ *noun, pl* **-ists** [*count*] : a person who works to protect the natural world from pollution and other threats
– **en·vi·ron·men·tal·ism** /ɪnˌvaɪrənˈmɛntəˌlɪzəm/ *noun* [*noncount*]

en·vi·rons /ɪnˈvaɪrənz/ *noun* [*plural*] : the area that is around a place (such as a city) ▪ We bought a guide to New York and (its) *environs*. ▪ a town and its immediate *environs*

en·vis·age /ɪnˈvɪzɪʤ/ *verb* **-ag·es; -aged; -ag·ing** [+ *obj*] : to picture (something) in your mind : ENVISION ▪ I *envisage* a day when proper health care will be available to everyone.
✧ *Envisage* is used in U.S. English but it is more common in British English.

en·vi·sion /ɪnˈvɪʒən/ *verb* **-sions; -sioned; -sion·ing** [+ *obj*] *chiefly US* : to think of (something that you believe might exist or happen in the future) : to picture (something) in your mind ▪ The inventor *envisioned* many uses for his creation. ▪ She *envisioned* a better life for herself.

en·voy /ˈɛnˌvoɪ, ˈɑːn-/ *noun, pl* **en·voys** [*count*] : a person who is sent by one government to represent it in dealing with another government ▪ diplomatic *envoys* ▪ a special *envoy*

[1]en·vy /ˈɛnvi/ *noun* [*noncount*]
1 : the feeling of wanting to have what someone else has ▪ my *envy* of his success ▪ Their exotic vacations inspired *envy* in/among their friends. ▪ We watched with *envy* as the yacht slid past us. ▪ They were ***green with envy***. [=they were filled with envy; they were very envious] ▪ Her beautiful hair was an ***object of envy***. [=people felt envy because of her beautiful hair] — sometimes used humorously after a noun that indicates an object of envy ▪ My neighbor's new lawn mower has given me a bad case of lawn mower *envy*. [=I'm very envious of my neighbor's new lawn mower]
2 : someone or something that causes envy — used in the phrase ***the envy of*** ▪ She was *the envy of* all her friends. [=all her friends envied her] ▪ Our car was *the envy of* the neighborhood. [=the neighbors envied us for our car]

[2]envy *verb* **-vies; -vied; -vy·ing** [+ *obj*] : to feel a desire to have what someone else has : to feel envy because of (someone or something) ▪ I *envy* you for your large group of friends. ▪ They *envied* his success. = They *envied* him for his success. ▪ I *envy* the way you've made so many friends. ▪ I don't *envy* you your dental problems. [=I'm glad that I don't have your dental problems]

en·zyme /ˈɛnˌzaɪm/ *noun, pl* **-zymes** [*count*] *technical* : a chemical substance in animals and plants that helps to cause natural processes (such as digestion)
– **en·zy·mat·ic** /ˌɛnzəˈmætɪk/ *adj*

eon (*US*) *or chiefly Brit* **ae·on** /ˈiːˌɑːn/ *noun, pl* **eons** [*count*] : a very long period of time — usually plural ▪ Over the *eons*, the river changed its course many times. ▪ (*informal*) How have you been? I haven't seen you in *eons*! [=*ages*]

ep·au·let (*chiefly US*) *or chiefly Brit* **ep·au·lette** /ˌɛpəˈlɛt/ *noun, pl* **-lets** [*count*] : a decorative piece on the shoulder of a uniform

ephem·era /ɪˈfɛmərə/ *noun* [*plural*] : things that are important or useful for only a short time : items that were not meant to have lasting value ▪ He has a large collection of old menus and other *ephemera*.

ephem·er·al /ɪˈfɛmərəl/ *adj* [*more* ~; *most* ~] : lasting a very short time ▪ His fame turned out to be *ephemeral*. [=*short-lived*]

[1]ep·ic /ˈɛpɪk/ *noun, pl* **-ics** [*count*]
1 : a long poem that tells the story of a hero's adventures ▪ Homer's ancient Greek *epic* "The Odyssey"
2 : a long book, movie, etc., that usually tells a story about exciting events or adventures

[2]epic *adj*
1 : telling a story about a hero or about exciting events or adventures ▪ an *epic* poem ▪ an *epic* film/novel
2 [*more* ~; *most* ~] : very great or large and usually difficult or impressive ▪ The football game was an *epic* battle between two great teams. ▪ The bridge was an *epic* achievement. ▪ The company is engaged in an *epic* struggle for survival. ▪ an accomplishment of *epic* proportions ▪ undertaking an *epic* journey

epi·cen·ter (*US*) *or Brit* **epi·cen·tre** /ˈɛpɪˌsɛntə/ *noun, pl* **-ters** [*count*] : the part of the earth's surface that is directly above the place where an earthquake starts

ep·i·cure /ˈɛpɪˌkjuə/ *noun, pl* **-cures** [*count*] *formal* : a person who appreciates fine food and drink : GOURMET

ep·i·cu·re·an /ˌɛpɪkjʊˈriːjən, ˌɛpɪˈkjuriːjən/ *adj* : involving an appreciation of fine food and drink : of or relating to an epicure ▪ a person of *epicurean* tastes ▪ *epicurean* delights/pleasures
– **epicurean** *noun, pl* **-reans** [*count*] ▪ affluent *epicureans* [=*epicures*]

ep·i·dem·ic /ˌɛpəˈdɛmɪk/ *noun, pl* **-ics** [*count*]
1 *medical* : an occurrence in which a disease spreads very quickly and affects a large number of people ▪ a flu *epidemic* ▪ the AIDS *epidemic*
2 : a sudden quickly spreading occurrence of something harmful or unwanted ▪ a crime *epidemic* ▪ an *epidemic* of bankruptcies
– **epidemic** *adj* ▪ an *epidemic* disease ▪ The violence has now reached *epidemic* proportions.

ep·i·de·mi·ol·o·gy /ˌɛpəˌdiːmiˈɑːləʤi/ *noun* [*noncount*] *medical* : the study of how disease spreads and can be controlled
– **ep·i·de·mi·o·log·i·cal** /ˌɛpəˌdiːmijəˈlɑːʤɪkəl/ *also US* **ep·i·de·mi·o·log·ic** /ˌɛpəˌdiːmijəˈlɑːʤɪk/ *adj* – **ep·i·de·mi·ol·o·gist** /ˌɛpəˌdiːmiˈɑːləʤɪst/ *noun, pl* **-gists** [*count*]

epi·der·mis /ˌɛpəˈdəməs/ *noun* [*noncount*] *medical* : the outer layer of skin
– **epi·der·mal** /ˌɛpəˈdəməl/ *adj* ▪ *epidermal* tissues

epi·du·ral /ˌɛpəˈdurəl, *Brit* ˌɛpəˈdjuərəl/ *noun, pl* **-rals** [*count*] *medical* : an injection of a substance into a person's spine to cause the lower part of the body to become unable to feel pain • Many women undergoing childbirth are given *epidurals.*

ep·i·gram /ˈɛpəˌgræm/ *noun, pl* **-grams** [*count*] : a short and clever poem or saying
– **ep·i·gram·mat·ic** /ˌɛpəgrəˈmætɪk/ *adj* • *epigrammatic* poetry – **ep·i·gram·ma·tist** /ˌɛpəˈgræmətɪst/ *noun, pl* **-tists** [*count*]

ep·i·lep·sy /ˈɛpəˌlɛpsi/ *noun* [*noncount*] *medical* : a disorder of the nervous system that can cause people to suddenly become unconscious and to have violent, uncontrolled movements of the body

[1]**ep·i·lep·tic** /ˌɛpəˈlɛptɪk/ *adj, medical* : having epilepsy • *epileptic* patients : resulting from epilepsy • an *epileptic* seizure

[2]**epileptic** *noun, pl* **-tics** [*count*] *medical* : a person who has epilepsy

ep·i·logue /ˈɛpəˌlɑːg/ *noun, pl* **-logues** [*count*] : a final section or speech after the main part of a book, play, or musical composition — sometimes used figuratively • His final years were a peaceful *epilogue* to a life of adventure. — compare PROLOGUE

epiph·a·ny /ɪˈpɪfəni/ *noun, pl* **-nies**
1 ***Epiphany*** [*singular*] : a Christian festival held on January 6 in honor of the coming of the three kings to the infant Jesus Christ
2 [*count*] : a moment in which you suddenly see or understand something in a new or very clear way • Seeing her father again when she was an adult was an *epiphany* that changed her whole view of her childhood. • She experienced an *epiphany.*

epis·co·pal /ɪˈpɪskəpəl/ *adj*
1 : of or relating to a bishop or to bishops as a group • an *episcopal* conference • *episcopal* teachings
2 ***Episcopal*** : of or relating to either the Protestant Episcopal Church in the U.S. or the Episcopal Church in Scotland • an *Episcopal* [=*Episcopalian*] church/clergyman

Epis·co·pa·lian /ɪˌpɪskəˈpeɪljən/ *noun, pl* **-lians** [*count*] : a member of either the Protestant Episcopal Church in the U.S. or the Episcopal Church in Scotland • She was raised as an *Episcopalian.*
– **Episcopalian** *adj* • an *Episcopalian* family • an *Episcopalian* [=*Episcopal*] church/clergyman – **Epis·co·pa·lian·ism** /ɪˌpɪskəˈpeɪljəˌnɪzəm/ *noun* [*noncount*]

ep·i·sode /ˈɛpəˌsoʊd/ *noun, pl* **-sodes** [*count*]
1 : an event or a short period of time that is important or unusual • It was a brief romantic *episode* in a life devoted to work. • He tried to forget the whole embarrassing *episode.* • a painful *episode* from my childhood
2 : a television show, radio show, etc., that is one part of a series • Millions of people are expected to watch the show's final *episode.* • a special holiday *episode*
3 : an occurrence of an illness • The patient has experienced recurrent/repeated *episodes* [=*bouts*] of severe infection. • a fainting *episode*

ep·i·sod·ic /ˌɛpəˈsɑːdɪk/ *adj, formal*
1 a : made up of many different events or episodes • He led an *episodic* life. [=a life in which many different and unusual things happened] **b** : telling about many separate events • an *episodic* novel
2 : happening or appearing at different times • an *episodic* illness

epis·tle /ɪˈpɪsəl/ *noun, pl* **epis·tles** [*count*]
1 ***Epistle** in the Bible* : any one of the letters to the early Christians that are part of the New Testament • St. Paul's *Epistle* to the Romans
2 *formal* : LETTER • He penned lengthy *epistles* to her.

epis·to·lary /ɪˈpɪstəˌleri, *Brit* ɪˈpɪstələri/ *adj, formal*
1 : of or relating to a letter : suitable to a letter • an *epistolary* writing style
2 : written in the form of a series of letters • an *epistolary* novel

ep·i·taph /ˈɛpəˌtæf/ *noun, pl* **-taphs** [*count*] : something written or said in memory of a dead person; *especially* : words written on a gravestone • The *epitaph* reads "In loving memory of John Gray: husband, father, soldier."

ep·i·thet /ˈɛpəˌθɛt/ *noun, pl* **-thets** [*count*]
1 : a word or phrase that describes a person or thing • His charitable works have earned him the epithet "Mr. Philanthropy."
2 : an offensive word or name that is used as a way of abusing or insulting someone • Many were offended by her use of racial *epithets.* • a group of angry people hurling *epithets* at one another

epit·o·me /ɪˈpɪtəmi/ *noun, pl* **-mes** [*count*] : a perfect example : an example that represents or expresses something very well — usually used in the phrase ***the epitome of*** • Your response was *the epitome of* good sense. • In his tailored suit and fashionable haircut, he was *the* (very) *epitome of* style.

epit·o·mize *also Brit* **epit·o·mise** /ɪˈpɪtəˌmaɪz/ *verb* **-mizes; -mized; -miz·ing** [+ *obj*] : to be a perfect example or representation of (something) : to be the epitome of (something) • He *epitomizes* laziness. • This student's struggles *epitomize* the trouble with our schools.

ep·och /ˈɛpək, *Brit* ˈiːˌpɒk/ *noun, pl* **-ochs** [*count*] : a period of time that is very important in history • The Civil War era was an *epoch* in 19th-century U.S. history. • The development of the steam engine marked an important *epoch* in the history of industry. — compare ERA
– **ep·och·al** /ˈɛpəkəl, *Brit* ˈɛˌpɒkəl/ *adj* • an *epochal* [=*epoch-making*] invention/event

epoch–making *adj* : very important in history : causing an important change in history • The steam engine was an *epoch-making* [=*epochal*] development in the history of industry.

ep·oxy /ɪˈpɑːksi/ *noun* [*noncount*] : a type of glue — called also *epoxy resin*

Ep·som salt /ˈɛpsəm-/ *noun, pl* **~ salts** [*count*] : a bitter salt that is used in medicine — usually plural

equa·ble /ˈɛkwəbəl/ *adj* [*more* ~; *most* ~] *formal* : tending to remain calm : free from sudden or harsh changes • an *equable* temperament • an *equable* [=*mild*] climate • a calm, *equable* fellow — compare EQUITABLE
– **eq·ua·bly** /ˈɛkwəbli/ *adv* • He accepted the criticism *equably.* [=he was not upset by the criticism]

[1]**equal** /ˈiːkwəl/ *adj*
1 a : the same in number, amount, degree, rank, or quality • an *equal* number of apples and oranges • officers of *equal* rank • issues of *equal* importance = issues that are *equal* in importance • We divided the profits into three *equal* shares. • The play combines tragedy and comedy in *equal* measure/proportions. • The opposing candidate has demanded *equal* time on television. • "... all men are created *equal*..." —*U.S. Declaration of Independence* (1776) • people from different cultures learning to live together ***on equal terms*** [=learning to live together as equals] • making it possible for poor children to compete ***on an equal footing*** [=in conditions where they have an equal chance] with other children — often + *to* • In one night he earned an amount *equal to* an entire month's salary. • issues that are *equal* in importance *to* the most serious problems we face **b** : having the same mathematical value • The fractions ½ and ²⁄₄ are *equal.* — often + *to* • ½ is *equal to* ²⁄₄.
2 : not changing : the same for each person • providing *equal* opportunities for children of all races • We need to have *equal* academic standards for male and female students. • *equal* rights • (*US*) an ***equal opportunity*** employer = (*Brit*) an ***equal opportunities*** employer [=an employer who does not discriminate against people because of their race, religion, etc.]
3 *formal* : able to do what is needed — + *to* • He says that he's *equal to* the task. [=he's capable of completing the task]
all/other things being equal see THING

[2]**equal** *noun, pl* **equals** [*count*] : someone or something that is as good, skillful, valuable, etc., as another person or thing • I consider him my *equal.* • They say they are producing wine that is the *equal* of the best wines in the world. [=that is as good as the best wines in the world] • We are all *equals* here. • He has no *equal* at chess. = He is ***without equal*** at chess. [=no one plays chess as well as he does]
first among equals see [1]FIRST

[3]**equal** *verb* **equals**; *US* **equaled** *or chiefly Brit* **equalled**; *US* **equal·ing** *or chiefly Brit* **equal·ling**
1 [*linking verb*] — used to say that one amount or number is the same as another • His salary *equals* mine. • Three plus two *equals* five.
2 [+ *obj*] **a** : to be as good as (something else) • Nothing can ever *equal* that experience. **b** : to produce something that is as good as (something else) or to do something as well as (someone else) • See if you can *equal* that! • a weight lifter attempting to *equal* his rival's performance • No one can *equal* him in chess.
3 [+ *obj*] : to have the same force, effect, etc., as (something else) — usually used as *(be) equaled* • His arrogance *is equaled* only by his vanity. [=he is both extremely arrogant and vain]

equal·i·ty /ɪˈkwɑːləti/ *noun [noncount]* : the quality or state of being equal : the quality or state of having the same rights, social status, etc. ▪ racial/gender *equality* ▪ the ideals of liberty and *equality* ▪ women's struggle for *equality* — opposite INEQUALITY; compare EQUIVALENCE

equal·ize *also Brit* **equal·ise** /ˈiːkwəˌlaɪz/ *verb* **-iz·es; -ized; -iz·ing**

1 : to make (something) equal or to become equal [+ *obj*] They are hoping to *equalize* pay for workers with similar jobs. ▪ We need to *equalize* educational opportunities for all children. [=to give equal educational opportunities to all children] [*no obj*] Educational opportunities have not yet *equalized.*

2 : to make (something) even or to become even [+ *obj*] trying to *equalize* the pressure [*no obj*] The pressure soon *equalized.*

3 [*no obj*] *Brit, sports* : to tie the score ▪ Their best chance to *equalize* [=(*US*) *tie*] came in the 60th minute. — see also EQUALIZER

– equal·i·za·tion *also Brit* **equal·i·sa·tion** /ˌiːkwələˈzeɪʃən, *Brit* ˌiːkwəˌlaɪˈzeɪʃən/ *noun [noncount]*

equal·iz·er *also Brit* **equal·is·er** /ˈiːkwəˌlaɪzɚ/ *noun, pl* **-ers** *[count]*

1 : something that makes people or things equal ▪ Education can be the great *equalizer.* [=education can give poor people an equal chance]

2 *sports* : a score (such as a point, goal, or run) that ties a game ▪ He scored the *equalizer* in the 60th minute.

equal·ly /ˈiːkwəli/ *adv*

1 : in an equal or even manner ▪ The money will be distributed *equally* among the winners. ▪ sharing the work *equally*

2 : to an equal degree or extent ▪ My opinions are *equally* valid. ▪ She's respected *equally* by the young and old. ▪ The two projects are *equally* important. ✧ ***Equally*** is sometimes used to introduce a statement that is added to and just as important as a previous statement. ▪ We need to be concerned about his rise to power. *Equally,* the influence of his opponents cannot be ignored.

equally as informal — used to say that one thing is as important, good, etc., as another thing ▪ One project is *equally as* [=*just as*] important as the other.

equal sign *noun, pl* ~ **signs** *[count]* : a symbol = used to show that two numbers are equal ▪ ½ = ²⁄₄ — called also *equals sign*

equa·nim·i·ty /ˌiːkwəˈnɪməti, ˌɛkwəˈnɪməti/ *noun [noncount] formal* : calm emotions when dealing with problems or pressure ▪ She accepted her misfortunes with *equanimity.* [=she did not become upset; she remained calm]

equate /ɪˈkweɪt/ *verb* **equates; equat·ed; equat·ing** [+ *obj*] : to say or think that (two things) are equal or the same ▪ You shouldn't *equate* those two things. — often + *with* or *and* ▪ He *equates* disagreement *with/and* disloyalty. ▪ You shouldn't *equate* material wealth *with* happiness.

equate to [*phrasal verb*] ***equate to (something)*** : to be the same as or similar to (something) ▪ Disagreement doesn't *equate to* [=*equal*] disloyalty.

equa·tion /ɪˈkweɪʒən/ *noun, pl* **-tions**

1 [*count*] *mathematics* : a statement that two expressions are equal (such as 8 + 3 = 11 or 2x – 3 = 7) ▪ solve an *equation*

2 [*count*] : a complicated situation or issue — usually singular ▪ Helping a troubled teenager is more difficult when drugs are part of the *equation.* [=when drugs are involved] ▪ The southern states will be an important part of the election *equation.*

3 [*noncount*] : the act of regarding two things as the same : the act of equating things ▪ the *equation* of material wealth with/and happiness

equa·tor /ɪˈkweɪtɚ/ *noun*

the equator : an imaginary circle around the middle of the Earth that is the same distance from the North Pole and the South Pole ▪ The city of Quito, Ecuador, lies very close to *the equator.* ▪ Is it near *the equator?*

equa·to·ri·al /ˌiːkwəˈtorijəl, ˌɛkwəˈtorijəl/ *adj* : of or relating to the equator : located at or near the equator ▪ *equatorial* regions/countries ▪ *equatorial* Africa ▪ the *equatorial* climate

¹eques·tri·an /ɪˈkwɛstrijən/ *adj* : of or relating to the riding of horses ▪ *equestrian* sports ▪ an *equestrian* competition

²equestrian *noun, pl* **-ans** *[count]* : a person who rides horses

equi·dis·tant /ˌiːkwəˈdɪstənt, ˌɛkwəˈdɪstənt/ *adj* : of equal distance : located at the same distance ▪ Points on a circle are *equidistant* from its center. ▪ Montreal is roughly *equidistant* from New York, Boston, and Toronto.

equi·lat·er·al triangle /ˌiːkwəˈlætərəl-, ˌɛkwəˈlætərəl-/ *noun, pl* ~ **-angles** *[count] mathematics* : a triangle in which all three sides are the same length

equi·lib·ri·um /ˌiːkwəˈlɪbrijəm, ˌɛkwəˈlɪbrijəm/ *noun [noncount]*

1 : a state in which opposing forces or actions are balanced so that one is not stronger or greater than the other ▪ Supply and demand were in *equilibrium.* ▪ chemical *equilibrium*

2 : a state of emotional balance or calmness ▪ It took me several minutes to recover my *equilibrium.* [=*composure*]

¹equine /ˈiːˌkwaɪn, ˈɛˌkwaɪn/ *adj*

1 : of or relating to horses ▪ an *equine* disease ▪ *equine* grace

2 : resembling a horse ▪ an *equine* face — compare EQUESTRIAN

²equine *noun, pl* **equines** *[count] formal* : HORSE

equi·nox /ˈiːkwəˌnɑːks, ˈɛkwəˌnɑːks/ *noun, pl* **-nox·es** *[count]* : a day when day and night are the same length ✧ There are two equinoxes in the year: the ***spring*** (or ***vernal***) ***equinox***, which occurs around March 21, and the ***autumn*** (or ***autumnal***) ***equinox***, which occurs around September 23. — compare SOLSTICE

equip /ɪˈkwɪp/ *verb* **equips; equipped; equip·ping** [+ *obj*]

1 a : to provide (someone) with necessary materials or supplies ▪ More money was needed to train and *equip* the troops. ▪ *Equipped* with a hoe and a shovel, I headed for the garden. **b** : to provide (something) with a particular feature or ability ▪ All of the buses are *equipped* with air-conditioning. [=all of the buses have air-conditioning] ▪ specially/fully *equipped* aircraft

2 : to prepare (someone) for a particular activity or problem ▪ Her training has *equipped* her to deal with emergencies. ▪ She is well-*equipped* to deal with emergencies. ▪ Those students are not *equipped* for the challenges of college.

equip·ment /ɪˈkwɪpmənt/ *noun [noncount]*

1 : supplies or tools needed for a special purpose ▪ sports/stereo/laboratory *equipment* ▪ The photographer came early to set up his *equipment.* ▪ I'm looking for a hobby that doesn't require a lot of fancy *equipment.* ▪ an expensive piece of medical *equipment*

2 : the act of equipping someone or something ▪ Not enough funds were provided for the *equipment* of the troops.

eq·ui·ta·ble /ˈɛkwətəbəl/ *adj [more ~; most ~] formal* : just or fair : dealing fairly and equally with everyone ▪ They reached an *equitable* settlement of their dispute. ▪ fighting for a more *equitable* distribution of funds ▪ an *equitable* system of taxation — compare EQUABLE

– eq·ui·ta·bly /ˈɛkwətəbli/ *adv*

eq·ui·ty /ˈɛkwəti/ *noun, pl* **-ties**

1 [*noncount*] *formal* : fairness or justice in the way people are treated ▪ In making these decisions we should be governed by the principle of *equity.*

2 *finance* **a** [*noncount*] : the value of a piece of property (such as a house) after any debts that remain to be paid for it (such as the amount of a mortgage) have been subtracted ▪ We've been slowly paying off our mortgage and building up *equity* in our house. ▪ a ***home equity loan*** [=a loan based on the amount of equity you have in your home] **b** [*count*] : a share in a company : a share of a company's stock — usually plural ▪ Half of his money is invested in bonds and the other half in *equities.*

equiv·a·lence /ɪˈkwɪvələns/ *noun [noncount] formal* : the quality or state of being alike : the quality or state of having the same value, function, meaning, etc. ▪ the *equivalence* of the two propositions — compare EQUALITY

equiv·a·len·cy /ɪˈkwɪvələnsi/ *noun [noncount]*

1 : EQUIVALENCE

2 *chiefly US* : a level of achievement that is considered to be on the same level as finishing a course of study — often used before another noun ▪ He went to night school and got his high school *equivalency* certificate. [=a certificate that is equivalent to a high school degree]

¹equiv·a·lent /ɪˈkwɪvələnt/ *adj* : having the same value, use, meaning, etc. ▪ Those less-known companies manufacture *equivalent* products at cheaper prices. ▪ I haven't taken English 202, but I took an *equivalent* course at another university. ▪ an *equivalent* amount of money ▪ two words of *equivalent* meaning = two words that are *equivalent* in meaning — often + *to* ▪ 100 milligrams of calcium, which is *equivalent to* three glasses of milk ▪ Allowing him to leave prison now would be *equivalent to* [=would amount to, would be the

same as] saying that his crime was not serious.
– **equiv·a·lent·ly** *adv* ▪ The two products are priced *equivalently*.

²equivalent *noun, pl* **-lents** [*count*] : something that has the same value, use, meaning, etc., as another thing ▪ a Chinese word for which English has no (exact) *equivalent* ▪ His newspaper column is the journalistic *equivalent* of candy.

equiv·o·cal /ɪˈkwɪvəkəl/ *adj* [*more* ~; *most* ~] *formal*
1 : having two or more possible meanings : AMBIGUOUS ▪ an *equivocal* term ▪ He responded to reporters' questions with *equivocal* answers. — opposite UNEQUIVOCAL
2 : not easily understood or explained ▪ The experiment produced *equivocal* results. ▪ *equivocal* evidence ▪ *equivocal* behavior
– **equiv·o·cal·ly** /ɪˈkwɪvəkli/ *adv*

equiv·o·cate /ɪˈkwɪvəˌkeɪt/ *verb* **-cates; -cat·ed; -cat·ing** [*no obj*] *formal* : to use unclear language especially to deceive or mislead someone ▪ The applicant seemed to be *equivocating* when we asked him about his last job. ▪ When asked about her tax plan, the candidate didn't *equivocate*.
– **equiv·o·ca·tion** /ɪˌkwɪvəˈkeɪʃən/ *noun, pl* **-tions** [*noncount*] The candidate spoke without *equivocation* about her tax plan. [*count*] His answers were filled with evasions and *equivocations*. – **equiv·o·ca·tor** /ɪˈkwɪvəˌkeɪtɚ/ *noun, pl* **-tors** [*count*]

er /ˈəː, ˈɚ: *usually with a prolonged vowel*/ *interj* — used when you are speaking and you are not sure what to say ▪ "What's the answer?" "Well, *er*, I just don't know."

ER *abbr* emergency room

¹-er /ɚ/ *adj suffix or adv suffix* — used to form the comparative form of adjectives and adverbs of one syllable ▪ fast*er* ▪ hott*er* ▪ dri*er* — used to form the comparative of some adjectives and adverbs of two or more syllables ▪ shallow*er* ▪ earli*er* — compare -EST

²-er /ɚ/ *also* **-ier** /iɚ, jɚ/ *or* **-yer** /jɚ/ *noun suffix*
1 a : person having a particular job ▪ hatt*er* ▪ furri*er* ▪ law*yer* ▪ jail*er* b : person or thing belonging to or associated with something ▪ old-tim*er* ▪ high school*er* ▪ prison*er* c : native of : resident of ▪ New York*er* ▪ cottag*er* d : thing that has ▪ double-deck*er*
2 : person or thing that does or performs a specified action ▪ report*er* ▪ play*er* ▪ sharpen*er* ▪ do-good*er*
3 : person who is ▪ foreign*er* ▪ Western*er*

era /ˈerə, *Brit* ˈɪərə/ *noun, pl* **eras** [*count*] : a period of time that is associated with a particular quality, event, person, etc. ▪ the Victorian *era* ▪ the Christian *era* ▪ the *era* of the horse and buggy ▪ We're just now entering an *era* of great prosperity. ▪ His death marks the end of an *era*. — compare EPOCH

erad·i·cate /ɪˈrædəˌkeɪt/ *verb* **-cates; -cat·ed; -cat·ing** [+ *obj*] *formal* : to remove (something) completely : to eliminate or destroy (something harmful) ▪ The disease has now been completely *eradicated*. ▪ His ambition is to *eradicate* poverty in/from his community.
– **erad·i·ca·tion** /ɪˌrædəˈkeɪʃən/ *noun* [*noncount*] ▪ working for the *eradication* of poverty

erase /ɪˈreɪs, *Brit* ɪˈreɪz/ *verb* **eras·es; erased; eras·ing**
1 [+ *obj*] : to remove (something that has been recorded) from a tape (such as a videotape or audiotape) or a computer disk ▪ The recording can be *erased* and the tape used again. ▪ Several important files were accidentally *erased*.; *also* : to remove recorded material from (a tape or disk) ▪ You can *erase* the tape/disk and use it again.
2 *chiefly US* a : to remove (something written) by rubbing or scraping so that it can no longer be seen [+ *obj*] She *erased* the wrong answer from her paper and filled in the correct one. ▪ I *erased* the chalk marks from the blackboard. [*no obj*] These marks won't *erase*. [=can't be erased] b : to remove something written from (a surface) ▪ *erase* [=*clean*] the blackboard
3 [+ *obj*] : to remove any thought or memory of (something) ▪ Time has *erased* the event from her memory. [=she has completely forgotten the event]
– **eras·able** /ɪˈreɪsəbəl, *Brit* ɪˈreɪzəbəl/ *adj* ▪ an *erasable* tape

eras·er /ɪˈreɪsɚ, *Brit* ɪˈreɪzə/ *noun, pl* **-ers** [*count*] *chiefly US* : a small piece of rubber or other material that is used to erase something you have written or drawn — called also (*Brit*) *rubber*; see picture at OFFICE

era·sure /ɪˈreɪʃɚ, *Brit* ɪˈreɪʒə/ *noun, pl* **-sures** : an act of erasing something [*noncount*] accidental *erasure* of the tape [*count*] (*chiefly US*) ▪ There were many errors and *erasures* in the typescript.

ere /ˈeɚ/ *prep or conj, old-fashioned or literary* : BEFORE ▪ *ere* nightfall ▪ *ere long* [=soon]

¹erect /ɪˈrɛkt/ *adj*
1 [*more* ~; *most* ~] : straight up and down ▪ an *erect* [=*upright*] pole ▪ *erect* trees ▪ She sat *erect*, listening for her name. ▪ The soldiers stood *erect*.
2 : in a state of erection because of sexual excitement : swollen and stiff ▪ an *erect* penis ▪ *erect* nipples
– **erect·ly** *adv* ▪ standing/sitting *erectly* – **erect·ness** /ɪˈrɛktnəs/ *noun* [*noncount*] ▪ the *erectness* of her posture

²erect *verb* **erects; erect·ed; erect·ing** [+ *obj*]
1 : to build (something) by putting together materials ▪ The settlers *erected* [=*built*] a stone wall. ▪ The city *erected* a statue in his honor. — sometimes used figuratively ▪ He has had to overcome many obstacles *erected* by his political enemies. ▪ *erect* a civilization
2 : to set or place (something) so that it stands up ▪ *erect* a flagpole ▪ They *erected* a marker over the grave.

erec·tile /ɪˈrɛktl̩, ɪˈrɛkˌtajəl/ *adj, technical* : of or relating to an erection (sense 1) ▪ *erectile* dysfunction [=a problem that makes a man unable to get an erection]

erec·tion /ɪˈrɛkʃən/ *noun, pl* **-tions**
1 [*count*] : the state in which a body part (such as the penis) becomes firm and swollen because of sexual excitement; *also* : the penis when it is in such a state ▪ get/have an *erection*
2 [*noncount*] : the act or process of building or erecting something ▪ the *erection* of a new apartment building

er·go /ˈeɚgoʊ, ˈɚgoʊ/ *adv, formal* : THEREFORE, HENCE ▪ The products are poorly constructed; *ergo*, they break easily.

er·go·nom·ics /ˌɚgəˈnɑːmɪks/ *noun*
1 [*noncount*] : a science that deals with designing and arranging things so that people can use them easily and safely
2 [*plural*] : the parts or qualities of something's design that make it easy to use ▪ *Ergonomics* are a crucial consideration when designing an office ▪ The car's *ergonomics* are outstanding.
– **er·go·nom·ic** /ˌɚgəˈnɑːmɪk/ *adj* [*more* ~; *most* ~] ▪ *ergonomic* chairs/injuries/factors ▪ The binoculars have a comfortable *ergonomic* shape. – **er·go·nom·i·cal·ly** /ˌɚgəˈnɑːmɪkli/ *adv* ▪ *ergonomically* designed office furniture

er·mine /ˈɚmən/ *noun, pl* **ermine** *or* **er·mines**
1 [*count*] *US* : a small animal that has a long body and fur that turns white in winter — compare STOAT
2 [*noncount*] : the white fur of an ermine ▪ an *ermine* coat

erode /ɪˈroʊd/ *verb* **erodes; erod·ed; erod·ing** : to gradually destroy (something) or to be gradually destroyed by natural forces (such as water, wind, or ice) [+ *obj*] Crashing waves have *eroded* the cliffs along the beach. — often used as *(be) eroded* ▪ The shoreline *was* badly *eroded* by last winter's storms. — often used figuratively ▪ Years of mismanagement have *eroded* the quality of their products. ▪ The value of your savings can be *eroded* by inflation. [*no obj*] The shoreline has *eroded* badly. — often used figuratively ▪ Support for the new law has been *eroding* steadily.

erog·e·nous /ɪˈrɑːdʒənəs/ *adj* [*more* ~; *most* ~] : producing sexual excitement or pleasure when touched : sexually sensitive ▪ ***erogenous zones*** [=sensitive areas on the body that cause sexual arousal when they are touched]

ero·sion /ɪˈroʊʒən/ *noun* [*noncount*] : the gradual destruction of something by natural forces (such as water, wind, or ice) : the process by which something is eroded or worn away ▪ Landscapers planted grass to stop the *erosion* of the hillside. ▪ Centuries of *erosion* by wind have carved grooves in the rocks. — often used figuratively ▪ the *erosion* of moral standards ▪ an *erosion* of support for the new law ▪ Many companies fear further *erosion* of liberal trade policies.
– **ero·sion·al** /ɪˈroʊʒənl/ *adj, technical* ▪ *erosional* areas/periods/processes – **ero·sive** /ɪˈroʊsɪv/ *adj* [*more* ~; *most* ~] *technical* ▪ the *erosive* effect of water ▪ *erosive* processes

erot·ic /ɪˈrɑːtɪk/ *adj* [*more* ~; *most* ~] : relating to sex ▪ *erotic* dreams/fantasies/feelings ▪ an *erotic* [=*sexual*] relationship : causing sexual feelings ▪ *erotic* literature/art ▪ *erotic* beauty ▪ an *erotic* dance
– **erot·i·cal·ly** /ɪˈrɑːtɪkli/ *adv*

erot·ica /ɪˈrɑːtɪkə/ *noun* [*noncount*] : works of art or literature that deal with sex and are meant to cause sexual feelings : erotic works ▪ a collection of *erotica*

erot·i·cism /ɪˈrɑːtəˌsɪzəm/ *noun* [*noncount*] : a quality that causes sexual feelings ▪ the subtle *eroticism* of his films ▪ an actress known for her smoldering *eroticism*

err /ˈeɚ, ˈɚ/ *verb* **errs; erred; err·ing** [*no obj*] *formal* : to

E

make a mistake ▪ I may have *erred* in my calculations. ▪ The court *erred* in refusing to allow bail. ▪ ***To err is human.*** [=it is normal for people to make mistakes]

err on the side of ✧ To *err on the side of* something, such as caution, is to use or show more of it than may be needed so that you can be sure that you are using or showing enough of it. ▪ It's better to *err on the side of* generosity [=to be too generous] than to be too stingy. ▪ We chose to ***err on the side of caution*** [=to be very cautious] when planning our investments.

er·rand /ˈerənd/ *noun, pl* **-rands** [*count*] **:** a short journey that you take to do or get something ▪ He was sent out on an urgent *errand.* ▪ We were there on an ***errand of mercy*** to help provide medical care for the refugees. — often used with *run* ▪ I have to *run* some *errands* for my mom this afternoon. — sometimes used with *do* ▪ She had a bunch of *errands* to *do* before dinner. ✧ A ***fool's errand*** is an errand that does not need to be done or that cannot be done successfully.

errand boy *noun, pl* **~ boys** [*count*] *US* **:** a person whose job is to run errands for important people ▪ He worked his way up from *errand boy* to regional sales manager. ✧ *Errand boy* is often used figuratively to criticize people by suggesting that they are controlled by someone more powerful. ▪ The governor is nothing more than an *errand boy* for the big companies in his state.

er·rant /ˈerənt/ *adj*
1 *always used before a noun* **a :** behaving wrongly ▪ an *errant* [=*unfaithful*] husband ▪ an *errant* cop [=a policeman who has broken the law] **b** *US* **:** going outside the proper area ▪ an *errant* calf ▪ an *errant* motorboat **c** *US, sports* **:** not going in the intended direction **:** not accurate ▪ an *errant* throw/pass/shot
2 : wandering to different places in search of adventure ▪ an *errant* knight — see also KNIGHT-ERRANT

Do not confuse *errant* with *arrant.*

er·rat·ic /ɪˈrætɪk/ *adj* [*more ~; most ~*] **:** acting, moving, or changing in ways that are not expected or usual **:** not consistent or regular ▪ His behavior seemed *erratic.* ▪ The light flashes at *erratic* [=*irregular, random*] intervals. ▪ He's an *erratic* [=*inconsistent*] shooter. ▪ *erratic* [=*fluctuating*] oil prices
— er·rat·i·cal·ly /ɪˈrætɪkli/ *adv* ▪ behaving/moving/acting *erratically*

er·ro·ne·ous /ɪˈrounijəs/ *adj* [*more ~; most ~*] *formal* **:** not correct ▪ We received *erroneous* information. ▪ an *erroneous* diagnosis/theory
— er·ro·ne·ous·ly *adv* ▪ The paper reported *erroneously* [=*incorrectly*] that he had died.

er·ror /ˈerɚ/ *noun, pl* **-rors**
1 : something that is not correct **:** a wrong action or statement **:** MISTAKE [*count*] I made an *error* in my calculations. ▪ They uncovered several *errors* in his report to the committee. ▪ The paper contains numerous spelling *errors.* ▪ The computer displayed an ***error message.*** [=a message indicating that an error has occurred] ▪ The project was a ***comedy of errors.*** [=there were many errors made throughout the project] ▪ The company has admitted that it made an ***error in judgment*** [=a poor decision] in trying to expand too quickly. [*noncount*] horrifying cases of hospital *error* ▪ The accident was caused by ***human error.*** [=by a mistake made by a person] — see also *trial and error* at ¹TRIAL
2 [*count*] **:** a mistake made by a person who is playing a sport (such as baseball or tennis) ▪ The shortstop was charged with an *error.*

***in error* 1 :** not correct ▪ I believe your conclusion is *in error.* [=*incorrect, mistaken*] ▪ The judge was *in error* when she allowed the evidence to be admitted. **2 :** in a way that is not correct ▪ My earlier statement was made *in error.* [=my earlier statement was incorrect] ▪ The evidence was admitted *in error.* [=*incorrectly, mistakenly*]

margin of/for error see MARGIN

the error of your ways ✧ To see, recognize, acknowledge, etc., *the error of your ways* is to admit that you have been doing something wrong or behaving badly and to stop doing it. ▪ Congress recognized the *error of its ways* and repealed the law. ▪ He publicly acknowledged *the error of his ways* and asked for forgiveness.

— er·ror·less /ˈerɚləs/ *adj*

er·satz /ˈeɚˌsɑːts, *Brit* ˈeəˌzæts/ *adj* [*more ~; most ~*] **:** copied from something else and usually not as good as the original **:** FAKE ▪ an apartment complex designed as an *ersatz* Mediterranean villa

erst·while /ˈɚstˌwajəl/ *adj, always used before a noun, formal* **:** in the past **:** FORMER ▪ *erstwhile* friends [=people who were friends in the past] ▪ *erstwhile* allies/enemies/lovers

er·u·dite /ˈerəˌdaɪt/ *adj* [*more ~; most ~*] **:** having or showing knowledge that is learned by studying ▪ an *erudite* [=*learned*] scholar/professor/librarian ▪ an *erudite* essay
— er·u·dite·ly *adv*

er·u·di·tion /ˌerəˈdɪʃən/ *noun* [*noncount*] **:** impressive knowledge that is learned by studying ▪ a scholar of remarkable *erudition* ▪ an amazing display of *erudition* [=*learning*]

erupt /ɪˈrʌpt/ *verb* **erupts; erupt·ed; erupt·ing** [*no obj*]
1 : to send out rocks, ash, lava, etc., in a sudden explosion ▪ The volcano *erupted* with tremendous force.; *also* **:** to come out in a sudden explosion — *+ from* ▪ Tons of ash *erupted from* the volcano. ▪ Steam *erupted from* the geyser.
2 : to happen or begin suddenly and violently ▪ War could *erupt* [=*break out*] in that part of the world at any time. ▪ Riots *erupted* last summer. ▪ A bitter dispute has *erupted* among the members of the team.
3 : to begin doing something (such as shouting or applauding) suddenly — usually *+ in, into,* or *with* ▪ The crowd *erupted in* applause when she finished her speech. ▪ The audience *erupted into/with* laughter.
4 : to appear suddenly on the skin ▪ A rash has *erupted* on his back.
5 *of a tooth* **:** to come out through the gum ▪ permanent teeth *erupting*
— erup·tion /ɪˈrʌpʃən/ *noun, pl* **-tions** [*count*] a volcanic *eruption* ▪ a sudden *eruption* of violence ▪ a skin *eruption* [=a rash that has erupted on the skin] [*noncount*] trying to prevent *eruption* of violence **— erup·tive** /ɪˈrʌptɪv/ *adj, technical* ▪ *eruptive* volcanic activity

-ery /əri/ *noun suffix*
1 : qualities considered as a group **:** character ▪ snobb*ery*
2 : place of doing, keeping, producing, or selling (something) ▪ fish*ery* ▪ bak*ery*
3 : collection ▪ fin*ery*
4 : state or condition ▪ slav*ery*

¹-es /əz, ɪz *after* s, z, ʃ, ʧ; z *after* v *or a vowel*/ *noun plural suffix* — used to form the plural of most nouns that end in *s, x, z, sh, ch,* or a final *y* that changes to *i* ▪ glass*es* ▪ box*es* ▪ waltz*es* ▪ bush*es* ▪ peach*es* ▪ lad*ies* — compare ¹-S

²-es *verb suffix* — used to form the third person singular present tense of most verbs that end in *s, x, z, sh, ch,* or a final *y* that changes to *i* ▪ bless*es* ▪ mix*es* ▪ fizz*es* ▪ hush*es* ▪ catch*es* ▪ def*ies* — compare ²-S

es·ca·late /ˈɛskəˌleɪt/ *verb* **-lates; -lat·ed; -lat·ing**
1 : to become worse or to make (something) worse or more severe [*no obj*] The conflict has *escalated* into an all-out war. ▪ a time of *escalating* tensions/violence [*+ obj*] We are trying not to *escalate* the violence.
2 : to become greater or higher or to make (something) greater or higher [*no obj*] Salaries of leading executives have continued to *escalate.* ▪ an effort to combat *escalating* [=*rising*] costs [*+ obj*] The cold weather has *escalated* fuel prices.
— es·ca·la·tion /ˌɛskəˈleɪʃən/ *noun* [*count, noncount*]

es·ca·la·tor /ˈɛskəˌleɪtɚ/ *noun, pl* **-tors** [*count*] **:** a moving set of stairs that carries people up or down from one level of a building to another

es·ca·pade /ˈɛskəˌpeɪd/ *noun, pl* **-pades** [*count*] **:** an exciting, foolish, or dangerous experience or adventure ▪ a madcap/drunken/comic *escapade* ▪ As a teenager he embarked on a series of ill-advised *escapades.* ▪ sexual/erotic *escapades*

¹es·cape /ɪˈskeɪp/ *verb* **-capes; -caped; -cap·ing**
1 [*no obj*] **a :** to get away from a place (such as a prison) where you are being held or kept ▪ The prisoner *escaped* (from jail). ▪ an ***escaped convict*** [=a convict who has escaped from prison] **b :** to get away from a dangerous place or situation ▪ The boat sank but the crew *escaped* (unharmed). ▪ They managed to *escape* from the burning building.
2 : to get away from something that is difficult or unpleasant [*+ obj*] He needed a vacation to *escape* the routine of daily life. ▪ She moved to the city to *escape* the memory of her mother's death. ▪ trying to help people to *escape* poverty [*no obj*] trying to help people to *escape* from poverty ▪ This vacation will give us a chance to *escape* (from the routine of daily life). ▪ *escape* from reality
3 : to avoid something **:** to not experience something (such as disease or injury) [*+ obj*] He succeeded in *escaping* punishment for many years. ▪ A few passengers somehow *escaped* injury. ▪ *escaped* being injured ▪ She barely/narrowly *escaped* death/disaster when her car slid off the road. ▪ Many

cases of fraud **escape detection.** [=are not detected] [*no obj*] Several passengers *escaped* without injury. • She narrowly **escaped with her life.** [=she narrowly avoided death]
4 [+ *obj*] **:** to fail to be remembered or noticed by (someone) • His name *escapes* me. [=I can't remember his name] • Nothing *escapes* her. = Nothing *escapes* her notice.
5 [*no obj*] **:** to come out from somewhere • A bit of light *escaped* through the cracks. **:** to leak out • Gas is *escaping* from the tank.
6 *literary* **:** to come out or be spoken without being intended [+ *obj*] A sigh of relief *escaped* her. [=she sighed in relief without realizing that she was doing it] [*no obj*] A sigh *escaped* from her lips.
escape the ax see [1]AX
there is no escaping — used to say that something is certainly true, real, etc., and cannot be avoided or denied • *There's no escaping* the conclusion [=it is necessary to conclude] that he lied about his involvement. • *There's no escaping* the fact that this system needs to be replaced.

[2]**escape** *noun, pl* **-capes**
1 [*count*] **:** an act of escaping from a place, situation, etc. • The prisoners attempted a daring *escape*. • He celebrated his *escape* from his boring job with a long vacation. • He made his *escape*. = He ***made good his escape.*** [=he succeeded in escaping] • She had a ***lucky escape*** when she wasn't injured in the accident. • She managed to avoid serious injury, but it was a ***narrow escape.***
2 [*count*] **:** a way of escaping from a place, situation, etc. • The door was locked; there was no *escape*. • Gardening offered an *escape* from her busy life. — see also FIRE ESCAPE
3 : an occurrence in which an amount of liquid or gas passes out through a hole or crack in a container [*count*] an accidental *escape* of poisonous gases [*noncount*] trying to prevent further *escape* of liquid

escape artist *noun, pl* **~ -ists** [*count*] **:** a person (such as an entertainer) who is good at escaping • Harry Houdini became famous as an *escape artist*.

escape clause *noun, pl* **~ clauses** [*count*] **:** a part of a contract that allows you to get out of the contract in a particular situation

es·cap·ee /ɪˌskeɪˈpiː/ *noun, pl* **-ees** [*count*] **:** a person who has escaped **:** a prisoner who has escaped • an *escapee* from the local jail

escape hatch *noun, pl* **~ hatches** [*count*] **:** a door or hatch that can be used to get out of something in an emergency • the *escape hatch* of a submarine

escape mechanism *noun, pl* **~ -nisms** [*count*] **:** a way of behaving or thinking that is used to avoid unpleasant facts or problems • She uses humor as an *escape mechanism*. • Football gives him an *escape mechanism* for his anger.

es·cap·ism /ɪˈskeɪˌpɪzəm/ *noun* [*noncount*] **:** an activity or form of entertainment that allows people to forget about the real problems of life • The movie is pure *escapism*. [=*fantasy*] • Reading romantic novels is for her a form of *escapism*.
– es·cap·ist /ɪˈskeɪpɪst/ *adj* • *escapist* fiction • the film's *escapist* appeal

es·carp·ment /ɪˈskɑɚpmənt/ *noun, pl* **-ments** [*count*] **:** a long cliff or steep slope that separates two flat or slightly sloped areas

es·chew /ɛˈʃuː, ɛsˈʧu/ *verb* **es·chews; es·chewed; es·chew·ing** [+ *obj*] *formal* **:** to avoid (something) especially because you do not think it is right, proper, etc. • They now *eschew* the violence of their past. • a psychologist who *eschews* the traditional methods of psychotherapy

[1]**es·cort** /ˈɛsˌkoɚt/ *noun, pl* **-corts** [*count*]
1 a : a person or group of people who go with someone to give protection guidance • Visitors are not allowed to enter the building without an *escort*. • a police *escort* — sometimes used after *under* • The prisoner was taken to the court *under* police *escort*. [=with a police escort] **b :** a group of vehicles, ships, or planes that provide protection • The bombers were protected by a fighter *escort*.
2 a *formal* **:** a man who goes with a woman to a social event • Everyone was surprised when she arrived at the party without an *escort*. **b :** a woman or a man who is hired to go with someone to a social event — often used before another noun • an *escort* agency/service

[2]**es·cort** /ɪˈskoɚt/ *verb* **-corts; -cort·ed; -cort·ing** [+ *obj*] **:** to go with (someone or something) to give protection or guidance • He *escorted* [=*guided, led*] me to the library upstairs. • Several fighters *escorted* the bombers back to base.

Es·ki·mo /ˈɛskəˌmoʊ/ *noun, pl* **Eskimo** *or* **Es·ki·mos** [*count*] **:** a member of a group of people of Alaska, northern Canada, Greenland, and northeastern Siberia ✧ The word *Eskimo* is now considered offensive by some people. — compare INUIT

ESL /ˌiːˌɛsˈɛl/ *noun* [*noncount*] **:** the teaching of English to people who speak a different language and who live in a country where English is the main language spoken ✧ *ESL* is an abbreviation of "English as a second language."

esoph·a·gus (*US*) *or Brit* **oe·soph·a·gus** /ɪˈsɑːfəgəs/ *noun, pl* **-a·gi** /-ˌgaɪ/ [*count*] *medical* **:** the tube that leads from the mouth through the throat to the stomach — see picture at HUMAN

es·o·ter·ic /ˌɛsəˈterɪk/ *adj* [*more ~; most ~*]
1 : only taught to or understood by members of a special group • *esoteric* knowledge **:** hard to understand • *esoteric* subjects/concepts
2 : limited to a small number of people • *esoteric* pursuits • *esoteric* religious sects
– es·o·ter·i·cal·ly /ˌɛsəˈterɪkli/ *adv*

esp. *abbr* especially

ESP /ˌiːˌɛsˈpiː/ *noun* [*noncount*] **:** EXTRASENSORY PERCEPTION

es·pe·cial /ɪˈspɛʃəl/ *adj, always used before a noun, formal* **:** more than usual **:** SPECIAL • This is a matter of *especial* importance.

es·pe·cial·ly /ɪˈspɛʃəli/ *adv* [*more ~; most ~*]
1 : more than usually **:** VERY, EXTREMELY • He was *especially* concerned about the contract. • an *especially* good essay • There is nothing *especially* radical about that idea. • Winning this tournament was *especially* satisfying. • The food was not *especially* good. [=not very good]
2 a — used to indicate something that deserves special mention • She can't be sure she will win, *especially* at this early stage of the campaign. • The appetizers and *especially* [=*particularly*] the soup were delicious. • *Especially* in the beginning, they had many doubts. **b :** for a particular purpose or person • The facility was built *especially* [=*specifically*] for research. • I made this pie *especially* for you.
not especially informal — used to say that you are not very interested in doing something • "Would you like to go to a movie?" "No, *not especially*."

es·pi·o·nage /ˈɛspijəˌnɑːʒ/ *noun* [*noncount*] **:** the things that are done to find out secrets from enemies or competitors **:** the activity of spying • He was charged with several counts of *espionage*. • international/industrial *espionage* • an *espionage* novel/thriller

es·pla·nade /ˈɛspləˌnɑːd, *Brit* ˌɛspləˈneɪd/ *noun, pl* **-nades** [*count*] **:** a level, open area; *especially* **:** an area for walking or driving along a shore • a tree-lined *esplanade* by the river

es·pous·al /ɪˈspaʊzəl/ *noun* [*singular*] *formal* **:** the act of expressing support for a cause or belief **:** the act of espousing something — + *of* • His *espousal of* socialism has been a surprise to many former colleagues.

es·pouse /ɪˈspaʊz/ *verb* **-pous·es; -poused; -pous·ing** [+ *obj*] *formal* **:** to express support for (a cause, belief, etc.) • The new theory has been *espoused* by many leading physicists. • Those *espousing* unpopular views were often excluded.
– es·pous·er *noun, pl* **-ers** [*count*] • an *espouser* [=*supporter, proponent*] of liberal causes

espres·so /ɛˈsprɛsoʊ/ *noun, pl* **-sos :** strong coffee that is made by forcing steam through finely ground roasted coffee beans [*noncount*] a cup of *espresso* [*count*] Two *espressos*, [=cups of espresso] please.

es·prit de corps /ɪˌspriːdəˈkoɚ/ *noun* [*noncount*] **:** feelings of loyalty, enthusiasm, and devotion to a group among people who are members of the group • The troops showed great *esprit de corps*.

es·py /ɪˈspaɪ/ *verb* **-pies; -pied; -py·ing** [+ *obj*] *formal + literary* **:** to see or notice (someone or something) • ". . . the next thing he *espies* may be the lady." —Shakespeare, *A Midsummer Night's Dream* (1595)

Esq. *abbr* esquire

es·quire /ˈɛˌskwajɚ, *Brit* ɪˈskwajə/ *noun, pl* **-quires** [*count*] — used as a title of courtesy after a name; in writing usually used in its abbreviated form *Esq.* • John Smith, *Esq.* ✧ The use of *Esq.* after a man's name was once common in British English but is now considered somewhat old-fashioned. In U.S. English, *Esq.* is used in writing after the name of an attorney, and it is used for both men and women. • Sheila Jones, *Esq.*

[1]**es·say** /ˈɛˌseɪ/ *noun, pl* **-says** [*count*] **:** a short piece of writ-

ing that tells a person's thoughts or opinions about a subject • Your assignment is to write a 500-word *essay* on one of Shakespeare's sonnets. • The book is a collection of his previously unpublished *essays* on/about a variety of topics.

[2]**es·say** /ɛˈseɪ/ *verb* **-says; -sayed; -say·ing** [+ *obj*] *formal* : to try to do, perform, or deal with (something) • He at first *essayed* [=*tried, attempted*] a career as a writer. • There is no hint as to which of the approaches *essayed* in this book will prove most useful. — sometimes followed by *to* + *verb* • He *essayed* [=*tried, attempted*] *to restore* an emphasis on classical languages.

es·say·ist /ˈɛˌsejɪst/ *noun, pl* **-ists** [*count*] : a writer of essays • a 17th-century *essayist*

es·sence /ˈɛsn̩s/ *noun*
1 [*singular*] : the basic nature of a thing : the quality or qualities that make a thing what it is • The *essence* of love is unselfishness. • The book's illustrations capture the *essence* of the story. • Competition is the (very) *essence* of capitalism.
2 [*noncount*] : a substance that contains in very strong form the special qualities (such as the taste and smell) of the thing from which it is taken • *essence* of peppermint/lemon
in essence : at the most basic level • He was *in essence* [=*basically, essentially, fundamentally*] an honest person. • *In essence*, I believe that a real solution is not possible.
of the essence : of the greatest importance • Time/speed is *of the essence* when dealing with a medical emergency.

[1]**es·sen·tial** /ɪˈsɛnʃəl/ *adj* [*more* ~; *most* ~]
1 : extremely important and necessary • As a fighter pilot, he knows that good vision is *essential*. • Reservations are *essential* [=*necessary, needed*] if you plan to eat there on a Saturday. — often + *to* or *for* • The river is *essential to* the region's economy. • Food is *essential* [=*necessary*] *for* life. — often followed by *to* + *verb* • It is *essential to use* the proper technique. • It's *essential to arrive* on time. — often + *that* • It's *essential that* we arrive on time.
2 : very basic : FUNDAMENTAL • Free speech is an *essential* right of citizenship. • The *essential* problem with this plan is that it will cost too much. • There's no *essential* difference between the two products.
— **es·sen·tial·ly** /ɪˈsɛnʃəli/ *adv* [*more* ~; *most* ~] • All action movies have *essentially* [=*basically, fundamentally*] the same plot. • What he says is *essentially* true. — **es·sen·tial·ness** /ɪˈsɛnʃəlnəs/ *noun* [*noncount*]

[2]**essential** *noun, pl* **-tials** [*count*] : something that is basic or necessary : something essential — usually plural • the *essentials* for success • He tried to teach them the *essentials* of physics in just a week. • a computer stripped down to its *essentials* • We only had enough room to pack the ***bare essentials***. [=the things that are absolutely necessary]

essential oil *noun, pl* ~ **oils** [*count*] : an oil that comes from a plant, that smells like the plant it comes from, and that is used in perfumes and flavorings

-est /əst, ɪst/ *adj suffix or adv suffix* — used to form the superlative of most adjectives and adverbs of one syllable • sweet*est* • fatt*est* • lat*est* — used to form the superlative of some adjectives and adverbs of two or more syllables • lucki*est* • often*est* — compare -ER

es·tab·lish /ɪˈstæblɪʃ/ *verb* **-lish·es; -lished; -lish·ing** [+ *obj*]
1 **a** : to cause (someone or something) to be widely known and accepted • *establish* a claim • The film *established* her as a star. • She *established* a reputation as a hard worker. • The word is now *established* as part of the English language. • The company has *established* itself as a leader in the industry. **b** : to put (someone or something) in a position, role, etc., that will last for a long time • As a young doctor he worked hard to *establish* himself in the community. • They want to *establish* their children in the family business.
2 **a** : to begin or create (something that is meant to last for a long time) • *establish* [=*found*] a school • The city was *established* [=*founded*] in the 18th century. **b** : to succeed in making or creating (something) • He was never able to *establish* [=*build, forge*] a close relationship with his son. • She *established* a system of tracking expenses more accurately. • We need to *establish* [=*set*] more realistic goals for ourselves. • The two countries *established* a mutual trade agreement.
3 **a** : to make the truth or existence of (something) clear or certain : to show that (something) is true or real • He was unable to *establish* [=*prove*] his innocence. • Research has *established* [=*demonstrated, shown*] that he played an important role in the negotiations. • *establishing* a link between diet and cancer **b** : to find out (something) • Investigators are trying to *establish* if/whether anyone knew about these problems before the accident. • I was unable to *establish* why these changes were made.

established *adj*
1 : accepted and used by many people • You need to follow *established* [=*standard*] procedures/practices. • a well-*established* principle • He challenged the ***established order***. [=the way things are usually done in society, in an organization, etc.]
2 : successful for a long period of time • an *established* author/artist • an *established* law firm
3 *of a church or religion* : officially recognized and accepted by the government of a country • an *established* church — often used in British English to refer to the Church of England • a leader of the *Established Church*

es·tab·lish·ment /ɪˈstæblɪʃmənt/ *noun, pl* **-ments**
1 [*count*] : a place or organization where people live or do business • a dry-cleaning *establishment* • a business *establishment*
2 [*noncount*] : the act of establishing something or someone: such as **a** : the act of starting something that will last for a long time • the *establishment* of a business/school/church/settlement **b** : the act of causing something or someone to be widely known and accepted • the *establishment* of a scientific fact
3 **a** *or* ***Establishment*** [*singular*] *often disapproving* : the people in business, government, etc., who have power over the other people in a society • She dislikes *establishment* types. • an anti*establishment* campaign — usually used with *the* • We spent our youth rebelling against *the Establishment*. • He accepted a boring job and became a member of *the Establishment*. **b *the establishment*** : the part of a particular group that has power or control • His novels were disliked by *the* literary *establishment*. • *the* medical *establishment*

es·tate /ɪˈsteɪt/ *noun, pl* **es·tates**
1 [*count*] **a** : all of the things that a person owns • His *estate* is worth millions of dollars. **b** : the things left by someone who has died • He inherited the *estate* from his parents.
2 [*count*] : a large piece of land with a large house on it • a country *estate* • the grounds of the *estate* — see also REAL ESTATE
3 [*count*] *Brit* : a group of buildings that were built for a particular purpose (such as housing or industry) on an area of land • a council *estate* [=buildings built by a local government council] — see also INDUSTRIAL ESTATE
4 [*count*] *Brit* : ESTATE CAR, STATION WAGON
5 [*noncount*] *formal* : a particular state or condition • the *estate* [=*state*] of matrimony
— see also FOURTH ESTATE

estate agent *noun, pl* ~ **agents** [*count*] *Brit* : REAL ESTATE AGENT

estate car *noun, pl* ~ **cars** [*count*] *Brit* : STATION WAGON

estate tax *noun, pl* ~ **taxes** [*count, noncount*] : a tax that you pay on the money and other property that comes to you because someone has died : a tax on an estate that you inherit — called also (*Brit*) *death duty*, (*chiefly US*) *death tax*

[1]**es·teem** /ɪˈstiːm/ *noun* [*noncount*] *formal*
1 : respect and affection • She has won *esteem* for her work with cancer patients. • His movies have always enjoyed critical *esteem*. [=have always been praised by critics] • Please accept this gift as a token of my *esteem*. [=as a sign of my affection and respect]
2 — used to say how much someone or something is admired and respected • His movies have fallen in critical *esteem*. [=are admired less now than they were before] — often used after *hold* • He *holds* his father in high *esteem*. [=he respects and admires his father] • That type of job is *held* in low *esteem* [=is poorly regarded] by most people. — see also SELF-ESTEEM

[2]**esteem** *verb* **es·teems; es·teemed; es·teem·ing** [+ *obj*] *formal* : to think very highly or favorably of (someone or something) — usually used as *(be) esteemed* • She *is* (highly) *esteemed* for her work with cancer patients. • an actor *esteemed* [=*admired*] by all his peers • an *esteemed* author/artist/colleague

esthete, esthetic *variant spellings of* AESTHETE, AESTHETIC

es·ti·ma·ble /ˈɛstəməbəl/ *adj* [*more* ~; *most* ~] *formal* : deserving respect : ADMIRABLE • She has written an *estimable* novel. • We owe thanks to our *estimable* colleague.

[1]**es·ti·mate** /ˈɛstəmət/ *noun, pl* **-mates**
1 [*count*] : a guess that you make based on the information

you have about the size, amount, etc., of something • According to government *estimates*, current oil reserves are 10 percent lower than they were a year ago. • One conservative *estimate* is that he stole five million dollars. • At a (very) rough *estimate*, the job will take three months.
2 [*count*] **: a statement about how much a job will cost** • We solicited several *estimates* for the project. • The contractor's *estimate* for the job seemed high.
3 : an opinion or judgment about how good or bad something is [*singular*] He has a high *estimate* [=*opinion, estimation*] of his own abilities. [*noncount*] The company's products are, by general *estimate*, poorly made.

[2]**es·ti·mate** /ˈɛstəˌmeɪt/ *verb* **-mates; -mat·ed; -mat·ing** [+ *obj*] **: to give or form a general idea about the value, size, or cost of (something) : to make an estimate of (something)** • They *estimated* the distance at/as about three miles. • We need to *estimate* how much paint we'll need for the job. • The cost of the project has been *estimated* at/as about 10 million dollars. • He *estimates* that current oil reserves are 20 percent lower than they were a year ago. • Damage from the hurricane is *estimated* (to be) in the billions of dollars.
– estimated *adj* • An *estimated* 50,000 people were in attendance. **– es·ti·ma·tor** /ˈɛstəˌmeɪtɚ/ *noun, pl* **-tors** [*count*]

es·ti·ma·tion /ˌɛstəˈmeɪʃən/ *noun, pl* **-tions**
1 [*singular*] *formal* **: a judgment or opinion about something** • My *estimation* of his films was never very high. [=I never thought his films were very good] • This is not, ***in my estimation***, an efficient use of our resources. • She went down *in her supporters' estimation* after she voted against the plan.
2 a [*noncount*] **: the act of judging the size, amount, cost, etc., of something : the act of estimating something** • Planning the project requires careful cost *estimation*. • By his own *estimation* [=*estimate*] he had wrecked six different cars. **b** [*count*] **: a guess about the size, amount, cost, etc., of something** • My *estimation* [=(more commonly) *estimate*] of the amount of materials we needed was wrong.

es·trange /ɪˈstreɪnʤ/ *verb* **-trang·es; -tranged; -trang·ing** [+ *obj*] *formal*
1 : to cause someone to be no longer friendly or close to another person or group — usually + *from* • His political beliefs have *estranged* him *from* his family. — often used as *(be) estranged* • They *are estranged from* their children. • an ***estranged couple*** [=a married couple who no longer live together] • her ***estranged husband*** [=her husband, who no longer lives with her] • an ***estranged wife*** [=a wife who no longer lives with her husband]
2 : to cause someone to be no longer involved or connected with something — usually + *from* • This decision *estranged* her *from* the church. • He felt *estranged from* his past life.
– es·trange·ment /ɪˈstreɪnʤmənt/ *noun* [*noncount*] • His *estrangement from* his family was deeply painful.

es·tro·gen (*US*) *or Brit* **oes·tro·gen** /ˈɛstrəʤən, *Brit* ˈiːstrəʤən/ *noun* [*noncount*] *medical* **: a substance (called a hormone) that occurs naturally in women** ✧ Estrogen plays an important role in the development of the female characteristics of a woman's body.
– es·tro·gen·ic (*US*) *or Brit* **oes·tro·gen·ic** /ˌɛstrəˈʤɛnɪk, *Brit* ˌiːstrəˈʤɛnɪk/ *adj, technical* • *estrogenic* chemicals

es·tu·ary /ˈɛsʧəˌweri, *Brit* ˈɛsʧuəri/ *noun, pl* **-ar·ies** [*count*] **: an area where a river flows into the sea**

ETA *abbr* estimated time of arrival • The flight's *ETA* is 5:00 p.m. [=the flight is expected to arrive at around 5:00 p.m.]

e–tail /ˈiːˌteɪl/ *noun* [*noncount*] **: the business of using the Internet to sell products directly to the people who will use them** • growing opportunities in *e-tail* — often used before another noun • an *e-tail* store/site • *e-tail* sales
– e–tail·er /ˈiːˌteɪlɚ/ *noun, pl* **-ers** [*count*] • a book *e-tailer* [=an online bookstore]

et al. /ˌɛtˈɑːl, ˌɛtˈæl/ *abbr* and others — used to shorten a list of names • a paper written by Jones, Smith, *et al.* ✧ The abbreviation *et al.* comes from a Latin phrase that means "and others."

etc. *abbr* et cetera

et cet·era /ɛtˈsɛtərə/ **: and other things of the same kind : and so forth — in writing usually used in its abbreviated form *etc.*** • They accuse us of being fat, stupid, lazy, *etc.* • He brought a tent, sleeping bag, *etc.*, when he came to visit.

etch /ˈɛʧ/ *verb* **etch·es; etched; etch·ing** [+ *obj*] **: to produce a pattern, design, etc., by using a powerful liquid (called an acid) to cut the surface of metal or glass** • *etched* an identification number on the back of the television • glass that has been *etched* with an identification number — often used figuratively • That trip is *etched* in her memory. [=she will never forget that trip] • Pain/sorrow was *etched* [=was shown very clearly] on his face.
– etch·er *noun, pl* **-ers** [*count*] • a skillful painter and *etcher*

etching /ˈɛʧɪŋ/ *noun, pl* **-ings** [*count*] **: a picture made by putting ink on an etched piece of metal and then pressing paper against the metal**

eter·nal /ɪˈtɚnl/ *adj*
1 : having no beginning and no end in time : lasting forever • *eternal* life • *eternal* damnation • *eternal* bliss • the *eternal* flames of hell • light an ***eternal flame*** [=a small fire that is kept burning as a symbol to show that something will never end]
2 : existing at all times : always true or valid • *eternal* [=*timeless*] truths • in search of *eternal* wisdom
3 : seeming to last forever • When will his *eternal* whining stop?
– eter·nal·ly *adv* • I will be *eternally* grateful for your help. • *eternally* young

eter·ni·ty /ɪˈtɚnəti/ *noun*
1 [*noncount*] **: time without an end** • She promised to love him for all *eternity*. [=to love him forever]
2 [*noncount*] **: a state that comes after death and never ends** • They believed that sinners would spend *eternity* in hell.
3 [*singular*] **: time that seems to be without an end** • I waited (for) an *eternity* for my car to be fixed. • We suffered through an *eternity* of delays during the lawsuit.

-eth see -TH

eth·a·nol /ˈɛθəˌnɑːl/ *noun* [*noncount*] *technical* **:** ALCOHOL 1 **— used especially to refer to alcohol when it is used as a fuel** • a car that uses a mixture of *ethanol* and gasoline for fuel

ether /ˈiːθɚ/ *noun* [*noncount*]
1 : a liquid that burns easily, that is used to turn solid substances into liquid, and that was used in medicine in the past to prevent patients from feeling pain during operations
2 *the ether* : the air : the sky • The balloon disappeared into *the ether*. • plucked an answer out of *the ether* [=*out of thin air*] — used especially when describing electronic signals that travel through the air • broadcasting radio signals ***into the ether*** • sent a message ***over/through the ether***

ethe·re·al /ɪˈθirijəl/ *adj* [*more* ~; *most* ~] *formal*
1 a : in heaven • *ethereal* heights **b : resembling heaven : seeming to belong to another world** • The windows give the church an *ethereal* glow. • *ethereal* music
2 : very delicate • an *ethereal* ballet dancer • *ethereal* elegance • His writing is filled with *ethereal* [=*airy*] abstractions.
– ethe·re·al·ly *adv* • an *ethereally* beautiful image

Ether·net /ˈiːθɚˌnɛt/ *noun* [*noncount*] *technical* **: a system of wires and devices for connecting computers so that they can work together**

eth·ic /ˈɛθɪk/ *noun, pl* **-ics**
1 [*count*] **: rules of behavior based on ideas about what is morally good and bad** • the Protestant/Puritan *ethic* — usually plural • legal/medical *ethics* • government/journalistic/professional *ethics* • His *ethics* are questionable. [=some of the things he does may be morally wrong] • The company has its own ***code of ethics***. [=its own set of rules about good and bad behavior]
2 *ethics* [*noncount*] **: an area of study that deals with ideas about what is good and bad behavior : a branch of philosophy dealing with what is morally right or wrong** • *Ethics* is his chosen field of study.
3 [*count*] **: a belief that something is very important — usually singular** • a peace *ethic* • People here have a strong ***work ethic***. [=a strong belief in the importance and value of work]

eth·i·cal /ˈɛθɪkəl/ *adj*
1 : involving questions of right and wrong behavior : relating to ethics • *ethical* [=*moral*] principles/standards • *ethical* theories/problems
2 [*more* ~; *most* ~] **: following accepted rules of behavior : morally right and good** • Some doctors feel that this procedure is not medically *ethical*. • favoring the *ethical* [=*humane*] treatment of animals — opposite UNETHICAL
– eth·i·cal·ly /ˈɛθɪkli/ *adv* • behaving *ethically* [=in a way that is right and good] • *ethically* dubious behavior [=behavior that may be morally wrong] • Her involvement in the case was *ethically* wrong.

[1]**eth·nic** /ˈɛθnɪk/ *adj*
1 : of or relating to races or large groups of people who have the same customs, religion, origin, etc. • The U.S. has a wide variety of *ethnic* groups made up of immigrants or their de-

scendants. ▪ *ethnic* Germans/Chinese [=people whose culture or background is German/Chinese] ▪ *ethnic* violence/fighting [=violence/fighting between different ethnic groups] ▪ ***ethnic minorities*** [=people who belong to an ethnic group that is a relatively small part of a population]
2 : associated with or belonging to a particular race or group of people who have a culture that is different from the main culture of a country ▪ an *ethnic* neighborhood ▪ *ethnic* customs ▪ I love *ethnic* food/restaurants.
– eth·ni·cal·ly /ˈɛθnɪkli/ *adv* ▪ an *ethnically* diverse population **– eth·nic·i·ty** /ɛθˈnɪsəti/ *noun, pl* **-ties** [*count*] people of different *ethnicities* [=people who belong to different ethnic groups] [*noncount*] groups separated by race and *ethnicity*

[2]ethnic *noun, pl* **-nics** [*count*] *chiefly US* **:** a person who belongs to a particular ethnic group — used chiefly in newspapers and magazines ▪ trying to win the votes of blacks and of white *ethnics* ▪ urban *ethnics*

ethnic cleansing *noun* [*noncount*] **:** the practice of removing or killing people who belong to an ethnic group that is different from the ruling group in a country or region

eth·no·cen·tric /ˌɛθnoʊˈsɛntrɪk/ *adj* [*more ~; most ~*] *disapproving* **:** having or based on the idea that your own group or culture is better or more important than others ▪ The review was criticized for its *ethnocentric* bias.
– eth·no·cen·tric·ity /ˌɛθnoʊsɛnˈtrɪsəti/ *noun* [*noncount*] **– eth·no·cen·trism** /ˌɛθnoʊˈsɛnˌtrɪzəm/ *noun* [*noncount*]

eth·nog·ra·phy /ɛθˈnɑːgrəfi/ *noun* [*noncount*] **:** the study of human races and cultures
– eth·nog·ra·pher /ɛθˈnɑːgrəfɚ/ *noun, pl* **-phers** [*count*] **– eth·no·graph·ic** /ˌɛθnəˈgræfɪk/ *adj* ▪ *ethnographic* research **– eth·no·graph·i·cal·ly** /ˌɛθnəˈgræfɪkli/ *adv*

ethos /ˈiːˌθɑːs/ *noun* [*singular*] *formal* **:** the guiding beliefs of a person, group, or organization ▪ The company made environmental awareness part of its business *ethos*. ▪ They are working to keep a democratic *ethos* alive in the community. ▪ an *ethos* of arrogance

eth·yl alcohol /ˈɛθəl-/ *noun* [*noncount*] *technical* **:** ETHANOL

et·i·quette /ˈɛtɪkət/ *noun* [*noncount*] **:** the rules indicating the proper and polite way to behave ▪ Her failure to respond to the invitation was a serious breach of *etiquette*. ▪ a book of *etiquette* ▪ telephone *etiquette* [=the proper way to behave when speaking on the telephone]

-ette *noun suffix*
1 : little one ▪ kitchen*ette*
2 : female ▪ major*ette*

et·y·mol·o·gy /ˌɛtəˈmɑːləʤi/ *noun, pl* **-gies**
1 [*count*] **:** an explanation of where a word came from **:** the history of a word ▪ According to its *etymology*, the English word "dope" comes from the Dutch word "doop" (which means "sauce"). ▪ Several different *etymologies* have been proposed.
2 [*noncount*] **:** the study of word histories ▪ an expert in *etymology*
– et·y·mo·log·i·cal /ˌɛtəməˈlɑːʤɪkəl/ *adj* ▪ *etymological* research ▪ an *etymological* dictionary/expert **– et·y·mo·log·i·cal·ly** /ˌɛtəməˈlɑːʤɪkli/ *adv* ▪ The words are related *etymologically*. **– et·y·mol·o·gist** /ˌɛtəˈmɑːləʤɪst/ *noun, pl* **-gists** [*count*] ▪ a brilliant *etymologist*

EU *abbr* European Union

eu·ca·lyp·tus /ˌjuːkəˈlɪptəs/ *noun, pl* **-tus·es** *also* **-ti** /ˌjuːkəˈlɪpˌtaɪ/ [*count*] **:** a type of tree that grows naturally in western Australia and that is grown in other places for the products (such as wood and oil) that it provides

Eu·cha·rist /ˈjuːkərəst/ *noun*
the Eucharist **:** a Christian ceremony in which bread is eaten and wine is drunk as a way of showing devotion to Jesus Christ **:** COMMUNION ▪ celebrate *the Eucharist*
– Eu·cha·ris·tic /ˌjuːkəˈrɪstɪk/ *adj*

eu·gen·ics /juˈʤɛnɪks/ *noun* [*noncount*] **:** a science that tries to improve the human race by controlling which people become parents

eu·lo·gize *also Brit* **eu·lo·gise** /ˈjuːləˌʤaɪz/ *verb* **-giz·es; -gized; -giz·ing** [+ *obj*] **:** to say or write good things about (someone or something); *especially* **:** to praise (someone who has died) in a eulogy ▪ He was *eulogized* at his funeral as a great actor and a good friend.
– eu·lo·gist /ˈjuːləʤɪst/ *noun, pl* **-gists** [*count*] ▪ described by his *eulogist* as a great actor

eu·lo·gy /ˈjuːləʤi/ *noun, pl* **-gies** [*count*] **:** a speech that praises someone who has died ▪ He delivered a moving *eulogy* at his father's funeral. ✧ *Eulogy* can refer to any speech expressing praise, but it almost always refers to a funeral speech. — compare ELEGY

eu·nuch /ˈjuːnək/ *noun, pl* **eu·nuchs** [*count*] **:** a man who has had his sexual organs removed

eu·phe·mism /ˈjuːfəˌmɪzəm/ *noun, pl* **-misms** [*count*] **:** a mild or pleasant word or phrase that is used instead of one that is unpleasant or offensive ▪ using "eliminate" as a *euphemism* for "kill"
– eu·phe·mis·tic /ˌjuːfəˈmɪstɪk/ *adj* [*more ~; most ~*] ▪ *euphemistic* language **– eu·phe·mis·ti·cal·ly** /ˌjuːfəˈmɪstɪkli/ *adv* ▪ The prison was *euphemistically* referred to as a "correctional facility."

eu·pho·ni·ous /juˈfoʊnijəs/ *adj* [*more ~; most ~*] *formal* **:** having a pleasant sound ▪ a *euphonious* name ▪ *euphonious* harmonies

eu·pho·ria /juˈforijə/ *noun* [*noncount*] **:** a feeling of great happiness and excitement ▪ The initial *euphoria* following their victory in the election has now subsided. ▪ The drug produces intense feelings of *euphoria*.
– eu·phor·ic /juˈforɪk/ *adj* [*more ~; most ~*] ▪ a *euphoric* mood ▪ feeling *euphoric* ▪ *euphoric* effects of a drug **– eu·phor·i·cal·ly** /juˈforɪkli/ *adv*

Eur·asian /juˈreɪʒən/ *adj*
1 : of or relating to both Europe and Asia ▪ a *Eurasian* empire ▪ a *Eurasian* species of bird
2 : having ancestors from both Europe and Asia ▪ a *Eurasian* child
– Eurasian *noun, pl* **-asians** [*count*]

eu·re·ka /juˈriːkə/ *interj* — used to express excitement when a discovery has been made ▪ He held up the gold and shouted "*Eureka*! I have found it!"

eu·ro /ˈjuroʊ/ *noun, pl* **-ros** *also* **-ro** [*count*] **:** a monetary unit used by countries of the European Union since 1999 ▪ was sold for 100,000 *euros*

Euro- *or* **Eur-** *combining form* **:** Europe **:** European **:** European and ▪ *Euro*-American relations ▪ *Eur*asian

Eu·ro·pe·an /ˌjurəˌpiːjən/ *noun, pl* **-ans** [*count*]
1 : a person born, raised, or living in Europe; *also* **:** a native or resident of the continent of Europe rather than Britain
2 : a person who is descended from Europeans
– European *adj* ▪ *European* history

eu·tha·na·sia /ˌjuːθəˈneɪʒə/ *noun* [*noncount*] **:** the act or practice of killing someone who is very sick or injured in order to prevent any more suffering ▪ a physician who refuses to practice *euthanasia* — called also *mercy killing*

evac·u·ate /ɪˈvækjəˌweɪt/ *verb* **-ates; -at·ed; -at·ing**
1 [+ *obj*] **:** to remove (someone) from a dangerous place ▪ People who live along the coast are being *evacuated* as the hurricane approaches. ▪ During World War II, children were *evacuated* from London to the country.
2 : to leave (a dangerous place) [+ *obj*] Residents were ordered to *evacuate* the building. [*no obj*] Residents have been ordered to *evacuate*.
3 [+ *obj*] *medical* **:** to pass (solid waste) from your body ▪ *evacuate* your bowels
– evac·u·a·tion /ɪˌvækjəˈweɪʃən/ *noun, pl* **-tions** [*noncount*] Many nations are assisting in the *evacuation* of the refugees. [*count*] repeated *evacuations* of the embassy

evac·u·ee /ɪˌvækjəˈwiː/ *noun, pl* **-ees** [*count*] **:** a person who has been removed from a dangerous place **:** a person who has been evacuated ▪ One hundred *evacuees* spent the night at a school during the storm.

evade /ɪˈveɪd/ *verb* **evades; evad·ed; evad·ing** [+ *obj*]
1 a : to stay away from (someone or something) ▪ The criminals have so far managed to *evade* the police. ▪ They have ***evaded capture/arrest***. [=have avoided being captured/arrested] ▪ His criminal activities somehow ***evaded detection***. [=were not detected] **b :** to avoid dealing with or facing (something) ▪ a politician skilled at *evading* difficult questions ▪ The governor has been accused of *evading* the issue. **c :** to avoid doing (something required) ▪ illegally *evading* taxes [=failing to pay taxes]
2 a : to not be understood by (someone) ▪ Their purpose in doing this *evades* me. [=I don't understand their purpose] **b :** to fail to be achieved by (someone) ▪ Up to now, success has *evaded* [=*eluded*] me.
– evad·er *noun, pl* **-ers** [*count*] ▪ tax *evaders*

eval·u·ate /ɪˈvæljəˌweɪt/ *verb* **-ates; -at·ed; -at·ing** [+ *obj*] **:** to judge the value or condition of (someone or something) in a careful and thoughtful way ▪ We need to *evaluate* our options. ▪ *evaluate* a job candidate ▪ *evaluate* a training program as effective/ineffective

– **eval·u·a·tion** /ɪˌvæljəˈweɪʃən/ *noun, pl* **-tions** [*count*] make/do an *evaluation* of the program ▪ He's been ordered to undergo/have/get a psychiatric *evaluation*. ▪ teacher *evaluations* [*noncount*] The program will be undergoing careful *evaluation*. – **eval·u·a·tive** /ɪˈvæljəˌweɪtɪv, *Brit* ɪˈvæljuətɪv/ *adj, formal* ▪ *evaluative* procedures/criteria – **eval·u·a·tor** /ɪˈvæljəˌweɪtɚ/ *noun, pl* **-tors** [*count*]

ev·a·nes·cent /ˌɛvəˈnɛsn̩t/ *adj* [*more* ~; *most* ~] *formal + literary* : lasting a very short time ▪ *evanescent* fame

– **ev·a·nes·cence** /ˌɛvəˈnɛsn̩s/ *noun* [*noncount*]

evan·gel·i·cal /ˌiːˌvænˈʤɛlɪkəl/ *adj* [*more* ~; *most* ~]

1 : of or relating to a Christian sect or group that stresses the authority of the Bible, the importance of believing that Jesus Christ saved you personally from sin or hell, and the preaching of these beliefs to other people ▪ the *evangelical* movement ▪ She is an *evangelical* Christian.

2 : having or showing very strong and enthusiastic feelings ▪ He spoke about the project with *evangelical* zeal.

– **evangelical** *or* **Evangelical** *noun, pl* **-cals** [*count*] ▪ She is an *Evangelical*. – **evan·gel·i·cal·ly** /ˌiːˌvænˈʤɛlɪkli/ *adv*

evan·ge·list /ɪˈvænʤəlɪst/ *noun, pl* **-lists** [*count*]

1 : a person and especially a preacher who tries to convince people to become Christian — see also TELEVANGELIST

2 : someone who talks about something with great enthusiasm ▪ an *evangelist* of space exploration ▪ software *evangelists*

3 *or* ***Evangelist*** **:** a writer of any of the Gospels in the Bible ▪ St. John the *Evangelist*

– **evan·ge·lism** /ɪˈvænʤəlɪzəm/ *noun* [*noncount*] ▪ television *evangelism* – **evan·ge·lis·tic** /ɪˌvænʤəˈlɪstɪk/ *adj* [*more* ~; *most* ~] ▪ He spoke with *evangelistic* [=*evangelical*] zeal. ▪ the *evangelistic* movement

evan·ge·lize *also Brit* **evan·ge·lise** /ɪˈvænʤəˌlaɪz/ *verb* **-liz·es; -lized; -liz·ing :** to try to convert (a group or area) to a different religion (especially Christianity) [+ *obj*] The missionaries set out to *evangelize* the world. — often used figuratively ▪ They *evangelized* their neighbors about the importance of saving energy. [*no obj*] They were *evangelizing* about the importance of saving energy.

– **evan·ge·li·za·tion** *also Brit* **evan·ge·li·sa·tion** /ɪˌvænʤələˈzeɪʃən, *Brit* ɪˌvænʤəˌlaɪˈzeɪʃən/ *noun* [*noncount*]

evap·o·rate /ɪˈvæpəˌreɪt/ *verb* **-rates; -rat·ed; -rat·ing**

1 : to change from a liquid into a gas [*no obj*] Let the liquid start to *evaporate*. [+ *obj*] The heat *evaporated* the water.

2 [*no obj*] **:** to go away suddenly : to disappear or vanish ▪ The opportunity *evaporated* before he could act on it.

– **evap·o·ra·tion** /ɪˌvæpəˈreɪʃən/ *noun* [*noncount*] ▪ water loss through *evaporation* – **evap·o·ra·tive** /ɪˈvæpəˌreɪtɪv/ *adj, technical* ▪ *evaporative* cooling – **evap·o·ra·tor** /ɪˈvæpəˌreɪtɚ/ *noun, pl* **-tors** [*count*] ▪ The boiling takes place in machines called *evaporators*.

evaporated milk *noun* [*noncount*] : canned milk from which most of the water has been removed — compare CONDENSED MILK

eva·sion /ɪˈveɪʒən/ *noun, pl* **-sions**

1 a [*noncount*] **:** the act of avoiding something that you do not want to do or deal with : the act of evading something ▪ He was arrested for tax/draft *evasion*. **b** [*count*] **:** a way of avoiding something ▪ They came up with an *evasion* of the law to keep all the land for themselves.

2 [*count*] **:** a statement or action that avoids directly dealing with something (such as a difficult problem or question) ▪ His reply was nothing but careful *evasions*.

eva·sive /ɪˈveɪsɪv/ *adj* [*more* ~; *most* ~]

1 : not honest or direct ▪ She gave an *evasive* answer.

2 : done to avoid harm, an accident, etc. ▪ They took *evasive* action to avoid capture. ▪ an *evasive* maneuver

– **eva·sive·ly** *adv* ▪ She answered *evasively*. – **eva·sive·ness** *noun* [*noncount*]

eve /ˈiːv/ *noun, pl* **eves** [*count*]

1 *literary* **:** EVENING ▪ one pleasant summer's *eve* ▪ ". . . from noon to dewy *eve* . . ." —John Milton, *Paradise Lost* (1667)

2 : the evening or the day before a special day — usually singular ▪ New Year's *Eve* ▪ Christmas *Eve*

3 : the period of time just before an important event — used in the phrase ***on the eve of*** ▪ The students were nervous *on the eve of* their graduation.

[1]**even** /ˈiːvən/ *adj*

1 [*more* ~; *most* ~] **a :** having a flat, smooth, or level surface ▪ We finally reached *even* ground after the long climb. ▪ The ground became more *even*. [=*level*] **b :** not having breaks or bumps ▪ an *even* coastline ▪ The transition was *even* [=*smooth*] and slow.

2 : located next to someone or something else ▪ They slowed down and waited for him to draw *even*. — often + *with* ▪ The houses are lined up *even with* each other. [=lined up so that neither one is in front of or behind the other]

3 : not changing : staying the same ▪ She spoke with a calm, *even* voice. ▪ the *even* beat of the drum ▪ He was maintaining an *even* [=*constant*] speed.

4 a [*more* ~; *most* ~] **:** equal and fair : not giving an advantage to one side or group ▪ an *even* trade ▪ He favors a more *even* distribution of wealth. ▪ Everyone should have an *even* chance. **b :** having nothing owed by either side ▪ Here's the money I owe you. Now we're *even*. [=now we don't owe each other anything] **c :** not likely to be won easily by one side or another ▪ an *even* match

5 a *of a number* **:** able to be divided by two into two equal whole numbers ▪ 2, 4, 6, and 8 are *even* numbers; 1, 3, 5, and 7 are odd numbers. **b :** marked by an even number ▪ the *even* and odd pages of a book **c** *always used before a noun* **:** not more or less than a stated amount ▪ That'll cost you an *even* dollar. [=that'll cost you exactly one dollar] ▪ an *even* dozen

6 — used to say that something is as likely to happen as to not happen ▪ He stands an *even* [=*fifty-fifty*] chance of winning. ▪ Our chances of success or failure are about *even*.

break even see [1]BREAK

get even **:** to do something bad or unpleasant to someone who has treated you badly or unfairly ▪ He vowed that he would *get even* (with them) for the way he'd been treated.

on an even keel see [1]KEEL

– **even·ly** *adv* ▪ The money was distributed *evenly*. ▪ The committee was *evenly* divided. ▪ The two teams are *evenly* matched. ▪ Apply pressure slowly and *evenly*. – **even·ness** /ˈiːvənnəs/ *noun* [*noncount*] ▪ the *evenness* of the lighting/distribution/match

[2]**even** *adv*

1 — used to stress something that is surprising or unlikely ▪ It's so simple that *even* a child can do it. ▪ Not only did she stay in business, she *even* managed to make a profit. ▪ They've changed everything about the place, *even* the color! ▪ They've changed the doors, the carpets, the color, *even*!

2 — used to stress the difference between two things that are being compared ▪ His first book was good, but this one is *even* better. ▪ An *even* bigger change came the next year.

3 — used after a negative word (such as *not* or a contraction of *not*) to stress the smallness of an amount or effort ▪ Not only didn't they help, they didn't *even* offer to help! ▪ We thought he'd be interested in the painting, but he didn't *even* glance at it. ▪ She didn't *even* give him a second thought.

4 — used to stress something that goes beyond what has just been mentioned in some way (such as by being stronger or more specific) ▪ They were willing, *even* eager, to help. ▪ The disease can cause brain damage and *even* death.

even as **:** at the same time as ▪ They are finishing the job *even as* we speak. [=they are finishing the job right now]

even if — used to stress that something will happen despite something else that might prevent it ▪ I'm going to the party *even if* it rains. [=whether or not it rains]

even now/then **1** — used to stress that something is or was happening at a particular time ▪ They are *even now* preparing for his arrival. [=they are preparing for his arrival right now] ▪ Enemy troops were *even then* approaching the city. **2** — used to stress that something (such as a person's attitude or behavior) was or is very surprising and unexpected ▪ We showed her the proof, but *even then*, she wouldn't admit she was wrong. ▪ Despite all that went wrong, he insists *even now* that he would do it again.

even so — used to introduce a statement that is somehow different from what has just been said ▪ These problems are not as bad as they were. *Even so*, there is much more work to be done.

even though — used as a stronger way to say "though" or "although" ▪ She stayed with him *even though* he often mistreated her. ▪ I'm going *even though* it may rain.

[3]**even** *verb* **evens; evened; even·ing** [+ *obj*] **:** to make (something) equal ▪ He *evened* [=*tied*] the set at two games apiece. — see also *even the score* at [1]SCORE

even out [*phrasal verb*] **1 :** to become level ▪ After a long climb the ground *evened out*. [=*leveled out*] **2** ***even (something) out*** *or* ***even out (something)*** **:** to make (something)

E

even and smooth • Let me *even out* the rug. **3** ***even out*** *or* ***even (something) out*** *or* ***even out (something)*** **: to reach a balanced or middle state between extremes over a period of time** • The economy had good periods and bad periods, but it all *evened out* by the end of the year. • Any variations will be *evened out* eventually.

even·hand·ed /ˌivənˈhændəd/ *adj* [*more* ~; *most* ~] **: not favoring one side or group over another : FAIR** • *evenhanded* justice • I thought it was an *evenhanded* assessment/analysis/treatment of her performance.

– even·hand·ed·ly *adv* **– even·hand·ed·ness** *noun* [*noncount*]

[1]**eve·ning** /ˈiːvnɪŋ/ *noun, pl* **-nings** [*count*]

1 : the last part of the day and early part of the night • We're going out to dinner this *evening*. • He devotes his *evenings* to charity work. • They left on the *evening* of July 26. **— often used before another noun** • an *evening* walk • We watched the ***evening news***. [=a news program broadcast in the evening] • I'm taking two ***evening classes***. [=classes for adult students that are scheduled in the evening]

2 : an event or activity that happens during an evening • We're looking forward to an *evening* at the theater. • several fun-filled *evenings* of poker

3 *literary* **: a late part of something (such as a person's life)** • He met her in the *evening* of his life.

[2]**evening** *present participle of* [3]EVEN

evening gown *noun, pl* ~ **gowns** [*count*] **: a long, formal dress that is worn to evening parties or events — called also** *evening dress*; **see color picture on page C15**

evenings /ˈiːvnɪŋz/ *adv, US* **: in the evening** • He has to work *evenings*.

evening star *noun*

the evening star **: the planet Venus when it can be seen in the western sky at sunset or just after sunset — compare** MORNING STAR

event /ɪˈvɛnt/ *noun, pl* **events** [*count*]

1 a : something (especially something important or notable) that happens • The article recounted the *events* of the past year. • the last major/big *event* of the summer • He had no memory of the *events* that happened afterwards. • The accident was caused by an unusual ***sequence/chain/series of events***. • It's difficult to predict the ***course of events*** [=to predict what will happen] with any confidence. **— see also** CURRENT EVENTS **b : a planned occasion or activity (such as a social gathering)** • She likes to arrive at social *events* early. • upcoming *events* • a sporting *event* • a calendar of *events* **— see also** MEDIA EVENT, NONEVENT

2 : any one of the contests in a sports program • track-and-field *events* • It's the only *event* on the golf tour that she hasn't yet won. • the main *event*

at all events *or* ***in any event*** **— used to say that what is being said is true no matter what other things may or may not happen or be true** • It's possible that she was too nervous to pay close attention. *At all events* [=*in any case, anyway*], she does not have all the details quite right. • It is curious, *in any event*, why their decision bothers him so much.

in the event *chiefly Brit* **: when something that was planned or thought about actually happened** • We thought the weather might delay us, but, *in the event* [=*as it turned out*], we were able to leave on time.

in the event of **: if (something) happens** • *In the event of* rain [=if it rains], the ceremony will be held indoors. • I can call for help *in the event of* an emergency.

in the event (that) **: if it happens that (something occurs) : IF** • *In the event* you (should) decide not to continue your subscription, you may cancel it at any time. • The insurance policy will provide you with a regular income *in the* (unlikely) *event that* you are injured.

overtaken by events **see** OVERTAKE

even–tempered *adj* [*more* ~; *most* ~] **: not easily upset or made angry** • a very *even-tempered* girl

event·ful /ɪˈvɛntfəl/ *adj* [*more* ~; *most* ~] **: having many important things happening** • an *eventful* [=*busy*] day • He led a short but *eventful* life. • It was an extremely *eventful* period in American history.

– event·ful·ly *adv* • The day began *eventfully*. **– event·ful·ness** *noun* [*noncount*]

even·tu·al /ɪˈvɛntʃəwəl/ *adj* **: coming or happening at a later time** • our *eventual* success • She lost to the *eventual* champion. [=the person who would later become champion] • This plant reaches an *eventual* height of 15 feet. [=this plant will grow to be 15 feet high]

even·tu·al·i·ty /ɪˌvɛntʃəˈwæləti/ *noun, pl* **-ties** [*count*] *formal* **: something that might happen : a possible event or occurrence** • He planned carefully and was ready for any *eventuality*.

even·tu·al·ly /ɪˈvɛntʃəwəli, ɪˈvɛntʃəli/ *adv* **: at some later time : in the end** • *Eventually*, I did get better and returned to work. • I am sure that we'll succeed *eventually*. • Her constant campaigning *eventually* got her the nomination. • This plant *eventually* reaches a height of 15 feet.

ev·er /ˈɛvɚ/ *adv*

1 : at any time • The crime rate is higher now than it has *ever* been. • He's forgotten all he's *ever* learned about history. • Have you *ever* been to France? • She's doing fine and is as pretty as *ever*. • No one has *ever* seen a better example of woodwork. • We need your help now more than *ever* (before). • Has this *ever* been done before? • That was my best vacation *ever*. [=the best vacation I have ever had] • Did it *ever* occur to you that I might like more myself? • He's a born politician if *ever* I saw one. [=he is certainly a born politician] • That was the worst movie I *ever* saw. • I don't *ever* want to do that again. = (*informal*) I don't want to *ever* do that again. = I don't want to do that again, *ever*!

2 *formal* **: at all times** • He is *ever* [=*always*] faithful. • moving *ever* westward • a guard who is *ever* watchful = an *ever*-watchful guard

3 : to a greater degree • Technology in recent years has become *ever* more sophisticated. • The deadline draws *ever* closer. • Millions of farmers were forced into *ever*-deeper debt during the Great Depression.

4 — used after words like ***where, who, how,*** **and** ***why*** **to make a question more forceful** • How *ever* can I (possibly) thank you? • What *ever* happened to my former classmates? • Where *ever* did I put my keys? • "I can't do that." "Why *ever* not?" • Who *ever* would want to go there? **— also used in indirect questions** • I can't imagine who *ever* would want to go there!

5 *US, informal* **— used to give stress to what follows** • Wow, was he *ever* funny! [=he was very funny] • Am I *ever* embarrassed! [=I am very embarrassed]

as ever **: as has always been true : as usual** • The problem, *as ever*, is to find a better way to control spending.

ever after *old-fashioned* **: from that time forward** • She remembered him fondly *ever after*. ✧ **Fairy tales sometimes end by saying that the characters in the story** ***lived happily ever after***. • The prince saved the queen and they all *lived happily ever after*. **The phrase** ***live happily ever after*** **is also used to describe real people who are being compared in some way to characters in a fairy tale.** • His biography tells the story of a poor boy who grew up to be a millionaire and *lived happily ever after*.

ever and anon *old-fashioned + literary* **: at different times : now and then** • *Ever and anon* [=*every so often*] there came the sound of bells.

ever since **1 : continually or often from a past time until now** • We both liked the idea and have been working on it *ever since*. [=*since then*] • I went to the festival its first year and have been returning *ever since*. **2 : continually from the time in the past when : SINCE** • She's wanted to be a firefighter *ever since* she was a young girl.

ever so *informal* **: VERY** • Thank you *ever so* much. • I'm *ever so* glad that you got better. • The violin was ***ever so slightly*** out of tune.

ever such *chiefly Brit, informal* **— used as a more forceful way to say "such"** • He's *ever such* a nice person! [=he's a very nice person]

for ever (and ever) **: FOREVER** • I'll love you *for ever and ever*!

hardly/scarcely ever **: almost never : RARELY** • She *hardly ever* sings anymore. • I *scarcely ever* think of them now.

never ever *informal* **— used especially in speech as a more forceful way to say "never"** • He *never ever* wanted to grow up. • I promise to *never ever* do it again.

rarely/seldom ever **: almost never : RARELY** • We *seldom ever* dine out these days. • She *rarely ever* drinks wine. ✧ **Some people regard** ***rarely ever*** **and** ***seldom ever*** **as incorrect, but these phrase are common in speech and in informal writing.**

rarely/seldom if ever **— used as a more forceful way to say "rarely" or "seldom"** • I have *seldom if ever* been so embarrassed. ✧ ***Rarely if ever*** **and** ***seldom if ever*** **can be written both with or without commas** • Such radical opinions have *rarely, if ever*, been heard here before. • She *rarely if ever* sings anymore.

Yours ever *or* ***Ever yours*** *Brit* — used as a way to end an informal letter • *Yours ever*, Robert

ev•er•green /ˈɛvɚˌgriːn/ *adj* : having leaves that remain green all year long • Most pines are *evergreen* trees. • *evergreen* forests/leaves

– evergreen /ˈɛvɚˌgriːn/ *noun, pl* **-greens** [*count*] • Most pine trees are *evergreens*.

ev•er•last•ing /ˌɛvɚˈlæstɪŋ, *Brit* ˌɛvəˈlɑːstɪŋ/ *adj* : lasting forever • *everlasting* love = love *everlasting* • To his *everlasting* credit, he never once gave in to temptation.

– ev•er•last•ing•ly *adv* • We are *everlastingly* hopeful.

ev•ery /ˈɛvri/ *adj*

1 : including each person or thing in a group or series • I heard *every* word you said. • He devotes *every* spare moment to his hobby. • His *every* move was carefully watched. • She's beautiful in *every* way/respect. • Ceramics of *every* kind were on display. • We have *every* reason to believe (that) he's telling the truth. [=we have no reason not to believe him] • He looked closely at ***every last one*** [=every one] of them. • They were questioning ***every little thing*** [=*everything*] she said. • He provided them with guidance ***every step of the way***. [=throughout the entire process] • ***Every time*** [=*whenever*] I go there I learn something new. • We're ***making every effort*** [=we're doing all that we can] to solve the problem.

2 a — used to describe how often some repeated activity, event, etc., happens or is done • She drives to town *every* few days. • *Every* day she starts work at 8 a.m. • The fair is held ***every other/second*** year. [=the fair is held one year, not held the next year, held the following year, and so on] **b** — used to describe how far apart the things in a series of things are placed from each other • They placed a marker *every* 20 yards or so. **c** — used in phrases like ***one in every three*** to describe how common something is • problems that affect *one in every three* people

3 : not lacking in any way • I have *every* [=*complete, total*] confidence in you.

at every turn see ²TURN

each and every see ¹EACH

every bit see ¹BIT

every expectation of see EXPECTATION

every man for himself see ¹MAN

every now and then/again *or* ***every once in a while*** *or* ***every so often*** : sometimes but not often : from time to time : OCCASIONALLY • We still see each other *every now and then*. • They would get together *every now and again*. • *Every so often* she'd come in to check on him.

every which way *US, informal* **1** : in every direction • Bullets were flying *every which way*. **2** : in a disorderly manner • The papers were stacked *every which way*.

ev•ery•body /ˈɛvriˌbʌdi, ˈɛvriˌbɑːdi, *Brit* ˈɛvriˌbɒdi/ *pronoun*

1 : every person : EVERYONE • The president waved to *everybody* in the crowd. • *Everybody* hates to hear bad news.

2 : every important person • *Everybody* will be there.

ev•ery•day /ˈɛvriˌdeɪ/ *adj, always used before a noun* : used or seen every day : suitable for every day • *everyday* clothes • Don't let the problems of *everyday* life get you down. • She uses a variety of *everyday* [=*familiar, ordinary*] objects in her art. • *everyday* [=*ordinary*] people

ev•ery•man *or* **Ev•ery•man** /ˈɛvriˌmæn/ *noun* [*singular*] : the typical, ordinary person • an actor who is seen as the image of *everyman*

ev•ery•one /ˈɛvriˌwʌn/ *pronoun* : every person : EVERYBODY • He hated the movie but *everyone* else enjoyed it. • Not *everyone* got the joke.

ev•ery•place /ˈɛvriˌpleɪs/ *adv, US* : EVERYWHERE • We've been seeing them *everyplace*. • We see them *everyplace* we go.

ev•ery•thing /ˈɛvriˌθɪŋ/ *pronoun*

1 a : every thing there is : all that exists • People will buy *everything* she paints. • I didn't agree with *everything* he said. • What do you buy for the man who has *everything*? **b** : all that is related to a particular subject • Tell us *everything* that happened. • He denied *everything* about the incident. ♦ The phrase ***everything from (something) to (something)*** is used to show the wide range of things that are included in something. • The company makes *everything from golf tees to diapers*. • Her paintings have been called *everything from childish to brilliant*.

2 : all that is important • To him, money is *everything*. [=he only cares about money] • She means *everything* to me.

3 *informal* : the things that are happening in a person's life • How's *everything*? • *Everything* is fine. • We're pretty happy with *everything* right now. ♦ Phrases like ***How's everything?*** and ***How's everything going?*** are used, especially in U.S. English, as informal ways to say "How are you?"

and everything *informal* : and other things like that • I like being out in the forest with all the birds and trees *and everything*. • He has a lot on his mind, what with his health problems *and everything*.

carry everything before you see ¹CARRY

ev•ery•where /ˈɛvriˌweɚ/ *adv* : in or to every place • *Everywhere* we went, people were friendly. • His new book is anxiously awaited by fans *everywhere*. • I seem to hear his music *everywhere* these days! • We went *everywhere* we could.

evict /ɪˈvɪkt/ *verb* **evicts; evict•ed; evict•ing** [+ *obj*] : to force (someone) to leave a place • His landlord has threatened to *evict* him if he doesn't pay the rent soon. • They were *evicted* from their apartment.

– evic•tion /ɪˈvɪkʃən/ *noun, pl* **-tions** [*noncount*] He was threatened with *eviction* for failing to pay the rent. [*count*] unlawful *evictions*

¹ev•i•dence /ˈɛvədəns/ *noun, pl* **-denc•es**

1 a [*noncount*] : something which shows that something else exists or is true • There is no *evidence* that these devices actually work. • He has been unable to find *evidence* to support his theory. • She first showed/gave *evidence* of her abilities [=she first showed her abilities] at an early age. • Investigators could find no *evidence* linking him to the crime. • He denies that he was involved, despite (abundant/ample) *evidence* to the contrary. [=despite evidence indicating that he was involved] **b** [*count*] *chiefly US, somewhat formal* : a visible sign of something — usually plural • They found many *evidences* of neglect.

2 [*noncount*] : material that is presented to a court of law to help find the truth about something • The jury had a great deal of *evidence* to sort through before reaching a verdict. • There is not a scrap/shred of *evidence* in her favor. • circumstantial *evidence* • Anything you say may be used as/in *evidence* against you. • The letter was admitted in *evidence*. = (*chiefly US*) The letter was admitted into *evidence*. [=the letter was accepted by the court as evidence] • You may be asked to ***give evidence*** [=*testify*] at the trial. — see also STATE'S EVIDENCE

in evidence : easily seen • Her charm was very much *in evidence* throughout the meeting. • Their former confidence is now ***nowhere in evidence***. [=nowhere to be seen, entirely absent]

²evidence *verb* **-denc•es; -denced; -denc•ing** [+ *obj*] *formal* : to offer or show evidence of (something) : to show or indicate (something) • certificates *evidencing* stock ownership — often used as *(be) evidenced* • The effectiveness of the program *is* clearly *evidenced* [=*shown*] by the recent decrease in drug-related crimes throughout the city.

as (is) evidenced by : as is clearly shown by • She has become known for the power of her writing, *as (is) evidenced by* the popularity of her new book. • There clearly were settlements here, *as evidenced by* these remains.

ev•i•dent /ˈɛvədənt/ *adj* [*more* ~; *most* ~] : clear to the sight or mind : OBVIOUS • She spoke with *evident* anguish about the death of her son. • The problems have been *evident* for quite some time. — compare SELF-EVIDENT

ev•i•dent•ly /ˈɛvədəntli, ˌɛvəˈdɛntli/ *adv*

1 : in a way that can be easily seen or noticed : in an evident way • He was *evidently* [=*obviously*] uncomfortable. • *Evidently* you and I have different feelings on this issue. • "We seem to have different feelings on this issue." "*Evidently*!"

2 — used to describe something that appears to be true based on what is known • Ancient Spartans were *evidently* taught to prefer death to dishonor. • *Evidently* [=*apparently*] nobody saw them leave.

¹evil /ˈiːvəl/ *adj* **evil•er; evil•est** [*or more* ~; *most* ~]

1 : morally bad • an *evil* villain • *evil* spirits • *evil* deeds

2 a : causing harm or injury to someone • She drank an *evil* potion. **b** : marked by bad luck or bad events • The city has fallen on *evil* days/times. **c** : very unpleasant or offensive • an *evil* smell • an *evil* temper **d** : showing that something bad will happen • It was an *evil* omen.

– evil•ly *adv* • He grinned *evilly*. **– evil•ness** *noun* [*noncount*]

²evil *noun, pl* **evils**

1 [*noncount*] : the force of things that are morally bad • the

battle of good versus *evil* • He believed that the world was full of *evil*. [=*wickedness*]
2 [*count*] **: something that is harmful or bad — usually plural** • They were talking about the *evils* of alcohol. • all the *evils* that plague us ✧ The ***lesser of two evils*** or the ***lesser evil*** is the better choice between two unpleasant choices. • Since neither candidate is appealing, voters are forced to choose the *lesser of two evils*. • Which candidate would be the *lesser evil*? ✧ A ***necessary evil*** is a bad or unwanted thing that has to be done or accepted to achieve some good result. • He thinks of taxes as a *necessary evil*.

evil·do·er /ˌiːvəlˈduːwɚ/ *noun, pl* **-ers** [*count*] **: a person who does bad or evil things** • The sheriff is protecting the community from *evildoers*.
– evil·do·ing /ˌiːvəlˈduːwɪŋ/ *noun, pl* **-ings** [*noncount*] no evidence of *evildoing* [=*wrongdoing*] [*count*] his defense of his *evildoings*

evil eye *noun*
the evil eye **: a look that is thought to be able to harm someone** • He gave her *the evil eye*.

evil–mind·ed /ˌiːvəlˈmaɪndəd/ *adj* [*more* ~; *most* ~] **: thinking bad or evil thoughts : having a morally bad mind or character** • an *evil-minded* villain
– evil–mind·ed·ness *noun* [*noncount*]

evince /ɪˈvɪns/ *verb* **evinc·es; evinced; evinc·ing** [+ *obj*] *formal* **: to show (something) clearly** • She *evinced* an interest in art at an early age.

evis·cer·ate /ɪˈvɪsəˌreɪt/ *verb* **-ates; -at·ed; -at·ing** [+ *obj*] *formal* **: to take out the internal organs of (an animal) : DISEMBOWEL** • tools used for *eviscerating* [=*gutting*] fish — often used figuratively • Opponents charge that the amendment would *eviscerate* [=badly weaken] the new law.

evo·ca·tion /ˌiːvoʊˈkeɪʃən/ *noun, pl* **-tions : the act of bringing something into the mind or memory : the act of evoking something** [*count*] rich *evocations* of the sights, sounds, and smells of the carnival [*noncount*] the *evocation* of a simpler time

evoc·a·tive /ɪˈvɑːkətɪv/ *adj* [*more* ~; *most* ~] **: bringing thoughts, memories, or feelings into the mind** • He wrote a powerful and *evocative* biography. — often + *of* • His photographs are *evocative of* the solitude of the desert.

evoke /ɪˈvoʊk/ *verb* **evokes; evoked; evok·ing** [+ *obj*]
1 : to bring (a memory, feeling, image, etc.) into the mind • The old house *evoked* memories of his childhood. • His photographs *evoke* the isolation and solitude of the desert.
2 : to cause (a particular reaction or response) to happen • His wisecrack *evoked* [=*elicited*] snickers from around the classroom. • Her remarks have *evoked* [=*provoked*] an angry response.

ev·o·lu·tion /ˌɛvəˈluːʃən/ *noun* [*noncount*]
1 *biology* **a : a theory that the differences between modern plants and animals are because of changes that happened by a natural process over a very long time** • the theory of *evolution* **b : the process by which changes in plants and animals happen over time** • changes brought about by *evolution*
2 : a process of slow change and development • an important step in the *evolution* of computers • We have been able to watch her *evolution* [=*growth*] into a world-class runner.
– ev·o·lu·tion·ary /ˌɛvəˈluːʃəˌneri/ *adj* • *evolutionary* changes/development/history **– ev·ol·u·tion·ist** /ˌɛvəˈluːʃənɪst/ *noun, pl* **-ists** [*count*] • a brilliant *evolutionist*

evolve /ɪˈvɑːlv/ *verb* **evolves; evolved; evolv·ing : to change or develop slowly often into a better, more complex, or more advanced state : to develop by a process of evolution** [*no obj*] Some believe that birds *evolved* from dinosaurs. = Some believe that dinosaurs *evolved* into birds. • Her company has *evolved* from a hobby into a thriving business. [+ *obj*] Some flowers have *evolved* remarkable means of insect pollination.

ewe /ˈjuː/ *noun, pl* **ewes** [*count*] **: a female sheep** — compare [1]LAMB, [1]RAM

ew·er /ˈjuːwɚ/ *noun, pl* **ew·ers** [*count*] **: a type of pitcher or jug that is shaped like a vase and that was used in the past for holding water**

ex /ˈɛks/ *noun, pl* **ex·es** [*count*] *informal* **: a former husband, wife, boyfriend, or girlfriend** • I ran into my *ex* at the mall yesterday.

ex- /ɛks/ *prefix* **: former** • *ex*-president • *ex*-girlfriend • *ex*-husband

ex·ac·er·bate /ɪgˈzæsɚˌbeɪt/ *verb* **-bates; -bat·ed; -bat·ing** [+ *obj*] **: to make (a bad situation, a problem, etc.) worse** • The proposed factory shutdown would only *exacerbate* our unemployment problems. • His angry comments have *exacerbated* tensions in the negotiation process.
– ex·ac·er·ba·tion /ɪgˌzæsɚˈbeɪʃən/ *noun* [*noncount*] • the *exacerbation* of symptoms/problems/tensions

[1]exact /ɪgˈzækt/ *adj*
1 : fully and completely correct or accurate • the *exact* time • an *exact* copy/duplicate/replica/reproduction • Those were his *exact* words. • The *exact* cause of the fire is still under investigation. • We don't know the *exact* nature of the problem. • Predicting the path of hurricanes is not an *exact* science.
2 [*more* ~; *most* ~] **: very careful and accurate** • The police have an *exact* description of the killer. • Please take the most *exact* measurements possible. • *exact* [=*precise*] instruments • He is very *exact* in the way he solves a problem.
exact opposite **: the complete opposite** • I realize now that I have tried to make my work the *exact opposite* of my father's. [=to make my work as different as possible from my father's] • He used to be romantic, but now he's the *exact opposite*. [=now he is not at all romantic]
exact same or ***US same exact*** **— used as a more forceful way to say "same"** • We grow the *exact same* vegetables in our garden every year. • They showed up at the party in the *same exact* outfits.
to be exact **— used to indicate that a statement is accurate and specific** • that afternoon, June 22, *to be exact* • They had many children—seven, *to be exact*. • He came a long way—from Nome, Alaska, *to be exact*—to attend the wedding.
– exact·ness *noun* [*noncount*] • mathematical *exactness* [=*precision*]

[2]exact *verb* **-acts; -act·ed; -act·ing** [+ *obj*] *formal*
1 : to demand and get (something, such as payment or revenge) especially by using force or threats • They would not rest until they had *exacted* revenge. • He was able to *exact* a promise from them.
2 — used in phrases like *exact a terrible toll* and *exact a high/heavy price* to say that something has caused a lot of suffering, loss, etc. • The war has *exacted a terrible toll*. • These mistakes have *exacted a heavy price*.

ex·act·ing /ɪgˈzæktɪŋ/ *adj* [*more* ~; *most* ~] **: requiring much time, attention, or effort from someone : very difficult or demanding** • an *exacting* process/teacher/task • He has very *exacting* standards/requirements.
– ex·act·ing·ly *adv* • *exactingly* high standards

ex·ac·ti·tude /ɪgˈzæktəˌtuːd, *Brit* ɪgˈzæktəˌtjuːd/ *noun* [*noncount*] *formal* **: the quality or state of being accurate and correct** • She was able to recall the event with remarkable *exactitude*. [=*exactness, precision*]

ex·act·ly /ɪgˈzæktli/ *adv* [*more* ~; *most* ~]
1 — used to stress that something is accurate, complete, or correct • The mansion has *exactly* 33 rooms. • I know *exactly* where they went. • The two rooms are *exactly* the same size. • When *exactly* are they supposed to arrive? = *Exactly* when are they supposed to arrive?
2 *informal* **— used in speech to say that what someone has said is exactly correct or that you agree with it completely** • "So you think we should take an earlier flight?" "*Exactly*." [=yes, that's exactly what I think] • "It's just not worth the trouble." "*Exactly*." — see also NOT EXACTLY (below)
3 : in a correct or precise way • The levers need to be *exactly* positioned. **: in a way that agrees completely with what is needed** • You need to do *exactly* [=*just, precisely*] as you're told.
4 : in every way • That was *exactly* the wrong thing to do. • He is *exactly* what a good student ought to be.
not exactly *informal* **1 — used in speech as a mild way of saying "no" especially to indicate that what someone has said is not completely correct or true** • "He's your boss, isn't he?" "*Not exactly*." • "Did everything go the way you planned it?" "*Not exactly*." **2 — used as a humorous or ironic way to say "not"** • He's *not exactly* the smartest guy I've ever met. [=he is not very smart]

ex·ag·ger·ate /ɪgˈzæʤəˌreɪt/ *verb* **-ates; -at·ed; -at·ing**
1 : to think of or describe something as larger or greater than it really is [+ *obj*] The book *exaggerates* the difficulties he faced in starting his career. • It's impossible to *exaggerate* the importance of this discovery. [*no obj*] He tends to *exaggerate* when talking about his accomplishments.
2 [+ *obj*] **: to make (something) larger or greater than normal** • He *exaggerated* his movements so we could see them more clearly.

– **exaggerated** *adj* [*more* ~; *most* ~] ▪ He has a very/greatly *exaggerated* idea of his own importance. ▪ a very *exaggerated* gesture – **ex·ag·ger·at·ed·ly** *adv* [*more* ~; *most* ~] ▪ an *exaggeratedly* large gesture – **ex·ag·ger·a·tion** /ɪgˌzæʤəˈreɪʃən/ *noun, pl* **-tions** [*count*] The report was filled with *exaggerations* and outright lies. [*noncount*] She told us what happened without *exaggeration*. [=without exaggerating] – **ex·ag·ger·a·tor** /ɪgˈzæʤəˌreɪtɚ/ *noun, pl* **-tors** [*count*] ▪ He's an *exaggerator*, if not an outright liar.

ex·alt /ɪgˈzɑːlt/ *verb* **-alts; -alt·ed; -alt·ing** [+ *obj*]
1 *formal* : to raise (someone or something) to a higher level ▪ His behavior has *exalted* the power and prestige of his office.
2 a *formal* : to praise (someone or something) highly ▪ The essay *exalts* the simple beauty of the country. ▪ We *exalt* thee, O Lord. **b** : to present (something) in a way that is very favorable or too favorable ▪ His new film *exalts* [=*glorifies*] military power. ▪ He shamelessly *exalts* his own role in the peace process.

Do not confuse *exalt* with *exult*.

– **exalted** *adj* [*more* ~; *most* ~] ▪ She rose to an *exalted* [=very high] position in the company. ▪ an *exalted* feeling [=a very happy feeling] ▪ He had an *exalted* [=very high] opinion of his own work. – **exalting** *adj* [*more* ~; *most* ~] ▪ The movie is an *exalting* [=*uplifting*] experience.

ex·al·ta·tion /ˌɛgˌzɑːlˈteɪʃən/ *noun* [*noncount*] *formal*
1 : the act of raising someone or something in importance : the act of exalting someone or something or the state of being exalted ▪ the *exaltation* [=*glorification*] of athletic skill
2 : a strong sense of happiness, power, or importance ▪ feelings of joy and *exaltation*

ex·am /ɪgˈzæm/ *noun, pl* **-ams** [*count*]
1 *US* : EXAMINATION 1b ▪ an annual physical *exam*
2 : EXAMINATION 2 ▪ Your final *exam* will count for half of the semester's grade.

ex·am·i·na·tion /ɪgˌzæməˈneɪʃən/ *noun, pl* **-tions**
1 a : the act of looking at something closely and carefully : the act of examining something [*noncount*] On closer/further *examination*, the painting appears to be a fake. ▪ The victim's clothes were sent to the lab for *examination*. ▪ The policy is ***under examination***. [=is being examined] [*count*] The police made/performed a rigorous *examination* of the evidence at the crime scene. **b** [*count*] : a close and careful study of someone or something to find signs of illness or injury ▪ medical/eye *examinations* ▪ The court ordered that the defendant undergo a psychiatric *examination*. ▪ an ***examination table*** [=a table in a doctor's office on which a patient lies to be examined]
2 [*count*] : a test to show a person's progress, knowledge, or ability ▪ I have to study for the history *examination*. ▪ an *examination* in/on history ▪ I took an *examination*. = (*Brit*) I did/sat an *examination*. ▪ an ***entrance examination*** [=a test to see if someone should be admitted to a school]
3 [*noncount*] *law* : the act of questioning a witness in a court of law ▪ procedures that are not allowed during *examination* of witnesses — see also CROSS-EXAMINATION

ex·am·ine /ɪgˈzæmən/ *verb* **-ines; -ined; -in·ing** [+ *obj*]
1 : to look at (something) closely and carefully in order to learn more about it, to find problems, etc. ▪ An accountant has been hired to *examine* the company's books. ▪ We need to *examine* [=*consider*] this question more carefully. ▪ The police *examined* the evidence carefully.
2 : to test or look carefully at (something or someone) for signs of illness or injury ▪ You should have your eyes *examined*. ▪ He was *examined* by several doctors, who found nothing wrong with him. ▪ the ***examining room*** [=a room in a doctor's office where the doctor examines patients]
3 *law* : to question (someone) closely ▪ *examine* a witness — see also CROSS-EXAMINE
– **ex·am·in·er** *noun, pl* **-ers** [*count*] ▪ photo *examiners* — see also MEDICAL EXAMINER

ex·am·ple /ɪgˈzæmpəl/ *noun, pl* **-am·ples**
1 : a person or way of behaving that is seen as a model that should be followed [*count*] He was inspired by the *example* of his older brother. [=he wanted to do what his older brother did] ▪ You should try to follow her *example*. [=try to do as she does] ▪ Let that be an *example* to you! [=let that show you what you should or should not do] ▪ He set a good/bad *example* for the rest of us. ▪ It's up to you to ***set an example***. [=to behave in a way that shows other people how to behave] [*noncount*] She chooses to ***lead by example***. [=to lead by behaving in a way that shows others how to behave]
2 [*count*] **a** : someone or something that is mentioned to help explain what you are saying or to show that a general statement is true ▪ She gave/offered several *examples* to show that the program is effective. **b** : something or someone chosen from a group in order to show what the whole group is like ▪ We've chosen three *examples* of contemporary architecture for closer study. ▪ a classic *example* of a Persian rug ▪ a fine/prime *example* of the artist's work
3 [*count*] **a** : a phrase or sentence that shows how a word is used ▪ The dictionary includes thousands of *examples*. **b** : something (such as a problem that a student has to solve) that is used to teach how a rule or process works ▪ arithmetic *examples*
for example — used when you are mentioning a specific person or thing that helps to explain what you are saying or to show that a general statement is true ▪ Things are getting better. Last year, *for example* [=*for instance*], the company achieved record sales in Europe. ▪ It was obvious that her memory was failing. *For example*, she would often forget where she put her car keys. ▪ A lot of my friends were there—John and Linda, *for example*.
make an example of ✧ If you *make an example of* a person who has done something wrong, you punish that person as a way of warning other people not to do the same thing. ▪ Although it was only his first offense, the judge decided to *make an example of him* and sentence him to prison.

ex·as·per·ate /ɪgˈzæspəˌreɪt, *Brit* ɪgˈzɑːspəreɪt/ *verb* **-ates; -at·ed; -at·ing** [+ *obj*] : to make (someone) very angry or annoyed ▪ The criticism of his latest movie is sure to *exasperate* his admirers. ▪ We were *exasperated* by the delays.
– **exasperated** *adj* [*more* ~; *most* ~] ▪ The delays left us feeling tired and *exasperated*. ▪ an *exasperated* smile – **ex·as·per·at·ed·ly** *adv* ▪ smiling/sighing *exasperatedly* – **exasperating** *adj* [*more* ~; *most* ~] ▪ *exasperating* delays ▪ He wants everyone to know how *exasperating* his job can be. – **ex·as·per·at·ing·ly** *adv* ▪ His lectures were *exasperatingly* dull.

ex·as·per·a·tion /ɪgˌzæspəˈreɪʃən, *Brit* ɪgˌzɑːspəˈreɪʃən/ *noun* [*noncount*] : the state of being very annoyed or upset ▪ They had all experienced the *exasperation* and frustration of holiday shopping. ▪ He sighed in *exasperation*.

ex·ca·vate /ˈɛkskəˌveɪt/ *verb* **-vates; -vat·ed; -vat·ing** [+ *obj*]
1 : to uncover (something) by digging away and removing the earth that covers it ▪ They *excavated* an ancient city. ▪ It is the first site to be *excavated* in this area.
2 a : to dig a large hole in (something) ▪ They began *excavating* the backyard for their new pool. **b** : to form (a hole, tunnel, etc.) by digging ▪ *excavate* a tunnel **c** : to dig out and remove (dirt, soil, etc.) ▪ The excess dirt was carefully *excavated*.
– **ex·ca·va·tion** /ˌɛkskəˈveɪʃən/ *noun, pl* **-tions** [*count, noncount*]

ex·ca·va·tor /ˈɛkskəˌveɪtɚ/ *noun, pl* **-tors** [*count*]
1 : a person who digs up things that have been buried for a long time ▪ The *excavators* found ancient tools at the site.
2 : STEAM SHOVEL

ex·ceed /ɪkˈsiːd/ *verb* **-ceeds; -ceed·ed; -ceed·ing** [+ *obj*]
1 : to be greater or more than (something) ▪ The cost must not *exceed* 10 dollars. ▪ The cost *exceeded* our estimate. ▪ The demand for new housing has already *exceeded* the supply. : to be better than (something) ▪ Their accomplishments far *exceeded* [=*surpassed*] our expectations. ▪ He's trying to match or *exceed* last year's sales.
2 : to go beyond the limit of (something) ▪ Lawyers argue that the court *exceeded* [=*overstepped*] its authority in ordering a new trial.

ex·ceed·ing·ly /ɪkˈsiːdɪŋli/ *adv, somewhat formal* : VERY, EXTREMELY ▪ an *exceedingly* fine job ▪ The weather was *exceedingly* cold. ▪ The crime rate is *exceedingly* high.

ex·cel /ɪkˈsɛl/ *verb* **ex·cels; ex·celled; ex·cel·ling**
1 [*no obj*] : to be better than others — usually + *at* or *in* ▪ He *excelled at* whatever role he played. ▪ She *excels in* sports.
2 [+ *obj*] : to be or do better than (others) ▪ She *excels* everyone else in sports. ▪ (*Brit*) She really ***excelled herself*** [=she did much better than usual] in her last race!

ex·cel·lence /ˈɛksələns/ *noun* [*noncount*] : extremely high quality ▪ The school is known for the *excellence* of its teachers. ▪ an award for academic *excellence* ▪ setting a high standard of *excellence* — see also PAR EXCELLENCE

Ex·cel·len·cy /ˈɛksələnsi/ *noun, pl* **-cies** [*count*] — used as a title for some high government and church officials ▪ your

Excellency ▪ their *Excellencies* the Ambassadors of India and Indonesia

ex·cel·lent /ˈɛksələnt/ *adj* : very good : extremely good ▪ Her new movie has received *excellent* reviews. ▪ He is an *excellent* role model for young men everywhere. ▪ That dinner was *excellent*. ▪ The car is in *excellent* condition. ▪ She enjoys *excellent* health. ▪ "At last we're making a profit!" "(That's) *Excellent*!"

– **ex·cel·lent·ly** *adv* ▪ The food was delicious and *excellently* prepared.

[1]**ex·cept** /ɪkˈsɛpt/ *also* **ex·cept·ing** /ɪkˈsɛptɪŋ/ *prep* : not including (someone or something) : other than (something or someone) ▪ The stores will be open daily *except* Sundays. ▪ *Excepting* [=*with the exception of*] one student, no one could answer the questions correctly. ▪ Everyone was invited *except* [=*but*] me.

except for **1** : not including (someone or something) : other than (someone or something) ▪ I got all As on my report card, *except for* a B in Latin. ▪ *Except for* that one typo, there were no mistakes. ▪ Everyone was invited *except for* [=*but*] me. **2** : if not for (someone or something) ▪ They would all have died *except for* [=*but for*] her and her quick thinking. [=it was only because of her that they did not die]

[2]**except** *conj*

1 — used to introduce a statement that indicates the only person or thing that is not included in or referred to by a previous statement ▪ Take no orders *except* from me. [=take orders only from me] ▪ Employees were not allowed to leave *except* in an emergency. [=unless there was an emergency] ▪ She didn't leave the house all weekend, *except* to go to church. [=she only left the house to go to church] ▪ He does nothing *except* [=*but*] complain. [=all he does is complain]

2 — used to introduce a statement that explains the reason why something is not possible, will not happen, etc. ▪ We'd go, *except* (that) it's too far. ▪ I would buy a new suit, *except* I don't have enough money.

[3]**except** *verb* **-cepts; -cept·ed; -cept·ing** [+ *obj*] *formal* : to leave out (someone or something) : to not include (someone or something) ▪ Children were *excepted* from the study. ▪ Everyone was included in the study—children *excepted*. [=except for children] ▪ I don't like lawyers—***present company excepted***, of course! [=although I don't like lawyers, I make an exception in your case]

ex·cep·tion /ɪkˈsɛpʃən/ *noun, pl* **-tions** [*count*]

1 : someone or something that is different from others : someone or something that is not included ▪ I like all his books, with one *exception*. [=I like all but one of his books] ▪ The decision was supported by almost everyone, the single/sole *exception* being me. [=everyone supported the decision but me] ▪ Her parties are always elegant, and last night's party was ***no exception***. [=last night's party was also elegant]

2 : a case where a rule does not apply ▪ There will be no *exceptions* to this rule. ▪ We'll ***make an exception*** [=allow the rule not to be followed] this time.

take exception : to object to something : to feel or express disagreement with or opposition to something — usually + *to* ▪ I *take exception to* the tone of her remarks. [=I am offended by the tone of her remarks]

without exception — used to say that a statement is true in all or almost all cases ▪ *Without exception*, his books have been widely read and admired. ▪ The critics have praised her films almost *without exception*. [=the critics have praised almost every one of her films]

with the exception of : not including (someone or something) ▪ It's all here, *with the exception of* [=*except for, except*] the sweater. ▪ *With the* (notable) *exception of* the bland soup, the food was very good. ▪ Everyone should be there, *with the* (possible) *exception of* my brother.

ex·cep·tion·able /ɪkˈsɛpʃənəbəl/ *adj* [*more* ~; *most* ~] *formal* : likely to cause objection or offense ▪ an unpleasant and highly *exceptionable* [=*objectionable*] piece of writing — opposite UNEXCEPTIONABLE

ex·cep·tion·al /ɪkˈsɛpʃənl/ *adj* [*more* ~; *most* ~]

1 : not usual : unusual or uncommon ▪ an *exceptional* [=unusually large] amount of rain ▪ We're bending the rules for this *exceptional* situation. ▪ *exceptional* circumstances

2 : unusually good : much better than average ▪ an *exceptional* student in math ▪ The seafood dishes at this restaurant are *exceptional*. ▪ *exceptional* skill

3 : mentally or physically disabled ▪ a separate school for *exceptional* children

– **ex·cep·tion·al·ly** *adv* ▪ an *exceptionally* hardy plant ▪ The film was *exceptionally* good.

[1]**ex·cerpt** /ˈɛkˌsəpt, ˈɛgˌzəpt/ *noun, pl* **-cerpts** [*count*] : a small part of a longer written work ▪ She read an *excerpt* from the play. ▪ I've read only *excerpts* of/from *Moby-Dick*, never the whole book.

[2]**ex·cerpt** /ˌɛkˈsəpt, ˌɛgˈzəpt/ *verb* **-cerpts; -cerpt·ed; -cerpt·ing** [+ *obj*] : to include (part of a longer written work) in something else — usually used as *(be) excerpted* ▪ This article *was excerpted* from the *New York Times*. ▪ Portions of her novel *were excerpted* in a literary magazine.

[1]**ex·cess** /ɪkˈsɛs, ˈɛkˌsɛs/ *noun, pl* **-cess·es**

1 [*singular*] : an amount that is more than the usual or necessary amount ▪ They were equipped with an *excess* of provisions. ▪ The tests found an *excess* of sodium in his blood. ▪ an *excess* of enthusiasm/zeal ▪ There was an *excess* of 10 bushels (over what was needed to fill the bin). ▪ Eating anything ***in excess*** [=in overly large amounts] can be bad for you.

2 a [*noncount*] : behavior that is considered wrong because it goes beyond what is usual, normal, or proper ▪ He lived a life of *excess*. **b** ***excesses*** [*plural*] : actions or ways of behaving that go beyond what is usual or proper ▪ The movie embraces all the worst *excesses* of popular American culture. ▪ the violent *excesses* of the military regime ▪ He apologized for his past *excesses*.

in excess of : more than (an amount) ▪ Annual repairs cost *in excess of* [=*over*] $50,000. ▪ traveling at speeds *in excess of* 100 mph

to excess : more than is usual, normal, or proper ▪ He often eats *to excess*. [=*excessively*] ▪ college students who drink *to excess* [=who drink too much]

[2]**excess** *adj, always used before a noun* : more than is usual, allowed, or needed ▪ *excess* baggage ▪ Basketball provided an outlet for their *excess* energy. ▪ She is trying to eliminate *excess* fat and calories from her diet.

ex·ces·sive /ɛkˈsɛsɪv/ *adj* [*more* ~; *most* ~] : going beyond what is usual, normal, or proper ▪ an *excessive* display of wealth ▪ She was reprimanded for her *excessive* tardiness. [=for being tardy too often] ▪ High fever, nausea, and *excessive* sweating are some of the symptoms. ▪ He drinks *excessive* amounts of coffee. [=he drinks too much coffee]

– **ex·ces·sive·ly** *adv* ▪ a dog who barks *excessively* ▪ drinking *excessively* [=*to excess*]

[1]**ex·change** /ɪksˈʧeɪnʤ/ *noun, pl* **-chang·es**

1 : an occurrence in which people give things of similar value to each other : the act of giving or taking one thing in return for another thing [*noncount*] the *exchange* [=*exchanging*] of goods [*count*] an *exchange* of goods ▪ an *exchange* of prisoners ▪ an even/fair *exchange* of property

2 [*count*] **a** : an occurrence in which people direct something at each other ▪ an *exchange* of glances ▪ an angry *exchange* of insults ▪ an *exchange* of blows [=a fistfight] **b** : an occurrence in which people give information to each other ▪ a useful *exchange* of information/knowledge/ideas **c** : an occurrence in which people use weapons against each other ▪ an *exchange* of gunfire ▪ threats of a nuclear *exchange*

3 [*count*] : an occurrence in which people talk to each other for a short time : a brief conversation ▪ a friendly *exchange*, *especially* : an angry conversation ▪ a heated *exchange* ▪ a bitter *exchange*

4 [*count*] **a** : a place where things or services are traded ▪ the student book *exchange* **b** : an office or building in which telephone calls are connected ▪ a telephone *exchange*

in exchange ✧ If you give something to a person and get something *in exchange*, that person also gives something of similar value to you. ▪ If I give you this, what will you give me *in exchange*? ▪ She bought me dinner ***in exchange for*** helping her move. [=she bought me dinner as a way of paying me for helping her move]

— see also FOREIGN EXCHANGE, STOCK EXCHANGE

[2]**exchange** *verb* **-changes; -changed; -chang·ing** [+ *obj*]

1 : to give something and receive something in return ▪ We *exchanged* addresses and promised we'd write each other often. ▪ We *exchange* gifts [=give gifts to each other] at the holidays. ▪ These coupons can be *exchanged* for food. ▪ I'll *exchange* [=*trade, swap*] my orange for your pear.

2 : to direct (words, looks, etc.) at each other ▪ They *exchanged* glances. [=they looked quickly at each other] ▪ They *exchanged* greetings [=they greeted each other] when they met. ▪ They *exchanged* insults/blows. [=they insulted/hit each other] ▪ soldiers *exchanging* fire [=shooting at each other]

3 : to return (a product) to a store and have it replaced by

another product : to trade (something that has been purchased) for something else ▪ I'd like to *exchange* this sweater for a smaller one. ▪ The vase had a crack in it, so he *exchanged* it (for an unbroken one). ▪ Can I *exchange* this vase? = Can you *exchange* this cracked vase for me?
– ex·change·able /ɪksˈʧeɪnʤəbəl/ *adj* ▪ *exchangeable* merchandise

exchange rate *noun, pl* **~ rates** [*count*] : a number that is used to calculate the difference in value between money from one country and money from another country — called also *rate of exchange*

exchange student *noun, pl* **~ -dents** [*count*] : a student from one country who attends a school in another country ▪ I went to Germany as an *exchange student.*

Ex·che·quer /ˈɛksˌʧɛkɚ, ɪksˈʧɛkɚ/ *noun* [*singular*] : a department of the British government which manages the money that is used to run the government : TREASURY — now used chiefly in the title *the Chancellor of the Exchequer*

¹ex·cise /ˈɛkˌsaɪz/ *noun, pl* **-cis·es** [*count*] : a tax on certain things that are made, sold, or used within a country ▪ an *excise* imposed on a number of goods — called also *excise tax*

²ex·cise /ɪkˈsaɪz/ *verb* **-cis·es; -cised; -cis·ing** [+ *obj*] *formal* : to remove (something) by cutting it out ▪ *excise* a tumor ▪ All of the scandalous parts had been *excised* [=*deleted*] from the diary.
– ex·ci·sion /ɪkˈsɪʒən/ *noun, pl* **-sions** [*noncount*] surgical *excision* of the tumor [*count*] The diary was published with numerous *excisions.* [=*deletions*]

excise tax *noun, pl* **~ taxes** [*count*] : ¹EXCISE

ex·cit·able /ɪkˈsaɪtəbəl/ *adj* [*more ~; most ~*] : easily excited ▪ an *excitable* dog/child
– ex·cit·abil·i·ty /ɪkˌsaɪtəˈbɪləti/ *noun* [*noncount*]

ex·cite /ɪkˈsaɪt/ *verb* **-cites; -cit·ed; -cit·ing** [+ *obj*]
1 : to cause feelings of enthusiasm in (someone) : to make (someone) feel energetic and eager to do something ▪ ideas that *excite* young people ▪ Our announcement *excited* the children. ▪ It *excites* me [=it arouses me sexually] when you dress like that.
2 : to cause (a particular emotion or reaction) to be felt or to happen ▪ *excite* admiration/suspicion/discussion ▪ The posters *excited* much interest in the show.
3 : to increase the activity of (something, such as nerve tissue) ▪ a chemical that *excites* [=*stimulates*] the nerve cells in the brain

excited *adj* [*more ~; most ~*] : very enthusiastic and eager about something ▪ They were *excited* about/over the trip. ▪ We were *excited* (to hear) that they were getting married. ▪ The children were *excited* before the school play.
– ex·cit·ed·ly *adv* ▪ He talked *excitedly* about visiting his old friends.

ex·cite·ment /ɪkˈsaɪtmənt/ *noun, pl* **-ments**
1 [*noncount*] : a feeling of eager enthusiasm and interest : the state of being excited ▪ Our *excitement* was building/growing/mounting as the end of the game approached. ▪ His hands shook with *excitement.* ▪ The child cried out in *excitement.*
2 a : exciting activity [*noncount*] a trip filled with *excitement* and adventure ▪ We had some *excitement* this morning. [=something exciting happened this morning] [*count*] She talked about the *excitements* of her new life. **b** [*singular*] : a quality that causes feelings of eager enthusiasm : an exciting quality ▪ This job loses its *excitement* after a while.

exciting /ɪkˈsaɪtɪŋ/ *adj* [*more ~; most ~*] : causing feelings of interest and enthusiasm : causing excitement ▪ an *exciting* discovery ▪ an *exciting* trip to Africa ▪ an *exciting* account of her adventures ▪ This isn't a very *exciting* book.
– ex·cit·ing·ly *adv* ▪ an *excitingly* close election

ex·claim /ɪkˈskleɪm/ *verb* **-claims; -claimed; -claim·ing**
1 [+ *obj*] : to say (something) in an enthusiastic or forceful way ▪ "I won!" she *exclaimed.* ▪ "Here he comes!" someone *exclaimed.*
2 [*no obj*] : to cry out or speak suddenly or with strong feeling ▪ She *exclaimed* in delight over/at the Christmas tree. ▪ The children *exclaimed* with wonder when they saw the elephant.

ex·cla·ma·tion /ˌɛkskləˈmeɪʃən/ *noun, pl* **-tions** [*count*] : a sharp or sudden cry : a word, phrase, or sound that expresses a strong emotion ▪ Her unexpected announcement caused a few *exclamations* of surprise. ▪ an *exclamation* of pain ▪ *exclamations* of delight
– ex·clam·a·to·ry /ɪkˈsklæməˌtori, *Brit* ɪkˈsklæmətri/ *adj* ▪ *exclamatory* outbursts

exclamation point *noun, pl* **~ points** [*count*] *US* : a punctuation mark ! used to show a forceful way of speaking or a strong feeling — often used figuratively ▪ His victory in the final game ***put an exclamation point on*** a brilliant year. [=ended a brilliant year in a very exciting way] — called also (*chiefly Brit*) *exclamation mark*

ex·clude /ɪkˈsklu:d/ *verb* **-cludes; -clud·ed; -clud·ing** [+ *obj*]
1 a : to prevent (someone) from doing something or being a part of a group ▪ You can share files with some people on the network while *excluding* others. — often + *from* ▪ Don't *exclude* your little sister *from* the game. ▪ Until 1920, women were *excluded from* the right to vote in the U.S. — opposite INCLUDE **b** : to leave out (something) : to not include (something) ▪ The prices on the menu *exclude* tax. — often + *from* ▪ Certain words should be *excluded from* polite conversation. [=should not be used in polite conversation] — opposite INCLUDE
2 : to think that (something, such as a possibility) is not worth attention ▪ We can't altogether/entirely *exclude* [=*discount*] the possibility that the economy will soon improve.
– ex·clu·sion /ɪkˈsklu:ʒən/ *noun, pl* **-sions** [*noncount*] the *exclusion* of women from the priesthood ▪ He spent all his time with colleagues ***to the exclusion of*** [=in a way that excluded] his own family. [*count*] *exclusions* noted in the insurance policy

excluding *prep* : not including (someone or something) ▪ The store is open all week, *excluding* [=*except for*] Sundays.

see also FOREIGN EXCHANGE, STOCK EXCHANGE

¹ex·clu·sive /ɪkˈsklu:sɪv/ *adj*
1 : not shared : available to only one person or group ▪ We have *exclusive* use of the beach. [=we are the only ones who can use the beach] ▪ The company has *exclusive* rights to (use) the logo. ▪ an *exclusive* interview
2 [*more ~; most ~*] **a** : only allowing in people from a high social class ▪ He belongs to an *exclusive* club. ▪ an *exclusive* hotel ▪ an *exclusive* party — opposite INCLUSIVE **b** : available to only a few people because of high cost ▪ *exclusive* suburban neighborhoods ▪ She attended an *exclusive* private school. ▪ one of the city's most *exclusive* restaurants
3 : full and complete ▪ They gave their *exclusive* attention to the job.
exclusive of *formal* : not including (something) ▪ for five days *exclusive of* today ▪ There is a sale on all merchandise *exclusive of* jewelry.
– see also MUTUALLY EXCLUSIVE
– ex·clu·sive·ly *adv* ▪ a restaurant that *exclusively* [=*only*] serves vegetarian cuisine = a restaurant that serves vegetarian cuisine *exclusively* ▪ The store's customers were almost *exclusively* [=*all*] male. **– ex·clu·sive·ness** *noun* [*noncount*] ▪ The club has been criticized for its *exclusiveness.* [=*exclusivity*]

²exclusive *noun, pl* **-sives** [*count*] : a news story that appears in only one newspaper or that is broadcast by only one television or radio station

ex·clu·siv·i·ty /ˌɛkˌsklu:ˈsɪvəti/ *noun* [*noncount*] : the quality or state of being exclusive : the quality of being limited to people of wealth or high social class ▪ The private school's *exclusivity* [=*exclusiveness*] was part of its appeal for many parents. ▪ a symbol of wealth and *exclusivity*

ex·com·mu·ni·cate /ˌɛkskəˈmju:nəˌkeɪt/ *verb* **-cates; -cat·ed; -cat·ing** [+ *obj*] : to not allow (someone) to continue being a member of the Roman Catholic church ▪ He was *excommunicated* (from the church) for his radical practices.
– ex·com·mu·ni·ca·tion /ˌɛkskəˌmju:nəˈkeɪʃən/ *noun, pl* **-tions** [*count, noncount*]

ex·co·ri·ate /ɛkˈskoriˌeɪt/ *verb* **-ates; -at·ed; -at·ing** [+ *obj*] *formal* : to criticize (someone or something) very harshly ▪ He was *excoriated* as a racist. ▪ The candidates have publicly *excoriated* each other throughout the campaign.
– ex·co·ri·a·tion /ɛkˌskoriˈeɪʃən/ *noun, pl* **-tions** [*count, noncount*]

ex·cre·ment /ˈɛkskrəmənt/ *noun* [*noncount*] *formal* : solid waste passed out of the body : FECES

ex·crete /ɪkˈskri:t/ *verb* **-cretes; -cret·ed; -cret·ing** [+ *obj*] *formal* : to pass (waste matter) from the body or from an organ in the body ▪ *excrete* sweat ▪ The kidneys *excrete* toxins.

ex·cre·tion /ɪkˈskri:ʃən/ *noun, pl* **-tions** *formal*
1 [*noncount*] : the act or process of passing waste from the body : the process of excreting waste ▪ The kidneys are organs of *excretion.* ▪ *excretion* of sweat
2 [*count*] : waste passed from the body : excreted matter ▪ bodily *excretions*

ex•cre•to•ry /ˈɛkskrəˌtori/ *adj, formal* : of or relating to excretion ▪ *excretory* organs ▪ *excretory* functions

ex•cru•ci•at•ing /ɪkˈskruːʃiˌeɪtɪŋ/ *adj [more ~; most ~]*
1 : very painful : causing great mental or physical pain ▪ I have an *excruciating* headache. ▪ an *excruciating* moment of embarrassment
2 a : very severe ▪ *excruciating* shyness **b** : extreme or excessive ▪ They described their vacation in *excruciating* detail.
– **ex•cru•ci•at•ing•ly** *adv* ▪ an *excruciatingly* painful condition ▪ The speech was *excruciatingly* long. ▪ *excruciatingly* slow

ex•cul•pate /ˈɛkˌskʌlˌpeɪt/ *verb* **-pates; -pat•ed; -pat•ing** [+ *obj*] *formal* : to prove that someone is not guilty of doing something wrong ▪ The court *exculpated* him after a thorough investigation.
– **ex•cul•pa•tion** /ˌɛkˌskʌlˈpeɪʃən/ *noun [noncount]* – **ex•cul•pa•to•ry** /ɛkˈskʌlpəˌtori, *Brit* ɛkˈskʌlpətri/ *adj* ▪ *exculpatory* evidence

ex•cur•sion /ɪkˈskɚʒən/ *noun, pl* **-sions** *[count]* : a short trip especially for pleasure ▪ a fishing *excursion* ▪ They went on a brief *excursion* to the coast. — often used figuratively ▪ Her brief *excursion* into politics [=her brief political career] ended badly.

¹**ex•cuse** /ɪkˈskjuːz/ *verb* **-cus•es; -cused; -cus•ing** [+ *obj*]
1 : to forgive someone for making a mistake, doing something wrong, etc., ▪ Please *excuse* [=*pardon*] my clumsiness. ▪ His boss *excused* the mistake but told him to be more careful next time. ▪ Please *excuse* me for not calling sooner.
2 a : to say that (someone) is not required to do something ▪ I was *excused* from jury duty. ▪ The teacher *excused* the class from homework that day. **b** : to allow (someone, such as a child) to leave ▪ I've finished my dinner. May I (please) be *excused*? [=allowed to leave the dinner table]
3 : to be an acceptable reason for (something) : JUSTIFY ▪ Nothing can *excuse* that kind of rudeness. ▪ Her father's illness *excused* her absence.
excuse me ✧ *Excuse me* is used as a polite way of starting to say something. It can be used when you are interrupting someone, trying to get someone's attention, or disagreeing with someone. ▪ *Excuse me*, but may I say something? ▪ *Excuse me*, but do you mind if I shut the window? ▪ *Excuse me*, do you know where I can find Maple Street? ▪ *Excuse me*, but I don't think those figures are entirely accurate. It is also used as a polite apology for a minor fault or offense, such as laughing, coughing, or burping, and, in U.S. English, for getting in someone's way or bumping into someone. ▪ Oh, *excuse me*. [=*pardon me, I beg your pardon*] I didn't notice you standing there. The phrase is also used, especially in U.S. English, as a polite way of asking someone to repeat something. ▪ *Excuse me*? [=*pardon me*?; *I beg your pardon*?] I didn't hear the last part of what you were saying. In informal use, *excuse me* is often used in an annoyed way when someone has suggested that you have done something wrong and you do not feel that you have. ▪ "You were supposed to be home an hour ago." "Well, *excuse me*! I had to fix a flat tire."
excuse yourself : to say politely that you have to leave ▪ *Excusing himself*, he quickly rose from the table and left the room.
– **ex•cus•able** /ɪkˈskjuːzəbəl/ *adj* ▪ Such minor errors are *excusable*.

²**ex•cuse** /ɪkˈskjuːs/ *noun, pl* **-cus•es**
1 a *[count]* : a reason that you give to explain a mistake, bad behavior, etc. ▪ What's your *excuse* for being so late? ▪ She had no valid *excuse* for not finishing her homework. ▪ He's always making *excuses* for himself. ▪ a lame/flimsy excuse **b** ***excuses*** *[plural]* : reasons that you give to explain politely why you cannot do something, why you have to leave, etc. ▪ I won't be able to come to the wedding. Please give my *excuses* to your cousin. [=please tell your cousin that I'm sorry I won't be able to come] ▪ I ***made my excuses*** and left.
2 *[count]* : something (such as a condition or set of conditions) that explains improper behavior and makes it acceptable — usually used in negative statements ▪ There is no *excuse* for child abuse. ▪ His youth is no *excuse* for his irresponsible behavior.
3 *[count]* : a reason for doing something ▪ His birthday gives us a good *excuse* for a party. ▪ She'll use any *excuse* [=*pretext*] to wallow in self-pity.
4 *[count]* : a poor example — + *for* ▪ He's a ***poor/sad excuse for*** a father. [=he's a bad father] ▪ That pile of junk is a ***sorry excuse for*** a car!

ex–di•rec•to•ry /ˌɛksdəˈrɛktəri *Brit* ˌɛksdaɪˈrɛktri/ *adj, Brit, of a telephone number* : not shown in a telephone directory : UNLISTED ▪ an *ex-directory* number
– **ex–directory** *adv* ▪ He went *ex-directory* after becoming famous.

ex•e•cra•ble /ˈɛksɪkrəbəl/ *adj [more ~; most ~] formal* : very bad ▪ Living conditions in the slums were *execrable*. ▪ *execrable* taste
– **ex•e•cra•bly** /ˈɛksɪkrəbli/ *adv* ▪ an *execrably* written novel

ex•e•crate /ˈɛksəˌkreɪt/ *verb* **-crates; -crat•ed; -crat•ing** [+ *obj*] *formal* : to dislike and criticize (someone or something) very strongly ▪ She came to *execrate* the hypocritical values of her upper-class upbringing.
– **ex•e•cra•tion** /ˌɛksəˈkreɪʃən/ *noun, pl* **-tions** *[count, noncount]*

ex•e•cute /ˈɛksɪˌkjuːt/ *verb* **-cutes; -cut•ed; -cut•ing** [+ *obj*]
1 : to kill (someone) especially as punishment for a crime ▪ He was captured, tried, and *executed* for murder.
2 a : to do (something that you have planned to do or been told to do) : CARRY OUT ▪ They carefully *executed* the plan. ▪ *execute* an order **b** : to do or perform (an action or movement that requires skill) ▪ The pilot *executed* an emergency landing. ▪ The quarterback *executed* the play perfectly.
3 *law* : to do what is required by (a legal document or command) ▪ *execute* a decree ▪ *execute* the provisions of the will
4 : to make or produce (a work of art) ▪ a statue *executed* in bronze ▪ a painting *executed* in bright colors

ex•e•cu•tion /ˌɛksɪˈkjuːʃən/ *noun, pl* **-tions**
1 : the act of killing someone especially as punishment for a crime *[noncount]* *execution* by lethal injection ▪ He is in prison awaiting *execution*. *[count]* gangland *executions* [=murders done by gangsters]
2 *[noncount]* : the act of doing or performing something ▪ We put the plan into *execution*. [=we executed the plan] ▪ The quarterback's *execution* of the play was perfect. ▪ Her ideas were brilliant, but her *execution* (of them) was sloppy. ▪ skillful *execution* of the dance steps ▪ (*law*) the *execution* of a will [=the act of doing the things that are required by a will]

ex•e•cu•tion•er /ˌɛksɪˈkjuːʃənɚ/ *noun, pl* **-ers** *[count]* : a person who performs executions : a person who executes people who have been sentenced to death

¹**ex•ec•u•tive** /ɪgˈzɛkjətɪv/ *noun, pl* **-tives**
1 *[count]* : a person who manages or directs other people in a company or organization ▪ a sales *executive* ▪ The television network's *executives* decided not to air the controversial show. ▪ a phone company *executive* ▪ The President is the chief *executive* of the U.S.
2 ***the executive*** : the executive branch of a government ▪ matters of policy controlled by *the executive*

²**executive** *adj, always used before a noun*
1 a : relating to the job of managing or directing other people in a company or organizaton ▪ She has good *executive* skills. ▪ He has an *executive* position in the company. **b** : of, relating to, or used by the people who manage or direct a company or organization ▪ the *executive* committee ▪ the *executive* dining room ▪ *executive* offices ▪ an *executive* jet [=a private jet airplane used by important executives]
2 : responsible for making sure laws are carried out and for managing the affairs of a nation ▪ In the U.S., the President is the head of the ***executive branch*** of government. — compare JUDICIAL, LEGISLATIVE

executive order *noun, pl* ~ **-ders** *[count]* : an order that comes from the U.S. President or a government agency and must be obeyed like a law

ex•ec•u•tor /ɪgˈzɛkjətɚ/ *noun, pl* **-tors** *[count]* : someone who is named in a will as the person who will make sure that the instructions in the will are properly followed ▪ He named his daughter as his *executor*.

ex•em•plar /ɪgˈzɛmˌplɑɚ/ *noun, pl* **-plars** *[count] formal*
1 : an admired person or thing that is considered an example that deserves to be copied ▪ cited Joan of Arc as the *exemplar* of courage
2 : a typical example ▪ He is an *exemplar* of this new breed of politician.

ex•em•pla•ry /ɪgˈzɛmpləri/ *adj [more ~; most ~]*
1 : extremely good and deserving to be admired and copied ▪ We congratulated him on his *exemplary* [=*outstanding, excellent*] work. ▪ an *exemplary* school ▪ an *exemplary* citizen
2 *formal* : serving as an example of something — + *of* ▪ a style *exemplary of* romanticism

ex•em•pli•fy /ɪg'zɛmplə,faɪ/ *verb* **-fies; -fied; -fy•ing** [+ *obj*] : to be a very good example of (something) : to show (something) very clearly • His works *exemplify* the taste of the period. • a style *exemplifying* romanticism • The city's economic growth is *exemplified* by the many new buildings that are currently under construction.
– **ex•em•pli•fi•ca•tion** /ɪg,zɛmpləfə'keɪʃən/ *noun, pl* **-tions** [*count, noncount*]

[1]**ex•empt** /ɪg'zɛmpt/ *adj* : not required to do something that others are required to do — usually + *from* • He was *exempt from* military service. • She was *exempt from* physical education requirements because of her health problems. — see also TAX-EXEMPT

[2]**exempt** *verb* **-empts; -empt•ed; -empt•ing** [+ *obj*] : to say that (someone or something) does not have to do something that others are required to do : to make (someone or something) exempt — usually + *from* • He was *exempted from* military service because of his heart condition.

ex•emp•tion /ɪg'zɛmpʃən/ *noun, pl* **-tions**
1 : freedom from being required to do something that others are required to do — usually + *from* [*noncount*] They were granted *exemption from* military service [=they were not required to join the military] because of their religious beliefs. [*count*] They were granted *exemptions from* military service.
2 [*count*] : a source or amount of income that is not taxed • You can claim a tax *exemption* for each of your dependents.

[1]**ex•er•cise** /'ɛksɚ,saɪz/ *noun, pl* **-cis•es**
1 a [*noncount*] : physical activity that is done in order to become stronger and healthier • Get plenty of fresh air and *exercise*. • Swimming is my favorite kind of *exercise*. • I need to get more *exercise*. [=I need to exercise more frequently] • She plays tennis chiefly for (the) *exercise*. — often used before another noun • an *exercise* class/video/machine • *exercise* balls/mats **b** [*count*] : a particular movement or series of movements done to become stronger and healthier • knee *exercises* • She did stretching *exercises* before her daily run.
2 [*count*] : something that is done or practiced to develop a particular skill • arithmetic *exercises* • vocal *exercises* • Do the writing *exercise* at the end of each chapter.
3 [*count*] : an activity that has a specified quality or result • The negotiations have gotten nowhere, and I see no reason to continue with this pointless *exercise*. — usually + *in* • Waiting for the letter to come was an *exercise in* patience. • an *exercise in* public relations • The negotiations turned out to be an ***exercise in futility***. [=the negotiations were not successful or worthwhile]
4 ***exercises*** [*plural*] **a** *chiefly US* : a ceremony for students who have graduated from a school • graduation/commencement *exercises* **b** : military activities done for training • conducting naval *exercises* in the Mediterranean
5 [*noncount*] *somewhat formal* : the use of an ability or power that you have • We can avoid these problems by the *exercise* of a little common sense. [=by using a little common sense] • the *exercise* of self-control

[2]**exercise** *verb* **-cis•es; -cised; -cis•ing**
1 [*no obj*] : to do physical activities in order to make yourself stronger and healthier • It's important to *exercise* every day. • He eats right and *exercises* regularly.
2 [+ *obj*] **a** : to use (a body part) again and again in order to make it stronger • *exercise* a muscle • Bicycle riding *exercises* the leg muscles. **b** : to cause (an animal) to walk, run, etc., : to give exercise to (an animal) • The stable boys *exercise* the horses every morning.
3 [+ *obj*] : to use (an ability, power, etc.) • He didn't *exercise* good judgment. • We just need to *exercise* common sense. • She has been reluctant to *exercise* her authority. • *Exercise* caution when using these chemicals.

exercise bike *noun, pl* ~ **bikes** [*count*] : STATIONARY BIKE — called also *exercise bicycle*

ex•ert /ɪg'zɚt/ *verb* **-erts; -ert•ed; -ert•ing** [+ *obj*]
1 : to use (strength, ability, etc.) • He had to *exert* all of his strength to move the stone. • She hasn't been reluctant to *exert* [=*exercise*] her authority.
2 : to cause (force, effort, etc.) to have an effect or to be felt • The company *exerted* [=*put*] pressure on local politicians. • He *exerts* a lot of influence on the other members of the committee. • the force *exerted* by the machine
exert yourself : to make an effort to do something • Don't *exert yourself* too much. • She's always willing to *exert herself* to help other people.

ex•er•tion /ɪg'zɚʃən/ *noun, pl* **-tions** : physical or mental effort [*noncount*] He was panting from the *exertion* of climbing the stairs. • an easy sport that requires little physical *exertion* [*count*] Their *exertions* [=*efforts*] were rewarded when they won the championship.

ex gra•tia /,ɛks'greɪʃijə/ *adj or adv, chiefly Brit* — used to describe something that is done or given freely rather than because it is required by a law • They made an *ex gratia* payment to the accident victim.

ex•hale /eks'heɪl/ *verb* **-hales; -haled; -hal•ing** : to breathe out [*no obj*] She inhaled deeply and *exhaled* slowly, trying to relax. [+ *obj*] He *exhaled* a sigh. — sometimes used figuratively • The pipe *exhaled* a cloud of smoke. — opposite INHALE
– **ex•ha•la•tion** /,ɛkshə'leɪʃən/ *noun, pl* **-tions** [*count, noncount*] • (an) *exhalation* of breath

[1]**ex•haust** /ɪg'zɑːst/ *verb* **-hausts; -haust•ed; -haust•ing** [+ *obj*]
1 : to use all of someone's mental or physical energy : to tire out or wear out (someone) completely • If you keep working these long hours, you're just going to *exhaust* yourself. = Working these long hours will just *exhaust* you.
2 a : to completely use up (something, such as supplies or money) • If they keep spending this way, they'll *exhaust* their savings. **b** : to try all of (something) • They've ***exhausted (all) the possibilities***. [=they've tried everything they can]
3 : to consider or talk about (a subject) thoroughly or completely • He can talk about baseball for hours and still feel that he hasn't ***exhausted the subject/topic***.
– **exhausted** *adj* [*more* ~; *most* ~] • The children were *exhausted* after their day at the beach. • She collapsed on her bed, totally *exhausted*. – **exhausting** *adj* [*more* ~; *most* ~] • It was an *exhausting* day at the beach. • We have an *exhausting* amount of work to do. – **ex•haust•ing•ly** *adv* • They worked *exhaustingly* long hours.

[2]**exhaust** *noun, pl* **-hausts**
1 [*noncount*] : the mixture of gases produced by an engine • diesel *exhaust* from passing trucks • *exhaust* fumes • smog from automobile *exhaust*
2 [*count*] : a pipe or system of pipes through which exhaust is released • There's a problem with the car's *exhaust*. — called also *exhaust pipe*, (*chiefly US*) *tailpipe*

ex•haus•tion /ɪg'zɑːstʃən/ *noun* [*noncount*]
1 : the state of being extremely tired : the state of being exhausted • physical/nervous *exhaustion* • She collapsed in *exhaustion*. • He worked to the point of complete/total *exhaustion*. — see also HEAT EXHAUSTION
2 : the act of using all of something : the act of exhausting something • the *exhaustion* of our natural resources

ex•haus•tive /ɪg'zɑːstɪv/ *adj* [*more* ~; *most* ~] : including all possibilities : very thorough • *exhaustive* research • an *exhaustive* study/search • The list was long but not *exhaustive*.
– **ex•haus•tive•ly** *adv* • an *exhaustively* researched report – **ex•haus•tive•ness** *noun* [*noncount*]

[1]**ex•hib•it** /ɪg'zɪbət/ *verb* **-its; -it•ed; -it•ing** [+ *obj*]
1 : to make (a painting, sculpture, etc.) available for people to see • They will be *exhibiting* a collection of paintings. • He proudly *exhibited* his trophy.
2 *somewhat formal* : to show or reveal (something) • He first *exhibited* an interest in music when he was very young. • The patient *exhibited* signs of the disease. • She *exhibited* no fear.
– **ex•hib•i•tor** /ɪg'zɪbətɚ/ *noun, pl* **-tors** [*count*] • The craft show attracts *exhibitors* from around the country.

[2]**exhibit** *noun, pl* **-its** [*count*]
1 a : an object or a collection of objects that have been put out in a public space for people to look at : something shown in an exhibition • The show includes dozens of interesting *exhibits*. **b** *chiefly US* : EXHIBITION 2a • Have you seen the new photography *exhibit*? • a school art *exhibit*
2 : an object that is used as evidence in a court of law • introduced the weapons into evidence as *exhibits* A and B ✧ The phrase ***exhibit A*** is sometimes used to refer to someone or something that is being mentioned as evidence or proof of something, as if in a court of law. • He says that the new regulations have hurt small businesses, and he offers his own company as *exhibit A*.
on exhibit : being publicly shown in an exhibition • The photographs are *on exhibit* in the museum's west wing. • The painting went *on exhibit* last week. • The painting was put *on exhibit*.

ex•hi•bi•tion /,ɛksə'bɪʃən/ *noun, pl* **-tions**
1 [*singular*] : an act of showing some quality or trait — + *of* • a notable *exhibition of* courage • give/provide an *exhibition of* bad manners

2 a [*count*] : an event at which objects (such as works of art) are put out in a public space for people to look at : a public show of something • There were several famous paintings at the *exhibition*. • an *exhibition* of early American crafts **b** [*noncount*] : the act of showing something in public • helping to promote artists by *exhibition* of their paintings

3 [*count*] : a public display of athletic skill • a fencing *exhibition* • an *exhibition* baseball game [=an unofficial game that does not count in the standings]

make an exhibition of yourself : to behave in a foolish or embarrassing way in public • He got drunk at the wedding and *made an exhibition of himself* in front of everyone.

on exhibition : being publicly shown in an exhibition • The coin collection will be (placed/put) *on exhibition* [=*on exhibit*] next week.

ex·hi·bi·tion·ism /ˌɛksəˈbɪʃəˌnɪzəm/ *noun* [*noncount*] *disapproving* : behavior that is meant to attract attention to yourself • shameless *exhibitionism*

– **ex·hi·bi·tion·ist** /ˌɛksəˈbɪʃənɪst/ *noun, pl* **-ists** [*count*]

– **exhibitionist** *or* **ex·hi·bi·tion·ist·ic** /ˌɛksəˌbɪʃəˈnɪstɪk/ *adj* [*more* ~; *most* ~] • *exhibitionist* behavior

ex·hil·a·rate /ɪgˈzɪləˌreɪt/ *verb* **-rates; -rat·ed; -rat·ing** [+ *obj*] : to cause (someone) to feel very happy and excited — usually used as *(be) exhilarated* • We *were exhilarated* by the news of his success.

– **exhilarated** *adj* [*more* ~; *most* ~] • I feel *exhilarated*!

– **exhilarating** *adj* [*more* ~; *most* ~] • an *exhilarating* ski trip • *exhilarating* news

ex·hil·a·ra·tion /ɪgˌzɪləˈreɪʃən/ *noun* [*noncount*] : a feeling of great happiness and excitement • I felt a kind of *exhilaration* when I reached the top of the mountain.

ex·hort /ɪgˈzoət/ *verb* **-horts; -hort·ed; -hort·ing** [+ *obj*] *formal* : to try to influence (someone) by words or advice : to strongly urge (someone) *to do* something • He *exhorted* his people *to take back* their land. • She *exhorted* her listeners *to support* the proposition.

– **ex·hor·ta·tion** /ˌɛkˌsoəˈteɪʃən/ *noun, pl* **-tions** [*count, noncount*]

ex·hume /ɪgˈzuːm, *Brit* ɪgˈzjuːm/ *verb* **-humes; -humed; -hum·ing** [+ *obj*] *formal* : to remove (a body) from the place where it is buried • The victim's body will be *exhumed* [=*disinterred*] so that a new autopsy can be performed.

– **ex·hu·ma·tion** /ˌɛkshjuˈmeɪʃən/ *noun, pl* **-tions** [*count, noncount*]

ex·i·gen·cy /ˈɛksəʤənsi/ *noun, pl* **-cies** *formal* : something that is necessary in a particular situation [*count*] — usually plural • Administrative *exigencies* [=*needs*] have led to some changes in the structure of the committee. • the *exigencies* of war [*noncount*] They are motivated by political *exigency* [=*necessity*] rather than by principal.

ex·i·gent /ˈɛksəʤənt/ *adj* [*more* ~; *most* ~] *formal*

1 : requiring immediate attention : needing to be dealt with immediately • *exigent* circumstances

2 : expecting much time, attention, effort, etc., from other people : DEMANDING • *exigent* bosses/clients

[1]**ex·ile** /ˈɛgˌzajəl, ˈɛkˌsajəl/ *noun, pl* **-iles**

1 a [*noncount*] : a situation in which you are forced to leave your country or home and go to live in a foreign country • They hoped that his *exile* would be temporary. — often used after *in* or *into* • forced *into exile* • He went *into exile* to avoid capture and execution by the government. • He now lives *in exile* in the United States. — sometimes used figuratively • She went *into* political *exile* [=she stopped being involved in politics] after the last election. **b** [*count*] : a period of time during which someone has lived in exile • a five-year *exile*

2 [*count*] : a person who has been forced to live in a foreign country : a person who is in exile • Many chose to live as *exiles* rather than face persecution. — see also TAX EXILE

[2]**exile** *verb* **-iles; -iled; -il·ing** [+ *obj*] : to force (someone) to go to live in a distant place or foreign country : to force (someone) into exile — usually used as *(be) exiled* • The President *was exiled* by military rulers soon after the coup. • an *exiled* writer • dissidents *exiled* to Siberia

ex·ist /ɪgˈzɪst/ *verb* **-ists; -ist·ed; -ist·ing** [*no obj*]

1 : to have actual being : to be real • She believes that ghosts really do *exist*. • It's the largest galaxy known to *exist*. • Does life *exist* on Mars? • The Internet didn't *exist* then. • Those ideas only *exist* in your mind. [=they are only in your mind] • We shouldn't ignore the problems that *exist* in our own community.

2 : to continue to be or to live • as long as doubt *exists* [=*persists*] • Racism still *exists* in our society. • The organization may soon cease to *exist* if more funding isn't provided. • We cannot *exist* [=*live*] without oxygen. • They *exist* [=*survive, subsist*] on a diet of fruit, nuts, and leaves.

– **existing** *adj* • ignore *existing* problems • making changes to the *existing* structure [=the structure that is there now]

ex·ist·ence /ɪgˈzɪstəns/ *noun, pl* **-enc·es**

1 [*noncount*] : the state of existing: such as **a** : the fact of having actual being : the state of being real • the *existence* of ghosts • She began to doubt the *existence* of God. • the largest animal/building in *existence* [=the largest animal/building that exists] • We shouldn't deny the *existence* of these problems. [=we shouldn't deny that these problems are present or real] • long before the country had ***come into existence*** [=begun to exist; come to have actual being] • The company has since gone ***out of existence***. [=it no longer exists] **b** : the state of continuing to be or to live • The organization is engaged in a struggle for (its) *existence*. • I owe my very *existence* [=*life*] to their courage. [=I am alive because of their courage]

2 [*count*] : a particular way of living — usually singular • They enjoyed a comfortable *existence*. • They pursued their meager *existence* in a poor rural area.

ex·ist·ent /ɪgˈzɪstənt/ *adj, formal* : having existence : present or real • The resort is no longer *existent*. [=it doesn't exist anymore] : existing now • I think we should improve *existent* parks rather than create new ones. — opposite NONEXISTENT

[1]**exit** /ˈɛgzət, ˈɛksət/ *noun, pl* **exits** [*count*]

1 : something (such as a door) that is used as a way to go out of a place • Use the emergency *exit* in case of fire. • There are 12 *exits* in the building. • We can't get out this way: the sign says "No *Exit*." • the *exit* door — sometimes used figuratively • The deal provides an *exit* for the company. [=a way for the company to stop being involved in something] — compare [1]ENTRANCE 2 ✧ In U.S. English a door or passage that leads outside or to an exit door is marked ***Exit***, while in British English it is often marked ***Way Out***.

2 a : the act of going out or away from something • Her *exit* [=*departure*] was not noticed at the time. • He ***made*** a quick ***exit***. [=he left quickly] • We *made* an early *exit* from the show. [=we left the show early] **b** : the act of leaving a situation, competition, etc. • Most fans were surprised by the team's early *exit* from the tournament. [=surprised that the team lost and was out of the tournament at an early stage] • The company needs to have an ***exit strategy***. [=a plan for ending its involvement when it wants or needs to end it]

3 : a special road by which vehicles leave a highway • Take the first *exit*. • *exit* ramps

[2]**exit** *verb* **exits; exit·ed; exit·ing**

1 : to go out of a place or situation : to make an exit [*no obj*] We can *exit* (out) through the back door. [+ *obj*] *exit* a building • *exit* the parking lot • The team *exited* the tournament early. — opposite ENTER

2 [+ *obj*] : to cause (a computer program) to stop when you have finished using it • Save your work and then *exit* the program.

exit poll *noun, pl* ~ **polls** [*count*] : a method of predicting the result of an election by asking people who they voted for as they leave the place where they voted

ex·o·dus /ˈɛksədəs/ *noun, pl* **-dus·es** [*count*] : a situation in which many people leave a place at the same time — usually singular • The war caused a mass *exodus* of refugees.

ex of·fi·cio /ˌɛksəˈfɪʃiˌoʊ/ *adv, formal* : because of your job, office, or position • The Vice President serves *ex officio* as president of the Senate. [=being vice president means that you are also the president of the Senate]

– **ex officio** *adj* • *ex officio* members of the council

ex·on·er·ate /ɪgˈzɑːnəˌreɪt/ *verb* **-ates; -at·ed; -at·ing** [+ *obj*] *formal* : to prove that someone is not guilty of a crime or responsible for a problem, bad situation, etc. • Her attorney claims that this new evidence will *exonerate* [=*clear*] the defendant completely. — sometimes + *of* or *from* • evidence that will *exonerate* her *of/from* the charges

– **ex·on·er·a·tion** /ɪgˌzɑːnəˈreɪʃən/ *noun* [*noncount*] • A review of the evidence led to her complete *exoneration*.

ex·or·bi·tant /ɪgˈzoəbətənt/ *adj* [*more* ~; *most* ~] : going far beyond what is fair, reasonable, or expected : too high, expensive, etc. • *exorbitant* fees/costs/prices/expenses • They were charged *exorbitant* rates for phone calls.

– **ex·or·bi·tant·ly** *adv* • *exorbitantly* expensive meals • *exorbitantly* high prices

ex·or·cise *also* **ex·or·cize** /ˈɛksəˌsaɪz/ *verb* **-cis·es** *also*

-ciz·es; **-cised** *also* **-cized**; **-cis·ing** *also* **-ciz·ing** [+ *obj*] : to force (an evil spirit) to leave • The movie is about a priest who tries to *exorcise* demons from a young girl. — often used figuratively • She tried hard to *exorcise* her feelings of guilt. • His charitable works seem to be an effort to *exorcise* the ghosts/demons of his past. [=to make up for the bad things he did in the past]
– **ex·or·cism** /ˈɛksəˌsɪzəm/ *noun, pl* **-cisms** [*noncount*] the *exorcism* of demons [*count*] a priest performing *exorcisms* – **ex·or·cist** /ˈɛksəˌsɪst/ *noun, pl* **-cists** [*count*]

¹ex·ot·ic /ɪgˈzɑːtɪk/ *adj* [*more* ~; *most* ~]
1 : very different, strange, or unusual • *exotic* colors/flavors • an *exotic* locale • She's known for her *exotic* tastes.
2 *of a plant or animal* : not living or growing naturally in a particular area : from another part of the world • *exotic* plants • *exotic* fish/birds
– **ex·ot·i·cal·ly** /ɪgˈzɑːtɪkli/ *adv* • *exotically* flavored teas – **ex·ot·i·cism** /ɪgˈzɑːtəˌsɪzəm/ *noun* [*noncount*] – **ex·ot·ic·ness** /ɪgˈzɑːtɪknəs/ *noun* [*noncount*]

²exotic *noun, pl* **-ics** [*count*] : a plant or animal that does not live or grow naturally in a particular area • Some native species are being crowded out by *exotics*.

ex·pand /ɪkˈspænd/ *verb* **-pands**; **-pand·ed**; **-pand·ing**
1 a [*no obj*] : to increase in size, range, or amount : to become bigger • The liquid *expands* and contracts with changes in temperature. • the *expanding* universe • His business has *expanded* to serve the entire state. • The coffee shop may *expand* into a full restaurant. **b** [+ *obj*] : to cause (something) to increase in size, range, or amount : to make (something) bigger • He has *expanded* his business to serve the entire state. • There are plans to *expand* the airport. • The police have decided to *expand* their investigation. • She plans to *expand* the lecture series into a book. • This trip will give you an opportunity to *expand* [=*broaden*] your horizons. [=to learn more about the world] • *expand* your knowledge
2 [+ *obj*] : to write (something) in full form • *Expand* the abbreviation "deg." to "degree."
expand on/upon [*phrasal verb*] ***expand on/upon (something)*** : to speak or write about (something) in a more complete or detailed way • She declined to *expand on* her earlier statement. • Please *expand* [=*elaborate*] *on* that idea. • Researchers will *expand upon* their data in a new study.
– **ex·pand·able** /ɪkˈspændəbəl/ *adj* [*more* ~; *most* ~] • *expandable* computer memory [=computer memory that can be easily increased]

ex·panse /ɪkˈspæns/ *noun, pl* **-pans·es** [*count*] : a large and usually flat open space or area • The explorer gazed across the vast Arctic *expanse*. — usually + *of* • the vast/broad *expanse of* the ocean • an *expanse of* desert • great *expanses of* pavement

ex·pan·sion /ɪkˈspænʃən/ *noun, pl* **-sions**
1 [*noncount*] : the act of becoming bigger or of making something bigger : the act of expanding • territorial *expansion* • The league is undergoing *expansion*. • economic *expansion* • the *expansion* of a lecture series into a book
2 [*count*] : a more complete and detailed written work or set of comments based on something shorter • This book is an *expansion* of a lecture series. — often + *on* or *upon* • Her remarks today were an *expansion on* her earlier comments regarding the budget.

ex·pan·sion·ism /ɪkˈspænʃəˌnɪzəm/ *noun* [*noncount*] : the belief that a country should grow larger : a policy of increasing a country's size by expanding its territory
– **ex·pan·sion·ist** /ɪkˈspænʃənɪst/ *adj* • *expansionist* policies – **expansionist** *noun, pl* **-ists** [*count*]

ex·pan·sive /ɪkˈspænsɪv/ *adj* [*more* ~; *most* ~]
1 *formal* : talking a lot • He was unusually *expansive* at the press conference. • She was in an *expansive* mood.
2 a : covering or including many things : very broad or wide • The law was *expansive* in its scope. • a more *expansive* treatment of the topic **b** : covering a large space or area • the hotel's *expansive* dining room • The house has *expansive* views of the valley. • an *expansive* gesture [=a broad gesture]
3 : growing quickly or steadily : marked by expansion • an *expansive* economy
– **ex·pan·sive·ly** *adv* – **ex·pan·sive·ness** *noun* [*noncount*]

ex·pat /ˈɛksˌpæt/ *noun, pl* **-pats** [*count*] *informal* : EXPATRIATE

ex·pa·ti·ate /ɛkˈspeɪʃiˌeɪt/ *verb* **-ates**; **-at·ed**; **-at·ing** [*no obj*] *formal* : to speak or write about something in a way that includes a lot of details or uses many words — usually + *on* or *upon* • an essay *expatiating on/upon* the legislative process

ex·pa·tri·ate /ɛkˈspeɪtrijət, *Brit* ɛkˈspætriət/ *noun, pl* **-ates** [*count*] : a person who lives in a foreign country • American *expatriates* living in Paris
– **expatriate** *adj, always used before a noun* • *expatriate* writers

ex·pect /ɪkˈspɛkt/ *verb* **-pects**; **-pect·ed**; **-pect·ing**
1 [+ *obj*] : to think that something will probably or certainly happen • We *expect* (that) the economy will improve. = We *expect* the economy to improve. • As *expected*, the election was very close. • Costs have been higher than *expected*. = Costs have been higher than they were *expected* to be. • It's *expected* that the new products will be available next month. • Prices are *expected* to rise. • He's opposed to the new law, as you might *expect*. • I *expect* (that) she won't like the news. • We were half/fully *expecting* [=we thought there was a reasonable/good chance] that the game would be canceled. • Good things sometimes happen when you least *expect* them. — often followed by *to* + *verb* • She *expects to go* to college. • I *expect to do well* on the exam. • Who do you *expect to win*? = Who do you *expect* will win?
2 [+ *obj*] : to think that (someone or something) will arrive or that (something) will happen • We *expect* them (to arrive) any minute now. • We *expect* rain tomorrow. = We *expect* it to rain tomorrow. • I'll *expect* your letter (to arrive) next week. • I'm *expecting* a phone call. • The *expected* delivery date is next month.
3 [+ *obj*] : to consider (something) to be reasonable, required, or necessary • He's a teacher who *expects* hard work from his students. • Her latest film lacks the quality that we've come to *expect* (from her). • We *expected* more from/of you. • This is not the kind of behavior I *expected* of you. • He *expects* a great deal from/of himself and from/of other people. • I don't think it's too much to *expect* that you should get to work on time. • The supplier *expects* to be paid on time. • We *expect* you to pay your debts. • "England *expects* every man to do his duty." —Lord Nelson (1805)
4 *always used in progressive tenses* [*no obj*] : to be pregnant • She's *expecting*. : to be due to give birth • She's *expecting* next month. [=she will probably give birth next month; her baby will probably be born next month]
5 [+ *obj*] *informal* : to suppose or think — usually used after *I* • *I expect* [=*guess*] that these problems occur in other places too. • She feels the same way, *I expect*. • "Does she feel the same way?" "*I expect* so/not."
– **ex·pect·able** /ɪkˈspɛktəbəl/ *adj* [*more* ~; *most* ~] • an *expectable* [=*predictable*] reaction

ex·pect·an·cy /ɪkˈspɛktənsi/ *noun* [*noncount*] : a feeling that something is going to happen : the feeling that you have when you are expecting something • We were all in a state of (nervous) *expectancy*, awaiting the results of the vote. • an air of *expectancy* — see also LIFE EXPECTANCY

ex·pect·ant /ɪkˈspɛktənt/ *adj*
1 [*more* ~; *most* ~] : feeling or thinking that something will happen : expecting something • An *expectant* crowd waited for her arrival.
2 *always used before a noun* : expecting the birth of a child : soon to become a parent • *expectant* parents • an *expectant* mother
– **ex·pect·ant·ly** *adv* • The crowd waited *expectantly* for her arrival.

ex·pec·ta·tion /ˌɛkˌspɛkˈteɪʃən/ *noun, pl* **-tions**
1 : a belief that something will happen or is likely to happen [*count*] Their *expectation* was [=they expected] that the plan would succeed. • The company has *expectations* of making a profit next year. [*noncount*] I saved the files in the *expectation* that they would be useful in the future. • There is widespread *expectation* that the strike will be settled soon. • The crowd waited ***in expectation of*** her arrival. ✧ To have ***every expectation of*** something is to feel very sure that it will happen. • They have *every expectation of* success. [=they believe they will succeed]
2 [*count*] : a feeling or belief about how successful, good, etc., someone or something will be — usually plural • *Expectations* for the team were high. [=people expected the team to do very well] • We've had to lower our *expectations* for the festival. [=to expect that the festival will not be as successful, big, etc., as we originally thought it would be] • We need to have more realistic *expectations* about when the house will be finished. [=to accept that the house will not be finished as soon as we thought it would be] • We're living in a time of diminished/rising *expectations*. • He found it hard ***to live up to***

their expectations. [=to do as well as they expected him to do] • The company failed to ***match/meet expectations.*** [=to be as successful as people thought it would be] • The restaurant has succeeded ***beyond*** (all) ***expectations.*** = The restaurant has ***exceeded expectations.*** [=it is more successful than people thought it would be] • Company earnings were ***not up to expectations.*** = Earnings ***fell short of expectations.*** [=the company did not earn as much money as people thought it would earn] • ***Contrary to expectations,*** all of the birds survived. = ***Against*** (all) ***expectations,*** the birds survived. [=the birds survived although people did not think they would]

[1]**ex·pe·di·ent** /ɪk'spiːdijənt/ *adj* [*more* ~; *most* ~] *often disapproving* : providing an easy and quick way to solve a problem or do something • They found it *expedient* to negotiate with the terrorists. • a politically *expedient* solution • Do the right thing, not the *expedient* thing.
– **ex·pe·di·ent·ly** *adv* • We want to resolve this issue as *expediently* [=*quickly*] as possible. – **ex·pe·di·ence** /ɪk'spiːdijəns/ *or* **ex·pe·di·en·cy** /ɪk'spiːdijənsi/ *noun* [*noncount*] • political *expedience/expediency* • for reasons of *expediency*

[2]**expedient** *noun, pl* **-ents** [*count*] : an easy and quick way to solve a problem or do something : an expedient solution • The government chose short-term/temporary *expedients* instead of a real economic policy. • We can solve this problem by the simple *expedient* of taking out another loan.

ex·pe·dite /'ɛkspəˌdaɪt/ *verb* **-dites; -dit·ed; -dit·ing** [+ *obj*] *formal* : to cause (something) to happen faster • They've asked the judge to *expedite* the lawsuits. • We'll do what we can to *expedite* the processing of your insurance claim. — compare EXPEDITIOUS

ex·pe·di·tion /ˌɛkspə'dɪʃən/ *noun, pl* **-tions** [*count*]
1 : a journey especially by a group of people for a specific purpose (such as to explore a distant place or to do research) • organize/mount/launch a mountain-climbing *expedition* • a scientific *expedition* to Antarctica — also used in a playful way to refer to a short trip for a specific purpose • a shopping *expedition* • fishing *expeditions* ✧ The phrase ***fishing expedition*** is sometimes used in a disapproving way, especially in U.S. English, to describe a situation in which a person or group looks for evidence that someone has done something wrong without having a good reason to believe the evidence exists. • Critics charge that the government investigation is a politically motivated *fishing expedition.*
2 : a group of people who travel together to a distant place : a group of people who go on an expedition • The (members of the) *expedition* discovered an ancient burial site.

ex·pe·di·tion·ary /ˌɛkspə'dɪʃəˌneri, *Brit* ˌɛkspə'dɪʃənri/ *adj*
1 : relating to an expedition • *expeditionary* missions
2 : sent to fight in a foreign country • an ***expeditionary force***

ex·pe·di·tious /ˌɛkspə'dɪʃəs/ *adj* [*more* ~; *most* ~] *formal* : acting or done in a quick and efficient way • Both sides hoped for an *expeditious* [=*prompt*] resolution of the dispute.
– **ex·pe·di·tious·ly** *adv* • The insurer handled the claim *expeditiously.* [=*promptly*]

ex·pel /ɪk'spɛl/ *verb* **-pels; -pelled; -pel·ling** [+ *obj*]
1 : to officially force (someone) to leave a place or organization • The club may *expel* members who do not follow the rules. • She was *expelled* from school for bad behavior.
2 : to push or force (something) out • *expel* air from the lungs

ex·pend /ɪk'spɛnd/ *verb* **-pends; -pend·ed; -pend·ing** [+ *obj*] *formal*
1 : to use or spend (something) • You can only lose weight by *expending* [=*using, using up*] more calories than you take in. • *expend* [=*spend*] funds
2 : to use (time, energy, effort, etc.) for a particular purpose • Are we willing to *expend* the time and resources required to solve the problem? — often + *on* • We need to *expend* more time and resources *on* solving the problem. — sometimes followed by *in* + *-ing verb* • We need to *expend* more time and resources *in finding* a solution to the problem.

ex·pend·able /ɪk'spɛndəbəl/ *adj* : easily replaced : not worth saving • employees whose jobs are considered *expendable* : not meant to be saved : meant to be used and thrown away • an *expendable* rocket • *expendable* [=*disposable*] supplies

ex·pen·di·ture /ɪk'spɛndɪtʃɚ/ *noun, pl* **-tures** *formal*
1 a : an amount of money that is spent on something [*count*] Your income should exceed your *expenditures.* [=you should earn more money than you spend] • an increase in military *expenditures* [*noncount*] an increase in military *expenditure* **b** : an amount of time, energy, effort, etc., that is used to do something [*count*] vast *expenditures* of time and effort [*noncount*] The energy *expenditure* was significant.
2 a [*noncount*] : the act of spending money • the *expenditure* of funds for the new school **b** : the act of using something (such as time or effort) for a particular purpose [*noncount*] greater *expenditure* of effort [*count*] The project will require an *expenditure* of effort on everyone's part.

ex·pense /ɪk'spɛns/ *noun, pl* **-pens·es**
1 [*noncount*] : the amount of money that is needed to pay for or buy something • I'd like to save the time and *expense* [=*cost*] of redoing the whole thing. • I don't think a first-class ticket is worth the added/extra *expense.* — often used after *at* • These items were imported *at* great/considerable/enormous *expense.* [=it cost a lot to import them] • We were able to fix the problem *at* very little *expense.* [=for very little money] • The repairs were made *at* no *expense* to us. [=without costing us anything] — see also AT SOMEONE'S EXPENSE (below) ✧ If you ***spare no expense***, you spend as much money as you need to in order to make something as good as possible. • When they go on vacation, they *spare no expense.* • They *spared no expense* in building the house.
2 [*count*] : an amount of money that must be spent especially regularly to pay for something • The annual fee is simply an *expense* of doing business. — usually plural • Their *expenses* [=*expenditures*] were getting far ahead of their income. • We need to find a way to control *expenses.* • cutting back on *expenses* • legal/medical/household *expenses* [=*costs*] • I'm concerned about the project's hidden *expenses.* • You'll have to pay your own travel/traveling *expenses.* • an ***all-expenses paid*** trip [=a journey for which all costs are already paid]
3 [*count*] : something on which money is spent • A new car is a major *expense.* • My new computer was a business *expense.* [=something I had to buy in order to do business]
at someone's expense **1** : paid for by someone • a fancy dinner *at my parents' expense* • a stadium built *at the taxpayers' expense* = a stadium built *at taxpayer expense* [=with money from taxes] • The tour is free, but all meals are *at your own expense.* [=you must pay for your meals] **2** ✧ If someone makes a joke about you or laughs at you, the joke or laughter is said to be ***at your expense.*** • Everyone had a good laugh *at my expense.*
at the expense of : in a way that harms (something or someone) • Malls flourished *at the expense of* small stores downtown. • She acquired power *at the expense of* friendships. • He argues that the tax cut will benefit the rich *at the expense of* the poor.
go to (the) expense : to spend money on something • Why *go to the expense* of installing something you'll never use? • She *went to* great *expense* to have this party.

expense account *noun, pl* ~ **accounts** [*count*] : an arrangement that allows an employee (such as someone who is traveling for business) to pay for things using the company's money instead of the employee's money • He charged dinner to his *expense account.* • She put the tickets on her *expense account.*

ex·pen·sive /ɪk'spɛnsɪv/ *adj* [*more* ~; *most* ~] : costing a lot of money • an *expensive* hobby • an *expensive* car • *expensive* clothes • The lights were *expensive* to install. • They live in an *expensive* neighborhood. [=a neighborhood in which houses, apartments, etc., cost a lot to buy or rent] • Her decision to leave the company proved to be an *expensive* mistake. [=a mistake that caused her to lose a lot of money] • an *expensive* shop [=a shop that sells expensive things] • He has *expensive* tastes. [=he likes expensive things]
– **ex·pen·sive·ly** *adv* • He dresses *expensively.*

[1]**ex·pe·ri·ence** /ɪk'spirijəns/ *noun, pl* **-enc·es**
1 [*noncount*] : the process of doing and seeing things and of having things happen to you • The best way to learn is by *experience.* • the *experience* of pain/love
2 [*noncount*] **a** : skill or knowledge that you get by doing something • We need someone with *experience.* • She gained/acquired a lot of *experience* at that job. • I know that from personal/firsthand *experience.* • Do you have *experience* doing this kind of work? [=have you done this kind of work?] • I have little *experience* (dealing) with these kinds of issues. **b** : the length of time that you have spent doing something (such as a particular job) • She has five years' *experience* as a computer programmer.
3 [*count*] : something that you have done or that has happened to you • He wrote about his *experiences* as a pilot. •

That *experience* is one I'd rather forget! • She had a frightening *experience*.

²experience *verb* **-enc·es; -enced; -enc·ing** [+ *obj*] : to do or see (something) or have (something) happen to you • Have you ever *experienced* [=*suffered*] the loss of a pet? • That was one of the worst days I've ever *experienced*. : to feel or be affected by (something) • The patient has been *experiencing* pain in her left shoulder.

experienced /ɪkˈspirijənst/ *adj* [*more* ~; *most* ~] : having skill or knowledge from doing something : having experience • an *experienced* driver • The job calls for someone who is more *experienced*. • *experienced* at/in teaching

¹ex·per·i·ment /ɪkˈsperəmənt/ *noun, pl* **-ments**
1 : a scientific test in which you perform a series of actions and carefully observe their effects in order to learn about something [*count*] Students will carry out simple laboratory *experiments*. • perform/conduct/do/run an *experiment* • a failed *experiment* • They did some *experiments* with magnets. • a series of *experiments* on rats [=done to rats] [*noncount*] These theories have not yet been confirmed by *experiment*.
2 [*count*] : something that is done as a test : something that you do to see how well or how badly it works • I'd like to paint the room a different color, just as an *experiment*. [=to see if it looks good or not] • an *experiment* in living more frugally • the city's *experiment* with a longer school year

²ex·per·i·ment /ɪkˈsperəˌment/ *verb* **-ments; -ment·ed; -ment·ing** [*no obj*] : to make or do an experiment: such as **a** : to do a scientific test in which you perform a series of actions and carefully observe their effects • They *experimented* with magnets. • researchers *experimenting* on rats **b** : to try a new activity or a new way of doing or thinking about something • an artist who's always *experimenting* [=trying new things] — usually + *with* • He's been *experimenting with* various materials. • She *experimented with* different kinds of weaving. • The school is *experimenting with* a longer school year. • teenagers *experimenting with* drugs [=using illegal drugs to find out if they like them]
– ex·per·i·men·ta·tion /ɪkˌsperəmənˈteɪʃən/ *noun* [*noncount*] • scientific *experimentation* with/on rats • artistic *experimentation* **– ex·per·i·ment·er** /ɪkˈsperəˌmentɚ/ *noun, pl* **-ers** [*count*]

ex·per·i·men·tal /ɪkˌsperəˈmentl/ *adj* [*more* ~; *most* ~]
1 : relating to a scientific experiment or to scientific experiments in general • *experimental* data/evidence • *experimental* approaches/conditions • *experimental* animals [=animals that are used in experiments]
2 : made or done in order to see how well something works • an *experimental* treatment • *experimental* drugs/techniques • Plans for new city bus routes are still in the *experimental* stage. [=they are not final yet; they are being tested] • The fuel is being used on an *experimental* basis.
3 : using a new way of doing or thinking about something • *experimental* art/films
– ex·per·i·men·tal·ly *adv* • The theory was only recently *experimentally* confirmed. [=confirmed in an experiment] • The technique/fuel is being used *experimentally*.

¹ex·pert /ˈɛkˌspɚt/ *noun, pl* **-perts** [*count*] : a person who has special skill or knowledge relating to a particular subject • a computer *expert* • She was an acknowledged *expert* on/in child development. • an *expert* at planning dinner parties

²expert *adj* [*more* ~; *most* ~] : having or showing special skill or knowledge because of what you have been taught or what you have experienced • We received some *expert* advice. • an *expert* poker player • an *expert* opinion • The company has become *expert* at/in adapting its products for new clients. • *expert* testimony • an ***expert witness*** [=a witness in a court of law who is an expert on a particular subject]
– ex·pert·ly *adv* • The furniture was *expertly* constructed. **– ex·pert·ness** *noun* [*noncount*]

ex·per·tise /ˌɛkspɚˈtiːz/ *noun* [*noncount*] : special skill or knowledge : the skill or knowledge an expert has • His *expertise* on defense will help the team. • her *expertise* in legal matters • The company has no environmental *expertise*. [=the company does not have experience with environmental problems, matters, etc.] • This question falls outside my ***area of expertise*** [=the subject area I know a lot about]

ex·pi·ate /ˈɛkspiˌeɪt/ *verb* **-ates; -at·ed; -at·ing** [+ *obj*] *formal* : to do something as a way to show that you are sorry about doing something bad • trying to find a way to *expiate* [=*atone for*] his guilt/sin
– ex·pi·a·tion /ˌɛkspiˈeɪʃən/ *noun* [*noncount*] • *expiation* of his guilt/sin

ex·pi·ra·tion /ˌɛkspəˈreɪʃən/ *noun* [*noncount*]
1 : the fact of coming to an end or no longer being valid after a period of time : the fact of expiring • the patent's *expiration* • one month after the *expiration* of the contract
2 *medical* : the act of breathing out • inhalation and *expiration* [=*exhalation*]

expiration date *noun, pl* ~ **dates** [*count*]
1 : the date when something (such as a credit card or driver's license) can no longer legally or officially be used • What is the *expiration date* on your credit card? [=when does your credit card expire?] — called also (*Brit*) *expiry date*
2 : the date when something (such as milk or medicine) can no longer be sold because it may no longer be good or effective • Check the *expiration date* on the bottle to make sure the medicine is still good. — called also (*Brit*) *expiry date*

ex·pire /ɪkˈspajɚ/ *verb* **-pires; -pired; -pir·ing**
1 [*no obj*] : to end : to no longer be valid after a period of time • This offer *expires* (on) March 1. • My driver's license has *expired*.
2 [*no obj*] *formal* : to die • She *expired* after a long illness.
3 /ɛkˈspajɚ/ [+ *obj*] *medical* : to breathe out (air) : EXHALE • measuring the volume of air *expired* from the lungs
time expires ✧ When *time expires* in a game, the clock shows that there is no more time and play stops. • They scored seconds before *time expired*.

ex·pi·ry /ɪkˈspajəri/ *noun* [*noncount*] *chiefly Brit* : the fact of expiring : EXPIRATION • the *expiry* of the waiting period

expiry date *noun, pl* ~ **dates** [*count*] *Brit* : EXPIRATION DATE

ex·plain /ɪkˈspleɪn/ *verb* **-plains; -plained; -plain·ing**
1 [+ *obj*] : to make (something) clear or easy to understand • I need a lawyer to *explain* this contract to me. • The professor *explained* the poem to the class. • She *explained* how the machine worked. • I *explained* to them that I would be available by phone.
2 : to tell, show, or be the reason for or cause of something [+ *obj*] Scientists could not *explain* the strange lights in the sky. • I don't know how to *explain* the dog's strange behavior. • "I need to rest," I *explained* to them. = I *explained* to them that I needed to rest. • We asked him to *explain* his reasons to us. • Can you *explain* why no one was informed earlier? • Well, that *explains* it! • That *explains* why we we're so far behind schedule. [*no obj*] Give me a chance to *explain*.
explain away [*phrasal verb*] ***explain away (something) or explain (something) away*** **1** : to make (something) seem less important by telling how it happened, what caused it, etc. • It will be hard for his lawyers to *explain away* this new evidence. • She tried to *explain* her symptoms *away* by insisting she was just overtired. **2** : to give a reason for (a fault, a mistake, etc.) so that you will not be blamed for it • They've tried to *explain away* the delays, citing computer problems.
explain yourself **1** : to give a reason for your behavior • She had a hard time *explaining herself* after the theft was revealed. • I don't think that I should have to *explain myself* to you. **2** : to say something clearly so that it can be understood • Let me try to *explain myself* more clearly.
hasten to explain see HASTEN
– ex·plain·able /ɪkˈspleɪnəbəl/ *adj* [*more* ~; *most* ~] • He thought all behavior was *explainable* in terms of genetics.

ex·pla·na·tion /ˌɛkspləˈneɪʃən/ *noun, pl* **-tions**
1 [*noncount*] : the act or process of making something clear or easy to understand • Some of the more technical terms need/require *explanation*. [=they need to be explained] : the act or process of telling, showing, or being the reason for or cause of something • She declined the offer without (further) *explanation*. • Some of his actions defy *explanation*. [=cannot be explained] • The company offered little ***by way of explanation*** for the delays. [=as a way of explaining why there were delays]
2 [*count*] : something (such as a statement or fact) that explains something • The professor's *explanation* was that the poem is really a parody. — often + *for* or *of* • Did the company offer an *explanation for* the delays? • There are several possible *explanations for* the current oil shortage. • a likely/probable/possible/plausible *explanation of* how the accident occurred

ex·plan·a·to·ry /ɪkˈsplænəˌtori, *Brit* ɪkˈsplænətri/ *adj* : made or included in order to explain something • There are *explanatory* notes at the front of the book. — compare SELF-EXPLANATORY

ex·ple·tive /ˈɛksplətɪv, *Brit* ɪkˈspliːtɪv/ *noun, pl* **-tives**

[*count*] : a word or phrase (such as "Damn it!") that people sometimes say when they are angry or in pain; *especially* : one that is offensive • Angry *expletives* filled the air. • *Expletives* were deleted from the transcript of their conversation.

ex·pli·ca·ble /ɛkˈsplɪkəbəl, ˈɛksplɪkəbəl/ *adj, formal* : possible to explain : EXPLAINABLE • phenomena *explicable* by the laws of physics • his least *explicable* mistake — opposite INEXPLICABLE

ex·pli·cate /ˈɛkspləˌkeɪt/ *verb* **-cates; -cat·ed; -cat·ing** [+ *obj*] *formal* : to explain or analyze (something, such as an idea or work of literature) • an essay *explicating* a theory • *explicate* a poem

— **ex·pli·ca·tion** /ˌɛkspləˈkeɪʃən/ *noun, pl* **-tions** [*count, noncount*]

E

ex·plic·it /ɪkˈsplɪsət/ *adj* [*more* ~; *most* ~]

1 : very clear and complete : leaving no doubt about the meaning • They were given *explicit* instructions. • Changes to the property can't be done without their *explicit* consent. • The law is very *explicit* about how these measures should be enacted. — opposite IMPLICIT

2 a : showing or referring very openly to nudity, violence, or sexual activity • *explicit* photographs • They're concerned about exposing children to (sexually) *explicit* films. • a song with *explicit* lyrics **b** : openly shown • The movie contains scenes of *explicit* violence. • two people engaging in *explicit* sex • sexually *explicit* conduct

— **ex·plic·it·ly** *adv* • We *explicitly* asked for a room with a view. • The building was *explicitly* restricted to official personnel. — **ex·plic·it·ness** *noun* [*noncount*] • sexual *explicitness*

ex·plode /ɪkˈsploʊd/ *verb* **-plodes; -plod·ed; -plod·ing**

1 : to suddenly break apart in a violent way with parts flying outward [*no obj*] The bomb could *explode* [=*blow up, detonate*] at any minute. • One of the shells failed to *explode*. • an *exploding* volcano [+ *obj*] *explode* [=*blow up, detonate*] a bomb — compare IMPLODE

2 [*no obj*] **a** : to change in a very sudden and violent way • These occasional skirmishes may soon *explode* into all-out war. **b** : to move with sudden speed and force • The horses *exploded* [=*burst*] out of the starting gate. • The birds suddenly *exploded* into flight. • We *exploded* [=*burst*] into action. **c** : to be affected by something very suddenly • The building *exploded* in/into flames/fire. • The audience *exploded* with/in/into laughter. [=everyone burst out laughing]

3 a [*no obj*] : to express emotion in a sudden and violent way • She looked like she was ready to *explode* with anger. **b** [+ *obj*] : to say (something) in a sudden and angry way • "Damn you!" she *exploded*.

4 [+ *obj*] : to show that (something, such as a belief or theory) is false • Science has *exploded* many old theories. • The book *explodes* a number of myths/legends about his youth.

5 [*no obj*] : to increase very quickly • The deer population has recently *exploded*. • the *exploding* [=*soaring, rising*] costs of childcare • The book has *exploded* in popularity.

exploded *adj, technical* : showing the parts of something separately but in correct relationship to each other • an *exploded* view/diagram of an engine

[1]ex·ploit /ˈɛkˌsplɔɪt/ *noun, pl* **-ploits** [*count*] : an exciting act or action — usually plural • performing heroic *exploits* [=*feats*] • He enjoys talking about his youthful *exploits*. [=*adventures*] • a book about his sexual *exploits*

[2]ex·ploit /ɪkˈsplɔɪt/ *verb* **-ploits; -ploit·ed; -ploit·ing** [+ *obj*]

1 : to get value or use from (something) • He has never fully *exploited* his talents. • Top athletes are able to *exploit* their opponents' weaknesses. • We need to *exploit* [=*take advantage of*] this opportunity/situation. • *exploit* natural resources

2 : to use (someone or something) in a way that helps you unfairly • They were accused of *exploiting* [=*taking advantage of*] migrant workers. • She said the tragedy had been *exploited* by the media.

— **ex·ploit·able** /ɪkˈsplɔɪtəbəl/ *adj* [*more* ~; *most* ~] • *exploitable* resources — **ex·ploi·ta·tion** /ˌɛkˌsplɔɪˈteɪʃən/ *noun* [*noncount*] • a victim of *exploitation* — **ex·ploit·er** *noun, pl* **-ers** [*count*]

ex·plo·ra·tion /ˌɛkspləˈreɪʃən/ *noun, pl* **-tions** : the act of exploring something [*noncount*] space *exploration* • a topic for scholarly *exploration* • the early *exploration* of the West [*count*] early *explorations* of the West

ex·plor·a·to·ry /ɪkˈsplorəˌtori, *Brit* ɪkˈsplɒrətri/ *adj* [*more* ~; *most* ~] : done or created to find something or to learn more about something • *exploratory* drilling for oil • an *exploratory* committee • He underwent ***exploratory surgery***. [=surgery done to find and identify a problem]

ex·plore /ɪkˈsploɚ/ *verb* **-plores; -plored; -plor·ing**

1 [+ *obj*] **a** : to look at (something) in a careful way to learn more about it : to study or analyze (something) • Researchers are *exploring* how language is acquired by children. **b** : to talk or think about (something) in a thoughtful and detailed way • The book *explores* a number of controversial issues. • You need to *explore* your feelings on this subject more carefully. • We *explored* various options/alternatives/possibilities. **c** : to learn about (something) by trying it • an opportunity to *explore* different activities • The children were encouraged to *explore* mathematics.

2 [+ *obj*] : to travel over or through (a place) in order to learn more about it or to find something • I decided to go out and *explore* the town. • They were sent to *explore* unknown regions of Africa.

3 [*no obj*] : to make a careful search *for* something by traveling to different places • companies *exploring for* oil

4 [+ *obj*] : to touch (something) to learn more about it • The doctor *explored* the wound.

— **ex·plor·er** *noun, pl* **-ers** [*count*] • Arctic *explorers*

ex·plo·sion /ɪkˈsploʊʒən/ *noun, pl* **-sions** [*count*]

1 : the sudden, loud, and violent release of energy that happens when something (such as a bomb) breaks apart in a way that sends parts flying outward • The filmmakers staged the car's *explosion*. • The island was rocked by a series of volcanic *explosions*. • set off an *explosion*

2 a : a sudden and very fast increase • The region has experienced a population *explosion*. • an *explosion* of interest **b** : a sudden expression of some strong emotion • an *explosion* of anger **c** : a sudden occurrence of laughter • His comments prompted an *explosion* of laughter from the crowd.

[1]ex·plo·sive /ɪkˈsploʊsɪv/ *adj*

1 a [*more* ~; *most* ~] : able to cause an explosion • a highly *explosive* substance : used for exploding something • an *explosive* charge • *explosive* devices **b** : relating to an explosion or caused by an explosion • the bomb's *explosive* force

2 [*more* ~; *most* ~] **a** : tending to get angry very easily • an *explosive* personality • He has an *explosive* temper. **b** : likely to become violent very suddenly • The police are trying to defuse a very *explosive* [=*volatile*] situation. **c** : happening suddenly and quickly • The region has experienced *explosive* [=*rapid*] population growth.

[2]explosive *noun, pl* **-sives** [*count*] : a substance (such as dynamite) that is used to cause an explosion : an explosive substance • the danger of working with ***high explosives*** [=very powerful explosives]

ex·po·nent /ɪkˈspoʊnənt, ˈɛkˌspoʊnənt/ *noun, pl* **-nents** [*count*]

1 a : someone who supports a particular cause, belief, etc. • He was a leading *exponent* [=*supporter, proponent*] of the civil rights movement. **b** : someone who is known for a particular method, style, etc. • She has become one of America's foremost *exponents* of the romantic style in interior design.

2 *mathematics* : a symbol that is written above and to the right of a number to show how many times the number is to be multiplied by itself • The *exponent* 3 in 10^3 indicates 10 x 10 x 10.

ex·po·nen·tial /ˌɛkspəˈnɛnʧəl/ *adj*

1 [*more* ~; *most* ~] : very fast : increasingly rapid • The business has experienced several years of *exponential* growth. • Prices have increased at an *exponential* rate. ✧ ***Exponential*** growth is literally growth that becomes faster and faster as it continues. In ordinary use, however, ***exponential*** is understood to mean simply "very fast" when it is used with words like ***growth*** and ***increase***.

2 *mathematics* : including or using an exponent • 10^3 is an *exponential* expression.

— **ex·po·nen·tial·ly** /ˌɛkspəˈnɛnʧəli/ *adv* • Prices have increased *exponentially*. • *exponentially* rapid growth

[1]ex·port /ɛkˈspoɚt/ *verb* **-ports; -port·ed; -port·ing** [+ *obj*] : to send a product to be sold in another country • countries that *export* oil to the U.S. — opposite IMPORT

— **ex·port·able** /ɛkˈspoɚtəbəl/ *adj* • *exportable* goods — **ex·por·ta·tion** /ˌɛkˌspoɚˈteɪʃən/ *noun* [*noncount*] • the *exportation* [=*export*] of oil — **ex·port·er** /ɛkˈspoɚtɚ/ *noun, pl* **-ers** [*count*] • a leading *exporter* of soybeans

[2]ex·port /ˈɛkˌspoɚt/ *noun, pl* **-ports**

1 [*count*] : something that is exported : a product that is sent to another country to be sold there • *Exports* to China have risen this year.

2 [*noncount*] : the act of exporting something • goods for *export* [=*exportation*] • the *export* of wines
– **export** *adj, always used before a noun* • the *export* market • *export* crops

ex·pose /ɪkˈspoʊz/ *verb* **-pos·es; -posed; -pos·ing** [+ *obj*]
1 : to leave (something) without covering or protection • The shingles had fallen off, *exposing* the wood underneath. — often + *to* • The colors will fade if they are *exposed to* sunlight.
2 : to cause (someone) to experience something or to be influenced or affected by something — + *to* • He wants to *expose* his students *to* great works of literature. • The workers were *exposed to* dangerous chemicals. [=they were placed in conditions that left them unprotected from dangerous chemicals] • She hasn't yet been *exposed to* measles. • Children are being *exposed to* violence on television. • His mistakes have *exposed* him *to* ridicule. [=he has been ridiculed because of his mistakes]
3 a : to reveal (something hidden, dishonest, etc.) • Undercover investigators *exposed* the scam. **b** : to reveal the crimes or faults of (someone) • They threatened to *expose* him. — often + *as* • They *exposed* him *as* a fraud.
4 : to let light fall on (film in a camera) in order to create a photograph • The film had not been properly *exposed*. — compare OVEREXPOSE, UNDEREXPOSE
expose yourself : to show your sexual organs in public • He was arrested for *exposing himself* (to women) in the park.

ex·po·sé /ˌɛkspoʊˈzeɪ, *Brit* ɛkˈspəʊzeɪ/ *noun, pl* **-sés** [*count*] : a news report or broadcast that reveals something illegal or dishonest to the public • a newspaper *exposé* of government corruption • The show aired an *exposé* on the candidate's financial indiscretions.

exposed /ɪkˈspoʊzd/ *adj* : not protected or covered • an *exposed* hillside • *exposed* wiring • an *exposed* beam

ex·po·si·tion /ˌɛkspəˈzɪʃən/ *noun, pl* **-tions**
1 *formal* : the act of explaining something : clear explanation [*noncount*] The subject requires some *exposition*. [*count*] a clear *exposition* of his ideas
2 [*count*] : a public show or exhibition • the great Paris *Exposition* of 1899 • have/hold/mount an international *exposition*

ex·pos·i·to·ry /ɪkˈspɑːzəˌtori, *Brit* ɪkˈspɒzətri/ *adj, chiefly US, somewhat formal* — used to describe writing that is done to explain something • *expository* prose • I'm taking an ***expository writing*** class this semester.

ex·pos·tu·late /ɪkˈspɑːstʃəˌleɪt/ *verb* **-lates; -lat·ed; -lat·ing** [*no obj*] *formal* : to disagree with something or argue against it • She *expostulated* (with us) at length on/about/concerning the proposed law.
– **ex·pos·tu·la·tion** /ɪkˌspɑːstʃəˈleɪʃən/ *noun, pl* **-tions** [*count, noncount*]

ex·po·sure /ɪkˈspoʊʒɚ/ *noun, pl* **-sures**
1 [*noncount*] : the fact or condition of being affected by something or experiencing something : the condition of being exposed *to* something • *exposure to* heat/cold • *exposure to* infection/danger • children's *exposure to* violence on television • He risks *exposure to* ridicule by saying such things in public.
2 [*noncount*] : the act of revealing secrets about someone or something • They threatened him with (public) *exposure*. — often + *of* • *exposure of* his criminal past.
3 [*noncount*] : public attention and notice • The candidates are competing for television/media *exposure*.
4 [*count*] *photography* **a** : the amount of time during which light is allowed to enter a camera in order to produce a photograph • a three-second *exposure* **b** : a section of a film used for a single photograph • This roll of film has 24 *exposures*.
5 [*noncount*] *medical* : a condition that results from being outside in cold weather for a long time • The climbers nearly died of *exposure*.
6 [*count*] : a position that provides a view in a specified direction • The room has a southern *exposure*.
– see also INDECENT EXPOSURE

ex·pound /ɪkˈspaʊnd/ *verb* **-pounds; -pound·ed; -pound·ing** *formal* : to explain or state (something) : to give details about (something) [+ *obj*] The article *expounds* the virtues of a healthy diet. [*no obj*] When asked to *expound*, he had no comment. — often + *on* • The article *expounds on* the virtues of a healthy diet.

[1]**ex·press** /ɪkˈsprɛs/ *verb* **-press·es; -pressed; -press·ing** [+ *obj*]
1 a : to talk or write about (something that you are thinking or feeling) • He *expressed* an interest in meeting her. • We *expressed* (to them) our thoughts/feelings/views on the subject. • She *expressed* surprise at his rude behavior. **b** : to make (your thoughts and feelings) known by doing something other than talking or writing • Her love of nature is *expressed* [=*shown, reflected*] in her paintings/music. • Words ***can't (even begin to) express*** how grateful I am.
2 : to show (an amount, quantity, etc.) by a sign or a symbol • The results can be *expressed* as a percentage. • The length, *expressed* in centimeters, is 29.
3 *chiefly US* : to send (a package, letter, etc.) so that it will be delivered more quickly than usual : to send (something) by express • They *expressed* the package to us.
4 : to cause (something) to come out by squeezing or pressing • a room where nursing mothers can *express* [=*pump*] milk for their babies
express itself/themselves *of feelings* : to become known or seen as the result of a particular action • His rage and frustration *expressed* [=*showed, manifested*] *themselves* as/in/through temper tantrums.
express yourself : to say or show your thoughts and feelings • He has a hard time *expressing himself*. • She felt that she hadn't *expressed herself* correctly. • He *expressed himself* in song.
– **ex·press·ible** /ɪkˈsprɛsəbəl/ *adj* • The depth of my gratitude is not *expressible* in words.

[2]**express** *adj, always used before a noun*
1 : said or given in a clear way • My *express* [=*explicit*] orders were for you to go directly home.
2 : of a particular kind • I came for that *express* [=*specific*] purpose.
3 a : traveling at high speed with few stops • an *express* train/bus/elevator — compare [1]LOCAL 2 **b** : delivered faster than usual • an *express* shipment **c** : designed or intended to be used for fast movement or travel • *express* roads • the *express* lane at the grocery store
– **ex·press·ly** *adv* • Smoking is *expressly* [=*explicitly*] forbidden.

[3]**express** *noun, pl* **-presses**
1 [*noncount*] : a system for delivering things (such as letters and packages) quickly • He sent the package to us by *express*.
2 [*count*] : a train or bus that travels quickly with few stops • He takes the *express* to work. — compare [2]LOCAL 1

[4]**express** *adv* : by a system that delivers letters and packages quickly : by express • They sent the package *express*.

ex·pres·sion /ɪkˈsprɛʃən/ *noun, pl* **-sions**
1 : the act of making your thoughts, feelings, etc., known by speech, writing, or some other method : the act of expressing something [*noncount*] freedom of *expression* [=freedom to say and show what you feel and believe] • Dance is a form of artistic/creative *expression*. • She is always looking for new ways to ***give expression to*** [=to express] her ideas. • Her competitive spirit ***found expression*** [=was expressed] in sports. [*count*] an *expression* of affection • *expressions* of anger — see also SELF-EXPRESSION
2 [*count*] : a word or phrase • a slang *expression* • He uses some very odd *expressions*. • The *expression* "to make fun of" means "to ridicule." ✧ People say ***excuse/pardon/forgive the expression*** when they are using a word or phrase that might offend or annoy someone. • When you first told me your plan, I thought you were, *pardon the expression*, crazy. • I'm so glad that you've decided to join us. In fact, I'm tickled pink, (if you'll) *excuse the expression*.
3 [*count*] : the way someone's face looks that shows emotions and feelings • Judging from her *expression*, I think the gift was a complete surprise. • We saw his *expression* change from angry/anger to sad/sadness. • facial *expressions* • She wore/had a smug *expression*.
4 [*noncount*] : a way of doing something (such as speaking or singing) that shows emotions and feelings • I told him to read the poem with more *expression*.
5 [*count*] *mathematics* : a symbol or a combination of symbols and signs representing a quantity or process • 10^3 is an exponential *expression*.
– **ex·pres·sion·less** /ɪkˈsprɛʃənləs/ *adj* • an *expressionless* face – **ex·pres·sion·less·ly** *adv* • staring *expressionlessly* at the camera – **ex·pres·sion·less·ness** *noun* [*noncount*]

ex·pres·sive /ɪkˈsprɛsɪv/ *adj* [*more* ~; *most* ~]
1 : showing emotions and feelings clearly and openly • an *expressive* performance • She has very *expressive* features. [=her feelings are shown very clearly on her face] • an *expressive* silence/gesture

2 : showing or expressing something — *+ of* ▪ His work is *expressive of* his personality. [=his work epxresses his personality]

3 : of or relating to expression ▪ the *expressive* function of language

– **ex·pres·sive·ly** *adv* ▪ singing *expressively* – **ex·pres·sive·ness** *noun [noncount]* ▪ the *expressiveness* of her features

ex·press·way /ɪkˈsprɛsˌweɪ/ *noun, pl* **-ways** *[count] US* **:** a large highway that may be entered and left only at certain places

ex·pro·pri·ate /ɪkˈsproupriˌeɪt/ *verb* **-ates; -at·ed; -at·ing** *[+ obj] formal* **:** to take (someone's property) — used especially when a government takes property for public use ▪ The land was *expropriated* by the state.

– **ex·pro·pri·a·tion** /ɪkˌsproupriˈeɪʃən/ *noun, pl* **-tions** *[count, noncount]*

ex·pul·sion /ɪkˈspʌlʃən/ *noun, pl* **-sions**

1 : the act of forcing someone to leave a place (such as a country or a school) **:** the act of expelling someone *[count]* The government engaged in mass *expulsions*. *[noncount]* He was threatened with *expulsion* (from the school) if his grades didn't improve.

2 *[noncount]* **:** the act of forcing something out **:** the act of expelling something ▪ the *expulsion* of air from the lungs

ex·punge /ɪkˈspʌnʤ/ *verb* **-pung·es; -punged; -pung·ing** *[+ obj] formal* **:** to remove (something) completely ▪ The criminal charges were *expunged* [=*deleted, erased*] from his record. ▪ They hoped to *expunge* [=*erase*] the memory of that tragic event.

ex·pur·gate /ˈɛkspɚˌgeɪt/ *verb* **-gates; -gat·ed; -gat·ing** *[+ obj] formal* **:** to change (a written work) by removing parts that might offend people ▪ They felt it was necessary to *expurgate* his letters before publishing them.

– **expurgated** *adj* ▪ an *expurgated* edition of his letters

– **ex·pur·ga·tion** /ˌɛkspɚˈgeɪʃən/ *noun [count, noncount]*

ex·quis·ite /ɛkˈskwɪzət, ˈɛkskwɪzət/ *adj [more ~; most ~]*

1 : finely done or made ▪ *exquisite* workmanship ▪ a move executed with *exquisite* precision **:** very beautiful or delicate ▪ *exquisite* flowers ▪ Her singing voice is truly *exquisite*.

2 : very sensitive or fine ▪ They have *exquisite* [=excellent] taste in furniture. ▪ The scenes are described in *exquisite* detail. [=with a lot of very fine details]

3 : extreme or intense ▪ *exquisite* pain/agony ▪ He chose his words with *exquisite* care.

– **ex·quis·ite·ly** *adv* ▪ an *exquisitely* prepared meal – **ex·quis·ite·ness** *noun [noncount]*

ex·tant /ˈɛkstənt, *Brit* ɛkˈstænt/ *adj, formal* **:** in existence **:** still existing ▪ *extant* bird species **:** not destroyed or lost ▪ There are few *extant* records from that period. ▪ one of the oldest buildings still *extant*

ex·tem·po·ra·ne·ous /ɛkˌstɛmpəˈreɪnijəs/ *adj [more ~; most ~]* **:** made up or done without special preparation — usually used to describe public speaking ▪ He made an *extemporaneous* speech. ▪ *extemporaneous* remarks

– **ex·tem·po·ra·ne·ous·ly** *adv* ▪ speaking *extemporaneously*

ex·tend /ɪkˈstɛnd/ *verb* **-tends; -tend·ed; -tend·ing**

1 a *[+ obj]* **:** to cause (something, such as your arm or leg) to straighten out or to stretch out ▪ *Extend* your arms (out) in front of you. ▪ He *extended* a hand in greeting. ▪ sitting with both legs fully *extended* ▪ The table measures eight feet long when it is fully *extended*. **b** *[no obj]* **:** to become longer or to be able to become longer ▪ The table *extends* to eight feet in length. ▪ The table *extends* easily.

2 *[no obj]* **:** to continue in a specified direction or over a specified distance, space, or time ▪ Their jurisdiction *extended* over the whole area. [=included the whole area] ▪ The woods *extend* for miles to the west. ▪ Their knowledge of the family's history *extends* back to colonial times. ▪ Their influence *extends* well beyond their immediate circle of friends. ▪ The organization soon *extended* [=*reached*] across the country. ▪ His popularity *extends* from coast to coast.

3 *[no obj]* **:** to involve or include a specified person or thing — *+ to* ▪ His interests *extend to* art and literature. ▪ The offer doesn't *extend to* nonmembers.

4 *[+ obj]* **:** to make (something) longer or greater ▪ She *extended* her visit by a couple of weeks. ▪ measures that might *extend* [=*prolong*] the patient's life ▪ They scored twice in the third inning to *extend* [=*increase*] their lead to 6–0.

5 *[+ obj]* **a :** to offer (something, such as an apology) to someone ▪ *extend* an invitation — usually *+ to* ▪ I'd like to *extend* my apologies [=I'd like to apologize] *to* everyone here. ▪ They *extended* a warm welcome *to* us. [=they welcomed us warmly] **b :** to make (something) available — usually *+ to* ▪ The store *extends* credit only *to* its regular customers. ▪ It was many years before these rights were *extended to* women. ▪ They plan to *extend* the service *to* people in rural areas.

extend yourself **:** to work hard **:** to do things that require effort ▪ She's always willing to *extend herself* for others. ▪ an actor who *extends himself* by choosing difficult roles

– **ex·tend·able** *or* **ex·tend·ible** /ɪkˈstɛndəbəl/ *adj* ▪ a two-year contract, *extendable* to five years ▪ a chair with *extendable* legs – **ex·tend·er** /ɪkˈstɛndɚ/ *noun, pl* **-ers** *[count]*

ex·tend·ed /ɪkˈstɛndəd/ *adj, always used before a noun*

1 : longer than usual or typical **:** unusually long ▪ We went on an *extended* [=*lengthy*] vacation. ▪ a period of *extended* hospitalization = an *extended* period of hospitalization

2 : going beyond the usual, original, or basic version of something ▪ Do you want the *extended* service warranty? [=a warranty that covers more things or lasts for a longer period of time] ▪ The word has developed several *extended* [=*additional*] meanings/senses.

extended family *noun, pl* ~ **-lies** *[count]* **:** a family that includes not only parents and children but also other relatives (such as grandparents, aunts, or uncles) — compare NUCLEAR FAMILY

ex·ten·sion /ɪkˈstɛnʃən/ *noun, pl* **-sions**

1 : the act of extending something: such as **a :** the act of making something longer or greater *[noncount]* *extension* of the patient's life *[count]* He's asking for a contract *extension*. **b :** the act of straightening or stretching something (such as an arm or a leg) *[count]* He did some leg *extensions*. [=exercises in which you extend your legs] *[noncount]* Make sure that the muscles get the proper amount of *extension*.

2 *[count]* **:** extra time allowed for doing something ▪ I missed the deadline but was granted an *extension*.

3 *[count]* **:** something (such as an interest or activity) that develops from something else — *+ of* ▪ Writing screenplays was a natural/logical *extension of* his career as a novelist and his longtime interest in film. ✧ The phrase ***by extension*** is used to say that what follows comes from or is connected with something that has already been mentioned. ▪ The new measures benefit taxpayers and, *by extension*, the economy. ▪ He disliked authority and, *by extension*, all government officials.

4 *[count]* **a :** a part that is added on to something to make it larger or longer ▪ They built an *extension* on their house. ▪ a road *extension* **b :** EXTENSION CORD

5 *[count]* **:** an extra telephone that is connected to the main line ▪ We've added another *extension* in our daughter's bedroom.; *also* **:** a telephone number that connects to a particular extension ▪ I dialed her *extension*, but she wasn't at her desk. ▪ *Extension* 365, please.

extension cord *noun, pl* ~ **cords** *[count] US* **:** an electric cord that is used to make another electric cord reach farther — called also *extension, (Brit) extension lead*

ex·ten·sive /ɪkˈstɛnsɪv/ *adj [more ~; most ~]* **:** large in size or amount **:** very full or complete ▪ an *extensive* [=*comprehensive*] reading list ▪ He's had *extensive* [=*considerable*] training in this area. ▪ The storm caused *extensive* damage. ▪ *extensive* repairs ▪ an *extensive* series of tests

– **ex·ten·sive·ly** *adv* ▪ She has written *extensively* on this subject. – **ex·ten·sive·ness** *noun [noncount]*

ex·tent /ɪkˈstɛnt/ *noun [noncount]*

1 : the range, distance, or space that is covered or affected by something or included in something ▪ She tried to determine the *extent* of the damage. ▪ the full *extent* of human knowledge ▪ They underestimated the *extent* [=*size*] of the problem. ▪ He questions the *extent* to which these remedies are needed.

2 : the point or limit to which something extends or reaches ▪ We reached the southernmost *extent* [=*end*] of the peninsula. ▪ He swore to prosecute them ***to the fullest extent of the law***. [=as fully as the law allows] ▪ ***To what extent*** [=how far, how much] can they be trusted?

3 — used to indicate the degree to which something exists, happens, or is true ✧ If you say that something is true ***to an extent, to some extent***, or ***to a certain extent***, you mean that it is partly but not completely true. ▪ *To an extent*, they're both right. ▪ Some critics claim that the government is at fault, and, *to a certain extent*, that's true. Something that is true ***to a large extent*** or ***to a great extent*** is mostly true. ▪ These traits are *to a large extent* inherited. [=these traits are mostly inherited] The phrases ***to the extent that, to that extent***, and ***to a greater/lesser extent*** are often used to describe the effect or importance of something in relation to something else. ▪ *To the extent that* he encouraged their bad behavior, he's to blame for it. [=he's partly to blame for their bad behavior because he encouraged it] ▪ He encouraged their bad behavior, and *to that extent* he's to blame for it. ▪ He studied only *to the extent that* was required to pass the exam. [=he studied just enough to pass the exam] ▪ This new tax affects the middle class and, *to a lesser extent*, the rich. ▪ This new tax affects everyone *to a greater or lesser extent*. [=it affects some people more than it does other people] *To the extent that* or ***to such an extent that*** can also be used to say that something is true to a very extreme degree. ▪ He was fearful *to the extent that* he refused to leave his house. [=he was so fearful that he refused to leave his house] ▪ She has changed *to such an extent that* you wouldn't recognize her.

ex·ten·u·at·ing /ɪkˈstɛnjəˌweɪtɪŋ/ *adj* — used to describe something (such as an unusual situation) that makes something (such as a crime or a mistake) seem less serious or deserving of blame; usually used in the phrase ***extenuating circumstances*** ▪ The company claims that its failure to deliver the materials on time is due to bad weather and other *extenuating circumstances*.

[1]ex·te·ri·or /ɛkˈstirijɚ/ *adj*
1 a : located on the outside of something ▪ an *exterior* [=*outer*] surface ▪ *exterior* walls **b :** suited for use on outside surfaces ▪ *exterior* paint ▪ *exterior* lights
2 : shown on the outside or surface ▪ They're more concerned with *exterior* [=*external*] beauty than interior/inner strength. — opposite [1]INTERIOR

[2]exterior *noun, pl* **-ors** [*count*]
1 : an outer part or surface ▪ The building has a rather plain *exterior*. — opposite [2]INTERIOR
2 : the way someone looks or seems to other people : a person's outward appearance — usually singular ▪ Although she was nervous, she maintained a calm *exterior*. [=she looked calm] ▪ Underneath that tough *exterior*, he's really very sentimental.

ex·ter·mi·nate /ɪkˈstɚməˌneɪt/ *verb* **-nates; -nat·ed; -nat·ing** [+ *obj*] **:** to destroy or kill (a group of animals, people, etc.) completely ▪ We made arrangements to have the termites *exterminated*. ▪ The invaders nearly *exterminated* the native people.
– ex·ter·mi·na·tion /ɪkˌstɚməˈneɪʃən/ *noun, pl* **-tions** [*count, noncount*] ▪ *extermination* of household pests **– ex·ter·mi·na·tor** /ɪkˈstɚməˌneɪtɚ/ *noun, pl* **-tors** [*count*] ▪ We hired an *exterminator* to get rid of the termites.

ex·ter·nal /ɪkˈstɚnl̩/ *adj*
1 : located, seen, or used on the outside or surface of something ▪ the *external* features of the building ▪ the *external* signs of the disease ▪ This medication is intended only for *external* use. [=for use on the skin] — opposite INTERNAL
2 : coming from outside ▪ *external* pressures ▪ *external* stimuli — opposite INTERNAL
3 : existing or occurring outside your mind ▪ *external* reality — opposite INTERNAL
4 : concerning relationships with foreign countries ▪ *external* [=*foreign, international*] affairs — opposite INTERNAL
– ex·ter·nal·ly *adv*

ex·ter·nals /ɪkˈstɚnl̩z/ *noun* [*plural*] *formal* **:** the way something looks on the surface or from the outside : external appearances ▪ We should not judge them solely on the basis of *externals*.

ex·tinct /ɪkˈstɪŋkt/ *adj*
1 : no longer existing ▪ an *extinct* (species of) animal ▪ Many of these old traditions have since become *extinct*.
2 : no longer active ▪ an *extinct* volcano

ex·tinc·tion /ɪkˈstɪŋkʃən/ *noun, pl* **-tions :** the state or situation that results when something (such as a plant or animal species) has died out completely [*noncount*] the *extinction* of all life in the region ▪ Several bird species are threatened with *extinction*. = Several bird species are ***on the brink of extinction***. ▪ the *extinction* of many old traditions [*count*] Mass *extinctions* of prehistoric animals are known to have occurred.

ex·tin·guish /ɪkˈstɪŋgwɪʃ/ *verb* **-guish·es; -guished; -guish·ing** [+ *obj*]
1 : to cause (something) to stop burning ▪ The fire department was called in to *extinguish* the blaze. ▪ He *extinguished* his cigarette in the ashtray.
2 : to cause the end or death of (something) ▪ They ruthlessly *extinguished* all resistance. ▪ News of the conflict *extinguished* our hopes for a peaceful resolution.
– ex·tin·guish·er *noun, pl* **-ers** [*count*] — see also FIRE EXTINGUISHER

ex·tir·pate /ˈɛkstɚˌpeɪt/ *verb* **-pates; -pat·ed; -pat·ing** [+ *obj*] *formal* **:** to destroy or remove (something) completely ▪ Such ingrained behavior can never be completely *extirpated*. [=*eradicated*]
– ex·tir·pa·tion /ˌɛkstɚˈpeɪʃən/ *noun* [*noncount*]

ex·tol *also US* **ex·toll** /ɪkˈstoʊl/ *verb* **-tols** *also US* **-tolls; -tolled; -tol·ling** [+ *obj*] **:** to praise (someone or something) highly ▪ They *extolled* [=*lauded*] the virtues of education. ▪ The health benefits of exercise are widely *extolled*.

ex·tort /ɪkˈstoɚt/ *verb* **-torts; -tort·ed; -tort·ing** [+ *obj*] **:** to get (something, such as money) from a person by the use of force or threats ▪ The criminals *extorted* large sums of money from their victims. ▪ He was arrested for *extorting* bribes. ▪ He claimed that the confession had been *extorted* (from him) by the police.
– ex·tort·er *noun, pl* **-ers** [*count*]

ex·tor·tion /ɪkˈstoɚʃən/ *noun* [*noncount*] **:** the crime of getting money from someone by the use of force or threats ▪ He was arrested and charged with *extortion*. ▪ committing/practicing *extortion*
– ex·tor·tion·ist /ɪkˈstoɚʃənɪst/ *noun, pl* **-ists** [*count*]

[1]ex·tra /ˈɛkstrə/ *adj*
1 *always used before a noun* **:** more than is usual or necessary : ADDITIONAL ▪ a sandwich with *extra* mayonnaise ▪ She got a part-time job to earn some *extra* money. ▪ He gave us an *extra* week to finish the job. ▪ There's no *extra* charge for breakfast. ▪ Room service is/costs an *extra* $5. = You have to pay an *extra* $5 for room service.
2 : costing more : requiring additional payment ▪ Breakfast is included in the price, but room service is *extra*. [=you have to pay more for room service]
go the extra mile see MILE

[2]extra *adv*
1 : beyond the usual size or amount ▪ *extra* long ▪ *extra* large eggs ▪ You have to pay $5 *extra* for room service.
2 *somewhat informal* **:** very or unusually ▪ The food was *extra* good. ▪ The roads are slippery, so be *extra* careful. ▪ This is an *extra* special occasion. ▪ She tried *extra* hard.

[3]extra *noun, pl* **-tras** [*count*]
1 : something that is added especially to make a product, service, etc., more appealing ▪ The package deal includes some nice *extras*. ▪ The bill doesn't include any hidden *extras*. [=extra costs]
2 : a person hired to act in a group scene in a movie ▪ Thousands of *extras* were hired for the battle scene.

extra- *prefix* **:** outside or beyond ▪ an *extra*marital affair — opposite INTRA-

extra–base hit *noun, pl* **~ hits** [*count*] *baseball* **:** a double, triple, or home run

[1]ex·tract /ɪkˈstrækt/ *verb* **-tracts; -tract·ed; -tract·ing** [+ *obj*]
1 : to remove (something) by pulling it out or cutting it out ▪ He *extracted* a credit card from his wallet. ▪ I had to have a tooth *extracted*. ▪ The tumor was surgically *extracted*.
2 a : to get (information, a response, etc.) from someone who does not want to give it ▪ We finally *extracted* a confession from him. ▪ *extract* a promise **b :** to get (something, such as information) *from* something ▪ Investigators were able to *extract* useful information *from* the company's financial records. ▪ They are hoping to *extract* new insights *from* the test results.
3 : to get (a substance) *from* something by the use of a machine or chemicals ▪ The machines *extract* the juice *from* the apples. ▪ oil *extracted from* sunflower seeds ▪ venom *extracted from* poisonous snakes
4 : to choose and take out (parts of a written work) for a separate use ▪ He *extracted* [=*excerpted*] a few lines from a favorite poem for use in his speech.
extract yourself **:** to remove yourself from a difficult situation ▪ He has been unable to *extract himself* from his legal difficulties.
– ex·tract·able /ɪkˈstræktəbəl/ *adj* **– ex·trac·tor** /ɪkˈstræktɚ/ *noun, pl* **-tors** [*count*] ▪ a tooth *extractor* ▪ a juice *extractor*

[2]ex·tract /ˈɛkˌstrækt/ *noun, pl* **-tracts**
1 : a substance that you get from something by using a machine or chemicals [*noncount*] The recipe calls for a tablespoon of vanilla *extract*. [*count*] herbal *extracts*
2 [*count*] **:** a short piece of writing that is taken from a longer

work (such as a book) ▪ The anthology includes *extracts* [=*excerpts*] from the works of several well-known authors.

ex·trac·tion /ɪkˈstrækʃən/ *noun, pl* **-tions**
1 : the act or process of getting something by pulling it out, forcing it out, etc. **:** the act of extracting something [*count*] tooth *extractions* and other dental procedures [*noncount*] the *extraction* of teeth by dentists ▪ the *extraction* of juices from plant matter
2 [*noncount*] — used after *of* to describe the origin of a person or family ▪ a family *of* Italian *extraction* [=a family whose ancestors came to another country from Italy]

ex·tra·cur·ric·u·lar /ˌɛkstrəkəˈrɪkjələ/ *adj* — used to describe extra activities (such as sports) that can be done by the students in a school but that are not part of the regular schedule of classes ▪ *extracurricular* activities
– **extracurricular** *noun, pl* **-lars** [*count*] ▪ The school offers a variety of *extracurriculars.* [=extracurricular activities]

ex·tra·dite /ˈɛkstrəˌdaɪt/ *verb* **-dites; -dit·ed; -dit·ing** [+ *obj*] *law* **:** to send (a person who has been accused of a crime) to another state or country for trial ▪ He will be *extradited* from the U.S. to Canada to face criminal charges there. ▪ The prisoner was *extradited* across state lines.
– **ex·tra·di·tion** /ˌɛkstrəˈdɪʃən/ *noun, pl* **-tions** [*noncount*] The accused terrorists are awaiting *extradition.* [*count*] The government has agreed to the *extraditions* of the accused terrorists.

ex·tra·mar·i·tal /ˌɛkstrəˈmerətl/ *adj* **:** happening outside of a marriage — used to describe sexual relations between a married person and someone who is not that person's husband or wife ▪ an *extramarital* [=*adulterous*] affair

ex·tra·ne·ous /ɛkˈstreɪnijəs/ *adj* **:** not forming a necessary part of something ▪ She sped up the process by eliminating all *extraneous* steps. **:** not important ▪ *extraneous* [=*irrelevant*] information/details

ex·traor·di·nary /ɪkˈstroədəˌneri, *Brit* ɪkˈstrɔːdənri/ *adj* [*more ~; most ~*]
1 : very unusual **:** very different from what is normal or ordinary ▪ The researchers made an *extraordinary* discovery. ▪ It's an *extraordinary* situation. ▪ *extraordinary* rudeness/insensitivity ▪ The race is an *extraordinary* event. ▪ They convened an *extraordinary* [=*special*] meeting of the Security Council.
2 : extremely good or impressive ▪ She was a woman of *extraordinary* [=*great, remarkable*] intelligence. ▪ The child has *extraordinary* [=*exceptional*] abilities. ▪ The food was *extraordinary.*
– **ex·traor·di·nar·i·ly** /ɪkˌstroədəˈnerəli, *Brit* ɪkˈstrɔːdənrəli/ *adv* ▪ an *extraordinarily* intelligent person ▪ *extraordinarily* good/bad weather

extra point *noun, pl* **~ points** [*count*] *American football* **:** a point scored after a touchdown by kicking the ball between the goalposts or by carrying or throwing it a short distance into the end zone

ex·trap·o·late /ɪkˈstræpəˌleɪt/ *verb* **-lates; -lat·ed; -lat·ing** *formal* **:** to form an opinion or to make an estimate about something from known facts [+ *obj*] We can *extrapolate* the number of new students entering next year by looking at how many entered in previous years. — often + *from* ▪ They *extrapolated* these results *from* their research. [*no obj*] With such a small study it is impossible to *extrapolate* accurately. — often + *from* ▪ She *extrapolated from* last year's data to arrive at her estimate.
– **ex·trap·o·la·tion** /ɪkˌstræpəˈleɪʃən/ *noun, pl* **-tions** [*count, noncount*]

ex·tra·sen·so·ry perception /ˌɛkstrəˈsɛnsəri-/ *noun* [*singular*] **:** the ability to know things (such as what another person is thinking or what will happen in the future) that cannot be known by normal use of the senses — called also *ESP*

ex·tra·ter·res·tri·al /ˌɛkstrətəˈrɛstrijəl/ *adj* **:** coming from or existing outside the planet Earth ▪ *extraterrestrial* life ▪ *extraterrestrial* beings/intelligence
– **extraterrestrial** *noun, pl* **-als** [*count*] ▪ a movie about an *extraterrestrial* [=an extraterrestrial being]

ex·trav·a·gance /ɪkˈstrævɪgəns/ *noun, pl* **-ganc·es**
1 [*noncount*] **:** the act or practice of spending a lot of money **:** wasteful or careless spending ▪ The reorganization of the department was aimed at reducing *extravagance.* ▪ his *extravagance* with money
2 [*count*] **:** a special purchase that costs more than you usually spend ▪ That coat is an *extravagance* that you can't afford. ▪ Going to the play will be our one *extravagance* for this vacation.
3 [*noncount*] **:** the quality of something that is very expensive or fancy **:** an extravagant quality ▪ I was shocked by the *extravagance* of their lifestyle. ▪ The church is known for the *extravagance* of its architecture.

ex·trav·a·gant /ɪkˈstrævɪgənt/ *adj* [*more ~; most ~*]
1 a : more than is usual, necessary, or proper ▪ He went to *extravagant* [=*elaborate, extreme*] lengths to impress his boss. ▪ The brunch featured an *extravagant* [=*lavish*] assortment of entrees. ▪ *extravagant* praise ▪ The company has been making *extravagant* claims/promises about the drug's effectiveness. **b :** very fancy ▪ an *extravagant* display ▪ The film is notable for its *extravagant* settings and special effects.
2 a : very expensive and not necessary ▪ an *extravagant* purchase ▪ We're going on a less *extravagant* vacation this year. **b :** spending a lot of money ▪ On my income, I can't afford to be *extravagant.* [=I can't afford to buy expensive things that I don't need] ▪ Her *extravagant* spending has to stop.
– **ex·trav·a·gant·ly** *adv* ▪ Her work was praised *extravagantly.* ▪ an *extravagantly* expensive wedding

ex·trav·a·gan·za /ɪkˌstrævəˈgænzə/ *noun, pl* **-zas** [*count*] **:** a very large and exciting show or event ▪ a musical *extravaganza*

extravert *variant spelling of* EXTROVERT

¹ex·treme /ɪkˈstriːm/ *adj*
1 : very great in degree ▪ The plant is sensitive to *extreme* heat and cold. ▪ They are living in *extreme* poverty. ▪ If you have to go out in the storm, use *extreme* caution. [=be very careful] ▪ *Extreme* accuracy is required. ▪ *extreme* old age
2 [*more ~; most ~*] **:** very serious or severe ▪ She went on an *extreme* diet. ▪ Many thought that the punishment was too *extreme* for the crime. ▪ *extreme* weather conditions ▪ This situation calls for *extreme* [=*drastic*] measures. ▪ The plan was rejected as too *extreme.* ▪ This is an *extreme* example of what can happen when a company grows too quickly.
3 [*more ~; most ~*] **:** very far from agreeing with the opinions of most people **:** not moderate ▪ He has *extreme* opinions when it comes to politics. ▪ Members of the *extreme* right/left opposed the legislation.
4 *always used before a noun* **:** in the farthest possible position ▪ In the photo, she is at/on the *extreme* right/left. [=she is in the position that is farthest to the right/left] ▪ The city is in the *extreme* northern part of the state.
5 *sports* **a :** unusual and dangerous ▪ *extreme* sports ▪ He is a fan of *extreme* skiing/snowboarding. **b** *always used before a noun, US* **:** involved in an unusually dangerous sport **:** competing in an extreme sport ▪ an *extreme* athlete ▪ He is an *extreme* snowboarder/skier.
go to extreme lengths see LENGTH
– **ex·treme·ly** *adv* ▪ It is *extremely* [=*very*] hot/cold in here. ▪ She is *extremely* generous. ▪ The story has an *extremely* complicated plot. ▪ It is *extremely* [=*highly, very*] unlikely that we will know anyone there.

²extreme *noun, pl* **ex·tremes** [*count*]
1 : either one of two opposite conditions, feelings, positions, etc., that are thought of as being far from what is normal or reasonable ▪ After spending lavishly for years, the company has now gone to the opposite/other *extreme* and has cut expenses drastically. ▪ His mood changed/swung ***from one extreme to the other.*** — often plural ▪ experiencing *extremes* of emotion ▪ The temperature in the desert ranges between *extremes* of heat and cold. ▪ Their political views represent the *extremes* within the party. ▪ There are people at both *extremes* within the party.
2 : an amount or degree that is far beyond what is normal or reasonable ▪ The movie changes the story to such an *extreme* [=changes it so much] that it's hardly recognizable. ▪ They are being pushed/driven to ridiculous *extremes.* [=being forced to do much more than seems reasonable] ✧ If you ***carry/take (something) to extremes*** or ***go to extremes,*** you do much more than most people would consider reasonable or normal. ▪ The problems in our school system can be solved without *going to* (such) *extremes.* ▪ Problems can occur when people *carry/take dieting to extremes.*
in the extreme *formal* **:** to the greatest possible degree — used to make a statement more forceful ▪ I'm finding it difficult *in the extreme* [=very/extremely difficult] to deal with this situation.

ex·trem·ism /ɪkˈstriːˌmɪzəm/ *noun* [*noncount*] **:** belief in and support for ideas that are very far from what most people consider correct or reasonable ▪ political *extremism*

ex·trem·ist /ɪkˈstriːmɪst/ *noun, pl* **-ists** [*count*] : someone who has extreme ideas about politics, religion, etc. ▪ *Extremists* in the party view him as too conservative. ▪ A group of *extremists* took several hostages.
– **extremist** *adj* [*more ~; most ~*] ▪ *extremist* tendencies/beliefs

ex·trem·i·ty /ɪkˈstrɛməti/ *noun, pl* **-ties**
1 [*count*] : a hand or foot — usually plural ▪ You will feel the effects of the cold in your *extremities*. [=hands and feet]
2 [*count*] : the farthest limit, point, or part of something ▪ We lived on the island's westernmost *extremity*. [=the part of the island that is farthest to the west]
3 *formal* : a very great or extreme degree or amount of something (such as emotion or pain) [*noncount*] The *extremity* of her grief is impossible to imagine. [*count*] They endured *extremities* of suffering. [=they endured extreme suffering]

ex·tri·cate /ˈɛkstrəˌkeɪt/ *verb* **-cates; -cat·ed; -cat·ing** [+ *obj*] : to free or remove (someone or something) *from* something (such as a trap or a difficult situation) ▪ Several survivors were *extricated from* the wreckage. ▪ They *extricated* the tractor *from* the mud. ▪ She hasn't been able to *extricate* herself *from* her legal problems.

ex·trin·sic /ɛkˈstrɪnzɪk/ *adj, formal* : not part of something : coming from the outside of something ▪ You have to consider any *extrinsic* factors in the success of the business. ▪ *extrinsic* circumstances — opposite INTRINSIC

ex·tro·vert *also* **ex·tra·vert** /ˈɛkstrəˌvɚt/ *noun, pl* **-verts** [*count*] : a friendly person who likes being with and talking to other people : an outgoing person — opposite INTROVERT
– **ex·tro·vert·ed** *also* **ex·tra·vert·ed** /ˈɛkstrəˌvɚtəd/ *adj* [*more ~; most ~*] ▪ He is the most *extroverted* [=*outgoing*] member of the family.

ex·trude /ɪkˈstruːd/ *verb* **ex·trudes; ex·trud·ed; ex·trud·ing** [+ *obj*] *technical*
1 : to force, press, or push (something) out ▪ The machine *extrudes* enough molten glass to fill the mold.
2 : to shape (something) by forcing it through a hole ▪ The plastic is *extruded* as a strong, continuous sheet. ▪ a toy made from *extruded* plastic

ex·u·ber·ant /ɪgˈzuːbərənt, *Brit* ɪgˈzjuːbərənt/ *adj* [*more ~; most ~*]
1 : very lively, happy, or energetic : filled with energy and enthusiasm ▪ His *exuberant* personality makes him fun to be around. ▪ *exuberant* music
2 : existing in large amounts : very plentiful ▪ *exuberant* blossoms
– **ex·u·ber·ance** /ɪgˈzuːbərəns, *Brit* ɪgˈzjuːbərəns/ *noun* [*noncount*] ▪ youthful *exuberance* – **ex·u·ber·ant·ly** *adv* ▪ an *exuberantly* joyful performance

ex·ude /ɪgˈzuːd/ *verb* **exudes; ex·ud·ed; ex·ud·ing**
1 a [+ *obj*] : to produce a liquid or smell that flows out slowly ▪ Pine trees *exude* a sticky substance. ▪ The flowers *exuded* a sweet fragrance. **b** [*no obj*] : to flow out slowly — usually + *from* ▪ Moisture *exuded from* the walls of the cave. ▪ A sticky substance *exuded* [=*oozed*] *from* the pine tree.
2 [+ *obj*] : to show (a quality, emotion, etc.) very clearly or strongly ▪ She *exudes* authority/charm. [=she has a great deal of authority/charm] ▪ They *exuded* elegance/confidence.

ex·ult /ɪgˈzʌlt/ *verb* **-ults; -ulted; -ulting**
1 [*no obj*] : to feel or show great happiness — often + *at, in,* or *over* ▪ The team *exulted in* their victory. ▪ She *exulted over* her students' test scores.
2 [+ *obj*] : to say (something) in a very excited and happy way ▪ "That was the best meal I've ever had!" he *exulted*.

Do not confuse *exult* with *exalt*.

ex·ult·ant /ɪgˈzʌltənt/ *adj* [*more ~; most ~*] : very happy and excited ▪ The crowd let out an *exultant* cheer. ▪ Researchers are *exultant* over/about the new discovery.
– **ex·ult·ant·ly** *adv*

ex·ul·ta·tion /ˌɛkˌsʌlˈteɪʃən, ˌɛgˌzʌlˈteɪʃən/ *noun* [*noncount*] : a feeling of great happiness and excitement : an exultant feeling ▪ The crowd cheered in *exultation*.

-ey see -Y

[1]eye /ˈaɪ/ *noun, pl* **eyes**
1 [*count*] : the part of the body that you see with ▪ Her *eyes* slowly became accustomed to the dark. ▪ He wears a patch over one *eye*. ▪ I have something in my *eye*. ▪ He has (a pair of) bright blue *eyes*. ▪ bright/sad/sleepy *eyes* ▪ She has good/strong/bad/weak *eyes*. [=*eyesight*] ▪ Her ***eyes lit up*** [=she

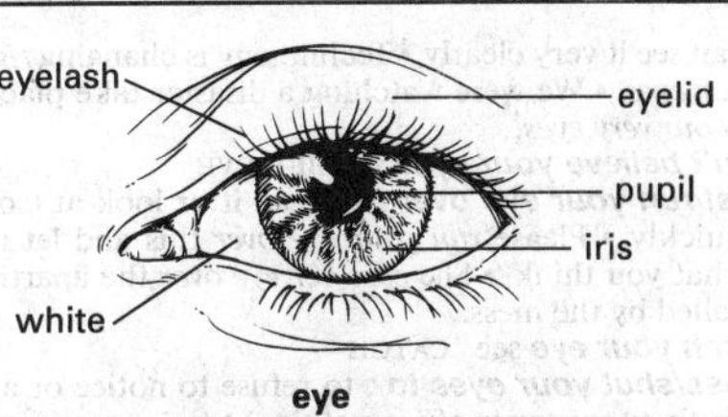

eye

looked excited and happy] when he showed her the ring. ▪ His ***eyes were popping out of his head*** with astonishment [=he looked very astonished] when he saw how big it was! ▪ He punched him ***right between the eyes***. [=punched him hard in the face] ▪ She looked me (right) ***in the eye*** [=she looked directly at me] and told me I was fired. ▪ The garden is ***a feast for the eyes***. [=the garden is very beautiful] ▪ The display was very pleasing ***to the eye***. [=pleasing to look at] ▪ I measured the distance ***by eye***. = I measured the distance ***with my eye***. [=by looking at it to get a rough idea of its size] ▪ Their daughter came home from school ***with tears in her eyes***. [=she was crying] ▪ Seeing her again ***brought tears to my eyes***. = Seeing her again ***brought a tear to my eye***. [=made me shed tears] ▪ He ***had/kept half an eye on*** [=he occasionally looked at] the TV while he read the paper.
2 [*singular*] **a** : an ability to understand and appreciate something seen ▪ Only a trained *eye* can tell the difference between the original painting and a good copy. ▪ For decorating, they rely on her discerning/discriminating/expert *eye*. ▪ He has an artist's *eye* for color. ✧ If you ***have an eye for*** something or ***a good/keen/sharp eye for*** something, you have a special ability to recognize a particular thing or quality. ▪ He *has a keen eye for* detail. ▪ He *has a good eye* for quality. **b** — used to describe the way something looks to you ▪ It looks a little awkward to my *eye*. [=it looks awkward to me] **c** : a way of looking at or judging something ▪ He reviewed the proposal with a jaundiced/critical *eye*. ▪ The biographer ***cast a cold/critical/skeptical eye*** on the artist's life.
3 [*count*] — used to describe where someone is looking ▪ Her *eye* was attracted to the bright colors in the painting. ▪ She ***dropped her eyes*** [=she looked down] when he looked at her. = Her ***eyes fell*** when he looked at her. ▪ He ***averted his eyes*** [=he looked away] when she approached him. ▪ I saw something moving ***out of the corner of my eye***. [=to the side of where I was looking] ▪ Her ***eyes fell on*** [=she noticed] a piece of evidence no one had noticed before. ▪ ***All eyes were on her*** [=everyone was looking at her] as she entered the room. ▪ She ***fixed her eyes on*** me [=she kept looking or staring at me] for a long time before answering.
4 [*count*] : a way of looking at or thinking about something ▪ We need to look at this problem with a fresh *eye*. [=to look at the problem in a new way] ▪ ***Beauty is in the eye of the beholder***. [=different people have different ideas about what is beautiful] — often plural ▪ He was guilty in the *eyes* of the police. [=the police considered him guilty] ▪ He was handsome in her *eyes*. [=she thought he was handsome] ▪ In the *eyes* [=*opinion*] of many, he is the best person for the job.
5 [*count*] : the hole through the top of a needle ▪ the *eye* of a needle
6 [*count*] : a loop that a hook fits into to fasten or attach something
7 [*count*] : an area on a potato from which a new plant can grow : a bud on a potato
8 [*count*] : the center of a storm (such as a hurricane) where there is little wind or rain and sometimes there is clear sky ▪ The *eye* of the storm should reach the coast by morning.

all eyes : watching something or someone closely : very attentive ▪ She was *all eyes* as I opened the box.

an eye for an eye *or* ***an eye for an eye and a tooth for a tooth*** — used to say that a person who has committed a crime should be given punishment that is the same as or as serious as the crime ▪ The ancient code of law called for punishment in the form of *an eye for an eye*.

as far as the eye could see : as far as could be seen ▪ The crowd stretched away *as far as the eye could see*.

a sight for sore eyes see [1]SIGHT

a twinkle in your eye see [1]TWINKLE

bawl your eyes out see BAWL

before your eyes *or* ***in front of your eyes*** ✧ If something happens (*right*) *before your eyes* or *in front of your (very) eyes*, it happens in a very open and visible way so that you

can see it very clearly. ▪ Technology is changing *right before our eyes.* ▪ We were watching a disaster take place *in front of our very eyes.*
can't believe your eyes see BELIEVE
cast/run your eye over : to read it or look at (something) quickly. ▪ Please *run your eye over* this and let me know what you think. ▪ She *cast her eye over* the apartment, appalled by the mess.
catch your eye see [1]CATCH
close/shut your eyes to : to refuse to notice or accept the truth or existence of (something) : to ignore (something) ▪ Our legislators have *closed their eyes to* the poverty that surrounds them.
cock an/your eye see [2]COCK
cry your eyes out see [1]CRY
easy on the eyes see [1]EASY
eyes in the back of your head ✧ When people are surprised that you have seen or noticed something that is behind you, they may say that you have *eyes in the back of your head.* ▪ How did you know we were here? You must have *eyes in the back of your head*!
feast your eyes on see [2]FEAST
for your eyes only : intended to be seen only by you ▪ This memo is *for your eyes only.*
give (someone) the eye *informal* : to look at (someone) in a way that shows sexual attraction ▪ Several men were *giving her the eye* across the bar.
have/keep an/your eye out for : to be looking for (someone or something) : to hope to see or find (someone or something) ▪ I'm *keeping my eye out for* a good cheap used car. ▪ He'll be here soon, so *keep your eye out for* him.
have an eye to/toward : to have (something) in your thoughts as a goal or purpose ▪ She *has an eye to* attending graduate school. [=she hopes to attend graduate school]
(have) stars in your eyes see [1]STAR
have your eye on **1** : to watch (someone or something) closely ▪ I'll *have my eye on* the kids while they're swimming. **2** : to be thinking about buying (something) ▪ I *have my eye on* a new car. ▪ She's *had her eye on* that house for a long time.
in a pig's eye *US slang* — used to express strong disagreement ▪ You want me to apologize to him? *In a pig's eye*! [=*Never!*]
in the blink of an eye see [2]BLINK
in the public eye : in a position that receives a lot of public notice and attention ▪ The job requires someone who is comfortable being *in the public eye.*
in the twinkle/twinkling of an eye : in a very short time : very quickly ▪ He was back *in the twinkle/twinkling of an eye.*
in your mind's eye ✧ If you see something *in your mind's eye*, you imagine or remember how it looks. ▪ I can still see the old playground *in my mind's eye.*
keep an/your eye on : to watch or take care of (someone or something) ▪ Will you *keep an eye on* my suitcase (for me) while I get something to eat?
keep your eye on the ball see [1]BALL
keep your eyes glued to *informal* : to watch (something) very closely for a long time ▪ They *kept their eyes glued to* the television, waiting for more news about the accident.
keep your eyes open *or* ***keep your eyes peeled*** *or Brit* ***keep your eyes skinned*** *informal* : to look or watch closely in order to see or find (something) ▪ We *kept our eyes peeled* for a sign that would tell us where to turn.
lay/set eyes on *or Brit* ***clap eyes on*** : to see or look at (someone or something) ▪ I hope never to *lay eyes on* him again! ▪ We liked the house from the moment we *set eyes on* it. [=the moment when we first saw it]
make eyes at *informal* : to look at (someone) in a way that shows sexual attraction ▪ Some guy was *making eyes at* her from across the room.
more than meets the eye ✧ If something is *more than meets the eye* or there is ***more to something than meets the eye***, there is more to it than there appears to be at first. ▪ There is *more to this proposal than meets the eye.*
my eye *informal* — used to express surprise or mild disagreement ▪ A diamond, *my eye*! That's glass!
not bat an eye see [4]BAT
only have eyes for : to only be attracted to (a particular person) : to only feel love for (someone) ▪ He *only has eyes for* you.
open someone's eyes : to cause someone to notice or be aware of something important ▪ The experience really *opened his eyes* and changed the way he felt about his life. — often + *to* ▪ It's time they *opened their eyes to* the truth. ▪ His film helped *open people's eyes to* the problem.
open your eyes : to begin to notice or be aware of something important ▪ You need to *open your eyes* and face the truth. — often + *to* ▪ We have to *open our eyes to* these problems and stop ignoring them.
pull the wool over someone's eyes see WOOL
roving eye see ROVING
run your eye down : to quickly read or look at (something, such as a list) ▪ She *ran her eye down* the list looking for her name.
see eye to eye : to have the same opinion : AGREE — usually used in negative statements ▪ They don't *see eye to eye* (with each other) on this issue.
take your eyes off : to stop looking at (someone or something) ▪ I *took my eyes off* the road for one second. ▪ She was so beautiful, he ***couldn't take his eyes off*** her.
the apple of someone's eye see APPLE
turn a blind eye see [1]BLIND
under the eye of : while being watched by (someone) ▪ Students work ***under the watchful/vigilant eye of*** their teacher.
up to your eyes : deeply involved in or affected by something ▪ We're *up to our eyes* in work. [=we are very busy] ▪ They're *up to their eyes* in debt.
with an eye to/toward : with (something) in your thoughts as a goal or purpose ▪ They hired him *with an eye toward* increased sales. ▪ They bought the house *with an eye toward* its restoration. ▪ He took the job ***with an eye to the future.*** [=he took the job because he felt it would help him in the future]
with your/both eyes open : fully aware of what could happen ▪ I went into the job *with my eyes (wide) open.* ▪ If you do this, you need to do it *with both eyes open.*
with your eyes shut/closed *informal* : with little or no effort : very easily ▪ She could run that company *with her eyes shut.*
your eyes are bigger than your stomach ✧ If *your eyes are bigger than your stomach*, you have taken more food than you can possibly eat. ▪ I can't finish my meal—I guess *my eyes were bigger than my stomach*!
— see also BLACK EYE, EVIL EYE, PRIVATE EYE, RIB EYE, SEEING EYE

[2]eye *verb* **eyes; eyed; eye·ing** *or* **ey·ing** [+ *obj*] : to watch or look at (someone or something) in a very close or careful way ▪ I saw someone *eyeing* me from across the street. ▪ The manager *eyed* us (up and down) as we walked into the restaurant.

[1]eye·ball /ˈaɪˌbɑːl/ *noun, pl* **-balls** [*count*] : the entire round part of the eye
up to your eyeballs *informal* : deeply involved in something ▪ We're *up to our eyeballs* in work. [=we are very busy]

[2]eyeball *verb* **-balls; -balled; -ball·ing** [+ *obj*] *informal* : to look at or stare at (someone or something) ▪ The police *eyeballed* [=*eyed*] the suspects. ▪ The children were *eyeballing* the desserts.

eye·brow /ˈaɪˌbraʊ/ *noun, pl* **-brows** [*count*] : the line of hair that grows over your eye — see picture at FACE ✧ To ***raise an/your eyebrow*** is to move your eyebrow up in a way that shows surprise or mild disapproval. To ***raise eyebrows*** is to cause other people to react in this way. These phrases are often used figuratively. ▪ No one *raised an eyebrow* [=no one expressed surprise] when he announced that he was planning to run for governor. ▪ His recent public statements have *raised* (a few) *eyebrows.* [=people have reacted with surprise and disapproval to his recent public statements]

eye candy *noun* [*noncount*] *informal* : someone or something that is attractive but is not serious or interesting ▪ A lot of the material on their Web site is just *eye candy.*

eye–catch·ing /ˈaɪˌkætʃɪŋ, ˈaɪˌkɛtʃɪŋ/ *adj* [*more* ~; *most* ~] : very noticeable because of being unusual or attractive ▪ The movie features *eye-catching* special effects. ▪ an *eye-catching* advertisement ▪ *eye-catching* colors/styles — see also *catch your eye* at [1]CATCH
– eye–catch·ing·ly *adv*

eye chart *noun, pl* ~ **charts** [*count*] : a chart that has numbers and letters of different sizes and that is used for testing someone's vision

eye contact *noun* [*noncount*] : a situation in which two people are looking directly into each other's eyes ▪ He maintained *eye contact* with me throughout the conversation. ▪

The speaker *made eye contact* with audience members. ▪ The jury *avoided eye contact* with the defendant as the verdict was read.

eyed /ˈaɪd/ *adj* **:** having an eye or eyes of a specified kind or number — used in combination ▪ a brown-*eyed* boy ▪ one-*eyed*

eye·drop·per /ˈaɪˌdrɑːpɚ/ *noun, pl* **-pers** [*count*] **:** a small tube that is used to measure out drops of liquid **:** DROPPER

eye·ful /ˈaɪˌfʊl/ *noun* [*singular*] *informal*

1 : something that is very surprising, attractive, etc., to look at ▪ The view of the mountains is an *eyeful.*

2 : an attractive person **:** a beautiful woman ▪ She's a real *eyeful!*

get/have an eyeful ✧ If you *get/have an eyeful* of something or if someone ***gives you an eyeful*** of something, you see it very clearly or you see a lot of it or too much of it. ▪ They wanted to see nature and *got an eyeful* during the camping trip. These phrases often refer to seeing something shocking, such as a person who is naked. ▪ I opened the door to the locker room and *got quite an eyeful.*

eye·glass /ˈaɪˌglæs, *Brit* ˈaɪˌglɑːs/ *noun, pl* **-glass·es**

1 [*count*] *old-fashioned* **:** a single lens that is worn over your eye to help you see **:** MONOCLE

2 ***eyeglasses*** [*plural*] *chiefly US* **:** a pair of lenses set into a frame and worn over your eyes to help you see **:** GLASSES ▪ She left her *eyeglasses* at work.

eye·lash /ˈaɪˌlæʃ/ *noun, pl* **-lash·es** [*count*] **:** any one of the hairs that grow along the top of the eyelid ▪ She has beautiful dark *eyelashes.* [=*lashes*] ▪ false *eyelashes* — see picture at EYE

not bat an eyelash see [4]BAT

eye·let /ˈaɪlət/ *noun, pl* **-lets** [*count*] **:** a small hole or opening in a material (such as cloth or leather) for a string or rope to pass through; *also* **:** a metal or plastic ring that strengthens such an opening

eye level *noun* [*singular*] **:** a level that is as high as a person's eyes ▪ He hung the picture at *eye level.* ▪ The hook is just above *eye level.*

eye·lid /ˈaɪˌlɪd/ *noun, pl* **-lids** [*count*] **:** either one of the two movable pieces of skin that cover your eye when it is closed ▪ the upper/lower *eyelid* of the left eye — see picture at EYE

not bat an eyelid see [4]BAT

eye·lin·er /ˈaɪˌlaɪnɚ/ *noun, pl* **-ers** [*count, noncount*] **:** a type of makeup used to put a dark line around the eyes

eye–open·er /ˈaɪˌoʊpənɚ/ *noun, pl* **-ers** [*count*] *informal* **:** something that shows or teaches you something in a surprising way ▪ Traveling abroad can be a real *eye-opener* to many people. ▪ They say her biography is quite an *eye-opener.* ▪ The speech was an *eye-opener* for us. — see also *open your eyes* at [2]OPEN

– eye–open·ing /ˈaɪˌoʊpənɪŋ/ *adj* [*more* ~; *most* ~] ▪ Traveling abroad was an *eye-opening* experience. ▪ The movie has some *eye-opening* special effects.

eye·piece /ˈaɪˌpiːs/ *noun, pl* **-piec·es** [*count*] **:** the part of a telescope or microscope that you look through

eye shadow *noun, pl* ~ **-ows** [*count, noncount*] **:** a type of colored makeup that is put on the eyelids — see picture at GROOMING

eye·sight /ˈaɪˌsaɪt/ *noun* [*noncount*] **:** the ability to see **:** sight or vision ▪ He wears glasses because his *eyesight* is not good. ▪ failing *eyesight* ▪ keen *eyesight*

eye socket *noun, pl* ~ **-ets** [*count*] **:** either one of the hollow places in the skull that hold the eyeballs

eye·sore /ˈaɪˌsoɚ/ *noun, pl* **-sores** [*count*] **:** an ugly object or building ▪ The shack is a real *eyesore.*

eye·strain /ˈaɪˌstreɪn/ *noun* [*noncount*] **:** a tired and unpleasant feeling in your eyes ▪ After looking at the computer screen all day she had *eyestrain* and a stiff neck.

eye·tooth /ˈaɪˈtuːθ/ *noun, pl* **-teeth** /-ˈtiːθ/ [*count*] **:** a pointed tooth **:** CANINE ✧ If you say you would ***give your eyeteeth*** for something, it means that you want to do or have it very much. ▪ Many journalists would *give their eyeteeth* for an opportunity like this.

eye·wash /ˈaɪˌwɑːʃ/ *noun* [*noncount*]

1 : a liquid used for washing the eyes

2 *informal + old-fashioned* **:** foolish words **:** NONSENSE ▪ He says he'll quit his job, but we know that's just *eyewash.*

eyewear *noun* [*noncount*] **:** glasses, sunglasses, etc. ▪ protective *eyewear* ▪ a shop that specializlzed in fashionable *eyewear*

eye·wit·ness /ˈaɪˈwɪtnəs/ *noun, pl* **-ness·es** [*count*] **:** a person who sees something happen and is able to describe it ▪ The police are hoping to locate an *eyewitness* to the shooting. ▪ He was able to give an *eyewitness* account of the shooting.

eyrie *chiefly Brit spelling of* AERIE

e–zine /ˈiːˌziːn/ *noun, pl* **-zines** [*count*] **:** an electronic magazine **:** a magazine that is on the Internet

F

[1]f *or* **F** /ˈɛf/ *noun, pl* **f's** *or* **fs** *or* **F's** *or* **Fs** /ˈɛfs/

1 : the sixth letter of the English alphabet [*count*] The word "foot" begins with an *f.* [*noncount*] The word "foot" begins with *f.*

2 : a musical note or key referred to by the letter F **:** the fourth tone of a C-major scale [*count*] play/sing an *F* [*noncount*] the key of *F*

3 [*count*] **:** a grade that is given to a student who is doing very poor work ▪ I got an *F* on the test.

[2]f *abbr* **1** female **2** feminine **3** forte — used in music

F *abbr* Fahrenheit ▪ Water freezes at 32 degrees *F.*

fa *or chiefly Brit* **fah** /ˈfɑː/ *noun* [*noncount*] *music* **:** the fourth note of a musical scale ▪ do, re, mi, *fa,* sol, la, ti

FAA *abbr* Federal Aviation Administration ▪ a ruling by the *FAA* ▪ an *FAA* official ✧ The Federal Aviation Administration is a part of the U.S. federal government that is responsible for controlling the use of aircraft.

fab /ˈfæb/ *adj, informal + old-fashioned* **:** extremely good **:** FABULOUS ▪ We had a *fab* time.

fa·ble /ˈfeɪbəl/ *noun, pl* **fa·bles**

1 [*count*] **:** a short story that usually is about animals and that is intended to teach a lesson ▪ Aesop's *fables* ▪ a *fable* about busy ants

2 : a story or statement that is not true [*count*] The story that he won the battle single-handedly is a mere *fable.* [*noncount*] He combines fact and *fable* to make a more interesting story.

fa·bled /ˈfeɪbəld/ *adj*

1 : told about in old stories ▪ a *fabled* [=*legendary*] underwater city

2 [*more* ~; *most* ~] **:** widely known **:** FAMOUS ▪ She served us some of her *fabled* cherry pie.

fab·ric /ˈfæbrɪk/ *noun, pl* **-rics**

1 : woven or knitted material **:** CLOTH [*noncount*] The curtains are made of expensive *fabric.* ▪ a *fabric* store [*count*] scarves made of woven *fabrics*

2 [*singular*] **:** the basic structure of something ▪ the *fabric* of society ▪ the *fabric* of the community

fab·ri·cate /ˈfæbrɪˌkeɪt/ *verb* **-cates; -cat·ed; -cat·ing** [+ *obj*]

1 : to make or build (something) ▪ Only the largest parts were *fabricated* at the factory. ▪ Their plan is to *fabricate* the house out of synthetic materials.

2 : to create or make up (something, such as a story) in order to trick people ▪ a story *fabricated* to sell magazines ▪ She was accused of *fabricating* data. ▪ *fabricated* evidence

– fab·ri·ca·tion /ˌfæbrɪˈkeɪʃən/ *noun, pl* **-tions** [*noncount*] the *fabrication* of parts ▪ the *fabrication* of evidence [*count*] his *fabrications* [=*lies*] about his military service ▪ The story was a total/complete *fabrication.* **– fab·ri·ca·tor** /ˈfæbrɪˌkeɪtɚ/ *noun, pl* **-tors** [*count*]

fabric softener *noun, pl* ~ **-ers** [*count, noncount*] **:** a product that is used to make clothes softer when they are washed or dried in a machine — called also (*Brit*) *conditioner*

fab·u·lous /ˈfæbjələs/ *adj*
1 [*more ~; most ~*] **a :** very good • I had a *fabulous* time. • The weather has been *fabulous*. **b :** very large in amount or size • *fabulous* wealth/riches • He is making *fabulous* amounts of money.
2 *literary* **:** not real • *fabulous* beasts **:** told about in a story • a *fabulous* [=*mythical*] creature
– fab·u·lous·ly *adv* • *fabulously* rich • a *fabulously* successful executive **– fab·u·lous·ness** *noun* [*noncount*]

fa·cade *or* **fa·çade** /fəˈsɑːd/ *noun, pl* **-cades** *or* **-çades** [*count*]
1 : the front of a building • the *facade* of the bank • the windowless *façade* of the skyscraper • a brick *facade*
2 : a way of behaving or appearing that gives other people a false idea of your true feelings or situation • They were trying to preserve the *facade* of a happy marriage. • I could sense the hostility lurking behind her polite *facade*.

F

[1]face /ˈfeɪs/ *noun, pl* **faces** [*count*]
1 : the front part of the head that has the eyes, nose, and mouth on it • He has a round *face*. • He punched me (right) in the *face*. • His *face* is familiar but I can't remember his name. • I'll never forget the look on her *face*. • She slapped him in the *face*. = She slapped his *face*. • He fell flat on his *face*. • a bearded/freckled/tanned *face* • a fresh/youthful *face* • *face* cream • *face* powder • Her ***face lit up*** [=she looked pleased and happy] when she saw him. • Her ***face fell*** [=she looked unhappy] when I told her the bad news. • I don't know how he can ***show his face*** around here. [=how he can stand being seen here] • Why the ***long face***? [=why do you look so unhappy?] • He was ***wearing a silly grin/smile on his face***. [=he was grinning/smiling in a silly way] • She angrily told him to ***wipe that smile off his face***. [=to stop smiling] • Her guilt was ***written all over her face***. [=the expression on her face showed her guilt very clearly] • The answer to the problem was ***staring me in the face*** all along. [=the answer was obvious but I did not see it]
2 : a facial expression • a happy/sad *face* • a friendly/smiling *face* • She tried to ***put on a brave face*** [=she tried to appear brave or calm] despite the pain of the injury. • It was hard to ***keep a straight face***. [=it was hard not to laugh] • You ***should have seen his face*** when we shouted "Surprise!" [=he had a shocked, surprised, etc., look on his face] — see also POKER FACE
3 : PERSON • I didn't recognize any of the *faces* around the table. • There are lots of new *faces* around the office. • It's good to see a ***familiar face***. [=a person that I know]
4 a : the way something appears when it is first seen or thought about — usually singular • ***On the face of it***, her proposal seems ridiculous. [=when you first hear about her proposal it seems ridiculous, although it may not be ridiculous when you learn more about it] • Her proposal seems ridiculous ***on its face***. **b :** the way something is seen or thought of by people — usually singular • If she wins the election it will change the *face* of American politics. ✧ To ***put a brave/good/positive face on*** something or to ***put the best face on*** something is to talk about it or describe it in a way that makes it seem as good as possible. • She can *put a positive face on* the worst situations. • He was disappointed by the results of the election, but tried to *put the best face on* the situation by saying he had come closer to winning than people expected.
5 a : a front or outer surface of something • the *face* of a cliff = a cliff *face* • the *face* of a building • the *face* of a golf club • a species that has vanished from ***the face of the earth*** [=a species that is no longer found anywhere in the world] • If you ask me, he's the biggest fool ***on the face of the earth***. [=in the world] **b :** a surface or side that is marked or prepared in some way • the *face* of a document **c :** a side of a coin • Which *face* will the coin land on—heads or tails? **d :** the part of a clock or watch that shows the time • a clock *face* **e** *mathematics* **:** any one of the flat surfaces of a solid shape • A cube is a solid with six square *faces*.
a slap in the face see [2]SLAP
as plain as the nose on your face see [1]NOSE
blue in the face see [1]BLUE
cross someone's face see [2]CROSS
cut off your nose to spite your face see [1]NOSE
egg on your face see [1]EGG
***face to face* 1** — used to describe a situation in which two people are together and looking at each other • They were sitting *face to face*. • I've spoken with him on the phone but I've never met him *face to face*. [=I've never met him] • We've never had a *face-to-face* meeting. — often + *with* • I've never been *face to face with* him before. **2 :** very close to something dangerous, difficult, etc. — + *with* • The actors were *face to face with* real flames. • She came *face to face with* death. [=she nearly died] • When she visited the school she was brought *face to face with* the problems encountered by teachers every day.
fly in the face of see [1]FLY
game face ✧ In informal U.S. English, if you are ***wearing your game face*** or ***have your game face on***, you have a serious look on your face which shows that you are ready to compete in a game, sport, competition, etc. • He was *wearing his game face* in the finals.
get out of someone's face *US, informal* **:** to go away and stop bothering someone **:** to leave someone alone • *Get out of my face!* • Hey, *get out of your sister's face* and go play somewhere else!
in someone's face* 1 :** in a direct way that shows anger or disrespect for someone • She laughed *in his face*. • He slammed the door *in my face*. **2** ✧ In informal U.S. English, if you ***are/get in someone's face, you are criticizing or shouting at someone in a very direct and angry way. • The coach *got in my face* because I was late for practice. — see also IN-YOUR-FACE
in the face of **:** while in a situation in which you have to deal with (something or someone that is dangerous, difficult, etc.) • Their defeat seemed certain *in the face of* such a powerful opponent. • She showed great courage *in the face of* danger. [=she showed great courage when she was faced with danger] • She succeeded *in the face of* [=*despite*] great difficulties.
just another face in the crowd see [2]CROWD
laugh on the other side of your face see [1]LAUGH
lose face **:** to cause other people to have less respect for you **:** to lose other people's respect • She was afraid that she would *lose face* if she admitted her mistake.
make a face *or chiefly Brit* ***pull a face* 1 :** to make a facial expression that shows dislike or disgust • He *made a face* when I mentioned her name. **2 :** to make a silly or amusing facial expression • She tried to get me to laugh by *making a face* when I looked at her. • He was entertaining the children by *making* (funny) *faces*.
pretty face see [1]PRETTY
put a human face on see [1]HUMAN
save face **:** to avoid having other people lose respect for you • He tried to *save face* by working overtime.
shut your face see [1]SHUT
stare (someone) in the face see [1]STARE
stuff your face see [2]STUFF
to someone's face **:** directly to someone • If you have something to say about me, you should say it *to my face*. [=say it directly to me rather than to someone else]

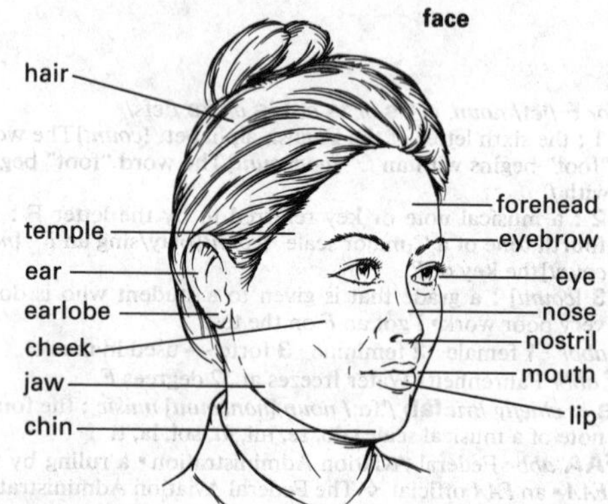

[2]face *verb* **fac·es; faced; fac·ing**
1 a : to stand or sit with your face and body turned toward (something or someone) [+ *obj*] The teacher *faced* the class. • She turned around to *face* the window. • He sat *facing* the wall. [*no obj*] Turn and *face* to the east. **b :** to have the front part toward (something) [+ *obj*] The house *faces* the park. • The living room *faces* the afternoon sun. [*no obj*] My shoe was lying in the corner with its sole *facing* upward. • The flower opens *facing* skyward. **c :** to be on the page that is opposite to (another page) [+ *obj*] Look at the illustration that *faces* page 132. = Look at the illustration *facing* page

132. [*no obj*] Look at the illustration on the *facing* page.
2 [+ *obj*] **a** : to deal with (something bad or unpleasant) in a direct way ▪ Only by *facing* your problems can you hope to overcome them. ▪ You must stand and *face* the danger. ▪ He'll have to *face* the consequences of his decision. **b** : to admit that (something) is true or real ▪ It was time to *face* the truth. ▪ We have to *face* the possibility that the economy will get worse before it gets better. ▪ We have to *face* reality.
3 [+ *obj*] **a** : to have (something bad or unpleasant) as a problem or possibility : to be confronted by (something) ▪ This is not the first time she has *faced* adversity. ▪ Because of the drought, thousands of people are now *facing* starvation. ▪ He finds himself *facing* criminal charges for his role in the conspiracy. ▪ She *faced* a difficult choice. [=she had to make a difficult choice] **b** : to be a problem for (someone) : to require the attention of (someone) ▪ There were many important questions *facing* them. ▪ We can't ignore the problems that *face* us. **c** : to force (someone) to see and deal with something in a direct way ▪ He couldn't deny his involvement when the police *faced* [=*confronted*] him with the evidence. — usually used as *(be) faced* ▪ He *was faced* with the evidence. ▪ We *are faced* with two unpleasant options. ▪ We can't ignore the problems that we *are faced* with.
4 [+ *obj*] **a** : to meet with (someone) despite shame, fear, or embarrassment ▪ I don't know if I can *face* him again after treating him so badly. **b** : to meet (someone) in a competition : to compete or fight against (someone) ▪ The team has to *face* a tough opponent in its next game. ▪ It was the first time that these two fighters had *faced* each other in the ring. ▪ The pitcher struck out the first three batters he *faced*.
5 [+ *obj*] : to cover the front or the surface of (something) ▪ They *faced* the building with marble. ▪ a chimney *faced* with red brick ▪ a brick-*faced* chimney
face facts or face the fact(s) : to admit that something is true ▪ The time has come to *face the fact* that the government's policies aren't working. ▪ The time has come to *face the facts* and admit that the government's policies aren't working. ▪ Let's *face facts*—our plan isn't working.
face off [*phrasal verb*] *chiefly US* : to be involved in or become involved in a conflict, dispute, or competition ▪ The protesters were *facing off* with/against the police. ▪ They *faced off* in a nationally televised debate. ▪ two teams that *faced off* in the play-offs last year — see also FACE-OFF
face the music : to accept and deal with the unpleasant result of something you have said or done ▪ He knows that he'll be criticized for making a bad decision, and he's ready to *face the music*.
face up to [*phrasal verb*] ***face up to (something)*** : to deal with (something bad or unpleasant) in a direct way ▪ She has to *face up to* [=*face*] her problems now, or else they'll only get worse. ▪ We need to *face up to* our fears.
(let's) face it — used to say that something is true and cannot be denied ▪ *Face it*, a lot of people don't even bother to vote. ▪ *Let's face it*, most of us don't get enough exercise.

face card *noun, pl* ~ **cards** [*count*] : a king, queen, or jack in a deck of cards — called also (*chiefly Brit*) *court card*, (*Brit*) *picture card*

face·cloth /ˈfeɪsˌklɑːθ/ *noun, pl* **-cloths** [*count*] : WASHCLOTH

-faced /ˌfeɪst/ *combining form*
1 : having a particular kind of face ▪ a fresh-*faced* girl ▪ freckle-*faced* [=having a face with many freckles]
2 : having a particular kind of surface or front ▪ a brick-*faced* house

face·down /ˌfeɪsˈdaʊn/ *adv* : with the face down ▪ The cards were dealt *facedown*. ▪ lying/floating *facedown* ▪ He fell *facedown* in the sand.

face·less /ˈfeɪsləs/ *adj, usually disapproving*
1 : not having any unusual and interesting qualities ▪ the *faceless* masses ▪ a *faceless* corporation
2 : not identified : ANONYMOUS ▪ a decision made by *faceless* bureaucrats ▪ a *faceless* accuser

face–lift /ˈfeɪsˌlɪft/ *noun, pl* **-lifts** [*count*]
1 : surgery to make a person's face look younger (such as by removing wrinkles) ▪ She's planning to get a *face-lift*.
2 : changes made to something to make it more attractive or modern ▪ The hotel was given a million-dollar *face-lift*. ▪ The new landscaping has given the park a much-needed *face-lift*.

face mask *noun, pl* ~ **masks** [*count*] : a mask or protective covering that goes over your face or part of your face ▪ gas delivered to the patient via *face mask* ▪ (*American football*) The lineman grabbed the running back's *face mask*.

face–off /ˈfeɪsˌɑːf/ *noun, pl* **-offs** [*count*]
1 *ice hockey* : a method of beginning play by dropping the puck between two players ▪ a *face-off* at center ice
2 *chiefly US* : a meeting of opponents : a conflict or fight ▪ a legal *face-off* ▪ a diplomatic *face-off* between Communist and non-Communist nations — see also *face off* at ²FACE

face–sav·ing /ˈfeɪsˌseɪvɪŋ/ *adj, always used before a noun* : done to keep someone from looking foolish ▪ a *face-saving* gesture ▪ They needed a *face-saving* way out of the confrontation. — see also *save face* at ¹FACE

fac·et /ˈfæsət/ *noun, pl* **-ets** [*count*]
1 : a part or element *of* something ▪ Each *facet of* the problem requires careful attention. ▪ the different *facets of* our culture ▪ Which *facet of* his character is most appealing?
2 : a small, flat surface on a jewel ▪ the *facets* of a diamond
– fac·et·ed /ˈfæsətəd/ *adj* ▪ a *faceted* jewel — see also MULTIFACETED

face time *noun* [*noncount*] *US, informal*
1 : time spent meeting with someone ▪ He hoped to get more *face time* with the president.
2 : time spent at the place where you work especially before or after normal working hours ▪ Some bosses think lots of *face time* is a sign of loyalty to the company.
3 : the amount of time someone spends appearing on television ▪ a celebrity who has been getting a lot of *face time*

fa·ce·tious /fəˈsiːʃəs/ *adj* [*more* ~; *most* ~] — used to describe speech that is meant to be funny but that is usually regarded as annoying, silly, or not proper ▪ I was just being *facetious*. ▪ a *facetious* remark
– fa·ce·tious·ly *adv* ▪ She was speaking *facetiously*. **– fa·ce·tious·ness** *noun* [*noncount*]

face·up /ˈfeɪsˈʌp/ *adv* : with the face up ▪ The cards were dealt *faceup*. ▪ lying/floating *faceup*

face value *noun, pl* ~ **values** [*count*] : the value that is printed or shown on something (such as a coin or bill) ▪ We paid $100 for tickets that had a *face value* of $50.
at face value **1** : for the price that is printed on something ▪ We bought the tickets *at face value*. **2** ✧ Something that is ***taken/accepted at face value*** is regarded as true or genuine without being questioned or doubted. ▪ After all his lying, nothing he says now should be ***taken at face value***. [=accepted as true]

facia *variant spelling of* FASCIA 3

¹fa·cial /ˈfeɪʃəl/ *adj* : of or relating to a person's face ▪ *facial* expressions ▪ *facial* features ▪ *facial* hair

²facial *noun, pl* **-cials** [*count*] : a beauty treatment to make a person's face look and feel better ▪ a deep-cleaning *facial*

facie see PRIMA FACIE

fac·ile /ˈfæsəl, *Brit* ˈfæsaɪl/ *adj* [*more* ~; *most* ~] *formal*
1 *disapproving* : too simple : not showing enough thought or effort ▪ a *facile* explanation ▪ This problem needs more than just a *facile* solution.
2 *always used before a noun, disapproving* : done or achieved in a way that is too easy ▪ a *facile* [=*effortless*] victory
3 *always used before a noun, chiefly US, approving* : working, moving, or performing well and very easily ▪ He is a wonderfully *facile* writer.
– fac·ile·ly *adv*

fa·cil·i·tate /fəˈsɪləˌteɪt/ *verb* **-tates; -tat·ed; -tat·ing** [+ *obj*] *formal*
1 : to make (something) easier : to help cause (something) ▪ Cutting taxes may *facilitate* economic recovery. ▪ Her rise to power was *facilitated* by her influential friends.
2 : to help (something) run more smoothly and effectively ▪ The moderator's role is to *facilitate* the discussion by asking appropriate questions.
– fa·cil·i·ta·tion /fəˌsɪləˈteɪʃən/ *noun* [*noncount*] ▪ the *facilitation* of discussion **– fa·cil·i·ta·tor** /fəˈsɪləˌteɪtɚ/ *noun, pl* **-tors** [*count*] ▪ the *facilitator* of a discussion

fa·cil·i·ty /fəˈsɪləti/ *noun, pl* **-ties**
1 a [*count*] : something (such as a building or large piece of equipment) that is built for a specific purpose ▪ a large manufacturing *facility* ▪ a new sewage-treatment *facility* ▪ The injured child was rushed to a ***medical facility***. [=a hospital] ▪ a ***correctional facility*** [=a prison] **b** [*count*] : something that makes an action, operation, or activity easier — usually plural ▪ The resort offers a wide range of *facilities* for young and old alike. **c** ***facilities*** [*plural*] *informal* : BATHROOM ▪ The *facilities* are at the end of the corridor.
2 : skill and ease in doing something [*singular*] He had a great *facility* for writing. [*noncount*] He had great *facility* with words. ▪ She handled the crisis with *facility*.

F

fac·ing /ˈfeɪsɪŋ/ *noun, pl* **-ings** **:** a layer of material that is placed on the surface or front of something to improve its appearance [*noncount*] a house with brick *facing* [*count*] ornamental window *facings* ▪ a suit with red *facings* at the collar and the cuffs

fac·sim·i·le /fækˈsɪməli/ *noun, pl* **-les** [*count*]
1 : an exact copy ▪ A *facsimile* of the world's first computer was exhibited in the museum.
2 *formal* **:** ¹FAX 1
reasonable facsimile ◇ A ***reasonable facsimile*** is a copy that is not exact but is fairly close. ▪ The house is a *reasonable facsimile* of his original home. This phrase is sometimes used in a joking way. ▪ I can speak French, or at least a *reasonable facsimile* of French. [=I can speak French but not very well]

fact /ˈfækt/ *noun, pl* **facts**
1 [*count*] **:** something that truly exists or happens **:** something that has actual existence ▪ Rapid electronic communication is now a *fact.* — often used in the phrase ***the fact that*** ▪ It's hard to accept *the fact that* she's gone. [=it's hard to accept that she's gone] ▪ What they're proposing is impractical, apart from *the fact that* it's also illegal. ▪ In spite of *the fact that* he was sick [=although he was sick], I went to visit him.
2 : a true piece of information [*count*] The book is filled with interesting *facts* and figures. ▪ Those are the (cold) hard *facts* of the case. ▪ I ***know for a fact*** that he did it. [=I am sure that he did it] ▪ He did it, and ***that's a fact*** ▪ There's no doubt that he did it. ***The facts speak for themselves*** [=the facts make it clear that he did it] [*noncount*] It can sometimes be hard to separate ***fact from fiction*** [=to know what is true and what is false]
after the fact **1** *law* **:** after a crime has been committed ▪ She was charged with being an ***accessory after the fact*** [=she was charged with helping someone who had committed a crime after the crime was committed] **2 :** after something has happened **:** AFTERWARD ▪ They informed me of their decision only *after the fact.* [=after they had already made their decision]
as a matter of fact — used to stress the truth of a statement ▪ "Do you know her personally?" "*As a matter of fact,* I do."
bend (the) facts see ¹BEND
in fact **1 :** in truth — used to stress that a statement is true although it may be surprising or unlikely ▪ painters who are *in fact* anything but unsophisticated ▪ He looks younger, but he is *in* (actual) *fact* almost 60 years old. ▪ They know each other; *in fact,* they're close friends. = They know each other; they're close friends, *in fact.* **2** *also* ***in point of fact*** — used to introduce a true statement which shows that another statement is not true or accurate ▪ He claims that he supported the bill, but *in fact* he voted against it. [=the truth is that he voted against it] ▪ She says that she doesn't know him, but *in point of fact* they have been seen together many times.
is that a fact? — used to respond to a statement that is thought to be surprising or unlikely ▪ "He looks much younger, but he's actually almost 60 years old." "*Is that a fact?*" [=I am surprised he is 60 years old] ▪ "A lot of people agree with me." "*Is that a fact?*" [=I doubt that a lot of people agree with you]
the fact is/remains — used to stress that a statement is true and that its truth is not affected or changed by a previous statement ▪ He may not have meant it, but *the fact remains* that he committed a crime. ▪ The company has struggled recently, but *the fact is* that they are still making a profit.
the fact of the matter see ¹MATTER

fact–finding *adj, always used before a noun* **:** done or created in order to learn the facts that relate to a particular situation or event ▪ a *fact-finding* mission ▪ a *fact-finding* panel

fac·tion /ˈfækʃən/ *noun, pl* **-tions** [*count*] **:** a group within a larger group that has different ideas and opinions than the rest of the group ▪ The committee soon split into *factions.* ▪ warring *factions*
– fac·tion·al /ˈfækʃənl/ *adj* ▪ *factional* strife/violence/maneuvering **– fac·tion·al·ism** /ˈfækʃənəˌlɪzəm/ *noun* [*noncount*] ▪ a political party split by *factionalism* and infighting

fact of life *noun, pl* **facts of life**
1 [*count*] **:** something that exists and that cannot be changed or ignored ▪ For new parents, lack of sleep is just a *fact of life.*
2 ***the facts of life*** **:** the facts about sex that are told to children ▪ He explained *the facts of life* to his son.

fac·toid /ˈfækˌtoɪd/ *noun, pl* **-toids** [*count*] **:** a brief and usually unimportant fact ▪ The book is really just a collection of interesting *factoids.*

¹fac·tor /ˈfæktɚ/ *noun, pl* **-tors** [*count*]
1 : something that helps produce or influence a result **:** one of the things that cause something to happen ▪ There were several *factors* contributing to their recent decline. ▪ Poor planning was a major *factor* in the company's failure. ▪ Cost was the ***decisive/deciding/determining factor*** in their decision. [=the most important reason for their decision]
2 a *mathematics* **:** a number that evenly divides a larger number ▪ 6, 4, 3, and 2 are *factors* of 12. **b :** an amount by which another amount is multiplied or divided ▪ Costs increased/decreased by a *factor* of 10. [=costs were 10 times higher/lower than they had been]
— see also RH FACTOR, RISK FACTOR

²factor *verb* **-tors; -tored; -tor·ing** [+ *obj*]
1 : to consider or include (something) in making a judgment or calculation — + *in* or *into* ▪ In doing our calculations we need to *factor in* inflation. ▪ We need to *factor* inflation *into* our calculations.
2 : to not consider or include (something) in making a judgment or calculation — + *out* ▪ Even after *factoring out* inflation, the costs have increased greatly.

fac·to·ry /ˈfæktəri/ *noun, pl* **-ries** [*count*] **:** a building or group of buildings where products are made ▪ an automobile *factory* ▪ She got a job in/at the *factory.* — often used before another noun ▪ *factory* workers/gates — often used figuratively ▪ The college was well-known as a football *factory.* [=a school known more for its football teams and players than for its students and teachers] ▪ the Hollywood studios that were the dream *factories* of the American film industry

factory floor *noun*
the factory floor **:** the part of a factory where products are made ▪ There's talk ***on the factory floor*** [=among the ordinary workers in the factory] about a possible strike.

fac·to·tum /fækˈtoutəm/ *noun, pl* **-tums** [*count*] *formal* **:** a person whose job involves doing many different types of work ▪ He was the office *factotum.*

fac·tu·al /ˈfæktʃəwəl/ *adj*
1 [*more ~; most ~*] **:** limited to, involving, or based on facts ▪ *factual* knowledge/information ▪ She tried to separate what is *factual* [=*true, real*] from what is not. ▪ That statement is not *factual.* ▪ a report filled with ***factual errors***
2 : of or relating to facts ▪ the *factual* aspects of the case
– fac·tu·al·ly *adv* ▪ a *factually* incorrect statement

fac·ul·ty /ˈfækəlti/ *noun, pl* **-ties**
1 a [*noncount*] **:** the group of teachers in a school or college ▪ She's a member of the Harvard *faculty.* — often used before another noun ▪ *faculty* members ▪ a *faculty* meeting **b** ***faculty*** [*plural*] *US* **:** faculty members or teachers ▪ The school hired more *faculty.* ▪ a meeting with students and *faculty*
2 a [*count*] **:** one of the powers of your mind or body ▪ the *faculty* of hearing/speech ▪ It was sad to see that his ***mental faculties*** [=his ability to think clearly] had begun to fail. ▪ She needs to learn to develop her ***critical faculties*** [=her ability to make judgments about what is good or true] **b** [*singular*] **:** a natural talent for doing something ▪ She has a *faculty* for making friends.
3 [*count*] **:** a department in a college or university ▪ The *Faculty* of Arts and Sciences ▪ the *Faculty* of Law

fad /ˈfæd/ *noun, pl* **fads** [*count*] **:** something (such as an interest or fashion) that is very popular for a short time ▪ She's always interested in the latest *fads.* ▪ a *fad* diet
– fad·dish /ˈfædɪʃ/ *adj* [*more ~; most ~*] ▪ a *faddish* psychological treatment

fad·dist /ˈfædɪst/ *noun, pl* **-dists** [*count*] **:** a person who becomes very interested or enthusiastic about different things for a short time **:** a person who becomes involved in fads ▪ a food *faddist* [=someone who becomes very enthusiastic about different types of food as they become popular]

¹fade /ˈfeɪd/ *verb* **fades; fad·ed; fad·ing**
1 [*no obj*] **a :** to lose strength or freshness ▪ The flowers were *fading* in the vase. **:** to become weaker ▪ the *fading* light of late afternoon ▪ She was *fading* fast from the effects of the pneumonia. ▪ Her hearing gradually *faded* (away) as she grew older. ▪ His voice *faded* off into a whisper. = His voice *faded* to a whisper. **b :** to disappear gradually ▪ We watched the ship gradually *fade* from view as it sailed away. ▪ The smile *faded* from his face. ▪ Hopes for a quick end of the crisis are *fading* fast. ▪ Their reasons for leaving have *faded* from memory. ▪ He's trying to recapture the *faded* glory of his youth. ▪ The band's popularity has *faded* in recent years.

2 : to become less bright **:** to lose color [*no obj*] The fabric will *fade* unless you protect it from the sunlight. ▪ The colors of the photograph have *faded* with time. [+ *obj*] Exposure to the elements has *faded* the car's finish. ▪ blue jeans *faded* by wear ▪ She was wearing *faded* blue jeans.
3 [*no obj*] **:** to change gradually in loudness, strength, or appearance — used to describe a radio signal, a picture in a movie, etc. ▪ As the hero rides into the sunset, the screen ***fades to black*** [=the image gradually changes until the screen is completely black] — often + *in* or *out* ▪ One scene *fades out* as the next *fades in*. ▪ The radio signal *faded out* as we got further from the station. ▪ The sound of her voice gradually *faded out*.

[2]fade *noun, pl* **fades** [*count*] **:** a gradual change from one picture to another in a movie or television program ▪ The movie ends with a *fade* to black.

fade–in /ˈfeɪdˌɪn/ *noun, pl* **-ins** [*count*] **:** the gradual appearance of an image at the beginning of a scene in a movie or television program ▪ The film begins with a *fade-in* of a girl's head on a pillow.

fade–out /ˈfeɪdˌaʊt/ *noun, pl* **-outs** [*count*] **:** the gradual disappearance of an image at the end of a scene in a movie or television program ▪ The movie ends with a slow *fade-out* to a black screen.

fae•ces *chiefly Brit spelling of* FECES

[1]fag /ˈfæg/ *noun, pl* **fags** [*count*] *US, informal + offensive* **:** a homosexual man — compare [2]FAG

[2]fag *noun, pl* **fags** [*count*] *Brit, informal* **:** CIGARETTE — compare [1]FAG

fag end *noun, pl* **~ ends** [*count*] *Brit, informal* **:** the last and usually least appealing or interesting part of something ▪ He came in right at the *fag end* [=*tail end*] of the meeting.

fagged /ˈfægd/ *adj* [*more ~; most ~*] *Brit, informal* **:** very tired ▪ He was too *fagged* [=*exhausted*] even to eat.

fag•got /ˈfægət/ *noun, pl* **-gots** [*count*] *US, informal + offensive* **:** a homosexual man

fah *chiefly Brit spelling of* FA

Fahr•en•heit /ˈferənˌhaɪt/ *adj* **:** relating to or having a scale for measuring temperature on which the boiling point of water is at 212 degrees above zero and the freezing point is at 32 degrees above zero ▪ the *Fahrenheit* scale ▪ It was 70 degrees *Fahrenheit* outside. — abbr. *F*; compare CELSIUS

[1]fail /ˈfeɪl/ *verb* **fails; failed; fail•ing**
1 a : to not succeed **:** to end without success [*no obj*] He *failed* in his first attempt but succeeded in his second attempt. ▪ The rebellion *failed* completely. ▪ an experiment that *failed* = a *failed* experiment ▪ a marriage that is *failing* = a *failing* marriage ▪ The drought caused the crops to *fail*. [=the crops did not grow successfully because of the drought] ▪ He only bothers to read the directions ***if/when all else fails***. [=if/when everything else he has attempted has failed] [+ *obj*] — followed by *to + verb* ▪ She *failed to finish* the race. ▪ He *failed to achieve* all that he hoped to achieve. **b** [*no obj*] **:** to not succeed as a business **:** to become bankrupt ▪ His first company *failed*, but his second company succeeded. ▪ The bank *failed*. ▪ a *failed* bank
2 a [+ *obj*] **:** to not do (something that you should do or are expected to do) — followed by *to + verb* ▪ He *failed to act* on the advice of his staff. [=he should have acted on their advice but he didn't] ▪ He *failed to mention* his new girlfriend when he spoke to his parents. **b :** to not do something [+ *obj*] — followed by *to + verb* ▪ I turned on the switch but the light *failed to go on*. ▪ It never *fails to surprise* me that people can be so gullible. [=I am always surprised that people can be so gullible] ▪ Her public appearances rarely *fail to attract* huge crowds. [=her public appearances almost always attract huge crowds] ▪ It never *fails to rain* [=it always rains] when I plan to take a day off. ▪ I ***fail to see/understand*** [=I don't see/understand] why we need to change the current system. [=I don't think we need to change it] [*no obj*] ***It never fails***. I plan to take a day off, and it rains. [=whenever I plan to take a day off, it rains]
3 [+ *obj*] **:** to not do or provide something that is needed by (someone) ▪ He felt that he had *failed* her when she needed him most. ▪ The government has *failed* the voters. ▪ In the face of continued threats, his ***courage failed him***. [=he lost courage, he became afraid] ▪ He wanted to express his appreciation for all they had done, but ***words failed him***. [=he did not know what to say]
4 a : to be unsuccessful in passing (an examination, a course of study, etc.) [+ *obj*] He *failed* the test/exam. ▪ He *failed* chemistry. [*no obj*] He *failed* in chemistry. ▪ *Failing* students must repeat the course. **b** [+ *obj*] **:** to decide that (someone) has not passed an examination or course of study ▪ The teacher *failed* several students. ▪ He received a ***failing grade/mark*** in chemistry. [=his teacher gave him a grade/mark that showed he failed chemistry]
5 [*no obj*] **a :** to stop working ▪ The power *failed*. ▪ The plane's engine *failed*, forcing an emergency landing. ▪ His kidneys *failed*. **b :** to lose strength **:** to become weak or weaker ▪ Her health/eyesight is starting to *fail*. ▪ Her children are concerned about her *failing* health/eyesight.

[2]fail *noun*
without fail **1** — used to stress that something always happens ▪ Every day, *without fail*, he has toast and coffee for breakfast. **2** — used to stress that something will definitely happen ▪ She promised that she would be there *without fail*. [=she would definitely be there]

[1]fail•ing /ˈfeɪlɪŋ/ *noun, pl* **-ings** [*count*] **:** a weakness or problem in a person's character, behavior, or ability ▪ He has some minor *failings*.

[2]failing *prep, formal* **:** in the absence of (something) **:** WITHOUT ▪ *Failing* progress in the peace process, war seems likely. ▪ We could try to persuade them by arguing or, ***failing that*** [=if that does not happen or succeed], we could threaten to cancel the deal.

fail–safe /ˈfeɪlˌseɪf/ *adj* [*more ~; most ~*] **:** certain not to fail ▪ Of course, no system is entirely *fail-safe*. ▪ He was looking for a *fail-safe* source of money. ▪ a *fail-safe* device/mechanism [=a device/mechanism that will not break]

fail•ure /ˈfeɪljɚ/ *noun, pl* **-ures**
1 : the act or result of failing: such as **a :** a lack of success in some effort [*count*] He became discouraged by his repeated *failures* in business. [*noncount*] He was often crippled by his fear of *failure*. ▪ He was trying to rescue the business from *failure*. [=*bankruptcy*] — opposite SUCCESS **b :** a situation or occurrence in which something does not work as it should [*count*] The storm caused power *failures* [=*outages*] in many parts of the city. ▪ a *failure* [=*lapse*] of memory [*noncount*] The accident was caused by engine *failure*. ▪ The patient was suffering from heart/kidney *failure*. **c :** an occurrence in which someone does not do something that should be done — followed by *to + verb* [*count*] The accident was caused by a *failure to use* proper procedures. [*noncount*] She was criticized for *failure to follow* directions. **d :** an occurrence in which crops do not grow and produce food in the normal way [*noncount*] The drought caused crop *failure*. [*count*] a serious crop *failure*
2 [*count*] **:** a person or thing that has failed ▪ He felt like a *failure* when he wasn't accepted into law school. ▪ The scheme was a complete *failure*. — opposite SUCCESS

[1]faint /ˈfeɪnt/ *adj* **faint•er; -est**
1 : not clearly seen, heard, tasted, felt, etc. ▪ We heard a *faint* noise. ▪ a *faint* smell/odor/aroma ▪ the *faint* glow of a distant light ▪ There was a *faint* smile on her lips. ▪ a *faint* [=*weak*] radio signal
2 : very slight or small ▪ There's just a *faint* chance/possibility that the weather will improve by tomorrow. ▪ a *faint* hope ▪ a *faint* reminder of their former greatness ▪ He ***didn't have the faintest idea/notion*** what she was talking about. [=he did not know what she was talking about] ▪ She showed ***not the faintest interest*** in him. [=she showed no interest at all in him]
3 *not used before a noun* **:** weak and dizzy ▪ I'd better lie down; I feel *faint*. ▪ She felt *faint* from/with hunger.
damn with faint praise see [2]DAMN
faint of heart **:** lacking the courage to face something difficult or dangerous — usually used in the phrase ***not for the faint of heart*** ▪ This is a difficult climb that is *not for the faint of heart*. — see also FAINTHEARTED
– faint•ly *adv* ▪ He was smiling *faintly*. ▪ The room still smelled *faintly* of perfume. ▪ She looked *faintly* [=*somewhat, slightly*] familiar. ▪ He was *faintly* [=*barely*] aware of her presence. **– faint•ness** *noun* [*noncount*] ▪ the *faintness* of distant stars

[2]faint *verb* **faints; faint•ed; faint•ing** [*no obj*] **:** to suddenly become unconscious ▪ He always *faints* at the sight of blood. ▪ She almost *fainted* from the pain. ▪ She suffers from *fainting* spells.

faint•heart•ed /ˈfeɪntˈhɑɚtəd/ *adj* [*more ~; most ~*] **:** feeling or showing a lack of courage ▪ *fainthearted* people ▪ She gave him a *fainthearted* response. — usually used in the phrase ***not for the fainthearted*** ▪ a dangerous job that is *not for the fainthearted* ▪ a frightening movie that is *not for the*

F

fainthearted — see also *faint of heart* at [1]FAINT
– **faint·heart·ed·ly** *adv*

[1]fair /ˈfeɚ/ *adj* **fair·er; -est**
1 : agreeing with what is thought to be right or acceptable • We received *fair* treatment. • *fair* elections • a *fair* fight • a *fair* bargain/deal/trade • I'm just trying to get a *fair* price for the house. [=I'm not trying to get more money for the house than most people think is right] • That's a *fair* question, and it deserves an honest reply. • The workers claim that they are not being paid ***fair wages***. [=they are being paid less than they should be paid] • It's ***only fair*** [=it is the right thing] to tell him the truth. • I washed the dishes yesterday, so it's *only fair* (that) you to do them today. • He gets his ***fair share*** of attention too. [=he gets a reasonable amount of attention] • She's had more than her *fair share* of trouble. [=she has had a lot of trouble]
2 : treating people in a way that does not favor some over others • He is known as a very *fair* man. • I try to be *fair* to/with my children. • He claims that the competition wasn't *fair*. • It's not *fair* that she gets to leave early and I don't. • Sometimes life isn't *fair*. • a *fair* and impartial jury • a bargain/deal/trade that is *fair* to/for everyone • All she wants is a ***fair chance***. [=the same chance everyone else gets]
3 : not too harsh or critical • "What a bad movie!" "***Be fair***! Parts of it are actually pretty funny." • I can't say I liked the movie, but, ***to be fair***, parts of it are pretty funny. • She did poorly on the test, but, *to be fair*, so did a lot of other people.
4 a : not very good or very bad : of average or acceptable quality • Her work has been *fair* to good. • The quality of her work has been only *fair*. • I think our waiter did a *fair* job. • The patient has been upgraded from serious to *fair* condition. • The food was ***fair to middling***. [=just average; not especially good] **b** *approving* : reasonably good : good although usually not excellent • The team has a *fair* [=*pretty good*] chance of winning the championship this year. • He does a pretty *fair* [=*good*] imitation of the President. • He was able to give us a *fair* idea of the problems involved. • It's a *fair* bet that the weather will improve soon. • "I'm guessing that he's about 50 years old." "That's a *fair* guess, but he's actually almost 60." **c** *always used before a noun* : reasonably large — used to describe an amount or size that is not small although it is also not extremely large • There were a *fair* number of new participants at the convention. • Researchers now know a *fair* amount about the earliest humans. • He lives a *fair* distance from here.
5 : not stormy or cloudy • *fair* skies • *fair* weather
6 *of a person's hair, skin, etc.* **:** having a light color • *fair* hair/skin • a person of *fair* complexion • a *fair*-skinned person — opposite DARK
7 *literary + old-fashioned* **:** attractive or pleasing to look at • We're happy to welcome you to our *fair* [=*lovely*] city. • a *fair* maid/maiden • Who's the *fairest* of them all?
8 *baseball* **:** in the area between the foul lines • The ball was caught in *fair* territory. ✧ A ***fair ball*** is a batted ball that lands in the area between the foul lines. — compare FOUL
a fair bit see [1]BIT
a fair shake see [2]SHAKE
all's fair in love and war — used to describe a situation in which people do not follow the usual rules of behavior and do things that are normally considered unfair • Sure, it was underhanded to steal his customers, but *all's fair in love and war*.
bid fair see [1]BID
fair and square : in an honest and fair manner • He won the election *fair and square*.
fair crack of the whip see [2]CRACK
fair enough *informal* — used to say that something is reasonable or fair • "I'll wash the dishes today, and you can wash them tomorrow." "*Fair enough*." • "He needs more time." "*Fair enough*, but we can't wait too much longer."
fair's fair *informal* — used to say that something was done or should be done because it is fair • *Fair's fair*: I washed the dishes yesterday, so it's your turn to do them today.
fair to say ✧ A comment that is *fair to say* is reasonable and is not expected to cause argument. • The key concept in this book, I think it is *fair to say*, is freedom. • She's not entirely to blame, but it's (only) *fair to say* that she handled the situation badly.
fair warning : enough warning to be able to avoid something bad • I'm giving you *fair warning* that you had better not discuss politics at dinner tonight.
it's a fair cop see [1]COP
– **fair** *adv* • He claims that his opponent wasn't ***playing fair***. [=wasn't playing according to the rules] – **fair·ness** *noun* [*noncount*] • She questioned the *fairness* of the decision. • In the interest of *fairness*, let's not mention any names. • She did poorly, but ***in all fairness*** [=to be fair to her], she was tired.

[2]fair *noun, pl* **fairs** [*count*]
1 : a large public event at which there are various kinds of competitions, games, rides, and entertainment; *especially, US* : such an event at which farm products and farm animals are shown and judged • She showed her horse at the annual county/state *fair*.
2 : an event at which many people gather to buy things or to get information about a product or activity • a book *fair* • a craft *fair* • a ***job fair*** [=an event where employers offer information about their companies to people who are looking for jobs]
3 : an event at which different things (such as crafts or food) are sold usually for charity • The church is having a *fair* to raise money for the new school.

fair game *noun* [*noncount*] : someone or something that can be chased, attacked, or criticized • Celebrities are *fair game* for the tabloids. • The tourists were *fair game* for the pickpockets. • Even her retirement savings were *fair game* for her creditors.

fair·ground /ˈfeɚˌgraʊnd/ *noun, pl* **-grounds** [*count*] : an outdoor area where fairs, circuses, and exhibitions are held

fair–haired /ˈfeɚˈheɚd/ *adj*
1 : having light or blond hair • a *fair-haired* child
2 *chiefly US* **:** especially well-liked or admired — usually used in the phrase ***fair-haired boy*** • an athlete who was once the fans' *fair-haired boy*

fair·ly /ˈfeɚli/ *adv* [*more* ~; *most* ~]
1 : to some degree or extent but not very or extremely : to a reasonable or moderate extent • a *fairly* easy job • It's still *fairly* early. • a *fairly* simple procedure • It's a *fairly* common disease.
2 : in a way that is right or proper : in a fair way • She treats everyone *fairly*. • I told the story as *fairly* as possible. • He reports *fairly* on the issues. • He beat me ***fairly and squarely***.
3 — used for emphasis before a verb that is being used figuratively • The situation *fairly* screamed for someone to intervene.
4 *literary + old-fashioned* **:** in a favorable or pleasing way • a town *fairly* situated on a hill

fair–mind·ed /ˈfeɚˌmaɪndəd/ *adj* [*more* ~; *most* ~] : having or showing an honest and fair way of thinking • a *fair-minded* man • *fair-minded* reporting
– **fair–mind·ed·ness** *noun* [*noncount*]

fair play *noun* [*noncount*] : a way of behaving or of treating other people that is honest and fair • The court's decision goes against my sense of *fair play*. [=the court's decision does not seem fair to me] — see also *turnabout is fair play* at TURNABOUT

fair sex *noun*
the fair sex also the fairer sex *old-fashioned* — used to refer to all women as a group • a member of *the fair sex*

fair·way /ˈfeɚˌweɪ/ *noun, pl* **-ways** [*count*] : the part of a golf course that has short grass and that lies between a tee and a green • Her shot landed at the left side of the *fairway*. — compare ROUGH

fair–weath·er /ˈfeɚˌwɛðɚ/ *adj, always used before a noun, disapproving* : loyal or helpful only during times of success and happiness • They are *fair-weather* friends. [=they are friends when you are successful but not when you fail] • *fair-weather* fans

fairy /ˈferi/ *noun, pl* **fair·ies** [*count*]
1 *in stories* **:** a creature that looks like a very small human being, has magic powers, and sometimes has wings • a good *fairy* • a *fairy* princess — see also TOOTH FAIRY
2 *informal + offensive* **:** a homosexual man
– **fairy·like** /ˈferiˌlaɪk/ *adj*

fairy cake *noun, pl* ~ **cakes** [*count*] *Brit* : CUPCAKE

fairy godmother *noun, pl* ~ **-thers** [*count*] *in stories* : a woman with magic powers who saves a person from trouble

fairy·land /ˈferiˌlænd/ *noun, pl* **-lands** [*count*]
1 *in stories* **:** a place where fairies live
2 : a beautiful or magical place • a winter *fairyland* of snow-covered trees

fairy tale *noun, pl* ~ **tales** [*count*]
1 : a simple children's story about magical creatures • the *fairy tale* about the sleeping princess — sometimes used figuratively • Their marriage is a real-life *fairy tale*. [=they have a

very happy marriage] ▪ a *fairy-tale* romance — called also *fairy story*
2 : a false story that is meant to trick people ▪ Everything he told us about his happy marriage was just a *fairy tale.*

fait ac·com·pli /ˈfeɪtəˌkɑːmˈpliː/ *noun, pl* **faits ac·com·plis** /ˈfeɪtəˌkɑːmˈpliː/ [*count*] *formal* **:** something that has been done and cannot be changed ▪ By the time we learned about the decision, it was already a *fait accompli.*

faith /ˈfeɪθ/ *noun, pl* **faiths**
1 [*noncount*] **:** strong belief or trust in someone or something ▪ His supporters have accepted his claims with blind/unquestioning *faith*. ▪ Our *faith* in the government has been badly shaken by the recent scandals. ▪ His parents have always ***had faith in*** him. = His parents have never ***lost faith in*** him. [=his parents have always believed that he is a person who deserves to be trusted and who will succeed] ▪ I ***have no faith*** in politicians. = I ***put/have little faith in*** politicians. [=I do not trust politicians] ▪ Lending him the money to start his own business was an ***act of faith***. ▪ It requires a giant ***leap of faith*** for us to believe that she is telling the truth. — see also BAD FAITH, GOOD FAITH
2 a [*noncount*] **:** belief in the existence of God **:** strong religious feelings or beliefs ▪ religious *faith* ▪ Nothing is more important to her than her *faith* in God. ▪ She says that her *faith* has given her the courage to deal with this tragedy. ▪ He says he has ***found faith***. [=he has begun to believe in God or has developed strong religious beliefs] **b** [*count*] **:** a system of religious beliefs **:** RELIGION ▪ people of all *faiths* ▪ the Christian/Jewish/Muslim *faith*
accept/take (something) on faith **:** to accept (something) as true without proof or evidence that it is true ▪ I'm not willing to *take her statements on faith*. ▪ I'll *accept it on faith* that he knows the truth.
an article of faith **:** something that is believed without being questioned or doubted ▪ For many it is an *article of faith* that the economy will begin to improve soon.
break faith with **:** to stop supporting or being loyal to (someone) **:** to betray (someone) ▪ He has accused the government of *breaking faith with* its supporters.
keep faith with **:** to continue supporting or being loyal to (someone) ▪ He has *kept faith with* his old political allies.
keep the faith **:** to continue to believe in, trust, or support someone or something when it is difficult to do so ▪ The team has been playing poorly, but its devoted fans have *kept the faith*. [=they have continued to support the team]

faith·ful /ˈfeɪθfəl/ *adj* [*more ~; most ~*]
1 : having or showing true and constant support or loyalty ▪ a *faithful* friend/companion ▪ *faithful* friendship ▪ the team's *faithful* fans ▪ a *faithful* dog — often + *to* ▪ Despite his problems, his friends have remained *faithful to* him. ▪ She has always remained *faithful to* the values she learned as a child.
2 : deserving trust **:** keeping your promises or doing what you are supposed to do ▪ a *faithful* worker/servant ▪ She has provided the company with many years of *faithful* service. — often + *to* ▪ He began to keep a journal and was *faithful to* it for years. [=he continued to write in his journal for many years] ▪ He was not *faithful to* his word. [=he did not do what he said he would]
3 : not having sex with someone who is not your wife, husband, girlfriend, or boyfriend ▪ a *faithful* husband/wife ▪ He insists that he has always been *faithful* to his wife.
4 : exact and accurate ▪ The movie was a *faithful* adaptation of the book. ▪ a *faithful* copy — often + *to* ▪ The movie is *faithful to* the book. [=the story told in the movie closely matches the story told in the book]
the faithful **1 :** the people who believe or participate in a religion ▪ *The faithful* gather here each year to celebrate together. **2 :** the people who are loyal members or supporters of a group or organization ▪ *The faithful* come out and cheer for the team every year. ▪ The convention was packed with *the* Republican/Democratic *faithful*.
– faith·ful·ly /ˈfeɪθfəli/ *adv* ▪ My friends have supported me *faithfully*. ▪ He *faithfully* submitted all the proper forms. ▪ The model *faithfully* [=*accurately*] reproduces the original building. **– faith·ful·ness** *noun* [*noncount*]

faith healing *noun* [*noncount*] **:** a way of treating diseases by using prayer and religious faith
– faith healer *noun, pl* **~ -ers** [*count*]

faith·less /ˈfeɪθləs/ *adj* [*more ~; most ~*] **:** not able to be trusted ▪ a *faithless* friend/employee/servant
– faith·less·ly *adv* **– faith·less·ness** *noun* [*noncount*]

fa·ji·ta /fəˈhiːtə/ *noun, pl* **-tas** [*count*] **:** a Mexican food that consists of cooked strips of meat served with a flour tortilla and fillings (such as tomatoes, onions, and peppers) — usually plural ▪ steak *fajitas*

¹fake /ˈfeɪk/ *adj* **:** not true or real ▪ *fake* emotions ▪ She's a *fake* friend. **:** meant to look real or genuine but not real or genuine ▪ That blood is clearly *fake*. ▪ *fake* fur/leather ▪ He was wearing a *fake* mustache.

²fake *noun, pl* **fakes** [*count*]
1 : a copy of something that is meant to look like the real thing in order to trick people ▪ Experts says that the antique/painting/signature is a *fake*.
2 : a person who pretends to have some special knowledge or ability or pretends to be someone else ▪ He told everyone he was a lawyer, but he was just a *fake*.
3 *US, sports* **:** a movement (such as a pretended kick, pass, or step) that is meant to trick an opponent ▪ The runner made a *fake* to the left and then cut to the right.

³fake *verb* **fakes; faked fak·ing**
1 [+ *obj*] **a :** to make (something) seem real or true in order to trick someone ▪ He *faked* a heart attack. ▪ *fake* an emotion ▪ She *faked* her own death. [=she tricked people into thinking that she had died] **b :** to change (something) in order to trick people ▪ He *faked* the test results. **c :** to make a copy of (something) in order to trick people ▪ She *faked* her father's signature. ▪ He *faked* a rare first edition.
2 *US, sports* **a** [+ *obj*] **:** to pretend to do (something) in order to trick an opponent ▪ The quarterback *faked* a handoff and then threw a pass downfield. **b** [+ *obj*] **:** to trick (an opponent) by pretending to do something ▪ The runner *faked* the defender by stepping to his left and then cutting to the right. — often + *out* ▪ He *faked out* the defender. **c** [*no obj*] **:** to make a false movement in order to deceive an opponent ▪ The runner *faked* left and then cut to the right.
3 [+ *obj*] **:** to pretend to know or to be able to do (something) ▪ He didn't know the words to the song, so he had to *fake* them.
fake it *informal* **:** to pretend to be something that you are not or to have some knowledge or ability that you do not really have ▪ He acts like he's my friend, but I can tell that he's just *faking it*. ▪ He didn't know the words to the song, so he had to *fake it*.
fake out [*phrasal verb*] ***fake (someone) out*** *or* ***fake out (someone)*** *chiefly US, informal* **:** to deliberately deceive (someone) **:** FOOL ▪ Don't believe him when he says he'll help you. He's just trying to *fake* you *out*. — see also ³FAKE 2b (above)
– fak·er *noun, pl* **-ers** [*count*] ▪ You're not hurt, you *faker*.

fal·con /ˈfælkən, ˈfɑːlkən/ *noun, pl* **-cons** [*count*] **:** a type of hawk that can fly very fast and is sometimes trained to hunt

fal·con·er /ˈfælkənɚ, ˈfɑːlkənɚ/ *noun, pl* **-ers** [*count*] **:** a person who hunts with hawks or trains hawks for hunting

fal·con·ry /ˈfæːlkənri, ˈfɑːlkənri/ *noun* [*noncount*] **:** the sport of hunting with hawks

¹fall /ˈfɑːl/ *verb* **falls; fell** /ˈfɛl/; **fall·en** /ˈfɑːlən/; **fall·ing** [*no obj*]
1 a : to come or go down quickly from a high place or position ▪ An apple *fell* from the tree. ▪ A vase *fell* off the shelf. ▪ Rain *fell* from the sky. ▪ the sound of the *falling* rain **b :** to come or go down suddenly from a standing position ▪ She slipped and *fell* on the ice. ▪ He *fell* flat on his face. ▪ She was afraid that I would trip and *fall*. ▪ He *fell* down the stairs. ▪ One of the sailors had *fallen* overboard. ▪ a *fallen* tree — often + *down* or *over* ▪ She *fell down* and hurt herself. ▪ The tree *fell over* during the storm. **c :** to let yourself come or go down to a lower position ▪ He *fell* [=*dropped, sank*] to his knees and asked for forgiveness. ▪ He *fell* back/forward onto the bed.
2 a : to come down at a particular place after moving through the air ▪ The shot *fell* a great distance from its target. — often + *on* ▪ A ray of light *fell on* the table. — sometimes used figuratively ▪ music *falling on* the ear **b :** to slope downward — usually + *away* ▪ The ground *falls away* to the east. ▪ The sides of the ridge *fall away* steeply. **c :** to hang down ▪ Her hair *fell* loosely over her shoulders.
3 a : to become lower ▪ The tide rose and *fell*. ▪ The temperature *fell* after dark. ▪ His heart rate *fell* (off) dramatically. ▪ The value of the stock has *fallen* drastically. **b :** to become less ▪ Participation in the group has *fallen*. [=*declined*] — often + *off* ▪ Participation in the group has *fallen off*. ▪ Factory production has *fallen off*. **c :** to lose value **:** to suffer a decline in prices ▪ Stocks *fell* several points in early trading today. ▪ The market is continuing to *fall*. **d :** to become less

F

loud ▪ His voice *fell* (to a whisper). ▪ The music rose and *fell*. **4 a** *of a glance or the eyes* **: to become lowered** ▪ Her eyes *fell*. [=she looked down] **b** *of the face* **: to begin to look ashamed or disappointed** ▪ His face *fell* [=he looked disappointed] when he heard the news.
5 *of night or darkness* **: to arrive or begin** ▪ Darkness *falls* early in the winter. ▪ Night has *fallen*.
6 a : to be wounded or killed in battle ▪ Many men *fell* on the battlefield that day. **b : to be captured or defeated** ▪ The fortress *fell* on the third day of the siege. **c : to experience ruin or failure** ▪ A great civilization *fell* in less than a century. ▪ a *fallen* [=*disgraced*] leader ▪ We will stand or *fall* together. ▪ a politician who has *fallen* from power ▪ The coalition government *fell* after only six months in office.
7 a : to happen at a specified time ▪ Christmas *falls* on a Friday this year. ▪ The worst weather of the year *fell* during his vacation. **b — used when something (such as a responsibility) comes or passes to someone in a way that does not involve choice** ▪ It *fell* to me [=it was my responsibility] to tell them about the car accident. ▪ Responsibility for the damage *falls* with the other driver. ▪ The estate *fell* to his brother. [=his brother inherited the estate] **c : to have a specified proper place** ▪ The accent *falls* on the second syllable. ▪ The comma *falls* inside the quotation mark.
8 : to belong in a particular category or range ▪ This word *falls* within the class of verbs. ▪ Her political views *fall* somewhere between liberal and conservative. ▪ His creative output *falls* into three distinct categories.
9 a — used when someone's body or mind passes from one condition or state to another ▪ She *fell* ill/sick. ▪ He *fell* asleep. **b — used when something passes to a different and usually a less active or less desirable state or condition** ▪ The crowd *fell* silent. ▪ This word has *fallen* [=*gone*] out of use. = This word has *fallen* into disuse. [=this word is no longer used] ▪ His theories have now *fallen* into disrepute/disfavor. ▪ The machinery has *fallen* into disrepair.
10 : to start doing something in a very active and energetic way — + *to* ▪ She came in and *fell* immediately *to* work.

(as) easy as falling off a log see [1]EASY
fall afoul of see AFOUL OF
fall (all) over yourself **: to be very eager or too eager** ▪ Fans were *falling over themselves* trying to meet the basketball star. ▪ Reviewers are *falling all over themselves* to praise her latest novel.
fall apart [*phrasal verb*] **1 : to break into parts in usually a sudden and unexpected way** ▪ The pie was *falling apart* as I tried to serve it. **— often used figuratively** ▪ I feel as if my family is *falling apart*. ✧ Something that is ***falling apart*** is in very bad condition. ▪ My old car is *falling apart*. ▪ The house was *falling apart* when we bought it. **2 : to become unable to live in a normal way because you are experiencing a lot of confusion or emotional pain** ▪ She began to *fall apart* when her son was imprisoned.
fall away [*phrasal verb*] **: to become gradually less : to disappear gradually** ▪ The sound of the parade *fell away* in the distance.
fall back [*phrasal verb*] **1 : to move back away from something dangerous or threatening : RETREAT** ▪ The crowd *fell back* when the police arrived. ▪ The guerrillas *fell back* across the border after a brief battle with the army. **2 *fall back on (something) also fall back upon (something)* : to use (something) for help or protection when you are in a bad situation** ▪ When her health insurance was canceled she had nothing to *fall back on*. ▪ They had to *fall back on* their emergency supplies when the snow storm blocked the road to town.
fall behind [*phrasal verb*] **1 : to fail to move or go forward as quickly as others** ▪ We had to stop several times so that the slower hikers wouldn't *fall* (too far) *behind*. **2 : to fail to do something as quickly as planned or required — often + *with*** ▪ We've been *falling* further *behind with* our work. **— often + *on*** ▪ I am *falling behind on* my homework. ▪ We *fell behind on* our car payments.
fall down on the job **: to do a job badly** ▪ The people who are supposed to be keeping the city clean have been *falling down on the job*.
fall flat **: to produce no response or result** ▪ All of his jokes *fell flat*. [=no one laughed at his jokes]
fall for [*phrasal verb*] **1 *fall for (someone)* : to feel a strong attraction for (someone) : to fall in love with (someone)** ▪ He *fell for* her the moment he saw her. ▪ He *fell for* her hard. = He *fell* hard *for* her. = He *fell for* her like a ton of bricks. [=he became deeply in love with her] **2 *fall for (something)* : to be fooled by (something, such as a trick)** ▪ I can't believe you *fell for* that old trick.
fall foul of see [1]FOUL
fall from grace see [1]GRACE
fall in [*phrasal verb*] **1 : to break apart and fall down in an inward direction** ▪ The roof *fell in*. **2 : to take your place in a military formation** ▪ The troops were ordered to *fall in*. **— compare FALL OUT (below)**
fall in/into line **: to start to do what you are told or required to do** ▪ Several of the older companies have refused to *fall in line* (with the new regulations). ▪ It was weeks before the new prisoner *fell into line*.
fall in love, fall out of love see [1]LOVE
fall into [*phrasal verb*] **1 : to be caught in (a trap)** ▪ We *fell into* a trap. **2 : to begin to do or experience (something) or to be affected by (something) without wanting or trying to** ▪ He *fell* deeply *into* debt. ▪ She *fell into* her career almost accidentally. ▪ She ***fell into the habit*** of going out for ice cream every night.
fall into place **: to fit together : to make sense** ▪ The pieces of the puzzle/mystery are finally starting to *fall into place*.
fall into step see [1]STEP
fall into the hands of **: to come to be held or possessed by (someone)** ▪ Officials are concerned that the stolen weapons may *fall into the hands of* terrorists. [=that terrorists may get/obtain the stolen weapons]
fall into the wrong hands **: to come to be held or possessed by the wrong person or group** ▪ There could be a disaster if the weapons *fell into the wrong hands*.
fall into your lap see [1]LAP
fall in with [*phrasal verb*] **1 *fall in with (someone)* : to begin to spend time with (someone)** ▪ Their daughter *fell in with* a bad crowd. **2 *fall in with (something)* : to accept and act in agreement with (something)** ▪ They readily *fell in with* our plans.
fall off [*phrasal verb*] **: to stop being attached to something** ▪ The handle was so loose that it almost *fell off*. **— see also [1]FALL 3b (above)**
fall on/upon [*phrasal verb*] **1 *fall on/upon (something)* a : to begin to experience (something) : to meet with (an experience)** ▪ We *fell on* hard times after I lost my job. ▪ The company *fell upon* some unexpected competition. **b : to notice (something) especially without wanting or trying to** ▪ Her eyes/glance *fell on* the letter on his desk. **2 *fall on/upon (someone)* : to attack (someone) suddenly** ▪ They *fell on* the enemy soldiers and killed every one of them.
fall on deaf ears see [1]EAR
fall on your feet see [1]FOOT
fall out [*phrasal verb*] **1** *of a tooth or hair* **: to stop being attached to the body** ▪ The cancer treatments made her hair *fall out*. **2 : to have an argument** ▪ They *fell out* [=*fought, argued*] over money. ▪ He had *fallen out* [=*quarreled*] with his neighbor. **— see also FALLING-OUT 3 : to leave your place in a military formation** ▪ The soldiers were ordered to *fall out*. **— compare FALL IN (above)**
fall over backward see [1]BACKWARD
fall prey to see [1]PREY
fall short **1 : to fail to be as good or successful as expected or hoped for** ▪ In comparison to her previous novel, this one *falls short*. [=this one is not as good] **— often + *of*** ▪ Her current book *falls short of* her previous novel. ▪ The cruise ***fell short of our expectations***. [=the cruise was not as good as we expected it to be] **2 : to fail to reach a goal** ▪ Their efforts *fell short*. **— often + *of*** ▪ Their efforts *fell* (far) *short of* (achieving) their goal.
fall through [*phrasal verb*] **: to fail or stop in a sudden or final way** ▪ Contract negotiations have *fallen through*. ▪ Our vacation plans have *fallen through*.
fall through/between the cracks see [2]CRACK
fall through the net see [1]NET
fall to pieces see [1]PIECE
fall under [*phrasal verb*] ***fall under (something)*** **: to be influenced or affected by (something)** ▪ He *fell under* her influence. ▪ *fall under* a spell ▪ He has *fallen under* suspicion. [=people have begun to suspect him of doing something]
fall victim to see VICTIM
let the chips fall where they may see [1]CHIP

[2]**fall** *noun, pl* **falls**
1 [*count*] **: the act of falling: such as a : the act of coming or going down from a high position or from a standing position** ▪ a *fall* from a horse ▪ She's had/suffered several bad *falls* in recent years. ▪ a *fall* of three feet ▪ He slipped on the ice and hurt his hand when he tried to ***break his fall***. [=to stop him-

self from falling] **b** : the act of becoming lower • the rise and *fall* of the tide
2 *US* : the season between summer and winter : the season when leaves fall from trees : AUTUMN [*count*] She went off to college in the *fall*. • an unusually warm *fall* [*noncount*] in early/late *fall* • Several weeks of *fall* remain before winter begins. • When *fall* came he planted grass. — often used before another noun • our *fall* catalog • a new *fall* coat • *fall* colors/foliage • the *fall* harvest
3 [*count*] : a decrease in the size, amount, degree, activity, or value of something • a *fall* in the price of oil
4 a [*singular*] : loss of power or greatness • the rise and *fall* [=*collapse*] of an empire **b** [*singular*] : the surrender or capture of a place that is being attacked • the *fall* of Troy • The *fall* of the fort caused the local civilians to flee. **c** [*singular*] : loss of innocence or goodness • a *fall* from virtue **d** ***the Fall*** : the event in the Bible when Adam and Eve are forced to leave the Garden of Eden because they have sinned against God • after *the Fall*
5 [*count*] : an area on a river or stream where water runs steeply downward — usually plural • Bears hunted for fish in the rocky *falls*. [=*waterfall*] • Niagara *Falls*
be riding for a fall see [1]RIDE
fall from grace see [1]GRACE
– see also FREE FALL, WINDFALL

fal·la·cious /fəˈleɪʃəs/ *adj* [*more* ~; *most* ~] *formal* : containing a mistake : not true or accurate • a *fallacious* [=*false*] set of assumptions • *fallacious* [=*misleading*] arguments
– **fal·la·cious·ly** *adv* – **fal·la·cious·ness** *noun* [*noncount*]

fal·la·cy /ˈfæləsi/ *noun, pl* **-cies**
1 [*count*] : a wrong belief : a false or mistaken idea • popular *fallacies* about medicine • It's a *fallacy* (to believe) that the Earth is flat.
2 [*noncount*] : the quality of being false or wrong • The *fallacy* of their ideas about medicine soon became apparent.

fall guy *noun, pl* ~ **guys** [*count*] *informal* : a person who is blamed for something done by others : SCAPEGOAT • His lawyers will argue that he was set up as a/the *fall guy* for crimes he had no part in.

fal·li·ble /ˈfæləbəl/ *adj* [*more* ~; *most* ~] : capable of making mistakes or being wrong • *fallible* human beings — opposite INFALLIBLE
– **fal·li·bil·i·ty** /ˌfæləˈbɪləti/ *noun* [*noncount*] • She acknowledged her *fallibility*. • scientific *fallibility*

fall·ing–out /ˌfɑːlɪŋˈaʊt/ *noun, pl* **fall·ings–out** [*count*] : a serious argument or disagreement • The two actors barely spoke after their bitter *falling-out*. • He had a *falling-out* with his parents over money. — see also *fall out* at [1]FALL

falling star *noun, pl* ~ **stars** [*count*] : METEOR

fall·out /ˈfɑːˌlaʊt/ *noun* [*noncount*]
1 : the radioactive particles that are produced by a nuclear explosion and that fall through the atmosphere • radioactive *fallout* • a ***fallout shelter*** [=a shelter built underground to protect people from radioactive fallout]
2 : a bad effect or result of something • concerned about the possible political *fallout* from the scandal

fal·low /ˈfæloʊ/ *adj*
1 : not used for growing crops : not planted • *fallow* land/fields • allowing several fields to ***lie fallow***
2 : not active or productive • a writer who has been going through a ***fallow period*** [=a period in which he has done no writing] • There were too many promising ideas ***lying fallow*** [=not being used] at the company.

false /ˈfɑːls/ *adj*
1 : not real or genuine — used to say that something is not really what it seems to be • *false* documents • *false* teeth/hair/eyelashes • a trunk with a *false* bottom
2 : not true or accurate • Indicate whether each of the following statements is true or *false*.; *especially* : deliberately untrue : done or said to fool or deceive someone • *false* testimony • *false* accusations/statements • a *false* promise • *false* advertising • He registered at the hotel under a *false* name. • The loan was obtained ***on/under false pretenses***. [=by pretending that a certain condition or circumstance was true]
3 : based on mistaken ideas • Your conclusion is based on *false* [=*incorrect*] assumptions. • *false* confidence/pride • *false* expectations/hopes • The dog gave her a *false* sense of security. [=made her feel safe when she was not really safe]
4 a : not faithful or loyal • a *false* friend **b** : not sincere • *false* modesty • *false* sympathy
5 : sudden or deceptive in a threatening way • The police warned him not to make any ***false moves/movements***. [=movements that are not expected and that may be threatening or dangerous]
– **false·ly** *adv* • He was *falsely* accused of stealing. • The suspect stated *falsely* that she was working that day. – **false·ness** *noun* [*noncount*]

false alarm *noun, pl* ~ **alarms** [*count*]
1 : an alarm (such as a fire alarm) that is set off when it is not needed • A *false alarm* drew firefighters to the school.
2 : something that causes people to wrongly believe that something bad or dangerous is going to happen • The report that the factory would be closing was a *false alarm*. • He thought he might be having a heart attack, but his chest pains were just a *false alarm*.

false arrest *noun, pl* ~ **-rests** [*count, noncount*] : an arrest that is not legally justified • He's suing the police for *false arrest*.

false·hood /ˈfɑːlsˌhʊd/ *noun, pl* **-hoods**
1 [*count*] : an untrue statement : LIE • a politician accused of spreading (malicious) *falsehoods* about his opponent
2 [*noncount*] : the quality of not being true or accurate : false quality • the *falsehood* [=(more commonly) *falseness, falsity*] of these accusations • the line between truth and *falsehood*

false start *noun, pl* ~ **starts** [*count*]
1 : the mistake of starting too soon in a race • If someone makes/commits a *false start*, the race is immediately stopped and the runners have to start again.
2 : an unsuccessful attempt to begin something (such as a career or a project) • After several *false starts*, the researchers were finally able to identify the virus causing the epidemic.

fal·set·to /fɑlˈsɛtoʊ/ *noun, pl* **-tos** [*count, noncount*] : a very high voice used by a man (such as a male singer) • He sang in (a) *falsetto*. • a *falsetto* voice
– **falsetto** *adv* • singing *falsetto*

fals·ie /ˈfɑːlsi/ *noun, pl* **-sies** [*count*] *informal*
1 : a piece of material (such as rubber) that is worn under a bra to make the breast appear larger — usually plural • a woman wearing *falsies*
2 : false eyelashes — usually plural • Instead of mascara, she wore *falsies*.

fal·si·fy /ˈfɑːlsəˌfaɪ/ *verb* **-fies; -fied; -fy·ing** [+ *obj*] : to make (something) false : to change (something) in order to make people believe something that is not true • He was caught *falsifying* financial accounts.
– **fal·si·fi·ca·tion** /ˌfɑːlsəfəˈkeɪʃən/ *noun, pl* **-tions** [*count, noncount*]

fal·si·ty /ˈfɑːlsəti/ *noun, pl* **-ties** *formal*
1 [*noncount*] : the quality of not being true or accurate : the quality of being false • The army would not comment on the truth or *falsity* [=*falseness*] of the report.
2 [*count*] : an untrue statement • spreading *falsities* [=(more commonly) *falsehoods, lies*] over the Internet

fal·ter /ˈfɑːltɚ/ *verb* **-ters; -tered; -ter·ing** [*no obj*]
1 : to stop being strong or successful : to begin to fail or weaken • The business was *faltering* due to poor management. • Their initial optimism has *faltered*. • signs that the economy is *faltering*
2 : to begin to walk or move in an unsteady way • Her steps began to *falter*.
3 : to feel doubt about doing something • He never *faltered* [=*wavered*] in his determination to go to college.
4 ✧ If your ***voice falters***, you are unable to speak normally because you are unsure about what to say or because you are feeling strong emotions. • Her *voice faltered* when she spoke about her parents.
– **faltering** *adj* • a *faltering* economy • They are trying to save their *faltering* [=*failing*] marriage. • He was only able to take a few *faltering* steps.

fame /ˈfeɪm/ *noun* [*noncount*] : the condition of being known or recognized by many people • He died at the height of his *fame*. • The book tells the story of her sudden rise to *fame*. • He gained/found *fame* as an actor. • The house was once occupied by Noah Webster of dictionary *fame*. [=Noah Webster, who was famous for his dictionary] • achieving/earning/winning international/worldwide *fame* • She went to Hollywood seeking *fame* and fortune. — see also HALL OF FAME
claim to fame see [2]CLAIM

famed /ˈfeɪmd/ *adj* : known and usually liked by many people : FAMOUS • a *famed* writer • a bowl of the restaurant's *famed* chili — often + *for* • a restaurant *famed for* its chili

F

fa·mil·ial /fəˈmɪljəl/ *adj*
1 : of or relating to a family ▪ *familial* relationships : suggesting a family ▪ The company has created a *familial* atmosphere in its offices.
2 *medical* : tending to affect members of the same family ▪ a *familial* disease

fa·mil·iar /fəˈmɪljə/ *adj* [*more* ~; *most* ~]
1 a : frequently seen, heard, or experienced ▪ a *familiar* joke/sight ▪ *familiar* surroundings ▪ The essay covers *familiar* ground/territory. ▪ It's a sad but (all too) *familiar* story. ▪ She has become a *familiar* figure in the world of politics. — often + *to* ▪ surroundings that are more *familiar to* us ▪ foods that are already *familiar to* most Americans **b** — used to say that something is easy for you to recognize because you have seen, heard, or experienced it many times in the past ▪ He spotted a *familiar* face in the crowd. ▪ a *familiar* voice **c** : possibly known but not clearly remembered ▪ He looked *familiar* [=he looked like someone I had seen before] but I couldn't remember his name. ▪ Her name is/sounds/seems (vaguely) *familiar*.
2 a : relaxed and informal ▪ She spoke in a *familiar* way about her past. ▪ an essay written in a *familiar* style **b** : appropriate for use with people you know well ▪ a *familiar* way of addressing someone **c** : too friendly ▪ They felt the waiter was being overly *familiar*. — often + *with* ▪ He avoids being overly/too *familiar with* his employees.
familiar with : having some knowledge about (something) ▪ We are *familiar with* the situation. [=we know about the situation] ▪ I'm not very *familiar with* that area.
— fa·mil·iar·ly *adv* ▪ The coach patted him *familiarly* on the back. ▪ Locals refer to the Maple Leaf restaurant *familiarly* [=*informally*] as 'The Leaf.'

fa·mil·iar·i·ty /fəˌmɪliˈerəti/ *noun* [*noncount*]
1 : the state of being familiar with something : the state of having knowledge about something — usually + *with* ▪ His *familiarity with* local issues helped him during the campaign. ▪ The job requires *familiarity with* current software. ✧ The expression ***familiarity breeds contempt*** means that knowing a lot about someone or something can cause you to like that person or thing less.
2 : a friendly and informal way of acting or talking ▪ He spoke to everyone with the easy/relaxed *familiarity* of an old friend.

fa·mil·iar·ize *also Brit* **fa·mil·iar·ise** /fəˈmɪljəˌraɪz/ *verb* **-iz·es; -ized; -iz·ing** [+ *obj*] : to give (someone) knowledge about something : to make (someone) familiar *with* something ▪ The visit was meant to *familiarize* [=*acquaint*] students *with* the library. ▪ I've been slowly *familiarizing* myself *with* the neighborhood.
— fa·mil·iar·i·za·tion *also Brit* **fa·mil·iar·i·sa·tion** /fəˌmɪljərəˈzeɪʃən, *Brit* fəˌmɪljəˌraɪˈzeɪʃən/ *noun* [*noncount*]

[1]fam·i·ly /ˈfæmli/ *noun, pl* **-lies**
1 a : a group of people who are related to each other ✧ This sense of *family* can refer to a group that consists of parents and their children or it can refer to a bigger group of related people including grandparents, aunts, uncles, cousins, etc. It is often used specifically of a group of related people who live together in one house. [*count*] There were a lot of *families* at the circus. ▪ a close/close-knit *family* ▪ The show is fun for the whole/entire *family*. ▪ the royal *family* ▪ a single-parent *family* ▪ a death in the *family* ▪ There are several doctors on his mother's side of the *family*. ▪ She wants to spend more time with her *family*. ▪ my sister and other members of my ***immediate family*** [=the group that includes my parents, my brothers and sisters, and me] ▪ After his father's death he became the ***head of the family***. ▪ She's a ***friend of the family***. ▪ a ***two-family house/dwelling*** [=a house that has separate areas for two families to live in] [*noncount*] He spent a quiet evening at home with *family*. ▪ trying to find a balance between work and *family* ▪ She was surrounded by friends and *family*. [=family members] ▪ He has *family* in California. [=he has relatives who live in California] ✧ To be treated ***like one of the family*** or ***like family*** is to be treated in a very warm and kind way, like a member of someone's family. ▪ They treat their guests *like family*. ✧ You can informally describe someone as a member of your family by saying that he or she ***is family***. ▪ You're always welcome here because *you're family*. ▪ My brother has a lot of faults, but we forgive him because *he's family*. ✧ If something ***runs in the family*** or ***runs in someone's family***, it occurs in all or many members of a family. ▪ Musical talent *runs in her family*. [=many or all of the people in her family have musical talent] — see also EXTENDED FAMILY, NUCLEAR FAMILY **b** [*count*] : a person's children ▪ He's devoted to his wife and *family*. ▪ My sister and her husband want to have a big/large *family*. [=to have many children] ▪ They want to ***raise a family***. [=to have children] ▪ They want to ***start a family*** [=to begin having children] soon. **c** [*count*] : a group of related people including people who lived in the past ▪ My *family* came to America from Italy. ▪ Their *family* has lived here for many generations.

> ***usage*** In U.S. English, *family* is used with a singular verb. ▪ His *family* has always supported him. In British English, *family* can also be used with a plural verb. ▪ His *family* have always supported him.

2 [*count*] : a group of people who resemble a family in some way ▪ We like to think that the people who work here are all one big, happy *family*.
3 [*count*] : a group of things that are alike in some way ▪ a *family* of languages/instruments
4 [*count*] : a group of related plants or animals ▪ Peaches, apples, and roses belong to one *family*. ▪ a plant that belongs to the cabbage *family* ▪ Despite their large size, crows are members of the songbird *family*.
5 [*count*] : a group of criminals who work together in an organized way ▪ the suspected head of a crime *family*

[2]family *adj, always used before a noun*
1 : of or relating to a family ▪ *family* members ▪ a *family* picnic ▪ the *family* business/car ▪ He enjoys ***family life*** [=he enjoys spending time with his wife and children] ▪ an old ***family friend*** [=*friend of the family*]
2 : designed or suitable for both children and adults ▪ a *family* restaurant ▪ *family* entertainment ▪ *family* [=*wholesome*] values
the family jewels see JEWEL

family doctor *noun, pl* ~ **-tors** [*count*] : a doctor who treats the members of a family : a doctor who provides general medical care for people of all ages — called also *family practitioner*

family leave *noun* [*noncount*] : a period of time when an employee has permission to be away from a job in order to deal with family matters (such as caring for a baby or a sick family member)

family man *noun, pl* ~ **men** [*count*] : a man who has a wife and children; *especially* : a man who enjoys spending a lot of time with his wife and children

family name *noun, pl* ~ **names** [*count*] : the name shared by the people in a family : SURNAME ▪ Her *family name* is Smith.

family planning *noun* [*noncount*] : the use of birth control to determine the number of children there will be in a family and when those children will be born

family practice *noun* [*noncount*] : the work of providing general medical care for people of all ages ▪ She plans to enter *family practice* when she graduates from med school. — called also *family medicine*

family practitioner *noun, pl* ~ **-ers** [*count*] : FAMILY DOCTOR

family room *noun, pl* ~ **rooms** [*count*]
1 *US* : a large, informal room in a family's house that is designed as a place for children and parents to spend time playing and relaxing
2 *Brit* : a room in a pub in which children are allowed

family tree *noun, pl* ~ **trees** [*count*] : a drawing or chart that shows how the different members of a family are related to each other ▪ A framed *family tree* hung on the wall.

fam·ine /ˈfæmən/ *noun, pl* **-ines** : a situation in which many people do not have enough food to eat [*count*] The *famine* affected half the continent. [*noncount*] millions killed by war, drought, and *famine*

fam·ished /ˈfæmɪʃt/ *adj* [*more* ~; *most* ~] *informal* : very hungry ▪ What's for supper? I'm *famished*.

fa·mous /ˈfeɪməs/ *adj* [*more* ~; *most* ~] : known or recognized by very many people : having fame ▪ an internationally *famous* hotel ▪ a *famous* entertainer/explorer/athlete/politician — often + *for* or *as* ▪ The hotel is (justly) *famous for* its luxury. ▪ The hotel is *famous as* the place where the treaty was signed. — see also WORLD-FAMOUS

fa·mous·ly /ˈfeɪməsli/ *adv*
1 : in a way that is known by many people : in a famous manner ▪ The executive *famously* insisted on riding the bus to work every day. ▪ the team's *famously* passionate fans [=fans who are famous for being passionate]
2 ✧ People who ***get on/along famously*** like each other and

family

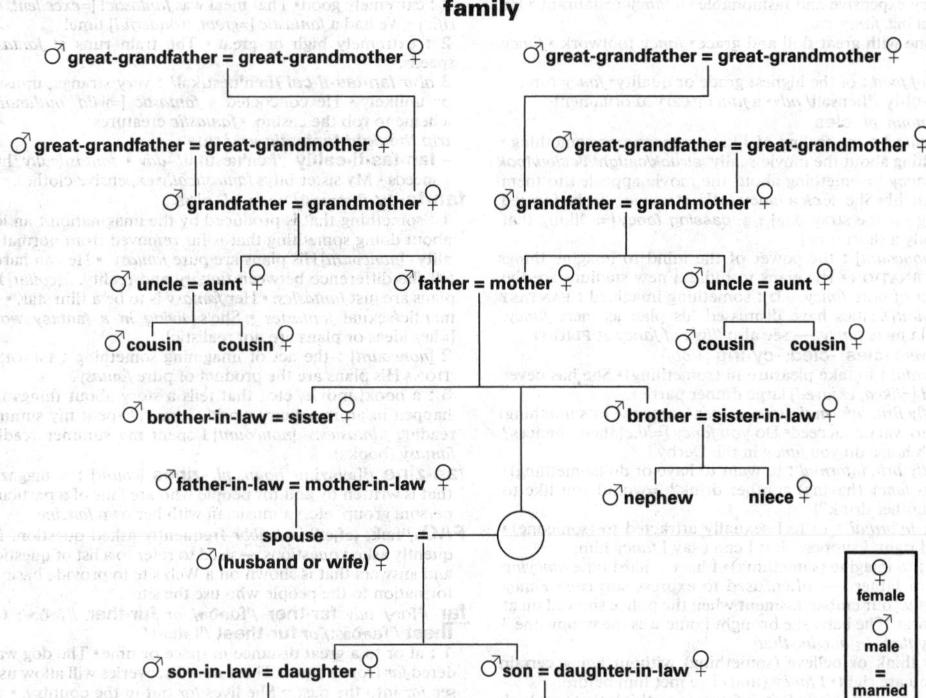

enjoy each other's company very much. • They've always *gotten along famously* (together).

[1]fan /ˈfæn/ *noun, pl* **fans** [*count*] **:** a machine or device that is used to move the air and make people or things cooler: such as **a :** a flat device that is held in your hand and waved back and forth in front of your face **b :** an electrical machine that has turning blades • The engine was cooled by an electric *fan*. — see picture at CAR

hit the fan *informal* **:** to cause a lot of anger and trouble — used especially to describe what happens when people find out about something that makes them very angry • I don't want to be there when it *hits the fan*. — often used in the impolite phrase ***when the shit hits the fan***

— compare [3]FAN

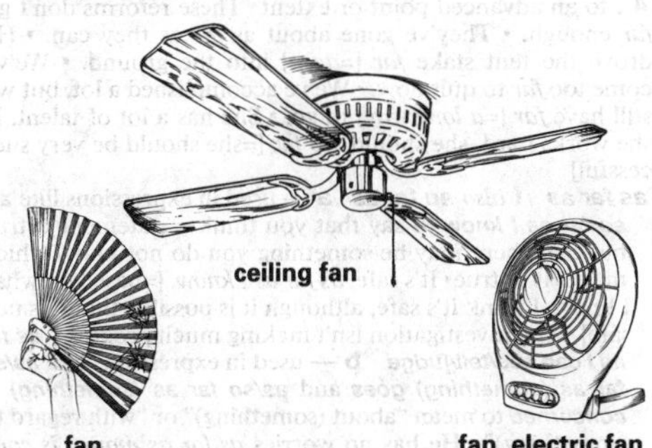
ceiling fan

fan

fan, electric fan

[2]fan *verb* **fans; fanned; fan·ning**

1 [+ *obj*] **:** to move air on or toward (someone or something) with a fan • He *fanned* himself with a newspaper while he waited for the bus. ✧ To *fan a fire* is literally to blow air onto a fire so that it will burn more strongly. In figurative use the phrase ***fan the fires/flames*** means to make an emotional situation more dangerous, so that people become angrier and more likely to act in a violent way. • They are *fanning the flames* of hate. • The rebels did all they could to *fan the fires* of revolution. [=to encourage revolution]

2 *baseball, informal* **:** to strike out [+ *obj*] The pitcher has *fanned* six batters in the first three innings. [*no obj*] The batter *fanned* on a curveball.

fan out [*phrasal verb*] ***fan out or fan out (something) or fan (something) out*** **:** to spread apart or to cause (something) to spread apart • The police *fanned out* across the park in search of the suspect. • He *fanned out* his fingers.

[3]fan *noun, pl* **fans** [*count*] **:** a person who likes and admires someone (such as a famous person) or something (such as a sport or a sports team) in a very enthusiastic way • I am a huge baseball *fan*. • sports *fans* • He's her biggest/greatest *fan*. • He is not a *fan* of insurance companies. [=he doesn't like insurance companies] — compare [1]FAN

fa·nat·ic /fəˈnætɪk/ *noun, pl* **-ics** [*count*]

1 : a person who is very enthusiastic about something • I became a boating *fanatic*.

2 *disapproving* **:** someone who has extreme ideas about politics, religion, etc. • a religious *fanatic* [=*extremist*]

— fanatic *or* **fa·nat·i·cal** /fəˈnætɪkəl/ *adj* [*more* ~; *most* ~] • a *fanatic* supporter • *fanatical* zeal/devotion/loyalty — often + ***about*** • She's *fanatical about* her job. • He is *fanatical about* boating. **— fa·nat·i·cal·ly** /fəˈnætɪkli/ *adv* • She was *fanatically* devoted to her job. **— fa·nat·i·cism** /fəˈnætəˌsɪzəm/ *noun* [*noncount*] • religious *fanaticism*

fan belt *noun, pl* **~ belts** [*count*] **:** a band of material (such as rubber) that moves to provide power to the fan that cools the engine in a car

fan·ci·er /ˈfænsijɚ/ *noun, pl* **-ers** [*count*] **:** a person who likes something or has an interest in something • a cat *fancier* [=a person who fancies/likes cats] • a wine *fancier*

fan·ci·ful /ˈfænsɪfəl/ *adj* [*more* ~; *most* ~]

1 : coming from the imagination • a *fanciful* tale of a monster in the woods

2 : showing imagination **:** unusual and appealing • They gave all their children *fanciful* names. • *fanciful* architecture

— fan·ci·ful·ly /ˈfænsɪfli/ *adv* • *fancifully* [=*imaginatively*] named children

fan club *noun, pl* **~ clubs** [*count*] **:** an organization for people who admire a famous person, group, etc. • members of the singer's *fan club*

[1]fan·cy /ˈfænsi/ *adj* **fan·ci·er; -est**

1 : not plain or ordinary • a *fancy* dress • a *fancy* hairdo • *fancy* decorations

F

2 : very expensive and fashionable ▪ a *fancy* restaurant ▪ He drives a big, *fancy* car.
3 : done with great skill and grace ▪ *fancy* footwork ▪ *fancy* diving
4 *US, of food* **:** of the highest grade or quality ▪ *fancy* tuna
– fan·ci·ly /ˈfænsəli/ *adv* ▪ a *fancily* carved ornament

²fancy *noun, pl* **-cies**
1 [*singular*] **:** the feeling of liking someone or something ▪ Something about the movie really ***struck/caught/tickled/took their fancy*** [=something about the movie appealed to them very much] ▪ She ***took a fancy to*** the stray dog. [=she formed a liking for the stray dog] ▪ a ***passing fancy*** [=a liking that lasts only a short time]
2 a [*noncount*] **:** the power of the mind to imagine things **:** IMAGINATION ▪ His plans to build a new stadium are the product of pure *fancy*. **b :** something imagined **:** FANTASY [*noncount*] Critics have dismissed his plan as mere *fancy*. [*count*] a mere *fancy* — see also *flight of fancy* at FLIGHT

F

³fancy *verb* **-cies; -cied; -cy·ing** [+ *obj*]
1 *informal* **:** to take pleasure in (something) ▪ She has never *fancied* [=*liked, enjoyed*] large dinner parties.
2 *chiefly Brit, informal* **:** to consider (someone or something) likely to win or succeed ▪ Do you *fancy* [=*like*] their chances? ▪ Which horse do you *fancy* in the Derby?
3 *chiefly Brit, informal* **:** to want to have or do (something) ▪ Do you *fancy* (having) another drink? [=would you like to have another drink?]
4 *Brit, informal* **:** to feel sexually attracted to (someone) ▪ He's all right, I suppose, but I can't say I *fancy* him.
5 *Brit* **:** to imagine (something) ▪ I have a hard time *fancying* you as a father. — often used to express surprise ▪ *Fancy* [=*imagine*] our embarrassment when the police showed up at the door. ▪ "The baby she brought home was the wrong one." "***Fancy that***" [=*imagine that*]
6 : to think or believe (something) without being certain that you are right ▪ I *fancy* (that) I've met him before.
fancy yourself *chiefly Brit, informal* **:** to think that you look good or that you are very special or important ▪ They really *fancy themselves* after only one hit song! ▪ I never thought I'd *fancy myself* in a kilt.

fancy dress *noun* [*noncount*] *chiefly Brit* **:** special clothes that you wear to a party where people are dressed to look like famous people, characters, etc. ▪ Everyone wore *fancy dress* for the ball. ▪ a *fancy-dress* ball/party [=a costume ball/party]

fan·cy–free /ˌfænsiˈfriː/ *adj* **:** having no responsibilities **:** not held back by ties to other people — usually used in the phrase ***footloose and fancy-free*** ▪ He felt *footloose and fancy-free* after he left college.

fan·dan·go /fænˈdæŋgoʊ/ *noun, pl* **-gos** [*count*] **:** a fast Spanish dance

fan·fare /ˈfænˌfeɚ/ *noun, pl* **-fares**
1 [*noncount*] **:** a lot of talk or activity showing that people are excited about something ▪ The new jet was introduced with great *fanfare*.
2 [*count*] **:** a short piece of music played loudly with trumpets especially to announce that someone is arriving

fang /ˈfæŋ/ *noun, pl* **fangs** [*count*] **:** a long, sharp tooth ▪ the *fangs* of a rattlesnake ▪ a tiger baring/showing its *fangs*
– fanged /ˈfæŋd/ *adj* ▪ a *fanged* monster [=a monster that has fangs]

fan letter *noun, pl* ~ **-ters** [*count*] **:** a letter sent to a famous person by a fan ▪ She sent a *fan letter* to her favorite star.

fan light *noun, pl* ~ **lights** [*count*]
1 *US* **:** a window in the shape of a half circle that is placed over a door or another window
2 *Brit* **:** TRANSOM 2

fan mail *noun* [*noncount*] **:** letters that are sent to a famous person by fans **:** fan letters ▪ The band gets a lot of *fan mail*.

fan·ny /ˈfæni/ *noun, pl* **-nies** [*count*] *informal*
1 *US* **:** the part of the body that you sit on **:** BUTTOCKS ▪ I'd like to give him a good kick in the *fanny*!
2 *Brit, offensive* **:** a woman's sexual organs

fanny pack *noun, pl* ~ **packs** [*count*] *US* **:** a small bag for carrying things that is worn with a strap which goes around a person's waist

fan·ta·size *also Brit* **fan·ta·sise** /ˈfæntəˌsaɪz/ *verb* **-siz·es; -sized; -siz·ing :** to imagine doing things that you are very unlikely to do **:** to have fantasies [*no obj*] — often + *about* ▪ He *fantasized about* quitting his job and becoming a painter. [+ *obj*] She *fantasized* that she had won a million dollars.

fan·tas·tic /fænˈtæstɪk/ *adj* [*more* ~; *most* ~]
1 : extremely good ▪ That meal was *fantastic*! [=*excellent, terrific*] ▪ We had a *fantastic* [=*great, wonderful*] time!
2 : extremely high or great ▪ The train runs at *fantastic* speeds.
3 *also* **fan·tas·ti·cal** /fænˈtæstɪkəl/ **:** very strange, unusual, or unlikely ▪ He concocted a *fantastic* [=*wild, outlandish*] scheme to rob the casino. ▪ *fantastic* creatures
trip the light fantastic see ²TRIP
– fan·tas·ti·cal·ly /fænˈtæstɪkli/ *adv* ▪ *fantastically* high speeds ▪ My sister buys *fantastically* expensive clothes.

fan·ta·sy /ˈfæntəsi/ *noun, pl* **-sies**
1 : something that is produced by the imagination **:** an idea about doing something that is far removed from normal reality [*noncount*] His plans are pure *fantasy*. ▪ He can hardly tell the difference between *fantasy* and reality. [*count*] His plans are just *fantasies*. ▪ Her *fantasy* is to be a film star. ▪ romantic/sexual *fantasies* ▪ She's ***living in a fantasy world*** [=her ideas or plans are not realistic]
2 [*noncount*] **:** the act of imagining something **:** IMAGINATION ▪ His plans are the product of pure *fantasy*.
3 : a book, movie, etc., that tells a story about things that happen in an imaginary world [*count*] I spent my summer reading *fantasies*. [*noncount*] I spent my summer reading *fantasy* (books).

fan·zine /ˈfænˌziːn/ *noun, pl* **-zines** [*count*] **:** a magazine that is written by and for people who are fans of a particular person, group, etc. ▪ a musician with her own *fanzine*

FAQ /ˈfæk, ˌɛfˌeɪˈkjuː/ *abbr* frequently asked question, frequently asked questions — used to refer to a list of questions and answers that is shown on a Web site to provide basic information to the people who use the site

¹far /ˈfɑɚ/ *adv* **far·ther** /ˈfɑɚðɚ/ *or* **fur·ther** /ˈfɚðɚ/; **far·thest** /ˈfɑɚðəst/ *or* **fur·thest** /ˈfɚðəst/
1 : at or to a great distance in space or time ▪ The dog wandered *far* from home. ▪ These new discoveries will allow us to see *far* into the past. ▪ She lives *far* out in the country. ▪ the *far* distant future ▪ The house is set *far* back from the road. ▪ The deadline is not *far* off/away. ▪ regions *far* to the north ▪ a town not *far* from Chicago ▪ "Where's the park?" "It's not *far* (from here)." ▪ He still lives not *far* from where he was born. ▪ She doesn't like being so *far* (away) from home.
2 : to a great extent ▪ It's *far* [=*much, a lot*] easier to deal with these problems now. ▪ a *far* better choice ▪ The car is *far* too expensive. ▪ The two sides are still *far* apart. [=a long way apart] ▪ His policies are *far* different from those of his predecessor. ▪ People are now living *far* longer. ▪ "It is a *far, far* better thing that I do than I have ever done . . . " —Charles Dickens, *A Tale of Two Cities* (1859)
3 : to or at a particular distance, point, or degree ▪ Those birds aren't usually seen this *far* north. ▪ They have offices as *far* west as Ohio. ▪ People come to this museum from as *far* away as California. ▪ The word was used as *far* back as the 17th century. ▪ The hills extend ***as far as the eye can see***
4 : to an advanced point or extent ▪ These reforms don't go *far* enough. ▪ They've gone about as *far* as they can. ▪ He drove the tent stake *far* [=*deep*] into the ground. ▪ We've come too *far* to quit now. ▪ We've accomplished a lot, but we still have *far* [=*a long way*] to go. ▪ She has a lot of talent. If she works hard, she should ***go far***. [=she should be very successful]
as far as **1** *also* ***so far as*** **a** — used in expressions like ***as/so far as I know*** to say that you think a statement is true but that there may be something you do not know which makes it untrue ▪ It's safe, *as far as I know*. [=based on what I know, I think it's safe, although it is possible that it is not safe] ▪ The investigation isn't making much progress, ***as far as I can see/tell/judge*** **b** — used in expressions like ***as/so far as (something) goes*** and ***as/so far as (something) is concerned*** to mean "about (something)" or "with regard to (something)" ▪ He has no worries *as far as money is concerned*. [=he has no worries about money] ▪ *As far as the weather is concerned*, we've been having nothing but rain for the past week. **c** — used in expressions like ***as/so far as (someone) is concerned*** to mean "in someone's opinion" ▪ *As far as I'm concerned* [=in my opinion], everything he says is a lie. ▪ *As far as she's concerned*, he's perfect. **2** *informal* **:** with regard to (something or someone) ▪ He's here. *As far as* [=*as for*] the others, they'll arrive later. [=the others will arrive later]
by far **:** by a great extent or degree ▪ Frank was *by far* the best runner. = Frank was the best runner *by far*.
far and away **:** by a great extent or degree **:** by far ▪ The col-

lege is *far and away* the best one in the area. ▪ Frank was *far and away* the best runner.

far and wide **1 :** in every direction ▪ We searched *far and wide* [=*everywhere*] for the lost cat. **:** in many different places **:** very widely ▪ He's known *far and wide* for his skill as a cook. **2 :** distant places ▪ People came ***from far and wide*** to attend the fair.

far be it from me **:** it would not be correct or appropriate for me — followed by *to + verb* ▪ *Far be it from me to tell* you how to do your job. [=I should not tell you how to do your job] — often used when you are about to give advice or criticism and you know that you have no real right to say what you are going to say ▪ *Far be it from me to interfere,* but I don't know why you keep dating that guy.

far from **:** certainly not **:** not at all ▪ The trip was *far from* a failure. [=the trip was not a failure at all] ▪ He was *far from* (being) friendly. [=he was not at all friendly] ▪ It is *far from* certain that the strike will be settled soon. ▪ The investigation is *far from* complete. ▪ She argues that the new law, *far from* being an aid to small businesses, will actually hurt them. ▪ "Was the movie disappointing?" "*Far from* it! We had a great time!"

far gone *informal* **:** in a very bad, weak, or confused condition because of being sick, tired, drunk, etc. ▪ He had been drinking for a couple of hours, so he was pretty *far gone* by then. ▪ She was too *far gone* to understand what we were asking her.

far off **:** very wrong **:** very far from being correct ▪ He was not *far off* in his predictions.

few and far between see [1]FEW

from far and near *or* ***from near and far*** **:** from distant places and from near places **:** from many different places ▪ people came *from far and near*

how far **1 :** to what extent or degree ▪ She didn't know *how far* to trust him. [=she didn't know how much she could trust him] **2** — used to ask about the distance between places ▪ *How far* is it (from here) to the station, please?

in so far as see INSOFAR AS

so far **1 :** until the present time **:** to this point ▪ He has written only two books *so far.* ✧ The phrase ***so far, so good*** is used to say that something (such as a project or an activity) has proceeded well or without problems until now. ▪ "How's the work on your house going?" "There's a lot more to do, but *so far, so good.*" **2 :** to a certain point, degree, or distance ▪ Intelligence will only take you *so far* without effort. [=intelligence by itself is not enough for success; effort is also needed]

so far as see AS FAR AS 1 (above)

thus far **:** until the present time **:** so far ▪ *Thus far* the results have been disappointing.

[2]**far** *adj, always used before a noun* **farther** *or* **further; farthest** *or* **furthest**

1 : very distant in space or time ▪ the *far* corners of the world ▪ the *far* horizon ▪ the *far* reaches of outer space ▪ the *far* past

2 — used to refer to the side, end, etc., that is more distant ▪ There is a fishing camp on the *far* side of the lake, but nothing on the near side. ▪ the *far* bank of the river ▪ a table at the *far* end of the room

a far cry from see [2]CRY

the far left **:** the group of people whose political views are the most liberal ▪ His nomination is opposed by members of *the far left.*

the far right **:** the group of people whose political views are the most conservative ▪ His nomination is opposed by members of *the far right.*

far·away /ˈfɑrəˌweɪ/ *adj* **:** very distant ▪ My grandfather told us tales of *faraway* lands. ✧ If you have a ***faraway look*** in your eyes, you are not paying attention to what is happening around you; you appear to be thinking about something that is far away. ▪ Don't bother talking to her when she gets that *faraway look* in her eyes.

farce /ˈfɑɚs/ *noun, pl* **farc·es**

1 a [*count*] **:** a funny play or movie about ridiculous situations and events **b** [*noncount*] **:** the style of humor that occurs in a farce ▪ an actor with a talent for *farce*

2 [*count*] *disapproving* **:** something that is so bad that it is seen as ridiculous ▪ This trial is a *farce.* [=*travesty*] ▪ The election turned out to be a complete/utter *farce.* [=*fiasco*]

– far·ci·cal /ˈfɑɚsɪkəl/ *adj* [*more* ~; *most* ~] ▪ a *farcical* [=*ludicrous, ridiculous*] situation

[1]**fare** /ˈfeɚ/ *verb* **fares; fared; far·ing** [*no obj*] **:** to do something well or badly ▪ How did you *fare* [=*do*] on your exam? ▪ The team hasn't *fared* [=*done*] well in recent weeks.

[2]**fare** *noun, pl* **fares**

1 [*count*] **:** the money a person pays to travel on a bus, train, boat, or airplane or in a taxi ▪ I need some coins for the bus *fare.* — see also AIRFARE, CARFARE

2 [*count*] **:** a passenger who pays a fare ▪ The taxi driver picked up his *fares* at the airport.

3 [*noncount*] **:** a specified kind of food ▪ Less expensive *fare* is available at the restaurant across the street. — sometimes used figuratively to refer to things shown on television, in movies, etc. ▪ Many parents dislike the violent *fare* [=the violent programs/material] on television.

Far East *noun*

the Far East **:** the countries of eastern and southeastern Asia (such as China, Japan, North Korea, South Korea, and Vietnam) — compare MIDDLE EAST, NEAR EAST

[1]**fare·well** /feɚˈwɛl/ *interj, formal + literary* **:** [1]GOODBYE ▪ *Farewell,* good friend, until we meet again.

[2]**farewell** *noun, pl* **-wells** [*count*] *formal + literary*

1 : something that you say to a person who is leaving **:** GOODBYE ▪ She bid/wished me *farewell.* ▪ They said their *farewells* and headed home. ▪ a fond *farewell*

2 : an act of leaving ▪ I will take my *farewell* of this place tomorrow. [=I will leave this place tomorrow]

[3]**farewell** /ˈfeɚˌwɛl/ *adj, always used before a noun* **:** done when someone is leaving, ending a career, etc. ▪ The band gave a *farewell* concert. ▪ a *farewell* party/speech/performance

[4]**farewell** /feɚˈwɛl/ *verb* **-wells; -welled; -well·ing** [*+ obj*] *chiefly Australia + New Zealand* **:** to bid farewell to (someone who is leaving) ▪ The retiring teacher was *farewelled* by the whole school at a special assembly.

far–fetched /ˈfɑɚˈfɛʧt/ *adj* [*more* ~; *most* ~] **:** not likely to happen or be true ▪ The movie features a *far-fetched* plot to kidnap the President.

far–flung /ˈfɑɚˈflʌŋ/ *adj* [*more* ~; *most* ~]

1 : covering a very large area ▪ a *far-flung* [=*vast*] media empire

2 : located in a very distant place ▪ a *far-flung* trading post in the Arctic

[1]**farm** /ˈfɑɚm/ *noun, pl* **farms** [*count*]

1 : a piece of land used for growing crops or raising animals ▪ She grew up on a dairy *farm.* ▪ Running a *farm* is hard work. ▪ a vegetable *farm*

2 : an area of water where fish, oysters, etc., are raised ▪ a fish *farm* ▪ an oyster *farm*

buy the farm see [1]BUY

[2]**farm** *verb* **farms; farmed; farm·ing :** to use land for growing food or raising animals [*+ obj*] My uncle has been *farming* this land for 60 years. ▪ *farm* 200 acres [*no obj*] My uncle has been *farming* on this land for 60 years.

farm out [*phrasal verb*] ***farm (something) out*** *or* ***farm out (something)*** **:** to send out (work) to be done by others ▪ The company decided to *farm out* the job of upgrading their Web site.

farm·er /ˈfɑɚmɚ/ *noun, pl* **-ers** [*count*] **:** a person who runs a farm ▪ My uncle has been a *farmer* for 60 years. ▪ hog *farmers* ▪ a cotton *farmer*

farm·hand /ˈfɑɚmˌhænd/ *noun, pl* **-hands** [*count*] **:** a person who is hired to work on a farm

farm·house /ˈfɑɚmˌhaʊs/ *noun, pl* **-hous·es** [*count*] **:** a house on a farm

farming *noun* [*noncount*] **:** the job or business of running a farm

farm·land /ˈfɑɚmˌlænd/ *noun* [*noncount*] **:** land used or suitable for farming ▪ 50 acres of rich *farmland*

farm·stead /ˈfɑɚmˌstɛd/ *noun, pl* **-steads** [*count*] **:** a farm with its buildings

farm team *noun, pl* ~ **teams** [*count*] *baseball* **:** a minor-league baseball team that is associated with a major-league team

farm·yard /ˈfɑɚmˌjɑɚd/ *noun, pl* **-yards** [*count*] **:** BARNYARD

far–off /ˈfɑɚˌɑːf/ *adj* **:** very far away in time or space ▪ tales of *far-off* lands ▪ Some *far-off* day you will thank me.

far–out /ˈfɑɚˌaʊt/ *adj* [*more* ~; *most* ~] *informal* **:** very strange or unusual ▪ My sister wears some pretty *far-out* clothes.

far–reach·ing /ˈfɑɚˌriːʧɪŋ/ *adj* [*more* ~; *most* ~] **:** affecting many people or things **:** having a wide range or influence ▪ The court issued a *far-reaching* decision. ▪ The theory has *far-reaching* implications for the future of the planet.

far·sight·ed /ˈfɑɚˌsaɪtəd/ *adj* [*more ~; most ~*]
1 *chiefly US* **:** able to see things that are far away more clearly than things that are near ▪ He wears glasses because he is *farsighted.* [=(*Brit*) *longsighted*] — compare NEARSIGHTED
2 a : able to predict what will or might happen in the future ▪ plans made by *farsighted* city leaders **b :** made or done while thinking about what will happen in the future ▪ *farsighted* investments ▪ a *farsighted* plan/approach — opposite SHORTSIGHTED
– **far·sight·ed·ly** *adv* – **far·sight·ed·ness** *noun* [*noncount*] ▪ She had her eyes tested for *farsightedness.* ▪ the *farsightedness* of city leaders

[1]fart /ˈfɑɚt/ *verb* **farts; fart·ed; fart·ing** [*no obj*] *informal + impolite* **:** to release gas from the anus
fart around *informal + impolite* **:** to waste time **:** to spend time doing activities that have no serious purpose ▪ Quit *farting around* [=*messing around, fooling around*] and finish your work!

[2]fart *noun, pl* **farts** [*count*] *informal + impolite*
1 : a release of gas from the anus
2 : an annoying or unpleasant person ▪ a cranky old *fart*

[1]far·ther /ˈfɑɚðɚ/ *adv* **:** to or at or to a more distant place or time or a more advanced point **:** FURTHER ▪ drive *farther* north ▪ It's *farther* away than I'd thought. ▪ I tried to read the book, but I got no *farther* [=*further*] than the first chapter. ▪ You think I don't like you? ***Nothing could be farther from the truth.*** [=it is completely untrue that I don't like you; I like you very much]

[2]farther *adj, always used before a noun* **:** more distant **:** FURTHER ▪ the *farther* side of town

[1]far·thest /ˈfɑɚðəst/ *adv*
1 : to or at the greatest distance in space or time **:** FURTHEST ▪ He chose the seat *farthest* from the door. ▪ We had a contest to see who could hit a golf ball the *farthest.*
2 : to the most advanced point **:** FURTHEST ▪ This plan goes *farthest* toward achieving our goal.
3 *chiefly US* **:** by the greatest degree or extent **:** MOST, FURTHEST ▪ Of all the paintings, this one is the *farthest* removed from reality.

[2]farthest *adj, always used before a noun* **:** most distant in space or time **:** FURTHEST ▪ the *farthest* frontier ▪ the *farthest* reaches of space — often used figuratively ▪ Food is the *farthest* thing from my mind right now. [=I am not thinking about food at all]

far·thing /ˈfɑɚðɪŋ/ *noun, pl* **-things** [*count*] **:** a former British coin that had a value equal to ¼ of a penny

fas·cia /ˈfeɪʃijə/ *noun, pl* **-cias** [*count*]
1 *technical* **:** a long, thin board that covers the area where a wall joins a roof — called also *fascia board*
2 /ˈfæʃijə/ *medical* **:** a sheet of tissue that covers or connects parts inside the body (such as muscles)
3 *also* **fa·cia** /ˈfeɪʃə/ *Brit* **:** DASHBOARD

fas·ci·nate /ˈfæsəˌneɪt/ *verb* **-nates; -nat·ed; -nat·ing :** to cause (someone) to be very interested in something or someone [+ *obj*] His strange behavior *fascinated* the children. = He *fascinated* the children with his strange behavior. ▪ Her paintings *fascinate* me. = I'm *fascinated* by/with her paintings. ▪ a question that *fascinates* both biologists and anthropologists [*no obj*] Her paintings never fail to *fascinate.*
– **fas·ci·na·tion** /ˌfæsəˈneɪʃən/ *noun* [*noncount*] the children's growing *fascination* with his strange behavior [=their increasing strong interest in his behavior] ▪ I've studied her paintings with *fascination.* [=a strong desire to look at and think about them] [*singular*] Her paintings have/hold a real *fascination* for me. [=they interest me deeply]

fas·ci·nat·ing /ˈfæsəˌneɪtɪŋ/ *adj* [*more ~; most ~*] **:** very interesting or appealing ▪ a *fascinating* book ▪ Her paintings are *fascinating.* ▪ It's *fascinating* (to watch) how a child's language skills develop.
– **fas·ci·nat·ing·ly** *adv*

fas·cism /ˈfæˌʃɪzəm/ *noun* [*noncount*]
1 *or* ***Fas·cism*** **:** a way of organizing a society in which a government ruled by a dictator controls the lives of the people and in which people are not allowed to disagree with the government ▪ the rise of *Fascism* in Europe before World War II
2 : very harsh control or authority ▪ corporate *fascism*
– **fas·cist** *or* **Fas·cist** /ˈfæʃɪst/ *noun, pl* **-cists** [*count*] ▪ notorious *fascists* – **fascist** *or* **Fascist** *adj* ▪ a *Fascist* state
– **fas·cist·ic** *or* **Fas·cist·ic** /fæˈʃɪstɪk/ *adj* [*more ~; most ~*] ▪ a *fascistic* organization

[1]fash·ion /ˈfæʃən/ *noun, pl* **-ions**
1 a : a popular way of dressing during a particular time or among a particular group of people [*count*] Jewelry and clothing *fashions* vary with the season. [*noncount*] Long, full skirts were (all/very much) the *fashion* in those days. ▪ *fashion*-conscious shoppers [=shoppers who know what styles are popular] ▪ Short skirts are currently ***in fashion.*** [=are currently popular] ▪ Short skirts have come back ***into fashion.*** ▪ Those ruffled blouses went ***out of fashion*** years ago. **b** [*noncount*] **:** the business of creating and selling clothes in new styles ▪ the world of *fashion* — often used before another noun ▪ the *fashion* industry ▪ She reads all the *fashion* magazines. [=magazines about the newest fashions] ▪ We attended a ***fashion show.*** [=a show at which people who design clothes show their new designs] — see also HIGH FASHION **c *fashions*** [*plural*] **:** clothes that are popular ▪ She always wears the latest *fashions.*
2 : a style, way of behaving, etc., that is popular in a particular time and place [*count*] Literary *fashions* have changed in recent years. [*noncount*] Action movies are (all) the *fashion* in Hollywood these days. = Action movies are ***in fashion*** in Hollywood these days. ▪ Her theories have fallen/gone ***out of fashion.*** [=are no longer popular]
3 : a specified way of acting or behaving — usually used after *in* [*singular*] His friends noticed that he was behaving *in* a strange *fashion.* [=behaving strangely] ▪ We started the meeting *in* an orderly *fashion.* [*noncount*] We all lined up *in* orderly *fashion.*
after a fashion **:** to a slight or minor degree **:** SOMEWHAT ▪ I can play the piano *after a fashion,* but I can't play anything difficult.

[2]fashion *verb* **-ions; -ioned; -ion·ing** [+ *obj*] **:** to form (something) into something else ▪ Students *fashioned* the clay into small figures. **:** to make (something) from something else ▪ figures *fashioned* [=*formed*] from clay ▪ She used the scraps of fabric to *fashion* a little doll's dress. ▪ a table *fashioned* out of an old door

fash·ion·able /ˈfæʃənəbəl/ *adj* [*more ~; most ~*]
1 : currently popular ▪ *fashionable* clothes [=clothes that are popular; clothes that are in fashion] ▪ She wore a sleek black dress and *fashionable* [=*stylish*] shoes. ▪ *fashionable* cars ▪ a *fashionable* café ▪ It isn't *fashionable* to express such an opinion these days.
2 : dressing and acting in a way that is currently popular ▪ *fashionable* people who know all the right restaurants
– **fash·ion·ably** /ˈfæʃənəbli/ *adv* ▪ She was *fashionably* dressed, as usual. ▪ He arrived at the party *fashionably* late. [=he arrived at the party slightly late, which is the fashionable thing to do]

fash·ion·is·ta /ˌfæʃəˈni:stə/ *noun, pl* **-tas** [*count*] *informal* **:** a person who designs, sells, or is very interested in clothing fashions

fashion plate *noun, pl* **~ plates** [*count*] **:** a person who dresses in the current fashions **:** a fashionable person ✧ The term *fashion plate* is often used in a disapproving way to describe someone who cares too much about fashion.

[1]fast /ˈfæst, *Brit* ˈfɑ:st/ *adj* **fast·er; -est**
1 [*more ~; most ~*] **a :** moving or able to move quickly ▪ She's a very *fast* runner. ▪ a *fast* car ▪ a *fast* pitch ▪ maintaining a *fast* [=*quick*] pace ▪ blazingly/blindingly *fast* **b :** happening quickly **:** taking a short amount of time ▪ a *fast* race ▪ We're off to a *fast* start. ▪ We're now experiencing a *faster* rate of inflation. ▪ I'd like to take a *fast* [=(more commonly) *quick*] look at my records. **c :** operating quickly ▪ a *fast* computer **d :** doing something or able to do something quickly ▪ a *fast* learner **e :** allowing movement at a great speed ▪ a *fast* road ▪ We took the *faster* route. — see also FAST LANE, FAST TRACK
2 *of a clock or watch* **:** showing a time that is later than the correct time ▪ My watch is (ten minutes) *fast.*
3 *photography* **:** allowing photographs to be taken very quickly or when there is very little light ▪ *fast* film
4 *informal* **a :** tricky and unfair ▪ Be careful that he doesn't ***pull a fast one*** *on* you. [=that he doesn't trick or deceive you] **b :** earned or gotten quickly and often in a dishonest way ▪ She's always looking to make a *fast* buck. ▪ *fast* money **c :** quick and not safe to trust ▪ He gave us a lot of *fast* talk about how he was going to solve all our problems. — see also FAST-TALK
5 *old-fashioned + humorous* **a :** actively seeking excitement or pleasure **:** WILD ▪ He runs with a pretty *fast* crowd. ▪ *fast* living **b** *of women* **:** very willing to have sex ▪ a typical West-

ern filled with outlaws, gamblers, and *fast* women
6 a : placed, tied, or attached in a way that is not easily moved • Make the rope *fast* [=tie the rope securely] to the anchor. **b :** closed tightly • Make sure the door is *fast*. [=(more commonly) *shut fast*] **c :** impossible to change — used in the phrase ***hard and fast*** • There are no *hard and fast* rules to be followed when you plan a vacation. [=there are many ways to plan a vacation] **d :** not likely to fade • *fast* colors
7 : very loyal or faithful • They became ***fast friends.***
fast and furious **:** in a very fast and forceful way : with one thing following another very quickly ✧ The phrase *fast and furious* is used both as an adjective and as an adverb. • The action was *fast and furious*. • The questions were coming at me *fast and furious*. • The jokes were flying *fast and furious*.
play fast and loose see [1]PLAY

[2]fast *adv* **faster; -est**
1 : with great speed • The boss expects this to be done this afternoon, so you'd better work *fast*. • You're driving too *fast*! • He ran as *fast* as he could. • a *fast*-paced story **:** in a very short time : very quickly • This is *fast* becoming a national problem. • You need to act *fast* to take advantage of this offer. • species that are *fast* disappearing = species that are disappearing *fast* • I don't know what caused the accident. It all happened so *fast*. — opposite SLOW, SLOWLY
2 a : in a quick and intelligent way • She's a woman who can think *fast* in a crisis. • You catch on *fast*. **b :** quickly and in a way that is meant to deceive or persuade someone • He's going to have to talk *fast* to get himself out of this mess. — see also FAST-TALK
3 : in a way that is not easily moved or changed • The window was stuck *fast*. • She held *fast* to her belief in justice. • We must stand *fast* and not surrender!
fast and furious see [1]FAST
fast asleep see ASLEEP
going/getting nowhere fast *informal* ✧ To be *going/getting nowhere fast* is to be failing to make progress or to produce a desired result. • The plan for a new stadium is *going nowhere fast*.
not so fast *informal* — used in speech to say that you disagree with what someone has said or to tell someone to stop or slow down • "This proves they're wrong." "*Not so fast*. There's other evidence to consider." • "The discussion is closed." "*Not so fast*. I have a few more things to say."

[3]fast *verb* **fasts; fast·ed; fast·ing** [*no obj*] **:** to eat no food for a period of time • She always *fasts* on Yom Kippur. • Patients must *fast* for six hours before having the procedure.
– fasting *noun* [*noncount*] • periods of *fasting* • a time of *fasting* and prayer

[4]fast *noun, pl* **fasts** [*count*] **:** a period of time when you do not eat any food : a time of fasting • He went on a *fast* [=he ate nothing] for several days. • We broke our *fast* just after sunset. • observing a ***fast day*** [=a day on which people do not eat any food because of their religion]

fast·ball /ˈfæstˌbɑːl, *Brit* ˈfɑːstˌbɔːl/ *noun, pl* **-balls** [*count*] *baseball* **:** a pitch that is thrown at full speed : a very fast pitch • He struck him out with a *fastball*.

fast break *noun, pl* **~ breaks** [*count*] *basketball* **:** a quick movement toward the net in an attempt to score before the opposing players can reach their defensive positions

fas·ten /ˈfæsn̩, *Brit* ˈfɑːsn̩/ *verb* **fas·tens; fas·tened; fas·ten·ing**
1 a [+ *obj*] **:** to attach (something) or join (two things or two parts of something) especially by using a pin, nail, etc. • *fastening* clothes on/onto a clothesline • He *fastened* the dog's leash to a post and went into the store. • two boards *fastened* together by/with nails • a decorative clasp that could be used to *fasten* a cape or cloak **b** [*no obj*] *of parts of something* **:** to become attached or joined • a shoe that *fastens* with a buckle • This dress *fastens* in the back.
2 a [+ *obj*] **:** to put something in a position or location in such a way that it will not move • *Fasten* your seat belt. • She twisted her hair into a bun and *fastened* it with bobby pins. • Make sure the lid is tightly *fastened*. **b :** to close and lock (something, such as a window or door) [+ *obj*] Make sure that the doors and windows are all (securely) *fastened*. [*no obj*] The lock was so damaged it wouldn't *fasten*.
3 : to grip and hold something with (your hand, teeth, etc.) [+ *obj*] He *fastened* his hands on/around my arm and wouldn't let go. • The dog *fastened* its teeth on my sleeve. [*no obj*] His hands *fastened* on/around my arm.
fasten on [*phrasal verb*] ***fasten (something) on (something) or fasten on (something)*** **:** to direct (something, such as your eyes or attention) to (something) • They *fastened* their eyes *on* the distant ship. [=they looked at it steadily] • She *fastened* her attention *on* the problem. [=she gave all her attention to the problem] • They had *fastened* the blame *on* the wrong man. [=they had blamed the wrong man] • She *fastened* [=*pinned*] (all) her hopes *on* getting the job.
fasten onto [*phrasal verb*] ***fasten onto (something)*** **:** to grip and tightly hold (something) • The stranger *fastened onto* my arm and wouldn't let go. — often used figuratively • Once he *fastens onto* a subject he just won't let it drop.
– fas·ten·er /ˈfæsnɚ, *Brit* ˈfɑːsnə/ *noun, pl* **-ers** [*count*] • windows held shut by rusty *fasteners*

fas·ten·ing /ˈfæsn̩ɪŋ, *Brit* ˈfɑːsn̩ɪŋ/ *noun, pl* **-ings** [*count*] **:** something that fastens one thing to another thing • a coat with button and loop *fastenings*

fast food *noun, pl* **~ foods :** food that is prepared and served quickly : food from a restaurant that makes and serves food very quickly [*noncount*] They eat a lot of *fast food*. [*count*] Most *fast foods* are high in calories.
– fast–food *adj, always used before a noun* • a *fast-food* restaurant

[1]fast–for·ward /ˌfæstˈforwɚd, *Brit* ˌfɑːstˈfɔːwəd/ *noun* [*noncount*]
1 : a function that causes a recording (such as a videotape) to go forward at a speed that is faster than normal • Hit the *fast-forward* button. — opposite [2]REWIND
2 : a state in which something is quickly developing or progressing • Taking those classes put her career in *fast-forward*.

[2]fast–forward *verb* **-wards; -ward·ed; -ward·ing**
1 [+ *obj*] **:** to cause (a recording) to go forward at a speed that is faster than normal • We *fast-forwarded* the tape to get to the last song. — opposite [1]REWIND
2 [*no obj*] **:** to move forward through time quickly • He wished he could *fast-forward* to the future, when he would no longer be a student.

fas·tid·i·ous /fæˈstɪdijəs/ *adj* [*more ~; most ~*]
1 : very careful about how you do something • He is *fastidious* about keeping the house clean. • a *fastidious* dresser/scholar
2 : liking few things : hard to please • a *fastidious* eater/diner
3 : wanting to always be clean, neat, etc. • She was too *fastidious* to do anything that might get her dirty.
– fas·tid·i·ous·ly *adv* • a *fastidiously* researched book • *fastidiously* dressed **– fas·tid·i·ous·ness** *noun* [*noncount*] • She's known for her *fastidiousness* as a scholar.

fast lane *noun, pl* **~ lanes**
1 [*count*] **:** a section of a highway for cars that are traveling at high speeds • I pulled into the *fast lane* to pass the truck.
2 [*singular*] **:** a way of living that makes you very busy or that is full of excitement and often danger — usually used in the phrase ***life in the fast lane*** • He likes to live *life in the fast lane*, going from one wild party to the next.

fast·ness /ˈfæstnəs, *Brit* ˈfɑːstnəs/ *noun, pl* **-ness·es** [*count*] *literary* **:** a place that is difficult to get to or that can be easily defended if it is attacked • a remote mountain *fastness* [=*stronghold, fortress*]

fast–talk /ˈfæstˌtɑːk, *Brit* ˈfɑːstˌtɔːk/ *verb* **-talks; -talked; -talk·ing** [+ *obj*] *informal* **:** to influence or persuade (someone) by talking quickly in a confident and often dishonest way • The salesperson *fast-talked* him into buying the car for more than it was worth. • He *fast-talked* the old woman out of a large piece of her property. — see also [1]FAST 4c
– fast–talk·er *noun, pl* **-ers** [*count*] **– fast–talking** *adj* • a *fast-talking* salesperson

fast track *noun* [*singular*] **:** a process or way of proceeding that produces a desired result quickly • The proposed law is ***on a fast track*** to/for approval. [=it is being given special treatment so that it will be approved quickly] • She hoped that her college degree would put her ***on the fast track*** to success in the business world. [=would make it possible for her to succeed quickly in the business world]
– fast–track /ˈfæstˌtræk, *Brit* ˈfɑːstˌtræk/ *verb* **-tracks; -tracked; -track·ing** [+ *obj*] • The proposed new law *is* being *fast-tracked* for approval. **– fast–track** *adj, always used before a noun* • *fast-track* approval • *fast-track* careers

[1]fat /ˈfæt/ *adj* **fat·ter; fat·test**
1 : having a lot of extra flesh on your body : having a lot of body fat • The dog is getting *fat* because you feed him too much. • a cute, *fat* baby • I can't believe I've let myself get so *fat*. • a movie that has a lot of ***fat jokes*** [=jokes about fat people] ✧ *Fat* can be an insulting word when it is used to de-

scribe a person. ▪ She called him a big, *fat* slob. ▪ She's gotten really *fat*. [=(more politely) *big, heavy*] — opposite [1]THIN

2 : having a full, rounded form ▪ a *fat* belly ▪ a *fat*, juicy peach ✧ A ***fat lip*** is a lip that is swollen because of injury, especially from being punched. ▪ He threatened to give me a *fat lip*. [=he threatened to punch me]

3 : unusually wide or thick ▪ a *fat* book of poems ▪ a *fat* envelope ▪ a truck with *fat* tires

4 *informal* **:** containing, providing, or costing a large amount of money ▪ a *fat* bank account ▪ He signed a *fat* contract. ▪ The company offered her a *fat* salary. ▪ a *fat* check [=a check for a large amount of money] ▪ He had to pay a *fat* [=*big*] fine.

5 *informal + disapproving* **:** successful or wealthy ▪ The company grew *fat* on profits during the war.

6 *baseball* **:** easy to hit ▪ a *fat* pitch right down the middle of the plate

big fat — used for emphasis ▪ That's a *big fat* lie! ▪ Come here and give me a *big fat* kiss. ▪ He came home with a *big fat* F [=a failing grade] on his report card.

fat chance see [1]CHANCE

it ain't over until/till the fat lady sings see LADY

– fat·ness *noun* [*noncount*] ▪ body *fatness*

[2]fat *noun, pl* **fats**

1 [*noncount*] **:** the soft flesh on the bodies of people and animals that helps keep the body warm and is used to store energy ▪ people with excess body *fat* ▪ a diet and exercise program to help you gain muscle and lose *fat* ▪ exercises that ***burn fat*** = ***fat-burning*** exercises [=exercises that make your body use the fat it has stored] — see also BABY FAT

2 : an oily solid or liquid substance in food [*noncount*] Nuts contain a lot of *fat*. ▪ milk/bacon *fat* ▪ Trim the *fat* from the meat before you cook it. ▪ foods that are high in *fat* = foods with a high *fat* content ▪ reducing dietary *fat* ▪ a diet low in *fat* [=a low-fat diet] [*count*] a diet low in *fats* ▪ saturated *fats* ▪ *fats* like butter and olive oil — see also DEEP FAT

3 [*noncount*] **:** an amount that is more than what is usual or needed **:** EXCESS ▪ trim the *fat* off/from the budget

chew the fat see [1]CHEW

live off/on the fat of the land ✧ To *live off/on the fat of the land* is to live very well, enjoying the best things that are available without having to work hard to get those things. ▪ They retired several years ago and have been *living on the fat of the land* ever since.

fa·tal /ˈfeɪtl̩/ *adj* [*more* ~; *most* ~]

1 : causing death ▪ a *fatal* accident ▪ a disease that is often *fatal* ▪ a *fatal* blow ▪ a chemical that can be *fatal* to birds

synonyms see [1]DEADLY

2 : causing ruin or failure ▪ She made a *fatal* mistake/error. ▪ The plan contained a *fatal* flaw. [=a flaw that would cause it to fail] ▪ a *fatal* weakness

– fa·tal·ly *adv* ▪ *fatally* shot/wounded

fa·tal·ism /ˈfeɪtəˌlɪzəm/ *noun* [*noncount*] **:** the belief that what will happen has already been decided and cannot be changed ▪ Many people seem to have developed a sense of *fatalism* about the war.

– fa·tal·ist /ˈfeɪtəlɪst/ *noun, pl* **-ists** [*count*] ▪ He's a *fatalist* about the future. **– fa·tal·is·tic** /ˌfeɪtəˈlɪstɪk/ *adj* [*more* ~; *most* ~] ▪ a *fatalistic* attitude/philosophy **– fa·tal·is·ti·cal·ly** /ˌfeɪtəˈlɪstɪkli/ *adv*

fa·tal·i·ty /feɪˈtæləti/ *noun, pl* **-ties**

1 [*count*] **:** a death that results from a disaster, accident, etc. ▪ The car crash caused one *fatality* and several serious injuries. ▪ war *fatalities*

2 [*noncount*] **:** a tendency to result in death ▪ a disease with a high ***fatality rate*** [=a disease that frequently causes death]

fat cat *noun, pl* ~ **cats** [*count*] *informal + disapproving* **:** an important, wealthy, or powerful person ▪ The best seats in the theater were reserved for the *fat cats*. ▪ political *fat cats*

– fat–cat *adj, always used before a noun* ▪ *fat-cat* business executives

fat city *noun* [*noncount*] *US slang* **:** a very comfortable condition or situation in life ▪ He thinks he's going to win the lottery, and then he'll be in *fat city*.

fate /ˈfeɪt/ *noun, pl* **fates**

1 [*noncount*] **:** a power that is believed to control what happens in the future ▪ They thought they would never see each other again, but *fate* brought them back together. ▪ a surprising turn/twist/quirk of *fate*

2 [*count*] **:** the things that will happen to a person or thing **:** the future that someone or something will have ▪ The boy disappeared, and his *fate* was unknown [=no one knew what happened to him] for many years. ▪ Exile was his *fate*. = It was his *fate* to be exiled. [=he was exiled] ▪ The two companies suffered a common *fate*. [=the same thing happened to both companies] ▪ One company went bankrupt, and a similar *fate* befell the other. ▪ her sad/unhappy/tragic *fate* ▪ Congress will decide the bill's *fate* tomorrow. [=will vote to accept or reject the bill tomorrow] ▪ Her ***fate was sealed*** by the marriage arrangement made in her youth. ▪ She regarded poverty as ***a fate worse than death***. [=as worse than dying] ▪ Like his father, he ***met his fate*** [=he died] on the battlefield.

synonyms see DESTINY

tempt fate see TEMPT

fat·ed /ˈfeɪtəd/ *adj* **:** certain to do or be something ▪ The two of them seemed *fated* [=*destined*] for each other. ▪ He felt he was *fated* to be famous.; *especially* **:** certain to die or suffer in a particular way ▪ a kingdom *fated* [=*doomed*] to collapse ▪ a character *fated* to die young — see also ILL-FATED

fat farm *noun, pl* ~ **farms** [*count*] *chiefly US, informal* **:** a place where people go to lose weight by eating a special diet, exercising, etc.

fate·ful /ˈfeɪtfəl/ *adj* **:** having important results ▪ She made the *fateful* [=*momentous*] decision to go back home to face her mother. ▪ His life changed on that *fateful* November evening. **:** producing a serious and usually bad result ▪ Hundreds perished on that *fateful* day. ▪ Her campaign took a *fateful* turn.

– fate·ful·ly *adv*

fat–free *adj* **:** containing no fat ▪ The cereal is *fat-free*. ▪ *fat-free* milk

fat·head /ˈfætˌhɛd/ *noun, pl* **-heads** [*count*] *informal* **:** a stupid person ▪ Don't be such a *fathead*!

– fat·head·ed /ˈfætˈhɛdəd/ *adj* [*more* ~; *most* ~] ▪ a *fatheaded* [=*stupid*] idea/person **– fat·head·ed·ness** *noun* [*noncount*]

[1]fa·ther /ˈfɑːðɚ/ *noun, pl* **-thers** [*count*]

1 : a male parent ▪ He became a *father* when he was 30. ▪ He's the *father* of three small children. ▪ He has been like a *father* to me. ▪ the foal's *father* ▪ He's a ***single father***. [=a father who does not have a wife or partner] ✧ The expression ***like father, like son*** means that a son is like his father in character, behavior, etc. ▪ "He's very stubborn." "Well, *like father, like son*." [=his father is also stubborn] — see also BIRTH FATHER, GRANDFATHER, STEPFATHER

2 : a man who is thought of as being like a father ▪ He was a *father* to me after my own father died.

3 ***Father*** **:** GOD 1 ▪ heavenly *Father* — see also OUR FATHER

4 *formal* **:** a person who was in someone's family in past times **:** ANCESTOR, FOREFATHER — usually plural ▪ She inherited the land on which her *fathers* toiled. ▪ the faith of his *fathers*

5 : a man who invents or begins something — usually singular ▪ the *father* of modern science ▪ George Washington is the *father* of our country. — see also FOUNDING FATHER

6 *old-fashioned* **:** an older man who is one of the leaders of a city, town, etc. — usually plural ▪ Will the city *fathers* agree to it?

7 : a priest especially in the Roman Catholic Church or the Orthodox Church — used especially as a title or as a form of address ▪ *Father* Fitzgerald ▪ Good morning, *Father*. — see also HOLY FATHER

– fa·ther·hood /ˈfɑːðɚˌhʊd/ *noun* [*noncount*] ▪ a young man who didn't yet seem ready for *fatherhood* **– fa·ther·less** /ˈfɑːðɚləs/ *adj* ▪ a *fatherless* child

[2]father *verb* **-thers; -thered; -ther·ing** [+ *obj*]

1 : to become the father of (a child) **:** to make a woman pregnant so that she gives birth to (a child) ▪ He *fathered* three children.

2 *of a man* **:** to invent, create, or produce (something) ▪ He was praised for *fathering* a plan to improve the city's schools.

Father Christmas *noun* [*singular*] *Brit* **:** SANTA CLAUS

father figure *noun, pl* ~ **-ures** [*count*] **:** an older man who is respected and admired like a father ▪ The coach was a stern, wise *father figure* to his players.

fa·ther–in–law /ˈfɑːðɚənˌlɑː/ *noun, pl* **fa·thers–in–law** /ˈfɑːðɚzənˌlɑː/ [*count*] **:** the father of your husband or wife

fa·ther·land /ˈfɑːðɚˌlænd/ *noun, pl* **-lands** [*count*] **:** the country where you were born or where your family came from — usually singular ▪ He fought to protect his *fatherland*. — often used with *the* ▪ Her grandmother told them stories of *the fatherland*. ✧ *Fatherland* can refer to any country, but it is often associated especially with Germany. — compare MOTHERLAND

fa·ther·ly /ˈfɑːðɚli/ *adj* [*more* ~; *most* ~] : of a father • *fatherly* [=*paternal*] responsibilities : resembling a father • a *fatherly* old man : showing the affection or concern of a father • *fatherly* advice • He took a *fatherly* interest in the careers of younger writers.

Father's Day *noun, pl* ~ **Days** [*count, noncount*] : the third Sunday in June treated as a special day for honoring fathers

¹fath·om /ˈfæðəm/ *noun, pl* **-oms** [*count*] : a unit of length equal to six feet (about 1.8 meters) used especially for measuring the depth of water • The water here is five *fathoms* deep.

²fathom *verb* **-oms; -omed; -om·ing** [+ *obj*] : to understand the reason for (something) • I couldn't *fathom* why she made such a foolish decision. = I couldn't *fathom* her reasons for making such a foolish decision. • (*Brit*) I couldn't **fathom out** her reasons. — see also UNFATHOMABLE

¹fa·tigue /fəˈtiːg/ *noun, pl* **-tigues**
1 [*noncount*] : the state of being very tired : extreme weariness • We were overcome by *fatigue* after the long journey. • The drug's side effects include headache and *fatigue*.
2 ***fatigues*** [*plural*] : the uniform that soldiers wear when they are doing physical work • soldiers wearing combat boots and *fatigues* • army/military *fatigues*
3 [*noncount*] *technical* : the tendency of a material (such as metal) to break after being bent or moved many times • The cracks in the engine were caused by metal *fatigue*.

²fatigue *verb* **-tigues; -tigued; -tigu·ing** [+ *obj*] : to make (someone) tired — usually used as *(be) fatigued* • We *were fatigued* by the long journey.
– **fatigued** *adj* [*more* ~; *most* ~] • He always left work feeling somewhat *fatigued*. [=*tired*] • mentally *fatigued*
– **fatiguing** *adj* [*more* ~; *most* ~] • a very *fatiguing* [=*tiring*] journey • an emotionally *fatiguing* experience

fat·so /ˈfætsoʊ/ *noun, pl* **-soes** [*count*] *informal + offensive* : a fat person

fat·ten /ˈfætn̩/ *verb* **-tens; -tened; -ten·ing** /ˈfætnɪŋ/
1 [+ *obj*] : to make (someone or something) fat • *fatten* (up) pigs for slaughter
2 [*no obj*] : to become fat — usually + *up* • Bears need to *fatten up* for the winter.
– **fattening** *adj* [*more* ~; *most* ~] • Sauces made with cream are very *fattening*. [=they are very likely to make people fat] • I'm trying to avoid *fattening* foods.

¹fat·ty /ˈfæti/ *adj* **fat·ti·er; -est** [*more* ~; *most* ~] : containing fat and especially a large amount of fat • a rather *fatty* steak • *fatty* tissue • I try to avoid *fatty* foods.
– **fat·ti·ness** *noun* [*noncount*]

²fatty *noun, pl* **-ties** [*count*] *informal + offensive* : a fat person

fatty acid *noun, pl* ~ **acids** [*count*] : an acid that is naturally in fats and various oils

Fat Tuesday *noun* [*noncount*] *US* : SHROVE TUESDAY

fa·tu·ity /fəˈtuːwəti, *Brit* fəˈtjuːəti/ *noun, pl* **-it·ies** *formal*
1 [*noncount*] : a foolish or stupid quality : a fatuous quality • the *fatuity* of these policies
2 [*count*] : something foolish or stupid : a fatuous remark • politicians exchanging *fatuities* about the need for campaign reform

fat·u·ous /ˈfætʃuwəs/ *adj* [*more* ~; *most* ~] : foolish or stupid • *fatuous* remarks • *fatuous* notions
– **fat·u·ous·ly** *adv* – **fat·u·ous·ness** *noun* [*noncount*] • the *fatuousness* of the remarks

fau·cet /ˈfɑːsət/ *noun, pl* **-cets** [*count*] *US* : a device that is used to control the flow of water from a pipe • turn on/off the *faucet* [=*tap*] — see pictures at BATHROOM, KITCHEN

¹fault /ˈfɑːlt/ *noun, pl* **faults**
1 [*count*] **a** : a bad quality or part of someone's character : a weakness in character • He loved her despite her many *faults*. [=*failings*] • Lack of courage is his worst *fault*. • In spite of her *faults*, she's a loyal friend. = For all her *faults*, she's a loyal friend. **b** : a problem or bad part that prevents something from being perfect : a flaw or defect • We discussed the book's strengths and *faults*. [=*weaknesses*] • If the book has a *fault*, it's that it's too long.
2 [*noncount*] : responsibility for a problem, mistake, bad situation, etc. • The accident was not her *fault*. [=she did not cause the accident; she should not be blamed for the accident] • It's all my *fault*. [=I am responsible] • It's your own *fault* you missed that bus. • Through no *fault* of his own, he won't be able to attend the meeting.
3 [*count*] *tennis* : a mistake that results in a bad serve • She committed too many *faults* to win the match. — see also DOUBLE FAULT
4 [*count*] *geology* : a break in the Earth's crust • Frequent earthquakes have occurred along the San Andreas *Fault*.
at fault : deserving blame for something bad : RESPONSIBLE • She's not *at fault* for the accident. • It will be difficult to determine who's really *at fault*.
find fault see ¹FIND
to a fault : to a great or excessive degree • generous *to a fault* [=very generous or too generous] • honest *to a fault*
– **fault·less** /ˈfɑːltləs/ *adj* • a *faultless* [=*perfect, flawless*] performance – **fault·less·ly** *adv* • She performed *faultlessly*.
– **fault·less·ness** *noun* [*noncount*]

²fault *verb* **faults; fault·ed; fault·ing** [+ *obj*]
1 : to criticize (something) • One critic *faulted* the book as (being) too long.
2 : to blame or criticize (someone) • The truck driver was *faulted* for the accident. • Many have *faulted* her for not acting sooner. • I can't *fault* him for trying to protect his family.

fault·find·er /ˈfɑːltˌfaɪndɚ/ *noun, pl* **-ers** [*count*] : a person who criticizes someone or something often in a way that is not fair or reasonable • *Faultfinders* were quick to point out inconsistencies in the study. — see also *find fault* at ¹FIND
– **fault·find·ing** /ˈfɑːltˌfaɪndɪŋ/ *noun* [*noncount*] • constant *faultfinding* – **fault·find·ing** *adj* • a *faultfinding* analysis

faulty /ˈfɑːlti/ *adj* **fault·i·er; -est** [*also more* ~; *most* ~] : having a mistake, fault, or weakness : IMPERFECT • a *faulty* argument • a *faulty* design • The report is based on *faulty* [=*inaccurate*] statistics.
– **fault·i·ly** /ˈfɑːltəli/ *adv* • *faultily* designed parts – **fault·i·ness** /ˈfɑːltinəs/ *noun* [*noncount*] • the *faultiness* of the design

faun /ˈfɑːn/ *noun, pl* **fauns** [*count*] : a creature in Roman mythology that is part human and part goat

fau·na /ˈfɑːnə/ *noun, pl* **fau·nas** *also* **fau·nae** /ˈfɑːˌniː/ *biology* : all the animals that live in a particular area, time period, or environment [*noncount*] studying the diverse *fauna* of the island • aquatic *fauna* • prehistoric *fauna* [*count*] studying the *faunas* of different islands — compare FLORA
– **fau·nal** /ˈfɑːnl/ *adj* • *faunal* diversity

faux pas /ˈfoʊˌpɑː/ *noun, pl* **faux pas** /ˈfoʊˌpɑːz/ [*count*] : an embarrassing social mistake • Arriving too early would be a serious/major *faux pas*. • making/committing a *faux pas*

fa·va bean /ˈfɑːvə-/ *noun, pl* ~ **beans** [*count*] *chiefly US* : a large, flat, pale green seed that is eaten as a vegetable — called also (*chiefly Brit*) *broad bean*

fave /ˈfeɪv/ *noun, pl* **faves** [*count*] *informal* : FAVORITE 1 • I like all the actors on the show, but he's my *fave*.
– **fave** *adj, always used before a noun* • my *fave* actor

¹fa·vor (*US*) *or Brit* **fa·vour** /ˈfeɪvɚ/ *noun, pl* **-vors**
1 [*count*] : a kind or helpful act that you do for someone • do/grant a friend a *favor* = do a *favor* for a friend = grant a *favor* to a friend • Can I ask you (for) a *favor*? • I drove her to the airport because I owed her a *favor*. • She's willing to help you but only as a *favor* to me. • I'm here as a (special) *favor* to my sister. • Don't do me any *favors*. I don't need your help. • I've learned to be grateful for small *favors*. • He treats them well, and they ***return the favor***. [=they also treat him well] • ***Do me a favor*** [=do what I want you to do; do what you should do] and get home on time for once. • You can ***do yourself a favor*** [=you can make things easier for yourself] by arriving early at the airport. • The company made campaign donations in exchange/return for ***political favors***. [=political acts/decisions that helped the company] • He was arrested for soliciting ***sexual favors*** [=sex acts done in exchange for something, such as money] from a prostitute.
2 [*noncount*] **a** : approval, support, or popularity • Her ideas have found/gained *favor* with many young people. [=many young people like/support her ideas] • He's trying to earn the boss's *favor* by working late. • Her theories have lost *favor*. = Her theories have fallen from *favor*. = Her theories are no longer ***in favor***. = Her theories are now ***out of favor***. [=they are no longer popular] • a style that has come ***into favor*** [=become popular] • The committee ***looks with favor on*** the project. [=the committee regards the project favorably; the committee likes and approves of the project] **b** : preference for one person, group, etc., over another • The judge showed *favor* for/toward the defendant. • The students naturally showed *favor* toward their own school's team.
3 [*count*] *US* : a small gift given to the people who come to a party : PARTY FAVOR • Small boxes of candy were given out as *favors* at the wedding.

court someone's favor or ***court favor with someone*** see ²COURT

curry favor see ²CURRY

in favor of **1 :** wanting or approving of (something) • All *in favor of* (having) a party [=everyone who wants to have a party], raise your hands. • Not surprisingly, most voters are *in favor of* the tax cuts. • a politician who is *in favor of* the death penalty **2 :** in a way that tries to persuade people to support (something) • He argued *in favor of* the tax cuts. [=he argued for the tax cuts] **3 :** choosing (something) instead of something else : preferring (something) • She turned down the scholarship *in favor of* a pro career. • The original proposal was rejected *in favor of* a new design. **4 :** in support of (someone) : in a way that helps or benefits (someone) • The judge ruled *in favor of* the defendant.

in someone's favor **1 :** in support of (someone) : in a way that helps or benefits (someone) • We hope the final decision will be *in our favor*. • The judge ruled *in our favor*. **2 :** in a state of being liked or approved of by (someone) • She did extra work to get back *in the teacher's favor*.

odds are in favor ✧ If the ***odds are in your favor***, you are likely to win or succeed. • We don't know what the decision will be, but we think *the odds are in our favor*. ✧ If ***the odds are in favor of something***, that thing is likely to happen. • *The odds are in favor of* a major storm this weekend.

²**favor** (*US*) *or Brit* **favour** *verb* **-vors; -vored; -vor·ing** [+ *obj*]

1 a : to prefer (someone) especially in an unfair way : to show that you like or approve of (someone) more than others • The teacher clearly *favors* you. • He claims that his parents *favor* his sister (over him). **b :** to approve of or support (something) • Most voters *favor* these tax cuts. • Her father *favored* the idea of her going to law school. **c :** to regard (someone or something) as most likely to succeed or win • They won the championship last year, and most forecasters *favor* them to win again this year.

2 *formal* **:** to give something to (someone) : to present (someone) *with* something • The author *favored* us *with* a copy [=gave us a copy] of his latest book. • She will now *favor* us *with* a song. [=she will now sing or play a song for us] • He did not *favor* us *with* a reply. [=he did not reply to us]

3 : to treat (an injured leg, foot, etc.) gently or carefully • It was obvious that she was *favoring* her left leg. [=she was walking carefully in a way that showed that her left leg was injured]

4 *formal* **:** to make (something) possible or easy : to help (something) to succeed • Darkness *favored* the attack. • The weather *favored* our plans for a picnic.

5 : to look like (a parent or other relative) • He *favors* [=*resembles*] his mother.

fa·vor·able (*US*) *or Brit* **fa·vour·able** /ˈfeɪvərəbəl/ *adj* [*more* ~; *most* ~]

1 a : showing approval • The new play got many *favorable* reviews. • He was given a *favorable* recommendation. **b :** expressing approval : giving or providing what is desired • They gave a *favorable* answer to our request. [=they said they would grant our request] **c :** giving a result that helps, benefits, or shows approval of someone • a *favorable* comparison = a comparison *favorable* to someone

2 : producing feelings of approval • She made a very *favorable* [=*good*] impression on her future colleagues.

3 a : tending to help : tending to produce a desired result • a *favorable* wind • The plants grow rapidly under *favorable* [=*advantageous*] conditions. **b :** showing that a desired result is likely • Early test results were *favorable*.

– fa·vor·ably (*US*) *or Brit* **fa·vour·ably** /ˈfeɪvərəbli/ *adv* • The play was *favorably* reviewed. • I was very *favorably* impressed by the candidate. • They responded *favorably* to our request. • The wine compares *favorably* with some that are far more expensive. • The patient responded *favorably* [=*well*] to the medicine.

fa·vored (*US*) *or Brit* **fa·voured** /ˈfeɪvəd/ *adj* [*more* ~; *most* ~]

1 : given special advantages over others • She enjoys a *favored* position in the company. : preferred over others • a *favored* location

2 : considered most likely to win • The team is heavily *favored* to win the championship.

¹**fa·vor·ite** (*US*) *or Brit* **fa·vour·ite** /ˈfeɪvrət/ *adj, always used before a noun* **:** most liked • Red is my *favorite* color. [=red is the color I like most] • What's your *favorite* movie?

²**favorite** (*US*) *or Brit* **favourite** *noun, pl* **-ites** [*count*]

1 : a person or a thing that is liked more than others : a favorite person or thing • Of all his books, do you have a *favorite*? • She's always been the teacher's *favorite*. [=*pet*] • That movie is my *favorite*. • That movie is a great *favorite* with audiences everywhere.

2 : a person, team, etc., that is considered most likely to win • He's the (heavy/clear) *favorite* in the election. = He's the (heavy/clear) *favorite* to win the election. • She always bets (on) the *favorite* [=bets for the horse that is favored to win] when she goes to the races.

favorite son *noun, pl* ~ **sons** [*count*] **:** a well-known man (such as a political candidate or a celebrity) who is very popular in the area where he lives now or where he lived as a child • an athlete who is one of New York's *favorite sons*

fa·vor·it·ism (*US*) *or Brit* **fa·vour·it·ism** /ˈfeɪvrəˌtɪzəm/ *noun* [*noncount*] **:** the unfair practice of treating some people better than others • He accused the teacher of showing *favoritism* in assigning grades. • political *favoritism*

¹**fawn** /ˈfɑːn/ *verb* **fawns; fawned; fawn·ing** [*no obj*] *disapproving* **:** to try to get the approval of an important or powerful person by giving that person praise, special attention, etc. • a sports star surrounded by *fawning* fans — usually + *over* or *on* • The waiters were *fawning* (all) *over* the celebrity. • She doesn't seem to mind being *fawned on* by her fans.

²**fawn** *noun, pl* **fawns**

1 [*count*] **:** a young deer; *especially* : a deer that is less than a year old

2 [*noncount*] **:** a light brown color : TAN

¹**fax** /ˈfæks/ *noun, pl* **fax·es**

1 a [*noncount*] **:** a system for sending and receiving printed materials (such as documents and drawings) and photographs using telephone lines • She sent me a copy of her report ***by fax*** **b** [*count*] **:** a machine used in this system — called also *fax machine*; see picture at OFFICE

2 [*count*] **:** something (such as a document or a photograph) that is sent or received by fax • She sent me a *fax* of her report. • I received your *faxes*.

²**fax** *verb* **faxes; faxed; fax·ing** [+ *obj*] **:** to send (something, such as a document or photograph) by fax to someone • She *faxed* me a copy of her report. = She *faxed* a copy of her report to me.

faze /ˈfeɪz/ *verb* **faz·es; fazed; faz·ing** [+ *obj*] **:** to cause (someone) to feel afraid or uncertain • Nothing *fazes* [=*daunts*] her. • You'll never succeed as a writer if you let a little bit of criticism *faze* you.

Do not confuse *faze* with *phase*.

FBI *abbr* Federal Bureau of Investigation • The crime is being investigated by the *FBI*. — often used before another noun • an *FBI* agent • an *FBI* laboratory ✧ The Federal Bureau of Investigation is a part of the U.S. federal government that is responsible for investigating crimes.

FCC *abbr* Federal Communications Commission • the chairman of the *FCC* ✧ The Federal Communications Commission is a part of the U.S. federal government that controls radio and television broadcasting.

FDA *abbr* Food and Drug Administration • a new medicine that has not yet been approved by the *FDA* ✧ The Food and Drug Administration is a part of the U.S. federal government that tests, approves, and sets standards for foods, drugs, chemicals, and household products.

FDIC *abbr* Federal Deposit Insurance Corporation • payments made by the *FDIC* ✧ The Federal Deposit Insurance Corporation is a part of the U.S. federal government that provides insurance against loss of money that people have deposited in banks.

fe·al·ty /ˈfiːjəlti/ *noun, pl* **-ties** [*count*] *old-fashioned + literary* **:** loyalty to a person, group, etc. • He swore/pledged *fealty* to the king.

¹**fear** /ˈfiə/ *noun, pl* **fears**

1 : an unpleasant emotion caused by being aware of danger : a feeling of being afraid [*noncount*] He was trembling with *fear*. • an old story that still has the power to inspire *fear* [=to make people feel afraid] • unable to walk the streets without *fear* of being mugged • They regarded their enemies with *fear* and hatred/loathing. • I've been trying to overcome my *fear* of flying. • He won't say anything ***for fear of*** losing his job. [=because he is afraid of losing his job] • She ***lived in fear*** of being caught. = She *lived in fear* that she would be caught. [=she was always afraid that she would be caught] • They *lived in* (constant) *fear* of air raids during the war. • an accident that ***struck fear into the hearts of*** [=frightened] skiers everywhere [*count*] The doctor's diagnosis confirmed our worst *fears*. • The government is trying to allay/alleviate/ease *fears* of a recession. • Employees expressed *fears* that the company would go out of business. • He told us about all his hopes and *fears*. • She has a morbid *fear* of cats. ✧ If you are ***in fear of your life*** or (*US*) ***in fear for your life***, you are afraid of being killed. • She claimed that she shot the burglar because she was *in fear for her life*.

2 [*noncount*] : a feeling of respect and wonder for something very powerful • *fear* of God ✧ To ***put the fear of God into*** someone is to frighten someone very badly. • The bad economic news has *put the fear of God into* investors.

no fear *Brit, informal* — used in speech to say that there is no reason to be afraid or worried • "Are you going to tell her the truth?" "*No fear* [=*never fear, fear not*], mate: she won't hear a thing from me!"

> ***synonyms*** FEAR, DREAD, ALARM, and FRIGHT mean painful emotion felt because of danger. FEAR is the most general word and suggests a continuing emotional state. • people living in *fear* of violent crimes DREAD suggests a strong feeling of not wanting to accept or deal with something bad or unpleasant. • the *dread* felt by people awaiting bad news ALARM may suggest a strong emotion caused by an unexpected or immediate danger. • They view the worsening food shortage with *alarm*. FRIGHT suggests a feeling caused by something unexpected and often suggests a brief emotion. • The creaking door gave them a *fright*.

²fear *verb* **fears; feared; fear·ing**

1 [+ *obj*] : to be afraid of (something or someone) • She *fears* [=(more commonly) *is afraid of*] the water. • He was a cruel king who was *feared* and hated by his subjects. • ". . . the only thing we have to *fear* is fear itself" —Franklin D. Roosevelt, Inaugural Address (1933) — sometimes followed by *to* + *verb* • Many people *feared to go out* at night.

2 [+ *obj*] : to expect or worry about (something bad or unpleasant) • His parents *feared* (that) he would drop out of school. • She went to her doctor, *fearing* (that) she might have cancer. • The questions weren't as difficult as he had *feared* (they might be). • When we heard there had been an accident, we ***feared the worst***. [=we feared that the worst possible thing had happened] ✧ The formal phrase ***I fear*** is used when you are worried that something bad or unpleasant has happened or is true. • *I fear* that we're already too late. • These problems have no easy solution, *I fear*.

3 [*no obj*] : to be afraid and worried • There's no need to *fear*. • Having problems with your computer? ***Never fear*** [=don't worry]—help is readily available. • ***Fear not*** [=don't be afraid]—I'll protect you.

4 [+ *obj*] : to feel respect and wonder for something very powerful • *fear* God

fear for [*phrasal verb*] ***fear for (something or someone)*** : to feel concern for (something or someone) : to worry about (something or someone) • They *feared for* their lives [=they were afraid that they might be killed] as they felt the first trembles of the earthquake. • She *feared for* her husband's safety. [=she worried that her husband might not be safe]

fear·ful /ˈfiəfəl/ *adj* [*more* ~; *most* ~]

1 : feeling fear • He plays the role of a timid and *fearful* clerk. — often + *of* • *fearful* [=*afraid*] *of* danger • He was *fearful of* being left behind. = He was *fearful* that he would be left behind. — sometimes + *for* • She was *fearful for* their safety. [=she was afraid that they were not safe]

2 : showing or caused by fear • a *fearful* glance

3 : very bad or extreme • a *fearful* waste • *fearful* cold • They won the war but at a *fearful* cost.

4 : causing fear • I spent a *fearful* night alone in the woods.

– fear·ful·ly *adv* • *fearfully* cold • She glanced *fearfully* out the window. **– fear·ful·ness** *noun* [*noncount*]

fear·less /ˈfiələs/ *adj* [*more* ~; *most* ~] : not afraid : very brave • a *fearless* warrior

– fear·less·ly *adv* • They ventured *fearlessly* into unknown lands. • The actor strode *fearlessly* across the stage. **– fear·less·ness** *noun* [*noncount*] • *fearlessness* in the face of danger

fear·some /ˈfiəsəm/ *adj* [*more* ~; *most* ~] : causing fear : very frightening • tales of a *fearsome* [=*scary*] monster • a *fearsome* opponent

– fear·some·ly *adv* • growling *fearsomely* • *fearsomely* [=*very, extremely*] ambitious • a *fearsomely* difficult problem **– fear·some·ness** *noun* [*noncount*]

fea·si·ble /ˈfiːzəbəl/ *adj* [*more* ~; *most* ~] : possible to do • This plan for a new town library is not economically *feasible*. [=it costs too much money] • looking for a *feasible* way to create new jobs • a *feasible* goal

– fea·si·bil·i·ty /ˌfiːzəˈbɪləti/ *noun* [*noncount*] • She questions the *feasibility* of the plan. • a ***feasibility study*** [=a study to show if something can be done] **– fea·si·bly** /ˈfiːzəbli/ *adv*

¹feast /ˈfiːst/ *noun, pl* **feasts** [*count*]

1 : a special meal with large amounts of food and drink • give/have the annual Thanksgiving *feast* • Every guest brought a different dish to the party, and we had quite a *feast*. : a large formal dinner • There were hundreds of guests at the royal wedding *feast*. — often used figuratively • a *feast* of colors • The carnival provided a veritable *feast* of sights and sounds. • The garden is ***a feast for the eyes***. [=the garden is very beautiful]

2 : a religious festival • the *feast* of the Nativity • a ***movable feast*** [=a religious festival that is on a different date each year]

²feast *verb* **feasts; feast·ed; feast·ing** [*no obj*] : to eat large amounts of food — usually + *on* • We *feasted on* steak and potatoes.

feast your eyes on : to look at (something or someone) with great pleasure • We *feasted our eyes on* the colors of the autumn landscape.

feat /ˈfiːt/ *noun, pl* **feats** [*count*] : an act or achievement that shows courage, strength, or skill • a performer known for her astonishing acrobatic *feats* • *feats* of strength • an exceptional *feat* of the human intellect • Writing that whole report in one night was quite a *feat*. • It was no mean/small/easy *feat*.

¹feath·er /ˈfɛðɚ/ *noun, pl* **-ers** [*count*] : any one of the light growths that make up the outer covering of the body of a bird • duck *feathers* • tail/wing *feathers* • downy *feathers* • a tuft of *feathers* • a *feather* pillow = a pillow filled with *feathers* • Her suitcase felt ***as light as a feather***. [=extremely light] • When I found out I had won, ***you could have knocked me over with a feather***. [=I was extremely surprised or astonished]

a feather in your cap : an achievement or honor that you can be proud of • The promotion was *a feather in his cap*.

of a feather : of the same kind or nature — usually used in the phrase ***birds of a feather*** • Those two guys are *birds of a feather*. [=they are very much alike] ✧ The expression ***birds of a feather flock together*** means that people who are alike tend to do things together.

ruffle feathers see ¹RUFFLE

– feath·ered /ˈfɛðɚd/ *adj* • She likes to refer to birds as "our *feathered* friends." • a *feathered* hat **– feath·er·less** *adj* • a bird with *featherless* legs

²feather *verb* **-ers; -ered; -er·ing** [+ *obj*] : to put a feather in or on (something) • *feather* an arrow

feather your (own) nest : to make yourself richer in a dishonest or improper way : to do things to increase your own wealth, comfort, etc. • She was accused of *feathering her own nest* with the company's money.

tar and feather see ²TAR

feather bed *noun, pl* ~ **beds** [*count*] : a bed with a mattress that is filled with feathers

feath·er·brained /ˈfɛðɚˌbreɪnd/ *adj* [*more* ~; *most* ~] *informal* : very foolish or silly • a *featherbrained* idea • a *featherbrained* fool

¹feath·er·weight /ˈfɛðɚˌweɪt/ *noun, pl* **-weights** [*count*] : someone or something that weighs very little; *especially* : a boxer who weighs more than 118 pounds (53.5 kilograms) but less than 126 pounds (57 kilograms)

²featherweight *adj, always used before a noun* : weighing very little : very light • a *featherweight* fabric • *featherweight* aircraft

fea·thery /ˈfɛðəri/ *adj* [*more* ~; *most* ~] : extremely light and soft or delicate : like a feather • a plant with *feathery* leaves • a *feathery* brushstroke

¹fea·ture /ˈfiːtʃɚ/ *noun, pl* **-tures** [*count*]

1 : an interesting or important part, quality, ability, etc. • This year's models include several new safety *features*. • This camera has several *features* that make it easy to use. • The car has some interesting new design *features*. • His plan combines the best *features* of the earlier proposals.

2 : a part of the face (such as the eyes, nose, or mouth) • Her eyes are her best *feature*. — usually plural • attractive facial *features* • He has handsome *features*. [=he has a handsome face] • She has striking/delicate/refined *features*.

3 : a movie that is made to be shown in a theater for entertainment : a full-length movie • Tonight's *feature* is a new romantic comedy. • He starred in his first ***feature film*** a year ago. • a ***feature-length*** motion picture [=a movie that is about two hours long] — see also DOUBLE FEATURE

4 : a special story or section in a newspaper or magazine • The paper ran a *feature* on/about urban violence. • a *feature* writer/editor = (*chiefly US*) a *features* writer/editor

– fea·ture·less /ˈfiːtʃɚləs/ *adj* • a *featureless* plain • a *featureless* expanse of rocks and sand

²feature *verb* **-tures; -tured; -tur·ing** [+ *obj*]

1 : to have or include (someone or something) as an important part • The building *features* a state-of-the-art security system. • The new menu *features* several low-fat entrees. • The show now *features* a new singer.

2 : to discuss or mention (something or someone) in a noticeable way **:** to give particular attention to (someone or something important) • The evening news report *featured* the story of the murder. • The newspaper *featured* health care on its front page. — often used as *(be) featured* • She *was featured* in an article on local businesswomen.

feature in [*phrasal verb*] ***feature in (something)*** **:** to be a part of (something) • Health care *features* prominently *in* the new bill. • a character who *features in* many of his novels

– featured *adj* • He'll be appearing as the *featured* speaker [=the main speaker] at the conference. • She had a *featured* role [=an important role] in the movie. • The *featured* software is on sale through next month.

Feb. *abbr* February

fe·brile /ˈfɛˌbrajəl, *Brit* ˈfiːˌbraɪl/ *adj* [*more* ~; *most* ~] *medical* **:** including or caused by fever **:** FEVERISH • a *febrile* illness — often used figuratively • a writer with a *febrile* [=very active] imagination

Feb·ru·ary /ˈfɛbjəˌweri, ˈfɛbrəˌweri/ *noun, pl* **-ar·ies** *or* **-arys :** the second month of the year [*noncount*] in (early/middle/mid-/late) *February* • early/late in *February* • We arrived on *February* the fourth. = (*US*) We arrived on *February* fourth. = We arrived on the fourth of *February*. [*count*] Sales are up (for) this *February* in comparison with the previous two *Februaries*. — abbr. *Feb.*

fe·ces (*US*) *or Brit* **fae·ces** /ˈfiːˌsiːz/ *noun* [*plural*] **:** solid waste that is released from the body **:** EXCREMENT

– fe·cal (*US*) *or Brit* **fae·cal** /ˈfiːkəl/ *adj* • *fecal* matter

feck·less /ˈfɛkləs/ *adj* [*more* ~; *most* ~] **:** having or resulting from a weak character or nature • She can't rely on her *feckless* son. • *feckless* behavior

– feck·less·ness *noun* [*noncount*]

fe·cund /ˈfɛkənd/ *adj* [*more* ~; *most* ~] *formal* **:** producing or able to produce many babies, young animals, or plants **:** FERTILE • *fecund* fields • a *fecund* breed of cattle — sometimes used figuratively • She has a *fecund* [=(more commonly) *fertile*] imagination. • a *fecund* source of ideas

– fe·cun·di·ty /fɪˈkʌndəti/ *noun* [*noncount*]

¹fed *past tense and past participle of* ¹FEED

²fed *or* **Fed** /ˈfɛd/ *noun, pl* **feds** *or* **Feds** [*count*] *US, informal* **:** an official who works for a branch of the U.S. government **:** a federal agent, officer, or official — usually plural • He got into trouble with the *feds*. • was investigated by the *Feds*

the Fed *US, informal* **:** the group of officials (***the Federal Reserve Board***) who control the U.S. government's central banking system (***the Federal Reserve System***). • *The Fed* has decided to cut interest rates.

fed·er·al /ˈfɛdərəl/ *adj*

1 a : of or relating to a form of government in which power is shared between a central government and individual states, provinces, etc. • a *federal* government/system **b :** of or relating to the central government • *federal* laws/funds/employees • a *federal* district • We pay *federal*, state, and local taxes. • The ruling was overturned by a *federal* appeals court.

2 *or* ***Federal*** **:** of, relating to, or loyal to the federal government during the American Civil War • *Federal* soldiers • a *Federal* stronghold — compare CONFEDERATE, UNION

3 ***Federal US*** **:** of or popular during the early years of the U.S. government • the *Federal* period • furniture made in the *Federal* style

– fed·er·al·ly *adv*

Federal *noun, pl* **-als** [*count*] *US*

1 : a supporter of the government of the U.S. in the American Civil War; *especially* **:** a soldier in the federal armies — compare CONFEDERATE

2 *formal* **:** a federal agent or officer — usually plural • Local police sought help from the *federals*. [=(less formally) *feds*]

federal case *noun, pl* **~ cases** [*count*] *US, law* **:** a legal case that will be decided in a U.S. federal court

make a federal case out of *US, informal* **:** to become very upset or angry about (something that is not important) • I agree that he shouldn't have said that, but there's no reason to *make a federal case out of* it. [=*make a big deal about it*] • Do you have to *make a federal case out of* it every time I come home late?

fed·er·al·ist /ˈfɛdərəlɪst/ *noun, pl* **-ists** [*count*]

1 *or* ***Federalist*** **:** a supporter of federal government; *especially, US* **:** a supporter of the U.S. Constitution

2 ***Federalist US*** **:** a member of a major political party in the early years of the U.S. that wanted a strong central government

– fed·er·al·ism *or* **Federalism** /ˈfɛdərəˌlɪzəm/ *noun* [*noncount*] **– federalist** *or* **Federalist** *adj* • the *Federalist* period

fed·er·al·ize *also Brit* **fed·er·al·ise** /ˈfɛdərəˌlaɪz/ *verb* **-izes; -ized; -iz·ing** [+ *obj*] *chiefly US*

1 : to join (states, nations, etc.) together in or under a federal system of government • a *federalized* government

2 : to cause (something) to be under the control of a federal government • The measure *federalizes* several state programs. • newly *federalized* crimes

– fed·er·al·i·za·tion *also Brit* **fed·er·al·i·sa·tion** /ˌfɛdərələˈzeɪʃən, *Brit* ˌfɛdərəˌlaɪˈzeɪʃən/ *noun* [*noncount*]

fed·er·ate /ˈfɛdəˌreɪt/ *verb* **-ates; -at·ed; -at·ing** [+ *obj*] **:** to join (organizations, states, etc.) in a federation • The independent provinces were *federated* to form a nation. • a *federated* state

fed·er·a·tion /ˌfɛdəˈreɪʃən/ *noun, pl* **-tions**

1 [*count*] **a :** a country formed by separate states that have given certain powers to a central government while keeping control over local matters **b :** an organization that is made by loosely joining together smaller organizations • a *federation* of labor unions • a *federation* of women's clubs

2 [*noncount*] **:** the act of joining together separate organizations or states • the *federation* of the states

fe·do·ra /fɪˈdorə/ *noun, pl* **-ras** [*count*] **:** a type of soft hat for men that has a wide brim — see picture at HAT

fed up *adj* [*more* ~; *most* ~] *informal* **:** very tired of something **:** angry about something that has continued for a long time • We've had one delay after another, and I'm starting to feel/get pretty *fed up*. — usually + *with* • I'm *fed up with* all these delays. • Consumers are *fed up with* rising gas prices. — sometimes + *of* in British English • I'm *fed up of* all these delays.

fee /ˈfiː/ *noun, pl* **fees** [*count*]

1 : an amount of money that must be paid • The admission/entrance *fee* is $10. • a credit card with no annual *fee* • The tuition *fees* went up this year. • We returned the library book late and had to pay a ***late fee***. ***synonyms*** see ¹PRICE

2 : an amount that is paid for work done by a doctor, lawyer, etc. • His insurance covers the doctor's *fee*. • They paid a fortune in legal *fees*.

fee·ble /ˈfiːbəl/ *adj* **fee·bler** /ˈfiːbəlɚ/; **-blest** /ˈfiːbələst/ [*also more* ~; *most* ~]

1 : very weak • a *feeble* old man • She's still *feeble* from her long illness. • We heard a *feeble* cry for help. • Business is suffering because of the *feeble* economy. ***synonyms*** see WEAK

2 : not good enough **:** not successful or effective • a *feeble* joke • He made a *feeble* attempt/effort to explain his behavior. • He offered a *feeble* excuse for his behavior. • "Dislike" is too *feeble* a word for how she feels about him.

– fee·ble·ness /ˈfiːbəlnəs/ *noun* [*noncount*] • the *feebleness* of his excuse **– fee·bly** /ˈfiːbli/ *adv* • She smiled *feebly*. • He *feebly* attempted to explain his behavior.

fee·ble·mind·ed /ˌfiːbəlˈmaɪndəd/ *adj* [*more* ~; *most* ~]

1 *often offensive* **:** having less than normal intelligence • a *feebleminded* person

2 : foolish or stupid **:** not sensible • a *feebleminded* approach/solution

– fee·ble·mind·ed·ness *noun* [*noncount*]

¹feed /ˈfiːd/ *verb* **feeds; fed** /ˈfɛd/; **feed·ing**

1 a [+ *obj*] **:** to give food to (someone or something) • Don't *feed* the animals. • He was too weak to *feed* himself. • We *feed* the plants with a special fertilizer twice a week. • We *fed* the horses with/on apples, oats, and hay. **b** [+ *obj*] **:** to give (something) as food to someone or something • They *fed* [=*gave, served*] us breakfast before we left. = They *fed* breakfast to us before we left. • The children *fed* apples to the horses. — sometimes used figuratively • He was *feeding* information to the enemy. [=he was secretly giving information to the enemy] **c** [+ *obj*] **:** to produce or provide food for (someone or something) ▪ These supplies could *feed* a small army for a week. ▪ He doesn't earn enough to *feed* a family of four. ▪ helping to *feed* and clothe poor children **d** [*no obj*] **:** EAT — usually used of animals ▪ We spotted some ducks *feeding* in a nearby pond. ▪ They are studying the *feeding* habits of sharks. ▪ a favorite ***feeding ground*** [=an area where animals feed]

2 [+ *obj*] **a :** to provide what is needed for the continued growth, operation, or existence of (something) ▪ They used the wood to *feed* the fire. ▪ The streams *feed* the creek. ▪ The motor is *fed* by an electrical current. **b :** to supply (material to be used) to a machine ▪ The logs are *fed* into the mill for processing. ▪ She *fed* the data into the computer. ▪ The camera *feeds* the images to a monitor.

3 [+ *obj*] **:** to give support or strength to (something, such as a feeling) ▪ He *fed* their hopes with false promises. ▪ fears *fed* by ignorance ▪ Her early success only served to *feed* her ambition.

4 [+ *obj*] **:** to make (something) move through an opening ▪ The procedure involves *feeding* a tube down the patient's throat. ▪ She *fed* more coins into the slot.

5 [+ *obj*] *sports* **:** to pass a ball or puck to (a team member) especially for a shot at the goal ▪ He *fed* the ball to a teammate for an easy basket.

bite the hand that feeds you see [1]BITE

feed back [*phrasal verb*] ***feed back*** or ***feed back (something)*** or ***feed (something) back*** *Brit* **:** to give helpful information or criticism to someone about a performance, product, etc. **:** to provide feedback — usually + *to* or *into* ▪ My music *feeds back into* my work. ▪ Decide how your staff should *feed back to* you. ▪ Computer users can *feed* their views *back to* the software companies.

feed off [*phrasal verb*] ***feed off (something)*** **:** to gain strength, energy, or support from (something) ▪ She *fed off* the crowd's enthusiasm. ▪ His anger *fed off* his jealousy. ▪ We are able to *feed off* each other's ideas.

feed on/upon [*phrasal verb*] ***feed on/upon (something)*** **:** to eat (something) as food — usually used of animals ▪ Owls *feed on* insects, birds, and small mammals.

feed (someone) a line *informal* **:** to tell (someone) a story or an explanation that is not true ▪ He *fed me a line* about how he was late because his car broke down.

feed up [*phrasal verb*] ***feed (someone) up*** *Brit, informal* **:** to make (someone) stronger or less thin by giving them large meals ▪ His mother *fed him up* after his illness. — see also FED UP

feed your face *slang* **:** to eat a lot of food ▪ He sat there for an hour, just *feeding his face*.

[2]**feed** *noun, pl* **feeds**

1 a [*noncount*] **:** food for animals ▪ cattle *feed* **b** [*count*] *informal* **:** a large meal ▪ a good *feed* **c** [*count*] *Brit* **:** FEEDING ▪ the baby's last *feed*

2 [*count*] **:** a part of a machine or system that sends material or electricity to other parts ▪ There's a jam in the paper *feed*. ▪ We had to cut off the main power *feed*.

3 [*count*] **:** a television program that is sent to a station for broadcasting ▪ They're showing a live satellite *feed* of the event.

4 [*count*] *sports* **:** the action of passing a ball or puck to a team member who is in position to score ▪ He scored off/on a *feed* from the left wing.

– see also CHICKEN FEED

feed·back /ˈfiːdˌbæk/ *noun* [*noncount*]

1 : helpful information or criticism that is given to someone to say what can be done to improve a performance, product, etc. ▪ The company uses customer *feedback* to improve its products. ▪ He asked for some *feedback* from his boss.

2 *technical* **a :** something (such as information or electricity) that is returned to a machine, system, or process ▪ The computer makes adjustments based on *feedback* from the sensors. **b :** an annoying and unwanted sound caused by signals being returned to an electronic sound system ▪ We were getting some *feedback* from the microphone.

feed·bag /ˈfiːdˌbæg/ *noun, pl* **-bags** [*count*] *US* **:** a bag that is used for feeding an animal — called also (*Brit*) *nose bag*

put/tie/strap on the feedbag *US, informal* **:** to begin eating ▪ He's always ready to *strap on the feedbag* when it's time for dinner.

feed·er /ˈfiːdɚ/ *noun, pl* **-ers** [*count*]

1 a : a device for supplying food to animals ▪ a wooden bird *feeder* **b :** a person who supplies food for animals ▪ a pigeon *feeder* holding a bag of stale bread

2 : a road, railway, etc., that connects to a larger road, railway, etc. — often used before another noun ▪ a *feeder* road/route/line

3 : a part that sends materials into a machine or system

4 : a person or thing that eats or feeds in a specified way ▪ a messy *feeder* ▪ a gluttonous *feeder* ▪ plants that are heavy *feeders*; *also* **:** an animal that eats a specified kind of food ▪ This species is a carrion *feeder*. — see also BOTTOM FEEDER

feeding *noun, pl* **-ings** [*count*] *US* **:** the act of giving food to a person (such as a baby) or an animal ▪ When was the baby's last *feeding*? [=(*Brit*) *feed*]

feeding frenzy *noun, pl* **~ -zies** [*count*] **:** a state of wild activity in which the animals in a group are all trying to eat something ▪ sharks in a *feeding frenzy* — often used figuratively ▪ There has been a *feeding frenzy* among publishers to obtain the rights to her story.

[1]**feel** /ˈfiːl/ *verb* **feels; felt** /ˈfɛlt/; **feel·ing**

1 [+ *obj*] **:** to be aware of (something that affects you physically, such as pain, heat, or an object touching your body) ▪ He *felt* a sudden pain in his leg. ▪ I could *feel* the warmth of the sun. ▪ I *felt* someone tap my shoulder. ▪ I could *feel* him pulling my hair. [=I could feel that he was pulling my hair] ▪ Do you *feel* a draft? ▪ I'm the kind of person who really ***feels the heat/cold***. [=hot/cold weather bothers me more than it bothers most people]

2 [*linking verb*] — used to describe or ask about someone's physical or mental state ▪ I *feel* dizzy/faint. ▪ How *are* you *feeling* today? = How do you *feel* today? ▪ I *feel* bad/good/sick/well/fine. ▪ I hope you *feel* better soon. [=I hope you will stop feeling ill soon] ▪ He's been *feeling* a little depressed lately. ▪ You can *feel* proud of what you've accomplished. ▪ I *feel* responsible for the accident. [=I feel that I was responsible for the accident; I feel that the accident was my fault] ▪ I *feel* confident that we'll win. ▪ You may *feel* different tomorrow. [=your mood/thinking may change tomorrow] ▪ She *felt* hurt by their indifference. ▪ I *feel* certain/sure that we can solve these problems. ▪ I *feel* like a fool. = (*chiefly Brit*) I *feel* a fool. ▪ I didn't ***feel like myself*** yesterday. = I didn't ***feel myself*** yesterday. [=I didn't feel well yesterday] ▪ I ***feel as if/though*** I'm falling. = (*informal*) I ***feel like*** I'm falling. ▪ (You can) ***Feel free*** to leave whenever you like. [=you are free to leave whenever you like] ✧ If you ***feel like*** doing something, you want to do it. ▪ Do you *feel like* (taking) a walk? ▪ I *feel like* crying. ▪ "Why won't you come?" "Because I don't *feel like* it." ▪ He does whatever he *feels like* (doing). ▪ I don't *feel like* talking about it. [=I don't want to talk about it]

3 a [+ *obj*] **:** to touch (something) with your fingers to see what it is like ▪ She *felt* the fabric to see if it was wool. **b** [+ *obj*] **:** to find (something) by touching with your fingers ▪ Your ribs are bruised, but I don't *feel* any broken bones. **c** [*no obj*] **:** to search for something by reaching or touching usually with your fingers — often + *for* ▪ The doctor *felt for* any possible fractures in the patient's bruised ribs. ▪ He *felt for* the switch. — often + *around* or (*Brit*) *about* ▪ He *felt around* in the dark for the light switch. ▪ He *felt around* under the table with his foot. **d** *not used in progressive tenses* [*linking verb*] — used to describe the quality that something has when it is touched ▪ This *feels* like wool (to me)—but it may not be. ▪ The silk *feels* smooth (to me).

4 [+ *obj*] **:** to believe or think (something) ▪ He *feels* that they behaved badly. ▪ They *felt* (that) it would be foolish to continue. ▪ I *feel* (that) I really ought to say something. ▪ He *felt* it necessary to say something. = He *felt* that it was necessary to say something.

5 [*no obj*] **:** to have an opinion ▪ How do you *feel* about this proposal? [=what do you think of this proposal; what is your opinion of this proposal?] ▪ Their votes reflect how they *feel* toward poor people. ✧ If you ***feel strongly***, you have a strong or definite opinion about something. ▪ We *feel* (very) *strongly* that they've been treated unfairly. ▪ If you *feel* that *strongly* (about it), we won't go.

6 [+ *obj*] **:** to be aware of (something) in your mind or emotions ▪ He *felt* his son's ingratitude, and he resented it. ▪ She could *feel* [=*sense*] the presence of an intruder in the house. ▪ I *feel* the urge to speak. ▪ I ***feel the need*** to try again. [=I think I/we should try again] ▪ ***I feel your pain***. [=I am aware of how (much) you must have suffered]

7 [+ *obj*] **a :** to experience the effect of (something) ▪ He *felt* the medicine starting to work. ▪ I'm really ***feeling my age*** lately. [=I am feeling the effects of growing older] **b :** to experience (something) ▪ Many people will *feel* the impact of this decision. [=many people will be affected by this decision] ▪ I *felt* pleasure in her company. [=I enjoyed being with her] ▪ He *felt* no remorse for what he had done. ▪ She *feels* con-

F

tempt for her political enemies. **c** : to be hurt by (something) ▪ They *felt* the insult deeply. [=they were deeply hurt by the insult] ▪ She *felt* the loss/death of her mother.

8 *not used in progressive tenses* [*linking verb*] **a** — used to describe the quality that something has or the feeling that something causes ▪ It just doesn't *feel* [=*seem*] right to be doing this. ▪ It *feels* like spring today. ▪ It *feels* strange that I'm here again. = It *feels* strange to be here again. ▪ This place really *feels* like home. ▪ It *feels* as if it's going to rain. = (*chiefly US*) It *feels* like rain. **b** : to have a specified physical quality ▪ My eyes *feel* dry. ▪ His hands *felt* cool.

feel for [*phrasal verb*] ***feel for (someone)*** : to have sympathy or pity for (someone) ▪ I *feel* (deeply) *for* you, but there's nothing I can do to help. — see also [1]FEEL 3c (above)

feel no pain *chiefly US, informal* : to be drunk ▪ He had been at the bar for several hours and he was clearly *feeling no pain*. [=he was very drunk]

feel out [*phrasal verb*] ***feel (someone) out*** : to talk to or question (someone) in an indirect way in order to find out if something you want to do or get will be possible ▪ He tried to *feel* us *out* to see if we'd loan him more money.

feel up [*phrasal verb*] ***feel (someone) up*** or ***feel up (someone)*** *informal* : to touch (someone who does not want to be touched) for sexual pleasure ▪ She says he *felt* her *up*.

feel your best see [3]BEST

feel your oats see OAT

feel your way **1** : to move forward carefully by putting your hands in front of you so that you can feel anything that blocks you ▪ He *felt his way* through the darkened room. **2** : to move toward a goal very slowly and carefully ▪ In the early days of the project they were just *feeling their way* (along), trying not to make mistakes.

[2]**feel** *noun* [*singular*]

1 a : the quality of a thing that is experienced by touching it ▪ It had a greasy *feel*. [=it felt greasy] ▪ the *feel* of old leather **b** : a particular quality ▪ The restaurant's decor has an Asian *feel* (to/about it). ▪ Although the table is brand-new, it has the look and *feel* of an antique.

2 a : an understanding of something ▪ We walked around to get the *feel* of the town. [=to find out what the town was like] — usually + *for* ▪ We walked around to get a *feel for* the town. ▪ After living in France for 20 years, she has a *feel for* the way the French think. ▪ We're trying to get a *feel for* what's needed. **b** : an ability to use something or do something in a skillful way — usually + *for* ▪ He's been practicing for several weeks and he's starting to get a *feel for* the instrument. ▪ She has a *feel for* language.

3 : a feeling or sensation ▪ He liked the *feel* of the sun on his face.

4 *Brit* : an act of feeling or touching something ▪ They had a *feel* of the old leather. [=they felt the old leather]

by feel **1** : by feeling with your hands when you cannot see ▪ It was too dark too see anything, so she had to find the door knob *by feel*. **2** : by being guided by your physical feelings, your senses, etc., instead of by rules or directions ▪ an athlete who plays *by feel*

cop a feel see [2]COP

feel·er /ˈfiːlɚ/ *noun, pl* **-ers** [*count*]

1 : a movable part (such as an antenna) of an animal or insect that is used for touching things

2 : a suggestion or question to find out the thoughts or opinions of other people ▪ I haven't had a definite job offer yet, but I've received a few *feelers*. [=I've been asked if I am interested in a new job] — usually plural ▪ The companies have been ***putting out feelers*** about a merger. [=the companies have been quietly asking about the possibility of a merger]

feel–good /ˈfiːlˌgʊd/ *adj, always used before a noun* : producing good or happy feelings ▪ a *feel-good* movie

feel·ing /ˈfiːlɪŋ/ *noun, pl* **-ings**

1 : an awareness by your body of something in it or on it : SENSATION [*count*] a *feeling* of pain/nausea ▪ I noticed tingling *feelings* in my fingers. ▪ She had a queasy *feeling* in her stomach. ▪ I had the *feeling* of something crawling across my foot. ▪ We enjoyed the *feeling* of walking barefoot in the sand. [*noncount*] He had no *feeling* in his right leg.

2 a : an emotional state or reaction [*count*] *feelings* of joy/sorrow/anger/love ▪ He's been troubled by *feelings* of guilt. ▪ There's no point in trying to hide your *feelings*. ▪ She's always had a kindly *feeling* towards them. = She always had kindly *feelings* towards them. ▪ I hope this decision won't cause any ***bad/ill feelings***. [=cause any feelings of anger, dislike, etc.] ▪ I have a ***good feeling*** about this project. [=I expect this project to go well] ▪ He has ***ambivalent/mixed feelings*** about his new job [=he has both good and bad feelings about his new job] ▪ ***warm feelings*** [=good, pleasant, or friendly feelings] ▪ "I could really use a vacation." "I ***know the feeling***." [=I know how you feel] ▪ The new security patrols gave residents ***a feeling of*** safety. [=the patrols made them feel safe] ▪ *a feeling of* comfort ▪ I didn't mean to insult you—***no hard feelings***, right? [=you're not angry, are you?] ▪ You ***hurt my feelings***. [=you upset me; you made me feel bad] ▪ We pretended to like his artwork in order to ***spare his feelings***. [=to avoid hurting his feelings] [*noncount*] They complained ***with feeling*** [=in a way that showed they were feeling strong emotion] about her decision. ▪ He spoke *with feeling* about the injustice he had seen. **b** [*noncount*] : thoughts of wanting to help someone who is sick, hungry, in trouble, etc. : SYMPATHY ▪ Have you no *feeling* for the plight of the homeless? — see also FELLOW FEELING

3 a [*count*] : an opinion or belief ▪ What's your *feeling* on/about this subject? = What are your *feelings* on/about this subject? ▪ I can see that you have strong *feelings* about this subject. ▪ I get the *feeling* [=*impression*] that you think I don't know what I'm doing. ▪ My *feeling* is that we need to hire more people. ▪ She ***shared her feelings*** with us on a variety of subjects. [=told us her opinions about a variety of subjects] ✧ If you ***have a/the feeling*** that something might happen or be true, you think it might happen or be true even though you have no definite reason to think so. ▪ He *had the feeling* (that) he was being watched, although he didn't see anyone. ▪ I *had a feeling* you'd say that. ▪ I *have a* nagging/funny *feeling* that I've forgotten something. ▪ I *have a* sneaky/sneaking *feeling* that my guess was wrong. ▪ Do you ever *have the feeling* [=*have the sense, have the impression*] (that) you're being watched? **b** [*noncount*] : an opinion or a way of thinking that is shared by many people ▪ Anti-war *feeling* has reached an all-time high. = There is strong *feeling* against the war. [=many people are opposed to the war]

4 [*singular*] : the general quality or character of a place or thing ▪ The story has an eerie *feeling*. [=*feel, quality*] ▪ a big city with a small-town *feeling* [=*feel, atmosphere*]

5 [*noncount*] : the quality of a work of art or performance that shows the emotion of the artist or performer ▪ You need to play this passage with more *feeling*. [=*expression*]

6 [*singular*] : an ability to understand the nature of something : [2]FEEL 2 ▪ a painter with a good *feeling* for color

have feelings for : to feel love or affection for (someone) ▪ Even though they're divorced, it's obvious that they still *have* (tender) *feelings for* each other.

feel·ing·ly /ˈfiːlɪŋli/ *adv* [*more* ~; *most* ~] : in an emotional manner ▪ She wrote *feelingly* about the tragedy.

feet *plural of* [1]FOOT

feet·first /ˌfiːtˈfɚst/ *adv* : with the feet leading ▪ She jumped into the pool *feetfirst*. — compare HEADFIRST

feign /ˈfeɪn/ *verb* **feigns**; **feigned**; **feign·ing** [+ *obj*] : to pretend to feel or be affected by (something) ▪ He would often *feign* [=*fake*] illness to get out of class. ▪ He *feigned* being ill. ▪ *feign* death/surprise/madness/sleep/ignorance

– feigned *adj* ▪ She greeted him with *feigned* nonchalance.

[1]**feint** /ˈfeɪnt/ *noun, pl* **feints** [*count*] *sports* : a quick movement that you make to trick an opponent ▪ The boxer made a *feint* with his right, then followed with a left hook.

[2]**feint** *verb* **feints**; **feint·ed**; **feint·ing** [*no obj*] *sports* : to pretend to make an attack as a trick to fool your opponent : to make a feint ▪ He *feinted* with his right, then followed with a left hook.

feisty /ˈfaɪsti/ *adj* **feist·i·er**; **-est** [*also more* ~; *most* ~] : not afraid to fight or argue : very lively and aggressive ▪ The novel features a *feisty* heroine. ▪ Even her opponents admire her *feisty* spirit.

– feist·i·ness *noun* [*noncount*] ▪ They admire her *feistiness*.

feld·spar /ˈfɛldˌspɑɚ/ *noun* [*noncount*] : a very common type of mineral

fe·lic·i·ta·tion /fɪˌlɪsəˈteɪʃən/ *noun, pl* **-tions** *formal* : CONGRATULATION 2 [*noncount*] a message of *felicitation* [*plural*] They offered their heartfelt *felicitations*. ▪ *Felicitations* to you and your family on this happy occasion.

fe·lic·i·tous /fɪˈlɪsətəs/ *adj* [*more* ~; *most* ~] *formal* : very well suited for some purpose or situation : APPROPRIATE ▪ a *felicitous* combination of flavors ▪ a *felicitous* phrase

– fe·lic·i·tous·ly *adv* ▪ expressing himself *felicitously* **– fe·lic·i·tous·ness** *noun* [*noncount*]

fe·lic·i·ty /fɪˈlɪsəti/ *noun, pl* **-ties** *formal*

1 [*noncount*] : great happiness ▪ domestic/marital *felicity*

2 [*count*] : something that is pleasing and well chosen —

usually plural • He admired the movie for its stylistic *felicities*. • *felicities* of phrasing
3 [*noncount*] : a talent for speaking or writing in a very effective way • I've always admired his *felicity* with words.

[1]**fe·line** /ˈfiːˌlaɪn/ *adj*
1 : of or relating to the cat family • a *feline* species • *feline* diseases
2 [*more ~; most ~*] : resembling a cat : like a cat's • *feline* eyes • They move with *feline* agility/grace.

[2]**feline** *noun, pl* **-lines** [*count*] *formal* : a feline animal : CAT • domesticated *felines*

[1]**fell** *past tense of* [1]FALL

[2]**fell** /ˈfɛl/ *verb* **fells; felled; fell·ing** [+ *obj*]
1 : to cut down (a tree) • using an ax to *fell* a tree
2 : to beat or knock down (someone or something) • He's strong enough to *fell* an ox. — often used figuratively • Their father was *felled* [=*killed*] by a heart attack at age 55.

[3]**fell** *adj, formal + literary* : very fierce or cruel • a *fell* enemy/purpose
in one fell swoop *also* ***at one fell swoop*** : with a single, quick action or effort • The court has dismissed all of the charges against him *in one fell swoop*.

[4]**fell** *noun, pl* **fells** [*count*] *Brit*
1 : a hill in the north of England
2 : a high field or moor in the north of England

fel·la /ˈfɛlə/ *noun, pl* **-las** [*count*] *informal*
1 : a male person : FELLOW • He's not a bad *fella*.
2 : BOYFRIEND • She has a new *fella*.

fel·la·tio /fəˈleɪʃiˌoʊ/ *noun* [*noncount*] : the act of stimulating a man's penis with the mouth for sexual pleasure

[1]**fel·low** /ˈfɛloʊ/ *noun, pl* **-lows** [*count*]
1 *informal + somewhat old-fashioned* **a** : a male person : a boy or man • *fellows* and girls at a party • He seems like an amiable *fellow*. [=*guy*] • a fine *fellow* • a young *fellow* like you • Your son's a bright little *fellow*. **b** : a male companion of a girl or woman : BOYFRIEND • She's found herself a new *fellow*.
2 *old-fashioned* : a member of a group of people who have shared interests, activities, etc. — usually plural • He's eager to rejoin his *fellows*. • She wants to protect the good reputation she enjoys among her *fellows*.
3 *or* ***Fellow*** **a** : a member of a literary, artistic, or scientific organization • a *fellow* of the American College of Surgeons • a *Fellow* of the Royal Society/Academy **b** : a senior member of some British colleges and universities
4 *chiefly US* : an advanced student at a university who is given money to pay for food, housing, etc. : a graduate student who has been granted a fellowship • a postdoctoral *fellow* • a teaching/research *fellow* [=a graduate student who gets money in exchange for teaching/research] • a medical *fellow*

[2]**fellow** *adj, always used before a noun* — used to describe people who belong to the same group or class or who share a situation, experience, etc. • He attended the concert with a *fellow* student. [=someone who is a student, as he is] • her *fellow* employees/citizens — see also FELLOW MAN, FELLOW TRAVELER

fellow feeling *noun* [*noncount*] : a feeling of shared interest or understanding • There's a sense of sympathy and *fellow feeling* among members of the group.

fellow man *noun, pl* **~ men** [*count*] : a person other than yourself : a fellow human being — usually used with *my, our, his, her*, etc., to refer to other people in general • He has always tried to be of service to *his fellow man*. [=to other people] • We have to learn to love *our fellow man*.

fel·low·ship /ˈfɛləˌʃɪp/ *noun, pl* **-ships**
1 [*noncount*] : a friendly relationship among people • People came to the community dinner to share good food and good *fellowship*. [=*company, companionship*]
2 [*noncount*] : the relationship of people who share interests or feelings • traditions that bind us together in *fellowship*
3 [*count*] : a group of people who have similar interests • a youth *fellowship* • a *fellowship* of writers
4 [*count*] **a** : an amount of money to pay for food, housing, etc., that is given to a graduate student who teaches or does research at a university • She applied for a research *fellowship* in physics. • He came to the university on a teaching *fellowship*. **b** : the position of a fellow at a university or college • He holds a *fellowship* at the university.

fellow traveler (*US*) *or Brit* **fellow traveller** *noun, pl* **~ -ers** [*count*]
1 : someone who is traveling in the same group or on the same train, airplane, etc., as you • I struck up a conversation with one of my *fellow travelers*.
2 : someone who shares the opinions and beliefs of the people in a group or organization (especially the Communist Party) but does not belong to that group or organization • He was not a member of the Communist Party or even a *fellow traveler*.

fel·on /ˈfɛlən/ *noun, pl* **-ons** [*count*] : a criminal who has committed a serious crime (called a felony) • a convicted *felon*

fel·o·ny /ˈfɛləni/ *noun, pl* **-nies** [*count*] *law* : a serious crime (such as murder or rape) • The crime is considered a *felony* under state law. • He received a *felony* conviction. = He was convicted of committing a *felony*. • He was convicted of *felony* murder/theft. — compare MISDEMEANOR
— fe·lo·ni·ous /fɛˈloʊnijəs/ *adj* • *felonious* assault **— fe·lo·ni·ous·ly** *adv* • charged with *feloniously* assaulting a police officer

[1]**felt** *past tense and past participle of* [1]FEEL

[2]**felt** /ˈfɛlt/ *noun* [*noncount*] : a soft, heavy cloth made by pressing together fibers of wool, cotton, or other materials • She made her son's costume from scraps of *felt*. • a *felt* hat

felt–tip /ˈfɛltˌtɪp/ *noun, pl* **-tips** [*count*] : a pen that has a writing point made of felt — called also *felt-tip pen*; see picture at OFFICE

fem *abbr* female; feminine

[1]**fe·male** /ˈfiːˌmeɪl/ *adj*
1 a : of or relating to the sex that can produce young or lay eggs • a *female* bird/mammal/insect • *female* [=*women*] athletes • a study of *female* [=*women's*] sexuality **b** [*more ~; most ~*] : characteristic of girls or women • a *female* [=*feminine*] voice/name **c** : having members who are all girls or women • a *female* choir
2 *of a plant* : having only seed-producing flowers • a *female* holly
3 *technical* : having a hole that another part (called a male part) fits into • Most extension cords have a male plug on one end and a *female* plug on the other.
— fe·male·ness *noun* [*noncount*]

[2]**female** *noun, pl* **-males** [*count*]
1 : a woman or a girl : a female person • She attended a school where there were more males than *females*.

> ***usage*** The use of *female* to mean "woman" or "girl" now occurs most commonly in scientific or technical language. • According to the study, males scored about the same as *females*. • The suspect was described as a white *female* aged about 30. In other contexts, it is often seen as a humorous or mildly insulting word. • The shopping mall was mobbed by herds of adolescent *females*. • He referred to his angry coworkers as "a bunch of spiteful *females*."

2 : an animal that can produce young or lay eggs : a female animal • *Females* of this species weigh 8 to 10 pounds.
3 : a plant that can produce seed or fruit : a female plant

[1]**fem·i·nine** /ˈfɛmənən/ *adj*
1 [*more ~; most ~*] : of, relating to, or suited to women or girls • a *feminine* look/appearance • *feminine* beauty/mystique • the *feminine* [=*female*] figure • *feminine* hygiene • The book examines the subject from a *feminine* perspective. • They've added some *feminine* touches to the decor. • He has a rather *feminine* [=*effeminate*] voice. — compare [1]MASCULINE
2 *grammar, in some languages* : of or belonging to the class of words (called a gender) that ordinarily includes most of the words referring to females • a *feminine* noun • the *feminine* gender • The *feminine* form of the Spanish adjective "lindo" is "linda." — compare [1]MASCULINE, [1]NEUTER
— fem·i·nin·i·ty /ˌfɛməˈnɪnəti/ *noun* [*noncount*] • old-fashioned notions about masculinity and *femininity*

[2]**feminine** *noun, pl* **-nines** [*count*] *grammar, in some languages* : a word or form of the feminine gender • The *feminine* of the Spanish adjective "lindo" is "linda."

fem·i·nism /ˈfɛməˌnɪzəm/ *noun* [*noncount*]
1 : the belief that men and women should have equal rights and opportunities
2 : organized activity in support of women's rights and interests
— fem·i·nist /ˈfɛmənɪst/ *noun, pl* **-nists** [*count*] • liberal *feminists* **— feminist** *adj* • the *feminist* movement • *feminist* theory

femme fa·tale /ˌfɛmfəˈtæl/ *noun, pl* **femmes fa·tales** /ˌfɛmfəˈtælz/ [*count*] : a very attractive woman who causes

F

trouble or unhappiness for the men who become involved with her

fe·mur /ˈfiːmɚ/ *noun, pl* **fe·murs** *also* **fem·o·ra** /ˈfɛmərə/ [*count*] *medical* : the long bone in the upper part of the leg — called also *thighbone*; see picture at HUMAN
– **fem·o·ral** /ˈfɛmərəl/ *adj, always used before a noun* ▪ the *femoral* artery [=an artery that lies near the femur]

fen /ˈfɛn/ *noun, pl* **fens** [*count*] : low land that is completely or partly covered by water ▪ bogs and *fens*

[1]**fence** /ˈfɛns/ *noun, pl* **fenc·es** [*count*]
1 : a structure like a wall built outdoors usually of wood or metal that separates two areas or prevents people or animals from entering or leaving ▪ We put up a *fence* around our yard. — see picture at HOUSE; see also CHAIN-LINK FENCE
2 *informal* : a person who buys stolen property from thieves and sells it
mend fences see [1]MEND
on the fence : unable to decide about something ▪ He tried to persuade those still (sitting) *on the fence* to vote in his favor.
the grass is always greener on the other side (of the fence) see [1]GRASS
– **fence·less** *adj*

[2]**fence** *verb* **fences; fenced; fenc·ing**
1 [+ *obj*] **a** : to put a fence around (a place or area) ▪ They've decided to *fence* (in) the yard. ▪ She *fenced* (off) a corner of the property to use as a garden. ▪ a house with a *fenced*-in yard **b** : to keep (something or someone) in or out with a fence ▪ He *fenced* (in) the sheep so they wouldn't wander too far.
2 [*no obj*] : to fight with swords : to practice the art or sport of fencing ▪ Do you *fence*? — sometimes used figuratively ▪ candidates *fencing* with each other in their televised debates
3 [+ *obj*] *informal* : to sell (stolen property) to someone who buys and sells stolen property as an illegal business : to sell (stolen property) to a fence ▪ He stole watches and *fenced* them on the street.
– **fenc·er** *noun, pl* **-ers** [*count*] ▪ A skilled *fencer* advances as his opponent retreats.

fencing *noun* [*noncount*]
1 : the art or sport of fighting with swords
2 : material that is used for making fences ▪ barbed-wire *fencing*

fend /ˈfɛnd/ *verb* **fends; fend·ed; fend·ing**
fend for yourself : to do things without help : to do basic activities by yourself ▪ They had to *fend for themselves* while their mother was away. ▪ He's been *fending for himself* since his wife died.
fend off [*phrasal verb*] ***fend off (someone or something)*** *or* ***fend (someone or something) off*** : to defend yourself against (someone or something) ▪ They succeeded in *fending off* the attack/attackers. ▪ They have had to *fend off* allegations of voter fraud.

fend·er /ˈfɛndɚ/ *noun, pl* **-ers** [*count*]
1 *US* : a part of a vehicle that covers a wheel — called also (*Brit*) *wing*; see picture at CAR
2 *US* : a curved piece of metal that covers a wheel of a motorcycle or bicycle — called also (*Brit*) *mudguard*
3 : a low metal frame or screen placed in front of an open fireplace

fender bender *noun, pl* ~ **-ers** [*count*] *US, informal* : a minor car accident ▪ She had a *fender bender*. = She was in a *fender bender*.

feng shui /ˈfʌŋˈʃwiː/ *noun* [*noncount*] : a Chinese system for positioning a building and the objects within a building in a way that is thought to agree with spiritual forces and to bring health and happiness

fen·nel /ˈfɛnl̩/ *noun* [*noncount*] : a garden plant that is grown for its seeds, stems, and leaves

fe·ral /ˈferəl/ *adj*
1 : of, relating to, or resembling a wild beast ▪ *feral* instincts ▪ They led a *feral* existence.
2 — used to describe an animal (such as a cat or dog) that has escaped and become wild ▪ *feral* cats

[1]**fer·ment** /fɚˈmɛnt/ *verb* **-ments; -ment·ed; -men·ting** : to go through a chemical change that results in the production of alcohol [*no obj*] The wine *ferments* in oak barrels. — sometimes used figuratively ▪ He let the plan *ferment* [=*develop*] in his mind. [+ *obj*] Yeast *ferments* the sugar in the juice.
– **fer·men·ta·tion** /ˌfɚmənˈteɪʃən/ *noun* [*noncount*] ▪ Grape juice becomes wine through *fermentation*. ▪ the process of *fermentation*

[2]**fer·ment** /ˈfɚˌmɛnt/ *noun* [*noncount*] : a situation in which there is much excitement and confusion caused by change ▪ The city was in a state of *ferment* after the election.

fern /ˈfɚn/ *noun, pl* **ferns** [*count*] : a type of plant that has large, delicate leaves and no flowers
– **fern·like** /ˈfɚnˌlaɪk/ *adj* – **ferny** /ˈfɚni/ *adj* ▪ a plant with *ferny* foliage ▪ a *ferny* courtyard

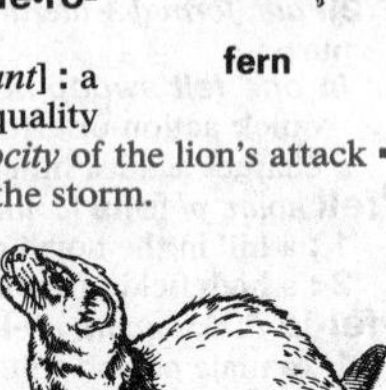
fern

fe·ro·cious /fəˈroʊʃəs/ *adj* [*more* ~; *most* ~]
1 : very fierce or violent ▪ *ferocious* animals ▪ A *ferocious* wind swept the beach. ▪ He had a *ferocious* [=*savage*] look in his eye.
2 : very great or extreme ▪ The competition among the students was *ferocious*. ▪ *ferocious* heat ▪ a *ferocious* appetite
– **fe·ro·cious·ly** *adv* ▪ *ferociously* strong winds ▪ a *ferociously* hot day – **fe·ro·cious·ness** *noun* [*noncount*]

fe·roc·i·ty /fəˈrɑːsəti/ *noun* [*noncount*] : a very fierce or violent quality : the quality or state of being ferocious ▪ the *ferocity* of the lion's attack ▪ We were stunned by the *ferocity* of the storm.

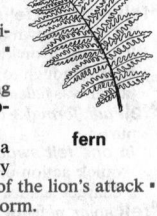

[1]**fer·ret** /ˈferət/ *noun, pl* **-rets** [*count*] : a small animal that is related to the weasel and is used for hunting rodents

ferret

[2]**ferret** *verb* **-rets; -ret·ed; -ret·ing**
ferret out [*phrasal verb*] ***ferret out (something)*** *or* ***ferret (something) out*** : to find (something, such as information) by careful searching ▪ He's good at *ferreting out* the facts. ▪ *ferret out* answers/problems

Fer·ris wheel /ˈferəs-/ *noun, pl* ~ **wheels** [*count*] *chiefly US* : a very large upright wheel that has seats around its edge where people sit while the wheel turns ✧ Ferris wheels are rides that are found at amusement parks. — called also (*Brit*) *big wheel*

Ferris wheel

fer·rous /ˈferəs/ *adj, technical* : of, relating to, or containing iron ▪ *ferrous* metal/materials

fer·rule /ˈferəl/ *noun, pl* **-rules** [*count*] : a usually metal ring or cap that is placed around the end of a wooden stick or handle to strengthen it

[1]**fer·ry** /ˈferi/ *verb* **-ries; -ried; -ry·ing** [+ *obj*] : to carry or move (someone or something) on a vehicle (such as a boat or a car) usually for a short distance between two places ▪ The cars were *ferried* across the river. ▪ They *ferry* supplies to the island. ▪ A bus *ferries* visitors from the parking lot to the entrance gate. = A bus *ferries* visitors between the parking lot and the entrance gate.

[2]**ferry** *noun, pl* **-ries** [*count*]
1 : FERRYBOAT ▪ *Ferries* to both islands depart daily. ▪ You can get there by *ferry*. ▪ a *ferry* service/ride
2 : a place where a ferryboat operates ▪ We'll meet you at the *ferry*.

fer·ry·boat /ˈferiˌboʊt/ *noun, pl* **-boats** [*count*] : a boat that is used to carry people and things for a short distance between two places : a boat that ferries people and things

fer·ry·man /ˈferimən/ *noun, pl* **-men** /-mən/ [*count*] : a person (especially a man) who operates a ferry

fer·tile /ˈfɚtl̩/ *adj*
1 [*more* ~; *most* ~] : producing many plants or crops : able to support the growth of many plants ▪ *fertile* [=*rich*] farmland/soil
2 [*more* ~; *most* ~] **a** : producing a large amount of something ▪ an area that is a *fertile* breeding ground for political extremism ▪ This subject remains a *fertile* field for additional

investigation. **b :** producing many ideas ▪ He has a *fertile* mind. ▪ her *fertile* imagination
3 a : able to produce children, young animals, etc. ▪ healthy, *fertile* women/men ▪ a *fertile* cow/bull **b :** able to grow or develop ▪ a *fertile* egg

fer·til·i·ty /fəˈtɪləti/ *noun* [*noncount*] **:** the state or condition of being fertile: such as **a :** the ability to produce young ▪ She studied the effects of pollution on the *fertility* of the local fish population. ▪ The doctor ordered a test of his/her *fertility*. — often used before another noun ▪ a *fertility* test/drug ▪ a *fertility* god/idol **b :** the ability to support the growth of many plants ▪ The area is known for its soil *fertility*. **c :** the ability to produce many ideas ▪ the *fertility* of his imagination

fer·til·ize *also Brit* **fer·til·ise** /ˈfətəˌlaɪz/ *verb* **-iz·es; -ized; -iz·ing**
1 [+ *obj*] **a :** to make (an egg) able to grow and develop ▪ A single sperm *fertilizes* an egg. **b :** to make (a plant or flower) able to produce seeds ▪ Bees *fertilize* plants as they collect nectar from flowers.
2 : to make (soil, land, etc.) richer and better able to support plant growth by adding chemicals or a natural substance (such as manure) [+ *obj*] He *fertilizes* the lawn every year. [*no obj*] The soil is so rich there is no need to *fertilize*.
– fer·til·i·za·tion *also Brit* **fer·til·i·sa·tion** /ˌfətələˈzeɪʃən/ *noun* [*noncount*]

fer·til·iz·er *also Brit* **fer·til·is·er** /ˈfətəˌlaɪzə/ *noun, pl* **-ers :** a substance (such as manure or a special chemical) that is added to soil to help the growth of plants [*noncount*] We only use organic *fertilizer* in our gardens. [*count*] They use chemical *fertilizers* on their lawn.

fer·vent /ˈfəvənt/ *adj* [*more ~; most ~*] **:** felt very strongly ▪ He is known for his *fervent* [=*passionate, zealous*] nationalism. **:** having or showing very strong feelings ▪ They entered a *fervent* [=*heated*] debate over the death penalty. ▪ a *fervent* admirer/supporter/opponent
– fer·vent·ly *adv* ▪ *fervently* enthusiastic supporters

fer·vid /ˈfəvəd/ *adj* [*more ~; most ~*] *somewhat formal* **:** having or showing feelings that are very strong or too strong ▪ *fervid* fans
– fer·vid·ly *adv*

fer·vor (*US*) *or Brit* **fer·vour** /ˈfəvə/ *noun* [*noncount*] **:** a strong feeling of excitement and enthusiasm ▪ The *fervor* surrounding her campaign continued right through election day. ▪ The novel captures the revolutionary *fervor* of the period. ▪ religious *fervor*

fess /ˈfɛs/ *verb* **fess·es; fessed; fess·ing**
fess up [*phrasal verb*] *chiefly US, informal* **:** to admit that you have done something wrong **:** CONFESS ▪ At first he denied everything, but eventually he *fessed up*. ▪ He finally *fessed up* about his involvement. = He finally *fessed up* to being involved.

fes·ter /ˈfɛstə/ *verb* **-ters; -tered; -ter·ing** [*no obj*]
1 : to become painful and infected ▪ His wounds *festered* for days before he got medical attention. ▪ a *festering* sore
2 : to become worse as time passes ▪ His feelings of resentment have *festered* for years. ▪ We should deal with these problems now instead of allowing them to *fester*.

fes·ti·val /ˈfɛstəvəl/ *noun, pl* **-vals** [*count*]
1 : a special time or event when people gather to celebrate something ▪ Each year, a *festival* was held to celebrate the harvest. ▪ The town has a summer *festival* in the park.
2 : an organized series of performances ▪ a film/jazz *festival*

fes·tive /ˈfɛstɪv/ *adj*
1 [*more ~; most ~*] **:** cheerful and exciting **:** suited to a celebration or holiday ▪ The house looks very *festive* during the holidays. ▪ She was in a *festive* mood. ▪ The reunion will be a *festive* occasion.
2 *Brit* **:** of or relating to Christmas ▪ the ***festive season***

fes·tiv·i·ty /fɛˈstɪvəti/ *noun, pl* **-ties**
1 [*noncount*] **:** celebration and enjoyment ▪ The decorations give the hall an air of *festivity*.
2 *festivities* [*plural*] **:** enjoyable activities at the time of a holiday or other special occasion **:** festive activities ▪ The *festivities* will include a parade, a concert, and games for children. ▪ We enjoyed the New Year's Eve *festivities*.

[1]**fes·toon** /fɛˈstuːn/ *verb* **-toons; -tooned; -toon·ing** [+ *obj*] **:** to cover or decorate (something) with many small objects, pieces of paper, etc. ▪ We *festooned* the halls with leaves and white lights. ▪ The balcony is *festooned* in/with ivy. ▪ His office is *festooned* with newspaper clippings.

[2]**festoon** *noun, pl* **-toons** [*count*] **:** a long chain or strip of something (such as flowers or cloth) that is hung as a decoration — usually plural ▪ walls covered with *festoons* of flowers

fe·ta /ˈfɛtə/ *noun* [*noncount*] **:** a type of white Greek cheese that is made from sheep's or goat's milk ▪ *feta* cheese

fe·tal (*US*) *or Brit* **foe·tal** /ˈfiːtl̩/ *adj* **:** of or relating to a developing animal or human being that is not yet born **:** of or relating to a fetus ▪ a *fetal* heartbeat ▪ a *fetal* pig

fetal position (*US*) *or Brit* **foetal position** *noun* [*singular*] **:** a position in which you lie on your side with both legs and both arms bent and pulled up to your chest and with your head bowed forward

fetch /ˈfɛtʃ/ *verb* **fetch·es; fetched; fetch·ing**
1 : to go after and bring back (someone or something) [+ *obj*] Wait here while I *fetch* [=*get*] the doctor. ▪ Please *fetch* me a drink. = Please *fetch* a drink for me. ▪ If you throw the ball the dog will *fetch* it. [*no obj*] Hunting dogs are trained to *fetch*.
2 [+ *obj*] **:** to be sold for (an amount of money) ▪ This table should *fetch* quite a bit at auction. ▪ The house *fetched* more than we expected.
fetch and carry **:** to do the kind of jobs that servants do for someone ▪ I won't *fetch and carry* for you all day.
fetch up [*phrasal verb*] *chiefly Brit, informal* **:** to reach or come to a place, condition, or situation that was not planned or expected ▪ She traveled throughout Europe and eventually *fetched up* [=*ended up*] in Italy.

fetching /ˈfɛtʃɪŋ/ *adj* [*more ~; most ~*] *somewhat old-fashioned* **:** attractive or pleasing ▪ a *fetching* smile ▪ You look very *fetching* in that outfit.
– fetch·ing·ly *adv* ▪ *fetchingly* dressed

[1]**fete** *or* **fête** /ˈfeɪt, ˈfɛt/ *noun, pl* **fetes** [*count*]
1 *US* **:** a large party or celebration
2 *Brit* **:** an outdoor event for raising money that usually includes competitions and things for sale ▪ won a prize at the church/village *fete*

[2]**fete** *or* **fête** *verb* **fetes** *or* **fêtes; fet·ed** *or* **fêt·ed; fet·ing** *or* **fêt·ing** [+ *obj*] **:** to honor (a person) or celebrate (something) with a large party or public celebration ▪ They *feted* the winning team with banquets and parades. — often used as *(be) feted* ▪ She *was feted* for her contributions to science.

fet·id /ˈfɛtəd/ *adj* [*more ~; most ~*] **:** having a strong, unpleasant smell ▪ a *fetid* pool of water ▪ the *fetid* odor of rotting vegetables

fe·tish /ˈfɛtɪʃ/ *noun, pl* **-tish·es** [*count*]
1 : a strong and unusual need or desire for something ▪ He has a *fetish* for secrecy.
2 : a need or desire for an object, body part, or activity for sexual excitement ▪ a shoe/foot/leather *fetish*
3 : an object that is believed to have magical powers ▪ He wore a *fetish* to ward off evil spirits.
– fe·tish·ism /ˈfɛtɪʃˌɪzəm/ *noun* [*noncount*] ▪ sexual *fetishism* **– fe·tish·ist** /ˈfɛtɪʃɪst/ *noun, pl* **-ists** [*count*] ▪ a foot *fetishist* [=a person who has a foot fetish]

fet·lock /ˈfɛtˌlɑːk/ *noun, pl* **-locks** [*count*] **:** a part at the back of a horse's leg above the hoof

fet·ter /ˈfɛtə/ *verb* **-ters; -tered; -ter·ing** [+ *obj*]
1 *formal* **:** to prevent (someone or something) from moving or acting freely ▪ He found himself *fettered* by responsibilities. ▪ restrictions that *fetter* [=*hinder*] creativity
2 *old-fashioned* **:** to put chains around someone's feet to prevent motion ▪ *fetter* [=*shackle*] a prisoner

fet·ters /ˈfɛtəz/ *noun* [*plural*]
1 *formal* **:** something that prevents someone or something from moving or acting freely ▪ She longs to be free of the *fetters* [=*constraints*] of family obligations.
2 : chains placed around a person's feet to restrict motion ▪ a prisoner in *fetters* [=*shackles*]

fet·tle /ˈfɛtl̩/ *noun* [*singular*] *informal* **:** a person's physical state or condition — usually used in the phrase ***in fine fettle*** ▪ He seems to be *in fine fettle* this morning. [=he seems to be feeling very well; he seems very fit and cheerful]

fet·tuc·ci·ne *or* **fet·tuc·ci·ni** *or* **fet·tu·ci·ne** *or* **fet·tu·ci·ni** /ˌfɛtəˈtʃiːni/ *noun* [*noncount*] **:** a type of pasta that is shaped like long, thin ribbons

fe·tus *or chiefly Brit* **foe·tus** /ˈfiːtəs/ *noun, pl* **-tus·es** [*count*] **:** a human being or animal in the later stages of development before it is born — compare EMBRYO

feud /ˈfjuːd/ *noun, pl* **feuds** [*count*] **:** a long and angry fight or quarrel between two people or two groups ▪ The workers' *feud* with management concerns health benefits and pay increases. ▪ Because of a family *feud*, they did not see each other for a decade. — see also BLOOD FEUD
– feud *verb* **feuds; feud·ed; feud·ing** [*no obj*] ▪ They

feuded (with each other) for years. ▪ The estate is not settled because the family is still *feuding* over the will.

feu·dal /ˈfjuːdl/ *adj* **:** of or relating to feudalism ▪ the *feudal* system ▪ a *feudal* law/lord

feu·dal·ism /ˈfjuːdəˌlɪzəm/ *noun* [*noncount*] **:** a social system that existed in Europe during the Middle Ages in which people worked and fought for nobles who gave them protection and the use of land in return

fe·ver /ˈfiːvɚ/ *noun, pl* **-vers**
1 a : a body temperature that is higher than normal [*count*] He has had a *fever* for two days. = He has been running a *fever* for two days. [*noncount*] The symptoms of the disease include headache and *fever*. **b** [*count*] **:** a disease that causes an increase in body temperature ▪ She caught a *fever*. — see also HAY FEVER, RHEUMATIC FEVER, SCARLET FEVER, YELLOW FEVER
2 [*singular*] **a :** a state of excited emotion or activity ▪ We waited in a *fever* of anticipation. ▪ He had us all in a *fever* with worry. — see also CABIN FEVER, SPRING FEVER **b :** a state of great enthusiasm or interest ▪ Every fall the town develops football *fever*. [=the town becomes very excited about football]

fever blister *noun, pl* **~ -ters** [*count*] *US* **:** COLD SORE

fe·vered /ˈfiːvɚd/ *adj* [*more ~; most ~*]
1 : having or affected by a fever — usually used in the phrase ***fevered brow*** ▪ She wiped the sweat from his *fevered brow*.
2 : very excited or active ▪ *fevered* activity/experimentation ▪ a *fevered* imagination

fe·ver·ish /ˈfiːvərɪʃ/ *adj* [*more ~; most ~*]
1 a : having a fever **:** suffering from a higher than normal body temperature caused by illness ▪ She was feeling tired and *feverish*. **b :** of or relating to a fever ▪ a *feverish* nightmare ▪ He had a *feverish* appearance.
2 : involving intense emotion or activity **:** feeling or showing great or extreme excitement ▪ We waited for the announcement with *feverish* [=*eager*] anticipation. ▪ *feverish* [=*hectic*] activity
– fe·ver·ish·ly *adv* ▪ We worked *feverishly* to prepare for the party.

fever pitch *noun* **:** a state of extreme excitement or activity [*singular*] I worked myself up to/into a *fever pitch* of enthusiasm. ▪ New allegations brought interest in the scandal to a *fever pitch*. [*noncount*] Demand for the new car soon reached *fever pitch*.

[1]few /ˈfjuː/ *adj* **few·er; -est**
1 : not many ▪ *Few* people came. ▪ the next/last/past *few* weeks ▪ I know (very) *few* people in the class. ▪ Music is one of my (very) *few* pleasures. ▪ He caught *fewer* fish than the rest of us. ▪ There are *fewer* children at the school this year. ▪ Not many people came, but the *few* people who did enjoyed themselves. ▪ *Few* (if any) people understand me.
2 : not many but some — used in the phrase ***a few*** ▪ Only/Just *a few* people came. ▪ We went out for *a few* drinks after work. ▪ I know *a few* people in the class. ▪ The train leaves in *a few* minutes. ✧ The phrases ***quite a few*** and, less commonly, ***not a few*** or (*chiefly Brit*) ***a good few*** all mean "fairly many." ▪ *Quite a few* students from our high school go on to college.
as few as — used to suggest that a number or amount is surprisingly small ▪ The procedure is recommended by *as few as* [=*only*] one out of five doctors. ▪ *As few as* half the students passed the test.
***few and far between* :** not common or frequent ▪ Really good movies are *few and far between*. [=there are not many really good movies] ▪ Opportunities like that are *few and far between*.
***no fewer than* :** at least — used to suggest that a number or amount is surprisingly large ▪ *No fewer than* 1,000 people attended the meeting. ▪ *No fewer than* 80 percent of registered voters turned out for the primary.
of few words ✧ A person *of few words* is someone who does not talk very much. ▪ a man/woman *of few words*

[2]few *pronoun*
1 : not many people or things ▪ (Very) *Few* came. ▪ His stories may be entertaining, but *few* (if any) are true. = They may be entertaining, but *few* (if any) of his stories are true. ▪ There are many students in the class, but I know very *few* (of them). ▪ "Never . . . was so much owed by so many to so *few*." —Sir Winston Churchill, Speech (August, 1940)
2 : some people or things — used in the phrase ***a few*** ▪ *A few* came. ▪ I bought several magazines and I read *a few* (of them). ▪ Unfortunately, *a few* of the people who came failed to enjoy themselves. ▪ We gave away most of the photographs but we kept *a few* (of them). ▪ They sold *a few* of the books. ▪ She met *a few* of my relatives. ✧ The phrases ***quite a few*** and, less commonly, ***not a few*** or (*chiefly Brit*) ***a good few*** all mean "fairly many." ▪ Not all our students go on to college, but *quite a few* (of them) do. [=a large number of our students do]
3 : a small number of people or things that are chosen or regarded as special or unusual in some way ▪ A select *few* will receive advance tickets. ▪ A sophisticated movie like this only appeals to the discriminating *few*.
***have a few** or **have a few too many informal* :** to have too many alcoholic drinks ▪ We could tell from his slurred speech that he'd *had a few*. ▪ It looks like she *had a few too many*.

[1]few·er /ˈfjuːwɚ/ *adj* **:** not so many **:** a smaller number of ▪ I take *fewer* (and *fewer*) vacations every year. ▪ He teaches (many) *fewer* classes than I do. ***usage*** see [1]LESS

[2]fewer *pronoun* **:** a smaller number of people or things ▪ *Fewer* came than were expected. ▪ Few know and (even) *fewer* care about local history. ▪ *Fewer* than 50 percent of registered voters turned out for the primary.

fez /ˈfɛz/ *noun, pl* **fez·zes** [*count*] **:** a type of round red hat that has a flat top and no brim ✧ Fezzes are worn by men in some Middle Eastern countries.

fez

fi·an·cé /ˌfiːˌɑːnˈseɪ, fiˈɑːnˌseɪ/ *noun, pl* **-cés** [*count*] **:** a man that a woman is engaged to be married to ▪ Let me introduce my *fiancé*.

fi·an·cée /ˌfiːˌɑːnˈseɪ, fiˈɑːnˌseɪ/ *noun, pl* **-cées** [*count*] **:** a woman that a man is engaged to be married to ▪ My *fiancée* and I will be married in June.

fi·as·co /fiˈæskoʊ/ *noun, pl* **-coes** [*count*] **:** a complete failure or disaster ▪ The party turned into a complete/utter *fiasco*. ▪ a political *fiasco*

fi·at /ˈfiːət, ˈfaɪˌæt/ *noun, pl* **-ats** *formal* **:** an official order given by someone who has power **:** an order that must be followed [*count*] a judicial *fiat* [*noncount*] He runs the company ***by fiat*** ▪ government *by fiat*

[1]fib /ˈfɪb/ *noun, pl* **fibs** [*count*] *informal* **:** an untrue statement about something minor or unimportant ▪ I have to admit that I told a *fib* when I said I enjoyed the movie. ▪ Is she telling *fibs* again?

[2]fib *verb* **fibs; fibbed; fib·bing** [*no obj*] *informal* **:** to tell a fib **:** to make an untrue statement about something minor or unimportant ▪ I *fibbed* when I said that I enjoyed the movie. ▪ He *fibbed* about his weight.

fi·ber (*US*) *or Brit* **fi·bre** /ˈfaɪbɚ/ *noun, pl* **-bers**
1 [*noncount*] **:** plant material that cannot be digested but that helps you to digest other food ▪ It's important to get enough *fiber* in your diet. ▪ dietary *fiber* ▪ What foods do you recommend as good sources of *fiber*? ▪ foods that are high in *fiber*
2 a : a thin thread of natural or artificial material that can be used to make cloth, paper, etc. [*count*] The fabric is made from a mix of synthetic *fibers*. ▪ The natural *fibers* allow the fabric to breathe. [*noncount*] The paper is made from both cotton and wood *fiber*. **b :** material (such as cloth) that is made from thin threads **:** something made of fibers [*count*] Nylon is a very strong man-made *fiber*. [*noncount*] The police examined hair and bits of *fiber* found in the victim's car.
3 [*count*] **:** a long, thin piece of material that forms a type of tissue in your body ▪ muscle/nerve *fibers*
4 [*noncount*] *formal* **:** strength or toughness of character ▪ cultural changes that have weakened the ***moral fiber*** of our nation's youth
***with every fiber of your being* :** with all of your effort or desire ▪ She wanted to be a doctor *with every fiber of her being*. ▪ He fought *with every fiber of his being* for freedom.

fi·ber·board (*US*) *or Brit* **fi·bre·board** /ˈfaɪbɚˌboɚd/ *noun* [*noncount*] **:** a type of board made by pressing fibers of wood into stiff sheets

fi·ber·glass (*US*) *or Brit* **fi·bre·glass** /ˈfaɪbɚˌglæs, *Brit* ˈfaɪbəˌglɑːs/ *noun* [*noncount*] **:** a light and strong material that is made from thin threads of glass and that is used in making various products — often used before another noun ▪ a *fiberglass* boat

fiber optics (*US*) *or Brit* **fibre optics** *noun* [*noncount*] *technical* **:** the use of thin threads of glass or plastic to carry

very large amounts of information in the form of light signals
– fi·ber–op·tic *(US)* or *Brit* **fi·bre–op·tic** /ˈfaɪbɚˌɑːptɪk/ *adj, technical* ▪ a *fiber-optic* cable/network

fi·brous /ˈfaɪbrəs/ *adj* [*more ~; most ~*] **:** containing, made of, or resembling fibers ▪ He had surgery to remove *fibrous* scar tissue in his knee. ▪ The vegetable has a *fibrous* [=*stringy, tough*] texture.

fib·u·la /ˈfɪbjələ/ *noun, pl* **-lae** /-li/ *or* **-las** [*count*] *medical* **:** the outer one of the two bones below the knee in a person's leg — see picture at HUMAN

fick·le /ˈfɪkəl/ *adj* [*more ~; most ~*]
1 : changing often ▪ *fickle* weather
2 *disapproving* **:** changing opinions often ▪ *fickle* friends/supporters ▪ He blames poor sales on *fickle* consumers.
– fick·le·ness *noun* [*noncount*] ▪ the *fickleness* of the weather

fic·tion /ˈfɪkʃən/ *noun, pl* **-tions**
1 [*noncount*] **:** written stories about people and events that are not real **:** literature that tells stories which are imagined by the writer ▪ She mainly writes *fiction.* ▪ great works of *fiction* — compare NONFICTION; see also SCIENCE FICTION
2 : something that is not true [*noncount*] His explanation of what happened was pure *fiction.* [=was completely untrue] [*count*] She believes the *fiction* that crime rates are up.
– fic·tion·al /ˈfɪkʃənl̩/ *adj* ▪ a *fictional* character/place ▪ She wrote a *fictional* account of a family living during the war.

fic·tion·al·ize *also Brit* **fic·tion·al·ise** /ˈfɪkʃənəˌlaɪz/ *verb* **-iz·es; -ized; -iz·ing** [+ *obj*] **:** to change (a true story) into fiction by changing or adding details ▪ The book is a *fictionalized* account of their travels. ▪ Her books are based in fact, but she *fictionalizes* many of the events.
– fic·tion·al·i·za·tion *also Brit* **fic·tion·al·i·sa·tion** /ˌfɪkʃənələˈzeɪʃən, *Brit* ˌfɪkʃənəˌlaɪˈzeɪʃən/ *noun, pl* **-tions** [*count, noncount*] ▪ the *fictionalization* of a true story

fic·ti·tious /fɪkˈtɪʃəs/ *adj* **:** not true or real ▪ a *fictitious* story ▪ The characters in the book are all *fictitious.* ▪ She gave a *fictitious* address on the application.

¹fid·dle /ˈfɪdl̩/ *noun, pl* **fid·dles** [*count*] *informal*
1 : VIOLIN ▪ an expert with/on the *fiddle*
2 *Brit* **:** a dishonest way of getting money **:** SWINDLE, SCAM ▪ arrested for a tax *fiddle*
fit as a fiddle see ¹FIT
play second fiddle **:** to have a less important position or status than someone or something else **:** to be regarded or treated as less important ▪ a former star athlete who is not happy to *play second fiddle* as he nears the end of his career — often + *to* ▪ He's not happy to *play second fiddle to* the younger players on the team.

²fiddle *verb* **fid·dles; fid·dled; fid·dling** /ˈfɪdlɪŋ/
1 [*no obj*] *informal* **:** to play a violin ▪ Nero *fiddled* while Rome burned. — used especially to describe playing folk music, country music, etc., on a violin ▪ a *fiddling* competition
2 [+ *obj*] *chiefly Brit, informal* **:** to secretly change (something, such as information) in a harmful or dishonest way ▪ *fiddle* [=*fudge*] the accounts/books
fiddle around or *chiefly Brit* ***fiddle about*** [*phrasal verb*] **:** to spend time in activity that does not have a real purpose ▪ They spent hours just *fiddling* [=*fooling*] *around* when they should have been working.
fiddle with [*phrasal verb*] ***fiddle with (something)*** **1 :** to move or handle (something) with your hands or fingers in a nervous way ▪ She was nervously *fiddling with* her pen as she waited for the test to start. **2 :** to change or handle (something, such as the controls of a machine) in a way that shows you are not sure what to do ▪ He was *fiddling* [=*tinkering*] *with* the controls of the television, trying to get it to work. **3 :** to change (something) in a harmful or foolish way ▪ It became clear that someone had *fiddled* [=*tampered*] *with* the equipment.
– fid·dler /ˈfɪdlɚ/ *noun, pl* **fid·dlers** [*count*] ▪ an expert/champion *fiddler* ▪ (*Brit*) ***tax fiddlers*** [=people who lie to avoid paying taxes]

fid·dle·sticks /ˈfɪdl̩ˌstɪks/ *interj, informal + old-fashioned* — used to express mild anger or disagreement ▪ "I had nothing to do with it." "Oh, *fiddlesticks*! I know you did."

fid·dly /ˈfɪdli/ *adj* **fid·dli·er; -dli·est** [*or more ~; most ~*] *chiefly Brit, informal* **:** awkward or difficult to handle because of many small parts or details ▪ connecting up all the wires and the other *fiddly* bits

fi·del·i·ty /fəˈdɛləti/ *noun* [*noncount*]
1 a : the quality of being faithful to your husband, wife, or sexual partner ▪ She began to doubt her husband's *fidelity.* [=to wonder if he was having an affair with another woman] ▪ sexual *fidelity* — often + *to* ▪ his *fidelity to* his wife — opposite INFIDELITY **b :** the quality of being faithful or loyal to a country, organization, etc. — usually + *to* ▪ No one can doubt his *fidelity* [=*devotion*] *to* his country.
2 : the degree to which something matches or copies something else — + *to* ▪ The movie's director insisted on total *fidelity to* the book. [=insisted that the story told in the movie should accurately copy the story told in the book]
3 : the degree to which a device (such as a CD player, radio, or television) correctly reproduces sounds, pictures, etc. ▪ music with much higher *fidelity* than on cassettes ▪ a printer with outstanding color *fidelity* [=a printer that produces very accurate colors] — see also HIGH FIDELITY

fidg·et /ˈfɪʤət/ *verb* **-ets; -et·ed; -et·ing** [*no obj*] **:** to make a lot of small movements because you are nervous, bored, etc. **:** to move or act in a nervous or restless way ▪ He was constantly *fidgeting* in his chair.
fidget with [*phrasal verb*] ***fidget with (something)*** **:** to move or handle (something) with your hands and fingers in a nervous way ▪ He was *fidgeting* [=*fiddling*] *with* his tie before the presentation.

fidg·ety /ˈfɪʤəti/ *adj* [*more ~; most ~*] **:** moving a lot because of nervousnees, boredom, etc. **:** tending to fidget ▪ He grew more *fidgety* with each passing hour. ▪ Coffee makes me *fidgety.* [=*jumpy, restless*]

fi·du·ci·ary /fəˈduːʃiˌeri, *Brit* fɪˈdjuːʃiəri/ *adj, formal* **:** relating to or involving trust (such as the trust between a customer and a professional) ▪ a *fiduciary* capacity/duty ▪ a bank's *fiduciary* obligations

fief /ˈfiːf/ *noun, pl* **fiefs** [*count*] **:** a large area of land that was ruled over by a lord in medieval times **:** a feudal estate — sometimes used figuratively ▪ a politician's *fief* [=*fiefdom*]

fief·dom /ˈfiːfdəm/ *noun, pl* **-doms** [*count*] **:** an area over which a person has control ▪ The coaches viewed their school districts as personal *fiefdoms.*

¹field /ˈfiːld/ *noun, pl* **fields** [*count*]
1 a : an open area of land without trees or buildings ▪ He gazed out across the *fields.* ▪ a grassy/muddy *field* ▪ green *fields* ▪ an open *field* — see also ICE FIELD **b :** an area of land that has a special use ▪ farm *fields* ▪ a *field* of wheat = a wheat *field* ▪ cotton/tobacco *fields* — see color picture on page C7; see also OIL FIELD
2 : an area of work, study, etc. ▪ She hopes to find work in the health *field.* ▪ She is a pioneer/leader in the *field* of genetic research. ▪ a lawyer who is eminent in his *field* ▪ working in his chosen *field* ▪ *fields* of learning/interest/study ▪ a fascinating *field* of endeavor
3 a : an area of land that is used for sports ▪ football/athletic/baseball/soccer *fields* ▪ a ball *field* ▪ The home team ***took the field***. [=ran out onto the field to begin play] ▪ Spectators are not allowed on the ***field of play***. [=*playing field*] ▪ The team has been tough to beat on its ***home field***. [=its own field where it plays in front of its fans] ✧ In a baseball or cricket game, when one team is batting the other team is ***in the field***. — see also CENTER FIELD, FIELD EVENT, LEFT FIELD, PLAYING FIELD, RIGHT FIELD, TRACK AND FIELD **b** ✧ In basketball a shot taken ***from the field*** is a shot taken during ordinary play rather than a free throw. ▪ They shot well *from the field* but they missed too many free throws.
4 : the area where work is done away from a laboratory, office, etc. ▪ archaeologists/salesmen working in the *field* — often used before another noun ▪ She will be doing *field* research in South America. ▪ *field* studies ▪ The product has been tested under *field* conditions of actual use. ▪ *field* workers — see also FIELD-TEST, FIELDWORK
5 : the group of people, horses, teams, etc., that are in a race or other competition ▪ a race with a large *field* of runners ▪ The presidential election has attracted a large *field* of candidates. ▪ She was ***leading/trailing the field*** by a wide margin. — often used figuratively ▪ The company is working hard to ***stay/keep ahead of the field***. [=to continue to be more successful than its competitors]
6 : a place where battles and other military activities happen ▪ the *field* of battle ▪ soldiers in the *field* — see also BATTLEFIELD, LANDING FIELD, MINEFIELD
7 : a region or space in which an effect or force (such as gravity, electricity, or magnetism) exists ▪ an electric/magnetic *field*
8 : an area in which a particular type of information is

F

placed ▪ You must complete all *fields* before submitting the form. ▪ (*computers*) The database is separated into several different *fields*.

9 : FIELD OF VISION ▪ Nothing moved within his visual *field*. — see also FIELD OF VIEW

play the field see [1]PLAY

[2]**field** *verb* **fields; field·ed; field·ing** [+ *obj*]

1 *baseball or cricket* **:** to catch or stop and throw a ball ▪ The shortstop *fielded* the ground ball. ▪ a *fielding* error; *also* **:** to play (a position) on a baseball team ▪ a shortstop who *fields* his position flawlessly

2 a : to deal with or respond to (something, such as a telephone call or a request) ▪ Last week she *fielded* two offers on her house. ▪ His secretary will *field* requests for more information. **b :** to give an answer to (a question) ▪ The senator *fielded* the reporters' questions.

3 : to put (a team, army, etc.) into the field to compete or fight ▪ They expect to *field* a strong team this year. ▪ the greatest fighting force that any nation has ever *fielded*

field day *noun, pl* **~ days** [*count*] **:** a day of outdoor sports and athletic competition for school children ▪ the fifth grade's annual *field day*

have a field day **:** to get a lot of pleasure and enjoyment from doing something — used especially to describe getting enjoyment from criticizing someone, making fun of someone, etc. ▪ If word of his involvement in this scandal ever leaks out, the newspapers are going to *have a field day*. ▪ Journalists have *had a field day with* this scandal.

field·er /ˈfiːldɚ/ *noun, pl* **-ers** [*count*] *baseball or cricket* **:** a player who is in the field while the opposing team is batting

field event *noun, pl* **~ events** [*count*] **:** an event in a track meet that is not a race ▪ a discus thrower who excelled at all the *field events*

field glasses *noun* [*plural*] **:** BINOCULARS

field goal *noun, pl* **~ goals** [*count*]

1 *American football* **:** a score of three points made by kicking the ball between the goalposts ▪ He kicked a 20-yard *field goal*. ▪ They've won three games by less than a *field goal*. [=by fewer than three points]

2 *basketball* **:** BASKET 2b ▪ a three-point *field goal*

field guide *noun, pl* **~ guides** [*count*] **:** a book that helps you to identify birds, plants, animals, rocks, etc. ▪ a *field guide* to the birds

field hand *noun, pl* **~ hands** [*count*] *US* **:** a person who is hired to work on a farm **:** FARMHAND

field hockey *noun* [*noncount*] *US + Canada* **:** a game that is played on a field in which each team uses curved sticks to try to hit the ball into the opponent's goal — called also (*chiefly Brit*) *hockey*; compare ICE HOCKEY

field house *noun, pl* **~ houses** [*count*] *US* **:** a large building that is used for athletic events and that usually has seats for spectators

field marshal *noun, pl* **~ -shals** [*count*] **:** the highest ranking military officer in the British Army

field mouse *noun, pl* **~ mice** [*count*] **:** a type of mouse that lives in open fields

field of view *noun, pl* **fields of view** [*count*]

1 : the area that can be seen when you look through a telescope, a pair of binoculars, etc. ▪ the telescope's *field of view*

2 : FIELD OF VISION

field of vision *noun, pl* **fields of vision** [*count*] **:** the area that you can see without moving your eyes ▪ He ran right through my *field of vision*. ▪ She has a blind spot in the middle of her *field of vision*.

field·stone /ˈfiːldˌstoun/ *noun, pl* **-stones** [*count*] **:** a stone that is taken from a field and used in its natural form ▪ They used plain *fieldstones* as grave markers. — often used before another noun ▪ a *fieldstone* fireplace

field–test /ˈfiːldˌtɛst/ *verb* **-tests; -test·ed; -test·ing** [+ *obj*] **:** to test (something, such as a product) by using it in the actual conditions it was designed for ▪ These products need to be thoroughly *field-tested* before we can begin using them.
— **field test** *noun, pl* **~ tests** [*count*] ▪ doing a *field test* of the prototype

field trip *noun, pl* **~ trips** [*count*] **:** a visit to a place (such as a museum or zoo) that is made by students to learn about something ▪ We took a class *field trip* to the power plant. ▪ We went on a *field trip*.

field·work /ˈfiːldˌwɚk/ *noun* [*noncount*] **:** the work of gathering information by going into the field (sense 4) ▪ an anthropologist who has done *fieldwork* in the South Pacific

fiend /ˈfiːnd/ *noun, pl* **fiends** [*count*]

1 a : an evil spirit **:** a demon or devil **b :** a very evil or cruel person ▪ a murderous *fiend* ▪ a *fiend* in human form

2 *informal* **a :** a person who is very enthusiastic about something **:** FANATIC ▪ He's a real golf *fiend*. ▪ a fresh air *fiend* ▪ He's a *fiend* for physical fitness. [=he is very devoted to physical fitness] **b :** a person who is addicted to a drug or to a kind of behavior ▪ a dope/drug *fiend* [=*addict*] ▪ a sex *fiend*

like a fiend *chiefly US, informal* — used to say that someone does a lot of something ▪ She's been working *like a fiend*. [=working very hard] ▪ He smokes *like a fiend*.

fiend·ish /ˈfiːndɪʃ/ *adj* [*more ~; most ~*]

1 : very evil or cruel ▪ a *fiendish* murderer ▪ He takes a *fiendish* delight in hurting people. ▪ a *fiendish* contraption ▪ a *fiendish* [=*diabolical*] plot to destroy the world

2 : extremely bad, unpleasant, or difficult ▪ *fiendish* weather ▪ a *fiendish* problem
— **fiend·ish·ly** *adv* ▪ a *fiendishly* clever plot ▪ a *fiendishly* hot sun ▪ a *fiendishly* coldhearted murderer ▪ *fiendishly* complex tools and machinery — **fiend·ish·ness** *noun* [*noncount*] ▪ a plot of incredible *fiendishness*

fierce /ˈfiɚs/ *adj* **fierc·er; -est**

1 a : very violent ▪ He was killed in a *fierce* battle. ▪ a *fierce* assault/attack ▪ *fierce* combat/fighting **b :** eager to fight or kill ▪ a *fierce* tiger/warrior ▪ a *fierce* fighter

2 : having or showing a lot of strong emotion **:** very strong or intense ▪ a *fierce* argument/struggle ▪ The proposal has faced *fierce* opposition. ▪ The two teams have had a *fierce* rivalry for many years. ▪ *fierce* enthusiasm ▪ He's admired for his *fierce* independence. ▪ She's a *fierce* competitor. ▪ You could see the *fierce* determination in her eyes.

3 : very harsh or powerful ▪ a *fierce* desert wind ▪ a *fierce* heat wave ▪ a *fierce* storm/squall ▪ She was suffering through *fierce* [=*excruciating*] pain.

something fierce *US, informal* **:** very badly or very much ▪ I miss her *something fierce*. [=*tremendously*] ▪ I need a vacation *something fierce*.
— **fierce·ly** *adv* [*more ~; most ~*] ▪ He has been *fiercely* denounced by his former associates. ▪ a *fiercely* partisan/independent voter ▪ the *fiercely* hot sun ▪ *fiercely* protective/loyal — **fierce·ness** *noun* [*noncount*]

fi·ery /ˈfajəri/ *adj* **fi·er·i·er; -est** [*or more ~; most ~*]

1 : having or producing fire ▪ the *fiery* [=*blazing*] interior of the furnace ▪ He was killed in a *fiery* crash/explosion. ▪ a *fiery* volcano

2 *of food* **:** tasting very hot and spicy ▪ *fiery* chili peppers ▪ a *fiery* sauce

3 a : having or showing a lot of strong and angry emotion ▪ a *fiery* speech/sermon ▪ a *fiery* young politician ▪ *fiery* determination **b :** easily made angry ▪ He has a *fiery* temper. [=he becomes angry very easily]

4 : having the color of fire ▪ a *fiery* sunset ▪ a *fiery* red/orange color
— **fi·er·i·ness** *noun* [*noncount*]

fi·es·ta /fiˈɛstə/ *noun, pl* **-tas** [*count*] **:** a public celebration in Spain and Latin America with parades and dances in honor of a saint

fife /ˈfaɪf/ *noun, pl* **fifes** [*count*] **:** a musical instrument that looks like a small flute

fif·teen /ˌfɪfˈtiːn/ *noun, pl* **-teens** [*count*] **:** the number 15
— **fifteen** *adj* ▪ *fifteen* dollars — **fifteen** *pronoun* ▪ Only *fifteen* (of them) showed up on time. — **fif·teenth** /ˌfɪfˈtiːnθ/ *noun, pl* **-teenths** [*count*] ▪ the *fifteenth* of September ▪ one *fifteenth* of the total — **fifteenth** *adj* ▪ the *fifteenth* day — **fifteenth** *adv* ▪ Their boat finished *fifteenth*.

[1]**fifth** /ˈfɪθ, ˈfɪfθ/ *noun, pl* **fifths**

1 [*singular*] **:** number five in a series ▪ The bill is due on the *fifth* of each month.

2 [*count*] **:** one of five equal parts of something ▪ She donated a *fifth* of her income to charity.

3 [*count*] **:** a unit of measure for alcoholic liquor that is equal to one fifth of a U.S. gallon (approximately 750 ml); *also* **:** a bottle that holds this amount of liquor ▪ bought a *fifth* of whiskey

take/plead the Fifth *chiefly US* **:** to refuse to answer questions in a court of law because your answers might be harmful to you or might show that you have committed a crime ▪ When called to testify, he *took the Fifth*. — often used figuratively ▪ He *took the Fifth* [=he refused to answer] when his wife asked him where he'd spent the night. ✧ The phrase *take/plead the Fifth* refers to the Fifth Amendment of the U.S. Constitution, which says that citizens of the U.S. cannot be required to give testimony that could be used against them in a court of law.

²fifth *adj* : occupying the number five position in a series ▪ the *fifth* dancer in the line ▪ the *fifth* annual awards banquet
– **fifth** *adv* ▪ the nation's *fifth* largest city ▪ She finished *fifth* in the race.

fifth wheel *noun, pl* ~ **wheels** [*count*] *informal* : an extra person who is not needed in a group ▪ He felt more and more like a *fifth wheel* at the office.

fif·ty /ˈfɪfti/ *noun, pl* **-ties**
1 [*count*] : the number 50
2 *fifties* [*plural*] **a** : the numbers ranging from 50 to 59 **b** : a set of years ending in digits ranging from 50 to 59 ▪ She is in her *fifties*. ▪ He fondly remembers growing up in the *fifties*. [=1950–1959]
3 [*count*] *US* : a fifty-dollar bill ▪ The bill for dinner came to $43, and she gave him a *fifty*.
– **fif·ti·eth** /ˈfɪftiəθ/ *adj* ▪ their *fiftieth* wedding anniversary – **fiftieth** *noun, pl* **-eths** [*count*] ▪ one *fiftieth* of the total – **fifty** *adj* ▪ *fifty* cars in the parking lot – **fifty** *pronoun* ▪ *Fifty* (of them) were wounded in battle. – **fif·ty·ish** /ˈfɪftijɪʃ/ *adj* ▪ He looked *fiftyish*. [=about 50 years old]

fif·ty–fif·ty /ˌfɪftiˈfɪfti/ *adj*
1 : shared equally ▪ a *fifty-fifty* split [=an equal split] ▪ a *fifty-fifty* blend of cotton and polyester
2 : equally good and bad ▪ We have a *fifty-fifty* chance of succeeding. [=we are as likely to succeed as we are to fail]
– **fifty–fifty** *adv* ▪ They divided/split the expenses *fifty-fifty*. [=*equally*]

fig /ˈfɪg/ *noun, pl* **figs** [*count*]
1 : a sweet fruit that grows on a tree and that is usually eaten dry — see color picture on page C5
2 *informal + old-fashioned* : anything at all — usually used in negative statements ▪ He ***doesn't care a fig*** [=doesn't care at all] about what others think. ▪ I ***don't give a fig*** whether he comes or goes.

fig. *abbr* figure

¹fight /ˈfaɪt/ *verb* **fights; fought** /ˈfɑːt/; **fight·ing**
1 a : to use weapons or physical force to try to hurt someone, to defeat an enemy, etc. : to struggle in battle or physical combat [*no obj*] The soldiers *fought* bravely. ▪ When he was young he was always *fighting*. ▪ He *fought* like a tiger. ▪ The U.S. and Germany *fought* in World Wars I and II. — often + *against* ▪ The U.S. *fought against* Germany in World Wars I and II. [+ *obj*] They vowed to *fight* the invaders of their homeland. ▪ The U.S. *fought* Germany in World Wars I and II. **b** [+ *obj*] : to be involved in (a battle, struggle, etc.) ▪ *fight* [=*wage*] a war/battle for independence ▪ *fighting* a duel ▪ I think we're ***fighting a losing battle***. [=we are trying to do something that we will not be able to do]
2 [*no obj*] : to argue in an angry way ▪ He and his wife are always *fighting* over/about money. ▪ They *fight* (with each other) all the time.
3 [*no obj*] : to try hard *to do* something that is difficult ▪ They were *fighting* [=*struggling*] *to stay* awake/alive. ▪ We were *fighting to protect* our jobs.
4 a : to work hard to defeat, end, or prevent something [*no obj*] *fighting* against poverty ▪ *fighting* against AIDS/cancer/crime [+ *obj*] *fighting* poverty ▪ The company *fought* the takeover attempt. ▪ His lawyers have vowed that they will *fight* the court's decision. ▪ *fight* a fire ▪ *fight* crime **b** [+ *obj*] : to struggle against (something) ▪ I've been *fighting* a cold all week. ▪ We had to *fight* traffic [=to drive through a lot of traffic] all the way home.
5 [+ *obj*] : to try not to be affected by (a feeling, urge, etc.) ▪ He was *fighting* the urge/impulse to laugh. [=he was trying not to laugh]
6 : to participate in the sport of boxing [*no obj*] He will *fight* for the heavyweight title next month. [+ *obj*] He has *fought* several worthy opponents. ▪ He *fought* several difficult matches on his way to the title.

fight back [*phrasal verb*] **1** : to attack or try to defeat someone who is attacking or trying to defeat you ▪ We can't just let them make these accusations against us. We need to *fight back*! **2** : to make a new effort against an opponent ▪ They fell behind early in the game, but they were able to *fight back* and tie the score in the second half. — see also FIGHTBACK **3** ✧ Someone who is ***fighting back tears*** is trying very hard not to cry. ▪ He was *fighting back tears* as he announced his resignation.

fight fire with fire : to fight against an opponent by using the same methods or weapons that the opponent uses

fight for [*phrasal verb*] ***fight for (something)*** **1** : to fight in support of (something) ▪ young soldiers *fighting for* their country ▪ This is a cause that's worth *fighting for*. **2** : to fight or struggle to get, keep, or achieve (something) ▪ The team is *fighting for* a spot in the play-offs. ▪ The two armies *fought* all night *for* control of the fort. ▪ We are *fighting for* our rights as citizens. ▪ They had to *fight for* survival. ▪ When they brought him to the hospital, he was ***fighting for breath***. [=he was struggling to breathe] ▪ Her condition is very serious. She's ***fighting for her life***. [=she is struggling to survive; she is in danger of dying]

fight it out **1** : to be in a fight ▪ People were *fighting it out* over parking spaces. **2** : to end a dispute by fighting or arguing ▪ This matter won't be settled until the lawyers *fight it out* in court.

fight like cats and dogs (*chiefly US*) *or Brit* ***fight like cat and dog*** *informal* : to fight or argue a lot or in a very forceful and angry way ▪ a married couple who are always *fighting like cats and dogs*

fight off [*phrasal verb*] ***fight (someone or something) off*** *or* ***fight off (someone or something)*** : to defend yourself against (someone or something) by fighting or struggling : to avoid being harmed or overcome by (someone or something) by fighting or struggling ▪ They *fought off* the attack/attackers. ▪ I'm trying to *fight off* a cold.

fight on [*phrasal verb*] : to continue fighting ▪ He vowed that he would *fight on* alone.

fight shy of see ¹SHY

fight the good fight : to try very hard to do what is right ▪ He has always *fought the good fight* against oppression.

fight with [*phrasal verb*] ***fight with (someone or something)*** **1** : to fight against (someone or something) ▪ He *fought with* his wife over/about money. ▪ The U.S. *fought with* Germany in World Wars I and II. ▪ He *fought with* several worthy opponents. **2** : to fight on the same side as (someone or something) ▪ The U.S. *fought* (together) *with* the Soviet Union in World War II. **3** : to fight by using (something, such as a weapon) ▪ They were *fighting with* knives. ▪ They *fought with* their fists.

fight your way : to move forward or make progress by pushing, fighting, or struggling ▪ He *fought his way* through the crowd. ▪ They've had to *fight their way* through a lot of red tape to get the project approved.

– **fighting** *adj* ▪ a powerful *fighting* force ▪ a *fighting* ship ▪ They admired his *fighting* [=*aggressive*] spirit. — see also *fighting chance* at ¹CHANCE ✧ ***Fighting words*** are angry or insulting words that are likely to cause a fight. ✧ In U.S. English, someone who is ***fighting mad*** is angry enough to fight. ▪ Some voters are *fighting mad* about the outcome of the election. – **fighting** *noun* [*noncount*] ▪ *Fighting* has broken out along the border. ▪ There are reports of (heavy) *fighting* between rival factions.

²fight *noun, pl* **fights**
1 [*count*] : a violent physical struggle between opponents ▪ A *fight* broke out in the bar. ▪ a bar *fight* ▪ a street *fight* ▪ a knife *fight* [=a fight using knives] ▪ When he was young he was always getting into *fights*. ▪ It would be foolish to ***pick a fight*** [=start a fight] with that guy. ▪ a ***pillow fight*** [=a playful fight using pillows as weapons] ▪ a ***food fight*** [=a playful fight in which people throw food at each other] ▪ a ***snowball fight*** — see also BULLFIGHT, DOGFIGHT, FIREFIGHT, FISTFIGHT, GUNFIGHT
2 [*count*] : an argument or quarrel ▪ He got into another *fight* with his wife about money.
3 [*count*] : a boxing match ▪ a *fight* for the heavyweight title — see also PRIZEFIGHT
4 [*count*] : a struggle to achieve a goal or to defeat something or someone ▪ We didn't win, but at least we put up a good *fight*. ▪ They are leading/joining the *fight* against cancer. ▪ the *fight* to defeat cancer ▪ He's in the *fight* of his political life in this election. ▪ She's ***in a fight for her life***. [=she is struggling to stay alive]
5 [*noncount*] : a willingness to fight ▪ full of *fight*

fight·back /ˈfaɪtˌbæk/ *noun, pl* **-backs** [*count*] *Brit* : a new effort to win or succeed after being close to defeat or failure : COMEBACK ▪ The team staged a *fightback* in the second half. — see also *fight back* at ¹FIGHT

fight·er /ˈfaɪtɚ/ *noun, pl* **-ers** [*count*] : someone or something that fights: such as **a** : a warrior or soldier ▪ nationalist *fighters* — see also FREEDOM FIGHTER **b** : BOXER 1 ▪ a championship *fighter* **c** : someone who does not give up : someone who continues fighting or trying ▪ Despite everything, you'll survive because you're a (real) *fighter*! **d :** a fast airplane that has weapons for destroying enemy aircraft • a jet *fighter* • a *fighter* plane • a *fighter* pilot

fig leaf *noun, pl* ~ **leaves** [*count*]
1 : the leaf of a fig tree ✧ In works of art, such as paintings and sculptures, naked people have sometimes been shown with a fig leaf covering their sexual organs.
2 : something that prevents embarrassment or criticism by covering or hiding something • Opponents claim that the humanitarian goals of the project are just a *fig leaf*, and that its real purpose is to make money.

fig·ment /ˈfɪgmənt/ *noun, pl* **-ments** [*count*] **:** something produced by the imagination **:** something that does not really exist — usually used in the phrase ***figment of your imagination*** • I thought I heard her voice, but I guess it was just a *figment of my imagination*.

fig·u·ra·tive /ˈfɪgjərətɪv/ *adj*
1 *of words, language, etc.* **:** used with a meaning that is different from the basic meaning and that expresses an idea in an interesting way by using language that usually describes something else **:** not literal • The phrase "know your ropes" means literally "to know a lot about ropes," while its *figurative* meaning is "to know a lot about how to do something." • *figurative* language
2 : showing people and things in a way that resembles how they really look **:** not abstract • *figurative* art

fig·u·ra·tive·ly /ˈfɪgjərətɪvli/ *adv* **:** in a figurative way **:** with a meaning that is different from the basic or literal meaning and that expresses an idea by using language that usually describes something else • He's a sailor who knows his ropes, literally and *figuratively*. • In the phrase "know your ropes," the word "ropes" is being used *figuratively*.

[1]**fig·ure** /ˈfɪgjɚ, *Brit* ˈfɪgə/ *noun, pl* **-ures** [*count*]
1 a : a symbol that represents a number **:** DIGIT • He has a six-*figure* salary. [=he has a salary of at least $100,000] **b :** a value that is expressed in numbers • Are you sure of your *figures*? • I came up with a very different *figure*. • No precise/exact/official *figures* are available yet. • The company had yearly sales *figures* of half a million units. ✧ If you ***have a good head for figures***, you are good at making calculations with numbers. If you ***have no head for figures***, you are bad at making calculations with numbers. • She *has a good head for figures*, so I'm not surprised that she became an accountant.
2 a : a person or animal that can be seen only as a shape or outline • We could barely make out some *figures* moving in the mist. **b :** the shape or form of a person's body • the human *figure* • the male/female *figure* ✧ *Figure* in this sense usually refers to women rather than men. • She has a very shapely *figure*. [=*body*] • a full *figure* • a slim, youthful *figure* • She likes to wear clothes that show off her *figure*. **c** ✧ The phrases ***a fine figure of a man*** and (less commonly) ***a fine figure of a woman*** describe someone who is tall and has a strong and well-formed body. • The football coach is *a fine figure of a man*.
3 : a drawing, scupture, etc., that represents the form of a person or animal • The vase is decorated with *figures* of birds and fish. • The walls of the cave are covered with drawings of human and animal *figures*. • a male/female *figure* • a collection of bronze/carved *figures* • a cardboard *figure* • a cartoon *figure* — see also STICK FIGURE
4 : a person who has a specified status or who is regarded in a specified way • a noted/familiar/popular/prominent sports *figure* • He began by writing letters to well-known *figures* in journalism. • a mysterious/shadowy *figure* • She's a key *figure* in the organization. • He has become a ***figure of contempt***. [=someone who is regarded with contempt] • a ***figure of fun/ridicule*** [=someone who is laughed at or ridiculed] • a ***figure of authority*** = an ***authority figure*** [=a person who has authority over other people] — see also ACTION FIGURE, FATHER FIGURE, MOTHER FIGURE
5 a : a diagram or picture • Turn your attention to the *figure* on page 15. — abbr. *fig.* **b** *mathematics* **:** a combination of points, lines, or surfaces in geometry • A circle is a closed plane *figure*. • geometric *figures*

[2]**figure** *verb* **-ures; -ured; -ur·ing**
1 [+ *obj*] **:** to expect or think (something) • I *figured* (that) they would lose. [=I expected them to lose] • I *figured* [=*thought*] he'd get tired of it in a few days. • The media *figured* that she would be the appointee. = The media *figured* her to be the appointee. • "They lost." "I *figured* as much." • (*US*) He *figured* [=*expected*] to lose money in the deal.
2 *US, informal* **a** [+ *obj*] **:** to understand or find (something, such as a reason) by thinking • Their reasons for doing this are hard to *figure*. [=*figure out*] • I've finally *figured* [=*figured out*] a way to manage my time better. • We've got to *figure* [=*find*] a way out of this mess. **b** [*no obj*] **:** to appear likely *to do* something • She *figures to finish* by noon. • He doesn't *figure to win*. [=he probably won't win]
3 [*no obj*] **:** to be or appear important **:** to have an important part *in* something • The debate over tax rates *figured* prominently *in* the last election.
4 [+ *obj*] **:** to calculate (an amount, cost, etc.) • He *figured* the cost at about $10,000. • The cost in dollars is easily *figured*.
5 [*no obj*] *chiefly US, informal* **:** to seem reasonable, normal, or expected • His explanation just doesn't *figure*. [=*add up, make sense*] • ***It figures*** [=it is not surprising] that he would be late today. • "He's late." "Well, *it figures*." • ***That figures***. [=that doesn't surprise me]

figure in [*phrasal verb*] **1** ***figure (something) in*** *or* ***figure in (something)*** *US* **:** to include (something) while making calculations • When they were preparing a budget, they forgot to *figure in* [=*factor in*] occasional travel expenses. **2** ***figure in (something)*** **:** to be involved in (something, such as an activity) • persons who *figured in* the robbery

figure into [*phrasal verb*] ***figure into (something)*** *US* **:** to be included as a part of (something) • Age may *figure into* the equation.

figure on [*phrasal verb*] ***figure on (something)*** *US, informal* **1 :** to expect to get or have (something) • They weren't *figuring on* the extra income. **2 :** to plan to do (something) • I *figure on* going [=I plan to go] downtown later today.

figure out [*phrasal verb*] **1** ***figure out (something)*** *or* ***figure (something) out*** **a :** to understand or find (something, such as a reason or a solution) by thinking • I'm trying to *figure out* a way to do it. • He claims he has it all *figured out*. • I finally *figured* it *out*. • I can't *figure out* why he does these crazy things. **b :** to find an answer or solution for (something, such as a problem) • *figure out* [=*solve*] a math problem **2** ***figure (someone) out*** *or* ***figure out (someone)*** **:** to understand the behavior of (someone) • He does these crazy things, and I just can't *figure* him *out*.

go figure *US, informal* — used to say that something is surprising or hard to understand • After losing their first six games, they won the next ten. *Go figure*.

figure eight *noun, pl* ~ **eights** [*count*] *US* **:** something that is shaped like the numeral 8 • The skater traced a *figure eight* on the ice. — called also (*Brit*) *figure-of-eight*

fig·ure·head /ˈfɪgjɚˌhɛd, *Brit* ˈfɪgəˌhɛd/ *noun, pl* **-heads** [*count*]
1 : a carved figure (as of a woman) on a ship's bow • an elaborately carved *figurehead*
2 : a person who is called the head or chief of something but who has no real power • The king is merely a *figurehead*; the government is really run by elected officials.

figure–of–eight *noun, pl* **figures–of–eight** [*count*] *Brit* **:** FIGURE EIGHT

figure of speech *noun, pl* **figures of speech** [*count*] **:** a phrase or expression that uses words in a figurative way rather than in a plain or literal way • "You are the apple of my eye" is a *figure of speech*.

figure skate *noun, pl* ~ **skates** [*count*] **:** a special skate that is used for figure skating — see picture at SKATE

figure skating *noun* [*noncount*] **:** ice-skating in which the skaters perform various jumps, spins, and dance movements
– **figure skater** *noun, pl* ~ **-ers** [*count*] • a champion *figure skater*

fig·u·rine /ˌfɪgjəˈriːn/ *noun, pl* **-rines** [*count*] **:** a small figure or model of a person made of wood, plastic, etc.

fil·a·ment /ˈfɪləmənt/ *noun, pl* **-ments** [*count*]
1 : a thin thread or hair • a slender *filament* • algae covered with tiny *filaments*
2 : a thin wire in a light bulb that glows when electricity passes through it
– **fil·a·men·tous** /ˌfɪləˈmɛntəs/ *adj, technical* • *filamentous* algae

fil·bert /ˈfɪlbɚt/ *noun, pl* **-berts** [*count*] *chiefly US* **:** HAZELNUT

filch /ˈfɪltʃ/ *verb* **filch·es; filched; filch·ing** [+ *obj*] *informal* **:** to steal (something that is small or that has little value) • He *filched* a pack of gum when no one was looking.

[1]**file** /ˈfajəl/ *noun, pl* **files** [*count*]
1 a : a device (such as a box, folder, or cabinet) in which documents that you want to keep are stored so that they can be found easily • He put each memo in its proper *file*. **b :** a

collection of documents that have information you want to keep and that are stored so that they can be found easily • The FBI has a large *file* on his activities. • She noticed that two employees' *files* were missing from the cabinet. ✧ Something that is ***on file*** is stored in a file. • We'll keep your resume *on file* in case a suitable job becomes available. • The company has several thousand customers *on file*.
2 : a collection of computer data that forms a single unit and that is given a particular name • You should save the *file* frequently as you do your work. • a word-processing *file* • He accidentally deleted some important *files*.
– compare ³FILE, ⁵FILE

²file *verb* **files; filed; filing**
1 [+ *obj*] **:** to put (a document) in a place where it can be found easily **:** to place (something) in a file • He *filed* each recipe for future reference. • I'm not sure what name this letter should be *filed* under. — often + *away* • She *filed away* each of his letters.
2 : to give (something, such as an official form or a legal document) to someone in authority so that it can be considered, dealt with, approved, etc. [+ *obj*] She had to *file* [=*submit*] dozens of forms to get a loan. • *file* a lawsuit • *file* a tax return • The policeman *filed* his report. [*no obj*] + *for* • She has *filed for* divorce/bankruptcy.
3 [+ *obj*] **:** to send (a story or report) to a newspaper • He *filed* a story incorrectly indicating that the strike was over.
– compare ⁴FILE, ⁶FILE
– fil·er /ˈfaɪlɚ/ *noun, pl* **-ers** [*count*] • tax *filers* claiming deductions • typists and *filers*

³file *noun, pl* **files** [*count*] **:** a metal tool that has sharp ridges and that is used to make rough surfaces smooth — see picture at CARPENTRY; see also NAIL FILE — compare ¹FILE, ⁵FILE

⁴file *verb* **files; filed; fil·ing** [+ *obj*] **:** to make something smooth by using a file • He *filed* away/down the rough edges. • She *filed* the rough edges off her nails with a nail file. • She *filed* her nails. — compare ²FILE, ⁶FILE

⁵file *noun, pl* **files** [*count*] **:** a row of people, animals, or things that form a line • a *file* of soldiers • soldiers marching in *file* — compare ¹RANK; see also RANK AND FILE, SINGLE FILE — compare ¹FILE, ³FILE

⁶file *verb* **files; filed; filing** [*no obj*] **:** to walk in a line • The inmates *filed* past on their way to the mess hall. • The customers *filed* out at closing time. — compare ²FILE, ⁴FILE

file cabinet *noun, pl* ~ **-nets** [*count*] *US* **:** a piece of furniture that is used for storing documents so that they can be found easily — called also *filing cabinet*; see picture at OFFICE

fil·i·al /ˈfɪlijəl/ *adj, formal* **:** of or relating to a son or daughter • *filial* duties **:** appropriate for a son or daughter • *filial* obedience/devotion

fil·i·bus·ter /ˈfɪləˌbʌstɚ/ *noun, pl* **-ters** [*count*] *chiefly US* **:** an effort to prevent action in a legislature (such as the U.S. Senate or House of Representatives) by making a long speech or series of speeches • They engaged in a *filibuster* that lasted for over a week.
– filibuster /ˈfɪləˌbʌstɚ/ *verb* **-ters; -tered; -ter·ing** [*no obj*] They are *filibustering* to delay the vote. [+ *obj*] They *filibustered* the bill for over a week.

fil·i·gree /ˈfɪləˌgriː/ *noun* [*noncount*] **:** decoration that consists of delicate and complicated designs made of fine gold or silver wire • a surface decorated with *filigree* and pearls
– fil·i·greed /ˈfɪləˌgriːd/ *adj* • *filigreed* ornaments/balconies/tableware

¹fil·ing /ˈfaɪlɪŋ/ *noun, pl* **-ings** [*count*] **:** a small piece that is removed when something is smoothed or rubbed with a file — usually plural • iron *filings* — compare ²FILING

²filing *noun, pl* **-ings**
1 [*count*] **:** the act of giving an official form or document to someone in authority in order to begin a legal process • *Filings* for bankruptcy are declining.
2 [*noncount*] **:** the job or activity of storing documents in a file • She does all the typing and *filing* in our office. — sometimes used before another noun • a *filing* clerk
– compare ¹FILING

filing cabinet *noun, pl* ~ **-nets** [*count*] **:** FILE CABINET

¹fill /ˈfɪl/ *verb* **fills; filled; fill·ing**
1 a [+ *obj*] **:** to make (something) full • May I *fill* your glass for you? • *fill* (up) a glass with water • He told the gas station attendant to *fill* it/her up. [=to fill the tank of his car with gasoline] • Clothes *filled* the closet. • She *filled* her house with antiques. • His massive body *filled* the doorway. • He has enough books to *fill* a library. • Two hundred people *filled* the room. • *fill* a sheet of paper with writing • Tears *filled* her eyes. [=she began to cry] • Joy *filled* her heart. [=she became very joyful] • He *filled* her head with lies [=he told her many lies] about his military service. • pastries *filled* with meat = meat-*filled* pastries • a vase *filled* with flowers • stadiums *filled* with cheering fans • The theater was ***filled to capacity***. [=completely full] ✧ If something ***fills you*** or ***fills your heart*** with an emotion, it makes you feel that emotion very strongly. • The thought of leaving *fills me* with sadness. [=makes me very sad] • I'm *filled* with shame [=I'm very ashamed] when I think of how I treated her. • The news *filled their hearts* with hope. [=made them very hopeful] **b** [*no obj*] **:** to become full • Her eyes *filled* with tears. [=she began to cry] • Her heart *filled* with joy. [=she became very joyful] • The rivers have *filled* and are close to flooding. • The stadium *filled* more than an hour before the game.
2 [+ *obj*] **:** to spread all through (an area, the air, etc.) • Smoke *filled* the room. • Laughter *filled* the air. • The smell of fried onions *filled* the house. • Tension *filled* the air as we waited for further news.
3 [+ *obj*] **:** to spend or use (time) • She likes to *fill* (up) her day with small chores. • Since he retired he doesn't know how to *fill* his time. • a **fun-filled** afternoon [=an afternoon filled with fun; a very enjoyable afternoon]
4 : to make (someone) full with food and drink — usually + *up* [+ *obj*] foods that won't *fill* you *up* [*no obj*] We *filled up* on sandwiches before leaving for the game.
5 [+ *obj*] **:** to place material inside of (a hole, crack, etc.) in order to repair a surface • *fill* a crack with putty • workers *filling* potholes • *fill* a cavity in a tooth = *fill* a tooth [=put filling in a cavity/tooth] — often used figuratively • He's trying to ***fill the gaps*** in his record collection. [=trying to get the records he needs to make his collection complete] • These new discoveries will help to *fill a gap* in our knowledge of how the human body ages. • Some other player will have to ***fill the void*** left by his retirement.
6 [+ *obj*] **:** to do or provide what is needed for (something) • *fill* [=*fulfill*] all requirements • *fill* a need
7 [+ *obj*] **a :** to perform the work of (an office, position, etc.) • *fill* [=*hold, occupy*] the office of president • A new representative will be appointed to *fill* his vacated seat. **b :** to hire a person for a job that has become available • The company hopes to *fill* several vacancies in its marketing department. • *fill* a job opening
8 [+ *obj*] **:** to provide the things that are asked for in (something, such as an order) • *fill* an order • (*US*) *fill* a prescription [=(*Brit*) make up a prescription]
fill in [*phrasal verb*] **1 *fill (something) in* or *fill in (something)* a :** to complete (a document) by providing necessary information • *fill in* an application • *fill in* an order form • Please ***fill in the blanks***. [=put information in the blank spaces] — sometimes used figuratively • At the end of the movie, the narrator goes back and *fills in* (all) *the blanks*. [=the narrator provides missing information about the movie's plot] **b :** to provide (more information) • Just tell me the most important parts—you can *fill in* the details later. **2 *fill (someone) in* or *fill in (someone)* :** to provide information to (someone) • I missed the meeting so I need someone to *fill* me *in* (on what happened). • She *filled* us *in* on the details. **3 *fill in* :** to take the place of (someone who is away for a time) • He can't be here today, so he asked me to *fill in*. — often + *for* • He asked me to *fill in for* him. — see also FILL-IN
fill out [*phrasal verb*] **1 :** to increase in size **:** to become larger and heavier • The tree looks weak now but should begin to *fill out* in a few years. • It was easier to find clothes that fit him once he began to *fill out*. **2 *fill (something) out* or *fill out (something)* *chiefly US* :** to complete (something, such as a form) by providing necessary information • *fill out* [=*fill in*] a form • *fill out* an application
***fill someone's shoes* :** to take someone's place or position • No one will be able to *fill her shoes* after she retires.
fill the bill see ¹BILL

²fill *noun* [*noncount*]
1 : a full amount **:** all that someone wants or needs ✧ If you have ***eaten/drunk your fill***, you have eaten/drunk all that you want. • I'm going to *eat my fill*. ✧ If you have ***had your fill of*** something, you do not want to do or have any more of it. • We've *had our fill of* dance music for one night.
2 : material that is used to fill something • They delivered a truckload of *fill* for the trench.

fill·er /ˈfɪlɚ/ *noun, pl* **-ers**
1 [*noncount*] **a :** a substance that is added to a product to

increase its size or weight **b :** material that is used to fill holes and cracks in a surface **c :** extra material that is added to something (such as a newspaper page or a recording) to fill space that would otherwise be empty ▪ Those extra songs were just *filler* to make the CD longer.
2 [*count*] **:** a sound, word, or phrase (such as "um" or "you know?") that people say during a pause when they are speaking

[1]**fil·let** *also US* **fi·let** /ˈfɪlət, fɪˈleɪ/ *noun, pl* **-lets** [*count*] **:** a piece or slice of boneless meat or fish ▪ catfish *fillets* ▪ a juicy *fillet* of beef

[2]**fillet** *verb* **fil·lets; fil·leted** /ˈfɪlətəd, fɪˈleɪd/; **fil·let·ing** [+ *obj*] **:** to cut (meat or fish) into fillets ▪ He carefully *filleted* the fish with a sharp knife. ▪ slices of *filleted* pork

fill–in /ˈfɪlˌɪn/ *noun, pl* **-ins** [*count*] **:** someone who takes the place of another person who is away for a short time **:** someone who fills in for someone else ▪ She performed well as the emergency *fill-in*. [=*replacement, substitute*]

[1]**fill·ing** /ˈfɪlɪŋ/ *adj* [*more ~; most ~*] *of food* **:** causing you to feel full ▪ a very *filling* meal ▪ *filling* foods

[2]**filling** *noun, pl* **-ings**
1 [*count*] **:** material that is used to fill something ▪ a *filling* for a tooth
2 : a food mixture that is used to fill something (such as pastry or a sandwich) [*count*] pies with fruit *fillings* [*noncount*] pies that need more *filling*

filling station *noun, pl* **~ -tions** [*count*] **:** GAS STATION

fil·lip /ˈfɪləp/ *noun, pl* **-lips** [*count*] **:** an added part or feature that makes something more interesting or exciting ▪ a structural *fillip* that will add much to the appearance of the building ▪ lent a *fillip* of danger to the sport

fil·ly /ˈfɪli/ *noun, pl* **-lies** [*count*] **:** a young female horse — compare COLT, FOAL

[1]**film** /ˈfɪlm/ *noun, pl* **films**
1 [*noncount*] **:** a special material that is used for taking photographs ▪ Have you bought any *film* for the camera? ▪ We haven't had the *film* developed yet. ▪ We shot four rolls of *film* on our trip. [=we filled four rolls of film with pictures]
2 a : MOVIE [*count*] He's interested in making *films* about war. ▪ *film* critics/reviewers/criticism ▪ We'll start the *film* at 10:00. [*noncount*] The accident was captured ***on film***. [=was recorded by a movie or video camera] **b** [*noncount*] **:** the process, art, or business of making movies ▪ He studied *film* in college. ▪ her career in *film*
3 [*count*] **:** a thin layer on or over the surface of something ▪ the protective *film* over a shark's eye ▪ A *film* of ice covered the sidewalk.

[2]**film** *verb* **films; filmed; film·ing**
1 [+ *obj*] **:** to make a movie of (something) **:** to photograph (an event, scene, etc.) with a movie or video camera ▪ Television news crew members came to *film* the interview. ▪ She *filmed* the children playing.
2 [*no obj*] **:** to make a movie ▪ We'll begin *filming* [=*shooting*] next week.
– filming *noun* [*noncount*] ▪ *Filming* will begin next week. ▪ two weeks of *filming*

film·go·er /ˈfɪlmˌgowɚ/ *noun, pl* **-ers** [*count*] **:** a person who often goes to movies or who is at a particular movie **:** MOVIEGOER

film·mak·er /ˈfɪlmˌmeɪkɚ/ *noun, pl* **-ers** [*count*] **:** a person (such as a director or producer) who makes movies ▪ a major *filmmaker*

film noir /-ˈnwɑɚ/ *noun, pl* **films noir** /ˌfɪlmzˈnwɑɚ/ [*count*] **:** a movie about crime that uses dark shadows and lighting to show the complicated moral nature of the subject; *also* [*noncount*] **:** this style of film

film·strip /ˈfɪlmˌstrɪp/ *noun, pl* **-strips** [*count*] **:** a long piece of film used for showing a series of pictures on a screen individually and not as a movie

filmy /ˈfɪlmi/ *adj* **film·i·er; -est :** very thin and light ▪ *filmy* curtains ▪ *filmy* fabric

filo *variant spelling of* PHYLLO

[1]**fil·ter** /ˈfɪltɚ/ *noun, pl* **-ters** [*count*]
1 : a device that is used to remove something unwanted from a liquid or gas that passes through it ▪ She smokes cigarettes with *filters*. ▪ a water *filter*
2 : a device that prevents some kinds of light, sound, electronic noises, etc., from passing through ▪ He placed a red *filter* on the camera lens. ▪ digital *filters* that stop high-frequency sounds
3 *computers* **:** software that prevents someone from looking at or receiving particular kinds of material through the Internet ▪ a spam *filter* [=a program that keeps you from seeing spam or unwanted e-mail]

[2]**filter** *verb* **-ters; -tered; -ter·ing**
1 [+ *obj*] **a :** to pass (something, such as a gas or liquid) through a filter to remove something unwanted ▪ They've begun *filtering* their water to remove impurities. **b :** to remove (something unwanted) by using a filter ▪ a device that *filters* impurities from water ▪ sunglasses that *filter* ultraviolet light — often + *out* ▪ sunglasses that *filter out* ultraviolet light — often used figuratively ▪ The purpose of the first interview is to *filter out* people who are not good candidates for the job.
2 *always followed by an adverb or preposition* [*no obj*] **a :** to move through or into something in small amounts or in a gradual way ▪ Sunlight *filtered* through the leaves. ▪ His ideas have *filtered* down to his children. **b :** to come or go slowly in small groups or amounts ▪ The crowd *filtered* into the arena. ▪ The crowd *filtered* out (of the arena). ▪ Early election returns have begun to *filter* in.

filth /ˈfɪlθ/ *noun* [*noncount*]
1 : a large and very unpleasant amount of dirt ▪ He emerged from the cellar covered in *filth*. **:** very dirty conditions ▪ the *filth* of the slaughterhouse ▪ living in *filth* and squalor
2 : something that is very offensive or disgusting and often is about sex ▪ magazines full of *filth*

[1]**filthy** /ˈfɪlθi/ *adj* **filth·i·er; -est**
1 : very dirty ▪ *filthy* clothes ▪ *filthy* streets
2 a : very offensive or disgusting and usually about sex ▪ a *filthy* movie/joke ▪ He has a *filthy* mouth. [=he uses language that is very offensive] **b :** very evil **:** morally wrong ▪ *filthy* tactics ▪ That's a *filthy* lie! **c :** very bad ▪ He has a *filthy* temper. [=he gets angry very easily] ▪ She's in a *filthy* mood. ▪ (*chiefly Brit*) We've been having *filthy* weather.
– filth·i·ness /ˈfɪlθinəs/ *noun* [*noncount*] ▪ the *filthiness* of the streets

[2]**filthy** *adv, informal* **:** VERY ▪ He's ***filthy rich***. [=he's extremely rich; he has so much money that his wealth is disgusting or offensive] ▪ Her clothes were ***filthy dirty***. [=extremely dirty]

fil·tra·tion /fɪlˈtreɪʃən/ *noun* [*noncount*] *technical* **:** the act or process of removing something unwanted from a liquid, gas, etc., by using a filter ▪ water *filtration*

fin /ˈfɪn/ *noun, pl* **fins** [*count*]
1 : a thin flat part that sticks out from the body of a fish and is used in moving or guiding the fish through water ▪ a fish with blue scales and spiny *fins* ▪ a shark *fin*
2 : a part on a machine (such as a car or airplane) that is shaped like a fish's fin ▪ a car from the 1950s with *fins* on the back — see also TAIL FIN
– finned /ˈfɪnd/ *adj* ▪ a *finned* creature [=a fish]

fi·na·gle /fəˈneɪgəl/ *verb* **-na·gles; -na·gled; -na·gling** [+ *obj*] *informal*
1 : to get (something) in a clever or dishonest way ▪ He *finagled* an invitation to the conference by claiming to be a reporter. = He *finagled* his way into the conference by claiming to be a reporter.
2 : to trick (someone) in order to get something ▪ A con man *finagled* my neighbor out of four hundred dollars.
– fi·na·gler /fəˈneɪglɚ/ *noun, pl* **-glers** [*count*]

[1]**fi·nal** /ˈfaɪnl/ *adj*
1 *always used before a noun* **a :** happening or coming at the end ▪ the *final* act of the play ▪ They won their *final* four games. ▪ in the *final* minutes/moments/seconds of the game ▪ Our last/previous stop was Bangkok, but our *final* destination is Tokyo. ▪ The plans are undergoing *final* review. ▪ *final* exams [=exams at the end of a class or term] ▪ I'd like to add one *final* note. [=make one last statement] **b :** happening as a result **:** happening at the end of a process ▪ What was the *final* score? ▪ The *final* product was not what we had expected. ▪ the *final* results
2 — used to say that something will not to be changed or done again ▪ This is my *final* offer. ▪ You can't come with us, and that's *final*! ▪ All sales are *final*. ▪ Is that your *final* answer?
in the final analysis see ANALYSIS
the final straw see STRAW
the final word see [1]WORD

[2]**final** *noun, pl* **-nals**
1 [*count*] **:** the last competition (such as a game or race) or set of competitions in a series ▪ He was defeated in the (men's) *final*. — usually plural ▪ He won in the quarterfinals and semifinals but was defeated in the *finals*.
2 a finals [*plural*] **:** the examinations that happen at the end

of a class, term, or course of study • He passed his *finals.* • He failed his history *finals.* **b** [*count*] *US* **:** an examination at the end of a class • He failed his history *final.*

fi·na·le /fəˈnæli, fəˈnɑːli/ *noun, pl* **-les** [*count*] **:** the last part of something (such as a musical performance, play, etc.) • She sung a very difficult song for the *finale.* • the TV show's season *finale* [=the last program of the season] — see also GRAND FINALE

fi·nal·ist /ˈfaɪnəlɪst/ *noun, pl* **-ists** [*count*] **:** a person who competes in the last part of a competition • They interviewed all of the *finalists* before making a decision. • a *finalist* in the tennis tournament

fi·nal·i·ty /faɪˈnæləti/ *noun* [*noncount*] **:** the quality or state of being final or finished and not able to be changed • the *finality* of death • "It won't work," he said, with an air of *finality.*

fi·nal·ize *also Brit* **fi·nal·ise** /ˈfaɪnəˌlaɪz/ *verb* **-iz·es; -ized; -iz·ing** [+ *obj*] **:** to put (something, such as a plan or an agreement) in a final or finished form • They are *finalizing* their divorce this week. • We bought our tickets and *finalized* our vacation plans.
– **fi·nal·i·za·tion** *also Brit* **fi·nal·i·sa·tion** /ˌfaɪnələˈzeɪʃən, *Brit* ˌfaɪnəˌlaɪˈzeɪʃən/ *noun* [*noncount*]

fi·nal·ly /ˈfaɪnl̩i/ *adv*
1 : at the end of a period of time • He won't rest until the killer is *finally* found. **:** after a long time • After years of arguing, the two brothers *finally* made up. • I *finally* found my wallet. • They're *finally* here. • "They're here." "*Finally!*" • We're *finally* starting to see some results.
2 a — used to describe the last action or event in a series of actions or events • He slowly stood up, cleared his throat, and *finally* began to speak. **b** — used to introduce a final statement or series of statements • *Finally* [=*in conclusion, lastly*], I'd like to thank all who cooperated in this project.
3 : in a final manner **:** in a way that cannot be changed • The dispute has not yet been *finally* settled.

[1]fi·nance /ˈfaɪˌnæns, fəˈnæns/ *noun, pl* **-nanc·es**
1 [*noncount*] **:** the way in which money is used and handled • She's taking a course on personal *finance*; *especially* **:** the way in which large amounts of money are used and handled by governments and companies • an expert in *finance* who predicts global economic disaster • corporate *finance* — see also HIGH FINANCE
2 *finances* [*plural*] **a :** money available to a government, business, or person • The library closed due to a lack of *finances.* **b :** matters relating to money and how it is spent or saved • His *finances* were in bad shape. [=he did not have enough money] • Her health problems have put a serious strain on her *finances.* [=she lacks money because of an unusual number of health expenses]

[2]fi·nance /fəˈnæns, ˈfaɪˌnæns/ *verb* **-nanc·es; -nanced; -nanc·ing** [+ *obj*]
1 : to provide money for (something or someone) • His parents *financed* his college education. • The study was *financed* by a government grant. • They *financed* him to study abroad.
2 : to buy (something) by borrowing money that will be paid back over a period of time • *finance* a new car
– **financing** *noun* [*noncount*] • Public *financing* paid for the new stadium. • The car dealer offers *financing.* [=you can get a loan through the car dealer to pay for a car that you buy there]

finance company *noun, pl* ~ **-nies** [*count*] **:** a company that makes small loans to people — called also (*Brit*) *finance house*

fi·nan·cial /fəˈnænʃəl/ *adj* **:** relating to money • The company is headed for *financial* disaster. • a family struggling with *financial* problems • I would like some *financial* advice before I buy this house. • You can get a loan at a ***financial institution***. [=a company that deals with money; a bank]
– **fi·nan·cial·ly** *adv* • He has made some smart investments, so he's doing very well *financially.* • a *financially* stable organization

financial aid *noun* [*noncount*] *US* **:** money that is given or lent to students in order to help pay for their education • She needed *financial aid.*

financial year *noun, pl* ~ **years** [*count*] *Brit* **:** FISCAL YEAR

fin·an·cier /ˌfɪnənˈsiɚ, *Brit* fəˈnænsiə/ *noun, pl* **-ciers** [*count*] **:** a person who controls the use and lending of large amounts of money • A group of powerful *financiers* bought out the company.

finch /ˈfɪntʃ/ *noun, pl* **finch·es** [*count*] **:** a small bird with a short, thick beak

[1]find /ˈfaɪnd/ *verb* **finds; found** /ˈfaʊnd/; **find·ing**
1 [+ *obj*] **a :** to discover (something or someone) without planning or trying to **:** to discover (something or someone) by chance • He *found* a dollar on the ground. • The well diggers *found* a number of Native American artifacts. • She *finds* [=*meets*] interesting people wherever she goes. **b** ◊ Something or someone that ***is found*** in a specified place exists there or lives there. • Many artifacts can *be found* in this area. [=there are many artifacts in this area] • Polar bears *are found* in the Northern Hemisphere.
2 [+ *obj*] **:** to get or discover (something or someone that you are looking for) • After an hour of searching, I finally *found* my glasses. • *find* a missing person • We need to *find* a suitable person for the job. • I *found* a job for him. = I *found* him a job. • My glasses are ***nowhere to be found***. = I can't *find* my glasses.
3 [+ *obj*] **a :** to discover or learn (something) by studying about it • She *found* the answer at last. • They claim to have *found* a more efficient way to run the business. • researchers trying to *find* a cure for cancer **b :** to get (something needed or wanted) by effort • You must *find* time to do it. • I *found* a way to pay for college without taking out any loans. • She *found* the courage to address the crowd. • I hope you can ***find it in your heart*** to forgive me. = I hope you can ***find it in yourself*** to forgive me. [=I hope you can forgive me]
4 [+ *obj*] **a :** to regard (someone or something you have met, seen, experienced, etc.) in a specified way • I *found* him (to be) a very sensible man. = I *found* him very sensible. • Students often *find* this book (to be) useful. • I *find* it hard to concentrate [=it is hard for me to concentrate] with that music playing. • The travel arrangements were ***found wanting***. [=the travel arrangements were criticized] **b :** to be affected by (something) in a specified way • He *finds* laughing/laughter painful. = He *finds* it painful to laugh. **c :** to feel (a pleasing emotion) • He *finds* pleasure in her company. • They didn't win, but the team *found* some satisfaction in having played so well.
5 [+ *obj*] **a :** to discover (someone) in a specified state • He *found* them waiting for him. • I *found* her relaxing by the pool. • He was *found* dead the next morning. • The crisis *found* them unprepared. [=they were unprepared when the crisis occurred] **b :** to become aware that you are doing something or that you are in a particular place or situation • I often *find* myself thinking about her. • When he awoke, he *found* himself in an unfamiliar room. [=he saw that he was in an unfamiliar room] • I *found* myself agreeing with him. [=I found that I agreed with him]
6 [+ *obj*] **:** to begin to have (something) • The new product *found* few buyers. [=few people bought it] • It took a while before his unusual brand of comedy *found* an audience. • These ideas have ***found approval/favor*** [=been accepted; become well-liked] among many young people. • His doctrines ***found acceptance*** [=were accepted] among scholars.
7 *law* **a** [+ *obj*] **:** to make a decision about the guilt or innocence of (someone) • The jury *found* her guilty. • She was *found* innocent. **b :** to decide the result of a court case [+ *obj*] The jury *found* a verdict of guilty. [*no obj*] The jury *found* for the defendant. [=the jury's decision was in favor of the defendant] • The jury *found* against her.

find common cause see [1]CAUSE

find fault **:** to criticize someone or something • No matter what she did, her husband was always *finding fault.* — usually + *with* • Her husband *found fault with* everything she did. — see also FAULTFINDER

find its mark/target **:** to hit a target that was aimed for • The bullet *found its mark.* — often used figuratively • Her angry reaction showed that his criticisms had *found their mark.*

find out [*phrasal verb*] **1** ***find out (something)*** **:** to learn (something) by making an effort • I'd like to *find out* more about the school's psychology program. • We need to *find out* where the meeting is being held. • I don't know when the game starts, but I'll *find out.* **2** ***find out about (something)*** **:** to become aware of (something) • Her mother *found out about* her smoking habit. **3** ***find (someone) out*** **:** to learn the unpleasant truth about (someone) • He pretended to be a respectable citizen, but we *found* him *out* at last. • Luckily, he was *found out* before he could do any harm.

find your bearings see BEARING

find yourself **:** to learn what you truly value and want in life

• He left school and traveled to Europe, saying that he wanted to *find himself.*

find your voice : to begin speaking or expressing your thoughts : to be able to speak or to express yourself as a writer • I couldn't speak for a moment, but then I *found my voice.* • a young novelist who has *found her voice*

find your way **1** : to look for and find where you need to go in order to get somewhere • I *found my way* home without any problems. • She got lost trying to *find her way* back to the hotel. — often used figuratively • He's still *finding his way* as an actor. [=he's still learning what he needs to do to succeed as an actor] **2** : to go or arrive somewhere by chance or after a time of wandering • The settlers eventually *found their way* to California.

[2]**find** *noun, pl* **finds** [*count*] : something or someone that has been found; *especially* : a valuable person or thing that has been found or discovered • That antique she bought at the flea market was a real *find.* • That new secretary of yours is a real *find!*

find·er /ˈfaɪndɚ/ *noun, pl* **-ers** [*count*] : a person who finds something that was lost

finders keepers (losers weepers) — used especially in children's speech to say that you can keep what you have found and do not need to give it back to the person who has lost it

find·ing /ˈfaɪndɪŋ/ *noun, pl* **-ings** [*count*]

1 : a legal decision : VERDICT • The Supreme Court overturned the lower court's *finding.*

2 : the results of an investigation — usually plural • He published his *findings* in a medical journal.

[1]**fine** /ˈfaɪn/ *adj* **fin·er; -est**

1 a *not used before a noun* : good, acceptable, or satisfactory : OK • That's *fine* with me. • "Is there anything wrong?" "No, everything's *fine.*" • The house looks *fine* to me. • "Would you like more coffee?" "No, I'm *fine,* thanks." [=I am happy with the amount of coffee I have now] • "Would you like more coffee?" "No, this is *fine,* thanks." [=no, this is as much as I want] • That's just ***fine and dandy*** with me. [=that is fine with me; I approve of that] ✧ *Fine* is often used as a response to show acceptance or approval. • "I have to leave early, all right?" "*Fine.*" **b** — used in an ironic way to refer to things that are not good or acceptable • This is a *fine* mess we're in. • "Those kids are no good." "You're a ***fine one to talk,*** considering all the trouble you caused when you were young." [=you should not say bad things about others because those same things could be said about you]

2 a *always used before a noun* : very good • I think that's a *fine* idea. • You did a *fine* job. • The house is in *fine* shape. • This is a *fine* example of what can go wrong when one person is given too much power. • They make a *fine* pair. [=they are well suited to each other] • She has a *fine* grasp of the problem. [=she understands the problem very well] • He was in *fine* form. [=he performed very well] **b** *always used before a noun* : deserving praise, admiration, or respect • He's a *fine* young man. • a *fine* musician • a *fine* mind

3 *not used before a noun* : well or healthy : not sick or injured • I feel *fine.* • "Did you hurt yourself?" "No, I'm *fine.*"

4 *of weather* : sunny and pleasant • a *fine* spring day • The weather has been *fine* lately.

5 a : very thin • *fine* thread/wire/yarn • Her head was covered with *fine,* silky hair. **b** : very sharp or narrow • a knife with a *fine* edge • a pen/brush with a *fine* tip : having a sharp point • a *fine* pen/brush **c** : made up of very small pieces, drops, etc. • *fine* sand/dust/powder • *fine* gravel • a *fine* mist/spray **d** : very small • The print was so *fine* that I could barely read it. • very *fine* details on the sculpture — see also FINE PRINT **e** : having very small holes • a *fine* mesh **f** : small and delicate • She has *fine* features. [=her eyes, nose, and mouth are small and delicate]

6 a : small and done with a lot of care and accuracy • *fine* measurements • *fine* movements **b** : small and difficult to see or understand : SUBTLE • a *fine* distinction • He's still learning the *finer* points of the job. • Some very *fine* legal points were involved. • There's a ***fine line*** [=a very small difference] between being helpful and being intrusive.

7 a *always used before a noun* : expensive and of high quality • *fine* dining • *fine* china **b** : formal and graceful • *fine* handwriting • His manners are very *fine.* [=*refined*]

a fine figure of a man/woman see [1]FIGURE

chance would be a fine thing see [1]CHANCE

finest hour see HOUR

not to put too fine a point on it — used in an ironic way to introduce a very strong and usually critical statement • *Not to put too fine a point on it,* (but) his suggestions have been worthless.

– fine·ly /ˈfaɪnli/ *adv* • The onions should be *finely* chopped. [=should be chopped in small pieces] • a *finely* judged response that was just right • a *finely* balanced election that could go either way **– fine·ness** /ˈfaɪnnəs/ *noun* [*noncount*] • the *fineness* of the thread • *fineness* of detail

[2]**fine** *adv, somewhat informal*

1 : not badly or poorly : well enough • She did *fine* on the test. • My mother is doing *fine,* thank you. • Everything was going *fine.* • That suits me *fine.* • This'll do *fine* for now.

2 : in an elegant and graceful way • She talks and walks so *fine,* just like a great lady.

3 *used after a verb* : in small pieces • The onions should be chopped *fine.* [=*finely*]

[3]**fine** *noun, pl* **fines** [*count*] : an amount of money that you pay as a punishment for breaking a law or rule • He had to pay a heavy *fine* for speeding. • a *fine* of $500 • The judge imposed a *fine* on him.

[4]**fine** *verb* **fines; fined; fin·ing** [+ *obj*] : to require (someone) to pay a fine as a punishment • He was *fined* for speeding. • The judge *fined* him $35.

fine art *noun, pl* ~ **arts**

1 : a type of art (such as painting, sculpture, or music) that is done to create beautiful things [*noncount*] a collector of *fine art* [*plural*] She studies painting in the department of *fine arts.* • We saw the sculpture at the Museum of *Fine Arts.*

2 [*singular*] : an activity that requires skill and care • the *fine art* of gourmet cooking — often used in a humorous or ironic way • He has mastered the *fine art* of flattery.

fine print *noun* [*noncount*] : the part of an agreement or document that contains important details and that is sometimes written in small letters • Read the *fine print* before you sign the contract. — see also [1]FINE 5d

fin·ery /ˈfaɪnəri/ *noun* [*noncount*] *somewhat formal* : clothes, jewels, etc., that are expensive and beautiful • wedding *finery* • She was proud to show off her new evening *finery.*

[1]**fi·nesse** /fəˈnɛs/ *noun* [*noncount*] : skill and cleverness that is shown in the way someone deals with a situation, problem, etc. • She handled the interview questions with *finesse.*

[2]**finesse** *verb* **-ness·es; -nessed; -ness·ing** [+ *obj*] : to handle, deal with, or do (something) in an indirect and skillful or clever way • He managed to *finesse* a deal through bargaining. • She is just trying to *finesse* the issue.

fin·est /ˈfaɪnəst/ *noun* [*plural*] *US, informal* : the police officers of a specified city or area • He's a member of New York's *finest.* [=he's a police officer in New York]

fine–tooth comb /ˈfaɪnˌtuːθ-/ *noun, pl* ~ **combs** [*count*] : a comb with many small teeth

go over/through (something) with a fine-tooth comb : to examine something very closely • The police are *going over the evidence with a fine-tooth comb.*

fine–tune /ˈfaɪnˈtuːn/ *verb* **-tunes; -tuned; -tun·ing** [+ *obj*] : to make small changes to (something) in order to improve the way it works or to make it exactly right • *fine-tune* a TV set • *fine-tune* the temperature of the room • They're *fine-tuning* interest rates to achieve economic growth without inflation.

[1]**fin·ger** /ˈfɪŋgɚ/ *noun, pl* **-gers**

1 [*count*] : one of the five long parts of the hand that are used for holding things; *especially* : one of the four that are not the thumb • Don't stick your *fingers* in the cookie batter! • He slipped the ring onto her *finger.* • The baby held onto my thumb with her tiny *fingers.* • She ran her *fingers* through his hair. • He drummed his *fingers* on the table impatiently. — see also FOREFINGER, INDEX FINGER, LITTLE FINGER, MIDDLE FINGER, RING FINGER

2 [*count*] **a** : something that is long and thin and looks like a finger • a *finger* of land extending into the sea • a *finger* of flame **b** : the part of a glove into which a finger is placed

3 ***the finger*** *US, informal* : an obscene gesture made by pointing the middle finger up, keeping the other fingers down, and turning the palm towards you • She was so mad, she ***gave him the finger.*** • Some angry driver ***flipped me the finger*** on the highway this morning.

all fingers and thumbs *informal* : very clumsy • Sorry I dropped the vase; I'm *all fingers and thumbs* today.

cross your fingers see [2]CROSS

finger on the pulse ✧ If you ***have/keep your finger on the pulse of*** something, you know about the latest things that are happening. • He claims that he *has/keeps his finger on the pulse of* the computer industry. [=that he is very aware what is happening in the computer industry]

have a finger in a/the pie : to have an interest or share in something • a sharp talent agent who *has a finger in* nearly every *pie* in show business

itchy finger see ITCHY

keep your fingers crossed see ²CROSS

lay a finger on informal : to touch or hit (someone) — usually used in negative statements • I don't know what he's complaining about. I never *laid a finger on him.*

lift a finger : to make an effort to do something — usually used in negative statements • I have so many chores to do, and my sister won't *lift a finger* to help me. • He never *lifted a finger* to try to improve his failing grades.

point an accusing finger at or ***point a/the finger at*** : to accuse or blame (someone) • He was quick to *point an accusing finger at* his coworkers. • Let's stop *pointing fingers at* each other and just solve the problem!

put/stick two fingers up at someone *Brit, informal* : to make an obscene gesture by holding up the index finger and the middle finger of one hand in the shape of a V while keeping the palm turned inward

put your finger on : to find out the exact nature of (something) : IDENTIFY • I feel that something is wrong but I can't quite *put my finger on* the problem.

the finger of blame/suspicion — used to say that someone is being blamed or suspected • He was shocked to realize that the *finger of suspicion* was now pointed at him. [=that he was now suspected]

work your fingers to the bone : to work very hard • She had to *work her fingers to the bone* to make enough money to raise her kids.

wrap (someone) around your (little) finger see ¹WRAP

– fin·gered /ˈfɪŋgɚd/ *adj* — used in combination • three-*fingered* **– fin·ger·like** /ˈfɪŋgɚˌlaɪk/ *adj*

²**finger** *verb* **-gers; -gered; -ger·ing** [+ *obj*]

1 : to touch (something) with your fingers • She *fingered* the silk. • She *fingered* her necklace.

2 *chiefly US, informal* : to identify (someone) as the person who has committed a crime • He was *fingered* as a suspect.

finger food *noun, pl* ~ **foods** [*count, noncount*] *US* : a piece of food that is meant to be picked up with the fingers and eaten

fin·ger·ing /ˈfɪŋgərɪŋ/ *noun* [*noncount*] : the way in which the fingers are used and positioned in order to play a musical instrument

fin·ger·nail /ˈfɪŋgɚˌneɪl/ *noun, pl* **-nails** [*count*] : the hard covering at the end of your fingers • I trimmed and filed my *fingernails.* • He had dirt under his *fingernails.* • Quit biting/chewing your *fingernails.* — see picture at HAND

finger paint *verb* ~ **paints;** ~ **painted;** ~ **painting** [*no obj*] *chiefly US* : to paint a picture using only your hands or fingers instead of a brush • The kids will *finger paint* today.

– finger paint *noun, pl* ~ **paints** [*count*] • I have to buy some *finger paints* for my classroom. **– finger painting** *noun* [*noncount*] • Today's activity is *finger painting.*

finger–pointing *noun* [*noncount*] : the act of blaming someone for a problem instead of trying to fix or solve it • This administration refuses to engage in *finger-pointing.*

¹**fin·ger·print** /ˈfɪŋgɚˌprɪnt/ *noun, pl* **-prints** [*count*]

1 a : the mark that is made by pressing the tip of a finger on a surface • Detectives found his *fingerprints* all over the gun. • Everyone has a unique *fingerprint.* — sometimes used figuratively • This project has his *fingerprints* all over it. [=it is obvious that he was very involved in this project] **b** : a mark of this kind made in ink for the purpose of identifying a person — usually plural • The police took her *fingerprints* for their files. — called also *print*

2 : something (such as genetic material) that can be used to identify a person • a DNA *fingerprint*

²**fingerprint** *verb* **-prints; -print·ed; -print·ing** [+ *obj*] : to take the fingerprints of (someone, such as a criminal) for the purpose of identification • He was arrested, taken to the police station, and *fingerprinted.*

– fingerprinting *noun* [*noncount*] • He was arrested and taken to the police station for *fingerprinting.*

fin·ger·tip /ˈfɪŋgɚˌtɪp/ *noun, pl* **-tips** [*count*] : the very end of a finger — usually plural • He tapped on the tabletop with his *fingertips.*

at your fingertips : easily available : easy to find or use • The librarian has all the information *at his fingertips.*

to your fingertips *chiefly Brit* : in every way • He is a gentleman *to his fingertips.*

fin·icky /ˈfɪnɪki/ *adj* [*more* ~; *most* ~]

1 : very hard to please • a *finicky* eater • My teacher is *finicky* about grammar.

2 : requiring a lot of care or attention • a complicated and *finicky* recipe

¹**fin·ish** /ˈfɪnɪʃ/ *verb* **-ish·es; -ished; -ish·ing**

1 a : to reach the end of (something) : to stop doing (something) because it is completed [+ *obj*] He *finished* (giving) his speech and sat down. • He hasn't *finished* his work yet. = He hasn't *finished* working yet. • You can't watch TV until you *finish* your homework. [*no obj*] He started his homework two hours ago and he still hasn't *finished.* • I'll wait here until you *finish.* = I'll wait here until you have *finished.* — compare FINISHED 1a **b** : to be done with building or creating (something) [+ *obj*] They hope to *finish* their new home by winter. [*no obj*] They're building a new home and they hope to *finish* by winter. — compare FINISHED 1b **c** : to cause something to end or stop : to reach the end of something [+ *obj*] The chairman *finished* the meeting at noon. [*no obj*] The meeting *finished* [=*ended*] at noon. • The meeting *finished* on a positive note.

2 [+ *obj*] **a** : to cause the ruin or failure of (someone or something) • These allegations could *finish* his career as a politician. = These allegations could *finish* him as a politician. — compare FINISHED 2b **b** : to kill (someone or something already wounded) — usually + *off* • The crowd in the arena shouted for the gladiator to *finish off* his opponent. **c** : to defeat or exhaust (someone) completely — usually + *off* • Climbing so many stairs just about *finished* me *off.*

3 [+ *obj*] : to use, eat, or drink all that is left of (something) • They *finished* (off/up) the pie before I got a chance to have a slice. • I've had enough wine. You can *finish* (off) the rest of the bottle.

4 : to end a race, competition, etc., in a specified position or manner [*no obj*] The horse I bet on *finished* third. • The horse *finished* in third place. • Our team started poorly but *finished* well. [+ *obj*] The horse I bet on *finished* the race in third place. • Our team *finished* the season in first place.

5 [+ *obj*] : to put a final coat or surface on (something) • He *finished* the table with varnish.

finishing touch : one of the last things done to make something complete — usually plural • They're ***putting the finishing touches*** on their new home. • He's *putting the finishing touches* on his latest novel.

finish with [*phrasal verb*] **1** ***finish with (something)*** : to have no further need for (something) : to stop using (something) • Could I see the newspaper when you *finish with* it? **2** ***finish with (someone)*** : to stop being involved with (someone) : to end a romantic relationship with (someone) • She and her boyfriend had another fight, and now she says she's going to *finish with* him once and for all. — compare FINISHED 2a **3** ***finish with (someone or something)*** : to stop dealing with, working on, or punishing (someone or something) • When I *finish with* him he'll be sorry! • I haven't *finished with* you yet! — see also FINISHED

²**finish** *noun, pl* **-ish·es**

1 [*singular*] : the last part of something : END, CONCLUSION • a suspense film with a perfect surprise *finish* • The race was close ***from start to finish.*** [=from the beginning to the end] • The race had a ***close/tight finish.*** [=the winner of the race won by a very small amount] • It was a ***fight to the finish.*** [=the fight went on until one side was completely defeated] — see also PHOTO FINISH

2 [*count*] : the final coating on a surface or the appearance produced by such a coating • The table had a shiny *finish.* • I need to put one more coat of *finish* on the chair.

– fin·ish·er *noun, pl* **-ers** [*count*]

finished *adj*

1 a *not used before a noun* : having reached the end of an activity, job, etc. • He started his homework two hours ago and he still isn't *finished.* • I'll wait here until you're *finished.* — compare ¹FINISH 1a **b** : not requiring more work : entirely done or completed • The job is finally *finished.* • We were pleased with the *finished* product. • The house has a ***finished basement/attic.*** [=a basement/attic that has floors, ceilings, and walls like the rooms in the main part of the house] — compare ¹FINISH 1b

2 *not used before a noun* **a** : having reached the end of a romantic relationship • We're *finished*! I never want to see you again! • She says she's *finished* with that guy. **b** : no longer able to continue : completely ruined or defeated • This scandal means that his career is *finished*. — compare [1]FINISH 2a

finishing line *noun, pl* ~ **lines** [*count*] *Brit* : FINISH LINE

finishing school *noun, pl* ~ **schools** [*count*] : a private school where girls from wealthy families are taught proper behavior and manners

finish line *noun, pl* ~ **lines** [*count*] *US* : a line that marks the end of a race — called also (*Brit*) *finishing line*

fi•nite /ˈfaɪˌnaɪt/ *adj*

1 : having limits ▪ a *finite* number of possibilities : having a limited nature ▪ the earth's *finite* supply of natural resources ▪ the *finite* human life span

2 *grammar* : of or relating to a verb form that shows action that takes place at a particular time (such as the past) ▪ a *finite* verb such as "is" or "are" — opposite NONFINITE

– **fi•nite•ly** *adv*

[1]**fink** /ˈfɪŋk/ *noun, pl* **finks** [*count*] *chiefly US, informal*

1 : a person who is strongly disliked ▪ She says her boss is a rotten *fink*.

2 : a person who gives information to the police or to some other authority about the bad behavior or criminal activity of someone else

[2]**fink** *verb* **finks; finked; fink•ing**

fink on [*phrasal verb*] ***fink on (someone)*** *US, informal* : to tell someone about the bad behavior or criminal activity of (another person) ▪ The other gang members will kill him if they find out that he *finked on* them (to the police).

Finn /ˈfɪn/ *noun, pl* **Finns** [*count*] : a person born, raised, or living in Finland

[1]**Finn•ish** /ˈfɪnɪʃ/ *adj* : of or relating to Finland, its people, or the Finnish language ▪ *Finnish* lakes/customs/grammar

[2]**Finnish** *noun* [*noncount*] : the chief language of the people of Finland

fiord *variant spelling of* FJORD

fir /ˈfɚ/ *noun, pl* **firs**

1 [*count*] : a tall evergreen tree

2 [*noncount*] : the wood of a fir tree

[1]**fire** /ˈfajɚ/ *noun, pl* **fires**

1 [*noncount*] : the light and heat and especially the flame produced by burning ▪ Stay away from the *fire*.

2 : an occurrence in which something burns : the destruction of something (such as a building or a forest) by fire [*count*] The shack was destroyed by a *fire*. ▪ Two people died in that terrible *fire*. ▪ How did the *fire* start? ▪ Police think he ***set a fire*** [=deliberately started a fire] in the bedroom. ▪ Firefighters ***put the fire out***. = Firefighters ***put out the fire***. [=firefighters stopped the fire from burning] [*noncount*] The shack ***caught (on) fire*** [=began to burn] when it was struck by lightning. ▪ Someone ***set fire to*** the shack. [=deliberately caused the shack to burn]

3 [*count*] : a controlled occurrence of fire created by burning something (such as wood or gas) in a special area (such as in a fireplace or stove) ▪ We warmed our hands over the *fire*. ▪ She built a *fire* in the fireplace. ▪ The *fire* went out and he had to light it again. — see also CAMPFIRE

4 [*noncount*] : the shooting of weapons ▪ We heard heavy rifle *fire* in the distance. ▪ He shot at the police officer and the police officer ***returned his fire***. [=the police officer shot back at him] ▪ He and the police officer ***exchanged fire***. [=shot at each other] ▪ He was caught in the ***line of fire*** and killed. ▪ The troops ***opened fire on*** [=began shooting at] the enemy. ▪ ***Hold your fire***! [=don't shoot] ▪ ***Cease fire***! [=stop shooting] ▪ Several soldiers were killed by ***friendly fire***. [=they were accidentally killed by weapons fired from their own side]

5 [*noncount*] : very heavy or harsh criticism ▪ The company has drawn/taken (heavy) *fire* for its use of child labor overseas.

6 [*noncount*] : strong emotion, anger, enthusiasm, etc. ▪ I admire her *fire* for teaching and helping children. ▪ young lovers with their hearts full of *fire* [=*passion*]

7 [*count*] *Brit* : a small device that uses gas or electricity to heat a room ▪ Turn on/off the *fire*.

baptism of/by fire see BAPTISM

fan a fire, fan the fire see [2]FAN

fight fire with fire see [1]FIGHT

from/out of the frying pan (and) into the fire see FRYING PAN

hang fire see [1]HANG

irons in the fire see [1]IRON

light a fire under see [3]LIGHT

like a house on fire see [1]HOUSE

on fire 1 : in the process of burning ▪ The house was *on fire*. 2 : feeling very strong enthusiasm, love, etc. ▪ He was *on fire* with enthusiasm. ▪ young lovers with their hearts *on fire* 3 : very successful ▪ The team has been *on fire*, winning 10 of its last 11 games. — see also *set the world on fire* at [1]WORLD

play with fire see [1]PLAY

under fire 1 : being shot at by the enemy ▪ The civilians panicked when they realized they were *under fire*. ▪ As a soldier he showed extraordinary skill and courage *under fire*. 2 : exposed to criticism : being criticized ▪ He is *under fire* from his political opponents. ▪ The company has ***come under fire*** [=has been criticized] for using child labor overseas.

where there's smoke, there's fire or ***there's no smoke without fire*** see [1]SMOKE

[2]**fire** *verb* **fires; fired; fir•ing**

1 a : to shoot a weapon [+ *obj*] *fire* a bullet ▪ She *fired* the arrow at the target. ▪ He *fired* the gun. ▪ He *fired* several shots at the police. [*no obj*] He *fired* at the police. ▪ The gun failed to *fire*. ▪ The soldiers *fired* on/at the enemy. ▪ The officers were told to ***fire at will***. [=to shoot when they felt that they should] — often used figuratively ▪ Reporters *fired* questions at her. [=they asked her many questions in a quick and forceful way] b [+ *obj*] : to throw (something) with speed and force ▪ The shortstop *fired* the ball to first base. ▪ The angry mob *fired* rocks at him. ▪ The boxer *fired* a left jab at his opponent's chin.

2 [+ *obj*] : to give life or energy to (something or someone) ▪ The story *fired* his imagination.

3 [+ *obj*] : to dismiss (someone) from a job ▪ She had to *fire* several workers. — usually used as *(be/get) fired* ▪ He *got/was fired* (from his job) after missing work.

4 [*no obj*] : to begin working ▪ The engine/cylinders failed to *fire*. — sometimes used figuratively ▪ The team got off to a slow start, but now it's ***firing on all cylinders***. [=it's now playing very well]

5 [+ *obj*] *technical* : to heat (a clay pot, dish, etc.) in an oven in order to make it very hard ▪ She will *fire* the pots later today.

fire away *informal* — used in speech to tell someone to begin asking you questions ▪ "We have some questions we'd like to ask you." "OK. *Fire away*."

fire back [*phrasal verb*] : to answer someone quickly and usually angrily ▪ After his statement, his opponent *fired back*. — often + *at* ▪ He *fired back at* his critics.

fire off [*phrasal verb*] ***fire (something) off*** or ***fire off (something)*** : to write and send (something, such as a letter or memo) in a quick and often angry way ▪ He *fired off* a letter of complaint. ▪ She *fired* an e-mail *off* to her lawyer.

fire up [*phrasal verb*] 1 ***fire (something) up*** or ***fire up (something)*** a : to start (something) by lighting a fire ▪ We *fired up* the grill for the barbecue. b : to cause (something) to start working ▪ I *fired up* my computer and got down to work. ▪ Before we start working let's *fire up* the coffeemaker. 2 ***fire (someone) up*** or ***fire up (someone)*** : to fill (someone) with energy or enthusiasm ▪ The coach *fired up* the players with a pep talk. — usually used as *(be/get) fired up* ▪ We *were fired up* for the concert.

– **firing** *noun, pl* **firings** [*count, noncount*] ▪ the hiring and *firing* of employees ▪ The pot must cool before its second *firing*.

fire alarm *noun, pl* ~ **alarms** [*count*] : a device that makes a loud sound to warn people when there is a fire ▪ Someone set off the *fire alarm*.

fire ant *noun, pl* ~ **ants** [*count*] : a type of ant that gives a very painful bite

fire•arm /ˈfajɚˌɑɚm/ *noun, pl* **-arms** [*count*] : a small gun ▪ revolvers, rifles, and other *firearms*

fire•ball /ˈfajɚˌbɑːl/ *noun, pl* **-balls** [*count*] : a huge mass of fire ▪ The house erupted into a *fireball*. ▪ a nuclear *fireball*

fire•bomb /ˈfajɚˌbɑːm/ *noun, pl* **-bombs** [*count*] : a bomb that causes a fire when it explodes

– **firebomb** *verb* **-bombs; -bombed; -bomb•ing** [+ *obj*] ▪ Rioters *firebombed* the courthouse.

fire•brand /ˈfajɚˌbrænd/ *noun, pl* **-brands** [*count*] : a person who tries to get people to become angry and to do things for a political or social cause ▪ a political *firebrand*

fire•break /ˈfajɚˌbreɪk/ *noun, pl* **-breaks** [*count*] : an area of land that has had plants and trees removed to stop the spread of a fire

fire–breath•ing /ˈfajɚˌbriːðɪŋ/ *adj, always used before a noun*

1 : able to produce a stream of fire from the mouth • a story about a *fire-breathing* dragon
2 : very angry and emotional in speech, manner, or behavior • a *fire-breathing* politician • a *fire-breathing* orator

fire brigade *noun, pl* ~ **-gades** [*count*]
1 *US* : a group of people who work to put out a fire
2 *Brit* : FIRE DEPARTMENT

fire·bug /ˈfajɚˌbʌg/ *noun, pl* **-bugs** [*count*] *US, informal* : a person who starts destructive fires

fire·crack·er /ˈfajɚˌkrækɚ/ *noun, pl* **-ers** [*count*] : a small paper cylinder that is filled with an explosive and that produces a loud noise when it explodes • boys setting off *firecrackers*

-fired /ˌfajɚd/ *combining form* : using a particular kind of fuel • a gas-*fired* furnace • a coal-*fired* power plant

fire department *noun, pl* ~ **-ments** [*count*] *US* : an organization for preventing and putting out fires — called also (*Brit*) *fire brigade*

fire drill *noun, pl* ~ **drills** [*count*] : an activity in which people practice leaving a place quickly so that they will know what to do if there is a fire

fire–eat·er /ˈfajɚˌiːtɚ/ *noun, pl* **-ers** [*count*] : a performer who pretends to eat fire

fire engine *noun, pl* ~ **-gines** [*count*] : a truck that has equipment for putting out fires — called also (*US*) *fire truck*

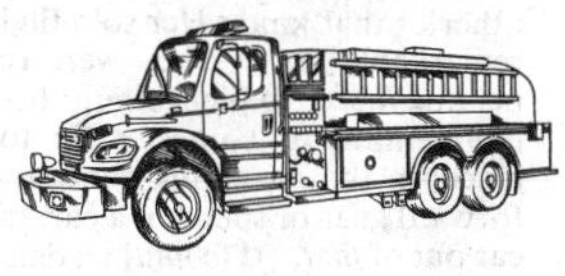
fire engine

fire escape *noun, pl* ~ **-capes** [*count*] : a stairway or ladder that can be used to escape from a burning building

fire extinguisher *noun, pl* ~ **-ers** [*count*] : a metal container filled with chemicals that is used to put out a fire

fire extinguisher

fire·fight /ˈfajɚˌfaɪt/ *noun, pl* **-fights** [*count*] : a battle in which people shoot guns • a *firefight* between police and bank robbers; *especially* : a usually short and fast gunfight between opposing military units

fire·fight·er /ˈfajɚˌfaɪtɚ/ *noun, pl* **-ers** [*count*] : a member of a group that works to put out fires
– **fire·fight·ing** *noun* [*noncount*] • *firefighting* equipment

fire·fly /ˈfajɚˌflaɪ/ *noun, pl* **-flies** [*count*] : a small flying insect that produces a soft light — called also (*US*) *lightning bug*

fire·house /ˈfajɚˌhaʊs/ *noun, pl* **-houses** [*count*] *US* : FIRE STATION

fire hydrant *noun, pl* ~ **-drants** [*count*] : a pipe usually in the street that provides water especially for putting out fires — called also *hydrant*, (*US*) *fireplug*

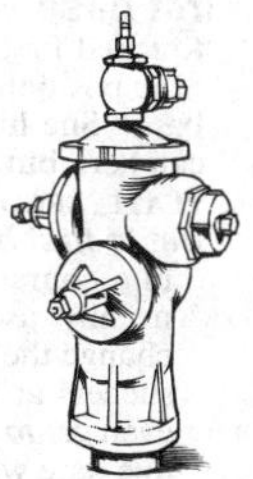
fire hydrant

fire·light /ˈfajɚˌlaɪt/ *noun* [*noncount*] : the light produced by a fire in a fireplace, stove, etc. • The *firelight* gave the room a warm glow. • At night, he read by *firelight*.

fire·man /ˈfajɚmən/ *noun, pl* **-men** /-mən/ [*count*] : a man who is a member of group that works to put out fires

fire·place /ˈfajɚˌpleɪs/ *noun, pl* **-plac·es** [*count*] : a specially built place in a room where a fire can be built • a stone/brick *fireplace* — see picture at LIVING ROOM

fire·plug /ˈfajɚˌplʌg/ *noun, pl* **-plugs** [*count*] *US* : FIRE HYDRANT

fire·pow·er /ˈfajɚˌpawɚ/ *noun* [*noncount*]
1 : the amount or strength of military weapons that can be used against an enemy • The army didn't have the *firepower* to defeat the invaders. • They had enough *firepower*.
2 : effective power or force • intellectual *firepower*

[1]**fire·proof** /ˈfajɚˌpruːf/ *adj* : not easily burned : not able to catch fire • firefighters in *fireproof* suits

[2]**fireproof** *verb* **-proofs**; **-proofed**; **-proof·ing** [+ *obj*] : to make (something) safe from fire • The building was not *fireproofed*.

fire sale *noun, pl* ~ **sales** [*count*]
1 : a sale of products that have been damaged by fire
2 : a sale at very low prices • The company is having a *fire sale* of its old office equipment.

fire screen *noun, pl* ~ **screens** [*count*] *US* : a metal screen that is placed in front of a fireplace

[1]**fire·side** /ˈfajɚˌsaɪd/ *noun, pl* **-sides** [*count*] : a place next to a fire : an area close to a fireplace, campfire, etc. • We sat chatting at the *fireside*.

[2]**fireside** *adj, always used before a noun* : having an informal or friendly quality • a *fireside* chat

fire station *noun, pl* ~ **-tions** [*count*] : a building in which the members of a fire department and the equipment used to put out fires are located — called also (*US*) *firehouse*

fire·storm /ˈfajɚˌstoɚm/ *noun, pl* **-storms** [*count*]
1 : a very large fire that destroys everything in its path and produces powerful winds • The bombing left the city engulfed in a *firestorm*.
2 : a large amount of anger and criticism • His proposal set off a political *firestorm*. • a *firestorm* of public protest

fire·trap /ˈfajɚˌtræp/ *noun, pl* **-traps** [*count*] : a building that is difficult to get out of and is likely to have a deadly fire • The factory was a *firetrap* and dozens of workers died before rescuers could reach them.

fire truck *noun, pl* ~ **trucks** [*count*] *US* : FIRE ENGINE

fire wall *noun, pl* ~ **walls** [*count*]
1 : a very thick wall that keeps fire from spreading
2 *usually* ***firewall*** : a computer program or piece of equipment that keeps people from using or connecting to a computer or a computer network without permission

fire·wood /ˈfajɚˌwʊd/ *noun* [*noncount*] : wood used to make a fire : wood used as fuel • They chopped enough *firewood* to last the winter.

fire·work /ˈfajɚˌwɚk/ *noun, pl* **-works**
1 a [*count*] : a small device that explodes to make a display of light and noise — usually plural • setting off some *fireworks* **b fireworks** [*plural*] : a display where fireworks are exploded • Are you going to stay for the *fireworks*? • a *fireworks* display
2 fireworks [*plural*] : a display of anger • We expect a few *fireworks* during the presidential debate.

firing line *noun, pl* ~ **lines**
1 [*count*] : a line of soldiers who are shooting at an enemy • a brave soldier who was never far behind the *firing line*
2 [*singular*] : a place or position in which someone is not protected from attack or criticism — used especially in the phrase (*US*) ***on the firing line*** or *Brit* ***in the firing line*** • School administrators are not *on the firing line* every day like the teachers are.

firing squad *noun, pl* ~ **squads** [*count, noncount*] : a group of soldiers whose job is to shoot a prisoner who has been sentenced to death • The traitor was executed by (a) *firing squad*.

[1]**firm** /ˈfɚm/ *adj* **firm·er**; **-est**
1 : fairly hard or solid : not soft • *firm* flesh • *firm* muscles • a *firm* mattress • a *firm* stomach • a *firm* cheese
2 : set, placed, or attached in a way that is not easily moved • a *firm* base/foundation — often used figuratively • He believes that his argument is ***on firm ground/footing***. [=that he has good support, evidence, etc., for his argument]
3 : not weak or uncertain • a *firm* [=*strong*] handshake/grip • She has a *firm* grasp of the basic principles. • They insist on maintaining *firm* control over the project. • He spoke to her in a soft but *firm* voice. • The time has come for us to take a *firm* stand. • The children need gentle but *firm* handling.
4 a : not likely to change or be changed • We've made *firm* [=*definite*] plans for next weekend. • a *firm* price/estimate/offer • The dollar remained *firm* against the euro. • reaching a *firm* conclusion/decision • They haven't set a *firm* date for their wedding. • The campaign has taken a *firm* hold on the public's imagination. **b :** having or showing true and constant support for something or someone • I'm a *firm* [=*strong*] believer in the value of exercise. = I have a *firm* belief in the value of exercise. • Those two are *firm* friends. [=they are very close friends]

hold firm see [1]HOLD
stand firm see [1]STAND
– **firm·ly** *adv* • They stood *firmly* [=*steadfastly, solidly*] behind their boss. • He pulled the hat down *firmly* over his ears. • I *firmly* [=*strongly*] believe in the value of exercise. • She's got her feet *firmly* (planted) on the ground. [=she is a practical and sensible person] – **firm·ness** *noun* [*noncount*] • the *firmness* of the mattress • the *firmness* of the price/estimate/offer

[2]firm *verb* **firms; firmed; firm·ing**
1 [+ *obj*] **:** to put (something, such as a plan) into a final form — usually + *up* ▪ We still need to *firm up* our vacation plans.
2 [+ *obj*] **:** to make (something) harder or more solid **:** to make (something) less loose ▪ I've been doing exercises to *firm* (up) and strengthen my stomach muscles. ▪ She *firmed* [=*tightened*] her grip on the racket.
3 [+ *obj*] **:** to make (something) stronger ▪ Her early failures only *firmed* [=*strengthened*] her resolve (to succeed).
4 [*no obj*] **:** to become less likely to change or become weaker ▪ The market is *firming*. — often + *up* ▪ The market is *firming up*. ▪ Imports are rising and prices are *firming up*.
– **firming** *adj* ▪ a *firming* cream [=a cream that makes your skin less loose]

[3]firm *noun, pl* **firms** [*count*] **:** a business organization ▪ a law *firm* ▪ a consulting *firm* [=*company*]

fir·ma·ment /ˈfɚməmənt/ *noun* [*noncount*] *formal + literary* **:** the sky ▪ meteors flashing across the *firmament* — sometimes used figuratively to refer to an area of interest or activity ▪ He was once the brightest star in the literary *firmament*.

firm·ware /ˈfɚmˌweɚ/ *noun* [*noncount*] *computers* **:** computer programs that are contained permanently in a device

[1]first /ˈfɚst/ *adj*
1 : coming before all others in time, order, or importance ▪ She won *first* prize. ▪ We sat in the *first* row. ▪ his *first* wife ▪ her *first* book/child ▪ in the *first* century ▪ his *first* offense ▪ her *first* kiss ▪ She succeeded on her *first* attempt/try. ▪ He was (the) *first* in line. ▪ We will correct these errors at the *first* opportunity. [=as soon as it is possible to do so] ▪ English is not my *first* [=*native*] language. [=it is not the language I learned first; I learned to speak another language before I learned to speak English] ▪ She's in *first* grade. [=the first level in school after kindergarten] ▪ I still remember the *first* time I saw her. ▪ You should leave at the *first* [=*earliest*] hint of trouble. ▪ My *first* [=*initial*] impulse was to say no. ▪ This is a matter of the *first* [=*highest*] importance. ▪ Your *first* [=*main*] concern should be to get well. ▪ the captain and the ***first mate*** [=the officer on a ship who is most important after the captain] ▪ She was accused of murder ***in the first degree***. [=first-degree murder; the most serious kind of murder]
2 — used to refer to the lowest forward gear or speed of a vehicle ▪ I couldn't get the car out of *first* gear.
3 : having or playing the main part in a group of instruments ▪ *first* violin
at first blush *or* ***at first glance*** *also* ***at first sight*** **:** when first seen or considered ▪ *At first blush*, the proposal seems ridiculous. ▪ It appears *at first glance/sight* to be a simple matter of hiring more people.
at first hand **:** in a direct way **:** FIRSTHAND ▪ I had a chance to verify his claims *at first hand*.
first among equals ✧ A person who is *first among equals* is the leader of a group of people but is officially considered equal in rights and status to the other members of the group. ▪ As a director, he encourages collaboration and considers himself only (the) *first among equals*.
first thing **1** ***the first thing*** **:** anything at all — used in negative statements ▪ He doesn't know/understand *the first thing* about the problems we've been having. **2 :** before anything else **:** right away **:** very early ▪ I'll be back *first thing* (on) Monday morning. ▪ She promised to call *first thing* in the morning.
first things first — used to say that you should do the things that are most important before doing other things ▪ I know you're eager to start shopping for a car, but *first things first*—you need to find out how much you can afford to spend. ▪ You must set priorities and learn how to ***put first things first***.
in the first flush of see [1]FLUSH
in the first instance see INSTANCE
in the first place see [1]PLACE
love at first sight see [1]LOVE

[2]first *adv*
1 a : before any other in time, order, or importance ▪ I have to pay him *first*. ▪ She finished *first* in the race. = She came in *first* in the race. = (*Brit*) She came *first* in the race. ▪ You go *first*. ▪ He said it *first*. ▪ These problems are not as simple as they *first* appear. **b :** for the first time ▪ I loved her when I *first* saw her. ▪ We met *first* at a party. = We *first* met at a party. ▪ This word was *first* recorded in the 19th century. **c :** before doing other things ▪ We'll get started soon, but *first* we have to make sure everyone is here.
2 — used to introduce a statement that is the first in a series of statements ▪ *First*, let me explain my reasons for calling this meeting. ▪ I want to talk about several things in this meeting. *First*, the schedule. Second, . . . — often used in the phrases ***first of all*** and ***first off*** ▪ Let me explain, *first of all*, why I called this meeting. ▪ *First off*, there's some confusion we have to clear up.
come first **:** to be more important than other things ▪ My career is important, but my family *comes first*.
first and foremost **:** at the most basic level ▪ He is *first and foremost* [=*primarily, fundamentally*] a teacher.
first and last **:** at the most basic level **:** in all respects ▪ This is *first and last* a matter of national security.
first come, first served *or* ***first come, first serve*** — used to say that the people who arrive earliest get served or treated before the people who arrive later ▪ The campsites are *first come, first served*, so we'd better get there early. = The campsites are assigned on a *first-come-first-serve* basis, so we'd better get there early. ▪ "Aren't there any cookies left?" "Sorry—*first come, first served*."
– see also FEETFIRST, HEADFIRST

[3]first *noun, pl* **firsts**
1 : something that is first: such as **a** [*count*] **:** an occurrence, achievement, etc., that happens or exists before any other of that kind ▪ Her solo flight across the Atlantic was a remarkable *first*. ▪ They were responsible for several engineering *firsts*. **b** [*noncount*] **:** the position of the winner in a competition or contest ▪ He took *first* [=finished in first place] in the pie-eating contest. **c** [*noncount*] **:** the lowest forward gear or speed of a car, truck, etc. ▪ I couldn't get the car out of *first*. **d** [*count*] **:** a degree of the highest level from a British university ▪ take/get a *first* in English
2 [*noncount*] *baseball* **:** FIRST BASE ▪ a runner on *first* ▪ Who's playing *first*?
at first **:** when something first happens or begins to happen **:** when you first notice or consider something ▪ We didn't like each other *at first*. [=when we met] ▪ *At first* I thought she was crying, but then I realized she was actually laughing. ▪ The book bored me *at first*. [=*initially*]
from the first **:** from the beginning ▪ I've loved her *from the first*.

[4]first *pronoun*
1 : the first one or ones ▪ They were among the *first* in line. ▪ It was the *first* of many delays. ▪ I'll be the *first* to admit when I've done something wrong. ▪ He was the *first* to arrive. ▪ She was born on the *first* of May. [=on May 1] ▪ The son of King Charles the *First* became King Charles the Second.
2 : the first time ▪ She's not coming? Well, that's the *first* I've heard of it! [=I did not know that before now]

first aid *noun* [*noncount*] **:** emergency treatment given to a sick or injured person ▪ She gave him *first aid* for his sprained ankle. ✧ A ***first aid kit*** is a set of materials and tools used for giving first aid.

first base *noun* [*singular*] *baseball* **:** the base that must be touched first by a base runner ▪ a runner on *first base*; *also* **:** the position of the player who defends the area around first base ▪ She hit a ground ball to *first base*. ▪ He used to be a catcher, but now he plays *first base*. — compare HOME PLATE, SECOND BASE, THIRD BASE
get to first base *chiefly US, informal* **:** to make the first step in a course or process that you hope will lead further — usually used in negative statements ▪ Her proposal to change the tax laws never *got to first base*. [=never had any success at all] ▪ He kept asking her out, but he couldn't even *get to first base*. [=she would not agree to go on even one date with him]

first base·man /-ˈbeɪsmən/ *noun, pl* ~ **-men** /-ˌmɛn/ [*count*] *baseball* **:** the player who defends the area around first base ▪ an all-star *first baseman*

first·born /ˈfɚstˈboɚn/ *adj* **:** born first ▪ their *firstborn* [=*eldest, oldest*] child
– **firstborn** *noun, pl* **-borns** [*count*] ▪ Parents often spoil their *firstborns*.

first class *noun* [*noncount*] **:** the best or highest group or class: such as **a :** the best of usually three kinds of service you can have when you travel ▪ flying in *first class* **b :** a class of mail in the U.S. that includes letters and postcards **c :** a class of mail in the U.K. that includes letters and packages which are delivered sooner than ordinary second-class mail but cost more to send

first–class /ˈfɚstˈklæs, *Brit* ˈfəːstˈklɑːs/ *adj*
1 : of or relating to first class ▪ passengers in the *first-class*

cabin • raising the rates for *first-class* mail
2 : of the best quality : of the highest excellence • a *first-class* telescope/meal • *first-class* [=*excellent, superior*] work
– **first–class** *adv* • They insist on flying *first-class.* • I'd like to send this package *first-class.*

first cousin *noun, pl* ~ **-ins** [*count*] : a child of your aunt or uncle : COUSIN 1a • He's her *first cousin.* = He and she are *first cousins.* — compare SECOND COUSIN

first–de•gree /ˈfəstdɪˈgriː/ *adj, always used before a noun*
1 *US* : of the most serious type : deserving the harshest punishment • *first-degree* murder/theft/arson
2 : of the least harmful or mildest type • He suffered a *first-degree* burn. — compare SECOND-DEGREE, THIRD-DEGREE

first down *noun, pl* ~ **downs** [*noncount*] *American football* : the first of a series of usually four downs in which a team must gain 10 yards to keep the ball • They have *first down* on the 20-yard line.; *also* [*count*] : the right to start a new series of downs after a gain of 10 or more yards • The pass was completed for a *first down.*

first edition *noun, pl* ~ **-tions** [*singular*] : the first set of printed copies of a book • There were many errors in the book's *first edition.*; *also* [*count*] : a single copy from such a set • She owns a valuable *first edition* of *Huckleberry Finn.*

first family *noun, pl* ~ **-lies** [*count*]
1 *or* ***First Family*** : the family of the U.S. president • The *First Family* will be vacationing on a ranch this year.
2 : a family that has great importance, influence, or success in a specified activity or profession • He and his sons are considered the *first family* of jazz.

first floor *noun, pl* ~ **floors** [*count*]
1 *US* : the floor of a building that is at ground level : GROUND FLOOR
2 *Brit* : the floor of a building that is immediately above the ground floor

first•hand /ˈfəstˈhænd/ *adj* : coming directly from actually experiencing or seeing something • He gave a *firsthand* account of the battle. • She draws on *firsthand* experiences for her novel. — compare SECONDHAND; see also *at first hand* at [1]FIRST
– **firsthand** *adv* • He knows *firsthand* how difficult school can be.

first lady *noun, pl* ~ **ladies** [*count*]
1 *or* ***First Lady*** : the wife of the U.S. president • The President and the *First Lady* attended the concert.
2 : a woman who has great importance, influence, or success in a specified activity or profession • the *first lady* of American dance

first lieutenant *noun, pl* ~ **-ants** [*count*]
1 : an officer in the U.S. Army, Air Force, or Marine Corps who ranks below a captain
2 : a naval officer who is responsible for keeping a ship in good condition

first light *noun* [*noncount*] : the time when light is first seen in the morning : DAWN • She was up at *first light.*

first–line /ˈfəstˈlaɪn/ *adj, always used before a noun, chiefly US*
1 : used or chosen first • *first-line* treatment/therapy
2 : available to be used immediately • *first-line* troops

first•ly /ˈfəstli/ *adv* — used to introduce a statement that is the first in a series of statements • *Firstly,* we need to consider the issue of providing people with affordable health care. ✧ *Firstly* is chiefly used to begin lists and is usually followed by *secondly, thirdly,* etc. • I have several concerns. *Firstly,* the lack of funding. Secondly, . . . ✧ In U.S. English, *first* is more common than *firstly* in this use. • I have several concerns. *First,* the lack of funding. Second, . . . — compare LASTLY, SECONDLY, THIRDLY

first name *noun, pl* ~ **names** [*count*] : the name that comes first in someone's full name • Children at the school call their teachers by their *first names.* — compare LAST NAME, MIDDLE NAME, SURNAME
– **first–name** *adj* ✧ People who are ***on a first-name basis*** (*US*) or ***on first-name terms*** (*Brit*) know each other well and address each other by their first names. • He was *on a first-name basis* with his boss. • They know most of the officials *on a first-name basis.* — sometimes used figuratively • She was *on a first-name basis* with adversity. [=she experienced a lot of adversity]

first offender *noun, pl* ~ **-ers** [*count*] *law* : a person who is convicted for the first time of committing a crime • Because he was a *first offender,* he was put on probation rather than sentenced to jail.

first person *noun* [*noncount*]
1 : a set of words or word forms (such as pronouns or verb forms) that refer to the person who is speaking or writing — often used before another noun • *Me* is the objective case of the *first person* singular pronoun *I,* and *us* is the objective case of the *first person* plural pronoun *we.*
2 : a writing style that uses first person pronouns and verbs • She always wrote in the *first person.* • The sentence "I was born in Maine" is written in the *first person.* — compare SECOND PERSON, THIRD PERSON

first–rate /ˈfəstˈreɪt/ *adj* : of the best quality : EXCELLENT • a *first-rate* chef/book/education • The service was *first-rate.*

first–run /ˈfəstˈrʌn/ *adj, always used before a noun* : available for the public to see for the first time • *first-run* movies

first strike *noun, pl* ~ **strikes** [*count*] : a nuclear attack against an enemy before the enemy can attack • launch a *first strike*
– **first–strike** *adj, always used before a noun* • a *first-strike* capability/threat

first–string /ˈfəstˈstrɪŋ/ *adj, US, sports* : most skillful • the *first-string* quarterback/catcher ✧ The *first-string* players on a team play first in the game because they are considered the best players. This term is also sometimes used figuratively. • The newspaper sent its *first-string* [=*best*] critic to review the play. — compare SECOND-STRING

first–time *adj, always used before a noun*
1 : doing something for the first time • *first-time* home buyers [=people who are buying a home for the first time] • a *first-time* visitor • a *first-time* author [=a person who has written a book for the first time]
2 : done for the first time • The punishment for a *first-time* offense of this kind is a fine.

first world *or* **First World** *noun* [*singular*] : the countries of the world that have many industries and relatively few poor people : the rich nations of the world — compare THIRD WORLD

fis•cal /ˈfɪskəl/ *adj* : of or relating to money and especially to the money a government, business, or organization earns, spends, and owes • *fiscal* policy/responsibility • a *fiscal* crisis • a *fiscal* conservative • the *fiscal* health of the university/orchestra
– **fis•cal•ly** *adv* • *fiscally* sound policies • *fiscally* conservative

fiscal year *noun, pl* ~ **years** [*count*] *chiefly US* : a 12-month period used by a government, business, or organization to calculate how much money is being earned, spent, etc. • Sales were up in the last *fiscal year.* • Our *fiscal year* runs from October 1 to September 30. — called also (*Brit*) *financial year*; compare CALENDAR YEAR

[1]**fish** /ˈfɪʃ/ *noun, pl* **fish** *or* **fish•es**
1 [*count*] : a cold-blooded animal that lives in water, breathes with gills, and usually has fins and scales • a small *fish* • an ocean/river *fish* [=a kind of fish that lives in an ocean/river] — see color picture on page C8

> ***usage*** When you are talking about more than one fish, the plural *fish* is more commonly used than *fishes.* • We caught several *fish.* When you are talking about more than one kind or species of fish, both *fishes* and *fish* are used. • varieties of tropical *fish* • all the *fishes* of the sea

2 [*noncount*] : the meat of a fish eaten as food • We're having *fish* for dinner.

a big fish in a small pond (*chiefly US*) *or Brit* ***a big fish in a little pond*** : a person who is very well known or important in a small group of people but who is not known or important outside that group • In school he was a *big fish in a small pond,* but once he moved to the city he was just another struggling actor.

a fish out of water : a person who is in a place or situation that seems unnatural or uncomfortable • He's a small-town boy who feels like *a fish out of water* here in the big city.

drink like a fish see [1]DRINK

fish in the sea *informal* — used to say that there are many more people available for a romantic relationship • "I know you're sad because you and your boyfriend broke up, but he's ***not the only fish in the sea.***" "You're right. There are ***many/plenty more fish in the sea.***"

fish to fry *informal* : things to do or deal with • We'll have to address that problem tomorrow. Right now ***we've got other/bigger fish to fry.*** [=we've got other/bigger problems that we need to give our attention to]

neither fish nor fowl : a person or thing that does not belong to a particular class or category • The movie is *neither fish nor fowl*—it's not really a comedy, but it's too light-hearted to be called a drama.

odd/queer fish *Brit, informal* : a strange or unusual person • She's really quite an *odd fish*.

– see also COLD FISH, *kettle of fish* at KETTLE

– fish·less /ˈfɪʃləs/ *adj* • a *fishless* lake **– fish·like** /ˈfɪsˌlaɪk/ *adj* • a *fishlike* tail

²fish *verb* **fish·es; fished; fish·ing**

1 a [*no obj*] : to catch or try to catch fish • I love to *fish*. • We spent the afternoon *fishing* for trout. **b** [+ *obj*] : to catch or try to catch fish in (a river, stream, etc.) • They *fished* the stream all morning.

2 [*no obj*] : to search for something by feeling : to use your hand to try to find something • She was *fishing* around in her purse for her keys.

fish for [*phrasal verb*] ***fish for (something)*** : to ask for or try to get (something, such as praise or attention) in an indirect way • I think he offers apologies for his cooking as a way of *fishing for* compliments. [=as a way of getting people to say that they like the food he cooks] • *fishing for* answers

fish or cut bait *US, informal* : to stop hesitating and choose to do or not do something • It's time for the company to *fish or cut bait*. We either take the job or turn it down.

fish out [*phrasal verb*] ***fish (something) out*** or ***fish out (something)*** **1** : to pull (something) out of water or some other liquid • The police *fished* the car *out* of the harbor. • She *fished* the sugar packet *out* of her iced tea. **2** : to pull (something) out from a container, bag, etc. • She reached into her purse and *fished out* her keys.

fish and chips *noun* : a meal that consists of fried fish and french-fried potatoes — used with both singular and plural verbs • The restaurant's *fish and chips* is/are delicious.

fish·bowl /ˈfɪsˌboʊl/ *noun, pl* **-bowls** [*count*]

1 : a bowl used for keeping live fish

2 *chiefly US* : a place or condition in which there is no privacy • Being a politician these days means living in a *fishbowl*—every part of your life is open to public view.

fish cake *noun, pl* ~ **cakes** [*count*] : a round fried cake made of a mixture of fish and mashed potatoes

fish·er·man /ˈfɪʃɚmən/ *noun, pl* **-men** /-mən/ [*count*] : a person (especially a man) who catches fish

fish·er·wom·an /ˈfɪʃɚˌwʊmən/ *noun, pl* **-wom·en** /-ˌwɪmən/ [*count*] : a woman who catches fish

fish·ery /ˈfɪʃəri/ *noun, pl* **-er·ies** [*count*]

1 : a part of the ocean where fish and other sea creatures are caught • an oyster *fishery* • a salmon *fishery* • coastal *fisheries*

2 : a business that catches and sells fish • small commercial *fisheries*

fish–eye lens *noun, pl* ~ **lenses** [*count*] *photography* : a camera lens that shows an extremely wide area with curved edges

fish farm *noun, pl* ~ **farms** [*count*] : a place where fish are raised for food

fish finger *noun, pl* ~ **-gers** [*count*] *Brit* : FISH STICK

fish fry *noun, pl* ~ **fries** [*count*] *US* : a meal or event at which the main food served is fried fish • a community *fish fry*

fish·hook *noun, pl* **-hooks** [*count*] : a small curved piece of metal that is attached to the end of a piece of fishing line and used to catch fish — see picture at HOOK

fishing *noun* [*noncount*] : the sport or business of catching fish • The *fishing* was pretty good today. • I'm ***going fishing*** this weekend. — often used before another noun • I bought a *fishing* pole/rod and some *fishing* line. • a store that sells *fishing* gear — see also FLY-FISHING, ***fishing expedition*** at EXPEDITION

fish·mong·er /ˈfɪʃˌmɑːŋgɚ, ˈfɪʃˌmʌŋgɚ/ *noun, pl* **-ers** [*count*] *chiefly Brit* : a person or shop that sells fish • You can get fresh cod at the *fishmonger's*.

fish·net /ˈfɪʃˌnɛt/ *noun, pl* **-nets**

1 [*count*] : a net for catching fish

2 [*noncount*] : a type of fabric that has many small holes like a net — usually used before another noun • *fishnet* stockings • a *fishnet* shirt

fish slice *noun, pl* ~ **slices** [*count*] *Brit* : SPATULA

fish stick *noun, pl* ~ **sticks** [*count*] *US* : a long and thin piece of fish that is breaded and cooked

fish story *noun, pl* ~ **stories** [*count*] *US* : an exaggerated story : a story that is so strange or surprising that it seems very unlikely to be true • He told a ridiculous *fish story* about a swarm of giant mosquitoes.

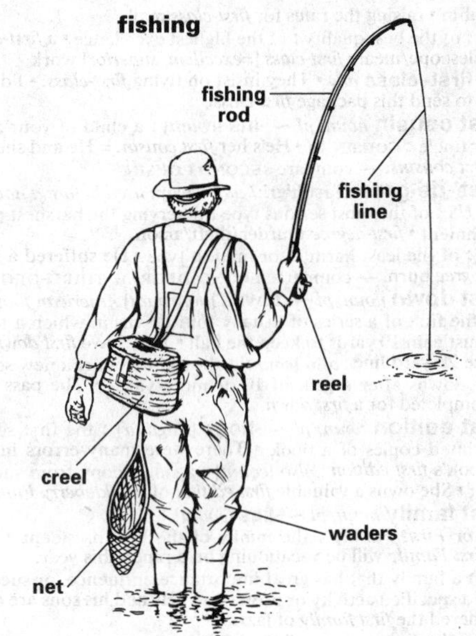

fish·tail /ˈfɪʃˌteɪl/ *verb* **-tails; -tailed; -tail·ing** [*no obj*] *chiefly US, of a car, truck, etc.* : to slide in an uncontrolled way with the rear end going from side to side • The car *fish-tailed* on the icy curve.

fish·wife /ˈfɪʃˌwaɪf/ *noun, pl* **-wives** /-ˌwaɪvz/ [*count*] *old-fashioned*

1 : a woman who sells fish

2 : a rude and rough woman

fishy /ˈfɪʃi/ *adj* **fish·i·er; -est**

1 : of or relating to fish; *especially* : tasting or smelling like a fish • a *fishy* odor/taste

2 *informal* : causing doubt or suspicion : likely to be bad, untrue, dishonest, etc. • That story sounds/smells *fishy* [=*suspicious, dubious*] to me. • There's something *fishy* about that guy.

fis·sion /ˈfɪʃn/ *noun* [*noncount*]

1 *physics* : a process in which the nucleus of a heavy atom is split apart ✧ A large amount of energy is released when fission occurs. — called also *nuclear fission*; compare FUSION

2 *biology* : a kind of reproduction in which a cell or body divides into two or more parts and each part grows into a whole new individual

fis·sure /ˈfɪʃɚ/ *noun, pl* **-sures** [*count*] : a narrow opening or crack • rock *fissures* • a *fissure* in the Earth's crust • a deep *fissure* in the ice — sometimes used figuratively • ideological *fissures* in a political party

– fis·sured /ˈfɪʃɚd/ *adj* [*more* ~; *most* ~] • a heavily *fissured* rock face

fist /ˈfɪst/ *noun, pl* **fists** [*count*] : the hand with its fingers bent down into the palm • He pounded his *fist* on the table in anger. • She pounded on the door with both *fists*. • a clenched *fist* • make a *fist* • He defiantly shook his *fist* at the policeman.

hand over fist see ¹HAND

make a good fist of *Brit, informal* : to do (something) well • Despite her inexperience, she *made a* remarkably *good fist of* chairing the meeting.

make a poor fist of *Brit, informal* : to do (something) badly • He *made a poor fist of* explaining his reasons.

rule with an iron fist see ²RULE

fist·fight /ˈfɪstˌfaɪt/ *noun, pl* **-fights** [*count*] : a fight in which people hit each other with their fists • A *fistfight* broke out in the stands. • He often gets into *fistfights*.

fist·ful /ˈfɪstˌfʊl/ *noun, pl* **-fuls** [*count*]

1 : an amount that can be held in one hand : HANDFUL • a *fistful* of coins

2 : a somewhat large number or amount • She has won a *fistful* of awards.

fist·i·cuffs /ˈfɪstɪˌkʌfs/ *noun* [*plural*] *old-fashioned* : a fight with fists • engaging in *fisticuffs* • It was a loud debate that ended in *fisticuffs*. — sometimes used figuratively ▪ legal *fisticuffs*

[1]fit /ˈfɪt/ *adj* **fit·ter; -test**

1 a : proper or acceptable : morally or socially correct — often + *for* ▪ a movie *fit* [=*suitable*] *for* the whole family ▪ This is not a *fit* subject *for* discussion with children. ▪ a subject not *fit for* discussion — often followed by *to* + *verb* ▪ a subject not *fit to be* discussed **b :** suitable for a specified purpose — often + *for* ▪ This water is not *fit for* drinking. ▪ The building is no longer *fit for* human habitation. — often followed by *to* + *verb* ▪ This water is not *fit to drink*. ▪ The building is no longer *fit for* people *to live* in.

2 a : physically healthy and strong ▪ physically *fit* ▪ He felt overmatched against *fitter* [=*healthier*], stronger players. ▪ Patients are encouraged to get/keep *fit*. ▪ Are you *fit* enough to walk there? **b** *Brit slang* **:** sexually attractive : SEXY

3 : having the necessary skills — usually + *for* ▪ I just don't think he's *fit* [=*qualified*] *for* this job.

4 : made ready : put in a suitable state — usually + *for* ▪ get the ship *fit* [=*prepared*] *for* sea

fit as a fiddle *also Brit* ***fit as a flea*** *informal* **:** in good physical condition : very healthy and strong ▪ I feel (as) *fit as a fiddle* this morning.

fit for a king **:** good enough even for a king : very good ▪ a meal (that is) *fit for a king*

fit to be tied *informal* **:** very angry or upset ▪ Dad was *fit to be tied* when my sister came home late last night.

fit to burst *chiefly Brit, informal* **:** very much ▪ laugh/shout *fit to burst*

fit to kill *US, informal* **:** in an impressive way that attracts attention ▪ He was dressed *fit to kill*.

see/think fit ◊ To *see fit* or *think fit* to do something is to choose to do it because you think it is right or appropriate. ▪ She can spend her money as she *sees fit*. [=she can spend her money as she chooses] ▪ She let him do his job as he *thought fit*. ▪ They might *see fit* [=*choose, decide*] to make some adjustments.

– fit·ness *noun* [*noncount*] ▪ No one questioned her *fitness* for the job. ▪ The program promotes healthy eating and ***physical fitness***. [=being healthy through exercise]

[2]fit *verb* **fits; fit·ted** *or chiefly US* **fit; fit·ting**

1 *not used in progressive tenses* **:** to be the right size and shape for (someone or something) [+ *obj*] The suit *fits* him perfectly. ▪ I hope this key *fits* the lock. ▪ The two pieces *fit* each other perfectly. [*no obj*] These shoes *fit* perfectly. ▪ This calculator will *fit* nicely/neatly in your shirt pocket. ▪ pants that *fit* tightly/loosely = tight-*fitting*/loose-*fitting* pants ▪ The two pieces *fit* together perfectly. ◊ Something that ***fits (you) like a glove*** fits (you) very well. ▪ That suit *fits him like a glove*. ◊ The phrase ***one size fits all*** describes a hat, piece of clothing, etc., that is made in a size that is supposed to fit everyone. This phrase is commonly used figuratively. ▪ The school recognizes that a *one size fits all* approach won't work for these children. [=these children need to be taught in a way that considers the needs and abilities of each child]

2 *not used in progressive tenses* **a** [*no obj*] **:** to go into or through a particular space ▪ All these groceries won't *fit* in the trunk of my car. = These groceries won't all *fit* in the trunk of my car. ▪ How many people can *fit* in a phone booth? ▪ The box was too large to *fit* through the door. **b** [+ *obj*] **:** to cause (something) to go into or through a particular space ▪ I can't *fit* all these groceries into the trunk of my car. ▪ We weren't able to *fit* the box through the door.

3 *past tense and past participle* ***fitted*** [+ *obj*] **a :** to measure (someone) in order to choose clothes that are the right size and shape for that person — usually used as *(be) fitted* ▪ I'm *being fitted* [=*measured*] for a new suit tomorrow. **b :** to change the shape or form of (a piece of clothing) for a particular person ▪ *fitting* the jacket to the customer

4 [+ *obj*] **:** to find time to meet with (someone) or do (something) — usually + *in* or *into* ▪ I'll try to *fit* you *into* my schedule. ▪ The doctor can *fit* you *in* this afternoon. [=the doctor can meet with you this afternoon] ▪ She's got a lot of meetings to *fit in* this morning.

5 [*no obj*] **:** to belong in a particular situation, place, or group ▪ It's a good school, but I feel like I just don't *fit* here. — usually + *in* ▪ I was looking for a group that I could *fit in* with. ▪ No matter how hard she tried, she just didn't *fit in*. ▪ He *fit* right *in* at school. ▪ That chair *fits in* well with the rest of the office.

6 *not used in progressive tenses* [+ *obj*] **a :** to be suitable or appropriate for (someone or something) ▪ The nickname *fits* [=*suits*] him very well. ▪ The punishment should *fit* the crime. **b :** to make (someone or something) suitable or appropriate *for* or *to* something ▪ Her previous experience *fitted* [=*qualified*] her *for* the job. ▪ Let us *fit* the punishment *to* the crime.

7 *not used in progressive tenses* [+ *obj*] **:** to be in agreement with (something or someone) ▪ Their story doesn't *fit* the facts. ▪ He *fits* [=*matches*] the description perfectly. = The description *fits* him perfectly.

8 *past tense and past participle* ***fitted*** [+ *obj*] **:** to supply equipment for (something) ▪ a lab *fitted* with the latest equipment ▪ The camera can be *fitted* with many different lenses. — often + *out* or *up* ▪ *fit out* an expedition ▪ an old ocean liner *fitted up* as a hospital ship

fit the bill see [1]BILL

if the cap fits see [1]CAP

if the shoe fits see [1]SHOE

– fit·ter /ˈfɪtɚ/ *noun, pl* **-ters** [*count*] ▪ a shoe/boot *fitter* [=a person whose job is to help you find a shoe/boot that fits] — see also PIPE FITTER

[3]fit *noun, pl* **fits** [*count*] **:** the way something fits : the way something suits the size and shape of your body or goes into or through a particular space ▪ The *fit* of this shirt is a bit tight. ▪ a loose/snug *fit* ▪ It's a tight *fit* but I think we can get the box through the door. ▪ a comfortable *fit* ▪ That dress is a good *fit* for you. [=that dress fits you well; it is the right size and shape for your body] — compare [4]FIT

[4]fit *noun, pl* **fits** [*count*]

1 : an uncontrolled expression of strong emotion ▪ He threw a *fit* [=he became very angry and upset] when they accused him of cheating. ▪ She has/throws a *fit* [=*tantrum*] when she doesn't get what she wants.

2 : a sudden occurrence *of* some activity, emotion, etc. ▪ a *fit of* anger ▪ a *fit of* coughing = a coughing *fit* ▪ He apologized profusely in a *fit of* remorse. ▪ The joke sent the audience into ***fits of laughter***. [=it made the people in the audience laugh a lot]

3 : an abnormal state in which you become unconscious and your body moves in an uncontrolled and violent way ▪ an epileptic *fit* [=(more commonly) *seizure*]

by fits and starts *or* ***in fits and starts*** **:** by stopping and starting again : in a way that is not constant or steady ▪ Their courtship was gradual, proceeding *by fits and starts*. ▪ Progress came only *in fits and starts*.

in fits *Brit, informal* **:** laughing very much : in fits of laughter ▪ The audience was *in fits*. [=*in stitches*]

— compare [3]FIT

fit·ful /ˈfɪtfəl/ *adj* [*more* ~; *most* ~] **:** not regular or steady ▪ He had a few *fitful* hours of sleep. ▪ Several *fitful* attempts at negotiation have failed. ▪ making slow, *fitful* progress

– fit·ful·ly *adv* ▪ progressing *fitfully* ▪ He slept *fitfully* [=*restlessly*] for a few hours. **– fit·ful·ness** *noun* [*noncount*]

fit·ted /ˈfɪtəd/ *adj* **:** shaped for a precise fit ▪ a *fitted* sheet; *especially* **:** designed to match the shape of a person's body ▪ He was wearing a *fitted* shirt.

[1]fit·ting /ˈfɪtɪŋ/ *adj* [*more* ~; *most* ~] **:** of a kind that is appropriate for the situation or purpose ▪ It was a *fitting* end to their rivalry. ▪ It seemed only *fitting* [=*proper, right*] that she should win her final tournament. ▪ a *fitting* memorial/tribute

– fit·ting·ly *adv* ▪ *Fittingly* [=*appropriately*], she won her final tournament.

[2]fitting *noun, pl* **-tings** [*count*]

1 : the act of putting on clothes to see if they fit properly ▪ I have a *fitting* for my wedding dress this afternoon.

2 : a small part ▪ a pipe *fitting* ▪ brass/electrical *fittings*

3 *Brit* **:** something (such as a refrigerator or a bookcase) that is in a house or building but can be removed if the house or building is sold — usually plural ▪ pay extra for fixtures and *fittings*

fitting room *noun, pl* ~ **rooms** [*count*] **:** a room in a store in which customers can put on a piece of clothing to see if it fits before they buy it — called also *dressing room*

five /ˈfaɪv/ *noun, pl* **fives**

1 [*count*] **:** the number 5

2 [*count*] **:** the fifth in a set or series ▪ the *five* of clubs ▪ page *five*

3 [*noncount*] **:** five o'clock ▪ I get off work at *five*. ▪ The store is open until *five*.

4 [*count*] **a** *US* **:** a five-dollar bill ▪ The total cost was $3.83 and she gave him a *five*. **b** *Brit* **:** a five-pound note : FIVER

– five *adj* ▪ *five* years **– five** *pronoun* ▪ *Five* (of them) are missing.

five–and–dime /ˌfaɪvənˈdaɪm/ *noun, pl* **-dimes** [*count*] *US, old-fashioned* **:** a store that sells inexpensive things ▪ the local *five-and-dime* — called also *dime store, five-and-ten* /-ˈtɛn/

five·fold /ˈfaɪvˌfoʊld/ *adj* : five times as great or as many • There has been a *fivefold* increase in membership this year.
– **five·fold** /ˈfaɪvˈfoʊld/ *adv* • Membership has increased *fivefold.*

five–o'clock shadow *noun, pl* ~ **-ows** [*count*] : the beginning of a beard that you can see late in the afternoon on the face of a man who has not shaved since morning

fiv·er /ˈfaɪvɚ/ *noun, pl* **-ers** [*count*] *Brit, informal* : a five-pound note

five–spice powder *noun* [*noncount*] : a mixture of spices that is used in Chinese cooking

five–star /ˈfaɪvˈstɑɚ/ *adj, always used before a noun* : of the best quality • a *five-star* hotel

[1]**fix** /ˈfɪks/ *verb* **fix·es; fixed; fix·ing** [+ *obj*]
1 a : to make (something) whole or able to work properly again : to repair (something) • He *fixed* the fence last weekend. • I need to *fix* this dent in my car. • *fix* a leaky faucet **b :** to deal with or correct (a problem) • Your proposals won't *fix* [=*solve*] anything. • People expect the schools to *fix* whatever is wrong with their kids.
2 : to attach (something) in such a way that it will not move • All tables on the ship will be *fixed* to the floor. : to connect or join (things) physically • *fix* [=*attach, fasten*] this sign to your door • The table was *fixed* firmly to the floor. • The scarf was *fixed* in place with a pin. — sometimes used figuratively • I want to *fix* this moment in my mind forever. [=I want to remember this moment forever]
3 a : to set or place (something) definitely • They haven't yet *fixed* the date of their wedding. • They *fixed* the price at $10. • illegal price *fixing* **b :** to find out (something) with certainty • Investigators are still attempting to *fix* the exact time of the accident. • We're trying to *fix* [=*get a fix on*] the ship's location. **c :** to arrange the details of something • My lawyer ***fixed it*** [=made arrangements] so I wouldn't have to go to court.
4 *chiefly US* **a :** to make (something, such as a meal) ready • *fix* [=*prepare, make*] dinner • Can I *fix* [=*make*] you a drink? = Can I *fix* a drink for you? **b** *informal* **:** to make (someone's hair, makeup, etc.) neat or attractive • We had to wait 10 minutes while she *fixed* her hair. • *fixing* her lipstick/makeup
5 : to control or affect (something, such as a game or election) in a dishonest way • They were accused of *fixing* games in college. • The election was *fixed.* • *fix* a parking ticket [=arrange for someone to not have to pay a fine for parking illegally]
6 : to change the appearance of (someone's face, nose, etc.) through surgery • She wants to get her nose *fixed.*
7 *informal* **:** to do something to punish (someone who has treated you badly or unfairly) • They thought they could cheat me, but I *fixed* them good. • I'll *fix* you!
8 *US* **:** to make (an animal) unable to reproduce : to neuter or spay (an animal) • You should have your dog/cat *fixed.*
9 *US, informal + old-fashioned* **:** to be or get ready *to do* something • They were *fixing to leave.* • It looks like it's *fixing to rain.* [=it's about to rain] ✧ This sense of *fix* is sometimes used humorously to suggest the speech of cowboys in western movies.
10 *technical* **:** to change (nitrogen) into a stable or useful form • bacteria that *fix* nitrogen

fix on/upon [*phrasal verb*] ***fix on/upon (something)*** **1 :** to direct your attention or thoughts toward (something) : to focus on (something) • He has *fixed on/upon* the idea of going back to school. • All eyes *fixed on* her as she entered the room. [=everyone looked at her as she entered the room] **2 :** to make a decision about or choose (something) • After weeks of discussion, they've finally *fixed on* a solution.

fix (someone) with a stare/look (etc.) **:** to look directly at (someone) usually in an angry way • She *fixed him with an* angry *stare.* [=she stared at him angrily]

fix up [*phrasal verb*] **1** ***fix up (something) or fix (something) up*** **:** to improve the appearance or condition of (something, such as a building) by repairing it, making changes to it, etc. • We spent thousands of dollars *fixing up* our house. — see also FIXER-UPPER **2** ***fix (someone or something) up*** *chiefly US* **:** to make (someone or something) more attractive or fancy • I need a few minutes to *fix* myself *up* before we leave. • She got herself all *fixed up* [=*dressed up, spruced up*] for the party. **3** ***fix (someone) up*** **a :** to provide (someone) with something that is needed or wanted • They can *fix* you *up* with a rental car at the airport. **b :** to provide a possible boyfriend or girlfriend for (someone) : to arrange a date for (someone) • My mother tried to *fix* me *up* with one of her friends' sons.

fix your eyes/gaze (etc.) on/upon **:** to look at (someone or something) steadily • Everyone *fixed their eyes on* her as she entered the room.

fix your hopes/sights (etc.) on/upon **:** to direct your hopes, efforts, etc., toward (something) • They *fixed their sights on* winning the championship. • She ***has her hopes fixed on*** a career in journalism. [=she hopes/wants to have a career in journalism]

if it ain't broke, don't fix it see [2]BROKE

– **fix·able** /ˈfɪksəbəl/ *adj* • All the car's problems are *fixable.*
– **fix·er** /ˈfɪksɚ/ *noun, pl* **-ers** [*count*]

[2]**fix** *noun, pl* **fix·es** [*count*]
1 : a difficult or embarrassing situation • I found myself in an awful *fix.* [=*mess, predicament*]
2 : something that solves a problem : SOLUTION • There's no easy *fix* to this problem. • a quick *fix*
3 : the act of dishonestly controlling or affecting something (such as a game or election) • The result was unexpected, and some people suspect a *fix.* • (*US*) It was obvious early in the game that ***the fix was in.*** [=the outcome of the game was being controlled or affected in a dishonest way]
4 : an amount of an illegal drug that someone wants or needs to have • He was desperately in search of his next *fix.* — often used figuratively • I got my nostalgia *fix* at my class reunion. • an ice-cream *fix*
5 a : the exact position of something (such as a ship or an airplane) • an accurate *fix* • We're trying to ***get a fix on*** the ship's location. [=trying to find or determine the ship's exact location] **b :** an accurate understanding of something • Voters are still trying to ***get a fix on*** her character. • Analysts are reading reports to *get a fix on* how the market will perform.

fix·ate /ˈfɪkˌseɪt/ *verb* **-ates; -at·ed; -at·ing** [*no obj*] **:** to look at or think about something constantly : to give all of your attention to something — usually + *on* or *upon* • Why do journalists *fixate on* scandals?
– **fixated** *adj* [*more* ~; *most* ~] • Why are journalists are so ***fixated on*** scandals? – **fix·a·tion** /fɪkˈseɪʃən/ *noun, pl* **-tions** [*count*] • The band is my latest music *fixation.* [=the music I am thinking about constantly most recently] • the media's ***fixation on*** scandals • society's *fixation on* [=*obsession with*] race

fixed /ˈfɪkst/ *adj*
1 a — used to describe something that does not change • a *fixed* interest rate • They are trying to live on a *fixed* income. • They have no *fixed* schedule. • Each contestant is allowed a *fixed* amount of time. • *fixed* costs/fees/prices • a *fixed* stare/expression/smile • *fixed* ideas about right and wrong **b :** placed or attached in a way that does not move easily • a small mirror *fixed* to the wall • That day remains *fixed* in my memory. • All eyes were *fixed on* her as she entered the room. [=everyone looked at her as she entered the room]
2 *informal* **:** having something needed • They were well ***fixed for*** food. [=they had a good supply of food] • How are you *fixed for* money? [=do you have enough money?] • He's ***fixed for life.*** [=he has enough money to live comfortably for the rest of his life]
– **fix·ed·ly** /ˈfɪksədli/ *adv* • They stared *fixedly* at me.

fix·er–up·per /ˈfɪksɚˌʌpɚ/ *noun, pl* **-pers** [*count*] *US, informal* **:** a house, apartment, etc., that is in bad condition and needs to be repaired • Their first house was a one-bedroom *fixer-upper.* — see also *fix up* at [1]FIX

fix·ings /ˈfɪksənz/ *noun* [*plural*] *US, informal* **:** foods that are traditionally served with the main dish of a particular meal • For Thanksgiving dinner my mother always made turkey with all the *fixings.* [=potatoes, vegetables, etc.]

fix·i·ty /ˈfɪksəti/ *noun, formal* **:** the state or quality of not changing [*noncount*] looking for safety and *fixity* [=*stability*] in the ever-changing world [*singular*] a *fixity* of purpose

fix·ture /ˈfɪkstʃɚ/ *noun, pl* **-tures** [*count*]
1 : something (such as a light, toilet, sink, etc.) that is attached to a house or building and that is not removed when the house or building is sold — usually plural • bathroom *fixtures* • lighting *fixtures* — compare [2]FITTING 3
2 : a person or thing that has been part of something or involved in something for a long time • He's been a *fixture* in the parade for many years. • She hopes the new educational program will become a permanent *fixture* at the zoo.
3 *Brit, sports* **:** a game played at a particular time and place •

I attended all their home *fixtures* [=(US) games] last year.

¹fizz /ˈfɪz/ *verb* **fizz·es; fizzed; fizz·ing** [*no obj*] : to make a sound like many small bubbles popping • The soda *fizzed*.

²fizz *noun, pl* **fizz·es**

1 [*noncount*] : a sound like many small bubbles popping • the characteristic *fizz* of champagne

2 [*noncount*] : energy and liveliness • All the *fizz* was gone from their relationship.

3 a [*count*] : a drink with many small bubbles • a gin *fizz* **b** [*noncount*] *Brit, informal* : CHAMPAGNE • a glass of *fizz*

– fizzy /ˈfɪzi/ *adj* **fizz·i·er; -est** • a *fizzy* [=*bubbly, carbonated*] soft drink • *fizzy* enthusiasm

fiz·zle /ˈfɪzəl/ *verb* **fiz·zles; fiz·zled; fiz·zling** [*no obj*] *informal* : to gradually fail or end

> ***usage*** In U.S. English *fizzle* can be used by itself or with *out*. • The project ended up *fizzling*. • He had a great rookie season and then just *fizzled out*. In British English, *fizzle* is almost always followed by *out*. • Dance crazes tend to *fizzle out* quickly.

– fizzle *noun, pl* **fizzles** [*count*] • She felt responsible for her team's recent *fizzle*. [=*failure, flop*]

fjord *also* **fiord** /fiˈoɚd/ *noun, pl* **fjords** *also* **fiords** [*count*] : a narrow part of the ocean between cliffs or steep hills or mountains • the *fjords* of Norway

FL *abbr* Florida

Fla *abbr* Florida

flab /ˈflæb/ *noun* [*noncount*] *informal* : extra soft flesh on a person's body : excess body fat • stomach/arm *flab* — sometimes used figuratively • cutting jobs to eliminate corporate *flab*

– flab·by /ˈflæbi/ *adj* **flab·bi·er; -est** • *flabby* arms • *flabby* [=*soft*] muscles • She writes in a *flabby* [=*loose*] style that ruins the narrative. **– flab·bi·ness** /ˈflæbinəs/ *noun* [*noncount*] • the *flabbiness* of his muscles • moral/intellectual *flabbiness*

flab·ber·gast /ˈflæbɚˌgæst, *Brit* ˈflæbəˌgɑːst/ *verb* **-gasts; -gast·ed; -gast·ing** [+ *obj*] : to shock or surprise (someone) very much • It *flabbergasts* me to see how many people still support them. — often used as *(be) flabbergasted* • We *were flabbergasted* by/at the news that he'd won the game.

– flabbergasting *adj* [*more* ~; *most* ~] • *flabbergasting* news

flac·cid /ˈflæsəd/ *adj* [*more* ~; *most* ~]

1 : not firm : not hard or solid • *flaccid* muscles/tissue • a *flaccid* handshake

2 : lacking strength or force : WEAK • *flaccid* leadership • a *flaccid* response

¹flack /ˈflæk/ *noun, pl* **flacks** [*count*] *US, informal + disapproving* : a person whose job is to make people like or be interested in someone or something • a public relations *flack* • campaign *flacks* [=*publicists, press agents*]

²flack *variant spelling of* FLAK

¹flag /ˈflæg/ *noun, pl* **flags** [*count*]

1 : a piece of cloth with a special design that is used as a symbol of a nation or group • raise/lower the American *flag* • The *flag* was flying [=the flag was raised up on a pole] over the fort. ✧ To ***fly/show/wave the flag*** is to display the flag of your country as a sign of patriotism.

2 : a piece of cloth used as a signal or to attract attention • waving a *flag* of surrender/truce • a checkered *flag* • The referee threw a penalty *flag*. — see also RED FLAG, WHITE FLAG

– compare ⁴FLAG

²flag *verb* **flags; flagged; flag·ging** [+ *obj*]

1 : to signal (someone or something that is moving past you) to stop especially by raising or waving your hand • *flag* a taxi • I *flagged* the waiter for the check. — often + *down* • We should *flag* someone *down* and ask for directions.

2 : to mark (something, such as a page or section of a book) so that it can be easily seen or found • She *flagged* several pages for me to review.

3 *American football* : to signal that you are giving a penalty to (a player) by throwing a penalty flag • He was *flagged* for holding.

– compare ³FLAG

³flag *verb* **flags; flagged; flag·ging** [*no obj*]

1 : to become weak • Our interest *flagged* as the speaker droned on. • The good news boosted my *flagging* spirits. • Her energy shows no sign of *flagging* after all these years.

2 : to become less interesting, attractive, or valuable • He's trying to revive his *flagging* career. • *flagging* stock prices

– compare ²FLAG

⁴flag *noun, pl* **flags** [*count*] : FLAGSTONE — compare ¹FLAG

Flag Day *noun* [*singular*] : June 14 observed in the U.S. as the anniversary of the day the American flag was officially accepted in 1777

flag·el·late /ˈflæʤəˌleɪt/ *verb* **-lates; -lat·ed; -lat·ing** [+ *obj*] *formal* : to hit (yourself or another person) with a whip as punishment or as part of a religious ritual — sometimes used figuratively • He *flagellated* [=severely criticized] himself for years for allowing the business to fail. — see also SELF-FLAGELLATION

– flag·el·la·tion /ˌflæʤəˈleɪʃən/ *noun* [*noncount*] • ritual *flagellation*

flag football *noun* [*noncount*] : a form of American football in which the player with the ball is not tackled but instead must stop when another player removes a piece of cloth that is attached to the player's waist

flag·on /ˈflægən/ *noun, pl* **-ons** [*count*] *old-fashioned* : a container for liquids that usually has a handle, spout, and lid • a pewter *flagon*; *also* : the amount in a flagon • We drank a whole *flagon* of wine.

flag·pole /ˈflægˌpoʊl/ *noun, pl* **-poles** [*count*] : a tall pole from which a flag hangs : a pole used to display a flag

fla·grant /ˈfleɪgrənt/ *adj* [*more* ~; *most* ~] : very bad : too bad to be ignored • a *flagrant* violation • *flagrant* abuse of the law • her *flagrant* disregard for other people's rights • a *flagrant* error

– fla·grant·ly *adv* • *flagrantly* violating our rights

flag·ship /ˈflægˌʃɪp/ *noun, pl* **-ships** [*count*]

1 : the ship that carries the commander of a group of ships • the *flagship* of the Atlantic fleet

2 : the best, largest, or most important one of a group of things (such as products, stores, etc.) — often used before another noun • the company's *flagship* store • The next game will be broadcast on our *flagship* station.

flag·staff /ˈflægˌstæf, *Brit* ˈflægˌstɑːf/ *noun, pl* **-staffs** [*count*] : FLAGPOLE

flag·stone /ˈflægˌstoʊn/ *noun, pl* **-stones** [*count*] : a hard, flat piece of stone that is used for making paths • a walkway paved with *flagstones* — often used before another noun • a *flagstone* path

flag–wav·ing /ˈflægˌweɪvɪŋ/ *noun* [*noncount*] *usually disapproving* : words and actions that show very strong support for your government usually in a way that seems foolish or excessive • The essay is little more than *flag-waving*. — sometimes used before another noun • *flag-waving* rhetoric/patriotism

– flag–wav·er /ˈflægˌweɪvɚ/ *noun, pl* **-wav·ers** [*count*]

¹flail /ˈfleɪl/ *verb* **flails; flailed; flail·ing**

1 : to move or swing your arms or legs in a wild and uncontrolled way [+ *obj*] They were *flailing* their arms to drive away the insects. [*no obj*] The wounded animal lay on the ground, *flailing* helplessly. • He was wildly *flailing* about/around on the dance floor. • He *flailed* away at the ball. [=he swung wildly at the ball]

2 [+ *obj*] : to strike or hit (something or someone) in a wild and uncontrolled way • The bird's wings *flailed* the water.

²flail *noun, pl* **flails** [*count*] : a long-handled tool that was used in the past for beating wheat so that the grain would become separated from the wheat

flair /ˈfleɚ/ *noun* [*singular*]

1 : a natural ability to do something — usually + *for* • He has a *flair for* storytelling. • She has a *flair for* the dramatic. [=she tends to behave or talk in a very dramatic way]

2 : an unusual and appealing quality or style • a restaurant with a European *flair*

flak *also* **flack** /ˈflæk/ *noun* [*noncount*]

1 : exploding shells that are shot at enemy aircraft from guns on the ground

2 *informal* : harsh criticism • He caught/drew heavy *flak* for his decision to oppose the new school. • He took a lot of *flak* from the other kids for his unusual appearance.

¹flake /ˈfleɪk/ *noun, pl* **flakes** [*count*]

1 : a small, thin piece of something • delicate *flakes* of snow • white *flakes* of dandruff • soap *flakes* — see also CORNFLAKES, SNOWFLAKE

2 *chiefly US, informal* : a strange or unusual person : ODDBALL • He's a nice guy but he's a bit of a *flake*.

²flake *verb* **flakes; flaked; flak·ing** [*no obj*]

1 : to break apart into small, thin pieces • Bake the fish until it *flakes* easily when tested with a fork.

2 : to form loose, thin pieces that fall off ▪ The old fence was falling apart, and its paint was *flaking* (off).

flak jacket *noun, pl* ~ **-ets** [*count*] **:** a special jacket that is worn by soldiers, police officers, etc., for protection against flak or bullets — called also *flak vest*

flaky /ˈfleɪki/ *adj* **flak·i·er; -est**
1 : tending to form or break apart into thin pieces ▪ pie with a crisp, *flaky* crust **:** consisting of flakes ▪ *flaky* snow
2 *chiefly US, informal* **:** unusual or strange ▪ a *flaky* idea ▪ He's a nice guy but he's a little *flaky*.
– **flak·i·ness** *noun* [*noncount*]

flam·bé /flɑmˈbeɪ/ *verb* **-bés; -béed; -bé·ing** [+ *obj*] **:** to pour an alcoholic liquid on (a food) and light it so that flames are produced ▪ The crepes were *flambéed* with brandy.
– **flambé** *adj* — used after a noun ▪ trout *flambé*

flam·boy·ant /flæmˈbojənt/ *adj* [*more* ~; *most* ~] **:** having a very noticeable quality that attracts a lot of attention ▪ a *flamboyant* performer ▪ the *flamboyant* gestures of the conductor ▪ wearing *flamboyant* clothes ▪ *flamboyant* colors
– **flam·boy·ance** /flæmˈbojəns/ *noun* [*noncount*] ▪ youthful *flamboyance* ▪ the *flamboyance* of her clothes – **flam·boy·ant·ly** *adv* ▪ *flamboyantly* dressed

F

[1]**flame** /ˈfleɪm/ *noun, pl* **flames**
1 [*count*] **:** the hot, glowing gas that can be seen when a fire is burning ▪ the *flame* of a candle ▪ We built a fire and roasted marshmallows over the *flames*. ▪ They tried to put out the fire, but the *flames* grew higher.
2 : a state of burning brightly [*count*] The engine suddenly ***burst/exploded into flames***. [=the engine suddenly began burning] ▪ The entire building was ***in flames***. [=was on fire; was burning] ▪ The curtains caught on fire and the cabin ***went up in flames***. [=was destroyed by fire] [*noncount*] The engine *burst/exploded into flame*.
3 [*count*] **:** strongly felt emotion — usually plural ▪ the *flames* of passion
4 [*count*] *informal* **:** a person you have a romantic relationship with **:** SWEETHEART ▪ She refuses to answer questions about her current *flame*. ▪ He's an old *flame* from her high-school days. ▪ a former *flame*
5 [*count*] **:** an angry or insulting e-mail message
fan the flames see [2]FAN

[2]**flame** *verb* **flames; flamed; flam·ing**
1 [*no obj*] **:** to burn with a flame **:** to produce a flame ▪ A fire *flamed* in the oven. — often + *up* ▪ The overheated pan *flamed up* suddenly.
2 [*no obj*] *literary* **:** to feel or express strong or angry emotion ▪ He *flamed* with indignation.
3 [*no obj*] *literary* **:** to shine brightly **:** GLOW ▪ The sun *flamed* through the clouds. ▪ color *flaming* in her cheeks
4 [+ *obj*] **:** to send an angry or insulting e-mail message to (someone) ▪ He got/was *flamed* for expressing a controversial political opinion on the Internet.
flame out [*phrasal verb*] **1** *of a jet engine* **:** to stop working suddenly ▪ The plane nearly crashed when one of its engines *flamed out* shortly after takeoff. **2** *US, informal* **:** to fail or end in a very sudden way ▪ His career *flamed out* after the failure of his last movie. — see also FLAMEOUT

fla·men·co /fləˈmɛŋkoʊ/ *noun* [*count, noncount*] **:** a fast and lively Spanish dance; *also* **:** music that is played for this type of dance

flame·out /ˈfleɪmˌaʊt/ *noun, pl* **-outs** [*count*]
1 : a sudden stopping of a jet engine
2 *US, informal* **:** a very sudden and complete failure ▪ Fans were disappointed by the team's *flameout* in the play-offs.
– see also *flame out* at [2]FLAME

flame·proof /ˈfleɪmˌpruːf/ *adj* **:** not easily damaged by flames **:** FIREPROOF ▪ *flameproof* clothing

flame·throw·er /ˈfleɪmˌθrowɚ/ *noun, pl* **-ers** [*count*]
1 : a weapon that shoots a stream of burning liquid
2 *baseball, informal* **:** a pitcher who throws the ball very fast **:** a fastball pitcher

flam·ing /ˈfleɪmɪŋ/ *adj*
1 : having a bright or glowing red or orange color ▪ the *flaming* sunset sky ▪ *flaming* red hair
2 : burning with bright flames ▪ a *flaming* torch
3 : very intense or strongly felt ▪ *flaming* passion
4 *informal* — used to make an angry or critical statement more forceful ▪ They're a couple of *flaming* idiots.

fla·min·go /fləˈmɪŋgoʊ/ *noun, pl* **-gos** *also* **-goes** [*count*] **:** a large tropical bird that has pink or red wings and a very long neck and legs — see color picture on page C9

flam·ma·ble /ˈflæməbəl/ *adj* [*more* ~; *most* ~] **:** capable of being set on fire and of burning quickly ▪ a *flammable* liquid ▪ a highly *flammable* fabric
– **flam·ma·bil·i·ty** /ˌflæməˈbɪləti/ *noun* [*noncount*]

flan /ˈflæn/ *noun, pl* **flans** [*count, noncount*]
1 *chiefly US* **:** a type of sweet dessert made of a smooth, thick custard covered with caramel
2 : an open pie containing any of various fillings ▪ a mushroom *flan*

flange /ˈflænʤ/ *noun, pl* **flang·es** [*count*] **:** an edge that sticks out from something (such as a wheel) and is used for strength, for guiding, or for attachment to another object
– **flanged** /ˈflænʤd/ *adj* ▪ a *flanged* wheel

[1]**flank** /ˈflæŋk/ *noun, pl* **flanks** [*count*]
1 : the area on the side of an animal (such as a horse) between the ribs and the hip ▪ She gently patted the horse's *flank*. — see picture at HORSE
2 : the right or left side of a military formation ▪ They attacked the enemy on both *flanks*.
3 : the side of something ▪ the eastern *flank* of a volcano

[2]**flank** *verb* **flanks; flanked; flank·ing** [+ *obj*] **:** to be located on both sides of (something or someone) ▪ Guards *flanked* the entrance. — usually used as *(be) flanked* ▪ The bed *was flanked* by two small tables. ▪ a celebrity *flanked* by muscular bodyguards — see also OUTFLANK

flank·er /ˈflæŋkɚ/ *noun, pl* **-ers** [*count*] *American football* **:** a player on the offensive team whose position is toward the side and behind the line of scrimmage

flan·nel /ˈflænl/ *noun*
1 [*noncount*] **:** a soft cloth made of wool or cotton ▪ shirts made of bright-colored *flannel* — often used before another noun ▪ a *flannel* shirt ▪ a *flannel* suit ▪ *flannel* pajamas
2 ***flannels*** [*plural*] **:** pants made of flannel ▪ He wore a dark blazer and gray *flannels*.
3 [*count*] *Brit* **:** WASHCLOTH
4 [*noncount*] *Brit, informal* **:** foolish or meaningless words ▪ Cut out all that *flannel* and tell us what really happened!

flan·nel·ette /ˌflænəˈlɛt/ *noun* [*noncount*] *Brit* **:** a light and soft cotton cloth

[1]**flap** /ˈflæp/ *noun, pl* **flaps** [*count*]
1 : a flat piece of material that is attached to something on one side and that can be easily moved ▪ She opened the tent *flap* and crawled outside. ▪ the inside *flap* of a book's cover ▪ a loose *flap* of skin
2 : the movement or sound of something that is moving up and down or back and forth ▪ the soft *flap* [=*flapping*] of the flag in the breeze ▪ the steady *flap* [=*beat*] of the bird's wings
3 *informal* **a :** a state or situation in which many people are excited or upset ▪ He was widely criticized during the recent *flap* [=*uproar*] about his controversial new book. **b** *chiefly Brit* **:** a state in which someone is very upset ▪ He got ***in a flap*** [=he became upset] over the delays in the schedule.
4 : a movable part of an airplane wing that can be raised or lowered and that is used to increase lift

[2]**flap** *verb* **flaps; flapped; flap·ping :** to move (something) up and down or back and forth [+ *obj*] birds *flapping* their wings ▪ The breeze *flapped* the sails. [*no obj*] The flag *flapped* in the breeze. ▪ The bird's wings were *flapping*.

flap·doo·dle /ˈflæpˌduːdl/ *noun* [*noncount*] *chiefly US, informal* **:** foolish words **:** NONSENSE ▪ The speech was a lot of *flapdoodle* about the economy.

flap·jack /ˈflæpˌʤæk/ *noun, pl* **-jacks** [*count*]
1 *US* **:** PANCAKE
2 *Brit* **:** a thick, sweet cake made of oatmeal usually with molasses or honey

flap·per /ˈflæpɚ/ *noun, pl* **-pers** [*count*] **:** a young woman in the 1920s who dressed and behaved in a way that was considered very modern

[1]**flare** /ˈfleɚ/ *verb* **flares; flared; flar·ing**
1 [*no obj*] **:** to shine or burn suddenly and briefly ▪ A match *flared* (up) in the darkness.
2 [*no obj*] **:** to become suddenly excited, angry, or active ▪ ***Tempers flared*** [=people became angry] during the debate. — often + *up* ▪ The fighting *flared up* again after a two-week lull. ▪ She *flared up* [=became very angry] at her brother. ▪ Her asthma has *flared up* again. [=her asthma has become suddenly active or worse again]
3 : to open or spread outward [*no obj*] pants that *flare* at the bottom ▪ the bull's *flaring* nostrils — often + *out* ▪ The skirt *flares out* at the knee. [+ *obj*] The bull *flared* its nostrils.

[2]**flare** *noun, pl* **flares**
1 [*count*] **:** a light that shines brightly and briefly ▪ the sudden *flare* of the match

2 [*count*] : a very bright light that is used to give a signal, to light up something, or to attract attention ▪ When the crew saw *flares*, they knew the other ship was in trouble.; *also* : a device that produces such a light
3 [*count*] : a sudden expression of anger : FLARE-UP ▪ a *flare* of temper
4 [*count*] : a shape or part that spreads outward ▪ the *flare* at the bottom of the vase
5 ***flares*** [*plural*] : pants with legs that become wider at the bottom : BELL-BOTTOMS

flare–up /ˈfleɚˌʌp/ *noun, pl* **-ups** [*count*]
1 : a sudden occurrence of flame ▪ The fire is smoldering and there is still a danger of *flare-ups*.
2 : a sudden occurrence or expression of anger ▪ a *flare-up* of temper during the debate ▪ a moody teenager prone to emotional *flare-ups*
3 : an occurrence in which something (such as violence or a disease) suddenly begins or becomes worse ▪ She had another *flare-up* of her asthma. ▪ There has been a *flare-up* of violence along the border.

[1]flash /ˈflæʃ/ *verb* **flash·es; flashed; flash·ing**
1 : to shine or give off bright light suddenly or in repeated bursts [*no obj*] Thunder rumbled and lightning *flashed*. ▪ Cameras *flashed* as the celebrities passed. ▪ A car was sitting on the side of the road with its lights *flashing*. [+ *obj*] She *flashed* her car's headlights (at us) and honked her horn.
2 a : to appear quickly or suddenly [*no obj*] A message *flashed* on the screen. [+ *obj*] The screen *flashed* a message in black letters. **b** [*no obj*] : to move or pass very quickly ▪ A car *flashed* by. ▪ An idea *flashed* into/through his mind. [=he suddenly had an idea]
3 [*no obj*] *of the eyes* : to show strong emotion ▪ Her eyes *flashed* with anger.
4 [+ *obj*] : to show (something) briefly ▪ The mugger *flashed* a knife and demanded their wallets. ▪ The officer *flashed* his badge. ▪ She *flashed* a shy smile.
5 *informal* : to show your sexual organs to (someone) suddenly and briefly in public [+ *obj*] A strange man *flashed* her on the subway. [*no obj*] He was arrested for *flashing*. — see also FLASHER

[2]flash *noun, pl* **flashes**
1 [*count*] : a sudden bright light ▪ A brilliant/blinding *flash* lit up the sky. ▪ a *flash* of lightning = a lightning *flash*
2 [*count*] : a sudden appearance or occurrence of something ▪ a *flash* of insight ▪ a *flash* of color ▪ a *flash* of wit ▪ a *flash* of anger ▪ The idea for the movie came to her in a *flash* of inspiration. — see also HOT FLASH
3 [*noncount*] *usually disapproving* : a fancy or exciting quality or appearance that is meant to attract attention to something that is usually not very good or interesting ▪ They relied on gimmicks and *flash* to get people's attention. ▪ a show with a lot of *flash* but little substance
4 : a device that is used to produce a brief and very bright flash of light for taking photographs [*count*] a camera with a *flash* ▪ Use the *flash* when you're taking pictures indoors. [*noncount*] a picture taken using *flash* ▪ *flash* photography [=photography that is done with a flash] — see picture at CAMERA; compare FLASHBULB
5 [*count*] : NEWSFLASH
(as) quick as a flash *informal* : very quickly ▪ The waitress brought our order *as quick as a flash*.
flash in the pan : a person or thing that fails after being very popular or successful for a brief time ▪ He was a *flash in the pan* whose second album didn't sell very well.
in a flash *informal* : very quickly or suddenly ▪ I'll be back *in a flash*. ▪ The idea came to me *in a flash*.

[3]flash *adj*
1 *always used before a noun* : beginning suddenly and lasting only a short time ▪ a ***flash fire*** ▪ a ***flash flood*** [=a sudden flood that is caused by heavy rain and that lasts a short time]
2 *always used before a noun, US, informal* : very talented ▪ a *flash* athlete
3 [*more* ~; *most* ~] *Brit, informal + disapproving* : FLASHY, SHOWY ▪ a *flash* car

flash·back /ˈflæʃˌbæk/ *noun, pl* **-backs**
1 : a part of a story or movie that describes or shows something that happened in the past [*count*] The character's childhood was described in a series of *flashbacks*. [*noncount*] events shown ***in flashback***
2 [*count*] : a strong memory of a past event that comes suddenly into a person's mind ▪ He's having *flashbacks* of/to his days in the war.

flash·bulb /ˈflæʃˌbʌlb/ *noun, pl* **-bulbs** [*count*] : an electric bulb that produces a very bright flash of light for taking photographs — compare [2]FLASH 5

flash card *noun, pl* ~ **cards** [*count*] : a card that has words, numbers, or pictures on it and that is used to help students learn about a subject

flash·er /ˈflæʃɚ/ *noun, pl* **-ers** [*count*]
1 : a light that shines briefly and repeatedly : ▪ emergency *flashers* ▪ We noticed a car at the side of the road with its *flashers* on.
2 *informal* : a man who shows his sexual organs in public

flash·light /ˈflæʃˌlaɪt/ *noun, pl* **-lights** [*count*] *US* : a small electric light that can be carried in your hand and that runs on batteries — called also (*Brit*) *torch*

flashlight

flash point *noun, pl* ~ **points** [*count*] : a point, place, or situation in which sudden anger or violence could happen ▪ The city became a *flash point* as political tensions grew. ▪ The situation reached a *flash point* when union leaders urged the workers to protest.

flashy /ˈflæʃi/ *adj* **flash·i·er; -est** *usually disapproving* : bright or fancy in a way that is meant to attract attention : GAUDY ▪ rich young men who drive *flashy* cars ▪ *flashy* glamour ▪ *flashy* colors/clothes ▪ a *flashy* dresser ▪ *flashy* ads
– flash·i·ly /ˈflæʃəli/ *adv* ▪ *flashily* dressed **– flash·i·ness** /ˈflæʃinəs/ *noun* [*noncount*]

flask /ˈflæsk, *Brit* ˈflɑːsk/ *noun, pl* **flasks** [*count*]
1 : a container that is shaped like a flattened bottle and that is used to carry alcohol ▪ a *flask* of whiskey — called also *hip flask*
2 : a glass bottle used in scientific laboratories
3 *Brit* : THERMOS

[1]flat /ˈflæt/ *adj* **flat·ter; flat·test**
1 : having a smooth, level, or even surface : not having curves or bumps ▪ *flat* ground ▪ the *flat* top of the table ▪ the *flat* landscape of the prairie ▪ a *flat* stomach ▪ a *flat* wall
2 : having a wide, smooth surface and little thickness ▪ Coins are usually round and *flat*. ▪ small, *flat* computer disks ▪ a *flat* piece of wood
3 *of a shoe heel* : very low and wide ▪ *flat* heels; *also, of a shoe* : having a flat heel or no heel ▪ wearing *flat* shoes
4 : spread out on or along a surface ▪ The soldiers were lying *flat* on the ground. ▪ He was (lying) *flat* on his back.
5 : very clear and definite : ABSOLUTE ▪ a *flat* refusal ▪ His comments were a *flat* contradiction of his sister's statement.
✧ In British English the expression ***and that's flat!*** is used to stress that a statement or decision is definite and will not be changed. ▪ I'm not going to do it *and that's flat*! [=*and that's that*]
6 a : not changing in amount ▪ They charged a *flat* rate for their services. ▪ a *flat* [=*fixed*] fee ▪ Ticket sales have been/remained *flat*. [=have not increased or decreased] ▪ *flat* profits ▪ a *flat* tax [=a tax that is paid at the same rate by everyone] **b** : not having much business activity ▪ The market is very *flat* for this time of year.
7 : not having much interest or energy : DULL ▪ *flat* writing ▪ a *flat* performance ▪ He spoke in a *flat*, tired voice.
8 *of a drink* : no longer having bubbles ▪ This beer is *flat*. = This beer has gone *flat*. ▪ *flat* ginger ale ▪ *flat* champagne
9 *of a tire* : not having enough air ▪ I got a *flat* tire from a nail in the street. ▪ The tire was (slightly) *flat*.
10 *music* **a** : lower than the true pitch ▪ Her singing was slightly *flat*. **b** : lower than a specified note by a semitone ▪ B *flat* [=a note that is a semitone lower than B] — compare [1]NATURAL 8, [1]SHARP 13
11 *of lighting conditions* : not producing strong shadows ▪ a portrait taken in *flat* lighting
12 : not shiny ▪ *flat* paint
13 *Brit, of a battery* : no longer producing electricity : DEAD ▪ The battery has gone *flat*. [=(*US*) the battery is dead; the battery has died]
(as) flat as a pancake *informal* : very flat ▪ The land there is *as flat as a pancake*. ▪ The tire was *flat as a pancake*.
– flat·ly *adv* ▪ He *flatly* refuses to talk about it. ▪ Lay the map *flatly* on the desk. ▪ She has *flatly* denied the accusations.
– flat·ness *noun* [*noncount*]

[2]flat *noun, pl* **flats** [*count*]

1 : a level area of land — usually plural • salt *flats* • tidal *flats*
2 : a flat part or surface • the *flat* of your hand • the *flat* of a sword
3 a : a musical note that is one semitone lower than a specified note • B *flat* **b** : a written symbol ♭ that is placed before a note to show that it should be played a semitone lower — compare ²NATURAL, ³SHARP
4 *US* : a shallow box in which young plants are grown
5 *chiefly US* : a shoe or slipper that has a flat heel or no heel — usually plural • She wore a casual dress and *flats* to the show.
6 *chiefly Brit* : an apartment typically on one floor • They moved out of their old *flat*. — compare APARTMENT
7 : a tire that does not have enough air • I drove over a nail and got a *flat*. • fix a *flat*

³flat *adv*
1 a : on or against a flat surface • Lay the map *flat* on the desk. **b** : in the position of someone or something that is lying spread out on the ground or another surface • He slipped and landed/fell *flat* on his back/face.
2 : exactly or precisely — used to describe something that happens quickly • He got there in two minutes *flat*. • in 10 seconds *flat* • She finished her homework ***in nothing flat***. [=in no time at all; very quickly]
3 *informal* : completely or absolutely • We asked for more time but they turned us down *flat*. • (*US*) If you ask me, what they're doing is *flat* wrong. • I'm ***flat broke***. [=I have no money] — see also FLAT OUT
4 : below the correct musical pitch • He sang slightly *flat*. — compare ²SHARP 2
fall flat see ¹FALL

¹flat·bed /ˈflæt͵bɛd/ *adj, always used before a noun* : having a flat surface on which work is placed • a *flatbed* scanner • a *flatbed* printing press

²flatbed *noun, pl* **-beds** [*count*] *chiefly US* : a truck or trailer that has a body which is shaped like a platform or shallow box

flat·car /ˈflæt͵kɑɚ/ *noun, pl* **-cars** [*count*] *chiefly US* : a railroad car without sides or a roof that is used for carrying goods

flat·fish /ˈflæt͵fɪʃ/ *noun, pl* **-fish** [*count*] : a fish (such as a halibut, flounder, or sole) that has a flat body and swims on its side with both eyes on the upper side

flat foot *noun* [*count*]
1 *pl* ~ ***feet*** : a foot that is flat on the bottom so the entire sole rests upon the ground — usually plural • He has *flat feet*.
2 *usually* **flat·foot** /ˈflæt͵fʊt/ *pl* **-foots** *US slang, old-fashioned* : POLICE OFFICER

flat–foot·ed /ˈflæt͵fʊtəd/ *adj*
1 a : having flat feet • a *flat-footed* man **b** : walking or moving in a slow and awkward way • a clumsy, *flat-footed* new recruit
2 *chiefly US, informal* : not ready or prepared — usually used in the phrase ***catch flat-footed*** • The surprise announcement of his candidacy *caught* his opponents *flat-footed*. [=his opponents were not prepared for his announcement]

flat·mate /ˈflæt͵meɪt/ *noun, pl* **-mates** [*count*] *chiefly Brit* : a person who shares a flat (sense 6) with someone : ROOMMATE

flat out *adv, informal*
1 *chiefly US* : in a very clear and direct way • I told him *flat out* that I have no intention of marrying him. • We asked for more time but they refused us *flat out*.
2 : at the fastest possible speed • The car does 180 mph *flat out*. • We've been working *flat out*. [=as hard as possible] • He was running *flat out*. [=as fast as possible]
3 *usually* **flat-out** *US, informal* — used to make a statement more forceful • This class is just *flat-out* confusing. • The movie was *flat-out* lousy. • She *flat-out* [=*completely*] missed the target.

flat–out /ˈflæt͵aʊt/ *adj, always used before a noun, informal*
1 *chiefly US* : absolute and complete • It was a *flat-out* lie. • a *flat-out* refusal
2 : greatest possible : MAXIMUM • a *flat-out* effort

flat–pan·el /ˈflætˈpænl/ *adj, always used before a noun* : FLAT-SCREEN • a computer with a *flat-panel* display • a *flat-panel* monitor • *flat-panel* TVs

flat–screen /ˈflæt͵skriːn/ *adj, always used before a noun* — used to describe a television, computer monitor, etc., that has a thin and flat screen • We bought a new *flat-screen* TV.

flat·ten /ˈflætn̩/ *verb* **-tens; -tened; -ten·ing**
1 a [+ *obj*] : to make (something) flat or flatter • He opened the map and *flattened* it (out) against the tabletop. • He *flattened* himself against the wall. [=he pressed himself against the wall so that he was as close to it as possible] **b** [*no obj*] : to become flat or flatter • The dough *flattened* smoothly/easily. • The land *flattens* (out) as you approach the coast.
2 [+ *obj*] **a** : to knock down (something or someone) • Dozens of houses were *flattened* by the tornado. • The boxer was *flattened* in the seventh round. **b** *informal* : to defeat (a competitor) easily or completely • The team got *flattened* in the first round of the play-offs.
3 [*no obj*] : to go to and stay at a lower level • Prices are expected to *flatten* after the holiday shopping season. — often + *out* • Student performance *flattened out* after the second month of the school year.

flat·ter /ˈflætɚ/ *verb* **-ters; -tered; -ter·ing** [+ *obj*]
1 : to praise (someone) in a way that is not sincere • He *flattered* her with comments about her youthful appearance. • His comments *flattered* her. • You're just *flattering* me.
2 : to cause (someone) to feel pleased by showing respect, affection, or admiration • It *flattered* her to be asked to sing at their wedding. — usually used as *(be) flattered* • She *was flattered* when they asked her to sing. • I'm *flattered* that he asked me out, but he isn't my type.
3 a : to show or describe (someone or something) in a way that is very favorable or too favorable • That portrait *flatters* him. [=that portrait makes him look better than he really does] **b** : to cause (someone or something) to look as attractive as possible • That dress really *flatters* your figure.
flatter yourself : to believe something about yourself that makes you feel pleased or proud • Don't *flatter yourself*—you don't sing any better than we do. • I *flatter myself* on my skill in dancing. = I *flatter myself* that I'm a good dancer.
– **flat·ter·er** /ˈflætərɚ/ *noun, pl* **-ers** [*count*] • an insincere *flatterer* – **flattering** *adj* [*more* ~; *most* ~] She wasn't fooled by his *flattering* comments. • a very *flattering* portrait • a *flattering* dress – **flat·ter·ing·ly** /ˈflætərɪŋli/ *adv* • a *flatteringly* favorable portrait

flat·tery /ˈflætəri/ *noun* [*noncount*] : praise that is not sincere • He tried to win his teacher's favor with *flattery*. • ***Flattery will get you nowhere***. [=you will not succeed by flattering me]

flat·top /ˈflæt͵tɑːp/ *noun, pl* **-tops** [*count*]
1 *US* : AIRCRAFT CARRIER
2 : a haircut in which the hair is very short on the sides and flat and evenly cut on top

flat·u·lence /ˈflætʃələns, *Brit* ˈflætjələns/ *noun* [*noncount*] : the presence of too much gas or air in the stomach or intestines • symptoms include nausea, *flatulence*, and cramps
– **flat·u·lent** /ˈflætʃələnt, *Brit* ˈflætjələnt/ *adj* [*more* ~; *most* ~]

flat·ware /ˈflæt͵weɚ/ *noun* [*noncount*] *US* : forks, spoons, and knives used for serving and eating food : SILVERWARE

flaunt /ˈflɑːnt/ *verb* **flaunts; flaunt·ed; flaunt·ing** [+ *obj*]
1 : to show (something) in a very open way so that other people will notice • She liked to *flaunt* her wealth by wearing furs and jewelry. • Their motto seems to be, "***If you've got it, flaunt it!***" [=you should not be afraid to show your good features and talents]
2 : to show a lack of respect for (something, such as a rule) : FLOUT • They openly *flaunted* the rules.

> ***usage*** The use of *flaunt* to mean "flout" is common, but it is considered by many people to be incorrect.

flau·tist /ˈflɑːtɪst/ *noun, pl* **-tists** [*count*] : a person who plays a flute : FLUTIST

¹fla·vor (*US*) *or Brit* **fla·vour** /ˈfleɪvɚ/ *noun, pl* **-vors**
1 a : the quality of something that you can taste [*count*] This dish has an unusual *flavor*. • the hot, spicy *flavors* of Mexican food [*noncount*] a dish with unusual *flavor* **b** [*count*] : a particular type of taste • They sell 20 different *flavors* of ice cream. • Grape is my favorite bubble gum *flavor*. **c** [*noncount*] : a good or appealing taste • The dish lacks *flavor*. • The stew is full of *flavor*.
2 *chiefly US* : a substance that is added to food or drink to give it a desired taste : FLAVORING [*count*] artificial *flavors* [*noncount*] She added vanilla *flavor* to the custard.
3 a [*count*] : a particular quality that something has • I like the Italian *flavor* of the neighborhood. • The film has an avant-garde *flavor*. **b** [*noncount*] : an appealing quality • Her performance adds *flavor* to the show.
4 [*count*] *informal* : a type or version of something • different

flavors of software ✧ The ***flavor of the month*** is someone or something that is popular and gets a lot of attention for a brief time. ▪ Education reform seems to have become the *flavor of the month* among politicians.
– **fla·vor·ful** *(US) or Brit* **fla·vour·ful** /ˈfleɪvɚfəl/ *adj [more ~; most ~]* ▪ food that is *flavorful* as well as nutritious ▪ *flavorful* recipes – **fla·vor·less** *(US) or Brit* **fla·vour·less** /ˈfleɪvɚləs/ *adj* ▪ *flavorless* food – **fla·vor·some** *(US) or Brit* **fla·vour·some** /ˈfleɪvɚsəm/ *adj [more ~; most ~]* ▪ *flavorsome [=flavorful]* recipes

²flavor *(US) or Brit* **flavour** *verb* **-vors; -vored; -vor·ing** *[+ obj]* : to give or add flavor to (something) ▪ We *flavored* the cookies with cinnamon. ▪ I *flavored* the salad with herbs.
– **flavored** *(US) or Brit* **fla·voured** *adj* ▪ *flavored* coffee ▪ cherry-*flavored* candies

fla·vor·ing *(US) or Brit* **fla·vour·ing** /ˈfleɪvərɪŋ/ *noun, pl* **-ings** : a substance that is added to a food or drink to give it a desired taste *[count]* We used ginger and other natural *flavorings.* ▪ add more *flavorings [noncount]* add more *flavoring*

flaw /ˈflɑː/ *noun, pl* **flaws** *[count]*
1 : a small physical problem (such as a crack) that makes something less valuable : DEFECT ▪ There was a *flaw* in the vase. ▪ He inspected the fabric for *flaws.*
2 : a small fault or weakness ▪ Several critics pointed out the *flaws* in the book's plot. ▪ Vanity was the one *flaw* in his character. ▪ There are a few *flaws* in your argument.
– **flaw·less** /ˈflɑːləs/ *adj* ▪ an attractive woman with *flawless* skin ▪ a *flawless [=perfect]* performance – **flaw·less·ly** *adv* ▪ She performed *flawlessly.* – **flaw·less·ness** *noun [noncount]*

flawed /ˈflɑːd/ *adj [more ~; most ~]* : having a mistake, fault, or weakness ▪ a *flawed* but decent man ▪ fatally/badly *flawed* reasoning ▪ a *flawed* but powerful performance

flax /ˈflæks/ *noun [noncount]*
1 : a plant that has blue flowers and that is grown for its fiber and its seed ✧ The fiber of flax is used to make linen and the seed is used to make linseed oil.
2 : the fiber of the flax plant

flax·en /ˈflæksən/ *adj, literary* : having a pale yellow color ▪ *flaxen* hair

flay /ˈfleɪ/ *verb* **flays; flayed; flay·ing** *[+ obj]* : to beat or whip (someone or something) in a very violent and severe way — usually used figuratively ▪ He was *flayed* [=severely criticized] by the media for his thoughtless comments.

flea /ˈfliː/ *noun, pl* **fleas** *[count]* : a very small insect that lives on animals and that has strong legs used for jumping ▪ The dog has *fleas.* ▪ a *flea* bite
fit as a flea see ¹FIT

flea·bag /ˈfliːˌbæg/ *noun, pl* **-bags** *[count] US, informal* : a cheap and dirty hotel — usually used before another noun ▪ a *fleabag* hotel

flea collar *noun, pl* **~ -lars** *[count]* : a collar for dogs and cats that contains a substance which kills fleas

flea market *noun, pl* **~ -kets** *[count]* : a usually outdoor market in which old and used goods are sold

¹fleck /ˈflɛk/ *noun, pl* **flecks** *[count]* : a small spot or mark ▪ a brown cloth with *flecks* of yellow ▪ The police found *flecks* of blood on his clothes.

²fleck *verb* **flecks; flecked; flecking** *[+ obj]* : to put a small spots or marks of something on different parts of (a surface) ▪ She *flecked* the canvas with blue paint. — usually used as *(be) flecked* ▪ a brown beard *flecked* with gray [=a brown beard that has many small areas or spots of gray] ▪ snow *flecked* with mud = mud-*flecked* snow

fled *past tense and past participle of* FLEE

fledge /ˈflɛʤ/ *verb* **fledg·es; fledged; fledg·ing** *[no obj] of a bird* : to develop the feathers necessary for flying ▪ The young birds haven't yet *fledged.*

fledg·ling /ˈflɛʤlɪŋ/ *noun, pl* **-lings** *[count]*
1 : a young bird that has just become able to fly ▪ a female bird feeding her *fledglings* ▪ a *fledgling* robin
2 : someone or something that is getting started in a new activity — usually used before another noun ▪ a *fledgling* company with only four employees ▪ a *fledgling* novelist

flee /ˈfliː/ *verb* **flees; fled** /ˈflɛd/; **flee·ing**
1 *[no obj]* : to run away from danger ▪ They *fled* for their lives. [=they fled to save their lives] ▪ The family *fled* from Nazi Germany to Britain in 1936.
2 *[+ obj]* : to run away from (a place) ▪ He was accused of trying to *flee* the scene of the accident. ▪ Many people *fled* the city to escape the fighting. ▪ He was forced to *flee* the country.

¹fleece /ˈfliːs/ *noun, pl* **fleec·es**
1 *[count]* : the woolly coat of a sheep
2 a *[noncount]* : a soft cloth that is used to make warm clothes ▪ warm *fleece* jackets **b** *[count] chiefly Brit* : a jacket made from this cloth
– **fleecy** /ˈfliːsi/ *adj* **fleec·i·er; -est** ▪ *fleecy* white clouds ▪ soft, *fleecy* fabric

²fleece *verb* **fleeces; fleeced; fleec·ing** *[+ obj] informal* : to deceive and take money from (someone) : CHEAT ▪ Don't let that salesman *fleece* you. ▪ an unsuspecting tourist *fleeced* by a scam artist

¹fleet /ˈfliːt/ *noun, pl* **fleets** *[count]*
1 a : a group of military ships that are controlled by one leader ▪ He was the commander of the Pacific *fleet.* **b** : all of a country's military ships ▪ the British *fleet*
2 : a group of ships or vehicles that move or work together or that are controlled or owned by one company ▪ a fishing *fleet* ▪ The company has a large *fleet* of delivery trucks. ▪ a *fleet* of taxis

²fleet *adj* **fleet·er; -est** *literary* : very fast ▪ a *fleet* runner ▪ She is vey ***fleet of foot***. [=she is able to run very fast]
– **fleet·ly** *adv* ▪ running *fleetly* – **fleet·ness** *noun [noncount]* ▪ *fleetness* of foot

fleet–foot·ed /ˈfliːtˌfʊtəd/ *adj [more ~; most ~]* : able to run fast ▪ a *fleet-footed* runner

fleet·ing /ˈfliːtɪŋ/ *adj [more ~; most ~]* : not lasting : lasting for only a short time ▪ autumn's *fleeting* beauty ▪ I caught a *fleeting* glimpse of the comet. ▪ Her fame was *fleeting.*

Fleet Street /ˈfliːt-/ *noun [singular]* — used as a name for London newspapers and journalists ▪ *Fleet Street* is speculating about his political future following the scandal. ✧ The term *Fleet Street* comes from the name of a street in London where many newspapers were once located.

Flem·ish /ˈflɛmɪʃ/ *noun [noncount]* : the Germanic language that is spoken by people in northern Belgium and that is now officially called Dutch
– **Flemish** *adj*

¹flesh /ˈflɛʃ/ *noun [noncount]*
1 : the soft parts of the body of an animal or person ▪ the flabby white *flesh* of his belly
2 : the skin of a person ▪ a disease that causes sores on the *flesh* ▪ sun-tanned *flesh* ▪ ***flesh-colored*** [=having the color of a white person's skin] ▪ The memory of all that blood was enough to ***make my flesh crawl/creep***. [=to make me feel disgusted, afraid, etc.]
3 : parts of an animal used as food : MEAT ▪ cooked rabbit *flesh* ▪ *flesh*-eating mammals
4 : the soft part of a fruit that is eaten ▪ the soft, sweet *flesh* of a peach
5 : the physical nature of a person rather than the mind or spirit ▪ pleasures of the *flesh* [=physical pleasures, such as eating, drinking, and having sex] ▪ sins of the *flesh* ▪ "The spirit indeed is willing, but the *flesh* is weak." —Matthew 26:41(KJV) — see also *the spirit is willing but the flesh is weak* at ¹SPIRIT
a thorn in the/your flesh see THORN
flesh and blood **1** : a human being — often used when talking about human weakness ▪ There's a limit to what I can do—I'm only *flesh and blood.* ▪ It was more than *flesh and blood* can bear. **2** : someone who is closely related to you : a person in your family — usually used in the phrase ***your own flesh and blood*** ▪ How could you do something so cruel to *your own flesh and blood?*
go the way of all flesh *literary* : to die
in the flesh ✧ If you see someone *in the flesh* you see that person directly rather than in a picture, on television, etc. ▪ I saw him *in the flesh* just three days ago. ▪ She was excited to see the President *in the flesh.*
pound of flesh see ¹POUND
press the flesh see ²PRESS

²flesh *verb* **flesh·es; fleshed; flesh·ing**
flesh out *[phrasal verb]* ***flesh (something) out*** *or* ***flesh out (something)*** : to provide more information about (something) : to make (something) more complete by adding details ▪ You need to *flesh out* your plan with more details. ▪ She *fleshes out* the characters in her novels very well.

flesh·pot /ˈflɛʃˌpɑːt/ *noun, pl* **-pots** *[count] informal + humorous* : a place where people are entertained in ways that relate to physical pleasures (such as drinking and sex) — usually plural ▪ visiting the *fleshpots* of the city

flesh wound *noun, pl* ~ **wounds** [*count*] : a wound that injures the skin and flesh but does not go deep into the body

fleshy /ˈflɛʃi/ *adj* **flesh·i·er; -est**
1 : having a large amount of flesh • a large, *fleshy* nose • the *fleshy* part of the thigh • a *fleshy* face • *fleshy* arms
2 : soft and thick • the *fleshy* texture of the melon • *fleshy* fruit • a plant with *fleshy* leaves
– **flesh·i·ness** *noun* [*noncount*]

flew *past tense of* [1]FLY

[1]**flex** /ˈflɛks/ *verb* **flex·es; flexed; flex·ing**
1 [+ *obj*] **a** : to bend (a body part) • *flexing* a leg • *flex* your fingers **b** : to move or tighten (a muscle) • He *flexed* the muscles of his right arm.
2 [*no obj*] : BEND • a material that *flexes* easily
flex your muscles : to show your strength or power • The election will give us a chance to *flex our* political *muscles*.

[2]**flex** *noun, pl* **flexes** [*count*] *Brit* : [1]CORD 2 • buy a new *flex* for the toaster

flex·i·ble /ˈflɛksəbəl/ *adj* [*more* ~; *most* ~]
1 : capable of bending or being bent • *flexible* branches swaying in the breeze • a material that is both strong and *flexible* • She's been doing exercises to become stronger and more *flexible*.
2 **a** : easily changed • Our schedule for the weekend is very *flexible*. : able to change or to do different things • This computer program has to be *flexible* to meet all our needs. **b** : willing to change or to try different things • Whatever you want to do is fine with me. I'm *flexible*. — opposite INFLEXIBLE
– **flex·i·bil·i·ty** /ˌflɛksəˈbɪləti/ *noun* [*noncount*] • She's been exercising to improve her *flexibility*. • He shows remarkable *flexibility* as an actor. [=he can play a wide range of roles] – **flex·i·bly** /ˈflɛksəbli/ *adv*

flex·time (*US*) /ˈflɛksˌtaɪm/ *or chiefly Brit* **flexi·time** /ˈflɛksɪˌtaɪm/ *noun* [*noncount*] : a system in which employees are required to work a certain number of hours but are allowed to choose their own times for starting and finishing work

[1]**flick** /ˈflɪk/ *noun, pl* **flicks** [*count*] : a short, quick movement • with a *flick* of his thumb • a *flick* of the wrist • She turned on the light with a *flick* [=*flip*] of a switch. — compare [3]FLICK

[2]**flick** *verb* **flicks; flicked; flick·ing**
1 **a** : to move (something) with a short, quick movement [+ *obj*] *flick* a switch • The snake *flicked* its tongue in and out. • a cow *flicking* its tail back and forth • She *flicked* her hair back over her shoulder. [*no obj*] The snake's tongue *flicked* in and out. **b** [+ *obj*] : to cause (something) to fly through the air by making a quick movement with your hand, finger, or thumb • She *flicked* an ash into the ashtray. • He *flicked* his cigarette butt out the window.
2 [+ *obj*] : to turn (something) *on* or *off* with a switch • *flick on* the TV • *flick off* the lights
3 [+ *obj*] : to hit (someone or something) with a short quick movement • The boys were *flicking* each other with towels.

[3]**flick** *noun, pl* **flicks** [*count*] *informal* : MOVIE • the new action *flick* • a ***skin flick*** [=a movie featuring nude people] • (*Brit*) go to ***the flicks*** [=go to a movie theater; (*US*) go to the movies] — compare [1]FLICK

[1]**flick·er** /ˈflɪkɚ/ *verb* **-ers; -ered; -er·ing** [*no obj*]
1 : to burn or glow in an unsteady way : to produce an unsteady light • A TV was *flickering* in the background. • The overhead light kept *flickering* off and on. • a *flickering* candle/flame
2 : to appear or pass briefly or quickly • Thoughts *flickered* through his mind. • A smile *flickered* across her face.

[2]**flicker** *noun, pl* **-ers** [*count*]
1 : a quick and unsteady movement of light • the *flicker* of candlelight
2 : a sudden quick movement • the *flicker* of an eyelash
3 : a very small amount *of* something : a slight hint or suggestion *of* something (such as an emotion or quality) • a *flicker of* interest • His writing doesn't show the faintest *flicker of* imagination or originality. • There was a faint *flicker of* a smile on her face. • a *flicker of* recognition/hope

flick–knife /ˈflɪkˌnaɪf/ *noun, pl* **-knives** [*count*] *Brit* : SWITCHBLADE

fli·er *or* **fly·er** /ˈflajɚ/ *noun, pl* **-ers** [*count*]
1 : a person or animal that flies • These birds are graceful *fliers*. • Charles Lindbergh was the first *flier* [=*pilot*] to fly solo across the Atlantic. • a fearful/nervous *flier* [=airplane passenger] • a ***frequent flier*** [=a person who flies often on a particular airline] ◊ The usual spelling of this sense in U.S. English is *flier*. The usual British spelling is *flyer*.
2 *usually* **flyer** : a piece of paper that has something printed on it (such as an advertisement or an announcement) and that is given to many people • They distributed *flyers* announcing the concert throughout the city.
take a flier *US, informal* : to do something that could have either good or bad results : to do something risky • He *took a flier* in politics soon after getting his degree. — often + *on* • Investors have been unwilling to *take a flier on* [=to invest money in] such a small and unproven company.

flight /ˈflaɪt/ *noun, pl* **flights**
1 [*noncount*] **a** : the act of flying : the act of moving through the air by the use of wings • the *flight* of a bee • a bird ***in flight*** [=a bird that is flying] **b** : the act of moving through the air or through outer space • the *flight* of a bullet/baseball • the *flight* of a rocket to the moon
2 [*count, noncount*] : the act of running away in order to escape from danger • the *flight* of refugees
3 [*count*] **a** : a journey on an airplane • an overnight *flight* • a transatlantic *flight* • a direct/nonstop *flight* **b** : the airplane that is making a journey • Our *flight* leaves at noon. • They boarded *Flight* 101.
4 [*count*] : a group of similar birds, airplanes, etc., that are flying through the air together • a *flight* of geese
5 [*count*] : a series of stairs going from one level or floor to another • Her apartment is five *flights* up. • He fell down a *flight* of stairs.
flight of fancy also flight of imagination/fantasy : an idea, story, etc., that shows great imagination but is very unlikely to be true or practical • The book is filled with *flights of fancy* about the future of the computer industry.
put (someone) to flight *formal* + *old-fashioned* : to cause (someone) to leave or run away • The rebels were *put to flight* by the advancing army.
take flight **1** : to leave or run away from danger • Fearing arrest, they *took flight* and hid in the mountains. **2** *US* : to begin flying • The bird *took flight* [=*took wing*] when we tried to approach it. **3** *US* : to begin a period of rapid activity, development, or growth • The idea really *took flight* [=*took off*] and soon it seemed everyone was copying it.

flight attendant *noun, pl* ~ **-dants** [*count*] : a person whose job is to help passengers who are traveling in an airplane — compare STEWARD, STEWARDESS

flight deck *noun, pl* ~ **decks** [*count*]
1 : the top deck of an aircraft carrier
2 : the area where the pilots sit in a large airplane • The captain spoke to the passengers from the *flight deck*. [=*cockpit*]

flight·less /ˈflaɪtləs/ *adj* : unable to fly • *flightless* birds

flight lieutenant *noun, pl* ~ **-nants** [*count*] : an officer in the British Air Force

flight path *noun, pl* ~ **paths** [*count*] : the route that an airplane, spaceship, etc., travels along through the air or space • No other planes were on their *flight path*. • a missile's *flight path*

flight plan *noun, pl* ~ **plans** [*count*] : a written statement that tells when and where an aircraft will fly • The pilot filed a *flight plan* before taking off.

flight recorder *noun, pl* ~ **-ers** [*count*] : a device on an aircraft that records information (such as airspeed and altitude) about a flight ◊ If an aircraft crashes, its flight recorder can be used to help find out what caused it to crash. — called also *flight data recorder*

flighty /ˈflaɪti/ *adj* **flight·i·er; -est** [*also more* ~; *most* ~]
1 : not serious or dependable : likely to forget things or to change opinions, plans, etc., without reason • an actress who specializes in playing silly, *flighty* women
2 : easily excited or frightened • *flighty* [=*skittish*] racehorses • *flighty* investors
– **flight·i·ness** /ˈflaɪtinəs/ *noun* [*noncount*]

[1]**flim·flam** /ˈflɪmˌflæm/ *noun* [*noncount*] *informal*
1 : dishonest behavior meant to take money or property from someone — usually used before another noun • He lost all his money to a ***flimflam artist/man***. [=a criminal who steals money from people by tricking them; a con man]
2 : foolish or deceptive words : NONSENSE • The report is just a lot of corporate *flimflam*.

[2]**flimflam** *verb* **-flams; -flammed; -flamm·ing** [+ *obj*] *informal* : to trick (someone) in order to steal money • Investors now realize that they have been *flimflammed*. [=*conned*]

flim·sy /ˈflɪmzi/ *adj* **flim·si·er; -est** [*also more* ~; *most* ~]
1 : easily broken, torn, etc. : not strong or solid • a *flimsy* building • *flimsy* construction • a *flimsy* piece of material

2 : not likely to be true or to be believed ▪ a *flimsy* [=*weak*] excuse ▪ They have only the *flimsiest* of evidence against him. ▪ a movie with a *flimsy* plot

– flim·si·ly /ˈflɪmzəli/ *adv* [*more* ~; *most* ~] ▪ *flimsily* [=*weakly*] constructed **– flim·si·ness** /ˈflɪmzinəs/ *noun* [*noncount*]

flinch /ˈflɪntʃ/ *verb* **flinch·es; flinched; flinch·ing** [*no obj*]

1 : to move suddenly because you are afraid of being hit or hurt ▪ He *flinched* when I tapped him on the shoulder.

2 : to show fear : to hesitate from doing something unpleasant or dangerous ▪ She met danger without *flinching.* ▪ The bill was much higher than expected, but he paid it without *flinching.* — often + *at* or *from* ▪ He didn't *flinch at* paying the bill. ▪ She never *flinched from* danger.

– flinch *noun* [*singular*] ▪ She met danger without a *flinch.*

¹fling /ˈflɪŋ/ *verb* **flings; flung** /ˈflʌŋ/; **fling·ing** [+ *obj*]

1 : to throw or push (something) in a sudden and forceful way ▪ He *flung* his shoe across the room. ▪ She *flung* the door open and stormed into the room. ▪ *fling* open a window ▪ They *flung* their hats into the air. — often used figuratively ▪ They were *flinging* abuse at each other. [=they were angrily shouting insults at each other] ▪ They *flung* him into prison. [=put him in prison] ▪ The crowd was *flung* into confusion. [=the crowd suddenly became very confused]

2 : to forcefully move (yourself or a part of your body) in a specified way ▪ She *flung* herself into his arms. ▪ He *flung* his arms around her. ▪ I *flung* back my head and laughed. ▪ He leaned back and *flung* his leg over the arm of the chair. ▪ She *flung* herself onto the couch.

fling caution to the wind see ¹CAUTION

***fling yourself into* :** to begin doing or working on (something) with great energy and enthusiasm ▪ He *flung himself into* (composing/performing) his music.

²fling *noun, pl* **flings** [*count*]

1 : a brief sexual relationship ▪ She ***had a fling*** with her boss.

2 : a short period of time spent doing enjoyable and exciting things ▪ They had time for one last *fling* before going back to school.

give (something) a fling or ***have a fling at (something)* :** to try something without being very serious about it or without worrying about whether or not you will succeed ▪ He had always thought about starting his own business, and he decided to *give it a fling.* ▪ He *had a* brief *fling at* starting his own business.

flint /ˈflɪnt/ *noun, pl* **flints**

1 a [*noncount*] **:** a hard type of rock that produces a small piece of burning material (called a spark) when it is hit by steel **b** [*count*] **:** a piece of flint

2 [*count*] **:** a piece of metal used for producing a spark ▪ the *flint* in a cigarette lighter

flinty /ˈflɪnti/ *adj* **flint·i·er; -est :** not soft or gentle in manner or appearance : having a very serious quality or manner ▪ a *flinty* and determined hero ▪ *flinty* determination ▪ *flinty* eyes ▪ a ***flinty-eyed*** bureaucrat

– flint·i·ness *noun* [*noncount*]

¹flip /ˈflɪp/ *verb* **flips; flipped; flip·ping**

1 [+ *obj*] **:** to turn (something) over by throwing it up in the air with a quick movement ▪ *flip* a coin

2 : to cause (something) to turn or turn over quickly [+ *obj*] She was sitting in the waiting room, *flipping* the pages of a magazine. ▪ He *flipped* his car (over) on the interstate. ▪ They *flipped* the turtle (over) onto its back. ▪ *flip* a pancake ▪ (*informal*) He got a job ***flipping burgers*** [=working as a cook in a fast-food restaurant] [*no obj*] His car *flipped* over on the interstate. ▪ She was sitting in the waiting room, *flipping* [=*leafing*] through magazines.

3 [+ *obj*] **a :** to move (something) with a quick light movement : FLICK ▪ *flip* a switch **b :** to turn (something) *on* or *off* with a switch ▪ *flip on* the radio/TV

4 [+ *obj*] **:** to throw (something) with a quick movement ▪ *Flip* me the ball. = *Flip* the ball to me.

5 [*no obj*] *informal* **:** to become very excited or angry ▪ You'll *flip* when you hear this! ▪ Take the trash out before your father *flips.* — see also FLIP OUT (below)

6 : to change or move through (channels, stations, etc.) quickly [+ *obj*] He *flipped* the channel back to the golf tournament. ▪ I spent the afternoon *flipping* channels. [*no obj*] He kept *flipping* [=*switching*] to another channel.

flip open [*phrasal verb*] ***flip open*** or ***flip open (something)*** or ***flip (something) open* :** to open or to cause (something) to open with a quick movement ▪ Her notebook *flipped open.* ▪ She *flipped open* her notebook.

flip out [*phrasal verb*] *informal* **:** to become crazy or very excited or angry ▪ I *flipped out* when I saw how they had changed my work. ▪ She's going to *flip out* when she sees the great present I got her. — see also ¹FLIP 5 (above)

flip someone off or ***flip someone the bird*** *US slang* **:** to make an offensive gesture at someone by pointing the middle finger upward while keeping the other fingers folded down ▪ angry drivers *flipping each other the bird* [=*giving each other the bird/finger*]

flip your lid also *chiefly US* ***flip your wig*** *informal* **:** to become crazy or very angry ▪ His mother *flipped her lid* when she saw what a mess he'd made.

²flip *noun, pl* **flips** [*count*]

1 : the act of flipping something : a quick turn, toss, or movement ▪ the *flip* of a coin ▪ She turned on the lights with the *flip* of a switch.

2 : an athletic movement in which someone jumps in the air and rolls forward or backward : a somersault in the air ▪ a back *flip*

³flip *adj* **flip·per; flip·pest** [*or more* ~; *most* ~] *informal* **:** not serious : FLIPPANT ▪ a *flip* answer/attitude

flip chart *noun, pl* **~ charts** [*count*] **:** a chart that consists of a series of large pieces of paper which are attached at the top and which are used to present information to an audience by turning over one piece of paper at a time

¹flip–flop /ˈflɪpˌflɑːp/ *noun, pl* **-flops** [*count*]

1 : a type of loose rubber sandal ▪ She wore *flip-flops* to the beach. — see picture at SHOE

2 *chiefly US, informal* **:** a sudden change of opinion ▪ a politician accused of doing *flip-flops* on important social issues

²flip–flop *verb* **-flops; -flopped; -flop·ping** [*no obj*] *chiefly US, informal* **:** to suddenly or frequently change your opinion ▪ a politician accused of *flip-flopping* on social issues

flip·pant /ˈflɪpənt/ *adj* [*more* ~; *most* ~] **:** lacking proper respect or seriousness ▪ He made/gave a *flippant* response to a serious question.

– flip·pan·cy /ˈflɪpənsi/ *noun* [*noncount*] ▪ Many people were offended by the *flippancy* of his responses. **– flip·pant·ly** *adv* ▪ He responded *flippantly.*

flip·per /ˈflɪpɚ/ *noun, pl* **-pers** [*count*]

1 : one of two flat body parts that stick out from the side of a seal, whale, etc., and are used by the animal for swimming

2 : a flat rubber shoe that has a very wide front and that is used for swimming — see picture at SCUBA DIVING

flip side *noun, pl* **~ sides** [*count*]

1 : the side of a record that has a song which is not as popular and well known as the one on the other side ▪ That song was on the *flip side* of their first single.

2 : the bad or unpleasant part or result of something ▪ Loss of privacy is the *flip side* of fame.

the flip side of the coin see ¹COIN

¹flirt /ˈflɚt/ *verb* **flirts; flirt·ed; flirt·ing** [*no obj*]

1 : to behave in a way that shows a sexual attraction for someone but is not meant to be taken seriously ▪ He likes to *flirt.* ▪ They were *flirting* all night. — usually + *with* ▪ He *flirts with* every attractive woman he meets. ▪ He was *flirting with* her. ▪ They were *flirting with* each other.

2 : to think about something or become involved in something in a way that is usually not very serious — + *with* ▪ She's been *flirting* [=*toying*] *with* the idea of going back to school. ▪ He *flirted with* communism when he was young.

3 : to come close to reaching or experiencing something — + *with* ▪ The temperature *flirted with* [=*approached*] 100 yesterday. ▪ They were *flirting with* [=*risking*] death/disaster. ▪ The company has been *flirting with* bankruptcy. [=the company has been close to going bankrupt]

– flir·ta·tion /ˌflɚˈteɪʃən/ *noun, pl* **-tions** [*count*] ▪ They had a brief *flirtation.* — often + *with* ▪ He had a casual *flirtation with* her. ▪ his youthful *flirtation with* communism

²flirt *noun, pl* **flirts** [*count*] **:** a person who enjoys flirting with other people : a flirtatious person ▪ He admits that he's a terrible *flirt.* [=that he flirts a lot]

flir·ta·tious /ˌflɚˈteɪʃəs/ *adj* [*more* ~; *most* ~] **:** feeling or showing a sexual attraction for someone that is usually not meant to be taken seriously ▪ feeling *flirtatious* ▪ a *flirtatious* smile ▪ a *flirtatious* mood

– flir·ta·tious·ly *adv* ▪ smiling *flirtatiously* **– flir·ta·tious·ness** *noun* [*noncount*] ▪ the *flirtatiousness* of her smile

¹flit /ˈflɪt/ *verb* **flits; flit·ted; flit·ting** [*no obj*] **:** to move or fly quickly from one place or thing to another ▪ butterflies *flitting* around the garden ▪ The hummingbird *flitted* from flower to flower. ▪ She was always *flitting* around the kitchen. ▪

F

writers who *flit* [=*bounce*] from topic to topic

²flit *noun* — ***do a moonlight flit*** see ¹MOONLIGHT

¹float /ˈflout/ *verb* **floats; float·ed; float·ing**

1 [*no obj*] **a :** to rest on top of a liquid ▪ She was *floating* on her back. ▪ ice *floating* in the river ▪ Will this material sink or *float*? **b :** to be carried along by moving water or air ▪ The raft *floated* downstream. ▪ dust *floating* through the air

2 [+ *obj*] **a :** to cause (something) to rest on top of a liquid **:** to cause (something) to float ▪ The incoming tide will eventually *float* the ship off the reef. **b :** to cause or allow (something) to be carried or moved by moving water ▪ They *floated* the logs down the river.

3 [*no obj*] **:** to move or go in a gentle, graceful, or quiet way ▪ She *floated* gracefully across the stage. ▪ His voice *floated* to the back of the room. — sometimes used figuratively ▪ She *floated* off to sleep.

4 [*no obj*] **:** to live without having any serious purpose or goal ▪ He *floated* through life without ever settling down.

5 [+ *obj*] **:** to suggest (an idea, plan, etc.) for acceptance ▪ Someone *floated* this idea for a new book.

6 [+ *obj*] *US* **:** to make arrangements for (a loan) ▪ They may have to *float* a loan to raise the money for renovations. ▪ Could you *float* me a loan? [=could you lend money to me?]

7 [+ *obj*] *finance* **:** to sell (shares in a company) in the market ▪ The company has announced plans to raise capital by *floating* a new issue of securities next month.

8 *of a government* **:** to allow the value of a currency when it is exchanged for other types of currency to change freely [+ *obj*] *float* a currency [*no obj*] allow a currency to *float*

floating on air see ¹AIR

²float *noun, pl* **floats** [*count*]

1 : something that floats: such as **a :** a light object that is attached to a fishing line **b :** a floating platform near a shore for use by swimmers or boats **c :** a structure that holds up an airplane on water

2 : a vehicle with a platform used to carry an exhibit in a parade ▪ We are building a *float* for the homecoming parade.

3 *US* **:** a soft drink with ice cream floating in it ▪ a root beer *float*

4 *Brit* **:** an amount of money that is kept available for making change in a shop

— see also MILK FLOAT

floating *adj*

1 : continually moving or changing position ▪ the *floating* population

2 : having no fixed value or rate ▪ *floating* currencies ▪ *floating* interest rates

3 *Brit* **:** not associated with a particular political party **:** not certain to vote for a particular candidate or party in an election ▪ *floating* voters

¹flock /ˈflɑːk/ *noun, pl* **flocks** [*count*]

1 : a group of birds or animals (such as sheep) ▪ a *flock* of birds/sheep

2 : a large number of people ▪ a *flock* of tourists

3 : the members of a church ▪ a priest caring for his *flock*

²flock *verb* **flocks; flocked; flock·ing** [*no obj*] **:** to gather or move in a crowd ▪ Thousands of people *flocked* to the beach each weekend.

birds of a feather flock together see ¹FEATHER

floe /ˈflou/ *noun, pl* **floes** [*count*] **:** a sheet or mass of floating ice **:** ICE FLOE

flog /ˈflɑːg/ *verb* **flogs; flogged; flog·ging** [+ *obj*] **:** to beat or whip (someone) severely ▪ The sailors were *flogged* for attempting a mutiny. — sometimes used figuratively ▪ He is being *flogged* [=harshly criticized] in the press for his failure to take action.

flog a dead horse see ¹HORSE

— **flogging** /ˈflɑːgɪŋ/ *noun, pl* **-gings** [*noncount*] *Flogging* was a common form of punishment in those days. [*count*] They gave him a good *flogging*. [=they beat/whipped him severely]

¹flood /ˈflʌd/ *noun, pl* **floods**

1 [*count*] **:** a large amount of water covering an area of land that is usually dry ▪ A *flood* inundated the whole area. ▪ the devastating *flood* of 1936 ▪ The water has risen to *flood* level.

2 ***the Flood*** **:** a flood described in the Bible as covering the earth in the time of Noah

3 [*singular*] **:** a large amount of things that come or happen at the same time ▪ We've received a *flood* of mail. ▪ a *flood* of phone calls ▪ a *flood* of criticism ▪ a *flood* of tears ▪ Seeing her again brought back a *flood* of memories.

in flood ✧ A river that is *in flood* has so much water in it that it may flow over its banks and flood the land next to it. ▪ After a week of rain, the river is *in (full) flood*. The phrase ***in full flood*** is sometimes used figuratively to describe the time when something is most active, successful, etc. ▪ a political movement that was *in full flood* in the 1980s

²flood *verb* **floods; flood·ed; flood·ing**

1 a : to cover (land) with a flood [+ *obj*] Heavy rains *flooded* the valley. [*no obj*] The rivers are close to *flooding*. **b** [*no obj*] **:** to become filled or covered by a flood ▪ The valley *flooded* after the heavy rains. ▪ The plain *floods* every spring.

2 [+ *obj*] **a :** to fill (something) completely ▪ Light *flooded* the room. ▪ The room was *flooded* with light. **b :** to cause (something) to receive or take in a large amount of things at the same time ▪ The company plans to *flood* the market with this product. ▪ The office has been *flooded* with phone calls.

3 [*no obj*] **:** to go or come in large numbers or as a large amount ▪ The phone calls have been *flooding* in. ▪ Refugees *flooded* into the camp. ▪ Light *flooded* into the room. ▪ Memories came *flooding* into my mind.

4 : to cause too much fuel to go into (an engine) [+ *obj*] He wasn't able to start the car because he had *flooded* the engine. [*no obj*] The car's engine *flooded*.

flood·gate /ˈflʌdˌgeɪt/ *noun, pl* **-gates** [*count*] **:** a gate for controlling the flow of water from a lake, river, reservoir, etc. — often used figuratively ▪ Many people fear that the court's latest ruling will ***open the floodgates*** for/to a host of new lawsuits. [=will cause/allow a large number of new lawsuits] ▪ Once the ***floodgates have opened***, there will be no way to stop all the lawsuits.

flood·light /ˈflʌdˌlaɪt/ *noun, pl* **-lights** [*count*] **:** a light that shines brightly over a wide area ▪ The yard was lit by *floodlights*. — sometimes used figuratively ▪ The company has been exposed to the *floodlight* of publicity.

— **flood·lit** /ˈflʌdˌlɪt/ *adj* ▪ a *floodlit* stadium

flood·plain /ˈflʌdˌpleɪn/ *noun, pl* **-plains** [*count*]

1 : an area of low, flat land along a stream or river that may flood

2 : an area of land built up from soil left by floods

flood tide *noun, pl* **~ tides** [*count*]

1 : a rising tide

2 : a very large amount of something ▪ The company has been subjected to a *flood tide* [=*flood*] of criticism for its hiring policies.

flood·wa·ter /ˈflʌdˌwɑːtɚ/ *noun, pl* **-ters** [*count*] **:** the water of a flood — usually plural ▪ The *floodwaters* have at last started to recede.

¹floor /ˈfloɚ/ *noun, pl* **floors**

1 [*count*] **:** the part of a room on which you stand ▪ Keep your feet on the *floor*. ▪ washing the kitchen *floor* ▪ a marble/tile/hardwood *floor*

2 [*count*] **a :** the lower inside surface of something (such as a vehicle) ▪ the *floor* of a car **b :** the area of ground at the bottom of something — usually singular ▪ the ocean *floor* ▪ the forest *floor*

3 [*count*] **:** a level in a building ▪ She lives on the second *floor* of a five-story building. ▪ His office is located on the fourth *floor*. — see also FIRST FLOOR, GROUND FLOOR

4 [*count*] **:** a large indoor space where people gather for some activity — usually singular ▪ the *floor* of the convention/legislature ▪ the factory *floor* ▪ the dance *floor* ▪ buying and selling shares on the *floor* of the exchange

5 [*singular*] **:** the people who are gathered in a place for a public meeting ▪ He will now take questions from the *floor*.

6 [*count*] **:** a lower limit — usually singular ▪ establishing a *floor* for wages and prices ▪ The value of the stock has dropped/gone/fallen ***through the floor***. [=to a very low level] — opposite CEILING

have the floor **:** to have the right to speak at a public meeting ▪ May I *have the floor*?

hold the floor **:** to be the person who is speaking at a public meeting ▪ The senator *held the floor* for several hours.

on the cutting-room floor see CUTTING ROOM

take the floor **1 :** to begin speaking at a public meeting ▪ After Senator Smith was finished addressing the assembly, Senator White *took the floor*. **2 :** to go out onto a dance floor to begin dancing ▪ Several couples *took the floor*.

wipe the floor with see ¹WIPE

²floor *verb* **floors; floored; floor·ing** [+ *obj*]

1 : to cover (a surface) with material to make a floor — usually used as *(be) floored* ▪ The lobby *is floored* with marble.

2 a : to knock (someone) to the floor or ground ▪ He *floored*

me with his first punch. **b** *informal* : to surprise, shock or amaze (someone) very much • The news just *floored* me. — often used as *(be) floored* • I *was floored* by the news. • She *was floored* by his knowledge of the subject.
3 *US, informal* : to press (the accelerator of a vehicle) to the floor — usually used in the phrase ***floor it*** • When the light turned green, he *floored it.* [=he pressed the accelerator all the way down and sped away]

floor·board /ˈfloɚˌboɚd/ *noun, pl* **-boards** [*count*]
1 : a board in a floor — usually plural • creaky *floorboards* • wide pine *floorboards*
2 *US* : the floor of a vehicle

floor·ing /ˈflorɪŋ/ *noun* [*noncount*] : material used for floors • marble/tile/hardwood *flooring*

floor lamp *noun, pl* ~ **lamps** [*count*] : a tall lamp that stands on the floor — called also *(Brit) standard lamp*; see picture at LIGHTING

floor–length *adj* : reaching to the floor • a *floor-length* gown/mirror

floor plan *noun, pl* ~ **plans** [*count*] : a plan that shows the position of the rooms in a building • Before construction began, we adjusted the building's *floor plan* to take advantage of the view. • a house with an unusual *floor plan* — called also *ground plan*

floor show *noun, pl* ~ **shows** [*count*] : a series of acts by performers in a nightclub

floo·zy *or* **floo·zie** /ˈflu:zi/ *noun, pl* **-zies** [*count*] *informal* + *old-fashioned* : a usually young woman whose behavior is not morally correct or proper • chasing some *floozy* around
✧ *Floozy* is an insulting word. In U.S. English, *floozy* is the more common spelling; in British English, *floozie* is more common.

¹flop /ˈflɑ:p/ *verb* **flops; flopped; flop·ping** [*no obj*]
1 : to fall, lie, or sit down in a sudden, awkward, or relaxed way • He *flopped* down onto the bed. • She *flopped* into the chair with a sigh.
2 *informal* : to fail completely • The play *flopped.* [=(US) *bombed*] • All of their attempts have *flopped* miserably.
3 : to swing or move in a loose, awkward, or uncontrolled way • The curtains were *flopping* around in the breeze.
– see also FLIP-FLOP

²flop *noun, pl* **flops** [*count*]
1 *informal* : a complete failure • The movie was a total *flop.*
2 : the sound made when someone or something suddenly falls, lies, or sits down • It fell to the ground with a *flop.*
– see also BELLY FLOP

flop·house /ˈflɑ:pˌhaʊs/ *noun, pl* **-hous·es** [*count*] *chiefly US, informal* : a very inexpensive hotel for poor people who do not have anywhere else to live • a crowded *flophouse* — called also *(chiefly Brit) doss-house*

¹flop·py /ˈflɑ:pi/ *adj* **flop·pi·er; -est** : soft and flexible • a *floppy* hat

²floppy *noun, pl* **-pies** [*count*] : FLOPPY DISK

floppy disk *noun, pl* ~ **disks** [*count*] : a small, thin, square case with a flexible disk inside on which data for a computer can be stored — compare HARD DISK

flo·ra /ˈflorə/ *noun, pl* **-ras** *biology* : all the plants that live in a particular area, time, period, or environment [*noncount*] an amazing variety of coastal *flora* • aquatic *flora* [*count*] the *floras* of different coastal regions — compare FAUNA

flo·ral /ˈflorəl/ *adj* [*more* ~; *most* ~] : of or relating to flowers • a *floral* display/design [=a display/design that has pictures of flowers] • a *floral* pattern in wallpaper • The wine has a *floral* aroma. • a *floral* arrangement — see color picture on page C12
– **floral** *noun, pl* **-rals** [*count*] • Her most famous paintings are her *florals.* [=paintings in which flowers are the main subject]

flo·ret /ˈflorət/ *noun, pl* **-rets** [*count*] : a group of flower buds that are part of a vegetable • broccoli/cauliflower *florets* — see color picture on page C4

flor·id /ˈflorəd/ *adj* [*more* ~; *most* ~]
1 : very fancy or too fancy • *florid* writing
2 : having a red or reddish color • a *florid* [=*ruddy*] complexion • a *florid* face
– **flor·id·ly** *adv* • *floridly* written

flo·rist /ˈflorɪst/ *noun, pl* **-rists** [*count*] : a person whose job or business is to sell flowers and plants

¹floss /ˈflɑ:s/ *noun* [*noncount*]
1 : DENTAL FLOSS
2 : soft silk or cotton thread used for sewing

²floss *verb* **floss·es; flossed; floss·ing** : to use dental floss to clean your teeth [*no obj*] My dentist told me I should *floss* more often. [+ *obj*] *floss* your teeth

flo·ta·tion /floʊˈteɪʃən/ *noun* [*noncount*] : the act, process, or state of floating or of causing or allowing something to float • fills the tanks with air for *flotation* • the *flotation* of a currency • *(Brit)* the *flotation* of a company [=the act or process of selling shares in a company to the public] • a (personal) ***flotation device*** [=a life preserver]

flo·til·la /floʊˈtɪlə/ *noun, pl* **-las** [*count*] : a group of small ships

flot·sam /ˈflɑ:tsəm/ *noun* [*noncount*] : floating pieces, parts, etc., from a ship that has been wrecked • *flotsam* washed up on the shore — often used figuratively • bits of *flotsam* gathered from yard sales • human *flotsam* [=people who have no home or who have been forced to leave their homes] — often used in the phrase ***flotsam and jetsam*** • He spends a lot of time sorting through the *flotsam and jetsam* that come(s) across his desk each day. — compare JETSAM

¹flounce /ˈflaʊns/ *verb* **flounc·es; flounced; flounc·ing** [*no obj*]
1 : to move with exaggerated motions • an actress *flouncing* around on the stage • a *flouncing* walk
2 *chiefly Brit* : to walk or move quickly in a way that shows anger or annoyance • He *flounced* out of the room and slammed the door behind him.

²flounce *noun, pl* **flounces** [*count*] *chiefly Brit* : a quick way of walking or moving that shows anger or annoyance — usually singular • leave the room with a *flounce* — compare ³FLOUNCE

³flounce *noun, pl* **flounces** [*count*] : a strip of cloth that is attached to a piece of clothing by one edge — compare ²FLOUNCE
– **flounced** *adj* • *flounced* blouses • a *flounced* skirt
– **flouncy** /ˈflaʊnsi/ *adj* **flounc·i·er; -est** • a *flouncy* skirt

¹floun·der /ˈflaʊndɚ/ *noun, pl* **flounder** *or* **floun·ders** [*count*] : a type of fish that has a flat body and that is eaten as food — see color picture on page C8

²flounder *verb* **-ders; -dered; -der·ing** [*no obj*]
1 : to move in an awkward way with a lot of difficulty and effort : STRUGGLE • The horses were *floundering* through the deep snow. • He was *floundering* around in the pool like an amateur.
2 a : to be unsure about what to do or say • After watching me *flounder* for a few minutes, my instructor took over. **b** : to have a lot of problems and difficulties • The team has been *floundering* [=*struggling*] since the start of the season.

¹flour /ˈflawɚ/ *noun, pl* **flours** : powder made from a grain (especially wheat) that is used in cooking for making bread, cakes, etc. [*noncount*] a five-pound bag of *flour* [*count*] mix the two *flours* together
– **flour·less** /ˈflaʊɚləs/ *adj* • a *flourless* cake

²flour *verb* **flours; floured; flour·ing** [+ *obj*] : to cover (something) with flour • a *floured* board • The fish should be lightly *floured* before it's fried.

¹flour·ish /ˈflɚrɪʃ/ *verb* **-ish·es; -ished; -ish·ing**
1 [*no obj*] : to grow well : to be healthy • plants and animals that *flourished* here thousands of years ago
2 [*no obj*] : to be very successful : to do very well • Regional markets have *flourished* in recent years. • a decorative style that *flourished* in the 1920s • a *flourishing* business
3 [+ *obj*] : to hold up and show (something) in an excited or proud way • Dressed as a pirate, he entered the stage *flourishing* his sword.

²flourish *noun, pl* **-ishes** [*count*]
1 : something that is added as a detail or decoration • the floral *flourishes* in the living room • a house with many clever little *flourishes* • Her writing style is simple and clear, without unnecessary *flourishes.*
2 a : a dramatic or fancy way of doing something • Dinner was served with a *flourish.* **b** : a sudden smooth movement that is likely to be noticed • He waved his sword with a *flourish.* • She opened the door with a *flourish.* • With a *flourish* of her pen, she signed the bill into law.
3 : a short and exciting piece of music played by trumpets : FANFARE • a *flourish* of trumpets

floury /ˈflawəri/ *adj* [*more* ~; *most* ~]
1 : of or resembling flour • a *floury* coating
2 : covered with flour • He wiped his *floury* hands on his pants.

flout /ˈflaʊt/ *verb* **flouts; flout·ed; flout·ing** [+ *obj*] : to break or ignore (a law, rule, etc.) without hiding what you are doing or showing fear or shame ▪ Despite repeated warnings, they have continued to *flout* the law. ▪ *flouting* authority ▪ *flouting* convention — compare FLAUNT

[1]flow /ˈfloʊ/ *verb* **flows; flowed; flow·ing** [*no obj*]

1 *of liquid, gas, or electricity* : to move in a steady and continuous way ▪ rivers *flowing* into the sea ▪ a gently *flowing* [=*running*] stream ▪ She opened the faucet and the water began to *flow* freely. ▪ a device that measures the amount of electricity *flowing* through a circuit — often used figuratively ▪ Excitement was *flowing* through the crowd.

2 a : to move in a continuous and smooth way ▪ Traffic has been *flowing* smoothly/steadily from east to west. ▪ The grain *flowed* smoothly down the elevator chute. **b** : to move, come, or go continuously in one direction ▪ Requests have *flowed* into the office. ▪ Money has continued to *flow* in.

3 a : to proceed in a smooth and easy way ▪ Conversation *flowed* freely. **b** *of a drink* : to be drunk freely ▪ The wine *flowed* freely throughout the evening. [=people drank wine throughout the evening]

4 : to hang down in a loose and graceful way ▪ Her long hair *flowed* down over her shoulders.

5 : to be caused or produced by something : to come *from* something ▪ the wealth that *flows from* trade

6 *of a tide* : to move in toward the land : RISE ▪ The tide ebbs and *flows* twice every 24 hours.

– flowing *adj* ▪ a long, *flowing* dress ▪ her *flowing* hair

[2]flow *noun, pl* **flows**

1 [*singular*] : an act of flowing ▪ a sudden *flow* of tears : the movement of something that is flowing ▪ a steady/smooth *flow* of traffic ▪ The doctor was trying to stop/staunch the *flow* of blood. ▪ We want to encourage the free *flow* of ideas. ▪ the westward *flow* of settlers ▪ We've been receiving a constant *flow* of phone calls.

2 [*count*] : a large area of mud or some other material that is flowing or that was formed by flowing ▪ a mud *flow* ▪ an ancient lava *flow* [=an area of rock that was created by flowing lava]

3 [*noncount*] : the amount of something that flows in a certain time ▪ measuring blood *flow* to the brain — see also CASH FLOW

ebb and flow see [1]EBB

go against the flow : to do things that do not agree with what most other people are doing ▪ She has her own way of thinking and she's not afraid to *go against the flow*.

go with the flow : to relax and accept what is happening without trying to change things or do something different or difficult ▪ When I'm on vacation, I just like to take it easy and *go with the flow*.

in full flow *chiefly Brit* **1** — used to describe someone who is talking continuously in a very enthusiastic way ▪ He can talk for hours when he's *in full flow*. **2** — used to describe the time when something is most active, successful, etc. ▪ When we arrived the party was already *in full flow*.

flow chart *noun, pl* ~ **charts** [*count*] : a chart that shows each step of a process using special symbols that are connected by lines

[1]flow·er /ˈflawɚ/ *noun, pl* **-ers**

1 [*count*] **a** : the part of a plant that is often brightly colored, that usually lasts a short time, and from which the seed or fruit develops ▪ The plant is known for its large white *flowers*. [=*blossoms*] ▪ The tree ***came into flower*** early this year. [=the flowers on the tree bloomed early this year] ▪ The bushes should be ***in flower*** soon. [=the flowers should be blooming soon] ▪ These plants are very fragrant when they are *in* (full) *flower*. — sometimes used figuratively. ▪ His interest in history *came into flower* [=*developed*] while he was just a boy. ▪ She entered the movement after it was *in full flower*. [=after it was fully developed] — see color picture on page C6 **b** : a small plant that is grown for its beautiful flowers ▪ We planted *flowers* in the garden. ▪ *Flowers* line the walkway. ▪ a *flower* garden **c** : a cut stem of a plant with its flower ▪ He sent her a bouquet of *flowers*. ▪ He wore a single *flower* in his lapel.

2 [*singular*] *literary* : the best part of something — used in the phrase ***the flower of*** ▪ *The flower of* a generation was lost in that war. [=the best members of a generation died in that war] ▪ He wrote his best works while ***in the flower of his youth***. [=when he was young]

[2]flower *verb* **-ers; -ered; -er·ing** [*no obj*]

1 : to produce flowers : BLOOM, BLOSSOM ▪ This tree *flowers* in early spring. ▪ The plant will *flower* every other year.

2 : to develop or grow in a successful way ▪ His genius *flowered* at the university. ▪ a political movement that began to *flower* during the 1960s

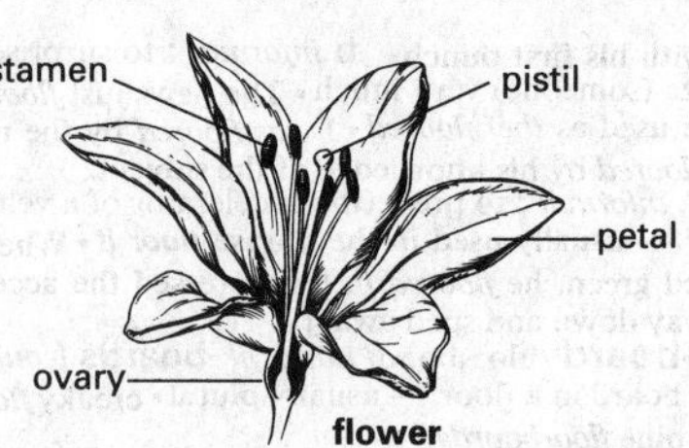

flower

flower bed *noun, pl* ~ **beds** [*count*] : an area where flowers are planted

flower child *noun, pl* ~ **children** [*count*] : a young person in the 1960s and 1970s who rejected the traditional values of society : HIPPIE

flow·ered /ˈflawɚd/ *adj* : decorated with flowers or with pictures of flowers ▪ *flowered* silk ▪ *flowered* wallpaper ▪ a *flowered* dress

flower girl *noun, pl* ~ **girls** [*count*] *US* : a young girl who carries flowers at a wedding

[1]flowering *adj* : having or producing many flowers ▪ a *flowering* branch ▪ *flowering* plants/shrubs/trees

[2]flowering *noun* [*singular*] : the development of something ▪ We witnessed the gradual *flowering* of his talent. [=we saw his talent gradually develop] ▪ a period that saw the *flowering* of the civil rights movement

flow·er·pot /ˈflawɚˌpɑːt/ *noun, pl* **-pots** [*count*] : a container (such as a clay or plastic pot) in which plants are grown

flower power *noun* [*noncount*] : the belief that war is wrong and that people should love each other and lead peaceful lives — used especially to refer to the beliefs and culture of young people (called hippies) in the 1960s and 1970s

flow·ery /ˈflawɚri/ *adj* **flow·er·i·er; -est** [*also more* ~; *most* ~]

1 a : filled with flowers ▪ *flowery* fields **b** : decorated with pictures of flowers ▪ We put two *flowery* prints in the dining room. ▪ a *flowery* dress **c** : smelling like a flower : having a sweet smell like a flower ▪ *flowery* perfume/wine

2 *of language* : very fancy or too fancy or elaborate ▪ He gave a long, *flowery* speech. ▪ *flowery* prose

flown *past participle of* [1]FLY

fl. oz. *abbr* fluid ounce; fluid ounces

flu /ˈfluː/ *noun* [*noncount*] : a common disease that is caused by a virus and that causes fever, weakness, body aches, and breathing problems : INFLUENZA ▪ He came down with a bad bout/attack/case of the *flu*. ▪ catch/get the *flu* ▪ She has the *flu*. = (*Brit*) She has *flu*. — often used before another noun ▪ the *flu* season ▪ a *flu* shot ▪ a *flu* epidemic

flub /ˈflʌb/ *verb* **flubs; flubbed; flub·bing** [+ *obj*] *US, informal* : to fail to do (something) correctly : BOTCH ▪ The ball went right to him but he *flubbed* the catch. ▪ The actress *flubbed* several lines.

– flub *noun, pl* **flubs** [*count*] ▪ a politician known for his verbal *flubs* [=*mistakes, blunders*]

fluc·tu·ate /ˈflʌktʃəˌweɪt/ *verb* **-ates; -at·ed; -at·ing** [*no obj*] : to change level, strength, or value frequently ▪ Oil prices *fluctuated* [=became higher, lower, etc.] throughout the year. ▪ *fluctuating* prices ▪ His popularity has *fluctuated* during his term in office. ▪ In the desert, the temperature *fluctuates* dramatically.

– fluc·tu·a·tion /ˌflʌktʃəˈweɪʃən/ *noun, pl* **-tions** [*count*] Small *fluctuations* in prices are to be expected. [*noncount*] He reported some *fluctuation* in/of real estate values.

flue /ˈfluː/ *noun, pl* **flues** [*count*] : a channel or pipe in a chimney for carrying flame and smoke to the outer air

flu·en·cy /ˈfluːwənsi/ *noun* [*noncount*]

1 : the ability to speak easily and smoothly ▪ She speaks with great *fluency*.; *especially* : the ability to speak a foreign language easily and effectively ▪ Students must demonstrate *fluency* in a foreign language to earn a degree.

2 : the ability to do something in a way that seems very easy ▪ a dancer known for her *fluency* and grace ▪ He plays the piano with speed and *fluency*.

flu·ent /ˈfluːwənt/ *adj* [*more* ~; *most* ~]

1 a : able to speak a language easily and very well ▪ a *fluent* speaker ▪ a *fluent* speaker of Chinese — often + *in* ▪ He is *fluent in* Chinese. **b** ✧ Language that is *fluent* is language that is spoken easily and very well. ▪ She speaks *fluent* Spanish and a little French.

2 : done in a smooth and easy way • We admired their *fluent* [=*fluid*] movement across the dance floor. • a *fluent* performance

– **flu·ent·ly** *adv* • He speaks seven languages *fluently*.

[1]fluff /ˈflʌf/ *noun* [*noncount*]
1 : something light and soft: such as **a :** small balls or pieces of thread, fiber, or dust • Her sweater was covered with *fluff*. **b :** soft fur or feathers
2 *chiefly US, informal* **:** something that has little importance or interest • The movie was pure *fluff*. • Her latest article has the usual *fluff* about movie stars and gossip.

[2]fluff *verb* **fluffs; fluffed; fluff·ing** [+ *obj*]
1 : to shake or move (something, such as a pillow) so that it is fuller, lighter, or softer • Would you like me to *fluff* (up) your pillows? • The wind *fluffed* his hair. • The bird spread its wings and *fluffed* (up) its feathers.
2 *informal* **:** to do (something) badly **:** FLUB • The golfer *fluffed* another shot. • The actor kept *fluffing* the same line.

fluffy /ˈflʌfi/ *adj* **fluff·i·er; -est**
1 : covered with soft material • the *fluffy* fur of a kitten • *fluffy* young chicks • a *fluffy* wool blanket
2 : light and soft or airy • Beat the egg whites until they are *fluffy*. • furniture with big *fluffy* cushions • a favorite *fluffy* sweater **:** having a light and soft appearance • a *fluffy* white cloud

[1]flu·id /ˈfluːwəd/ *adj* [*more ~; most ~*]
1 : capable of flowing freely like water • *fluid* lava • a substance in a *fluid* state
2 — used to describe something that can change easily or that changes often • Boundaries between the farms were very *fluid*. • a *fluid* situation
3 : having or showing a smooth and easy style **:** GRACEFUL • a dancer's *fluid* movements • the sculpture's *fluid* lines
– **flu·id·i·ty** /fluˈɪdəti/ *noun* [*noncount*] • The extreme *fluidity* of the situation has made it impossible to predict the outcome. • She plays the violin with great *fluidity*. – **flu·id·ly** *adv* • moving *fluidly*

[2]fluid *noun, pl* **-ids :** a substance that is able to flow freely **:** a liquid substance [*count*] Please check the *fluids* in the car's engine. • She needs to drink plenty of *fluids*. [*noncount*] *Fluid* leaked from the car's engine. • a bottle of yellow *fluid*

fluid ounce *noun, pl* **~ ounces** [*count*]
1 *US* **:** a unit of liquid measurement equal to 1/16 of a U.S. pint or about 29.6 milliliters
2 *Brit* **:** a unit of liquid measurement equal to 1/20 of a British pint or about 28.4 milliliters

fluke /ˈfluːk/ *noun, pl* **flukes** [*count*] *informal* **:** something that happens because of luck **:** an unexpected or unusual thing that happens by accident • Her second championship shows that the first one was no mere *fluke*. • By some strange *fluke* we ended up working for the same company.

flung *past tense and past participle of* [1]FLING

flunk /ˈflʌŋk/ *verb* **flunks; flunked; flunk·ing** *US, informal*
1 : to get a failing grade in (something, such as an examination or course) **:** FAIL [+ *obj*] If I *flunk* this class, I have to take it over again. • *flunk* a test [*no obj*] If I *flunk*, I have to take this class over again.
2 [+ *obj*] **:** to give a failing grade to (someone) **:** FAIL • The teacher had to *flunk* two students.
flunk out [*phrasal verb*] *US, informal* **:** to be required to leave a school because you have failed your courses • He tried going to college, but he *flunked out* after one year. — often + *of* • He *flunked out of* college.

flun·ky *or* **flun·key** /ˈflʌŋki/ *noun, pl* **-kies** *or* **-keys** [*count*] *informal + disapproving* **:** a person who does small jobs for someone powerful or important • If he can't go himself, he'll send one of his *flunkies*.

flu·o·res·cent /flʊˈresn̩t/ *adj*
1 : producing light when electricity flows through a tube that is filled with a type of gas • a *fluorescent* light/lamp
2 : very bright • *fluorescent* colors/clothing • *fluorescent* tape/paint
– **flu·o·res·cence** /flʊˈresn̩s/ *noun* [*noncount*]

flu·o·ri·date /ˈflurəˌdeɪt/ *verb* **-dates; -dat·ed; -dat·ing :** to add fluoride to (water or toothpaste) — often used as *(be) fluoridated* • The drinking water here is *fluoridated*. • *fluoridated* toothpaste
– **flu·o·ri·da·tion** /ˌflurəˈdeɪʃən/ *noun* [*noncount*]

flu·o·ride /ˈfloəˌaɪd/ *noun* [*noncount*] **:** a chemical that is sometimes added to drinking water and toothpaste to help keep teeth healthy

flur·ry /ˈflɚri/ *noun, pl* **-ries** [*count*]
1 : a brief and light snowfall • We had a few *flurries* yesterday. • a snow *flurry*
2 a : a brief period of excitement or activity — + *of* • There was a *flurry of* trading in the stock exchange. • The incident could create a *flurry of* interest in safety issues. **b :** a large amount of something that happens or comes suddenly — + *of* • a *flurry* [=*barrage*] *of* publicity • There was a *flurry of* requests for more information.

[1]flush /ˈflʌʃ/ *noun, pl* **flush·es** [*count*]
1 : redness on a person's face because of emotion, heat, etc. • A *flush* spread over her face at the mention of his name. — see also HOT FLUSH
2 : the act of cleaning a toilet with a flow of water **:** the act of flushing a toilet • We could hear the *flush* of a toilet somewhere in the building. • give the toilet a *flush*
3 : a sudden feeling or strong emotion — + *of* • a *flush of* grief/pleasure • He felt a *flush of* pride in his son's victory.
in the (first) flush of **:** in the early and exciting time of (something) • She published her first novel while still *in the flush of* youth. [=while still young] • Everyone felt hopeful *in the first flush of* victory.
– compare [6]FLUSH

[2]flush *verb* **flushes; flushed; flush·ing**
1 : to cause a strong flow of water to clean (a toilet) [+ *obj*] *flush* the toilet [*no obj*] The toilet *flushes* automatically. ✧ If you ***flush something down the toilet*** you get rid of it by putting it in the toilet bowl and flushing the toilet. • Police suspect that the drugs were *flushed down the toilet*.
2 [+ *obj*] **a :** to clean (something) with a flow of water or some other liquid • *Flush* the wound immediately with water. • The doctor *flushed* her eye with a special solution. — often + *out* • He *flushed out* the car's radiator. • *flush out* the system **b :** to remove (something) with a flow of liquid • They *flushed* impurities from the system. = They *flushed* impurities out of the system. • He used a hose to *flush* the leaves from the gutters.
3 [*no obj*] **:** to become red in the face because of heat, emotion, etc. • She *flushed* with anger/embarrassment. • Her face *flushed* at the mention of his name.
– compare [3]FLUSH

[3]flush *verb* **flushes; flushed; flushing** [+ *obj*] **:** to cause or force (someone or something) to leave a hiding place • The police *flushed* the suspects from the building. — usually + *out* • The police *flushed out* the suspects. • The birds were *flushed out* of the tree. — sometimes used figuratively • The committee succeeded in *flushing out* [=*finding*] several good candidates. • The agency *flushed out* a surprising number of tax evaders. — compare [2]FLUSH

[4]flush *adj, not used before a noun*
1 : even or level with another surface • The paneling and the wall should be *flush* (with each other).
2 *informal* **:** having a large amount of money • He just got paid and he was feeling *flush*. — often + *with* • Right now the town is *flush with* money. [=the town has more money than usual]

[5]flush *adv*
1 : in order to be level or even with another surface — + *with* • He arranged the books *flush with* the edge of the shelf.
2 : in a very forceful way **:** in a way that makes very solid contact • He landed a punch *flush* [=*squarely*] on my chin. • She placed her hands *flush* against the door and pushed with all her might. • He hit the ball *flush*.

[6]flush *noun, pl* **flushes** [*count*] **:** a set of cards that a player has in a card game (such as poker) that are all of the same suit (such as diamonds) • She won the pot with a *flush*. — see also ROYAL FLUSH — compare [1]FLUSH

flushed *adj* **:** red because of heat or emotion • a *flushed* face • *flushed* cheeks ✧ If you are ***flushed with*** some emotion, such as pride or excitement, you feel that emotion very strongly. • He was *flushed with* pride at his daughter's graduation. ✧ If you are ***flushed with success***, you are very happy and excited because you have succeeded in doing something. • *Flushed with success* after winning the election, she made plans for some dramatic new programs in the coming year.

flus·ter /ˈflʌstɚ/ *verb* **-ters; -tered; -ter·ing :** to make (someone) nervous and confused [+ *obj*] The interruption *flustered* the speaker. • Nothing *flusters* her. [*no obj*] Some speakers *fluster* more easily than others.

flustered *adj* [*more ~; most ~*] **:** upset or nervous • She seemed *flustered* when he asked about her past. • Don't do anything to get him *flustered*. • He was too *flustered* to speak.

F

flute /ˈfluːt/ *noun, pl* **flutes** [*count*]
1 : a musical instrument that is shaped like a thin pipe and that is played by blowing across a hole near one end — see picture at WOODWIND
2 : a tall, thin glass that is used for drinking champagne

flut·ed /ˈfluːtəd/ *adj* **:** decorated with a series of long, rounded lines that are cut into the surface • The mansion has six *fluted* columns across the porch.
– **flut·ing** /ˈfluːtɪŋ/ *noun* [*noncount*] • columns with *fluting*

flut·ist /ˈfluːtɪst/ *noun, pl* **-ists** [*count*] *US* **:** a flute player **:** FLAUTIST

[1]**flut·ter** /ˈflʌtɚ/ *verb* **-ters; -tered; -ter·ing**
1 *of a bird or insect* **a :** to move or flap the wings quickly without flying [+ *obj*] The bird was *fluttering* its wings. [*no obj*] The bird's wings were *fluttering*. **b** [*no obj*] **:** to fly lightly with quick beats of the wings • We watched the butterflies *fluttering* in the garden.
2 : to move with quick, light movements [*no obj*] Leaves *fluttered* to the ground. • The breeze made the curtains *flutter*. [+ *obj*] The breeze *fluttered* the curtains. • She *fluttered* her eyelashes at him.
3 [*no obj*] **:** to move or behave in a nervous and excited way • She nervously *fluttered* around the office. ✧ If your ***heart/stomach flutters***, you become very nervous or excited. • Her *heart fluttered* when she saw the letter in the mail. • Just the mention of his name ***makes my stomach flutter***.

[2]**flutter** *noun, pl* **-ters**
1 [*count*] **:** a quick, light movement • With a *flutter* of wings, the birds settled into the nest. • The *flutter* of the flame cast shadows on the ceiling.
2 [*singular*] **:** a state of excitement or confusion • He was in a *flutter* until he found his keys. • The news of her resignation caused quite a *flutter*. • a *flutter* of excitement
3 [*count*] *Brit, informal* **:** a small bet • have a *flutter* on a horse in the second race
4 [*noncount*] *technical* **:** quick changes in the pitch of recorded sound • The stereo is designed to minimize *flutter*.

flux /ˈflʌks/ *noun* [*noncount*]
1 : a series of changes **:** continuous change • Language is in a state of constant *flux*. = Language is constantly in a state of *flux*. [=language is changing constantly]
2 *technical* **:** a substance used for helping to melt or join metals

[1]**fly** /ˈflaɪ/ *verb* **flies; flew** /ˈfluː/; **flown** /ˈfloʊn/; **fly·ing**
1 [*no obj*] **:** to move through the air with wings • A bird *flew* in through the open window. • insects *flying* over the water
2 [*no obj*] **:** to move through the air especially at a high speed • We watched as clouds *flew* across the sky. • Waves crashed on the rocks and spray *flew* up into the air. • Bullets were *flying* in all directions. • He tripped and ***went flying*** (through the air). — often used figuratively • ***Rumors are flying*** [=there are a lot of rumors] that he'll be announcing his candidacy soon. • ***Accusations are flying.*** [=people are making a lot of accusations]
3 a : to control an airplane, helicopter, etc., as it moves through the air **:** to be the pilot of an aircraft [+ *obj*] *fly* a plane • He *flies* jets. [*no obj*] He learned to *fly* while he was in the Air Force. • She *flies* for a major airline. • She's taking *flying* lessons. **b** [+ *obj*] **:** to journey over (something, such as an ocean) by flying an airplane • Charles Lindbergh was the first person to *fly* the Atlantic solo.
4 a [*no obj*] **:** to travel in an aircraft or spacecraft • They *flew* to California for vacation. • I'm *flying* to Canada to visit my family. • He insists on *flying* first-class. • A doctor *flew* in from the mainland. • She *flew* on a shuttle mission last year. **b** [+ *obj*] **:** to travel by flying on (a particular airline) • He always *flies* the same airline. [=he always flies on the same airline] **c** [+ *obj*] **:** to carry (someone or something) to a place in an aircraft • Supplies were *flown* to the disaster area. • They *fly* cargo around the world. • A doctor was *flown* in from the mainland.
5 a : to show (something, such as a flag) by putting it in a high place [+ *obj*] We *flew* a banner across the entrance. [*no obj*] A flag *flies* in front of the building. = There is a flag *flying* in front of the building. — see also *fly the flag* at [1]FLAG **b** [+ *obj*] **:** to cause (something, such as a kite) to fly in the air • Children were *flying* kites in the park. — see also *go fly a kite* at KITE
6 [*no obj*] **:** to move or go quickly • She *flew* to the window when she heard the car. • The door *flew* open and he rushed into the room. • I *flew* up the stairs to answer the phone. • I must *fly* or I'll be late for my appointment. • That horse really *flies*. • Cars were *flying* past us on the highway.
7 [*no obj*] **:** to move freely • As she ran, her hair *flew* in every direction.
8 [*no obj*] **:** to pass very quickly • Time *flies*. • Our vacation *flew* by before we knew it.
9 [*no obj*] *chiefly US, informal* **:** to be approved or accepted — usually used in negative statements • This plan will never *fly*. • His budget proposals didn't *fly* with voters. [=voters didn't like his proposals]
as the crow flies see [1]CROW
fly at [*phrasal verb*] ***fly at (someone)*** **:** to attack (someone) with sudden violence • He *flew at* me in a rage.
fly high *informal* **1 :** to be very happy and excited • She was *flying high* after her excellent exam results. **2 :** to be very successful • After some difficult years, the company is *flying high* again.
fly in the face of *also US* ***fly in the teeth of*** **:** to fail completely to agree with (something) **:** to oppose or contradict (something) directly • His explanation *flies in the face of* the evidence. [=his explanation is not supported at all by the evidence] • a theory that *flies in the face of* logic [=a theory that is not logical at all] • a policy that *flies in the face of* reason [=a policy that is extremely unreasonable]
fly into [*phrasal verb*] ***fly into (something)*** **:** to be overcome by (sudden extreme emotion) • He *flew into* a rage. [=he suddenly became very angry] • They *flew into* a panic. [=they suddenly panicked]
fly off the handle *informal* **:** to lose control of your emotions **:** to become very angry • He tends to *fly off the handle* when people disagree with him.
fly the coop *informal* **:** to leave suddenly or secretly **:** to escape or go away • In the morning the suspect had *flown the coop*. • All their children have *flown the coop*. [=have moved away from home]
let fly *or* ***let fly with*** *informal* **:** to throw (something) in a forceful way • The quarterback *let fly* (with) a long pass. — often used figuratively • She *let fly* (with) a few angry words. [=she shouted a few angry words]
– compare [2]FLY

[2]**fly** *verb* **flies; flied; fly·ing** [*no obj*] *baseball* **:** to hit a fly ball • The batter *flied* to left field. • He *flied* out to left field. [=he made an out by hitting a fly ball that was caught by the left fielder] — compare [1]FLY

[3]**fly** *noun, pl* **flies** [*count*]
1 : a small insect that has two wings • swat a *fly* • the buzz of a *fly*
2 : a hook that is designed to look like an insect and that is used for catching fish • an artificial *fly* — see also FLY-FISHING
drop like flies *also* ***die like flies*** *informal* ✧ If people or animals are ***dropping/dying like flies***, they are dropping or dying very quickly in large numbers. • The heat was so intense that people were *dropping like flies*. [=many people were fainting from the heat] • Horses and cattle *dropped/died like flies* during the drought. These phrases are often used figuratively. • Candidates were *dropping like flies* during the early part of the campaign.
fly in the ointment **:** someone or something that causes problems • We're almost ready to start work. Getting the permit is the only *fly in the ointment*.
fly on the wall **:** someone who secretly watches or listens to other people • I would like to be a *fly on the wall* during the negotiations. [=I would like to be able to hear what is being said during the negotations]
no flies on *chiefly Brit, informal* ✧ If ***there are no flies on*** you, you are a smart person who is quick to undertand things and not easily fooled.
wouldn't hurt a fly ✧ Someone who *wouldn't hurt a fly* is too gentle to want to hurt anyone. • He looks big and dangerous, but he *wouldn't hurt a fly*.
– compare [4]FLY

[4]**fly** *noun, pl* **flies** [*count*]
1 : an opening in a piece of clothing (such as a pair of trousers, shorts, or a skirt) that is hidden by a fold of cloth and that is closed by a zipper or a row of buttons • He zipped/buttoned his *fly*. — sometimes plural in British English • He zipped his *flies*. — see color picture on page C16
2 *baseball* **:** FLY BALL • He hit a *fly* to the left fielder.
on the fly **1 :** quickly and often without preparation • You'll have to make decisions *on the fly*. **2 :** through the air **:** without hitting the ground • The home run went 450 feet *on the fly*. **3 :** while something else is also being done

on a computer • software that handles formatting *on the fly* — compare ³FLY

fly·away /ˈflajəˌweɪ/ *adj, of hair* : very thin and light : difficult to keep tidy • *flyaway* hair

fly ball *noun, pl* ~ **balls** [*count*] *baseball* : a baseball that is hit high into the air • He hit a long *fly ball* to left field. — compare GROUND BALL

fly·blown /ˈflaɪˌbloʊn/ *adj, chiefly Brit* : in poor and dirty condition • a *flyblown* old building : made dirty by flies : not suitable for eating • *flyblown* food

fly·boy /ˈflaɪˌbɔɪ/ *noun, pl* **-boys** [*count*] *US, informal + old-fashioned* : a man who is a pilot in the Air Force

fly·by /ˈflaɪˌbaɪ/ *noun, pl* **-bys** [*count*]
1 *US* : a usually low flight past a group of people at an air show, during a parade, etc., by an aircraft or group of aircraft — called also *flyover, (Brit) fly-past*
2 : a flight of a spacecraft past a planet, moon, etc.

fly–by–night /ˈflaɪbaɪˌnaɪt/ *adj, always used before a noun, informal* : trying to make money quickly by using dishonest or illegal methods • a *fly-by-night* insurance company

fly·catch·er /ˈflaɪˌkætʃɚ, ˈflaɪˌkɛtʃɚ/ *noun, pl* **-ers** [*count*] : a type of bird that catches and eats flying insects

flyer *variant spelling of* FLIER

fly–fish·ing /ˈflaɪˌfɪʃɪŋ/ *noun* [*noncount*] : the activity of catching fish by using artificial flies • do some *fly-fishing* • He plans to ***go fly-fishing*** this weekend.

¹fly·ing /ˈflajɪŋ/ *adj* : moving or able to move in the air • *flying* insects • *flying* clouds • a story about a *flying* car
with flying colors : with complete or great success • She passed the exam *with flying colors.* • They came through the ordeal *with flying colors.*

²flying *noun* [*noncount*] : the activity of traveling in an aircraft • She doesn't enjoy *flying.*

flying buttress *noun, pl* ~ **-tresses** [*count*] : a structure that supports a wall or building from the outside

flying fish *noun, pl* ~ **fish** *or* ~ **fishes** [*count*] : a type of fish that has long fins which look like wings and that is able to jump out of the water and glide through the air

flying machine *noun, pl* ~ **-chines** [*count*] : a machine that is able to fly; *especially* : an airplane from the time when airplanes had recently been invented

flying officer *noun, pl* ~ **-cers** [*count*] : an officer in the British Air Force

flying saucer *noun, pl* ~ **-cers** [*count*] : a flying object that people say they have seen in the sky, that is usually round like a saucer or disc, and that is believed by some people to be a spaceship from another world : UFO

flying start *noun, pl* ~ **starts** [*singular*] : a good or fast start • The meeting ***got off to a flying start.*** • The restaurant ***made a flying start*** by filling up on opening night.

fly·leaf /ˈflaɪˌliːf/ *noun, pl* **-leaves** /-ˌliːvz/ [*count*] : an empty page at the beginning or end of a book

fly·over /ˈflaɪˌoʊvɚ/ *noun, pl* **-overs** [*count*]
1 *US* : FLYBY 1
2 *Brit* : OVERPASS

fly·pa·per /ˈflaɪˌpeɪpɚ/ *noun* [*noncount*] : a long piece of sticky paper that is used for catching and killing flies

fly–past /ˈflaɪˌpæst, *Brit* ˈflaɪˌpɑːst/ *noun, pl* **-pasts** [*count*] *Brit* : FLYBY 1

fly·speck /ˈflaɪˌspɛk/ *noun, pl* **-specks** [*count*]
1 : a very small piece of waste matter from a fly
2 *informal* : something that is very small • She grew up in a *flyspeck* of a town.

fly·swat·ter /ˈflaɪˌswɑːtɚ/ *noun, pl* **-ers** [*count*] : a device used for killing flies and other insects that consists of a flat piece of plastic or other material attached to a handle

fly·weight /ˈflaɪˌweɪt/ *noun, pl* **-weights** [*count*] : a fighter in a class of boxers who dos not weigh more than 112 pounds (51 kilograms)

fly·wheel /ˈflaɪˌwiːl/ *noun, pl* **-wheels** [*count*] : a heavy wheel that is part of a machine and that controls the speed of machinery

FM /ˈɛfˌɛm/ *noun* [*noncount*] : a system for sending radio signals in which the number of radio waves per second is changed in order to send information in the form of sound ✧ *FM* is an abbreviation of "frequency modulation." — compare AM
– FM *adj* • an *FM* radio/station • This station is *FM* only.

¹foal /ˈfoʊl/ *noun, pl* **foals** [*count*] : a young horse; *especially* : a horse that is less than one year old — compare COLT, FILLY

²foal *verb* **foals; foaled; foal·ing** [*no obj*] : to give birth to a foal • The mare will *foal* in June.

¹foam /ˈfoʊm/ *noun* [*noncount*]
1 : a mass of small bubbles that are formed in or on a liquid • As I poured the beer, *foam* bubbled up in the glass.
2 : a substance that is like a thick liquid made of many small bubbles • The fire extinguisher is filled with *foam.* • a can of shaving *foam*
3 : a soft material that is used to make many products : FOAM RUBBER — often used before another noun • a *foam* mattress/pillow
– foam·i·ness /ˈfoʊminəs/ *noun* [*noncount*] **– foamy** /ˈfoʊmi/ *adj* **foam·i·er; -est** • a *foamy* glass of beer

²foam *verb* **foams; foamed; foam·ing** [*no obj*] : to produce foam • The soda *foamed* in the glass. • The mixture will bubble and *foam* when you add the yeast.
foam at the mouth **1** : to produce foam from the mouth because of illness or excitement • The dog was *foaming at the mouth.* **2** *informal* : to be very angry about something • He was *foaming at the mouth* with rage.

foam rubber *noun* [*noncount*] : a soft and light rubber material that has many small holes throughout it and is used to make various products • The mattress/pad is (made of) *foam rubber.* — often used before another noun • a *foam-rubber* mattress/pad

¹fob /ˈfɑːb/ *noun, pl* **fobs** [*count*]
1 : a short chain attached especially to a pocket watch
2 : a small object that is a decoration on a watch chain or a key ring

²fob *verb* **fobs; fobbed; fob·bing**
fob off [*phrasal verb*] ***fob (someone or something) off*** *or* ***fob off (someone or something)*** *informal* **1** : to cause (someone) to accept something that is false, badly made, etc., instead of what is wanted — + *with* • He thought he could *fob* me *off with* some weak excuse about being too busy to talk. **2** : to present or offer (something fake or false) *as* genuine or true • They're trying to *fob off* science fiction *as* truth. [=trying to make people believe that something that is science fiction is true] **3** *US* : to give (someone or something not wanted) to someone else : to palm off (someone or something) — often + *on* • The child's father was always *fobbing* her *off on* relatives and babysitters.

fo·cal /ˈfoʊkəl/ *adj, always used before a noun* : having central or great importance • a *focal* figure in the movement

focal length *noun, pl* ~ **lengths** [*count*] *technical* : the distance from the surface of a lens to the point of focus (sense 3)

focal point *noun, pl* ~ **points** [*count*]
1 : a center of activity, interest, or attention • This port was the *focal point* of trade two centuries ago. • The new school curriculum was the *focal point* [=*focus*] of the debate.
2 *technical* : ¹FOCUS 3

¹fo·cus /ˈfoʊkəs/ *noun, pl* **fo·ci** /ˈfoʊˌsaɪ/ *also* **fo·cus·es**
1 [*count*] : a subject that is being discussed or studied : the subject on which people's attention is focused — usually singular • The *focus* of our discussion/debate/attention will be drug abuse. • The scandal became the primary *focus* of the day's news coverage. • The study's main *focus* is adults with sleep disorders.
2 : a main purpose or interest [*noncount*] He's successful, but he feels that his life lacks *focus.* [*singular*] His life lacks a *focus.*
3 [*count*] *technical* : a point at which rays of light, heat, or sound meet or from which they move apart or appear to move apart; *especially* : the point at which an image is formed by a mirror, a lens, etc.
4 [*noncount*] **a** : a state in which something (such as a camera, a telescope, or a person's eyes) produces a clear picture or image • bringing the binoculars ***into focus*** [=focusing the binoculars; adjusting the binoculars so that the image seen through them is clear and sharp] • It took him a few seconds after he woke up to bring his eyes *into focus.* [=to focus his eyes] • The binoculars were not ***in focus.*** = The binoculars were ***out of focus.*** [=the binoculars were not focused] **b** : a state in which the small details of a picture or image can be clearly seen • It was a nice picture—the family was ***in focus*** and everyone was smiling. • Unfortunately, several of the pictures were ***out of focus.*** — see also SOFT FOCUS **c** : a state or condition in which something can be clearly understood • She tried to bring the important issues ***into focus.*** [=she tried to say clearly what the important issues were]

[2]focus *verb* **-cuses** *also* **-cus·ses; -cused** *also* **-cussed; -cus·ing** *also* **-cus·sing**
1 [+ *obj*] **:** to cause (something, such as attention) to be directed at something specific — + *on* ▪ The crime has *focused* public attention *on* the problem of parole. ▪ We need to *focus* our efforts *on* getting the work done.
2 [*no obj*] **:** to direct your attention or effort at something specific ▪ She has an amazing ability to *focus* for hours at a time. — often + *on* ▪ We need to *focus on* getting the work done. ▪ The day's news coverage *focused* primarily/mainly *on* the scandal.
3 : to adjust (something, such as a lens or a camera) to make an image clear [+ *obj*] *focus* a telescope ▪ I wasn't able to *focus* the camera. ▪ He *focused* his binoculars on a distant ship. [=he looked through his binoculars at a distant ship] [*no obj*] I wasn't able to get the camera to *focus*. ◊ If you ***focus your eyes*** on something or if your ***eyes focus*** on something, you look at that thing so that you can see it clearly. ▪ Everyone *focused their eyes* on her [=everyone looked at her] when she entered the room. ▪ His *eyes* were *focused* on the road. = He kept his *eyes focused* on the road.
4 *technical* **:** to cause (light) to come together at a point [+ *obj*] *focus* rays of light [*no obj*] laser beams that *focus* at a single point

focused *also* **focussed** *adj* [*more* ~; *most* ~]
1 : giving attention and effort to a specific task or goal ▪ They are making a *focused* effort to win support for the proposal.
2 : having very clear and definite goals and ambitions ▪ She's a very *focused* and determined young woman.

focus group *noun, pl* ~ **groups** [*count*] **:** a small group of people whose opinions about something (such as a politician or a new product) are studied to learn the opinions that can be expected from a larger group

fod·der /ˈfɑːdɚ/ *noun* [*noncount*]
1 : food given to horses, cows, etc. ▪ grain used for *fodder*
2 : material that is used for a particular purpose ▪ His antics always make good *fodder* for the gossip columnists. ▪ She often used her friends' problems as *fodder* for her novels. — see also CANNON FODDER

foe /ˈfoʊ/ *noun, pl* **foes** [*count*] **:** an enemy ▪ political *foes* ▪ Many considered him a *foe* of democracy. ▪ Her ability was acknowledged by friend and *foe* alike.

foetal, foetus *chiefly Brit spellings of* FETAL, FETUS

[1]fog /ˈfɑːg/ *noun*
1 : many small drops of water floating in the air above the ground, the sea, etc. [*noncount*] Heavy *fog* made it difficult to see the road. ▪ a patch/blanket of *fog* ▪ ocean *fog* [*count*] a climate marked by heavy *fogs* ▪ The *fog* reduced visibility to a quarter of a mile.
2 [*singular*] **:** a state of mental confusion ▪ This problem has me in a *fog*. ▪ an alcohol-induced *fog*

[2]fog *verb* **fogs; fogged; fog·ging**
1 a [+ *obj*] **:** to cover or fill (something) with small drops of water **:** to make (something) foggy ▪ The steam from the pot was *fogging* the window near the stove. ▪ The cold air *fogged* (up) his glasses. ▪ The bathroom was all *fogged up* after my shower. **b** [*no obj*] **:** to become foggy ▪ His glasses were *fogging*. — often + *up* ▪ His glasses were *fogging up*. ▪ The weather is *fogging up*.
2 [+ *obj*] **:** to make (someone or something) confused ▪ politicians who try to *fog* the issue instead of taking a stand ▪ drugs that *fog* [=*cloud*] your mind/judgment

fog·bound /ˈfɑːg͵baʊnd/ *adj*
1 : unable to move or travel because of fog ▪ a *fogbound* ship ▪ *fogbound* travelers
2 : covered by fog ▪ a *fogbound* coast

fogey *chiefly Brit spelling of* FOGY

fog·gy /ˈfɑːgi/ *adj* **fog·gi·er; -est**
1 a : having or filled with fog ▪ a gray, *foggy* morning ▪ *foggy* weather ▪ a *foggy* valley **b :** covered with small drops of water ▪ a *foggy* mirror ▪ *foggy* glasses
2 : not clear **:** vague or confused ▪ I don't remember what her name was—my memory is a little *foggy*. ▪ I haven't the *foggiest* [=*faintest*] idea what she's talking about. [=I don't understand what she is talking about at all] ▪ "Where did I put my keys?" "***I haven't the foggiest***." [=*I have no idea*; I don't know]
– fog·gi·ly /ˈfɑːgəli/ *adv* **– fog·gi·ness** /ˈfɑːginəs/ *noun* [*noncount*]

Foggy Bottom *noun* [*singular*] *informal* **:** the U.S. Department of State

fog·horn /ˈfɑːg͵hoɚn/ *noun, pl* **-horns** [*count*] **:** a horn on a boat, ship, etc., that makes a loud, deep sound and is used in foggy weather to warn nearby ships — often used figuratively to describe someone with a very loud voice ▪ He has a *foghorn* voice. [=a voice like a foghorn]

fog lamp *noun, pl* ~ **lamps** [*count*] **:** a very bright light on the front of a vehicle that is used to help the driver see better in fog — called also *fog light*

fo·gy (*chiefly US*) *or chiefly Brit* **fo·gey** /ˈfoʊgi/ *noun, pl* **fogies** [*count*] **:** a person with old-fashioned ideas — usually used with *old* ▪ Maybe I'm just an *old fogy*, but I don't think this kind of music is appropriate for children.
– fo·gy·ish (*chiefly US*) *or chiefly Brit* **fo·gey·ish** /ˈfoʊgijɪʃ/ *adj* ▪ a *fogyish* old man

foi·ble /ˈfoɪbəl/ *noun, pl* **foi·bles** [*count*] **:** a minor fault in someone's character or behavior — usually plural ▪ We all have our little *foibles*. ▪ He was amused by the *foibles* of his eccentric neighbor.

foie gras /ˈfwɑːˈgrɑː/ *noun* [*noncount*] **:** a food made from the liver of a goose **:** PÂTÉ DE FOIE GRAS

[1]foil /ˈfojəl/ *verb* **foils; foiled; foil·ing** [+ *obj*]
1 : to prevent (someone) from doing something or achieving a goal **:** DEFEAT ▪ Police managed to *foil* the burglars. — often used as *(be) foiled* ▪ He *was foiled* by his opponents once again. ▪ She *was foiled* by her own indecision.
2 : to prevent (something) from happening or being successful ▪ Police *foiled* an attempted robbery. ▪ Her accident *foiled* her dreams of becoming a dancer.

[2]foil *noun, pl* **foils**
1 [*noncount*] **:** a very thin and light sheet of metal ▪ Cover the dish with aluminum *foil*. ▪ kitchen *foil* [=foil used to wrap or cover food] ▪ candy wrapped in *foil* — see also SILVER FOIL, TINFOIL
2 [*count*] **:** someone or something that is different from another person or thing in a useful or appealing way — usually + *for* or *to* ▪ He acted as a *foil for* the comedian. [=he acted very serious to make the comedian seem funnier] ▪ That dark blue dress is good *foil for* her blonde hair. ▪ His reserved manner was a perfect *foil for/to* her bubbly personality.
3 [*count*] **:** a sword that has a light, thin blade and that is used in the sport of fencing

foist /ˈfoɪst/ *verb* **foists; foist·ed; foist·ing** [+ *obj*] **:** to force someone to accept (something that is not good or not wanted) — usually + *on* or *upon* ▪ scams that *foist* high funeral expenses *on* grieving customers ▪ He *foisted* his prejudices *upon* his young students. ▪ phony paintings *foisted* (off) *on* naïve buyers

[1]fold /ˈfoʊld/ *verb* **folds; fold·ed; fold·ing**
1 : to bend one part of (something) over or against another part [+ *obj*] He *folded* the paper in half and then unfolded it again. ▪ *Fold* the flaps open/shut. ▪ He *folded* the blanket and laid it at the foot of the bed. ▪ She *folded* over the edge of the fabric to make a hem. ▪ a piece of paper *folded* into the shape of a bird [*no obj*] The paper *folded* easily. ▪ The map *folds* neatly/flat so you can fit it in a pocket.
2 : to reduce the length or size of something (such as a piece of furniture) by moving parts of it so that they lie close together [+ *obj*] We *folded* (up) the lawn chair and put it in the trunk. [*no obj*] The lawn chair *folded* (up) easily. ▪ The bed *folds* (away) into a space in the wall.
3 [+ *obj*] **a :** to put your arm or hand over your other arm or hand in a way that keeps them together ▪ She *folded* [=*crossed*] her arms across her chest. ▪ She *folded* her hands on her lap. ▪ He *folded* his arms around her. ▪ hands *folded* in prayer **b :** to bend (a leg, a knee, an elbow, etc.) ▪ He sat with his legs *folded* under him.
4 [+ *obj*] *literary* **:** to put your arms around (someone) **:** EMBRACE ▪ She *folded* him in her arms.
5 [+ *obj*] **:** to add (a food ingredient) to a mixture by gently and repeatedly lifting one part over another ▪ *Fold* the egg whites into the chocolate mixture.
6 [*no obj*] **:** to fail completely **:** COLLAPSE ▪ The business *folded*.
7 [*no obj*] **:** to accept defeat in a card game (such as poker) by removing your cards from the game ▪ Realizing that she probably wasn't bluffing, he decided to *fold*.

[2]fold *noun, pl* **folds** [*count*]
1 : a line or mark made by bending one part of something over another part and pressing at the bent edge **:** a line or mark made by folding something **:** CREASE ▪ the *fold* in a newspaper
2 : a part of something (such as cloth or skin) that lies or

hangs over another part ▪ hidden in the *folds* of the curtain ▪ the *folds* of her dress ▪ He had *folds* of flab around his middle.

3 : the act of folding something ▪ She made a paper airplane by using a simple series of *folds*.

4 *technical* : a bend produced in a rock layer by pressure

— compare ³FOLD

³fold *noun, pl* **folds**

1 [*count*] : an enclosed area for sheep

2 ***the fold*** : a group of people who have a shared faith or interest ▪ His former colleagues would be glad to welcome him back into *the fold*.

— compare ²FOLD

-fold /ˌfoʊld/ *suffix*

1 : multiplied by (a specified number) : times ▪ a twelve*fold* increase ▪ It will repay you ten*fold*.

2 : having (so many) parts ▪ a three*fold* problem

fold·away /ˈfoʊldəˌweɪ/ *adj, always used before a noun* : designed to be folded for storage : FOLDING ▪ a *foldaway* bed/table

fold·er /ˈfoʊldɚ/ *noun, pl* **-ers** [*count*]

1 : a folded cover or large envelope for holding documents — see picture at OFFICE

2 : a collection of files or documents that are stored together on a computer

fol·de·rol /ˈfɑːldəˌrɑːl/ *noun* [*noncount*] *chiefly US, informal + old-fashioned* : foolish language, behavior, or ideas : NONSENSE ▪ I wish we could just discuss these questions without having to go through all the *folderol* of a formal meeting.

fold·ing /ˈfoʊldɪŋ/ *adj, always used before a noun* : able to be folded into a smaller shape : designed to be folded ▪ *folding* chairs ▪ a *folding* door

folding money *noun* [*noncount*] *informal* : PAPER MONEY ▪ He always carries a lot of *folding money*.

fold·out /ˈfoʊldˌaʊt/ *noun, pl* **-outs** [*count*] : a large folded page in a book or magazine ▪ The book includes special maps in the form of *foldouts*. ▪ The book includes *foldout* maps.

fo·liage /ˈfoʊlijɪʤ/ *noun* [*noncount*] : the leaves of a plant or of many plants ▪ a tree with pretty *foliage* ▪ the thick green *foliage* of the jungle ▪ colorful autumn *foliage*

¹folk /ˈfoʊk/ *noun*

1 ***folks*** [*plural*] **a** *chiefly US, informal* : people in general ▪ *Folks* say that house is haunted. ▪ Some *folks* think the law should be changed. **b** — used to talk to a group of people in a friendly and informal way ▪ Do you *folks* need any help? ▪ That's all for today, *folks*—see you tomorrow!

2 *or chiefly US* ***folks*** [*plural*] *informal* : a certain kind of people ▪ a home for old *folks* ▪ He doesn't much care for city *folk*. [=people who live in a city] ▪ country *folk* ▪ the distinctive speech of *folks* from the South

3 ***folks*** [*plural*] *chiefly US, informal* : family members ▪ I'll be spending the holidays with my *folks*.; *especially* : PARENTS ▪ His *folks* gave him everything a kid could want.

4 [*noncount*] : FOLK MUSIC ▪ My favorite kind of music is *folk*.

²folk *adj, always used before a noun* : of or relating to the common people of a country or region ▪ *folk* customs ▪ *folk* art ▪ a *folk* dance ▪ a *folk* remedy

folk hero *noun, pl* **~ -roes** [*count*] : a person who is greatly admired by many people of a particular kind or in a particular place ▪ He has become a *folk hero* in his home state because of the work he has done to help poor children.

folk·lore /ˈfoʊkˌloɚ/ *noun* [*noncount*]

1 : traditional customs, beliefs, stories, and sayings ▪ The coyote appears in a great deal of Native American *folklore*. ▪ the rich *folklore* of Louisiana

2 : ideas or stories that are not true but that many people have heard or read ▪ He can't tell the difference between fact and *folklore*.

— **folk·lor·ist** /ˈfoʊkˌlorɪst/ *noun, pl* **-ists** [*count*] ▪ a *folklorist* who has collected many folktales

folk music *noun* [*noncount*] : the traditional music of the people in a country or region ▪ Irish *folk music*; *also* : a type of popular music that is based on traditional music and that does not use electric instruments

folk·sing·er /ˈfoʊkˌsɪŋɚ/ *noun, pl* **-ers** [*count*] : a person who sings folk songs

folk song *noun, pl* **~ songs** [*count*] : a song created by the people of a country or region : a song sung in folk music

folksy /ˈfoʊksi/ *adj* **folks·i·er; -est** *informal* : friendly or informal in manner or style ▪ a *folksy* politician ▪ an entertainer with a *folksy* manner ▪ *folksy* charm

— **folks·i·ness** /ˈfoʊksinəs/ *noun* [*noncount*]

folk·tale /ˈfoʊkˌteɪl/ *noun, pl* **-tales** [*count*] : a traditional story ▪ West African *folktales* that continue to be passed from generation to generation through storytelling

fol·li·cle /ˈfɑːlɪkəl/ *noun, pl* **-li·cles** [*count*] : a tiny hole in the skin from which a hair grows

fol·low /ˈfɑːloʊ/ *verb* **-lows; -lowed; -low·ing**

1 a : to go or come after or behind (someone or something) [+ *obj*] She *followed* us into the kitchen. ▪ The dog *followed* the children home. ▪ The exit is right this way. Just *follow* me. [*no obj*] The children went home and the dog *followed* behind. ▪ If one sheep goes through the gate, the rest will *follow*. **b** [+ *obj*] : to go after or behind (someone) secretly and watch to find out what happens ▪ He hired a private detective to *follow* his wife everywhere. [=to secretly find out where she went and what she did] ▪ *follow* a suspect ▪ I think that someone is *following* us. = I think we're being *followed*.

2 a : to come after (something) in time or place or as part of a series [+ *obj*] Spring *follows* winter. = Winter *is followed* by spring. ▪ The number 15 *follows* 14. ▪ Her accident was *followed* by a long period of recovery. [*no obj*] First came the student speeches, and the presentation of awards *followed*. ▪ (*formal*) The war ended. ***There followed*** [=*then came*; then there was] a long period of rebuilding. **b** [+ *obj*] : to have or do something after (something else) — + *with* ▪ I *followed* my dinner *with* a liqueur. [=I had a liqueur after dinner] ▪ The actor *followed* his success as Othello *with* a triumph as Macbeth.

3 a : to happen after and as a result of (something) [+ *obj*] Rioting *followed* the unjust verdict. [*no obj*] If you work hard, success will/must surely *follow*. **b** [*no obj*] : to be true or seem to be true because of something ▪ From the evidence given, several conclusions *follow*. = Several conclusions *follow* from the evidence given. [=we can make several conclusions based on the evidence given] — often + *that* ▪ From the evidence given, it *follows that* the accused is guilty. ▪ Just because he's done some bad things, does/must it *follow that* he's a bad person? [=does it mean that he is a bad person?]

4 [+ *obj*] **a** : to be guided by (something) ▪ You should *follow* [=*obey*] your conscience. ▪ *follow* your instincts ▪ *follow* my advice ▪ She must learn to *follow* instructions. ▪ We must *follow* the evidence wherever it leads. ▪ You should ***follow her example***. = You should *follow* the example she set. [=you should do what she did] **b** : to do the same thing as (someone) ▪ She *followed* her father (by going) into medicine. = She *followed* her father by becoming a doctor.

5 [+ *obj*] : to move forward on (a road, a path, etc.) ▪ *Follow* that path, and you will come to a log cabin. ▪ You should *follow* the main highway until you see signs for the stadium. — often used figuratively ▪ His friends all went to college, but he chose to *follow* a different path. [=to do something different] ▪ Do recessions *follow* a predictable cycle/pattern?

6 [+ *obj*] *of a road, path, etc.* : to be on or next to (something) for a distance ▪ The path *follows* the river pretty closely. ▪ The road *follows* the curve of the hill.

7 [+ *obj*] **a** : to keep your eyes or attention on (something) ▪ *Follow* the bouncing ball. **b** : to give close attention to what happens in (something) ▪ He *followed* her career with interest. ▪ *follow* football ▪ The book *follows* his political career from its humble beginnings to his election as president. **c** *Brit* : to be a fan of (a team) : SUPPORT ▪ He *follows* Manchester United.

8 : to understand the sense or logic of (something or someone) [+ *obj*] I found it hard to *follow* the twists and turns of the movie's complicated plot. ▪ I'm sorry—I don't *follow* your argument/reasoning. = I'm sorry—I don't *follow* you. [=I don't understand you] [*no obj*] I'm sorry—I don't *follow*. [=I don't understand]

a hard/tough act to follow : someone or something that has been so successful that it is very difficult for the person or thing coming next to be as good ▪ Yesterday's thrilling victory will be *a tough act to follow*.

as follows — used to introduce a list, a statement, instructions, etc. ▪ The names of the finalists are *as follows*: Mary, James, and George. ▪ Proceed *as follows*: go straight ahead to Martin Street and then turn left.

follow around *or Brit* ***follow about*** [*phrasal verb*] ***follow (someone) around/about*** : to go wherever (someone) goes ▪ The little boy *followed* his mother *around* all day.

follow in someone's footsteps see FOOTSTEP

follow someone's lead see ²LEAD

follow suit **1** *in card games* : to play a card of the same suit (such as hearts or spades) as the card that was played just before ▪ Jane played a spade, and Roger *followed suit.* **2** : to do the same thing that someone else has just done ▪ His brother went to medical school, and he *followed suit.* ▪ After one airline lowers their fares, the other airlines usually *follow suit.*

follow the path/line of least resistance see RESISTANCE

follow through [*phrasal verb*] **1** ***follow through or follow (something) through*** : to complete an activity or process that has been started ▪ He always starts the school year off studying and working hard, but he doesn't *follow through.* [=he doesn't continue to study and work hard] ▪ He doesn't *follow* his good intentions *through.* [=although he makes plans to do things, he doesn't actually do them] — often + *on* or *with* ▪ He doesn't *follow through on* his good intentions. ▪ We feared they would *follow through on/with* their threat. [=we feared that they would do what they threatened to do] **2** *sports* : to keep your arms, legs, etc., moving after you hit or kick a ball : to complete a stroke or swing ▪ You should *follow through* on your backhand. ▪ Don't forget to *follow through* when you putt. — see also FOLLOW-THROUGH

follow up [*phrasal verb*] **1** ***follow up (something) or follow (something) up or follow up*** : to follow (something) with something similar, related, or additional — + *with* or *by* ▪ He *followed up* his early findings *with* another study. ▪ After you submit your job application, you should *follow* it *up by* making a phone call. ▪ Her first book was a big success, and she *followed up with* another best seller. **2** ***follow up (something) or follow (something) up or follow up or chiefly US follow up on (something)*** **a** : to try to get more information about (something) ▪ The police *followed up (on)* the leads. ▪ The references in the book were too vague to *follow up.* **b** : to do something in response to (something) : to take appropriate action about (something) ▪ Police *followed up* the complaints with several arrests. ▪ He complained several times, but the police never *followed up.* ▪ He says that the police failed to *follow up on* his complaints. — see also FOLLOW-UP

follow your nose *informal* **1** : to go in a straight or obvious course ▪ Just *follow your nose* until you get there; you can't miss it. **2** : to proceed without a definite plan : to do what seems right or best without careful planning ▪ You don't need my advice—just *follow your nose.* **3** : to go toward the place where a smell is coming from ▪ I *followed my nose* to the kitchen, where dinner was cooking.

fol·low·er /ˈfɑːləwɚ/ *noun, pl* **-ers** [*count*]

1 a : someone who supports and is guided by another person or by a group, religion, etc. ▪ the candidate's loyal/faithful *followers* ▪ The party drew most of its *followers* from among young people. ▪ *followers* of Christianity/Islam **b** : a person who likes and admires (someone or something) very much : FAN ▪ The band has a large group of *followers.*

2 : someone who does what other people say to do ▪ He had a reputation of being a *follower*, not a leader.

¹fol·low·ing /ˈfɑːləwɪŋ/ *adj*

1 : coming next ▪ She found a good job, and moved into a new house the *following* year. ▪ We met again the *following* day. — opposite PRECEDING, PREVIOUS

2 : listed or shown next ▪ Trains will leave at the *following* times: 2 p.m., 4 p.m., and 8 p.m. ▪ If you have questions or comments, please write to us at the *following* address: P.O. Box 234, . . .

²following *noun, pl* **-ings** [*count*] : a group of followers or fans ▪ The band has a large and devoted *following* in Japan. ▪ The movement quickly gained/attracted/built a *following* among young people.

³following *prep* : immediately after (something) ▪ *Following* the lecture, refreshments were served. ▪ We were tired for a few days *following* our trip.

⁴following *pronoun*

the following : the following one or ones — used to introduce a list, a quotation, etc. ▪ The finalists are *the following*: Mary, James, and George. = *The following* are the finalists: Mary, James, and George. ▪ Our address is *the following* [=*as follows*]: P.O. Box 234, . . . ▪ *The following* are the times of departing trains: 2 p.m., 4 p.m., and 8 p.m.

fol·low–on /ˈfɑːloʊˌɑːn/ *noun, pl* **-ons** [*count*] : something that happens or is done to continue or add to something previous — usually singular ▪ The new project is a natural *follow-on* to last year's success.

– follow–on *adj, always used before a noun* ▪ a *follow-on* product

follow–the–leader (*US*) *or Brit* **follow–my–leader** *noun* [*noncount*] : a children's game in which everyone follows and does what the child who is chosen to be the leader does

fol·low–through /ˈfɑːloʊˌθruː/ *noun, pl* **-throughs**

1 [*count*] *sports* : the part of a stroke, swing, or kick that happens after a ball is hit ▪ He has a good backswing, but he's a little weak on the *follow-through.*

2 [*singular*] : the act of completing an action or process ▪ He makes a lot of promises, but there's no *follow-through.* [=he does not do what he promises to do] — see also *follow through* at FOLLOW

fol·low–up /ˈfɑːloʊˌʌp/ *noun, pl* **-ups** [*count*] : something that continues or completes a process or activity ▪ A week after the story broke, the newspaper printed a *follow-up.* ▪ As a *follow-up* to last week's show, tonight we'll show the other side of the story. — see also *follow up* at FOLLOW

– follow–up *adj, always used before a noun* ▪ After you submit your job application, you should make a *follow-up* phone call. ▪ He had a *follow-up* appointment a week after his surgery.

fol·ly /ˈfɑːli/ *noun, pl* **-lies**

1 [*noncount*] **a** : the lack of good sense or judgment : FOOLISHNESS ▪ the *folly* of driving fast on steep, winding roads ▪ his *folly* in thinking that he would not be noticed ▪ The *folly* of such an action should be apparent to everyone. **b** : a foolish act or idea : foolish behavior [*noncount*] Their pranks were just youthful *folly.* [=the kinds of foolish things that young people often do] [*count*] engaging in youthful *follies* ▪ the *follies* of the modern world

2 [*count*] : a very unusual or fancy building that was built in a garden for decoration or amusement in the past

3 ***follies*** [*plural*] *chiefly US* : a large public show or entertainment with many performers ▪ the famous Ziegfeld *Follies* of the 1920s ▪ ice *follies* [=a show with ice-skaters skating to music]

fo·ment /ˈfoʊˌmɛnt/ *verb* **-ments**; **-ment·ed**; **-ment·ing** [+ *obj*] *formal* : to cause or try to cause the growth or development of (something bad or harmful) : INCITE ▪ *foment* rebellion/war/revolution ▪ He was accused of *fomenting* violence.

– fo·ment·er *noun, pl* **-ers** [*count*]

fond /ˈfɑːnd/ *adj* **fond·er**; **-est**

1 : feeling or showing love or friendship : AFFECTIONATE ▪ a *fond* admirer ▪ She still has *fond* feelings for him. ▪ She has *fond* [=*cherished, warm*] memories of their time together. ▪ a *fond* smile ▪ Absence makes the heart grow *fonder.* ▪ He wished them a ***fond farewell.***

2 : strongly felt ▪ their *fondest* wishes ▪ the *fond* hope that the situation would change

fond of : having a liking for or love of (someone or something) ▪ She is still *fond of* him. [=she still likes/loves him] ▪ She grew quite *fond of* him. ▪ I'm *fond of* skiing. [=I like to ski; I enjoy skiing] ▪ She's *fond of* asking silly questions. [=she asks a lot of silly questions]

– fond·ness /ˈfɑːndnəs/ *noun* [*noncount*] his parents' *fondness* [=*affection*] for each other [*singular*] a *fondness* [=*liking*] for fine wine

fon·dle /ˈfɑːndl/ *verb* **fon·dles**; **fon·dled**; **fon·dling** [+ *obj*]

1 : to touch or handle (something) in a gentle way ▪ *fondle* a coin ▪ She *fondled* [=*caressed*] the dog's ear.

2 : to touch (someone) in a sexual way ▪ She claims that her boss tried to *fondle* her at the office Christmas party.

fond·ly /ˈfɑːndli/ *adv*

1 : in a loving way ▪ She speaks *fondly* [=*affectionately*] of you. ▪ She remembers their time together *fondly.*

2 : in a hopeful but not reasonable way ▪ He *fondly* [=*foolishly*] imagines that his plan will be a success.

fon·due /fɑnˈduː, *Brit* ˈfɒnˌdjuː/ *noun, pl* **-dues** : a dish that people prepare for themselves at the table by putting small pieces of food (such as bread, meat, or fruit) in a hot liquid (such as melted and flavored cheese or melted chocolate) [*noncount*] dipped his bread into the (cheese) *fondue* [*count*] dip fruit in melted chocolate to have a chocolate *fondue*

¹font /ˈfɑːnt/ *noun, pl* **fonts** [*count*]

1 *religion* : a container that holds the water which is used for baptizing a child

2 *US* : a source from which something comes : FOUNT ▪ a *font* of knowledge/wisdom

– compare ²FONT

font

serif type		**sans serif type**
English	roman	English
English	italic	*English*
English	bold	**English**

²font *noun, pl* **fonts** [*count*] *technical* : a set of letters, numbers, and punctuation marks that are all one size and style ▪ The book's small *font* was difficult to read. ▪ a boldface *font* — called also (*Brit*) *fount* — compare ¹FONT

food /ˈfuːd/ *noun, pl* **foods**
1 a [*noncount*] : the things that people and animals eat ▪ a farmer who grows his own *food* ▪ drought victims who don't have enough *food* to eat ▪ She gave *food* and drink to the hungry travelers. ▪ good/great/delicious *food* **b** : a particular kind of food [*noncount*] Italian *food* ▪ cat *food* ▪ frozen *food* ▪ What is your favorite *food*? [*count*] an important *food* ▪ fruits, vegetables, and other healthy *foods* ▪ frozen *foods* — see also FAST FOOD, HEALTH FOOD, JUNK FOOD, WHOLE FOOD
2 [*noncount*] : substances taken in by plants and used for growth ▪ plant *food*
food for thought : something that should be thought about or considered carefully ▪ The unexpected test results have given us *food for thought*.

food bank *noun, pl* ~ **banks** [*count*] *US* : a place like a store that has free food for poor people

food chain *noun, pl* ~ **chains** [*count*] : a series of types of living things in which each one uses the next lower member of the series as a source of food — usually used with *the* ▪ Sharks eat fish that are lower in *the food chain*. ▪ animals that are at the top/bottom of *the food chain* — often used figuratively ▪ directors and producers at the top of *the* Hollywood *food chain* [=very powerful and successful directors and producers] ▪ *the* corporate *food chain*

food court *noun, pl* ~ **courts** [*count*] : an area within a building (such as a shopping mall) where there are many small restaurants that share a large area of tables for their customers

food·ie /ˈfuːdi/ *noun, pl* **-ies** [*count*] *informal* : a person who enjoys and cares about food very much ▪ The restaurant is very popular among *foodies*.

food poisoning *noun* [*noncount*] : sickness caused by bacteria or chemicals in food

food processor *noun, pl* ~ **-sors** [*count*] : an electric kitchen device that is used for cutting and mixing food — see picture at KITCHEN

food stamp *noun, pl* ~ **stamps** [*count*] *US* : a small document that is given by the government to poor people and that can be used to buy food

food·stuff /ˈfuːdˌstʌf/ *noun, pl* **-stuffs** [*count*] *technical* : a substance that is used as food ▪ grain and other *foodstuffs* [=*foods*]

¹fool /ˈfuːl/ *noun, pl* **fools** [*count*]
1 : a person who lacks good sense or judgment : a stupid or silly person ▪ those *fools* who ride motorcycles without wearing helmets ▪ Only a *fool* would ask such a silly question. ▪ You'd be a *fool* to believe what he tells you. ▪ You're making yourself look like a *fool*. ▪ ***A fool and his money are soon parted***. [=a foolish person spends money too quickly on unimportant things] ▪ ***Any fool*** can see [=anyone can see] that he's lying. ▪ I never thought you'd be ***fool enough*** to believe him. = I never thought you'd be enough of a *fool* to believe him. ▪ (*informal*) Only that ***fool of a*** brother [=that foolish brother] of yours would ask such a silly question! ▪ (*informal*) Some (damn/damned) *fool of a* driver kept trying to pass me! ▪ ***Fools rush in*** (***where angels fear to tread***). [=it is foolish to take action if you do not know much about what you are doing] ▪ (*Brit, informal*) (***The***) ***more fool you*** if you believe him. = (*The*) *more fool you* for believing him. [=you would be a fool to believe him] ▪ (*Brit, informal*) *More fool him* for trusting her. ▪ ***There's no fool like an old fool***. [=a foolish old person is especially foolish because an old person should have learned from experience not to make the kind of mistakes a young person makes] ✧ A smart or clever person can be described as ***no fool*** or as ***nobody's fool***. ▪ He may not look very smart, but he's *no fool*. ▪ Don't try to trick her—she's *nobody's fool*.
2 *US, informal* : a person who enjoys something very much ▪ He's a dancing *fool*. [=he loves to dance] ▪ He's ***a fool for*** candy. [=he loves to eat candy]
3 *chiefly Brit* : a dessert made with cooked fruit and cream or a thick sauce ▪ a strawberry *fool*
4 : JESTER
act/play the fool : to behave in a silly or foolish way ▪ If you keep *playing the fool* by asking silly questions, people won't take you seriously.
make a fool of yourself : to behave in a very foolish or silly way ▪ He got drunk at the party and *made a fool of himself*. ▪ He's *making a fool of himself* over that woman.
make a fool (out) of : to cause (someone) to look stupid or foolish ▪ She *made a fool of me* by insulting me in front of my friends.
— see also APRIL FOOLS' DAY

²fool *verb* **fools; fooled; fool·ing**
1 [*no obj*] : to speak or act in a way that is not serious : JOKE, KID ▪ I was only *fooling*. ▪ When she first told us that she was getting married, we thought she was *fooling*.
2 [+ *obj*] : to make (someone) believe something that is not true : to trick (someone) ▪ His disguise didn't *fool* anybody. ▪ "He's an expert in his field." "Well, you sure ***could have fooled me***!" [=I doubt that he is really an expert in his field] ▪ He really ***had me fooled***. ▪ Stop ***fooling yourself***—she doesn't really love you. — often + *into* ▪ He *fooled* me *into* thinking I could trust him. ▪ We *were fooled into* thinking there was no danger. — sometimes used figuratively ▪ *fool* the eye *into* seeing colors that aren't there
fool around *also Brit* ***fool about*** [*phrasal verb*] *informal* **1** : to do things that are not useful or serious : to waste time ▪ We *fooled around* [=*messed around*] outdoors for a while, but then went inside to get some work done. ▪ He decided it was time to stop *fooling around* and settle down and get married. ▪ Wow, he's already done everything he promised. He ***doesn't fool around***, does he? [=he gets things done quickly] **2** : to have sex with someone who is not your husband, wife, or regular partner ▪ His wife discovered that he was *fooling around* (on her). [=that he was having sex with another woman] — often + *with* ▪ His wife discovered that he was *fooling around with* his secretary. **3** ***fool around/about with (something)*** **a** : to use or do (something) in a way that is not very serious ▪ I'm not really a painter; I just like to *fool around with* paints. **b** : to handle or play with (something) in a careless or foolish way ▪ Stop *fooling* [=*fiddling, messing*] *around with* the stereo. ▪ Don't *fool around with* that gun.
fool with [*phrasal verb*] *informal* **1** ***fool with (something)*** **a** : to handle or play with (something) in a careless way : to fool around with (something) ▪ Don't *fool with* [=*mess with*] that gun. **b** : to deal with or be involved with (something that causes or that could cause trouble) ▪ The company doesn't want to *fool with* [=*mess with, be bothered with*] small distributors. **2** ***fool with (someone)*** : to deal with (someone) in a way that may cause anger or violence ▪ I wouldn't want to *fool with* [=*mess with*] that guy.

³fool *adj, always used before a noun, US, informal* : FOOLISH ▪ The dog was barking its *fool* head off. ▪ Some *fool* driver kept trying to pass me!

fool·ery /ˈfuːləri/ *noun* [*noncount*] *old-fashioned* : foolish or silly behavior ▪ an amusing bit of *foolery*

fool·har·dy /ˈfuːlˌhɑɚdi/ *adj* [*more* ~; *most* ~] : foolishly doing things that are too dangerous or risky ▪ a *foolhardy* explorer ▪ *foolhardy* investors
— **fool·har·di·ness** /ˈfuːlˌhɑɚdinəs/ *noun* [*noncount*]

fool·ish /ˈfuːlɪʃ/ *adj* [*more* ~; *most* ~] : having or showing a lack of good sense or judgment : STUPID, SILLY ▪ a *foolish* decision/mistake ▪ He was wearing a *foolish* grin. ▪ She's been taking *foolish* risks. ▪ Those flashy clothes make her look *foolish*. ▪ She must feel *foolish* wearing those flashy clothes. ▪ I never thought you'd be *foolish* enough to believe him.
— **fool·ish·ly** *adv* ▪ He *foolishly* ignored his parents' advice.
— **fool·ish·ness** *noun* [*noncount*]

fool·proof /ˈfuːlˌpruːf/ *adj* [*more* ~; *most* ~] : done, made, or planned so well that nothing can go wrong ▪ *foolproof* directions ▪ a *foolproof* plan ▪ DNA fingerprinting gives police a virtually *foolproof* way to link a suspect to a crime scene.

fool's gold *noun* [*noncount*] : a mineral that looks like gold

fool's paradise *noun* [*singular*] : a state of happiness that is based on mistaken beliefs or false ideas ▪ We are headed for economic trouble, and anyone who thinks otherwise is living in a *fool's paradise*.

foos·ball /ˈfuːzˌbɑːl/ *noun* [*noncount*] : a table game resembling soccer in which the ball is moved by turning rods to which small figures of players are attached — called also (*US*) *table soccer*, (*Brit*) *table football*

[1]foot /ˈfʊt/ *noun, pl* **feet** /ˈfiːt/

1 [*count*] : the part of the leg on which an animal or person stands and moves : the part of the leg below the ankle • He was wearing boots on his *feet*. • tracks made by the *feet* of a bird • standing on one *foot* • The people in the crowd began to stamp their *feet*. • She was walking around the house in (her) bare *feet*. [=she was not wearing any shoes or socks] • She was ***in her stockinged/stocking feet***. [=she was wearing socks but no shoes] • It's a long hike, but we'll get there if we just keep ***putting one foot in front of the other***. [=if we just keep walking] • ***Wipe your feet*** [=rub the bottoms of your shoes on the doormat] when you come in. — often used before another noun • a *foot* pump [=a pump that is operated by being pressed with the foot] • a *foot* brake • an area that gets a lot of ***foot traffic*** [=an area where many people walk] — see also ATHLETE'S FOOT, CLUBFOOT, COLD FEET, FLAT FOOT

2 *pl also* **foot** [*count*] : a unit of measurement equal to ⅓ yard (0.3048 meter) or 12 inches • a 10-*foot* pole = a pole 10 *feet* long • He's six *feet* tall. • He's six *feet*, three inches tall. = He's six *foot* three. • a plant that grows three *feet* tall = a three-*foot*-tall plant

3 [*singular*] **a** : the lowest part of something : BOTTOM • They camped at the *foot* of the mountain. • at the *foot* of the stairs **b** : the end of something that is opposite to the end that is called the head • the *foot* of the bed [=the end where your feet are when you are lying on the bed] • the *foot* of the table

4 [*count*] : a basic unit of rhythm in a line of poetry made up of a group of syllables that are accented in a certain way • Each line of the poem has five *feet*.

at someone's feet : close to someone's feet • His dog was lying *at his feet*. — sometimes used figuratively • He was young and fearless, and he felt the world was *at his feet*. [=felt that he could do great things in the world] • She claimed that men fell *at her feet*. [=that men often fell in love with her]

be run/rushed off your feet *Brit* : to be very busy • We *are run off our feet* trying to fill orders.

drag your feet see [1]DRAG

feet of clay ✧ A person who was admired in the past but who has serious faults or flaws can be described as having *feet of clay*. • a former political leader who turned out to have *feet of clay*

find your feet : to start to be comfortable in a new situation : to begin to be confident or successful • They quickly *found their feet* in their adopted country. • I was away for a long time, so it will take me a while to *find my feet* again.

get/start off on the right foot : to begin a relationship well • I want to *get off on the right foot* with your parents.

get/start off on the wrong foot : to begin a relationship badly • They *got off on the wrong foot* when they first met and they've disliked each other ever since.

get your feet wet see [1]WET

get your foot in the door : to make the first step toward a goal by gaining entry into an organization, a career, etc. • He took a job as a secretary to *get his foot in the door*.

hand and foot see [1]HAND

have one foot in the grave : to be close to dying because of old age or illness

have/keep your feet on the ground : to be a sensible and practical person • Even after she became famous, she always *kept her feet on the ground*.

let the grass grow under your feet see [1]GRASS

light on your feet see [4]LIGHT

my foot *informal + somewhat old-fashioned* — used to express surprise or disagreement • Fair, *my foot*! That contest wasn't fair!

off your feet : not in a standing position : in or into a sitting or lying position • The blow knocked me *off my feet*. • The doctor suggested that he stay *off his feet* [=that he avoid standing and walking] as much as possible.

on foot : by walking • The refugees traveled *on foot*.

on your feet **1** : in a standing position • I've been *on my feet* all day. • He jumped over the wall and landed *on his feet*. • They say that no matter how a cat falls, it always manages to land *on its feet*. • By the end of the day the workers were ***dead on their feet***. [=very tired but still standing, working, etc.] ✧ In figurative use, to ***land on your feet*** or *Brit* ***fall on your feet*** is to be lucky and be in good condition or in a good situation after having a bad or difficult experience. • He lost his job but *landed on his feet* when he was hired by another company just a few days later. **2** : in a good position or condition • The business is finally/back *on its feet*. **3** : in a healthy condition after an illness or injury • She should be out of the hospital and (back) *on her feet* again in a couple of weeks. **4** : quickly and while actively doing something • Good debaters can think *on their feet*.

put a foot wrong : to make a mistake • He never *put a foot wrong* during the campaign.

put your best foot forward **1** *US* : to behave very well so that someone will like you and approve of you • When I visited my girlfriend's parents I tried to be very polite and *put my best foot forward*. **2** *Brit* : to try as hard as possible to do something difficult • I've got to *put my best foot forward* [=do my best] to meet this deadline.

put your feet up *informal* : to sit and relax : to not work or be active • I'm going to go home and *put my feet up*.

put your foot down **1** : to deal with someone in a harsh or strict way • When my son broke his curfew for the third time, I knew it was time to *put my foot down*. **2** *Brit* : to make a car go faster

put your foot in your mouth (*chiefly US*) *or* ***put your foot in it*** *informal* : to say something that causes someone to be embarrassed, upset, or hurt especially when you did not expect that reaction • I really *put my foot in it* when I asked her about her job. I didn't know she'd just been fired.

set foot in : to enter (a place) • That was the last time she ever *set foot in* this house.

set foot on : to walk on (something) • Neil Armstrong was the first man to *set foot on* the surface of the moon.

shoot yourself in the foot see [1]SHOOT

stand on your own two feet : to support yourself without help from other people • You can't live with your parents forever. It's time to get a place of your own and learn to *stand on your own two feet*.

sweep (someone) off his/her feet see [1]SWEEP

the shoe is on the other foot *or Brit* ***the boot is on the other foot*** — used to say that a situation has changed to the opposite of what it was before • I used to boss my little sister around. Now *the shoe is on the other foot*. [=now she bosses me around] • *The shoe is on the other foot* and he is the one asking for help this time.

to your feet : to a standing position • I got/rose *to my feet* [=I stood up] and left. • His inspirational speech brought the crowd *to its feet*. • Everyone in the courtroom came *to their feet* when the judge entered.

two left feet ✧ A person who dances badly can be described as having *two left feet*. • My wife is a good dancer, but I've got *two left feet*.

under your feet *chiefly Brit* : in the way : UNDERFOOT • I can't get any work done with those kids *under my feet*.

vote with your feet see [1]VOTE

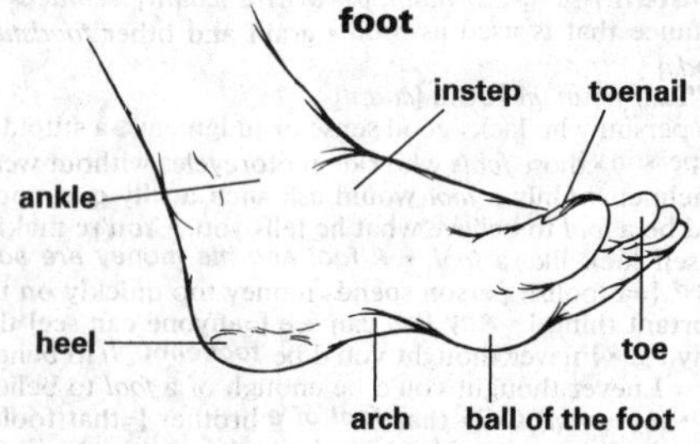

[2]foot *verb* **foots; foot·ed; foot·ing**

foot the bill : to pay for something • His parents *footed the bill* for his college education. • It was a business lunch, so the company is *footing the bill*.

foot·age /ˈfʊtɪʤ/ *noun* [*noncount*]

1 : scenes or action recorded on film or video • Some disturbing *footage* of the war was shown on the evening news.

2 : the size of something measured in feet • calculating the square *footage* of the room [=calculating the size of the room in square feet]

foot–and–mouth disease *noun* [*noncount*] : a serious

and often deadly disease of animals (such as cows and sheep)

foot•ball /ˈfʊtˌbɑːl/ *noun, pl* **-balls**
1 [*noncount*] : any one of several games in which two teams try to get a ball to the goals at each end of a large field: such as **a** *US* : an American game that is played between two teams of 11 players each and in which the ball is moved forward by running or passing ▪ He played a lot of *football* in high school and college. **b** : a similar Canadian game between two teams of 12 players each **c** *Brit* : SOCCER **d** *Brit* : RUGBY
2 [*count*] : a ball filled with air that is used in the game of football — see picture at BALL
political football : an issue that politicians argue about and try to use for their advantage ▪ This issue is too important to be treated as a *political football*.

foot•ball•er /ˈfʊtˌbɑːlɚ/ *noun, pl* **-ers** [*count*] *chiefly Brit* : a person who plays soccer ✧ In U.S. English, a person who plays soccer is usually called a *soccer player*. A person who plays American football is called a *football player*.

footboard /ˈfʊtˌboɚd/ *noun, pl* **-boards** [*count*] : an upright board at the foot of a bed

foot•bridge /ˈfʊtˌbrɪʤ/ *noun, pl* **-bridg•es** [*count*] : a bridge for people who are walking ▪ We built a wooden *footbridge* over the creek.

foot–drag•ging /ˈfʊtˌdrægɪŋ/ *noun* [*noncount*] : failure to do something quickly because you do not want to do it ▪ bureaucrats criticized for *foot-dragging* on important issues

foot•ed /ˈfʊtəd/ *adj* : having a foot or feet of a specified kind or number — usually used in combination ▪ a four-*footed* animal ▪ flat-*footed* ▪ fleet-*footed* — see also SUREFOOTED

foot•er /ˈfʊtɚ/ *noun, pl* **-ers** [*count*]
1 : someone or something that is a specified number of feet tall or long — usually used in combination ▪ two players on the team who are seven-*footers* ▪ The putt was a six-*footer*. [=a six-foot putt]
2 : a word, phrase, etc., that is placed at the bottom of every page of a document — compare HEADER

foot•fall /ˈfʊtˌfɑːl/ *noun, pl* **-falls** [*count*] *literary* : the sound of a footstep ▪ She heard *footfalls* echoing in the hall.

foot fault *noun, pl* ~ **faults** [*count*] *tennis* : the mistake of not keeping your feet behind the baseline when you serve

foot•gear /ˈfʊtˌgiɚ/ *noun* [*noncount*] : FOOTWEAR ▪ Hikers need to wear appropriate *footgear*.

foot•hill /ˈfʊtˌhɪl/ *noun, pl* **-hills** [*count*] : a hill next to a higher mountain or group of mountains — usually plural ▪ the *foothills* of the Rockies

foot•hold /ˈfʊtˌhoʊld/ *noun, pl* **-holds** [*count*]
1 : a place where your foot may be placed when you are climbing a cliff, a mountain, etc. — compare TOEHOLD 1
2 : a position that makes it possible to begin an activity or effort ▪ The army gained a *foothold* on the island. ▪ The company has secured a *foothold* in the market.

foot•ie (*Brit*) *or Australia* **footy** /ˈfʊti/ *noun* [*noncount*] *informal* : SOCCER

foot•ing /ˈfʊtɪŋ/ *noun*
1 [*singular*] **a** : the ability of your feet to stay where you put them as you walk, run, etc. ▪ The loose stones made it difficult for me to maintain/keep my *footing*. [=to avoid slipping or falling] ▪ He lost his *footing* and fell down the slope. **b** : the condition of the ground that makes it easy or hard for your feet to stay where you put them as you walk or run ▪ Be careful. The *footing* is slippery there.
2 [*singular*] **a** — used to describe the kind of relationship that exists between people, countries, etc.; usually used with *on* ▪ a nation that is *on* a friendly *footing* with its neighbors [=a nation that has friendly relations with its neighbors] ▪ They all started *on* an equal *footing* (with one another). = They all started *on* the same *footing*. [=none of them had an advantage when they started] **b** : the base or foundation on which something is established : BASIS — usually used with *on* ▪ put the business *on* a firm financial *footing*
3 [*count*] : the base or foundation on which a structure is built — usually plural ▪ the *footings* of a building/bridge ▪ pour concrete *footings* for a garage

foot•lights /ˈfʊtˌlaɪts/ *noun* [*plural*] : a row of lights across the front of a stage floor that shine on the performers

foot•lock•er /ˈfʊtˌlɑːkɚ/ *noun, pl* **-ers** [*count*] *US* : a strong box that is kept at the foot of a soldier's bed and that is used for storing personal property

foot•loose /ˈfʊtˌluːs/ *adj* [*more* ~; *most* ~] : able to act or move freely : not held back by ties to other people ▪ *footloose* bachelors ▪ When she was 20, she was ***footloose and fancy-free***, with no family or serious career to tie her down.

foot•man /ˈfʊtmən/ *noun, pl* **-men** /-mən/ [*count*] : a male servant who lets visitors into a house and serves food at the dinner table

foot•note /ˈfʊtˌnoʊt/ *noun, pl* **-notes** [*count*]
1 : a note with added information that is placed below the text on a printed page
2 : someone or something that is remembered or regarded as a minor or unimportant part of an event, work, etc. ▪ a movement now regarded as a *footnote* to history
— **foot•not•ed** /ˈfʊtˌnoʊtəd/ *adj* ▪ The book is heavily *footnoted*. [=the book includes many footnotes]

foot•path /ˈfʊtˌpæθ, *Brit* ˈfʊtˌpɑːθ/ *noun, pl* **-paths** [*count*]
1 : a narrow path that people walk on ▪ a *footpath* winding through the garden
2 *Brit* : SIDEWALK

foot•print /ˈfʊtˌprɪnt/ *noun, pl* **-prints** [*count*]
1 : a track or mark left by a foot or shoe ▪ The child left her tiny *footprints* in the snow. ▪ He walked into the kitchen with his boots on, making/leaving muddy *footprints* on the floor.
2 : the amount of space that is covered on a surface by something (such as a computer) ▪ The new model has a smaller *footprint* than the older model.

foot•race /ˈfʊtˌreɪs/ *noun, pl* **-rac•es** [*count*] : a running race

foot•rest /ˈfʊtˌrɛst/ *noun, pl* **-rests** [*count*] : something that you put your feet on to raise them off the floor or ground when you are sitting ▪ a recliner chair with a padded *footrest* attached

foot•sie *also US* **foot•sy** /ˈfʊtsi/ *noun*
play footsie *informal* **1** : to secretly touch another person's foot with your own foot as a way of showing sexual attraction ▪ He was *playing footsie* with her under the dining room table. **2** : to secretly work with or help someone in a way that is dishonest or wrong ▪ world leaders *playing footsie* with terrorists

foot soldier *noun, pl* ~ **-diers** [*count*]
1 : a soldier who marches and fights on foot : INFANTRYMAN
2 : a person who does active and difficult work for an organization or cause ▪ *foot soldiers* in the war against drugs

foot•sore /ˈfʊtˌsoɚ/ *adj* [*more* ~; *most* ~] : having feet that are sore from walking ▪ tired and *footsore* soldiers

foot•step /ˈfʊtˌstɛp/ *noun, pl* **-steps** [*count*]
1 : a movement made by your foot as you walk or run : STEP ▪ She slowly took one *footstep* toward the frightened animal.
2 : the distance covered by a step : PACE ▪ It's five *footsteps* from the bedroom to the bathroom.
3 : the sound of a foot making a step — usually plural ▪ We could hear the approaching *footsteps*.
follow in someone's footsteps : to do the same things that another person has done before ▪ She *followed in her father's footsteps* by becoming a doctor.

foot•stool /ˈfʊtˌstuːl/ *noun, pl* **-stools** [*count*] : a low, small piece of furniture that you can put your feet on when you are sitting

footsy *variant spelling of* FOOTSIE

foot•wear /ˈfʊtˌweɚ/ *noun* [*noncount*] : things (such as shoes and boots) that are worn on your feet ▪ sneakers, loafers, and other casual *footwear*

foot•work /ˈfʊtˌwɚk/ *noun* [*noncount*]
1 : the activity of moving or walking from place to place ▪ The investigation required a lot of *footwork*.
2 : movement of the feet in a sport, dance, etc. ▪ He used quick *footwork* to dodge his opponent. ▪ The tango involves some fancy *footwork*.
3 : active and skillful movement or activity to achieve a goal ▪ He knows that getting enough votes for the proposal is going to require some fancy political *footwork*.

footy *Australia spelling of* FOOTIE

fop /ˈfɑːp/ *noun, pl* **fops** [*count*] *old-fashioned + disapproving* : a man who cares too much about how he looks or dresses ▪ He's an eccentric *fop*.
— **fop•pish** /ˈfɑːpɪʃ/ *adj* [*more* ~; *most* ~] ▪ *foppish* fashions

[1]for /ˈfoɚ, fɚ/ *prep*
1 a — used to indicate the place someone or something is going to or toward ▪ He just left *for* the office. ▪ We're heading *for* home. ▪ When's the next train *for* [=to] London? **b** — used to indicate the person or thing that something is sent or

given to • Are there any letters *for* me? • This present is *for* you. • She baked a cake *for* me.

2 a — used to indicate the thing that something is meant to be used with • There's a separate slot *for* out-of-town mail. • Are these the tires *for* this car? • The scenery *for* the play is beautiful. • This food is *for* the party. **b** — used to indicate the person or type of person who should use or have something • The store sells suits *for* tall men. • This is just right *for* me. • That job is not *for* me. [=that job would not suit me] • Who's the best/right person *for* the job?

3 a — used to indicate the use of something • an instrument *for* measuring speed **b** — used to indicate why something is done • She's dressing *for* dinner. • Squirrels were storing nuts *for* the winter. • He's making plans *for* retirement. • studying *for* examinations • They shouted the news *for* all to hear. [=so that all could hear it]

4 — used to indicate the person that a statement refers to • Seeing her again must be difficult *for* him. — often followed by *to + verb* • It's time *for* us *to get* busy. • *For* him *to confess* would be painful. • That's too heavy *for* you *to carry*. • (*chiefly US*) I'd hate *for* you *to miss* the show. [=I'd hate it if you missed the show]

5 a : in order to help or cause (something) • We are working *for* the good of humanity. • This is *for* your own good. [=to help you] • They believe that they are acting ***for the best***. [=they are doing what is best] **b :** in order to get (something) • *For* more information, call our main office. • Everybody ran *for* safety/shelter when the shooting started.

6 : in favor of (someone or something) • Which candidate are you *for*? • You're either *for* [=*with*] me or you're against me. • the case *for* and the case against disarmament • I am ***all for*** [=completely in favor of] freedom of speech.

7 : because of (something) • He shouted *for* joy. • He wept *for* sorrow. • He was decorated *for* bravery.

8 — used to indicate the person or thing toward which feelings, thoughts, etc., are directed • He was hungry *for* praise. • They are longing *for* home. • I can't help feeling sorry *for* him. • She has a taste *for* spicy food. [=she enjoys spicy food]

9 a — used to indicate an amount of time or space • You can see *for* miles from the top of the hill. • She won't be here *for* long. • She won't get here *for* hours (yet). • We're staying there *for* the summer. **b** — used to indicate the time when something happens or will happen • The wedding is planned *for* next April. • We've invited her *for* 8 p.m. **c** — used to indicate the time that a statement refers to • That's all *for* now/today.

10 a : in place of (someone or something else) : instead of (someone or something else) • Would you go to the store *for* me? • Johnson is now batting *for* Smith. **b :** as a representative of (someone) • His lawyer will act *for* him in this affair. • I'm sure I speak *for* everyone here when I say "Well Done!" **c :** in order to help or serve (someone or something) • What else can I do *for* you? • Let me carry that *for* you. • They fought and died *for* their country.

11 : in order to cure or treat (an illness, injury, disease, etc.) • You should take something *for* that cough.

12 — used to indicate the amount or value of something • a check *for* $100

13 — used to indicate the meaning of a word • The French word *for* "good" is "bon."

14 — used to indicate the food that is eaten at a meal • I ordered eggs *for* breakfast. • What did you have *for* dinner?

15 : as an employee, member, player, etc., of (something) • She works *for* the government. • He plays *for* Denver.

16 *chiefly US* **:** with the name of (someone) • He was named *for* [=*after*] his grandfather. [=he was given the same name as his grandfather]

17 — used to indicate the parts of a list or series • *For* one thing, we have no money; *for* another, we have no time. • People don't buy it because, *for* one thing, the price is too high.

18 — used to refer to something that is surprising or unexpected when compared to something else • He's tall *for* his age. [=he is taller than you would expect someone his age to be] • It's been very cool *for* May. • That was a good score *for* him. = *For* him, that was a good score.

19 — used to indicate the relationship between numbers or amounts that are being compared • *For* every good writer there are a dozen bad ones.

20 — used in various emphatic phrases • ***I for one*** will vote for him. [=I will definitely vote for him] • ***For the last time***, will you stop that noise! • I wish you'd be sensible ***for once***.

for all* 1 :** in spite of (something) • You don't convince me *for all* your clever arguments. • *For all* his education, he's pretty dumb when it comes to home repair. **2** — used in phrases like ***for all someone knows and ***for all someone cares*** to say that someone does not know, care, etc., about something • *For all I know*, she's still there. [=she may still be there, but I don't know] • *For all he cares*, we might as well be dead! [=he doesn't care if we're dead or not]

for ever (and ever) see EVER

for real see [1]REAL

if not for see [1]IF

in for *informal* **:** certain to experience (something) • She's *in for* a big surprise.

in for it *or Brit* ***for it*** *informal* **:** certain to be punished • If his parents find out what he's done, he'll be *in for it*.

in order for see [1]ORDER

***not for (someone) to do something* :** not the right or duty of (someone) to do something • It is *not for you to say* that she can't go. [=it is not appropriate for you to say she can't go; you cannot decide that she cannot go]

once and for all see [1]ONCE

that's/there's . . . for you *informal* — used say that something is very good, very disappointing, or very common • They brought me the package on Christmas Day! Now *that's real service for you*! [=bringing the package on Christmas Day was excellent service] • They didn't even send me a Christmas card! *There's gratitude for you*! [=they were very ungrateful not to send me a Christmas card] • He stays up late, playing video games and listening to music. *That's a teenager for you*. [=that's how a typical teenager behaves]

[2]for *conj, formal + literary* **:** BECAUSE — used to introduce a statement that explains why a preceding statement is true • They were certainly there, *for* I saw them.

fora *plural of* FORUM

[1]for·age /ˈforɪʤ/ *verb* **-ag·es; -aged; -ag·ing** [*no obj*]

1 *of an animal* **:** to eat growing grass or other plants **:** GRAZE • The cows were *foraging* in the pasture.

2 : to search *for* something (such as food or supplies) • He had to *forage for* firewood. • squirrels *foraging for* acorns

– for·ag·er *noun, pl* **-ers** [*count*]

[2]forage *noun* [*noncount*] **:** grasses and other plants that are eaten by animals (such as cows) • The grass serves as *forage* for livestock. • a good *forage* crop

for·ay /ˈfoɚˌeɪ/ *noun, pl* **-ays** [*count*]

1 : a sudden invasion or attack **:** RAID • a *foray* into enemy territory

2 : an attempt to do something especially for the first time • This book marks the novelist's first *foray* into nonfiction. [=his first attempt at writing nonfiction]

3 : a short journey • We made a quick *foray* into town for some supplies.

[1]for·bear /foɚˈbeɚ/ *verb* **-bears; -bore** /-ˈboɚ/; **-borne** /-ˈboɚn/; **-bear·ing** *formal* **:** to choose not to do (something that you could do) **:** to avoid doing or saying (something) [+ *obj*] He carefully *forbore* any mention of her name for fear of upsetting them. • We decided to *forbear* provoking him any further. [*no obj*] We decided to *forbear* from provoking him any further. • He *forebore* to mention her name.

– forbearing *adj* [*more* ~; *most* ~] • He was very *forbearing* toward them. [=he treated them in a very patient way]

[2]forbear *variant spelling of* FOREBEAR

for·bear·ance /foɚˈberəns/ *noun* [*noncount*] *formal* **:** the quality of someone who is patient and able to deal with a difficult person or situation without becoming angry • He showed great *forbearance* in his dealings with them.

for·bid /fɚˈbɪd/ *verb* **-bids; -bade** /-ˈbæd, -ˈbeɪd/ *or* **-bad** /-ˈbæd/; **-bid·den** /-ˈbɪdn̩/; **-bid·ding** [+ *obj*]

1 : to order (someone) not to do something • I *forbid* you to go! • She was *forbidden* by her parents to marry him. • She was *forbidden* from marrying him.

2 *formal* **:** to say that (something) is not allowed • The museum *forbids* flash photography. • The company's rules *forbid* dating among employees.

God/heaven forbid — used in speech to say that you hope a bad thing will not happen • This is the number you should call if, *God forbid*, you should get into an accident. • *Heaven forbid* that something bad should happen.

forbidden *adj* **:** not permitted or allowed • Smoking is *forbidden*. • *forbidden* foods • a *forbidden* pleasure

forbidden fruit *noun, pl* **~ fruits** [*count*] **:** something that is attractive because it is not allowed • For dieters, dessert becomes a/the *forbidden fruit*.

forbidding *adj* [*more* ~; *most* ~] **:** not friendly or appealing

: having a frightening or threatening appearance • a harsh and *forbidding* landscape • a *forbidding* scowl
– **for·bid·ding·ly** *adv* • a *forbiddingly* harsh landscape • He scowled *forbiddingly*.

[1]force /ˈfoɚs/ *noun, pl* **forc·es**
1 [*noncount*] : physical strength, power, or effect • The front of the car took the full *force* of the collision. • instruments used to measure the *force* of the wind
2 [*noncount*] : power or violence used on a person or thing • The police were accused of using excessive *force* when they made the arrest. • We discourage the use of *force*. • a show of *force* • He used brute *force* to open the door. • He took the purse from her ***by force***. [=he used physical power to take her purse] • He feels that this conflict can only be resolved ***by force of arms***. [=by using weapons; by military action]
3 [*noncount*] : strength or power that is not physical • I was impressed by the *force* of her personality. • lending *force* to his arguments [=making his arguments more effective/persuasive] • These regulations do not have the *force* of law. [=they do not have the power that laws have] • She succeeded by/through sheer ***force of will***. [=because she was so determined to succeed] • Through/By ***force of circumstance(s)*** [=because of conditions that cannot be controlled], the company has had to lay off several hundred workers. • Even after he retired, he still woke up early every day ***by/from force of habit***. [=he woke up early every day because he was in the habit of doing so]
4 *technical* : a natural power or effect that is able to change the speed or direction of something [*noncount*] the *force* of gravity [*count*] gravitational/electromagnetic *forces* — see also CENTRIFUGAL FORCE
5 [*count*] : something (such as rain or wind) that occurs in nature and that can be very powerful — usually plural • The cliff was gradually eroded by the *forces* of nature. • natural *forces* — sometimes used figuratively • She gets people to do whatever she wants: she's ***a force of nature***. [=she's a very powerful person who cannot be easily controlled]
6 [*count*] **a** : a group of soldiers trained to fight in a war • a *force* of 20,000 soldiers • He belonged to an elite fighting *force*. • The enemy *forces* had us surrounded. • ground *forces* • allied/rebel *forces* — see also AIR FORCE **b** [*count*] : a group of people who do a particular job or are available for a particular purpose • our country's labor/work *force* • The company has a very large sales *force*. • security *forces* — see also TASK FORCE **c** ***the Force*** *informal* : POLICE FORCE • After graduating from high school, he joined *the Force*. **d** ***the forces*** *Brit* : ARMED FORCES • Will the new defense policy weaken *the forces*?
7 [*count*] : a person or group that has the power to do something or make something happen • The organization has been a strong *force* for good. [=has done a lot of good things] • He has been the driving/motivating *force* behind these changes. [=he has been the person who has caused these changes to occur] • He has become a ***force to be reckoned with*** [=a person who has power and influence] in politics.
8 — used to describe the strength of a wind • damage caused by a *force* 9 gale • The house was flattened by hurricane-*force* winds. • Storm-*force* winds [=very strong winds] are expected tonight.
9 [*count*] *baseball* : FORCE-OUT • a *force* at second base
in force **1** : in large numbers • Picnickers were out *in force* today. [=there were many picnickers out today] **2** *of a law, rule, etc.* : actually working or operating • The ban remains *in force*. [=*in effect*] • The resolution remains ***in full force***.
into force : into the condition of actually working or operating • The law came/went *into force* [=*into effect*] last year. • The regulations have not yet been put/brought *into force*.
join forces *also* ***combine forces*** : to begin working together in order to achieve something • We must all *join forces* to prevent violence. — often + *with* • The company has *joined forces with* local environmental groups.
moving force see MOVING
– see also TOUR DE FORCE

[2]force *verb* **forces; forced; forc·ing** [+ *obj*]
1 : to make (someone) do something that he or she does not want to do • They *forced* us to work long hours without pay. • He was *forced* to resign from office. = He was *forced* out of office. • I really have to ***force myself*** [=to make a great effort] to get up and go to work these days.
2 a : to make it necessary for (someone) *to do* something • The flooding *forced* hundreds of residents *to flee* their homes. • After seeing the evidence, I was *forced to admit* my error. • I am *forced to conclude* that more funding will be necessary. • The pilot was *forced to land* when one of the plane's engines caught fire. **b** : to make (something) necessary • The scandal *forced* his resignation. • Lack of time may eventually *force* a compromise. **c** : to cause the occurrence of (something that other people do not want to happen) • They are trying to *force* a vote on this issue.
3 a : to move (someone or something) by physical effort • The runner was *forced* out of bounds. • Their car was *forced* off the road. • After hours of fighting, they were able to *force* back the enemy. • The pressure *forces* the water to the surface. • A pump *forces* air into the chamber. • The medicine tasted awful, but I managed to ***force it down***. [=to swallow it by making an effort] • If the key doesn't fit the lock, don't ***force it***. [=don't use too much physical strength to make the key go into the lock] **b** : to cause (something) to open by using physical effort or violence • They *forced* (open) the door. • It was clear that the door/lock had been *forced*.
4 : to produce (something, such as a smile) by making an effort • She *forced* a smile.
5 *baseball* : to cause (a runner) to be put out by means of a force-out • He was *forced* (out) at second base.
force on/upon [*phrasal verb*] ***force (someone or something) on/upon (someone)*** : to cause (someone or something that is not wanted) to be accepted by (someone) • They resent having these decisions *forced on* them. • I don't like the way he keeps *forcing* himself *on* us. [=the way he keeps coming to be with us when we do not want to be with him]
force someone's hand : to make it necessary for someone to do something • She'd intended to postpone her decision, but events *forced her hand*.
force (something) down someone's throat see THROAT
force the issue see [1]ISSUE
force your way : to move ahead by pushing and making people move out of your way • They *forced their way* into the room. • He *forced his way* through the crowd.

forced /ˈfoɚst/ *adj*
1 a : caused by necessity • The plane had engine problems and had to make a *forced* landing in a field. [=the plane was forced to land in a field] **b** : obtained by using power or force • a *forced* confession
2 : done with effort : not natural or sincere • *forced* laughter

forced labor *noun* [*noncount*]
1 : very hard physical work that someone is forced to do • The prisoners endured years of *forced labor*.
2 : a group of people who are made to work very hard for no money; *also* : a system that allows this • The railroad was built with/by *forced labor*.

force–feed *verb* **-feeds; -fed; -feed·ing** [+ *obj*]
1 : to make (a person or animal) eat by physically putting food down the throat
2 : to force (someone) to read, listen to, or learn (something) • *force-feed* students the classics = *force-feed* the classics to students

force field *noun, pl* **~ fields** [*count*] *chiefly US* : an area in which a particular force (such as magnetism) exists and can be felt — often used figuratively • No one could break through the protective *force field* legislators put up around the proposed bill.

force·ful /ˈfoɚsfəl/ *adj* [*more ~; most ~*]
1 : having a strong and confident quality • He has a very *forceful* personality. • She's a confident and *forceful* leader.
2 : expressed in a way that is effective and that influences people's thoughts and ideas • They have made a *forceful* argument in favor of changing the system.
3 : done with military or physical force • The government has threatened to use more *forceful* measures if necessary.
– **force·ful·ly** *adv* • speaking *forcefully* – **force·ful·ness** *noun* [*noncount*] • the *forcefulness* of her argument/personality

force–out /ˈfoɚsˌaʊt/ *noun, pl* **-outs** [*count*] *baseball* : a play in which a runner who is forced to run to the next base is put out when the player who has the ball touches the base • a *force-out* at second base — called also *force, force play*

for·ceps /ˈfoɚˌseps/ *noun, pl* **forceps** [*count*] : a medical tool that is used for grasping or holding things • He removed the splinter with a (pair of) *forceps*. — usually plural • He removed the splinter with *forceps*. • a *forceps* delivery/birth [=a birth/delivery in which forceps are used to help deliver the baby]

forc·i·ble /ˈfoɚsəbəl/ *adj* : made or done by physical force or violence • the *forcible* removal of the rioters • (*chiefly US*)

The door showed signs of ***forcible entry***. [=the door looked as if someone had forced it open]

– **forc·i·bly** /ˈfoɚsəbli/ *adv* ▪ The rioters were *forcibly* removed from the scene.

[1]**ford** /ˈfoɚd/ *verb* **fords; ford·ed; ford·ing** [+ *obj*] : to cross (an area of water) by walking or riding across a shallow part ▪ *ford* a river/stream

– **ford·able** /ˈfoɚdəbəl/ *adj* ▪ a *fordable* river

[2]**ford** *noun, pl* **fords** [*count*] : a shallow part of a river, stream, etc., that may be crossed by walking or driving across it

[1]**fore** /ˈfoɚ/ *noun*

to the fore : in or into a place of importance ▪ The recent publicity has brought the issue *to the fore*. [=has brought a great deal of attention to the issue] ▪ The issue has come *to the fore*.

[2]**fore** *adv* : toward or at the front part of a boat, ship, or airplane ▪ The plane's exits are located *fore* and aft. — compare [1]AFT

[3]**fore** *adj* : located at the front of a boat, ship, or airplane ▪ the *fore* and aft cabins/exits

fore- *combining form*

1 : earlier ▪ *foresee*

2 a : located at the front ▪ the dog's *foreleg* **b** : front or lower part of (something specified) ▪ She bruised her *forearm*.

[1]**fore·arm** /ˈfoɚˌɑɚm/ *noun, pl* **-arms** [*count*] : the part of the arm between the elbow and the wrist — see picture at HUMAN

[2]**forearm** /foɚˈɑɚm/ *verb* **-arms; -armed; -arm·ing**

forewarned is forearmed see FOREWARN

fore·bear *also* **for·bear** /ˈfoɚˌbeɚ/ *noun, pl* **-bears** [*count*] *formal* : a member of your family in the past : ANCESTOR ▪ His *forebears* fought in the American Civil War.

fore·bod·ing /foɚˈboʊdɪŋ/ *noun, pl* **-ings** : a feeling that something bad is going to happen [*noncount*] She was filled with a sense of *foreboding*. [*count*] It seems that her *forebodings* were justified.

[1]**fore·cast** /ˈfoɚˌkæst, *Brit* ˈfɔːˌkɑːst/ *verb* **-casts; -cast** *also* **-cast·ed; -cast·ing** [+ *obj*] : to say that (something) will happen in the future : to predict (something, such as weather) after looking at the information that is available ▪ They're *forecasting* rain for this weekend. ▪ The company is *forecasting* reduced profits. ▪ Experts *forecast* that the economy will slow in the coming months.

– **fore·cast·er** *noun, pl* **-ers** [*count*] ▪ weather *forecasters* ▪ economic *forecasters*

[2]**forecast** *noun, pl* **-casts** [*count*] : a statement about what you think is going to happen in the future ▪ weather *forecasts* ▪ economic *forecasts*

fore·cas·tle /ˈfoʊksəl/ *noun, pl* **-cas·tles** [*count*] *technical* : the front part of the upper deck of a ship where the sailors usually live

fore·close /foɚˈkloʊz/ *verb* **-clos·es; -closed; -clos·ing** : to take back property because the money owed for the property has not been paid [*no obj*] They've been unable to make their mortgage payments, and the bank has threatened to *foreclose*. — often + *on* ▪ The bank has threatened to *foreclose on* their property/mortgage. [+ *obj*] The bank has threatened to *foreclose* their mortgage.

– **fore·clo·sure** /foɚˈkloʊʒɚ/ *noun, pl* **-sures** [*count, noncount*]

fore·court /ˈfoɚˌkoɚt/ *noun, pl* **-courts** [*count*]

1 : the area near the net in tennis

2 *chiefly Brit* : a large, flat, open area in front of a building

fore·doomed /foɚˈduːmd/ *adj, formal* : certain to fail ▪ Their efforts were *foredoomed* to failure.

fore·fa·ther /ˈfoɚˌfɑːðɚ/ *noun, pl* **-thers** [*count*]

1 : a person (especially a man) who was in your family in past times : ANCESTOR — usually plural ▪ The town is named after one of his *forefathers*.

2 : a person (especially a man) from an earlier time who helped to create or start something modern or important — usually plural ▪ our country's *forefathers*

fore·fin·ger /ˈfoɚˌfɪŋgɚ/ *noun, pl* **-gers** [*count*] : the finger that is next to the thumb — called also *index finger*; see picture at HUMAN

fore·foot /ˈfoɚˌfʊt/ *noun, pl* **-feet** /-ˌfiːt/ [*count*] : either one of the front feet of a four-footed animal

fore·front /ˈfoɚˌfrʌnt/ *noun, pl* **-fronts** [*count*] : the most important part or position — usually singular ▪ Their company is ***at/in the forefront*** of research in this area. [=their company is a leader in research in this area] ▪ The discussion has brought the issue of health care ***to the forefront***. [=has made the issue very important or well-known]

foregather *variant spelling of* FORGATHER

forego *variant spelling of* FORGO

fore·go·ing /foɚˈgowɪŋ/ *adj, formal* : already mentioned ▪ The *foregoing* [=*preceding, above*] examples illustrate my point.

the foregoing *formal* : the things that have just been mentioned ▪ It should be clear from *the foregoing* that a new system is needed.

fore·gone /ˈfoɚˌgɑːn/ *adj*

a foregone conclusion : something in the future that is certain to happen or be true ▪ It was a *foregone conclusion* that he would take over the business after his father retired. ▪ Most people felt that the outcome of the trial was a *foregone conclusion*. [=they felt sure that the trial would end in a certain way]

[1]**fore·ground** /ˈfoɚˌgraʊnd/ *noun, pl* **-grounds**

1 [*count*] : the part of a scene or picture that is nearest to and in front of the viewer — usually singular ▪ Objects in the *foreground* seem larger than those in the background.

2 [*singular*] : an important position ▪ We want the issue to be in the *foreground*.

[2]**fore·ground** *verb* **-grounds; -ground·ed; -ground·ing** [+ *obj*] : to make (something) more important ▪ Public discussion has *foregrounded* the issue of health care.

fore·hand /ˈfoɚˌhænd/ *noun, pl* **-hands** [*count*] *sports* : a way of hitting a ball in tennis and similar games in which the palm of the hand holding the racket is turned in the direction of the ball ▪ She hit a *forehand* across the court. — often used before another noun ▪ a *forehand* stroke/shot — compare BACKHAND

fore·head /ˈfoɚˌhɛd, ˈfɑrəd/ *noun, pl* **-heads** [*count*] : the part of the face above the eyes — see picture at FACE

for·eign /ˈforən/ *adj*

1 : located outside a particular place or country and especially outside your own country ▪ They've visited several *foreign* countries. ▪ a ***foreign correspondent*** [=a journalist who reports from a foreign country]

2 : coming from or belonging to a different place or country ▪ We don't get many *foreign* visitors. ▪ Have you studied any *foreign* languages? ▪ She has a *foreign* accent. ▪ a *foreign*-born resident [=a resident who was born in a foreign country]

3 : relating to or dealing with other nations ▪ matters of *foreign* policy ▪ the ministry of *foreign* affairs ▪ *foreign* aid/trade — see also FOREIGN OFFICE

4 : coming from outside : not normally found in the place or part where it is located ▪ Dust and other *foreign* bodies can irritate the eyes. ▪ The sample contained a *foreign* object.

5 [*more* ~; *most* ~] : not known or familiar ▪ a *foreign* concept — often + *to* ▪ That concept is completely *foreign to* me. ▪ That is *foreign to* my experience.

– **for·eign·ness** /ˈforənnəs/ *noun* [*noncount*] ▪ the *foreignness* of this concept

for·eign·er /ˈforənɚ/ *noun, pl* **-ers** [*count*] : a person who is from a country that is not your own

foreign exchange *noun* [*noncount*] *finance*

1 : the process by which people in different countries pay each other by exchanging different types of money

2 : money from foreign countries ▪ Our country has to export more in order to earn more *foreign exchange*.

Foreign Legion *noun*

the Foreign Legion : a part of the French Army that is made up of soldiers who are not French

Foreign Office *noun*

the Foreign Office : a government department especially in Great Britain that deals with foreign affairs ✧ The official name of the British Foreign Office is now the *Foreign and Commonwealth Office*.

Foreign Secretary *noun, pl* ~ **-taries** [*count*] *Brit* : the official in Great Britain and other countries who is in charge of how the country relates to and deals with foreign countries

Foreign Service *noun*

the Foreign Service : a part of the U.S. State Department that hires people (such as diplomats) to represent the government in foreign countries

fore·know·ledge /ˌfoɚˈnɑːlɪʤ/ *noun* [*noncount*] *formal* : knowledge of something before it happens or exists ▪ He denied any *foreknowledge* of the crime.

fore·leg /ˈfoɚˌlɛg/ *noun, pl* **-legs** [*count*] : a front leg of an animal

fore·lock /ˈfoɚˌlɑːk/ *noun, pl* **-locks** [*count*] : a piece of hair growing from the front of the head
tug/touch your forelock *Brit, disapproving* : to be too concerned with pleasing someone who you think is powerful or important

fore·man /ˈfoɚmən/ *noun, pl* **-men** /-mən/ [*count*]
1 : the member of a jury who is the leader
2 : a person who is in charge of a group of workers ✧ *Foreman* can refer to women as well as men, but it is more commonly used for men.

¹fore·most /ˈfoɚˌmoʊst/ *adj* : most important ▪ He is the *foremost* [=*leading*] authority/scholar on the American Civil War period. ▪ Safety is their *foremost* [=*primary*] concern.

²foremost *adv*
1 : in the first or most important position ▪ The building's designers put safety *foremost.* [=(more commonly) *first*]
2 : at the most basic or important level ▪ Though he has many other interests, he is *foremost* [=*primarily*] an authority on the American Civil War period.
first and foremost see ²FIRST

fore·name /ˈfoɚˌneɪm/ *noun, pl* **-names** [*count*] *chiefly Brit, formal* : FIRST NAME

fo·ren·sic /fəˈrɛnsɪk/ *adj, law*
1 : relating to the use of scientific knowledge or methods in solving crimes ▪ *forensic* medicine ▪ *forensic* science/experts
2 *somewhat formal* : relating to, used in, or suitable to a court of law ▪ a lawyer's *forensic* skills [=a lawyer's skills at arguing a case in a court of law]

fo·ren·sics /fəˈrɛnsɪks/ *noun* [*noncount*]
1 : the study or science of solving crimes by using scientific knowledge or methods ▪ a career in *forensics*
2 : the results of a scientific test done to help solve a crime ▪ The *forensics* showed he was at the scene of the crime.

fore·play /ˈfoɚˌpleɪ/ *noun* [*noncount*] : sexual actions (such as kissing and touching) that people do with each other before they have sex

fore·run·ner /ˈfoɚˌrʌnɚ/ *noun, pl* **-ners** [*count*]
1 : someone or something that comes before another ▪ a simple machine that was the *forerunner* of today's computers
2 : a sign of something that is going to happen ▪ I had that strange feeling that's the *forerunner* of a cold.

fore·see /foɚˈsiː/ *verb* **-sees**; **-saw** /-ˈsɑː/; **-seen** /-ˈsiːn/; **-see·ing** [+ *obj*] *somewhat formal* : to see or become aware of (something that has not yet happened) ▪ We couldn't have *foreseen* the consequences of our actions. ▪ He *foresees* a day when all war will cease. ▪ She *foresaw* the company's potential and invested early on.
– fore·see·able /foɚˈsiːjəbəl/ *adj* ▪ a *foreseeable* consequence ▪ We have no plans to sell our house ***in/for the foreseeable future*** [=*soon*]

fore·shad·ow /foɚˈʃædoʊ/ *verb* **-shad·ows**; **-shad·owed**; **-shad·ow·ing** [+ *obj*] : to give a suggestion of (something that has not yet happened) ▪ Her early interest in airplanes *foreshadowed* her later career as a pilot. ▪ The hero's predicament is *foreshadowed* in the first chapter.
– foreshadowing *noun, pl* **-ings** [*count, noncount*] ▪ The first chapter contains *foreshadowings* of what will happen later.

fore·short·en /foɚˈʃoɚtn̩/ *verb* **-ens**; **-ened**; **-en·ing** [+ *obj*]
1 : to cause (something) to appear shorter than it really is because it is in the foreground of a drawing, painting, etc. ▪ The parts that extend towards the viewer are *foreshortened.*
2 *somewhat formal* : to make (something) shorter ▪ His athletic career was *foreshortened* [=(more commonly) *shortened, cut short*] by a knee injury.

fore·sight /ˈfoɚˌsaɪt/ *noun* [*noncount*] : the ability to see what will or might happen in the future ▪ They had the *foresight* to invest the money wisely. ▪ His career choice shows a lack of *foresight.*
– fore·sight·ed /ˈfoɚˌsaɪtəd/ *adj* [*more* ~; *most* ~] ▪ *foresighted* investors/investments **– fore·sight·ed·ness** *noun* [*noncount*]

fore·skin /ˈfoɚˌskɪn/ *noun, pl* **-skins** [*count*] : a fold of skin that covers the end of the penis

for·est /ˈforəst/ *noun, pl* **-ests** : a thick growth of trees and bushes that covers a large area [*count*] a vast *forest* [*noncount*] Fires destroyed acres of *forest.* — often used before another noun ▪ *forest* fires ▪ the *forest* floor — often used figuratively ▪ The candidate was surrounded by a *forest* of microphones. — see color picture on page C7; see also RAIN FOREST
not see the forest for the trees see TREE

fore·stall /foɚˈstɑːl/ *verb* **-stalls**; **-stalled**; **-stall·ing** [+ *obj*]
1 : to stop (something) from happening or to cause (something) to happen at a later time ▪ Negotiations failed to *forestall* the conflict. ▪ His comments were meant to *forestall* criticism of his proposal.
2 : to act before (someone else) in order to prevent something ▪ He *forestalled* critics by offering a defense of the project.

for·est·ed /ˈforəstəd/ *adj* [*more* ~; *most* ~] : covered or filled with trees ▪ a heavily *forested* [=*wooded*] area

for·est·er /ˈforəstɚ/ *noun, pl* **-ers** [*count*] : a person whose job is to take care of forests by planting trees, cutting down trees, etc.

forest green *noun* [*noncount*] *chiefly US* : a dark green — see color picture on page C2

forest ranger *noun, pl* ~ **-ers** [*count*] *US* : RANGER 1

for·est·ry /ˈforəstri/ *noun* [*noncount*] : the science and practice of caring for forests ▪ She studied *forestry* in college.

fore·taste /ˈfoɚˌteɪst/ *noun, pl* **-tastes** [*count*] *somewhat formal* : a small or short experience of something that will not be fully experienced until later ▪ The sudden cold snap gave us a *foretaste* [=*taste*] of winter. ▪ These layoffs are only a *foretaste* of what's to come.

fore·tell /foɚˈtɛl/ *verb* **-tells**; **-told** /-ˈtoʊld/; **-tell·ing** [+ *obj*] *formal + literary* : to describe (something) before it happens : PREDICT ▪ We cannot *foretell* the future. ▪ Economists *foretold* impending disaster.

fore·thought /ˈfoɚˌθɑːt/ *noun* [*noncount*] : careful thinking or planning about the future ▪ Her decision showed a lack of *forethought.* ▪ With a little *forethought*, you can save yourself a lot of work later on.

¹for·ev·er /fəˈrɛvɚ/ *adv*
1 a : for an endless time : for all time ▪ He promised that he'd love her *forever.* [=*eternally*] ▪ She was convinced that she would live *forever.* **b** : for a very long time ▪ I've been waiting *forever* for the doctor.
2 : at all times : CONSTANTLY ▪ a dog that was *forever* chasing cars ▪ He's *forever* asking silly questions.
for ever (and ever) see EVER

²forever *noun* [*noncount*] : an extremely long time : a time that seems to last forever ▪ After what seemed like *forever*, I was able to see the doctor. ▪ It ***took forever*** to find his keys.

fore·warn /foɚˈwoɚn/ *verb* **-warns**; **-warned**; **-warn·ing** [+ *obj*] : to warn (someone) before something happens — usually used as *(be) forewarned* ▪ They had *been forewarned* of the danger. ▪ *Be forewarned*: there will be a test on Monday. ✧ The expression ***forewarned is forearmed*** means that when you are warned about something, you are prepared to deal with it.

fore·wo·man /ˈfoɚˌwʊmən/ *noun, pl* **-wo·men** /-ˌwɪmən/ [*count*] : a woman who is the leader of a jury

fore·word /ˈfoɚˌwɚd/ *noun, pl* **-words** [*count*] : a section at the beginning of a book that introduces the book and is usually written by someone other than the book's author

¹for·feit /ˈfoɚfət/ *verb* **-feits**; **-feit·ed**; **-feit·ing** : to lose or give up (something) as a punishment or because of a rule or law [+ *obj*] He *forfeited* his right to a trial by jury. ▪ If the money is not claimed within six months, it will be *forfeited* to the town. [=the owner of the money will lose any right to it] ▪ They didn't have enough players, so they ended up having to *forfeit* the game (to the other team). [*no obj*] They didn't have enough players, so they ended up having to *forfeit.*

²forfeit *noun, pl* **-feits** : something that is lost or given up as punishment or because of a rule or law [*count*] — usually singular ▪ The judge declared the property a *forfeit.* ▪ They were required to pay a *forfeit.* [*noncount*] We won the game ***by forfeit*** [=we won because the other team forfeited the game]

³forfeit *adj, not used before a noun, formal* : given up or taken away as a punishment or because of a rule or law ▪ If the money is not claimed within six months, it will be *forfeit* to the town. [=the owner of the money will lose any right to it, and it will be given to the town]

for·fei·ture /ˈfoɚfəʧɚ/ *noun, pl* **-tures** [*count, noncount*] *law* : the act of giving up something as punishment or because of a rule or law : the act of forfeiting something ▪ *forfeiture* of assets ▪ money subject to *forfeiture*

for·gath·er *or* **fore·gath·er** /foɚˈgæðɚ/ *verb* **-ers**; **-ered**; **-ering** [*no obj*] *formal* : to come together as a group : GATH-

ER • Members of the organization are planning to *forgather* in the city for their annual meeting.

forgave *past tense of* FORGIVE

[1]**forge** /ˈfoɚʤ/ *verb* **forg·es; forged; forg·ing** [+ *obj*]
1 : to form something by heating and shaping metal • *forging* hooks out of pieces of iron = *forging* pieces of iron into hooks
2 : to form or create (something, such as an agreement or relationship) through great effort • The two countries have *forged* a strong alliance. • They were able to *forge* a peaceful relationship.
3 : to make or copy (something, such as a document or signature) falsely in order to deceive someone • *forge* a check • *forge* a signature • a *forged* passport
– compare [3]FORGE
– forg·er *noun, pl* **-ers** [*count*] • a check *forger* • a professional art *forger*

[2]**forge** *noun, pl* **forges** [*count*] **:** a place where objects are made by heating and shaping metal

[3]**forge** *verb* **forges; forged; forg·ing** [*no obj*]
1 : to move forward slowly and steadily • The hikers *forged* through the snow. — usually + *ahead* • The ship *forged ahead* through heavy seas.
2 : to move with a sudden increase of speed and power • On the last lap, he *forged* into the lead. — often + *ahead* • The company has *forged ahead* of its competitors.
– compare [1]FORGE

forg·ery /ˈfoɚʤəri/ *noun, pl* **-er·ies**
1 [*noncount*] **:** the crime of falsely making or copying a document in order to deceive people • check *forgery*
2 [*count*] **:** something that is falsely made or copied in order to deceive people **:** something that is forged • These paintings are *forgeries*. [=*fakes*]

for·get /fɚˈgɛt/ *verb* **-gets; -got** /-ˈgɑːt/; **-got·ten** /-ˈgɑːtn/ *or* **-got; -get·ting**
1 : to be unable to think of or remember (something) [+ *obj*] He *forgot* the address. • I keep *forgetting* her name. • The pain and misery are impossible to *forget*. • She *forgot* how to set up the tent. • I'll never *forget* the first time we met. • Don't *forget* that you have to turn off the light when you leave. — often followed by *to + verb* • I *forgot to pay* the bill. [*no obj*] "Did you pay the bill?" "I *forgot*." — often + *about* • I *forgot* (all) *about* paying the bill.
2 [+ *obj*] **:** to fail to remember to bring or take (something) • When he got to the restaurant he realized that he had *forgotten* his wallet. [=he had left his wallet at home]
3 a *or* ***forget about*** [+ *obj*] **:** to stop thinking or caring about (someone) • He was once a famous actor, but now most people have *forgotten* (*about*) him. • You shouldn't *forget* (*about*) your old friends. • He's now a *forgotten* hero. • He's a *forgotten* man in the world of politics. **b** *or* ***forget about*** [+ *obj*] **:** to stop thinking or caring about (something) on purpose • We need to *forget* (*about*) our differences and learn to get along. • "I'm sorry I'm late." "That's OK. *Forget* (*about*) it." [=don't worry about it] • If you're hoping to hear from him soon, *forget* it, it's not going to happen. • *Forget about* finding a way to escape—there's no way out of here. • "Have you seen my keys?" "No. Did you leave them in your other jacket?" "No, I thought . . . Oh, *forget* it, here they are." **c** [*no obj*] **:** to stop remembering or caring about something • We've had our differences in the past, but now it's time to ***forgive and forget***.
forget yourself **:** to lose control of your emotions because of anger, excitement, etc. **:** to behave in a way that is not proper or acceptable • She *forgot herself* and said some things that she later regretted.

for·get·ful /fɚˈgɛtfəl/ *adj* [*more* ~; *most* ~]
1 : tending to forget things **:** forgetting things often or easily • He became *forgetful* in his old age.
2 — used to say that someone has forgotten something • She has been ***forgetful of*** her duties. [=she has forgotten/neglected her duties]
– for·get·ful·ly *adv* • He *forgetfully* left the lights on. **– for·get·ful·ness** *noun* [*noncount*] • His *forgetfulness* grew worse in his old age.

for·get–me–not /fɚˈgɛtmiˌnɑːt/ *noun, pl* **-nots** [*count*] **:** a type of small plant that has bright blue flowers

for·get·ta·ble /fɚˈgɛtəbəl/ *adj* [*more* ~; *most* ~] **:** likely to be forgotten **:** not worth remembering • It was an extremely *forgettable* performance. — opposite UNFORGETTABLE

for·giv·able /fɚˈgɪvəbəl/ *adj* [*more* ~; *most* ~] **:** able to be forgiven **:** deserving forgiveness • a *forgivable* error/mistake • Her actions in this case are completely *forgivable*. [=*excusable*] — opposite UNFORGIVABLE
– for·giv·ably /fɚˈgɪvəbli/ *adv*

for·give /fɚˈgɪv/ *verb* **-gives; -gave** /-ˈgeɪv/; **-giv·en** /-ˈgɪvən/; **-giv·ing**
1 : to stop feeling anger toward (someone who has done something wrong) **:** to stop blaming (someone) [+ *obj*] *forgive* your enemies • Can you ever *forgive* me for being so selfish? • I've never *forgiven* myself for the way I treated her. • We must ask God to *forgive* us for our sins. • He ***can be forgiven*** for feeling this way. [=it is understandable that he feels this way; he should not be blamed for feeling this way] [*no obj*] When he feels he's been insulted, he finds it hard to ***forgive and forget***.
2 [+ *obj*] **:** to stop feeling anger about (something) **:** to forgive someone for (something wrong) • He finds it hard to *forgive* an insult. • We must ask God to *forgive* our sins.
3 [+ *obj*] **:** to stop requiring payment of (money that is owed) • The government has agreed to *forgive* some of the debt.
forgive me — used in speech as a polite way of starting to say something that may seem rude or unpleasant • *Forgive me* (for saying so), but I don't think you understood my point. • *Forgive me*, but something has come up and I have to leave right away.
– for·giv·er *noun, pl* **-ers** [*count*] • a *forgiver* of sins

for·give·ness /fɚˈgɪvnəs/ *noun* [*noncount*]
1 : the act of forgiving someone or something • I ask (for) your *forgiveness*. [=I ask you to forgive me] • *forgiveness* of our sins
2 : the attitude of someone who is willing to forgive other people • She treats us with kindness and *forgiveness*.

forgiving *adj* [*more* ~; *most* ~]
1 : able or willing to forgive someone or something • a person with a *forgiving* nature — sometimes + *of* • As a teacher, she was *forgiving of* her students' mistakes.
2 — used to describe something that produces good results even when it is not used perfectly • The tennis racket is designed to be *forgiving*. [=designed to produce good shots even when the ball is not hit perfectly] — opposite UNFORGIVING

for·go *or* **fore·go** /foɚˈgoʊ/ *verb* **-goes; -went** /-ˈwɛnt/; **-gone** /-ˈgɑːn/; **-go·ing** [+ *obj*] **:** to give up the use or enjoyment of (something) • *forgo* an opportunity • She is planning to *forgo* her right to a trial and simply plead guilty. ✧ The past tense *forwent* is now rare or formal.

forgot *past tense of* FORGET

forgotten *past participle of* FORGET

for in·stance /fɚˈɪnstəns/ *noun, pl* ~ **-stanc·es** [*count*] *US, informal* **:** EXAMPLE • Let me give you a *for instance*. — see also *for instance* at INSTANCE

[1]**fork** /ˈfoɚk/ *noun, pl* **forks** [*count*]
1 a : a small tool with two or more pointed parts (called prongs or tines) used for picking up and eating food • a salad *fork* — see picture at PLACE SETTING **b :** a garden tool with two or more prongs used for lifting and digging soil — see also PITCHFORK
2 a : a place where something (such as a road or river) divides into two parts • a *fork* in the road **b :** either one of the parts that a road, river, etc., divides into • take the left *fork* • the north *fork* of the river
3 : a part or tool that divides into two parts • the front *fork* of a bicycle — see also TUNING FORK

[2]**fork** *verb* **forks; forked; fork·ing**
1 [*no obj*] *of a road, river, etc.* **:** to divide into two parts • The road *forks* to the north and south.
2 [+ *obj*] *informal* **:** to pay or give (money) — usually + *over* or *out* • He had to *fork over* half his paycheck. • The company *forked out* thousands of dollars to repair the damage.
3 [+ *obj*] **:** to lift or throw (something) with a fork • They *forked* the hay into the loft.

forked /ˈfoɚkt/ *adj* **:** divided into two parts at one end **:** shaped like the letter Y • a bird with a deeply *forked* tail • *forked* lightning • the *forked* tongue of a snake
speak/talk with (a) forked tongue **:** to speak in a dishonest way that is meant to deceive people • His colleagues accused him of *speaking with a forked tongue*.

fork·ful /ˈfoɚkˌfʊl/ *noun, pl* **-fuls** [*count*] **:** the amount held by a fork • a *forkful* of mashed potatoes

fork·lift /ˈfoɚkˌlɪft/ *noun, pl* **-lifts** [*count*] **:** a machine that is used for lifting and moving heavy objects — called also *forklift truck*; see picture at CONSTRUCTION

for·lorn /fɚˈloɚn/ *adj* [*more* ~; *most* ~]
1 : sad and lonely • a *forlorn* old widow

2 : empty and in poor condition ▪ a *forlorn* landscape ▪ a *forlorn* abandoned factory
3 : not having much chance of success : nearly hopeless ▪ a *forlorn* cause/hope ▪ He led a *forlorn* [=*desperate*] attack against the enemy.
– **for·lorn·ly** *adv* ▪ She wandered *forlornly* through the deserted neighborhood.

[1]**form** /ˈfoɚm/ *noun, pl* **forms**
1 [*count*] **a** : a type or kind of something ▪ Coal is a *form* of carbon. ▪ a rare/deadly *form* of cancer ▪ a popular *form* of entertainment ▪ different *forms* of life = different life *forms* [=different types of living beings] ▪ an ancient *form* of music ▪ an art *form* **b** : one of several or many different ways in which something is seen, experienced, or produced ▪ The medicine can be taken in the *form* of a liquid or pill. = The medicine can be taken in pill or liquid *form*. ▪ His essays are now available in book *form*. [=his essays have been published in a book] ▪ the written/spoken *form* of the language ▪ Antisocial behavior can take many *forms*. [=there are many different types of antisocial behavior] ▪ Most of his wealth is in the *form* of stocks. [=most of his wealth consists of stocks]
2 **a** : the shape of something [*count*] the building's massive *form* [*noncount*] a style of architecture that emphasizes *form* over function **b** [*count*] : something that can be seen only as a shape or outline ▪ The shadowy *forms* of several people were visible through the smoke. **c** [*count*] : bodily shape : FIGURE ▪ the human/female *form*
3 [*count*] : a document with blank spaces for filling in information ▪ a tax *form* ▪ an application *form* ▪ fill out a *form*
4 [*noncount*] *somewhat old-fashioned* : a way of behaving that is judged as proper or improper ▪ It's considered ***bad/poor form*** to arrive so early. = It's not considered ***good form*** to arrive so early. [=it is not proper to arrive so early]
5 [*noncount*] **a** : a manner or style of performing ▪ an athlete with good *form* ▪ She would be a better swimmer/golfer if she improved her *form*. **b** : condition for performing ▪ an athlete in top *form* [=*shape*] **c** — used to describe how well or badly someone is performing ▪ She was really in great *form* at the party, telling jokes and dancing. ▪ He was ***at the top of his form***. [=he was performing extremely well] ▪ (*chiefly Brit*) He's been playing poorly in recent months, but now he's back ***on form***. [=now he's playing well again] ▪ (*chiefly Brit*) She was a little ***off form***.
6 : the way in which the parts of a piece of writing or music or of a work of art are arranged [*noncount*] the *form* and content of a poem/essay [*count*] The sonnet is a poetical *form*. ▪ symphonic *forms*
7 [*count*] : any one of the different ways in which a word may be written or spoken ▪ the plural/possessive *form* of a noun ▪ the inflected *forms* of a verb — see also COMBINING FORM
8 [*noncount*] : a grade in a British secondary school or in some American private schools ▪ students in the sixth *form*
as a matter of form — used to say that something is done because it is polite, usual, or required ▪ He was asked to participate only *as a matter of form*.
form of address see [2]ADDRESS
in any way, shape, or form see [1]WAY
take form : to begin to develop : to start to exist or be seen ▪ a political movement that first *took form* in the 1960s ▪ The new stadium is gradually *taking form*. [=being built]
true to form ✧ Something or someone that is (or runs, holds, etc.) ***true to form*** behaves or proceeds in the usual and expected way. ▪ Her latest movie is/runs *true to form*. ▪ *True to form*, he was 20 minutes late for the meeting.

[2]**form** *verb* **forms; formed; form·ing**
1 [+ *obj*] : to cause (something) to have a particular shape or form ▪ She *formed* [=*made*] the dough into balls.
2 [+ *obj*] : to get, create, or develop (something) over a period of time ▪ *form* a habit ▪ The friendship that they *formed* in school lasted a lifetime. ▪ *form* an opinion ▪ Her early experiences played an important role in *forming* her personality. ▪ His ideas were not yet fully *formed*.
3 **a** : to begin to exist or to be seen [*no obj*] Fog often *forms* [=*develops*] in this valley. ▪ The drug can help prevent blood clots from *forming*. ▪ Beads of sweat *formed* on his forehead. ▪ A plan was gradually *forming* in my mind. [+ *obj*] A plan was gradually ***forming itself*** in my mind. **b** [*no obj*] : to gather together in a group ▪ An angry crowd was *forming* in the streets. ▪ insects *forming* into swarms
4 [+ *obj*] : to make or create (something) ▪ Water vapor condenses to *form* clouds. ▪ The two traditions have merged to *form* a new culture. ▪ A thin layer of plastic *forms* a protective coating over the surface. ▪ They have *formed* a council to investigate the incident. ▪ *form* a government/company/coalition/partnership ▪ Mix the wet and dry ingredients until they *form* a paste. ▪ Our footprints *formed* a lovely pattern in the wet sand.
5 [*linking verb*] : to be something ▪ one of several products that *form* [=*make up, constitute*] the foundation/basis of the company's success ▪ These principles *form* [=*are*] the essence of his philosophy. ▪ These books *form* the backbone of his collection.
6 [+ *obj*] : to be arranged in (a shape) ▪ The chairs *formed* a semicircle. : to move or be moved into (a shape) ▪ a substance capable of *forming* different shapes ▪ The dancers *formed* a line. = The dancers ***formed themselves*** into a line.

[1]**for·mal** /ˈfoɚməl/ *adj*
1 [*more* ~; *most* ~] : requiring or using serious and proper clothes and manners ▪ We attended a *formal* dinner. ▪ a *formal* occasion/event ▪ They are *formal* with people they don't know well.; *also* : suitable for a formal occasion ▪ a *formal* dress ▪ wearing *formal* clothes — opposite INFORMAL
2 [*more* ~; *most* ~] *of language* : suitable for serious or official speech and writing ▪ He spoke to them in *formal* Spanish. ▪ a *formal* word — opposite INFORMAL
3 **a** : made or done in an official and usually public way ▪ He wrote up a *formal* statement of his political beliefs. ▪ She received *formal* recognition for her volunteer work. ▪ He has made a *formal* announcement of his candidacy. **b** : done in a proper way according to the law ▪ a *formal* contract ▪ They seem to be interested in buying the house, but they haven't yet made a *formal* offer.
4 : arranged in a very orderly and regular way ▪ a *formal* garden — opposite INFORMAL
5 [*more* ~; *most* ~] : showing great concern for behaving in a proper and serious way ▪ He has a very stiff and *formal* manner.
6 : received in a school ▪ His *formal* education ended when he dropped out of high school. ▪ He lacks *formal* schooling.
7 : relating to the form of something (such as a piece of writing) rather than the content ▪ the *formal* aspects of a poem
– **for·mal·ly** *adv* ▪ dressed *formally* ▪ They behave very *formally* with people they don't know well. ▪ He *formally* announced his candidacy.

[2]**formal** *noun, pl* **-mals** [*count*] *US* : a social gathering (such as a dance) that requires formal dress and manners : a formal event

form·al·de·hyde /foɚˈmældəˌhaɪd/ *noun* [*noncount*] *chemistry* : a chemical that is used to prevent decay in the dead bodies of people and animals

for·mal·ism /ˈfoɚməˌlɪzəm/ *noun* [*noncount*] : a method, style, way of thinking, etc., that shows very careful attention to traditional forms and rules ▪ artistic/musical *formalism*
– **for·mal·ist** /ˈfoɚməlɪst/ *noun, pl* **-ists** [*count*] – **for·mal·ist** *or* **for·mal·is·tic** /ˌfoɚməˈlɪstɪk/ *adj* [*more* ~; *most* ~] ▪ *formalist* notions about art

for·mal·i·ty /foɚˈmæləti/ *noun, pl* **-ties**
1 : a formal quality [*noncount*] Her use of old-fashioned language lends an air of *formality* to her writing. ▪ He failed to appreciate the *formality* of the occasion. [*singular*] a *formality* of expression
2 [*count*] : something that is required or usual but that has little true meaning or importance ▪ They haven't approved the loan yet, but that's just a mere/pure *formality*.
3 [*count*] : a formal part, activity, etc. — usually plural ▪ the *formalities* of courtship ▪ Let's skip the *formalities* and get right down to business.

for·mal·ize *also Brit* **for·mal·ise** /ˈfoɚməˌlaɪz/ *verb* **-iz·es; -ized; -iz·ing** [+ *obj*] : to make (something) formal : to give proper or official form to (something) ▪ The company has *formalized* its hiring practices. ▪ Congress *formalized* the policy by making it law.
– **for·mal·i·za·tion** *also Brit* **for·mal·i·sa·tion** /ˌfoɚmələˈzeɪʃən, *Brit* ˌfɔːməˌlaɪˈzeɪʃən/ *noun* [*noncount*]

[1]**for·mat** /ˈfoɚˌmæt/ *noun, pl* **-mats**
1 : the form, design, or arrangement of something (such as a book, magazine, or television or radio program) [*count*] the book's large-print *format* ▪ The radio station recently changed its *format* from jazz to classical. [=the radio station now plays classical music instead of jazz] [*noncount*] The journals are available in electronic *format*.
2 : the way in which information is stored on a computer disk [*count*] different file *formats* [*noncount*] The file is saved in MP3 *format*.

²format *verb* **-mats; -mat·ted; -mat·ting** [+ *obj*]
1 : to arrange (something) in a particular format • The book is *formatted* in several different styles. • The data was improperly *formatted.*
2 : to prepare (a computer disk) so that it can store information in a particular format • *format* a floppy disk

for·ma·tion /foɚˈmeɪʃən/ *noun, pl* **-tions**
1 [*noncount*] **:** the act of forming or creating something • the *formation* [=*development*] of new ideas • The book explains the *formation* of the planets.
2 [*count*] **:** something that is formed or created • an interesting cloud *formation* • new word *formations* • rock *formations*
3 : an orderly arrangement or group of people, ships, or airplanes — often used after *in* [*noncount*] The soldiers were marching *in formation.* • jets flying *in formation* [*count*] The team ran on the field and lined up *in* a punt *formation.*

for·ma·tive /ˈfoɚmətɪv/ *adj* [*more* ~; *most* ~]
1 — used to describe the time when someone or something is growing or being formed • The movement was then still in its *formative* stages. • His family traveled widely during his *formative* years. [=when he was young]
2 : helping to develop something • This experience had a *formative* influence on his art. • a *formative* experience

for·mer /ˈfoɚmɚ/ *adj, always used before a noun*
1 — used to say what someone or something was in the past • a *former* congressman • her *former* husband • two *former* friends
2 : existing in the past • They hope to restore the old theater to its *former* glory. [=to make it as good as it was in the past] • She is now just a shadow of her *former* self. [=she is not the same person she once was]
the former **:** the first one of two things or people that have been mentioned • Of these two options, *the former* is less expensive, while the latter is less risky. • If offered a choice between death and exile, he said that he would choose *the former.* [=he would choose death] — compare ***the latter*** at LATTER

for·mer·ly /ˈfoɚmɚli/ *adv* **:** at an earlier time **:** in the past • He was *formerly* a congressman. • a privilege *formerly* [=*previously*] available only to the rich • Istanbul was *formerly* [=*once*] known as Constantinople.

form–fit·ting /ˈfoɚm,fɪtɪŋ/ *adj* **:** matching the shape of a person's body **:** fitting very tightly or closely • a *form-fitting* dress

For·mi·ca /foɚˈmaɪkə/ *trademark* — used for various plastic products that are used especially for covering surfaces

for·mi·da·ble /ˈfoɚmədəbəl, foɚˈmɪdəbəl/ *adj* [*more* ~; *most* ~]
1 : very powerful or strong **:** deserving serious attention and respect • a *formidable* enemy/opponent/weapon
2 : very difficult to deal with • The mountains were a *formidable* barrier. • a *formidable* challenge/task
3 : large or impressive in size or amount • He has mastered a *formidable* amount of material.
– for·mi·da·bly /ˈfoɚmədəbli, foɚˈmɪdəbli/ *adv* • a *formidably* long list

form·less /ˈfoɚmləs/ *adj* **:** having no regular form or shape • a *formless* [=*shapeless*] pile
– form·less·ness *noun* [*noncount*]

form letter *noun, pl* **~ -ters** [*count*] **:** a letter that has a standard form and is sent to many people • The bank sent out thousands of *form letters* offering its credit card.

for·mu·la /ˈfoɚmjələ/ *noun, pl* **-las** *also* **-lae** /-ˌliː/
1 [*count*] **a :** a plan or method for doing, making, or achieving something • His investment strategy is based on a simple *formula.* • This has proven to be a winning *formula.* — often + *for* • a *formula for* success/happiness • There is no ***magic formula*** [=no simple and certain method] *for* achieving success in the business world. **b :** a list of the ingredients used for making something (such as a medicine or a drink) • The product is made using a secret *formula* that the company refuses to reveal.
2 [*count*] **a** *mathematics* **:** a general fact or rule expressed in letters and symbols • The *formula* for the area of a rectangle is l X w. [=length times width] **b** *chemistry* **:** a series of letters, numbers, and symbols showing the chemicals that a compound is made of • The *formula* for water is H_2O. • chemical *formulas*
3 [*noncount*] *US* **:** a liquid that usually contains milk and that is used for feeding a baby • infants drinking *formula* instead of their mother's milk
4 [*count*] **a :** a set of words that are commonly used in a way that does not seem original or sincere **:** a conventional statement • Politicians often resort to familiar *formulas* when discussing controversial issues. **b :** a common way of creating or telling a story in a movie, book, etc. • the narrative *formula* offered in so many movies • All her books are written according to a familiar *formula.*

for·mu·la·ic /ˌfoɚmjəˈlejɪk/ *adj* [*more* ~; *most* ~]
1 : produced according to a formula **:** not new or original • a *formulaic* movie/novel/plot
2 : commonly used • a *formulaic* [=*set, fixed*] phrase such as "Sincerely yours" at the end of a letter

for·mu·late /ˈfoɚmjəˌleɪt/ *verb* **-lates; -lat·ed; -lat·ing** [+ *obj*] **:** to create, invent, or produce (something) by careful thought and effort • A long-range plan is being *formulated.* [=*devised*] • *formulate* a rule/theory/principle • a carefully *formulated* response • a plastic specially *formulated* to resist high temperatures
– for·mu·la·tion /ˌfoɚmjəˈleɪʃən/ *noun, pl* **-tions** [*count, noncount*] • the *formulation* of a new drug • a drug available in several *formulations* **– for·mu·la·tor** /ˈfoɚmjəˌleɪtɚ/ *noun, pl* **-tors** [*count*] • Darwinism was named after its *formulator,* Charles Darwin.

for·ni·cate /ˈfoɚnəˌkeɪt/ *verb* **-cates; -cat·ed; -cat·ing** [*no obj*] *formal + disapproving* **:** to have sexual intercourse ✧ *Fornicate* refers to sexual intercourse that occurs between people who are not married to each other. It is a word that is associated with legal language and the language of the Bible.
– for·ni·ca·tion /ˌfoɚnəˈkeɪʃən/ *noun* [*noncount*] • laws forbidding *fornication* • commit *fornication* **– for·ni·ca·tor** /ˈfoɚnəˌkeɪtɚ/ *noun, pl* **-tors** [*count*]

for–prof·it /ˈfoɚˈprɑːfət/ *adj, always used before a noun* **:** existing or done for the purpose of making a profit • a *for-profit* company/venture

for·sake /fɚˈseɪk/ *verb* **-sakes; -sook** /-ˈsʊk/; **-sak·en** /-ˈseɪkən/; **-sak·ing** [+ *obj*] **:** to give up or leave (someone or something) entirely • All my friends have *forsaken* [=*abandoned*] me. • She *forsook* [=*left*] acting for a teaching career.

for·swear /foɚˈsweɚ/ *verb* **-swears; -swore** /-ˈswoɚ/; **-sworn** /-ˈswoɚn/; **-swear·ing** [+ *obj*] *formal* **:** to promise to give up (something) or to stop doing (something) • She *forswore* her allegiance to the old regime. • He *foreswore* cigarettes/smoking as his New Year's resolution.

for·syth·ia /fɚˈsɪθijə, *Brit* fəˈsaɪθiə/ *noun, pl* **-ias** *also* **-ia** [*count, noncount*] **:** a type of bush that produces bright yellow flowers in the early spring

fort /ˈfoɚt/ *noun, pl* **forts** [*count*] **:** a strong building or group of buildings where soldiers live • They captured the *fort* after a long battle.
hold the fort *or US* ***hold down the fort*** **:** to be in charge of a place while the person who is usually in charge is away • You can stay here and *hold the fort* while I go to the store.

¹forte /ˈfoɚt, ˈfoɚˌteɪ/ *noun, pl* **fortes** [*count*] **:** something that a person does well • Drawing was always your *forte.* [=*strength*]

²for·te /ˈfoɚˌteɪ/ *adv, music* **:** in a loud manner • violins playing a passage *forte* — abbr. *f*
– forte *adj* • a *forte* passage

forth /ˈfoɚθ/ *adv, literary*
1 : out into notice or view **:** OUT • a flow of lava bursting *forth* from the earth • The snow is gone and the flowers are ready to spring *forth.* • He went *forth* to spread the news.
2 : onward or forward in time or place • She stretched *forth* her hands in prayer. • ***from that day forth*** [=from that time onward]
and so forth see ¹SO
bring forth see BRING
call forth see ¹CALL
hold forth see ¹HOLD
put forth see ¹PUT
sally forth see ²SALLY
set forth see ¹SET
— see also BACK AND FORTH

forth·com·ing /foɚθˈkʌmɪŋ/ *adj*
1 *always used before a noun* **:** appearing, happening, or arriving soon • the *forthcoming* [=*approaching*] holidays • He read an excerpt from his *forthcoming* [=soon to be published] autobiography.
2 *not used before a noun* **:** readily available • No help has been *forthcoming* from the government. [=the government has not provided any help]
3 *not used before a noun* [*more* ~; *most* ~] **:** honest and open • He was more *forthcoming* about his past than they expect-

ed. ▪ She has been less than *forthcoming* about her involvement in the scandal.

forth·right /ˈfoɚθˌraɪt/ *adj* [*more* ~; *most* ~] **:** honest and direct **:** providing answers or information in a very clear and direct way ▪ a *forthright* answer/person
– forth·right·ly *adv* ▪ He explained his opinions publicly and *forthrightly*. **– forth·right·ness** *noun* [*noncount*]

forth·with /foɚθˈwɪθ/ *adv, formal* **:** without delay **:** IMMEDIATELY ▪ The court ordered the company to cease operations *forthwith*.

for·ti·fi·ca·tion /ˌfoɚtəfəˈkeɪʃən/ *noun, pl* **-tions**
1 [*noncount*] **:** the act of building military defenses to protect a place against attack **:** the act of fortifying something ▪ They began the *fortification* and reconstruction of the city.
2 [*count*] **:** a structure (such as a wall or tower) that is built to protect a place — usually plural ▪ The city was protected by massive *fortifications*.

for·ti·fy /ˈfoɚtəˌfaɪ/ *verb* **-fies; -fied; -fy·ing** [+ *obj*]
1 : to strengthen (a place) by building military defenses (such as walls, trenches, etc.) ▪ *fortify* a city against attack ▪ a heavily *fortified* town/border ▪ a city *fortified* by high walls
2 a : to make (someone or something) stronger ▪ *fortify* [=*strengthen*] the body against illness ▪ Support for his theories has been *fortified* by the results of these experiments. **b :** to make (yourself) feel stronger or less fearful ▪ He took a deep breath to *fortify* himself before stepping onto the stage.
3 : to improve the usefulness or quality of (something) by adding something to it **:** ENRICH ▪ *fortify* soil with fertilizer ▪ milk *fortified* with vitamin D

for·tis·si·mo /foɚˈtɪsəˌmoʊ/ *adv, music* **:** very loudly ▪ violins playing *fortissimo*
– fortissimo *adj* ▪ a *fortissimo* passage

for·ti·tude /ˈfoɚtəˌtuːd, *Brit* ˈfɔːtəˌtjuːd/ *noun* [*noncount*] *formal* **:** mental strength and courage that allows someone to face danger, pain, etc. ▪ She has endured disappointments with *fortitude* and patience. ✧ The phrase ***intestinal fortitude*** is used informally in U.S. English as a humorous replacement for "guts," which means "courage." ▪ They accused him of lacking *intestinal fortitude*. [=of being a coward]

fort·night /ˈfoɚtˌnaɪt/ *noun, pl* **-nights** [*count*] *chiefly Brit* **:** a period of 14 days **:** two weeks ▪ They stayed with us for a *fortnight*.

fort·night·ly /ˈfoɚtˌnaɪtli/ *adj, chiefly Brit* **:** happening or appearing once every two weeks ▪ a *fortnightly* [=*biweekly*] meeting/magazine
– fortnightly *adv* ▪ It happens *fortnightly*.

for·tress /ˈfoɚtrəs/ *noun, pl* **-tress·es** [*count*] **:** a place that is protected against attack **:** a fortified place ▪ a mountaintop *fortress*
– for·tress·like /ˈfoɚtrəsˌlaɪk/ *adj*

for·tu·i·tous /foɚˈtuːwətəs, *Brit* fɔːˈtjuːətəs/ *adj* [*more* ~; *most* ~] *formal*
1 : happening by chance ▪ His presence there was entirely *fortuitous*. ▪ a *fortuitous* circumstance/discovery
2 : having or showing good luck **:** FORTUNATE ▪ You could not have arrived at a more *fortuitous* time.

> ***usage*** Sense 2 of *fortuitous* is commonly used, but many people regard it as an error.

– for·tu·i·tous·ly *adv*

for·tu·nate /ˈfoɚtʃənət/ *adj* [*more* ~; *most* ~]
1 : having good luck **:** enjoying good fortune **:** LUCKY ▪ How *fortunate* we were to find that restaurant! ▪ They were (very) *fortunate* to have his help. ▪ It's *fortunate* (for us) that these documents have been preserved. ▪ We're *fortunate* in having these opportunities. = We're *fortunate* to have these opportunities. ▪ We should try to help others who are less *fortunate* than ourselves. ▪ They were *fortunate* (enough) to escape injury when their car crashed. = It was *fortunate* that they escaped injury when their car crashed.
2 : coming or happening because of good luck ▪ a *fortunate* discovery/outcome — opposite UNFORTUNATE

for·tun·ate·ly /ˈfoɚtʃənətli/ *adv* [*more* ~; *most* ~] — used to say that something good or lucky has happened ▪ *Fortunately* [=*luckily*], the plane was able to land safely. ▪ *Fortunately* (for us), these documents have been preserved. ▪ No one was injured, *fortunately*. — opposite UNFORTUNATELY

for·tune /ˈfoɚtʃən/ *noun, pl* **-tunes**
1 a [*count*] **:** a very large amount of money — usually singular ▪ He won/made a *fortune* (by) gambling. ▪ Their house is worth a *fortune*. ▪ They spent a ***small fortune*** [=a surprisingly or unexpectedly large amount of money] on redecorating their house. ▪ She ***made her/a fortune in*** real estate. **b** [*noncount*] *somewhat formal* **:** a great amount of money or possessions **:** WEALTH ▪ He is a man of considerable *fortune*. [=he is a wealthy man] ▪ He hoped to achieve fame and *fortune*.
2 [*noncount*] **:** something that happens by chance **:** LUCK ▪ Our meeting here was a real stroke of (good) *fortune*. ▪ They had the good *fortune* to escape injury when their car crashed.
3 *fortunes* [*plural*] **:** the good and bad things that happen to someone ▪ The book follows the *fortunes* of two families through the years. ▪ the *fortunes* of war
4 [*count*] **:** the future that someone or something will have ▪ She said that she could tell my *fortune*. [=could tell what would happen to me in the future] ▪ I had my *fortune* told.
— see also SOLDIER OF FORTUNE

fortune cookie *noun, pl* ~ **-ies** [*count*] **:** a thin cookie served in Chinese restaurants that contains a slip of paper on which a message (such as a prediction about your future) is printed

fortune hunter *noun, pl* ~ **-ters** [*count*] **:** a person who is trying to become very wealthy especially by marrying a wealthy person

for·tune–tell·er /ˈfoɚtʃənˌtɛlɚ/ *noun, pl* **-ers** [*count*] **:** a person who claims to use special powers to tell what will happen to someone in the future **:** a person who tells people's fortunes
– for·tune–tell·ing /ˈfoɚtʃənˌtɛlɪŋ/ *noun* [*noncount*]

for·ty /ˈfoɚti/ *noun, pl* **for·ties**
1 [*count*] **:** the number 40
2 *forties* [*plural*] **a :** the numbers ranging from 40 to 49 ▪ The temperature outside is in the high *forties*. **b :** a set of years ending in digits ranging from 40 to 49 ▪ She is in her *forties*. ▪ She found some old record albums from the *forties*. [=from 1940–1949]
– for·ti·eth /ˈfoɚtijəθ/ *noun, pl* **-eths** [*count*] ▪ one *fortieth* of the total **– fortieth** *adj* ▪ his *fortieth* birthday **– forty** *adj* ▪ *forty* days **– forty** *pronoun* ▪ *forty* of her classmates **– for·ty·ish** /ˈfoɚtijɪʃ/ *adj* ▪ He was tall, *fortyish* [=about 40 years old], and had glasses and brown hair.

for·ty–five /ˌfoɚtiˈfaɪv/ *noun, pl* **-fives** [*count*]
1 : a small gun **:** a type of pistol — usually written .45
2 : a small record with one song on each side — usually written 45

forty winks *noun* [*plural*] *informal* **:** a short sleep **:** a brief nap ▪ I had time to catch *forty winks* before the flight.

fo·rum /ˈforəm/ *noun, pl* **forums** *also* **fo·ra** /ˈforə/ [*count*]
1 : a meeting at which a subject can be discussed ▪ *Forums* were held to determine how to handle the situation. ▪ The town has scheduled a public *forum* to discuss the proposal. ▪ an open *forum*
2 : a place or opportunity for discussing a subject ▪ The club provides a *forum* for people who share an interest in local history. ▪ an online *forum*
3 : a large public place in an ancient Roman city that was used as the center of business

[1]for·ward /ˈfoɚwɚd/ *also chiefly Brit* **for·wards** /ˈfoɚˌwɚdz/ *adv*
1 : toward the front **:** to or toward what is ahead or in front ▪ a sudden movement *forward* ▪ moved/pushed backward and *forward* ▪ Her long hair fell *forward* as she bent to tie her shoes. ▪ He pushed the throttle *forward*. ▪ She took a small step *forward*.
2 : toward the future ▪ Remember to set the clock *forward* [=*ahead*] (by) an hour. ▪ The narrative moves backward and *forward* in time. ▪ from that time *forward* ▪ Economists expect these trends to ***carry forward*** [=continue in the same way] into the next quarter.
3 : to or toward a more advanced state or condition ▪ Our plans are moving *forward*. [=our plans are progressing] ▪ The technology has taken a big step/leap *forward*. ▪ I don't want to ***go forward*** [=*proceed*] without a contract. ▪ We're *going forward* with the sale of the house. [=continuing to make the sale happen; not stopping the sale]
bring forward see BRING
come forward see [1]COME
forward of formal **:** in a position that is ahead of (something) **:** in front of (something) ▪ The valves are located just *forward of* the fuel tanks.
know something backward and forward see [1]KNOW
look forward to see [1]LOOK
put forward see [1]PUT
put your best foot forward see [1]FOOT

F

²forward *adj*
1 *always used before a noun* **:** near or belonging to the front part of something • the *forward* deck of a boat
2 *always used before a noun* **a :** moving or directed ahead or toward the front • a sudden *forward* movement • a *forward* somersault **b :** moving toward the future or toward a more advanced state or condition • the *forward* movement of history/technology
3 [*more* ~; *most* ~] **:** too confident or direct in social situations • a *forward* [=*brash*] manner/question • a very *forward* young woman
– for·ward·ness *noun* [*noncount*] • the *forwardness* of his manner/question

³forward *verb* **-wards; -ward·ed; -ward·ing** [+ *obj*]
1 a : to send (something you have received, such as a letter) to someone else • Your letter will be *forwarded* to the appropriate department. • *forward* an e-mail (message) to someone = *forward* someone an e-mail (message) **b :** to send (something that has arrived, such as a letter) to another place • Please *forward* my mail to my new address. — see also FORWARDING ADDRESS
2 : to help (something) make progress or continue to a more advanced state • He's always happy to *forward* [=*promote, advance*] a friend's career.
– see also FAST-FORWARD

⁴forward *noun, pl* **-wards** [*count*] *sports* **:** a player who plays near the opponent's goal • a soccer/basketball/hockey *forward*

forwarding address *noun, pl* ~ **-dress·es** [*count*] **:** an address that you give to someone when you move to a different place so that any mail that comes to your old address can be sent to you • She didn't leave a *forwarding address*.

forw·ard–look·ing /ˈfoɚwɚdˌlʊkɪŋ/ *adj* [*more* ~; *most* ~] *approving* **:** relating to the future • *forward-looking* [=*innovative*] ideas/plans/products **:** planning for the future • *forward-looking* [=*farsighted*] engineers/politicians/industrialists — opposite BACKWARD-LOOKING

forward pass *noun, pl* ~ **passes** [*count*] *American football* **:** a pass made in the direction of the opponents' goal

for·ward–think·ing /ˈfoɚwɚdˌθɪŋkɪŋ/ *adj* [*more* ~; *most* ~] **:** thinking about the future **:** FORWARD-LOOKING • a *forward-thinking* company

fos·sil /ˈfɑːsəl/ *noun, pl* **-sils** [*count*]
1 : something (such as a leaf, skeleton, or footprint) that is from a plant or animal which lived in ancient times and that you can see in some rocks • a dinosaur *fossil* — sometimes used before another noun • *fossil* [=*fossilized*] footprints
2 *informal* **:** a person whose ideas are very old-fashioned or out-of-date • He says the school's directors are a bunch of old *fossils*. [=*fogies*]

fossil fuel *noun, pl* ~ **fuels :** a fuel (such as coal, oil, or natural gas) that is formed in the earth from dead plants or animals [*count*] oil and other *fossil fuels* [*noncount*] sources of *fossil fuel*

fos·sil·ize *also Brit* **fos·sil·ise** /ˈfɑːsəˌlaɪz/ *verb* **-iz·es; -ized; -iz·ing :** to become a fossil or to cause (something) to become a fossil [*no obj*] Few animals ever *fossilize*. [+ *obj*] The mud helped to preserve and *fossilize* the wood.
– fos·sil·i·za·tion *also Brit* **fos·sil·i·sa·tion** /ˌfɑːsələˈzeɪʃən, *Brit* ˌfɒsəˌlaɪˈzeɪʃən/ *noun* [*noncount*]

fossilized *also Brit* **fos·sil·ised** *adj*
1 : having been changed into a fossil • *fossilized* dinosaur eggs • *fossilized* bones
2 *disapproving* **:** very old-fashioned and unlikely to change • *fossilized* attitudes about the rights of women

¹fos·ter /ˈfɑːstɚ/ *verb* **-ters; -tered; -ter·ing**
1 [+ *obj*] **:** to help (something) grow or develop • We are trying to *foster* [=*encourage, promote*] a sense of community. • Such conditions *foster* the spread of the disease.
2 : to provide the care that a parent usually gives to a child **:** to be or become the foster parent of a child [+ *obj*] Would you consider *fostering* a child? [*no obj*] (*chiefly Brit*) Would you consider *fostering*?

²foster *adj, always used before a noun* — used to describe a situation in which for a period of time a child lives with and is cared for by people who are not the child's parents • They are *foster* parents to three *foster* children. • She's in ***foster care***. = She's in a ***foster home***. [=she is living in a home with and being taken care of by foster parents]

fought *past tense and past participle of* ¹FIGHT

¹foul /ˈfawəl/ *adj* **foul·er; -est** [*or more* ~; *most* ~]
1 : very unpleasant to taste or smell • the *foul* odor of rotten eggs • *foul* breath/air • The medicine left a *foul* taste in my mouth. • a *foul*-smelling chemical
2 : morally bad **:** very evil • a *foul* crime
3 : very bad or unpleasant • He was in a *foul* [=angry] mood. • The weather has been *foul* all week. • They do their job in fair weather and *foul*. [=in good weather and bad weather]
4 : indecent and offensive • *foul* [=*dirty*] language • She has a ***foul mouth***. [=she uses foul language; she speaks in an indecent and offensive way] — see also FOUL-MOUTHED
5 : very unfair **:** not morally or socially acceptable • He's determined to get what he wants, whether by fair means or *foul*. — see also FOUL PLAY
6 *baseball* **:** outside the area between the foul lines • *foul* territory • a *foul* grounder ✧ A ***foul ball*** is a batted ball that lands in the area outside the foul lines. — compare ¹FAIR 8
fall foul of **:** to get into trouble because of (the law, a rule, etc.) • After leaving school she *fell foul of* the law. [=she got into trouble with the law; she was arrested for committing a crime] • companies that *fall foul of* labor laws
– foul·ly *adv* • He was *foully* [=*brutally*] murdered. **– foul·ness** *noun* [*noncount*] • the *foulness* of the water/air/odor • the *foulness* of his crimes/mood

²foul *noun, pl* **fouls** [*count*]
1 *sports* **:** an action that is against the rules and for which a player is given a penalty • She committed three *fouls*. = She was charged with three *fouls*. • a basketball player in ***foul trouble*** [=a player who has committed several fouls; a player who is close to fouling out] — see also PERSONAL FOUL, PROFESSIONAL FOUL, TECHNICAL FOUL, *foul out* at ³FOUL
2 *baseball* **:** a batted ball that lands outside the foul lines **:** a foul ball • He hit several *fouls* in a row. — see also *foul out* at ³FOUL
cry foul see ¹CRY

³foul *verb* **fouls; fouled; foul·ing**
1 [+ *obj*] **:** to make (a substance, place, etc.) dirty • pollutants that *foul* the air • *fouling* [=*befouling*] the sacred waters
2 *sports* **a** [*no obj*] **:** to commit a foul • She *fouled* on her first long jump attempt. **b** [+ *obj*] **:** to commit a foul against (another player) • The other team has *fouled* him [=hit him, held him, etc.] repeatedly. • He was *fouled* as he attempted the shot.
3 [+ *obj*] *baseball* **:** to hit (a pitched ball) so that it lands outside the foul lines • He kept *fouling* pitches/balls into the stands. — often + *off* • He *fouled off* several pitches in a row.
4 [+ *obj*] **:** to become twisted around (something) so that it cannot move, be used, etc. • The anchor's rope *fouled* the propeller.
foul out [*phrasal verb*] **1** *basketball* **:** to be forced to leave a game because you have made too many fouls • She *fouled out* (of the game) without scoring a point. **2** *baseball, of a batter* **:** to make an out by hitting a foul fly ball ball that is caught by a fielder • The batter *fouled out* to the first baseman.
foul up [*phrasal verb*] *informal* **1** ***foul (something) up*** **:** to ruin or spoil (something) • The weather has *fouled up* our plans. **:** to ruin or spoil (something) by making a mistake or being careless • She *fouled up* [=*ruined, messed up*] our plans by forgetting to make the reservations. **2** ***foul up*** **:** to make mistakes **:** to fail at something because you have made a mistake or been careless • Whenever I try to be clever, I usually *foul up*. [=*mess up*] — see also FOUL-UP

foul line *noun, pl* ~ **lines** [*count*]
1 *baseball* **:** either one of two straight lines that go from home plate through first and third base on to the edge of the outfield • The ball landed just inside the right-field *foul line*.
2 *basketball* **:** a line from which a player shoots free throws

foul–mouthed /ˈfaulˌmauθt/ *adj* [*more* ~; *most* ~] **:** using indecent or offensive language **:** having a foul mouth • *foul-mouthed* students

foul play *noun* [*noncount*]
1 : criminal violence or murder • She is still missing, and the police now suspect that she may have been a victim of *foul play*. [=that she may have been murdered or harmed in some way] • There is no evidence of *foul play*.
2 : unfair or dishonest acts • The company's deal with the government has brought ***cries/accusations of foul play*** [=claims that there have been unfair or dishonest acts] from its competitors.

foul shot *noun, pl* ~ **shots** [*count*] *basketball* **:** FREE THROW

foul–up /ˈfaulˌʌp/ *noun, pl* **-ups** [*count*] *informal* **:** a problem caused by someone making a mistake or being careless •

They had to deal with yet another administrative *foul-up.* — see also *foul up* at [3]FOUL

[1]**found** *past tense and past participle of* [1]FIND

[2]**found** /ˈfaʊnd/ *verb* **founds; found·ed; found·ing** [+ *obj*]

1 : to begin or create (something that is meant to last for a long time) : ESTABLISH • *found* a colony/museum/college • The college was *founded* in 1793.

2 : to provide support for something — usually used as *(be) founded* • His suspicions *were founded* [=*based*] on nothing more than rumor. — see also UNFOUNDED, WELL-FOUNDED

foun·da·tion /faʊnˈdeɪʃən/ *noun, pl* **-tions**

1 [*count*] **a** : a usually stone or concrete structure that supports a building from underneath • The inspector discovered a crack in the house's *foundation.* • pour/lay/dig the *foundation* **b** : something (such as an idea, a principle, or a fact) that provides support for something • He insists that these charges are without *foundation.* [=are unfounded] • These charges have no *foundation* in fact. [=there are no facts that support these charges] • The book explains the moral *foundations* on which her political career was built. • These problems threaten the very *foundations* of modern society. • The scandal has shaken the government to its *foundations.* • Her early research ***laid the foundation*** [=provided the basis] for many important medical discoveries.

2 [*count*] : an organization that is created and supported with money that people give in order to do something that helps society • They established a *foundation* to help orphaned children. • set up a *foundation* • a charitable/nonprofit/private *foundation*

3 [*count, noncount*] : a special cream that is the color of your skin and that you spread on your face and neck before putting on other makeup

4 [*noncount*] : the act of founding something • the *foundation* of a new school

[1]**found·er** /ˈfaʊndɚ/ *noun, pl* **-ers** [*count*] : a person who creates or establishes something that is meant to last for a long time (such as a business or school) : a person who founds something • the *founder* of a newspaper empire • He's the son of the company's *founder.*

[2]**foun·der** /ˈfaʊndɚ/ *verb* **-ers; -dered; -der·ing** [*no obj*]

1 : to experience failure : to be unsuccessful : FAIL • Her career *foundered,* and she moved from job to job for several years. • Their marriage is *foundering.* • trying to save a *foundering* career/marriage

2 *of a boat or ship* : to fill with water and sink • a *foundering* ship

founding father *noun, pl* ~ **-thers** [*count*]

1 : a person who helps to create or establish something : a person who founds something • He is now recognized as one of the *founding fathers* [=*founders*] of the environmental movement.

2 *or* ***Founding Father*** : a man who had an important part in creating the government of the U.S.; *specifically* : a member of the American Constitutional Convention of 1787 • a tribute to Benjamin Franklin, Thomas Jefferson, and the other *Founding Fathers*

founding member *noun, pl* ~ **-bers** [*count*] : an original member of a group (such as a club or corporation) — called also (*US*) *charter member,* (*Brit*) *founder member*

found·ling /ˈfaʊndlɪŋ/ *noun, pl* **-lings** [*count*] : a baby that is found after being left by its parents

found·ry /ˈfaʊndri/ *noun, pl* **-ries** [*count*] : a building or factory where metals are produced

fount /ˈfaʊnt/ *noun, pl* **founts** [*count*]

1 *somewhat old-fashioned + literary* : the source *of* something • Our tour guide was a *fount of* information about the city's history. • a *fount of* knowledge/justice/wisdom • (*humorous*) You know the answer to that one too? Why, you're a regular *fount of* wisdom. [=you know everything]

2 *Brit* : [2]FONT

foun·tain /ˈfaʊntn̩/ *noun, pl* **-tains** [*count*]

1 **a** : a device or structure that sends a stream of water into the air in a garden, park, etc. • an elaborate marble *fountain* • The crowd gathered around the *fountain* in the plaza.; *also* : the water that rises from a fountain • a *fountain* of water — see also DRINKING FOUNTAIN, SODA FOUNTAIN **b** : something that rises into the air like a fountain of water • a *fountain* of flame/sparks

2 : the source *of* something • She is a *fountain* [=*fount*] *of* knowledge/wisdom. • an endless *fountain of* inspiration

foun·tain·head /ˈfaʊntn̩ˌhɛd/ *noun, pl* **-heads** [*count*] *literary* : the origin or source of something • the *fountainhead* of the faith

fountain of youth *noun, pl* **foun·tains of youth** [*count*]

1 *or* ***Fountain of Youth*** *in stories and legends* : a fountain with magic water ✧ According to legend, anyone who drinks water from the Fountain of Youth will live forever.

2 : a source of the kind of energy or health that young people usually have • Exercise is good for you, but it's not a perfect *fountain of youth.*

fountain

fountain pen *noun, pl* ~ **pens** [*count*] : a pen with ink inside that flows to a special metal tip (called a nib)

four /ˈfoɚ/ *noun, pl* **fours**

1 [*count*] : the number 4

2 [*count*] : the fourth in a set or series • the *four* of hearts

3 [*noncount*] : four o'clock • "What time is it?" "It's *four.*" • I leave each day at *four.*

— see also ALL FOURS

— **four** *adj* • waiting for *four* hours — **four** *pronoun* • *Four* (of them) are broken.

4x4 *also* **four–by–four** /ˈfoɚbaɪˌfoɚ/ *noun, pl* **4x4s** *also* **four–by–fours** [*count*] *US* : a vehicle (such as a truck) that has four wheels and four-wheel drive

four·fold /ˈfoɚˌfould/ *adj* : four times as great or as many • There has been a *fourfold* increase in membership this year.

— **fourfold** *adv* • Membership has increased *fourfold.*

4–H /ˈfoɚˈeɪʧ/ *adj* : of or relating to a government program in the U.S. that teaches farming skills and good citizenship to young people • a *4-H* club

four–letter word *noun, pl* ~ **words** [*count*]

1 : an offensive word and especially an offensive word that has four letters : DIRTY WORD 1 • a book that contains a lot of *four-letter words*

2 : a word, subject, or idea that is disliked by some people : DIRTY WORD 2 • "Tax" is a *four-letter word* as far as he's concerned.

401(k) /ˌfoɚˌouˌwʌnˈkeɪ/ *noun, pl* **401(k)s** [*count*] *US* : a method by which the workers in a company can save money for their retirement by having an amount of money saved from their paychecks over a long period of time

four–post·er /ˌfoɚˈpoustɚ/ *noun, pl* **-ers** [*count*] : a bed with tall posts at each of its four corners — called also *four-poster bed*

four·score /ˈfoɚˈskoɚ/ *adj, formal + old-fashioned* : EIGHTY • "*Fourscore* and seven [=87] years ago . . ." —Abraham Lincoln, Gettysburg Address (1863)

four·some /ˈfoɚsəm/ *noun, pl* **-somes** [*count*] : a group of four people or things • a *foursome* of golfers = a golfing *foursome*

four·square /ˈfoɚˈskweɚ/ *adj*

1 : having a square shape • *foursquare* houses/buildings

2 [*more* ~; *most* ~] *formal* : strong and direct : FORTHRIGHT • her *foursquare* support for the proposal

— **foursquare** *adv* • They are lined up *foursquare* [=*firmly, forthrightly*] against him. • She came out *foursquare* [=*strongly*] in support of the proposal.

four–star /ˈfoɚˈstaɚ/ *adj, always used before a noun* : of very high quality • a *four-star* hotel/restaurant

four·teen /foɚˈtiːn/ *noun, pl* **-teens** [*count*] : the number 14

— **fourteen** *adj* • *fourteen* days — **fourteen** *pronoun* • *Fourteen* (of them) are gone. — **four·teenth** /foɚˈtiːnθ/ *noun, pl* **-teenths** [*count*] • The bill is due on the *fourteenth* (of the month). • one *fourteenth* of the total — **fourteenth** *adj* • I finished (the race) in *fourteenth* place. — **fourteenth** *adv* • I finished *fourteenth* in the race. • the nation's *fourteenth* largest city

[1]**fourth** /ˈfoɚθ/ *noun, pl* **fourths**

1 [*singular*] : number four in a series • I'll be flying in on the *fourth.* [=the fourth day of the month] • He got a base hit in the *fourth.* [=the fourth inning]

2 [*count*] : one of four equal parts of something • cut the cake into *fourths* • She drank a *fourth* of the bottle.

3 [*noncount*] : the fourth forward gear or speed of a car, truck, etc. • He shifted into *fourth.*

4 ***the Fourth*** : INDEPENDENCE DAY • watching fireworks on *the Fourth*

[2]fourth *adj*
1 : occupying the number four position in a series • on the *fourth* day • the book's *fourth* edition • her *fourth* goal of the season
2 — used to refer to one of the forward gears or speeds of a vehicle • *fourth* gear
– **fourth** *adv* • She finished *fourth* in the race. • the *fourth* highest mountain

fourth estate *or* **Fourth Estate** *noun [singular]* : the people and organizations who report the news : journalists as a group • a member of ***the Fourth Estate***

Fourth of July *noun [singular]* : INDEPENDENCE DAY

four–wheel /ˈfoɚˌwiːl/ *also* **four–wheeled** /ˈfoɚˌwiːld/ *adj, always used before a noun* : having four wheels • a *four-wheel* vehicle

four–wheel drive *noun [noncount]* : a system that applies engine power directly to all four wheels of a vehicle • a truck equipped with *four-wheel drive*

fowl /ˈfawəl/ *noun, pl* **fowl** *also* **fowls**
1 a *[count]* : a bird (such as a chicken) that is raised for food — usually plural • raising domestic *fowl* • The young *fowl/fowls* are fully independent when they hatch. **b** *[noncount]* : the meat of such a bird used as food • roasted *fowl*
2 *[count] old-fashioned + humorous* : a bird of any kind • I spotted a long-legged *fowl* by the water's edge. — see also GUINEA FOWL, WATERFOWL, WILDFOWL
neither fish nor fowl see [1]FISH

[1]fox /ˈfɑːks/ *noun, pl* **fox·es**
1 a *[count]* : a small wild animal that is related to dogs and that has a long pointed nose and a bushy tail **b** *[noncount]* : the fur of a fox — often used before another noun • a *fox* coat
2 *[count]* : a clever person • He's a wily/sly old *fox*. • She's ***crazy like a fox***. [=she seems foolish or strange but is actually very clever]
3 *[count] US, informal* : an attractive person • She's a real *fox*. [=she's a very attractive woman]

fox

[2]fox *verb* **foxes; foxed; fox·ing** *[+ obj] chiefly Brit*
1 : to trick or fool (someone) • They *foxed* me into telling the secret. — compare OUTFOX
2 : to confuse (someone) • The problem had us *foxed*!

fox·glove /ˈfɑːksˌglʌv/ *noun, pl* **-gloves** *[count]* : a tall plant that has many white or purple bell-shaped flowers growing on its stem

fox·hole /ˈfɑːksˌhoʊl/ *noun, pl* **-holes** *[count]* : a hole dug for a soldier to sit or lie in for protection from the enemy

fox·hound /ˈfɑːksˌhaʊnd/ *noun, pl* **-hounds** *[count]* : a type of quick and strong dog that is often trained to hunt foxes

fox·hunt·ing /ˈfɑːksˌhʌntɪŋ/ *noun [noncount]* : an activity in which people riding horses hunt foxes by using specially trained dogs

fox terrier *noun, pl* **~ -ers** *[count]* : a type of small and lively dog

fox–trot /ˈfɑːksˌtrɑːt/ *noun, pl* **-trots** *[count]* : a formal dance that includes slow walking steps and quick running steps; *also* : the music for this dance • The band played a *fox-trot*.

foxy /ˈfɑːksi/ *adj* **fox·i·er; -est**
1 : resembling or suggesting a fox • a narrow *foxy* face
2 : very clever • a *foxy* politician/strategy
3 *US, informal* : physically attractive : SEXY • a *foxy* lady

foy·er /ˈfojɚ, ˈfoɪˌeɪ/ *noun, pl* **-ers** *[count]*
1 : an open area in a public building (such as a hotel or theater) near the entrance : a lobby or entrance hall
2 *US* : an open area near the entrance in someone's home

fr. *abbr* **1** father **2** franc **3** from

Fr. *abbr* **1** France; French **2** Friday

fra·cas /ˈfreɪkəs, *Brit* ˈfræˌkɑː/ *noun, pl* **fra·cas·es** *(US) or Brit* **fracas** *[count]* : a noisy argument or fight — usually singular • a drunken *fracas* • a minor *fracas*

frac·tion /ˈfrækʃən/ *noun, pl* **-tions** *[count]*
1 *mathematics* : a number (such as ½ or ¾) which indicates that one number is being divided by another; *also* : a number (such as 3.323) that consists of a whole number and a decimal
2 : a part or amount of something • a *fraction* of an inch/second • We've described only a small *fraction* [=*portion*] of the available options. • The new program will provide similar benefits at a *fraction* of the cost (of the old one). [=at much less cost; for much less money] • The new technology allows us to complete the job in a *fraction* of the time [=in much less time] it formerly took.

frac·tion·al /ˈfrækʃənl/ *adj*
1 *mathematics* : of or relating to a fraction • *fractional* numbers
2 a : very small • There has been a *fractional* rise in the price of the stock. • There is only a *fractional* improvement in the new version. • a *fractional* amount **b** : not complete • *fractional* [=*partial*] ownership
– **frac·tion·al·ly** *adv* • The stock's price rose *fractionally*. [=*slightly*]

frac·tious /ˈfrækʃəs/ *adj [more ~; most ~]*
1 : causing trouble : hard to manage or control • *fractious* [=*unruly*] children • The *fractious* crowd grew violent.
2 : full of anger and disagreement • a *fractious* relationship • *fractious* negotiations • a *fractious* political campaign
– **frac·tious·ness** *noun [noncount]*

[1]frac·ture /ˈfræktʃɚ/ *noun, pl* **-tures** *[count]* : the result of breaking something : a crack or break • a *fracture* in the Earth's crust; *especially* : a broken bone • She suffered a wrist *fracture* when she slipped on the ice. — see also COMPOUND FRACTURE, SIMPLE FRACTURE, STRESS FRACTURE

[2]fracture *verb* **-tures; -tured; -tur·ing**
1 *[+ obj]* **a** : to cause a crack or break in (something hard, such as a bone) • She *fractured* [=*broke*] her wrist when she slipped on the ice. **b** *[no obj] of something hard* : to crack or break • Her wrist *fractured* when she fell on the ice.
2 : to damage or destroy (something) or to be damaged or destroyed in a sudden or violent way *[+ obj]* Their happiness was *fractured* by an unforeseen tragedy. • These problems may *fracture* the unity of the two parties. *[no obj]* Their fragile happiness/unity *fractured* all too soon.

fractured *adj*
1 : having a crack or break • a badly *fractured* [=*broken*] wrist • a *fractured* skull/rib • *fractured* rocks
2 : spoken with many mistakes : not fluent • They couldn't understand my *fractured* [=*broken*] French.
3 : damaged or destroyed in a sudden or violent way • *fractured* happiness/unity

frag·ile /ˈfrædʒəl, ˈfræˌdʒajəl/ *adj [more ~; most ~]* : easily broken or damaged • the flower's *fragile* petals • Her health has always been very *fragile*. • *fragile* bones • an artist with a *fragile* ego • He is in an emotionally *fragile* state. : very delicate • her *fragile* beauty : not strong • The two countries have formed a *fragile* coalition. • a *fragile* cease-fire
– **fra·gil·i·ty** /frəˈdʒɪləti/ *noun [noncount]* • the *fragility* of her health

[1]frag·ment /ˈfrægmənt/ *noun, pl* **-ments** *[count]*
1 : a broken part or piece of something • bone *fragments* • a pottery *fragment* • The dish lay in *fragments* on the floor.
2 : an incomplete part • I could only hear *fragments* of their conversation. — see also SENTENCE FRAGMENT

[2]frag·ment /ˈfrægˌmɛnt, *Brit* frægˈmɛnt/ *verb* **-ments; -ment·ed; -ment·ing** : to break or to cause (something) to break into parts or pieces *[no obj]* The party is *fragmenting* into warring factions. *[+ obj]* These issues are *fragmenting* our society. • The property is being *fragmented* into subdivisions.
– **frag·men·ta·tion** /ˌfrægmənˈteɪʃən/ *noun [noncount]* • the increasing *fragmentation* of society – **fragmented** *adj [more ~; most ~]* • We live in an increasingly *fragmented* society. • a *fragmented* market

frag·men·tary /ˈfrægmənˌteri, *Brit* ˈfrægməntri/ *adj [more ~; most ~]* : made up of parts or pieces : made up of fragments • discovering *fragmentary* remains of primitive animals • *fragmentary* [=*incomplete*] evidence/fossils/memories • *fragmentary* information/knowledge

fra·grance /ˈfreɪgrəns/ *noun, pl* **-granc·es** *[count]*
1 : a pleasant and usually sweet smell • a flower with a lovely *fragrance*
2 : a perfume or cologne • the company's newest *fragrance*

fra·grant /ˈfreɪgrənt/ *adj [more ~; most ~]* : having a pleasant and usually sweet smell • a *fragrant* flower • The soup was *fragrant* with herbs and spices.

fraîche see CRÈME FRAÎCHE

fraidy–cat /ˈfreɪdiˌkæt/ *noun, pl* **-cats** *[count] US, informal*

: SCAREDY-CAT — used mainly by children or when speaking to children • Don't be such a *fraidy-cat!*

frail /ˈfreɪl/ *adj* **frail·er; -est**
1 : having less than a normal amount of strength or force **:** very weak • a *frail* child • a *frail* old man • I could barely hear her *frail* [=*weak*] voice. • In his old age his health became increasingly *frail*. ***synonyms*** see WEAK
2 : easily damaged or destroyed • a small and *frail* ship
– frail·ness *noun* [*noncount*] • the *frailness* [=(more commonly) *frailty*] of his health

frail·ty /ˈfreɪlti/ *noun, pl* **-ties**
1 [*noncount*] **:** physical weakness **:** the quality or state of being frail • the old man's *frailty* • the *frailty* of her voice/health
2 : weakness of character that causes a person to do things that are morally wrong [*noncount*] He is not immune to human *frailty*. [=he sometimes fails to do what is fair, honest, etc.] [*count*] We can no longer be surprised by the *frailties* of our political leaders.

¹frame /ˈfreɪm/ *noun, pl* **frames**
1 [*count*] **:** the basic structure and shape of the body of a person or animal • She had to extend every inch of her five-foot *frame* [=*body*] to reach the top shelf. • her petite/slight/thin/wiry *frame* • his large/lanky/lean *frame*
2 [*count*] **:** an arrangement of parts that support and form the basic shape of something • the *frame* of a house • a bicycle *frame* • the car's steel *frame*
3 a [*count*] **:** an open structure that holds something (such as glass or a picture) • a picture/window/door *frame* — see also COLD FRAME **b** ***frames*** [*plural*] **:** the plastic or metal structure that holds the lenses of eyeglasses • I need new *frames* for my glasses.
4 [*count*] **a :** one of the pictures in the series of pictures that make up a film • The film runs at eight *frames* per second. — see also FREEZE-FRAME **b :** one of the drawings in the series of drawings that make up a comic strip
5 [*count*] *computers* **:** a section of a Web page that is like a small separate page **:** a section of a Web page that has its own scroll bar
6 [*count*] *Brit* **:** ¹RACK 6
in the frame *Brit, informal* **:** in the position of being considered for something • a job candidate who is still *in the frame*
out of the frame *Brit, informal* **:** no longer in the position of being considered for something • a job candidate who is *out of the frame*
– see also TIME FRAME

²frame *verb* **frames; framed; fram·ing** [+ *obj*]
1 a : to put (something) inside an open structure that holds it **:** to put (something) in a frame • *frame* a picture • a *framed* photograph • paintings *framed* with/in wood • steel-*framed* spectacles **b :** to be around the edge of (something) — usually used as *(be) framed* • a house *framed* by a white picket fence • The child's face *was framed* by brown curls.
2 : to produce (something written or spoken) • It was the first state to *frame* a written constitution. **:** to express (a question, answer, etc.) in words • She *framed* her questions carefully. • He took the time to *frame* a thoughtful reply.
3 : to make (an innocent person) appear to be guilty of a crime • She claims that she was *framed*. — see also FRAME-UP
– fram·er *noun, pl* **-ers** [*count*] • a picture *framer* • the *framers* of the U.S. Constitution [=the people who wrote the U.S. Constitution]

frame of mind *noun, pl* **frames of mind** [*count*] **:** the way someone is feeling **:** a person's emotional state **:** MOOD • Wait until he's in a better *frame of mind*. • a cheerful/happy/relaxed *frame of mind* • a serious/somber *frame of mind*

frame of reference *noun, pl* **frames of reference** [*count*] **:** a set of ideas, conditions, experiences, etc., that affect how something is thought about or understood • Each person experiences art through his or her own *frame of reference*. • Her biographer tries to provide a *frame of reference* in which her work can be analyzed.

frame–up /ˈfreɪm,ʌp/ *noun, pl* **-ups** [*count*] *informal* **:** a plan to make an innocent person appear to be guilty of a crime • She's the victim of a *frame-up*. — see also ²FRAME 3

frame·work /ˈfreɪm,wɚk/ *noun, pl* **-works** [*count*]
1 : the basic structure of something • These influences threaten the very *framework* of our society. **:** a set of ideas or facts that provide support for something • The book provides a general *framework* for understanding modern politics. • He questions the study's theoretical *framework*.
2 : a supporting structure **:** a structural frame • An iron *framework* surrounds the sculpture. • The panels are attached to the building's steel *framework*.

franc /ˈfræŋk/ *noun, pl* **francs** [*count*] **:** a basic unit of money that is used in some countries where French is spoken and that was formerly used in France, Luxembourg, and Belgium; *also* **:** a coin or bill representing one franc

¹fran·chise /ˈfræn,ʧaɪz/ *noun, pl* **-chis·es** [*count*]
1 : the right to sell a company's goods or services in a particular area • She was granted an exclusive *franchise* in the city's west end.; *also* **:** a business that is given such a right • They just opened a new fast-food *franchise* down the street.
2 : the right to vote • The U.S. did not extend the *franchise* to women until the early 20th century.
3 *US, sports* **:** a team that is a member of a professional sports league • He's the best player in the history of the *franchise*. ✧ In U.S. and Canadian English, a ***franchise player*** is the best and most important player on a particular professional sports team.

²franchise *verb* **-chises; -chised; -chis·ing** [+ *obj*] **:** to offer the right to sell (your company's goods or services) in a particular area • Most of the restaurants are owned by the company, but 15 are *franchised* restaurants. [=are owned and operated by people who have a franchise]

fran·chi·see /,fræn,ʧaɪˈziː/ *noun, pl* **-sees** [*count*] **:** someone who has been given the right to sell a company's goods or services in a particular area **:** a person who has been granted a franchise

Fran·co- /,fræŋkoʊ/ *combining form*
1 : French • *Franco*-German
2 : France, French culture, or the French • a *Franco*phile [=a person who greatly likes and admires France and French things] • a *Franco*phobe [=a person who dislikes France and French things]

Fran·co–Amer·i·can /,fræŋkowəˈmerəkən/ *noun, pl* **-cans** [*count*] **:** an American whose family comes originally from France
– Franco–American *adj*

Fran·co·phone /ˈfræŋkə,foʊn/ *adj* **:** having French as the main language • the region's *Francophone* population • a *Francophone* neighborhood in an English-speaking country
– Francophone *noun, pl* **-phones** [*count*] • a neighborhood that includes many *Francophones* [=people who speak French as their main language]

¹frank /ˈfræŋk/ *adj* **frank·er; -est** [*also more ~; most ~*] — used to say that someone is speaking or writing in a very direct and honest way • She gave me some very *frank* criticism. • Don't be afraid to be perfectly/completely *frank* with me. • To be brutally *frank* with you, I don't think you're good enough. • We had a full and *frank* discussion.
– frank·ness *noun* [*noncount*] • She spoke with surprising *frankness*.

²frank *noun, pl* **franks** [*count*] *US, informal* **:** FRANKFURTER, HOT DOG • We ate *franks* and beans for lunch.

frank·furt·er /ˈfræŋk,fɚtɚ/ *noun, pl* **-ers** [*count*] **:** HOT DOG 1

frank·in·cense /ˈfræŋkən,sɛns/ *noun* [*noncount*] **:** a substance that is burned for its sweet smell and that was used in religious ceremonies in ancient times

frank·ly /ˈfræŋkli/ *adv* **:** in an honest and direct way • You can speak *frankly* to us. — often used to introduce a statement that tells your true opinion, reason, etc. • *Frankly*, I think your essay needs more work. [=I am being honest when I tell you that your essay needs more work]

fran·tic /ˈfræntɪk/ *adj* [*more ~; most ~*]
1 : feeling or showing a lot of fear and worry • *frantic* cries for help • The girl was *frantic* with fear/worry. • They made a *frantic* search for the missing child. • a *frantic* phone call
2 : having a lot of wild and hurried activity • They were making *frantic* preparations for the party. • a *frantic* attempt/effort to finish on schedule
– fran·ti·cal·ly /ˈfræntɪkli/ *adv* • searching *frantically*

frat /ˈfræt/ *noun, pl* **frats** [*count*] *US, informal* **:** FRATERNITY 1 — often used before another noun • a ***frat party*** [=a party given by a fraternity] • a ***frat boy*** [=a member of a fraternity]

fra·ter·nal /frəˈtɚnl̩/ *adj*
1 : of or relating to brothers • *fraternal* love
2 : made up of members who share an interest or purpose • He belonged to a *fraternal* organization.
3 : friendly or brotherly • There was a *fraternal* feeling among the troops.
– fra·ter·nal·ly *adv*

F

fraternal twin *noun, pl* ~ **twins** [*count*] : either member of a pair of twins that are produced from different eggs and may not have the same sex or appearance — compare IDENTICAL TWIN

fra·ter·ni·ty /frəˈtənəti/ *noun, pl* **-ties**
1 [*count*] : an organization of male students at a U.S. college — compare SORORITY
2 [*count*] : a group of people who have the same job, interests, etc. • the racing *fraternity* [=people who are involved or interested in racing] • the legal *fraternity*
3 [*noncount*] *formal* : the feeling of friendship that exists between people in a group • an atmosphere of *fraternity* and cooperation

frat·er·nize *also Brit* **frat·er·nise** /ˈfrætəˌnaɪz/ *verb* **-niz·es; -nized; -niz·ing** [*no obj*] : to be friendly with someone : to spend time with someone in a friendly way especially when it is considered wrong or improper to do so • It is usually unwise to *fraternize* with your employees. • The soldiers were caught *fraternizing* (with the enemy).
– frat·er·ni·za·tion *also Brit* **frat·er·ni·sa·tion** /ˌfrætənəˈzeɪʃən, *Brit* ˌfrætənaɪˈzeɪʃən/ *noun* [*noncount*] **– frat·er·niz·er** *also Brit* **frat·er·nis·er** /ˈfrætəˌnaɪzə/ *noun, pl* **-ers** [*count*]

frat·ri·cide /ˈfrætrəˌsaɪd/ *noun, pl* **-cides** [*count*] : the crime of murdering your own brother or sister; *also* : a person who has committed this crime — compare MATRICIDE, PATRICIDE
– frat·ri·cid·al /ˌfrætrəˈsaɪdl/ *adj*

fraud /ˈfrɑːd/ *noun, pl* **frauds**
1 : the crime of using dishonest methods to take something valuable from another person [*noncount*] He was found guilty of bank *fraud*. • credit card *fraud* [*count*] He was the victim of an elaborate *fraud*. — see also WIRE FRAUD
2 [*count*] **a** : a person who pretends to be what he or she is not in order to trick people • He claimed he was a licensed psychologist, but he turned out to be a *fraud*. **b** : a copy of something that is meant to look like the real thing in order to trick people • The UFO picture was proved to be a *fraud*.

fraud·ster /ˈfrɑːdstə/ *noun, pl* **-sters** [*count*] *chiefly Brit* : a person who commits fraud

fraud·u·lent /ˈfrɑːʤələnt/ *adj* [*more* ~; *most* ~] : done to trick someone for the purpose of getting something valuable • Corrupt leaders were chosen in a *fraudulent* election. • *fraudulent* use of a credit card • a *fraudulent* claim • the victim of a *fraudulent* scheme
– fraud·u·lence /ˈfrɑːʤələns/ *noun* [*noncount*] **– fraud·u·lent·ly** *adv*

fraught /ˈfrɑːt/ *adj* : causing or having a lot of emotional stress or worry : ANXIOUS • a *fraught* silence/atmosphere ♢ *Fraught* in this sense is more common in British English than in U.S. English.
fraught with : full of (something bad or unwanted) • The situation was *fraught with* danger. [=very dangerous] • The paper was poorly researched and *fraught with* errors.

[1]**fray** /ˈfreɪ/ *noun, pl* **frays** [*count*] : a fight, struggle, or disagreement that involves many people • He threw himself into the *fray*. • He joined/entered the political *fray*.
above the fray : not directly involved in an angry or difficult struggle or disagreement • His political aides handled the controversy while he remained *above the fray*.

[2]**fray** *verb* **frays; frayed; fray·ing** : to cause (a cloth or other material) to become worn down at the end or edge : to separate the threads of (a material) [+ *obj*] She *frayed* the edges of her cutoff jeans. = She *frayed* her cutoff jeans at the edges. [*no obj*] The cuffs of the old shirt were *fraying*. — often used figuratively • Her temper was starting to *fray*. [=she was beginning to get angry] • His nerves were *frayed/fraying*. • their *frayed/fraying* friendship

[1]**fraz·zle** /ˈfræzəl/ *verb* **fraz·zles; fraz·zled; fraz·zling** [+ *obj*] *informal* : to make (someone) very nervous or upset • He's a clever player who knows how to *frazzle* his opponents. • *frazzle* someone's nerves
– frazzled *adj* [*more* ~; *most* ~] • feeling very tired and *frazzled* • *frazzled* nerves

[2]**frazzle** *noun*
to a frazzle *informal* **1** : to a very tired or nervous condition • By the end of the day, the waitress was ***worn to a frazzle***. [=was exhausted] **2** *Brit* : to a state of being hard, dry, and easily broken • The toast had been ***burned to a frazzle***. [=*burned to a crisp*]

[1]**freak** /ˈfriːk/ *noun, pl* **freaks** [*count*]
1 a *disapproving* : a very strange or unusual person • Who's that *freak* [=*weirdo*] with the green hair? • eccentric, artistic types whom many regarded as *freaks* • a hippie *freak* **b** *old-fashioned + sometimes offensive* : a person or animal that is physically abnormal • a circus *freak* • I had a terrible rash on my face, and I felt like a *freak*. • a *freak* show
2 *informal* : a person who is very interested or active in something specified • a magazine for computer *freaks* [=*enthusiasts*] • a fitness *freak* • a movie *freak* — see also CONTROL FREAK, NEAT FREAK
3 *informal* : a person who uses a specified illegal drug • a speed *freak*
4 : something (such as an event) that is very unusual or unexpected • Through some incredible ***freak of fate*** [=strange event] they survived the shipwreck. — see also FREAK OF NATURE

[2]**freak** *adj, always used before a noun* : not natural, normal, or likely • He was the victim of a *freak* accident. • a *freak* occurrence

[3]**freak** *verb* **freaks; freaked; freak·ing** *informal*
1 [+ *obj*] : to make (someone) very upset • He was a little *freaked* by the accident. — usually + *out* • He was a little *freaked out* by the accident. • It *freaks* me *out* to see people being so violent. • She was *freaked out* by what you said.
2 [*no obj*] : to become very upset • She really *freaked* when you said that. — often + *out* • She really *freaked out*. • He *freaked out* when he saw his girlfriend kiss another guy.

freaking /ˈfriːkn̩, ˈfriːkɪŋ/ *adj, US, informal + impolite* — used to make an angry statement more forceful • Give me the *freaking* keys!
– freaking *adv* • She is so *freaking* annoying!

freak·ish /ˈfriːkɪʃ/ *adj* [*more* ~; *most* ~] : very strange or abnormal • *freakish* weather • a *freakish* twist of fate
– freak·ish·ly *adv* • He has a *freakishly* large nose. • *freakishly* hot weather **– freak·ish·ness** *noun* [*noncount*]

freak of nature *noun, pl* **freaks of nature** [*count*] : a person or thing that is very unusual or abnormal • He's an amazing athlete—a real *freak of nature*. • The storm that destroyed the house was a *freak of nature*.

freaky /ˈfriːki/ *adj* **freak·i·er; -est** *informal* : strange or unusual • That book was kind of *freaky*. • a *freaky* kid wearing a weird hat

[1]**freck·le** /ˈfrekəl/ *noun, pl* **freck·les** [*count*] : a small, brownish spot on someone's skin • a pale, redheaded girl with *freckles* across her cheeks • a *freckle*-faced girl

[2]**freckle** *verb* **freckles; freck·led; freck·ling** : to be or become marked with freckles or spots [*no obj*] His skin *freckles* but doesn't tan. [+ *obj*] Tiny black spots *freckled* the walls.
– freckled *adj* [*more* ~; *most* ~] • She has a *freckled* face. [=she has many freckles on her face]

[1]**free** /ˈfriː/ *adj* **fre·er fre·est**
1 : not costing any money • They're giving out *free* tickets to the show. • The school newsletter is *free*. • *free* advice • *free* drinks/food • The tickets are ***free for the taking***. [=anyone who wants one can take one] • The store is offering a calculator as a ***free gift*** [=something that is given to people to help get new customers for a business]
2 a : not held as a slave or prisoner • After 10 years in jail, he was finally a *free* man. — often used after *set* • After 10 years, they finally *set* him *free*. **b** : not physically held by something • The animal struggled to get *free* of/from the trap. • His legs became caught in the net, and he was unable to get himself *free*.
3 : able to do what you want to do : able to move, go, or act without being stopped — followed by *to + verb* • You are *free to leave*. • You're (entirely) *free to do* whatever you want to do. • We were *free to choose* from among several options.
4 a : not controlled by a harsh ruler or laws • He dreamed of a day when his people would be *free*. • a *free* society • I can say whatever I want to say. This is a *free* country. **b** : not limited by government control • *free* competition • *free* and democratic elections • *free* speech — see also FREE ENTERPRISE, FREE MARKET, FREE TRADE
5 a : not limited by fear, uncertainty, etc. : OPEN • a *free* expression of opinions • a *free* exchange of ideas • Children are often *freer* and more imaginative than adults in their writing. **b** : not limited in any way • Your password allows you to have *free* access to the system. • The ships were allowed *free* passage into and out of the port. — see also FREE HAND, FREE LOVE, *free rein* at REIN
6 : not having, including, or suffering from something unpleasant, painful, or unwanted — usually + *from* or *of* • *free*

from worry/disease • The product is guaranteed to be *free of/from* major defects. • The speech was *free of* political rhetoric. • writing that is *free of* jargon — sometimes used in combination • jargon-*free* writing • sugar-*free* chewing gum • After struggling with her addiction for many years, she is finally drug-*free*. [=she has finally stopped using drugs] — see also SCOT-FREE

7 a : not required to be doing something **:** having nothing that must be done instead • I'm *free* tomorrow night. • We're having a party next Saturday. Are you *free*? **b** *of time* **:** not being used for work or other activities • Wednesday is her only *free* afternoon. • I wish I had more *free* time. • He spends a lot of his *free* time [=time when he is not working on his job] tinkering with his car.

8 a : not being used • I'm going to call my mother as soon as the phone is *free*. • "Excuse me: is this seat *free*?" "I'm sorry: it's taken." • There's not enough *free* space on my computer's hard drive to install the software. **b :** not holding anything • He waved at us with his *free* hand. **c :** not attached to anything • She held onto the *free* end of the rope.

9 : not covered or filled with things **:** CLEAR • We'll need a lot of *free* floor space for the dancing lesson. • The hallway should be kept *free* of clutter.

10 : giving, doing, or saying something very often • He seems to be very *free* about giving people his advice. = He seems to be very ***free with*** his advice. = [=he seems to give his advice very often, even when it is not wanted] • She's very *free with* her money. = She's a *free* spender. [=she spends her money freely; she spends a lot of money without worrying about trying to save it] • (*chiefly Brit*) He had a habit of ***making free with*** other people's money. [=of using other people's money freely]

11 *of a translation* **:** not closely following or matching the original language **:** not exact • This is a very *free* [=*loose*] translation of the original poem.

(as) free as a bird **:** completely free • After he left school he felt *as free as a bird*.

feel free — used to tell someone that there is no reason to hesitate about doing something • *Feel free* to call me if you have any questions.

for free **:** without charge **:** at no cost • If you buy two boxes of cereal, you'll get another box *for free*. [=without paying any more money]

free and easy **1 :** very informal and relaxed • a teacher with a *free and easy* manner • a *free and easy* atmosphere **2 :** not strict or careful enough • They have been too *free and easy* in accepting political contributions.

– free·ly *adv* • He *freely* admitted that he had lied. • We passed *freely* through the gate. • Wine flowed *freely*. • She spends money *freely*.

²free *adv*

1 : in a free way • The gate opened, and the animals ran *free*. **2 :** without charge **:** at no cost • Children will be admitted *free*. [=*for free*] • Buy one, get one *free*.

break free see ¹BREAK

free and clear **:** without owing any money • I've paid off my mortgage and now I own the property *free and clear*. [=I no longer owe any money for the property]

free of charge **:** without charge **:** at no cost • He offered his services *free of charge*. [=without receiving money]

home free see ²HOME

³free *verb* **frees; freed; free·ing** [+ *obj*] **:** to cause (someone or something) to be free: such as **a :** to release (a person or animal) from a prison, cage, etc. • The government has agreed to *free* all political prisoners (from jail). • The gunman *freed* two of the hostages. • The animals were *freed* from their cages. **b :** to release (someone or something) from being physically held or blocked • His legs became tangled in the net, and he was unable to *free* himself. • He was unable to *free* his legs from the net. • The animal struggled to *free* itself from the trap. **c :** to cause or allow (someone or something) to stop having or being affected by something unpleasant, painful, or unwanted — + *from* or *of* • He has struggled to *free* himself *from* debt. • The new road will help to *free* the city *of* traffic jams. • patients trying to *free* themselves *from* dependence on drugs **d :** to make (something) available for use • I'll see if I can *free* (up) some time on my schedule next week so that we can meet. • We need to delete more files to *free* (up) space on the computer's hard drive. **e :** to give more free time to (someone) • Hiring an assistant has *freed* him to spend more time with his family. **f :** to remove limits from (someone or something) • She encourages her students to *free* their imaginations.

free on bail, freed on bail see ¹BAIL

free agent *noun, pl* **~ agents** [*count*]

1 : a person who is able to act freely without being controlled by someone else

2 : a professional athlete (such as a baseball player) who is free to sign a contract to play for any team

– free agency *noun* [*noncount*] • an athlete who has become eligible for *free agency*

free·base /ˈfriːˌbeɪs/ *noun* [*noncount*] **:** a form of cocaine that can be smoked

– freebase *verb* **-bas·es; -based; -bas·ing** [*no obj*] a drug addict who *freebases* [+ *obj*] a drug addict who *freebases* cocaine

free·bie *or* **free·bee** /ˈfriːbi/ *noun, pl* **-bies** *or* **-bees** [*count*] *informal* **:** something that is given for free • On the store's opening day, the manager gave out hats, small toys, and other *freebies*.

free·born /friːˈboɚn/ *adj* **:** not born in slavery • a *freeborn* citizen

free·dom /ˈfriːdəm/ *noun, pl* **-doms**

1 [*noncount*] **:** the state of being free: such as **a :** the power to do what you want to do **:** the ability to move or act freely • religious *freedom* • academic *freedom* • He thinks children these days have too much *freedom*. • She has the *freedom* to do as she likes. • *freedom* of choice • ***freedom of speech/expression*** [=the right to express your opinions freely] • ***freedom of the press*** [=the right to publish books, newspapers, etc., without being controlled by the government] **b :** the state of not being a slave, prisoner, etc. • a political prisoner struggling to win his *freedom* **c :** the state of not having or being affected by something unpleasant, painful, or unwanted — + *from* • *freedom from* care • *freedom from* pain/fear • *freedom from* responsibility **d :** the right to use something or go somewhere without being controlled • *freedom* of the seas

2 [*count*] **:** a political right • an important *freedom* • basic human *freedoms*

freedom fighter *noun, pl* **~ -ers** [*count*] **:** a person who is part of an organized group fighting against a cruel and unfair government or system

free enterprise *noun* [*noncount*] **:** a system in which private businesses are able to compete with each other with little control by the government — called also *private enterprise*

free fall *noun, pl* **~ falls**

1 [*noncount*] **:** the state or condition of falling through the air toward the ground • a parachutist in *free fall* [=a parachutist who is falling through the air before the parachute opens]

2 a [*noncount*] **:** the condition of quickly becoming lower, less, or fewer • Sales were in *free fall*. • Stock prices have gone into *free fall*. [=they are going down very quickly] **b** [*count*] **:** a fast or continuing drop • There has been a *free fall* in stock prices. [=stock prices have gone down very quickly]

free–float·ing /ˈfriːˈfloʊtɪŋ/ *adj* **:** not connected or attached to anything • *free-floating* ideas **:** not directed at or caused by anything specific • *free-floating* anxiety

free–for–all /ˈfriːfəˌrɑːl/ *noun, pl* **-alls** [*count*] **:** an uncontrolled fight or competition that involves many people • A fight between two players quickly turned into a *free-for-all* involving all the players on both teams. — often used figuratively to describe a wild and noisy disagreement • The press conference turned into a *free-for-all*.

free–form /ˈfriːˈfoɚm/ *adj, always used before a noun* **:** created or done in any way you choose **:** not required to have particular patterns or forms • *free-form* dancing

free·hand /ˈfriːˌhænd/ *adj, always used before a noun* **:** done without special tools or instruments • She took a course in *freehand* drawing. • a *freehand* sketch

– freehand *adv* • She drew the picture *freehand*.

free hand *noun*

a free hand **:** the freedom to do things and make decisions without being controlled by another • Her father gave her *a free hand* in running the family business. [=her father let her run the family business as she wanted to]

free kick *noun, pl* **~ kicks** [*count*] *soccer* **:** a kick that is made without being stopped or slowed by an opponent and that is allowed because of a foul by an opponent

free·lance /ˈfriːˌlæns/ *adj* **:** earning money by being hired to work on different jobs for short periods of time rather than by having a permanent job with one employer • a *freelance* writer • a *freelance* worker; *also* **:** done or produced by a

freelance worker • a *freelance* job • looking for *freelance* work • I wrote a *freelance* article for a nature magazine.
– freelance *adv* • working *freelance* **– freelance** *verb* **-lanc•es; -lanced; -lanc•ing** [*no obj*] • a writer who *freelances*

free•load /ˈfriːˌloʊd/ *verb* **-loads; -load•ed; -load•ing** [*no obj*] *informal + disapproving* **:** to get or ask for things (such as food, money, or a place to live) from people without paying for them • He often *freeloads* [=*mooches*] off his relatives.
– free•load•er *noun, pl* **-ers** [*count*] • a lazy *freeloader*

free love *noun* [*noncount*] **:** the practice of having sex with many people instead of with just one partner

free•man /ˈfriːmən/ *noun, pl* **-men** /-mən/ [*count*] **:** a free man **:** a man who is not a slave

free market *noun, pl* **~ -kets** [*count*] **:** an economic market or system in which prices are based on competition among private businesses and not controlled by a government
– free–market *adj, always used before a noun* • a *free-market* economy • *free-market* principles

Free•ma•son /friːˈmeɪsn̩/ *noun, pl* **-sons** [*count*] **:** a member of a large organization of men who have secret rituals and who give help to other members — called also *Mason*
– Free•ma•son•ry /friːˈmeɪsn̩ri/ *noun* [*noncount*] • learning about the origins of *Freemasonry*

free–range /ˈfriːˌreɪnʤ/ *adj* **:** allowed to move around freely **:** not kept in cages • *free-range* chickens; *also* **:** coming from free-range animals • *free-range* eggs

free ride *noun, pl* **~ rides** [*count*] **:** special treatment that involves giving away something that is valuable or expensive • The state university offered him a *free ride* for all four years of college—his football scholarship would cover tuition, room and board, and other expenses. • companies getting a *free ride* at the taxpayer's expense

free spirit *noun, pl* **~ -its** [*count*] *usually approving* **:** a person who thinks and acts in a free way without worrying about normal social rules • Their daughter is a real *free spirit*.

free•stand•ing /friːˈstændɪŋ/ *adj* **:** standing alone without being attached to or supported by something else • a *free-standing* wall

free•style /ˈfriːˌstajəl/ *noun* [*singular*]
1 : a competition (such as a swimming race) in which the competitors are allowed to use different styles or methods • the one-mile *freestyle* — often used before another noun • a *freestyle* race • *freestyle* skating
2 : [2]CRAWL 2

free•think•er /ˈfriːˈθɪŋkɚ/ *noun, pl* **-ers** [*count*] **:** a person who forms his or her own opinions about important subjects (such as religion and politics) instead of accepting what other people say
– free•think•ing /ˈfriːˈθɪŋkɪŋ/ *adj*

free throw *noun, pl* **~ throws** [*count*] **:** a basketball shot worth one point that must be made from behind a special line and that is given because of a foul by an opponent • make/miss a *free throw* — called also *foul shot*

free trade *noun* [*noncount*] **:** a system of trade between nations in which there are no special taxes placed on imports

free verse *noun* [*noncount*] **:** poetry that does not rhyme and does not have a regular rhythm

free•ware /ˈfriːˌweɚ/ *noun* [*noncount*] **:** computer software that can be used at no cost — compare SHAREWARE

free•way /ˈfriːˌweɪ/ *noun, pl* **-ways** [*count*] *US* **:** a wide highway that is built for fast travel

free•wheel•ing /ˌfriːˈwiːlɪŋ/ *adj* **:** free and loose in style or manner **:** not held back by rules, duties, or worries • a *free-wheeling* young adventurer • She led a *freewheeling* life in the city. **:** not controlled or limited • a *freewheeling* discussion/investigation • *freewheeling* competition

free will *noun* [*noncount*]
1 : the ability to choose how to act • I do this ***of my own free will*** [=I do this because I want to do it; no one is forcing me to do this]
2 : the ability to make choices that are not controlled by fate or God • He argues that all humans have *free will*.

[1]**freeze** /ˈfriːz/ *verb* **freez•es; froze** /ˈfroʊz/; **fro•zen** /ˈfroʊzn̩/; **freez•ing**
1 : to be become a hard substance (such as ice) because of cold [*no obj*] Water *freezes* (in)to ice. • The pond *froze* over. [=the surface of the pond froze] • The pond *froze* solid. [=the water in the pond froze completely] [+ *obj*] The low temperature *froze* the river (over).
2 [*no obj*] **:** to be very cold • The children are going to *freeze* out there without their coats. • She nearly ***froze to death***. [=nearly died from the cold]
3 : to become blocked or unable to move because of ice [*no obj*] The water pipes *froze*. • My car doors *froze*. [+ *obj*] The cold weather *froze* the water pipes.
4 : to preserve (food) by storing it in a very cold place [+ *obj*] We *froze* the leftovers. [=we put the leftovers in the freezer] [*no obj*] Some vegetables don't *freeze* well.
5 a [*no obj*] **:** to stop moving **:** to become completely still • The guard ordered him to *freeze*. • The deer *froze* in the road as the car approached it. **b** [*no obj*] **:** to become unable to do or say anything • She *froze* (up) when the teacher asked her a difficult question. **c** [*no obj*] **:** to stop working • The engine suddenly *froze*. • My computer has *frozen* (up) again. **d** [+ *obj*] **:** to cause (a person or animal) to stop moving • A fake by the quarterback *froze* the defender. • The lights of the approaching car *froze* the deer.
6 [+ *obj*] **a :** to stop (something, such as prices or wages) from changing or increasing • The government *froze* prices on certain materials. • The struggling company had to *freeze* wages and eliminate several jobs. **b :** to stop (money or property) from being used, spent, etc. • The government has *frozen* foreign assets.
freeze out [*phrasal verb*] ***freeze out (someone)*** *or* ***freeze (someone) out*** **:** to not allow (someone) to be included in an activity or group • a politician who is being *frozen out* by former supporters who accuse him of betraying the party
frozen stiff see [2]STIFF
when hell freezes over see HELL
– freezing *adj or adv* • Turn up the heat—I'm *freezing* (to death)! [=I'm very cold] • It's *freezing* in here! • The weather has been *freezing* [=very cold] lately. • *freezing* weather • It's ***freezing cold*** [=very cold] in here!

[2]**freeze** *noun, pl* **freezes** [*count*]
1 : a period in which the weather is very cold **:** a time when temperatures are below 32°F or 0°C • The *freeze* destroyed many oranges.
2 : a stop in the increase, decrease, or change of prices or wages • a six-month wage *freeze* = a six-month *freeze* on wages • a price *freeze*

freeze–dry /ˈfriːzˈdraɪ/ *verb* **-dries; -dried; -dry•ing** [+ *obj*] **:** to preserve (something, such as food) by a process that both dries and freezes it • a process used to *freeze-dry* food
– freeze–dried *adj* • *freeze-dried* foods • *freeze-dried* coffee

freeze–frame /ˈfriːzˈfreɪm/ *noun, pl* **-frames :** a still, unchanging picture produced in a movie or video [*count*] The movie ended with a *freeze-frame* of the child waving at his mother. [*noncount*] The VCR allows you to fast-forward, reverse, or put the picture in *freeze-frame*.
– freeze–frame *verb* **-frames; -framed; -fram•ing** [+ *obj*] • *freeze-frame* an image

freez•er /ˈfriːzɚ/ *noun, pl* **-ers** [*count*] **:** a device or room for freezing food or keeping it frozen • a *freezer* compartment • Don't forget to put the ice cream back in the *freezer*. — see picture at KITCHEN

freezing point *noun, pl* **~ points** [*count*] **:** the temperature at which a liquid freezes • The *freezing point* of water is 0 degrees Celsius and 32 degrees Fahrenheit.

[1]**freight** /ˈfreɪt/ *noun, pl* **freights**
1 [*noncount*] **a :** goods that are carried by ships, trains, trucks, or airplanes • trains that carry both passengers and *freight* • The *freight* arrived by steamboat. **b :** the system by which goods are carried from one place to another • The order was shipped by *freight*.
2 [*noncount*] **:** the amount of money paid for carrying goods • paid the full *freight* — sometimes used figuratively in U.S. English • parents struggling to ***pay the freight*** [=to pay] for their children's college education • He warns that taxpayers will end up *paying the freight* for the new stadium.
3 [*count*] *US* **:** FREIGHT TRAIN • an eastbound *freight*

[2]**freight** *verb* **freights; freight•ed; freight•ing** [+ *obj*]
1 : to send (goods) from one place to another • cargo *freighted* by airplane
2 : to cause (something) to have or carry many things **:** to load or burden (something) — usually used as *(be) freighted* • an essay *freighted* with complex arguments [=an essay that has too many complex arguments]

freight car *noun, pl* **~ cars** [*count*] *US* **:** a railroad car that is used for carrying goods — called also (*Brit*) *wagon*

freight•er /ˈfreɪtɚ/ *noun, pl* **-ers** [*count*] **:** a large ship that is used to carry goods — see picture at SHIP

freight train *noun, pl* **~ trains** [*count*] **:** a train that carries goods : a train that carries freight

[1]French /ˈfrɛntʃ/ *adj* : of or relating to France, its people, or their language ▪ *French* cuisine ▪ *French* literature

[2]French *noun*
1 [*noncount*] : the language of the French people ▪ learned to speak *French*
2 ***the French*** : the people of France : French people ▪ the customs of *the French*
pardon my French see [1]PARDON

French bean *noun, pl* ~ **beans** [*count*] *Brit* : GREEN BEAN

French bread *noun* [*noncount*] : a type of crusty bread that is baked in long, thin loaves

French Canadian *noun, pl* ~ **-ians** [*count*] : a Canadian whose family comes originally from France ▪ the *French Canadians* of Quebec and other provinces
– **French–Canadian** *adj*

French door *noun, pl* ~ **doors** [*count*] *chiefly US* : FRENCH WINDOW

French dressing *noun* [*noncount*]
1 *US* : a creamy salad dressing that is flavored with tomatoes
2 *chiefly Brit* : a salad dressing made of vinegar and oil with spices

french–fried *adj, chiefly US* : fried in deep fat ▪ *french-fried* onions ▪ *french-fried* potatoes

french fry *or* **French fry** *noun, pl* ~ **fries** [*count*] *chiefly US* : a long, thin piece of potato that is fried in deep fat — called also (*Brit*) *chip,* (*US*) *fry*

French horn *noun, pl* ~ **horns** [*count*] : a brass musical instrument that has a long tube which forms a circle and has a wide opening at one end — see picture at BRASS INSTRUMENT

French kiss *noun, pl* ~ **kisses** [*count*] : a kiss made with the mouths open and the tongues touching

French•man /ˈfrɛntʃmən/ *noun, pl* **-men** /-mən/ [*count*] : a French man

French polish *noun* [*noncount*] *Brit* : a kind of liquid (called a varnish) that is used on wood to make it shiny

French toast *noun* [*noncount*] : bread that is covered in a mixture of eggs and milk and fried at low heat ▪ a slice of *French toast*

French window *noun, pl* ~ **-dows** [*count*] : a pair of windows that have many small panes and that reach to the floor and open in the middle like doors

French•wom•an /ˈfrɛntʃˌwʊmən/ *noun, pl* **-wom•en** /-ˌwɪmən/ [*count*] : a French woman

fre•net•ic /frɪˈnɛtɪk/ *adj* [*more* ~; *most* ~] : filled with excitement, activity, or confusion : wild or frantic ▪ The celebration was noisy and *frenetic.* ▪ *frenetic* activity
– **fre•net•i•cal•ly** /frɪˈnɛtɪkli/ *adv* ▪ a *frenetically* fast pace ▪ dancing *frenetically*

fren•zied /ˈfrɛnzid/ *adj* [*more* ~; *most* ~] : very excited or upset ▪ *frenzied* dancing ▪ The screams of the fans grew more *frenzied* as the concert progressed.
– **fren•zied•ly** *adv*

fren•zy /ˈfrɛnzi/ *noun, pl* **-zies** [*count*] : great and often wild or uncontrolled activity ▪ the buying *frenzy* just before Christmas ▪ The partygoers worked themselves (up) into a *frenzy.* ▪ a *frenzy* of shopping — see also FEEDING FRENZY

fre•quen•cy /ˈfri:kwənsi/ *noun, pl* **-cies**
1 [*noncount*] : the fact or condition of happening often : common occurrence ▪ the alarming *frequency* of serious automobile accidents caused by young drivers ▪ The *frequency* of student errors was frustrating to the young teacher.
2 [*noncount*] : the number of times that something happens during a particular period ▪ The *frequency* of our visits decreased [=our visits occurred less often] during the school year. ▪ Our visits decreased in *frequency.* ▪ Errors were occurring with increasing *frequency.* ▪ high/low *frequency*
3 *technical* : the number times that something (such as a sound wave or radio wave) is repeated in a period of time (such as a second) [*noncount*] a sound wave of high/low *frequency* [*count*] waves having very different *frequencies* from one another ▪ high/low *frequencies* ▪ a current having a *frequency* of 60 hertz ▪ a radio *frequency* of 30 megahertz

[1]fre•quent /ˈfri:kwənt/ *adj* [*more* ~; *most* ~]
1 : happening often ▪ We made *frequent* trips to town. ▪ a *frequent* [=*common, usual*] occurrence ▪ This bus makes *frequent* stops. — opposite INFREQUENT
2 : acting or returning regularly or often ▪ She was a *frequent* visitor to the museum. ▪ He is one of our most *frequent* customers. — opposite INFREQUENT
– **fre•quent•ly** *adv* ▪ I see her *frequently.* ▪ This list is updated *frequently.*

[2]fre•quent /friˈkwɛnt/ *verb* **-quents; -quent•ed; -quent•ing** [+ *obj*] : to visit or go to (a place) often ▪ He began *frequenting* cheap bars. ▪ a neighborhood *frequented* by tourists ▪ a restaurant *frequented* by local politicians
– **fre•quent•er** *noun, pl* **-ers** [*count*] ▪ a *frequenter* of cheap bars

fres•co /ˈfrɛskoʊ/ *noun, pl* **-coes**
1 [*noncount*] : the art of painting on wet plaster ▪ scenes done in *fresco*
2 [*count*] : a painting that is done on wet plaster ▪ a ceiling *fresco*

[1]fresh /ˈfrɛʃ/ *adj* **fresh•er; -est**
1 a : newly produced, made, gathered, etc. : not preserved by being frozen, canned, etc. ▪ *fresh* vegetables = vegetables *fresh* from the farm = farm-*fresh* vegetables ▪ You can use either *fresh* or dried basil for this recipe. ▪ *fresh* fish [=fish that were caught and killed very recently] **b** : not old, spoiled, etc. ▪ *fresh* bread = bread *fresh* from the oven = oven-*fresh* bread ▪ The meat was kept *fresh* in the refrigerator. ▪ a bouquet of *fresh* flowers
2 a : clean and pure ▪ *fresh* air ▪ *fresh* flavors ▪ *fresh* colors **b** : not having an unpleasant smell, taste, etc. ▪ *fresh* breath **c** : not worn or dirty ▪ He changed into a *fresh* shirt. ▪ She brought a *fresh* change of clothes.
3 : full of life and energy ▪ She rose *fresh* from a good night's sleep. ▪ She always seems to be (as) ***fresh as a daisy.*** [=very fresh; not at all tired]
4 : not containing salt ▪ *fresh* water
5 a : newly made, experienced, or received ▪ a *fresh* wound **b** : replacing something old or used ▪ Can I get you a *fresh* drink? ▪ I used a *fresh* piece of paper. ▪ Let's ***make a fresh start.*** [=let's start again] **c** : remaining clear : not faded ▪ I'd like to take the test soon, while the information is still ***fresh in my mind.*** [=while I still remember the information clearly] ▪ memories that remained *fresh* **d** : new and original ▪ She offered *fresh* insight into the problem. ▪ a young writer with *fresh* ideas ▪ Let's try a *fresh* approach to this problem.
6 a : behaving or talking in a rude or impolite way ▪ Don't be/get *fresh* with the teacher. ▪ a very *fresh* kid **b** *old-fashioned* : behaving or talking in a way that shows sexual attraction to someone ▪ He tried to get *fresh* with me.
7 *of wind* : fairly strong ▪ a *fresh* breeze
a breath of fresh air see BREATH
fresh from *or* ***fresh out of*** : having recently left or come from (a place, such as a school) ▪ new employees *fresh out of* college ▪ a young doctor *fresh from* medical school
fresh off the boat see [1]BOAT
– **fresh•ly** *adv* ▪ a *freshly* baked pie ▪ *freshly* polished boots
– **fresh•ness** *noun* [*count, noncount*] ▪ The fruit had been shipped a great distance, and lacked flavor and *freshness.* ▪ Several critics praised the *freshness* of her style.

[2]fresh *adv* : just recently : NEWLY, FRESHLY ▪ This bread was baked *fresh.* — usually used in combination ▪ *fresh*-baked bread ▪ *fresh*-laid eggs
fresh out (of something) *US, informal* — used to say that you do not have any more of something ▪ "Are there any bagels left?" "I'm sorry, we're *fresh out (of them).*" ▪ I'm *fresh out of* ideas. [=I don't have any more ideas] ▪ We're *fresh out of* time.

fresh•en /ˈfrɛʃən/ *verb* **-ens; -ened; -en•ing**
1 [+ *obj*] : to make (something) fresh : to cause (something) to be more pleasant ▪ We tried to *freshen* (up) the room [=to give the room a brighter appearance] with some color. ▪ a mint that *freshens* the breath
2 [+ *obj*] *chiefly US, informal* : to pour more of a usually alcoholic drink into someone's glass ▪ Can I ***freshen your drink?***
3 [*no obj*] *of wind* : to become stronger ▪ The wind/breeze suddenly *freshened.*
freshen up [*phrasal verb*] : to wash yourself in order to feel clean and fresh ▪ After my walk, I *freshened up* with a shower.
– **fresh•en•er** /ˈfrɛʃənɚ/ *noun, pl* **-ers** [*count*] ▪ an air/room *freshener* [=something used to make the air in a room smell fresher or more pleasant] ▪ a breath *freshener*

fresh•er /ˈfrɛʃɚ/ *noun, pl* **-ers** [*count*] *Brit, informal* : a university freshman

fresh–faced /ˈfrɛʃˈfeɪst/ *adj* : having a young, healthy, and innocent appearance ▪ *fresh-faced* young students

fresh•man /ˈfrɛʃmən/ *noun, pl* **-men** /-mən/ [*count*]

F

1 : a student in the first year of high school or college • My daughter's a *freshman* at UCLA. — often used before another noun • She had a successful *freshman* year. — compare SOPHOMORE, JUNIOR, SENIOR
2 *chiefly US* : someone who is starting a job or activity : BEGINNER • He was the best *freshman* in professional basketball this year. — often used before another noun • a *freshman* congressman

fresh•wa•ter /ˈfrɛʃˈwɑːtɚ/ *adj, always used before a noun* : of, relating to, or living in water that is not salty • *freshwater* fish • a *freshwater* stream — compare SALTWATER

[1]fret /ˈfrɛt/ *verb* **frets; fret•ted; fret•ting** [*no obj*] : to worry or be concerned • I was sure we wouldn't get there in time, but she told me not to *fret*. • Don't *fret*. We won't miss the plane. • It turned out that it was nothing to *fret* about/over.

[2]fret *noun* [*singular*] *informal* : a state of being worried or upset • Don't get in (such) a *fret*! We won't miss the plane. — compare [3]FRET

[3]fret *noun, pl* **frets** [*count*] : any one of a series of ridges on the neck of some stringed musical instruments (such as a guitar) — compare [2]FRET
– **fret•less** *adj* • a *fretless* bass – **fretted** *adj* • *fretted* instruments

fret•ful /ˈfrɛtfəl/ *adj* [*more ~; most ~*]
1 : upset and worried • a *fretful* child
2 : not relaxing or restful • He fell into a *fretful* sleep.
– **fret•ful•ly** *adv* • He was sleeping *fretfully*. – **fret•ful•ness** *noun* [*noncount*] • the child's *fretfulness*

fret•work /ˈfrɛtˌwɚk/ *noun* [*noncount*] : patterns or decoration on a surface made by cutting into or through the surface

Freud•i•an /ˈfrɔɪdijən/ *adj*
1 : of, relating to, or following the theories of Sigmund Freud • *Freudian* psychology • a *Freudian* psychologist
2 : relating to or coming from very deeply hidden desires or feelings • a *Freudian* compulsion • a *Freudian* joke
– **Freudian** *noun, pl* **-ians** [*count*] • The psychologist considers himself a *Freudian*.

Freudian slip *noun, pl* **~ slips** [*count*] : a mistake in speech that shows what the speaker is truly thinking • He meant to say "I'm glad you're here," but what came out was a *Freudian slip*: "I'm mad you're here."

Fri. *abbr* Friday

fri•a•ble /ˈfrajəbəl/ *adj* [*more ~; most ~*] *technical* : easily broken into smaller pieces • *friable* soil
– **fri•a•bil•i•ty** /ˌfrajəˈbɪləti/ *noun* [*noncount*]

fri•ar /ˈfrajɚ/ *noun, pl* **-ars** [*count*] : a member of a men's Roman Catholic group who is poor and studies or teaches about Christianity

fric•as•see /ˈfrɪkəˌsiː, *Brit* ˈfrɪkəˌseɪ/ *noun, pl* **-sees** [*count, noncount*] : a dish of small pieces of meat cooked in liquid and served in a thick white sauce • chicken *fricassee*

fric•a•tive /ˈfrɪkətɪv/ *noun, pl* **-tives** [*count*] *linguistics* : a sound made by forcing air out of your mouth through a narrow opening that is made using the lips, teeth, or tongue • The sounds /f v θ ð s z ʃ ʒ h/ are English *fricatives*.
– **fricative** *adj* • a *fricative* consonant

fric•tion /ˈfrɪkʃən/ *noun* [*noncount*]
1 a : the act of rubbing one thing against another • *Friction* causes heat. • the *friction* of sandpaper on wood **b** : the force that causes a moving object to slow down when it is touching another object • Oil in a car engine reduces/lessens *friction*.
2 : disagreement or tension between people or groups of people • It was difficult to reach an agreement because of the *friction* between the two sides.
– **fric•tion•al** /ˈfrɪkʃənl/ *adj, technical* • *frictional* heating
– **fric•tion•less** /ˈfrɪkʃənləs/ *adj* • a *frictionless* surface

Fri•day /ˈfraɪˌdeɪ/ *noun, pl* **-days** : the day of the week between Thursday and Saturday [*count*] She was here last *Friday*. • My birthday falls on a *Friday* this year. • (*Brit*) I'll arrive on the Monday and leave on the *Friday*. • The class meets on *Fridays*. [=every Friday] [*noncount*] I will arrive on *Friday*. = (*chiefly US*) I will arrive *Friday*. • I'll arrive on Monday and leave on *Friday*. — abbr. *Fri.*; see also GOOD FRIDAY
– **Fridays** *adv* • He works late *Fridays*. [=he works late every Friday]

fridge /ˈfrɪʤ/ *noun, pl* **fridg•es** [*count*] : REFRIGERATOR • Please put the milk in the *fridge*. ✧ In U.S. English, *fridge* is informal, but in British English it is the usual word for a refrigerator.

fridge–freezer *noun, pl* **-ers** [*count*] *Brit* : a kitchen appliance that includes both a refrigerator and a freezer ✧ In U.S. English, this appliance is usually called a *refrigerator*.

fried /ˈfraɪd/ *adj*
1 : cooked in hot oil • *fried* fish
2 *US, informal* : not able to think clearly because you are very tired • Sorry, I'm just *fried* today.

fried rice *noun* [*noncount*] *chiefly US* : a dish of rice that is cooked and then fried with soy sauce and vegetables, meat, or beaten eggs

friend /ˈfrɛnd/ *noun, pl* **friends** [*count*]
1 : a person who you like and enjoy being with • I'd like you to meet my *friend*. • She is such a good/close/dear *friend* (of mine). • We're fast *friends*. = We're the best of *friends*. • He's no *friend* of mine. • He has always been a good *friend* to me. [=he has always helped or supported me as a good friend should] • She's my ***best friend***. [=my closest friend] • We are ***childhood friends***. [=we have been friends since we were children] • ***old friends*** [=people who have been friends for a long time] • She is an ***old family friend***. = She is an ***old friend of the family***. [=she has known and spent time with the family over many years] • We are ***just friends***. [=we are not in a romantic relationship] • He wants to ***be friends with*** my younger sister. [=he wants to be my sister's friend] • She ***is best friends with*** my younger sister. [=she is my youngest sister's closest friend] ✧ *Friend* is sometimes used in a humorous or ironic way to refer to someone who is annoying or disliked. • Has our *friend* with the rude attitude been bothering you lately? • Don't look now. Here comes your *friend*.
2 : a person who helps or supports someone or something (such as a cause or charity) • She is a *friend* of the environment. [=she supports environmental causes] • The strikers knew they had a *friend* in the senator. [=knew that the senator supported them] • Are you *friend* or foe? [=do you support us or oppose us?]
3 ***Friend*** : QUAKER
a friend in need is a friend indeed — used to say that a friend who will help you when you need help is a true friend
friends in high places ✧ To ***have friends in high places*** is to know people with social or political influence or power. • She got the job because she has *friends in high places*.
make friends : to become someone's friend • Sometimes it is hard for children to *make* new *friends*. — often + *with* • She's very good at *making friends with* people from all walks of life.
man's best friend see [1]MAN

friend•less /ˈfrɛndləs/ *adj, literary* : not having any friends : not having anyone who can help you • He was *friendless* and alone.

[1]friend•ly /ˈfrɛndli/ *adj* **friend•li•er; -est** [*also more ~; most ~*]
1 a : acting like a friend : kind and helpful • *friendly* neighbors • The local people are very *friendly* to/toward visitors. • It was *friendly* of him to offer to help us. **b** : having or showing the feelings that friends have for each other • His *friendly* smile was reassuring. • They maintained a *friendly* correspondence. • They are ***friendly with*** their new neighbors. [=they are friends with their new neighbors]
2 : showing support or approval — usually + *to* or *toward* • The boss is *friendly to* new ideas. • He accuses his political opponents of being overly *friendly toward* special interests.
3 : giving help : making the process of doing something easier • A *friendly* breeze helped us sail the boat into the harbor.
4 : cheerful or pleasant • The *friendly* glow of the fire was welcome after our hike through the snowy mountains.
5 : not an enemy : not hostile • That nation was not *friendly* (to us). • *friendly* competitors • They have enjoyed a *friendly* rivalry for many years.; *specifically* : involving or coming from your own military forces • *friendly* planes • Several soldiers were killed by ***friendly fire***. [=they were accidentally killed by weapons fired from their own side]
6 a : easy to use or understand • *friendly* computer software • a customer-*friendly* telephone system — see also USER-FRIENDLY **b** : not harmful • environmentally *friendly* products = eco-*friendly* products [=products that do not harm the environment]
7 : done for enjoyment or exercise instead of for money or prizes • a *friendly* game of tennis/poker • a *friendly* preseason match
– **friend•li•ness** *noun* [*noncount*] • She appreciated the

friendliness of her neighbors. ▪ There was *friendliness* and warmth in his eyes.

[2]**friendly** *noun, pl* **-lies** [*count*] *Brit* : a game between sports teams that is done for fun and not as part of a regular playing season ▪ a preseason *friendly*

friendly society *noun, pl* ~ **-ties** [*count*] *Brit* : an association in which members pay money to receive benefits when they are old or sick

friend·ship /ˈfrɛndˌʃɪp/ *noun, pl* **-ships**
1 : the state of being friends : the relationship between friends [*count*] They have a long-standing *friendship*. [=they have been friends for a long time] ▪ They struck up a *friendship*. [=they became friends] ▪ She formed many lasting *friendships* [=she made and kept many friends] during her time in college. ▪ a *friendship* between two countries [*noncount*] They have enjoyed many years of *friendship*.
2 [*noncount*] : a friendly feeling or attitude : kindness or help given to someone ▪ He was encouraged by the *friendship* his coworkers showed him.

frier *variant spelling of* FRYER

frieze /ˈfri:z/ *noun, pl* **friez·es** [*count*] : a decorative band or border usually on the top of a building or wall

frig·ate /ˈfrɪgət/ *noun, pl* **-ates** [*count*] : a small and fast military ship

frig·ging /ˈfrɪgɪŋ/ *adv, informal + impolite* — used to make an angry statement more forceful ▪ That was so *frigging* stupid!
– **frigging** *adj* ▪ I failed the *frigging* test.

fright /ˈfraɪt/ *noun, pl* **frights**
1 a [*noncount*] : fear caused by sudden danger : sudden fear ▪ Her eyes were wide with *fright*. ▪ He was paralyzed with/by *fright*. [=he was so afraid that he couldn't move] ▪ I almost died of *fright*. [=I was extremely afraid or terrified] ▪ I approached very slowly, but the hawk ***took fright*** [=became afraid] and flew away. **b** [*count*] : a feeling of sudden fear — usually singular ▪ When you jumped out from behind the door it gave me such a *fright*! [=it made me feel very afraid] ***synonyms*** see [1]FEAR
2 [*count*] *old-fashioned* : something that looks strange, shocking, ugly, etc. — usually singular ▪ You can't go out like that. Your hair ***looks a fright***! [=your hair looks very messy or unattractive]
— see also STAGE FRIGHT

fright·en /ˈfraɪtn̩/ *verb* **-ens**; **-ened**; **-en·ing**
1 [+ *obj*] : to cause (someone) to become afraid ▪ The story really *frightened* me. ▪ The child was badly *frightened* by the mask. ▪ The story nearly ***frightened me to death***. = The story nearly ***frightened the life out of*** me. [=the story frightened me very badly]
2 [*no obj*] : to become afraid ▪ She doesn't *frighten* easily.
frighten away/off [*phrasal verb*] ***frighten (someone or something) away/off*** : to cause (someone or something) to go away or stay away because of fear ▪ The dog *frightened* the prowler *away*. ▪ Tourists have been *frightened off* by the violence in the city.
frighten into [*phrasal verb*] ***frighten (someone) into (doing something)*** : to cause (someone) to do (something) because of fear ▪ The insurance agent tried to *frighten* her *into* buying the most expensive flood insurance. ▪ They *frightened* the boy *into* confessing his crime.
frighten out of [*phrasal verb*] ***frighten (someone) out of (doing something)*** : to keep (someone) from (doing something) because of fear ▪ Bad economic news has *frightened* people *out of* putting their money in the stock market.
– **frightened** *adj* [*more* ~; *most* ~] ▪ Are you *frightened* [=*afraid*] of dogs? ▪ a badly/very *frightened* child
– **frightening** *adj* [*more* ~; *most* ~] ▪ There were *frightening* noises outside my tent. ▪ a *frightening* mask – **fright·en·ing·ly** *adv* ▪ The car came *frighteningly* close to the guardrail. ▪ It is *frighteningly* [=*extremely*] easy to mislead voters.

fright·ful /ˈfraɪtfəl/ *adj* [*more* ~; *most* ~] *somewhat old-fashioned*
1 : causing fear ▪ As he fell, he let out a *frightful* scream. ▪ a *frightful* illness that causes extreme pain
2 : very bad or shocking ▪ The children made a *frightful* mess of the kitchen. ▪ Many critics have expressed shock at the song's *frightful* lyrics.
3 : very strong ▪ a *frightful* thirst

fright·ful·ly /ˈfraɪtfəli/ *adv, somewhat old-fashioned*
1 : in a shocking way ▪ The cost of living here is *frightfully* expensive.
2 : VERY ▪ She's *frightfully* good at her work. ▪ That's a *frightfully* clever solution.

frig·id /ˈfrɪʤəd/ *adj* [*more* ~; *most* ~]
1 : very cold ▪ The *frigid* gusts of wind stung their faces. ▪ *frigid* air/water
2 : not friendly or loving : lacking emotional warmth ▪ She was born into an emotionally *frigid* family. ▪ He looked at them with a *frigid* [=*cold*] stare.
3 *of a woman* : not wanting to have sex : not enjoying sex
– **fri·gid·i·ty** /frɪˈʤɪdəti/ *noun* [*noncount*] ▪ the *frigidity* of the climate ▪ sexual problems such as impotence and *frigidity* – **frig·id·ly** *adv* ▪ a *frigidly* cold gust of wind

frill /ˈfrɪl/ *noun, pl* **frills** [*count*]
1 : a strip of cloth that is gathered into folds on one edge and attached to something (such as clothing or curtains) as a decoration ▪ The dress had *frills* around the hem and sleeves.
2 : something that is added but is not necessary ▪ He likes plain food without any *frills*. — see also NO-FRILLS

frilly /ˈfrɪli/ *adj* **frill·i·er**; **-est** [*also more* ~; *most* ~]
1 : having frills ▪ a *frilly* dress ▪ *frilly* curtains
2 : looking like a frill : having wavy edges ▪ a plant with *frilly* leaves

[1]**fringe** /ˈfrɪnʤ/ *noun, pl* **fring·es**
1 [*count*] : a border made of hanging threads used to decorate the edge of something (such as clothing, rugs, and curtains) ▪ a lampshade with a *fringe*
2 [*count*] : a narrow area along the edge of something ▪ a *fringe* of moss around the tree — often plural ▪ Scientists were measuring temperatures at the outer *fringes* of the atmosphere.
3 [*singular*] : an area of activity that is related to but not part of whatever is central or most widely accepted ▪ a party on the political *fringe* : a group of people with extreme views or unpopular opinions ▪ the conservative/liberal *fringe* — often used before another noun ▪ a *fringe* topic ▪ published in a *fringe* journal ▪ *fringe* theater ▪ the *fringe* element ▪ *fringe* activists — see also LUNATIC FRINGE
4 [*count*] *Brit* : the front section of hair cut short and worn over the forehead : BANGS — usually singular ▪ She wears her hair in a *fringe*.
on the fringe(s) : on the outer edge of something ▪ They lived *on the fringe* of the forest. — often used figuratively ▪ He has been working for years *on the fringes* of the entertainment industry.

[2]**fringe** *verb* **fringes**; **fringed**; **fring·ing** [+ *obj*]
1 : to decorate (something) with a fringe ▪ a *fringed* leather vest
2 : to go along or around (something) ▪ A jungle *fringed* the shore.

fringe benefit *noun, pl* ~ **-fits** [*count*] : something extra (such as vacation time) that is given by an employer to workers in addition to their regular pay

frip·pery /ˈfrɪpəri/ *noun, pl* **-peries** *somewhat formal + old-fashioned* : something that is not necessary or not serious [*noncount*] The design is simple and devoid of needless *frippery*. [*count*] needless *fripperies*

Fris·bee /ˈfrɪzbi/ *trademark* — used for a plastic disc that you throw to someone who tries to catch it as part of a game

frisk /ˈfrɪsk/ *verb* **frisks**; **frisked**; **frisk·ing** [+ *obj*] : to pass your hands over (someone) to search for something that may be hidden in clothing ▪ All visitors to the prison are *frisked* (for weapons) before they're allowed to enter.

frisky /ˈfrɪski/ *adj* **frisk·i·er**; **-est** [*more* ~; *most* ~]
1 : very playful or lively ▪ *frisky* kittens ▪ The kids were *frisky* after all that candy.
2 *informal* : sexually playful or excited ▪ feeling *frisky*
– **frisk·i·ly** /ˈfrɪskəli/ *adv* ▪ kittens playing *friskily* on the lawn – **frisk·i·ness** *noun* [*noncount*] ▪ the *friskiness* of the kittens

fris·son /friˈsoun/ *noun, pl* **-sons** [*count*] *somewhat formal* : a sudden strong feeling or emotion ▪ a *frisson* of surprise

[1]**frit·ter** /ˈfrɪtɚ/ *noun, pl* **-ters** [*count*] : a small piece of food that has been coated in a flour and egg mixture and fried ▪ apple/corn *fritters*

[2]**fritter** *verb* **-ters**; **-tered**; **-ter·ing**
fritter away [*phrasal verb*] ***fritter away (something) or fritter (something) away*** : to spend or use up (something) in a slow and usually foolish way ▪ He *frittered* the afternoon *away*. ▪ He *frittered away* his fortune on gambling.

fritz /ˈfrɪts/ *noun*
on the fritz *US, informal* : not working properly ▪ We can't listen to music because the stereo is *on the fritz*.

fri·vol·i·ty /frɪˈvɑːləti/ *noun, pl* **-ties**
1 [*noncount*] : a lack of seriousness : the quality or state of being silly or frivolous ▪ He has no patience for *frivolity*.
2 [*count*] : something that is unnecessary or silly ▪ He spends money on the latest fashions and other *frivolities*.

friv·o·lous /ˈfrɪvələs/ *adj* [*more* ~; *most* ~]
1 : not important : not deserving serious attention ▪ She thinks window shopping is a *frivolous* activity. ▪ a *frivolous* lawsuit [=a lawsuit about something that is not important]
2 : silly and not serious ▪ a *frivolous* conversation
– **friv·o·lous·ly** *adv* ▪ She was spending money *frivolously*.
– **friv·o·lous·ness** *noun* [*noncount*]

frizz /ˈfrɪz/ *noun* [*noncount*] : very tightly curled hair ▪ She used gel on her hair to control the *frizz*.
– **frizz** *verb* **frizz·es**; **frizzed**; **frizz·ing** [*no obj*] ▪ Humidity makes my hair *frizz*. – **frizzy** /ˈfrɪzi/ *adj* **frizz·i·er**; **-est** ▪ *frizzy* hair

fro /ˈfroʊ/ *adv* see TO AND FRO

F

frock /ˈfrɑːk/ *noun, pl* **frocks** [*count*]
1 *old-fashioned* : a woman's or girl's dress ▪ wearing an old *frock* ▪ a party *frock*
2 : a long outer garment worn by some Christian monks and friars

frock coat *noun, pl* ~ **coats** [*count*] *old-fashioned* : a long coat worn by men especially in the 19th century

frog /ˈfrɑːg/ *noun, pl* **frogs** [*count*]
1 : a small animal that spends much of the time in water and has smooth skin, webbed feet, and long back legs for jumping — compare TOAD
2 *Frog informal + offensive* : a French person ✧ This sense is very offensive and should be avoided.
a frog in your throat ✧ If you have *a frog in your throat*, you are unable to speak normally because your throat is dry.

frog

toad

frog·man /ˈfrɑːg,mæn/ *noun, pl* **-men** /-,mɛn/ [*count*] : a person (especially a man in the military or police) who uses special equipment to work underwater for long periods of time

frog–march /ˈfrɑːg,maɚʧ/ *verb* **-march·es**; **-marched**; **-march·ing** [+ *obj*] *chiefly Brit* : to grab and force (someone) to walk forward by pushing from behind ▪ They *frog-marched* him out the door.

[1]**frol·ic** /ˈfrɑːlɪk/ *verb* **-ics**; **-icked**; **-ick·ing** [*no obj*] : to play and move about happily : ROMP ▪ We watched the seals as they *frolicked* in the harbor. ▪ children *frolicking* in the yard

[2]**frolic** *noun, pl* **-ics** : an enjoyable time or activity [*count*] We went out for a *frolic* in the sun. [*noncount*] an evening of fun and *frolic*

frol·ic·some /ˈfrɑːlɪksəm/ *adj* [*more* ~; *most* ~] : very lively and playful ▪ *frolicsome* children

from /ˈfrʌm, ˈfrɑːm, frəm/ *prep*
1 — used to indicate the starting point of a physical movement or action ▪ He drove here *from* the city. ▪ He set out *from* town this morning. ▪ She took a fall *from* a horse. ▪ The cat came out *from* under the table.
2 — used to indicate the place that something comes out of ▪ He took a dime *from* [=*out of*] his pocket.
3 — used to indicate the place where someone lives or was born ▪ My family is/comes originally *from* Italy. ▪ Where are you *from*? = Where do you come *from*?
4 — used to indicate the starting or central point of any activity ▪ She looked at me *from* under her glasses. ▪ He spoke *from* the heart. ▪ She watched us *from* across the street.
5 — used to indicate the starting point in measuring something ▪ The meeting is scheduled for a week *from* today. ▪ It's 20 miles *from* here to the nearest town. ▪ They were married three years *from* that day. ▪ *From* childhood (onward) he displayed unusual musical talent.
6 — used to indicate a physical separation between two things ▪ An ocean separates America *from* Europe.
7 — used to indicate something that is removed, released, blocked, or prevented ▪ This lotion provides protection *from* the sun. ▪ relief *from* anxiety ▪ They asked him to refrain *from* interrupting. ▪ They have no right to exclude her *from* membership. ▪ The dictator fell *from* power. ▪ subtract 3 *from* 9
8 — used to indicate change to a different state or condition ▪ Things have gone *from* bad to worse. ▪ They were transformed *from* raw recruits into trained soldiers.
9 — used to indicate the material that is used to make something ▪ Wine is made *from* grapes. ▪ a doll made *from* cloth
10 — used to indicate the source of something ▪ I'm expecting a call *from* my lawyer. ▪ All his problems have come *from* that one bad decision. ▪ She received a letter *from* home. ▪ reading aloud *from* a book ▪ He inherited a love of music *from* his father. ▪ I bought a book *from* him. [=he sold a book to me] ▪ The painting was done directly *from* nature. ▪ She drew it *from* memory.
11 — used to indicate the basis or cause of something ▪ We conclude *from* this that no changes are necessary. ▪ He's suffering *from* a bad cold. ▪ They were weak *from* hunger. ▪ I could tell she was angry *from* [=*by*] the look on her face.
12 — used to indicate the lowest point, amount, etc., in a range ▪ These parts cost (anywhere/anything) *from* $5 to $10. ▪ It's anywhere *from* $50,000 on up. [=it is at least $50,000 and could be more]
13 — used to indicate the group or number of people or things out of which someone or something is chosen or selected ▪ She was chosen *from* a large number of competitors.
as from see [2]AS

frond /ˈfrɑːnd/ *noun, pl* **fronds** [*count*] : a large, long leaf ▪ palm *fronds*

[1]**front** /ˈfrʌnt/ *noun, pl* **fronts**
1 [*count*] : the forward part or surface of something : the part of something that is seen first — usually singular ▪ the *front* of a shirt ▪ the *front* of the house [=the part facing the street] ▪ The jacket zips down the *front*. [=has a zipper that goes from the collar to the waist to open and close it] ▪ There's a picture on the *front* of the box. [=on the part of the box that usually faces out and that you see first] — see also SHOP FRONT, STOREFRONT
2 [*count*] : a place, position, or area that is most forward or is directly ahead — usually singular ▪ The teacher asked her to come (up) to the *front* of the classroom. ▪ She was sitting in the *front* of the bus.
3 [*count*] : the part of your body that faces forward and includes your face and chest — usually singular ▪ The baby rolled onto his *front*.
4 [*count*] : the part of a book, magazine, etc., that includes the first few pages — usually singular ▪ You'll find that information in the *front* of the book.
5 [*singular*] : a way of behaving that is meant to hide your true feelings, thoughts, etc. ▪ I can't believe that your anger was all just a *front*! [=that you were pretending to be angry] ▪ She ***put up a good/brave front***, but I know she was very disappointed. [=she acted as if she was not disappointed]
6 [*count*] : someone or something that hides or protects an illegal activity ▪ The business is a *front* for organized crime.
7 [*count*] **a** : an area where military forces are fighting ▪ The general is sending more troops to the *front*. — see also HOME FRONT **b** : an area or field of activity — usually singular ▪ We are making progress on the educational *front*. ▪ Not much has been happening on the political *front*.
8 [*count*] *weather* : the place where two large areas of air that are of different temperatures come together — see also COLD FRONT, WARM FRONT
front to back of a piece of clothing : with the front where the back should be ▪ He accidentally put the sweater on *front to back*. [=*back to front, backwards*]
in front **1** : in a forward position : in an area at the front of something ▪ There was room for one passenger *in front*, so the rest of us sat in back. **2** : in the leading position in a race or competition ▪ She's still *in front*, but the other runners are catching up to her. — often used after *out* ▪ She's still *out in front*.
in front of **1** : directly before or ahead of (something or someone) ▪ A tree stood *in front of* the house. ▪ A deer ran (out) *in front of* the car. ▪ They are frightened of what lies *in front of* them. [=what is in the future] **2** : in the presence of (someone) ▪ We shouldn't argue *in front of* the children.
out front **1** : in the area directly before or ahead of something (such as a building) ▪ There was a small statue on the lawn *out front*. **2** : in the audience ▪ There are about 20,000 screaming fans *out front*.
united front : a group of people or organizations that join together to achieve a shared goal ▪ We've decided to

present a *united front* against these proposals.

up front **1** : in or at the most forward position ▪ They told us we could sit *up front*. **2** *informal* : before beginning to do something : in advance ▪ He'll do the work, but he insists on being paid *up front*. **3** *informal* : in a direct and honest way ▪ They told me *up front* that my chances of being selected weren't good. — see also UP-FRONT

²front *adj, always used before a noun*

1 : of or relating to the front : located at the front ▪ There's a small statue on the *front* lawn. ▪ He keeps his wallet in his *front* pocket. ▪ the *front* entrance/hall ▪ She likes to sit in the *front* [=*first*] row. = She likes *front*-row seats. ▪ the *front* door [=the door in the front of a building that is usually the main entrance] ▪ The story appeared on the *front* page [=the first page] of the newspaper. ▪ We checked into the hotel at the ***front desk***. [=the desk in a building where visitors are greeted] ▪ There is a dent in the car's **front end**. [=the part of a vehicle that faces forward]

2 *golf* — used to refer to the first 9 holes of an 18-hole golf course ▪ He was two over par on the *front* nine.

front and center *US* : in the most important position or area ▪ These issues are *front and center* in voters' minds.

³front *verb* **fronts; front·ed; front·ing**

1 : to have the face or front toward (something) [+ *obj*] The house *fronts* Main Street. [*no obj*] The house *fronts* on/onto Main Street.

2 [+ *obj*] **a** : to be the leader or lead singer of (a musical group) ▪ He is now *fronting* a different band. **b** *Brit* : to host or present (a radio or TV program) ▪ He *fronts* a talk show.

3 [+ *obj*] *US, informal* : to give (someone) the money needed to do something (such as to start a business) ▪ The record company will *front* (them) the money to record the album.

front·age /ˈfrʌntɪʤ/ *noun* [*noncount*] : the part of a building or of the land that a building is on that runs along a river, road, etc. ▪ We have 200 feet of *frontage* on Main Street.

frontage road *noun, pl* ~ **roads** [*count*] *US* : SERVICE ROAD

front·al /ˈfrʌntl/ *adj, always used before a noun*

1 : relating to the front of something : directed at the front ▪ a *frontal* attack

2 : relating to or showing the front of the human body ▪ (full) *frontal* nudity

– fron·tal·ly *adv* ▪ The enemy attacked them *frontally*.

front bench *noun, pl* ~ **bench·es** [*count*] *Brit* : the front row of seats on both sides in a British legislature (such as the House of Commons) where the leaders sit; *also* : the leaders themselves ▪ He challenged the views of his party's *front bench*. ▪ the party's *front-bench* spokesman — compare BACKBENCH

– front–bench·er /ˈfrʌntˈbɛnʧɚ/ *noun, pl* **-ers** [*count*] ▪ He has been a *front-bencher* for 20 years.

front burner *noun*

on the front burner *chiefly US* : in the position of something that will receive immediate attention and action ▪ The President has put tax cuts *on the front burner*. — compare BACK BURNER

front–end loader *noun, pl* ~ **-ers** [*count*] *chiefly US* : a vehicle with a large scoop in front that is used for digging and loading loose material — called also *front loader*; see picture at CONSTRUCTION

fron·tier /ˌfrʌnˈtiɚ, *Brit* ˈfrʌntɪə/ *noun, pl* **-tiers** [*count*]

1 : a border between two countries ▪ the *frontier* between Canada and the U.S.

2 : a distant area where few people live ▪ They were sent on an expedition to explore the western *frontier*. ▪ *frontier* life

3 : the limits of knowledge in a particular field — usually plural ▪ the *frontiers* of science ▪ a discovery at the very *frontiers* of our understanding

fron·tiers·man /ˌfrʌnˈtiɚzmən, *Brit* ˈfrʌntɪəzmən/ *noun, pl* **-men** /-mən/ [*count*] : a person (especially a man) who lives on the frontier (sense 2)

fron·tis·piece /ˈfrʌntəˌspiːs/ *noun, pl* **-piec·es** [*count*] : a picture in the front of a book ✧ The *frontispiece* of a book comes before and usually faces the title page.

front line *noun, pl* ~ **lines** [*count*]

1 : an area where soldiers are fighting : ¹FRONT 7a ▪ troops on the *front line* = *front-line* troops

2 : the most important and active position in a job or field of activity ▪ These researchers are on/at the *front line* of defense against cancer. ▪ She has been working on the *front lines* to educate the poor.

front loader *noun, pl* ~ **loaders** [*count*] *US* : FRONT-END LOADER

front matter *noun* [*noncount*] : the pages at the beginning of a book before the main part ▪ The conventions of the book are explained in the *front matter*. — compare BACK MATTER

front office *noun* [*noncount*] : the people who manage a business or organization (such as a professional sports team) ▪ Many fans blame the team's poor performance on bad decisions made by the *front office*. — often used before another noun ▪ a *front-office* job ▪ *front-office* decisions

front–page /ˈfrʌntˈpeɪʤ/ *adj, always used before a noun*

1 : printed on the front page of a newspaper ▪ a *front-page* story/photograph

2 : very important ▪ *front-page* news ▪ a *front-page* political event

front room *noun, pl* ~ **rooms** [*count*] : LIVING ROOM

front–run·ner /ˈfrʌntˌrʌnɚ/ *noun, pl* **-ners** [*count*] : the person or thing that is most likely to win a race or competition ▪ the presidential *front-runner*

front–wheel drive *noun* [*noncount*] : a system that applies engine power to the front wheels of a vehicle ▪ a car with *front-wheel drive*

frosh /ˈfrɑːʃ/ *noun, pl* **frosh·es** [*count*] *US, informal + old-fashioned* : FRESHMAN

¹frost /ˈfrɑːst/ *noun, pl* **frosts**

1 [*noncount*] : a thin layer of ice that forms on the ground, on grass, etc., when the air becomes cold ▪ The grass was covered with *frost*. ▪ light/heavy *frost* ▪ *Frost* formed on the window.

2 [*count*] : the occurrence of weather that is cold enough to cause water to freeze and frost to form ▪ These plants should bloom until the first *frost* of the season. ▪ We had an early/late *frost*. ▪ a killing *frost* [=weather that is so cold that the frost kills plants]

²frost *verb* **frosts; frost·ed; frost·ing**

1 a [+ *obj*] : to cover (something) with frost ▪ The cold had *frosted* the windows. **b** [*no obj*] : to become covered with frost ▪ The windows *frosted* (up).

2 [+ *obj*] *chiefly US* : to cover (something, such as a cake) with frosting (sense 1) ▪ I have to *frost* the birthday cake.

3 [+ *obj*] *chiefly US* : to make small strips of your hair lighter so the top layer of your hair is lighter than the rest of it ▪ She *frosts* her bangs.

frost·bite /ˈfrɑːstˌbaɪt/ *noun* [*noncount*] : a condition in which part of your body (such as your fingers or toes) freezes or almost freezes ▪ minor *frostbite* ▪ He wore gloves to prevent *frostbite*.

frost·ed /ˈfrɑːstəd/ *adj*

1 : having a dull surface that looks as if it is covered with frost ▪ *frosted* glass

2 *chiefly US, of hair* : having very small strips on the top layer of your hair that are lighter than the rest of your hair ▪ She has *frosted* bangs.

frost·ing /ˈfrɑːstɪŋ/ *noun, pl* **-ings** [*count*]

1 *chiefly US* : a sweet, creamy mixture that is used to cover cakes ▪ We put *frosting* on the cupcakes. — called also *icing*

2 : a dull surface on metal or glass

frosty /ˈfrɑːsti/ *adj* **frost·i·er; -est**

1 : cold enough to produce frost ▪ a *frosty* night

2 : covered with frost ▪ *frosty* windows

3 : unfriendly or cold ▪ a *frosty* stare ▪ We received a *frosty* welcome.

– frost·i·ly /ˈfrɑːstəli/ *adv* ▪ She was glaring *frostily* at us. **– frost·i·ness** *noun* [*noncount*] ▪ There's some *frostiness* [=*coolness*] between them. ▪ the *frostiness* of the night

¹froth /ˈfrɑːθ/ *noun* [*noncount*]

1 : bubbles that form in or on a liquid ▪ *froth* on the waves

2 : something that is appealing but that has no serious value or interest ▪ news shows full of *froth*

– froth·i·ness /ˈfrɑːθinəs/ *noun* ▪ the *frothiness* of the cream **– frothy** /ˈfrɑːθi/ *adj* ▪ the *frothy* waves ▪ a *frothy* comedy

²froth *verb* **froths; frothed; froth·ing** [*no obj*] : to produce or form froth ▪ The water *frothed* as the waves broke along the shore.

froth at the mouth **1** : to produce froth from the mouth because of illness or excitement ▪ The dog was *frothing* [=*foaming*] *at the mouth*. **2** *informal* : to be very angry about something ▪ She was *frothing* [=*foaming*] *at the mouth* with rage.

frou–frou /ˈfruːˌfruː/ *adj* [*more* ~; *most* ~] *chiefly US, informal* : very heavily decorated and fancy ▪ *frou-frou* designs

¹frown /ˈfraʊn/ *noun, pl* **frowns** [*count*] : a serious facial expression that usually shows anger, displeasure, or concentration ▪ She was wearing a *frown*. [=she was frowning]

[2]**frown** *verb* **frowns; frowned; frown·ing** [*no obj*] : to make a frown in anger, concentration, etc. ▪ She was *frowning* when she entered the room, so I knew that she was annoyed about something.

frown on/upon [*phrasal verb*] ***frown on/upon (something)*** : to disapprove of (something) ▪ The company *frowns on* dating among employees. ▪ Public expressions of affection are *frowned upon* in many cultures.

– **frown·ing·ly** /ˈfraʊnɪŋli/ *adv* ▪ She stared *frowningly*.

frow·sy *also* **frow·zy** /ˈfraʊzi/ *adj* **frow·si·er** *also* **frow·zi·er; -est** *US, informal* : having a messy or dirty appearance ▪ a *frowsy* old sweater ▪ *frowsy* hair

froze *past tense of* [1]FREEZE

frozen *past participle of* [1]FREEZE

frozen yogurt *noun, pl* ~ **-gurts** [*count, noncount*] *chiefly US* : a sweet frozen dessert that is like ice cream but is made with yogurt

fruc·tose /ˈfrʌkˌtoʊs/ *noun* [*noncount*] : a very sweet kind of sugar that is found in fruit juices and honey

fru·gal /ˈfruːgəl/ *adj* [*more* ~; *most* ~]

1 : careful about spending money or using things when you do not need to : using money or supplies in a very careful way ▪ He's a *frugal* shopper. — often + *with* ▪ She's very *frugal with* her money.

2 : simple and plain ▪ a *frugal* meal of bread and cheese

– **fru·gal·i·ty** /fruˈgæləti/ *noun* [*noncount*] ▪ He's admired for his *frugality*. – **fru·gal·ly** /ˈfruːgəli/ *adv* ▪ She's trying to live *frugally*.

[1]**fruit** /ˈfruːt/ *noun, pl* **fruits**

1 a : a usually sweet food (such as a blueberry, orange, or apple) that grows on a tree or bush [*count*] apples, oranges, and other *fruits* [*noncount*] a bowl/piece of *fruit* — often used before another noun ▪ *fruit* salad [=a mixture of fruits cut into small pieces] ▪ *fruit* juice ▪ a *fruit* tree [=a tree that bears fruit] — see color picture on page C5; see also FORBIDDEN FRUIT **b** [*count*] *technical* : the part of a plant that has the seeds in it (such as the pod of a pea, a nut, a grain, or a berry)

2 [*count*] : a result or reward that comes from some action or activity — usually plural ▪ They're finally able to enjoy the *fruits* of their labors. ▪ We hope that we'll be able to share in the *fruits* of victory.

3 [*count*] : something that exists naturally in the world and is useful to people — usually plural ▪ We need to remember that the *fruits* of the earth belong to us all.

bear fruit see [2]BEAR

the fruit of someone's loins see LOIN

[2]**fruit** *verb* **fruits; fruit·ed; fruit·ing** [*no obj*] *technical* : to produce fruit ▪ When will the trees *fruit*?

fruit bat *noun, pl* ~ **bats** [*count*] : a large bat that eats fruit and lives in hot parts of the world

fruit·cake /ˈfruːtˌkeɪk/ *noun, pl* **-cakes** [*count*]

1 : a very sweet cake that contains nuts, fruits, and spices

2 *informal* : a foolish, strange, or crazy person : NUT ▪ He's a real *fruitcake*. = He's ***as nutty as a fruitcake***.

fruit fly *noun, pl* ~ **flies** [*count*] : a small fly that eats fruit or rotting vegetables

fruit·ful /ˈfruːtfəl/ *adj* [*more* ~; *most* ~] : producing a good result : very productive ▪ We had a *fruitful* discussion about the problems with the schedule. ▪ a *fruitful* meeting ▪ *fruitful* ideas/methods/suggestions — compare FRUITLESS

– **fruit·ful·ly** *adv* ▪ These problems could be *fruitfully* addressed. – **fruit·ful·ness** *noun* [*noncount*]

fru·i·tion /fruˈɪʃən/ *noun* [*noncount*] : the state of being real or complete — used after *come to* or *bring to* ▪ His plans have finally *come to fruition*. [=he has finally done the things that he planned to do] ▪ She was never able to *bring* her dreams *to fruition*. [=she was never able to achieve her dreams]

fruit·less /ˈfruːtləs/ *adj* : producing no good results : not successful ▪ They made a *fruitless* attempt to find a solution. ▪ It would be *fruitless* to continue. ▪ a *fruitless* argument — compare FRUITFUL

– **fruit·less·ly** *adv* ▪ They argued *fruitlessly*. – **fruit·less·ness** *noun* [*noncount*]

fruit machine *noun, pl* ~ **-chines** [*count*] *Brit* : SLOT MACHINE

fruity /ˈfruːti/ *adj* **fruit·i·er; -est**

1 : tasting or smelling like fruit ▪ a *fruity* smell/taste ▪ a *fruity* wine

2 *US, informal* : strange or crazy ▪ She acts a little *fruity*.

3 *Brit, of a voice* : rich and deep

frump /ˈfrʌmp/ *noun, pl* **frumps** [*count*] *disapproving* : a woman who wears unattractive clothes or does not make an effort to appear attractive ▪ an old *frump*

frumpy /ˈfrʌmpi/ *adj* **frump·i·er; -est** : dressed in an unattractive way ▪ a *frumpy* housewife; *also, of clothing* : old and unattractive ▪ That's a *frumpy* dress.

frus·trate /ˈfrʌˌstreɪt/ *verb* **-trates; -trat·ed; -trat·ing** [+ *obj*]

1 : to cause (someone) to feel angry, discouraged, or upset because of not being able to do something ▪ It *frustrated* him to miss so many games because of injuries. ▪ We've been *frustrated* by bureaucratic delays.

2 : to prevent (efforts, plans, etc.) from succeeding ▪ Bureaucratic delays have *frustrated* our efforts to resolve this problem. : to keep (someone) from doing something ▪ The lack of investors has *frustrated* them in their efforts to expand the company.

frustrated *adj*

1 [*more* ~; *most* ~] : very angry, discouraged, or upset because of being unable to do or complete something ▪ By the end of the day, we were all feeling very tired and *frustrated*. ▪ They were getting pretty *frustrated* with/at the delay. ▪ sexually *frustrated* [=wanting to have sex but not able to; not satisfied sexually]

2 *always used before a noun* : trying to do something or gain a skill but not successful ▪ He works in an office, but he's really a *frustrated* actor/writer. [=a person who wants to be an actor/writer but is not]

frus·trat·ing /ˈfrʌˌstreɪtɪŋ/ *adj* [*more* ~; *most* ~] : causing feelings of anger and annoyance ▪ All these delays have been very *frustrating*.

– **frus·trat·ing·ly** *adv* ▪ *frustratingly* long delays

frus·tra·tion /ˌfrʌˈstreɪʃən/ *noun, pl* **-tions**

1 a [*noncount*] : a feeling of anger or annoyance caused by being unable to do something : the state of being frustrated ▪ He shook his head in *frustration*. ▪ These bureaucratic delays have been causing us a lot of *frustration*. **b** [*count*] : something that causes feelings of anger and annoyance : something that frustrates someone ▪ These delays have proven to be a major *frustration*. ▪ We've been experiencing a lot of *frustrations*.

2 [*noncount*] : the act of preventing the success of something : the act of frustrating something ▪ He was angry about the *frustration* of his plans.

[1]**fry** /ˈfraɪ/ *verb* **fries; fried; fry·ing** : to cook (food) in fat or oil [+ *obj*] They *fried* (up) some chicken for dinner. ▪ They *fried* us some chicken. = They *fried* some chicken for us. ▪ We had *fried* eggs and ham for breakfast. [*no obj*] We could smell the onions *frying*. — see also DEEP-FRY, PANFRY, STIR-FRY

fish to fry see [1]FISH

[2]**fry** *noun, pl* **fries** [*count*] *US* : FRENCH FRY — usually plural ▪ steak and *fries* [=(*Brit*) *chips*] ▪ Would you like an order of *fries* with your hamburger? — see also FISH FRY, STIR-FRY — compare [3]FRY

[3]**fry** *noun* [*plural*] : very young fish — see also SMALL FRY — compare [2]FRY

fry·er /ˈfrajɚ/ *noun, pl* **-ers** [*count*]

1 : a deep pan for frying foods

2 *chiefly US* : a young chicken that is suitable for frying — compare BROILER, ROASTER

frying pan *noun, pl* ~ **pans** [*count*] : a metal pan that has a long handle and is used for frying — called also (*chiefly US*) *skillet*; see picture at KITCHEN

from/out of the frying pan (and) into the fire ✧ If you have gone or jumped *from* or *out of the frying pan (and) into the fire*, you have gone from a bad situation or problem to a worse one.

fry pan *noun, pl* ~ **pans** [*count*] *US* : FRYING PAN

fry–up /ˈfraɪˌʌp/ *noun, pl* **-ups** [*count*] *Brit* : a dish or meal of fried food

ft. *abbr* **1** feet; foot **2** fort

FTC *abbr* Federal Trade Commission ▪ The company is being investigated by the *FTC*. ✧ The Federal Trade Commission is a part of the U.S. federal government that is responsible for preventing unfair or deceptive business practices.

FTP /ˌɛfˌtiːˈpiː/ *noun* [*noncount*] : a system for sending files from one computer to another computer over the Internet ▪ files sent by *FTP* ✧ *FTP* is an abbreviation of "file transfer protocol."

fuch•sia /ˈfjuːʃə/ *noun, pl* **-sias** [*count, noncount*]
1 : a type of bush that has large pink, red, purple, or white flowers — see color picture on page C6
2 : a bright reddish-purple color — see color picture on page C3

[1]**fuck** /ˈfʌk/ *verb* **fucks; fucked; fuck•ing** ✧ *Fuck* is an extremely offensive word in all of its uses and should be avoided.
1 *offensive + obscene* **a** [*no obj*] : to have sex **b** [+ *obj*] : to have sex with (someone)
2 [+ *obj*] *offensive* : to cheat or mistreat (someone) • They really *fucked* me (over) when they sold me that car.
3 *offensive* — used to express anger, disgust, etc. • I'm tired of waiting. *Fuck* it, let's get out of here. • If you don't like it—*fuck you*! • Oh *fuck*, they've left without us!
fuck off [*phrasal verb*] *offensive* — used as an angry command to tell someone to go away
fuck up [*phrasal verb*] *offensive* **1** : to act stupidly : to make mistakes • You really *fucked up* this time, getting to work so late. **2** ***fuck up (something) or fuck (something) up*** : to ruin (something) by being stupid or careless • You really *fucked up* our schedule! **3** ***fuck up (someone) or fuck (someone) up*** : to cause (someone) to become confused, crazy, etc. • The war really *fucked* him *up*.
fuck with [*phrasal verb*] *offensive* **1** ***fuck with (something)*** : to handle (something) carelessly : to mess with (something) • Don't you dare *fuck with* my stereo. **2** ***fuck with (someone)*** : to treat (someone) wrongly : to mess with (someone) • Don't *fuck with* me!

[2]**fuck** *noun, pl* **fucks**
1 [*count*] *offensive + obscene* : an act of sexual intercourse
2 [*count*] *offensive + obscene* : a sexual partner
3 *offensive* **a** [*singular*] : anything at all — usually used in negative statements • I don't ***give/care a fuck*** about their problems. **b** [*noncount*] — used with *the* as a way to make an angry statement or question more forceful • What *the fuck* do they want from me? • Shut *the fuck* up!
4 [*count*] *US, offensive* : FUCKER • He's a stupid *fuck*.

fuck all *noun* [*noncount*] *Brit, offensive* : NOTHING • You've done *fuck all* to help me!

fuck•er /ˈfʌkɚ/ *noun, pl* **-ers** [*count*] *offensive* : an annoying person or thing • That little *fucker* is going to get it from me!

fuck•ing /ˈfʌkɪŋ/ *adj, offensive* — used to make an angry statement more forceful • He's such a *fucking* idiot!
– fucking *adv, offensive* • She thinks she's so *fucking* cool.

fud•dy–dud•dy /ˈfʌdiˌdʌdi/ *noun, pl* **-dies** [*count*] *informal + disapproving* : a person with old-fashioned or conservative ideas and attitudes • He's just an old *fuddy-duddy*.

[1]**fudge** /ˈfʌʤ/ *verb* **fudg•es; fudged; fudg•ing**
1 a [+ *obj*] : to fail to deal with (something) in an open and direct way • Politicians have been known to *fudge* the issues. **b** [*no obj*] : to speak or act in a way that is meant to avoid dealing with a problem directly — often + *on* • The company *fudged on* how it would deal with the problem.
2 [+ *obj*] : to change (something) in order to trick people • The treasurer *fudged* the figures. • It was later discovered that the researchers had *fudged* their data. • *fudge* the facts

[2]**fudge** *noun, pl* **fudges**
1 [*noncount*] : a soft, sweet brown candy • We bought three kinds of *fudge*. • chocolate *fudge*
2 [*count*] : a statement that does not deal with a problem or issue in a direct way • His response to these charges has been a series of denials and *fudges*.
hot fudge *US* : a hot, thick, chocolate sauce that is usually served on ice cream • a *hot-fudge* sundae [=an ice-cream sundae made with hot fudge]
– fudgy /ˈfʌʤi/ *adj* **fudg•i•er; -est** *chiefly US* • *fudgy*, chewy brownies

[1]**fu•el** /ˈfjuːwəl/ *noun, pl* **fuels**
1 [*count, noncount*] : a material (such as coal, oil, or gas) that is burned to produce heat or power • a gallon of *fuel* • a 16-gallon *fuel* tank • I had the *fuel* pump replaced on my car. — often used figuratively • Breakfast is my *fuel* to get through the morning. — see also FOSSIL FUEL
2 [*noncount*] : something that gives support or strength to something (such as argument or angry feelings) • These latest scandals will provide further *fuel* for his political opponents. • These latest accusations will only add *fuel* to the controversy. • The controversy continues to rage, and these latest accusations will only ***add fuel to the fire***.

[2]**fuel** *verb* **fuels;** *US* **fueled** *or Brit* **fuelled;** *US* **fuel•ing** *or Brit* **fuel•ling**
1 a [+ *obj*] : to supply (something) with fuel • The airplanes were *fueled* in midair. **b** [*no obj*] : to take in fuel • The airplanes *fueled (up)* in midair.
2 [+ *obj*] **a** : to give support or strength to (something) • The criticism she has faced has only *fueled* her determination to succeed. **b** : to provide the necessary conditions for (something) • Inflation was *fueled* by high prices. • The strong economy has *fueled* the construction of new homes.
fuel up [*phrasal verb*] : to put fuel into a car, airplane, etc. • They *fueled up* for their long journey home.

fug /ˈfʌg/ *noun* [*noncount*] *chiefly Brit* : the unpleasant air in a room that is very crowded, smoky, etc. • They sat in the dense *fug* of a smoky bar.

[1]**fu•gi•tive** /ˈfjuːʤətɪv/ *noun, pl* **-tives** [*count*] : a person who is running away to avoid being captured • They discovered that the slave was a *fugitive*; *especially* : a person who is trying to escape being arrested by the police — often + *from* • He's a *fugitive from* the law. • She has been charged with helping a ***fugitive from justice***.

[2]**fugitive** *adj, always used before a noun*
1 : running away to avoid being captured • a *fugitive* slave
2 *literary* : lasting a very short time • As he daydreamed, *fugitive* thoughts/dreams passed through his mind.

fugue /ˈfjuːg/ *noun, pl* **fugues** [*count*] : a piece of music in which tunes are repeated in complex patterns

[1]**-ful** /fəl/ *adj suffix*
1 : full of • pride*ful* • event*ful*
2 : characterized by • peace*ful* • success*ful*
3 : having the qualities of • master*ful*
4 : tending or likely to • forget*ful* • help*ful*

[2]**-ful** /fʊl/ *noun suffix* : the number or amount that fills or would fill • a room*ful* • a cup*ful* • a spoon*ful*

ful•crum /ˈfʊlkrəm, ˈfʌlkrəm/ *noun, pl* **ful•crums** *also* **ful•cra** /ˈfʊlkrə, ˈfʌlkrə/ [*count*] *technical* : the support on which a lever moves when it is used to lift something

ful•fill (*US*) *or Brit* **ful•fil** /fʊlˈfɪl/ *verb, US* **fulfills** *or Brit* **fulfils; ful•filled; ful•fill•ing** [+ *obj*]
1 : to do what is required by (something, such as a promise or a contract) • *fulfill* a promise/vow • He *fulfilled* his pledge to cut taxes. • She failed to *fulfill* her obligations.
2 a : to succeed in doing or providing (something) • They haven't yet *fulfilled* [=*met, satisfied*] the requirements needed to graduate. • The program is intended to *fulfill* the basic needs of children in the community. • The committee was disbanded after it had *fulfilled* its purpose. [=after it had done what it was intended to do] **b** : to succeed in achieving (something) : to make (something, such as a dream) true or real • If we could have that house, our dreams would be *fulfilled*. • He *fulfilled* his childhood wish to become a professional baseball player. • She *fulfilled* her life's ambition when she started her own business. • Their vacation failed to *fulfill* their expectations. [=their vacation was not as good as they expected it to be] • With the money she earned in the stock market, she was finally able to *fulfill* her dreams. [=she was finally able to do the things she had always dreamed of doing] • He has a lot of talent, but he hasn't really *fulfilled* [=*lived up to, reached*] his potential.
3 : to make (someone or yourself) happy by achieving or doing something that was wished for • Her work *fulfills* her. • He's trying to *fulfill* himself as an artist.
– ful•fill•ment (*US*) *or Brit* **ful•fil•ment** /fʊlˈfɪlmənt/ *noun* [*noncount*] • the *fulfillment* of a promise/dream/contract • She found *fulfillment* by starting her own business.

fulfilled *adj* [*more* ~; *most* ~]
1 : feeling happy and satisfied about life : feeling that your abilities and talents are being fully used • She wants to find a career that will allow her to feel *fulfilled*.
2 : providing happiness and satisfaction • She wants to lead a more *fulfilled* life.

fulfilling *adj* [*more* ~; *most* ~] : providing happiness and satisfaction • My time in college was a happy and *fulfilling* period in my life. • The work has been very *fulfilling*.

[1]**full** /ˈfʊl/ *adj* **full•er; -est**
1 : containing or holding as much or as many as possible • a *full* bottle • The disk is *full*. • The plane was carrying a *full* load of passengers. • The theater was *full* to capacity. — often + *of* • a bottle *full of* milk • a bin *full of* corn
2 *always used before a noun* **a** : not lacking anything : complete in number, amount, etc. • We bought a *full* set of dishes. • They waited for three *full* months. • He has a *full* array of stereo equipment. • The soldiers were wearing *full* combat

F

gear. • This will be his first *full* season with the team. ✧ The phrase ***a full*** is often used to stress the large size of an amount. • He won the match by *a full* seven strokes. • It was *a full* three months before they made a decision. • He's *a full* foot taller than his wife. **b : not limited in any way** • His theories have not yet found *full* acceptance. • I have *full* [=*complete*] confidence in your honesty. • I hope that you'll give us your *fullest* cooperation. • Please give me your *full* attention. • We need to take *full* advantage of this opportunity. • She's expected to make a *full* recovery. • They're not making *full* use of these resources. • He's now a *full* member of the club. = He now has *full* membership in the club. • the rights of *full* citizenship • a *full* professor • We're still waiting to hear the *full* story of what happened. • She deserves *full* credit for meeting the deadline. **c : not reduced or shortened** • He doesn't like having to pay *full* price. • We could feel the *full* impact of every bump. • What is your *full* name? **d : existing or working at the highest or greatest degree : developed as much as possible** • The flowers were in *full* bloom. • The machine was running at *full* power/speed. • The factory is operating at *full* capacity. • The tree has not yet reached *full* size. • The stereo was at *full* volume. [=was playing as loudly as possible] • After the meeting, he had a *fuller* understanding of the job. • It'll be a few minutes before you feel the *full* effect of the drug. • He hasn't yet realized his *full* potential as a writer.

3 a *always used before a noun* **: including many things** • She has a *full* range of interests. [=she is interested in many different things] • The store carries a *full* line of products. **b : involving many activities** • We have a *full* schedule of events planned. • We have a *full* day of work ahead of us. **: very active** • She lived a very *full* and satisfying life.

4 : having a rounded shape : not thin or narrow • She has a *full* face. • a woman with a *full* figure = a *full*-figured woman • *full* lips

5 : having or containing a great number or amount *of* something • The room was *full of* pictures. • Despite his problems, he was still *full of* hope. • *full of* enthusiasm • food *full of* flavor • He says the charges against him are *full of* lies.

6 a : having eaten all that is wanted • No dessert for me, thank you. I'm *full*. [=(*chiefly Brit*) *full up*] **b** *always used before a noun* **: large enough to satisfy hunger** • I like to start the day with a *full* breakfast. • a *full* meal

7 a : having a large amount of material • a *full* skirt/dress **b : having a large amount of hair** • He has a *full* [=*thick*] head of hair. • a *full* beard

8 : thinking *of* something all the time • He was *full of* his own concerns. ✧ If you are ***full of yourself***, you think of yourself more than you should. • She is certainly very *full of herself*.

9 : having a strong and pleasing quality • a food/wine of *full* flavor • His voice is a *full*, rich baritone.

10 *of the moon* **: appearing as a bright circle** • The moon is *full* tonight.

full blast see [1]BLAST

full count see [2]COUNT

full of beans see BEAN

full of crap/shit *informal + offensive* **: not to be believed : saying things that are not true** • That guy is *full of shit*.

full of it *informal + sometimes offensive* **: not to be believed** • His story was so exaggerated that I thought he was *full of it*. • Oh, you're so *full of it*.

full steam/speed ahead **— used to say that something is being done with as much speed and power as possible** • The work started slowly, but now it's *full steam ahead*. • The campaign is ***going full speed ahead***

have your hands full see [1]HAND

not playing with a full deck see [1]DECK

to the fullest **: in a very active and energetic way** • She likes to live life *to the fullest*.

– full·ness *also* **ful·ness** *noun* [*noncount*] • the *fullness* of her voice • The conditioner added *fullness* to her hair. • I expected it would happen ***in the fullness of time*** [=it would happen eventually]

[2]full *adv*

1 : as much as possible : entirely or completely • The cup was filled *full* to the brim.

2 : directly or squarely • The ball hit him *full* in the chest. • He kissed her *full* on the lips.

full out **: with as much effort as possible** • He was running *full out*. — see also FULL-OUT

full well *formal* **: very well** • I ***knew full well*** who they were. • You *know full well* that it won't be possible for me to go.

[3]full *noun*

in full **: entirely or completely** • The receipt indicated that their bill had been paid *in full*. • Please write your name and address *in full*. [=please write your full name and address]

to the full **1 : to a great or complete degree** • I enjoyed the performance *to the full*. **: as much as possible** • We need to exploit this opportunity *to the full*. **2 : in a very active and energetic way** • She likes to live life *to the full*.

full·back /ˈfʊlˌbæk/ *noun, pl* **-backs** [*count*]

1 *American football* **: a player on offense who lines up behind the line of scrimmage and who runs with the ball and blocks**

2 : a defensive player in games like soccer and field hockey who is usually positioned near the goal

full beam *noun* [*noncount*] *Brit* **:** HIGH BEAM • The car's headlights were on *full beam*.

full–blood·ed /ˈfʊlˌblʌdəd/ *adj, always used before a noun*

1 : having parents who are of the same race or origin • Both his parents were Irish, so he was a *full-blooded* Irishman. • a *full-blooded* Cherokee

2 a : full of enthusiasm, energy, etc. • a *full-blooded* socialist **b : fully developed** • They started a *full-blooded* revolution.

full–blown /ˈfʊlˈbloʊn/ *adj* **: having all of the qualities that are associated with a particular thing or type of person : fully developed** • a *full-blown* recession • *full-blown* AIDS • The movie made him a *full-blown* star.

full–bod·ied /ˈfʊlˌbɑːdid/ *adj* [*more* ~; *most* ~] **: having a strong and pleasant flavor** • a *full-bodied* wine

full circle *adv* **: through a series of changes that lead back to an original position or situation or to an opposite position or situation** • Now that she's back on the stage, her career has ***come/gone full circle*** [=her career began on the stage, and now she has returned to it]

full–court press *noun, pl* ~ **presses** [*count*]

1 *basketball* **: a very aggressive way of playing defense over all areas of the court**

2 *US* **: a very aggressive effort or attack usually involving many people** • The bill's supporters are mounting/launching a *full-court press* to assure its passage.

full–cream *adj, Brit* **: containing cream** • *full-cream* milk [=(*US*) whole milk] • *full-cream* cheese

full dress *noun* [*noncount*] **: special clothes that are worn for a ceremony or for important social occasions** • The Army required *full dress* be worn to the event. • The officers were in *full dress*. • *full-dress* uniforms

full–dress *adj, always used before a noun* **: involving attention to every detail : very complete or full** • a *full-dress* investigation/biography

full–fat *adj, always used before a noun, Brit* **: having no fat removed** • *full-fat* dairy products

full–fledged /ˈfʊlˈflɛʤd/ *adj, always used before a noun, chiefly US*

1 : fully developed • The conflict widened into a *full-fledged* war. • a *full-fledged* recession

2 : meeting all the necessary requirements to be something • a *full-fledged* lawyer/member

full–grown *adj* **: having reached full growth or development : fully grown or mature** • *full-grown* animals/trees • a *full-grown* man

full house *noun, pl* ~ **houses** [*count*]

1 : a theater or concert hall that is filled with spectators • a singer performing before a *full house*

2 : a set of cards that a player has in a poker game containing three cards of one value and two cards of another value • A hand with three kings and two tens is a *full house*.

full–length /ˈfʊlˌlɛŋθ/ *adj*

1 : showing all of a person's body from the head to the feet • a *full-length* mirror • a *full-length* portrait

2 : reaching to the end of your legs or arms • a *full-length* dress • a shirt with *full-length* sleeves

3 : having the normal length : not shortened • They staged a *full-length* version of the play.

full marks *noun* [*plural*] *Brit*

1 : praise given for an achievement • *Full marks* to Mary for her excellent suggestion! [=Mary should be praised for her excellent suggestion]

2 : the highest score that you can get on a test — see also *full marks for effort* at EFFORT

full moon *noun* [*singular*] **: the moon when it appears as a bright circle** — compare HALF-MOON, NEW MOON

full–on /ˈfʊlˌɑːn/ *adj, always used before a noun* **: not limited**

in any way • Her new album is *full-on* funk. : fully developed • a *full-on* barroom brawl

full–out /ˈfʊlˌaʊt/ *adj, always used before a noun*
1 : made or done with as much effort as possible : ALL-OUT • a *full-out* sprint — see also *full out* at [2]FULL
2 : fully developed • a *full-out* war

full–scale /ˈfʊlˌskeɪl/ *adj, always used before a noun*
1 : having the same size as the original • They built a *full-scale* replica of the ship. • a *full-scale* model
2 : not limited in any way : using everything that can be used • a *full-scale* war • a *full-scale* investigation

full–ser•vice /ˈfʊlˈsɚvəs/ *adj, always used before a noun* : offering all the necessary or expected services • a *full-service* bank/restaurant • a *full-service* health resort

full–size /ˈfʊlˌsaɪz/ *adj*
1 : having the same size as the original : FULL-SCALE • a *full-size* model
2 *US, of a bed* : having a size of 54 inches by 75 inches (about 1.4 by 1.9 meters) — compare KING-SIZE, QUEEN-SIZE, TWIN-SIZE

full stop *noun, pl* ~ **stops** [*count*] *Brit* : [1]PERIOD 5a

full–term /ˈfʊlˌtɚm/ *adj* : lasting for the normal length of time • a *full-term* pregnancy; *also* : born after a pregnancy that lasts for the normal length of time • a *full-term* baby

full–time *adj*
1 a : working the full number of hours considered normal or standard • *full-time* employees **b :** done during the full number of hours considered normal or standard • a *full-time* job — compare PART-TIME
2 : requiring all of or a large amount of your time • Taking care of children is a *full-time* job.
– full–time *adv* • She worked *full-time* at the office. **– full–tim•er** /ˈfʊlˈtaɪmɚ/ *noun, pl* **-ers** [*count*] • Some of the employees are *full-timers*, but most of them are part-timers.

ful•ly /ˈfʊli/ *adv*
1 : in every way or detail : completely or entirely • He *fully* recovered from the operation. • They will never *fully* appreciate their luck. • The house is *fully* furnished. • When will the tree be *fully* grown? — sometimes used with *more* and *most* • I've never felt *more fully* alive. • We need to understand these problems *more fully* before we can find a solution to them. • The father is the *most fully* developed character in the novel. — see also *fully booked* at [2]BOOK
2 : AT LEAST — used to stress the large size of a number or amount • *Fully* 90 percent of us attended the meeting. • Next year, *fully* three-quarters of the jobs will be unfilled.

ful•ly–fledged /ˌfʊliˈflɛʤd/ *adj, Brit* : FULL-FLEDGED

ful•mi•nate /ˈfʊlməˌneɪt, ˈfʌlməˌneɪt/ *verb* **-nates; -nat•ed; -nat•ing** [*no obj*] *formal* : to complain loudly or angrily • She was *fulminating* about/over/at the dangers of smoking. • The editorial *fulminated* against the proposed tax increase.
– ful•mi•na•tion /ˌfʊlməˈneɪʃən, ˌfʌlməˈneɪʃən/ *noun, pl* **-tions** [*count*] a *fulmination* against the proposed tax increase [*noncount*] The proposed tax increase has been the subject of much anger and *fulmination*.

ful•some /ˈfʊlsəm/ *adj* [*more* ~; *most* ~] *formal* : expressing something (such as praise or thanks) in a very enthusiastic or emotional way — often used in a disapproving way to describe words that seem excessive or insincere • They were *fulsome* in their praise of her efforts. • a *fulsome* apology
– ful•some•ly *adv* • *fulsomely* praised

fum•ble /ˈfʌmbəl/ *verb* **fum•bles; fum•bled; fum•bling**
1 [*no obj*] : to search for something by reaching or touching with your fingers in an awkward or clumsy way • She *fumbled* in her pocket for her keys. • He *fumbled* (around) for the light switch. — often used figuratively • She *fumbled* for an answer but couldn't think of one.
2 : to handle something in an awkward or clumsy way [*no obj*] — usually + *with* • She *fumbled with* her keys as she tried to unlock the door. [+ *obj*] They *fumbled* a good opportunity to take control of the market.
3 *sports* : to fail to catch or hold the ball [*no obj*] He was hit hard and *fumbled* on the 20-yard line. [+ *obj*] He *fumbled* the ball on the 20-yard line.
– fumble *noun, pl* **fumbles** [*count*] • (*American football*) He had one *fumble* during last week's game. **– fum•bler** *noun, pl* **-blers** [*count*] **– fumbling** *adj* • He made a *fumbling* attempt to explain his behavior.

[1]fume /ˈfjuːm/ *noun, pl* **fumes** [*count*] : smoke or gas that smells unpleasant — usually plural • automobile exhaust *fumes*

[2]fume *verb* **fumes; fumed; fum•ing**
1 a [*no obj*] : to show or feel anger • She's still *fuming* about/over/at not being invited to the party. • We sat there waiting for him, *fuming* with anger at the delay. **b** [+ *obj*] : to say (something) in an angry way • "They made these changes without even asking our opinion," one employee *fumed*.
2 : to produce or give off (smoke, fumes, etc.) [+ *obj*] The volcano was *fuming* thick black smoke. [*no obj*] The volcano was *fuming*.

fu•mi•gate /ˈfjuːməˌgeɪt/ *verb* **-gates; -gat•ed; -gat•ing** [+ *obj*] : to remove germs, insects, etc., from (a room or building) with smoke or gas that destroys them • All the hospital rooms had to be *fumigated*. • We had to *fumigate* our apartment to get rid of the ants.
– fu•mi•ga•tion /ˌfjuːməˈgeɪʃən/ *noun, pl* **-tions** [*count, noncount*] **– fu•mi•ga•tor** /ˈfjuːməˌgeɪtɚ/ *noun, pl* **-tors** [*count*]

[1]fun /ˈfʌn/ *noun* [*noncount*]
1 : someone or something that is amusing or enjoyable : an enjoyable experience or person • The game was a lot of *fun*. [=the game was very enjoyable] • She's *fun* to be with. = It's *fun* to be with her. = It's *fun* being with her. [=her company is enjoyable] • Picnics are great *fun* [=are very enjoyable] in good weather.
2 : an enjoyable or amusing time • We had *fun* at the movie. [=we enjoyed ourselves at the movie; we enjoyed the movie] • I can't remember when I've had so much *fun*. • a vacation filled with *fun* = a *fun*-filled vacation • a *fun*-loving couple [=a couple who love to have fun]
3 : the feeling of being amused or entertained • He plays cards just for *fun*. = He plays cards just for the *fun* of it. • Sickness takes all the *fun* out of life.
a figure of fun : a person who people laugh at and make jokes about in an unkind way • He was a *figure of fun* around town.
in fun : in a joking way : in a way that is not serious • Don't take offense: I was only saying it *in fun*.
make fun of : to laugh at and make jokes about (someone or something) in an unkind way • The other kids were *making fun of* me. • They *made fun of* the way he talked.
more fun than a barrel (full) of monkeys see [1]BARREL
poke fun at : to make a joke about (someone or something) usually in a friendly way • I like to *poke fun at* my boss, but he's really not a bad guy.

[2]fun *adj, always used before a noun, sometimes* **fun•ner**; *sometimes* **fun•nest** *informal* : providing amusement : amusing or enjoyable • Our vacation was a *fun* time. • She's a *fun* person to be with. • The park is a *fun* place to visit. • We had a *fun* time at the movie.

[3]fun *verb* **funs; funned; fun•ning** [*no obj*] *US, informal* : to speak or act in a way that is not serious • I don't want you to get angry; I was only *funning*. [=(more commonly) *joking, fooling*] • He's just *funning* with you.

fun and games *noun* [*plural*] : activity that is meant to be enjoyable rather than serious • The family reunion was full of *fun and games*. — often used in a disapproving way to describe activity that is considered silly and not useful • The convention is just an excuse for journalistic *fun and games*.

[1]func•tion /ˈfʌŋkʃən/ *noun, pl* **-tions**
1 : the special purpose or activity for which a thing exists or is used [*count*] The *function* of the heart is to pump blood through the body. • He believes that the true *function* of art is to tell the truth. • What *functions* do these programs fulfill/perform/serve? • infants learning to control their bodily *functions* [*noncount*] The instrument is chiefly used to measure and record heart *function*. • The design achieves a perfect blend of ***form and function***.
2 [*count*] : the job or duty of a person • His job combines the *functions* of a manager and a worker. • Her chief/main/primary/principal *function* is to provide expert legal advice.
3 [*count*] : a large ceremony or social event • They went to several *functions* during their college reunion weekend. • a social *function*
4 [*count*] **a :** something (such as a quality or measurement) that is related to and changes with something else • Height is ***a function of*** age in children. [=the height of children increases as their age increases] **b :** something that results from something else • His personal problems are ***a function of*** [=a result of] his drinking.

[2]function *verb* **-tions; -tioned; -tion•ing** [*no obj*]
1 : to work or operate • The new machine *functions* well. • His bad health has prevented him from being able to *func-*

tion effectively in recent weeks. • Her heart now seems to be *functioning* normally. • The computer network is not yet fully *functioning.* • Stress may interfere with (the) normal *functioning* of the immune system.

2 : to have a specified function, role, or purpose : SERVE — usually + *as* • Teachers also *function as* counselors. • The couch was designed to also *function as* a bed.

func·tion·al /ˈfʌŋkʃənl/ *adj*

1 : designed to have a practical use • They worked outside, so they preferred wearing *functional* clothes. • The building's design is not only *functional* but also beautiful. • *functional* and decorative pottery

2 *medical* **:** affecting the way a part of your body works • a *functional* heart disorder

3 : working properly • The flashlight was still *functional* after I dropped it. • The computer network is fully *functional.*

4 : of or relating to the use or function of something • the *functional* differences between the departments

– func·tion·al·ly *adv*

func·tion·al·i·ty /ˌfʌŋkʃəˈnæləti/ *noun, pl* **-ties**

1 [*noncount*] **:** the quality of having a practical use **:** the quality of being functional • a design that is admired both for its beauty and for its *functionality*

2 : the particular use or set of uses for which something is designed [*noncount*] The cameras are comparable in price and *functionality.* [*count*] a device with new *functionalities*

func·tion·ary /ˈfʌŋkʃəˌneri, *Brit* ˈfʌŋkʃənri/ *noun, pl* **-ar·ies** [*count*] **:** a person who works for a government or political party • He was a party *functionary* during the political campaign.

function key *noun, pl* **~ keys** [*count*] **:** any one of a set of keys on a computer keyboard that have special uses

function word *noun, pl* **~ words** [*count*] *linguistics* **:** a word (such as a preposition or a conjunction) that is used mainly to show grammatical relationships between other words

[1]fund /ˈfʌnd/ *noun, pl* **funds**

1 [*count*] **:** an amount of money that is used for a special purpose • the library's book *fund* • The *fund* was established to aid the poor. • a pension *fund* — see also MUTUAL FUND, SLUSH FUND, TRUST FUND

2 funds [*plural*] **:** available money • All her *funds* were in a checking account. • His *funds* were getting lower as he continued to look for a job. • raising campaign *funds* • I'm a little short of *funds* right now. [=I don't have much money right now]

3 [*singular*] **:** an amount of something that is available for use **:** a supply of something • The comedian had a large *fund* of jokes.

[2]fund *verb* **funds; fund·ed; fund·ing** [+ *obj*] **:** to provide money for (something) • The group *funded* three new scholarships. • Who *funds* the company pension plan? • The program is *funded* by the state. = The program is state-*funded.* • The plan is fully *funded.* [=the plan is provided with all the money it requires]

– funding *noun* [*noncount*] • The program relies on *funding* from the state. = The program relies on state *funding.*

[1]fun·da·men·tal /ˌfʌndəˈmɛntl/ *adj* [*more ~; most ~*]

1 : forming or relating to the most important part of something **:** BASIC • The Constitution ensures our *fundamental* rights. • There's a *fundamental* difference between these two political parties. • a *fundamental* truth/concept/belief — often + *to* • beliefs that are *fundamental to* our society

2 : of or relating to the basic structure or function of something • These ideas are of *fundamental* importance. • The revolution brought about a *fundamental* change in the country. • We need to make some *fundamental* changes in the way we do business. • We need to address these problems on a more *fundamental* level.

[2]fundamental *noun, pl* **-tals** [*count*] **:** one of the basic and important parts of something **:** a fundamental part — usually plural • Reading, writing, and arithmetic are the *fundamentals* of education. • the *fundamentals* of algebra

fun·da·men·tal·ist /ˌfʌndəˈmɛntəlɪst/ *noun, pl* **-ists** [*count*] **:** a person who strictly and literally follows a set of rules and laws especially about religion • a religious *fundamentalist*

– fun·da·men·tal·ism /ˌfʌndəˈmɛntəˌlɪzəm/ *noun* [*noncount*] • religious *fundamentalism* **– fundamentalist** *adj* • *fundamentalist* beliefs

fun·da·men·tal·ly /ˌfʌndəˈmɛntḷi/ *adv* **:** at the most basic level • All people are *fundamentally* the same. = *Fundamentally,* all people are the same. • *fundamentally* important principles • I disagree with some of her points, but *fundamentally* she's right. • His plan is *fundamentally* different.

fund–rais·er /ˈfʌndˌreɪzɚ/ *noun, pl* **-ers** [*count*]

1 : a person who collects money for a political party, charity, school, etc.

2 : a social event held to collect money for a political party, charity, school, etc.

fund–rais·ing /ˈfʌndˌreɪzɪŋ/ *noun* [*noncount*] **:** activity done to collect money for a political party, charity, school, etc. • political *fund-raising* • a *fund-raising* dinner/campaign

fu·ner·al /ˈfjuːnərəl/ *noun, pl* **-als** [*count*] **:** a ceremony held for a dead person • Only family attended the *funeral.* • His *funeral* will be held on Friday. • a *funeral* procession/service • His cousin made the *funeral* arrangements.

it's your funeral *informal* — used to say that you will have to deal with the unpleasant result of your actions • Tell the boss she's wrong if you like: *it's your funeral!*

funeral director *noun, pl* **~ -tors** [*count*] **:** a person whose job is to arrange and manage funerals **:** UNDERTAKER

funeral home *noun, pl* **~ homes** [*count*] **:** a place where dead people are prepared for burial or cremation and where wakes and funerals are held — called also (*US*) *funeral parlor*

fu·ne·re·al /fjuˈnirijəl/ *adj* **:** very sad and serious **:** suggesting a funeral • a *funereal* silence • *funereal* music

fun·fair /ˈfʌnˌfeɚ/ *noun, pl* **-fairs** [*count*] *Brit* **:** an outdoor event at which there are various kinds of games, rides, and entertainment

fun·gal /ˈfʌŋgəl/ *adj* **:** of, relating to, or caused by a fungus • a *fungal* disease/infection

fungi *plural of* FUNGUS

fun·gi·cide /ˈfʌnʤəˌsaɪd, ˈfʌŋgəˌsaɪd/ *noun, pl* **-cides** [*count, noncount*] **:** a substance that kills fungi

fun·gus /ˈfʌŋgəs/ *noun, pl* **fun·gi** /ˈfʌnˌʤaɪ, ˈfʌŋˌgaɪ/ *also* **fun·gus·es** [*count*] **:** any one of a group of related plants (such as molds, mushrooms, or yeasts) that have no flowers and that live on dead or decaying things

fun house *noun, pl* **~ houses** [*count*] *US* **:** a building in an amusement park with many features that amuse and surprise people as they walk or ride through it

fu·nic·u·lar /fjʊˈnɪkjəlɚ/ *noun, pl* **-lars** [*count*] **:** a railway going up and down a mountain that carries people in cars pulled by a moving cable

[1]funk /ˈfʌŋk/ *noun, pl* **funks** [*count*] *chiefly US, informal* **:** a condition in which you are unable to think or behave normally because you are sad, depressed, etc. — usually singular • She seems to be coming out of her *funk.* — usually used after *in* or *into* • He had been *in* a (blue) *funk* since failing the exam. • She went *into* a dark/deep *funk* after she lost her job. — sometimes used figuratively • The country is *in* an economic *funk.* [=the country's economy is doing poorly] — compare [2]FUNK

[2]funk *noun* [*noncount*] **:** a type of popular music that has a strong beat and that combines traditional forms of African-American music (such as blues, gospel, or soul) — compare [1]FUNK

funky /ˈfʌŋki/ *adj* **funk·i·er; -est**

1 : having the style or feeling of funk music • *funky* music • The music had a *funky* beat.

2 *informal* **:** stylish or appealing in an unusual way • We had dinner at a *funky* little Italian restaurant. • a *funky* bar

3 *US* **:** having a strange or unpleasant odor • Something in the closet smells a little *funky.*

[1]fun·nel /ˈfʌnl/ *noun, pl* **-nels** [*count*]

1 : a device shaped like a hollow cone with a tube extending from the point ✧ A funnel is used for pouring something (such as a liquid) into a narrow opening.

2 : something that is shaped like a funnel • the *funnel* cloud of a tornado

3 : a large pipe on a ship through which smoke or steam comes out

funnel

[2]funnel *verb, always followed by an adverb or preposition* **-nels;** *US* **-neled** *or Brit* **-nelled;** *US* **-nel·ing** *or Brit* **-nel·ling**

1 : to pass through a funnel or a narrow opening [*no obj*] Winds *funneled* through the canyon. • Smoke *funneled* up the chimney. • The crowd *funneled* through the doors. [+ *obj*] He *funneled* the gas into the tank.

2 [+ *obj*] **:** to send (something, such as money) to someone or something in usually an indirect or secret way • They *fun-*

neled money into the campaign. • The information was being secretly *funneled* to the head of the organization.

fun·nies /ˈfʌniz/ *noun*

the funnies *US, informal* : the comic strips in a newspaper : the part of a newspaper that has comic strips • They enjoyed reading *the funnies* [=*the comics*] in the Sunday newspapers.

[1]**fun·ny** /ˈfʌni/ *adj* **fun·ni·er; -est**

1 : causing laughter • He told a *funny* story. • He's a very *funny* guy. • What's so *funny*? • What are you laughing at? There's nothing *funny* about it. • It's not that *funny*. • a *funny* story/movie

2 *informal* : odd or strange • There's something *funny* going on here. • She has some *funny* ideas about how to run a company. • "I can't find my keys." "That's *funny*—they were here a minute ago." • "That's *funny*." "Do you mean *funny* peculiar/strange or *funny* ha-ha?" [=by "funny" do you mean "odd" or "amusing"?] • My car has been making a *funny* noise lately. • A *funny* thing happened to me the other day. • a *funny*-looking hat • It feels *funny* to be back here again. • It's *funny* that you should say that—I was just thinking the same thing myself. • *Funny*, things didn't turn out the way we planned. [=it's odd that things didn't turn out the way we planned]

3 *not used before a noun, informal* : not well : somewhat ill • My stomach feels *funny*. • I feel a little *funny*. • (*chiefly Brit*) After the accident he went a bit *funny* in the head.

4 *informal* : not honest : meant to deceive someone • The guard told his prisoner not to try anything *funny*. • Fake bidding and other ***funny business*** [=dishonest activity] occurred during the auction.

– fun·ni·ly /ˈfʌnəli/ *adv* • There's something *funnily* [=*oddly*] familiar about him. • *Funnily* (enough), she never even mentioned our first meeting.

[2]**funny** *adv, informal* : in an odd or strange way • He's been acting *funny* lately. • She looked at me *funny*.

funny bone *noun, pl* **~ bones** [*count*] : a place at the back of your elbow where you feel a painful tingling sensation when it is hit • I hit my *funny bone* on the edge of the table. — called also (*US*) *crazy bone* ✧ Something that ***tickles your funny bone*** is amusing to you. • Parts of the movie really *tickled my funny bone*.

funny farm *noun*

the funny farm *informal + humorous* : a hospital for people who are mentally ill ✧ *The funny farm* is now often considered offensive.

fun·ny·man /ˈfʌniˌmæn/ *noun, pl* **-men** /-ˌmɛn/ [*count*] *informal* : a man who is funny; *especially* : a professional comedian

funny money *noun* [*noncount*] *informal* : fake money : counterfeit money

funny papers *noun* [*plural*] *US, informal* : FUNNIES

fur /ˈfɚ/ *noun, pl* **furs**

1 [*noncount*] : the hairy coat of an animal especially when it is soft and thick • The cat has black-and-white *fur*. • The rabbit's *fur* is soft.

2 a : the fur of an animal used for clothing [*noncount*] Her gloves are lined with *fur*. [*count*] He made his fortune trading *furs* in the 17th century. — often used before another noun • a *fur* coat/collar **b** [*count*] : a piece of clothing (such as a coat) made with fur • Her new *fur* is a full-length mink coat. **c** [*noncount*] : a material that looks and feels like the fur of an animal • a teddy bear with soft *fur* • fake/imitation *fur*

3 [*noncount*] *Brit* : a hard material that forms in metal pipes, boilers, etc. : SCALE

fur flies *informal* ✧ When (the) ***fur flies***, someone becomes very angry or upset. • When she finds our about this, *fur* will *fly*. [=she will be very angry]

– furred /ˈfɚd/ *adj* • a thickly *furred* animal • (*Brit*) a thickly *furred* boiler

fu·ri·ous /ˈfjʊrijəs/ *adj* [*more ~; most ~*]

1 : very angry • She's *furious* at/over how slowly the investigation is proceeding. • I was *furious* with/at them for printing the story. • a *furious* argument

2 a : very powerful or violent • a *furious* storm **b** : very active or fast • We worked all night at a *furious* pace.

fast and furious see [1]FAST

– fu·ri·ous·ly *adv* • She shouted at him *furiously*. • working *furiously* [=at a furious pace]

furl /ˈfɚl/ *verb* **furls; furled; furl·ing** [*+ obj*] : to wrap or roll (something, such as a sail or a flag) close to or around something • They *furled* the sails.

fur·long /ˈfɚˌlɑːŋ/ *noun, pl* **-longs** [*count*] : a unit of distance equal to 220 yards (about 201.2 meters) or ⅛ of a mile — used chiefly in horse racing

[1]**fur·lough** /ˈfɚˌloʊ/ *noun, pl* **-loughs** [*count*]

1 : a period of time when a soldier is allowed to leave the place where he or she is stationed • a four-week *furlough*

2 *US* : a period of time when an employee is told not to come to work and is not paid • *furloughs* of federal workers • Each employee will have a one-day *furlough* every month.

3 *US* : a period of time when a prisoner is allowed to leave prison

on furlough : having a furlough : allowed or required to leave because of a furlough • soldiers going home *on furlough* • workers/prisoners *on furlough*

[2]**furlough** *verb* **-loughs; -loughed; -lough·ing** [*+ obj*]

1 : to grant a furlough to (someone) • *furlough* a soldier • (*US*) The prison will *furlough* certain inmates.

2 *US* : to put (a worker) on furlough • The company will consider *furloughing* a small number of workers.

fur·nace /ˈfɚnəs/ *noun, pl* **-nac·es** [*count*] : an enclosed container in which heat is produced: such as **a** : one for melting metals • stoke a *furnace* — see also BLAST FURNACE **b** *chiefly US* : one for heating a building or apartment — called also (*chiefly Brit*) *boiler*

fur·nish /ˈfɚnɪʃ/ *verb* **-nish·es; -nished; -nish·ing** [*+ obj*]

1 : to provide (a room or building) with furniture • The inn is beautifully *furnished*. • He has enough money to *furnish* the apartment nicely. — often + *with* • We are *furnishing* the office *with* contemporary pieces. • She *furnished* her home *with* antiques.

2 a : to supply or give (something) to someone or something : PROVIDE • We'll *furnish* the food for the party. • Can he *furnish* the information to us? **b** : to supply or give to (someone) something that is needed or wanted : PROVIDE — + *with* • Students are *furnished with* all the necessary materials for the course. • Can he *furnish* us *with* the information?

– furnished *adj* • He moved from a *furnished* room to an unfurnished apartment.

fur·nish·ings /ˈfɚnɪʃɪŋz/ *noun* [*plural*] : pieces of furniture, curtains, rugs, and decorations for a room or building • The room has very comfortable *furnishings*.

fur·ni·ture /ˈfɚnɪtʃɚ/ *noun* [*noncount*] : chairs, tables, beds, etc., that are used to make a room ready for use • They bought some new *furniture* for the house. • The office *furniture* is wearing out. • a large piece of *furniture*

fu·ror (*US*) /ˈfjʊɚˌoɚ, ˈfjʊrɚ/ *also chiefly Brit* **fu·rore** /ˈfjʊɚˌoɚ, *Brit* fjʊˈrɔːri/ *noun* [*singular*] : a situation in which many people are very angry and upset • The book caused/created a *furor* across the country. • Amid a public *furor*, the senator continues to deny the allegations.

fur·ri·er /ˈfɚrijɚ/ *noun, pl* **-ers** [*count*] : a person who sells or makes fur clothing

[1]**fur·row** /ˈfɚroʊ/ *noun, pl* **-rows** [*count*]

1 : a long and narrow cut in the ground • We plowed *furrows* in the field.

2 : a narrow line or wrinkle in the skin of a person's face • When he frowns a deep *furrow* forms in his brow.

plough a furrow *Brit, literary* ✧ If you ***plough your own furrow***, you do something that is different from what other people do. • She was not afraid to *plough her own furrow*. [=to act independently; to do something no one else has done] If you ***plough the same furrow***, you do the same thing someone else does. • He was not content to *plough the same furrow* as his father. If you ***plough a lone/lonely furrow***, you do something alone or do something that no one else will do. • She has had to *plough a lone/lonely furrow* in her pursuit of reform.

[2]**furrow** *verb* **-rows; -rowed; -row·ing** : to make furrows in (something) [*+ obj*] plows *furrowing* the fields • He *furrowed* his brow. [*no obj*] His forehead *furrows* when he frowns.

– furrowed *adj* • a *furrowed* brow/forehead • a *furrowed* field

fur·ry /ˈfɚri/ *adj* **fur·ri·er; -est**

1 : covered with fur • My children love *furry* animals.

2 a : covered with something that looks or feels like fur • The plant has *furry* leaves. • *furry* slippers **b** : resembling fur • *Furry* mold was growing on the cheese.

[1]**fur·ther** /ˈfɚðɚ/ *adv*

1 : to or at a more distant place or time : FARTHER • He lives *further* (away) from the office than his boss. • We need to look back *further* into the past to find the cause of these problems. ▪ I've never been *further* west than St. Louis. ▪ Their house is *further* up/down the street. ▪ The road ended and we couldn't go any *further*. [=we couldn't go beyond that point]

2 : to a greater degree or extent ▪ We need to research/look *further* into this matter. ▪ The police have been reluctant to take their investigation any *further*. ▪ I do not want anything *further* [=*more*] to do with this mess. ▪ I don't know anything *further* [=*more*] about what really happened. ▪ The interview ended before they could question me *further*. [=*more*] ▪ Interest rates fell *further*. [=*more*] ▪ "They are not our friends." "I would go even *further* and say they are our enemies." ▪ Some people claim that he is an arrogant man, but ***nothing could be further from the truth***. [=it is completely untrue to say that he is an arrogant man] ▪ Some people expect him to retire, but he says that ***nothing could be further from his mind***. [=he has no intention of retiring] ▪ Don't worry, what you've told me will ***go no further***. [=I will not tell anyone else what you have told me]

3 *formal* **:** in addition to what has been said **:** FURTHERMORE ▪ I had enough money to invest. I realized, *further*, that the risk was small.

further to *Brit, formal* — used in a letter to refer to a subject discussed in a previous letter or conversation ▪ *Further to* my letter of last Wednesday, may I remind you that the money outstanding has still not been paid.

²further *adj*

1 : ADDITIONAL, MORE ▪ *Further* study/research is needed. ▪ He will undergo *further* questioning. ▪ If you need *further* information/details, you can call me. ▪ We do not expect any *further* deliveries today. ▪ I have nothing *further* to say. ▪ There is a *further* problem: do we have enough money? ▪ The library will be closed ***until further notice***. [=until some time in the future which has not yet been decided or stated]

2 : more distant **:** FARTHER ▪ We parked in the *further* lot. ▪ There is more damage to the *further* part of the fence.

³further *verb* **-thers; -thered; -ther·ing** [+ *obj*] **:** to help the progress of (something) **:** to cause (something) to become more successful or advanced ▪ He will do all he can to *further* [=*promote*] the cause. ▪ What can I do to *further* [=*advance*] my career? ▪ Their efforts greatly *furthered* the state of research. ▪ The funds are to be used to *further* the public good.

fur·ther·ance /ˈfɚðərəns/ *noun* [*noncount*] *formal* **:** the act of helping something to become more successful or advanced **:** ADVANCEMENT ▪ They made the *furtherance* of science their life's work. ▪ His main concern is with the *furtherance* [=*promotion*] of his own agenda.

further education *noun* [*noncount*] *Brit* **:** courses of study for adults **:** CONTINUING EDUCATION

fur·ther·more /ˈfɚðɚˌmoɚ/ *adv, formal* **:** in addition to what has been said **:** MOREOVER — used to introduce a statement that supports or adds to a previous statement ▪ These findings seem plausible. *Furthermore*, several studies have confirmed them. ▪ She always arrives on time. Her work, *furthermore*, has always been excellent.

¹furth·est /ˈfɚðəst/ *adv*

1 : to or at the greatest distance in space or time **:** FARTHEST ▪ The best table is *furthest* from the kitchen. ▪ Who can run (the) *furthest* in five minutes?

2 : to the most advanced point **:** FARTHEST ▪ She went the *furthest* [=she made the greatest effort] to research the issue.

3 : by the greatest degree or extent **:** MOST ▪ Of all his paintings, this one is the *furthest* removed from reality.

²furthest *adj, always used before a noun* **:** most distant in space or time **:** FARTHEST ▪ Their ideas fall at the *furthest* extremes of the political spectrum. ▪ He says that retiring is ***the furthest thing from his mind***. [=he is not thinking at all about retiring; he has no intention of retiring]

fur·tive /ˈfɚtɪv/ *adj* [*more* ~; *most* ~] **:** done in a quiet and secret way to avoid being noticed ▪ He cast a *furtive* glance in our direction. ▪ We exchanged *furtive* smiles across the table. ▪ *furtive* movements

— **fur·tive·ly** *adv* ▪ He looked *furtively* at the clock. ▪ She slipped *furtively* out of the room. — **fur·tive·ness** *noun* [*noncount*]

fu·ry /ˈfjuri/ *noun, pl* **-ries**

1 : violent anger **:** RAGE [*noncount*] I could see the *fury* in her eyes. ▪ Nothing could contain his *fury* over their accusations. ▪ He turned away from them in *fury*. [*singular*] ✧ If you are ***in a fury***, you are very angry. ▪ She rose *in a fury* and stalked out of the room. ✧ If you ***fly into a fury***, you become very angry. ▪ He *flew into a fury* [=*flew into a rage*] and began shouting at them. ***synonyms*** see ¹ANGER

2 [*noncount*] **:** wild and dangerous force ▪ The hurricane unleashed its *fury* on hundreds of homes and businesses.

sound and fury see ¹SOUND

¹fuse /ˈfju:z/ *noun, pl* **fus·es** [*count*] **:** a device that causes electricity to stop flowing when a current becomes too strong ▪ The lights went out when the *fuse* blew. ▪ change a *fuse*

blow a fuse *informal* **:** to become very angry or upset ▪ The boss *blew a fuse* when the shipment didn't arrive on time.

— compare ²FUSE

²fuse *noun, pl* **fuses** [*count*]

1 : a string that is connected to an explosive device (such as a bomb or firecracker) and that is set on fire to cause the device to explode ▪ light a *fuse*

2 *also US* **fuze :** a mechanical or electrical device that causes a weapon (such as a bomb or torpedo) to explode

a short fuse *informal* ✧ If you ***have a short fuse*** or you are ***on a short fuse***, you become angry very quickly. ▪ The boss is known to be *on a short fuse*.

— compare ¹FUSE

³fuse *verb* **fuses; fused; fus·ing**

1 : to join or become joined because of heat or a chemical reaction [*no obj*] During the reaction the atoms *fuse* (together). ▪ The melted metals *fused* (with each other). [+ *obj*] Particles are *fused* to form a new compound. ▪ He *fused* the wires (together).

2 : to join or combine (different things) together [+ *obj*] His compositions *fuse* jazz and rhythm and blues elements. ▪ Their approach *fused* ideas from several disciplines. [*no obj*] Dreams and reality *fuse* (together) in her latest film. = Dreams *fuse* with reality in her latest film.

3 *Brit* **:** to stop working because a fuse has blown [*no obj*] The light *fused* and left us in the dark. [+ *obj*] I must have *fused* the light by accident.

fuse box *noun, pl* **~ boxes** [*count*] **:** a box that contains the fuses for the electrical system in a building

fu·se·lage /ˈfju:səˌlɑ:ʒ, *Brit* ˈfju:zəˌlɑ:ʒ/ *noun, pl* **-lag·es** [*count*] **:** the main part of an airplane **:** the part of an airplane that holds the crew, passengers, and cargo — see picture at AIRPLANE

fu·sil·lade /ˈfju:səˌlɑ:d, *Brit* ˌfju:zəˈleɪd/ *noun* [*singular*] **:** a large number of shots that are fired very quickly ▪ A *fusillade* of bullets filled the courtyard. — often used figuratively ▪ She faced a *fusillade* [=*barrage, flurry*] of accusations. ▪ a *fusillade* of obscenities

fu·sion /ˈfju:ʒn̩/ *noun, pl* **-sions**

1 : a combination or mixture of things [*count*] a *fusion* of different methods ▪ a *fusion* of musical styles ▪ The show is a *fusion* of news and entertainment. [*noncount*] The *fusion* of different cultural influences is evident in her sculpture.

2 [*noncount*] *physics* **:** a process in which the nuclei of atoms are joined ▪ a *fusion* reactor/reaction ✧ A large amount of energy is released when fusion occurs. — called also *nuclear fusion*; compare FISSION

3 [*noncount*] **:** a type of popular music that combines different styles (such as jazz and rock)

4 [*noncount*] **:** food prepared by combining methods and ingredients from different areas of the world — called also *fusion cuisine*

¹fuss /ˈfʌs/ *noun*

1 : activity or excitement that is unusual and that often is not wanted or necessary [*noncount*] They got down to business without any *fuss*. ▪ What is all the *fuss* about? [*singular*] Her new novel has caused quite a *fuss*. — often used with *make* ▪ We'd love to come to dinner, but please don't *make* a *fuss*. [=don't do a lot of extra things that you would not usually do] ▪ (*US*) Everyone *made* such a *fuss* over the baby. = (*Brit*) Everyone *made* such a *fuss* of the baby. [=everyone paid a lot of excited attention to the baby]

2 : an expression of anger or complaint especially about something that has little importance [*noncount*] She accepted the new assignment without any *fuss*. [=she did not complain about the new assignment] — often used with *make* ▪ She accepted the new assignment without *making* any *fuss*. [*singular*] I don't want to *make* a *fuss*, but this soup is cold.

²fuss *verb* **fuss·es; fussed; fuss·ing** [*no obj*]

1 : to be or become upset or worried ▪ She'll *fuss* the whole time we're gone. ▪ I told him not to *fuss*. ✧ In informal British English, someone who is ***not fussed*** is not bothered or worried. ▪ We can eat at either restaurant: I'm *not fussed*. =

I'm *not fussed* about which restaurant we eat at.
2 *US* **:** to show that you are annoyed or unhappy ▪ The baby *fussed* all day. ▪ Stop *fussing* and get to work! ▪ He's *fussing* about his new assignment.
fuss over [*phrasal verb*] ***fuss over (someone or something)*** **:** to pay a lot of attention to (someone or something) in a nervous or excited way ▪ Everyone *fussed over* the baby. ▪ He spent hours *fussing over* the details of the speech. ▪ I don't want anyone to *fuss over* me.
fuss with [*phrasal verb*] ***fuss with (something)*** **:** to move or handle (something) in a nervous or uncertain way **:** to fiddle with (something) ▪ He *fussed with* his tie the whole time we were talking. ▪ She's always *fussing with* her hair.

fuss·bud·get /ˈfʌsˌbʌʤət/ *noun, pl* **-gets** [*count*] *US, informal + disapproving* **:** a person who worries or complains about small things **:** a fussy person ▪ a grumpy old *fussbudget*

fuss·pot /ˈfʌsˌpɑːt/ *noun, pl* **-pots** [*count*] *chiefly Brit, informal + disapproving* **:** FUSSBUDGET

fussy /ˈfʌsi/ *adj* **fuss·i·er; -est**
1 : very careful or too careful about choosing or accepting things **:** hard to please ▪ a *fussy* shopper ▪ She's always been *fussy* [=*picky*] about food. ▪ I'm not *fussy* about where we eat. ▪ This plant is not *fussy* about soil quality. [=this plant will grow well even in poor soil]
2 *US* **:** often upset or unhappy ▪ a very *fussy* baby
3 *disapproving* **:** too fancy or complicated ▪ a *fussy* dress ▪ *fussy* curtains/wallpaper ▪ The room was cluttered and *fussy*.
– fuss·i·ly /ˈfʌsəli/ *adv* **– fuss·i·ness** *noun* [*noncount*]

fus·ty /ˈfʌsti/ *adj* **fus·ti·er; -est**
1 : full of dust and unpleasant smells **:** not fresh **:** MUSTY ▪ a *fusty* cottage ▪ The trunk was full of *fusty* clothing.
2 : very old-fashioned ▪ *fusty* notions about art

fu·tile /ˈfjuːtl̩, ˈfjuːˌtajəl/ *adj* [*more ~; most ~*] **:** having no result or effect **:** pointless or useless ▪ All our efforts proved *futile*. ▪ a *futile* and foolish gesture ▪ They made a *futile* [=*vain*] attempt to control the flooding.
– fu·tile·ly *adv* **– fu·til·i·ty** /fjuˈtɪləti/ *noun* [*noncount*] ▪ His speech focused on the *futility* of violence. ▪ They demonstrated the *futility* of the plan. ▪ an exercise in *futility*

fu·ton /ˈfuːˌtɑːn/ *noun, pl* **-tons** [*count*] **:** a mattress that is used on the floor or in a frame as a bed, couch, or chair

[1]**fu·ture** /ˈfjuːʧɚ/ *noun, pl* **-tures**
1 a [*noncount*] **:** the period of time that will come after the present time ▪ (*Brit*) He promises to do better ***in future***. [=*from now on*; from this time onward] — usually used with *the* ▪ (*US*) He promises to do better in *the future*. ▪ We're making plans for *the future*. ▪ They will hire more people sometime in *the future*. ▪ What do you think you will be doing in *the future*? ▪ What does/will *the future* hold for you? ▪ *the* near/immediate *future* ▪ *the* foreseeable *future* ▪ Changes are expected ***in the not too distant future***. [=*soon*] **b *the future*** **:** the events that will happen after the present time ▪ It's impossible to predict *the future*.
2 [*count*] **:** the condition or situation of someone or something in the time that will come ▪ He has a promising *future* (ahead of him). ▪ Their *future* looks bright. ▪ The company faces an uncertain *future*. ▪ The *future* was already decided for her. ▪ There is ***no future for you*** in this business. = You ***have no future*** in this business. [=there is no chance that you will succeed in this business]
3 *the future* *grammar* **:** FUTURE TENSE
4 *futures* [*plural*] *finance* **:** goods or shares that are bought at prices which are agreed to now but that are delivered at a later time ▪ He made a fortune trading in oil *futures*.
mortgage the/your future see [2]MORTGAGE

[2]**future** *adj, always used before a noun*
1 : coming after the present time **:** existing in the future ▪ We cannot predict *future* events. ▪ *Future* generations will benefit from this research. ▪ You should keep these instructions ***for future reference***. [=so that you can refer to them when you need to in the future]
2 — used to say what someone or something will be ▪ He met his *future* wife [=the woman who would become his wife] at college. ▪ the country's *future* king

future perfect *noun* [*noncount*] *grammar* **:** a verb tense that is used to refer to an action that will be completed by a specified time in the future ▪ The *future perfect* in English is formed with "will have" and "shall have," as in "They will have left by the time we arrive."

future tense *noun, pl* **~ tenses** [*count*] *grammar* **:** a verb tense that is used to refer to the future ▪ The *future tense* in English is formed with "will" or "shall." ▪ a verb in the *future tense*

fu·tur·ist /ˈfjuːʧərɪst/ *noun, pl* **-ists** [*count*] **:** a person who tries to tell what the future will be like

fu·tur·is·tic /ˌfjuːʧəˈrɪstɪk/ *adj*
1 [*more ~; most ~*] **:** very modern ▪ *futuristic* furniture/designs ▪ The new offices are very *futuristic*.
2 a : relating to or telling about events in the future ▪ a *futuristic* novel/story **b :** existing in the future ▪ The film depicts a *futuristic* society.

fu·tu·ri·ty /fjuˈtʊrəti, *Brit* fjuˈtjʊərəti/ *noun* [*noncount*] *formal* **:** the quality of being or happening in the future ▪ In English we can express *futurity* with "will" and "shall."

fu·tur·olo·gy /ˌfjuːʧəˈrɑːləʤi/ *noun* [*noncount*] **:** the study of what might happen in the future
– fu·tur·olo·gist /ˌfjuːʧəˈrɑːləʤɪst/ *noun, pl* **-ists** [*count*]

fuze *US variant spelling of* [2]FUSE 2

fuzz /ˈfʌz/ *noun*
1 [*noncount*] **:** short, soft hairs ▪ The baby's head is covered with/in *fuzz*. ▪ the *fuzz* on a peach
2 [*noncount*] **:** small, light pieces of cloth or other soft material ▪ The blanket is covered with *fuzz*.
3 *the fuzz* *old-fashioned slang* **:** the police ▪ He was arrested by *the fuzz*.

fuzzy /ˈfʌzi/ *adj* **fuzz·i·er; -est**
1 : covered with short, soft hairs, fur, etc. **:** covered with fuzz ▪ a *fuzzy* sweater/blanket ▪ The plant has *fuzzy* leaves. ▪ a *fuzzy* stuffed toy
2 a : not clear **:** not sharp or distinct ▪ The picture in the newspaper is *fuzzy*. [=*blurred, blurry*] ▪ Without my glasses everything looks *fuzzy*. ▪ The line between our areas of responsibility is *fuzzy*. **b :** not clear in thought ▪ I think his reasoning is a little *fuzzy*.
3 *US, informal* **:** pleasant or comforting — usually used with *warm* ▪ Seeing her again after all these years gave me a *warm, fuzzy* feeling. ▪ His personality is not exactly *warm* and *fuzzy*. — see also WARM FUZZIES
– fuzz·i·ly /ˈfʌzəli/ *adv* **– fuzz·i·ness** *noun* [*noncount*]

fuzzy logic *noun* [*noncount*] *technical* **:** a system of logic in which statements do not have to be entirely true or false

fwd. *abbr* forward

f–word /ˈɛfˌwɚd/ *noun*
the f-word or ***the F-word*** — used as a way to refer to the offensive word "fuck" without saying it or writing it ▪ He got in trouble for using *the f-word* on television.

-fy /faɪ/ *verb suffix* **:** cause to become ▪ beauti*fy* ▪ puri*fy*

FYI *abbr* for your information — used when you are providing someone with interesting or useful information in a note, an e-mail message, etc. ▪ *FYI*, the meeting has been postponed to next week.

G

g *or* **G** /ˈʤiː/ *noun, pl* **g's** *or* **gs** *or* **G's** *or* **Gs**
1 : the seventh letter of the English alphabet [*count*] There are two *g's* in "bigger." [*noncount*] words that end in *g*
2 : a musical note or key referred to by the letter G **:** the fifth tone of a C-major scale [*count*] play/sing a *G* [*noncount*] The song is in the key of *G*.
3 [*count*] **:** the force of gravity at the Earth's surface ▪ An astronaut can experience three *g's* [=an amount of force equal to three times the normal force of gravity] during liftoff.
4 [*count*] *slang* **:** one thousand dollars **:** GRAND ▪ a couple of *g's*

g *abbr* gram

G — used as a special mark to indicate that people of all ages may see a particular movie in a movie theater ▪ The movie is rated *G*. — compare NC-17, PG, PG-13, R, X; see also G-RATED

GA *abbr* Georgia

[1]**gab** /ˈgæb/ *verb* **gabs; gabbed; gab·bing** [*no obj*] *informal* : to talk a lot in an informal way usually about things that are not important or serious ▪ They stayed up late *gabbing* (away) on the phone. ▪ *gabbing* about the weather
– **gab·ber** *noun, pl* **-bers** [*count*] ▪ talk radio *gabbers*

[2]**gab** *noun* [*noncount*] *informal* : informal talk ▪ a steady stream of *gab* ✧ A person with (*US*) ***the gift of gab*** or *Brit* ***the gift of the gab*** is someone who talks a lot or who is good at talking to people. ▪ a salesman with *the gift of gab*

gab·ar·dine /ˈgæbɚˌdiːn/ *noun* [*noncount*] : a smooth, stiff type of cloth that is often used for suits ▪ a jacket made of *gabardine* — often used before another noun ▪ a *gabardine* suit/coat

gab·ble /ˈgæbəl/ *verb* **gab·bles; gab·bled; gab·bling** /ˈgæblɪŋ/ [*no obj*] *chiefly Brit* : to talk quickly and in a way that is difficult to understand ▪ I could hear my aunts *gabbling* [=*babbling*] in the kitchen.
– **gabble** *noun* [*noncount*] I could hear the *gabble* of my aunts in the kitchen. [*singular*] a *gabble* of voices

gab·by /ˈgæbi/ *adj* **gab·bi·er; -est** *informal* : talking a lot : very talkative ▪ a *gabby* talk show host

gab·fest /ˈgæbˌfɛst/ *noun, pl* **-fests** [*count*] *US, informal*
1 : a long conversation ▪ a *gabfest* between friends
2 : a gathering for people to talk ▪ the group's annual *gabfest*

ga·ble /ˈgeɪbəl/ *noun, pl* **ga·bles** [*count*] : a section of a building's outside wall that is shaped like a triangle and that is formed by two sections of the roof sloping down — see picture at HOUSE
– **ga·bled** /ˈgeɪbəld/ *adj* ▪ *gabled* houses [=houses that have gables] ▪ a *gabled* roof [=a roof that forms a gable or gables]

gad /ˈgæd/ *verb* **gads; gad·ded; gad·ding**
gad about/around [*phrasal verb*] ***gad about/around*** *or* ***gad about/around (somewhere)*** : to move or travel without a plan or purpose ▪ He spent several months *gadding about* Europe after college.

gad·a·bout /ˈgædəˌbaʊt/ *noun, pl* **-bouts** [*count*] *sometimes disapproving* : a person who goes to many places and social events for pleasure ▪ a wealthy young *gadabout*

gad·fly /ˈgædˌflaɪ/ *noun, pl* **-flies** [*count*] : someone who annoys people by being very critical ▪ a political *gadfly* [=a person who criticizes politicians, political decisions, etc.]

gad·get /ˈgæʤət/ *noun, pl* **-gets** [*count*] : a small, useful device ▪ a clever *gadget* ▪ The kitchen is equipped with all the latest *gadgets*. ▪ cell phones, pagers, and other *gadgets*

gad·get·ry /ˈgæʤətri/ *noun* [*noncount*] : small, useful devices ▪ The kitchen is equipped with the latest *gadgetry*. [=*gadgets*] ▪ electronic *gadgetry* ▪ (*disapproving*) newfangled *gadgetry* [=new gadgets that are difficult to use, understand, etc.]

Gael·ic /ˈgeɪlɪk, ˈgælɪk/ *adj*
1 : of or relating to the Celtic people of Scotland and Ireland ▪ *Gaelic* politicians/folklore
2 : of or relating to the Celtic language of Scotland and Ireland ▪ *Gaelic* idioms
– **Gaelic** *noun* [*noncount*] ▪ The poems are written in *Gaelic*.

gaff /ˈgæf/ *noun, pl* **gaffs** [*count*]
1 : a spear or hook used for lifting heavy fish
2 : a pole that supports the top of a sail on some sailboats
3 *Brit slang* : someone's home ▪ Why not come round to my *gaff* for a few drinks?
blow the gaff *Brit slang* : to reveal a secret especially in a public way — usually + *on* ▪ The report *blows the gaff on* a series of illegal actions by the government.

gaffe /ˈgæf/ *noun, pl* **gaffes** [*count*] : a mistake made in a social situation ▪ He realized that he had committed/made an awful/embarrassing *gaffe* when he mispronounced her name. ▪ a verbal/diplomatic *gaffe*

gaf·fer /ˈgæfɚ/ *noun, pl* **-fers** [*count*] : a person who is in charge of the lights that are used when making a movie, television show, etc.

[1]**gag** /ˈgæg/ *verb* **gags; gagged; gag·ging**
1 [+ *obj*] : to put something (such as a piece of cloth) into or over a person's mouth in order to prevent that person from speaking, calling for help, etc. ▪ The hostages were ***bound and gagged*** [=their hands and feet were tied and their mouths were gagged]
2 [+ *obj*] : to prevent (someone) from speaking freely or expressing opinions ▪ The government is trying to *gag* the press.
3 [*no obj*] **a** : to vomit or feel as if you are about to vomit : to feel as if what is in your stomach is going to come up into your mouth ▪ The smell (almost) made me *gag*. — often + *on* ▪ She was *gagging on* the fumes. [=the fumes were causing her to gag] **b** : to be unable to breathe because something is stuck in your throat : CHOKE — often + *on* ▪ He *gagged on* a hot dog.

[2]**gag** *noun, pl* **gags** [*count*]
1 **a** : something said or done to make people laugh : JOKE ▪ The movie relies on simpleminded *gags* for laughs. ▪ a typical sitcom *gag* ▪ (*chiefly Brit*) The comedian told a few *gags*. — sometimes used before another noun ▪ a *gag* line ✧ A ***running gag*** is a joke that is repeated many times in slightly different ways. ▪ Her fake news reports were a *running gag* on the show. ✧ A ***sight gag*** is a joke that does not involve speaking. ▪ The movie is full of outrageous *sight gags*. **b** *chiefly US* : something done as a playful trick : PRANK ▪ They hid his clothes as a *gag*.
2 : something (such as a piece of cloth) that is put into or over someone's mouth in order to prevent speech ▪ They tied up the hostages and put *gags* in their mouths.
3 : something done to prevent people from speaking freely or expressing opinions ▪ The government is trying to put a *gag* on the press. — see also GAG ORDER, GAG RULE

ga·ga /ˈgɑːˌgɑː/ *adj* [*more ~; most ~*] *informal*
1 : extremely enthusiastic about or interested in something or someone ▪ I can't understand how anyone could be so *gaga* over/about golf. ▪ She's *gaga* over her boss's nephew. [=she's very attracted to her boss's nephew] — often used after *go* ▪ She's *gone gaga* over her boss's nephew. ▪ Critics have *gone gaga* over the movie.
2 : crazy or foolish ▪ He thinks that most artists are at least a little bit *gaga*.

gage *variant spelling of* GAUGE

gag·gle /ˈgægəl/ *noun, pl* **gag·gles** [*count*]
1 : a group of geese : a flock of geese
2 : a group of people ▪ a noisy *gaggle* of photographers/reporters/tourists

gag order *noun, pl* **~ -ders** [*count*] *chiefly US, law* : an order by a judge or court saying that the people involved in a legal case cannot talk about the case or anything related to it in public ▪ The judge has issued a *gag order*. — called also (*Brit*) *gagging order*

gag rule *noun, pl* **~ rules** [*count*] *US* : a rule saying that people are not allowed to speak freely or express their opinions about a particular subject ▪ The law prohibits insurance companies from imposing *gag rules* that limit communication between doctors and their patients.

gai·ety /ˈgejəti/ *noun* [*noncount*] *old-fashioned* : a happy and lively quality ▪ The party had none of the *gaiety* we've seen in past years. ▪ the *gaiety* of the carnival

gai·ly /ˈgeɪli/ *adv* [*more ~; most ~*] *old-fashioned*
1 : in a happy and lively way ▪ chatting/playing/laughing *gaily*
2 : in a bright and colorful way ▪ *gaily* dressed crowds ▪ a *gaily* painted vase ▪ a *gaily* colored poster

[1]**gain** /ˈgeɪn/ *verb* **gains; gained; gain·ing**
1 [+ *obj*] **a** : to get (something wanted or valued) ▪ They stand to *gain* an advantage over their competitors by getting an early start. ▪ What do you hope to *gain* from/by this? ▪ *gain* control of/over the territory ▪ Investigators are trying to *gain* access to the group's financial records. ▪ We were unable to *gain* admission/entrance/entry to the club. ▪ We need to *gain* a better understanding of the problem. ▪ They had nothing to lose and everything to *gain*. ▪ He first *gained* attention/recognition/fame as a young writer. ▪ Her theories are slowly *gaining* acceptance. ▪ She's *gaining* confidence in herself. [=she is becoming more confident] ▪ I took the job to *gain* experience. **b** : to win (something) in a competition, battle, etc. ▪ He is still hoping to *gain* the party's nomination. ▪ *gain* a victory **c** : to gradually get (something) or more of (something) as time passes ▪ He *gained* 40 pounds over five years, and then lost it all in two. ▪ *gain* weight ▪ The baby is quickly *gaining* strength in her legs.
2 [+ *obj*] : to cause (someone) to have (something) ▪ His recent behavior has *gained* [=*earned*] him a reputation for stubbornness. ▪ Her hard work *gained* her their respect. [=she has gained their respect through hard work; they respect her now because of her hard work]
3 **a** : to increase in (something) [+ *obj*] This event *gains* pop-

ularity [=becomes more popular] each year. • The plane was *gaining* altitude. • Some of the stocks are *gaining* value, while others are losing value. [*no obj*] Some of the stocks are *gaining*, while others are losing. — usually + *in* • This event *gains in* popularity each year • The stocks are *gaining in* value. **b** [+ *obj*] : to increase in value by (a specified amount) • The stocks *gained* three percent last month. **c** [*no obj*] : to increase in value when compared to something else • The dollar *gained* against the pound last month.

4 [*no obj*] : to get an advantage • The company hopes to *gain* [=*profit*] from the new regulations.

5 [+ *obj*] *American football* : to move the ball (a specified distance) down the field • They *gained* five yards on the last play.

6 *of a clock or watch* : to show a time that is later than the correct time : to run fast [*no obj*] The clock *gains* by less than a second a year. [+ *obj*] The clock *gains* less than a second a year.

7 [+ *obj*] *formal* : to arrive at (a place) especially after much effort • The tired swimmer *gained* the shore at last.

gain a/the jump on see ²JUMP

gain ground see ¹GROUND

gain on [*phrasal verb*] ***gain on (someone or something)*** : to come nearer to (someone or something that is ahead of you in a race or competition) • She was still leading at the halfway point, but the other runners were *gaining on* her.

gain time : to cause something to be delayed so that more time is available to do what is needed • His lawyers are delaying the trial to *gain time* to prepare their defense.

– gain·er *noun, pl* **-ers** [*count*] • a stock that was one of the year's biggest *gainers* [=one of the stocks that increased the most in value]

²gain *noun, pl* **gains**

1 [*count*] : something wanted or valued that is gotten : something that is gained • ill-gotten *gains* [=money and other valuable things gotten through dishonest methods]; *especially* : money gotten through some activity or process : PROFIT • financial/stock-market *gains* • economic *gains* — see also CAPITAL GAIN

2 [*noncount*] : something that is helpful : advantage or benefit • He acted only for his own personal/political *gain*. [=he acted only to benefit himself]

3 : an increase in amount, size, or number [*count*] a *gain* in weight • impressive *gains* [=*improvements*] in performance • They hope to make big *gains* in Congress in the coming election. [=they hope that many more members of their party will be elected to Congress] [*noncount*] The medication can cause nausea and weight *gain*.

4 [*count*] *American football* : the distance the ball is moved down the field during a play • They picked up a five-yard *gain* on first down.

no pain, no gain *also* ***no gain without pain*** *informal* — used to say that it is necessary to suffer or work hard in order to succeed or make progress

gain·ful /ˈgeɪnfəl/ *adj* [*more ~; most ~*] : paying money • people seeking *gainful* [=*paid*] employment • a *gainful* occupation • *gainful* activity

– gain·ful·ly *adv* • *gainfully* employed

gain·say /ˌgeɪnˈseɪ/ *verb* **gain·says** /ˌgeɪnˈseɪz, ˌgeɪnˈsɛz/; **gain·said** /ˌgeɪnˈseɪd, ˌgeɪnˈsɛd/; **gain·say·ing** [+ *obj*] *formal* : to deny or disagree with (something) : to show or say that (something) is not true — used in negative statements • There is no *gainsaying* such evidence. [=the truth of such evidence cannot be denied]

gait /ˈgeɪt/ *noun, pl* **gaits** [*count*] : a particular way of walking • He has an awkward *gait*. • an easy/unsteady *gait*

gai·ter /ˈgeɪtɚ/ *noun, pl* **-ters** [*count*] : a cloth or leather covering worn over the lower part of the leg especially to keep the legs and ankles dry when hiking — usually plural • a pair of *gaiters*

gal /ˈgæl/ *noun, pl* **gals** [*count*] *chiefly US, informal* : a girl or woman • She's a fun *gal*. • I want to see all you guys and *gals* out on the dance floor! • I've grown rather fond of the old *gal*.

gal. *abbr* gallon

ga·la /ˈgeɪlə, *Brit* ˈgɑːlə/ *noun, pl* **-las** [*count*] : a public party or celebration • a grand *gala* celebrating the town's centennial — often used before another noun • a *gala* event/affair/celebration

gal·axy /ˈgæləksi/ *noun, pl* **-ax·ies**

1 *astronomy* **a** [*count*] : any one of the very large groups of stars that make up the universe • the formation of *galaxies* • a giant/spiral *galaxy* **b** ***the Galaxy*** : the galaxy in which we live : MILKY WAY

2 [*count*] : a large group of important or well-known people or things • The event was attended by a *galaxy* of artists.

– ga·lac·tic /gəˈlæktɪk/ *adj, astronomy* • *galactic* objects

gale /ˈgeɪl/ *noun, pl* **gales** [*count*]

1 : a very strong wind • The boat was damaged in a strong *gale*. • The winds approached *gale* force. • *gale*-force winds

2 : a sudden occurrence of laughter, tears, etc. • The audience erupted in *gales* of laughter. • a *gale* of laughter/tears

¹gall /ˈgɑːl/ *noun* [*noncount*] : extreme confidence expressed in a way that is impolite : NERVE • I can't believe she just said that to me. What *gall*! — often used in the phrase ***have the gall*** • He *had the gall* to think that he could replace her. • I can't believe she *had the* (unmitigated) *gall* to ask for another day off.

²gall *verb* **galls**; **galled**; **gall·ing** [+ *obj*] : to make (someone) feel annoyed or angry • It *galls* me that such a small group of people can have so much power. — see also GALLING

gal·lant *adj* [*more ~; most ~*]

1 /ˈgælənt/ : showing courage : very brave • The defenders of the fort made a *gallant* stand. • a *gallant* knight • They failed to reach the summit, but they made a *gallant* attempt.

2 /ˈgælənt/ : large and impressive • a *gallant* ship

3 /gəˈlænt, gəˈlɑːnt/ : having or showing politeness and respect for women • He greeted her with a *gallant* bow. • He offered her his seat in a *gallant* gesture.

– gal·lant·ly *adv* • The troops marched *gallantly* into battle. • He *gallantly* offered her his seat.

gal·lant·ry /ˈgæləntri/ *noun* [*noncount*]

1 : very brave behavior : COURAGE • He was awarded several medals for *gallantry* [=*heroism, valor*] in battle. • I so admire the *gallantry* [=*spirit, courage*] with which she fought the disease.

2 : polite attention shown by a man to a woman • Many women were charmed by his old-fashioned *gallantry*.

gall·blad·der /ˈgɑːlˌblædɚ/ *noun, pl* **-ders** [*count*] *medical* : the organ in the body in which bile from the liver is stored — see picture at HUMAN

gal·le·on /ˈgælijən/ *noun, pl* **-ons** [*count*] : a large sailing ship used especially by the Spanish in the 1500s and 1600s

gal·lery /ˈgæləri/ *noun, pl* **-ler·ies** [*count*]

1 a : a room or building in which people look at paintings, sculptures, etc. • an art *gallery* • the National *Gallery* **b** : a business that sells paintings, sculptures, etc. • She owns a *gallery* downtown.

2 : a group or collection of people or things • The movie features a *gallery* of weird characters. — see also ROGUES' GALLERY

3 a : the highest section of seats in a theater **b** : the people sitting in the gallery **c** : the people who are watching a tennis or golf match

play to the gallery : to do things that you think will be popular among many people instead of doing what you think is right • a governor who refuses to *play to the gallery*

— see also SHOOTING GALLERY

gal·ley /ˈgæli/ *noun, pl* **-leys** [*count*]

1 : the kitchen of a ship or airplane

2 : a long, low ship that was moved by oars and sails and that was used in ancient times by the Egyptians, Greeks, and others • a slave *galley* [=a galley rowed by slaves]

Gal·lic /ˈgælɪk/ *adj* : of or relating to France or French people • a *Gallic* [=*French*] pop star; *especially* : typical of French people • our host's *Gallic* charm

gall·ing /ˈgɑːlɪŋ/ *adj* [*more ~; most ~*] : causing someone to feel angry or annoyed • Their refusal to meet with me was extremely *galling*. [=*annoying*] • This is a *galling* defeat.

gal·li·vant /ˈgæləˌvænt/ *verb* **-vants**; **-vant·ed**; **-vant·ing** [*no obj*] *somewhat informal + often disapproving* : to go or travel to many different places for pleasure • They've been *gallivanting* all over town. • He's been *gallivanting* around the country when he ought to be looking for a job.

gal·lon /ˈgælən/ *noun, pl* **-lons** [*count*]

1 *US* : a unit of liquid measurement equal to four U.S. quarts or 3.785 liters

2 *Brit* : a unit of liquid measurement equal to four British quarts or 4.546 liters

¹gal·lop /ˈgæləp/ *noun, pl* **-lops**

1 : the way a horse or similar animal moves when it is running fast and all four of its feet leave the ground at the same time — often used after *at* [*noncount*] The horse was *at* full *gallop*. [*singular*] He mounted his horse and took off *at* a *gallop*. — sometimes used figuratively ▪ The course covers early American history *at a gallop*. [=very quickly; in a short amount of time]

2 [*count*] **:** a ride or run at a gallop ▪ We went for a *gallop* through the countryside. — sometimes used figuratively ▪ The course begins with a quick *gallop* through early American history. — compare [1]CANTER, [2]TROT

[2]**gallop** *verb* **-lops; -loped; -lop·ing**

1 a [*no obj*] *of a horse or similar animal* **:** to run very fast **:** to run at a gallop ▪ The horse *galloped* toward us. **b** [*no obj*] **:** to ride on a galloping horse ▪ He mounted his horse and *galloped* off to sound the alarm. **c** [+ *obj*] **:** to make (a horse) gallop ▪ She *galloped* her horse toward us.

2 [*no obj*] **:** to run or move quickly ▪ I grabbed my books and *galloped* out the door. ▪ The program *gallops* through early American history.

gal·lop·ing /ˈgæləpɪŋ/ *adj, always used before a noun* **:** quickly developing or increasing ▪ *galloping* inflation

gal·lows /ˈgæloʊz/ *noun, pl* **-lows** [*count*] **:** a structure on which a criminal who has been sentenced to death is killed by being hanged ▪ He was sentenced to death on the *gallows*. ▪ She was ***sent to the gallows*** [=she was sentenced to death]

G

gallows humor *noun* [*noncount*] **:** humor that relates to very serious or frightening things (such as death and illness)

gall·stone /ˈgɑːlˌstoʊn/ *noun, pl* **-stones** [*count*] *medical* **:** a hard object like a small stone that sometimes forms in the gallbladder and that can cause great pain

ga·loot /gəˈluːt/ *noun, pl* **-loots** [*count*] *US slang* **:** a man or boy; *especially* **:** one who is foolish or awkward ▪ You big *galoot*! ▪ a clumsy *galoot*

ga·lore /gəˈloɚ/ *adj, always used after a noun, informal* **:** in large numbers or amounts ▪ The store promises bargains *galore* [=promises that there will be many bargains] during its weekend sale.

ga·losh·es /gəˈlɑːʃəz/ *noun* [*plural*]

1 *old-fashioned* **:** tall rubber shoes that are worn over other shoes in wet weather to keep your feet dry — compare RUBBERS

2 : rubber boots worn in wet weather to keep the feet dry

ga·lumph /gəˈlʌmf/ *verb* **-lumphs; -lumphed; -lumph·ing** [*no obj*] *informal* **:** to move in a loud and clumsy way ▪ I could hear him *galumphing* around in the attic.

gal·van·ic /gælˈvænɪk/ *adj*

1 *technical* **:** relating to or producing a direct current of electricity ▪ a *galvanic* cell ▪ *galvanic* corrosion

2 [*more ~; most ~*] **:** causing people to feel or react strongly ▪ a *galvanic* performance/performer ▪ Her performance had a *galvanic* effect on the audience.

gal·va·nize *also Brit* **gal·va·nise** /ˈgælvəˌnaɪz/ *verb* **-niz·es; -nized; -niz·ing** [+ *obj*]

1 a : to cause (people) to become so excited or concerned about an issue, idea, etc., that they want to do something about it ▪ an issue that *galvanized* the public (to take action) **b :** to cause (a force that is capable of causing change) to become active ▪ The group is hoping to *galvanize* public opinion against the proposed law. ▪ The Web site has *galvanized* support for the project.

2 *technical* **:** to cover (steel or iron) with a layer of zinc to prevent it from rusting ▪ a factory where steel is *galvanized*

– **galvanized** *adj* ▪ *galvanized* nails ▪ *galvanized* steel

gam·bit /ˈgæmbət/ *noun, pl* **-bits** [*count*]

1 : a planned series of moves at the beginning of a game of chess ✧ A gambit usually involves losing a piece, such as a pawn, in order to gain an advantage later in the game.

2 : something done or said in order to gain an advantage or to produce a desired result ▪ a conversational *gambit* ▪ Their ***opening gambit*** [=their first move] in the negotiations was to demand a wage hike.

[1]**gam·ble** /ˈgæmbəl/ *verb* **gam·bles; gam·bled; gam·bling**

1 [*no obj*] **:** to play a game in which you can win or lose money or possessions **:** to bet money or other valuable things ▪ I like to *gamble*. ▪ He's been drinking and *gambling* heavily. ▪ *gambling* at cards — often + *on* ▪ She likes to *gamble on* football games.

2 [+ *obj*] **a :** to risk losing (an amount of money) in a game or bet ▪ He would often *gamble* hundreds of dollars on a hand of poker. **b :** to risk losing (something valuable or important) in order to do or achieve something ▪ She *gambled* [=*risked*] everything she owned to start the business. — often + *on* ▪ The company is *gambling* [=*betting, risking*] everything *on* this strategy.

3 : to do something that could have the good result that you want or a bad result that you cannot control [*no obj*] The mayor is *gambling* with the city's future. ▪ people who lost money *gambling* in the stock market — often + *on* ▪ Many people are willing to *gamble on* the new treatment. [=are willing to try the new treatment because they hope it will help them] [+ *obj*] The mayor is *gambling* that the new policies will help rather than hurt the city.

gamble away [*phrasal verb*] ***gamble away (something)*** *or* ***gamble (something) away*** **:** to lose (something, such as money) by gambling ▪ She *gambled away* her inheritance. ▪ *gambling away* the city's future

– **gam·bler** /ˈgæmblɚ/ *noun, pl* **-blers** [*count*] ▪ The casino attracts many wealthy *gamblers*. ▪ a compulsive *gambler*

[2]**gamble** *noun, pl* **gambles** [*count*] **:** something that could produce a desired result or a bad or unpleasant result **:** RISK ▪ Starting her own business was a *gamble*, but it paid off. ▪ She thought about starting her own business, but she decided it was too much of a *gamble*. ▪ He was ***taking a*** (big) ***gamble*** [=doing something that could produce a (very) bad or unpleasant result] ▪ Many people are willing to *take a gamble* on the new treatment. [=to try the new treatment]

gambling *noun* [*noncount*] **:** the practice or activity of betting money **:** the practice of risking money in a game or bet ▪ He was arrested for illegal *gambling*. ▪ legalized *gambling* ▪ compulsive *gambling* — often used before another noun ▪ a *gambling* casino ▪ a *gambling* resort ▪ She has a *gambling* problem. ▪ a *gambling* game

gam·bol /ˈgæmbəl/ *verb* **-bols;** *US* **-boled** *or Brit* **-bolled;** *US* **-bol·ing** *or Brit* **-bol·ling** [*no obj*] **:** to run or jump in a lively way ▪ lambs *gamboling* in the meadow

– **gambol** *noun, pl* **-bols** [*count*] ▪ a playful *gambol*

[1]**game** /ˈgeɪm/ *noun, pl* **games**

1 [*count*] **a :** a physical or mental activity or contest that has rules and that people do for pleasure ▪ a card *game* ▪ party *games* [=activities people do at parties for pleasure] ▪ word *games* [=games or puzzles that involve words] ▪ computer *games* ▪ poker and other gambling *games* ▪ Baseball is my favorite *game*. [=*sport*] **b :** a particular occurrence of a game ▪ Do you want to play a *game* (of tennis/cards)? ▪ She scored a goal to tie the *game*. ▪ They won/lost the *game*. ▪ We played a few *games* of chess. ▪ That was a good *game*! **c :** one of the games that are part of a larger contest (such as a tennis match) ▪ She won the first two *games*, but lost the set and the match. — see also BALL GAME, BOARD GAME, FUN AND GAMES, GUESSING GAME, PARLOR GAME, PERFECT GAME, RETURN GAME, SHELL GAME, VIDEO GAME, *game of chance* at [1]CHANCE, *game of skill* at SKILL

2 games [*plural*] **a :** playful activities ▪ children playing at their *games* **b** *or* **Games :** an organized series of athletic contests; *specifically* **:** the Olympics ▪ Let the *Games* begin.

3 a [*singular*] **:** the way someone plays in a sport ▪ They are known to play a very rough *game*. ▪ She has a strong all-around *game*. ▪ She needs to improve her *game* if she wants to win the championship. ▪ Champions can raise/lift their *game* [=can play better] when they're in danger of losing. **b** [*count*] **:** a skill that is used in playing a particular game or sport ▪ a football team with a strong running/passing *game*

4 [*count*] **a :** an activity that is being compared to a game or contest ▪ He's a loser in the *game* of love. [=he is not successful in romantic relationships] ▪ the *game* of life ▪ They're playing a dangerous *game* by refusing to negotiate. ▪ He's trying to ***beat them at their own game*** [=he's trying to gain an advantage over them by using the same methods that they use] ▪ the ***mating game*** [=the effort to find a sexual partner] — see also WAITING GAME, WAR GAME, *the name of the game* at [1]NAME **b :** a type of work **:** a business or profession ▪ She's spent the last 30 years in the newspaper *game*. ▪ the money *game* ▪ the ***fight game*** [=professional boxing] — see also WAR GAME

5 [*count*] **:** something that is not meant to be taken seriously ▪ Politics for her is just a *game*. ▪ Was our entire relationship just a *game* to you?

6 [*count*] **:** a usually dishonest or unfair plan for doing something ▪ I've seen through your little *game* and I know what you're really after! ▪ What's his *game*? [=what is his real reason for doing the things he is doing?] ✧ To ***give the game away*** is to make a secret plan or activity known. ▪ We can't let him know anything about it. He's too likely to *give the game away*. ✧ If ***the game is up***, a dishonest plan or activity has been discovered and will no longer be allowed to continue. ▪ Okay, *the game is up*. [=*the jig is up*] We know you forged the letters.

7 [*noncount*] : animals that are hunted • wild *game* • small *game* — often used before another noun • a *game* bird/fish [=a bird or fish that may be legally hunted or caught] • a ***game preserve*** [=an area of land in which hunting and fishing are carefully controlled] • a ***game warden*** [=a person who makes sure that hunting and fishing laws are obeyed] — often used figuratively • The police aren't interested in these small-time drug dealers; they're after much bigger *game*. — see also BIG GAME

ahead of the game : in a position or situation in which you are likely to succeed, win, etc. • The company has stayed *ahead of the game* by meeting new government standards before they go into effect.

early/late in the game : at an early/late time in a game or sport • She scored a goal *early in the game*. [=near the beginning of the game] — often used figuratively • It's too *late in the game* to change the date of the meeting. [=it's no longer reasonable to change the date; the meeting is too soon for the date to be changed] • She got into the computer industry *early in the game*. [=when the industry was new]

got game ✧ In informal U.S. English, someone who has *got game* is very good at playing a particular game or sport, such as basketball.

head/mind games : actions that are meant to confuse or upset someone in order to get an advantage • I couldn't handle the *head games* that came with the job anymore. • She's known for playing *mind games* with her opponents.

on the game *Brit, informal* : working as a prostitute • I didn't know she was *on the game*.

on/off your game ✧ If you are *on your game*, you are playing a sport or game well; if you are *off your game*, you are playing poorly. • She's really *on her game* tonight. [=she's playing very well] • Sorry I missed that shot. I'm *off my game* today. [=I'm not playing as well as I usually do] These phrases are also used figuratively. • He seemed a little *off his game* during the sales presentation this morning.

play games 1 : to treat someone in a dishonest or unfair way in order to get an advantage • Stop *playing games* (with me) and tell me what really happened! • I'm trying to be honest with you. I'm not interested in *playing games*. 2 : to behave in a way that is not serious • Let's stop *playing games* and get down to business.

the only game in town : the only available, desirable, or valuable thing • For serious home cooks, this stove is *the only game in town*. [=it is the only stove that serious home cooks should want to have] • Our company is no longer *the only game in town*. [=we now have competition; another company/business is doing what we do]

²game *adj* **gam·er; -est**

1 : willing or ready to do something • "Do you feel like going to the movies tonight?" "Sure, I'm *game*." • They were *game* for anything. = They were *game* to try anything.

2 : showing a willingness to work hard, keep trying, etc. : showing determination • They remained *game* [=*determined*] to the end. • She lost despite a *game* effort.

– **game·ly** *adv* [*more* ~; *most* ~] • She smiled *gamely* for the camera.

game ball *noun, pl* ~ **balls** [*count*] *US* : a ball that is given to a player or coach who did something impressive to help win a game in American football, basketball, etc.

game hen *noun, pl* ~ **hens** [*count*] : a young, small hen used especially for roasting

game·keep·er /ˈgeɪmˌkiːpɚ/ *noun, pl* **-ers** [*count*] : a person who is in charge of the breeding and protection of animals that are hunted on private land

game plan *noun, pl* ~ **plans** [*count*]

1 : a plan for playing a game (such as American football or soccer)

2 : a plan for doing or achieving something • The governor is developing a *game plan* to lure businesses to the region.

game point *noun, pl* ~ **points** [*count*] *sports* : a situation in tennis or another game in which the player who wins the next point will win the game; *also* : the point itself — compare MATCH POINT

gam·er /ˈgeɪmɚ/ *noun, pl* **-ers** [*count*] *US*

1 : a person who plays games and especially video or computer games • video *gamers*

2 *informal* : a person who is game; *especially* : an athlete who tries very hard to win games, competitions, etc. • He's a real *gamer*.

game show *noun, pl* ~ **shows** [*count*] : a television program in which people try to win prizes in a game • He was a contestant on a *game show*. = He was a *game-show* contestant.

games·man·ship /ˈgeɪmzmənˌʃɪp/ *noun* [*noncount*] *usually disapproving*

1 : the practice of winning a game or contest by doing things that seem unfair but that are not actually against the rules • They blur the line between *gamesmanship* and cheating.

2 : the clever use of skills or tricks to succeed or do something • corporate/political *gamesmanship*

gam·ete /ˈgæˌmiːt/ *noun, pl* **-etes** [*count*] *technical* : one of the cells that join together to begin making a person or other creature

gamey *variant spelling of* GAMY

ga·mine /gæˈmiːn/ *noun, pl* **-mines** [*count*] : an attractive and usually thin and small woman or girl who often shows a playful desire to cause trouble • a movie about a French *gamine*

– **gamine** *adj* • She was girlish and *gamine*.

gam·ing /ˈgeɪmɪŋ/ *noun* [*noncount*]

1 : the activity of playing computer games • He does a lot of *gaming* online.

2 : the act or activity of gambling • casino *gaming*

gam·ma /ˈgæmə/ *noun, pl* **-mas** [*count*] : the third letter of the Greek alphabet — Γ or γ

gamma rays *noun* [*plural*] : powerful invisible rays that are sent out from some radioactive substances — called also *gamma radiation*

gam·mon /ˈgæmən/ *noun* [*noncount*] *Brit* : smoked or salted meat from the side or leg of a pig • a *gammon* steak

gam·ut /ˈgæmət/ *noun* [*singular*] : a range or series of related things • She experienced the full *gamut* of human emotions. • Her emotions ***ran the gamut*** from joy to despair. [=she felt emotions ranging from joy to despair]

gamy *or* **gam·ey** /ˈgeɪmi/ *adj* **gam·i·er; -est** : having the flavor of meat from wild animals especially when it is slightly spoiled • *gamy* meat • The deer tasted *gamy*.

– **gam·i·ness** /ˈgeɪminəs/ *noun* [*noncount*]

¹gan·der /ˈgændɚ/ *noun, pl* **-ders** [*count*] : a male goose

what's good for the goose is good for the gander see ¹GOOSE

– compare ²GANDER

²gander *noun* [*singular*] *informal* : a look at something • I'd like to stop by and ***take/have a gander*** at your new car. — compare ¹GANDER

¹gang /ˈgæŋ/ *noun, pl* **gangs** [*count*]

1 : a group of criminals • a *gang* of drug dealers • a *gang* of thieves — see also CHAIN GANG

2 : a group of young people who do illegal things together and who often fight against other gangs • street *gangs* • He is in a *gang*. • He was shot by a member of a rival *gang*. • *gang* violence

3 *informal* : a group of people who are friends and who do things together • The *gang's* all here. • the *gang* at the office

²gang *verb* **gangs; ganged; gang·ing**

gang up [*phrasal verb*] *informal* : to form a group to attack, oppose, or criticize someone — usually + *on* • His classmates *ganged up on* him and beat him up pretty badly. — sometimes + *against* • Everyone *ganged up against* her.

gang bang *noun, pl* ~ **bangs** [*count*] *informal + impolite* : an occurrence in which several men have sex with the same woman one after another

gang·bust·ers /ˈgæŋˌbʌstɚz/ *noun*

like gangbusters *US, informal* 1 : very well or successfully • The team got off to a slow start, but recently they have been coming on *like gangbusters*. [=they have been doing very well] 2 : very quickly • The company has been growing *like gangbusters*.

gang·land /ˈgæŋˌlænd/ *noun* [*singular*] : the violent world of organized crime — usually used before another noun • a *gangland* shooting

gan·gling /ˈgæŋglɪŋ/ *adj* [*more* ~; *most* ~] *chiefly Brit* : GANGLY • a *gangling* teenager

gan·gli·on /ˈgæŋglijən/ *noun, pl* **-glia** /-glijə/ *also* **-gli·ons** [*count*] *medical* : a mass of nerve cells

gan·gly /ˈgæŋgli/ *adj* **gan·gli·er; -est**

1 : tall, thin, and awkward • a *gangly* teenager

2 : long and thin • *gangly* legs

gang·plank /ˈgæŋˌplæŋk/ *noun, pl* **-planks** [*count*] : a board or other structure that people walk on to get on or off a ship

gang rape *noun, pl* ~ **rapes** [*count*] : a crime in which one woman is raped by several men one after another

G

– **gang–rape** *verb* **-rape; -raped; -raping** [+ *obj*]

gan·grene /ˈgæŋˌgriːn/ *noun* [*noncount*] *medical* **:** the decay of flesh that occurs in a part of the body that no longer has blood flowing to it ▪ When *gangrene* set in, the soldier's leg had to be amputated.

– **gan·gre·nous** /ˈgæŋgrənəs/ *adj* ▪ a *gangrenous* foot

gang·sta /ˈgæŋstə/ *noun, pl* **-stas** [*count*] *US, informal*

1 : a member of a street gang

2 : a person who performs gangsta rap music

gangsta rap *noun* [*noncount*] **:** a type of rap music with lyrics about the violence and drug use of street gangs

– **gangsta rapper** *noun, pl* ~ **-pers** [*count*]

gang·ster /ˈgæŋstɚ/ *noun, pl* **-sters** [*count*] **:** a member of a group of violent criminals

gang·way /ˈgæŋˌweɪ/ *noun, pl* **-ways**

1 [*count*] **:** GANGPLANK

2 [*count*] *Brit* **:** a passage between sections of seats in a theater, airplane, etc. **:** AISLE

3 — used to tell people in a crowd to move aside so that someone can pass through ▪ "*Gangway*!" the man shouted as he pushed his way through the crowd.

G

gan·ja /ˈgɑːnʤə/ *noun* [*noncount*] *slang* **:** MARIJUANA

gan·net /ˈgænət/ *noun, pl* **gan·nets** *also* **gannet** [*count*] **:** a large ocean bird that eats fish

gantlet *variant spelling of* [1]GAUNTLET

gaol, gaol·bird, gaol·break, gaol·er *Brit spellings of* JAIL, JAILBIRD, JAILBREAK, JAILER

gap /ˈgæp/ *noun, pl* **gaps** [*count*]

1 a : a space between two people or things ▪ The child had a *gap* between her two front teeth. ▪ The *gap* between the lead runner and the rest of the field continued to widen. **b :** a hole or space where something is missing ▪ The sheep got through a *gap* in the fence.

2 : a missing part ▪ There are unexplained *gaps* in his story. ▪ The class filled in the *gaps* in my knowledge of biology.

3 : a part or period in which nothing happens ▪ She had taken several years off to raise a family, so there was a large *gap* in her work history.

4 : a difference between two people, groups, or things — often + *between* ▪ There is a widening *gap between* the rich and the poor. ▪ We hope to ***close the gap between*** well-funded suburban schools and the struggling schools in poorer communities. ▪ His work ***bridges the gap between*** popular fiction and serious literature. [=his work has qualities of both popular fiction and serious literature] — see also CREDIBILITY GAP, GENERATION GAP

gape /ˈgeɪp/ *verb* **gapes; gaped; gap·ing** [*no obj*]

1 : to open widely ▪ Her mouth ***gaped open.***

2 : to look at someone or something with your mouth open in surprise or wonder — often + *at* ▪ The crowd *gaped at* the princess as she passed by. ▪ What are you *gaping at*?

synonyms see [1]GAZE

gap·ing /ˈgeɪpɪŋ/ *adj* **:** wide open **:** very large ▪ a ***gaping wound*** ▪ a ***gaping hole***

gap–toothed /ˈgæpˌtuːθt/ *adj* **:** having a large space between two teeth ▪ a *gap-toothed* child/smile/grin

gap year *noun, pl* ~ **years** [*count*] **:** a year that you spend traveling, working, etc., before continuing your studies ▪ She decided to take a *gap year* between high school and college.

[1]**ga·rage** /gəˈrɑːʒ, *Brit* ˈgærɪʤ/ *noun, pl* **-rag·es** [*count*]

1 : a building or part of a building in which a car, truck, etc., is kept ▪ a house with a two-car *garage* — see picture at HOUSE; see also PARKING GARAGE

2 : a shop where vehicles are repaired ▪ My car was making a strange noise, so I brought it to the *garage*.

[2]**garage** *verb* **-rages; -raged; -rag·ing** [+ *obj*] **:** to put or keep (a car, truck, etc.) in a garage ▪ He *garaged* the car for the winter.

garage band *noun, pl* ~ **bands** [*count*] **:** a group of people who play rock music together and typically practice in a garage

garage sale *noun, pl* ~ **sales** [*count*] *chiefly US* **:** a sale of used furniture, clothing, etc., held at the seller's home — called also (*US*) *tag sale,* (*US*) *yard sale*

[1]**garb** /ˈgɑɚb/ *noun* [*noncount*] **:** a particular style or type of clothing ▪ traditional academic *garb* ▪ dressed in ceremonial *garb* ▪ prison *garb*

[2]**garb** *verb* **garbs; garbed; garb·ing** [+ *obj*] **:** to dress (someone) *in* a particular type of clothing — usually used as *(be) garbed* ▪ He *was garbed in* a black robe. [=he was wearing a black robe]

gar·bage /ˈgɑɚbɪʤ/ *noun* [*noncount*]

1 *chiefly US* **a :** things that are no longer useful or wanted and that have been thrown out **:** TRASH ▪ The park was littered with *garbage*. ▪ Please take out the *garbage*. ▪ Raccoons were going through the *garbage*. — often used to refer specifically to food waste that is being thrown out ▪ the smell of rotting *garbage* **b :** a container where people put things that are being thrown out ▪ Throw the can in the *garbage*.

2 *informal* **:** something that is worthless, unimportant, or of poor quality ▪ Maybe you should read a book instead of watching that *garbage* [=*rubbish*] on TV.

3 *informal* **:** foolish or untrue words or ideas **:** NONSENSE ▪ If you ask me, what he said is a bunch/load of *garbage*.

garbage can *noun, pl* ~ **cans** [*count*] *US* **:** a container for garbage — called also (*US*) *garbage pail,* (*Brit*) *waste bin*

garbage disposal *noun, pl* ~ **-als** [*count*] *US* **:** a device in a kitchen sink that grinds up food waste so it can be washed down the drain — called also (*Brit*) *waste disposal unit*

gar·bage·man /ˈgɑɚbɪʤˌmæn/ *noun, pl* **-men** [*count*] *US* **:** a person who collects and removes garbage — called also (*US*) *garbage collector,* (*Brit*) *binman,* (*Brit*) *dustman*

garbage truck *noun, pl* ~ **trucks** [*count*] *US* **:** a truck used to take away garbage that people put outside their houses, buildings, etc., in bags or cans — called also (*Brit*) *dustcart*; see picture at TRUCK

gar·ban·zo /gɑɚˈbɑːnˌzoʊ, *Brit* gɑˈbænˌzəʊ/ *noun, pl* **-zos** [*count*] *US* **:** CHICKPEA

garbanzo bean *noun, pl* ~ **beans** [*count*] *US* **:** CHICKPEA

gar·ble /ˈgɑɚbəl/ *verb* **gar·bles; gar·bled; gar·bling** [+ *obj*] **:** to cause (a word, name, message, etc.) to be unclear or confusing ▪ He was so nervous he *garbled* her name [=he said her name incorrectly] when he introduced her.

– **garbled** *adj* ▪ We could not understand him because of his *garbled* speech. ▪ a *garbled* phone message

[1]**gar·den** /ˈgɑɚdn/ *noun, pl* **-dens**

1 [*count*] *US* **:** an area of ground where plants (such as flowers or vegetables) are grown ▪ We planted a small *garden* in our backyard. ▪ a vegetable/rose *garden* ▪ a *garden* hose/cart/rake/path ▪ a ***garden party*** [=a party that takes place in a garden or in a large yard with gardens] — see color picture on page C6

2 [*count*] *Brit* **:** [1]YARD 1 ▪ They were sitting out in the back *garden*.

3 [*count*] **:** a public area with many plants and trees ▪ a botanical/public *garden* — often plural ▪ Kew *Gardens*

4 [*count*] *US* **:** a large stadium or building for sports or entertainment — used in names ▪ They went to the hockey game at Madison Square *Garden*.

5 ***Gardens*** [*plural*] *chiefly Brit* — used in street names ▪ Belsize *Gardens*

common-or-garden see [1]COMMON

lead someone down/up the garden path see [1]LEAD

[2]**garden** *verb* **-dens; -dened; -den·ing** [*no obj*] **:** to work in a garden **:** to take care of the plants in a garden ▪ He likes to *garden*.

– **gar·den·er** /ˈgɑɚdənɚ/ *noun, pl* **-ers** [*count*] ▪ She's a talented *gardener*. ▪ He hired a *gardener* to take care of his estate. – **gardening** *noun* [*noncount*] ▪ Her hobbies include bicycling and *gardening*.

garden chair *noun, pl* ~ **chairs** [*count*] *Brit* **:** LAWN CHAIR

gar·de·nia /gɑɚˈdiːnjə/ *noun, pl* **-nias** [*count*] **:** a large white or yellowish flower that has a pleasant smell

Garden of Eden *noun* [*singular*] **:** EDEN 1

garden–variety *adj, always used before a noun, US* **:** not unusual **:** ordinary or common ▪ He doesn't have the flu—just a *garden-variety* cold. ▪ The movie is a *garden-variety* thriller.

gar·gan·tuan /gɑɚˈgænʧəwən/ *adj* [*more* ~; *most* ~] **:** very large in size or amount **:** GIGANTIC ▪ a creature of *gargantuan* proportions ▪ a *gargantuan* appetite

[1]**gar·gle** /ˈgɑɚgəl/ *verb* **gar·gles; gar·gled; gar·gling :** to clean your throat and mouth with a liquid that you move around in your throat and then spit out [*no obj*] He *gargled* with salt water. ▪ She *gargles* every morning. [+ *obj*] He *gargled* the salt water, then spit it out.

[2]**gargle** *noun, pl* **gargles :** a liquid used for gargling [*count*] a medicinal *gargle* used for sore throats [*noncount*] (*Brit*) treating a sore throat with *gargle*

gar·goyle /ˈgɑɚˌgojəl/ *noun, pl* **-goyles** [*count*] **:** a strange or ugly human or animal figure that sticks out from the roof of a building (such as a church) ✧ Gargoyles are stone sculp-

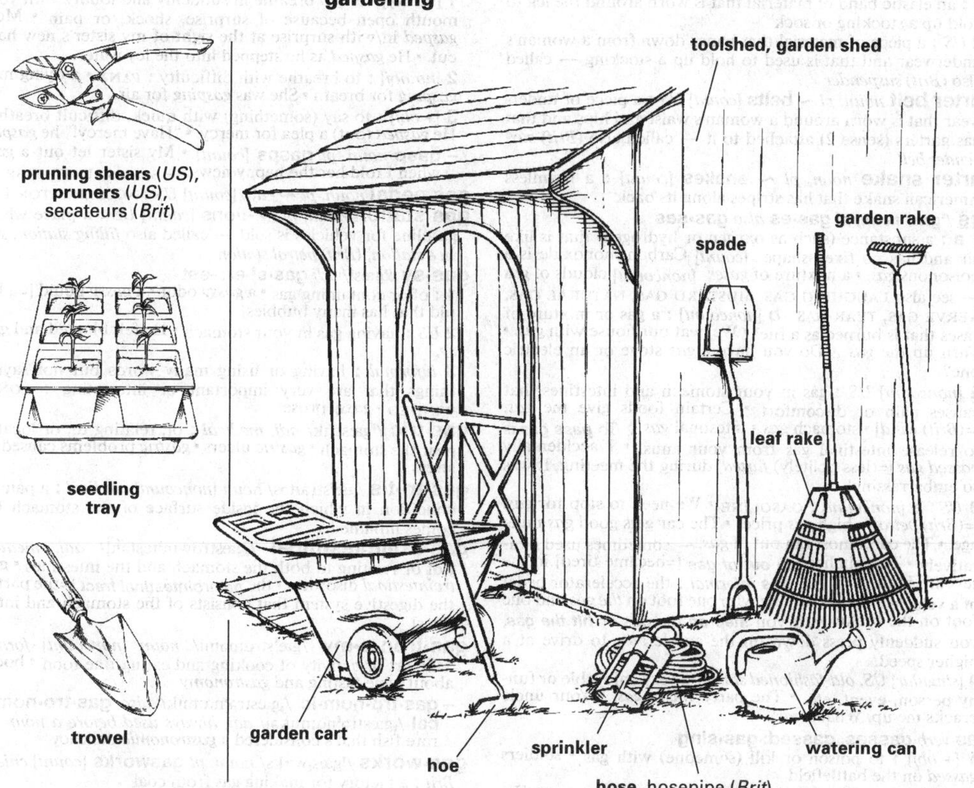

tures that are used to cause rainwater to flow away from the sides of a building.

gar·ish /ˈgerɪʃ/ *adj* [*more* ~; *most* ~] **:** too bright or colorful • a *garish* [=*gaudy*] dress covered with sequins • *garish* neon signs

– gar·ish·ly *adv* • a *garishly* decorated room • *garishly* dressed **– gar·ish·ness** *noun* [*noncount*]

¹gar·land /ˈgaɚlənd/ *noun, pl* **-lands** [*count*] **:** a ring or rope that is made of leaves, flowers, or some other material and that is used as a decoration • They placed a *garland* of flowers around her neck.

²garland *verb* **-lands; -land·ed; -land·ing** [+ *obj*] **:** to put a garland on (someone or something) — usually used as *(be) garlanded* • The winner *was garlanded* with flowers. — often used figuratively • The book has *been garlanded* with praise. [=has received a lot of praise]

gar·lic /ˈgaɚlɪk/ *noun* [*noncount*] **:** a plant that is related to the onion and that has small sections (called cloves) which have a strong taste and smell and are used for flavoring foods • The recipe calls for two cloves of *garlic*, minced. • a pasta dish flavored with basil and *garlic* • ***garlic bread*** [=bread toasted and flavored with butter and garlic] • a ***garlic press*** [=a tool used to crush garlic] — see color picture on page C4

– gar·licky /ˈgaɚlɪki/ *adj* [*more* ~; *most* ~] • a strong, *garlicky* dish • *garlicky* breath

gar·ment /ˈgaɚmənt/ *noun, pl* **-ments** [*count*] *somewhat formal* **:** a piece of clothing • expensive silk *garments*

garment bag *noun, pl* ~ **bags** [*count*] **:** a bag that folds in half and is used to carry suits and dresses when you are traveling

gar·ner /ˈgaɚnɚ/ *verb* **-ners; -nered; -ner·ing** [+ *obj*] *formal*

1 : to collect or gather (something) • She *garnered* more evidence to support her theory. • The senator has spent much time *garnering* financial support for his upcoming campaign.

2 : to get or receive (something wanted or valued) • The novel has *garnered* much praise and several awards. • The band has *garnered* [=*gained*] a large following.

gar·net /ˈgaɚnət/ *noun, pl* **-nets**

1 [*count*] **:** a dark red stone that is used in jewelry — see color picture on page C11

2 [*noncount*] **:** a dark red color

garni see BOUQUET GARNI

¹gar·nish /ˈgaɚnɪʃ/ *verb* **-nish·es; -nished; -nish·ing** [+ *obj*] **:** to put something on (food) as a decoration — usually + *with Garnish* the cake *with* chocolate curls. • The fish was *garnished with* parsley leaves.; *also* **:** to be added as a decoration to (food) • Chocolate curls *garnished* the cake.

²garnish *noun, pl* **-nishes** [*count, noncount*] **:** something (such as small pieces of fruit, chopped herbs, etc.) that is put on food as a decoration

garotte *variant spelling of* GARROTTE

gar·ret /ˈgerət/ *noun, pl* **-rets** [*count*] **:** a usually small and unpleasant room or space area just below the roof of a building • an artist's *garret* [=a garret where a struggling artist lives in poverty]

¹gar·ri·son /ˈgerəsən/ *noun, pl* **-sons** [*count*]

1 : a military camp, fort, or base • troops defending the *garrison* • a *garrison* town

2 : a group of soldiers who are living at a garrison • a *garrison* of 5,000 men

²garrison *verb* **-sons; -soned; -son·ing** [+ *obj*]

1 : to send soldiers to (a place) in order to defend it • *garrison* a town

2 : to send (soldiers) to live in and defend a place — often used as *(be) garrisoned* • The men *were garrisoned* in town.

¹gar·rote *or* **ga·rotte** /gəˈrɑːt/ *noun, pl* **-rotes** *or* **-rottes** [*count*] **:** a device (such as a piece of wire with a handle at each end) that is used to strangle someone

²garrote *or* **garotte** *verb* **-rotes** *or* **-rottes; -rot·ed** *or* **-rott·ed; -rot·ing** *or* **-rott·ing** [+ *obj*] **:** to strangle (someone) with a garrote • The victim was *garroted*.

gar·ru·lous /ˈgerələs/ *adj* [*more* ~; *most* ~] **:** tending to talk a lot **:** very talkative • He became more *garrulous* after drinking a couple of beers.

gar·ter /ˈgaɚtɚ/ *noun, pl* **-ters** [*count*]

1 : an elastic band of material that is worn around the leg to hold up a stocking or sock
2 *US* : a piece of material that hangs down from a woman's underwear and that is used to hold up a stocking — called also *(Brit) suspender*

garter belt *noun, pl* ~ **belts** [*count*] *US* : a piece of underwear that is worn around a woman's waist and hips and that has garters (sense 2) attached to it — called also *(Brit) suspender belt*

garter snake *noun, pl* ~ **snakes** [*count*] : a harmless American snake that has stripes along its back

[1]**gas** /ˈgæs/ *noun, pl* **gas·es** *also* **gas·ses**
1 a : a substance (such as oxygen or hydrogen) that is like air and has no fixed shape [*count*] Carbon monoxide is a poisonous *gas*. • a mixture of *gases* [*noncount*] clouds of *gas* — see also LAUGHING GAS, MUSTARD GAS, NATURAL GAS, NERVE GAS, TEAR GAS **b** [*noncount*] : a gas or mixture of gases that is burned as a fuel • We heat our house with *gas*. • Turn up the *gas*. • Do you have a *gas* stove or an electric one?
2 [*noncount*] *US* : gas in your stomach and intestines that causes pain or discomfort • Certain foods give me *gas*. [=(*Brit*) *wind*] • stomach *gas* • intestinal *gas* ✧ To ***pass gas*** is to release intestinal gas from your anus. • I accidentally *passed gas* [=(less politely) *farted*] during the meeting. It was so embarrassing!
3 *US* **a** [*noncount*] : GASOLINE • We need to stop for *gas*. [=(*Brit*) *petrol*] • high *gas* prices • The car gets good *gas* mileage. • The car almost ran out of *gas*. — sometimes used figuratively • The pitcher ***ran out of gas*** [=became tired] in the seventh inning. **b** ***the gas informal*** : the accelerator pedal of a vehicle • He was driving with one foot on *the gas* and one foot on the brake. ✧ If you ***step on the gas*** or ***hit the gas***, you suddenly press down on the accelerator to drive at a higher speed.
4 [*singular*] *US, old-fashioned slang* : a very enjoyable or funny person, event, etc. • The party was a *gas*. • Your uncle cracks me up. What a *gas*!

[2]**gas** *verb* **gasses; gassed; gas·sing**
1 [+ *obj*] : to poison or kill (someone) with gas • soldiers *gassed* on the battlefield
2 *US* : to put gasoline in (a car, truck, etc.) [+ *obj*] We stopped to *gas* the car. — usually + *up* • The car is all *gassed up*. [*no obj*] — + *up* • We *gassed up* before getting on the highway.

gas·bag /ˈgæsˌbæg/ *noun, pl* **-bags** [*count*] *US, informal* : a person who talks too much : WINDBAG

gas chamber *noun, pl* ~ **-bers** [*count*] : a room in which prisoners are killed by poisonous gas

gas·eous /ˈgæʃəs/ *adj* : having the form of gas • *gaseous* fuels • an odorless, *gaseous* element • a substance changing from a liquid to a *gaseous* state

gas–guz·zler /ˈgæsˈgʌzlɚ/ *noun, pl* **-zlers** [*count*] *US, informal* : a usually large vehicle that uses a lot of gasoline
– gas–guz·zling /ˈgæsˈgʌzlɪŋ/ *adj, always used before a noun* • *gas-guzzling* SUVs

[1]**gash** /ˈgæʃ/ *noun, pl* **gash·es** [*count*] : a long, deep cut • The dog had a bad *gash* in his leg. • The iceberg made a *gash* in the hull of the ship.

[2]**gash** *verb* **gashes; gashed; gash·ing** [+ *obj*] : to make a long, deep cut in (something) • The knife slipped and *gashed* his finger.

gas·ket /ˈgæskət/ *noun, pl* **-kets** [*count*] : a piece of rubber or some other material that is used to make a tight seal between two parts that are joined together
blow a gasket **1** *of a car, engine, etc.* : to develop a very bad leak in a gasket **2** *informal, of a person* : to become very angry • When the boss found out that the shipment was late, he *blew a gasket*.

gas·light /ˈgæsˌlaɪt/ *noun, pl* **-lights**
1 [*noncount*] : light made by burning gas (sense 1b) • streets illuminated by *gaslight*
2 [*count*] : a lamp that uses gas as fuel — called also *gas lamp*
– gas·lit /ˈgæsˌlɪt/ *adj* • a *gaslit* street

gas mask *noun, pl* ~ **masks** [*count*] : a mask used to protect the face and lungs against poisonous gases

gas·o·hol /ˈgæsəˌhɑːl/ *noun* [*noncount*] *technical* : a mixture of gasoline and ethanol that is used as a fuel for engines

gas·o·line /ˈgæsəˌliːn/ *noun* [*noncount*] *US* : a liquid made from petroleum and used especially as a fuel for engines — called also *(US) gas, (Brit) petrol*

gasp /ˈgæsp, *Brit* ˈgɑːsp/ *verb* **gasps; gasped; gasp·ing**
1 [*no obj*] **a** : to breathe in suddenly and loudly with your mouth open because of surprise, shock, or pain • Mom *gasped* in/with surprise at the sight of my sister's new haircut. • He *gasped* as he stepped into the icy water.
2 [*no obj*] : to breathe with difficulty : PANT • a dying man *gasping* for breath • She was *gasping* for air.
3 [+ *obj*] : to say (something) with quick, difficult breaths • He *gasped* (out) a plea for mercy. • "Have mercy!" he *gasped*.
– gasp *noun, pl* **gasps** [*count*] • My sister let out a *gasp* when I told her the happy news. — see also LAST-GASP

gas pedal *noun, pl* ~ **-als** [*count*] *US* : ACCELERATOR 1

gas station *noun, pl* ~ **-tions** [*count*] *US* : a place where gasoline for vehicles is sold — called also *filling station, service station, (Brit) petrol station*

gas·sy /ˈgæsi/ *adj* **gas·si·er; -est**
1 : of or containing gas • a *gassy* odor • a *gassy* liquid [=a liquid that has many bubbles]
2 *US* : having gas in your stomach • He felt bloated and *gassy*.
3 *informal* : having or using many words but not saying things that are very important or interesting : LONG-WINDED • *gassy* prose

gas·tric /ˈgæstrɪk/ *adj, medical* : of, relating to, or located near the stomach • *gastric* ulcers • *gastric* problems caused by stress

gas·tri·tis /gæˈstraɪtəs/ *noun* [*noncount*] *medical* : a painful condition in which the inside surface of the stomach becomes inflamed

gas·tro·in·tes·ti·nal /ˌgæstrowɪnˈtɛstənl/ *adj, medical* : of or relating to both the stomach and the intestines • *gastrointestinal* disorders • the ***gastrointestinal tract*** [=the part of the digestive system that consists of the stomach and intestines]

gas·tron·o·my /gæˈstrɑːnəmi/ *noun* [*noncount*] *formal* : the art or activity of cooking and eating fine food • books about wine tasting and *gastronomy*
– gas·tro·nom·ic /ˌgæstrəˈnɑːmɪk/ *also* **gas·tro·nom·i·cal** /ˌgæstrəˈnɑːmɪkəl/ *adj, always used before a noun* • a rare fish that's considered a *gastronomic* delicacy

gas·works /ˈgæsˌwɚks/ *noun, pl* **gasworks** [*count*] *chiefly Brit* : a factory for making gas from coal

gate /ˈgeɪt/ *noun, pl* **gates** [*count*]
1 : a place in a wall or a fence that has a movable part which can be opened or closed like a door • The car drove through the *gate* and up the long driveway. • The prison *gates* are always guarded.; *also* : the movable part itself • He pushed the *gate* open. — see also PEARLY GATES, STARTING GATE
2 : a device that can be opened and closed to control the flow of water or other liquids • the canal *gates*
3 : an area at an airport where passengers arrive and leave • When she got off the plane, her mother was waiting for her at the *gate*. • Flight 213 is now boarding at *Gate* 6.
4 a : the number of people who buy tickets for a sports event • The game drew/attracted a large *gate*. **b** : the amount of money received from selling tickets to a sports event • A portion of the *gate* for today's game will be donated to charity.

gat·ed /ˈgeɪtəd/ *adj*
1 : having a gate • a *gated* entrance
2 : having guarded or locked gates so that only some people are allowed to enter • They live in a ***gated community***. [=a group of expensive homes that are surrounded by a gated wall or fence]

gate·house /ˈgeɪtˌhaʊs/ *noun, pl* **-hous·es** [*count*] : a small building near a gate at the entrance of a park, large house, etc.

gate·keep·er /ˈgeɪtˌkiːpɚ/ *noun, pl* **-ers** [*count*] : a person who guards a gate • the palace *gatekeeper* — sometimes used figuratively • teachers who consider themselves the *gatekeepers* of knowledge

gate·way /ˈgeɪtˌweɪ/ *noun, pl* **-ways** [*count*] : an opening in a wall or fence that can be closed by a gate • Mourners slowly passed though the *gateway* of the cemetery. — often used figuratively • Studying is the *gateway* to success. • Make London your *gateway* to Europe!

gateway drug *noun, pl* ~ **drugs** [*count*] : a drug (such as alcohol or marijuana) that is thought to lead to the use of more dangerous drugs (such as cocaine or heroin)

[1]**gath·er** /ˈgæðɚ/ *verb* **-ers; -ered; -er·ing**
1 [+ *obj*] **a** : to bring (things or people) together into a group • The children *gathered* their toys (together) and put them away. • Give me just a minute to *gather* my things and

then we can leave. • The coach *gathered* her players together. • She *gathered* her hair into a ponytail. **b** : to choose and collect (things) • We *gathered* (up) wood for the fire. • The child was *gathering* flowers to give to his mother. • She has been *gathering* poems (together) for/into a collection. **c** : to get or take (things) from different people or places and bring them together • The police are continuing to *gather* evidence relating to the crime. • Volunteers have been *gathering* contributions for the new library.

2 [*no obj*] : to come together to form a group • A crowd began to *gather* on the sidewalk. • The players *gathered* together to hear the coach's game plan. — often + *around* or *round* • Everyone *gathered around* him as he began to speak. • He asked us to *gather round.*

3 [+ *obj*] : to get more of (something, such as speed) gradually • The bicyclists *gathered* speed as they went downhill. • The campaign has begun to ***gather momentum/strength***. [=has begun to be more popular and effective] — see also *gathering dust* at [1]DUST

4 [*no obj*] : to increase in amount or strength • Clouds had begun to *gather* overhead. • We hurried home in the *gathering* darkness. • the *gathering* storm • the *gathering* [=*worsening*] crisis

5 [+ *obj*] **a** : to prepare yourself to use (your courage, strength, etc.) in order to do something difficult • He *gathered* his courage and finally spoke up. • Despite her injury, she *gathered* her strength and was able to finish the race. **b** : to prepare (yourself, your thoughts, etc.) before doing something difficult • He paused to ***gather himself*** before stepping out onto the stage. • I barely had time to ***gather my thoughts/wits*** before replying.

6 *not used in progressive tenses* [+ *obj*] : to believe that something is probably true because of what you have heard or learned • I *gather* (from her comments) that she's read a great deal about this topic. = From what I (can) *gather*, she's read a great deal about this topic. • "She's read a great deal about this topic." "So I *gather!*"

7 [+ *obj*] : to pull (someone or something) close to your body • He *gathered* the child (up) in his arms. • She *gathered* her cloak around her before stepping outside.

8 [+ *obj*] *sewing* : to pull (cloth) along a line of stitches to form folds • I *gathered* the fabric to make small pleats.

– **gath•er•er** /ˈgæðərɚ/ *noun, pl* **-ers** [*count*] • a *gatherer* of data/information • hunters and *gatherers* [=people who gather food]

[2]**gather** *noun, pl* **-ers** [*count*] : a fold formed when cloth is pulled together — usually plural • a shirt with *gathers* at the shoulders

gath•er•ing /ˈgæðərɪŋ/ *noun, pl* **-ings**

1 [*count*] : an occasion when people come together as a group • I see my cousins only at occasional family *gatherings*. • dinner parties and other social *gatherings* • a *gathering* of political leaders

2 [*noncount*] : the act or process of gathering something • hunting and food *gathering* • the *gathering* of data

ga•tor /ˈgeɪtɚ/ *noun, pl* **-tors** [*count*] *US, informal* : ALLIGATOR

GATT *abbr* General Agreement on Tariffs and Trade

gauche /ˈgoʊʃ/ *adj* **gauch•er; -est** [*also more* ~; *most* ~] : having or showing a lack of awareness about the proper way to behave : socially awkward • a *gauche* young man • He has *gauche* manners. • Would it be *gauche* of me to ask her how old she is?

– **gauche•ness** *noun* [*noncount*] *chiefly Brit* • the *gaucheness* of his manner

gau•cho /ˈgaʊˌʧoʊ/ *noun, pl* **-chos** [*count*] : a cowboy in South America

gaudy /ˈgɑːdi/ *adj* **gaud•i•er; -est**

1 : too bright and heavily decorated • *gaudy* jewelry/colors • The showgirls wore *gaudy* costumes.

2 *informal* : very large or impressive • They bought the house for a *gaudy* sum. • (*disapproving*) He collected fancy cars and other *gaudy* symbols of wealth. • The team had a *gaudy* [=*dazzling*] 10–0 record at the start of the season.

– **gaud•i•ly** /ˈgɑːdəli/ *adv* • *gaudily* dressed clowns • *gaudily* painted statues – **gaud•i•ness** /ˈgɑːdinəs/ *noun* [*noncount*] • the *gaudiness* of the mansion

[1]**gauge** *also US* **gage** /ˈgeɪʤ/ *noun, pl* **gaug•es** *also* **gag•es**

1 [*count*] : an instrument that is used for measuring something • a temperature/rain *gauge* • the fuel/gas *gauge*

2 [*count*] : something that can be used to measure or judge something else — usually singular; often + *of* • He does not believe that these tests are an accurate *gauge of* intelligence. • Home sales provide a *gauge of* the state of the economy.

3 [*noncount*] : the distance between the rails of a railroad • a standard/broad/narrow *gauge* railroad

4 [*noncount*] : the thickness of something (such as a sheet of metal) or the diameter of wire or a screw • 20-*gauge* wire • heavy *gauge* aluminum

5 [*noncount*] : the size of a shotgun based on how big the inside of the barrel is • a 12-*gauge* shotgun

[2]**gauge** *also US* **gage** *verb* **gauges** *also* **gages**; **gauged** *also* **gaged**; **gaug•ing** *also* **gag•ing** [+ *obj*]

1 : to make a judgment about (something) • Home sales provide a useful way of *gauging* the overall state of the economy. • He accurately *gauged* the mood of the voters. • I was *gauging* her reaction to the news.

2 : to measure (something) exactly • instruments for *gauging* temperature and humidity

gaunt /ˈgɑːnt/ *adj* **gaunt•er; -est**

1 : very thin usually because of illness or suffering • a small *gaunt* man • He left the hospital looking tired and *gaunt.*

2 *literary* : plain and unpleasant in appearance : desolate and gloomy • *gaunt* leafless trees • a *gaunt* factory on the edge of town

– **gaunt•ness** *noun* [*noncount*]

[1]**gaunt•let** *also US* **gant•let** /ˈgɑːntlət/ *noun, pl* **-lets** [*count*] : a situation in which someone is attacked, criticized, questioned, etc., by many people — usually used in the phrase ***run the gauntlet*** • Soldiers in the past were sometimes punished by being forced to *run the gauntlet*. [=to run between two rows of men who would hit them with clubs] • He had to *run the gauntlet* of reporters waiting outside the court. — compare [2]GAUNTLET

[2]**gauntlet** *noun, pl* **-lets** [*count*]

1 : a metal glove worn with a suit of armor by soldiers in the Middle Ages

2 : a long, heavy glove worn to protect the hand

pick/take up the gauntlet : to show that you are willing and ready to fight, argue, or compete with someone or to do something that is difficult but necessary : to accept or respond to a challenge • The time has come for Congress to *pick up the gauntlet* and do something about this problem.

throw down the gauntlet : to say or show that you are ready to fight, argue, or compete with someone : to challenge someone • The company *threw down the gauntlet* and told the union that this offer for a contract was final.

– compare [1]GAUNTLET

– **gaunt•let•ed** /ˈgɑːntlətəd/ *adj* • a *gauntleted* hand

gauze /ˈgɑːz/ *noun* [*noncount*]

1 : a very thin cloth : cloth so thin that you can see through it • red *gauze* curtains

2 : loosely woven cotton that is used as a bandage • He wrapped the wound in *gauze*. • a *gauze* pad [=a small square of folded gauze]

gauzy /ˈgɑːzi/ *adj* **gauz•i•er; -est**

1 : light and thin : made of or resembling gauze • *gauzy* curtains/dresses

2 *US* : not clear : HAZY • *gauzy* images • *gauzy* memories

gave *past tense of* [1]GIVE

gav•el /ˈgævəl/ *noun, pl* **-els** [*count*] : a small hammer that someone (such as a judge) bangs on a table to get people's attention in a meeting or in a court of law

gawk /ˈgɑːk/ *verb* **gawks; gawked; gawk•ing** [*no obj*] *informal* : to stare at someone or something in a rude or stupid way • a crowd of *gawking* tourists — often + *at* • She just stood there *gawking at* the celebrities as they arrived for the ceremony. • Celebrities are used to being *gawked at.*

– **gawk•er** *noun, pl* **-ers** [*count*] • a crowd of *gawkers*

gawky /ˈgɑːki/ *adj* **gawk•i•er; -est** *informal* : awkward and clumsy • a tall, *gawky* teenager

– **gawk•i•ly** /ˈgɑːkəli/ *adv* • He moves *gawkily*. – **gawk•i•ness** *noun* [*noncount*] • his teenage *gawkiness*

gawp /ˈgɑːp/ *verb* **gawps; gawped; gawp•ing** [*no obj*] *chiefly Brit, informal* : to stare at someone or something in a rude or stupid way : GAWK

– **gawp•er** /ˈgɑːpɚ/ *noun, pl* **-ers** [*count*]

[1]**gay** /ˈgeɪ/ *adj* **gay•er; -est** [*or more* ~; *most* ~]

1 a : sexually attracted to someone who is the same sex : HOMOSEXUAL • My uncle is *gay*. **b** *always used before a noun* : of, relating to, or used by homosexuals • the *gay* rights movement • The march celebrates *gay* pride. [=pride in being gay] • a *gay* bar

2 *old-fashioned* : happy and excited • *gay* and carefree children : cheerful and lively • The band was playing a *gay* tune. • a *gay* festival/reception

3 *old-fashioned* : very bright in color : COLORFUL • the *gayest* of the spring flowers — see also GAILY

– gay·ness *noun* [*noncount*] • He is no longer trying to hide his *gayness*. [=*homosexuality*] • the *gayness* [=(more commonly) *gaiety*] of the colors

²gay *noun, pl* **gays** [*count*] : a person and especially a man who is homosexual • a bar that is frequented by *gays* • *gays* and lesbians

¹gaze /ˈgeɪz/ *verb, always followed by an adverb or preposition* **gaz·es; gazed; gaz·ing** [*no obj*] : to look at someone or something in a steady way and usually for a long time • He *gazed* out the window at the snow. • She *gazed* intently/longingly into his eyes.

> ***synonyms*** GAZE, GAPE, STARE, and GLARE mean to look at something or someone for a long time. GAZE suggests looking steadily at something with feelings of interest, wonder, or admiration. • She was *gazing* at the moon. GAPE suggests looking in wonder or surprise with your mouth open. • tourists *gaping* at celebrities STARE suggests looking with your eyes open wide, often in a rude way. • Don't *stare* at him, it's not polite. GLARE suggests looking in an angry way. • The speaker *glared* at the people in the audience who were talking.

²gaze *noun, pl* **gazes** [*count*] : a long and steady look • He fixed his *gaze* out the window. [=he gazed out the window] • She looked at him with a calm, steady *gaze*. • He ***dropped/lifted his gaze*** [=he looked down/up] • She calmly ***met his gaze*** [=looked back at him while he looked at her] — sometimes used figuratively • He has his *gaze* firmly fixed on the future. [=he is thinking about the future]

ga·ze·bo /gəˈziːˌboʊ/ *noun, pl* **-bos** [*count*] : a small building in a garden or park that is open on all sides

gazebo

ga·zelle /gəˈzɛl/ *noun, pl* **gazelles** *also* **ga·zelle** [*count*] : a small animal that is a kind of antelope and that is very graceful and fast

ga·zette /gəˈzɛt/ *noun, pl* **-zettes** [*count*] : NEWSPAPER usually used in the names of newspapers • The Daily *Gazette*

gaz·et·teer /ˌgæzəˈtiɚ/ *noun, pl* **-teers** [*count*] : a book or list that is arranged in alphabetical order and gives information about places

ga·zil·lion /gəˈzɪljən/ *noun, pl* **-lions** [*count*] *US, informal* : a very large number • He made *gazillions* (of dollars) in real estate.

– gazillion *adj* • a *gazillion* years • He made a *gazillion* dollars in real estate.

gaz·pa·cho /gəˈspɑːˌʧoʊ/ *noun* [*noncount*] *chiefly US* : a spicy cold soup that is made with chopped vegetables (such as tomatoes, cucumbers, peppers, and onions)

GB *abbr* **1** gigabyte **2** Great Britain

GDP *abbr* gross domestic product

¹gear /ˈgiɚ/ *noun, pl* **gears**

1 [*noncount*] **a** : supplies, tools, or clothes needed for a special purpose • fishing *gear* • I somehow managed to pack all my *gear* into one suitcase. • soldiers in full combat *gear* • wearing protective *gear* • rain *gear* [=waterproof clothes worn in the rain] — see also FOOTGEAR, HEADGEAR, LANDING GEAR **b** *informal* : CLOTHES • She wears trendy *gear*.

gears

2 a [*count*] : a toothed wheel in a machine • a complicated arrangement of *gears* and shafts **b** : a part that connects the engine of a vehicle or the pedals of a bicycle to the wheels and controls the speed at which the wheels turn [*count*] a car with four forward *gears* [*noncount*] Halfway up the hill, my bike slipped ***out of gear***. • He put the car ***in/into gear*** [=he moved the lever that controls the car's gears into the position that allows the car to begin moving] and drove away. • (*US*) She shifted *into* low/high *gear*. = (*Brit*) She changed *into* bottom/top *gear*. [=she changed to a gear that allows for a slower/faster rate of speed] — see also REVERSE GEAR

change/shift/switch gears (*US*) *or Brit* ***change gear*** : to move from one level or area of activity to another • He once again *changed gears* in his career. • She's decided to *shift gears*, quit her job, and go back to school.

get in gear *or* ***get (something) in gear*** *informal* : to start working or doing something in a more energetic and effective way • We need to *get in gear* [=*get going*] if we want to finish this project on time. • She finally *got* her career *in gear*. [=finally started to be successful in her career] • (*US, informal* + *impolite*) He angrily told him to ***get his ass in gear***. [=to get going, to start moving or doing something much more quickly]

in/into high gear see HIGH GEAR

²gear *verb* **gears; geared; gear·ing** [+ *obj*] : to make (something) suitable for a particular use or type of person — usually used as *(be) geared* • The book *is geared* toward children. [=the book is intended to be used by children] • software *geared* to the needs of the first-time user • The program *is geared* for/to/toward a young audience. • The system *is geared* [=*designed*] to handle several tasks at once.

gear up [*phrasal verb*] ***gear up*** *or* ***gear (someone) up*** *or* ***gear up (someone)*** : to get ready or to cause (someone) to get ready for something or to do something • The team is *gearing up* for a comeback. • Manufacturers are *gearing up* to produce more merchandise. • The coach is *gearing up* the team for a comeback. • The team is *geared up* for a win.

gear·box /ˈgiɚˌbɑːks/ *noun, pl* **-box·es** [*count*] : a box in a car, truck, etc., that contains the gears • a five-speed *gearbox* [=(more commonly) *transmission*]

gear·head /ˈgiɚˌhɛd/ *noun, pl* **-heads** [*count*] *US, informal* : a person who is very interested in mechanical or technical things (such as cars or computers) • *gearheads* discussing hardware upgrades

gear·ing /ˈgirɪŋ/ *noun* [*noncount*] *technical* : the parts that transfer motion from one part of a machine to another • a *gearing* mechanism

gear·shift /ˈgiɚˌʃɪft/ *noun, pl* **-shifts** [*count*] *US* : a lever or other device that is moved to change gears in a car, on a bicycle, etc. — called also (*Brit*) *gear lever*, (*Brit*) *gearstick*, (*US*) *shifter*; see pictures at BICYCLE, CAR; compare STICK SHIFT

gear·stick /ˈgiɚˌstɪk/ *noun, pl* **-sticks** [*count*] *Brit* : GEARSHIFT

gecko /ˈgɛkoʊ/ *noun, pl* **geck·os** *also* **geck·oes** [*count*] : a small tropical lizard

gecko

GED /ˌjiːˌiːˈdiː/ *noun, pl* **GEDs** [*count*] *US*

1 : a test that is taken by an adult who did not finish high school to show that the person being tested has as much knowledge of basic math, science, English, etc., as a high school graduate • I had to take the *GED* yesterday. • *GED* test ✧ *GED* in this sense is an abbreviation of "General Educational Development."

2 : an official document that is given to a person who has taken and passed the GED • The job requires a high school diploma or *GED*. ✧ *GED* in this sense is an abbreviation of "general equivalency diploma."

gee /ˈʤiː/ *interj, chiefly US* — used especially to show surprise, enthusiasm, or disappointment • *Gee*, that sounds like fun. • *Gee*, that's too bad.

gee–gee /ˈʤiːˌʤiː/ *noun, pl* **-gees** [*count*] *Brit, informal* : HORSE — used especially by children or when referring informally to horse racing • have a bet on the *gee-gees*

geek /ˈgiːk/ *noun, pl* **geeks** [*count*] *chiefly US, informal*

1 : a person who is socially awkward and unpopular : a usually intelligent person who does not fit in with other people • He was a real *geek* in high school.

2 : a person who is very interested in and knows a lot about a particular field or activity • She's a computer *geek*.

– geeky /ˈgiːki/ *adj* **geek·i·er; -est** • I was a *geeky* kid.

– geek·i·ness *noun* [*noncount*] • I liked her in spite of her *geekiness*.

geese *plural of* ¹GOOSE

gee whiz /ˌʤiːˈwɪz/ *interj, US, old-fashioned* — used especially to show surprise or enthusiasm• *Gee whiz*, I didn't expect to see you here!

gee–whiz /ˈʤiːˌwɪz/ *adj, always used before a noun, chiefly US*
1 : very impressive or amazing• *gee-whiz* gadgets/technology
2 : showing or feeling excitement and wonder• *gee-whiz* enthusiasm

geez *or* **jeez** /ˈʤiːz/ *interj, informal* — used to express surprise, anger, or annoyance• *Geez*, it's cold out here. • *Geez*, I didn't think the food would be this bad.

gee·zer /ˈgiːzɚ/ *noun, pl* **-zers** [*count*] *informal*
1 *US* : an old man• a group of old *geezers* playing cards
2 *Brit* : GUY, BLOKE• Some *geezer* asked me for a light.

Gei·ger counter /ˈgaɪgɚ-/ *noun, pl* ~ **-ers** [*count*] : an instrument used for finding and measuring radioactivity

gei·sha /ˈgeɪʃə/ *noun, pl* **gei·shas** *also* **geisha** [*count*] : a Japanese girl who is trained to entertain men with singing, conversation, etc. — called also *geisha girl*

[1]**gel** /ˈʤɛl/ *noun, pl* **gels** [*count, noncount*] : a thick substance that is like jelly and that is used in various products• hair *gels* [=gels used for styling hair] • shower *gel* [=soap that is in a gel form]

[2]**gel** *verb* **gels; gelled; gel·ling**
1 [*no obj*] : to change into a gel : to change into a thick substance that is like jelly• The mixture will *gel* as it cools.
2 [*no obj*] : to become clear and definite : JELL• Our plans are finally starting to *gel.*
3 [+ *obj*] : to style (hair) with gel• She *gelled* her hair.

gel·a·tin (*chiefly US*) *or chiefly Brit* **gel·a·tine** /ˈʤɛlətən/ *noun* [*noncount*]
1 : a clear substance that is made by boiling animal bones or tissues and that is used in making jelly
2 : a food made with gelatin• a fruity *gelatin* dessert
— **ge·lat·i·nous** /ʤəˈlætənəs/ *adj* [*more* ~; *most* ~]• a *gelatinous* mass • a *gelatinous* texture

geld /ˈgɛld/ *verb* **gelds; geld·ed; geld·ing** [+ *obj*] : to remove the testicles of (a male animal and especially a horse or bull)• a *gelded* horse

geld·ing /ˈgɛldɪŋ/ *noun, pl* **-ings** [*count*] : a male horse that has had its testicles removed • a six-year-old *gelding* — compare STALLION

gem /ˈʤɛm/ *noun, pl* **gems** [*count*]
1 : a valuable stone that has been cut and polished for use in jewelry — see color picture on page C11
2 : something that is admired for its beauty or excellence• The house is a *gem* of colonial architecture. • He pitched a *gem* of a game. • Her most recent novel is a real *gem.*

Gem·i·ni /ˈʤɛməni, ˈʤɛməˌnaɪ/ *noun, pl* **-nis**
1 [*noncount*] : the third sign of the zodiac that comes between Taurus and Cancer and has a pair of twins as its symbol — see picture at ZODIAC
2 [*count*] : a person born under the sign of Gemini : a person born between May 21st and June 21st• His girlfriend is a *Gemini.*

gem·stone /ˈʤɛmˌstoun/ *noun, pl* **-stones** [*count*] : a stone that can be used in jewelry when it is cut and polished

Gen. *abbr* General• *Gen.* Smith

gen·darme /ˈʒɑːnˌdɑɚm/ *noun, pl* **-darmes** [*count*] : a police officer; *especially* : a police officer in a country where French is spoken

gen·der /ˈʤɛndɚ/ *noun, pl* **-ders**
1 [*count*] : the state of being male or female : SEX• Please state your name, birth date, and *gender.* • *gender* differences • ***gender-specific*** language [=words that refer only to men or only to women] • ***gender-neutral*** language [=words that do not refer to either sex but only to people in general]
2 *grammar* : one of the categories (masculine, feminine, and neuter) into which words (such as nouns, adjectives, and pronouns) are divided in many languages [*noncount*] The adjective and noun must agree in number and *gender.* [*count*]Some languages do not use *genders.*

gender–bending *noun* [*noncount*] : the act of dressing and behaving like a member of the opposite sex• a pop star famous for his *gender-bending*
— **gender bender** *noun, pl* ~ **-ers** [*count*]• He's known as a *gender bender.* — **gender–bending** *adj* • a *gender-bending* comedy • a *gender-bending* pop star

gene /ˈʤiːn/ *noun, pl* **genes** [*count*] *biology* : a part of a cell that controls or influences the appearance, growth, etc., of a living thing• She inherited a good set of *genes* from her parents. • dominant/recessive *genes*

ge·ne·al·o·gy /ˌʤiːniˈɑːləʤi, ˌʤiːniˈæləʤi/ *noun, pl* **-gies**
1 [*noncount*] : the study of family history• an expert in *genealogy*
2 [*count*] : the history of a particular family showing how the different members of the family are related to each other• They've been researching their *genealogies.*
— **ge·ne·a·log·i·cal** /ˌʤiːnijəˈlɑːʤɪkəl/ *adj* • *genealogical* relationships/history • a *genealogical* expert — **ge·ne·al·o·gist** /ˌʤiːniˈɑːləʤɪst, ˌʤiːniˈæləʤɪst/ *noun, pl* **-gists** [*count*]• She's an expert *genealogist.*

gene pool *noun, pl* ~ **pools** [*count*] *biology* : all of the genes in a particular group of people or animals• the *gene pool* of a species

genera *plural of* GENUS

[1]**gen·er·al** /ˈʤɛnrəl/ *adj*
1 *always used before a noun* : of, relating to, or affecting all the people or things in a group• They have issued a *general* warning/order. • a *general* alarm : involving or including many or most people• The *general* mood here is optimistic. [=most people here are optimistic] • The *general* consensus is that we should go ahead. • It's a story with *general* interest. = It's a *general*-interest story. [=it is a story that will interest many or most people]
2 a [*more* ~; *most* ~] : relating to the main or major parts of something rather than the details : not specific• The witness was able to provide a very *general* description of the thief. • She began her talk with some *general* observations about the state of the industry. • The book provides a good *general* introduction to the subject. • My concerns are all *general*—nothing specific. • The details of the new plan are different, but it's based on the same *general* concept/idea. • My *general* impression was that things were going well. **b** *always used before a noun* — used to indicate that a description relates to an entire person or thing rather than a particular part• The building was in good *general* shape. • Her *general* [=*overall*] health is good.
3 *always used before a noun* : not exact : APPROXIMATE • They were found in the same *general* area. • I'm going in the *general* direction of the store.
4 *always used before a noun* : ordinary, normal, or usual• Their ***general practice*** in such cases is to offer a deal. = As a ***general rule***, they offer a deal in such cases. [=they usually/generally offer a deal in such cases]
5 : of the basic or usual kind : not special or specialized• a *general* hospital • a science book for the *general* reader [=the reader who is not a scientist] • a doctor practicing *general* medicine [=basic health care that is not specialized]
6 *always used before a noun* : of high rank : having wide authority or responsibility• a *general* manager • a *general* contractor [=a contractor who is in charge of a building project] — see also ATTORNEY GENERAL, INSPECTOR GENERAL

[2]**general** *noun*
in general **1** : in a general way — used to say that a statement describes your general feeling or opinion• *In general*, I like the way things have gone. **2** : as a whole• It had an impact not just on young people, but on people *in general.* [=on all or most people] **3** : in most cases : USUALLY• *In general* [=*generally*], it takes about a month for the shipment to arrive.
— compare [3]GENERAL

[3]**general** *noun, pl* **-als** [*count*] : a military officer of very high rank — compare [2]GENERAL

general admission *noun* [*noncount*] : a situation in which a customer pays a fee to get into an event (such as a concert or baseball game) but is not assigned to a specific seat• Reserved seating is $20; *general admission* is $10.

general delivery *noun* [*noncount*] *US* : a department in a post office that keeps a person's mail until that person comes to the post office to get it• The letter is addressed to *general delivery.* — called also (*Brit*) *poste restante*

general election *noun, pl* ~ **-tions** [*count*] : a regular election that involves voters and candidates throughout an entire country

gen·er·al·ist /ˈʤɛnrəlɪst/ *noun, pl* **-ists** [*count*] : a person who knows something about a lot of subjects• The staff includes both *generalists* and specialists.

gen·er·al·i·ty /ˌʤɛnəˈræləti/ *noun, pl* **-ties** *formal*
1 [*count*] : a statement that is not specific or detailed• He spoke in *generalities* as he discussed his plans for the future.
2 [*noncount*] : the quality or state of being general rather than specific or detailed• I noticed the *generality* of the lan-

guage he used in discussing his plans.
3 [*noncount*] *Brit* : the biggest part of a group : MAJORITY • The *generality* of the students [=most of the students] will go on to university.

gen·er·al·i·za·tion *also Brit* **gen·er·al·i·sa·tion** /ˌʤɛnrələˈzeɪʃən, *Brit* ˌʤɛnrəˌlaɪˈzeɪʃən/ *noun, pl* **-tions** *often disapproving*
1 [*count*] : a general statement : a statement about a group of people or things that is based on only a few people or things in that group • He made several sweeping/broad *generalizations* about women.
2 [*noncount*] : the act or process of forming opinions that are based on a small amount of information • She was prone to *generalization*.

gen·er·al·ize *also Brit* **gen·er·al·ise** /ˈʤɛnrəˌlaɪz/ *verb* **-iz·es; -ized; -iz·ing**
1 [*no obj*] : to make a general statement or form a general opinion; *especially* : to state an opinion about a larger group that is based on a smaller number of people or things within that group • She tends to *generalize*. — often + *about* • She is always *generalizing about* men.
2 [+ *obj*] *formal* : to apply (something specific, such as a theory or rule) to larger group — often used as *(be) generalized* • The theory can *be generalized* to other branches of science as well.

generalized *also Brit* **generalised** *adj* [*more* ~; *most* ~] : not specific : not limited to a particular area, part, etc. • The patient has been experiencing *generalized* pain. • *generalized* anxiety

gen·er·al·ly /ˈʤɛnrəli/ *adv*
1 [*more* ~; *most* ~] : in a general way : in a way that is not detailed or specific • He talked *generally* about his plans. • I had a *generally* good day.
2 : in most cases : USUALLY • *Generally* [=*in general*], his suggestions have been well-received. • It *generally* takes about a month for the shipment to arrive. • When stocks are up, bonds are *generally* down. • Writers *generally* oppose censorship. = *Generally* (speaking), writers oppose censorship.
3 : by or to most people • a *generally* used phrase • This town is *generally* regarded as a good place to raise kids.

general practitioner *noun, pl* ~ **-ers** [*count*] : a person (especially a doctor) whose work is not limited to a special area : a person who is not a specialist • Our family doctor is a *general practitioner*. — abbr. *G.P.*

general public *noun*
the general public : all the people of an area, country, etc. • The park is open to *the general public*.

general-purpose *adj, always used before a noun* : able to be used for many purposes : not limited to a single purpose • a *general-purpose* vehicle • *general-purpose* film — compare ALL-PURPOSE

general store *noun, pl* ~ **stores** [*count*] : a store usually in a small town that sells many different things including groceries

gen·er·ate /ˈʤɛnəˌreɪt/ *verb* **-ates; -at·ed; -at·ing** [+ *obj*]
1 : to produce (something) or cause (something) to be produced • windmills used to *generate* electricity • *generate* heat • This business should *generate* a lot of revenue. • We hope to *generate* some new ideas at the meeting. • a computer-*generated* list [=a list that was made by a computer program]
2 : to be the cause of or reason for (something, such as interest or excitement) • His theories have *generated* a great deal of interest among other scientists. • Her comments have *generated* a good deal of excitement/controversy. • They have been unable to *generate* much support for their proposals.
— **gen·er·a·tive** /ˈʤɛnrətɪv/ *adj, technical* • *generative* power

gen·er·a·tion /ˌʤɛnəˈreɪʃən/ *noun, pl* **-tions**
1 [*count*] **a** : a group of people born and living during the same time • She was worshipped by a *generation* of moviegoers. • He was a hero to *generations* of students. • We need to preserve these resources for future *generations*. • His books are popular among members of the younger/older *generation*. • (*US*) The current *generation* is changing the way things are done. = (*Brit*) The current *generation* are changing the way things are done. **b** : the people in a family born and living during the same time • That family has lived in the same house for four *generations*. • The house has been passed down in the family from *generation* to *generation*. • first- and second-*generation* immigrants [=people who immigrated and their children]
2 [*count*] : the average length of time between the birth of parents and the birth of their children • She's a *generation* [=around 20–30 years] older than most of her colleagues. • He has held that position for a *generation*. • No one dreamed that such things would be possible a *generation* ago.
3 [*count*] : a group of things that are developed from an earlier type • The company claims to be developing the next *generation* of portable computers.
4 [*noncount*] : the act or process of making or producing something : the act or process of generating something • the *generation* of heat • the *generation* of new ideas

gen·er·a·tion·al /ˌʤɛnəˈreɪʃənəl/ *adj, always used before a noun* : of or relating to different generations of people • *generational* differences • The family was divided along *generational* lines.
— **gen·er·a·tion·al·ly** *adv* • culturally and *generationally* diverse

generation gap *noun* [*singular*] : the differences in opinions, values, etc., between younger people and older people

Generation X *noun* [*noncount*] : the group of people in the U.S. who were born during the late 1960s and the 1970s
— **Generation Xer** /-ˈɛksɚ/ *noun, pl* ~ **Xers** [*count*] • a TV show that appeals to *Generation Xers*

gen·er·a·tor /ˈʤɛnəˌreɪtɚ/ *noun, pl* **-tors** [*count*] : something that produces something • This new product will be a major revenue *generator*.; *especially* : a machine that produces electricity • a backup *generator* for the store

[1]**ge·ner·ic** /ʤəˈnerɪk/ *adj* [*more* ~; *most* ~]
1 : of or relating to a whole group or class • "Flu" is sometimes used as a *generic* term/name for any illness caused by a virus.
2 : not sold or made under a particular brand name • *generic* drugs
3 *biology* : of or relating to a genus
— **ge·ner·i·cal·ly** /ʤəˈnerɪkli/ *adv* • "Flu" is sometimes used *generically* for any illness caused by a virus.

[2]**generic** *noun, pl* **-ics** [*count*] : a product (such as a drug) that is not sold or made under a particular brand name : a generic product • You can substitute *generics* for brand-name drugs on this health plan.

gen·er·os·i·ty /ˌʤɛnəˈrɑːsəti/ *noun* [*noncount*] : the quality of being kind, understanding, and not selfish : the quality of being generous • She is admired for the *generosity* of her spirit. = She is admired for her *generosity* of spirit. [=she is admired because she is a kind person who cares about other people]; *especially* : willingness to give money and other valuable things to others • her *generosity* toward/to the poor

gen·er·ous /ˈʤɛnərəs/ *adj* [*more* ~; *most* ~]
1 : freely giving or sharing money and other valuable things • a *generous* benefactor • The school raised the money through donations from *generous* alumni. • He was *generous* with both his time and his money. • She has always been very *generous* toward/to the poor.
2 : providing more than the amount that is needed or normal : abundant or ample • a *generous* supply • This restaurant is known for its *generous* portions. • a *generous* helping of mashed potatoes • a *generous* donation
3 : showing kindness and concern for others • She has a *generous* heart/spirit. • He has *generous* sympathy for unemployed workers.
— **gen·er·ous·ly** *adv* • He *generously* insisted on paying for dinner. • She tipped the waiter *generously*. • a *generously* [=*lavishly*] illustrated book

gen·e·sis /ˈʤɛnəsəs/ *noun* [*noncount*] *somewhat formal* : the beginning of something : ORIGIN • a book about the *genesis* of the civil rights movement

gene therapy *noun* [*noncount*] *medical* : a way of treating some disorders and diseases that usually involves replacing bad copies of genes with other genes • advances in the science of *gene therapy*

ge·net·ic /ʤəˈnɛtɪk/ *adj* : of, relating to, or involving genes • a *genetic* disease • *genetic* material • ***genetic fingerprinting*** [=using genes or parts of genes to identify a person, such as a criminal]
— **ge·net·i·cal·ly** /ʤəˈnɛtɪkli/ *adv* • *genetically* modified food • a *genetically* inherited illness • *genetically* related offspring

genetic engineering *noun* [*noncount*] : the science of making changes to the genes of a plant or animal to produce a desired result • The crops were made resistant to disease by *genetic engineering*.
— **genetic engineer** *noun, pl* ~ **-neers** [*count*] • *Genetic engineers* have introduced a new disease-resistant soybean.

ge·net·i·cist /ʤəˈnɛtəsɪst/ *noun, pl* **-cists** [*count*] : a scientist who studies genetics

ge·net·ics /ʤəˈnɛtɪks/ *noun* [*noncount*] : the scientific study of how genes control the characteristics of plants and animals

Ge·ne·va Convention /ʤəˈni:və-/ *noun*
the Geneva Convention : an international law that explains how people who are wounded or taken prisoner during a war are supposed to be treated

ge·nial /ˈʤi:nijəl/ *adj* [*more* ~; *most* ~] : cheerful and pleasant • a *genial* host • a host with a *genial* manner • He was *genial* to/toward everyone.
– **ge·nial·i·ty** /ˌʤi:niˈæləti/ *noun* [*noncount*] • the *geniality* of his manner – **ge·nial·ly** /ˈʤi:njəli/ *adv* • We were chatting *genially* [=*pleasantly*] on the phone.

ge·nie /ˈʤi:ni/ *noun, pl* **-nies** [*count*] *in stories* : a magic spirit that looks like a person, often lives in a lamp or bottle, and serves the person who calls it • He rubbed the magic lamp to summon the *genie*.

gen·i·tal /ˈʤɛnətl/ *adj, always used before a noun* : of or relating to the sexual organs • a *genital* disease/wart • *genital* tissue

gen·i·ta·lia /ˌʤɛnəˈteɪljə/ *noun* [*plural*] : GENITALS

gen·i·tals /ˈʤɛnətlz/ *noun* [*plural*] : sexual organs; *especially* : the sexual organs on the outside of the body • male/female *genitals*

gen·i·tive /ˈʤɛnətɪv/ *noun* [*noncount*] *grammar* : the form of a noun or pronoun when it is used to show that someone or something owns, controls, or is associated with someone or something else • a noun in the *genitive*
– **genitive** *adj* • the *genitive* case

ge·nius /ˈʤi:njəs/ *noun, pl* **-nius·es**
1 [*count*] **a** : a very smart or talented person : a person who has a level of talent or intelligence that is very rare or remarkable • Albert Einstein and Isaac Newton were great scientific *geniuses*. • a musical/artistic/creative *genius* • You don't have to be a *genius* to see that this plan will never work. **b** : a person who is very good at doing something • He was a *genius* at handling the press.
2 a [*noncount*] : great natural ability : remarkable talent or intelligence • She's now widely recognized as an artist of *genius*. • He's admired for his comic/artistic/scientific *genius*. **b** [*singular*] : a great or unusual talent or ability — usually + *for* • She has a *genius for* knowing what will sell. • He had a *genius for* getting into trouble. [=he often got into trouble]
3 [*singular*] **a** : a very clever or smart quality • The (sheer) *genius* of his theory was not immediately recognized. **b** : a part of something that makes it unusually good or valuable • My plan is simple—that's the *genius* of it. • The *genius* of these new computers is their portability.
a stroke of genius : a brilliant and successful idea or decision • Deciding to relocate the company was *a stroke of genius*.

geno·cide /ˈʤɛnəˌsaɪd/ *noun* [*noncount*] : the deliberate killing of people who belong to a particular racial, political, or cultural group
– **geno·cid·al** /ˌʤɛnəˈsaɪdl/ *adj*

genre /ˈʒɑ:nrə/ *noun, pl* **genres** [*count*] : a particular type or category of literature or art • a literary/film/musical *genre* • This book is a classic of the mystery *genre*.

gent /ˈʤɛnt/ *noun, pl* **gents** [*count*] *informal + old-fashioned* : GENTLEMAN • He's a real *gent*. • ladies and *gents* ✧ In U.S. English, *gent* is likely to refer to a man who is British. • Our host in London was a delightful old *gent*. — see also GENTS

gen·teel /ʤɛnˈti:l/ *adj* [*more* ~; *most* ~]
1 a *somewhat old-fashioned* : of or relating to people who have high social status : ARISTOCRATIC • a person of *genteel* upbringing • She was born into a *genteel* family. **b** : pretending or trying to have the qualities and manners of people who have high social status • an elderly woman living in *genteel* poverty • speaking in a *genteel* accent
2 : having a quietly appealing or polite quality • They lived in a more *genteel* era. • the *genteel* manners of an old southern gentleman • *genteel* grace
– **gen·teel·ly** *adv* – **gen·teel·ness** *noun* [*noncount*]

gen·tile *or* **Gen·tile** /ˈʤɛnˌtajəl/ *noun, pl* **-tiles** [*count*] : a person who is not Jewish
– **gentile** *or* **Gentile** *adj*

gen·til·i·ty /ʤɛnˈtɪləti/ *noun* [*noncount*]
1 : high social status • Education was considered a mark of *gentility*.
2 : a quietly appealing and polite quality or manner : a genteel quality or manner • He's a model of good taste and *gentility*. [=*courtesy*]

gen·tle /ˈʤɛntl/ *adj* **gen·tler** /ˈʤɛntlɚ/; **gen·tlest** /ˈʤɛntləst/ [*also more* ~; *most* ~]
1 : having or showing a kind and quiet nature : not harsh or violent • a very *gentle* man/dog • a dog that is *gentle* with children • Your mother has a *gentle* manner/voice/smile. • *gentle* eyes • a *gentle* sense of humor • a ***gentle giant*** [=a large but gentle person or animal]
2 a : not hard or forceful • a *gentle* rain/breeze/wind • *gentle* movements • a *gentle* push • Apply *gentle* [=*soft*] pressure to the area. • I heard a *gentle* knock at the door. **b** : not strong or harsh in effect or quality • a *gentle* soap = a soap that is *gentle* on the skin • It's a delicate problem that requires *gentle* handling/treatment. • The job requires a *gentle* touch. • The cold snap was a *gentle* reminder that winter was coming. • *gentle* flavors
3 : not steep or sharp • a *gentle* slope/hill • a *gentle* curve
– **gen·tle·ness** /ˈʤɛntl̩nəs/ *noun* [*noncount*] • the *gentleness* of his manner • the *gentleness* of the breeze – **gent·ly** /ˈʤɛntli/ *adv* • She spoke to him *gently*. • The vase is very fragile, so handle it *gently*.

gen·tle·folk /ˈʤɛntl̩ˌfoʊk/ *noun* [*plural*] *old-fashioned* : people who have high social status

gen·tle·man /ˈʤɛntl̩mən/ *noun, pl* **-men** /-mən/ [*count*]
1 : a man who treats other people in a proper and polite way • A true *gentleman* would never engage in such behavior.
2 : MAN — used especially in polite speech or when speaking to a group of men • Please show this *gentleman* to his seat. • Good evening, ladies and *gentlemen*.
3 *old-fashioned* : a man of high social status • He's a *gentleman* by birth. • a ***gentleman farmer*** [=a gentleman who farms for pleasure]
– **gen·tle·man·li·ness** /ˈʤɛntl̩mənlinəs/ *noun* [*noncount*] – **gen·tle·man·ly** /ˈʤɛntl̩mənli/ *adj* [*more* ~; *most* ~] • *gentlemanly* conduct

gentleman's agreement *or* **gentlemen's agreement** *noun, pl* ~ **-ments** [*count*] : an informal agreement based on trust rather than on a legal document

gen·tle·wom·an /ˈʤɛntl̩ˌwʊmən/ *noun, pl* **-wom·en** /-ˌwɪmən/ [*count*] *old-fashioned* : a woman of high social status

gen·tri·fy /ˈʤɛntrəˌfaɪ/ *verb* **-fies**; **-fied**; **-fy·ing** [+ *obj*] : to change (a place, such as an old neighborhood) by improving it and making it more appealing to people who have money • As the neighborhood became *gentrified*, the people who had lived there for many years could no longer afford it.
– **gen·tri·fi·ca·tion** /ˌʤɛntrəfəˈkeɪʃən/ *noun* [*noncount*] • a neighborhood undergoing *gentrification*

gen·try /ˈʤɛntri/ *noun*
the gentry *old-fashioned* : people of high social status • a member of *the gentry* [=*the aristocracy*] • ***the landed gentry*** [=wealthy people who own land]

gents /ˈʤɛnts/ *noun* [*singular*] *Brit, informal* : MEN'S ROOM — usually used with *the* • Can you tell me where *the gents* is, please? — compare LADIES

gen·u·flect /ˈʤɛnjəˌflɛkt/ *verb* **-flects**; **-flect·ed**; **-flect·ing** [*no obj*]
1 : to kneel on one knee and then rise again as an act of respect • They *genuflected* before the altar in the church.
2 *disapproving* : to obey someone with power in a way that is seen as weak • politicians *genuflecting* [=*kowtowing*] to wealthy businessmen
– **gen·u·flec·tion** *also Brit* **gen·u·flex·ion** /ˌʤɛnjəˈflɛkʃən/ *noun, pl* **-tions** [*count, noncount*]

gen·u·ine /ˈʤɛnjəwən/ *adj* [*more* ~; *most* ~]
1 : actual, real, or true : not false or fake • *genuine* leather • The signature is *genuine*. [=*authentic*] • There has been a *genuine* improvement in the economy in recent months. — often used in the phrase ***the genuine article*** to refer to someone or something that is not a copy or substitute • Don't fall for cheap imitations; this is *the genuine article*. • A lot of people pretend to be cowboys, but he's *the genuine article*. [=he's a real cowboy]
2 : sincere and honest • *genuine* emotions • She showed a *genuine* interest in our work. • He has always shown a *genuine* concern for poor people. • a *genuine* desire to help others • She seems to be a very *genuine* person.
– **gen·u·ine·ly** *adv* • He was *genuinely* concerned. – **gen·u·ine·ness** *noun* [*noncount*] • the *genuineness* of the leather • the *genuineness* of her interest

ge·nus /ˈʤi:nəs/ *noun, pl* **gen·era** /ˈʤɛnərə/ [*count*] *biology*

: a group of related animals or plants that includes several or many different species

Gen X /ˈʤɛnˈɛks/ *noun* [*noncount*] : GENERATION X — often hyphenated and used before a noun ▪ a *Gen-X* celebrity
– **Gen Xer** /ˈʤɛnˈɛksɚ/ *noun, pl* ~ **Xers** [*count*]

geo- /ʤiːjoʊ/ *combining form* : earth : ground : soil ▪ *geology*

geo•cen•tric /ˌʤiːoʊˈsɛntrɪk/ *adj* : having or relating to the Earth as the center ▪ the old *geocentric* theory that the Sun goes round the Earth ▪ a *geocentric* universe — compare HELIOCENTRIC

ge•og•ra•phy /ʤiˈɑːgrəfi/ *noun, pl* **-phies**
1 [*noncount*] : an area of study that deals with the location of countries, cities, rivers, mountains, lakes, etc.
2 : the natural features (such as rivers, mountains, etc.) of a place [*noncount*] studying the *geography* of the western United States [*count*] regional *geographies*
– **ge•og•ra•pher** /ʤiˈɑːgrəfɚ/ *noun, pl* **-phers** [*count*] ▪ She's a professional *geographer*. – **geo•graph•ic** (*chiefly US*) /ˌʤiːjəˈgræfɪk/ *or* **geo•graph•i•cal** /ˌʤiːjəˈgræfɪkəl/ *adj* ▪ a large *geographic* area ▪ *geographical* names – **geo•graph•i•cal•ly** /ˌʤiːjəˈgræfɪkli/ *adv*

ge•ol•o•gy /ʤiˈɑːləʤi/ *noun* [*noncount*]
1 : a science that studies rocks, layers of soil, etc., in order to learn about the history of the Earth and its life
2 : the rocks, land, processes of land formation, etc., of a particular area ▪ learning about the *geology* of Hawaii
– **geo•log•ic** (*chiefly US*) /ˌʤiːjəˈlɑːʤɪk/ *or* **geo•log•i•cal** /ˌʤiːjəˈlɑːʤɪkəl/ *adj* ▪ the *geologic* features of an area ▪ ***geologic time*** [=the period of time during which the earth has existed] – **geo•log•i•cal•ly** /ˌʤiːjəˈlɑːʤɪkli/ *adv* – **ge•ol•o•gist** /ʤiˈɑːləʤɪst/ *noun, pl* **-gists** [*count*]

ge•om•e•try /ʤiˈɑːmətri/ *noun* [*noncount*] : a branch of mathematics that deals with points, lines, angles, surfaces, and solids
– **geo•met•ric** /ˌʤiːjəˈmɛtrɪk/ *also* **geo•met•ri•cal** /ˌʤiːjəˈmɛtrɪkəl/ *adj* ▪ *geometric* shapes/patterns – **geo•met•ri•cal•ly** /ˌʤiːjəˈmɛtrɪkli/ *adv*

geo•phys•ics /ˌʤiːjəˈfɪzɪks/ *noun* [*noncount*] : a branch of science that deals with the physical movements and forces of the Earth (such as its climate and oceans)

geo•pol•i•tics /ˌʤiːjoʊˈpɑːləˌtɪks/ *noun*
1 [*noncount*] : the study of how geography and economics have an influence on politics and on the relations between nations
2 [*plural*] : the political and geographic parts of something ▪ The *geopolitics* of war are often complex.
– **geo•po•lit•i•cal** /ˌʤiːjoʊpəˈlɪtɪkəl/ *adj* ▪ *geopolitical* interests – **geo•po•lit•i•cal•ly** /ˌʤiːjoʊpəˈlɪtɪkli/ *adv*

Geor•gian /ˈʤoɚʤən/ *adj* : of or relating to the time from 1714 to 1830 when England was ruled by four kings named George ▪ an example of *Georgian* architecture

geo•ther•mal /ˌʤiːjoʊˈθɚməl/ *adj* : of, relating to, or using the natural heat produced inside the Earth ▪ *geothermal* power; *also* : produced by such heat ▪ *geothermal* steam

ge•ra•ni•um /ʤəˈreɪnijəm/ *noun, pl* **-ums** [*count*] : a plant that is grown for its red, white, pink, or purple flowers — see color picture on page C6

ger•bil /ˈʤɚbəl/ *noun, pl* **-bils** [*count*] : a small animal that is often kept as a pet — see picture at RODENT

[1]**ge•ri•at•ric** /ˌʤeriˈætrɪk/ *adj*
1 *always used before a noun, medical* : of or relating to the process of growing old and the medical care of old people : of or relating to geriatrics ▪ *geriatric* patients/medicine ▪ *geriatric* illnesses ▪ a *geriatric* ward
2 [*more* ~; *most* ~] *informal* : OLD ▪ a *geriatric* dog ▪ children who think that anyone over the age of 40 is *geriatric* ▪ a *geriatric* [=old and outdated] computer ▪ *geriatric* airplanes

[2]**geriatric** *noun, pl* **-rics** [*count*] : an old person — usually plural ▪ providing medical care for *geriatrics*

ge•ri•at•rics /ˌʤeriˈætrɪks/ *noun* [*noncount*] : a branch of medicine that deals with the problems and diseases of old people ▪ a doctor who specializes in *geriatrics*

germ /ˈʤɚm/ *noun, pl* **germs** [*count*]
1 *biology* : a very small living thing that causes disease ▪ the *germ* that causes tuberculosis
2 a : the origin or basis of something ▪ the *germ* of an idea
b : a very small amount of something ▪ a *germ* of truth
3 *biology* : something that can grow to become a whole animal, plant, etc., or one of its parts ▪ a *germ* cell ▪ the *germ* layers of an embryo — see also WHEAT GERM

Ger•man /ˈʤɚmən/ *noun, pl* **-mans**
1 [*count*] : a person born, raised, or living in Germany : a person whose family is from Germany
2 [*noncount*] : the language of Germany that is also spoken in Austria, parts of Switzerland, and other places
– **German** *adj* ▪ *German* food/literature

ger•mane /ʤɚˈmeɪn/ *adj* [*more* ~; *most* ~] *formal* : relating to a subject in an appropriate way : RELEVANT ▪ Her com-

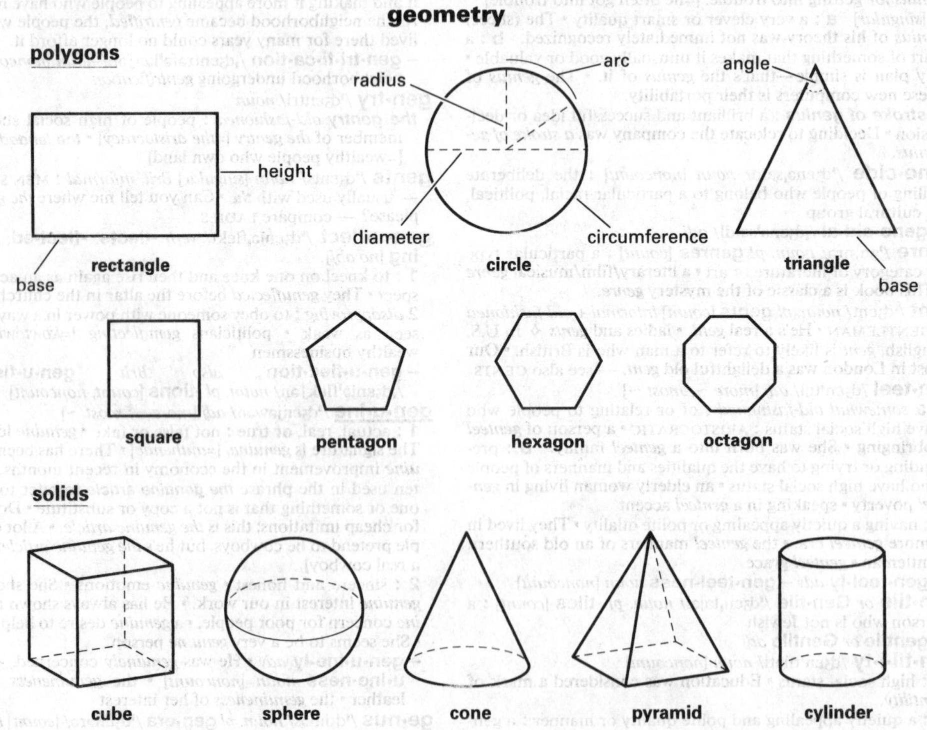

ments were not *germane* (to the discussion). ▪ facts *germane* to the dispute
– ger·mane·ly *adv*
Ger·man·ic /ʤɚˈmænɪk/ *adj*
1 : of or relating to Germans ▪ their *Germanic* homeland ▪ *Germanic* music/influence/tribes
2 : of or relating to the German language or to other closely related languages ▪ *Germanic* languages, such as German, English, Dutch, and the Scandinavian languages
German mark *noun, pl* **~ marks** [*count*] **:** DEUTSCHE MARK
German measles *noun* [*noncount*] **:** a disease that is less severe than typical measles but that can harm an unborn child if the mother gets the disease when she is pregnant — called also *rubella*
German shepherd *noun, pl* **~ -herds** [*count*] **:** a large dog that is often used in police work and as a guide dog for blind people — called also (*Brit*) *Alsatian*; see picture at DOG
ger·mi·nate /ˈʤɚməˌneɪt/ *verb* **-nates; -nat·ed; -nat·ing**
1 [*no obj*] *of a seed* **:** to begin to grow ▪ waiting for the seeds to *germinate* [=*sprout*] ▪ The seeds *germinated* quickly. — often used figuratively ▪ The idea has been *germinating* [=*forming, developing*] in his mind for some time.
2 [+ *obj*] **:** to cause (a seed) to begin to grow ▪ methods used by gardeners to *germinate* seeds
– ger·mi·na·tion /ˌʤɚməˈneɪʃən/ *noun* [*noncount*] ▪ seed *germination* ▪ the *germination* of an idea
germ warfare *noun* [*noncount*] **:** BIOLOGICAL WARFARE
ger·on·tol·o·gy /ˌʤerənˈtɑːləʤi/ *noun* [*noncount*] *technical* **:** the scientific study of old age and of the process of becoming old
– ge·ron·to·log·i·cal /ʤəˌrɑːntəˈlɑːʤɪkəl/ *adj* ▪ *gerontological* research **– ger·on·tol·o·gist** /ˌʤerənˈtɑːləʤɪst/ *noun, pl* **-gists** [*count*]
ger·ry·man·der *verb* **-ders; -dered; -der·ing** /ˈʤeriˌmændɚ/ [+ *obj*] **:** to divide (a state, school district, etc.) into political units that give one group an unfair advantage ▪ *gerrymandering* urban districts to give rural voters a majority
ger·und /ˈʤerənd/ *noun, pl* **-unds** [*count*] *grammar* **:** an English noun formed from a verb by adding *-ing* ▪ In the sentence "Learning can be fun," "learning" is a *gerund*.
ge·stalt /gəˈstɑːlt, gəˈʃtɑːlt/ *noun* [*singular*] *psychology* **:** something that is made of many parts and yet is somehow more than or different from the combination of its parts ▪ the *gestalt* of human consciousness; *broadly* **:** the general quality or character of something ▪ the *gestalt* [=*feel, atmosphere*] of the place ▪ the *gestalt* [=*spirit*] of the era
ges·ta·tion /ʤɛˈsteɪʃən/ *noun* [*noncount*]
1 : the time when a person or animal is developing inside its mother before it is born; *also* **:** the process of development that happens during this time ▪ in the last weeks of *gestation* [=*pregnancy*]
2 : the process by which something (such as an idea) forms and develops ▪ the *gestation* of new ideas ▪ The book has been in *gestation* for a long time.
ges·tic·u·late /ʤɛˈstɪkjəˌleɪt/ *verb* **-lates; -lat·ed; -lat·ing** [*no obj*] **:** to move your arms and hands especially when speaking in an angry or emotional way ▪ He was *gesticulating* [=*gesturing*] wildly during his speech.
– ges·tic·u·la·tion /ʤɛˌstɪkjəˈleɪʃən/ *noun, pl* **-tions** [*count*] strange *gesticulations* [=*gestures*] [*noncount*] communication by means of *gesticulation*
[1]**ges·ture** /ˈʤɛsʧɚ/ *noun, pl* **-tures** [*count*]
1 : a movement of your body (especially of your hands and arms) that shows or emphasizes an idea or a feeling ▪ Specific *gestures* can indicate particular moods. ▪ an obscene *gesture* ▪ His arm was raised in a *gesture* of defiance.
2 : something said or done to show a particular feeling or attitude ▪ a thoughtful/polite/friendly *gesture* ▪ a *gesture* of goodwill ▪ The president's visit was mainly a ***symbolic gesture***. [=an act that has no purpose or effect other than to show support, respect, etc.]
[2]**gesture** *verb* **-tures; -tured; -tur·ing** [*no obj*] **:** to make a gesture **:** to move your hands, arms, etc., to express an idea or feeling ▪ She *gestured* towards the fireplace. ▪ He *gestured* at his audience. ▪ The room was filled with angry people shouting and *gesturing*. ▪ He *gestured* (to his partner) that it was time to leave. ▪ He *gestured* to/for his partner to leave.
ge·sund·heit /gəˈzʊntˌhaɪt/ *interj, chiefly US* — used to wish good health to someone who has sneezed
get /ˈgɛt/ *verb* **gets; got** /ˈgɑːt/; **got** *or US* **got·ten** /ˈgɑːtn/; **get·ting**
1 [+ *obj*] **:** to obtain (something): such as **a :** to receive or be given (something) ▪ He *got* a new bicycle for his birthday. ▪ I never did *get* an answer to my question. ▪ I *got* a letter from my lawyer. ▪ She *got* a phone call from her sister. ▪ Did you *get* my message? ▪ Can I *get* [=*catch*] a ride to town with you? [=will you give me a ride to town?] ▪ You need to *get* your mother's permission to go. **b :** to obtain (something) through effort, chance, etc. ▪ She hasn't been able to *get* a job. ▪ It's nearly impossible to *get* [=*make*] a reservation at that restaurant. ▪ If you want to be successful you need to *get* a good education. ▪ It took us a while to *get* the waiter's attention. ▪ She *got* a look at the thief. [=she managed to look at the thief] **c :** to obtain the use or services of (something) ▪ It took us a while to *get* a taxi. ▪ It's hard to *get* good help these days. **d :** to earn or gain (something) ▪ How much does he *get* [=*make*] a week? ▪ I *got* $50 when I sold my old bicycle. = I *got* $50 for my old bicycle. ▪ He's *gotten* a bad reputation (for himself). = He's *gotten* himself a bad reputation. ▪ I *got* an "A" on my history exam! **e :** to win (something) ▪ She *got* first prize in the essay contest.
2 [+ *obj*] **:** to buy or pay for (something) ▪ He *got* (himself) a new car at a great price. ▪ "Did you *get* that dress at the mall?" "Yes, and I *got* it for only $20." ▪ Do you *get* [=subscribe to] the local newspaper? ▪ I'll *get* the next round of drinks. ▪ He offered to *get* the check, but I insisted on *getting* it myself. ▪ He *got* a beautiful necklace for his wife. = He *got* his wife a beautiful necklace.
3 [+ *obj*] **:** to go somewhere and come back with (something or someone) ▪ I'll *get* a pencil from the desk. ▪ Can I *get* anything for you? = Can I *get* you anything? ▪ Someone has to (go) *get* the boss from the airport and bring her back here.
4 [+ *obj*] **:** to send or take (something or someone) *to* a person or place ▪ I have to *get* an important message *to* her at once! ▪ We have to *get* him *to* the hospital immediately.
5 a *always followed by an adverb or preposition* [+ *obj*] **:** to cause (someone or something) to move or go ▪ He quickly *got* himself and his luggage through customs. ▪ She *got* the car out of the garage. ▪ I could barely *get* [=*fit*] the luggage into the car's trunk. ▪ I can't *get* this ring on/off my finger. **b** *always followed by an adverb or preposition* [*no obj*] **:** to move or go ▪ He *got* on the horse and rode away. ▪ We *got* on/off the bus. ▪ They quickly *got* [=*passed*] through customs. ▪ She never *got* out of the house last weekend. ▪ He lost weight to be able to *get* [=*fit*] into his jeans again. ▪ He *got* between them to keep them from fighting. ▪ Ouch! *Get* off my foot! **c** *always followed by an adverb* [*no obj*] **:** to arrive at a place ▪ When did you *get* here/there? ▪ He *got* home last night.
6 [+ *obj*] **:** to begin to have (a feeling, an idea, etc.) ▪ I *got* a funny feeling when I saw her again. ▪ He somehow *got* the idea that I was lying to him. ▪ I *got* the impression that he wasn't interested. ▪ One thing led to another, and—well, ***you get the picture/idea***. [=you can easily guess the rest]
7 [+ *obj*] **a :** to become affected by (a disease) ▪ I *got* a bad cold when I was on vacation. ▪ Clean the wound carefully so you don't *get* an infection. **b :** to suffer (an injury) ▪ He *got* a broken nose in a fight. ▪ Where/how did you *get* that bruise on your leg?
8 [+ *obj*] **:** to have or experience (something) ▪ We've been *getting* a lot of rain recently. ▪ I finally *got* a good night's sleep last night. [=I finally slept well last night] ▪ The inn doesn't *get* many visitors these days. ▪ "Do people often ask if you're Irish?" "Yes, I *get* that a lot." [=people ask me that often] ▪ ***You get*** [=there are] so many crazy drivers these days.
9 [+ *obj*] **:** to cause (a particular reaction) ▪ That joke always *gets* a laugh. ▪ Her comments *got* an angry reaction.
10 *always followed by an adverb* **a** [*no obj*] **:** to make progress in some activity ▪ He hasn't *gotten* far with the essay. [=he hasn't made much progress with the essay] ▪ You won't *get* anywhere with flattery. [=you won't succeed by using flattery] ▪ At last we're ***getting somewhere*** (with our work)! — see also GET AHEAD (below) **b** [+ *obj*] **:** to cause or help (someone) to make progress ▪ All that effort didn't really *get* us very far. ▪ Flattery will ***get you nowhere***. = Flattery ***won't get you anywhere***.
11 [+ *obj*] **:** to cause (someone or something) to be in a specified position or condition ▪ He *got* his feet wet when he stepped in a puddle. ▪ He *got* his nose broken in a fight. [=his nose was broken in a fight] ▪ I told you not to *get* yourself dirty. ▪ You nearly *got* us both killed! ▪ I need to *get* [=*have*] my hair cut. ▪ She finally *got* her office organized. ▪ He promised to *get* the work done quickly. [=to do the work quickly] ▪ When you're making a measurement be careful to ***get it right***. [=to do it correctly] ▪ Let me ***get this straight*** [=let me

G

be sure that I understand this correctly]: are you saying that you won't help us?
12 [+ *obj*] **: to cause (someone or something) to do something — usually followed by *to + verb*** • I can't *get* the children *to behave.* • How can I *get* you *to understand* that this isn't a good idea? • He *got* the computer *to work* again. — **sometimes + *-ing verb*** • He *got* the computer *working* again.
13 [*no obj*] **: to start *doing* something** • We *got talking* about old times. — see also GET TO 1a (below)
14 [*no obj*] **: to have or be given the chance *to do* something : to be able *to do* something** • She never *got to go* to college. • Why do I never *get to drive* the car? • She hopes she'll finally *get to spend* more time working on her garden this year.
15 [+ *obj*] **: to deal with (something that needs attention): such as a : to answer (a telephone)** • Would somebody please *get* the phone? **b : to open (a door)** • If you'll *get* the door for me, I'll carry that box inside. • There's someone at the door. Would you please ***get it***? [=open the door and deal with the person who knocked]
16 [+ *obj*] **a : to understand (something or someone)** • I just don't *get* the point of what you're saying. • He didn't *get* the joke. • I don't *get* what you mean. • Oh, now I ***get it*** [=*understand*] • He's a strange guy. I just don't *get* him. • Don't ***get me wrong*** [=don't misunderstand what I am saying] • I ***get your drift*** [=I understand what you are saying] **b : to hear and understand (something)** • I didn't quite *get* [=*catch*] his name.
17 a [*linking verb*] **: BECOME 1** • My hands *got* dirty when I was working in the garden. • I *get* very nervous when I have to speak in public. • I *got* sick last week but I'm feeling better now. • I just can't *get* used to this cold weather. • She sent her sick friend a "*Get* Well Soon" card. • I should go; it's *getting* late. • (*Brit, informal*) Your daughter's *getting* quite a big girl now! • We need to finish by 5 o'clock, so we'd better ***get busy*** [=begin to work] • You've never heard of the Internet? Come on, now. ***Get with it*** [=become up-to-date in your knowledge] ✧ People say ***how stupid/lucky (etc.) can you get*** to mean that someone or something is unusually stupid, lucky, etc. • He tried to rob a policeman. *How stupid can you get*? [=he was very stupid to try to rob a policeman] • Just look at that dress! *How tacky can you get*? [=that dress is very tacky] **b** [*no obj*] **: to change in a specified way as time passes — followed by *to + verb*** • Your daughter is *getting to be* [=is becoming] quite a big girl now!
18 [*no obj*] **: to do something specified — followed by *to + verb*** • Once you *get to know* him, you will like him.
19 [*auxiliary verb*] **— used like *be* with the past participle of some verbs to form passive constructions** • They *got* [=*were*] married last month. • He *got* [=*was*] paid for his work. • She *got* arrested for fraud. • I nearly *got* killed.
20 [+ *obj*] **a : to have (a meal)** • We *got* dinner at an Italian restaurant last night. **b : to prepare (a meal)** • On weekends, my wife sleeps late while I *get* breakfast.
21 [+ *obj*] **: to receive (punishment)** • He *got* five years in prison for his crime. • (*informal*) If you don't stop misbehaving you're going to ***get it*** when your father gets home! [=your father is going to punish you]
22 [+ *obj*] **: to grip and hold (something or someone)** • The dog *got* the thief by the leg. • He *got* [=*grabbed*] me around/by the neck and wouldn't let go.
23 [+ *obj*] **: to find and catch (someone)** • The Royal Canadian Mounted Police always *get* their man! [=they always capture the man they are trying to capture]
24 [+ *obj*] **: to hit (someone)** • The bullet *got* him in the leg.
25 [+ *obj*] **a : to hurt or cause trouble for (someone)** • He's convinced that his ex-wife is out to *get* him. • I'll *get* you if it's the last thing I do! **b : to cause the death of (someone)** • He had heart problems for many years, but it was pneumonia that *got* him in the end.
26 [+ *obj*] *informal* **a : to bother or annoy (someone)** • It really *gets* me that such a foolish man has so much influence. • What *gets* me is all these delays! — see also GET TO 2a (below) **b : to make (someone) sad** • The end of that movie always *gets* me. — see also GET TO 2b (below) **c : to cause (someone) to be fooled or unable to think of an answer** • Well, you *got* [=*fooled, tricked*] me that time. That was very clever. • That's a good question. ***You've got me (there)*** [=I don't know the answer]
27 [+ *obj*] **: to make a phone call and hear or speak to (a person or answering machine)** • Where were you? I've been trying to *get* [=*reach*] you (on the phone) all day! • When I tried to call him I *got* his answering machine. [=the phone was answered by his answering machine]
28 [+ *obj*] **: to receive (a radio or TV station or channel)** • We don't *get* this channel at home.
29 [+ *obj*] **: to produce or provide (a level of performance)** • Our new car *gets* [=*delivers*] excellent gas mileage.
30 [+ *obj*] *informal* **: to notice (someone or something)** • Did you *get* the way he looked at you? **— often used to direct someone's attention to a person or thing that is seen as foolish, surprising, etc.** • Just *get* him in his new pants! • She showed up at the party in—***get this***—a $3,000 designer dress!
get about see GET AROUND (below)
get above yourself see ²ABOVE
get across [*phrasal verb*] **1 : to be clearly expressed to and understood by someone** • I hope my point has finally *gotten across* to you. [=I hope you finally understand what I am trying to say] **2 *get (something) across or get across (something)* : to express (something) clearly so that it is understood** • I don't know if I was able to *get* my point *across* to you. • a politician who is trying hard to *get* his message *across* (to the voters)
get after [*phrasal verb*] ***get after (someone) US, informal* : to tell (someone) repeatedly to do something** • His parents are always *getting after* him about doing his homework. = His parents are always *getting after* him to do his homework.
get ahead [*phrasal verb*] **: to become more successful** • a book about how to *get ahead* in the business world
get along [*phrasal verb*] **1 : to be or remain friendly** • We *get along* well enough, but we're not really close friends. • My brother and my uncle don't really *get along* (with each other). **2 : to make progress while doing something** • How are you *getting along* with your work? [=how's your work coming along?] • He never showed up, but we managed to *get along* [=*get by*] without him. **3 : to leave a place** • I really must be *getting along*. [=*going, leaving*] **4 : to become old** • Her parents are ***getting along in years***.
get around [*phrasal verb*] **1** *or chiefly Brit* ***get about*** **: to go, walk, or travel to different places** • She *gets around* a lot because of her job. • He's having trouble *getting around* because of his sore knee. **2** *or chiefly Brit* ***get round*** *or* ***get about*** **: to become known by many people** • People will be shocked when the news about her arrest *gets around*. • Word *got around* that he was resigning. **3 *get around (something)* *or chiefly Brit* *get round (something)* : to avoid being stopped by (something) : to avoid having to deal with (something)** • I'm sure we can find a way to *get around* these problems. • ***There's no getting around*** the fact that the current system isn't working. [=there is no way to deny that the current system isn't working] **4 *get around to (something)* *or chiefly Brit* *get round to (something)* : to do or deal with (something that you have not yet done or dealt with)** • Don't you think it's about time you *got around to* tidying your room? • I've been meaning to call her, but I just haven't *gotten around to* it. [=I haven't called her] • Sooner or later we'll have to *get around to* the subject of taxation.
get at [*phrasal verb*] **1 *get at (something or someone)* : to reach (something or someone)** • The valve is hard to *get at* unless you have a special tool. • An angry mob tried to *get at* him but the police protected him. **2 *get at (something)* : to find out (information that is hidden or hard to know)** • How can we ever *get at* the truth? **3 *get at (something)* : to say or suggest (something) in an indirect way — usually used as *getting at*** • Just what are you *getting at*? [=what are you suggesting?] **4 *get at (someone) Brit* : to criticize (someone) repeatedly** • He says his teachers are always *getting at* [=(*US*) *getting on*] him unfairly. • He's always being *got at* by his teachers. **5 *get at it US, informal* : to start doing something** • You have a lot of work to do so you'd better *get at it*. [=*get to it*]
get away [*phrasal verb*] **1 : to go away from a place** • I'll be busy at work all day and I can't *get away* until tonight. **— often used figuratively** • The company is having problems because they've ***gotten away from*** the things they do best. [=they have stopped doing the things they do best] **2 : to go away from your home for a vacation** • I'm taking some time off because I really need to *get away* for a few days. • We went on a cruise to ***get away from it all***. **3 : to avoid being caught : to escape** • The robbers *got away* (from the police) in a fast car. **— often + *with*** • The robbers *got away with* a lot of stolen jewelry. **— sometimes used figuratively** • You can't *get away* from the facts. = ***There's no getting away from*** the facts. [=you can't avoid or deny the facts; the facts are known and cannot be ignored] — see also GETAWAY **4 *get away with (something)* a :** to not be crit-

icized or punished for (something) ▪ She's incredibly rude. I don't know how she *gets away with* it. — often used figuratively ▪ There's a chance of rain, but I think I can probably *get away with* leaving my umbrella at home. [=I probably will not need my umbrella] ▪ It would be nice to have more food for the party, but I think we can *get away with* what we have. [=I think what we have is enough and will not cause problems for us] **b** : to be given only slight or mild punishment for a crime or for doing something wrong ▪ The policeman stopped her for speeding but let her *get away with* just a warning. — see also *get away with murder* at [1]MURDER

get back [*phrasal verb*] **1** : to return to a place after going away ▪ When did you *get back* from your vacation? ▪ We *got back* to the office in the early afternoon. **2** : to return to an activity, condition, etc. — usually + *to* ▪ Things are finally *getting back to* normal. ▪ Let's *get back to* the topic we were discussing yesterday. ▪ It's time to ***get back to work*** [=to start working again] **3** ***get (something) back or get back (something)*** : to get or obtain (something you have lost) again : to recover (something) ▪ He *got* his old job *back* after a long struggle. ▪ Someone stole his wallet but he *got* it *back* from the police. **4** ***get (someone) back or get back at (someone) or Brit get your own back informal*** : to do something bad or unpleasant to someone who has treated you badly or unfairly ▪ I'll *get* you *back* for what you did to me! ▪ After he lost his job, he vowed that he would find a way to *get back at* his old boss. **5** ***get back to (someone)*** **a** : to talk to or write to (someone) at a later time in order to give more information, answer a question, etc. ▪ He *got back to* me (by e-mail) in a few days with a new offer. ▪ "How much will it cost?" "I'm not sure. I'll have to *get back to* you on that." **b** : to call (someone) back on the telephone ▪ "There's someone on the phone for you, sir." "Tell them I can't take their call now but I'll *get back to* them as soon as I can."

get back to (the) basics see [2]BASIC

get behind [*phrasal verb*] **1** : to fail to do something as quickly as required or expected ▪ We've been *getting* further (and further) *behind* (schedule). ▪ We *got behind* with our car payments. **2** ***get behind (someone or something)*** : to support (someone or something) ▪ The proposal may succeed if a few more people *get behind* it.

get by [*phrasal verb*] **1** : to do enough or to do well enough to avoid failure ▪ He's doing very well in his history classes, but he's barely *getting by* in math. **2** : to be able to live or to do what is needed by using what you have even though you do not have much ▪ We don't have a lot of money, but we *get by*. — often + *on* ▪ How can you *get by on* such a small salary? — often + *with* ▪ We *got by with* a minimum of clothing when we went camping.

get cracking see [1]CRACK

get down [*phrasal verb*] **1** ***get (someone) down*** : to cause (someone) to become sad or depressed ▪ The weather was really *getting* her *down*. ▪ Talking about politics always *gets* me *down*. **2** ***get (something) down or get down (something)*** **a** : to swallow (something) : to eat or drink (something) ▪ You'll feel better once you *get* this medicine *down*. **b** : to write (something) down ▪ If you have a good idea, you should *get* it *down* (in writing) so that you won't forget it. **3** *informal* : to play music or dance with skill and enthusiasm ▪ She likes to *get down* on the dance floor. **4** ***get down to (something)*** **a** : to start to do (something) : to begin to give your attention or effort to (something) ▪ It's time to stop delaying and *get down to* work. ▪ Let's ***get down to business*** **b** : to talk about or describe (something) in a very simple and accurate way ▪ ***When you get right down to it*** this movie is just not very good.

get even see [1]EVEN

get going **1** : to leave ▪ We ought to *get going* if we don't want to be late. **2** : to start doing something ▪ You should *get going* on that assignment. **3 a** : to start talking ▪ Once he *gets going* about the war you can't shut him up. **b** : to cause (someone) to start talking ▪ Don't *get* him *going* about the war or you'll never shut him up!

get hold of see [2]HOLD

get in [*phrasal verb*] **1 a** : to enter a place ▪ The burglar *got in* through an unlocked window. **b** : to arrive at a place ▪ The train *got in* late. **c** : to arrive home ▪ Her husband was out late last night. He didn't *get in* until almost midnight. **2** : to become involved in an activity ▪ The people who have become rich in this business are the ones who *got in* at the beginning. **3** : to be chosen or elected for office ▪ The mayor *got in* by a very slim margin. **4** ***get in or get (someone) in*** : to be accepted or to cause (someone) to be accepted as a student, member, etc. ▪ It's a very good school. I hope your daughter *gets in*. ▪ I hope you *get* your daughter *in*. **5** ***get (someone) in*** : to have (someone) come to your home, business, etc., to do work ▪ We had to *get* a doctor/plumber *in* to deal with the emergency. **6** ***get (something) in or get in (something)*** **a** : to do or say (something) by making an effort ▪ He managed to *get* a few good punches *in* before they stopped the fight. ▪ May I ***get a word in*** here? [=may I say something here?] — see also *get a word in edgewise* at EDGEWISE **b** : to send or deliver (something) to the proper person or place ▪ Did you *get* your assignment *in* on time? **c** : to do (something) in the amount of time that is available ▪ I was able to *get in* a few hours of reading last night. ▪ I hope we can *get in* a visit to the art museum the next time we're in the city. **d** : to harvest (a crop) and put it in a safe or dry place ▪ It's time to *get* the crop/harvest *in*. ▪ We'd better *get* the hay *in* before it rains. **7** ***get in on (something)*** : to become involved in (something) ▪ It sounds like an interesting project and I'd like to *get in on* it. **8** ***get in with (someone)*** : to become friends with (someone) ▪ She *got in with* [=*fell in with*] a bad crowd and got into trouble. ▪ He managed to ***get in good with*** the boss. [=he got the boss to like him]

get into [*phrasal verb*] **1** ***get into (a place)*** **a** : to enter (a place) ▪ The burglar *got into* the house through an unlocked window. **b** : to arrive at (a place) ▪ The train *got into* New York late last night. **2** ***get into (something)*** **a** : to become involved in (an activity) ▪ The people who have become rich in this business are the ones who *got into* it at the beginning. **b** : to begin to be interested in and to enjoy (something) ▪ It's only recently that I've really *gotten into* music. ▪ I tried reading the book, but I just couldn't *get into* it. **3** ***get into (something) or get (someone) into (something)*** **a** : to be accepted or to cause (someone) to be accepted as a student, member, etc. ▪ I hope your daughter *gets into* the school. ▪ I hope you *get* your daughter *into* the school. **b** : to become involved or to cause (someone) to become involved in (something bad, such as trouble or a fight) ▪ He *got into* a lot of trouble when he was a teenager. ▪ They *got into* an argument. ▪ His friends *got* him *into* trouble. **4** ***get into (something)*** : to talk about (something) ▪ I'll tell you what happened, but I don't want to *get into* [=*go into*] all the reasons for why it happened. **5** ***got into (someone)*** : to affect the behavior of (someone) — used to say that someone is behaving in an unusual way and you don't know why ▪ I don't know what has *gotten into* him lately. ▪ She never used to be so rude to people. ***What got into her?*** [=why is she behaving this way?]

get lost see [2]LOST

get lucky see LUCKY

get moving see [1]MOVE

get off [*phrasal verb*] **1** : to leave at the start of a journey ▪ We *got off* early on our camping trip. — often used figuratively in the phrase ***get off to a good/bad (etc.) start*** ▪ He and I *got off to a bad start*, but now we get along well. ▪ The project *got off to a slow start*. — see also *get off on the right/wrong foot* at [1]FOOT **2** ***get off or get (someone) off*** **a** : to not be punished for a crime : to be judged not guilty of a crime ▪ He's been arrested several times, but he always *gets off*. : to help (someone) to be judged not guilty ▪ His lawyer *got* him *off*. **b** : to be given or to help (someone) to be given only a slight punishment for a crime ▪ She *got off* lightly. — usually + *with* ▪ He *got off with* a light sentence. ▪ His lawyer tried to *get* him *off with* a light sentence. — sometimes used figuratively ▪ It was a bad accident. You're lucky that you *got off with* just a broken leg—you could have been killed! **3** : to stop being on or against someone or something ▪ *Get off*—you're hurting me! ▪ I took the subway and *got off* at the downtown station. — see also GET 5a b (above) **4** ***get off (something) or get (someone) off (something)*** : to stop talking about (something) or to cause (someone) to stop talking about (something) ▪ We somehow *got off* (the subject of) work and started talking about our personal lives. ▪ I tried to change the subject, but I couldn't *get* her *off* it. **5** ***get off or get off work*** : to finish working and leave the place where you work ▪ I *get off* early on Fridays. ▪ I *got off work* early last Thursday so I could see the parade. **6** ***get (something) off or get off (something)*** **a** : to write and send (a letter, an e-mail message, etc.) ▪ I'll *get* the letter *off* (to them) tomorrow. **b** : to shoot (something) from a gun ▪ The policeman *got off*

G

[=*fired*] several shots before the criminal escaped. — sometimes used figuratively • He managed to *get off* a few good jokes in his speech. **7** ***get off or get (someone) off chiefly Brit*** : to fall asleep or to help (someone, such as a baby) to fall asleep • I had just *got off* [=*dropped off*] when the doorbell rang. = I had just **got off to sleep** when the doorbell rang. • I just *got* the baby *off to sleep*. **8** ***get off or get (someone) off US, informal*** : to have an orgasm or to cause (someone) to have an orgasm **9** ***get off on (something) informal + sometimes disapproving*** : to enjoy or be excited by (something) especially in a sexual way • He's one of those guys who seem to *get off on* making other people feel guilty. **10** ***get off with (someone) Brit, informal*** : to have sex with (someone) : to begin a sexual relationship with (someone) • She found out he'd *gotten off with* another woman. **11** *informal* **a** ✧ To ***tell someone where to get off*** is to criticize or disagree with someone in a very direct and angry way. • I was sick of listening to his constant complaints, so I *told him where to get off*. **b** *US* ✧ If you ***don't know where someone gets off*** (doing something), you are angry because someone has done something that is not right. • I *don't know where he gets off* telling me what to do. = ***Where does he get off*** telling me what to do? [=he has no right to tell me what to do]

get on [*phrasal verb*] **1** ***get on with (something)*** : to continue doing (something) • I didn't mean to interrupt you. I'll let you *get on with* your work. • You need to stop feeling sorry for yourself and just ***get on with your life***. [=return to doing the things you do in your normal life] • This introduction is taking forever. I wish they'd just ***get on with it***. [=stop delaying and get to the interesting or important part] **2** *chiefly Brit* : to be or remain friendly : to get along • They've never really *got on* (with each other). • We *get on* well enough, but we're not really close friends. **3** *chiefly Brit* **a** : to make progress while doing something • How is your daughter *getting on* in/at school? • We can *get on* [=*get along, get by, manage*] just fine without them. **b** : to achieve greater success : to get ahead • an ambitious young woman trying to *get on* in business **4** ***get on (something) US*** : to start to do or deal with (something) • "These files need to be organized." "I'll *get on* it right away." **5** ***get on (someone) US*** : to criticize (someone) repeatedly • His boss has been *getting on* him about the quality of his work. • She's always ***getting on his case*** about cleaning his room. [=she's always telling him to clean it] **6** ***get it on US slang*** : to have sex **7** *informal* **a** ***get on or get on in years*** : to grow old • My grandmother is *getting on* [=*aging*] a bit, but she's still very active. **b** : to become late • It's *getting on*, and we really ought to go. **8** ***get on for (something) Brit, informal*** : to move toward becoming (a specified age, time, etc.) • He's *getting on for* 70. [=he's approaching 70; he is nearly 70] • It was *getting on for* noon.

get onto *or* **get on to** [*phrasal verb*] **1** ***get onto (something) or get on to (something)*** : to start to do or deal with (something) • "We need someone to send out the invitations." "I'll *get onto* [=*get on*] it right away." : to start to talk about something • How did we *get onto* this topic? **2** ***get onto (someone) or get on to (someone) Brit*** : to speak to or write to (someone) about a particular problem, job, etc. • I'll *get onto* [=*get in touch with*] the doctor/plumber straightaway and see if he'll come round.

get out [*phrasal verb*] **1 a** : to leave or escape from a place, a vehicle, etc. • He was trapped in the burning building/car, but he was somehow able to *get out* (of it) alive. — used as an angry way to tell someone to leave • *Get out*! I never want to see you again! **b** ***get (someone) out*** : to cause or help (someone) to leave or escape • The firemen managed to *get* him *out* (of the burning building) alive. **c** ***get (something) out or get out (something)*** : to remove (something) from storage so that it can be used • It's raining. I'd better *get out* the umbrella. **2** : to go to places outside your home for social occasions, events, etc. • You spend too much time at home. You need to *get out* more. **3** : to become known • Their secret *got out*. • Word *got out* that she was resigning. **4** ***get (something) out or get out (something)*** : to say (something) by making an effort • He managed to *get out* a few words before he collapsed. **5** *US, informal* — used in speech to show that you are surprised by something or do not believe it • "They gave the job to Jane." "*Get out*!" = "***Get out of here***!" **6** ***get out of (something) or get (someone or something) out of (something)*** **a** : to avoid doing (something) or to help (someone) to avoid doing (something) • I didn't want to go to the lecture, but I couldn't *get out of* it. • He tried to *get out of* doing his homework. • My sister said she could *get* me *out of* going to the party if I really didn't want to go **b** : to stop having (a habit) or to cause (someone) to stop having (a habit) • I used to exercise every day, but I *got out of* the habit. • All the extra work I've been doing has *gotten* me *out of* the habit of exercising. **c** : to stop being in or involved in (something) or to cause (someone or something) to stop being in or involved in (something) • The company has decided to *get* (itself) *out of* the computer business. • She *got* her money *out of* the stock market. **7** ***get (something) out of (something or someone)*** : to take (something) from (something or someone) • The police officer *got* the gun *out of* the suspect's hand. • The police officer *got* a confession *out of* the suspect. **8** ***get (something) out of (something)*** : to gain (something) from (something) • What do you hope to *get out of* this experience?

get over [*phrasal verb*] **1** ***get over (something)*** **a** : to stop being controlled or bothered by (something, such as a problem or feeling) • You need to *get over* [=*overcome*] your fear of being lied to. **b** : to stop feeling unhappy about (something) • She's disappointed about their decision, but she'll *get over* it eventually. **c** *informal* — used to say that you are very surprised or impressed by something • I just can't *get over* how much weight you've lost! **2** ***get over (an illness)*** : to become healthy again after (an illness) • He had a bad cold, and he still hasn't *gotten over* it completely. **3** ***get over (someone)*** : to stop feeling unhappy after ending a relationship with (someone) • He broke up with his girlfriend a couple of months ago, and he still hasn't *gotten over* her. **4** ***get (something) over*** **a** ***or get (something) over with*** : to cause or experience the end of (something) : to finish (something) • I just want to *get* this ordeal *over*! = I just want to *get* this ordeal *over with*! = I just want to ***get*** this ordeal ***over and done with***! [=I want this ordeal to end] **b** ***or get over (something) chiefly Brit*** : to express (something) clearly so that it is understood • I don't know if I was able to *get* my message *over* [=*across*] to them.

get real see [1]REAL

get rid of see RID

get rolling see [1]ROLL

get round see GET AROUND (above)

get the best of see [3]BEST

get the better of see [3]BETTER

get there : to reach a goal : to do what you are trying to do • We haven't made a profit yet, but we'll *get there* eventually. [=we'll make a profit eventually] : to come closer to reaching a goal • We haven't made a profit yet, but we're *getting there*.

get through [*phrasal verb*] **1 a** *chiefly US* : to finish a job or activity • When you *get through* (with that job), I've got something else for you to do. **b** ***get through (something)*** : to do or finish (something, such as an amount of work) • We *got through* [=*covered*] all of the material that we wanted to cover. • There's still a lot of paperwork to be *gotten through*. **c** ***get through (something) or get (someone) through (something)*** : to complete or to help (someone) to complete (a test, an exam, etc.) successfully • She studied hard and *got through* [=*passed*] her exams. • The extra hours of study are what *got* her *through* her exams. **2** ***get through or get through (something) or get (something) through (something)*** : to pass through or beyond something that blocks you or slows you down • Traffic was very heavy, but we managed to *get through* (it). • Rescuers are having trouble *getting through* to the flood victims. : to cause (something) to pass through or beyond something • Traffic was very heavy, but we managed to *get* our truck *through* (it). • Rescuers are having trouble *getting* supplies *through* to the flood victims. **3** ***get through (something) or get (someone) through (something)*** : to have the experience of living through (something that is difficult, dangerous, etc.) • It was a very difficult time in our marriage, but we *got through* it. • I don't know how those early settlers managed to *get through* [=*survive*] the winter. : to help (someone) to live through (something) • It was pure determination that *got* them *through* that crisis. **4** ***get through (something) chiefly Brit*** : to spend or use all of (something) • He *got through* [=*went through*] all the money he inherited in just a few years. • They *got through* [=*went through*] three bottles of wine with dinner. **5 a** ***get through or get through to (someone)*** : to be clearly expressed to and understood by someone • I hope my message has finally *gotten through to* you. [=I hope you finally understand my message] • I think my message finally *got through*. **b** ***get through to (someone)*** *or* ***get (something) through to (someone)*** : to express something clearly so that it is understood by (someone) • I've talked to him many times, but I just can't seem to *get through to* him. • I hope I've finally *gotten* my message *through to* him. **6** ***get through*** *or* ***get through to (someone)*** : to make a successful telephone call to someone • I tried to call home but I couldn't *get through*. • Where were you? I've been trying to *get through to* you (on the phone) all day! **7** ***get through*** *or* ***get through (something)*** : to be accepted or approved by an official group • The bill finally *got through* [=*passed*] and eventually became a law. • The bill finally *got through* [=*passed*] Congress and eventually became a law.

get to [*phrasal verb*] **1** ***get to (something)*** **a** : to start (*doing* something) • She sometimes *gets to worrying* over her health. • We *got to talking* about old times. **b** : to deal with (something) • The letter is on my desk, but I haven't *gotten to* it yet. • I'll *get to* the accounts as soon as I can. **2** ***get to (someone)*** **a** : to bother or annoy (someone) • All these delays are starting to *get to* me. — see also GET 26a (above) **b** : to make (someone) feel sad • The movie's sad ending really *got to* me. — see also GET 26b (above) **c** *chiefly US* : to change or influence the behavior of (someone) wrongly or illegally by making threats, paying money, etc. • The witness changed his story. Someone must have *gotten to* him. **3** ***get to (somewhere)*** : to go to or reach (somewhere) • We *got to* the station/airport just in time.

get together [*phrasal verb*] **1 a** : to meet and spend time together • I'd like to *get together* with you soon. • He often *gets together* with his friends after work. **b** : to begin to have a sexual or romantic relationship • He and his wife first *got together* in college. **c** ***get (people) together*** : to cause (people) to meet or to have a relationship • Their shared interest in photography is what *got* them *together*. **2** : to agree to do or accept something — often + *on* • The two sides have been unable to *get together on* a new contract. **3** ***get together (things or people)*** *or* ***get (things or people) together*** : to collect (things) or gather (people) into one place or group • He *got together* [=*assembled*] a great art collection. • The government *got together* a group of experts to study the problem. • We're still trying to *get together* [=*obtain*] the money we need to buy a new car. **4** ***get your act together*** *or* ***get yourself together*** *or* ***get it together*** *informal* **a** *or* ***get your life together*** : to begin to live in a good and sensible way : to stop being confused, foolish, etc. • His life got much better when he stopped drinking and *got his act together*. **b** : to begin to function in a skillful or effective way • The company finally *got its act together* and started making a profit this year.

get to sleep : to start sleeping : to fall asleep • She finally *got to sleep* after midnight.

get to work : to start working • We need to stop delaying and *get to work*.

get up [*phrasal verb*] **1** ***get up*** *or* ***get (someone) up*** : to rise or to cause (someone) to rise after lying or sleeping in a bed • I *got up* [=got out of bed] early this morning. • I woke up early but I didn't *get up* till later. • The alarm clock *got* me *up* earlier than usual. **2** : to stand up • He *got up* to greet her when she entered the room. **3** ***get (something) up*** *or* ***get up (something)*** **a** : to produce (something, such as courage) in yourself by trying or making an effort • He couldn't *get up* the courage to ask her out on a date. • She was so tired she could hardly *get up* the energy to make dinner. **b** : to prepare or organize (something that involves a group of people) • They're trying to *get up* a petition to have the movie theater reopened. **4** ***get it up*** *slang* : to get an erection

get up on the wrong side of the bed see [1]BED

get what's coming to you see [1]COME

get wind of see [1]WIND

get your bearings see BEARING

get your goat see GOAT

have got see HAVE

get·away /ˈgetəˌweɪ/ *noun, pl* **-aways** [*count*]
1 : the act of getting away or escaping • The robbers made a clean *getaway*. [=*escape*] • He drove the ***getaway car*** [=the car used by criminals to leave the scene of a crime]
2 a : a short vacation • We're planning a weekend *getaway* to the mountains. **b** : a place where people go for a short vacation • The resort advertises itself as the perfect island *getaway*. — see also *get away* at GET

get–go /ˈgɪtˌgoʊ, ˈgetˌgoʊ/ *noun*
from the get-go *US, informal* : from the very beginning • She didn't like me *from the get-go*. • They were involved in the project *from the get-go*.

get·out /ˈgetˌaʊt/ *noun, pl* **-outs** [*count*] *Brit, informal* : an excuse that lets you avoid doing something (such as a duty) • Is there no *getout* I can use to avoid attending the meeting? — see also ALL GET-OUT, *get out* 6 at GET

get–to·geth·er /ˈgettəˌgeðɚ/ *noun, pl* **-ers** [*count*] : an informal social gathering • There is a family *get-together* this weekend. • She's hosting a *get-together* for her classmates.

get·ter /ˈgetɚ/ *noun, pl* **-ters** [*count*] : someone or something that receives, gets, or is given something • the top vote *getter* [=the person who receives the most votes] • a real attention *getter*

get·up /ˈgetˌʌp/ *noun, pl* **-ups** [*count*] *informal* : an unusual outfit or costume • He came onstage in a cowboy *getup*. • a guy in a crazy *getup*

get–up–and–go /ˌgetˌʌpnˈgoʊ/ *noun* [*noncount*] *informal* : energy and enthusiasm • full of *get-up-and-go* • I'm not as young as I used to be, but I still have plenty of *get-up-and-go*.

gew·gaw /ˈgu:ˌgɑ:/ *noun, pl* **-gaws** [*count*] : a small thing that has little value • collectible/childish *gewgaws* [=*trinkets*]

gey·ser /ˈgaɪzɚ, *Brit* ˈgi:zə/ *noun, pl* **-sers** [*count*]
1 : a hole in the ground that shoots out hot water and steam • The water from the *geyser* rises as high as 75 feet.; *also* : the column of water and steam that comes from a geyser • *geysers* rising as high as 75 feet • The water shot into the sky in an enormous *geyser*.
2 *Brit* : a device for heating water in a bathroom or kitchen

ghast·ly /ˈgæstli, *Brit* ˈgɑ:stli/ *adj* **ghast·li·er; -est**
1 : very shocking or horrible • a *ghastly* [=*gruesome, hideous*] crime/ritual • Her behavior was truly *ghastly*. [=*dreadful, appalling*]
2 : very bad : TERRIBLE, AWFUL • You're making a *ghastly* mistake. • His room was a *ghastly* mess. • I feel *ghastly*. [=I feel very unwell]
– ghast·li·ness *noun* [*noncount*] • the *ghastliness* of the crime **– ghastly** *adv* • Her face was *ghastly* [=*ghostly*] pale/white.

gher·kin /ˈgɚkən/ *noun, pl* **-kins** [*count*] : a small cucumber that is used to make pickles

ghet·to /ˈgetoʊ/ *noun, pl* **-tos** *also* **-toes** [*count*]
1 : a part of a city in which members of a particular group or race live usually in poor conditions • a Jewish *ghetto*
2 : the poorest part of a city • He grew up in the *ghetto*. — sometimes used figuratively • The program has been banished to the *ghetto* of late-night television.

ghetto blaster *noun, pl* **~ -ers** [*count*] *informal* : BOOM BOX

ghet·to·ize *also Brit* **ghet·to·ise** /ˈgetoʊˌaɪz/ *verb* **-iz·es; -ized; -iz·ing** [+ *obj*]
1 : to place (someone or something) in a ghetto • *ghettoized* minorities — often used figuratively • a program *ghettoized* to late-night television
2 : to turn (something) into a ghetto • Parts of the city that had been *ghettoized* are now being restored.

[1]**ghost** /ˈgoʊst/ *noun, pl* **ghosts**
1 [*count*] : the soul of a dead person thought of as living in an unseen world or as appearing to living people • a house haunted by *ghosts* • He looks like he's just seen a *ghost*. [=he looks frightened] — sometimes used figuratively • She is still haunted by the *ghosts* of her past. [=she is still troubled by bad memories of the past]
2 [*singular*] : a very small amount or trace — usually + *of* • I thought I detected the *ghost of* a smile [=a very faint smile] on her lips. • He doesn't have/stand ***a ghost of a chance*** of winning. [=he has no chance of winning]
give up the ghost *informal* : to die — often used figuratively • After years of service my car finally *gave up the ghost*.

[2]**ghost** *verb* **ghosts; ghost·ed; ghost·ing** [+ *obj*] : GHOSTWRITE • She *ghosted* the mayor's autobiography.

ghost·ly /ˈgoʊstli/ *adj* **ghost·li·er; -est** [*or more* ~; *most* ~] : of or relating to a ghost • A *ghostly* figure appears in the house at night. : suggesting a ghost • a *ghostly* fog • leading a *ghostly* existence • a *ghostly* white gown
– ghost·li·ness *noun* [*noncount*] **– ghostly** *adv* • Her face was *ghostly* pale/white.

ghost story *noun, pl* **~ -ries** [*count*] : a frightening story about ghosts

ghost town *noun, pl* **~ towns** [*count*] : a town that no longer has any people living in it : an abandoned town • Af-

G

ter all the gold was mined, the place became a *ghost town*.

ghost·write /ˈgoustˌraɪt/ *verb* **-writes**; **-wrote** /-ˌrout/; **-writ·ten** /-ˌrɪtn̩/; **-writ·ing** [+ *obj*] **:** to write (something, such as a book) for someone else using that person's name ▪ She was hired to *ghostwrite* the mayor's autobiography. ▪ *ghostwritten* books/articles
– **ghost·writ·er** *noun, pl* **-ers** [*count*]

ghoul /ˈguːl/ *noun, pl* **ghouls** [*count*] **:** an evil creature in frightening stories that robs graves and eats dead bodies
– **ghoul·ish** /ˈguːlɪʃ/ *adj* [*more ~; most ~*] ▪ a *ghoulish* [=*fiendish*] laugh ▪ He took a *ghoulish* [=*sinister*] delight in their troubles. – **ghoul·ish·ly** *adv* ▪ laughing *ghoulishly* – **ghoul·ish·ness** *noun* [*noncount*] ▪ the *ghoulishness* of his laughter

GI /ˌdʒiːˈaɪ/ *noun, pl* **GI's** *or* **GIs** [*count*] **:** a member or former member of the U.S. armed forces — often used before another noun ▪ *GI* bill/rations

[1]**gi·ant** /ˈdʒajənt/ *adj* [*more ~; most ~*] **:** very large **:** much larger or more powerful than normal ▪ a *giant* photograph/machine/wrestler ▪ a *giant* corporation ▪ a *giant*-size box of detergent

[2]**giant** *noun, pl* **-ants** [*count*]
1 : a legendary creature usually thought of as being an extremely large and powerful person ▪ the land of the *giants*
2 : a person or thing that is very large, powerful, or successful ▪ a big baby who grew up to be a *giant* of a man [=a very large man] ▪ The company has become a *giant* of the automotive industry. [=it has become very large and successful] ▪ an American literary *giant*

giant panda *noun, pl* **~ -das** [*count*] **:** PANDA 1

giant sequoia *noun, pl* **~ -quoias** [*count*] **:** a very tall evergreen tree that grows in the western U.S. — called also *sequoia*

giant squid *noun, pl* **~ squid** *or* **~ squids** [*count*] **:** a very large type of squid

giant tortoise *noun, pl* **~ -toises** [*count*] **:** a large plant-eating tortoise ✧ Giant tortoises were once common on islands in the Pacific and Indian oceans, but they are now rare.

gib·ber /ˈdʒɪbɚ/ *verb* **-bers**; **-bered**; **-ber·ing** [*no obj*] **:** to talk in a fast or foolish way ▪ What are they *gibbering* about now? ▪ Calm down! You sound like a *gibbering* idiot!

gib·ber·ish /ˈdʒɪbərɪʃ/ *noun* [*noncount*] **:** foolish, confused, or meaningless words ▪ His lecture seemed like nothing but *gibberish*. [=*nonsense*] ▪ She was talking *gibberish* in her sleep.

gib·bon /ˈgɪbən/ *noun, pl* **-bons** [*count*] **:** a small ape of southeastern Asia that has long arms and legs and lives mostly in trees — see picture at APE

gibe *or* **jibe** /ˈdʒaɪb/ *noun, pl* **gibes** *or* **jibes** [*count*] **:** an insulting or critical remark that is meant to hurt someone or make someone appear foolish ▪ The other children made cruel *gibes* about her weight. ▪ He used his speech as an opportunity to take/make *gibes* at his political opponents.

gib·let /ˈdʒɪblət/ *noun, pl* **-lets** [*count*] **:** an organ (such as the heart or liver) of a bird that is cooked and eaten as food — usually plural ▪ gravy with *giblets*

gid·dy /ˈgɪdi/ *adj* **gid·di·er**; **-est**
1 : playful and silly ▪ *giddy* children ▪ *giddy* antics ▪ a *giddy* atmosphere
2 : feeling or showing great happiness and joy ▪ The news made him positively *giddy*. ▪ He was *giddy* with delight. ▪ The room was filled with *giddy* laughter.
3 *always used before a noun* **:** causing dizziness ▪ *giddy* heights ▪ *giddy* panoramic views — often used figuratively ▪ Her second book lifted her to *giddy* heights of literary fame. [=made her extremely famous]
– **gid·di·ly** /ˈgɪdəli/ *adv* ▪ He was talking *giddily* [=*excitedly*] about his business plan. – **gid·di·ness** /ˈgɪdinəs/ *noun* [*noncount*] ▪ youthful *giddiness* [=*silliness, lightheartedness*]

[1]**gift** /ˈgɪft/ *noun, pl* **gifts** [*count*]
1 : something that is given to another person or to a group or organization ▪ The money was a *gift*, not a loan. ▪ a birthday/Christmas/anniversary/wedding *gift* [=*present*] ▪ We always exchange *gifts* [=we give each other gifts] on our anniversary. ▪ a generous/lavish/small *gift* ▪ a ***charitable gift*** [=something, such as money, that is given to a charity]
2 : a special ability ▪ She considers her voice a God-given *gift*. ▪ He's an athlete with many physical *gifts*. [=*talents*] — often + *for* ▪ He has a *gift for* expressing himself. ▪ a *gift for* playing the piano ▪ an actor with a *gift for* comedy — sometimes + *of* ▪ She claimed to have the *gift of* prophecy.
God's gift *informal + disapproving* — used to describe the attitude of people who think that they are very talented, attractive, etc. ▪ He thinks he's *God's gift* to the world. [=he thinks very highly of himself; he is very vain or conceited]
look a gift horse in the mouth see [1]HORSE
the gift of gab see [2]GAB

[2]**gift** *verb* **gifts**; **gift·ed**; **gift·ing** [+ *obj*] **:** to present (someone) *with* a gift ▪ The foundation has *gifted* the museum *with* an important collection of paintings. [=(more commonly) the foundation has given the museum an important collection of paintings] — see also GIFTED

gift certificate *noun, pl* **~ -cates** [*count*] *US* **:** a piece of paper that is worth a certain amount of money and is given to someone to be used like money to pay for things (such as the products or services of a particular business) ▪ a $10 *gift certificate* — called also *(Brit) gift token, (Brit) gift voucher*

gift·ed /ˈgɪftəd/ *adj* [*more ~; most ~*] **:** having great natural ability **:** TALENTED ▪ He's an extremely *gifted* student/athlete. ▪ a school for *gifted* children
gifted with ✧ To be *gifted with* something is to have it as a special ability or quality. ▪ She is *gifted with* a talent for playing the piano. ▪ He is *gifted with* a good sense of humor.

gift shop *noun, pl* **~ shops** [*count*] **:** a store (such as a small store in a museum) that sells things which might be given people as gifts

[1]**gift wrap** *noun* [*noncount*] **:** decorative paper that is used for wrapping gifts ▪ a roll of *gift wrap*

[2]**gift wrap** *verb* **~ wraps**; **~ wrapped**; **~ wrapping** [+ *obj*] **:** to wrap (a gift) in decorative paper ▪ The store will *gift wrap* your purchases for you.
– **gift–wrapped** *adj* ▪ a *gift-wrapped* box ▪ a *gift-wrapped* bottle of wine

[1]**gig** /ˈgɪg/ *noun, pl* **gigs** [*count*] *informal* **:** a job for a musician, an actor, etc. ▪ He was finally able to book a *gig* [=to arrange a performance or series of performances] at the nightclub. ▪ a talk-show *gig* ▪ her last acting *gig*; *broadly, US* **:** JOB ▪ I have a part-time job, but I really need a full-time *gig*.

[2]**gig** *verb* **gigs**; **gigged**; **gig·ging** [*no obj*] *informal* **:** to work as a musician ▪ He *gigged* in a band during the summer.

giga·byte /ˈgɪgəˌbaɪt/ *noun, pl* **-bytes** [*count*] **:** a unit of computer information equal to 1,073,741,824 bytes ▪ a six-*gigabyte* hard drive — abbr. *GB*; compare KILOBYTE, MEGABYTE

gi·gan·tic /dʒaɪˈgæntɪk/ *adj* [*more ~; most ~*] **:** extremely large ▪ *Gigantic* [=*huge, monstrous*] waves were crashing on the beach. ▪ a *gigantic* [=*immense, enormous*] corporation ▪ He made a *gigantic* [=*huge*] mistake when he quit his job.

gig·gle /ˈgɪgəl/ *verb* **gig·gles**; **gig·gled**; **gig·gling** [*no obj*] **:** to laugh in a nervous or childlike way ▪ She *giggled* like a little kid. ▪ We were all joking and *giggling* nervously as we waited for the ceremony to begin.
– **giggle** *noun, pl* **giggles** [*count*] ▪ trying to suppress a *giggle* ▪ I had an attack of the *giggles*. [=I was unable to stop giggling] ▪ *(Brit)* Going to the circus would be a bit of a *giggle*. [=would be amusing or enjoyable] – **gig·gly** /ˈgɪgəli/ *adj* [*more ~; most ~*] ▪ *giggly* children ▪ a *giggly* laugh

gig·o·lo /ˈdʒɪgəˌlou/ *noun, pl* **-los** [*count*] **:** a man who is paid by a woman to be her lover and companion

Gi·la monster /ˈhiːlə-/ *noun, pl* **~ -sters** [*count*] **:** a large orange and black poisonous lizard of the southwestern U.S.

gild /ˈgɪld/ *verb* **gilds**; **gild·ed** /ˈgɪldəd/ *or* **gilt** /ˈgɪlt/; **gild·ing** [+ *obj*] **:** to cover (something) with a thin layer of gold ▪ *gild* a statue
gild the lily **:** to add decoration to something that is already beautiful **:** to try to improve something that does not need to be improved ▪ Putting ice cream on this delicious cake is just *gilding the lily*.
– **gilded** *adj* ▪ a *gilded* sculpture/mask/design ✧ A ***gilded age*** is a time of great success and wealth. The capitalized form ***Gilded Age*** is used when referring specifically to a period from about 1870–90 in American history. ▪ a novel about life in New York during the *Gilded Age* ✧ ***Gilded youth*** are wealthy young people who enjoy many things that other people do not have. – **gild·er** *noun, pl* **-ers** [*count*] ▪ a *gilder's* workshop

[1]**gill** /ˈgɪl/ *noun, pl* **gills** [*count*] **:** the body part that a fish uses for breathing
to the gills *informal* **1 :** as full as possible ▪ The car was packed *to the gills* for our vacation. **2 :** very thoroughly or completely ▪ I'm fed up *to the gills* with his whining! ▪ a theater equipped *to the gills* with new sound equipment
– compare [2]GILL

[2]**gill** /ˈdʒɪl/ *noun, pl* **gills** [*count*] **:** a unit of liquid measure equal to ¼ pint ▪ He measured out one *gill*. [=(*US*) four fluid

ounces; (*Brit*) 5 fluid ounces] — compare [1]GILL

[1]**gilt** /ˈgɪlt/ *noun, pl* **gilts**

1 [*noncount*] : a thin layer of gold or of something like gold • She covered the frame with *gilt*.

2 [*count*] *Brit* : a stock or bond that is considered to be a very safe investment : a gilt-edged security — usually plural • She has/keeps her money in *gilts*.

[2]**gilt** *adj, always used before a noun*

1 : having a golden color • a *gilt* marble surface • *gilt* paint

2 : covered with gilt • a *gilt* plate • *gilt* buttons

[3]**gilt** *past tense and past participle of* GILD

gilt–edged /ˈgɪltˌɛʤd/ *adj* : having the best quality or rating • *gilt-edged* securities [=stocks and bonds that are the safest kind of investment]

[1]**gim·me** /ˈgɪmi/ — used in writing to represent the sound of the phrase *give me* when it is spoken quickly • Just *gimme* the money. ✧ The pronunciation represented by *gimme* is common in informal speech. The written form should be avoided except when trying to represent or record such speech.

[2]**gimme** *noun, pl* **-mes** [*count*] *US, informal* : something that is easily done, achieved, won, etc. • (*golf*) This putt is no *gimme*. [=this is not an easy putt] • They expected the game to be a *gimme*. [=they expected to win the game easily]

gim·mick /ˈgɪmɪk/ *noun, pl* **-micks** [*count*] *often disapproving* : a method or trick that is used to get people's attention or to sell something • a marketing *gimmick* [=*ploy*] • The proposal to cut taxes was just an election *gimmick* to win votes. – **gim·micky** /ˈgɪmɪki/ *adj* [*more* ~; *most* ~] • a flashy, *gimmicky* movie with no real substance

gim·mick·ry /ˈgɪmɪkri/ *noun* [*noncount*] *disapproving* : the use of gimmicks • a lot of marketing *gimmickry* and hype

gimpy /ˈgɪmpi/ *adj* **gimp·i·er; -est** [*also more* ~; *most* ~] *US, informal* : having an injury that makes walking difficult or painful • a *gimpy* football player • a *gimpy* leg/foot

gin /ˈʤɪn/ *noun, pl* **gins**

1 [*count, noncount*] : a clear alcoholic drink that is flavored with juniper berries

2 [*noncount*] : GIN RUMMY

– see also COTTON GIN

[1]**gin·ger** /ˈʤɪnʤɚ/ *noun* [*noncount*]

1 **a** : the strongly flavored root of a tropical plant that is used in cooking **b** : a spice made from ginger • The recipe calls for a teaspoon of *ginger*.

2 *chiefly Brit* : a light reddish or reddish-brown color

– **ginger** *adj, chiefly Brit* • The child has *ginger* [=reddish-brown] hair. – **gin·gery** /ˈʤɪnʤəri/ *adj* [*more* ~; *most* ~] • a *gingery* sauce

[2]**ginger** *verb* **-gers; -gered; -ger·ing**

ginger up [*phrasal verb*] ***ginger up (someone or something) or ginger (someone or something) up*** *Brit, informal* : to make (someone or something) more exciting or lively • *ginger* a group *up* by proposing a new strategy

ginger ale *noun, pl* ~ **ales** [*count, noncount*] : a soft drink that is flavored with ginger

gin·ger·bread /ˈʤɪnʤɚˌbrɛd/ *noun* [*noncount*] : a cake or cookie made with molasses and ginger — often used before another noun • *gingerbread* cookies • We made ***gingerbread men*** [=gingerbread cookies shaped like people] for the holidays. • a ***gingerbread house*** decorated with candy

ginger group *noun, pl* ~ **groups** [*count*] *Brit* : a group that is part of a larger group (such as a political party) and that tries to make other members accept and support their ideas • a left-wing *ginger group* within the Labour Party

gin·ger·ly /ˈʤɪnʤɚli/ *adv* [*more* ~; *most* ~] : very carefully • She *gingerly* placed the cake down on the table. • It's a delicate subject, and we need to approach it *gingerly*.

gin·ger·snap /ˈʤɪnʤɚˌsnæp/ *noun, pl* **-snaps** [*count*] : a hard cookie that is flavored with ginger — called also (*Brit*) *ginger nut*

ging·ham /ˈgɪŋəm/ *noun* [*noncount*] : a cotton cloth that often is marked with a pattern of colored squares • a red and white *gingham* tablecloth

gin·gi·vi·tis /ˌʤɪnʤəˈvaɪtəs/ *noun* [*noncount*] *medical* : a disease in which the gums become red, swollen, and sore

gink·go *also* **ging·ko** /ˈgɪŋkoʊ/ *noun, pl* **-goes** *or* **-gos** *also* **-koes** *or* **-kos** [*count*] : a large Chinese tree that has fan-shaped leaves

ginkgo bi·lo·ba /-ˌbaɪˈloʊbə/ *noun* [*noncount*] : a product made from the leaves of the ginkgo tree that is used as a medicine

gin rummy *noun* [*noncount*] : a card game that is played by two players who are each dealt 10 cards

gin·seng /ˈʤɪnˌsɛŋ/ *noun* [*noncount*] : a Chinese herb that is used as a medicine

Gipsy *variant spelling of* GYPSY

gi·raffe /ʤəˈræf, *Brit* ʤəˈrɑːf/ *noun, pl* **gi·raffes** *or* **giraffe** [*count*] : a very tall African animal that has an extremely long neck and legs

giraffe

gird /ˈgɚd/ *verb* **girds; gird·ed** /ˈgɚdəd/ *also* **girt** /ˈgɚt/; **gird·ing** : to prepare yourself to fight or to do something difficult — usually + *for* [*no obj*] Both sides are *girding for* battle. [+ *obj*] Both sides are ***girding themselves for*** battle. • The company is ***girding (up) its loins for*** what could be a long strike.

gird·er /ˈgɚdɚ/ *noun, pl* **-ers** [*count*] : a strong beam used to build buildings, bridges, etc.

[1]**gir·dle** /ˈgɚdḷ/ *noun, pl* **gir·dles** [*count*] : something that wraps or circles around something else; *specifically* : a tight piece of clothing worn especially in the past by women under other clothes to make the area around the waist look thinner

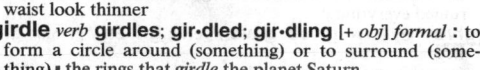

[2]**girdle** *verb* **girdles; gir·dled; gir·dling** [+ *obj*] *formal* : to form a circle around (something) or to surround (something) • the rings that *girdle* the planet Saturn

girl /ˈgɚl/ *noun, pl* **girls**

1 [*count*] **a** : a female child • It's a *girl*! = She gave birth to a baby *girl*. • a nine-year-old *girl* • Ever since I was a (little/young) *girl*, I've wanted to travel. **b** : DAUGHTER • Is this your little *girl*? • She's our oldest/youngest *girl*.

2 [*count*] **a** : a young woman • a group of teenage *girls* • a 19-year-old *girl* • His parents hope he'll soon find a nice *girl*, settle down, and get married. • When she was younger, she was a real ***party girl***. [=a young woman who enjoys parties] • She's a big star now, but her fans still think of her as the ***girl next door***. [=a wholesome young woman from a middle-class family] **b** : a usually young woman from a specified kind of place • a city/country *girl* = a *girl* from the city/country • a local/hometown *girl*

3 *informal* **a** ***the girls*** : the female friends or work partners of a woman viewed as a group • Wait till *the girls* back home hear about this! • Our boss thinks of herself as just one of *the girls*. • She went out dancing with *the girls*. **b** [*count*] : a woman of any age — often used as a friendly way for one woman to address another woman • *Girl*, you will not believe what just happened to me! **c** [*count*] : a woman or girl who does a particular job or activity • a shop *girl* • They just hired a new *girl* to do the filing. ✧ The use of *girl* to refer to an adult woman is often considered offensive, especially when it is used this way by a man. — see also BALL GIRL, CALL GIRL, CHORUS GIRL, COVER GIRL, OFFICE GIRL, PAPERGIRL, POSTER GIRL, SCHOOLGIRL

4 [*count*] *informal + old-fashioned* : GIRLFRIEND • I took my *girl* out to the movies last night.

– **girl·hood** /ˈgɚlˌhʊd/ *noun* [*noncount*] • She lost touch with the friends of her *girlhood*. • her *girlhood* friends – **girl·ish** /ˈgɚlɪʃ/ *adj* [*more* ~; *most* ~] • a *girlish* voice • her *girlish* figure – **girl·ish·ly** *adv* • She smiled *girlishly* at him. – **girl·ish·ness** *noun* [*noncount*] • the *girlishness* of her voice/figure

girl Friday *noun, pl* ~ **-days** [*count*] *informal + old-fashioned* : a woman who does many different jobs in an office : a female office assistant

girl·friend /ˈgɚlˌfrɛnd/ *noun, pl* **-friends** [*count*]

1 : a woman that someone is having a romantic or sexual relationship with • My *girlfriend* and I have only been dating for a couple of months. — compare BOYFRIEND

2 : a female friend • She spends hours talking on the phone with her *girlfriends*.

Girl Guide *noun, pl* ~ **Guides** [*count*] : a member of a worldwide organization for girls ages 7 through 18 that is similar to the Girl Scouts in the United States — called also *Guide*

girl·ie *also* **girly** /ˈgɚli/ *adj*

1 *always used before a noun* : featuring attractive young women who are wearing little or no clothing • a *girlie* show/magazine

2 : having a quality that is considered suitable for girls or

women and not suitable for men or boys • She likes to wear *girlie* pink dresses. • a *girlie* voice

Girl Scout *noun, pl* ~ **Scouts** [*count*] : a member of a U.S. organization for girls ages 5 through 17 ✧ Girl Scouts participate in group activities, learn skills, and are encouraged to have good morals and be good citizens. — called also *Scout*; compare BOY SCOUT, BROWNIE, CUB SCOUT, GIRL GUIDE

gi·ro /ˈʤiəˌoʊ, *Brit* ˈʤajəˌrəʊ/ *noun, pl* **-ros** [*count*] *Brit* : a check paid by the government to someone who is sick or does not have a job

girt *past participle of* GIRD

girth /ˈgəθ/ *noun, pl* **girths**

1 : the size of someone or something measured around the middle [*noncount*] The tree is about two meters in *girth*. • a person of large *girth* [*count*] a *girth* of about two meters

2 [*count*] : a band or strap placed around the body of an animal (such as a horse) to hold something (such as a saddle) on its back

gist /ˈʤɪst/ *noun*

the gist : the general or basic meaning of something said or written — usually + *of* • *The gist of* her argument was that the law was unfair. • I didn't read the whole article, but I ***got the gist of*** it. [=I understood the main points of it]

git /ˈgɪt/ *noun, pl* **gits** [*count*] *Brit slang* : a stupid or worthless person (especially a man) • That *git* of a brother of yours has ruined everything!

[1]**give** /ˈgɪv/ *verb* **gives**; **gave** /ˈgeɪv/; **giv·en** /ˈgɪvən/; **giv·ing**

1 [+ *obj*] **a** : to cause or allow someone to have (something) as a present : to make a present of (something) • She *gave* him a camera for Christmas. • Someone *gave* me a present. = Someone *gave* a present to me. = I was *given* a present. = A present was *given* (to) me. • Are you *giving* this to me or only lending it? **b** : to cause or allow (something valued or needed) to go to another person, group, etc. : DONATE [+ *obj*] She has *given* money to many worthy/good causes. • They're asking people to *give* money for a new hospital. • *give* blood [*no obj*] Please *give* to our charity. • We already *gave* at the office. • It is better to *give* than to receive.

2 [+ *obj*] : to put (something) into someone's hand • He picked up the letter and *gave* [=*handed*] it to me. • He *gave* me the letter. : to cause someone to hold or possess (something) for a specified reason • He *gave* me a letter to mail for him. = He *gave* a letter to me to mail for him. • He *gave* her his coat to hold.

3 [+ *obj*] **a** : to provide someone with (something wanted or needed) • She has *given* me a lot of help/support/encouragement. [=she has helped/supported/encouraged me a lot] • They *gave* me a job. [=they hired me] • He *gave* me a head start. • I'll *give* you a lift/ride to the station. [=I'll drive you to the station in my car] : to allow someone to have (something wanted or needed) • I know I can do it if you'll just *give* me a chance. • They *gave* her another opportunity. • Her boss has *given* her a lot of responsibility/authority. • They *gave* him the best room available. • The law *gives* all citizens the right to vote. = The law *gives* the right to vote to all citizens. **b** : to allow someone to have or take (an amount of time) • Just *give* me a few more minutes and I'll be ready. • The doctor *gave* him two weeks to pay his bill.

4 [+ *obj*] **a** : to treat or regard someone or something with (a particular attitude, feeling, etc.) • She *gave* her friend her complete confidence. = She *gave* her complete confidence to her friend. [=she trusted her friend completely] • He *gave* the company his loyalty. [=he was loyal to the company] • They've worked hard. You should *give* them some respect. [=you should respect them] **b** : to direct (something) toward someone • She *gave* him an angry look. [=she looked at him angrily] • He *gave* her a smile. [=he smiled at her]

5 [+ *obj*] **a** : to tell (information) to someone • Just *give* me the facts. • They weren't able to *give* us the information we needed. • The witness was reluctant to *give* evidence. • He *gave* his name as "John Smith." [=he said his name was "John Smith"] • The drawing *gives* [=*shows*] the dimensions of the room. • The book *gives* [=*provides*] a brief history of the industry. **b** : to express or say (something) to someone • You have no right to *give* me orders. • They *gave* him careful instructions on how to proceed. • *Give* them my regards. = *Give* my regards to them. • His parents *gave* him a lecture about the importance of studying. • The coach *gave* the team a pep talk. • I ***give you my word*** [=I swear; I promise], I knew nothing about their plans. • Just ***give it to me straight*** [=just say what you are going to say to me in a direct way] ✧ The informal phrase ***don't give me that*** is used in speech to show annoyance when someone tells you something that you do not believe or accept. • "It's not my fault that we're late." "*Don't give me that*! You were the one who said we didn't have to leave early!" **c** : to show (something) • a young artist who has *given* evidence/signs of real talent • She *gave* (us) no hint/indication that she was upset or worried. **d** : to offer (something) for consideration or acceptance • He declined to *give* an opinion. • Can you *give* an example? • He *gave* no reason for his absence.

6 [+ *obj*] : to say that someone has or deserves (something) • He *gives* the credit for his success to his wife. [=he credits his wife for his success]

7 [+ *obj*] **a** : to cause someone to have or experience (something, such as an emotion, a problem, etc.) • My car has been *giving* [=*causing*] me a lot of trouble lately. • I like Mexican food, but it *gives* me indigestion. • a book that *gives* pleasure to the reader • All that noise is *giving* me a headache. [=I'm getting a headache from all that noise] • It *gave* me a shock to see how sick he is. • Her encouragement *gave* me a lot of self-confidence. [=made me feel very self-confident] **b** : to cause someone to become affected by (something, such as an illness) • His sister *gave* him the measles. [=he got/caught the measles from his sister] • Hearing the joke *gave* him the giggles. [=hearing the joke made him giggle] **c** : to cause someone or something to have (a quality) • His quiet manner *gives* him a mysterious air. • The large windows *give* the room an open feeling. **d** : to cause something to be affected by (something) • He argues that the tax cuts would *give* a considerable stimulus/boost to the economy.

8 [+ *obj*] : to cause someone to get or take (a medicine) • The doctor *gave* the patient a pill. • The doctor *gave* him an injection. • The drug is usually *given* intravenously.

9 [+ *obj*] **a** : to present (a show, speech, etc.) in public • *give* a concert/lecture/talk/speech/reading/performance **b** : to provide (something) as entertainment or as a social gathering • *give* [=*throw*] a party • *give* a formal dinner

10 [+ *obj*] : to do (an action) • She *gave* the door a push. [=she pushed the door] • He *gave* her a hug. [=he hugged her] • He *gave* a cynical smile. [=he smiled cynically] • She picked up the package and *gave* it a shake. [=she shook the package] • The referee *gave* [=*made*] the signal to start the game. • The ship *gave* a sudden lurch. [=the ship lurched suddenly]

11 [+ *obj*] **a** : to cause someone to experience or suffer (a form of punishment) • His father *gave* the boy a whipping. • The judge *gave* him life (imprisonment) for murder. **b** : to cause someone to undergo or do (something) • The teacher *gave* the class a test.

12 ✧ To ***give something thought/consideration (etc.)*** is to think about it. • We've *given* your proposal a lot of thought and careful consideration. [=we've thought about your proposal a lot and considered it carefully]

13 ✧ To ***give someone a call/ring/buzz/bell*** is to make a telephone call to someone. • I'll *give you a call* later.

14 ✧ If you try to do something, you ***give it a try*** or (informally) ***give it a go/shot/stab***. • I've never gone skiing before, but I'm willing to *give it a try*.

15 ✧ If you would ***give anything*** or ***give your right hand/arm*** to do or to have something, you want to do or have it very much. • I'd *give anything* to be able to sing like that!

16 [+ *obj*] : to make (something, such as your hand) available for someone • She *gave* [=*offered*] her hand to him to shake/kiss. = She *gave* him her hand to shake/kiss. [=she held out her hand toward him so that he could shake/kiss it] • She *gave* him her arm [=she linked her arm in his arm] and they walked together into the room. ✧ When a woman ***gives her hand in marriage to*** a man, she marries him. This is a formal and somewhat old-fashioned expression.

17 [+ *obj*] **a** : PAY • I wouldn't *give* a penny for that old bike! • If you have an extra ticket, I'll *give* you $20 for it. **b** : SELL • I'm willing to *give* you the ticket for $20.

18 [+ *obj*] : to say or judge that someone or something will last for (an amount of time) • The doctor *gave* him only a few weeks to live. [=the doctor said that he would live for only a few weeks] • Their marriage will never work. I *give* it/them six months—tops!

19 [+ *obj*] *informal* : to admit (something) to or about someone • He made an effort, I'll *give* him that (much). [=I'll admit that he made an effort] • I don't really like his movies, but he's a talented actor, ***I'll give you that*** [=I admit that he is a talented actor]

20 [+ *obj*] : to have or produce (something) as a product, result, or effect • medical procedures that *give* better results • Cows *give* milk.

21 [+ *obj*] *formal* **:** to cause someone to believe or think (something) — followed by *to + verb* • They *gave* [=*led*] me *to understand* that they'd be arriving later. ✧ To ***give someone an idea/impression (etc.)*** is to cause someone to believe or think something. • Whatever *gave you the idea* (that) he loved you?! [=whatever made you think that he loved you?] • I'm sorry if I *gave you the wrong impression*. [=I'm sorry if I misled you; I'm sorry if you got the wrong impression from me] • I don't know what *gave her the notion* that she could treat people that way.

22 [*no obj*] **a :** to bend because of force, pressure, or strain • The branch *gave* [=*sagged*] under his weight, but it didn't break. **b :** to break because of force, pressure, or strain • The branch suddenly *gave* [=*gave way*] under his weight, and he fell to the ground.

23 [*no obj*] **:** to stop trying to resist or oppose something **:** to give in or submit to pressure • Both sides refuse to *give* [=refuse to accept or agree to the demands of the other side] in this dispute. • For the strike to be settled, ***something has (got) to give***! [=one side or the other has to give in]

24 [+ *obj*] **a** — used to indicate a possible or assumed state or condition • *Give* him his books and his music and he's happy. [=he is happy if he has his books and his music] • (If) *Given* better conditions, she'd do the work even better. = She'd do the work even better (if) *given* better conditions. = If she were *given* better conditions, she'd do the work even better. **b** — used to say what you want to have or would prefer to have • ". . . *give* me liberty, or *give* me death!" [=I would rather die than live without liberty] —Patrick Henry, Speech (1775) • The country's OK—but *give* me the city any day! [=I prefer the city]

25 [+ *obj*] *informal* — used in phrases like ***give a damn*** to say that you do not care at all about something • He angrily told her that he didn't *give a damn* what she did.

give as good as you get *informal* **:** to be as forceful in fighting or arguing against others as they are in fighting or arguing against you • She can *give as good as she gets* in an argument with just about anybody.

give away [*phrasal verb*] **1** ***give (something) away or give away (something)*** **a :** to make a present of (something) • For a limited time only our store is *giving away* [=*giving*] a free can of soda to each and every one of our customers! • Our prices are so cheap we're practically *giving away* everything in our store! **b :** to lose (something) in a careless way • He virtually *gave* the election *away* when he made a racist remark. • The pitcher *gave* the game *away* by walking four batters in a row. **c :** to allow (something hidden or secret) to become known • The way she looked at him *gave away* her real feelings for him. • Please don't *give away* [=*reveal*] how the trick is done. — see also GIVEAWAY, GIVEAWAY PRICE, *give the game away* at [1]GAME **2** ***give (someone) away also give away (someone)*** **a :** to bring (the bride) to the groom at a wedding • Traditionally, it's the father of the bride who *gives* his daughter *away* at the wedding. **b :** to reveal the truth about (someone) • His fellow conspirators *gave* him *away* to the police. [=they betrayed him to the police] • His accent *gave* him *away* as a northerner. [=his accent showed that he was a northerner]

give back [*phrasal verb*] ***give (something) back or give back (something)*** **:** to cause someone to have (something) again **:** to return or restore (something) to someone • He *gave back* the money he found to the person who'd lost it. • Her encouragement helped to *give* me *back* my self-confidence. [=her encouragement helped me to get my self-confidence back] • They agreed to *give* him his old job *back*. — see also GIVEBACK

give birth see BIRTH

give chase see [1]CHASE

give ground see [1]GROUND

give in [*phrasal verb*] **1 :** to stop trying to fight or resist something **:** to agree to do or accept something that you have been resisting or opposing • The strike has been going on for weeks, and neither side seems willing to *give in*. — often + *to* • He refused to *give in to* their demands. [=he refused to do what they demanded that he do] **2** ***give (something) in or give in (something) Brit*** **:** to give (something) to a person who has authority to review or accept it • *give in* [=(*US*) *hand in*] an assignment

give it a rest, give (something) a rest see [2]REST

give me a break, give (someone) a break see [2]BREAK

give of [*phrasal verb*] ***give of yourself or give of your time*** *formal* **:** to use your time and effort to help others • They freely *gave of their time* when their help was needed.

give off [*phrasal verb*] ***give off (something)*** **:** to send (light, energy, etc.) out from a source • The telescope can detect light *given off* [=*emitted*] by distant galaxies. • The garbage *gave off* an unpleasant smell. • The chimneys *gave off* thick, black smoke.

give on to also give onto [*phrasal verb*] ***give on to (something) also give onto (something) Brit*** **:** to provide a view of or a passage to (something) • The door *gives* directly *on to* the garden. • The rooms *give onto* a hall.

give or take — used to indicate that the stated amount is approximate and might be increased or decreased by a specified amount • He ran a mile, *give or take* a few yards. • The movie lasted three hours, *give or take* a few minutes either way. • (*informal*) He ran a mile, *give or take*. [=he ran about a mile]

give out [*phrasal verb*] **1 :** to stop working • The plane's engine sputtered and *gave out*, forcing an emergency landing. • His voice *gave out*. [=he was unable to talk] • His courage finally *gave out*. [=he lost his courage] **2 :** to become used up • Our supply of fuel had almost *given out* [=*run out*] entirely. **3** ***give out (something)*** **:** to produce (noise, light, etc.) • The brakes *gave out* a loud squeal. • The woodstove *gives out* a lot of heat. **4** ***give (something) out or give out (something)*** **:** to give (something) to many people **:** to hand out (something) • They *gave out* copies of the newsletter. • He's always *giving out* unwanted advice.

give over [*phrasal verb*] *Brit, informal* **:** to stop doing something that is annoying or unpleasant • Oh, *give over*! I'm tired of your complaints! — often + *-ing verb* • They eventually *gave over bothering* me [=stopped bothering me] and let me alone.

give over to [*phrasal verb*] ***give (something) over to (someone)*** **1 :** to give (something) to (someone) to have, use, do, etc. • She has *given* most of her work *over* to her assistant. **2** ***give (yourself) over to (something)*** **:** to allow (yourself) to be fully affected by, controlled by, or involved in (something) • He *gave himself over to* despair. [=he was overcome by despair] • She *gave herself over* completely *to* her work. [=she devoted all of her attention and energy to her work] **3** ✧ Something that is ***given over to*** a specified purpose is used for that purpose. • One of the upstairs rooms is *given over to* storage. • Much of her time recently has been *given over to* researching her family history.

give place to see [1]PLACE

give rise to see [2]RISE

give up [*phrasal verb*] **1 :** to stop an activity or effort **:** to admit that you cannot do something and stop trying **:** QUIT • He vowed that he would never *give up*. • I *give up*! I don't know what more I can do to please my girlfriend! • "How many prime numbers are there between 1 and 100? Well, do you *give up*?" "OK, I *give up*!" **2** ***give (something) up or give up (something)*** **a :** to stop having, doing, or using (something) • He was forced to *give up* his job. • She refused to *give up* trying. • My doctor urged me to *give up* smoking/cigarettes. • Rescuers have not yet *given up* hope that more survivors will be found. • He *gave up* his seat to an elderly woman. [=he got out of his seat so that an elderly woman could sit there] **b :** to stop trying to do (something) • We did our best to repair the engine, but in the end we had to *give it up* as impossible. **c** *sports* **:** to allow (a score, a hit, etc.) by an opposing team or player • The defense *gave up* two touchdowns in the first quarter. • The pitcher didn't *give up* a hit till the ninth inning. **3** ***give (yourself) up*** **:** to surrender (yourself) as a prisoner • The fugitive eventually *gave himself up* (to the police/authorities). **4** ***give (someone) up*** **a :** to stop trying to improve the condition of (someone) because it seems hopeless • The teacher *gave him up* as a hopeless case. • The doctors ***gave him up for dead***. [=the doctors said that he was certain to die] **b :** to stop having hope of seeing (someone) • We'd *given* you *up* (for lost) hours ago! **5** ***give (yourself) up to (something)*** **:** to allow (yourself) to be fully affected by, controlled by, or involved in (something) • He *gave himself up to* despair. • She *gave herself up* completely *to* her work. **6** ***give up on (someone)*** **a :** to stop trying to improve the condition of (someone) • He has gotten in trouble many times, but his parents have never *given up on* him. • Please don't *give up on* me. I promise I'll do better. **b :** to stop having hope of seeing (someone) • We'd *given up on* you hours ago! **7** ***give up on (something)*** **:** to stop trying to do or achieve (something) • They have *given up on* their plan to build a new factory. • She hasn't *given up on* trying to convince her husband to buy a new car.

give up the ghost see [1]GHOST

give way see [1]WAY

What gives? informal — used to ask the reason for something • You've been acting weird all week. *What gives?* [=why are you acting weird?]

[2]**give** *noun* [*noncount*] : the ability of a material to bend or stretch • This fabric has a lot of *give.* [=this fabric is very flexible]

give–and–take /ˌgɪvənˈteɪk/ *noun* [*noncount*]

1 : the process by which people reach an agreement with each other by giving up something that was wanted and agreeing to some of the things wanted by the other person • A successful marriage requires a lot of *give-and-take* between husband and wife.

2 *US* : the act or process of exchanging ideas or comments • She enjoys a lot of friendly *give-and-take* with her customers.

give·away /ˈgɪvəˌweɪ/ *noun, pl* **-aways**

1 [*singular*] : something (such as a movement or a facial expression) that clearly shows the truth or existence of something that had not been known • The way she looked at him was a ***dead giveaway*** that they were more than just friends.

2 [*count*] **a** : something that is given away free • The store is offering coffee mugs as free *giveaways* to attract new customers. **b** : an event at which things are given away • The store is staging a promotional *giveaway* to attract new customers. — see also *give away* at [1]GIVE

giveaway price *noun, pl* ~ **prices** [*count*] : a very low price • We're selling everything in our store at low, low *giveaway prices.*

give·back /ˈgɪvˌbæk/ *noun, pl* **-backs** [*count*] *US, business* : a previous gain (such as increased wages or benefits) that is given back to a company by workers as part of an agreement • The union had to agree to certain *givebacks* in order to save the jobs of all its members. — see also *give back* at [1]GIVE

[1]**given** /ˈgɪvən/ *adj* — used to refer to a particular time, place, etc., that has been, will be, or might be specified • You'll have to finish the exam within a *given* (amount of) time. • They agreed to meet again at a *given* location. • Climate has a great effect on the types of plants found in any *given* area. • You never know what might happen on any *given* night.

given to — used to say that a person often behaves in a specified way • a man (very) much *given to* swearing/profanity [=a man who swears often] • She is *given to* behaving selfishly. = She is *given to* selfishness.

take (something) as given : to regard or accept (something) as true or real • I think we can *take* their support *as given.* = I think we can *take* (it) *as given* that they will support us. [=I think we can assume that they will support us]

[2]**given** *noun, pl* **-ens** [*count*] : something that is regarded or accepted as true or real : a basic fact or assumption • In our system it is a *given* that all are equal before the law. • I think we can ***take (it) as a given*** that they will support us.

[3]**given** *prep* — used to indicate something that is being assumed or considered • *Given* the bad conditions under which the work was done, she has done it very well. = *Given* the fact that the work was done under bad conditions, she has done it very well. • *Given* a value of 5 for x, what is 2x? — often used in the phrase ***given that*** • Even *given that* the house is not in perfect condition, it's still a great buy!

given name *noun, pl* ~ **names** [*count*] *US* : FIRST NAME

giv·er /ˈgɪvɚ/ *noun, pl* **-ers** [*count*] : someone who gives something to another person • a *giver* of orders • a *giver* of unwanted advice — often used in combination • care*givers*

giz·mo /ˈgɪzˌmoʊ/ *noun, pl* **-mos** [*count*] *informal* : a usually small mechanical or electronic device : GADGET • He broke the *gizmo* he uses to open and close his garage door.

giz·zard /ˈgɪzɚd/ *noun, pl* **-zards** [*count*] : a part in the stomach of a bird in which food is broken down into small pieces

gla·cial /ˈgleɪʃəl/ *adj*

1 : of or relating to glaciers • *glacial* flow/ice : produced or caused by glaciers • a *glacial* lake • *glacial* erosion

2 [*more ~; most ~*] : very cold : FRIGID • a *glacial* wind — sometimes used figuratively • a *glacial* stare

3 [*more ~; most ~*] : very slow • Progress on the bill has been *glacial.* • a *glacial* pace

— **gla·cial·ly** *adv* • *glacially* slow progress

gla·cier /ˈgleɪʃɚ, *Brit* ˈglæsiə/ *noun, pl* **-ciers** [*count*] : a very large area of ice that moves slowly down a slope or valley or over a wide area of land

glad /ˈglæd/ *adj* **glad·der; -dest** [*also more ~; most ~*]

1 *not used before a noun* : feeling pleasure, joy, or delight • We're *glad* [=*happy*] that he won. • We're *glad* you could come. • I'm *glad* (that) things turned out so well. = I'm *glad* about how things turned out. — sometimes + *of* • She was *glad of* [=*grateful for*] the help her brother provided. — sometimes + *for* • I'm *glad for* the chance to help. — sometimes followed by *to* + *verb* • I'm so *glad to see* you! • I'm *glad to have* the chance to help.

2 *not used before a noun* : very willing *to do* something • I'll be *glad to answer* any questions you may have. • I'd be (only too) *glad to lend* you the money.

3 *always used before a noun, old-fashioned* : causing happiness and joy : PLEASANT • The mail brought *glad* news/tidings from our friends in England. • We've been through some sad times and some *glad* times.

— **glad·ly** *adv* • I'll *gladly* answer any questions you may have. • "Will you take questions from the audience?" "*Gladly!*" — **glad·ness** *noun* [*noncount*] • The news of their wedding fills my heart with *gladness.*

glad·den /ˈglædn̩/ *verb* **-dens; -dened; -den·ing** [+ *obj*] *old-fashioned* : to make (someone) glad • We were *gladdened* by the news. = It *gladdened* us to hear the news. • Her news will ***gladden the hearts*** of her family and friends. [=will make her family and friends happy]

glade /ˈgleɪd/ *noun, pl* **glades** [*count*] : a grassy open space in a forest

glad–hand /ˈglædˌhænd/ *verb* **-hands; -hand·ed; -hand·ing** [+ *obj*] : to give a friendly welcome or greeting to (people) as a way of getting approval • politicians *glad-handing* voters

glad·i·a·tor /ˈglædiˌeɪtɚ/ *noun, pl* **-tors** [*count*] : a man in ancient Rome who fought against another man or animal for public entertainment

— **glad·i·a·to·ri·al** /ˌglædijəˈtorijəl/ *adj* • *gladiatorial* combat

glad·i·o·lus /ˌglædiˈoʊləs/ *noun, pl* **glad·i·o·li** /ˌglædiˈoʊli/ *or* **glad·i·o·lus·es** *or US* **gladiolus** [*count*] : a plant with long, stiff leaves and brightly colored flowers

glad rags *noun* [*plural*] *chiefly Brit, informal + old-fashioned* : a person's best clothes • He put on his *glad rags* to go to the party.

glam /ˈglæm/ *adj* [*more ~; most ~*] *informal* : GLAMOROUS • *glam* celebrities

glam·or·ize *also Brit* **glam·or·ise** /ˈglæməˌraɪz/ *verb* **-iz·es; -ized; -iz·ing** [+ *obj*] : to make (something) seem exciting and attractive • The movie was criticized for *glamorizing* crime and violence. • a novel that *glamorizes* war

glam·or·ous /ˈglæmərəs/ *adj* [*more ~; most ~*] : very exciting and attractive : full of glamour • She looked *glamorous* in her formal black gown. • She wore a *glamorous* black gown. • *glamorous* movie stars • A private investigator's job isn't as *glamorous* as people think.

— **glam·or·ous·ly** *adv*

glam·our *also US* **glam·or** /ˈglæmɚ/ *noun* [*noncount*] : a very exciting and attractive quality • She left her hometown, attracted to the *glamour* of the big city. • an acting career filled with glitz and *glamour* • the *glamour* of the movie business • She's a serious actress and not just another ***glamour girl*** [=a beautiful woman who wears sexy and attractive clothing and makeup] • He's one of the ***glamour boys*** of the football league. [=he's a very popular and attractive player who gets a lot of attention]

glam·our–puss /ˈglæmɚˌpʊs/ *noun, pl* **-puss·es** [*count*] *informal + disapproving* : a person (especially a woman) who is very attractive but not talented, smart, serious, etc. • a self-absorbed *glamour-puss* • a *glamour-puss* celebrity

[1]**glance** /ˈglæns, *Brit* ˈglɑːns/ *verb* **glanc·es; glanced; glanc·ing** [*no obj*]

1 *always followed by an adverb or preposition* : to look at someone or something very quickly • *Glancing* down, she noticed her shoe was untied. • I *glanced* at my watch. • He sat quietly, *glancing* through a magazine. • She *glanced* up from her book when he entered the room.

2 : to hit something and bounce off at an angle — usually + *off* • The arrow *glanced off* the shield. • Sunlight *glanced off* the surface of the pond.

— **glanc·ing** /ˈglænsɪŋ, *Brit* ˈglɑːnsɪŋ/ *adj, always used before a noun* • A rock struck the windshield with a ***glancing blow.*** [=a rock glanced off the windshield]

²glance *noun, pl* **glances** [*count*] **:** a quick look ▪ They exchanged *glances.* [=looked at each other quickly] ▪ He gave me a quick/passing *glance* over his shoulder. ▪ I took/had a *glance* at the newspaper this morning. ▪ He stole/darted a *glance* at her [=he looked at her quickly] as she walked by.
at a glance **:** with a quick look ▪ She was able to identify the problem *at a glance.*
at first glance see ¹FIRST

gland /ˈglænd/ *noun, pl* **glands** [*count*] **:** an organ in the body that makes a substance (such as saliva, sweat, or bile) which is used by the body ▪ sweat *glands* ▪ the pituitary *gland*

glan·du·lar /ˈglænʤələ/ *adj* **:** of or relating to glands ▪ *glandular* activity/cancer

glandular fever *noun* [*noncount*] *chiefly Brit, medical* **:** MONONUCLEOSIS

¹glare /ˈgleɚ/ *verb* **glares; glared; glar·ing** [*no obj*]
1 : to shine with a harsh, bright light ▪ The sun *glared* down relentlessly. ▪ The white snow *glared* in the morning sunlight.
2 : to look directly at someone in an angry way ▪ The teacher *glared* at him as he walked in late. ***synonyms*** see ¹GAZE

²glare *noun, pl* **glares**
1 : a harsh, bright light [*singular*] There was a *glare* coming off the water. [*noncount*] I was blinded by the *glare* of the approaching headlights. ▪ I shielded my eyes from/against the *glare* of the sun. ▪ The car's headlights are designed to cut down on *glare.* — sometimes used figuratively to suggest the idea of a very bright light shining on someone who is being given a lot of public attention ▪ He grew tired of living in the *glare* of the television cameras. ▪ After the success of her first film, she could not escape ***the glare of publicity.***
2 [*count*] **:** an angry look ▪ She responded to the reporters' questions with an angry/icy *glare.*

glaring /ˈglerɪŋ/ *adj*
1 [*more ~; most ~*] **:** very obvious or noticeable ▪ a *glaring* mistake/error/omission ▪ a *glaring* example of racism
2 : shining with a harsh, bright light ▪ the *glaring* noonday sun
3 : having a look of anger ▪ *glaring* eyes
– **glar·ing·ly** *adv* ▪ a *glaringly* obvious mistake

¹glass /ˈglæs, *Brit* ˈglɑːs/ *noun, pl* **glass·es**
1 [*noncount*] **:** a hard usually transparent material that is used for making windows and other products ▪ He broke the *glass.* — often used before another noun ▪ a *glass* bowl/bottle — see also PLATE GLASS, STAINED GLASS
2 [*count*] **a :** a drinking container made out of glass ▪ The waiter filled our *glasses* with water. ▪ an elegant wine *glass* ✧ The expression ***raise a glass*** or ***raise your glasses*** is used to tell people to hold up their glasses and drink a toast as a way to wish someone happiness, success, etc. **b :** the amount held by a glass container ▪ She drank two *glasses* of water.
3 ***glasses*** [*plural*] **:** a pair of glass or plastic lenses set into a frame and worn over the eyes to help a person see ▪ I have to wear *glasses* [=*spectacles,* (*US*) *eyeglasses*] for reading. ▪ I have to wear reading *glasses.* ▪ She was wearing dark *glasses* with thick black frames. ▪ horn-rimmed *glasses* — see also FIELD GLASSES, MAGNIFYING GLASS, OPERA GLASSES
people who live in glass houses shouldn't throw stones — used to say that people who have faults should not criticize other people for having the same faults
under glass **:** in a glass container ▪ Most of the articles in the museum are preserved *under glass.*
– see also HOURGLASS, LOOKING GLASS
– **glass·ful** /ˈglæsˌfʊl, *Brit* ˈglɑːsˌfʊl/ *noun, pl* **-fuls** [*count*] ▪ had another *glassful* [=more commonly, *glass*] of beer

²glass *verb* **glasses; glassed; glass·ing** [+ *obj*] **:** to fit, protect, or enclose (something) with glass — usually + *in* ▪ The porch is *glassed in.*

glass·blow·ing /ˈglæsˌblowɪŋ, *Brit* ˈglɑːsˌbləwɪŋ/ *noun* [*noncount*] **:** the art of shaping a piece of hot, melted glass by blowing air into it through a tube
– **glass·blow·er** /ˈglæsˌblowɚ, *Brit* ˈglɑːsˌbləwə/ *noun, pl* **-ers** [*count*]

glass ceiling *noun, pl* **~ -ings** [*count*] **:** an unfair system or set of attitudes that prevents some people (such as women or people of a certain race) from getting the most powerful jobs — usually singular ▪ women executives trying to break through the *glass ceiling*

glass·mak·er /ˈglæsˌmeɪkɚ, *Brit* ˈglɑːsˌmeɪkə/ *noun, pl* **-ers** [*count*] **:** a person who makes glass

glass·ware /ˈglæsˌweɚ, *Brit* ˈglɑːsˌweə/ *noun* [*noncount*] **:** things made of glass ▪ a cabinet that holds *glassware*

glassy /ˈglæsi, *Brit* ˈglɑːsi/ *adj* **glass·i·er; -est**
1 : smooth and shiny **:** resembling glass ▪ the *glassy* surface of the lake ▪ a hard, *glassy* substance
2 : not shiny or bright **:** dull and lifeless ▪ *glassy* eyes ▪ He was gazing out the window with a *glassy* stare.

glau·co·ma /glaʊˈkoʊmə, glɑˈkoʊmə/ *noun* [*noncount*] *medical* **:** a disease in which pressure inside the eye causes gradual loss of vision

¹glaze /ˈgleɪz/ *verb* **glaz·es; glazed; glaz·ing**
1 [+ *obj*] **:** to give a smooth and shiny coating to (something) ▪ The storm *glazed* the trees with ice. ▪ *Glaze* the tart with melted jam. ▪ *glazed* ceramic pots ▪ a *glazed* doughnut [=a doughnut with a smooth, sugary coating]
2 [*no obj*] **:** to become dull and lifeless — usually + *over* ▪ His eyes *glazed over* [=he began to look very bored and tired] as the speech droned on.

²glaze *noun, pl* **glazes :** a liquid mixture that is put on the surface of something and that becomes shiny and smooth when it is dry [*count*] The pot is covered with a bright red *glaze.* ▪ doughnuts with a chocolate *glaze* [*noncount*] The pot needs more *glaze.*

gla·zier /ˈgleɪʒɚ, *Brit* ˈgleɪziə/ *noun, pl* **-ziers** [*count*] **:** a person who puts glass in window frames

¹gleam /ˈgliːm/ *noun, pl* **gleams**
1 [*count*] **:** a small, bright light ▪ He saw the *gleam* of a flashlight in the distance.
2 [*singular*] **:** a bright or shining quality ▪ the rich *gleam* of the polished wood
3 [*count*] **:** a small amount or sign of something ▪ a *gleam* [=*glimmer*] of hope
4 [*count*] **:** a small amount of emotion (such as happiness or excitement) that can be seen in someone's eyes ▪ Her father had a *gleam* in his eyes as he told the story.

²gleam *verb* **gleams; gleamed; gleam·ing** [*no obj*] **:** to shine brightly ▪ The sun *gleamed* on the water. ▪ His eyes were *gleaming* with delight.

glean /ˈgliːn/ *verb* **gleans; gleaned; glean·ing**
1 [+ *obj*] **a :** to gather or collect (something) in a gradual way ▪ She *gleaned* her data from various studies. ▪ He has a collection of antique tools *gleaned* from flea markets and garage sales. **b :** to search (something) carefully ▪ They spent days *gleaning* the files for information.
2 : to gather grain or other material that is left after the main crop has been gathered [*no obj*] They spent hours *gleaning* in the wheat fields. [+ *obj*] *gleaning* stray ears of corn ▪ *gleaning* a vineyard
– **glean·er** *noun, pl* **-ers** [*count*]

glean·ings /ˈgliːnɪŋz/ *noun* [*plural*] **:** information, grain, etc., that is gathered ▪ the *gleanings* of long hours of research

glee /ˈgliː/ *noun* [*noncount*] **:** a strong feeling of happiness **:** great pleasure or satisfaction ▪ They were dancing with/in *glee.* ▪ He could hardly contain his *glee* over his victory.
– **glee·ful** /ˈgliːfəl/ *adj* [*more ~; most ~*] ▪ a *gleeful* smile
– **glee·ful·ly** /ˈgliːfəli/ *adv* ▪ smiling *gleefully*

glee club *noun, pl* **~ clubs** [*count*] **:** a group of people who sing together especially as a social activity in a school or college

glen /ˈglɛn/ *noun, pl* **glens** [*count*] **:** a narrow valley

glib /ˈglɪb/ *adj* **glib·ber; -best** [*also more ~; most ~*] *disapproving*
1 : said or done too easily or carelessly **:** showing little preparation or thought ▪ Politicians need to do more than provide *glib* answers to difficult questions. ▪ *glib* generalizations ▪ the actor's *glib* portrayal of a drug addict
2 : speaking in a smooth, easy way that is not sincere ▪ *glib* politicians
– **glib·ly** *adv* ▪ He talks *glibly* of returning to school, but I know he doesn't have the discipline. – **glib·ness** *noun* [*noncount*]

glide /ˈglaɪd/ *verb* **glides; glid·ed; glid·ing**
1 *always followed by an adverb or preposition* [*no obj*] **:** to move in a smooth way ▪ The swans *glided* over the surface of the lake. ▪ We watched the skiers *glide* down the slope.
2 *of an airplane* **:** to fly without engine power [*no obj*] The pilot/plane *glided* to a safe landing after the engine failed. [+ *obj*] The pilot *glided* the plane to a safe landing.
– **glide** *noun* [*singular*] ▪ the graceful *glide* of the swan ▪ The plane went into a *glide.*

glid·er /ˈglaɪdɚ/ *noun, pl* **-ers** [*count*] **:** an aircraft that is similar to an airplane but without an engine — compare HANG GLIDER

¹glim·mer /ˈglɪmɚ/ *noun, pl* **-mers** [*count*]
1 : a weak, unsteady light ▪ the *glimmer* of a distant star

G

2 a : a faint idea or suggestion of something ▪ Their first meeting with the new boss gave them a *glimmer* of what they could expect. **b** : a small amount or sign of something ▪ a *glimmer* of light ▪ a *glimmer* of hope ▪ I saw a *glimmer* [=*glint*] of recognition in her eyes.

²glimmer *verb* **-mers; -mered; -mer·ing** [*no obj*] : to shine in a weak, faint, or unsteady way ▪ Candles *glimmered* in the windows of the inn. ▪ Moonlight *glimmered* on the pond. ▪ *glimmering* light

glim·mer·ing /ˈglɪmərɪŋ/ *noun, pl* **-ings** [*count*] : GLIMMER ▪ a faint *glimmering* of light ▪ *glimmerings* of hope

¹glimpse /ˈglɪmps/ *verb* **glimps·es; glimpsed; glimps·ing** [+ *obj*] : to look at or see (something or someone) for a very short time ▪ We *glimpsed* him through the window as his car sped past. — sometimes used figuratively ▪ The book allows us to *glimpse* the future of the computer industry.

²glimpse *noun, pl* **glimpses** [*count*] : a brief or quick view or look ▪ We caught/got/had a *glimpse* of him through the window as his car sped past. ▪ my first *glimpse* of [=my first look at] the city — often used figuratively ▪ The book offers a *glimpse* into the future of the computer industry.

¹glint /ˈglɪnt/ *verb* **glints; glint·ed; glint·ing** [*no obj*] : to shine in small bright flashes ▪ The sun *glinted* off the tops of the waves. ▪ The waves *glinted* in the sunlight.

²glint *noun, pl* **glints** [*count*]
1 : a small flash of light ▪ He saw *glints* of sunlight on the river's surface.
2 : a small amount of emotion seen in a person's eyes ▪ I thought I detected a *glint* [=*glimmer*] of recognition when I met her. ▪ He had a playful *glint* in his eyes. = He had a *glint* of playfulness in his eyes.

glis·ten /ˈglɪsn̩/ *verb* **-tens; -tened; -ten·ing** [*no obj*] : to shine with light reflected off a wet surface ▪ Rain made the streets *glisten*. ▪ The streets *glistened* in the rain. ▪ Her eyes *glistened* with tears/emotion. ▪ a long beach of *glistening* sand

glitch /ˈglɪʧ/ *noun, pl* **glitch·es** [*count*] *informal* : an unexpected and usually minor problem ▪ *Glitches* in the speaker's schedule caused some delays.; *especially* : a minor problem with a machine or device (such as a computer) ▪ A technical *glitch* caused a temporary shutdown. ▪ computer/software *glitches*

¹glit·ter /ˈglɪtɚ/ *verb* **-ters; -tered; -ter·ing** [*no obj*] : to shine brightly : to shine with bright points of light ▪ The sequins on her dress *glittered* in the sun. ▪ Her eyes *glittered* with intelligence and amusement.

²glitter *noun* [*noncount*]
1 : light that shines in small, bright points ▪ the *glitter* of diamonds
2 : an appealing, fancy, and exciting quality : a glamorous quality ▪ He was drawn to the *glitter* of the city's nightlife.
3 : small, shiny objects used to decorate a surface
— **glit·tery** /ˈglɪtəri/ *adj* [*more* ~; *most* ~] ▪ a *glittery* gown/nightclub

glit·te·ra·ti /ˌglɪtəˈrɑːti/ *noun* [*plural*] *informal* : people who are famous, wealthy, and attractive — usually used with *the* ▪ She's frequently seen at parties attended by *the* Hollywood *glitterati*. ▪ His new restaurant is popular among *the glitterati*.

glittering *adj* [*more* ~; *most* ~]
1 : shining brightly ▪ *glittering* stars
2 a : very attractive or appealing in a fancy or exciting way ▪ The party was attended by a *glittering* array of celebrities. ▪ *glittering* prizes **b** *chiefly Brit* : very successful or impressive ▪ a *glittering* triumph ▪ a *glittering* career

glitz /ˈglɪts/ *noun* [*noncount*] *often disapproving* : a very fancy and attractive quality that is associated with rich or famous people ▪ She grew tired of the *glitz* and glamour of Hollywood life. ▪ The casino was all *glitz*.
— **glitzy** /ˈglɪtsi/ *adj* **glitz·i·er; -est** ▪ a *glitzy* casino

gloam·ing /ˈgloʊmɪŋ/ *noun*
the gloaming *literary* : the low light that is seen in the evening as the sun sets ▪ Fireflies twinkled in *the gloaming*. [=in the twilight; at dusk]

gloat /ˈgloʊt/ *verb* **gloats; gloat·ed; gloat·ing** [*no obj*] : to show in an improper or selfish way that you are happy with your own success or another person's failure ▪ After such a tough campaign, they're *gloating* over their victory in the election. ▪ All right, you won. There's no need to *gloat* (about it). ▪ a *gloating* remark/look
— **gloat·ing·ly** *adv* ▪ They spoke *gloatingly* about their victory.

glob /ˈglɑːb/ *noun, pl* **globs** [*count*] *informal* : a large, round drop of something soft or wet : BLOB ▪ A *glob* of ice cream was stuck to his mustache. ▪ *globs* of whipped cream

glob·al /ˈgloʊbəl/ *adj*
1 : involving the entire world ▪ the *global* economy ▪ *global* fame ▪ English is becoming a *global* language.
2 : involving all of something and especially a computer system, file, etc. ▪ The program allows users to do *global* searches through all the available data.
— **glob·al·ly** /ˈgloʊbəli/ *adv* ▪ The game will be televised *globally*. [=throughout the world] ▪ a *globally* recognized problem

glob·al·ize *also Brit* **glob·al·ise** /ˈgloʊbəˌlaɪz/ *verb* **-iz·es; -ized; -iz·ing**
1 [+ *obj*] : to make (something) cover, involve, or affect the entire world ▪ The economy has become *globalized*. ▪ *globalize* a company's operations
2 [*no obj*] *of a business* : to begin to operate throughout the world ▪ The company is planning to *globalize*.
— **glob·al·i·za·tion** *also Brit* **glob·al·i·sa·tion** /ˌgloʊbələˈzeɪʃən, *Brit* ˌgləʊbəˌlaɪˈzeɪʃən/ *noun* [*noncount*] ▪ the *globalization* of the economy/company

global village *noun* [*singular*] : the world seen as a community in which people are connected by computers, television, etc., and all depend on one another

global warming *noun* [*noncount*] : the recent increase in the world's temperature that is believed to be caused by the increase of certain gases (such as carbon dioxide) in the atmosphere ▪ World leaders will address the problem of *global warming*. — compare GREENHOUSE EFFECT

globe /ˈgloʊb/ *noun, pl* **globes**
1 [*count*] : an object that is shaped like a large ball with a map of the world on it ▪ She has a *globe* in her office.
2 ***the globe*** : the earth ▪ satellites circling *the globe* ▪ His fame has spread around *the globe*.
3 [*count*] : a round object : SPHERE ▪ The tree was decorated with colorful glass *globes*.
— **glob·u·lar** /ˈglɑːbjəlɚ/ *adj* ▪ *globular* [=*round*] fruit ▪ a *globular* shape

globe–trot·ter /ˈgloʊbˌtrɑːtɚ/ *noun, pl* **-ters** [*count*] : a person who frequently travels to different places around the world
— **globe–trot·ting** /ˈgloʊbˌtrɑːtɪŋ/ *noun* [*noncount*] ▪ a life of *globe-trotting* — **globe–trotting** *adj* ▪ a *globe-trotting* diplomat

glob·ule /ˈglɑːˌbjuːl/ *noun, pl* **-ules** [*count*] : a tiny ball of something (such as a thick liquid) ▪ *globules* of fat/mercury

glock·en·spiel /ˈglɑːkənˌʃpiːl/ *noun, pl* **-spiels** [*count*] : a musical instrument that has a line of flat metal bars of different sizes that are hit with two special sticks

glom /ˈglɑːm/ *verb* **gloms; glommed; glom·ming** [+ *obj*] *US, informal* : to take or get (something) ▪ The book consists of a collection of humorous essays *glommed* [=*taken*] from popular magazines.
glom on to or glom onto [*phrasal verb*] ***glom on to (something or someone) or glom onto (something or someone)***
1 : to take (something) for your own use ▪ He *glommed on to* other people's ideas as if they were his own. **2** : to become strongly attached to or associated with (someone or something) ▪ The coating *gloms on to* the plastic during heating. ▪ He *glommed onto* me at the party, and I was stuck talking to him all night. **3** : to become aware of (something) ▪ Other businesses have not yet *glommed on to* the potential of this new technology.

gloom /ˈgluːm/ *noun* [*noncount*]
1 : partial or total darkness ▪ The painting captures the *gloom* of a foggy night. ▪ He walked away, disappearing into the *gloom*. ▪ the *gloom* of the forest
2 : a feeling of sadness ▪ He was often subject to periods of *gloom*. ▪ A cloud of *gloom* has descended over the city. ▪ The papers are filled with stories of ***gloom and doom***. [=with sad and tragic stories]

gloomy /ˈgluːmi/ *adj* **gloom·i·er; -est** [*also more* ~; *most* ~]
1 : somewhat dark ▪ a *gloomy* hallway : not bright or sunny ▪ We've had a week of *gloomy* weather.
2 : causing feelings of sadness ▪ The news continues to be *gloomy*. ▪ a *gloomy* landscape : not hopeful or promising ▪ She doesn't agree with their *gloomy* economic forecasts. ▪ His book paints a *gloomy* picture of the prospects for peace.
3 : sad or depressed ▪ I've never seen you looking so *gloomy*.
— **gloom·i·ly** /ˈgluːməli/ *adv* ▪ They *gloomily* surveyed the fire damage. — **gloom·i·ness** /ˈgluːminəs/ *noun* [*noncount*] ▪ the *gloominess* of the hallway/weather/future

glop /ˈglɑːp/ *noun, pl* **glops** *chiefly US, informal* : a thick, wet mixture or quantity of something unpleasant [*noncount*] I remember the *glop* they used to feed us for school lunch. [*count*] She always puts big *glops* [=*globs*] of ketchup on her fries.
– **glop·py** /ˈglɑːpi/ *adj* **glop·pi·er; -est** • a *gloppy* mess

glorified *adj, always used before a noun* — used to say that someone or something that seems to be impressive is actually not very important, powerful, etc. • His title is Assistant to the Director, but he's really just a *glorified* errand boy.

glo·ri·fy /ˈglorəˌfaɪ/ *verb* **-fies; -fied; -fy·ing** [+ *obj*]
1 : to honor or praise (a god or goddess) • *Glorify* and give thanks to God.
2 : to make (something) seem much better or more important than it really is • The film *glorifies* violence. [=the film makes violence seem exciting or appealing]
– **glo·ri·fi·ca·tion** /ˌglorəfəˈkeɪʃən/ *noun* [*noncount*] • Critics object to the film's *glorification* of violence.

glo·ri·ous /ˈglorijəs/ *adj* [*more* ~; *most* ~]
1 : having or deserving glory, fame, or honor • He had a long and *glorious* military career. • The old ruins give only a hint of the city's *glorious* past. • The government has described the battle as a *glorious* victory.
2 : very beautiful or delightful • Our room had a *glorious* view of the mountains. • a *glorious* sunset • *glorious* music • What a *glorious* day!
– **glo·ri·ous·ly** *adv* • a *gloriously* beautiful sunset — sometimes used for emphasis • They were all *gloriously* [=*extremely*] drunk. – **glo·ri·ous·ness** *noun* [*noncount*]

[1]**glo·ry** /ˈglori/ *noun, pl* **-ries**
1 [*noncount*] **a** : public praise, honor, and fame • As a young soldier he dreamed of winning military *glory*. • He now has only a few trophies to remind him of the *glory* of his athletic career. • He claimed that everything he did was done for the ***greater glory*** of his country. [=was done to bring honor to his country] • Neither candidate has exactly ***covered himself in/with glory*** [=neither candidate has been very successful or impressive] during this campaign. • They are ***basking in the glory*** of their success. [=they are enjoying the attention that has been given to them because of their success] — see also REFLECTED GLORY **b** : praise of a god or goddess • Let us give *glory* to God. • *Glory* be to God.
2 [*count*] : something that brings praise or fame to someone or something : something that is a source of great pride • The *glory* of the town is its fountain. • an art exhibit showing off the *glories* of ancient civilizations • He intends this movie to be the ***crowning glory*** [=the final, most successful part or achievement] of his career as a filmmaker.
3 [*noncount*] **a** : a state of great happiness or satisfaction • When she's on stage, she's ***in her glory***. [=she is at her best; she is most happy] **b** : a state of great success or beauty • The new owners are trying to restore the company/building to its former *glory*. • The beautiful art reminds us of the *glory* of the empire. • The autumn leaves are ***in their glory*** now. [=they are at their most beautiful stage now] • He was there ***in all his glory***. [=he was there looking very well or impressive]
glory be! *old-fashioned* — used to express surprise or happiness • You're pregnant? Well, *glory be*!
glory days/years : a time in the past that is remembered for great success or happiness • The team's *glory days* are long gone. • His *glory years* as an actor are now far behind him.
go to (your) glory *old-fashioned* : to die • remembering those who have *gone to their glory*
no guts, no glory see [1]GUT
– see also MORNING GLORY

[2]**glory** *verb* **-ries; -ried; -ry·ing**
glory in [*phrasal verb*] ***glory in (something)*** : to feel or show great joy or pleasure because of (something) • They *gloried in* their country's success.

[1]**gloss** /ˈglɑːs/ *noun*
1 [*singular*] : the brightness of a smooth and shiny surface • He polished the car to a high *gloss*. [=until it was very shiny]
2 : an attractive quality or appearance that hides the way a person or thing really is [*noncount*] He was all *gloss* and no substance. [*singular*] Her ruthless ambition was covered by a thin *gloss* of good manners.
3 [*noncount*] : a type of makeup that is used to add shine and often color to the lips • lip *gloss*
– compare [3]GLOSS

[2]**gloss** *verb* **gloss·es; glossed; gloss·ing**
gloss over [*phrasal verb*] ***gloss over (something)*** : to treat or describe (something, such as a serious problem or error) as if it were not important • He *glossed over* the accident. • The problems were ignored or *glossed over*.
– compare [4]GLOSS

[3]**gloss** *noun, pl* **glosses** [*count*] : a brief explanation of the meaning of a word used in a text • The book's introductory chapters include helpful *glosses* for/of many unfamiliar terms. — compare [1]GLOSS

[4]**gloss** *verb* **glosses; glossed; glossing** [+ *obj*] : to give the meaning of (a word or phrase used in a text) • Many unfamiliar terms are *glossed* in the book's introduction. • Scholars have *glossed* this term as (meaning) "chisel." — compare [2]GLOSS

glos·sa·ry /ˈglɑːsəri/ *noun, pl* **-ries** [*count*]
1 : a list that gives definitions of the hard or unusual words found in a book
2 : a dictionary of the special terms in a particular field or job

[1]**glossy** /ˈglɑːsi/ *adj* **gloss·i·er; -est** [*also more* ~; *most* ~] : having a shiny, smooth surface • a *glossy* magazine cover • *glossy* paint • a plant with *glossy* green leaves
– **gloss·i·ness** *noun* [*noncount*]

[2]**glossy** *noun, pl* **gloss·ies** [*count*]
1 : a photograph with a shiny surface • an 8x10 [=8-inch by 10-inch] *glossy*
2 *chiefly Brit* : a popular magazine that is printed on smooth and shiny paper — usually plural • The *glossies* were filled with stories about his affair.

glottal stop *noun, pl* ~ **stops** [*count*] *linguistics* : a speech sound made by briefly stopping the flow of air through the vocal cords

glot·tis /ˈglɑːtəs/ *noun, pl* **-tis·es** [*count*] *medical* : the opening between the vocal cords in your throat
– **glot·tal** /ˈglɑːtl/ *adj*

glove /ˈglʌv/ *noun, pl* **gloves** [*count*]
1 : a covering for the hand that has separate parts for each finger • a pair of *gloves* • latex/leather/rubber *gloves* — compare MITTEN; see also KID GLOVES
2 a *baseball* : a padded leather covering for the hand that is used to catch the ball and that has individual thumb and finger sections • a fielder's *glove* — compare MITT **b** : a very thick, padded covering for the hand that is worn in the sport of boxing • a boxing *glove* — often used figuratively in the phrases ***take off the gloves*** and ***the gloves are off*** to say that people are beginning to criticize or attack each other in a very harsh and direct way • The candidates have *taken off the gloves* and started to make personal attacks against each other. • It's the end of the campaign, and *the gloves are off*.
fit (you) like a glove see [2]FIT
hand in glove see [1]HAND
– **gloved** /ˈglʌvd/ *adj* • a *gloved* hand [=a hand wearing a glove]

glove compartment *noun, pl* ~ **-ments** [*count*] : a small storage area in front of the front seat of a car, truck, etc. — called also *glove box*; see picture at CAR

glove puppet *noun, pl* ~ **-pets** [*count*] *Brit* : HAND PUPPET

[1]**glow** /ˈglou/ *verb* **glows; glowed; glow·ing** [*no obj*]
1 a : to shine with low light and heat but usually without flame • The coals *glowed* in the fireplace. • The fireplace

glowed with the dying coals. **b :** to shine with a steady light ▪ The lamp *glowed* (brightly/softly) in the window. ▪ This toy *glows* in the dark.
2 a : to have a warm, reddish color from exercise, emotion, etc. — often + *with* ▪ Her face was *glowing with* embarrassment. **b :** to look happy, excited, or healthy — usually + *with* ▪ Her parents *glowed with* pride [=they looked very happy and proud] as she was given her diploma. ▪ The children were *glowing with* pleasure/excitement.

²glow *noun [singular]*
1 : a soft and steady light ▪ We could see the *glow* of the lamp in the window. ▪ The town's lights cast a *glow* on the horizon.
2 : a pink color in your face from exercising, being excited, etc. ▪ the rosy *glow* of health
3 a : a pleasant feeling ▪ He felt a *glow* as he remembered the day they first met. ▪ Their problems were all forgotten in the *glow* of victory. **b :** physical warmth or heat ▪ She felt the *glow* from the fireplace.

glow·er /ˈglawɚ/ *verb* **-ers; -ered; -er·ing** *[no obj]* **:** to look at someone or something in an angry way ▪ The librarian *glowered* at us when she heard us laughing. — sometimes used figuratively ▪ a *glowering* [=*dark, forbidding*] sky
– glower *noun, pl* **-ers** *[count]* ▪ The librarian looked at us with a *glower* of annoyance.

glowing *adj [more ~; most ~]*
1 : very enthusiastic **:** full of praise ▪ Her previous boss gave her a *glowing* recommendation. ▪ The book has received *glowing* reviews. ▪ They spoke about their trip ***in glowing terms***. [=they described their trip in a very enthusiastic way]
2 : having a warm color ▪ She has a *glowing* complexion.
– glow·ing·ly /ˈglowɪŋli/ *adv* ▪ They spoke *glowingly* about their trip.

glow·worm /ˈgloʊˌwɚm/ *noun, pl* **-worms** *[count]* **:** a type of insect that produces a small amount of light from its body

glu·cose /ˈgluːˌkoʊs/ *noun [noncount] technical* **:** a type of sugar that is found in plants and fruits

¹glue /ˈgluː/ *noun, pl* **glues :** a substance used to stick things tightly together *[noncount]* a tube of *glue* *[count]* The hardware store offers several different *glues*.
stick like glue see ²STICK
– glu·ey /ˈgluːwi/ *adj* **glu·i·er; -est** ▪ a *gluey* [=*sticky*] mess

²glue *verb* **glues; glued; glu·ing** *also* **glue·ing** *[+ obj]*
1 : to make (something) stick to something else by using glue ▪ I *glued* the pieces of the cup back together. ▪ I *glued* the handle (back) on/onto the cup.
2 : to stay in one place because of interest, shock, excitement, etc. — usually used as *glued to* ▪ He spends his days *glued to* the television. [=he watches television all day] ▪ We spent several anxious hours *glued to* the phone as we waited for news of her condition. ▪ a thriller that will keep you *glued to* your seat
keep your eyes glued to see ¹EYE

glum /ˈglʌm/ *adj* **glum·mer; -mest :** sad or depressed ▪ There's no need to look so *glum*—things will get better soon. ▪ There was a *glum* silence in the room.
– glum·ly *adv* ▪ "It's no good," he said *glumly*. **– glum·ness** *noun [noncount]*

¹glut /ˈglʌt/ *noun, pl* **gluts** *[count]* **:** too much of something **:** a supply of something that is much more than is needed or wanted — usually singular ▪ a *glut* of oil on the market

²glut *verb* **gluts; glut·ted; glut·ting** *[+ obj]* **:** to fill (something) with more of something than is needed or wanted ▪ The market is *glutted* with oil.

glu·ten /ˈgluːtn̩/ *noun [noncount]* **:** a substance in wheat and flour that holds dough together

glu·ti·nous /ˈgluːtnəs/ *adj [more ~; most ~]* **:** STICKY ▪ *glutinous* rice

glut·ton /ˈglʌtn̩/ *noun, pl* **-tons** *[count]*
1 : a person who eats too much
2 : someone who wants a large amount of something — + *for* ▪ She's a *glutton for* gossip. ▪ That guy's a real ***glutton for punishment***. [=he seems to enjoy things that other people dislike]
– glut·ton·ous /ˈglʌtənəs/ *adj [more ~; most ~]* ▪ He's a *gluttonous* little boy. **– glut·ton·ous·ly** *adv* ▪ eating *gluttonously*

glut·tony /ˈglʌtəni/ *noun [noncount]* **:** the act or habit of eating or drinking too much

glyc·er·in *also* **glyc·er·ine** /ˈglɪsərən/ *noun [noncount] technical* **:** a thick, sweet, clear liquid used in making medicines, food, soap, etc.

gm *abbr* gram

GM *abbr* **1** general manager **2** genetically modified

G–man /ˈʤiːˌmæn/ *noun, pl* **G–men** /ˈʤiːˌmɛn/ *[count] US, informal + old-fashioned* **:** a special agent of the U.S. Federal Bureau of Investigation **:** an FBI agent ▪ a movie about gangsters and *G-men*

GMO *abbr* genetically modified organism ▪ This food is *GMO*-free.

GMT *abbr* Greenwich Mean Time

gnarled /ˈnɑrəld/ *adj [more ~; most ~]*
1 *of wood* **:** having many twists and hard bumps or knots ▪ *gnarled* branches ▪ an ancient *gnarled* tree
2 : bumpy or twisted ▪ the old man's *gnarled* fingers/hands

gnarly /ˈnɑɚli/ *adj* **gnarl·i·er; -est**
1 : GNARLED ▪ *gnarly* branches
2 *US slang* **a :** very difficult or bad ▪ a *gnarly* situation ▪ a *gnarly* accident **b :** very good ▪ some *gnarly* guitar playing

gnash /ˈnæʃ/ *verb* **gnash·es; gnashed; gnash·ing**
gnash your teeth **1 :** to grind your teeth together ▪ He *gnashed* his teeth in his sleep. **2 :** to show you are angry, upset, etc. ▪ His opponents have been *gnashing their teeth* in/with frustration [=they have been showing their frustration] since he won the election. ▪ His election has caused some ***weeping and gnashing of teeth*** among his opponents.

gnat /ˈnæt/ *noun, pl* **gnats** *[count]* **:** a small fly that bites people and animals

gnaw /ˈnɑː/ *verb* **gnaws; gnawed; gnaw·ing**
1 : to bite or chew (something) repeatedly *[+ obj]* The dog was *gnawing* a bone. *[no obj]* He nervously *gnawed* on his fingernails. ▪ Rabbits have *gnawed* at the hedge.
2 *[+ obj]* **:** to make (a hole in something) by chewing ▪ Rabbits had *gnawed* a hole in the hedge. ▪ Squirrels had *gnawed* their way into the attic. [=they had entered the attic by chewing a hole]
gnaw at *[phrasal verb]* ***gnaw at (someone)*** **:** to be a source of worry or concern to (someone) ▪ This problem has been *gnawing at* me day and night. ▪ She says she's fine, but I can see that something is *gnawing at* her.

gnawing *adj, always used before a noun [more ~; most ~]* **:** causing feelings of doubt or worry that last for a long time ▪ I have a *gnawing* suspicion that he won't be there. ▪ *gnawing* doubts

gnoc·chi /ˈnɑːki/ *noun [plural]* **:** small balls of dough made from potatoes or flour that are boiled in water and usually served with a sauce in Italian cooking

gnome /ˈnoʊm/ *noun, pl* **gnomes** *[count]*
1 *in stories* **:** a small creature who lives inside the earth and guards treasure ✧ A gnome looks like a little man and is often shown wearing a pointed hat.
2 : a statue that looks like a gnome and is often used outside in a garden ▪ a garden *gnome*

gno·mic /ˈnoʊmɪk/ *adj [more ~; most ~] formal* **:** said or written using few words that are difficult to understand ▪ He made *gnomic* utterances concerning death. ▪ *gnomic* writing/wisdom

GNP *abbr* gross national product

gnu /ˈnuː/ *noun, pl* **gnu** *or* **gnus** *[count]* **:** WILDEBEEST

¹go /ˈgoʊ/ *verb* **goes** /ˈgoʊz/; **went** /ˈwɛnt/; **gone** /ˈgɑːn/; **go·ing** /ˈgowɪŋ/
1 *[no obj]* **a :** to move or travel to a place ▪ He *went* to the window and looked out at the yard. ▪ She *goes* to the office every morning and comes home in the evening. ▪ I'm tired. Let's *go* home. ▪ She *went* downstairs to the kitchen. ▪ The train *goes* from New York to Chicago. ▪ Halt! ***Who goes there***? [=who is there?; who is coming this way?] **b :** to travel to and stay in (a place) for a particular amount of time ▪ I *went* with my family to Rome last year. ▪ We're *going to* Iowa for a week. **c :** to move or travel in a particular way or for a particular distance ▪ The car was *going* too fast. ▪ How much farther do we have to *go*? ▪ She *went* a long way to see him. ▪ We *went* many miles that day. ▪ *Go* straight for two blocks, then *go* right/left at the light. ▪ The street is blocked, so we'll have to *go* around.— often used figuratively ▪ Their relationship doesn't seem to be *going* anywhere. [=doesn't seem to be making any progress] ▪ ***Where do we go from here***? [=what do we do now?] ▪ We've accomplished a lot, but we still have ***a long way to go***. [=we have much more to do] ▪ She has a lot of talent. If she works hard, she should ***go far***. [=she should be very successful] ▪ These changes will ***go a long way*** toward solving the dispute. ▪ Would you ***go so far*** as to call them dishonest? [=would you say that they are dishonest?] ▪ This time you've ***gone too far***! [=you've done

something that cannot be allowed]
2 a [*no obj*] **: to move to or be at a place (such as an office or school) for work, study, etc. — + *to*** ▪ She *goes to* church on Sunday. ▪ She *goes to* work from 9 a.m. to 5 p.m. ▪ Their son is *going to* college in Florida. [=he is attending a college in Florida] ▪ He *went to* prison for his crimes. **b** [*no obj*] **: to do something that involves moving or traveling to a place — often + *on*** ▪ We're *going on* vacation next week. ▪ The thieves *went on* a crime spree. **— often + *-ing verb*** ▪ The neighbors *went running* [=the neighbors ran] when they heard the screams. ▪ I like to *go walking/swimming/shopping*. [=I like to walk/swim/shop] **— see also GO FOR 5 (below) c** [*no obj*] **: to move or travel to a place for a particular purpose** ▪ I *went* to see them last week. ▪ We *went* to see a movie last night. = We *went* to a movie last night. ▪ Are you *going* to the wedding? [=do you plan to attend the wedding?] ▪ I may *go* to see them next week. = I may *go* and see them next week. = (*US*) I may *go* see them next week. ✧ **In informal spoken English, *go and* is used to emphasize a following verb. It usually expresses anger or annoyance.** ▪ Now you've *gone and* ruined it! ▪ They *went and* changed it! ▪ *Go and* get me a towel! ✧ **In U.S. English, *go* by itself is also sometimes used this way.** ▪ Why did you have to *go* ruin it?! ▪ *Go* get me a towel! **d** [+ *obj*] *informal* **: to engage in (*doing* something)** ▪ Don't *go telling* everyone what happened. [=don't tell everyone what happened] ▪ He *went blabbing* the news all over the place.
3 [*no obj*] **a : to leave a place** ▪ It's getting late. I should *go* now. ▪ It's time to *go*. ▪ I was just *going* when the phone rang. **b : to leave a job, position, etc.** ▪ Pack up your desk and *go*. ▪ She's retiring soon, and it'll be sad for all of us to see her *go*.
4 : to lie or move along a particular route or in a particular direction [*no obj*] The road *goes* from the town to the lake. ▪ His land *goes* almost all the way down to the river. [+ *obj*] Are you *going* my way? [=are you going in the same direction that I'm going in?] ▪ The car *went* the length of the street and then turned around. **— often used figuratively** ▪ She *went* the conventional route [=she did the conventional thing] by going straight to college after high school. ▪ He has always ***gone his own way***. [=he has always done the things he wants to do instead of the things that most people do]
5 [*no obj*] **: to provide a way to get to a place** ▪ That door *goes* to the cellar. [=you can get to the cellar by going through that door] ▪ Where does this road *go*?
6 [*no obj*] **: to be sent** ▪ The message *went* by e-mail to all members of the staff.
7 [*no obj*] **: to be lost, used, or spent** ▪ I don't know where the money *goes*. ▪ I put my keys here a few minutes ago, and now they're *gone*. = (*Brit*) I put my keys here a few minutes ago, and now they've *gone*. **— often used with *all*** ▪ The money was *all gone* by Friday. = *All* (of) the money was *gone* by Friday. ▪ "Is there any ice cream left?" "No, it's *all gone*."
8 [*no obj*] **: to die** ▪ She *went* peacefully at about midnight.
9 [*no obj*] **a *of time* : to pass** ▪ The time/day seemed to *go* very quickly/slowly. **b : to happen in a particular way** ▪ The evening *went* well/badly. ▪ She worked hard to make the party *go* according to plan. ▪ ***The way things are going*** [=if things keep happening this way], I may get laid off. ▪ We lost the game, but ***that's the way it/life goes***. [=it is a fact that bad or disappointing things will happen sometimes]
10 [*no obj*] *informal* **— used to talk or ask about how you are feeling** ▪ "How are things *going*? = How's everything *going*? = How's it *going*?" "Everything's *going* well/fine/great."
11 [*no obj*] **: to be given up, thrown away, etc.** ▪ I want to keep these, but that one can *go*. ▪ These old boxes ***have got to go***. = These old boxes ***have to go***. [=we have to get rid of these old boxes]
12 *always followed by an adverb or preposition* [*no obj*] **a : to be sold** ▪ The house *went* for a good price. ▪ The cabinets *go* for about $400. ▪ The painting will *go* to the highest bidder **b : to be willing to pay a certain price for something** ▪ I'll *go* as high as $100, but not over that.
13 [*no obj*] **: to fail or become weak because of use, age, etc.** ▪ His hearing has started to *go*. ▪ The batteries in the flashlight are *going* and will have to be changed.
14 [*no obj*] **: to break because of force or pressure** ▪ The dam/roof is weakening and it could *go* at any time.
15 [*no obj*] **: to start doing something** ▪ Everyone's here, so I think we're ready to *go*. = (*US, informal*) I think we're ***good to go***. [=I think we're ready to start] **— see also *get going* at GET**
16 [*no obj*] **— used to describe the result of a contest, election, decision, etc.** ▪ The election *went* in her favor. [=she won the election] ▪ The verdict *went* against him.
17 [*no obj*] **: to work in the usual or expected way** ▪ I couldn't get the car to *go*. ▪ I kept working on the engine until I finally got it *going*. [=I finally got it to work/run] **— see also *keep going* at [1]KEEP**
18 a [*linking verb*] **: to become — used to describe a change** ▪ The building has *gone* condo. [=the building has become a condominium] ▪ British currency *went* decimal in 1971. **— used especially to describe a change that is not wanted** ▪ The tire *went* flat. ▪ The bread has *gone* stale. ▪ The company *went* bankrupt. ▪ Everything keeps *going* wrong. **b** [*no obj*] **: to change** ▪ The leaves here *go* from green to red in the fall. ▪ The situation *went* from bad to worse.
19 [*linking verb*] **— used to describe someone's or something's condition** ▪ I like to *go* barefoot in the summer. ▪ There was nothing to eat, so we had to *go* hungry. ▪ My letters have *gone* unanswered. [=have not been answered] ▪ Her excellent work has not *gone* unnoticed/unappreciated. [=someone has noticed/appreciated her excellent work]
20 [*no obj*] *informal* **: to make a particular movement** ▪ Can you *go* like this with your eyebrows? [=can you move your eyebrows like this?]
21 [*no obj*] **— used to talk about a story, song, etc.** ▪ I can't remember how the story *goes*. [=I can't remember what happens in the story] ▪ The story/rumor/legend *goes* that he left home poor and came back rich. ▪ The tune *goes* like this.
22 [*no obj*] **a : to be able to fit in or through a space** ▪ Will these clothes *go* in your suitcase? [=is there enough room for these clothes in your suitcase?] ▪ The box was too big to *go* [=*fit*] through the door. **b : to have a usual or proper place or position : BELONG** ▪ These books *go* on the top shelf. ▪ Where do your keys *go*?
23 [*no obj*] **: to have authority : to require you to do what is said or demanded** ▪ ***What she says goes***! [=she is the boss; you have to do what she tells you to do]
24 [*no obj*] *informal* **: to use the toilet** ▪ One of the children said he had to *go*. **— see also *go to the bathroom* at BATHROOM**
25 : to make a sound [*no obj*] The bell *went* and the class came to an end. ▪ The music was *going* full blast. [=the music was being played as loud as possible] [+ *obj*] The gun *went* bang. ▪ The cow *went* "moo."
26 [+ *obj*] *informal* **: to say (something) — used in describing what people said in a conversation** ▪ So she *goes*, "Did you write this?" and I *go*, "Mind your own business!"
27 [*no obj*] ***of a sports team or player* : to have a specified record** ▪ The team *went* 11–2 last season. [=the team won 11 games and lost 2 games last year] ▪ The shortstop *went* two for four in yesterday's game. [=the shortstop had two hits in four times at bat in yesterday's game]
***anything goes* : anything is acceptable : there are no rules for behavior, dress, etc.** ▪ She dresses conservatively at work, but on the weekends, *anything goes*.
***as (someone or something) goes* — used to compare someone or something with someone or something else of the same kind** ▪ *As lectures go*, it was very interesting.
***be going Brit* : to be available** ▪ There *are* no jobs *going* right now.
***be going to* — used to talk about what will happen or could happen** ▪ It*'s going to* be cold tomorrow. [=it will be cold tomorrow] ▪ It*'s going to* rain: if you don't take an umbrella, you*'re going to* get soaked. ▪ I *am* not *going to* tolerate [=I won't tolerate] any more bad behavior! ▪ I *was* just *going to* call him. [=I was about to call him] **— see also GONNA**
***come and go* see [1]COME**
***easy come, easy go* see [2]EASY**
go about* [*phrasal verb*] *go about (something)* 1 : to start to do (something)** ▪ I'd like to fix this old radio but I don't know how to *go about* (doing) it. **2 : to do (something)** ▪ Despite the threat of war, most people are just quietly ***going about their business. [=most people are just doing the things that they usually do]
***go a bundle on* see [1]BUNDLE**
***go after* [*phrasal verb*] 1 *go after (someone)* a : to follow and try to stop or catch (someone)** ▪ When the boy ran out the door, his mother quickly *went after* him. ▪ The police *went after* the escaped criminal. **b : to try to find and punish (someone)** ▪ The government is *going after* people who cheat on their taxes. **2 *go after (something or someone)* : to try to get (something or someone)** ▪ If you want the job, you should just *go after* it. ▪ She accused her friend of *going after* her husband.
***go against* [*phrasal verb*] 1 *go against (something)* : to not agree with (something)** ▪ I won't do anything that *goes*

against my conscience/beliefs/principles. ▪ values that *go against* those of society **2 *go against (someone or something)*** **a :** to oppose (someone or something) ▪ He was surprised when some of his former supporters *went against* him. ▪ He was reluctant to *go against* his parents' wishes. [=he was reluctant to do something that his parents did not want him to do] **b :** to compete against (a player or team) in a contest or game ▪ The Red Sox will be *going against* the Yankees in tonight's game. **3 *go against (someone)* :** to not be good for (someone) : to not produce the result that is wanted by (someone) ▪ Everything seemed to be *going against* her but she didn't give up hope. ▪ The verdict *went against* the defendant. [=the verdict was not in favor of the defendant]

go ahead [*phrasal verb*] **1 :** to do or begin to do something ▪ Instead of waiting for approval, they just *went ahead* and started working on the project. **:** to do something after planning to do it or after getting permission to do it ▪ Despite the bad weather, they decided to *go ahead* with the party. ▪ My boss told me to *go ahead* (with the work). ▪ "Could I sit here?" "Sure, *go* (right) *ahead*." ▪ "I probably shouldn't have any more cake." "Oh, *go ahead*. It won't kill you." — see also GO-AHEAD **2 :** to happen or proceed ▪ Despite the weather, the party *went ahead* as planned. ▪ After a brief delay, the work is now *going ahead* again. **3 :** to go or travel to a place before the other person or group that is with you ▪ I'll *go* (on) *ahead* and make sure that everything's ready when you arrive.

go all out **:** to do something with as much effort as possible ▪ When he has a party, he likes to *go all out*. [=have a big and expensive party] ▪ Her company always *went all out* [=did everything possible] to make the customer happy. — see also ALL-OUT

go all the way see [1]WAY

go along [*phrasal verb*] **1 :** to continue or proceed ▪ The project is *going along* smoothly. ▪ On this job there's a lot to learn—but I'm sure you'll pick it up as you *go along*. ▪ He was just making up the story as he *went along*. **2 :** to go or travel with someone ▪ They were going to the fair so I asked whether I could *go along*. — often + *with* ▪ I asked whether I could *go along with* them. **3 :** to agree to do or accept what other people want ▪ We tried to convince him to support us but he refused to *go along*. — usually + *with* ▪ He refused to *go along with* us. ▪ He refused to *go along with* our plan. **4 :** to be part of something — + *with* ▪ If I want the job I have to accept the stress that *goes along with* it.

go ape see [3]APE

go around or *chiefly Brit* ***go round*** [*phrasal verb*] **1 a** *always followed by an adverb or preposition* **:** to go to different places ▪ She and her friends *go around* (together) to lots of clubs. = She *goes around* with her friends to lots of clubs. **b** *chiefly Brit* **:** to travel *to* a place that is nearby ▪ I *went round* [=*went over*] *to* his flat. **c** — used to describe the way a person often dresses or behaves ▪ She *goes around* (dressed) in a miniskirt. ▪ You can't *go around* treating people so rudely. **2 *go around* or *go around (a place)* :** to go or pass from one person to another person ▪ There's a rumor *going around* (the office) that the boss is about to get fired. ▪ An amusing story is *going around*. ▪ There's a nasty cold *going around*: I hope you don't catch it. **3 *go around* or *go around (something or someone)* :** to be long enough to pass all the way around (something or someone) ▪ This belt isn't long enough to *go around* (my waist). **4** ✧ If people want something and there is ***enough/plenty to go around***, there is enough for all of the people who want it or need it. ▪ There aren't *enough jobs to go around*. **5 *what goes around comes around informal*** — used to say that if you treat other people badly you will eventually be treated badly by someone else

go at [*phrasal verb*] **1 a *go at (someone)* :** to attack (someone) ▪ They *went at* each other viciously. **b *go at it* :** to fight or argue ▪ Our neighbors were arguing again last night. They *went at it* for almost an hour. **2 *go at (something)* :** to make an effort to do or deal with (something) ▪ They had to *go at* the problem from many different angles before they finally solved it. ▪ It was a tough job, and I was impressed by the energetic way he *went at* it.

go away [*phrasal verb*] **1 a :** to leave a place or person ▪ She angrily told him to *go away* and stop bothering her. **b :** to leave your home for a period of time ▪ They're *going away* on vacation. ▪ After graduating from high school, he *went away* to college. ▪ a *going-away* present/party [=a present/party for someone who is leaving to live, study, or travel in a distant place] **2 :** to stop existing or happening : to end ▪ I just wish there was some way to make the pain *go away*.

go back [*phrasal verb*] **1 a :** to return to a place ▪ I forgot my purse and had to *go back* for it. ▪ What was it like to *go back* after so many years? ▪ After college she *went back* home. ▪ *Go back* inside! You'll catch cold. **b :** to begin doing something again — + *to* ▪ I turned off the alarm and *went back to* sleep. ▪ He waved hello, then *went* right *back to* work. ▪ She *went back to* eating her dinner. ✧ The phrase ***there's no going back*** means that you have done or decided something and cannot change it. ▪ I've already signed the contract, so *there's no going back* now. **2 a :** to have existed for a particular amount of time or since a particular period ▪ These ruins *go back* hundreds of years. — often + *to* ▪ a tradition that *goes back* [=*dates back*] *to* colonial times **b :** to have known each other for a particular amount of time ▪ We *go back* 30 years. ▪ He and I ***go back a long way***. = He and I ***go way back***. [=he and I have known each other for many years] **c :** to think or talk about something from the past ▪ To fully understand the issues, we have to *go back* a few years. — often + *to* ▪ I'd like to *go back to* your earlier comment. [=I'd like to discuss it further] **3 *go back on (something)* :** to not do what is required by (something, such as a promise) ▪ She *went back on* her promise to help us. [=she failed to keep her promise] ▪ I would never *go back on* my word.

go before [*phrasal verb*] **1 *go before (someone)* :** to happen or exist at an earlier time than (someone) ▪ We owe a great debt of gratitude to those who *went before* us. **2 *go before (someone or something)* :** to be considered by (someone or something) for an official decision or judgment ▪ The contestants will *go before* the judges tomorrow. ▪ The case *went before* the court.

go beyond [*phrasal verb*] ***go beyond (something)* :** to do more than (something) ▪ She *went beyond* the call of duty. [=she did more than was required] ▪ We need to *go beyond* merely talking about the problem.

go by [*phrasal verb*] **1** *of time* **:** to pass ▪ The morning seemed to *go by* very quickly/slowly. ▪ Many years have *gone by* since the last time I saw her. ▪ They have many happy memories of days *gone by*. [=bygone days, days/times in the past] **2 *go by (something)*** **a :** to be guided or directed by (something, such as a rule) ▪ That's a good rule to *go by*. **b :** to form an opinion from (something) ▪ She may be guilty but we have very little evidence to *go by*. ▪ You can't always *go by* appearances. [=you can't always judge people or things by the way they look] **3 *go by (a name)* :** to be known by (a name) ▪ His name is Edwin but he *goes by* Ed. [=people call him Ed] **4 *go by* or *go by (somewhere)* :** to go somewhere in order to visit someone ▪ I *went by* (her house) to see her after school.

go down [*phrasal verb*] **1 :** to fall or crash to the ground ▪ The airplane *went down* when one of its engines caught fire. ▪ The boxer took a punch and *went down* hard. **2 :** to sink into the water ▪ The ship *went down* after hitting an iceberg. **3 a :** to drop to a lower level ▪ Prices are expected to *go down* soon. ▪ The quality of his work has been *going down*. ▪ She had a fever yesterday, but it *went down* this morning. **b :** to become less or smaller ▪ It may take a few hours for the swelling to *go down*. **4 :** to become less bright ▪ The lights *went down* [=the lights were turned down] as the movie started. **5** *of the sun or moon* **:** to stop being visible in the sky : to set ▪ The sun comes up in the morning and *goes down* at night. **6 a** — used to say how easy or hard it is to eat or drink something ▪ The medicine *went down* easily. [=it was easy to swallow the medicine] ▪ I took a sip but it *went down* the wrong way. [=I choked on my drink] **b** — used to say how easy or hard it is to accept or agree to something ▪ His suggestion didn't *go down* [=*go over*] very well with his boss. [=his boss didn't like his suggestion] **7 :** to lose or fail ▪ Last year's champion *went down* in the first round of the tournament this year. ▪ The regime finally *went down* [=*fell*] in a wave of popular protest. **8** *of a computer, system, etc.* **:** to stop working ▪ The network *went down* this morning. **9 :** to be remembered or talked about as an important person, event, etc. ▪ He will *go down* as one of the greatest leaders this country has ever known. ▪ His name will ***go down in history***. **10** *Brit, informal* **:** to be sent to prison ▪ He *went down* [=went to jail] for six years for the robbery. **11** *somewhat informal* **:** to travel to a place (especially one that is nearby or to the south) ▪ I need to *go down* to the store for milk. ▪ We *went down* south to visit relatives. **12** *slang* **:** to happen ▪ We need to find out what's *going down*. [=(more commonly) *going on*] **13** ***go down on (someone)*** *slang* **:** to perform oral sex on (someone) **14** ***go down with (an illness)*** *Brit* **:** to begin to have or suffer from (an illness) ▪ He *went down with* [=*caught, came down with*] measles.

go easy, go easy on/with see ²EASY

go figure see ²FIGURE

go for [*phrasal verb*] **1 a** ***go for (someone)*** **:** to attack (someone) ▪ My dog *went for* the intruder. **b** ***go for (something)*** **:** to try to get (something) ▪ *go for* the prize ▪ If you want to achieve success, you have to stop hesitating and just ***go for it***! **2** ***go for (something)*** **:** to accept or agree to (something, such as a plan or suggestion) ▪ I asked her to lend us some money, but she wouldn't *go for* it. [=she wouldn't agree to lend us money] **3** ***go for (someone or something)*** *informal* **a :** to like or be attracted to (someone or something) ▪ When I see how she looks at him, I can tell she really *goes for* him. ▪ I don't really *go for* modern art. ▪ I ***could go for*** [=I would like] a cup of coffee right now. **b :** to relate to or apply to (someone or something) ▪ The rule *goes for* you, too. [=the rule also applies to you] ▪ "I'd like ice cream for desert." "That *goes for* me too." [=I'd like ice cream too] ▪ The economy here has been growing stronger, and ***the same goes for*** [=the same is true for] many other areas. **4** ***go for (a price)*** **:** to be sold for (a particular price) ▪ The painting *went for* more than a million dollars. **5** ***go for (a walk, a drive, etc.)*** **:** to do an activity (such as walking or driving a car) that usually involves going somewhere ▪ She *went for* a walk/stroll after dinner. ▪ On Saturday mornings we like to *go for* a drive out in the countryside. ▪ Would anyone like to *go for* a swim? **6** ✧ If you ***have something going for you***, you have a talent, skill, etc., that helps you. ▪ She's not as young as some of the other athletes, but experience helps, and she *has that going for* her. [=she has an advantage because of her experience] ▪ You should be more confident in yourself. You ***have a lot going for you***! [=you have many talents, abilities, etc.]

go great guns see ¹GUN

go in [*phrasal verb*] **1** *of the sun or moon* **:** to become hidden by a cloud ▪ The afternoon got cooler after the sun *went in*. **2** ***go in for (something)*** **:** to like or be interested in (something) ▪ She doesn't *go in for* sports. **3** ***go in on (something)*** *US, informal* **:** to help pay for (something, such as a present) ▪ Are you going to *go in on* the gift for her? ▪ We all *went in on* the gift together. [=we all gave some money towards buying the gift] **4** ***go in with (someone)*** **:** to join (someone) in a business, project, etc. ▪ His brother-in-law *went in with* him on his new business.

go into [*phrasal verb*] ***go into (something)*** **1 a :** to start to be in (a different state or condition) ▪ After she lost her job she *went into* a deep depression. [=she became very depressed] ▪ The criminal has ***gone into hiding***. [=the criminal is hiding] ▪ After losing the election, she ***went into seclusion***. — see also *go into effect* at ¹EFFECT **b :** to start to move in (a different and usually bad way) ▪ The car *went into* a skid. [=the car began to skid] ▪ The plane *went into* a tailspin. **2 :** to start to do (something) as a job or career ▪ He wants to *go into* the priesthood. [=he wants to become a priest] ▪ Their daughter is planning to *go into* medicine. [=to be a doctor; to get a job in the medical field] ▪ Both his sons have *gone into* the army. [=joined the army] ▪ His dream is to ***go into business*** for himself. [=to start his own business] **3 a :** to talk about (something) ▪ I'll try to tell the story without *going into* too many details. = I'll try not to *go into* too much detail. **:** to talk about the details of (something) ▪ Having *gone into* the causes of the French Revolution, the book then discusses its effects. ▪ "I've had a long day." "What happened?" "I'll tell you later. I don't feel like *going into* it right now." **b :** to try to get information about (something) — usually used as *(be) gone into* ▪ A problem like that should really *be gone into* [=*looked into*] carefully. **4 :** to be used for (something) ▪ Lots of time, energy, and money have *gone into* (completing) the project. **5** *mathematics* — used to say how many times a number can be multiplied to produce a larger number ▪ 6 *goes into* 18 three times. [=18 divided by 6 equals 3]

go it alone see ²ALONE

go off [*phrasal verb*] **1 a** *of a bomb* **:** to explode ▪ The building was evacuated before the bomb *went off*. **b** *of a gun* **:** to shoot ▪ The gun *went off* accidentally. **c** *of an alarm* **:** to begin to make a sudden loud noise ▪ I woke up when the alarm *went off*. **2** *of lights, electricity, etc.* **:** to stop working ▪ The lights in the building suddenly *went off*. **3 :** to leave a place for a new place ▪ He *went off* to join the army after graduating from high school. ▪ She *went off* to America. **4 a :** to occur or happen ▪ The meeting *went off* as scheduled. [=the meeting happened when it was scheduled to happen] **b :** to happen a particular way ▪ The party *went off* well. [=the party was a success] ▪ The meeting *went off* poorly. **5** *US, informal* **:** to begin shouting at someone in an angry way — usually + *on* ▪ Her boss *went off on* her because she was late again. **6** ***go off (someone or something)*** *Brit* **:** to stop liking (someone or something) ▪ She used to like him but now she's *gone off* him completely. ▪ My boss has *gone off* the idea, so it's been cancelled. **7** *chiefly Brit* **a** ***go off with (someone)*** **:** to leave (a spouse, partner, etc.) for someone else ▪ He left his wife and *went off with* [=*ran off with*] some young thing. **b** ***go off with (something)*** **:** to take (something that belongs to someone else) away with you **:** STEAL ▪ Someone *went off with* my pencil/wallet.

go on [*phrasal verb*] **1 :** to continue: such as **a :** to continue on a journey ▪ We stopped briefly in Detroit, and then *went on* to Chicago. **b :** to continue as time passes ▪ Life *goes on*. ▪ How much longer will the meeting *go on*? [=*last*] **c :** to continue doing something ▪ She *went on* working [=she continued to work] after everyone else had stopped. **d :** to continue talking ▪ He *went on* (and on) about how unfairly he had been treated. [=he talked about it for a long time] **:** to talk too much or too long about something ▪ She's always *going on* about the importance of a good diet. **e :** to continue to be in the same situation or relationship ▪ We can't *go on* like this. **2 :** to go or travel to a place before another person or group that is with you ▪ You *go on* (ahead). I'll come later. **3 :** to do or say something else after you have finished doing or saying something — usually + *to* ▪ He accepted the nomination and *went on to* win the election. ▪ After I finished reading the first book I immediately *went on to* the next one. ▪ He *went on to* say that further tax increases would be necessary. ▪ Everyone expected that she would ***go on to greater things***. [=that she would become very successful] **4 :** to happen ▪ What's *going on*? ▪ No one knows exactly what *went on* during their private meeting. — see also GOINGS-ON **5** *of lights, electricity, etc.* **:** to begin to work or function ▪ The lights *went on* briefly and then went out again. **6 :** to form an opinion or conclusion from something — used in the phrase ***to go on*** ▪ There's very little evidence *to go on*. [=there's very little evidence that can be used to form an opinion] **7 a** — used in speech to urge someone to do something ▪ *Go on* (and try it): you might actually like it! ▪ "I probably shouldn't have any more ice cream." "Oh, *go on*! It won't hurt you to have a little more." **b** *chiefly Brit, informal + old-fashioned* — used in speech to express disbelief ▪ "I used to be a spy." "Oh, *go on*." ▪ A spy? ***Go on with you***, then. [=I don't believe you] **8** ***go on at (someone)*** *chiefly Brit, informal* **:** to criticize (someone) often or repeatedly ▪ Quit *going on at* me all the time! — see also *going on* at ²GOING

go one better **1 :** to achieve more **:** to move to a higher or better level ▪ She qualified for the finals, then *went one better* and took first place. **2** ***go (someone or something) one better*** **:** to do better or more than (someone or something) **:** to outdo (someone or something) ▪ The company has *gone* its competitors *one better* by offering new customers a special discount.

go out [*phrasal verb*] **1 :** to leave your home for an activity ▪ I'm *going out* for a walk. I'll be back soon. ▪ We're *going out* to get some lunch. ▪ On Saturday nights he *goes out* drinking with his friends. **2 :** to be sent from a person or place ▪ The message *went out* by e-mail to all members of the staff. ▪ Word has *gone out* that snow is expected. ▪ ***Our thoughts and prayers go out to*** all the victims of this tragedy. [=we are thinking of and praying for all the victims of this tragedy] **3 :** to stop being popular or fashionable ▪ That hairstyle *went out* years ago. ▪ Short skirts have ***gone out of fashion***. **4 a :** to meet someone for a romantic social activity **:** to go on a date with someone ▪ They *went out* a couple of times, but it was never serious. **b :** to have a continuing romantic relationship with someone ▪ I've been *going out* with her for quite a while now. = We've been *going out* for quite a while now. **5 :** to stop working ▪ The electricity suddenly *went out*; *especially* **:** to stop shining or burning ▪ The fire/candle *went out*. ▪ All the lights suddenly *went out*. **6** *chiefly US* **:** to try to become a member of a team, group, etc. — usually + *for* ▪ He *went out for* football last year. = He *went out for* the football team last year. • She *went out* [=*tried out*] *for* the school play. **7** *of the tide* **:** to drop to a lower level • The tide is *going out* [=(more formally) *ebbing*] now. **8 :** to be broadcast on the radio, television, etc. • A distress call *went out* three hours ago. — often + *over* • Warnings about the approaching storm *went out over* the radio.

go over [*phrasal verb*] **1 :** to move or travel to a particular place or person • He *went over* and stood by the window. • He *went over* and hugged her. • I think I see Jane. Let's *go over* and say hello. — often + *to* • He *went over to* the window. • He *went over to* her and hugged her. **2 :** to change sides in a disagreement, competition, etc. — usually + *to* • After several years of supporting us, he *went over to* our competitors. **3** *US* **:** to be accepted or received in a particular way • He tried to make a joke but it *went over* badly. [=no one thought his joke was funny] • Her proposal didn't *go over* very well. — often + *with* • Her proposal didn't *go over* very well *with* the boss. [=the boss didn't like her proposal] **4** ***go over (something)*** **a :** to talk about or think about (something) carefully • He *went over* all the arguments before making up his mind. • We *went over* the accident again and again in our minds. **b :** to look at or study (something) again in order to correct it, learn it, etc. • The students were told to *go over* their essays. • Let's *go over* the instructions. • an actress *going over* her lines

go the distance see [1]DISTANCE

go there *informal* **:** to start to talk or think about something — usually used in negative statements • "Do you remember when we were dating?" "Let's not *go there.*" = "I don't want to *go there.*" = "Don't *go there.*" [=I don't want to talk about that]

go through [*phrasal verb*] **1** ***go through (something)*** **a :** to study or look at (something) in a careful way • The book *goes through* every detail of the French Revolution. • Let's *go through* the plan one more time. **b :** to look in or at (something) in order to find something **:** to search in or through (something) • I found him *going through* my closet. **c :** to experience (something) • He's *going through* a painful divorce. • I understand what you're *going through.* • In order to learn the job well, you have to *go through* several months of training. • The book has already *gone through* four editions. [=the publishers have already released four editions of the book] **d :** to spend or use all of (something) • He *went through* all the money he inherited. • They *went through* three bottles of wine with dinner. **e :** to occur throughout (something) • A note of despair *goes through* the narrative. [=there is a note of despair throughout the narrative] ✧ If something (such as an idea or a song) is ***going through your head/mind***, you are thinking about it or remembering it. • I don't know what was *going through her mind* [=I don't know what her thoughts were; I don't know why she did this] when she agreed to help him. • That song keeps *going through my head.* **f :** to do (something) • It took him about an hour to *go through* his usual morning routine. • Before we practice the next section, let's *go through* the chorus once again. — see also *go through the motions* at [1]MOTION **2** ✧ Something (such as a law or contract) that ***goes through*** is officially accepted and approved. • The bill is expected to *go through* easily. • The proposed deal failed to *go through.* • The bill ***went through Congress/Parliament*** [=was passed by Congress/Parliament] without difficulty and soon became law. **3** ***go through with (something)*** **:** to do (something that you have thought or talked about) • He was always threatening to quit his job, but I never thought he'd actually *go through with* it. [=I never thought he would actually do it]

go to [*phrasal verb*] **1** ***go to (something)*** **:** to begin to be in (a particular state, condition, or situation) • You need to ***go to sleep.*** • The countries ***went to war.*** **2** ***go to (someone or something)*** **:** to be given to (someone or something) • First prize *went to* the team from Chicago. • The property will *go to* his wife if he dies before she does. **3** ***go to (trouble or expense)*** *chiefly US* **:** to do something that causes you (trouble or expense) • You shouldn't *go to all this trouble* just for me. • They *went to a lot of expense* [=they spent a lot of money] to make sure that the job was done correctly.

go together [*phrasal verb*] **1** *not used in progressive tenses* **:** to be suited to or appropriate for each other • The tie and his suit *go together* well. — see also GO WITH 2 (below) **2** *somewhat old-fashioned* **:** to have a continuing romantic relationship • They've been *going together* for several years. — see also GO WITH (below)

go to show/prove **:** to help show or prove something • Her success ***goes to show*** that if you work hard, you can make your dreams come true.

go toward(s) [*phrasal verb*] ***go toward(s) (something)*** **:** to help pay for (something) • My extra income is *going towards* a new car. • Your donations will *go toward* better sanitation for refugees.

go under [*phrasal verb*] **1 :** to sink below the surface of the water • The ship *went under* after being struck by a torpedo. **2 :** to fail **:** to not succeed • The company has been losing money and is in danger of *going under.*

go up [*phrasal verb*] **1 :** to rise to a higher level • Prices are expected to *go up* soon. **2 :** to become brighter • The lights *went up* [=the lights were turned up] when the movie ended. **3 :** to be built • A new store is *going up* downtown. **4 :** to travel *to* a place (especially one that is to the north) • We *went up to* the lake for the weekend.

go with [*phrasal verb*] **1** ***go with (someone)*** **:** to have a continuing romantic relationship with (someone) **:** to date (someone) • I've been *going with* her for quite a while now. — see also GO OUT 4b (above), GO TOGETHER 2 (above) **2** ***go with (something)*** **a :** to be suitable for or appropriate with (something) • The skirt she's wearing doesn't really *go with* [=*match*] her blouse. • The tie *goes* (well) *with* his suit. • Do you think this wine will *go* well *with* dinner? — see also GO TOGETHER 1 (above) **b :** to exist or occur as a necessary part of (something) • If I want the job I have to accept the stress that *goes with* it. • There are a lot of responsibilities that *go with* starting your own business. — see also *go with the territory* at TERRITORY **3** ***go with (someone or something)*** **:** to choose or use (someone or something) • After thinking about who to offer the job to, they decided to *go with* the more experienced candidate. • The golfer *went with* an iron off the tee. [=the golfer used an iron for her tee shot]

go without [*phrasal verb*] ***go without or go without (something)*** **:** to not have (something) **:** to live or continue without having (something) • How long can you *go without* sleeping/sleep? • If you can't afford a new car, you'll just have to *go without.*

here goes (nothing) see [1]HERE

here/there you go (again) *informal* — used to say that something is happening again or in the same way that it has happened before • *There you go*, making a big deal out of nothing. • When I saw his name in the headlines I thought, "*Here we go again.*"

how goes it? — used as an informal greeting • Hi Paul. *How goes it*? [=how are you?]

ready, set, go see [1]READY

there go/goes *informal* — used to say that something is no longer available or possible • Look at that traffic jam! *There goes* our only chance of arriving on time. [=our only chance of arriving on time is gone/lost] • It's supposed to rain this weekend, so *there go* our plans for a barbecue. [=we won't be able to have a barbecue]

to go **1 :** still remaining • There are only three more days *to go* until my birthday! **2** *US, of food* **:** sold to be taken away and eaten somewhere else • "I'd like a hamburger." "For here or *to go*?" "*To go.*"

[2]go *noun, pl* **goes**

1 [*count*] **:** an attempt to do something • "I can't get the window open." "Let me ***have a go*** (at it)." [=let me try to do it] • She's been thinking about learning to fly for many years, and she's finally decided to ***give it a go.*** [=she's finally decided to try doing it] • (*chiefly Brit*) He managed to finish the work ***in/at one go.*** [=in one attempt, without stopping] • (*chiefly Brit*) I don't know if this new medicine will help, but I think it's ***worth a go.*** [=it's worth a try]

2 [*singular*] *US, informal* **:** permission to do something • My boss gave the project a *go.* [=my boss gave permission for the project to go ahead] ✧ In informal U.S. English, if you say that something ***is a go***, you mean that it will or can happen in the way that was planned or hoped for. • The rocket launch *is a go.* • After many delays, we finally received word that the project *is a go.* If you say ***all systems (are) go***, you mean that everything is working correctly so that something can continue or proceed in the planned or expected way. • NASA officials have declared *all systems go* for the rocket launch. • The problems have been fixed, and now *all systems are go.*

3 [*noncount*] *chiefly Brit, informal* **:** energy that makes someone want to do many things • a young reporter who's full of *go* — see also GET-UP-AND-GO

4 [*count*] *Brit* : a turn in a game or other activity ▪ It's your *go*: they've had several *goes* already.
all go *Brit, informal* : full of activity : very busy ▪ In this office it's *all go* all day without a break.
have a go at *Brit, informal* : to attack or criticize (someone) ▪ The press is *having a go at* the Prime Minister.
make a go of : to succeed in doing (something) ▪ He tried starting his own business, but he wasn't able to *make a go of* it. [=he wasn't able to succeed]
no go *US, informal* — used to say that something will not be allowed or cannot be done ▪ We tried and tried to get the computer running but it was just *no go*. ▪ I asked my boss for more time to finish the project, but she said *no go*. [=she said I could not have more time]
on the go **1** : very active or busy ▪ a housewife and mother who's always *on the go* **2** *chiefly Brit* : happening or going ▪ They have several projects *on the go* at the same time.

[1]**goad** /ˈgoʊd/ *verb* **goads; goad·ed; goad·ing** [+ *obj*] : to urge or force (someone) to do something ▪ He was *goaded* (on) by a sense of duty. ▪ The threat of legal action should *goad* them into complying/compliance.

[2]**goad** *noun, pl* **goads** [*count*]
1 : a pointed rod used to make an animal move forward
2 : someone or something that urges or forces someone to do something ▪ The threat of legal action is a powerful *goad* to companies that have ignored the regulations.

[1]**go–ahead** /ˈgowəˌhɛd/ *noun*
the go-ahead : permission to do something ▪ We've finally been ***given the go-ahead*** for the project. ▪ The company ***received/got the go-ahead*** to manufacture the new drug. — see also *go ahead* at [1]GO

[2]**go–ahead** *adj, always used before a noun*
1 *US, sports* : allowing a team to take the lead in a game ▪ He scored the *go-ahead* run/touchdown/goal.
2 [*more* ~; *most* ~] *Brit* : having a lot of energy and desire to try new ideas and methods ▪ a vigorous *go-ahead* company — see also *go ahead* at [1]GO

goal /ˈgoʊl/ *noun, pl* **goals** [*count*]
1 : something that you are trying to do or achieve ▪ He set a *goal* for himself of exercising at least three times a week. ▪ Her primary/long-term *goal* is to get a college degree. ▪ We all share/have a common *goal*. ▪ She pursued her *goal* of starting her own business. ▪ The company has instituted several new policies with the *goal* of reducing waste. ▪ achieve/accomplish/reach/realize a *goal*
2 a : an area or object into which a ball or puck must be hit, kicked, etc., to score points in various games (such as soccer and hockey) ✧ If you are the player who guards the goal in a sport like hockey or soccer, your position is ***in goal***. ▪ He has played brilliantly *in goal* so far this year. ✧ In U.S. English, a shot or kick that is ***on goal*** is directed at the goal. ▪ They had a dozen shots *on goal* in the second period. **b** : the act of hitting, kicking, etc., a ball or puck into a goal or the score that results from doing this ▪ Last month he had 10 *goals* and six assists. ▪ She scored the winning *goal* in the game's final minute. ▪ The team was ahead by a *goal* [=was ahead by one] when the third period started. — see also FIELD GOAL
– **goal·less** /ˈgoʊlləs/ *adj* ▪ After playing the first half, both teams were still *goalless*. [=neither team had scored a goal]

goal·ie /ˈgoʊli/ *noun, pl* **-ies** [*count*] : a player who defends the goal in a game (such as soccer or hockey)

goal·keep·er /ˈgoʊlˌkiːpɚ/ *noun, pl* **-ers** [*count*] : a player who defends the goal in various games (especially soccer) — compare GOALTENDER
– **goal·keep·ing** /ˈgoʊlˌkiːpɪŋ/ *noun* [*noncount*]

goal line *noun, pl* **~ lines** [*count*] : a line that must be crossed to score a goal in soccer, hockey, football, etc.

goal mouth *noun, pl* **~ mouths** [*count*] : the area directly in front of the goal in soccer, hockey, etc.

goal·post /ˈgoʊlˌpoʊst/ *noun, pl* **-posts** [*count*] : one of two upright posts that form part of the goal in various games (such as soccer, hockey, and football)
move/shift the goalposts *Brit* : to change the rules or requirements in a way that makes success more difficult

goal·tend·er /ˈgoʊlˌtɛndɚ/ *noun, pl* **-ers** [*count*] *US* : a player who defends the goal in various games (especially hockey) — compare GOALKEEPER
– **goal·tend·ing** /ˈgoʊlˌtɛndɪŋ/ *noun* [*noncount*]

go–around /ˈgowəˌraʊnd/ *noun, pl* **-arounds** [*count*] *chiefly US, informal* : GO-ROUND

goat /ˈgoʊt/ *noun, pl* **goats**
1 [*count*] : a small animal that is related to the sheep
2 ***the goat*** *US* : a person who is blamed for a loss or failure ▪ In the last inning, a home run can make you the hero, and a strikeout can make you *the goat*.

goat

get your goat *informal* ✧ If something *gets your goat*, it upsets you or irritates you. ▪ The way she's always correcting other people really *gets my goat*!
old goat *informal* — used as an insulting way to refer to an old man ▪ She got married to some rich *old goat*.
separate the sheep from the goats see [1]SEPARATE

goat cheese *noun, pl* **~ cheeses** [*count, noncount*] *chiefly US* : a cheese that is made from goat's milk

goa·tee /goʊˈtiː/ *noun, pl* **-tees** [*count*] : a small pointed beard on a man's chin — see picture at BEARD
– **goa·teed** /goʊˈtiːd/ *adj* ▪ a *goateed* man

goat·herd /ˈgoʊtˌhɚd/ *noun, pl* **-herds** [*count*] : a person who watches over a herd of goats

goat·skin /ˈgoʊtˌskɪn/ *noun, pl* **-skins** [*count, noncount*] : leather made from the skin of a goat ▪ *goatskin* gloves

[1]**gob** /ˈgɑːb/ *noun, pl* **gobs**
1 [*count*] : a lump of something ▪ There's a *gob* of gum stuck to the bottom of my shoe.
2 ***gobs*** [*plural*] *US, informal* : a large amount of something ▪ They make *gobs* of money. ▪ She wore *gobs* of makeup.
— compare [2]GOB

[2]**gob** *noun, pl* **gobs** [*count*] *Brit slang* : MOUTH ▪ Shut your *gob*! — compare [1]GOB

gob·bet /ˈgɑːbət/ *noun, pl* **-bets** [*count*] *chiefly Brit* : a small lump or piece of something ▪ *gobbets* of meat : a small amount of something ▪ *gobbets* of information

[1]**gob·ble** /ˈgɑːbəl/ *verb* **gob·bles; gob·bled; gob·bling** [+ *obj*]
1 : to swallow or eat (something) quickly ▪ We *gobbled* our meal and rushed back to work. — usually + *down* or *up* ▪ He *gobbled down* a sandwich. ▪ The children are afraid that monsters will *gobble* them *up*.
2 : to take (something) quickly or suddenly — usually + *up* ▪ The local bank was *gobbled up* by a national conglomerate.
– compare [2]GOBBLE

[2]**gobble** *verb* **gobbles; gobbled; gobbling** [*no obj*] : to make the sound that a male turkey makes ▪ The actor *gobbled* like a turkey and quacked like a duck. — compare [1]GOBBLE
– **gobble** *noun, pl* **gobbles** [*count*] ▪ We heard the *gobble* of a turkey.

gob·ble·dy·gook *also* **gob·ble·de·gook** /ˈgɑːbəldiˌguk/ *noun* [*noncount*] *informal* : speech or writing that is complicated and difficult to understand ▪ The report is just a bunch of *gobbledygook*.

gob·bler /ˈgɑːblɚ/ *noun, pl* **-blers** [*count*] : a male turkey

go–be·tween /ˈgoʊbəˌtwiːn/ *noun, pl* **-tweens** [*count*] : a person who talks to people or groups who disagree in order to help deal with or end the disagreement ▪ He'll act/serve as a *go-between* during the negotiations.

gob·let /ˈgɑːblət/ *noun, pl* **-lets** [*count*] : a container used for drinking liquids that has a round bowl on top of a stem attached to a flat base

gob·lin /ˈgɑːblən/ *noun, pl* **-lins** [*count*] *in stories* : an ugly and sometimes evil creature that likes to cause trouble

gob·smacked /ˈgɑːbˌsmækt/ *adj* [*more* ~; *most* ~] *Brit, informal* : very surprised or shocked : DUMBSTRUCK ▪ I was (really) *gobsmacked* by the news!

god /ˈgɑːd/ *noun*
1 ***God*** [*singular*] **a** : the perfect and all-powerful spirit or being that is worshipped especially by Christians, Jews, and Muslims as the one who created and rules the universe ▪ Does she believe in *God*? ▪ (May) *God* bless us all. ▪ (May) *God* rest her soul. [=I pray that God will give her soul peace now that she has died] ▪ I pray to *God* that no one was seriously injured in the accident. — see also MAN OF GOD **b** ✧ *God* is used informally by itself and in phrases to make a statement or question more forceful or to express surprise, anger, etc. These uses are common but are considered offensive by some people. ▪ *God*, it's hot out today. ▪ ***Good God***, that's a lot of food! ▪ ***God Almighty***, is it that late already? ▪ ***My God***, what were you thinking?! ▪ ***Oh my God***! I can't believe it! ▪ ***By God***, I refuse to give up! ▪ ***For God's sake***, what

do you want from me? • Who ***in God's name*** [=*on earth, in heaven's name*] could that be? • Where *in God's name* have you been? • I ***swear to God***, if you're not ready in five minutes, I'm leaving without you. • I ***wish to God*** you would stop complaining.

2 [*count*] : a spirit or being that has great power, strength, knowledge, etc., and that can affect nature and the lives of people : one of various spirits or beings worshipped in some religions • the *gods* and goddesses of ancient Egypt • a Hindu *god* • a myth about the *god* of war • an offering for the *gods* — often used informally to suggest that what happens to someone is controlled by gods or by luck • The *gods* smiled/frowned on us. = The *gods* were/weren't on our side [=we had good/bad luck; things went well/badly for us] • (*humorous*) The golf *gods* seem to like you today. [=you are playing golf very well today] • Her sudden arrival was ***a gift from the gods***. [=a very lucky and helpful thing]

3 [*count*] **a** : a person and especially a man who is greatly loved or admired • a professor who was regarded as a kind of *god* • a guitar *god* like Jimi Hendrix **b** : a person who is very important or powerful in a particular field — usually plural • a talented writer who never found favor with the *gods* of the literary world

4 [*singular*] : something that is regarded as one of the most important things in someone's life • He made a *god* of money. [=he worshipped money; he regarded money as more important than it really is]

5 ***the gods*** *Brit* : the highest and cheapest seats in a theater • The people in *the gods* can be the hardest to please.

act of God see [1]ACT
for the love of God see [1]LOVE
God bless you see BLESS
God forbid see FORBID
God help someone see [1]HELP
God knows see [1]KNOW
God's gift see [1]GIFT
God willing — used to say what you hope and expect to do or happen if no problems occur • We'll be able to move into our new house next week, *God willing*. • *God willing*, I'll finish my degree this year.
in the lap of the gods see [1]LAP
play God see [1]PLAY
put the fear of God into see [1]FEAR
so help me God see [1]HELP
thank God see THANK
(there) but for the grace of God (go I) see [1]GRACE
– god·like /ˈgɑːdˌlaɪk/ *adj*

god–aw·ful /gɑdˈɑːfəl/ *adj* [*more* ~; *most* ~] *informal* + *sometimes offensive* : very bad or unpleasant : AWFUL • *god-awful* [=*terrible*] weather • a *god-awful* [=*hideous*] hat

god·child /ˈgɑːdˌʧajəld/ *noun, pl* **-child·ren** /-ˌʧɪldrən/ [*count*] : a child that you promise to help teach and guide in religious matters when you become the child's godparent in a Christian baptism ceremony • My niece is also my *godchild*.

god·damn *also* **god·dam** /ˌgɑːdˌdæm/ *or* **god·damned** /ˌgɑːdˌdæmd/ *adj, always used before a noun, informal* + *impolite* : DAMN • I don't want to hear another *goddamn* lie. • He's nothing but a *goddamn* fool!

> ***usage*** *Goddamn* is an angry word that many people find offensive.

– god·damn *also* **god·dam** /ˌgɑːdˌdæm/ *or* **goddamned** /ˌgɑːdˌdæmd/ *adv* • It's too *goddamn* late to be talking about this. **– god·damn** *also* **god·dam** /ˈgɑːdˈdæm/ *noun* [*singular*] • I don't give a *goddamn* what you think. [=I don't care at all about what you think] **– god·damn** *also* **god·dam** /ˈgɑːdˈdæm/ *interj* • *Goddamn*! That sauce is hot! **– god·damn** *also* **god·dam** /ˈgɑːdˈdæm/ *verb* [+ *obj*] • *Goddamn* these detours! • I'll be *goddamned* if I let this stop me. [=I will not let this stop me] • ***Goddamn it***. They're gone.

god·daugh·ter /ˈgɑːdˌdɑːtɚ/ *noun, pl* **-ters** [*count*] : a female godchild

god·dess /ˈgɑːdəs/ *noun, pl* **-dess·es** [*count*]
1 : a female god (sense 2) • a *goddess* of ancient Greece
2 : a woman who is greatly loved or admired • The actress, who is already a *goddess* in her own country, is finally getting recognition here.

god·fa·ther /ˈgɑːdˌfɑːðɚ/ *noun, pl* **-thers** [*count*]
1 : a man who is a godparent • Her uncle is her *godfather*.
2 a : a man who invents or begins something • Many people regard him as the *godfather* of rock and roll. **b** *usually* ***Godfather*** : the leader of a group of criminals who belong to a secret criminal organization (such as the Mafia)

God–fear·ing /ˈgɑːdˌfirɪŋ/ *adj* [*more* ~; *most* ~] — used to describe religious people who try to obey the rules of their religion and to live in a way that is considered morally right • They are hardworking, *God-fearing* people.

god·for·sak·en /ˈgɑːdfɚˌseɪkən/ *adj, always used before a noun* [*more* ~; *most* ~] *of a place* : not at all interesting or appealing and usually located far from interesting people and places • a *godforsaken* little town • Who would want to visit such a *godforsaken* place?

God–giv·en /ˈgɑːdˈgɪvən/ *adj* : received as a gift from God • She has a *God-given* [=*natural*] talent for making friends. • *God-given* athletic skills

God·head /ˈgɑːdˌhɛd/ *noun*
the Godhead *formal* : GOD 1; *especially* : God as considered by Christians to be made up of the Father, Son, and Holy Spirit • praying to *the Godhead*

god·less /ˈgɑːdləs/ *adj* [*more* ~; *most* ~] *disapproving* : not believing in God • a *godless* people/society • a *godless* place [=a place where no one believes in God] • *godless* ideologies
– god·less·ness *noun* [*noncount*]

god·ly /ˈgɑːdli/ *adj* **god·li·er; -est** [*or more* ~; *most* ~] *old-fashioned* : believing in God and in the importance of living a moral life • a *godly* person • She lived a *godly* life.
– god·li·ness *noun* [*noncount*] • ***Cleanliness is next to godliness***. [=it is almost as important to be clean as it is to be good]

god·moth·er /ˈgɑːdˌmʌðɚ/ *noun, pl* **-ers** [*count*] : a woman who is a godparent • Her aunt is also her *godmother*. — see also FAIRY GODMOTHER

god·par·ent /ˈgɑːdˌperənt/ *noun, pl* **-ents** [*count*] : a person who promises to help teach and guide someone in religious matters as part of a Christian baptism ceremony : a godfather or godmother • My aunt and uncle are also my *godparents*.

god·send /ˈgɑːdˌsɛnd/ *noun, pl* **-sends** [*count*]
1 : something that provides great and usually unexpected help when it is needed — usually singular • The treatment is a *godsend* for people who suffer from this condition.
2 : a very helpful person — usually singular • I didn't want to hire her but she's turned out to be a real *godsend*.

god·son /ˈgɑːdˌsʌn/ *noun, pl* **-sons** [*count*] : a male godchild

God·speed /ˈgɑːdˈspiːd/ *noun* [*noncount*] *formal* + *old-fashioned* — used to wish success to someone who is going away • We wish you *Godspeed*. — sometimes used as an interjection • Goodbye and *Godspeed* to you.

go·er /ˈgowɚ/ *noun, pl* **-ers** [*count*] *informal*
1 *chiefly Brit* : someone or something that goes or moves fast • The horse is a real *goer*.
2 *Brit* : a woman who has sex with many men • She had a reputation as a bit of a *goer*.

-goer *combining form, pl* **-goers** [*count*] : someone who often goes to a particular kind of place, event, etc. • movie*goers* • church*goers* : someone who goes to a particular event or activity • party*goers*

goes see GO

go·fer /ˈgoufɚ/ *noun, pl* **-fers** [*count*] *informal* : a person whose job is to do various small and usually boring jobs for other people

go–get·ter /ˈgouˈgɛtɚ/ *noun, pl* **-ters** [*count*] *informal* : a person who works very hard and who wants very much to succeed • She's always been a real *go-getter*.
– go–get·ting /ˈgouˌgɛtɪŋ/ *adj, always used before a noun* • a *go-getting* attitude

gog·gle /ˈgɑːgl/ *verb* **gog·gles; gog·gled; gog·gling** [*no obj*] *informal* : to look at something or someone with your eyes very open in a way that shows that you are surprised, amazed, etc. • He *goggled* in amazement at the huge statue.

gog·gle–eyed /ˈgɑːglˌaɪd/ *adj, informal* : with the eyes very open in a way that shows surprise, amazement, etc. • He stared at me *goggle-eyed*. • a *goggle-eyed* child

gog·gles /ˈgɑːglz/ *noun* [*plural*] : special eyeglasses that fit close to your face and that are worn to protect your eyes • swimming/ski *goggles* • safety *goggles*

go–go /ˈgouˌgou/ *adj, always used before a noun*
1 — used to describe a woman who performs as a dancer to fast, energetic, popular music in a nightclub • *go-go* dancers • *go-go* girls
2 *chiefly US* : relating to or involved in a time when many

businesses are growing quickly and it is possible to make a lot of money • He made a fortune during the market's *go-go* years. • a *go-go* economy

[1]go·ing /ˈgowɪŋ/ *noun, pl* **-ings**
1 [*count*] : the act of leaving a place — usually singular • We were disappointed to learn of her *going*. [=*departure*]
2 [*noncount*] **a** : the condition of the ground for walking, running, etc. • The muddy ground made for slippery *going*. [=the muddy ground was slippery] • Debris in the street made the *going* difficult. • The *going* got better as we neared the town. **b** — used to describe a situation in which you are trying to make progress or do something • It's been ***slow going*** so far [=progress has been slow so far], but the project should speed up soon. • The report is pretty ***hard/heavy going***. [=it is quite difficult to understand] • This is a big job, and it's going to be ***rough/tough going*** [=hard work; a difficult situation] for a while. • What will you do ***when the going gets tough***? [=when it becomes difficult to continue or to make progress] • You know what they say—***when the going gets tough, the tough get going***. [=when there are problems, strong people work hard to solve them] • (*chiefly Brit*) Let's get what we can ***while the going is good***. [=while there is a good opportunity]
3 [*noncount*] *chiefly Brit* : forward movement, speed, or progress • She wrote four books in two years, and that's pretty good *going* by any standards!
comings and goings : the activity of people arriving at and leaving a place • I sat and watched the *comings and goings* of the other museum visitors.

[2]going *adj*
1 *always used after a noun, informal* : living or existing • He's the best novelist *going*. • They make the best chili *going*. [=the best chili that there is]
2 *always used before a noun* : current or usual — used to describe an amount of money (such as a price or salary) • What's the *going* price? • They offered to pay the ***going rate*** [=the rate usually paid] for her services.
going on : coming closer to (something, such as an age) • Their daughter is six years old *going on* seven. • It's *going on* 10 years since I saw him last. [=I haven't seen him for almost 10 years]

-going *combining form* : often or regularly going to a particular kind of place, event, etc. • the theater*going* public [=the people who often go to see plays performed] • church*going* people

going concern *noun, pl* ~ **-cerns** [*count*] : a business that is making a profit • They had a difficult start, but they've turned the restaurant into a *going concern*.

go·ing–over /ˌgowɪŋˈouvɚ/ *noun* [*singular*]
1 : a careful examination • I'll give the documents a (thorough) *going-over*. [=I'll read the documents carefully]
2 *informal* : a severe beating • They threatened to give him a (good) *going-over* if he didn't cooperate.
— see also *go over* at [1]GO

go·ings–on /ˌgowɪŋzˈɑːn/ *noun* [*plural*] : actions or events that are occurring : things that are happening • We heard about all the strange *goings-on* [=*happenings*] at the office. — see also *go on* at [1]GO

goi·ter (*US*) *or chiefly Brit* **goi·tre** /ˈgoɪtɚ/ *noun, pl* **-ters** [*count, noncount*] *medical* : a swelling on the front of the neck caused by the thyroid gland becoming too large

go–kart /ˈgouˌkaɚt/ *noun, pl* **-karts** [*count*] : a small car that has one or two seats and an open top and that is used especially for racing

[1]gold /ˈgould/ *noun, pl* **golds**
1 [*noncount*] : a soft yellow metal that is very valuable and that is used especially in jewelry • diamonds in a setting of 24-karat *gold* • What is the price of *gold*? • miners digging for *gold* • solid/pure *gold* — see also FOOL'S GOLD
2 [*noncount*] : gold coins • a bag of *gold* — often used figuratively • All the *gold* [=*money, wealth*] in the world won't make you happy. • She's chasing after a ***pot of gold*** (at the end of the rainbow). [=something impossible to get or achieve]
3 [*count, noncount*] : a deep yellow color — see color picture on page C2
4 [*count*] : GOLD MEDAL • She hopes to bring home a *gold*. • She is ***going for the gold***. [=trying to win the gold medal]
(as) good as gold : very good • The children were *as good as gold* this morning. • His word is *as good as gold*. [=you can always trust him to do what he says he will do]
strike gold see [1]STRIKE
worth your weight in gold : very useful, valuable, or important • Good teachers are *worth their weight in gold*. • An experience like that is *worth its weight in gold*.

[2]gold *adj*
1 : made of or from gold • *gold* jewelry • *gold* bullion
2 : having a gold color • the *gold* [=*golden*] glow of the sun • *gold* paint

gold digger *noun, pl* ~ **-gers** [*count*] *informal* : a woman who becomes or tries to become romantically involved with a rich man in order to get money and gifts from him

gold·en /ˈgouldən/ *adj*
1 : made of gold • a *golden* idol • *golden* jewelry
2 [*more* ~; *most* ~] : having the deep yellow color of gold • *golden* hair • fields of *golden* wheat
3 [*more* ~; *most* ~] : very happy and successful • The memoir recounts the *golden* times in her life. • a *golden* era — see also GOLDEN AGE, GOLDEN YEARS
4 [*more* ~; *most* ~] : very excellent : SUPERB, WONDERFUL • This is a ***golden opportunity***. [=a wonderful opportunity; an excellent chance to do or get something]
5 : very talented, popular, and successful — used in the phrases ***golden boy*** and ***golden girl*** • He was once the *golden boy* of tennis, but now few people remember his name. • She's the *golden girl* of the newspaper business.
6 [*more* ~; *most* ~] : having a rich and smooth sound • a smooth *golden* voice
7 *not used before a noun, informal* : in a very good or fortunate position or situation • If the bank approves the loan, we're *golden*.
8 *always used before a noun* : of or relating to the 50th anniversary of an important event (such as a marriage) • They will celebrate their ***golden (wedding) anniversary*** this year. = (*Brit*) They will celebrate their ***golden wedding*** this year. • a ***golden jubilee*** — compare DIAMOND, SILVER
golden goose *or* ***the goose that lays the golden egg*** see [1]GOOSE
silence is golden see [1]SILENCE

golden age *noun, pl* ~ **ages** [*count*] : a time of great happiness, success, and achievement • the *golden age* of art/literature • a *golden age* for our country

gold·en–ag·er /ˈgouldənˈeɪʤɚ/ *noun, pl* **-ers** [*count*] *US* : an old and often retired person : SENIOR CITIZEN • a club for *golden-agers*

golden eagle *noun, pl* ~ **eagles** [*count*] : a very large bird that lives in the northern parts of the world and that is dark brown with yellow feathers on the back of its head and neck

golden handcuffs *noun* [*plural*] : the salary and benefits that stop a highly paid employee from choosing to leave a job

golden handshake *noun, pl* ~ **-shakes** [*count*] : a large amount of money that a company gives to an employee who is leaving the company

golden oldie *noun, pl* ~ **-ies** [*count*] *informal* : a song, recording, or television show that was very popular in the past • The radio station plays *golden oldies* from the 1950s.

golden parachute *noun, pl* ~ **-chutes** [*count*] : a large amount of money that a company pays to an executive who is being forced to leave the company

golden raisin *noun, pl* ~ **-sins** [*count*] *US* : a dried grape that is a brownish-yellow color and is used for food — called also (*chiefly Brit*) *sultana*

golden retriever *noun, pl* ~ **-ers** [*count*] : a type of dog that has long yellowish-brown fur — see picture at DOG

gold·en·rod /ˈgouldənˌrɑːd/ *noun* [*noncount*] : a type of wild plant that has large groups of yellow flowers

golden rule *noun, pl* ~ **rules**
1 ***the Golden Rule*** : a general rule for how to behave that says that you should treat people the way you would like other people to treat you • I try to live by *the Golden Rule*.
2 [*count*] : an important rule to follow when you do something • The *golden rule* in sales is to know your customer.

golden years *noun* [*plural*] : the late years in someone's life : the time of life when someone is old • My grandparents were active well into their *golden years*. [=*old age*]

gold·finch /ˈgouldˌfɪnʧ/ *noun, pl* **-finch·es** [*count*]
1 : a small mostly yellow American bird — see color picture on page C9
2 : a small European bird that has red on its head and yellow and black wings

gold·fish /ˈgouldˌfɪʃ/ *noun, pl* **goldfish** [*count*] : a small usually orange fish that people often keep in ponds or in fishbowls or tanks as a pet

G

goldfish bowl *noun, pl* ~ **bowls** [*count*] : a place or condition in which there is no privacy • celebrities who cannot escape from the *goldfish bowl* of constant publicity

gold leaf *noun* [*noncount*] : a very thin sheet of gold used especially to decorate a surface • a frame covered with *gold leaf*

gold medal *noun, pl* ~ **-dals** [*count*] : a medal made of gold that is awarded as the prize for first place in a sports competition • He won three *gold medals* in the Olympics. — compare BRONZE MEDAL, SILVER MEDAL

gold mine *noun, pl* ~ **mines** [*count*]
1 : a place where gold is dug from the ground : a mine that produces gold
2 : something that has or produces a lot of something desired (such as money) • When she was the manager, the restaurant was a (real/veritable) *gold mine*! [=it was very profitable] • The library is a *gold mine* of information.

gold–plat•ed /ˈgoʊldˈpleɪtəd/ *adj* : covered with a thin layer of gold • a *gold-plated* serving tray

gold record *noun, pl* ~ **-cords** [*count*] : an award that is given to a singer or musical group for selling a lot of recordings — compare PLATINUM RECORD

gold rush *noun, pl* ~ **rushes** [*count*] : a situation in which many people go quickly to a place where gold has been discovered because they hope to find more gold and become rich • the California *gold rush* of 1849

gold•smith /ˈgoʊldˈsmɪθ/ *noun, pl* **-smiths** [*count*] : a person who makes gold jewelry and other gold items

gold standard *noun*
the gold standard **1 :** a system in which a unit of money (such as the dollar) is equal to a particular amount of gold • It was the early 20th century, and the United States was still on *the gold standard*. **2 :** something that is considered to be the best and that is used to judge the quality or level of other, similar things • This car is *the gold standard* for luxury automobiles. • *the gold standard* of stylish resorts

golf /ˈgɑːlf/ *noun* [*noncount*] : an outdoor game in which players use special clubs (called golf clubs) to try to hit a small ball with as few strokes as possible into each of 9 or 18 holes • playing some *golf* • a round of *golf*
– golf *verb* **golfs; golfed; golfing** [*no obj*] • He likes to *golf*. [=to play golf] **– golf•er** *noun, pl* **-ers** [*count*] • She's an excellent *golfer*. **– golf•ing** /ˈgɑːlfɪŋ/ *noun* [*noncount*] • She enjoys photography and *golfing*. [=playing golf]

golf ball *noun, pl* ~ **balls** [*count*] : a small ball used in the game of golf — see picture at BALL

golf cart *noun, pl* ~ **carts** [*count*] : a small car that is used to carry golfers and their equipment around a golf course

golf club *noun, pl* ~ **clubs** [*count*]
1 : a special long stick with a larger part at the bottom that is used to hit the ball in golf • She bought a new set of *golf clubs*.
2 : an organization whose members play golf • He joined a *golf club* last year; *also* **:** the golf course where the members of such an organization play • I'll meet you at the *golf club*.

golf club

golf course *noun, pl* ~ **courses** [*count*] : a large area of land set up for the game of golf

gol•ly /ˈgɑːli/ *interj, old-fashioned* — used to express mild surprise • *Golly*, I never thought I'd see YOU here!

go•nad /ˈgoʊˌnæd/ *noun, pl* **-nads** [*count*] *technical* : a sex organ that produces sperm or eggs : a testicle or an ovary — called also *sex gland*

gon•do•la /ˈgɑːndələ/ *noun, pl* **-las** [*count*]
1 : a long narrow boat used on the canals of Venice
2 a : the part of a balloon or airship in which passengers or instruments are carried **b :** a vehicle that hangs from a cable and is used for carrying passengers (such as skiers) especially up a mountain

gon•do•lier /ˌgɑːndəˈliə/ *noun, pl* **-liers** [*count*] : a person who operates a gondola (sense 1)

[1]**gone** *past participle of* [1]GO

[2]**gone** /ˈgɑːn/ *adj, not used before a noun*
1 : not present : no longer at a place • How long will he be *gone*? [=*away, absent*] • She should have been back by now. She's been *gone* for more than an hour.
2 a : no longer existing • The days of the horse and buggy are (long) *gone*. **b :** no longer living • There was nothing we could do—he was already *gone*. [=*dead*]
3 *baseball* **:** hit over the fence for a home run • The outfielder went back to the fence and jumped, but the ball was *gone*.
4 *Brit, informal* **:** PREGNANT — used after a noun phrase indicating a length of time • She's six months *gone*. [=she became pregnant six months ago]
dead and gone see [1]DEAD
far gone see [1]FAR
gone on informal + old-fashioned : feeling strong or foolish love for (someone) • Those two are really *gone on* each other.

[3]**gone** *prep, Brit, informal* : AFTER, PAST • It was (just) *gone* six when he got back.

gon•er /ˈgɑːnə/ *noun, pl* **-ers** [*count*] *informal* : someone or something that is going to die or that can no longer be used • I thought we were all *goners* [=were going to die] when the plane's engine stopped. • This old computer is a *goner*. We'll have to get a new one.

gong /ˈgɑːŋ/ *noun, pl* **gongs** [*count*]
1 : a large metal disc that makes a deep ringing sound when it is struck with a padded hammer • They sounded a *gong* to summon us to dinner. — see picture at PERCUSSION
2 *Brit, informal* **:** a medal or award

gon•na /ˈgʌnə, gənə/ — used in writing to represent the sound of the phrase *going to* when it is spoken quickly • I'm *gonna* [=*going to*] get you if it's the last thing I do! ✧ The pronunciation represented by *gonna* is common in informal speech. The written form should be avoided except when trying to represent or record such speech.

gon•or•rhea (*US*) *or Brit* **gon•or•rhoea** /ˌgɑːnəˈriːjə/ *noun* [*noncount*] *medical* : a disease of the sex organs that is spread by sexual contact — called also (*slang*) *the clap*

gon•zo /ˈgɑːnzoʊ/ *adj, always used before a noun, chiefly US, informal* : having a very strange or unusual quality • *gonzo* humor • a *gonzo* comedian • ***gonzo journalism*** [=journalism that treats a subject in a very personal, unusual, and often shocking way]

goo /ˈguː/ *noun* [*noncount*] *informal* : a wet and sticky substance • What's this *goo* all over the stove? — often used figuratively • The movie is nothing but a lot of romantic/sentimental *goo*. [=the movie is too romantic/sentimental] — see also GOOEY

goo•ber /ˈguːbə/ *noun, pl* **-bers** [*count*] *US, informal* : PEANUT 1

[1]**good** /ˈgʊd/ *adj* **bet•ter** /ˈbɛtə/; **best** /ˈbɛst/
1 a : of high quality • The food was *good*. = It was *good* food. • You'll need *better* tools for this job. • The car is in *good* condition/shape. • There are some *good* restaurants in this neighborhood. • That was a *good* game. [=the game was exciting, people played well, etc.] • I'm afraid your work is just not *good* enough. • Keep up the *good* work. • "Would you hire her again?" "Yes, I would. She ***does good work***." • His most recent movie is ***no good***. [=it is boring, poorly made, etc.] **b :** of somewhat high but not excellent quality • The food was *good* but not great. • He has done *good* but not outstanding work.
2 : correct or proper • *good* manners • *good* grammar • She speaks very *good* English. [=she uses correct pronunciation, grammar, etc.]
3 a : pleasant, pleasing, or enjoyable • Did you have a *good* time at the party? • We're expecting *good* weather for the weekend. • The soup tastes/smells *good*. • food that is *good* to eat • It feels *good* to sit down after so much walking. • It's a *good* feeling to know that we were able to help. • *good* [=*happy*] memories • I want to make a *good* [=*favorable*] impression on my future in-laws. • his rugged *good* looks [=attractive appearance] • You look *good* in that dress. = That dress looks *good* on you. • You don't look so *good*. [=you look like you feel sick] Do you feel okay? • ***Have a good day***! = (*US, informal*) ***Have a good one***! [=I hope you have an enjoyable day] — see also GOOD LIFE, GOOD-LOOKING **b :** not having, marked by, or relating to problems, troubles, etc. • *good* and bad news • They've been together in *good* times and bad. • I had a *good* feeling about the meeting. • Things are looking pretty *good* for the company right now. • a *good* omen • I had the *good* luck/fortune to meet her when I was in New York. — see also *good luck* at [1]LUCK **c :** adequate or suitable • It's a *good* day for a sail. • We need to have a meeting. Is tomorrow *good* [=*convenient*] for you? • He's a *good* person to contact if you're ever in trouble. • I need tires that are *good* (for driving) in snow. • These tires aren't ***any good***. = These tires are ***no good***. **d :** sensible or reasonable • She has a very

good reason for being angry. ▪ He showed *good* judgment in buying a small car. ▪ She gave us some *good* advice. ▪ That's a very *good* question/point. ▪ She had the *good* sense to ask for help. [=she showed that she is able to think in a reasonable way by asking for help] ▪ It's a *good* idea to arrive early. ▪ "We'd better arrive early." "*Good* idea/thinking." **e : producing or likely to produce a pleasant or favorable result** ▪ a *good* deal/plan ▪ a *good* risk/investment ▪ a lot of *good* marketing ideas ▪ It's a *good* time to be investing in the stock market. ▪ Please accept our *best* wishes for your success. ▪ "The plane arrived on time." "That's *good*." ▪ Nothing *good* came of our efforts. ▪ It's a *good* thing (that) you answered so quickly. = It was *good* that you answered so quickly. **f : having a desired quality** ▪ We paid a *good* price [=a low price] for the tickets. ▪ The painting should fetch/bring a *good* price [=a high price] when it's sold. ▪ Did you get *good* [=*high*] grades in school? ▪ We found a *good* parking space near the restaurant. ▪ She has *good* taste in clothes. [=she likes clothes that are fashionable, of high quality, etc.] **g : expressing approval or praise** ▪ a movie that has been getting *good* reviews ▪ I've heard a lot of *good* things about you. **h — used in speech as a response** ▪ "I'm ready to go when you are." "*Good*. Let's get going." ▪ "I passed the exam!" "(Very) *Good*!" ▪ "I passed the exam!" "***Good for you***!" = (*chiefly Australia*) "***Good on you***!" [=well done]

4 a : not marked or affected by injury or disease : HEALTHY ▪ I went home early because I wasn't feeling too/very *good*. [=I wasn't feeling well; I was feeling sick] ▪ Her health is pretty *good*. = She's in pretty *good* health. ▪ The patient was reported to be in *good* condition following surgery. ▪ His hearing is still *good* but his eyesight is pretty poor/bad. ▪ my *good* arm/leg [=the arm/leg that is not injured or weak] **b : not causing harm or trouble : causing something desired** ▪ a *good* [=*healthy, healthful*] diet ▪ *good* nutrition ▪ You've been a *good* influence on the kids. ▪ *good* habits ▪ ***good cholesterol*** [=a type of cholesterol that helps prevent a disease that stops your blood from flowing easily] — **often + *for*** ▪ Regular exercise is *good for* you. [=regular exercise makes you healthier] ▪ Hot soup is *good for* a cold. [=hot soup makes you feel better when you have a cold] ▪ Being with friends is especially *good for* him right now.

5 a : not morally bad or wrong : morally proper or correct ▪ a *good* person ▪ *good* conduct/behavior ▪ a woman/man of *good* character ▪ Like most people, she has a *good* side and a bad side. ▪ My intentions were *good*. ▪ You did a *good* thing/deed when you helped that stranger. ▪ He lived a *good* life. ▪ It's hard to tell the ***good guys*** [=morally correct people/characters] from the bad guys in this movie. ▪ She is admired for her many ***good works***. [=for the many things she does to help poor people, sick people, etc.] ▪ You should stay away from that guy. He's ***no good***. [=he's a bad person] — see also GOOD LIFE **b : kind or helpful** ▪ You've always been so *good* to me. ▪ It was *good* of you to answer my request so quickly. — **sometimes used to formally make a request** ▪ ***Would you be good enough*** to show me the way? = ***Would you be so good*** as to show me the way? [=would you please show me the way?] **c : behaving properly : not causing trouble** ▪ a *good* dog ▪ The children were very *good* today.

6 a : having or showing talent or skill : doing or able to do something well ▪ She's a very *good* golfer. ▪ a *good* musician/doctor/cook ▪ He was really *good* in his last movie. [=he acted very well] ▪ I don't know if I'm *good* enough to make the team. ▪ I have a *good* memory. [=I am good at remembering things] ▪ a *good* sense of direction [=an ability to find your way easily in a new place] ▪ an agent with a ***good eye*** for new talent [=an agent who is good at finding talented people who are not yet known or famous] ▪ It's a great school where you know your kids are ***in good hands***. [=with people who are able to teach and take care of them well] ▪ I'm confident the café will be *in good hands* with you in charge. — **often + *at*** ▪ She's very *good at* (playing) golf. ▪ He's not very/any *good at* expressing his feelings. = He's ***no good at*** expressing his feelings. — **sometimes used in a joking way** ▪ I'm very/really *good at* saying the wrong thing. [=I often say things that make people uncomfortable, unhappy, etc.] — see also ***no good, not any good*** at ²GOOD **b : able to use something or to deal with something or someone well — + *with*** ▪ He's very *good with* his hands. [=he can easily make/do things with his hands] ▪ She's *good with* children. [=she manages and interacts with children well; children like her and behave well when they are with her] **c : having a tendency to do something — + *about*** ▪ He's *good about* writing everything down. [=he usually writes everything down] ▪ I'm trying to be *better about* exercising. [=I'm trying to exercise more often]

7 a : happy or pleased ▪ I ***feel good*** about what happened. [=I'm pleased by what happened] ▪ She *felt good* that she had remembered his birthday. = She *felt good* about remembering his birthday. ▪ Helping other people makes me *feel good*. ▪ She didn't *feel good* about having to fire her secretary. **b : cheerful or calm** ▪ She's in a *good* mood. [=a happy mood] ▪ He has a *good* temper. [=he is good-tempered; he doesn't become angry easily] ▪ Everyone was in *good* spirits.

8 ***not used before a noun*** **a — used to say how long something will continue or be valid** ▪ This offer is *good* only until the end of the month. ▪ This offer is ***good for*** the remainder of the month. ▪ Our old car should be *good for* a few more years. [=it should last a few more years; it should continue to operate for a few more years] **b : still suitable to eat or drink : not spoiled** ▪ Is the milk still *good* or has it gone bad?

9 — used in phrases like *good heavens* and *good God* to express surprise or anger or to make a statement or question more forceful ▪ *Good heavens*! You startled me! ▪ "Do you agree with him?" "*Good God*, no!" ▪ (*somewhat old-fashioned*) *Good gracious*, I completely forgot! — see also *good grief* at GRIEF

10 : causing laughter : FUNNY ▪ I heard a *good* joke the other day. ▪ "He says he's never met her." "That's a *good* one. [=that's amusing because it isn't true] I saw them together last week." ▪ She's always ***good for a laugh***. [=she is always funny]

11 a : large in size, amount, or quantity ▪ The store has a *good* selection of products. ▪ She won the election by a *good* [=*considerable*] margin. ▪ He makes *good* money as a lawyer. = He makes a *good* living as a lawyer. [=he earns a lot of money] ▪ They couldn't have succeeded without ***a good deal of*** luck. [=a lot of luck] ▪ Things could be ***a good deal*** worse. [=things could be much worse] ▪ Tourists have been coming to the area ***in good numbers***. [=many tourists have been coming to the area] ▪ an actress who has appeared in ***a good number of*** films [=in many films] **b : not less or fewer than a particular amount : at least — used in the phrase *a good*** ▪ He weighs *a good* 200 pounds. ▪ We waited *a good* hour. [=we waited at least an hour] ▪ There are *a good* 80 people here.

12 ***always used before a noun*** **: forceful or thorough** ▪ If you give the machine a *good* kick, it might start working again. ▪ Give the bottle a *good* shake before you open it. ▪ Take a *good* look at this. ▪ You just need (to get) a *good* night's sleep. ▪ We were scared when it happened, but we had a *good* laugh about it later.

13 : having a high social position or status ▪ He comes from a *good* family. ▪ She thinks her son is too *good* for me. ▪ It's a *good* neighborhood.

14 ***always used before a noun*** **a — used to describe people who know each other well and care about each other very much** ▪ She's a *good* [=*close*] friend of mine. = She and I are *good* friends. ▪ my *good* friend/pal/buddy Joe **b : showing true and constant support for someone** ▪ He's been a *good* friend to me. ▪ I'm trying to be a *better* sister. **c : belonging to and having loyalty to a group or organization** ▪ a *good* party member ▪ a *good* Catholic

15 ***not used before a noun, sports*** **a** ***of a serve or shot*** **: landing in the proper area of the court in tennis and similar games** ▪ I thought the ball/serve was *good* but my opponent said it was out. **b** ***of a shot or kick*** **: successfully done** ▪ (*basketball*) The first foul shot was *good*, but he missed the second one. ▪ (*American football*) The field goal was *good*. ▪ (*American football*) The field goal was ***no good***. [=the field goal was missed]

16 ***not used before a noun, informal*** **: not wanting or needing anything more** ▪ "Would you like more coffee?" "No, thanks. I'm *good*." ▪ "Here's the money I owed you. So we're *good* now, right?" "Yeah, we're *good*." [=we have settled our business; there is no longer any problem between us]

all in good time see ¹TIME

all well and good see ²WELL

as good as **: almost or nearly** ▪ The plan is *as good as* dead. ▪ Those people *as good as* ruined the school with their foolish ideas!

(as) good as gold see ¹GOLD

as good as it gets ***informal*** **1 — used to say that nothing better is possible or available** ▪ It's not a great restaurant, but in this part of the city, it's *as good as it gets*. **2 — used to say that something is very good and cannot be improved** ▪ There's nothing I enjoy more than spending time at home with my family. That's *as good as it gets*.

as good as new see ¹NEW

fight the good fight see [1]FIGHT
for good measure see [1]MEASURE
give as good as you get see [1]GIVE
good and /ˌgudn/ *chiefly US, informal* **1 :** VERY • I hit him *good and* hard. • He was *good and* angry. • I like my coffee *good and* hot. **2 :** completely or entirely • We'll leave when I'm *good and* ready.
good egg see [1]EGG
good for *somewhat informal* **:** able to provide or produce (something) • I'm *good for* a hundred dollars if you need a loan. — see also [1]GOOD 4b, 8a (above)
good for it *informal* **:** able to pay back a loan • Why won't you lend me the money? You know I'm *good for it.* [=you can trust me to pay it back]
good graces see [1]GRACE
good old *informal* — used before a noun to describe a familiar person or thing with affection or approval • *Good old* John: you can always count on him to help. • I don't need fancy shoes. I prefer *good old* sneakers. • They were talking about ***the good old days.*** [=happy times in the past] — see also GOOD OLD BOY
good riddance see RIDDANCE
good to go *US, informal* **:** ready to leave or to start doing something • We have all the tools and supplies we need, so we're *good to go.*
good word see [1]WORD
have it good **:** to be in a favorable position or situation • There's no reason for her to be so unhappy. She really *has it* (pretty) *good.* • He's ***never had it so good.*** [=he has never been in such a favorable situation]
have the good grace see [1]GRACE
hold good **:** to be true • The advice she gave us 10 years ago still *holds good* [=(more commonly) *holds true*] today.
if you know what's good for you **:** if you want to avoid trouble, problems, etc. • You'll take my advice *if you know what's good for you.* • She'll forget about the whole thing *if she knows what's good for her.*
in good company see COMPANY
in good part see [1]PART
make good **1 :** to become successful • It's a story about a kid from a small town trying to *make good* in the big city. ✧ If you ***make good your escape,*** you escape successfully. • The prisoners dug a tunnel under the fence and *made good their escape.* **2 :** to do something that you have promised or threatened to do • He *made good* his promise. — usually + *on* in U.S. English • He *made good on* his promise. • They *made good on* their threat and forced the company to go out of business. **3 a :** to pay for (something) — usually + *on* • The insurance company was required to *make good on* the loss. **b** *chiefly Brit* **:** to repair (something) • The contract obliges you to *make good* any damaged windows.
so far, so good see [1]FAR
too good to be true — used to say that something cannot be as good as it seems to be • The price of the car is *too good to be true.* There must be something wrong with it. • If it looks/seems *too good to be true,* it probably is. [=there is probably some cost or bad part you do not know about]
very good *formal* — used as a response to say you will do something that you have been told or asked to do • "Show the ambassador in." "*Very good,* sir."
what's good for the goose is good for the gander see [1]GOOSE
with (a) good grace see [1]GRACE

[2]**good** *noun, pl* **goods**

1 a [*noncount*] **:** morally good forces or influences • the battle of *good* versus evil • Teachers can be a strong force for *good.* • the difference between *good* and bad **b** [*count*] **:** something that is right or good • They had to sacrifice lesser *goods* for greater ones. • What is life's highest/greatest *good*?

2 ***the good*** **a** [*singular*] **:** the pleasant things that happen to people • You have to ***take the good with the bad.*** [=you have to accept both the good things and the bad things that happen to you] **b** [*singular*] **:** things that are morally proper or correct • Parents must teach their children the difference between *the good* and the bad. **c** [*plural*] **:** morally good people • She believes that *the good* go to heaven when they die and the bad go to hell. • Only *the good* die young.

3 [*noncount*] **:** the part of someone that is kind, honest, generous, helpful, etc. • They cherished the *good* [=*goodness*] in him, overlooking the bad. • She believes there is some *good* in everyone.

4 [*noncount*] **a :** something that helps someone or something to be better, stronger, etc. • She did it ***for the good of*** the community. [=to help the community] • citizens working together ***for the common/public good*** [=to help or benefit everyone] • I know you don't want to do this, but it's ***for your own good.*** [=it will make you stronger, better, etc.] • They talk too much *for their own good.* [=they hurt themselves by talking too much] **b :** a useful or favorable result • What *good* can possibly come of that? • No *good* came of our efforts. = Our efforts ***came to no good.*** [=our efforts did not produce a good or useful result] — see also NO GOOD (below)

5 **goods** [*plural*] **a :** products that are made or grown in order to be sold **:** things for sale • The store sells a variety of *goods.* • baked/canned *goods* • leather/paper *goods* • perishable *goods* such as milk, eggs, and produce • He's accused of selling stolen *goods.* • *goods* and services • a store that sells ***sporting goods*** [=products that are used for playing sports] — see also DAMAGED GOODS, DRY GOODS, DURABLE GOODS, WHITE GOODS **b :** things that are owned by a person • He sold all of his ***worldly goods.*** [=all of his possessions] **c** *Brit* **:** products carried by trains, trucks, etc. **:** FREIGHT — used before another noun • a *goods* lorry — see also GOODS TRAIN

be any good **:** to be useful or helpful • Would an apology *be any good*? [=*any use*]
deliver the goods *or chiefly Brit* ***come up with the goods*** *informal* **:** to produce the desired or promised results **:** to do what is wanted or expected • We knew we could count on him to *deliver the goods.* [=*get the job done*]
do good **1 :** to do kind or helpful things **:** to do things that help other people • She tried to make the community better by *doing good.* • She has *done* a lot of *good* in the community. — see also DO-GOODER **2 a :** to be useful or helpful — used with *any, much, some,* etc. • I tried to convince him to change his mind, but it didn't *do any good.* [=I was unable to convince him] • He's been exercising more and it seems to be *doing some good.* • You can try, but it probably won't *do much good.* • It might *do a little good.* **b :** to be useful to or helpful for someone or something • You should exercise more. It might *do you* (some) *good.* • Weeding regularly will *do* your garden *good.* [=will improve your garden] • The visit with her grandchildren ***did her a world/lot of good.*** = (*Brit*) The visit with her grandchildren ***did her a power of good.*** [=it was very good for her; it made her feel much better and happier] ✧ If you do not think that something is helpful, useful, or worth doing, you can ask ***What good does it do?, What good is it?, What's the good of it?,*** etc. • *What good does it to do* to bring an umbrella along [=why bring an umbrella along] if you are only going to leave it in the car? • *What good is* a college education when you can't get a job after you graduate? • *What's the good of* working hard if your boss doesn't give you any credit for it? • I could try talking to him, but *what good would that do/be*? He has already made up his mind.
for good *also* ***for good and all*** **:** forever • "When is she coming back?" "She's not coming back. She's gone *for good.*"
have/get the goods on *informal* ✧ To *have/get the goods on* someone is to have/get evidence showing that someone has done something wrong. • We can't arrest her until we *get the goods on her.*
in good with *US, informal* **:** in a favored position with (someone) • She's *in good with* the boss. [=the boss likes her]
it's an ill wind that blows no good see [1]ILL
no good *or* ***not any good*** **:** not effective or useful • I tried to convince him to change his mind, but it was *no good,* he wouldn't listen to me. • It's *no good* [=*no use*] talking to him. = It *isn't any good* talking to him. — see also BE ANY GOOD (above)
not much good **:** not very effective or useful • I tried to convince him to change his mind, but it *wasn't much good.*
to the good **1** — used to say that a particular result or effect is good or would be good; usually used after *all* • If the new policy requires the government to keep more accurate records, that's *all to the good.* [=that's a good thing; that's desirable] **2** — used to indicate an amount of gain or profit • In the end, we were $100 *to the good.* [=we gained $100]
up to no good *informal* **:** doing bad things or planning to do bad things • If you ask me, that woman's *up to no good.*

[3]good *adv, informal*
1 *chiefly US* : [1]WELL 1 • Things have been going *good* lately. • The team is doing *good* this year. • "How did you hit the ball today?" "*Good*." ✧ The use of *good* to mean "well" is considered wrong by many people. It occurs mainly in very informal speech.
2 *chiefly US* : completely and thoroughly • The other team whipped us *good*. • That was a funny joke you played on him. You really **got him good**. [=he was completely fooled by the joke] • "They sure soaked you with that bucket of water." "Yeah, they really *got me good*." [=I got completely soaked with water] • (*Brit*) Clean it up **good and proper**.
3 — used for emphasis before words like *long* and *many* • I haven't seen her for **a good long** time. [=a very long time] • There were **a good many** people [=a lot of people] at the meeting. • (*chiefly Brit*) Not all our students go on to university, but **a good few** [=*quite a few*] of them do.

good afternoon *interj, somewhat formal* — used to say hello to someone in the afternoon • *Good afternoon*! Thanks for calling.

Good Book *noun*
the Good Book : BIBLE 1a • As *the Good Book* says . . .

[1]good·bye *also* **good·by** /gʊdˈbaɪ/ *interj* — used to express good wishes when someone is leaving • *Goodbye*! See you later!

[2]goodbye *also* **goodby** *noun, pl* **-byes** *also* **-bys** [*count*]
1 : a remark or gesture made when someone is leaving • He said his *goodbyes* and left. • They said *goodbye* and went their separate ways. • They waved *goodbye* from the window. • She kissed him *goodbye*. — sometimes used figuratively • She **said goodbye to** her old job. [=she left her old job]
2 : a time or occasion when someone leaves • a tearful *goodbye* • I can't stand long *goodbyes*.
kiss (something) goodbye see [1]KISS

good day *interj, somewhat formal + old-fashioned* — used to say hello or goodbye to someone in the daytime • Welcome and *good day*.

good evening *interj, somewhat formal* — used to say hello to someone in the evening • *Good evening*, everyone.

good faith *noun* [*noncount*] : honesty in dealing with other people • You have no right to question my *good faith*. — often used before another noun • a *good-faith* effort — compare BAD FAITH
in good faith : in an honest and proper way • He bargained *in good faith*. • Both parties acted *in good faith*.

good–for–noth·ing /ˈgʊdfɚˌnʌθɪŋ/ *adj* [*more* ~; *most* ~] *informal* : of no use or value • I like Jane, but I can't stand that lazy *good-for-nothing* brother of hers.
– good–for–nothing *noun, pl* **-things** [*count*] • Her brother is a lazy *good-for-nothing*.

Good Friday *noun, pl* ~ **-days** [*count, noncount*] : the Friday before Easter that is observed by Christians as the anniversary of the death of Jesus Christ

good–heart·ed /ˈgʊdˈhɑɚtəd/ *adj* [*more* ~; *most* ~] : kind and generous • He's a *good-hearted* [=*kindhearted*] fellow. • She offered a *good-hearted* [=*well-meaning*] apology.

good–hu·mored (*US*) *or Brit* **good–hu·moured** /ˈgʊdˈhjuːməd/ *adj* [*more* ~; *most* ~] : pleasant and cheerful • She was still *good-humored* at the end of a tiring day. • He offered his comments in a *good-humored* manner.
– good–hu·mored·ly (*US*) *or Brit* **good–hu·moured·ly** *adv*

goodie *variant spelling of* GOODY

good·ish /ˈgʊdɪʃ/ *adj, chiefly Brit* : somewhat good • She did a *goodish* [=*fair*] amount of work. • a *goodish* wine

good life *noun*
the good life **1** *US* : the kind of life that people with a lot of money are able to have • She grew up poor, but now she's living *the good life*. • His idea of *the good life* includes owning several luxury cars. **2** : a happy and enjoyable life • She gave up a good job in the city to move to the country in search of *the good life*.

good–look·er /ˈgʊdˈlʊkɚ/ *noun, pl* **-ers** [*count*] *informal* : an attractive person • Your girlfriend's a real *good-looker*! [=she is very good-looking]

good–look·ing /ˈgʊdˈlʊkɪŋ/ *adj* [*more* ~; *most* ~] : having a pleasing or attractive appearance : pretty, handsome, or beautiful • a very *good-looking* woman/man

good·ly /ˈgʊdli/ *adj, always used before a noun* **good·li·er**; **-est** *somewhat old-fashioned* : large in size or amount • We expect a *goodly* [=*good*] number of people to show up. • He lives a *goodly* [=*considerable*] distance from his family. • a *goodly* sum

good morning *interj* — used to say hello to someone in the morning • *Good morning*. How are you today?

good name *noun, pl* ~ **names** [*count*] : a person's good reputation • I don't want the scandal to ruin my *good name*.

good–na·tured /ˈgʊdˈneɪtʃɚd/ *adj* [*more* ~; *most* ~] : friendly, pleasant, or cheerful • Her *good-natured* personality put us all at ease. • a *good-natured* competition — opposite ILL-NATURED
– good–na·tured·ly *adv*

good·ness /ˈgʊdnəs/ *noun* [*noncount*]
1 : the quality or state of being good: such as **a** : the quality or state of being kind, honest, generous, helpful, etc. • I believe there is (some) *goodness* in everyone. • Even if you don't agree, at least **have the goodness** to be polite! • She agreed to help him **out of the goodness of her heart**. [=because she is a kind and generous person] **b** : the quality or state of being useful or effective • If you cook the vegetables too long, they'll lose all their (natural) *goodness*.
2 — used to express mild surprise or shock • *Goodness*, it's hot out today! • *Goodness* (only) knows how it happened. • "Did you stop them?" "*Goodness* (gracious), no!" • Oh, **my goodness**! ✧ People use **I swear to goodness, I hope to goodness**, or **I wish to goodness** to add force to a statement. • *I wish to goodness* that you would hurry up!
for goodness' sake — used to express surprise or annoyance • Will you hurry up, *for goodness' sake*?
goodness knows see [1]KNOW

good night *interj* — used to express good wishes in the evening especially when someone is leaving or going to sleep • *Good night*. I'll see you in the morning.

good old boy *or* **good ol' boy** *or* **good ole boy** /ˈgʊdoʊlˌbɔɪ/ *noun, pl* ~ **boys** [*count*] *US, informal* : a white man from the southern U.S. who has interests, beliefs, etc., that are commonly associated with white southern men

Good Sa·mar·i·tan /-səˈmerətən/ *noun, pl* **-tans** [*count*] : a person who helps other people and especially strangers when they have trouble • We had a flat tire on the highway but fortunately a *Good Samaritan* stopped to help us change it.

good–sized /ˈgʊdˈsaɪzd/ *adj* : somewhat large • They live in a *good-sized* house. • a *good-sized* crowd

goods train *noun, pl* ~ **trains** [*count*] *Brit* : FREIGHT TRAIN

good–tem·pered /ˈgʊdˈtɛmpɚd/ *adj* [*more* ~; *most* ~] : usually calm and cheerful : not easily angered or upset • a *good-tempered* dog • The baby is very *good-tempered*. [=the baby has a very good temper]

good·will /ˌgʊdˈwɪl/ *noun* [*noncount*]
1 *or* **good will** : a kind, helpful, or friendly feeling or attitude • She has/feels *goodwill* toward all her coworkers. • They allowed him to keep the extra money as a gesture of *goodwill*. • trying to promote *goodwill* • people of *goodwill* — often used before another noun • a *goodwill* gesture • a *goodwill* ambassador on a *goodwill* tour/mission
2 *business* : the amount of value that a company's good reputation adds to its overall value • *goodwill* and other assets • loss of *goodwill*

goody *or* **good·ie** /ˈgʊdi/ *noun, pl* **good·ies** [*count*] *informal*
1 : something that tastes good • She gave each of the children a *goody* at snack time. — usually plural • The store sells cakes and pies and all kinds of other *goodies*.
2 : something that people want or like : something desirable • The company offers health insurance, paid vacation, and other *goodies* like stock options. • This song is an oldie but a *goodie*. • Each guest was given a **goody bag**. [=a bag containing a small gift]
3 *somewhat old-fashioned* — used in speech especially by children or when talking to children to show excitement and pleasure • "Are we going to the circus? *Goody*!"
4 *Brit* : a good person in a book, movie, etc. • He plays one of the *goodies* [=*good guys*] in his latest film and defeats all the baddies.

goody–goody /ˌgʊdiˈgʊdi/ *noun, pl* **-goodies** [*count*] *informal + disapproving* : a person (such as a child) whose good behavior and politeness are annoying because they seem to be excessive or not sincere • The other kids don't like her because she's a *goody-goody*. [=*goody two-shoes*] — often used before another noun • He can't stand *goody-goody* types.

goody two–shoes *or* **Goody Two–shoes** /ˈgʊdiˈtuː-

ˌfu:z/ *noun, pl* ~ **two–shoes** *or* ~ **Two–shoes** [*count*] *informal + disapproving* : GOODY-GOODY ▪ You didn't invite her to the party, did you? She's such a *goody two-shoes*.

goo•ey /ˈgu:wi/ *adj* **goo•ier; -est** *informal* : wet and sticky ▪ We had *gooey* hot fudge sundaes. ▪ a *gooey* mess — often used figuratively ▪ a *gooey* romantic comedy [=a very sentimental romantic comedy]

[1]**goof** /ˈgu:f/ *verb* **goofs; goofed; goof•ing** *chiefly US, informal* : to make a careless or stupid mistake : to make a goof [*no obj*] It was clear that someone had *goofed*. — often + *up* ▪ I really *goofed up* this time. [+ *obj*] — usually + *up* ▪ They both *goofed up* their lines.

goof around [*phrasal verb*] *chiefly US, informal* : to spend time doing silly or playful things ▪ The kids are *goofing around*, watching TV and hanging out.

goof off [*phrasal verb*] *chiefly US, informal* : to spend time doing things that are not useful or serious ▪ He spent the day *goofing off* instead of working. — see also GOOF-OFF

goof on [*phrasal verb*] ***goof on (someone or something)*** *US slang* : to make jokes about (someone or something) in a way that is either playful or unkind ▪ They're just *goofing on* [=*kidding with, teasing*] you.

[2]**goof** *noun, pl* **goofs** [*count*] *chiefly US, informal*
1 : a silly or stupid person ▪ Don't be such a *goof*.
2 : a careless or stupid mistake ▪ I'll admit it's my *goof*. ▪ I made a major *goof*.

goof•ball /ˈgu:fˌbɑ:l/ *noun, pl* **-balls** [*count*] *US, informal* : a silly or stupid person : GOOF

goof–off /ˈgu:fˌɑ:f/ *noun, pl* **-offs** [*count*] *chiefly US, informal* : a person who avoids work or responsibility : someone who goofs off a lot ▪ *goof-offs* who never do any work

goofy /ˈgu:fi/ *adj* **goof•i•er; -est** [*also more* ~; *most* ~] *informal* : crazy or silly ▪ She was making *goofy* faces at us in class. ▪ a *goofy* grin/smile ▪ He's a *goofy* guy. ▪ an actress known for her *goofy* charm
– **goof•i•ly** /ˈgu:fəli/ *adv* ▪ He smiled *goofily*. – **goof•i•ness** /ˈgu:finəs/ *noun* [*noncount*] ▪ a moment of *goofiness* in an otherwise serious interview

goo•gly–eyed /ˈgu:gliˌaɪd/ *adj* : having eyes that stick out ▪ a *googly-eyed* monster ▪ a *googly-eyed* frog : having eyes that are very open or staring because of amazement, admiration, etc. ▪ *googly-eyed* lovers ▪ *googly-eyed* fans

goon /ˈgu:n/ *noun, pl* **goons** [*count*] *informal*
1 *chiefly US* : a person who is hired to threaten, beat up, or kill someone : THUG ▪ He was beat up by a couple of *goons*.
2 *chiefly Brit* : a stupid person

goop /ˈgu:p/ *noun* [*noncount*] *informal* : a sticky or greasy substance ▪ I stepped in some *goop*.

[1]**goose** /ˈgu:s/ *noun, pl* **geese** /ˈgi:s/
1 [*count*] : any one of many different kinds of birds that swim, that are larger than ducks, and that have a long neck and webbed feet ▪ a flock/gaggle of *geese*
2 [*count*] : a female goose — compare GANDER
3 [*noncount*] : the meat of a goose used as food ▪ roast *goose*
4 [*count*] *informal + old-fashioned* : a foolish or silly person — usually singular ▪ You silly *goose*.

cook someone's goose see [2]COOK

the golden goose or the goose that lays the golden egg : something that is a very good source of money or business ▪ The city's leaders don't want to do anything that could ***kill the golden goose*** of tourism.

what's good for the goose is good for the gander (*US*) *or chiefly Brit* ***what's sauce for the goose is sauce for the gander*** — used to say that one person or situation should be treated the same way that another person or situation is treated ▪ If he can go out with his friends at night, then she should be able to, too. *What's good for the goose is good for the gander.*

wouldn't say boo to a goose see [1]BOO
– see also WILD GOOSE CHASE

[2]**goose** *verb* **goos•es; goosed; goos•ing** [+ *obj*] *US, informal*
1 : to touch or pinch (someone) on the buttocks
2 : to increase the activity or amount of (something) ▪ They hope the new product will help to *goose* (up) profits.

goose•ber•ry /ˈgu:sˌberi, *Brit* ˈgʊzbri/ *noun, pl* **-ries** [*count*]
1 : a small green berry that has a sour taste — see color picture on page C5
2 *Brit, informal* : an extra person who is present when two other people (such as lovers) want to be alone together — used especially in the phrase ***play gooseberry*** ▪ He was left to *play gooseberry* while the other two talked and laughed all evening.

goose bumps *noun* [*plural*] *chiefly US, informal* : small bumps on your skin that are caused by cold, fear, or a sudden feeling of excitement ▪ I get *goose bumps* every time I think about it. ▪ It gives me *goose bumps*. — called also *goose flesh*, (*chiefly Brit*) *goose pimples*

goose egg *noun, pl* ~ **eggs** [*count*] *US, informal* : a score of zero ▪ The two teams matched *goose eggs* [=they both scored no runs] for five innings. ▪ They put another *goose egg* up on the scoreboard.

goose•neck /ˈgu:sˌnek/ *noun, pl* **-necks** [*count*] : a flexible metal pipe

goose step *noun* [*singular*] : a way of marching by kicking your legs forward very high and not bending your knees
– **goose–step** /ˈgu:sˌstep/ *verb* **-steps; -stepped; -stepping** [*no obj*] ▪ The soldiers *goose-stepped* past the general in the parade.

GOP /ˌʤi:ˌoʊˈpi:/ *noun*
the GOP : the Republican Party of the U.S. ▪ longtime members of *the GOP* — often used as *GOP* before another noun ▪ a *GOP* governor ▪ attending the *GOP* convention ✧ *GOP* is an abbreviation of "Grand Old Party."

go•pher /ˈgoʊfɚ/ *noun, pl* **-phers** [*count*] : an American animal that is similar to a large rat and that lives in the ground

gopher ball *noun, pl* ~ **balls** [*count*] *baseball, informal* : a pitch that a batter hits for a home run ▪ a pitcher who has thrown eight *gopher balls* so far this year

Gor•di•an knot /ˈgoɚdijən-/ *noun, pl* ~ **knots** [*count*] : a complicated and difficult problem ▪ a *Gordian knot* of legal troubles

cut the Gordian knot : to solve a difficult problem in a very direct way by doing something forceful or extreme

[1]**gore** /ˈgoɚ/ *noun* [*noncount*]
1 : thick blood from a wound
2 : violent images or scenes that show a lot of blood ▪ The movie contains excessive violence, *gore*, and profanity. ▪ blood and *gore*

[2]**gore** *verb* **gores; gored; gor•ing** [+ *obj*] *of an animal* : to wound (a person or another animal) with a horn or tusk ▪ The bull *gored* him. — usually *(be) gored* ▪ He *was gored* by a bull.

[1]**gorge** /ˈgoɚʤ/ *noun, pl* **gorg•es** [*count*]
1 : a deep, narrow area between hills or mountains
2 ✧ If ***your gorge rises*** you feel sick, disgusted, or angry. ▪ My *gorge rises* [=I feel very angry] when I think of children living in such bad conditions. ▪ a disgusting odor that ***made my gorge rise*** [=made me feel like vomiting]

[2]**gorge** *verb* **gorg•es; gorged; gorg•ing**
1 : to eat large amounts of food — usually + *on* [*no obj*] We *gorged on* chips and cookies. [+ *obj*] We ***gorged ourselves on*** chips and cookies.
2 [+ *obj*] : to fill (something) completely — usually used as *(be) gorged* ▪ tissue *gorged* with blood

gor•geous /ˈgoɚʤəs/ *adj* [*more* ~; *most* ~]
1 : very beautiful or attractive ▪ Your baby is absolutely *gorgeous*! ▪ a *gorgeous* young man/woman ▪ a *gorgeous* red dress
2 : very enjoyable or pleasant ▪ *gorgeous* summer afternoons
– **gor•geous•ly** *adv* ▪ The book is *gorgeously* illustrated.
– **gor•geous•ness** *noun* [*noncount*]

Gor•gon /ˈgoɚgən/ *noun, pl* **-gons** [*count*] : any one of the three sisters in Greek mythology who had snakes for hair and who could turn anyone who looked at them into stone ▪ Medusa the *Gorgon*

Gor•gon•zo•la /ˌgoɚgənˈzoʊlə/ *noun* [*noncount*] : an Italian cheese that contains blue mold and that has a strong flavor

go•ril•la /gəˈrɪlə/ *noun, pl* **-las** [*count*]
1 : a type of very large ape that has black fur and that comes from Africa — see picture at APE
2 *informal* : a large, strong, and usually ugly or frightening man ▪ She hired some *gorilla* as her bodyguard.

800-pound gorilla *US, informal* : someone or something that is very powerful and difficult to control or ignore ▪ Their company is the *800-pound gorilla* of the computer industry.

gorm•less /ˈgoɚmləs/ *adj* [*more* ~; *most* ~] *Brit, informal* : very stupid or foolish ▪ a *gormless* fool

go–round /ˈgoʊˌraʊnd/ *noun, pl* **-rounds** [*count*] *chiefly US, informal* : one of a series of repeated actions or events ▪ I missed their show (on) the first *go-round*. [=the first time they came here] — called also *go-around*

gory /ˈgori/ *adj* **gor·i·er; -est :** having or showing a lot of violence and blood ▪ a *gory* crime scene ▪ *gory* horror movies
gory detail(s) *informal* ✧ To describe something ***in gory detail*** or to give ***(all) the gory details*** about something is to tell all the small details about something that is unpleasant or interesting in a shocking way. ▪ The murder was described *in gory detail*. ▪ Please, spare us *the gory details*. [=do not tell us all the unpleasant facts]

gosh /ˈgɑːʃ/ *interj, informal* — used to express surprise or mild anger ▪ "*Gosh*, is she OK?" ▪ "Oh *gosh*, that's beautiful!" ▪ *Gosh* darn it!

gos·ling /ˈgɑːzlɪŋ/ *noun, pl* **-lings** [*count*] **:** a young goose

go–slow /ˌgoʊˈsloʊ/ *noun, pl* **-slows** [*count*] *Brit* **:** an action in which workers protest against an employer by working slowly

gos·pel /ˈgɑːspəl/ *noun, pl* **-pels**
1 *or* **Gospel** [*singular*] **:** the teachings of the Christian religion — usually used with *the* ▪ preaching/spreading *the Gospel* [=telling people about Christianity]
2 ***Gospel*** [*count*] **:** any one of the first four books of the Christian Bible that tell of the life of Jesus Christ ▪ a reading from the *Gospel* of St. John
3 [*singular*] **:** an idea or set of ideas that someone believes and often tries to make other people believe ▪ She's always spreading/preaching the *gospel* of good health. [=telling people about the importance of good health]
4 [*noncount*] **:** something that is believed to be definitely true ▪ These myths are ***accepted/taken as gospel*** [=believed to be true] by many teenagers. ▪ I didn't do it, and that's ***the gospel truth***. [=the absolute truth; a completely true statement]
5 [*noncount*] **:** a type of Christian music that was created by African-Americans in the southern U.S. ▪ She sings *gospel*. ▪ a *gospel* choir — called also *gospel music*

gos·sa·mer /ˈgɑːsəmɚ/ *noun* [*noncount*]
1 : a piece of a spider's web
2 *literary* **:** a very light or delicate material ▪ a butterfly's wings of *gossamer* — often used before another noun ▪ *gossamer* wings/petals ▪ *gossamer* fabric

¹gos·sip /ˈgɑːsəp/ *noun, pl* **-sips**
1 [*noncount*] **a :** information about the behavior and personal lives of other people ▪ Have you heard the latest (piece of) *gossip* about their divorce? ▪ He had been ***spreading gossip*** about his coworkers. **b :** information about the lives of famous people ▪ the latest news and *gossip* from the entertainment industry ▪ She writes a *gossip* column in the paper. ▪ a *gossip* columnist
2 [*count*] **:** a person who often talks about the private details of other people's lives ▪ He's a terrible *gossip*.
3 [*count*] *chiefly Brit* **:** a conversation about the personal lives of other people ▪ I like having a good *gossip* now and then.
– gos·sipy /ˈgɑːsəpi/ *adj* [*more* ~; *most* ~] *informal* ▪ a *gossipy* magazine/writer

²gossip *verb* **-sips; -siped; -sip·ing** [*no obj*] **:** to talk about the personal lives of other people ▪ They spent the afternoon *gossiping* on the phone. ▪ They often *gossip* with each other about their neighbors.
– gos·sip·er *noun, pl* **-ers** [*count*] ▪ a malicious *gossiper*

gos·sip·mon·ger /ˈgɑːsəpˌmɑːŋgɚ, ˈgɑːsəpˌmʌŋgɚ/ *noun, pl* **-gers** [*count*] *disapproving* **:** a person who enjoys talking about other people's private lives **:** a person who spreads gossip

got *past tense and past participle of* GET

¹got·cha /ˈgɑːʧə/ — used in writing to represent the sound of the phrase *got you* when it is spoken quickly ▪ She ran after him, grabbed him by the arm, and said "*Gotcha*!" [=I got you; I caught you] ▪ "We'll have to leave soon, so be ready." "*Gotcha*." [=I have got you; I understand] ✧ The pronunciation represented by *gotcha* occurs only in very informal speech. The written form should be avoided except when you are trying to represent or record such speech.

²got·cha *noun, pl* **-chas** [*count*] *US, informal* **:** an unexpected problem or usually unpleasant surprise ▪ The program has a few *gotchas* in store for unsuspecting computer users.

goth /ˈgɑːθ/ *noun, pl* **goths**
1 [*noncount*] **:** a type of rock music with words that express sad, depressing, or frightening ideas
2 [*count*] **:** a person who listens to or performs goth music, wears mostly black clothing, uses black and white makeup, and often has dyed black hair

Goth·ic /ˈgɑːθɪk/ *adj*
1 : of or relating to a style of writing that describes strange or frightening events that take place in mysterious places ▪ *Gothic* novels
2 : of or relating to a style of architecture that was popular in Europe between the 12th and 16th centuries and that uses pointed arches, thin and tall walls, and large windows ▪ a *Gothic* cathedral

go–to /ˈgoʊˌtuː/ *adj, always used before a noun, US, informal* **:** always helpful **:** producing desired results or information when needed ▪ She's the team's *go-to* player [=she is the player that the team relies on] when they need to score late in the game. ▪ He's the ***go-to guy*** in the office for tax information.

got·ta /ˈgɑːtə/ — used in writing to represent the sound of the phrase *got to* when it is spoken quickly ▪ "We've *gotta* go." [=we have got to go] ▪ "I *gotta* [=have got to] get a new pair of shoes." ✧ The pronunciation represented by *gotta* is common in informal speech. The written form should be avoided except when you are trying to represent or record such speech.

gotten *past participle of* GET

Gou·da /ˈguːdə/ *noun* [*noncount*] **:** a Dutch cheese that has a mild taste

¹gouge /ˈgaʊʤ/ *verb* **goug·es; gouged; goug·ing** [+ *obj*]
1 a : to cut a deep hole in (something) ▪ The lamp fell and *gouged* the table. **b :** to make (a deep hole) in something ▪ A bomb had *gouged* a large crater in the street.
2 *US, informal* **:** to make (someone) pay too much money for something ▪ They feel that they are being *gouged* by the oil companies. ▪ The company has been *gouging* [=*overcharging*] its customers for years. ▪ They have been accused of ***price gouging***. [=making their customers pay too much money]
gouge out [*phrasal verb*] ***gouge out (something) or gouge (something) out*** **1 :** to remove (something) by digging or cutting ▪ The impact of the accident *gouged* a big piece *out* of the wall. ▪ He threatened to *gouge* my eyes *out*. **2 :** to make (a hole or path) by digging or cutting ▪ The river *gouged out* a wide path between the mountains.
– goug·er *noun, pl* **-ers** [*count*] *chiefly US* ▪ a price *gouger*

²gouge *noun, pl* **gouges** [*count*]
1 : a metal tool with a curved, sharp end that is used to cut and shape wood
2 : a deep cut or hole ▪ The accident left a big *gouge* in the side of the car.

gou·lash /ˈguːˌlɑːʃ, *Brit* ˈguːˌlæʃ/ *noun*
1 [*noncount*] **:** a dish of meat, vegetables, and paprika that is slowly cooked in liquid ▪ Hungarian *goulash*
2 [*singular*] **:** a mixture of different things ▪ a *goulash* of facts and figures

gourd /ˈgoɚd, ˈguɚd/ *noun, pl* **gourds** [*count*] **:** any one of several types of fruits that have a hard shell and that are used for decoration and not for eating
out of your gourd *US, informal* **:** CRAZY ▪ That guy is completely *out of his gourd*. [=(more commonly) *out of his mind*] — sometimes used to give emphasis ▪ I was bored *out of my gourd*. [=I was very bored]
– gourd·like /ˈgoɚdˌlaɪk, ˈguɚdˌlaɪk/ *adj* [*more* ~; *most* ~] ▪ a *gourdlike* fruit

gour·mand /ˈguɚˌmɑːnd/ *noun, pl* **-mands** [*count*] **:** a person who loves to eat and drink **:** a person who eats and drinks too much

gourmet /ˈguɚˌmeɪ, guɚˈmeɪ/ *noun, pl* **-mets** [*count*] **:** a person who enjoys and knows a lot about good food and wine
– gour·met *adj, always used before a noun* ▪ a *gourmet* meal [=a meal of very high quality; a meal that appeals to gourmets] ▪ *gourmet* foods ▪ a *gourmet* cook/chef [=an excellent cook/chef who makes gourmet meals]

gout /ˈgaʊt/ *noun* [*noncount*] **:** a disease that causes painful swelling of the joints especially in the toes
– gouty /ˈgaʊti/ *adj* **gout·i·er; -est** ▪ *gouty* toes

gov *abbr* **1 gov.** government **2 Gov.** governor ▪ *Gov.* Jerry Brown **3** government institution — used in Internet addresses ▪ http://www.whitehouse.gov

gov·ern /ˈgʌvɚn/ *verb* **-erns; -erned; -ern·ing**
1 : to officially control and lead (a group of people) **:** to make decisions about laws, taxes, social programs, etc., for (a country, state, etc.) [+ *obj*] Members of the party have *governed* [=*ruled*] the country for the last 20 years. ▪ The tribe is *governed* by a 10-member council. ▪ They want to form their own country and *govern* themselves. [*no obj*] The scandal limited her ability to *govern* effectively. ▪ How would he *govern* if he were elected president?

2 [+ *obj*] : to control the way that (something) is done • She suggested changing the state's laws *governing* the sale of alcohol. • The council *governs* fishing in the region.
3 [+ *obj*] : to control or guide the actions of (someone or something) • We will be studying the forces that *govern* the Earth's climate. • Tradition *governs* all aspects of their lives. • He allows himself to be *governed* by his emotions.
– gov·ern·able /ˈgʌvɚnəbəl/ *adj* [*more* ~; *most* ~] • a *governable* city

gov·er·nance /ˈgʌvɚnəns/ *noun* [*noncount*] *formal* : the way that a city, company, etc., is controlled by the people who run it • They have very different approaches to the *governance* of the city. • corporate *governance*

gov·ern·ess /ˈgʌvɚnəs/ *noun, pl* **-ess·es** [*count*] : a woman who is paid to care for and teach a child in the child's house

governing *adj, always used before a noun*
1 : controlling and making decisions for a country, organization, etc. • She is currently the leader of the *governing* party. • a five-member *governing* board/council/body
2 : controlling or guiding the actions of someone or something • Tradition is the *governing* factor in the lives of these people. • Their *governing* principle is to provide their customers with the best possible products. — see also SELF-GOVERNING

gov·ern·ment /ˈgʌvɚmənt/ *noun, pl* **-ments**
1 [*count*] : the group of people who control and make decisions for a country, state, etc. • The *government* has been slow to react to the crisis. • She works for the federal *government*. • the national/central *government* • We need to improve relations with foreign *governments*. • the British *government* • a corrupt/powerful/weak *government* — often used before another noun • They have promised to reduce *government* spending. • a *government* agency/official/program • *government* policies and regulations ✧ In British English, *government* is used with both singular and plural verbs. • *The government* is/are working on the problem.— see also LOCAL GOVERNMENT, STUDENT GOVERNMENT
2 [*noncount*] **a** : a particular system used for controlling a country, state, etc. • He is a firm believer in democratic/representative *government*. **b** : the process or manner of controlling a country, state, etc. • We learned about different methods/systems of *government*. • The country has been damaged by many years of weak/corrupt *government*.— see also BIG GOVERNMENT
– gov·ern·men·tal /ˌgʌvɚnˈmɛntl̩/ *adj* • *governmental* agencies • The law provides *governmental* protection for investors.**– gov·ern·men·tal·ly** /ˌgʌvɚnˈmɛntl̩i/ *adv* • *governmentally* funded programs

gov·er·nor /ˈgʌvn̩ɚ/ *noun, pl* **-nors** [*count*]
1 *or* ***Governor*** : a person who is the leader of the government of a state, province, etc. • the *governor* of the state of Florida • *Governor* Jones— abbr. *Gov.*; see also LIEUTENANT GOVERNOR
2 **a** : a person who is part of a group of people who control a large organization, school, etc. • He was the chairman of the board of *governors* at the school. **b** *chiefly Brit* : a person who is in charge of a school, prison, or other large organization or institution • the *governor* of the Bank of England • the school *governor* • a prison *governor* [=(*US*) *warden*]
3 *Brit, informal* : a man who has authority over other people : BOSS • Wait here while I get the *governor*.

gov·er·nor·ship /ˈgʌvn̩ɚˌʃɪp/ *noun, pl* **-ships**
1 [*noncount*] : the job of a governor • a candidate for the *governorship*
2 [*count*] : the period when a person is a governor • The state has done well during her *governorship*.

govt. (*chiefly US*) *or Brit* **govt** *abbr* government

gown /ˈgaʊn/ *noun, pl* **gowns** [*count*]
1 : a long, formal dress that a woman wears especially during a special event • The bride wore a lovely lace wedding *gown*. • a red ***evening gown*** [=a gown that is worn to events in the evening] • a beautiful ***ball gown*** [=a gown that is worn to large formal parties for dancing]
2 : a loose piece of clothing that covers most of the body • a ***hospital gown*** [=a robe worn by a patient in a hospital] — see also DRESSING GOWN, NIGHTGOWN
3 : a loose piece of clothing that is worn over other clothes during an official event by a judge, a priest, a student, etc.

G.P. (*chiefly US*) *or Brit* **GP** *abbr* general practitioner

GPA *abbr, US* grade point average

GPS /ˌʤiːˌpiːˈɛs/ *noun* [*noncount*] : a radio system that uses signals from satellites to tell you where you are and to give you directions to other places • The car comes with *GPS*. ✧ *GPS* is an abbreviation of "Global Positioning System."

[1]grab /ˈgræb/ *verb* **grabs; grabbed; grab·bing**
1 : to quickly take and hold (someone or something) with your hand or arms [+ *obj*] She *grabbed* his wrist. = She *grabbed* him by the wrist. • I have to go back in the house and *grab* my car keys. • He tried to *grab* the ball out of her hands. = He tried to *grab* it (away) from her. • He ***grabbed hold of*** a tree branch [=he grabbed a tree branch] and pulled himself out of the water. [*no obj*] The little boy ***grabbed onto*** his mother's leg and wouldn't let go.
2 [+ *obj*] : to take or get (something) in a quick and informal way • *Grab* me a beer, please. = *Grab* a beer for me, please. • I'll *grab* a taxi and meet you there. • Let's *grab* a bite to eat before the movie starts. • ***Grab a seat***. [=sit down] I'll be with you in a minute.
3 [+ *obj*] *informal* **a** : to get the attention or interest of (someone or something) • The store had a lot of nice stuff, but nothing really *grabbed* me. • The play *grabs* the audience from the opening scene. • ***How does that grab you***? [=what do you think of that idea?] **b** : to get or be given (something, such as attention) • One player in particular has been *grabbing* a lot of attention lately. • A new cancer treatment ***grabbed (the) headlines*** [=it was given much attention in the news] this week.
4 [+ *obj*] : to take (something) usually in an unfair way • They tried to *grab* the largest portion of the money for themselves. • He *grabbed* the company (away) from its founders.
grab at/for [*phrasal verb*] ***grab at/for (someone or something)*** : to quickly stretch out your hand and try to touch or hold (something or someone) • People were *grabbing at* her as she walked through the crowd. • He *grabbed for* the ball and missed.— often used figuratively • We *grabbed at* the chance to go. • political parties *grabbing for* power
– grab·ber *noun, pl* **-bers** [*count*] • That outfit is a real attention *grabber*. • a headline *grabber*

[2]grab *noun, pl* **grabs** [*count*]
1 : a quick attempt to take or get something — usually singular; often + *for* • He is a member of a group that has broken away from the party's leaders in a *grab for* power. • a *grab for* attention • She ***made a grab for*** the last cookie. [=she tried to grab the last cookie]
2 : the act of taking something in a forceful or illegal way • an illegal land *grab*
up for grabs : available for anyone to try to get • Several positions on the team are still *up for grabs*. • With the election just a few weeks away, a lot of voters are still *up for grabs*.

grab bag *noun, pl* ~ **bags** [*count*] *US*
1 : a bag that holds many small gifts and that you reach into in order to pull one out without knowing what it is — compare LUCKY DIP
2 *informal* : a group or mixture of different things • Congress has proposed a *grab bag* of tax cuts.

grab·by /ˈgræbi/ *adj* **grab·bi·er; -est** *informal* : tending to take things in a quick and selfish way : GREEDY • a *grabby* government/corporation • You need to learn to share and not be so *grabby*.

[1]grace /ˈgreɪs/ *noun, pl* **grac·es**
1 [*noncount*] : a way of moving that is smooth and attractive and that is not stiff or awkward • She walked across the stage with effortless *grace*.
2 **a** [*noncount*] : a controlled, polite, and pleasant way of behaving • She handles her problems with *grace* and dignity. • He has shown remarkable *grace* during this crisis. ✧ People say you ***have the (good) grace*** to do something when they approve of what you do and consider it to be polite and proper. • She *has the grace* [=she is polite/nice enough] to listen to everyone's complaints. • At least he *had the good grace* to admit that he was wrong. **b** ***graces*** [*plural*] : skills that are needed for behaving in a polite way in social situations • She is quite lovable despite her lack of ***social graces***.
3 [*noncount*] **a** : help or kindness that God gives or shows to people • Let us give thanks for God's *grace*. • By the *grace* of God, no one was seriously hurt. ✧ People use the phrase ***(there) but for the grace of God (go I)*** to say that they could be in the same bad situation as someone else. • I saw a homeless person on the street and thought "*there but for the grace of God go I*." [=I am lucky not to be homeless also] **b** : a state of being pleasing to God • She tried to live her life in God's *grace*. • He died in a ***state of grace***. [=he died after he asked God to forgive his sins]

4 [*noncount*] **:** a short prayer that is said before a meal • They asked her to *say grace* at dinner.

5 ***Grace*** [*noncount*] — used as a title for a duke, a duchess, or an archbishop; used with *his, her,* or *your* • *His Grace* the Duke • Yes, *Your Grace.*

airs and graces see [1]AIR

fall from grace ✧ If you *fall from grace* or experience a *fall from grace*, you no longer enjoy the success or good reputation that you once had, usually because you have done something wrong. • The governor *fell from grace* after being accused of tax fraud. • The book tells of his *fall from grace.*

in someone's good graces ✧ If you are *in someone's good graces*, that person likes you and has a good opinion of you. • He works late to stay *in* his boss's *good graces.*

with bad/ill grace **:** in a way that shows that you are not happy about something **:** in an unpleasant way • They agreed to the compromise *with bad grace.*

with good grace **:** in a polite and pleasant way • She accepted his advice *with good grace.* [=*graciously*] • They lost the game *with good grace.*

— see also COUP DE GRÂCE, SAVING GRACE

[2]**grace** *verb* **graces; graced; grac·ing** [+ *obj*] *formal* **:** to decorate or add beauty to (something) • Several marble statues *grace* the courtyard. • Her face has *graced* [=*appeared on*] the cover of many magazines.

grace (a person, group, etc.) with your presence **:** to come to a place to be with (a person, group, etc.) — usually used humorously • He finally decided to *grace us with his presence* [=he finally showed up] 10 minutes after dinner started. • Will you be *gracing the meeting with your presence*? [=will you be coming to the meeting?]

grace·ful /ˈgreɪsfəl/ *adj* [*more* ~; *most* ~]

1 : moving in a smooth and attractive way • He has become a very *graceful* dancer. • the *graceful* movements of a ballerina

2 : having a smooth and pleasing shape or style • She was a *graceful* young woman with delicate features. • the long, *graceful* neck of a swan • His writing is clear and *graceful.*

3 : polite or kind • There was no *graceful* way to say no to their offer.

— **grace·ful·ly** *adv* • The dancers moved *gracefully* across the stage. • She has aged *gracefully.* [=she has continued to be healthy and young looking as she has gotten older]

— **grace·ful·ness** *noun* [*noncount*]

grace·less /ˈgreɪsləs/ *adj* [*more* ~; *most* ~]

1 : awkward or clumsy • *graceless* movements

2 : having a style or shape that is not attractive or pleasing • Her writing can be *graceless* and awkward at times. • a massive, *graceless* building

3 : not kind or polite • She was criticized for her *graceless* [=*rude*] refusal to help.

— **grace·less·ly** *adv* • a *gracelessly* written book • She *gracelessly* refused to help. — **grace·less·ness** *noun* [*noncount*] • the *gracelessness* of her refusal

grace period *noun, pl* ~ **-ods** [*count*] **:** an amount of extra time that someone is given to pay a bill, finish a project, etc. • The terms of the loan allow for a ten-day *grace period.*

gra·cious /ˈgreɪʃəs/ *adj* [*more* ~; *most* ~]

1 : very polite in a way that shows respect • It was very *gracious* [=*kind, courteous*] of him to offer us a place to stay. • a *gracious* hostess • Thank you for your *gracious* hospitality.

2 : having or showing the attractive things (such as charm, good taste, and comfort) that are associated with having a lot of money • The magazine promotes *gracious* living. • a *gracious* mansion

3 *old-fashioned* — used as an interjection to express mild surprise or for emphasis • *Gracious,* I never expected to see you here! • Good *gracious,* No. • Goodness *gracious,* I hope it works.

— **gra·cious·ly** *adv* • He *graciously* offered us a place to stay. — **gra·cious·ness** *noun* [*noncount*]

grack·le /ˈgrækəl/ *noun, pl* **grack·les** [*count*] **:** a common American bird that has shiny black feathers

grad /ˈgræd/ *noun, pl* **grads** [*count*] *US, informal* **:** GRADUATE • college *grads*

— **grad** *adj, always used before a noun* • He's still in *grad* school. • *grad* students [=students in graduate school]

gra·da·tion /greɪˈdeɪʃən/ *noun, pl* **-tions** [*count*] **:** a small difference between two points or parts that can be seen in something that changes gradually — often + *of* • subtle *gradations of* color/meaning

[1]**grade** /ˈgreɪd/ *noun, pl* **grades** [*count*]

1 *US* **a :** a level of study that is completed by a student during one year • Our son is in (the) fourth/twelfth *grade.* **b :** the students in the same year of study at a school • The fifth *grade* will perform their annual play this week.

2 : a number or letter that indicates how a student performed in a class or on a test • (*US*) I got a good *grade* on my math test. = (*Brit*) I got a good *grade* in my maths test. • a *grade* of 90 percent or better • Her *grades* are up/better this semester. • passing/failing *grades*

3 a : a particular level of quality • an expensive *grade* of leather • government *grades* for beef **b :** a particular position or rank in an organization • junior *grade* officers — see also HIGH-GRADE, LOW-GRADE

4 *US* **:** a place where the ground slopes up or down **:** GRADIENT • a steep six percent *grade*

make the grade **:** to be good enough or perform well enough to succeed • Many people apply for these positions, but only a few *make the grade.*

[2]**grade** *verb* **grades; grad·ed; grad·ing** [+ *obj*]

1 *chiefly US* **:** to give a grade to (a student or a student's work) • Students will be *graded* on their reading ability. • She hasn't finished *grading* the exams.

2 : to give a rating to (something) • How would you *grade* your meal on a scale from one to five?

3 : to separate (things) into groups or classes according to a particular quality • The eggs are *graded* according to size.

4 : to give (a surface) a desired degree of slope • They *graded* the new highway.

grade A *adj* **:** of the highest quality • a *grade A* performance

grade point average *noun, pl* ~ **-ages** [*count*] *US* **:** a number that indicates a student's average grade — abbr. *GPA*

grad·er /ˈgreɪdə/ *noun, pl* **-ers** [*count*]

1 *US* **:** a student in a particular grade in school • a sixth *grader* [=a student in the sixth grade]

2 : a person who grades students or their work • Her students say that she's a tough/easy *grader.*

3 : a machine used for grading a surface • a road *grader*

grade school *noun, pl* ~ **schools** [*count, noncount*] *US* **:** ELEMENTARY SCHOOL

grade–school·er /ˈgreɪdˌskuːlə/ *noun, pl* **-ers** [*count*] *US* **:** a child in elementary school

gra·di·ent /ˈgreɪdijənt/ *noun, pl* **-ents** [*count*] **:** a place where the ground slopes up or down **:** SLOPE • a steep *gradient*

grad·u·al /ˈgrædʒəwəl/ *adj* [*more* ~; *most* ~]

1 : moving or changing in small amounts **:** happening in a slow way over a long period of time • We noticed a *gradual* change in temperature. • The hospital has made *gradual* improvements in health care.

2 : not steep • a *gradual* slope

— **grad·u·al·ly** *adv* • The population *gradually* increased. • The temperature changed *gradually.* • The cat moved *gradually* forward.

[1]**grad·u·ate** /ˈgrædʒəˌweɪt/ *verb* **-ates; -at·ed; -at·ing**

1 a [*no obj*] **:** to earn a degree or diploma from a school, college, or university • He *graduated* from the university last June. • They both *graduated* with honors. • She *graduated* with a degree in history. • He joined the navy after *graduating* from high school. • a *graduating* class of 300 students ✧ In British English, *graduate* refers only to earning a college or university degree. In U.S. English, *graduate* is also used for other schools (such as high schools). **b** [+ *obj*] *US, of a school, college, or university* **:** to award a degree or diploma to (a student) — usually used as *(be) graduated* • He *was graduated* from the university last June. **c** [+ *obj*] *US, informal* **:** to earn a degree or diploma from (a school, college, or university) • He joined the navy after *graduating* high school.

2 [*no obj*] **:** to move *from* one level *to* another usually higher level • The word has *graduated from* slang *to* accepted use. • My nephew has *graduated from* baby food *to* solid food. • The former child actor has finally *graduated* [=*moved on*] *to* more serious roles.

[2]**grad·u·ate** /ˈgrædʒəwət/ *noun, pl* **-ates** [*count*] **:** a person who has earned a degree or diploma from a school, college, or university • a college *graduate* • (*US*) a high school *graduate* • an engineering *graduate* [=a person with a degree in engineering] • recent Harvard *graduates* — often + *of* • She's a *graduate of* Harvard. ✧ In British English, only a person who has earned a college or university degree is called a *graduate.*

[3]**graduate** *adj, always used before a noun, US* **:** of or relating to a course of studies taken at a college or university after

earning a bachelor's degree or other first degree : POSTGRADUATE • He is taking *graduate* classes at the university. • *graduate* students/school

grad·u·at·ed /ˈgræʤəˌweɪtəd/ *adj, always used before a noun*
1 : marked with lines for measuring • a *graduated* cylinder [=a tall, narrow container used for measuring liquids] • a *graduated* thermometer
2 a : gradually increasing • a series of bowls in *graduated* sizes • *graduated* payments **b** *of a tax* : increasing in rate as the thing being taxed (such as income) increases • a *graduated* income tax

grad·u·a·tion /ˌgræʤəˈweɪʃən/ *noun, pl* **-tions**
1 [*noncount*] : the act of receiving a diploma or degree from a school, college, or university : the act of graduating • He joined the navy after *graduation.* • We had a party to celebrate her *graduation* from high school.
2 [*count*] : a ceremony at which degrees or diplomas are given out • They took lots of pictures at their son's *graduation.*

graf·fi·ti /grəˈfi:ti/ *noun* [*noncount*] : pictures or words painted or drawn on a wall, building, etc. • The walls of the old building are covered with *graffiti.* • a piece of *graffiti*

G

¹graft /ˈgræft, *Brit* ˈgrɑ:ft/ *noun, pl* **grafts** [*count*]
1 *technical* : a part of a plant that is placed on another plant in such a way that it attaches to and grows with the plant; *also* : the place where such an attachment is made • You will need to cut off any new shoots that grow below the *graft.*
2 *medical* : a piece of skin, muscle, or bone that is attached to a part of the body to repair a damaged area • a skin *graft*; *also* : an operation that is done to make such an attachment • perform a bone *graft* on the patient
– compare ³GRAFT, ⁴GRAFT

²graft *verb* **grafts; graft·ed; graft·ing** [+ *obj*]
1 a *technical* : to attach (a part of a plant) to another plant • a type of apple that is grown by being *grafted* onto/to the roots of a different species **b** *medical* : to attach (a piece of skin, muscle, or bone) to a part of the body • The surgeon was able to *graft* skin over the scar.
2 : to make (something) become a part of (something else) — usually + *onto* • the difficulties of trying to *graft* modern technology *onto* traditional societies
– compare ⁵GRAFT

³graft *noun* [*noncount*] *chiefly US* : dishonest activity in which people with power (such as political leaders) use their position and influence to get money and advantages • The newspaper published a series of articles exposing *graft* in the city government. — compare ¹GRAFT, ⁴GRAFT

⁴graft *noun* [*noncount*] *Brit, informal* : hard work or effort • He succeeded because of years of ***hard graft.*** — compare ¹GRAFT, ³GRAFT

⁵graft *verb* **grafts; graft·ed; graft·ing** [*no obj*] *Brit, informal* : to work hard : LABOR • He spent years *grafting* to get where he is today. — compare ²GRAFT

gra·ham cracker /ˈgræm-/ *noun, pl* **~ -ers** [*count*] *US* : a slightly sweet type of cracker

grail /ˈgreɪl/ *noun, pl* **grails** [*count*] : HOLY GRAIL

grain /ˈgreɪn/ *noun, pl* **grains**
1 a [*noncount*] : the seeds of plants (such as wheat, corn, and rice) that are used for food • bread made from whole wheat *grain* • The machine grinds *grain* into flour.; *also* [*count*] : a single seed of wheat, corn, rice, etc. • a *grain* of rice **b** : a plant that produces grain [*count*] The farm grows a variety of *grains.* [*noncount*] fields planted with *grain*
2 [*count*] **a** : a small, hard piece of something • a *grain* of sand/salt — see also *take (something) with a grain of salt* at ¹SALT **b** : a very small amount of something • Anyone with a *grain* of sense knows that she's lying. • There is not a *grain* of truth in what he said.
3 [*count*] **a** : the way the lines or fibers in something (such as wood) are arranged — usually singular • She sanded the wood in the direction of the *grain.* **b** : the way that the surface of something feels when it is touched — usually singular • The wood has a fine/coarse *grain.*
4 [*count*] : a unit of weight equal to 0.0648 grams
against the grain **1** ✧ To ***be/go against the grain*** is to be different or to act in a way that is different from what is normal or usual. • It takes courage to *go against the grain* and stand up for what you believe in. **2** ✧ If something ***goes against your grain,*** it does not seem right or natural to you. • It *goes against his grain* to question the boss's judgment.
– **grained** /ˈgreɪnd/ *adj* • beautifully *grained* wood • coarse-*grained* leather

grain elevator *noun, pl* **~ -tors** [*count*] : ELEVATOR 2

grainy /ˈgreɪni/ *adj* **grain·i·er; -est** [*also more ~; most ~*]
1 : not smooth or fine • The mustard has a *grainy* texture. • He has a *grainy* [=*rough*] voice.
2 *of a photograph* : not clear or sharp because of having a picture formed from many dots that are large enough to be seen • a *grainy* photograph
– **grain·i·ness** *noun* [*noncount*] • the *graininess* of the mustard/picture

gram *also Brit* **gramme** /ˈgræm/ *noun, pl* **grams** [*count*] : a unit of weight in the metric system that is equal to 1/1000 kilogram

gram·mar /ˈgræmə/ *noun, pl* **-mars**
1 : the set of rules that explain how words are used in a language [*noncount*] the rules of *grammar* • English *grammar* can be hard to master. • a *grammar* lesson • comparing English and Japanese *grammar* [*count*] comparing the *grammars* of English and Japanese
2 [*noncount*] : speech or writing judged by how well it follows the rules of grammar • "Him and I went" is bad/poor *grammar.* • I know some German, but my *grammar* isn't very good.
3 [*count*] : a book that explains the grammar rules of a language • an English *grammar*

gram·mar·i·an /grəˈmerijən/ *noun, pl* **-ans** [*count*] : a person who knows a lot about grammar

grammar school *noun, pl* **~ schools** [*count, noncount*]
1 : a school in the U.S. for young children : ELEMENTARY SCHOOL
2 : a school in Britain for children over age 11 who have passed an entrance exam

gram·mat·i·cal /grəˈmætɪkəl/ *adj*
1 : of or relating to grammar • a *grammatical* error • *grammatical* rules
2 : following the rules of grammar • That sentence is not *grammatical.*
– **gram·mat·i·cal·ly** /grəˈmætɪkli/ *adv* • That sentence is *grammatically* incorrect.

gramme *Brit spelling of* GRAM

Gram·my /ˈgræmi/ *service mark* — used for a small statue that is given as an award to someone (such as a musician) who works in the business of recording music

gram·o·phone /ˈgræməˌfoʊn/ *noun, pl* **-phones** [*count*] *old-fashioned* : RECORD PLAYER

gramps /ˈgræmps/ *or* **gramp** /ˈgræmp/ *noun, pl* **gramps** [*count*] *informal* : GRANDFATHER

gran /ˈgræn/ *noun, pl* **grans** [*count*] *informal* : GRANDMOTHER

gra·na·ry /ˈgreɪnəri, *Brit* ˈgrænəri/ *noun, pl* **-ries** [*count*] : a building in which grain is stored

¹grand /ˈgrænd/ *adj* **grand·er; -est**
1 : involving or including many people or things : very large in scope • He thinks everything the government does is part of some *grand* conspiracy. • the beauty of nature's *grand* design : intended to have an important or impressive result • When they bought the house, they had *grand* [=*big*] plans for renovating it. ✧ Something that happens or is done ***on a grand scale*** involves a great amount of money, effort, space, people, or things. • War forces us to face death *on a grand scale.* • Pollution affects nature *on a grand scale.*
2 a : impressive because of size, importance, etc. • The neighborhood includes many *grand* old homes. • His job is much less *grand* than his title makes it sound. • This room is only used for *grand* occasions. [=very important and formal occasions] • My great aunt lived to ***the grand old age of*** 103. • (*humorous*) He retired at *the grand old age of* 37. **b** : intended to impress people • Despite its *grand* name, the hotel is small and somewhat seedy. • He made some *grand* statements about the company's future. • They celebrated their anniversary ***in grand style.*** • He planned to ***make a grand entrance,*** driving up to the house in a fancy red sports car.
3 *always used before a noun* : having higher rank than others of the same kind • We won the *grand* prize. • the *grand* champion • a *Grand* Duke/Duchess
4 *informal* : very good • We are having *grand* weather this summer. • We had a *grand* time at the picnic.
– **grand·ly** *adv* • She *grandly* announced that the ceremony was about to begin.

²grand *noun, pl* **grand** [*count*] *informal* : a thousand dollars or pounds • He bought a used car for about five *grand*. — compare [3]GRAND

[3]**grand** *noun, pl* **grands** [*count*] : GRAND PIANO • a concert *grand* — compare [2]GRAND

grand·ba·by /ˈgrændˌbeɪbi/ *noun, pl* **-bies** [*count*] *informal* : a grandchild who is a baby

grand·child /ˈgrændˌʧajəld/ *noun, pl* **-chil·dren** /-ʧɪldrən/ [*count*] : a child of your son or daughter

grand·dad *also* **gran·dad** /ˈgrænˌdæd/ *noun, pl* **-dads** [*count*] *informal* : GRANDFATHER

grand·dad·dy *also* **gran·dad·dy** /ˈgrænˌdædi/ *noun, pl* **-dies** [*count*] *informal*
1 : GRANDFATHER
2 : someone or something that is the first or oldest one in a particular area or field — usually + *of* • The company is the ***granddaddy of*** computer manufacturers.

grand·daugh·ter /ˈgrænˌdɑːtɚ/ *noun, pl* **-ters** [*count*] : a daughter of your son or daughter

grande dame /ˈgrɑːnˈdɑːm/ *noun, pl* **grandes dames** /ˈgrɑːnˈdɑːm/ *also* **grande dames** /ˈgrɑːnˈdɑːm/ [*count*] : a usually old woman who is highly admired or respected — often + *of* • She is the ***grande dame of*** the American theater.

gran·deur /ˈgrænʤɚ/ *noun* [*noncount*] : a great and impressive quality • His paintings capture the beauty and *grandeur* of the landscape. • They are restoring the hotel to its original/former *grandeur*. — see also *delusions of grandeur* at DELUSION

grand·fa·ther /ˈgrændˌfɑːðɚ/ *noun, pl* **-thers** [*count*] : the father of your father or mother

grandfather clause *noun, pl* ~ **clauses** [*count*] *US, law* : a part of a law which says that the law does not apply to certain people and things because of conditions that existed before the law was passed • Because of a *grandfather clause*, the strict emission standards only apply to new cars.

grandfather clock *noun, pl* ~ **clocks** [*count*] : a tall clock that stands on the floor

grand finale *noun, pl* ~ **-les** [*count*] : a very exciting or impressive ending of a performance or show • All of the performers came on stage for the opera's *grand finale*.

gran·dil·o·quent /grænˈdɪləkwənt/ *adj* [*more* ~; *most* ~] *formal* : using words that are intended to sound very impressive and important • *grandiloquent* language • He's fond of making *grandiloquent* pronouncements about art. • a *grandiloquent* speaker
– **gran·dil·o·quence** /grænˈdɪləkwəns/ *noun* [*noncount*]
– **gran·dil·o·quent·ly** *adv*

gran·di·ose /ˈgrændiˌous/ *adj* [*more* ~; *most* ~] *disapproving* : seeming to be impressive or intended to be impressive but not really possible or practical • He was full of *grandiose* ideas. • *grandiose* plans/schemes
– **gran·di·ose·ly** *adv*

grand jury *noun, pl* ~ **juries** [*count*] *US, law* : a group of people who look at the evidence against someone who has been accused of a crime in order to decide if there should be a trial

grand·kid /ˈgrændˌkɪd/ *noun, pl* **-kids** [*count*] *US, informal* : GRANDCHILD

grand larceny *noun* [*noncount*] *US, law* : the crime of stealing something that is very valuable — called also *grand theft*; compare PETIT LARCENY

grand·ma /ˈgræˌmɑː/ *noun, pl* **-mas** [*count*] *informal* : GRANDMOTHER

grand marshal *noun, pl* ~ **-shals** [*count*] *chiefly US* : a person who is honored by being made the leader of a parade

grand master *noun, pl* ~ **-ters** [*count*] : an expert player in chess who has scored very high in international competition

grand·moth·er /ˈgrændˌmʌðɚ/ *noun, pl* **-ers** [*count*] : the mother of your father or mother

grand old man *noun, pl* ~ **men** [*count*] : a highly respected and admired man who has had a long career in a particular field • the ***grand old man*** of the American theater

grand opening *noun, pl* ~ **-ings** [*count*] : a special celebration held to mark the opening of a new business or public place (such as a park or stadium)

grand opera *noun, pl* ~ **-eras** [*count, noncount*] : serious opera in which all the words are sung

grand·pa /ˈgræmˌpɑː/ *noun, pl* **-pas** [*count*] *informal* : GRANDFATHER

grand·par·ent /ˈgrændˌperənt/ *noun, pl* **-ents** [*count*] : a parent of your father or mother

grand piano *noun, pl* ~ **-anos** [*count*] : a very large piano used for concerts

Grand Prix /ˈgrɑːnˈpriː/ *noun, pl* **Grand Prix** *or* **Grands Prix** /ˈgrɑːnˈpriː/ [*count*] : one of a series of international car races; *also* : a similar race or competition in another sport (such as sailing)

grand slam *noun, pl* ~ **slams** [*count*]
1 *baseball* : a home run that is hit with three runners on base
2 *or* ***Grand Slam*** : the achievement of winning of all the major events of a sport (such as tennis or golf) in one season — usually singular • a golfer trying to win the *Grand Slam*
3 : the achievement of winning of all the tricks in one hand of a card game (such as bridge) • He made a *grand slam*.

grand·son /ˈgrændˌsʌn/ *noun, pl* **-sons** [*count*] : a son of your son or daughter

[1]**grand·stand** /ˈgrændˌstænd/ *noun, pl* **-stands** [*count*] : a usually roofed structure with seats for people to sit on while they are watching a race or sporting event

[2]**grandstand** *adj, always used before a noun, US* : done in a way that is intended to impress the people who are watching • The outfielder made a *grandstand* play out of what should have been a routine catch.

[3]**grandstand** *verb* **-stands; -stand·ed; -stand·ing** [*no obj*] *US, disapproving* : to behave or speak in a way that is intended to impress people and to get public approval • a politician who *grandstands* to the public = a *grandstanding* politician
– **grand·stand·er** *noun, pl* **-ers** [*count*] – **grand·standing** *noun* [*noncount*] • He has been accused of political *grandstanding*.

grand theft *noun* [*noncount*] *US, law* : GRAND LARCENY

grand total *noun, pl* ~ **-tals** [*count*] : a final total reached by adding together other total amounts — usually singular • They have managed to raise a *grand total* of $15 million in the past two years. ✧ *Grand total* is often used in a humorous or critical way to refer to a total that is unusually small. • A *grand total* of two people have signed up for the class. • They scored a *grand total* of three points in the first quarter.

grand tour *noun, pl* ~ **tours** [*count*]
1 *or* ***Grand Tour*** : a journey to the different countries of Europe that in the past was part of the education of wealthy young people from Britain and the U.S.
2 : a tour that is given to show people around a place • They offered to give us a/the *grand tour* of their new house.

gran·ite /ˈgrænət/ *noun* [*noncount*] : a very hard type of rock that is used in buildings and monuments

gran·ny *also* **gran·nie** /ˈgræni/ *noun, pl* **-nies** [*count*] *informal* : GRANDMOTHER

granny flat *noun, pl* ~ **flats** [*count*] *Brit* : IN-LAW APARTMENT

granny knot *noun, pl* ~ **knots** [*count*] : a type of knot that looks similar to a square knot but is much less strong

gra·no·la /grəˈnoulə/ *noun, pl* **-las** [*count, noncount*] *chiefly US* : a mixture of oats and other ingredients (such as brown sugar, raisins, coconut, or nuts) that is eaten especially for breakfast or as a snack • a bowl of *granola* • a ***granola bar*** [=a bar of granola that is eaten as a snack]

[1]**grant** /ˈgrænt, *Brit* ˈgrɑːnt/ *verb* **grants; grant·ed; grant·ing** [+ *obj*]
1 a : to agree to do, give, or allow (something asked for or hoped for) • The mayor refused to *grant* my request for an interview. • The court *granted* the motion for a new trial. • She *granted* me an interview. [=she agreed to let me interview her] • She rarely *grants* interviews. [=she rarely agrees to be interviewed] • I cannot *grant* you that wish. **b** : to give (something) legally or formally • The government has agreed to *grant* the refugees asylum. = The government has agreed to *grant* asylum to the refugees. • We haven't yet been *granted* access to the archive. • The country was *granted* independence in 1950. • The judge *granted* custody of the children to their mother. — see also *grant bail* at [1]BAIL
2 : to admit (something) although it does not agree with or support your opinion • I *grant* that he's a talented writer, but I just don't find his books very interesting. • The house is not in perfect condition, I *grant* you [=I admit that the house is not in perfect condition], but it's still a great deal. • The house is not perfect, I *grant* you that. — often used in the form *granted* or *granting* to introduce a clause • *Granted* that she's been under a lot of stress lately, her behavior is still surprising. [=I admit that she has been under a lot of stress lately, but I am still surprised by her behavior] • Even *granting* that you may be right [=even if you are right], I still think we

G

need to consider other solutions. — often used in the form *granted* as an adverb • *Granted*, the house is not in perfect condition, but it's still a great deal. • "The house is not in very good condition." "*Granted* [=I admit that what you say is true]—but it's still a great deal."

take for granted **1** ***take (something) for granted*** : to believe or assume that (something) is true or probably true without knowing that it is true • We *took* our invitation to the party *for granted*. = We ***took it for granted*** that we'd be invited to the party. [=we assumed we'd be invited and did not think about the possibility that we wouldn't be] **2** ***take (someone or something) for granted*** : to fail to properly notice or appreciate (someone or something that is helpful or important to you) • We often *take* our freedom *for granted*. • Being apart from my family for so long has made me realize that I've been *taking* them *for granted*. • I'm tired of being *taken for granted*.

[2]**grant** *noun, pl* **grants** [*count*]
1 : an amount of money that is given to someone by a government, a company, etc., to be used for a particular purpose (such as scientific research) • Her study is being funded by a federal *grant*. • a research *grant* • They wrote a *grant* proposal to get funding for the project.
2 : an area of land that is given to someone by a government • a land *grant*

gran·u·lar /ˈgrænjələ/ *adj* [*more* ~; *most* ~] **:** made of or appearing to be made of small pieces or granules • *granular* rock • fruit with a *granular* [=*grainy*] texture • a *granular* [=*bumpy*] leather surface

gran·u·lat·ed /ˈgrænjəˌleɪtəd/ *adj* **:** formed into small grains or pieces • *granulated* sugar

gran·ule /ˈgrænˌjuːl/ *noun, pl* **-ules** [*count*] **:** a small grain or piece of something • coffee *granules* • salt/sugar *granules*

grape /ˈgreɪp/ *noun, pl* **grapes** [*count*] **:** a green, dark red, or purplish-black berry that is used to make wine or is eaten as a fruit • a bunch of seedless *grapes* — see color picture on page C5; see also SOUR GRAPES

grape·fruit /ˈgreɪpˌfruːt/ *noun, pl* **grapefruit** *or* **grapefruits** [*count, noncount*] **:** a large yellow citrus fruit — see color picture on page C5

grape·vine /ˈgreɪpˌvaɪn/ *noun, pl* **-vines** [*count*]
1 : a climbing plant on which grapes grow
2 : an informal way of spreading information or rumors through conversation — usually singular • The office *grapevine* isn't always a reliable source of information. • I heard about the new position ***through the grapevine***. • The word ***on the grapevine*** is that a new treatment has been discovered.

[1]**graph** /ˈgræf, *Brit* ˈgrɑːf/ *noun, pl* **graphs** [*count*] **:** a drawing that uses a series of dots, lines, etc., to show how much or how quickly something changes • She drew/plotted a *graph* showing the rise and fall in temperature during the month.

[2]**graph** *verb* **graphs; graphed; graph·ing** [+ *obj*] *mathematics* **:** to show (something) with a graph • Students were asked to *graph* each equation.

-graph /ˌgræf, *Brit* ˌgrɑːf/ *noun combining form*
1 : something that is written or drawn • an auto*graph*
2 : a machine that records or sends information • a seismo*graph* • a tele*graph*

[1]**graph·ic** /ˈgræfɪk/ *adj*
1 [*more* ~; *most* ~] **:** shown or described in a very clear way — used especially to refer to things that are unpleasant or shocking • The reporter provided a *graphic* account of the plane crash. • The movie was controversial because of its *graphic* [=*explicit*] violence. • *graphic* sex • *graphic* language
2 *always used before a noun* **:** relating to the artistic use of pictures, shapes, and words especially in books and magazines • *graphic* design • a *graphic* artist/designer

[2]**graphic** *noun, pl* **-ics**
1 ***graphics*** [*plural*] **:** pictures or images on the screen of a computer, television, etc. • computer *graphics*
2 [*count*] **:** a picture, drawing, or graph used as a decoration or to make something (such as magazine article) easier to understand • She illustrated her talk with a *graphic* showing state population growth.

graph·i·cal /ˈgræfɪkəl/ *adj, technical*
1 : relating to or involving pictures, shapes, or letters especially on the screen of a computer • a *graphical* computer display — see also GRAPHICAL USER INTERFACE
2 : using a drawing (called a graph) to show how much or how quickly something changes • a *graphical* representation of rainfall amounts

graph·i·cal·ly /ˈgræfɪkli/ *adv*
1 : in a very clear way that usually includes unpleasant or shocking details • The crash was *graphically* described.
2 : in a graph • The information was presented *graphically*.

graphical user interface *noun, pl* ~ **-faces** [*count*] **:** a program that allows a person to work easily with a computer by using a mouse to point to small pictures and other elements on the screen — abbr. *GUI*

graphic novel *noun, pl* ~ **-els** [*count*] **:** cartoon drawings that tell a story and are published as a book

graph·ite /ˈgræˌfaɪt/ *noun* [*noncount*] **:** a shiny black substance that is used in pencils

graph paper *noun, pl* ~ **-ers** [*count*] **:** paper that is covered with squares formed by lines that run from top to bottom and side to side

-graphy /grəfi/ *noun combining form* **:** a way of writing or showing something • photo*graphy* • carto*graphy* • mammog*raphy*

grap·ple /ˈgræpəl/ *verb* **grap·ples; grap·pled; grap·pling** [*no obj*]
1 : to hold and fight with another person • The wrestlers *grappled* [=*wrestled*] on the mat. — usually + *with* • The wrestlers *grappled with* each other.
2 : to try to solve a problem **:** to deal with a problem — + *with* • Every parent has to *grapple with* [=*cope with*] a variety of serious issues. • The company has been *grappling with* supply problems.
— grap·pler /ˈgræpələ/ *noun, pl* **-plers** [*count*] • a famous *grappler* [=*wrestler*]

[1]**grasp** /ˈgræsp, *Brit* ˈgrɑːsp/ *verb* **grasps; grasped; grasp·ing** [+ *obj*]
1 : to take and hold (something) with your fingers, hands, etc. • I *grasped* the end of the rope and pulled as hard as I could. • I *grasped* the rope by its end. • His arthritis is so bad he can barely *grasp* a pencil. — often used figuratively • We need to *grasp* [=*seize*] this opportunity while we can.
2 : to understand (something that is complicated or difficult) • They failed to *grasp* [=*comprehend*] the importance of talking to their children about the dangers of taking drugs. • They don't (fully) *grasp* the implications of these changes.

grasp at [*phrasal verb*] ***grasp at (something)*** **:** to try to take or get (something) in an eager or desperate way • They were ready to *grasp at* any possible solution. • He *grasped at* the opportunity to speak with her.

grasp at straws see STRAW

grasp for [*phrasal verb*] ***grasp for (something)*** **:** to try in a desperate or awkward way to get (something) • His sudden decision to quit the race has left his supporters *grasping for* explanations. • *grasping for* attention

grasp the nettle see [2]NETTLE

— grasp·able /ˈgræspəbəl, *Brit* ˈgrɑːspəbəl/ *adj* • an easily *graspable* idea

[2]**grasp** *noun* [*singular*]
1 : a usually strong hold • I kept a firm *grasp* on the rope. [=I held the rope firmly with my hand] • The ball slipped/fell from her *grasp*. [=she dropped the ball]
2 : an understanding of something • She has a good/firm/thorough *grasp* of mathematics. [=she understands mathematics well] • The author shows a weak/feeble/shaky *grasp* of military strategy. • His motives are ***beyond my grasp***. [=I can't understand his motives] • We're still trying to ***get a grasp on*** [=to gain a good understanding of] the situation.
3 a : the distance that can be reached by your arms and hands **:** REACH • The books on the top shelf are just beyond my *grasp*. • She moved the toy to within the baby's *grasp*. • He tried to grab the rolling ball, but it ***eluded his grasp***. [=he could not reach it] **b :** the ability to get or find something • Success is almost ***within our grasp***. [=we are very close to success] • She felt the solution was *within her grasp*.
4 : power or control • The land was in the *grasp* [=*grip*] of a tyrant. • He had the country in his *grasp*.

grasping /ˈgræspɪŋ, *Brit* ˈgrɑːspɪŋ/ *adj* [*more* ~; *most* ~] **:** wanting money and possessions too much **:** GREEDY • Her *grasping* children fought over her property when she died.

[1]**grass** /ˈgræs, *Brit* ˈgrɑːs/ *noun, pl* **grass·es**
1 a [*noncount*] **:** plants that have narrow green leaves, that are eaten by cows, sheep, horses, etc., and that are commonly grown on lawns and in gardens • a field of *grass* • blades/tufts of *grass* • It's time to mow/cut the *grass*. [=mow/cut the lawn] • Keep off the *grass*. [=don't walk on the lawn] — often used before another noun • *grass* clippings • *grass* seed • a *grass* hut/skirt [=a hut/skirt made from grass] **b** [*count*] **:** a particular type of grass • ornamental *grasses* • wild *grasses*

2 [*noncount*] *slang* : MARIJUANA ▪ They were smoking some *grass.*
3 [*count*] *Brit slang* : a person who gives information to the police about the criminal activity of other people : a police informer — see also SUPERGRASS
let the grass grow under your feet : to wait before doing something or to do something slowly — used in negative statements ▪ He has never been one to *let the grass grow under his feet.* [=he has never been slow about doing things; he gets things done quickly]
put (someone) out to grass *Brit* : to force (someone) to leave a job because of old age ▪ I'm not ready to be *put out to grass* [=*put out to pasture*] just yet.
the grass is always greener on the other side (of the fence) — used to say that the things you do not have always seem more appealing than the things you do have
– grass·like /ˈgræsˌlaɪk, *Brit* ˈgrɑːsˌlaɪk/ *adj* ▪ *grasslike* vegetation **– grassy** /ˈgræsi, *Brit* ˈgrɑːsi/ *adj* **grass·i·er; -est** ▪ a *grassy* field

²grass *verb* **grasses; grassed; grass·ing** [+ *obj*] : to cover (an area) with grass ▪ a large *grassed* area — often + *over* ▪ The land was cleared and *grassed over.*
grass on/up [*phrasal verb*] ***grass on (someone)*** *also* ***grass (someone) up*** *Brit slang* : to tell the police about the criminal activity of (someone) ▪ He refused to *grass on* [=*inform on*] his friends. ▪ Someone *grassed* him *up.*

grass·hop·per /ˈgræsˌhɑːpɚ, *Brit* ˈgrɑːsˌhɒpə/ *noun, pl* **-pers** [*count*] : a plant-eating insect that has long legs used for jumping — see color picture on page C10

grass·land /ˈgræsˌlænd, *Brit* ˈgrɑːsˌlænd/ *noun, pl* **-lands** [*count, noncount*] : land covered with grasses and other soft plants but not with bushes and trees

grass roots *noun* [*plural*] : the ordinary people in a society or organization : the people who do not have a lot of money and power ▪ He has been criticized for losing touch with the party's *grass roots.* ▪ Many people in/at the *grass roots* are still angry about the election.
– grass·roots /ˈgræsˌruːts, *Brit* ˈgrɑːsˌruːts/ *adj, always used before a noun* ▪ A *grassroots* environmental movement has sprung up. ▪ The young candidate hoped to gather votes at the *grassroots* level in his own neighborhood.

¹grate /ˈgreɪt/ *noun, pl* **grates** [*count*] : a metal frame with bars across it that is used in a fireplace or to cover an opening

²grate *verb* **grates; grat·ed; grat·ing**
1 [+ *obj*] : to cut (food) into very small pieces by rubbing it against a special tool (called a grater) ▪ I'll beat the eggs while you *grate* the cheese. ▪ *grate* chocolate/carrots ▪ The recipe calls for half a cup of *grated* cheese.
2 [*no obj*] : to make a harsh, unpleasant noise by rubbing against something ▪ metal *grating* against metal ▪ I hear a loud *grating* sound whenever I step on the brake.
3 [*no obj*] : to have an annoying effect ▪ His negative attitude begins to *grate* after a while. [=his attitude becomes very irritating after a while] — often + *on* ▪ His negative attitude is starting to *grate on* me. [=starting to bother or irritate me] ▪ Her shrill voice can really *grate on* your nerves/ear.
– grating *adj* [*more* ~; *most* ~] ▪ She has a very *grating* [=*annoying, irritating*] voice.

G–rat·ed /ˈdʒiːˈreɪtəd/ *adj, US, of a movie* : having a rating of G : suitable to be seen by children : having no violence, offensive language, or sexual activity ▪ a *G-rated* film — often used figuratively ▪ She's an actress with a *G-rated* public image. [=people think she is a wholesome person] ▪ some *G-rated* fun for the whole family

grate·ful /ˈgreɪtfəl/ *adj* [*more* ~; *most* ~] : feeling or showing thanks ▪ She was *grateful* (that) she didn't have to work on the holiday. ▪ the *grateful* [=*thankful*] recipient of a new heart ▪ The college sent us a *grateful* acknowledgment of our donation. : feeling or showing thanks to someone for some helpful act ▪ I'm *grateful* to you for your help. ▪ He's *grateful* for the attention. ▪ I'm *grateful* (to you) for this opportunity. = I'm *grateful* to have this opportunity. = I'm *grateful* that I have this opportunity. ▪ a *grateful* smile — opposite UNGRATEFUL
– grate·ful·ly *adv* ▪ The college *gratefully* [=*thankfully*] acknowledges your donation. **– grate·ful·ness** *noun* [*noncount*] ▪ expressing my *gratefulness* [=(more commonly) *gratitude*] for this opportunity

grat·er /ˈgreɪtɚ/ *noun, pl* **-ers** [*count*] : a tool that has a rough metal surface with small holes and is used to cut food into small pieces ▪ a cheese *grater* — see picture at KITCHEN

grat·i·fy /ˈgrætəˌfaɪ/ *verb* **-fies; -fied; -fy·ing** [+ *obj*] *formal*
1 : to make (someone) happy or satisfied ▪ A guilty verdict would *gratify* the victim's relatives. ▪ It *gratifies* [=*pleases*] me to see how well the book is doing. — often used as *(be) gratified* ▪ He's *gratified* by the response he's been getting.
2 : to do or give whatever is wanted or demanded by (someone or something) ▪ He's only concerned with *gratifying* his own desires. ▪ *gratify* a whim ▪ I'll be happy to *gratify* [=*satisfy*] your curiosity.
– grat·i·fi·ca·tion /ˌgrætəfəˈkeɪʃən/ *noun, pl* **-tions** [*noncount*] He's only concerned with selfish *gratification* of his own desires. [*count*] Her life now offers few *gratifications.* [=few sources of satisfaction or pleasure] **– gratified** *adj* [*more* ~; *most* ~] ▪ He's very/highly *gratified* that his students have done so well. ▪ She was *gratified* to see her ideas become so widely accepted.

gratifying *adj* [*more* ~; *most* ~] : giving pleasure or satisfaction ▪ It was a *gratifying* victory. ▪ The response has been *gratifying.* ▪ It's been very *gratifying* (to me) to see how well the book has done.
– grat·i·fy·ing·ly *adv*

gra·tin /ˈgrɑːtn̩, *Brit* ˈgrætæn/ *noun, pl* **-tins** [*count*] : a dish that has bread crumbs or cheese on top and is cooked in an oven — see also AU GRATIN

grat·ing /ˈgreɪtɪŋ/ *noun, pl* **-ings** [*count*] : a frame with bars across it that is used to cover an opening

gra·tis /ˈgrætəs/ *adv* — used to indicate that no money is paid for something ▪ The food was supplied *gratis* [=*for free; at no cost; without charge*] by a local caterer.
– gratis *adj* ▪ The food was *gratis.* [=*free*] ▪ *gratis* hotel accommodations

grat·i·tude /ˈgrætəˌtuːd, *Brit* ˈgrætəˌtjuːd/ *noun* [*noncount*] : a feeling of appreciation or thanks ▪ Let me express my sincere *gratitude* for all your help. ▪ We remember with *gratitude* those who died defending our country. ▪ We owe them a ***debt of gratitude*** [=we should be grateful to them] for all the help they've given us. — opposite INGRATITUDE

gra·tu·i·tous /grəˈtuːwətəs, *Brit* grəˈtjuːətəs/ *adj* [*more* ~; *most* ~] *formal* : not necessary or appropriate ▪ The film was criticized for its *gratuitous* violence. ▪ *gratuitous* insults
– gra·tu·i·tous·ly *adv* ▪ a *gratuitously* violent film **– gra·tu·i·tous·ness** *noun* [*noncount*]

gra·tu·i·ty /grəˈtuːwəti, *Brit* grəˈtjuːəti/ *noun, pl* **-ties** [*count*]
1 *formal* : an amount of money given to a person (such as a waiter or waitress) who has performed a service : TIP ▪ A 15 percent *gratuity* is automatically added to the restaurant bill.
2 *Brit* : an amount of money given to a retiring soldier or employee

¹grave /ˈgreɪv/ *noun, pl* **graves** [*count*]
1 : a hole in the ground for burying a dead body ▪ dig a *grave* ▪ The casket was lowered into the *grave.* ▪ He was buried in a shallow *grave.* ▪ We went to the cemetery to visit my aunt's *grave.* [=to visit the place where my aunt's body is buried] ▪ A headstone marks her son's *grave.* ▪ ***grave robbers*** [=people who dig up a buried body to steal the things that were buried with it] ✧ When people think that a dead person would be very shocked or upset to see something that is happening now, they say that person is or must be ***turning/spinning in his/her grave*** or *US* ***turning over in his/her grave*** or *US* ***rolling (over) in his/her grave.*** ▪ The company founder must be *turning in his grave* because of the changes we've made.
2 — used to talk about death ▪ She took her secrets with her to the *grave.* [=she died without telling anyone her secrets] ▪ He believes that there is life ***beyond the grave.*** [=that there is life after death] ▪ A hard life ***drove him to an early grave.*** [=caused him to die when he was fairly young] ▪ She ***went to her grave*** [=she died] a lonely and bitter woman.
dig your own grave see ¹DIG
from (the) cradle to (the) grave see ¹CRADLE
have one foot in the grave see ¹FOOT

²grave *adj* **grav·er; -est** [*also more* ~; *most* ~]
1 *formal* : very serious : requiring or causing serious thought or concern ▪ This violation of school rules is a *grave* matter. ▪ His carelessness could have *grave* consequences. ▪ They have placed themselves in *grave* danger. ▪ I have *grave* doubts about this plan. ▪ suffering from a *grave* illness
2 : serious and formal in appearance or manner ▪ The judge issued his ruling with a *grave* expression.
3 /ˈgrɑːv/ *of an accent mark* : having the form ` ▪ The French word *père* is written with a *grave* accent over the first *e.*

G

— compare ACUTE 7
– **grave·ly** *adv* ▪ My mother is *gravely* [=*seriously*] ill. ▪ He shook his head *gravely*.

grave·dig·ger /ˈgreɪvˌdɪgɚ/ *noun, pl* **-gers** [*count*] : a person whose job it is to dig graves

grav·el /ˈgrævəl/ *noun* [*noncount*] : small pieces of rock ▪ a layer of *gravel* — often used before another noun ▪ a *gravel* road [=a road with a top surface made of gravel] ▪ a *gravel* pit [=a large hole in the ground where gravel has been dug up]

grav·el·ly /ˈgrævəli/ *adj* [*more* ~; *most* ~]
1 : containing or covered with gravel ▪ *gravelly* soil
2 : having a rough sound ▪ a *gravelly* voice

grav·en image /ˈgreɪvən-/ *noun, pl* ~ **-ages** [*count*] : an object (such as a statue) that is worshipped as a god or in place of a god

grave·stone /ˈgreɪvˌstoun/ *noun, pl* **-stones** [*count*] : a stone that marks the place where a dead person is buried and that usually has the person's name and birth and death dates on it : HEADSTONE, TOMBSTONE

grave·yard /ˈgreɪvˌjɑɚd/ *noun, pl* **-yards** [*count*]
1 : a place where people are buried : CEMETERY ✧ *Graveyard* usually refers to a small cemetery, such as one that is next to a church.
2 : a place where old things are left or thrown away ▪ an automobile *graveyard*
whistle past the graveyard see [2]WHISTLE

graveyard shift *noun, pl* ~ **shifts** [*count*] *chiefly US* : a scheduled period of work that begins late at night and ends in the morning

grav·i·tas /ˈgrævəˌtɑːs/ *noun, formal* : a very serious quality or manner [*noncount*] The new leader has an air of *gravitas* that commands respect. ▪ a comic actress who lacks the *gravitas* for dramatic roles [*singular*] The new leader has a certain *gravitas*.

grav·i·tate /ˈgrævəˌteɪt/ *verb* **-tates; -tat·ed; -tat·ing** [*no obj*]
1 : to move or tend to move *to* or *toward* someone or something ▪ The guests *gravitated toward* the far side of the room. ▪ The conversation *gravitated to/toward* politics.
2 : to be attracted *to* or *toward* something or someone ▪ Voters have started *gravitating to* him as a possible candidate. ▪ Many young people now *gravitate toward* careers in the computer industry.

grav·i·ta·tion /ˌgrævəˈteɪʃən/ *noun* [*noncount*]
1 *technical* **:** the natural force that causes things to fall towards the earth : GRAVITY
2 : movement to or toward someone or something ▪ the *gravitation* of young people to/toward computer careers
– **grav·i·ta·tion·al** /ˌgrævəˈteɪʃənl/ *adj, technical* ▪ the Earth's *gravitational* field – **grav·i·ta·tion·al·ly** *adv, technical*

grav·i·ty /ˈgrævəti/ *noun* [*noncount*]
1 : a very serious quality or condition : the condition of being grave or serious ▪ They didn't seem to understand the *gravity* [=*seriousness*] of the situation. ▪ He uttered the oath with proper *gravity*. [=*solemnity*]
2 *technical* **:** the natural force that tends to cause physical things to move towards each other : the force that causes things to fall towards the Earth ▪ attempting to defy *gravity* ▪ the force of *gravity* — see also CENTER OF GRAVITY

gra·vy /ˈgreɪvi/ *noun, pl* **-vies**
1 [*count, noncount*] **:** a sauce made from the juices of cooked meat ▪ mashed potatoes with *gravy* ▪ a *gravy* boat [=a container for serving gravy]
2 [*noncount*] *chiefly US, informal* **:** something valuable or pleasing that is more than what is earned or expected ▪ The bonus he received in addition to his salary was pure *gravy*.

gravy train *noun, pl* ~ **trains** [*count*] *informal* : something (such as a business or a government program) that provides money to many people without requiring much work or effort ▪ They're trying to get on board the *gravy train*. ▪ ride the *gravy train*

[1]**gray** (*US*) *or chiefly Brit* **grey** /ˈgreɪ/ *adj* **gray·er; -est**
1 : having a color between black and white : having a color that is like the color of smoke ▪ a *gray* sweater/suit ▪ *gray* hair
2 : having gray hair ▪ What will you do when you are old and *gray*? ▪ My friends have all gone *gray*.
3 : lacking brightness: such as **a :** cloudy and dark ▪ It was a *gray* winter day. ▪ a cold, *gray* dawn **b :** very boring or ordinary ▪ leading a *gray* existence **c :** having or showing little life or energy ▪ the *gray* faces of the people in the crowd
– **gray·ness** (*US*) *or chiefly Brit* **grey·ness** *noun* [*noncount*] ▪ the *grayness* of the dawn

[2]**gray** (*US*) *or chiefly Brit* **grey** *noun, pl* **grays**
1 [*count, noncount*] **:** a color that is between black and white : a color that is like the color of smoke ▪ wearing *gray* ▪ shades of *gray* — see color picture on page C1
2 [*count*] **:** something (such as an animal) that is gray
– **gray·ish** (*US*) *or chiefly Brit* **grey·ish** /ˈgrejɪʃ/ *adj*

[3]**gray** (*US*) *or chiefly Brit* **grey** *verb* **grays; grayed; gray·ing** [*no obj*]
1 : to become gray ▪ His hair is *graying*. = He has *graying* hair.
2 : to become older ▪ The population is *graying*.

gray area *noun, pl* ~ **areas** [*count*] : an area or situation in which it is difficult to judge what is right and what is wrong ▪ There are no *gray areas* in the rules. ▪ a legal *gray area*

gray matter *noun* [*noncount*] : the tissue that makes up the brain — often used figuratively to refer to a person's intelligence ▪ His books are enjoyable, but they don't do much to challenge the reader's *gray matter*. [=*intelligence*]

[1]**graze** /ˈgreɪz/ *verb* **graz·es; grazed; graz·ing**
1 a *of an animal* **:** to eat grass or other plants that are growing in a field, pasture, etc. [*no obj*] The cattle *grazed* (on grass) in the field. ▪ *grazing* cattle [+ *obj*] Fields *grazed* by cattle. **b** [+ *obj*] **:** to cause (animals) to graze ▪ We *grazed* our cattle on the front pasture.
2 [*no obj*] **:** to eat small amounts of food at many times during the day ▪ She *was grazing* on snacks all afternoon.
— compare [2]GRAZE

[2]**graze** *verb* **grazes; grazed; grazing** [+ *obj*]
1 : to touch or hit (something) while moving past it ▪ The car's wheel *grazed* the curb. ▪ He was *grazed* by a bullet.
2 : to injure (the skin, a part of the body, etc.) by scraping against something ▪ She *grazed* her knee when she fell.
— compare [1]GRAZE

[3]**graze** *noun, pl* **grazes** [*count*] : an injury on your skin that is caused because it moves against something ▪ She had a slight *graze* on her knee from falling.

[1]**grease** /ˈgriːs/ *noun* [*noncount*]
1 : melted animal fat ▪ hamburger/bacon *grease*
2 : an oily substance ▪ axle *grease* — see also ELBOW GREASE
a/the squeaky wheel gets the grease see [1]WHEEL

[2]**grease** *verb* **greas·es; greased; greas·ing** [+ *obj*] : to put a thin layer of grease or oil on (something) ▪ *Grease* the pan before you put the cake batter in.
grease the palm of (someone) *or US* ***grease the hand of (someone)*** : to give (someone) money for doing something illegal or dishonest for you ▪ They had to *grease the palms of* a few inspectors at city hall to get the permits they needed to start building.
like greased lightning see [1]LIGHTNING

grease monkey *noun, pl* ~ **-keys** [*count*] *informal* : a person who repairs machines (such as car engines) : MECHANIC ✧ *Grease monkey* is usually considered an insulting word.

grease·paint /ˈgriːsˌpeɪnt/ *noun* [*noncount*] : makeup worn by actors in the theater

grease·proof paper /ˈgriːsˈpruːf-/ *noun* [*noncount*] *Brit* : WAX PAPER

greasy /ˈgriːsi/ *adj* **greas·i·er; -est**
1 a : covered with grease or oil : dirty from grease or oil ▪ *greasy* clothes/hair/fingers **b** *chiefly Brit* **:** wet and slippery ▪ *greasy* roads
2 : containing or cooked with a large amount of fat ▪ My doctor told me to avoid *greasy* food. ▪ *greasy* potato chips

greasy spoon *noun, pl* ~ **spoons** [*count*] *informal* : a small and cheap restaurant ▪ We ate at some *greasy spoon* near the bus station.

[1]**great** /ˈgreɪt/ *adj* **great·er; -est**
1 a : very large in size : very big ▪ all creatures *great* and small — usually used before a noun ▪ a *great* beast ▪ We were surprised by the *great* size of the auditorium. ▪ They traveled through a *great* stretch of wilderness. ▪ a *great* cloud of smoke ▪ A *great* crowd had formed in the city square. ▪ the *Great* Wall of China ▪ the *Great* Lakes ▪ (*US*) The house has a large ***great room***. [=a large room used for several different purposes] ▪ (*informal*) They live in a ***great big*** house. [=a very large house] ▪ (*chiefly Brit*) a ***huge/whopping great*** elephant **b** — used in the names of animals that are larger than similar animals ▪ the *great* white shark ▪ the *great* horned owl
2 : very large in amount or extent ▪ The project will require a *great* amount of time and money. ▪ He lived to a *great* age.

[=he lived to be very old] • The show was a *great* [=*big, huge*] success. • It's been a *great* [=*long*] while since we last saw them. • He amassed a *great* [=*large*] fortune. • The building was restored at *great* expense. • a *great* quantity of fish • He explained in *great* [=*much*] detail how they had met. • These topics need to be discussed in *greater* [=*more*] depth and at *greater* length. • Our speed/strength/power became *greater* (and *greater*) as we went on. • He made ***a great deal of*** money. [=he made a large amount of money] • Things could be ***a great deal*** worse. [=things could be much worse] • He is supported by ***the great majority*** of voters. [=by most voters]
3 a : very strong • The low cost of these products gives them *great* appeal. • There is a very *great* need for reform. • They're in no *great* hurry to finish. • There is a *great* demand for his services. • She takes a *great* [=*considerable*] interest in everything her children do. • an actress of *great* charm • with *great* [=strongly felt] sadness/admiration/love • Is there any love *greater* than that between parent and child? • The whole matter must be treated ***with great care***. [=very carefully] • His comments are true ***to a great extent***. [=most of his comments are true] • This new tax affects everyone ***to a greater or lesser degree/extent***. [=to some degree/extent] **b** — used for emphasis before a noun that describes someone • I've always been a *great* admirer of his work. [=I have always admired his work very much] • They are *great* friends. [=they are very friendly] • I'm a *great* believer in the value of patience. [=I believe very much in the value of patience] **c :** very important • This room is only used for *great* occasions. [=grand occasions, very important and formal occasions] **d :** very bad **:** very extreme or severe • The storm caused *great* damage/destruction. • He was obviously in *great* pain/discomfort. • She has suffered a *great* loss. • It would be a *great* mistake to ignore these problems. • a *great* disaster/misfortune • *great* difficulties • a very *great* error
4 : better than good: such as **a :** of the highest quality • *great* (works of) art/literature • *great* music **b :** very important and admired • a *great* poet/artist • a *great* leader/scientist/thinker/woman • He was a *great* but flawed man. • a *great* discovery/invention • *great* achievements **c :** very talented or successful • My brother is a *great* golfer. • She's a *great* judge of character. • My brother is ***great at*** (playing) golf. [=my brother plays golf very well] • She is *great at* Chinese cooking. **d** *informal* **:** very enjoyable, favorable, etc. **:** EXCELLENT • "How was the movie?" "It was (really) *great*!" • It was the *greatest*. • The movie got *great* reviews. • We are having *great* weather this summer. • We had a *great* time on our vacation. • a *great* party/lecture/performance • an actress with *great* [=very good-looking] legs • It's *great* to see you again. = It's *great* seeing you again. • This restaurant is *great* for a quick meal. = This is a *great* restaurant for a quick meal. • The food tastes *great*! • *Great* work, everybody! • "I've passed the exam!" "That's *great*!" — often used in the phrases ***feel great*** and ***look great*** • You *look great* in that hat. = That hat *looks great* on you. • Things aren't *looking* so *great* at this point. • He came home early because he wasn't *feeling* too *great*. [=he wasn't feeling well] • I *feel great* just being with her! — sometimes used in an ironic way to describe something that is very bad or upsetting • "I can't find the tickets." "That's (just) *great*! What are we supposed to do now?" • Oh, *great*. Now I've lost the tickets.
5 *always used before a noun* **:** more distant in a family relationship by one generation • My *great* aunt/uncle is my father's/mother's aunt/uncle. — usually used in combination • My *great*-grandfather is my grandfather's father. • My *great-great*-grandmother is my *great*-grandfather's mother. • a gift sent to *Great*-Uncle Mike
a great one for *informal* ✧ If you are *a great one for* (doing) something, you do it often or enjoy doing it very much. • He's *a great one for* (playing) golf. • She's *a great one for* getting other people to do her work.
go great guns see ¹GUN
go to great pains see ¹PAIN
great with child *old-fashioned + literary* **:** PREGNANT
no great shakes see ²SHAKE
– great·ness *noun* [*noncount*] • the *greatness* of the need for reform • Shakespeare achieved true/real/genuine *greatness* as a writer.

²great *adv* **greater; -est** *informal* **:** very well • We had some problems at first, but now things are going just *great*. • Keep up the good work. You're doing *great*!

³great *noun, pl* **greats** [*count*] **:** a very successful or admired person — usually plural • She is among the *greats* of literature. • He is one of the all-time *greats* in baseball.

great ape *noun, pl* **~ apes** [*count*] **:** ¹APE 1

Great Dane *noun, pl* **~ Danes** [*count*] **:** a very large type of dog

Great·er /ˈgreɪtɚ/ *adj* **:** consisting of a central city and the surrounding areas that are connected with it — always used before the name of a place • *Greater* London • *Greater* New York • *Greater* Tokyo

great·ly /ˈgreɪtli/ *adv* [*more ~; most ~*] **:** to a great extent or degree **:** very much • She has contributed *greatly* to our success. • They don't seem to be *greatly* bothered by the delay. • I've always admired his work *greatly*. = I've always *greatly* admired his work.

Great Power *noun, pl* **~ Powers** [*count*] **:** a very powerful country

Great Scott /-ˈskɑːt/ *interj, old-fashioned* — used to express surprise • *Great Scott*, is it that late already?!

Gre·cian /ˈgriːʃən/ *adj* **:** of or relating to ancient Greece • a *Grecian* sculpture/urn

greed /ˈgriːd/ *noun* [*noncount*] **:** a selfish desire to have more of something (especially money) • He was a ruthless businessman, motivated by naked ambition and *greed*. • corporate *greed* — sometimes + *for* • He made no effort to conceal his *greed for* money and power.

greedy /ˈgriːdi/ *adj* **greed·i·er; -est**
1 : having or showing a selfish desire to have more of something (such as money or food) **:** having greed • He was a ruthless and *greedy* businessman. • There's no need to get *greedy*—there's plenty for everyone. • He blames all his problems on *greedy* lawyers. — often + *for* • The children were *greedy for* more candy. • *greedy for* money
2 : very eager to have something — + *for* • He was *greedy for* a promotion. • The company is *greedy for* publicity.
– greed·i·ly /ˈgriːdəli/ *adv* • She *greedily* insisted on special benefits at work. • eating and drinking *greedily* **– greed·i·ness** /ˈgriːdinəs/ *noun* [*noncount*] • I was surprised by the children's *greediness*.

Greek /ˈgriːk/ *noun, pl* **Greeks**
1 [*count*] **a :** a person born, raised, or living in Greece • the ancient *Greeks* • modern *Greeks* **b :** a person whose family is from Greece
2 [*noncount*] **:** the language of the Greeks ✧ In informal English you can describe something that you do not understand by saying ***It's (all) Greek to me.***
– Greek *adj* • *Greek* culture/mythology • the *Greek* alphabet [=the alphabet used for writing Greek]

¹green /ˈgriːn/ *adj* **green·er; -est**
1 : having the color of growing grass • *green* leaves • a *green* sweater
2 a : covered by green grass or other plants • *green* fields **b :** consisting of green plants or of the leaves of plants • a *green* salad
3 : feeling envy — usually used in the phrase ***green with envy*** • His brother's success made him *green with envy*.
4 a : not ripe yet • *green* tomatoes **b :** not having training, knowledge, or experience • *green* troops • When she arrived at the company she was still very *green* but eager to learn.
5 *informal* **:** having a pale or sick appearance • Our flight hit some turbulence, and half the passengers started turning *green*. — often used in the phrase ***green around/about the gills*** • The passengers were looking *green around the gills*.
6 : trying to protect or meant to protect the natural world **:** concerned with protecting the environment • She only buys products from *green* companies. • companies that use *green* practices [=companies that do things in a way that helps to protect the environment] • finding *greener* methods of waste disposal
greener pastures see ¹PASTURE
– green·ish /ˈgriːnɪʃ/ *adj* • *greenish* eyes **– green·ness** /ˈgriːnnəs/ *noun* [*noncount*] • the *greenness* of the leaves/troops

²green *noun, pl* **greens**
1 : a color that is like the color of growing grass [*noncount*] shades of *green* [*count*] a mixture of blues and *greens* — see color picture on page C1
2 greens [*plural*] **:** the leaves of plants used for food • turnip *greens* • salad *greens* — see color picture on page C4
3 [*count*] **a :** a large area covered with growing grass in the center of a town or village • The town *green* was the center of activity. **b** *golf* **:** an area covered with very short grass around the hole into which the ball must be played • It took him four shots to get to the *green*. — called also *putting green*
4 *or* **Green** [*count*] **:** a person who tries to protect the natural

G

world; *especially* : a person who belongs to a political party that has the protection of the environment as its main goal

green·back /ˈgriːnˌbæk/ *noun, pl* **-backs** [*count*] *informal* : a piece of U.S. paper money

green bean *noun, pl* ~ **beans** [*count*] : a type of bean whose long green seed cases are eaten as a vegetable when they are young and tender — see color picture on page C4; compare STRING BEAN

green card *noun, pl* ~ **cards** [*count*] : a card indicating that a person from a foreign country can live and work in the U.S.

green·ery /ˈgriːnəri/ *noun* [*noncount*] : green leaves or plants ▪ The restaurant was adorned with *greenery*. ▪ the lush *greenery* of the islands

green–eyed monster *noun*
the green-eyed monster informal : jealousy thought of as a monster that bites or attacks people ▪ She was bitten by *the green-eyed monster*. [=she became jealous] ▪ *The green-eyed monster* reared its (ugly) head [=I became jealous] when my ex-wife began dating someone else.

green fingers *noun* [*plural*] *Brit* : an unusual ability to make plants grow ▪ She has *green fingers*. [=(*US*) *a green thumb*]

green·fly /ˈgriːnˌflaɪ/ *noun, pl* **green·flies** *or* **greenfly** [*count*] *Brit* : a type of small, green insect that damages plants

green·gro·cer /ˈgriːnˌgrousə/ *noun, pl* **-cers** [*count*] *chiefly Brit* : a person who works in or owns a store that sells fresh vegetables and fruit ▪ I bought the fruit from the *greengrocer*. = I bought the fruit at the *greengrocer's*.

green·horn /ˈgriːnˌhoən/ *noun, pl* **-horns** [*count*] *informal* : a person who lacks experience and knowledge ▪ He's not the most sophisticated businessman you'll ever meet, but he's no *greenhorn*.

[1]**green·house** /ˈgriːnˌhaʊs/ *noun, pl* **-hous·es** [*count*] : a building or part of a building that has glass walls and a glass roof and that is used for growing plants

greenhouse

[2]**greenhouse** *adj, always used before a noun* : relating to or caused by the warming of the Earth's atmosphere that is caused by air pollution : relating to or caused by the greenhouse effect ▪ *greenhouse* warming ▪ carbon dioxide and other ***greenhouse gases*** [=gases that cause the greenhouse effect]

greenhouse effect *noun*
the greenhouse effect : the warming of the Earth's atmosphere that is caused by air pollution ✧ *The greenhouse effect* occurs when warmth from the sun is trapped in the Earth's atmosphere by a layer of gases (such as carbon dioxide) and water vapor.

green light *noun*
the green light : permission to start or continue something (such as a project) ▪ His boss finally gave him *the green light* [=*the go-ahead*] to start the new project.

green onion *noun, pl* ~ **-ions** [*count*] *US* : a young onion that is pulled from the ground before the bulb has become large — called also (*US*) *scallion*, (*chiefly Brit*) *spring onion*; see color picture on page C4

Green Paper *noun, pl* ~ **-pers** [*count*] *Brit* : a government document that suggests solutions to a problem and that is intended to cause discussion before a law is made — compare WHITE PAPER

green pepper *noun, pl* ~ **-pers** [*count*] : a type of hollow vegetable (called a pepper) that is green and that is eaten raw or cooked

green·room /ˈgriːnˌruːm/ *noun, pl* **-rooms** [*count*] : a room in a theater or television studio where performers can relax before or after they perform

green·sward /ˈgriːnˌswaəd/ *noun, pl* **-swards** [*count*] *old-fashioned + literary* : an area of ground that is covered with green grass

green tea *noun* [*noncount*] : a type of tea that is light in color

green thumb *noun* [*singular*] *US* : an unusual ability to make plants grow ▪ Thanks to my mother's *green thumb* [=(*Brit*) *green fingers*], we usually had vegetables fresh from the garden.
– green–thumbed /ˈgriːnˈθʌmd/ *adj* ▪ a *green-thumbed* gardener

Green·wich mean time /ˈgrɪnɪʤ-, ˈgrɛnɪʧ-/ *noun* [*singular*] : the time in Greenwich, England, that is used as the basis of standard time throughout the world — called also (*US*) *Greenwich time*

greet /ˈgriːt/ *verb* **greets; greet·ed; greet·ing** [+ *obj*]
1 : to meet (someone who has just arrived) with usually friendly and polite words and actions : WELCOME ▪ My husband *greeted* our guests at the door. ▪ She *greeted* him warmly. ▪ She *greeted* him with open arms.
2 : to react to (someone or something) in a specified way — often + *with* ▪ Her idea was *greeted with* enthusiasm.
3 : to appear to (someone who has just arrived) : to be seen or experienced by (someone) ▪ A chaotic scene *greeted* them. — often used as *(be) greeted* ▪ We *were greeted* by a snowstorm when we arrived at the airport.

greet·er *noun, pl* **-ers** [*count*] : someone who greets people as they enter a place ▪ He was hired as a professional *greeter*, welcoming customers to the store.

greeting *noun, pl* **-ings**
1 : something that is said or done to show people that you are happy to meet or see them [*count*] He addressed the members of the delegation with a formal *greeting*. ▪ The delegates exchanged *greetings*. [*noncount*] He held out his hand ***in greeting***. [=as a way to greet someone]
2 [*count*] : a message that expresses good wishes to someone — usually plural ▪ My sister sends you *greetings*. ▪ holiday/season's *greetings*

greeting card *noun, pl* ~ **cards** [*count*] *US* : a decorated card with a message of good wishes that is sent or given to someone on a special occasion ▪ holiday *greeting cards* — called also (*Brit*) *greetings card*; see picture at MAIL

greetings *interj* — used to greet someone who has just arrived ▪ *Greetings*! I'm glad you were able to come.

gre·gar·i·ous /grɪˈgerijəs/ *adj* [*more* ~; *most* ~]
1 : enjoying the company of other people ▪ She is outgoing and *gregarious*. ▪ a *gregarious* personality
2 *biology* : tending to live in groups ▪ *gregarious* animals
– gre·gar·i·ous·ly *adv* **– gre·gar·i·ous·ness** *noun* [*noncount*]

Gre·go·ri·an calendar /grɪˈgorijən-/ *noun* [*singular*] : the calendar system that is used by most people in the world today ✧ The Gregorian calendar was introduced in 1582 by Pope Gregory XIII. It is now used throughout the world for legal and business purposes.

Gregorian chant *noun, pl* ~ **chants** [*count, noncount*] : a type of religious music from the Middle Ages that is sung without instruments

grem·lin /ˈgrɛmlən/ *noun, pl* **-lins** [*count*] : a small imaginary creature that is blamed when something (such as a machine) does not work properly ▪ As expected, the new computer network has had its share of *gremlins*. [=there have been problems with the new computer network]

gre·nade /grəˈneɪd/ *noun, pl* **-nades** [*count*] : a small bomb that is designed to be thrown by someone or shot from a rifle ▪ a hand *grenade* ▪ a *grenade*-launcher

grenade

gren·a·dine /ˌgrɛnəˈdiːn/ *noun* [*noncount*] : a sweet liquid that is made from a type of red fruit (called a pomegranate) and that is used in alcoholic drinks

grew *past tense of* GROW

grey *chiefly Brit spelling of* GRAY

grey·hound /ˈgreɪˌhaʊnd/ *noun, pl* **-hounds** [*count*] : a tall, thin dog that runs very fast and that is often used in races

grid /ˈgrɪd/ *noun, pl* **grids** [*count*]
1 : a metal frame with bars running across it that is used to cover an opening
2 : a pattern of lines that cross each other to form squares on a piece of paper, a map, etc. ▪ The students plotted points on a *grid*. ▪ The city streets form a *grid*.
3 : a network of electrical wires and equipment that supplies electricity to a large area

grid·dle /ˈgrɪdl/ *noun, pl* **grid·dles** [*count*] : a flat surface or pan on which food is cooked

griddle cake *noun, pl* ~ **cakes** [*count*] *chiefly US* : PANCAKE

grid·iron /ˈgrɪdˌajɚn/ *noun, pl* **-irons** [*count*]
1 : a metal grid for cooking food over a fire
2 *US, informal* : the field on which American football is played • The book recounts his many moments of glory on the *gridiron*. — often used before another noun • *gridiron* glory

grid·lock /ˈgrɪdˌlɑːk/ *noun*
1 : a situation in which streets are so full that vehicles cannot move [*noncount*] An accident caused *gridlock* at rush hour yesterday. [*singular*] We were caught in a *gridlock*.
2 : a situation in which no progress can be made [*noncount*] Disagreements about funding have caused legislative *gridlock* in Congress. [*singular*] a legislative *gridlock*
– **grid·locked** /ˈgrɪdˌlɑːkt/ *adj* • *gridlocked* streets • Congress remains *gridlocked*.

grief /ˈgriːf/ *noun, pl* **griefs**
1 a [*noncount*] : deep sadness caused especially by someone's death • He has been unable to recover from his *grief* at/over his son's death. • She was overcome with/by *grief*. **b** [*count*] : a cause of deep sadness • the joys and *griefs* of our lives
2 [*noncount*] *informal* **a** : trouble or annoyance • I've had enough *grief* for one day. • Trying to fix the computer isn't worth the *grief*. **b** : annoying or playful criticism • He's taken/gotten/had a lot of *grief* from his friends. • His friends have been ***giving him a lot of grief***.
come to grief : to experience failure, disaster, etc. • The boat *came to grief* on the rocks. • Their plans for opening a restaurant *came to grief* when they failed to get a loan.
good grief *informal* — used to express surprise or annoyance • "He's burned the toast." "*Good grief!* Can't he do anything right?"

grief–strick·en /ˈgriːfˌstrɪkən/ *adj* [*more* ~; *most* ~] : very sad : deeply affected by grief • The death of his son has left him *grief-stricken*.

griev·ance /ˈgriːvəns/ *noun, pl* **-anc·es**
1 : a feeling of having been treated unfairly [*noncount*] He has a deep sense of *grievance* against his former employer. [*count*] She has been ***nursing a grievance*** all week.
2 [*count*] : a reason for complaining or being unhappy with a situation • In the petition, the students listed their many *grievances* against the university administration.
3 [*count*] : a statement in which you say you are unhappy or not satisfied with something • The union has filed a formal *grievance* [=*complaint*], accusing the company of unfair labor practices. • Several customers came to the front desk to ***air their grievances***.

grieve /ˈgriːv/ *verb* **grieves; grieved; griev·ing**
1 [+ *obj*] : to cause (someone) to feel sad or unhappy • It *grieves* me to see my brother struggling like this. • Her decision to live overseas *grieved* her mother.
2 : to feel or show grief or sadness [*no obj*] People need time to *grieve* after the death of a family member. • The children are still *grieving* for their mother. = The children are *grieving* over their mother's death. • a *grieving* widow [+ *obj*] The children are still *grieving* the death of their mother.

griev·ous /ˈgriːvəs/ *adj* [*more* ~; *most* ~] *formal* : causing great sadness, suffering, or pain : very serious or severe • the *grievous* cost of war • He took a foolish financial risk and suffered a *grievous* loss. • *grievous* bodily harm • a *grievous* error/mistake
– **griev·ous·ly** *adv* • Several passengers were *grievously* injured in the bus accident.

grif·fin *also* **grif·fon** *or* **gryph·on** /ˈgrɪfən/ *noun, pl* **griffins** *also* **grif·fons** *or* **gryph·ons** [*count*] *in stories* : an animal that is half eagle and half lion

[1]**grill** /ˈgrɪl/ *noun, pl* **grills** [*count*]
1 a : a metal frame that is used to cook food over hot coals or an open fire • She put the hamburgers on the *grill*. **b** : a cooking device with a grill • a portable gas *grill* **c** : an electric device in which food is cooked between two hot surfaces
2 : a restaurant that serves grilled or broiled foods • a Mexican *grill* — often used in the names of restaurants • Jackie's Bar and *Grill*
3 : a dish of grilled or broiled food • a seafood *grill* • a mixed *grill* [=a dish of various grilled meats]
4 *Brit* : BROILER 1

[2]**grill** *verb* **grills; grilled; grill·ing** [+ *obj*]
1 *chiefly US* **a** : to cook (food) on a metal frame over fire • We're planning to *grill* some chicken and burgers at the cookout. **b** : to fry or toast (something, such as a sandwich) on a hot surface • a *grilled* cheese sandwich
2 *Brit* : to cook (food) directly over or under high heat : BROIL
3 *informal* : to ask (someone) a series of difficult and unpleasant questions : to question (someone) intensely • The police *grilled* [=*interrogated*] the suspect for hours. • Her parents *grilled* her when she came home late.
– **grilling** /ˈgrɪlɪŋ/ *noun, pl* **-ings** [*noncount*] These steaks are perfect for *grilling*. [*count*] The police gave him a *grilling* about his possible involvement in the robbery.

grill

grille *also* **grill** /ˈgrɪl/ *noun, pl* **grilles** *also* **grills** [*count*] : a metal frame with bars running across it that is used to cover or protect something • The vent was covered with a *grille*. • The truck has a large metal *grille* at the front. — see picture at CAR

grim /ˈgrɪm/ *adj* **grim·mer; -mest**
1 : unpleasant or shocking to see or think about • Hikers made a *grim* discovery when they came across a dead body in the woods. • The accident serves as a *grim* reminder of the dangers of drinking and driving.
2 : causing feelings of sadness or worry : gloomy or depressing • a *grim* winter • The prognosis is *grim*—doctors do not expect her to live longer than six months. • He paints a *grim* picture of the prospects for peace.
3 : having a very serious appearance or manner • His face looked *grim*, and we knew his news wouldn't be good. • a *grim* smile • a *grim* taskmaster
4 : strongly felt and serious • *grim* determination
– **grim·ly** *adv* • She spoke *grimly* of the scarcity of jobs.
– **grim·ness** *noun* [*noncount*]

grim·ace /ˈgrɪməs/ *noun, pl* **-ac·es** [*count*] : a facial expression in which your mouth and face are twisted in a way that shows disgust, disapproval, or pain • The patient made/gave a painful *grimace* as the doctor examined his wound.
– **grimace** *verb* **-aces; -aced; -ac·ing** [*no obj*] • The patient *grimaced* in pain when his wound was touched.

grime /ˈgraɪm/ *noun* [*noncount*] : dirt that covers a surface • The windows were coated with *grime*.
– **grimy** /ˈgraɪmi/ *adj* **grim·i·er; -est** • *grimy* [=*dirty*] windows

Grim Reaper *noun*
the Grim Reaper : death thought of as a man or skeleton holding a scythe and wearing a dark cloak with a hood • a visit from *the Grim Reaper*

grin /ˈgrɪn/ *verb* **grins; grinned; grin·ning** [*no obj*] : to smile widely • She continued to tease her brother, *grinning* wickedly. • He was ***grinning from ear to ear***. [=he was grinning very broadly]
grin and bear it : to accept something that you do not like because you have no choice • I don't agree with their decision, but all I can do is *grin and bear it*.
– **grin** *noun, pl* **grins** [*count*] • He had/wore a foolish/sheepish/big *grin* on his face.

grinch /ˈgrɪntʃ/ *noun, pl* **grinch·es** [*count*] *US, informal* : an unpleasant person who spoils other people's fun or enjoyment • Only a *grinch* would complain about the movie's silly plot.

[1]**grind** /ˈgraɪnd/ *verb* **grinds; ground** /ˈgraʊnd/; **grind·ing**
1 [+ *obj*] **a** : to crush or break (something) into very small pieces by rubbing it against a rough surface or using a special machine • *Grind* (up) the coffee beans into a fine powder. • The corn is *ground* into meal. **b** : to cut (meat) into small pieces by putting it through a special machine • *Grind* (up) the turkey meat. — usually used in U.S. English in the form *ground* to describe meat that has been cut into very small pieces • a recipe made with *ground* turkey • a pound of ***ground beef*** [=(*US*) *hamburger*, (*Brit*) *mince*]
2 : to make (something) sharp or smooth by rubbing it against a hard surface [+ *obj*] *grind* an ax [*no obj*] The steel *grinds* to a sharp edge. — see also *ax to grind* at [1]AX
3 a [+ *obj*] : to cause (things) to rub against each other in a forceful way that produces a harsh noise • She kept *grinding* the car's gears. • He *grinds* his teeth in his sleep. **b** [*no obj*] : to make a harsh noise caused by rubbing • I could hear the gears *grinding*.
4 [+ *obj*] : to rub or press (something) against a hard surface •

She *ground* (out) her cigarette on the pavement. ▪ Dirt was *ground* into the carpet.

grind along [*phrasal verb*] **1** : to continue in a slow and steady way ▪ The traffic *ground along* through the city streets. ▪ The economy continues to *grind along*. **2** ***grind along (something)*** : to continue moving down or along (something) in a slow and steady way ▪ The traffic was *grinding along* the streets.

grind away [*phrasal verb*] **1** : to work or study in a steady, determined way ▪ She was *grinding away* at her studies. **2** ***grind away (something) or grind (something) away*** : to remove (a part of something) by rubbing something rough against it ▪ He uses a special tool to *grind away* the stone.

grind down [*phrasal verb*] **1** ***grind down (something) or grind (something) down*** : to make (something hard) smaller and smoother by gradually rubbing off tiny bits ▪ The old dog's teeth had been *ground down* by use. **2** ***grind down (someone or something) or grind (someone or something) down*** : to weaken or destroy (someone or something) gradually ▪ Poverty *ground* her spirit *down*. ▪ These people have been *ground down* by years of oppression.

grind on [*phrasal verb*] : to continue for a long time — used to describe something unpleasant ▪ The war *ground on* for many more months.

grind out [*phrasal verb*] ***grind out (something) or grind (something) out*** : to produce (something, especially something of low quality) quickly as part of a continuous process ▪ He *grinds out* [=*churns out*] a new novel every year.

***grind to a halt** or **come to a grinding halt** of a machine* : to stop working or moving forward ▪ The machinery slowly *ground to a halt*. — often used figuratively ▪ Without more money, work on the project will soon *grind to a halt*. [=*stop*] ▪ The project *came to a grinding halt*.

²grind *noun, pl* **grinds**

1 [*singular*] : boring or difficult work ▪ I need a break from the daily *grind*. ▪ the dull *grind* of office work

2 [*count*] *US* : a person who works or studies too much ▪ In college he had a reputation as a *grind* [=(*Brit*) *swot*] who never went to parties.

3 [*count*] — used to describe the size of the pieces of something that has been ground ▪ a fine/coarse *grind* of coffee

4 [*count*] : the act of rotating the hips in a sexual way ▪ dancers doing the bump and *grind* — compare BUMP

grind·er /ˈgraɪndɚ/ *noun, pl* **-ers** [*count*]

1 : a person or thing that grinds something ▪ a coffee *grinder* — see also ORGAN-GRINDER

2 *US* : SUBMARINE SANDWICH

grinding *adj, always used before a noun* [*more* ~; *most* ~] : very harsh or difficult : continuing without getting any better ▪ *grinding* poverty

grind·stone /ˈgraɪnˌstoʊn/ *noun, pl* **-stones** [*count*] : a stone disc that can be turned like a wheel and that is used for sharpening tools, smoothing rough edges, etc.

nose to the grindstone ✧ If *your nose is to the grindstone*, you are doing hard, continuous work. ▪ You'll do well at school if you just ***keep your nose to the grindstone***.

grin·go /ˈgrɪŋˌgoʊ/ *noun, pl* **-gos** [*count*] *informal + offensive* : a foreign person in a Latin-American country; *especially* : an American person

¹grip /ˈgrɪp/ *verb* **grips; gripped; grip·ping** [+ *obj*]

1 : to grab or hold (something) tightly ▪ The little boy *gripped* his mother's hand tightly. ▪ I *gripped* the door handle and pulled as hard as I could.

2 : to get and hold the interest or attention of (someone) ▪ The story really *grips* the reader. ▪ The scandal has *gripped* the nation.

²grip *noun, pl* **grips**

1 [*count*] **a** : the act of grabbing or holding something — often + *on* ▪ She tightened her *grip on* the handlebars as she coasted down the hill. ▪ I got a good *grip on* the door handle and pulled. ▪ He loosened/relaxed/lost his *grip on* the rope. — see also DEATH GRIP **b** : a way or style of holding something ▪ a loose/tight *grip* ▪ His tennis instructor showed him the proper backhand *grip*. ▪ a golfer with an incorrect *grip*

2 [*singular*] **a** : power or control ▪ He has the country in his *grip*. [=he controls the country] ▪ He has been doing all he can to maintain/tighten his *grip* on the company's finances. ✧ To be ***in the grip of*** something unpleasant is to be unable to stop or escape its effect or influence. ▪ The country is *in the grip of* a recession. ▪ We're still *in the grip of* winter. **b** : an understanding of something — often + *on* ▪ She has a good *grip on* local politics. [=she understands local politics well] ▪ He can't seem to ***get a grip on*** [=gain a good understanding of] calculus.

3 [*count*] : a part for holding something ▪ a knife with a wooden *grip* [=*handle*] ▪ I need new *grips* for my golf clubs.

come to grips with** or Brit **get to grips with : to begin to understand or deal with (something, such as a problem) in a direct or effective way ▪ The government needs to *come to grips with* the unemployment problem.

***get a grip on yourself** or **get a grip** informal* : to get control of your thoughts and emotions and stop behaving in a foolish or uncontrolled way ▪ *Get a grip on yourself!* This is no time to be hysterical!

lose your grip** informal* : to lose control of your thoughts and emotions : to lose your ability to think or behave in a normal way ▪ I've never seen him so confused and indecisive—he really seems to be *losing his grip*. ▪ The patient seems to be ***losing his grip on reality. [=confusing what is real and what is not real]

gripe /ˈgraɪp/ *verb* **gripes; griped; grip·ing** *informal* : to complain about something [*no obj*] All of the workers were *griping* about the new regulations. [+ *obj*] The students *griped* that they had too much homework.

– gripe *noun, pl* **gripes** [*count*] ▪ I'm sick of listening to their *gripes*. [=*complaints*]

gripping *adj, always used before a noun* [*more* ~; *most* ~] : very interesting and exciting ▪ a *gripping* story about a slave's escape to freedom

– grip·ping·ly /ˈgrɪpɪŋli/ *adv* ▪ a *grippingly* exciting story

gris·ly /ˈgrɪzli/ *adj* **gris·li·er; -est** [*also more* ~; *most* ~] : causing horror or fear : very shocking ▪ a *grisly* [=*gruesome*] murder ▪ The jurors saw *grisly* photos of the crime scene.

grist /ˈgrɪst/ *noun*

grist for your/the mill** (US) or Brit **grist to your/the mill : something that can be used for a particular purpose ▪ Now that he's a writer, he regards his difficult childhood experiences as *grist for the mill*. [=he regards them as material that he can use as a writer]

gris·tle /ˈgrɪsəl/ *noun* [*noncount*] : tough matter in meat that is difficult to eat ▪ a cheap piece of meat, full of *gristle* and fat

– gris·tly /ˈgrɪsəli/ *adj* **gris·tli·er; -est** [*also more* ~; *most* ~] ▪ *gristly* meat

¹grit /ˈgrɪt/ *noun* [*noncount*]

1 : very small pieces of sand or stone ▪ He shook out his shoes to remove the small rocks and *grit*.

2 *informal* : mental toughness and courage ▪ Through resourcefulness and *grit*, the pioneers survived the winter.

²grit *verb* **grits; grit·ted; grit·ting**

grit your teeth **1** : to press or rub your teeth together ▪ He *gritted* his teeth in anger/pain. **2** : to show courage and determination when you are dealing with problems or challenges ▪ Starting your own business can be very tough, but you just have to *grit your teeth* and keep working at it.

grits /ˈgrɪts/ *noun* [*plural*] : a type of ground corn that is eaten especially in the southern U.S. ▪ We had sausage and *grits* for breakfast.

grit·ty /ˈgrɪti/ *adj* **grit·ti·er; -est** [*also more* ~; *most* ~]

1 : containing very small pieces of sand or stone : containing grit ▪ *gritty* vegetables

2 *informal* : having or showing a lot of courage and determination ▪ the story's *gritty* heroine ▪ I admire her *gritty* determination to succeed.

3 : harsh and unpleasant ▪ The book describes the *gritty* realities of life on the streets. ▪ He gave us all of the *gritty* details of his divorce.

— see also NITTY-GRITTY

griz·zle /ˈgrɪzəl/ *verb* **griz·zles; griz·zled; griz·zling** *Brit, informal*

1 [*no obj*] : to make a continuous, quiet, crying sound : WHIMPER ▪ a *grizzling* baby

2 : to complain in a weak or annoying way [*no obj*] He is always *grizzling* about the weather. [+ *obj*] He always *grizzles* that the weather is bad.

grizzled *adj* : having gray hair ▪ He had thinning hair and a *grizzled* beard. ▪ a *grizzled* war veteran

griz·zly /ˈgrɪzli/ *noun, pl* **-zlies** [*count*] : GRIZZLY BEAR

grizzly bear *noun, pl* ~ **bears** [*count*] : a very large and powerful bear of western North America — see picture at BEAR

groan /ˈgroʊn/ *verb* **groans; groaned; groan·ing**

1 a [*no obj*] : to make a deep sound because of pain or some strong emotion (such as grief or disappointment) ▪ The wounded man *groaned* in/with pain. ▪ She *groaned* when she saw the bill. • She *groaned* silently/inwardly when she saw the bill. [=she was upset when she saw the bill but she did not actually groan] **b** [+ *obj*] **:** to say (something that expresses annoyance or unhappiness) • "Oh, no," she *groaned*, "I'm going to have to start all over." • She *groaned* that she would have to start all over.

2 [*no obj*] **:** to complain about something • Merchants are *groaning* over slow holiday sales. • He's always *moaning and groaning* about his salary.

3 [*no obj*] **:** to make a deep sound caused especially by weight or pressure • The chair *groaned* under his weight. • *groaning* bookshelves = bookshelves *groaning* with (the weight of their) books [=bookshelves filled with books]

– groan *noun, pl* **groans** [*count*] • She let out a *groan* when she saw the bill. • We could hear the *groans* of the wounded man. • a *groan* of despair

gro·cer /ˈgrousɚ/ *noun, pl* **-cers** [*count*] **:** a person who sells food and other supplies for people's houses • Ask your local *grocer* if he sells organic fruits and vegetables. • I bought the fruit and vegetables at the *grocer's*. [=grocery store]

gro·cery /ˈgrousri/ *noun, pl* **-cer·ies**

1 [*count*] *chiefly US* **:** GROCERY STORE

2 *groceries* [*plural*] **:** food sold by a grocer **:** food bought at a store • She stopped to pick up some *groceries* for supper.

– grocery *adj, always used before a noun* • *grocery* bags/shopping • a *grocery* cart/clerk

grocery store *noun, pl* **~ stores** [*count*] *chiefly US* **:** a store that sells food and household supplies **:** SUPERMARKET — called also *grocery*

grog /ˈgrɑːg/ *noun* [*noncount*]

1 : an alcoholic drink containing liquor (such as rum) mixed with water

2 *chiefly Australia and New Zealand, informal* **:** any alcoholic drink (such as beer)

grog·gy /ˈgrɑːgi/ *adj* **grog·gi·er; -est** [*also more ~; most ~*] **:** not able to think or move normally because of being tired, sick, etc. • I'm still a little *groggy* from my nap. • The medicine sometimes makes patients *groggy*.

– grog·gi·ly /ˈgrɑːgəli/ *adv* • He got out of bed and staggered *groggily* to the bathroom. **– grog·gi·ness** /ˈgrɑːginəs/ *noun* [*noncount*] • Patients may experience some *grogginess* after taking the medicine.

groin /ˈgroɪn/ *noun, pl* **groins** [*count*] **:** the area of the body where your legs come together — see picture at HUMAN

grom·met /ˈgrɑːmət/ *noun, pl* **-mets** [*count*] **:** a metal or plastic ring that is used to strengthen a small hole in a piece of cloth or leather **:** EYELET

¹groom /ˈgruːm/ *noun, pl* **grooms** [*count*]

1 : a man who has just married or is about to be married — called also *bridegroom*; compare BRIDE

2 : a person who takes care of horses

²groom *verb* **grooms; groomed; groom·ing** [+ *obj*]

1 : to clean and care for (an animal) • The horses are being *groomed* for the competition. • The cat was *grooming* itself in the corner. [=the cat was cleaning itself by licking its fur]

2 a : to make (someone) neat and attractive • She spent

G

grooming

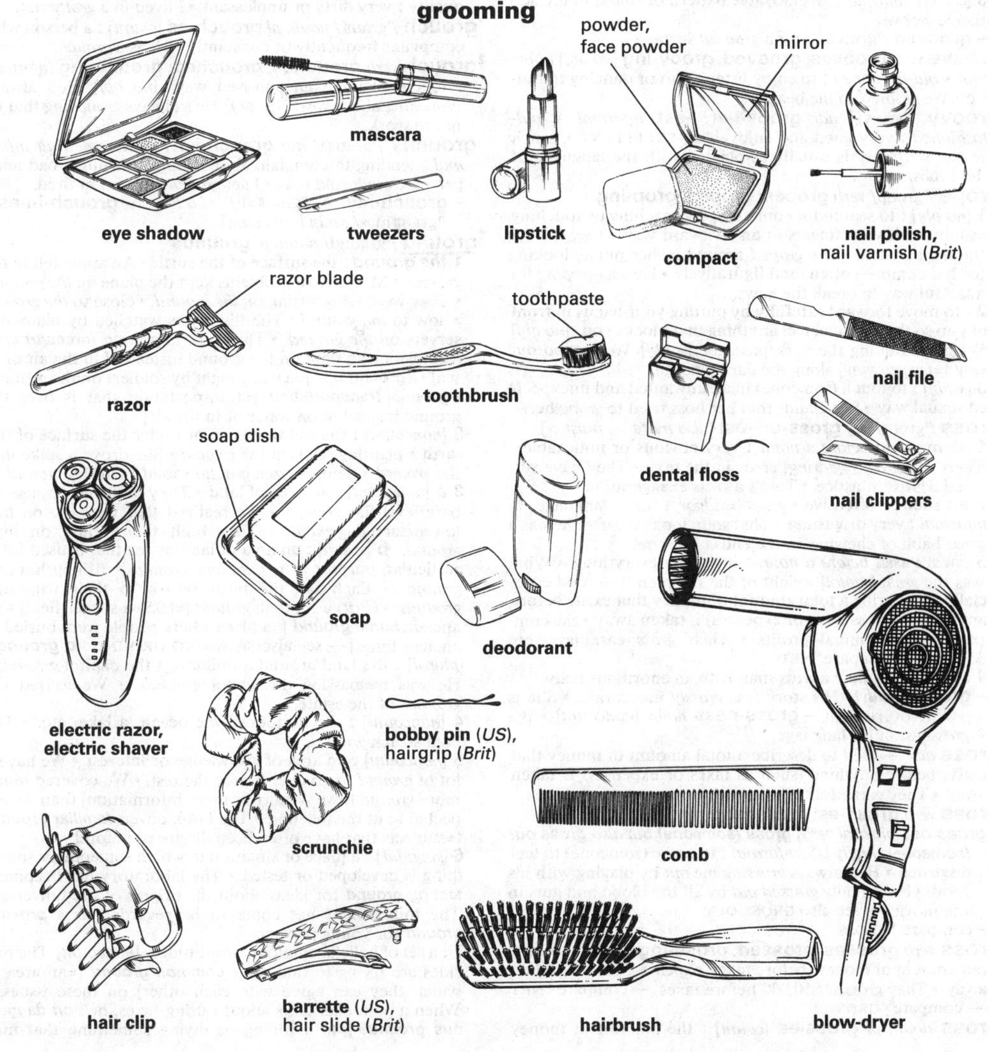

hours *grooming* herself. ▪ She always seems to be perfectly *groomed* and neatly dressed. **b :** to make (something) neat, smooth, or attractive ▪ a carefully *groomed* lawn ▪ perfectly *groomed* ski slopes — see also WELL-GROOMED
3 : to prepare (someone) for a particular job or position ▪ He is being *groomed* to take over the company.
– grooming *noun [noncount]* ▪ Horses need a lot of *grooming.* ▪ She spends an hour each morning on personal *grooming.* [=care of her hair, skin, nails, etc.] — see picture on previous page

groom·er /ˈgruːmɚ/ *noun, pl* **-ers** *[count]* **:** a person who cleans and cares for an animal ▪ a dog *groomer*

grooms·man /ˈgruːmzmən/ *noun, pl* **-men** /-mən/ *[count] chiefly US* **:** a male friend or relative who helps a groom at his wedding ▪ He asked his two closest college friends to be his *groomsmen.* — compare BEST MAN, BRIDESMAID, MAID OF HONOR, MATRON OF HONOR

¹groove /ˈgruːv/ *noun, pl* **grooves**
1 *[count]* **:** a long, narrow cut or low area in a surface ▪ the *grooves* on a vinyl record ▪ The door slides along a *groove* in the doorframe.
2 *[singular] informal* **a** *US* **:** a state in which you are able to do something well and easily especially because you are doing it often ▪ It's not hard to do a little studying each day once you get into a/the *groove.* [=*routine*] ▪ He's a great pitcher when he's in a/the *groove.* ▪ She hasn't yet found her *groove.* **b** *chiefly Brit* **:** a dull routine that does not change **:** RUT ▪ They've gotten ***stuck in a groove*** in their jobs.
3 *[count] informal* **:** an enjoyable pattern of sound in music ▪ dance *grooves*
– grooved /ˈgruːvd/ *adj* ▪ a *grooved* surface

²groove *verb* **grooves; grooved; groov·ing** *[no obj] informal + old-fashioned* **:** to enjoy listening to or dancing to music ▪ We *grooved* to the beat.

groovy /ˈgruːvi/ *adj* **groov·i·er; -est** *informal + old-fashioned* **:** very good and enjoyable **:** EXCELLENT ▪ *groovy* music ✧ *Groovy* is usually associated with the language of the 1960s.

grope /ˈgroup/ *verb* **gropes; groped; grop·ing**
1 *[no obj]* **:** to search for something by reaching or touching usually with your fingers in an awkward way ▪ I *groped* for the light switch. ▪ She *groped* around in her purse, looking for her comb. — often used figuratively ▪ He was *groping* for a tactful way to break the news.
2 : to move forward carefully by putting your hands in front of you so that you can feel anything that blocks you *[no obj]* We *groped* along the dark passage. *[+ obj]* We ***groped our way*** [=*felt our way*] along the dark passage.
3 *[+ obj]* **:** to touch (someone) in an unwanted and unexpected sexual way ▪ She claims that her boss tried to *grope* her.

¹gross /ˈgrous/ *adj* **gross·er; -est** *[also more ~; most ~]*
1 *always used before a noun* **:** very obvious or noticeable ▪ There is a *gross* [=*glaring*] error in the text. ▪ They have suffered a *gross* injustice. ▪ That's a *gross* exaggeration.
2 a : rude or offensive ▪ *gross* [=*vulgar, coarse*] language **b** *informal* **:** very disgusting ▪ That soup looks *gross.* ▪ She has a *gross* habit of chewing on the ends of her hair.
3 *always used before a noun* **:** including everything ▪ What was the *gross* [=*total*] weight of the shipment? — used especially to describe a total amount of money that exists before anything (such as taxes or expenses) is taken away ▪ the company's *gross* annual profits ▪ Their *gross* earnings were $50,000. — compare ³NET
4 : very big or fat ▪ a *gross* man with an enormous belly
– gross·ly *adv* ▪ His story was *grossly* inaccurate. ▪ She is *grossly* overweight. **– gross·ness** *noun [noncount]* ▪ the *grossness* of his language

²gross *adv* — used to describe a total amount of money that exists before anything (such as taxes or expenses) is taken away ▪ They earned $50,000, *gross.*

³gross *verb* **gross·es; grossed; gross·ing**
gross out *[phrasal verb]* ***gross (someone) out*** *also* ***gross out (someone)*** *chiefly US, informal* **:** to cause (someone) to feel disgusted ▪ He's always *grossing* me *out* by playing with his food. ▪ I was really *grossed out* by all the blood and guts in the movie. — see also GROSS-OUT
– compare ⁴GROSS

⁴gross *verb* **grosses; grossed; gross·ing** *[+ obj]* **:** to earn (an amount of money) before taxes, expenses, etc., are taken away ▪ They *grossed* $50,000 before taxes. — compare ⁴NET — compare ³GROSS

⁵gross *noun, pl* **gross·es** *[count]* **:** the amount of money earned before taxes, expenses, etc., are taken away ▪ They give five percent of their *gross* to charity every year. — compare ⁵NET — compare ⁶GROSS

⁶gross *noun, pl* **gross** *[count]* **:** a group of 144 things **:** 12 dozen ▪ a *gross* of pencils ▪ selling pencils by the *gross* — compare ⁵GROSS

gross domestic product *noun, pl* **~ -ucts** *[count, noncount]* **:** the total value of the goods and services produced by the people of a nation during a year not including the value of income earned in foreign countries — abbr. *GDP*

gross national product *noun, pl* **~ -ucts** *[count, noncount]* **:** the total value of the goods and services produced by the people of a nation during a year — abbr. *GNP*

gross–out /ˈgrousˌaut/ *noun, pl* **-outs** *[count] chiefly US, informal* **:** something that is very disgusting **:** something that grosses you out ▪ The last scene in the movie is a real *gross-out.* ▪ *gross-out* humor

gro·tesque /grouˈtɛsk/ *adj [more ~; most ~]*
1 : very strange or ugly in a way that is not normal or natural ▪ animals with *grotesque* deformities ▪ a *grotesque* villain ▪ The actors wore dark capes and *grotesque* masks.
2 : extremely different from what is expected or usual ▪ a *grotesque* distortion of the facts
– gro·tesque·ly *adv* ▪ *grotesquely* deformed **– gro·tesque·ness** *noun [noncount]*

grot·to /ˈgrɑːtou/ *noun, pl* **-toes** *also* **-tos** *[count]* **:** a small cave

grot·ty /ˈgrɑːti/ *adj* **grot·ti·er; -est** *Brit, informal* **:** of poor quality **:** very dirty or unpleasant ▪ I lived in a *grotty* flat.

¹grouch /ˈgrautʃ/ *noun, pl* **grouch·es** *[count]* **:** a person who complains frequently or constantly ▪ He is a *grouch.*

²grouch *verb* **grouches; grouched; grouch·ing** *informal* **:** to complain in an annoyed way *[no obj]* He's always *grouching* about work. *[+ obj]* He's always *grouching* that he has to work.

grouchy /ˈgrautʃi/ *adj* **grouch·i·er; -est** *somewhat informal* **:** tending to complain about things **:** having a bad temper ▪ a *grouchy* old man ▪ I get *grouchy* when I'm tired.
– grouch·i·ly /ˈgrautʃəli/ *adv* **– grouch·i·ness** /ˈgrautʃinəs/ *noun [noncount]*

¹ground /ˈgraund/ *noun, pl* **grounds**
1 ***the ground*** **:** the surface of the earth ▪ An apple fell to *the ground.* ▪ Mechanical problems kept the plane on *the ground.* ▪ They were lying/sitting on *the ground.* ▪ close to *the ground* = low to *the ground* ▪ The flight was watched by many observers on *the ground.* ▪ They sent in ***ground forces/troops***. [=soldiers who fight on the ground instead of in the air or at sea] ▪ a ***ground war*** [=a war fought by soldiers on the ground] ▪ ***ground transportation*** [=transportation that is over the ground instead of on water or in the air]
2 *[noncount]* **:** the soil that is on or under the surface of the earth ▪ planting seeds in the *ground* ▪ She drove a spike into the *ground.* ▪ damp/frozen *ground* ▪ solid/firm/dry *ground*
3 a *[noncount]* **:** an area of land ▪ They built their house on bare/level/flat *ground.* ▪ We realized that we were on hallowed/sacred *ground.* ▪ They built their house on high *ground.* **b** *[count]* **:** an area of land or sea that is used for a particular purpose ▪ a camping *ground* ▪ fishing/hunting *grounds* ▪ Each fall the birds return to their wintering *grounds.* ▪ (*Brit*) a football *ground* [=(*US*) a soccer field] ▪ an ancient ***burial ground*** [=a place where people were buried in ancient times] — see also SPAWNING GROUND **c** ***grounds*** *[plural]* **:** the land around a building ▪ the capitol *grounds* ▪ He was trespassing on school *grounds.* ▪ We toured the *grounds* of the estate.
4 *[noncount]* **:** the bottom of the ocean, a lake, etc. ▪ The boat struck *ground.*
5 *[noncount]* **:** an area of knowledge or interest ▪ We have a lot of *ground* to go over before the test. ▪ We covered much more *ground* [=we went over more information] than we expected to at the meeting. ▪ The book covers ***familiar ground***. [=subjects that have often been discussed before]
6 *[singular]* **:** a place or situation in which someone or something is developed or tested ▪ The laboratory has become a ***testing ground*** for ideas about the origins of the universe. ▪ The tournament has come to be regarded as a ***proving ground*** for young players.
7 : a set of beliefs, opinions, or attitudes *[noncount]* The two sides are trying to find some ***common ground*** [=an area in which they can agree with each other] on these issues. ▪ When a politician talks about raising taxes, he's ***on dangerous ground***. [=he is doing or saying something that may

cause anger or criticism] [*singular*] The two sides continue to look for a ***middle ground*** [=a middle position] between two extremes. — see also HIGH GROUND
8 [*count*] : a reason for doing or thinking something — usually plural • The company has been accused of discriminating on the *grounds* of race. • We have no *grounds* for believing that the crisis will end soon. • Her husband's infidelity was *grounds* for divorce. • Many critics have objected to the proposal ***on the grounds that*** [=because] it would be too costly. • The law was rejected *on the grounds that* it was not constitutional. = The law was rejected on constitutional *grounds.*
9 ***grounds*** [*plural*] : very small pieces of crushed coffee beans • coffee *grounds*
10 [*count*] *US* : a wire or metal object that makes an electrical connection with the earth — usually singular • This metal bracket provides the *ground.* — called also (*Brit*) *earth*
11 [*count*] : the area behind or around a design • The wallpaper has red tulips on a white *ground.* [=*background*]
above ground : on top of the earth's surface • The bird's nest is located high *above ground.*
below ground : under the earth's surface • The seeds should be planted a few inches *below ground.*
break ground **1** : to dig into the ground at the start of building something • Workers *broke ground* on the new stadium last week. **2** *or* ***break new ground*** : to make new discoveries • Critics say that the study does not *break* (any) *new ground* in the search for a cure for cancer.
burn to the ground see [1]BURN
down to the ground *Brit, informal* : completely or perfectly • The job ***suits her down to the ground.*** [=suits her perfectly]
from the ground up **1** : completely or thoroughly • The car has been redesigned *from the ground up.* **2** : from a point at which nothing has been done : from the very beginning • They built the resort *from the ground up.*
gain ground *or* ***make up ground*** : to move faster so that you come closer to someone or something that is in front of you • She was trailing in the race, but she was beginning to *gain ground* (on the leaders). — often used figuratively • Alternative forms of energy are quickly *gaining ground.* [=becoming more popular or successful] • The company has been *gaining ground on* [=*catching up with*] its competitors. • The campaign is trying to *make up ground* by advertising heavily in key states.
get off the ground **1** : to begin to operate or proceed in a successful way • *The project* never really *got off the ground.* **2** ***get (something) off the ground*** : to cause (something) to begin to operate or proceed in successful way • We're still trying to *get* this project *off the ground.*
give ground : to move backward when you are being attacked : RETREAT • The troops were forced to *give ground.* — often used figuratively • The controversy has continued, and both sides are still refusing to *give ground.*
have/keep your feet on the ground see [1]FOOT
hit the ground running see [1]HIT
hold/stand your ground : to not change your position when you are being attacked : to not retreat • The troops managed to *hold their ground* despite a fierce enemy attack. — often used figuratively • The company has managed to *hold its ground* in the marketplace. • The president has continued to *stand his ground* despite criticism.
into the ground **1** : to the point of being very tired or exhausted • She's been working/running/driving herself *into the ground.* **2** : to the point of complete failure or ruin • He ran that company *into the ground.* [=he destroyed that company] • She drove that old car *into the ground.* [=she drove it until it would not run anymore]
lose ground : to move slower so that you are farther away from someone or something that is in front of you • She was beginning to *lose ground* (to the leaders) in the race.— often used figuratively • The political party *lost ground* [=became less popular or successful; did not do well] in the election. • The company is *losing ground to* [=falling behind; not doing as well as] its competitors.

[2]**ground** *verb* **grounds; ground·ed; ground·ing**
1 [+ *obj*] : to provide a basis or reason for (something) — usually used as *(be) grounded* • She discussed the principles on which her philosophy *is grounded.* [=*based, founded*] • It turned out that our fears *were* well *grounded.* [=there was a good reason for our fears]— often + *in* • These practices *are* solidly *grounded* [=*based*] *in* tradition. • a theory *grounded* [=*based*] *in* fact
2 : to cause a ship or boat to hit the ground below the water so that it cannot move [+ *obj*] They *grounded* the ship on a sandbar. • a *grounded* ship [*no obj*] The ship *grounded* on a sandbar. [=(more commonly) the ship ran aground on a sandbar]
3 [+ *obj*] : to prevent (an aircraft or a pilot) from flying • The plane was *grounded* by mechanical problems. • Bad weather *grounded* his flight. • a pilot *grounded* by health problems
4 [+ *obj*] : to stop (a child) from leaving the house to spend time with friends as a form of punishment • Her parents threatened to *ground* her for a week. [=her parents threatened to keep her from going out with her friends for a week] • Sorry, I can't go out, I'm *grounded.*
5 [+ *obj*] *US* : to connect (a wire, a device, etc.) electrically to the ground for safety • The wire was not properly *grounded.* [=(*Brit*) *earthed*]
6 [*no obj*] *baseball* : to hit a ground ball • He *grounded* to the shortstop. • He ***grounded out*** [=made an out by hitting a ground ball] to the shortstop.
7 [+ *obj*] *American football* : to throw (a football) to the ground in order to avoid being tackled • The quarterback was penalized for intentionally *grounding* the ball.
ground in [*phrasal verb*] ***ground (someone) in (something)*** : to give (someone) basic knowledge about (something) • The study helped to *ground* them *in* the methods of research. — often used as *(be) grounded in* • She *is* well/solidly *grounded in* mathematics. [=she has a good basic knowledge of mathematics]

[3]**ground** *past tense and past participle of* [1]GRIND

ground ball *noun, pl* ~ **balls** [*count*] *baseball* : a ball that is hit by the batter and that rolls or bounces along the ground • He hit a *ground ball* to the shortstop. — called also *grounder*; compare FLY BALL

ground·break·ing /ˈgraʊndˌbreɪkɪŋ/ *adj* [*more* ~; *most* ~] : introducing new ideas or methods • She was honored for her *groundbreaking* work in nuclear physics. • a *groundbreaking* new book

ground cloth *noun, pl* ~ **cloths** [*count*] *US* : a piece of waterproof material that is used under tents, sleeping bags, etc., by people who are sleeping outdoors — called also (*Brit*) *ground sheet*

ground cover *noun, pl* ~ **covers** [*count, noncount*] : a low plant or group of plants used in a garden to cover the ground • Ivy is often used as (a) *ground cover.*

ground crew *noun, pl* ~ **crews** [*count*] : a group of people at an airport who take care of and repair aircraft — called also (*Brit*) *ground staff*

ground·ed /ˈgraʊndəd/ *adj* [*more* ~; *most* ~] — used to describe a person who is sensible and has a good understanding of what is really important in life • He's trying to stay *grounded* despite all the fame and praise. • She comes from a very *grounded* family.

ground·er /ˈgraʊndɚ/ *noun, pl* **-ers** [*count*] *baseball* : GROUND BALL • He hit a *grounder* to the shortstop.

ground floor *noun, pl* ~ **floors** [*count*] : the floor of a building that is at ground level — called also (*US*) *first floor*
in on the ground floor ✧ If you ***are/get in on the ground floor*** of something (such as a new business or project), you become involved in it at the very beginning. • He was able to *get in on the ground floor* of the computer industry.

ground·hog /ˈgraʊndˌhɑːg/ *noun, pl* **-hogs** [*count*] : WOODCHUCK

Groundhog Day *noun* [*singular*] : February 2 observed in the U.S. as a day that indicates whether winter will end soon ✧ Tradition says that if a groundhog sees its shadow because the sun is shining on February 2, the winter will last six more weeks, and if it does not see its shadow because of cloudy weather, the winter will end soon.

ground·ing /ˈgraʊndɪŋ/ *noun* [*singular*] : training or instruction that gives someone basic knowledge of a particular subject • It is clear he has a solid *grounding* in the issues. [=that he knows about and understands the issues] • The job requires a thorough *grounding* in the history of the region. • classes that give students a good moral *grounding*

ground·less /ˈgraʊndləs/ *adj* [*more* ~; *most* ~] : not based on facts • The charges against him were (completely) *groundless.* • Doubts about how the new system would work proved (to be) *groundless.* • *groundless* fears
— **ground·less·ly** *adv* — **ground·less·ness** *noun* [*noncount*] • the *groundlessness* of their fears

ground–level *adj, always used before a noun* : occurring or

lying at or near the ground • *ground-level* winds/temperatures • a *ground-level* window
– **ground level** *noun [singular]* • a window located at *ground level*

ground·nut /ˈgraʊndˌnʌt/ *noun, pl* **-nuts** *[count] chiefly Brit* : PEANUT 1

ground plan *noun, pl* ~ **plans** *[count]* : FLOOR PLAN

ground rule *noun, pl* ~ **rules** *[count]*
1 : a basic rule about what should be done in a particular situation, event, etc. — usually plural • We need to lay out the *ground rules* for tonight's meeting.
2 *chiefly US, sports* : a special rule about how a game is played on a particular field, court, or course — usually plural • The coaches and umpires discussed the *ground rules*.

ground sheet *noun, pl* ~ **sheets** *[count] Brit* : GROUND CLOTH

grounds·keep·er /ˈgraʊndzˌkiːpɚ/ *noun, pl* **-ers** *[count] US* : a person who takes care of a large area of land (such as a sports field or a park) — called also *(chiefly Brit) groundsman*

grounds·man /ˈgraʊndzmən/ *noun, pl* **-men** /-mən/ *[count] chiefly Brit* : GROUNDSKEEPER

G

ground staff *noun, pl* ~ **staffs** *[count] Brit*
1 : the people who take care of a large area of land (such as a sports field) — usually singular
2 : GROUND CREW

ground stroke *noun, pl* ~ **strokes** *[count] tennis* : a stroke made by hitting a ball that has bounced off the ground — compare VOLLEY

ground·swell /ˈgraʊndˌswel/ *noun, pl* **-swells** *[count]* : a fast increase in the amount of public support for something (such as a political cause or candidate) — usually + *of* • They hope to create a *groundswell of* support for her candidacy. • a *groundswell of* enthusiasm

ground·wa·ter /ˈgraʊndˌwɑːtɚ/ *noun [noncount]* : water that is underground • There were concerns about contaminated *groundwater*.

ground·work /ˈgraʊndˌwɚk/ *noun [noncount]* : something that is done at an early stage and that makes later work or progress possible — often used with *lay* or *do* • His discoveries *laid* the *groundwork* [=*foundation*] for further research. • He *did* the *groundwork* for further research.

ground zero *noun [noncount]*
1 : the point on the earth's surface directly above, below, or at which an explosion (especially a nuclear explosion) occurs
2 : the central point in an area of fast change or intense activity • *ground zero* in the battle over immigration laws
3 : the beginning state or starting point • We're going to have to go right back to *ground zero* [=*square one*] and start all over again.

[1]**group** /ˈgruːp/ *noun, pl* **groups** *[count]*
1 a : a number of people or things that are together or in the same place • It'll be easier if we go there as a *group*. • She presented the idea to the *group*. • We like to let these students work ***in groups*** whenever possible. — often + *of* • A large *group of* people were waiting for him at the airport. • a *group of* tourists • a small *group of* islands ◊ In British English *group* is used with both singular and plural verbs. • A large *group* was/were waiting for him. **b** : a number of people who are connected by some shared activity, interest, or quality • She belongs to an environmental/youth *group*. • ethnic/religious *groups* • She joined a discussion *group*. • A select *group* of scientists has been invited to the conference. • The disease was seen in all ***age groups***. [=groups made up of people who are the same age] • a ***group discussion*** [=a discussion involving a group of people] — see also FOCUS GROUP, INTEREST GROUP, NEWSGROUP, PRESSURE GROUP, SUPPORT GROUP **c** : a number of things that are related in some way • the four food *groups* • a *group* of languages
2 : a number of musicians who play together regularly • a rock/musical *group* [=*band*]

[2]**group** *verb* **groups; grouped; group·ing**
1 [+ *obj*] : to put (people or things) in a group — often + *together* • She *grouped* the toys *together* by type. — often used as *(be) grouped* • English and Dutch can *be grouped together* as Germanic languages. • The children *were grouped* by age.
2 [*no obj*] : to form a group — often + *around* or *together* • The students *grouped around* the table. • The children *grouped together* near their teachers.

grou·per /ˈgruːpɚ/ *noun, pl* **grou·pers** *also* **grouper** *[count]* : a large fish that lives at the bottom of warm seas

group home *noun, pl* ~ **homes** *[count] US* : a place where people who need special care or attention live together in a group • a *group home* for young adults with disabilities

group·ie /ˈgruːpi/ *noun, pl* **-ies** *[count] informal*
1 a : a fan of a music group who follows the group on concert tours **b** : a fan of an athlete or celebrity who tries to see the athlete or celebrity as often as possible
2 : an enthusiastic supporter or follower of something • a science-fiction *groupie* • a political *groupie*

group·ing /ˈgruːpɪŋ/ *noun, pl* **-ings**
1 *[count]* : a set of people or things combined in a group • They arranged the furniture in a *grouping* around the fireplace. — often + *of* • The garden has several large *groupings of* carefully selected plants. • a *grouping of* stars/islands
2 *[noncount]* : the act or process of combining people or things into groups • the *grouping* of English with other Germanic languages

group practice *noun, pl* ~ **-tices** *[count, noncount]* : a group of doctors, dentists, etc., who all work in the same building and share office costs • He is in (a) *group practice* with three other doctors.

group therapy *noun [noncount]* : a method for helping people with mental or emotional problems by having them discuss their problems together in a group

[1]**grouse** /ˈgraʊs/ *noun, pl* **grouse** *[count]* : a small bird that is often hunted

[2]**grouse** *verb* **grous·es; groused; grous·ing** *informal* : to complain about something *[no obj]* She's been *grousing* to her boss about the working conditions. [+ *obj*] Fans have *groused* that the higher prices are unfair.
– **grous·er** *noun, pl* **-ers** *[count]*

[1]**grout** /ˈgraʊt/ *noun [noncount] technical* : material used for filling spaces or cracks between tiles

[2]**grout** *verb* **grouts; grout·ed; grout·ing** [+ *obj*] *technical* : to fill the cracks in (something) with grout • I need to *grout* the bathroom tiles.

grove /ˈgroʊv/ *noun, pl* **groves** *[count]* : a small group of trees • a *grove* of oaks; *especially* : a group of trees that produce fruit or nuts • an orange *grove* • a pecan *grove* — sometimes used in street names • Evans *Grove* • Oak *Grove*

grov·el /ˈgrɑːvəl, ˈgrʌvəl/ *verb* **grov·els**; *US* **grov·eled** *or Brit* **grov·elled**; *US* **grov·el·ing** *or Brit* **grov·el·ling** *[no obj]*
1 : to kneel, lie, or crawl on the ground • The peasants *groveled* before the king.
2 : to treat someone with too much respect or fear in a way that shows weakness in order to be forgiven or to gain approval or favor • He had to *grovel* to get her to accept his apology. • He made a *groveling* apology to his girlfriend.
– **grov·el·er** *(US) or Brit* **grov·el·ler** *noun, pl* **-ers** *[count]*

grow /ˈgroʊ/ *verb* **grows; grew** /ˈgruː/; **grown** /ˈgroʊn/; **grow·ing**
1 *[no obj]* : to become larger : to increase in size, amount, etc. • The city is *growing* rapidly/dramatically. • The list of chores to do this weekend keeps *growing*. — often + *in* • The sport is *growing in* popularity. [=is becoming more popular] • The school has *grown* (considerably/greatly) *in* size. • His followers continue to *grow in* number. [=to become more numerous]
2 *[no obj]* : to become better or improved in some way : to become more developed, mature, etc. • She *grew* intellectually and emotionally in her first year at college. • It's wonderful to see how she has *grown* as a person since going to college.
3 *[no obj]* : to become larger and change from being a child to being an adult as time passes : to pass from childhood to adulthood • It can be hard to watch our children change as they *grow*. • He's still just a *growing* boy. • She's *grown* (by) at least an inch since the last time I saw her.
4 a *[no obj] of a plant* : to exist and develop • These trees *grow* only in the jungle. • As the tree *grew* taller, the branches began to touch the house. • This plant does well in difficult *growing* conditions. [=conditions in which it is difficult for most plants to grow] • The flowers ***grow wild*** [=grow naturally without being planted or cared for by humans] along the highway. **b** [+ *obj*] : to cause (a plant) to grow : to cultivate or raise (a plant) • She *grows* tomatoes in her garden. • The plant is *grown* for its colorful flowers.
5 *of hair, fingernails, etc.* : to become longer *[no obj]* She's letting her hair *grow* a little. • His fingernails *grow* quickly. [+ *obj*] She's *growing* her hair long. • He tried to *grow* a beard/mustache. [=to have a beard/mustache by letting the hair on his face grow] — see also GROW OUT 1 (below)

6 a *always followed by an adjective* [*linking verb*] **:** BECOME • He suddenly *grew* pale. • He had *grown* tired of hearing about their problems. • She *grew* fat due to her lack of exercise. • He's worried about *growing* old. • These diseases are *growing* more common. • We have *grown* accustomed to his angry outbursts. **b** [*no obj*] **:** to have or form an opinion, attitude, etc., after time passes — followed by *to + verb* • She's *grown to like* her new job. • I *grew to admire* her very much. • I *grew to feel* that these problems were not important. • She *grew to hate* him for his selfishness.

7 [*+ obj*] **:** to cause (something, such as a business) to develop or get bigger • These changes should allow us to *grow* the company while reducing waste. • He claims that his proposals will help *grow* the economy.

grow apart [*phrasal verb*] **:** to become less friendly or emotionally close as time passes **:** to become distant from someone • My wife and I have *grown apart* over the years.

grow from [*phrasal verb*] ***grow from (something)*** **:** to come from or originate from (something) • The company *grew from* an idea he had in college.

grow into [*phrasal verb*] ***grow into (something)*** **1 :** to become (something) as time passes • She has *grown into* an accomplished and charming young woman. • His small company has *grown into* a huge international corporation. **2 :** to become large enough for (a certain size of clothing) • Ben will *grow into* Billy's shoes in a year or two.

grow on [*phrasal verb*] ***grow on (someone)*** **:** to become more appealing to (someone) as time passes • Try the dish again—it *grows on* you. • I didn't like him at first, but he's starting to *grow on* me.

grow on trees *informal* **:** to exist in large amounts **:** to be easy to get • Good jobs don't *grow on trees.* [=good jobs are hard to get] • He acts as if money *grows on trees.*

grow out [*phrasal verb*] **1** ***grow (something) out*** *or* ***grow out (something)*** **:** to allow (something) to get longer • She's *growing out* her hair.— see also GROW 5 (above) **2** ***grow out of (something)*** **a :** to develop or come from (a source) • The project *grew out of* a simple suggestion. • This new theory *grew out of* their earlier research. **b :** to become too large for (a certain size of clothing) • He quickly *grew out of* his clothes.— see also OUTGROW **c :** to stop doing or having (something) because you are older and more mature • She hoped to *grow out of* her bad habits. • He's wild now, but he'll *grow out* of it.

grow up [*phrasal verb*] **1 a :** to become an adult • She wants to be a firefighter when she *grows up.*— used to describe where you lived, what you did, etc., when you were a child • I *grew up* in the city. • We *grew up* poor, but we always had food on the table. • He *grew up* playing music. [=he played music when he was a child] **b :** to stop thinking and behaving in a childish way • It's time for him to *grow up* and start accepting his responsibilities. • Oh, *grow up!*— see also GROWN-UP **2 :** to begin to exist and develop as time passes • A number of villages and cities *grew up* along the river. • A rivalry *grew up* between the villages.

– grow·er /ˈgrowɚ/ *noun, pl* **-ers** [*count*] • corn/fruit *growers* • This plant is known as a fast *grower.*– **growing** *adj, always used before a noun* • There is *growing* acceptance of the new plan. • the *growing* popularity of this film • There's a *growing* sense that he may be right.

growing pains *noun* [*plural*]

1 : pains in the legs of children who are growing

2 : the problems that are experienced as something (such as a business or a project) grows larger or more successful • a young company/city dealing with *growing pains*

growing season *noun, pl* **~ -sons** [*count*] **:** the period of the year that is warm enough for plants to grow

¹growl /ˈgrawəl/ *verb* **growls; growled; growl·ing**

1 [*no obj*] **a** *of an animal* **:** to make a deep threatening sound • I could hear a dog *growling* behind me. • a *growling* dog— often + *at* • The dog *growled at* me. **b :** to make a low sound like the sound of a growling animal • My stomach's been *growling* all morning. • The engine *growled.*

2 a [*+ obj*] **:** to say (something) in an angry way • "What do you want?" he *growled.* **b** [*no obj*] **:** to complain in an angry way • He's always *growling* about the government.

²growl *noun, pl* **growls** [*count*] **:** a deep sound made by an animal • The dog gave a menacing *growl; also* **:** a similar sound • He answered my question with a *growl.* • We could hear a *growl* of thunder in the distance.

– growly /ˈgrauli/ *adj* **grow·li·er; -est** • a *growly* voice

¹grown *past participle of* GROW

²grown /ˈgroun/ *adj, always used before a noun* **:** no longer a child **:** ADULT • It's a job that requires a *grown* man. • She has two *grown* children [=two children who are now adults] from a previous marriage.— see also FULL-GROWN

¹grown–up /ˈgrounˌʌp/ *adj* [*more ~; most ~*]

1 : no longer young **:** fully grown • Their children are all *grown-up* now. [=are adults now]

2 *somewhat informal* **a :** suitable for adults • a *grown-up* movie/party • This book is a little too *grown-up* for him. • a young girl with *grown-up* tastes **b :** like an adult • How *grown-up* you look! • They're *grown-up* [=*mature*] enough to deal with the situation.

²grown–up *noun, pl* **-ups** [*count*] *somewhat informal* **:** a person who is fully grown **:** ADULT • Her books appeal to both children and *grown-ups.*

growth /ˈgrouθ/ *noun, pl* **growths**

1 [*noncount*] **:** the process of growing: such as **a :** natural increase in size • He had a *growth* spurt when he was 16 years old. • She's concerned that the medication might slow/stunt her child's *growth.*— often + *of* • the *growth of* facial hair • the *growth of* a crystal **b :** the process of forming or developing something • He discovered a substance that promotes the *growth* of new blood vessels. **c :** an increase in the number, amount, or size of something • The city has undergone explosive *growth* in recent years. • rapid *growth* • slow/steady *growth* • the *growth* of civilization • population/economic *growth* • Children's books are a ***growth area*** [=an area of business that is becoming larger and more successful] in the publishing industry. • Children's publishing is a ***growth industry***. [=a business that is becoming larger and more successful] • The company has limited ***growth potential***. [=the company is not likely to grow much larger] **d :** the development of a person's mind, emotions, etc. • He sees his college years as an opportunity for personal *growth.* • emotional/intellectual *growth*

2 : a result or product of growing [*noncount*] It's important to prune the bush every year to encourage new *growth.* • Their profits have averaged five percent *growth* in the last four years. [*singular*] The tree has an average annual *growth* of almost a foot. • a thick *growth* of underbrush

3 [*count*] *medical* **:** an abnormal mass of tissue (such as a tumor) • a cancerous *growth*

¹grub /ˈgrʌb/ *noun, pl* **grubs**

1 [*count*] **:** the young form of an insect in which it looks like a small worm

2 [*noncount*] *informal* **:** FOOD 1 • Let's go get some *grub.*

²grub *verb* **grubs; grubbed; grub·bing** [*no obj*]

1 : to dig in the ground for something that is difficult to find or remove • animals *grubbing* for roots

2 *informal* **:** to search for something **:** to try hard to get or find something • Everyone was *grubbing* for whatever food they could find. • students *grubbing* for better grades— see also MONEY-GRUBBER, MONEY-GRUBBING

grub·by /ˈgrʌbi/ *adj* **grub·bi·er; -est** *informal* **:** dirty or messy • He lives in a *grubby* little apartment. • *grubby* clothes • Keep your *grubby* hands off me! [=do not touch me]

– grub·bi·ness /ˈgrʌbinəs/ *noun* [*noncount*] • the *grubbiness* of his clothes

¹grudge /ˈgrʌʤ/ *noun, pl* **grudg·es** [*count*] **:** a strong feeling of anger toward someone that lasts for a long time • She still has/holds/bears a *grudge* against him for the way he treated her in school. • He has nursed/harbored a *grudge* against his former boss for years. • I don't bear him any *grudges.*

grudge match **:** a contest or fight between players, teams, etc., who dislike each other • The race had turned into a *grudge match* between the two teams.

²grudge *verb* **grudges; grudged; grudg·ing** [*+ obj*]

1 : to give, do, or allow (something) in a reluctant or unwilling way **:** BEGRUDGE • I don't *grudge* paying my share.

2 : to dislike or feel angry toward (someone) for something • I don't *grudge* her the opportunities she has been given.

grudg·ing /ˈgrʌʤɪŋ/ *adj* [*more ~; most ~*] **:** said, done, or given in an unwilling or doubtful way • Her theories have begun to win *grudging* acceptance in the scientific community. • He has earned the *grudging* admiration/respect of his rivals.

– grudg·ing·ly *adv* • Her theories have been *grudgingly* accepted. • They *grudgingly* gave him permission.

gru·el /ˈgruːwəl/ *noun* [*noncount*] **:** a thin food made by boiling oatmeal or some other grain in water or milk • a bowl of *gruel*

gru·el·ing (*US*) *or Brit* **gru·el·ling** /ˈgruːwəlɪŋ/ *adj* [*more*

~; *most* ~] : very difficult : requiring great effort ▪ a *grueling* race ▪ His schedule is *grueling*.

grue·some /ˈgruːsəm/ *adj* [*more* ~; *most* ~] : causing horror or disgust ▪ The police report described the scene in *gruesome* detail. ▪ a *gruesome* murder
– grue·some·ly *adv* ▪ She was *gruesomely* murdered. **– grue·some·ness** *noun* [*noncount*]

gruff /ˈgrʌf/ *adj* **gruff·er; gruff·est**
1 : rough or very serious in manner or speech ▪ Don't be fooled by his *gruff* manner—he's really very kind. ▪ his *gruff* charm ▪ a *gruff* old man
2 *of a voice* : low and rough ▪ He spoke in a *gruff* voice.
– gruff·ly *adv* ▪ He answered their questions *gruffly*. **– gruff·ness** *noun* [*noncount*] ▪ Don't be fooled by his *gruffness*—he's really very kind.

grum·ble /ˈgrʌmbəl/ *verb* **grum·bles; grum·bled; grum·bling**
1 : to complain quietly about something : to talk in an unhappy way [*no obj*] There's been a lot of *grumbling* among the employees. ▪ Some of the customers have been *grumbling* about poor service. ▪ Fans *grumbled* about the team's poor play. [+ *obj*] "When are we going to leave?" he *grumbled*.
2 [*no obj*] : to make a low, heavy sound : RUMBLE ▪ His stomach was *grumbling*. ▪ We could hear thunder *grumbling* in the distance.
– grumble *noun, pl* **grumbles** [*count*] ▪ We could hear the *grumble* of thunder in the distance. **– grum·bler** /ˈgrʌmbələ/ *noun, pl* **-blers** [*count*] ▪ He tries to ignore the *grumblers* and just do his job. **– grum·bling** *noun, pl* **-blings** [*count, noncount*] ▪ Your *grumbling* needs to stop.

grump /ˈgrʌmp/ *noun, pl* **grumps** [*count*] *informal* : a person who is often angry or who often complains ▪ Our neighbor is an old *grump*.

grumpy /ˈgrʌmpi/ *adj* **grump·i·er; -est** *informal* : easily annoyed or angered : having a bad temper or complaining often ▪ Our neighbor is a *grumpy* old man. ▪ I was feeling *grumpy* after my long flight.
– grump·i·ly /ˈgrʌmpəli/ *adv* ▪ "Leave me alone," he said *grumpily*. **– grump·i·ness** /ˈgrʌmpinəs/ *noun* [*noncount*]

grunge /ˈgrʌnʤ/ *noun* [*noncount*]
1 : a type of loud rock music that was popular especially in the early 1990s ▪ I'm a fan of *grunge*. ▪ a *grunge* band; *also* : the fashions associated with this type of music ▪ the *grunge* look
2 *US, informal* : heavy dirt ▪ I cleared the *grunge* out of the drains.

grun·gy /ˈgrʌnʤi/ *adj* **grun·gi·er; -est** *chiefly US, informal* : [1]DIRTY ▪ After working in the garden all day, I felt sweaty and *grungy*. ▪ a *grungy* pair of jeans ▪ a *grungy* movie theater

[1]**grunt** /ˈgrʌnt/ *noun, pl* **grunts** [*count*]
1 : a short, low sound from the throat ▪ the *grunt* of a pig ▪ I could hear the *grunts* of the movers as they lifted the heavy furniture. ▪ He answered her with a *grunt*.
2 *informal* : a U.S. soldier especially in the Vietnam War ▪ He was a *grunt* who worked his way up to become an officer.
3 *US, informal* : a person who does ordinary and boring work ▪ He's just a *grunt* in the attorney's office. — often used in the phrase ***grunt work*** ▪ She resents having to do all the *grunt work* for her boss.

[2]**grunt** *verb* **grunts; grunt·ed; grunt·ing**
1 [*no obj*] : to make a short, low sound : to make a grunt ▪ The workers were *grunting* with effort as they lifted the heavy furniture. ▪ The pigs *grunted*. ▪ He *grunted* in agreement.
2 [+ *obj*] : to say (something) with a grunt ▪ She *grunted* a few words in reply, then turned and walked away.

Gru·yère /gruˈjeə/ *noun* [*noncount*] : a type of hard cheese from Switzerland with a nutty flavor

gryphon *variant spelling of* GRIFFIN

G–string /ˈʤiːˌstrɪŋ/ *noun, pl* **G–strings** [*count*] : a narrow strip of cloth that passes between the legs and is held up by a string around the waist

Gt. *or* **Gt** *abbr, chiefly Brit* great — used in place-names ▪ *Gt.* Britain

gua·ca·mo·le /ˌgwɑːkəˈmoʊli/ *noun* [*noncount*] : a Mexican food made of mashed avocado usually mixed with chopped tomatoes and onion

gua·no /ˈgwɑːnoʊ/ *noun* [*noncount*] : waste material from birds and bats that is used to help plants grow

[1]**guar·an·tee** /ˌgerənˈtiː/ *noun, pl* **-tees** [*count*]
1 : a usually written promise: such as **a** : a promise that the quality of something (such as a product that is being sold) will be as good as expected ▪ The washer comes with a *guarantee* against major defects. ▪ The software comes with a ***money-back guarantee***. [=a promise that the money you spend on a product will be returned if the product is not good enough] **b** : a promise that something is true or real ▪ They wanted a *guarantee* that the document was authentic.
2 : a promise that something will happen or be done ▪ They want the new contract to include a *guarantee* of job security. ▪ The U.S. Constitution includes *guarantees* against unreasonable searches. ▪ He cited the First Amendment *guarantee* of free speech.
3 : a thing that makes something sure to happen or exist — often used in negative constructions ▪ There is no *guarantee* that they will approve the contract. [=there is no way to be sure that they will approve it] ▪ There's no *guarantee* they'll get here on time. ▪ She took the job even though there was no *guarantee* of permanent employment.
4 : something valuable that the owner will allow to be taken if a promise is not kept or a loan is not paid back ▪ We used our house as a *guarantee* for the loan. [=we said that the bank could take our house if we did not pay back the loan]

[2]**guarantee** *verb* **-tees; -teed; -tee·ing** [+ *obj*]
1 a : to make a usually written promise that whatever you are selling, doing, etc., is what you say it is ▪ The washer is *guaranteed* against defects for one year. ▪ They *guarantee* that the diamonds they sell are top quality. **b** : to promise to pay for (something) if another person fails to pay for it ▪ He offered to personally *guarantee* the loan. ▪ The investment was *guaranteed* by the bank.
2 a : to say (something) with great confidence ▪ I *guarantee* that you'll be satisfied. ▪ He *guaranteed* us that everything would go according to plan. **b** : to make (something) certain ▪ We can't *guarantee* your safety. = We can't *guarantee* (you) that you'll be safe. ▪ Money doesn't *guarantee* a happy life. **c** : to say that (something) will certainly happen ▪ He *guaranteed* a victory in the championship game.

guar·an·teed *adj*
1 : protected or promised by a guarantee ▪ a *guaranteed* annual wage ▪ a *guaranteed* annuity
2 : certain to happen or to do something — followed by *to + verb* ▪ If we don't take an umbrella, it's *guaranteed to rain*. [=it will certainly rain] ▪ He's *guaranteed to reject* my ideas.

guar·an·tor /ˌgerənˈtoə/ *noun, pl* **-tors** [*count*] *finance* : a person who promises to pay back a loan if the original borrower does not pay it back

guar·an·ty /ˈgerənti/ *noun, pl* **-ties** [*count*]
1 *law* : a formal promise to pay a debt ▪ a loan *guaranty* [=*guarantee*] — often used in the names of financial companies ▪ He worked for the Morgan *Guaranty* Trust Company.
2 : something that protects or maintains the existence of something else ▪ the *guaranty* [=*guarantee*] of free speech

[1]**guard** /ˈgɑəd/ *noun, pl* **guards**
1 [*noncount*] : a state in which someone is carefully looking for possible danger, threats, problems, etc. ▪ There were dozens of police officers ***standing/keeping guard*** along the parade route. ▪ Several soldiers were ***on guard*** [=watching and ready to respond if needed] at the gate. ▪ The soldiers were ***on their guard***. [=they were watching and ready to respond] ▪ We need to be ***on guard against*** attack. [=we need to be alert so we are not attacked; we should be prepared to be attacked] ▪ He always ***has/keeps his guard up*** [=is careful and alert] during negotiations. ▪ She never ***lets down her guard***. = She never ***lets her guard down***. [=she never relaxes and stops being careful and alert]
2 a [*count*] : a person whose job or duty is to watch and protect someone or something ▪ There were several (armed) *guards* stationed at the gate. ▪ (*US*) a prison *guard* [=someone who watches prisoners to prevent their escape] — see also SECURITY GUARD **b** [*count*] : a group of people (such as soldiers) who protect a person or place ▪ the palace *guard* ▪ Tourists gather every day to watch the changing of the *guard* at Buckingham Palace. **c** ***the Guards*** : soldiers who protect a king or queen ▪ *the* Royal Horse *Guards* — see also COLOR GUARD, HONOR GUARD, OLD GUARD, REARGUARD
3 [*count*] **a** : something that keeps an unwanted result or effect from happening — often + *against* ▪ The wound should be thoroughly cleaned as a *guard against* infection. — see also SAFEGUARD **b** : a special part or device that protects someone or something from injury or damage ▪ The *guard* must be in place before operating the meat slicer. ▪ a mouth/shin *guard*
4 [*count*] **a** *American football* : either one of two players

who play in positions on either side of the center **b** *basketball* **:** either one of two players who usually play away from the basket and control their team's play when they are trying to score points — see also POINT GUARD
5 [*count*] *Brit* **:** CONDUCTOR 2
off guard **:** in an unprepared state **:** not ready • They've been bluffing, trying to keep him *off guard*. • Her angry response ***caught me off guard***. [=surprised me] • We were ***thrown off guard*** [=surprised] by their early arrival.
under guard **:** in the position of someone (such as a prisoner) who is being watched by a guard • He was arrested and placed *under guard*. [=he was arrested and watched carefully so he would not escape]

²guard *verb* **guards; guard·ed; guard·ing** [+ *obj*]
1 : to watch (someone) in order to prevent escape • Two policemen were assigned to *guard* the prisoner.
2 : to protect (someone or something) from danger or attack • soldiers *guarding* the president • A tank *guarded* the bridge from/against enemy attack. • A police officer was stationed outside to *guard* the door/entrance.
3 : to be careful about not telling or talking about (something, such as a secret) • They jealously *guard* their secrets. • He *guards* his privacy. • Her whereabouts are a tightly/closely *guarded* secret.
4 *sports* **:** to try to keep (an opponent) from scoring (especially in basketball) • He was assigned to *guard* their best player.
guard against [*phrasal verb*] ***guard against (something)*** **:** to try to keep (something) from happening • Clean the wound to *guard against* infection. • That's the sort of thinking we have to *guard against*. • We need to *guard against* waste.

guard dog *noun, pl* ~ **dogs** [*count*] **:** a dog that is trained to protect a place **:** WATCHDOG

guarded /ˈgɑɚdəd/ *adj* [*more* ~; *most* ~] **:** very careful about giving information, showing feelings, etc. • They're being very *guarded* about their plans. [=they are not saying much about their plans] • a *guarded* answer • *guarded* [=*cautious*] optimism
– guard·ed·ly *adv* • *guardedly* optimistic

guard·house /ˈgɑɚdˌhaʊs/ *noun, pl* **-hous·es** [*count*] **:** a building for soldiers who are watching something (such as an entrance)

guard·i·an /ˈgɑɚdijən/ *noun, pl* **-ans** [*count*]
1 : someone or something that watches or protects something — often + *of* • The historical society sees itself as the *guardian of* the town's traditions. • a usage criticized by people who consider themselves *guardians of* proper English
2 *law* **:** someone who takes care of another person or of another person's property • After the death of her parents, her uncle was appointed as her legal *guardian*.
– guard·i·an·ship /ˈgɑɚdijənˌʃɪp/ *noun* [*noncount*] • their *guardianship* of the town's traditions • The court granted *guardianship* to her uncle.

guardian angel *noun, pl* ~ **-gels** [*count*]
1 : an angel believed to watch and protect someone
2 : a helpful or protective person • He has become a *guardian angel* for struggling young artists.

guard·rail /ˈgɑɚdˌreɪl/ *noun, pl* **-rails** [*count*]
1 *US* **:** a strong metal bar along the side of a road that prevents vehicles from driving off the road — called also (*Brit*) *crash barrier*
2 : a strong bar or fence that prevents people from falling off a deck, bridge, etc.

guards·man /ˈgɑɚdzmən/ *noun, pl* **-men** /-mən/ [*count*]
1 : a U.S. soldier in the National Guard or the Coast Guard • *Guardsmen* were deployed to the region.
2 : a British soldier in the Guards

guard's van *noun, pl* ~ **vans** [*count*] *Brit* **:** CABOOSE

gua·va /ˈgwɑːvə/ *noun, pl* **-vas**
1 [*count, noncount*] **:** the sweet yellow fruit of a tropical American tree
2 [*count*] **:** a tree that produces guavas

gu·ber·na·to·ri·al /ˌguːbɚnəˈtorijəl/ *adj* **:** of or relating to the governor of a U.S. state or to the position of governor • a *gubernatorial* candidate • the *gubernatorial* campaign/election

guer·ril·la *also* **gue·ril·la** /gəˈrɪlə/ *noun, pl* **-las** [*count*] **:** a member of a usually small group of soldiers who do not belong to a regular army and who fight in a war as an independent unit • The *guerrillas* controlled half the country. — often used before another noun • *guerrilla* warfare/raids/attacks

¹guess /ˈgɛs/ *verb* **guess·es; guessed; guess·ing**
1 a : to form an opinion or give an answer about something when you do not know much or anything about it [+ *obj*] Can you *guess* how many people were there? • He *guessed* that it would rain today. • It was colder and windier than I had *guessed* it would be. • She can only *guess* what he meant. • I'm *guessing* that she won't come. [=I don't think she'll come] • I never would have *guessed* [=I am very surprised] that you could be so selfish. [*no obj*] I had to choose one, and I *guessed* right/wrong. • If you can't think of an answer, *guess*. • "I just heard why he left her." "Let me *guess*—another woman." • As you might have *guessed*, her parents are not happy about her decision. • We can only *guess* at what really happened. ✧ *Guess* is used in phrases like ***guess what*** or ***guess who*** as an informal way of indicating that you have surprising news. • "*Guess what*!" "What?" "I bought a new car." • "*Guess who* I saw yesterday!" "Who?" "My old boyfriend from high school." • *Guess where* I'm going on my vacation! • You'll never *guess what* happened to me today. [=you will be surprised by what happened to me today] **b** [+ *obj*] **:** to guess (something) correctly **:** to make a correct conclusion about (someone or something) by chance • She *guessed* my age on her first try. • It took us a while to *guess* the answer to the riddle. ✧ The phrase ***you guessed it*** is used as an informal way of saying that what follows is just what you would expect. • We had lunch at Smith's Café, which is owned by, *you guessed it*, John Smith.
2 [+ *obj*] *chiefly US, informal* **:** to suppose or think (something) — usually used following the pronoun *I* • *I guess* you're right. • *I guess* this means that we can't go. • What saved her, *I guess* [=I imagine], was her quick wit. • *I guess* you could say that it was all his fault. ✧ In responding to a question, the phrase ***I guess (so)*** is used as an informal way of agreeing or saying "yes" when you are not certain or not very excited or interested. • "Are you hungry?" "*I guess*." • "This one looks better, doesn't it?" "*I guess so*." ✧ The phrase ***I guess not*** is used as an informal way of agreeing with a negative statement or of saying "no." • "That wasn't a very smart thing to do, was it?" "*I guess not*." — see also SECOND-GUESS
keep (someone) guessing *or chiefly US* ***leave (someone) guessing*** **:** to make it impossible for someone to know what will happen next • The many twists and turns in the plot will *keep readers guessing* until the last page. • He likes to *leave us guessing* about his plans.
– guess·er *noun, pl* **-ers** [*count*] • a lucky *guesser*

²guess *noun, pl* **guesses** [*count*] **:** an attempt to give an opinion or answer about something when you do not know much about it or are not sure about it • I'm not sure how old he is, but I'm willing to hazard/venture a *guess*. • My *guess* is that he'll change his story when he realizes how much trouble he's in. • There might be about 20 people there, but that's just a (rough) *guess*. • If you don't know the answer, ***make a guess***. = (*US*) If you don't know the answer, ***take a guess***. = (*chiefly Brit*) If you don't know the answer, ***have a guess***. • "How many people will be there?" "I don't know. ***Your guess is as good as mine***." [=I don't know any more than you do] • "I have no idea how many peanuts are in the jar." "Take a ***wild guess***." [=a guess based on no knowledge or information] ✧ An ***educated/informed guess*** is a guess that is probably close to being correct because it is based on some amount of knowledge. • Forecasters will be making an *educated guess* about the demand for electricity this summer.
anybody's/anyone's guess ✧ Something that is *anybody's/anyone's guess* is something that is very uncertain or that no one knows. • What causes these changes is *anybody's guess*. [=no one knows what causes these changes] • It's *anyone's guess* what his next book will be about.

guessing game *noun, pl* ~ **games** [*count*] **:** a game in which the player has to correctly guess the answer — often used figuratively • Making a diagnosis in such cases can be a real *guessing game*. • Reporters continue to play a *guessing game* as they wait to hear her final decision. [=they continue to guess about what her final decision will be]

guess·ti·mate /ˈgɛstəˌmeɪt/ *verb* **-mates; -mat·ed; -mat·ing** [+ *obj*] *informal* **:** to make a quick estimate of (something) • He used a simple formula to *guesstimate* the amount of material he would need for the job.
– guess·ti·mate /ˈgɛstəmət/ *noun, pl* **-mates** [*count*] • He made a *guesstimate* of how much material he needed.

guess·work /ˈgɛsˌwɚk/ *noun* [*noncount*] **:** the act or process of finding an answer by guessing • This book takes the *guesswork* out of buying a home. [=it gives you the informa-

G

tion you need so that you can be sure about what to do] • Calculating the drug's long-term effects is pure *guesswork.*

guest /ˈgɛst/ *noun, pl* **guests** [*count*]
1 : a person who is invited to visit or stay in someone's home • Our *guests* should be arriving soon. • a dinner/party *guest* • an overnight *guest*
2 : a person who is invited to a place or an event as a special honor • Only invited *guests* are allowed inside the banquet hall. • He played at the country club as a *guest* of one of the members. • She will be the ***guest of honor*** [=the person who is being specially honored] at the annual banquet. • He was the ***guest speaker*** [=a person invited to a gathering to give a speech] at the awards ceremony. • The ***guest list*** [=the list of people who are being invited] for the party is getting long.
3 : a customer at a hotel, restaurant, etc. • Our *guests* receive the finest quality service. • Frequent *guests* receive a discount. • ***Paying guests*** [=guests who have paid to stay in or use something] may use the fitness room.
4 : a usually well-known person who is invited to appear or perform on a program, at an event, etc. • They frequently appeared as *guests* on TV talk shows. • a celebrity *guest* — often used before another noun • a *guest* star • He made several *guest* appearances/shots on the series.
be my guest — used in speech to say that someone is welcome to do or take something • "Could I borrow your pen?" "Sure, *be my guest.*"

guest book *noun, pl* ~ **books** [*count*] **:** a book of blank pages in which guests at an event (such as a wedding or funeral) or a place (such as an art gallery) sign their names

guest·house /ˈgɛst,haʊs/ *noun, pl* **-hous·es** [*count*]
1 *chiefly US* **:** a building that is separate from the main house of a property and that is used for guests • The estate includes a small *guesthouse.*
2 *chiefly Brit* **:** a small hotel; *also* **:** a private house that accepts paying guests

guest room *noun, pl* ~ **rooms** [*count*] **:** a bedroom for guests — called also *guest bedroom*

guest worker *noun, pl* ~ **-kers** [*count*] **:** a person from one country who lives and works for a time in another country

guff /ˈgʌf/ *noun* [*noncount*] *informal*
1 : foolish nonsense • His latest book has a lot of *guff* about conspiracies of one kind or another.
2 *chiefly US* **:** annoying or playful criticism • His friends have given him a lot of *guff* about his hair. • She doesn't take *guff* from anybody.

guf·faw /gəˈfɑː/ *verb* **-faws; -fawed; -faw·ing** [*no obj*] **:** to laugh loudly • The reporters were *guffawing* at all his jokes.
– guffaw *noun, pl* **-faws** [*count*] • Her remark sparked *guffaws* around the room. • He let out a loud *guffaw.*

GUI *abbr* graphical user interface

guid·ance /ˈgaɪdn̩s/ *noun* [*noncount*]
1 : help or advice that tells you what to do **:** the act or process of guiding someone or something • I couldn't have done it without her *guidance.* • We need more *guidance* on how to handle these unusual cases. • expert *guidance* • moral/spiritual *guidance*
2 : the process of controlling the flight of something (such as a missile) • There are problems with the missile's *guidance* (system).

guidance counselor *noun, pl* ~ **-lors** [*count*] *US* **:** a person who gives help and advice to students about educational and personal decisions

¹guide /ˈgaɪd/ *noun, pl* **guides** [*count*]
1 a : a person who leads or directs other people on a journey • We hired a *guide* for our trip to the mountains. • a river *guide* **b :** a person who shows and explains the interesting things in a place • a museum *guide* • a tour *guide*
2 : a person who helps to direct another person's behavior, life, career, etc. • He was my friend and my *guide* in the early years of my career.
3 : something that helps to direct a person's actions, thoughts, etc. • They used the stars as a *guide* to find their way back. • If past experience is any *guide*, we're in for a long and difficult project. • Let your conscience be your *guide.* [=do what your conscience says is right]
4 : a book, magazine, etc., that provides information about a particular subject • a street *guide* • The book is intended to be a *guide* for new parents. • a dining/restaurant *guide* — often + *to* • a *guide to* teenage slang • I bought him a *guide to* Poland. — see also FIELD GUIDE
5 ***Guide*** *Brit* **:** GIRL GUIDE

²guide *verb* **guides; guid·ed; guid·ing** [+ *obj*]
1 : to direct or lead (someone) • She *guided* them outside. • He *guided* us around the city. — often + *through* or *to* • Staff members are available to *guide* visitors *through* the exhibits. • We were *guided to* our seats by an usher. • You'll need an experienced lawyer to *guide* you *through* the legal system.
2 a : to direct or control the path or course of (something) • He claims that there were unknown forces *guiding* the outcome of the election. • He carefully *guided* the ship into the harbor. • She *guided* her team to victory. **b :** to direct or influence the thoughts or behavior of (someone) • Let your conscience *guide* you. • Her example helped to *guide* me toward a career in medicine. • In his work, he has always been *guided* by a desire to help other people. • programs to help *guide* teenagers away from drug use • She had a *guiding* influence on my decision. • His ***guiding principle*** when he built his house was that bigger was better.

guide·book /ˈgaɪd,bʊk/ *noun, pl* **-books** [*count*] **:** a book of information for travelers

guided *adj* **:** led by a guide • a *guided* tour of the factory

guided missile *noun, pl* ~ **-siles** [*count*] **:** a missile whose course may be changed during flight

guide dog *noun, pl* ~ **dogs** [*count*] **:** a dog that is specially trained to lead and help blind people

guide·line /ˈgaɪd,laɪn/ *noun, pl* **-lines** [*count*] **:** a rule or instruction that shows or tells how something should be done — usually plural • The government has issued new *guidelines* for following a healthy and balanced diet. • calling for stricter *guidelines* • Here are some basic *guidelines* for helping you choose a dishwasher.

guide·post /ˈgaɪd,poʊst/ *noun, pl* **-posts** [*count*] *chiefly US* **:** a post next to a trail or road that has a sign on it with directions for travelers • The *guidepost* said that the camp was to the left. — often used figuratively • There are few *guideposts* to help young parents. • *guideposts* for raising children

guide word *noun, pl* ~ **words** [*count*] **:** either one of the words that are at the top of a page in a dictionary or similar book and that show the first and last words on the page

guild /ˈgɪld/ *noun, pl* **guilds** [*count*] **:** an organized group of people who have joined together because they share the same job or interest • the local artists' *guild*; *especially* **:** an association of people who made or sold goods in the Middle Ages

guil·der /ˈgɪldɚ/ *noun, pl* **-ders** [*count*] **:** a basic unit of money that was formerly used in the Netherlands; *also* **:** a coin or bill representing one guilder — called also *gulden*

guile /ˈgajəl/ *noun* [*noncount*] **:** the use of clever and usually dishonest methods to achieve something • When they couldn't win by honest means, they resorted to *guile.* [=*duplicity*]

guile·less /ˈgajəlləs/ *adj* [*more* ~; *most* ~] **:** very innocent **:** NAIVE • a *guileless* person/smile

¹guil·lo·tine /ˈgɪlə,tiːn/ *noun, pl* **-tines** [*count*] **:** a machine with a heavy blade that was used in the past to cut off the heads of people who had been sentenced to death

²guillotine *verb* **-tines; -tined; -tin·ing** [+ *obj*] **:** to cut off the head of (someone) with a machine that drops a heavy blade on the person's neck **:** to kill (someone) with a guillotine — usually used as *(be) guillotined* • people *guillotined* during the French Revolution

guilt /ˈgɪlt/ *noun, pl* **guilts**
1 [*noncount*] **:** responsibility for a crime or for doing something bad or wrong • The jury determines the defendant's *guilt* or innocence. • an admission of *guilt* • His *guilt* in the matter was indisputable. • It was clear that the *guilt* lay with him. — opposite INNOCENCE
2 : a bad feeling caused by knowing or thinking that you have done something bad or wrong [*noncount*] I was overwhelmed by feelings of *guilt.* [=*shame*] • a strong sense of *guilt* • She feels *guilt* over something that happened before she was born! • *guilt*-ridden people [=people who feel a lot of guilt] [*count*] our secret *guilts* and insecurities
– guilt·less /ˈgɪltləs/ *adj* [*more* ~; *most* ~] • He's not entirely to blame, but he's not *guiltless* [=*innocent*], either. • a *guiltless* pleasure [=a pleasure that does not make you feel guilty]

guilt trip *noun, pl* ~ **trips** [*count*] *informal* **:** a feeling of guilt that you get when someone suggests that you have done something wrong or that you are not doing something that you should • "I guess you're just too busy to call." "I don't need the *guilt trip*, Mom. If you want me to call more often, just say so." ▪ The speaker ***laid/put a (big) guilt trip on*** us [=tried to make us feel bad or sorry] by describing in detail how much waste the average American generates.

guilty /ˈgɪlti/ *adj* **guilt·i·er; -est** [*also more* ~; *most* ~]
1 : responsible for committing a crime or doing something bad or wrong ▪ Do you think he's innocent or *guilty*? ▪ Will the defendant plead *guilty* or not *guilty*? ▪ Police have not been able to identify the ***guilty party.*** [=the person who committed the crime] ▪ The state will prove that the defendants are ***guilty as charged.*** [=that they committed the crime they are accused of committing] ▪ (*informal*) They're ***(as) guilty as sin.*** [=completely/very guilty] — often + *of* ▪ The jury found her *guilty of* manslaughter. ▪ The only thing I'm *guilty of* is bad taste. — sometimes used informally in a joking way ▪ "Did you plan this party?" "*Guilty as charged.*" [=yes, I did] — opposite INNOCENT
2 a : showing that you know you have done something bad or wrong ▪ The children exchanged *guilty* looks. ▪ He was acting like someone with a *guilty* conscience. **b :** feeling bad because you have done something bad or wrong or because you believe you have done something bad or wrong ▪ There's no need to feel *guilty* about it. ▪ Chocolate is one of my ***guilty pleasures.*** [=something that I enjoy even though eating it causes feelings of guilt]
– guilt·i·ly /ˈgɪltəli/ *adv* ▪ She hung her head *guiltily*.

guin·ea /ˈgɪni/ *noun, pl* **-eas** [*count*] **:** an old British coin worth 21 shillings

guinea fowl *noun, pl* ~ **fowl** *or* ~ **fowls** [*count*] **:** a gray-and-white spotted bird that is commonly raised for food

guinea hen *noun, pl* ~ **hens** [*count*] **:** a female guinea fowl

guinea pig *noun, pl* ~ **pigs** [*count*]
1 : a small animal that is often kept as a pet — see picture at RODENT
2 : a person or thing used for testing something ▪ He volunteered to act as a *guinea pig* in the experiment.

guise /ˈgaɪz/ *noun, pl* **guis·es**
1 [*count*] **:** one of several or many different ways in which something is seen, experienced, or produced ▪ They serve the same basic dish in various *guises*. [=*forms*]
2 [*singular*] **:** a way of seeming or looking that is not true or real ▪ She swindles people ***under the guise of*** friendship. [=by pretending to be their friend] ▪ a story about a demon ***in the guise of*** an angel [=a demon disguised as an angel; a demon made to look like an angel]

gui·tar /gɪˈtɑɚ/ *noun, pl* **-tars** [*count*] **:** a musical instrument that is held against the front of your body and that has usually six strings which are played with your fingers or with a pick ▪ an acoustic/electric *guitar* ▪ I'm learning to play the *guitar*. = (*US*) I'm learning to play *guitar*. ▪ a *guitar* player — see picture at STRINGED INSTRUMENT
– gui·tar·ist /gɪˈtɑrɪst/ *noun, pl* **-ists** [*count*] ▪ She's a very talented *guitarist*.

gulch /ˈgʌlʧ/ *noun, pl* **gulch·es** [*count*] *chiefly US* **:** a small, narrow valley with steep sides **:** RAVINE

gul·den /ˈguːldən/ *noun, pl* **gul·dens** *or* **gulden** [*count*] **:** GUILDER

gulf /ˈgʌlf/ *noun, pl* **gulfs** [*count*]
1 : a large area of ocean that is partly surrounded by land — often used in proper names ▪ the *Gulf* of Mexico ▪ the Persian *Gulf* — often used before another noun ▪ They have a home on the *Gulf* Coast. [=the coast of the Gulf of Mexico] ▪ the (Persian) *Gulf* region ▪ the *Gulf* states [=the U.S. states next to the Gulf of Mexico or the countries next to the Persian Gulf]
2 : a difference between two people, groups, or things — often + *between* ▪ The report examines the (widening) *gulf* [=*gap, divide*] *between* the state's rich and poor schools. ▪ The program is intended to help ***bridge the gulf*** *between* younger and older generations.

Gulf War syndrome *noun* [*noncount*] **:** a group of medical problems experienced by people who fought in the war in the Persian Gulf in 1991

[1]gull /ˈgʌl/ *noun, pl* **gulls** [*count*] **:** a large, common, usually gray and white bird that lives near the ocean **:** SEAGULL

[2]gull *verb* **gulls; gulled; gull·ing** [+ *obj*] *old-fashioned* **:** to fool or trick (someone) ▪ I was *gulled* [=*deceived*] by their false promises of easy money.

gul·let /ˈgʌlət/ *noun, pl* **-lets** [*count*] **:** the tube that leads from the mouth through the throat to the stomach **:** ESOPHAGUS ▪ the fish's *gullet*

gull·ible /ˈgʌləbəl/ *adj* [*more* ~; *most* ~] **:** easily fooled or cheated; *especially* **:** quick to believe something that is not true ▪ I'm not *gullible* enough to believe something that outrageous. ▪ They sell overpriced souvenirs to *gullible* tourists.
– gull·ibil·i·ty /ˌgʌləˈbɪləti/ *noun* [*noncount*] **– gull·ibly** /ˈgʌləbli/ *adv*

gul·ly *also* **gul·ley** /ˈgʌli/ *noun, pl* **-lies** *also* **-leys** [*count*] **:** a long, narrow cut or low area in the ground that water moves through when it rains

gulp /ˈgʌlp/ *verb* **gulps; gulped; gulp·ing**
1 [+ *obj*] **:** to eat or swallow (something) quickly or in large amounts ▪ She told him not to *gulp* his food. — often + *down* ▪ Don't *gulp down* your dinner like that. ▪ They *gulped down* a couple of beers and left.
2 : to take (air) into your lungs quickly [+ *obj*] The exhausted racers lay on the ground, *gulping* air. [*no obj*] The exhausted racers were *gulping* for air.
3 : to swallow because of strong emotion (such as fear or shock) [*no obj*] I *gulped* nervously before beginning my speech. [+ *obj*] "That's a lot of money," she *gulped*. ▪ He ***gulped back*** tears as he thanked the rescuers.
– gulp *noun, pl* **gulps** [*count*] ▪ He ate it in one *gulp*. ▪ We gobbled up the cookies between *gulps* of coffee. ▪ She took several *gulps* of air. **– gulp·er** *noun, pl* **-ers** [*count*] ▪ coffee *gulpers*

[1]gum /ˈgʌm/ *noun, pl* **gums** [*count*] **:** the flesh that surrounds the roots of your teeth — usually plural ▪ The dentist said my *gums* are swollen/inflamed. — see picture at MOUTH — compare [3]GUM

[2]gum *verb* **gums; gummed; gum·ming** [+ *obj*] *US* **:** to chew (something) with the gums because you do not have teeth ▪ The baby *gummed* her food. — compare [4]GUM

[3]gum *noun, pl* **gums**
1 a [*noncount*] **:** CHEWING GUM ▪ a stick/piece of *gum* ▪ a pack of *gum* — see also BUBBLE GUM **b** [*count*] *Brit* **:** GUMDROP ▪ fruit *gums*
2 [*count, noncount*] **:** a sticky substance in some kinds of plants that is hard when it dries
by gum *informal* + *old-fashioned* — used to show that you are surprised or determined ▪ I looked it up, and *by gum*, she was right! ▪ *By gum*, I really mean it this time!
– compare [1]GUM

[4]gum *verb* **gums; gummed; gumming**
gum up [*phrasal verb*] ***gum (something) up*** *or* ***gum up (something)*** *informal* **:** to prevent (something) from working or flowing properly ▪ Don't use that paper with the copier; you'll *gum* it *up*. ▪ The highway construction has really *gummed up* traffic. ▪ The bearings are all *gummed up* [=*clogged up*] with mud. — often used in phrase ***gum up the works*** ▪ Some dirt got inside the gears and *gummed up the works*. ▪ The new regulations have really *gummed up the works* in the office.
– compare [2]GUM

gum·bo /ˈgʌmboʊ/ *noun, pl* **-bos** [*count, noncount*] **:** a thick soup made in the southern U.S. with meat or seafood and usually okra ▪ a bowl of real Cajun *gumbo* — sometimes used figuratively ▪ a cultural *gumbo* [=a mixture of cultures]

gum·drop /ˈgʌmˌdrɑːp/ *noun, pl* **-drops** [*count*] *US* **:** a sweet, chewy candy — called also (*Brit*) *gum*

gum·my /ˈgʌmi/ *adj* **gum·mi·er; -est** [*also more* ~; *most* ~] **:** made of, containing, or covered with gum or a sticky or chewy substance ▪ *gummy* candy ▪ How did you get your hands so *gummy*? ▪ a *gummy* [=*sticky*] substance
– gum·mi·ness *noun* [*noncount*]

gump·tion /ˈgʌmpʃən/ *noun* [*noncount*] *informal* **:** courage and confidence ▪ It took a lot of *gumption* to speak up for yourself like that.

gum·shoe /ˈgʌmˌʃuː/ *noun, pl* **-shoes** [*count*] *US, informal* + *old-fashioned* **:** a person whose job is to find information about someone or something **:** a private detective — used especially to imitate the language of old detective novels ▪ The movie's main character is a hard-boiled *gumshoe*.

gum tree *noun*
up a gum tree *Brit, informal* **:** in a very difficult situation that you cannot get out of ▪ If they don't deliver the parts we need, we'll really be *up a gum tree*! [=*up the creek*]

[1]gun /ˈgʌn/ *noun, pl* **guns** [*count*]
1 : a weapon that shoots bullets or shells ▪ big/heavy *guns* ▪ He pulled/drew a *gun* on us. [=he took out a gun and pointed it at us] ▪ a loaded *gun* [=a gun that has bullets in it] ▪ fire/shoot a *gun* ▪ carry a *gun* ▪ a *gun* battle between gang members and the police ▪ She claimed that the *gun* went off acci-

dentally. ▪ a toy *gun* — see also AIR GUN, BB GUN, HANDGUN, MACHINE GUN, SHOTGUN, STUN GUN, SUBMACHINE GUN
2 : STARTING GUN
3 : a tool or device that looks like a gun ▪ a grease/spray/radar *gun*
— see also BIG GUN, HIRED GUN, SMOKING GUN, TOP GUN, WATER GUN, YOUNG GUN
***go great guns** informal* : to do something or proceed in a very quick, effective, and successful way ▪ The new program has been *going great guns* since it began last spring.
hold/put a gun to someone's head : to force someone to do something by using threats ▪ You don't have to go if you don't want to. No one's *holding a gun to your head*.
***jump the gun** informal* : to start or do something too soon ▪ Several racers *jumped the gun*. [=started to race before the starting gun was fired] ▪ The newspaper *jumped the gun* [=acted too soon] and announced the wrong candidate as winner of the election.
stick to your guns : to continue to have a particular opinion, plan, etc., when other people criticize you and say that you are wrong ▪ Despite criticism from the press, the governor is *sticking to her guns* on this issue.
***under the gun** chiefly US* : in a situation in which you are getting a lot of criticism or pressure or in which you have only a short amount of time to do something ▪ We were *under the gun* to finish the project on time. ▪ Those responsible for the error suddenly found themselves *under the gun*.
with (all/both) guns blazing : while firing guns ▪ They stepped out from behind the building *with guns blazing*. — often used figuratively ▪ The team came out *with all guns blazing* in the second half. [=the team was playing very forcefully and well]

[2]**gun** *verb* **guns; gunned; gun·ning** [+ *obj*] *informal*
1 *US* : to cause (a car or a car's engine) to go very fast by pressing the accelerator ▪ She let the car coast down the hill, then *gunned* it. ▪ He *gunned* the engine.
2 *US* : to throw (something) very hard ▪ The shortstop *gunned* the ball to first base.
gun down [*phrasal verb*] ***gun down (someone) or gun (someone) down*** : to shoot (someone) with a gun ▪ He was *gunned down* in the street.
gun for [*phrasal verb*] **1** ***gun for (something)*** : to try to get or achieve (something) in a very determined way ▪ The team is *gunning for* its third straight championship this year. ▪ That guy is *gunning for* my job. **2** ***gun for (someone)*** : to try to hurt or defeat (someone) ▪ Her political enemies will be *gunning for* her if she runs for reelection.

gun·boat /ˈgʌnˌboʊt/ *noun, pl* **-boats** [*count*] : a small ship with guns
gunboat diplomacy : the threat to use military force against a country as a way of forcing the country to do something

gun control *noun* [*noncount*] : laws that control how guns are sold and used and who can own them

gun dog *noun, pl* **~ dogs** [*count*] *Brit* : BIRD DOG

gun·fight /ˈgʌnˌfaɪt/ *noun, pl* **-fights** [*count*] : a fight in which people shoot guns at each other ▪ There was a *gunfight* between the rival gangs.
— **gun·fight·er** /ˈgʌnˌfaɪtɚ/ *noun, pl* **-ers** [*count*]

gun·fire /ˈgʌnˌfajɚ/ *noun* [*noncount*] : the firing of guns ▪ We heard *gunfire* in the distance. ▪ There was (an exchange of) *gunfire* between the gangs. [=they shot guns at each other]

gunge /ˈgʌnʤ/ *noun* [*noncount*] *Brit, informal* : [1]GUNK ▪ The old windows were covered in *gunge*.
— **gun·gy** /ˈgʌnʤi/ *adj* **gun·gi·er; -est**

gung ho /ˈgʌŋˈhoʊ/ *adj* [*more* ~; *most* ~] *sometimes disapproving* : extremely excited and enthusiastic about doing something ▪ We were really *gung ho* about joining the team. ▪ *gung ho* recruits

[1]**gunk** /ˈgʌŋk/ *noun* [*noncount*] *chiefly US, informal* : material that is dirty, sticky, or greasy ▪ The engine was all full of *gunk*. ▪ I need to wipe this *gunk* off my hands.
— **gunky** /ˈgʌŋki/ *adj* **gunk·i·er; -est** ▪ Your hands are all *gunky*! ▪ a *gunky* residue

[2]**gunk** *verb* **gunks; gunked; gunk·ing**
gunk up [*phrasal verb*] ***gunk up (something) or gunk (something) up** US, informal* : to cause (something) to be dirty, sticky, or greasy ▪ Don't *gunk up* your hair with a lot of styling products. ▪ The mechanism gets *gunked up* if you don't clean it regularly.

gun·man /ˈgʌnmən/ *noun, pl* **-men** /-mən/ [*count*] : a person (especially a man) who uses a gun to shoot someone or to try to shoot someone ▪ They were shot by an unknown *gunman*.

gun moll *noun, pl* **~ molls** [*count*] *chiefly US, old-fashioned* : MOLL

gun·ner /ˈgʌnɚ/ *noun, pl* **-ners** [*count*]
1 : a soldier who operates a large gun
2 *Brit* : a soldier in the British artillery

gun·nery /ˈgʌnəri/ *noun* [*noncount*] : the use of large military guns or the study of how such guns can be used effectively — often used before another noun ▪ *gunnery* practice ▪ a *gunnery* range

gun·ny·sack /ˈgʌniˌsæk/ *noun, pl* **-sacks** [*count*] *US* : a large bag made of rough, heavy cloth (such as burlap)

gun·point /ˈgʌnˌpoɪnt/ *noun*
at gunpoint — used to describe a situation in which someone is being threatened by a person with a gun ▪ They forced us out of the car *at gunpoint*. ▪ They were robbed/held *at gunpoint*.

gun·pow·der /ˈgʌnˌpaʊdɚ/ *noun* [*noncount*] : a dry explosive substance that is used in guns and to break open sections of rock or earth for mining, building roads, etc.

gun·ship /ˈgʌnˌʃɪp/ *noun, pl* **-ships** [*count*] : a military aircraft with rockets and machine guns ▪ a helicopter *gunship*

gun·shot /ˈgʌnˌʃɑːt/ *noun, pl* **-shots**
1 : bullets fired from a gun [*noncount*] death/murder by *gunshot* [*count*] He was killed by a *gunshot* to the head. — often used before another noun ▪ *gunshot* wounds/victims
2 [*count*] : the firing of a gun ▪ We heard several *gunshots*.
3 [*noncount*] : the distance that a bullet fired from a gun can travel — usually used in the phrase ***within gunshot*** ▪ The target was *within gunshot* (range).

gun·sling·er /ˈgʌnˌslɪŋɚ/ *noun, pl* **-ers** [*count*] : someone (such as a character in a story, movie, or television show) who is known for being able to handle and shoot a gun extremely well ▪ a *gunslinger* in the Wild West

gun

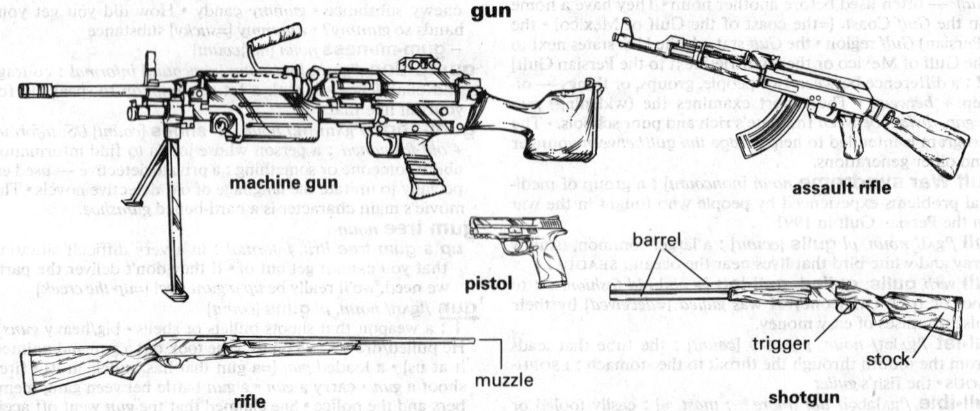

gun·smith /ˈgʌnˌsmɪθ/ *noun, pl* **-smiths** [*count*] : a person who designs, makes, or repairs guns

gun·wale /ˈgʌnl/ *noun, pl* **-wales** [*count*] : the upper edge of a ship's or boat's side — see picture at BOAT

***to the gunwales** informal + old-fashioned* : as full as possible • The car was loaded *to the gunwales* with gifts.

gup·py /ˈgʌpi/ *noun, pl* **-pies** [*count*] : a small tropical fish

gur·gle /ˈgəgəl/ *verb* **gur·gles; gur·gled; gur·gling** [*no obj*]

1 : to make the quiet sound of water moving over rocks, through a pipe, etc. • Nearby a stream was *gurgling.* [=*bubbling, bubbling*] • The water *gurgled* through the pipes.

2 : to make a sound like a liquid boiling or bubbling • I was so hungry that you could hear my stomach *gurgling.*

3 *of a baby* : to make happy and quiet sounds • The baby *gurgled* contentedly.

– gurgle *noun, pl* **gurgles** [*noncount*] the *gurgle* of running water [*count*] You could hear the creaks and *gurgles* of the pipes. • the *gurgles* of the baby

gur·ney /ˈgəni/ *noun, pl* **-neys** [*count*] *US* : a bed on a frame with wheels that is used for moving people who are sick or injured • a hospital *gurney*

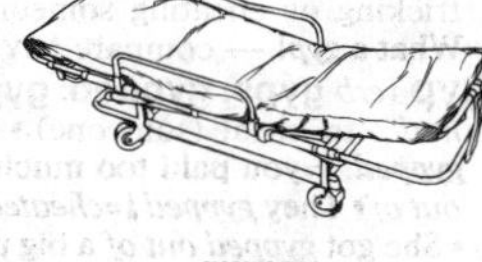
gurney

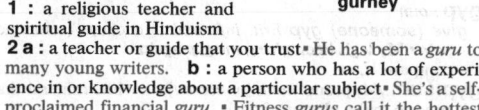

gu·ru /ˈguru/ *noun, pl* **-rus** [*count*]

1 : a religious teacher and spiritual guide in Hinduism

2 a : a teacher or guide that you trust • He has been a *guru* to many young writers. **b** : a person who has a lot of experience in or knowledge about a particular subject • She's a self-proclaimed financial *guru.* • Fitness *gurus* call it the hottest new exercise trend of the year.

¹gush /ˈgʌʃ/ *verb* **gush·es; gushed; gush·ing**

1 a [*no obj*] : to flow out very quickly and in large amounts • Oil *gushed* from the well. • Blood *gushed* from the wound. **b** [+ *obj*] : to produce a large amount of (a quickly flowing liquid) • The well *gushed* oil.

2 *often disapproving* **a** [*no obj*] : to speak in an extremely enthusiastic way • I'm tired of hearing her *gush* about her boyfriend. • Everyone has been *gushing* over/about the baby. **b** [+ *obj*] : to say (something) in an extremely enthusiastic way • "Oh, your baby is so cute!" they *gushed.*

²gush *noun, pl* **gushes** [*count*] : a sudden outward flow of a large amount of liquid • A *gush* of oil came out of the well. — sometimes used figuratively • a sudden *gush* of emotion

gush·er /ˈgʌʃɚ/ *noun, pl* **-ers** [*count*] : someone or something that gushes; *especially* : an oil well that produces a large and forceful flow of oil

gushy /ˈgʌʃi/ *adj* **gush·i·er; -est** [*also more ~; most ~*] *informal + usually disapproving* : very emotional or enthusiastic • *gushy* praise

gus·set /ˈgʌsət/ *noun, pl* **-sets** [*count*] : a piece of cloth usually in the shape of a triangle that is sewn into something (such as the underneath part of a sleeve) to make it wider or stronger

gus·sy /ˈgʌsi/ *verb* **gus·sies; gus·sied; gus·sy·ing**

***gussy up** [phrasal verb] **gussy (someone or something) up** or **gussy up (someone or something)** US, informal* **1** : to put fancy clothes, jewelry, etc., on (someone) — usually used as *(be) gussied up* • She *was* all *gussied up* [=*dressed up*] for the party. **2** : to make (something) more attractive, impressive, or fancy • The streets were *gussied up* with lights and garlands for the festival. • I made a basic tomato soup and then added fresh herbs to *gussy* it *up.*

¹gust /ˈgʌst/ *noun, pl* **gusts** [*count*] : a sudden strong wind • His hat was blown off by a sudden *gust* (of wind). • Today's weather will be windy, with *gusts* of up to 40 miles per hour. — often used figuratively • *gusts* of laughter • a *gust* of emotion

– gust·i·ness /ˈgʌstinəs/ *noun* [*noncount*] • the *gustiness* of the winds **– gusty** /ˈgʌsti/ *adj* **gust·i·er; -est** • a *gusty* day • *gusty* winds

²gust *verb* **gusts; gust·ed; gust·ing** [*no obj*] *of wind* : to blow strongly for a short time : to blow in gusts • The forecast calls for winds *gusting* up to 40 miles per hour.

gus·ta·to·ry /ˈgʌstəˌtori, *Brit* ˈgʌstətri/ *adj, formal* : relating to taste or the sense of taste • *gustatory* pleasures/delights

gus·to /ˈgʌstoʊ/ *noun* [*noncount*] : great enjoyment, energy, and enthusiasm — usually used in the phrase ***with gusto*** • She ate her dinner *with gusto.* • He played the role of the villain *with gusto.*

¹gut /ˈgʌt/ *noun, pl* **guts**

1 ***guts*** [*plural*] **a** : the internal organs of an animal • the *guts* of the fish • fish *guts* [=*entrails*] **b** *informal* : the inside parts of something • the *guts* of a machine **c** *informal* : the most important parts of something • the *guts* of a business deal

2 ***guts*** [*plural*] *informal* : COURAGE • That decision took a lot of *guts.* • I didn't have the *guts* to do it. ✧ The expression ***no guts, no glory*** is sometimes used in informal U.S. English to mean that if you do not have courage, you will never achieve success and fame.

3 [*count*] *informal* — used to talk about feelings, ideas, etc., that come from your emotions and from what seems true or right rather than from logic or reason • She knew in her *gut* that he was lying. • He knew he had to trust his *gut* [=*instincts*] and do what felt right. • What does your *gut* tell you to do?

4 [*count*] *informal* : a person's stomach or the part of the body that contains the stomach : BELLY • Her cruel remark was like a kick in the *gut.* • He has a big *gut.*

5 [*count*] : INTESTINE • a problem affecting the *gut*

6 [*noncount*] : CATGUT • a violin with *gut* strings

blood and guts : violent acts or images • a movie with lots of *blood and guts*

***bust a gut** also **bust your gut** informal* **1** : to work or try extremely hard • We're going to have to *bust a gut* to finish this project on time. **2** *US* : to laugh in an uncontrolled way • I thought I'd *bust a gut* (laughing) when you showed up in that silly outfit.

***hate someone's guts** informal* : to hate or dislike someone very much • That guy really *hates my guts.*

***spill your guts** informal* : to tell your secrets or private feelings to another person • What makes some people want to *spill their guts* on national television?

²gut *adj, always used before a noun*

1 : relating to or based on emotions : not based on logic or reason • a *gut* feeling/reaction • *gut* instinct

2 : affecting people's emotions • *gut* issues

³gut *verb* **guts; gut·ted; gut·ting** [+ *obj*]

1 : to remove the internal organs from (a fish or an animal) • The salmon is already *gutted* and filleted.

2 a : to destroy the inside of (a structure) • Fire *gutted* the building. — often used as *(be) gutted* • The building *was* completely *gutted* by fire. **b** : to destroy the power of (something) : to make (something) no longer effective • Critics claim that these reforms will *gut* the law.

gut·less /ˈgʌtləs/ *adj* [*more ~; most ~*] *informal* : lacking courage : COWARDLY • a *gutless* wimp

gutsy /ˈgʌtsi/ *adj* **guts·i·er; -est** [*also more ~; most ~*] *informal*

1 : very tough or brave • the book's *gutsy* heroine : showing courage • That was a very *gutsy* decision.

2 : having a strong and appealing flavor • *gutsy* stews • a rich *gutsy* wine

gutted *adj, Brit, informal* : very disappointed • "How did you feel when you didn't win the championship?" "I was absolutely *gutted!*"

¹gut·ter /ˈgʌtɚ/ *noun, pl* **-ters**

1 [*count*] **a** : a long, hollow device that is attached to the edges of a roof to catch rain and carry it away from a building — see picture at HOUSE **b** : a low area at the side of a road that is used to catch water and carry it away from the road

2 [*count*] : a long, narrow low section along the sides of a bowling lane

3 ***the gutter*** **a** : the lowest or poorest conditions of human life • He squandered all his money and wound up in *the gutter.* [=a state of severe poverty] **b** *US, informal* — used to refer in usually a joking way to thoughts that relate to sex • Get your mind out of *the gutter.* [=stop thinking that everything relates to sex]

²gutter *adj, always used before a noun* : of the worst kind : offensive or immoral • *gutter* language • *gutter* politics • (*Brit*) the ***gutter press*** [=newspapers that print shocking stories about the personal lives of people]

gut·tur·al /ˈgʌtərəl/ *adj* : formed or pronounced in the throat • *guttural* sounds • a *guttural* grunt

– gut·tur·al·ly *adv*

gut–wrench·ing /ˈgʌtˌrɛnʧɪŋ/ *adj* [*more ~; most ~*] *infor-*

G

mal : causing great mental or emotional pain • *gut-wrenching* decisions

guv /ˈgʌv/ *noun, Brit, informal* — used by a man to address another man (such as a customer) • "Where to, *guv*?" asked the taxi driver.

guy /ˈgaɪ/ *noun, pl* **guys** *informal*
1 [*count*] : a man • He seems like a nice *guy*. • Who's that *guy* she's with? • It's hard to tell the ***good guys*** [=the heroes] from the ***bad guys*** [=the villains] in this movie. — see also FALL GUY, LITTLE GUY, MR. NICE GUY, WISE GUY
2 ***guys*** [*plural*] *chiefly US* — used to refer to two or more people • Quiet down, *guys*—I'm trying to get some sleep here! • ***You guys*** [=you both/all] should come visit us sometime. • Would *you guys* like anything else?

guz·zle /ˈgʌzəl/ *verb* **guz·zles; guz·zled; guz·zling** /ˈgʌzlɪŋ/ *informal* : to drink (something, such as beer or liquor) quickly or in large amounts [*+ obj*] She spends her days smoking cigarettes and *guzzling* (down) coffee. [*no obj*] Sip, don't *guzzle*. — sometimes used figuratively • devices that *guzzle* electricity • cars that *guzzle* gasoline ✧ In British English, *guzzle* is used for both eating and drinking.
— **guz·zler** /ˈgʌzələ/ *noun, pl* **-zlers** [*count*] • beer *guzzlers* — see also GAS-GUZZLER

gym /ˈdʒɪm/ *noun, pl* **gyms**
1 [*count*] : GYMNASIUM, HEALTH CLUB • He works out at the *gym*. • a membership at the *gym* = a *gym* membership
2 [*noncount*] : sports and exercise taught as a subject in school : PHYSICAL EDUCATION • Students are required to take *gym*. — often used before another noun • *gym* class • *gym* shoes [=*sneakers*] — see also JUNGLE GYM

gym·na·si·um /dʒɪmˈneɪzijəm/ *noun, pl* **-ums** [*count*] : a room or building that has equipment for sports activities or exercise

gym·nast /ˈdʒɪmˌnæst/ *noun, pl* **-nasts** [*count*] : a person who performs various physical exercises on a mat or on special equipment as part of an athletic competition : a person who participates in the sport of gymnastics

gym·nas·tics /dʒɪmˈnæstɪks/ *noun*
1 [*noncount*] **a** : physical exercises for developing strength and balance • **They limbered up by practicing some *gymnastics* on the mat.** **b** : a sport in which athletes are judged on how well they perform various physical exercises on a mat or on special equipment • **She won an Olympic gold medal in *gymnastics*.** • **He teaches *gymnastics* at the local high school.**
2 [*plural*] : an activity that requires unusual ability or effort • **The singer's vocal *gymnastics* are impressive.** • **It makes sense, but only after some complicated mental *gymnastics*.**
— **gym·nas·tic** /dʒɪmˈnæstɪk/ *adj* • *gymnastic* moves • a *gymnastic* exhibition

gy·ne·col·o·gy (*US*) *or chiefly Brit* **gy·nae·col·o·gy** /ˌgaɪnəˈkɑːlədʒi/ *noun* [*noncount*] *medical* : the scientific study of the reproductive system of women and its diseases — compare OBSTETRICS
— **gy·ne·co·log·i·cal** (*US*) *or chiefly Brit* **gy·nae·co·log·i·cal** /ˌgaɪnɪkəˈlɑːdʒɪkəl/ *adj* • **a *gynecological* examination**
— **gy·ne·col·o·gist** (*US*) *or chiefly Brit* **gy·nae·col·o·gist** /ˌgaɪnəˈkɑːlədʒɪst/ *noun, pl* **-gists** [*count*]

¹gyp /ˈdʒɪp/ *noun* [*singular*] *chiefly US, informal* : an act of tricking or cheating someone • **Is that all they give you? What a *gyp*!** — compare ³GYP

²gyp *verb* **gyps; gypped; gyp·ping** [*+ obj*] *chiefly US, informal* : to cheat (someone) • **You paid $100? You got/were *gypped*. [=you paid too much; you were cheated]** — often + *out of* • **They *gypped* [=*cheated*] us *out of* hundreds of dollars.** • **She got *gypped out of* a big promotion.**

³gyp *noun*
give (someone) gyp *Brit, informal* : to cause (someone) pain • **My leg's been *giving me gyp* again.**
— compare ¹GYP

gyp·sum /ˈdʒɪpsəm/ *noun* [*noncount*] : a white mineral that is used to make plaster of paris

Gyp·sy *also* **Gip·sy** /ˈdʒɪpsi/ *noun, pl* **-sies** [*count*] : a member of a group of people who originally came from northern India and now live mostly in Asia, Europe, and North America ✧ The Gypsy people are known for moving from place to place instead of living in one place for a long time.

gypsy moth *noun, pl* **~ moths** [*count*] : a type of moth

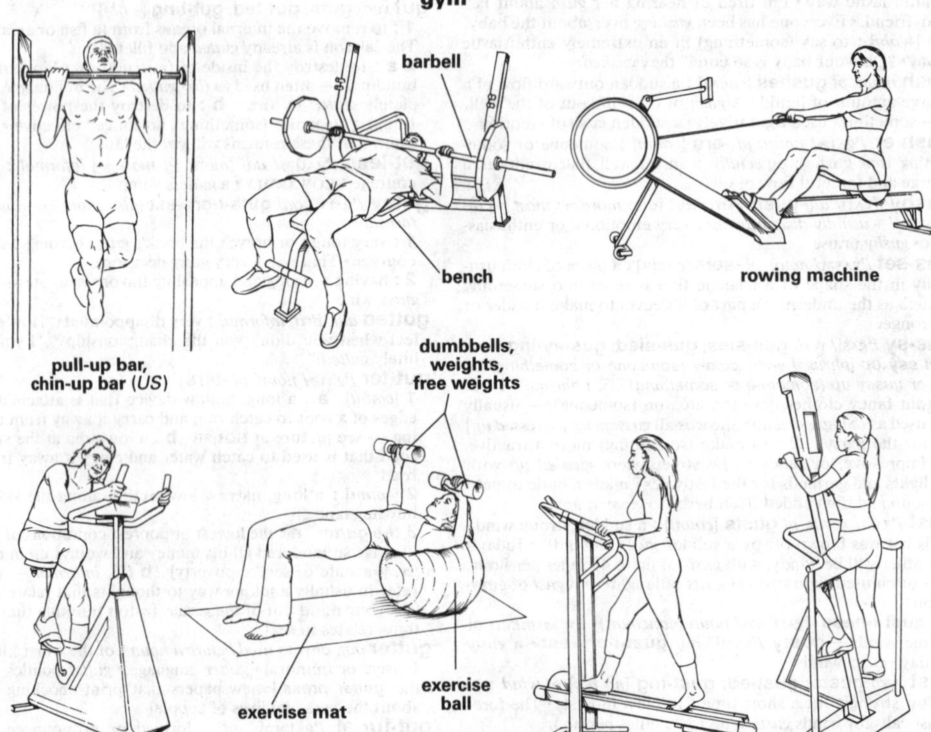

whose caterpillar does great damage to trees by eating the leaves

gy·rate /ˈʤaɪˌreɪt, *Brit* ʤaɪˈreɪt/ *verb* **-rates; -rat·ed; -rat·ing** [*no obj*] : to move back and forth with a circular motion • They *gyrated* to the music. — sometimes used figuratively • The markets have been *gyrating* [=*fluctuating*] wildly.
– **gy·ra·tion** /ʤaɪˈreɪʃən/ *noun, pl* **-tions** [*count*] their *gyrations* on the dance floor • market *gyrations* [=*fluctuations*] [*noncount*] the *gyration* of the dancers

[1]**gy·ro** /ˈʤaɪˌroʊ/ *noun, pl* **-ros** [*count*] : GYROSCOPE — compare [2]GYRO

[2]**gy·ro** /ˈjiːˌroʊ/ *noun, pl* **-ros** [*count*] : a Greek food that consists of a pita wrapped around a filling of usually lamb, onion, tomato, and a yogurt sauce — compare [1]GYRO

gyroscope

gy·ro·scope /ˈʤaɪrəˌskoʊp/ *noun, pl* **-scopes** [*count*] : a wheel that spins quickly and is held in a frame that allows it to tilt in any direction ✧ Gyroscopes are used in steering devices on ships, airplanes, etc., and in other instruments. Some gyroscopes are used as toys.
– **gy·ro·scop·ic** /ˌʤaɪrəˈskɑːpɪk/ *adj* • *gyroscopic* instruments

H

h *or* **H** /ˈeɪʧ/ *noun, pl* **h's** *or* **hs** *or* **H's** *or* **Hs** /ˈeɪʧəz/ : the eighth letter of the English alphabet [*count*] The word "hand" begins with an *h*. [*noncount*] The word "hand" begins with *h*.

ha /ˈhɑː/ *interj* — used especially to express surprise or a feeling of pleasure that you have when you do something or find out about something • *Ha*! And you thought I couldn't do it!

ha·be·as cor·pus /ˈheɪbijəsˈkoɚpəs/ *noun* [*noncount*] *law* : an order to bring a jailed person before a judge or court to find out if that person should really be in jail • apply for a writ of *habeas corpus*

hab·er·dash·er /ˈhæbɚˌdæʃɚ/ *noun, pl* **-ers** [*count*] *old-fashioned*
1 *US* : a person who owns or works in a shop that sells men's clothes
2 *Brit* : a person who owns or works in a shop that sells small items (such as needles and thread) that are used to make clothes

hab·er·dash·ery /ˈhæbɚˌdæʃəri/ *noun, pl* **-er·ies**
1 [*noncount*] : goods sold by a haberdasher
2 [*count*] : a haberdasher's shop

hab·it /ˈhæbət/ *noun, pl* **-its**
1 : a usual way of behaving : something that a person does often in a regular and repeated way [*count*] It was his *habit* to take a nap after dinner every evening. • It's important that parents teach their children good study/eating *habits*. • He fell/got into some bad *habits* after graduating from college. • It's never easy to ***break/kick a bad habit***. • ***Old habits die hard***. [=it is hard to stop doing things that you have been doing for a long time] — often followed by *of* + *-ing verb* • He had a *habit of coughing* when he was nervous. • He has an annoying/irritating *habit of cracking* his knuckles. • Things have a nasty *habit of not turning out* the way you expect them to. [=things often do not turn out the way you expect them to] [*noncount*] He still gets up early every day from *habit*. • She always closed the door softly out of *habit*. • He reached into his pocket for his keys ***by/from force of habit***. [=he did it without thinking because it is what he usually does] • I'm a ***creature of habit***. [=I always do the same things in the same way] ✧ If you are ***in the habit of*** doing something, you do it often or usually. • I'm *in the habit of* reading before I go to bed. ✧ If you say that you are ***not in the habit of*** doing something, you mean that you do not do it or that you do not usually do it. • I'm *not in the habit of* getting involved in other people's arguments. • I'm *not in the habit of* making predictions, but I don't think there's much doubt about who will win this election. ✧ To ***get in/into the habit of*** doing something means to do something in a regular or repeated way so that it becomes a habit. • I had *gotten into the habit of* reading before going to bed. • She *got in the habit of* leaving her keys on the counter so she wouldn't forget them. ✧ To ***fall/slip into the habit of*** doing something is to begin to do something in a regular way without realizing that you are doing it. • It's easy to *fall into the habit of* not eating enough for breakfast. ✧ If you ***make a habit of*** doing something or ***make it a habit to*** do something, you do it often. • They have *made a habit of* criticizing each other whenever possible. • The team has *made a habit of* winning the crucial games. • Yes, you can leave work early today, but don't *make a habit of* it.
2 [*count*] : a strong need to use a drug, to smoke cigarettes, etc. • He hasn't been able to kick his cocaine *habit*. • I used to have a three-pack-a-day cigarette *habit*. [=I used to smoke three packs of cigarettes a day]
3 [*count*] : a piece of clothing worn by members of a religious group • a monk's/nun's *habit*

hab·it·able /ˈhæbətəbəl/ *adj* : suitable or fit to live in • The house is not *habitable*.

hab·i·tat /ˈhæbəˌtæt/ *noun, pl* **-tats** [*count*] : the place or type of place where a plant or animal naturally or normally lives or grows • a creature's natural *habitat* • tropical *habitats*

hab·i·ta·tion /ˌhæbəˈteɪʃən/ *noun, pl* **-tions**
1 [*noncount*] : the act of living in a place • The house was not fit for human *habitation*.
2 [*count*] *formal* : a place where someone lives • a wilderness area with few *habitations*

hab·it–form·ing /ˈhæbətˌfoɚmɪŋ/ *adj* [*more* ~; *most* ~] : causing a strong need to regularly have something (such as a drug) or do something • Heroin is a *habit-forming* [=*addictive*] drug. • Eating chocolate can be *habit-forming*.

ha·bit·u·al /həˈbɪʧəwəl/ *adj*
1 : done regularly or repeatedly • He was fired for his *habitual* lateness. • *habitual* drug use • They went for their *habitual* evening walk.
2 *always used before a noun* : doing something regularly or repeatedly • She was a *habitual* liar. [=she always lied] • *habitual* criminals/offenders
– **ha·bit·u·al·ly** *adv* • He was *habitually* late.

ha·bit·u·ate /həˈbɪʧəˌweɪt/ *verb* **-ates; -at·ed; -at·ing** [+ *obj*] *formal* : to cause (a person or animal) to become familiar with and used to a particular place, situation, etc. — + *to* • The dog slowly became *habituated to* its new home. = The dog slowly *habituated* itself *to* its new home.
– **ha·bit·u·a·tion** /həˌbɪʧəˈweɪʃən/ *noun* [*noncount*]

ha·bi·tué /həˈbɪʧəˌweɪ/ *noun, pl* **-tu·és** [*count*] : a person who is often at a specified place • a *habitué* of bars • racetrack *habitués*

ha·ci·en·da /ˌhɑːsiˈɛndə, *Brit* ˌhæsiˈɛndə/ *noun, pl* **-das** [*count*] : a large estate in a country where people speak Spanish

[1]**hack** /ˈhæk/ *verb* **hacks; hacked; hack·ing**
1 : to cut (something or someone) many times and usually in a rough and violent way. [+ *obj*] *He hacked* [=*chopped*] the tree down with an ax. = He *hacked* down the tree with an ax. • The victim had been *hacked* to death. • The table had been *hacked* to pieces. [*no obj*] He *hacked* (away) at the tree with an ax. — see also HACK OFF (below)
2 [+ *obj*] : to make (a path) by cutting plants • They used a machete to *hack* a path through the jungle. • They ***hacked their way*** through the jungle.
3 [+ *obj*] *informal* : to manage or deal with (something) successfully — usually used in negative statements • He just *couldn't hack* the new job. — often used in the phrase ***hack it*** • After two weeks at the new job, he decided that he just *couldn't hack it*.
4 [*no obj*] : to cough loudly • I could hear him *hacking* (away) all night long. • The patient has a ***hacking cough***. [=a loud, dry cough]
5 *computers* : to secretly get access to the files on a computer or network in order to get information, cause damage,

etc. [*no obj*] — + *into* ▪ She was trying to *hack into* the network. ▪ Someone *hacked into* the company's financial records. [+ *obj*] The Web site had been *hacked*.

hack off [*phrasal verb*] **1** ***hack (something) off or hack off (something)*** : to cut (something) off in a rough and violent way ▪ She used an ax to *hack* the dead branch *off* (the tree). **2** ***hack (someone) off also hack off (someone) informal*** : to make (someone) angry and annoyed ▪ It really *hacks* me *off* to see people treated so unfairly. — see also HACKED OFF

²hack *noun, pl* **hacks** [*count*]

1 : the act of hitting something roughly with an ax, knife, etc. ▪ He took a *hack* at the branch.

2 *baseball, informal* : SWING ▪ He took a *hack* at a high fastball and popped it up.

3 : a loud, dry cough ▪ a smoker's *hack*

– compare ³HACK

³hack *noun, pl* **hacks** [*count*]

1 *disapproving* **a** : a writer who produces a large amount of work mainly to make money ▪ a *hack* writer **b** : someone who does work that is not important or original ▪ a political *hack*

2 *US, old-fashioned + informal* : TAXI; *also* : the driver of a taxi : CABDRIVER

3 a : a horse that can be hired for use **b** : an old, worn-out horse

– compare ²HACK

H

hacked off *adj* [*more ~; most ~*] *informal* : angry or irritated ▪ He was really *hacked off* when they lost the game.

hack·er /ˈhækɚ/ *noun, pl* **-ers** [*count*]

1 *computers* : a person who secretly gets access to a computer system in order to get information, cause damage, etc. : a person who hacks into a computer system

2 *US, informal* : a person who plays a sport badly ▪ My friends and I have been playing golf for years, but we're still just a bunch of *hackers*. ▪ a tennis *hacker*

hack·les /ˈhækəlz/ *noun* [*plural*] : hairs along the neck and back of an animal — often used figuratively with *raise* or *rise* to describe something that makes people angry or annoyed ▪ The court ruling is sure to ***raise some hackles*** [=sure to upset some people] ▪ Their arrogant attitude is what really ***made my hackles rise*** [=really made me angry]

hack·neyed /ˈhæknid/ *adj* [*more ~; most ~*] : not interesting, funny, etc., because of being used too often : not fresh or original ▪ *hackneyed* phrases/jokes

hack·saw /ˈhækˌsɑː/ *noun, pl* **-saws** [*count*] : a saw used for cutting metal — see picture at CARPENTRY

had *past tense and past participle of* HAVE

had·dock /ˈhædək/ *noun, pl* **haddock** [*count, noncount*] : a fish that lives in the Atlantic Ocean and that is often eaten as food — see color picture on page C8

Ha·des /ˈheɪˌdiːz/ *noun* [*noncount*]

1 : the home of the dead in Greek mythology

2 *or* ***hades informal*** — used as a more polite way of saying "hell" ▪ It's hotter than *hades* today.

hadn't /ˈhædn̩t/ — used as a contraction of *had not* ▪ They *hadn't* arrived at the party yet. ▪ *Hadn't* we better be going now?

haemoglobin, haemophilia, haemophiliac, haemorrhage, haemorrhoid *Brit spellings of* HEMOGLOBIN, HEMOPHILIA, HEMOPHILIAC, HEMORRHAGE, HEMORRHOID

hag /ˈhæg/ *noun, pl* **hags** [*count*] *offensive* : an ugly, evil, or unpleasant old woman

hag·gard /ˈhægɚd/ *adj* [*more ~; most ~*] : looking very thin and tired especially from great hunger, worry, or pain ▪ She looked tired and *haggard*. ▪ We were shocked by his *haggard* appearance.

hag·gis /ˈhægəs/ *noun, pl* **-gis·es** [*count, noncount*] : a Scottish dish made from the organs of a sheep that are chopped up, mixed with suet, onions, oatmeal, and seasonings, and boiled in the stomach of the sheep

hag·gle /ˈhægəl/ *verb* **hag·gles; hag·gled; hag·gling** [*no obj*] : to talk or argue with someone especially in order to agree on a price ▪ I dislike having to *haggle* (with a salesman) over/about the price of a new car. ▪ She is good at *haggling*.

– hag·gler /ˈhægəlɚ/ *noun, pl* **hag·glers** [*count*] ▪ a skillful *haggler*

ha·gi·og·ra·phy /ˌhægiˈɑːgrəfi/ *noun, pl* **-phies** *disapproving* : a book about someone's life that makes it seem better than it really is or was : a biography that praises someone too much [*count*] a *hagiography* about a famous politician [*noncount*] The book gives a good idea of his virtues without resorting to *hagiography*.

ha ha *or* **ha–ha** /ˈhɑːˈhɑː/ *interj* — used to represent laughter ▪ "*Ha ha*! That's a good one!" he chuckled. — often used in an ironic way ▪ Oh, *ha ha*. That's very funny. [=that's not really funny at all]

hai·ku /ˈhaɪˌku/ *noun, pl* **haiku** *also* **hai·kus** : a Japanese form of poetry or a poem written in this form [*noncount*] a master of *haiku* [*count*] He has written many beautiful *haiku*. ✧ A haiku has three lines, with the first line containing five syllables, the second line containing seven syllables, and the third line containing five syllables again.

¹hail /ˈheɪl/ *noun*

1 [*noncount*] : pieces of ice that fall from clouds like rain ▪ Many cars were damaged by *hail* during the storm.

2 [*singular*] : a large number *of* small hard objects (such as bullets or stones) flying or falling together ▪ They were gunned down in a *hail of* bullets. ▪ a *hail of* pellets — often used figuratively ▪ The court's decision was met with a *hail of* criticism. [=was strongly criticized by many people]

²hail *verb* **hails; hail·ed; hail·ing** [*no obj*] — used with *it* to say that hail is falling ▪ *It's hailing* outside. [=hail is falling from the sky] — compare ³HAIL

³hail *verb* **hails; hailed; hailing** [+ *obj*]

1 : to speak of or welcome (someone or something) with praise or enthusiasm ▪ The town *hailed* him as a hero when he returned with the championship trophy. ▪ His supporters have *hailed* [=strongly praised] his decision to run for reelection. — often used as *(be) hailed* ▪ She is *being hailed* [=*acclaimed*] for her generosity. ▪ The new drug has *been* widely *hailed* as a great breakthrough.

2 : to call out in order to stop or get the attention of (someone or something) ▪ We *hailed* the passing ship. ▪ He *hailed* a taxi for me. — see also HAILING DISTANCE

hail from [*phrasal verb*] ***hail from (a place)*** : to have been born or raised in (a place) : to come from (a place) ▪ He *hails from* a small town in western Kansas.

– compare ²HAIL

hailing distance *noun* [*noncount*] : the distance within which it is possible to hear someone who is calling out ▪ They were within *hailing distance* of each other.

Hail Mary /-ˈmeri/ *noun, pl* **~ Marys** [*count*]

1 : a Roman Catholic prayer to the Virgin Mary

2 *American football* : a long forward pass thrown into or close to the end zone as playing time runs out ▪ He threw up a *Hail Mary* at the end of the first half. ▪ a *Hail Mary* pass

hail·stone /ˈheɪlˌstoun/ *noun, pl* **-stones** [*count*] : a piece of hail

hail·storm /ˈheɪlˌstoɚm/ *noun, pl* **-storms** [*count*] : a storm that produces hail

hair /ˈheɚ/ *noun, pl* **hairs**

1 a [*count*] : a thin threadlike growth from the skin of a person or animal ▪ He plucked a *hair* from his arm. ▪ There are dog/cat *hairs* all over my coat. **b** [*noncount*] : a covering or growth of hairs ▪ The *hair* on her arms is blond. ▪ He has a lot of *hair* on his chest. ▪ facial/pubic *hair* **c** [*noncount*] : the covering of hairs on a person's head ▪ He got his *hair* cut last week. ▪ Your *hair* looks nice. ▪ She has long/black/straight *hair*. ▪ He has a thick/full head of *hair*. ▪ a balding man who is losing his *hair* ▪ a lock/strand of *hair* ▪ *hair* conditioners/curlers ▪ a *hair* dryer ▪ I'm having a ***bad hair day*** [=my hair does not look nice today]

2 [*singular*] *informal* : a very small distance or amount ▪ He won the race by a *hair*. ▪ He was a *hair* off on the count.

hair of the dog (that bit you) informal : an alcoholic drink that is taken by someone to feel better after having drunk too much at an earlier time

hide or hair, hide nor hair see ²HIDE

in your hair informal ✧ Someone who is *in your hair* is bothering or annoying you. ▪ His wife says that since he retired he's *in her hair* all day because he's at home so much.

keep your hair on Brit, informal — used to tell someone not to become too excited or upset

let your hair down informal : to relax and enjoy yourself ▪ We work hard all week, so when Friday comes we like to *let our hair down* a little and have some fun.

make your hair curl informal ✧ If something *makes your hair curl*, it frightens, shocks, or surprises you. ▪ I've heard stories about that guy that would *make your hair curl*.

make your hair stand on end informal ✧ If something *makes your hair stand on end*, it frightens you. ▪ Just hearing his voice *makes my hair stand on end*.

not have a hair out of place informal : to have a very neat appearance ▪ a politician who *never has a hair out of place*

not turn a hair informal : to remain calm even though something frightening or shocking has happened ▪ Most people would have been very nervous in that situation, but she *never turned a hair*.

out of your hair informal ✧ Someone who is *out of your hair* is no longer bothering or annoying you. ▪ Let me take the children *out of your hair* while you cook dinner.

pull your hair out or ***tear your hair out informal*** : to be very worried or upset about something ▪ We've been *tearing our hair out* trying to decide what to do.

split hairs : to argue about small details or differences that are not important ▪ His lawyers are *splitting hairs* over the wording of his contract. — see also HAIRSPLITTING

– haired /ˈheɚd/ *adj* ▪ a long-*haired* cat ▪ a dark-*haired* person **– hair·less** /ˈheɚləs/ *adj* ▪ a *hairless* breed of cat

hair·brush /ˈheɚˌbrʌʃ/ *noun, pl* **-brush·es** [*count*] : a brush for the hair — see picture at GROOMING

hair·cut /ˈheɚˌkʌt/ *noun, pl* **-cuts** [*count*] : the act or result of cutting and shaping someone's hair ▪ The girls got *haircuts* yesterday. ▪ He just had a *haircut*. ▪ Do you like my *haircut*? ▪ a short *haircut*

– hair·cut·ter /ˈheɚˌkʌtɚ/ *noun, pl* **-ers** [*count*]

hair·do /ˈheɚˌduː/ *noun, pl* **-dos** [*count*] : a way of cutting and arranging someone's hair ▪ a stylish *hairdo*

hair·dress·er /ˈheɚˌdrɛsɚ/ *noun, pl* **-ers** [*count*] : a person who cuts and shapes hair

– hair·dress·ing /ˈheɚˌdrɛsɪŋ/ *noun* [*noncount*] ▪ She is taking classes in *hairdressing*.

hair·grip /ˈheɚˌgrɪp/ *noun, pl* **-grips** [*count*] *Brit* : BOBBY PIN

hair·line /ˈheɚˌlaɪn/ *noun, pl* **-lines** [*count*]

1 : a thin line or crack ▪ The plate had a *hairline* running across it. — often used before another noun ▪ a *hairline* crack ▪ He suffered a *hairline* fracture of his shin bone.

2 : the line where your hair starts on your forehead ▪ He has a receding *hairline*.

hair·net /ˈheɚˌnɛt/ *noun, pl* **-nets** [*count*] : a net worn over someone's hair to keep it in place

hair·piece /ˈheɚˌpiːs/ *noun, pl* **-piec·es** [*count*] : a section of real or false hair that is worn to cover a bald spot on your head or to make your hair look longer, thicker, or a different color

hair·pin /ˈheɚˌpɪn/ *noun, pl* **-pins** [*count*]

1 : a pin that is worn in your hair; *especially* : a pin shaped like a U that is worn to hold your hair in place

2 : an extremely sharp turn in a road that is shaped like a U — often used before another noun ▪ a *hairpin* turn/curve

hair–rais·ing /ˈheɚˌreɪzɪŋ/ *adj* [*more* ~; *most* ~] : very frightening or exciting ▪ a *hair-raising* adventure/story

– hair–rais·ing·ly *adv*

hair's breadth or *US* **hair·breadth** /ˈheɚˌbrɛtθ/ *noun* [*singular*] : a very small distance or amount ▪ He came within a *hair's breadth* of winning the race. [=he came very close to winning the race] — often used before another noun ▪ a *hair-breadth* escape [=a very narrow escape]

hair slide *noun, pl* ~ **slides** [*count*] *Brit* : BARRETTE

hair·split·ter /ˈheɚˌsplɪtɚ/ *noun, pl* **-ters** [*count*] : a person who argues about differences that are too small to be important

hair·split·ting /ˈheɚˌsplɪtɪŋ/ *noun* [*noncount*] : the act of arguing about differences that are too small to be important ▪ The lawyers have been engaging in legalistic *hairsplitting*. — see also *split hairs* at HAIR

– hairsplitting *adj* ▪ lawyers making *hairsplitting* distinctions

hair·style /ˈheɚˌstajəl/ *noun, pl* **-styles** [*count*] : HAIRDO

hair·styl·ing /ˈheɚˌstaɪlɪŋ/ *noun* [*noncount*] : the act or job of cutting and arranging people's hair ▪ the latest trends in *hairstyling*

– hair·styl·ist /ˈheɚˌstaɪlɪst/ *noun, pl* **-ists** [*count*] ▪ a professional *hairstylist*

hair trigger *noun, pl* ~ **-gers** [*count*] : a trigger on a gun that needs very little pressure to cause the gun to shoot

hair–trig·ger /ˈheɚˌtrɪgɚ/ *adj, always used before a noun* : becoming angry very easily ▪ He has a *hair-trigger* temper.

hairy /ˈheri/ *adj* **hair·i·er; -est** [*also more* ~; *most* ~]

1 : covered with a lot of hair ▪ *hairy* arms ▪ a *hairy* chest

2 *informal* : causing fear or tension : dangerous or stressful ▪ The taxi ride got a little *hairy*. ▪ When the deadline approaches, things can get a little *hairy*.

– hair·i·ness /ˈherinəs/ *noun* [*noncount*]

hajj /ˈhæʤ/ *noun* [*singular*] : a journey to Mecca that is a religious duty for Muslims

hake /ˈheɪk/ *noun, pl* **hake** [*count, noncount*] : a large fish that lives in the Atlantic Ocean and is often eaten as food

ha·lal /həˈlɑːl/ *adj*

1 : accepted by Muslim law as fit for eating ▪ *halal* meat

2 : selling or serving halal food ▪ a *halal* butcher ▪ a *halal* restaurant

hal·cy·on /ˈhælsijən/ *adj, always used before a noun, literary* : very happy and successful — used to refer to a happy and successful time in the past that is remembered as being better than today ▪ She looks back fondly recalling the ***halcyon days/years*** of her career, when she was just out of college.

hale /ˈheɪl/ *adj* **hal·er; hal·est** [*also more* ~; *most* ~] : healthy and strong — usually used in the phrase ***hale and hearty*** ▪ His mother remains *hale and hearty* in her old age.

[1]**half** /ˈhæf, *Brit* ˈhɑːf/ *noun, pl* **halves** /ˈhævz, *Brit* ˈhɑvz/

1 : one of two equal or nearly equal parts into which something can be divided [*count*] She broke each cookie into *halves*. ▪ "Which *half* do you want?" "I'll take the smaller *half*." ▪ Two *halves* make a whole. [*noncount*] The price has been reduced ***by half***. [=by 50 percent; by an amount that is

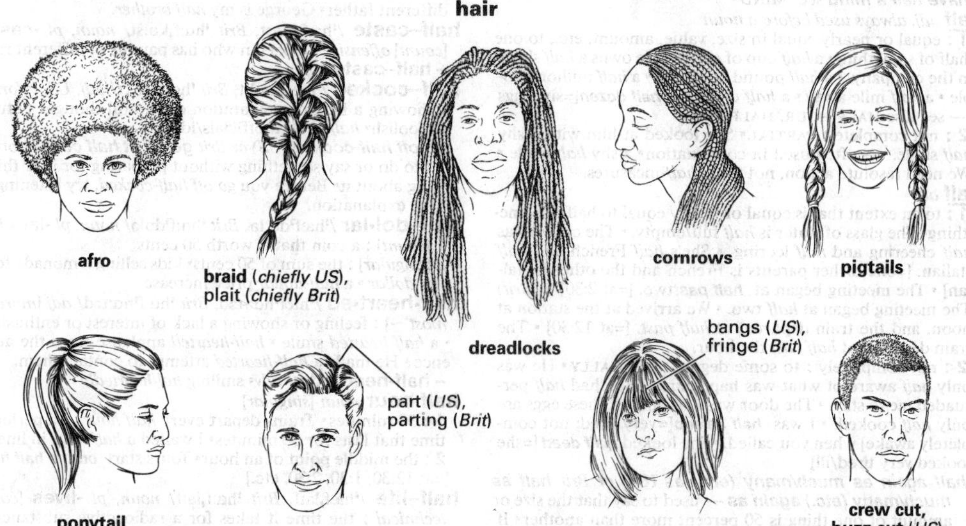

equal to one half of the original] — see also BETTER HALF, OTHER HALF

2 a [*count*] : either of the two equal periods of playing time in sports like football and basketball • The team fell behind in the first *half* but rallied in the second *half* to win the game. **b** ***the half*** : the time when the first half of a game ends • The score was tied at *the half*. [=at halftime]

3 [*count*] *Brit, informal* : half a pint of a drink (such as beer) • "What's yours?" "A *half* of lager, please."

and a half **1** — used in measurements of time, distance, weight, etc., to indicate one half of the unit of measurement • My daughter is two and a *half* (years old). [=two years and six months old] • The fish was a foot *and a half* long. [=one foot and six inches long] • ten *and a half* pounds [=ten pounds and eight ounces] **2** *informal* — used to say that something is very good, large, difficult, etc. • That was a meal *and a half*! [=that was a very big meal] • Renovating a house is a job *and a half*. [=is a very difficult job]

by halves *informal* : in an incomplete way — used in negative statements to say that someone does things with a lot of energy and effort • She never does anything *by halves*—it's all or nothing!

go halves *also* ***go half and half*** : to share the cost of something equally • We decided to *go halves* (with each other) on the expenses.

in half : into two equal parts : into two halves • She cut the apple *in half*.

the half of it *informal* — used to say that a situation is even worse than you think it is or than it seems to be • "It sounds like you've been having some problems." "You don't know *the half of it*!" • Sales are down but that's only *the half of it*—the company is closing several stores.

too . . . by half *chiefly Brit, informal* — used to say that someone or something has too much of a particular quality usually in a way that is annoying • an arrogant politician who is ***too clever by half***

²half *pronoun* : a number or amount that is equal to one half of a total • "Do you want the whole piece?" "*Half* would be enough, please." • Thirty students took the exam; *half* (that number) passed. [=15 students passed] • *Half* of 30 is/equals 15. • I seem to spend *half* (of) the day on the phone. • She gave *half* (of) her money to charity. • *Half* a million people live in this area. • Do you want *half* (of) my sandwich? • *Half* the time the kids are outside playing. [=the kids are often outside playing] • Getting to your destination is *half* the fun of a vacation. = Getting there is *half* the fun. • *Half* the problem is that we do not have enough employees to handle the increased workload. • I waited for ***half an hour*** [=30 minutes] • Please wait (for) ***half a minute/second*** [=for a moment] while I try to connect you. • ***half a dozen*** [=six] eggs • He's always chasing women ***half his age*** [=women who are much younger than he is]

half the battle see ¹BATTLE

have half a mind see ¹MIND

³half *adj, always used before a noun*

1 : equal or nearly equal in size, value, amount, etc., to one half of something • a *half* cup of coffee • He owns a *half* share in the company. • a *half* pound of cheese • a *half* million people • a *half* mile away • a *half* circle • a ***half dozen*** [=six] eggs — see also HALF HOUR, HALF PRICE

2 : not complete : PARTIAL • She looked at him with a shy *half* smile. — often used in combination • a shy *half*-smile • We need resolute action, not timid *half*-measures.

⁴half *adv*

1 : to an extent that is equal or nearly equal to half of something • The glass of water is *half* full/empty. • The crowd was *half* cheering and *half* jeering. • She's *half* French and *half* Italian. [=one of her parents is French and the other is Italian] • The meeting began at ***half past*** two. [=at 2:30] = (*Brit*) The meeting began at *half* two. • We arrived at the station at noon, and the train departed at *half past*. [=at 12:30] • The train departed at *half past* the hour.

2 : not completely : to some degree : PARTIALLY • He was only *half* aware of what was happening. • She had *half* persuaded me to stay. • The door was *half* open. • These eggs are only *half* cooked. • I was ***half asleep*** [=very tired; not completely awake] when you called. • She looked ***half dead*** [=she looked very tired/ill]

half again as much/many (etc.) as (*US*) *or Brit* ***half as much/many (etc.) again as*** — used to say that the size or amount of one thing is 50 percent more than another • If 100 people were expected and 150 came, *half again as many* people came *as* were expected. • This dress costs *half again as much as* that one.

half as big/much/good (etc.) as — used to say that the size, amount, or quality of one thing is half or nearly half that of another • The bush is *half as tall as* the tree. [=the tree is twice as tall as the bush] • This dress costs *half as much as* that one. • If 100 people were expected and 50 came, only *half as many* people came *as* were expected. • If he can play the guitar *half as well as* he can sing, he should have quite a career. [=he will have a very successful career if he can play the guitar well, even if he doesn't play as well as he sings] • The sequel isn't *half as good as* the original movie. [=the original movie was much better than the sequel]

half off — used to say that something is being sold at half the original price • Peaches are *half off* today.

not half **1** : not nearly • He's *not half* the fool you think he is. = He's *not half* so foolish as you think he is. [=he is much smarter than you think he is] • an aging baseball player who is *not half* the hitter he once was [=he is not nearly as good as a hitter as he once was] **2** *Brit, informal* — used to emphasize a statement or description • She *doesn't half* swear! [=she swears a lot] • It's *not half* cold today! [=it is very cold today] • "Is it cold out?" "*Not half*!" [=yes, it is very cold]

not half bad *informal* : surprisingly good • Her singing was *not half bad*. [=not bad at all] • The food there is *not half bad*. [=pretty good]

half–and–half /ˌhæfn̩ˈhæf, *Brit* ˌhɑːfn̩ˈhɑːf/ *noun* [*noncount*] *US* : a mixture of cream and whole milk • She usually puts *half-and-half* in her coffee.

half–assed (*US*) /ˈhæfˈæst, *Brit* ˈhɑːfˈæst/ *or Brit* **half–arsed** /ˈhæfˈɑɚst, *Brit* ˈhɑːfˈɑːst/ *adj* [*more* ~; *most* ~] *informal + impolite*

1 : poorly done or planned • He did a *half-assed* job.

2 : stupid or foolish • a *half-assed* remark

half•back /ˈhæfˌbæk, *Brit* ˈhɑːfˌbæk/ *noun, pl* **-backs** [*count*]

1 *American football* : a player on offense who lines up next to the fullback and who runs with the ball and blocks

2 : a defensive player in games like soccer and field hockey who is positioned in front of the fullback

half–baked /ˈhæfˈbeɪkt, *Brit* ˈhɑːfˈbeɪkt/ *adj* [*more* ~; *most* ~] *informal* : not well planned : foolish or stupid • a *half-baked* idea

half bath *noun, pl* ~ **baths** [*count*] *US* : a bathroom that has a sink and toilet but no bathtub or shower

half–breed /ˈhæfˌbriːd, *Brit* ˈhɑːfˌbriːd/ *noun, pl* **-breeds** [*count*] *offensive* : a person who has parents of different races; *especially* : a person who has a Native American parent and a white parent

– half–breed *adj*

half brother *noun, pl* ~ **-ers** [*count*] : a brother with the same father but a different mother or the same mother but a different father • George is my *half brother*.

half–caste /ˈhæfˌkæst, *Brit* ˈhɑːfˌkɑːst/ *noun, pl* **-castes** [*count*] *offensive* : a person who has parents of different races

– half–caste *adj*

half–cocked /ˈhæfˌkɑːkt, *Brit* ˈhɑːfˈkɒkt/ *adj, US, informal* : showing a lack of preparation or careful thought : stupid or foolish • *half-cocked* officials/ideas

go off half-cocked (*US*) *or Brit* ***go off at half cock*** *informal* : to do or say something without preparing for it or thinking about it • Before you *go off half-cocked*, try listening to the explanation.

half–dol•lar /ˈhæfˈdɑːlɚ, *Brit* ˈhɑːfˈdɒlə/ *noun, pl* **-lars** *US*

1 [*count*] : a coin that is worth 50 cents

2 [*singular*] : the sum of 50 cents • kids selling lemonade for a *half-dollar* • a *half-dollar* price increase

half•heart•ed /ˈhæfˈhɑɚtəd, *Brit* ˈhɑːfˈhɑːtəd/ *adj* [*more* ~; *most* ~] : feeling or showing a lack of interest or enthusiasm • a *half-hearted* smile • *half-hearted* applause from the audience • He made a *half-hearted* attempt to contact them.

– half•heart•ed•ly *adv* • smiling *halfheartedly*

half hour *noun* [*singular*]

1 : 30 minutes • Trains depart every *half hour*. : a period of time that lasts for 30 minutes • I waited a *half hour* in line.

2 : the middle point of an hour • Tours start ***on the half hour*** [=at 12:30, 1:30, 2:30, etc.]

half–life /ˈhæfˌlaɪf, *Brit* ˈhɑːfˌlaɪf/ *noun, pl* **-lives** [*count*] *technical* : the time it takes for a radioactive substance to lose half its radioactivity • a *half-life* of 200,000 years — often used figuratively to describe how long something remains useful or popular • Slang usually has a short *half-life*. [=slang usually is popular for only a short time]

half–light /ˈhæfˌlaɪt, *Brit* ˈhɑːfˌlaɪt/ *noun* [*noncount*] : dim grayish light • the *half-light* of early morning

half–mast /ˈhæfˈmæst, *Brit* ˈhɑːfˈmɑːst/ *noun* [*noncount*] : the position in the middle of a mast or pole ✧ A flag is flown ***at half-mast*** or lowered ***to half-mast*** to show respect for a person who has died.

half–moon /ˈhæfˌmuːn, *Brit* ˈhɑːfˌmuːn/ *noun, pl* **-moons**
1 [*singular*] : the moon when only half of it can be seen — compare FULL MOON, NEW MOON
2 [*count*] : something that is shaped like a half-moon • The pattern consists of circles and *half-moons*. • *half-moon* earrings [=earrings that are shaped like half-moons]

half note *noun, pl* ~ **notes** [*count*] *US* : a musical note equal in time to half of a whole note — called also (*Brit*) *minim*

half·pen·ny /ˈheɪpni/ *noun, pl* **-nies** /ˈheɪpniz/ [*count*] *Brit* : a former British coin worth one half of a penny

half–pipe /ˈhæfˌpaɪp, *Brit* ˈhɑːfˌpaɪp/ *noun, pl* **-pipes** [*count*] : a curved structure with high sides that is used for doing tricks on a skateboard, snowboard, etc.

half price *noun* [*noncount*] : half of the original price • I bought these shoes at *half price*. = I paid *half price* for these shoes.
– half–price *adj* • *half-price* items • All winter coats are *half-price* today. **– half–price** *adv* • Reserve now and fly *half-price*.

half shell *noun*
on the half shell : served in one of the two halves of the shell • oysters *on the half shell*

half sister *noun, pl* ~ **-ters** [*count*] : a sister with the same father but a different mother or the same mother but a different father • Emily is my *half sister*.

half–staff /ˈhæfˈstæf, *Brit* ˈhɑːfˈstɑːf/ *noun* [*noncount*] *US* : HALF-MAST

half step *noun, pl* ~ **steps** [*count*] *US, music* : SEMITONE

half·time /ˈhæfˌtaɪm, *Brit* ˈhɑːfˌtaɪm/ *noun* [*noncount*] : the period of rest between the end of the first half and the beginning of the second half in games like football and basketball • The score was tied at *halftime*. • The coaches discussed strategy during *halftime*.

half·tone /ˈhæfˌtoun, *Brit* ˈhɑːfˌtəʊn/ *noun, pl* **-tones** [*count*] *technical*
1 : a shade of gray in a photograph • using software to lighten/darken the picture's *halftones*
2 : an image printed by a method that creates many small dots

half–truth /ˈhæfˌtruːθ, *Brit* ˈhɑːfˌtruːθ/ *noun, pl* **-truths** [*count*] : a statement that is only partly true and that is intended to deceive people • I'm tired of all these *half-truths*—I want to know the real story.

half·way /ˈhæfˈweɪ, *Brit* ˈhɑːfˈweɪ/ *adj*
1 : in the middle between two points • She was leading at the *halfway* mark/point of the race. • We're *halfway* toward completing the project.
2 *always used before a noun, informal* : not total or complete : PARTIAL • They're only offering *halfway* measures, not a real solution.
meet (someone) halfway see [1]MEET
– halfway *adv* • I was *halfway* home when I realized I had forgotten my briefcase. • The project isn't done yet, but we're *halfway* there. • He stopped *halfway* up the stairs. • We left *halfway* through the speech. • (*informal*) I'm willing to eat anywhere as long as the food is ***halfway decent*** [=fairly good]

halfway house *noun, pl* ~ **houses**
1 [*count*] : a place where people who have recently left a prison, mental hospital, etc., can live until they are considered ready to live by themselves
2 [*singular*] *chiefly Brit* : something that combines the qualities or features of two different things • The car is the perfect *halfway house* between a family caravan and luxury sedan.

half–wit /ˈhæfˌwɪt, *Brit* ˈhɑːfˌwɪt/ *noun, pl* **-wits** [*count*] *informal* : a foolish or stupid person • He says the people he works with are a bunch of *half-wits*.
– half–wit·ted /ˈhæfˈwɪtəd, *Brit* ˈhɑːfˈwɪtəd/ *adj* [*more* ~; *most* ~]

hal·i·but /ˈhæləbət/ *noun, pl* **halibut** [*count, noncount*] : a large fish of the Atlantic and Pacific oceans that is often eaten as food

hal·i·to·sis /ˌhæləˈtousəs/ *noun* [*noncount*] *medical* : the condition of having breath that smells bad : bad breath

hall /ˈhɑːl/ *noun, pl* **halls** [*count*]
1 : a usually long, narrow passage inside a building with doors that lead to rooms on the sides • The bathroom is down the *hall*. • Her office is at the end of the *hall*.
2 : the area inside the entrance of a building • I'll meet you in the front *hall*. • The front door opens onto a large *hall*.
3 a : a large room or building for meetings, entertainment, etc. • We rented a *hall* for the wedding reception. • a concert/dining/dance *hall* • a ***lecture hall*** [=*auditorium*] — often used in proper names • Carnegie *Hall* • the Hampden County *Hall* of Justice — see also CITY HALL, MESS HALL, MUSIC HALL, TOWN HALL **b** : a building where students live at a college or university : DORMITORY • (*US*) a ***residence hall*** = (*Brit*) a ***hall of residence***
4 *Brit* : a large, impressive house — used in proper names • The family owned Locksley *Hall* for generations.
the halls of power see [1]POWER
– see also STUDY HALL

[1]**hal·le·lu·jah** /ˌhæləˈluːjə/ *interj* — used to express praise, joy, or thanks especially to God • *Hallelujah*! Praise the Lord! • It's the weekend! *Hallelujah*!

[2]**hallelujah** *noun, pl* **-jahs** [*count*] : a shout or song of praise or thanks to God

hall·mark /ˈhɑːlˌmaɚk/ *noun, pl* **-marks** [*count*]
1 : a quality, ability, etc., that is typical of a particular person or thing • He had all the *hallmarks* of a great baseball player. • Humor is one of the *hallmarks* of her style. • The murder bore all the *hallmarks* of a serial killer's work. — compare EARMARK
2 : an official mark that is put on gold and silver objects in Britain to indicate their purity

Hall of Fame *noun, pl* **Halls of Fame** [*count*] *chiefly US* : a place that is like a museum with exhibits honoring the famous people and events related to a particular activity (such as a sport) • We visited the Basketball *Hall of Fame*.; *also* : the group of people who are honored in such a place • He was elected as a member of the Baseball *Hall of Fame*.
– Hall of Fam·er /ˌhɑːləˈfeɪmɚ/ *noun, pl* ~ **-ers** [*count*] • *Hall of Famers* [=members of the Hall of Fame] will be at the event to sign autographs.

hal·lowed /ˈhæloud/ *adj* [*more* ~; *most* ~]
1 : holy or blessed • The church stands on *hallowed* ground.
2 : highly respected • *hallowed* customs/traditions

Hal·low·een /ˌhæləˈwiːn, ˌhɑːləˈwiːn/ *noun, pl* **-eens** [*count, noncount*] : the night of October 31 when children dress up as ghosts, witches, monsters, etc., and go to houses to ask for candy — compare TRICK OR TREAT

hal·lu·ci·nate /həˈluːsəˌneɪt/ *verb* **-nates; -nat·ed; -nat·ing** : to see or sense something or someone that is not really there : to have hallucinations [*no obj*] The patient may *hallucinate* if she has a fever. [+ *obj*] His thirst caused him to *hallucinate* (that there was) an oasis in the desert.

hal·lu·ci·na·tion /həˌluːsəˈneɪʃən/ *noun, pl* **-tions** [*count*] : something (such as an image, a sound, or a smell) that seems real but does not really exist and that is usually caused by mental illness or the effect of a drug • He could not tell if what he was seeing was real or if it was a *hallucination*. • He has been having *hallucinations* due to the medication.
– hal·lu·ci·na·to·ry /həˈluːsənəˌtori, *Brit* həˈluːsənətri/ *adj* • *hallucinatory* drugs [=drugs that cause hallucinations] • *hallucinatory* images

hal·lu·ci·no·gen /həˈluːsənəʤən/ *noun, pl* **-gens** [*count*] : a substance (such as a drug) that causes people to see or sense things that are not real : a substance that causes hallucinations
– hal·lu·ci·no·gen·ic /həˌluːsənəˈʤɛnɪk/ *adj* • *hallucinogenic* drugs

hall·way /ˈhɑːlˌweɪ/ *noun, pl* **-ways** [*count*]
1 : HALL 1 • Her office is at the end of the *hallway*.
2 : HALL 2 • I'll meet you in the front *hallway*.

ha·lo /ˈheɪlou/ *noun, pl* **-los** *or* **-loes** [*count*]
1 : a circle of light that is shown in a religious painting, drawing, etc., around the head of a holy figure (such as an angel, saint, or god) — often used figuratively • the child's *halo* of golden curls • The scandal has tarnished the candidate's *halo*. [=has damaged his reputation as a morally good person]

H

2 : a bright circle seen around the sun or the moon

[1]**halt** /ˈhɑːlt/ *verb* **halts; halt•ed; halt•ing**

1 [+ *obj*] : to stop (something or someone) from moving or continuing • The project had to be *halted* due to lack of funds. • They voted to *halt* expansion of the shopping mall. • The strike *halted* subways and buses.

2 [*no obj*] : to stop moving or happening • The troops *halted* outside the city. • The fighting *halted* briefly. • The project *halted* when funding ran out. • The guard shouted, "*Halt!* Who goes there?"

[2]**halt** *noun, pl* **halts**

1 [*singular*] : the stopping or ending of movement, progress, or action • The contract ***brought a halt to*** [=*ended*] the strike. • They ***put a halt to*** the rumors. • The chairman ***called a halt to*** [=*stopped*] the proceedings. • The car skidded/slowed ***to a halt*** • The project ***came to a (grinding) halt*** = The project ***ground to a halt*** [=the project stopped completely] • The project came to a ***screeching/crashing halt*** [=the project stopped suddenly and completely]

2 [*count*] *Brit* : a small railroad stop at which there is no station

hal•ter /ˈhɑːltɚ/ *noun, pl* **-ters** [*count*]

1 : a set of straps placed around a horse's head so that the horse can be led or tied

2 : a piece of clothing worn on a woman's upper body that is held in place by straps around the neck and back and that leaves the back, arms, and shoulders bare — called also *halter top*; see color picture on page C14

halting /ˈhɑːltɪŋ/ *adj* [*more* ~; *most* ~] : stopping often because of not being sure about what to say or do : not steady • She answered in a *halting* voice. • The baby took a few *halting* steps. • Progress in the negotiations has been *halting*.

— **halt•ing•ly** *adv*

halve /ˈhæv, *Brit* ˈhɑːv/ *verb* **halves; halved; halv•ing** [+ *obj*]

1 : to divide (something) into two equal parts : to divide (something) into halves • He *halved* the sandwich.

2 : to reduce (something) to one half of the original amount or size • The store is *halving* the price of many summer items.

halves *plural of* [1]HALF

[1]**ham** /ˈhæm/ *noun, pl* **hams**

1 : meat from the leg of a hog that is often prepared by smoking or salting [*noncount*] a piece/slice of *ham* • We're having *ham* for dinner. • a *ham* sandwich [*count*] a delicious *ham*

2 [*count*] *informal* **a** *disapproving* : a bad actor who performs in an exaggerated way • He was once a fine actor, but now he's just an old *ham*. • a *ham* actor **b** : someone who enjoys performing and who tends to behave in an exaggerated or playful way when people are watching • Cameras bring out the *ham* in her.

3 [*count*] : someone who operates an amateur radio station — often used before another noun • *ham* radio • a *ham* radio operator

[2]**ham** *verb* **hammed; ham•ming**

ham it up *informal* : to act or behave in an exaggerated or playful way • She likes to *ham it up* for the camera.

ham•burg /ˈhæmˌbɚg/ *noun, pl* **-burgs** [*count*] *US, informal* : HAMBURGER

ham•burg•er /ˈhæmˌbɚgɚ/ *noun, pl* **-ers**

1 [*count*] : a flat, usually round cake of finely chopped beef that is cooked and served usually in a roll or bun • They served hot dogs and *hamburgers* at the cookout.

2 [*noncount*] : beef that has been cut into very small pieces : ground beef • Add the cooked *hamburger* to the sauce. — called also (*Brit*) *mince*

ham–fist•ed /ˈhæmˌfɪstəd/ *adj* [*more* ~; *most* ~] : awkward or clumsy : HAM-HANDED • a *ham-fisted* performance

ham–hand•ed /ˈhæmˌhændəd/ *adj* [*more* ~; *most* ~] : awkward or clumsy • The actress gave a *ham-handed* performance. • a *ham-handed* attempt at humor • The apology was rather *ham-handed*.

ham•let /ˈhæmlət/ *noun, pl* **-lets** [*count*] : a small village

[1]**ham•mer** /ˈhæmɚ/ *noun, pl* **-mers**

1 [*count*] **a** : a tool that has a heavy metal head attached to a handle and that is used for hitting nails or breaking things apart — see picture at CARPENTRY; see also SLEDGEHAMMER **b** : a similar tool made usually of wood and used especially for hitting a surface to make a loud noise • an auctioneer's *hammer*

2 [*count*] : the part of a gun that strikes a charge causing the gun to shoot

3 [*count*] : a piece inside a piano that strikes a string to produce a sound

4 [*count*] : a stick that is shaped like a hammer and that is used to play a musical instrument

5 **a** [*count*] : a heavy metal ball with a flexible handle that people throw as a sport **b** ***the hammer*** : an event in which people compete by throwing a hammer • He won a gold medal in *the hammer*. — called also *the hammer throw*

hammer and tongs : in a very forceful and energetic way • Our neighbors were arguing again last night. They were ***going at it hammer and tongs***.

under the hammer — used to describe something that is being sold at an auction • Some valuable paintings ***went/came under the hammer*** today.

[2]**hammer** *verb* **-mers; -mered; -mer•ing**

1 **a** : to force (something) into a particular place or shape by hitting it with a hammer [+ *obj*] He *hammered* the dent out of the fender. • I *hammered* [=*drove*] the nails into the wall. • The copper was *hammered* [=*pounded*] into a flat sheet. [*no obj*] The carpenters were *hammering* all afternoon. **b** [+ *obj*] : to attach (something) with a hammer and nails • The workers are *hammering* the studs to the frame.

2 *informal* **a** [+ *obj*] : to hit (something or someone) in a very forceful way • The batter *hammered* the ball over the fence. • Someone tried to *hammer* him over the head with a club. • Many towns were *hammered* by the hurricane. **b** : to hit (something) hard and repeatedly [+ *obj*] The typist's fingers were *hammering* the keys. • He was *hammering* [=*pounding, banging*] the door with his fists. [*no obj*] He was *hammering* at/on the door. • The rain *hammered* down on the roof. **c** [*no obj*] : to beat very quickly and forcefully • My heart was *hammering*. [=*pounding*]

3 [+ *obj*] *informal* : to defeat (an opponent) very easily • The home team was *hammered* 9–0.

4 [+ *obj*] *informal* : to harm or criticize (someone or something) severely — often used as *(be) hammered* • Local businesses are *being hammered* by the new shopping mall. • He is *being hammered* by his political opponents for his failure to cut taxes.

5 [*no obj*] : to keep talking about something or trying to do something — usually + *at* • He kept *hammering at* the need for tax relief throughout his speech. — often + *away* • I know we can solve this problem if we just keep *hammering away* (*at* it).

hammer into [*phrasal verb*] ***hammer (something) into (someone)*** : to force (something) to be learned very well by (someone) by repeating it again and again • They are constantly trying to *hammer* good manners *into* their children. • She *hammered* it *into* me that I could succeed.

hammer out [*phrasal verb*] ***hammer out (something)*** or ***hammer (something) out*** : to produce (something, such as an agreement) by a lot of discussion or argument • After hours of discussion, we finally *hammered out* an agreement/deal. • We'll *hammer* the details *out* later.

hammered *adj, not used before a noun* [*more* ~; *most* ~] *slang* : very drunk • They got/were *hammered* last night.

ham•mer•ing /ˈhæmərɪŋ/ *noun, pl* **-ings**

1 : the sound made when something is being hit by a hammer, by rain, etc. [*noncount*] Loud *hammering* was coming from next door. • We could hear the *hammering* of the rain on the roof. [*singular*] We could hear a loud *hammering* from next door.

2 [*singular*] *informal* — used to say that someone or something has been very forcefully hit, damaged, criticized, etc. • The old church ***got/took quite a hammering*** [=was badly damaged] during the storm. • The governor *took a hammering* from the media for his decision. • Our team *got/took quite a hammering* [=was badly beaten] in yesterday's game.

hammer throw *noun*

the hammer throw : [1]HAMMER 5b

ham•mock /ˈhæmək/ *noun, pl* **-mocks** [*count*] : a type of bed that consists of a piece of cloth hung between two trees, poles, etc.

hammock

[1]**ham•per** /ˈhæmpɚ/ *verb* **-pers; -pered; -per•ing** [+ *obj*] : to slow the movement, progress, or action of (someone or something) • Bad weather could *hamper* our search efforts. = Bad weather

could *hamper* us in our search efforts. • The project was *hampered* by budget restraints. • Construction is *hampering* traffic on the highway.

²hamper *noun, pl* **-pers** [*count*] : a large basket usually with a cover: such as **a** : a basket for food • a picnic *hamper* **b** *US* : a basket for holding dirty clothes until they can be washed • a clothes *hamper* — see picture at BATHROOM

ham·ster /ˈhæmstɚ/ *noun, pl* **-sters** [*count*] : a small animal that is often kept as a pet

¹ham·string /ˈhæmˌstrɪŋ/ *noun, pl* **-strings** [*count*]
1 : a tendon at the back of a person's knee
2 : a muscle at the back of a person's upper leg • This exercise will strengthen your *hamstrings.* = This exercise will strengthen your *hamstring* muscles.

²hamstring *verb* **-strings; -strung** /-ˌstrʌŋ/; **-string·ing** [+ *obj*] : to damage or ruin the force or effectiveness of (something or someone) • The mayor tried to *hamstring* our efforts by cutting the budget. • The company claims it is being *hamstrung* by government regulations.

¹hand /ˈhænd/ *noun, pl* **hands**
1 [*count*] **a** : the body part at the end of your arm that includes your fingers and thumb • These gloves will keep your *hands* warm. • She put her *hands* over her eyes. • He sat quietly with his *hands* folded in his lap. **b** — used in some phrases to refer to a person • I'm afraid this job will need ***more than one pair of hands*** [=more than one person] • It's a big job, but ***many hands make light work*** [=if many people work on it, it will be easier to do]
2 hands [*plural*] : power, possession, or control • The maps were in the *hands* of the enemy. [=the enemy had the maps] • The land between these mountains remains in private *hands.* [=is privately owned]
3 [*singular*] : physical help : assistance in doing something • Do you need a *hand*? • I'll be happy to ***lend a hand*** [=*help*] — often + *with* • Can you ***give/lend me a hand with*** [=help me with] this suitcase? • Let me *give you a hand with* that. — see also HELPING HAND
4 [*count*] : a long, thin part that points to a number on a clock or dial • Many clocks have a second *hand,* a minute *hand,* and an hour *hand.*
5 [*noncount*] *somewhat old-fashioned* : a promise of marriage • He asked for her *hand* (in marriage). [=he asked her to marry him] • She offered her *hand* in marriage to him. [=she said that she would marry him] • She gave him her *hand* in marriage. [=she married him]
6 [*singular*] : the act of hitting your hands together to show approval, appreciation, etc. : the act of applauding • Let's give him a big *hand!* [=a big round of applause]
7 [*count*] **a** : the cards that are held by a player in a card game • He studied his *hand* before deciding how much to bet. — often used figuratively • The program is designed to help children who have been dealt a cruel *hand* in life. [=children who have suffered or had bad things happen to them] • Even her critics say her chances of succeeding are great since she has been dealt such a strong *hand.* [=she is in a strong position] — see also *overplay your hand* at OVERPLAY **b** : a single round of play in a card game • He lost the first *hand* but won the next two.
8 [*count*] **a** : a hired worker • factory *hands* • The cowboys were simply ***hired hands*** with no ownership rights. — see also FARMHAND, OLD HAND, STAGEHAND **b** : a member of a ship's crew — usually plural • All *hands* on deck!
9 [*count*] : someone who performs or produces something (such as a work of art) — usually singular • These two portraits are by the same *hand.* [=by the same artist]
10 [*singular*] : a particular way or style of doing or handling something • The *hand* of a master is evident in these sculptures. [=these sculptures were obviously done by a very skillful artist] • He runs the business with a firm *hand.* • a cook who has a ***heavy hand*** with the salt [=who uses too much salt] — see also HEAVY-HANDED
11 [*singular*] *old-fashioned* : the way a person's writing looks : a type of handwriting • a note written in an elegant *hand*
12 [*count*] : a unit of measure equal to 4 inches (about 10.16 centimeters) and used especially to measure the height of horses • a horse that is 15 *hands* high

a bird in the hand is worth two in the bush see BIRD
a show of hands see ²SHOW
at first hand see ¹FIRST
at hand : close in distance or time • She likes to keep the phone (close) *at hand.* • We need to address the problem *at hand* [=the particular problem we are dealing with] and not argue about these other issues.
at the hand(s) of : by or through the action of (someone or something) • They were treated badly *at the hands of* the prison guards. • The people had suffered *at the hands of* a cruel dictator.
by hand **1** : with the hands • The stone was carved *by hand.* **2** : from one person directly to another • I delivered the document to his office *by hand.*
by the hand : by holding someone's hand • I took him *by the hand* and led him through the crowd. — sometimes used figuratively • You can't expect me to lead you *by the hand* through every difficult situation.
by your own hand : by your own actions • She ***died by her own hand*** [=she killed herself; she committed suicide]
change hands see ¹CHANGE
eat out of someone's hand see EAT
fall into the hands of see ¹FALL
fall into the wrong hands see ¹FALL
force someone's hand see ²FORCE
get your hands dirty see ¹DIRTY
get/lay your hands on : to find, get, or control (someone or something) • I'm still trying to *lay my hands on* my car keys. • He couldn't wait to *get his hands on* her money. • Wait until I *get my hands on* you. [=you will be in trouble when I catch you]
give your right hand see ¹GIVE
good with your hands : skillful at things that require the use of your hands • He's always been *good with his hands.*
grease the hand of see ²GREASE
hand and foot **1** — used to describe someone whose hands and feet are tied to prevent escape or movement • The prisoner was bound/tied *hand and foot.* **2** ✧ To ***wait on someone hand and foot*** is to provide everything that someone needs or wants. • I can't stand the way they *wait on her hand and foot!*
hand in glove : very closely • We are working *hand in glove* with the police to recover the stolen property.
hand in hand **1** : holding hands : grasping another person's hand • They walked on the beach *hand in hand.* **2** — used to say that two people or things are very closely connected or related • In a film, the images and sounds go *hand in hand.* • The chef works *hand in hand* [=very closely] with a nutritionist.
hand over fist *informal* — used to say that someone is earning or losing money very quickly or in large amounts • They were making/earning money *hand over fist.*
hands are tied ✧ If ***your hands are tied*** you cannot do anything about a situation because you do not have the power to act freely. • I'd like to help you, but my *hands are tied.* • The judge says her *hands are tied* because the law requires a harsh sentence in such cases.
hands off — used as a command to tell someone not to touch something • *Hands off* my property! • "Those cookies look delicious." "*Hands off*! We're saving them for later."
hand to mouth : without much money : in poverty • They have been living *hand to mouth* since he lost his job. = It's been *hand to mouth* since he lost his job. — see also HAND-TO-MOUTH
hat in hand (*US*) *or Brit* ***cap in hand*** : asking or begging for something in a respectful way • He came to me, *hat in hand,* asking if I could get him a job at the company.
have a hand in : to be involved in (something) • She *had a hand in* designing the new highway. • Did he *have a hand in* this decision?
have someone in the palm of your hand see ¹PALM
have your hands full : to be very busy • She'll *have her hands full* with the new baby.
heavy on your hands see ²HEAVY
hold hands *or* ***hold someone's hand*** **1** : to hold a person's hand in one of your hands for a period of time • two people *holding hands* • He *held hands* with his daughter. • He *held her hand* as they walked. **2** : to guide someone through a process by carefully explaining each step • I don't need you to *hold my hand.*
in good/safe hands : being taken care of very well • With her in charge, the office is *in good hands.* [=she will do the job well] • You're *in safe hands* with us. [=you will be safe with us]
in hand **1** : in your possession or control • We started our hike with compass and map *in hand.* • He has the situation ***well in hand*** [=he is in control of the situation] ✧ To ***take someone in hand*** is to begin to guide or direct someone who has been behaving badly. • You need someone to *take*

H

you in hand, young lady, and show you how to behave! **2** *chiefly Brit* : available for use • If we work at this rate we'll have a month *in hand* before our deadline is up!

join hands see JOIN

keep your hand in informal : to continue to be involved in some activity • He retired several years ago, but he still comes by the office occasionally because he likes to *keep his hand in* (the business).

keep/get your hands off (of) : to not touch (something) • *Keep your hands off* the cookies! We're saving them for later. — often used figuratively • The military is asking lawmakers to *keep their hands off* [=not change] the defense budget.

know (something) like the back of your hand see [1]KNOW

lay a hand on : to touch or harm (someone) • He claims that he never *laid a hand on* her.

off your hands : no longer in your possession or no longer your responsibility • If you don't want those golf clubs anymore, I'll be glad to take them *off your hands*. [=I'll be glad to take them] • She's trying to find a way to get some of that extra work *off her hands*.

on hand **1** : available for use • We have plenty of water *on hand*. **2** : present and available to do something • Five musicians were *on hand* to accompany her. • A priest was *on hand* to console them.

on the one hand, on the other hand — used to introduce statements that describe two different or opposite ideas, people, etc. • *On the one hand*, I think the price is fair, but *on the other* (*hand*), I really can't afford to spend that much money. • He's a good guy. His brother, *on the other hand*, is a very selfish man.

on your hands — used to say that you have something or are responsible for something • With all that extra work *on her hands* she'll need all the help she can get. • Once this project is over she should have some ***time on her hands***. [=free time] — see also *blood on your hands* at BLOOD

on your hands and knees : with your hands and knees on the ground : in a crawling position • She went down *on her hands and knees*.

out of hand **1** : very quickly without serious thought • He rejected the plan *out of hand*. • Suggestions that the hearing should be delayed were dismissed *out of hand*. **2** : not controlled • The kids were (getting) *out of hand*. [=were behaving in a wild and uncontrolled way] • He warns that technology is getting *out of hand*.

out of your hands — used to say that you cannot control something • The decision is *out of my hands*.

play into someone's hands see [1]PLAY

putty in your hands see [1]PUTTY

safe pair of hands Brit : someone who can be trusted with responsibility or a job • The next leader of the party should be a *safe pair of hands*.

sit on your hands see [1]SIT

take (something) into your (own) hands : to take control of something • The judge had no sympathy for people who insisted on *taking the law into their own hands*. [=trying to punish criminals themselves instead of allowing the legal system to do it] • After months of waiting for something to happen, he decided to *take matters into his own hands*.

to hand : available for use • I don't have all the latest data (immediately) *to hand*.

try your hand : to try to do something — usually + *at* • She wanted to *try her hand at* photography.

turn your hand to : to begin doing (something) usually in a skillful way : to start (a new activity, field of study, etc.) • an actress who has *turned her hand to* directing • After he left publishing, he *turned his hand to* law.

wash your hands of see [1]WASH

with your bare hands : using only your hands and no tools or weapons • He tried to kill me *with his bare hands*.

– see also FIRSTHAND, HANDS DOWN, SECONDHAND, SLEIGHT OF HAND, UPPER HAND

[2]**hand** *verb* **hands; hand·ed; hand·ing** [+ *obj*] : to give (something) to someone using your hands • He *handed* her a letter. = He *handed* a letter to her. • *Hand* me that picture.

hand back [*phrasal verb*] ***hand (something) back*** *or* ***hand back (something)*** : to return (something) by handing it to someone • He *handed* the letter *back* (to her) without reading it. • The clerk *handed back* my credit card.

hand down [*phrasal verb*] ***hand (something) down*** *or* ***hand down (something)*** **1** : to pass (something) from a person who is older (such as a parent) to a person who is younger (such as a child) • She will *hand* the diamond ring *down* to

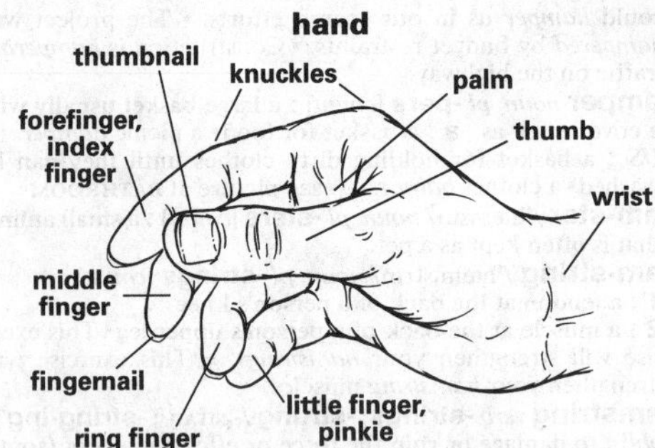

her niece. • The farm was *handed down* from generation to generation. **2** *chiefly US, law* : to form and express (a decision or opinion) in writing • The Supreme Court has *handed down* its decision.

hand in [*phrasal verb*] ***hand (something) in*** *or* ***hand in (something)*** : to give (something) to a person who will review or accept it • Students should *hand* their papers *in* on Thursday. • He *handed in* his resignation.

hand it to informal : to give credit to (someone) for doing something • I've got to *hand it to* you. You did a great job planning the party.

hand off [*phrasal verb*] ***hand (something) off*** *or* ***hand off (something) US*** : to give (something) to another person • (*American football*) The quarterback *handed off* the ball to the halfback. • She *handed* the job *off* to her assistant.

hand on [*phrasal verb*] ***hand (something) on*** *or* ***hand on (something) formal*** : to pass (something) from one person to another • These stories have been *handed on* from generation to generation.

hand out [*phrasal verb*] ***hand (something) out*** *or* ***hand out (something)*** : to give (something) to several or many people • They will *hand out* [=*distribute*] copies of the newsletter today. • He's always *handing out* advice to the people he works with. • She *handed* flyers *out* at the grocery store.

hand over [*phrasal verb*] ***hand (someone or something) over*** *or* ***hand over (someone or something)*** : to give up control or possession of (something or someone) • They demanded that he *hand* the documents *over* to them. • They agreed to *hand over* their hostages.

hand·bag /ˈhændˌbæg/ *noun, pl* **-bags** [*count*] : a woman's small bag or purse used for carrying personal things and money — see picture at BAG

hand baggage *noun* [*noncount*] : HAND LUGGAGE

hand·ball /ˈhændˌbɑːl/ *noun, pl* **-balls**

1 [*noncount*] : a game for two or four players who use their hands to hit a ball against a wall

2 [*count*] : the ball used in handball

hand·bas·ket /ˈhændˌbæskət/ *noun*

go to hell in a handbasket US, informal : to become completely ruined • He's convinced that the country is ***going to hell in a handbasket***.

hand·bill /ˈhændˌbɪl/ *noun, pl* **-bills** [*count*] *somewhat old-fashioned* : a small printed advertisement or announcement that is given out to many people by hand

hand·book /ˈhændˌbʊk/ *noun, pl* **-books** [*count*] : a small book that gives useful information about a particular subject • a *handbook* of English • a writer's *handbook*

hand brake *noun, pl* **~ brakes** [*count*]

1 : a brake that is operated by pushing or pulling a lever with your hand

2 : PARKING BRAKE

[1]**hand·craft** /ˈhændˌkræft, *Brit* ˈhændˌkrɑːft/ *verb* **-crafts; -craft·ed; -craft·ing** [+ *obj*] : to make (something) by using your hands • She *handcrafted* a set of bowls out of red clay.
– **handcrafted** *adj* • a *handcrafted* [=*handmade*] set of bowls • a beautiful *handcrafted* bed

[2]**handcraft** *noun, pl* **-crafts** [*count*] : HANDICRAFT

hand·cuff /ˈhændˌkʌf/ *verb* **-cuffs; -cuffed; -cuf·fing** [+ *obj*] : to put handcuffs on (someone) • *handcuff* a prisoner

hand·cuffs /ˈhændˌkʌfs/ *noun* [*plural*] : a set of two metal rings that are joined together and locked around a person's wrists • Police put *handcuffs* on the prisoner.

hand–eye coordination *noun* [*noncount*] : the way that your hands and sight work together so you are able to do things that require speed and accuracy (such as catching or hitting a ball) • an athlete with good *hand-eye coordination*

hand·ful /ˈhænd,fʊl/ *noun, pl* **-fuls**
1 [*count*] : an amount that you can hold in your hand • The children collected seashells by the *handful.* — often + *of* • a *handful of* strawberries
2 [*singular*] : a small amount or number — often + *of* • Only a *handful of* people showed up for the lecture.
3 [*singular*] *informal* : someone or something that is difficult to control • Our dog is a real *handful.*

hand·gun /ˈhænd,gʌn/ *noun, pl* **-guns** [*count*] : a small gun (such as a revolver or a pistol) designed to be held and shot with one hand

[1]**hand·held** /ˈhænd,held/ *adj, always used before a noun* : designed to be used while being held in your hands • a *handheld* movie camera

[2]**handheld** *noun, pl* **-helds** [*count*] : a small electronic device or computer that fits in your hand

hand·hold /ˈhænd,hoʊld/ *noun, pl* **-holds** [*count*] : a place or part on a surface that you can hold on to with your hand while climbing a cliff, mountain, etc.

hand–hold·ing /ˈhænd,hoʊldɪŋ/ *noun* [*noncount*] : patient attention, support, or instruction • New computer users often require a good deal of *hand-holding.* — see also *hold hands* at [1]HAND

[1]**hand·i·cap** /ˈhændi,kæp/ *noun, pl* **-caps** [*count*]
1 *sometimes offensive* : a physical or mental condition that may limit what a person can do : a physical or mental disability • a mental/physical *handicap* ✧ Some people consider the word *handicap* offensive in this sense and prefer the word *disability.*
2 : a problem, situation, or event that makes progress or success difficult • His shyness was a *handicap* in his job.
3 *golf* : a number that shows a golfer's level of skill and that is used to allow golfers of different abilities to compete with each other • She's been practicing a lot and her *handicap* has gone down from 18 to 12.
4 : a horse race in which some horses are required to carry more weight so that all the horses in the race will have an equal chance of winning

[2]**handicap** *verb* **-caps; -capped; -cap·ping** [+ *obj*]
1 : to make success or progress difficult for (someone) — usually used as *(be) handicapped* • He *was handicapped* by his extreme shyness.
2 *US* : to make a judgment about the likely winner of a race or contest • *handicap* the horses in a race = *handicap* a race • It's very hard to *handicap* the election at this point.
– hand·i·cap·per /ˈhændi,kæpɚ/ *noun, pl* **-pers** [*count*]

hand·i·capped /ˈhændɪ,kæpt/ *adj*
1 [*more ~; most ~*] *sometimes offensive* : having a physical or mental condition that limits what a person can do : having a handicap • He has been *handicapped* since his motorcycle accident. • physically/mentally *handicapped* ✧ Some people consider the word *handicapped* offensive in this sense and prefer *disabled.*
2 : designed or reserved for disabled people • *handicapped* parking spaces • a *handicapped* entrance

hand·i·craft /ˈhændi,kræft, *Brit* ˈhændi,krɑːft/ *noun, pl* **-crafts** [*count*]
1 : an activity that involves making something in a skillful way by using your hands • Her favorite *handicraft* is sewing.
2 : an object made by skillful use of your hands — usually plural • The street is lined with vendors selling *handicrafts.* — called also *handcraft*

hand·i·ly /ˈhændəli/ *adv* [*more ~; most ~*] : without trouble : very easily • He won the card game *handily.*

hand·i·work /ˈhændɪ,wɚk/ *noun* [*noncount*]
1 : work that is done by using your hands • They admired the potter's beautiful *handiwork.*
2 : something done by a particular person or group • I think all of these problems are her *handiwork.*

hand·ker·chief /ˈhæŋkɚʧəf/ *noun, pl* **-chiefs** *also* **-chieves** /ˈhæŋkɚʧəfs/ [*count*] : a small cloth used for wiping your face, nose, or eyes — called also *(informal) hankie*

[1]**han·dle** /ˈhændl/ *noun, pl* **han·dles** [*count*]
1 : a part of something that is designed to be held by your hand • He held the shovel by the/its *handle.* • The *handles* on the bag were torn. • a door *handle* [=the part that you turn with your hand to open a door] — see picture at BAG; see also LOVE HANDLES
2 *slang* : [1]NICKNAME • What's your *handle*?
fly off the handle see [1]FLY
get/have a handle on *informal* : to understand (something) • I can't quite *get a handle on* the way this machine works. • It seemed like she *had a* good *handle on* the situation. [=she understood the situation and was able to deal with it]
– han·dled /ˈhændḷd/ *adj* — usually used in combination • a wooden-*handled* basket

[2]**handle** *verb* **handles; han·dled; han·dling**
1 [+ *obj*] **a** : to touch, feel, hold, or move (something) with your hand • *Handle* the fruit carefully or it will bruise. • The baked potatoes were too hot to *handle* with our bare hands. **b** : to manage or control (something) with your hands • He knows how to *handle* a motorcycle. • He *handles* his motorcycle well. • She learned how to *handle* a weapon.
2 [+ *obj*] : to do the work required for (something) • She *handles* all the bookkeeping. • The system is *handled* by the main computer. • She's proven that she can *handle* anything. • The airport *handles* both passenger and cargo flights.
3 [+ *obj*] : to deal with (a person, situation, etc.) successfully • She couldn't *handle* being away from her children for more than a couple of days. • He's having a hard time *handling* the pressure of his new job. • A good politician knows how to *handle* the press. • Do you think he can *handle* the truth?
4 [+ *obj*] : to express thoughts about (something) in a piece of music, writing, or art • The class discussed how the author *handled* [=*dealt with*] the theme of loneliness in the novel.
5 [+ *obj*] : to be involved with the buying or selling of (something) • They own a store that *handles* rugs. • He was arrested for *handling* stolen goods.
6 [*no obj*] — used to describe how easy or difficult it is to control a vehicle • I'm looking for a car that *handles* well in the snow. • "How does his motorcycle *handle*?" "It *handles* very well."
handle yourself : to behave • She closely watched how the boys *handled themselves* at the ceremony. • She *handled herself* well under very difficult circumstances. — see also HANDLING

han·dle·bar /ˈhændḷ,baɚ/ *noun, pl* **-bars** [*count*] : a straight or bent bar with a handle at each end that is used to steer a bicycle, motorcycle, etc. — usually plural • Keep both hands on the *handlebars.* — see picture at BICYCLE

handlebar mustache *noun, pl* **~ -taches** [*count*] : a thick, long mustache that curves upward at the ends

han·dler /ˈhændlɚ/ *noun, pl* **-dlers** [*count*]
1 : a person who trains or controls an animal • a dog *handler* and breeder
2 : a person who carries or handles something • a baggage *handler* • food *handlers*
3 *chiefly US* : a person who guides, helps, or manages a political or public figure • a politician and his *handlers*

han·dling /ˈhændlɪŋ/ *noun* [*noncount*]
1 a : the act of touching, feeling, holding, or moving something • These items require careful *handling.* **b** : the way that someone deals with a person, event, situation, etc. — often + *of* • His *handling of* the situation could not have been worse. • The media's *handling of* the tragedy has been criticized.
2 : the act or process of packing and shipping something to someone (such as a customer) • There are additional charges for shipping and *handling.*
3 : the way a vehicle moves when it is driven or ridden • The car's *handling* was smooth.

hand luggage *noun* [*noncount*] : small pieces of luggage that a passenger can carry onto an airplane • You are entitled to one piece of *hand luggage* per flight.

hand·made /ˈhændˈmeɪd/ *adj* : made with the hands or by using hand tools • a *handmade* rug • *handmade* furniture

hand·maid /ˈhænd,meɪd/ *noun, pl* **-maids** [*count*] : HANDMAIDEN

hand·maid·en /ˈhænd,meɪdṇ/ *noun, pl* **-ens** [*count*] *somewhat old-fashioned* : a female servant or maid — usually used figuratively • He feels that government has become the *handmaiden* of corporate interests. [=the government only serves corporate interests]

hand–me–down /ˈhændmi,daʊn/ *adj* : owned or used by someone else before you : SECONDHAND — used especially of clothing • He was wearing an old, *hand-me-down* jacket. — sometimes used figuratively • He has some old-fashioned, *hand-me-down* notions about the role of women.
– hand–me–down *noun, pl* **-downs** [*count*] • Her closet was full of *hand-me-downs* from her older sisters.

hand·off /ˈhænd,ɑːf/ *noun, pl* **-offs** [*count*] *American football* : an act of handing the ball to another player • He fum-

H

bled the ball while attempting a *handoff.* — see also *hand off* at ²HAND

hand·out /ˈhændˌaʊt/ *noun, pl* **-outs** [*count*]
1 : something (such as food, clothing, or money) that is given to someone who is poor • He sat on the sidewalk asking for a *handout.* • The family wasn't interested in government *handouts.* — see also *hand out* at ²HAND
2 : a document that is given to people • The *handouts* had all the major points of his speech outlined on them. • advertising *handouts*

hand·over /ˈhændˌoʊvɚ/ *noun* [*singular*] **:** the act or process of giving control of someone or something to another person, country, etc. • the *handover* of power from the old government to the new government — see also *hand over* at ²HAND

hand·pick /ˌhændˈpɪk/ *verb* **-picks; -picked; -pick·ing** [+ *obj*]
1 : to pick (something, such as a fruit) by using your hand • They run a farm where you can *handpick* fresh strawberries. • a box of *handpicked* strawberries
2 : to choose (something or someone) carefully by yourself instead of letting someone else do it • The executive *handpicked* her successor.

hand puppet *noun, pl* **~ -pets** [*count*] *US* **:** a puppet that fits over your hand like a glove and is moved by the fingers and hand of its wearer — called also (*Brit*) *glove puppet*

hand·rail /ˈhændˌreɪl/ *noun, pl* **-rails** [*count*] **:** a narrow bar placed on the side of a walkway or a flight of stairs that you can hold as you walk

hand·saw /ˈhændˌsɑː/ *noun, pl* **-saws** [*count*] **:** a saw designed to be used with one hand

hands down /ˈhændzˈdaʊn/ *adv, informal*
1 : without much effort **:** very easily • She could win any race *hands down.*
2 : without any doubt **:** DEFINITELY • It's *hands down* the best movie of the year.
– hands–down /ˈhændzˌdaʊn/ *adj, informal* • the *hands-down* favorite to win

hand·set /ˈhændˌsɛt/ *noun, pl* **-sets** [*count*] **:** the part of a telephone that you hold near your ear and mouth for listening and speaking — see picture at TELEPHONE

hands–free *adj, always used before a noun* **:** designed to be used without being held in your hands • a *hands-free* cell phone

hand·shake /ˈhændˌʃeɪk/ *noun, pl* **-shakes** [*count*] **:** the act of grasping someone's right hand with your right hand and moving it up and down **:** the act of shaking hands • She greeted him with a *handshake.* ; *also* **:** the manner in which a person shakes hands • He has a firm/weak *handshake.* ✧ A handshake is often the way people greet each other, but it is also used when people part from each other or when they have made an agreement. • The deal was sealed with a *handshake.* — see also GOLDEN HANDSHAKE

hands–off /ˈhændzˈɑːf/ *adj, always used before a noun* **:** allowing people to do what they want to do without bothering or stopping them • His *hands-off* approach to teaching allows students to choose the focus of their studies.

hand·some /ˈhænsəm/ *adj* **hand·som·er; -est** [*also more* ~; *most* ~]
1 : pleasing to look at **:** ATTRACTIVE • It was a *handsome* house situated on a large lot. • The book includes many *handsome* illustrations. ; *especially, of a person* **:** having a pleasing appearance that causes romantic or sexual feelings in someone • a *handsome* face • I predict that someone tall, dark, and *handsome* is going to come into your life. ✧ Men are more frequently described as *handsome* than women. ***synonyms*** see BEAUTIFUL
2 *always used before a noun* **:** large in size or amount • He inherited a *handsome* fortune. • He made a *handsome* profit on the sale of the house. • They made *handsome* [=*generous*] contributions to charity.
3 *always used before a noun* **:** done or achieved in an impressive way • The book is a *handsome* tribute to a great poet. • (*chiefly Brit*) She won a *handsome* victory in the election.
– hand·some·ly *adv* • The book is *handsomely* illustrated with ink drawings. • He was *handsomely* [=*generously*] rewarded for his loyalty. **– hand·some·ness** *noun* [*noncount*] • an actor known for his rugged *handsomeness*

hands–on /ˈhændzˈɑːn/ *adj*
1 *always used before a noun* **a :** gained by actually doing something rather than learning about it from books, lectures, etc. • New employees are given hours of *hands-on* training. • They need *hands-on* experience with the machinery. **b :** involving or allowing the use of your hands or touching with your hands • The children's museum is full of *hands-on* displays. • *hands-on* activities
2 [*more* ~; *most* ~] **:** actively and personally involved in something (such as running a business) • He felt strongly that the staff needed a more *hands-on* manager. • She's always been very *hands-on* when it comes to running the restaurant.

hand·spring /ˈhændˌsprɪŋ/ *noun, pl* **-springs** [*count*] **:** a fast movement in which you jump forward or backward, land on your hands, swing your legs up and over your body, and then land on your feet • He did a *handspring* on the lawn.

hand·stand /ˈhændˌstænd/ *noun, pl* **-stands** [*count*] **:** the act of balancing on your hands with the body and legs straight up in the air

hand–to–hand /ˈhændtəˈhænd/ *adj, always before a noun* **:** involving physical contact between people — used to describe fighting that is done with the hands or with knives, clubs, etc., instead of guns, arrows, etc. • *hand-to-hand* combat

hand–to–mouth /ˈhændtəˈmaʊθ/ *adj* **:** having only enough money to survive • After the factories closed, many people lived a *hand-to-mouth* existence. [=many people were poor] — see also *hand to mouth* at ¹HAND

hand tool *noun, pl* **~ tools** [*count*] **:** a small tool (such as a hammer or wrench) that usually does not use electricity

hand towel *noun, pl* **~ -els** [*count*] **:** a small towel for drying your hands — see picture at BATHROOM

hand·work /ˈhændˌwɚk/ *noun* [*noncount*] **:** work done with your hands and not by a machine • She wore a beaded dress that required many hours of *handwork.*

hand·wo·ven /ˈhændˈwoʊvən/ *adj* **:** woven by hand **:** woven using a machine (called a loom) that is not powered by electricity • *handwoven* cloth/fabrics

hand–wring·ing /ˈhændˌrɪŋɪŋ/ *noun* [*noncount*] *disapproving* **:** worried talk or behavior • There has been a lot of silly *hand-wringing* over the latest hike in interest rates.
– hand·wring·er /ˈhændˌrɪŋɚ/ *noun, pl* **-ers** [*count*]

hand·writ·ing /ˈhændˌraɪtɪŋ/ *noun, pl* **-ings** [*count, noncount*] **:** the way a person's writing looks • Her *handwriting* is nearly impossible to read.
handwriting (is) on the wall see ¹WALL

hand·writ·ten /ˈhændˌrɪtn̩/ *adj* **:** written with a pen or pencil and not with a computer or typewriter • a *handwritten* note

handy /ˈhændi/ *adj* **hand·i·er; -est** [*also more* ~; *most* ~]
1 a : very useful or helpful • a *handy* cookbook/gadget • a *handy* little tool • The extra batteries for the flashlight ***came in handy*** [=were useful] when the electricity went off. **b :** near or close • He always liked to keep a dictionary *handy.* [=*on hand, nearby*] • (*Brit*) My flat is ***handy for*** [=near to] the underground.
2 : clever or skillful in using your hands, doing small jobs, etc. • She's *handy* with a needle and thread. • He's *handy* around the house.

handy·man /ˈhændiˌmæn/ *noun, pl* **-men** /-ˌmɛn/ [*count*] **:** a person (especially a man) who is skillful at doing small jobs (such as household repairs)
handyman's special *US, informal* **:** a house that is being sold at a low price because it needs many repairs

¹hang /ˈhæŋ/ *verb* **hangs; hung** /ˈhʌŋ/ *or in sense 3* **hanged; hang·ing**
1 a : to attach or place something so that it is held up without support from below [+ *obj*] He *hung* the painting on the wall. • We *hung* paper lanterns from the trees. • My grandmother used to *hang* the wash on a clothesline. [*no obj*] A photograph of her family *hangs* on the wall. • Several of her paintings are *hanging* in the Museum of Modern Art. • Your coat is *hanging* in the closet. • The curtains *hang* all the way (down) to the floor. — see also HANG UP 2 (below) **b** [+ *obj*] **:** to decorate (a surface) by hanging something (such as a picture) on it — usually used as *(be) hung* • The walls *are hung* with paintings. [=there are paintings hanging on the walls] **c** [+ *obj*] **:** to put (wallpaper) on a wall • They plan to *hang* wallpaper in the hallway.
2 [*no obj*] **:** to be in a lowered position • He let his arm *hang* down into the water. • We *hung* [=*leaned*] over the side of the boat and waved. • Her hair *hung* loose/limply.
3 *past tense and past participle usually* ***hanged*** **a :** to kill (someone) by using a rope that goes around the neck and holds the person's body in the air without any support from below [+ *obj*] They will *hang* him in the county jailhouse. •

He was *hanged* for his crimes. ▪ He *hanged* himself. [*no obj*] He *hanged* for his crimes. **b** *old-fashioned* — used to express surprise, anger, etc. ▪ We need those supplies now, *hang* the cost! [=we need them no matter how much they cost] ▪ ***I'll be hanged*** if I'll do anything to help him. [=I won't do anything to help him]

4 [*no obj*] **:** to float over a place or object for a long time ▪ Storm clouds were *hanging* low overhead. ▪ Smoke *hung* above the crowd. ▪ The smell of perfume *hung* in the air around her.

5 [*no obj*] — used to say that a decision has not yet been made ▪ The decision is still *hanging*. — see also HUNG JURY, HUNG PARLIAMENT

6 [*no obj*] *US, informal* **:** to be or stay somewhere for a period of time without doing much ▪ We were *hanging* [=*hanging around/out*] at Suzee's.

7 [+ *obj*] *chiefly US, informal* **:** to make (a turn) especially while driving ▪ *Hang* a right at the stoplight.

8 [*no obj*] *baseball, of a pitch* **:** to fail to curve in the desired way ▪ a *hanging* curveball

a peg to hang something on see [1]PEG

hang around *or Brit* ***hang about/round*** [*phrasal verb*] *informal* **1** ***hang around/about/round or hang around/about/round (a place)*** **:** to be or stay in a place for a period of time without doing much ▪ We just *hung around* all afternoon, listening to music. ▪ They *hung around* the theater after the play was over. **2** ***hang around/about/round with (someone)*** **:** to spend time relaxing, talking, or doing things with (someone) ▪ She *hangs around with* older kids. ▪ Who does he usually *hang around with*?

hang back [*phrasal verb*] **1 :** to be or stay behind others ▪ The little girl followed the older children but *hung back* a little. **2 :** to be unwilling to do something because of nervousness, fear, etc. ▪ When there's work to be done, she doesn't *hang back*.

hang by a thread **:** to be in a very dangerous situation or state **:** to be very close to death, failure, etc. ▪ The patient's life was *hanging by a thread*. [=the patient was very close to dying]

hang fire *chiefly Brit* **:** to be delayed ▪ The project has been *hanging fire* for several years. ▪ The decision is *hanging fire*.

hang in [*phrasal verb*] **1** *chiefly US, informal* **:** to keep working or trying in a difficult situation ▪ She says she'll *hang in* until she makes the business work. ▪ She did her best to *hang in* against some of the more experienced swimmers. — often used in the phrase ***hang in there*** ▪ *Hang in there*, kid! Don't quit! **2** ***hang in the air*** **:** to be incomplete or uncertain ▪ The design of the new currency is still *hanging in the air*.

hang loose see [2]LOOSE

hang on [*phrasal verb*] **1 :** to keep happening or continuing ▪ He had a terrible cold that *hung on* all spring. **2 :** to wait or stop briefly ▪ "Can we go now?" "*Hang on*, I'll be ready in just a minute." **3** ***hang on or hang on (to) (someone or something)*** **:** to hold or grip someone or something tightly ▪ *Hang on* or you'll fall! ▪ *Hang on* tight! ▪ The children *hung on* his arm. ▪ *Hang on to* your purse. ▪ The children *hung on to* his arm. **4** ***hang on to (something)*** **:** to keep (something) ▪ You should *hang on to* those old coins; they could be valuable. **5 a** ***hang on (something)*** **:** to be determined or decided by (something) **:** to depend on (something) ▪ The decision *hangs on* one vote. **b** ***hang (something) on (something)*** **:** to base (a story, theory, etc.) on (something) ▪ There weren't enough facts *on* which to *hang* a newspaper story. ▪ You can't *hang* your case *on* her testimony. **6** ***hang on someone's every word*** **:** to listen very carefully or closely to (someone) ▪ The children *hung on* the teacher's *every word*.

hang out [*phrasal verb*] **1** *informal* **:** to be or stay somewhere for a period of time without doing much ▪ The gang *hangs out* at the corner store. ▪ Our dog spends all his time *hanging out* [=*hanging around*] on the front porch. — see also HANGOUT **2** ***hang out with (someone)*** *informal* **:** to spend time relaxing, talking, or doing something with (someone) **:** to hang around with (someone) ▪ He spent a couple of days *hanging out with* his old friends. **3** ***hang (something) out or hang out (something)*** **:** to hang (something wet) outside to dry ▪ I *hung* the laundry *out* on the clothesline. ▪ I *hung out* the sheets to dry. **4** ***hang (someone or something) out to dry*** *informal* **:** to leave (someone or something) in a helpless or unprotected state ▪ When things got tough, the company *hung* us *out to dry*.

hang out your shingle see [1]SHINGLE

hang over [*phrasal verb*] ***hang over (someone)*** **:** to be a threat or danger to (someone) **:** to cause (someone) to feel worried or guilty ▪ They are glad that the deadline is no longer *hanging over* them. ▪ I can't relax with that test ***hanging over my head***. [=I can't relax until after I take that test] — see also HANGOVER

hang tight [*phrasal verb*] *US, informal* **:** to wait before doing anything ▪ Investors are being advised to *hang tight* until the stock market rebounds.

hang together [*phrasal verb*] *informal* **1 :** to stay with someone ▪ If we just *hang together* a while longer, I know that we can work out our problems. **2 :** to work in a logical and effective way ▪ The movie starts out well, but the story doesn't *hang together* after the first hour.

hang tough *chiefly US, informal* **:** to keep working or trying to succeed in a difficult situation ▪ The team *hung tough* through the whole game, but lost in the end.

hang up [*phrasal verb*] **1** ***hang up or hang up (something) or hang (something) up*** **:** to end a telephone connection by putting the handset on its base or by turning the telephone off ▪ "Is he still on the phone?" "No, he *hung up*." ▪ Let me talk to her before you *hang up* the phone. — often + *on* ▪ I can't believe he *hung up on* me! [=that he suddenly hung up while I was talking to him on the phone] **2** ***hang (something) up or hang up (something)*** **:** to put (something) on a hook or hanger ▪ *Hang up* your coat, please. — see also [1]HANG 1a (above) **3** ***hang up (something)*** *informal* **:** to stop doing (something) **:** to finish using (something) for the last time — used figuratively ▪ She decided to *hang up* her running shoes [=she decided to quit running] and to start riding her bike instead. **4** ***hang it up*** *US, informal* **:** to stop doing something ▪ After all this time, you're just going to *hang it up*? [=*quit*] — see also HUNG UP

hang with [*phrasal verb*] ***hang with (someone)*** *US, informal* **1 :** to spend time with (someone) ▪ He's just been *hanging with* his friends. **2 :** to stay close to (someone) **:** to keep up with (someone) ▪ He *hung with* the leaders for the first half of the race, but then he began to fall behind.

hang your hat see HAT

hang your head **:** to have your head turned downward because of shame or embarrassment ▪ He *hung his head* in shame.

let it all hang out see [1]LET

thereby hangs a tale — used to suggest that there is a story about something that has just been mentioned ▪ I realized where I had seen him before—and *thereby hangs a tale*.

[2]**hang** *noun* [*singular*] **:** the way in which something hangs ▪ the *hang* of a skirt

get the hang of *informal* **:** to learn the skills that are needed to do (something) ▪ He was finally *getting the hang of* his job. [=he was finally beginning to understand and become skillful in his job] ▪ She's *getting the hang of* driving.

give a hang *informal* **:** to be concerned or worried about something — usually used in negative statements ▪ I don't *give a hang* [=I don't care] what they say.

hang·ar /ˈhæŋɚ/ *noun, pl* **-ars** [*count*] **:** a building where aircraft are kept

hang·dog /ˈhæŋˌdɑːg/ *adj* [*more ~; most ~*] **:** sad or depressed ▪ He came home with a *hangdog* expression/look on his face.

hang·er /ˈhæŋɚ/ *noun, pl* **-ers** [*count*] **:** a usually curved piece of metal, plastic, or wood that is used for hanging clothing

hang·er–on /ˈhæŋɚˌɑːn/ *noun, pl* **hang·ers–on** [*count*] **:** someone who spends a lot of time around a person, place, or group in order to get something (such as fame, money, or power) ▪ a star who is always surrounded by *hangers-on*

hang glider *noun, pl* **~ -ers** [*count*] **:** a small aircraft that consists of a metal frame covered with strong cloth and that is flown through the air by a person who hangs beneath it; *also* **:** a person who flies a hang glider

– hang gliding *noun* [*noncount*] ▪ I've always wanted to try *hang gliding*.

hang·ing /ˈhæŋɪŋ/ *noun, pl* **-ings**

1 : the act of killing someone by hanging that person from a rope tied around the neck [*count*] The *hanging* was scheduled for 3 o'clock. [*noncount*] He was sentenced to death by *hanging*.

2 [*count*] **:** something (such as a curtain) that is hung on a wall especially for decoration — often plural ▪ There were several antique wall *hangings* in the house.

hang·man /ˈhæŋmən/ *noun, pl* **-men** /-mən/ [*count*] **:** a person who kills criminals by hanging them

hang·nail /ˈhæŋˌneɪl/ *noun, pl* **-nails** [*count*] **:** a small piece of skin hanging loose at the side or bottom of a fingernail

hang·out /ˈhæŋˌaʊt/ *noun, pl* **-outs** [*count*] *informal* **:** a place where a person spends a lot of time ▪ The park was their favorite *hangout*. — see also *hang out* at [1]HANG

hang·over /ˈhæŋˌoʊvɚ/ *noun, pl* **-overs** [*count*] **:** a sick feeling or condition that comes after drinking too much alcohol at an earlier time ▪ She woke up with a *hangover*.

hang time *noun* [*noncount*] *US, informal* **:** the amount of time that something (especially a ball that is hit, kicked, or thrown) remains in the air ▪ He got some amazing *hang time* on that pass.

hang–up /ˈhæŋˌʌp/ *noun, pl* **-ups** [*count*] *informal* **:** something that causes you to feel worried, afraid, embarrassed, etc. ▪ We all have our *hang-ups*. — often + *about* ▪ He has a lot of *hang-ups about* money.

hank /ˈhæŋk/ *noun, pl* **hanks** [*count*] **:** an amount of yarn, thread, etc., that has been wound into a large loop or loose ball — compare SKEIN

han·ker /ˈhæŋkɚ/ *verb* **-kers; -kered; -ker·ing** [*no obj*] *informal + old-fashioned* **:** to have a strong or constant desire for something ▪ She is still *hankering* after [=*longing for*] a return to the good old days. = She is still *hankering* to return to the good old days. ▪ By the middle of the winter, they were *hankering* for a warm day.

– hankering *noun* [*singular*] *informal + old-fashioned* ▪ They had/felt a *hankering* for ice cream. ▪ She had a *hankering* to buy a new car.

han·kie *or* **han·ky** /ˈhæŋki/ *noun, pl* **-kies** [*count*] *informal* **:** HANDKERCHIEF

han·ky–pan·ky /ˌhæŋkiˈpæŋki/ *noun* [*noncount*] *informal*

1 : sexual activity ▪ We thought there was some *hanky-panky* going on between him and his secretary.

2 : dishonest or suspicious activity ▪ They accused the company of financial *hanky-panky*.

Ha·nuk·kah *also* **Cha·nu·kah** /ˈhɑːnəkə/ *noun, pl* **-kahs** [*count, noncount*] **:** an eight-day Jewish holiday that is celebrated in November or December

hap·haz·ard /ˌhæpˈhæzɚd/ *adj* [*more ~; most ~*] **:** having no plan, order, or direction ▪ We were given a *haphazard* tour of the city. ▪ a *haphazard* procedure

– hap·haz·ard·ly *adv* ▪ Books and papers were scattered *haphazardly* on the desk.

hap·less /ˈhæpləs/ *adj, always used before a noun* [*more ~; most ~*] *somewhat formal + literary* **:** having no luck **:** very unfortunate ▪ She plays the *hapless* heroine who is unlucky in love.

– hap·less·ly *adv* ▪ the movie's *haplessly* ineffectual hero

hap·pen /ˈhæpən/ *verb* **-pens; -pened; -pen·ing** [*no obj*]

1 : to take place especially without being planned **:** OCCUR ▪ Mistakes/Accidents will *happen*. ▪ Something like that was bound to *happen* sooner or later. ▪ You never know what's going to *happen* when they get together. ▪ What *happened* at school today? ▪ "What's *happening*?" "They're installing new equipment."

2 *not used in progressive tenses* **a :** to do or be something by chance — followed by *to + verb* ▪ The children *happened to be* asleep when we called. ▪ I *happened to overhear* their conversation. ▪ I *happen to know* his brother. ▪ Do you *happen to know* the way to the station? **b** — used with *it* to describe something that occurs by chance ▪ *It* (so) *happened* that the children were asleep when we called. ▪ *It happened* to rain that day. ▪ As *it happened*, it rained that day. ▪ *It* (just so) *happens* that I know his brother. **c** — used to make an angry or forceful statement; followed by *to + verb* ▪ The woman you've been looking at *happens to be* my wife! ▪ I *happen to think* that the movie was actually very good.

happen along *or* ***happen by*** [*phrasal verb*] *US, literary + old-fashioned* **:** to come to or by a place by chance ▪ He was about to leave when his old girlfriend *happened by*.

happen into [*phrasal verb*] ***happen into (a place)*** *US* **:** to enter (a place) by chance ▪ She *happened into* the room just as the music started.

happen on/upon [*phrasal verb*] ***happen on/upon (someone or something)*** *literary + old-fashioned* **:** to find or meet (someone or something) by chance ▪ She *happened on* a little cottage in the woods. ▪ I *happened upon* them at the grocery store.

happen to [*phrasal verb*] ***happen to (someone or something)*** **:** to affect or involve (someone or something) as the result of an event or action ▪ An odd thing *happened to* me on my way to the office last week. ▪ I wonder what/whatever *happened to* that guy. [=I wonder where that guy has gone and what he has been doing]; *especially* **:** to affect (someone or something) in a bad or harmful way ▪ I promise nothing will *happen to* you. ▪ What *happened to* the car? There's a big scratch on the fender.

[1]**happening** *noun, pl* **-ings** [*count*] **:** an event or occurrence — often plural ▪ There were strange *happenings* at the inn.

[2]**happening** *adj* [*more ~; most ~*] *informal* **:** fashionable or popular ▪ This is quite a *happening* town on the weekends.

hap·pen·stance /ˈhæpənˌstæns/ *noun, pl* **-stances** *formal + literary* **:** something that happens by chance [*noncount*] Our meeting was pure *happenstance*. ▪ We met each other by *happenstance*. [*count*] It was an agreeable *happenstance* that we met.

hap·pi·ly /ˈhæpəli/ *adv* [*more ~; most ~*]

1 : in a happy way or state ▪ They have been *happily* married for 12 years. ▪ The story ended *happily*. ▪ She giggled *happily*. ▪ They lived *happily* ever after.

2 — used to say that something good or lucky has happened ▪ *Happily*, no one was injured. [=I am happy to say that no one was injured]

3 : in a very willing way ▪ He says he'll *happily* [=*gladly*] postpone the appointment. ▪ We *happily* accept credit cards.

hap·pi·ness /ˈhæpinəs/ *noun, pl* **-ness·es**

1 [*noncount*] **:** the state of being happy **:** JOY ▪ They made a toast to long life and *happiness*. ▪ They found *happiness* together.

2 [*count*] *somewhat formal* **:** an experience that makes you happy ▪ I wish the them every *happiness*. [=I hope that they will be very happy]

hap·py /ˈhæpi/ *adj* **hap·pi·er; -est**

1 a : feeling pleasure and enjoyment because of your life, situation, etc. ▪ She was a very *happy* child. ▪ I can see that you're not *happy* in your work. [=I can see that you do not enjoy your work] ▪ You don't look *happy*. What's the problem? ▪ We're all one big, *happy* family here. ▪ I'd do anything to make/keep her *happy*. ▪ She's *happy* playing with her toys. = She's *happy* when she plays with her toys. **b :** showing or causing feelings of pleasure and enjoyment ▪ I could hear the children's *happy* laughter in the other room. ▪ She had a very *happy* childhood. ▪ They've had a very *happy* marriage. ▪ remembering *happier* times ▪ a *happy* event/occasion ▪ I was glad the movie had a ***happy ending***. **c** *not used before a noun* **:** pleased or glad about a particular situation, event, etc. ▪ We are so *happy* that you were able to come to the party. ▪ They are not at all *happy* about the rise in taxes. ▪ He's not *happy* with the way the project is going. ▪ It's great that he won the scholarship. I'm very ***happy for*** him. [=I am glad something good happened to him] **d :** very willing to do something — usually followed by *to + verb* ▪ I would be *happy to assist* you.

2 — used as part of a greeting or wish for someone on a special holiday or occasion ▪ *Happy* birthday, Mom! ▪ *Happy* Holidays!

3 *always used before a noun* **:** lucky or fortunate ▪ We were brought together by a series of *happy* accidents. ▪ a *happy* coincidence

4 *always used before a noun* **:** fitting or suitable ▪ a *happy* choice of words ▪ He was a *happy* choice for chairman of the committee.

(as) happy as a clam see [1]CLAM

happy medium see [1]MEDIUM

happy returns see [2]RETURN

– see also TRIGGER-HAPPY

happy camper *noun, pl* **~ -ers** [*count*] *chiefly US, informal* **:** someone who is pleased or happy ▪ I was one *happy camper* when I heard the news. — often used in negative statements ▪ When she found out that the report wasn't ready, she was not a *happy camper*. [=she was angry or upset]

hap·py–go–lucky /ˌhæpigoʊˈlʌki/ *adj* [*more ~; most ~*] **:** not worried about anything ▪ He's always been a *happy-go-lucky* guy. ▪ She has a *happy-go-lucky* disposition.

happy hour *noun, pl* **~ hours** [*count, noncount*] **:** a time at a bar when drinks are sold at a lower price than usual ▪ *Happy hour* runs from 5:00 to 7:00.

[1]**ha·rangue** /həˈræŋ/ *noun, pl* **-rangues** [*count*] **:** a forceful or angry speech ▪ He delivered a long *harangue* about the evils of popular culture.

[2]**harangue** *verb* **-rangues; -rangued; -rangu·ing** [*+ obj*] **:** to speak to (someone) in a forceful or angry way **:** to deliver a harangue to (someone) ▪ He *harangued* us for hours

about the evils of popular culture.

ha·rass /hə'ræs, 'herəs/ *verb* **-rass·es; -rassed; -rass·ing** [+ *obj*]

1 : to annoy or bother (someone) in a constant or repeated way • She was constantly *harassed* by the other students. • He claims that he is being unfairly *harassed* by the police. • He was accused of ***sexually harassing*** his secretary. [=of making unwanted sexual comments to her]

2 : to make repeated attacks against (an enemy) • The troops *harassed* the defeated army throughout its retreat.

– harassed *adj* [*more* ~; *most* ~] • She looked very *harassed* and distraught. **– ha·rass·ment** /hə'ræsmənt, 'herəsmənt/ *noun* [*noncount*] • police *harassment* • children subjected to *harassment* by bullies • He was accused of ***sexual harassment.***

har·bin·ger /'hɑɚbənʤɚ/ *noun, pl* **-gers** [*count*] **:** something that shows what is coming — usually + *of* • The warm weather is a *harbinger of* spring. • Is this news a *harbinger of* better days to come? • a *harbinger of* death/doom

¹har·bor (*US*) *or Brit* **har·bour** /'hɑɚbɚ/ *noun, pl* **-bors** [*count*]

1 : a part of the ocean, a lake, etc., that is next to land and that is protected and deep enough to provide safety for ships

2 : a place of safety and comfort **:** HAVEN — often used in the phrase ***safe harbor*** • She can always find (a) *safe harbor* in her home.

²harbor (*US*) *or Brit* **har·bour** *verb* **-bors; -bored; -bor·ing** [+ *obj*]

1 : to give shelter to (someone) **:** to hide and protect (someone) • It is illegal to *harbor* an escaped convict.

2 : to have (something, such as a thought or feeling) in your mind for a long time • He still *harbors* deep feelings of resentment toward his former employer. • I don't *harbor* any illusions about our chances for success. • *harbor* a grudge • *harbor* doubts/bitterness

3 : to hold or contain (something) • She studies the genetic material *harbored* in a cell's nucleus. • Some of these animals may *harbor* disease that could affect humans.

¹hard /'hɑɚd/ *adj* **hard·er; -est**

1 : very firm or solid **:** not easy to bend, cut, etc. **:** not soft • *hard* ground • a *hard* bench/floor/shell • *hard* cheese/rubber • This bread is (as) ***hard as a rock.*** [=very hard] — opposite SOFT

2 : physically or mentally difficult **:** not easy • That test was *hard.* • a *hard* task • *hard* work • She was asked a lot of *hard* questions. • We're going to have to make some *hard* choices/decisions. • It's *hard* to solve this problem. = This is a *hard* problem (to solve). = This problem is *hard* (to solve). • He's a *hard* guy to figure out. = He's a guy who's *hard* to figure out. = It's *hard* to figure that guy out. • It was very *hard* to find a replacement for her. • Their story is *hard* to believe. • It's *hard* not to worry about her. • It's *hard* to tell/know what she's thinking. • He was sentenced to five years of ***hard labor.*** [=time in prison spent in intense physical labor]

3 a : difficult to experience **:** severe or harsh • He has learned a *hard* lesson. • It's been a *hard* winter. [=a very cold winter with harsh weather] **:** having a lot of pain, trouble, or worries • She has had a very *hard* life. = Life has been very *hard* for her. • I had a *hard* [=*tough*] day at the office. • We've been having some *hard* [=*poor, bad*] luck. ✧ ***Hard times*** are times when there is a lot of trouble, poverty, worry, or failure. • She's stuck with them through all the *hard times.* • The region has been experiencing some economic *hard times.* • After years of success, their business has ***fallen on hard times.*** **b :** having a harmful or destructive effect • His health has suffered from years of *hard* living. • This old bicycle has obviously gotten some *hard* use.

4 : working or doing something with a lot of energy • She's a *hard* [=*diligent, energetic*] worker.

5 : very forceful • The plane made a *hard* [=*jarring*] landing. • He hit a *hard* line drive past the shortstop. • A *hard* rain was falling. • He was knocked out by a *hard* right to the jaw. **:** quick and forceful • *hard* acceleration • *hard* braking • a *hard* left turn

6 : done with a lot of careful thought and attention **:** thorough or intense • The jeweler gave the gem a long *hard* look. [=the jeweler looked at the gem very closely and carefully] • Investors are taking a very *hard* look at how the company does business.

7 : able to be clearly seen and measured **:** not able to be questioned or doubted • Those are the (cold) *hard* facts of the case. • She is still collecting *hard* data on the software's performance. • It's an interesting theory, but there is no *hard* evidence that supports it.

8 a : not seeming to care about other people or to feel kindness or affection • He's a *hard* man. • a *hard* taskmaster • She has an extremely *hard* [=*unfeeling*] heart. • He's ***as hard as nails.*** [=he's very hard or tough] — opposite SOFT **b :** not gentle or friendly • *hard* [=*harsh*] words

9 : holding extreme political views • a member of the *hard* [=*far, extreme*] right/left

10 : relating to serious matters • They only report *hard* news. — opposite SOFT

11 a : containing a large amount of alcohol • *hard* liquor • the *hard* stuff **b :** containing alcohol • *hard* cider/lemonade

12 : powerful and extremely harmful to the health • cocaine and other *hard* drugs — opposite SOFT

13 *of water* **:** containing many minerals and therefore unable to make bubbles with soap • *hard* water — opposite SOFT

14 : having clear, sharp lines • trying to soften the *hard* edges of the image

15 : very bright and unpleasant • *hard* lighting • the cold, *hard* light of day

16 : sounding like the "c" in "cold" or the "g" in "geese" • The "g" in "gorilla" is *hard*, but the "g" in "giant" is soft. • the *hard* "c" in "cat" — opposite SOFT

17 *informal* **:** physically strong • *hard* [=*muscular*] bodies

a hard act to follow see FOLLOW

a hard nut (to crack) see NUT

a hard row to hoe see ¹ROW

between a rock and a hard place see ²ROCK

drive a hard bargain see ¹BARGAIN

give (someone) a hard time **:** to criticize or annoy someone • They *gave him a hard time* about quitting the team.

hard feelings **1** ✧ If you have *hard feelings*, you feel dislike or anger toward someone who you think has mistreated you. • She felt/had no *hard feelings* towards him. • The court's decision has caused a lot of *hard feelings.* **2** ✧ The phrase ***no hard feelings*** is used in speech to say that you are not upset or to ask if someone else is upset. • "I'm sorry I broke our date last night." "That's OK; *no hard feelings.*" • "So, we're still friends, right? *No hard feelings*?"

hard knocks see ²KNOCK

hard of hearing **:** not able to hear well • He has become a little *hard of hearing* in his old age.

hard on **1 a :** causing damage or strain to (something) • Reading in dim light is *hard on* your eyes. [=it puts a strain on your eyes; it is not good for them] • This kind of work can be *hard on* your back. **b :** causing stress or worry to (someone) • These past few months have been *hard on* everyone, but things should get better soon. **2 :** treating or judging (someone) in a harsh or critical way • Don't be too *hard on* the boy. [=don't judge or treat the boy too harshly] • She is sometimes too *hard on* herself. • There's no need to be so *hard on* yourself—you did the best you could.

hard up *informal* **1 :** lacking money • We're pretty *hard up* these days. **2 :** having not enough of something — + *for* • She always seems to be *hard up for* cash. • He's *hard up for* friends. [=he has few friends]

have a hard time ✧ If you *have a hard time* doing something or with something, it is difficult for you. • She's *having a hard time* adjusting to college life. • The school has *had a hard time* recruiting substitute teachers. • He's been *having a hard time* with his research paper.

play hard to get see ¹PLAY

the hard way **:** in a way that involves difficult or painful experiences • He found out *the hard way* that crime doesn't pay. [=he found out by being punished for his crimes] • She insisted on doing things *the hard way.*

²hard *adv* **hard·er; -est**

1 : with a lot of effort or energy • You have to work *hard* in order to succeed. • I know how *hard* she tried. • She ran as *hard* as she could. • working/studying/fighting *hard* • We've thought ***long and hard*** about this problem. ✧ If you are ***hard at work*** (on something) you are doing work with a lot of effort and energy. • You shouldn't disturb her while she's *hard at work.* • We're *hard at work* on the new project.

2 : in a very forceful way • He hit the ball *hard.* • a *hard*-hit ball • The ball hit him *hard* on the wrist. • He pressed his nose *hard* against the window. • swallowing *hard* • She pushed *hard* against the door, but it wouldn't open. • The wind was blowing *hard.* • The snow/rain came down *hard.* • The dog bit down *hard* on the thief's hand. **:** in a loud and forceful way • She was breathing *hard.* • laughing/crying *hard* ✧ If you are ***hit hard*** or ***hard hit*** by something or if something ***hits***

H

you hard, it affects you powerfully in a very painful or shocking way. ▪ His business was *hit hard* by the recession. ▪ Her sudden death *hit them hard*. ✧ If you ***take something hard*** you are very upset or hurt by it. ▪ She *took it hard* [=she was very upset] when he left. ▪ We *took* the defeat *hard*.
3 a : in a very direct and intense way ▪ He looked *hard* into her eyes. **b :** in an extreme or complete way ▪ He fell *hard* for the girl next door.
die hard see [1]DIE
hard by *old-fashioned* **:** next to ▪ The school stood *hard by* a church.
hard done by *Brit* **:** treated harshly or unfairly ▪ He felt very *hard done by* when he was laid off after many years of faithful service.
hard on the heels of see [1]HEEL

hard–and–fast /ˌhɑɚdn̩ˈfæst, *Brit* ˌhɑːdn̩ˈfɑːst/ *adj* — used to say that something (such as a rule) cannot be changed ▪ a *hard-and-fast* rule

hard–ass /ˈhɑɚdˌæs/ *noun, pl* **-ass•es** [*count*] *chiefly US, informal + impolite* **:** a very tough person who treats other people harshly ▪ He has a reputation for being a *hard-ass*.
– hard–assed /ˈhɑɚdˌæst/ *adj* [*more ~; most ~*] ▪ a *hard-assed* cop/journalist

hard•back /ˈhɑɚdˌbæk/ *noun, pl* **-backs :** HARDCOVER [*count*] The store sells only *hardbacks*. [*noncount*] The book is sold only in *hardback*. ▪ a *hardback* edition

hard•ball /ˈhɑɚdˌbɑːl/ *noun* [*noncount*] *chiefly US, informal*
1 : BASEBALL
2 : forceful and sometimes dishonest methods used to get something you want — often used after *play* ▪ He's not afraid to *play* political *hardball*. [=to use tough and perhaps dishonest methods to meet a political goal] ▪ *hardball* tactics/politics

hard–bit•ten /ˈhɑɚdˈbɪtn̩/ *adj* [*more ~; most ~*] **:** tough and experienced ▪ *hard-bitten* journalists ▪ a *hard-bitten* cynic/skeptic

hard–boiled /ˈhɑɚdˈbojəld/ *adj*
1 *of an egg* **:** boiled until all the inside parts have become solid ▪ *hard-boiled* eggs — compare SOFT-BOILED
2 a [*more ~; most ~*] **:** not feeling or showing emotions such as affection or kindness **:** emotionally tough ▪ a *hard-boiled* detective **b** *chiefly US* **:** having a tough detective as the main character ▪ a *hard-boiled* novel ▪ *hard-boiled* fiction

hard•bound /ˈhɑɚdˌbaʊnd/ *adj, chiefly US, of a book* **:** having a stiff or hard cover ▪ *hardbound* books [=hardcovers] — compare SOFTBOUND

hard candy *noun, pl* **~ -dies** [*count, noncount*] **:** a small, hard piece of candy with a sweet and usually fruity flavor — called also (*Brit*) *boiled sweet*

hard cash *noun* [*noncount*] **:** money that a person has and can use immediately **:** money in the form of bills and coins rather than checks or credit cards ▪ He wanted *hard cash* for his watch.

hard–charging *adj* [*more ~; most ~*] *US* **:** very aggressive, determined, or ambitious **:** HARD-DRIVING ▪ a *hard-charging* young executive

hard–cooked *adj, US* **:** HARD-BOILED 1 ▪ *hard-cooked* eggs

hard copy *noun, pl* **~ cop•ies** [*count*] *computers* **:** a printed copy of a document ▪ print a *hard copy* of the report

hard core *noun* [*singular*] **:** a small number of very active and enthusiastic members of a group **:** the most devoted and active members of a group ▪ He knows that he can count on the support of a *hard core* of party loyalists.

hard–core /ˈhɑɚdˈkoɚ/ *adj* [*more ~; most ~*]
1 : very active and enthusiastic ▪ He knows that he can count on his *hard-core* supporters. ▪ *hard-core* fans
2 : showing or describing sex acts very openly ▪ *hard-core* pornography — compare SOFT-CORE

hard•cov•er /ˈhɑɚdˈkʌvɚ/ *noun, pl* **-ers** *US* **:** a book that has stiff or hard covers [*count*] She bought several *hardcovers*. [*noncount*] His first novel was published in *hardcover* last spring. — often used before another noun ▪ the book's *hardcover* [=*hardbound*] edition — called also *hardback*; compare PAPERBACK, SOFTCOVER

hard currency *noun, pl* **~ -cies** [*count, noncount*] **:** money that comes from a country with a strong government and economy and that is not likely to lose its value

hard disk *noun, pl* **~ disks** [*count*] *computers* **:** a disk that is not flexible and that is used to store computer data ▪ Remember to save the file to your *hard disk*. — compare FLOPPY DISK, HARD DRIVE

hard–drinking *adj* [*more ~; most ~*] — used to describe a person who often drinks a lot of alcohol ▪ He had a troubled relationship with his violent, *hard-drinking* father.

hard drive *noun, pl* **~ drives** [*count*] *computers* **:** a device that is used for storing computer data and that contains one or more hard disks ▪ an external/removable *hard drive*

hard–driv•ing /ˈhɑɚdˈdraɪvɪŋ/ *adj* [*more ~; most ~*] **:** very aggressive, determined, or ambitious ▪ a *hard-driving* businesswoman/entrepreneur

hard–earned *adj* [*more ~; most ~*] **:** achieved or acquired through a lot of effort or hard work ▪ Someone stole all her *hard-earned* money. ▪ a *hard-earned* victory

hard–edged /ˈhɑɚdˈɛʤd/ *adj* [*more ~; most ~*] **:** having a tough or sharp quality ▪ Critics have praised her *hard-edged* satire. ▪ *hard-edged* realism ▪ a *hard-edged* campaigner

hard•en /ˈhɑɚdn̩/ *verb* **-ens; -ened; -en•ing**
1 : to become hard or firm or to make (something) hard or firm [*no obj*] It will take several hours for the concrete to *harden* (into a solid block). ▪ The gel *hardens* quickly. ▪ The presence of certain substances in the blood can cause the arteries to *harden*. [+ *obj*] These additives are designed to *harden* the steel. ▪ substances that can *harden* the arteries
2 : to become more definite and strongly felt or to make (something) more definite and strongly felt [*no obj*] Opposition to the goverment has *hardened* as news of further scandals has leaked out. [+ *obj*] The news has *hardened* opposition to the government.
3 [+ *obj*] **:** to make (someone) hard **:** to make (someone) less emotional and less likely to feel sorry for other people ▪ He had been *hardened* by his years of military service.
4 [*no obj*] **:** to begin to be or seem harsh, angry, serious, etc. ▪ Her voice/manner *hardened* as she spoke of her determination to win.
harden your heart ✧ If you *harden your heart* or if something *hardens your heart*, you stop having kind or friendly feelings for someone. ▪ She *hardened her heart* against him.
– hard•en•er /ˈhɑɚdnɚ/ *noun, pl* **-ers** [*count*] ▪ a metal *hardener* **– hardening** *noun* [*noncount*] ▪ *hardening* of the arteries

hardened *adj* [*more ~; most ~*]
1 — used to describe something that has become hard ▪ *hardened* arteries ▪ a *hardened* patch of skin
2 : very tough because of harsh experiences **:** not having the kind of emotions (such as fear, sorrow, etc.) that most people feel in difficult or dangerous situations ▪ a *hardened* criminal ▪ It's so dangerous that even *hardened* journalists won't go there. ✧ If you become ***hardened to*** something, you are no longer saddened or shocked when you see or experience it. ▪ New doctors quickly become *hardened to* the terrible injuries suffered by accident victims.

hard–eyed /ˈhɑɚdˌaɪd/ *adj* [*more ~; most ~*] **:** looking at things in a very critical way without emotion ▪ a *hard-eyed* realist ▪ *hard-eyed* scrutiny

hard–fought *adj* [*more ~; most ~*]
1 : requiring a lot of effort or hard work ▪ He won a *hard-fought* campaign for reelection.
2 : achieved or acquired through a lot of effort or hard work ▪ a *hard-fought* [=*hard-earned*] victory/triumph

hard hat *noun, pl* **~ hats** [*count*] **:** a hat that is worn by workers at a building site to protect their heads from falling objects — see picture at HAT

hard•head•ed /ˈhɑɚdˈhɛdəd/ *adj* [*more ~; most ~*]
1 : not willing to change ideas or opinions **:** very stubborn ▪ He was always *hardheaded* about getting his way. ▪ a *hardheaded* old man
2 : having or involving careful and practical thoughts and ideas that are not influenced by emotions **:** practical and realistic ▪ We need to take a more *hardheaded* approach to these problems. ▪ She gave him some *hardheaded* advice. ▪ a *hardheaded* judgment/analysis
– hard•head•ed•ly *adv* ▪ dealing *hardheadedly* with the facts **– hard•head•ed•ness** *noun* [*noncount*] ▪ the *hardheadedness* of the old man

hard–heart•ed /ˈhɑɚdˈhɑɚtəd/ *adj* [*more ~; most ~*] **:** having or showing no kindness or sympathy for other people ▪ a *hard-hearted* businessman ▪ a *hard-hearted* decision
– hard–heart•ed•ness *noun* [*noncount*]

hard–hit•ting /ˈhɑɚˈhɪtɪŋ/ *adj* [*more ~; most ~*] **:** very effective or forceful ▪ a *hard-hitting* interview/documentary ▪ a *hard-hitting* [=*aggressive*] investigative reporter

hard line *noun* [*singular*] **:** a strict and forceful way of behaving when you are dealing with other people — usually used after *take* ▪ She is known for *taking* a *hard line* with terrorists. [=for dealing with terrorists in a forceful way] ▪ The government has *taken* a *hard line* in treaty negotiations.

– hard–line /ˈhɑɚdˈlaɪn/ *adj* ▪ a *hard-line* [=very strict] conservative **– hard–lin•er** /ˈhɑɚˈlaɪnɚ/ *noun, pl* **-ers** [*count*] ▪ conservative/liberal *hard-liners*

hard–luck /ˈhɑɚdˌlʌk/ *adj, always used before a noun*
1 : of or relating to bad luck ▪ a *hard-luck* story
2 *chiefly US* **:** experiencing or having bad luck ▪ He was the *hard-luck* [=*unlucky*] loser of last night's match.

hard•ly /ˈhɑɚdli/ *adv*
1 a : BARELY, SCARCELY — used to say that something was almost not possible or almost did not happen ▪ She could *hardly* bear to look at him. ▪ I could *hardly* believe my eyes. [=it was difficult to believe what I was seeing] ▪ I can *hardly* believe it! ▪ She was *hardly* able to control her excitement. **b :** almost not at all ▪ We *hardly* knew them. ▪ It *hardly* matters what I think. ▪ The changes in service have *hardly* been noticed. **c :** almost not ▪ There are *hardly* any new features in this software. ▪ *Hardly* anyone showed up for the meeting. ▪ *Hardly* a day goes by when I don't think about you. **d** — used to say that something reached a specifed condition or happened only a short time before ▪ I had *hardly* [=*barely*] arrived when the telephone rang.
2 : certainly not ▪ The news is *hardly* surprising. = The news is *hardly* a surprise. [=the news is not surprising at all] ▪ This is *hardly* a new idea for a movie. ▪ "Is this a new idea for a movie?" "*Hardly*! I've seen dozens of movies just like it."
hardly ever see EVER

hard•ness /ˈhɑɚdnəs/ *noun* [*noncount*] **:** the quality or state of being hard ▪ the *hardness* of a diamond ▪ The wood's *hardness* makes it suitable for carving. ▪ There was a *hardness* [=*toughness*] in her voice I hadn't heard before.

hard–nosed /ˈhɑɚdˈnoʊzd/ *adj* [*more* ~; *most* ~]
1 : very tough ▪ She can be very *hard-nosed* in her business dealings. ▪ a *hard-nosed* football player
2 : not influenced by emotions **:** practical and realistic **:** HARDHEADED ▪ *hard-nosed* science/realism ▪ a *hard-nosed* analysis

hard–on /ˈhɑɚdˌɑːn/ *noun, pl* **-ons** [*count*] *impolite* **:** an erection of the penis

hard–pressed /ˈhɑɚdˈprɛst/ *adj* [*more* ~; *most* ~]
1 — used to say that it is difficult to do something; followed by *to + verb* ▪ You would be *hard-pressed to find* a better solution. [=it would be difficult to find a better solution] ▪ He was *hard-pressed to prove* the claims he'd made.
2 : in a bad situation because you do not have enough money, time, etc. ▪ a financially *hard-pressed* public school system ▪ *hard-pressed* nations/voters/farmers — sometimes + *for* ▪ families that are *hard-pressed for* time/money ▪ He's *hard-pressed for* space [=he does not have much space] in his new apartment.

hard put *adj* [*more* ~; *most* ~] **:** HARD-PRESSED — used to say that it is difficult to do something; followed by *to + verb* ▪ He was *hard put to describe* their musical style. [=it was difficult for him to describe their musical style] ▪ I would be *hard put to find* an explanation. — sometimes used in the phrase ***hard put to it*** ▪ She was *hard put to it* to say what the story was about. [=she found it hard to say what the story was about]

hard rock *noun* [*noncount*] **:** loud rock music that has a heavy regular beat — compare SOFT ROCK

hard rocker *noun, pl* ~ **-ers** [*count*] **:** someone who plays or performs hard rock

hard science *noun, pl* ~ **-ences** [*count, noncount*] **:** a science (such as chemistry, physics, or astronomy) that deals with things that can be observed and measured
– hard scientist *noun, pl* ~ **-ist** [*count*]

hard•scrab•ble /ˈhɑɚdˌskræbəl/ *adj* [*more* ~; *most* ~] *US*
1 : having poor soil ▪ a *hardscrabble* farm ▪ *hardscrabble* prairies
2 : having harsh and difficult conditions because of poverty ▪ a *hardscrabble* childhood ▪ He lived a *hardscrabble* life. ▪ a *hardscrabble* cotton town

hard sell *noun* [*singular*]
1 : an aggressive way of selling something — usually used with *the* ▪ He gives every customer *the hard sell*. — compare SOFT SELL
2 *US* **:** something that is difficult to sell **:** something that others are not willing or likely to accept ▪ Such an expensive project will be a *hard sell* during these slow economic times.

hard•ship /ˈhɑɚdˌʃɪp/ *noun, pl* **-ships**
1 [*noncount*] **:** pain and suffering ▪ He had suffered through considerable/great *hardship*. ▪ The city has been experiencing a period of financial/economic *hardship*.
2 [*count*] **:** something that causes pain, suffering, or loss ▪ They had to endure the *hardships* of life on the frontier.

hard shoulder *noun, pl* ~ **-ders** [*count*] *Brit* **:** [1]SHOULDER 5

hard•top /ˈhɑɚdˌtɑːp/ *noun, pl* **-tops** [*count*] **:** a car that has a metal top which cannot be removed — compare CONVERTIBLE

hard•ware /ˈhɑɚdˌweɚ/ *noun* [*noncount*]
1 : things (such as tools or parts of machines) that are made of metal ▪ a *hardware* store
2 : equipment used for a particular purpose ▪ military *hardware* [=guns, tanks, etc.] *especially* **:** computer equipment ▪ She bought some new *hardware* for her system. — compare SOFTWARE

hard–wearing *adj* [*more* ~; *most* ~] *Brit* **:** lasting for a long time **:** DURABLE ▪ *hard-wearing* boots

hard•wired /ˈhɑɚdˌwajɚd/ *adj* **:** having permanent electronic circuits and connections ▪ a *hardwired* network — often used figuratively ▪ Humans are *hardwired* for speech. = Speech is *hardwired* in/into the human brain. ▪ Mothers are *hardwired* to protect their children.

hard–won /ˈhɑɚdˈwʌn/ *adj* [*more* ~; *most* ~] **:** HARD-EARNED ▪ a *hard-won* victory ▪ our *hard-won* reputation for quality

hard•wood /ˈhɑɚdˌwʊd/ *noun, pl* **-woods**
1 [*count, noncount*] **:** the wood of a tree (such as an oak or maple) that is heavy and hard ▪ They used expensive *hardwoods* for the flooring. — often used before another noun ▪ *hardwood* floors
2 [*count*] **:** a tree that produces hardwood ▪ oaks, maples, and other *hardwoods* — often used before another noun ▪ *hardwood* forests — compare SOFTWOOD

hard•work•ing /ˈhɑɚdˈwɚkɪŋ/ *adj* [*more* ~; *most* ~] **:** using a lot of time and energy to do work **:** INDUSTRIOUS ▪ a *hardworking* young woman [=a young woman who works hard]

har•dy /ˈhɑɚdi/ *adj* **har•di•er; -est**
1 : able to live through difficult conditions (such as a cold winter or a drought) ▪ a *hardy* rose ▪ the *hardiest* plants/animals
2 : strong and able to accept difficult or unpleasant conditions ▪ Most of the soldiers were *hardy* young men. ▪ *Hardy* fans stuck with the team through good times and bad. ▪ Only the *hardiest* pilgrims made the journey.
– har•di•ness /ˈhɑɚdinəs/ *noun* [*noncount*] ▪ the *hardiness* of the rose ▪ cattle bred for *hardiness*

[1]hare /ˈheɚ/ *noun, pl* **hares** *also* **hare** [*count*] **:** a fast animal that resembles a rabbit

[2]hare *verb* **hares; hared; har•ing** [*no obj*] *Brit, informal* **:** to run or go very quickly ▪ He came *haring* round the corner at top speed.

hare•brained /ˈheɚˈbreɪnd/ *adj* [*more* ~; *most* ~] *informal* **:** very silly or foolish ▪ a *harebrained* scheme/idea/plan

hare•lip /ˈheɚˈlɪp/ *noun, pl* **-lips** [*count*] *old-fashioned + often offensive* **:** CLEFT LIP

har•em /ˈherəm/ *noun, pl* **-ems** [*count*]
1 a : a house or part of a house in which the women of a Muslim household live **b :** the women who live in a harem in a Muslim household
2 *informal* **:** a group of women who are associated with one man ▪ the pop star and his *harem*

har•i•cot bean /ˈherɪˌkoʊ-/ *noun, pl* ~ **beans** [*count*] *Brit* **:** NAVY BEAN

hark /ˈhɑɚk/ *verb* **harks; harked; hark•ing** [*no obj*] *old-fashioned + literary* **:** LISTEN — usually used as a command ▪ "*Hark*! I hear a rustling of the leaves." —H. D. Thoreau, *Walden* (1854) ▪ "*Hark*, she speaks!" —Shakespeare, *Macbeth* (1605–06)
hark back to [*phrasal verb*] ***hark back to (something)*** **1 :** to return to or remember (something in the past) ▪ He always *harks back to* the good old days of his youth. **2 :** to look or seem like (something in the past) ▪ The movie has a style that *harks back to* the golden age of Hollywood.

har•le•quin /ˈhɑɚlɪkwən/ *noun, pl* **-quins** [*count*]
1 : a pattern of diamond-shaped figures of different colors — usually used before another noun ▪ fabric decorated with a *harlequin* pattern ▪ *harlequin* ice cream
2 *or* ***Harlequin*** **:** a comic character in old stories and plays who wears a mask and colorful clothes with a diamond pattern

H

har·lot /ˈhɑɚlət/ *noun, pl* **-lots** [*count*] *old-fashioned + disapproving* : PROSTITUTE

[1]**harm** /ˈhɑɚm/ *noun* [*noncount*] : physical or mental damage or injury : something that causes someone or something to be hurt, broken, made less valuable or successful, etc. ▪ No *harm* was done. ▪ I never meant to do/cause you any *harm*. [=I never meant to harm/hurt you in any way] ▪ They threatened him with bodily *harm*. ▪ The scandal has done irreparable/lasting/great *harm* to his reputation. ▪ I want to be sure that no *harm* will come to her. = I want to be sure that she won't come to any *harm*. [=that she won't be hurt in any way] ▪ She'll do anything to protect her children from *harm*. ▪ They have suffered serious physical/psychological *harm*. ▪ These new regulations could cause lasting *harm* to small businesses. ▪ He claims that he didn't mean any *harm*. [=that he didn't mean to hurt or bother anyone] ▪ What's the *harm* in letting her leave early? = I don't see any *harm* in letting her leave early. = There's no *harm* in letting her leave early. [=letting her leave early will not hurt anyone or cause a bad result] ▪ He thinks the treatment may ***do more harm than good*** [=be more harmful than helpful]

harm's way : a dangerous place or situation ▪ As a war correspondent, she never hesitated to put herself in *harm's way*. ▪ The soldiers were sent into *harm's way*. ▪ The tug towed the sailboat out of *harm's way*.

no harm done *informal* — used to tell someone that no apology or concern is necessary because no damage has been done ▪ "I'm so sorry about forgetting to call earlier." "That's OK. *No harm done*."

[2]**harm** *verb* **harms; harmed; harm·ing** [+ *obj*] : to cause hurt, injury, or damage to (someone or something) : to cause harm to (someone or something) ▪ He would never intentionally *harm* his children. ▪ She is trying to destroy weeds without *harming* [=*damaging*] her crops. ▪ chemicals that could *harm* the environment ▪ The scandal has seriously *harmed* his reputation. ***synonyms*** see INJURE

harm·ful /ˈhɑɚmfəl/ *adj* [*more* ~; *most* ~] : causing or capable of causing damage or harm ▪ The chemical kills *harmful* [=*dangerous*] bacteria. ▪ They claim that the drug has no *harmful* [=*bad*] side effects. — often + *to* ▪ These conditions can be *harmful to* plant/animal life.

— **harm·ful·ly** *adv* — **harm·ful·ness** *noun* [*noncount*]

harm·less /ˈhɑɚmləs/ *adj* [*more* ~; *most* ~] : not causing harm : unable to cause harm : not dangerous ▪ a *harmless* snake ▪ His ideas seem *harmless* enough. : not meant to cause harm or offense ▪ We're just having a bit of *harmless* fun. ▪ It was just a *harmless* joke. — sometimes + *to* ▪ These chemicals are deadly to insects but they are supposed to be *harmless to* animals and people.

— **harm·less·ly** *adv* ▪ The incident began *harmlessly* enough but soon escalated into a riot. — **harm·less·ness** *noun* [*noncount*]

har·mon·ic /hɑɚˈmɑːnɪk/ *adj, technical* : of or relating to musical harmony rather than melody or rhythm ▪ two different *harmonic* styles

— **har·mon·i·cal·ly** /hɑɚˈmɑːnɪkli/ *adv* ▪ a piece that is *harmonically* simple but melodically complex

har·mon·i·ca /hɑɚˈmɑːnɪkə/ *noun, pl* **-cas** [*count*] : a small musical instrument that is played with your mouth ✧ A harmonica has many small openings that produce different sounds when air is blown or sucked through them.

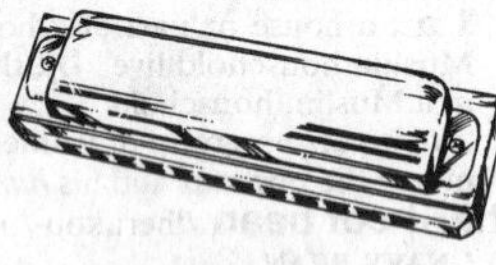
harmonica

har·mo·ni·ous /hɑɚˈmounijəs/ *adj* [*more* ~; *most* ~]

1 *music* : having a pleasing mixture or combination of notes ▪ a *harmonious* song ▪ *harmonious* voices

2 : having parts that are related or combined in a pleasing way ▪ The living room was decorated in *harmonious* colors. ▪ a *harmonious* combination of flavors

3 : not experiencing disagreement or fighting ▪ a *harmonious* family ▪ The two countries have maintained a *harmonious* [=friendly and peaceful] relationship for many years. ▪ *harmonious* relations

— **har·mo·ni·ous·ly** *adv* ▪ Their voices blended together *harmoniously*. ▪ flavors/colors blending with each other *harmoniously* ▪ people living together *harmoniously* — **har·mo·ni·ous·ness** *noun* [*noncount*] ▪ the *harmoniousness* of their voices

har·mo·nize *also Brit* **har·mo·nise** /ˈhɑɚməˌnaɪz/ *verb* **-niz·es; -nized; -niz·ing**

1 [*no obj*] : to play or sing different musical notes that sound pleasing together : to play or sing in harmony ▪ A group of singers were *harmonizing* on the street corner.

2 [*no obj*] : to be combined or go together in a pleasing way : to be in harmony ▪ The flavors *harmonize* (with one another) beautifully. ▪ Their beliefs did not always *harmonize*.

3 [+ *obj*] : to cause (two or more things) to be combined or to go together in a pleasing or effective way ▪ The singers *harmonized* their voices beautifully. ▪ a recipe that *harmonizes* flavors from different parts of the world ▪ The background music is not *harmonized* with the action on-screen.

— **har·mo·ni·za·tion** *also Brit* **har·mo·ni·sa·tion** /ˌhɑɚmənəˈzeɪʃən, *Brit* ˌhɑːməˌnaɪˈzeɪʃən/ *noun* [*noncount*]

har·mo·ny /ˈhɑɚməni/ *noun, pl* **-nies**

1 : the combination of different musical notes played or sung at the same time to produce a pleasing sound [*noncount*] She taught him how to sing *harmony*. [=how to sing notes that combined with other notes in a pleasing way] — often used after *in* ▪ She taught him to sing *in harmony*. ▪ They sang *in* perfect *harmony*. [*count*] a song with complicated *harmonies* and rhythms

2 [*singular*] : a pleasing combination or arrangement of different things ▪ a *harmony* of flavors/colors ✧ When things are ***in harmony*** or when one thing is ***in harmony with*** something else, they go together well or they agree with each other very well. ▪ Every part was moving *in* perfect *harmony*. ▪ The two machines are linked and working *in harmony*. ▪ That principle is not *in harmony with* our ideals. ✧ When people are ***in harmony*** or ***in harmony with*** each other, they live together in a peaceful and friendly way. ▪ She lives *in harmony with* her neighbors. ✧ To bring something ***into harmony with*** something else is to change it so that it agrees with or matches something else. ▪ Our proposal has been revised to bring it *into harmony with* their requirements. ✧ When things are ***out of harmony*** or when one thing is ***out of harmony with*** something else, they do not agree or combine well. ▪ The modern furnishings seem *out of harmony with* the Victorian architecture. ▪ The governor's statement is totally *out of harmony with* the mayor's earlier comments.

[1]**har·ness** /ˈhɑɚnəs/ *noun, pl* **-ness·es** [*count*]

1 : a set of straps that are placed on an animal (such as a horse) so that it can pull something heavy

2 : a set of straps that are used to connect a person to something (such as a parachute or a seat) ▪ The pilot strapped himself into his *harness* before takeoff. ▪ a safety *harness*

in harness *Brit* : working at a job : on duty ▪ I was back *in harness* on Monday, handling paperwork at my desk.

[2]**harness** *verb* **-ness·es; -nessed; -ness·ing** [+ *obj*]

1 a : to put a harness on (an animal) ▪ *harness* the horses **b** : to attach (an animal) to something with a harness ▪ The horses were *harnessed* to the wagon.

2 : to use (something) for a particular purpose ▪ Engineers are finding new ways to *harness* the sun's energy to heat homes. ▪ The company is *harnessing* technology to provide better service to its customers. ▪ They *harnessed* the power of the waterfall to create electricity. ▪ *harness* anger to fight injustice

3 : to connect or join (things) together ▪ She *harnessed* several computers (together) to work as one large computer.

harness racing *noun* [*noncount*] *US* : the sport of racing two-wheeled carts that are pulled by horses

[1]**harp** /ˈhɑɚp/ *noun, pl* **harps** [*count*] : a musical instrument that has strings stretched across a large open frame and that is played with your fingers ▪ pluck/play a *harp* — see picture at STRINGED INSTRUMENT

— **harp·ist** /ˈhɑɚpɪst/ *noun, pl* **-ists** [*count*] ▪ a talented *harpist*

[2]**harp** *verb* **harps; harped; harp·ing**

harp at [*phrasal verb*] ***harp at (someone)*** *US, informal* : to tell (someone) constantly or repeatedly to do something ▪ My mother was always *harping at* me to clean my room.

harp on [*phrasal verb*] *US* ***harp on (something)*** *or Brit* ***harp on about (something)*** *informal* : to talk about (a subject) constantly or repeatedly in an annoying way ▪ She's always *harping on* the importance of a good diet. ▪ He seems to enjoy *harping on* my shortcomings.

har·poon /hɑɚˈpuːn/ *noun, pl* **-poons** [*count*] : a long weapon used especially for hunting large fish or whales

— **harpoon** /hɑɚˈpuːn/ *verb* **-poons; -pooned; -poon·ing** [+ *obj*] ▪ They *harpooned* the whale. [=killed the whale with a harpoon] – **har·poon·er** *noun, pl* **-ers** [*count*]

harp·si·chord /ˈhɑɚpsɪˌkoɚd/ *noun, pl* **-chords** [*count*] **:** a musical instrument that is similar to a piano but with strings that are plucked rather than struck — see picture at KEYBOARD

– **harp·si·chord·ist** /ˈhɑɚpsɪˌkoɚdɪst/ *noun, pl* **-ists** [*count*] ▪ a famous *harpsichordist*

har·py /ˈhɑɚpi/ *noun, pl* **-pies** [*count*]

1 ***Harpy*** **: an evil creature in Greek mythology that is part woman and part bird**

2 : an angry and unpleasant woman : SHREW

har·ri·dan /ˈherədən/ *noun, pl* **-dans** [*count*] *old-fashioned + literary* **: an angry and unpleasant woman : HARPY, SHREW**

har·ried /ˈherid/ *adj* [*more ~; most ~*] **: bothered by many problems or worries : very worried or anxious** ▪ *harried* shoppers/travelers

har·ri·er /ˈherijɚ/ *noun, pl* **-ers** [*count*] **: a type of hawk**

har·row·ing /ˈherowɪŋ/ *adj* [*more ~; most ~*] **: very painful or upsetting** ▪ She gives a *harrowing* account/description of her battle with cancer. ▪ They managed to escape after several *harrowing* encounters with the enemy. ▪ a *harrowing* ordeal/experience

– **har·row·ing·ly** *adv* ▪ a *harrowingly* honest description

har·rumph /həˈrʌmf/ *verb* **-rumphs; -rumphed; -rumph·ing** *informal* **: to say (something) in a disapproving or complaining way — used to suggest that the person who is speaking is very serious, pompous, etc.** [+ *obj*] "These charges are absurd," he *harrumphed.* [*no obj*] They stood around *harrumphing* about the current state of politics.

harsh /ˈhɑɚʃ/ *adj* **harsh·er; -est** [*also more ~; most ~*]

1 a : unpleasant and difficult to accept or experience ▪ The climate there is very *harsh.* ▪ We've had an extremely *harsh* winter. ▪ a *harsh* environment ▪ It's time for her to face the *harsh* realities of this situation. ▪ The accident serves as a *harsh* reminder of the importance of wearing a seat belt. **b : having an unpleasant or harmful effect because of great strength or force : too intense or powerful** ▪ *harsh* colors ▪ a *harsh* [=*shrill*] whistle/voice ▪ The lighting in the room was very *harsh.* ▪ *harsh* chemicals/detergents

2 a : severe or cruel : not kind ▪ *harsh* discipline ▪ a *harsh* disciplinarian ▪ The state has established *harsh* penalties for drug dealers. ▪ She has been criticized for her *harsh* treatment of his students. ▪ He was sentenced to a *harsh* prison term. **b : very critical : strongly negative** ▪ He had *harsh* words for his opponent. ▪ *harsh* language ▪ She has faced some extremely *harsh* criticism. ▪ He has been one of her *harshest* critics.

– **harsh·ly** *adv* [*more ~; most ~*] ▪ She promised to deal *harshly* with all criminals. ▪ He treats his students *harshly.* ▪ The room was *harshly* lit. – **harsh·ness** *noun* [*noncount*]

hart /ˈhɑɚt/ *noun, pl* **harts** [*count*] *chiefly Brit* **: a male deer : STAG;** *especially* **: a male red deer** — compare ²HIND

¹har·vest /ˈhɑɚvəst/ *noun, pl* **-vests** [*count*]

1 : the season when crops are gathered from the fields or the activity of gathering crops ▪ The beginning of the *harvest* varies from year to year. ▪ It is time for the *harvest.* ▪ *harvest* time

2 : the amount of crops that are gathered ▪ They prayed for a bountiful *harvest.* ▪ We had enormous *harvests* of corn this year.; *also* **: the amount of a natural product gathered in a single season** ▪ the salmon/timber *harvest* — sometimes used figuratively ▪ The government will reap a bitter *harvest* of discontent [=many people will be extremely unhappy and angry] if it fails to meet the people's needs.

²harvest /ˈhɑɚvəst/ *verb* **-vests; -vest·ed; -vest·ing** [+ *obj*]

1 : to gather (a crop) ▪ It is time to *harvest* the wheat.

2 : to gather or collect (something) for use ▪ They want to *harvest* timber in these woods. — sometimes used figuratively ▪ She has *harvested* the rewards/fruits of her labors.

har·vest·er /ˈhɑɚvəstɚ/ *noun, pl* **-ers** [*count*]

1 : a person who gathers crops or other natural products

2 : a large machine that is used for harvesting crops

harvest moon *noun* [*singular*] **: the full moon in autumn**

has see HAVE

has–been /ˈhæzˌbɪn/ *noun, pl* **-beens** [*count*] *informal* **: a person who is no longer popular or successful** ▪ They called him a washed-up old *has-been.* ▪ a famous child actor who had become a *has-been* at 25 — often used before another noun ▪ a *has-been* singer

¹hash /ˈhæʃ/ *verb* **hash·es; hashed; hash·ing**

hash out [*phrasal verb*] *US, informal* ***hash out (something)*** *or* ***hash (something) out*** **1** *or* ***hash over (something)*** *or* ***hash (something) over*** **: to talk about (something)** ▪ The detectives *hashed out* their theories about who committed the murder. ▪ They've spent quite a bit of time *hashing over* the problem. ▪ We need to sit down and *hash* things *out.* [=talk about things; discuss the situation] **2 a : to find (a solution) by talking** ▪ Their lawyers *hashed out* a resolution. **b : to solve (a problem) by talking** ▪ We were finally able to *hash out* our differences.

²hash *noun, pl* **hashes** [*count, noncount*] **: a dish of chopped meat mixed with potatoes and baked or fried** ▪ corned beef *hash*

make a hash of *informal* **: to ruin (something) by making many mistakes** ▪ He *made a hash* of the whole project!

– compare ³HASH, ⁴HASH

³hash *noun* [*noncount*] *informal* **: HASHISH** — compare ²HASH, ⁴HASH

⁴hash *noun, pl* **hashes** [*count*] *Brit* **: ³POUND** — compare ²HASH, ³HASH

hash browns *noun* [*plural*] **: boiled potatoes that have been cut up, mixed with chopped onions and fat, and fried until brown** — called also *hash brown potatoes, hashed brown potatoes, hashed browns*

hash·ish /ˈhæˌʃiːʃ, hæˈʃiːʃ/ *noun* [*noncount*] **: an illegal drug that comes from the hemp plant and that is usually smoked or chewed**

hash sign *noun, pl* **~ signs** [*count*] *Brit* **: ³POUND**

hasn't /ˈhæzn̩t/ — used as a contraction of *has not* ▪ The mail *hasn't* arrived yet.

hasp /ˈhæsp, *Brit* ˈhɑːsp/ *noun, pl* **hasps** [*count*] **: a device that is used to fasten a door, lid, etc.** ✧ A hasp is a metal strap that fits over a metal loop and is held by a pin or lock.

¹has·sle /ˈhæsəl/ *verb* **has·sles; has·sled; has·sling** *informal*

1 [+ *obj*] **: to bother or annoy (someone) constantly or repeatedly** ▪ Other kids were always *hassling* her because she was overweight. ▪ I'm sick of being *hassled* by telemarketers.

2 [*no obj*] *US* **: to argue or fight** ▪ I don't have time to *hassle* with you about this! Just do what I tell you to do!

²hassle *noun, pl* **hassles** [*count*] *informal*

1 : something that is annoying or that causes trouble ▪ All this paperwork is a *hassle.* ▪ They've had to deal with flight delays and all of the other *hassles* of holiday travel. ▪ Cooking is too much of a *hassle* tonight. [=it is too much trouble; I do not have enough time, energy, etc., to do it]

2 *US* **: a fight or argument** ▪ He got into a *hassle* with his landlord.

has·sock /ˈhæsək/ *noun, pl* **-socks** [*count*]

1 : a cushion that you kneel on while praying

2 *US* **: a cushion or soft stool that is used as a seat or for resting your feet** ▪ a sofa and *hassock* [=(more commonly) *ottoman*]

haste /ˈheɪst/ *noun* [*noncount*] **: speed of motion or action : quickness or eagerness that can result in mistakes** ▪ The application had been approved with undue *haste.* — often used with *in* ▪ He left *in haste* [=*hurriedly, in a hurry*], so I didn't get a chance to talk to him. ▪ She sent the letter *in haste* and later regretted it. ▪ *In* their *haste* to leave for the airport, they forgot their passports.

haste makes waste *US* — used to say that doing something too quickly causes mistakes that result in time, effort, materials, etc., being wasted

make haste *old-fashioned* **: to move, act, or go quickly : HURRY** ▪ "You will be too late, if you do not *make haste.*" —Jane Austen, *Persuasion* (1817)

has·ten /ˈheɪsn̩/ *verb* **has·tens; has·tened; has·ten·ing**

1 [+ *obj*] **: to cause (something) to happen more quickly** ▪ A factory was built, *hastening* [=*accelerating*] the town's growth. ▪ His death was *hastened* by alcohol abuse.

2 [*no obj*] *old-fashioned* **: to move or act quickly** ▪ When she heard the baby crying, she *hastened* [=*hurried*] up the stairs.

hasten to add/say/explain (etc.) **: to immediately say something in order to prevent confusion or misunderstanding** ▪ The company announced that the initial tests look promising, but they *hastened to add* that there is still much more testing to be done. ▪ Let me *hasten to point out* that these changes will not affect our existing clients.

hasty /ˈheɪsti/ *adj* **hast·i·er; -est** [*also more ~; most ~*]

1 a : done or made very quickly ▪ I made a *hasty* sketch of the scene. ▪ Seeing the dog, the cat made/beat a *hasty* retreat up a tree. **b : done or made too quickly** ▪ We don't want to make any *hasty* decisions. ▪ a *hasty* marriage

2 : acting too quickly : RASH ▪ He later realized that he was

too *hasty* in his decision to quit.
– hast·i·ly /ˈheɪstəli/ *adv* ▪ She *hastily* gathered her things and left. ▪ a *hastily* made decision **– hast·i·ness** *noun* [*noncount*] ▪ the *hastiness* [=*haste*] of his decision

hat /ˈhæt/ *noun, pl* **hats** [*count*] : a covering for the head that often has a brim and a rounded or flat top ▪ a straw *hat* — see also COWBOY HAT, HARD HAT, TOP HAT
at the drop of a hat see [1]DROP
hang your hat ✧ The place where you *hang your hat* is the place where you live or stay. ▪ I'm looking for a new place to *hang my hat*.
hat in hand see [1]HAND
***hats off to** informal* — used to give praise or credit to someone ▪ *Hats off to* Susan for doing such a great job.
I'll eat my hat see EAT
keep (something) under your hat : to keep (something) secret : to not tell anyone about (something) ▪ I'll tell you what happened, but you have to *keep it under your hat*.
pass the hat : to collect money usually for a particular purpose ▪ They *passed the hat* at one of their meetings and collected almost $200. ▪ *passing the hat* for families affected by the disaster
***take your hat off to** informal* : to give (someone) praise or credit ▪ I (have to) *take my hat off to* her. She did a great job.
talk through your hat see [1]TALK
throw/toss your hat in/into the ring : to announce that you are going to try to win a contest (such as an election) ▪ Yet another candidate has *thrown his hat into the ring*.
tip your hat see [1]TIP
wear many hats : to have many jobs or roles ▪ She *wears many hats*: she's a doctor, a musician, and a writer.
— see also OLD HAT

hat·band /ˈhæt,bænd/ *noun, pl* **-bands** [*count*] : a decorative piece of cloth that goes around the base of some hats

hat·box /ˈhæt,bɑːks/ *noun, pl* **-box·es** [*count*] : a round container for storing or carrying hats

[1]**hatch** /ˈhætʃ/ *noun, pl* **hatch·es** [*count*]
1 a : an opening in the deck of a ship or in the floor, wall, or roof of a building ▪ He squeezed into/through the *hatch* and crawled below deck. **b** : the covering of such an opening ▪ He lifted the *hatch*.
2 : a small door or opening in an airplane or spaceship — see also ESCAPE HATCH
batten down the hatches see [1]BATTEN
***down the hatch** informal* ✧ If something goes *down the hatch*, you swallow it. ▪ a whiskey that goes *down the hatch* smoothly

[2]**hatch** *verb* **hatches; hatched; hatch·ing**
1 a [*no obj*] *of a bird, insect, fish, etc.* : to come out of an egg : to be born by coming out of an egg ▪ We watched the chicks *hatch*. **b** [+ *obj*] : to cause (a young bird, insect, fish, etc.) to come out of an egg — usually used as *(be) hatched* ▪ newly *hatched* chicks
2 a [*no obj*] *of an egg* : to break open as a young bird, insect, fish, etc., is born ▪ The eggs will soon *hatch*. **b** [+ *obj*] : to cause (an egg) to hatch ▪ a hen *hatching* her eggs
3 [+ *obj*] : to create or produce (something, such as an idea or a plan) usually in a secret way ▪ They *hatched* a plot to overthrow the government. ▪ *hatch* (up) a scheme

hatch·back /ˈhætʃ,bæk/ *noun, pl* **-backs** [*count*] : a door that opens upward on the back of a car; *also* : a car that has such a door — see picture at CAR

hatch·ery /ˈhætʃəri/ *noun, pl* **-eries** [*count*] : a place where people raise young chicken, fish, etc., from eggs ▪ a salmon *hatchery*

hatch·et /ˈhætʃət/ *noun, pl* **-ets** [*count*] : a small ax that has a short handle
bury the hatchet : to agree to stop arguing or fighting : to end a disagreement and become friendly ▪ After all these years, they've finally *buried the hatchet*.

hatchet job *noun, pl* **~ jobs** [*count*] *informal* : a very harsh and unfair spoken or written attack ▪ The reviewers did a *hatchet job* on her latest book. [=the reviewers criticized her latest book very harshly or unfairly]

hatchet man *noun, pl* **~ men** [*count*] : a person whose job is to do harsh and unpleasant things that other people do not want to do ▪ She doesn't criticize her opponent's character directly. She has her *hatchet men* in the media do it for her. ▪ He was fired by his boss's *hatchet man*.

hatch·ling /ˈhætʃlɪŋ/ *noun, pl* **-lings** [*count*] : a recently hatched animal : a very young bird, fish, etc., that has just come out from an egg

hatch·way /ˈhætʃ,weɪ/ *noun, pl* **-ways** [*count*] : an opening or passage into an enclosed space (such as a cellar or an attic)

[1]**hate** /ˈheɪt/ *noun, pl* **hates** : a very strong feeling of dislike [*noncount*] You could see the *hate* [=*hatred*] in his eyes. ▪ These crimes are motivated by prejudice and *hate*. [*count*] They have been unable to overcome their *hates* and fears.— sometimes used before another noun ▪ The organization gets a lot of ***hate mail*** [=extremely angry letters, e-mail, etc.] from people who disagree with their policies. ▪ a ***hate crime*** [=a crime done against someone because of the person's race, religion, etc.] ▪ ***Hate speech*** [=speech expressing hatred of a particular group of people] is not allowed at school. — opposite LOVE

[2]**hate** *verb* **hates; hat·ed; hat·ing**
1 : to dislike (someone) very strongly : to feel hate for (someone) [+ *obj*] He was a cruel tyrant who was *hated* and feared by his people. ▪ She *hated* them for betraying her. ▪ They were political rivals who truly/bitterly *hated* each other. ▪ What is it that you *hate* about him most? ▪ a *hated* ene-

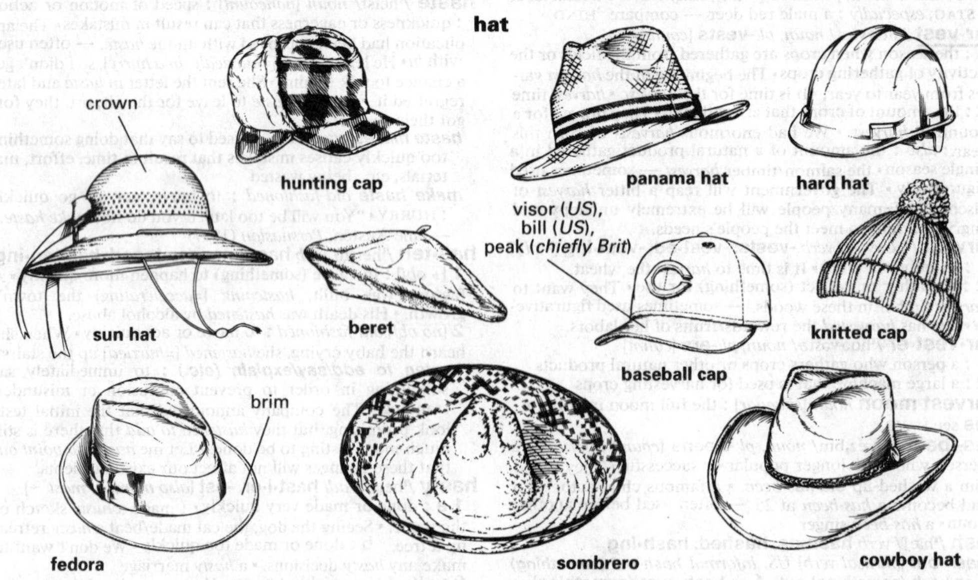

my *[no obj]* children whose families have taught them to *hate* — opposite LOVE

2 *[+ obj]* **:** to dislike (something) very strongly **:** to find (something) very unpleasant ▪ She *hates* [=really dislikes] cold weather. ▪ I *hate* spinach. ▪ I *hate* doing this. ▪ I *hate* having to do this. = I *hate* it when I have to do this. ▪ They *hate* being apart from each other. ▪ I *hate* the idea of leaving my mother alone all week. ▪ She *hates* cooking. — often followed by *to + verb* ▪ They *hate to be* apart from each other. ▪ She *hates to cook*. — opposite LOVE

3 *[+ obj]* — used to apologize for doing something or to express regret or guilt ▪ I *hate* bothering you [=I'm sorry to bother you], but would you mind moving your car? ▪ I'd *hate* it if they got the wrong idea. [=I would feel regret if they misunderstood] — often followed by *to + verb* ▪ I *hate to bother* you [=I'm sorry to bother you], but would you mind moving your car? ▪ I *hate to say* it, but I don't think he has much chance of winning. ▪ I'd *hate* (for) them *to get* the wrong idea.

hate someone's guts see [1]GUT

– hat·er *noun, pl* **-ers** *[count]* ▪ a cat *hater* [=a person who hates cats]

hate·ful /ˈheɪtfəl/ *adj [more ~; most ~]*

1 : very bad or evil **:** causing or deserving hate ▪ a *hateful* crime

2 : full of hate ▪ *hateful* enemies/people **:** showing hate ▪ *hateful* comments/words

– hate·ful·ly *adv* ▪ It's not clear if the comments were meant *hatefully* or not. **– hate·ful·ness** *noun [noncount]* ▪ the *hatefulness* of the crime

hat·mak·er /ˈhætˌmeɪkɚ/ *noun, pl* **-ers** *[count]* **:** a person whose job is to make hats

hat·pin /ˈhætˌpɪn/ *noun, pl* **-pins** *[count]* **:** a kind of pin used especially in the past by women to fasten hats to their hair

ha·tred /ˈheɪtrəd/ *noun, pl* **-treds :** a very strong feeling of dislike **:** HATE *[noncount]* He had an irrational fear and *hatred* of foreigners. ▪ She makes no attempt to conceal her *hatred* for her opponents. ▪ This troubled city is filled with *hatred*, prejudice, crime, and fear. *[count]* The war was fueled by *hatreds* that were centuries old.

hat·ter /ˈhætɚ/ *noun, pl* **-ters** *[count]* **:** a person who makes, sells, or repairs hats

mad as a hatter *informal + old-fashioned* **:** severely mentally ill **:** CRAZY ▪ He's a nice fellow, but *mad as a hatter*.

hat trick *noun, pl* **~ tricks** *[count]* **:** three goals scored by one player in a game of ice hockey, soccer, etc. ▪ score a *hat trick* — often used figuratively ▪ She scored a *hat trick* when her last three novels all won prizes.

haugh·ty /ˈhɑːti/ *adj* **haugh·ti·er; -est :** having or showing the insulting attitude of people who think that they are better, smarter, or more important than other people ▪ *haughty* [=*arrogant*] aristocrats ▪ He rejected their offer with a tone of *haughty* disdain. ▪ a *haughty* attitude

– haugh·ti·ly /ˈhɑːtəli/ *adv* ▪ *haughtily* disdainful **– haugh·ti·ness** /ˈhɑːtinəs/ *noun [noncount]*

[1]**haul** /ˈhɑːl/ *verb* **hauls; hauled; haul·ing** *[+ obj]*

1 *always followed by an adverb or preposition* **a :** to pull or drag (something) with effort ▪ *Haul* the ropes in. = *Haul* in the ropes. ▪ They *hauled* the boat up onto the beach. ▪ The car was *hauled* away/off to the junkyard. **b :** to move or carry (something) with effort ▪ We used buckets to *haul* water up from the river. ▪ She *hauled* herself to her feet and limped home. ▪ I'm tired of *hauling* this heavy camera around with me.

2 *always followed by an adverb or preposition* **:** to force (someone) to go or come to a place ▪ The police caught him and *hauled* him (in) to the station. ▪ The prisoner was *hauled* away in handcuffs. ▪ They *hauled* her off to court/jail.

3 : to carry (someone or something) in a vehicle ▪ The cattle were *hauled* by rail. ▪ The company has a fleet of trucks that are used to *haul* freight.

haul ass *US, informal + impolite* **:** to move quickly ▪ You'd better *haul ass* or you'll miss your flight.

haul in *[phrasal verb]* ***haul in (something) or haul (something) in*** *US, sports* **:** to catch (a ball or pass) ▪ He *hauled in* a long touchdown pass.

haul off and *US, informal* **:** to suddenly do (something specified) — followed by a verb that expresses some kind of usually violent action ▪ She *hauled off and* punched him in the face.

haul on *[phrasal verb]* ***haul on (something)*** **:** to forcefully pull (something) ▪ *haul on* the reins

haul over the coals see COAL

– haul·er *(US)* /ˈhɑːlɚ/ *or Brit* **haul·i·er** /ˈhɑːlijɚ/ *noun, pl* **-ers** *[count]* ▪ cattle *haulers*

[2]**haul** *noun, pl* **hauls** *[count]*

1 : the act of pulling or dragging something with effort **:** the act of hauling something ▪ each *haul* of the rope

2 : a usually large amount of something that has been stolen, collected, or won ▪ a burglar's *haul* ▪ Authorities seized the drugs in one of the biggest drug *hauls* in the history of the county. ▪ The kids always collect a substantial *haul* of candy on Halloween.

3 : a distance to be traveled ▪ It's just a short *haul* from our cabin to the beach. — see also LONG HAUL

haunch /ˈhɑːntʃ/ *noun, pl* **haunch·es** *[count]* **:** the upper part of a person's or animal's leg; *especially* **:** the upper part of an animal's rear leg used as meat ▪ a *haunch* of venison

on your haunches **:** sitting on or close to your heels with your knees bent ▪ The girl was sitting/squatting *on her haunches* in the sand, searching for shells.

[1]**haunt** /ˈhɑːnt/ *verb* **haunts; haunt·ed; haunt·ing** *[+ obj]*

1 *of a ghost* **:** to visit or live in (a place) ▪ Spirits *haunted* the house. ▪ Some people believe that the ghost of an old sea captain *haunts* the beach.

2 : to eventually cause problems for (someone) as time passes ▪ If you ignore the problem, it will ***come back to haunt you***. ▪ Their failure to plan ahead is now *coming back to haunt them*.

3 : to keep coming back to the mind of (someone) especially in a way that makes the person sad or upset ▪ The tune *haunted* me all day. ▪ He was *haunted* by his memories of the war. [=he could not forget his memories of the war]

4 : to visit (a place) often ▪ She spent much of her vacation *haunting* bookstores and antique shops.

[2]**haunt** *noun, pl* **haunts** *[count]* **:** a place that you go to often ▪ The restaurant became one of her favorite *haunts*. ▪ I went back to visit my old childhood *haunts*. [=the places I often went to when I was a child]

haunted *adj*

1 : lived in or visited by ghosts ▪ Everyone says that the inn is *haunted*. ▪ a *haunted* house

2 : troubled or upset ▪ a mysterious young woman who always has a *haunted* expression on her face

haunting *adj [more ~; most ~]* **:** sad or beautiful in a way that is difficult to forget ▪ The old prison camp is a *haunting* reminder of the country's dark past. ▪ the *haunting* sounds of the violin ▪ the *haunting* beauty of her voice

– haunt·ing·ly *adv* ▪ her *hauntingly* beautiful voice

haute cou·ture /ˌoutkuˈtuɚ, *Brit* ˌəʊtkuˈtjʊə/ *noun [noncount] somewhat formal* **:** the people and companies that create clothes that are very expensive and fashionable; *also* **:** the clothes they create ▪ a fashion designer who's a renowned master of *haute couture* ▪ celebrities wearing *haute couture* ▪ *haute couture* fashions/designers/models

haute cui·sine /ˌoutkwɪˈziːn/ *noun [singular]* **:** cooking that is done in a very skillful and complicated way

have /ˈhæv, əv; *in "have to" meaning "must" usually* ˈhæf/ *verb* **has** /ˈhæz, əz; *in "has to" meaning "must" usually* ˈhæs/; **had** /ˈhæd, əd/; **hav·ing** /ˈhævɪŋ/ ✧ For many senses of *have*, the phrase *have got* can also be used. Each sense, idiom, or phrasal verb below in which this phrase can occur includes the note "—also ***have got***." See "have got" (below) for more information.

1 *not used in progressive tenses [+ obj]* **a :** to own, use, or hold (something) ▪ Do they *have* a new car? ▪ You can *have* it until I get back. ▪ She *has* a red bike, and I *have* a blue one. ▪ She got another part-time job and now she *has* two jobs. ▪ I'm looking for the newspaper. Do you *have* it? ▪ He *had* the newspaper right in his hand. ▪ I used to *have* a necklace like that, but I lost it. ▪ She used to share a room with her sister, but now she *has* her own room. — also used for things that cannot be seen or touched ▪ Do you *have* an appointment? ▪ Do you *have* any experience in this line of work? [=have you done this kind of work before?] ▪ She *has* so many things that she wants to do. ▪ They *have* a deadline that must be met. — also ***have got*** ▪ *Have* they *got* a new car? ▪ She*'s got* two jobs. ▪ *Have* you *got* it? ▪ I*'ve got* an appointment. — see also MUST-HAVE **b** ✧ If you ***have (something) to do, finish (etc.)***, there is something that you must do or want to do in order to complete a task. ▪ We *have* things *to do*. = (*chiefly Brit*) We*'ve* things *to do*. ▪ I *have* several more pages *to read*. ▪ She *has* six more rows *to knit*. ▪ "But I *have* promises *to keep* . . ." —Robert Frost, "Stopping by Woods on a Snowy Evening" (1923) — also ***have got*** ▪ We*'ve got* things *to do*.

H

2 *not used in progressive tenses* [+ *obj*] — used to say that something is available or not available • They *had* nothing to eat or drink, nothing to wear, and nowhere to live. • We didn't want to do it, but we *had* no choice/alternative. • You *have* a tremendous opportunity, and you should make the most of it. • The group will *have* enough tickets for everyone. • Do you *have* any spare change? • Do you ***have a minute/moment/second***? [=are you available for a short time right now?] I have a few things I'd like to discuss with you. • Give me a call when you ***have a few minutes/moments***. [=when you have a short period of time available] • I don't ***have the time*** to talk right now. [=I am too busy to talk right now] — also ***have got*** • I ***haven't got the time*** to talk right now. • ***Have*** you ***got a minute/moment/second***? — see also HAVE THE TIME (below)
3 *not used in progressive tenses* [+ *obj*] — used to describe a quality, skill, feature, etc., of a person or thing • She *has* an impressive knowledge of French. [=she knows French very well] • He *has* a way with words. [=he uses words/language very effectively] • She *has* a good outlook on life. • The car *has* power brakes. • That country *has* a king; this country *has* a president. • All the children in that family *have* red hair. • A man who *had* a foreign accent [=a man with a foreign accent] was asking to see you. • The museum *has* interesting exhibits. • I *have* a fear of spiders. [=I am afraid of spiders] — also ***have got*** • He*'s got* a way with words. • The car*'s got* power brakes.
4 *not used in progressive tenses* [+ *obj*] **:** to include or contain (something or someone) • The list *has* my name on it. [=my name is on the list] • April *has* 30 days. [=there are 30 days in April; April is a month with 30 days] • The club *has* 100 members. — also ***have got*** • The list *has got* my name on it. • The club*'s got* 100 members.
5 [+ *obj*] **a :** to give birth to (a child) • She *had* her first child when she was 25. • She's going to be *having* another baby soon. **b** *not used in progressive tenses* **:** to be the parent of (a child) • She and her husband *have* three children. • They *have* a son. — also ***have got*** • They*'ve got* a son and a daughter.
6 *not used in progressive tenses* [+ *obj*] — used to describe a relationship between people • I *have* two sisters and a brother. • She *has* many friends and few enemies. • I wouldn't want to *have* him as an enemy. [=I wouldn't want him to be my enemy] • Do you *have* a big family? [=is your family big?; are there many people in your family?] • Does he *have* a girlfriend? • They *have* [=*employ*] a housekeeper. • We *have* many satisfied clients. • I *have* a customer who comes in every Tuesday and orders a tuna sandwich. — also ***have got*** • I*'ve got* two sisters and a brother.
7 *not used in progressive tenses* [+ *obj*] **:** to tightly hold (someone) • The dog *has* him by the leg. [=the dog is tightly holding his leg in its mouth] • She *had* me by the arm and wouldn't let go. — also ***have got*** • The dog*'s got* him by the leg.
8 *not used in progressive tenses* [+ *obj*] **:** to get (something) • Whenever she sees the latest new electronic gadget, she needs to *have* it. • This piano is the best to be *had*. [=it is the best that can be bought or owned]
9 *not used in progressive tenses* [+ *obj*] **:** to receive or be given (something) • We *had* some bad/good news yesterday. • I *had* a letter from my cousin last week. • "Waiter, can I *have* the check, please?" "I'll bring it right away." • Could I please *have* your attention? [=would you please give me your attention?] • Can I *have* a moment of your time? [=can I speak to you for a moment?]
10 *not used in progressive tenses* [+ *obj*] — used to describe the position of a person or thing • He *had* his hands behind his back. [=his hands were behind his back] • She *had* her back to the door and didn't see me enter the room. • He *has* a bodyguard with/near him whenever he goes out in public. • The house *has* a large tree next to it. [=there is a large tree next to the house] — also ***have got*** • The house *has got* a large tree next to it.
11 [+ *obj*] **:** to cause or produce (something, such as an effect) • The defeat *had* a terrible effect/impact on the team's spirits. • Her decision might *have* serious consequences.
12 [+ *obj*] **a :** to experience (something) • "Are you *having* fun?" "Yes, I'm *having* a wonderful time!" • Everyone *had* a good time at the party. = A good time was *had* by all (at the party). • She's *had* many strange things happen to her recently. = She's been *having* a lot of strange things happen to her recently. • I've *had* a bad/tough/long day. • I'm *having* trouble getting this computer to work. [=I am unable to get it to work] • I've *had* a good life. • We've *had* another setback. • She *had* [=*suffered*] a heart attack at the age of 50. **b** *not used in progressive tenses* **:** to experience or be affected by (an illness or injury) • I *have* a cold. • My uncle *has* diabetes. • She *has* a broken leg. — also ***have got*** • I*'ve got* a cold. • She*'s got* a broken leg. **c :** to experience (an emotion or feeling) • I *have* many regrets. [=I regret many things] • I *have* complete confidence in your abilities. = I don't *have* any doubts about your abilities. — also ***have got*** • I*'ve got* many regrets. • I *haven't got* any doubts about your abilities.
13 *not used in progressive tenses* [+ *obj*] — used to describe a person's thoughts, ideas, etc. • Everyone *has* a different opinion about what to do. • I *have* a few thoughts on the matter. • "What time is it?" "***I have no idea***." = "***I've no idea***." [=I don't know] • "Was it hard?" "***You have no idea*** (how hard it was)!" [=it was extremely hard] • I ***don't have a clue***. = I ***haven't a clue***. [=I don't know] — also ***have got*** • Everyone*'s got* a different opinion. • I ***haven't got a clue***.
14 [+ *obj*] **:** to perform (an action) **:** to do or participate in (an activity) • Did you *have* a good nap? • I was *having* a nap [=I was napping] when a loud noise woke me up. • We need to *have* a long talk. • I *have* soccer practice every Tuesday. • Please don't interrupt us when we are *having* a conversation. • (*Brit*) *Have* a sleep/lie-down. • (*Brit*) *Have* a think. • ***Have a look*** at this. [=look at this] • I *had a* (good) *look*, but I couldn't find the problem. • Let me ***have a try***. [=let me try]
15 [+ *obj*] **:** to provide (something) as entertainment or as a social gathering • We're *having* [=*giving, throwing*] a party on Saturday. Can you come? • We're *having* a little get-together. • The museum is *having* [=*holding*] an exhibition of her work. = She's *having* an exhibition of her work at the museum. [=the museum is exhibiting her work]
16 [+ *obj*] **a :** to cause, tell, or ask (someone) to do something • *Have* her call me [=tell her to call me on the telephone] when she gets back. • *Have* my assistant schedule another appointment for you. • You should *have* someone check that out for you. • She's *having* the children stay with us for the weekend. [=the children are staying with us for the weekend because she wants them to] • He *had* the barber cut his hair short. [=he got the barber to cut his hair short] • What would you *have* me do? [=what do you want me to do?] • They ***would have us believe*** [=they want/expect us to believe] that all these problems can be fixed by raising taxes. **b :** to cause (something) to be changed, removed, added, or affected in a specified way • I *had* my nose straightened by a plastic surgeon. • He *had* his hair cut short by a barber. • The doctor said I should *have* this mole removed. • We are *having* new windows installed. • I just *had* new tires put on the car. **c** — used when you hire someone to do something or when you go to a place (such as hospital or a mechanic's shop) so that something can be done • She's *having* surgery next week. • I *had* an X-ray. • When was the last time you *had* a checkup? • We're *having* some work done on the house. • The car should *have* regular maintenance checks. [=someone should check the car regularly]
17 [+ *obj*] — used to say that someone (such as a guest or a worker) is at your home or is coming to your home • We're *having* guests this weekend. • I'd love to come for a visit, if you'll *have* me. [=if you would welcome me as a guest] • We're going to *have* a plumber in to look at the furnace. • She *has* guests to/for dinner several times a week. • I *had* my friends back to my place for drinks after the movie. — see also HAVE OVER (below)
18 *not used in progressive tenses* [+ *obj*] **a :** to cause (something) to be in a specified state or condition • He *had* dinner ready by the time she came back. • It's hard to think when she *has* the radio on so loud. • He *had* the computer working again very quickly. • Please *have* your assignment ready/done/finished/completed by tomorrow. — also ***have got*** • She*'s got* the radio on so loud. • *Have* you *got* your assignment ready? [=is your assignment ready?] **b** — used when something that belongs to someone or something is damaged, destroyed, or taken • I *had* [=*got*] my nose broken in a fight. [=my nose was broken in a fight] • She *had* her car stolen last week. [=her car was stolen last week] • The house *had* its roof torn off in the hurricane.
19 [+ *obj*] **:** to allow (something) — used in negative statements • We'll *have* no more of that behavior! = We can't *have* that sort of behavior! = We can't *have* you behaving like that! = We can't be *having* you behave like that!
20 *not used in progressive tenses* [+ *obj*] **:** to accept (someone) • Who will we *have* as our leader?; *specifically* **:** to accept (someone) as a husband or wife • I'll marry her if she'll *have* me! • She wouldn't *have* him.
21 a *not used in progressive tenses* [+ *obj*] **:** to be able to con-

trol, capture, or defeat (someone) • We *have* him now! He can't possibly escape! — also **have got** • We*'ve got* him now! **b** ✧ The phrases ***You have me there*** and ***There you have me*** or (more commonly and informally) ***You've/You got me (there)*** are used in speech to mean "I don't know." • "How on earth can he justify his behavior?" "*You have me there.*" • "When exactly was the company founded?" "*There you have me.*" • "Why did she leave?" "*You got me.*" The phrase *You got me* is sometimes shortened to ***Got me*** in very informal speech. • "When does the movie start?" "*Got me.*"

22 [+ *obj*] **a** : to eat or drink (something) • We *had* steak for dinner last night. • We'll be *having* [=*eating*] dinner at six. • Will you *have* a drink with me? • Would you like to *have* some black pepper on your salad? • "What will you *have* (to drink)?" "(I'll *have*) A glass of red wine, please." • Did you *have* dessert yet? • *Have* some cake. It's delicious! **b** : to smoke (something) • She *had* a cigarette while she was waiting for the bus. **c** — used to say how you want food or drink to be cooked or prepared • I'd like to *have* my steak well done, please. • I usually *have* [=*take*] my coffee black.

23 *not used in progressive tenses* [+ *obj*] *informal* : to have sex with (someone) • He claims that he's *had* dozens of women.

24 [*auxiliary verb*] — used with the past participle to form the perfect tenses of verbs • We *have* been friends for many years. • She *has* bought a new car. • They *had* already left by the time we arrived. • I *have* not seen that movie yet. • *Has* the rain stopped? • I *have* never been so embarrassed! = Never *have* I been so embarrassed! • *Having* never been to Chicago, I really don't know much about it.

> ***usage*** When *have* is used as an auxiliary verb, the shortened forms ***'ve*** for ***have***, ***'s*** for ***has***, and ***'d*** for ***had*** are common in informal writing and usual in speech. • I*'ve* already seen that movie. • I*'ve* never been so embarrassed! • We*'ve* been friends for years. • She*'s* bought a new car. • They*'d* already left by the time we arrived. The negative forms ***haven't, hasn't,*** and ***hadn't*** are also common in informal writing and usual in speech. • I *haven't* seen that movie yet. • *Hasn't* the rain stopped? • We *hadn't* arrived yet when they left.

be had : to be tricked or fooled by someone • She doesn't want to buy a used car because she's worried about *being had* by a dishonest salesman. • I don't trust them. I think we've *been had.* [=I think they have tricked us]

have against [*phrasal verb*] ***have (something) against (someone or something)*** : to have (something) as a reason for not liking (someone or something) • She *has* a grudge *against* her former boss. • What *do you have against* him? [=why do you dislike him?] • I ***have nothing against*** her personally—it's her friends I don't like. — also **have got** • She*'s got* a grudge *against* her former boss. • What *have* you *got against* him?

have back [*phrasal verb*] **1** ***have (something) back*** : to receive (something that is returned to you) • If I lend you this book, can I *have* it *back* by next Tuesday? • How I wish I could *have* my youth *back* (again)! **2** ***have (someone) back*** **a** : to be with (someone who has returned) again • Welcome home! It's great to *have* you *back* (with us again)! • We'd love to *have* you *back* for another visit. • He longs to *have* her *back* in his life. • The doctor said he'd like to *have* me *back* for more tests next week. **b** : to allow (someone) to return • He wants to return to his wife, but she won't *have* him *back.*

have done with *old-fashioned* : to stop doing (something) : to bring (something) to an end • Let us *have done with* name-calling.

have got : HAVE

> ***usage*** Examples of *have got* are shown above and below for each sense, idiom, and phrasal verb in which it occurs. Note that *have got* is used only in the present tense. It is common in place of *have* in informal writing, and it is usual in ordinary speech. The contracted forms ***'s*** for ***has*** and ***'ve*** for ***have*** are commonly used for the first part of this phrase. • He *has* it. = He *has got* it. = (more commonly) He*'s got* it. • We *have* to go. = We *have got* to go. = (more commonly) We*'ve got* to go. The usual negative forms of *have got* are ***haven't got*** and ***hasn't got.*** • We do not *have* it. = We *have* not *got* it. = (more commonly) We *haven't got* it. • She doesn't *have* a chance. = She *hasn't got* a chance.

have had it *informal* **1 a** : to be too old or damaged to be used • We need a new stove. This one *has had it.* • My old dictionary *has* just about *had it.* Time to get a new one. **b** : to be so tired or annoyed that you will no longer allow or accept something • That's it. I*'ve had it.* I won't pay these kinds of fees any more. • I've been working all day and I*'ve had it.* **c** : to be angry about something that has continued for a long time • I*'ve had it* (up to here) with all these delays! [=I am fed up with all these delays; I am very annoyed by all these delays] **2** : to be completely ruined or defeated • After this scandal, he*'s had it* as a politician. [=he will no longer be able to be a politician] • His political career *has had it.* [=his political career is finished/ruined]

have it 1 — used to say that what is being reported is a rumor, a story, etc. • ***Rumor/word has it*** [=a rumor says] that the company will be going out of business. • ***Legend has it*** [=*according to legend*] George Washington slept here. **2** — used to describe a person's condition or situation • He's *had it* pretty tough since his wife died. [=his life has been difficult since his wife died] • You've never *had it* so good (as you *have it* now)! • We *have it* pretty good right now. — also **have got** • We*'ve got* it pretty good right now.

have it in for : to want to hurt or cause problems for (someone you do not like) • She's *had it in for* me for a long time. — also **have got** • She*'s got it in for* me.

have it in you : to have the ability to do something • His last performance was wonderful; I didn't know he *had it in him*! [=I didn't know he was capable of such a performance] • I don't think she *has it in her* to be cruel. [=I don't think she's capable of being cruel] — also **have got** • I don't think she*'s got it in her* to be cruel.

have it out : to settle a disagreement by talking or arguing • If you don't like the way he's treated you, you should *have it out* with him instead of just brooding about it.

have mercy/pity : to treat someone with mercy or pity • The prisoner begged the judge to *have mercy.* — usually + *on* • The prisoner begged the judge to *have mercy on* him.

have on [*phrasal verb*] **1** ***have (something) on or have on (something)*** : to be wearing (something) • She *has on* a new suit. • He **had nothing on.** [=he was naked] — also **have got** • She*'s got on* a new suit. **2** ***have (something) on (you)*** *informal* : to be carrying (something) • Do you *have* any spare change *on* you? • I don't *have* my wallet *on* me: I left it at home. — also **have got** • *Have* you *got* any spare change *on* you? **3** ***have (something) on*** : to keep (a device or machine) operating • They *have* the radio *on* all the time. **4** ***have (something) on*** *chiefly Brit* : to have plans for (something) • Do you *have* anything *on* for tomorrow? [=do you have any plans for tomorrow?] • What do you *have on* for tomorrow? [=what are your plans for tomorrow?] — also **have got** • *Have* you *got* anything *on* for tomorrow? **5** ***have (someone) on*** *Brit, informal* : to trick or fool (someone) in a joking way — usually used as ***(be) having (someone) on*** • He said he knew the Prime Minister, but I think he *was* just *having* me *on.* [=he was joking; he was just putting me on] **6** ***have nothing on (someone) or not have anything on (someone)*** : to have no evidence showing that someone has committed a crime or done something bad • The police were suspicious, but they *had nothing on* her. • If the police *don't have anything on* you, they have to let you go. — also **have got** • They *haven't got anything on* me. • They*'ve got nothing on* me. **7** ***have nothing on (someone or something)*** : to have less of a particular quality than (someone or something) • The winters here are bad, but they *have nothing on* the winters I remember when I was a child. [=they are not as bad as the winters I remember; the winters I remember were worse] • He says Houston *has nothing on* Chicago [=Houston is not as good as Chicago] when it comes to fine restaurants. — also **have got** • Houston*'s got nothing on* Chicago.

have over [*phrasal verb*] ***have (someone) over*** — used to say that someone is coming to your home as a guest • We're *having* some friends *over* for dinner tonight. — see also HAVE 17 (above)

have (someone or something) (all) to yourself : to be in a situation in which you are not required to share someone or something with anyone else • We *have the entire evening to ourselves.* [=we have no plans to do anything with anyone else this evening] • She *has the house all to herself* this weekend. [=she is the only one staying in the house this weekend] • I'm happy to *have you to myself* tonight; it will give us a chance to talk privately.

have the time ✧ If someone asks you if you *have the time*, that person is asking if you know what time it is. • "Do you *have the time*?" [=can you tell me what time it is?] "Yes, it's

H

10 minutes past 3." — also ***have got*** ▪ *Have* you *got* the time? — see also HAVE 2 (above)

have to **:** MUST: such as **a** — used to say that something is required or necessary ▪ You *have to* follow the rules. ▪ You *have to* stop. [=you must stop; I command you to stop] ▪ I told him what he *had to* do. [=what he must do] ▪ We *have to* correct these problems soon or the project will fail. ▪ I *have to* remember to stop at the store. ▪ "Do you *have to* go?" "Yes, I'm afraid I really *have to*." ▪ If you *have to* go, at least wait until the storm is over. ▪ Do what you *have to* (do). ▪ I didn't want to do it but I *had to*. — also ***have got to*** ▪ You*'ve got to* stop. ▪ I*'ve got to* go now. ✧ Note the difference in meaning between ***not have to*** and ***must not***. ▪ You *don't have to* do it. [=it is not necessary for you to do it] ▪ You *must not* do it. [=you are not allowed to do it; you are forbidden to do it] **b** — used to say that something is required by a rule or law ▪ All passengers *have to* exit at the next stop. — also ***have got to*** ▪ All passengers *have got to* exit at the next stop. **c** — used to say that something is desired or should be done ▪ You *have to* read this book. It's fantastic! ▪ You *have to* come visit us soon. [=we would like to have you visit us soon] ▪ You really *have to* see the doctor about that cough. [=I urge you to see the doctor; I really think you need to see the doctor] — also ***have got to*** ▪ You*'ve got to* come visit us soon. **d** — used to say that something is very likely ▪ It *has to* be close to noon. ▪ She *has to* be the most beautiful woman I've ever seen. [=I think she is the most beautiful woman I've ever seen] ▪ He *has to* have a lot of money to live the way he does. ▪ The bus *has to* be coming soon. ▪ There *has to* be some mistake. — also ***have got to*** ▪ It*'s got to* be close to noon. ▪ There*'s got to* be some mistake. **e** — used in various spoken phrases to emphasize a statement ▪ ***I have to say***, I was surprised to hear from him. ▪ She's a talented actress, ***you have to admit***. ▪ ***I have to admit***, I expected better results. ▪ ***It has to be said*** that the movie was not very good. ▪ ***I have to warn you***, this will not be easy. — also ***have got to*** ▪ ***I've got to say***, I was surprised to hear from him. ▪ She's a talented actress, ***you've got to admit***. **f** — used in questions or statements that express annoyance or anger ▪ Do you *have to* be so unreasonable? ▪ Why does it always *have to* rain on the weekend? ▪ Naturally it *has to* rain on the day when we planned a picnic. — also ***have got to*** ▪ It*'s got to* rain on the day when we planned a picnic.

have to do with see [1]DO

have with [*phrasal verb*] **1** ***have (someone) with (you)*** **:** to be with (someone) ▪ They *had* their grandchildren *with* them when they arrived. [=they arrived with their grandchildren] **2** ***have (something) with (you)*** **:** to be carrying (something) with (you) ▪ I don't *have* my wallet *with* me.

I have it — used to say that you suddenly remember, understand, or have found something; usually ***I've got it*** ▪ Now, what was his name? Tony? Tom? No, *I've got it*! Tim. His name was Tim.

I'll have you know — used to emphasize something in a somewhat annoyed or angry way ▪ "Did your son go to college?" "Did he go to college? *I'll have you know* that he was given a full scholarship to Harvard!"

there you have it — used to say that something has just been shown, described, or stated in a very clear and definite way ▪ "But we can't spend more money unless we have more money to spend!" "Precisely. *There you have it*."

what have you see [1]WHAT

you had to be there — used to say that people cannot understand something because they did not experience it or see it themselves ▪ I know it sounds weird, but it was so funny. I guess *you had to be there*.

ha·ven /ˈheɪvən/ *noun, pl* **-vens** [*count*] **:** a place where you are protected from danger, trouble, etc. ▪ The shelter offers/provides a *haven* from abusive spouses. ▪ The inn is a *haven* for weary travelers. ▪ This national park provides a ***safe haven*** for wildlife. — see also TAX HAVEN

have–nots /ˈhævˌnɑːts/ *noun*

the have-nots **:** people who have little money and few possessions **:** poor people — usually used in the phrase ***the haves and the have-nots*** ▪ the gap between *the haves and the have-nots* [=between rich people and poor people]

haven't /ˈhævənt/ — used as a contraction of *have not* ▪ We *haven't* tried the new restaurant yet.

haves /ˈhævz/ *noun*

the haves **:** people who have a lot of money and possessions **:** wealthy people — usually used in the phrase ***the haves and the have-nots*** ▪ the gap between *the haves and the have-nots* [=between rich people and poor people]

hav·oc /ˈhævək/ *noun* [*noncount*] **:** a situation in which there is much destruction or confusion ▪ the *havoc* of war ▪ A powerful tornado ***wreaked havoc*** on [=caused great destruction to] the small village. ▪ The disease can ***play havoc*** with the body's immune system. ▪ Several small children can ***create/cause havoc*** in a house.

haw /ˈhɑː/ *verb* **haws; hawed; haw·ing**

hem and haw see [3]HEM

[1]**hawk** /ˈhɑːk/ *noun, pl* **hawks** [*count*]

1 : a bird that kills other birds and animals for food — see color picture on page C9

2 : a person who supports war or the use of military force ▪ The *hawks* voted against the proposed cuts in military spending. — compare DOVE

watch (someone or something) like a hawk **:** to watch (someone or something) very carefully ▪ The storeowner *watches those teenagers like a hawk* whenever they come in because she's afraid they're going to steal something.

— **hawk·ish** /ˈhɑːkɪʃ/ *adj* [*more ~; most ~*] ▪ a *hawkish* politician

[2]**hawk** *verb* **hawks; hawked; hawk·ing** [+ *obj*] **:** to offer (something) for sale especially by calling out or by going from one person to another **:** PEDDLE ▪ Vendors were *hawking* soda and hot dogs. ▪ *hawking* newspapers — compare [3]HAWK

— **hawk·er** *noun, pl* **-ers** [*count*] ▪ a newspaper *hawker*

[3]**hawk** *verb* **hawks; hawked; hawking** [+ *obj*] **:** to clear (material) from your throat by coughing, making a noise with your voice, etc. — usually + *up* ▪ *hawking up* phlegm — compare [2]HAWK

haw·ser /ˈhɑːzɚ/ *noun, pl* **-sers** [*count*] *technical* **:** a very thick rope or cable for towing or tying up a ship

haw·thorn /ˈhɑːˌθoɚn/ *noun, pl* **-thorns** [*count*] **:** a type of bush or small tree with white or pink flowers and small red fruits

hay /ˈheɪ/ *noun* [*noncount*]

1 : grass that has been cut and dried to be used as food for animals ▪ a bale of *hay*

2 *US, informal* **:** a small amount of money — usually used in negative statements ▪ They made over a million dollars last year, and that ***ain't hay***! [=that is a lot of money]

a roll in the hay see [3]ROLL

hit the hay see [1]HIT

make hay (while the sun shines) **:** to get value or use from an opportunity while it exists **:** to not waste an opportunity ▪ These good economic conditions won't last forever, so investors need to *make hay while the sun shines*.

hay fever *noun* [*singular*] *medical* **:** a sickness that is like a cold and that is caused by breathing in plant pollen

hay·field /ˈheɪˌfiːld/ *noun, pl* **-fields** [*count*] **:** a field where grass is grown for hay

hay·loft /ˈheɪˌlɑːft/ *noun, pl* **-lofts** [*count*] **:** the upper part of a barn where hay is stored

hay·mak·er /ˈheɪˌmeɪkɚ/ *noun, pl* **-ers** [*count*] *chiefly US, informal* **:** a powerful hit with the fist **:** a very hard punch ▪ He was knocked down by a *haymaker* to his jaw. ▪ throw/deliver a *haymaker*

hay·rick /ˈheɪˌrɪk/ *noun, pl* **-ricks** [*count*] *chiefly Brit* **:** HAYSTACK

hay·ride /ˈheɪˌraɪd/ *noun, pl* **-rides** [*count*] *US* **:** an informal event in which a group of people ride for pleasure in a wagon, sleigh, or open truck that is partly filled with straw or hay

hay·stack /ˈheɪˌstæk/ *noun, pl* **-stacks** [*count*] **:** a large pile of hay

a needle in a haystack see [1]NEEDLE

hay·wire /ˈheɪˌwajɚ/ *adj, informal* **:** not working properly ▪ a *haywire* immune system — usually used in the phrase ***go haywire*** ▪ The disease has caused her immune system to *go haywire*. [=to stop working properly] ▪ The old radio *went haywire*. ▪ The stock market has *gone* completely *haywire*.

[1]**haz·ard** /ˈhæzɚd/ *noun, pl* **-ards**

1 [*count*] **:** a source of danger ▪ Young people should be educated about the *hazards* of excessive drinking. [=about how drinking too much alcohol is harmful] ▪ That old staircase is a safety *hazard*. [=it is dangerous; someone could get hurt by using it] ▪ a fire *hazard* [=something that could cause a fire] ▪ a health *hazard* = a *hazard* to your health [=something that could make you sick] ▪ Hand injuries are an ***occupational***

hazard for typists. [=typists are likely to have hand injuries because of the work they do] ▪ a ***traffic hazard*** [=something that could cause an accident involving a car, bicycle, etc.]
2 [*count*] *golf* : something on a golf course (such as a pond or an area of sand) that makes hitting the ball into the hole more difficult ▪ a water *hazard*
3 *hazards* [*plural*] : HAZARD LIGHTS

²hazard *verb* **-ards; -ard•ed; -ard•ing** [+ *obj*]
1 : to risk losing (something, such as money) in an attempt to get, win, or achieve something ▪ His friend asked him to *hazard* a small sum in a business venture.
2 : to offer (something, such as a guess or an opinion) even though you may be wrong ▪ She was unwilling to *hazard* [=*venture*] a guess as to the outcome of the election. ▪ *hazard* an opinion

hazard lights *noun* [*plural*] : special lights on a vehicle that flash on and off and are used to warn other drivers of a dangerous situation (such as when the vehicle is not working properly) — called also *hazards*

haz•ard•ous /ˈhæzɚdəs/ *adj* [*more* ~; *most* ~] : involving risk or danger : DANGEROUS ▪ It was a *hazardous* voyage. ▪ These are *hazardous* chemicals that can cause death if inhaled. ▪ *hazardous* driving habits — sometimes + *to* ▪ Smoking can be *hazardous to* your health.
– haz•ard•ous•ly *adv*

hazard pay *noun* [*noncount*] *US* : extra money that someone is paid for doing work that is dangerous — called also (*US*) *danger pay,* (*Brit*) *danger money*

haze /ˈheɪz/ *noun* [*singular*]
1 : dust, smoke, or mist that has filled the air so that you cannot see clearly ▪ The bar was filled with a smoky *haze.* ▪ a *haze* of smoke
2 : a state of confusion ▪ She stumbled around in a drug-induced *haze.*
– hazed /ˈheɪzd/ *adj* ▪ the pale, *hazed* sky — usually used in combination ▪ the smoke-*hazed* sky/bar ▪ a drug-*hazed* state

ha•zel /ˈheɪzəl/ *noun, pl* **-zels**
1 [*count*] : a kind of bush or small tree that produces nuts
2 [*count, noncount*] : a color that combines light brown with green and gray
– see also WITCH HAZEL
– hazel *adj* ▪ *hazel* eyes

ha•zel•nut /ˈheɪzəlˌnʌt/ *noun, pl* **-nuts** [*count*] : the nut of a hazel — called also (*US*) *filbert*; see picture at NUT

haz•ing /ˈheɪzɪŋ/ *noun* [*noncount*] *US* : the practice of playing unpleasant tricks on someone or forcing someone to do unpleasant things ✧ *Hazing* is done as part of a ritual that people (such as college students) must go through before they are allowed to become members of a group (such as a fraternity).
– haze /ˈheɪz/ *verb* **haz•es; hazing; hazed** [+ *obj*] ▪ Varsity team members *hazed* the new players by leading them around campus on leashes.

hazy /ˈheɪzi/ *adj* **haz•i•er; -est**
1 : partly hidden, darkened, or clouded by dust, smoke, or mist : hidden by haze ▪ We had only a *hazy* view of the mountain. ▪ *hazy* sunshine; *also* : having or filled with haze ▪ *hazy* weather
2 a : not clear in thought or meaning : VAGUE ▪ He gave us a *hazy* account of how he had spent the last two weeks. ▪ She has only *hazy* memories of the accident. **b** : not certain ▪ I'm a little *hazy* [=*unclear*] on/about the details.
– haz•i•ly /ˈheɪzəli/ *adv* ▪ *hazily* remembered **– haz•i•ness** /ˈheɪzinəs/ *noun* [*noncount*] ▪ the *haziness* of the view/memories

H–bomb /ˈeɪtʃˌbɑːm/ *noun, pl* **-bombs** [*count*] : HYDROGEN BOMB

HDTV *abbr* high-definition television

¹he /ˈhiː, i/ *pronoun*
1 : that male — used to indicate a male person or animal that is the subject of a verb ▪ *He* is my father. ▪ Ask your brother where *he* is going. ▪ *He* has been planning this trip since January. ▪ (*on the telephone*) "Hello, I'd like to speak with Jim." "This is *he.*" [=I (the person who answered the phone) am Jim] — compare SHE
2 : that person — used in a general sense or when the sex of the person is unknown ▪ Everyone should do the best *he* can. ▪ Tell whoever is in there that *he* had better come out. ▪ *He* who laughs last, laughs best. ✧ This use of *he* was common in the past but is now often avoided because it is considered sexist.

²he /ˈhiː/ *noun* [*singular*] : a boy, man, or male animal ▪ "Somebody called when you were out, but I can't remember who." "Was it a *he* or a she?" — sometimes used in combination ▪ a *he*-goat

¹head /ˈhɛd/ *noun, pl* **heads** *or in sense 7* **head**
1 [*count*] : the part of the body containing the brain, eyes, ears, nose, and mouth ▪ She patted the dog on the *head.* ▪ He nodded his *head* in agreement. ▪ The ceiling's low—watch your *head*! ▪ *head* injuries ▪ They were covered ***from head to foot/toe*** in mud. [=they were completely covered in mud] ▪ He has a ***full head of hair.*** [=he has a full amount of hair on his head] — see picture at HUMAN; see also TALKING HEAD
2 [*count*] : a person's mental ability : mind or intellect ▪ You shouldn't let your heart rule your *head.* [=you should be guided by reason and not by your emotions] ▪ She did some quick calculations ***in her head.*** [=without writing anything; mentally] ▪ I keep hearing that song *in my head.* = That song keeps running through my *head.* = I can't get that song ***out of my head.*** ▪ It never even ***entered my head*** to run for office. [=I never thought of running for office] ▪ The problem is ***all in his head.*** [=the problem is not real; he's just imagining it] ▪ Don't go ***putting ideas in/into his head.*** [=don't cause him to have ideas or suspicions that he would not have himself] ▪ You should ***put that idea out of your head.*** [=you should stop thinking about that idea] ▪ She always says the first thing that ***comes/pops into her head.*** [=the first thing that she thinks of] ▪ I'm sure we can solve this problem if we just ***use our heads.*** [=think carefully] ▪ That guy should ***have his head examined.*** = That guy is ***not right in the head.*** [=that guy is crazy] ▪ You need a ***cool/calm head*** [=an ability to remain calm] to deal with someone like him. ▪ a ***clear head*** [=an ability to think clearly] ✧ If you have ***a good head on your shoulders,*** you are intelligent and have good judgment. ▪ You don't have to worry about her—she's got *a good head on her shoulders.* ✧ When you ***get/take it into your head*** to do something, you suddenly decide to do it in a way that seems foolish or surprising. ▪ He's *taken it into his head* to try skydiving. ▪ I somehow *got it into my head* to run for public office. ✧ If you ***get it into your head*** that something is true, you begin to believe something even though there is no good reason for believing it. ▪ She's somehow *gotten it into her head* that I don't like her. [=she believes that I don't like her although I do like her]
3 [*count*] : a person who has a specified mental or emotional quality ▪ A fight was avoided when ***cooler heads prevailed.*** [=when calmer or less angry people were able to convince others not to fight] — see also HOTHEAD, SOREHEAD
4 [*singular*] : a distance equal to the length of a head ▪ The horse won the race by a *head.* ▪ I'm a *head* taller than you.
5 [*count*] : the front side of a coin : the side of a coin that shows a picture of a person's head ▪ the *head* of a penny — usually used in the plural to refer to one of the two choices you can make when a coin is thrown in the air to decide something ▪ I call *heads.* ▪ Is it *heads* or tails? [=did the coin land with heads or tails facing up?] ▪ It landed *heads* up. — compare ¹TAIL 3
6 *head* [*plural*] : individual animals ▪ 100 *head* of cattle
7 [*count*] **a** : an end of something that is like a head in shape or position — usually singular; often + *of* ▪ She placed the pillows at the *head of* the bed. ▪ We arrived early so that we'd be at the *head* [=*front*] *of* the line. ▪ The chairman sat at the *head of* the table. ▪ the *head* [=*top*] *of* a nail/pin/screw — compare FOOT **b** : the part of an object that hits or touches something else ▪ a grinding *head* ▪ the hammer's *head* — often + *of* ▪ the *head of* a spear ▪ the *head of* a golf club — see also ARROWHEAD, SPEARHEAD, WARHEAD
8 [*noncount*] : the position of being a leader ▪ She's ***at the head of*** her class. [=she is the best student in her class]
9 [*count*] **a** : a person who leads or directs a group or organization ▪ Have you met the new department *head*? — often + *of* ▪ She is the *head of* our sales division. ▪ *heads of* families/households ▪ ***heads of state*** [=leaders of countries] — often used before another noun ▪ the restaurant's *head* cook ▪ the team's *head* coach **b** *chiefly Brit* : HEAD TEACHER
10 [*count*] : a tight mass of leaves or flowers on a plant ▪ The flower *heads* on the plant are very large. ▪ a *head* of cabbage/lettuce ▪ a *head of* garlic
11 [*count*] : the place where a stream or river begins — usually singular ▪ the *head* of the Nile
12 [*singular*] : pressure caused by the water or steam in a machine ✧ When an engine has a ***full head of steam,*** it has built up a full amount of power. This phrase is often used figuratively to describe something that is moving forward in a fast and powerful way. ▪ The project started slowly, but

now we have a *full head of steam*.

13 [*count*] : the bubbles that form on the top of some liquids (such as beer) — usually singular • the foamy *head* on a beer

14 [*singular*] : the point at which a situation becomes very serious or when action is required • Things ***came to a head*** when the workers threatened to go on strike. • These new revelations ***brought*** the scandal ***to a head***.

15 [*count*] : a small, inflamed area on the skin with a spot in the middle — see also BLACKHEAD

a big/swelled head *informal* : an overly high opinion of yourself • All those compliments have given him a *big head*. [=have made him very conceited]

a head : for each person • The price is $20 *a head*.

a price on someone's head see [1]PRICE

bang heads together see [1]BANG

bite someone's head off see [1]BITE

butt heads see [3]BUTT

count heads see [1]COUNT

eyes in the back of your head see [1]EYE

get it through someone's head : to cause someone to learn and remember something • She's finally *gotten it through their heads* that she doesn't eat meat.

get it through your head : to accept or understand (something) • He can't seem to *get it through his head* that I'm not interested in working with him.

get your head round *Brit* : to understand (something) • She couldn't *get her head round* why he had to leave.

go over someone's head : to discuss something with a person who is higher in rank than someone else • He *went over his supervisor's head* to complain about the policy to the company's president. [=he complained about the policy to the company's president rather than his supervisor]

go to your head **1** *of an alcoholic drink* : to make you feel drunk • I just had one glass of wine, but it ***went straight to my head***. **2** : to make you believe that you are better than other people • He has never let his fame *go to his head*.

have a head for : to have an ability to understand or deal with (something) • She's always *had a* (good) *head for* business. • (*Brit*) He ***has a head for heights***. [=he is not afraid of heights; being up high does not bother him]

have/get your head (screwed) on right/straight *informal* : to think or act in a smart and sensible way • She's young, but it's clear that she *has her head screwed on right*. • You think that's a good idea? You need to *get your head screwed on straight*.

head and shoulders above — used to say that someone or something is much better than others • They ***are/stand head and shoulders above*** the competition.

head in the sand ✧ If you ***bury/have/hide (etc.) your head in the sand***, you ignore something unpleasant that you should be dealing with. • He can't just *bury his head in the sand* every time there's a problem.

head over heels : very deeply in love • We were *head over heels* (in love). • He ***fell head over heels for*** some girl he met at school. • (*US*) He ***went head over heels for*** her.

heads roll *informal* ✧ If you say that ***heads will roll*** or (less commonly) ***heads are going to roll***, you mean that people will be severely punished or will lose their jobs because of something that has happened. • When the boss finds out about the mistake, *heads will roll*.

hit the nail on the head see [1]HIT

hold up your head *or* ***hold your head (up) high*** : to be proud : to not feel ashamed • Even though they lost the game, they can still *hold up their heads* because they tried their best.

keep your head : to remain calm • She has shown that she can *keep her head* in a crisis.

keep your head above water : to avoid financial failure while having money problems • We have so much debt that we're barely able to *keep our heads above water*.

keep your head down *informal* : to behave in a quiet way that does not attract attention • a politician who is *keeping his head down* and trying to avoid controversy

knock heads see [1]KNOCK

knock someone's head off see [1]KNOCK

knock some sense into someone's head see [1]SENSE

knock (something) on the head see [1]KNOCK

lose your head : to become very upset or angry • He *lost his head* and said some things he regrets.

not make head or/nor tail of *or US* ***not make heads or/nor tails (out) of*** *informal* : to be unable to understand (something) • I *couldn't make heads or tails of* her reaction. • His handwriting was so bad that we *couldn't make heads or tails out of* it.

off the top of your head see [1]TOP

off your head *Brit, informal* : crazy or foolish • He's not just eccentric—he's completely *off his head*! • He's gone *off his head* over some girl.

on your head **1** : with the upper and lower parts of your body reversed in position • Can you ***stand on your head***? **2** : in or into great disorder • News of the discovery ***turned*** the scientific world ***on its head***. **3** — used to say that you will be blamed for something • If we miss our deadline, it will be *on your head*. [=it will be your fault]

out of your head *informal* : unable to act or think in a reasonable and controlled way because of drunkenness or strong emotion • He was (drunk) *out of his head*. [=he was extremely drunk] • Her parents were *out of their heads* with worry [=were extremely worried and upset] when she didn't come home on time.

over your head : beyond your understanding or ability • The technical details were *over my head*. [=too complicated for me to understand] • That joke went right *over my head*. [=I did not get that joke] • We realized after we started the business that we were (in) *over our heads*. [=we were trying to do something that was too difficult]

per head : for each person • The price is $20 *per head*.

put/stick/raise your head above the parapet see PARAPET

put your heads together : to think of a solution to a problem with another person • I'm sure we can solve this problem if we just *put our heads together*.

rear/raise its ugly head ✧ If something bad *rears/raises its ugly head*, it suddenly becomes obvious or causes trouble. • Inflation threatened to *rear its ugly head*.

scratch your head *informal* : to be confused about something and unable to understand the reason for it • His odd behavior left us all *scratching our heads*.

scream/shout/yell/laugh (etc.) your head off *informal* : to scream/shout/yell/laugh (etc.) very loudly or for a long time • She was *screaming her head off*. • You can *shout your head off* at him, but he still won't listen. • If they saw me dressed like this, they'd *laugh their heads off*.

shake your head see [1]SHAKE

two heads are better than one — used to say that it is easier for two people who help each other to solve a problem than it is for one person to solve a problem alone

turn heads : to attract attention or notice • The car's sleek design is bound to *turn heads*.

[2]head *verb* **heads; head•ed; head•ing**

1 [+ *obj*] **a** : to be the leader of (something) • She *heads* the committee. • The group was *headed* by the church pastor. • He was accused of *heading* the revolt. — often + *up* • The research committee was *headed up* by several leading scientists. **b** : to be first on (a list) • He *heads* [=*tops*] the list of candidates for the job.

2 *always followed by an adverb or preposition* [*no obj*] : to go in a specified direction or toward a specified place • She turned around and *headed* (for) home. • I hopped in the car and *headed* down the street. • After lunch, we *headed* back to the office. • She *headed* out early this morning. • The birds have already started *heading* south for the winter. ✧ To be ***heading*** or ***headed*** somewhere is to be going or directed somewhere. • Where are you *heading*? = Where are you *headed*? [=where are you going?] • The ship was *heading/headed* out to sea. — often + *for* • We were on a plane *headed for* Hawaii. — often used figuratively • The economy may be *heading* into a recession. • If you keep acting like this, you'll be *heading/headed for* trouble!

3 [+ *obj*] *soccer* : to hit (the ball) with your head • The forward *headed* the ball into the goal.

head off [*phrasal verb*] **1** : to go to another place • I'll see you later—I'm *heading off*. • He *headed off* to work. **2** ***head (someone) off*** *or* ***head off (someone)*** : to stop (someone) from moving forward • We can *head* them *off* at the pass. **3** ***head (something) off*** *or* ***head off (something)*** : to prevent (something) from happening • They tried to *head off* the crisis by raising interest rates.

head•ache /ˈhɛdˌeɪk/ *noun, pl* **-aches**

1 : an ache or pain in the head [*count*] I'm starting to get a *headache*. [*noncount*] The symptoms include fever and *headache*. — see also SPLITTING HEADACHE

2 [*count*] : a difficult or annoying situation or problem • The city's biggest *headache* is traffic. • Managing your finances can be a real *headache*.

– head·achy /ˈhɛdˌeɪki/ *adj* [*more* ~; *most* ~] ▪ I was feeling tired and *headachy*.

head·band /ˈhɛdˌbænd/ *noun, pl* **-bands** [*count*] : a band of cloth or some other material worn on or around your head

head·board /ˈhɛdˌboɚd/ *noun, pl* **-boards** [*count*] : an upright board at the end of a bed where you rest your head — see picture at BED

head boy *noun, pl* ~ **boys** [*count*] *Brit* : an older male student in a British school who is chosen to have special duties and to represent the school

head case *noun, pl* ~ **cases** [*count*] *informal* : a person who has mental or emotional problems : a crazy person ▪ Her brother's a real *head case*.

head·cheese /ˈhɛdˌʧi:z/ *noun* [*noncount*] *US* : a food made from parts of the head, feet, and sometimes the tongue and heart of a pig — called also (*Brit*) *brawn*

head cold *noun, pl* ~ **colds** [*count*] : a cold that mainly affects areas in your nose, throat, etc., and that makes breathing difficult

head count *noun, pl* ~ **counts** [*count*] : an act of counting the number of people at a place, event, etc. ▪ She ***did a head count*** to make sure all the students were on the bus.

head·dress /ˈhɛdˌdrɛs/ *noun, pl* **-dress·es** [*count*] : a decorative covering for your head ▪ The dancers wore ceremonial *headdresses*.

head·ed /ˈhɛdəd/ *adj* : having a head or heads of a specified type or number — usually used in combination with another adjective ▪ a curly-*headed* child [=a child with curly hair] ▪ a red-*headed* actress ▪ a two-*headed* ax — see also WRONG-HEADED

head·er /ˈhɛdɚ/ *noun, pl* **-ers** [*count*]
1 : a word, phrase, etc., that is placed at the beginning of a document, passage, etc., or at the top of a page ▪ a column *header* ▪ an e-mail *header* [=lines at the beginning of an e-mail message giving information about the message's origin, etc.] — see picture at TABLE; compare FOOTER
2 *informal* : a fall in which your head hits the ground ▪ She tripped on the rock and ***took a header***.
3 *soccer* : a shot or pass made by hitting the ball with your head ▪ He scored with a *header* past the goalie.
– see also DOUBLEHEADER

head·first /ˈhɛdˈfɚst/ *adv*
1 : with the head leading ▪ She dove into the water *headfirst*. — compare FEETFIRST
2 : without taking time to think about your actions ▪ She rushed into the relationship *headfirst*.
– headfirst *adj* ▪ a *headfirst* dive/slide

head·gear /ˈhɛdˌgiɚ/ *noun* [*noncount*] : things (such as hats and helmets) that are worn on your head ▪ The law requires cyclists to wear protective *headgear*. ▪ Her preferred form of *headgear* is a big, floppy hat.

head girl *noun, pl* ~ **girls** [*count*] *Brit* : an older female student in a British school who is chosen to have special duties and to represent the school

head–hunt·ing /ˈhɛdˌhʌntɪŋ/ *noun* [*noncount*] : the activity of finding people who are suited for a particular job — often used before another noun ▪ They retained a *head-hunting* firm to fill the position of chief executive officer.
– head·hunt·er /ˈhɛdˌhʌntɚ/ *noun, pl* **-ers** [*count*] ▪ Corporations often use *headhunters* to find candidates for executive positions.

head·ing /ˈhɛdɪŋ/ *noun, pl* **-ings** [*count*]
1 : the direction in which a ship or aircraft points ▪ What is your current *heading*?
2 : a word, phrase, etc., that is placed at the beginning of a document, passage, etc., or at the top of a page ▪ We organized all the recipes under different subject *headings*. ▪ a chapter *heading* — see picture at TABLE
3 : a name or label used for a group of people or things ▪ His paintings usually fall/go/come ***under the heading of*** realism.

head·lamp /ˈhɛdˌlæmp/ *noun, pl* **-lamps** [*count*] : HEADLIGHT

head·land /ˈhɛdlənd/ *noun, pl* **-lands** [*count*] : a narrow area of land that sticks out into the sea : PROMONTORY

head·less /ˈhɛdləs/ *adj* : having no head ▪ a *headless* pin ▪ a *headless* body

head·light /ˈhɛdˌlaɪt/ *noun, pl* **-lights** [*count*] : a light on the front of a vehicle (such as a car or motorcycle) — see picture at CAR

¹head·line /ˈhɛdˌlaɪn/ *noun, pl* **-lines**
1 [*count*] : the title written in large letters over a story in a newspaper ▪ The story of his arrest appeared beneath the *headline* "Caught!" ▪ She only had time to scan the *headlines* before she had to rush out the door.
2 *headlines* [*plural*] : the major news stories reported in newspapers, magazines, or television news programs ▪ Surprising developments have kept the murder investigation ***in the headlines*** for several weeks. ▪ He ***made/grabbed headlines*** [=became the subject of major news] with his recent antismoking campaign. ▪ She has ***grabbed/hit/made the headlines*** by making public accusations of corruption within the government. ▪ The murder investigation has been ***in the headlines*** for several weeks.

²headline *verb* **-lines; -lined; -lin·ing** [+ *obj*]
1 : to provide (a newspaper story) with a headline — usually used as *(be) headlined* ▪ The story of his arrest *was headlined* "Caught!"
2 *US* : to be the main performer in (a show or concert) ▪ The band is *headlining* the music festival.

head·lin·er /ˈhɛdˌlaɪnɚ/ *noun, pl* **-ers** [*count*] : the main performer in a show or concert ▪ He was the *headliner* at a local night club.

head·lock /ˈhɛdˌlɑ:k/ *noun, pl* **-locks** [*count*] : a method of holding someone by putting your arm around the person's head ▪ He had me in a *headlock*.

head·long /ˈhɛdˈlɑ:ŋ/ *adv*
1 : with the head leading : HEADFIRST ▪ I dove *headlong* to the floor.
2 : without taking time to think about your actions — usually + *into* ▪ We rushed *headlong into* marriage.
– head·long /ˈhɛdˌlɑ:ŋ/ *adj, always used before a noun* ▪ a *headlong* dive ▪ We made a *headlong* rush for the door.

head·man /ˈhɛdˈmæn/ *noun, pl* **-men** /-ˈmɛn/ [*count*] : a man who is the leader of a tribe or village : CHIEF

head·mas·ter /ˈhɛdˈmæstɚ, *Brit* ˈhɛdˈmɑ:stə/ *noun, pl* **-ters** [*count*]
1 : a man who is the head of a U.S. private school
2 : a man who is the head of a British school

head·mis·tress /ˈhɛdˈmɪstrəs/ *noun, pl* **-tress·es** [*count*]
1 : a woman who is the head of a U.S. private school
2 : a woman who is the head of a British school

head–on /ˈhɛdˈɑ:n/ *adv*
1 : with the head or front hitting first ▪ The two cars collided *head-on*.
2 : in a very direct way ▪ She decided to confront/meet the challenge *head-on*.
– head–on *adj, always used before a noun* ▪ a *head-on* collision/confrontation

head·phones /ˈhɛdˌfounz/ *noun* [*plural*] : a device that is worn over your ears and used for listening to music, the radio, etc., without having other people hear it ▪ a pair/set of *headphones*

head·piece /ˈhɛdˌpi:s/ *noun, pl* **-piec·es** [*count*] : a usually decorative covering for the head ▪ The bride wore a veil with a beaded *headpiece*.

head·quar·tered /ˈhɛdˌkwoɚtɚd/ *adj, not used before a noun* : having headquarters in a certain place : based in a particular location ▪ The company is *headquartered* in Springfield, Massachusetts.

head·quar·ters /ˈhɛdˌkwoɚtɚz/ *noun* [*plural*] : a place from which something (such as a business or a military action) is controlled or directed ✧ *Headquarters* is plural in form but is used with both plural and singular verbs. ▪ The company's *headquarters* is/are in Atlanta.

head·rest /ˈhɛdˌrɛst/ *noun, pl* **-rests** [*count*] : the part of a seat or chair that supports your head — see picture at CAR

head·room /ˈhɛdˌru:m/ *noun* [*noncount*] : the space between the top of your head and a ceiling or roof when you are standing or sitting ▪ There isn't much *headroom* in the basement. [=the ceiling is low in the basement] ▪ He's looking for a car with a lot of *headroom*.

head·scarf /ˈhɛdˌskɑɚf/ *noun, pl* **-scarves** [*count*] : a piece of cloth worn over a woman's or girl's head

head·set /ˈhɛdˌsɛt/ *noun, pl* **-sets** [*count*]
1 : a pair of headphones
2 : a device that holds an earphone and a microphone in place on a person's head
– see picture on next page

head·stand /ˈhɛdˌstænd/ *noun, pl* **-stands** [*count*] : the act of positioning your body so that your head and hands are on the floor and your legs and feet are straight up in the air ▪

headset

She can do a *headstand*. [=she can stand on her head]

head start *noun, pl* ~ **starts** [*count*]

1 : an advantage given to a someone at the beginning of a race • They gave me a five-minute *head start*.

2 : an advantage that you have or get when you are starting to do something • She took some extra classes to get a *head start* in/on her career. • His natural athletic talent gave him a *head start* on/over his peers.

head·stone /ˈhɛdˌstoʊn/ *noun, pl* **-stones** [*count*] **:** a stone that marks the place where a dead person is buried and that usually has the person's name and birth and death dates on it — called also *gravestone, tombstone*

head·strong /ˈhɛdˌstrɑːŋ/ *adj* [*more* ~; *most* ~] **:** not willing to do what other people want **:** very stubborn • The child is very *headstrong*. • He is known for his *headstrong* behavior.

heads up *interj, US, informal* — used to tell someone to look up because of possible danger • He shouted, "*Heads up*!" as he threw the ball.

[1]**heads–up** /ˈhɛdzˈʌp/ *noun* [*singular*] *US, informal* **:** a message that tells or warns someone about something that is going to happen • She ***gave him a heads-up*** that the company's president will be visiting the office.

[2]**heads–up** *adj, always used before a noun, US, informal* **:** showing that you are very aware of what is happening around you **:** ALERT • a *heads-up* play by the first baseman

head table *noun, pl* ~ **tables** [*count*] **:** the table at which the most important people sit during a formal meal

head teacher *noun, pl* ~ **-ers** [*count*] *Brit* **:** the person who is in charge of a school

head–to–head *adv* **:** in a direct competition or contest • The two teams will compete *head-to-head* for the championship. • He'll ***go head-to-head*** with his toughest opponent in the upcoming debate.

– head–to–head *adj, always used before a noun* • a *head-to-head* competition

head·wait·er /ˈhɛdˈweɪtɚ/ *noun, pl* **-ers** [*count*] **:** a waiter who is in charge of other waiters in a restaurant

head·wa·ters /ˈhɛdˌwɑːtɚz/ *noun* [*plural*] **:** the beginning and upper part of a stream or river • the *headwaters* of the Amazon

head·way /ˈhɛdˌweɪ/ *noun*

make headway **:** to move forward or make progress • The wind kept the boat from *making headway* toward shore. • The boat *made* little *headway* [=moved forward very little] against the strong wind. • We're gradually *making headway* with the project. • They've recently *made* some *headway* in their search for a cure.

head·wind /ˈhɛdˌwɪnd/ *noun, pl* **-winds** [*count*] **:** a wind that is blowing toward something (such as a ship or an airplane) as it moves forward — compare TAILWIND

head·word /ˈhɛdˌwɚd/ *noun, pl* **-words** [*count*] **:** a word placed at the beginning of an entry in a dictionary, encyclopedia, etc.

heady /ˈhɛdi/ *adj* **head·i·er; -est**

1 : causing feelings of excitement or dizziness **:** having a powerful effect on your senses • a *heady* wine/aroma • The plane soared to *heady* heights.

2 : very excited and happy • They were *heady* with their newfound success.

heal /ˈhiːl/ *verb* **heals; healed; heal·ing**

1 [*no obj*] **:** to become healthy or well again • The cut *healed* slowly. • You've got to give the injury time to *heal*. • After the divorce, he needed some time to *heal*.

2 [+ *obj*] **:** to make (someone or something) healthy or well again • The ointment will help *heal* the wound. • *heal* the sick • Only time will ***heal the rift/breach*** between the two families. [=make the two families become friendly again]

– heal·er /ˈhiːlɚ/ *noun, pl* **-ers** [*count*] • Native American *healers* • Time is a great *healer*. **– healing** *adj* • The tree sap is believed to have *healing* powers. • the *healing* process **– healing** *noun* [*noncount*] • traditional methods of *healing* — see also FAITH HEALING

[1]**health** /ˈhɛlθ/ *noun* [*noncount*]

1 a : the condition of being well or free from disease • We nursed him back to *health*. • My aunt is quite elderly, but she still has her *health*. [=she is still healthy] • She is ***the picture of health***. [=she is very healthy] ✧ If you ***drink (to) someone's health***, you take a drink as a wish for that person to be healthy. **b :** the overall condition of someone's body or mind • He's in good/poor *health* these days. • He has continued to enjoy good *health* in his old age. • Her *health* is excellent. = She is in the best of *health*. • Smoking is bad for your *health*. • He is concerned about his sister's mental *health*.

2 : the condition or state of something • We must protect the *health* of our oceans. • The economy is in a period of robust financial *health*. • Investors are worried about the company's *health*.

give (someone or something) a clean bill of health see [1]BILL

[2]**health** *adj, always used before a noun*

1 : of or relating to medical care • She works in the *health* field. • *health* insurance/services • He was treated at the *health* center.

2 : relating to or affecting the condition of your body or mind • *health* education • Have you had any *health* problems recently? • These chemicals pose a *health* hazard/risk.

health care *noun* [*noncount*] **:** the prevention or treatment of illness by doctors, dentists, psychologists, etc.

– health–care *adj, always used before a noun* • *health-care* workers

health club *noun, pl* ~ **clubs** [*count*] **:** a private club where people go to exercise

health farm *noun, pl* ~ **farms** [*count*] *chiefly Brit* **:** SPA 1b

health food *noun, pl* ~ **foods :** a food that is believed to be good for your health **:** a food that has no artificial ingredients [*noncount*] He eats only *health food*. • She shops at the *health-food* store. [*count*] The restaurant offers a variety of *health foods*.

health·ful /ˈhɛlθfəl/ *adj* [*more* ~; *most* ~] **:** good for your health **:** HEALTHY • *healthful* living • a *healthful* lifestyle/diet • The meal was both *healthful* and satisfying.

– health·ful·ly *adv* **– health·ful·ness** *noun* [*noncount*]

health spa *noun, pl* ~ **spas** [*count*] **:** SPA 1b

healthy /ˈhɛlθi/ *adj* **health·i·er; -est** [*also more* ~; *most* ~]

1 a : having good health **:** not sick or injured **:** WELL • *healthy* babies • tips for staying *healthy* **b :** showing good health • a *healthy* complexion • He has a *healthy* [=*hearty, large*] appetite.

2 : good for your health **:** HEALTHFUL • a *healthy* lifestyle/diet • *healthy* living • Those foods aren't *healthy* (for you). = It's not *healthy* (for you) to eat those foods.

3 : doing well **:** successful or growing • a *healthy* economy • The company is financially *healthy*.

4 : large in size or amount • A *healthy* number of her poems were published in the magazine. • She has a *healthy* bank account. • This line of work requires a *healthy* dose of self-discipline. • His business earns a *healthy* profit.

5 : sensible or natural • The students have a *healthy* curiosity about the world. • a *healthy* respect for dangerous animals

– health·i·ly /ˈhɛlθəli/ *adv* • living *healthily* • *healthily* active people **– health·i·ness** /ˈhɛlθinəs/ *noun* [*noncount*] **– healthy** *adv, informal* • He eats *healthy*. • She lives *healthy* by exercising and eating right.

[1]**heap** /ˈhiːp/ *noun, pl* **heaps** [*count*]

1 : a large, disordered pile of things • He dumped the grass clippings into the compost *heap*. • a *heap* of old newspapers • She left her dirty clothes ***in a heap*** on the floor. — see also SCRAP HEAP

2 *informal* **:** a great number or large amount of something • He's in a *heap* of trouble! — often plural • They've got *heaps* of money.

3 *informal* **:** an old car that is in poor condition • I can't believe he's still driving that old *heap*.

at the bottom/top of the heap — used to describe a person's level of success, position in society, etc. • Quite a few people applied for the job, but his past work experience put him *at the top of the heap*. [=made him the strongest candidate of the group] • People *at the bottom of the heap* [=poor people] will not be helped much by the new tax cuts.

collapse/fall (etc.) in a heap **:** to fall very suddenly to the ground and lie there • Overcome by heat exhaustion, he *collapsed/fell in a heap*.

²heap *verb* **heaps; heaped; heap·ing** [+ *obj*]

1 a : to put (something) in a large pile • He *heaped* the leaves (up) beside the fence. • They *heaped* food on our plates. [=they put a lot of food on our plates] — often used as *(be) heaped* • Books and magazines *were heaped* in a corner. • Bags of flour *were heaped* (up) on the counter. **b :** to put a pile or heap on or in (something) — + *with* • They *heaped* our plates *with* food. • She brought out a basket *heaped with* fruit. [=filled with a large amount of fruit]

2 : to give (something, such as praise, blame, etc.) in large amounts — + *on* or *upon* • The critics *heaped* scorn *on* our efforts. [=the critics were very scornful of our efforts] • He was embarrassed by all the praise being *heaped upon* him.

heaped *adj, Brit* **:** HEAPING • a *heaped* plateful • a *heaped* tablespoon

heaping *adj, US*

1 : holding a large pile of something • I ate three *heaping* platefuls of rice and beans.

2 : holding as much as can be held • Add one *heaping* tablespoon of sugar.

hear /ˈhiɚ/ *verb* **hears; heard** /ˈhɚd/; **hear·ing**

1 *not used in progressive tenses* **a :** to be aware of (sound) through the ear [+ *obj*] Do you *hear* that music? • I can't *hear* you. = I can't *hear* what you are saying. • I couldn't *hear* a word of what he said over all that noise. • I thought I *heard* him leave. • He was *heard* leaving. = He was *heard* to leave. [*no obj*] Would you turn the volume up a little? I can't *hear*. • She doesn't *hear* well. [=her ability to hear sounds is poor; her hearing is poor] **b** [+ *obj*] **:** to listen to (someone or something) • I *heard* her in concert a few years ago. • Have you ever *heard* Wagner sung/performed in English? • The committee will *hear* witnesses today.

2 : to be told (something) [+ *obj*] I *hear* he's leaving town. • "Is he leaving town?" "So I've *heard*." = "So I *hear*." • "Is he leaving town?" "That's what I'm *hearing*." [=that's what people are saying] • I don't know what happened. I'll let you know if I *hear* anything. • I've *heard* it said that smoking is bad for your health. • He *heard* it on the radio. • (*old-fashioned*) I ***hear tell*** that he's leaving town. • ***Have you heard the one/joke about*** the traveling salesman and the farmer's daughter? [*no obj*] Didn't you *hear*? There's a storm heading our way. — often + *about* • A week passed before they *heard about* the incident. • Frankly, I'm sick of *hearing about* his problems.

3 [+ *obj*] **:** to give attention to (someone or something) • Lord, *hear* our prayers.

4 [+ *obj*] *law* **:** to listen to and make a judgment about (a court case) • The judge will *hear* the case.

be hearing things **:** to hear sounds that are not real • She swears she heard someone open the door, but I think she's just *hearing things*.

hear from [*phrasal verb*] ***hear from (someone)*** **:** to receive a letter, a telephone call, etc., from (someone) • We *heard from* them yesterday. • I haven't *heard from* her lately. • I haven't *heard* anything *from* her lately.

Hear! Hear! — used during a speech or meeting to say that you agree with what someone else has just said

hear of [*phrasal verb*] ***hear of (someone or something)*** **:** to be aware of the existence of (someone or something) **:** to know about (someone or something) • He's supposed to be a famous actor, but this is the first time I've ever (even) *heard of* him. [=the first time I have heard his name] • I've never *heard of* such a thing! • If I *hear of* a job opening, I'll let you know. — see also NOT HEAR OF (below)

hear out [*phrasal verb*] ***hear (someone) out*** **:** to listen to (someone who wants to tell you something) • I know you don't agree but *hear* me *out*.

hear yourself think *informal* — used to say that you cannot think clearly because of loud talking, music, etc. • That music is so loud I *can't hear myself think*.

I hear what you're saying *informal* — used to say that you understand what someone is telling you • I *hear what you're saying* but I still disagree.

make your presence heard see PRESENCE

make yourself heard see ¹MAKE

never/not hear the end of it *informal* — used to say that someone will keep talking about something for a long time • If it turns out that he's right, we'll *never hear the end of it*. [=he will keep reminding us that he was right]

not hear of **:** to not allow (something) • We tried to pay him for his help, but he would*n't hear of* it. [=he wouldn't allow us to pay] — see also HEAR OF (above)

you could hear a pin drop see ¹PIN

hear·er /ˈhirɚ/ *noun, pl* **-ers** [*count*] **:** a person who hears or listens to someone or something • Different *hearers* may interpret the same phrase differently.

hear·ing /ˈhirɪŋ/ *noun, pl* **-ings**

1 [*noncount*] **:** the sense through which a person or animal is aware of sound **:** the ability to hear • Her *hearing* is good/poor. • He suffered some loss of *hearing* in his right ear. • She is ***hearing-impaired*** [=not able to hear well] — see also *hard of hearing* at ¹HARD

2 [*noncount*] **:** the distance within which someone's voice can be heard • She stayed ***within hearing*** of her mother's voice. [=she stayed close enough to her mother to hear her voice]

3 [*count*] **:** an opportunity to explain why you did, said, or believe something — usually singular • They agreed to give both sides ***a fair hearing*** [=they agreed to listen to and consider statements from both sides]

4 [*count*] **:** a meeting or session at which evidence and arguments about a crime, complaint, etc., are presented to a person or group who will have to decide on what action should be taken • The judge has granted them a *hearing*. • The committee held public *hearings* on the bill.

hearing aid *noun, pl* **~ aids** [*count*] **:** an electronic device worn in or on the ear to help a person who has hearing problems to hear better

hear·say /ˈhiɚˌseɪ/ *noun* [*noncount*] **:** something heard from another person **:** something that you have been told • You can't judge them solely on the basis of *hearsay*. • They're supposedly getting married soon, but that's just *hearsay*. • (*law*) ***hearsay evidence*** [=evidence presented by a witness that is based on another person's statement]

hearse /ˈhɚs/ *noun, pl* **hears·es** [*count*] **:** a large car that is used for carrying a coffin to a grave

heart /ˈhɑɚt/ *noun, pl* **hearts**

1 [*count*] **:** the organ in your chest that pumps blood through your veins and arteries • I could feel my *heart* pounding/racing. • He has a bad/weak *heart*. — often used before another noun • He suffers from a *heart* condition. • *heart* failure/disease/surgery • a *heart* murmur • Aerobic exercise increases your ***heart rate*** [=*pulse*] — see picture at HUMAN; see also CORONARY HEART DISEASE, OPEN-HEART

2 [*count*] **:** the front part of your chest • He put his hand on his *heart*. • (*literary*) She clutched the child to her *heart*. [=*breast, bosom*]

3 a [*count*] **:** the heart thought of as the place where emotions are felt • You shouldn't let your *heart* rule your head. [=you should be guided by reason and not by your emotions] • When she heard the news, her *heart* filled with joy/sorrow. • You're a man ***after my own heart*** [=we have similar likes and dislikes] • He offered to help us ***out of the goodness of his heart*** [=because he is a good person and not because he wanted to get anything for himself] • He ***wears his heart on his sleeve*** [=he shows his emotions very openly] • She's not too smart, but at least her ***heart is in the right place*** [=she is a kind person who is trying to do good things] • I just ***didn't have the heart*** to tell her that I didn't like her singing. [=I couldn't tell her because I knew that she would be hurt by what I said] • The idea ***struck fear into their hearts*** [=made them very afraid] • I decided to ***follow my heart*** [=to do what I truly wanted to do] and take up acting. • ***My heart goes out to*** [=I feel very sorry for] the families of the victims. • Her ***heart's desire*** [=greatest wish] was to become a movie star. • She just couldn't ***find it in her heart to*** forgive them. • I ***felt in my heart*** that our relationship was never meant to be. • I think she knows ***in her heart*** that they're right. = I think she knows it ***in her heart of hearts*** [=she knows it even though she does not want to admit it] • They said they'd try to fix the problem, but I could see that ***their hearts (just) weren't in it*** [=they did not really feel much interest or enthusiasm about doing it] **b :** a kind or generous feeling for other people [*noncount*] a ruler without *heart* [*count*] a ruler without a *heart* • He has a kind *heart*. [=he treats people kindly] • He has a cold/hard *heart*. [=he treats people in a harsh or unfriendly way] • She has ***a big heart*** = She is ***all heart*** = She has ***a heart of gold*** [=she is a very kind person] • She has ***a heart of stone*** [=she does not care at all about the feelings of other people] • ***Have a heart*** Can't you see he needs help? — see also CHANGE OF HEART, HEART-TO-HEART, LONELY HEARTS

4 [*noncount*] **:** feelings of love or affection • It's best not to interfere in ***matters/affairs of the heart*** [=romantic matters/

affairs] ▪ He was determined to ***win/steal/capture her heart***. [=to win her love]

5 [*noncount*] **:** emotional strength that allows you to continue in a difficult situation ▪ The team has shown a lot of *heart*.

6 a ***the heart*** **:** the central or most important part of something ▪ deep in *the heart* of the forest ▪ Their offices are in *the heart* of the city. ▪ Let's get right to *the heart of* the matter. **b** [*count*] **:** the central part of some vegetables ▪ artichoke *hearts* ▪ *cabbage* hearts

7 [*count*] **:** a shape that looks like a simple drawing of a heart and that is used as a symbol of love and affection ▪ The child decorated the card with *hearts* and flowers.

8 a [*count*] **:** a playing card that is marked with a red heart ▪ one *heart*, two diamonds, and two clubs — see picture at PLAYING CARD **b** ***hearts*** [*plural*] **:** the suit in a deck of playing cards that consists of cards marked by hearts ▪ the king of *hearts* — compare CLUB, DIAMOND, SPADE

absence makes the heart grow fonder see ABSENCE

at heart **1 :** at the most basic level ▪ I'm really a romantic *at heart*. ▪ She's 81 years old, but she's still ***young at heart***. [=she behaves and thinks like a much younger person] **2 :** as a main concern ▪ We ***have your best interests at heart***. [=we want to do what is best for you]

break someone's heart **:** to cause someone to feel great sorrow or sadness ▪ He *broke her heart* when he left her for another woman. ▪ Her boyfriend left her with a *broken heart*. ▪ It *breaks my heart* to think of how those children have suffered.

by heart **:** from memory ▪ She knows the entire poem *by heart*. [=she has learned the poem and can recite it from memory] ▪ He learned the speech *by heart*.

close/dear/near to your heart **:** very personally and emotionally important to you ▪ This topic is one that's very *close to my heart*. [=I care very much about this subject] ▪ The school is very ***near and dear to her heart***.

cross my heart see [2]CROSS

cry your heart out see [1]CRY

do your heart good **:** to make you feel very happy ▪ It *does his heart good* to know that his daughters have become friends.

eat your heart out see EAT

faint of heart see [1]FAINT

from the bottom of your heart *or* ***from the/your heart*** **:** in a very sincere way ▪ He thanked us *from the bottom of his heart*. ▪ When I said you were my best friend, I meant it *from the bottom of my heart*. ▪ His speech at the memorial service was ***straight from the heart***.

harden your heart see HARDEN

have your heart set on (something) *or* ***set your heart on (something)*** ✧ When you *have your heart set on something* or when you *set your heart on something*, you want it very much. ▪ She *has her heart set on* a new bicycle.

heart in your mouth *informal* ✧ If ***your heart is in your mouth***, you are very excited or nervous about something. ▪ He waited for her arrival with *his heart in his mouth*.

heart is knocking see [1]KNOCK

heart skips a beat *informal* ✧ When you say that your ***heart skipped a beat*** or that something ***made your heart skip a beat***, it means that you suddenly became very surprised, excited, or nervous about something. ▪ When I learned I was on live television, my *heart skipped a beat*. ▪ The news was enough to *make his heart skip a beat*.

heavy heart **:** a feeling of sadness ▪ It is with a *heavy heart* that I bring you this bad news.

know your own heart see [1]KNOW

light heart **:** a feeling of happiness ▪ He left for home with a *light heart*.

lose heart **:** to begin to feel that you cannot do something that you have been trying to do **:** to become discouraged ▪ They never *lost heart*, even in the face of adversity.

lose your heart **:** to fall in love with someone ▪ He met a beautiful woman and *lost his heart*. — usually + *to* ▪ She *lost her heart to* a dashing young artist.

open your heart **1 :** to talk in a very open and honest way about your feelings ▪ He *opened his heart* (to her) and told her how he really felt. **2 :** to begin to be generous and kind ▪ We should all *open our hearts* and do something to help those poor children.

pour your heart out see POUR

sick at heart **:** very sad and upset ▪ The idea of children suffering from hunger made him *sick at heart*.

sing/dance/play (etc.) your heart out **:** to sing/dance/play (etc.) with great energy or effort ▪ The band *played their hearts out* in hopes of winning the prize.

take heart **:** to begin to feel better and more hopeful **:** to stop feeling sad or discouraged ▪ *Take heart*; things will get better soon.

take (something) to heart **:** to be deeply affected or hurt by something ▪ He *took their criticism* (very much) *to heart*.

to your heart's content **:** until you feel satisfied **:** as long or as much as you want ▪ They let him eat and drink *to his heart's content*. ▪ Let's go somewhere where we can talk *to our hearts' content*.

warm the cockles of your heart see COCKLE

with all your heart **:** in a very sincere and deeply felt way ▪ I love him *with all my heart*. ▪ She tried *with all her heart* to please them.

your heart bleeds for ✧ If *your heart bleeds for* someone, you feel great sadness or pity for that person.

your heart leaps ✧ When *your heart leaps*, you become very happy or joyful about something. ▪ *Our hearts leapt* when we heard that she had won.

your heart melts ✧ When *your heart melts*, you begin to feel love, affection, or sympathy for someone or something. ▪ When he saw the puppies, *his heart melted*. ▪ It would have *melted your heart* to see her lying in that hospital bed. ▪ A warm smile *melts the heart*.

your heart sinks ✧ When *your heart sinks*, you become sad or disappointed about something. ▪ *My heart sank* when I saw the sad expression on her face.

heart·ache /ˈhɑɚtˌeɪk/ *noun, pl* **-aches :** a strong feeling of sadness [*count*] I've had more than my share of *heartaches* in my life. [*noncount*] If you ignore the problem, you'll just cause yourself more *heartache* [=*grief*] later on.

heart attack *noun, pl* **~ -tacks** [*count*] **:** a sudden painful and dangerous condition in which your heart stops beating properly ▪ Her chest pains turned out to be caused by a minor *heart attack*. ▪ He died of a massive *heart attack*. ▪ He fell off the swing and ***nearly gave me a heart attack***. [=scared me very badly]

heart·beat /ˈhɑɚtˌbiːt/ *noun, pl* **-beats** [*count*] **:** the action or sound of the heart as it pumps blood ▪ The patient had a rapid *heartbeat*. ▪ irregular *heartbeats*

in a heartbeat *US, informal* **:** in a very brief time **:** without any delay or hesitation ▪ Even though the job was difficult, he says he'd agree to do it again *in a heartbeat*.

heart·break /ˈhɑɚtˌbreɪk/ *noun, pl* **-breaks :** a very strong feeling of sadness, disappointment, etc. [*count*] He recently suffered a string of romantic *heartbreaks*. [*noncount*] She's had more than her share of *heartbreak*. [=her heart has been broken many times]

heart·break·er /ˈhɑɚtˌbreɪkɚ/ *noun, pl* **-ers** [*count*] **:** someone or something that causes you to feel very sad, disappointed, etc. **:** someone or something that breaks your heart ▪ a handsome actor who has a reputation as a *heartbreaker* [=as someone who breaks the hearts of many women] ▪ The team's most recent loss was a real *heartbreaker*.

heart·break·ing /ˈhɑɚtˌbreɪkɪŋ/ *adj* [*more* ~; *most* ~] **:** causing great sadness, disappointment, etc. ▪ She wrote a *heartbreaking* story about the death of her grandfather. ▪ It was *heartbreaking* to know that there was nothing I could do. ▪ The team suffered another *heartbreaking* defeat.

— **heart·break·ing·ly** *adv* [*more* ~; *most* ~] ▪ a *heartbreakingly* tragic movie

heart·bro·ken /ˈhɑɚtˌbroʊkən/ *adj* [*more* ~; *most* ~] **:** filled with great sadness ▪ She is *heartbroken* [=*brokenhearted*] that things turned out so badly.

heart·burn /ˈhɑɚtˌbɚn/ *noun* [*noncount*] **:** an unpleasant hot feeling in your chest caused by something that you ate ▪ I like spicy food, but it gives me *heartburn*.

heart·en /ˈhɑɚtn̩/ *verb* **-ens; -ened; -en·ing** [+ *obj*] **:** to cause (someone) to feel more cheerful or hopeful ▪ The team's victory has *heartened* its fans. — usually used as *(be) heartened* ▪ The team's fans *were heartened* by the victory.

— **heartening** *adj* [*more* ~; *most* ~] ▪ It was ***heartening* to** see him looking so happy. ▪ We've received some *heartening* news.

heart·felt /ˈhɑɚtˌfɛlt/ *adj* [*more* ~; *most* ~] **:** deeply felt **:** very sincere ▪ You have our *heartfelt* thanks/sympathy/congratulations. ▪ Our most *heartfelt* wish is for our children to be happy.

hearth /ˈhɑɚθ/ *noun, pl* **hearths** [*count*] **:** the floor in front of or inside a fireplace ▪ They swept the ashes from the *hearth*. ▪ (*literary*) They longed for the comforts of ***hearth and home***. [=the comforts of home]

heart–healthy /ˈhaɚtˌhɛlθi/ *adj* [*more* ~; *most* ~] *chiefly US* : good for the health of your heart ▪ a *heart-healthy* diet ▪ *heart-healthy* foods

heart·i·ly /ˈhaɚtəli/ *adv* [*more* ~; *most* ~]
1 : in an enthusiastic and energetic way : in a hearty way ▪ The children ate *heartily.* [=they ate a lot of food] ▪ We all laughed *heartily.* ▪ I *heartily* recommend the movie.
2 : completely or fully ▪ I'm *heartily* sick of their complaints. ▪ I'll be *heartily* [=*very*] glad when this job is done. ▪ They *heartily* agreed.

heart·land /ˈhaɚtˌlænd/ *noun, pl* **-lands** [*count*]
1 a : a central area of land ▪ We drove into Scotland's *heartland.* **b** : the central area of the U.S. which is known for traditional values ▪ a politician who is popular in the American *heartland*
2 : an area that is the center of an industry or activity ▪ the *heartland* of high technology

heart·less /ˈhaɚtləs/ *adj* [*more* ~; *most* ~] : very cruel ▪ a *heartless* person/act
– **heart·less·ly** *adv* ▪ She rescues pets that have been *heartlessly* abandoned. – **heart·less·ness** *noun* [*noncount*]

heart·rend·ing /ˈhaɚtˌrɛndɪŋ/ *adj* [*more* ~; *most* ~] : causing great sadness or sorrow ▪ a *heartrending* [=*heartbreaking*] story/cry
– **heart·rend·ing·ly** *adv*

heart·sick /ˈhaɚtˌsɪk/ *adj* [*more* ~; *most* ~] : very sad or disappointed ▪ They were absolutely *heartsick* over/about the loss of their home. ▪ I was *heartsick* to learn of their divorce.

heart–stop·ping /ˈhaɚtˌstɑːpɪŋ/ *adj, always used before a noun* [*more* ~; *most* ~] : extremely shocking or exciting ▪ a *heart-stopping* adventure ▪ *heart-stopping* views of the canyon

heart·strings /ˈhaɚtˌstrɪŋz/ *noun* [*plural*] : deep emotions ▪ That movie really ***tugs/pulls at your heartstrings***. [=makes you emotional] ▪ a writer who knows how to ***play on his readers' heartstrings***

heart·throb /ˈhaɚtˌθrɑːb/ *noun, pl* **-throbs** [*count*] : an attractive and usually famous man ▪ the latest teen *heartthrob*

[1]**heart–to–heart** /ˈhaɚttəˈhaɚt/ *adj* : very sincere and honest ▪ The two of them had a *heart-to-heart* talk. [=they spoke to each other about their feelings very honestly]

[2]**heart–to–heart** *noun, pl* **-hearts** [*count*] : an honest, serious, and private conversation ▪ He had a *heart-to-heart* with his son about the facts of life.

heart·warm·ing /ˈhaɚtˌwaɚmɪŋ/ *adj* [*more* ~; *most* ~] : causing pleasant feelings of happiness ▪ The movie is a *heartwarming* story about a boy and his dog. ▪ It's *heartwarming* to see how his neighbors have helped him.

hearty /ˈhaɚti/ *adj* **heart·i·er**; **-est** [*also more* ~; *most* ~]
1 : done or expressed in a very open, cheerful, and energetic way ▪ He gave us all a *hearty* welcome/greeting. ▪ Our plan won their *hearty* [=*wholehearted*] approval. ▪ a *hearty* laugh/handshake
2 : strong, healthy, and active ▪ *hearty* young men and women ▪ His grandmother remains ***hale and hearty*** in her old age. ▪ All of the children have ***hearty appetites***. = All of the children are ***hearty eaters***. [=all of the children eat large amounts of food]
3 : large enough to satisfy hunger ▪ a *hearty* meal ▪ *hearty* soups
– **heart·i·ness** *noun* [*noncount*]

[1]**heat** /ˈhiːt/ *noun, pl* **heats**
1 [*noncount*] : energy that causes things to become warmer ▪ The sun's *heat* melted the snow. ▪ the intense *heat* of a fire ▪ She applied *heat* to the sore muscles in her leg. ▪ body *heat*
2 [*noncount*] : hot weather or temperatures ▪ a period of high *heat* and humidity ▪ The crops were damaged by drought and extreme *heat.* ▪ the desert's ***dry heat*** [=hot temperatures with little moisture in the air] — often used with *the* ▪ She doesn't like *the heat.* ▪ The runners performed well despite *the* 90-degree *heat.* ▪ These flowers tend to wilt in *the heat* of summer. ▪ They found a place to rest during *the* midday/afternoon *heat.* ▪ They rested during ***the heat of the day***. [=the hottest part of the day]
3 a : the level of temperature that is used to cook something [*count*] — usually singular ▪ The meat was cooked at a high *heat* for 10 minutes. ▪ Reduce the *heat* to low and simmer. [*noncount*] Cook the milk over low/gentle/medium *heat.* **b** [*singular*] : a source of heat used for cooking something : the hot part of an oven, stove top, etc. ▪ Remove the pan from the *heat.*
4 [*singular*] *chiefly US* : a system that is used to provide warmth to a room or building ▪ The house uses electric/gas/oil/solar *heat.* [=*heating*] ▪ Would you please turn up/down the *heat*? [=(*Brit*) *heating*]
5 [*noncount*] **a** : strong and often angry feelings ▪ It's a topic that generates a lot of *heat.* ▪ He responded with some *heat* [=he responded in an angry way] to the accusations. **b** : the time when emotions are most strongly felt — used in phrases like ***in the heat of passion, in the heat of the moment***, etc. ▪ The crime was committed *in the heat of passion.* [=when the criminal was very angry] ▪ She said things in *the heat of the moment* [=when she was angry for a short period of time] that she later regretted. — see also *in the heat of (the) battle* at [1]BATTLE
6 [*noncount*] *chiefly US, informal* **a the heat** : pressure to do something ▪ The administration is ***putting the heat on*** legislators to approve the tax bill. ▪ She's at her best when ***the heat is on***. [=when she feels a lot of pressure; when she needs to finish something quickly] ▪ The company has ***turned up the heat on*** [=has put extra pressure on] its employees to finish the job quickly. ✧ The expression ***if you can't stand/take the heat, get out of the kitchen*** means that you should not try to do a difficult job if you cannot deal with the pressure and problems that are part of the job. **b** : criticism or abuse ▪ He will likely take/get a lot of *heat* for his decision.
7 [*count*] : one of several races or contests that are held in order to decide who will be in the final race or contest ▪ The top two finishers in each *heat* will move on to the finals. — see also DEAD HEAT
in heat (*US*) ***or Brit on heat*** — used to describe a female animal that is ready to have sex and is able to become pregnant ▪ The cat is *in heat.* ▪ like a dog *in heat* ▪ an animal that is ***coming into heat*** [=beginning to be in heat]
more heat than light ✧ To produce or generate *more heat than light* means to cause anger without helping to make something better understood. ▪ Her first book on the issue generated *more heat than light.*
pack heat *US slang, old-fashioned + humorous* : to carry a gun ▪ a thug who was *packing heat*
– see also PRICKLY HEAT
– **heat·less** /ˈhiːtləs/ *adj* ▪ *heatless* buildings

[2]**heat** *verb* **heats**; **heat·ed**; **heat·ing** [+ *obj*] : to cause (something) to become warm or hot ▪ I *heated* the vegetables in the microwave. ▪ They *heat* their house with a wood stove.
heat up [*phrasal verb*] **1** : to become warm or hot ▪ The morning started out cold but it *heated up* quickly. **2** : to become more active, intense, or angry ▪ Their conversation started to *heat up.* [=(*Brit*) *hot up*] ▪ Competition between the two companies is *heating up.* **3** ***heat (something) up*** *or* ***heat up (something)*** : to cause (something) to become warm or hot ▪ Could you *heat up* the vegetables, please? — see also PREHEAT

heat·ed /ˈhiːtəd/ *adj*
1 : including a system that provides warmth ▪ a *heated* pool/apartment
2 [*more* ~; *most* ~] : marked by excited or angry feelings ▪ a *heated* argument/debate/dispute ▪ Their conversation/discussion quickly became *heated.*
– **heat·ed·ly** *adv* ▪ He *heatedly* denied the rumors.

heat·er /ˈhiːtɚ/ *noun, pl* **-ers** [*count*] : a machine that heats water or air ▪ a water *heater* — see also SPACE HEATER

heat exhaustion *noun* [*noncount*] *medical* : a condition that happens when someone is too active in extremely hot conditions and that causes a person to sweat and feel very weak, dizzy, etc. — called also (*chiefly US*) *heat prostration*; compare HEATSTROKE

heath /ˈhiːθ/ *noun, pl* **heaths** [*count*] : an area of land that is covered with grass and small shrubs

hea·then /ˈhiːðən/ *noun, pl* **hea·thens** *or* **heathen** [*count*] *old-fashioned + often offensive* : a person who is not religious or who does not practice Christianity, Judaism, or Islam
– **heathen** *adj* ▪ *heathen* gods/practices ▪ a *heathen* people/nation

heath·er /ˈhɛðɚ/ *noun, pl* **-ers** [*count*] : a low-growing plant of northern areas that has small leaves and tiny white or purplish-pink flowers

Heath Rob·in·son /ˌhiːθˈrɑːbənsən/ *adj, always used before a noun, Brit* : RUBE GOLDBERG ▪ a *Heath Robinson* contraption/device

heating *noun* [*noncount*] : a system that is used to provide warmth to a room or building ▪ a house with electric *heating* [=*heat*] ▪ (*Brit*) Would you please turn up/down the *heating*? [=(*US*) *heat*] ▪ The house has ***central heating***. [=a system that heats all parts of a building]

H

heat lightning *noun [noncount] chiefly US* : flashes of light in the sky that happen without the sound of thunder and that are produced by distant lightning

heat•proof /ˈhiːtˌpruːf/ *adj* : not able to be burned or melted ▪ a *heatproof* bowl/dish/plate

heat prostration *noun [noncount] chiefly US, medical* : HEAT EXHAUSTION

heat rash *noun, pl* ~ **rashes** *[count, noncount] medical* : a skin rash that people sometimes get during hot weather : PRICKLY HEAT

heat resistant *adj [more ~; most ~]* : not easily burned or melted ▪ *heat resistant* cooking utensils

heat–seeking *adj, always used before a noun* : designed to follow the heat from an airplane or rocket in order to destroy it ▪ *heat-seeking* missiles

heat•stroke /ˈhiːtˌstroʊk/ *noun [noncount] medical* : a serious condition that happens when someone has been in high temperatures for a long time and that causes a person to stop sweating, have a very high body temperature, and become exhausted or unconscious — compare HEAT EXHAUSTION, SUNSTROKE

heat wave *noun, pl* ~ **waves** *[count]* : a period of unusually hot weather

[1]**heave** /ˈhiːv/ *verb* **heaves; heaved; heav•ing**

1 : to lift or pull (something) with effort *[+ obj]* We *heaved* the box (up) onto the table. ▪ I tried to *heave* myself (up) out of the chair. ▪ She *heaved* the door shut. *[no obj]* — usually + *on* ▪ The sailors started *heaving on* the rope.

2 *[+ obj] US* : to throw (something) with effort ▪ *heave* a rock ▪ The quarterback *heaved* the ball down the field.

3 *[+ obj]* : to breathe in and breathe out (a sigh) in a slow or loud way ▪ She sat down and *heaved* a sigh of relief.

4 *[no obj]* **a** : to move up and down repeatedly ▪ He stopped running and stood there with his chest *heaving*. ▪ The boat *heaved* up and down with the waves. **b** : to be pushed up ▪ The roads have begun to *heave* with frost.

5 *[no obj] informal* : VOMIT ▪ The smell made me want to *heave*. ✧ If your ***stomach is heaving***, you feel like vomiting.

heave into view *or* ***heave in/into sight*** *past tense and past participle* **hove** : to slowly move closer and become visible ▪ A ship *hove into view* on the horizon.

heave to *[phrasal verb] past tense and past participle* **hove** *of a boat or ship* : to stop moving ▪ The ship *hove to*.

— see also HEAVING

[2]**heave** *noun, pl* **heaves** *[count]*

1 : an act of lifting or pulling something with effort ▪ We lifted the box onto the table with a *heave*. ▪ He gave the rope a mighty *heave*.

2 : a forceful throw ▪ The quarterback uncorked a mighty *heave*.

— see also DRY HEAVES

heave–ho /ˈhiːvˈhoʊ/ *noun*

the (old) heave-ho *informal* : the act of causing someone to leave a job, place, or relationship ▪ The team's coach ***gave him the heave-ho*** [=made him leave the team] ▪ We ***got the old heave-ho*** [=we got kicked out; we had to leave] when we couldn't pay the rent on our apartment.

heav•en /ˈhɛvən/ *noun, pl* **-ens**

1 *or* **Heaven** *[singular]* : the place where God lives and where good people go after they die according to some religions ▪ She prayed to God in *Heaven*. ▪ He hopes to go to *Heaven* when he dies. ▪ Our baby is a gift from *heaven*.

2 *[noncount]* : something that is very pleasant or good ▪ The week at the beach was (sheer/pure) *heaven*. ▪ *(chiefly US)* The cake tastes ***like heaven*** [=it is delicious] ▪ Her voice sounded *like heaven*. [=it sounded very beautiful]

3 ***the heavens*** : the sky ▪ the brightest star in *the heavens* ▪ ***The heavens opened (up)*** [=it began to rain] and the game had to be stopped.

4 — used informally by itself and in phrases to make a statement or question more forceful or to express surprise, anger, etc. ▪ "Have you ever committed a crime?" "*Heavens*, no!" ▪ ***Good heavens*** You startled me. ▪ ***Heaven's above*** I haven't seen you in a while. ▪ ***My heavens*** [=(more commonly) *my goodness*] you've grown! ▪ Who ***in heaven's name*** [=*on earth, in God's name*] could that be? ▪ Where *in heaven's name* have you been? ▪ ***For heaven's sake*** turn down that music!

(a) heaven on earth : a very pleasant or enjoyable place or situation ▪ We spent our vacation in *a* real *heaven on earth*. ▪ The time we spent together was *heaven on earth*.

heaven forbid see FORBID

heaven help someone see [1]HELP

heaven knows see [1]KNOW

made in heaven : very good and successful ▪ Theirs was ***a marriage made in heaven*** ▪ Our partnership is ***a match made in heaven***

move heaven and earth see [1]MOVE

thank heaven/heavens see THANK

to high heaven *informal* : very much, very badly, etc. ▪ The kids were laughing and screaming *to high heaven*. [=very loudly] ▪ This whole situation ***stinks to high heaven*** [=it stinks; it is very bad or wrong]

— see also HOG HEAVEN, SEVENTH HEAVEN

heav•en•ly /ˈhɛvənli/ *adj*

1 *always used before a noun* : appearing or occurring in the sky ▪ the moon, stars, and other ***heavenly bodies***

2 *always used before a noun* : of or relating to heaven : divine or blessed ▪ *heavenly* angels/choirs ▪ *heavenly* grace

3 *[more ~; most ~] informal* : very pleasant or good ▪ The weather was *heavenly*. ▪ a *heavenly* dessert

heav•en–sent /ˈhɛvənˌsɛnt/ *adj* : very lucky or helpful ▪ a *heaven-sent* opportunity ▪ Her advice was *heaven-sent*.

heav•en•ward /ˈhɛvənwəd/ *also chiefly Brit* **heav•en•wards** /ˈhɛvənwədz/ *adv* : toward the sky ▪ Lift your eyes *heavenward*.

heavi•ly /ˈhɛvəli/ *adv [more ~; most ~]*

1 : to a great degree : very much ▪ *heavily* salted foods ▪ *heavily* armored vehicles ▪ *heavily* populated/forested areas ▪ He relies *heavily* on his wife for advice. ▪ These artists borrow *heavily* from Picasso. ▪ Our flowers were *heavily* damaged by a late spring frost. ▪ She drank and smoked *heavily* for years. ▪ The decision weighs *heavily* on my mind. [=the decision is difficult and causes me to feel worried]

2 : in a slow or heavy way ▪ He sat down *heavily* on the couch. ▪ He was leaning *heavily* on the table. ▪ She sighed *heavily* then said "Okay, I'll do it."

heaving *adj, Brit* : filled with people and activity ▪ The shop was *heaving* [=*teeming*] with customers.

[1]**heavy** /ˈhɛvi/ *adj* **heavi•er; -est**

1 a : having great weight : difficult to lift or move ▪ "Is that box too *heavy* for you to lift?" "No, it's not very *heavy*." ▪ a *heavy* suitcase ▪ *heavy* pots and pans ▪ The truck was carrying a *heavy* load. — opposite LIGHT **b** : large in size and weight ▪ The man was six feet tall with a *heavy* build. ▪ a tall, *heavy* [=(less politely) *fat*] man

2 : having a particular weight ▪ How *heavy* is it? [=how much does it weigh?]

3 a : greater in amount or degree than usual ▪ Turnout for the election is expected to be *heavy*. ▪ We got caught in *heavy* traffic. **b** : strong ▪ *heavy* perfume ▪ *heavy* winds **c** : great in amount ▪ *Heavy* rains caused flooding in the area. ▪ *heavy* bleeding/sweating ▪ She was wearing sunglasses and *heavy* makeup. ▪ The storm caused *heavy* damage to the building. ▪ The company is facing *heavy* losses this quarter. ▪ We suffered *heavy* casualties. [=many deaths or injuries] ▪ a day of *heavy* fighting **d** : difficult to accept or bear ▪ They are paying a *heavy* price for their mistakes. ▪ It is a *heavy* burden for one person to bear. : harsh or severe ▪ The stress has taken a *heavy* toll on his health. ▪ *heavy* fines/penalties **e** : great in degree or effect ▪ He came under *heavy* attack/fire for his comments. ▪ She is the *heavy* favorite to win. ▪ the country's *heavy* reliance on oil ▪ *(chiefly Brit)* He caught a *heavy* cold. — opposite LIGHT

4 : involving a lot of physical effort ▪ an hour of *heavy* exercise/exertion ▪ Why do I have to do all the ***heavy work***? ▪ I hurt my back and couldn't do any ***heavy lifting*** — sometimes used figuratively ▪ He does all the *heavy lifting* [=difficult work] while his partner gets the recognition. — opposite LIGHT

5 : very loud or forceful ▪ The song has a *heavy* beat. ▪ There was a *heavy* knock at the door. ▪ *heavy* footsteps ▪ He delivered a ***heavy blow*** to his opponent. — often used figuratively ▪ The new government was dealt a *heavy blow*. — opposite LIGHT

6 : important and serious ▪ We were having a *heavy* conversation about our son's future. ▪ This is pretty *heavy* stuff. ▪ doing some *heavy* reading/thinking ▪ a *heavy* thinker — opposite LIGHT

7 : difficult to move or lift up because of tiredness ▪ My legs became *heavier* with every step. ▪ Her eyelids grew *heavy*.

8 : dense and thick : having a lot of hair, trees, etc., in a small area ▪ He has a *heavy* beard. ▪ The animals have shed their *heavy* winter coats. ▪ areas of forest and *heavy* brush ▪ *heavy* fog/smoke ▪ *heavy* clay soil — opposite LIGHT

9 : made of thick material ▪ a *heavy* winter coat ▪ *heavy* blankets

10 : having too much heat, moisture, etc., and not enough fresh air ▪ The air was *heavy* and still. ▪ The air in the room was *heavy* with smoke. ▪ the *heavy* odor of wet dogs

11 a : showing signs of rain or snow ▪ sailing in *heavy* weather ▪ a *heavy* sky ▪ *heavy* clouds **b :** having large waves ▪ *heavy* seas

12 : deep and loud ▪ She let out a *heavy* sigh. ▪ the *heavy* breathing of a tired runner ✧ The phrase ***heavy breathing*** is sometimes used in a joking way to refer to sexual activity. ▪ a night of *heavy breathing*

13 a : eating, drinking, or using large amounts of something ▪ a *heavy* eater/drinker/smoker ▪ a cook who has a ***heavy hand*** with the salt [=who uses too much salt] **b :** done often and in large amounts ▪ *heavy* alcohol consumption ▪ Years of *heavy* smoking had destroyed her lungs. — opposite LIGHT

14 a : very rich, dense, or thick ▪ fruit in *heavy* syrup ▪ The bread was a little *heavy*. **b :** making your stomach feel full ▪ *heavy* desserts ▪ a *heavy* breakfast of pancakes and sausage — opposite LIGHT

15 a : large and powerful ▪ *heavy* machinery/equipment ▪ the army's tanks and *heavy* artillery ▪ He flew *heavy* bombers in World War II. **b** *of a group of soldiers* **:** having more weapons and armor than other groups ▪ *heavy* infantry/cavalry — opposite LIGHT

16 *of a person's accent* **:** very easy to notice ▪ She spoke French/English/German with a *heavy* [=*thick*] accent.

heavy date *chiefly US, humorous* **:** an important romantic date ▪ He has a *heavy date* tonight.

heavy going **:** difficult to do or finish ▪ The cold made the race *heavy going* for many runners. ▪ The book is really *heavy going* at the beginning.

heavy heart ✧ If you have a *heavy heart*, you are sad. ▪ I announced my decision to leave with a *heavy heart*.

heavy on **:** having or using a large amount of (something) ▪ His movies are light/low on talk and *heavy on* action. ▪ She tends to be *heavy on* the salt. [=she uses a lot of salt]

heavy sleeper **:** someone who does not wake up easily

heavy with **:** carrying or having a large amount of (something) ▪ The trees are *heavy with* fruit. ▪ Her comments were *heavy with* irony.

hot and heavy see [1]HOT

make heavy weather of *Brit, informal* **:** to treat (something) in a way that makes it seem more important or difficult than it really is ▪ an actor who *makes heavy weather of* what should be a simple scene

– heavi·ness *noun* [*noncount*] the *heaviness* of the table [*singular*] He felt a sudden *heaviness* [=a feeling of pressure] in his chest. — often used figuratively ▪ There was a *heaviness* [=a feeling of sadness] in his heart.

[2]heavy *adv* **:** in a heavy way **:** HEAVILY ▪ The smoke hung/lay *heavy* in the air. ▪ The decision weighs *heavy* on my mind. [=the decision is difficult and causes me to feel worried]

go heavy on **:** to use a lot of (something) ▪ *Go heavy on* the sauce, please.

heavy on your hands ✧ If time hangs or lies *heavy on your hands*, it passes very slowly. ▪ Time hung *heavy on his hands*.

[3]heavy *noun, pl* **heav·ies** [*count*]

1 : a bad person in a movie or play **:** VILLAIN ▪ He played the *heavy* in film after film.

2 *US, informal* **:** a person or thing that is serious, important, or powerful **:** HEAVYWEIGHT ▪ The conference will be attended by several media *heavies*. ▪ They have become one of the industry *heavies*.

heavy cream *noun* [*noncount*] *US* **:** very thick cream — called also (*Brit*) *double cream*

heavy–du·ty /ˈhɛviˈduːti, *Brit* ˈhɛviˈdjuːti/ *adj* [*more* ~; *most* ~]

1 : designed to do difficult work without breaking ▪ *heavy-duty* vehicles/machines

2 *US* **:** very intense or serious ▪ *heavy-duty* efforts ▪ a *heavy-duty* conservative ▪ I need to do some *heavy-duty* studying. ▪ Her plan is facing some *heavy-duty* opposition.

heavy goods vehicle *noun, pl* ~ **-hicles** [*count*] *Brit* **:** HGV

heavy–hand·ed /ˈhɛviˈhændəd/ *adj* [*more* ~; *most* ~]

1 : dealing with people or problems in a severe or harsh way **:** too strict or controlling ▪ Their efforts to keep the peace have been *heavy-handed*. ▪ *heavy-handed* tactics/measures

2 : awkward or clumsy **:** showing a lack of skill ▪ Her love songs tend to be a bit *heavy-handed*. ▪ a writer with a *heavy-handed* style

– heavy–hand·ed·ly *adv* **– heavy–hand·ed·ness** *noun* [*noncount*]

heavy hitter *noun, pl* ~ **-ters** [*count*] *US, informal* **:** an important or powerful person or thing ▪ She spoke to a room full of political *heavy hitters*. ▪ Their company is one of the industry's *heavy hitters*.

heavy industry *noun* [*noncount*] **:** the production of goods (such as coal or steel) that are used to make other goods — compare LIGHT INDUSTRY

heavy metal *noun, pl* ~ **-als**

1 [*noncount*] **:** a type of loud rock music that has a strong beat ▪ He listens to *heavy metal*.

2 [*count, noncount*] *technical* **:** a metal that is very dense and heavy ▪ lead, gold, and other *heavy metals*

heavy·set /ˌhɛviˈsɛt/ *adj* [*more* ~; *most* ~] **:** having a heavy and often somewhat fat body **:** THICKSET ▪ a short, *heavyset* man

heavy·weight /ˈhɛviˌweɪt/ *noun, pl* **-weights** [*count*]

1 : a fighter in the heaviest class of boxers **:** a boxer who weighs more than 175 pounds (79.5 kilograms) — often used before another noun ▪ They are fighting for the *heavyweight* title. ▪ the *heavyweight* champion of the world

2 : someone or something that is very important and powerful ▪ Their company is one of the industry's *heavyweights*.

3 : something that is heavy — often used before another noun ▪ *heavyweight* paper ▪ *heavyweight* cotton/wool/silk

He·bra·ic /hɪˈbrejɪk/ *adj* **:** of or relating to the Hebrews or their language or culture ▪ *Hebraic* traditions ▪ *Hebraic* texts/music

He·brew /ˈhiːbruː/ *noun, pl* **-brews**

1 [*count*] **:** a member of an ancient group of people who lived mostly in the kingdom of Israel and practiced Judaism

2 [*noncount*] **a :** the language of the ancient Hebrews **b :** the language of modern Israel

– Hebrew *adj* ▪ the *Hebrew* people/Bible

heck /ˈhɛk/ *noun* [*noncount*] *informal* — used as a more polite form of *hell* ▪ Oh, *heck*, I forgot my keys. ▪ "Did you give her any money?" "*Heck*, no!" ▪ They were mad ***as heck***. ▪ I decided to go just ***for the heck of it***. ▪ It was one ***heck of a*** good fight. ▪ Where ***in (the) heck*** did I put my keys? ▪ My back hurts ***like heck***. ▪ Let's get ***the heck*** out of here. ▪ ***What the heck*** was that? ▪ *What the heck*, let's try it.

heck·le /ˈhɛkəl/ *verb* **heck·les; heck·led; heck·ling :** to interrupt (someone, such as a speaker or performer) by shouting annoying or rude comments or questions [+ *obj*] Several protesters were *heckling* the speaker at the rally. ▪ The players were being *heckled* by the fans. [*no obj*] People in the crowd were booing and *heckling* as she tried to speak.

– heck·ler /ˈhɛklɚ/ *noun, pl* **-lers** [*count*] ▪ There were several *hecklers* at the rally. **– heckling** *noun* [*noncount*] ▪ She was upset by the crowd's *heckling*.

hect·are /ˈhɛkˌteɚ/ *noun, pl* **-ares** [*count*] **:** a unit of area in the metric system that is equal to 10,000 square meters or 2.47 acres

hec·tic /ˈhɛktɪk/ *adj* [*more* ~; *most* ~] **:** very busy and filled with activity ▪ We both had *hectic* days at work. ▪ She maintains a *hectic* schedule as a journalist and mother. ▪ a *hectic* lifestyle

– hec·ti·cal·ly /ˈhɛktɪkli/ *adv* ▪ *hectically* busy

hec·tor /ˈhɛktɚ/ *verb* **-tors; -tored; -tor·ing** [+ *obj*] **:** to criticize or question (someone) in a threatening way ▪ The judge ordered the attorney to stop *hectoring* the witness.

– hectoring *adj* [*more* ~; *most* ~] ▪ a *hectoring* tone of voice

he'd /ˈhiːd, id/ — used as a contraction of *he had* or *he would* ▪ He thought *he'd* [=*he had*] better be leaving. ▪ *He'd* [=*he would*] have done the same thing himself.

[1]hedge /ˈhɛʤ/ *noun, pl* **hedg·es** [*count*]

1 : a row of shrubs or small trees that are planted close to each other in order to form a boundary

2 : something that provides protection or defense — usually + *against* ▪ She invests her money as a *hedge against* inflation. ▪ *hedges against* loss/disappointment/uncertainty/failure

[2]hedge *verb* **hedges; hedged; hedg·ing**

1 [+ *obj*] **:** to surround (an area) with a hedge ▪ The garden is *hedged* by flowering shrubs.

2 : to avoid giving a promise or direct answer [*no obj*] She *hedged* when she was asked to support the campaign. [+ *obj*] He *hedged* his earlier comments about the need for new management.

hedge against [*phrasal verb*] ***hedge against (something)*** **:** to protect yourself from (something) ▪ They *hedge against* inflation by investing their money. ▪ looking for ways to *hedge against* risk/failure

hedge around *or* ***hedge about*** [*phrasal verb*] ***hedge (something) around/about*** *Brit* : to limit or restrict (something) — usually used as *(be) hedged*; usually + *with* or *by* ▪ Their offer *is* so *hedged around with* conditions [=so restricted by conditions] that it hardly seems worthwhile. ▪ a rule that *is hedged about* by exceptions

hedge in [*phrasal verb*] **1** ***hedge in (something)*** *or* ***hedge (something) in*** : to form a boundary around (something) ▪ a field *hedged in* [=*surrounded*] by trees **2** ***hedge in (someone)*** *or* ***hedge (someone) in*** : to surround or restrict (someone) in a way that prevents free movement or action ▪ We have been *hedged in* by their rules and regulations.

hedge your bets : to do things that will prevent great loss or failure if future events do not happen as you plan or hope ▪ They decided to *hedge their bets* by putting half their money in stocks and the other half in bonds.

hedge fund *noun, pl* ~ **funds** [*count*] *finance* : a group of investors who take financial risks together in order to try to earn a lot of money

hedge•hog /ˈhɛʤˌhɑːg/ *noun, pl* **-hogs** [*count*] : a small, brown animal of Europe, Asia, and Africa that has sharp spines on its back and that can roll itself up into a ball

hedgehog

hedge•row /ˈhɛʤˌroʊ/ *noun, pl* **-rows** [*count*] : a row of shrubs or trees that form the boundary of an area

he•do•nism /ˈhiːdəˌnɪzəm/ *noun* [*noncount*] : the belief that pleasure or happiness is the most important goal in life
– **he•do•nis•tic** /ˌhiːdəˈnɪstɪk/ *adj* ▪ a *hedonistic* lifestyle
– **he•do•nis•ti•cal•ly** /ˌhiːdəˈnɪstɪkli/ *adv*

he•do•nist /ˈhiːdənɪst/ *noun, pl* **-nists** [*count*] : a person who believes that pleasure or happiness is the most important goal in life

hee•bie–jee•bies /ˌhiːbiˈʤiːbiz/ *noun*
the heebie-jeebies *informal* : nervous feelings ▪ He gave me *the heebie-jeebies.* [=he made me feel nervous] ▪ I got *the heebie-jeebies* when I saw him looking at me.

¹heed /ˈhiːd/ *verb* **heeds; heed•ed; heed•ing** [+ *obj*] : to pay attention to (advice, a warning, etc.) ▪ She failed to *heed* the warnings. ▪ We must *heed* the words of our leaders [=listen to our leaders' advice] and make peace. ▪ Many people have *heeded* his call to volunteer. [=listened to him and volunteered]

²heed *noun* [*noncount*] : attention or notice — often used with *pay* or *take* ▪ She *pays* no *heed* to the concerns of others. ▪ She does not *pay* their concerns any *heed.* ▪ Sailors *take heed.* [=listen to this warning] A storm is on the way. ▪ He failed to ***take heed of*** our advice. = He failed to ***pay heed to*** our advice. [=he failed to follow our advice]

heed•less /ˈhiːdləs/ *adj* [*more* ~; *most* ~] : not paying careful attention ▪ They remain *heedless of* their own safety. ▪ the *heedless* use of natural resources ▪ *heedless* waste
– **heed•less•ly** *adv*

¹heel /ˈhiːl/ *noun, pl* **heels**
1 [*count*] : the back part of your foot that is below the ankle — see picture at FOOT
2 a [*count*] : the part of a shoe or sock that covers the heel of your foot **b** [*count*] : the part of the bottom of a shoe or boot that is under the heel of your foot ▪ shoes with low/high/cushioned *heels* — see picture at SHOE; see also HIGH HEELS, SPIKE HEELS, STILETTO HEEL **c** ***heels*** [*plural*] *informal* : shoes with high heels ▪ She does not like wearing *heels.*
3 [*count*] : the part of the inside of your hand that is closest to your wrist ▪ She scraped the *heel* of her hand.
4 [*count*] : the end of a loaf of bread
5 [*count*] *old-fashioned* : a bad or selfish man ▪ I felt like a *heel* when I couldn't stop to help.

at someone's heels : following someone very closely ▪ The dog was (nipping) *at my heels.* ▪ He once had a big lead in the campaign, but now the other candidates are nipping *at his heels.*

cool your heels see ²COOL
dig in your heels see ¹DIG
drag your heels see ¹DRAG
head over heels see ¹HEAD
kick up your heels see ¹KICK

on someone's or something's heels **1** ✧ If you are ***(close/hard/hot) on someone's or something's heels,*** you are chasing or following that person or thing very closely. ▪ The police were *hot on his heels.* **2** ✧ If something comes or follows ***close/hard/hot on something's heels*** or ***close/hard/hot on the heels of something,*** it happens very soon afterward. ▪ Her decision drew much criticism, and so did the explanation that followed *hard on its heels.* ▪ Her second movie followed *close on the heels of* her successful film debut. ▪ His resignation comes *hard on the heels of* the announcement that the company is going bankrupt.

spin/turn on your heel : to turn away from someone in a very quick or sudden way ▪ He told us he had nothing more to say, then he *turned on his heel* and walked away.

take to your heels : to begin to run away ▪ They *took to their heels* when they saw the policeman approaching.

to heel **1** : to a position that is close behind ▪ She called the dog *to heel.* [=she told the dog to return close to her] ▪ The dog came *to heel.* **2** : into a controlled or obedient condition ▪ We hope these measures will help to ***bring*** inflation ***to heel.*** [=will help to control inflation] ▪ The President is trying to *bring to heel* his opponents in the legislature. [=to force his opponents to do what he wants them to do] ▪ They are not likely to ***come to heel.***

under heel ✧ If you are ***under the heel of someone*** or ***under someone's heel*** or *US* ***under heel,*** you are completely controlled by another person, group, etc. ▪ They put us *under their heel.* ▪ They kept us *under heel.*

— see also ACHILLES' HEEL, DOWN-AT-THE-HEELS, WELL-HEELED

²heel *verb* **heels; heeled; heel•ing** [*no obj*]
1 — used as a command to tell a dog to walk next to you ▪ *Heel!* Good dog.
2 *of a boat or ship* : to lean to one side ▪ The boat *heeled* (over) in the strong wind.

¹heft /ˈhɛft/ *noun* [*noncount*]
1 : weight or heaviness ▪ the *heft* of a good hammer
2 *chiefly US* : importance or influence ▪ She uses her political *heft* [=(more commonly) *clout*] to get bills passed.

²heft *verb* **hefts; heft•ed; heft•ing** [+ *obj*] *chiefly US* : to lift (something) up ▪ He *hefted* the suitcase (up) onto the bed.

hefty /ˈhɛfti/ *adj* **heft•i•er; -est**
1 : large and heavy ▪ He was a tall, *hefty* man. ▪ a *hefty* book : big and strong ▪ *hefty* football players
2 : very large ▪ Her boss gave her a *hefty* raise. ▪ The new equipment comes with a *hefty* price tag. [=it is expensive] ▪ a *hefty* amount/fee/payment/sum ▪ a *hefty* dose of irony
3 : very forceful ▪ He gave the door a *hefty* kick/shove.
– **heft•i•ly** /ˈhɛftəli/ *adv* – **heft•i•ness** /ˈhɛftinəs/ *noun* [*noncount*]

he•gem•o•ny /hɪˈʤɛməni, *Brit* hɪˈgɛməni/ *noun* [*noncount*] *formal* : influence or control over another country, a group of people, etc. ▪ They discussed the national government's *hegemony* over their tribal community.

heif•er /ˈhɛfɚ/ *noun, pl* **-ers** [*count*] : a young female cow; *especially* : one that has not had a calf

height /ˈhaɪt/ *noun, pl* **heights**
1 : a measurement of how tall a person or thing is : the distance from the bottom to the top of a person or thing [*count*] What's the *height* of the building? ▪ These bushes grow to *heights* of up to five feet. [*noncount*] a woman of average *height* ▪ We were measured for *height* and weight. ▪ The ride has a *height* requirement. You have to be four feet tall to ride. ▪ He is six feet ***in height.*** [=(more commonly) he is six feet tall] ▪ She rose/stood (up) to her ***full height.*** [=she stood straight up] — see picture at GEOMETRY
2 [*noncount*] : the condition of being tall ▪ I was surprised by his *height.*
3 [*count*] : the distance above a level or surface ▪ The land reaches a *height* of 600 feet above sea level. ▪ The *height* of the ceiling is eight feet. [=the ceiling is eight feet above the floor; the ceiling is eight feet high]
4 [*count*] **a** : a great distance above the ground ▪ It was frightening to look down from such a dizzying/great *height.* — usually plural ▪ I'm afraid of *heights.* **b** : an area that is higher than the areas around it ▪ The soldiers left the *height* they were defending. — usually plural; often used in the names of places ▪ We used to live in Washington *Heights.* ▪ the Golan *Heights*
5 [*singular*] : the most advanced or extreme point of some-

thing • During the *height* of the violence, dozens of people lost their lives. • He was ***at the height of*** his fame when he died. [=he died when he was most famous] • ***At its height,*** their civilization was the greatest in the world.

6 *heights* [*plural*] : very good or successful levels • Her popularity rose/soared to great *heights*. • They have taken the company to new *heights*.

7 *the height of* — used to say that something is an extreme example of something • It was *the height of* stupidity to quit the team. [=it was extremely stupid to quit the team] • *the height of* arrogance/folly/hypocrisy • Long skirts are now *the height of* fashion. [=are now extremely fashionable] • *the height of* style/luxury

height·en /ˈhaɪtn̩/ *verb* **-ens; -ened; -en·ing** : to increase the amount, degree, or extent of (something) : INCREASE [+ *obj*] The plan will only *heighten* tensions between the two groups. • This tragedy has *heightened* our awareness of the need for improved safety measures. [*no obj*] Tensions between the two groups have *heightened*.

– heightened *adj* • The meeting now has *heightened* [=*more, greater*] significance.

hei·nie /ˈhaɪni/ *noun, pl* **-nies** [*count*] *US slang* : the part of the body you sit on : BUTTOCKS • Get off your *heinie* and do some work.

hei·nous /ˈheɪnəs/ *adj* [*more* ~; *most* ~] : very bad or evil : deserving of hate or contempt • These murders were especially *heinous*. • people accused of committing *heinous* crimes/acts

– hei·nous·ly *adv* **– hei·nous·ness** *noun* [*noncount*]

heir /ˈeɚ/ *noun, pl* **heirs** [*count*]

1 : a person who has the legal right to receive the property of someone who dies • His *heirs* could inherit millions of dollars. — often + *to* • She is the sole *heir to* her family's fortune.

2 : a person who has the right to become a king or queen or to claim a title when the person holding it dies • The king left no *heirs* when he died.

heir apparent *noun, pl* **heirs apparent** [*count*]

1 : an heir whose right to receive money, property, or a title cannot be taken away • The Prince of Wales is (the) *heir apparent* to the throne of England.

2 : a person who is very likely to have a job or position after the person who has it now leaves • The coach named her assistant as her *heir apparent*.

heir·ess /ˈerəs/ *noun, pl* **-ess·es** [*count*] : a girl or woman who is an heir; *especially* : a girl or woman who inherits a large amount of money

heir·loom /ˈeɚˌluːm/ *noun, pl* **-looms** [*count*]

1 : a valuable object that is owned by a family for many years and passed from one generation to another • a priceless family *heirloom*

2 *US* : an old type of plant that is still available because individual people have continued to grow it for many years — usually used before another noun • *heirloom* tomatoes • *heirloom* roses

heist /ˈhaɪst/ *noun, pl* **heists** [*count*] *chiefly US, informal* : an act of stealing something from a bank or store • bank *heists* • a jewel *heist*

– heist *verb* **heists; heist·ed; heist·ing** [+ *obj*] • The jewels were *heisted* [=*stolen*] last night.

held *past tense of* [1]HOLD

helices *plural of* HELIX

he·li·cop·ter /ˈheləˌkɑːptɚ/ *noun, pl* **-ters** [*count*] : an aircraft that can stay in the air without moving forward and that has metal blades that turn around on its top

helicopter

he·lio·cen·tric /ˌhiːlijouˈsentrɪk/ *adj* : having or relating to the sun as the center • Galileo proposed the *heliocentric* theory that the Earth goes around the sun. — compare GEOCENTRIC

he·li·pad /ˈheləˌpæd/ *noun, pl* **-pads** [*count*] : a special area where a helicopter can take off and land • The building has a *helipad* on its roof.

he·li·port /ˈheləˌpoɚt/ *noun, pl* **-ports** [*count*] : a small airport that is designed for use by helicopters

he·li·um /ˈhiːlijəm/ *noun* [*noncount*] : a chemical element that is a colorless gas, that is lighter than air, and that is often used to fill balloons

he·lix /ˈhiːlɪks/ *noun, pl* **-li·ces** /ˈheləˌsiːz/ *also* **-lix·es** [*count*] : the shape formed by a line that curves around and along a central line : SPIRAL — see also DOUBLE HELIX

– he·li·cal /ˈhelɪkəl/ *adj*

hell /ˈhel/ *noun*

1 *or* **Hell** [*singular*] : the place where the devil lives and where evil people go after they die according to some religions

2 : a very difficult or unpleasant situation or experience [*noncount*] Getting the loan approved was pure/sheer *hell*. • He ***went through hell*** during his divorce. • She had to *go through hell* to get where she is today. [*singular*] Living with the disease can be a ***hell on earth***. • The pain has made her life a ***living hell***.

3 *informal + impolite* — used to express anger, annoyance, etc. • *Hell*, I don't know why he did it! • But, *hell*, why not? • Oh, *hell*, I forgot my keys. • "Did you give her any money?" "*Hell*, no!"

all hell breaks loose *informal* — used to describe what happens when violent, destructive, and confused activity suddenly begins • I heard people shouting at each other, and suddenly *all hell broke loose*.

as hell *informal + somewhat impolite* — used to make a statement more forceful • It was (as) funny *as hell*. [=it was very funny] • They were mad *as hell*. • We've been working as hard *as hell* to finish on schedule. • "Can you finish on schedule?" "We'll ***sure as hell*** try."

catch hell *chiefly US, informal + somewhat impolite* : to be yelled at or criticized in a very angry and severe way • She *caught hell* (from her boss) for coming in late.

come hell or high water *informal* — used to say that something will definitely happen or be done even though other events or situations might make it difficult • I will be there on time, *come hell or high water*.

for the hell of it *informal + somewhat impolite* : for the fun of doing something : without having a particular reason • Just *for the hell of it*, I decided to go. • He likes to start arguments *for the hell of it*.

from hell *informal + somewhat impolite* — used to describe someone or something that is very bad or unpleasant • It was the vacation *from hell*: everything that could go wrong, did. • bosses *from hell*

give (someone) hell *informal + somewhat impolite* : to yell at or criticize (someone) in an angry way • Her boss *gave her hell* for coming in late. • *Give them hell*, John!

go to hell *informal + impolite* **1** — used to show that you are very angry with someone • I'm not coming, so you can just *go to hell*! • He told his boss to *go to hell*. **2** : to become completely ruined : to fail completely • The economy is *going to hell*.

go to hell in a handbasket see HANDBASKET

hell of a *informal + somewhat impolite* **1** — used to make a statement more forceful • It was one *hell of a* good fight. [=it was a very good fight] • He is one *hell of a* nice guy. **2** : very good • She's a *hell of a* player. [=she's a very good player] **3** : very bad or difficult • We've been having a *hell of a* time trying to finish on schedule. • This is a *hell of a* mess we're in.

hell on *US, informal + somewhat impolite* — used to describe something that causes a lot of damage or trouble • Running can be *hell on* your knees. [=can do a lot of harm to your knees] • His constant traveling was *hell on* their relationship.

hell to pay see [1]PAY

in hell *informal + impolite* **1** — used to make a statement more forceful • There is no way *in hell* I'm going! • We don't have a hope *in hell* [=we have no hope] of getting out of this mess. **2** *or* ***in the hell*** *US* — used to make a question more forceful • What *in hell* is wrong now? • How *in the hell* did that happen?

like a bat out of hell see [3]BAT

like hell *informal + impolite* **1** : very much • My back hurts *like hell*. **2** : with a lot of energy and speed • We've been working *like hell* since morning. • When I say "go," run *like hell*. **3** : very bad • This place looks *like hell*. **4** — used to say in an angry and forceful way that you will not do something, do not agree, etc. • "You're coming with me!" "*Like hell* I am!" • "It's your fault!" "*Like hell* it is!"

play hell with *or Brit* ***play merry hell with*** : to cause many problems for (someone or something) : to have a very bad effect on (someone or something) • High oil prices are

H

playing hell with the nation's economy.

raise hell *informal + somewhat impolite* **1** : to complain in a loud or angry way ▪ People are *raising hell* about the new law. **2** : to behave wildly and make a lot of noise ▪ He and his friends used to get drunk and ***raise hell*** on the weekends. — see also HELL-RAISER

the hell *informal + impolite* **1** — used to make a statement or question more forceful ▪ Let's get *the hell* out of here. ▪ (*chiefly US*) They moved way *the hell* up north. ▪ How *the hell* did you do that? ▪ Who *the hell* do you think you are? ▪ What *the hell* is going on? **2** — used to say in an angry and forceful way that you will not do something, do not agree, etc. ▪ "You said you'd pay for it." "*The hell* I did!" [=I never said that] ▪ "It's your fault!" "*The hell* it is!" — see also WHAT THE HELL (below)

the hell out of *informal + impolite* — used for emphasis after words like *scare, frighten*, and *beat* ▪ That movie *scared the hell out of* me. [=scared me very badly] ▪ The boxer *beat the hell out of* his opponent.

to hell and back *informal* ✧ Someone who goes *to hell and back* experiences a very difficult or unpleasant situation often for a long time. ▪ She's been *to hell and back* since her daughter became ill.

to hell with or ***the hell with*** *informal + impolite* — used to say in a forceful and angry way that you do not care about someone or something. ▪ They want me to stop, but *to hell with* them! I'll do what I want to do!

what the hell *informal + impolite* **1** — used to express anger, surprise, etc. ▪ *What the hell*! Just what do you think you're doing!? **2** — used to say that you are not worried about or bothered by something ▪ So I figured, *what the hell*, let's give it a try. ▪ We lost a little money, but *what the hell*, it's not a big deal.

when hell freezes over *informal + impolite* — used to say that you think that something will never happen ▪ I'll apologize *when hell freezes over*. [=I'll never apologize]

he'll /ˈhiːl, hɪl/ — used as a contraction of *he will* ▪ *He'll* be here soon.

hel·la·cious /ˌhɛˈleɪʃəs/ *adj* [*more* ~; *most* ~] *chiefly US, informal* : very difficult, large, or powerful ▪ Traffic is *hellacious* this time of day. ▪ *hellacious* winds

hell–bent /ˈhɛlˌbɛnt/ *adj* [*more* ~; *most* ~] : very determined to do something especially when the results might be bad — usually + *on* ▪ He's *hell-bent on* (getting) revenge. ▪ They seem to be *hell-bent on* starting a war. — sometimes followed by *to* + *verb* in U.S. English ▪ They seem to be *hell-bent to start* a war.

Hel·len·ic /hɛˈlɛnɪk/ *adj* : of or relating to ancient Greek culture

hell·fire /ˈhɛlˌfajɚ/ *noun* [*noncount*] : the fire of Hell ▪ a minister who preaches *hellfire* and damnation [=who talks about how bad people will be tortured in Hell]

hell·hole /ˈhɛlˌhoʊl/ *noun, pl* **-holes** [*count*] *informal* : a very dirty or unpleasant place ▪ The factory is a *hellhole*.

hel·lion /ˈhɛljən/ *noun, pl* **-lions** [*count*] *US, informal* : a person (especially a child) who behaves badly ▪ My children can act like little *hellions* when they're bored.

hell·ish /ˈhɛlɪʃ/ *adj* [*more* ~; *most* ~] : very bad, unpleasant, or shocking ▪ We've been having *hellish* weather lately. ▪ *hellish* living conditions ▪ The battlefield was a *hellish* scene of death and destruction.

– hell·ish·ly *adv*

hel·lo /həˈloʊ/ *noun, pl* **-los**

1 — used as a greeting ▪ *Hello* there! How are you? ▪ *Hello*, my name is Linda.

2 [*count*] : the act of saying the word *hello* to someone as a greeting ▪ We exchanged *hellos*. [=we said hello to each other] ▪ They welcomed us with a warm *hello*.

3 — used when you are answering the telephone ▪ *Hello*. Who's this? [=who is calling?] ▪ *Hello*. May I speak to Linda, please?

4 — used to get someone's attention ▪ *Hello*? Is anybody here?

5 — used to express surprise ▪ Well, *hello*! What do we have here?

hell–rais·er /ˈhɛlˌreɪzɚ/ *noun, pl* **-ers** [*count*] *informal + disapproving* : a person who behaves badly or causes trouble for others ▪ He said that the protesters were just a bunch of *hell-raisers*.

– hell–rais·ing /ˈhɛlˌreɪzɪŋ/ *adj* ▪ a group of *hell-raising* teenagers **– hell–raising** *noun* [*noncount*] ▪ He did a lot of *hell-raising* when he was younger.

hell·uva /ˈhɛləvə/ — used in writing to represent the sound of the phrase *hell of a* ▪ He's a *helluva* nice guy. [=he's a very nice guy]

helm /ˈhɛlm/ *noun, pl* **helms**

1 [*count*] : a handle or wheel that is used to steer a ship or boat ▪ The ship's captain ***took the helm***. [=steered the ship] ▪ The ship's captain was ***at the helm***. [=steering the ship]

2 [*singular*] : a position of full control or authority in an organization ▪ She ***took the helm*** of the university. ▪ He left after only a year ***at the helm*** [=*in charge*] of the corporation.

hel·met /ˈhɛlmət/ *noun, pl* **-mets** [*count*] : a hard hat that is worn to protect your head — see also CRASH HELMET, PITH HELMET

– hel·met·ed /ˈhɛlmətəd/ *adj* ▪ *helmeted* warriors

helms·man /ˈhɛlmzmən/ *noun, pl* **-men** /-mən/ [*count*] : a person (especially a man) who steers a ship or boat

helms·per·son /ˈhɛlmzˌpɚsn̩/ *noun, pl* **-sons** [*count*] : a person who steers a ship or boat

¹help /ˈhɛlp/ *verb* **helps**; **helped**; **help·ing**

1 : to do something that makes it easier for someone to do a job, to deal with a problem, etc. : to aid or assist someone [+ *obj*] Let me *help* you with that box. = Let me *help* you lift/carry that box. ▪ *help* a child with her homework = *help* a child (to) do her homework ▪ I *helped* her up/down the stairs. [=I gave her support so that she could go up/down the stairs] ▪ *Help* me! I'm drowning! [*no obj*] Don't blame me: I was only trying to *help*! ▪ She *helped* (to) set the table. ▪ *Help*! Somebody call the police!

2 : to make something less severe : to make something more pleasant or easier to deal with [+ *obj*] Rest *helps* a cold. ▪ She took an aspirin to *help* her headache. ▪ Some color would really *help* [=*improve*] this room. ▪ Humor often *helps* a tense situation. [*no obj*] Yelling doesn't *help*. ▪ It's not much money, but ***every little bit helps***. — often followed by *to* + *verb* ▪ It *helps to know* you care. [=I feel better because I know that you care]

3 [+ *obj*] **a** : to give (yourself or another person) food or drink ▪ There's plenty of food, so ***help yourself***. [=take as much food as you would like] — often + *to* ▪ He *helped* his neighbor *to* a glass of wine. ▪ *Help* yourself *to* whatever you'd like. **b** *informal* : to take something for (yourself) without permission ▪ He saw the money lying on the table, and he *helped himself*. [=he took the money] — usually + *to* ▪ He *helped himself to* the money.

can help ✧ If you ***can help something***, you can prevent it from happening. ▪ *Can* I *help it* [=is it my fault] if no one listens to my advice? ▪ There will be no more layoffs. At least ***not if I can help it***. [=if I can prevent it; if it is up to me]

cannot help **1** ✧ If you ***cannot help yourself***, you cannot control your actions or stop yourself from doing something. ▪ I know I shouldn't eat any more, but I *can't help myself*. ▪ They knew they shouldn't go, but they *couldn't help themselves*. **2** ✧ If you ***cannot help something***, you cannot stop it or prevent it. ▪ I *can't help loving you*. ▪ I know I shouldn't be angry, but I *can't help it*—it's just the way I feel. **3** ✧ If you ***cannot help doing something*** or ***cannot help but do something***, you cannot stop yourself from doing it. ▪ I *couldn't help having some dessert*. ▪ We *couldn't help laughing*. = We *couldn't help but laugh*. **4** ✧ Something that ***cannot be helped*** cannot be avoided. ▪ It's too bad that we have to leave, but it *can't be helped*.

God/Lord/heaven help (someone) — used to express strong feelings of worry or concern about what is happening or could happen ▪ If he ever gets control of the country, *Lord help us*! ▪ *Heaven help you* [=you will be in trouble] when he finds out you dented the car.

help off/on [*phrasal verb*] ***help (someone) off/on with (something)*** : to do something that makes it easier for (someone) to put on or take off (clothing, shoes, etc.) ▪ Let me *help* you *off with* your boots. ▪ He *helped* her *on with* her coat.

help out [*phrasal verb*] ***help out*** or ***help (someone) out*** or ***help out (someone)*** : to do something so another person's job or task is easier ▪ I can't do this myself. Won't someone please *help* me *out*? ▪ I sometimes *help out* in the kitchen. ▪ He *helped out* with the bills whenever he could. [=he helped pay the bills whenever he could]

so help me (God) — used to stress that a statement is serious and truthful ▪ I'm going on a diet and, *so help me*, this time I'll stick to it!

²help *noun, pl* **help**

1 [*noncount*] **a** : activities or efforts that make it easier to do a job, deal with a problem, etc. ▪ He thanked us for our *help*. ▪ I could use some *help* with the dishes. ▪ We could hear shouts for *help* coming from the house. ▪ a ***help menu/screen*** [=a part of a computer program that gives instructions and information about how to use the program] **b :** something (such as money or advice) that is given to someone who needs it ▪ I couldn't have bought this house without financial *help*. [=without money given to me by someone else] ▪ She is very unhappy and needs some serious/professional *help*. [=she should see a counselor or psychologist to help her with her problems]

2 [*singular*] **:** someone or something that makes it easier to do a job, deal with a problem, etc. ▪ She has always been a real *help* (to me) in times of trouble. ▪ He's been more of a hindrance than a *help*.

3 [*noncount*] **a :** the fact of being useful to someone ▪ You've been (of) no *help* at all to me. [=you haven't helped me at all] **b :** the state of being helped ▪ Is there any *help* for us? [=is there anything that can be done to help us?] ▪ The situation is ***beyond help*** [=nothing can be done to improve the situation] ▪ (*Brit*) There was ***no help for it*** but to tell her parents. [=there was no way to avoid telling her parents]

4 [*plural*] **:** servants or paid workers ▪ We need to hire additional *help*. ▪ The *help* have already left for the day. ▪ It's hard to find good *help*. ▪ (*US*) I looked through the ***help wanted*** ads. [=the part of the newspaper in which jobs are advertised]

help desk *noun, pl* **~ desks** [*count*] **:** a group of people who provide help and information usually for electronic or computer problems — usually singular ▪ Call the *help desk* if you have trouble with the software.

help·er /ˈhɛlpɚ/ *noun, pl* **-ers** [*count*] **:** someone who helps another person with a job or task ▪ The carpenter measured the wall while one of his *helpers* brought in the tools.

help·ful /ˈhɛlpfəl/ *adj* [*more ~; most ~*]

1 : making it easier to do a job, deal with a problem, etc. **:** giving help ▪ A *helpful* neighbor shoveled our walkway. ▪ She offered us *helpful* [=*useful*] suggestions. ▪ a *helpful* hint

2 : willing to help other people ▪ a kind and *helpful* person

come in helpful see *come in* at [1]COME

– help·ful·ly *adv* ▪ He *helpfully* offered to carry the groceries for me. **– help·ful·ness** *noun* [*noncount*] ▪ I appreciate your *helpfulness*.

help·ing /ˈhɛlpɪŋ/ *noun, pl* **-ings** [*count*] **:** an amount of food that is put on a plate at one time **:** a portion of food **:** SERVING ▪ He had two *helpings* of carrots. ▪ Can I give you a second *helping*? — sometimes used figuratively ▪ He needed a generous *helping* of self-confidence to ask for a raise.

helping hand *noun, pl* **~ hands** [*count*] **:** help or assistance ▪ I'm always willing to lend/give a *helping hand*. [=I am always willing to help]

helping verb *noun, pl* **~ verbs** [*count*] *grammar* **:** AUXILIARY VERB

help·less /ˈhɛlpləs/ *adj* [*more ~; most ~*]

1 : not protected **:** not able to defend yourself ▪ a *helpless* little baby ▪ The civilians were *helpless* against their attackers.

2 : unable to do something to make a situation, task, etc., better or easier ▪ Firefighters were *helpless* against the blaze. ▪ I feel *helpless*. Isn't there anything I can do?

3 a : not able to be controlled ▪ *helpless* laughter/rage **b :** not able to control something (such as laughter or anger) ▪ The crowd was ***helpless with*** laughter. ▪ He was *helpless with* rage.

– help·less·ly *adv* ▪ We stood by *helplessly* while the fire destroyed the house. ▪ They were laughing *helplessly*. **– help·less·ness** *noun* [*noncount*] ▪ feelings of *helplessness* and despair

help·line /ˈhɛlpˌlaɪn/ *noun, pl* **-lines** [*count*] **:** a telephone service that offers help or information ▪ Call our toll-free *helpline* for more information.

help·mate /ˈhɛlpˌmeɪt/ *noun, pl* **-mates** [*count*] *old-fashioned + literary* **:** a person who is a companion and helper; *especially* **:** WIFE

help·meet /ˈhɛlpˌmiːt/ *noun, pl* **-meets** [*count*] *old-fashioned + literary* **:** HELPMATE

[1]**hel·ter–skel·ter** /ˌhɛltɚˈskɛltɚ/ *adv*

1 : in a confused and careless way ▪ The children raced *helter-skelter* through the house.

2 : in no particular order ▪ magazines stacked *helter-skelter* on her desk

– helter–skelter *adj* ▪ a *helter-skelter* rush through the train station

[2]**helter–skelter** *noun, pl* **-ters** [*count*] *Brit* **:** a slide that twists around a tower at an amusement park

[1]**hem** /ˈhɛm/ *noun, pl* **hems** [*count*] **:** the edge of a piece of cloth that is folded back and sewn down ▪ shorten the *hem* of the dress/skirt/trousers — see color picture on page C12

[2]**hem** *verb* **hems; hemmed; hem·ming** [+ *obj*] **:** to sew down a folded edge of cloth on (something) **:** to give (something) a hem ▪ *hem* the dress/skirt/trousers ▪ The curtains need to be *hemmed*.

hem in [*phrasal verb*] ***hem (someone or something) in*** or ***hem in (someone or something)*** **:** to surround (someone or something) very closely or in a way that makes movement or escape difficult — usually used as *(be) hemmed in* ▪ The town *is hemmed in* by mountains on all sides. ▪ He *was hemmed in* by reporters as he tried to leave the courthouse. — often used figuratively ▪ He felt *hemmed in* by the school's rules. [=he felt that the rules prevented him from acting freely]

– compare [3]HEM

[3]**hem** *verb* **hems; hemmed; hemming**

hem and haw *chiefly US, informal* **1 :** to stop often and change what you are saying during speech because you are not sure of what to say or are trying to avoid saying something ▪ The question surprised her and she *hemmed and hawed* a bit before answering. **2 :** to take a long time before you make a decision about what to do ▪ The city council *hemmed and hawed* for a year before deciding to build the new school.

– compare [2]HEM

he–man /ˈhiːˌmæn/ *noun, pl* **-men** /-ˌmɛn/ [*count*] *informal* **:** a man who is very strong and masculine ▪ He plays another *he-man* in his latest action movie.

hemi·sphere /ˈhɛməˌsfiɚ/ *noun, pl* **-spheres** [*count*]

1 : a half of the Earth ▪ the ***Northern/Southern Hemisphere*** [=the half of the Earth that is north/south of the equator] ▪ the ***Eastern Hemisphere*** [=the half of the Earth that is east of the Atlantic Ocean and that includes Europe, Africa, Asia, and Australia] ▪ the ***Western Hemisphere*** [=the half of the Earth that is west of the Atlantic Ocean and that includes North and South America]

2 : half of a sphere **:** half of a round object

3 *technical* **:** either of the two halves of the brain ▪ a tumor in the right/left ***cerebral hemisphere***

– hemi·spher·ic /ˌhɛməˈsfirɪk/ *or* **hemi·spher·i·cal** /ˌhɛməˈsferɪkəl/ *adj, technical* ▪ a *hemispherical* structure

hem·line /ˈhɛmˌlaɪn/ *noun, pl* **-lines** [*count*] **:** the bottom edge of a dress, skirt, or coat ▪ The *hemline* falls just above the knee. ▪ I shortened/raised the *hemline* on the dress.

hem·lock /ˈhɛmˌlɑːk/ *noun, pl* **-locks**

1 [*count, noncount*] **:** an evergreen tree with soft wood

2 [*noncount*] **a :** a type of poisonous plant that has small white flowers **b :** a deadly drug or drink made from this plant ▪ Socrates died after drinking *hemlock*.

he·mo·glo·bin (*US*) *or Brit* **hae·mo·glo·bin** /ˈhiːməˌgloubən/ *noun* [*noncount*] *technical* **:** the part of blood that contains iron, carries oxygen through the body, and gives blood its red color

he·mo·phil·ia (*US*) *or Brit* **hae·mo·phil·ia** /ˌhiːməˈfɪlijə/ *noun* [*noncount*] *medical* **:** a serious disease that causes a person who has been cut or injured to keep bleeding for a very long time

he·mo·phil·i·ac (*US*) *or Brit* **hae·mo·phil·i·ac** /ˌhiːməˈfɪliˌæk/ *noun, pl* **-acs** [*count*] **:** a person who has hemophilia

[1]**hem·or·rhage** (*US*) *or Brit* **haem·or·rhage** /ˈhɛmərɪʤ/ *noun, pl* **-rhag·es** *medical* **:** a condition in which a person bleeds too much and cannot stop the flow of blood [*count*] The patient suffered a cerebral *hemorrhage*. [*noncount*] There is a possibility of *hemorrhage* with the procedure. — sometimes used figuratively ▪ The company has suffered a financial *hemorrhage*. [=the company has lost large amounts of money]

– hem·or·rhag·ic (*US*) *or Brit* **haem·or·rhag·ic** /ˌhɛməˈræʤɪk/ *adj, medical* ▪ a *hemorrhagic* fever [=a fever that causes hemorrhaging]

[2]**hemorrhage** (*US*) *or Brit* **haemorrhage** *verb* **-rhages; -rhaged; -rhag·ing**

1 [*no obj*] *medical* **:** to bleed in a very fast and uncontrolled way ▪ The patient began to *hemorrhage* after the surgery.

2 [+ *obj*] **:** to lose (people, money, etc.) in a very fast and uncontrolled way ▪ The company is *hemorrhaging* money. [=the company is losing very large amounts of money]

– hemorrhaging (*US*) *or Brit* **haem·or·rhag·ing** *noun*

H

[*noncount*] • The patient has internal *hemorrhaging*.

hem·or·rhoid (*US*) *or Brit* **haem·or·rhoid** /ˈhɛmˌrɔɪd/ *noun, pl* **-rhoids** [*count*] : a swollen and painful area located at or near the anus — usually plural • a patient who suffers from *hemorrhoids*

hemp /ˈhɛmp/ *noun* [*noncount*] : a plant that is used to make thick ropes and some drugs (such as hashish and marijuana)

hen /ˈhɛn/ *noun, pl* **hens** [*count*]
1 : an adult female chicken — compare ROOSTER
2 : a female bird of any kind

hence /ˈhɛns/ *adv, formal*
1 : for this reason • He was a newcomer and *hence* [=*consequently, therefore*] had no close friends here. • He knew he could not win the election—*hence* his decision to withdraw. • The company lost a great deal of money. *Hence*, the CEO was asked to resign.
2 : later than the present time • a week *hence* [=a week from now] • What will life be like a century *hence*?

hence·forth /ˈhɛnsˌfoɚθ/ *adv, formal* : from this time forward : starting now • *Henceforth*, supervisors will report directly to the manager. • She announced that *henceforth* she would be running the company.

hence·for·ward /hɛnsˈfoɚwɚd/ *adv, formal* : HENCEFORTH

H

hench·man /ˈhɛntʃmən/ *noun, pl* **-men** /-mən/ [*count*] *disapproving* : a trusted follower or supporter who performs unpleasant, wrong, or illegal tasks for a powerful person (such as a politician or criminal) • a gangster surrounded by his *henchmen*

hen·house /ˈhɛnˌhaus/ *noun, pl* **-hous·es** [*count*] : a covered shelter for chickens or other birds

hen·na /ˈhɛnə/ *noun* [*noncount*] : a reddish-brown dye used especially for coloring hair or skin

hen party *noun, pl* **~ -ties** [*count*] *Brit, informal* : a party for women only; *especially* : a party for a woman who is about to be married — called also *hen night*

hen·pecked /ˈhɛnˌpɛkt/ *adj, informal* — used to describe a man who is constantly controlled and criticized by his wife • a *henpecked* husband

hep /ˈhɛp/ *adj* **hep·per; hep·pest** [*also more ~; most ~*] *US slang, old-fashioned* : having or showing knowledge about the newest things in music, fashion, etc. : HIP • a *hep* cafe • She's *hep*. ✧ ***Hep*** **is often associated with people who played and listened to jazz music in the mid-20th century.**

hep·a·ti·tis /ˌhɛpəˈtaɪtəs/ *noun* [*noncount*] *medical* : a serious disease of the liver that causes fever and makes your skin and eyes yellow

hep·cat /ˈhɛpˌkæt/ *noun, pl* **-cats** [*count*] *US slang, old-fashioned* : a person who knows about the newest things in music, fashion, etc. : a hip person • a cool *hepcat* ✧ ***Hepcat*** **often refers to someone who played or listened to jazz music in the mid-20th century.**

hep·ta·gon /ˈhɛptəˌgɑːn/ *noun, pl* **-gons** [*count*] *mathematics* : a flat shape that has seven sides and seven angles
– hep·tag·o·nal /hɛpˈtægənəl/ *adj* • a *heptagonal* shape/room

hep·tath·lon /hɛpˈtæθlən/ *noun, pl* **-lons** [*count*] : an athletic contest for women that consists of seven running, jumping, and throwing events • She won a gold medal in the *heptathlon*.

¹her /ˈhɚ, ɚ/ *adj, always used before a noun, possessive form of* SHE : relating to or belonging to a certain woman, girl, or female animal • She bought *her* own house. • *Her* parents will visit soon. • What is *her* name? : made or done by a certain woman, girl, or female animal • I would like to read some of *her* essays. • She was jailed for *her* crime. • It's *her* turn to play. — sometimes used figuratively to refer to something thought of as female (such as a ship, car, machine, or country) • The ship is in port to have *her* hull repaired. • the United States and *her* allies — see also HERS

²her *pronoun, objective form of* SHE — used to refer to a certain woman, girl, or female animal as the object of a verb or a preposition • Tell *her* I said hello. • Did you invite *her*? • I gave the book to *her*. • a gift for *her* • The dress fits her sister as well as *her*.

¹her·ald /ˈhɛrəld/ *verb* **-alds; -ald·ed; -ald·ing** [*+ obj*]
1 : to be a sign of (something that is beginning to happen or will happen soon) • Rain *heralds* the arrival of spring. • The technology *heralded* a new age of space exploration.
2 : to greet (someone or something) with enthusiasm — usually used as *(be) heralded* • This achievement will *be heralded* all over the world. • She is *being heralded* as the year's best new author. ✧ **Someone or something that is *much-heralded* receives a large amount of praise or admiration.** • a *much-heralded* film

²herald *noun, pl* **-alds** [*count*] *formal*
1 : a sign that something will happen • The early flowers are *heralds* of spring.
2 : an official messenger in the past • Mercury was the *herald* of the Roman gods.

her·ald·ry /ˈhɛrəldri/ *noun* [*noncount*] *formal* : the activity of creating or studying coats of arms and of tracing and recording family histories
– he·ral·dic /hɛˈrældɪk/ *adj* • crosses and other *heraldic* devices

herb /ˈɚb, *Brit* ˈhəːb/ *noun, pl* **herbs** [*count*] : a plant or a part of a plant that is used as medicine or to give flavor to food • a dish seasoned with chopped fresh *herbs* • rosemary, sage, and other *herbs* — see color picture on page C6

her·ba·ceous /hɚˈbeɪʃəs/ *adj*
1 : relating to herbs • *herbaceous* flavors/aromas
2 : relating to a type of plant that has a soft stem • *herbaceous* plants/perennials • a ***herbaceous border*** [=a garden of flowering plants that die in the autumn and grow again in the spring]

herb·al /ˈɚbəl, *Brit* ˈhəːbəl/ *adj, always used before a noun* : made of or relating to herbs • *herbal* tea/supplements • a doctor who practices ***herbal medicine*** [=the use of herbs to treat illness]

herb·al·ist /ˈɚbəlɪst, *Brit* ˈhəːbəlɪst/ *noun, pl* **-ists** [*count*] : a person who grows, sells, or uses herbs to treat illness

herb doctor *noun, pl* **~ -tors** [*count*] *chiefly US* : a person who uses herbs to treat illness

her·bi·cide /ˈhɚbəˌsaɪd/ *noun, pl* **-cides** [*count, noncount*] : a chemical used to destroy plants or stop plant growth

her·bi·vore /ˈhɚbəˌvoɚ/ *noun, pl* **-vores** [*count*] : an animal that only eats plants
– her·biv·o·rous /ˌhɚˈbɪvərəs/ *adj* • *herbivorous* animals

her·cu·le·an *or* **Her·cu·le·an** /ˌhɚkjəˈliːjən/ *adj* [*more ~; most ~*] : very large, difficult, powerful, etc. • a *herculean* task/effort • *Herculean* strength • They took on the *herculean* job of restoring the house after the fire. • a problem of *herculean* proportions

¹herd /ˈhɚd/ *noun, pl* **herds**
1 [*count*] : a group of animals that live or are kept together • *herds* of cattle/horses/elephants • The *herd* grazed peacefully in the pasture.
2 a [*count*] : a large group of people • A *herd* of shoppers waited anxiously for the store to open. **b *the herd*** : common people : people as a group • *the* common *herd* • He always sticks with *the herd*. [=he always does what other people do; he does not think for himself] • I refuse to ***follow the herd***. [=do what other people do]
ride herd on see ¹RIDE

²herd *verb* **herds; herd·ed; herd·ing**
1 [*+ obj*] : to gather and move (a group of animals) • *herd* cattle • The horses were *herded* into the corral.
2 a [*+ obj*] : to move (people) in a group • We left the hotel and were *herded* onto a bus. • They *herded* the students into the auditorium. **b** [*no obj*] : to form a group or move as a group • The commuters *herded* onto the train.
– herd·er /ˈhɚdɚ/ *noun, pl* **-ers** [*count*]

herds·man /ˈhɚdzmən/ *noun, pl* **-men** /-mən/ [*count*] : a person (especially a man) who watches over a herd of cows, sheep, etc.

¹here /ˈhiɚ/ *adv*
1 a : in this place : at this location • I like it *here*. • I'm *here* to help you. • Turn *here*. • Hello—is anyone *here*? • I'm sure I left my glasses (right) *here*. • They have lived *here* for 30 years. • Please sign *here*. [=at the place indicated by the speaker] • At last we're *here*! = *Here* we are at last! [=we have finally arrived] • "Hey, where are you?" "I'm ***over/out/down/up/in here***." • I'm planning to be ***back here*** by 6:00. — used in speech when something is found • Have you seen my glasses? Oh, *here* they are. • Ah, *here*'s the book I've been looking for. **b :** to or into this place • Come *here*. • I've come *here* to help you. • Bring the book *here*. • He rode his bicycle *here* this morning. • When will you get *here*? • *Here* comes the bus. [=the bus is coming right now]
2 a : at this point in a process, activity, story, etc. • *Here* the author introduces a new character. • The speaker paused *here* for a moment. • *Here* the film changes from black-and-white to color. **b :** in the matter that is being considered

: in this case ▪ *Here* we agree. ▪ The essential conflict *here* is their different ways of cutting costs. **c** : appearing or happening now ▪ *Here*'s your chance for a new career. ▪ Winter is *here* at last.

3 a *informal* — used to make a statement about the present situation or subject more forceful ▪ Hey, I'm trying to work *here*! ▪ We're talking about a lot of money *here*! ▪ Let's get serious *here*! **b** *informal* — used after a noun to emphasize which person, thing, etc. you are referring to ▪ This book *here* is the one I was talking about. ▪ My brother *here* just bought a new car. **c** — used when you are giving something to someone ▪ *Here*'s my phone number. ▪ "Could you pass the salt?" "Sure, ***here you are***." = "Sure, ***here it is***." = "Sure, ***here you go***."

from here on (out) *US, informal* : from this time forward ▪ *From here on out*, I'm making all the decisions.

here and now : at the present time ▪ Instead of dwelling on the past, we need to deal with the problems that exist *here and now*. — often used in the phrase ***the here and now*** ▪ We need to deal with the problems that exist in *the here and now*. [=the problems that exist in the present]

here and there : in different places ▪ Books and papers were strewn *here and there*. ▪ He's traveled *here and there*.

here goes *or chiefly US* ***here goes nothing*** *informal* — used when you are about to try doing something new, difficult, or unpleasant ▪ It's hard to explain, but *here goes*. [=I will try to explain] ▪ I've never skied before, so *here goes nothing*.

here is — used in speech and informal writing to introduce a person, subject, or action ▪ *Here is* what I think we should do. ▪ *Here's* the thing/problem—I already told her I would go. ▪ *Here is* the latest election news. ▪ *Here's* how you should hold the golf club.

here's to — used to express good wishes for someone, to say you are pleased about something, etc., before you drink something; used for making a toast to someone or something ▪ *Here's to* the new couple. May they find great happiness together. ▪ Thank you all for your hard work. And now, *here's to* another successful year!

here, there, and everywhere *informal* : in many different places : all over ▪ I've been looking for you *here, there, and everywhere*.

here to stay : likely to last or be present for a long time ▪ She's convinced that her bad luck is *here to stay*.

here we go *informal* — used when something is just beginning to happen or move ▪ *"Here we go,"* I said as the roller coaster began to climb the first hill.

here you go (again) see [1]GO

neither here nor there : not important or interesting ▪ What I think is really *neither here nor there*. You have to make up your own mind.

out of here *or* ***outta here*** *informal* — used to say that you are leaving ▪ It's five o'clock, so I am ***out of here***. [=I am leaving this place]

up to here see [2]UP

[2]**here** *interj*

1 — used to say that you are present ▪ When he calls your name, say *"here."* ▪ "John Smith?" *"Here!"*

2 — used for emphasis or to attract someone's attention ▪ *Here*, let me help you with that. ▪ (*chiefly Brit*) *Here*, what are you doing with my bike?

3 — used in calling a pet to you ▪ *Here*, boy! Good dog!

[3]**here** *noun* [*noncount*]

1 : this place ▪ get away ***from here***

2 : this point ▪ I've done my part. ***You take it from here.*** [=you are responsible from now on]

here·abouts /ˈhirəˌbaʊts/ *also US* **here·about** /ˈhirəˌbaʊt/ *adv, informal* : near or around this place : in this area ▪ We don't see a lot of snow *hereabouts*. — compare THEREABOUTS

[1]**here·af·ter** /hiɚˈæftɚ, *Brit* hɪərˈɑːftə/ *adv, formal*

1 : after this : from now on ▪ *Hereafter* the two companies will operate in full partnership. — often used in legal documents ▪ my client, *hereafter* the plaintiff [=my client, who will be called "the plaintiff" from this point onward]

2 : in a future time or state ▪ We don't know what will happen *hereafter*.

[2]**hereafter** *noun*

the hereafter : an existence that comes after life ends : life after death ▪ belief in *the hereafter*

here·by /hiɚˈbaɪ/ *adv, formal* : by means of this act, these words, this document, etc. ▪ I *hereby* declare the Olympic Games officially open. ▪ The sum will *hereby* be charged to your account. ▪ The parties to the lawsuit *hereby* agree to settle the matter out of court.

he·red·i·tary /həˈrɛdəˌteri, *Brit* həˈrɛdətri/ *adj*

1 : passed or able to be passed from parent to child before birth ▪ *hereditary* traits/diseases ▪ He suffers from a rare *hereditary* condition.

2 *formal* **a** : passing from a person who has died to that person's child or younger relative ▪ The position is *hereditary*. [=*inherited*] ▪ a *hereditary* monarchy **b** : holding a position or title that was passed on from your parent or an older relative ▪ a *hereditary* ruler/monarch

he·red·i·ty /həˈrɛdəti/ *noun* [*noncount*] *formal* : the natural process by which physical and mental qualities are passed from a parent to a child ▪ *Heredity* plays no part in the disease.

here·in /hiɚˈɪn/ *adv, formal*

1 : in this book, document, etc. ▪ For an explanation of the abbreviations used *herein*, see the section entitled "Abbreviations in this Work."

2 : in this statement, fact, or detail — used to introduce something that is related to the main subject and that is usually followed by an explanation ▪ The company faces more competition every year. *Herein* lies the challenge. In order to maintain our current standing, we have to increase sales.

here·in·af·ter /ˌhirəˈnæftɚ, *Brit* ˌhɪərəˈnɑːftə/ *adv, formal* : [1]HEREAFTER 1

her·e·sy /ˈherəsi/ *noun, pl* **-sies** : a belief or opinion that does not agree with the official belief or opinion of a particular religion [*noncount*] They were accused of *heresy*. [*count*] He was preaching dangerous *heresies*. — often used figuratively ▪ To disagree with the party leadership was *heresy*.

her·e·tic /ˈherəˌtɪk/ *noun, pl* **-tics** [*count*] : someone who believes or teaches something that goes against accepted or official beliefs ▪ The church regards them as *heretics*.

— **he·ret·i·cal** /həˈrɛtɪkəl/ *adj* ▪ *heretical* ideas/writings ▪ It would be *heretical* to suggest changing company policy.

here·to /hiɚˈtuː/ *adv, formal* : to this document ▪ I attach *hereto* my revisions.

here·to·fore /ˈhiɚtəˌfoɚ/ *adv, formal* : until this time : before now ▪ *Heretofore* her writing has never displayed such depth of feeling. ▪ This technology has created *heretofore* unimaginable possibilities.

here·with /hiɚˈwɪθ, hiɚˈwɪð/ *adv, formal* : with this : included with this note, letter, document, etc. ▪ You will find my check *herewith*. ▪ *Herewith* are your instructions. ▪ I enclose *herewith* my revisions.

her·i·ta·ble /ˈherətəbəl/ *adj, formal*

1 : able to be passed from parent to child before birth ▪ a *heritable* disease

2 *law* : able to be passed from a parent or older relative to a child ▪ a *heritable* title

her·i·tage /ˈherətɪʤ/ *noun, pl* **-tag·es** [*count*] : the traditions, achievements, beliefs, etc., that are part of the history of a group or nation — usually singular ▪ a nation with a rich *heritage* of folklore ▪ His Polish *heritage* was very important to him. ▪ These battlefields are an important part of our *heritage* and should be preserved.

herky–jerky /ˈhɚkiˈʤɚki/ *adj* [*more* ~; *most* ~] *US, informal* : not smooth or graceful : marked by sudden movements or changes ▪ a *herky-jerky* dance ▪ a film criticized for its *herky-jerky* editing

her·maph·ro·dite /hɚˈmæfrəˌdaɪt/ *noun, pl* **-dites** [*count*] : a person, plant, or animal that has both male and female parts

— **hermaphrodite** *adj* ▪ *hermaphrodite* populations — **her·maph·ro·dit·ic** /hɚˌmæfrəˈdɪtɪk/ *adj* ▪ *hermaphroditic* species

her·met·ic /hɚˈmɛtɪk/ *adj, formal* : closed tightly so that no air can go in or out ▪ *hermetic* [=(more commonly) *airtight*] seals

— **her·met·i·cal·ly** /hɚˈmɛtɪkli/ *adv* ▪ *hermetically* sealed containers

her·mit /ˈhɚmət/ *noun, pl* **-mits** [*count*] : a person who lives in a simple way apart from others especially for religious reasons

her·mit·age /ˈhɚmətɪʤ/ *noun, pl* **-ag·es** [*count*]

1 : a place where a hermit lives

2 : a house or building that is far away from other houses, buildings, or people ▪ On weekends he escapes to his *hermitage* in the mountains.

hermit crab *noun, pl* ~ **crabs** [*count*] **:** a type of crab that lives in the empty shell of another animal (such as a snail)

her·nia /ˈhənijə/ *noun, pl* **-ni·as** *medical* **:** a painful condition in which an organ (such as the intestine) pushes through the muscles that are around it [*count*] He has a *hernia*. [*noncount*] He was treated for *hernia*. — called also *rupture*

he·ro /ˈhirou/ *noun, pl* **heroes** *or in sense 3* **heros** [*count*]
1 a : a person who is admired for great or brave acts or fine qualities ▪ He returned from the war a national *hero*. ▪ the *hero* of a rescue ▪ She was a *hero* for standing up to the government. **b :** a person who is greatly admired ▪ a football *hero* ▪ His father has always been his *hero*. ▪ He has always been a *hero* to his son. ✧ *Hero* can refer to either a man or a woman, but it is often used to refer specifically to a man. The specific word for a woman who is brave and admired is *heroine*. — see also FOLK HERO
2 : the chief male character in a story, play, movie, etc. ▪ The *hero* [=*protagonist*] of the film is a fisherman.
3 *pl usually* **heros** *US* **:** SUBMARINE SANDWICH

he·ro·ic /hɪˈrowɪk/ *adj*
1 : of or relating to heroes ▪ the *heroic* age ▪ *heroic* legends
2 [*more* ~; *most* ~] **:** having or showing great courage ▪ It was *heroic* of those women to fight for the right to vote. ▪ The soldiers received medals for their *heroic* actions.
3 [*more* ~; *most* ~] **:** very large or great in size, amount, etc. ▪ Despite *heroic* efforts to save the business, it ultimately went bankrupt. ▪ a political battle of *heroic* proportions ▪ *Heroic* [=*drastic*] measures may be required to save the patient.
– he·ro·i·cal·ly /hɪˈrowɪkli/ *adv* ▪ women who fought *heroically* for the right to vote

he·ro·ics /hɪˈrowɪks/ *noun* [*plural*] **:** actions that show courage **:** heroic acts or behavior ▪ Despite his *heroics* on the football field, he has had a troubled life. — often used to describe heroic actions that are regarded as foolish ▪ We need to be cautious now. This is no time for *heroics*.

her·o·in /ˈherəwən/ *noun* [*noncount*] **:** a powerful illegal drug that is made from morphine

her·o·ine /ˈherəwən/ *noun, pl* **-ines** [*count*]
1 : a woman who is admired for great or brave acts or fine qualities ▪ The town remembered her as the *heroine* of the flood and erected a statue in her honor.
2 : the chief female character in a story, play, movie, etc. ▪ a tragic *heroine*

her·o·ism /ˈherəˌwɪzəm/ *noun* [*noncount*] **:** great courage ▪ acts/feats of *heroism* ▪ women who showed *heroism* by fighting for their right to vote

her·on /ˈherən/ *noun, pl* **-ons** [*count*] **:** a large bird that has long legs and a long neck and bill — see color picture on page C9

hero sandwich *noun, pl* ~ **-wiches** [*count*] *US* **:** SUBMARINE SANDWICH

hero worship *noun* [*noncount*] **:** foolish or excessive admiration of someone ▪ He objects to the unthinking *hero worship* of great athletes by their fans.
– hero–worship *verb* **-ships; -shipped** *also US* **-shiped; -ship·ping** *also US* **-ship·ing** [+ *obj*] ▪ As a child he *hero-worshipped* his older brother.

her·pes /ˈhəˌpiːz/ *noun* [*noncount*] **:** a disease that causes painful spots on the skin

her·ring /ˈherɪŋ/ *noun, pl* **herring** *or* **herrings** [*count, noncount*] **:** a fish that lives in the northern Atlantic Ocean and is often eaten as food — see also RED HERRING

her·ring·bone /ˈherɪŋˌboun/ *noun* [*noncount*] **:** a pattern used on cloth that consists of rows of parallel lines that slant in opposite directions to form V shapes — usually used before another noun ▪ a *herringbone* pattern/design ▪ a *herringbone* jacket

hers /ˈhəz/ *pronoun*
1 : that which belongs to or is connected with her **:** her one **:** her ones ▪ The book is *hers*. [=the book belongs to her; it is her book] ▪ *Hers* is the book on the left. [=her book is the one on the left] ▪ a former professor ***of hers*** [=one of her former professors] ▪ That face *of hers* [=her face] is hard to forget.
2 *Brit, informal* **:** her home ▪ Let's go back to *hers* for a drink.

her·self /həˈsɛlf/ *pronoun*
1 : that same woman, girl, or female animal: **a** — used as the object of a verb or preposition to refer to a woman, girl, or female animal that has already been mentioned ▪ She considers *herself* lucky. ▪ She accepted the award for her coworkers and *herself*. ▪ She is proud of *herself* for finishing college. ▪ She wrapped the blanket around *herself*. ▪ "I wonder what he meant?" she said/thought to *herself*. ▪ She had the house (all) to *herself*. [=she was alone in the house] ▪ She wanted to see it ***for herself*** [=she wanted to see it rather than have someone tell her about it, describe it to her, etc.] **b** — used for emphasis to refer again to a woman, girl, or female animal that has already been mentioned ▪ She told me *herself* that she would be here. ▪ It's hard to believe that she was young once *herself*. ▪ My father wanted my mother to see a doctor, but she *herself* didn't think it was necessary. ▪ We were welcomed by the company president *herself*. ▪ She was nervous about meeting them, but I told him to just ***be herself*** [=to behave like she normally does]
2 : her normal or healthy self ▪ She was *herself* again after a good night's sleep. ▪ She's not *herself* today; something's bothering her.
by herself **1 :** without any help from other people ▪ She shoveled the driveway *by herself*. ▪ She did her homework (all) *by herself*. **2 :** with nobody else **:** ALONE ▪ The grandmother still lives in the house *by herself*. ▪ She went to the store *by herself*.

hertz /ˈhəts/ *noun, pl* **hertz** [*count*] *technical* **:** a unit used for measuring the frequency of sound waves — abbr. *Hz*

he's /ˈhiːz, iz/ — used as a contraction of *he is* or *he has* ▪ *He's* [=*he is*] tall. ▪ *He's* [=*he has*] told me that before.

hes·i·tant /ˈhɛzətənt/ *adj* [*more* ~; *most* ~] **:** slow to act or speak especially because you are nervous or unsure about what to do **:** feeling or showing hesitation ▪ She took a *hesitant* step back from the door. ▪ He seems *hesitant* about accepting the job. — sometimes followed by *to + verb* ▪ He seems *hesitant to accept* the job.
– hes·i·tan·cy /ˈhɛzəntənsi/ *noun* [*noncount*] ▪ We were surprised by his *hesitancy* about accepting the job. **– hes·i·tant·ly** *adv* ▪ She *hesitantly* stepped back from the door. ▪ He *hesitantly* asked a stranger for directions.

hes·i·tate /ˈhɛzəˌteɪt/ *verb* **-tates; -tat·ed; -tat·ing**
1 [*no obj*] **:** to stop briefly before you do something especially because you are nervous or unsure about what to do ▪ She *hesitated* and waited for her friend to say something. ▪ He *hesitated* about/over accepting the job.
2 [+ *obj*] **:** to be unwilling *to do* something because of doubt or uncertainty ▪ I sometimes *hesitate to say* what I am really thinking. ▪ I *hesitated to come* without being asked. ▪ I wouldn't *hesitate to ask* for your help if I felt I needed it. ▪ Don't *hesitate to call* if there is a problem.
he who hesitates is lost — used to say that it is important to make decisions and do things in a quick and definite way
– hes·i·ta·tion /ˌhɛzəˈteɪʃən/ *noun* [*noncount*] A moment's *hesitation* could have cost him his life. ▪ He showed no *hesitation* about/over accepting the job. ▪ I would do it again ***without hesitation*** [=with no delay or doubts] [*count*] After several brief *hesitations* he proceeded.

hes·sian /ˈhɛʃən, *Brit* ˈhɛsiən/ *noun* [*noncount*] *Brit* **:** BURLAP

het·ero·dox /ˈhɛtərəˌdɑːks/ *adj* [*more* ~; *most* ~] *formal* **:** not agreeing with established beliefs or standards **:** UNORTHODOX ▪ a *heterodox* religious thinker ▪ *heterodox* ideas
– het·ero·doxy /ˈhɛtərəˌdɑːksi/ *noun, pl* **-dox·ies** [*count, noncount*]

het·er·o·ge·neous /ˌhɛtərəˈʤiːnijəs/ *adj* [*more* ~; *most* ~] *formal* **:** made up of parts that are different ▪ an ethnically *heterogeneous* population — opposite HOMOGENEOUS
– het·ero·ge·ne·ity /ˌhɛtəroudʒəˈniːjəti/ *noun* [*noncount*]

het·ero·sex·u·al /ˌhɛtərouˈsɛkʃəwəl/ *adj*
1 : sexually attracted to people of the opposite sex ▪ a *heterosexual* male
2 : based on sexual attraction to people of the opposite sex ▪ *heterosexual* behavior — compare BISEXUAL, HOMOSEXUAL
– heterosexual *noun, pl* **-als** [*count*] ▪ male *heterosexuals*
– het·ero·sex·u·al·i·ty /ˌhɛtərouˌsɛkʃəˈwæləti/ *noun* [*noncount*]

het up /ˈhɛtˈʌp/ *adj* [*more* ~; *most* ~] *informal + somewhat old-fashioned* **:** very excited or upset ▪ John can get all/very *het up* about/over politics. ▪ What are you so *het up* about?

heu·ris·tic /hjuˈrɪstɪk/ *adj, formal* **:** using experience to learn and improve ▪ *heuristic* writing techniques ▪ *heuristic* methods ▪ *heuristic* computer programs
– heuristic *noun, pl* **-tics** [*count*] ▪ The program uses *heuristics* [=heuristic methods] to continually improve its performance.

hew /ˈhjuː/ *verb* **hews; hewed; hewed** *or* **hewn** /ˈhjuːn/; **hew·ing** [+ *obj*] **:** to shape (something) by cutting with a sharp tool (such as an ax) • They *hewed* logs to build a cabin. • The walls are built of stones *hewn* by skilled craftsmen. • roughly *hewn* logs — sometimes used figuratively • Settlers *hewed* a town from the wilderness. • His father *hewed* a fortune from the railroads. — see also ROUGH-HEWN

hew to [*phrasal verb*] ***hew to (something)*** *US* **: to follow or obey (something)** • Everyone must *hew to* the rules/standards. • He is a politician who has always *hewed* [=*adhered*] closely *to* the party line.

hex /ˈhɛks/ *noun, pl* **hex·es** [*count*] *chiefly US* **: a magical spell that is meant to cause bad luck for someone** • He claimed that a witch had put a *hex* on him.

– **hex** /ˈhɛks/ *verb* **hexes; hexed; hex·ing** [+ *obj*] • He claimed that someone had *hexed* him.

hexa·gon /ˈhɛksəˌgɑːn, *Brit* ˈhɛksəgən/ *noun, pl* **-gons** [*count*] *mathematics* **: a flat shape that has six angles and six sides** — see picture at GEOMETRY

– **hex·ag·o·nal** /hɛkˈsægənl/ *adj* • a *hexagonal* room

hey /ˈheɪ/ *interj*

1 — used to attract someone's attention or to express surprise, joy, or anger • *Hey* (there), it's good to see you! • *Hey*, wait for me! • *Hey*, what are you doing with my car! • *Hey* you!—get away from there!

2 — used to indicate that something is not important, that you are not upset about something, etc. • I thought she was my friend, but, *hey*, it's not the first time I've been wrong. • "We lost." "*Hey*, you can't win them all." • "I'm sorry to be so late." "*Hey*, don't worry about it."

hey·day /ˈheɪˌdeɪ/ *noun, pl* **-days** [*count*] **: the time when someone or something is most successful, popular, etc.** — usually singular • In the *heyday* of big cars nobody cared how much gas cost. • That's when he was in his *heyday*.

hey presto *interj, Brit* **:** PRESTO • A wave of the hand and, *hey presto*, it's gone!

HGV /ˌeɪtʃˌʤiːˈviː/ *noun, pl* **HGVs** [*count*] *Brit* **: a large truck** ✧ *HGV* is an abbreviation of "heavy goods vehicle."

hi /ˈhaɪ/ *interj* **— used as an informal way of saying "hello"** • *Hi*, how are you? • Aren't you going to ***say hi to*** [=*greet*] him?

HI *abbr* Hawaii

hi·a·tus /haɪˈeɪtəs/ *noun, pl* **-tus·es : a period of time when something (such as an activity or program) is stopped** [*count*] The band is making an album again after a five-year *hiatus*. [*noncount*] (*US*) The television network put the show ***on hiatus*** [=it stopped broadcasting the show] for several months. = The show went *on hiatus* for several months.

hi·ba·chi /hɪˈbɑːʧi/ *noun, pl* **-chis** [*count*] *chiefly US* **: a small grill (sense 1b) for cooking food over charcoal**

hi·ber·nate /ˈhaɪbɚˌneɪt/ *verb* **-nates; -nat·ed; -nat·ing** [*no obj*] *of an animal* **: to spend the winter sleeping or resting** • bears *hibernating* in their dens

– **hi·ber·na·tion** /ˌhaɪbɚˈneɪʃən/ *noun* [*noncount*] • bears in *hibernation*

hi·bis·cus /haɪˈbɪskəs/ *noun, pl* **hibiscus** *or* **hi·bis·cus·es** [*count, noncount*] **: a type of shrub that has large colorful flowers**

hic·cup *also* **hic·cough** /ˈhɪˌkʌp/ *noun, pl* **-cups** *also* **-coughs**

1 a [*count*] **: a sound in your throat that is caused by a sudden, uncontrolled movement of muscles in your chest after you have eaten or drunk too much or too quickly b *hiccups*** [*plural*] **: a condition in which you make hiccups repeatedly** • The baby has (the) *hiccups*. • I got the *hiccups*.

2 [*count*] *informal* **: a small problem, change, or delay** • Our computer problems were caused by a *hiccup* in the power supply. • The stock market has continued to rise, except for a slight *hiccup* earlier this month.

– **hiccup** *also* **hiccough** /ˈhɪˌkʌp/ *verb* **-cups** *also* **-coughs; -cuped** *also* **-cupped** *or* **-coughed; -cup·ing** *also* **-cup·ping** *or* **-cough·ing** [*no obj*] • Someone in the audience started *hiccuping*.

hick /ˈhɪk/ *noun, pl* **hicks** [*count*] *US, informal + disapproving* **: an uneducated person from a small town or the country** • We felt like a bunch of *hicks* when we went to the city for the first time. — often used before another noun • a *hick* town [=a town where the people are hicks]

hick·o·ry /ˈhɪkəri/ *noun, pl* **-ries**

1 [*count*] **: a type of tree that has very hard wood and that produces nuts which can be eaten** — called also *hickory tree*

2 [*noncount*] **: the wood of a hickory tree**

[1]hidden *past participle of* [1]HIDE

[2]hidden *adj*

1 : not seen or known • a *hidden* [=*concealed*] microphone/camera • His suggestions have a *hidden* [=*secret*] purpose. • *hidden* motives • He's accused of having a ***hidden agenda***. [=a secret plan]

2 : not easily found or recognized • There was a *hidden* flaw in the airplane's design. • the *hidden* costs in buying a home • searching for *hidden* meanings • a *hidden* valley

[1]hide /ˈhaɪd/ *verb* **hides; hid** /ˈhɪd/; **hid·den** /ˈhɪdn/ *or* **hid; hid·ing** /ˈhaɪdɪŋ/

1 [+ *obj*] **a : to put (something) in a place where it cannot be seen or found** • She *hid* the gifts under the bed. • His records were *hidden* (away) in the back room. **b : to prevent (something) from being seen** • Clouds *hid* the sun all day. • She *hid* her face in her hands. [=she covered her face with her hands] • They live in a house *hidden* among the trees. • a house *hidden* (from view) by trees

2 a [*no obj*] **: to go to or stay at a place where you cannot be seen or found** • She *hid* under the bed. • The prisoners *hid* (out) down by the river after escaping. • criminals *hiding* (out) from the police • Photographers were *hiding* behind the fence. • He has nowhere to *hide*. — sometimes used figuratively • He tried to *hide* from his responsibilities. [=he tried to avoid his responsibilities] • She has been accused of *hiding* behind her reputation [=using her reputation to protect herself] instead of answering the charges openly. **b** [+ *obj*] **: to put (someone or yourself) in a place that cannot be seen or found** • She *hid* him/herself under the bed. • She *hid* him from the police.

3 [+ *obj*] **: to keep (something) from being known** • She tried to *hide* the fact that she was looking for another job. • You shouldn't try to *hide* your feelings (from me). • He made no attempt to *hide* his anger. • You can ask me anything. I have nothing to *hide*.

hide your light under a bushel see BUSHEL

[2]hide *noun, pl* **hides** [*count*]

1 : the skin of a usually large animal • cattle *hides*

2 *informal* **— used to talk about protecting or saving yourself or someone else from harm** • He betrayed his friend to protect his own *hide*. [=to protect himself] • Thanks for helping me out—you really ***saved my hide***! [=kept me from being harmed; saved me]

3 *chiefly Brit* **:** [3]BLIND 2

hide or hair *or* ***hide nor hair*** *informal* **: any sign of a particular person or thing** • He hasn't seen *hide or hair* of his son [=hasn't seen his son at all] since he went off to college. • We haven't seen *hide nor hair* of a gas station.

tan someone's hide *informal + old-fashioned* **: to beat or whip (someone) very badly** • He threatened to *tan my hide* if I didn't do what he told me to do.

hide–and–go–seek *noun* [*noncount*] *US* **:** HIDE-AND-SEEK

hide–and–seek *noun* [*noncount*] **: a children's game in which everyone hides from one player who tries to find them** • play *hide-and-seek*

hide·away /ˈhaɪdəˌweɪ/ *noun, pl* **-aways** [*count*] **: a hidden place : a place where someone goes to be alone** • The resort is a perfect romantic *hideaway* for young couples.

hide·bound /ˈhaɪdˌbaʊnd/ *adj* [*more* ~; *most* ~] *disapproving* **: not willing to accept new or different ideas** • a *hidebound* conservative • *hidebound* traditions [=old traditions that are out-of-date and should be changed]

hid·eous /ˈhɪdijəs/ *adj* [*more* ~; *most* ~] **: very ugly or disgusting** • The room was filled with *hideous* furniture. • a *hideous* deformity/crime • He let out a *hideous* [=*frightful*] laugh.

– **hid·eous·ly** *adv* • Her face was *hideously* deformed by the fire. – **hid·eous·ness** *noun* [*noncount*]

hide·out /ˈhaɪdˌaʊt/ *noun, pl* **-outs** [*count*] **: a place where someone (such as a criminal) hides to avoid being found or captured** • a secret *hideout*

[1]hid·ing /ˈhaɪdɪŋ/ *noun* [*noncount*] **: the state of being hidden** • She ***went into hiding*** [=she went to a secret place where she would not be found by the people who were looking for her] to avoid reporters and television cameras. • He has been ***in hiding*** for years. • He ***came out of hiding*** to answer the rumors. — compare [2]HIDING

[2]hiding *noun, pl* **-ings** [*count*] *chiefly Brit, informal* **: a severe beating** — usually singular • My father threatened to give me a good *hiding*. — sometimes used figuratively • They gave us a good *hiding* [=they defeated us badly] in that game.

on a hiding to nothing *Brit, informal* **: on the way to failure : certain to fail**

– compare [1]HIDING

hiding place *noun, pl* ~ **places** [*count*] : a place where someone or something is hidden or can be hidden • My favorite *hiding place* when I was a kid was in the attic.

hi·er·ar·chy /ˈhajəˌrɑɚki/ *noun, pl* **-chies** [*count*]
1 : a group that controls an organization and is divided into different levels • The church *hierarchy* faced resistance to some of their/its decisions.
2 : a system in which people or things are placed in a series of levels with different importance or status • He was at the bottom of the corporate *hierarchy*. • a rigid *hierarchy* of social classes
– **hi·er·ar·chi·cal** /ˌhajəˈrɑɚkɪkəl/ *also* **hi·er·ar·chic** /ˌhajəˈrɑɚkɪk/ *adj* [*more* ~; *most* ~] • The army has a rigid *hierarchical* structure. – **hi·er·ar·chi·cal·ly** /ˌhajəˈrɑɚkɪkli/ *adv* • The church is organized *hierarchically*.

hi·ero·glyph /ˈhajərəˌglɪf/ *noun, pl* **-glyphs** [*count*] : a written character that looks like a picture : a character used in hieroglyphics

hieroglyphs

hi·ero·glyph·ic /ˌhajərəˈglɪfɪk/ *noun, pl* **-ics** [*count*] : HIEROGLYPH
– **hieroglyphic** *adj* • *hieroglyphic* writing

hi·ero·glyph·ics /ˌhajərəˈglɪfɪks/ *noun* [*plural*] : a system of writing (such as the one used in ancient Egypt) that uses characters that look like pictures

hi–fi /ˈhaɪˈfaɪ/ *noun, pl* **-fis**
1 [*noncount*] : HIGH FIDELITY
2 [*count*] *somewhat old-fashioned* : a piece of electronic equipment for reproducing sound in a clear and accurate way • We bought a *hi-fi* for the bedroom.
– **hi–fi** *adj* • *hi-fi* sound reproduction • a *hi-fi* system • *hi-fi* equipment

hig·gle·dy–pig·gle·dy /ˌhɪgəldiˈpɪgəldi/ *adv, informal* : in a messy way : without order • All the dishes were stacked *higgledy-piggledy* next to the sink.
– **higgledy–piggledy** *adj* • a *higgledy-piggledy* assortment of things

[1]**high** /ˈhaɪ/ *adj* **high·er; -est**
1 a : rising or extending upward a great distance • *high* mountains/peaks • a *high* [=*tall*] building • a *high* fly ball — opposite LOW **b** : extending or reaching upward more than other things of the same kind • *high* boots • a *high* collar • a *high* fence • *high* [=*tall*] grass — opposite LOW **c** : located far above the ground or another surface • *high* clouds/altitudes • The sun was *high* [=far above the horizon] in the eastern sky. • The apartment has *high* ceilings. • The cat was found *high* (up) in the tree. • The airplane was *high* above the clouds. — opposite LOW **d** : having a specified height • The bush is six feet *high*. • a building 100 stories *high* • The grass was knee-*high*. [=the grass reached a person's knees] • waist-*high* water — see also SKY-HIGH **e** *always used before a noun* : rising above surrounding land • They have a home in the *high* country. • the *high* plains • The houses are built on *high* ground. — opposite LOW
2 a : greater than usual in amount, number, or degree • They were traveling at a *high* (rate of) speed. = They were traveling at *high* speed. • They reached speeds as *high* as 100 mph. • He's being treated for *high* blood pressure. • *high* cholesterol • a *high* fever • She earns a *high* salary. • *high* anxiety • *high* heat/humidity/temperatures • *high* interest rates • *high* intelligence • His books are in *high* demand. • We liked the house, but the price was too *high*. • He has received *high* praise for his efforts to help the homeless. • They are paying him a *high* compliment. — opposite LOW **b** : near or at the top of a range • Temperatures were in the *high* 80s. [=were around 87–89] — opposite LOW
3 a : very favorable • He holds you in *high* regard/esteem. = He has a *high* opinion of you. [=he thinks highly of you; he regards you favorably] • They started their trip with *high* hopes/expectations. [=they started their trip hoping/expecting that it would go well] • Hopes are *high* that the strike will be settled soon. • All the children were ***in high spirits*** [=were very happy and excited] on the last day of school. — opposite LOW **b** : very good • We manufacture products of *high* quality. • He got *high* marks/grades throughout college. • *high* morale • Our vacation ended ***on a high note***. [=it ended in a pleasant or enjoyable way] • Our trip to the museum was the ***high point*** [=the most enjoyable part] of our vacation. — opposite LOW **c** : morally good • She is a woman of *high* character. • *high* ideals/principles • *high* standards of conduct — opposite LOW
4 : above others in power, importance, etc. • *high* officials = officials of *high* rank = *high*-ranking officials • The decision will be reviewed by a *higher* court. • Losing weight is a *high* priority for him. • He has friends ***in high places***. [=he has friends who have power and influence] • He is ***high on the list*** of possible candidates for the job. [=he is considered to be a very good choice for the job] — opposite LOW
5 : not low in sound • a *high* voice : occurring near the top of the musical scale • a *high* note — opposite LOW
6 *always used before a noun* : very strong or forceful • *high* winds/explosives
7 : having qualities that appeal to intelligent people • *high* art • *high* comedy — opposite LOW
8 *always used before a noun* : filled with the most activity • The rates at the resort are more expensive during (the) *high* season. [=the season when it is most busy or popular] • The town is filled with tourists in ***high summer***. [=in the middle of summer]
9 *always used before a noun* : of or relating to people who have and spend a lot of money on travel, good food, etc. : rich and luxurious • *high* society/living • the *high* life
10 : very exciting or intense • *high* adventure • The hostage crisis has provided many moments of ***high drama***. [=many highly dramatic moments]
11 *of a river, stream, etc.* : rising farther up the banks than usual : having more water than usual • The river is *high*. — opposite LOW
12 *not used before a noun, informal* : intoxicated by alcohol or drugs • All he wanted to do was to ***get high***. • He was ***as high as a kite***. [=very high; very drunk or intoxicated] — often + *on* • He was *high on* cocaine.

come hell or high water see HELL
high and mighty *informal* **1** : having or showing the insulting attitude of people who believe that they are better or more important than other people • He's not so *high and mighty* now that he needs our help. • I can't stand her when she ***acts/gets (all) high and mighty*** like that. **2** ***the high and (the) mighty*** : people who are important and powerful • She likes to rub elbows with *the high and mighty*.
high in : containing a large amount of (something) • These vegetables are *high in* nitrogen. • a diet *high in* fiber
high on *US, informal* : excited or enthusiastic about (someone or something) • The coach is very *high on* this new player. • Party leaders are *high on* her prospects.
in high dudgeon see DUDGEON
it's high time *informal* ✧ If *it's high time* to do something, it is time to do something that should have been done a long time ago. • *It's high time* we made some changes around here. • *It's high time* (that) you cleaned your room.
pay a high price see [1]PAY
to high heaven(s) see HEAVEN

> ***synonyms*** HIGH, TALL, and LOFTY mean being above the usual level in height. HIGH is used for things and not people, and it refers to distance from the ground or some other surface. • A *high* fence surrounded the house. TALL is used for both people and things. • *tall* buildings • She is *tall* for her age. LOFTY is a literary word that is used for something that rises to a very great or impressive height. • *lofty* mountains

[2]**high** *adv* **high·er; -est**
1 : at or to a high place or level • The painter climbed *high* on the ladder. • The hawks were circling *high* in the air/sky. • The letters were stacked *high* on the table. • a *high*-flying airplane • If you want to be successful, you have to ***aim high***. [=you have to be ambitious]
2 : at a high rate • Don't value yourself too *high*. [=*highly*] • a *high*-paid lawyer
3 : at a high price • buy low and sell *high*
4 *informal* : in a rich manner : in the manner of people who have and spend a lot of money • He is living pretty *high*.

be riding high see [1]RIDE
fly high see [1]FLY
high and dry : in a helpless position : without help or protection • The company suddenly went out of business and left its customers *high and dry*.
high and low : EVERYWHERE • They've searched/looked *high and low* for a new car that they can afford.
high off the hog or ***high on the hog*** *US, informal* : in a luxurious style • Those movie stars live pretty *high off the hog*.
hold your head (up) high see [1]HEAD

run high see [1]RUN
set the bar higher see [1]BAR

[3]high *noun, pl* **highs**
1 [*count*] : a high point or level • Oil prices reached a new *high* last winter. • an all-time/record *high* • She achieved a career *high* in points [=she scored more points than she ever had before] in last night's game. • The *high* [=the highest temperature] today was 75. • The forecast is for showers with *highs* in the 70s. • He talked about the ***highs and lows*** [=the good parts and bad parts] of his college years.
2 [*noncount*] *US* : a gear that is used for faster speeds of travel in a vehicle • He shifted into *high.* — called also *(US) high gear*
3 [*count*] *informal* : a state of intoxication produced by a drug • The *high* only lasted a few minutes.
4 [*count*] *weather* : an area of high atmospheric pressure • A strong *high* brought clear skies and warm temperatures.
from on high **1 a** : from God or heaven • He claimed to have heard a voice *from on high.* **b** : from people with power or authority • orders *from on high* **2** : from a high place • We looked down *from on high* at the lush valley.
on a high informal : feeling happy and excited • He was *on a high* after receiving the promotion.
on high : in the sky : up above • the clouds *on high* • in heaven • the gods *on high*

high·ball /ˈhaɪˌbɑːl/ *noun, pl* **-balls** [*count*] *US, somewhat old-fashioned* : a drink of alcoholic liquor mixed with water or another liquid and served in a tall glass

high beam *noun, pl* **~ beams** *US* : the setting of a vehicle's headlights that makes the brightest light [*noncount*] The car's headlights were on *high beam.* [*plural*] Turn off your *high beams.* — called also *(Brit) full beam*; compare LOW BEAM

high·born /ˈhaɪˈboən/ *adj, formal* : born into a family with very high social status • a *highborn* lady

high·brow /ˈhaɪˌbraʊ/ *adj* [*more ~; most ~*] *often disapproving* : interested in serious art, literature, ideas, etc. • The book was a popular success, but it was trashed by *highbrow* literary critics. : relating to or intended for people who are interested in serious art, literature, ideas, etc. • It's an art film that you can see only at *highbrow* theaters. — compare MIDDLEBROW, LOWBROW
– **highbrow** /ˈhaɪˌbraʊ/ *noun, pl* **-brows** [*count*] • The book is generally looked down upon by literary *highbrows.*

high chair *noun, pl* **~ chairs** [*count*] : a child's chair that has long legs so that the child sits at the height of a dining table

high–class /ˈhaɪˈklæs, *Brit* ˈhaɪˈklɑːs/ *adj* **high·er–class; high·est–class** [*also more ~; most ~*] : very fancy, wealthy, or expensive • I felt out of place at such a *high-class* party. • a *high-class* neighborhood • The restaurant is trying to attract a *higher-class* clientele. — compare LOWER-CLASS

high command *noun* [*singular*] : the most powerful and important leaders of an organization or military force • the Republican *high command*

High Court *noun* [*singular*] : SUPREME COURT

high day *noun, pl* **~ days** [*count*] *Brit* : a day when a religious festival or holiday is observed : HOLY DAY — usually used in the phrase ***high days and holidays***

high–definition *adj, always used before a noun, of a television* : having a very clear picture and a wide screen • a new *high-definition* TV — see also HDTV

high–end /ˈhaɪˈɛnd/ *adj* **high·er–end; high·est–end** [*also more ~; most ~*] *US* : higher in price and of better quality than most others • He designs clothes that are available only at *high-end* [=*upscale*] boutiques and department stores. • This is a *high-end* camera with lots of extra features.

high·er /ˈhajɚ/ *adj, always used before a noun*
1 : far above the ground • The forecast is for strong winds at *higher* elevations.
2 : located toward the north • in the *higher* latitudes
3 : above another or others in position, rank, or order • *higher* and lower courts
4 : more advanced or developed • *higher* and lower animals

higher education *noun* [*noncount*] : education or learning at a college or university • Students and their parents worry about the rising cost of *higher education.*

higher learning *noun* [*noncount*] : education or learning at a college or university • He founded a prestigious ***institution of higher learning*** [=a college or university]

higher power *noun, pl* **~ powers** [*count*] : a spirit or being (such as God) that has great power, strength, knowledge, etc., and that can affect nature and the lives of people • belief in a *higher power*

high·er–up /ˌhajɚˈʌp/ *noun, pl* **-ups** [*count*] *informal* : a person in an organization or government who has a lot of power and authority • Her hard work and clever ideas impressed the *higher-ups* and earned her a promotion.

high·fa·lu·tin /ˌhaɪfəˈluːtn̩/ *adj* [*more ~; most ~*] *informal* : seeming or trying to seem great or important • I enjoy the opera, but not all of the *highfalutin* [=*pretentious*] people it seems to attract. • a *highfalutin* way of talking

high fashion *noun* [*noncount*]
1 : the newest fashions that are usually bought by only a small number of people • boutiques that sell *high fashion* to the very wealthy
2 : HAUTE COUTURE

high fidelity *noun* [*noncount*] : the very good quality that some recorded sounds or copied images have
– **high–fidelity** *adj* • *high-fidelity* [=*hi-fi*] recordings • *high-fidelity* sound • *high-fidelity* speakers

high finance *noun* [*noncount*] : activities (such as buying companies and investing in stocks) that involve large amounts of money • the world of *high finance*

high five *noun, pl* **~ fives** [*count*] *chiefly US, informal* : a gesture in which you slap the palm of your hand against the palm of someone else's hand in the air usually to show that you are happy about a victory or accomplishment • People began cheering and giving each other *high fives.*
– **high–five** *verb* **-fives; -fived; -fiv·ing** *US, informal* [*no obj*] People were cheering and *high-fiving* when the election results were announced. [*+ obj*] People cheered and *high-fived* each other.

high–fli·er *or* **high–fly·er** /ˈhaɪˈflajɚ/ *noun, pl* **-ers** [*count*] : a person who is very successful or very determined to succeed in business, politics, etc. • young *high-fliers* in the computer industry

high–flown /ˈhaɪˈfloʊn/ *adj* [*more ~; most ~*] *disapproving* : using fancy words that are meant to sound important and impressive • Her books are filled with abstract ideas and *high-flown* language. • *high-flown* rhetoric

high–fly·ing /ˈhaɪˈflajɪŋ/ *adj, always used before a noun* [*more ~; most ~*]
1 : flying far above the ground • *high-flying* airplanes
2 : very successful or determined to succeed • a *high-flying* young executive • a *high-flying* company

high gear *noun* [*singular*] *US* : [3]HIGH 2 • She shifted the car into *high gear.*
in/into high gear : in or into a state of great or intense activity • The project is now *in high gear.* [=*(Brit) top gear*] • Fuel prices are expected to rise as the summer travel season ***kicks/moves into high gear.***

high–grade /ˈhaɪˈgreɪd/ *adj* **high·er–grade; high·est–grade**
1 : of a very good quality • *high-grade* paper/steel
2 : medically serious : relating to a dangerous medical condition • a *high-grade* tumor/fever

high ground *noun*
the high ground : a position in which you have an advantage over others • They claim to have *the* (intellectual) *high ground* in this debate. [=they claim to have the (intellectually) better position] — often used in the phase ***the moral high ground*** • These countries lost/ceded *the moral high ground* [=they stopped being morally better than others; they lost the right to consider themselves morally better than others] when they entered the war to protect their economic interests. • She believes she has *the moral high ground* on this issue. [=she believes her position on the issue is the morally correct one]

high–hand·ed /ˈhaɪˈhændəd/ *adj* [*more ~; most ~*] : not having or showing any interest in the rights, opinions, or feelings of other people • arrogant and *high-handed* public officials • She's notorious for her *high-handed* treatment of employees.
– **high–hand·ed·ly** *adv* • treating her employees *high-handedly* – **high–hand·ed·ness** *noun* [*noncount*]

high–heeled *adj, always used before a noun, of a shoe or boot* : having a tall heel • *high-heeled* pumps

high heels *noun* [*plural*] : women's shoes that have tall heels • For the party she wore a black silk dress and *high heels.* — see picture at SHOE

High Holiday *noun, pl* **~ -days** [*count*] : either one of two important Jewish holidays: **a** : ROSH HASHANAH **b** : YOM KIPPUR

H

high horse *noun [singular] informal* ✧ If you are on ***a/your high horse***, you are talking or behaving in a way that shows that you think you are better than other people or that you know more about something than other people do. ▪ I'm not going to get up on *a high horse* and tell you that you're wrong for doing this. ▪ Oh, climb/get (down) off *your high horse*. You don't know any more about it than the rest of us.

high jinks /ˈhaɪˌʤɪŋks/ *noun [plural]* : wild or playful behavior ▪ It's a silly movie about adolescent *high jinks*.

high jump *noun*

be (in) for the high jump *Brit, informal* : to be certain to be punished ▪ If the boss finds out what we've done, *we're (in) for the high jump*! [=*we're in for it*; *we're in trouble*]

the high jump : an athletic event in which people compete by trying to jump over a bar high above the ground ▪ He won the gold medal in *the high jump*.

high jump

– **high jumper** *noun, pl* ~ **-ers** *[count]*

high·land /ˈhaɪlənd/ *noun, pl* **-lands** *[count]* : an area where there are many mountains or where the land is high above the level of the sea — usually plural ▪ a home in the *highlands* ▪ the Scottish *Highlands* [=the mountainous area in the northern part of Scotland] — compare LOWLAND

– **highland** *adj, always used before a noun* ▪ a *highland* region/village – **high·land·er** /ˈhaɪləndɚ/ *noun, pl* **-ers** *[count]* ▪ rivalries between *highlanders* and lowlanders

high–lev·el /ˈhaɪˈlɛvəl/ *adj, always used before a noun* **high·er–level; high·est–level** : of great importance or high rank ▪ These military secrets are known only to a few *high-level* government officials.

[1]**high·light** /ˈhaɪˌlaɪt/ *noun, pl* **-lights** *[count]*

1 : something (such as an event or a detail) that is very interesting, exciting, or important : the best part of something ▪ I missed the game, but I saw the *highlights* on the evening news. ▪ The jazz concert was the *highlight* [=*high point*] of our trip. — compare LOWLIGHT

2 : a light spot or area ▪ brown hair with (natural) gold *highlights* ▪ She added *highlights* to her hair. [=she dyed parts of her hair a lighter color than the rest] ▪ (*technical*) the *highlights* of a photograph/picture/painting

[2]**highlight** *verb* **-lights; -light·ed; -light·ing** *[+ obj]*

1 a : to make or try to make people notice or be aware of (someone or something) : to direct attention to (someone or something) ▪ Unfortunately, the media insisted upon *highlighting* his troubled past. ▪ The speech *highlighted* [=*emphasized*] the importance of improving education in rural communities. **b** : to be a very interesting, exciting, or important part of (something) ▪ Our trip was *highlighted* by a great jazz concert we attended.

2 : to mark (something, such as text) with a bright color ▪ The students *highlighted* important vocabulary words in their textbooks. ▪ Important names and dates in each chapter are *highlighted*. ▪ (*computers*) Use your mouse to *highlight* the text that you want to revise.

high·light·er /ˈhaɪˌlaɪtɚ/ *noun, pl* **-ers** *[count]* : a special pen with brightly colored ink that you can see through ✧ People use highlighters to mark parts of a page so that those parts will be easy to see.

high·ly /ˈhaɪli/ *adv [more ~; most ~]*

1 a : to a great degree ▪ She is one of the most *highly* respected journalists in the country. ▪ This is a *highly* [=*very*] sensitive matter. ▪ *highly* accomplished/successful ▪ That idea seems *highly* [=*extremely*] unlikely to me. **b** : in an amount or number that is greater than usual : to a high degree ▪ a *highly* paid [=high-paid] executive ▪ *highly* priced items

2 : in an approving way : with approval ▪ He speaks *highly* [=*favorably*] of you. ▪ They regard her *highly*.

highly strung *adj [more ~; most ~] chiefly Brit* : HIGH-STRUNG

high–mind·ed /ˈhaɪˈmaɪndəd/ *adj [more ~; most ~]* : having or showing intelligence and a strong moral character ▪ a *high-minded* person ▪ *high-minded* intentions ▪ a novel with *high-minded* themes

– **high–mind·ed·ly** *adv* ▪ speaking *high-mindedly* – **high–mind·ed·ness** *noun [noncount]*

High·ness /ˈhaɪnəs/ *noun, pl* **-ness·es** *[count]* — used as a title for a member of a royal family; used with *his, her,* or *your* ▪ *Her Highness* the Queen ▪ *His* Royal *Highness* the Prince of Wales ▪ *Your Highness*

high noon *noun [singular]*

1 *somewhat old-fashioned* : exactly noon ▪ The duel was to take place at *high noon*.

2 : the time when a fight or contest will happen or be decided ▪ We are approaching *high noon* of the election campaign.

3 : the most important or active time of something ▪ the *high noon* of her career

high–octane *adj*

1 *of engine fuel* : of a good quality that allows an engine to run efficiently ▪ *high-octane* gasoline

2 *informal* : very powerful, strong, or effective ▪ *high-octane* football ▪ *high-octane* coffee [=coffee that contains a lot of caffeine]

high performance *adj, always used before a noun* : better, faster, or more efficient than others ▪ *high performance* cars/airplanes/boats ▪ *high performance* running shoes

high–pitched /ˈhaɪˈpɪʧt/ *adj* **high·er–pitched; high·est–pitched** *[also more ~; most ~]* : making a high sound : HIGH ▪ She has a *high-pitched* voice. ▪ The car's brakes produced a *high-pitched* squeal.

high–pow·ered /ˈhaɪˈpawɚd/ *also* **high–pow·er** /ˈhaɪˈpawɚ/ *adj*

1 *of a person* : very successful, important, and powerful ▪ a *high-powered* executive

2 : very energetic or forceful ▪ a *high-powered* performance by a rock musician

3 *of a machine or device* : very powerful ▪ *high-powered* computers ▪ *high-power* lasers

high–pressure *adj, always used before a noun*

1 : using or involving forceful methods to sell something ▪ a *high-pressure* salesman ▪ *high-pressure* sales tactics

2 *[more ~; most ~]* : causing or involving a lot of mental or emotional stress : very stressful ▪ She has a *high-pressure* job on Wall Street. ▪ the *high-pressure* world of advertising

3 a : having or using a lot of force or pressure from air, water, etc. ▪ a *high-pressure* hose ▪ gas stored in a *high-pressure* container **b** *of weather* : having a high atmospheric pressure ▪ A *high-pressure* system will bring us better weather later this week. ▪ a *high-pressure* center/area

high priest *noun, pl* ~ **priests** *[count]*

1 *informal* : a person (especially a man) who is a leader in a particular profession, subject, etc. — often + *of* ▪ the *high priest of* psychotherapy ▪ the *high priest of* horror fiction

2 : an important priest in some religions

high priestess *noun, pl* ~ **-esses** *[count]*

1 *informal* : a woman who is a leader in a particular profession, subject, etc. — often + *of* ▪ a *high priestess of* the civil rights movement ▪ the *high priestess of* the blues

2 : an important priestess in some religions

high–profile *adj [more ~; most ~]* : attracting a lot of attention in newspapers, on television, etc. ▪ a *high-profile* legal case ▪ a *high-profile* athlete ▪ She has a very *high-profile* job.

high–ranking *adj, always used before a noun* **high·er–ranking; high·est–ranking** : having a high rank or position ▪ *high-ranking* officials

high–rise /ˈhaɪˈraɪz/ *adj, always used before a noun*

1 *of a building* : very tall : having many floors or stories ▪ a *high-rise* apartment building

2 : made up of high-rise buildings ▪ a *high-rise* district

– **high rise** *noun, pl* ~ **rises** *[count]* ▪ My apartment is in the *high rise* on the corner.

high–risk *adj*

1 : likely to result in failure, harm, or injury : having a lot of risk ▪ a *high-risk* [=*dangerous*] activity ▪ *high-risk* investments

2 : more likely than others to get a particular disease, condition, or injury ▪ *high-risk* patients ▪ patients in the *high-risk* group

high road *noun, pl* ~ **roads** *[count] old-fashioned* : a main road

the high road **1** *chiefly US* : a morally proper way of doing something ▪ Several local news programs reported the rumor, but the city newspaper ***took the high road*** [=behaved properly] and waited to see if anyone could confirm the story. **2** : an easy way to do something ▪ The book claims to teach *the high road* to financial success.

high roller *noun, pl* ~ **-ers** *[count] informal*

1 : a rich person who spends a lot of money ▪ a *high roller* known for his lavish parties

2 : a person who gambles large amounts of money ▪ The casino offers special deals to attract *high rollers.*

high school *noun, pl* **~ schools**

1 *[count, noncount]* **:** a school in the U.S. and Canada for older children ▪ She's in *high school.* = She goes to *high school.* = She attends *high school.* ▪ He graduated from Manchester *High School.* — often used before another noun ▪ the *high school* track team ▪ *high-school* students ✧ Children in the U.S. and Canada attend high school for their last three or usually four years of schooling before possibly going to a college or university. — compare ELEMENTARY SCHOOL, JUNIOR HIGH SCHOOL, MIDDLE SCHOOL

2 *[singular]* — used in the U.K. in the names of secondary schools ▪ She sat A levels at Slough *High School* for Girls.

high schooler *noun, pl* **-ers** *[count] US* **:** a high-school student

high seas *noun [plural]* **:** the open part of a sea or ocean **:** the part of a sea or ocean that is away from land ▪ The ship was attacked on the *high seas.*

high–security *adj, always used before a noun* **:** carefully locked, protected, or guarded ▪ a *high-security* prison/facility

High Sheriff *noun, pl* **~ -iffs** *[count] Brit* **:** SHERIFF 2

high–sound·ing /ˈhaɪˈsaʊndɪŋ/ *adj [more ~; most ~] disapproving* **:** using words that are meant to sound important and impressive ▪ *high-sounding* rhetoric/language

high–speed /ˈhaɪˈspiːd/ *adj*

1 : designed to go or move very fast ▪ *high-speed* trains

2 : going or moving very fast ▪ The robbers led the police on a *high-speed* chase. ▪ a *high-speed* Internet connection

high–spir·it·ed /ˈhaɪˈspirətəd/ *adj [more ~; most ~]* **:** full of energy or enthusiasm **:** LIVELY ▪ a *high-spirited* group of school children ▪ She gave a *high-spirited* performance.

– high–spir·it·ed·ness *noun [noncount]*

high street *noun, pl* **~ streets** *[count] Brit* **:** a town's main street where there are many shops, banks, etc. ▪ 74 *High Street* — often used before another noun ▪ *high street* shops/retailers

high–strung /ˈhaɪˈstrʌŋ/ *adj [more ~; most ~] chiefly US* **:** very nervous or easily upset ▪ stories of *high-strung* performers who place unreasonable demands on the people who work with them ▪ Dogs of this breed are often *high-strung.* [=(*chiefly Brit*) *highly strung*]

high·tail /ˈhaɪˌteɪl/ *verb* **-tails; -tailed; -tail·ing**

hightail it *US, informal* **:** to leave a place as quickly as possible ▪ When we heard the night watchman, we *hightailed it* out of there as quick as we could.

high tea *noun, pl* **~ teas** *[count, noncount] chiefly Brit* **:** an early evening meal at which tea and often cold meat and sandwiches are usually served

high–tech *also* **hi–tech** /ˈhaɪˈtɛk/ *adj [more ~; most ~]* **:** relating to or using new electronic devices and technology ▪ *high-tech* devices/materials ▪ *high-tech* solutions ▪ *high-tech* businesses ▪ The methods they use are very *high-tech.*

high tech *also* **hi–tech** *noun [noncount]* **:** HIGH TECHNOLOGY

high technology *noun [noncount]* **:** the use or creation of new scientific methods or materials especially when they involve computers or electronic devices ▪ advances in *high technology* ▪ This region has become a center of *high technology.* — often used before another noun ▪ *high-technology* [=*high-tech*] products/industries

high–tension *adj, always used before a noun* **:** having or using a very powerful flow of electricity **:** HIGH-VOLTAGE ▪ *high-tension* wires

high–test *adj* **:** HIGH-OCTANE ▪ *high-test* fuel ▪ *high-test* vodka

high tide *noun, pl* **~ tides** *[count, noncount]* **:** the tide when the water is at its highest level ▪ At *high tide* the water covers the rocks completely. — sometimes used figuratively ▪ He became involved in social issues at the *high tide* of the civil rights movement. [=at the most active and important time of the civil rights movement] — compare LOW TIDE

high–toned /ˈhaɪˌtoʊnd/ *adj [more ~; most ~] chiefly US*

1 : having a high moral or intellectual tone or quality ▪ a *high-toned* movie/play ▪ *high-toned* moral themes

2 : HIGH-SOUNDING ▪ *high-toned* phrases

high–top /ˈhaɪˌtɑːp/ *adj, always used before a noun, chiefly US, of a shoe or sneaker* **:** extending up over the ankle ▪ *high-top* sneakers

– high–tops /ˈhaɪˌtɑːps/ *noun [plural]* ▪ The kids wore jeans and *high-tops.* [=high-top sneakers]

high treason *noun [noncount]* **:** TREASON ▪ The conspirators were hanged for *high treason.*

high–up *noun, pl* **-ups** *[count] Brit* **:** HIGHER-UP

high–volt·age /ˈhaɪˈvoʊltɪʤ/ *adj, always used before a noun*

1 : having or using a very powerful flow of electricity ▪ *high-voltage* wires

2 *[more ~; most ~]* **:** having or showing a lot of energy ▪ a *high-voltage* [=*dynamic, electric*] performance/performer

high water *noun*

come hell or high water see HELL

high–water mark *noun, pl* **~ marks** *[count]*

1 : the time when something is most active, successful, etc. **:** PEAK ▪ It was the *high-water mark* of her career.

2 : the highest level that water from a river, ocean, etc., reaches especially during a flood

high·way /ˈhaɪˌweɪ/ *noun, pl* **-ways** *[count] chiefly US* **:** a main road that connects cities, towns, etc. ▪ I had heard there was a traffic jam on the *highway,* so I took the side roads. — compare EXPRESSWAY, FREEWAY, INTERSTATE

high·way·man /ˈhaɪˌweɪmən/ *noun, pl* **-men** /-mən/ *[count]* **:** a man especially in the past who stopped travelers on roads and robbed them

highway robbery *noun [noncount] US, informal* **:** the practice of charging a price that is very high and usually unfair for something ▪ Charging that much to see a movie is *highway robbery!*

high wire *noun, pl* **~ wires** *[count]* **:** a rope or wire on which a performer walks and does tricks high up in the air to entertain people especially as part of a circus **:** a high tightrope — usually singular ▪ walking/performing on the *high wire* — often used before another noun ▪ a ***high-wire act*** [=a circus performance on a high wire] — sometimes used figuratively to refer to something that is difficult or dangerous ▪ The company is walking a financial *high wire.* [=behaving in a financially risky way] ▪ a financial *high-wire act*

hi·jack /ˈhaɪˌʤæk/ *verb* **-jacks; -jacked; -jack·ing** *[+ obj]*

1 a : to stop and steal (a moving vehicle) ▪ He *hijacked* a truck, threatening the driver at gunpoint. **b :** to steal (something) from a moving vehicle that you have stopped ▪ A band of robbers *hijacked* the load of furs from the truck.

2 : to take control of (an aircraft) by force ▪ A group of terrorists *hijacked* the plane.

3 : to take or take control of (something) for your own purposes ▪ The organization has been *hijacked* by radicals.

– hijack *noun, pl* **-jacks** *[count]* ▪ recent airline *hijacks*
– hi·jack·er *noun, pl* **-ers** *[count]* ▪ airline *hijackers*
– hijacking *noun, pl* **-ings** *[count]* ▪ recent airline *hijackings*

[1]hike /ˈhaɪk/ *verb* **hikes; hiked; hik·ing**

1 : to walk a long distance especially for pleasure or exercise **:** to go on a hike *[no obj]* We spent the afternoon *hiking* around the lake. ▪ She *hiked* 10 miles in the hot desert sun. ▪ We *hiked* (up) to the camp. *[+ obj]* We *hiked* some of the shorter trails. ▪ Our neighbors spent their vacation *hiking* the Rockies.

2 *[+ obj]* **:** to suddenly increase the cost, amount, or level of (something) ▪ The state keeps *hiking* the tax on cigarettes. ▪ There's talk of *hiking* the eligibility age.

3 *[+ obj]* **:** to pull or lift (something, such as yourself or part of your clothing) with a quick movement ▪ I *hiked* myself onto the ledge. — usually + *up* ▪ She *hiked up* her long skirt and stepped over the hedge.

4 *[+ obj] American football* **:** to pass (the ball) back to the quarterback at the start of a play **:** SNAP ▪ The center *hiked* the ball too soon, and the quarterback fumbled.

– hik·er *noun, pl* **-ers** *[count]* ▪ The *hikers* wandered away from the trail and got lost. **– hiking** *adj* ▪ *hiking* boots **– hiking** *noun [noncount]* ▪ My hobbies include *hiking* and photography. ▪ Our neighbors like to ***go hiking*** in the mountains.

[2]hike *noun, pl* **hikes** *[count]*

1 : a usually long walk especially for pleasure or exercise ▪ We went for a *hike* around the lake. ▪ a 10-mile *hike*

2 : a usually sudden increase in the cost, level, or amount of something ▪ The school lost a number of students after the tuition *hike.* ▪ a price/tax/wage *hike*

take a hike *US, informal + impolite* — used in speech as an angry way of telling someone to leave

hi·lar·i·ous /hɪˈlerijəs/ *adj [more ~; most ~]* **:** very funny ▪ Some people don't like his comedy, but I think he's *hilarious.*

H

▪ She gave us a *hilarious* account of her first days as a teacher. ▪ a *hilarious* comedy

— **hi·lar·i·ous·ly** *adv* ▪ a *hilariously* irreverent comedy

hi·lar·i·ty /hɪˈlerəti/ *noun* [*noncount*] **:** noisy fun or laughter ▪ My attempt to carve the turkey was a source of great *hilarity* at the dinner table.

hill /ˈhɪl/ *noun, pl* **hills**

1 [*count*] **:** a usually rounded area of land that is higher than the land around it but that is not as high as a mountain ▪ She watched the sun set behind the *hills*. ▪ The house was built at the very top of the *hill*.

2 [*count*] **:** an area of sloping ground on a road, path, etc. ▪ Our driveway is a long, steep *hill*. ▪ He came barreling down the *hill* at 65 miles per hour.

3 [*count*] **:** a pile of something **:** HEAP, MOUND ▪ The plows came and cleared the streets, forming a *hill* of snow on the street corner.

4 ***the Hill*** *US, informal* — used to refer to the U.S. Congress ▪ a proposed new law that is being debated on *the Hill* [=on Capitol Hill]

a hill of beans *chiefly US, informal* **:** something that has little or no value — used in negative statements ▪ These proposals don't amount to *a hill of beans*. = These proposals aren't worth *a hill of beans*. [=these proposals have no value; they are useless]

over the hill *informal* **:** old and no longer successful, attractive, etc. ▪ an athlete who's *over the hill* ▪ an *over-the-hill* actor

hill·bil·ly /ˈhɪlˌbɪli/ *noun, pl* **-lies** [*count*] *US, usually disapproving* **:** a person who lives in the country far away from cities and who is often regarded as someone who lacks education, who is stupid, etc. ▪ Other kids called her a *hillbilly* because of her accent and her simple clothes.

hillbilly music *noun* [*noncount*] *US* **:** COUNTRY MUSIC

hill·ock /ˈhɪlək/ *noun, pl* **-ocks** [*count*] **:** a small hill

hill·side /ˈhɪlˌsaɪd/ *noun, pl* **-sides** [*count*] **:** the side of a hill ▪ Streams of rainwater rushed down the *hillside*. — often used before another noun ▪ a *hillside* neighborhood

hill·top /ˈhɪlˌtɑːp/ *noun, pl* **-tops** [*count*] **:** the top of a hill ▪ They built their house on a *hilltop*. — often used before another noun ▪ a *hilltop* view ▪ a *hilltop* town

hilly /ˈhɪli/ *adj* **hill·i·er**; **-est :** having many hills ▪ *hilly* terrain ▪ *hilly* roads.

— **hill·i·ness** *noun* [*noncount*]

hilt /ˈhɪlt/ *noun, pl* **hilts** [*count*] **:** the handle of a sword or dagger

to the hilt **:** as much as possible **:** to the greatest possible limit or extent ▪ The farm was mortgaged (up) *to the hilt*. ▪ She played the role *to the hilt*.

him /ˈhɪm, ɪm/ *pronoun, objective form of* HE

1 — used to refer to a certain man, boy, or male animal as the object of a verb or preposition ▪ I hadn't heard from my brother in a while, so I gave *him* a call. ▪ Do you know *him*? ▪ His mother punished *him* for hitting his little sister. ▪ I often play basketball with *him*.

2 — used to indicate either a male or female object of a verb or preposition in general statements or when the sex of the person is unknown ▪ If any student misbehaves, send *him* to the office. ✧ This use of *him* was common in the past but is now often avoided because it is considered sexist.

him·self /hɪmˈself/ *pronoun*

1 : that same man, boy, or male animal: **a** — used as the object of a verb or preposition to refer to a man, boy, or male animal that has already been mentioned ▪ He accidentally cut *himself* while shaving. ▪ He bought *himself* a new wallet. = He bought a new wallet for *himself*. ▪ He doesn't consider *himself* old. = He doesn't think of *himself* as (being) old. ▪ The cat washed *himself*. ▪ He wrote a note to *himself*. ▪ He had the house (all) *to himself*. [=he was alone in the house] ▪ "It's almost morning," he said to *himself*. ▪ He wanted to see it ***for himself*** [=he wanted to see it rather than have someone tell him about it, describe it to him, etc.] **b** — used for emphasis to refer again to a man, boy, or male animal that has already been mentioned ▪ He told me *himself* that he was broke. = He *himself* told me (that) he was broke. ▪ He reminded them that he was young once *himself*. ▪ The proposal was made by the governor *himself*. ▪ The composer *himself* conducted the symphony.

2 : that same person — used to indicate either a male or female object of a verb or preposition ▪ Everyone must fend for *himself*. [=all people must fend for themselves] ✧ This use of *himself* was common in the past but is now often avoided because it is considered sexist.

3 : his normal or healthy self ▪ After a good night's sleep, he felt like *himself* again. ▪ He's not *himself* today; something must be bothering him. ▪ He was nervous about meeting them, but I told him to just ***be himself*** [=to behave like he normally does]

by himself **1 :** without any help from other people ▪ He shoveled the driveway *by himself*. ▪ He did his homework (all) *by himself*. **2 :** with nobody else **:** ALONE ▪ He lives in the house *by himself*. ▪ He likes to travel *by himself*.

every man for himself see [1]MAN

[1]**hind** /ˈhaɪnd/ *adj, always used before a noun* **:** at or near the back of something ▪ The dog stood on his *hind* [=*rear*] legs, begging for food.

[2]**hind** *noun, pl* **hinds** [*count*] *chiefly Brit* **:** a female deer **:** DOE; *especially* **:** a female red deer — compare HART

hin·der /ˈhɪndɚ/ *verb* **-ders**; **-dered**; **-der·ing** [+ *obj*] **:** to make (something, such as a task or action) slow or difficult ▪ Their journey was *hindered* [=*impeded, slowed*] by snow and high winds. ▪ The witness refused to cooperate, *hindering* the investigation. ▪ The country's economic growth is being *hindered* by the sanctions. ▪ It's not clear whether the change will help or *hinder* our project.

hinder from [*phrasal verb*] ***hinder (someone or something) from (something)*** **:** to stop (someone) from (doing something) ▪ Financial troubles *hindered* [=*prevented*] him *from* going on the trip. ▪ Unfortunately, her ignorance has never *hindered* [=*stopped*] her *from* giving her opinion.

Hin·di /ˈhɪndi/ *noun* [*singular*] **:** an official language of India

— **Hindi** *adj* ▪ *Hindi* grammar

hind·quar·ter /ˈhaɪndˌkwoɚtɚ/ *noun, pl* **-ters** [*count*] **:** the back left or right part of the body of an animal with four feet — usually plural ▪ the dog's/horse's *hindquarters*

hin·drance /ˈhɪndrəns/ *noun, pl* **-dranc·es**

1 [*count*] **:** a person or thing that makes a situation difficult **:** a person or thing that hinders someone or something ▪ She wanted to sign up for the class, but the cost was a *hindrance*. [=the class cost too much] ▪ Is my presence here a help or a *hindrance*? — often + *to* ▪ I'm afraid you're more of a *hindrance to* me than a help at this point. ▪ These sanctions are a *hindrance to* the country's economic growth.

2 [*noncount*] **:** the act of making it difficult for someone to act or for something to be done **:** the act of hindering someone or something ▪ He should be allowed to live where he chooses ***without hindrance*** = (*chiefly Brit*) He should be allowed to live where he chooses ***without let or hindrance***

hind·sight /ˈhaɪndˌsaɪt/ *noun* [*noncount*] **:** the knowledge and understanding that you have about an event only after it has happened ▪ It's easy for us to say that the war was wrong, but we have the advantage/benefit of *hindsight*. ▪ ***In hindsight***, it's clear that there were alternatives. = ***With hindsight***, we clearly see that there were alternatives. — see also *twenty-twenty hindsight* at TWENTY-TWENTY

Hin·du /ˈhɪnˌduː/ *noun, pl* **-dus** [*count*] **:** a follower of Hinduism

— **Hindu** *adj* ▪ *Hindu* philosophy ▪ They are *Hindu*. [=they are Hindus]

Hin·du·ism /ˈhɪnˌduːˌɪzəm/ *noun* [*singular*] **:** the main religion of India which includes the worship of many gods and the belief that after you die you return to life in a different form

[1]**hinge** /ˈhɪnʤ/ *noun, pl* **hing·es** [*count*] **:** a usually metal piece that attaches a door, gate, or cover to something and allows it to open and close — see picture at DOOR

[2]**hinge** *verb* **hinges**; **hinged**; **hing·ing** [+ *obj*] **:** to attach (a door, gate, or cover) by hinges — usually used as *(be) hinged* ▪ a storage trunk with a *hinged* lid

hinge on *also* ***hinge upon*** [*phrasal verb*] ***hinge on/upon (something)*** **:** to be determined or decided by (something) **:** to depend on (something) ▪ The outcome of the election *hinges on* how the candidates perform in the debate.

[1]**hint** /ˈhɪnt/ *noun, pl* **hints** [*count*]

1 : a small piece of information that helps you guess an answer or do something more easily ▪ I can't tell you the answer, but I'll give you a *hint*. [=*clue*] ▪ The book includes helpful *hints* [=*tips*] for inexperienced cooks.

2 : information about something given in an indirect way ▪ Her face gave me a *hint* of what she was thinking.; *especially* **:** a statement that suggests something that you do not want to say in a direct way ▪ He's been ***dropping hints*** that he'd like to be invited to the party. [=he has been saying things that show that he wants to be invited] ▪ When she told me how much work she had to do, I ***got/took the hint*** [=I understood what she was suggesting] and left. • "I have a lot of work to do." "OK, I'll leave. I can ***take a hint***."

3 : a very small amount of something • The sauce has a subtle *hint* of garlic. • It was late March, but there was still a *hint* [=*trace*] of winter in the air. • He had a *hint* of a German accent. • They'll betray you at the first *hint* of trouble.

²hint *verb* **hints; hint·ed; hint·ing** : to say (something) or give information about (something) in an indirect way [+ *obj*] — usually + *that* • He's been *hinting that* he might run for mayor. [*no obj*] I keep *hinting*, but she's not catching on. I think I need to be more direct. • The boss *hinted* about possible layoffs.

hint at [*phrasal verb*] ***hint at (something)*** : to talk about (something) in an indirect way • He's been *hinting at* the possibility of running for mayor. = He's been *hinting at* a mayoral run. • The history textbook only *hinted at* the racial prejudice of that era. • What is she *hinting at*?

hin·ter·land /ˈhɪntɚˌlænd/ *noun, pl* **-lands** [*count*] : an area that is not close to any cities or towns : a remote region • a/the rural *hinterland* ✧ *Hinterland* is usually singular in British English but is often plural in U.S. English. • She had grown up in the city and knew nothing of life in the *hinterlands*.

¹hip /ˈhɪp/ *noun, pl* **hips** [*count*] : the part of your body between your waist and legs on each side • She stood with her hands on her *hips*. — see picture at HUMAN

joined at the hip *informal* — used to describe two people who are often or usually together • She and her sister used to be *joined at the hip* [=*inseparable*] when they were kids.

shoot from the hip see ¹SHOOT

– compare ²HIP

– hipped /ˈhɪpt/ *adj* • a wide-*hipped* woman [=a woman with wide hips]

²hip *noun, pl* **hips** [*count*] : ROSE HIP — compare ¹HIP

³hip *adj* **hip·per; hip·pest** [*also more ~; most ~*] *informal*

1 : knowing about and following the newest styles, fashions, etc. • He tried to learn about the latest bands so he could impress his *hip* new college friends.

2 : very popular or fashionable • She knows how to get into all of the *hippest* clubs and restaurants.

hip to *informal* : aware of (something) • He's *hip to* what's going on in the jazz world.

– hip·ness /ˈhɪpnəs/ *noun* [*noncount*]

⁴hip *interj* — used in a cheer • *Hip, hip,* hooray!

hip bone *noun, pl* **~ bones** [*count*] : the large bone between your waist and your legs that has sides that spread outward to form the hips — see picture at HUMAN

hip flask *noun, pl* **~ flasks** [*count*] : FLASK 1

hip–hop /ˈhɪpˌhɑːp/ *noun* [*noncount*] : rap music • I listen to *hip-hop* and reggae. • a *hip-hop* artist; *also* : the culture associated with rap music

hip·pie *also* **hip·py** /ˈhɪpi/ *noun, pl* **-pies** [*count*] : a usually young person who rejects established social customs (such as by dressing in an unusual way or living in a commune) and who opposes violence and war; *especially* : a young person of this kind in the 1960s and 1970s • longhaired *hippies* • draft-dodging *hippies* • She used to be a *hippie*, but she's fairly conservative now. • an old/aging *hippie* [=an old person who still lives like the hippies of the 1960s and 1970s] • The band appeals to a new generation of *hippies*. — often used before another noun • the *hippie* generation/movement • my *hippie* days [=the time when I was a hippie]

hip·po /ˈhɪpoʊ/ *noun, pl* **-pos** [*count*] *somewhat informal* : HIPPOPOTAMUS

hip·po·pot·a·mus /ˌhɪpəˈpɑːtəməs/ *noun, pl* **-mus·es** *or* **-mi** /-ˌmaɪ/ [*count*] : a large African animal that has an extremely large head and mouth and short legs and that spends most of its time in water

hip·ster /ˈhɪpstɚ/ *noun, pl* **-sters** [*count*] *informal* : a person who follows the latest styles, fashions, etc. : a hip person • a movie that appeals equally to *hipsters* and suburbanites

¹hire /ˈhajɚ/ *verb* **hires; hired; hir·ing**

1 a *chiefly US* : to give work or a job to (someone) in exchange for wages or a salary [+ *obj*] She had very little office experience, so the company wouldn't *hire* her. • a *hired* hand/worker • We *hired* someone to clean the office once a week. [*no obj*] The company isn't *hiring* right now. **b** [+ *obj*] : to use or get the services of (someone) to do a particular job • You should *hire* [=(more formally) *employ*] a lawyer to look over the contract.

2 [+ *obj*] *chiefly Brit* : to pay to use (something) : RENT • *hire* a hall • a *hired* car

hire out [*phrasal verb*] **1** ***hire out (something) or hire (something) out*** *chiefly Brit* : to allow someone to use (something) in exchange for money • The hotel *hires out* [=*rents out*] boats to guests. **2** ***hire out or hire (yourself) out*** *US, informal* : to take a job : to work for wages or a salary • She *hired out* as a cook. • He's a teacher most of the year, but in the summer he *hires himself out* as a tour guide.

– hiring *noun* [*noncount*] • Who's in charge of the *hiring* and firing of the office staff? • the company's *hiring* practices

²hire *noun, pl* **hires**

1 [*count*] *US, informal* : someone who has been hired for a job • The company has a few new *hires*.

2 [*noncount*] *Brit* : RENTAL • The *hire* of a car and other equipment will of course incur a supplementary charge. • a car-*hire* firm — often used before another noun • a *hire* car [=a car that is or can be rented; a rental car]

for hire **1 a** : available to be used in exchange for money • They have boats (available) *for hire*. [=*for rent*] **b** : available to do work in exchange for money • Several people in the neighborhood responded to the "gardener *for hire*" signs she posted. **2** : in exchange for money • He says he'll do farm work *for hire*.

on hire *chiefly Brit* : kept to be used by people in exchange for money • The boats are *on hire* to the guests from the management.

hired gun *noun, pl* **~ guns** [*count*] *chiefly US*

1 : a person who is paid to kill someone

2 : a person who is hired to do a specific job and especially one that some people consider to be morally wrong • business executives and the *hired guns* they pay to polish their images

hire·ling /ˈhajɚlɪŋ/ *noun, pl* **-lings** [*count*] *disapproving* : a person who is paid for doing a job that is not respected or that is considered morally wrong • She's one of the political *hirelings* who run the candidate's campaign.

hire purchase *noun* [*noncount*] *Brit* : INSTALLMENT PLAN • They bought the furniture on *hire purchase*.

hir·sute /ˈhɚˌsuːt, *Brit* ˈhəːˌsjuːt/ *adj* [*more ~; most ~*] *formal + often humorous* : having a lot of hair especially on the face or body : HAIRY • his *hirsute* chest

¹his /ˈhɪz, ɪz/ *adj, always used before a noun, possessive form of* HE

1 : relating to or belonging to a certain man, boy, or male animal • He bought *his* own house. • *His* house is out in the country. • What is *his* name? • He sat quietly at *his* desk. : made or done by a certain man, boy, or male animal • I would like to read some of *his* essays. • He was jailed for three years for *his* crime. • It's *his* turn to play.

2 — used to refer to a person of either sex in general statements or when the sex of the person is unknown • Each student should do *his* own work. [=each student should do his or her own work; all students should do their own work] ✧ This use of *his* was common in the past but is now often avoided because it is considered sexist.

²his /ˈhɪz/ *pronoun*

1 : that which belongs to or is connected with him : his one : his ones • The book is *his*. [=the book belongs to him; it is his book] • My eyes are blue and *his* are brown. • The red car is mine; *his* is the green one. • Are you a friend ***of his***? [=are you his friend?] • That face *of his* [=his face] is hard to forget.

2 *Brit, informal* : his home • Let's go back to *his* [=*his place*] after the show.

His·pan·ic /hɪˈspænɪk/ *adj* : coming originally from an area where Spanish is spoken and especially from Latin America • *Hispanic* people; *also* : of or relating to Hispanic people • *Hispanic* culture

– Hispanic *noun, pl* **-ics** [*count*]

¹hiss /ˈhɪs/ *noun, pl* **hiss·es** [*count*] : a sound like a long "s" • The air escaped from the balloon with a *hiss*. • the *hiss* of a snake • the boos and *hisses* of the audience

²hiss *verb* **hisses; hissed; hiss·ing**

1 [*no obj*] : to produce a sound like a long "s" : to make a hiss • The radiator *hissed* as it let off steam. • a *hissing* noise

2 : to show that you dislike or disapprove of someone (such as a performer or speaker) by making a hiss [*no obj*] The audience booed and *hissed* (at him) when he came on stage. [+ *obj*] The audience *hissed* him off the stage.

3 [+ *obj*] : to say (something) in a loud or angry whisper • "Leave me alone!" he *hissed*.

hissy fit /ˈhɪsi-/ *noun, pl* **~ fits** [*count*] *informal* : an uncontrolled expression of strong emotion : FIT • She threw/had a *hissy fit* [=she became very angry and upset] when I told her she couldn't go.

his·ta·mine /ˈhɪstəˌmiːn/ *noun, pl* **-mines** [*count*] *medical* : a chemical substance in the body that causes the symptoms that people experience when they are allergic to something — compare ANTIHISTAMINE

his·to·ri·an /hɪˈstorijən/ *noun, pl* **-ans** [*count*] : a person who studies or writes about history • a military *historian*

his·tor·ic /hɪˈstorɪk/ *adj*

1 a [*more* ~; *most* ~] : famous or important in history • a/an *historic* event • *historic* landmarks **b** [*more* ~; *most* ~] : having great and lasting importance • It's wonderful to see so many people here on this *historic* occasion. • She returned safely from her *historic* flight into space. • The court made a *historic* decision last week. **c** : happening or existing in the past • *historic* interest rates • They know of many *historic* volcanic eruptions in the area. **d** : considered in comparison with the past • Unemployment is at a *historic* low. [=an all-time low; the rate of unemployment is lower than it has ever been]

2 : of or relating to history or the past : HISTORICAL • the *historic* importance of the river • *historic* artifacts/relics

his·tor·i·cal /hɪˈstorɪkəl/ *adj*

1 : of or relating to history • He strove for *historical* accuracy in the movie. • *historical* research/facts • a ***historical museum*** [=a museum that shows objects relating to the history of a place] • a ***historical society*** [=a group of people who work to preserve the history of a place]

2 : based on history • a/an *historical* novel [=a novel that tells a story about events and people in the past] • *historical* fiction

3 : arranged in the order that things happened or came to be : CHRONOLOGICAL • The kings are listed in *historical* order.

— his·tor·i·cal·ly /hɪˈstorɪkli/ *adv* • The movie is not *historically* accurate. • *historically* significant events • *Historically* [=*in the past*], the school has had a strong sports program.

his·to·ry /ˈhɪstəri/ *noun, pl* **-ries**

1 [*noncount*] : the study of past events • I studied *history* in college. • a professor of medieval/American *history* — see also NATURAL HISTORY

2 [*noncount*] **a** : events of the past • They were one of the greatest teams in *history*. • the dawn of recorded *history* [=the beginning of the time when important events in the past were written down] • These problems have occurred throughout (human) *history*. • It was one of the most destructive storms in modern/recent *history*. • It was a period in American *history* when most people lived and worked on farms. • Her discoveries have earned her a place in *history*. [=she will be remembered in the future because of her discoveries] • How will *history* judge the policies of the current administration? [=how will the policies be regarded in the future?] • ***History has shown*** that such attempts have always failed. [=such attempts have always failed in the past] • They believe that they will succeed because ***history is on their side***. [=because other people have succeeded in the past in similar situations] • You can't ***rewrite history***. [=you can't change what has happened in the past] • A talent scout spotted her behind the counter at a soda fountain and ***the rest is history***. [=the rest of the story about her success is well-known] • They won the championship last year. Will ***history repeat itself*** this year? [=will the same thing happen again?] **b** : past events that relate to a particular subject, place, organization, etc. • He gave us a tour of the building and told us about the company's *history*. [=about how the company began and how it has developed over time] • The company has been successful throughout its *history*. [=throughout the entire time of its existence] • Nothing like this has occurred before in the company's 20-year *history*. [=in the 20 years that the company has existed] • There is quite a bit of *history* [=much has happened] in this old house. • The *history* of space exploration is a fascinating topic. • The school can ***trace its history*** back to the early 19th century. [=the school has existed since the early 19th century]

3 [*count*] : a written record of important events that have happened since the beginning of something • He wrote a well-known *history* of the British empire. • The book begins with a brief/short *history* of the Internet.

4 [*count*] : an established record of past events, actions, etc. — usually singular • The patient has no (prior) *history* of heart problems. [=she has not had heart problems in the past] • The prisoner has a *history* of violence. [=the prisoner has been violent in the past] • a patient's ***medical history*** [=a record of past medical problems and treatments] • a worker's ***employment history*** [=a record of jobs that a worker has had] • It's hard to buy a car if you don't have any ***credit history***. [=if you have not borrowed and repaid money in the past] • They have a ***family history*** of heart disease. [=many people in their family have suffered from heart disease in the past]

5 [*noncount*] *informal* : someone or something that is finished • Their winning streak was *history*. [=their winning streak was finished/over] • His boss told him that if he was late one more time, he would be *history*. [=he would be fired]

ancient history see ANCIENT

go down in history : to be remembered as a very important person or event • The discovery of the structure of DNA will *go down in history*.

make history : to do something that is very important or famous and that will be remembered as part of history • They *made history* by discovering the structure of DNA.

his·tri·on·ic /ˌhɪstriˈɑːnɪk/ *adj* [*more* ~; *most* ~] *disapproving* : too emotional or dramatic • *histrionic* behavior/gestures

— his·tri·on·i·cal·ly /ˌhɪstriˈɑːnɪkli/ *adv*

his·tri·on·ics /ˌhɪstriˈɑːnɪks/ *noun* [*plural*] *disapproving* : behavior that is too emotional or dramatic : histrionic behavior • a tennis player known for his *histrionics* on the court • He told the story simply, without any *histrionics*.

[1]hit /ˈhɪt/ *verb* **hits; hit; hit·ting**

1 a : to move your hand, a bat, etc., quickly so that it touches someone or something in a forceful or violent way [+ *obj*] She told her son to stop *hitting* his sister. • She *hit* him hard with her purse. • He *hit* the fence with a stick. = He *hit* a stick against/on the fence. • The boxers *hit* each other with their fists. [*no obj*] The boxers were *hitting* furiously at each other. **b** [+ *obj*] : to cause (something, such as a ball) to move by hitting it forcefully with a bat, racket, etc. • He *hit* a fastball (over the fence) for a home run. • She *hit* the ball right to the shortstop. **c** : to touch (something or someone) in a forceful or violent way after moving at a high speed [+ *obj*] The ball *hit* the house. • The plate shattered when it *hit* the floor. • The tank was *hit* by enemy fire. • He was *hit* by a car. • The ship *hit* an iceberg. [*no obj*] The plate shattered when it *hit*. **d** [+ *obj*] : to cause or allow (something, such as part of your body) to touch something in a forceful or violent way • I accidentally *hit* my head on/against the side of the door while I was getting into the car. • She *hit* her elbow on the edge of the table.

2 a [+ *obj*] : to attack (something or someone) • Our plan is to *hit* the enemy before they can *hit* us. **b** : to affect (something or someone) in a harmful or damaging way [+ *obj*] The ship was *hit* by a sudden storm. • A powerful earthquake *hit* the city. • Many families have been ***hit hard*** by the layoffs. = Many families have been ***hard hit*** by the layoffs. [=many families have been badly affected/hurt by the layoffs] • If you really want to teach your son a lesson you should ***hit him where it hurts*** and take away his cell phone. [*no obj*] Many people were unprepared when the storm *hit*. • The layoffs have *hit hard* here.

3 [+ *obj*] **a** : to come to (something) by chance or accident while you are moving • We *hit* a west wind coming out of port. • I was late because I *hit* a traffic jam on the way over. **b** : to begin to have or experience (problems, trouble, etc.) • The project went smoothly at first, but then we started to *hit* [=*encounter*] some problems.

4 [+ *obj*] *informal* : to become suddenly or completely clear to (someone) : STRIKE • It suddenly *hit* [=*occurred to*] me that I was doing something wrong. [=I suddenly realized that I was doing something wrong] • The importance of the victory hasn't really *hit* her yet. • I was just about to give up when the solution *hit* me. • When you meet him, the first thing that *hits* you [=the first thing that you notice] is his air of confidence. • The smell *hit* me [=I noticed the smell] as soon as I opened the door.

5 [+ *obj*] : to get or come to (a goal, level, etc.) : REACH • He *hit* 100 mph on his motorcycle. • They expect the temperature to *hit* 90 this afternoon. • Sales *hit* $100 million last year alone. • Gold prices *hit* an all-time high last week. • a singer who can *hit* the high notes • He kept digging until he *hit* [=*struck*] water. • The stock market ***hit bottom***. [=reached an extremely low point] • (*informal*) Next year he'll ***hit the big four-oh/five-oh***. [=turn 40/50 years of age]

6 [+ *obj*] *informal* : to arrive or appear at, in, or on (a place) • We *hit* [=went to] the beach nearly every day this summer. • They got up early and headed out to *hit* the (ski) slopes. [=to go skiing] • The magazine's new issue *hits* newsstands tomorrow. [=the new issue becomes available on newsstands tomorrow] ▪ The new product should *hit* the shelves/market soon. = The new product should *hit* stores soon. [=the new product should be available in stores soon] ▪ These new illegal drugs only recently ***hit the street*** [=became available for illegal purchase]

7 [+ *obj*] *informal* **a :** to turn (something) on or off with a switch ▪ Could someone please ***hit the lights?*** **b :** to move (a switch) to an on or off position ▪ The lights came on when she ***hit the switch*** **c :** to push down on (the brake pedal or accelerator in a vehicle) in a sudden and forceful way ▪ I had to ***hit the brakes*** hard to avoid an accident. ▪ She suddenly *hit* the accelerator and sped away. = (*US*) She suddenly ***hit the gas*** and sped away.

8 a : to succeed in hitting (something aimed at) with a shot, throw, etc. [+ *obj*] *hit* the bull's-eye ▪ *hit* the target — sometimes used figuratively ▪ Her criticism really ***hit the mark*** [=her criticism was very accurate] [*no obj*] The first shot *hit* but the second shot missed. **b** [+ *obj*] **:** to succeed in making (a shot) ▪ She *hit* [=*made, sank*] 40 percent of her shots last season. ▪ She *hit* her first basket but then missed the next one. **c** [+ *obj*] **:** to succeed in making a pass to (another player) ▪ The quarterback *hit* the wide receiver (with a pass) for a touchdown.

9 a [*no obj*] **:** to try to hit the ball with a bat in baseball, cricket, or a similar game ▪ It's your turn to *hit*. [=*bat*] **b** [+ *obj*] **:** to produce (a home run, a ground ball, etc.) by batting ▪ He *hit* 30 home runs last year. ▪ He *hit* a ground ball to the shortstop. ▪ She *hit* a double to left field. **c** [*no obj*] **:** to have a specified batting average ▪ This year he's *hitting* [=*batting*] .300. [=his batting average is .300] **d :** to hit the pitches thrown by (a pitcher) [+ *obj*] He has *hit* this pitcher well/poorly in the past. [*no obj*] He has *hit* well/poorly against this pitcher in the past.

10 *not used in progressive tenses* [+ *obj*] *informal* **:** to deal another card to (a player in blackjack) ▪ *Hit* me. [=deal another card to me]

hit a nerve see NERVE

hit a/the wall see [1]WALL

hit back [*phrasal verb*] **:** to attack or criticize someone who has attacked or criticized you ▪ If you hit me, I'll *hit back*. ▪ The team *hit back* with a touchdown of their own. — often + *at* ▪ The Senator *hit back at* his critics.

hit home see [2]HOME

hit it *informal* — used to tell a group of musicians to begin playing ▪ *Hit it*, boys! [=let's begin playing music]

hit it big or hit big see BIG

hit it off *informal* **:** to become friends **:** to get along well ▪ The two of them *hit it off* (with each other) immediately. ▪ Though we work together, we've never really *hit it off*.

hit on/upon [*phrasal verb*] **1** ***hit on (someone)*** *US, informal* **:** to talk to (someone) in order to try to start a sexual relationship ▪ She's always being/getting *hit on* at the gym. ▪ Some drunk at the bar was *hitting on* her. **2** ***hit on/upon (something)*** **:** to succeed in finding (something, such as a solution) ▪ She thought about the problem for days before she finally *hit on* a solution. ▪ He *hit on* a new way to do things. ▪ We *hit upon* the answer accidentally.

hit out at [*phrasal verb*] ***hit out at (someone)*** *informal* **:** to make an angry attack against (someone) ▪ The singer *hit out at* [=(more commonly) *lashed out at*] her critics.

hit someone for six see SIX

hit the books see [1]BOOK

hit the buffers see [1]BUFFER

hit the deck or hit the dirt or hit the ground **:** to drop down to the ground or floor suddenly ▪ She *hit the deck* when the gunfire started.

hit the fan see [1]FAN

hit the ground running **:** to begin an effort or activity in a quick, energetic, and effective way ▪ The new administration *hit the ground running* after the inauguration.

hit the hay or hit the sack *informal* **:** to go to bed ▪ I'm tired. I'm going to *hit the hay*.

hit the jackpot see JACKPOT

hit the nail on the head *informal* **:** to be exactly right ▪ He *hit the nail on the head* with that analysis.

hit the panic button see PANIC BUTTON

hit the road see ROAD

hit the roof or hit the ceiling *informal* **:** to become very angry or upset ▪ His parents really *hit the roof* when they found out he had flunked out of school.

hit the skids see [2]SKID

hit the spot see [1]SPOT

hit the streets or US hit the pavement *informal* **:** to go out in search of something or for a specific purpose ▪ I grabbed the classifieds and *hit the pavement*, looking for a new job. ▪ The reporters *hit the streets* to interview passersby. — see also [1]HIT 6 (above)

hit the town see TOWN

hit the trail see [2]TRAIL

hit up [*phrasal verb*] ***hit (someone) up or hit up (someone)*** *US, informal* **:** to ask (someone) *for* something (such as money) ▪ She's waiting for the right moment to *hit up* her father *for* a loan. [=to ask her father for a loan] ▪ I donated money to that charity a few months ago, and they're already *hitting* me *up for* more.

hit your stride see [2]STRIDE

know what hit you see [1]KNOW

[2]**hit** *noun, pl* **hits** [*count*]

1 a : an act of hitting someone or something ▪ The player was penalized for an illegal *hit* from behind. ▪ The torpedo made a direct *hit*. **b** — used to describe being hit by something (such as a bullet, bomb, punch, etc.); usually used with *take* ▪ The bunker *took* a direct *hit* from the bombers. ▪ The plane *took* some *hits*, but the pilot was able to fly back to the base. — often used figuratively ▪ His pride *took* a *hit*. [=his pride was hurt] ▪ The company *took a* public relations *hit* when it lost the lawsuit. [=the company's public image was damaged when it lost the lawsuit] ▪ She *took* a big financial *hit* when the stock market fell. [=she lost a lot of money]

2 a : something that is very successful ▪ The show was a (smash/big) *hit*. ▪ The album is a collection of the group's greatest *hits*. [=the group's most popular and successful songs] — often used before another noun ▪ a *hit* record/song ▪ a *hit* movie — see also ONE-HIT WONDER **b :** someone or something that is liked by someone very much ▪ The pony ride was/made a big *hit* at the party. — usually + *with* ▪ The pony ride was a big *hit with* the kids at the party. [=the kids at the party enjoyed the pony ride very much]

3 : a successful effort to reach a desired goal or result ▪ His business ventures have been a mixture of *hits* and misses. [=some of his business ventures have been successful and some have failed]

4 *baseball* **:** BASE HIT ▪ He got/had two *hits* in last night's game.

5 *computers* **a :** an act of connecting to a particular Web site ▪ The site had/got over a million *hits* last month. [=people connected to the site more than a million times last month] **b :** a successful attempt to find something in a search of a computer database or the Internet ▪ A search for his name in the newspaper's database produced/found more than 30 *hits*.

6 *informal* **:** a single dose of an illegal drug ▪ Can I get a *hit*? ▪ He ***took a hit*** of LSD.

7 *informal* **:** a planned murder done by a paid killer ▪ an attempted *hit* on the gang's leader — see also HIT MAN

– hit·less /ˈhɪtləs/ *adj* ▪ a *hitless* musical group [=a musical group that has not had any hit songs] ▪ She has gone/been *hitless* [=has not had any base hits] in her last three games. ▪ He pitched six *hitless* innings. [=six innings in which no batter got a base hit]

hit–and–miss /ˌhɪtn̩ˈmɪs/ *adj* **:** sometimes successful and sometimes not **:** not always good or successful ▪ The company has relied on a *hit-and-miss* [=*hit-or-miss*] approach to developing new products.

[1]**hit–and–run** /ˌhɪtn̩ˈrʌn/ *adj, always used before a noun*

1 : involving a driver who does not stop after causing an accident ▪ a *hit-and-run* accident ▪ Police are looking for an unidentified *hit-and-run* driver.

2 : involving quick action by someone who then leaves or runs away quickly ▪ *hit-and-run* raids along the border

[2]**hit–and–run** *noun, pl* **-runs** [*count*] *baseball* **:** a play in which a base runner begins running as soon as a pitch is thrown and the batter tries to hit the pitch — often used before another noun ▪ a *hit-and-run* play

[1]**hitch** /ˈhɪʧ/ *verb* **hitch·es; hitched; hitch·ing**

1 [+ *obj*] **:** to attach, fasten, or connect (something) with a hook, knot, etc. ▪ *hitch* a trailer to a car ▪ He *hitched* his horse to a post outside the saloon. = He tied his horse to a ***hitching post*** outside the saloon.

2 *informal* **:** HITCHHIKE [*no obj*] He *hitched* across the country last summer. [+ *obj*] He *hitched* his way across the country last summer.

get hitched *informal* **:** to get married ▪ He's *getting hitched* to his college sweetheart.

hitch a ride or chiefly Brit hitch a lift *informal* **:** to get a ride in a passing vehicle • Her car broke down, so she had to *hitch a ride/lift* with a passing truck.

hitch up [*phrasal verb*] ***hitch (something) up*** *or* ***hitch up (something)*** : to pull (a piece of clothing) up with a quick movement • She *hitched* her skirt *up* above her knees.

hitch your wagon to (someone or something) see WAGON

[2]**hitch** *noun, pl* **hitches** [*count*]

1 : a hidden problem that makes something more complicated or difficult to do • It sounded like a good plan, but there was just one *hitch*. [=*catch*] • The plan ***went off without a hitch***.

2 : a device that is used to connect one thing (such as a plow or trailer) to another (such as a tractor, car, or animal) • a trailer *hitch*

3 *US, informal* : a period of service in the military, at a job, etc. • He went back to college after doing his *hitch* in the army. • a seven-year *hitch* at the newspaper

4 : a type of simple knot that is used to hold or fasten something for a short time

hitch•hike /ˈhɪʧˌhaɪk/ *verb* **-hikes; -hiked; -hik•ing** : to get a ride in a passing vehicle by holding out your arm with your thumb up as you stand on the side of the road [*no obj*] Her car broke down, so she had to *hitchhike* back home. [+ *obj*] He *hitchhiked* his way across the country last summer.

– hitch•hik•er *noun, pl* **-ers** [*count*]

hi–tech *variant spelling of* HIGH TECH

hith•er /ˈhɪðɚ/ *adv, old-fashioned + literary* : to this place • come *hither* [=come here] • She has been very busy, traveling ***hither and yon***. [=here and there; traveling to many different places] • traveling/wandering ***hither and thither*** [=here and there] — see also COME-HITHER

hith•er•to /ˈhɪðɚˌtuː/ *adv, formal* : until now : before this time • The biography reveals some *hitherto* [=*formerly, previously*] unknown facts about his early life.

hit list *noun, pl* ~ **lists** [*count*] : a list of people, organizations, etc., that a person or group plans to oppose or eliminate • the gunman's *hit list* • Excess spending is at the top of the governor's *hit list*. [=it is the first thing the governor plans to eliminate]

hit man *noun, pl* ~ **men** [*count*] : a person who is paid to kill someone • She hired a *hit man* to kill her ex-husband. • Mafia *hit men*

hit–or–miss /ˌhɪtɚˈmɪs/ *adj* : not carefully planned or directed • a *hit-or-miss* [=*hit-and-miss*] method of finding answers • a *hit-or-miss* procedure/proposition

hit•ter /ˈhɪtɚ/ *noun, pl* **-ters** [*count*] : a person who hits someone or something; *especially, baseball* : a player who is trying to hit the ball • The pitcher walked the first *hitter*. [=*batter*] • He's a good fielder but a poor *hitter*. — see also DESIGNATED HITTER, HEAVY HITTER, PINCH HITTER

HIV /ˌeɪʧˌaɪˈviː/ *noun* [*noncount*] *medicine* : a virus that causes AIDS • The patient is ***HIV positive/negative***. ✧ *HIV* is an abbreviation of "human immunodeficiency virus."

[1]**hive** /ˈhaɪv/ *noun, pl* **hives** [*count*]

1 a : a nest for bees — called also *beehive* **b** : the bees living in a hive

2 : a place filled with busy activity • The house was a ***hive of activity*** as we prepared for the party.

[2]**hive** *verb* **hives; hived; hiv•ing**

hive off [*phrasal verb*] *chiefly Brit* **1 a** : to separate from a group • The youngest campers *hived off* into another room. **b** ***hive off (someone or something)*** *or* ***hive (someone or something) off*** : to separate (someone or something) from a group • They *hived off* the youngest campers into another room. **2** ***hive off (something)*** *or* ***hive (something) off*** : to give control of (something) to another person or group • The new owners *hived off* the best parts of the company to another part of their corporate empire.

hives /ˈhaɪvz/ *noun* [*noncount*] *medicine* : a condition in which an area of your skin becomes red and itchy • I broke out in *hives* after being stung by the bee.

hi•ya /ˈhajə/ *interj, informal* : HI • "*Hiya*, sweetheart."

HM *abbr* Her Majesty, Her Majesty's, His Majesty, His Majesty's

hmm *also* **hm** /ˈm̩, ˈhm̩/ *interj* — used to represent a sound made by someone who is thinking about what to say or do • I thought to myself, *hmm*, what's the best way to take advantage of this opportunity?

HMO /ˌeɪʧˌɛmˈoʊ/ *noun, pl* **HMOs** [*count*] *US* : an organization that provides health care to people who make regular payments to it and who agree to use the doctors, hospitals, etc., that belong to the organization ✧ *HMO* is an abbreviation of "health maintenance organization." — compare PPO

HMS *abbr* Her Majesty's ship; His Majesty's ship

[1]**ho** /ˈhoʊ/ *interj*

1 — used to attract attention • "Land *ho*!" [=I see land]

2 ***ho ho*** *or* ***ho ho ho*** — used to represent laughter • *Ho ho ho*! Merry Christmas! — often used in an ironic way • *Ho ho*. That's very funny. [=that's not really funny at all]

[2]**ho** *noun, pl* **hos** *or* **hoes** *also* **ho's** [*count*] *US slang, offensive* : WHORE

hoa•gie /ˈhoʊgi/ *noun, pl* **-gies** [*count*] *US* : SUBMARINE SANDWICH • She had a meatball *hoagie* for lunch.

[1]**hoard** /ˈhoɚd/ *noun, pl* **hoards** [*count*] : a large amount of something valuable that is kept hidden • a *hoard* of jewels • a squirrel's *hoard* of nuts

Do not confuse *hoard* with *horde*.

[2]**hoard** *verb* **hoards; hoard•ed; hoard•ing** [+ *obj*] : to collect and hide a large amount of (something valuable) • *hoarding* money/food

– hoard•er *noun, pl* **-ers** [*count*]

hoarding /ˈhoɚdɪŋ/ *noun, pl* **-ings** [*count*] *Brit* : BILLBOARD

hoarse /ˈhoɚs/ *adj* **hoars•er; -est** : having a harsh or rough sound or voice • She could only speak in a *hoarse* whisper. • The cold made me a little *hoarse*. — see also *shout yourself hoarse* at [1]SHOUT

– hoarse•ly *adv* **– hoarse•ness** *noun* [*noncount*]

hoary /ˈhori/ *adj* **hoar•i•er; -est**

1 a : very old • *hoary* [=*ancient*] legends • a *hoary* tale of revenge **b** : not interesting, funny, etc., because of being used too often : not fresh or original • a *hoary* cliché/joke

2 *literary* : having gray or white hair • He bowed his *hoary* head. • a man *hoary* with age

[1]**hoax** /ˈhoʊks/ *noun, pl* **hoax•es** [*count*] : an act that is meant to trick or deceive people • The bomb threat is probably a *hoax*, but we should still evacuate the building. • She was the victim of a cruel *hoax*.

[2]**hoax** *verb* **hoaxes; hoaxed; hoax•ing** [+ *obj*] : to trick or deceive (someone) — usually used as *(be) hoaxed* • People *were hoaxed* by the Web site.

– hoax•er *noun, pl* **-ers** [*count*]

hob /ˈhɑːb/ *noun, pl* **hobs** [*count*] *Brit* : COOKTOP

hob•ble /ˈhɑːbəl/ *verb* **hob•bles; hob•bled; hob•bling**

1 [*no obj*] : to walk with difficulty because of injury or weakness • She picked up her cane and *hobbled* across the room.

2 [+ *obj*] : to slow the movement, progress, or action of (someone or something) • Critics say that his policies will *hobble* [=*hamper*] economic growth. • She is sometimes *hobbled* by self-doubt. • He has been *hobbled* by a knee injury.

3 [+ *obj*] : to keep (an animal) from straying or wandering by tying two legs together • *hobble* a horse

hob•by /ˈhɑːbi/ *noun, pl* **-bies** [*count*] : an activity that a person does for pleasure when not working • She collects stamps as a *hobby*. • He has many *hobbies*, including photography and gardening.

– hob•by•ist /ˈhɑːbijɪst/ *noun, pl* **-ists** [*count*] • The camera is perfect for professionals as well as *hobbyists*.

hob•by•horse /ˈhɑːbiˌhoɚs/ *noun, pl* **-hors•es** [*count*]

1 : a subject that someone speaks about or complains about often • Once he ***gets on his hobbyhorse*** and starts talking about taxes, you can't get him to discuss anything else. • She's been ***riding that hobbyhorse*** for months.

2 : a stick with a horse's head at one end that a child pretends to ride

hob•gob•lin /ˈhɑːbˌgɑːblən/ *noun, pl* **-lins** [*count*]

1 : an ugly or evil creature that plays tricks in children's stories

2 : something that causes fear or worry • intimidated by the *hobgoblins* of etiquette

hob•nail boot /ˈhɑːbˌneɪl-/ *or* **hob•nailed boot** /ˈhɑːbˌneɪld-/ *noun, pl* ~ **boots** [*count*] : a heavy boot with short nails driven into the bottom to protect against wear

hob•nob /ˈhɑːbˌnɑːb/ *verb* **-nobs; -nobbed; -nob•bing** [*no obj*] : to spend time with someone (such as a famous or wealthy person) in a friendly way • He loves to *hobnob* with celebrities.

ho•bo /ˈhoʊboʊ/ *noun, pl* **-boes** *also* **-bos** [*count*] *US* : a person who has no place to live and no money and who travels to many different places ▪ an old *hobo* [=*tramp*] riding on a freight train

Hob·son's choice /ˈhɑːbsənz-/ *noun, pl* ~ **choices** [*count*] : a situation in which you are supposed to make a choice but do not have a real choice because there is only one thing you can have or do ▪ He jokingly referred to dinner as a *Hobson's choice* between soup and salad or salad and soup.

¹hock /ˈhɑːk/ *noun, pl* **hocks** [*count*]
1 : a small piece of meat from the leg of a pig ▪ ham *hocks*
2 : the part of the rear leg of a four-footed animal (such as a horse) that is like the human ankle — see picture at HORSE
– compare ²HOCK, ⁴HOCK

²hock *noun* [*noncount*] *informal*
1 : the state of being in the possession of a pawnbroker ✧ An item that is **in hock** has been exchanged for money in an arrangement with a pawnbroker. If the money is returned, the item will be returned, or else the pawnbroker may sell it to someone else. When the item is returned it is **out of hock**. ▪ His gold watch is *in hock*. ▪ She got her earrings *out of hock*.
2 : the state of owing money to someone or something : DEBT ▪ He is **in hock** to his boss for several thousand dollars. [=he owes his boss several thousand dollars] ▪ She had to go **into hock** to pay for her college tuition. ▪ He's trying to get **out of hock**.
– compare ¹HOCK, ⁴HOCK

³hock *verb* **hocks; hocked; hock·ing** [+ *obj*] : to give (something that you own) to a pawnbroker in exchange for money : to put (something) in hock ▪ He *hocked* [=*pawned*] his gold watch to help pay for his medical bills.

⁴hock *noun, pl* **hocks** [*count, noncount*] *Brit* : a type of German white wine — compare ¹HOCK, ²HOCK

hock·ey /ˈhɑːki/ *noun* [*noncount*]
1 *chiefly US* : ICE HOCKEY
2 *chiefly Brit* : FIELD HOCKEY

hockey skate *noun, pl* ~ **skates** [*count*] : a special skate used for ice hockey — see picture at SKATE

ho·cus–po·cus /ˌhoʊkəsˈpoʊkəs/ *noun* [*noncount*] : language or activity that is meant to trick or confuse people ▪ He misled voters with his political *hocus-pocus*.

hodge·podge /ˈhɑːʤˌpɑːʤ/ *noun* [*singular*] *chiefly US* : a mixture of different things ▪ a *hodgepodge* of styles — called also (*Brit*) *hotchpotch*

¹hoe /ˈhoʊ/ *noun, pl* **hoes** [*count*] : a garden tool that has a flat blade on a long handle — see picture at GARDENING

²hoe *verb* **hoes; hoed; hoe·ing** : to work on (something, such as a garden or a crop) with a hoe [+ *obj*] The garden has to be *hoed*. [*no obj*] She was *hoeing* in the garden all day.

hoe·down /ˈhoʊˌdaʊn/ *noun, pl* **-downs** [*count*] *US* : an informal country party where people do square dances

¹hog /ˈhɑːg/ *noun, pl* **hogs** *also* **hog** [*count*]
1 a *chiefly US* : a pig ▪ a *hog* farmer **b** *Brit* : a male pig that has had its sex organs removed and that is raised for meat
2 *informal* **a** : a selfish or greedy person ▪ Don't be such a *hog*! Other people have to eat too! — see also ROAD HOG **b** : something that takes or uses a large amount or too much of something ▪ This car is a gas *hog*. [=it uses a lot of gasoline] ▪ The new software is a real memory *hog*.
go hog wild *US, informal* : to do something in an extreme or excessive way : to go wild ▪ They *went hog wild* with special effects in this movie.
go (the) whole hog *informal* : to do something in a very thorough and complete way ▪ If we're going to have a party, we might as well *go the whole hog* and hire a band.
high off/on the hog see ²HIGH

²hog *verb* **hogs; hogged; hog·ging** [+ *obj*] *informal* : to take, keep, or use (something) in a way that prevents other people or things from having or using it ▪ He's been *hogging* the remote control all night. ▪ Stop *hogging* the road. [=stop driving in a way that does not allow room for other cars to pass] ▪ I hate when she *hogs* the bathroom. [=she stays in the bathroom for a long time when other people want to use it]

hog heaven *noun* [*noncount*] *US, informal* : a very pleasing or satisfying state or situation ▪ We had plenty of food, good wine, and beautiful weather. We were in *hog heaven*.

hog·wash /ˈhɑːgˌwɑːʃ/ *noun* [*noncount*] *informal* : foolish or meaningless talk : NONSENSE ▪ You wouldn't believe the *hogwash* he was spouting at us. ▪ His argument is *hogwash*.

ho hum /ˈhoʊˈhʌm/ *interj* — used to show that you are bored, not interested, etc. ▪ As another election campaign gets started, most voters seem to be saying, "*Ho hum*, here we go again."

ho–hum /ˈhoʊˈhʌm/ *adj* [*more* ~; *most* ~] *informal* : having or showing no excitement or enthusiasm ▪ He's been leading a very *ho-hum* [=*dull, boring*] existence. ▪ I don't see how you could be so *ho-hum* [=*indifferent*] about this movie.

hoick /ˈhoɪk/ *verb* **hoicks; hoicked; hoick·ing** [+ *obj*] *Brit, informal* : to lift or pull (something) with a quick movement : YANK ▪ He *hoicked* up his trousers and waded in.

hoi pol·loi /ˌhoɪpəˈloɪ/ *noun* [*plural*] : ordinary people : people who are not rich, famous, etc. — usually used with *the* ▪ aristocrats who treated *the hoi polloi* with contempt

¹hoist /ˈhoɪst/ *verb* **hoists; hoist·ed; hoist·ing** [+ *obj*]
1 : to raise (something) especially by using ropes or machinery ▪ *hoist* the sail/flag ▪ The steel girders were *hoisted* into place and securely welded. ▪ The engine was *hoisted* out with a winch. ▪ The cargo was *hoisted* up onto the ship.
2 *chiefly US, informal* : ¹DRINK ▪ He stopped at a bar after work to *hoist* a few beers with his friends.
3 *basketball, informal* : to take (a shot) ▪ She *hoisted* a last-second shot that would have won the game if it had gone in.
hoist by/on/with your own petard see PETARD

²hoist *noun, pl* **hoists** [*count*] : a machine used for lifting heavy loads

hoi·ty–toi·ty /ˌhoɪtiˈtoɪti/ *adj* [*more* ~; *most* ~] *chiefly US, informal* : having or showing the insulting attitude of people who think that they are better, smarter, or more important than other people ▪ a bunch of *hoity-toity* snobs

hok·ey /ˈhoʊki/ *adj* **hok·i·er; -est** *US, informal* + *disapproving*
1 : obviously fake : PHONY ▪ She gave us some *hokey* excuse for being late.
2 : very silly, old-fashioned, or sentimental : CORNY ▪ a *hokey* melodrama

ho·kum /ˈhoʊkəm/ *noun* [*noncount*] *informal*
1 *chiefly US* : foolish or untrue words or ideas : NONSENSE ▪ Everyone knows his story is pure *hokum*.
2 : writing, music, etc., that is too dramatic or sentimental and not very original ▪ His new film is yet another piece of Hollywood *hokum*.

¹hold /ˈhoʊld/ *verb* **holds; held** /ˈhɛld/; **hold·ing**
1 [+ *obj*] **a** : to have or keep (something) in your hand, arms, etc. ▪ *Hold* the rail so you won't fall. ▪ He was *holding* his hat (in his hand). ▪ He was *holding* a large package in his arms. ▪ Would you *hold* this for me? ▪ She showed him the correct way to *hold* the racket. ▪ She *held* his hand. = She *held* him by the hand. **b** : to put your arms around (someone) : to embrace or hug (someone) ▪ Some people just don't like to be *held*. ▪ He *held* her close/tight and kissed her.
2 a [+ *obj*] : to put or keep (something or someone) in a specified place or position ▪ He *held* the pen in his mouth while he dialed the number. ▪ *Hold* the pen upright when you write. ▪ She picked up the trophy and *held* it over her head. ▪ You have to *hold* the button down for several seconds. ▪ I *held* the door open for her. ▪ *Hold* your arms at your sides. **b** [+ *obj*] : to keep (something or someone) in the same place or position ▪ I need someone to *hold* this string while I finish tying the knot. ▪ She *held* the ladder steady while he climbed up it. ▪ It took six guards to *hold* him (down). ▪ The board was *held* in place/position by a couple of nails. ▪ The Federal Reserve has been *holding* interest rates down/up. ▪ The cover was **held on** by a piece of tape. **c** [*no obj*] : to remain in the same place or position ▪ The anchor *held*. ▪ The line of soldiers *held* under constant attack. ▪ Please **hold still** for a moment. ▪ His weight has **held steady** for several months now.
3 [*no obj*] : to continue to be good ▪ We arrived late but our luck *held* and we were able to get tickets. ▪ We hope the weather *holds* through the weekend.
4 [+ *obj*] **a** : to own or possess (something) ▪ The bank *holds* (the) title to the car. ▪ Do you *hold* any shares/stock in the company? **b** : to have or keep (a job, a position, etc.) ▪ She has never before *held* public office. ▪ It's been a struggle for him to *hold* a job. ▪ In the last election the Democratic party managed to *hold* several seats but lost others. ▪ President Franklin Roosevelt **held office** for 12 years. = Franklin Roosevelt *held* the office of president for 12 years. **c** : to succeed in keeping (something that is being attacked) ▪ The troops were able to *hold* the bridge. ▪ The line of soldiers **held their position/ground** and fought off the attack. **d** : to have (something that you have achieved or earned) ▪ She *holds* a master's degree in chemistry. ▪ a swimmer who *holds* several world records
5 [+ *obj*] : to support the pressure or weight of (something or

H

someone) ▪ The floor will *hold* 10 tons. ▪ I don't know if the roof can *hold* all that snow.

6 [+ *obj*] **a :** to have or keep (a belief, a feeling, etc.) in your mind ▪ There's no need for him to *hold* [=*bear*] a grudge against me. ▪ I don't *hold* any resentment toward/against him. ▪ a belief *held* by many = a widely *held* belief ▪ I will always *hold* that memory in my heart. **b** *somewhat formal* **:** to consider or judge (someone or something) in a specified way ▪ They *hold* me responsible. **— often + *for*** ▪ He should be *held* accountable *for* his actions. ▪ The store can't be *held* liable *for* damage to your vehicle. **— often followed by *to* + *verb*** ▪ The court *held* his actions *to be* grounds for a lawsuit. [=the court said/ruled that his actions were grounds for a lawsuit] ▪ His latest book is generally/widely *held* [=*considered*] *to be* the best one. ▪ "We *hold* these truths *to be* self-evident. . . ." —U.S. Declaration of Independence (1776) **c** *not used in progressive tenses, somewhat formal* **:** to have or express (an opinion, belief, etc.) **— + *that*** ▪ I *hold* [=*believe*] *that* such problems should be dealt with at the federal level. ▪ The Supreme Court *held* [=*ruled*] *that* the trial court had acted properly. **— sometimes used figuratively** ▪ Tradition *holds that* [=it is traditional that] the oldest member of the family be seated first.

7 [+ *obj*] **:** to cause (a meeting, class, sale, etc.) to take place ▪ A sale will be *held* next weekend. ▪ Free elections will be *held* next month. ▪ We will *hold* [=*have*] the meeting at 2 o'clock. ▪ The President has decided to *hold* [=*give*] a press conference. ▪ They're *holding* an art show at the gallery. ▪ The two sides will *hold* [=*have*] talks/discussions to resolve the dispute.

8 [+ *obj*] **a :** to contain (something) ▪ The box *holds* his collection of old photographs. **b** *not used in progressive tenses* **:** to have enough room for (an amount) ▪ The disk can *hold* 1.44 megabytes of data. ▪ How much water can that bucket *hold*? ▪ The bottle *holds* two liters. ▪ The dining room *holds* 500 people.

9 [+ *obj*] **:** to continue to have (someone's interest or attention) ▪ The speaker wasn't able to *hold* [=*keep*] our interest/attention for long.

10 [+ *obj*] **:** to have (a specified quality, feature, etc.) ▪ His eyes *held* [=*had*] a quizzical look. ▪ She has always *held* a special place in my heart. [=I have always had special feelings for her] ▪ This hotel has long *held* [=*claimed*] a place among the world's finest. [=has long been considered one of the world's finest] **— often + *for*** ▪ Music *holds* great appeal *for* many people. [=music appeals greatly to many people] ▪ His job *holds* no surprises *for* him. [=nothing about his job surprises him] ▪ Her paintings *hold* a real fascination *for* me. [=her paintings fascinate me] ▪ No one can know what the future *holds* (*for* us). [=no one can know what will happen (to us) in the future] ▪ These experiments *hold* great promise *for* future cancer research.

11 [+ *obj*] **:** to stop doing (something) or wait to do (something) ▪ Tell the men to ***hold their fire*** [=not shoot] until I give the order. ▪ ***Hold everything*** [=wait; stop] We're not doing this right. ▪ ***Hold it*** right there. [=stop right there] Where do you think you're going?

12 [+ *obj*] **a :** to keep (something) available for later use ▪ A room at the hotel will be *held* for us for 24 hours. ▪ We will *hold* these flight reservations for you until tomorrow. **b :** to delay the handling of (something, such as a telephone call) for a time ▪ Please *hold* all my calls while I'm in the meeting.

13 [+ *obj*] **:** to prevent (something, such as a vehicle) from leaving ▪ The train was *held* until the track was cleared. ▪ Would you *hold* the elevator for me? ▪ *Hold* that taxi!

14 [+ *obj*] *chiefly US* **:** to not use or include (something) in preparing food ▪ I'd like a roast beef sandwich on rye, and *hold* the mustard please. [=do not put any mustard on the sandwich]

15 [+ *obj*] **:** to force (someone) to stay in a place (such as a prison) ▪ The police are *holding* him for questioning. ▪ Terrorists are *holding* the passengers hostage. ▪ They're being *held* hostage/captive/prisoner. **— sometimes used figuratively** ▪ He was *held* captive by his own fears.

16 [+ *obj*] **:** to continue moving on (a course) without change ▪ The ship continued to *hold* its course.

17 [+ *obj*] *of a vehicle* **:** to stay on (a road) in a safe and secure way when being driven at high speeds ▪ The car *holds* the road well when turning quickly.

18 [*no obj*] **:** to be true **:** to remain valid ▪ Her advice still *holds* [=*applies*] today. ▪ The general rule *holds* in most cases. **— often used in the phrases *hold true* and (less commonly) *hold good*** ▪ The general rule *holds true* in most cases. ▪ Their son needs support and understanding. The same *holds true* for all children. ▪ The advice she gave us 10 years ago still *holds good* today.

19 : to wait to speak to someone on the telephone [*no obj*] All operators are currently busy. Please *hold*. [+ *obj*] All operators are busy. Please ***hold the line*** for a minute.

hold a candle to see CANDLE

hold against [*phrasal verb*] ***hold (something) against (someone)*** **:** to use (something) as a reason to have a bad opinion of (someone) ▪ He lied to her once, and she still *holds it against him*. ▪ Nobody is going to *hold it against you* if you don't come. [=no one is going to be angry or upset with you if you don't come]

hold a gun to someone's head see [1]GUN

hold all the aces see [1]ACE

hold (all/all of) the cards see [1]CARD

hold back [*phrasal verb*] **1 a :** to stop yourself from doing something ▪ She wanted to introduce herself to him but she *held back* out of shyness. **b :** to make a less than complete effort ▪ She could have beaten him in the race, but she *held back* and let him win. [=she did not run as fast as she could have so that he would win] **c *hold (someone) back*** **:** to stop (someone) from doing something ▪ Once he starts talking, ***there's no holding him back*** [=it's very hard to get him to stop talking] **2 *hold (something) back or hold back (something)*** **a :** to not allow (something) to be seen or known by someone ▪ He was unable to *hold back* his tears. [=to keep from crying] ▪ The government *held back* [=*withheld*] some crucial information from the media. ▪ I know you're angry, so don't *hold* anything *back* (from me). [=tell me everything] **b :** to keep (something) ▪ He *held* several thousand dollars *back* in case of an emergency. **c :** to delay (something) ▪ The company *held back* the first shipment of the new product until it was completely ready. **3 *hold (someone or something) back or hold back (someone or something)*** **:** to stop (someone or something) from moving forward **:** to stop (someone or something) from advancing to the next level, grade, or stage ▪ She might have been more successful, but bad health *held* her *back*. ▪ He was *held back* [=*kept back*] in first grade.

hold court see [1]COURT

hold down [*phrasal verb*] **1 *hold (something) down or hold down (something)*** **a :** to stop (something) from being or becoming too high ▪ Could you please *hold* the noise *down*? I'm trying to read. ▪ The company is trying to *hold down* costs/expenses/prices. **b :** to continue to have (a job) ▪ It's been a struggle for him to *hold down* [=*keep*] a job. **2 *hold (someone) down or hold down (someone)*** **:** to stop (someone) from doing something or advancing to a higher level, position, etc. ▪ We need to free ourselves of the unfair restrictions that are *holding us down*.

hold firm **:** to refuse to change what you have been doing or believing ▪ They are *holding firm* on their refusal to proceed. ▪ Despite opposition, she has *held firm* to her decision.

hold forth [*phrasal verb*] *formal* **:** to speak about something for a long time ▪ He *held forth* about/on the need for reform in his country.

hold hands or hold someone's hand see [1]HAND

hold in [*phrasal verb*] ***hold (something) in or hold in (something)*** **:** to stop (an emotion) from being expressed ▪ Don't *hold* your feelings *in*. Let them out.

hold off [*phrasal verb*] **1 a :** to wait to do something ▪ You need to decide now. You can't *hold off* any longer. ▪ He *held off* as long as he could. **— often + *on*** ▪ She decided to *hold off on* her vacation for a while longer. ✧ If you ***hold off doing*** something or ***hold off on doing*** something, you wait to do it at a later time. ▪ He *held off on* announcing his decision. **b :** to not happen until later ▪ The rain *held off* until we got home. [=it didn't rain until we got home] **2 *hold (someone) off or hold off (someone)*** **:** to stop (someone) from coming near someone or something ▪ Her bodyguard *held off* the crowd. [=kept the crowd away from her] **3 *hold (something) off or hold off (something)*** **:** to defend against (something) successfully **:** WITHSTAND ▪ The soldiers *held off* the attack. ▪ Our team *held off* a late rally by the other team.

hold on [*phrasal verb*] **1 :** to have or keep your hand, arms, etc., tightly around something ▪ He was *holding on* [=*hanging on*] for dear life. ▪ *Hold on* (tight). It's going to get bumpy. ▪ The steps are slippery; you'd better *hold on* to the railing. **2 :** to succeed in keeping a position, condition, etc. ▪ I hope we can *hold on* until help arrives. ▪ They were able to *hold on* for a 10–9 victory. **3 :** to wait or stop briefly ▪ "Can we go now?" "*Hold on*, I'll be ready in just a minute." **4** ***hold on to (something)*** : to keep possession of (something) ▪ She's trying very hard to *hold on to* her money. ▪ He has managed to *hold on to* his lead in the polls. : to not lose or give up (something) ▪ Despite all his troubles, he has somehow *held on to* his faith in himself.

hold out [*phrasal verb*] **1 a** : to continue to exist or be available ▪ I don't know how much longer our supply of food will *hold out*. [=*last*] ▪ You should do it while your courage is still *holding out*. ▪ I'm going to keep writing as long as my money *holds out*. **b** : to continue to work ▪ My old car is still *holding out*. **2** : to continue to oppose someone or defend against something : to refuse to surrender or give in ▪ The troops were able to *hold out* until help arrived. ▪ Many of the strikers are still *holding out*. — see also HOLDOUT **3** ***hold out (something)*** *or* ***hold (something) out*** **a** : to reach outward with (something, such as your hand) ▪ He *held out* [=*extended*] his hand in greeting. ▪ She *held out* the car keys and asked him to drive. — sometimes used figuratively ▪ I *held out* the hand of friendship to my enemies. [=I offered friendship to my enemies] **b** : to say that there is a good reason to have (something, such as hope) ▪ The doctor didn't *hold out* [=*offer*] much hope for her recovery. [=the doctor didn't say that there was much hope for her recovery] **c** : to say that (a possibility) exists ▪ The mayor has *held out* the possibility that the library will be expanded in the future. [=has said that it is possible that the library will be expanded] **4** ***hold out for (something)*** : to refuse to accept or agree to something in order to get (something) ▪ The workers are *holding out for* higher pay. ▪ The wide receiver is *holding out for* a new contract. **5** ***hold out on (someone)*** *informal* : to keep something (such as information) from (someone) ▪ She didn't tell me she was rich; she's been *holding out on* me.

hold over [*phrasal verb*] **1** ***hold over (something)*** *or* ***hold (something) over*** **a** : to cause (something) to happen later ▪ A vote on the proposal has been *held over* [=*delayed, postponed*] until tomorrow. **b** *US* : to cause (something) to continue beyond a normal or planned time ▪ The movie is being *held over* for two more weeks. [=the movie will continue to be shown for two more weeks] **2** ***hold (something or someone) over*** *or* ***hold over (something or someone)*** : to keep (something or someone) from an earlier time ▪ He is the only player to have been *held over* from their previous team. — see also HOLDOVER **3** ***hold (something) over (someone)*** : to use your knowledge of (something) to influence or control the behavior of (someone) ▪ She knows about his criminal past and has been *holding* it *over* him [=she has been threatening to tell other people about his criminal past] to force him to cooperate.

hold the bag (*US*) *or Brit* ***hold the baby*** *informal* : to be given all of the blame or responsibility that should be shared with others ▪ His friends ran away and he was stuck/left *holding the bag*.

hold the fort see FORT

hold the line see [1]LINE

hold to [*phrasal verb*] **1 a** ***hold to (something)*** : to continue to have or follow (a plan, purpose, etc.) ▪ He has *held to* his plan of exercising regularly. : to not change (a decision, belief, etc.) ▪ Despite opposition, she has **held to** her decision. **b** ***hold (someone) to (something)*** : to force (someone) to do what is required by (something, such as a promise) ▪ You made a promise and I'm going to *hold* you *to* it. ▪ He was *held to* an impossible standard. [=he was required to meet very high expectations] **2** ***hold (someone) to (something)*** : to prevent (an opponent) from having or getting more than (a specified number of scores or shots) ▪ Our team *held* the other team *to* just three runs. ▪ The defense *held* him *to* only one shot attempt in the first half.

hold together [*phrasal verb*] **1** : to stay joined together or in one piece ▪ The empire *held together* for many decades. **2** ***hold (something) together*** *or* ***hold together (something)*** : to cause (something) to stay joined together or in one piece ▪ The coach hopes to *hold* the team *together* for at least one more season. ▪ The box was *held together* by a strong glue.

hold up [*phrasal verb*] **1** : to continue in the same condition without failing or losing effectiveness or force ▪ The sales team was *holding up* well under the stress. ▪ The nurse came in to see how I was *holding up*. ▪ Their music still *holds up* 20 years later. **2** ***hold (something) up*** *or* ***hold up (something)*** : to raise (something) ▪ He *held up* his hand. **3** ***hold up (something or someone)*** *or* ***hold (something or someone) up*** **a** : to delay, stop, or slow the movement, progress, or action of (something or someone) : DELAY ▪ Their decision was *held up* for months. ▪ A major accident *held* traffic *up* for hours. ▪ She was late for the meeting because she got *held up* in traffic. — see also HOLDUP **b** : to use a gun to rob (a person, store, etc.) ▪ Someone *held up* the gas station. ▪ He was *held up* by a masked robber. — see also HOLDUP **c** : to cause (someone or something) to be noticed for a particular reason ▪ His work has been *held up* to ridicule. [=his work has been ridiculed] ▪ Experts have been *holding* these programs *up* as examples of government waste.

hold water see [1]WATER

hold with [*phrasal verb*] ***hold with (something)*** : to agree with or approve of (something) — usually used in negative statements ▪ I don't *hold with* all these newfangled notions!

hold your breath see BREATH

hold your ground see [1]GROUND

hold your horses see [1]HORSE

hold your liquor see LIQUOR

hold your nose see [1]NOSE

hold your own : to do well in a difficult situation ▪ It was a tough interview, but she managed to *hold her own*. ▪ She's been *holding her own* against cancer.

hold your tongue *also* ***hold your peace*** : to keep silent : to not say anything about something ▪ It was difficult, but he somehow managed to *hold his tongue*.

H

[2]**hold** *noun, pl* **holds**

1 : the act of holding or gripping something [*count*] — usually singular ▪ He had/kept a tight *hold* on the rope. ▪ He loosened/tightened his *hold* on the handle. [*noncount*] He ***took hold of*** the rope. [=he took the rope and held it] ▪ She ***grabbed hold of*** his arm. [=she grabbed his arm] — often used figuratively ▪ The idea of being an actress first *took/grabbed hold of* her when she was in college. [=she first became excited by the idea when she was in college] ▪ Jealousy *took hold of* him. [=he began to feel very jealous]

2 [*count*] : a way of holding your opponent in wrestling ▪ The wrestler applied an illegal *hold*. — see also CHOKE HOLD, STRANGLEHOLD

3 [*singular*] **a** : power that is used to control something or someone [*noncount*] His ideas have lost their *hold* on/over the public. [=the public is no longer interested in his ideas] ▪ The law has no *hold* over her. ▪ He is trying to tighten his *hold* on the company's finances. [=to gain greater control of the company's finances] ▪ He has a *hold* on her. [=he has power over her; he controls her] **b** : an understanding of something — usually + *on* ▪ It's hard to ***get a hold on*** the cause of these problems.

4 [*count*] : something that can be held or stepped on for support while you are climbing ▪ She searched for *holds* in the rock. — see also FOOTHOLD, HANDHOLD, TOEHOLD

5 [*singular*] : an order that something is to be kept for a particular person or time ▪ I asked the library to ***put a hold on*** the book for me. [=to hold the book for me]

6 [*count*] : an area on a ship or airplane where cargo is stored

cop hold of see [2]COP

get hold of *or chiefly US* ***get a hold of*** **1** : to get possession of (something) : to succeed in getting (something) ▪ Somehow she managed to *get hold of* the band's new album before it came out. ▪ Where did you *get hold of* that idea? [=what led you to believe that idea?] **2** : to find and talk to (someone) : to contact (someone) ▪ I need to talk to my lawyer, but I haven't been able to *get hold of* him. ▪ I've been trying to *get a hold of* [=*get in touch with*] my lawyer for days. **3** ***get hold of yourself*** *or chiefly US* ***get a hold of yourself*** : to get control of your thoughts and emotions and stop behaving in a foolish or uncontrolled way ▪ *Get a hold of yourself* and tell me what happened.

lay hold of **1** : to take and hold (something) : GRAB ▪ *Lay hold of* that rope and pull. **2** : to understand (something) ▪ The idea is difficult to *lay hold of*.

no holds barred ✧ If there are *no holds barred*, there are no limits or rules for what can and cannot be done in a particular situation. — see also NO-HOLDS-BARRED

on hold **1** : in the state of waiting to speak to someone on the telephone ▪ The person I wanted to speak to wasn't available, so the operator put my call *on hold*. ▪ They kept me *on hold* for hours! **2** : in the state of being delayed for a time ▪ Our vacation plans are *on hold*. = Our vacation plans have been **put on hold**.

take hold *or chiefly US* ***take a hold*** : to become effective, established, or popular • The change in the law has not yet *taken hold.* • new ideas that have recently *taken hold* in the fashion industry

hold·all /ˈhouldˌɑːl/ *noun, pl* **-alls** [*count*] *chiefly Brit* : CARRYALL

hold·er /ˈhouldɚ/ *noun, pl* **-ers** [*count*]
1 : a person who holds or owns something • She is the *holder* of an honorary degree. • the *holder* of a world record • the ticket *holder* — see also CARDHOLDER, OFFICEHOLDER, RECORD HOLDER, SHAREHOLDER, STOCKHOLDER
2 : a device that holds something • a cigarette/cup *holder*

[1]hold·ing /ˈhouldɪŋ/ *noun, pl* **-ings**
1 [*count*] : property (such as land or stocks) that is owned by someone — usually plural • She has been selling many of her *holdings* in the stock market.
2 [*noncount*] *sports* : the illegal act of using your hands or arms to slow or stop the movement of an opponent in sports like ice hockey and American football • penalized 10 yards for *holding*

[2]holding *adj, always used before a noun*
1 : causing or intended to cause a temporary stop or delay • The troops were engaged in a *holding* action until reinforcements could arrive. • a *holding* operation
2 — used to describe a place where someone or something is kept for a time before being moved somewhere else • The prisoner was placed in a *holding* cell. • a *holding* tank/pen

holding company *noun, pl* ~ **-ies** [*count*] *business* : a company whose main business is owning more than half of another company's stock

holding pattern *noun, pl* ~ **-terns** [*count*] : a course flown by an aircraft while waiting for permission to land • Our plane was in a *holding pattern* for almost an hour because of the fog. — sometimes used figuratively • The company has put production in a *holding pattern* [=has temporarily stopped production] while better testing methods are developed.

hold·out /ˈhouldˌaʊt/ *noun, pl* **-outs** [*count*]
1 a : a person who refuses to reach an agreement until certain terms are met : a person who holds out • He says he might be a *holdout* at the start of the next season if the team doesn't agree to pay him more. **b** : an act of holding out for something • He is expected to end his three-week *holdout* and join the team tomorrow.
2 : a person who continues to do or use something after others have stopped doing or using it • A few *holdouts* still use typewriters, but nearly everybody uses computers now.
– see also *hold out* at [1]HOLD

hold·over /ˈhouldˌouvɚ/ *noun, pl* **-overs** [*count*] *US* : someone or something that remains or is kept from an earlier time • He is the only *holdover* from their last championship team. • This policy is a *holdover* from the previous administration. — see also *hold over* at [1]HOLD

hold·up /ˈhouldˌʌp/ *noun, pl* **-ups** [*count*]
1 : a usually brief delay • a traffic *holdup* • Hey, what's the *holdup*? [=what is the reason for the delay?] — see also *hold up* at [1]HOLD
2 : a robbery that is done using a gun • There have been a series of *holdups* at local banks.

[1]hole /ˈhoul/ *noun, pl* **holes**
1 [*count*] : an opening into or through something • I have a *hole* in my sock. • He fixed the *hole* in the roof. • a bullet *hole* • make/poke/drill a *hole* • a mouse *hole* in the wall
2 [*count*] **a** : a hollow place in the ground • The dog dug a deep/shallow *hole*. — see also FOXHOLE, SWIMMING HOLE, WATER HOLE **b** : a place in the ground where an animal lives • a rabbit *hole*
3 [*count*] *golf* **a** : the cup into which the ball is hit • Her putt rolled right into the *hole*. **b** : one of the separate parts of a golf course that includes a tee and a green • She made a birdie on the seventh *hole*. • The course has 18 *holes*.
4 [*count*] : a flaw or weakness • There are plenty of *holes* in the theory. • There are a couple of *holes* in their defense. • The police were unable to poke any *holes* in his story. [=to find evidence showing that his story was not true] — see also LOOPHOLE
5 [*singular*] *informal* **a** : a difficult or embarrassing situation • He's in trouble and needs someone to help get/dig him out of this *hole*. [=*fix, jam*] • They found themselves ***in a hole***, trailing by 10 points with not much time left in the game. **b** *US* : the state of owing or losing money • She gave them a loan to help get them out of their financial *hole*. [=*debt*] • He was hundreds of dollars ***in the hole*** [=he owed hundreds of dollars] by the end of the night.
6 [*count*] — used to describe a situation in which someone or something is gone or missing • When their daughter went to college, it left/made a big *hole* in their lives. [=they missed their daughter very much when she went to college]
7 *informal* **a** [*count*] : a dirty and unpleasant place • I can't believe he lives there! It's such a *hole*! — see also HELLHOLE **b** ***the hole*** *US* : a prison cell where a prisoner who is being punished is kept alone • He spent a month in *the hole*. [=(more formally) in solitary confinement]
8 [*count*] **a** *baseball* : an open area between two fielders • He hit a grounder that went through the *hole* between the first and second basemen. • He hit a sharp ground ball into ***the hole***. [=the area between the shortstop and third baseman] **b** *American football* : an open area between defenders that allows an offensive player to move the ball forward • a running back skilled at finding *holes*

an ace in the hole see [1]ACE

like a hole in the head *informal* ✧ If you do not need something at all, you can say that you need it *like a hole in the head*. • She already has too many shoes. She needs another pair *like a hole in the head*.

punch holes in *informal* : to weaken (an argument, idea, etc.) by proving that parts of it are wrong • Lawyers tried to *punch holes in* her argument.

[2]hole *verb* **holes; holed; hol·ing** *golf* : to hit (the ball) into the hole [+ *obj*] She *holed* a long putt for a birdie. [*no obj*] — + *out* • She waited for her partner to *hole out* [=to finish putting the ball into the hole] before she putted.

hole up [*phrasal verb*] *informal* : to stay in a place hidden or apart from other people • The criminals *holed up* in a downtown motel for a few days. • The band *holed up* in the recording studio to record their album. ✧ You can *hole up* in a place or ***be/stay holed up*** in a place. • The band *was/stayed holed up* in the recording studio.

hole in one *noun, pl* **holes in one** [*count*] *golf* : a score of one on a hole in golf • She got/made/had a *hole in one* on the eighth hole. — called also (*US*) *ace*

hole–in–the–wall *noun, pl* **holes–in–the–wall** [*count*] *informal*
1 *chiefly US* : a small place (such as a bar or restaurant) that is not fancy or expensive • We had dinner at some *hole-in-the-wall* downtown.
2 *Brit* : ATM

hol·ey /ˈhouli/ *adj* [*more* ~; *most* ~] *informal* : having holes • *holey* socks

[1]hol·i·day /ˈhɑːləˌdeɪ, *Brit* ˈhɒlədi/ *noun, pl* **-days**
1 [*count*] : a special day of celebration • a religious *holiday* : a day when most people do not have to work • July 4 is a national *holiday* in the U.S. • The stock market is closed tomorrow because it's a *holiday*. — often used before another noun • *holiday* gifts/parties • Do you have any plans for the ***holiday weekend***? [=a weekend that is preceded or followed by a holiday] ✧ In U.S. English, ***the holiday season*** and ***the holidays*** refer to the time from November until the beginning of January during which many holidays are celebrated. • How are you celebrating *the holiday season*? • I'm looking forward to going home for *the holidays*. — see also BANK HOLIDAY, LEGAL HOLIDAY
2 *Brit* : VACATION [*noncount*] She'll have four weeks' *holiday* next year. • She spent two weeks ***on holiday*** [=(*US*) *on vacation*] in Italy. [*count*] We're planning on taking a *holiday* in the Caribbean. — often plural • She went to the Caribbean for her *holidays*. • He spent the summer *holidays* in Spain.

[2]holiday *verb* **-days; -dayed; -day·ing** [*no obj*] *Brit* : to spend a holiday in or at a particular place : VACATION • She likes *holidaying* in the Caribbean.

holiday–maker *noun, pl* **-ers** [*count*] *Brit* : VACATIONER

ho·li·er–than–thou /ˌhoulijəðənˈðaʊ/ *adj* [*more* ~; *most* ~] *disapproving* : having or showing the annoying attitude of people who believe that they are morally better than other people • a *holier-than-thou* attitude

ho·li·ness /ˈhoulinəs/ *noun*
1 [*noncount*] : the quality or state of being holy • the *holiness* of this sacred place
2 ***Holiness*** [*count*] — used in the titles of high religious officials • His *Holiness* the pope • Does Your *Holiness* require anything else?

hol·is·tic /houˈlɪstɪk/ *adj* [*more* ~; *most* ~] : relating to or concerned with complete systems rather than with individual parts • *Holistic* medicine attempts to treat both the mind

H

and the body. ▪ We need to take a more *holistic* approach to improving our schools.

hol·lan·daise /ˌhɑːlənˈdeɪz/ *noun* [*noncount*] : a rich sauce made of butter, egg yolks, and lemon juice or vinegar — called also *hollandaise sauce*

hol·ler /ˈhɑːlɚ/ *verb* **-lers; -lered; -ler·ing** *chiefly US, informal*

1 : to call out loudly : SHOUT [*no obj*] He was *hollering* across the fields to his workers. ▪ They were screaming and *hollering* at each other all night. [+ *obj*] He *hollered* (out) orders to his workers. ▪ She *hollered* across the street, "Did you hear the news?" ▪ Someone was *hollering* my name.

2 [*no obj*] : to make loud or angry complaints ▪ People always *holler* about tax increases.

– holler *noun, pl* **-lers** [*count*] ▪ If you need any help, just give (me) a *holler*. [=just let me know if you need any help]

[1]**hol·low** /ˈhɑːloʊ/ *adj* **hol·low·er; -est**

1 : having nothing inside : not solid ▪ a *hollow* log

2 : curved inward or down ▪ *hollow* [=*sunken*] cheeks ▪ There was a *hollow* spot in the field.

3 : not having real value or meaning ▪ They achieved a *hollow* victory over a team missing its best players. [=their victory was not an important or impressive one since the other team was missing its best players] ▪ She made *hollow* promises. [=she made promises she would not keep] ▪ Their threats ***ring hollow***. = Their threats ***have a hollow ring***. [=their threats do not seem truthful or sincere]

4 ✧ A sound that is ***hollow*** is like the sound made when you hit something that is empty inside. ▪ He heard a *hollow* sound when he knocked on the wall.

5 : weak and without any emotion ▪ "It's useless," he said in a *hollow* voice. ▪ a *hollow* laugh

– hol·low·ly /ˈhɑːləli/ *adv* ▪ "It's useless," he said *hollowly*. **– hol·low·ness** *noun* [*noncount*] ▪ the *hollowness* of her promises

[2]**hollow** *noun, pl* **-lows** [*count*]

1 : a place or area (especially on the ground) that is lower than the area around it ▪ a grassy *hollow*

2 : an empty space inside of something ▪ The owls nested in the *hollow* of a tree.

in the hollow of your hand ✧ If you hold something *in the hollow of your hand*, you hold it in your palm with your hand curved like a cup ▪ I held the bead *in the hollow of my hand*.

[3]**hollow** *verb* **-lows; -lowed; -low·ing** [+ *obj*] : to remove the inside of (something) ▪ They *hollowed* the log to make a canoe. — often used as *(be) hollowed* ▪ a *hollowed* tree

hollow out [*phrasal verb*] ***hollow (something) out or hollow out (something)*** **1** : to remove the inside of (something) : to make an empty space in (something) ▪ The kids were *hollowing out* pumpkins. ▪ a *hollowed-out* log **2** : to form (something) by digging or cutting the inside of something ▪ Workers *hollowed out* a tunnel through the mountain. ▪ He *hollowed out* a bowl from the wood.

hol·ly /ˈhɑːli/ *noun, pl* **-lies** [*count, noncount*] : a tree or bush with dark green leaves and bright red berries; *also* : the branches of this plant which are used for decoration especially at Christmas

hol·ly·hock /ˈhɑːliˌhɑːk/ *noun, pl* **-hocks** [*count*] : a tall plant with rounded leaves and brightly colored flowers

[1]**Hol·ly·wood** /ˈhɑːliˌwʊd/ *noun* [*singular*] : the American movie industry ▪ an actor who has had a long career in *Hollywood* ✧ Hollywood is a part of Los Angeles, California, where the American movie industry is based.

[2]**Hollywood** *adj, always used before a noun*

1 : relating to or characteristic of people in the American movie industry ▪ the *Hollywood* lifestyle

2 : relating to or typical of a movie made in Hollywood ▪ a story with a *Hollywood* ending [=a happy ending; an ending like the one you often see in movies]

ho·lo·caust /ˈhoʊləˌkɑːst, ˈhɑːləˌkɑːst/ *noun, pl* **-causts** *formal*

1 ***the Holocaust*** : the killing of millions of Jews and other people by the Nazis during World War II ▪ The museum is devoted to *the Holocaust*. ▪ Her parents were survivors of *the Holocaust*. = Her parents were *Holocaust* survivors. ▪ a *Holocaust* memorial

2 [*count*] : an event or situation in which many people are killed and many things are destroyed especially by fire ▪ There were fears of a nuclear *holocaust*.

ho·lo·gram /ˈhoʊləˌgræm, ˈhɑːləˌgræm/ *noun, pl* **-grams** [*count*] : a special kind of picture that is produced by a laser and that looks three-dimensional

hols /ˈhɑːlz/ *noun* [*plural*] *Brit, informal + old-fashioned* : VACATION ▪ Where did you have your *hols*?

Hol·stein /ˈhoʊlˌstiːn/ *noun, pl* **-steins** [*count*] *US* : a black-and-white cow used for milk

hol·ster /ˈhoʊlstɚ/ *noun, pl* **-sters** [*count*] : a leather case that you wear on your body and that holds a small gun

ho·ly /ˈhoʊli/ *adj* **ho·li·er; -est**

1 a : connected to a god or a religion ▪ a *holy* temple ▪ a *holy* relic worn by one of the saints ▪ the *Holy* Bible **b** : religious and morally good ▪ a *holy* man

2 *informal* — used in phrases that show surprise or excitement ▪ ***Holy cow***! [=*Wow*!] ▪ ***Holy mackerel***! You got your hair cut! ▪ ***Holy smoke***!

3 *informal* — used for emphasis ▪ That boy is a ***holy terror***. [=he is very difficult to control] ▪ He gave them ***holy hell***. [=he scolded them in a very angry way]

Holy Communion *noun* [*noncount*] *formal* : COMMUNION

holy day *noun, pl* **~ days** [*count*] : a day when a religious festival or holiday is observed

Holy Family *noun*

the Holy Family : Jesus Christ, his mother Mary, and her husband Joseph

Holy Father *noun* [*singular*] — used to refer to the Pope

Holy Ghost *noun*

the Holy Ghost : HOLY SPIRIT

Holy Grail *noun, pl* **~ Grails**

1 *or* ***holy grail*** [*count*] : something that you want very much but that is very hard to get or achieve ▪ Finding a cure for cancer is the *holy grail* of medical researchers.

2 ***the Holy Grail*** : the cup that is said to have been used by Jesus Christ and that was sought by knights during the Middle Ages

Holy Land *noun*

the Holy Land : the area in the Middle East where the events of the Bible happened ▪ We visited *the Holy Land*.

holy of holies *noun*

1 ***the holy of holies*** : the most holy part of a Jewish temple

2 [*singular*] *humorous* : something (such as a place or event) that is thought of as very special and which only a few people are allowed to use, see, etc. ▪ His trophy room is the *holy of holies* where only his closest friends are allowed.

holy orders *noun* [*plural*] : the position of a Christian priest, bishop, etc. ▪ He ***took holy orders***. [=became a priest]

Holy Spirit *noun*

the Holy Spirit : God in the form of a spirit in Christianity ▪ the Father, the Son, and the *Holy Spirit* — called also *the Holy Ghost*

Holy Trinity *noun*

the Holy Trinity : TRINITY 1

holy war *noun, pl* **~ wars** [*count*] : a war that is fought to defend or spread one group's religious beliefs

holy water *noun* [*noncount*] : water that has been blessed by a priest

Holy Week *noun* [*noncount*] : the week before Easter in the Christian church

hom·age /ˈɑːmɪʤ, *Brit* ˈhɑːmɪʤ/ *noun*

1 [*noncount*] : respect or honor ▪ People bowed ***in homage to*** [=as a sign of respect for] the king as he passed by. ▪ Her paintings ***pay homage to*** [=*honor*] women artists of the past.

2 [*singular*] : something that is done to honor someone or something ▪ Her book is a/an *homage* to her favorite city.

hom·bre /ˈɑːmbreɪ/ *noun, pl* **-bres** [*count*] *US, informal* : a man : GUY ▪ He is one tough *hombre*. [=he is very tough]

[1]**home** /ˈhoʊm/ *noun, pl* **homes**

1 : the place (such as a house or apartment) where a person lives [*count*] Right now his *home* is a small apartment. ▪ People are concerned about protecting their *homes*. ▪ (*chiefly US*) The neighborhood is filled with expensive new *homes*. [=*houses*] ▪ They've started on a major ***home-improvement*** project. [=a project to make their house better, bigger, more modern, etc.] ▪ They have a ***second/vacation home*** on the lake. [*noncount*] There's no place like *home*. ▪ Let's stay at *home* tonight. [=let's not go out tonight] ▪ I must have left my notes at *home*. ▪ We're a long way from *home*. [=we are not close to our house] ▪ I will be ***away from home*** [=I will not be at my house] for two weeks. ▪ He has no place to ***call home***. [=he does not have a place to live] ▪ He ***works at/from home***. [=he does his work in his house and not in an office building] — see also AT HOME (below), MOBILE HOME, MOTOR HOME

H

2 [*count*] : a family living together in one building, house, etc. • She made a good *home* for her husband and children. • She came from a troubled *home*. [=a family with many problems] • He comes from a ***broken home***. [=a family in which the parents have divorced] • She ***lived at home*** [=she lived with her parents or family] until she got married. • He ***left home*** [=left his parent's house and lived in his own house] after graduating from high school.

3 **a** : a place where something normally or naturally lives or is located [*count*] Australia is the *home* [=*habitat*] of the kangaroo. [*noncount*] The islands are *home* to many species of birds. **b** [*count*] : the place where something began or was created — usually + *of* • The restaurant advertises itself as the *home of* the "Big Burger." **c** [*count*] : a place where something is placed, stored, etc. • Can you find *homes* for these files in your office?

4 : the place where someone lives or originally comes from : the place to which you feel most strongly attached [*noncount*] New York will always be *home* to me. • They ***made their home*** [=they settled] on the banks of the Mississippi. • *People* ***back home*** [=in his hometown; in the place he is from] would never believe how much he has changed. [*count*] He has fond memories of his boyhood *home*. [=the place where he lived as a boy]

5 [*count*] : the place where an organization, a company, etc., is located and operates • This building will be the orchestra's new *home*. • The big television networks have their *homes* in the same city.

6 [*count*] : a place where people who are unable to care for themselves live and are cared for • an orphan's *home* • an old people's *home* • She doesn't want to put her mother ***in a home***. — see also NURSING HOME, REST HOME

7 [*noncount*] : a place that you try to reach in some games (such as baseball) • He was tagged out at *home*. — see also HOME PLATE

at home **1** : in your own country and not a foreign country • We face serious threats both *at home* and abroad. **2** *sports* : in a team's own stadium, park, etc. : in the place where a team is based • The team's next six games are *at home*. [=in its own stadium] • The team has done much better *at home* [=in its home games] than on the road. — see also [1]HOME 1 (above) **3** : relaxed and comfortable • She feels *at home* on the stage. • They ***made me feel (right) at home*** my first day at the new job. • Come on in and ***make yourself at home***. [=do what you need to do to feel relaxed and comfortable] • The professor is equally ***at home in*** politics and history. [=knows a lot about both politics and history] • I've never really felt/been completely ***at home with*** [=comfortable and confident about using] all these newfangled machines.

charity begins at home see CHARITY

home away from home (*US*) *or Brit* ***home from home*** : a place that is as pleasant and comfortable as your own home • Whenever he came to the city, his brother's place was like a *home away from home*.

home sweet home ◇ You say *home sweet home* to show that you are happy when you return to your home after being away from it.

— **home·like** /ˈhoʊmˌlaɪk/ *adj* [*more* ~; *most* ~] *chiefly US* • an inn with a *homelike* atmosphere

[2]**home** *adv*

1 : to or at the place where you live • She called *home* to say she would be late for dinner. • He's sending money *home* from a job overseas. • She is on her way *home*. • It's great to be back *home*. • (*chiefly US*) They're never *home* when I try to see them. • I can't wait to ***come/go/get home***. • (*chiefly US*) Let's ***stay home*** tonight. [=let's not go out tonight] • He ***brings/takes home*** about $750 a week. [=the amount of money he gets after paying taxes, health insurance, etc., is about $750 each week]

2 **a** : into a finished or final position • He used a hammer to drive the nail *home*. • shove the bolt *home* [=all the way into its place] **b** *sports* : to, toward, or into a goal • He fired the puck *home*. [=he shot the hockey puck into the goal]

bring home the bacon see BACON

bring (something) home : to make (something) very clear and obvious in usually a forceful or unpleasant way — usually + *to* • The importance of regular exercise was *brought home to him* when his best friend developed heart problems.

close to home see [2]CLOSE

come home to : to become very clear and obvious to (someone) in usually a forceful or unpleasant way • The truth about her marriage *came home to her* when he left her.

come home to roost see [2]ROOST

drive your point home : to say something in a very strong or forceful way : to make a point very forcefully • He *drove his point home* during the debate.

hit/strike home : to become very clear and obvious in usually a forceful or unpleasant way • The truth about their marriage finally *hit home*.

home free (*US*) *or Brit* ***home and dry*** *informal* : sure of succeeding, winning, etc. : no longer in danger of failing • If we can meet this next deadline, we'll be *home free*.

nothing to write home about see WRITE

ram home see [2]RAM

till/until the cows come home see [1]COW

[3]**home** *adj, always used before a noun*

1 : of or relating to a home or family • She has a happy *home* life. • Please give us your *home* phone number. • What is your *home* address?

2 : designed to be used in your home • a *home* entertainment system : done or made in your home • *home* cooking — often used in combination • He couldn't wait to have a ***home-cooked*** meal. [=a meal made and eaten at home] — see also HOME MOVIE, HOME VIDEO

3 *sports* : at a team's own field, stadium, arena, etc. • the *home* team • *home* games • The team opens its *home* season in just two weeks. — compare AWAY, ROAD

4 *chiefly Brit* : of, relating to, or coming from within your own country : DOMESTIC • We can make a profit on *home* sales alone. • the *home* market

home brew see [2]BREW

[4]**home** *verb* **homes; homed; hom·ing**

home in on [*phrasal verb*] ***home in on (someone or something)*** : to find and move directly toward (someone or something) • The missile was *homing in on* its target. — often used figuratively • Researchers are *homing in on* the cause of the disease.

home base *noun, pl* ~ **bases**

1 [*count*] : the place in which someone or something lives or operates — usually singular • The company's *home base* is in New York. • (*informal*) She returned to her *home base* [=she went back home] after a long month of traveling.

2 [*noncount*] *baseball* : HOME PLATE

home·body /ˈhoʊmˌbɑːdi/ *noun, pl* **-bod·ies** [*count*] *informal* : a person who likes to stay home • He's a *homebody* who hates parties.

home·bound /ˈhoʊmˌbaʊnd/ *adj*

1 : unable to leave your house because of age, injury, etc. • They deliver meals to *homebound* people.

2 : going home • *Homebound* travelers were stranded at the airport. • *homebound* traffic • a *homebound* train

home·boy /ˈhoʊmˌbɔɪ/ *noun, pl* **-boys** [*count*] *US slang*

1 : a boy or man from your own neighborhood or hometown • He dedicated his win to his *homeboys* back home.

2 : a member of your gang • He was hanging out with his *homeboys*. — called also *homey*

home·buy·er /ˈhoʊmˌbajɚ/ *noun, pl* **-ers** [*count*] : someone who buys a house, apartment, etc. • The books has helpful information for first-time *homebuyers*. [=for people who are buying their first home]

home·com·ing /ˈhoʊmˌkʌmɪŋ/ *noun, pl* **-ings**

1 [*count*] : the act of returning to your home or to a place that is like your home • A large crowd gathered at the airport for the soldiers' *homecoming*.

2 *or* ***Homecoming*** [*count, noncount*] *US* **a** : an annual celebration for people who attended a college or university • *Homecoming* weekend **b** : an annual celebration for high-school students that includes sports games and a formal dance • Who's taking you to *Homecoming*? = Who's taking you to the *Homecoming* dance?

home economics *noun* [*noncount*] : a subject or class that teaches cooking, sewing, and other skills that are useful in the home • She learned to sew in *home economics*. — called also (*US, informal*) *home ec*

home fries *noun* [*plural*] *US* : potatoes that have been cut into small pieces and fried — called also *home fried potatoes*

home front *noun*

the home front : the people who stay in a country and work while that country's soldiers are fighting in a war in a foreign country • During the war we had to keep up morale ***on the home front***. [=keep up morale among the people living and working in our home country]

home·girl /ˈhoʊm,gəl/ *noun, pl* **-girls** [*count*] *US slang*
1 : a girl or woman from your own neighborhood or hometown • She was happy to be back home with her *homegirls.*
2 : a girl or woman who is one of your friends

home·grown /ˈhoʊmˈgroʊn/ *adj*
1 : grown or made at home or in your local area • The family sells their *homegrown* vegetables at the local market.
2 : raised in or coming from your local area • The music festival will feature some *homegrown* talent this year.

home help *noun, pl* ~ **helps** [*count*] *Brit* **:** a person whose job is to help ill or elderly people in their homes with cooking, cleaning, etc.

home·land /ˈhoʊm,lænd/ *noun, pl* **-lands** [*count*]
1 : the country where someone was born or grew up • He returned to his *homeland* for the first time in many years.
2 : a usually large area where a particular group of people can live • The rebels are fighting for an independent *homeland.* • the Department of *Homeland* Security [=a department in the U.S. government that is responsible for the safety of the U.S. and its citizens]

home·less /ˈhoʊmləs/ *adj* **:** having no place to live • *homeless* people • We volunteer at the *homeless* shelter. [=a building where homeless people can sleep and get food]
the homeless **:** homeless people **:** people who have no place to live • a shelter for *the homeless*
– home·less·ness *noun* [*noncount*]

home loan *noun, pl* ~ **loans** [*count*] **:** [1]MORTGAGE

home·ly /ˈhoʊmli/ *adj* **home·li·er; -est**
1 *US* **:** not pretty or handsome **:** plain or unattractive • She has a *homely* face. • He's a bit *homely* but nice.
2 *Brit* **:** plain and simple in an appealing or pleasant way • the *homely* appeal of farm life • The hotel has a *homely* [=(*US*) *homey*] atmosphere.
– home·li·ness *noun* [*noncount*]

home·made /ˈhoʊmˈmeɪd/ *adj* **:** made in the home and not in a factory, store, etc. • *homemade* bread — compare STORE-BOUGHT

home·mak·er /ˈhoʊm,meɪkə/ *noun, pl* **-ers** [*count*] *chiefly US* **:** a wife who does work (such as sewing, cleaning, or cooking) at home and usually does not have another job outside the home **:** HOUSEWIFE • TV commercials often show happy *homemakers.*
– home·mak·ing /ˈhoʊm,meɪkɪŋ/ *noun* [*noncount*] • the challenges of *homemaking*

home movie *noun, pl* ~ **-ies** [*count*] **:** a movie that you make for people to watch in your home and that is usually of your family or a family event • We watched *home movies* of the family reunion. — compare HOME VIDEO

home office *noun, pl* ~ **-fices**
1 [*count*] **:** a room in your house where you do office work • When I began working from home, I set up a *home office.*
2 ***the Home Office*** *Brit* **:** the department in the British government that deals with the law, the police, and prisons, and that decides which people can come into the country

ho·me·op·a·thy *also Brit* **ho·moe·op·a·thy** /,hoʊmiˈɑːpəθi/ *noun* [*noncount*] **:** a system for treating illnesses that uses very small amounts of substances that would in larger amounts produce symptoms of the illnesses in healthy people
– ho·meo·path *also Brit* **ho·moeo·path** /ˈhoʊmijə,pæθ/ *noun, pl* **-paths** [*count*] Maybe you should see a *homeopath.* **– ho·meo·path·ic** *also Brit* **ho·moeo·path·ic** /,hoʊmijəˈpæθɪk/ *adj* • *homeopathic* medicine/treatments

home·own·er /ˈhoʊm,oʊnə/ *noun, pl* **-ers** [*count*] **:** a person who owns a home, apartment, etc. • The new law should provide tax relief for *homeowners.* • Do you have ***homeowner's insurance***? [=insurance that covers damage to your house or the things inside your house]

home page *noun, pl* ~ **pages** [*count*] **:** the part of a Web site that is seen first and that usually contains links to other parts of the site • They have designed a simpler *home page* that is easier to use.

home plate *noun* [*noncount*] *baseball* **:** the base that a runner must touch in order to score • The runner was tagged out at *home plate.* — called also *home base*

hom·er /ˈhoʊmə/ *noun, pl* **-ers** [*count*] *baseball, informal* **:** HOME RUN • He hit three *homers* in yesterday's game.
– homer *verb* **-ers; -ered; -er·ing** [*no obj*] • He *homered* three times in yesterday's game.

home·room /ˈhoʊm,ruːm/ *noun, pl* **-rooms** *US* **:** a classroom where students go at the beginning of each school day [*count*] They were assigned to different *homerooms.* [*noncount*] He was late for *homeroom.*

home rule *noun* [*noncount*] **:** government of a place (such as a country or territory) by the people who live there instead of by another country • The citizens petitioned for *home rule.*

home run *noun, pl* ~ **runs** [*count*] *baseball* **:** a hit that allows the batter to go around all the bases and score a run • He hit three *home runs.* — compare DOUBLE, SINGLE, TRIPLE

home·school /ˈhoʊm,skuːl/ *verb* **-schools; -schooled; -school·ing** *US* **:** to teach your children at home instead of sending them to a school [+ *obj*] They *homeschooled* both their children. [*no obj*] Parents who *homeschool* are meeting on Thursday.
– homeschooling *noun* [*noncount*] • They believe in *homeschooling.*

home·school·er /ˈhoʊm,skuːlə/ *noun, pl* **-ers** [*count*] *US*
1 : a child who is taught at home instead of in a school • Both of their children were *homeschoolers.*
2 : a parent who teaches a child at home instead of sending the child to a school • His parents are *homeschoolers.*

home·sick /ˈhoʊm,sɪk/ *adj* [*more* ~; *most* ~] **:** sad because you are away from your family and home • He was/got *homesick* when he went to college. • She was *homesick* for her mother's cooking.
– home·sick·ness *noun* [*noncount*]

home·spun /ˈhoʊm,spʌn/ *adj* [*more* ~; *most* ~] **:** plain and simple • People enjoy his folksy, *homespun* manner.

[1]**home·stead** /ˈhoʊm,stɛd/ *noun, pl* **-steads** [*count*]
1 : a house and the farmland it is on • They decided to farm the old *homestead.*
2 *US* **:** a piece of government land that a person could acquire by living on it and farming it when the western part of the U.S. was being settled

[2]**homestead** *verb* **-steads; -stead·ed; -stead·ing** *US* **:** to settle on goverment land and farm it [*no obj*] They *homesteaded* in Alaska. [+ *obj*] They *homesteaded* the territory in the 1860s.
– home·stead·er /ˈhoʊm,stɛdə/ *noun, pl* **-ers** [*count*]

home·stretch /ˈhoʊmˈstrɛʧ/ *noun, pl* **-stretch·es** [*count*] **:** the part of a racetrack between the last turn and the finish line • The horses are in the *homestretch.* — often used figuratively • The presidential race remains extremely close as we enter the *homestretch.* [=as we near the finish] — called also (*Brit*) *home straight*

home theater *noun, pl* ~ **-ters** [*count*] **:** an entertainment system for your home that usually includes a large television, a DVD player or VCR, and a sound system with many speakers

home·town /ˈhoʊmˈtaʊn/ *noun, pl* **-towns** [*count*] **:** the city or town where you were born or grew up • She returned to her *hometown* to stay after college. • *hometown* friends

home truth *noun, pl* ~ **truths** [*count*] **:** an unpleasant fact about someone or something — usually plural • She was all ready to tell him some hard *home truths.* • The doctor told me the *home truths* about the dangers of smoking.

home video *noun, pl* ~ **videos**
1 [*noncount*] *US* **:** movies that are sold on videotapes or DVDs and are meant to be watched on television at home • the latest releases in *home video* • the *home video* market
2 [*count*] **:** a home movie that is recorded with a video camera • We watched a *home video* of their wedding.

home visit *noun, pl* ~ **-its** [*count*] *Brit* **:** HOUSE CALL

home·ward /ˈhoʊmwəd/ *also chiefly Brit* **home·wards** /ˈhoʊmwədz/ *adv* **:** in the direction of home • He struggled *homeward* in the rain. • I am ***homeward bound*** [=going home]
– homeward *adj* • a *homeward* voyage/journey

home·work /ˈhoʊm,wək/ *noun* [*noncount*]
1 : work that a student is given to do at home • Please do/finish your *homework.* • She started her algebra *homework.* — compare CLASSWORK
2 : research or reading done in order to prepare for something — used in the phrase ***do your homework*** • The candidate *did his homework* [=studied the issues] before the debate.

[1]**hom·ey** /ˈhoʊmi/ *adj* **hom·i·er; -est** [*or more* ~; *most* ~] *chiefly US* **:** comfortable or familiar like home • a *homey* [=(*Brit*) *homely*] restaurant with a warm fireplace • a *homey* atmosphere
– hom·ey·ness *or* **hom·i·ness** *noun* [*noncount*] • We

liked the *homeyness* of the restaurant.

[2]**homey** *noun, pl* **-ies** *[count] US slang* : HOMEBOY

ho·mi·cid·al /ˌhɑːməˈsaɪdl/ *adj*
1 : likely to kill someone ▪ a *homicidal* maniac
2 : of or relating to murder ▪ a *homicidal* obsession ▪ *homicidal* thoughts

ho·mi·cide /ˈhɑːməˌsaɪd/ *noun, pl* **-cides** *chiefly US* **:** the act of killing another person : MURDER *[count]* The number of *homicides* increased last year. *[noncount]* He has been arrested for *homicide*.

hom·i·ly /ˈhɑːməli/ *noun, pl* **hom·i·lies** *formal*
1 *[count]* **:** a usually short talk on a religious or moral topic ▪ The priest gave a brief *homily* on forgiveness.
2 : advice that is often not wanted *[count]* We had to listen to another one of his *homilies* about the value of public service. *[noncount]* a politician with a fondness for *homily*

hom·ing /ˈhoumɪŋ/ *adj, always used before a noun*
1 : returning home ▪ an animal with a ***homing instinct*** [=an ability to return home from a great distance]
2 *technical* **:** able to find and follow a target ▪ A *homing* device guides the missile to the target. ▪ a *homing* torpedo

homing pigeon *noun, pl* **~ -geons** *[count]* **:** a pigeon that is trained to return home from a great distance

hom·i·ny /ˈhɑːməni/ *noun [noncount]* **:** a food made from dried corn ▪ We had pork and *hominy* stew.

H

ho·mo /ˈhoumou/ *noun, pl* **-mos** *[count] informal + offensive* **:** a homosexual person

ho·mo·ge·neous /ˌhouməˈʤiːnjəs/ *adj [more ~; most ~] somewhat formal* **:** made up of the same kind of people or things ▪ a racially *homogeneous* neighborhood [=a neighborhood in which all the people belong to the same race] ▪ a fairly *homogeneous* collection of examples — compare HETEROGENEOUS
– ho·mo·ge·ne·ity /ˌhouməʤəˈniːjəti/ *noun [noncount] formal* ▪ racial/economic/cultural *homogeneity*

ho·mog·e·nize *also Brit* **ho·mog·e·nise** /houˈmɑːʤəˌnaɪz/ *verb* **-niz·es; -nized; -niz·ing** *[+ obj] formal*
1 : to treat (milk) so that the fat is mixed throughout instead of floating on top
2 : to change (something) so that its parts are the same or similar ▪ The new curriculum is an attempt to *homogenize* education throughout the county.
– ho·mog·e·ni·za·tion *also Brit* **ho·mog·e·ni·sa·tion** /houˌmɑːʤənəˈzeɪʃən, *Brit* həuˌmɒʤəˌnaɪˈzeɪʃən/ *noun [noncount]* ▪ the *homogenization* of society **– homogenized** *also Brit* **homogenised** *adj* ▪ a carton of *homogenized* milk ▪ an increasingly *homogenized* society

ho·mog·e·nous /houˈmɑːʤənəs/ *adj [more ~; most ~]* **:** HOMOGENEOUS

ho·mo·graph /ˈhɑːməˌgræf, *Brit* ˈhɒməˌgrɑːf/ *noun, pl* **-graphs** *[count]* **:** a word that is spelled like another word but that is different in origin, meaning, or pronunciation ▪ The words "bow" for a part of a ship and "bow" for a weapon that shoots arrows are *homographs*.

hom·onym /ˈhɑːməˌnɪm/ *noun, pl* **-nyms** *[count]* **:** a word that is spelled and pronounced like another word but is different in meaning ▪ The noun "bear" and the verb "bear" are *homonyms*.

ho·mo·phobe /ˈhouməˌfoub/ *noun, pl* **-phobes** *[count]* **:** a person who hates or is afraid of homosexuals or treats them badly
– ho·mo·pho·bia /ˌhouməˈfoubijə/ *noun [noncount]* ▪ She was accused of *homophobia*. **– ho·mo·pho·bic** /ˌhouməˈfoubɪk/ *adj [more ~; most ~]* ▪ *homophobic* remarks

ho·mo·phone /ˈhɑːməˌfoun/ *noun, pl* **-phones** *[count]* **:** a word that is pronounced like another word but is different in meaning, origin, or spelling ▪ "To," "too," and "two" are *homophones*.

Ho·mo sa·pi·ens /ˌhoumouˈseɪpijənz, *Brit* ˌhəuməuˈsæpiənz/ *noun, pl* **Homo sapiens** *technical* **:** the species of human beings that exist today *[noncount]* All people are members of *Homo sapiens*. *[plural]* All *Homo sapiens* [=human beings] share certain characteristics.

ho·mo·sex·u·al /ˌhouməˈsɛkʃəwəl/ *adj, somewhat formal*
1 : sexually attracted to people of the same sex ▪ a *homosexual* man
2 : based on or showing a sexual attraction to people of the same sex ▪ *homosexual* behavior ▪ a *homosexual* affair — compare BISEXUAL, HETEROSEXUAL
– homosexual *noun, pl* **-als** *[count]* ▪ bias against *homosexuals* **– ho·mo·sex·u·al·i·ty** /ˌhouməˌsɛkʃəˈwæləti/ *noun [noncount]* ▪ He is very open about his *homosexuality*.

hon /ˈhʌn/ *noun, informal* — used to address someone you love ▪ Hey, *hon*, would you get the door for me? ✧ *Hon* is a short form of *honey*.

Hon. *also Brit* **Hon** *abbr* honorable — used in titles ▪ the *Hon*. Judge Smith presiding

hon·cho /ˈhɑːnʧou/ *noun, pl* **-chos** *[count] chiefly US, informal* **:** a person who is in charge of other people ▪ corporate *honchos* ▪ Talk to the ***head honcho***. [=the person with the most authority]

hone /ˈhoun/ *verb* **hones; honed; hon·ing** *[+ obj]*
1 : to sharpen (something, such as a knife) with a stone ▪ *hone* a blade
2 : to make (something, such as a skill) better or more effective ▪ She *honed* her language skills by reading and writing every day.
hone in on *[phrasal verb] US* **:** to find and go directly toward (someone or something) ▪ The missile was *honing in on* [=*homing in on*] its target. — usually used figuratively ▪ Researchers are *honing in on* the cause of the disease. ✧ Although *hone in on* is widely used, many people regard it as an error for *home in on*.

[1]**hon·est** /ˈɑːnəst/ *adj [more ~; most ~]*
1 a : good and truthful : not lying, stealing, or cheating ▪ They are *honest* people. ▪ He says that it's impossible to find an *honest* politician. ▪ These criminals pose a danger to *honest* citizens. — opposite DISHONEST **b :** showing or suggesting a good and truthful character ▪ He has an *honest* face. — opposite DISHONEST
2 : not hiding the truth about someone or something : not meant to deceive someone ▪ Just give me an *honest* answer. ▪ an *honest* reply ▪ If you want my *honest* opinion, you should get a job. ▪ To be perfectly/quite *honest*, I don't want to go. ▪ You shouldn't be afraid of a little *honest* criticism. [=criticism that is based on facts] ▪ I'd be less than *honest* [=I would be lying] if I told you there won't be problems. ▪ He gave us a painfully/brutally/refreshingly *honest* account of his childhood. ▪ I don't think these people are being ***honest with me***. [=I don't think they're telling me the truth] — opposite DISHONEST
3 a : not deserving blame : not done with the intent of hurting or harming anyone ▪ It was an *honest* error/mistake. **b :** done using your own work or effort ▪ He still goes to the office every morning and puts in an *honest* day's work. **:** not gotten by cheating, lying, etc. ▪ He's just trying to earn an ***honest living***. [=he is trying to earn a good amount of money for his hard work] ▪ These people work hard, and they deserve an ***honest wage***. [=an amount of money that is fair for the work that is done]
4 : plain and good : not fancy ▪ The restaurant prides itself on serving simple, *honest* food.
make an honest woman of (someone) *or* ***make (someone) an honest woman*** *old-fashioned + humorous* **:** to marry (a woman, especially a woman you have already had sex with) ▪ When will he finally *make an honest woman of* her?

[2]**honest** *adv, informal* — used to stress that a statement is true ▪ I didn't do it—*honest* I didn't! ▪ She is not my friend, *honest*. — sometimes used in the phrases ***honest to God*** or ***honest to goodness*** ▪ *Honest to God*, I wasn't there that night. ▪ He told you that? *Honest to goodness*? [=*really*?; *honestly*?] — see also HONEST-TO-GOODNESS

hon·est·ly /ˈɑːnəstli/ *adv [more ~; most ~]*
1 a : without cheating or lying : in an honest way ▪ Officials counted the votes *honestly*. ▪ The bank has always dealt *honestly* with me. ▪ I can *honestly* say that I have never seen that man before today. ▪ He spoke *honestly* about the mistakes he had made. **b :** in a genuine way : without pretending ▪ He was *honestly* [=*truly*] frightened by what the doctor told him. ▪ She *honestly* believes that she has been mistreated.
2 — used to stress that a statement is true ▪ *Honestly*, I don't know how you can raise kids and work too. ▪ I *honestly* don't know what to do.
3 *informal* — used to express annoyance or disapproval ▪ *Honestly*! Is that the best you can do?!

honest–to–goodness *adj, always used before a noun, chiefly US, informal* **:** REAL ▪ He is an *honest-to-goodness* legend. ▪ an *honest-to-goodness* movie star

hon·es·ty /ˈɑːnəsti/ *noun [noncount]* **:** the quality of being fair and truthful : the quality of being honest ▪ She is admired for her kindness and her *honesty*. ▪ He demands *honesty* from everyone who works for him. ▪ He didn't even have enough *honesty* to tell me he was leaving.

honesty is the best policy — used to say that telling the truth is better than lying even when it is hard to do ▪ He realized *honesty is the best policy* and told them what really happened to their car.

in all honesty — used to stress that a statement is true ▪ *In all honesty*, I don't know what you're talking about. ▪ I don't like him, but *in all honesty*, I don't know why.

hon·ey /ˈhʌni/ *noun, pl* **-eys**

1 [*noncount*] : a thick, sweet substance made by bees ▪ She likes *honey* in her tea.

2 *informal* — used to address someone you love ▪ "*Honey*, would you pass the salt?" ▪ *Honey*, I'm home!

3 [*singular*] *chiefly US, informal* : something that is very good ▪ The shortstop made a *honey* of a play. [=he made a very good play] ▪ Your car is a real *honey*.

land of milk and honey see [1]LAND

hon·ey·bee /ˈhʌniˌbiː/ *noun, pl* **-bees** [*count*] : a bee that makes honey — see color picture on page C10

hon·ey·comb /ˈhʌniˌkoʊm/ *noun, pl* **-combs** : a group of wax cells with six sides that are built by honeybees in their hive and that contain young bees or honey [*noncount*] a piece of *honeycomb* [*count*] One of the *honeycombs* was empty.

hon·ey·combed /ˈhʌniˌkoʊmd/ *adj* : having many holes or open spaces ▪ The car bumper includes a special *honeycombed* plastic. ▪ The rock is *honeycombed* with caves.

hon·ey·dew melon /ˈhʌniˌduː-, *Brit* ˈhʌniˌdjuː-/ *noun, pl* ~ **-ons** [*count*] : a type of large fruit (called a melon) that has a hard, smooth skin and green flesh — see color picture on page C5

[1]**hon·ey·moon** /ˈhʌniˌmuːn/ *noun, pl* **-moons** [*count*]

1 : a trip or vacation taken by a newly married couple ▪ Where are you going on your *honeymoon*? ▪ a *honeymoon* cruise

2 : a pleasant period of time at the start of something (such as a relationship or a politician's term in office) when people are happy, are working with each other, etc. ▪ The *honeymoon* (period) between the business partners was brief.

[2]**honeymoon** *verb* **-moons; -mooned; -moon·ing** [*no obj*] : to go on a honeymoon ▪ They *honeymooned* in Niagara Falls. ▪ a *honeymooning* couple

– hon·ey·moon·er *noun, pl* **-ers** [*count*] ▪ The resort attracts many *honeymooners*.

hon·ey·suck·le /ˈhʌniˌsʌkəl/ *noun, pl* **-suck·les** [*count, noncount*] : a type of shrub that has bright, colorful flowers

[1]**honk** /ˈhɑːŋk/ *verb* **honks; honked; honk·ing**

1 [*no obj*] *of a goose* : to make a loud sound ▪ We could hear the geese *honking* overhead.

2 a [*no obj*] *of a horn* : to make a loud sound ▪ a *honking* horn **b** : to cause (a horn) to honk [+ *obj*] The people in the cars behind us kept *honking* [=*blowing*, (*Brit*) *hooting*] their horns. [*no obj*] I *honked* at the car in front of me.

[2]**honk** *noun, pl* **honks** [*count*] : the loud sound made by a goose; *also* : a similar loud sound ▪ the *honk* of a horn

hon·ky *or* **hon·kie** /ˈhɑːŋki/ *noun, pl* **-kies** [*count*] *US, informal + offensive* : a white person

hon·ky–tonk /ˈhɑːŋkiˌtɑːŋk/ *noun, pl* **-tonks**

1 [*noncount*] **a** : a type of lively music usually performed on a piano **b** *US* : a type of country music with a heavy beat

2 [*count*] *US* : a cheap nightclub or dance hall that often features country music

– honky–tonk *adj, always used before a noun* ▪ a *honky-tonk* piano/song

[1]**hon·or** (*US*) *or Brit* **hon·our** /ˈɑːnɚ/ *noun, pl* **-ors**

1 [*noncount*] : respect that is given to someone who is admired ▪ These people deserve to be treated with *honor*. ▪ The team brought *honor* to the school. ▪ Please welcome our ***guest of honor***. [=the person who is being specially honored] ▪ He was given a ***place of honor*** at the table. [=a seat for someone who is being specially honored] ▪ The trophy has a *place of honor* [=a special position for something that is highly valued] on the mantel. ▪ They're having a dinner ***in honor of*** the new coach. = They're having a dinner ***in the new coach's honor***. [=they are having a dinner as a way to show respect and admiration for the new coach] ▪ The building was named *in honor of* the city's founder. ▪ He wore his ethnic heritage as a ***badge of honor***. [=he was proud of his ethnic heritage and did not try to hide it]

2 [*noncount*] **a** : good reputation : good quality or character as judged by other people ▪ He was prepared to fight to defend/protect/uphold his family's *honor*. **b** : high moral standards of behavior ▪ She has a keen sense of *honor*. ▪ a code of *honor* ▪ He would not do it as a matter of *honor*. ▪ He's a man of *honor*.

3 [*singular*] *formal* **a** : a special opportunity to do something that makes you proud — usually + *of* ▪ She was given/granted the *honor of* christening the ship. ▪ I have the *honor of* informing you that you have won first prize. ▪ May I have the *honor of* this dance? [=(more commonly) will you dance with me?] **b** : something that shows that other people have respect for you ▪ It was an *honor* to be invited. ▪ It's a great *honor* (for me) to be here with you tonight. ▪ I hope you'll ***do me the honor*** of accepting this invitation. [=it will make me feel happy and proud if you accept this invitation]

4 [*count*] : something (such as a title or medal) that is given to a person as a sign of respect and admiration ▪ She has received/won many *honors* and awards for her charitable works. ▪ Charitable organizations have been heaping *honors* on him. ▪ He was buried with ***full military honors***. [=a special military ceremony for a person who has died] — see also MEDAL OF HONOR

5 [*singular*] : an admired person who is a source of pride and respect for the other members of a group, organization, etc. — used in the phrase ***an honor to*** ▪ She was *an honor to* [=*a credit to*] her profession.

6 ***Honor*** [*count*] — used as a title for a judge or mayor ▪ Please welcome His *Honor*, the mayor. ▪ We request a recess, Your *Honor*.

7 ***honors*** [*plural*] **a** : special credit or recognition given to students who have successfully done work at a high level ▪ She graduated with (top/high) *honors*. **b** : a special course of study for students who want to take classes at a high level ▪ *honors* classes/courses ▪ an *honours* degree from a British university

do the honors : to do the actions performed by a host or hostess ▪ My mother cooks a big turkey for Thanksgiving every year, and my father *does the honors* at the table. [=my father carves and serves the turkey] ▪ The Ambassador *did the honors* by introducing the guest speaker.

lap of honour see [3]LAP

on your honor *formal* — used to say that you promise to do something ▪ *On my honor*, I will do my duty.

word of honor see [1]WORD

– see also MAID OF HONOR

[2]**honor** (*US*) *or Brit* **honour** *verb* **-ors; -ored; -or·ing** [+ *obj*]

1 a : to regard or treat (someone) with respect and admiration : to show or give honor to (someone) ▪ You should *honor* [=*respect*] your parents. ▪ When we got married, we promised to love and *honor* each other. ▪ We were *honored* with/by the queen's presence. ▪ (*often humorous*) Thank you for *honoring* us with your presence. [=thank you for coming here] **b** : to show admiration for (someone or something) in a public way : to give a public honor to (someone or something) ▪ She has been *honored* by several organizations for her charitable works. ▪ We need to find an appropriate way to *honor* these brave people. ▪ They're holding a dinner at which she is being *honored* (with an award) as player of the year. ▪ They have established a scholarship as a way to *honor* his memory/achievements.

2 a : to do what is required by (something, such as a promise or a contract) ▪ He claims that the company failed to *honor* [=*fulfill*] the contract/warranty. ▪ *honor* a warranty **b** : to accept (something) as payment ▪ *honor* a credit card ▪ *honor* a check **c** : to repay (a debt) ▪ They are accused of failing to *honor* their debts.

– honored *adj* ▪ He was welcomed as an *honored* guest. ▪ I feel *honored* to have been invited. ▪ an *honored* tradition

hon·or·able (*US*) *or Brit* **hon·our·able** /ˈɑːnərəbəl/ *adj*

1 [*more* ~; *most* ~] **a** : deserving honor and respect ▪ The college has a long and *honorable* history. ▪ an *honorable* profession **b** : having or showing honesty and good moral character ▪ an *honorable* man ▪ It is not *honorable* of you to behave like that. **c** : fair and proper : not deserving blame or criticism ▪ They are trying to find an *honorable* way out of this dispute. ▪ He assured her that his intentions were *honorable*. ▪ He received an ***honorable discharge*** from the army. — opposite DISHONORABLE

2 ***Honorable*** **a** — used as a title for some government officials ▪ the *Honorable* Senator/Judge — abbr. *Hon.* **b** *Brit* — used as a title for the children of some members of the nobility; abbr. *Hon.*

– hon·or·ably (*US*) *or Brit* **hon·our·ably** /ˈɑːnərəbli/ *adv*

• He served *honorably* in the war. • He was *honorably* discharged from the service.

honorable mention *noun, pl* ~ **-tions** [*count*] : an award or special praise given to someone who has done something extremely well but who has not won any of the official prizes

hon•o•rar•i•um /ˌɑːnəˈrerijəm/ *noun, pl* **-ia** /-ijə/ *also* **-i•ums** [*count*] *formal* : an amount of money paid for a service • We are willing to offer a small *honorarium* that we hope you will accept for judging the competition.

hon•or•ary /ˈɑːnəˌreri, *Brit* ˈɑːnərəri/ *adj*
1 : given as a sign of honor or achievement • He was awarded an *honorary* degree/title.
2 *always used before a noun* **a** : regarded as one of a group although not officially elected or included • He's an *honorary* member of the club. **b** : holding a position for which no payment is given : not paid • He is the *honorary* president/chairman of the commission.

hon•or•ee /ˌɑːnəˈriː/ *noun, pl* **-ees** [*count*] *US* : a person who is being given an honor • Three *honorees* were chosen for the Hall of Fame.

honor guard *noun, pl* ~ **guards** [*count*] *chiefly US* : a person or group that is the guard at a formal or ceremonial event (such as a military funeral or a parade)

hon•or•if•ic /ˌɑːnəˈrɪfɪk/ *adj* : giving or expressing honor or respect • an *honorific* name/title
– honorific *noun, pl* **-ics** [*count*] • The title "Excellency" was used as an *honorific.*

honor roll *noun, pl* ~ **rolls** [*count*] *US* : a list of people who deserve to be honored; *especially* : a list of students who have received good grades in school — called also (*Brit*) *roll of honour*; compare DEAN'S LIST

honor society *noun, pl* ~ **-ties** [*count*] *US* : a group of students who are honored for receiving good grades

honor system *noun, pl* ~ **-tems** [*singular*] *chiefly US* : a system in which people are trusted to follow rules and to act in an honest way • Customers are on the *honor system* to pay for any software they choose to purchase.

honour, honourable *Brit spellings of* HONOR, HONORABLE

hooch /ˈhuːʧ/ *noun* [*noncount*] *chiefly US slang* : alcoholic liquor especially when it is cheap or made illegally • a bottle of *hooch*

¹hood /ˈhʊd/ *noun, pl* **hoods** [*count*]
1 a : a soft covering for the head and neck often attached to a coat or cape **b** : a cloth covering worn over the entire head to hide a person's face • Witnesses reported that the bandits were wearing *hoods.* — see color picture on page C15
2 a : a cover that is used to protect or shield something (such as part of a machine or a camera lens) • The photographer used a lens *hood* to cut down on glare. **b** *US* : the movable metal covering over the engine of an automobile • What kind of engine do you have under the *hood*? • a *hood* ornament — called also (*Brit*) *bonnet*; see picture at CAR **c** *US* : a device attached above a cooking surface that is used for carrying off smoke and fumes • a range *hood*
– compare ²HOOD, ³HOOD

²hood *noun, pl* **hoods** [*count*] *US, informal* : HOODLUM • a gang of *hoods* — compare ¹HOOD, ³HOOD

³hood *noun, pl* **hoods** [*count*] *US slang* : a neighborhood; *especially* : a poor neighborhood in a large city • his friends in ***the hood*** • programs to help kids living in *the hood* — compare ¹HOOD, ²HOOD

-hood /-ˌhʊd/ *noun suffix*
1 : state : condition : quality • likeli*hood* • false*hood* • child*hood* • adult*hood*
2 : people sharing a condition or character • brother*hood*

hood•ed /ˈhʊdəd/ *adj*
1 : having a hood • a *hooded* jacket/sweatshirt : wearing a hood • a *hooded* figure
2 *of an animal* : having a head that is colored or formed in a way that looks like a hood • a *hooded* duck/cobra
3 — used to describe eyes that are half closed • He looked at us with *hooded* eyes.

hood•ie /ˈhʊdi/ *noun, pl* **-ies** [*count*] *informal* : a hooded sweatshirt

hood•lum /ˈhuːdləm, ˈhʊdləm/ *noun, pl* **-lums** [*count*] : a tough and violent criminal : THUG • a small-time *hoodlum*

hood•wink /ˈhʊdˌwɪŋk/ *verb* **-winks; -winked; -wink•ing** [+ *obj*] *informal* : to deceive or trick (someone) • Don't let yourself be *hoodwinked* into buying things you don't need.

hoo•ey /ˈhuːwi/ *noun* [*noncount*] *chiefly US, informal* : foolish talk or writing : NONSENSE • Don't waste your money on that book—it's a lot of *hooey.*

¹hoof /ˈhʊf/ *noun, pl* **hooves** /ˈhuːvz, ˈhʊvz/ *also* **hoofs** [*count*] : the hard covering on the foot of an animal (such as a horse or pig) — see picture at HORSE; see also CLOVEN HOOF
on the hoof **1** *of an animal* : while still living : before being killed for meat • The cattle cost $1.20 a pound *on the hoof.* **2** *informal, of people* : while doing something else • She ate lunch *on the hoof* to get the report done on time.
– hoofed /ˈhʊft/ *adj* • *hoofed* animals

²hoof *verb* **hoofs; hoofed; hoof•ing** [*no obj*] *US, informal* : to dance as a performer • The cast was *hoofing* on the stage.
hoof it *informal* : to move or travel on foot : to walk or run • We quickly *hoofed it* down to the subway station.
– hoof•er /ˈhʊfɚ/ *noun, pl* **-ers** [*count*] • a talented *hoofer* [=*dancer*] on Broadway

hoof–and–mouth disease *noun* [*noncount*] : FOOT-AND-MOUTH DISEASE

hoof•beat /ˈhʊfˌbiːt/ *noun, pl* **-beats** [*count*] : the sound made when an animal's hoof hits the ground

hoo–ha *also* **hoo–hah** /ˈhuːˌhɑː/ *noun* [*noncount*] *informal* + *usually disapproving* : great excitement or concern about something • Despite all the initial *hoo-ha*, people came to accept the new building.

¹hook /ˈhʊk/ *noun, pl* **hooks** [*count*]
1 : a curved or bent tool for catching, holding, or pulling something • He baited the *hook* [=*fishhook*] with a worm. • a coat/picture *hook*
2 : a ball or shot in golf and other games that curves to the side instead of going straight • She hit a *hook* into the left rough.
3 *boxing* : a punch coming from the side of the body instead of going straight forward • He threw a right/left *hook* to his opponent's body. — compare JAB, UPPERCUT
4 *basketball* : HOOK SHOT
5 *baseball, informal* — used to describe the action of removing a pitcher from a game • He ***got the hook*** [=he was removed] after allowing three runs in the second inning. • The manager ***gave him the hook***
6 : something (such as part of a song) that attracts people's attention • The song has a catchy *hook.* • They used the commercial as a *hook* to get people to visit their Web site.
by hook or by crook *informal* : by any possible means • She was determined to succeed *by hook or by crook.*
hook, line and sinker *informal* : without hesitation or doubt : COMPLETELY • He gave them some ridiculous explanation, and they fell for it *hook, line and sinker.* [=they believed his explanation completely]
off the hook **1** *informal* — used to describe someone who has avoided trouble or punishment; usually used with *get* or *let* • He counted on his friends to *get* him *off the hook.* [=to protect him from trouble or punishment] • I wasn't going to *let* her *off the hook* so easily. **2** *of a telephone* : with the receiver not resting in its usual position • They took the phone *off the hook* so that it wouldn't ring.
on the hook for *US, informal* : owing money for (something) : responsible for (something) • He's still *on the hook for* the cost of the repairs.
ring off the hook see ³RING
sling your hook see ¹SLING

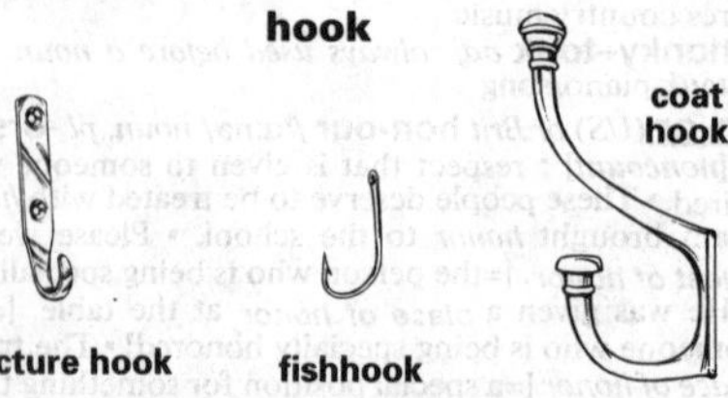

²hook *verb* **hooks; hooked; hook•ing**
1 *always followed by an adverb or preposition* **a** [+ *obj*] : to connect or attach (something) with a hook • The train cars were *hooked* together. • My sweater was *hooked* on a branch. • I *hooked* the door shut. **b** [*no obj*] : to be attached by hooks • The dress *hooks* in the back. • The two parts *hooked* together.
2 [+ *obj*] : to catch (something, such as a fish) with a hook • He *hooked* a large fish.

3 *always followed by an adverb or preposition* [+ *obj*] : to bend (a part of your body, such as an arm) and place it around something • He *hooked* his arm around my neck. • She *hooked* her fingers around the doorknob. • He *hooked* his thumb through a loop of his pants.
4 [*no obj*] : to curve like a hook • The bird's beak *hooks* downward.
5 *sports* : to hit or kick (a ball or shot) in a way that causes it to curve to the side : to hit a hook [+ *obj*] (*golf*) She *hooked* her drive into the rough. • (*American football*) The kicker *hooked* the ball to the left and missed the field goal. [*no obj*] (*golf*) The ball *hooked* into the rough.
hook into [*phrasal verb*] ***hook into (something)*** *informal* : to become connected to (something, such as a computer network or a source of electrical power) • We don't have the hardware we need to *hook into* the network.
hook up [*phrasal verb*] **1** *informal* : to join together to do something • The two men *hooked up* to form a new company. — often + *with* • She *hooked up with* a guitarist and drummer. **2** *chiefly US, informal* : to meet at a place • We are planning to *hook up* after the game. — often + *with* • We plan to *hook up with* our friends after the game. **3** ***hook (someone) up*** *chiefly US, informal* **a** : to cause (someone) to have a friendly or romantic relationship *with* someone • They *hooked him up with* some new friends. [=they introduced him to some new friends] • She tried to *hook* him *up with* [=*fix him up with*] one of her friends. **b** : to provide (someone) with something that is needed or wanted • Don't worry. I'll *hook* you *up*.— usually + *with* • She *hooked me up with* some great tickets. **4** ***hook up (something or someone)*** *or* ***hook (something or someone) up*** : to attach (something or someone) to a device by means of electrical connections • *hook up* the wires/speakers • The patient was *hooked up* to a monitor/respirator. — see also HOOKUP

hooked *adj*
1 : shaped like a hook • the bird's *hooked* beak
2 *not used before a noun, informal* **a** : addicted to a drug — usually + *on* • He was *hooked on* cocaine. **b** : very interested in and enthusiastic about something • Her friends talked her into playing golf, and now she's *hooked*.— usually + *on* • He's *hooked on* skiing. • She got *hooked on* the show after watching one episode.

hook·er /ˈhʊkɚ/ *noun, pl* **-ers** [*count*] *informal* : PROSTITUTE

hook shot *noun, pl* **~ shots** [*count*] *basketball* : a shot made by swinging the ball up and over your head with a long movement of your arm

hook·up /ˈhʊkˌʌp/ *noun, pl* **-ups** [*count*] : an arrangement or part by which pieces of equipment can be connected • The interview will be broadcast through a satellite *hookup*. • The cabin has electric and water *hookups*. • telephone/computer/Internet *hookups*— see also *hook up* at ²HOOK

hooky *also* **hook·ey** /ˈhʊki/ *noun*
play hooky *US, informal* : to be away from school without permission : to not be at school when you should be • He was *playing hooky* [=*skipping school*] with his friends.

hoo·li·gan /ˈhuːlɪgən/ *noun, pl* **-gans** [*count*] : a usually young man who does noisy and violent things as part of a group or gang • The windows were broken by a gang of teenage *hooligans*. • soccer *hooligans* [=violent soccer fans who fight against other soccer fans]
– hoo·li·gan·ism /ˈhuːlɪgəˌnɪzəm/ *noun* [*noncount*]

hoop /ˈhuːp/ *noun, pl* **hoops** [*count*]
1 a : a circular object : a large ring • She wore gold *hoops* as earrings. = She wore ***hoop earrings***. **b** : a large metal ring used for holding together the sides of a barrel **c** : a large ring used by performers or for play — see also HULA-HOOP
2 *basketball* **a** : a metal ring that the ball must go through in order to score points • He grabbed the rebound and put the ball back up through the *hoop*. [=*basket, net*] **b** *informal* : a successful shot • They scored a quick *hoop* [=*basket, bucket*] on a fast break. **c** *US, informal* : BASKETBALL • *hoop* fans — usually plural • *hoops* fans • Let's play/shoot some *hoops*. • a game of *hoops* • college/pro *hoops*
3 : an arch through which the ball must be hit in the game of croquet : WICKET
jump through hoops see ¹JUMP

hoop·la /ˈhuːˌplɑː/ *noun* [*noncount*] *chiefly US, informal* + *usually disapproving* : talk or writing that is designed to get people excited about and interested in something • Many people have grown tired of all the *hoopla* surrounding the opening of the new theater.

hooray *variant spelling of* HURRAH

hoose·gow /ˈhuːsˌgaʊ/ *noun*
the hoosegow *US, informal* + *humorous* : PRISON, JAIL • The cops threatened to throw him in *the hoosegow*.

¹**hoot** /ˈhuːt/ *noun, pl* **hoots** [*count*]
1 : the loud, deep sound made by an owl; *also* : a similar loud, deep sound • (*Brit*) the *hoot* [=*honk*] of a car's horn
2 : a loud laugh or call made by a person • *hoots* of laughter • The announcement was met with *hoots* of derision/scorn.
3 *informal* : an amusing person or thing — usually singular • Your father is a *hoot*. • Wasn't that a *hoot*?
give a hoot *also* ***care a hoot*** *informal* : to care at all about someone or something — used in negative statements • I don't *care a hoot* about what they say. • I don't ***give two hoots*** about his problems.

²**hoot** *verb* **hoots; hoot·ed; hoot·ing**
1 [*no obj*] *of an owl* : to make a hoot • We could hear an owl *hooting* in the woods.
2 *Brit* **a** [*no obj*] *of a horn* : to make a loud sound : HONK • a *hooting* horn **b** *Brit* : to cause (a horn) to hoot [+ *obj*] The people in the cars behind us kept *hooting* [=(*US*) *honking*] their horns. [*no obj*] I *hooted* at the car in front of me.
3 : to call out or laugh loudly [*no obj*] The crowd booed and *hooted* when it was announced that the show was canceled. [+ *obj*] The crowd *hooted* its disapproval. • The speaker was ***hooted down*** by a small group of protesters. [=the protesters loudly shouted at the speaker so that the speaker could not be heard] • The speaker was ***hooted off*** the platform by a small group of protesters.

hoot·er /ˈhuːtɚ/ *noun, pl* **-ers**
1 [*count*] : a person or device that hoots
2 hooters [*plural*] *US, informal* + *impolite* : a woman's breasts
3 [*count*] *Brit slang* : ¹NOSE 1 • He has an enormous *hooter*.

hoo·ver /ˈhuːvɚ/ *verb* **-vers; -vered; -ver·ing** *Brit* : VACUUM [*no obj*] I spent the morning *hoovering*. [+ *obj*] She *hoovered* the carpet.

hooves *plural of* ¹HOOF

¹**hop** /ˈhɑːp/ *verb* **hops; hopped; hop·ping**
1 [*no obj*] : to move by a quick jump or series of jumps • He *hopped* over the hot sand. • We crossed the stream by *hopping* from one rock to another. • A frog was *hopping* along the edge of the pond. • I sprained my ankle and had to *hop* (on one foot) back to the house to get help.
2 [+ *obj*] : to jump over (something) • *hop* a puddle/fence
3 *always followed by an adverb or preposition* [*no obj*] *informal* **a** : to move or go quickly • I *hopped* out of bed, got dressed, and headed off to work. • I need to *hop* into the shower [=I need to take a quick shower] before we go. • He *hopped* in the car and drove off. • She *hopped* on the train/elevator/plane. **b** : to go from place to place without staying long at any one place • We spent the evening *hopping* from one night club to another. • She's been *hopping* from job to job for years.
4 *informal* **a** [+ *obj*] *US* : to ride on (an airplane, train, etc.) • She *hopped* [=*took*] the first available flight to New York. **b** *always followed by an adverb or preposition* [*no obj*] : to make a short trip especially in an airplane • They plan to *hop* down/over to the conference.— see also HOPPING
hop it *Brit, informal* : to go away quickly • She told her brother to *hop it* [=*beat it*] and leave her alone.
hop to it *informal* : to act or move quickly • The car was ready to leave and he was told to *hop to it*.

²**hop** *noun, pl* **hops** [*count*]
1 a : a short, quick jump • She did a little *hop* to the left. **b** : the bounce of a ball • The shortstop fielded the ball on the second *hop*.
2 *old-fashioned* : a social event with dancing • a ***sock hop*** [=a social event of the 1950s in the U.S. at which teenagers danced in their socks]
3 *informal* **a** : a short flight in an airplane • a *hop* down to Philadelphia **b** *chiefly US* : a short trip • a quick *hop* to the grocery store
a hop, skip, and (a) jump *informal* : a short distance • Her house is just *a hop, skip, and jump* from mine.
– see also HIP-HOP

¹**hope** /ˈhoʊp/ *verb* **hopes; hoped; hop·ing** : to want something to happen or be true and think that it could happen or be true [*no obj*] No one knows yet if anyone survived the crash. At this point, we can only *hope*. • "Will you be able to come to the party?" "I ***hope so***." [=I want to go to the party

but am not sure that I will be able to] • "Will you have to miss the party?" "I **hope not**" [=I do not want to miss the party] — often + *for* • He's *hoping for* a promotion. • An apology is the best/most we can *hope for*. • She was *hoping for* an invitation to the party. • She finally got her *hoped-for* promotion. • All we can do is **hope for the best** [=hope that things will turn out as well as possible] [+ *obj*] She *hoped* that she would be invited to the party. = She *hoped* to receive an invitation to the party. • We all *hope* (that) things will be better soon. = We're all *hoping* (that) things will be better soon. • They *hope* to succeed. • I *hope* (that) she remembers. • I *hope* you're feeling better soon. • That's what she *hoped* would happen. • It is (to be) *hoped* that the strike will end soon. • Let's *hope* that the strike ends soon. • I *hope* I haven't bored you. • Everyone in your family is well, I *hope*.

here's hoping *informal* — used to say that you hope something will happen • *Here's hoping* (that) it doesn't rain.

hope against hope : to hope for something when you know that it will probably not happen or be true • We're *hoping against hope* that they survived the crash.

²hope *noun, pl* **hopes**

1 : the feeling of wanting something to happen and thinking that it could happen : a feeling that something good will happen or be true [*noncount*] When they started their life together, they were young and full of *hope*. • Rescuers have not yet abandoned/lost *hope* that more survivors will be found. • The drug has brought/given *hope* to thousands of sufferers. [*count*] We allowed ourselves to entertain *hopes* that the crisis would end soon. • The goal raised/lifted the *hopes* of the team. • The *hope* is that there will be a settlement soon. • The lawyers do not want to raise false *hopes* of an early settlement. • Our *hopes* are fading/dwindling. • We had ***high hopes*** of winning the game. [=we felt we had a very good chance of winning the game] • You shouldn't ***get your hopes up*** [=feel so hopeful] • She went back to the restaurant ***with hopes of*** finding her purse there. = She went back to the restaurant ***with the hope of*** finding her purse there. [=because she thought and hoped that she might find her purse there] • He told them the truth ***with the hope that*** they would understand.

2 [*noncount*] : the chance that something good will happen • She believes there's *hope* of/for a cure. [=that a cure is possible] • He had little/no *hope* of attending college. • The latest reports hold out *hope* for a possible end to this crisis. • They have a ***glimmer/ray of hope*** [=a small chance] of winning. • His condition is ***beyond hope*** [=his condition is hopeless]

3 [*singular*] : someone or something that may be able to provide help : someone or something that gives you a reason for hoping • He's our last/best *hope*. • At this point their only *hope* is that someone will offer to buy the company. • What *hope* is there for someone like me?

4 [*count*] : something that is hoped for • All my *hopes* have been fulfilled at last. • Our fondest *hope* is that our children will be happy and healthy. • We all have *hopes* and dreams for the future. • We have great *hopes* for the coming year.

fix your hopes on/upon see ¹FIX

in (the) hope of/that or ***in hopes of/that*** : with the hope that something will happen or could happen • He returned to the crime scene *in (the) hope of* finding further evidence. • He waited *in hopes that* she would show up.

live in hope *chiefly Brit* : to hope for something when you know that it will probably not happen or be true • We *live in hope* that there will be some survivors of the crash.

pin (all) your hopes on see *pin on* at ²PIN

hope chest *noun, pl* **~ chests** [*count*] *US, old-fashioned* : a chest or box in which a young woman keeps things (such as silverware and linen) that she will use after she gets married

¹hope·ful /ˈhoʊpfəl/ *adj* [*more* ~; *most* ~]

1 : full of hope • The mood is sad rather than *hopeful*. • a *hopeful* message : feeling or showing hope • He was *hopeful* that things would get better soon. • I still feel *hopeful* about the future. • She is *hopeful* of winning the race. • a *hopeful* tone of voice

2 : giving someone feelings of hope • There are *hopeful* signs that the crisis may end soon. • The movie has a *hopeful* ending. • Investigators report that there have been some *hopeful* developments in the case.

– hope·ful·ness *noun* [*noncount*]

²hopeful *noun, pl* **-fuls** [*count*] : a person who hopes to do something • a presidential *hopeful* [=a person who hopes to become president] • young *hopefuls* in Hollywood

hope·ful·ly /ˈhoʊpfəli/ *adv*

1 : in a hopeful manner • They gazed up at us *hopefully*.

2 : it is hoped : I hope : we hope • *Hopefully*, it won't rain tomorrow. [=I hope that it won't rain tomorrow] • *Hopefully*, things will get better soon.

hope·less /ˈhoʊpləs/ *adj* [*more* ~; *most* ~]

1 : having or feeling no hope • He felt confused and *hopeless* after losing his job.

2 a *always used before a noun* : unable to be changed • She's a *hopeless* romantic. **b** *informal* : unable to be helped or improved : very bad • We were the most *hopeless* group of golfers you ever saw. • We were *hopeless* at (playing) golf.

3 : giving no reason for hope • a *hopeless* situation • He's very ill, but his condition isn't *hopeless*.

4 : unable to be solved or done : IMPOSSIBLE • a *hopeless* problem/task

– hope·less·ly /ˈhoʊpləsli/ *adv* • He stared *hopelessly* out the window. — used especially to add force to a statement • He's a *hopelessly* naive person. • She was *hopelessly* addicted to tobacco. • They fell *hopelessly* in love. **– hope·less·ness** *noun* [*noncount*] • feelings of *hopelessness*

hopped–up /ˈhɑːptˈʌp/ *adj* [*more* ~; *most* ~] *US, informal*

1 : showing or feeling the effects of a drug • a *hopped-up* addict • She was *hopped-up* on morphine.

2 : very energetic or excited • *hopped-up* music • The cast was *hopped-up* on opening night.

3 : having more than usual power • a *hopped-up* [=souped-up] engine

hop·per /ˈhɑːpɚ/ *noun, pl* **-pers**

1 [*count*] : someone or something that hops • (*informal*) a job *hopper* [=someone who keeps changing jobs] • The third baseman caught a *hopper*. [=a ball that bounced on the ground]

2 [*count*] : a container that is used for pouring material (such as grain or coal) into a machine or opening

3 ***the hopper*** *US* **a** : a box that bills are put into before they are considered by a legislature **b** : a mix of things to be considered or done • The company has several new product ideas in *the hopper*.

¹hop·ping /ˈhɑːpɪŋ/ *noun* [*noncount*] *informal* : the activity of going from one place to another place of the same kind — usually used in combination • Every night they went club-*hopping*. [=they went to a number of different clubs every night] • gallery-*hopping* • bar-*hopping*

²hopping *adj, informal* : very busy or active • The bar was *hopping*. • The boss kept me *hopping* all day.

³hopping *adv, informal* : very or extremely — used in the phrase ***hopping mad*** • Many employees are *hopping mad* over the new contract.

hop·py /ˈhɑːpi/ *adj* : having the taste or smell of hops • a *hoppy* beer/flavor

hops /ˈhɑːps/ *noun* [*plural*] : the dried flowers of a plant that are used to give a bitter flavor to beer and ale

¹hop·scotch /ˈhɑːpˌskɑːtʃ/ *noun* [*noncount*] : a child's game in which players hop through a series of squares drawn on the ground

²hopscotch *verb* **-scotch·es**; **-scotched**; **-scotch·ing** [*no obj*] *chiefly US, informal* : to move from one place to another • The tour *hopscotched* from city to city. • We *hopscotched* across the country.

horde /ˈhoɚd/ *noun, pl* **hordes** [*count*] *usually disapproving* : a large group of people • A *horde* of tourists entered the museum. • *Hordes* of reporters were shouting questions.

Do not confuse *horde* with *hoard*.

ho·ri·zon /həˈraɪzn/ *noun, pl* **-zons**

1 ***the horizon*** : the line where the earth or sea seems to meet the sky • We sailed toward *the horizon*. • The sun rose slowly over/above *the* eastern *horizon*. — see color picture on page C7

2 [*count*] **a** : the limit or range of a person's knowledge, understanding, or experience • Reading ***broadens/expands our horizons*** **b** : the limit of what is possible in a particular field or activity • These discoveries have opened up new *horizons* in the field of cancer research.

on the horizon : coming in the near future • Scientists believe that a major breakthrough is *on the horizon*.

hor·i·zon·tal /ˌhorəˈzɑːntl/ *adj* : positioned from side to side rather than up and down : parallel to the ground • a *horizontal* line/beam — compare VERTICAL

– horizontal *noun, pl* **-tals** [*count*] • a design with strong *horizontals* [=horizontal lines or parts] **– hor·i·zon·tal·ly**

/ˌhorəˈzɑːntḷi/ *adv* ▪ The line extends *horizontally*.

hor·mone /ˈhoɚˌmoʊn/ *noun, pl* **-mones** [*count*] : a natural substance that is produced in the body and that influences the way the body grows or develops ▪ sex *hormones* ▪ a *hormone* deficiency
– **hor·mon·al** /hoɚˈmoʊnl/ *adj* ▪ *hormonal* changes – **hormonally** *adv* ▪ *hormonally* controlled changes

hormone replacement therapy *noun* [*noncount*] *medical* : the use of the hormone estrogen to treat symptoms of menopause

¹horn /ˈhoɚn/ *noun, pl* **horns**
1 [*count*] **a** : one of the hard pointed parts that grows on the head of some animals (such as cattle, goats, or sheep) **b** [*count*] : a hard pointed part that grows on the nose of a rhinoceros **c** [*noncount*] : the hard material of which horns are made ▪ utensils made of *horn*
2 [*count*] : something that is shaped like a horn ▪ a saddle *horn*
3 [*count*] **a** : a brass musical instrument (such as a trumpet or trombone) — see also ENGLISH HORN, FRENCH HORN **b** : an instrument made from an animal's horn that is used for music or for producing loud signals
4 [*count*] : a device that makes a loud noise ▪ The driver in the car behind me blew/honked his *horn*. — see picture at CAR
5 ***the horn*** *US slang* : ¹TELEPHONE ▪ When he heard there was trouble, he ***got on the horn*** to the police. [=he phoned the police]
blow your own horn *or* ***toot your own horn*** *US, informal* : to talk about yourself or your achievements especially in a way that shows that you are proud or too proud ▪ We've had a very successful year, and I think we have a right to *blow our own horn* [=(*Brit*) *blow our own trumpet*] a little.
lock horns see ²LOCK
on the horns of a dilemma : in a situation in which you have to choose between things that are unpleasant or undesirable
pull in your horns *also* ***draw in your horns*** : to begin to behave in a more careful way; *especially* : to spend or invest money more carefully ▪ The bad economic news has caused many investors to *pull in their horns*.
take the bull by the horns see ¹BULL
– **horn·less** /ˈhoɚnləs/ *adj* ▪ a *hornless* animal

²horn *verb* **horns; horned; horn·ing**
horn in [*phrasal verb*] *US, informal + usually disapproving* : to add your comment or opinion to a conversation or discussion that you have been listening to ▪ Whenever I start to talk, he always *horns in*. — usually + *on* ▪ He always *horns in on* the conversation.

horned /ˈhoɚnd/ *adj* : having horns or parts that look like horns ▪ a *horned* dinosaur ▪ *horned* cattle ▪ a *horned* owl [=an owl that has feathers on its head that look like ears or horns]

hor·net /ˈhoɚnət/ *noun, pl* **-nets** [*count*] : a flying insect that has a powerful sting

hornet's nest *noun* [*singular*]
1 : a situation or place in which there are many dangers ▪ The principal entered the *hornet's nest* of angry parents.
2 : an angry reaction ▪ His comments stirred up a *hornet's nest* of angry opposition and criticism.

horn–rimmed glasses *noun* [*plural*] : eyeglasses with frames made of a plastic that resembles horn (sense 1c)

horn–rims /ˈhoɚnˌrɪmz/ *noun* [*plural*] : HORN-RIMMED GLASSES

horny /ˈhoɚni/ *adj* **horn·i·er; -est** [*also more ~; most ~*]
1 : made of horn (sense 1c) or a similar substance ▪ a *horny* growth
2 : hard and tough ▪ *horny* skin
3 *informal* : sexually excited ▪ *horny* teenagers

horo·scope /ˈhorəˌskoʊp/ *noun, pl* **-scopes** [*count*] : advice and future predictions based on the date of a person's birth and the positions of the stars and planets ▪ She checked the newspaper for her *horoscope*.

hor·ren·dous /həˈrɛndəs/ *adj* [*more ~; most ~*] : very bad or unpleasant : HORRIBLE ▪ *horrendous* crimes ▪ Her taste in clothes is *horrendous*. ▪ a *horrendous* traffic jam
– **hor·ren·dous·ly** *adv*

hor·ri·ble /ˈhorəbəl/ *adj* [*more ~; most ~*]
1 : causing horror : very shocking and upsetting ▪ He suffered a *horrible* death. ▪ The crime scene was too *horrible* to describe. ▪ a *horrible* accident
2 : very bad or unpleasant ▪ a *horrible* [=*disgusting*] smell ▪ That was a *horrible* [=*terrible, awful*] movie. ▪ The team had a *horrible* season last year. ▪ He realized that he had made a *horrible* mistake.
– **hor·ri·bly** /ˈhorəbli/ *adv* ▪ He died *horribly*. ▪ He was *horribly* disfigured in the fire. ▪ Something had gone *horribly* wrong.

hor·rid /ˈhorəd/ *adj* [*more ~; most ~*]
1 : very shocking or bad ▪ People there are living in *horrid* conditions. ▪ a *horrid* [=*horrible*] crime
2 : very unpleasant ▪ The medicine was *horrid*. ▪ He's a *horrid* little man.
– **hor·rid·ly** *adv*

hor·ri·fic /hoɚˈrɪfɪk/ *adj* [*more ~; most ~*] : causing horror or shock ▪ a *horrific* crime
– **hor·ri·fic·al·ly** *adv* ▪ a *horrifically* brutal murder ▪ *horrifically* expensive

hor·ri·fy /ˈhorəˌfaɪ/ *verb* **-fies; -fied; -fy·ing** [+ *obj*] : to cause (someone) to feel horror or shock : to greatly upset and shock (someone) ▪ The details of the crime *horrified* the nation. ▪ They were *horrified* by/at the movie's violence.
– **horrified** *adj* [*more ~; most ~*] ▪ He was *horrified* to realize that his comments had been overheard. ▪ She had a *horrified* look on her face. – **horrifying** *adj* [*more ~; most ~*] ▪ a *horrifying* experience – **hor·ri·fy·ing·ly** *adv* ▪ a *horrifyingly* brutal crime

¹hor·ror /ˈhorɚ/ *noun, pl* **-rors**
1 [*noncount*] : a very strong feeling of fear, dread, and shock ▪ There was a look of *horror* on her face. ▪ He saw ***to his horror*** that he couldn't escape. [=he was horrified to see that he couldn't escape] ▪ The crowd watched ***in horror*** as the fire spread.
2 [*noncount*] : the quality of something that causes feelings of fear, dread, and shock : the horrible or shocking quality or character *of* something ▪ His friends were shocked by the *horror of* his death. ▪ the *horror of* war
3 : something that causes feelings of fear, dread, and shock : something that is shocking and horrible [*count*] His crimes were unspeakable *horrors*. ▪ His memoirs recount the *horrors* of the war. [*noncount*] tales of *horror*
4 [*count*] *chiefly Brit, informal* : a child who behaves very badly ▪ Their children are perfect little *horrors*!
have a horror of : to have a strong dislike for or fear of (something) ▪ Some students seem to *have a horror of* using the dictionary. ▪ Like many teenagers, she *has a horror of* being seen in public with her parents. ▪ He *has a horror of* being caught unprepared.
horror of horrors *informal + humorous* — used to describe something as shocking or horrible ▪ There was no television at the cabin, so—*horror of horrors*!—we had to spend the evenings reading books and playing board games.
shock horror see ³SHOCK

²horror *adj, always used before a noun* : intended to cause feelings of fear or horror ▪ a *horror* movie ▪ He writes *horror* novels.

horror show *noun, pl* **~ shows** [*count*] *informal* : something that is difficult to deal with or watch because it is so bad, unpleasant, etc. ▪ The trial has been a *horror show*.

horror story *noun, pl* **~ -ries** [*count*] *informal*
1 : a story about an actual event or experience that is very unpleasant ▪ We've all heard *horror stories* about airlines losing people's luggage.
2 : an experience that is very unpleasant ▪ Her childhood was a *horror story*.

hors d'oeuvre /oɚˈdɚv/ *noun, pl* **hors d'oeuvres** [*count*] : a food served in small portions before the main part of a meal ▪ a tray of assorted *hors d'oeuvres*

¹horse /ˈhoɚs/ *noun, pl* **hors·es**
1 [*count*] : a large animal that is used for riding and for carrying and pulling things ▪ ride/mount a *horse* — often used before another noun ▪ a *horse* farm ▪ *horse* people [=people who raise or have a special interest in horses] — compare COLT, FILLY, FOAL, GELDING, MARE, PONY, STALLION; see also QUARTER HORSE, RACEHORSE, WORKHORSE
2 [*count*] **a** : a frame used to support a piece of wood while it is being cut with a saw : SAWHORSE **b** : a large piece of equipment used in gymnastics : POMMEL HORSE
3 ***horses*** [*plural*] *informal* **a** *US* : HORSEPOWER ▪ a car with 275 *horses* **b** ***the horses*** : horse races ▪ He lost a lot of money on *the horses*.
4 [*count*] *US, informal* : an athlete who is strong and who helps a team to win — usually plural ▪ a team with the *horses* to win the pennant [=a team with the good players needed to win the pennant]

H

a horse of a different color *chiefly US, informal* : a very different thing or issue ▪ That's what we'll do when he gets here. But if he doesn't show up . . . well, that's *a horse of a different color.*

beat a dead horse (*chiefly US*) *or* ***flog a dead horse*** *informal* **1** : to keep talking about a subject that has already been discussed or decided ▪ I don't mean to *beat a dead horse*, but I still don't understand what happened. **2** : to waste time and effort trying to do something that is impossible ▪ Is it just *beating a dead horse* to ask for another recount of the votes?

change horses in midstream : to choose a different leader or policy during a time when serious problems are being dealt with ▪ a politician whose slogan for reelection is "Don't *change horses in midstream*"

eat a horse *informal* ✧ Someone who is very hungry can be described as being hungry enough to *eat a horse.* ▪ I didn't eat today and now I'm so hungry I could *eat a horse*.

from the horse's mouth *informal, of information* : from the original source or person and therefore thought to be true ▪ I know it's hard to believe but I heard it (straight) *from the horse's mouth*.

hold your horses *informal* — used to tell someone to slow down, stop, or wait for a short time ▪ "Hurry up. We need to get going." "*Hold your horses*. I'll be ready in a minute."

look a gift horse in the mouth : to look in a critical way at something that has been given to you ▪ I noticed the guitar wasn't made of real wood, but I didn't say anything because you shouldn't *look a gift horse in the mouth*.

put the cart before the horse see [1]CART

the wrong horse ✧ If you choose/pick/back (etc.) *the wrong horse*, you choose or support someone or something that is not successful. ▪ The company has been losing money, and many investors are beginning to feel that they may have backed *the wrong horse*.

– see also CHARLEY HORSE, DARK HORSE, HIGH HORSE, HOBBYHORSE, ONE-HORSE, ROCKING HORSE, SEA HORSE, STALKING HORSE, TROJAN HORSE

[2]**horse** *verb* **horses; horsed; hors·ing**

horse around *or Brit* ***horse about*** [*phrasal verb*] *informal* : to play in a rough or loud way : to engage in horseplay ▪ They were *horsing around* instead of studying. ▪ He *horsed around* with the kids for a while.

[1]**horse·back** /ˈhoɚsˌbæk/ *noun*

on horseback : on the back of a horse ▪ Before the invention of the automobile, people often traveled *on horseback*. [=they traveled by riding horses]

[2]**horseback** *adj, always used before a noun* : on the back of a horse ▪ a **horseback rider** [=a person riding on a horse] ▪ Do you enjoy **horseback riding**? [=the activity of riding horses]

– **horseback** *adv, chiefly US* ▪ riding *horseback*

horse chestnut *noun, pl* ~ **-nuts** [*count*] : a tree with flowers that grow in large bunches and large brown seeds; *also* : the seed of a horse chestnut tree

horse–drawn *adj* : pulled by a horse or by a group of horses ▪ a *horse-drawn* carriage

horse·feath·ers /ˈhoɚsˌfɛðɚz/ *noun* [*noncount*] *US, old-fashioned slang* : foolish or untrue words : NONSENSE ▪ He thought the story was a lot of *horsefeathers*.

horse·fly /ˈhoɚsˌflaɪ/ *noun, pl* **-flies** [*count*] : a type of large biting fly

horse·hair /ˈhoɚsˌheɚ/ *noun* [*noncount*] : hair from the mane or tail of a horse

– **horsehair** *adj* ▪ *horsehair* fabric ▪ a *horsehair* couch/sofa [=a couch/sofa filled with horsehair]

horse laugh *noun, pl* ~ **laughs** [*count*] *informal* : a loud laugh

horse·man /ˈhoɚsmən/ *noun, pl* **-men** /-mən/ [*count*]

1 : a person (especially a man) who rides horses ▪ a skillful *horseman*

2 : a person (especially a man) who breeds or raises horses — compare HORSEWOMAN

– **horse·man·ship** /ˈhoɚsmənˌʃɪp/ *noun* [*noncount*] ▪ a camp where children learn *horsemanship* [=learn how to ride horses]

horse opera *noun, pl* ~ **-eras** [*count*] *chiefly US, old-fashioned* : [2]WESTERN ▪ the star of many *horse operas*

horse·play /ˈhoɚsˌpleɪ/ *noun* [*noncount*] : rough or loud play : energetic and noisy playful activity ▪ The lamp got broken when the kids were engaging in a little *horseplay*.

horse·pow·er /ˈhoɚsˌpawɚ/ *noun, pl* **horsepower** : a unit used to measure the power of engines [*noncount*] We need an engine with greater/more *horsepower*. [=a more powerful engine] [*count*] an engine with 200 *horsepower* — often used figuratively ▪ intellectual *horsepower*

horse race *noun, pl* ~ **races** [*count*]

1 : an event in which horses race and people bet on which horse will win

2 *chiefly US* : a close contest ▪ The election is sure to become a *horse race* by early summer.

– **horse·rac·ing** /ˈhoɚsˌreɪsɪŋ/ *noun* [*noncount*] ▪ He lost a lot of money betting on *horseracing*.

horse·rad·ish /ˈhoɚsˌrædɪʃ/ *noun, pl* **-ish·es**

1 [*count*] : a tall plant whose root is used for making a sauce

2 [*noncount*] : a strong sauce made from the root of the horseradish plant — often used before another noun ▪ a spicy *horseradish* sauce

horse's ass *noun, pl* ~ **asses** [*count*] *US, informal + impolite* : a very stupid or foolish person : ASS ▪ She angrily told him to stop acting like a *horse's ass*.

horse sense *noun* [*noncount*] *informal* : the ability to make good judgments or decisions : common sense ▪ He credits his success to good old-fashioned *horse sense*.

horse·shit /ˈhoɚsˌʃɪt/ *noun* [*noncount*] *US, informal + offensive* : NONSENSE, BULLSHIT

horse·shoe /ˈhoɚsˌʃuː/ *noun, pl* **-shoes**

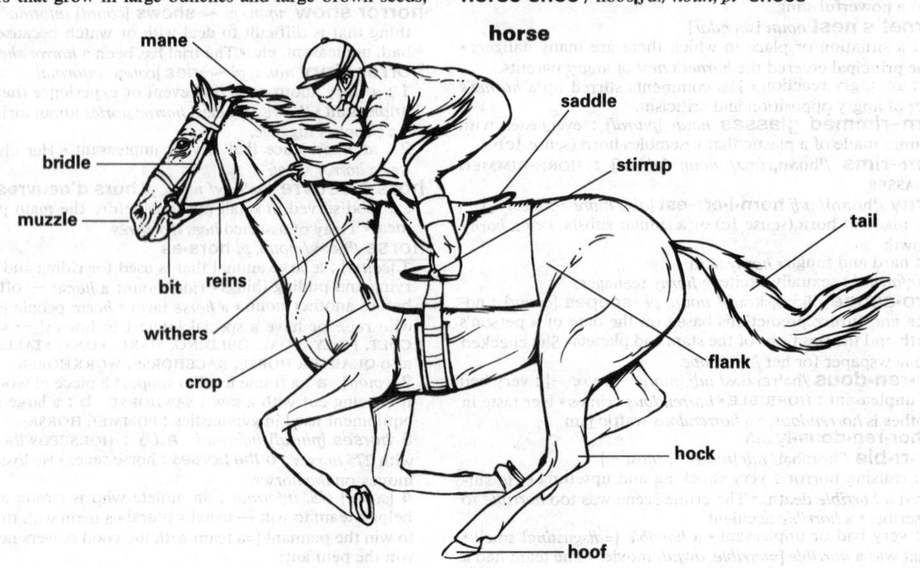

H

1 [*count*] **a** : a U-shaped band of iron nailed to the bottom of a horse's hoof as a shoe **b** : something shaped like a horseshoe • The lake was a *horseshoe* surrounded by tall pine trees.
2 ***horseshoes*** [*plural*] *US* : a game in which players try to get horseshoes around a stake in the ground by throwing them at the stake from a certain distance

horse show *noun, pl* ~ **shows** [*count*] : an event where people bring horses to compete against one another

horse trade *noun, pl* ~ **trades** [*count*] : a clever and often secret agreement made by powerful people who are usually trying to get an advantage over others • a political *horse trade*
– **horse trader** *noun, pl* ~ **-ers** [*count*] • a politician who is known as a clever *horse trader* – **horse trading** *noun* [*noncount*] • political *horse trading*

horse·whip /ˈhoɚsˌwɪp/ *verb* **-whips; -whipped; -whipping** [+ *obj*] : to hit (someone) with a whip • He thinks that any government official who steals public money should be *horsewhipped.*

horse·wom·an /ˈhoɚsˌwʊmən/ *noun, pl* **-wom·en** /-ˌwɪmən/ [*count*]
1 : a woman who rides horses
2 : a woman who breeds or manages horses — compare HORSEMAN

hors·ey *or* **horsy** /ˈhoɚsi/ *adj* **hors·i·er; -est**
1 : of, relating to, or involved with horses • *horsey* people [=people who own or are interested in horses] • a *horsey* family
2 : suggesting a horse or horses • a *horsey* face

hor·ti·cul·ture /ˈhoɚtəˌkʌltʃɚ/ *noun* [*noncount*] : the science of growing fruits, vegetables, and flowers — compare AGRICULTURE
– **hor·ti·cul·tur·al** /ˌhoɚtəˈkʌltʃərəl/ *adj* • *horticultural* books – **hor·ti·cul·tur·ist** /ˌhoɚtəˈkʌltʃərɪst/ *or chiefly Brit* **hor·ti·cul·tur·al·ist** /ˌhoɚtəˈkʌltʃrəlɪst/ *noun, pl* **-ists** [*count*] • They had several *horticulturists* on staff to care for the orchard.

ho·san·na /hoʊˈzænə, hoʊˈzɑːnə/ *noun, pl* **-nas** [*count*] : an expression of enthusiastic praise • The book was met with hearty *hosannas* from literary critics. [=literary critics praised the book enthusiastically] — sometimes used as an interjection • *Hosanna* in the highest!

¹hose /ˈhoʊz/ *noun*
1 *pl* ***hos·es*** : a long, usually rubber tube that liquids or gases can flow through [*count*] There are several *hoses* stored in the shed. • a ***fire hose*** [=a hose used to spray water on a fire] • a ***garden hose*** [=a hose used to water a garden] [*noncount*] We need another 50 feet of *hose.* — see pictures at GARDENING, SCUBA DIVING
2 ***hose*** [*plural*] : clothes (such as stockings, socks, and pantyhose) that are worn on the legs and feet • women's *hose* — called also *hosiery*

²hose *verb* **hos·es; hosed; hos·ing** [+ *obj*]
1 : to spray or wash (something) with water from a hose — usually + *down* or *off* • At the end of the day he *hosed down/off* the sidewalk outside his shop.
2 *US slang* : to cheat or trick (someone) • We got *hosed.*

hose·pipe /ˈhoʊzˌpaɪp/ *noun, pl* **-pipes** [*count*] *Brit* : ¹HOSE 1

ho·siery /ˈhoʊʒəri, *Brit* ˈhəʊzjəri/ *noun* [*noncount*] : ¹HOSE 2 • a shop that sells *hosiery*

hos·pice /ˈhɑːspəs/ *noun, pl* **-pic·es** [*count*]
1 : a place that provides care for people who are dying • She chose to go to a *hospice* instead of a hospital. — often used before another noun • He was placed in *hospice* care for the last three months of his life. • a *hospice* program
2 *somewhat old-fashioned* : a place where travelers can stay : INN; *especially* : an inn kept by people in a religious organization

hos·pi·ta·ble /hɑˈspɪtəbəl, ˈhɑːspɪtəbəl/ *adj* [*more* ~; *most* ~]
1 : generous and friendly to guests or visitors • The people of that country are very *hospitable.* — often + *to* • They were very *hospitable to* their guests. — opposite INHOSPITABLE
2 : having an environment where plants, animals, or people can live or grow easily • It's a hearty plant that grows in even the least *hospitable* climates. • elderly people moving to Florida for its *hospitable* climate — often + *to* • The climate here is *hospitable to* many species. — opposite INHOSPITABLE
3 : ready or willing to accept or consider something — usually + *to* • a person/company known for being *hospitable* [=*open*] *to* new ideas
– **hos·pi·ta·bly** /hɑˈspɪtəbli, ˈhɑːspɪtəbli/ *adv* • Their guests are always treated *hospitably.*

hos·pi·tal /ˈhɑːˌspɪtl/ *noun, pl* **-tals** [*count*] : a place where sick or injured people are given care or treatment and where children are often born • (*US*) She's in the *hospital.* = (*Brit*) She's in *hospital.* • (*US*) She was admitted to the *hospital* yesterday. = (*Brit*) She was admitted to *hospital* yesterday. [=she was hospitalized yesterday] • (*US*) She'll be discharged from the *hospital* tomorrow. = (*Brit*) She'll be discharged from *hospital* tomorrow. — often used before another noun • *hospital* beds • a *hospital* gown

hos·pi·tal·i·ty /ˌhɑːspəˈtæləti/ *noun* [*noncount*]
1 : generous and friendly treatment of visitors and guests : hospitable treatment • It was refreshing to be met with such *hospitality* after our long journey.
2 : the activity of providing food, drinks, etc. for people who are the guests or customers of an organization — often used before another noun • a job in the *hospitality* business/industry • entertaining potential clients in a ***hospitality suite***

hos·pi·tal·ize *also Brit* **hos·pi·tal·ise** /ˈhɑːspɪtəˌlaɪz/ *verb* **-iz·es; -ized; -iz·ing** [+ *obj*] : to place (someone) in a hospi-

hospital

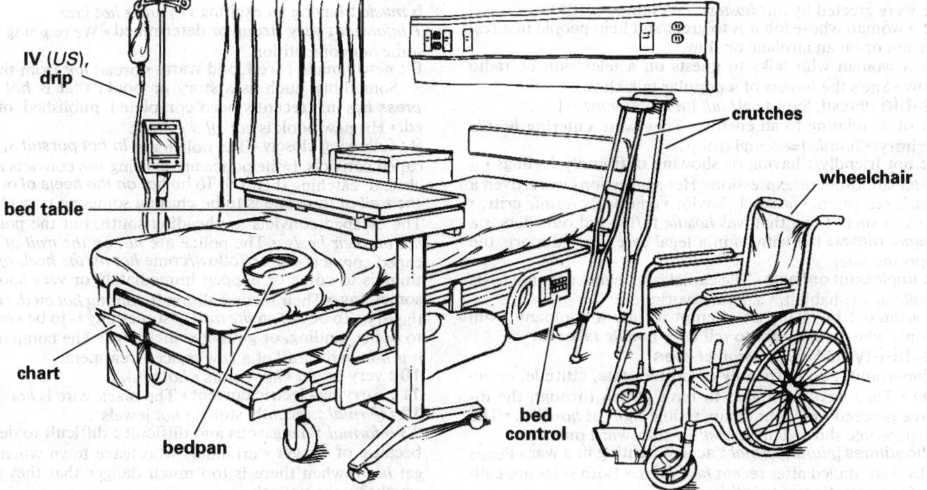

tal for care or treatment ▪ The doctor wants to *hospitalize* her for a few days so that he can run some tests. — usually used as *(be) hospitalized* ▪ He *was hospitalized* after the accident.
– **hos·pi·tal·i·za·tion** *also Brit* **hos·pi·tal·i·sa·tion** /ˌhɑːspɪtələˈzeɪʃən, *Brit* ˌhɑːspɪtəˌlaɪˈzeɪʃən/ *noun, pl* **-tions** [*count*] He was released after a brief *hospitalization*. [*noncount*] Her injuries were not serious enough to require *hospitalization*.

[1]host /ˈhoʊst/ *noun, pl* **hosts** [*count*]
1 : a person (especially a man) who is entertaining guests socially or as a job ▪ We were greeted at the front door by our *host*. — compare HOSTESS
2 : a person who talks to guests on a television or radio show ▪ He/she is the *host* of the talk show. ▪ a game-show *host*
3 : an animal or plant in which another animal or plant lives and gets its food or protection ▪ A tick can often carry diseases, making it a danger to its *hosts*. ▪ a human *host* — compare PARASITE 1
play host to ✧ A place or organization that *plays host to* an event (such as a meeting or convention) provides the things that are needed for that event. ▪ Each year, the city *plays host to* [=*hosts*] the film festival for one week. ▪ The mall was *playing host to* [=*hosting*] an auto show.
– compare [3]HOST

[2]host *verb* **hosts; host·ed; host·ing** [+ *obj*] : to be the host for (a social event, a group of people, etc.) ▪ He/she is going to *host* the music awards. ▪ They *hosted* a dinner party on Saturday.

[3]host *noun, pl* **hosts** [*count*] : a great amount or number ▪ a (whole) *host* of options — compare [1]HOST

Host /ˈhoʊst/ *noun*
the Host : a round, thin piece of bread used in the Christian Communion ceremony

hos·tage /ˈhɑːstɪʤ/ *noun, pl* **-tag·es** [*count*] : a person who is captured by someone who demands that certain things be done before the captured person is freed ▪ The terrorists demanded a plane and a pilot in exchange for the *hostages*. ▪ The *hostage* crisis is now entering its second week. ▪ The passengers were ***taken hostage***. ▪ They were ***held hostage*** for several days. — sometimes used figuratively ▪ a neighborhood being *held hostage* to fear [=a neighborhood controlled or dominated by fear]
a hostage to fortune ✧ In British English, *a hostage to fortune* is something (such as a promise or an action) that someone has made or done that may cause problems in the future. In U.S. English, this phrase is much less common and is usually understood to mean a person whose future success or failure is controlled by luck or fortune.

hos·tel /ˈhɑːstl̩/ *noun, pl* **-tels** [*count*]
1 : an inexpensive place for usually young travelers to stay overnight — called also *youth hostel*
2 *Brit* : a shelter for homeless people

hos·tel·ry /ˈhɑːstl̩ri/ *noun, pl* **-ries** [*count*] *old-fashioned* : an inn, pub, or hotel

host·ess /ˈhoʊstəs/ *noun, pl* **-ess·es** [*count*]
1 : a woman who is entertaining guests socially or as a job ▪ We were greeted by our *hostess*. — compare HOST
2 : a woman whose job it is to greet and help people in a restaurant or on an airplane or ship
3 : a woman who talks to guests on a television or radio show ▪ She's the *hostess* of a popular talk show.

hos·tile /ˈhɑːstl̩, ˈhɑːˌstajəl/ *adj* [*more ~; most ~*]
1 : of or relating to an enemy ▪ They were entering *hostile* territory. ▪ *hostile* [=*enemy*] troops
2 : not friendly : having or showing unfriendly feelings ▪ a *hostile* atmosphere/expression ▪ Her suggestions were given a *hostile* reception. ▪ *hostile* behavior ▪ an openly *hostile* critic ▪ It was a small town that was *hostile* to/toward outsiders. ▪ a ***hostile witness*** [=a witness in a legal case who supports the opposing side]
3 : unpleasant or harsh ▪ The camel is specially adapted to its *hostile* desert habitat. ▪ a *hostile* workplace
4 *business* : involving an attempt to buy a company from people who do not want to sell it ▪ a ***hostile takeover***

hos·til·i·ty /hɑˈstɪləti/ *noun, pl* **-ties**
1 [*noncount*] : an unfriendly or hostile state, attitude, or action ▪ They were both glad to have gotten through the divorce proceedings without any visible signs of *hostility*. ▪ The townspeople showed open *hostility* to/toward outsiders.
2 ***hostilities*** [*plural*] *formal* : acts of fighting in a war ▪ Peace talks were stalled after recent *hostilities*. ▪ Both sides are calling for a cessation of *hostilities*.

[1]hot /ˈhɑːt/ *adj* **hot·ter; hot·test**
1 a : having a high temperature ▪ *hot* August nights ▪ *hot* and humid weather ▪ taking a *hot* bath/shower ▪ a *hot* climate/country ▪ It is/gets *hot* in the summer and cold in the winter. ▪ The baked potatoes were too *hot* to handle with our bare hands. ▪ We worked all afternoon in/under the *hot* sun. ▪ The chicken was fried in *hot* oil. ▪ Your forehead feels *hot*. I think you might have a fever. ▪ a blazing/sizzling/steaming *hot* afternoon ▪ boiling/burning/fiery *hot* — see also RED-HOT, WHITE-HOT **b** : having a feeling of high body heat ▪ I was feeling *hot* and tired. **c** *of food or drink* : heated to a hot or warm temperature : served at a hot or warm temperature ▪ *hot* cereal ▪ a *hot* meal ▪ a selection of *hot* beverages — see also PIPING HOT
2 *informal* **a** : currently liked or wanted by many people ▪ The new toys are so *hot* that stores can't keep them in stock. ▪ a *hot* new restaurant ▪ He's considered a *hot* [=*appealing, desirable*] prospect. : currently very active or strong ▪ Her new book is a *hot* seller. ▪ She spoke about the latest *hot* trends in the computer industry. : currently causing a lot of interest or discussion ▪ reporters pursuing a *hot* story ▪ a *hot* concept/idea ▪ His decision has been a *hot* topic of conversation. ✧ Something or someone that is a ***hot commodity/item/property*** is currently very valuable or popular. ▪ Exotic mushrooms are a *hot commodity*. ▪ The success of her latest movie has made her a *hot property* in Hollywood. ▪ Computer games are a *hot item* in stores this year. **b** : very good — usually used in negative statements ▪ I don't think that's such a *hot* idea. [=I don't think it's a good idea] ▪ He came home early because he wasn't feeling too *hot*. [=he wasn't feeling well] ▪ Things aren't looking so *hot* at this point. **c** : having a period of unusual success or good luck ▪ The team has been *hot* recently. = The team has recently been on a ***hot streak***. [=the team has been winning a lot recently] ▪ ***When you're hot, you're hot***. [=when you are having good luck, you keep winning or succeeding repeatedly]
3 a : marked by anger or strong feelings ▪ a *hot* [=*heated*] argument ▪ His decision has been a topic of *hot* debate. ▪ This is an area of *hot* dispute. ✧ An issue or topic that is ***too hot to handle*** causes so much anger or controversy that people avoid discussing or dealing with it. **b** *always used before a noun* : easily excited or angered ▪ He's known for his *hot* [=*bad*] temper. **c** : ANGRY ▪ He was starting to get pretty *hot* about the delays. ▪ You shouldn't allow these little delays to get you all ***hot and bothered***. [=to make you angry and upset] — see also HOT UNDER THE COLLAR (below)
4 *of food* : having a spicy or peppery flavor ▪ *hot* chilis ▪ *hot* sauce/mustard ▪ Do you prefer your curry *hot* or mild?
5 *informal* **a** : sexually excited by or interested in someone — + *for* ▪ Everyone knows she's *hot for* the new guy in her office. **b** : sexually attractive ▪ The girl he's dating is really *hot*. ▪ He was voted the *hottest* [=*sexiest*] actor in Hollywood. **c** : exciting in a sexual or romantic way ▪ He's nervous because he has a ***hot date*** tonight. **d** *of sex* : very intense or exciting ▪ *hot* sex **e** : EAGER — usually followed by *to* + *verb* ▪ She's *hot to party*. — sometimes + *for* ▪ The students are *hot for* reform.
6 *music* : having an exciting rhythm ▪ *hot* jazz
7 *informal* : very strong or determined ▪ We're going to face some *hot* competition.
8 : newly made : fresh and warm ▪ bread *hot* from the oven ✧ Something, such as a story or book, that is ***hot off the press*** has just recently been completed, published, or printed. ▪ His new book is *hot off the press*.
9 : following closely ▪ The police are ***in hot pursuit*** of the escaped convicts. [=the police are chasing the convicts and are close to catching them] ✧ To be ***hot on the heels of*** or ***hot on the trail of*** someone is to be chasing someone very closely. ▪ The escaped convicts are heading south, but the police are *hot on their heels*. ▪ The police are *hot on the trail of* the escaped convicts. To be/follow/come *hot on the heels of* something is to come or happen immediately or very soon after something. ▪ Their second album is coming *hot on the heels of* the first. To be *hot on the trail of* something is to be very close to doing, finding, or getting something. ▪ The company says it is *hot on the trail* of a new cancer treatment.
10 : very bright ▪ *hot* colors ▪ *hot* pink
11 : carrying electric current ▪ The black wire is *hot*.
12 *informal* : recently stolen ▪ *hot* jewels
13 *informal* : dangerous and difficult : difficult to deal with because of danger ▪ criminals who leave town when things get *hot* [=when there is too much danger that they will be caught by the police]

blow hot and cold see [1]BLOW
hot and heavy *informal* : sexually intense, active, or exciting • They have a very *hot and heavy* relationship.
hot on *informal* : strongly favoring or liking (something) • The company president is very *hot on* [=*big on*] the idea of developing new products.
hot tip *informal* : a valuable piece of information about something (such as the stock market or a horse race) that can help someone get money or an advantage
hot to trot *informal* : very eager to have sex • a movie about a couple of college students who are *hot to trot*
hot under the collar *informal* : angry or upset • He tends to get a little *hot under the collar* when his wife keeps him waiting.
like a hot knife through butter see [1]KNIFE
strike while the iron is hot see [1]STRIKE
– hot·ly *adv* • a *hotly* contested election • a *hotly* debated issue • He *hotly* denied any involvement in the controversy.
– hot·ness *noun* [*noncount*] • the *hotness* [=*spiciness*] of the pepper

[2]hot *verb* **hots; hot·ted; hot·ting**
hot up [*phrasal verb*] *Brit* : to become more intense or lively • The controversy has *hotted up* [=*heated up*] again.

hot air *noun* [*noncount*] *informal* : talk that is meant to sound important but does not mean very much • She's full of *hot air*.

hot–air balloon *noun, pl* **~ -loons** [*count*] : a large balloon that is filled with heated air and that floats in the sky with a basket underneath for people to ride in

hot·bed /ˈhɑːtˌbɛd/ *noun, pl* **-beds** [*count*] : a place where something grows or develops easily : a place where something happens very commonly • The neighborhood has become a *hotbed* of crime. [=a place where many crimes occur] • a *hotbed* of research • a *hotbed* of political unrest

hot–blood·ed /ˈhɑːtˈblʌdəd/ *adj* [*more ~; most ~*] : becoming angry or excited very easily • a *hot-blooded* young man

hot button *noun, pl* **~ -tons** [*count*] : an issue that causes people to feel strong emotions (such as anger) and to argue with each other • The film is considered very controversial for all the *hot buttons* it pushes. • a political *hot button*
– hot–button *adj, always used before a noun* • The budget is a real *hot-button* issue right now.

hot·cake /ˈhɑːtˌkeɪk/ *noun, pl* **-cakes** [*count*] *chiefly US* : PANCAKE
like hotcakes *informal* : at a very fast rate : very quickly • The new record is selling/going *like hotcakes*.

hot chocolate *noun, pl* **~ -lates** [*count, noncount*] : a hot drink that is chocolate-flavored • a cup of *hot chocolate* — called also *hot cocoa*

hotch·potch /ˈhɑːʧˌpɑːʧ/ *noun* [*singular*] *Brit* : HODGEPODGE

hot dog /ˈhɑːtˌdɑːg/ *noun, pl* **~ dogs** [*count*]
1 : a small cooked sausage that is mild in flavor and is usually served in a long roll (called a hot dog bun)
2 *US, informal* : a person (such as an athlete) who performs or plays in a way that is meant to attract attention : a person who hotdogs • The other players on the team don't like him because he's such a *hot dog*.
3 *US, old-fashioned + humorous* — used to express approval or pleasure • "She said we could go!" "*Hot dog*!"

hot·dog /ˈhɑːtˌdɑːg/ *verb* **-dogs; -dogged; -dog·ging** [*no obj*] *US, informal* : to perform or play in a way that is meant to attract attention • *hotdogging* skiers • His opponents have accused him of *hotdogging* after he scores a touchdown.
– hot·dog·ger /ˈhɑtˌdɑgɚ/ *noun, pl* **-ers** [*count*] • They've accused him of being a *hotdogger*. [=*hot dog*]

ho·tel /hoʊˈtɛl/ *noun, pl* **-tels** [*count*] : a place that has rooms in which people can stay especially when they are traveling : a place that provides food, lodging, and other services for paying guests • check into a *hotel* • check out of a *hotel*

ho·tel·i·er /hoʊˈtɛljɚ/ *noun, pl* **-iers** [*count*] : a person who owns or operates a hotel

hot flash *noun, pl* **~ flashes** [*count*] *US* : a sudden brief hot feeling experienced especially by women during menopause

hot flush *noun, pl* **~ flushes** [*count*] *Brit* : HOT FLASH

hot·foot /ˈhɑːtˌfʊt/ *verb* **-foots; -foot·ed; -foot·ing** [*no obj*] *informal* : to go quickly — usually + *it* • We had to *hotfoot it* [=*hurry*] back home to get there in time for dinner.

hot·head /ˈhɑːtˌhɛd/ *noun, pl* **-heads** [*count*] *informal* : a person who gets angry easily : a hotheaded person • Working on the project with such a *hothead* has been unpleasant.

hot·head·ed /ˈhɑːtˈhɛdəd/ *adj* [*more ~; most ~*] *informal* : easily angered • a *hotheaded* boss; *also* : very angry • He wrote a *hot-headed* letter.

hot·house /ˈhɑːtˌhaʊs/ *noun, pl* **-hous·es** [*count*] : a heated building used for growing plants — compare GREENHOUSE
– hothouse *adj, always used before a noun* • *hothouse* tomatoes [=tomatoes grown in a hothouse]

hot line *noun, pl* **~ lines** [*count*]
1 : a telephone service for the public to use to get help in emergencies • a suicide prevention *hot line*
2 : a telephone connection that allows leaders of different countries to talk to each other directly and that is always kept ready for use • They set up a *hot line* between Washington and Moscow.

hot pants *noun* [*plural*] : very short and tight shorts for women

hot plate *noun, pl* **~ plates** [*count*] : a small portable device with a metal plate used for cooking or heating food

hot pot *noun, pl* **~ pots** [*count, noncount*] *chiefly Brit* : a mixture of meat and vegetables cooked together with liquid in a single pot

hot potato *noun, pl* **~ -toes** [*count*] *informal* : an issue or question about which people have different opinions and feel very strongly • He tried to avoid taking a strong stand on political *hot potatoes* like abortion.

hot rod *noun, pl* **~ rods** [*count*] *informal* : a car that has been changed so that it can be driven and raced at very fast speeds

hots /ˈhɑːts/ *noun*
the hots *informal* : strong feelings of sexual attraction *for* someone • Everyone knows she has *the hots for* the new guy in her office. [=she is very attracted to the new guy in her office]

hot seat *noun*
the hot seat : the position of someone who is in trouble or is being asked many difficult or embarrassing questions • When the company ran into financial trouble, it was the accountant who found herself in *the hot seat*.

hot·shot /ˈhɑːtˌʃɑːt/ *noun, pl* **-shots** [*count*] *informal* : a talented and successful person • The company has hired a couple of young *hotshots* to revamp its advertising campaign. : someone who is successful or skillful in a showy or flashy way • That guy thinks he's a real *hotshot*. — often used before another noun • They've hired a *hotshot* lawyer.

hot spot *noun, pl* **~ spots** [*count*] *informal*
1 : a very popular or active place • The new restaurant is the latest *hot spot* in town. • a vacation *hot spot*
2 : a place where there is much danger or fighting • This part of the country is a *hot spot* of rebel activity. • a global *hot spot* [=an area in the world where war is possible or likely]

hot spring *noun, pl* **~ springs** [*count*] : a place where hot water flows out of the ground — usually plural • We hiked to the *hot springs*.

hot stuff *noun* [*noncount*] *informal*
1 : someone or something that is unusually good or popular • I remember when that guy was *hot stuff*. [=I remember when he was very popular] • His music was *hot stuff* back in those days.
2 : a person who is considered hot (sense 5b) : a sexually attractive person • The new guy in her office is *hot stuff*.

hot–tem·pered /ˈhɑːtˈtɛmpɚd/ *adj* [*more ~; most ~*] : becoming angry very easily : having or showing a hot temper • a *hot-tempered* political activist • a *hot-tempered* reply

hot ticket *noun, pl* **~ -ets** [*count*] *US, informal* : someone or something that is very popular • The musical is this season's *hot ticket*. • She's a *hot ticket* on the lecture circuit.

hot·tie /ˈhɑːti/ *noun, pl* **-ties** [*count*] *informal* : a sexually attractive person • His girlfriend is a real *hottie*.

hot tub *noun, pl* **~ tubs** [*count*] : a large tub of hot water in which people sit to relax or spend time together

hot water *noun* [*noncount*] *informal* : a difficult situation : TROUBLE — used with *in* or *into* • He's *in hot water* [=*in trouble*] with the IRS for failing to report his income. • The book got her *into hot water* with people on both sides of the issue. [=the book made people on both sides of the issue angry at her]

hot–water bottle *noun, pl* **~ bottles** [*count*] : a rubber container that is filled with hot water and used to warm a bed or a part of your body

hot–wire /ˈhɑːtˌwajɚ/ *verb* **-wires; -wired; -wir·ing** [+ *obj*] *informal* : to start (a car or the engine of a car) by connecting wires in the electrical system without using a key • His car was stolen when somebody broke a window and *hot-wired* the engine.

[1]**hound** /ˈhaʊnd/ *noun, pl* **hounds** [*count*]

1 : a dog; *especially* : a type of dog that has a very good sense of smell and is trained to hunt

2 : a person who is very determined to get something especially for a collection : a very enthusiastic collector • autograph *hounds*

[2]**hound** *verb* **hounds; hound·ed; hound·ing** [+ *obj*] : to chase or bother (someone or something) in a constant or determined way • He is being *hounded* by the press. • They *hounded* me with questions. • They *hounded* me for my autograph. • *hound* a politician out of office

hour /ˈawɚ/ *noun, pl* **hours**

1 [*count*] : one of the 24 equal parts of a day : 60 minutes • She wasn't supposed to eat for six *hours* before the operation. • You'll be paid by the *hour* for/on this job. • The job pays ten dollars an *hour*. • We've been waiting (for) an *hour*. • She exercises for a full/good/solid *hour* every day. • He practiced the piano for *hours* at a time. = He spent *hours* practicing the piano. • She was half an *hour* late. • They arrived a few *hours* later. • A project like that can take *hours* (to finish). • The project required long/endless *hours* of work. • He spent ***all his waking hours*** [=all of the hours in the day that he was awake] working on the project. • (*Brit*) She has been working ***all the hours God sends*** [=she has been working very long hours] • He's ***counting the hours*** until his retirement. [=he is waiting eagerly for his retirement] • We talked for ***hours and hours*** = We talked for ***hours on end*** = We talked for many *hours*. • She grew more nervous ***with each passing hour*** [=as each hour passed] • The mood changed ***from hour to hour*** — see also HALF HOUR, QUARTER HOUR

2 [*count*] **a** : the time shown on a clock or watch • The *hour* [=*time*] is half past ten. [=10:30] • We arrived just as the clock struck the *hour*. [=we arrived at exactly 12:00, 1:00, 2:00, etc.] • (*US*) The program is scheduled to start ***at the top of the hour*** [=at the beginning of the hour; at 12:00, 1:00, 2:00, etc.] • The next train will leave ***on the hour*** [=at the beginning of the next hour] • Trains leave the station ***every hour on the hour*** [=at the beginning of each hour; at 12:00, 1:00, 2:00, etc.] • Trains leave the station every hour at ten minutes ***before the hour*** [=trains leave at 12:50 (10 minutes to one), 1:50 (ten minutes to two), etc.] • Trains leave every hour at ten minutes ***past the hour*** = (*chiefly US*) Trains leave every hour at ten minutes ***after the hour*** [=trains leave at 1:10, 2:10, etc.] **b** : a particular time during the day • a late *hour* • What are you doing here at this *hour*? [=why are you here at such a late hour?] • at the midnight *hour* [=at midnight] • These animals are most active in the *hour* just before sunrise. • You can call me at any *hour* of the day or night. • People began arriving in the early *hours* of the morning. • The park is open during daylight *hours*. • We arrived at ***the appointed hour*** [=we arrived at the time that had been agreed upon] • They serve breakfast ***at all hours*** = They serve breakfast at any *hour*. [=at any time of day] • These animals are active *at all hours* of the day. [=throughout the day] • They were up ***till/until all hours*** [=they were up very late] • The store is open ***twenty-four hours a day*** [=the store is open all day and night] ✧ The ***wee/small/early hours*** are the very early hours of the morning. • They studied into the *wee hours*. • The negotiations lasted into the *small hours* (of the morning).

3 a [*count*] : the time of a specified activity • She likes to go for a walk during her lunch *hour*. • the breakfast/dinner *hour* • the cocktail *hour* — see also ELEVENTH HOUR, HAPPY HOUR, RUSH HOUR, ZERO HOUR **b** [*count*] : a particular time or period of time • The ***hour of reckoning*** had come. [=the moment of truth had come; the time when something would be decided had come] • They helped us in our ***hour of need*** [=the time when we were most in need of help] ✧ The ***man/woman (etc.) of the hour*** is a person who is being honored or praised or who is enjoying success at a particular time. • The success of his latest film has made him the *man of the hour* in Hollywood. ✧ Someone's or something's ***darkest hour*** is a time of great trouble or danger. • They helped us in our *darkest hour*. ✧ Someone's or something's ***finest hour*** is a time of great success, courage, or heroism. • The troops triumphed in our country's *finest hour*. **c hours** [*plural*] : a time scheduled or used for a particular purpose or activity • School *hours* are from 8 a.m. to 4 p.m. • She works regular/normal *hours*. [=she works a regular schedule; she works during the day on Monday through Friday] • She has been working longer *hours*. [=she has been working for more hours than usual each day] • ***Visiting hours*** on this hospital ward are between 2 p.m. and 6 p.m. • Personal phone calls are not allowed during ***business/office hours*** • He enjoys reading and relaxing in his ***off hours*** [=the time when he is not working] • We ***keep early hours*** out here in the country. [=we go to bed early] • She has been ***keeping late hours*** at the office. [=she has been working late]

4 [*count*] : the distance that can be traveled in an hour • She lives two *hours* away. • Her house is two *hours* north of here. • Her house is two *hours'* drive from here. = Her house is a two-*hour* drive from here.

5 hours [*plural*] — used to refer to time when time is being measured on a 24-hour clock • In the military, 4:00 p.m. is called 1600 *hours*.

after hours or *Brit* ***out of hours*** : after the regular hours of work or operation • The professor gave out his phone number so students could reach him *after hours*.

an/per hour — used in measurements that describe the speed of something • The speed limit is 65 miles *per hour*. • a fastball thrown at 88 miles *an hour*

hour·glass /ˈawɚˌglæs, *Brit* ˈawəˌglɑːs/ *noun, pl* **-glass·es** [*count*] : a device for measuring time ✧ An hourglass is a glass container with an upper part and a lower part connected by a narrow opening. The upper part contains sand which flows into the lower part in a specified amount of time (such as an hour).

– **hourglass** *adj, always used before a noun* • an *hourglass* shape

hour hand *noun, pl* ~ **hands** [*count*] : the short hand that marks the hours on a watch or clock — compare MINUTE HAND, SECOND HAND

hour·ly /ˈawɚli/ *adj*

1 : happening every hour • *hourly* bus service

2 a : paid for one hour of work • an *hourly* wage [=an amount paid for each hour of work] **b** : paid by the hour : earning an hourly wage • *hourly* workers

– **hourly** *adv* • The news was updated *hourly*. [=every hour]

[1]**house** /ˈhaʊs/ *noun, pl* **hous·es** /ˈhaʊzəz/

1 a [*count*] : a building in which a family lives • Would you like to come to my *house* for dinner? • a two-family *house* • I spent the weekend just puttering around the *house*. — often used before another noun • *house* pets/plants • a *house* guest • *house* parties **b** [*singular*] : the people who live in a house • He made enough noise to wake the whole *house*.

2 [*count*] **a** : a structure or shelter in which animals are kept — see also BIRDHOUSE, DOGHOUSE, HENHOUSE **b** : a building in which something is stored • a carriage *house* — see also BOATHOUSE, WAREHOUSE

3 [*count*] : a building where students or members of a religious group live • a fraternity *house*

4 a [*count*] : a group of people who meet to discuss and make the laws of a country • The bill has been approved by both *houses* of Congress. • The two *houses* of the U.S. Congress are the Senate [=the upper house] and the House of Representatives. [=the lower house] • The two *houses* of the British Parliament are the House of Lords [=the upper house] and the House of Commons. [=the lower house] **b** ***the House*** : HOUSE OF REPRESENTATIVES • They hope to win enough seats in the election to regain control of *the House*. — see also HOUSE OF COMMONS, HOUSE OF LORDS

5 [*count*] **a** : a specified kind of business • a publishing *house* • fashion *houses* • an investment banking *house* • a brokerage *house* **b** : a place or building where a specified kind of activity or entertainment occurs • an auction *house* • a ***house of God/worship*** [=a place, such as a church, where people go for religious services] • (*US*) a ***movie house*** [=a cinema, (*US*) a movie theater] : a place where an illegal activity occurs • a gambling *house* • a *house* of prostitution — see also OPERA HOUSE **c** : a particular kind of restaurant • We had dinner at the local fish *house*. • a seafood *house* • Oyster stew is a ***specialty of the house*** [=a special dish that is featured in a restaurant] ✧ A ***house wine*** is a basic wine that is always available in a restaurant. A ***house salad*** and a ***house (salad) dressing*** are the regular salad and dressing in a U.S. restaurant. • Would you like the *house salad* or a spinach salad? • The *house dressing* is a creamy vinaigrette. — see also COFFEEHOUSE, STEAK HOUSE

6 [*count*] : the audience in a theater or concert hall • They had a full/packed *house* on opening night. • When the movie ended, ***there wasn't a dry eye in the house***. [=everyone had tears in their eyes] ✧ To ***bring down the house*** or to ***bring the house down*** is to get great approval and applause or laughter from an audience. ▪ His performance *brought down the house* night after night.

7 *House* [*count*] **:** a royal or noble family including ancestors and all the people who are related to them ▪ the *House* of Tudor

8 [*noncount*] **:** a type of electronic dance music with a heavy, regular beat — called also *house music*

clean house *US* **1 :** to clean the floors, furniture, etc., inside a house ▪ He *cleans house* on Tuesdays. **2 :** to make important basic changes in an organization, business, etc., in order to correct problems ▪ After the corruption was revealed, the police chief decided it was time to *clean house*.

(from) house to house ✧ If you go *(from) house to house*, you go to each house or apartment in an area and do or ask for something. ▪ Volunteers went *from house to house* asking for donations. — see also HOUSE-TO-HOUSE

house in order ✧ To put/get/set (etc.) your *house in order* is to improve or correct the way you do things. ▪ We should *get our* (own) *house in order* before we criticize others for their mistakes. ▪ The company needs to *get its financial house in order*. [=to correct its financial problems]

keep house **:** to do the work that is needed to take care of a house ▪ When I started living on my own I had no idea how to cook or *keep house*. ▪ You need someone to *keep house* for you. — see also HOUSEKEEPER, HOUSEKEEPING

like a house on fire *informal* **:** extremely well ▪ Those two got on/along *like a house on fire*. [=they liked each other very much] ▪ (*US*) The business started out *like a house on fire*. [=the business started very successfully]

on the house **:** without charge **:** FREE ▪ The drinks are *on the house*.

people who live in glass houses shouldn't throw stones see [1]GLASS

play house ✧ When children *play house* they pretend that they are adults and that they are doing the things that adults do in a house, such as cooking and serving food. ▪ She always loved *playing house* with her little sister.

set up house **:** to become settled in a house where you are going to live ▪ They moved to California and *set up house* in a suburb of Los Angeles.

– house•ful /ˈhausˌful/ *noun, pl* **-fuls** [*count*] ▪ a *houseful* of guests

[2]**house** /ˈhauz/ *verb* **hous•es; housed; hous•ing** [+ *obj*]

1 : to provide shelter or a living space for (someone) ▪ More prisons are needed to *house* the growing number of inmates. — often used as *(be) housed* ▪ The soldiers *were housed* in poorly heated huts.

2 : to be a shelter for (something) **:** to store or contain (something) ▪ The museum *houses* an impressive collection of jewels. — often used as *(be) housed* ▪ The paintings *are* now *housed* in the National Gallery.

3 : to surround or enclose (something) in order to protect it ▪ The carpenter built casing to *house* the hot water pipes.

house arrest *noun* [*noncount*] *law* **:** the condition of being forced to stay in your home rather than in prison as a form of punishment — often used with *under* ▪ He was placed *under house arrest* until the trial.

house•boat /ˈhausˌbout/ *noun, pl* **-boats** [*count*] **:** a boat that is also used as a house

house•bound /ˈhausˌbaund/ *adj* **:** unable to leave your home ▪ She has been *housebound* since she fell.

house•break /ˈhausˌbreɪk/ *verb* **-breaks; -broke** /-ˌbrouk/; **-bro•ken** /-ˌbroukən/; **-break•ing** [+ *obj*] *US* **:** to train (an animal) to urinate or defecate outside the home or in an acceptable place indoors ▪ She's trying to *housebreak* [=(*chiefly Brit*) *house-train*] a puppy.

house•break•ing /ˈhausˌbreɪkɪŋ/ *noun* [*noncount*] **:** the act of forcefully entering someone's house in order to commit a crime (such as robbery)

– house•break•er /ˈhausˌbreɪkɚ/ *noun, pl* **-ers** [*count*]

housebroken *adj, US, of an animal* **:** trained to urinate or defecate outside the home or in an acceptable place indoors ▪ Pigs are said to make very good pets once they are *housebroken*. [=(*chiefly Brit*) *house-trained*]

house call *noun, pl* **~ calls** [*count*] *chiefly US* **:** a visit by a doctor to someone's house ▪ Does your doctor make *house calls*?

house cat *noun, pl* **~ cats** [*count*] **:** a cat that is kept as a pet

house•clean•ing /ˈhausˌkliːnɪŋ/ *noun* [*singular*] **:** the act or activity of cleaning the inside of a house or apartment and its furniture, appliances, etc. ▪ We gave the place a thorough *housecleaning*.

house•coat /ˈhausˌkout/ *noun, pl* **-coats** [*count*] **:** an informal and often long and loose piece of clothing that is worn by a woman at home

house•dress /ˈhausˌdres/ *noun, pl* **-dress•es** [*count*] *chiefly US* **:** an informal dress that is usually worn only while cleaning or doing other housework

house•fly /ˈhausˌflaɪ/ *noun, pl* **-flies** [*count*] **:** a common fly that lives in or near people's houses — see color picture on page C10

house•guest /ˈhausˌgest/ *noun, pl* **-guests** [*count*] **:** a person who visits and usually stays in someone's home overnight ▪ We have *houseguests* this weekend.

[1]**house•hold** /ˈhausˌhould/ *noun, pl* **-holds** [*count*] **:** the people in a family or other group that are living together in one house ▪ At that time, not many *households* had telephones. ▪ This form should be filled out by the ***head of the household***. [=the person in the house who is responsible for making decisions and earning money]

[2]**household** *adj, always used before a noun*

1 : of or relating to a house or to the people living in a house ▪ *household* appliances/chores

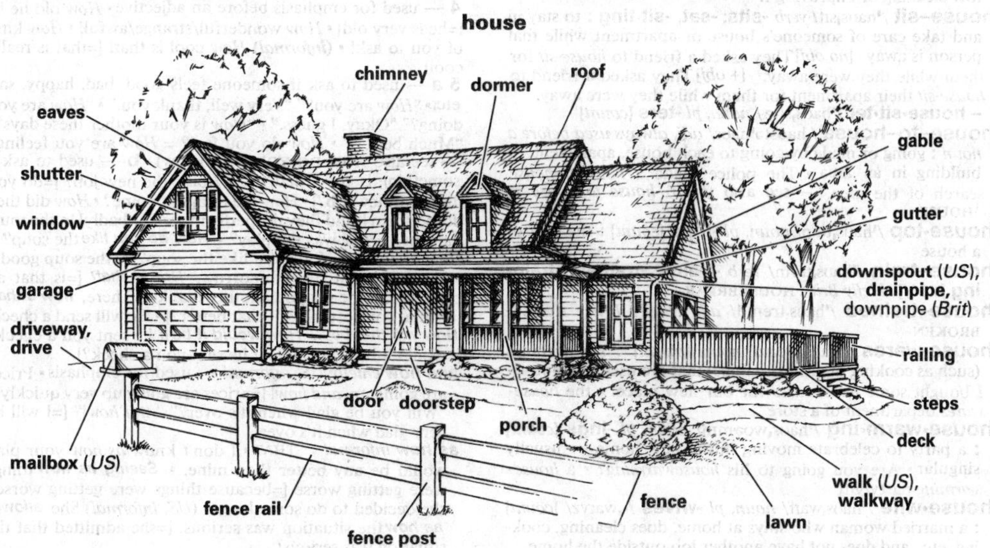

2 : known to many people : familiar or common • a famous actor who has become a ***household name*** [=a person or thing whose name is very well-known]

house·hold·er /ˈhaʊsˌhoʊldɚ/ *noun, pl* **-ers** [*count*] *chiefly Brit, formal* : someone who lives in a house, apartment, etc.

house·hus·band /ˈhaʊsˌhʌzbənd/ *noun, pl* **-bands** [*count*] : a married man who stays at home, does cleaning, cooking, etc., and does not have another job outside the home

house·keep·er /ˈhaʊsˌkiːpɚ/ *noun, pl* **-ers** [*count*] : a person whose job is to manage the cooking, cleaning, etc., in a house

house·keep·ing /ˈhaʊsˌkiːpɪŋ/ *noun* [*noncount*]

1 : the work (such as cooking and cleaning) that is done in a house : HOUSEWORK • Who does your *housekeeping*? • *housekeeping* expenses

2 : the things that must be done regularly to keep something working properly • We took the computer offline to do some basic *housekeeping*.

house·maid /ˈhaʊsˌmeɪd/ *noun, pl* **-maids** [*count*] *chiefly Brit, old-fashioned* : a female servant who does cleaning, laundry, etc.

house·mate /ˈhaʊsˌmeɪt/ *noun, pl* **-mates** [*count*] : a person who lives in the same house with another person but is not a part of that person's family • In college, she lived in a house off campus with five *housemates*. • The TV belongs to my *housemate*.

H

house music *noun* [*noncount*] : HOUSE 8

house of cards *noun, pl* **houses of cards** [*count*] : a structure built by balancing playing cards on top of each other — often used figuratively to describe something (such as a plan) that is weak and can fail easily • Her elaborate scheme collapsed like a *house of cards*.

House of Commons *noun*

the House of Commons : the part of the British or Canadian Parliament whose members are elected by voters

House of Lords *noun*

the House of Lords : the part of the British Parliament whose members are not elected by voters

House of Representatives *noun*

the House of Representatives : the larger part of the U.S. Congress or of the Parliament of Australia or New Zealand — compare SENATE

house·paint·er /ˈhaʊsˌpeɪntɚ/ *noun, pl* **-ers** [*count*] : a person whose job is painting houses

house party *noun, pl* **~ -ties** [*count*] : a large party at someone's house that usually lasts for several days

house·plant /ˈhaʊsˌplænt, *Brit* ˈhaʊsˌplɑːnt/ *noun, pl* **-plants** [*count*] : a plant that is grown or kept indoors — see color picture on page C6

house–proud /ˈhaʊsˌpraʊd/ *adj* [*more ~; most ~*] *chiefly Brit* : proud of your house because you spend time and effort cleaning or improving it

house–sit /ˈhaʊsˌsɪt/ *verb* **-sits**; **-sat**; **-sit·ting** : to stay in and take care of someone's house or apartment while that person is away [*no obj*] They asked a friend to *house-sit* for them while they were away. [+ *obj*] They asked a friend to *house-sit* their apartment for them while they were away.
– **house·sit·ter** /ˈhaʊsˌsɪtɚ/ *noun, pl* **-ters** [*count*]

house–to–house /ˌhaʊstəˈhaʊs/ *adj, always used before a noun* : going or made by going to each house, apartment, or building in an area • The police made a *house-to-house* search of the area. — see also *(from) house to house* at [1]HOUSE

house·top /ˈhaʊsˌtɑːp/ *noun, pl* **-tops** [*count*] : the roof of a house

house–train /ˈhaʊsˌtreɪn/ *verb* **-trains**; **-trained**; **-train·ing** [+ *obj*] *chiefly Brit* : HOUSEBREAK

house–trained /ˈhaʊsˌtreɪnd/ *adj, chiefly Brit* : HOUSEBROKEN

house·wares /ˈhaʊsˌweɚz/ *noun* [*plural*] : small things (such as cooking utensils or lamps) that are used in a house • I bought some *housewares* for our new place. • the *housewares* department of a store

house·warm·ing /ˈhaʊsˌwoɚmɪŋ/ *noun, pl* **-ings** [*count*] : a party to celebrate moving into a new home — usually singular • Are you going to his *housewarming*? • a *housewarming* party/gift

house·wife /ˈhaʊsˌwaɪf/ *noun, pl* **-wives** /-ˌwaɪvz/ [*count*] : a married woman who stays at home, does cleaning, cooking, etc., and does not have another job outside the home

house·work /ˈhaʊsˌwɚk/ *noun* [*noncount*] : work (such as cleaning, cooking, or laundry) that is done to keep a house clean and running properly • I got up early and did some *housework*.

hous·ing /ˈhaʊzɪŋ/ *noun, pl* **-ings**

1 [*noncount*] : the houses, apartments, etc., in which people live • The cost of *housing* continued to rise. • The state should provide more/better *housing* for poor people. [=should provide poor people with more/better places to live] • low-income *housing* • *housing* costs — see also SOCIAL HOUSING

2 [*count*] : something that covers or protects something else (such as a mechanical part) • I had to remove the *housing* to inspect the vent.

housing development *noun, pl* **~ -ments** [*count*] *US* : a group of houses that are built near each other and sold or rented by one owner — called also *(Brit) housing estate*

housing project *noun, pl* **~ -jects** [*count*] *US* : a group of houses or apartments that are built for poor people — called also *(US) project*

hove *past tense and past participle of* [1]HEAVE

hov·el /ˈhʌvəl, ˈhɑːvəl/ *noun, pl* **-els** [*count*] : a small, poorly built and often dirty house

hov·er /ˈhʌvɚ, *Brit* ˈhɒvə/ *verb* **-ers**; **-ered**; **-er·ing** [*no obj*]

1 : to float in the air without moving in any direction • Watch as the hummingbird *hovers* over the flowers. • Helicopters *hovered* above us. • Bees *hovered* around the hive.

2 : to stay very close to a person or place • Waiters *hovered* near our table. • nervous mothers *hovering* over their children

3 *always followed by an adverb or preposition* **a** : to stay near a specified point or level • Unemployment rates were *hovering* around 10 percent. • Temperatures will continue to *hover* around freezing. **b** : to be or remain in a specified state or condition • The patient was *hovering* between life and death. • The country *hovers* on the brink of famine.

hov·er·craft /ˈhʌvɚˌkræft, *Brit* ˈhɒvəˌkrɑːft/ *noun, pl* **-craft** [*count*] : a vehicle that moves just above the surface of land or water on a cushion of air

[1]**how** /ˈhaʊ/ *adv*

1 : in what manner or way • *How* and where did you meet him? • *How* shall I address the President? • *How* will we pay for the trip? : by what means • "*How* did you get here?" "By bus." • "*How* did she die?" "She had cancer." • *How* do you know that? • *How* did you find us? • *How* could you have known?

2 : for what reason : WHY • *How* did you happen to move here? • "Is it going to rain?" "***How should/would I know?***" [=I don't know]

3 : to what degree, extent, or amount — used before an adjective or adverb • *How* handsome is he? • *How* much longer do we have to wait? = *How* much longer is the wait? • I don't know *how* good the service is at the new restaurant. • I'm not sure *how* old he is. • It's a pity *how* rarely we see each other.

4 — used for emphasis before an adjective • *How* old he is! [=he is very old] • *How* wonderful/strange/awful! • *How* kind of you to ask! • (*informal*) *How* cool is that! [=that is really cool]

5 a — used to ask if someone feels good, bad, happy, sad, etc. • "*How* are you?" "Very well, thank you." • "*How* are you doing?" "Okay, I guess." • "*How* is your mother these days?" "Much better." • *How* do you feel? = *How* are you feeling? — see also HOW DO YOU DO (below) **b** — used to ask if something is good, bad, etc. • *How's* the new job? [=do you like your new job?] • *How* are things at home? • *How* did they do/perform [=did they do/perform well or badly] in the tournament? • *How* was the play? • ***How do you like*** the soup? = *How* is the soup? [=do you like the soup?; is the soup good?] • I can bring it over tomorrow. ***How's that?*** [=is that all right?] • Let me get you another blanket. There, ***how's that?*** [=is that comfortable?; is that better?] • He will send a check. ***How will that be?*** = ***How would it be*** if he sent you a check? [=would it be acceptable if he sent you a check?]

and how *chiefly US, informal* — used for emphasis • Prices are going up, *and how*! [=prices are going up very quickly] • "Will you be glad when it's over?" "*And how*!" [=I will be very glad when it's over]

as how *informal* : [2]THAT • I don't know *as how* your plan would be any better than mine. • ***Seeing as how*** things were getting worse [=because things were getting worse], she decided to do something. • (*US, informal*) She ***allowed as how*** the situation was serious. [=she admitted that the situation was serious]

how about **1 :** does that include (someone) : what about • "We're all going to the beach." "*How about* Kenny?" **2** *informal* **a** — used to show that you are very impressed by someone or something • He won again! *How about* that guy! [=isn't that guy amazing/impressive?] **b** ***how about that*** *chiefly US* — used to show that you are surprised or pleased by something • He won again! *How about that*! [=what good news!; isn't that great?] **3** *also US (informal)* ***how's about*** **a** — used to make a suggestion about what could be done • We'll need to talk about this again. *How about* (meeting) next month? • *How about* [=*what about*] driving to the coast for the weekend? • *How about* another game? [=would you like to play another game?] • What should we do tonight? *How about* (seeing) a movie? • *How's about* some more pie? **b** — used to ask someone to give you something • *How about* a couple of dollars until payday? [=can you loan me a couple of dollars until payday?] • *How's about* (offering me) a drink? **c** — used to ask if someone will do something • Well, ***how about it***, are you coming? **4** — used to ask someone to tell you something in response to what you have just said • I like skiing and hiking. ***How about you?*** [=what sports do you like?] • I'm ready to go. *How about you?* [=are you ready, too?]

how can/could **1** — used to show you think that someone has done or said something shocking or wrong • "We don't need his help anyway." "*How can* you say that?!" [=it is very wrong of you to say that] • *How could* she just walk away from her children like that? **2** — used to express doubt that something will happen, is possible, etc. • *How could* I (ever/possibly) leave this job? • *How can* I (ever/possibly) thank you? [=I can never thank you enough; I am extremely grateful to you] **3** ***how could you*** *informal* — used to show disappointment in someone's actions, thoughts, words, etc. • You threw away my gift? Oh, *how could you*?

how come *chiefly US, informal* — used to ask why something has happened, is true, etc. • "He said he's not going." "*How come*?" [=why isn't he going?] • *How come* you're here so early? [=why are you here so early?] • *How come* no one told me?

how dare you see [1]DARE

how do you do *formal* : HELLO — used especially when you are first introduced to someone • *How do you do*, Miss Smith?

how do you like that — used for emphasis or to show surprise or disapproval • He's moving to Hawaii? Well, *how do you like that*! [=that's a surprise] • She canceled at the last minute. *How do you like that*?

how goes it? see [1]GO

how's everything (going) see EVERYTHING

how so : in what way : why do you think that • "This room looks different." "*How so*?" [=in what way does it look different?]

how's that (again) *informal* : WHAT — used to request that something be repeated or explained again • *How's that*? [=what did you say?] I didn't hear you. • I don't understand. *How's that again*?

how's that for *informal* — used for emphasis to describe someone or something you think is very impressive • He won first prize! *How's that for* a guy who almost didn't enter the contest at all! • They took care of everything for us. *How's that for* hospitality? [=that was very hospitable]

how will/would — used to express doubt that something will happen or is possible • *How will* we (ever) get everything done on time? • *How would* he manage without her? [=I don't know if he will be able to manage without her; I doubt he will manage without her]

[2]**how** *conj*

1 : in what manner or way • We asked *how* we could help. • Let me tell you *how* we'll pay for the trip. • The book tells the story of *how* the company was founded. • She explained *how* she came to live here. • I don't know *how* the service is at the new restaurant. • I remember *how* they fought. • It's strange *how* [=the way that] things happen. • Be careful *how* you talk; you could get fired. • And that's ***how it is***. [=that is the state of the situation] • They want to know ***how you're doing***. [=if you are happy, successful, etc.]

2 : THAT • She told us *how* she had to work hard. • He knows *how* you are a valued employee. • It's amazing *how* they completed the bridge so quickly.

3 : in whatever way : HOWEVER • He'll cook it *how* you like it.

how'd /ˈhaud/ — used as a contraction of *how would* or *how did* • *How'd* [=how did] you like your meal? • *How'd* [=how would] you like to go to the beach?

how·dy /ˈhaudi/ *interj, US* — used as an informal greeting • *Howdy*, folks.

[1]**how·ev·er** /hauˈɛvɚ/ *adv*

1 — used when you are saying something that is different from or contrasts with a previous statement • I'd like to go; *however*, I'd better not. [=I'd like to go, but I should not] • The forecast is bad. It's possible, *however*, that conditions could improve. • Sales are up this quarter. *However*, expenses have increased as well.

2 : to whatever degree or extent : no matter how — used before an adjective or adverb • *However* many people come [=whether a few people or many people come], we'll be ready. • She couldn't convince him, *however* hard [=no matter how hard] she tried.

3 — used as a more forceful way of saying *how* • *However* did you do that? [=how did you ever do that?]

[2]**however** *conj* : in whatever manner or way • Do it *however* you like. • I will help *however* I can.

how·it·zer /ˈhawətsɚ/ *noun, pl* **-zers** [*count*] : a large gun that is used to fire shells high into the air for a short distance

howl /ˈhawəl/ *verb* **howls; howled; howl·ing**

1 [*no obj*] *of a dog, wolf, etc.* : to make a long, loud cry that sounds sad • The dogs were *howling* at the moon.

2 [*no obj*] *of the wind* : to make a long, loud sound • The wind was *howling*.

3 [*no obj*] : to cry out loudly in pain, anger, amusement, etc. • He *howled* in agony. • The audience ***howled with laughter***. [=the audience laughed very loudly]

4 : to say something in a loud and angry way [+ *obj*] "I can't take it!" she *howled*. = She *howled* that she couldn't take it. [*no obj*] Activists are *howling* (in protest) over the court's decision. • protesters *howling* for change

– howl *noun, pl* **howls** [*count*] • We heard the dog's *howls*. • He let out a *howl* of protest. • *howls* of laughter

howl·er /ˈhaulɚ/ *noun, pl* **-ers** [*count*] *informal* : a stupid but funny mistake or error • The article was full of *howlers*.

howling /ˈhaulɪŋ/ *adj, always used before a noun*

1 : producing the long, low sound made by strong wind • a *howling* storm

2 *informal* : very great • The movie was a *howling* success.

how's /ˈhauz/ — used as a contraction of *how is* • *How's* your meal? • *How's* she doing?

[1]**how·so·ev·er** /ˌhausəˈwɛvɚ/ *adv, formal* : [1]HOWEVER

[2]**howsoever** *conj, formal* : [2]HOWEVER

[1]**how–to** /ˈhauˈtuː/ *adj, always used before a noun, chiefly US* : giving practical instruction or advice on how to do something yourself • *how-to* books on starting your own business

[2]**how–to** *noun, pl* **-tos** [*count*] *chiefly US* : a way of doing something yourself : instruction about how to do something • the *how-tos* of balancing a checkbook

hp *abbr* horsepower • a 200 *hp* engine

HQ *abbr* headquarters • Check in at camp *HQ* by 8:00.

hr *abbr* hour • a 35-*hr* work week

HR *abbr, US* **1** home run; home runs • He had three *HR* in the first game.

2 human resources • Talk to *HR* about benefits.

3 House of Representatives — used in the names of laws being voted on in the House of Representatives • Voting on *HR* 1740 will start next week.

HRH *abbr* Her Royal Highness; His Royal Highness

HS *abbr* high school • Springfield *HS*

ht. *abbr* height

HTML /ˌeɪʧˌtiːˌɛmˈɛl/ *noun* [*noncount*] : a computer language that is used to create documents or Web sites on the Internet • Do you know *HTML*?

http *abbr* hypertext transfer protocol; hypertext transport protocol — used in Internet addresses • *http://*www.Merriam-Webster.com

H_2O /ˌeɪʧˌtuːˈoʊ/ *technical* — the chemical symbol for water • two parts H_2O

hub /ˈhʌb/ *noun, pl* **hubs** [*count*]

1 : the central and most active part or place • the *hub* of the city • The island is a major tourist *hub*. [=a place where many tourists go] • She was at the *hub* of all the activity.

2 : the airport or the city through which an airline sends most of its flights • All of the airline's coast-to-coast flights pass through its *hub*.

3 : the center of a wheel, propeller, fan, etc. • The spokes attach to the *hub* of the wheel.

H

hub·bub /ˈhʌ̦bʌb/ *noun* [*noncount*]
1 : a loud mixture of sound or voices ▪ All the *hubbub* in the airport made it hard to hear the flight announcements.
2 : a situation in which there is much noise, confusion, excitement, and activity ▪ the *hubbub* surrounding the film star ▪ We went to the country to escape the *hubbub* of the city. ▪ What's all the *hubbub* about?

hub·by /ˈhʌbi/ *noun, pl* **-bies** [*count*] *informal* **:** HUSBAND

hub·cap /ˈhʌb̦kæp/ *noun, pl* **-caps** [*count*] **:** a removable plastic or metal cover on the center of a car or truck wheel — see picture at CAR

hu·bris /ˈhjuːbrəs/ *noun* [*noncount*] *formal + literary* **:** a great or foolish amount of pride or confidence ▪ His failure was brought on by his *hubris*.

huck·ster /ˈhʌkstɚ/ *noun, pl* **-sters** [*count*] *US, disapproving* **:** someone who sells or advertises something in an aggressive, dishonest, or annoying way

HUD /ˈhʌd/ *abbr, US* (Department of) Housing and Urban Development ▪ an official at *HUD* ✧ The Department of Housing and Urban Development is a part of the U.S. federal government that is responsible for policies that relate to providing housing for U.S. citizens.

¹hud·dle /ˈhʌdl/ *verb* **hud·dles; hud·dled; hud·dling** [*no obj*]
1 *always followed by an adverb or preposition* **:** to come close together in a group ▪ People were *huddling* (together) in doorways to get out of the rain. ▪ We *huddled* around the campfire. ▪ The sheep *huddled* together for warmth. ▪ "Give me your tired, your poor, your *huddled* masses yearning to breathe free . . ." —Emma Lazarus, "The New Colossus" (1883)
2 *always followed by an adverb or preposition* **:** to sit or lie in a curled or bent position ▪ The students *huddled* over their desks.
3 a : to come together to talk about something privately ▪ Union representatives are *huddling* to discuss the proposal. **b** *American football* **:** to gather in a huddle — often + *up* ▪ The players *huddled up*.

²huddle *noun, pl* **huddles** [*count*]
1 : a group of people or things that are close to each other ▪ sheep standing in a *huddle*
2 a : a private discussion or meeting ▪ The boss is in a *huddle* with the marketing director **b** *American football* **:** a group of players who have gathered away from the line of scrimmage for a short time to hear instructions for the next play ▪ The quarterback called the offense into a *huddle*.

hue /ˈhjuː/ *noun, pl* **hues** [*count*]
1 : a color or a shade of a color ▪ We decorated the room in *hues* of blue and green.
2 : kind or type ▪ politicians of every *hue* [=of every kind]

hue and cry *noun* [*singular*] **:** an angry protest about something ▪ There was a *hue and cry* in opposition to the film.

hued /ˈhjuːd/ *adj* **:** having a specified type of color ▪ brightly/richly *hued* [=*colored*] cloth ▪ *green-*hued

¹huff /ˈhʌf/ *verb* **huffs; huffed; huff·ing** [+ *obj*] **:** to say (something) in a way that shows you are annoyed or angry ▪ "The project is a complete waste of time," she *huffed*.
huff and puff **1 :** to breathe in a loud and heavy way because of physical effort ▪ He was *huffing and puffing* when he got to the top of the stairs. **2 :** to show you are annoyed or angry ▪ She'll *huff and puff* for a while, but she'll calm down later.

²huff *noun*
in a huff **:** in an angry or annoyed state ▪ They argued and she left *in a huff*. ▪ When he didn't get the promotion, he quit his job *in a huff*. [=he got angry and suddenly quit his job]

huffy /ˈhʌfi/ *adj* **huff·i·er; -est** *informal* **:** angry or annoyed ▪ Now, don't ***get huffy***—I was only teasing.
– huff·i·ly /ˈhʌfəli/ *adv* ▪ He *huffily* refused to answer.

¹hug /ˈhʌg/ *verb* **hugs; hugged; hug·ging**
1 : to put your arms around someone especially as a way of showing love or friendship [+ *obj*] I *hugged* him close. ▪ She *hugged* her daughter. [*no obj*] We *hugged* briefly, and then it was time to say goodbye.
2 [+ *obj*] **:** to hold (something) tightly with your arms ▪ I *hugged* my knees to my chest.
3 [+ *obj*] **:** to stay close to (something) ▪ The road *hugs* the river. ▪ The boat *hugged* the shore. ▪ body-*hugging* clothing [=clothes that are tight]
– hug·ga·ble /ˈhʌgəbəl/ *adj* [*more ~; most ~*] ▪ a cute, *huggable* puppy

²hug *noun, pl* **hugs** [*count*] **:** the act of putting your arms around someone or something as a way of showing love or friendship ▪ *hugs* and kisses ▪ He gave me a big *hug*. [=he hugged me]

huge /ˈhjuːʤ/ *adj* **:** very large **:** very great in size, amount, or degree ▪ a *huge* building/truck/garden ▪ The crowds were *huge*. ▪ Renovating the house is a *huge* undertaking. ▪ The store is having a *huge* sale tomorrow. ▪ The presentation was a *huge* success. [=the presentation was very successful]
– huge·ly *adv* ▪ a *hugely* popular movie

huh /ˈhʌ/ *interj, informal*
1 *chiefly US* — used at the end of a statement to ask whether someone agrees with you ▪ It's pretty good, *huh*?
2 — used when you have not heard or understood something that was said ▪ "His name is Cholmondely." "*Huh*?" [=*what*?]
3 — used to show surprise, disbelief, or disapproval ▪ "His wife left him." "*Huh*! I thought they had a happy marriage."

hu·la /ˈhuːlə/ *noun, pl* **-las** [*singular*] **:** a Hawaiian dance that has flowing hand and hip movements

Hula–Hoop /ˈhuːlə̦huːp/ *trademark* — used for a plastic hoop that is twirled around your body by moving your hips

hulk /ˈhʌlk/ *noun, pl* **hulks** [*count*]
1 : the main part of something (such as a ship, car, or building) that has been ruined and is no longer used ▪ The ship's rusting *hulk* is still visible on the rocks. ▪ the burned out *hulk* of the factory
2 *informal* **:** a large person ▪ He's a (great) *hulk of* a man. [=he's a very large man]

hulk·ing /ˈhʌlkɪŋ/ *adj, always used before a noun* **:** very large or heavy ▪ A *hulking* figure appeared in the doorway. ▪ *hulking* buildings

¹hull /ˈhʌl/ *noun, pl* **hulls** [*count*]
1 : the main part of a ship or boat **:** the deck, sides, and bottom of a ship or boat — see picture at BOAT
2 : the outer covering of a fruit, grain, or seed ▪ sesame seed *hulls*

²hull *verb* **hulls; hulled; hull·ing** [+ *obj*] **:** to remove the outer covering of (a fruit or seed) ▪ *hulling* seeds

hul·la·ba·loo /ˈhʌləbə̦luː/ *noun, informal*
1 : a very noisy and confused situation [*singular*] The announcement caused quite a *hullabaloo*. [*noncount*] The announcement caused a lot of *hullabaloo*.
2 : a situation in which many people are upset and angry about something [*singular*] There was a *hullabaloo* over his controversial statements. [*noncount*] There was a lot of *hullabaloo* over his controversial statements.

hum /ˈhʌm/ *verb* **hums; hummed; hum·ming**
1 [*no obj*] **:** to make a low continuous sound ▪ The garden was *humming* with bees. ▪ The refrigerator *hummed* in the background.
2 : to sing the notes of a song while keeping your lips closed [*no obj*] I was *humming* to myself. ▪ We *hummed* along to the music. [+ *obj*] Can you *hum* the tune for me? = Can you *hum* me the tune? ▪ I *hummed* a little song.
3 [*no obj*] **:** to be very active or busy ▪ By noon, the office was really *humming*. ▪ The restaurant *hums* on weekends.
– hum *noun* [*singular*] ▪ the *hum* of insects ▪ We could hear the *hum* of conversation from the next room.

¹hu·man /ˈhjuːmən/ *adj*
1 : of, relating to, or affecting people ▪ the *human* body ▪ the *human* brain ▪ *human* suffering ▪ problems that have occurred throughout *human* history ▪ The accident was blamed on ***human error***. [=the accident was blamed on a person's mistake rather than on the failure of a machine] ▪ a story that has ***human interest*** = a ***human-interest*** story [=a story that is appealing because it involves the experiences of real people] ▪ The need to be loved is simply part of ***the human condition***. [=part of being a person] ▪ an area where ancient ***human remains*** [=parts of the bodies of dead people] have been found
2 [*more ~; most ~*] **a :** typical of people ▪ a *human* failing/weakness ▪ *human* kindness ▪ *human* emotions ▪ His desire for revenge was very *human*. [=was very typical of the way people are] **b** [*more ~; most ~*] **:** having good or bad qualities that people usually have ▪ She is a very kind and *human* person. ▪ I once thought that he was perfect, but now I know that he's all too *human*. [=that he has the same problems, weaknesses, etc., that other people have] ✧ If you say that someone is ***only human***, you are saying that the mistakes someone has made could have been made by anyone. ▪ We do the best we can, but we're *only human*. **c :** looking or

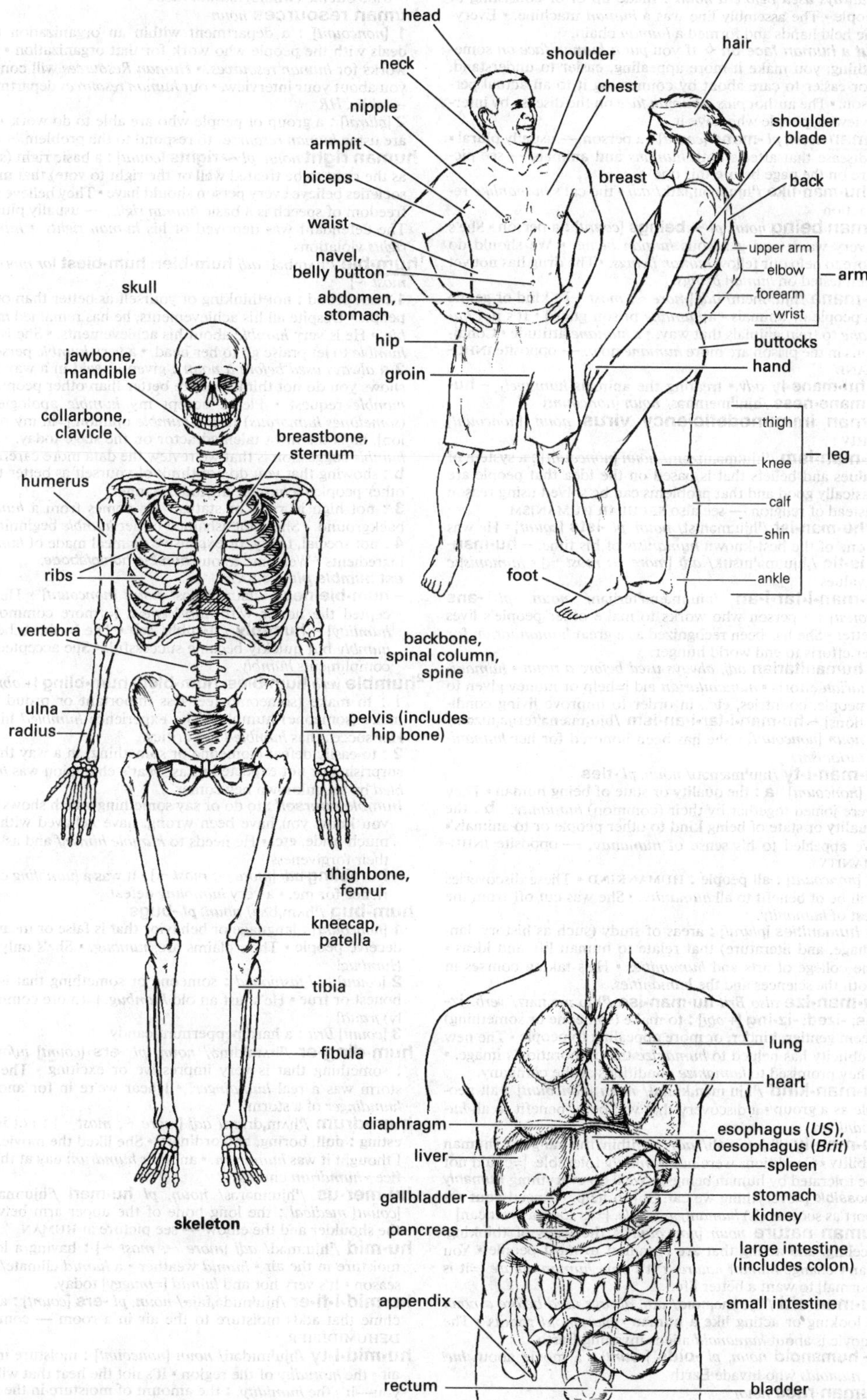
human
head
neck
nipple
armpit
biceps
waist
navel,
belly button
abdomen,
stomach
hip
groin
foot
hair
shoulder
chest
shoulder
blade
breast
back
upper arm
elbow
arm
forearm
wrist
buttocks
hand
thigh
leg
knee
calf
shin
ankle
skull
jawbone,
mandible
collarbone,
clavicle
breastbone,
sternum
humerus
ribs
vertebra
backbone,
spinal column,
spine
ulna
radius
pelvis (includes
hip bone)
thighbone,
femur
kneecap,
patella
tibia
fibula
skeleton
lung
heart
diaphragm
esophagus (*US*),
oesophagus (*Brit*)
liver
spleen
gallbladder
stomach
kidney
pancreas
large intestine
(includes colon)
appendix
small intestine
rectum
bladder

acting like a person ▪ The dog's expression was almost *human.* — compare INHUMAN
3 *always used before a noun* **: made up of or consisting of people** ▪ The assembly line was a *human* machine. ▪ Everyone held hands and formed a *human* chain.
put a human face on ✧ **If you *put a human face on* something, you make it more appealing, easier to understand, or easier to care about by connecting it to an actual person.** ▪ The author *puts a human face* on the disease by interviewing people who have it.

[2]**human** *noun, pl* **-mans** [*count*] **: a person — usually plural** ▪ a disease that affects both *humans* and animals — see picture on the page before this one
– **hu•man•like** /ˈhjuːmənˌlaɪk/ *adj* ▪ the cat's *humanlike* reaction

human being *noun, pl* ~ **beings** [*count*] **: a person** ▪ She's a very warm and generous *human being.* ▪ We should do more to help our fellow *human beings.* ▪ The drug has not yet been tested on *human beings.*

hu•mane /hjuːˈmeɪn/ *adj* [*more* ~; *most* ~] **: kind or gentle to people or animals** ▪ a *humane* prison guard ▪ It's not *humane* to treat animals that way. ▪ a *humane* attitude ▪ Conditions in the prison are more *humane* now. — opposite INHUMANE
– **hu•mane•ly** *adv* ▪ treating the animals *humanely* – **hu•mane•ness** /hjuːˈmeɪnnəs/ *noun* [*noncount*]

H

human immunodeficiency virus *noun* [*noncount*] **:** HIV

hu•man•ism /ˈhjuːməˌnɪzəm/ *noun* [*noncount*] **: a system of values and beliefs that is based on the idea that people are basically good and that problems can be solved using reason instead of religion** — see also SECULAR HUMANISM
– **hu•man•ist** /ˈhjuːmənɪst/ *noun, pl* **-ists** [*count*] ▪ He was one of the best-known *humanists* of his time. – **hu•man•is•tic** /ˌhjuːməˈnɪstɪk/ *adj* [*more* ~; *most* ~] ▪ *humanistic* values

hu•man•i•tar•i•an /hjuˌmænəˈterijən/ *noun, pl* **-ans** [*count*] **: a person who works to make other people's lives better** ▪ She has been recognized as a great *humanitarian* for her efforts to end world hunger.
– **humanitarian** *adj, always used before a noun* ▪ *humanitarian* efforts ▪ *humanitarian* aid [=help or money given to people, countries, etc., in order to improve living conditions] – **hu•man•i•tar•i•an•ism** /hjuˌmænəˈterijəˌnɪzəm/ *noun* [*noncount*] ▪ She has been honored for her *humanitarianism.*

hu•man•i•ty /hjuˈmænəti/ *noun, pl* **-ties**
1 [*noncount*] **a : the quality or state of being human** ▪ They were joined together by their (common) *humanity.* **b : the quality or state of being kind to other people or to animals** ▪ We appealed to his sense of *humanity.* — opposite INHUMANITY
2 [*noncount*] **: all people :** HUMANKIND ▪ These discoveries will be of benefit to all *humanity.* ▪ She was cut off from the rest of *humanity.*
3 ***humanities*** [*plural*] **: areas of study (such as history, language, and literature) that relate to human life and ideas** ▪ the college of arts and *humanities* ▪ He's taking courses in both the sciences and the *humanities.*

hu•man•ize *also Brit* **hu•man•ise** /ˈhjuːməˌnaɪz/ *verb* **-iz•es; -ized; -iz•ing** [+ *obj*] **: to make (someone or something) seem gentler, kinder, or more appealing to people** ▪ The new publicity has helped to *humanize* the corporation's image. ▪ They promised to *humanize* conditions at the company.

hu•man•kind /ˈhjuːmənˌkaɪnd/ *noun* [*noncount*] **: all people as a group** ▪ a discovery that will be of benefit to all *humankind*

hu•man•ly /ˈhjuːmənli/ *adv* **: within the range of human ability** ▪ Conditions were not *humanly* tolerable. [=could not be tolerated by human beings] ▪ We'll do everything ***humanly possible*** [=everything we can do] to help. ▪ I need your report as soon as (is) *humanly possible.* [=as soon as you can]

human nature *noun* [*noncount*] **: the ways of thinking, feeling, and acting that are common to most people** ▪ You can't change *human nature.* ▪ It's only *human nature* [=it is normal] to want a better life.

hu•man•oid /ˈhjuːməˌnoɪd/ *adj, always used before a noun* **: looking or acting like a human** ▪ *humanoid* robots ▪ The movie is about *humanoid* aliens invading Earth.
– **humanoid** *noun, pl* **-oids** [*count*] ▪ a movie about *humanoids* who invade Earth

human race *noun*
the human race **: all people : human beings as a group** ▪ the history of *the human race* ▪ destructive weapons that could wipe out *the* (whole) *human race*

human resources *noun*
1 [*noncount*] **: a department within an organization that deals with the people who work for that organization** ▪ She works for *human resources.* ▪ *Human Resources* will contact you about your interview. ▪ our *human resources* department — abbr. *HR*
2 [*plural*] **: a group of people who are able to do work** ▪ We are using *human resources* to respond to the problem.

human right *noun, pl* ~ **rights** [*count*] **: a basic right (such as the right to be treated well or the right to vote) that many societies believe every person should have** ▪ They believe that freedom of speech is a basic *human right.* — usually plural ▪ The defendant was deprived of his *human rights.* ▪ *human rights* violations

[1]**hum•ble** /ˈhʌmbəl/ *adj* **hum•bler; hum•blest** [*or more* ~; *most* ~]
1 : not proud : not thinking of yourself as better than other people ▪ Despite all his achievements, he has remained *humble.* ▪ He is very *humble* about his achievements. ▪ She is too *humble* to let praise go to her head. ▪ a very *humble* person
2 a *always used before a noun* **: given or said in a way that shows you do not think you are better than other people** ▪ a *humble* request ▪ Please accept my *humble* apologies. ▪ (*sometimes humorous*) In my *humble* opinion [=in my opinion], he is the most talented actor on the stage today. ▪ Her *humble* suggestion is that we review the data more carefully. **b : showing that you do not think of yourself as better than other people** ▪ a *humble* attitude/manner
3 : not high in rank or status ▪ He comes from a *humble* background. ▪ She's not ashamed of her *humble* beginnings.
4 : not special, fancy, or expensive ▪ a meal made of *humble* ingredients ▪ Welcome to our ***humble home/abode.***
eat humble pie see EAT
– **hum•ble•ness** /ˈhʌmbəlnəs/ *noun* [*noncount*] ▪ He accepted the honor with *humbleness.* [=(more commonly) *humility*] – **hum•bly** /ˈhʌmbli/ *adv* ▪ The business began *humbly* but quickly became successful. ▪ She accepted his compliments *humbly.*

[2]**humble** *verb* **hum•bles; hum•bled; hum•bling** [+ *obj*]
1 : to make (someone) feel less important or proud : to make (someone) humble ▪ The experience *humbled* him. ▪ Her success has *humbled* her critics.
2 : to easily defeat (someone or something) in a way that is surprising or not expected ▪ Last year's champion was *humbled* by an unknown newcomer.
humble yourself **: to do or say something which shows that you know you have been wrong, have behaved with too much pride, etc.** ▪ He needs to *humble himself* and ask for their forgiveness.
– **humbling** *adj* [*more* ~; *most* ~] ▪ It was a *humbling* experience for me. ▪ a very *humbling* defeat

hum•bug /ˈhʌmˌbʌg/ *noun, pl* **-bugs**
1 [*noncount*] **: language or behavior that is false or meant to deceive people** ▪ Their claims are *humbug.* ▪ She's only 30? *Humbug!*
2 [*count*] *old-fashioned* **: someone or something that is not honest or true** ▪ He's just an old *humbug.* [=(more commonly) *fraud*]
3 [*count*] *Brit* **: a hard peppermint candy**

hum•ding•er /ˈhʌmˈdɪŋɚ/ *noun, pl* **-ers** [*count*] *informal* **: something that is very impressive or exciting** ▪ The last storm was a real *humdinger!* ▪ I hear we're in for another *humdinger* of a storm!

hum•drum /ˈhʌmˌdrʌm/ *adj* [*more* ~; *most* ~] **: not interesting : dull, boring, and ordinary** ▪ She liked the movie, but I thought it was *humdrum.* ▪ another *humdrum* day at the office ▪ *humdrum* chores

hu•mer•us /ˈhjuːmərəs/ *noun, pl* **hu•meri** /ˈhjuːməˌraɪ/ [*count*] *medical* **: the long bone of the upper arm between the shoulder and the elbow** — see picture at HUMAN

hu•mid /ˈhjuːməd/ *adj* [*more* ~; *most* ~] **: having a lot of moisture in the air** ▪ *humid* weather ▪ a *humid* climate/day/season ▪ It's very hot and *humid* [=*muggy*] today.

hu•mid•i•fi•er /hjuˈmɪdəˌfajɚ/ *noun, pl* **-ers** [*count*] **: a machine that adds moisture to the air in a room** — compare DEHUMIDIFIER

hu•mid•i•ty /hjuˈmɪdəti/ *noun* [*noncount*] **: moisture in the air** ▪ the *humidity* of the region ▪ It's not the heat that will get you—it's the *humidity.* **: the amount of moisture in the air** ▪

The temperature is 67 degrees with *humidity* at 75 percent. ▪ an area of low/high *humidity*

hu·mil·i·ate /hjuˈmɪliˌeɪt/ *verb* **-ates**; **-at·ed**; **-at·ing** [+ *obj*] : to make (someone) feel very ashamed or foolish ▪ I hope I don't *humiliate* myself during the presentation. ▪ He accused her of trying to *humiliate* him in public. ▪ She was hurt and deeply *humiliated* by the lies he told about her.
– **humiliating** *adj* [*more* ~; *most* ~] ▪ It was a *humiliating* defeat. – **hu·mil·i·a·tion** /hjuˌmɪliˈeɪʃən/ *noun, pl* **-tions** [*noncount*] I can't take any more *humiliation*. [*count*] The loss would be one more *humiliation* for our team.

hu·mil·i·ty /hjuˈmɪləti/ *noun* [*noncount*] : the quality or state of not thinking you are better than other people : the quality or state of being humble ▪ He accepted the honor with *humility*. ▪ The ordeal taught her *humility*.

hum·mer /ˈhʌmɚ/ *noun, pl* **-mers** [*count*] *US, informal* : HUMMINGBIRD ▪ A *hummer* was feeding at the flowers.

hum·ming·bird /ˈhʌmɪŋˌbɚd/ *noun, pl* **-birds** [*count*] : a very small, brightly colored American bird that has wings which beat very fast — see color picture on page C9

hum·mock /ˈhʌmək/ *noun, pl* **-mocks** [*count*] : a small hill

hum·mus /ˈhʊməs/ *noun* [*noncount*] : a soft food made of ground chickpeas, garlic, and oil

hu·mon·gous *also* **hu·mun·gous** /hjuˈmʌŋgəs/ *adj* [*more* ~; *most* ~] *informal* : very large : HUGE ▪ a *humongous* dish of ice cream

[1]**hu·mor** (*US*) *or Brit* **hu·mour** /ˈhjuːmɚ/ *noun*
1 [*noncount*] **a** : a funny or amusing quality ▪ He didn't appreciate the *humor* of the situation. ▪ Someday, you'll see the *humor* in this. ▪ Everyone likes the gentle *humor* of his stories of family life. **b** : jokes, funny stories, etc., of a particular kind ▪ She doesn't care for ethnic *humor*. ▪ The book is a collection of American *humor*. — see also GALLOWS HUMOR
2 [*noncount*] : the ability to be funny or to be amused by things that are funny ▪ His *humor* is one of his most attractive qualities. ▪ She has a great ***sense of humor***. [=she says funny things and can see the funny side of things] ▪ He has no *sense of humor*. [=he does not find things amusing]
3 *formal* : the way someone feels emotionally [*singular*] She was in a good/bad *humor* [=(more commonly) *mood*] all day. [*noncount*] He answered the reporter's questions with charm and ***good humor***. [=in a friendly and cheerful way] — compare GOOD-HUMORED, ILL-HUMORED
– **hu·mor·less** (*US*) *or Brit* **hu·mour·less** /ˈhjuːmɚləs/ *adj* [*more* ~; *most* ~] ▪ a dour and *humorless* man ▪ The film is completely *humorless*.

[2]**humor** (*US*) *or Brit* **humour** *verb* **-mors**; **-mored**; **-mor·ing** [+ *obj*] : to try to please or satisfy (someone) by doing what is wanted ▪ The only way to get along with him is to *humor* him. ▪ I know you don't agree, but just *humor* me. [=listen to me]

hu·mor·ist /ˈhjuːmərɪst/ *noun, pl* **-ists** [*count*] : someone (such as a writer) who tells funny stories

hu·mor·ous /ˈhjuːmərəs/ *adj* [*more* ~; *most* ~] : causing laughter : FUNNY ▪ a *humorous* story ▪ a *humorous* writer ▪ The book is very *humorous*.
– **hu·mor·ous·ly** *adv* ▪ a *humorously* misleading sign

humour *Brit spelling of* HUMOR

[1]**hump** /ˈhʌmp/ *noun, pl* **humps** [*count*]
1 : a rounded lump on the surface of something: such as **a** : a raised, rounded part of a road ▪ a rough road with many *humps* [=*bulges*] and bumps **b** : a lump on the back of an animal (such as a camel) **c** : a lump on the back of a person whose spine is curved in an abnormal way
2 ***the hump*** *Brit, informal* : a state in which you are angry or upset ▪ She ***gets the hump*** when she loses. = Losing ***gives her the hump***. [=she becomes angry or upset when she loses]
over the hump *informal* : past the most difficult part of something (such as a project or job) ▪ A few more months of hard work should be enough to get/put us *over the hump* on this project.
– **humped** /ˈhʌmpt/ *adj* [*more* ~; *most* ~] ▪ a *humped* back

[2]**hump** *verb* **humps**; **humped**; **hump·ing** [+ *obj*]
1 *chiefly Brit* : to carry (something heavy) ▪ They had to *hump* [=*lug*] the supplies far into the jungle.
2 *offensive* : to have sex with (someone)

hump·back /ˈhʌmpˌbæk/ *noun, pl* **-backs** [*count*]
1 : HUMPBACK WHALE
2 a : HUNCHBACK 1 **b** *offensive* : HUNCHBACK 2
– **hump·backed** /ˈhʌmpˈbækt/ *adj* [*more* ~; *most* ~] ▪ a *humpbacked* fish

humpback whale *noun, pl* ~ **whales** [*count*] : a type of large whale that has a curved back and very long flippers

humungous *variant spelling of* HUMONGOUS

hu·mus /ˈhjuːməs/ *noun* [*noncount*] : a brown or black material in soil that is formed when plants and animals decay

[1]**hunch** /ˈhʌntʃ/ *verb* **hunch·es**; **hunched**; **hunch·ing**
1 [*no obj*] : to bend your body forward and down so that your back is rounded ▪ The generals were *hunched* [=*bent*] over the table reading a map.
2 [+ *obj*] : to raise (your shoulders or back) while bending your head forward especially to hide or protect your face ▪ He *hunched* his shoulders as he headed out into the storm.

[2]**hunch** *noun, pl* **hunches** [*count*] : a belief or idea about something (especially a future event) that is not based on facts or evidence ▪ My *hunch* is that the stock is going to go up in value. ▪ "How did you know I'd be here?" "It was just a *hunch*." ▪ I ***had a hunch*** [=*had a feeling*] (that) I'd see you here. ▪ She was ***acting on a hunch***. = (*chiefly US*) She was ***playing a hunch***.

hunch·back /ˈhʌntʃˌbæk/ *noun, pl* **-backs** [*count*]
1 : a back in which the spine is curved in an abnormal way
2 *offensive* : a person with a hunchback
– **hunch·backed** /ˈhʌntʃˈbækt/ *adj* ▪ a *hunchbacked* old man/woman

hun·dred /ˈhʌndrəd/ *noun, pl* **-dreds**
1 *pl* ***hundred*** [*count*] : the number 100 ▪ a/one *hundred* (of them) ▪ a *hundred* and one = one *hundred* and one = (*chiefly US*) a *hundred* one [=101] ▪ two/several *hundred* (of them)
2 ***hundreds*** [*plural*] **a** : an amount that is more than 200 ▪ *Hundreds* (and *hundreds*) (of them) came. = They came ***in the hundreds***. = (*chiefly Brit*) They came ***in their hundreds***. **b** — used to refer to a specified century ▪ The bridge was built some time in the sixteen-*hundreds*. [=the 1600s; the 17th century]
3 [*count*] : a very large number — usually plural ▪ I've seen that movie *hundreds* of times. [=many times]
4 [*count*] *US* : a hundred-dollar bill : a bill that is worth 100 dollars ▪ Can you give me change for a *hundred*? ▪ He paid with a couple of *hundreds*.
ninety-nine times out of a hundred *informal* : almost always ▪ *Ninety-nine times out of a hundred*, you can fix the problem by restarting the computer.
– **hundred** *adj, always used before a noun* ▪ a *hundred* employees [=100 employees] ▪ several *hundred* people ▪ We drove a few *hundred* miles today. ▪ I've seen that movie a *hundred* times. [=many times] – **hundreds** *pronoun* ▪ *Hundreds* (of them) came. – **hun·dredth** /ˈhʌndrədθ/ *noun, pl* **-dredths** [*count*] ▪ one *hundredth* of a second = one one-*hundredth* of a second [=$\frac{1}{100}$ second] – **hundredth** *adj* ▪ the *hundredth* person to join – **hundredth** *adv* ▪ the nation's *hundredth* largest city

hun·dred·weight /ˈhʌndrədˌweɪt/ *noun, pl* **-weight** *or* **-weights** [*count*] : a unit of weight equal to 100 pounds in the U.S. or to 112 pounds in the U.K.

hung *past tense and past participle of* [1]HANG

Hun·gar·i·an /ˌhʌŋˈgerijən/ *noun, pl* **-ans**
1 [*count*] : a person born, raised, or living in Hungary
2 [*noncount*] : the language of the Hungarian people
– **Hungarian** *adj* ▪ *Hungarian* food ▪ a *Hungarian* word

[1]**hun·ger** /ˈhʌŋgɚ/ *noun, pl* **-gers**
1 [*noncount*] **a** : a very great need for food : a severe lack of food ▪ She has been a leader in the fight against world *hunger*. ▪ Thousands of people there are ***dying from/of hunger***. [=dying because they do not have enough food; starving to death] **b** : an uncomfortable feeling in your stomach that is caused by the need for food ▪ One sandwich wasn't enough to satisfy his *hunger*. ▪ *hunger* pangs
2 [*count*] : a strong desire ▪ spiritual/sexual *hungers* : a strong desire *for* something or *to do* something ▪ Her students have a genuine *hunger for* knowledge. ▪ a *hunger to succeed* = a *hunger for* success — compare THIRST
from hunger *US, informal* : of very bad quality : very poorly done ▪ The film's scenery is beautiful, but the plot is (strictly) *from hunger*.

[2]**hunger** *verb* **-gers**; **-gered**; **-ger·ing** [*no obj*] *literary* : to have or feel a strong desire ▪ He *hungered* to succeed. — usually + *after* or *for* ▪ He *hungered after* success. ▪ The nation *hungers for* a strong leader. — compare THIRST

hunger strike *noun, pl* ~ **strikes** [*count*] : the act of refusing to eat as a way of showing that you strongly disagree with or disapprove of something ▪ She has threatened to ***go on a hunger strike*** [=refuse to eat] if her colleagues are not released from prison.

H

– **hunger striker** *noun, pl* ~ **-ers** [*count*]

hung jury *noun, pl* ~ **juries** [*count*] *law* **:** a jury whose members cannot agree about what the verdict should be ▪ The trial ended with a *hung jury* and the judge declared a mistrial.

hung over *adj* [*more* ~; *most* ~] **:** sick because you drank too much alcohol at an earlier time **:** suffering from a hangover ▪ He woke up groggy and *hung over.*

hung parliament *noun, pl* ~ **-ments** [*count*] *Brit* **:** a parliament in which no political party has a clear majority

hun·gry /ˈhʌŋgri/ *adj* **hun·gri·er; -est**

1 a : suffering because of a lack of food **:** greatly affected by hunger ▪ There are millions of *hungry* people throughout the world. ▪ Too many people in the world ***go hungry*** every day. [=suffer every day because they do not have enough food to eat] **b :** having an uncomfortable feeling in your stomach because you need food **:** feeling hunger ▪ That girl is always *hungry.* ▪ I'm *hungry.* When's dinner? ▪ I feel *hungry.*

2 *not used before a noun* **:** feeling a strong desire or need *for* something or *to do* something ▪ The prisoners' families were *hungry for* more information. ▪ They were *hungry to learn* more. ▪ *hungry for* success/attention/power — often used in combination ▪ power-*hungry* politicians

3 *always used before a noun* **:** showing hunger or desire ▪ *hungry* eyes ▪ a *hungry* look

4 : feeling a strong desire and determination to succeed ▪ The coach wants the players to stay *hungry.* [=to continue feeling a strong desire to win]

– **hun·gri·ly** /ˈhʌŋgrəli/ *adv* ▪ The dog stared *hungrily* at the food on the table.

hung up *adj* [*more* ~; *most* ~] *informal*

1 *US* **:** delayed for a time ▪ She got *hung up* at the airport. [=she had to be at the airport longer than she expected to be]

2 : thinking or worrying too much about something or someone ▪ Many people are *hung up* about their physical appearance. — usually + *on* ▪ He's still *hung up on* his ex-wife. ▪ students who are *hung up on* getting perfect grades

hunk /ˈhʌŋk/ *noun, pl* **hunks** [*count*]

1 : a large lump or piece of something ▪ a *hunk* of cheese/bread ▪ a steak cut into meaty *hunks*

2 *informal* **:** an attractive man ▪ That actor is such a *hunk*!

– **hunk·y** /ˈhʌŋki/ *adj* **hunk·i·er; -est** *informal* ▪ That actor is so *hunky!*

hun·ker /ˈhʌŋkɚ/ *verb* **-kers; -kered; -ker·ing** [*no obj*] *chiefly US* **:** to lower your body to the ground by bending your legs ▪ The hikers *hunkered* (down) under a cliff until the storm passed.

hunker down [*phrasal verb*] **:** to stay in a place for a period of time ▪ The leaders *hunkered down* at a country estate for difficult peace negotiations.

hunk·y–do·ry /ˌhʌŋkiˈdori/ *adj, not used before a noun* [*more* ~; *most* ~] *informal* **:** free of trouble or problems **:** FINE ▪ Everything is *hunky-dory* right now.

¹hunt /ˈhʌnt/ *verb* **hunts; hunt·ed; hunt·ing**

1 : to chase and kill (wild animals) for food or pleasure [+ *obj*] The wolf was *hunting* its prey. ▪ These birds have been *hunted* almost to extinction. ▪ a gun used for *hunting* squirrels [*no obj*] He likes to *hunt* and fish.

2 : to search for something or someone very carefully and thoroughly [*no obj*] She *hunted* around in the closet for a pair of shoes. — often + *for* ▪ The police are *hunting for* a killer. ▪ He's *hunting for* a new apartment. ▪ We went to the mall to *hunt for* bargains. [+ *obj*] Police *hunted* the escaped prisoners through several states. ▪ (*US*) We went to the mall to *hunt* bargains.

hunt down [*phrasal verb*] **1** ***hunt (something) down or hunt down (something)*** **:** to succeed in finding (something) ▪ It may take me a while to *hunt down* the phone number. **2** ***hunt (someone) down or hunt down (someone)*** **:** to find and capture (someone) ▪ The killer was *hunted down* with help from his relatives.

hunt out [*phrasal verb*] ***hunt (something) out or hunt out (something)*** **:** to find (something) after searching for it ▪ It took a while to *hunt out* the papers, but we finally found everything we needed.

hunt up [*phrasal verb*] ***hunt (someone or something) up or hunt up (someone or something)*** **:** to succeed in finding (someone or something) ▪ You can *hunt up* a good car at a fair price if you try.

²hunt *noun, pl* **hunts** [*count*]

1 : an occasion when people hunt wild animals ▪ They went on a *hunt.* ▪ a bear/fox/pheasant *hunt*

2 : an act of searching for something or someone ▪ We finally found a good restaurant after a long *hunt.* ▪ The *hunt* for the escaped convicts continues. = The *hunt* is still on for the escaped convicts. = The police are still ***on the hunt*** [=are still searching] for the escaped convicts. — see also SCAVENGER HUNT, TREASURE HUNT, WITCH HUNT

3 *chiefly Brit* **:** a group of people who hunt foxes together

in the hunt *US* **:** having a chance to win or succeed in a contest or competition ▪ At this point in the season, both teams are still *in the hunt.* [=both teams have a chance of winning the championship]

hunt–and–peck /ˌhʌntṇˈpɛk/ *noun* [*noncount*] *informal* **:** a method of typing that involves looking at the keyboard and using only one finger of each hand to press the keys

hunt·er /ˈhʌntɚ/ *noun, pl* **-ers** [*count*]

1 a : a person who hunts wild animals ▪ a deer *hunter* **b :** a person who searches for something ▪ My mother is a bargain-*hunter.* [=a person who searches for good prices on items to buy] ▪ job-*hunters* [=people trying to find jobs; job-seekers] — see also BOUNTY HUNTER

2 : a strong horse that people use when they hunt foxes

hunt·er–gath·er·er /ˈhʌntɚˈgæðɚrɚ/ *noun, pl* **-ers** [*count*] **:** a member of a culture in which people hunt animals and look for plants to eat instead of growing crops and raising animals ▪ a tribe of *hunter-gatherers*

hunt·ing /ˈhʌntɪŋ/ *noun* [*noncount*]

1 : the activity or sport of chasing and killing wild animals ▪ His hobbies include *hunting* and fishing. ▪ The law prohibits the *hunting* of migratory birds. ▪ big-game *hunting* ▪ She likes to ***go hunting.*** ▪ We *went hunting* for bear. = We *went* bear-*hunting.* — often used before another noun ▪ *hunting* boots ▪ a *hunting* accident ▪ the *hunting* season ▪ a *hunting* dog [=a dog people use when they hunt] — see also FOXHUNTING, HEAD-HUNTING

2 : the activity of searching for something ▪ bargain-*hunting* ▪ job-*hunting*

hunt·ress /ˈhʌntrəs/ *noun, pl* **-ress·es** [*count*] *literary* **:** a woman who hunts wild animals

hunts·man /ˈhʌntsmən/ *noun, pl* **-men** /-mən/ [*count*] *formal*

1 : a person (especially a man) who hunts wild animals

2 : a person (especially a man) who manages a group of people who are hunting wild animals

¹hur·dle /ˈhɚdḷ/ *noun, pl* **hur·dles**

1 a [*count*] **:** one of a series of barriers to be jumped over in a race **b** ***the hurdles*** **:** a race in which runners must jump over hurdles ▪ He won a medal in *the* high *hurdles.* — usually used with a singular verb ▪ *The hurdles* is his best event.

2 [*count*] **:** something that makes an achievement difficult ▪ The company faces severe financial *hurdles* this year. ▪ She overcame many *hurdles* [=*obstacles*] on her way to earning a college diploma.

hurdle

²hurdle *verb* **hur·dles; hur·dled; hur·dling** [+ *obj*]

1 : to jump over (something) while running ▪ The horse *hurdled* the fence.

2 : to deal with (a problem or difficulty) successfully ▪ She *hurdled* [=*overcame*] many obstacles on her way to earning a college diploma.

– **hur·dler** /ˈhɚdlɚ/ *noun, pl* **hur·dlers** [*count*]

hur·dy–gur·dy /ˌhɚdiˈgɚdi/ *noun, pl* **-dies** [*count*]

1 : a stringed musical instrument that is played by turning a handle

2 : BARREL ORGAN

hurl /ˈhɚrəl/ *verb* **hurls; hurled; hurl·ing** /ˈhɚlɪŋ/

1 [+ *obj*] **:** to throw (something) with force ▪ Someone *hurled* a rock through the window. ▪ He *hurled* a chair at me. ▪ It looked like she was going to *hurl* herself down the stairs.

2 [+ *obj*] **:** to say or shout (something, such as an insult) in a loud and forceful way ▪ The protesters *hurled* insults at us.

3 [*no obj*] *US slang* **:** VOMIT

– **hurl·er** /ˈhɚlɚ/ *noun, pl* **-ers** [*count*] ▪ a baseball team with several talented *hurlers* [=*pitchers*]

hur·ly–bur·ly /ˌhɚliˈbɚli/ *noun* [*noncount*] **:** a very active or confused state or situation ▪ the *hurly-burly* of politics ▪ We left the *hurly-burly* of city life and moved to the countryside.

hur·rah /hʊˈrɑː/ *or* **hoo·ray** /hʊˈreɪ/ *also* **hur·ray** /hʊˈreɪ/ *interj* — used to express joy, approval, or encouragement ▪ *Hurrah*! I got the job! ▪ Hip, hip, *hooray*! — sometimes + *for* ▪ *Hurrah for* the home team! — see also LAST HURRAH

hur·ri·cane /ˈhərəˌkeɪn, *Brit* ˈhʌrəkən/ *noun, pl* **-canes** [*count*] : an extremely large, powerful, and destructive storm with very strong winds that occurs especially in the western part of the Atlantic Ocean

hur·ried /ˈhərid/ *adj* [*more* ~; *most* ~]
1 : happening or done very quickly or too quickly ▪ The general was forced to make a *hurried* decision. ▪ She had a *hurried* meeting with her advisers before speaking to the press. ▪ a *hurried* meal/departure
2 : working very quickly or too quickly ▪ a *hurried* waitress
— **hur·ried·ly** /ˈhərədli/ *adv* ▪ a *hurriedly* scribbled note ▪ depart *hurriedly*

¹hur·ry /ˈhəri/ *verb* **-ries; -ried; -ry·ing**
1 [*no obj*] : to move, act, or go quickly ▪ Take your time. There's no need to *hurry*. ▪ She *hurried* off to her class. ▪ He *hurried* after her. ▪ They *hurried* past us. ▪ *Hurry* (back) home now. ▪ We *hurried* through the lesson so that we could finish early. ▪ We'll miss our flight if we don't *hurry*. = If we don't *hurry* we'll miss our flight. — often + *up* ▪ If we don't *hurry up* we'll miss our flight. ▪ *Hurry up*! We're going to be late!
2 [+ *obj*] **a** : to make (someone) move, act, or go quickly ▪ She hates to be *hurried* [=*rushed*] at dinner. ▪ The teacher *hurried* us through the lesson. — often + *up* ▪ Somebody needs to *hurry* them *up* so we can leave. ▪ Could you ***hurry it up*** a little please? [=could you please do what you are doing a little more quickly?] **b** [+ *obj*] : to carry or send (someone or something) more quickly than usual ▪ They *hurried* the children off to bed. ▪ A messenger *hurried* [=*rushed*] the package across town.
3 [+ *obj*] **a** : to increase the speed of (something) ▪ He heard the train coming and *hurried* his pace. [=he began to walk more quickly] **b** : to do (something) quickly or too quickly ▪ Don't *hurry* [=*rush*] your homework. ▪ The quarterback was forced to *hurry* his throw.
hurry up and wait *US, informal* — used to describe a situation in which you are forced to spend a lot of time waiting ▪ My father says that all he did in the army was *hurry up and wait*. — sometimes used as a noun phrase ▪ Traveling often involves a lot of *hurry up and wait*. [=a lot of waiting]

²hurry *noun* [*noncount*] : a need to do something more quickly than usual : RUSH ▪ "Come on, let's go." "What's the (big) *hurry*?" [=why do we need to hurry?] ▪ Why the *hurry*? ▪ Take your time. There's no (great) *hurry*. ▪ In her *hurry* to leave she forgot her briefcase.
in a hurry **1** : very quickly ▪ The weather got worse *in a hurry*. **2** : feeling a strong need to move, act, or go quickly ▪ He was *in* too much of *a hurry* to stop and say hello. ▪ teenagers who are *in a* (big) *hurry* to grow up [=who are eager to grow up; who want to grow up quickly] ▪ We're ***not in a/any hurry***. = We're ***in no hurry***. [=we do not need to hurry; we have plenty of time] — sometimes used to say that someone does not want to do something ▪ It was getting late, but our guests were *not in a/any hurry* to leave. = Our guests were *in no hurry* to leave. [=we wanted our guests to leave, but they did not seem to want to leave] ▪ I'm *in no* (particular/big/great) *hurry* to go to the dentist.

¹hurt /ˈhət/ *verb* **hurts; hurt; hurt·ing**
1 a [+ *obj*] : to cause pain or injury to (yourself, someone else, or a part of your body) ▪ Be careful with that knife or you could *hurt* yourself. ▪ Ouch! You're *hurting* my arm! ▪ I *hurt* my back (while) carrying a heavy box up the stairs. ▪ She was badly/seriously *hurt* in a car accident. ▪ My tooth/back still *hurts* me. ▪ Don't worry about the dog—he ***wouldn't hurt a fly***. [=the dog would never bite or attack anyone; the dog is very gentle] ***synonyms*** see INJURE **b** [*no obj*] : to be a source or cause of pain ▪ My tooth/back *hurts* (a lot/little). ▪ It *hurts* [=it is painful] to walk on hot pavement with bare feet. ▪ The injection didn't *hurt* at all. = It didn't *hurt* a bit. ▪ Ouch! That *hurts*! ▪ My arm *hurts* very badly. = (*informally*) My arm ***hurts like hell***. ▪ My leg *hurt*. = (*chiefly US*) My leg ***was hurting***. **c** [*no obj*] : to feel physical pain ▪ When I woke up this morning I *hurt* all over.
2 a [+ *obj*] : to make (someone) sad or upset : to cause (someone) to suffer emotionally ▪ Their lack of interest in her work *hurt* her deeply. ▪ You're only *hurting* yourself by holding a grudge against them. ▪ It *hurt* me to see her go. ▪ It *hurts* me to say this [=I don't enjoy saying this], but I just don't think you can do the job. ▪ I can't tell him the meal was bad because I don't want to ***hurt his feelings***. [=hurt him; make him sad or upset] **b** [*no obj*] : to feel emotional pain or distress ▪ My sister has really ***been hurting*** [=has been very upset and unhappy] since her boyfriend left her.
3 : to do harm to (someone or something) : to affect (someone or something) in a bad or harmful way : DAMAGE [+ *obj*] The lack of rain has *hurt* the corn crop. ▪ If we lose this game it will seriously *hurt* our chances of making the playoffs. ▪ These new regulations will *hurt* small businesses. ▪ *hurt* profits/sales ▪ There's no doubt that this scandal has *hurt* her image. ▪ Would it *hurt* you to cook dinner for once? = It wouldn't *hurt* you to cook dinner for once. [=you should cook dinner] ▪ As far as he's concerned, ***what he doesn't know can't/won't hurt him***. [=he would rather not know about something; he thinks that if he does not know about something, he cannot be damaged by it, blamed for it, etc.] [*no obj*] The company needs to cut spending, even if it *hurts*. — usually used in negative statements ▪ I know he's qualified for the job, but ***it doesn't hurt*** [=it helps] that the company president is his mother's best friend. ▪ It ***wouldn't hurt*** to try a little harder. [=you should try a little harder] ▪ We may not finish on time, but it ***won't hurt*** to try. [=we should try] ▪ "Should I ask her for a job?" "It ***couldn't/can't hurt*** (to ask)." [=she may give you a job if you ask]
4 [*no obj*] : to have many problems : to be in a bad situation or condition ▪ Those poor people ***are hurting*** and need our help. ▪ The local economy *is hurting* right now. [=it is doing poorly]
hurt for [*phrasal verb*] *US, informal* **1** ***hurt for (something)*** : to lack (something needed) ▪ Those children ***are hurting for*** attention. [=those children need to be given more attention] ▪ The company *is hurting for* money right now. **2** ***hurt for (someone)*** : to have sympathy or pity for (someone) ▪ I *hurt for* [=*feel for*] those poor people.

²hurt *adj* [*more* ~; *most* ~]
1 : having a physical injury ▪ Those who are most badly/seriously *hurt* [=*injured*] will be cared for first. ▪ She has a *hurt* back.
2 : feeling or showing emotional pain ▪ She gave him a *hurt* look. ▪ *hurt* [=*wounded*] pride ▪ I was/felt deeply *hurt* by their refusal to help. [=I was very sad or upset because they refused to help] ▪ His behavior at the party caused a lot of ***hurt feelings***. [=it made many people upset or sad]

³hurt *noun, pl* **hurts** : mental or emotional pain [*noncount*] Her sympathy eased the *hurt* he felt after his dog's death. ▪ It takes a long time to get past the *hurt* [=*suffering*] of a bitter divorce. [*count*] They felt a great *hurt* after their bitter divorce. ▪ She tried to put past *hurts* behind her.
put the/a hurt on *US, informal* : to injure or damage (someone or something) ▪ If we adopt a more aggressive strategy, we can really *put the hurt on* our competitors. ▪ They really *put a hurt on* him. [=hurt/injured him very badly]

hurt·ful /ˈhətfəl/ *adj* [*more* ~; *most* ~] : causing injury or emotional pain; *especially* : cruel or unkind ▪ She can't forgive him for the *hurtful* things he said. ▪ *hurtful* gossip ▪ Their comments were really *hurtful* to me.
— **hurt·ful·ly** *adv* ▪ He spoke *hurtfully* to her. — **hurt·ful·ness** *noun* [*noncount*]

hur·tle /ˈhətl̩/ *verb* **hur·tles; hur·tled; hur·tling**
1 *always followed by an adverb or preposition* [*no obj*] : to move or fall with great speed and force ▪ Boulders *hurtled* down the hill. ▪ comets *hurtling* through space ▪ We kept to the side of the road as cars and trucks *hurtled* past us. — often used figuratively ▪ a country *hurtling* toward disaster
2 [+ *obj*] : to cause (something or someone) to move or go with great speed and force : HURL ▪ The protesters *hurtled* bottles at the police. ▪ He *hurtled* himself into the crowd.

¹hus·band /ˈhʌzbənd/ *noun, pl* **-bands** [*count*] : a married man : the man someone is married to ▪ Have you met her *husband*? ▪ They were ***husband and wife*** [=a married couple] for almost 60 years. — compare WIFE

²husband *verb* **-bands; -band·ed; -band·ing** [+ *obj*] *formal* : to carefully use or manage (something, such as a resource) ▪ The country has *husbanded* its resources well.

hus·band·ry /ˈhʌzbəndri/ *noun* [*singular*] *formal* : the activity of raising plants or animals for food : FARMING ▪ crop *husbandry* — see also ANIMAL HUSBANDRY

¹hush /ˈhʌʃ/ *verb* **hush·es; hushed; hush·ing**
1 [+ *obj*] : to make (someone) quiet, calm, or still ▪ The woman in the seat behind me was trying to *hush* her baby. ▪ The judge *hushed* the spectators. — often used as *(be) hushed* ▪

The crowd *was hushed*. ▪ a *hushed* [=*quiet*] courtroom ▪ speaking in *hushed* [=*whispering*] tones
2 [*no obj*] **:** **to become quiet** ▪ The spectators *hushed* as the judge entered the courtroom. ▪ The room *hushed* [=people stopped talking, making noise, etc.] as the theater lights dimmed. **— usually used to tell someone to be quiet** ▪ *Hush*, children. I'm going to tell you a story.
hush up [*phrasal verb*] ***hush (something) up or hush up (something)*** **:** **to prevent people from knowing the truth about (something, such as a crime)** ▪ *hush up* a crime/scandal ▪ The city government tried to *hush* things *up* when the mayor was arrested.

²hush *noun* [*singular*] **:** **a time of silence, stillness, or calm especially after noise** ▪ A *hush* fell/came over the theater. = A *hush* settled/descended on the theater. [=the theater became quiet; people stopped talking, making noise, etc.]

hush–hush /ˈhʌʃˌhʌʃ/ *adj* [*more ~; most ~*] **:** **kept secret : known only to a few people** ▪ He wants to keep the relationship *hush-hush*. ▪ She works for a *hush-hush* government agency.

hush money *noun* [*noncount*] **:** **money paid so that someone will keep information secret : money that you pay someone to hush something up** ▪ He's accused of paying her *hush money* to keep their affair secret.

¹husk /ˈhʌsk/ *noun, pl* **husks** [*count*] **:** **a usually thin, dry layer that covers some seeds and fruits** ▪ a corn *husk* [=(*US*) *shuck*] **—** see color picture on page C4

²husk *verb* **husks; husked; husk·ing** [*+ obj*] **:** **to remove the thin, dry layer that covers some seeds and fruits : to remove the husk from (something)** ▪ Please *husk* [=(*US*) *shuck*] the corn while I set the table.

¹hus·ky /ˈhʌski/ *adj* **hus·ki·er; -est**
1 *of a voice* **:** **sounding somewhat rough** ▪ a *husky* [=*hoarse*] voice
2 : **large and strong** ▪ a *husky* [=*burly*] laborer

²husky *noun, pl* **hus·kies** [*count*] **:** **a large dog with thick fur that is used for pulling sleds —** see picture at DOG

hus·sy /ˈhʌsi/ *noun, pl* **-sies** [*count*] *old-fashioned + offensive* **:** **a girl or woman who does things that people consider immoral, improper, etc.** ▪ a brazen/wanton *hussy* ✧ *Hussy* **is now rarely used except in a joking way.**

hus·tings /ˈhʌstɪŋz/ *noun*
on the hustings **:** **making speeches, meeting people, etc., in order to get people to vote for you : campaigning for a political office** ▪ candidates who are (out) *on the hustings*
the hustings **:** **the political speeches, meetings, etc., that happen before an election** ▪ news reports from *the hustings*

¹hus·tle /ˈhʌsəl/ *verb* **hus·tles; hus·tled; hus·tling** /ˈhʌsəlɪŋ/
1 [*+ obj*] **:** **to quickly move or push (someone) often in a rough way** ▪ The guards *hustled* the prisoners into the jail. ▪ The star's manager *hustled* him out the back door of the theater to avoid the throngs of fans. ▪ She *hustled* the children (off) to school.
2 [*no obj*] *chiefly US* **a :** **to move or work in a quick and energetic way** ▪ If we want to catch that bus, we're going to have to *hustle*. [=*rush*] **b :** **to play a sport with a lot of energy and effort** ▪ He's not the most talented player on the team, but he always *hustles*.
3 *US, informal* **a :** **to get (something, such as money) in an illegal or improper way** [*+ obj*] She spent her mornings *hustling* change [=asking people for money] on the sidewalk. [*no obj*] *hustling* for money **b** [*+ obj*] **:** **to sell (something illegal, such as drugs)** ▪ He's been *hustling* drugs for a few years. **:** **to sell (something) in an illegal or improper way** ▪ They *hustle* diamonds, furs—whatever people are buying.
4 [*+ obj*] *informal* **a :** **to take something and especially money from (someone) by lying or doing something unfair : to swindle or cheat (someone)** ▪ She's accused of running an elaborate scam to *hustle* elderly people. **b** *chiefly US* **:** **to earn money by playing (a gambling game) and especially by playing against people who are less skillful than you are** ▪ He made a living by *hustling* pool.
5 [*no obj*] *US, informal* **:** **to work as a prostitute**
hustle up [*phrasal verb*] ***hustle up (something) or hustle (something) up*** *US, informal* **:** **to quickly get or find (something)** ▪ I'll try to *hustle up* [=*rustle up*] some tickets to tonight's game. ▪ Let's see if we can *hustle up* some grub. [=find something to eat]

²hustle *noun, pl* **hustles**
1 [*noncount*] **a :** **energetic activity** ▪ I enjoy the ***hustle and bustle*** of the city. **b** *chiefly US* **:** **effort and energy in playing a sport** ▪ The fans admire him for his *hustle*.
2 [*count*] *informal* **:** **a dishonest plan for getting money** ▪ She's always trying some kind of *hustle* [=*scam*] on the street.

hus·tler /ˈhʌslɚ/ *noun, pl* **hus·tlers** [*count*] **:** **a person who hustles: such as a** *chiefly US* **:** **a person who regularly earns money by playing a gambling game** ▪ a pool *hustler* **b** *chiefly US, informal* **:** PROSTITUTE

hut /ˈhʌt/ *noun, pl* **huts** [*count*] **:** **a small and simple house or building** ▪ a mud/wooden *hut* [=*shack*]

hutch /ˈhʌʧ/ *noun, pl* **hutch·es** [*count*]
1 *US* **:** **a piece of furniture that is used for displaying and storing dishes — called also (*Brit*) *dresser*, (*Brit*) *Welsh dresser***
2 : **an enclosed area or cage for an animal** ▪ a rabbit *hutch*

HVAC *abbr* **heating, ventilating, and air-conditioning; heating, ventilation, and air-conditioning**

hwy *abbr* **highway**

hy·a·cinth /ˈhajəsɪnθ/ *noun, pl* **-cinths** [*count*] **:** **a type of plant that is grown in gardens and has flowers that smell sweet**

hy·brid /ˈhaɪbrəd/ *noun, pl* **-brids** [*count*]
1 : **an animal or plant that is produced from two animals or plants of different kinds** ▪ a *hybrid* of two roses
2 : **something that is formed by combining two or more things** ▪ The band plays a *hybrid* of jazz and rock.
– hybrid ***adj, always used before a noun*** ▪ a *hybrid* rose/tree ▪ The car is a *hybrid* vehicle that uses both electricity and gasoline.

hy·dra /ˈhaɪdrə/ *noun, pl* **-dras**
1 ***Hydra*** [*singular*] **:** **a monster in Greek mythology that has many heads**
2 [*count*] **:** **a very complicated and serious problem that cannot be easily solved** ▪ trying to slay the *hydra* of inflation

hy·drant /ˈhaɪdrənt/ *noun, pl* **-drants** [*count*] **:** FIRE HYDRANT

¹hy·drate /ˈhaɪˌdreɪt/ *noun, pl* **-drates** [*count*] *technical* **:** **a substance that is formed when water combines with another substance**

²hydrate *verb* **-drates; -drat·ed; -drat·ing** [*+ obj*] *somewhat technical* **:** **to add water or moisture to (something)** ▪ lotions and creams that *hydrate* the skin **:** **to supply (something) with water** ▪ Drink fluids to *hydrate* the body. **— opposite** DEHYDRATE
– hydrated *adj* [*more ~; most ~*] ▪ Remember to stay *hydrated*. [=to drink enough water] **– hy·dra·tion** /haɪˈdreɪʃən/ *noun* [*noncount*]

hy·drau·lic /haɪˈdrɑːlɪk/ *adj*
1 : **operated by the pressure of a fluid** ▪ *hydraulic* brakes ▪ the airplane's *hydraulic* system
2 : **occurring or used in a hydraulic system** ▪ *hydraulic* fluid ▪ *hydraulic* pressure
– hy·drau·li·cal·ly /haɪˈdrɑːlɪkli/ *adv* ▪ *hydraulically* controlled brakes

hy·drau·lics /haɪˈdrɑːlɪks/ *noun* [*noncount*] **:** **the science that deals with ways to use liquid (such as water) when it is moving**

hy·dro·car·bon /ˈhaɪdroʊˌkɑɚbən/ *noun, pl* **-bons** [*count*] *technical* **:** **a substance (such as coal or natural gas) that contains only carbon and hydrogen**

hy·dro·chlo·ric acid /ˌhaɪdrəˈklorɪk-/ *noun* [*noncount*] *chemistry* **:** **a strong acid that is used especially in scientific experiments and in manufacturing**

hy·dro·elec·tric /ˌhaɪdrowɪˈlɛktrɪk/ *adj, technical* **:** **of or relating to the production of electricity by using machines that are powered by moving water** ▪ a *hydroelectric* dam ▪ *hydroelectric* power
– hy·dro·elec·tric·i·ty /ˌhaɪdrowɪˌlɛkˈtrɪsəti/ *noun* [*noncount*]

hy·dro·foil /ˈhaɪdrəˌfojəl/ *noun, pl* **-foils** [*count*] **:** **a very fast boat that rises partly out of the water when moving at high speeds**

hy·dro·gen /ˈhaɪdrəʤən/ *noun* [*noncount*] **:** **a chemical element that has no color or smell and that is the simplest, lightest, and most common element**

hy·dro·ge·nat·ed /ˌhaɪˈdrɑːʤəˌneɪtəd/ *adj, technical, of an oil or fat* **:** **having hydrogen added** ▪ *hydrogenated* fats/oils ▪ The study showed that ***partially hydrogenated*** oils increase the risk of heart disease.

hydrogen bomb *noun, pl* **~ bombs** [*count*] **:** **a bomb that produces an extremely powerful and destructive explosion when hydrogen atoms unite — called also *H-bomb***

hydrogen peroxide *noun [noncount]* : a liquid that is used to make things lighter in color or to kill bacteria

[1]**hy·dro·plane** /ˈhaɪdrəˌpleɪn/ *noun, pl* **-planes** *[count]* : a boat that is designed to move over the surface of water at very high speeds

[2]**hydroplane** *verb* **-planes; -planed; -plan·ing** *[no obj] US, of a vehicle* : to slide on a wet road because a thin layer of water on the road causes the tires to lose contact with it • The car started *hydroplaning* and skidded off the road.

hy·dro·pon·ics /ˌhaɪdrəˈpɑːnɪks/ *noun [noncount] technical* : a method of growing plants in water rather than in soil
– **hy·dro·pon·ic** /ˌhaɪdrəˈpɑːnɪk/ *adj* • *hydroponic* gardening/vegetables

hy·dro·pow·er /ˈhaɪdrəˌpawɚ/ *noun [noncount]* : electricity produced from machines that are run by moving water

hy·dro·ther·a·py /ˌhaɪdrəˈθerəpi/ *noun, pl* **-pies** *[count, noncount]* : the use of water in the treatment of disease or injury

hy·e·na /haɪˈiːnə/ *noun, pl* **-nas** *[count]* : a large animal of Asia and Africa that eats the flesh of dead animals • a pack of *hyenas* ✧ The call of the hyena sounds like very loud laughter, and the hyena is sometimes referred to as a ***laughing hyena***. A person who is laughing in a loud or foolish way is sometimes described as ***laughing like a hyena***.

hyena

hy·giene /ˈhaɪˌʤiːn/ *noun [noncount]* : the things that you do to keep yourself and your surroundings clean in order to maintain good health • Poor sanitation and *hygiene* caused many of the soldiers to get sick. • He has very poor personal *hygiene*. • Brushing your teeth regularly is an important part of good dental/oral *hygiene*.

hy·gien·ic /haɪˈʤiːnɪk, haɪˈʤɛnɪk/ *adj*
1 : relating to being clean and the the things that are done to maintain good health : of or relating to hygiene • For *hygienic* reasons, restaurants should wash silverware and drinking glasses more than once.
2 *[more ~; most ~]* : clean and likely to maintain good health : having or showing good hygiene • The *hygienic* conditions of the operating room are maintained by the nursing staff. • The prisoners' living quarters were not *hygienic*.
– **hy·gien·i·cal·ly** /haɪˈʤiːnɪkli, haiˈʤɛnɪkli/ *adv*

hy·gien·ist /haɪˈʤiːnɪst, haɪˈʤɛnɪst/ *noun, pl* **-ists** *[count]* : DENTAL HYGIENIST

hy·men /ˈhaɪmən/ *noun, pl* **-mens** *[count]* : a fold of tissue that partly covers the opening of the vagina

hymn /ˈhɪm/ *noun, pl* **hymns** *[count]* : a religious song : a song that praises God • sing a *hymn* of praise/thanksgiving • a book of *hymns* = a *hymn* book — sometimes used figuratively • This sentimental novel is a *hymn* to childhood and innocence. [=the novel praises childhood and innocence]

hym·nal /ˈhɪmnəl/ *noun, pl* **-nals** *[count]* : a book of hymns

[1]**hype** /ˈhaɪp/ *noun [noncount] informal + often disapproving* : talk or writing that is intended to make people excited about or interested in something or someone • There was a great deal of media *hype* surrounding the senator's announcement. • After months of promotional *hype*, the band finally released their new album.

[2]**hype** *verb* **hypes; hyped; hyp·ing** *[+ obj] informal + often disapproving* : to talk or write about (something or someone) in a way that is intended to make people excited or interested • He's being *hyped* (up) as the next big rap star. • Company executives have been *hyping* the new software for months.
hype up *[phrasal verb]* ***hype (someone) up*** or ***hype up (someone)*** *informal* : to make (someone) very excited • The announcer was trying to *hype* the crowd *up* before the show started. — often used as *hyped up* • I was so *hyped up*, I couldn't sleep.

hy·per /ˈhaɪpɚ/ *adj [more ~; most ~] informal* : very excited, nervous, or active • a *hyper* [=*hyperactive*] kid • I get a little *hyper* when I drink too much coffee.

hyper- /ˈhaɪpɚ/ *prefix*
1 : excessively or extremely • *hyper*active • *hyper*sensitive
2 : excessive or extreme • *hyper*sensitivity • *hyper*tension

hy·per·ac·tive /ˌhaɪpɚˈæktɪv/ *adj [more ~; most ~]* : extremely active or too active • *hyperactive* children • All of these wild characters are products of the author's *hyperactive* [=*overactive*] imagination.
– **hy·per·ac·tiv·i·ty** /ˌhaɪpɚˌækˈtɪvəti/ *noun [noncount]*

hy·per·bo·le /haɪˈpɚbəli/ *noun, pl* **-les** : language that describes something as better or worse than it really is *[noncount]* In describing his accomplishments, he's somewhat given to *hyperbole*. [=he tends to exaggerate his accomplishments] *[count]* The customer's letter of complaint was filled with *hyperboles* [=(more commonly) *exaggerations*] and outrageous claims.
– **hy·per·bol·ic** /ˌhaɪpɚˈbɑːlɪk/ *adj* • *hyperbolic* [=(more commonly) *exaggerated*] claims about his accomplishments

hy·per·crit·i·cal /ˌhaɪpɚˈkrɪtɪkəl/ *adj [more ~; most ~]* : criticizing other people or things too strongly or too often • a *hypercritical* boss • a *hypercritical* movie review

hy·per·drive /ˈhaɪpɚˌdraɪv/ *noun [noncount] chiefly US, informal* : a state of extremely fast activity • With only a few weeks left before the election, the campaign has shifted into *hyperdrive*. [=has shifted into overdrive; has become extremely active]

hy·per·in·fla·tion /ˌhaɪpərɪnˈfleɪʃən/ *noun [noncount]* : extremely rapid increase in the price of goods and services : extremely rapid economic inflation

hy·per·link /ˈhaɪpɚˌlɪŋk/ *noun, pl* **-links** *[count] computers* : a highlighted word or picture in a document or Web page that you can click on with a computer mouse to go to another place in the same or a different document or Web page

hy·per·mar·ket /ˈhaɪpɚˌmɑɚkət/ *noun, pl* **-ets** *[count] chiefly Brit* : a very large supermarket

hy·per·sen·si·tive /ˌhaɪpɚˈsensətɪv/ *adj* : very sensitive: such as **a** : having feelings that are very easily hurt • a *hypersensitive* child • She's *hypersensitive* about her past. **b** : very strongly and easily affected or harmed by something (such as a drug) • People who are *hypersensitive* to the chemical may have violent reactions even to small amounts.
– **hy·per·sen·si·tiv·i·ty** /ˌhaɪpɚsensəˈtɪvəti/ *noun [noncount]*

hy·per·ten·sion /ˌhaɪpɚˈtɛnʃən/ *noun [noncount] medical* : high blood pressure • He's being treated for *hypertension*.
– **hy·per·ten·sive** /ˌhaɪpɚˈtensɪv/ *adj* • *hypertensive* patients

hy·per·text /ˈhaɪpɚˌtɛkst/ *noun [noncount] computers* : an arrangement of the information in a computer database that allows a user to get information and to go from one document to another by clicking on highlighted words or pictures

hy·per·ven·ti·late /ˌhaɪpɚˈvɛntəˌleɪt/ *verb* **-lates; -lat·ed; -lat·ing** *[no obj]* : to breathe very quickly and deeply • The boy panicked and began *hyperventilating*. ✧ When you *hyperventilate* you breathe so quickly that you begin to feel dizzy. *Hyperventilate* is also sometimes used figuratively to describe a person who is becoming very upset or excited but not actually breathing quickly. • The latest economic news has prompted a lot of *hyperventilating* on Wall Street. [=people on Wall Street are very upset about the news]
– **hy·per·ven·ti·la·tion** /ˌhaɪpɚˌvɛntəˈleɪʃən/ *noun [noncount]*

hy·phen /ˈhaɪfən/ *noun, pl* **-phens** *[count]* : a punctuation mark - that is used to connect words or parts of words

hy·phen·ate /ˈhaɪfəˌneɪt/ *verb* **-ates; -at·ed; -at·ing** *[+ obj]* : to connect (words or parts of words) with a hyphen • In English, we *hyphenate* some compounds but not others.
– **hyphenated** *adj* • "Runner-up" is a *hyphenated* term.

hyp·no·sis /hɪpˈnoʊsəs/ *noun [noncount]* : a state that resembles sleep but in which you can hear and respond to questions or suggestions • He underwent *hypnosis* to treat his fear of water. • While ***under hypnosis***, she described the horrific accident in detail.

hyp·no·ther·a·py /ˌhɪpnoʊˈθerəpi/ *noun [noncount] medical* : the use of hypnosis to help people with emotional and psychological problems

[1]**hyp·not·ic** /hɪpˈnɑːtɪk/ *adj*
1 *always used before a noun* : of or relating to hypnosis • The psychologist put her into a *hypnotic* state.
2 *[more ~; most ~]* : having an effect like hypnosis: such as **a** : tending to cause sleep or relaxation • Riding in a car often has a *hypnotic* effect on babies. • the steady, *hypnotic* rhythm of the train **b** : attractive or interesting in a powerful or mysterious way • Her voice is powerful and *hypnotic*. [=*spellbinding, fascinating*] • a *hypnotic* personality
– **hyp·not·i·cal·ly** /hɪpˈnɑːtɪkli/ *adv* • chanting *hypnotically*

[2]**hypnotic** *noun, pl* **-ics** [*count*] *medical* : a drug that causes sleep

hyp·no·tism /ˈhɪpnəˌtɪzəm/ *noun* [*noncount*] : the act or practice of putting people into a state of hypnosis • a psychologist who employs *hypnotism* to treat his patients

hyp·no·tist /ˈhɪpnəˌtɪst/ *noun, pl* **-tists** [*count*] : a person who puts people into a state of hypnosis : a person who hypnotizes people

hyp·no·tize *also Brit* **hyp·no·tise** /ˈhɪpnəˌtaɪz/ *verb* **-tiz·es; -tized; -tiz·ing** [+ *obj*]

1 : to put (a person) into a state of hypnosis • The therapist *hypnotized* him and asked him questions about his traumatic experiences in the war. • a *hypnotized* patient

2 : to hold the attention of (someone) : to attract (someone) in a powerful or mysterious way • He can *hypnotize* people with his stare. — often used as *(be) hypnotized* • I *was hypnotized* [=*fascinated*] by her beauty.

– **hypnotizing** *adj* [*more* ~; *most* ~] • *hypnotizing* beauty

hypo- *prefix*

1 : under : beneath : down • *hypo*dermic

2 : less than normal or normally • *hypo*tension • *hypo*thermia

hy·po·chon·dria /ˌhaɪpəˈkɑːndrijə/ *noun* [*noncount*] : unusual or excessive concern about your health : a tendency to fear or imagine that you have illnesses that you do not actually have • She fueled her *hypochondria* by reading articles about rare diseases.

hy·po·chon·dri·ac /ˌhaɪpəˈkɑːndriˌæk/ *noun, pl* **-acs** [*count*] : a person who is often or always worried about being ill • My brother is a real *hypochondriac.* Every time he reads about some new disease, he thinks he has it.

hy·poc·ri·sy /hɪˈpɑːkrəsi/ *noun, pl* **-sies** *disapproving* : the behavior of people who do things that they tell other people not to do : behavior that does not agree with what someone claims to believe or feel [*noncount*] When his private letters were made public, they revealed his *hypocrisy.* • the *hypocrisy* of people who say one thing but do another [*count*] Teenagers often have a keen awareness of their parents' *hypocrisies.*

hyp·o·crite /ˈhɪpəˌkrɪt/ *noun, pl* **-crites** [*count*] *disapproving* : a person who claims or pretends to have certain beliefs about what is right but who behaves in a way that disagrees with those beliefs • the *hypocrites* who criticize other people for not voting but who don't always vote themselves

– **hyp·o·crit·i·cal** /ˌhɪpəˈkrɪtɪkəl/ *adj* [*more* ~; *most* ~] • It's *hypocritical* of you to demand respect from your students when you don't respect them in return. • a *hypocritical* remark • *hypocritical* politicians – **hyp·o·crit·i·cal·ly** /ˌhɪpəˈkrɪtɪkli/ *adv*

[1]**hy·po·der·mic** /ˌhaɪpəˈdəmɪk/ *adj, medical*

1 : going under the skin • a *hypodermic* injection

2 : used for putting fluids into or taking fluids out of the body by going under the skin • a ***hypodermic needle*** [=a thin, hollow needle used for giving people injections] • a ***hypodermic syringe***

[2]**hypodermic** *noun, pl* **-mics** [*count*] *medical* : a device that uses a thin, hollow needle for putting fluids into or taking fluids out of the body : SYRINGE

hy·po·ten·sion /ˌhaɪpoʊˈtɛnʃən/ *noun* [*noncount*] *medical* : low blood pressure

– **hy·po·ten·sive** /ˌhaɪpoʊˈtɛnsɪv/ *adj* • *hypotensive* patients

hy·pot·e·nuse /ˌhaɪˈpɑːtəˌnuːs, *Brit* ˌhaɪˈpɒtəˌnjuːz/ *noun, pl* **-nus·es** [*count*] *mathematics* : the long side opposite the right angle of a triangle

hy·po·ther·mia /ˌhaɪpoʊˈθəmijə/ *noun* [*noncount*] *medical* : a condition in which the temperature of your body is very low • She fell into the cold water and nearly died from *hypothermia.*

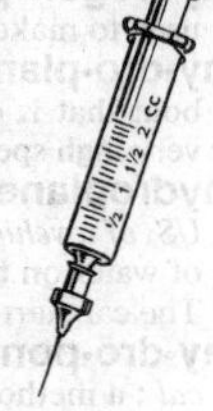
hypodermic

hy·poth·e·sis /ˌhaɪˈpɑːθəsəs/ *noun, pl* **-e·ses** /-əˌsiːz/ [*count*] : an idea or theory that is not proven but that leads to further study or discussion • Other chemists rejected his *hypothesis.* • put forward a *hypothesis* = advance a *hypothesis* • Their *hypothesis* is that watching excessive amounts of television reduces a person's ability to concentrate. • The results of the experiment did not support/confirm his *hypothesis.*

hy·poth·e·size *also Brit* **hy·poth·e·sise** /ˌhaɪˈpɑːθəˌsaɪz/ *verb* **-siz·es; -sized; -siz·ing** [+ *obj*] : to suggest (an idea or theory) : to make or suggest (a hypothesis) • Psychologists *hypothesized* that his odd behavior was caused by a chemical imbalance in the brain. • Biologists have *hypothesized* a relationship between the two species. [=biologists have suggested that there may be a relationship between the two species]

hy·po·thet·i·cal /ˌhaɪpəˈθɛtɪkəl/ *adj*

1 : involving or based on a suggested idea or theory : involving or based on a hypothesis • a *hypothetical* argument/discussion • The theory is *hypothetical.*

2 : not real : imagined as an example • She described a *hypothetical* case to clarify her point. • a *hypothetical* question/situation/example

– **hy·po·thet·i·cal·ly** /ˌhaɪpəˈθɛtɪkli/ *adv* • Suppose, *hypothetically,* that you were offered a large sum of money in exchange for revealing company secrets. Would you accept the offer? • We're just speaking *hypothetically.*

hys·ter·ec·to·my /ˌhɪstəˈrɛktəmi/ *noun, pl* **-mies** [*count, noncount*] *medical* : an operation to remove a woman's uterus • a surgeon who has performed many *hysterectomies*

hys·te·ria /hɪˈsterijə, hɪˈstirijə/ *noun* [*noncount*]

1 : a state in which your emotions (such as fear) are so strong that you behave in an uncontrolled way • A few of the children began to scream, and soon they were all caught up in the *hysteria.* • fits/attacks of *hysteria*

2 : a situation in which many people behave or react in an extreme or uncontrolled way because of fear, anger, etc. • Wartime *hysteria* led to many unfair accusations of treachery. • The spreading of the disease caused/produced ***mass hysteria*** in the village.

hys·ter·ic /hɪˈsterɪk/ *noun, pl* **-ics** [*count*] *usually disapproving* : a person who behaves or reacts in an extremely or foolishly emotional way : a hysterical person • He dismisses his critics as a bunch of *hysterics* who are always predicting disaster. — see also HYSTERICS

hys·ter·i·cal /hɪˈsterɪkəl/ *also* **hysteric** *adj* [*more* ~; *most* ~]

1 : feeling or showing extreme and uncontrolled emotion : marked by hysteria • crowds of screaming, *hysterical* fans • By the time the police arrived, the victim had become *hysterical.* • She burst into shrieks of *hysterical* laughter.

2 *informal* : very funny • I think his movies are *hysterical.*

– **hys·ter·i·cal·ly** /hɪˈsterɪkli/ *adv* • The child was crying/laughing *hysterically.* • His movies are *hysterically* funny.

hys·ter·ics /hɪˈsterɪks/ *noun* [*plural*] : uncontrolled laughter, crying, or extreme emotion : a fit of hysteria • My mother ***went into hysterics*** [=she became very upset] when she saw my tattoo. = My mother ***had hysterics*** when she saw my tattoo. • The audience was ***in hysterics*** [=was laughing very hard] throughout the movie.

Hz *abbr* hertz

I

i *or* **I** /ˈaɪ/ *noun, pl* **i's** *or* **is** *or* **I's** *or* **Is** /ˈaɪz/

1 : the ninth letter of the English alphabet [*count*] The word "ice" begins with an *i.* [*noncount*] The word "ice" begins with *i.*

2 [*count*] : the number one in Roman numerals

[1]**I** /ˈaɪ/ *pronoun* : the person who is speaking or writing — used as the subject of a verb • *I* feel fine • *I* think (that) we should leave now. • *I* like to drive. • *I* can do that myself. • You and *I* will be going to the movies together. • My brother and *I* are five years apart in age. • *I* am here. • Here *I* am. — compare ME, MINE, MY, WE ***usage*** see [1]ME

[2]**I** *abbr* island, isle

IA *abbr* Iowa

iamb /ˈaɪˌæm/ *noun, pl* **iambs** [*count*] *technical* : a unit of

rhythm in poetry that consists of one syllable that is not accented or stressed followed by one syllable that is accented or stressed (as in the words *away* or *above*)
– **iam·bic** /aɪˈæmbɪk/ *adj* ▪ *iambic* stanzas/poetry ▪ *iambic* pentameter

-ian see -AN

Ibe·ri·an /aɪˈbirijən/ *adj* **:** of or relating to Spain and Portugal ▪ the *Iberian* Peninsula ▪ *Iberian* peoples

ibex /ˈaɪˌbɛks/ *noun, pl* **ibex** *or* **ibex·es** [*count*] **:** a wild goat that lives chiefly in the mountains of Europe, Asia, and northeastern Africa

ibid *abbr* — used in formal writing to indicate that a reference is from the same source as a previous reference ✧ *Ibid* is an abbreviation of the Latin word "ibidem," which means "in the same place."

-ibility see -ABILITY

ibis /ˈaɪbəs/ *noun, pl* **ibis** *or* **ibis·es** [*count*] **:** a tall bird that has long legs and a long bill that curves downward

-ible see -ABLE

ibu·pro·fen /ˌaɪbjʊˈproʊfən/ *noun* [*noncount*] *medical* **:** a medicine that reduces pain and fever

1-ic /ɪk/ *adj suffix*
1 : having the character or form of ▪ panoram*ic* ▪ cherub*ic*
2 a : of or relating to ▪ chivalr*ic* **b :** coming from or containing ▪ acid*ic*
3 : in the manner of **:** like that of ▪ autocrat*ic*
4 : making use of ▪ electron*ic* ▪ atom*ic*

2-ic *noun suffix*
1 : someone belonging to or connected with ▪ academ*ic*
2 : someone affected by ▪ alcohol*ic*

-i·cal /ɪkəl/ *adj suffix* **:** 1-IC ▪ symmetr*ical* ▪ geolog*ical*

ICBM /ˌaɪˌsiːˌbiːˈɛm/ *noun, pl* **ICBM's** *or* **ICBMs** [*count*] **:** a type of missile that can fly from one continent to another ✧ *ICBM* is an abbreviation of "intercontinental ballistic missile."

1ice /ˈaɪs/ *noun, pl* **ic·es**
1 [*noncount*] **a :** frozen water ▪ The steps were coated with *ice.* ▪ a piece of *ice* ▪ *Ice* formed on the car's windows. ▪ The *ice* melted quickly in the hot sun. ▪ *ice* crystals/particles/sculptures ▪ *ice* cubes — see also DRY ICE **b :** a sheet of frozen water ▪ She skated out onto the *ice.* ▪ He almost fell through a hole in the *ice.* — see also BLACK ICE, CENTER ICE **c :** cubes or pieces of ice ▪ Fill the glass with *ice.*
2 a [*count, noncount*] *US* **:** a frozen dessert of crushed ice sweetened with fruit juice ▪ (a) raspberry *ice* **b** [*count*] *Brit, old-fashioned* **:** a serving of ice cream
3 [*noncount*] *US slang, old-fashioned* **:** diamonds or jewelry ▪ He gave her some *ice* for her birthday. ▪ She was dripping with *ice.* [=she was wearing a lot of diamond jewelry]
break the ice informal **:** to say or do something that helps people to relax and begin talking at a meeting, party, etc. ▪ He told a joke to *break the ice.* — see also ICEBREAKER 2
cut ice informal **:** to have importance to someone — usually + *with*; used in negative statements ▪ His opinion doesn't *cut* any *ice with* me. = His opinion *cuts* no *ice with* me. [=his opinion is not important to me]
on ice **1 :** on top of pieces of ice in order to be kept cool ▪ I'll put the champagne *on ice.* **2** *informal* **:** in the state of being delayed for a time ▪ We'll have to put/keep the project *on ice* until more funds become available. [=we'll have to stop working on the project until more funds become available] **3** *US, informal* **:** in a condition that makes victory certain ▪ With that last goal they ***put the game on ice.*** [=they iced the game; they made it certain that they would win the game]
on thin ice **:** in a dangerous situation **:** in a situation that may cause you to get into trouble ▪ In going against his father's wishes, he was (skating/walking) *on thin ice.*

2ice *verb* **ices; iced; ic·ing** [+ *obj*]
1 : to make (something) cold with ice ▪ *Ice* the glasses before you fill them. ▪ *ice* [=put ice on] a twisted ankle
2 : to cover (something, such as a cake) with icing ▪ *Ice* [=(*US*) *frost*] the cake after it has cooled.
3 *US, informal* **:** to make winning or getting (something) certain ▪ The last goal *iced* [=*clinched*] the game/win. ▪ His persuasive talk *iced* [=*secured*] the contract.
4 *ice hockey* **:** to shoot (the puck) down the rink and beyond the opponent's goal
5 *US slang, old-fashioned* **:** to kill or murder (someone) ▪ He had all his enemies *iced.*
ice over/up [*phrasal verb*] **:** to become covered with ice ▪ The freezing rain caused the roads to *ice over.* ▪ As the weather grew colder, the pond *iced over.* ▪ The wings of the plane *iced up* during the storm.

ice age *or* **Ice Age** *noun, pl* ∼ **ages** [*count*] **:** a time in the distant past when a large part of the world was covered with ice ▪ changes that occurred during the last *ice age* ▪ a valley formed during ***the Ice Age*** [=the most recent ice age]

ice ax *noun, pl* ∼ **axes** [*count*] **:** a cutting tool that is used in mountain climbing

ice·berg /ˈaɪsˌbɚg/ *noun, pl* **-bergs** [*count*] **:** a very large piece of ice floating in the ocean
the tip of the iceberg **:** a small part of something (such as a problem) that is seen or known about when there is a much larger part that is not seen or known about ▪ The news is shocking, but we may find out that the stories we've heard so far are just *the tip of the iceberg.*

iceberg lettuce *noun* [*noncount*] **:** a type of light green lettuce that is often eaten in salads — see color picture on page C4

ice·bound /ˈaɪsˌbaʊnd/ *adj* **:** surrounded or blocked by ice ▪ The harbor was *icebound.* ▪ The ship became *icebound.*

ice·box /ˈaɪsˌbɑːks/ *noun, pl* **-box·es** [*count*] *US, old-fashioned* **:** REFRIGERATOR

ice·break·er /ˈaɪsˌbreɪkɚ/ *noun, pl* **-ers** [*count*]
1 : a ship designed to clear a passage through ice
2 : something done or said to help people to relax and begin talking at a meeting, party, etc. ▪ using an old joke as a conversational *icebreaker* — see also *break the ice* at 1ICE

ice cap *noun, pl* ∼ **caps** [*count*] **:** a very large and thick sheet of ice that covers the North Pole, the South Pole, or another region ▪ the polar *ice cap*

ice–cold /ˈaɪsˈkoʊld/ *adj* **:** very cold ▪ My hands were *ice-cold.* ▪ *ice-cold* beer

ice cream /ˌaɪsˈkriːm/ *noun, pl* ∼ **creams :** a frozen food containing sweetened and flavored cream [*noncount*] What flavor of *ice cream* do you like? ▪ chocolate/vanilla *ice cream* [*count*] Would you like another *ice cream*? [=another serving of ice cream] — often used before another noun ▪ an *ice-cream* parlor/stand/soda

ice–cream cone *noun, pl* ∼ **cones** [*count*] **:** a thin, crisp cake that is shaped like a cone and used for holding ice cream; *also* **:** one filled with ice cream ▪ We each had an *ice-cream cone* for dessert.

iced *adj* **:** containing small pieces of ice or ice cubes ▪ *iced* coffee/tea

ice field *noun, pl* ∼ **fields** [*count*] **:** a large area of land covered with ice

ice fishing *noun* [*noncount*] **:** fishing that is done in winter through a hole that is cut in the ice on a lake, pond, etc.

ice floe *noun, pl* ∼ **floes** [*count*] **:** a large, flat area of ice floating in the ocean

ice hockey *noun* [*noncount*] **:** a game played on an ice rink in which two teams of six players on skates use curved sticks to try to shoot a puck into the opponent's goal — called also (*US*) *hockey*; compare FIELD HOCKEY

ice lolly *noun, pl* ∼ **lollies** [*count*] *Brit* **:** a piece of flavored ice that is eaten off a stick — compare POPSICLE

ice pack *noun, pl* ∼ **packs** [*count*]
1 : a container or bag filled with ice that is used to cool part of your body ▪ He had an *ice pack* on his sore elbow.
2 : a large area of ice on the ocean formed from pieces and sheets of ice that have been pushed together by wind and waves

ice pick *noun, pl* ∼ **picks** [*count*] **:** a sharp tool used for breaking off small pieces of ice

ice rink *noun, pl* ∼ **rinks** [*count*] **:** an often enclosed area that has a sheet of ice for ice-skating

ice sheet *noun, pl* ∼ **sheets** [*count*] **:** a very large and thick area of ice that covers a region

ice show *noun, pl* ∼ **shows** [*count*] **:** a show in which ice-skaters perform to music

ice skate *noun, pl* ∼ **skates** [*count*] **:** a shoe with a special blade on the bottom that is used for skating on ice ▪ a pair of *ice skates*

ice–skate /ˈaɪsˌskeɪt/ *verb* **-skates; -skat·ed; -skat·ing** [*no obj*] **:** to skate on ice ▪ I had never *ice-skated* before.
– **ice–skat·er** /ˈaɪsˌskeɪtɚ/ *noun, pl* **-ers** [*count*] ▪ There were several *ice-skaters* at the rink. – **ice–skating** *noun* [*noncount*] ▪ They use the frozen pond for *ice-skating.* ▪ Let's ***go ice-skating.***

ice storm *noun, pl* ∼ **storms** [*count*] **:** a storm in which falling rain freezes as it lands

ice water *noun [noncount] US* **:** water that has ice in it **:** very cold water ▪ a glass of *ice water* [=(*Brit*) iced water]
ice water in your veins US, informal ✧ If you have *ice water in your veins*, you remain very calm and controlled in a situation in which other people would become upset or afraid.

ic·i·cle /ˈaɪˌsɪkəl/ *noun, pl* **ic·i·cles** *[count]* **:** a hanging piece of ice formed when water freezes as it drips down from something (such as a roof)

ic·ing /ˈaɪsɪŋ/ *noun [noncount]* **:** FROSTING ▪ a cake with chocolate *icing*
icing on the cake **:** something extra that makes a good thing even better ▪ The concert itself was great, and getting to meet the band afterward was (the) *icing on the cake*.

icing sugar *noun [noncount] Brit* **:** POWDERED SUGAR

icky /ˈɪki/ *adj* **ick·i·er; -est** *[also more ~; most ~] informal* **:** having a very unpleasant quality ▪ The trail was *icky* with mud. ▪ an *icky* taste

icon /ˈaɪˌkɑːn/ *noun, pl* **icons** *[count]*
1 *computers* **:** a small picture on a computer screen that represents a program or function ▪ Click on the *icon* to open your e-mail program. — see picture at COMPUTER
2 a : a person who is very successful and admired ▪ He has become an *icon* in the movie business. ▪ a singer who has become a pop *icon* **b :** a widely known symbol ▪ The Statue of Liberty has become an American cultural *icon*.
3 *also* ***ikon*** **:** a religious image in the Orthodox Christian church
– icon·ic /aɪˈkɑːnɪk/ *adj [more ~; most ~]* ▪ He has achieved *iconic* status in the movie business.

I

icon·o·clast /aɪˈkɑːnəˌklæst/ *noun, pl* **-clasts** *[count] formal* **:** a person who criticizes or opposes beliefs and practices that are widely accepted
– icon·o·clasm /aɪˈkɑːnəˌklæzəm/ *noun [noncount]* ▪ The *iconoclasm* of his views made him unpopular. **– icon·o·clast·ic** /aɪˌkɑːnəˈklæstɪk/ *adj [more ~; most ~]* ▪ *iconoclastic* theories **– icon·o·clast·i·cal·ly** /aɪˌkɑːnəˈklæstɪkli/ *adv*

ico·nog·ra·phy /ˌaɪkəˈnɑːgrəfi/ *noun [noncount]* **:** the images or symbols related to something ▪ Christian *iconography* ▪ the *iconography* of the 1960s

-ics /ɪks/ *noun suffix*
1 : study **:** knowledge ▪ electron*ics* ▪ linguist*ics*
2 : characteristic actions or activities ▪ hero*ics* ▪ athlet*ics* ▪ acrobat*ics* ▪ gymnast*ics*

ICU *abbr* intensive care unit ▪ She spent several days in (the) *ICU* after the surgery.

icy /ˈaɪsi/ *adj* **ic·i·er; -est** *[also more ~; most ~]*
1 : covered with ice ▪ *icy* roads/sidewalks
2 : very cold ▪ *icy* weather ▪ an ***icy cold*** [=*ice-cold*] wind
3 : not friendly or kind ▪ an *icy* [=*cold, frigid*] stare
– ic·i·ly /ˈaɪsəli/ *adv* ▪ His manner was *icily* formal. **– ic·i·ness** /ˈaɪsinəs/ *noun [noncount]*

id /ˈɪd/ *noun, pl* **ids** *[count] psychology* **:** a part of a person's unconscious mind that relates to basic needs and desires — compare EGO, SUPEREGO

¹ID /ˈaɪˈdiː/ *noun, pl* **ID's** *or* **IDs :** a document, card, etc., that has your name and other information about you and that often includes your photograph *[noncount]* The guard insisted that we show him some *ID*. [=*identification*] *[count]* The guard insisted that we show him our *ID's*.

²ID *verb* **ID's** *or* **IDs; ID'd** *or* **IDed; ID'ing** *or* **IDing** *[+ obj] informal* **:** to find out the identity of (someone or something) **:** IDENTIFY ▪ The police have not yet *ID'd* the victim.

³ID *abbr* Idaho

I'd /ˈaɪd/ — used as a contraction of *I had* or *I would* ▪ *I'd* [=I had] already read the book. ▪ *I'd* [=I had] better leave. ▪ *I'd* [=I would] rather do it myself.

ID card *noun, pl* **~ cards** *[count]* **:** a card that has your name and other information about you and that often includes your photograph — called also *identification card, identity card*

-ide /aɪd/ *noun suffix, chemistry* **:** a chemical made up of two or more elements ▪ sulph*ide* ▪ cyan*ide*

idea /aɪˈdiːjə/ *noun, pl* **ideas**
1 *[count]* **:** a thought, plan, or suggestion about what to do ▪ My *idea* is to study law. ▪ Starting her own business seemed like a good *idea* at the time, but it turned out badly. ▪ I left with the *idea* that I'd come back later. = I left with the *idea* of coming back later. ▪ Whose *idea* was it to leave so early? ▪ My *idea* was that if we left early we could beat the crowd. ▪ Buying the car was a bad *idea*. ▪ I have some *ideas* for redecorating the room. ▪ He has an *idea* for a movie. ▪ I'm not sure what to do next. Do you have any *ideas*? ▪ She's always full of new *ideas*. ▪ It's a good *idea* to talk to people who have actually been there. ▪ ***There's/that's an idea***! = There's/that's a good *idea*! ▪ What's the next ***big idea*** in the fashion industry? ▪ Tom ***has the right idea***—while the rest of us are fighting traffic every day, he takes the train to work.
2 *[count]* **:** an opinion or belief ▪ That guy has some pretty strange *ideas*. ▪ "I thought he'd help us." "What gave you that *idea*?" ▪ Where did you get that *idea*? ▪ I thought we could handle this ourselves, but my boss ***had other ideas***. [=my boss did not agree]
3 : something that you imagine or picture in your mind *[count]* I formed a good *idea* of what the place is like by reading about it. ▪ A hamburger and a milkshake isn't exactly my *idea* of a gourmet meal! [=it is not what I imagine a gourmet meal to be] ▪ A quiet night at home is my *idea* of a good time. *[noncount]* Could you give us some *idea* of what to expect?
4 *[singular]* **:** an understanding of something **:** knowledge about something ▪ He has a clear *idea* of his responsibilities. [=he knows what his responsibilities are] ▪ Do you have any *idea* of what these repairs will cost? ▪ I ***have no idea*** what you're talking about. = I don't ***have the faintest/slightest idea*** what you're talking about. [=I do not know/understand at all what you're talking about] ▪ "Was it hard?" "***You have no idea*** (how hard it was)!" [=yes, it was very hard] ▪ All right, I ***get the idea***. [=I understand] ▪ I think he made a mistake, but don't ***get the wrong idea*** [=don't misunderstand me], I still think he has done a good job overall. ▪ I don't want to ***give you the wrong idea***.
5 *the idea* **:** the central meaning or purpose of something ▪ *The* whole *idea* [=*point, object*] of the game is to keep from getting caught. ▪ *The idea* [=*goal, aim*] is to get people to attend. ▪ I just don't get/understand ***the idea behind*** [=the reason for] this change in the rules. ▪ (*informal*) Hey! ***What's the big idea***!? [=why are you doing that?]
give someone ideas or ***put ideas in/into someone's head*** **:** to cause someone to think about doing something that probably should not be done ▪ Don't go *giving him ideas*. ▪ Don't *put ideas in/into his head* by telling him he'd be happier if he'd quit his job.

¹ide·al /aɪˈdiːl/ *adj* **:** exactly right for a particular purpose, situation, or person **:** PERFECT ▪ *ideal* weather ▪ the *ideal* man/woman ▪ It was an *ideal* spot for a vacation. ▪ She is an *ideal* candidate for the job. ▪ The conference provided us with an *ideal* opportunity to meet new people. ▪ In an *ideal* world [=a perfect world without problems] there would be no war. ▪ The conditions were ***far from ideal***. [=were not good at all]

²ideal *noun, pl* **-als** *[count]*
1 : an idea or standard of perfection or excellence ▪ an *ideal* of romantic love ▪ The organization has remained true to its *ideals*. [=has continued to work for and support the goals that it considers most worthwhile and important] ▪ He hasn't lived up to his high *ideals*.
2 : someone or something that is believed to be perfect **:** someone or something that you admire and want to imitate ▪ She considers the actress her *ideal*.

ide·al·ism /aɪˈdiːjəˌlɪzəm/ *noun [noncount]* **:** the attitude of a person who believes that it is possible to live according to very high standards of behavior and honesty ▪ youthful *idealism* ▪ political/religious/romantic *idealism*
– ide·al·ist /aɪˈdiːjəlɪst/ *noun, pl* **-ists** *[count]* ▪ The group was a mix of realists and *idealists*. **– ide·al·is·tic** /aɪˌdiːjəˈlɪstɪk/ *adj [more ~; most ~]* ▪ hopeful and *idealistic* students ▪ She was naïve and *idealistic*. **– ide·al·is·ti·cal·ly** /aɪˌdiːjəˈlɪstɪkli/ *adv*

ide·al·ize *also Brit* **ide·al·ise** /aɪˈdiːjəˌlaɪz/ *verb* **-iz·es; -ized; -iz·ing** *[+ obj]* **:** to think of or represent (someone or something) as being perfect ▪ She tends to *idealize* her job.
– ide·al·i·za·tion *also Brit* **ide·al·i·sa·tion** /aɪˌdiːjələˈzeɪʃən, *Brit* aɪˌdɪəˌlaɪˈzeɪʃən/ *noun, pl* **-tions** *[count, noncount]* ▪ The film presents the subject without (any) *idealization*. **– idealized** *also Brit* **idealised** *adj [more ~; most ~]* ▪ The movie presents a very *idealized* version of American life.

ide·al·ly /aɪˈdiːli/ *adv*
1 : in an ideal way **:** PERFECTLY ▪ His skills made him *ideally* suited for the job. ▪ They were *ideally* suited to one another. ▪ The ski slope was situated *ideally*.
2 — used to say what should happen or be done to produce the best results ▪ *Ideally*, each student should be taught indi-

vidually. ▪ *Ideally*, you should do these exercises daily.

iden·ti·cal /aɪˈdɛntɪkəl/ *adj*
1 : exactly the same ▪ We visited the *identical* place we stopped at last year
2 : exactly alike or equal ▪ They were wearing *identical* coats. ▪ The boxes were *identical* in shape. ▪ They drove virtually *identical* cars. ▪ The results were *identical* to/with those of the first test.
– iden·ti·cal·ly /aɪˈdɛntɪkli/ *adv* ▪ They were dressed *identically*. ▪ The two words are pronounced *identically*.

identical twin *noun, pl* ~ **twins** [*count*] **:** either member of a pair of twins that are produced from a single egg and who look exactly alike — compare FRATERNAL TWIN

iden·ti·fi·ca·tion /aɪˌdɛntəfəˈkeɪʃən/ *noun, pl* **-tions**
1 : the act of finding out who someone is or what something is **:** the act of identifying someone or something [*noncount*] A member of the family was brought in for *identification* of the body. ▪ The birds are tagged for easy *identification*. [*count*] The police have made a positive *identification* of the suspect.
2 [*noncount*] **:** something that shows who a person is **:** a document, card, etc., that has your name and other information about you and that often includes your photograph ▪ We were told to carry (some) personal *identification* at all times. ▪ He needed to show (his) *identification* before they would cash the check. ▪ You need two ***forms of identification***.
3 [*noncount*] **:** a feeling that you share and understand the problems or experiences of another person **:** the act of identifying *with* someone ▪ the movie audience's *identification with* the good guys ▪ They had/felt a (strong) sense of *identification with* their neighbors.

identification card *noun, pl* ~ **cards** [*count*] **:** ID CARD

identification parade *noun, pl* ~ **-ades** [*count*] *Brit* **:** LINEUP 3

iden·ti·fy /aɪˈdɛntəˌfaɪ/ *verb* **-fies; -fied; -fy·ing** [+ *obj*]
1 : to know and say who someone is or what something is ▪ She *identified* the dog as her lost pet. ▪ He was able to correctly *identify* the mushroom. ▪ The witness positively *identified* the suspect in the crime. ▪ She was easily *identified* by what she was wearing. [=it was easy to see who she was because of what she was wearing] ▪ He has a talent for *identifying* [=*recognizing*] good workers.
2 : to find out who someone is or what something is ▪ The corpse was *identified* on the basis of dental records. ▪ They could not *identify* the source of the quotation. ▪ They had no difficulty in *identifying* the problem. ▪ We began by *identifying* what we needed for the job. ▪ We need to *identify* the causes of unemployment.
3 : to show who someone is or what something is ▪ His clothes *identified* him as a clerk. [=his clothes showed that he was a clerk] ▪ an ***identifying mark/feature*** [=a mark/feature that shows who someone is or what something is]
identify with [*phrasal verb*] **1** ***identify (something) with (something)*** **:** to think of (something) as being the same as (something else) ▪ It is a mistake to *identify* [=*equate*] being healthy *with* being thin. **2** ***identify (someone) with (something)*** **:** to think of (someone) as being very closely associated with (something) — often used as *(be) identified with* ▪ She has always *been identified with* the civil rights movement. ▪ These groups *are identified with* conservation. **3** ***identify with (someone or something)*** **:** to think of yourself as having the same problems and feelings as someone ▪ Many readers *identify with* the characters in her novels. ▪ He could *identify with* the problems the athlete was having. [=he understood the problems because he had had similar problems himself]
identify yourself **:** to say who you are ▪ When the police asked his name, he refused to *identify himself*.
– iden·ti·fi·able /aɪˌdɛntəˈfajəbəl/ *adj* [*more* ~; *most* ~] ▪ a clearly/readily *identifiable* signature **– iden·ti·fi·ably** /aɪˌdɛntəˈfajəbli/ *adv* ▪ The band has an *identifiably* British sound.

iden·ti·ty /aɪˈdɛntəti/ *noun, pl* **-ties**
1 : who someone is **:** the name of a person [*count*] The *identity* of the criminal/victim is not known. ▪ The face of the witness was hidden in order to protect her *identity*. [=to keep her name from being known] ▪ The documents proved/established his *identity*. [=proved/established who he was] ▪ They produced their passports as proof of their *identities*. [*noncount*] You will need to show proof of *identity*. [=something that shows that you are who you say you are] ▪ They arrested the wrong man. It was a case of ***mistaken identity***.
2 : the qualities, beliefs, etc., that make a particular person or group different from others [*count*] As children grow, they establish their own *identities*. ▪ She did not want to be known only as the wife of her husband. She insisted on having her own *identity*. [=on being known for her own qualities, achievements, etc.] [*noncount*] people who seem to lack individual *identity* ▪ He has a strong sense of personal *identity*. [=a strong feeling about exactly the kind of person he is] ▪ His art reflects his cultural/racial *identity*.

identity card *noun, pl* ~ **cards** [*count*] **:** ID CARD

identity crisis *noun, pl* ~ **crises** [*count*] **:** a feeling of unhappiness and confusion caused by not being sure about what type of person you really are or what the true purpose of your life is ▪ He is suffering from an *identity crisis*.

identity parade *noun, pl* ~ **-rades** [*count*] *Brit* **:** LINEUP 3

identity theft *noun* [*noncount*] **:** the illegal use of someone else's personal identifying information (such as a Social Security number) in order to get money or credit ▪ How can we protect ourselves against *identity theft*?

ide·ol·o·gist /ˌaɪdiˈɑːləʤɪst/ *noun, pl* **-gists** [*count*] **:** IDEOLOGUE

ideo·logue /ˈaɪdijəˌlɑːg/ *noun, pl* **-logues** [*count*] *formal* + *often disapproving* **:** someone who very strongly supports and is guided by the ideology of a particular group ▪ conservative/liberal *ideologues*

ide·ol·o·gy /ˌaɪdiˈɑːləʤi/ *noun, pl* **-gies :** the set of ideas and beliefs of a group or political party [*count*] progressive/liberal/conservative *ideologies* ▪ the *ideology* of a totalitarian/capitalist society [*noncount*] He says that the election is not about *ideology*.
– ideo·log·i·cal /ˌaɪdijəˈlɑːʤɪkəl/ *adj* [*more* ~; *most* ~] ▪ The two groups divided along *ideological* lines. ▪ *ideological* conflicts **– ideo·log·i·cal·ly** /ˌaɪdijəˈlɑːʤɪkli/ *adv*

ides /ˈaɪdz/ *noun* [*plural*] **:** the 15th day of March, May, July, or October or the 13th day of any other month in the ancient Roman calendar ▪ "Beware the *ides* of March." —Shakespeare, *Julius Caesar* (1599)

id·i·o·cy /ˈɪdijəsi/ *noun, pl* **-cies**
1 [*noncount*] **:** extreme stupidity ▪ an act of sheer *idiocy*
2 [*count*] **:** something that is extremely stupid or foolish **:** an idiotic action or statement ▪ He was complaining again about the *idiocies* of the people he works for.

id·i·om /ˈɪdijəm/ *noun, pl* **-oms**
1 [*count*] **:** an expression that cannot be understood from the meanings of its separate words but that has a separate meaning of its own ▪ The expression "give way," meaning "retreat," is an *idiom*.
2 [*count, noncount*] **:** a form of a language that is spoken in a particular area and that uses some of its own words, grammar, and pronunciations **:** DIALECT
3 : a style or form of expression that is characteristic of a particular person, type of art, etc. [*count*] a poet's *idiom* ▪ rock and roll and other musical *idioms* [*noncount*] a feature of modern jazz *idiom*
– id·i·om·at·ic /ˌɪdijəˈmætɪk/ *adj* ▪ an *idiomatic* expression/phrase [=an expression/phrase that is an idiom] ▪ a use of language that is not *idiomatic* [=that does not sound natural or correct] **– id·i·om·at·i·cal·ly** /ˌɪdijəˈmætɪkli/ *adv* ▪ That phrase is *idiomatically* acceptable/correct.

id·io·syn·cra·sy /ˌɪdijəˈsɪŋkrəsi/ *noun, pl* **-sies** [*count*]
1 : an unusual way in which a particular person behaves or thinks ▪ Her habit of using "like" in every sentence was just one of her *idiosyncrasies*.
2 : an unusual part or feature of something ▪ The current system has a few *idiosyncracies*.
– id·io·syn·crat·ic /ˌɪdijoʊˌsɪnˈkrætɪk/ *adj* [*more* ~; *most* ~] ▪ She has an *idiosyncratic* [=*unusual*] singing voice. ▪ His taste in music was very *idiosyncratic*. ▪ an *idiosyncratic* writing style **– id·io·syn·crat·i·cal·ly** /ˌɪdijoʊˌsɪnˈkrætɪkli/ *adv*

id·i·ot /ˈɪdijət/ *noun, pl* **-ots** [*count*] **:** a very stupid or foolish person ▪ Don't be such an *idiot*! ▪ I really made an *idiot* of myself [=I acted very stupidly] at the party last night. ▪ Some *idiot* [=*fool*] of a driver kept trying to pass me!
– id·i·ot·ic /ˌɪdiˈɑːtɪk/ *adj* [*more* ~; *most* ~] ▪ an *idiotic* movie ▪ *idiotic* drivers ▪ My behavior last night was *idiotic*. **– id·i·ot·i·cal·ly** /ˌɪdiˈɑːtɪkli/ *adv*

id·i·ot–proof /ˈɪdijətˌpruːf/ *adj, informal* **:** extremely easy to use or do ▪ *idiot-proof* software

idiot savant *noun, pl* **idiots savants** *or* **idiot savants** [*count*] **:** SAVANT 2

[1]idle /ˈaɪdl/ *adj*
1 : not working, active, or being used ▪ *idle* workers [=workers who do not have jobs] ▪ The company's competitor's have not been *idle* [=they have been active/busy] in recent months. ▪ The factory has been lying/sitting/standing *idle* [=has not been used] for the past year. ▪ the ***idle rich*** [=rich people who do not have to work]
2 : not having any real purpose or value ▪ *idle* rumors/gossip ▪ There has been a lot of *idle* speculation about what might happen, but no one really knows. ▪ (*formal*) It is *idle* [=*useless, pointless*] to want what you cannot have. ▪ She said she would leave him, but he knew it was an ***idle threat***. [=he knew that she did not mean it]
3 : not having much activity ▪ the *idle* days of summer
4 *somewhat old-fashioned* **: trying to avoid work : LAZY** ▪ a careless and *idle* worker ▪ There was a group of *idle* boys standing on the corner.
– idle·ness /ˈaɪdl̩nəs/ *noun* [*noncount*]

[2]idle *verb* **idles; idled; idling**
1 *of an engine or vehicle* **: to run without being connected for doing useful work** [*no obj*] She left the engine *idling* for a few seconds before she turned it off. ▪ The cars *idled* in traffic. [+ *obj*] *idle* an engine
2 : to spend time doing nothing or nothing useful [*no obj*] A group of boys *idled* in the doorway. [+ *obj*] **— + *away*** ▪ We *idled away* the evening playing cards.
3 [+ *obj*] *US* **: to cause (someone or something) to stop working : to make (someone or something) idle** ▪ The factory closed, *idling* several hundred workers. ▪ Thousands of workers have been *idled* by the bad economy. ▪ The factory has been *idled* by the strike.

idler /ˈaɪdlə/ *noun, pl* **idlers** [*count*] *somewhat old-fashioned* **: someone who is lazy or does not work** ▪ a rich *idler*

idly /ˈaɪdli/ *adv* **: without much thought, effort, or concern** ▪ We sat *idly*, waiting for something to happen. ▪ I *idly* wondered what they were doing.

idol /ˈaɪdl/ *noun, pl* **idols** [*count*]
1 : a greatly loved or admired person ▪ a sports/teen/pop *idol* ▪ an actor who is the *idol* of millions ▪ a ***fallen idol*** [=a person who is no longer greatly admired] **— see also** MATINEE IDOL
2 : a picture or object that is worshipped as a god

idol·a·try /aɪˈdɑːlətri/ *noun* [*noncount*] **: the worship of a picture or object as a god**
– idol·a·trous /aɪˈdɑːlətrəs/ *adj* ▪ *idolatrous* worship

idol·ize *also Brit* **idol·ise** /ˈaɪdəˌlaɪz/ *verb* **-iz·es; -ized; -iz·ing** [+ *obj*] **: to love or admire (someone) very much or too much** ▪ The young boy *idolized* his father. [=he loved his father and thought that he never did anything wrong] ▪ an actor who is *idolized* by millions
– idol·i·za·tion *also Brit* **idol·i·sa·tion** /ˌaɪdələˈzeɪʃən, *Brit* ˌaɪdəˌlaɪˈzeɪʃən/ *noun* [*noncount*] ▪ The *idolization* of the novelist continued after his death.

idyll *also* **idyl** /ˈaɪdl/ *noun, pl* **idylls** *also* **idyls** [*count*] *literary*
1 : a simple poem or other piece of writing that describes peaceful country life
2 : a happy and enjoyable scene or experience ▪ a pastoral/romantic *idyll*

idyl·lic /aɪˈdɪlɪk/ *adj* [*more* ~; *most* ~] **: very peaceful, happy, and enjoyable** ▪ He had an *idyllic* childhood. ▪ an *idyllic* retreat/setting in the countryside ▪ an *idyllic* summer day
– idyl·li·cal·ly /aɪˈdɪlɪkli/ *adv* ▪ He had an *idyllically* happy childhood. ▪ The village is *idyllically* situated.

i.e. *abbr* **that is — used to introduce something that explains a preceding statement more fully or exactly** ▪ The medicine needs be taken for a short period of time; *i.e.*, three to five days. ✧ **The abbreviation *i.e.* comes from the Latin phrase "id est," which means "that is."**

-ie *also* **-y** /i/ *noun suffix, informal*
1 : little one ▪ boot*ie* ▪ bird*ie* **: dear little one** ▪ sonn*y*
2 : someone or something that is ▪ smart*y* ▪ bigg*ie* ▪ tough*ie*
3 : someone belonging to ▪ town*ie* **: someone having to do with** ▪ drugg*ie*

-ier see [2]-ER

[1]if /ˈɪf/ *conj*
1 — used to talk about the result or effect of something that may happen or be true ▪ *If* it rains, (then) we won't go to the park. ▪ *If* he actually did commit the crime, he deserves to be punished. ▪ *If* you believe that, you'll believe anything! ▪ Come to the party *if* you can. ▪ *If* you really want to know, you should ask. ▪ What will happen *if* I fail the test? ▪ You should study. ***If not***, you won't pass the test. = *If* you don't (study), you won't pass the test. ▪ Please arrive early ***if possible***. = Please arrive early *if* it is possible. ▪ I'll do the work myself ***if necessary***. = I'll do the work myself *if* it is necessary. ▪ ***If and when*** he comes, you can ask him. = ***When and if*** he comes, you can ask him.
2 — used to discuss the imaginary result or effect of something that did not happen or that is or was not true ▪ *If* you had studied, you would have passed the test. ▪ The situation would be funny *if* it weren't so tragic. = (*informal*) The situation would be funny *if* it wasn't so tragic. ▪ The harvest would have been good *if* it had rained. ▪ The news would be interesting *if* (it were) true, but it's not true.
3 — used to say that something must happen before another thing can happen ▪ He said he'll come to the party *if* she comes too. = (more strongly) He said he'll come to the party ***only if*** she comes too. = (most strongly) He says he'll come to the party ***if and only if*** she comes too.
4 — used to indicate a result that always occurs when something happens ▪ He gets angry *if* [=*when*] you disagree with him. ▪ The engine stalls *if* you let it get too hot.
5 : even though : ALTHOUGH ▪ It was an interesting *if* unbelievable story. ▪ Her actions were understandable, *if* not forgivable. ▪ He had to perform an annoying, *if* necessary, task. ▪ a fair, *if* tough, boss ▪ The weather was good, *if* not great.
6 — used to introduce a statement or question about something that is not certain ▪ I'll see *if* [=*whether*] I can come. ▪ Do you know *if* he'll come to the party? ▪ I wonder *if* it's true (or not). ▪ Frankly, I doubt *if* he'll pass the exams. ▪ She asked *if* the mail had come. ▪ We should determine/decide *if* it is safe to go swimming.
7 a — used to make a polite request or suggestion ▪ Would you mind *if* I sat here? [=may I sit here?] ▪ *If* you will/would (be good enough to) follow me, ladies and gentlemen, I'll take you to your seats. ▪ *If* I could make a suggestion, why don't we sit closer to the front of the theater? ▪ I'd like to stay a little longer, ***if you don't mind***. = I'd like to stay a little longer, ***if it's/that's all right with you***. **b — used to state an opinion in a polite way** ▪ You're looking particularly lovely today, ***if I may say so***.
8 — used in statements that describe feelings (such as regret) about a possible situation ▪ I'm sorry *if* you think I insulted you. ▪ I'd be sorry *if* you thought I had insulted you. ▪ I don't care *if* we're late.
9 — used in statements and questions that express doubt ▪ I met Brenda last week—*if* that is/was in fact her real name. ▪ *If* you're so smart, why aren't you rich?
10 — used to introduce an even stronger alternative to what has just been said ▪ These changes will have little ***if any*** impact on the problem. ▪ Few *if any* of the town's original settlers are left. ▪ Rarely, ***if ever***, does that happen. ▪ His efforts have helped to save thousands, ***if not*** millions, of lives. ▪ My car is as fast as yours *if not* (even) faster.
11 — used to express surprise about meeting someone when it is not expected ▪ So I went to the game and who should I see there ***if not*** [=*but*] my old friend Tom! ▪ Well, ***if it isn't*** my old friend Tom! ▪ So I went to the game and who did I see there ***if it wasn't*** my old friend Tom!
12 — used to emphasize the truth of a statement ▪ The idea is true *if* any idea has ever been! [=the idea is certainly true] ▪ "He claims that he's never met her." "Well, *if* that isn't the biggest load of nonsense I've ever heard!" [=that is a lot of nonsense; that is completely untrue] ▪ I'll get my revenge ***if it's the last thing I do***! [=I am determined to get my revenge]
as if see [2]AS
even if see [2]EVEN
***if anything* — used to make a statement that strongly disagrees or contrasts with a preceding statement** ▪ We don't see each other too often—*if anything* we don't see each other often enough! ▪ The economy has not improved. It has gotten worse, *if anything*.
if it comes to that see [1]COME
***if I were you* — used when giving advice to people about how they should behave** ▪ I'd study more *if I were you*. [=I think you should study more]
if not for* : in the absence of (something or someone) : WITHOUT** ▪ *If not for* modern medicine, fewer babies would survive. ▪ *If not for* him, I wouldn't be where I am today. **— often used in the phrases *if it were not for* and *if it had not been for ▪ *If it were not for* your donations, many more children would go hungry. ▪ *If it hadn't been for* him, I wouldn't be where I am today.
***if nothing else* : at least — used to stress that an approving statement is true even though a stronger statement might**

not be ▪ *If nothing else,* he's polite! ▪ The food was hot, *if nothing else.* [=the food may not have been very good, but at least it was hot]

if only — used to talk about something that you want to happen or be true ▪ *If only* she loved me in return! ▪ *If only* it would stop raining.

if you ask me — used in statements that express an opinion ▪ *If you ask me* [=in my opinion], he's a liar.

if you must see [1]MUST

what if see [1]WHAT

[2]**if** *noun, pl* **ifs** [*count*] **: something that is not certain : something that could either happen or not happen** ▪ There are too many *ifs* in this proposal. ▪ They could win if everyone plays his best, but ***that's a big if*** [=it is not likely that everyone will play his best] ▪ (*US*) She's the most qualified candidate, and there are no ***ifs, ands, or buts*** about it! = (*Brit*) She's the most qualified candidate, and there are no ***ifs and buts*** about it! [=it is certain that she is the most qualified candidate]

if·fy /ˈɪfi/ *adj* **if·fi·er; -est** [*also more ~; most ~*] *informal*

1 : having many uncertain or unknown qualities or conditions : not certain ▪ an *iffy* situation/proposal/decision ▪ It's *iffy* [=*doubtful*] whether he can play in the game.

2 : not certain to be good ▪ I'm hoping to play golf tomorrow, but the weather looks a bit *iffy.* [=there's a chance that the weather will be bad]

-i·fy /əˌfaɪ/ *verb suffix* **:** -FY

ig·loo /ˈɪˌgluː/ *noun, pl* **-loos** [*count*] **: a house made of blocks of snow or ice in the form of a dome**

ig·ne·ous /ˈɪgnijəs/ *adj, technical* **: formed when hot, liquid rock cools and becomes hard** ▪ *igneous* rock

ig·nite /ɪgˈnaɪt/ *verb* **-nites; -nit·ed; -nit·ing**

1 a [*+ obj*] **: to set (something) on fire : to cause (something) to burn :** LIGHT ▪ *ignite* a bonfire ▪ The fire was *ignited* by sparks. **b** [*no obj*] **: to begin burning : to catch fire** ▪ The paper *ignited* on contact with sparks. ▪ a material that *ignites* easily

2 [*+ obj*] **a : to give life or energy to (someone or something)** ▪ Three wins in a row *ignited* the team. ▪ The story *ignited* [=*fired*] her imagination. **b : to cause the sudden occurrence of (something)** ▪ Her comments have *ignited* [=*sparked*] a controversy. ▪ His proposal is *igniting* opposition.

– ig·nit·able /ɪgˈnaɪtəbəl/ *adj* ▪ a material that is easily *ignitable* ▪ *ignitable* fuel

ig·ni·tion /ɪgˈnɪʃən/ *noun, pl* **-tions**

1 [*count*] **a : the electrical system in an engine that causes the fuel to burn so that the engine begins working** ▪ There's a problem with the car's *ignition.* **b : the device that is used to start a car's engine — usually singular** ▪ Put the key in the *ignition.* ▪ Turn on/off the *ignition.* — see picture at CAR

2 [*noncount*] **: the act of causing something to start burning : the act of igniting something** ▪ *ignition* of the fire

ig·no·ble /ɪgˈnoʊbəl/ *adj* [*more ~; most ~*] *formal* **: not deserving respect : not noble or honorable** ▪ an *ignoble* past ▪ *ignoble* thoughts

– ig·no·bly /ɪgˈnoʊbli/ *adv* ▪ His career ended *ignobly.*

ig·no·min·i·ous /ˌɪgnəˈmɪnijəs/ *adj* [*more ~; most ~*] *formal* **: causing disgrace or shame** ▪ They suffered an *ignominious* [=*humiliating*] defeat.

– ig·no·min·i·ous·ly *adv* ▪ failed *ignominiously*

ig·no·mi·ny /ˈɪgnəˌmɪni/ *noun, pl* **-nies** *formal* **: a situation or event that causes you to feel ashamed or embarrassed** [*noncount*] She had to endure the *ignominy* of being forced to resign. [*count*] the small/petty *ignominies* that are a part of everyone's life

ig·no·ra·mus /ˌɪgnəˈreɪməs/ *noun, pl* **-mus·es** [*count*] **: a person who does not know much : an ignorant or stupid person** ▪ I can't believe they let an *ignoramus* like that run the company.

ig·no·rance /ˈɪgnərəns/ *noun* **: a lack of knowledge, understanding, or education : the state of being ignorant** [*noncount*] His racist attitudes were born out of *ignorance.* — often *+ of* ▪ *Ignorance of* the law is no excuse (for violating it). ▪ Their decisions were made ***in ignorance of*** [=*without knowing*] the true nature of the situation. ▪ When asked about the reasons for these drastic changes, she ***pleaded/pled ignorance*** [=she said that she did not know the reasons] [*singular*] an appalling *ignorance* about/of other cultures

ignorance is bliss — used to say that a person who does not know about a problem does not worry about it

ig·no·rant /ˈɪgnərənt/ *adj* [*more ~; most ~*]

1 : lacking knowledge or information ▪ He is an *ignorant* old racist. ▪ She was *ignorant* about the dangers of the drug. — often *+ of* ▪ They were *ignorant* [=*unaware*] *of* the facts. ▪ He remains *ignorant of* the changes. ▪ We were ***blissfully ignorant of*** the problems that had occurred.

2 : resulting from or showing a lack of knowledge ▪ It was an *ignorant* mistake. ▪ *ignorant* opinions

– ig·no·rant·ly *adv*

ig·nore /ɪgˈnoɚ/ *verb* **-nores; -nored; -nor·ing** [*+ obj*]

1 : to refuse to show that you hear or see (something or someone) ▪ She tried to *ignore* him but he wouldn't leave her alone. ▪ I'll *ignore* that last remark.

2 : to do nothing about or in response to (something or someone) ▪ If we continue to *ignore* these problems they will only get worse. ▪ They *ignored* the warning signs. ▪ *ignoring* the poor

igua·na /ɪˈgwɑːnə/ *noun, pl* **-nas** [*count*] **: a large lizard that lives in the tropical regions of Central and South America**

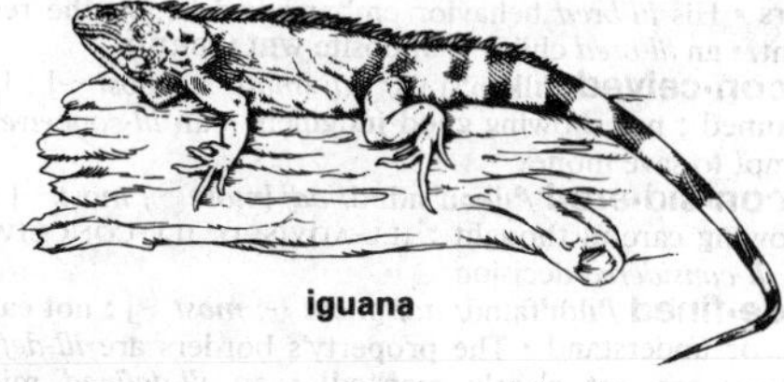

iguana

ikon *variant spelling of* ICON 3

il- see IN-

IL *abbr* Illinois

ilk /ˈɪlk/ *noun* [*singular*] **: sort or kind** ▪ The club attracts punk rockers and others of that *ilk.*

[1]**ill** /ˈɪl/ *adj*

1 a : not well or healthy : sick or unhealthy ▪ a chronically/critically/terminally *ill* patient ▪ mentally *ill* adults — **usually used after a verb** ▪ I felt *ill* [=*sick*] all afternoon. ▪ What's wrong? You look *ill.* ▪ He had been *ill* for several years. ▪ More than half of those exposed to the virus eventually become *ill.* ▪ She suddenly ***fell ill.*** = She was suddenly ***taken ill.*** = (*US*) She suddenly ***took ill.*** ▪ (*US*) The sight made her ***physically ill.*** [=the sight made her nauseated] ▪ (*US*) He became ***violently ill.*** [=he vomited] ✧ **The comparative form *iller* and the superlative form *illest* are sometimes used for this sense.** ▪ I have never seen him looking *iller.* [=*worse,* (*US*) *sicker*] ▪ That's the *illest* [=*worst,* (*US*) *sickest*] I have ever seen him. **b** *of health* **: not normal or good** ▪ Her *ill* [=*poor*] health forced her to retire early.

2 *always used before a noun* **: harmful or damaging** ▪ That dog can eat almost anything with no *ill* effects. ▪ They had been subjected to months of *ill* treatment.

3 *always used before a noun* **: not helpful or lucky** ▪ They seem to be plagued by *ill* [=*bad*] luck/fortune. ▪ an *ill* omen ✧ **The saying *it's an ill wind that blows no good* or *it's an ill wind that blows nobody (any) good* means that something that is bad in most ways is usually also good in some way.**

4 *always used before a noun* **: not kind or friendly** ▪ an angry customer's *ill* humor/temper ▪ We harbor no *ill* intentions toward them. ▪ Her comment caused some ***ill feeling/feelings.*** [=feelings of anger or resentment] — see also ILL WILL

ill repute see REPUTE

with ill grace see [1]GRACE

[2]**ill** *adv*

1 : in a bad or imperfect way : BADLY, POORLY ▪ He is being *ill* served by his advisers. — **often hyphenated** ▪ He is ***ill-equipped*** [=he does not have the experience or preparation that is needed] to handle so much responsibility. ▪ They were ***ill-prepared*** for the cold weather. ▪ Her arrival was ***ill-timed.*** [=she arrived at a bad time] ▪ a pet ***ill-suited*** for travel [=a pet that is difficult to take with you when you travel]

2 : in an unfavorable or unkind way ▪ Please don't think *ill* of me. ▪ He was a good man who never spoke *ill* of anyone. — see also *bode ill* at BODE

ill afford ✧ **If you can *ill afford* something, you should not do it or get it because it will cause problems.** ▪ We can *ill afford* more bad publicity. ▪ She bought a new car, which she could *ill afford.*

[3]**ill** *noun, pl* **ills**

1 [*noncount*] **: bad or unlucky things** ▪ She does not wish *ill* on/upon anyone. = She does not wish anyone *ill.* ▪ After the war, the country was changed, ***for good and for ill.*** [=in good ways and in bad ways]

2 a [*count*] : a sickness or disease • They claimed to have a cure for every *ill*. [=*ailment*] — usually plural • childhood *ills* **b** ***ills*** [*plural*] : troubles or problems • the *ills* of society

I'll /ˈajəl/ — used as a contraction of *I will* • *I'll* call you.

ill–ad•vised /ˌɪlədˈvaɪzd/ *adj* [*more ~; most ~*] : not wise or sensible : FOOLISH • an *ill-advised* decision • You would be *ill-advised* [=you would be making a mistake] to invest all your money in one company. — opposite WELL-ADVISED
– **ill–ad•vis•ed•ly** /ˌɪlədˈvaɪzədli/ *adv*

ill–assorted *adj* [*more ~; most ~*] : having a mixture of people or things that do not seem to belong together • the room's *ill-assorted* furniture

ill at ease *adj* [*more ~; most ~*] : not comfortable or relaxed : nervous or embarrassed • Their stares made us (feel) *ill at ease*. • He seemed *ill at ease* when we spoke with him.

ill–bred /ˈɪlˈbrɛd/ *adj* [*more ~; most ~*] *somewhat old-fashioned* : rude and impolite : having or showing bad manners • His *ill-bred* behavior embarrassed her at the restaurant. • an *ill-bred* child — opposite WELL-BRED

ill–con•ceived /ˈɪlkənˈsiːvd/ *adj* [*more ~; most ~*] : badly planned : not showing good judgment • an *ill-conceived* attempt to save money

ill–con•sid•ered /ˈɪlkənˈsɪdəd/ *adj* [*more ~; most ~*] : not showing careful thought : ILL-ADVISED, ILL-CONCEIVED • an *ill-considered* decision

ill–de•fined /ˈɪldɪˈfaɪnd/ *adj* [*more ~; most ~*] : not easy to see or understand • The property's borders are *ill-defined*. [=they are not clearly marked] • an *ill-defined* mission — opposite WELL-DEFINED

ill–dis•posed /ˈɪldɪˈspoʊzd/ *adj* [*more ~; most ~*] *formal* : not having a friendly or favorable feeling about someone or something — often + *to* or *toward* • She is *ill-disposed to* joining the organization. • Many people remain *ill-disposed toward* his plan. — opposite WELL-DISPOSED

il•le•gal /ɪˈliːgəl/ *adj*

1 : not allowed by the law : not legal • *illegal* [=*illicit, unlawful*] drugs • In this state, it is *illegal* for anyone under the age of 21 to drink alcohol. • an ***illegal alien/immigrant*** [=a foreign person who is living in a country without having official permission to live there]

2 : not allowed by the rules in a game • The team was penalized for an *illegal* play.

– **il•le•gal•i•ty** /ˌɪlɪˈgæləti/ *noun, pl* **-ties** [*noncount*] He claims that he was unaware of the *illegality* of these activities. [*count*] The campaign was accused of many fund-raising *illegalities*. [=illegal activities] – **il•le•gal•ly** /ɪˈliːgəli/ *adv* • She was parked *illegally* in a handicapped parking spot. • Her camera was *illegally* seized at the border. • people who are in the country *illegally*

il•leg•i•ble /ɪˈlɛʤəbəl/ *adj* [*more ~; most ~*] : not clear enough to read : not legible • *illegible* handwriting
– **il•leg•i•bil•i•ty** /ɪˌlɛʤəˈbɪləti/ *noun* [*noncount*] – **il•leg•i•bly** /ɪˈlɛʤəbli/ *adv* • He scribbled his name *illegibly* on the back of the envelope.

il•le•git•i•mate /ˌɪlɪˈʤɪtəmət/ *adj* : not legitimate: such as **a** : born to a father and mother who are not married • an *illegitimate* child **b** : not allowed according to rules or laws • They took over the government in an *illegitimate* [=*illegal*] seizure of power. • an *illegitimate* government **c** [*more ~; most ~*] : not reasonable or fair • She thinks that my concerns are *illegitimate*. • They were fired from their jobs for *illegitimate* reasons.

– **il•le•git•i•ma•cy** /ˌɪlɪˈʤɪtəməsi/ *noun* [*noncount*] • high rates of *illegitimacy* and teenage pregnancy • the *illegitimacy* of the government – **il•le•git•i•mate•ly** *adv*

ill–fat•ed /ˈɪlˈfeɪtəd/ *adj* [*more ~; most ~*] : ending in disaster : very unlucky • Everyone on the *ill-fated* trip died. • an *ill-fated* decision

ill–got•ten /ˈɪlˈgɑːtn/ *adj* : obtained in a dishonest or illegal way • an *ill-gotten* fortune • *ill-gotten* gains [=money and other valuable things gotten through dishonest methods]

ill–hu•mored (*US*) *or Brit* **ill–hu•moured** /ˈɪlˈhjuːməd/ *adj* [*more ~; most ~*] *somewhat formal* : easily angered or annoyed • *ill-humored* old men

il•lib•er•al /ɪˈlɪbrəl/ *adj* [*more ~; most ~*] *formal* : not allowing people to think and act as they choose : not liberal • an *illiberal* attitude toward sex • *illiberal* policies/views

il•lic•it /ɪˈlɪsət/ *adj*

1 : not allowed by law : unlawful or illegal • *illicit* drugs • He was arrested for selling *illicit* copies of the software.

2 : involving activities that are not considered morally acceptable • She had an *illicit* affair with her boss. • *illicit* sex
– **il•lic•it•ly** *adv* • The drug is sold *illicitly* on the streets.

ill–informed *adj*

1 : not having a lot of knowledge especially about current news and events • *ill-informed* political candidates

2 : not based on facts • an *ill-informed* decision/opinion — opposite WELL-INFORMED

il•lit•er•a•cy /ɪˈlɪtərəsi/ *noun, pl* **-cies**

1 [*noncount*] : the state of not knowing how to read or write • the government's efforts to reduce *illiteracy*

2 [*noncount*] : the state of not having knowledge about a particular subject • scientific *illiteracy* [=lack of knowledge about science] • cultural *illiteracy* • computer *illiteracy*

3 [*count*] : a mistake that is made in the use of language : an illiterate statement or expression • His letters contain many misspellings and *illiteracies*.

[1]**il•lit•er•ate** /ɪˈlɪtərət/ *adj* [*more ~; most ~*]

1 : not knowing how to read or write • an *illiterate* person • She didn't want anyone to know that she was *illiterate*. — opposite LITERATE

2 : having or showing a lack of knowledge about a particular subject • She is politically *illiterate* and has never voted in an election. • He's *illiterate* when it comes to computers. — opposite LITERATE

3 : not grammatically correct • an *illiterate* expression

[2]**illiterate** *noun, pl* **-ates** [*count*] : a person who is illiterate • His parents were *illiterates*. • a class for computer *illiterates*

ill–judged *adj* [*more ~; most ~*] *formal* : showing poor judgment or thinking • He lost all his money in an *ill-judged* attempt to start his own company.

ill–man•nered /ˈɪlˈmænəd/ *adj* [*more ~; most ~*] *formal* : having or showing bad manners : rude or impolite • an *ill-mannered* child • an *ill-mannered* remark — opposite WELL-MANNERED

ill–natured *adj* [*more ~; most ~*] *formal* : not friendly or pleasant • an *ill-natured* man • an *ill-natured* remark — opposite GOOD-NATURED

ill•ness /ˈɪlnəs/ *noun, pl* **-ness•es**

1 [*noncount*] : a condition of being unhealthy in your body or mind • Her body was not able to defend itself against *illness*. • Hundreds of soldiers died from *illness* and hunger. • He showed no signs of *illness*. • mental *illness*

2 [*count*] : a specific condition that prevents your body or mind from working normally : a sickness or disease • Scientists have not yet found a cure for this *illness*. • cancer, diabetes, and other *illnesses* • an acute/chronic *illness* • She died at the age of 60 after a brief/long *illness*.

il•log•i•cal /ɪˈlɑːʤɪkəl/ *adj* [*more ~; most ~*] : not showing good judgment : not thinking about things in a reasonable or sensible way : not logical • It is *illogical* to think that things will change on their own. • an *illogical* argument • You're being completely *illogical*.
– **il•log•i•cal•ly** /ɪˈlɑːʤɪkli/ *adv* • They *illogically* decided to stay.

ill–starred /ˈɪlˈstaəd/ *adj* [*more ~; most ~*] *literary* : very unlucky : certain to end in disaster • an *ill-starred* [=*ill-fated*] romance

ill–tem•pered /ˈɪlˈtɛmpəd/ *adj* [*more ~; most ~*]

1 : easily annoyed or angered : BAD-TEMPERED • We try to avoid our *ill-tempered* neighbor.

2 : showing that you are annoyed or angry • an *ill-tempered* reply

ill–timed *adj* [*more ~; most ~*] : done or happening at a time that is not good or suitable • an *ill-timed* question • The movie's release was *ill-timed*. — opposite WELL-TIMED

il•lu•mi•nate /ɪˈluːməˌneɪt/ *verb* **-nates; -nat•ed; -nat•ing** [*+ obj*]

1 : to supply (something) with light : to shine light on (something) • Candles *illuminate* [=*light*] the church. • the part of the moon *illuminated* by the sun

2 : to make (something) clear and easier to understand • A university study has *illuminated* the problem.
– **illuminating** *adj* [*more ~; most ~*] • The lecture was very *illuminating*. • an *illuminating* discussion

illuminated *adj*

1 : lit by bright lights • an *illuminated* entrance

2 *of an old book, document, etc.* : decorated with gold or colored designs and pictures • an *illuminated* manuscript from the Middle Ages

il•lu•mi•na•tion /ɪˌluːməˈneɪʃən/ *noun, pl* **-tions**

1 [*noncount*] : light that comes into a room, that shines on something, etc. • The room's only *illumination* [=*lighting*]

came from a small window. ▪ When taking photographs indoors, use a flash for *illumination*.
2 [*noncount*] *formal* **: knowledge or understanding** ▪ They traveled to the temple in search of spiritual *illumination*.
3 [*count*] **: a gold or colored decoration in an old book** ▪ an old manuscript with beautiful *illuminations*
4 *illuminations* [*plural*] *Brit* **: lights used as decorations** ▪ *Illuminations* were hung throughout the city.

il·lu·mine /ɪˈluːmən/ *verb* **-mines; -mined; -min·ing** [+ *obj*] *literary* **:** ILLUMINATE ▪ streets *illumined* by gaslight

ill–used *adj* [*more ~; most ~*] *formal* **: treated in a bad or unfair way** ▪ Some of the students felt *ill-used*. ▪ *ill-used* factory workers

il·lu·sion /ɪˈluːʒən/ *noun, pl* **-sions** [*count*]
1 : something that looks or seems different from what it is : something that is false or not real but that seems to be true or real ▪ The video game is designed to give the *illusion* that you are in control of an airplane. ▪ They used paint to create the *illusion* of metal. ▪ She says that all progress is just an *illusion*. — see also OPTICAL ILLUSION
2 : an incorrect idea : an idea that is based on something that is not true ▪ She had/harbored no *illusions* about how much work the project would require. [=she knew the project would require a lot of work] ▪ He was ***under the illusion*** [=he mistakenly believed] that he was a good player.

Do not confuse *illusion* with *allusion*.

il·lu·sion·ist /ɪˈluːʒənɪst/ *noun, pl* **-ists** [*count*] **: an entertainer who performs magic tricks :** MAGICIAN

il·lu·so·ry /ɪˈluːsəri/ *adj* [*more ~; most ~*] *formal* **: based on something that is not true or real : based on an illusion** ▪ an *illusory* hope ▪ an *illusory* sense of security

il·lus·trate /ˈɪləˌstreɪt/ *verb* **-trates; -trat·ed; -trat·ing** [+ *obj*]
1 : to give examples in order to make (something) easier to understand ▪ He *illustrated* his lecture with stories of his own experiences in the field. ▪ Please give a few examples to *illustrate* your point.
2 : to be proof or evidence of (something) ▪ These recent events *illustrate* [=*show, demonstrate*] the need for change in the country. ▪ The results *illustrate* how important it is to wear your seatbelt.
3 : to explain or decorate a story, book, etc., with pictures ▪ The students will write and *illustrate* their own stories. — often used as *(be) illustrated* ▪ The book *is illustrated* with many diagrams and charts.
– il·lus·tra·tor /ˈɪləˌstreɪtɚ/ *noun, pl* **-tors** [*count*] ▪ an *illustrator* of children's books

il·lus·tra·tion /ˌɪləˈstreɪʃən/ *noun, pl* **-tions**
1 [*count*] **: a picture or drawing in a book, magazine, etc.** ▪ The *illustration* on page 30 shows the parts of an engine. ▪ a book with many photographs and *illustrations*
2 [*count*] **: an example or story that is used to make something easier to understand** ▪ The *illustrations* that he provided in his speech were very effective.
3 [*noncount*] **: the act or process of illustrating something: such as a : the act or process of producing or providing pictures for a book, magazine, etc.** ▪ They selected photographs to use for the *illustration* of the book. **b : the act or process of giving examples to make something easier to understand** ▪ *Illustration* is the key to good communication. ▪ ***By way of illustration***, [=as an example] let us examine this poem.

il·lus·tra·tive /ɪˈlʌstrətɪv, *Brit* ˈɪləstrətɪv/ *adj, formal*
1 : used to illustrate or explain something ▪ *illustrative* examples/stories
2 : serving as an example of something ▪ Her struggle is *illustrative* of [=is a good example of] the difficulties facing women in her culture.

il·lus·tri·ous /ɪˈlʌstrijəs/ *adj* [*more ~; most ~*] *formal* **: admired and respected very much because a lot was achieved** ▪ He has had an *illustrious* military career. ▪ the company's *illustrious* history/past

ill will *noun* [*noncount*] **: an unfriendly feeling : a feeling of hatred or dislike** ▪ We bear/feel/harbor/have/hold no *ill will* toward each other.

im- see IN-

I'm /ˈaɪm/ — used as a contraction of *I am* ▪ *I'm* happy to meet you.

im·age /ˈɪmɪʤ/ *noun, pl* **-ag·es**
1 [*count*] **: a picture that is produced by a camera, artist, mirror, etc.** ▪ She studied her *image* in the mirror. ▪ The kids sat staring at the *images* on the TV screen. ▪ painters capturing *images* of war ▪ black-and-white *images* of the city — see also MIRROR IMAGE
2 [*count*] **: a mental picture : the thought of how something looks or might look** ▪ I can't get the *image* (of the accident) out of my mind. ▪ When you told the story I got this *image* (in my mind) of you as a child. ▪ His poem evokes *images* of the sea and warm summer days.
3 : the idea that people have about someone or something [*count*] She is worried about what motherhood will do to her *image* [=*reputation*] as a rock star. ▪ He is trying hard to improve/protect his *image*. ▪ The law suit has negatively affected the company's public *image*. ▪ a tarnished corporate *image* [*noncount*] a politician who cares more about *image* than about telling the truth
4 [*singular*] **a : the form or appearance of someone or something** ▪ "... God created man in his own *image* ..." —Genesis 1:27 (KJV) **b : someone who looks very much like another person** ▪ He's the (very/living) *image* of his father. [=he looks like his father] — see also SPITTING IMAGE **c : someone who looks very much like a certain kind of person** ▪ She was the (very) *image* of a successful businesswoman.
5 [*count*] **: an interesting or memorable way of showing or describing something in a book, movie, etc.** ▪ The book contains many striking/startling *images*.
6 [*count*] **: a statue or picture that is made to look like a person or thing** ▪ Her *image* still hangs on their living room wall. ▪ images carved in stone ▪ religious *images* — see also GRAVEN IMAGE

im·ag·ery /ˈɪmɪʤri/ *noun* [*noncount*]
1 *technical* **: pictures or photographs** ▪ They used ***satellite imagery*** [=pictures taken from satellites] to see the ice caps.
2 a : language that causes people to imagine pictures in their mind ▪ The book contains a great deal of sexual *imagery*. **b : pictures of people or things in a work of art** ▪ The movie was full of biblical/religious *imagery*. ▪ ***visual imagery***

imag·in·able /ɪˈmæʤənəbəl/ *adj* **: possible for people to imagine** ▪ Computers now allow us to do things that were hardly *imaginable* only a few years ago. ▪ The store has fruits of every kind *imaginable*. ▪ We tried every *imaginable* therapy. — **often used to give emphasis** ▪ We had the worst *imaginable* weather. = We had the worst weather *imaginable*. — opposite UNIMAGINABLE

imag·i·nary /ɪˈmæʤəˌneri, *Brit* ɪˈmæʤənri/ *adj* **: not real : existing only in your mind or imagination** ▪ The two groups were separated by an *imaginary* line down the middle of the room. ▪ an *imaginary* world of dragons and unicorns ▪ a child's *imaginary* friend

imag·i·na·tion /ɪˌmæʤəˈneɪʃən/ *noun, pl* **-tions**
1 a : the ability to imagine things that are not real : the ability to form a picture in your mind of something that you have not seen or experienced [*noncount*] You can find a solution if you use a little *imagination*. ▪ His plans to build a new stadium are the product of pure *imagination*. [=they are not based on reality; they are not likely to happen] [*count*] children with vivid/fertile/overactive *imaginations* ▪ The author does not tell us what happens to the characters. We have to use our *imagination*. ▪ He insists that these dangers are real and not just ***a figment of his imagination***. [=something that he has imagined] **b** [*noncount*] **: the ability to think of new things** ▪ Her painting shows a great deal of *imagination*. [=*creativity*] ▪ He's a competent writer, but he lacks *imagination*. ▪ He has no *imagination*.
2 [*noncount*] **: something that only exists or happens in your mind** ▪ Is it just my *imagination*, or is it getting warm in here?

by any/no stretch of the imagination see ²STRETCH

capture/catch someone's imagination **: to make someone very interested or excited** ▪ Her books have *captured the imaginations* of children from around the world. ▪ The story *caught the public imagination*. [=the public became very interested in the story]

leave (something) to the imagination **: to not show or describe all of the parts or details of (something)** ▪ Try to *leave something to the imagination*. ▪ The movie's sex scenes *leave nothing to the imagination*. [=they show everything] ▪ His explicit description of the crime scene *left little to the imagination*.

imag·i·na·tive /ɪˈmæʤənətɪv/ *adj*
1 [*more ~; most ~*] **: having or showing an ability to think of new and interesting ideas : having or showing imagination** ▪ an *imaginative* [=*creative*] filmmaker ▪ She wrote an *imaginative* story about life on the planet Venus. ▪ The restaurant's

I

menu is quite *imaginative*. • *imaginative* thinking/writing
2 *always used before a noun* **: of or relating to imagination** • a child's *imaginative* life
– imag·i·na·tive·ly *adv* • an *imaginatively* designed menu

imag·ine /ɪˈmæʤən/ *verb* **-ines; -ined; -in·ing** [+ *obj*]
1 a : to think of or create (something that is not real) in your mind • a writer who has *imagined* an entire world of amazing creatures **b : to form a picture or idea in your mind of (something that is not real or present)** • He asked us to *imagine* a world without poverty or war. • It's hard for me to *imagine* having children. **— often +** ***that*** • *Imagine that* you are relaxing on the beach. **— often +** ***what, why,*** **etc.** • It's hard to *imagine what* it would be like to be so wealthy. • I'm sure you can *imagine how* I felt. • I can't *imagine why* she would be so late. [=I do not understand why she is so late] • "Why is she so late?" "I can't *imagine*." **— sometimes used in phrases that express surprise** • Can you *imagine*! A person like him being elected mayor! [=it is surprising or ridiculous to think of a person like him being elected mayor] • Just *imagine* what such a change would mean! • "This tree is more than 300 years old." "***Imagine that!***" [=isn't that remarkable]
2 : to have or form (an idea or opinion that is not accurate or based on reality) • She *imagines* that she is very charming. = She *imagines* herself to be very charming. [=she thinks that she is charming but actually she is not charming] • He was *imagining* all sorts of terrible things happening. • "What was that sound? I think there's someone in the house!" "Oh, you're just ***imagining things.***"
3 : to think or believe (something) • I *imagine* it will snow at some point today. • It's difficult to *imagine* that these changes will really be effective. • The company will do better next year, I *imagine*. • It was worse than they had *imagined*.

im·ag·ing /ˈɪməʤɪŋ/ *noun* [*noncount*] **: the process of creating and showing images on a computer** • digital *imaging* technology • the *imaging* of a human heart **— see also** MAGNETIC RESONANCE IMAGING

imag·in·ings /ɪˈmæʤənɪŋz/ *noun* [*plural*] **: ideas, stories, etc. that are thought of in your mind but that are not true or real** • He has achieved a level of success beyond his wildest *imaginings*.

imam /ɪˈmɑːm/ *noun, pl* **imams** [*count*] **: a Muslim religious leader**

im·bal·ance /ɪmˈbæləns/ *noun, pl* **-anc·es** [*count*] **: a state or condition in which different things do not occur in equal or proper amounts** • There is an *imbalance* between his work life and family life. [=he needs to spend less time at work and more time with his family] • Her depression is caused by a chemical *imbalance* in the brain. • the problem of racial *imbalance* in schools

im·be·cile /ˈɪmbəsəl, *Brit* ˈɪmbəˌsiːl/ *noun, pl* **-ciles** [*count*] **: a very stupid person : an idiot or fool** • He drank too much and started acting like a complete *imbecile*.
– imbecile *or* **im·be·cil·ic** /ˌɪmbəˈsɪlɪk/ *adj* [*more* ~; *most* ~] • *imbecilic* behavior **– im·be·cil·i·ty** /ˌɪmbəˈsɪləti/ *noun, pl* **-ties** [*noncount*] the *imbecility* of his behavior [*count*] He was repeating all his usual *imbecilities* about politics.

imbed *variant spelling of* EMBED

im·bibe /ɪmˈbaɪb/ *verb* **-bibes; -bibed; -bib·ing** *formal + often humorous*
1 [+ *obj*] **: to drink (something)** • She *imbibed* vast quantities of coffee.
2 [*no obj*] **: to drink alcohol** • She never *imbibes* but isn't offended when others do.

im·bro·glio /ɪmˈbroʊlˌjoʊ/ *noun, pl* **-glios** [*count*] *formal* **: a complex dispute or argument** • a political/legal *imbroglio*

im·bue /ɪmˈbjuː/ *verb* **-bues; -bued; -bu·ing** [+ *obj*] **: to cause (someone or something) to be deeply affected by a feeling or to have a certain quality** • A feeling of optimism *imbues* her works. • His war experiences *imbued* in him [=caused him to feel] a strong sense of patriotism. **— usually +** ***with*** • His war experiences *imbued* him *with* a strong sense of patriotism. **— often used as** ***(be) imbued*** • He was *imbued with* a strong sense of patriotism. [=he felt very patriotic]

IMHO *abbr* in my humble opinion **— used in e-mail, chatrooms, etc., to indicate that what is being said is just an opinion**

im·i·tate /ˈɪməˌteɪt/ *verb* **-tates; -tat·ed; -tat·ing** [+ *obj*]
1 : to make or do something the same way as (something else) • Their competitors soon *imitated* [=*copied*] the idea. • Her style has been *imitated* by many other writers.
2 a : to do the same thing as (someone) • She's always *imitating* [=*copying*] her older sister. **b : to copy (someone's or something's behavior, sound, appearance, etc.)** • He's very good at *imitating* his father's voice. • She can *imitate* the calls of many different birds.
– im·i·ta·tor /ˈɪməˌteɪtɚ/ *noun, pl* **-tors** [*count*] • His style of directing has spawned/inspired a number of *imitators*.

[1]im·i·ta·tion /ˌɪməˈteɪʃən/ *noun, pl* **-tions**
1 : the act of copying or imitating someone or something [*noncount*] Children learn by *imitation* of adults. • The restaurant was designed ***in imitation of*** a Japanese temple. [*count*] He did a hilarious *imitation* of his father.
2 [*count*] **: something that is made or produced as a copy** • The real diamonds are in a museum. These are just *imitations*. • a cheap/poor *imitation* • The remake of the movie was a ***pale imitation*** [=an inferior version] of the original.

[2]imitation *adj, always used before a noun* **: made to look like something that is valuable : not genuine** • *imitation* pearls • *imitation* leather

im·i·ta·tive /ˈɪməˌteɪtɪv, *Brit* ˈɪmətətɪv/ *adj, formal* **: made or done to be like something or someone else** • *imitative* behavior • The architecture is *imitative* of a Japanese temple.

im·mac·u·late /ɪˈmækjələt/ *adj*
1 : perfectly clean • The house was always *immaculate*. [=*spotless*]
2 : having no flaw or error : PERFECT • She had an *immaculate* record of service.
– im·mac·u·late·ly *adv* • an *immaculately* dressed man

im·ma·te·ri·al /ˌɪməˈtirijəl/ *adj* **: not important or significant** • Whether or not he intended to cause problems is *immaterial*. • The fact that she is a woman is *immaterial* and irrelevant. **— often used in legal contexts** • The judge did not admit the evidence on the grounds that it was *immaterial*. **— opposite** [2]MATERIAL 2

im·ma·ture /ɪməˈtuɚ, ɪməˈʧɚ/ *adj* **: not mature: such as a : not fully developed or grown** • The flock included both adult and *immature* birds. • The fruit was still *immature*. [=*unripe*] **b** [*more* ~; *most* ~] **: acting in a childish way : having or showing a lack of emotional maturity** • emotionally *immature* adults • His teachers have complained about his *immature* behavior.
– im·ma·tu·ri·ty /ɪməˈturəti, ɪməˈʧɚəti/ *noun* [*noncount*] • His tantrums are a sign of *immaturity*.

im·mea·sur·able /ɪˈmɛʒərəbəl/ *adj, formal* **: very great in size or amount : impossible to measure** • The war has caused *immeasurable* damage. • The new medicine has brought about an *immeasurable* improvement in her life.
– im·mea·sur·ably /ɪˈmɛʒərəbli/ *adv* • Her life has improved *immeasurably*.

im·me·di·a·cy /ɪˈmiːdijəsi/ *noun* **: the quality that makes something seem important or interesting because it is or seems to be happening now** [*noncount*] Television coverage gave the war greater *immediacy* than it had ever before had. [*singular*] There is an *immediacy* to watching a live performance that you cannot get from hearing a recording.

im·me·di·ate /ɪˈmiːdijət/ *adj*
1 a : happening or done without delay • This requires your *immediate* attention. • The new restaurant was an *immediate* success. • This crisis calls for *immediate* action. • The response to the crisis was *immediate*. **b : happening or existing now** • The wildfire poses no *immediate* threat to any houses in the area. • The danger is not *immediate*. **c** *always used before a noun* [*more* ~; *most* ~] **: important now** • Our (most) *immediate* concern is to provide aid to the victims.
2 *always used before a noun* **a : close to a particular place** • They have evacuated everyone in the *immediate* area/vicinity of the wildfire. • outside the *immediate* neighborhood/surroundings **b : close to a particular time or event** • Many people suffered in the war's *immediate* aftermath. • The effect of the new policy will be unknown for the *immediate* future.
3 *always used before a noun* **: having no other person or thing in between** • Turn right onto Main Street and then take your *immediate* left. [=quickly turn onto the next street on your left] • He was sitting to my *immediate* right. • The company president will choose her *immediate* successor. • She was my *immediate* predecessor • He referred me to his *immediate* superior. • Hospital visits are limited to ***immediate family***. [=a person's parents, brothers and sisters, husband or wife, and children]
4 *always used before a noun* **: coming straight from a cause or reason** • The *immediate* [=*direct*] cause of death was pneu-

monia. ▪ There is an *immediate* connection between the two events.

[1]**im·me·di·ate·ly** /ɪˈmiːdijətli/ *adv*
1 *always followed by an adverb or preposition* **:** with no person or thing in between ▪ They live in the house *immediately* [=*directly*] behind this one. ▪ the person *immediately* to my left ▪ Dinner was served *immediately* after the ceremony.
2 : without any delay ▪ We need to leave *immediately.* [=*at once, right away*] ▪ The new law will become effective *immediately.* ▪ The cause of the problem was not *immediately* clear. [=is was not known right away]

[2]**immediately** *conj, Brit, formal* **:** immediately after **:** as soon as ▪ *Immediately* you fill out this form, we can start processing your request.

im·me·mo·ri·al /ˌɪməˈmorijəl/ *adj, formal + literary* **:** very old or ancient **:** from a time so long ago that it cannot be remembered ▪ the *immemorial* roots of human spirituality ▪ People have been creating art since ***time immemorial.*** [=a very long time ago] ▪ stories passed down from *time immemorial*
– im·me·mo·ri·al·ly /ˌɪməˈmorijəli/ *adv* ▪ an *immemorially* ancient custom

im·mense /ɪˈmɛns/ *adj* [*more ~; most ~*] **:** very great in size or amount ▪ He inherited an *immense* fortune. ▪ *immense* power/wealth ▪ Her movies continue to enjoy *immense* [=*enormous, tremendous*] popularity. ▪ She is an artist of *immense* talent.
– im·mense·ly *adv* ▪ *immensely* popular/successful/wealthy ▪ We enjoyed ourselves *immensely.* [=*very much*]

im·men·si·ty /ɪˈmɛnsəti/ *noun* [*noncount*] **:** extremely great size ▪ the *immensity* of the universe/ocean ▪ She couldn't understand the *immensity* of their problem.

im·merse /ɪˈmɚs/ *verb* **-mers·es; -mersed; -mers·ing** [+ *obj*]
1 : to put (something) in a liquid so that all parts are completely covered ▪ *Immerse* the fabric completely in the dye.
2 : to make (yourself) fully involved *in* some activity or interest ▪ She had *immersed* herself *in* writing short stories. ▪ He *immersed* himself *in* the culture of the island. — often used as *(be) immersed* ▪ He became completely/totally *immersed in* their culture. ▪ She *was immersed in* her work.

im·mer·sion /ɪˈmɚʒən/ *noun* [*noncount*]
1 : the act of putting someone or something completely in a liquid or the state of being completely in a liquid ▪ *immersion* in hot water
2 a : complete involvement in some activity or interest ▪ We were surprised by his complete *immersion* in the culture of the island. **b :** a method of learning a foreign language by being taught entirely in that language ▪ He learned French through *immersion.* ▪ I'm taking an *immersion* course in German.

im·mi·grant /ˈɪmɪgrənt/ *noun, pl* **-grants** [*count*] **:** a person who comes to a country to live there ▪ Millions of *immigrants* came to America from Europe in the 19th century. ▪ The city has a large *immigrant* population. ▪ an ***illegal immigrant*** [=a person who enters and lives in a country without official permission] — compare EMIGRANT, MIGRANT

im·mi·grate /ˈɪməˌgreɪt/ *verb* **-grates; -grat·ed; -grat·ing** [*no obj*] **:** to come to a country to live there — often + *to* ▪ My grandparents *immigrated* to America. — sometimes + *from* ▪ My grandparents *immigrated* from Hungary. — compare EMIGRATE, MIGRATE
– im·mi·gra·tion /ˌɪməˈgreɪʃən/ *noun* [*noncount*] ▪ waves of *immigration* from eastern Europe ▪ *immigration* policies

im·mi·nent /ˈɪmənənt/ *adj* [*more ~; most ~*] **:** happening very soon ▪ We are awaiting their *imminent* arrival. ▪ Their arrival is *imminent.* ▪ These patients are facing *imminent* death. ▪ The species is in *imminent* danger of extinction. [=the species is very close to becoming extinct]

Do not confuse *imminent* with *eminent.*

– im·mi·nence /ˈɪmənəns/ *noun* [*noncount*] ▪ the *imminence* of danger **– im·mi·nent·ly** *adv*

im·mo·bile /ɪˈmoubəl, ɪˈmouˌbajəl/ *adj*
1 : unable to move ▪ The tranquilizer made the animal *immobile.* ▪ The accident left her *immobile.*
2 : not moving ▪ The guard stood *immobile* [=*motionless*] by the gate.
– im·mo·bil·i·ty /ˌɪmouˈbɪləti/ *noun* [*noncount*] ▪ physical *immobility*

im·mo·bi·lize *also Brit* **im·mo·bi·lise** /ɪˈmoubəˌlaɪz/ *verb* **-liz·es; -lized; -liz·ing** [+ *obj*] **:** to keep (something or someone) from moving or working **:** to make (something or someone) immobile ▪ Doctors *immobilized* her wrist by putting it in a cast. ▪ I was *immobilized* by fear/uncertainty.
– im·mo·bi·li·za·tion *also Brit* **im·mo·bi·li·sa·tion** /ɪˌmoubələˈzeɪʃən/ *noun* [*noncount*] **– im·mo·bi·liz·er** *also Brit* **im·mo·bi·lis·er** /ɪˈmoubəˌlaɪzɚ/ *noun, pl* **-ers** [*count*] ▪ The car comes with an (engine) *immobilizer.* [=a device that prevents the engine from being started without a key]

im·mod·er·ate /ɪˈmɑːdərət/ *adj* [*more ~; most ~*] *formal* **:** going beyond reasonable limits **:** not moderate ▪ He talked to us about the dangers of *immoderate* [=*excessive*] drinking.
– im·mod·er·ate·ly *adv* ▪ He drinks *immoderately.*

im·mod·est /ɪˈmɑːdəst/ *adj* [*more ~; most ~*] **:** not modest: such as **a :** having or showing a high or too high opinion of yourself or your worth ▪ Although it might sound *immodest* of me to say so, I am very proud of what we have accomplished. **b** *of clothing* **:** showing a lot of your body in a way that is considered improper ▪ She wore a rather *immodest* [=*revealing*] dress to the party.
– im·mod·est·ly *adv* ▪ He *immodestly* named the company after himself. ▪ She was dressed *immodestly.* **– im·mod·es·ty** /ɪˈmɑːdəsti/ *noun* [*noncount*]

im·mo·late /ˈɪməˌleɪt/ *verb* **-lates; -lat·ed; -lat·ing** [+ *obj*] *formal* **:** to kill or destroy (someone or something) by fire ▪ a man who *immolated* himself as an act of protest
– im·mo·la·tion /ˌɪməˈleɪʃən/ *noun* [*noncount*]

im·mor·al /ɪˈmorəl/ *adj* [*more ~; most ~*] **:** not morally good or right **:** morally evil or wrong ▪ Don't condemn her: there was nothing *immoral* about what she did. ▪ It was *immoral* of her to tell lies like that. ▪ *immoral* behavior/acts — compare AMORAL, MORAL
– im·mo·ral·i·ty /ˌɪˌmoəˈræləti/ *noun* [*noncount*] ▪ sexual *immorality* ▪ the *immorality* of their behavior **– im·mor·al·ly** /ɪˈmorəli/ *adv*

[1]**im·mor·tal** /ɪˈmoətl/ *adj*
1 : not capable of dying **:** living forever ▪ the *immortal* soul ▪ *immortal* gods — opposite MORTAL
2 — used to say that something will last or be remembered forever ▪ *immortal* [=*everlasting*] fame ▪ his *immortal* [=*timeless*] melodies

[2]**immortal** *noun, pl* **-tals** [*count*]
1 : an immortal being (such as a god or goddess) — compare MORTAL
2 : a famous person who will never be forgotten ▪ baseball *immortals*

im·mor·tal·i·ty /ˌɪˌmoəˈtæləti/ *noun* [*noncount*] **:** the quality or state of someone or something that will never die or be forgotten **:** the quality or state of being immortal ▪ She believed in the *immortality* of the soul. ▪ He found/achieved *immortality* through his films. — opposite MORTALITY

im·mor·tal·ize *also Brit* **im·mor·tal·ise** /ɪˈmoətəˌlaɪz/ *verb* **-iz·es; -ized; -iz·ing** [+ *obj*] **:** to cause (someone or something) to be remembered forever ▪ The battle was *immortalized* in a famous poem. ▪ The explorers were *immortalized* when the mountains were named after them.

im·mov·able /ɪˈmuːvəbəl/ *adj*
1 : not able to be moved **:** firmly fixed in place ▪ an *immovable* object — opposite MOVABLE
2 : not able to be changed or persuaded ▪ He has remained *immovable* [=*steadfast*] in his opposition to the proposed law.

im·mune /ɪˈmjuːn/ *adj*
1 *not used before a noun* **a :** not capable of being affected by a disease — usually + *to* ▪ Most people are *immune to* the disease. **b :** not influenced or affected by something — + *to* ▪ They are *immune to* persuasion/criticism. ▪ She is *immune to* the power of advertising.
2 *not used before a noun* **:** having special protection *from* something that is required for most people by law ▪ The court ruled that he was *immune from* prosecution [=that he could not be prosecuted] because of his diplomatic status. ▪ *immune* [=*exempt*] *from* punishment
3 *always used before a noun* **:** of or relating to the body's immune system ▪ *immune* cells ▪ an *immune* response/reaction

immune system *noun, pl* **~ -tems** [*count*] **:** the system that protects your body from diseases and infections ▪ a strong/healthy *immune system*

im·mu·ni·ty /ɪˈmjuːnəti/ *noun*
1 *medical* **:** the power to keep yourself from being affected by a disease — usually + *to* [*noncount*] They have developed *immunity to* the virus. [*singular*] They have developed an *immunity to* the virus.

2 [*noncount*] : special protection from what is required for most people by law — usually + *from* ▪ He was granted *immunity from* prosecution. — see also DIPLOMATIC IMMUNITY

im·mu·nize *also Brit* **im·mu·nise** /ˈɪmjəˌnaɪz/ *verb* **-niz·es; -nized; -niz·ing** [+ *obj*] : to give (someone) a vaccine to prevent infection by a disease ▪ Many people had to be *immunized* after being exposed to the disease. — often + *against* ▪ All the children have been *immunized against* polio.
– **im·mu·ni·za·tion** *also Brit* **im·mu·ni·sa·tion** /ˌɪmjənəˈzeɪʃən, *Brit* ˌɪmjəˌnaɪˈzeɪʃən/ *noun, pl* **-tions** [*count, noncount*]

im·mu·no·de·fi·cien·cy /ˌɪmjəˌnoʊdɪˈfɪʃənsi/ *noun, pl* **-cies** [*count*] *medical* : a condition in which your body cannot produce enough of the substances or cells that it would normally produce to fight infection

im·mu·nol·o·gy /ˌɪmjəˈnɑːləʤi/ *noun* [*noncount*] : a science that deals with the ways in which the body protects itself from diseases and infections

im·mu·ta·ble /ɪˈmjuːtəbəl/ *adj, formal* : unable to be changed ▪ the *immutable* laws of nature ▪ *immutable* opposition
– **im·mu·ta·bil·i·ty** /ɪˌmjuːtəˈbɪləti/ *noun* [*noncount*] – **im·mu·ta·bly** /ɪˈmjuːtəbli/ *adv* ▪ She was not *immutably* opposed to the plan.

imp /ˈɪmp/ *noun, pl* **imps** [*count*]
1 : a small creature that plays harmful tricks in children's stories
2 : a child who causes trouble in a playful way : a mischievous child ▪ a lovable *imp* — see also IMPISH

¹im·pact /ˈɪmˌpækt/ *noun, pl* **-pacts**
1 : the act or force of one thing hitting another [*count*] No one could have survived such an *impact*. [*noncount*] The bomb exploded ***on/upon impact*** (with the ground). [=when it hit the ground]
2 [*count*] : a powerful or major influence or effect ▪ These warnings have been heard so often that they have lost their *impact*. ▪ The book had a huge *impact* when it first came out. ▪ We need to be concerned about the environmental *impacts* of all this construction. ▪ She expects to make an immediate *impact* at work. — often + *on* ▪ The stress of her job is having a negative *impact on* her health. [=is harming her health] ▪ We hope that these programs will have a positive *impact on* the community. [=will help the community]

²im·pact /ˌɪmˈpækt/ *verb* **-pacts; -pact·ed; -pact·ing**
1 : to have a strong and often bad effect on (something or someone) : AFFECT [+ *obj*] No one is sure how these changes will *impact* our relations with other countries. ▪ Both events negatively *impacted* her life. ▪ The tax increase will *impact* low-income families the most. [*no obj*] The poor economy is ***impacting on/upon*** small businesses.
2 [+ *obj*] *formal* : to hit (something) with great force ▪ A crater was formed at the point where the meteor *impacted* the planet's surface.

im·pact·ed /ɪmˈpæktəd/ *adj, of a tooth* : growing under another tooth ▪ *impacted* wisdom teeth

im·pair /ɪmˈpeɚ/ *verb* **-pairs; -paired; -pair·ing** [+ *obj*] : to make (something) weaker or worse ▪ Smoking can *impair* your health. ▪ Drinking *impairs* a person's ability to think clearly. ▪ His memory was so *impaired* by age that he often forgot where he was. ***synonyms*** see INJURE
– **im·paired** /ɪmˈpeɚd/ *adj* [*more* ~; *most* ~] ▪ The disease causes *impaired* vision/hearing in elderly people. — sometimes used in combination ▪ hearing-*impaired* people [=people with impaired hearing]

im·pair·ment /ɪmˈpeɚmənt/ *noun, pl* **-ments** : a condition in which a part of your body or mind is damaged and does not work well [*count*] a hearing/memory/visual *impairment* [*noncount*] The loud noise caused *impairment* of her hearing.

im·pa·la /ɪmˈpɑːlə/ *noun, pl* **im·pa·las** *or* **impala** [*count*] : a large brownish African animal

im·pale /ɪmˈpeɪl/ *verb* **-pales; -paled; -pal·ing** [+ *obj*] : to cause a pointed object to go into or through (someone or something) — often + *on* ▪ He slipped and *impaled* his leg *on* a metal spike. — usually used as *(be) impaled* ▪ The matador *was impaled* by the bull's horns. = The matador *was impaled on* the bull's horns.

im·pan·el *or* **em·pan·el** /ɪmˈpænl/ *verb* **-els;** *US* **-eled** *or Brit* **-elled;** *US* **-el·ing** *or Brit* **-el·ling** [+ *obj*] *law* : to choose people to serve on a jury ▪ *impanel* jurors = *impanel* a jury

im·part /ɪmˈpɑɚt/ *verb* **-parts; -part·ed; -part·ing** [+ *obj*] *formal*
1 : to give (something, such as a quality) to a thing ▪ Her presence *imparted* a sense of importance to the meeting. ▪ The oil *imparts* a distinctive flavor to the sauce. ▪ The chemicals *imparted* a bluish color to the paper.
2 : to make (something) known to someone ▪ He has clever ways of *imparting* [=*conveying, communicating*] knowledge to his students.

im·par·tial /ɪmˈpɑɚʃəl/ *adj* [*more* ~; *most* ~] : treating all people and groups equally : not partial or biased ▪ an *impartial* analysis of the case ▪ an *impartial* judge/jury/observer
– **im·par·tial·i·ty** /ɪmˌpɑɚʃiˈæləti/ *noun* [*noncount*] – **im·par·tial·ly** /ɪmˈpɑɚʃəli/ *adv*

im·pass·able /ɪmˈpæsəbəl/ *adj* : impossible to pass, cross, or travel over ▪ The roads were made *impassable* by the flood/snow.

im·passe /ˈɪmˌpæs, *Brit* æmˈpɑːs/ *noun, pl* **-pass·es** [*count*] : a situation in which no progress seems possible ▪ Negotiations are at an *impasse*. = Negotiations have reached/hit an *impasse*. ▪ An arbitrator was called in to break the *impasse*. ▪ She had reached an *impasse* in her career.

im·pas·sioned /ɪmˈpæʃənd/ *adj* [*more* ~; *most* ~] : showing or feeling very strong emotions ▪ Her lawyer made an *impassioned* argument in her defense. ▪ an *impassioned* speech/plea ▪ *impassioned* [=*passionate*] animal-rights activists

im·pas·sive /ɪmˈpæsɪv/ *adj* [*more* ~; *most* ~] : not showing emotion ▪ an *impassive* observer ▪ Her face/expression remained *impassive* throughout the trial.
– **im·pas·sive·ly** *adv* ▪ She sat *impassively* throughout the trial. – **im·pas·siv·i·ty** /ɪmˌpæˈsɪvəti/ *noun* [*noncount*]

im·pa·tient /ɪmˈpeɪʃənt/ *adj* [*more* ~; *most* ~]
1 a : not willing to wait for something or someone : not patient ▪ After months of delays, customers are becoming/growing *impatient*. ▪ Customers have grown *impatient* with/at the repeated delays. ▪ "Aren't you ready yet?" "Don't be so *impatient*. There's no need to hurry." — often + *for* ▪ He was *impatient for* the departure of his flight. ▪ She was becoming more *impatient for* the opportunity to begin working. **b** : wanting or eager *to do* something without waiting ▪ She was *impatient to leave*.
2 : showing that you do not want to wait : showing a lack of patience ▪ an *impatient* answer/gesture/look
– **im·pa·tience** /ɪmˈpeɪʃəns/ *noun* [*noncount*] ▪ He sighed with *impatience*. ▪ Her *impatience* with/at the many delays was obvious. ▪ Her *impatience* to leave was obvious. – **im·pa·tient·ly** *adv* ▪ Customers are waiting *impatiently* for the delays to end.

im·peach /ɪmˈpiːʧ/ *verb* **-peach·es; -peached; -peach·ing** [+ *obj*] *law*
1 : to charge (a public official) with a crime done while in office ▪ Congress will vote on whether or not to *impeach* the President. ▪ *impeach* a judge
2 *formal* : to cause doubts about the truthfulness of (a witness, testimony, etc.) ▪ The defense lawyers tried to *impeach* the witness's testimony by forcing him to admit that he had changed his story.
– **im·peach·able** /ɪmˈpiːʧəbəl/ *adj* ▪ an *impeachable* offense/crime – **im·peach·ment** /ɪmˈpiːʧmənt/ *noun, pl* **-ments** [*count, noncount*]

im·pec·ca·ble /ɪmˈpɛkəbəl/ *adj* [*more* ~; *most* ~] : free from fault or error ▪ The craftsmanship is *impeccable*. [=*flawless*] ▪ He speaks *impeccable* [=*perfect*] English. ▪ She has *impeccable* taste in music. ▪ His manners are *impeccable*.
– **im·pec·ca·bly** /ɪmˈpɛkəbli/ *adv* ▪ He behaved *impeccably*. ▪ She was *impeccably* dressed.

im·pe·cu·nious /ˌɪmpɪˈkjuːnijəs/ *adj* [*more* ~; *most* ~] *formal* : having little or no money : POOR ▪ an *impecunious* student

im·pede /ɪmˈpiːd/ *verb* **-pedes; -ped·ed; -ped·ing** [+ *obj*] : to slow the movement, progress, or action of (someone or something) ▪ He claims that economic growth is being *impeded* by government regulations. ▪ They were accused of *impeding* [=*blocking, hindering*] the administration of justice. ▪ The soldiers could not *impede* the enemy's advance.

im·ped·i·ment /ɪmˈpɛdəmənt/ *noun, pl* **-ments** [*count*]
1 : something that makes it difficult to do or complete something : something that interferes with movement or progress — often + *to* ▪ There were no legal *impediments to* the deal.
2 : a condition that makes it difficult to speak normally ▪ a speech *impediment*

im·pel /ɪmˈpɛl/ *verb* **-pels; -pelled; -pel·ling** [+ *obj*] : to cause (someone) to feel a strong need or desire to do something ▪ They were *impelled* [=*driven*] by their sense of adventure. • His interest in the American Civil War *impelled* him to make repeated visits to Gettysburg. • She felt *impelled* to give a speech after the performance.

im·pend·ing /ɪmˈpɛndɪŋ/ *adj, always used before a noun* **: happening or likely to happen soon** • She's worried about an *impending* business trip. • We need to prepare for their *impending* arrival.

im·pen·e·tra·ble /ɪmˈpɛnətrəbəl/ *adj [more ~; most ~]*
1 : impossible to pass or see through • an *impenetrable* wall/barrier/jungle • The fort's defenses were thought to be *impenetrable*. • *impenetrable* darkness/fog
2 : impossible to understand • an *impenetrable* mystery • an *impenetrable* secret code
– im·pen·e·tra·bil·i·ty /ɪmˌpɛnətrəˈbɪləti/ *noun [noncount]* **– im·pen·e·tra·bly** /ɪmˈpɛnətrəbli/ *adv* • an *impenetrably* complex mystery • an *impenetrably* thick wall

[1]**im·per·a·tive** /ɪmˈperətɪv/ *adj*
1 *[more ~; most ~] formal* **: very important** • an *imperative* duty • It is *imperative* that the public be informed about these dangers. = It is *imperative* to inform the public about these dangers.
2 *grammar* **: having the form that expresses a command rather than a statement or a question** • "Eat your spinach!" is an *imperative* sentence. • "Help" in the sentence "Help me!" is an *imperative* verb. • a verb in the *imperative* mood — compare DECLARATIVE, INDICATIVE, INTERROGATIVE, SUBJUNCTIVE
3 *formal* **: expressing a command in a forceful and confident way** • People resented his *imperative* tone of voice.

[2]**imperative** *noun, pl* **-tives**
1 *[count] formal* **: a command, rule, duty, etc., that is very important or necessary** • She considers it a moral *imperative* to help people in need. • legal *imperatives*
2 *grammar* **a** ***the imperative*** **: the form that a verb or sentence has when it is expressing a command** • "Eat your spinach!" is in *the imperative*. **b** *[count]* **: an imperative verb or sentence** • "Go" and "buy" are *imperatives* in the sentence "Please go to the store and buy some milk."

im·per·cep·ti·ble /ˌɪmpɚˈsɛptəbəl/ *adj [more ~; most ~]* **: impossible to see or notice** • *imperceptible* changes/differences • an almost *imperceptible* smile/breeze • These changes will be *imperceptible* to most people.
– im·per·cep·ti·bly /ˌɪmpɚˈsɛptəbli/ *adv*

[1]**im·per·fect** /ɪmˈpɚfɪkt/ *adj*
1 : having mistakes or problems : not perfect • an *imperfect* society • It's an *imperfect* solution to a difficult problem. • He had an *imperfect* understanding of the task. • *imperfect* [=*defective*] clothing
2 *grammar* **: of or relating to a verb tense used to express an incomplete action in the past or a state that continued for a period of time in the past** • In "He was singing when I came in," "was singing" is in the *imperfect* tense.
– im·per·fect·ly *adv* • an *imperfectly* patched hole

[2]**imperfect** *noun*
the imperfect *grammar* **: the imperfect tense of a verb** • a verb in *the imperfect*

im·per·fec·tion /ˌɪmpɚˈfɛkʃən/ *noun, pl* **-tions**
1 *[count]* **: a small flaw or bad part** • He detected several *imperfections* in the surface of the jewel. • She tried to hide the *imperfection* in the cloth. • skin *imperfections* [=*blemishes*]
2 *[noncount]* **: the state of being imperfect : lack of perfection** • human *imperfection*

im·pe·ri·al /ɪmˈpirijəl/ *adj, always used before a noun* **: of or relating to an empire or an emperor** • the Roman *imperial* age • a member of the *imperial* family/army • *imperial* power • the *imperial* palace

im·pe·ri·al·ism /ɪmˈpirijəˌlɪzəm/ *noun [noncount]*
1 : a policy or practice by which a country increases its power by gaining control over other areas of the world • British *imperialism* created the enormous British Empire.
2 : the effect that a powerful country or group of countries has in changing or influencing the way people live in other, poorer countries • Western *imperialism* • economic/cultural *imperialism*

im·pe·ri·al·ist /ɪmˈpirijəlɪst/ *noun, pl* **-ists** *[count]* **: a person who practices or supports imperialism**
– imperialist *adj* • *imperialist* power/expansion **– im·pe·ri·al·is·tic** /ɪmˌpirijəˈlɪstɪk/ *adj* • *imperialistic* aims/goals

im·per·il /ɪmˈperəl/ *verb* **-ils**; *US* **-iled** *or Brit* **-illed**; *US* **-il·ing** *or Brit* **-il·ling** *[+ obj] formal* **: to put (something or someone) in a dangerous situation : ENDANGER** • The toxic fumes *imperiled* the lives of the trapped miners. • The financial health of the company was *imperiled* by a string of bad investments. • a list of *imperiled* species

im·pe·ri·ous /ɪmˈpirijəs/ *adj [more ~; most ~] formal* **: having or showing the proud and unpleasant attitude of someone who gives orders and expects other people to obey them** • an *imperious* manner/tone/gesture • *imperious* bureaucrats
– im·pe·ri·ous·ly *adv* **– im·pe·ri·ous·ness** *noun [noncount]*

im·per·ish·able /ɪmˈperɪʃəbəl/ *adj, formal* **: never to be forgotten : lasting forever** • *imperishable* fame • an *imperishable* masterpiece

im·per·ma·nent /ɪmˈpɚmənənt/ *adj, formal* **: not lasting forever : not permanent** • an *impermanent* [=*temporary*] solution • *impermanent* materials
– im·per·ma·nence /ɪmˈpɚmənəns/ *noun [noncount]*

im·per·me·able /ɪmˈpɚmijəbəl/ *adj [more ~; most ~] technical* **: not allowing something (such as a liquid) to pass through** • an *impermeable* layer of rock • a fabric *impermeable* to moisture
– im·per·me·abil·i·ty /ɪmˌpɚmijəˈbɪləti/ *noun [noncount]*

im·per·mis·si·ble /ɪmˌpɚˈmɪsəbəl/ *adj, formal* **: not allowed or permitted : not permissible** • Such behavior is *impermissible* under the new guidelines. • an *impermissible* breach of etiquette
– im·per·mis·si·bly /ɪmˌpɚˈmɪsəbli/ *adv*

im·per·son·al /ɪmˈpɚsənəl/ *adj*
1 *[more ~; most ~]* **a : having or showing no interest in individual people or their feelings : lacking emotional warmth** • cold, *impersonal* cities • a giant *impersonal* corporation **b : not relating to or influenced by personal feelings** • We discussed the weather and other *impersonal* topics. • He maintained an *impersonal*, professional attitude.
2 *grammar* **: having no specified subject or no subject other than "it"** • "Rained" in "it rained" is an *impersonal* verb. • an *impersonal* sentence/construction
– im·per·son·al·ly /ɪmˈpɚsənəli/ *adv* • They were treated *impersonally*.

im·per·son·ate /ɪmˈpɚsəˌneɪt/ *verb* **-ates; -at·ed; -at·ing** *[+ obj]* **: to pretend to be (another person)** • He was arrested for *impersonating* a police officer. • a comedian with a talent for *impersonating* famous politicians and actors
– im·per·son·a·tion /ɪmˌpɚsəˈneɪʃən/ *noun, pl* **-tions** *[count]* He does a great *impersonation* of the President. *[noncount]* He was arrested for *impersonation* of a police officer.

im·per·son·a·tor /ɪmˈpɚsəˌneɪtɚ/ *noun, pl* **-tors** *[count]* **: a person who pretends to be someone else;** ***especially*** **: a person who entertains people by pretending to be another person** • an Elvis *impersonator* [=an entertainer who pretends to be Elvis Presley] • a female *impersonator* [=a male entertainer who plays the role of a woman]

im·per·ti·nent /ɪmˈpɚtn̩ənt/ *adj [more ~; most ~] formal* **: rude and showing a lack of respect** • She asked a few *impertinent* questions. • an *impertinent* young woman
– im·per·ti·nence /ɪmˈpɚtn̩əns/ *noun [noncount]* • I was shocked by the *impertinence* of her questions. **– im·per·ti·nent·ly** *adv*

im·per·turb·able /ˌɪmpɚˈtɚbəbəl/ *adj [more ~; most ~] formal* **: very calm : very hard to disturb or upset** • Although he seems outwardly *imperturbable*, he can get very angry at times. • an *imperturbable* demeanor/disposition
– im·per·turb·abil·i·ty /ˌɪmpɚˌtɚbəˈbɪləti/ *noun [noncount]* **– im·per·turb·ably** /ˌɪmpɚˈtɚbəbli/ *adv* • He sat there *imperturbably* as they insulted him.

im·per·vi·ous /ɪmˈpɚvijəs/ *adj [more ~; most ~]*
1 *technical* **: not allowing something (such as water or light) to enter or pass through** — usually + *to* • a substance *impervious to* light • a coat *impervious to* rain
2 *formal* **: not bothered or affected by something** — usually + *to* • He seems *impervious to* criticism.
– im·per·vi·ous·ness *noun [noncount]*

im·pet·u·ous /ɪmˈpɛtʃəwəs/ *adj [more ~; most ~]* **: acting or done quickly and without thought : controlled by emotion rather than thought : IMPULSIVE** • He's always been an *impetuous* young man. • an *impetuous* decision
– im·pet·u·os·i·ty /ɪmˌpɛtʃəˈwɑːsəti/ *noun [noncount]* **– im·pet·u·ous·ly** *adv* **– im·pet·u·ous·ness** *noun [noncount]*

im·pe·tus /ˈɪmpətəs/ *noun*
1 : a force that causes something (such as a process or activity) to be done or to become more active *[noncount]* His discoveries have given *impetus* to further research. • The move-

ment is now gaining/losing *impetus*. [=*momentum*] [*singular*] Her work provided the major *impetus* [=*stimulus*] behind the movement. — often + *for* • The tragic accident became an *impetus for* changing the safety regulations. — sometimes followed by *to* + *verb* • His discoveries have given researchers the *impetus to try* something new.

2 [*noncount*] *technical* **: a force that causes an object to begin moving or to continue to move**

im·pi·ety /ɪmˈpajəti/ *noun* [*noncount*] *formal* **: lack of respect for God : the quality or state of being impious** • accusations of *impiety*

im·pinge /ɪmˈpɪnʤ/ *verb* **-ping·es; -pinged; -ping·ing**

impinge on/upon [*phrasal verb*] ***impinge on/upon (something)*** *formal* **: to affect (something) in a way that is unwanted : to have a bad effect on (something)** • His lawyers argued that the publicity will *impinge on* the defendant's right to a fair trial. • Her work is *impinging on* [=*encroaching on, hindering*] her social life. • The government wants to avoid *impinging upon* the affairs of private citizens.

im·pi·ous /ˈɪmpijəs/ *adj* [*more* ~; *most* ~] *formal* **: feeling or showing a lack of respect for God : not pious** • *impious* books • He was fearful of seeming *impious*.

imp·ish /ˈɪmpɪʃ/ *adj* [*more* ~; *most* ~] **: having or showing a playful desire to cause trouble : playful and mischievous** • an *impish* grin/smile • an *impish* face/look

– imp·ish·ly *adv* • grinning *impishly* **– imp·ish·ness** *noun* [*noncount*] • his youthful *impishness*

im·pla·ca·ble /ɪmˈplækəbəl/ *adj* [*more* ~; *most* ~] **: opposed to someone or something in a very angry or determined way that cannot be changed** • He has an *implacable* hatred for his political opponents. • an *implacable* [=*unyielding*] opponent

– im·pla·ca·bly /ɪmˈplækəbli/ *adv* • They are *implacably* opposed to his proposals.

¹im·plant /ɪmˈplænt/ *verb* **-plants; -plant·ed; -plant·ing** [+ *obj*]

1 : to put (something) in a specified place • The police obtained permission to *implant* [=*plant*] a recording device in the suspect's home.; *especially, medical* **: to place (something) in a person's body by means of surgery** • a hearing aid that is surgically *implanted* in the ear

2 : to cause (something) to become a part of the way a person thinks or feels • She *implanted* a love of reading in her students. [=she taught her students to love reading]

– im·plant·able /ɪmˈplæntəbəl/ *adj* • *implantable* devices **– im·plan·ta·tion** /ˌɪmˌplænˈteɪʃən/ *noun, pl* **-tions** [*noncount*] the *implantation* of a hearing aid [*count*] (*chiefly US*) a surgeon who has performed many *implantations*

²im·plant /ˈɪmˌplænt/ *noun, pl* **-plants** [*count*] *medical* **: something placed in a person's body by means of surgery** • breast *implants*

im·plau·si·ble /ɪmˈplɑːzəbəl/ *adj* [*more* ~; *most* ~] **: not believable or realistic : not plausible** • She's been making *implausible* claims. • He gave an *implausible* excuse for showing up late for work. • The novel has an *implausible* ending.

– im·plau·si·bil·i·ty /ɪmˌplɑːzəˈbɪləti/ *noun* [*noncount*] • the *implausibility* of the novel's ending **– im·plau·si·bly** /ɪmˈplɑːzəbli/ *adv* • an *implausibly* happy ending • *Implausibly* (enough), the hero was saved at the last minute.

¹im·ple·ment /ˈɪmpləmənt/ *noun, pl* **-ments** [*count*] **: an object used to do work : TOOL** • farming *implements* • stone *implements* used in prehistoric times • a sharp-edged *implement* used to chop wood

> ***synonyms*** IMPLEMENT, TOOL, INSTRUMENT, and UTENSIL mean a device used for doing work. IMPLEMENT is a general word and may refer to anything that is needed to complete a task. • gardening *implements* such as rakes and hoes TOOL is also a general word but may suggest a device that is designed for a specific job and that requires some skill to be used properly. • carpenter's *tools* INSTRUMENT suggests a device that can be used for very precise work. • surgical *instruments* UTENSIL suggests a fairly simple device used for jobs in a person's house. • kitchen *utensils*

²im·ple·ment /ˈɪmpləˌmɛnt/ *verb* **-ments; -ment·ed; -ment·ing** [+ *obj*] **: to begin to do or use (something, such as a plan) : to make (something) active or effective** • The government *implemented* [=*carried out*] a series of reforms. • I wondered how I might best *implement* his plan. • Due to high costs, the program was never fully *implemented*.

– im·ple·men·ta·tion /ˌɪmpləmənˈteɪʃən/ *noun* [*noncount*] • *implementation* of the plan

im·pli·cate /ˈɪmpləˌkeɪt/ *verb* **-cates; -cat·ed; -cat·ing** [+ *obj*] **: to show that someone or something is closely connected to or involved in something (such as a crime)** • The evidence *implicated* many government officials in the conspiracy. [=the evidence showed that many government officials were involved in the conspiracy] • His business partner was *implicated* in the theft. • Scientists have discovered a gene that is *implicated* [=*involved*] in the development of Alzheimer's disease.

im·pli·ca·tion /ˌɪmpləˈkeɪʃən/ *noun, pl* **-tions**

1 [*count*] **: a possible future effect or result — usually plural** • We must consider the long-term *implications* of the new trade policies. [=we must consider the effect the policies may have in the future] • The closing of the factory has economic *implications* for the entire community. [=the closing will affect the economy of the entire community] • He needs to be aware of the political *implications* of his decision.

2 : something that is suggested without being said directly : something that is implied [*count*] I'm offended by his *implication* that women can't be good at mathematics. • I resent that/your *implication*! [*noncount*] He condemned the court and, ***by implication***, the entire legal system.

3 [*noncount*] **: the fact or state of being involved in or connected to something (such as a crime) : the fact or state of being implicated in something** • He was shocked by the *implication* of his partner in the theft.

im·plic·it /ɪmˈplɪsət/ *adj*

1 : understood though not clearly or directly stated • an *implicit* agreement/warning/promise • Their plans are based on the *implicit* [=*implied*] assumption that the proposal will be accepted. • There is a sense of moral duty *implicit* in her writings. — opposite EXPLICIT

2 : not affected by doubt : ABSOLUTE, COMPLETE • I have *implicit* trust/confidence/faith in her honesty.

– im·plic·it·ly *adv* • In his criticism of the court he *implicitly* condemns the entire legal system. • I trust her *implicitly*. [=*completely*]

im·plode /ɪmˈploʊd/ *verb* **-plodes; -plod·ed; -plod·ing** [*no obj*] **: to collapse inward in a very sudden and violent way** • an *imploding* star — **often used figuratively** • He warns that the nation's economy is about to *implode* under the weight of its debt. — compare EXPLODE

– im·plo·sion /ɪmˈploʊʒən/ *noun, pl* **-sions** [*count, noncount*]

im·plore /ɪmˈploɚ/ *verb* **-plores; -plored; -plor·ing** [+ *obj*] *formal*

1 a : to make a very serious or emotional request to (someone) : BEG • Don't go. I *implore* you. — **usually followed by** *to* + *verb* • She *implored* her son not *to go*. • He *implored* her *to think* of the children. **b : to say (something) as a serious or emotional request** • "Think of the children!" he *implored*.

2 : to ask or beg for (something) in a very serious or emotional way • He *implored* their help.

– imploring *adj* [*more* ~; *most* ~] • an *imploring* look • an *imploring* request for help **– im·plor·ing·ly** *adv* • "Don't go!" she said *imploringly*.

im·ply /ɪmˈplaɪ/ *verb* **-plies; -plied; -ply·ing** [+ *obj*]

1 : to express (something) in an indirect way : to suggest (something) without saying or showing it plainly • Your remark *implies* (to me) that you think I'm wrong. • Early reports *implied* that the judge's death was not an accident. • His words *implied* a threat. — compare INFER

2 : to include or involve (something) as a natural or necessary part or result • War *implies* fighting and death.

im·po·lite /ˌɪmpəˈlaɪt/ *adj* [*more* ~; *most* ~] **: not polite : RUDE** • It's *impolite* to talk during the performance. • He made some *impolite* comments about her appearance. • an *impolite* child • an *impolite* word

– im·po·lite·ly *adv* • They felt they were being treated *impolitely*. **– im·po·lite·ness** *noun* [*noncount*]

im·pon·der·a·ble /ɪmˈpɑːndərəbəl/ *adj, formal* **: not able to be measured or judged exactly** • the *imponderable* vastness of space

– imponderable *noun, pl* **-ables** [*count*] • the *imponderables* of human nature [=the mysteries of human nature; the questions about human nature that cannot be fully answered or understood]

¹im·port /ɪmˈpoɚt/ *verb* **-ports; -port·ed; -port·ing** [+ *obj*]

1 : to bring a product into a country to be sold • a dealer who *imports* cars from Italy to the U.S. — opposite EXPORT

2 *computers* **: to bring (something, such as data) into a file, system, etc., from another source** • software that makes it

simple to *import* digital photographs onto your hard drive
– imported *adj* • *imported* cars/coffee **– im·port·er** *noun, pl* **-ers** [*count*] • an *importer* of Italian cars

²im·port /ˈɪm͵poɚt/ *noun, pl* **-ports**
1 a [*count*] **: something that is imported : a product brought into a country to be sold there** • This car is an *import* from Italy. • They sell luxury *imports* from around the world. **b** [*noncount*] **: the act of importing something : IMPORTATION** • laws affecting the *import* of foreign goods • an *import* tax
2 [*noncount*] *formal* **: IMPORTANCE** • This is an issue of little *import* to voters. • a matter of great *import*
3 [*singular*] *formal* **: the meaning of something** • Researchers are still debating the *import* [=*meaning*] of the test results.

im·por·tance /ɪmˈpoɚtn̩s/ *noun* [*noncount*] **: the quality or state of being important : value or significance** • The teacher lectured the students on the *importance* of mutual respect. • a medical discovery of great/major *importance* [=a very important medical discovery] • He exaggerated the *importance* of his role in the rescue mission. • The negotiations have taken on added *importance* in the wake of the bomb attack. • a matter of little/minor *importance* • Nothing of *importance* [=nothing important] was decided.

im·por·tant /ɪmˈpoɚtn̩t/ *adj* [*more* ~; *most* ~]
1 : having serious meaning or worth • She's an *important* [=*significant*] part of the team. • Diet and exercise are *important* for health. **: deserving or requiring serious attention** • an *important* problem • In his editorial, he made several *important* points. • It's *important* that you remember to send these forms on time. = It's *important* for you to remember to send these forms on time. • Scientists have made an *important* discovery. • Doing her job well is *important* to her. • The new policy will help businesses and, more *important* [=*importantly*], it will create thousands of new jobs. [=it is more important that the new policy will create thousands of new jobs] • critically/crucially/vitally *important*
2 : having power, authority, or influence • He's one of the most *important* scholars in his field. • an *important* artist

im·por·tant·ly /ɪmˈpoɚtn̩tli/ *adv*
1 [*more* ~; *most* ~] **— used to say that something is important** • More *importantly*, [=it is more important that] the proposed law will have a harmful effect on funding for public schools.
2 a : in an important way • Her research has contributed *importantly* to our understanding of the disease. **b : in the manner of people who think that they are important : in an arrogant or pompous manner** • He strutted to and fro *importantly*, ordering everybody around.

im·por·ta·tion /͵ɪm͵poɚˈteɪʃən/ *noun* [*noncount*] **: the act of importing products** • illegal *importation* of weapons

im·por·tu·nate /ɪmˈpoɚʧənət/ *adj* [*more* ~; *most* ~] *formal*
1 : making repeated or annoying requests or demands • an *importunate* salesman
2 : causing annoyance or trouble • *importunate* demands
– im·por·tu·nate·ly *adv* • *importunately* demanding help

im·por·tune /͵ɪmpɚˈtuːn, *Brit* ͵ɪmpəˈtjuːn/ *verb* **-tunes; -tuned; -tun·ing** [+ *obj*] *formal* **: to ask (someone) for something or to do something in a repeated or annoying way : BEG** • He stood on the street corner, *importuning* passersby for help/money. • He *importuned* them to help.

im·pose /ɪmˈpoʊz/ *verb* **-pos·es; -posed; -pos·ing**
1 [+ *obj*] **a : to cause (something, such as a tax, fine, rule, or punishment) to affect someone or something by using your authority** • The judge *imposed* a life sentence. **— usually + *on* or *upon*** • The judge *imposed* a life sentence *on* the defendant. • *impose* [=*levy*] a tax *on* liquor • A curfew has been *imposed upon* the city's youth. **b : to establish or create (something unwanted) in a forceful or harmful way** • I needed to break free from the limits *imposed* by my own fear of failure.
2 [+ *obj*] **: to force someone to accept (something or yourself) — + *on* or *upon*** • He *imposed* his will *on* his subjects. [=he forced his subjects to do what he wanted them to do] • He *imposes* his personal beliefs *on* his employees. • I don't like having to ***impose myself*** *on* other people.
3 [*no obj*] **: to ask for or expect more than is fair or reasonable** • She asked if I wanted a ride, but I declined. I didn't want to *impose*. [=I didn't want to cause trouble or inconvenience for her] **— often + *on* or *upon*** • I didn't want to *impose on* her. = I didn't want to *impose on* her kindness. • You shouldn't *impose on/upon* your friend's good nature.

im·pos·ing /ɪmˈpoʊzɪŋ/ *adj* [*more* ~; *most* ~] **: very large or impressive** • He's an *imposing* man with a powerful voice. • an *imposing* building • an *imposing* figure
– im·pos·ing·ly *adv* • an *imposingly* large building

im·po·si·tion /͵ɪmpəˈzɪʃən/ *noun, pl* **-tions**
1 [*count*] **: a demand or request that is not reasonable or that causes trouble for someone** • Your kids can stay with me the night you're away—it's really not an *imposition*.
2 [*noncount*] **: the act of establishing or creating something in an official way : the act of imposing something** • the *imposition* of a life sentence on the defendant • the *imposition* of a tax on liquor

im·pos·si·bil·i·ty /ɪm͵pɑːsəˈbɪləti/ *noun, pl* **-ties**
1 [*count*] **: something that is impossible : something that cannot be done or that cannot happen** • The blizzard made travel an *impossibility*. • a logical/mathematical *impossibility*
2 [*noncount*] **: the quality or state of being impossible** • the *impossibility* of knowing what the future will bring

im·pos·si·ble /ɪmˈpɑːsəbəl/ *adj*
1 a : unable to be done or to happen : not possible • It's *impossible* to predict the future. • The heavy rain made it *impossible* to see the road. • It's logically/mathematically *impossible*. • It's physically *impossible* for a child to lift that much at once. • It's virtually/nearly/almost *impossible* to book a flight just before the holiday. • I find it *impossible* to believe [=I cannot believe] that he's telling the truth. • an *impossible* dream **b : very difficult** • an *impossible* [=*hopeless*] situation • These math problems are *impossible*!
2 [*more* ~; *most* ~] *of a person* **: very difficult to deal with : very irritating or annoying** • You refuse to help and then criticize me for not doing it right? You're *impossible*! • My boss is just an *impossible* woman.
the impossible **: something that cannot be done or that is very difficult** • Expecting people to do a good job in such a short time is asking *the impossible*.
– im·pos·si·bly /ɪmˈpɑːsəbli/ *adv* • The restaurants in this city are *impossibly* [=*extremely, ridiculously*] expensive. • *impossibly* high standards

im·pos·tor *or* **im·pos·ter** /ɪmˈpɑːstɚ/ *noun, pl* **-tors** *or* **-ters** [*count*] **: a person who deceives others by pretending to be someone else** • He claimed he was an experienced pilot, but he turned out to be an *impostor*.

im·pos·ture /ɪmˈpɑːsʧɚ/ *noun, pl* **-tures** *formal* **: the act of deceiving others by pretending to be someone else** [*noncount*] He was accused of *imposture*. [*count*] his elaborate *impostures*

im·po·tent /ˈɪmpətənt/ *adj*
1 [*more* ~; *most* ~] **: lacking power or strength** • an *impotent* political party
2 *of a man* **: unable to have sex : unable to get or keep an erection**
– im·po·tence /ˈɪmpətəns/ *noun* [*noncount*] • the *impotence* [=*weakness*] of the current regime • sexual *impotence* **– im·po·tent·ly** *adv* • We could only watch *impotently* [=*helplessly*] as the fire consumed our home.

im·pound /ɪmˈpaʊnd/ *verb* **-pounds; -pound·ed; -pound·ing** [+ *obj*] **: to use legal powers to get and hold (something)** • The police *impounded* her car because it was illegally parked. • *impound* evidence for a trial

im·pov·er·ish /ɪmˈpɑːvərɪʃ/ *verb* **-ish·es; -ished; -ish·ing** [+ *obj*]
1 : to make (someone) poor • The dictator enriched himself but *impoverished* his people.
2 : to use up the strength or richness of (something, such as land) • Poor farming practices *impoverished* the soil.
– impoverished *adj* [*more* ~; *most* ~] • the most *impoverished* areas [=the poorest areas] of the country • acres of *impoverished* soil **– im·pov·er·ish·ment** /ɪmˈpɑːvərɪʃmənt/ *noun* [*noncount*] • the *impoverishment* of the people/soil

im·prac·ti·ca·ble /ɪmˈpræktɪkəbəl/ *adj* [*more* ~; *most* ~] *formal* **: difficult or impossible to do or use : not practicable** • an *impracticable* plan • an *impracticable* solution
– im·prac·ti·ca·bil·i·ty /ɪm͵præktɪkəˈbɪləti/ *noun* [*noncount*] • the *impracticability* of his plan

im·prac·ti·cal /ɪmˈpræktɪkəl/ *adj* [*more* ~; *most* ~] **: not practical: such as a : not easy to do or use : not suitable for the situation** • Little sports cars are *impractical* for large families. • an attractive but completely *impractical* pair of shoes [=shoes that look nice but are not comfortable for walking] • an *impractical* plan/solution **b** *of a person* **: not sensible : not able to deal with practical matters effectively** • He was a dreamy and *impractical* young man.
– im·prac·ti·cal·i·ty /ɪm͵præktɪˈkæləti/ *noun, pl* **-ties** [*count*] They adopted the plan despite all its *impracticali-*

ties. [*noncount*] the *impracticality* of the plan – **im·prac·ti·cal·ly** /ɪmˈpræktɪkli/ *adv* ▪ an *impractically* large book

im·pre·ca·tion /ˌɪmprɪˈkeɪʃən/ *noun, pl* **-tions** [*count*] *formal* : an offensive word or phrase that people say when they are angry : CURSE ▪ He muttered *imprecations* under his breath.

im·pre·cise /ˌɪmprɪˈsaɪs/ *adj* [*more ~; most ~*] : not clear or exact : not precise ▪ *imprecise* language/measurements ▪ an *imprecise* description ▪ It's an *imprecise* translation of the original sentence.
– **im·pre·cise·ly** *adv* ▪ The passage had been translated *imprecisely.* – **im·pre·ci·sion** /ˌɪmprɪˈsɪʒən/ *noun* [*noncount*]

im·preg·na·ble /ɪmˈprɛgnəbəl/ *adj*
1 : not able to be captured by attack : very strong ▪ an *impregnable* fortress ▪ *impregnable* defenses
2 : not likely to be weakened or changed ▪ an *impregnable* reputation ▪ Her arguments seemed *impregnable.*

im·preg·nate /ɪmˈprɛgˌneɪt/ *verb* **-nates; -nat·ed; -nat·ing** [+ *obj*]
1 : to cause (a material) to be filled or soaked with something ▪ a cake *impregnated* with brandy
2 *technical* **:** to make (a woman or a female animal) pregnant
– **im·preg·na·tion** /ɪmˌprɛgˈneɪʃən/ *noun* [*noncount*]

im·pre·sa·rio /ˌɪmprəˈsɑriˌoʊ/ *noun, pl* **-ri·os** [*count*] : a person who manages a performance (such as a concert or play)

im·press /ɪmˈprɛs/ *verb* **-press·es; -pressed; -press·ing**
1 : to cause (someone) to feel admiration or interest [+ *obj*] He's trying to *impress* her. [=he is trying to win her admiration; he wants her to like him] ▪ The candidate *impressed* us with his qualifications. = The candidate's qualifications *impressed* us. ▪ What really *impressed* me was their enthusiasm. = It really *impressed* me that they were so enthusiastic. — often used as *(be) impressed* ▪ We *were* (favorably/deeply/very) *impressed* by/with his credentials. ▪ I *am impressed* that you can play the violin so well. ▪ I *was* particularly/especially *impressed* by their enthusiasm. [*no obj*] She's bright, ambitious, and eager to *impress.*
2 [+ *obj*] **:** to put (something) in someone's mind : to produce a clear idea or image of (something) — + *on* or *upon* ▪ The speaker tried to *impress* the dangers of drugs *on* the children. = The speaker tried to *impress on* the children how dangerous drugs can be. [=tried to make the children understand very clearly how dangerous drugs can be]
3 [+ *obj*] **:** to produce (something, such as a picture) by pushing something against a surface ▪ a design *impressed* on the book's cover

im·pres·sion /ɪmˈprɛʃən/ *noun, pl* **-sions** [*count*]
1 : the effect or influence that something or someone has on a person's thoughts or feelings ▪ Her words made a strong *impression* (on us). ▪ The candidate made a favorable/positive/good/bad *impression.* ▪ What was your *impression* of the candidate? [=what did you think of the candidate?] ▪ My first *impression* of him was that he was a kind and thoughtful young man. ▪ First *impressions* are important but can be misleading. ▪ In her journal, she recorded her *impressions* of the city. ▪ Her kindness left a lasting *impression* on her students. ▪ I was trying to make an *impression.* = I was trying to make a good *impression.* ▪ He's trying to avoid (giving) the *impression* that he's insensitive. ▪ a fleeting *impression*
2 : an idea or belief that is usually not clear or certain ▪ It was my *impression* [=I thought] that admission was free. ▪ I'm sorry if I gave you the wrong *impression.* [=I'm sorry if I misled you] ▪ I got/had the distinct *impression* that they didn't mean to stay long. ▪ They gave (us) the *impression* that they didn't mean to stay long. ▪ an erroneous/false/mistaken *impression* ▪ I was ***under the impression*** [=I thought] that admission was free.
3 : an appearance or suggestion of something ▪ The garden is designed in tiers to give/create the *impression* of steps. [=the garden is designed so that it looks like steps] ▪ His lifestyle conveyed the *impression* of great wealth. [=his lifestyle led people to believe that he was very wealthy]
4 : something (such as a design or a footprint) made by pressing or stamping a surface ▪ The child used her hand to make an *impression* in the mud.
5 : an imitation of a famous person that is done for entertainment ▪ He does a funny *impression* [=*impersonation*] of Elvis Presley.

im·pres·sion·able /ɪmˈprɛʃənəbəl/ *adj* [*more ~; most ~*] : easy to influence ▪ The teacher was accused of forcing his political beliefs on *impressionable* teenagers. ▪ The book had a profound effect on his *impressionable* young mind.
– **im·pres·sion·abil·i·ty** /ɪmˌprɛʃənəˈbɪləti/ *noun* [*noncount*] ▪ the *impressionability* of youth

im·pres·sion·ism *or* **Im·pres·sion·ism** /ɪmˈprɛʃəˌnɪzəm/ *noun* [*noncount*] : a style of painting that began in France around 1870, that uses spots of color to show the effects of different kinds of light, and that attempts to capture the feeling of a scene rather than specific details
– **impressionist** *or* **Impressionist** *adj* ▪ an *Impressionist* painting

im·pres·sion·ist /ɪmˈprɛʃənɪst/ *noun, pl* **-ists** [*count*]
1 *or* ***Impressionist*** **:** a painter who practices impressionism
2 : an entertainer who does impressions (sense 5)

im·pres·sion·is·tic /ɪmˌprɛʃəˈnɪstɪk/ *adj*
1 [*more ~; most ~*] **:** involving general feelings or thoughts rather than specific knowledge or facts ▪ He wrote an *impressionistic* account of the battle scene.
2 *chiefly US* **:** of or relating to impressionism ▪ an *impressionistic* painting
– **im·pres·sion·is·ti·cal·ly** /ɪmˌprɛʃəˈnɪstɪkli/ *adv* ▪ He wrote vaguely and *impressionistically* about his life.

im·pres·sive /ɪmˈprɛsɪv/ *adj* [*more ~; most ~*] : deserving attention, admiration, or respect : making a good impression ▪ He has an *impressive* vocabulary for a 10-year-old. ▪ Her first performance was very *impressive.* ▪ He has an *impressive* manner. ▪ a large and *impressive* [=*imposing*] building
– **im·pres·sive·ly** *adv* ▪ an *impressively* large vocabulary/building

im·pri·ma·tur /ˌɪmprəˈmɑːˌtuə/ *noun, pl* **-turs** [*count*] *formal* **:** official approval ▪ He gave the book his *imprimatur.*

¹im·print /ɪmˈprɪnt/ *verb* **-prints; -print·ed; -print·ing** [+ *obj*]
1 : to create a mark by pressing against a surface ▪ *imprint* [=*stamp*] a design on a sheet of paper ▪ wearing a T-shirt *imprinted* with the company logo
2 : to cause (something) to stay in your mind or memory ▪ The image of her beautiful face will always be *imprinted* on my mind. [=I will always remember her beautiful face] ▪ a picture *imprinted* in my memory

²im·print /ˈɪmˌprɪnt/ *noun, pl* **-prints** [*count*]
1 : a mark created by pressing against a surface : something imprinted or printed ▪ We saw an *imprint* of a bike tire on the dirt trail. ▪ a fossil *imprint* of a dinosaur's foot
2 : a strong effect or influence ▪ She was determined to ***put her imprint on*** the company. [=to use her ideas and influence to make the company better]
3 *technical* **:** a publisher's name on the title page of a book

im·pris·on /ɪmˈprɪzn̩/ *verb* **-ons; -oned; -on·ing** [+ *obj*] : to put (someone) in prison ▪ He was *imprisoned* for murder. ▪ He has threatened to *imprison* his political opponents. — sometimes used figuratively ▪ He has a brilliant mind *imprisoned* in an unhealthy body.
– **im·pris·on·ment** /ɪmˈprɪzn̩mənt/ *noun* [*noncount*] ▪ He was released after six months' *imprisonment.* ▪ sentenced to life *imprisonment*

im·prob·a·ble /ɪmˈprɑːbəbəl/ *adj* [*more ~; most ~*] : not probable : not likely to be true or to happen : UNLIKELY ▪ There really isn't enough evidence to prove that he committed the crime, so it's (highly) *improbable* that he'll be convicted. ▪ The team made an *improbable* comeback. ▪ an *improbable* story
– **im·prob·a·bil·i·ty** /ɪmˌprɑːbəˈbɪləti/ *noun* [*noncount*] the *improbability* of their success [*count*] The story includes a number of absurd *improbabilities.* [=improbable events or situations] – **im·prob·a·bly** /ɪmˈprɑːbəbli/ *adv* ▪ an *improbably* gifted child

im·promp·tu /ɪmˈprɑːmptu, *Brit* ɪmˈprɒmptju/ *adj* : not prepared ahead of time : made or done without preparation ▪ Two of my friends came by unexpectedly, and we had an *impromptu* little party in my kitchen. ▪ He made an *impromptu* speech about honor and responsibility.
– **impromptu** *adv* ▪ speaking *impromptu*

im·prop·er /ɪmˈprɑːpə/ *adj* [*more ~; most ~*] : not proper, right, or suitable: such as **a :** not correct ▪ The doctor gave him an *improper* diagnosis. ▪ *improper* grammar **b :** not following rules of acceptable behavior : legally or morally wrong ▪ They claim to have evidence of *improper* police conduct. ▪ *improper* use of public land **c :** not suitable for the situation : not appropriate ▪ This is an *improper* diet for a growing teenager. • *improper* dress/attire **d :** not polite • It would be *improper* for me to ask such a favor of her. • He made some *improper* remarks. • *improper* behavior

– **im·prop·er·ly** *adv* • He came to school *improperly* dressed. • She pronounced the word *improperly*. • behaving *improperly*

im·pro·pri·ety /ˌɪmprəˈprajəti/ *noun, pl* **-ties** *formal*
1 [*noncount*] **a :** rude or immoral behavior **:** improper behavior • He has a reputation for *impropriety*. • The judge excused herself from the case to avoid any appearance of *impropriety*. • She was shocked by the young man's *impropriety*. **b :** a rude or improper quality • She was shocked by the *impropriety* of his behavior/language.
2 [*count*] **:** a wrong or immoral act **:** an improper act • He has been accused of financial/sexual *improprieties*.

im·prov /ˈɪmˌprɑːv/ *noun* [*noncount*] *informal* **:** the act of performing without preparation **:** the act of improvising • a comedian with a talent for *improv* [=*improvisation*]

im·prove /ɪmˈpruːv/ *verb* **-proves; -proved; -prov·ing**
1 [+ *obj*] **:** to make (something) better • This operation will greatly/dramatically/significantly *improve* her chances of survival. • The advertising campaign has *improved* sales.
2 [*no obj*] **:** to become better • Maybe we'll buy a house when our financial situation *improves*. • Her writing has *improved* since the beginning of the school year. • The company has been having steadily *improving* sales.
improve on/upon [*phrasal verb*] ***improve on/upon (something)*** **:** to do better than (something previously done) • After months of study, I *improved on* my original score. • It'll be hard to *improve upon* the success they had last year.

– **improved** *adj* [*more* ~; *most* ~] • The campaign resulted in greatly *improved* sales. • She was voted the most *improved* player on the team.

im·prove·ment /ɪmˈpruːvmənt/ *noun, pl* **-ments**
1 [*noncount*] **:** the act of improving something **:** the act or process of making something better • Doctors were amazed by the sudden *improvement* in her medical condition. • His cooking needs *improvement*. = There's still ***room for improvement*** in his cooking.
2 [*count*] **a :** the quality of being better than before • I've noticed a significant *improvement* in your work since the spring. **b :** an addition or change that makes something better or more valuable • The editor made some *improvements* to/in the article before it was printed. • They spent the money on new kitchen cabinets and other ***home improvements***. ✧ An ***improvement on*** or (*chiefly US*) ***over*** something is a better version of it or a better way of doing it. • The food isn't fancy, but it's certainly an *improvement over* what we're served at school.

im·prov·i·dent /ɪmˈprɑːvədənt/ *adj* [*more* ~; *most* ~] *formal* **:** not providing or saving for the future **:** not wise or sensible regarding money • Her *improvident* habits left her with no retirement savings. • an *improvident* [=*irresponsible, unwise*] use of public money

– **im·prov·i·dence** /ɪmˈprɑːvədəns/ *noun* [*noncount*] • financial *improvidence*

im·pro·vise /ˈɪmprəˌvaɪz/ *verb* **-vis·es; -vised; -vis·ing**
1 : to speak or perform without preparation [*no obj*] If you forget any of your lines, try to *improvise*. • Good jazz musicians know how to *improvise*. [+ *obj*] He had to *improvise* his opening speech when he forgot his notes. • The trumpet player performed an *improvised* solo.
2 [+ *obj*] **:** to make or create (something) by using whatever is available • I wasn't expecting guests, so I had to *improvise* a meal with what I had in my refrigerator.

– **im·pro·vi·sa·tion** /ɪmˌprɑːvəˈzeɪʃən/ *noun, pl* **-tions** [*noncount*] an actor who is good at *improvisation* [*count*] His performance featured several clever *improvisations*.

– **im·pro·vi·sa·tion·al** /ɪmˌprɑːvəˈzeɪʃənl/ *also* **im·pro·vi·sa·to·ry** /ˌɪmprəˈvaɪzəˌtori, *Brit* ˌɪmprəˈvaɪzətri/ *adj* • an *improvisational* performance • *improvisational* theater

– **im·pro·vis·er** *also chiefly US* **im·pro·vis·or** /ˈɪmprəˌvaɪzə/ *noun, pl* **-ers** *also* **-ors** [*count*] • jazz *improvisers*

im·pru·dent /ɪmˈpruːdn̩t/ *adj* [*more* ~; *most* ~] *formal* **:** not wise or sensible **:** not prudent • She made some *imprudent* [=*foolish, unwise*] investments that she would later regret. • It's politically *imprudent* to stir up such controversy during an election year.

– **im·pru·dence** /ɪmˈpruːdn̩s/ *noun* [*noncount*] • financial *imprudence* – **im·pru·dent·ly** *adv* • She invested *imprudently*.

im·pu·dent /ˈɪmpjədənt/ *adj* [*more* ~; *most* ~] *formal* **:** failing to show proper respect and courtesy **:** very rude • The boy was punished for his *impudent* behavior/attitude. • an *impudent* [=*insolent, disrespectful*] soldier

– **im·pu·dence** /ˈɪmpjədəns/ *noun* [*noncount*] • The boy was punished for his *impudence*. – **im·pu·dent·ly** *adv* • He behaved *impudently*.

im·pugn /ɪmˈpjuːn/ *verb* **-pugns; -pugned; -pugn·ing** [+ *obj*] *formal* **:** to criticize (a person's character, intentions, etc.) by suggesting that someone is not honest and should not to be trusted • He *impugned* his rival's character. • Her motives have been scrutinized and *impugned*.

im·pulse /ˈɪmˌpʌls/ *noun, pl* **-puls·es** [*count*]
1 : a sudden strong desire to do something • He has to learn to control his *impulses*. • a natural/creative/sudden *impulse* • a generous *impulse* — often followed by *to* + *verb* • He had to resist the *impulse* [=*urge*] *to shout*. • My first/initial *impulse* was *to say* no. ✧ To do something ***on (an) impulse*** or ***on a sudden impulse*** is to do it suddenly and without thinking about it first. • He bought a new camera *on impulse*. • She quit her job *on a sudden impulse*. An ***impulse buy/purchase*** is something that is bought on impulse and that usually is not really needed. • The camera was an *impulse buy*. ***Impulse buying*** is the act or practice of buying things on impulse. • Shopping with a credit card can lead to *impulse buying*.
2 *technical* **:** a small amount of energy that moves from one area to another • an electrical *impulse* • a nerve *impulse* [=a wave of electrical energy that is carried through the nerves to the brain]

im·pul·sive /ɪmˈpʌlsɪv/ *adj* [*more* ~; *most* ~]
1 : doing things or tending to do things suddenly and without careful thought **:** acting or tending to act on impulse • She's *impulsive* and often does things that she later regrets.
2 : done suddenly and without planning **:** resulting from a sudden impulse • He needs to learn to control his *impulsive* behavior. • She made an *impulsive* decision to quit her job.

– **im·pul·sive·ly** *adv* • She *impulsively* decided to quit her job. • acting *impulsively* – **im·pul·sive·ness** *noun* [*noncount*] • Her *impulsiveness* gets her in trouble. • the *impulsiveness* of her decision

im·pu·ni·ty /ɪmˈpjuːnəti/ *noun* [*noncount*] **:** freedom from punishment, harm, or loss — usually used in the phrase ***with impunity*** • They broke the law *with* (complete/total) *impunity*. [=without fear of punishment; very freely and openly] • The rioters set fires and looted *with impunity*.

im·pure /ɪmˈpjuə/ *adj* [*more* ~; *most* ~] **:** not pure: such as **a :** DIRTY, UNCLEAN • *impure* water **b :** mixed with something else that is usually not as good • an *impure* chemical • selling *impure* drugs **c :** sexual in a way that is considered morally wrong • *impure* thoughts

im·pu·ri·ty /ɪmˈpjurəti/ *noun, pl* **-ties**
1 [*noncount*] **:** the quality or state of being impure • the *impurity* of the water • moral *impurity*
2 [*count*] **:** an unwanted substance that is found in something else and that prevents it from being pure • The syrup is strained to remove *impurities*. • The water is free of *impurities*.

im·pute /ɪmˈpjuːt/ *verb* **-putes; -put·ed; -put·ing** [+ *obj*] *formal* **:** to say or suggest that someone or something has or is guilty of (something) • They're trying to *impute* selfish motives *to* my actions. [=they're trying to say that my actions were motivated by selfishness] • He insists that he is not responsible for all the crimes that have been *imputed to* him. [=the crimes that he has been blamed for]

– **im·pu·ta·tion** /ˌɪmpjəˈteɪʃən/ *noun, pl* **-tions** [*noncount*] the *imputation* of blame [*count*] I deny all your *imputations* of blame.

¹in /ˈɪn, ən/ *prep*
1 — used to indicate location or position within something • We went for a swim *in* the lake. • They have a house *in* the country. • Albuquerque is *in* New Mexico. • There wasn't a cloud *in* the sky. • I like to read *in* bed. [=while sitting or lying on my bed] • He was wounded *in* the leg. • We had to stand *in* line for tickets. • Why don't you look it up *in* the dictionary? • There's something *in* my eye. [=between my eyelid and my eyeball] • There was fear *in* their eyes. [=I could tell they were afraid when I looked at their eyes] • I held her *in* my arms. • He saw his reflection *in* the mirror.
2 : to the inside of (a room, container, etc.) • She went *in* [=*into*] the house. • Don't come *in* here with those muddy feet! • I threw it *in* [=*into*] the garbage.
3 a — used to indicate that someone or something belongs

to or is included as part of something ▪ She used to play *in* [=as a member of] a band. ▪ There are 12 *in* a dozen. [=a dozen is equal to 12] **b — used to indicate the existence of something or someone within a story, movie, etc.** ▪ a character *in* a story ▪ a scene *in* a movie ▪ He saw it *in* a dream.
4 a : during (a period of time, a season, etc.) ▪ It happened *in* the 1930s. ▪ She likes to travel *in* [=*during*] the summer. ▪ Call us sometime *in* [=*during*] the morning/afternoon/evening. ▪ They plan to open *in* September. ▪ We haven't seen them *in* [=*for*] ages! ▪ Back *in* those days, we didn't have computers. ▪ an important moment *in* history ▪ Never *in* my life have I heard such a thing! ▪ I lost track of them *in* [=*during*] all the commotion/confusion. **b : at the end of (a period of time)** ▪ I'll be there *in* a minute. ▪ The movie is coming out *in* a few months. ▪ He got his degree *in* only three years. **c — used to indicate an approximate age or number** ▪ a woman *in* her thirties [=a woman who is between 30 and 39 years old] ▪ Our members number *in* the thousands. [=more than 2,000]
5 a — used to indicate the method, materials, or form of something ▪ a note written *in* pencil [=using a pencil] ▪ a note written *in* French ▪ a symphony *in* (the key of) C ▪ The book is bound *in* leather. ▪ They were covered *in* mud from head to toe. ▪ She gave us 50 dollars *in* cash. ▪ The measurements are listed *in* both inches and centimeters. ▪ The shirts come *in* three sizes. **b — used to indicate the color of something** ▪ I decorated the room *in* blues and grays. [=using different shades of blue and gray]
6 a — used to indicate the state or condition of someone or something ▪ We'll be *in* trouble if we can't get the brakes to work! [=we will experience a situation that is difficult, dangerous, etc.] ▪ She was *in* and out of trouble for many years. ▪ young people *in* love [=experiencing romantic love] ▪ Are you *in* much pain? ▪ I just stood there gaping *in* amazement. ▪ They're not *in* any danger. **b : to a specified state, condition, or form** ▪ They were always getting *in* [=*into*] trouble. ▪ The vase broke *in* [=*into*] pieces. ▪ They divided the money *in* [=*into*] thirds.
7 — used to indicate how people or things are arranged ▪ They stood *in* a circle. ▪ The chairs were placed *in* a row.
8 — used to indicate the conditions that are around someone or something ▪ I found her sitting *in* the dark. = I found her sitting *in* darkness. ▪ Don't just stand there *in* the rain!
9 : while or as a result of (doing something) ▪ *In* trying to please everyone, I ended up pleasing no one. ▪ Many mistakes were made *in* planning the project.
10 — used to indicate the manner or purpose of something ▪ "No way!" she said *in* reply. ▪ The remark was made *in* jest. ▪ They sure left *in* a hurry! ▪ We held a banquet *in* his honor. [=to honor him] ▪ They went *in* search of lost treasure. [=to search for lost treasure] ▪ She moved to the city *in* hopes of finding a better job. [=with the hope that she would find a better job] ▪ They increased the penalties *in* an attempt to discourage lawbreakers.
11 — used to make a statement or description more limited or specific in meaning ▪ They are slow *in* their movements. [=their movements are slow] ▪ The two are alike *in* some ways/respects. [=they have some similarities] ▪ It measures two feet *in* length. [=it is two feet long] ▪ The idea works *in* theory, but not *in* practice. ▪ *In* a way, it makes sense. [=it makes sense if you consider a particular fact, idea, etc.]
12 — used to indicate the person who is being described ▪ We've lost a valuable employee *in* Mike. ▪ *In* her, you have a true friend.
13 — used to indicate the object of a belief, opinion, or feeling ▪ Have a little faith *in* them! ▪ Do you believe *in* ghosts? [=do you think ghosts are real?] ▪ I really don't know what she sees *in* him. [=I don't know why she likes/loves him] ▪ I have no interest *in* sports. [=sports do not interest me]
14 — used to indicate a job or area of activity ▪ She has a job *in* marketing. ▪ I hear he's *in* advertising. [=he has a job that involves advertising] ▪ She's struggling *in* math.
15 — used to indicate the existence of something as a part of someone's character ▪ He has no pity *in* him. ▪ I tried to be tough with them, but I just ***didn't have it in me.*** [=I wasn't able to be tough with them]
16 : wearing (something) as clothes ▪ He showed up *in* his best suit. ▪ the boy *in* the red jacket ▪ a lady *in* black [=a lady wearing black clothes]
17 — used to describe how common something is by comparing a smaller number to a larger number ▪ This condition affects one *in* five [=1 in 5; one out of every five] Americans.

²in /ˈɪn/ *adv*
1 : to or toward the inside of something (such as a building) ▪ She went *in* and closed the door. ▪ I lost my keys and now I can't get *in*. ▪ Please come *in*! ▪ The burglars broke *in* through the kitchen window. ▪ The pool is deep. Be careful not to fall *in*. ▪ Is everyone *in* [=*inside*]? Then we can start. ▪ The shot went *in*. [=into the goal]
2 a : to or toward a place ▪ They flew *in* yesterday. ▪ The boss called us *in* for a conference. ▪ The fog was closing *in* fast. ▪ The tide is coming *in*. [=towards shore] ▪ Get your orders *in* early! **b : at the place where someone or something arrives after traveling** ▪ Is the train *in* yet? ▪ We expect to get *in* around noon. [=we expect to arrive around noon]
3 : at or inside a home, office, etc. ▪ The doctor is *in*. [=the doctor is in his/her office and is available to see patients] ▪ Are your parents *in*? [=are your parents at home?]
4 : at or to a location that is near to something or that seems near to something ▪ The coach told them to play closer *in*. [=nearer to the area where the most activity is happening or is expected to happen] ▪ Pull the car further *in*. [=closer to the curb, house, etc.]
5 a : in a way that will blend into or join with something ▪ Gradually mix *in* the flour. **b : to or at a proper or indicated place** ▪ I can't seem to fit this piece *in*. ▪ Please fill *in* your name and address on the application. **c : in a way that will agree or be in harmony** ▪ Do you think he'll fit *in* with the other kids?
6 : in a way that surrounds something or someone or prevents something or someone from leaving ▪ They fenced *in* the property. = They fenced the property *in*. [=they put a fence around the property] ▪ After the blizzard we were snowed *in* for a week. [=we could not leave our home because of the snow] **— sometimes used in combination** ▪ a house with a fenced-*in* yard
7 : in the position of someone who is involved or participating in something ▪ Count me *in*. [=include me in your plans] ▪ "Does anyone want to go to a movie tonight?" "Sure, I'm *in*." [=I want to go] ▪ She was ***in at the beginning/start***, when the company began.
8 : in or into a position or job ▪ They voted him *in* [=they elected him] by an overwhelming margin.
9 : in a friendly relationship *with* someone ▪ She was ***in with*** the city's most powerful people. [=she had friendly relationships with the city's most powerful people]; ***also* : in a specified sort of relationship** ▪ He got *in* good/bad *with* the boss. [=he was liked/disliked by the boss]
10 : present or in your possession and available for use ▪ Are all the votes/results *in*?
11 *sports* : inside the area where players or the ball must stay in sports like tennis, basketball, and American football : not out of bounds ▪ Her serve was just barely *in*.
all in informal **: very tired** ▪ I'm *all in*. I'm going to bed.
in for informal **: sure to experience (something)** ▪ Boy, is she *in for* a surprise! **— see also *have it in for* at HAVE**
in for it see ¹FOR
in on ✧ If you are *in on* something you have knowledge about it or are involved in it. ▪ They were all *in on* the scheme. ▪ The characters are convinced that they're on another planet, but the audience is *in on* the joke. [=the audience knows they are not on another planet] ▪ I let them *in on* our little secret. [=I told them our secret]
in that **— used to introduce a statement that explains or gives more specific information about what you have just said** ▪ The book is good, *in that* it's well written, but I didn't actually like reading it.

³in /ˈɪn/ *adj*
1 : popular or fashionable ▪ the *in* thing to do ▪ the *in* place to go ▪ Tall boots are *in* [=*in style*] this year.
2 : aware of and strongly influenced by what is new and fashionable ▪ It's what the *in* crowd is wearing this season. **— see also IN-GROUP, IN-JOKE**

⁴in /ˈɪn/ *noun, pl* **ins** [*count*] *chiefly US, informal* **: a way of becoming involved in something or of influencing someone** ▪ When you're trying to get started in show business, it helps to have an *in*. ▪ They must have an *in* with the boss. **— see also INS AND OUTS**

in. *abbr* inch, inches — see also INS.

IN *abbr* Indiana

in- *or* **il-** *or* **im-** *or* **ir-** *prefix* **: not** ▪ *in*conclusive ▪ *in*accurate ▪ *il*logical ▪ *im*moral ▪ *im*practical ▪ *ir*rational

in·abil·i·ty /ˌɪnəˈbɪləti/ *noun* **: the condition of not being able to do something : lack of ability** [*singular*] She has shown an *inability* to concentrate. [*noncount*] the *inability* of the government to cope with the problem

in ab·sen·tia /ˌɪnæbˈsɛnʃijə/ *adv, formal* : without being present ▪ They presented the award to him *in absentia.* [=they presented the award to him although he was not there to receive it himself] ▪ She was convicted of the crime *in absentia.*

in·ac·ces·si·ble /ˌɪnɪkˈsɛsəbəl/ *adj [more ~; most ~]* : difficult or impossible to reach, approach, or understand : not accessible ▪ The area is *inaccessible* by road. ▪ an *inaccessible* goal ▪ His prose is *inaccessible* to many readers.
– **in·ac·ces·si·bil·i·ty** /ˌɪnɪkˌsɛsəˈbɪləti/ *noun [noncount]* ▪ The town's *inaccessibility* discourages tourism. – **inac·cessibly** *adv*

in·ac·cu·ra·cy /ɪnˈækjərəsi/ *noun, pl* **-cies**
1 *[noncount]* : lack of correctness or exactness : lack of accuracy ▪ I pointed out the *inaccuracy* of his statement.
2 *[count]* : a statement that is not correct : an error or mistake ▪ The text is filled with *inaccuracies.*

in·ac·cu·rate /ɪnˈækjərət/ *adj [more ~; most ~]* : not correct or exact : having a mistake or error : not accurate ▪ The book makes several *inaccurate* [=*false, incorrect*] claims. ▪ an *inaccurate* quotation ▪ Our research isn't complete, so these figures are somewhat *inaccurate.* [=*inexact, approximate*]
– **in·ac·cu·rate·ly** *adv* ▪ She claims that the newspaper quoted her *inaccurately.*

in·ac·tion /ɪnˈækʃən/ *noun [noncount]* : failure to do something that should be done : lack of action or activity ▪ The protesters criticized the administration's *inaction* on environmental issues. ▪ We must consider the consequences of continued *inaction.*

in·ac·tive /ɪnˈæktɪv/ *adj [more ~; most ~]* : not active: such as **a** : not doing things that require physical movement and energy : not exercising ▪ *Inactive* people suffer higher rates of heart disease. **b** : not involved in the activities of a group or organization ▪ an *inactive* club member **c** : no longer being used ▪ an *inactive* mine : not currently being used ▪ the bank's *inactive* accounts **d** *of a volcano* : not capable of erupting **e** : not having a chemical effect ▪ *inactive* ingredients
– **in·ac·tive·ly** *adv* ▪ *inactively* traded stocks

in·ac·tiv·i·ty /ɪnˌækˈtɪvəti/ *noun [noncount]* : the state of not acting or moving : lack of activity ▪ His job involved long periods of (physical) *inactivity.*

in·ad·e·quate /ɪnˈædɪkwət/ *adj [more ~; most ~]* : not enough or not good enough : not adequate ▪ These supplies are *inadequate* to meet our needs. ▪ We were given very/woefully/wholly *inadequate* information. ▪ an *inadequate* leader ▪ I felt *inadequate* to the task. ▪ Her brother's success and popularity always made her feel *inadequate.*
– **in·ad·e·qua·cy** /ɪnˈædɪkwəsi/ *noun, pl* **-cies** *[noncount]* feelings of *inadequacy* *[count]* I'm fully aware of my own *inadequacies* as a parent. – **in·ad·e·quate·ly** *adv* ▪ He was *inadequately* prepared for adulthood.

in·ad·mis·si·ble /ˌɪnədˈmɪsəbəl/ *adj [more ~; most ~]* : not able to be allowed or considered in a legal case : not admissible ▪ The evidence was *inadmissible* in court.
– **in·ad·mis·si·bil·i·ty** /ˌɪnədˌmɪsəˈbɪləti/ *noun [noncount]*

in·ad·ver·tent /ˌɪnədˈvətənt/ *adj* : not intended or planned : ACCIDENTAL ▪ an *inadvertent* error/omission
– **in·ad·ver·tence** /ˌɪnədˈvətəns/ *noun [noncount]* ▪ mistakes made by/through *inadvertence* – **in·ad·ver·tent·ly** *adv* ▪ I *inadvertently* [=*accidentally, mistakenly*] dialed the wrong number.

in·ad·vis·able /ˌɪnədˈvaɪzəbəl/ *adj [more ~; most ~]* : not wise, sensible, or reasonable : not advisable ▪ The procedure is *inadvisable* because of the risks involved. ▪ It would be highly/very *inadvisable* to attempt to do this ourselves.
– **in·ad·vis·abil·i·ty** /ˌɪnədˌvaɪzəˈbɪləti/ *noun [noncount]*

in·alien·able /ˌɪnˈeɪljənəbəl/ *adj, formal* : impossible to take away or give up ▪ *inalienable* rights

in·amo·ra·ta /ɪˌnæməˈrɑːtə/ *noun, pl* **-tas** *[count] literary* : the woman that a man loves ▪ a story about a powerful politician and his *inamorata*

inane /ɪˈneɪn/ *adj [more ~; most ~]* : very silly or stupid ▪ I quickly tired of their *inane* comments/questions/chatter. ▪ The film's plot is *inane* and full of clichés.
– **inane·ly** *adv* ▪ an *inanely* simplistic idea ▪ She just sat there grinning *inanely* at the TV. – **inan·i·ty** /ɪˈnænəti/ *noun [noncount]* the *inanity* of their questions *[count]* the tiresome *inanities* [=inane comments or actions] of the political world

in·an·i·mate /ɪnˈænəmət/ *adj* : not living : not capable of life ▪ Stones are *inanimate.* ▪ an *inanimate* object — opposite [1]ANIMATE

in·ap·pli·ca·ble /ɪnˈæplɪkəbəl, ˌɪnəˈplɪkəbəl/ *adj, formal* : not able to be used in a particular situation : not applicable or relevant ▪ The rules are *inapplicable* [=*irrelevant*] in this instance.

in·ap·pro·pri·ate /ˌɪnəˈproupriјət/ *adj [more ~; most ~]* : not right or suited for some purpose or situation : not appropriate or suitable ▪ We won't tolerate such *inappropriate* behavior/conduct/language. ▪ Her informal manner seemed wholly/entirely *inappropriate* to/for the occasion. ▪ The movie's subject matter is *inappropriate* for small children (to see). = It's *inappropriate* for small children to see the movie. = It's *inappropriate* that small children should see the movie.
– **in·ap·pro·pri·ate·ly** *adv* ▪ They were dressed *inappropriately* for such a formal affair. – **in·ap·pro·pri·ate·ness** *noun [noncount]* ▪ We were shocked by the *inappropriateness* of his comments.

in·apt /ɪnˈæpt/ *adj [more ~; most ~] somewhat formal* : not appropriate or suitable : not apt ▪ an *inapt* [=*inappropriate*] analogy/metaphor/comparison ▪ His description of the experience as "weird" isn't altogether *inapt.* [=it is somewhat accurate] — compare INEPT
– **in·apt·ly** *adv* ▪ We had lunch at the *inaptly* named "Good Eats Diner." – **in·apt·ness** *noun [noncount]*

in·ar·gu·able /ɪnˈɑəgjəwəbəl/ *adj, chiefly US, somewhat formal* : certain or clearly true : not open to argument, doubt, or question ▪ It's an *inarguable* [=*indisputable, unquestionable*] fact.
– **in·ar·gu·ably** /ɪnˈɑəgjəwəbli/ *adv* ▪ She is *inarguably* [=*unquestionably, indisputably*] the world's foremost expert on the subject.

in·ar·tic·u·late /ˌɪnˌɑəˈtɪkjələt/ *adj [more ~; most ~]*
1 a : not able to express ideas clearly and effectively in speech or writing : not articulate ▪ He's smart, but somewhat *inarticulate.* ▪ an *inarticulate* drunk **b** : not able to speak ▪ I was almost *inarticulate* with rage.
2 a : not expressed clearly or easily understood ▪ an *inarticulate* explanation ▪ an *inarticulate* reply **b** : not understandable as spoken words ▪ an *inarticulate* cry ▪ *inarticulate* murmurs **c** : not able to be expressed ▪ *inarticulate* longings
– **in·ar·tic·u·late·ly** *adv* ▪ Her only response was to mumble *inarticulately.* – **in·ar·tic·u·late·ness** *noun [noncount]*

in·as·much as /ˌɪnəzˈmʌtʃəz/ *conj, formal* — used to introduce a statement that explains, limits, or gives more specific information about what you have just said ▪ They were lucky *inasmuch as* no one was hurt in the fire. ▪ They abide by the rules only *inasmuch as* [=*insofar as*] it suits them.

in·at·ten·tion /ˌɪnəˈtɛnʃən/ *noun [noncount]* : failure to carefully think about, listen to, or watch someone or something : lack of attention ▪ Many traffic accidents are the result of driver *inattention.* ▪ They lost several potential clients through their *inattention* to detail.
– **in·at·ten·tive** /ˌɪnəˈtɛntɪv/ *adj [more ~; most ~]* ▪ *inattentive* drivers ▪ *inattentive* behavior – **in·at·ten·tive·ly** *adv* ▪ I was listening *inattentively* and missed what she said. – **in·at·ten·tive·ness** *noun [noncount]* ▪ mistakes due to *inattentiveness* [=*inattention*]

in·au·di·ble /ɪnˈɑːdəbəl/ *adj* : impossible to hear : not audible ▪ She spoke so quietly that she was almost *inaudible.* ▪ The sound is *inaudible* to humans but can be heard by dogs.
– **in·au·di·bil·i·ty** /ɪnˌɑːdəˈbɪləti/ *noun [noncount]* – **in·au·di·bly** /ɪnˈɑːdəbli/ *adv* ▪ He whispered *inaudibly* to the person beside him.

in·au·gu·ral /ɪnˈɑːgjərəl/ *adj, always used before a noun*
1 : happening as part of an official ceremony or celebration when someone (such as a newly elected official) begins an important job : happening as part of an inauguration ▪ the President's *inaugural* address ▪ They attended the *inaugural* ball.
2 : happening as the first one in a series of similar events ▪ The new train will make its *inaugural* [=*first*] run next week.
– **inaugural** *noun, pl* **-rals** *[count] chiefly US* ▪ President Franklin D. Roosevelt's first *inaugural* [=*inauguration*]

in·au·gu·rate /ɪnˈɑːgjəˌreɪt/ *verb* **-rates; -rat·ed; -rat·ing** *[+ obj]*
1 : to introduce (someone, such as a newly elected official) into a job or position with a formal ceremony ▪ He was *inaugurated* (as President) on the 20th of January.
2 : to celebrate the fact that something (such as a new hospital or school) is officially ready to be used ▪ They *inaugurated* the new headquarters with a brief ceremony.
3 a : to be the beginning of (something, such as a period of

time) • This event *inaugurated* [=*introduced*] a new era in our history. **b :** to begin to use or have (something) for the first time • The airline will *inaugurate* [=*introduce*] five new routes this summer.

– in·au·gu·ra·tion /ɪnˌɑːgjəˈreɪʃən/ *noun, pl* **-tions** [*count*] presidential *inaugurations* • We attended the *inauguration* of the new museum. [=the event celebrating the fact that the new museum is officially ready to be used] [*noncount*] a discovery that led to (the) *inauguration* of a new era in our history

in·aus·pi·cious /ˌɪnˌɑːˈspɪʃəs/ *adj* [*more* ~; *most* ~] *formal* **:** not showing or suggesting that future success is likely **:** not auspicious • The team got off to an *inauspicious* [=*unpromising*] start/beginning with a series of early losses. • Despite its *inauspicious* beginnings, the company eventually became very profitable.

– in·aus·pi·cious·ly *adv* • His movie career started *inauspiciously* with several box-office flops.

in·au·then·tic /ˌɪnˌɑːˈθɛntɪk/ *adj* [*more* ~; *most* ~] **:** not real, accurate, or sincere **:** not authentic • Their Mexican dishes are tasty but somewhat *inauthentic*. [=they are not quite like real Mexican food]

– in·au·then·tic·ity /ˌɪnˌɑːˌθɛnˈtɪsəti/ *noun* [*noncount*]

in–be·tween /ˌɪnbɪˈtwiːn/ *noun, pl* **-tweens** [*count*] **:** a state or position that is in the middle between two other things **:** a middle position • The switch is either on or off; there's no *in-between*.

– in–between *adj* • available in small, large, and *in-between* sizes

in·board /ˈɪnˌboɚd/ *adj, technical* **:** located inside and towards the center of a boat, car, or airplane • an *inboard* engine/motor — compare OUTBOARD

– inboard *adv* • The wheels are *inboard* of the engines.

in·born /ˈɪnˈboɚn/ *adj* **:** existing from the time someone is born **:** natural or instinctive • Humans have the *inborn* [=*innate*] ability to adapt. • She has an *inborn* talent for music. • That kind of knowledge is acquired, not *inborn*.

in·bound /ˈɪnˌbaʊnd/ *adj* **:** traveling into a place **:** inward bound • *inbound* flights [=flights coming to an airport] • The bridge is closed to *inbound* traffic. [=traffic coming into a city or town] — opposite OUTBOUND

in·bounds pass /ˈɪnˈbaʊndz-/ *noun, pl* ~ **passes** [*count*] *basketball* **:** a pass to start play from a player who is standing out of bounds to a player who is on the court

in–box /ˈɪnˌbɑːks/ *noun, pl* **-box·es** [*count*]
1 *US* **:** a box or other container on a desk in which letters, notes, etc., that are sent to the desk are placed — called also (*Brit*) *in tray*; see picture at OFFICE; compare OUT-BOX
2 *computers* **:** a computer folder that holds new e-mail messages • There are five new messages in your *in-box*.

in·bred /ˈɪnˈbrɛd/ *adj*
1 : existing as a basic part of a person's nature or character • They have an *inbred* love of freedom.
2 : born from or produced by animals, plants, or people that are closely related **:** produced by inbreeding • *inbred* mice

in·breed·ing /ˈɪnˈbriːdɪŋ/ *noun* [*noncount*] **:** a process by which animals, plants, or people are born from or produced by closely related parents • genetic defects caused by *inbreeding*

in·built /ˈɪnˈbɪlt/ *adj, Brit* **:** BUILT-IN • It comes with several *inbuilt* features. • She has an *inbuilt* resistance to change.

Inc. *abbr* incorporated • Merriam-Webster *Inc.*

in·cal·cu·la·ble /ɪnˈkælkjələbəl/ *adj, formal* **:** not able to be calculated: such as **a :** very large or great • The extent of the damage is *incalculable*. • The collection is of *incalculable* value to historians. **b :** not able to be predicted • The future consequences of their decision are *incalculable*.

– in·cal·cu·la·bil·i·ty /ɪnˌkælkjələˈbɪləti/ *noun* [*noncount*]

– in·cal·cu·la·bly /ɪnˈkælkjələbli/ *adv* • an *incalculably* large amount of damage

in·can·des·cent /ˌɪnkənˈdɛsn̩t/ *adj*
1 a : white or glowing because of great heat • *incandescent* gas **b :** producing bright light when heated • an ***incandescent light bulb*** [=a light bulb whose light is produced by the glow of a wire heated by an electric current]
2 a : very impressive, successful, or intelligent • a play full of *incandescent* [=*brilliant*] performances **b :** happy and lively • children with *incandescent* [=*bright*] smiles
3 *Brit* **:** feeling or showing great anger • She was ***incandescent with rage***. [=she was very angry]

– in·can·des·cence /ˌɪnkənˈdɛsn̩s/ *noun* [*noncount*]

in·can·ta·tion /ˌɪnˌkænˈteɪʃən/ *noun, pl* **-tions :** a series of words used to make something magic happen [*count*] ritual prayers and *incantations* [*noncount*] trying to produce a miracle by *incantation*

in·ca·pa·ble /ɪnˈkeɪpəbəl/ *adj* [*more* ~; *most* ~] **:** not able to do something **:** not capable • an *incapable* assistant — usually + *of* • He seemed *incapable of* understanding the seriousness of the situation. • Some birds are physically *incapable of* flight. • She's completely *incapable of* telling a lie.

– in·ca·pa·bil·i·ty /ɪnˌkeɪpəˈbɪləti/ *noun* [*noncount*]

in·ca·pac·i·tate /ˌɪnkəˈpæsəˌteɪt/ *verb* **-tates; -tat·ed; -tat·ing** [+ *obj*] **:** to make (someone or something) unable to work, move, or function in the usual way **:** DISABLE • The class teaches you how to *incapacitate* an attacker. • The stroke left her completely *incapacitated*. • He was *incapacitated* by the pain. • a computer system *incapacitated* by software problems

– incapacitating *adj* • an *incapacitating* illness/injury **– in·ca·pac·i·ta·tion** /ˌɪnkəˌpæsəˈteɪʃən/ *noun* [*noncount*] • physical/mental *incapacitation*

in·ca·pac·i·ty /ˌɪnkəˈpæsəti/ *noun, pl* **-ties** *formal* **:** a lack or loss of the ability to do something in the usual or desired way [*noncount*] Who will run the company in the event of your death or *incapacity*? [=if you die or become unable to run it] [*count*] I'm aware of my weaknesses and *incapacities*. • They have a complete *incapacity* for dealing with numbers. [=they are not able to deal with numbers]

in·car·cer·ate /ɪnˈkɑɚsəˌreɪt/ *verb* **-ates; -at·ed; -at·ing** [+ *obj*] *formal* **:** to put (someone) in prison **:** IMPRISON — usually used as *(be) incarcerated* • They *were* both *incarcerated* for armed robbery.

– in·car·cer·a·tion /ɪnˌkɑɚsəˈreɪʃən/ *noun* [*noncount*] • They were each sentenced to six months' *incarceration*. [=*imprisonment*]

[1]in·car·nate /ɪnˈkɑɚnət/ *adj, formal* **:** having a human body • an *incarnate* deity • He treats her as though she's the devil *incarnate*. [=a human devil; a very evil person] • goodness/evil *incarnate*

[2]in·car·nate /ɪnˈkɑɚˌneɪt/ *verb* **-nates; -nat·ed; -nat·ing** [+ *obj*] *formal* **:** to represent (something, such as an idea or quality) in a clear and obvious way **:** EMBODY • He *incarnates* the nation's political ideals. = The nation's political ideals are *incarnated* in him.

in·car·na·tion /ˌɪnkɑɚˈneɪʃən/ *noun, pl* **-tions**
1 [*count*] **:** one of a series of lives that a person is believed to have had in the past in some religions • He claims that he was a Greek soldier in a previous *incarnation*. [=in a previous life; when he lived in the past as a different person] — often used figuratively • In an earlier *incarnation* [=an earlier phase of her life] she was a rock musician. • The TV and movie *incarnations* [=*versions*] of the story differ significantly. • The software's latest *incarnation* [=*version*] includes many new features. — compare REINCARNATION
2 [*count*] **:** a person who represents a quality or idea • She is the *incarnation* [=*embodiment*] of goodness. [=she is a very good person]
3 ***the Incarnation*** *in the Christian religion* **:** the belief in Jesus Christ as both God and a human being • the doctrine of *the Incarnation*

in·cau·tious /ɪnˈkɑːʃəs/ *adj* [*more* ~; *most* ~] *formal* **:** not careful about avoiding danger or risk **:** not cautious **:** CARELESS • He offended several people with his *incautious* remarks. • Their *incautious* behavior is going to get them into trouble someday.

– in·cau·tious·ly *adv* • an *incautiously* worded statement

in·cen·di·ary /ɪnˈsɛndiˌeri, *Brit* ɪnˈsɛndiəri/ *adj*
1 : containing chemicals that explode into flame **:** producing a fire • The fire was started by an *incendiary* bomb/device.
2 [*more* ~; *most* ~] **:** causing anger • They use *incendiary* [=*inflammatory*] rhetoric to get public attention. • *incendiary* words/language

[1]in·cense /ˈɪnˌsɛns/ *noun* [*noncount*] **:** a substance that is used often in religious ceremonies to produce a strong and pleasant smell when it is burned

[2]in·cense /ɪnˈsɛns/ *verb* **-cens·es; -censed; -cens·ing** [+ *obj*] **:** to make (someone) very angry • Her arrogance so *incensed* them that they refused to speak to her. • She *incensed* them with/by her arrogance. • We were *incensed* (to find) that such behavior was tolerated.

in·cen·tive /ɪnˈsɛntɪv/ *noun, pl* **-tives :** something that encourages a person to do something or to work harder [*count*] Our salespeople are given financial *incentives* for reaching their quotas. [=if they reach their quotas they are paid more money] ▪ The rising cost of electricity provides a strong/powerful *incentive* to conserve energy. ▪ The government offers special tax *incentives* for entrepreneurs. ▪ The company is offering a special low price as an ***added incentive*** for new customers. [*noncount*] employees who lack *incentive* — opposite DISINCENTIVE

in·cep·tion /ɪnˈsɛpʃən/ *noun, formal* **: the time at which something begins : BEGINNING, START** [*singular*] The project has been shrouded in controversy from/since its *inception*. ▪ Since its *inception*, the business has expanded to become a national retail chain. [*noncount*] We'll assist you at every stage from *inception* to completion.

in·ces·sant /ɪnˈsɛsn̩t/ *adj* **: continuing without stopping : not stopping — used to describe something that is unpleasant or annoying** ▪ The neighbors were bothered by the dog's *incessant* barking. ▪ Their *incessant* talking often distracts the other students.

– in·ces·sant·ly *adv* ▪ She pestered us *incessantly*.

in·cest /ˈɪnˌsɛst/ *noun* [*noncount*] **: sexual intercourse between people who are very closely related** ▪ commit *incest* ▪ the crime of *incest*

in·ces·tu·ous /ɪnˈsɛstʃəwəs/ *adj* [*more ~; most ~*] **: involving sexual intercourse between closely related people : involving incest** ▪ There were rumors that the father and daughter had had an *incestuous* relationship. **— often used figuratively** ▪ lobbyists who have an *incestuous* relationship [=an excessively close relationship] with politicians

– in·ces·tu·ous·ly *adv*

[1]**inch** /ˈɪntʃ/ *noun, pl* **inch·es** [*count*]

1 : a unit of measurement equal to 1/36 yard or 1/12 of a foot (2.54 centimeters) ▪ It measures six *inches* from top to bottom. ▪ an insect that is an *inch* long = an *inch*-long insect ▪ I'm five feet, two *inches* tall. = I'm five foot two (*inches*).

2 : a small amount, distance, or degree ▪ The bullet missed my head ***by inches***. [=the bullet came very close to hitting my head] ▪ I begged him to reconsider, but he wouldn't ***give/budge an inch***. [=he wouldn't make even a slight change in his opinion or attitude] ▪ I tried to improve the system, but she opposed me ***every inch of the way***. [=she opposed everything that I tried to do] ▪ We searched ***every inch of*** the house. [=we searched the house completely] ✧ The expression ***(if you) give them an inch, (and) they'll take a mile*** means that if you allow people to have a small amount of something that they want, they will take much more of it. ▪ The school is considering allowing older students to leave the campus for lunch on Fridays, but I'm concerned that *if we give them an inch, they'll take a mile*. [=students will leave campus more often]

every inch **: to the highest degree** ▪ He's *every inch* a winner. [=he's a winner in every way]

inch by inch **: by moving very slowly** ▪ We made our way *inch by inch* through the darkened corridor.

within an inch of **: almost to the point of (something)** ▪ She came *within an inch of* death/dying. [=she came very close to dying] ▪ They beat him (to) ***within an inch of his life***. [=they beat him so badly that he nearly died]

[2]**inch** *verb, always followed by an adverb or preposition* **inch·es; inched; inch·ing : to move very slowly or by a small amount in a specified direction or manner** [*no obj*] We *inched* along in heavy traffic. ▪ As she neared the finish line, she *inched* ahead of the other racers. ▪ Gas prices are *inching* up again. [+ *obj*] I *inched* the car into the garage.

in·cho·ate /ɪnˈkowət/ *adj* [*more ~; most ~*] *formal* **: not completely formed or developed yet : VAGUE** ▪ *inchoate* yearnings ▪ *inchoate* ideas

in·ci·dence /ˈɪnsədəns/ *noun, pl* **-denc·es** [*count*]

1 : the number of times something happens or develops : the rate at which something occurs ▪ The drug has been linked with a higher *incidence* of certain cancers. [=the drug seems to cause certain cancers; people who take the drug seem to be more likely to get certain cancers] ▪ an increased *incidence* of diabetes ▪ a high/low *incidence* of criminal behavior ▪ a disease with an *incidence* of one in 100,000 [=a disease that affects one person out of every 100,000]

2 *technical* **: the angle at which a ray (such as a ray of light) hits a surface** ▪ the angle of *incidence*

in·ci·dent /ˈɪnsədənt/ *noun, pl* **-dents**

1 : an unexpected and usually unpleasant thing that happens [*count*] We just want to put that embarrassing *incident* behind us. ▪ Two people were shot yesterday in two separate *incidents*. ▪ Aside from a few isolated *incidents*, the crowd was well-behaved. ▪ a shooting *incident* ▪ Many such *incidents* go unreported. [*noncount*] The suspects were arrested ***without incident***. [=without any unexpected trouble]

2 [*count*] **: an event or disagreement that is likely to cause serious problems in relations between countries** ▪ a border *incident* ▪ The bombing caused/provoked an international *incident*.

[1]**in·ci·den·tal** /ˌɪnsəˈdɛntl/ *adj* [*more ~; most ~*] **: happening as a minor part or result of something else** ▪ You may incur some *incidental* expenses on the trip. ▪ an *incidental* part of the job ▪ an *incidental* observation ▪ He writes *incidental* music for plays. **— often + *to*** ▪ This chapter is *incidental to* the plot.

[2]**incidental** *noun, pl* **-tals** [*count*] **: something that happens as a minor part or result of something else : something that is incidental — usually plural** ▪ We received a bill for tuition plus *incidentals*. [=incidental expenses] ▪ You should bring enough money to cover *incidentals* like cab fare and tips.

in·ci·den·tal·ly /ˌɪnsəˈdɛntli/ *adv*

1 : as something that is less interesting or important ▪ The report discusses the problem only *incidentally*. [=*in passing*] ▪ Not *incidentally*, the market slump was followed by widespread layoffs.

2 — used to introduce a statement that provides added information or that mentions another subject ▪ I recently met his wife who, *incidentally* [=*by the way*], is a well-known author. ▪ This product is the best—and, *incidentally* [=*by the way*], the most expensive—of its kind. ▪ *Incidentally* [=*by the way*], I saw Susan yesterday and she asked about you.

in·cin·er·ate /ɪnˈsɪnəˌreɪt/ *verb* **-ates; -at·ed; -at·ing** [+ *obj*] **: to burn (something) completely** ▪ The waste is *incinerated* in a large furnace.

– in·cin·er·a·tion /ɪnˌsɪnəˈreɪʃən/ *noun* [*noncount*] ▪ the *incineration* of hazardous materials

in·cin·er·a·tor /ɪnˈsɪnəˌreɪtɚ/ *noun, pl* **-tors** [*count*] **: a machine or container that is used for burning garbage, waste, etc.**

in·cip·i·ent /ɪnˈsɪpijənt/ *adj, always used before a noun, formal* **: beginning to develop or exist** ▪ The project is still in its *incipient* stages. ▪ an *incipient* romance [=a romance that is just beginning]

in·cise /ɪnˈsaɪz/ *verb* **-cis·es; -cised; -cis·ing** [+ *obj*] *formal* **: to cut or carve (letters, patterns, etc.) into a surface** ▪ The design is *incised* into the clay.; *also* **: to mark (a surface) by cutting or carving** ▪ The clay is *incised* to create a design.

– incised *adj* ▪ an *incised* pattern ▪ *incised* tablets

in·ci·sion /ɪnˈsɪʒən/ *noun, pl* **-sions** [*count*] **: a cut made in something;** *especially, medical* **: a cut made into the body during surgery** ▪ a small abdominal *incision*

in·ci·sive /ɪnˈsaɪsɪv/ *adj* [*more ~; most ~*] **: very clear and direct** ▪ an *incisive* analysis/commentary/observation **: able to explain difficult ideas clearly and confidently** ▪ She's known for her *incisive* mind and quick wit.

– in·ci·sive·ly *adv* ▪ an *incisively* funny film ▪ He has written *incisively* about the problem. **– in·ci·sive·ness** *noun* [*noncount*] ▪ the *incisiveness* of her analysis

in·ci·sor /ɪnˈsaɪzɚ/ *noun, pl* **-sors** [*count*] **: a tooth that has a sharp edge for biting : one of the four front teeth of the upper or lower jaw**

in·cite /ɪnˈsaɪt/ *verb* **-cites; -cit·ed; -cit·ing** [+ *obj*]

1 : to cause (someone) to act in an angry, harmful, or violent way ▪ The victim had done nothing to *incite* [=*provoke*] the attackers. **— often + *to*** ▪ They were clearly trying to *incite* the crowd *to* violence. **— often followed by *to* + *verb*** ▪ He *incited* the students *to riot*.

2 : to cause (an angry, harmful, or violent action or feeling) ▪ They were arrested and charged with *inciting* [=*provoking*] a riot. ▪ The news *incited* widespread fear and paranoia.

– in·cite·ment /ɪnˈsaɪtmənt/ *noun, pl* **-ments** [*count*] His words were an *incitement* to riot. [*noncount*] They were charged with *incitement* to violence.

in·ci·vil·i·ty /ˌɪnsəˈvɪləti/ *noun, pl* **-ties** *formal*

1 [*noncount*] **: a rude or impolite attitude or behavior : lack of civility** ▪ Never before have I been treated with such *incivility*! [=*rudeness*]

2 [*count*] **: a rude or impolite act** ▪ We chose to ignore their little insults and *incivilities*.

incl. *abbr* include; included; including; inclusive

in·clem·ent /ɪnˈklɛmənt, ˈɪnklәmənt/ *adj* [*more ~; most ~*] *formal* **: having rain and storms : STORMY** ▪ The game was postponed due to *inclement* weather. **— compare CLEMENT**

in·cli·na·tion /ˌɪnkləˈneɪʃən/ *noun, pl* **-tions**

1 : a feeling of wanting to do something : a tendency to do

something [*noncount*] She shows no/little *inclination* to give in to their demands. ▪ He's a loner ***by inclination***. [*count*] My first/initial/natural *inclination* was to say no, but I finally decided to do what she asked. ▪ We can either go now or plan to go later. What's your *inclination*? [=what are you inclined to do?; what do you want to do?] ▪ I have neither the time nor the *inclination* to learn about such matters. ▪ a person with artistic *inclinations* [=a person who wants to do artistic things] ▪ Her natural *inclination* [=*tendency*] is to do what other people are doing. ▪ The door has an *inclination* to stick. [=the door often sticks; the door tends to stick] ▪ He has an *inclination* to brag. = He has an *inclination* towards bragging. — opposite DISINCLINATION

2 [*count*] **: a slanting surface : SLOPE** ▪ a steep *inclination*

3 [*count*] **: the act of bending your head or body forward : the act of inclining your head or body** ▪ He acknowledged us with a slight *inclination* [=(more commonly) *nod*] of his head.

¹in·cline /ɪnˈklaɪn/ *verb* **-clines; -clined; -clin·ing**

1 : to bend forward or to cause (something) to bend forward [*no obj*] Her head *inclined* forward. [+ *obj*] He *inclined* [=(more commonly) *nodded*] his head slightly. ▪ She listened with her eyes closed and her head *inclined*.

2 [*no obj*] **: to lean or slope** ▪ The road *inclines* at an angle of about 12 degrees.

3 [+ *obj*] *formal* **: to cause (someone) to want to do something or to be likely to do something** ▪ His love of books *inclined* him toward a literary career.

4 *formal* **: to think or to cause (someone) to think that something is probably true or correct — followed by** *to + verb* [*no obj*] I *incline to agree* with you. [=(more commonly) I am inclined to agree with you] [+ *obj*] The evidence *inclines* me *to think* that she isn't guilty. [=makes me think that she probably isn't guilty] — see also INCLINED

²in·cline /ˈɪnˌklaɪn/ *noun, pl* **-clines** [*count*] **: a slanting surface : SLOPE** ▪ We drove up a steep *incline* to the summit. ▪ You can adjust the *incline* of the ramp. ▪ a slight *incline*

in·clined /ɪnˈklaɪnd/ *adj* [*more* ~; *most* ~]

1 *not used before a noun* **: wanting to do something or likely to do something** ▪ people who are *inclined* toward volunteering ▪ Feel free to leave early if you're ***so inclined***. [=if you want to] — usually followed by *to + verb* ▪ I'm *inclined to leave* early [=I would like to leave early], if that's OK with you. ▪ She didn't seem *inclined* [=*disposed*] *to help* us. ▪ He's *inclined to brag* about his accomplishments. [=he often brags about his accomplishments] ▪ The door is *inclined to stick*. [=the door often sticks]

2 — used with verbs like *agree, think, believe, suppose*, etc., **to express a thought or opinion that is not strong or certain** ▪ I'm *inclined to agree* with you. [=I think you are probably correct] ▪ We're *inclined to think* she was mistaken. [=we think she was probably mistaken] — see also ¹INCLINE 4

3 : having an interest in or a talent for something ▪ a special school for children who are ***inclined toward*** the arts — usually used after an adverb (such as *artistically, mechanically*, or *musically*) ▪ She's always been artistically *inclined*. [=she has always had a talent for art]

4 : having a slope ▪ an *inclined* surface

in·clude /ɪnˈkluːd/ *verb* **-cludes; -clud·ed; -clud·ing** [+ *obj*]

1 *not used in progressive tenses* **: to have (someone or something) as part of a group or total : to contain (someone or something) in a group or as a part of something** ▪ The speakers will *include* several experts on the subject. ▪ The price of dinner *includes* dessert. ▪ Admission to the museum is *included* in the tour package. — opposite EXCLUDE

2 : to make (someone or something) a part of something ▪ The results came in too late for us to *include* them in the study. ▪ He says he doesn't want to be *included* in the project. [=he doesn't want to participate in the project] — opposite EXCLUDE

– in·clu·sion /ɪnˈkluːʒən/ *noun, pl* **-sions** [*noncount*] I was surprised by the *inclusion* of his name in the credits. ▪ the *inclusion* of parents at the school board meeting [*count*] The collection has some surprising *inclusions*. [=it includes some surprising things]

included *adj, not used before a noun* **— used to say that someone or something is part of a group or total** ▪ Everyone, myself/me *included* [=everyone, including me], liked the book better than the movie. ▪ We should invite everyone, George *included*. ▪ The price is $122, tax *included*. [=including tax]

in·clud·ing /ɪnˈkluːdɪŋ/ *prep* **: having (someone or something) as part of a group or total** ▪ Everyone, *including* me, liked the book better than the movie. ▪ All his doctors, *including* the chief surgeon, agree on the diagnosis. ▪ It costs $7.99, not *including* sales tax. — opposite EXCLUDING

in·clu·sive /ɪnˈkluːsɪv/ *adj*

1 : covering or including everything ▪ an *inclusive* fee/tour ▪ an *inclusive* insurance policy — opposite EXCLUSIVE; see also ALL-INCLUSIVE

2 [*more* ~; *most* ~] **: open to everyone : not limited to certain people** ▪ an *inclusive* club ▪ an *inclusive* political movement — opposite EXCLUSIVE

3 *not used before a noun* **: including the stated limits and everything in between** ▪ a program for children seven to ten years of age *inclusive* [=children seven, eight, nine, and ten years of age] ▪ Our assignment is to read pages 10 to 20 *inclusive*. [=pages 10 to/through 20]

inclusive of *formal* **: including (something)** ▪ The price is *inclusive of* tax. [=the price includes tax]

– in·clu·sive·ly *adv* **– in·clu·sive·ness** *noun* [*noncount*] **– in·clu·siv·i·ty** /ɪnˌkluːˈsɪvəti/ *noun* [*noncount*] *formal*

in·cog·ni·to /ˌɪnˌkɑːgˈniːtoʊ/ *adv* **: with your true identity kept secret (as by using a different name or a disguise)** ▪ He travels *incognito*.

– incognito *adj* ▪ He remained *incognito* while living there. ▪ The food critic made an *incognito* visit to the restaurant.

in·co·her·ent /ˌɪnkoʊˈhirənt/ *adj* [*more* ~; *most* ~] **: not coherent: such as a : not able to talk or express yourself in a clear way that can be easily understood** ▪ The fever made her *incoherent*. ▪ He was very upset and practically *incoherent* after the accident. ▪ an *incoherent* patient **b : not logical or well-organized : not easy to understand** ▪ an *incoherent* story [=a story that does not make sense] ▪ The memo is completely *incoherent*.

– in·co·her·ence /ˌɪnkoʊˈhirəns/ *noun* [*noncount*] ▪ The patient experiences periods of *incoherence*. ▪ They criticized him for the *incoherence* of his writing. **– in·co·her·ent·ly** *adv* ▪ She responded *incoherently*.

in·come /ˈɪnˌkʌm/ *noun, pl* **-comes : money that is earned from work, investments, business, etc.** [*noncount*] Any *income* from investments must be reported. ▪ taxable *income* ▪ Farming is his main source of *income*. [*count*] Even on two *incomes*, we're having a hard time keeping up with our bills. ▪ He earns a good *income* as a consultant. ▪ What was the company's annual *income*? ▪ families with low/high *incomes* ▪ a two-*income* family [=a family in which both adults have jobs that provide income] ▪ ***low-income housing*** [=housing for people who have low incomes]

in·com·er /ˈɪnˌkʌmə/ *noun, pl* **-ers** [*count*] *Brit* **: a person who comes to a place to live**

income tax *noun, pl* ~ **taxes : a tax paid on the money that a person or business receives as income** [*noncount*] Federal *income tax* will be deducted from your pay. [*count*] The new law will lower *income taxes* for most taxpayers.

in·com·ing /ˈɪnˌkʌmɪŋ/ *adj, always used before a noun* **: coming in: such as a : arriving at or coming to a place** ▪ All *incoming* phone calls are monitored for quality control. ▪ *incoming* mail/messages ▪ *Incoming* [=*arriving*] flights were delayed by the storm. ▪ the *incoming* tide **b : taking a place or position that is being left by another person or group** ▪ the *incoming* president ▪ the *incoming* [=*new*] freshman class — opposite OUTGOING

in·com·mu·ni·ca·do /ˌɪnkəˌmjuːnəˈkɑːdoʊ/ *adj, not used before a noun, formal* **: not able to communicate with other people : in a situation or state that does not allow communication with other people** ▪ The prisoner was held/kept *incommunicado* for six weeks. ▪ She remained *incommunicado* while working on her book.

in·com·pa·ra·ble /ɪnˈkɑːmpərəbəl/ *adj* **: better than any other : having no equal** ▪ The quality of their products is *incomparable*. ▪ an *incomparable* musician ▪ an *incomparable* view of the valley

– in·com·pa·ra·bly /ɪnˈkɑːmpərəbli/ *adv* ▪ an *incomparably* beautiful view

in·com·pat·i·ble /ˌɪnkəmˈpætəbəl/ *adj* [*more* ~; *most* ~] **: not compatible: such as a : not able to exist together without trouble or conflict : not going together well** ▪ *incompatible* people [=people who do not get along well with each other] ▪ Their personalities were *incompatible*. ▪ *incompatible* colors ▪ a policy that is *incompatible* with my beliefs [=that does not agree with my beliefs] **b : not able to be used together** ▪ *incompatible* computer systems ▪ *incompatible* drugs

▪ This printer is *incompatible* with some PCs.

– **in·com·pat·i·bil·i·ty** /ˌɪnkəmˌpætəˈbɪləti/ *noun, pl* **-ties** [*noncount*] She sued for divorce on the grounds of *incompatibility*. ▪ software *incompatibility* ▪ *incompatibility* between drugs [*count*] Certain *incompatibilities* can prevent the program from running correctly.

in·com·pe·tence /ɪnˈkɑːmpətəns/ *noun* [*noncount*] **: lack of the ability to do something well : the quality or state of not being competent** ▪ mental *incompetence* ▪ Because of his *incompetence*, we won't make our deadline. ▪ She was fired for gross *incompetence*. — **opposite** COMPETENCE

in·com·pe·ten·cy /ɪnˈkɑːmpətənsi/ *noun* [*noncount*] **:** INCOMPETENCE

[1]**in·com·pe·tent** /ɪnˈkɑːmpətənt/ *adj* [*more ~; most ~*] **: not competent: such as a : lacking necessary ability or skills** ▪ an *incompetent* worker/doctor ▪ He is too *incompetent* to be trusted with such an important responsibility. ▪ The patient is mentally *incompetent*. **b** *law* **: not able to take part in a trial** ▪ The defendant was declared *incompetent* to stand trial. ▪ an *incompetent* witness

– **in·com·pe·tent·ly** *adv* ▪ The investigation was handled *incompetently*.

[2]**incompetent** *noun, pl* **-tents** [*count*] **: a person who is not able to do something well : an incompetent person** ▪ That department is full of *incompetents*.

in·com·plete /ˌɪnkəmˈpliːt/ *adj*

1 [*more ~; most ~*] **: lacking some part : not finished : not complete** ▪ an *incomplete* set of encyclopedias ▪ The sentence is *incomplete*. ▪ She handed in an *incomplete* assignment.

2 *American football, of a forward pass* **: not caught by the player the ball was thrown to** ▪ an *incomplete* pass

– **in·com·plete·ly** *adv* ▪ *incompletely* digested food ▪ an *incompletely* understood disease – **in·com·plete·ness** *noun* [*noncount*]

in·com·pre·hen·si·ble /ɪnˌkɑːmprɪˈhɛnsəbəl/ *adj* [*more ~; most ~*] **: impossible to understand : not comprehensible** ▪ I found his behavior utterly *incomprehensible*. ▪ It's *incomprehensible* to me that he could have acted that way. ▪ an *incomprehensible* theory/decision

– **in·com·pre·hen·si·bil·i·ty** /ɪnˌkɑːmprɪˌhɛnsəˈbɪləti/ *noun* [*noncount*] – **in·com·pre·hen·si·bly** /ɪnˌkɑːmprɪˈhɛnsəbli/ *adv*

in·com·pre·hen·sion /ɪnˌkɑːmprɪˈhɛnʃən/ *noun* [*noncount*] **: lack of understanding** ▪ She gave me a look of complete/utter *incomprehension*. ▪ He viewed the situation with *incomprehension*.

in·con·ceiv·able /ˌɪnkənˈsiːvəbəl/ *adj* **: impossible to imagine or believe : not conceivable** ▪ It's *inconceivable* (to me) that anyone could have survived such a violent crash. ▪ The fire caused an *inconceivable* amount of damage. ▪ After coming this far, to quit now would be *inconceivable*.

– **in·con·ceiv·ably** /ˌɪnkənˈsiːvəbli/ *adv* ▪ The fire caused an *inconceivably* large amount of damage.

in·con·clu·sive /ˌɪnkənˈkluːsɪv/ *adj* [*more ~; most ~*] **: not showing that something is certainly true : not conclusive** ▪ The results of the test were/proved *inconclusive*. ▪ *inconclusive* evidence ▪ an *inconclusive* argument ▪ The first two rounds of the boxing match were *inconclusive*.

– **in·con·clu·sive·ly** *adv* ▪ The first round ended *inconclusively*, with no clear winner.

in·con·gru·ous /ɪnˈkɑːŋgrəwəs/ *adj* [*more ~; most ~*] **: strange because of not agreeing with what is usual or expected** ▪ His outburst seemed *incongruous* to those who know him well. ▪ The style of the porch is *incongruous* with [=does not match] the style of the house overall. ▪ The modern sculpture seems *incongruous* [=*out of place*] among all the antiques.

– **in·con·gru·i·ty** /ˌɪnkənˈgruːwəti/ *noun, pl* **-ties** [*count, noncount*] – **in·con·gru·ous·ly** *adv*

in·con·se·quen·tial /ɪnˌkɑːnsəˈkwɛnʃəl/ *adj* [*more ~; most ~*] *formal* **: not important** ▪ *inconsequential* evidence/differences ▪ His opinion is *inconsequential*.

in·con·sid·er·able /ˌɪnkənˈsɪdərəbəl/ *adj, formal* **: not large enough in size or amount to be considered important — used in negative statements** ▪ a woman of ***not inconsiderable*** wealth [=a wealthy woman] ▪ It was a *not inconsiderable* accomplishment. [=it was not a trivial accomplishment; it was an important or impressive accomplishment] ▪ He played ***no inconsiderable*** role [=his role was important] in resolving the crisis.

in·con·sid·er·ate /ˌɪnkənˈsɪdərət/ *adj* [*more ~; most ~*] **: not thinking about the rights and feelings of other people : not considerate** ▪ an *inconsiderate* [=*thoughtless*] remark ▪ He was rude and *inconsiderate* to the waiter. ▪ There is no excuse for such *inconsiderate* behavior. — often + *of* ▪ It was *inconsiderate of* you to keep me waiting. ▪ She is very *inconsiderate of* her neighbors.

– **in·con·sid·er·ate·ly** *adv* ▪ He treats people *inconsiderately*.

in·con·sis·ten·cy /ˌɪnkənˈsɪstənsi/ *noun, pl* **-cies**

1 : the quality or fact of being inconsistent: such as a [*noncount*] **: the quality or fact of not staying the same at different times** ▪ Police noticed *inconsistency* in his two statements. ▪ Customers have been complaining about the *inconsistency* in the quality of service they have received. ▪ The team's biggest problem has been *inconsistency*: it has played well at times, but at other times it has played very poorly. **b : the quality or fact of having parts that disagree with each other** [*noncount*] There is some *inconsistency* in her argument. [*count*] Careful editing of the entire text has eliminated *inconsistencies* of style.

2 [*count*] **: a difference or disagreement between two statements which means that both cannot be true** ▪ We noted a major *inconsistency* in his story.

in·con·sis·tent /ˌɪnkənˈsɪstənt/ *adj* [*more ~; most ~*] **: not consistent: such as a : not always acting or behaving in the same way** ▪ His pitching has been very *inconsistent*. [=*unreliable*] ▪ Customers have been complaining about the *inconsistent* service they have received. **b : not continuing to happen or develop in the same way** ▪ The pain has been *inconsistent*. ▪ Her grades have been *inconsistent* this school year. **c : having parts that disagree with each other** ▪ Their descriptions of the accident were *inconsistent*. ▪ The results of the two experiments were *inconsistent*. ▪ She was *inconsistent* in her argument. [=her argument included parts that did not agree with one another] **: not in agreement *with* something** ▪ His statements were *inconsistent with* the truth. [=were not true] ▪ The decision was *inconsistent with* the company's policy.

– **in·con·sis·tent·ly** *adv* ▪ The team has been playing *inconsistently* all season.

in·con·sol·able /ˌɪnkənˈsoʊləbəl/ *adj* **: extremely sad and not able to be comforted** ▪ She was *inconsolable* when she learned that he had died.

– **in·con·sol·ably** /ˌɪnkənˈsoʊləbli/ *adv* ▪ The child cried *inconsolably*.

in·con·spic·u·ous /ˌɪnkənˈspɪkjəwəs/ *adj* [*more ~; most ~*] **: not very easy to see or notice : not conspicuous** ▪ an *inconspicuous* brick building ▪ She tried to remain as *inconspicuous* as possible so that no one would see her there.

– **in·con·spic·u·ous·ly** *adv* ▪ He always dressed *inconspicuously* in a gray suit.

in·con·stant /ɪnˈkɑːnstənt/ *adj* [*more ~; most ~*]

1 *literary* **: likely to change in feelings** ▪ an *inconstant* friend/lover

2 *formal* **: changing often** ▪ an *inconstant* world ▪ the *inconstant* nature of the business

in·con·test·able /ˌɪnkənˈtɛstəbəl/ *adj, formal* **: not able to be doubted or questioned :** INDISPUTABLE ▪ The evidence against him is *incontestable*. ▪ an *incontestable* fact

– **in·con·test·ably** /ˌɪnkənˈtɛstəbli/ *adv* ▪ They proved *incontestably* that the painting was an original. ▪ *incontestably* true

in·con·ti·nent /ɪnˈkɑːntənənt/ *adj, medical* **: not having control of your bladder or bowels** ▪ special products for *incontinent* patients

– **in·con·ti·nence** /ɪnˈkɑːntənəns/ *noun* [*noncount*]

in·con·tro·vert·ible /ɪnˌkɑːntrəˈvətəbəl/ *adj, formal* **: not able to be doubted or questioned :** INDISPUTABLE ▪ *incontrovertible* evidence/proof

– **in·con·tro·vert·ibly** /ɪnˌkɑːntrəˈvətəbli/ *adv* ▪ proved the point *incontrovertibly*

[1]**in·con·ve·nience** /ˌɪnkənˈviːnjəns/ *noun, pl* **-nienc·es**

1 [*noncount*] **: trouble or problems** ▪ I hope this delay doesn't cause you any *inconvenience*. ▪ Bridge repairs cannot be done without some *inconvenience* to the public.

2 [*count*] **: something that causes trouble or problems : something that is inconvenient** ▪ Parking in the city can be a major *inconvenience*. ▪ The delay was an *inconvenience*.

[2]**inconvenience** *verb* **-niences; -nienced; -nienc·ing** [+ *obj*] **: to cause trouble or problems for (someone)** ▪ I wouldn't want to *inconvenience* you. ▪ We were *inconvenienced* by the bad weather.

in·con·ve·nient /ˌɪnkənˈviːnjənt/ *adj* [*more ~; most ~*]

: causing trouble or problems : not convenient ▪ The restaurant is in an *inconvenient* location. ▪ I can call back if this is an *inconvenient* time to talk. = I can call back if it's *inconvenient* for you to talk now. ▪ an *inconvenient* delay
– **in·con·ve·nient·ly** *adv*

in·cor·po·rate /ɪnˈkoɚpəˌreɪt/ *verb* **-rates; -rat·ed; -rat·ing**
1 [+ *obj*] **: to include (something) as part of something else** ▪ This design *incorporates* the best features of our earlier models. ▪ a diet that *incorporates* many different fruits and vegetables — **often + *in* or *into*** ▪ The results of the study were *incorporated in* the final report. ▪ The committee recommended that we *incorporate* several new rules *into* the bylaws.
2 *business* **: to form into a corporation** [+ *obj*] The company was *incorporated* in 1981. [*no obj*] The company *incorporated in* 1981.
– **in·cor·po·ra·tion** /ɪnˌkoɚpəˈreɪʃən/ *noun* [*noncount*] ▪ the *incorporation* of different musical styles ▪ plans for the eventual *incorporation* of the company

in·cor·por·a·ted /ɪnˈkoɚpəˌreɪtəd/ *adj* **: formed into a legal corporation in the U.S.** ▪ The company is *incorporated* in the state of Delaware. — **often used in the names of corporations** ▪ Merriam-Webster, *Incorporated* — **abbr.** ***Inc.***

in·cor·po·re·al /ˌɪnkoɚˈporijəl/ *adj, formal* **: having no physical body or form** ▪ *incorporeal* spirits

in·cor·rect /ˌɪnkəˈrɛkt/ *adj* **: not correct: such as a : not true or accurate : WRONG** ▪ an *incorrect* answer ▪ The doctor's diagnosis was *incorrect*. ▪ The story in the newspaper is *incorrect*. ▪ *incorrect* information **b : having errors or mistakes** ▪ a grammatically *incorrect* sentence ▪ *incorrect* pronunciation/punctuation/spelling/usage **c : not proper or appropriate in a particular situation** ▪ Their behavior was *incorrect*. = It was *incorrect* of them to behave like that. ▪ The restaurant considers jeans and T-shirts *incorrect* attire for dinner. — **see also POLITICALLY INCORRECT**
– **in·cor·rect·ly** *adv* ▪ You filled out the form *incorrectly*. ▪ He answered several questions *incorrectly*. – **in·cor·rect·ness** *noun* [*noncount*]

in·cor·ri·gi·ble /ɪnˈkorədʒəbəl/ *adj* **: not able to be corrected or changed** ▪ an *incorrigible* gambler/optimist/prankster ▪ an *incorrigible* habit of playing practical jokes ▪ He is always the class clown and his teachers say he is *incorrigible*.
– **in·cor·ri·gi·bly** /ɪnˈkorədʒəbli/ *adv* ▪ *incorrigibly* [=*hopelessly, incurably*] romantic

in·cor·rupt·ible /ˌɪnkəˈrʌptəbəl/ *adj* [*more* ~; *most* ~] **: very honest : incapable of being corrupted** ▪ He was trusted, respected, and completely *incorruptible*. ▪ the town's *incorruptible* mayor
– **in·cor·rupt·ibil·i·ty** /ˌɪnkəˌrʌptəˈbɪləti/ *noun* [*noncount*]

[1]**in·crease** /ɪnˈkriːs/ *verb* **-creas·es; -creased; -creas·ing**
1 [*no obj*] **: to become larger or greater in size, amount, number, etc.** ▪ Sales *increased* [=*rose*] this year. ▪ The store is *increasing* [=*raising*] its prices. ▪ Skill *increases* with practice. ▪ The population is *increasing* [=*growing*] dramatically. ▪ The house *increased* in value.
2 [+ *obj*] **: to make (something) larger or greater in size, amount, number, etc.** ▪ They will soon *increase* [=*raise*] the price from $50 to $60. ▪ She *increased* her wealth substantially. ▪ The pilot *increased* speed. — **opposite DECREASE**
– **increased** *adj* ▪ These symptoms are associated with an *increased* risk of heart disease. – **increasing** *adj* ▪ There has been *increasing* criticism of his policies.

[2]**in·crease** /ˈɪnˌkriːs/ *noun, pl* **-creas·es**
1 : the act of becoming larger or of making something larger or greater in size, amount, number, etc. [*count*] a tax *increase* ▪ population *increases* ▪ *increases* in sales ▪ an *increase* in life expectancy [*noncount*] The employees expect some *increase* in wages. ▪ The construction will probably cause some *increase* in traffic delays.
2 [*count*] **: the amount by which something is made larger or greater** ▪ The report showed *increases* of between 20 and 30 percent. ▪ an *increase* of three dollars — **opposite DECREASE**
on the increase **: becoming more in size, amount, number, etc. : increasing** ▪ The number of college applications is *on the increase*. [=*on the rise*]

in·creas·ing·ly /ɪnˈkriːsɪŋli/ *adv* **: more and more : to an increasing degree** ▪ People are becoming *increasingly* aware of this problem. ▪ *Increasingly*, scientists are questioning the data. ▪ The situation grew *increasingly* hopeless.

in·cred·i·ble /ɪnˈkrɛdəbəl/ *adj* [*more* ~; *most* ~]
1 : difficult or impossible to believe ▪ The movie tells an *incredible* story of survival. ▪ an *incredible* coincidence ▪ I find his explanation pretty *incredible*. ▪ *Incredible* as it may seem, she's had no formal training as an artist. ▪ It's *incredible* to me that such a lazy person could be so successful.
2 : extremely good, great, or large ▪ a person of *incredible* [=*extraordinary*] skill/talent/intelligence ▪ a landscape of *incredible* beauty ▪ The new job is an *incredible* opportunity. ▪ We have put an *incredible* amount of work into this project.
– **in·cred·i·bly** /ɪnˈkrɛdəbli/ *adv* ▪ The snow fell *incredibly* fast. ▪ *Incredibly*, she has had no formal training as an artist. ▪ an *incredibly* [=*extremely*] dangerous sport ▪ The exam was *incredibly* difficult.

in·cre·du·li·ty /ˌɪnkrɪˈduːləti, *Brit* ˌɪnkrɪˈdjuːləti/ *noun* [*noncount*] **: a feeling that you do not or cannot believe or accept that something is true or real : DISBELIEF** ▪ The news of his death was met with expressions of *incredulity*.

in·cred·u·lous /ɪnˈkrɛdʒələs/ *adj* [*more* ~; *most* ~] **: not able or willing to believe something : feeling or showing a lack of belief** ▪ She listened to his explanation with an *incredulous* smile. ▪ He was *incredulous* at the news. ▪ Many people were *incredulous* that such a small fire could have caused so much damage.
– **in·cred·u·lous·ly** *adv* ▪ She listened *incredulously* as he explained his decision.

in·cre·ment /ˈɪŋkrəmənt/ *noun, pl* **-ments** [*count*] **: a usually small amount or degree by which something is made larger or greater** ▪ They increased the dosage of the drug in small *increments* over a period of several weeks. ▪ Fines increase in *increments* of $10. ▪ The volume is adjustable in 10 equal *increments*. ▪ (*Brit*) Employees receive an ***annual increment*** [=an annual raise in salary; an annual salary increase] of three percent.
– **in·cre·men·tal** /ˌɪŋkrəˈmɛntl/ *adj* ▪ *incremental* changes [=changes that occur in small amounts or very gradually] ▪ *incremental* additions – **in·cre·men·tally** /ˌɪŋkrəˈmɛntḷi/ *adv* ▪ The business grew *incrementally*.

in·crim·i·nate /ɪnˈkrɪməˌneɪt/ *verb* **-nates; -nat·ed; -nat·ing** [+ *obj*] **: to cause (someone) to appear guilty of or responsible for something (such as a crime)** ▪ Material found at the crime scene *incriminates* the defendant.
– **incriminating** *adj* [*more* ~; *most* ~] ▪ *incriminating* evidence ▪ a very *incriminating* conversation/document – **in·crim·i·na·tion** /ɪnˌkrɪməˈneɪʃən/ *noun* [*noncount*]

in·cu·bate /ˈɪŋkjəˌbeɪt/ *verb* **-bates; -bat·ed; -bat·ing**
1 a [+ *obj*] ***of a bird*** **: to sit on eggs so that they will be kept warm and will hatch** ▪ The female bird *incubates* the eggs. **b** [*no obj*] ***of an egg*** **: to be kept warm before hatching** ▪ The eggs needs to *incubate* for two weeks.
2 *technical* **: to keep (something) in the proper conditions for development** [+ *obj*] Researchers *incubated* the cells in the laboratory. [*no obj*] The cultures must *incubate* for five more days. ▪ The virus will *incubate* in the body for several days before the patient experiences any symptoms. — **sometimes used figuratively** ▪ The plan had been *incubating* [=*developing*] in his mind for several weeks.
– **in·cu·ba·tion** /ˌɪŋkjəˈbeɪʃən/ *noun, pl* **-tions** [*noncount*] The temperature must remain steady during *incubation*. ▪ a long ***incubation period*** [=a time during which something (such as an egg) is incubating or being incubated] [*count*] a long *incubation*

in·cu·ba·tor /ˈɪŋkjəˌbeɪtɚ/ *noun, pl* **-tors** [*count*]
1 : a device that is used to keep eggs warm before they hatch
2 *medical* **: a piece of equipment in which very weak or sick babies are placed for special care and protection after their birth**
3 *business* **: an organization or place that helps in the development of new businesses**

in·cul·cate /ɪnˈkʌlˌkeɪt, ˈɪnˌkʌlˌkeɪt/ *verb* **-cates; -cat·ed; -cat·ing** [+ *obj*] *formal* **: to cause (something) to be learned by (someone) by repeating it again and again** ▪ The teacher *inculcated* in her students the importance of good study habits. ▪ A sense of responsibility was *inculcated* in the students. = The students were *inculcated* with a sense of responsibility.

in·cum·ben·cy /ɪnˈkʌmbənsi/ *noun, pl* **-cies** *formal*
1 [*count*] **: the time during which a person holds a particular office or position** ▪ Hundreds of new jobs were created during her *incumbency*.
2 : the state of holding a particular office or position [*noncount*] the advantages of *incumbency* during an election [*count*] a politician seeking to keep his *incumbency*

[1]**in·cum·bent** /ɪnˈkʌmbənt/ *noun, pl* **-bents** [*count*] **: a person who holds a particular office or position** ▪ Voters will

have the chance to see the *incumbent* and her opponent in a series of three debates. • *Incumbents* often have an advantage in elections.

²incumbent /ɪnˈkʌmbənt/ *adj, always used before a noun, formal* : holding an office or position • the *incumbent* president/mayor/senator • *incumbent* members of Congress

incumbent on *or* incumbent upon *formal* : necessary as a duty for (someone) • It is *incumbent on* us to help. [=it is our duty to help] • It is *incumbent upon* all employees to participate. [=all employees are required to participate]

in•cur /ɪnˈkɚ/ *verb* **-curs; -curred; -cur•ring** [+ *obj*] *formal* : to cause yourself to have or experience (something unpleasant or unwanted) • *incur* expenses/debt • What did he do to *incur* such wrath?

in•cur•able /ɪnˈkjɚrəbəl/ *adj*
1 : impossible to cure : not curable • an *incurable* disease
2 : not likely to be changed • He's an *incurable* romantic. • an *incurable* gossip/optimist
– in•cur•ably /ɪnˈkjɚrəbli/ *adv* • *incurably* ill • *incurably* [=*hopelessly*] romantic

in•cu•ri•ous /ɪnˈkjɚrijəs/ *adj* [*more* ~; *most* ~] *formal* : having no desire to learn or know more about something or someone : not curious • She is remarkably *incurious* about the natural world.

in•cur•sion /ɪnˈkɚʒən/ *noun, pl* **-sions** [*count*] *formal* : a sudden invasion or attack : an act of entering a place or area that is controlled by an enemy • a military *incursion* • an *incursion* into enemy airspace — often used figuratively • an *incursion* of foreign traders into the domestic market • his only *incursion* [=*foray*] into the arts

in•debt•ed /ɪnˈdɛtəd/ *adj* [*more* ~; *most* ~] : owing something (such as money or thanks) to someone or something : in debt • heavily/deeply *indebted* countries/companies — often + *to* • The museum is deeply *indebted to* its many generous patrons. • She will forever be *indebted to* the hospital staff for saving her son's life.
– in•debt•ed•ness *noun* [*noncount*] — often + *to* • She readily acknowledges her great *indebtedness to* the hospital staff for saving her son's life.

in•de•cen•cy /ɪnˈdiːsn̩si/ *noun, pl* **-cies**
1 [*noncount*] : a morally or sexually offensive quality : an indecent quality • The book has been criticized for *indecency*. • I was shocked by the *indecency* of their language.
2 : behavior that is morally or sexually offensive : indecent behavior [*noncount*] He was arrested for public *indecency*. [=for doing something indecent in public, such as exposing his sexual organs] [*count*] He was accused of sexual *indecencies*.

in•de•cent /ɪnˈdiːsn̩t/ *adj* [*more* ~; *most* ~] : not decent: such as **a** : sexually offensive or shocking • *indecent* photos **b** *of clothes* : not covering enough of your body • *indecent* clothing **c** : using language that offends people : including behavior or ideas that people find offensive • an *indecent* joke • *indecent* language **d** : not appropriate or proper • He took *indecent* pleasure in her troubles.
– in•de•cent•ly *adv* • an *indecently* short skirt • *indecently* dressed

indecent assault *noun* [*noncount*] *law* : the crime of touching someone sexually without that person's permission

indecent exposure *noun* [*noncount*] *law* : the crime of showing your sexual organs to other people in public

in•de•ci•pher•able /ˌɪndɪˈsaɪfərəbəl/ *adj* [*more* ~; *most* ~] : impossible to read or understand : not decipherable • His handwriting is almost *indecipherable*. • an *indecipherable* code/message

in•de•ci•sion /ˌɪndɪˈsɪʒən/ *noun* [*noncount*] : difficulty in making a decision • They were paralyzed by *indecision*.

in•de•ci•sive /ˌɪndɪˈsaɪsɪv/ *adj* [*more* ~; *most* ~] : not decisive: such as **a** : not able to make choices quickly and confidently • an *indecisive* person • She's always been very *indecisive*. **b** : not settling something or making something final or certain • an *indecisive* battle • The meeting was *indecisive*.
– in•de•ci•sive•ly *adv* • The conflict ended *indecisively*.
– in•de•ci•sive•ness *noun* [*noncount*]

in•deed /ɪnˈdiːd/ *adv*
1 : without any question — used to stress the truth of a statement • *Indeed*, he is a great poet. = He is *indeed* a great poet. • This is *indeed* [=*certainly*] a matter of great importance. • They were *indeed* heroes, though they were never honored. • She does *indeed* work here. • I will *indeed* be there. • The problem is a serious one *indeed*. • "Do you know him?" "I do *indeed*." = "*Indeed* I do." • "Do you know him?" "***Yes, indeed!***" [=I certainly do] — often used after *very* • This is a very nice house *indeed*. • Thank you very much *indeed*.
2 — used in response to a statement that is regarded as doubtful or surprising • "I did my best." "Did you *indeed*?" • "The project is still on schedule." "Is it *indeed*?" • "He claims that it was just a misunderstanding." "*Indeed*?"
3 *formal* — used when making a statement that adds to or strengthens a previous statement • He likes to have things his own way; *indeed*, he can be very stubborn. • She is quite lovely, *indeed* a beauty. • Many people objected. *Indeed*, my uncle complained in writing. • It is possible—*indeed*, probable—that the crime was an inside job.
4 — used in a question that repeats and emphasizes a preceding question to show that you do not know the answer • "How can we help them?" "How, *indeed*?" • "When will they come here again?" "When, *indeed*?"
a friend in need is a friend indeed see FRIEND

in•de•fat•i•ga•ble /ˌɪndɪˈfætɪgəbəl/ *adj* [*more* ~; *most* ~] *formal* : able to work or continue for a very long time without becoming tired : TIRELESS • an *indefatigable* campaigner • a person of *indefatigable* patience/enthusiasm/optimism
– in•de•fat•i•ga•bly /ˌɪndɪˈfætɪgəbli/ *adv* • She works *indefatigably* on behalf of her clients.

in•de•fen•si•ble /ˌɪndɪˈfɛnsəbəl/ *adj* [*more* ~; *most* ~] : not defensible: such as **a** : not able to be thought of as good or acceptable • The company adopted an *indefensible* position on the issue. • His behavior is ethically *indefensible*. • Slavery is morally *indefensible*. **b** : not able to be kept safe from damage or harm • The city is in an *indefensible* location.

in•de•fin•able /ˌɪndɪˈfaɪnəbəl/ *adj* : impossible to describe or explain • He has an *indefinable* quality that draws people to him.
– in•de•fin•ably /ˌɪndiˈfaɪnəbli/ *adv*

in•def•i•nite /ɪnˈdɛfənət/ *adj* [*more* ~; *most* ~] : not definite: such as **a** : not certain in amount or length • We're stuck here for an *indefinite* period of time. • Their plans have been put on *indefinite* hold. **b** : not clear or certain in meaning or details : VAGUE • an *indefinite* answer/boundary • She is *indefinite* about her plans. • Our plans are *indefinite*.
– in•def•i•nite•ness *noun* [*noncount*] • the *indefiniteness* of their plans

indefinite article *noun, pl* ~ **-cles** [*count*] : the word *a* or *an* used in English to refer to a person or thing that is not identified or specified • In "I gave a book to the boy" the word "a" is an *indefinite article* and the word "the" is a definite article.; *also* : a word that has a similar use in another language

in•def•i•nite•ly /ɪnˈdɛfənətli/ *adv* : for a period of time that might not end • It's foolish to think that economic growth will continue *indefinitely*. [=*forever*] • Their vacation has been postponed *indefinitely*. [=until a later time that has not yet been decided]

indefinite pronoun *noun, pl* ~ **-nouns** [*count*] : a pronoun that does not refer to a specific person or thing • "Anyone," "something," and "few" are *indefinite pronouns*.

in•del•i•ble /ɪnˈdɛləbəl/ *adj* [*more* ~; *most* ~]
1 : impossible to remove or forget • Her performance made an *indelible* [=*unforgettable*] impression on me. • His achievements left an *indelible* [=*enduring*] mark on the era. • an *indelible* image
2 : producing marks that cannot be erased • an *indelible* pencil • *indelible* [=*permanent*] ink
– in•del•i•bly /ɪnˈdɛləbli/ *adv* • scenes/images *indelibly* captured on film • two names *indelibly* [=*permanently*] linked in the public mind

in•del•i•cate /ɪnˈdɛlɪkət/ *adj* [*more* ~; *most* ~] *formal* : not polite : having or showing bad manners or taste : RUDE • Many consider it *indelicate* to talk about such things in mixed company. • an *indelicate* question
– in•del•i•ca•cy /ɪnˈdɛlɪkəsi/ *noun, pl* **-cies** [*count, noncount*] • Everyone was shocked by the *indelicacy* [=*rudeness*] of his questions. **– in•del•i•cate•ly** *adv*

in•dem•ni•fy /ɪnˈdɛmnəˌfaɪ/ *verb* **-fies; -fied; -fy•ing** [+ *obj*] *law*
1 : to protect (someone) by promising to pay for the cost of possible future damage, loss, or injury • The policy *indemnifies* [=*insures*] you against/for any losses caused by fire. [=the policy promises that if fire destroys things that you own, you will be given money to buy new things]
2 : to give (someone) money or another kind of payment for some damage, loss, or injury • He was required to *indemnify* [=*compensate*] his neighbor for the damage he caused.

I

– **in·dem·ni·fi·ca·tion** /ɪnˌdɛmnəfəˈkeɪʃən/ *noun* [*noncount*] ▪ *indemnification* for loss/damages

in·dem·ni·ty /ɪnˈdɛmnəti/ *noun, pl* **-ties** *law*
1 [*noncount*] **:** a promise to pay for the cost of possible damage, loss, or injury ▪ an agreement providing *indemnity* against prosecution/loss — often used before another noun ▪ an *indemnity* plan/agreement
2 [*count*] **:** a payment made to someone because of damage, loss, or injury ▪ has paid $2 million in *indemnities*

[1]**in·dent** /ɪnˈdɛnt/ *verb* **-dents; -dent·ed; -dent·ing**
1 : to start (one or more lines of text) farther to the right than other lines of text [+ *obj*] The first line of each paragraph should be *indented*. [*no obj*] Don't forget to *indent* when starting a new paragraph.; *also* [+ *obj*] **:** to end (one or more lines of text) farther to the left than other lines of text ▪ The second paragraph is *indented* from the right margin.
2 [+ *obj*] **:** to make the edge of (something) go sharply inward **:** to create an indentation in (something) ▪ Many tiny inlets *indent* the coast. [=there are many tiny inlets along the coast]
3 [*no obj*] *Brit* **:** to order something from the person or place that can supply it ▪ We *indented* (on headquarters) for supplies.
– **in·dent·ed** *adj* [*more* ~; *most* ~] ▪ an *indented* paragraph ▪ deeply *indented* leaves ▪ an *indented* coastline

[2]**in·dent** /ˈɪnˌdɛnt/ *noun, pl* **-dents** [*count*] **:** a space at the beginning of a written line or paragraph ▪ Start each paragraph with an *indent*. ▪ a half-inch *indent*

in·den·ta·tion /ˌɪnˌdɛnˈteɪʃən/ *noun, pl* **-tions**
1 a [*count*] **:** a space at the beginning of a written line or paragraph **:** INDENT ▪ a smaller/larger *indentation* **b** [*noncount*] **:** the act of indenting a line or paragraph ▪ Our style guidelines call for *indentation* of the first line of each paragraph.
2 [*count*] **a :** a cut in or into the edge of something ▪ A slight *indentation* [=*notch*] was cut into the wood. **b :** an area where the edge of something goes sharply inward ▪ a coastline with many *indentations*
3 [*count*] **:** a small hole or inward curve made by pressure **:** DENT ▪ There were several small *indentations* in the surface of the table. ▪ bowl-shaped *indentations*

in·den·tured /ɪnˈdɛntʃəd/ *adj* **:** required by a contract to work for a certain period of time ▪ immigrants who came to the U.S. as *indentured* servants 200 years ago

in·de·pen·dence /ˌɪndəˈpɛndəns/ *noun*
1 : freedom from outside control or support **:** the state of being independent [*noncount*] They are fighting for *independence* from colonial rule. [=fighting because they want to stop being a colony ruled by another country] ▪ Her ambition is to achieve financial *independence*. [=to earn all the money she needs; to not depend on money given by anyone else] ▪ She asserted her *independence* from her parents by getting her own apartment. ▪ The country ***declared (its) independence***. [=said that it would no longer accept the rule of another country] ▪ a ***war of independence*** [=a war that is fought to gain independence] [*singular*] He has shown a fierce *independence* of spirit/thought.
2 [*noncount*] **:** the time when a country or region gains political freedom from outside control ▪ A month after *independence*, elections were held.

Independence Day *noun* [*noncount*] **:** a holiday celebrating the anniversary of a country's independence from another country that ruled it in the past; *especially* **:** July 4 celebrated as a legal holiday in the U.S. in honor of the day when the Declaration of Independence was signed in 1776

[1]**in·de·pen·dent** /ˌɪndəˈpɛndənt/ *adj*
1 : not dependent: such as **a :** not controlled or ruled by another country ▪ The country recently became *independent*. ▪ an *independent* nation **b :** not controlled by other people ▪ They have a good deal of *independent* authority. ▪ an *independent* investigator [=a person who is not directly involved in a situation or dispute and who is free to investigate problems and make judgments about what should be done] **c :** not requiring or relying on other people for help or support ▪ She has an *independent* income. ▪ She is a woman ***of independent means***. [=she has enough money to support herself without help from others] **d :** not associated with or owned by a larger business ▪ an *independent* record label ▪ an *independent* film studio ▪ an *independent* bookstore ▪ They hired an ***independent contractor*** [=a person hired to do work who controls how the work is done] to fix the roof.; *also* **:** produced by an independent company ▪ an *independent* film
2 : separate from and not connected to other people, things, etc. ▪ Another laboratory has provided *independent* confirmation of the test results. ▪ She is doing an ***independent study*** in Art History this semester. [=a course of study done by a student without an instructor or with help from an instructor but not as part of an organized class] ▪ This car has four-wheel ***independent suspension***. [=each of the four wheels has its own set of supports for the body of the car] — often + *of* ▪ The women enjoyed rights *independent of* their husbands. ▪ The speed of the particle is *independent of* its wavelength. [=is not connected/related to its wavelength]
3 [*more* ~; *most* ~] **:** acting or thinking freely instead of being guided by other people ▪ She is a very *independent* person. ▪ She has an *independent* mind/spirit. ▪ She's an *independent* thinker. ▪ They lead an *independent* life.
4 *politics* **:** not belonging to a political party ▪ *independent* voters ▪ an *independent* candidate
– **in·de·pen·dent·ly** *adv* ▪ They were working *independently* from/of one another. ▪ Every store is *independently* owned and operated. ▪ She's *independently* wealthy. ▪ He continues to live *independently* despite his injuries.

[2]**independent** *noun, pl* **-dents** [*count*]
1 : someone or something that is not connected to others of the same kind ▪ He started publishing a trendy *independent* [=an independent newspaper or magazine] that covers controversial topics. ▪ The school left the conference to become an *independent*. [=a school whose sports teams are not associated with a league]
2 *or* ***Independent*** *politics* **:** a person who does not belong to a political party ▪ She registered to vote as an *Independent*.

independent clause *noun, pl* ~ **clauses** [*count*] *grammar* **:** MAIN CLAUSE

in–depth /ɪnˈdɛpθ/ *adj* [*more* ~; *most* ~] **:** covering many or all important points of a subject **:** THOROUGH ▪ an *in-depth* investigation/analysis ▪ *in-depth* news coverage ▪ This film takes an *in-depth* look at life on the farm.

in·de·scrib·able /ˌɪndɪˈskraɪbəbəl/ *adj* **:** impossible to describe **:** very great or extreme ▪ *indescribable* beauty/joy/relief ▪ *indescribable* pain
– **in·de·scrib·ably** /ˌɪndɪˈskraɪbəbli/ *adv* ▪ an *indescribably* delicious meal

in·de·struc·ti·ble /ˌɪndɪˈstrʌktəbəl/ *adj* **:** impossible to break or destroy ▪ *indestructible* toys ▪ They claim that the watch is virtually/nearly *indestructible*. [=*unbreakable*] ▪ He was 20 years old and felt that he was *indestructible*. [=he felt that nothing could harm him]
– **in·de·struc·ti·bil·i·ty** /ˌɪndəˌstrʌktəˈbɪləti/ *noun* [*noncount*] ▪ He had a feeling of *indestructibility*.

in·de·ter·mi·nate /ˌɪndɪˈtəmənət/ *adj, formal* **:** not able to be stated or described in an exact way ▪ a man of *indeterminate* [=*uncertain*] age ▪ an *indeterminate* number of people ▪ an *indeterminate* color
– **in·de·ter·mi·na·cy** /ˌɪndɪˈtəmənəsi/ *noun* [*noncount*]
– **in·de·ter·mi·nate·ly** *adv* ▪ an *indeterminately* large number

[1]**in·dex** /ˈɪnˌdɛks/ *noun, pl* **in·dex·es** *or* **in·di·ces** /ˈɪndəˌsiːz/ [*count*]
1 *pl usually* ***indexes*** **:** an ordered list: such as **a :** an alphabetical list at the end of a book that shows the page where each thing in the list can be found ▪ Look up the recipe for potato soup in the *index*. ▪ Potato soup is listed under "soup" in the *index*. **b :** a group of related things that are in alphabetical or numerical order ▪ The card catalog is an *index* to the materials in the library.
2 : a sign or number that shows how something is changing or performing ▪ The price of goods is an *index* [=*indication*] of business conditions. **:** a number that indicates changes in the level of something (such as a stock market) when it rises or falls ▪ a stock *index* ▪ certain economic *indexes/indices* ▪ (*Brit*) an ***index-linked*** pension [=a pension that is linked to an index (such as the retail price index) so that it rises or falls as the index does] — see also CONSUMER PRICE INDEX, RETAIL PRICE INDEX
3 : a device used to point to something (such as a number) ▪ the *index* on a scale

[2]**index** *verb* **-dexes; -dexed; -dex·ing** [+ *obj*]
1 : to provide an index for (something, such as a book) — usually used as *(be) indexed* ▪ an *indexed* book [=a book that has an index]
2 : to list or include (something) in an index ▪ This search engine has *indexed* hundreds of millions of Web sites. — often used as *(be) indexed* ▪ Each term in the book *is indexed*.
3 : to link wages, benefits, etc., to a measurement of changes

in the price of goods and services so that they increase at the same rate — usually used as *(be) indexed to* ▪ Social security benefits *are indexed to* inflation. [=social security benefits increase when inflation occurs]

index card *noun, pl* **~ cards** [*count*] **: a thin paper card used especially for creating an alphabetical index**

index finger *noun, pl* **~ -gers** [*count*] **: the finger next to the thumb : FOREFINGER — see picture at HAND**

In•dia ink /ˈɪndijə/ *noun* [*noncount*] *US* **: black ink used especially for drawing — called also** *(Brit) Indian ink*

In•di•an /ˈɪndijən/ *noun, pl* **-ans** [*count*]

1 : a person born, raised, or living in India

2 *often offensive* **: NATIVE AMERICAN** ***usage*** **see NATIVE AMERICAN**

– Indian *adj* ▪ *Indian* culture/food/music ▪ a person of *Indian* descent ▪ an *Indian* word

Indian corn *noun* [*noncount*] *US*

1 : [1]CORN 1a

2 : corn that has seeds (called kernels) of several different colors on each ear and that is used for decoration

Indian summer *noun, pl* **~ -mers** [*count*]

1 : a period of warm weather in late autumn or early winter

2 : a happy or pleasant period near the end of someone's life, career, etc. ▪ She is in the *Indian summer* of her career.

in•di•cate /ˈɪndəˌkeɪt/ *verb* **-cates; -cat•ed; -cat•ing**

1 [+ *obj*] **: to show (something)** ▪ Our records *indicate* a depth of 3,000 feet here. ▪ Studies *indicate* (that) this chemical could cause cancer. ▪ The map *indicates* where the treasure is buried. **: to show that (something) exists or is true** ▪ There is nothing to *indicate* that the two events are connected. ▪ The size of his offer *indicates* that he is eager to buy the house. ▪ His hot forehead *indicates* a fever. = His hot forehead *indicates* that he has a fever.

2 [+ *obj*] **: to direct attention to (someone or something) usually by pointing** ▪ The general used a long ruler to *indicate* on the map exactly where the troops would land. ▪ We asked how to get to the rear entrance, and he *indicated* a path leading around the right side of the building.

3 [+ *obj*] **: to show or suggest that (something) is needed — usually used as** *(be) indicated* ▪ Further testing *is indicated.* [=is called for; is necessary] ▪ He feels that a different approach *is indicated.*

4 [+ *obj*] **: to represent or be a symbol of (something or someone)** ▪ A pronoun used as a direct object *indicates* the person or thing receiving the action. ▪ The markers *indicate* a distance of 50 yards. ▪ A new paragraph *indicates* a change in topic. ▪ In "my mother's coat," the apostrophe and "s" *indicate* possession.

5 [+ *obj*] **: to say or express (something) briefly** ▪ They have *indicated* their willingness/desire to cooperate. ▪ She *indicated* [=*wrote, said*] in her letter that she's planning to arrive next week. ▪ He nodded his head to *indicate* his approval. = He *indicated* his approval with a nod of his head.

6 [*no obj*] *Brit* **: to make a signal which shows that you are going to turn when you are driving a vehicle** ▪ You forgot to *indicate* [=*(US) signal*] before you made your turn.

in•di•ca•tion /ˌɪndəˈkeɪʃən/ *noun, pl* **-tions : something (such as a sign or signal) that points out or shows something** [*noncount*] She gave no *indication* that she was angry. = She gave no *indication* [=*hint*] of her anger. ▪ There is some *indication* [=*suggestion*] that the economy is recovering. [*count*] Her evaluation will give me a good *indication* of where I stand in the class. ▪ There were *indications* that he was thinking of changing jobs. ▪ There's ***every indication*** that the strike will end soon. [=it appears to be very likely that the strike will end soon]

[1]in•dic•a•tive /ɪnˈdɪkətɪv/ *adj*

1 *not used before a noun* [*more ~; most ~*] *formal* **: showing something : indicating something — usually +** *of* ▪ His bitter remarks are *indicative of* the resentment he stills feels over losing his job. [=his bitter remarks show that he still feels resentment over losing his job] ▪ Thin tree rings are *indicative of* slow growth. [=thin tree rings indicate that a tree has grown slowly]

2 *grammar* **: of or relating to the verb form that is used to state a fact that can be known or proved** ▪ In "I walked to school," the verb *walked* is in the *indicative* mood. ▪ an *indicative* verb form **— compare IMPERATIVE, SUBJUNCTIVE**

[2]indicative *noun*

the indicative *grammar* **: the form that a verb or sentence has when it is stating a fact that can be known or proved** ▪ a verb in *the indicative*

in•di•ca•tor /ˈɪndəˌkeɪtə/ *noun, pl* **-tors** [*count*]

1 : a sign that shows the condition or existence of something ▪ Economic *indicators* suggest that prices will go up. **— often +** *of* ▪ The size of the new building is an *indicator of* how much the company has grown. ▪ Her expression is usually a good/reliable *indicator of* how she's feeling.

2 a : a pointer or light that shows the state or condition of something ▪ a control panel with various *indicator* lights **b : a device that shows a measurement : GAUGE** ▪ an airspeed *indicator* **c** *Brit* **: TURN SIGNAL**

indices *plural of* **[1]INDEX**

in•dict /ɪnˈdaɪt/ *verb* **-dicts; -dict•ed; -dict•ing** [+ *obj*] *chiefly US, law* **: to formally decide that someone should be put on trial for a crime** ▪ A grand jury is expected to *indict* him for murder. **— often used as** *(be) indicted* ▪ She *was* arraigned in front of a judge and then *indicted* by a grand jury three weeks later. ▪ He has *been indicted* by the grand jury on murder charges.

– in•dict•able /ɪnˈdaɪtəbəl/ *adj* [*more ~; most ~*] ▪ an *indictable* offense/crime

in•dict•ment /ɪnˈdaɪtmənt/ *noun, pl* **-ments**

1 *chiefly US, law* **a** [*count*] **: an official written statement charging a person with a crime** ▪ The grand jury has handed down *indictments* against several mobsters. **b** [*noncount*] **: the act of officially charging someone with a crime : the act of indicting someone** ▪ No one was surprised by her *indictment.* ▪ He is ***under indictment*** [=he has been indicted] for perjury by two federal grand juries.

2 [*count*] **: an expression or statement of strong disapproval** ▪ She intended the film to be an *indictment* of the media.

in•die /ˈɪndi/ *adj, always used before a noun, informal* **: not connected with or created by a major producer of music or movies : INDEPENDENT** ▪ *indie* rock bands ▪ an *indie* (record) label ▪ the hit *indie* film of the year

– indie *noun, pl* **-dies** [*count*] ▪ This film is not like other low-budget *indies.*

in•dif•fer•ence /ɪnˈdɪfərəns/ *noun* **: lack of interest in or concern about something : an indifferent attitude or feeling** [*noncount*] She was amazed that some people could watch the trial with *indifference.* **— often +** *to* ▪ You can go or you can stay. It's a matter of complete *indifference to* me. [=I do not care at all if you go or stay] ▪ The government has shown complete/utter *indifference to* the struggles of organized labor. [*singular*] She watched them with a cool *indifference.*

in•dif•fer•ent /ɪnˈdɪfərənt/ *adj* [*more ~; most ~*]

1 : not interested in or concerned about something ▪ She was amazed that people could be so *indifferent* about the trial. [=could care so little about the trial] ▪ The movie was poorly received by an *indifferent* public. **— often +** *to* ▪ They seem to be *indifferent to* the problems of poor people.

2 : neither good nor bad : not very good ▪ She was tired and gave a rather *indifferent* [=*unimpressive*] performance. ▪ *indifferent* [=*mediocre*] leadership ▪ Was the food good, bad, or *indifferent?*

– in•dif•fer•ent•ly *adv* ▪ a biography received *indifferently* by the critics

in•dig•e•nous /ɪnˈdɪʤənəs/ *adj* **: produced, living, or existing naturally in a particular region or environment** ▪ He grows a wide variety of both *indigenous* [=*native*] and exotic plants. ▪ an *indigenous* culture/language ▪ There are several *indigenous* groups that still live in the area. **— sometimes +** *to* ▪ These birds are *indigenous to* South America.

– in•dig•e•nous•ly *adv*

in•di•gent /ˈɪndɪʤənt/ *adj* [*more ~; most ~*] *formal* **: lacking money : very poor** ▪ Because he was *indigent*, the court appointed a lawyer to defend him. ▪ The clinic provides free care for *indigent* patients.

in•di•gest•ible /ˌɪndaɪˈʤɛstəbəl/ *adj* [*more ~; most ~*]

1 : not capable of being used in the body as food ▪ *indigestible* carbohydrates **— sometimes +** *to* ▪ a substance that is *indigestible to* most mammals **— often used in an exaggerated way to describe bad or unappealing food** ▪ an *indigestible* meal

2 : difficult to understand : complicated or confusing ▪ Their presentation was an *indigestible* mass of information.

in•di•ges•tion /ˌɪndaɪˈʤɛsʧən/ *noun* [*noncount*] **: an unpleasant feeling (such as pain or a burning sensation) in your stomach or chest that is caused by difficulty in digesting food** ▪ The patient complained of *indigestion* and nausea. ▪ I like spicy foods but they always give me *indigestion.* ▪ an attack of *indigestion* ▪ acid *indigestion*

in•dig•nant /ɪnˈdɪgnənt/ *adj* [*more ~; most ~*] **: feeling or**

showing anger because of something that is unfair or wrong : very angry ▪ She wrote an *indignant* letter to the editor. ▪ He was/got/became very *indignant* about/over the changes. ▪ an *indignant* tone of voice
– **in·dig·nant·ly** *adv* ▪ She *indignantly* [=*angrily*] denied all the accusations.

in·dig·na·tion /ˌɪndɪgˈneɪʃən/ *noun* [*noncount*] : anger caused by something that is unfair or wrong ▪ The decision to close the factory has aroused the *indignation* of the townspeople. ▪ He adopted a tone of moral/righteous *indignation*.

in·dig·ni·ty /ɪnˈdɪgnəti/ *noun, pl* **-ties** : an act or occurrence that hurts someone's dignity or pride : an insulting or embarrassing act or occurrence [*count*] He remembers all the *indignities* he had to suffer in the early years of his career. ▪ We must endure the *indignities* of growing old. [*noncount*] He suffered the *indignity* of being forced to leave the courtroom. ▪ The *indignity* of it all was too much to bear.

in·di·go /ˈɪndɪˌgoʊ/ *noun* [*noncount*] : a deep purplish-blue color — see color picture on page C2
– **indigo** *adj* ▪ an *indigo* sky

in·di·rect /ˌɪndəˈrɛkt/ *adj*
1 [*more* ~; *most* ~] : not direct: such as **a** : not going straight from one point to another ▪ We took an *indirect* route. ▪ These plants grow best in bright *indirect* light/sun. **b** : not said or done in a clear and direct way ▪ He gave only vague, *indirect* answers to our questions. ▪ They used *indirect* methods of investigation. ▪ There were many *indirect* references to his earlier books. ▪ Looking at her watch was her *indirect* way of telling him it was time to leave. **c** : not having a clear and direct connection ▪ Poor nutrition may have been an *indirect* cause of the disease. ▪ The cigarette stubs were *indirect* evidence that someone had been smoking in the room.
2 *grammar* : stating what an original speaker said without exactly quoting the words ▪ "He said that he would call later," is an example of *indirect* speech/discourse since his actual words were "I'll call later." ▪ an *indirect* question such as "She asked whether the doctor had arrived" ▪ an *indirect* quotation
– **in·di·rect·ly** *adv* [*more* ~; *most* ~] ▪ He was *indirectly* involved in the robbery. ▪ The disease can be spread directly or *indirectly*. ▪ He answered our questions *indirectly*. – **in·di·rect·ness** *noun* [*noncount*]

indirect object *noun, pl* ~ **-jects** [*count*] *grammar* : a noun, pronoun, or noun phrase that occurs in addition to a direct object after some verbs and indicates the person or thing that receives what is being given or done ▪ In "He gave me the book," the direct object is "book" and the *indirect object* is "me." — compare DIRECT OBJECT

in·dis·cern·ible /ˌɪndɪˈsənəbəl/ *adj* [*more* ~; *most* ~] *formal* : impossible to see, hear, or know clearly ▪ Hidden under vines and moss, the crumbling wall was almost *indiscernible*. ▪ a change made for *indiscernible* reasons

in·dis·creet /ˌɪndɪˈskriːt/ *adj* [*more* ~; *most* ~] : not having or showing good judgment : revealing things that should not be revealed : not discreet ▪ He was *indiscreet* about his love affairs. [=he told people about his love affairs when he should have kept them secret]; *also* : not polite ▪ Should I ask you how you got that bruise, or would that be *indiscreet*? [=(more commonly) *impolite, rude*] ▪ an *indiscreet* question
– **in·dis·creet·ly** *adv* ▪ He spoke *indiscreetly* about his love affairs.

in·dis·cre·tion /ˌɪndɪˈskrɛʃən/ *noun, pl* **-tions**
1 [*noncount*] : lack of good judgment or care in behavior and especially in speech : lack of discretion ▪ He has been criticized for showing *indiscretion* in his remarks. [=for carelessly saying things that should not be said]
2 [*count*] : an act or remark that shows a lack of good judgment : an indiscreet act or remark ▪ She committed a few minor *indiscretions*. ▪ He describes his drug use in college as just a ***youthful indiscretion***. [=a minor mistake made by a young person]

in·dis·crim·i·nate /ˌɪndɪˈskrɪmənət/ *adj* [*more* ~; *most* ~] *disapproving*
1 : affecting or harming many people or things in a careless or unfair way ▪ They participated in the *indiscriminate* slaughter of countless innocent victims. ▪ He objects to the *indiscriminate* use of pesticides. ▪ an *indiscriminate* attack
2 : not careful in making choices ▪ She has been *indiscriminate* in choosing her friends.
– **in·dis·crim·i·nate·ly** *adv*

in·dis·pens·able /ˌɪndɪˈspɛnsəbəl/ *adj* [*more* ~; *most* ~] : extremely important and necessary ▪ She is an *indispensable* [=*essential*] part of the team. ▪ an *indispensable* employee/tool — often + *for* or *to* ▪ A calculator is an *indispensable* tool *for* solving these problems. ▪ She is *indispensable to* the team.
– **in·dis·pens·abil·i·ty** /ˌɪndɪˌspɛnsəˈbɪləti/ *noun* [*noncount*]

in·dis·posed /ˌɪndɪˈspoʊzd/ *adj* [*more* ~; *most* ~] *formal*
1 : slightly ill : not feeling well ▪ He was (somewhat) *indisposed* by/with a cold. — often used as a polite way of saying that someone is sick or unable to be present without giving a specific reason ▪ He was *indisposed* and unable to attend the banquet.
2 : not willing or likely to do something — followed by *to* + *verb* ▪ Officials are *indisposed to grant* their request. [=officials do not want to grant their request]

in·dis·po·si·tion /ɪnˌdɪspəˈzɪʃən/ *noun, formal*
1 [*count*] : a slight illness ▪ He blamed his absence on a minor *indisposition*.
2 [*singular*] : lack of willingness to do something — followed by *to* + *verb* ▪ The officials have shown an *indisposition to grant* their request.

in·dis·put·able /ˌɪndɪˈspjuːtəbəl/ *adj* [*more* ~; *most* ~] : impossible to question or doubt : not disputable ▪ He had *indisputable* [=*unquestionable*] proof that he had been there. ▪ Her success is *indisputable*. [=*undeniable*]
– **in·dis·put·ably** /ˌɪndɪˈspjuːtəbli/ *adv* ▪ an *indisputably* certain fact

in·dis·sol·u·ble /ˌɪndɪˈsɑːljəbəl/ *adj, formal* : impossible to destroy, break up, or get rid of ▪ an *indissoluble* contract ▪ They are bound together by/with *indissoluble* [=*permanent*] ties/bonds.
– **in·dis·sol·u·bil·i·ty** /ˌɪndɪˌsɑːljəˈbɪləti/ *noun* [*noncount*] – **in·dis·sol·u·bly** /ˌɪndɪˈsɑːljəbli/ *adv* ▪ They are *indissolubly* [=*permanently*] linked/connected.

in·dis·tinct /ˌɪndɪˈstɪŋkt/ *adj* [*more* ~; *most* ~] : not easily seen, heard, or recognized : not distinct or clear ▪ *indistinct* figures in the fog ▪ a far-off *indistinct* light ▪ The sound was *indistinct* [=*faint*] at first, then gradually became louder.
– **in·dis·tinct·ly** *adv* ▪ Her voice could only be heard *indistinctly*. [=*faintly*] – **in·dis·tinct·ness** *noun* [*noncount*]

in·dis·tin·guish·able /ˌɪndɪˈstɪŋgwɪʃəbəl/ *adj* : unable to be recognized as different : impossible to distinguish clearly from something else ▪ The copy and the original are practically *indistinguishable*. [=*identical*] — usually + *from* ▪ The copy is practically *indistinguishable from* the original. [=the copy and the original are so similar that it is almost impossible to see any difference between them]
– **in·dis·tin·guish·ably** /ˌɪndɪˈstɪŋgwɪʃəbli/ *adv* ▪ The flavors merged *indistinguishably* together.

¹in·di·vid·u·al /ˌɪndəˈvɪʤəwəl/ *adj*
1 *always used before a noun* : of, relating to, or existing as just one member or part of a larger group ▪ What are the *individual* traits/characteristics of the breed? ▪ The doctor carefully evaluates the *individual* needs of her patients. ▪ Students will receive as much *individual* attention as possible. ▪ The book is divided into *individual* [=*separate*] chapters. ▪ Each *individual* [=*particular*] case is different.
2 [*more* ~; *most* ~] : having a special and unusual quality that is easily seen ▪ She has a very *individual* style of writing. ▪ a pattern as *individual* as a fingerprint
3 *always used before a noun* : intended or designed for one person ▪ *individual* servings of dessert
– **in·di·vid·u·al·ly** *adv* ▪ Each student met *individually* [=*separately*] with the teacher. ▪ bowls *individually* crafted from wood ▪ *Individually* they don't amount to much, but as a group they're very powerful.

²individual *noun, pl* **-als** [*count*]
1 : a single person : a person who is considered separate from the rest of a group ▪ They promote a philosophy that sacrifices the rights of the *individual* for the public welfare.
2 : a particular person ▪ They are both rather odd *individuals*. ▪ Are you the *individual* I spoke with on the telephone? ▪ She's a very talented *individual*.
3 : a single member or part of a group ▪ The markings on tigers are unique to each *individual*.

in·di·vid·u·al·ism /ˌɪndəˈvɪʤəwəˌlɪzəm/ *noun* [*noncount*]
1 : the belief that the needs of each person are more important than the needs of the whole society or group ▪ a society that believes strongly in *individualism*
2 : the actions or attitudes of a person who does things without being concerned about what other people will think ▪ He was respected for his self-reliance and *individualism*.

in•di•vid•u•al•ist /ˌɪndəˈvɪʤəwəlɪst/ *noun, pl* **-ists** [*count*] **:** a person who does things without being concerned about what other people will think ▪ The school encourages children to be *individualists*.
– **in•di•vid•u•al•is•tic** /ˌɪndəˌvɪʤəwəˈlɪstɪk/ *also* **individualist** *adj* ▪ an *individualistic* approach to jazz music

in•di•vid•u•al•i•ty /ˌɪndəˌvɪʤəˈwæləti/ *noun* [*noncount*] **:** the quality that makes one person or thing different from all others ▪ She uses her clothing to express her *individuality*. ▪ materials that highlight the *individuality* of each piece in the collection

in•di•vid•u•al•ize *also Brit* **in•di•vid•u•al•ise** /ˌɪndəˈvɪʤəwəˌlaɪz/ *verb* **-iz•es; -ized; -iz•ing** [+ *obj*]
1 : to make (something) different from other things ▪ The author uses different styles to *individualize* the characters.
2 : to change (something) so that it fits each person's needs ▪ Teachers should *individualize* their lessons to address differences in their students. ▪ *individualized* computer programs
– **in•di•vid•u•al•i•za•tion** *also Brit* **in•di•vid•u•al•i•sa•tion** /ˌɪndəˌvɪʤəwələˈzeɪʃən, *Brit* ˌɪndəˌvɪʤəwəˌlaɪˈzeɪʃən/ *noun* [*noncount*] ▪ the *individualization* of lesson plans

individual retirement account *noun, pl* **~ -counts** [*count*] **:** IRA

in•di•vis•i•ble /ˌɪndəˈvɪzəbəl/ *adj, formal + literary* **:** impossible to divide or separate **:** not divisible ▪ an *indivisible* nation
– **in•di•vis•i•bil•i•ty** /ˌɪndəˌvɪzəˈbɪləti/ *noun* [*noncount*] ▪ He believes in the *indivisibility* of the mind and soul.

Indo- /ˈɪndoʊ/ *combining form* **:** Indian and ▪ He studies *Indo*-European languages.

in•doc•tri•nate /ɪnˈdɑːktrəˌneɪt/ *verb* **-nates; -nat•ed; -nat•ing** [+ *obj*] *disapproving* **:** to teach (someone) to fully accept the ideas, opinions, and beliefs of a particular group and to not consider other ideas, opinions, and beliefs ▪ The goal should be to teach politics, rather than to *indoctrinate* students in/with a narrow set of political beliefs.
– **in•doc•tri•na•tion** /ɪnˌdɑːktrəˈneɪʃən/ *noun* [*noncount*] ▪ the *indoctrination* of the new recruits

In•do–Eu•ro•pe•an /ˌɪndoʊˌjurəˈpiːjən/ *adj* **:** of or relating to a group of languages that includes many of the languages spoken in Europe, in the parts of the world colonized by Europeans, and in parts of Asia ▪ Hindi, Polish, and English are *Indo-European* languages.

in•do•lent /ˈɪndələnt/ *adj* [*more ~; most ~*] *formal* **:** not liking to work or be active **:** LAZY ▪ an *indolent* young man ▪ She is *indolent* and irresponsible.
– **in•do•lence** /ˈɪndələns/ *noun* [*noncount*] ▪ Some argue that television encourages *indolence*. – **in•do•lent•ly** *adv*

in•dom•i•ta•ble /ɪnˈdɑːmətəbəl/ *adj, formal* **:** impossible to defeat or discourage ▪ Her spirit was *indomitable*. [=*unconquerable*] ▪ her *indomitable* courage/strength/will
– **in•dom•i•ta•bly** /ɪnˈdɑːmətəbli/ *adv* ▪ *indomitably* courageous

in•door /ˈɪnˈdoɚ/ *adj, always used before a noun* **:** done, living, located, or used inside a building ▪ an *indoor* sport ▪ an *indoor* pet [=a pet that only lives inside] ▪ an *indoor* pool — compare OUTDOOR

in•doors /ˈɪnˈdoɚz/ *adv* **:** in, inside, or into a building ▪ The game will be played *indoors*. ▪ He worked *indoors* all afternoon. ▪ We went *indoors* when it began to rain. — compare OUTDOORS

indorse, indorsement *variant spellings of* ENDORSE, ENDORSEMENT

in•du•bi•ta•ble /ɪnˈduːbətəbəl, *Brit* ɪnˈdjuːbətəbəl/ *adj, formal* **:** certainly true **:** not able to be doubted ▪ an *indubitable* truth
– **in•du•bi•ta•bly** /ɪnˈduːbətəbli, *Brit* ɪnˈdjuːbətəbli/ *adv* ▪ He was *indubitably* [=*undoubtedly*] the most capable officer on the staff.

in•duce /ɪnˈduːs, *Brit* ɪnˈdjuːs/ *verb* **-duc•es; -duced; -duc•ing** [+ *obj*]
1 *somewhat formal* **:** to cause (someone or something) *to do* something ▪ The advertisement is meant to *induce* people *to eat* more fruit. ▪ No one knows what *induced* him *to leave*.
2 : to cause (something) to happen or exist ▪ medication to *induce* vomiting ▪ Her illness was *induced* by overwork. ▪ drug-*induced* sleep ▪ a stress-*induced* illness
3 *medical* **:** to give (a pregnant woman) special medicine in order to make her give birth ▪ The mother was *induced*. **:** to cause (labor or birth) to begin by giving special drugs to a pregnant woman ▪ They will *induce* labor to avoid complications.
– **in•duc•er** *noun, pl* **-ers** [*count*] *technical* ▪ He uses the herb as a sleep *inducer*.

in•duce•ment /ɪnˈduːsmənt, *Brit* ɪnˈdjuːsmənt/ *noun, pl* **-ments** *formal* **:** something that gives you a reason for doing something and makes you want to do it [*count*] Was his decision influenced by any illegal financial *inducements*? ▪ Employees were offered a bonus as an *inducement* to finish the project on schedule. [*noncount*] The low interest rate was little *inducement* for individuals to save money.

in•duct /ɪnˈdʌkt/ *verb* **-ducts; -duct•ed; -duct•ing** [+ *obj*]
1 : to have (someone) officially begin a new job, position, or government office — usually used as *(be) inducted*; usually + *into* ▪ The new president *was inducted into* office last year.
2 a : to officially make (someone) a member of a group or organization ▪ The club will *induct* six new members this year. — usually used as *(be) inducted*; usually + *into* ▪ She *was inducted into* the Basketball Hall of Fame. **b** *US* **:** to enroll (someone) for military training or service — usually used as *(be) inducted*; usually + *into* ▪ He *was inducted into* the army.
– **in•duct•ee** /ɪnˌdʌkˈtiː/ *noun, pl* **-ees** [*count*] *chiefly US* ▪ After the ceremony, we met the new *inductees*. [=the people who had just been inducted]

in•duc•tion /ɪnˈdʌkʃən/ *noun, pl* **-tions**
1 [*count*] **a :** the formal act or process of placing someone into a new job, position, government office, etc. ▪ Many people attended the bishop's *induction*. ▪ The *induction* ceremony was held at a banquet hall. **b** *US* **:** the formal act of making someone a member of the military ▪ the registration and *induction* of draftees
2 [*noncount*] *medical* **:** the act of giving a pregnant woman special drugs so that she will give birth ▪ *induction* of labor
3 [*noncount*] *technical* **:** a kind of reasoning that uses particular examples in order to reach a general conclusion about something
4 [*noncount*] *technical* **:** the process by which an electric current, an electric charge, or magnetism is produced in objects by being close to an electric or magnetic field

in•duc•tive /ɪnˈdʌktɪv/ *adj, technical* **:** using particular examples to reach a general conclusion about something ▪ *inductive* reasoning

in•dulge /ɪnˈdʌlʤ/ *verb* **-dulg•es; -dulged; -dulg•ing**
1 : to allow (yourself) to have or do something as a special pleasure [+ *obj*] It's my birthday. I'm going to *indulge* myself and eat whatever I want to eat. — often + *in* ▪ He *indulged* himself *in* the pleasure of a day spent entirely at the beach. [*no obj*] It's my birthday. I'm going to *indulge*. — often + *in* ▪ For our anniversary, we *indulged in* an expensive dinner.
2 [+ *obj*] **a :** to allow (someone) to have or do something even though it may not be proper, healthy, appropriate, etc. ▪ He knows that his aunt is always willing to *indulge* [=*spoil*] him. ▪ They always *indulged* their grandchildren's whims. [=they always allowed their grandchildren to do whatever they wanted to do] **b :** to patiently allow (someone) to do or say something ▪ Please *indulge* me while I review the topics we covered yesterday.
3 [+ *obj*] **:** to do the things that you want to do because of (a feeling, interest, desire, etc.) ▪ The museum is an excellent place to let children *indulge* their curiosity about dinosaurs. ▪ She bought a house with a big yard so that she could *indulge* her passion for gardening.
indulge in [*phrasal verb*] ***indulge in (something)*** **:** to become involved in (something, especially something that is considered wrong or improper) ▪ Both candidates have promised not to *indulge in* [=*take part in*] further personal attacks for the remainder of the campaign.

in•dul•gence /ɪnˈdʌlʤəns/ *noun, pl* **-genc•es**
1 [*noncount*] **:** the behavior or attitude of people who allow themselves to do what they want or who allow other people to do what they want ▪ She lived a life of selfish *indulgence*. ▪ They treated the sick boy with *indulgence*. = They showed great *indulgence* toward the sick boy. ▪ Ladies and gentlemen, I ask your *indulgence* [=*patience*] for a moment while my assistant prepares the next act. — see also SELF-INDULGENCE
2 [*noncount*] **:** the act of doing something that you enjoy but that is usually thought of as wrong or unhealthy ▪ his *indulgence* in forbidden pleasures
3 [*count*] **:** something that is done or enjoyed as a special pleasure ▪ She found that she couldn't afford the *indulgences* she had once enjoyed. ▪ For our anniversary we allowed ourselves the *indulgence* of an elegant dinner at our favorite res-

taurant. ▪ Good food is my only *indulgence*.

in·dul·gent /ɪnˈdʌlʤənt/ *adj [more ~; most ~]*
1 *sometimes disapproving* **: willing to allow someone to have or enjoy something even though it may not be proper, healthy, appropriate, etc.** ▪ These children are being spoiled by (overly) *indulgent* parents. ▪ He gave the child an *indulgent* smile. — see also SELF-INDULGENT
2 : done or enjoyed as a special pleasure ▪ an *indulgent* dessert
— **in·dul·gent·ly** *adv* ▪ She smiled *indulgently*.

in·dus·tri·al /ɪnˈdʌstrijəl/ *adj*
1 : of or relating to industry : of or relating to factories, the people who work in factories, or the things made in factories ▪ *industrial* development ▪ There are thousands of *industrial* uses for plastic. ▪ an *industrial* engineer ▪ He had an ***industrial accident***. [=an accident at work]
2 *[more ~; most ~]* **: having a developed industry : having factories that actively make a product** ▪ an *industrial* nation/region/city
3 : coming from or used in industry : made or used in factories ▪ *industrial* diamonds ▪ an *industrial* chemical; *also* **: stronger than most other products of its kind** ▪ an *industrial* cleaner
— **in·dus·tri·al·ly** *adv* ▪ *industrially* made glass ▪ Most crops are grown *industrially*. [=by large corporations and not individual farmers]

industrial action *noun, pl* **~ -tions** *[count] Brit* **:** JOB ACTION

industrial arts *noun [noncount] US* **: a subject that teaches students how to work with tools and machines** ▪ *Industrial arts* is her favorite class.

industrial estate *noun, pl* **~ -tates** *[count] Brit* **:** INDUSTRIAL PARK

in·dus·tri·al·ism /ɪnˈdʌstrijəˌlɪzəm/ *noun [noncount]* **: a social system in which industry and factories are the basis of a country's economy**

in·dus·tri·al·ist /ɪnˈdʌstrijəlɪst/ *noun, pl* **-ists** *[count]* **: someone who owns or manages an industry** ▪ a meeting of *industrialists* to discuss environmental issues

in·dus·tri·al·ize *also Brit* **in·dus·tri·al·ise** /ɪnˈdʌstrijəˌlaɪz/ *verb* **-iz·es; -ized; -iz·ing : to build and operate factories and businesses in a city, region, country, etc.** *[+ obj]* The government hopes to *industrialize* some of the agricultural regions. *[no obj]* This region *industrialized* [=this region gained industry] before the rest of the country.
— **in·dus·tri·al·i·za·tion** *also Brit* **in·dus·tri·al·i·sa·tion** /ɪnˌdʌstrijələˈzeɪʃən, *Brit* ɪnˌdʌstrijəˌlaɪˈzeɪʃən/ *noun [noncount]* ▪ The country is in the early stages of *industrialization*. — **industrialized** *also Brit* **industrialised** *adj* ▪ *industrialized* regions/nations

industrial park *noun, pl* **~ parks** *[count] US* **: an area outside of a town or city that is designed especially for factories or offices — called also** *(Brit)* ***industrial estate***

industrial relations *noun [plural]* **: the ways in which businesses relate to and deal with workers, the government, and the public**

Industrial Revolution *noun*
the Industrial Revolution **: the major social and economic changes that occurred in Britain, Europe, and the U.S. in the late 18th and early 19th centuries when new machinery, new sources of power, and new ways of manufacturing products were developed**

industrial–strength *adj, often humorous* **: stronger, more powerful, or more intense than others of its kind** ▪ She was wearing *industrial-strength* boots. ▪ He served us *industrial-strength* coffee.

in·dus·tri·ous /ɪnˈdʌstrijəs/ *adj [more ~; most ~]* **: working very hard : not lazy** ▪ He is an *industrious* worker.
— **in·dus·tri·ous·ly** *adv* ▪ She was working *industriously*.
— **in·dus·tri·ous·ness** *noun [noncount]* ▪ He was praised for his *industriousness*.

in·dus·try /ˈɪndəstri/ *noun, pl* **-tries**
1 a *[noncount]* **: the process of making products by using machinery and factories** ▪ He favors policies that promote *industry*. **b** *[count]* **: a group of businesses that provide a particular product or service** ▪ the automobile/oil/computer *industry* ▪ the tourist/entertainment *industry* ▪ She invested in several large *industries*. ▪ She became so popular that a whole *industry* grew up around her and her image. — see also CAPTAIN OF INDUSTRY, COTTAGE INDUSTRY
2 *[noncount]* **: the habit of working hard and steadily** ▪ She is admired for her *industry*. [=industriousness]

ine·bri·at·ed /ɪˈniːbriˌeɪtəd/ *adj [more ~; most ~] formal* **: affected by drinking too much alcohol :** DRUNK ▪ He was clearly *inebriated* when he left the bar.
— **ine·bri·a·tion** /ɪˌniːbriˈeɪʃən/ *noun [noncount]* ▪ public *inebriation* [=drunkenness]

in·ed·i·ble /ɪnˈɛdəbəl/ *adj* **: not suitable or safe to eat : not edible** ▪ *inedible* mushrooms ▪ The steak was overcooked, but not *inedible*.

in·ef·fa·ble /ɪnˈɛfəbəl/ *adj, formal* **: too great, powerful, beautiful, etc., to be described or expressed** ▪ She felt *ineffable* [=inexpressible] joy at the sight of her children. ▪ His paintings have an *ineffable* [=indescribable] beauty.
— **in·ef·fa·bly** /ɪnˈɛfəbli/ *adv* ▪ an *ineffably* beautiful film

in·ef·fec·tive /ˌɪnəˈfɛktɪv/ *adj [more ~; most ~]* **: not producing or having the effect you want : not effective** ▪ The treatment was *ineffective* against the disease. ▪ an *ineffective* law/leader
— **in·ef·fec·tive·ly** *adv* ▪ She argued her point *ineffectively*.
— **in·ef·fec·tive·ness** *noun [noncount]* ▪ He has been criticized for his *ineffectiveness* as a leader.

in·ef·fec·tu·al /ˌɪnəˈfɛkʧəwəl/ *adj [more ~; most ~]* **: not producing or able to produce the effect you want** ▪ an *ineffectual* politician ▪ an *ineffectual* struggle
— **in·ef·fec·tu·al·ly** /ˌɪnəˈfɛkʧəwəli/ *adv* ▪ They struggled *ineffectually* for reform.

in·ef·fi·cien·cy /ˌɪnəˈfɪʃənsi/ *noun, pl* **-cies : the lack of ability to do something or produce something without wasting materials, time, or energy : the quality or state of being inefficient** *[noncount]* The candidate blamed her opponent for the local government's *inefficiency*. *[count]* She claims that money can be saved by reducing *inefficiencies*.

in·ef·fi·cient /ˌɪnəˈfɪʃənt/ *adj [more ~; most ~]* **: not capable of producing desired results without wasting materials, time, or energy : not efficient** ▪ an *inefficient* worker ▪ The delivery system was very *inefficient*. ▪ an *inefficient* use of fuel
— **in·ef·fi·cient·ly** *adv* ▪ The engine uses fuel *inefficiently*.

in·el·e·gant /ɪnˈɛləgənt/ *adj [more ~; most ~] somewhat formal* **: not graceful, attractive, or polite : not elegant** ▪ an *inelegant* dancer ▪ *inelegant* language
— **in·el·e·gance** /ɪnˈɛləgəns/ *noun [noncount] formal* — **in·el·e·gant·ly** *adv* ▪ an *inelegantly* named car

in·el·i·gi·ble /ɪnˈɛləʤəbəl/ *adj* **: not allowed to do or be something : not eligible** ▪ Previously *ineligible* patients may now be able to participate in the study. ▪ She was *ineligible* for the contest. = She was *ineligible* to participate in the contest. ▪ They are *ineligible* for a loan.
— **in·el·i·gi·bil·i·ty** /ɪnˌɛləʤəˈbɪləti/ *noun [noncount]*

in·eluc·ta·ble /ˌɪnɪˈlʌktəbəl/ *adj, formal* **: not able to be avoided or changed** ▪ You cannot escape an *ineluctable* [=unavoidable] fate. ▪ an *ineluctable* conclusion
— **in·eluc·ta·bly** /ˌɪnɪˈlʌktəbli/ *adv*

in·ept /ɪˈnɛpt/ *adj [more ~; most ~]*
1 : lacking skill or ability ▪ an *inept* mechanic ▪ He was completely *inept* at sports. ▪ a socially *inept* teenager [=a teenager who is shy or awkward around other people]
2 : showing a lack of skill or ability : not done well ▪ *inept* planning ▪ He made an *inept* attempt to apologize. — compare INAPT
— **in·ept·ly** *adv* ▪ It was *ineptly* done. — **in·ept·ness** *noun [noncount]* ▪ the *ineptness* of the coaching staff

in·ep·ti·tude /ɪˈnɛptəˌtuːd, *Brit* ɪˈnɛptəˌtjuːd/ *noun [noncount]* **: a lack of skill or ability** ▪ The team's poor play is being blamed on the *ineptitude* of the coaching staff. ▪ social *ineptitude*

in·equal·i·ty /ˌɪnɪˈkwɑːləti/ *noun, pl* **-ties : an unfair situation in which some people have more rights or better opportunities than other people** *[noncount]* social/sexual/economic/racial *inequality* ▪ They discussed the problem of *inequality* between students. ▪ He accused the company of *inequality* in its hiring practices. *[count]* He has proposed a new system designed to remove *inequalities* in health care. ▪ the *inequalities* of education/income

in·eq·ui·ta·ble /ɪnˈɛkwətəbəl/ *adj [more ~; most ~] formal* **: not fair or equal :** UNFAIR ▪ They protested the *inequitable* treatment of employees.
— **in·eq·ui·ta·bly** /ɪnˈɛkwətəbli/ *adv* ▪ The law is being applied *inequitably*. [=unfairly]

in·eq·ui·ty /ɪnˈɛkwəti/ *noun, pl* **-ties** *formal*
1 *[noncount]* **: lack of fairness : unfair treatment** ▪ She has been a leader in the fight against racial *inequity*. [=injustice]
2 *[count]* **: something that is unfair** ▪ the *inequities* in wages paid to men and women ▪ educational *inequities*

Do not confuse *inequity* with *iniquity*.

in·erad·i·ca·ble /ˌɪnɪˈrædɪkəbəl/ *adj, formal* : impossible to remove or forget ▪ an *ineradicable* problem ▪ She made an *ineradicable* impression on us.

in·ert /ɪˈnɚt/ *adj*
1 : unable to move ▪ an *inert* and lifeless body
2 [*more* ~; *most* ~] : moving or acting very slowly ▪ How does he propose to stimulate the *inert* economy and create jobs? ▪ a politically *inert* government
3 *chemistry* : not able to affect other chemicals when in contact with them : not chemically reactive ▪ an *inert* gas ▪ *inert* ingredients
– **in·ert·ly** *adv* ▪ He sat *inertly* in front of the television. – **in·ert·ness** *noun* [*noncount*] ▪ chemical *inertness*

in·er·tia /ɪˈnɚʃə/ *noun* [*noncount*]
1 a : lack of movement or activity especially when movement or activity is wanted or needed ▪ He blames governmental/bureaucratic *inertia* for the holdup. **b** : a feeling of not having the energy or desire that is needed to move, change, etc. ▪ After 10 years in an unsatisfying job she overcame her *inertia* and went back to school.
2 *physics* : a property of matter by which something that is not moving remains still and something that is moving goes at the same speed and in the same direction until another thing or force affects it
– **in·er·tial** /ɪˈnɚʃəl/ *adj, physics* ▪ an *inertial* sensor

in·es·cap·able /ˌɪnəˈskeɪpəbəl/ *adj* : impossible to deny or avoid ▪ It's an *inescapable* truth that these problems have no easy solution. ▪ an *inescapable* conclusion
– **in·es·cap·ably** /ˌɪnəˈskeɪpəbli/ *adv* ▪ an *inescapably* obvious truth

in·es·sen·tial /ˌɪnəˈsɛnʃəl/ *adj, formal* : not needed : not essential ▪ *inessential* details
– **inessential** *noun, pl* **-tials** [*count*]

in·es·ti·ma·ble /ɪnˈɛstəməbəl/ *adj, formal* : too great, valuable, or excellent to be measured ▪ He has made *inestimable* contributions to our society. ▪ *inestimable* value/worth

in·ev·i·ta·ble /ɪˈnɛvətəbəl/ *adj* : sure to happen ▪ the *inevitable* result ▪ Some criticism was *inevitable*. [=*unavoidable*]
the inevitable : something that is sure to happen ▪ They're just trying to delay/postpone *the inevitable*.
– **in·ev·i·ta·bil·i·ty** /ɪˌnɛvətəˈbɪləti/ *noun* [*noncount*] ▪ the *inevitability* of change – **in·ev·i·ta·bly** /ɪˈnɛvətəbli/ *adv* ▪ The changes *inevitably* resulted in criticism.

in·ex·act /ˌɪnɪgˈzækt/ *adj* [*more* ~; *most* ~] : not completely correct or precise : not exact ▪ The measurements were somewhat *inexact*, but they were close enough. ▪ an *inexact* word/calculation/description
– **in·ex·act·ness** *noun* [*noncount*]

in·ex·cus·able /ˌɪnɪkˈskjuːzəbəl/ *adj* : too bad or wrong to be excused or ignored ▪ her *inexcusable* rudeness ▪ The mistake was *inexcusable*.
– **in·ex·cus·ably** /ˌɪnɪkˈskjuːzəbli/ *adv* ▪ The salesperson was *inexcusably* rude. ▪ He behaved *inexcusably*.

in·ex·haust·ible /ˌɪnɪgˈzɑːstəbəl/ *adj* : impossible to use up completely : impossible to exhaust ▪ The world's supply of oil is not *inexhaustible*. ▪ He seems to have *inexhaustible* energy.
– **in·ex·haust·ibly** /ˌɪnɪgˈzɑːstəbli/ *adv* ▪ We do not have an *inexhaustibly* large supply of oil.

in·ex·o·ra·ble /ɪnˈɛksərəbəl/ *adj, formal* : not able to be stopped or changed ▪ an *inexorable* conclusion ▪ the *inexorable* rise of a political movement
– **in·ex·o·ra·bil·i·ty** /ɪnˌɛksərəˈbɪləti/ *noun* [*noncount*] – **in·ex·o·ra·bly** /ɪnˈɛksərəbli/ *adv* ▪ We are *inexorably* linked to the past. ▪ Will a break in negotiations lead *inexorably* to conflict?

in·ex·pen·sive /ˌɪnɪkˈspɛnsɪv/ *adj* [*more* ~; *most* ~] : low in price : not expensive ▪ The hotel room was surprisingly *inexpensive*. [=*cheap*] ▪ an *inexpensive* meal
– **in·ex·pen·sive·ly** *adv* ▪ Everything at that store is priced fairly *inexpensively*.

in·ex·pe·ri·ence /ˌɪnɪkˈspirijəns/ *noun* [*noncount*] : lack of experience ▪ He blames his mistakes on *inexperience*.
– **in·ex·pe·ri·enced** /ˌɪnɪkˈspirijənst/ *adj* [*more* ~; *most* ~] ▪ She's an *inexperienced* driver.

in·ex·pert /ɪnˈɛkspɚt/ *adj, formal* : not skillful at doing something ▪ an *inexpert* tailor ▪ The painting looks to be fake to my *inexpert* [=*untrained*] eye.
– **in·ex·pert·ly** *adv* ▪ It was *inexpertly* painted.

in·ex·pli·ca·ble /ˌɪnɪkˈsplɪkəbəl, ɪnˈɛksplɪkəbəl/ *adj* : not able to be explained or understood ▪ an *inexplicable* mystery ▪ He had a series of seemingly *inexplicable* accidents.
– **in·ex·pli·ca·bly** /ˌɪnɪkˈsplɪkəbli, ɪnˈɛksplɪkəbli/ *adv* ▪ The files have *inexplicably* disappeared.

in·ex·press·ible /ˌɪnɪkˈsprɛsəbəl/ *adj, somewhat formal* : too strong or great to be expressed or described ▪ *inexpressible* joy/pain
– **in·ex·press·ibly** /ˌɪnɪkˈsprɛsəbli/ *adv* ▪ an *inexpressibly* sad story

in ex·tre·mis /ˌɪnɪkˈstriːməs/ *adv, formal*
1 : at the point of death ▪ a patient *in extremis*
2 : in a very difficult situation ▪ They are helping a family *in extremis*.

in·ex·tri·ca·ble /ˌɪnɪkˈstrɪkəbəl, ɪnˈɛkstrɪkəbəl/ *adj, formal* : impossible to separate : closely joined or related ▪ He argues that there is an *inextricable* link between poverty and poor health.
– **in·ex·tri·ca·bly** /ˌɪnɪkˈstrɪkəbli, ɪnˈɛkstrɪkəbli/ *adv* ▪ He claims poverty is *inextricably* linked to poor health. ▪ Our lives are bound *inextricably* with others.

in·fal·li·ble /ɪnˈfæləbəl/ *adj*
1 : not capable of being wrong or making mistakes : not fallible ▪ I never claimed to be *infallible*. ▪ an *infallible* memory
2 : certain to work properly or succeed ▪ There is no *infallible* remedy to these problems.
– **in·fal·li·bil·i·ty** /ɪnˌfæləˈbɪləti/ *noun* [*noncount*] ▪ I never made any claims of *infallibility*. — see also PAPAL INFALLIBILITY – **in·fal·li·bly** /ɪnˈfæləbli/ *adv* ▪ The computer program can *infallibly* identify each type of file.

in·fa·mous /ˈɪnfəməs/ *adj* [*more* ~; *most* ~]
1 : well-known for being bad : known for evil acts or crimes ▪ an *infamous* traitor ▪ a city *infamous* for poverty and crime
2 : causing people to think you are bad or evil ▪ He committed an *infamous* crime. ▪ (*humorous*) We experienced some of the city's *infamous* weather.
– **in·fa·mous·ly** *adv* ▪ an *infamously* shocking crime

in·fa·my /ˈɪnfəmi/ *noun, pl* **-mies**
1 [*noncount*] : the condition of being known for having done bad things or for being evil ▪ He never escaped the *infamy* his crimes had earned him. ▪ a day of *infamy* [=an infamous day; a day on which something very bad happened]
2 [*count*] *formal* : an evil or terrible act — usually plural ▪ The book recounts the *infamies* committed by the regime.

in·fan·cy /ˈɪnfənsi/ *noun* [*noncount*]
1 : the first part of a child's life : the time in your life when you are a baby ▪ She was often sick during her *infancy*. ▪ a skill developed ***in infancy***
2 : a beginning : an early stage of development ▪ She has been a member of the church since its *infancy*. ▪ when the Internet was still ***in its infancy*** [=very new]

[1]in·fant /ˈɪnfənt/ *noun, pl* **-fants** [*count*] : a very young child : BABY ▪ The *infant* was healthy. ▪ a study of health problems that can affect young *infants* ▪ He showed us a picture of his *infant* daughter.

[2]infant *adj, always used before a noun*
1 : made or suitable for babies ▪ *infant* formula ▪ an *infant* bathtub
2 *Brit* : of, relating to, or for children between the ages of about four and seven ▪ children attending ***infant school*** [=a school for young children] ▪ She is an ***infant teacher***.
3 : very new and still developing ▪ our *infant* steel industry ▪ an *infant* navy

in·fan·ti·cide /ɪnˈfæntəˌsaɪd/ *noun* [*noncount*] : the act of killing a baby

in·fan·tile /ˈɪnfənˌtajəl/ *adj*
1 [*more* ~; *most* ~] *disapproving* : annoying and childish : very silly in a way that is not appropriate or polite ▪ His behavior was *infantile*. ▪ *infantile* jokes
2 *always used before a noun, medical* : affecting babies or very young children ▪ *infantile* diseases

infantile paralysis *noun* [*noncount*] *old-fashioned* : POLIO

in·fan·try /ˈɪnfəntri/ *noun* : the part of an army that has soldiers who fight on foot [*noncount*] He joined the *infantry* after leaving school. ▪ The *infantry* is coming. [*plural*] The *infantry* are coming. — compare CAVALRY

in·fan·try·man /ˈɪnfəntrimən/ *noun, pl* **-men** /-mən/ [*count*] : a soldier who is in the infantry

in·fat·u·at·ed /ɪnˈfæʧəˌweɪtəd/ *adj* : filled with foolish or very strong love or admiration — usually + *with* ▪ He was *infatuated with* his teacher. ▪ She became *infatuated with* the charms of city life.

in·fat·u·a·tion /ɪnˌfæʧəˈweɪʃən/ *noun, pl* **-tions** : a feeling of foolish or very strong love or admiration for someone or something [*noncount*] The attraction he felt for her was just *infatuation*, not true love. ▪ They condemn society's *infatuation* with Hollywood. [*count*] It was just an *infatuation*. ▪ She had a series of frivolous *infatuations* with younger men.

in·fect /ɪnˈfɛkt/ *verb* **-fects; -fect·ed; -fect·ing** [+ *obj*]

1 : to cause (someone or something) to become sick or affected by disease ▪ If you're sick you should stay home to avoid *infecting* other people in the office. ▪ The virus has *infected* many people. ▪ They were unable to prevent bacteria from *infecting* the wound. — often used as *(be) infected* ▪ He *was infected* by a coworker. ▪ He *was infected* with AIDS.

2 a : to cause (someone) to feel an emotion — usually + *with* ▪ She has *infected* everyone *with* her enthusiasm. [=her enthusiasm has made other people feel enthusiastic too] **b** *of an emotion* **:** to spread to (other people) ▪ Her enthusiasm has *infected* everyone.

3 *of a computer virus* **:** to cause (a computer or computer file) to stop working as it should ▪ The virus has *infected* many computers. ▪ All the computers in the office were *infected* by/with the same virus.

infected *adj*

1 a : containing germs that cause disease ▪ an *infected* wound **b :** having a disease caused by germs ▪ *infected* children

2 : affected by a computer virus ▪ an *infected* file/computer

in·fec·tion /ɪnˈfɛkʃən/ *noun, pl* **-tions**

1 [*noncount*] **:** the act or process of infecting someone or something **:** the state of being infected ▪ Poor hygiene can increase the danger of *infection*. ▪ The wound has so far remained free of *infection*. ▪ steps you can take to decrease your computer's risk of *infection*

2 [*count*] **:** a disease caused by germs that enter the body ▪ viral/bacterial *infections* ▪ a painful ear *infection*

in·fec·tious /ɪnˈfɛkʃəs/ *adj*

1 a : capable of causing infection ▪ viruses and other *infectious* agents **b** [*more ~; most ~*] **:** capable of being passed to someone else by germs that enter the body ▪ an acute *infectious* illness ▪ a highly *infectious* disease — compare CONTAGIOUS **c :** suffering from a disease that can be spread to other people by germs ▪ an *infectious* patient

2 [*more ~; most ~*] **:** capable of being easily spread to other people ▪ Their enthusiasm was *infectious*. [=*contagious*] ▪ She has an *infectious* grin. ▪ *infectious* laughter

– in·fec·tious·ly *adv* ▪ *infectiously* cheerful/enthusiastic

in·fer /ɪnˈfɚ/ *verb* **-fers; -ferred; -fer·ring** [+ *obj*]

1 : to form (an opinion) from evidence **:** to reach (a conclusion) based on known facts ▪ It's difficult to *infer* how these changes will affect ordinary citizens. — often + *from* ▪ She said she was pleased, but her true feelings could be *inferred from* the look of disappointment on her face. — often + *that* ▪ I *inferred from* his silence *that* he was angry about my decision. — compare IMPLY

2 *informal* **:** to hint or suggest (something) **:** IMPLY ▪ Are you *inferring* that I'm wrong? ✧ Many people regard this use of *infer* as an error, but it occurs commonly in spoken English.

in·fer·ence /ˈɪnfərəns/ *noun, pl* **-enc·es**

1 [*noncount*] **:** the act or process of reaching a conclusion about something from known facts or evidence ▪ Its existence is only known ***by inference***

2 [*count*] **:** a conclusion or opinion that is formed because of known facts or evidence ▪ The program uses records of past purchases to make/draw *inferences* about what customers will buy in the future. ▪ What *inference* can we draw from these facts?

¹in·fe·ri·or /ɪnˈfirijɚ/ *adj*

1 : of poor quality **:** low or lower in quality ▪ *inferior* goods/materials/products ▪ an *inferior* performer/performance ▪ These pearls are of *inferior* quality. — often + *to* ▪ These pearls are *inferior* (in quality) *to* others I have seen.

2 : of little or less importance or value ▪ They were considered a socially *inferior* group. ▪ He always felt *inferior* around his brother. — often + *to* ▪ He always felt *inferior to* his brother.

3 : low or lower in rank ▪ The judges voted to overturn a ruling made by an *inferior* court.

– in·fe·ri·or·i·ty /ɪnˌfiriˈorəti/ *noun* [*noncount*] ▪ the *inferiority* of the cheaper materials ▪ He had a sense of social *inferiority* among wealthy people.

²inferior *noun, pl* **-ors** [*count*] **:** a person of low rank or status ▪ She treated her employees as social *inferiors*.

inferiority complex *noun, pl* **~ -plexes** [*count*] **:** a belief that you are less worthy or important than other people ▪ His shyness is the result of an *inferiority complex*.

in·fer·nal /ɪnˈfɚnl/ *adj, always used before a noun*

1 *literary* **:** of or relating to hell ▪ the *infernal* regions of the dead

2 *informal + old-fashioned* **:** very bad or unpleasant ▪ Stop making that *infernal* racket! ▪ an *infernal* nuisance/pest

– in·fer·nal·ly /ɪnˈfɚnḷi/ *adv* ▪ an *infernally* [=*extremely*] difficult problem

in·fer·no /ɪnˈfɚnoʊ/ *noun, pl* **-nos** [*count*] **:** a very large and dangerous fire ▪ By the time help arrived, the fire had grown to a raging *inferno*.

in·fer·tile /ɪnˈfɚtḷ/ *adj* **:** not fertile: such as **a :** not able to reproduce **:** not able to produce children, young animals, etc. ▪ *infertile* married couples ▪ an *infertile* man/woman **b :** not suited for raising crops **:** unable to support the growth of plants ▪ *infertile* soil ▪ *infertile* land/fields

– in·fer·til·i·ty /ˌɪnˌfɚˈtɪləti/ *noun* [*noncount*] ▪ male/female *infertility* ▪ the *infertility* of the land

in·fest /ɪnˈfɛst/ *verb* **-fests; -fest·ed; -fest·ing** [+ *obj*] *of something harmful or unwanted* **:** to be in or over (a place, an animal, etc.) in large numbers ▪ Lice *infested* his scalp. — often used as *(be) infested* ▪ The area *was infested* with snakes/insects. [=there was a very large number of snake/insects in the area] ▪ The trees *were infested* by/with caterpillars. ▪ a neighborhood *infested* with crime ▪ shark-*infested* waters

– in·fes·ta·tion /ˌɪnˌfɛˈsteɪʃən/ *noun, pl* **-tions** [*count*] an *infestation* of caterpillars [*noncount*] There were signs of insect *infestation*.

in·fi·del /ˈɪnfədḷ/ *noun, pl* **-dels** [*count*] *disapproving* **:** a person who does not believe in a religion that someone regards as the true religion ▪ a holy war against the *infidels*

in·fi·del·i·ty /ˌɪnfəˈdɛləti/ *noun, pl* **-ties :** the act or fact of having a romantic or sexual relationship with someone other than your husband, wife, or partner [*noncount*] She was convinced that her husband was guilty of *infidelity*. [*count*] He has admitted to a number of marital *infidelities*.

in·field /ˈɪnˌfiːld/ *noun, pl* **-fields** [*count*]

1 a : the part of a baseball field that includes the area within and around the three bases and home plate ▪ He threw the ball across the *infield*. — often used before another noun ▪ an *infield* grounder ▪ an *infield* hit **b :** the part of a cricket field that is close to the wickets **c :** the players who are positioned in the infield ▪ The team has one of the best *infields* in the league. — compare OUTFIELD

2 *chiefly US* **:** the area that a racetrack or running track goes around **:** the area inside a track

– in·field·er /ˈɪnˌfiːldɚ/ *noun, pl* **-ers** [*count*] *US* ▪ a skillful *infielder* [=a baseball player who plays in the infield]

in·fight·ing /ˈɪnˌfaɪtɪŋ/ *noun* [*noncount*] **:** fighting or disagreement among the members of a group or organization ▪ political *infighting*

in·fil·trate /ɪnˈfɪlˌtreɪt, ˈɪnfɪlˌtreɪt/ *verb* **-trates; -trat·ed; -trat·ing** [+ *obj*]

1 a : to secretly enter or join (something, such as a group or an organization) in order to get information or do harm ▪ The gang was *infiltrated* by undercover agents. — sometimes used figuratively ▪ An attitude of cynicism has *infiltrated* the staff. [=the staff has become cynical] **b :** to cause (someone) to secretly enter or join a group, organization, etc. ▪ Attempts to *infiltrate* undercover agents into the gang have failed.

2 *technical* **:** to pass into or through (something) ▪ Water can easily *infiltrate* the soil.

– in·fil·tra·tion /ˌɪnfɪlˈtreɪʃən/ *noun* [*noncount*] ▪ the *infiltration* of undercover agents into the gang **– in·fil·tra·tor** /ɪnˈfɪlˌtreɪtɚ, ˈɪnfɪlˌtreɪtɚ/ *noun, pl* **-tors** [*count*] ▪ The gang discovered an *infiltrator* among its members.

in·fi·nite /ˈɪnfənət/ *adj*

1 : having no limits **:** ENDLESS ▪ *infinite* space ▪ an *infinite* series of numbers

2 : extremely large or great ▪ She has *infinite* patience when she's dealing with children. ▪ There seemed to be an *infinite* number of possibilities. ▪ an *infinite* variety of choices

– in·fi·nite·ly *adv* ▪ The universe is *infinitely* large. ▪ *infinitely* subtle variations ▪ an *infinitely* large number

in·fin·i·tes·i·mal /ɪnˌfɪnəˈtɛsəməl/ *adj* [*more ~; most ~*] **:** extremely small ▪ an *infinitesimal* moment in time ▪ an *infinitesimal* difference

– in·fin·i·tes·i·mal·ly /ɪnˌfɪnəˈtɛsəməli/ *adv* ▪ an *infinitesimally* small difference

in·fin·i·tive /ɪnˈfɪnətɪv/ *noun, pl* **-tives** [*count*] *grammar*

: the basic form of a verb ✧ In English the infinitive form of a verb is usually used with *to* ("I asked him *to go*") except with modal verbs like *should* and *could* ("He should *go*") and certain other verbs like *see* and *hear* ("I saw him *go*"). — see also SPLIT INFINITIVE

– infinitive *adj* ▪ an *infinitive* clause/form/phrase

in·fin·i·ty /ɪnˈfɪnəti/ *noun*

1 [*noncount*] **a :** the quality of having no limits or end : the quality of being infinite ▪ the *infinity* of space **b :** a space, amount, or period of time that has no limits or end ▪ The view tapers off into *infinity*. ▪ a series of numbers that continues to *infinity*

2 [*singular*] **:** a very great number or amount ▪ The night sky was filled with an *infinity* of stars. ▪ an *infinity* of choices

in·firm /ɪnˈfəm/ *adj* [*more ~; most ~*] **:** having a condition of weakness or illness that usually lasts for a long time and is caused especially by old age ▪ The clinic provides free care for elderly and *infirm* people who lack health insurance. ▪ mentally and physically *infirm*

the infirm **:** people who are weak, ill, etc. : infirm people ▪ providing care for the elderly and *the infirm*

in·fir·ma·ry /ɪnˈfəməri/ *noun, pl* **-ries** [*count*]

1 : a place where sick people stay and are cared for in a school, prison, summer camp, etc. ▪ One of the students became ill and was sent to the *infirmary*.

2 *Brit* **:** HOSPITAL — used especially in names ▪ the Edinburgh Royal *Infirmary*

in·fir·mi·ty /ɪnˈfəməti/ *noun, pl* **-ties**

1 [*noncount*] **:** the quality or state of being weak or ill especially because of old age ▪ In recent years she has had to reduce her schedule because of age and *infirmity*.

2 [*count*] **:** a disease or illness that usually lasts for a long time ▪ the *infirmities* of old age

in·flame /ɪnˈfleɪm/ *verb* **-flames; -flamed; -flam·ing** [*+ obj*]

1 a : to cause (a person or group) to become angry or violent ▪ His angry speech *inflamed* the mob. **b :** to make (something) more active, angry, or violent ▪ ideas that *inflame* the imagination ▪ His comments have *inflamed* an already tense situation. ▪ *inflaming* the passions of the mob

2 : to cause (a part of your body) to grow sore, red, and swollen ▪ a chemical that can *inflame* the skin

inflamed *adj* [*more ~; most ~*] *of a part of your body* **:** sore, red, and swollen from disease, injury, etc. ▪ an *inflamed* appendix ▪ *inflamed* skin

in·flam·ma·ble /ɪnˈflæməbəl/ *adj* [*more ~; most ~*]

1 : capable of being set on fire and of burning quickly : FLAMMABLE ▪ highly *inflammable* chemicals

2 : easily excited or angered ▪ an *inflammable* temper

in·flam·ma·tion /ˌɪnfləˈmeɪʃən/ *noun, pl* **-tions :** a condition in which a part of your body becomes red, swollen, and painful [*noncount*] The drug is used to reduce *inflammation*. [*count*] a chronic *inflammation* ▪ *inflammations* of the throat and ears

in·flam·ma·to·ry /ɪnˈflæməˌtori, *Brit* ɪnˈflæmətri/ *adj*

1 *medical* **:** causing or having inflammation ▪ *inflammatory* diseases ▪ chronic *inflammatory* conditions ▪ She had an acute *inflammatory* reaction to the drug. — compare ANTI-INFLAMMATORY

2 [*more ~; most ~*] **:** causing anger ▪ He incited the mob with an *inflammatory* speech. ▪ *inflammatory* remarks/language

in·flate /ɪnˈfleɪt/ *verb* **-flates; -flat·ed; -flat·ing**

1 a [*+ obj*] **:** to add air or gas to (something, such as a tire or a balloon) and make it larger ▪ We used a pump to *inflate* the raft. ▪ *inflate* [=*blow up*] a balloon **b** [*no obj*] **:** to become larger by being filled with air or gas ▪ The balloon slowly *inflated*. — opposite DEFLATE

2 [*+ obj*] **a :** to think or say that (something) is larger or more important than it really is ▪ His memoirs *inflate* [=*exaggerate*] his contributions to the war effort. **b :** to cause (a person's ego, reputation, etc.) to become too large or great ▪ All the publicity was *inflating* his ego. [=was making him too proud and conceited]

3 : to increase prices, costs, etc., in a way that is not normal or expected [*+ obj*] Economists warn that rapid economic growth could *inflate* prices. ▪ Increased competition has *inflated* salaries among professional athletes. [*no obj*] Rapid economic growth may cause prices to *inflate*.

– in·flat·able /ɪnˈfleɪtəbəl/ *adj* ▪ an *inflatable* raft

inflated *adj*

1 : filled and made larger with air or gas ▪ an *inflated* balloon/raft

2 a : too large or high ▪ He has an *inflated* opinion of his value to the company. [=he thinks he is more valuable than he really is] ▪ He has an *inflated* ego. [=he has an overly high opinion of himself] ▪ a writer with an *inflated* reputation ▪ *inflated* [=*exaggerated*] claims of greatness **b** *of language* **:** too serious or fancy ▪ an *inflated* style of writing ▪ *inflated* [=*overblown*] language

3 *of prices, wages, etc.* **:** too high : increased to a level that is not normal or proper ▪ She objects to the *inflated* salaries that many professional athletes now receive. ▪ *inflated* prices

in·fla·tion /ɪnˈfleɪʃən/ *noun* [*noncount*]

1 : an act of inflating something ▪ the *inflation* of a balloon : the state of being inflated ▪ It's important to maintain proper tire *inflation*. [=*pressure*]

2 : a continual increase in the price of goods and services ▪ The government has been unable to control/reduce/curb *inflation*. ▪ The rate of *inflation* is high/low/rising. ▪ The annual *inflation* rate is three percent. [=prices are rising three percent each year] ▪ economic *inflation*

in·fla·tion·ary /ɪnˈfleɪʃəˌneri, *Brit* ɪnˈfleɪʃənri/ *adj*

1 : of or relating to economic inflation ▪ *inflationary* theories ▪ *inflationary* increases

2 [*more ~; most ~*] **:** causing, experiencing, or affected by economic inflation : causing, experiencing, or affected by rising prices ▪ He blames the bad economy on the government's *inflationary* policies. ▪ *inflationary* pressures ▪ an *inflationary* environment/period

in·flect /ɪnˈflɛkt/ *verb* **-flects; -flect·ed; -flect·ing** *grammar* **:** to change the form of a word when using it in a particular way [*+ obj*] Most nouns in English are *inflected* for plural use by adding "-s" or "-es." [*no obj*] Most nouns in English *inflect* for plural use by adding "-s" or "-es." ▪ Most adjectives in English do not *inflect* for gender or number.

– inflected *adj* [*more ~; most ~*] ▪ Some languages are more (highly) *inflected* than others. [=the words in some languages change their forms for different uses more than the words in other languages] ▪ "Gone" and "went" are ***inflected forms*** of the verb "go."

in·flec·tion *also Brit* **in·flex·ion** /ɪnˈflɛkʃən/ *noun, pl* **-tions**

1 : a rise or fall in the sound of a person's voice : a change in the pitch or tone of a person's voice [*noncount*] She spoke with no *inflection*. [*count*] She read the lines with an upward/rising *inflection*. ▪ vocal *inflections*

2 *grammar* **a** [*noncount*] **:** a change in the form of a word that occurs when it has a particular use ▪ Most English adjectives do not require *inflection*. **b** [*count*] **:** a form of a word that occurs when it has a particular use : an inflected form ▪ "Gone" and "went" are *inflections* of the verb "go." **c** [*count*] **:** a part of a word (such as a suffix) that is used to change a word's form for a particular use ▪ English has fewer *inflections* than many other languages.

– in·flec·tion·al *also Brit* **in·flex·ion·al** /ɪnˈflɛkʃənl/ *adj* ▪ *inflectional* rules/forms

in·flex·i·ble /ɪnˈflɛksəbəl/ *adj* [*more ~; most ~*] **:** not flexible: such as **a :** not easily influenced or persuaded ▪ an *inflexible* judge **b :** not easily bent or twisted ▪ *inflexible* [=*stiff*] plastic **c :** not easily changed ▪ *inflexible* laws/rules ▪ an *inflexible* deadline/schedule

– in·flex·i·bil·i·ty /ɪnˌflɛksəˈbɪləti/ *noun* [*noncount*] ▪ the *inflexibility* of the schedule **– in·flex·i·bly** /ɪnˈflɛksəbli/ *adv*

in·flict /ɪnˈflɪkt/ *verb* **-flicts; -flict·ed; -flict·ing** [*+ obj*] **:** to cause someone to experience or be affected by (something unpleasant or harmful) ▪ These insects are capable of *inflicting* a painful sting. ▪ *inflict* a wound ▪ *inflict* pain/injury/punishment/damage — often + *on* or *upon* ▪ He shows no regret for the suffering he has *inflicted on/upon* these innocent people. ▪ They continue to *inflict* their strange ideas about nutrition *on/upon* their children.

– in·flic·tion /ɪnˈflɪkʃən/ *noun* [*noncount*] ▪ the *infliction* of a knife wound ▪ the *infliction* of pain/guilt/humiliation

in–flight /ˈɪnˈflaɪt/ *adj, always used before a noun* **:** made, done, or provided while you are flying in an airplane ▪ an *in-flight* meal/movie

in·flow /ˈɪnˌfloʊ/ *noun, pl* **-flows :** a flow or movement of something into a place, organization, etc. [*count*] The campaign has seen a massive *inflow* of funds/money/cash in recent months. [*noncount*] The vents provide improved *inflow* of air/water. — opposite OUTFLOW

¹in·flu·ence /ˈɪnˌfluːwəns/ *noun, pl* **-enc·es**

1 : the power to change or affect someone or something

: the power to cause changes without directly forcing them to happen [*noncount*] Recent years have seen a decline in the company's *influence* within the industry. • Her ideas have gradually gained *influence* in the company. • He used/wielded his *influence* to reform the company's policies. • She was ***under the influence*** of drugs. [=she was affected by drugs] • He came *under the influence* of new ideas [=he was influenced by new ideas] when he went away to college. • She has remained *under the influence* of her parents. — often + *on, upon,* or *over* • She claims that her personal problems played/had no/little *influence upon* her decision to resign. • His health problems may have had some *influence on* his decision. • Her parents still have a great deal of *influence over* her. • The chairman wields considerable *influence over* the board's decisions. [*singular*] Her parents are concerned that her new friends may have a bad *influence on* her. • Emily Dickinson has had a major *influence on* his poetry. • His health problems had a big *influence on* his decision. • They exert a strong cultural/economic *influence over* their neighbors in the region.

2 [*count*] : a person or thing that affects someone or something in an important way • My parents have been major *influences* in my life. • Emily Dickinson has been a major *influence* on his poetry. • Her parents are concerned that her new friends may be a bad *influence* on her. • The decision was affected by outside *influences*.

under the influence : affected by alcohol : DRUNK • He was arrested for driving *under the influence*.

²influence *verb* **-ences; -enced; -enc•ing** [+ *obj*] : to affect or change (someone or something) in an indirect but usually important way : to have an influence on (someone or something) • I was deeply/greatly *influenced* by my parents. • She claims that her decision to resign was not *influenced* by her personal problems. • No one knows how this decision will *influence* the outcome of the election. • He's accused of illegally attempting to *influence* the jury. — sometimes followed by *to + verb* • No one knows what may have *influenced* them *to commit* these crimes.

in•flu•en•tial /ˌɪnfluˈɛnʃəl/ *adj* [*more* ~; *most* ~] : having the power to cause changes : having influence • She became an (enormously/extremely) *influential* critic/writer. • a highly/very *influential* book • His theories have become more *influential* in recent years. • My parents have been the most *influential* people in my life. — sometimes + *in* • She has been *influential in* establishing programs to help the poor.

— **in•flu•en•tial•ly** /ˌɪnfluˈɛnʃəli/ *adv*

in•flu•en•za /ˌɪnfluˈɛnzə/ *noun* [*noncount*] *medical* : a common illness that is caused by a virus and that causes fever, weakness, severe aches and pains, and breathing problems • patients suffering from *influenza* [=*the flu*]

in•flux /ˈɪnˌflʌks/ *noun, pl* **-flux•es** [*count*]

1 : the arrival of a large number of people • The city is preparing for a large *influx* of tourists this summer.

2 : the arrival or inward flow of a large amount of something (such as money) • The company has had a sudden *influx* of capital.

in•fo /ˈɪnfoʊ/ *noun* [*noncount*] *informal* : INFORMATION • It contains a surprising amount of *info* for such a little book.

in•fo•mer•cial /ˈɪnfoʊˌmɚʃəl/ *noun, pl* **-cials** [*count*] *chiefly US* : a television program that is a long advertisement and that usually includes people talking about and using the product that is being sold

in•form /ɪnˈfoɚm/ *verb* **-forms; -formed; -form•ing**

1 : to give information to (someone) [+ *obj*] The book will entertain and *inform* you. • The arresting officer failed to *inform* the suspect of his rights. • He failed to *inform* the suspect that he had the right to remain silent. • We haven't yet been *informed* of/about her decision. • Frequent reports from the battlefield kept the general *informed* about how the attack was progressing. • I am sorry to have to *inform* [=*tell*] you that your flight has been delayed. [*no obj*] The book will both entertain and *inform*.

2 [+ *obj*] *formal* : to be or provide the essential quality of (something) : to be very noticeable in (something) • His Catholic upbringing *informs* all his writing.

inform on *also* ***inform against*** [*phrasal verb*] ***inform on/against (someone)*** : to give information about the secret or criminal activity of (someone) to the police • Despite pressure from the police he refused to *inform on* the other conspirators.

in•for•mal /ɪnˈfoɚməl/ *adj* [*more* ~; *most* ~] : not formal: such as **a** : having a friendly and relaxed quality • an *informal* party • We had an *informal* meeting over lunch. • an *informal* conversation • an *informal* writing style • He has an *informal* manner that puts people at ease. **b** : suited for ordinary use when you are relaxing • *informal* clothes • an *informal* dining area **c** *of language* : relaxed in tone : not suited for serious or official speech and writing • He spoke to them in *informal* Spanish/English. • The term is common in *informal* contexts. • *informal* language/speech/writing • an *informal* word **d** : done in a way that is not especially careful or scientific • He took an *informal* poll/survey among his coworkers.

— **in•for•mal•i•ty** /ˌɪnˌfoɚˈmæləti/ *noun* [*noncount*] • She liked the easy/casual *informality* of his manner. — **in•for•mal•ly** /ɪnˈfoɚməli/ *adv* • We met to discuss the situation *informally*. • speak/write *informally* • The word is used *informally* in this sense. • She was *informally* dressed in blue jeans.

in•for•mant /ɪnˈfoɚmənt/ *noun, pl* **-mants** [*count*]

1 : a person who gives information to the police about secret or criminal activities : INFORMER • The police were alerted to the plot by a paid *informant*.

2 *technical* : a person who gives information about his or her culture or language to a researcher • We learned the language with the help of a native *informant*.

in•for•ma•tion /ˌɪnfɚˈmeɪʃən/ *noun* [*noncount*]

1 : knowledge that you get about someone or something : facts or details about a subject • They're working to collect/gather *information* about the early settlers in the region. • The pamphlet provides a lot of *information* on/about/concerning recent changes to the tax laws. • detailed/specific *information* • He gave the police false/misleading *information* about his background. • The conference will give us an opportunity to exchange/share *information* with other researchers. • We can't make a decision until we have more/further/additional *information*. • The tests have not yet uncovered any new *information*. • I don't like having to reveal personal/private *information* when I fill in a job application. • He's accused of withholding useful/valuable/vital *information*. • ***My information is*** [=I have been told, I understand] that he will be arriving early this evening. • We enclose a price list ***for your information***. [=to provide you with information that we think will interest you] ✧ The phrase *for your information* is sometimes used informally in speech when responding to an annoying statement or question by someone who has accused or blamed you wrongly. • "Are these the best tickets you could get?" "*For your information*, I had to stand in line for two hours to get these!"

2 *US* : a service that telephone users can call to find out the telephone number for a specified person or organization : DIRECTORY ASSISTANCE • I couldn't remember his number so I had to call *information*.

— **in•for•ma•tion•al** /ˌɪnfɚˈmeɪʃənl̩/ *adj* • an *informational* brochure • *informational* books

information superhighway *noun*

the information superhighway : the Internet • He claims he can find out anything he needs to know on *the information superhighway*.

in•for•ma•tive /ɪnˈfoɚmətɪv/ *adj* [*more* ~; *most* ~] : providing information • a highly/very/most *informative* book

in•formed /ɪnˈfoɚmd/ *adj*

1 : having information • *Informed* sources told us of the new policy. • fully *informed* citizens/consumers/voters • Please keep me *informed* on any changes. [=please tell me about any changes when they happen]

2 : based on information • We need to spend more time researching our options so that we can make an *informed* choice/decision. — see also *informed guess* at ²GUESS

informed consent *noun* [*singular*] *medical* : a formal agreement that a patient signs to give permission for a medical procedure (such as surgery) after having been told about the risks, benefits, etc.

in•form•er /ɪnˈfoɚmɚ/ *noun, pl* **-ers** [*count*] : a person who gives information to the police about secret or criminal activities • He worked for the police/government as a paid *informer*. [=*informant*]

in•fo•tain•ment /ˌɪnfoʊˈteɪnmənt/ *noun* [*noncount*] : television programs that present information (such as news) in a way that is meant to be entertaining

in•frac•tion /ɪnˈfrækʃən/ *noun, pl* **-tions** [*count*] *formal* : an act that breaks a rule or law : VIOLATION • He was penalized for an *infraction* of the rules. = He was penalized for a rules *infraction*. • a minor ***traffic infraction***

in•fra dig /ˈɪnfrəˈdɪg/ *adj, chiefly Brit* : not appropriate for a person's social position : beneath someone's dignity ▪ Isn't it a bit *infra dig* to go to a launderette when you can afford a washing machine of your own?

in•fra•red /ˌɪnfrəˈrɛd/ *adj, technical* : producing or using rays of light that cannot be seen and that are longer than rays that produce red light ▪ *infrared* radiation/beams ▪ *infrared* photography

in•fra•struc•ture /ˈɪnfrəˌstrʌktʃɚ/ *noun, pl* **-tures** : the basic equipment and structures (such as roads and bridges) that are needed for a country, region, or organization to function properly [*noncount*] More money is needed to save the crumbling *infrastructure* of the nation's rural areas. ▪ We need to spend more money on maintaining and repairing *infrastructure*. [*count*] town/city *infrastructures*

– **in•fra•struc•tur•al** /ˈɪnfrəˌstrʌktʃərəl/ *adj* ▪ *infrastructural* maintenance and repair

in•fre•quent /ɪnˈfri:kwənt/ *adj* [*more ~; most ~*] : not happening often : not frequent ▪ an *infrequent* event ▪ We made *infrequent* stops/visits along the way. ▪ Problems with the network have become a ***not infrequent*** occurrence. [=have become a rather frequent occurrence]

– **infrequency** *noun* [*noncount*] ▪ She complained about the *infrequency* of her son's visits. [=she complained because her son did not visit her often] – **in•fre•quent•ly** *adv* ▪ a word that is *infrequently* used ▪ an error ***not infrequently*** made [=an error rather frequently made] by beginners

in•fringe /ɪnˈfrɪnʤ/ *verb* **-fring•es; -fringed; -fring•ing**

1 : to do something that does not obey or follow (a rule, law, etc.) [*+ obj*] *infringe* [=*violate*] a treaty/patent ▪ They claim that his use of the name *infringes* their copyright. [*no obj*] (*chiefly US*) — *+ on* or *upon* ▪ They claim that his use of the name *infringes on* their copyright.

2 : to wrongly limit or restrict (something, such as another person's rights) [*+ obj*] Her rights must not be *infringed*. [*no obj*] — *+ on* or *upon* ▪ He argues that the proposed law *infringes upon* our guaranteed right of free speech.

– **in•fringe•ment** /ɪnˈfrɪnʤmənt/ *noun, pl* **-ments** [*count*] repeated *infringements* of our rights [*noncount*] He faces charges of copyright *infringement*. – **in•fring•er** *noun, pl* **-ers** [*count*] ▪ a copyright *infringer*

in•fu•ri•ate /ɪnˈfjɚriˌeɪt/ *verb* **-ates; -at•ed; -at•ing** [*+ obj*] : to make (someone) very angry : to make (someone) furious ▪ His arrogance *infuriates* me! = It *infuriates* me that he is so arrogant! ▪ I was *infuriated* by his arrogance.

– **infuriated** *adj* [*more ~; most ~*] ▪ The sales clerk was being shouted at by an *infuriated* customer. – **infuriating** *adj* [*more ~; most ~*] ▪ He has an *infuriating* habit of ignoring me. – **in•fu•ri•at•ing•ly** /ɪnˈfjɚriˌeɪtɪŋli/ *adv* ▪ an *infuriatingly* arrogant man

in•fuse /ɪnˈfju:z/ *verb* **-fus•es; -fused; -fus•ing**

1 [*+ obj*] **a** : to cause (a person or thing) to be filled with something (such as a quality) ▪ She has *infused* her followers with confidence. **b** : to cause (something, such as a quality) to be added or introduced into a person or thing ▪ He has found ways to *infuse* new energy into his performances. ▪ She has *infused* confidence into her followers. ▪ His work is *infused* with anger.

2 : to allow something (such as tea or herbs) to stay in a liquid (such as hot water) in order to flavor the liquid [*no obj*] The tea should be allowed to *infuse* for several minutes. [*+ obj*] You should *infuse* the tea for several minutes.

in•fu•sion /ɪnˈfju:ʒən/ *noun, pl* **-sions**

1 [*count*] : the addition of something (such as money) that is needed or helpful ▪ The company has received an *infusion* of cash/capital/funds. = There has been an *infusion* of cash/capital/funds into the company. ▪ Her ideas have brought a new *infusion* of vitality to the organization.

2 a [*count*] : a drink made by allowing something (such as tea) to stay in a liquid (such as hot water) : a drink made by infusing something ▪ a strong *infusion* of tea ▪ herbal *infusions* **b** [*noncount*] : the act of infusing something ▪ a medicinal drink made by *infusion* of herbs

¹-ing /ɪŋ, ɪn/ *verb suffix or adj suffix* — used to form the present participle of a verb ▪ sail*ing* ▪ go*ing*

²-ing *noun suffix*

1 : action or process ▪ runn*ing* ▪ sleep*ing* ▪ meet*ing* ▪ draw*ing* ▪ wash*ing*

2 : product or result of an action or process ▪ a paint*ing* ▪ an engrav*ing*

3 : something used in or connected with making or doing (a specified thing) ▪ bedd*ing* ▪ roof*ing* ▪ scaffold*ing*

in•ge•nious /ɪnˈʤi:njəs/ *adj* [*more ~; most ~*] : very smart or clever : having or showing ingenuity ▪ The book has an *ingenious* plot. ▪ an *ingenious* device/plan/solution ▪ an *ingenious* person ▪ She was *ingenious* at finding ways to work more quickly. ▪ It was *ingenious* of him to arrange the schedule so precisely.

– **in•ge•nious•ly** *adv* ▪ an *ingeniously* clever design/solution

in•ge•nue (*US*) *or* **in•gé•nue** /ˈænʤəˌnu:, ˈɑ:nʤəˌnu:, *Brit* ˈænʒəˌnju:/ *noun, pl* **-nues** [*count*] : an innocent girl or young woman ▪ In her latest film she plays the part of an *ingenue*.

in•ge•nu•ity /ˌɪnʤəˈnu:wəti, *Brit* ˌɪnʤəˈnju:wəti/ *noun, pl* **-ities**

1 [*noncount*] : skill or cleverness that allows someone to solve problems, invent things, etc. ▪ She showed amazing *ingenuity* in finding ways to cut costs. ▪ It will take considerable/much/some *ingenuity* to fix these problems.

2 [*count*] : a clever device or method ▪ musical *ingenuities*

in•gen•u•ous /ɪnˈʤɛnjəwəs/ *adj* [*more ~; most ~*] : having or showing the innocence, trust, and honesty that young people often have ▪ an appealingly *ingenuous* young woman/man ▪ an *ingenuous* smile/response — compare DISINGENUOUS

– **in•gen•u•ous•ly** *adv* ▪ smiling *ingenuously* – **in•gen•u•ous•ness** *noun* [*noncount*]

in•gest /ɪnˈʤɛst/ *verb* **-gests; -gest•ed; -gest•ing** [*+ obj*] : to take (something, such as food) into your body : to swallow (something) ▪ The drug is more easily *ingested* in pill form. — sometimes used figuratively ▪ She *ingested* [=*absorbed*] large amounts of information very quickly.

– **in•ges•tion** /ɪnˈʤɛstʃən/ *noun* [*noncount*] ▪ the *ingestion* of food/alcohol

in•gle•nook /ˈɪŋgəlˌnʊk/ *noun, pl* **-nooks** [*count*] *chiefly Brit* : a space with a seat by the side of a large open fireplace

in•glo•ri•ous /ɪnˈglorijəs/ *adj* [*more ~; most ~*] *literary* : causing shame or disgrace ▪ an *inglorious* [=*disgraceful*] defeat/failure ▪ His command came to an *inglorious* [=*shameful*] end when he surrendered the fort.

– **in•glo•ri•ous•ly** *adv* ▪ His command ended *ingloriously*.

in•got /ˈɪŋgət/ *noun, pl* **-gots** [*count*] : a solid piece of metal that has been formed into a particular shape (such as a brick) so that it is easy to handle or store ▪ gold *ingots*

in•grained /ˈɪnˌgreɪnd/ *adj* [*more ~; most ~*] : existing for a long time and very difficult to change : firmly established ▪ an *ingrained* habit/tradition ▪ These attitudes are very deeply *ingrained* in the culture.

in•grate /ˈɪnˌgreɪt/ *noun, pl* **-grates** [*count*] *formal* : a person who does not show proper appreciation or thanks for something : an ungrateful person ▪ a spoiled *ingrate*

in•gra•ti•ate /ɪnˈgreɪʃiˌeɪt/ *verb* **-ates; -at•ed; -at•ing** [*+ obj*] *often disapproving* : to gain favor or approval for (yourself) by doing or saying things that people like — usually *+ with* ▪ She has tried to *ingratiate* herself *with* voters by promising a tax cut.

ingratiating *adj* [*more ~; most ~*] *often disapproving* : intended to gain someone's favor or approval ▪ an *ingratiating* smile/manner

– **in•gra•ti•at•ing•ly** *adv* ▪ smiling *ingratiatingly*

in•grat•i•tude /ɪnˈgrætəˌtu:d, *Brit* ɪnˈgrætəˌtju:d/ *noun* [*noncount*] : lack of proper appreciation or thanks for something (such as a kind or helpful act) : lack of gratitude ▪ He was hurt by his friends' *ingratitude*. [=*ungratefulness*] ▪ an act of *ingratitude*

in•gre•di•ent /ɪnˈgri:dijənt/ *noun, pl* **-ents** [*count*]

1 : one of the things that are used to make a food, product, etc. ▪ He uses only the finest/freshest *ingredients* in his cooking. ▪ the *ingredients* of a salad ▪ the *ingredients* in/of the soap

2 : a quality or characteristic that makes something possible ▪ Honesty is an essential *ingredient* of/for a successful marriage. ▪ The show has all the *ingredients* needed to attract a large audience.

in•gress /ˈɪnˌgrɛs/ *noun* [*noncount*] *formal* : a way to enter a place or the act of entering a place : ENTRANCE ▪ *Ingress* to and egress from the freeway were made difficult by the construction. — compare EGRESS

in•ground /ˈɪnˌgraʊnd/ *adj, always used before a noun, US* : located in the ground : not built above the ground ▪ an *inground* swimming pool — compare ABOVEGROUND, UNDERGROUND

in–group /ˈɪnˌgru:p/ *noun, pl* **-groups** [*count*] *usually disapproving* : a small group of people who share a particular interest or activity and who do not allow other people to join their group

in·grow·ing /ˈɪnˌgrowɪŋ/ *adj, always used before a noun, Brit* : INGROWN • an *ingrowing* toenail

in·grown /ˈɪnˌgroʊn/ *adj* : having a tip or edge that has grown back into the flesh • an *ingrown* toenail/hair

in·hab·it /ɪnˈhæbət/ *verb* **-its; -it·ed; -it·ing** [+ *obj*]
1 : to live in (a place) : to have a home in (a place) • Several hundred species of birds *inhabit* the island. • This part of the country is *inhabited* by native tribes. • The island is no longer *inhabited*. [=no people live there]
2 : to be present in (something) • There is a romantic quality that *inhabits* all her paintings. • The novel is *inhabited* by a cast of eccentric characters.
– in·hab·it·able /ɪnˈhæbətəbəl/ *adj* • The house is in such poor condition that it's barely *inhabitable*.

in·hab·it·ant /ɪnˈhæbətənt/ *noun, pl* **-ants** [*count*] : a person or animal that lives in a particular place • The city has more than a million *inhabitants*. [=*residents*]

in·hal·ant /ɪnˈheɪlənt/ *noun, pl* **-ants** [*count*] *medical* : a medicine or illegal drug that is breathed into the lungs • The medicine is now available as an *inhalant*.

in·hale /ɪnˈheɪl/ *verb* **-hales; -haled; -hal·ing**
1 : to breathe in [+ *obj*] This medicine can now be *inhaled*. • She *inhaled* the fresh country air. [*no obj*] He *inhaled* deeply and exhaled slowly, trying to relax. — opposite EXHALE
2 [+ *obj*] *US, informal* : to eat or drink (something) very quickly • After *inhaling* their dinner, the children ran out the door without even saying goodbye.
– in·ha·la·tion /ˌɪnhəˈleɪʃən/ *noun, pl* **-tions** [*count, noncount*] • (an) *inhalation* of chemical fumes • Several survivors of the fire are suffering from ***smoke inhalation***. [=a serious injury caused by breathing a lot of smoke]

in·hal·er /ɪnˈheɪlɚ/ *noun, pl* **-ers** [*count*] *medical* : a device used for inhaling a medicine

in·here /ɪnˈhiɚ/ *verb* **-heres; -hered; -her·ing**
inhere in [*phrasal verb*] ***inhere in (someone or something)*** *formal* : to be a natural part of (someone or something) • He believes that liberty *inheres in* [=(more commonly) *is inherent in*] humanity as a natural right. • Does selfishness *inhere in* each of us?

in·her·ent /ɪnˈhirənt, ɪnˈherənt/ *adj, formal* : belonging to the basic nature of someone or something • He has an *inherent* sense of fair play. • She believes strongly in the *inherent* [=*fundamental, natural*] goodness of all people. — often + *in* • She believes that goodness is *inherent in* all people. • There are a number of problems *inherent in* the design/plan.
– in·her·ent·ly *adv* • Are people *inherently* good? • There is nothing *inherently* illegal about what he did.

in·her·it /ɪnˈherət/ *verb* **-its; -it·ed; -it·ing** [+ *obj*]
1 : to receive (money, property, etc.) from someone when that person dies • She *inherited* the family business from her father. — compare DISINHERIT
2 a *biology* : to have (a characteristic, disease, etc.) because of the genes that you get from your parents when you are born • Baldness is *inherited* from the mother's side of the family. • She *inherited* her father's deep blue eyes. **b** : to get (a personal quality, interest, etc.) because of the influence or example of your parents or other relatives • She *inherited* a love of baseball/cooking from her dad.
3 a : to receive (something) from someone who had it previously • When my brother left for college, I *inherited* his old computer. **b** : to have to deal with (a situation, problem, etc.) when you take a job or position that someone else had before you • The company's new president will *inherit* some complicated legal problems. • When the coach quit, her assistant *inherited* a last-place team.
– in·her·it·able /ɪnˈherətəbəl/ *adj* • an *inheritable* disease
– inherited *adj* • an *inherited* estate • *inherited* [=*hereditary*] titles • an *inherited* disease/disorder **– in·her·i·tor** /ɪnˈherətɚ/ *noun, pl* **-tors** [*count*] • *inheritors* of the estate • The new coach is an *inheritor* of a great team legacy. • *inheritors* of a longtime family tradition

in·her·i·tance /ɪnˈherətəns/ *noun, pl* **-tanc·es**
1 [*count*] : money, property, etc., that is received from someone when that person dies • She began her own business with the *inheritance* she got from her grandfather. • He left sizable *inheritances* to his children. • an ***inheritance tax*** [=a tax on inherited property or money]
2 [*singular*] : something from the past that is still important or valuable • The buildings are part of the city's architectural *inheritance*. • our cultural *inheritance*
3 [*noncount*] : the act of inheriting something • the *inheritance* of an estate • the *inheritance* of a genetic trait

in·hib·it /ɪnˈhɪbət/ *verb* **-its; -it·ed; -it·ing** [+ *obj*]
1 : to keep (someone) from doing what he or she wants to do • You shouldn't allow fear of failure to *inhibit* you. • He was *inhibited* by modesty. • Fear can *inhibit* people from expressing their opinions.
2 : to prevent or slow down the activity or occurrence of (something) • drugs that are used to *inhibit* infection • Strict laws are *inhibiting* economic growth.
– in·hib·i·tor /ɪnˈhɪbətɚ/ *noun, pl* **-tors** [*count*] • a powerful *inhibitor* of infection • a growth *inhibitor*

inhibited *adj* [*more* ~; *most* ~] : unable to express thoughts and feelings freely • She wanted to feel less *inhibited*. • a shy, *inhibited* child — opposite UNINHIBITED

in·hi·bi·tion /ˌɪnhəˈbɪʃən/ *noun, pl* **-tions**
1 : a nervous feeling that prevents you from expressing your thoughts, emotions, or desires [*count*] — usually plural • After a few drinks, he lost his *inhibitions*. • a release/relaxation of *inhibitions* • She seems to have no *inhibitions* about stating her opinion. [*noncount*] She laughed loudly and without *inhibition*. • a loss of *inhibition*
2 [*noncount*] *technical* : the act of preventing or slowing the activity or occurrence of something • *inhibition* of muscle growth

in·hos·pi·ta·ble /ˌɪnhɑˈspɪtəbəl, ɪnˈhɑ:spɪtəbəl/ *adj* [*more* ~; *most* ~] : not hospitable: such as **a** : not generous and friendly to guests or visitors • It's very *inhospitable* of him to be so rude to strangers. — often + *to* • He was *inhospitable to* his guests. **b** : having an environment where plants, animals, or people cannot live or grow easily • an *inhospitable* [=*barren*] desert/habitat — often + *to* • soil *inhospitable to* plant growth **c** : not ready or willing to accept or consider something — usually + *to* • a person/company known for being *inhospitable* [=*closed*] *to* new ideas

in–house /ˈɪnˌhaʊs/ *adj, usually used before a noun* : created, done, or existing within a company or organization • *in-house* testing • an *in-house* investigation/adviser
– in–house *adv* • All the testing was done *in-house*.

in·hu·man /ɪnˈhju:mən/ *adj* [*more* ~; *most* ~]
1 a : very fierce or cruel • *inhuman* [=*savage*] punishment • a brutally *inhuman* tyrant • the most *inhuman* deeds/crimes **b** : having or showing no interest in individual people or their feelings : lacking emotional warmth • an *inhuman* [=*impersonal*] bureaucracy
2 : not good enough for people to use or live in : extremely poor, dirty, or unhealthy • *inhuman* living conditions
3 : unlike what might be expected from a human being • He let out an *inhuman* moan. • She had an almost *inhuman* desire to succeed. — compare NONHUMAN, SUBHUMAN
– in·hu·man·ly *adv* • an *inhumanly* cruel punishment

in·hu·mane /ˌɪnhju:ˈmeɪn/ *adj* [*more* ~; *most* ~] : not kind or gentle to people or animals : not humane • the *inhumane* [=*cruel*] treatment of prisoners
– in·hu·mane·ly *adv* • treating the animals *inhumanely*

in·hu·man·i·ty /ˌɪnhju:ˈmænəti/ *noun* [*noncount*] : the quality or state of being cruel to other people or to animals • She cannot understand man's *inhumanity* to man. [=she cannot understand why people treat each other in a cruel way] • the *inhumanity* [=*brutality*] of war

in·im·i·cal /ɪˈnɪmɪkəl/ *adj* [*more* ~; *most* ~] *formal*
1 : likely to cause damage or have a bad effect : HARMFUL — usually + *to* • habits *inimical to* health • Dry conditions can be *inimical to* plant life.
2 : not friendly • the judge's *inimical* glare

in·im·i·ta·ble /ɪˈnɪmətəbəl/ *adj* : impossible to copy or imitate • She delivered the speech in her own *inimitable* [=*unique*] style.

in·iq·ui·tous /ɪˈnɪkwətəs/ *adj* [*more* ~; *most* ~] *formal* : very unfair or evil • an *iniquitous* deed/war

in·iq·ui·ty /ɪˈnɪkwəti/ *noun, pl* **-ties** *formal*
1 [*noncount*] : the quality of being unfair or evil • a system plagued by corruption and *iniquity* [=*injustice*] • a notorious ***den of iniquity*** [=a place where immoral things are done]
2 [*count*] : something that is unfair or evil • the *iniquities* of slavery

Do not confuse *iniquity* with *inequity*.

[1]**ini·tial** /ɪˈnɪʃəl/ *adj, always used before a noun* : occurring at the beginning of something • The symptoms are mild in the

initial [=*early*] stages of the disease. • Her *initial* [=*first*] reaction was to say no, but she eventually agreed to help.

– ini·tial·ly /ɪˈnɪʃəli/ *adv* • The reason I *initially* [=*originally*] came here was to find work. • It turned out that the situation was not as serious as we had *initially* believed. • *Initially* [=*at first*], the symptoms are mild.

²initial *noun, pl* **-tials**

1 [*count*] **: a first letter of a name** • President Franklin D. Roosevelt's middle *initial* stood for "Delano."

2 ***initials*** [*plural*] **: the first letters of each of a person's names** • She put her *initials* on each page of the contract. • The *initials* F.D.R. stood for "Franklin Delano Roosevelt."

³initial *verb* **-tials**; *US* **-tialed** *or Brit* **-tialled**; *US* **-tial·ing** *or Brit* **-tial·ling** [+ *obj*] **: to mark (something) with your initials** • She *initialed* each page of the contract.

initial public offering *noun, pl* **~ -ings** [*count*] **: the first sale of a company's stock to the public : IPO**

¹ini·ti·ate /ɪˈnɪʃiˌeɪt/ *verb* **-ates; -at·ed; -at·ing** [+ *obj*]

1 *formal* **: to cause the beginning of (something) : to start or begin (something)** • *initiate* a new project • Doctors have *initiated* a series of tests to determine the cause of the problem. • The company *initiated* judicial proceedings against them.

2 : to formally accept (someone) as a member of a group or organization usually in a special ceremony • The new recruits will be *initiated* tomorrow night. • He was *initiated* into a secret society.

3 : to teach (someone) the basic facts or ideas about something — usually + *into* • They *initiated* her *into* the ways of the corporate world.

– ini·ti·a·tor /ɪˈnɪʃiˌeɪtɚ/ *noun, pl* **-tors** [*count*] • the *initiator* of the project

²ini·tiate /ɪˈnɪʃijət/ *noun, pl* **-tiates** [*count*] **: a person who is being formally accepted or who has been formally accepted as a member of a group or organization** • These secrets are known only to a small group of *initiates*.

ini·ti·a·tion /ɪˌnɪʃiˈeɪʃən/ *noun, pl* **-tions**

1 a [*noncount*] **: the process of being formally accepted as a member of a group or organization : the process of being initiated** • his *initiation* as a member of the club — often + *into* • her *initiation into* the sorority **b** [*count*] **: a ceremony or series of actions that makes a person a member of a group or organization** • crimes committed as part of gang *initiations* • an *initiation* rite/ritual

2 [*noncount*] **: the act of starting something : the beginning of something** • the *initiation* of therapy • the *initiation* of judicial proceedings

ini·tia·tive /ɪˈnɪʃətɪv/ *noun, pl* **-tives**

1 ***the initiative*** **: the power or opportunity to do something before others do** • If you want to meet her, you're going to have to ***take the initiative*** and introduce yourself. • The company has the opportunity to ***seize the initiative*** by getting its new products to the market before its competitors. • By failing to get its products to the market on schedule, the company has ***lost the initiative*** (to its competitors).

2 [*noncount*] **: the energy and desire that is needed to do something** • She has ability but lacks *initiative*. [=*drive*] ◇ If you do something ***on your own initiative***, you do it because you choose to, not because someone has told you to do it. • I'm doing this *on my own initiative*. [=because I want to] ◇ If you ***use your (own) initiative***, you decide for yourself what to do instead of waiting to be told by someone else. • You should *use your own initiative* to come up with a solution.

3 [*count*] **: a plan or program that is intended to solve a problem** • The governor has proposed a new *initiative* to improve conditions in urban schools. • anti-poverty *initiatives*

in·ject /ɪnˈʤɛkt/ *verb* **-jects; -ject·ed; -ject·ing** [+ *obj*]

1 a : to force a liquid medicine or drug into someone or something by using a special needle — often + *into* • The medicine is *injected* directly *into* the muscle. — often + *with* • The patients were *injected with* the vaccine. **b : to force (a liquid) into something** — usually + *into* • *inject* fuel *into* an engine — sometimes used in combination • a fuel-*injected* engine

2 a : to add (something) to something : to introduce (a particular quality) ***into*** **something** • She told a few jokes to *inject* a little humor *into* her speech. • We need to *inject* some life *into* this party. **b : to provide or add (something needed, such as money)** — + *into* • Several wealthy investors have *injected* money *into* the project.

– in·jec·tor /ɪnˈʤɛktɚ/ *noun, pl* **-tors** [*count*] • a fuel *injector*

in·jec·tion /ɪnˈʤɛkʃən/ *noun, pl* **-tions**

1 : the act or process of forcing a liquid medicine or drug into someone or something by using a special needle [*noncount*] The medicine cannot be taken orally; it must be given/administered ***by injection***. [*count*] Nurses give the *injections*. • an *injection* of a painkiller

2 : the act or process of forcing a liquid into something [*noncount*] an engine with ***fuel injection*** [=a system that injects fuel directly into the cylinders of an engine] [*count*] *injections* of fuel

3 [*count*] **: the addition of something (such as money) that is needed to support something** • The struggling company needed an *injection* of cash.

in–joke /ˈɪnˌʤoʊk/ *noun, pl* **-jokes** [*count*] **: a joke that is only understood by a particular group of people**

in·ju·di·cious /ˌɪnʤuˈdɪʃəs/ *adj* [*more* ~; *most* ~] *formal* **: not having or showing good judgment : not sensible or judicious** • an *injudicious* [=*unwise*] lawsuit • He made several *injudicious* comments to the press.

– in·ju·di·cious·ly *adv*

in·junc·tion /ɪnˈʤʌŋkʃən/ *noun, pl* **-tions** [*count*] *law* **: an order from a court of law that says something must be done or must not be done** • The group has obtained an *injunction* to prevent the demolition of the building. — often + *against* • The court has issued/granted an *injunction against* the strike.

in·jure /ˈɪnʤɚ/ *verb* **-jures; -jured; -jur·ing** [+ *obj*] **: to harm or damage (someone or something)** • She fell and *injured* herself. • She fell and slightly *injured* her arm. • The criticism *injured* [=*wounded*] his pride. • The scandal has *injured* [=*tarnished*] her reputation. • Several people were badly/seriously/critically *injured* in the accident. • He believes that the tax will *injure* [=*hurt*] small businesses.

> ***synonyms*** INJURE, HURT, HARM, DAMAGE, and IMPAIR mean to cause something or someone to no longer be healthy or in good condition. INJURE is usually used when the body of a person or animal has been harmed by something, such as an accident. • Two people were badly *injured* in the accident. • She *injured* her muscle/leg while running. HURT and HARM are both often used to mean the same thing as INJURE, but HURT often emphasizes physical or emotional pain. • He *hurt* his back and was unable to walk for a week. • I was *hurt* by their unkind remarks. HARM often emphasizes a bad change in health. • The plant is poisonous to humans but will not *harm* deer. DAMAGE is often used when something loses value or becomes less useful. • The table was *damaged* in shipping. • fruit trees *damaged* by frost • Very loud music may *damage* your ears. IMPAIR suggests that something has been made weaker or worse. • a disease that *impairs* memory/vision • Years of smoking had *impaired* his health.

injured *adj*

1 [*more* ~; *most* ~] **: suffering from an injury : physically hurt or harmed** • An ambulance took the *injured* boy to the hospital. • Her severely/badly *injured* arm took a long time to heal. • One of the players is *injured*.

2 *always used before a noun* **a** *law* **: having been treated unfairly** • A lawsuit is being filed on behalf of the *injured* party/person. **b : showing a feeling that you have been treated unfairly or insulted in some way** • He gave her an *injured* look.

the injured **: injured people** • *The injured* were treated at a nearby hospital.

in·ju·ri·ous /ɪnˈʤurijəs/ *adj* [*more* ~; *most* ~] *formal* **: causing injury : HARMFUL** • *injurious* behavior • The decision has had an *injurious* effect. — often + *to* • behavior *injurious to* others

– in·ju·ri·ous·ly *adv* • They have been *injuriously* affected by the decision.

in·ju·ry /ˈɪnʤəri/ *noun, pl* **-ries : harm or damage : an act or event that causes someone or something to no longer be fully healthy or in good condition** [*noncount*] Hikers need to take sensible precautions to prevent *injury*. • She's concerned about the risk of *injury* to her reputation. • The team has been weakened by illness and *injury*. • Careless use of these tools can cause serious bodily *injury*. • She survived the accident without *injury*. • an athlete who is ***injury-prone*** [=an athlete who is frequently injured] [*count*] She fell and suffered an *injury* to her arm. • His athletic career has been slowed by *injuries*. • minor/serious/severe *injuries*

add insult to injury see ²INSULT

do yourself an injury *chiefly Brit* **: to hurt yourself : to become injured because of your own actions** • If you keep on lifting those heavy weights, you'll *do yourself an injury*.

injury time *noun [noncount] Brit* : time that is added at the end of a game of hockey, soccer, etc., because of time lost when players are injured

in•jus•tice /ɪnˈʤʌstəs/ *noun, pl* **-tic•es** : unfair treatment : a situation in which the rights of a person or a group of people are ignored *[noncount]* The organization is devoted to fighting economic/racial/social *injustice*. ▪ protection against *injustice* *[count]* the *injustices* of apartheid ▪ The law is part of an effort to correct an old *injustice*. ▪ He suffered a great/terrible *injustice* [=*wrong*] at their hands.

do (someone or something) an injustice : to treat (someone or something) in an unfair way ▪ They *did her a* great/terrible/grave *injustice* by not allowing her to file a complaint. ▪ I think you *do the book an injustice* when you call it "trash." ▪ The weak punishment ***does an injustice to*** the criminal's victims.

[1]**ink** /ˈɪŋk/ *noun, pl* **inks**

1 : colored liquid that is used for writing or printing *[noncount]* Fill out the form using blue or black *ink*. ▪ The printer is out of *ink*. ▪ pen and *ink* drawings/sketches *[count]* We're using four different *inks* for this poster.

2 *[noncount] US slang* : public attention : PUBLICITY ▪ Her exploits have been getting a lot of *ink* lately. [=there have been many newspaper stories about her exploits lately]

3 *[noncount] biology* : the black liquid that is used by some sea creatures for protection ▪ squid *ink*

— see also RED INK

[2]**ink** *verb* **inks; inked; ink•ing** *[+ obj]*

1 : to put ink on (something) ▪ *ink* the printing block

2 *US, informal* **a** : to sign (a document) to show that you accept or agree with what is written on it ▪ They just *inked* a new partnership agreement/deal. **b** : to hire (someone) to do something by having that person sign a contract ▪ The team has *inked* [=*signed*] both players to a new contract.

ink in *[phrasal verb]* ***ink in (something) or ink (something) in*** : to write or draw (something) in ink ▪ She carefully *inked in* the letters.

in–kind /ˈɪnˈkaɪnd/ *adj, always used before a noun, US* : made up of something other than money ▪ The charity also accepts *in-kind* donations such as food or clothing.

ink–jet printer *noun, pl* **~ -ers** *[count] computers* : a printer that works by spraying small drops of ink onto paper — compare LASER PRINTER

in•kling /ˈɪŋklɪŋ/ *noun, pl* **-klings** *[count]* : a slight, uncertain idea about something : a slight amount of knowledge about something — usually singular ▪ I didn't have an *inkling* [=*clue*] of what it all meant. ▪ Nothing gave me any *inkling* that it would happen.

ink pad *noun, pl* **~ pads** *[count]* : a piece of soft material that is soaked with ink and used to get ink onto a rubber stamp

ink•well /ˈɪŋkˌwɛl/ *noun, pl* **-wells** *[count]* : a small container in the surface of a desk that was used in the past for holding ink

inky /ˈɪŋki/ *adj*

1 *literary* : very dark or black like ink ▪ the *inky* blackness/darkness of the sea

2 : made dirty by ink ▪ *inky* hands

in•laid /ˈɪnˈleɪd/ *adj*

1 : set into the surface of something in a decorative pattern ▪ *inlaid* designs/marble

2 : decorated with an inlaid design ▪ an *inlaid* box/tabletop

[1]**in•land** /ˈɪnˌlænd/ *adv* : in, into, or toward the middle of a country : away from the coast ▪ They traveled *inland* from the sea. ▪ They live *inland* about three miles.

[2]**inland** *adj [more ~; most ~]* : of, relating to, or in the part of a country that is away from the coast or boundaries ▪ *inland* transportation routes ▪ an *inland* sea

Inland Revenue *noun*

the Inland Revenue : the department of the British government that is responsible for collecting taxes — compare INTERNAL REVENUE SERVICE

in–law /ˈɪnˌlɑː/ *noun, pl* **-laws** *[count]* : a person you are related to because of your marriage; *especially* : the father or mother of your husband or wife — usually plural ▪ She was nervous when she met her *in-laws* for the first time.

in–law apartment *noun, pl* **~ -ments** *[count] US* : a small apartment that is part of or next to a house and that is used especially as a place for an older relative to live — called also *(US) mother-in-law apartment, (Brit) granny flat*

[1]**in•lay** /ɪnˈleɪ/ *verb* **-lays; -laid** /ɪnˈleɪd/; **-lay•ing** *[+ obj]* : to set pieces of wood, metal, etc., into the surface of (something) for decoration — often + *with* ▪ The desk is *inlaid with* ivory. ▪ The carpenter *inlaid* the furniture *with* intricate designs.

[2]**in•lay** /ˈɪnˌleɪ/ *noun, pl* **-lays** : material that is set into the surface of something for decoration : inlaid material *[noncount]* decorative/marble *inlay* *[count]* The cabinet doors are decorated with *inlays*.

in•let /ˈɪnˌlɛt/ *noun, pl* **-lets** *[count]*

1 : a narrow area of water that goes into the land from a sea or lake ▪ The coast is dotted with tiny *inlets*.

2 : an opening through which air, gas, or liquid can enter something (such as a machine) ▪ a gas/air *inlet*

in–line skate *noun, pl* **~ skates** *[count]* : a shoe with wheels set in a straight line on the bottom that is used for skating ▪ a pair of *in-line skates* — see picture at SKATE

— **in–line skater** *noun, pl* **~ -ers** *[count]* — **in–line skating** *noun [noncount]*

in lo•co pa•ren•tis /ɪnˈloʊkoʊpəˈrɛntəs/ *adv, law, formal* : in the place of a parent ▪ Some feel that the university should act *in loco parentis*. [=should be responsible for the students in the same way parents are responsible for their children]

in•mate /ˈɪnˌmeɪt/ *noun, pl* **-mates** *[count]* : a person who is kept in a prison or mental hospital ▪ prison *inmates*

in me•mo•ri•am /ˌɪnməˈmorijəm/ *prep, formal* : in memory of (someone who has died) — used especially on the stone that marks a grave

in•most /ˈɪnˌmoʊst/ *adj, always used before a noun* : INNERMOST ▪ She revealed her *inmost* thoughts and feelings.

inn /ˈɪn/ *noun, pl* **inns** *[count]*

1 : a house usually in the country where people can eat and rent a room to sleep in ▪ We stayed at a cozy/charming little *inn* in the country. — often used in the names of hotels ▪ We stayed at the Lakeside *Inn*.

2 *chiefly Brit* : a pub ▪ an old country *inn*

in•nards /ˈɪnədz/ *noun [plural] informal*

1 : the internal organs of a person or an animal ▪ the chicken's edible *innards*

2 : the inside parts of something ▪ the robot's complicated *innards* ▪ tinkering with the car's *innards*

in•nate /ɪˈneɪt/ *adj*

1 : existing from the time a person or animal is born ▪ an *innate* ability/talent ▪ She has an *innate* sense of rhythm.

2 : existing as part of the basic nature of something ▪ the *innate* problems of wireless communication

— **in•nate•ly** *adv* ▪ *innately* curious

in•ner /ˈɪnɚ/ *adj, always used before a noun*

1 : located toward the inside of something : not on or at the edge or outside of something ▪ She led the guests to an *inner* room. ▪ the *inner* face of the arch ▪ the *inner* lining of the jacket — opposite OUTER

2 : not known to or seen by most people ▪ the poem's *inner* meaning ▪ He wanted to experience the ***inner workings*** of the political campaign. [=the parts of the campaign that are only known by the people who work on it]

3 a : of or relating to a person's mind or spirit ▪ *inner* peace/conflict ▪ his *inner* life/self ▪ listening to her *inner* voice ▪ a person's *inner* beauty **b** : existing as a part of a person's character ▪ He's trying to get in touch with his *inner* artist. [=the part of his character that is artistic]

inner circle *noun, pl* **~ -cles** *[count]* : a small group of people who lead a government or an organization or who are close to its leader — usually singular ▪ The President has an ***inner circle*** of advisers.

inner city *noun, pl* **~ cities** *[count]* : the central section of a large city where mostly poor people live ▪ The mayor is trying to attract new businesses to the *inner city*.

— **inner–city** *adj, always used before a noun* ▪ *inner-city* kids/neighborhoods/schools/crime

inner ear *noun, pl* **~ ears** *[count] biology* : the part of the ear that is located within your head and that controls hearing and balance — compare OUTER EAR

in•ner•most /ˈɪnɚˌmoʊst/ *adj*

1 *always used before a noun* : most private and personal ▪ She revealed her *innermost* feelings/secrets.

2 : closest to the center or inside of something ▪ Jupiter's *innermost* moon ▪ the *innermost* part of the cave — opposite OUTERMOST

inner sanc•tum *noun, pl* **~ -tums** *[count] somewhat formal* : a very private room or place ▪ She was admitted to the building's *inner sanctum*. — often used figuratively • the *inner sanctum* of the CIA

inner tube *noun, pl* ~ **tubes** [*count*] : a round tube that holds air inside a tire

in·ning /ˈɪnɪŋ/ *noun, pl* **-nings** [*count*] *baseball* : one of the usually nine parts of a game in which each team bats until three outs are made • She hit a double in the fourth *inning*. • He pitched three *innings*.

innings /ˈɪnɪŋz/ *noun, pl* **innings** [*count*] *cricket* : one of the parts of a game in which a team or player bats

had a good innings *Brit, informal* — used to say that someone who has died lived a long life • We're sad she's gone, but she *had a good innings*.

inn·keep·er /ˈɪnˌkiːpɚ/ *noun, pl* **-ers** [*count*] *old-fashioned* : a person who owns or manages an inn

in·no·cence /ˈɪnəsəns/ *noun* [*noncount*] : the state of being innocent: such as **a** : the state of being not guilty of a crime or other wrong act • The defendant maintained/protested his *innocence*. [=he said that he was not guilty] • He vows that he will prove his *innocence* in court. — opposite GUILT **b** : lack of experience with the world and with the bad things that happen in life • the trusting *innocence* of childhood • The age of *innocence* was over. **c** *somewhat formal* : lack of knowledge about something • Your *innocence* [=(more commonly) *ignorance*] of the rules is no excuse for such behavior. • I mentioned ***in all innocence*** what turned out to be a very painful topic for her. [=I mentioned the topic without knowing that it was so painful for her to talk about it]

in·no·cent /ˈɪnəsənt/ *adj* [*more* ~; *most* ~]

1 : not guilty of a crime or other wrong act • He says that he is *innocent* of the crime. • She was found *innocent* of all charges. • A person accused of a crime is considered *innocent* until proven guilty. • Someone told your secret, but it wasn't me. I'm *innocent*. — opposite GUILTY

2 *always used before a noun* : not deserving to be harmed • an *innocent* victim • *innocent* bystanders

3 : lacking experience with the world and the bad things that happen in life • an *innocent* child

4 : not intended to cause harm or trouble • an *innocent* question • I made an *innocent* mistake; I'm sorry. • *innocent* [=*harmless*] fun

5 *not used before a noun, somewhat formal* : having no knowledge *of* something • He was entirely *innocent of* what had happened. [=he did not know what had happened]

– innocent *noun, pl* **-cents** [*count*] • a war that caused the death of thousands of *innocents* [=innocent people] • She was an *innocent* when it came to romance. **– in·no·cent·ly** *adv* • I *innocently* mentioned what turned out to be a very painful topic. • She smiled *innocently*. • Everything started out *innocently* [=*harmlessly*] enough.

in·noc·u·ous /ɪˈnɑːkjəwəs/ *adj* [*more* ~; *most* ~]

1 : not likely to bother or offend anyone : INOFFENSIVE • He told a few *innocuous* jokes. • an *innocuous* question

2 : causing no injury : HARMLESS • an *innocuous* gas

– in·noc·u·ous·ly *adv* **– in·noc·u·ous·ness** *noun* [*noncount*]

in·no·vate /ˈɪnəˌveɪt/ *verb* **-vates; -vat·ed; -vat·ing** : to do something in a new way : to have new ideas about how something can be done [*no obj*] The company plans to continue *innovating* and experimenting. [+ *obj*] The company *innovated* a new operating system.

– in·no·va·tor /ˈɪnəˌveɪtɚ/ *noun, pl* **-tors** [*count*] • She is known as a great/brilliant/gifted *innovator* in her field.

in·no·va·tion /ˌɪnəˈveɪʃən/ *noun, pl* **-tions**

1 [*count*] : a new idea, device, or method • She is responsible for many *innovations* in her field. • the latest *innovation* in computer technology

2 [*noncount*] : the act or process of introducing new ideas, devices, or methods • Through technology and *innovation*, they found ways to get better results with less work. • the rapid pace of technological *innovation*

in·no·va·tive /ˈɪnəˌveɪtɪv/ *adj* [*more* ~; *most* ~]

1 : introducing or using new ideas or methods • an *innovative* approach/solution to the problem • an *innovative* design

2 : having new ideas about how something can be done • a creative and *innovative* young designer

– in·no·va·tive·ly *adv*

in·no·va·to·ry /ˈɪnəvəˌtori, *Brit* ˈɪnəˌveɪtri/ *adj* [*more* ~; *most* ~] *Brit* : INNOVATIVE

in·nu·en·do /ˌɪnjəˈwɛndoʊ/ *noun, pl* **-dos** *or* **-does** : a statement which indirectly suggests that someone has done something immoral, improper, etc. [*count*] His reputation has been damaged by *innuendos* about his drinking and gambling. [*noncount*] His reputation has been damaged by *innuendo*. • The movie relies on sexual *innuendo* for its humor.

Innuit *variant spelling of* INUIT

in·nu·mer·a·ble /ɪˈnuːmərəbəl, *Brit* ɪˈnjuːmərəbəl/ *adj* : too many to be counted : very many • the *innumerable* [=*countless*] stars in the sky • There are *innumerable* errors in the book.

in·nu·mer·ate /ɪˈnuːmərət, *Brit* ɪˈnjuːmərət/ *adj* : unable to understand and do basic mathematics • an *innumerate* person

– in·nu·mer·a·cy /ɪˈnuːmərəsi, *Brit* ɪˈnjuːmərəsi/ *noun* [*noncount*]

in·oc·u·late /ɪˈnɑːkjəˌleɪt/ *verb* **-lates; -lat·ed; -lat·ing** [+ *obj*] *medical* : to give (a person or animal) a weakened form of a disease in order to prevent infection by the disease — often + *against* • All the children have been *inoculated against* smallpox.

– in·oc·u·la·tion /ɪˌnɑːkjəˈleɪʃən/ *noun, pl* **-tions** [*count, noncount*]

in·of·fen·sive /ˌɪnəˈfɛnsɪv/ *adj* [*more* ~; *most* ~] : not likely to offend or bother anyone : not offensive • The priest was a mild-mannered *inoffensive* fellow.

– in·of·fen·sive·ly *adv* • an *inoffensively* mild wine **– in·of·fen·sive·ness** *noun* [*noncount*]

in·op·er·a·ble /ɪnˈɑːpərəbəl/ *adj*

1 *medical* : not able to be corrected or removed by surgery • an *inoperable* tumor • a patient with *inoperable* cancer

2 *formal* : not capable of being used • The device makes the car *inoperable* when a key is not used to start it.

in·op·er·a·tive /ɪnˈɑːpərətɪv/ *adj, formal*

1 : not capable of being used • The accident had rendered the vehicle *inoperative*.

2 : having no force or effect • With the new federal law in place, the state law has become *inoperative*.

in·op·por·tune /ɪnˌɑːpɚˈtuːn, *Brit* ɪnˈɒpəˌtjuːn/ *adj* [*more* ~; *most* ~]

1 : not suitable or right for a particular situation : INCONVENIENT • He always shows up at the most *inopportune* times.

2 : done or happening at the wrong time • an *inopportune* sale of stocks

– in·op·por·tune·ly *adv*

in·or·di·nate /ɪnˈoɚdṇət/ *adj* : going beyond what is usual, normal, or proper • I waited an *inordinate* amount of time. • They have had an *inordinate* number of problems with the schedule.

– in·or·di·nate·ly *adv* • We had to wait an *inordinately* long time.

in·or·gan·ic /ˌɪnoɚˈgænɪk/ *adj* : made from or containing material that does not come from plants or animals • *inorganic* fertilizer • producing energy from *inorganic* materials — opposite ORGANIC

– in·or·gan·i·cal·ly /ˌɪnoɚˈgænɪkli/ *adv*

inorganic chemistry *noun* [*noncount*] : a branch of chemistry concerned with substances that contain little or no carbon — compare ORGANIC CHEMISTRY

in·pa·tient /ˈɪnˌpeɪʃənt/ *noun, pl* **-tients** [*count*] *medical* : a patient who stays for one or more nights in a hospital for treatment — often used before another noun • *inpatient* surgery [=surgery performed on inpatients] • *inpatient* care/treatment — compare OUTPATIENT

¹in·put /ˈɪnˌpʊt/ *noun, pl* **-puts**

1 [*noncount*] : advice or opinions that help someone make a decision • I need your *input* on what to have for dinner. • She provided some valuable *input* at the start of the project.

2 *technical* **a** [*noncount*] : information that is put into a computer • The computer gets its *input* from a keyboard or mouse. • an *input* device **b** [*noncount*] : something (such as power or energy) that is put into a machine or system • electrical *input* **c** [*count*] : the place at which information, power, etc., enters a computer, machine, or system • This VCR has several audio/video *inputs*.

3 : the act or process of putting something in or into something else [*singular*] The job will require a considerable *input* of money. [*noncount*] The data is ready for *input* into/to a computer. — compare OUTPUT

²input *verb* **-puts; -put·ted** *or* **-put; -put·ting** [+ *obj*] : to enter (information) into a computer • She *inputted* the sales figures into the spreadsheet. — compare OUTPUT

in·quest /ˈɪnˌkwɛst/ *noun, pl* **-quests** [*count*] *law* : an official investigation to find the reason for something (such as a person's death) • a coroner's *inquest* • The court has ordered an *inquest* into his death/disappearance.

in·quire *or chiefly Brit* **en·quire** /ɪnˈkwajɚ/ *verb* **-quires; -quired; -quir·ing** *somewhat formal* **:** to ask for information [*no obj*] When I *inquired*, they told me she was not here. — usually + *about* ▪ I called to *inquire about* the schedule. ▪ He was *inquiring about* a friend who used to work here. [+ *obj*] We *inquired* the way to the station. ▪ "So, what do you want?" he *inquired*.

inquire after [*phrasal verb*] ***inquire after (someone or something)*** **:** to ask for information about (someone or something) ▪ She *inquired after* my wife's health. ▪ He greeted us warmly and *inquired after* our families.

inquire into [*phrasal verb*] ***inquire into (something)*** **:** to gather or collect information about (something) ▪ A panel has been appointed to *inquire into* their activities. ▪ The commission should not have *inquired into* her personal life.

inquire of [*phrasal verb*] ***inquire of (someone)*** *formal* **:** to ask (someone) a question ▪ The police *inquired of* his neighbors if they knew where he was.

– in·quir·er *noun, pl* **-ers** [*count*]

inquiring *or chiefly Brit* **enquiring** *adj, always used before a noun* [*more ~; most ~*]

1 : asking questions **:** wanting to learn more ▪ He got a call from an *inquiring* journalist/reporter. ▪ She has an *inquiring* [=*inquisitive*] mind.

2 : showing a desire to ask a question or learn more ▪ an *inquiring* look/gaze

– in·quir·ing·ly /ɪnˈkwajərɪŋli/ *adv* ▪ She looked at him *inquiringly*. [=*questioningly*]

in·qui·ry *or chiefly Brit* **en·qui·ry** /ɪnˈkwaɪri, ˈɪnkwəri/ *noun, pl* **-ries**

1 [*count*] **:** a request for information ▪ She refused to answer *inquiries* from the media about her marriage. — often + *into* ▪ She was told that she could not make an *inquiry into* [=she could not ask about] the salaries of her coworkers.

2 [*count*] **:** an official effort to collect and examine information about something **:** INVESTIGATION ▪ judicial/legislative *inquiries* ▪ The board ordered an *inquiry* to determine whether the rules had been followed. — often + *into* ▪ The police are conducting an *inquiry into* (the circumstances of) his death. ✧ In British English, a person who is being questioned by the police as a suspect or a witness is said to be ***helping the police with their inquiries.***

3 [*noncount*] **:** the act of asking questions in order to gather or collect information ▪ Further *inquiry* showed that he had visited the city twice before. ▪ scientific/academic *inquiry* ▪ The police are pursuing a new ***line of inquiry.***

in·qui·si·tion /ˌɪnkwəˈzɪʃən/ *noun, pl* **-tions**

1 ***the Inquisition*** **:** an organization in the Roman Catholic Church in the past that was responsible for finding and punishing people who did not accept its beliefs and practices ▪ *the* Spanish *Inquisition*

2 [*count*] **:** a harsh and unfair investigation or series of questions ▪ His political enemies were conducting an *inquisition* into the details of his personal life.

in·quis·i·tive /ɪnˈkwɪzətɪv/ *adj* [*more ~; most ~*]

1 : tending to ask questions **:** having a desire to know or learn more ▪ She was very *inquisitive* [=*curious*] as a child. ▪ an *inquisitive* mind

2 *disapproving* **:** asking too many questions about other people's lives ▪ an overly *inquisitive* neighbor

– in·quis·i·tive·ly *adv* ▪ She looked at me *inquisitively*. **– in·quis·i·tive·ness** *noun* [*noncount*]

in·quis·i·tor /ɪnˈkwɪzətɚ/ *noun, pl* **-tors** [*count*]

1 : a person who asks many difficult questions in a harsh or unkind way ▪ He had to answer his *inquisitors'* questions or be thrown out of school.

2 : a member or officer of the Inquisition

– in·quis·i·to·ri·al /ɪnˌkwɪzəˈtorijəl/ *adj*

in·road /ˈɪnˌroʊd/ *noun, pl* **-roads** [*count*] — used to describe a situation in which someone or something becomes more successful or important often by making someone or something else less successful; usually plural ▪ We need to protect our company against the *inroads* of competitors. — usually used with *make* ▪ Despite the recent *inroads made* by competitors in the industry, the company is still doing well. ▪ The party hopes to *make* serious *inroads* in Congress. [=the party hopes that many more of its members will be elected to serve in Congress] ▪ The sport is *making inroads* in the U.S. [=it is becoming more popular in the U.S.]

in·rush /ˈɪnˌrʌʃ/ *noun* [*singular*] **:** a fast inward flow or movement into a place ▪ a sudden *inrush* of water/air

ins. *abbr* inches

in·sa·lu·bri·ous /ˌɪnsəˈluːbrijəs/ *adj* [*more ~; most ~*] *formal* **:** not clean or healthy ▪ the city's *insalubrious* air — opposite SALUBRIOUS

ins and outs /ˌɪnzənˈaʊts/ *noun*

the ins and outs **:** the details about how something works or is done — often + *of* ▪ I'm still learning all *the ins and outs of* American politics.

in·sane /ɪnˈseɪn/ *adj*

1 [*more ~; most ~*] **:** not sane: such as **a :** having or showing severe mental illness ▪ an *insane* person ▪ The murderer was found to be criminally *insane*.

> ***usage*** The use of *insane* to describe a person with severe mental illness is now often considered offensive. The phrase *mentally ill* is preferred. *Insane* in this sense now occurs chiefly in such legal phrases as *criminally insane* and *temporarily insane*.

b : unable to think in a clear or sensible way ▪ She was *insane* with jealousy/anger. **c** — used in the phrase ***drive/make (someone) insane*** to describe annoying or bothering someone very much. ▪ That noise is *driving* me *insane*. [=it is annoying me very much] ▪ It *makes me insane* [=I feel very annoyed] when people drive like that.

2 : wild and uncontrolled ▪ He had an *insane* look in his eyes.

3 [*more ~; most ~*] **:** very foolish or unreasonable **:** CRAZY ▪ She likes to drive at *insane* speeds. ▪ He had this *insane* idea that he could get rich by selling old computers.

4 : used for people who have severe mental illnesses ▪ an ***insane asylum*** [=(now more commonly) a mental hospital]

go insane **:** to become mentally ill **:** to go crazy ▪ She *went insane* and started thinking that everyone was trying to kill her. — usually used in an exaggerated way ▪ I must be *going insane*. I can't find my car keys anywhere. ▪ If you don't stop making that noise, I'm going to *go* (completely) *insane*!

the insane **:** insane people **:** people who have severe mental illness ▪ a hospital for *the insane* [=(now more commonly) the mentally ill]

– in·sane·ly *adv* ▪ Her boyfriend was *insanely* jealous.

in·san·i·tary /ɪnˈsænəˌteri/ *adj, chiefly Brit* **:** dirty and likely to cause disease **:** UNSANITARY ▪ *insanitary* living conditions ▪ an *insanitary* bathroom

in·san·i·ty /ɪnˈsænəti/ *noun, pl* **-ties**

1 [*noncount*] **:** severe mental illness **:** the condition of being insane ▪ She was found not guilty by reason of *insanity*. ▪ temporary *insanity*

2 : something that is very foolish or unreasonable [*noncount*] His friends thought his decision to quit his job was pure *insanity*. ▪ Please, no more violence. It's time to stop this *insanity*. [*count*] the *insanities* of modern life

in·sa·tia·ble /ɪnˈseɪʃəbəl/ *adj* [*more ~; most ~*] **:** always wanting more **:** not able to be satisfied ▪ an *insatiable* appetite/thirst ▪ Her desire for knowledge was *insatiable*.

– in·sa·tia·bly /ɪnˈseɪʃəbli/ *adv* ▪ an *insatiably* curious student

in·scribe /ɪnˈskraɪb/ *verb* **-scribes; -scribed; -scrib·ing** [+ *obj*]

1 : to write or cut (words, a name, etc.) on something — + *on* or *in* ▪ The winner's name is *inscribed on* the trophy. ▪ He *inscribed* a message *in* the book before giving it to his son. — sometimes used figuratively ▪ The image is *inscribed in* my memory. [=I remember the image very clearly]

2 : to write words, a name, etc., on (something) ▪ They *inscribed* the monument with the soldiers' names. ▪ The book was *inscribed* with the author's signature.

in·scrip·tion /ɪnˈskrɪpʃən/ *noun, pl* **-tions** [*count*] **:** words that are written on or cut into a surface ▪ The painting had an *inscription* that read, "To my loving wife." ▪ the *inscription* on a stone monument

in·scru·ta·ble /ɪnˈskruːtəbəl/ *adj* [*more ~; most ~*] *formal* **:** difficult to understand **:** causing people to feel curious or confused ▪ an *inscrutable* [=*mysterious*] expression/smile ▪ an *inscrutable* work of art ▪ He was a quiet, *inscrutable* man.

– in·scru·ta·bil·i·ty /ɪnˌskruːtəˈbɪləti/ *noun* [*noncount*] **– in·scru·ta·bly** /ɪnˈskruːtəbli/ *adv*

in·seam /ˈɪnˌsiːm/ *noun, pl* **-seams** [*count*] *US* **:** the line where two parts of a pair of pants are sewn together from the top of the inside of the leg to the bottom; *also* **:** the length of this line ▪ a 32-inch *inseam*

in·sect /ˈɪnˌsɛkt/ *noun, pl* **-sects** [*count*]

1 : a small animal that has six legs and a body formed of

three parts and that may have wings ▪ flies, bees, and other *insects* [=(*chiefly US, informal*) *bugs*] ▪ a swarm of flying *insects* — often used before another noun ▪ an *insect* bite ▪ Use plenty of *insect* spray/repellent to keep the mosquitoes from biting you. — see color picture on page C10
2 : an animal (such as a spider) that is similar to an insect — compare ARACHNID

in·sec·ti·cide /ɪnˈsɛktəˌsaɪd/ *noun, pl* **-cides** [*count, noncount*] **:** a chemical substance that is used to kill insects
– in·sec·ti·cid·al /ɪnˌsɛktəˈsaɪdl/ *adj*

in·sec·ti·vore /ɪnˈsɛktəˌvoɚ/ *noun, pl* **-vores** [*count*] *technical* **:** an animal that eats insects
– in·sec·tiv·o·rous /ˌɪnˌsɛkˈtɪvərəs/ *adj*

in·se·cure /ˌɪnsɪˈkjɚ/ *adj* [*more ~; most ~*] **:** not secure: such as **a :** not confident about yourself or your ability to do things well **:** nervous and uncomfortable ▪ I feel shy and *insecure* around strangers. — often + *about* ▪ She used to be *insecure about* her height. ▪ He felt *insecure about* the idea of becoming a father. ▪ Many young people are *insecure about* the future. [=they believe that bad things might happen in the future] **b :** not certain to continue or be successful for a long time ▪ an *insecure* investment ▪ He has always held low-paying, *insecure* jobs. [=jobs that people can lose easily] ▪ Most of these families are economically *insecure*. [=they do not have a dependable source of money] **c :** not locked or well protected ▪ One of the building's rear doors was *insecure*. ▪ The country's borders remain *insecure*.
– in·se·cu·ri·ty /ˌɪnsɪˈkjərəti/ *noun, pl* **-ties** [*noncount*] They share a sense of *insecurity* about the future. ▪ job/economic *insecurity* [*count*] the *insecurities* of teenagers

in·sem·i·nate /ɪnˈsɛməˌneɪt/ *verb* **-nates; -nat·ed; -nat·ing** [+ *obj*] *technical* **:** to put semen into (a woman or a female animal) in order to cause pregnancy ▪ She was ***artificially inseminated*** in January.
– in·sem·i·na·tion /ɪnˌsɛməˈneɪʃən/ *noun* [*noncount*] — see also ARTIFICIAL INSEMINATION

in·sen·si·ble /ɪnˈsɛnsəbəl/ *adj, formal*
1 [*more ~; most ~*] **:** not able to feel pain, emotions, etc. — often + *to* ▪ He was *insensible to* pain. ▪ *insensible to* fear
2 [*more ~; most ~*] **:** not aware of something — often + *of* ▪ They were *insensible* [=*unaware*] *of* the danger ahead.
3 : not conscious ▪ She was knocked *insensible* by the collision. ▪ They drank themselves *insensible*. [=they drank until they became unconscious]
– in·sen·si·bil·i·ty /ɪnˌsɛnsəˈbɪləti/ *noun* [*noncount*] ▪ his *insensibility* to pain **– in·sen·si·bly** /ɪnˈsɛnsəbli/ *adv* ▪ changes that occur *insensibly* [=without people being aware that they are occurring]

in·sen·si·tive /ɪnˈsɛnsətɪv/ *adj* [*more ~; most ~*] **:** not sensitive: such as **a :** showing that you do not know or care about the feelings of other people ▪ He's just a rude, *insensitive* jerk. ▪ a racially *insensitive* comment [=an offensive comment about a person's race] ▪ It was *insensitive* of her to say that. **b :** not responding to or caring about problems, changes, or needs ▪ an *insensitive* bureaucracy — often + *to* ▪ The government has been *insensitive to* the public's demands. ▪ Managers must not be *insensitive to* the needs of their employees. **c** *not used before a noun* **:** not greatly affected by something — usually + *to* ▪ He was *insensitive to* the risks involved in starting a business. ▪ *insensitive to* pain
– in·sen·si·tive·ly *adv* ▪ They had acted *insensitively*. **– in·sen·si·tiv·i·ty** /ɪnˌsɛnsəˈtɪvəti/ *noun* [*noncount*] ▪ racial *insensitivity*

in·sep·a·ra·ble /ɪnˈsɛpərəbəl/ *adj* **:** not able to be separated ▪ One problem is *inseparable* from the other. ▪ Growing up, the two of us were *inseparable*. [=we were very close friends; we spent a lot of time together] ▪ We were *inseparable* friends.
– in·sep·a·ra·bil·i·ty /ɪnˌsɛpərəˈbɪləti/ *noun* [*noncount*] **– in·sep·a·ra·bly** /ɪnˈsɛpərəbli/ *adv* ▪ Your future is *inseparably* linked/tied to ours.

¹in·sert /ɪnˈsɚt/ *verb* **-serts; -sert·ed; -sert·ing** [+ *obj*]
1 : to put (something) in something ▪ *Insert* your credit card here. ▪ You need to *insert* a comma between these two words. ▪ *insert* a space between paragraphs — often + *in* or *into* ▪ He *inserted* the key *in* the lock. ▪ She *inserted* a tape *in* the VCR. ▪ *insert* a word *in* a sentence ▪ Try *inserting* a couple of jokes *into* your speech to keep your audience's attention.
2 : to cause (someone) to be involved in an activity ▪ They tried to *insert* themselves into the conversation.

²in·sert /ˈɪnˌsɚt/ *noun, pl* **-serts** [*count*] **:** something that is put into something else ▪ shoe *inserts* ▪ The pot comes with an *insert* for steaming.; *especially* **:** a small section or piece of paper with information that is placed inside something ▪ advertising *inserts* in the Sunday paper ▪ Each box includes an *insert* explaining the product's proper use.

in·ser·tion /ɪnˈsɚʃən/ *noun, pl* **-tions**
1 [*noncount*] **:** the act or process of putting something into something else **:** the act or process of inserting something ▪ Treatment may include the *insertion* of a tube in his ear.
2 [*count*] **:** something (such as a comment) that is added to a piece of writing **:** something that is inserted ▪ The report contains a number of *insertions*.

in–ser·vice /ˈɪnˈsɚvəs/ *adj, always used before a noun* **:** happening while you are being paid to work ▪ a day of *in-service* training for teachers

¹in·set /ˈɪnˌsɛt/ *noun, pl* **-sets** [*count*]
1 : a small map or picture that is shown on or next to a larger map or picture in order to show more detail
2 : a piece of something that is added to something larger often for decoration ▪ The floor is decorated with an *inset* of marble tiles. ▪ velvet dresses with silk *insets*

²inset *verb* **-sets; -set; -set·ting** [+ *obj*]
1 : to put (something) in something larger for decoration, to give information, etc. ▪ *inset* a map in a larger map
2 : to put something into (something) often for decoration — usually used as *(be) inset* ▪ The ring *is inset* with diamonds. ▪ floors *inset* with marble tiles
– inset *adj* ▪ a table with an *inset* glass top ▪ an *inset* map/photograph

in·shore /ˈɪnˈʃoɚ/ *adj*
1 : moving toward the shore away from the water ▪ an *inshore* breeze
2 : located near the shore ▪ They fish in the shallow *inshore* waters of the Atlantic.
– inshore *adv* ▪ The animals move *inshore* to feed.

¹in·side /ɪnˈsaɪd, ˈɪnˌsaɪd/ *noun, pl* **-sides**
1 [*count*] **:** an inner side, edge, or surface of something — usually singular ▪ The door can only be locked from the *inside*. — often + *of* ▪ I had a sore on the *inside of* my mouth.
2 a ***the inside*** **:** an inner part of something (such as a building or machine) ▪ *The inside* of the church is quite beautiful. ▪ I've never seen *the inside* of a computer before. — often plural ▪ *the insides* of a computer **b** [*count*] *informal* **:** the inner parts (such as the heart and stomach) of a person's body — usually plural ▪ I felt like my *insides* were tied up in knots.
on the inside **1 :** on the inner side, edge, or surface of something ▪ The number 22 car tried to pass the leader *on the inside* (of the track). **2** *baseball* **:** on the side of home plate nearest the batter ▪ The next pitch was a fastball *on the inside*. **3** — used to describe how someone is feeling ▪ She may have seemed happy, but really she was sad *on the inside*. **4 :** in a position within an organization or group ▪ The bank robbers must have had help from someone *on the inside*. [=someone working for the bank that was robbed] **5 :** in prison ▪ He wondered what life was like *on the inside*.

²inside *adj, always used before a noun*
1 : located on or near the inner side, edge, or surface of something ▪ an *inside* wall/corner/door ▪ the *inside* edge of her foot ▪ (*baseball*) He struck out on an *inside* pitch.
2 a : coming from someone within a group or organization **:** relating to or having information that is known only to a special group of people ▪ *inside* sources/information ▪ He gave us an *inside* view of the situation. ▪ I got the *inside* story from a friend who works there. ▪ It's an ***inside joke***. [=a joke that is understood only by people with special knowledge about something] **b :** done by someone within a group or organization ▪ No one knows who robbed the bank, but the police suspect that it may have been an ***inside job***. [=that it may have been robbed by or with the help of someone who works in the bank]

³inside *prep*
1 : in or into the inner part of (something or someone) ▪ We waited *inside* the store. ▪ Several people were trapped *inside* the burning building. ▪ She kept her hands *inside* her pockets. ▪ His feelings were building up *inside* him.
2 a : within the borders or limits of (something) ▪ He lives *inside* the city limits. ▪ They make sure to stay *inside* the law. [=to not break any laws] ▪ She always kept well *inside* [=she drove slower than] the speed limit. **b :** before the end of (a period of time) ▪ Their marriage ended *inside* [=*within*] a year. ▪ We should hear the results *inside* [=in less than] an hour.

3 : belonging to (a group or organization) • Sources *inside* the company indicate that there are disagreements about the change in management.

inside of chiefly US : INSIDE • We waited *inside of* the store. • He lives *inside of* the city limits. • The results should be known *inside of* an hour. • information from sources *inside of* the company

⁴inside *adv*

1 : in the inner part of something • I cleaned my car *inside* and out. • The candy is chewy *inside*. • He keeps all his feelings locked up *inside*. [=he does not express his feelings]

2 : in or into the inner part of a building, room, etc. • We went/stayed *inside* during the storm. • Step *inside* and look at our menu.

3 *informal* **: in prison** • He got put *inside* for burglary.

***inside out* 1 : so that the inner surface becomes the outer surface** • He was wearing his socks *inside out*. • The wind blew my umbrella *inside out*. **2** *informal* **: very well and thoroughly** • She knows this area *inside out*.

turn (something) inside out *informal* **1 : to cause (a place) to become disorganized while you are trying to find something** • I *turned the closet inside out* and still couldn't find those shoes. **2 : to change (something) completely** • Her life was turned *inside out* after the accident.

in·sid·er /ɪnˈsaɪdɚ, ˈɪnˌsaɪdɚ/ *noun, pl* **-ers** *[count]* **: a person who belongs to a group or organization and has special knowledge about it** • Political *insiders* say that she is planning to run for president. • The book gives fans an *insider's* view of Hollywood. — opposite OUTSIDER

insider trading *noun [noncount] finance* **: the illegal activity of buying and selling a company's stocks while using secret information from a person who works for the company**

inside track *noun*

***the inside track* : a position that gives someone an advantage over others in a competition** • The owner's son has *the inside track* for the job. • She is on *the inside track* to get a promotion.

in·sid·i·ous /ɪnˈsɪdijəs/ *adj [more ~; most ~] formal* **: causing harm in a way that is gradual or not easily noticed** • Most people with this *insidious* disease have no idea that they are infected. • an *insidious* enemy

— in·sid·i·ous·ly *adv* • The disease progresses *insidiously*. **— in·sid·i·ous·ness** *noun [noncount]*

in·sight /ˈɪnˌsaɪt/ *noun, pl* **-sights**

1 *[noncount]* **: the ability to understand people and situations in a very clear way** • He is a leader of great *insight*.

2 : an understanding of the true nature of something *[noncount]* The author analyzes the problem with remarkable *insight*. — often + *into* • We need to gain *insight into* the politics of the region. *[count]* I had a sudden *insight*. • Her book provides us with fresh new *insights into* this behavior.

in·sight·ful /ˈɪnˌsaɪtfəl, ɪnˈsaɪtfəl/ *adj [more ~; most ~]* **: having or showing a very clear understanding of something : having or showing insight** • Her analysis of the problem was very *insightful*. • an *insightful* comment/remark • *insightful* leaders

— in·sight·ful·ly *adv* **— in·sight·ful·ness** *noun [noncount]*

in·sig·nia /ɪnˈsɪgnijə/ *noun, pl* **insignia** *or US* **in·sig·ni·as** *[count]* **: a badge or sign which shows that a person is a member of a particular group or has a particular rank** • Their jackets have the school's *insignia* on the front. • a military *insignia* — sometimes used figuratively • Both attacks bore the *insignia* of the terrorist group.

in·sig·nif·i·cant /ˌɪnsɪgˈnɪfɪkənt/ *adj [more ~; most ~]* **: small or unimportant : not significant** • They lost an *insignificant* amount of money. • *insignificant* details • Looking up at the stars always makes me feel so small and *insignificant*. • These problems are ***not insignificant***.

— in·sig·nif·i·cant·ly *adv* • an *insignificantly* small amount **— in·sig·nif·i·cance** /ˌɪnsɪgˈnɪfɪkəns/ *noun [noncount]* • feelings of *insignificance* • (*chiefly Brit*) Your financial debt ***pales into insignificance*** [=seems much smaller] when you compare it with mine.

in·sin·cere /ˌɪnsɪnˈsiɚ/ *adj [more ~; most ~]* **: not expressing or showing true feelings : not sincere** • He said he was sorry, but I could tell that he was being *insincere*. • *insincere* praise/flattery • an *insincere* apology

— in·sin·cere·ly *adv* • smiling *insincerely* **— in·sin·cer·i·ty** /ˌɪnsɪnˈserəti/ *noun [noncount]* • the *insincerity* of his apology

in·sin·u·ate /ɪnˈsɪnjəˌweɪt/ *verb* **-ates; -at·ed; -at·ing** *[+ obj]*

1 : to say (something, especially something bad or insulting) in an indirect way • Just what are you *insinuating*? [=*implying*] — often + *that* • Are you *insinuating that* I cheated!?

2 *formal* **: to gradually make (yourself) a part of a group, a person's life, etc., often by behaving in a dishonest way — usually + *into*** • He gradually *insinuated* himself *into* her life. • She has managed to *insinuate* herself *into* the city's highest social circles.

— insinuating *adj [more ~; most ~]* • He made an *insinuating* remark/comment about my weight.

in·sin·u·a·tion /ɪnˌsɪnjəˈweɪʃən/ *noun, pl* **-tions**

1 *[count]* **: a usually bad or insulting remark that is said in an indirect way** • I resent her *insinuation* that I can't do it without her help.

2 *[noncount]* **: the act of saying something bad or insulting in an indirect way** • He criticizes his opponents by *insinuation* rather than directly.

in·sip·id /ɪnˈsɪpəd/ *adj [more ~; most ~] formal*

1 : not interesting or exciting : dull or boring • an *insipid* movie/novel

2 : lacking strong flavor : BLAND • The soup was rather *insipid*.

— in·sip·id·ly *adv* **— in·si·pid·i·ty** /ˌɪnsəˈpɪdəti/ *noun [noncount]*

in·sist /ɪnˈsɪst/ *verb* **-sists; -sist·ed; -sist·ing**

1 : to demand that something happen or that someone do something *[no obj]* I didn't want to go, but she *insisted*. • "Come on, let's go." "Oh, all right, if/since you *insist*." *[+ obj]* — usually + *that* • She *insisted that* I (should) go. • The source for my story *insisted that* I not reveal his/her name.

2 *[+ obj]* **: to say (something) in a way that is very forceful and does not allow disagreement** • She *insists* the money is hers. — usually + *that* • She kept *insisting that* she was right. • He *insists that* these problems are not his fault. • Both men *insist that* they are innocent.

insist on also insist upon *[phrasal verb]* **1 *insist on/upon (something) or insist on/upon doing (something)* : to say or show that you believe that something is necessary or very important** • My source *insisted on* anonymity. • She *insists on* doing everything her own way. • They adamantly *insisted upon* (their) being included in the meeting. **2 *insist on/upon doing (something)*** *informal* **: to continue doing (something that other people think is annoying or unimportant)** • The people sitting next to us *insisted on* talking during the entire movie.

in·sis·tence /ɪnˈsɪstəns/ *noun [noncount]*

1 : the act of demanding something or saying something in a way that does not allow disagreement — often + *on* • I was surprised by their *insistence on* privacy. • her *insistence on* being honest — often + *that* • No one believed him despite his *insistence that* he was innocent. ✧ If you do something ***at the insistence of someone*** or ***at someone's insistence***, you do it because someone tells you that you must do it. • She was fired from her job *at the insistence of* the mayor. • He enrolled in the army *at his father's insistence*.

2 : the quality or state of being insistent • He spoke with great *insistence* of the need for reform. • the *insistence* of the crashing waves

in·sis·tent /ɪnˈsɪstənt/ *adj [more ~; most ~]*

1 : demanding that something happen or that someone do something • My friends were *insistent* that I go. = They were *insistent* on my going. [=they insisted that I go] • He was *insistent* about paying for dinner. [=he insisted on paying for dinner; he insisted that he should pay for dinner]

2 : happening for a long time and very difficult to ignore • an *insistent* drumbeat • We listened to the *insistent* crashing of waves on the beach.

— in·sis·tent·ly *adv* • He spoke very *insistently* of the need for reform.

in·so·far as /ˌɪnsəˈfɑɚ-/ *also* **in so far as** *conj, formal* **: to the extent or degree that** • She helped us *insofar as* she was able. [=she helped us as much as she could] • The news is good *insofar as* it suggests that a solution may be possible.

in·sole /ˈɪnˌsoul/ *noun, pl* **-soles** *[count]*

1 : the bottom of the inside of a shoe

2 : a thin piece of material that you put at the bottom of the inside of a shoe for comfort

in·so·lent /ˈɪnsələnt/ *adj [more ~; most ~] somewhat formal* **: rude or impolite : having or showing a lack of respect for other people** • an *insolent* [=*impudent, disrespectful*] child •

Insolent behavior will not be tolerated.
– **in·so·lence** /ˈɪnsələns/ *noun [noncount]* ▪ The boy was punished for his *insolence*. – **in·so·lent·ly** *adv*

in·sol·u·ble /ɪnˈsɑːljəbəl/ *adj*
1 *formal* **: not able to be solved or explained** ▪ a seemingly *insoluble* [=(less formally) *unsolvable*] dilemma/mystery/problem
2 *technical* **: not able to be dissolved in a liquid** ▪ a substance *insoluble* in water — **opposite** SOLUBLE

in·sol·vent /ɪnˈsɑːlvənt/ *adj* **: not having enough money to pay debts** ▪ The company has become *insolvent*. [=*bankrupt*] ▪ *insolvent* debtors
– **in·sol·ven·cy** /ɪnˈsɑːlvənsi/ *noun [noncount]*

in·som·nia /ɪnˈsɑːmnijə/ *noun [noncount]* **: the condition of not being able to sleep** ▪ She suffers from *insomnia*.

in·som·ni·ac /ɪnˈsɑːmniˌæk/ *noun, pl* **-ni·acs** *[count]* **: a person who is not able to sleep : a person with insomnia**

in·sou·ci·ance /ɪnˈsuːsijəns/ *noun [noncount] formal* **: a relaxed and calm state : a feeling of not worrying about anything** ▪ her youthful *insouciance* [=*nonchalance*]
– **in·sou·ci·ant** /ɪnˈsuːsijənt/ *adj [more ~; most ~]* ▪ his *insouciant* [=(less formally) *carefree*] charm

in·spect /ɪnˈspɛkt/ *verb* **-spects; -spect·ed; -spect·ing** *[+ obj]*
1 : to look at (something) carefully in order to learn more about it, to find problems, etc. ▪ The border guard *inspected* [=*examined*] their passports. ▪ She had the car *inspected* by a mechanic before she bought it. ▪ The candles are *inspected* for damage/defects before being packaged. ▪ After the storm, we went outside to *inspect* the damage.
2 : to officially visit a school, hospital, etc., in order to see if rules are being followed and things are in their proper condition ▪ He *inspected* the soldiers' barracks. ▪ *inspecting* a restaurant for health code violations

in·spec·tion /ɪnˈspɛkʃən/ *noun, pl* **-tions**
1 : the act of looking at something closely in order to learn more about it, to find problems, etc. : the act of inspecting something *[noncount]* Close *inspection* of the candles revealed some small defects. ▪ ***On closer inspection***, [=when it was examined more closely] the painting proved to be a fake. *[count]* The mechanic made/did a thorough *inspection* of the car. = The mechanic carried out a thorough *inspection*.
2 : an official visit to a school, hospital, etc., in order to see if rules are being followed and things are in their proper condition *[count]* Regular *inspections* are required of all restaurants in the area. *[noncount]* The barracks are ready for *inspection*.

in·spec·tor /ɪnˈspɛktɚ/ *noun, pl* **-tors** *[count]*
1 : a person whose job is to inspect something ▪ a building *inspector* ▪ safety/health *inspectors* [=people who make sure that a place or thing is safe/healthy]
2 : a police officer who is in charge of several police departments

inspector general *noun, pl* **inspectors general** *[count]* **: a person who is in charge of a group of inspectors or a system of inspection**

in·spi·ra·tion /ˌɪnspəˈreɪʃən/ *noun, pl* **-tions**
1 a *[noncount]* **: something that makes someone want to do something or that gives someone an idea about what to do or create : a force or influence that inspires someone** ▪ Where does the *inspiration* for your art come from? ▪ His paintings take/draw their *inspiration* from nature. ▪ Her early childhood provided (the) *inspiration* for her first novel. ▪ Her courage is a source of *inspiration* to us all. [=her courage makes us all want to be more courageous] ▪ Her most recent plays seem to lack *inspiration*. [=they are not very original or creative] ▪ ***divine inspiration*** [=inspiration that comes from God] **b** *[count]* **: a person, place, experience, etc., that makes someone want to do or create something** — usually singular ▪ His children are his greatest *inspiration*. ▪ Her courage is an *inspiration* to us all. ▪ She truly is an *inspiration*.
2 : a good idea *[singular]* She had a sudden *inspiration*. They would have the party outdoors! *[noncount]* Deciding to have the party outdoors was sheer *inspiration*.

in·spi·ra·tion·al /ˌɪnspəˈreɪʃənl/ *adj [more ~; most ~]* **: causing people to want to do or create something : giving inspiration** ▪ an *inspirational* speaker ▪ Her courage is *inspirational*.

in·spire /ɪnˈspajɚ/ *verb* **-spires; -spired; -spir·ing** *[+ obj]*
1 : to make (someone) want to do something : to give (someone) an idea about what to do or create ▪ He *inspired* generations of future scientists. ▪ Her courage has *inspired* us. — often followed by *to* + *verb* ▪ She has *inspired* us *to live* better lives. ▪ Her early childhood *inspired* her *to write* her first novel.
2 : to cause (something) to happen or be created ▪ His discoveries *inspired* a whole new line of scientific research. ▪ Her first novel was *inspired* by her early childhood.
3 : to cause someone to have (a feeling or emotion) ▪ The news *inspired* hope that the war might end soon. ▪ His unusual management style does not *inspire* confidence. [=it makes people worry about his ability to manage properly]

inspired *adj*
1 *[more ~; most ~]* **: very good or clever** ▪ She gave an *inspired* performance. ▪ He was an *inspired* choice for the role. ▪ an *inspired* guess — **opposite** UNINSPIRED
2 : having a particular cause or influence ▪ Her comments were politically *inspired*. [=they were made for political reasons] — often used in combination ▪ Italian-*inspired* architecture

inspiring *adj [more ~; most ~]* **: causing people to want to do or create something or to lead better lives** ▪ an *inspiring* leader ▪ His generosity is *inspiring*. ▪ an *inspiring* [=*inspirational*] true story of one family's struggles to overcome poverty — **opposite** UNINSPIRING
– **in·spir·ing·ly** *adv* ▪ He is *inspiringly* optimistic.

in·sta·bil·i·ty /ˌɪnstəˈbɪləti/ *noun [noncount]* **: the quality or state of being unstable: such as a : the state of being likely to change** ▪ Investors are worried about the current *instability* of the stock market. ▪ political/social *instability* **b : the tendency to change your behavior very quickly or to react to things in an extremely emotional way** ▪ The patient has a history of emotional/mental *instability*.

in·stall /ɪnˈstɑːl/ *verb* **-stalls; -stalled; -stall·ing**
1 : to make (a machine, a service, etc.) ready to be used in a certain place *[+ obj]* New locks were *installed* on all the doors. ▪ We thought about *installing* a new phone system. ▪ a newly *installed* door ▪ The computer comes with the software already *installed*. *[no obj]* The software *installs* easily/automatically on your hard drive.
2 *[+ obj]* **: to put (someone) in an official or important job** ▪ The college recently *installed* its first woman president.
3 *[+ obj]* **: to cause (someone) to be or stay in a particular place** ▪ He *installed* himself on the leather couch. [=he sat down on the couch and stayed there] ▪ They were temporarily *installed* in the guest bedroom.
– **in·stall·er** *noun, pl* **-ers** *[count]* ▪ a professional carpet *installer*

in·stal·la·tion /ˌɪnstəˈleɪʃən/ *noun, pl* **-tions**
1 *[noncount]* **: the act or process of making a machine, a service, etc., ready to be used in a certain place : the act of installing something** ▪ The cable company offers lower prices and free *installation*. ▪ These products are designed for easy *installation*.
2 *[singular]* **: a ceremony in which someone is put in an official or important job** ▪ Her *installation* as president will take place tomorrow.
3 *[count]* **: something (such as a piece of equipment) that is put together and made ready for use** ▪ The room contained the company's large computer *installation*.
4 *[count]* **: a place that is used for training soldiers, keeping military supplies and machinery, etc.** ▪ bases, forts, training camps, and other army *installations*
5 *[count]* **: a work of art that usually has several parts (such as a sculpture, lights, and sound) and that is usually shown in a large space**

in·stall·ment *(US) also chiefly Brit* **in·stal·ment** /ɪnˈstɑːlmənt/ *noun, pl* **-ments**
1 : any one of a series of small payments that you make over a long time until you have paid the total cost of something *[count]* He just paid the last *installment* of a $20,000 loan. ▪ We are paying for the computer in *installments*. *[noncount]* *(US)* We are paying ***on installment***.
2 *[count]* **: any one of several parts of a long book, television program, etc., that are published or shown over a period of time** ▪ The first *installment* of the five-part series will appear tonight at ten o'clock.

installment plan *noun, pl* **~ plans** *[count] US* **: a way of paying for something by making a series of small payments over a long time** ▪ We used an *installment plan* to buy the furniture. ▪ We bought it ***on the installment plan***. — called also *(Brit) hire purchase*

in·stance /ˈɪnstəns/ *noun, pl* **-stanc·es** *[count]* **: an example of a particular type of action or situation : an occasion of**

something happening ▪ an *instance* of great courage ▪ These delays are just another *instance* of bureaucratic inefficiency. ▪ We have seen too many *instances* [=*cases*] in which poor families have had to leave their homes. ▪ In most *instances* the disease can be controlled by medication. ▪ They have decided not to oppose the decision in this *instance*.

for instance : as an example : for example ▪ Lack of insurance is a problem for a lot of older people, like my grandmother, *for instance*. ▪ Now, take this car, *for instance*.

in the first instance *formal* : before other events happen : as the first thing in a series of actions ▪ You will be seen *in the first instance* by your own doctor who may then send you to a specialist.

[1]**in·stant** /ˈɪnstənt/ *noun, pl* **-stants** [*count*] : a very short period of time : MOMENT ▪ For an *instant*, I forgot where I was. ▪ The ride was over ***in an instant***. ▪ I knew it was him ***the instant (that)*** [=*as soon as*] I heard his voice. ▪ Come in the house, ***this instant***! [=*right now, immediately*]

[2]**instant** *adj*

1 : becoming something very quickly ▪ The movie was an *instant* hit/sensation/success. ▪ He became an *instant* celebrity with the publication of his first novel. ▪ Her trip made her an *instant* expert on the region. [=it made her believe that she knew everything about the region]

2 : happening or done without delay : IMMEDIATE ▪ We got an *instant* response from the company. ▪ The Internet provides *instant* access to an enormous amount of information. ▪ They took an *instant* dislike to each other. [=they immediately disliked each other] ▪ He expects *instant* gratification.

3 *of food* : able to be made very quickly : partially prepared by the manufacturer so that final preparation is quick and easy ▪ Is this coffee *instant* or regular? ▪ *instant* pudding/rice

in·stan·ta·neous /ˌɪnstənˈteɪnijəs/ *adj* : happening very quickly : happening in an instant ▪ We got an almost *instantaneous* response from the company. ▪ Their deaths were *instantaneous*.

– **in·stan·ta·neous·ly** *adv* ▪ They died *instantaneously*.

in·stant·ly /ˈɪnstəntli/ *adv* : without delay : IMMEDIATELY ▪ His voice is *instantly* recognizable. ▪ They *instantly* fell in love. ▪ She was killed *instantly* when her car hit a tree.

instant messaging *noun* [*noncount*] : a system for sending messages quickly over the Internet from one computer to another computer

– **instant message** *noun, pl* **~ -sages** [*count*] ▪ We sent each other *instant messages* all night.

instant replay *noun, pl* **~ -plays** *US* : a recording of an action in a sports event that can be shown on television immediately after the original play happens [*count*] They showed the winning goal again in an *instant replay*. [*noncount*] We watched the goal again on *instant replay*. — called also (*Brit*) *action replay*

in·stead /ɪnˈstɛd/ *adv* — used to say that one thing is done or that one thing or person is chosen when another is not chosen, cannot be done, etc. ▪ I was going to write you an e-mail, but I decided to call *instead*. ▪ I couldn't afford a new car. *Instead*, I bought a used one. ▪ I don't have any milk—do you mind juice *instead*? ▪ John couldn't attend the conference so Mary went *instead*. [=*in his place*] ▪ They didn't choose me: they chose her *instead*. ▪ She didn't want to live in the city and longed *instead* for the peace and quiet of the country. — often + *of* ▪ I decided to call *instead of* writing. [=to call and not write] ▪ *Instead of* buying a new car, I bought a used one. ▪ They chose her *instead of* [=*rather than; and not*] me. ▪ He had juice *instead of* milk.

in·step /ˈɪnˌstɛp/ *noun, pl* **-steps** [*count*]

1 : the raised middle part of the top of your foot between the toes and the ankle — see picture at FOOT

2 : the part of a shoe, sock, etc., that fits over the instep

in·sti·gate /ˈɪnstəˌgeɪt/ *verb* **-gates**; **-gat·ed**; **-gat·ing** [+ *obj*] : to cause (something) to happen or begin ▪ There has been an increase in the amount of violence *instigated* by gangs. ▪ She blamed him for *instigating* [=*starting*] the argument. ▪ The government has *instigated* an investigation into the cause of the accident.

– **in·sti·ga·tor** /ˈɪnstəˌgeɪtɚ/ *noun, pl* **-tors** [*count*] ▪ the *instigators* of the violence

in·sti·ga·tion /ˌɪnstəˈgeɪʃən/ *noun* [*noncount*] : the act of causing something to happen or begin : the act of instigating something ▪ the *instigation* of divorce proceedings ✧ Something that is done ***at the instigation of someone*** or ***at someone's instigation*** is done because that person causes it to be done. ▪ He was hired *at the instigation of* the company's president. ▪ The changes were made *at her instigation*.

in·still (*US*) *or Brit* **in·stil** /ɪnˈstɪl/ *verb* **-stills**; **-stilled**; **-still·ing** [+ *obj*] : to gradually cause someone to have (an attitude, feeling, etc.) ▪ *instill* character/discipline — usually + *in* or *into* ▪ They have *instilled* a love of music *in* their children. ▪ The coach is trying to *instill in/into* the players a feeling of confidence.

in·stinct /ˈɪnˌstɪŋkt/ *noun, pl* **-stincts**

1 a : a way of behaving, thinking, or feeling that is not learned : a natural desire or tendency that makes you want to act in a particular way [*count*] Our first *instinct* was to run. ▪ Cats possess a natural hunting *instinct*. ▪ Seeing the baby aroused all her maternal *instincts*. [*noncount*] The decision was based on (gut) *instinct*. — see also KILLER INSTINCT **b** : something you know without learning it or thinking about it [*count*] Her *instincts* told her that something was wrong. [=she believed that something was wrong even though there was no obvious reason to believe it] ▪ You have to learn to trust/follow your *instincts*. [=to trust your feelings about what is right or true even when you cannot be sure that it is right or true] ▪ He has been guided throughout his career by his political *instincts*. [*noncount*] Mere *instinct* alerted her to the danger. ▪ He knew ***by instinct*** what not to say. ▪ She seemed to know *by instinct* that something was wrong. — compare INTUITION

2 [*count*] : a natural ability ▪ He has a strong survival *instinct*. ▪ an athlete with good *instincts* — often + *for* ▪ He has a strong *instinct for* survival. ▪ She has a natural *instinct for* making the right decisions in her job. — sometimes followed by *to* + *verb* ▪ a strong *instinct to survive*

in·stinc·tive /ɪnˈstɪŋktɪv/ *adj* : relating to or based on instinct : based on feelings or desires that do not come from thinking or learning ▪ Cats have an *instinctive* desire to hunt. ▪ an *instinctive* reaction/response ▪ *instinctive* behavior

– **in·stinc·tive·ly** *adv* ▪ She felt *instinctively* that something was wrong. = *Instinctively*, she felt (that) something was wrong. ▪ He knew *instinctively* what not to say.

in·stinc·tu·al /ɪnˈstɪŋkʧəwəl/ *adj* : relating to or based on instinct : INSTINCTIVE ▪ *instinctual* behaviors

[1]**institute** *noun, pl* **-tutes** [*count*] : an organization created for a particular purpose (such as research or education) ▪ They founded an *institute* for research into the causes of mental illness. ▪ an art *institute* ▪ a technical *institute* ▪ the Massachusetts *Institute* of Technology

[2]**in·sti·tute** /ˈɪnstəˌtuːt, *Brit* ˈɪnstəˌtjuːt/ *verb* **-tutes**; **-tut·ed**; **-tut·ing** [+ *obj*] *formal* : to begin or create (something, such as a new law, rule, or system) ▪ By *instituting* these programs, we hope to improve our children's education. ▪ They have *instituted* new policies to increase public safety. ▪ The organization was *instituted* [=*established*] in 1910.

in·sti·tu·tion /ˌɪnstəˈtuːʃən, *Brit* ˌɪnstəˈtjuːʃən/ *noun, pl* **-tions**

1 [*count*] **a** : an established organization ▪ an educational/academic *institution* ▪ banks and other financial *institutions* ▪ an *institution* of higher learning **b** : a place where an organization takes care of people for a usually long period of time ▪ She committed herself to a ***mental institution***. [=a hospital for people with mental or emotional problems] ▪ a ***correctional institution*** [=a prison]

2 [*count*] **a** : a custom, practice, or law that is accepted and used by many people ▪ Family visits are a Thanksgiving *institution*. ▪ She's not interested in the *institution* of marriage. ▪ the *institution* of slavery **b** : someone or something that is very well known and established in a particular field or place ▪ He is an *institution* in local politics. [=he has participated in local politics for such a long time that people consider him to be a regular part of local politics] ▪ The play has become something of an *institution* on Broadway.

3 [*noncount*] : the act of beginning or creating something (such as a new law, rule, or system) : the act of instituting something ▪ the *institution* of new rules and regulations

– **in·sti·tu·tion·al** /ˌɪnstəˈtuːʃənl̩, *Brit* ˌɪnstəˈtjuːʃənl̩/ *adj* ▪ *institutional* power ▪ *institutional* funds ▪ *institutional* living ▪ *institutional* care

in·sti·tu·tion·al·ize *also Brit* **in·sti·tu·tion·al·ise** /ˌɪnstəˈtuːʃənəˌlaɪz, *Brit* ˌɪnstəˈtjuːʃənəˌlaɪz/ *verb* **-iz·es**; **-ized**; **-iz·ing** [+ *obj*]

1 : to cause (a custom, practice, law, etc.) to become accepted and used by many people : to establish (something) as an institution ▪ It will take time to *institutionalize* these reforms.

2 : to put (someone, such as a mentally ill person) in an institution (sense 1b) ▪ They had to *institutionalize* their youngest

son. • She was *institutionalized* for seven years.
– **in·sti·tu·tion·al·i·za·tion** *also Brit* **in·sti·tu·tion·al·i·sa·tion** /ˌɪnstəˌtuːʃənələˈzeɪʃən, *Brit* ˌɪnstəˌtjuːʃənəˌlaɪˈzeɪʃən/ *noun* [*noncount*]

institutionalized *also Brit* **institutionalised** *adj*
1 a : created and controlled by an established organization • *institutionalized* housing • *institutionalized* religion **b :** established as a common and accepted part of a system or culture • an *institutionalized* practice • *institutionalized* beliefs and values • protests against *institutionalized* racism
2 [*more* ~; *most* ~] — used to describe a person who has been living in an insitution (such as a prison) for a very long time and is no longer able to live an independent life in the outside world • After 20 years in prison, he had become completely *institutionalized*.

in–store /ˈɪnˈstoɚ/ *adj* **:** existing, happening, or available in a store • *in-store* displays/advertising • *in-store* cafés

in·struct /ɪnˈstrʌkt/ *verb* **-structs; -struct·ed; -struct·ing** [+ *obj*] *formal*
1 : to teach (someone) a subject, skill, etc. — usually + *in* or *on* • His friend *instructed* him *in* English. • Many doctors are *instructing* their patients *on* the importance of exercise. • She *instructed* us *on* how to interpret the text.
2 a : to give (someone) an order or command • She *instructed* us that we were to remain in our seats. — usually followed by *to + verb* • She *instructed* us *to remain* in our seats. — often used as *(be) instructed* • We were *instructed to remain* in our seats. **b** *law* **:** to give an order or an explanation of a law to (a jury) • The judge *instructed* the jury that they should disregard the testimony of the last witness.
3 *Brit* **:** to hire (a lawyer) to represent you in a legal case • She advised him to *instruct* a solicitor.

in·struc·tion /ɪnˈstrʌkʃən/ *noun, pl* **-tions**
1 [*count*] **a :** a statement that describes how to do something • You should read each *instruction* carefully. — usually plural • Our teacher gave us *instructions* for building the model. = Our teacher gave us *instructions* on how to build the model. • The manual provides complete/detailed *instructions* [=*directions*] for installing the software. • an *instruction* manual **b :** an order or command • Their *instruction* was to deliver the package by five o'clock. — usually plural • We had *instructions* not to admit anyone. • I gave you explicit *instructions* to be here by six o'clock. • Don't you know how to follow *instructions*? [=*directions*] • I did everything according to your *instructions*.
2 [*noncount*] **:** the action or process of teaching **:** the act of instructing someone • The after-school program offers/provides reading *instruction* to students who need it. — often + *in* • The students are receiving *instruction in* algebra.
3 [*count*] *computers* **:** a set of letters, numbers, etc., that tells a computer to do something • The computer can handle one million *instructions* per second.

in·struc·tion·al /ɪnˈstrʌkʃənl/ *adj, always used before a noun* **:** giving information about how to do or use something **:** providing instruction • We need more *instructional* materials in our classrooms. • *instructional* videos • These models are used for *instructional* purposes.

in·struc·tive /ɪnˈstrʌktɪv/ *adj* [*more* ~; *most* ~] **:** providing knowledge or information **:** helping to instruct someone • It was very *instructive* [=*informative, educational*] to watch the doctors work. • an interesting and *instructive* lesson

in·struc·tor /ɪnˈstrʌktɚ/ *noun, pl* **-tors** [*count*]
1 : a person who teaches a subject or skill **:** someone who instructs people • a swimming/driving *instructor*
2 *US* **:** a teacher in a college or university who is not a professor • He's a poetry *instructor* at a local community college.

in·stru·ment /ˈɪnstrəmənt/ *noun, pl* **-ments** [*count*]
1 : a tool or device used for a particular purpose • *instruments* of torture • The murder weapon was a ***blunt instrument***. [=an object without sharp edges or points]; *especially* **:** a tool or device designed to do careful and exact work • surgical/laboratory *instruments* ***synonyms*** see [1]IMPLEMENT
2 : a device that measures something (such as temperature or distance) • an *instrument* designed to measure the Earth's atmosphere • Part of her training as a pilot involved learning to fly by *instruments*. [=learning to fly only by looking at the instruments in the airplane]
3 : a device that is used to make music • The piano was his favorite musical *instrument*. • Do you play any *instruments*? — see also WIND INSTRUMENT
4 : someone or something that can be used to do or achieve something • Movies can be useful *instruments* of social change. [=movies can be used to cause social change] • She believed that she was an *instrument* of God. [=she believed that God was using her to do things; she believed that God was acting through her]
5 *law* **:** an official document that shows legal rights or duties • a mortgage *instrument* • stocks, bonds, and other ***financial instruments***

in·stru·men·tal /ˌɪnstrəˈmɛntl/ *adj*
1 [*more* ~; *most* ~] **:** very important in helping or causing something to happen or be done — often + *in* • He was *instrumental in* organizing the club. = He played an *instrumental* part/role *in* organizing the club. • Her influence was *instrumental in* bringing the painting to the museum.
2 *music* **:** written for or performed on musical instruments **:** not including singing • They played *instrumental* music at the wedding. • an *instrumental* version of a song
– **in·stru·men·tal·ly** /ˌɪnstrəˈmɛntḷi/ *adv* • an *instrumentally* and vocally beautiful song • He was *instrumentally* involved in the organization of the club.

in·stru·men·tal·ist /ˌɪnstrəˈmɛntḷɪst/ *noun, pl* **-ists** [*count*] **:** a person who plays a musical instrument • a talented *instrumentalist*

in·stru·men·ta·tion /ˌɪnstrəmənˈteɪʃən/ *noun* [*noncount*]
1 : a way of writing or arranging music so that it can be performed in a particular style or by particular instruments • jazz *instrumentation*
2 : a set of instruments • There was a problem with the airplane's *instrumentation*.

instrument panel *noun, pl* ~ **-els** [*count*] **:** a flat surface across the front of an airplane's cockpit that contains the instruments used to fly the plane — compare DASHBOARD

in·sub·or·di·nate /ˌɪnsəˈboɚdənət/ *adj* [*more* ~; *most* ~] *formal* **:** not obeying authority **:** refusing to follow orders • His behavior was unprofessional and *insubordinate*. • an *insubordinate* attitude
– **in·sub·or·di·na·tion** /ˌɪnsəˌboɚdəˈneɪʃən/ *noun* [*noncount*] • She was fired for gross *insubordination*.

in·sub·stan·tial /ˌɪnsəbˈstænʃəl/ *adj* [*more* ~; *most* ~] **:** not substantial: such as **a :** not large or important • Their contribution to the fund was *insubstantial*. • a very *insubstantial* [=*small*] amount of money • *insubstantial* differences **b :** not strong or solid • The scarf is beautiful but too thin and *insubstantial* [=*flimsy*] to keep you warm. **c :** not real **:** not made of a real substance • an *insubstantial* [=*imaginary*] place • as *insubstantial* as a ghost
– **in·sub·stan·ti·al·i·ty** /ˌɪnsəbˌstænʃiˈæləti/ *noun* [*noncount*] • the *insubstantiality* of the fabric/evidence

in·suf·fer·able /ɪnˈsʌfrəbəl/ *adj* [*more* ~; *most* ~] **:** very bad or unpleasant **:** too unpleasant to deal with or accept • I can't take any more of her *insufferable* arrogance. • He's an *insufferable* bore. • *insufferable* [=*unbearable, intolerable*] heat
– **in·suf·fer·ably** /ɪnˈsʌfrəbli/ *adv* [*more* ~; *most* ~] • an *insufferably* arrogant woman

in·suf·fi·cient /ˌɪnsəˈfɪʃənt/ *adj* [*more* ~; *most* ~] *somewhat formal* **:** not having or providing enough of what is needed **:** not sufficient • The case was thrown out because of *insufficient* evidence. — often followed by *to + verb* • There was *insufficient* evidence *to prove* their case. — often + *for* • His income was *insufficient for* the family's needs.
– **in·suf·fi·cien·cy** /ˌɪnsəˈfɪʃənsi/ *noun, pl* **-cies** [*count, noncount*] • an *insufficiency* [=*deficiency*] of evidence – **in·suf·fi·cient·ly** *adv* • *insufficiently* strong evidence

in·su·lar /ˈɪnsulɚ, *Brit* ˈɪnsjʊlə/ *adj* [*more* ~; *most* ~] **:** separated from other people or cultures **:** not knowing or interested in new or different ideas • an *insular* [=*isolated*] group • the *insular* world of boarding schools • an *insular* [=*narrow*] way of thinking
– **in·su·lar·i·ty** /ˌɪnsuˈlerəti, *Brit* ˌɪnsjʊˈlærəti/ *noun* [*noncount*] • the *insularity* of the boarding school world

in·su·late /ˈɪnsəˌleɪt, *Brit* ˈɪnsjʊˌleɪt/ *verb* **-lates; -lat·ed; -lat·ing**
1 : to add a material or substance to (something) in order to stop heat, electricity, or sound from going into or out of it [+ *obj*] They used a special type of fiberglass to *insulate* the attic. [*no obj*] a material that is able to *insulate* against cold
2 [+ *obj*] **:** to prevent (someone or something) from dealing with or experiencing something **:** to keep (someone or something) separate from something unpleasant, dangerous, etc. • The company has tried to *insulate* itself from the region's political turmoil. • I wish I could *insulate* my children from/against painful experiences.

– **insulated** *adj* ▪ *insulated* windows and doors ▪ an *insulated* ceiling ▪ *insulated* wires ▪ Our heating bills are high because our house is poorly *insulated*.

in·su·la·tion /ˌɪnsəˈleɪʃən, *Brit* ˌɪnsjʊˈleɪʃən/ *noun* [*noncount*]
1 : a material or substance that is used to stop heat, electricity, or sound from going into or out of something : a material that insulates something ▪ They used fiberglass *insulation*.
2 a : the quality or state of being insulated ▪ These materials provide the *insulation* needed in cold weather. **b** : the act of insulating something ▪ I hired them to do the *insulation* of the attic. [=to insulate the attic]

in·su·la·tor /ˈɪnsəˌleɪtɚ ˈɪnsjʊˌleɪtə/ *noun, pl* **-tors** [*count*] : a material that allows little or no heat, electricity, or sound to go into or out of something ▪ Metal is not a good *insulator*.

in·su·lin /ˈɪnsələn, *Brit* ˈɪnsjʊlən/ *noun* [*noncount*] *medical* : a substance that your body makes and uses to turn sugar into energy ✧ If your body does not produce enough insulin, you will develop diabetes. ▪ His *insulin* level is too low.

¹in·sult /ɪnˈsʌlt/ *verb* **-sults; -sult·ed; -sult·ing** [+ *obj*] : to do or say something that is offensive to (someone) : to do or say something that shows a lack of respect for (someone) ▪ She felt they had *insulted* her by repeatedly ignoring her questions. ▪ We were greatly *insulted* by his rudeness. ▪ They're understandably *insulted* when no one asks for their opinion on a matter that affects them so much. ▪ You're saying those photos are real? Don't ***insult my intelligence***. [=don't treat me as though I am stupid; don't expect me to believe those photos are real]

²in·sult /ˈɪnˌsʌlt/ *noun, pl* **-sults** [*count*] : a rude or offensive act or statement : something that insults someone ▪ The fans hurled/shouted *insults* at the referee as he walked off the field after the game. ▪ Their decision to cancel the project was an *insult* to all my hard work. ▪ They got into a fight over a minor *insult*. ▪ We could hear them angrily trading/exchanging *insults* (with each other). ▪ The assignment was an *insult* to our intelligence. [=the assignment was too simple]
add insult to injury : to do or say something that makes a bad situation even worse for someone ▪ Most people were forced to work longer hours each week, and to *add insult to injury*, the company decided not to give pay raises.

insulting *adj* [*more* ~; *most* ~] : rude or offensive : showing a lack of respect ▪ an *insulting* remark/attitude ▪ *insulting* language — sometimes + *to* ▪ jokes/lyrics that are *insulting to* women
– **in·sul·ting·ly** /ɪnˈsʌltɪŋli/ *adv* ▪ an *insultingly* simplistic plot

in·su·per·a·ble /ɪnˈsuːpərəbəl, *Brit* ɪnˈsjuːpərəbəl/ *adj* [*more* ~; *most* ~] *formal, of a problem, difficulty, etc.* : impossible to solve or get control of : impossible to overcome ▪ They succeeded despite some nearly *insuperable* [=*insurmountable*] difficulties. ▪ *insuperable* barriers

in·sup·port·able /ˌɪnsəˈpoɚtəbəl/ *adj* [*more* ~; *most* ~] *formal* : more or worse than can be dealt with or accepted ▪ *insupportable* [=*insufferable, intolerable*] behavior ▪ an *insupportable* [=*unbearable*] burden

in·sur·ance /ɪnˈʃərəns/ *noun* [*noncount*]
1 : an agreement in which a person makes regular payments to a company and the company promises to pay money if the person is injured or dies, or to pay money equal to the value of something (such as a house or car) if it is damaged, lost, or stolen ▪ life *insurance* ▪ *insurance* against theft or damage ▪ health/medical *insurance* ▪ auto *insurance* ▪ He was very glad that he had ***taken out insurance on*** the boat. [=that he had insured the boat] — see also NATIONAL INSURANCE
2 a : the amount of money a person regularly pays an insurance company as part of an insurance agreement ▪ What's the monthly *insurance* on your car? [=how much money do you pay each month for insurance for your car?] **b** : the amount of money that a person receives from an insurance company ▪ After the fire, we used the *insurance* (money) to buy a new house.
3 : the business of providing insurance ▪ She has a job in *insurance*. ▪ I work for an *insurance* company.
4 : protection from bad things that may happen in the future — usually + *against* ▪ Education provides *insurance against* instability in the job market. ▪ The contract provides *insurance against* future price changes.

insurance adjuster *noun, pl* ~ **-ers** [*count*] *US* : a person who works for an insurance company and whose job is to decide how much money the company will pay people when they are injured or when their property is damaged, lost, or stolen — called also (*Brit*) *loss adjuster*

insurance agent *noun, pl* ~ **agents** [*count*] : a person whose job is to provide people with insurance — called also *insurance broker*

insurance policy *noun, pl* ~ **-cies** [*count*] : ²POLICY

in·sure /ɪnˈʃɚ/ *verb* **-sures; -sured; -sur·ing** [+ *obj*]
1 a : to buy insurance for (something, such as property or health) ▪ He *insured* the boat. ▪ We *insured* our house against fire and flood damage. **b** : to provide insurance for (something, such as property or health) ▪ I found a company that will *insure* my car for less than I've been paying. ▪ This policy will *insure* your car against theft.; *also* : to provide (someone) with insurance ▪ She had difficulty finding a company that would *insure* her.
2 *US* : to make (something) sure, certain, or safe : ENSURE ▪ They take great care to *insure* the safety and security of their home. ▪ We hope that careful planning will *insure* success.
insure against [*phrasal verb*] **1** ***insure against (something)*** : to make (something bad) less likely to happen usually by planning and preparing ▪ Doctors recommend exercising to *insure against* health problems. ▪ Despite all of our planning, we can't *insure against* bad weather. **2** ***insure (someone) against (something)*** : to protect (someone) from (something bad) ▪ We can't *insure* our children *against* all life's problems.

insured *adj* : having insurance (sense 1) ▪ an *insured* person ▪ *insured* property ▪ All cars in this state must be *insured* in order to legally be driven. ▪ "I lost the ring." "Was it fully *insured*?" — often + *against* ▪ Was your ring *insured against* loss?
the insured *law* : a person who has insurance : a person whose life, health, or property is insured ▪ In the event of an injury, *the insured* will receive payment in 90 days.

in·sur·er /ɪnˈʃərɚ/ *noun, pl* **-ers** [*count*] : a company that provides insurance ▪ In this policy, the *insurer* agrees to pay for all medical expenses. ▪ the country's leading *insurers*

in·sur·gen·cy /ɪnˈsɚʤənsi/ *noun, pl* **-cies** : a usually violent attempt to take control of a government : a rebellion or uprising [*count*] The *insurgency* [=*insurrection*] has continued for three years. [*noncount*] a campaign of *insurgency*

in·sur·gent /ɪnˈsɚʤənt/ *noun, pl* **-gents** [*count*] : a person who fights against an established government or authority ▪ *Insurgents* are trying to gain control of the country's transportation system. — often used before another noun ▪ an *insurgent* group ▪ *insurgent* attacks

in·sur·mount·able /ˌɪnsɚˈmaʊntəbəl/ *adj* [*more* ~; *most* ~] *of a problem, difficulty, etc.* : impossible to solve or get control of : impossible to overcome ▪ They were faced with several *insurmountable* obstacles/problems. ▪ *insurmountable* debt
– **in·sur·mount·ably** /ˌɪnsɚˈmaʊntəbli/ *adv* ▪ *insurmountably* difficult

in·sur·rec·tion /ˌɪnsəˈrɛkʃən/ *noun, pl* **-tions** : a usually violent attempt to take control of a government [*count*] He led an armed *insurrection* [=*rebellion, uprising*] against the elected government. [*noncount*] acts of *insurrection*
– **in·sur·rec·tion·ary** /ˌɪnsəˈrɛkʃəˌneri, *Brit* ˌɪnsəˈrɛkʃn̩ri/ *adj* ▪ *insurrectionary* violence ▪ an *insurrectionary* group
– **in·sur·rec·tion·ist** /ˌɪnsəˈrɛkʃənɪst/ *noun, pl* **-ists** [*count*] ▪ a group of armed *insurrectionists*

in·tact /ɪnˈtækt/ *adj* : not broken or damaged : having every part ▪ The house survived the war *intact*. ▪ After 25 years, their friendship remained *intact*.

in·take /ˈɪnˌteɪk/ *noun, pl* **-takes**
1 : the amount of something (such as food or drink) that is taken into your body [*noncount*] You should limit your daily *intake* of fats and sugars. [*count*] a larger *intake* of fluids ▪ the recommended daily *intakes* of selected vitamins
2 [*count*] : the act of taking something (such as air) into your body ▪ a sudden *intake* of breath
3 [*count*] : a place or part where liquid or air enters something (such as an engine) ▪ the fuel *intake*
4 *Brit* : the number of things or people that are taken into something (such as an organization) [*count*] The new *intake* of Labour MPs includes many women. [*noncount*] The school's *intake* of students has increased in recent years.

in·tan·gi·ble /ɪnˈtænʤəbəl/ *adj* [*more* ~; *most* ~] : not made of physical substance : not able to be touched : not tangible ▪ Leadership is an *intangible* asset to a company. ▪ an *intangible* benefit
– **intangible** *noun, pl* **-gibles** [*count*] ▪ Success may depend upon such *intangibles* as talent and experience.

in·te·ger /ˈɪntɪʤɚ/ *noun, pl* **-gers** [*count*] *mathematics* **: any number that is not a fraction or decimal : any whole number or its negative** ▪ positive and negative *integers* ▪ Both 10 and -10 are *integers*. — compare WHOLE NUMBER

in·te·gral /ˈɪntɪgrəl/ *adj* [*more ~; most ~*] **: very important and necessary** ▪ Industry is an *integral* [=*essential*] part of modern society. ▪ She had become an *integral* part of their lives. — often + *to* ▪ His character is *integral* [=*essential*] *to* the story. ▪ Luck was *integral to* our success.

– **in·te·gral·ly** /ˈɪntɪgrəli/ *adv* ▪ She was *integrally* involved in their lives.

in·te·grate /ˈɪntəˌgreɪt/ *verb* **-grates; -grat·ed; -grat·ing**

1 [+ *obj*] **a : to combine (two or more things) to form or create something** ▪ The car's design successfully *integrates* art and/with technology. ▪ She *integrates* elements of jazz and rock in her music. **b : to make (something) a part of another larger thing — usually + *into*** ▪ He feels that these books should be *integrated into* the curriculum. [=should be included in the curriculum]

2 a : to make (a person or group) part of a larger group or organization — usually + *into* [+ *obj*] They have resisted efforts to *integrate* women *into* the military. [*no obj*] Many immigrants have found it difficult to *integrate into* American culture. **b : to end a policy that keeps people of different races apart in (a place, such as a school)** [+ *obj*] She has been a leader in the efforts to *integrate* [=*desegregate*] public schools. [*no obj*] a law requiring schools to *integrate* — opposite SEGREGATE

– **in·te·gra·tion** /ˌɪntəˈgreɪʃən/ *noun* [*noncount*] ▪ the *integration* of art and/with technology ▪ the *integration* of women into the military ▪ racial/social *integration*

integrated *adj* [*more ~; most ~*]

1 : having different parts working together as a unit ▪ an *integrated* system of hospitals ▪ an *integrated* company

2 : allowing all types of people to participate or be included : not segregated ▪ *integrated* schools ▪ an *integrated* neighborhood

integrated circuit *noun, pl* **~ -cuits** [*count*] *computers* **:** MICROCHIP

in·te·gra·tion·ist /ˌɪntəˈgreɪʃənɪst/ *noun, pl* **-ists** [*count*] **: a person who supports racial integration** ▪ *integrationists* versus segregationists

in·teg·ri·ty /ɪnˈtɛgrəti/ *noun* [*noncount*]

1 : the quality of being honest and fair ▪ He has a reputation for *integrity* [=*honesty*] in his business dealings. ▪ He's a man of the highest/greatest *integrity*. ▪ academic *integrity* ▪ I admire her artistic/personal *integrity*. ▪ She had the *integrity* to refuse to compromise on matters of principle.

2 : the state of being complete or whole ▪ Without music, the film loses its *integrity*. ▪ They are trying to preserve the cultural *integrity* of the community. ▪ The earthquake may have damaged the building's structural *integrity*.

in·tel·lect /ˈɪntəˌlɛkt/ *noun, pl* **-lects**

1 : the ability to think in a logical way [*noncount*] She is a woman of superior *intellect*. [*count*] She has a sharp/keen *intellect*. ▪ We were required to read a book every week in order to develop our *intellects*. ▪ music that appeals to the *intellect* while still satisfying the emotions

2 [*count*] **: a very smart person : a person whose intellect is well developed** ▪ He's recognized as one of the greatest *intellects* [=*minds*] currently working in this field.

¹in·tel·lec·tu·al /ˌɪntəˈlɛkʧəwəl/ *adj*

1 : of or relating to the ability to think in a logical way ▪ a child's *intellectual* development/growth ▪ *intellectual* challenges ▪ *intellectual* activities/exercises

2 [*more ~; most ~*] **a : involving serious study and thought** ▪ the social and *intellectual* life of the campus ▪ the library's commitment to ***intellectual freedom*** [=freedom that allows people to think about or study what they want] **b *of a person* : smart and enjoying serious study and thought** ▪ a rather *intellectual* poet

– **in·tel·lec·tu·al·ly** /ˌɪntəˈlɛkʧəwəli/ *adv* ▪ He has grown both emotionally and *intellectually*.

²intellectual *noun, pl* **-als** [*count*] **: a smart person who enjoys serious study and thought : an intellectual person** ▪ He thinks that he's an *intellectual*, but he doesn't know what he's talking about. ▪ She's a hard worker but she's no great *intellectual*. ▪ a café where artists and *intellectuals* mingle

intellectual property *noun* [*noncount*] *law* **: something (such as an idea, invention, or process) that comes from a person's mind** ▪ Any song that you write is your *intellectual property*. ▪ the protection of *intellectual property* rights [=the rights of a person who has thought of or invented something that other people want to use, profit from, etc.]

in·tel·li·gence /ɪnˈtɛləʤəns/ *noun* [*noncount*]

1 : the ability to learn or understand things or to deal with new or difficult situations ▪ She impressed us with her superior *intelligence*. ▪ a person of average/normal/high/low *intelligence* ▪ human *intelligence* — see also ARTIFICIAL INTELLIGENCE

2 : secret information that a government collects about an enemy or possible enemy ▪ military *intelligence* ▪ gathering *intelligence* about a neighboring country's activities — **often used before another noun** ▪ *intelligence* sources/operations ▪ a national *intelligence* agency; ***also* : a government organization that collects such information** ▪ He was appointed (as the) head of army *intelligence*.

intelligence quotient *noun, pl* **~ -tients** [*count*] **:** IQ

intelligence test *noun, pl* **~ tests** [*count*] **: a test designed to measure a person's intelligence**

in·tel·li·gent /ɪnˈtɛləʤənt/ *adj*

1 [*more ~; most ~*] **: having or showing the ability to easily learn or understand things or to deal with new or difficult situations : having or showing a lot of intelligence** ▪ highly/very *intelligent* [=*smart*] people ▪ She asked some *intelligent* questions. ▪ He's a hard worker but he's not very *intelligent*. ▪ an *intelligent* decision

2 : able to learn and understand things ▪ *intelligent* beings ▪ Dogs are *intelligent* animals. ▪ They are looking for signs of ***intelligent life*** [=creatures that can learn and understand things] on other planets.

3 : having an ability to deal with problems or situations that resembles or suggests the ability of an intelligent person ▪ *intelligent* software ▪ an *intelligent* machine

– **in·tel·li·gent·ly** *adv* ▪ He spoke/wrote *intelligently* about the changes that are needed. ▪ an *intelligently* designed computer system

in·tel·li·gen·tsia /ɪnˌtɛləˈʤɛntsijə, ɪnˌtɛləˈgɛntsijə/ *noun* [*singular*] **: a group of intelligent and well-educated people who guide or try to guide the political, artistic, or social development of their society — usually used with *the*** ▪ Her new book has been embraced by *the intelligentsia*. ▪ His proposals were ridiculed by *the intelligentsia*. ✧ ***Intelligentsia*** **can be used with either a singular or plural verb.** ▪ *The intelligentsia* has/have embraced her new book.

in·tel·li·gi·ble /ɪnˈtɛləʤəbəl/ *adj* [*more ~; most ~*] **: able to be understood** ▪ an *intelligible* plan ▪ the ability to make complex concepts *intelligible* to the average reader; ***especially* : clear enough to be heard, read, etc.** ▪ His diaries include passages that are barely *intelligible*. [=almost impossible to read] ▪ Very little of the recording was *intelligible*. — opposite UNINTELLIGIBLE

– **in·tel·li·gi·bil·i·ty** /ɪnˌtɛləʤəˈbɪləti/ *noun* [*noncount*] ▪ the *intelligibility* of the concepts – **in·tel·li·gi·bly** /ɪnˈtɛləʤəbli/ *adv* She has trouble speaking *intelligibly*. [=clearly, in a voice that is loud enough, etc.]

in·tem·per·ate /ɪnˈtɛmpərət/ *adj* [*more ~; most ~*] *formal* **: not temperate: such as a : having extreme conditions** ▪ an *intemperate* [=extremely hot/cold] climate/zone ▪ *intemperate* [=*severe, stormy*] weather **b : having or showing a lack of emotional calmness or control** ▪ He wrote an *intemperate* [=*angry*] letter to his congresswoman. ▪ an *intemperate* discussion **c *old-fashioned* : often drinking too much alcohol** ▪ an *intemperate* drinker

– **in·tem·per·ance** /ɪnˈtɛmpərəns/ *noun* [*noncount*] ▪ He later regretted the *intemperance* of his words. ▪ the *intemperance* of the weather

in·tend /ɪnˈtɛnd/ *verb* **-tends; -tend·ed; -tend·ing** [+ *obj*]

1 a : to plan or want to do (something) : to have (something) in your mind as a purpose or goal ▪ He *intended* that his daughter would inherit the business. = (*Brit*) He *intended* leaving the business to his daughter. ▪ I didn't *intend* any disrespect. — **usually followed by *to* + *verb*** ▪ I didn't *intend to show* any disrespect. ▪ He *intended to leave* the business to his daughter. ▪ She clearly *intends to stay* here. ▪ He didn't *intend to hurt* anybody. **b : to plan for or want (someone or something) to do or be something** ▪ We *intended* that she come with us. — **usually followed by *to* + *verb*** ▪ We *intended* her *to come* with us. ▪ They *intended* the wedding *to be* formal. ▪ If everything goes ***as intended*** [=if everything happens in the way that has been planned], he will graduate this spring.

2 a : to want (something that you control, provide, or have made) to be used for a particular purpose or by a particular person — often followed by *to* + *verb* ▪ The person who donated the computers *intended* them *to be used* in classrooms. — **often +** ***for*** ▪ The author *intended* the book *for* adults. — **usually used as** ***(be) intended*** ▪ The book *was intended for* adults. ▪ These computers *were intended* [=*meant*] *to be used* in classrooms. ▪ The bullet *was intended for* him. [=the person who shot the gun wanted the bullet to hit him] ▪ The film *was intended to educate* people. ▪ The program *is intended to make* life easier for working parents. — **sometimes +** ***as*** ▪ It *was* never *intended as* a substitute for the real thing. **b : to want (something) to express a particular meaning — usually used as** ***(be) intended*** ▪ What *was intended* by the author? [=what meaning was the author trying to express?] — **often +** ***as*** ▪ The comment *was* not *intended* [=*meant*] *as* an insult. ▪ The arrests were *intended as* a warning to other criminals. — **often followed by** ***to + verb*** ▪ The comment *was* not *intended to be* an insult.

¹intended *adj* **: in your mind as a purpose or goal** ▪ He was unable to pursue his *intended* career. [=the career that he wanted/planned to have] ▪ What's your *intended* destination? ▪ The book failed to reach its *intended* audience.

²intended *noun, pl* **-eds** [*count*] *old-fashioned* **: a person to whom someone is engaged to be married — usually singular** ▪ a young man and his *intended*

in·tense /ɪnˈtɛns/ *adj* [*more* ~; *most* ~]

1 : very great in degree : very strong ▪ *intense* [=*extreme*] heat/cold/pain/pressure ▪ He shielded his eyes from the *intense* flash of light. ▪ She has an *intense* dislike for/of her husband's friend. ▪ *intense* anger

2 a : done with or showing great energy, enthusiasm, or effort ▪ After many years of *intense* study, he received his medical degree. ▪ an *intense* effort ▪ School reform is a subject of *intense* debate. ▪ The work requires *intense* concentration. **b** *of a person* **: very serious** ▪ He was an *intense* young man who was very determined to do well in school.

– in·tense·ly *adv* ▪ an *intensely* ambitious woman ▪ The students competed *intensely* for the prize. ▪ He gazed at her *intensely*.

in·ten·si·fi·er /ɪnˈtɛnsəˌfajɚ/ *noun, pl* **-ers** [*count*] *grammar* **: a word (such as** ***really*** **or** ***very*****) that gives force or emphasis to a statement** ▪ "So" can function as an *intensifier*, as in "I'm *so* tired." — **called also** ***intensive***

in·ten·si·fy /ɪnˈtɛnsəˌfaɪ/ *verb* **-fies; -fied; -fy·ing**

1 [*no obj*] **: to become stronger or more extreme : to become more intense** ▪ We could hear the wind howling outside as the storm *intensified*. ▪ The fighting has *intensified*.

2 [+ *obj*] **: to make (something) stronger or more extreme : to make (something) more intense** ▪ They *intensified* their efforts to increase sales. ▪ an *intensified* search for survivors

– in·ten·si·fi·ca·tion /ɪnˌtɛnsəfəˈkeɪʃən/ *noun* [*noncount*] a process of *intensification* [*singular*] an *intensification* of violence

in·ten·si·ty /ɪnˈtɛnsəti/ *noun, pl* **-ties**

1 [*noncount*] **: the quality or state of being intense : extreme strength or force** ▪ the *intensity* of the sun's rays ▪ the *intensity* of the argument

2 : the degree or amount of strength or force that something has [*count*] hurricanes of different *intensities* [*noncount*] The noise grew in *intensity*. [=the noise became louder] ▪ The sun shone with great *intensity*.

¹in·ten·sive /ɪnˈtɛnsɪv/ *adj*

1 [*more* ~; *most* ~] **: involving very great effort or work** ▪ an *intensive* effort ▪ *intensive* study/research ▪ an *intensive* course in business writing

2 *grammar* **: giving force or emphasis to a statement** ▪ an *intensive* pronoun/adverb

3 *of farming* **: designed to increase production without using more land** ▪ *intensive* farming/agriculture

– see also CAPITAL-INTENSIVE, LABOR-INTENSIVE

– in·ten·sive·ly *adv* ▪ She trained *intensively* for two years.

²intensive *noun, pl* **-sives** [*count*] *grammar* **:** INTENSIFIER

intensive care *noun* [*noncount*] **: a section of a hospital where special medical equipment and services are provided for patients who are seriously injured or ill** ▪ patients in *intensive care* = patients in the ***intensive care unit*** [=*ICU*]; *also* **: the medical care provided in such a section** ▪ Her condition will require *intensive care*.

¹in·tent /ɪnˈtɛnt/ *noun, pl* **-tents** [*count*] **: the thing that you plan to do or achieve : an aim or purpose** ▪ She thinks I'm trying to make things difficult for her, but that's not my *intent*. ▪ What was the the writer's *intent*? ▪ The *intent* of the law is to protect consumers. ▪ He was charged with assault with *intent* to kill.

to all intents and purposes *also US* ***for all intents and purposes*** **— used to say that one thing has the same effect or result as something else** ▪ Their decision to begin bombing was, *to all intents and purposes*, a declaration of war.

²intent *adj* [*more* ~; *most* ~] **: showing concentration or great attention** ▪ an *intent* gaze

intent on/upon (something) **: giving all of your attention and effort to a specific task or goal** ▪ She seems *intent on* destroying our credibility. [=she seems to be determined to destroy our credibility] ▪ They were *intent on* their work. [=they were focused on their work]

– in·tent·ly *adv* ▪ She listened *intently* to the news report.

in·ten·tion /ɪnˈtɛnʃən/ *noun, pl* **-tions** [*count*] **: the thing that you plan to do or achieve : an aim or purpose** ▪ She announced her *intention* to run for governor. ▪ He seemed to think that I was trying to cause problems, but that was never my *intention*. ▪ He said he loved her, but he actually ***had no intention of*** marrying her. [=he did not intend to marry her] ▪ We ***have every intention of*** continuing with this project [=we intend to continue with this project], whatever the cost. ▪ He bought a dog ***with the intention of*** training it to attack intruders. ▪ He has ***good intentions***, but his suggestions aren't really helpful. ▪ Sometimes plans don't work out well, despite ***the best (of) intentions***. — **see also** WELL-INTENTIONED

in·ten·tion·al /ɪnˈtɛnʃənl/ *adj* **: done in a way that is planned or intended :** DELIBERATE ▪ an *intentional* drug overdose ▪ an *intentional* and premeditated killing ▪ I apologize for the omission of your name from the list. It was not *intentional*. — **opposite** UNINTENTIONAL

– in·ten·tion·al·ly *adv* ▪ Investigators suspect that the fire was set *intentionally*. ▪ The test is *intentionally* designed to trick students.

in·ter /ɪnˈtɚ/ *verb* **-ters; -terred; -ter·ring** [+ *obj*] *formal* **: to bury (a dead body)** ▪ a burial site where people have been *interred* for over a thousand years — **opposite** DISINTER

inter- /ˈɪntɚ/ *prefix*

1 : between : among : together ▪ *inter*lock ▪ *inter*twine ▪ *inter*relation ▪ *inter*relate

2 : involving two or more ▪ *inter*national ▪ *inter*departmental ▪ *inter*faith

in·ter·act /ˌɪntɚˈækt/ *verb* **-acts; -act·ed; -act·ing** [*no obj*]

1 : to talk or do things with other people ▪ They're quiet children who don't *interact* much. — **often +** ***with*** ▪ She *interacts with* other children at nursery school.

2 : to act together : to come together and have an effect on each other — often + ***with*** ▪ When these two drugs *interact* (*with* each other), the results can be deadly.

– in·ter·ac·tion /ˌɪntɚˈækʃən/ *noun, pl* **-tions** [*count*] social *interactions* ▪ the *interactions* between the two drugs [*noncount*] ways to encourage more *interaction* among children

in·ter·ac·tive /ˌɪntɚˈæktɪv/ *adj* [*more* ~; *most* ~]

1 : designed to respond to the actions, commands, etc., of a user ▪ *interactive* software ▪ an *interactive* Web site

2 : requiring people to talk with each other or do things together ▪ *interactive* learning

– in·ter·ac·tive·ly *adv* **– in·ter·ac·tiv·i·ty** /ˌɪntɚrækˈtɪvəti/ *noun* [*noncount*]

in·ter·agen·cy /ˌɪntɚˈeɪʤənsi/ *adj, always used before a noun* **: occurring between or involving different government agencies** ▪ an *interagency* task force

in·ter alia /ˌɪntɚˈeɪlijə/ *adv, formal* **: among other things** ▪ The collection of paintings included, *inter alia*, several Rembrandts and several Picassos. [=the collection included several Rembrandts, several Picassos, and other things as well]

in·ter·breed /ˌɪntɚˈbri:d/ *verb* **-breeds; -bred** /-ˈbrɛd/; **-breed·ing : to cause animals of two different species to produce young animals that are a mixture of the two species** [+ *obj*] *interbreed* horses with/and donkeys [*no obj*] horses *interbreeding* with donkeys

in·ter·cede /ˌɪntɚˈsi:d/ *verb* **-cedes; -ced·ed; -ced·ing** [*no obj*] *formal* **: to try to help settle an argument or disagreement between two or more people or groups** ▪ Their argument probably would have become violent if I hadn't *interceded*. **: to speak to someone in order to defend or help another person** ▪ When the boss accused her of lying, several other employees *interceded* on her behalf.

– in·ter·ces·sion /ˌɪntɚˈsɛʃən/ *noun, pl* **-sions** [*noncount*] Even the *intercession* of the United Nations failed to bring an end to the war. [*count*] She thanked them for their *intercessions* on her behalf.

in·ter·cept /ˌɪntɚˈsɛpt/ *verb* **-cepts; -cept·ed; -cept·ing** [+ *obj*]
1 : to stop and take someone or something that is going from one place to another place before that person or thing gets there ▪ Detectives have been *intercepting* her mail. ▪ The police *intercepted* him as he was walking out. ▪ *intercept* a secret message
2 *sports* **:** to catch or receive (a pass made by an opponent) ▪ He *intercepted* the pass/ball. ▪ (*American football*) The quarterback has been *intercepted* twice. [=two passes thrown by the quarterback have been intercepted]
– in·ter·cep·tion /ˌɪntɚˈsɛpʃən/ *noun, pl* **-tions** [*noncount*] They used a secret code because of the possibility of *interception* by spies. [*count*] He has made 143 passes without an *interception*.

in·ter·cep·tor /ˌɪntɚˈsɛptɚ/ *noun, pl* **-tors** [*count*] **:** a fast military plane or missile used to defend against enemy planes or enemy missiles

[1]**in·ter·change** /ˈɪntɚˌʧeɪnʤ/ *noun, pl* **-chang·es**
1 : the act of sharing or exchanging things [*count*] a friendly *interchange* [=*exchange*] of ideas [*noncount*] electronic data *interchange*
2 [*count*] **:** an area where two or more highways meet that is designed to allow traffic to move from one highway to another without stopping

[2]**in·ter·change** /ˌɪntɚˈʧeɪnʤ/ *verb* **-chang·es; -changed; -chang·ing** [+ *obj*] **:** to put each of two or more things in the place of the other ▪ We *interchanged* the two tires. ▪ We *interchanged* the front tire with the rear tire. [=we put the front tire on the rear and the rear tire on the front]

in·ter·change·able /ˌɪntɚˈʧeɪnʤəbəl/ *adj* **:** capable of being used in place of each other ▪ These words have similar meanings but they're not (freely) *interchangeable* (with each other).
– in·ter·change·abil·i·ty /ˌɪntɚˌʧeɪnʤəˈbɪləti/ *noun* [*noncount*] **– in·ter·change·ably** /ˌɪntɚˈʧeɪnʤəbli/ *adv* ▪ He uses the terms *interchangeably*.

in·ter·city /ˌɪntɚˈsɪti/ *adj, always used before a noun* **:** traveling or occurring between cities ▪ *intercity* rail services ▪ *intercity* trade

in·ter·col·le·giate /ˌɪntɚkəˈliːʤət/ *adj, always used before a noun, chiefly US* **:** involving or involved in competition between colleges ▪ *intercollegiate* sports/athletics

in·ter·com /ˈɪntɚˌkɑːm/ *noun, pl* **-coms** [*count*] **:** a system which allows a person speaking into a microphone to be heard on a speaker by people in a different room or area ▪ I heard my name called on the *intercom*. ▪ His secretary's voice came over the *intercom*, telling him that he had a visitor.

in·ter·com·mu·ni·ca·tion /ˌɪntɚkəˌmjuːnəˈkeɪʃən/ *noun* [*noncount*] **:** communication between people or groups ▪ *intercommunication* between employees

in·ter·con·nect /ˌɪntɚkəˈnɛkt/ *verb* **-nects; -nect·ed; -nect·ing :** to connect (two or more things) with each other [+ *obj*] The systems are *interconnected* with/by a series of wires. ▪ These political issues are closely *interconnected*. [=*related*] [*no obj*] The lessons are designed to show students how the two subjects *interconnect*. ▪ a series of *interconnecting* stories ▪ *interconnecting* rooms [=rooms that are connected to each other]
– in·ter·con·nec·tion /ˌɪntɚkəˈnɛkʃən/ *noun, pl* **-tions** [*count, noncount*]

in·ter·con·ti·nen·tal /ˌɪntɚˌkɑːntəˈnɛntl/ *adj*
1 : traveling or occurring between continents ▪ *intercontinental* flights/trade/travel
2 : capable of traveling from one continent to another ▪ an *intercontinental* ballistic missile [=*ICBM*]

in·ter·course /ˈɪntɚˌkoɚs/ *noun* [*noncount*]
1 : SEXUAL INTERCOURSE
2 *formal* **:** communication and actions between people ▪ the unspoken rules of social *intercourse*

in·ter·de·nom·i·na·tion·al /ˌɪntɚdɪˌnɑːməˈneɪʃənl/ *adj* **:** involving different religious groups ▪ an *interdenominational* service

in·ter·de·part·ment·al /ˌɪntɚdɪˌpɑɚtˈmɛntl/ *adj* **:** occurring between or involving different departments (as of a college) ▪ *interdepartmental* research

in·ter·de·pen·dent /ˌɪntɚdɪˈpɛndənt/ *adj* [*more* ~; *most* ~] **:** related in such a way that each needs or depends on the other **:** mutually dependent ▪ The two nations are politically independent but economically *interdependent*.
– in·ter·de·pen·dence /ˌɪntɚdɪˈpɛndəns/ *also* **in·ter·de·pen·den·cy** /ˌɪntɚdɪˈpɛndənsi/ *noun* [*noncount*] ▪ the economic *interdependence* of the two nations **– in·ter·de·pen·dent·ly** *adv* ▪ The nations' economies function *interdependently*.

in·ter·dis·ci·plin·ary /ˌɪntɚˈdɪsəpləˌneri/ *adj* **:** involving two or more academic, scientific, or artistic areas of knowledge **:** involving two or more disciplines ▪ *interdisciplinary* studies

[1]**in·ter·est** /ˈɪntrəst/ *noun, pl* **-ests**
1 a : a feeling of wanting to learn more about something or to be involved in something [*noncount*] She told us about her lifelong *interest* in music. ▪ I ***have no interest*** in politics. [=I am not interested in politics] ▪ The kids listened to the speaker for a little while, but then ***lost interest***. ▪ The speaker wasn't able to ***hold/keep their interest***. ▪ I've been following his career ***with*** (great) ***interest***. [*singular*] She took/had an active *interest* in the political debate. ▪ He expressed/showed an *interest* in learning more about photography. **b** [*noncount*] **:** a quality that attracts your attention and makes you want to learn more about something or to be involved in something ▪ The stories about his personal life add *interest* to the book. ▪ He looked through the available magazines, but found nothing ***of interest***. [=nothing interesting] ▪ I thought this article might be *of interest* to you. ▪ We visited many places *of interest* on our vacation. ▪ The price of the ticket was a matter *of interest* to everyone. ▪ a story that has ***human interest*** = a ***human-interest*** story [=a story that is interesting because it involves the experiences of real people]
2 [*count*] **:** something (such as a hobby) that a person enjoys learning about or doing ▪ Music is one of her many *interests*. ▪ She has a number of ***outside interests***. [=things that she enjoys doing when she is not working]
3 [*count*] — used when discussing what is the best or most helpful thing for someone ▪ It's in your (own) *interest* to keep silent. ▪ The judge decided that it would be in the (best) *interests* of the child to continue living with her mother. ▪ If he refuses to cooperate, he'll be acting against his own *interests*. [=he'll be acting in a way that is harmful to himself] ▪ a policy that is not ***in the national/public interest*** [=that is more likely to harm than to help the nation/public] ▪ The law is intended to ***protect/safeguard the interests of*** people who have no health insurance. ▪ He claims that he ***has her (best) interests at heart***. [=that he is concerned about her and wants to help her] ▪ ***In the interest of*** [=for the sake of] fairness, we decided to get everyone's opinion before making a decision.
4 [*noncount*] **a :** the money paid by a borrower for the use of borrowed money ▪ We pay six percent *interest* on the loan. ▪ The loan was repaid with *interest*. ▪ monthly *interest* payments/charges ▪ *interest* rates ▪ an ***interest-free*** loan [=a loan that the borrower does not have to pay any interest on] **b :** money paid to you by a bank for the money you have in a bank account ▪ He made about $500 in *interest* last year. — see also COMPOUND INTEREST, SIMPLE INTEREST
5 [*count*] **:** a legal share in a business or property ▪ They offered to buy out his *interest* in the company.
6 *interests* [*plural*] **:** a group financially involved in an industry or business ▪ This law is opposed by the oil *interests*. — see also SPECIAL INTEREST

[2]**interest** *verb* **-ests; -est·ed; -est·ing** [+ *obj*]
1 : to cause (someone) to want to learn more about something or to become involved in something ▪ Military history doesn't really *interest* me. ▪ It might *interest* you to know that the woman in this photograph is your great-grandmother. ▪ It *interested* me to learn that she had once lived in California.
2 : to persuade (someone) to have, take, or participate *in* (something) ▪ Can I *interest* you *in* a game of tennis? [=would you like to play tennis?] ▪ Could I *interest* you *in* another cup of coffee? [=would you like another cup of coffee?] ▪ The salesman tried to *interest* me *in* a more expensive computer.

interested *adj* [*more* ~; *most* ~]
1 a : wanting to learn more about something or to become involved in something ▪ The listeners were all greatly/very *interested* in the lecture. ▪ students who are *interested* in archaeology ▪ I'd be *interested* to learn more about his background. ▪ I'm *interested* to hear what you have to say. ▪ I was very *interested* to learn that she had once lived in California. **b :** having the desire to do or have something ▪ Are you *interested* in playing tennis? [=would you like to play tennis?] ▪ Would you be *interested* in another cup of coffee? [=would you like another cup of coffee?] ▪ I asked him if he wanted to play tennis, but he said he wasn't *interested*.
2 : having a direct or personal involvement in something ▪ The plan will have to be approved by all ***interested parties***.

interest group *noun, pl* ~ **groups** [*count*] : a group of people who try to influence politics or the policies of government, business, etc., in a way that helps their own interests — compare PRESSURE GROUP

in·ter·est·ing /ˈɪntrəstɪŋ/ *adj* [*more* ~; *most* ~] : attracting your attention and making you want to learn more about something or to be involved in something : not dull or boring • This is one of the most *interesting* books I've read all year. • It will be *interesting* to see how she decides to spend the money. • This building has an *interesting* history. • I don't find politics very *interesting*. • I found it *interesting* to learn that she had once lived in California. • Most of what he said wasn't *interesting* to me.

— **in·ter·est·ing·ly** *adv* • He was *interestingly* dressed. • *Interestingly* (enough), these animals rarely fight. [=it is interesting that these animals rarely fight]

[1]**in·ter·face** /ˈɪntəˌfeɪs/ *noun, pl* **-fac·es** [*count*]

1 : the place or area at which different things meet and communicate with or affect each other • the man-machine *interface* • the *interface* between engineering and science

2 a : a system that is used for operating a computer : a system that controls the way information is shown to a computer user and the way the user is able to work with the computer • The software has a user *interface* that's easy to operate. • a friendly/clunky *interface* **b :** an area or system through which one machine is connected to another machine • We installed an *interface* between the computer and the typesetting machine.

[2]**interface** *verb* **-faces; -faced; -fac·ing :** to connect or become connected : to connect by means of an interface [+ *obj*] *interface* a machine with a computer [*no obj*] the point at which the two machines *interface*

in·ter·faith /ˌɪntəˈfeɪθ/ *adj, always used before a noun* : involving people of different religions • an *interfaith* dialogue

in·ter·fere /ˌɪntəˈfiə/ *verb* **-feres; -fered; -fer·ing** [*no obj*] : to become involved in the activities and concerns of other people when your involvement is not wanted • I tried to offer advice without *interfering*. — often + *in* • I'm sick and tired of the way he's always *interfering in* my life. • We shouldn't *interfere* [=*meddle*] *in* the affairs of other countries.

interfere with [*phrasal verb*] **1 *interfere with (something)*** : to stop or slow (something) : to make (something) slower or more difficult • The drug might *interfere with* a child's physical development. • All of the noise was *interfering with* my concentration. [=was making it hard for me to concentrate] **2 *interfere with (someone)*** *Brit* : to touch (a child) in a sexual and improper way

— **interfering** *adj* • an *interfering* old busybody

— **interfering** *noun* [*noncount*] • I'm sick and tired of all his *interfering*.

in·ter·fer·ence /ˌɪntəˈfirəns/ *noun* [*noncount*]

1 : involvement in the activities and concerns of other people when your involvement is not wanted : the act of interfering • We had to put up with loud noise and constant *interference* from the neighbors. • *interference* in the affairs of another nation • trying to avoid governmental *interference*

2 : additional signals that weaken or block the main signal in a radio or television broadcast • It was hard to hear the radio program because of all the *interference*. • electrical *interference* • The TV picture had a lot of *interference*.

3 *sports* : the act of illegally hitting or getting in the way of an opponent • a hockey player receiving a penalty for *interference*

run interference *American football* : to run in front of the player who is carrying the ball in order to block opponents — often used figuratively • He was able to survive the scandal only because he had several clever assistants who *ran interference* for him.

in·ter·ga·lac·tic /ˌɪntəgəˈlæktɪk/ *adj, always used before a noun* : existing or occurring between galaxies • *intergalactic* space/travel

in·ter·gen·er·a·tion·al /ˌɪntəˌʤɛnəˈreɪʃənl/ *adj* : occurring between or involving people of different age groups • *intergenerational* conflicts

in·ter·gov·ern·men·tal /ˌɪntəˌgʌvənˈmentl/ *adj, always used before a noun* : occurring between or involving two or more governments • *intergovernmental* relations • an *intergovernmental* panel

[1]**in·ter·im** /ˈɪntərəm/ *noun* [*singular*] : a period of time between events : INTERVAL • The regulations are scheduled to change next winter, and ***in the interim*** [=*meanwhile*], we'll be working hard to make all of the appropriate changes.

[2]**interim** *adj, always used before a noun* : used or accepted for a limited time : not permanent • an *interim* solution • He served as the college's *interim* [=*temporary*] president while the committee searched for a permanent replacement.

[1]**in·te·ri·or** /ɪnˈtirijə/ *adj, always used before a noun*

1 a : located on the inside of something • an *interior* [=*inner*] surface • a large car with lots of *interior* room • *interior* walls **b :** suited for use in the inside or on inside surfaces • *interior* paint • *interior* lights. — opposite [1]EXTERIOR

2 : occurring in the mind • *interior* [=(more commonly) *inner*] thoughts • an ***interior monologue*** [=a section of a novel, story, or play in which a character's inner thoughts are expressed]

[2]**interior** *noun, pl* **-ors** [*count*]

1 : an inner part, area, or surface • a black car with gray leather *interior* • the *interior* of the house — opposite [2]EXTERIOR

2 : the part of a country that is far from the coast • They traveled deep into the *interior* of Australia.

3 : the events and activities of a country that involve the country itself rather than foreign countries • Secretary of the *Interior*

interior design *noun* [*noncount*] : the art or job of planning how the rooms of a building should be furnished and decorated — called also *interior decoration*

interior designer *noun, pl* ~ **-ers** [*count*] : a person whose job is to plan how the rooms of a building should be furnished and decorated — called also *interior decorator*

interj *abbr* interjection

in·ter·ject /ˌɪntəˈʤɛkt/ *verb* **-jects; -ject·ed; -ject·ing** *formal* : to interrupt what someone else is saying with (a comment, remark, etc.) [+ *obj*] "That's an interesting idea," he *interjected*, "but I don't think you've considered all of the details." • She listened to us, *interjecting* remarks every so often. [*no obj*] If I may *interject*, I have things I'd like to add.

in·ter·jec·tion /ˌɪntəˈʤɛkʃən/ *noun, pl* **-tions** [*count*] *grammar* : a spoken word, phrase, or sound that expresses sudden or strong feeling • *interjections* such as "oh," "alas," and "wow"

in·ter·lace /ˌɪntəˈleɪs/ *verb* **-lac·es; -laced; -lac·ing :** to join together (narrow things, such as strings or branches) by crossing them over and under each other [+ *obj*] *Interlace* the branches and bend them into a circle. [*no obj*] The vines *interlaced* with each other.

— **interlaced** *adj* • *interlaced* fibers/branches

in·ter·link /ˌɪntəˈlɪŋk/ *verb* **-links; -linked; -link·ing :** to connect (two or more things) together : LINK [+ *obj*] *interlink* Web sites [*no obj*] The Web sites *interlink*.

in·ter·lock /ˌɪntəˈlɑːk/ *verb* **-locks; -locked; -lock·ing** : to connect or lock (two or more things) together [+ *obj*] She *interlocked* her fingers with his. [*no obj*] The pieces of the puzzle *interlock* (with each other).

in·ter·loc·u·tor /ˌɪntəˈlɑːkjətə/ *noun, pl* **-tors** [*count*] *formal* : a person who is having a conversation with you • He often challenges his *interlocutors* [=the people he is speaking to] with difficult questions.

in·ter·lop·er /ˌɪntəˈloʊpə/ *noun, pl* **-ers** [*count*] : a person who is not wanted or welcome by the other people in a situation or place • I had hoped to help my neighbors, but they regarded me as an *interloper*.

in·ter·lude /ˈɪntəˌluːd/ *noun, pl* **-ludes** [*count*]

1 : a period of time between events or activities • She left for a brief *interlude*. • He has resumed his acting career after a two-year *interlude*.

2 : a brief romantic or sexual meeting or relationship • They always met in the city for their romantic *interludes*.

3 : a short piece of music that is played between the parts of a longer one, a drama, or a religious service • an orchestral *interlude* • a drama with musical *interludes*

in·ter·mar·ry /ˌɪntəˈmeri/ *verb* **-ries; -ried; -ry·ing** [*no obj*] : to marry a member of a different racial, social, or religious group • The settlers and the native people seldom *intermarried*.

— **in·ter·mar·riage** /ˌɪntəˈmerɪʤ/ *noun, pl* **-riag·es** [*count, noncount*]

in·ter·me·di·ary /ˌɪntəˈmiːdiˌeri/ *noun, pl* **-ar·ies** [*count*] : a person who works with opposing sides in an argument or dispute in order to bring about an agreement • He served as an *intermediary* between the workers and the executives.

— **intermediary** *adj* • He was an *intermediary* agent in the negotiations.

[1]**in·ter·me·di·ate** /ˌɪntəˈmiːdijət/ *adj*

1 : occurring in the middle of a process or series ▪ an *intermediate* stage of growth
2 : relating to or having the knowledge or skill of someone who is more advanced than a beginner but not yet an expert ▪ I'm taking *intermediate* French this year. ▪ an *intermediate* swimming class ▪ an *intermediate* swimmer

²intermediate *noun, pl* **-ates** [*count*] : a person who has the knowledge or skill of someone who is more advanced than a beginner but not yet an expert ▪ a class for *intermediates*

in·ter·ment /ɪnˈtɚmənt/ *noun, pl* **-ments** [*count, noncount*] *formal* : the act of burying a dead person

in·ter·mez·zo /ˌɪntɚˈmɛtˌsoʊ/ *noun, pl* **-zi** /-ˌsiː/ *or* **-zos** [*count*] : a short part of a musical work (such as an opera) that connects major sections of the work

in·ter·mi·na·ble /ɪnˈtɚmənəbəl/ *adj* [*more ~; most ~*] *disapproving* : having or seeming to have no end : continuing for a very long time ▪ an *interminable* war ▪ an *interminable* wait
– **in·ter·mi·na·bly** /ɪnˈtɚmənəbli/ *adv* ▪ an *interminably* long wait

in·ter·min·gle /ˌɪntɚˈmɪŋgəl/ *verb* **-min·gles; -min·gled; -min·gling** : to mix together [+ *obj*] In her short stories, science fiction and romance are *intermingled*. = In her short stories, science fiction is *intermingled* with romance. [*no obj*] In her short stories, science fiction and romance *intermingle*. ▪ The colors *intermingle* perfectly (with each other) in the painting.

in·ter·mis·sion /ˌɪntɚˈmɪʃən/ *noun, pl* **-sions** [*count*] : a short break between the parts of a performance (such as a play, movie, or concert) ▪ We'll return after a brief *intermission*. — called also (*Brit*) *interval*

in·ter·mit·tent /ˌɪntɚˈmɪtn̩t/ *adj* : starting, stopping, and starting again : not constant or steady ▪ The patient was having *intermittent* pains in his side. ▪ The forecast is for *intermittent* rain. ▪ There are reports of *intermittent* [=*sporadic*] fighting along the border.
– **in·ter·mit·tent·ly** *adv* ▪ It has been raining *intermittently* for the past several days.

in·ter·mix /ˌɪntɚˈmɪks/ *verb* **-mix·es; -mixed; -mix·ing** : to mix together [+ *obj*] When they talk, they often *intermix* English and/with Spanish. [*no obj*] groups of people that don't *intermix* (with one another)

¹in·tern /ˈɪnˌtɚn/ *noun, pl* **-terns** [*count*] *US*
1 : a student or recent graduate who works for a period of time at a job in order to get experience ▪ a teaching *intern*
2 : a person who works in a hospital in order to complete training as a doctor ▪ After medical school, he worked as an *intern* at the university hospital.

²intern *verb* **-terns; -terned; -tern·ing** [*no obj*] *US* : to work as an intern ▪ After medical school, he *interned* at the university hospital. — compare ³INTERN

³in·tern /ˈɪnˌtɚn, ɪnˈtɚn/ *verb* **-terns; -terned; -tern·ing** [+ *obj*] : to put (someone who has not been accused of a crime) in prison for political reasons especially during a war ▪ They are protesting the government's decision to *intern* citizens without evidence of wrongdoing. — compare ²INTERN

in·ter·nal /ɪnˈtɚnl/ *adj*
1 : existing or located on the inside of something ▪ the *internal* structure of the planet ▪ The theory has some *internal* inconsistencies. [=some parts of the theory are not consistent with other parts] — opposite EXTERNAL
2 : coming from inside ▪ *internal* pressures — opposite EXTERNAL
3 a : existing or occurring within your body ▪ a patient who is experiencing *internal* bleeding ▪ *internal* organs **b** : existing or occurring within your mind ▪ *internal* doubts ▪ *internal* thoughts — opposite EXTERNAL
4 a : existing or occurring within a country ▪ *internal* affairs ▪ the office of *internal* revenue — opposite EXTERNAL **b** : existing or occurring within an organization (such as a company or business) ▪ The new policy was spelled out in an *internal* memo
– **in·ter·nal·ly** *adv* ▪ an *internally* inconsistent theory ▪ a patient who is bleeding *internally* ▪ This medicine is to be taken *internally*. [=*orally*]

internal clock *noun, pl* **~ clocks** [*count*]
1 : BODY CLOCK
2 : a clock or timing device that is inside a computer

internal combustion engine *noun, pl* **~ -gines** [*count*] : a type of engine that is used for most vehicles : an engine in which the fuel is burned within engine cylinders

in·ter·nal·ize *also Brit* **in·ter·nal·ise** /ɪnˈtɚnəˌlaɪz/ *verb* **-iz·es; -ized; -iz·ing** [+ *obj*] : to make (something, such as an idea or an attitude) an important part of the kind of person you are ▪ They have *internalized* their parents' values.
– **in·ter·nal·i·za·tion** *also Brit* **in·ter·nal·i·sa·tion** /ɪnˌtɚnələˈzeɪʃən, *Brit* ɪnˌtəːnəˌlaɪˈzeɪʃən/ *noun* [*noncount*] ▪ *internalization* of moral standards

internal medicine *noun* [*noncount*] *US* : the work of a doctor who treats diseases that do not require surgery ▪ a doctor who specializes in *internal medicine*

Internal Revenue Service *noun*
the Internal Revenue Service : the department of the U.S. federal government that is responsible for collecting taxes — abbr. *IRS*; compare INLAND REVENUE

in·ter·na·tion·al /ˌɪntɚˈnæʃənl/ *adj*
1 : involving two or more countries : occurring between countries ▪ *international* trade ▪ studying *international* relations ▪ an *international* agreement ▪ *international* flights ▪ the *international* community ▪ *international* law
2 : made up of people or groups from different countries ▪ an *international* association of chemists
3 : active or known in many countries ▪ an *international* star ▪ She has achieved *international* fame/recognition.
– **in·ter·na·tion·al·ly** *adv* ▪ The process is now recognized *internationally*. ▪ an *internationally* televised event

international date line *noun*
the international date line : an imaginary line that runs through the Pacific Ocean from the North Pole to the South Pole and that marks the place where each day officially begins ▪ crossing *the international date line* — called also *date line*

in·ter·na·tion·al·ism /ˌɪntɚˈnæʃənəˌlɪzəm/ *noun* [*noncount*] : the belief that it is good for different countries to work together ▪ a proponent of economic *internationalism*
– **in·ter·na·tion·al·ist** /ˌɪntɚˈnæʃənəlɪst/ *noun, pl* **-ists** [*count*] – **internationalist** *adj* [*more ~; most ~*] ▪ adopting *internationalist* positions

in·ter·na·tion·al·ize *also Brit* **in·ter·na·tion·al·ise** /ˌɪntɚˈnæʃənəˌlaɪz/ *verb* **-iz·es; -ized; -iz·ing** : to place (something) under international control : to make (something) involve or affect two or more countries [+ *obj*] *internationalize* a business ▪ an *internationalized* economy [*no obj*] a business that has begun to *internationalize*
– **in·ter·na·tion·al·i·za·tion** *also Brit* **in·ter·na·tion·al·i·sa·tion** /ˌɪntɚˌnæʃənələˈzeɪʃən, *Brit* ˌɪntəˌnæʃənəˌlaɪˈzeɪʃən/ *noun* [*noncount*]

international relations *noun* [*noncount*] : an area of study or knowledge concerned with relations between different countries

in·ter·ne·cine /ˌɪntɚˈnɛˌsiːn, *Brit* ˌɪntəˈniːˌsaɪn/ *adj, always used before a noun, formal* : occurring between members of the same country, group, or organization ▪ a brutal *internecine* war/battle ▪ *internecine* feuds ▪ a political party that has suffered because of bitter *internecine* rivalries

In·ter·net /ˈɪntɚˌnɛt/ *noun*
the Internet : a system that connects computers throughout the world ▪ She spent hours surfing *the Internet*. — compare INTRANET, WORLD WIDE WEB
– **Internet** *adj, always used before a noun* ▪ an *Internet* connection ▪ an *Internet* site

Internet service provider *noun, pl* **~ -ers** [*count*] : ISP

in·ter·nist /ˈɪnˌtɚnɪst/ *noun, pl* **-nists** [*count*] *US, medical* : a doctor who specializes in diseases that do not require surgery : a doctor who specializes in internal medicine

in·tern·ment /ɪnˈtɚnmənt/ *noun* [*noncount*] : the act of putting someone in a prison for political reasons or during a war : the act of interning someone ▪ protesting the government's *internment* of citizens without evidence of wrongdoing : the state of being interned ▪ trying to escape *internment* — sometimes used before another noun ▪ *internment* camps

in·tern·ship /ˈɪnˌtɚnˌʃɪp/ *noun, pl* **-ships** [*count*]
1 : a position as an intern ▪ She got an *internship* at the city newspaper.
2 : the period of time when a person is an intern ▪ He will finish his *internship* in April.

in·ter·of·fice /ˌɪntɚˈɑːfəs/ *adj, always used before a noun, chiefly US* : going or happening between people who are part of the same company or organization ▪ an *interoffice* memo ▪ *interoffice* mail

in·ter·per·son·al /ˌɪntɚˈpɚsənəl/ *adj, always used before a noun* [*more ~; most ~*] : relating to or involving relations between people : existing or happening between people ▪ *interpersonal* communication ▪ *interpersonal* skills/relationships

in·ter·plan·e·tary /ˌɪntɚˈplænəˌteri/ *adj, always used before a noun, astronomy* **:** existing or occurring between planets ▪ *interplanetary* travel ▪ *interplanetary* space

in·ter·play /ˈɪntɚˌpleɪ/ *noun* **:** the ways in which two or more things, groups, etc., affect each other when they happen or exist together [*noncount*] — often + *between* or *of* ▪ the *interplay between* the old and the new ▪ enjoys the *interplay of* three very different flavors [*singular*] — + *of* ▪ a complex *interplay of* light and color

In·ter·pol /ˈɪntɚˌpoʊl, *Brit* ˈɪntəˌpɒl/ *noun* [*singular*] **:** an international police organization that works with the police of different countries to fight crime

in·ter·po·late /ɪnˈtɚpəˌleɪt/ *verb* **-lates; -lat·ed; -lat·ing** [+ *obj*] *formal* **:** to put (something) between other things or parts ▪ He smoothly *interpolates* fragments from other songs into his own.; *especially* **:** to put (words) into a piece of writing or a conversation ▪ He *interpolated* a very critical comment in/into the discussion.
– **in·ter·po·la·tion** /ɪnˌtɚpəˈleɪʃən/ *noun, pl* **-tions** [*count, noncount*]

in·ter·pose /ˌɪntɚˈpoʊz/ *verb* **-pos·es; -posed; -pos·ing** [+ *obj*] *formal*
1 : to place (someone or something) *between* two or more things or people ▪ The new system has *interposed* a bureaucratic barrier *between* doctors and patients. ▪ He tried to *interpose* himself *between* the people who were fighting.
2 : to interrupt a conversation with (a comment) ▪ Please allow me to *interpose* a brief observation.

in·ter·pret /ɪnˈtɚprət/ *verb* **-prets; -pret·ed; -pret·ing**
1 [+ *obj*] **:** to explain the meaning of (something) ▪ *interpret* a dream ▪ We need someone to *interpret* these results for us. ▪ How should we *interpret* the law/rules/decision?
2 [+ *obj*] **:** to understand (something) in a specified way ▪ I *interpreted* his behavior to mean that he disliked me. — often + *as* ▪ I *interpreted* his behavior *as* indicating that he disliked me. ▪ Her comment was meant to be *interpreted as* sarcasm.
3 [+ *obj*] **:** to perform (something, such as a song or a role) in a way that shows your own thoughts and feelings about it ▪ Every actor *interprets* the role of Hamlet a little differently.
4 [*no obj*] **:** to translate the words that someone is speaking into a different language **:** to repeat what someone says in a different language than the language originally used ▪ I'll need someone to *interpret* for me when I travel to China. — compare TRANSLATE
– **in·ter·pret·able** /ɪnˈtɚprətəbəl/ *adj* [*more ~; most ~*] ▪ These results are not easily *interpretable*.

in·ter·pre·ta·tion /ɪnˌtɚprəˈteɪʃən/ *noun, pl* **-tions**
1 : the act or result of explaining or interpreting something **:** the way something is explained or understood [*count*] We did not agree with his *interpretation* [=*explanation*] of the results. ▪ There were many *interpretations* of [=many ways to interpret] his behavior. ▪ a literal/loose *interpretation* of the law [*noncount*] The truth will only be found by careful *interpretation* of the evidence. ▪ His remarks need further *interpretation*. ✧ If something is ***open/subject to interpretation*** it can be understood in different ways ▪ Every art form is *subject to interpretation*.
2 [*count*] **:** a particular way of performing something ▪ an actor's *interpretation* of the role of Hamlet
– **in·ter·pre·tive** /ɪnˈtɚprətɪv/ *or* **in·ter·pre·ta·tive** /ɪnˈtɚprəˌteɪtɪv/ *adj* ▪ a series of *interpretive* essays

in·ter·pret·er /ɪnˈtɚprətɚ/ *noun, pl* **-ers** [*count*] **:** a person who translates the words that someone is speaking into a different language ▪ He has now learned English well enough that he can conduct interviews without an *interpreter*. ▪ He gave his statement ***through an interpreter***. [=an interpreter translated his statement]

in·ter·ra·cial /ˌɪntɚˈreɪʃəl/ *adj* **:** involving people of different races ▪ an *interracial* marriage

in·ter·re·late /ˌɪntərɪˈleɪt/ *verb* **-lates; -lat·ed; -lat·ing**
1 [*no obj*] **:** to have a close or shared relationship ▪ I like the way the characters *interrelate* in the novel. ▪ Linguists have found that language *interrelates* closely with culture.
2 [+ *obj*] **:** to make or show a relationship between (things or people) ▪ Linguists have tried to *interrelate* language with/and culture.
– **interrelated** *adj* [*more ~; most ~*] ▪ a number of *interrelated* topics ▪ Linguists have found that language and culture are closely *interrelated*. – **in·ter·re·lat·ed·ness** *noun* [*noncount*] – **in·ter·re·la·tion** /ˌɪntərɪˈleɪʃən/ *noun, pl* **-tions** [*count, noncount*] ▪ understanding the *interrelations* of/between/among different animal species – **in·ter·re·la·tion·ship** /ˌɪntərɪˈleɪʃənˌʃɪp/ *noun, pl* **-ships** [*count, noncount*] ▪ the *interrelationships* among all forms of life

in·ter·ro·gate /ɪnˈterəˌgeɪt/ *verb* **-gates; -gat·ed; -gat·ing** [+ *obj*] **:** to ask (someone) questions in a thorough and often forceful way ▪ *interrogate* a prisoner of war ▪ The suspect was *interrogated* (by the police) for several hours.
– **in·ter·ro·ga·tion** /ɪnˌterəˈgeɪʃən/ *noun, pl* **-tions** [*count, noncount*] ▪ He conducted a skillful *interrogation* of the witness. – **in·ter·ro·ga·tor** /ɪnˈterəˌgeɪtɚ/ *noun, pl* **-tors** [*count*] ▪ a skillful *interrogator*

¹in·ter·rog·a·tive /ˌɪntəˈrɑːgətɪv/ *adj*
1 *grammar* **a :** having the form of a question rather than a statement or command ▪ "Did you go to school today?" is an *interrogative* sentence. **b :** used to ask a question ▪ an *interrogative* pronoun such as "who" — compare DECLARATIVE, IMPERATIVE
2 *formal* **:** asking a question **:** having the form or force of a question ▪ She had an *interrogative* expression/look on her face. ▪ an *interrogative* tone of voice

²interrogative *noun, pl* **-tives** [*count*] *grammar* **:** a word (such as *who, what,* or *which*) that is used in asking a question
the interrogative **:** the form that a phrase or sentence has when it is asking a question ▪ "Is this sentence in *the interrogative*?" "Yes, it is."

in·ter·rupt /ˌɪntəˈrʌpt/ *verb* **-rupts; -rupt·ed; -rupt·ing**
1 : to ask questions or say things while another person is speaking **:** to do or say something that causes someone to stop speaking [+ *obj*] Please don't *interrupt* me (while I'm talking). [*no obj*] It's not polite to *interrupt*. ▪ Please don't *interrupt* (while I'm talking).
2 [+ *obj*] **:** to cause (something) to stop happening for a time ▪ His dinner was *interrupted* by a phone call. ▪ We *interrupt* this program to bring you a special announcement.
3 [+ *obj*] **:** to cause (something) to not be even or continuous **:** to change or stop the sameness or smoothness of (something) ▪ Every summer periods of cool weather occasionally *interrupt* the intense heat. — often used as *(be) interrupted* ▪ The intense heat *is* occasionally *interrupted* by periods of cool weather. ▪ a grassy plain *interrupted* by a lone tree
– **in·ter·rup·tion** /ˌɪntəˈrʌpʃən/ *noun, pl* **-tions** [*count*] The dynasty lasted several hundred years, with only a few *interruptions*. ▪ I wish it were possible to watch television without all the commercial *interruptions*. ▪ frequent/annoying *interruptions* [*noncount*] She spoke for an hour without *interruption*. ▪ There shouldn't be any *interruption* in/to your phone service.

in·ter·scho·las·tic /ˌɪntɚskəˈlæstɪk/ *adj, always used before a noun, US* **:** existing or done between schools ▪ *interscholastic* sports/athletics

in·ter·sect /ˌɪntɚˈsɛkt/ *verb* **-sects; -sect·ed; -sect·ing**
1 a [+ *obj*] **:** to divide (something) by passing through or across it **:** CROSS ▪ A dry stream bed *intersects* the trail in several places. ▪ Line A *intersects* line B. = Line B is *intersected* by line A. = Line A and line B *intersect* each other **b** [*no obj*] **:** to meet and cross at one or more points ▪ Line A *intersects* with line B. ▪ *intersecting* lines/paths/streets ▪ The two roads *intersect* at the edge of town.
2 [*no obj*] **:** to share some common area ▪ the place where politics and business *intersect* [=*overlap*] = the place where politics *intersects* with business

in·ter·sec·tion /ˌɪntɚˈsɛkʃən/ *noun, pl* **-tions**
1 [*count*] **:** the place or point where two or more things come together; *especially* **:** the place where two or more streets meet or cross each other ▪ The accident occurred at a busy *intersection*.
2 [*noncount*] **:** the act or process of crossing or intersecting ▪ two possible points of *intersection* ▪ the *intersection* of line A and/with line B

in·ter·sperse /ˌɪntɚˈspɚs/ *verb* **-spers·es; -spersed; -spers·ing** [+ *obj*]
1 : to put (something) at different places among other things ▪ You should *intersperse* these pictures evenly throughout the book. ▪ Some seagulls were *interspersed* among the ducks.
2 : to put things at different places within (something) — + *with* ▪ *intersperse* a book *with* illustrations — usually used as *(be) interspersed* ▪ The book *was* nicely *interspersed with* illustrations. ▪ The forecast calls for scattered showers *interspersed with* sunny periods. [=scattered showers with sunny periods between the showers]

¹in·ter·state /ˌɪntɚˈsteɪt/ *adj, always used before a noun* **:** relating to or connecting different states : existing or occurring between states especially in the U.S. • an *interstate* highway • *interstate* commerce/transportation

²in·ter·state /ˈɪntəˌsteɪt/ *noun, pl* **-states** [*count*] *US* : a major highway that connects two or more states : an interstate highway • You'll get there quicker if you take the *interstate*. • *Interstate* 90

in·ter·stel·lar /ˌɪntəˈstɛlə/ *adj, always used before a noun* : existing or occurring between stars • *interstellar* space/gas/dust

in·ter·stice /ɪnˈtəstəs/ *noun, pl* **-stic·es** /ɪnˈtəstəˌsiːz/ [*count*] *formal* : a small space that lies between things : a small break or gap in something — usually plural • the *interstices* [=*cracks*] of/between the bricks

in·ter·tid·al /ˌɪntəˈtaɪtl/ *adj, always used before a noun, technical* : of or relating to the area of the shore that is between the low point and the high point of the tide • animals that live in the *intertidal* zone

in·ter·tri·bal /ˌɪntəˈtraɪbəl/ *adj, always used before a noun* : existing or occurring between tribes • *intertribal* warfare/politics

in·ter·twine /ˌɪntəˈtwaɪn/ *verb* **-twines; -twined; -twin·ing**

1 : to twist (things) together [+ *obj*] — often used as *(be) intertwined* • The branches *are intertwined* (with each other) and grow into a solid wall. • Colored ribbons *were intertwined* in her hair. [*no obj*] The branches *intertwine* (with each other) to make a solid wall. • *intertwining* branches

2 : to be or become very closely involved with each other [*no obj*] He's always telling stories in which the present and the past *intertwine*. [+ *obj*] His fate is *intertwined* with hers.

in·ter·val /ˈɪntəvəl/ *noun, pl* **-vals** [*count*]

1 : a period of time between events : PAUSE • a three-month *interval* between jobs • There might be long *intervals* during/in which nothing happens. • The sun shone for brief *intervals* throughout the day.

2 *music* : the difference in pitch between two notes

3 *Brit* : INTERMISSION • There will be a 20-minute *interval* between acts one and two.

at intervals **1** : with an amount of space in between • There are signs *at* regular *intervals* along the outside wall. • The chairs were placed *at intervals* of two feet. **2** : with an amount of time in between • It recurs *at* (regular) *intervals* of every six months.

in·ter·vene /ˌɪntəˈviːn/ *verb* **-venes; -vened; -ven·ing** [*no obj*]

1 : to come or occur between two times or events • Twenty years *intervened* between their first and last meetings.

2 : to become involved in something (such as a conflict) in order to have an influence on what happens • The prisoner asked me to *intervene* with the authorities on his behalf. • The military had to *intervene* to restore order. — often + *in* • We need the courts to *intervene in* this dispute.

3 : to happen as an unrelated event that causes a delay or problem • We will leave on time unless some crisis *intervenes*.

– intervening *adj, always used before another noun* • They have spent the *intervening* years trying to figure out what happened. **– in·ter·ven·tion** /ˌɪntəˈvɛnʃən/ *noun, pl* **-tions** [*noncount*] praying for divine *intervention* • This situation called for military *intervention*. • The program is able to run without *intervention* by the user. • medical *intervention* [=*treatment*] [*count*] military *interventions*

in·ter·ven·tion·ism /ˌɪntəˈvɛnʃəˌnɪzəm/ *noun* [*noncount*] : a government policy or practice of doing things to directly influence the country's economy or the political affairs of another country • a proponent of aggressive economic *interventionism*

– in·ter·ven·tion·ist /ˌɪntəˈvɛnʃənɪst/ *adj* [*more ~; most ~*] • *interventionist* policies/government **– intervention·ist** *noun, pl* **-ists** [*count*] • a die-hard *interventionist*

in·ter·ver·te·bral disc /ˌɪntəˈvətəbrəl-/ *noun, pl* **~ discs** [*count*] : DISC 4

¹in·ter·view /ˈɪntəˌvjuː/ *noun, pl* **-views** [*count*]

1 : a meeting at which people talk to each other in order to ask questions and get information: such as **a** : a formal meeting with someone who is being considered for a job or other position • The company is holding *interviews* for several new jobs. ✧ If you ***have an interview***, you have an appointment to speak to someone who could hire you. • I *have a* job *interview* tomorrow morning. **b** : a meeting between a reporter and another person in order to get information for a news story • a journalist conducting/doing *interviews* with political leaders • an actor who has stopped ***giving/granting/doing interviews*** [=an actor who no longer talks to reporters]; *also* : a written or taped record of such a meeting • The *interview* will be shown on tonight's news. • This library has a large collection of his *interviews*. • a published *interview*

2 *US, informal* : a person who is interviewed : INTERVIEWEE • He is a very entertaining *interview*. • She's always been known as one of Hollywood's best/toughest *interviews*.

²interview *verb* **-views; -viewed; -view·ing**

1 [+ *obj*] : to question or talk with (someone) in order to get information or learn about that person • The company will start *interviewing* candidates for the job tomorrow. • Few of the people *interviewed* for the job seemed at all suitable. • She's been *interviewed* on television many times. • The police are *interviewing* [=*interrogating*] several witnesses.

2 [*no obj*] *US* : to participate in an interview for a position (such as a job) • He has *interviewed* with many companies, but he still hasn't found a job. — often + *for* • Several people are now *interviewing for* the position.

– in·ter·view·er *noun, pl* **-ers** [*count*] • an *interviewer* who is known for asking tough questions

in·ter·view·ee /ˌɪntəˌvjuːˈiː/ *noun, pl* **-ees** [*count*] : a person who is interviewed • He asked the *interviewee* some very personal questions.

in·ter·war /ˌɪntəˈwoə/ *adj, always used before a noun* : occurring between wars; *especially* : occurring between World War I and World War II • during the *interwar* years

in·ter·weave /ˌɪntəˈwiːv/ *verb* **-weaves; -wove** /ˌɪntəˈwoʊv/; **-woven** /ˌɪntəˈwoʊvən/; **-weav·ing** [+ *obj*] : to twist or weave (threads, fibers, etc.) together • The long strands of ribbon are *interwoven* (together). • a house built from poles *interwoven* with vines • a mat of *interwoven* fibers — often used figuratively • The two themes are *interwoven* throughout the poem. • He *interweaves* advice and amusing stories to create an entertaining book. • His life is closely *interwoven* with hers.

in·tes·tate /ɪnˈtɛˌsteɪt/ *adj, law* : not having made a will • He ***died intestate***. [=he did not have a will when he died]

in·tes·tine /ɪnˈtɛstən/ *noun, pl* **-tines** [*count*] : a long tube in the body that helps digest food after it leaves the stomach — see also LARGE INTESTINE, SMALL INTESTINE

– in·tes·ti·nal /ɪnˈtɛstənl/ *adj* • the *intestinal* tract/wall • *intestinal* tissue • *intestinal* gas • an *intestinal* disease — see also *intestinal fortitude* at FORTITUDE

in·ti·ma·cy /ˈɪntəməsi/ *noun, pl* **-cies**

1 : an intimate quality or state: such as **a** : emotional warmth and closeness [*noncount*] the *intimacy* of old friends • the *intimacy* of their relationship • a fear of *intimacy* [*singular*] He felt he achieved a certain *intimacy* with her. **b** [*noncount*] : a quality that suggests informal warmth or closeness • The band liked the *intimacy* of the nightclub.

2 [*noncount*] : sexual relations • sexual/physical *intimacy*

3 [*count*] : something that is very personal and private — usually plural • They shared *intimacies* about their private lives.

¹in·ti·mate /ˈɪntəmət/ *adj* [*more ~; most ~*]

1 : having a very close relationship : very warm and friendly • an *intimate* acquaintance • They remained *intimate* friends throughout their lives. • We have an *intimate* friendship with our neighbors. = We are ***on intimate terms*** with our neighbors. [=we are very close friends with our neighbors]

2 : very personal or private • *intimate* thoughts/feelings • *intimate* secrets • sharing an *intimate* moment • an *intimate* conversation • (*chiefly US*) a store that sells *intimate* apparel [=women's underwear and clothes for sleeping]

3 : involving sex or sexual relations • They are in an *intimate* and committed relationship. • He denies that they were ever *intimate*. = He denies that he was ever ***intimate with*** her. [=that he ever had sexual relations with her]

4 *of a place* : private and pleasant in a way that allows people to feel relaxed and comfortable • The room is small and *intimate*. • an *intimate* nightclub

5 : very closely related or connected : very close • There is an *intimate* connection/relationship between diet and health.

6 : very complete • She has an *intimate* [=very detailed] knowledge of the company. • The story is now known in *intimate* detail. • an *intimate* understanding of the process

– in·ti·mate·ly *adv* • She is *intimately* associated/involved with the production. • The problem is *intimately* connected with/to our culture. • *intimately* familiar with the experience • Diet and health are *intimately* [=very closely] related. • Their careers are *intimately* linked. • She knows the city *intimately*. [=very well]

[2]**in·ti·mate** /ˈɪntəmət/ *noun, pl* **-mates** [*count*] *somewhat formal* : a very close and trusted friend : an intimate friend • His coworkers knew him as "Robert," but his *intimates* called him "Robbie."

[3]**in·ti·mate** /ˈɪntəˌmeɪt/ *verb* **-mates; -mat·ed; -mat·ing** [+ *obj*] : to say or suggest (something) in an indirect way • He *intimated* (to us) that we should plan to arrive early.

— **in·ti·ma·tion** /ˌɪntəˈmeɪʃən/ *noun, pl* **-tions** [*count*] the earliest *intimations* [=*hints*] of spring • Even at the beginning, there were *intimations* [=*suggestions*] that the project was in trouble. [*noncount*] He hasn't given any *intimation* of his plans.

in·tim·i·date /ɪnˈtɪməˌdeɪt/ *verb* **-dates; -dat·ed; -dat·ing** [+ *obj*] : to make (someone) afraid • He tries to *intimidate* his opponents. • You shouldn't allow his reputation to *intimidate* you. — often used as *(be) intimidated* • Many people *are intimidated* by new technology. • Some people *are* easily *intimidated*. • She *was intimidated* by the size of the campus.

— **intimidated** *adj* [*more* ~; *most* ~] • I feel less *intimidated* now than I did when I started the job. — **intimidating** *adj* [*more* ~; *most* ~] • He is one of the most *intimidating* men I have ever met. • Speaking in front of a large audience can be very *intimidating*. — **in·tim·i·dat·ing·ly** /ɪnˈtɪməˌdeɪtɪŋli/ *adv* • The system is *intimidatingly* complex. — **in·tim·i·da·tion** /ɪnˌtɪməˈdeɪʃən/ *noun* [*noncount*] • *intimidation* of jurors/witnesses • enforcing agreement by *intimidation* or violence — **in·tim·i·da·tor** /ɪnˈtɪməˌdeɪtə/ *noun, pl* **-tors** [*count*]

intl. *or* **intnl.** *abbr* international

in·to /ˈɪntu, ˈɪntə/ *prep*

1 : to or toward the inside of (something) • She came *into* the room/house. • a medicine injected *into* the bloodstream • Please put the bowl *into* the sink/cupboard. • They were heading *into* town. • He jumped *into* the pool.

2 : in the direction of (something) • You should never look directly *into* [=*toward*] the sun. • She was just staring *into* space. • peering/looking *into* the past/future

3 — used to describe hitting or touching something or someone • He ran *into* [=*against*] a wall. • She bumped *into* me.

4 : to the state, condition, or form of (something) • She was shocked *into* silence. • come *into* being/existence • as day turns *into* night • I got *into* trouble again. • her slow descent *into* madness • converting sunlight *into* electricity • He translated the poem from Latin *into* English. • change dollars *into* euros • breaking up *into* smaller pieces

5 a — used to say that something or someone has become a part of something • They entered *into* an alliance. • He was born *into* a once-proud family. **b** — used to say that someone has become involved in something (such as a profession) • She wants to get *into* politics. • He decided to go *into* farming. [=he decided to be a farmer] **c** — used to say that someone has been forced or persuaded to do something • He was pressured *into* doing this by his boss. • I was talked *into* joining the class.

6 *informal* — used to say that someone is interested in and excited about (something) • He was never *into* sports. • I'm really *into* her music. • I usually enjoy her books, but I just couldn't get *into* this one.

7 — used to say how long something lasts • The party continued well/far/long/late *into* the night. • This snow should last well *into* the spring. • The heat wave will continue *into* next week.

8 : relating to or concerning (something) • an investigation *into* the causes of the accident

9 — used to describe dividing one number by another number • Six goes *into* 18 three times. • Dividing 3 *into* 6 gives 2.

be into (someone) for *US, informal* : to owe someone (an amount of money) • I'*m into him for* a thousand dollars.

in·tol·er·a·ble /ɪnˈtɑːlərəbəl/ *adj* [*more* ~; *most* ~] : too bad, harsh, or severe to be accepted or tolerated : not tolerable • The situation was totally *intolerable* [=*unacceptable*] to us. • *intolerable* [=*unbearable*] pain/behavior • She divorced him on the grounds of *intolerable* cruelty.

— **in·tol·er·a·bly** /ɪnˈtɑːlərəbli/ *adv* • *intolerably* cruel/dull/boring.

in·tol·er·ant /ɪnˈtɑːlərənt/ *adj*

1 [*more* ~; *most* ~] **a** : not willing to allow or accept something — often + *of* • He is *intolerant of* weakness/failure. • They were *intolerant* of his lifestyle. **b** *disapproving* : not willing to allow some people to have equality, freedom, or other social rights • an *intolerant* [=*bigoted*] racist

2 *medicine* : unable to take a certain substance into the body without becoming sick • people who are lactose *intolerant* [=unable to eat foods that contain lactose] — often + *of* • patients who are *intolerant of* certain drugs

— **in·tol·er·ance** /ɪnˈtɑːlərəns/ *noun* [*noncount*] • *intolerance* towards/to outsiders • fighting the forces of racism and *intolerance* • a campaign against religious *intolerance* • lactose *intolerance* — **in·tol·er·ant·ly** *adv*

in·to·na·tion /ˌɪntoʊˈneɪʃən/ *noun, pl* **-tions** : the rise and fall in the sound of your voice when you speak [*noncount*] identical sentences, differing only in *intonation* [*count*] sentences with different *intonations*

in·tone /ɪnˈtoʊn/ *verb* **-tones; -toned; -ton·ing** [+ *obj*]

1 : to speak (a prayer, poem, etc.) in a way that sounds like music or chanting • *intone* a prayer

2 : to say (something) in a slow and even voice • "Coming soon to a theater near you," the announcer *intoned*.

in to·to /ɪnˈtoʊˌtoʊ/ *adv, formal* : as a whole : totally or completely • The judge accepted/rejected the testimony *in toto*.

in·tox·i·cant /ɪnˈtɑːksɪkənt/ *noun, pl* **-cants** [*count*] *formal* : something (such as an acoholic drink) that causes people to become excited or confused and less able to control what they say or do : an intoxicating substance • The use of *intoxicants* and stimulants is prohibited. • He was driving under the influence of *intoxicants*.

in·tox·i·cate /ɪnˈtɑːksɪˌkeɪt/ *verb* **-cates; -cat·ed; -cat·ing** [+ *obj*] *somewhat formal*

1 *of alcohol, a drug, etc.* : to make (someone) unable to think and behave normally • The little bit of beer I drank was not enough to *intoxicate* me.

2 : to excite or please (someone) in a way that suggests the effect of alcohol or a drug — usually used as *(be) intoxicated* • He *was intoxicated* by the power of his position in the government. • He *was intoxicated* by her beauty.

— **in·tox·i·ca·tion** /ɪnˌtɑːksəˈkeɪʃən/ *noun* [*noncount*] • She drank to the point of *intoxication*. • He was arrested for public *intoxication*. [=for being drunk in public] • the *intoxication* of power

in·tox·i·cat·ed /ɪnˈtɑːksɪˌkeɪtəd/ *adj* [*more* ~; *most* ~] *somewhat formal* : affected by alcohol or drugs; *especially* : DRUNK • He appeared to be very *intoxicated*. • Driving while *intoxicated* is illegal.

intoxicating *adj* [*more* ~; *most* ~] *somewhat formal*

1 : causing intoxication; *especially* : able to make someone drunk • *intoxicating* beverages • the *intoxicating* effects of alcohol

2 : causing someone to have strong feelings of excitement or pleasure • the *intoxicating* power of his position in the government • her *intoxicating* beauty

in·tra- /ˈɪntrə/ *prefix*

1 : within something • *intra*mural — opposite EXTRA-

2 : in or into something • *intra*venous

in·trac·ta·ble /ɪnˈtræktəbəl/ *adj* [*more* ~; *most* ~] *formal*

1 : not easily managed, controlled, or solved • an *intractable* problem • an *intractable* mystery/question

2 : not easily relieved or cured • a patient experiencing *intractable* pain • an *intractable* infection/disease

— **in·trac·ta·bil·i·ty** /ɪnˌtræktəˈbɪləti/ *noun* [*noncount*] • the *intractability* of the problem/disease — **in·trac·ta·bly** /ɪnˈtræktəbli/ *adv* • an *intractably* complicated problem

in·tra·mu·ral /ˌɪntrəˈmjərəl/ *adj, US* : existing or occurring within a particular group or organization (such as a school) • *intramural* sports [=sports in which the students of one school compete against each other instead of competing against other schools]

in·tra·net /ˈɪntrəˌnɛt/ *noun, pl* **-nets** [*count*] *computers* : a network that works like the Internet but can only be used by certain people (such as the employees of a company) • a corporate *intranet*

in·tran·si·gent /ɪnˈtrænsəʤənt/ *adj* [*more* ~; *most* ~] *formal* : completely unwilling to change : very stubborn • *intransigent* enemies/opponents • He has remained *intransigent* in his opposition to the proposal.

— **in·tran·si·gence** /ɪnˈtrænsəʤəns/ *noun* [*noncount*] • fighting bureaucratic *intransigence* — **in·tran·si·gent·ly** *adv*

in·tran·si·tive /ɪnˈtrænsətɪv/ *adj, grammar, of a verb* : not taking or having a direct object • an *intransitive* verb • In "I ran" and "The bird flies," "ran" and "flies" are *intransitive*. — compare TRANSITIVE

– in•tran•si•tive•ly *adv* ▪ Some verbs can be used both *intransitively* and transitively.

in•tra•state /ˌɪntrəˈsteɪt/ *adj, always used before a noun* **: occurring within a state** ▪ *intrastate* commerce/trucking ▪ *intrastate* football rivals

in•tra•uter•ine /ˌɪntrəˈjuːtərən, ˌɪntrəˈjuːtəˌraɪn/ *adj, always used before a noun, medical* **: used or occurring within the uterus** ▪ an *intrauterine* growth

intrauterine device *noun, pl* **~ -vices** [*count*] *medical* **: a device that is inserted in the uterus and left there to prevent pregnancy — called also** *IUD*

in•tra•ve•nous /ˌɪntrəˈviːnəs/ *adj, always used before a noun* **: through, in, or into a vein : entering the body through a vein** ▪ *intravenous* feedings/drugs ▪ an *intravenous* needle

– in•tra•ve•nous•ly *adv* ▪ She is being given the medication *intravenously*.

in tray *noun, pl* **~ trays** [*count*] **:** IN-BOX

in•trep•id /ɪnˈtrɛpəd/ *adj* [*more ~; most ~*] *literary + often humorous* **: feeling no fear : very bold or brave** ▪ an *intrepid* explorer

in•tri•ca•cy /ˈɪntrəkəsi/ *noun, pl* **-cies**

1 [*noncount*] **: the quality or state of being complex or having many parts : the quality or state of being intricate** ▪ She admired the composition for its beauty and *intricacy*. ▪ the *intricacy* [=*complexity*] of the design/plan

2 [*count*] **: something that is complex or detailed : something intricate** ▪ I had trouble following all the *intricacies* in the plot. ▪ the *intricacies* of English grammar

in•tri•cate /ˈɪntrəkət/ *adj* [*more ~; most ~*] **: having many parts** ▪ *intricate* machinery ▪ an *intricate* [=*complex*] design/pattern ▪ The movie has an *intricate* plot.

– in•tri•cate•ly *adv* ▪ *intricately* woven fabric ▪ an *intricately* carved mantel

[1]in•trigue /ɪnˈtriːg/ *verb* **-trigues; -trigued; -trigu•ing**

1 [*+ obj*] **: to make (someone) want to know more about something : to cause (someone) to become interested** ▪ Your idea *intrigues* me. **— often used as** *(be) intrigued* ▪ She *was intrigued* with/by what he had to say.

2 [*no obj*] *formal* **: to make secret plans — usually +** *against* ▪ They were arrested for *intriguing against* the government.

[2]in•trigue /ˈɪnˌtriːg/ *noun, pl* **-trigues**

1 [*noncount*] **: the activity of making secret plans** ▪ a novel of *intrigue* and romance ▪ an administration characterized by *intrigue* and corruption

2 [*count*] **: a secret plan** ▪ political *intrigues*

in•trigu•ing /ɪnˈtriːgɪŋ/ *adj* [*more ~; most ~*] **: extremely interesting :** FASCINATING ▪ an *intriguing* idea/person/question ▪ The offer is very *intriguing*.

– in•trigu•ing•ly *adv*

in•trin•sic /ɪnˈtrɪnzɪk/ *adj* **: belonging to the essential nature of a thing : occurring as a natural part of something** ▪ the *intrinsic* value of a gem ▪ the *intrinsic* brightness of a star ▪ *intrinsic* beauty **— often +** *to* ▪ Creativity is *intrinsic to* human nature. **— opposite** EXTRINSIC

– in•trin•si•cal•ly /ɪnˈtrɪnzɪkli/ *adv* ▪ an *intrinsically* difficult language ▪ *intrinsically* evil/valuable

in•tro /ˈɪnˌtroʊ/ *noun, pl* **-tros** [*count*] *informal* **: a short introduction to something (such as a performance or a musical work)** ▪ a brief *intro*

in•tro•duce /ˌɪntrəˈduːs, *Brit* ˌɪntrəˈdjuːs/ *verb* **-duc•es; -duced; -duc•ing** [*+ obj*]

1 : to make (someone) known to someone else by name ▪ *introduce* two strangers ▪ He *introduced* his guest. ▪ Let me *introduce* myself: my name is John Smith. **— often +** *to* ▪ He *introduced* himself *to* the class. ▪ She *introduced* her mother *to* her friends.

2 a : to cause (something) to begin to be used for the first time ▪ They have been slow to *introduce* changes in procedure. **b : to make (something) available for sale for the first time** ▪ The designer is *introducing* a new line of clothes. **c : to present (something) for discussion or consideration** ▪ He *introduced* several issues during the meeting. ▪ New evidence was *introduced* at the trial. ▪ *introduce* a bill to Congress

3 : to bring (something, such as a type of plant or animal) to a place for the first time — often + *to* ▪ an Asian plant that has been *introduced to* America

4 : to speak briefly to an audience about (someone who is about to speak, perform, etc., or something that is about to begin) ▪ She *introduced* the speaker. ▪ He *introduced* the show's second act.

5 : to mention or refer to (something) for the first time ▪ The main topics are *introduced* in the first chapter.

6 : to cause (someone) to learn about or try (something) for the first time — + *to* ▪ The program *introduces* children *to* different sports. ▪ I was *introduced to* painting in college. ▪ The class *introduces* students *to* computer programming. ▪ She helped to *introduce* Americans *to* European fashions. = She helped to *introduce* European fashions *to* America.

7 : to put or insert (something) into something else ▪ *introduce* a needle into a vein ▪ The new carpet *introduces* some color into [=adds some color to] the living room. ▪ The rivalry *introduced* more drama to/into the competition.

in•tro•duc•tion /ˌɪntrəˈdʌkʃən/ *noun, pl* **-tions**

1 [*count*] **: the act of making a person known to others by name — usually plural** ▪ Once we finished the *introductions* [=once everyone was introduced], the meeting began. ▪ I'll ***make the introductions***. [=I'll introduce everyone]

2 [*noncount*] **: the act of introducing something: such as a : the act of bringing something into practice or use for the first time** ▪ the *introduction* of telephone service to the area **b : the act of making a product available for sale for the first time** ▪ Since its *introduction* last year, over a million copies of the software have been sold. **c : the act of presenting something for discussion or consideration** ▪ the *introduction* of evidence at the trial ▪ the *introduction* of a new topic for conversation ▪ the *introduction* of the bill to Congress ▪ She told the audience, ***by way of introduction***, that the research was completed a year ago. **d : the act of bringing something (such as a plant or animal) to a place for the first time** ▪ the *introduction* of an Asian plant species to America

3 [*count*] **: a statement made to an audience about someone who is about to speak, perform, etc., or something that is about to begin** ▪ After a brief *introduction*, the performer took the stage. ✧ A person who ***needs no introduction*** is well-known to the audience. ▪ Our speaker this evening *needs no introduction*.

4 [*count*] **a : the beginning part of a book, essay, speech, etc., that explains what will follow in the main part** ▪ Did you read the *introduction*? ▪ His *introduction* outlined the main points of the speech. **b : the beginning part of a piece of music**

5 [*count*] **: something (such as a book or a course of study) that provides basic information about a subject — +** *to* ▪ The book/course is an *introduction to* computer programming.

6 [*singular*] **: a person's first experience with something — +** *to* ▪ That concert was my *introduction to* her music. [=it was the first time I had heard her music]

7 [*count*] **: something that is added or introduced to something else** ▪ The plant is a recent *introduction* from Asia.

in•tro•duc•to•ry /ˌɪntrəˈdʌktəri/ *adj*

1 : providing information about someone who is about to speak, perform, etc., or something that is about to begin ▪ I'd like to make a few *introductory* remarks before we start the program. ▪ the book's *introductory* chapter

2 : providing basic information about a subject ▪ an *introductory* text ▪ a class in *introductory* physics

3 : intended to attract customers when a new product, service, etc., is introduced ▪ a special *introductory* offer/price

in•tro•spec•tion /ˌɪntrəˈspɛkʃən/ *noun* [*noncount*] **: the process of examining your own thoughts or feelings** ▪ a moment of quiet *introspection*

– in•tro•spec•tive /ˌɪntrəˈspɛktɪv/ *adj* [*more ~; most ~*] ▪ As a student, he was very quiet and *introspective*.

in•tro•vert /ˈɪntrəˌvət/ *noun, pl* **-verts** [*count*] **: a shy person : a quiet person who does not find it easy to talk to other people — opposite** EXTROVERT

– in•tro•vert•ed /ˈɪntrəˌvətəd/ *adj* [*more ~; most ~*] ▪ an *introverted* person/personality

in•trude /ɪnˈtruːd/ *verb* **-trudes; -trud•ed; -trud•ing** [*no obj*]

1 : to come or go into a place where you are not wanted or welcome ▪ Excuse me, sir. I don't mean to *intrude*, but you have a phone call. ▪ Would I be *intruding* if I came along with you? ▪ The plane *intruded* into their airspace.

2 : to become involved with something private in an annoying way ▪ Reporters constantly *intruded* into the couple's private life. ▪ He didn't want to *intrude* upon their conversation.

– in•tru•sion /ɪnˈtruːʒən/ *noun, pl* **-sions** [*count*] The phone call was an unwelcome *intrusion*. ▪ Please excuse the *intrusion*. We'll be finished shortly. ▪ They have grown tired of all the *intrusions* into their private lives. [*noncount*] These laws are meant to protect citizens from improper government *intrusion*. ▪ The animals are sensitive to human *intrusion* into their habitat.

in·trud·er /ɪnˈtruːdɚ/ *noun, pl* **-ers** [*count*]
1 : a person who is not welcome or wanted in a place ▪ The other children regarded him as an *intruder.*
2 : a person who enters a place illegally ▪ The police arrested the *intruder.*

in·tru·sive /ɪnˈtruːsɪv/ *adj* [*more* ~; *most* ~] **:** annoying someone by interfering with their privacy **:** intruding where you are not wanted or welcome ▪ a loud and *intrusive* person ▪ She tried to be helpful without being *intrusive.* ▪ *Intrusive* reporters disturbed their privacy. ▪ *intrusive* questions
– in·tru·sive·ness *noun* [*noncount*]

in·tu·it /ɪnˈtuːwət, *Brit* ɪnˈtjuːət/ *verb* **-its; -it·ed; -it·ing** [+ *obj*] *formal* **:** to know or understand (something) because of what you feel or sense rather than because of evidence **:** to know or understand (something) through intuition ▪ He was able to *intuit* the answer immediately. ▪ She *intuited* a connection between the two crimes.

in·tu·i·tion /ˌɪntuˈɪʃən, *Brit* ˌɪntjuˈɪʃən/ *noun, pl* **-tions**
1 [*noncount*] **:** a natural ability or power that makes it possible to know something without any proof or evidence **:** a feeling that guides a person to act a certain way without fully understanding why ▪ *Intuition* was telling her that something was very wrong. ▪ "How did you know I would drop by?" "Oh, I don't know. It must have been *intuition.*" ▪ I trusted my *intuition* [=*instincts*] and ended the relationship.
2 [*count*] **:** something that is known or understood without proof or evidence ▪ I had an *intuition* [=(more commonly) *feeling, hunch*] that you would drop by.

in·tu·i·tive /ɪnˈtuːwətɪv, *Brit* ɪnˈtjuːətɪv/ *adj* [*more* ~; *most* ~]
1 : having the ability to know or understand things without any proof or evidence **:** having or characterized by intuition ▪ She has an *intuitive* mind ▪ an *intuitive* person
2 : based on or agreeing with what is known or understood without any proof or evidence **:** known or understood by intuition ▪ She has an *intuitive* [=*instinctive*] understanding of the business. ▪ a doctor with an *intuitive* awareness of his patients' concerns
3 a : agreeing with what seems naturally right ▪ The argument makes *intuitive* sense. **b :** easily and quickly learned or understood ▪ The software has an *intuitive* interface.
– in·tu·i·tive·ly *adv* ▪ a chef who works *intuitively,* rather than from a recipe ▪ The solution is *intuitively* obvious.

In·u·it *also* **In·nu·it** /ˈɪnjuwət, ˈɪnuwət/ *noun, pl* **Inuit** *or* **In·u·its** *also* **Innuit** *or* **In·nu·its**
1 [*count*] **:** a member of a group of native people of northern North America and Greenland
2 [*noncount*] **:** the language of the Inuit people

in·un·date /ˈɪnənˌdeɪt/ *verb* **-dates; -dat·ed; -dat·ing** [+ *obj*]
1 : to cause (someone or something) to receive or take in a large amount of things at the same time ▪ Hundreds of letters *inundated* [=*flooded*] the office. — **often + *with*** ▪ The salesman *inundated* [=*overwhelmed*] them *with* information. — **often used as *(be) inundated*** ▪ The office *was inundated with* calls/letters. ▪ She *was inundated* [=*swamped*] *with* requests.
2 *formal* **:** to cover (something) with a flood of water **:** FLOOD ▪ Rising rivers could *inundate* low-lying areas. — **often used as *(be) inundated*** ▪ Low-lying areas could *be inundated* by rising rivers.
– in·un·da·tion /ˌɪnənˈdeɪʃən/ *noun, pl* **-tions** [*count, noncount*]

in·ure /ɪˈnuɚ, ɪˈnjuɚ/ *verb* **-ures; -ured; -ur·ing** [+ *obj*] *formal* **:** to cause (someone) to be less affected by something unpleasant **:** to cause (someone) to be less sensitive *to* something unpleasant ▪ Does violence on television *inure* children *to* violence in real life?
– inured *adj* **— + *to*** ▪ Are children *inured to* violence? ▪ We quickly became *inured to* his sarcasm.

in·vade /ɪnˈveɪd/ *verb* **-vades; -vad·ed; -vad·ing**
1 : to enter (a place, such as a foreign country) in order to take control by military force [+ *obj*] *invade* a country [*no obj*] The troops *invaded* at dawn.
2 a : to enter (a place) in large numbers [+ *obj*] Ants *invaded* the kitchen. ▪ Tourists *invaded* the town. [*no obj*] When tourists *invade,* the town is a very different place. **b** [+ *obj*] **:** to enter or be in (a place where you are not wanted) ▪ She was ***invading my space*** [=she was too close to me; she was in the place/space where I was or where I wanted to be]
3 : to spread over or into (something) in a harmful way [+ *obj*] The cancer eventually *invaded* the brain. ▪ Weeds had *invaded* the garden. ▪ Doubts *invaded* my mind. [=I began to have many doubts] [*no obj*] Bacteria *invaded* and caused an infection.
4 [+ *obj*] **:** to affect (something, such as your life or privacy) in an unwanted way ▪ He thinks people were happier before TV and the Internet *invaded* our lives. ▪ Photographers ***invaded her privacy.*** [=caused her to lose her privacy; intruded on her privacy]
– in·vad·er *noun, pl* **-ers** [*count*] ▪ The city was attacked by *invaders* from the north.

¹in·val·id /ɪnˈvæləd/ *adj* **:** not valid: such as **a :** having no force or effect ▪ The judge declared that the contract was *invalid.* **b :** not based on truth or fact **:** not logical or correct ▪ an *invalid* argument

²in·va·lid /ˈɪnvələd, *Brit* ˈɪnvəˌliːd/ *noun, pl* **-lids** [*count*] **:** a person who needs to be cared for because of injury or illness ▪ Her husband has become an *invalid.* — **often used before another noun** ▪ She cares for her *invalid* husband at home.

³in·va·lid /ˈɪnvələd, *Brit* ˈɪnvəˌliːd/ *verb* **-lids; -lid·ed; -lid·ing** [+ *obj*] *Brit* **:** to release (someone) from active military service because of illness or injury — **usually used as *(be) invalided*** ▪ He *was invalided* out of the army. ▪ He *was invalided* home.

in·val·i·date /ɪnˈvæləˌdeɪt/ *verb* **-dates; -dat·ed; -dat·ing** [+ *obj*] **:** to make (something) invalid: such as **a :** to weaken or destroy the effect of (something) ▪ actions that will *invalidate* the contract ▪ *invalidate* a marriage ▪ *invalidate* an election **b :** to show or prove (something) to be false or incorrect ▪ The study *invalidates* earlier theories. ▪ factors that may *invalidate* the test results

in·val·id·i·ty /ˌɪnvəˈlɪdəti/ *noun* [*noncount*] *formal*
1 : the state of having no force or effect **:** the state of being invalid ▪ the *invalidity* of the contract/election
2 *Brit* **:** the state or condition of being unable to work because of illness or injury **:** the state or condition of being an invalid ▪ an injured worker forced to live on *invalidity* benefit

in·valu·able /ɪnˈvæljəbəl/ *adj* [*more* ~; *most* ~] **:** extremely valuable or useful ▪ an *invaluable* experience ▪ Their help has been *invaluable* to us. ▪ *invaluable* information/advice

in·vari·able /ɪnˈverijəbəl/ *adj* **:** not changing or capable of change **:** staying the same **:** not variable ▪ an *invariable* routine
– in·vari·ably /ɪnˈverijəbli/ *adv* ▪ He is *invariably* [=*always*] courteous. ▪ The disease is *invariably* fatal.

in·va·sion /ɪnˈveɪʒən/ *noun, pl* **-sions**
1 : the act of invading something: such as **a :** the act of entering a place in an attempt to take control of it [*count*] The enemy launched/mounted an *invasion.* ▪ the *invasion* of Poland [*noncount*] The people live under a constant threat of *invasion.* **b :** the act of entering a place in large numbers especially in a way that is harmful or unwanted [*count*] The town is gearing up for the annual tourist *invasion.* ▪ an *invasion* of/by insects [*noncount*] protecting the house from insect *invasion*
2 ✧ An ***invasion of privacy*** is a situation in which someone tries to get information about a person's private life in an unwanted and usually improper way. ▪ I consider these questions to be an *invasion of my privacy.* ▪ Is drug testing an *invasion of privacy*?

in·va·sive /ɪnˈveɪsɪv/ *adj* [*more* ~; *most* ~]
1 : tending to spread ▪ The cancer is *invasive.* ▪ *invasive* plants
2 *medical* **:** involving entry into the body by cutting or by inserting an instrument ▪ an *invasive* medical procedure

in·vec·tive /ɪnˈvɛktɪv/ *noun* [*noncount*] *formal* **:** harsh or insulting words **:** rude and angry language ▪ a barrage/stream of racist *invective*

in·veigh /ɪnˈveɪ/ *verb* **-veighs; -veighed; -veigh·ing**
inveigh against [*phrasal verb*] ***inveigh against (someone or something)*** *formal* **:** to protest or complain about (something or someone) very strongly ▪ Employees *inveighed against* mandatory overtime.

in·vei·gle /ɪnˈveɪgəl/ *verb* **-vei·gles; -vei·gled; -vei·gling** [+ *obj*] *formal*
1 : to persuade (someone) to do something in a clever or deceptive way ▪ She *inveigled* him to write the letter. — **usually + *into*** ▪ They tried to *inveigle* her *into* taking the job.
2 : to get (something) in a clever or deceptive way ▪ We *inveigled* the information from him. ▪ He ***inveigled his way*** into a position of authority. [=he gained a position of authority by using trickery]

in·vent /ɪnˈvɛnt/ *verb* **-vents; -vent·ed; -ven·ting** [+ *obj*]
1 : to create or produce (something useful) for the first time

▪ Thomas Edison *invented* the phonograph. ▪ She is credited with *inventing* a procedure that has helped to save thousands of lives. ▪ *invent* a new word

2 : to create or make up (something, such as a story) in order to trick people ▪ She *invented* a clever excuse/story. ▪ We found out that he had *invented* the stories he told us about his military service.

– in·ven·tor /ɪnˈvɛntɚ/ *noun, pl* **-tors** [*count*] ▪ Thomas Edison was a great *inventor*.

in·ven·tion /ɪnˈvɛnʃən/ *noun, pl* **-tions**

1 : something invented: such as **a** [*count*] **:** a useful new device or process ▪ The light bulb was one of the most important *inventions* of the 19th century. **b :** something (such as a false story) that is made up [*count*] The stories he told about his military service were just *inventions*. [*noncount*] His explanation was pure *invention*. ▪ Parts of the movie were accurate, but much of it was *invention*.

2 [*noncount*] **:** the act of inventing something ▪ the *invention* of a new product ▪ the *invention* of a false story ▪ Don't believe everything she tells you. She's prone to *invention*. [=*exaggeration, lying*]

3 [*noncount*] **:** the ability to think of new ideas ▪ an artist with exceptional powers of *invention* — see also *necessity is the mother of invention* at [1]MOTHER

in·ven·tive /ɪnˈvɛntɪv/ *adj* [*more* ~; *most* ~] **:** having or showing an ability to think of new ideas and methods **:** creative or imaginative ▪ an *inventive* child/artist ▪ They have given their new company an *inventive* name.

– in·ven·tive·ly *adv* **– in·ven·tive·ness** *noun* [*noncount*]

[1]**in·ven·to·ry** /ˈɪnvənˌtori, *Brit* ˈɪnvəntri/ *noun, pl* **-ries**

1 [*count*] **:** a complete list of the things that are in a place ▪ an *inventory* of supplies ▪ We made an *inventory* of the library's collection.

2 *chiefly US* **:** a supply of goods that are stored in a place [*count*] The dealer keeps a large *inventory* of used cars and trucks. ▪ *Inventories* at both stores were low. [*noncount*] How can a small business afford to keep so much *inventory*?

3 [*noncount*] *chiefly US* **:** the act or process of making a complete list of the things that are in a place **:** the act or process of making an inventory ▪ We'll be doing *inventory* on the collection soon. — called also (*Brit*) *stocktaking*

[2]**inventory** *verb* **-ries; -ried; -ry·ing** [+ *obj*] **:** to make a complete list of (the things in a place) **:** to make an inventory of (something) ▪ We'll be *inventorying* the collection soon.

[1]**in·verse** /ɪnˈvɚs, ˈɪnˌvɚs/ *adj, always used before a noun*

1 — used to describe two things that are related in such a way that as one becomes larger the other becomes smaller ▪ The study indicates an *inverse* relationship between the unemployment rate and inflation. [=as the unemployment rate drops, inflation rises] ▪ My interest in his books declined in *inverse* proportion to his popularity. [=my interest declined as his books became more popular]

2 *technical* **:** opposite in nature or effect ▪ Addition and subtraction are *inverse* operations.

– in·verse·ly *adv*

[2]**inverse** /ɪnˈvɚs, ˈɪnˌvɚs/ *noun* [*singular*] *formal + technical* **:** something that is the opposite of something else ▪ the *inverse* of your argument

inversely proportional *adj* **:** related so that as one becomes larger the other becomes smaller ▪ The study indicates that the unemployment rate and inflation are *inversely proportional*. — compare DIRECTLY PROPORTIONAL

in·ver·sion /ɪnˈvɚʒən/ *noun, pl* **-sions**

1 *formal* **:** a change in the position, order, or relationship of things so that they are the opposite of what they had been [*count*] an *inversion* of the roles of parent and child [*noncount*] *Inversion* of the two words changes the meaning of the sentence.

2 [*count, noncount*] *weather* **:** a condition in which air close to the ground is cooler than the air above it ▪ (a) temperature *inversion*

in·vert /ɪnˈvɚt/ *verb* **-verts; -vert·ed; -ver·ting** [+ *obj*] *formal*

1 : to turn (something) upside down ▪ *invert* a bowl ▪ The lens *inverts* the image. ▪ The number 9 looks like an *inverted* 6. ▪ an *inverted* image

2 : to change the position, order, or relationship of things so that they are the opposite of what they had been ▪ *invert* the order of two words in a sentence

in·ver·te·brate /ɪnˈvɚtəbrət/ *noun, pl* **-brates** [*count*] **:** a type of animal that does not have a backbone ▪ Worms are *invertebrates*. — compare VERTEBRATE

– invertebrate *adj* ▪ *invertebrate* species

inverted comma *noun, pl* **~ -mas** [*count*] *Brit* **:** QUOTATION MARK

in·vest /ɪnˈvɛst/ *verb* **-vests; -vest·ed; -ves·ting**

1 : to use money to earn more money **:** to use your money to purchase stock in a company, to buy property, etc., in order to make future profit [*no obj*] She has always *invested* conservatively/aggressively. — often + *in* ▪ He made a fortune by *investing in* real estate. [+ *obj*] She *invested* her inheritance money. ▪ *invested* money — often + *in* ▪ He *invested* his savings *in* the business.

2 a : to spend (money) on building or improving something — usually + *in* [+ *obj*] The city will *invest* millions of dollars *in* two new schools. [*no obj*] The city plans to *invest* heavily *in* its educational system this year. **b** [+ *obj*] **:** to give your time or effort in order to do something or make something better — usually + *in* ▪ A lot of effort was *invested in* the project. ▪ We need to *invest* more time *in* educating our children. ▪ (*chiefly US*) She is ***deeply invested in*** this project [=she has given a lot of time and effort to this project and cares about it very much] and wants it to succeed.

3 [+ *obj*] *formal* **:** to provide (someone or something) *with* (something) ▪ The United States Constitution *invests* the President *with* certain powers. [=gives certain powers to the President] ▪ The emperor claimed to be *invested with* power by the gods. ▪ The promotion *invested* her *with* confidence. [=made her confident]

invest as [*phrasal verb*] ***invest (someone) as (something)*** *formal* **:** to give (someone) the power and authority of (a particular position or title) ▪ The group *invested* her *as* chairperson.

invest in [*phrasal verb*] ***invest in (something)*** *informal* **:** to spend money on (something useful or helpful to yourself) ▪ I am planning to *invest in* [=*buy, purchase*] a good coat.

– investing *noun* [*noncount*] ▪ I read a book on *investing* before I bought stocks and bonds. **– in·ves·tor** /ɪnˈvɛstɚ/ *noun, pl* **-tors** [*count*]

in·ves·ti·gate /ɪnˈvɛstəˌgeɪt/ *verb* **-gates; -gat·ed; -gat·ing**

1 : to try to find out the facts about (something, such as a crime or an accident) in order to learn how it happened, who did it, etc. [+ *obj*] The police are still *investigating* the murder. ▪ The accident was thoroughly *investigated*. [*no obj*] The manager promised to *investigate* when we pointed out an error on our bill.

2 [+ *obj*] **:** to try to get information about (someone who may have done something illegal) ▪ He was *investigated* for his involvement in the incident.

– in·ves·ti·ga·tion /ɪnˌvɛstəˈgeɪʃən/ *noun, pl* **-tions** [*count*] Police began an *investigation* into/of the incident. [*noncount*] The accident is ***under investigation***. [=being investigated] **– in·ves·ti·ga·tor** /ɪnˈvɛstəˌgeɪtɚ/ *noun, pl* **-tors** [*count*] ▪ *Investigators* revealed their findings.

in·ves·ti·ga·tive /ɪnˈvɛstəˌgeɪtɪv/ *adj, always used before a noun* **:** of, relating to, or involving investigation ▪ *investigative* methods/work/journalism/reporting

in·ves·ti·ga·to·ry /ɪnˈvɛstɪgəˌtori, *Brit* ɪnˈvɛstɪgətri/ *adj, always used before a noun* **:** INVESTIGATIVE

in·ves·ti·ture /ɪnˈvɛstəʧɚ/ *noun, pl* **-tures** [*count, noncount*] *formal* **:** a formal ceremony at which someone is placed in an office or given an official rank ▪ the *investiture* of the Prince of Wales

in·vest·ment /ɪnˈvɛstmənt/ *noun, pl* **-ments**

1 a : the act of using money to earn more money **:** the act of investing money [*noncount*] He became wealthy by shrewd *investment* of his money in the stock market. ▪ She got a good return on her *investment*. [=her investment earned a good profit] ▪ The company hopes to attract foreign *investment*. [=hopes that foreign people/companies will invest money in it] [*count*] Buying the house was a good *investment*. ▪ The financial company offers several kinds of *investments*. **b** [*count*] **:** an amount of money that is invested in something ▪ Her initial *investment* was $2,000.

2 [*count*] **:** something that you buy with the idea that it will increase in value, usefulness, etc. ▪ The house turned out to be a good *investment*. [=the house increased in value and they made a good profit when they sold it] ▪ A college education is a very good *investment*.

3 a : the act of spending money on something that is valuable or expected to be useful or helpful [*noncount*] The government has set aside money for *investment* in public transportation. [*count*] The company needs to make more *investments* in technology. **b** [*count, noncount*] **:** the act of giving your time or effort in order to accomplish something or make something better ▪ The project will require (a) substantial *investment* of time and energy.

in·vet·er·ate /ɪnˈvɛtərət/ *adj* [*more* ~; *most* ~] *formal* + *often disapproving*

1 : always or often doing something specified ▪ She's an *inveterate* reader/traveler. ▪ an *inveterate* liar

2 : always or often happening or existing ▪ her *inveterate* optimism ▪ his *inveterate* tendency to overlook the obvious

– in·vet·er·ate·ly *adv* ▪ *inveterately* optimistic

in·vid·i·ous /ɪnˈvɪdijəs/ *adj* [*more* ~; *most* ~] *formal* **:** unpleasant and likely to cause bad feelings in other people ▪ *invidious* remarks ▪ an *invidious* comparison/choice ▪ The boss made *invidious* distinctions between employees.

in·vig·i·late /ɪnˈvɪʤəˌleɪt/ *verb* **-lates; -lat·ed; -lat·ing** *Brit* **:** to watch students who are taking an examination **:** PROCTOR [+ *obj*] *invigilate* an exam [*no obj*] He was asked to *invigilate* next week.

– in·vig·i·la·tor /ɪnˈvɪʤəˌleɪtə/ *noun, pl* **-tors** [*count*]

in·vig·o·rate /ɪnˈvɪgəˌreɪt/ *verb* **-rates; -rat·ed; -rat·ing** [+ *obj*]

1 : to give life and energy to (someone) ▪ A brisk walk in the cool morning air always *invigorates* me. ▪ He was *invigorated* by the positive feedback.

2 : to cause (something) to become more active and lively ▪ The mayor has plans to *invigorate* the downtown economy.

– invigorating *adj* [*more* ~; *most* ~] ▪ an *invigorating* walk

in·vin·ci·ble /ɪnˈvɪnsəbəl/ *adj* **:** impossible to defeat or overcome **:** UNBEATABLE ▪ an *invincible* army ▪ The loss proved that the team is not *invincible*.

– in·vin·ci·bil·i·ty /ɪnˌvɪnsəˈbɪləti/ *noun* [*noncount*]

in·vi·o·la·ble /ɪnˈvajələbəl/ *adj, formal* **:** too important to be ignored or treated with disrespect ▪ an *inviolable* oath/law/right

– in·vi·o·la·bil·i·ty /ɪnˌvajələˈbɪləti/ *noun* [*noncount*] ▪ the *inviolability* of the law

in·vi·o·late /ɪnˈvajələt/ *adj, formal* **:** not harmed or changed ▪ These rights must remain *inviolate*.

in·vis·i·ble /ɪnˈvɪzəbəl/ *adj*

1 : impossible to see **:** not visible ▪ Sound waves are *invisible*. ▪ a thriller about an *invisible* man ▪ With the telescope we can see details of the planet's surface that are ordinarily *invisible*. ▪ It felt like I was *invisible* at the party. [=no one was paying any attention to me at the party] ▪ She feels as if her success is being blocked by an *invisible* barrier. ▪ Homelessness is no longer an *invisible* problem for this city. ▪ a letter written in ***invisible ink*** [=ink that can only be seen when it is specially treated in some way]

2 *chiefly Brit, finance* — used to describe money from foreign countries that is received from providing services (such as banking and tourism) rather than from selling products ▪ *invisible* earnings ▪ *invisible* exports

– in·vis·i·bil·i·ty /ɪnˌvɪzəˈbɪləti/ *noun* [*noncount*] **– in·vis·i·bly** /ɪnˈvɪzəbli/ *adv* ▪ a hearing aid that fits *invisibly* in the ear

in·vi·ta·tion /ˌɪnvəˈteɪʃən/ *noun, pl* **-tions**

1 [*count*] **:** a written or spoken request for someone to go somewhere or to do something ▪ We sent out more than 100 *invitations* for the party. ▪ He accepted/declined our *invitation*. ▪ an *invitation* to lunch/dinner ▪ a wedding *invitation* ▪ You have a ***standing/open invitation*** [=you are always welcome; you are always invited] to visit us any time.

2 [*noncount*] **:** the act of inviting someone ▪ She attended the fund-raiser ***at the invitation of*** the committee chairperson. [=she attended because she was invited by the committee chairperson] ▪ The event is ***by invitation only***. [=only people who have been invited to the event can attend it]

3 [*singular*] **:** something that encourages someone to do something or that makes something more likely to happen — + *to* ▪ She treated his request for help as an *invitation to* take control of his life. ▪ Leaving valuables unattended is an (open) *invitation to* thieves (to steal them). ▪ His letter to the newspaper was an *invitation to* criticism. ▪ Speeding is an *invitation to* disaster/trouble.

in·vi·ta·tion·al /ˌɪnvəˈteɪʃənl/ *adj, US, sports* **:** limited to people who have been invited to compete ▪ an *invitational* tournament

– invitational *noun, pl* **-als** [*count*] ▪ The tournament is an *invitational*.

[1]in·vite /ɪnˈvaɪt/ *verb* **-vites; -vit·ed; -vit·ing** [+ *obj*]

1 a : to ask (someone) to go somewhere or do something ▪ He *invited* a few friends (to come) over to his house after work. ▪ She *invited* them (to go) out to dinner. ▪ I visited their house once, but they've never *invited* me back. ▪ I'm planning to *invite* them for the weekend. ▪ Aren't you going to *invite* me in for a coffee? ▪ The event is limited to *invited* guests. **b :** to ask (someone) formally or politely to do something ▪ Employees are *invited* to apply for the new position. ▪ The college *invited* her to speak at the graduation ceremony. **c :** to request (something) formally or politely ▪ The company *invites* suggestions from customers.

2 : to make (something unwanted) more likely to happen ▪ behavior that *invites* criticism ▪ *invite* disaster by speeding

[2]in·vite /ˈɪnˌvaɪt/ *noun, pl* **-vites** [*count*] *informal* **:** INVITATION 1 ▪ Did you send out the *invites* to the party? ▪ Thanks for the *invite*!

in·vit·ing /ɪnˈvaɪtɪŋ/ *adj* [*more* ~; *most* ~] **:** attractive in a way that makes you want to do something, go somewhere, be near someone, etc. ▪ an *inviting* prospect ▪ The room is very *inviting*. [=*pleasant, cozy*] ▪ He has an *inviting* [=*friendly, warm*] smile.

– in·vit·ing·ly *adv* ▪ desserts arranged *invitingly* on the table

in vi·tro /ɪnˈviːtroʊ/ *adj, technical* **:** outside the body ▪ an *in vitro* study/test ▪ a baby conceived through ***in vitro fertilization*** [=fertilization of an egg outside the mother's body]

– in vitro *adv* ▪ an egg fertilized *in vitro*

in·vo·ca·tion /ˌɪnvəˈkeɪʃən/ *noun, pl* **-tions**

1 *formal* **:** the act of mentioning or referring to someone or something in support of your ideas **:** the act of invoking something — + *of* [*count*] his repeated *invocations of* the ancient philosophers [*noncount*] justifying his position by *invocation of* the past

2 *literary* **:** the act of asking for help or support especially from a god [*count*] The poem begins with an *invocation* of/to the Muses. [*noncount*] by *invocation* of God

3 [*count*] *US* **:** a prayer for blessing or guidance at the beginning of a service, ceremony, etc. ▪ They began the meeting with an *invocation*.

[1]in·voice /ˈɪnˌvoɪs/ *noun, pl* **-voic·es** [*count*] **:** a document that shows a list of goods or services and the prices to be paid for them **:** BILL ▪ Payment is due within 30 days after receipt of the *invoice*. — see also PRO FORMA INVOICE

[2]invoice *verb* **-voices; -voiced; -voic·ing** [+ *obj*] **:** to send or give (someone) a bill for a purchase or service **:** to submit an invoice to (someone) ▪ They will *invoice* you directly.

in·voke /ɪnˈvoʊk/ *verb* **-vokes; -voked; -vok·ing** [+ *obj*] *formal*

1 a : to mention (someone or something) in an attempt to make people feel a certain way or have a certain idea in their mind ▪ He *invoked* the memory/name of his predecessor. **b :** to refer to (something) in support of your ideas ▪ She *invoked* history to prove her point.

2 : to make use of (a law, a right, etc.) ▪ He *invoked* his Fifth Amendment privileges. ▪ The suspect *invoked* his right to an attorney.

3 : to ask for help or protection from (something or someone) ▪ They *invoked* God's mercy. ▪ *invoke* the authority of the court

in·vol·un·tary /ɪnˈvɑːlənˌteri, *Brit* ɪnˈvɒləntri/ *adj* **:** not voluntary: such as **a :** not done or made consciously ▪ Breathing and circulation are *involuntary* processes. ▪ *involuntary* bodily movements ▪ When the door burst open, she let out an *involuntary* shriek. **b :** not done by choice ▪ *involuntary* [=*forced*] labor ▪ The lawyer argued that the client's confession was *involuntary*. ▪ *involuntary* unemployment

– in·vol·un·tari·ly /ɪnˌvɑːlənˈterəli, *Brit* ɪnˈvɒləntrəli/ *adv*

in·volve /ɪnˈvɑːlv/ *verb* **-volves; -volved; -volv·ing** [+ *obj*]

1 a : to have or include (someone or something) as a part of something ▪ Does this *involve* me? ▪ The accident *involved* three cars. = Three cars were *involved* in the accident. ▪ He told us a story *involving* life on a farm. **b :** to cause (someone) to be included in some activity, situation, etc. **:** to cause (someone) to take part in something — usually + *in* ▪ I didn't intend to *involve* you *in* this mess. ▪ The teacher tried to *involve* all the children *in* the game. ▪ She ***involves herself in*** [=she participates in] everything they do. **c :** to cause (someone) to be associated *with* someone or something ▪ She remained *involved with* the organization for many years.

2 : to require (something) as a necessary part ▪ "Just what does this job *involve*?" "It *involves* [=*entails*] traveling and a lot of overtime." ▪ Renovating the house *involved* hiring a contractor.

3 : to affect (something) ▪ The disease continued to spread until it *involved* the entire jaw.

– in·volve·ment /ɪnˈvɑːlvmənt/ *noun [noncount]* ▪ *Involvement* with/in the community is important to him. ▪ Her *involvement* with the museum lasted over two decades. ▪ He denied any *involvement* in the crime. ▪ No one knew of their romantic *involvement.* [=no one knew that they had a romantic relationship]

in·volved /ɪnˈvɑːlvd/ *adj*

1 *[more ~; most ~]* **: very complicated** ▪ a long and *involved* story ▪ The instructions for assembling the toy are very *involved.* ▪ The process is quite *involved.*

2 *not used before a noun* **a : having a part in something : included in something** ▪ Those of us who were *involved* knew exactly what happened. **— often + *in*** ▪ He is *involved in* a lawsuit. ▪ I don't want to become *involved in* this argument. ▪ This department was not *involved in* the decision. **b** *[more ~; most ~]* **: actively participating in something** ▪ Students who stay *involved* get more out of the program. ▪ If you want to make things better, you need to get *involved.* **— often + *in*** ▪ You need to get *involved in* making things better. ▪ She was so *involved* [=*engrossed*] *in* her work that she didn't hear the phone ring. **c : having a romantic or sexual relationship** ▪ They quickly became romantically *involved.* ▪ No one knew that they were *involved.* **— often + *with*** ▪ She became romantically *involved with* a married man.

in·vul·ner·a·ble /ɪnˈvʌlnərəbəl/ *adj* **: impossible to harm, damage, or defeat** ▪ teenagers who think they are *invulnerable* ▪ The candidate seems to be in an *invulnerable* position. ▪ The team seems *invulnerable* this season. **— often + *to*** ▪ a city *invulnerable to* invasion

– in·vul·ner·a·bil·i·ty /ɪnˌvʌlnərəˈbɪləti/ *noun [noncount]*

[1]in·ward /ˈɪnwəd/ *adj [more ~; most ~]*

1 *always used before a noun* **: of or relating to a person's mind or spirit** ▪ *inward* [=(more commonly) *inner*] peace ▪ *inward* feelings

2 : directed or moving toward the inside of something ▪ an *inward* flow/curve **— opposite** OUTWARD

[2]inward *also chiefly Brit* **in·wards** /ˈɪnwədz/ *adv*

1 : toward the inside of something ▪ The window faces *inward* toward the courtyard. ▪ The door opens *inward.* **— opposite** OUTWARD

2 : toward the mind or spirit ▪ He turned his attention *inward.*

in·ward·ly /ˈɪnwədli/ *adv* **: in a way that is not openly shown or stated : on the inside** ▪ He chuckled/smiled/cursed *inwardly.* ▪ She was outwardly calm but *inwardly* nervous. **— opposite** OUTWARDLY

in–your–face /ˌɪnjəˈfeɪs/ *adj [more ~; most ~] informal* **: very direct and forceful : very aggressive** ▪ *in-your-face* advertising ▪ an *in-your-face* style of basketball **— see also** *in someone's face* at [1]FACE

io·dine /ˈajəˌdaɪn, *Brit* ˈajəˌdiːn/ *noun [noncount]* **: a chemical element that is used especially in medicine and photography**

ion /ˈaɪˌɑːn, ˈajən/ *noun, pl* **ions** *[count] technical* **: an atom or group of atoms that has a positive or negative electric charge from losing or gaining one or more electrons**

-ion *noun suffix*

1 a : act or process ▪ validat*ion* ▪ refrigerat*ion* ▪ rebell*ion* **b : result of an act or process** ▪ regulat*ion* ▪ reject*ion*

2 : state or condition ▪ perfect*ion*

io·ta /aɪˈoʊtə/ *noun [singular]* **: a very small amount — usually used in negative statements** ▪ That doesn't bother me one *iota.* [=that doesn't bother me at all] ▪ There isn't an *iota* of truth in what he says.

IOU /ˌaɪˌoʊˈjuː/ *noun, pl* **IOUs** *[count] informal* **: a usually written promise to pay a debt** ▪ I don't have any cash, so I'll have to give you an *IOU.* **— often used figuratively** ▪ The governor has acquired some political *IOUs* over the years. [=other people owe the governor political favors] ✧ *IOU* is from the pronunciation of the phrase "I owe you."

IPA /ˌaɪˌpiːˈeɪ/ *noun [noncount]* **: a system of symbols that represent all of the sounds made in speech** ✧ *IPA* is an abbreviation of "International Phonetic Alphabet."

IPO /ˌaɪˌpiːˈoʊ/ *noun, pl* **IPOs** *[count]* **: the first time a company's stock is offered for sale to the public** ✧ *IPO* is an abbreviation of "initial public offering."

ip·so fac·to /ˈɪpsoʊˈfæktoʊ/ *adv, formal* **: because of that fact : because of the fact that has just been mentioned** ▪ He thinks that anyone wearing a suit and tie is *ipso facto* a conservative. [=that anyone wearing a suit and tie must be a conservative]

IQ /ˌaɪˈkjuː/ *noun, pl* **IQs** *[count]* **: a number that represents your intelligence and that is based on your score on a special test** ▪ children with high *IQs* ▪ They wanted me to take an *IQ* test. ✧ *IQ* is an abbreviation of "intelligence quotient."

ir- see IN-

[1]IRA /ˌaɪˌɑɚˈeɪ/ *noun, pl* **IRAs** *[count] US* **: a special account in which you can save and invest money for your retirement without having to pay taxes on the money until a later time** ✧ *IRA* is an abbreviation of "individual retirement account."

[2]IRA *abbr* Irish Republican Army ▪ a representative of the *IRA* ▪ an *IRA* attack

iras·ci·ble /ɪˈræsəbəl/ *adj [more ~; most ~]* **: becoming angry very easily : having a bad temper** ▪ an *irascible* old football coach ▪ He has an *irascible* disposition/temper.

irate /aɪˈreɪt/ *adj [more ~; most ~]* **: very angry** ▪ *Irate* viewers called the television network to complain about the show. ▪ an *irate* neighbor

ire /ˈajɚ/ *noun [noncount]* **: intense anger** ▪ He directed his *ire* at the coworkers who reported the incident. ▪ The proposal has raised/roused/provoked the *ire* of environmentalists. [=has made environmentalists angry]

ir·i·des·cent /ˌirəˈdɛsn̩t/ *adj [more ~; most ~]* **: shining with many different colors when seen from different angles** ▪ an *iridescent* gemstone

– ir·i·des·cence /ˌirəˈdɛsn̩s/ *noun [noncount]* ▪ The stone shone with a beautiful *iridescence.*

iris /ˈaɪrəs/ *noun, pl* **iris·es** *[count]*

1 : the colored part of your eye — see picture at EYE

2 *pl* ***irises also iris*** **: a plant with long pointed leaves and large blue or yellow flowers — see color picture on page C6**

[1]Irish /ˈaɪrɪʃ/ *adj* **: of or relating to Ireland, its people, or the Gaelic language that is spoken in Ireland** ▪ *Irish* culture ▪ the *Irish* coast ▪ people of *Irish* descent ▪ *Irish* grammar

[2]Irish *noun, pl* **Irish**

1 *[plural]* **: the people of Ireland : Irish people** ▪ the *Irish* in America ▪ How many *Irish* are there in England?

2 *[noncount]* **: the Gaelic language of Ireland** ▪ Do you speak *Irish*?

Irish coffee *noun, pl* **~ -fees** *[count, noncount]* **: a drink of hot coffee with sugar, whiskey, and usually whipped cream**

Irish·man /ˈaɪrɪʃmən/ *noun, pl* **-men** /-mən/ *[count]* **: an Irish man**

Irish·wom·an /ˈaɪrɪʃˌwʊmən/ *noun, pl* **-wom·en** /-ˌwɪmən/ *[count]* **: an Irish woman**

irk /ˈɚk/ *verb* **irks; irked; irk·ing** *[+ obj]* **: to bother or annoy (someone)** ▪ Drivers were *irked* by the higher gasoline prices. ▪ It *irks* me to have to clean up after you.

irk·some /ˈɚksəm/ *adj [more ~; most ~]* **: annoying or irritating** ▪ the *irksome* task of cleaning up ▪ *irksome* rules

[1]iron /ˈajɚn/ *noun, pl* **irons**

1 *[noncount]* **: a heavy type of metal that is very common, occurs naturally in blood, and is used to make steel and in many products** ▪ The bars/chains are (made of) *iron.* ▪ She has an *iron* deficiency. [=she does not have enough iron in her blood] **— sometimes used figuratively** ▪ an athlete with legs/muscles of *iron* [=very strong legs/muscles] ▪ She has a will of *iron.* [=she has a very strong will] **— see also** CAST IRON, WROUGHT IRON

2 *[count]* **: a device with a flat metal base that is heated and is used to press wrinkles out of clothing** ▪ a heated *iron* **— see also** CURLING IRON, SOLDERING IRON, WAFFLE IRON

3 *[count]* **: a golf club that has a metal head and is identified by a number** ▪ a five-*iron* **— compare** WOOD

4 irons *[plural]* **: chains placed on a prisoner's arms or legs** ▪ They clapped/put the prisoner in *irons.* ▪ They slapped leg *irons* on him.

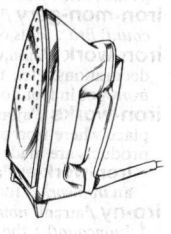

irons in the fire **: activities or projects that someone is involved in** ▪ Although he won't say exactly what he's working on now, he says he has quite a few *irons in the fire.*

pump iron see [2]PUMP

strike while the iron is hot see [1]STRIKE

iron

[2]iron *adj*

1 : made of iron ▪ *iron* bars/chains ▪ an *iron* fence

2 *always used before a noun* **: very strong** ▪ He has an *iron* constitution. [=he is very strong and healthy] ▪ She has an *iron* will. [=she is very determined to get what she wants] ▪ an *iron* grip

iron man **:** a man who is very strong and is able to do something (such as play a sport) for a long time without injury or illness

rule with an iron fist/hand, rule with a rod of iron see [2]RULE

[3]**iron** *verb* **irons; ironed; iron·ing :** to use a heated iron to make clothing or fabric smooth [+ *obj*] I *ironed* the shirt. [*no obj*] I *ironed* all morning.

iron out [*phrasal verb*] ***iron (something) out or iron out (something)*** **1 :** to remove (wrinkles) in cloth by using a heated iron ▪ She *ironed* the wrinkles *out* of the dress. ▪ Do you think we can *iron out* the creases in those curtains? **2 a :** to find a solution to (something) : to fix or correct (something) ▪ It'll take us a while longer to *iron out* the wrinkles/kinks in the network. [=to fix the small problems in the network] ▪ We haven't been able to *iron out* our differences. ▪ They're trying to ***iron things out***. [=work out their difficulties] **b :** to reach an agreement about (something) ▪ The final details of the contract still have to be *ironed out*.

Iron Age *noun*

the Iron Age **:** a period of time between about 3000 B.C. and 1000 B.C. in which people used iron to make weapons and tools ▪ *The Iron Age* followed the Bronze Age. ▪ an *Iron Age* tool — compare BRONZE AGE, STONE AGE

iron·clad /ˈajənˈklæd/ *adj*

1 : not able to be changed ▪ The company has an *ironclad* policy/rule against revealing secrets to competitors. ▪ an *ironclad* promise

2 : too strong to be doubted or questioned ▪ He has an *ironclad* alibi. ▪ *ironclad* proof/evidence

Iron Curtain *noun*

the Iron Curtain **:** the political and military barrier in the past that separated the communist countries of Europe from the rest of Europe ▪ a spy novel that takes place behind *the Iron Curtain*

iron·ic /ˌaɪˈrɑːnɪk/ *also* **iron·i·cal** /ˌaɪˈrɑːnɪkəl/ *adj* [*more ~; most ~*]

1 : using words that mean the opposite of what you really think especially in order to be funny ▪ an *ironic* remark ▪ She has an *ironic* sense of humor. ▪ an *ironic* writing style

2 : strange or funny because something (such as a situation) is different from what you expected ▪ It's *ironic* that computers break down so often, since they're meant to save people time. ▪ It is *ironic* that the robber's car crashed into a police station.

– iron·i·cal·ly /aɪˈrɑːnɪkli/ *adv* ▪ He wrote *ironically* [=in an ironic way] about his experiences during the war. ▪ *Ironically*, [=it is ironic that] the robber's car crashed into a police station.

iron·ing /ˈajənɪŋ/ *noun* [*noncount*]

1 : the activity of using an iron to smooth out clothes or fabric ▪ I hate *ironing*.

2 : clothes that need to be ironed ▪ a pile of *ironing*

ironing board *noun, pl* **~ boards** [*count*] **:** a flat, padded surface on which clothes are ironed

iron·mon·ger /ˈajənˌmɑːŋgɚ, ˈajənˌmʌŋgɚ/ *noun, pl* **-gers** [*count*] *Brit* **:** a person who sells iron or metal tools

iron·mon·gery /ˈajənˌmɑːŋgəri, ˈajənˌmʌŋgəri/ *noun* [*noncount*] *Brit* **:** tools or equipment used in a house or garden

iron·work /ˈajənˌwɚk/ *noun* [*noncount*] **:** fences, railings, decorations, etc., that are made of iron ▪ We admired the *ironwork* in front of the house.

iron·works /ˈajənˌwɚks/ *noun, pl* **ironworks** [*count*] **:** a place where iron or steel is processed or where iron or steel products are made

– iron·work·er /ˈajənˌwɚkɚ/ *noun, pl* **-ers** [*count*] ▪ He was an *ironworker* for 20 years.

iro·ny /ˈaɪrəni/ *noun, pl* **-nies**

1 [*noncount*] **:** the use of words that mean the opposite of what you really think especially in order to be funny ▪ a writer known for her clever use of *irony* ▪ "What a beautiful view," he said, his voice dripping with *irony*, as he looked out the window at the alley. ▪ She described her vacation with heavy *irony* as "an educational experience." — compare SARCASM

2 : a situation that is strange or funny because things happen in a way that seems to be the opposite of what you expected [*count*] It was a tragic *irony* that he made himself sick by worrying so much about his health. ▪ The (awful/bitter) *irony* is that in trying to forget her, he thought of her even more. ▪ That's just one of life's little *ironies*. [*noncount*] The *irony* of the situation was apparent to everyone. ▪ He has a strong sense of *irony*.

ir·ra·di·ate /ɪˈreɪdiˌeɪt/ *verb* **-ates; -at·ed; -at·ing** [+ *obj*] *technical* **:** to expose (someone or something) to radiation ▪ *irradiate* a tumor ▪ The food was *irradiated* to kill any germs.

– ir·ra·di·a·tion /ɪˌreɪdiˈeɪʃən/ *noun* [*noncount*] ▪ the *irradiation* of the tumor

ir·ra·tio·nal /ɪˈræʃənəl/ *adj* [*more ~; most ~*] **:** not rational: such as **a :** not thinking clearly : not able to use reason or good judgment ▪ He became *irrational* as the fever got worse. **b :** not based on reason, good judgment, or clear thinking ▪ She had an *irrational* fear of cats. ▪ an *irrational* prejudice

– ir·ra·tio·nal·i·ty /ɪˌræʃəˈnæləti/ *noun* [*noncount*] ▪ the *irrationality* of her fear **– ir·ra·tio·nal·ly** /ɪˈræʃənəli/ *adv* ▪ He was behaving *irrationally*.

ir·rec·on·cil·able /ɪˌrɛkənˈsaɪləbəl/ *adj* [*more ~; most ~*] *formal* **:** so different that agreement is not possible ▪ *irreconcilable* theories ▪ theories that are *irreconcilable* with each other ▪ They are filing for divorce, citing ***irreconcilable differences***. [=they cannot agree on most things or on important things]

– ir·rec·on·cil·ably /ɪˌrɛkənˈsaɪləbli/ *adv* ▪ The two sides are *irreconcilably* opposed.

ir·re·cov·er·able /ˌɪrɪˈkʌvərəbəl/ *adj, formal* **:** impossible to recover or get back ▪ The past is *irrecoverable*. ▪ an *irrecoverable* loss

ir·re·deem·able /ˌɪrɪˈdiːməbəl/ *adj, formal* **:** not able to be saved, helped, or made better : HOPELESS ▪ She does not believe that anyone is completely *irredeemable*. ▪ Without intervention, the country could fall into *irredeemable* chaos.

– ir·re·deem·ably /ˌɪrɪˈdiːməbli/ *adv* ▪ The government was *irredeemably* corrupt.

ir·re·duc·ible /ɪrɪˈduːsəbəl, *Brit* ˌɪrɪˈdjuːsəbəl/ *adj, formal* **:** not able to be made smaller or simpler ▪ They thought the world was made up of four *irreducible* elements: earth, air, fire, and water. ▪ an *irreducible* fraction

– ir·re·duc·ibly /ɪrɪˈduːsəbli, *Brit* ˌɪrɪˈdjuːsəbli/ *adv*

ir·re·fut·able /ˌɪrɪˈfjuːtəbəl, ɪˈrɛfjətəbəl/ *adj, formal* **:** not able to be proved wrong : not capable of being refuted ▪ There is *irrefutable* evidence that he committed these crimes.

– ir·re·fut·ably /ˌɪrɪˈfjuːtəbli, ɪˈrɛfjətəbli/ *adv* ▪ The evidence shows *irrefutably* that he committed these crimes.

[1]**ir·reg·u·lar** /ɪˈrɛgjələ/ *adj*

1 [*more ~; most ~*] **:** not normal or usual : not following the usual rules about what should be done ▪ His behavior as a teacher was highly *irregular*. ▪ Her application was handled in an *irregular* manner.

2 [*more ~; most ~*] **:** not even or smooth : not regular in form or shape ▪ an *irregular* outline ▪ a very jagged, *irregular* surface ▪ The stone has an *irregular* shape.

3 [*more ~; most ~*] **a :** happening or done at different times that change often ▪ She has been working *irregular* hours. [=she has been working for different amounts of time and at different times on different days] ▪ He has a very *irregular* schedule. **b :** not happening at times that are equally separated ▪ The festival has been held at *irregular* intervals. ▪ an *irregular* heartbeat

4 *grammar* **:** not following the normal patterns by which word forms (such as the past tenses of verbs) are usually created ▪ "Sell" is an *irregular* verb because its past tense is "sold."

5 *US* **:** not able to have normal bowel movements : CONSTIPATED

6 : not belonging to a country's official army ▪ *irregular* troops/soldiers

– ir·reg·u·lar·ly *adv* ▪ He has been behaving *irregularly*. ▪ an *irregularly* shaped stone

[2]**irregular** *noun, pl* **-lars** [*count*] **:** a soldier who does not belong to a country's official army

ir·reg·u·lar·i·ty /ɪˌrɛgjəˈlerəti/ *noun, pl* **-ties**

1 [*noncount*] **:** the quality or state of being irregular ▪ the *irregularity* of his behavior

2 [*count*] **a :** something that is irregular ▪ an *irregularity* [=a raised or rough area] on the surface of the jewel ▪ cardiac *irregularities* **b :** something that is not usual or proper and that usually indicates dishonest behavior — usually plural ▪ We uncovered *irregularities* in the town's finances.

3 [*noncount*] *US* **:** the state of not being able to have normal bowel movements : CONSTIPATION ▪ He is suffering from *irregularity*.

ir·rel·e·vant /ɪˈrɛləvənt/ *adj* [*more* ~; *most* ~] **:** not important or relating to what is being discussed right now **:** not relevant ▪ His comment is completely *irrelevant*. — sometimes + *to* ▪ Her comments were *irrelevant to* our discussion.
— **ir·rel·e·vance** /ɪˈrɛləvəns/ *also* **ir·rel·e·van·cy** /ɪˈrɛləvənsi/ *noun, pl* **-vancies** *also* **-vanc·es** [*noncount*] the *irrelevance* of his comments [*count*] He talked about the weather and other *irrelevancies*. — **ir·rel·e·vant·ly** *adv* ▪ He talked *irrelevantly* about the weather.

ir·re·li·gious /ˌɪrɪˈlɪʤəs/ *adj* [*more* ~; *most* ~] *formal*
1 : not believing in or practicing any religion ▪ *irreligious* people
2 : having or showing a lack of respect for religion ▪ *irreligious* remarks

ir·re·me·di·a·ble /ˌɪrɪˈmi:dijəbəl/ *adj, formal* **:** not able to be repaired or corrected ▪ There was an *irremediable* split between the two sides of the family.

ir·rep·a·ra·ble /ɪˈrɛprəbəl/ *adj, formal* **:** too bad to be corrected or repaired ▪ The oil spill did *irreparable* harm to the bay. ▪ The damage to their relationship was *irreparable*.
— **ir·rep·a·ra·bly** /ɪˈrɛprəbli/ *adv* ▪ His business was *irreparably* injured.

ir·re·place·able /ˌɪrɪˈpleɪsəbəl/ *adj* **:** too valuable or rare to be replaced **:** not replaceable ▪ *irreplaceable* works of art

ir·re·press·ible /ˌɪrɪˈprɛsəbəl/ *adj*
1 : impossible to hold back, stop, or control ▪ He has *irrepressible* curiosity.
2 : very lively and cheerful ▪ an *irrepressible* child ▪ She has an *irrepressible* sense of humor.
— **ir·re·press·ibly** /ˌɪrɪˈprɛsəbli/ *adv* ▪ He is *irrepressibly* cheerful.

ir·re·proach·able /ˌɪrɪˈprouʧəbəl/ *adj, formal* **:** not deserving criticism or blame **:** having no fault ▪ His conduct as a police officer was *irreproachable*. ▪ *irreproachable* manners
— **ir·re·proach·ably** /ˌɪrɪˈprouʧəbli/ *adv* ▪ He acted *irreproachably* at all times.

ir·re·sist·ible /ˌɪrɪˈzɪstəbəl/ *adj* [*more* ~; *most* ~] **:** impossible to resist especially because of strength or attractiveness ▪ The force of the waves was *irresistible*. ▪ She had an *irresistible* [=very strong] craving for chocolate. ▪ Women find him *irresistible*. [=women think he is very attractive]
— **ir·re·sist·ibly** /ˌɪrɪˈzɪstəbli/ *adv* ▪ He was *irresistibly* attracted to her.

ir·res·o·lute /ɪˈrɛzəˌlu:t/ *adj* [*more* ~; *most* ~] *formal* **:** not certain about what to do **:** not resolute ▪ He has been criticized as an *irresolute* [=*indecisive*] leader.
— **ir·res·o·lute·ly** *adv* ▪ He has wavered *irresolutely* from one opinion to another.

ir·re·spec·tive of /ˌɪrɪˈspɛktɪv-/ *prep, formal* **:** without thinking about or considering (something) ▪ They are protected by the law, *irrespective of* race. [=regardless of race]

ir·re·spon·si·ble /ˌɪrɪˈspɑ:nsəbəl/ *adj* [*more* ~; *most* ~] **:** not having or showing maturity or good judgment **:** not responsible ▪ He's too *irresponsible* to keep a job for more than a week. ▪ She made *irresponsible* comments that helped cause the riot. ▪ It would be *irresponsible* to ignore the threats.
— **ir·re·spon·si·bil·i·ty** /ˌɪrɪˌspɑ:nsəˈbɪləti/ *noun* [*noncount*] ▪ The students were criticized for their *irresponsibility*. — **ir·re·spon·si·bly** /ˌɪrɪˈspɑ:nsəbli/ *adv* [*more* ~; *most* ~] ▪ She acted *irresponsibly*. ▪ The funds were used *irresponsibly*.

ir·re·triev·able /ˌɪrɪˈtri:vəbəl/ *adj, somewhat formal* **:** impossible to recover or get back ▪ The data was *irretrievable* after the computer crashed. ▪ the *irretrievable* breakdown of a marriage
— **ir·re·triev·ably** /ˌɪrɪˈtri:vəbli/ *adv* ▪ Their pictures were *irretrievably* lost in the flood. ▪ Their marriage had broken down *irretrievably*.

ir·rev·er·ent /ɪˈrɛvərənt/ *adj* [*more* ~; *most* ~] **:** having or showing a lack of respect for someone or something that is usually treated with respect **:** treating someone or something in a way that is not serious or respectful ▪ He has a delightfully *irreverent* sense of humor. ▪ *irreverent* portrayals of nuns ▪ an *irreverent* comedian
— **ir·rev·er·ence** /ɪˈrɛvərəns/ *noun* [*noncount*] ▪ She's a comedian known for her *irreverence*. — **ir·rev·er·ent·ly** *adv* ▪ He joked *irreverently* about religion.

ir·re·vers·ible /ˌɪrɪˈvɚsəbəl/ *adj, somewhat formal* **:** impossible to change back to a previous condition or state ▪ He suffered an *irreversible* loss of vision. ▪ The crisis has done *irreversible* harm to the countries' relations.
— **ir·re·vers·ibly** /ˌɪrɪˈvɚsəbli/ *adv* ▪ Their relationship has been *irreversibly* harmed.

ir·rev·o·ca·ble /ɪˈrɛvəkəbəl/ *adj, formal* **:** not capable of being changed **:** impossible to revoke ▪ She has made an *irrevocable* decision. ▪ an *irrevocable* change
— **ir·rev·o·ca·bly** /ɪˈrɛvəkəbli/ *adv* ▪ Her life has been *irrevocably* changed.

ir·ri·gate /ˈirəˌgeɪt/ *verb* **-gates; -gat·ed; -gat·ing** [+ *obj*]
1 : to supply (something, such as land) with water by using artificial means (such as pipes) ▪ *irrigate* a field ▪ We *irrigate* our crops.
2 *medical* **:** to clean (a wound or a part of the body) with flowing liquid (such as water) ▪ The surgeon *irrigated* the wound.
— **ir·ri·ga·tion** /ˌirəˈgeɪʃən/ *noun* [*noncount*] ▪ *irrigation* of the fields/crops

ir·ri·ta·ble /ˈirətəbəl/ *adj* [*more* ~; *most* ~] **:** becoming angry or annoyed easily ▪ My father is always *irritable* after a nap. ▪ I came home from work feeling tired and *irritable*.
— **ir·ri·ta·bil·i·ty** /ˌirətəˈbɪləti/ *noun* [*noncount*] ▪ Side effects include fatigue and increased *irritability*. — **ir·ri·ta·bly** /ˈirətəbli/ *adv* ▪ "What's taking so long?" he asked *irritably*.

ir·ri·tant /ˈirətənt/ *noun, pl* **-tants** [*count*]
1 : something that makes part of your body sore and painful ▪ dust and other lung *irritants* ▪ skin *irritants*
2 : something that is unpleasant or annoying **:** something that irritates you ▪ The delay was a minor *irritant*.

ir·ri·tate /ˈirəˌteɪt/ *verb* **-tates; -tat·ed; -tat·ing** [+ *obj*]
1 : to make (someone) impatient, angry, or annoyed ▪ It's his arrogance that really *irritates* me. ▪ The other passengers were *irritated* by the child's rudeness.
2 : to make (part of your body) sore or painful ▪ Harsh soaps can *irritate* the skin.
— **irritated** *adj* [*more* ~; *most* ~] ▪ I've never seen him looking so *irritated*. ▪ an area of skin that is very *irritated* and sore — **irritating** *adj* [*more* ~; *most* ~] ▪ He's an *irritating* child. ▪ The child's rudeness was very *irritating* to us. ▪ Harsh soaps can be very *irritating* to the skin. — **ir·ri·tat·ing·ly** /ˈirəˌteɪtɪŋli/ *adv* ▪ He's an *irritatingly* rude child.
— **ir·ri·ta·tion** /ˌirəˈteɪʃən/ *noun* [*noncount*] You'll get over the *irritation* of being delayed. ▪ harsh soaps that can cause *irritation* of the skin [*count*] We had to put up with delays and other *irritations*. ▪ skin *irritations*

IRS *abbr* Internal Revenue Service ▪ He was being audited by the *IRS*.

is see BE

Is. *abbr* island

ISBN /ˌaɪˌɛsˌbi:ˈɛn/ *noun, pl* **ISBNs** [*count*] **:** a number that is given to a book when it is published and that is used to help identify the book — usually singular ▪ Can you give me the 10-digit *ISBN*? ✧ *ISBN* is an abbreviation of "International Standard Book Number."

-ise *Brit spelling of* -IZE

-ish *adj suffix* **:** almost or approximately ▪ The car is *greenish*. [=the car is a color that is almost green] ▪ She looks to be about *fiftyish*. [=she looks like she is around 50 years old]

Is·lam /ɪˈslɑ:m, ˈɪzˌlɑ:m/ *noun* [*noncount*]
1 : the religion which teaches that there is only one God and that Muhammad is God's prophet **:** the religion of Muslims
2 : the modern nations in which Islam is the main religion
— **Is·lam·ic** /ɪˈslɑ:mɪk, ɪzˈlɑ:mɪk/ *adj* ▪ *Islamic* faith/law ▪ the *Islamic* world

is·land /ˈaɪlənd/ *noun, pl* **-lands** [*count*]
1 : an area of land that is surrounded by water ▪ He lives on an *island* in the Caribbean. ▪ Long *Island* ▪ the Greek *islands* — see color picture on page C7
2 : an area or object that is separated from other things: such as **a :** a raised area within a road, parking lot, or driveway that is used to separate or direct traffic — called also *traffic island* **b** *chiefly US* **:** a separate raised area with a flat surface on which food is prepared in a kitchen ▪ a kitchen *island*

is·land·er /ˈaɪləndɚ/ *noun, pl* **-ers** [*count*] **:** a person born or living on an island ▪ Pacific *islanders*

isle /ˈajəl/ *noun, pl* **isles** [*count*] *literary* **:** ISLAND 1 ▪ a tropical *isle* — often used in proper nouns ▪ the British *Isles* ▪ the *Emerald Isle* [=Ireland]

is·let /ˈaɪlət/ *noun, pl* **-lets** [*count*] **:** a small island

ism /ˈɪzəm/ *noun, pl* **isms** [*count*] **:** a belief, attitude, style, etc., that is referred to by a word that ends in the suffix *-ism* ▪ Cubism, Impressionism, and other artistic *isms* ▪ ageism, racism, sexism, and all the other familiar *isms*

-ism /ˌɪzəm/ *noun suffix*

1 a : the act, practice, or process of doing something — used to form nouns from verbs that end in *-ize* ▪ critic*ism* ▪ plagiar*ism* ▪ hypnot*ism* **b :** behavior like that of a specified kind of person or thing ▪ hero*ism* **c :** unfair treatment of a group of people who have a particular quality ▪ rac*ism* ▪ sex*ism*

2 : the state or fact of being a specified kind of person or thing ▪ skeptic*ism* ▪ fanatic*ism*

3 *medical* **:** abnormal state or condition ▪ alcohol*ism* ▪ dwarf*ism*

4 : teachings or beliefs ▪ Buddh*ism* ▪ Marx*ism* ▪ social*ism* ▪ stoic*ism* ▪ real*ism*

5 a : a word that is from a specified source ▪ a Latin*ism* [=a word or phrase that comes from a Latin word or phrase] **b :** a word that has a specified quality ▪ a colloquial*ism*

isn't /ˈɪznt/ — used as a contraction of *is not* ▪ This *isn't* the way I expected it to be. ▪ She *isn't* coming to dinner.

iso·late /ˈaɪsəˌleɪt/ *verb* **-lates; -lat·ed; -lat·ing** [+ *obj*]

1 : to put or keep (someone or something) in a place or situation that is separate from others ▪ These policies will only serve to *isolate* the country politically and economically. ▪ Certain patients must be *isolated* in a separate ward. ▪ When he wants to work, he *isolates* himself in his office and won't talk to anyone. — often + *from* ▪ Certain patients must be *isolated from* the others in a separate ward.

2 a : to find and deal with (something, such as a problem) by removing other possibilities ▪ It may take several days to *isolate* the problem. [=to find out exactly what the problem is] **b** *technical* **:** to separate (something, such as a chemical) from another substance **:** to get (something) or an amount of (something) that is not mixed with or attached to anything else ▪ Scientists have *isolated* the gene/virus that causes the disease. — often + *from* ▪ The chemical/compound was originally *isolated from* a kind of seaweed.

iso·lat·ed *adj*

1 [*more* ~; *most* ~] **:** separate from others ▪ The town remains a very *isolated* community. ▪ The camp is located in an *isolated* area. ▪ *isolated* places/populations ▪ She felt *isolated* [=*alone*] in her new school. [=she felt unhappy because of being separated from people she knew]

2 : happening just once ▪ The arrest was an *isolated* incident in his youth. ▪ an *isolated* instance/case

3 : happening in different places and at different times ▪ There have been reports of *isolated* [=*sporadic*] outbreaks of the disease. ▪ a few *isolated* cases of vandalism

iso·la·tion /ˌaɪsəˈleɪʃən/ *noun* [*noncount*]

1 : the state of being in a place or situation that is separate from others **:** the condition of being isolated ▪ the *isolation* of the mountain community ▪ political and economic *isolation* ▪ a feeling of *isolation* [=*loneliness*]

2 : the act of separating something from other things **:** the act of isolating something ▪ *isolation* of the gene/virus

in isolation **:** apart from others ▪ The researchers work *in isolation*. ▪ Their culture developed *in isolation* [=*separately*] from the rest of the world.

iso·la·tion·ism /ˌaɪsəˈleɪʃəˌnɪzəm/ *noun* [*noncount*] **:** the belief that a country should not be involved with other countries **:** a policy of not making agreements or working with other countries

— **iso·la·tion·ist** /ˌaɪsəˈleɪʃənɪst/ *adj* [*more* ~; *most* ~] ▪ *isolationist* policies — **isolationist** *noun, pl* **-ists** [*count*]

iso·met·rics /ˌaɪsəˈmɛtrɪks/ *noun* [*plural*] **:** exercises in which muscles are made stronger by pushing against other muscles or against something that does not move

— **iso·met·ric** /ˌaɪsəˈmɛtrɪk/ *adj* ▪ an *isometric* exercise

isos·ce·les triangle /aɪˈsɑːsəˌliːz-/ *noun, pl* ~ **-angles** [*count*] *mathematics* **:** a triangle in which two sides have the same length

iso·tope /ˈaɪsəˌtoʊp/ *noun, pl* **-topes** [*count*] *chemistry* **:** any one of various forms in which the atoms of a chemical element can occur ▪ carbon *isotopes* ▪ radioactive *isotopes*

ISP /ˌaɪˌɛsˈpiː/ *noun, pl* **ISPs** [*count*] *computers* **:** a company which provides the services that make it possible for people using computers to connect to the Internet and to send and receive e-mail ✧ *ISP* is an abbreviation of "Internet service provider."

Is·rae·li /ɪzˈreɪli/ *noun, pl* **-lis** [*count*] **:** a person born, raised, or living in modern Israel

— **Israeli** *adj* ▪ *Israeli* politicians ▪ a team of *Israeli* scientists

Is·ra·el·ite /ˈɪzriːjəˌlaɪt, ˈɪzrəˌlaɪt/ *noun, pl* **-ites** [*count*] **:** a person who was born in or who lived in the ancient kingdom of Israel

is·su·ance /ˈɪʃəwəns/ *noun* [*noncount*] *formal* **:** the official act of making something available or of giving something to people to be used **:** the act of officially issuing something ▪ the *issuance* of stock ▪ a visa *issuance* ▪ the *issuance* of a search warrant

¹is·sue /ˈɪˌʃuː/ *noun, pl* **-sues**

1 [*count*] **:** something that people are talking about, thinking about, etc. **:** an important subject or topic ▪ She is concerned with a variety of social/moral/economic *issues*. ▪ Water purity is a public health *issue*. ▪ The President's speech addressed a number of important *issues*. ▪ campaign *issues* like education and defense ▪ The company insists that race was not an *issue* in its decision. [=that its decision was not related to race in any way] ▪ The *issue* is poverty, not race: to talk about race is simply to confuse the *issue*. ▪ The case involves some complicated legal *issues*. ▪ He should stop dodging/avoiding the *issue* and make a decision now.

2 [*count*] **:** the version of a newspaper, magazine, etc., that is published at a particular time ▪ There's an interesting article on page 12 of this *issue*. ▪ the most recent *issue* of the magazine/journal ▪ the current/latest *issue* ▪ The library has a large collection of ***back issues***. [=magazines, newspapers, etc., published before the current issue]

3 [*singular*] **:** the act of officially making something available or giving something to people to be used **:** the act of issuing something ▪ Several senators are calling for the *issue* [=*issuance*] of new guidelines. ▪ a government-*issue* gun [=a gun that the government has officially given to someone] — see also STANDARD-ISSUE

4 ***issues*** [*plural*] **:** problems or concerns ▪ the health *issues* associated with aging

at issue **:** being discussed or considered ▪ *At issue* is the city's budget plan for next year. ▪ What is *at issue* is not the candidate's private life but her politics.

force the issue **:** to force someone to do something or to make a decision about something ▪ They would never have addressed the problem if that newspaper article hadn't *forced the issue*. ▪ Neither side is willing to *force the issue*.

have issues *informal* **1 :** to have problems that make you unhappy and difficult to deal with ▪ He seemed nice enough at first, but it turns out he *has* (a lot of) *issues*. ▪ She *has* serious anger *issues*. [=she often gets so angry that she is difficult to deal with] **2 :** to have reasons for disliking someone or something **:** to disagree with or disapprove of someone or something — + *with* ▪ I *have* some *issues with* his behavior.

make an issue of **:** to argue about (something) or insist that (something) be treated as an important problem ▪ I knew they'd made a mistake, but I was too tired to *make an issue of* it. ▪ They kept *making an issue of* his smoking. [=they continued to criticize him because he smokes cigarettes]

take issue with **:** to disagree with (someone or something) ▪ She *took issue with* the conclusions reached by the study. ▪ I *take issue with* their whole approach to the problem.

without issue *law* **:** without having children ▪ He died *without issue*.

²issue *verb* **-sues; -sued; -su·ing**

1 [+ *obj*] **a :** to give (something) to someone in an official way ▪ The police have *issued* [=*handed out*] numerous tickets for speeding in recent days. **:** to give or supply (something) to (someone) ▪ The jail *issued* him an orange uniform. = (*Brit*) The jail *issued* him with an orange uniform. ▪ Each employee will be *issued* an identification card. **b :** to make (something) available to be sold or used ▪ The Post Office will *issue* a new first-class stamp. ▪ The company plans to raise money by *issuing* more stock. ▪ The bank will be *issuing* a new credit card. ▪ the bank's newly *issued* credit card

2 [+ *obj*] **:** to announce (something) in a public and official way ▪ The king *issued* a decree forbidding all protests. ▪ A severe storm warning has been *issued*. ▪ The police have *issued* a warrant for her arrest. ▪ *issue* a press release

3 [*no obj*] *formal* **:** to go, come, or flow out *from* some source ▪ A steady flow of lava *issued from* a crack in the rock.

— **is·su·er** *noun, pl* **-ers** [*count*] ▪ credit card *issuers* = *issuers* of credit cards

¹-ist /ɪst/ *noun suffix*

1 a : a person who does a specified action or activity ▪ typ*ist* **b :** a person who makes or produces something specified ▪ novel*ist* **c :** a person who plays a specified musical instrument ▪ pian*ist* ▪ violin*ist* **d :** a person who operates a specified machine or vehicle ▪ machin*ist* ▪ bicycl*ist*

2 : a person who has a specified job or skill • geolog*ist* • hairstyl*ist* • dental hygien*ist* • art*ist*
3 : a person who has particular beliefs — used to form nouns from related nouns that end in *-ism* • social*ist* • pur*ist* • popul*ist* • Method*ist* • Buddh*ist* • Darwin*ist*
4 : a person who has a particular quality — used to form nouns from related nouns that end in *-ism* • pessim*ist* • optim*ist* • ideal*ist*

²-ist *adj suffix* : of, relating to, or characterized by a specified quality — used to form adjectives from related nouns that end in *-ism* • an elit*ist* attitude

isth·mus /ˈɪsməs/ *noun, pl* **-mus·es** [*count*] : a narrow area of land that connects two larger land areas — often used in names • the *Isthmus* of Panama

-is·tic /ɪstɪk/ *also* **-is·ti·cal** /ɪstɪkəl/ *adj suffix* : of, relating to, or characterized by a (specified) quality — used to form adjectives from related nouns that end in *-ism* • altru*istic* • real*istic* • ego*tistical*

¹it /ˈɪt, ət/ *pronoun*
1 : that one just mentioned — used to refer to an object or substance • I caught the ball and threw *it* back. • He saw the car and immediately wanted to buy *it*. • She tasted the powder and *it* was sweet. — used to refer to a living thing whose sex is unknown or is being ignored • I don't know who *it* is. • "Who is *it*?" "*It's* only me." • There is a rosebush near the fence, and *it* is now blooming. • A fly landed on the table and I swatted *it*. • He heard the baby crying and brought *it* some milk. — used to refer to an idea, quality, emotion, etc. • Beauty is everywhere, and *it* is a source of great joy.
2 — used as the subject of a verb that describes a condition or occurrence • *It* is cold/hot/raining/snowing outside. • *It* is (getting) late/dark. • *It* will soon be summer. • What time is *it*? • *It* is ten (minutes) after four (o'clock). • *It* hurts when I sneeze. • *It* is almost summer. • *It* is only a short walk to the beach from here.
3 — used in the place of a noun, phrase, or clause that usually comes later • *It* hurts me to sneeze. [=to sneeze hurts me] • *It* is not necessary (for you) to repeat the whole thing. • *It* makes me happy just to think about her. • *It* is wonderful being back here again! • *It* is a long way to the next town. • *It* is said/believed that he died of a broken heart. • They made *it* clear that they needed our help. • I take *it* that there was some problem. • *It* is me you are looking for. = (*formal*) *It* is I you are looking for. • *It* was here that I lost my way. • *It* was in this city that the treaty was signed.
4 — used to refer to something that has been done or is being done or is going to be done • We're going to have to do *it* again. • Quit *it*! [=stop doing what you are doing] • You've been arguing all afternoon. Now cut *it* out! [=stop arguing] • Please do *it* right away. • Okay, go to *it*! [=do the thing you are going to do]
5 — used as a direct object with little or no meaning • We hoofed *it* all the way back to camp. [=we walked all the way back to camp] • We decided to rough *it* on vacation this year. [=to have our vacation somewhere where we would not have our normal comforts] • living *it* up [=doing exciting and enjoyable things; spending money freely while enjoying life] • She offered to come with me, but I decided to go *it* alone. [=to go by myself; to go alone]
6 : the general situation : things in general • How's *it* going? • *It* hasn't been the same since you left.
7 : something previously discussed or known • When the bell rings, *it* means that class is over.
ask for it see ASK
do it see ¹DO
in for it see ¹FOR
nothing to it see ¹NOTHING
out of it see ¹OUT
that is it or that's it informal **1** — used to say that something is finished or completed • Okay, *that's it*. You can go now. **2** — used to say that something is all that is needed or wanted • I came here to visit the museum and *that's it*. [=that is all I wanted to do here] **3** — used to say that something is correct • "I can't remember his name." "I think it was Brian Johnson." "Yes, *that's it*." **4** — used in an angry or annoyed way to say that you will not accept any more of something • *That's it*! I'm leaving!
this is it informal — used to say that this is the most important or final point • Well, *this is it*—the day we've been waiting for.

²it /ˈɪt/ *noun, pl* **its** [*count*] : the player in some children's games (such as hide-and-seek and tag) who performs the main action of the game (such as finding or catching other players) • You're *it*!

ital *abbr* italic, italicized

Ital *abbr* Italian

Ital·ian /ɪˈtæljən/ *noun, pl* **-ians**
1 [*count*] **a** : a person born, raised, or living in Italy **b** : a person whose family is from Italy
2 [*noncount*] : the language of the Italians
– **Italian** *adj* • *Italian* food/politics

Ital·ian·ate /ɪˈtæljənət/ *adj* : showing the influence of the art or culture of Italy • *Italianate* architecture • a beautiful *Italianate* painting/villa

Italian dressing *noun* [*noncount*] *US* : a salad dressing that is made of oil, vinegar, and herbs

¹ital·ic /ɪˈtælɪk/ *adj*
1 : having letters, numbers, etc., that slant upward to the right • *These words are italic.* • *italic* type — abbr. *ital*
2 ***Italic*** : of or relating to ancient Italy, the people who lived there, or the languages spoken there • *Italic* languages/dialects

²italic *noun, pl* **-ics** : letters, numbers, etc., that slant upward to the right : italic type [*noncount*] *These words are printed in italic.* [*plural*] The type should be set in *italics*. • *These words are printed in italics.* — abbr. *ital*; see picture at FONT

ital·i·cize *also Brit* **ital·i·cise** /ɪˈtæləˌsaɪz/ *verb* **-ciz·es; -cized; -ciz·ing** [+ *obj*] : to put letters, numbers, etc., in italics : to print (text) in italics • *italicize* a word • *italicized* text

¹itch /ˈɪtʃ/ *verb* **itch·es; itched; itch·ing** [*no obj*]
1 : to have or produce an unpleasant feeling on your skin or inside your mouth, nose, etc. that makes you want to scratch • My back really *itches*. • His eyes began to burn and *itch* because of his allergies. • My nose *itches*. [=I have an itchy nose] • This sweater makes me *itch*. • Most rashes *itch*.
2 *informal* : to have a strong desire *to do* something or *for* something — always used as *(be) itching* • I'*m itching to get started* in my garden again. [=I'm very eager to begin working in my garden again] • She *was itching for* a fight. • He seemed to *be itching for* an excuse to say something rude.
– **itching** *noun* [*noncount*] • Rashes can cause intense *itching*. • Symptoms include minor *itching* and redness. • This lotion should soothe/stop/relieve the *itching*. [=*itchiness*]

²itch *noun, pl* **itch·es** [*count*]
1 : an uncomfortable or unpleasant feeling on your skin or inside your mouth, nose, etc., that makes you want to scratch • I had a slight *itch* on my back. • Scratching only makes the *itch* worse.
2 *somewhat informal* : a constant and strong desire *for* something or *to do* something • She's always had an *itch for* adventure. • He has an *itch to travel*.
scratch the/an itch *chiefly US, informal* : to satisfy a desire or need for something • Sign up for a tour of Asia and *scratch the itch* to travel.

itchy /ˈɪtʃi/ *adj* **itch·i·er; -est**
1 a : feeling or having an itch • My eyes are/feel *itchy*. • *itchy* skin • an *itchy* back **b** : causing an itch • an *itchy* rash • This sweater is *itchy*.
2 *informal* : feeling a strong desire to do something, to change something, etc. • Voters are *itchy* for change. • He was *itchy* to get going. ♢ If you have ***itchy feet***, you have a strong desire to leave a place, job, etc., and go somewhere else. • She's had the same job for five years, and she's starting to get *itchy feet*. ♢ If you have an ***itchy finger*** or ***itchy fingers***, you have a strong desire to do or get something, especially something that other people think is wrong or dangerous. • a movie about a gunman who has an *itchy* (*trigger*) *finger* [=a gunman who wants to shoot his gun; a gunman who is eager or likely to shoot someone]
– **itch·i·ness** /ˈɪtʃinəs/ *noun* [*noncount*] • The chemical causes *itchiness* and inflammation if it gets on your skin.

it'd /ˈɪtəd/ — used as a contraction of *it would* and *it had* • We knew *it'd* [=*it would*] be dark soon. • *It'd* [=*it had*] been like that for a while.

-ite /aɪt/ *noun suffix*
1 : a person born, raised, or living in a specified area • suburban*ite* • New Jersey*ite*
2 : a follower or supporter of a specified person or group • Reagan*ite*

item /ˈaɪtəm/ *noun, pl* **items**
1 [*count*] : an individual thing : a separate part or thing • There are several *items* for sale. • an *item* [=*article*] of clothing • an *item* [=*article, piece*] of furniture • I need to buy a few household *items* like soap. • He always orders the most ex-

pensive *item* on the menu. • There are a lot of *items* on our agenda tonight, so let's start the meeting. — see also COLLECTOR'S ITEM, *hot item* at [1]HOT

2 [*count*] **:** a separate piece of news or information • I saw an *item* in today's paper about the mayor's campaign plans.

3 [*singular*] *informal* **:** two people who are in a romantic or sexual relationship • They were rumored to be an *item.* [=*a couple*]

item·ize *also Brit* **item·ise** /ˈaɪtəˌmaɪz/ *verb* **-iz·es; -ized; -iz·ing** [+ *obj*] **:** to create a detailed list of (things) • You'll need to *itemize* [=*list*] all of your deductions/expenses. • a list of *itemized* expenses

– **item·i·za·tion** *also Brit* **item·i·sa·tion** /ˌaɪtəməˈzeɪʃən, *Brit* ˌaɪtəˌmaɪˈzeɪʃən/ *noun* [*noncount*] • the *itemization* of all your expenses

itin·er·ant /aɪˈtɪnərənt/ *adj, always used before a noun* **:** traveling from place to place **:** staying in a place for only a short amount of time • an *itinerant* preacher/lecturer/performer

itin·er·ary /aɪˈtɪnəˌreri, *Brit* aɪˈtɪnərəri/ *noun, pl* **-ar·ies** [*count*] **:** the places you go to or plan to go to on a journey • We planned a detailed *itinerary.* • Our *itinerary* included stops at several famous cathedrals.; *also* **:** a document in which the places you will be going to are listed • I'll mail you a copy of my *itinerary* so you'll know where to reach me.

-i·tis /aɪtəs/ *noun suffix, medical* **:** inflammation of something specified • tonsil*litis* • bronch*itis* • laryng*itis* — sometimes used humorously to describe having too much of something • Hollywood has a bad case of sequel*itis* this summer. [=too many movies being shown this summer are sequels]

it'll /ˈɪtl/ — used as a contraction of *it will* • *It'll* be good to see her again. • *It'll* be dark soon.

its /ˈɪts, əts/ *adj, always used before a noun, possessive form of* IT **:** relating to or belonging to a certain thing, animal, etc. • the dog in *its* kennel • The landscape is beautiful in *its* own unique way. • Each region has *its* own customs. **:** made or done by a certain thing, animal, etc. • The company is hoping to increase *its* sales. — compare IT'S

it's /ˈɪts, əts/ — used as a contraction of *it is* and *it has* • *It's* [=*it is*] going to rain. • *It's* [=*it has*] been fun, but I must go now. • *It's* [=*it is*] a long way to the bottom. — compare ITS

it·self /ɪtˈsɛlf/ *pronoun*

1 : that same one: **a** — used as the object of a verb or preposition to refer to something that has already been mentioned • The cat washed *itself.* • History keeps repeating *itself.* • The problem should work *itself* out. • The chain folds back on *itself.* • The restaurant has built quite a reputation for *itself.* **b** — used for emphasis to refer to something that has already been mentioned • I found the envelope, but the letter *itself* was missing. • That *itself* was enough of an excuse. • The city *itself* is fairly small.

2 — used after a noun to say that someone or something has a lot of a particular quality • She was/seemed kindness *itself.* [=she was extremely kind] • Your cake is perfection *itself.* [=your cake is perfect]

by itself **1 :** on its own **:** without being directly controlled by a person • The computer shuts off *by itself* if you don't use it. • The sprinkler will turn on *by itself.* [=*automatically*] **2 :** with nothing nearby **:** ALONE • The house stood *by itself* at the end of the street.

in itself **:** in its own nature **:** when considered as something separate from other things • The idea was not *in itself* bad. • This is not *in itself* a new idea. **:** without anything else added • That's a story *in itself.* — see also *an end in itself* at [1]END

it·sy–bit·sy /ˈɪtsiˈbɪtsi/ *or* **it·ty–bit·ty** /ˈɪtiˈbɪti/ *adj, informal* **:** extremely small **:** TINY • a baby taking *itsy-bitsy* steps • an *itsy-bitsy* piece of cake

-ity /əti/ *noun suffix* **:** quality, state, or degree • availabil*ity* • stabil*ity* • absurd*ity* • complex*ity* • salin*ity*

IUD /ˌaɪˌjuːˈdiː/ *noun, pl* **IUDs** [*count*] *medical* **:** INTRAUTERINE DEVICE

[1]**IV** /ˌaɪˈviː/ *noun, pl* **IVs** [*count*] *US, medical* **:** a device that is used to allow a fluid (such as blood or a liquid medication) to flow directly into a patient's veins • The nurse started an *IV.* • The patient was hooked up to an *IV.* — see picture at HOSPITAL ✧ *IV* is an abbreviation of *intravenous.*

[2]**IV** *adj, always used before a noun, US* **:** INTRAVENOUS • *IV* drug users [=people who inject themselves with illegal drugs]

-ive /ɪv/ *adj suffix* **:** doing or tending to do something specified • exhaust*ive* • explos*ive*

I've /ˈaɪv, əv/ — used as a contraction of *I have* • The food was good, but *I've* had better. • It was the best movie *I've* ever seen. • *I've* got lots of work to do today. = (*chiefly Brit*) *I've* lots of work to do today.

ivied /ˈaɪvid/ *adj* **:** covered with ivy • the college's *ivied* walls

ivo·ry /ˈaɪvəri/ *noun, pl* **-ries**

1 [*noncount*] **:** a hard white substance that forms the tusks of elephants and other animals • a carved piece of *ivory*

2 [*noncount*] **:** a slightly yellowish white color — see color picture on page C2

3 [*count*] *informal* **:** a piano key — usually plural ✧ To ***tickle the ivories*** is to play the piano.

ivory tower *noun, pl* **~ -ers** [*count*] *disapproving* **:** a place or situation in which people make and discuss theories about problems (such as poverty and racism) without having any experience with those problems • The book was written by some college professor who's spent her entire professional life in an *ivory tower.* — often used before another noun • an *ivory-tower* intellectual

ivy /ˈaɪvi/ *noun, pl* **ivies** [*count, noncount*] **:** a plant that has long stems and that often grows on the outsides of buildings • walls covered with *ivy* = *ivy*-covered walls — called also *English ivy*; see color picture on page C6; see also POISON IVY

Ivy League *noun* [*singular*] **:** a group of eight colleges and universities in the eastern U.S. that have been respected for providing an excellent education for a long time — often used before another noun • an *Ivy League* diploma/degree • an *Ivy League* university/college ✧ The Ivy League consists of Harvard, Yale, Princeton, Columbia, Brown, and Cornell universities, the University of Pennsylvania, and Dartmouth College.

-ize *also Brit* **-ise** /aɪz/ *verb suffix*

1 a : to cause to become or become like something specified • American*ize* **:** to become or become like (something specified) • crystal*lize* • union*ize* **b :** to treat like something specified • idol*ize* • lion*ize* • commercial*ize*

2 : to talk or write about someone or something in a specified way • satir*ize* • romantic*ize*

3 : to make or suggest something specified • hypothes*ize* • theor*ize* • philosoph*ize*

4 : to place someone in something specified • hospital*ize* • institutional*ize*

J

j *or* **J** /ˈdʒeɪ/ *noun, pl* **j's** *or* **js** *or* **J's** *or* **Js :** the 10th letter of the English alphabet [*count*] a word that begins with a *j* [*noncount*] a word that begins with *j*

[1]**jab** /ˈdʒæb/ *verb* **jabs; jabbed; jab·bing**

1 : to push something sharp or hard quickly or suddenly into or toward someone or something [+ *obj*] The nurse *jabbed* the needle into his arm. = The nurse *jabbed* his arm with a needle. • She *jabbed* her elbow into my ribs. = She *jabbed* me in the ribs with her elbow. [*no obj*] He *jabbed* at the other player with his hockey stick.

2 : to be pushed quickly and suddenly into someone or a part of someone's body [+ *obj*] The needle *jabbed* his arm. [*no obj*] The needle *jabbed* into his arm.

[2]**jab** *noun, pl* **jabs** [*count*]

1 : a quick or sudden hit with something sharp or hard • She gave him a *jab* in the ribs. — sometimes used figuratively • In his speech, he ***took a jab at*** [=*criticized*] the senator.

2 *boxing* **:** a short, straight punch • He threw a right/left *jab* to his opponent's body. — compare HOOK, UPPERCUT

3 *Brit, informal* **:** an injection of something (such as medicine) into your body with a needle • a flu *jab* [=(*chiefly US*) *shot*]

jab·ber /ˈʤæbɚ/ *verb* **-bers; -bered; -ber·ing** *informal* **:** to talk in a fast, unclear, or foolish way [*no obj*] They *jabbered* away for hours. [+ *obj*] She rushed into the room *jabbering* something about a dog.

– jabber *noun* [*noncount*] • listening to their silly *jabber*

[1]jack /ˈʤæk/ *noun, pl* **jacks**

1 [*count*] **:** a device used for lifting something heavy (such as a car)

2 [*count*] **:** a playing card that has a picture of a soldier or servant and that is worth more than a ten and less than a queen • the *jack* of hearts/spades/clubs/diamonds — see picture at PLAYING CARD

3 [*count*] **:** a small opening where something connects with a wire to something else • a telephone/stereo *jack*

4 a [*count*] **:** a small usually metal object that has six points and that is used in the game of jacks **b** ***jacks*** [*plural*] **:** a child's game in which jacks are thrown and picked up while bouncing and catching a small ball • children playing *jacks*

5 [*noncount*] *US slang* **:** anything at all — used in negative statements • You don't know *jack*. = (*offensive*) You don't know ***jack shit***.

[2]jack *verb* **jacks; jacked; jack·ing**

jack in [*phrasal verb*] ***jack in (something) or jack (something) in*** *Brit, informal* **:** to stop doing (something) • He was building a new shed but *jacked* it *in*. • He *jacked in* [=*quit, gave up*] his job and became a hippie.

jack off [*phrasal verb*] *US, informal + impolite, of a man* **:** MASTURBATE

jack up [*phrasal verb*] ***jack up (something) or jack (something) up*** **1 :** to lift (something, such as a car) with a jack • He *jacked up* the car and changed the tire. **2** *informal* **:** to increase (something, such as a price) by a large amount • The restaurant has *jacked up* its prices in recent months.

jack·al /ˈʤækəl/ *noun, pl* **-als** [*count*] **:** a wild dog found in Africa and Asia

jackal

jack·ass /ˈʤækˌæs/ *noun, pl* **-ass·es** [*count*]

1 : a male donkey

2 *chiefly US, informal + impolite* **:** a stupid person **:** ASS • Some *jackass* spilled his drink on my shoes.

jack·boot /ˈʤækˌbuːt/ *noun, pl* **-boots** [*count*] **:** a heavy military boot that reaches above the knee — sometimes used figuratively • They suffered under the fascist *jackboot*. [=they suffered under fascist rule]

– jack·boot·ed /ˈʤækˌbuːtəd/ *adj* • *jackbooted* thugs

jack·et /ˈʤækət/ *noun, pl* **-ets** [*count*]

1 : a piece of clothing that is worn on your upper body over another piece of clothing (such as a shirt) **:** a usually short and light coat • a suit with a double-breasted *jacket* • a warm *jacket* — see color picture on page C15; see also DINNER JACKET, FLAK JACKET, LIFE JACKET, SPORTS JACKET, STRAITJACKET

2 : an outer covering: such as **a :** a paper cover that protects a book and that can be removed **:** DUST JACKET **b** *chiefly US* **:** a paper, cardboard, or plastic envelope for holding a record, CD, or DVD — called also *sleeve*

– see also YELLOW JACKET

jacket potato *noun, pl* **~ -toes** [*count*] *Brit* **:** a potato baked with its skin left on

Jack Frost *noun* — used as a way to refer to frost or cold weather • *Jack Frost* may arrive early this year.

jack·ham·mer /ˈʤækˌhæmɚ/ *noun, pl* **-ers** [*count*] *chiefly US* **:** a heavy tool used to break hard substances (such as concrete) into pieces by a repeated pounding action — called also *pneumatic drill*

jack–in–the–box /ˈʤækənðəˌbɑːks/ *noun, pl* **jack–in–the–box·es** *or* **jacks–in–the–box** [*count*] **:** a toy that is a small box containing a clown or other figure which jumps up when the box is opened

[1]jack·knife /ˈʤækˌnaɪf/ *noun, pl* **-knives** [*count*]

1 : a small knife that has a folding blade **:** POCKETKNIFE

2 : a dive in which you bend from the waist and touch your ankles and then straighten out

[2]jackknife *verb* **-knifes; -knifed; -knif·ing** [*no obj*] **:** to bend in the middle like a folding jackknife; *especially, of a large truck* **:** to have the back part slide out of control toward the front part • The truck *jackknifed* on the icy road.

jack–of–all–trades /ˌʤækəvˌɑːlˈtreɪdz/ *noun, pl* **jacks–of–all–trades** [*count*] **:** a person who has many skills **:** a person who can do many different jobs ✧ If you are a ***jack-of-all-trades, master of none***, you can do many things but are not an expert in any of them.

jack–o'–lan·tern /ˈʤækəˌlæntɚn/ *noun, pl* **-terns** [*count*] **:** a pumpkin that has had its insides removed and a face cut into it for Halloween ✧ You put a candle in a jack-o'-lantern so that light shines out through its eyes, nose, and mouth.

jack·pot /ˈʤækˌpɑːt/ *noun, pl* **-pots** [*count*] **:** a usually large amount of money won in a game of chance • The lottery *jackpot* is up to one million dollars.

hit the jackpot **1 :** to win all the money that can be won in a game of chance • He *hit the jackpot* on the slot machine. **2 :** to have unexpected success or good luck • He really *hit the jackpot* with his new restaurant. [=he became very successful with his new restaurant] • They *hit the jackpot* when they hired her. [=she is a very valuable employee]

jack·rab·bit /ˈʤækˌræbət/ *noun, pl* **-bits** [*count*] **:** a North American animal that resembles a large rabbit and that is very fast

Jac·o·be·an /ˌʤækəˈbiːjən/ *adj* **:** of or relating to James I of England or the time (1603–25) when he was king • *Jacobean* drama • a *Jacobean* mansion

Ja·cuz·zi /ʤəˈkuːzi/ *trademark* — used for a bathtub in which a pump causes water and air bubbles to move around your body

jade /ˈʤeɪd/ *noun* [*noncount*]

1 : a usually green stone that is used for jewelry — see color picture on page C11

2 : a light bluish-green color — called also *jade green*; see color picture on page C2

jad·ed /ˈʤeɪdəd/ *adj* [*more ~; most ~*] **:** feeling or showing a lack of interest and excitement caused by having done or experienced too much of something • He became *jaded* from years of work as a police officer. • a public *jaded* by political scandals • a *jaded* attitude

jag /ˈʤæg/ *noun, pl* **jags** [*count*] *chiefly US, informal* **:** a short period of time when you do something in an uncontrolled way • a crying *jag*

jag·ged /ˈʤægəd/ *adj* [*more ~; most ~*] **:** having a sharp, uneven edge or surface • a *jagged* mountain peak • *jagged* pieces of broken glass

jag·uar /ˈʤæˌgwɑɚ, *Brit* ˈʤægjəwə/ *noun, pl* **-uars** [*count*] **:** a large, brown, wild cat with black spots that lives in Central and South America — see picture at CAT

[1]jail *also Brit* **gaol** /ˈʤeɪl/ *noun, pl* **jails :** a place where people are kept when they have been arrested and are being punished for a crime [*count*] He was locked up in the county *jail*. [*noncount*] He was arrested and ***sent/sentenced to jail***. • He ***went to jail*** for his crimes. • He just got ***out of jail*** a few weeks ago. • He was kept ***in jail*** overnight.

> ***synonyms*** JAIL, PRISON, and PENITENTIARY all refer to places where criminals are kept. In U.S. English, *jail* usually refers to a small local place for holding criminals. • He was arrested for drunkenness and spent a night in the city *jail*. *Prison* refers to a much larger building for more serious criminals, such as murderers. • He was sentenced to 40 years in a state/federal *prison*. *Penitentiary* always refers to a large state or federal prison. • He is serving a life sentence at a federal *penitentiary*. In British English, there is no clear difference between *jail* and *prison*, and the word *penitentiary* is not now used.

[2]jail *also Brit* **gaol** *verb* **jails; jailed; jail·ing** [+ *obj*] **:** to put (a person) in jail — usually used as *(be) jailed* • He *was jailed* for assaulting a police officer.

jail·bird *also Brit* **gaol·bird** /ˈʤeɪlˌbɚd/ *noun, pl* **-birds** [*count*] *informal + old-fashioned* **:** a person who has often been in jail or prison

jail·break *also Brit* **gaol·break** /ˈʤeɪlˌbreɪk/ *noun, pl* **-breaks** [*count*] **:** an escape from jail or prison

jail·er *also* **jail·or** *or Brit* **gaol·er** /ˈʤeɪlɚ/ *noun, pl* **-ers** *also* **-ors** [*count*] *somewhat old-fashioned* **:** a person who is in charge of a jail or who guards the prisoners in a jail

jail·house /ˈʤeɪlˌhaʊs/ *noun, pl* **-hous·es** [*count*] *US* **:** [1]JAIL — usually used before another noun • a *jailhouse* informant [=an informant who is in jail]

ja·la·pe·ño *also* **ja·la·pe·no** /ˌhɑːləˈpeɪnjoʊ/ *noun, pl* **-ños** *also* **-nos** [*count*] **:** a small green pepper that is very hot and is used especially in Mexican cooking — called also *jalapeño pepper, jalapeno pepper*

ja·lopy /dʒəˈlɑːpi/ *noun, pl* **-lop·ies** [*count*] *informal* : an old car that is in poor condition ▪ He fixed up an old *jalopy.*

[1]jam /ˈdʒæm/ *verb* **jams; jammed; jam·ming**

1 a : to fill (a place) completely [*+ obj*] Thousands of people *jammed* the hall. = The hall was *jammed* [=*jam-packed, packed*] with thousands of people. [*no obj*] Thousands of people *jammed* into the hall. **b** [*+ obj*] **:** to fill (something, such as a door or a road) so that movement is slow or stopped ▪ People were *jamming* the exits after the concert. ▪ All the roads and bridges were *jammed* (with traffic). — sometimes used figuratively ▪ All the telephone lines were *jammed* with calls from angry customers.

2 a [*+ obj*] **:** to press or push (an object) into a tight place ▪ He *jammed* the book back into the bookcase. ▪ A piece of paper got/was *jammed* [=*stuck*] in the copy machine. **b :** to push (a part of your body, a lever, etc.) suddenly and forcefully [*+ obj*] She *jammed* her foot down hard on the brakes. [*no obj*] She ***jammed on the brakes.*** **c** [*+ obj*] **:** to cause (a part of your body) to be painfully crushed, squeezed, etc. ▪ I *jammed* my finger in the car door. = My finger got *jammed* in the car door. = I got my finger *jammed* in the car door. ▪ I *jammed* [=*stubbed*] my toe on the chair's leg.

3 a [*no obj*] **:** to stop working properly because something inside prevents movement ▪ The copy machine *jammed* (up) again. ▪ The lock/gun *jammed.* **b** [*+ obj*] **:** to cause (something) to stop working properly by preventing its parts from moving ▪ A piece of paper *jammed* the copy machine.

4 [*+ obj*] **:** to make (a radio signal or broadcast) impossible to understand by sending out signals or messages that weaken or block it ▪ *jam* a radio broadcast

5 [*no obj*] **:** to play music informally together without preparation ▪ We like to get together and *jam* (with each other).

6 [*+ obj*] *baseball* **:** to throw a pitch that is close to a batter and that the batter is unable to hit well ▪ The pitcher *jammed* him with an inside fastball.

[2]jam *noun, pl* **jams** [*count*]

1 : a situation in which a machine does not work properly because something inside prevents its parts from moving ▪ There's a paper *jam* in the printer.

2 : a situation in which something (such as a road) is so filled that movement is stopped or slowed ▪ I got stuck in a ***traffic jam*** on the way home from work. — see also LOGJAM

3 *informal* **:** a difficult situation ▪ He got in/into a real *jam* with his girlfriend. ▪ She asked her parents for money to help her get out of a *jam.*

– compare [3]JAM

[3]jam *noun, pl* **jams** [*count, noncount*] **:** a sweet food made of fruit and sugar thickened by boiling ▪ a jar of raspberry *jam*

money for jam see MONEY

– compare [2]JAM

jamb /ˈdʒæm/ *noun, pl* **jambs** [*count*] **:** a board that forms the side of a door or window — see also DOORJAMB

jam·ba·laya /ˌdʒʌmbəˈlajə, *Brit* ˌdʒæmbəˈlajə/ *noun* [*noncount*] **:** a spicy dish of rice cooked usually with ham, sausage, chicken, shrimp, or oysters

jam·bo·ree /ˌdʒæmbəˈriː/ *noun, pl* **-rees** [*count*]

1 : a large party or celebration with music and entertainment ▪ a country music *jamboree*

2 : a large gathering of Boy Scouts or Girl Scouts

jam·mies /ˈdʒæmiz/ *noun* [*plural*] *US, informal* **:** PAJAMAS ✧ *Jammies* is a word used mainly by children and when speaking to children.

jam·my /ˈdʒæmi/ *adj* **jam·mi·er; -est**

1 : resembling or suggesting jam ▪ *jammy* flavors

2 *Brit, informal* **:** having good luck **:** LUCKY ▪ He's a *jammy* bastard. [=lucky guy]

jam–packed /ˈdʒæmˈpækt/ *adj* **:** filled completely ▪ The theater was *jam-packed* (with people) for the performance.

jam session *noun, pl* ~ **-sions** [*count*] **:** a gathering or performance in which musicians play together informally without any preparation **:** a session in which musicians jam with each other

Jan. *abbr* January

Jane Doe /ˈdʒeɪnˈdoʊ/ *noun, pl* ~ **Does** [*count*] *US, law* — used as a name for a woman whose true name is not known or is being kept secret; compare JOHN DOE

jan·gle /ˈdʒæŋgəl/ *verb* **jan·gles; jan·gled; jan·gling**

1 [*no obj*] **:** to make a harsh ringing sound ▪ Coins *jangled* out of the machine.

2 [*+ obj*] **:** to cause (something) to make a harsh ringing sound ▪ He *jangled* his keys loudly outside the door.

jangle nerves ✧ If something *jangles your nerves*, it makes you feel very nervous and tense. ▪ The pressure of performing *jangled her nerves.* ▪ He took a deep breath to try to calm his *jangled nerves.*

– jangle *noun, pl* **jangles** [*count*] — usually singular ▪ the *jangle* of loose coins

jan·i·tor /ˈdʒænətɚ/ *noun, pl* **-tors** [*count*] *chiefly US* **:** a person who cleans a building and makes minor repairs — called also (*Brit*) *caretaker*

– jan·i·to·ri·al /ˌdʒænəˈtorijəl/ *adj*

Jan·u·ary /ˈdʒænjəˌweri/ *noun, pl* **-ar·ies :** the first month of the year [*noncount*] in (early/middle/mid-/late) *January* ▪ early/late in *January* ▪ They arrived on *January* the fourth. = (*US*) They arrived on *January* fourth. = They arrived on the fourth of *January.* [*count*] Sales are up (for) this *January* in comparison with the previous two *Januaries.* — abbr. *Jan.*

Jap /ˈdʒæp/ *noun, pl* **Japs** [*count*] *informal + offensive* **:** a Japanese person ✧ The word *Jap* is very offensive and should be avoided.

[1]Jap·a·nese /ˌdʒæpəˈniːz/ *noun*

1 ***the Japanese*** **:** the people of Japan **:** Japanese people ▪ the customs of *the Japanese*

2 [*noncount*] **:** the language of the Japanese ▪ He is learning to speak *Japanese.*

[2]Japanese *adj* **:** of or relating to Japan, its people, or their language ▪ *Japanese* history/food ▪ She is *Japanese.* ▪ The custom is *Japanese.*

Japanese beetle *noun, pl* ~ **beetles** [*count*] **:** a small green and brown beetle that is originally from Asia and that causes damage to plants in the U.S. — see color picture on page C10

[1]jar /ˈdʒɑɚ/ *noun, pl* **jars** [*count*]

1 a : a glass container that has a wide opening and usually a lid ▪ a pickle *jar* **b :** a clay container that has a wide opening ▪ a pottery *jar*

2 : the amount of something inside a jar ▪ We ate an entire *jar* of pickles.

jar

[2]jar *verb* **jars; jarred; jar·ring**

1 : to have a harsh or unpleasant effect on someone or something [*no obj*] — usually + *on* ▪ The loud music *jarred on* my ears. [*+ obj*] The attack *jarred* [=*shook, rattled*] her sense of security. ▪ The loss *jarred* his confidence in the team.

2 : to hit or shake (something) forcefully [*+ obj*] The earthquake *jarred* the tiles loose. ▪ He *jarred* [=*knocked*] the ball from his opponent's hands. [*no obj*] The tiles *jarred* loose in the earthquake.

3 [*+ obj*] **:** to make (someone) feel uneasy ▪ Visitors are often *jarred* [=*unsettled*] by the conditions at the hospital.

4 [*no obj*] *chiefly Brit* **:** to look bad or ugly together ▪ The two colors of the wallpaper *jar* [=*clash*] (with each other).

– jarring *adj* [*more* ~; *most* ~] ▪ It was *jarring* to see how frail she was. ▪ a *jarring* contrast

jar·gon /ˈdʒɑɚgən/ *noun* [*noncount*] *usually disapproving* **:** the language used for a particular activity or by a particular group of people ▪ legal/sports *jargon* ▪ medical *jargon* that the layman cannot understand ▪ an academic essay filled with *jargon*

jar·head /ˈdʒɑɚˌhɛd/ *noun, pl* **-heads** [*count*] *US slang* **:** a member of the United States Marine Corps

jas·mine /ˈdʒæzmən/ *noun* [*noncount*] **:** a plant that has flowers with a very pleasant and sweet smell

jaun·dice /ˈdʒɑːndəs/ *noun* [*noncount*] *medical* **:** a disease that causes a person's skin to turn yellow

jaun·diced /ˈdʒɑːndəst/ *adj* [*more* ~; *most* ~]

1 *medical* **:** having a disease that causes your skin to turn yellow **:** affected with jaundice ▪ a severely *jaundiced* patient

2 : feeling or showing dislike, distrust, or anger because of past experiences **:** likely to think that people, organizations, etc., are bad ▪ a *jaundiced* critic ▪ She has a very *jaundiced* view of politics and politicians.

jaunt /ˈdʒɑːnt/ *noun, pl* **jaunts** [*count*] **:** a brief trip taken for pleasure ▪ a four-day *jaunt* to the mountains

jaun·ty /ˈdʒɑːnti/ *adj* **jaun·ti·er; -est** [*also more* ~; *most* ~] **:** lively in manner or appearance ▪ *jaunty* tunes ▪ a *jaunty* greeting **:** having or suggesting a lively and confident quality ▪ He struck a *jaunty* pose for the camera. ▪ She was wearing a *jaunty* white cap.

– jaunt·i·ly /ˈdʒɑːntəli/ *adv* ▪ She posed *jauntily* for the camera. **– jaunt·i·ness** /ˈdʒɑːntinəs/ *noun* [*noncount*]

ja•va /ˈʤævə, ˈʤɑːvə/ *noun* [*noncount*] *US, informal* : COFFEE ▪ a hot cup of *java*

jav•e•lin /ˈʤævələn/ *noun, pl* **-lins**
1 [*count*] : a long spear that people throw as far as they can as a sport
2 ***the javelin*** : an event in which people compete by trying to throw a javelin farther than everyone else ▪ winner of *the javelin*

[1]**jaw** /ˈʤɑː/ *noun, pl* **jaws**
1 [*count*] **a** : either one of the two bones of the face where teeth grow ▪ He broke his upper/lower *jaw.* ▪ The crocodile tried to grab him in its *jaws.* [=*mouth*] ▪ the *jaws* of a tiger/shark — often used figuratively ▪ He barely escaped from ***the jaws of death.*** [=he barely escaped death] ▪ The team was able to snatch victory from ***the jaws of defeat*** [=the team won] by scoring in the final seconds of the game. — see picture at FACE **b** : the lower part of a person's face — usually singular ▪ I'd like to give that guy a punch in the *jaw.*
2 ***jaws*** [*plural*] : two parts of a machine or tool that open and close to hold or crush something ▪ the *jaws* of a vise
jaw drops ✧ If your *jaw drops,* you open your mouth in a way that shows you are very surprised or shocked. ▪ His *jaw dropped* when he heard who had won.

[2]**jaw** *verb* **jaws; jawed; jaw•ing** [*no obj*] *informal* : to talk in an angry way or for a very long time ▪ The coach was *jawing* with/at the referee. ▪ She was on the phone *jawing* with her sister all night.

jaw•bone /ˈʤɑːˌboun/ *noun, pl* **-bones** [*count*] : the bone that forms the lower jaw : MANDIBLE — see picture at HUMAN

jaw•break•er /ˈʤɑːˌbreɪkɚ/ *noun, pl* **-ers** [*count*] *US* : a round, hard candy

jaw•line /ˈʤɑːˌlaɪn/ *noun, pl* **-lines** [*count*] : the line of the face formed by the lower jaw : the bottom edge of a person's face ▪ He has a strong *jawline.*

jay /ˈʤeɪ/ *noun, pl* **jays** [*count*] : a noisy bird that is often brightly colored — see also BLUE JAY

jay•bird /ˈʤeɪˌbɚd/ *noun, pl* **-birds** [*count*] *US, informal + old-fashioned* : JAY
naked as a jaybird : completely naked ▪ He was standing at the window, *naked as a jaybird.*

jay•walk /ˈʤeɪˌwɑːk/ *verb* **-walks; -walked; -walk•ing** [*no obj*] : to cross a street carelessly or at an illegal or dangerous place ▪ The police officer warned us not to *jaywalk.*
– jay•walk•er *noun, pl* **-ers** [*count*] **– jaywalking** *noun* [*noncount*] ▪ She was arrested for *jaywalking.*

[1]**jazz** /ˈʤæz/ *noun* [*noncount*]
1 : a type of American music with lively rhythms and melodies that are often made up by musicians as they play ▪ He likes/plays *jazz.* ▪ She was listening to (some) *jazz.* — often used before another noun ▪ a *jazz* band/festival/musician
2 *informal* **a** : meaningless or foolish talk ▪ What's all this *jazz* about you leaving? **b** : similar things : STUFF ▪ She loves hiking, biking, ***and all that jazz.***

[2]**jazz** *verb* **jazz•es; jazzed; jazz•ing**
jazz up [*phrasal verb*] ***jazz up (something) or jazz (something) up informal*** : to make (something) more interesting, exciting, or attractive ▪ The company wants to *jazz up* its image. ▪ She tried to *jazz* the room *up* with a new rug.

jazzed *adj, not used before a noun* [*more ~; most ~*] *US, informal* : very excited ▪ He was really *jazzed* for the game. ▪ She was *jazzed* (up) to be playing in the band.

jazzy /ˈʤæzi/ *adj* **jazz•i•er; -est** [*also more ~; most ~*]
1 : having the qualities of jazz music ▪ *jazzy* tunes ▪ a *jazzy* piano solo
2 *informal* : bright, lively, or fancy in a way that is meant to attract attention ▪ *jazzy* decorations ▪ He wore a *jazzy* suit to the party. ▪ You're looking pretty *jazzy* [=*snazzy*] today.

J.D. *abbr* doctor of jurisprudence; doctor of law

jeal•ous /ˈʤɛləs/ *adj* [*more ~; most ~*]
1 : feeling or showing jealousy: such as **a** : feeling or showing an unhappy or angry desire to have what someone else has ▪ His success has made some of his old friends *jealous.* — often *+ of* ▪ Some of his old friends are *jealous* [=*envious*] *of* his success. = Some of his old friends are *jealous of* him because of his success. ▪ He feels *jealous of* his rich friends. **b** : feeling or showing unhappiness or anger because you think that someone you love (such as your husband or wife) likes or is liked by someone else ▪ a *jealous* husband ▪ She became very *jealous* whenever he talked to other women. ▪ He was in a *jealous* rage.
2 *somewhat formal* : very concerned about protecting or keeping something — *+ of* ▪ She was *jealous of* her good reputation. ▪ He has always been very *jealous of* his privacy.
– jeal•ous•ly *adv* ▪ He spoke *jealously* of his friend's success. ▪ He *jealously* accused his wife of flirting with other men. ▪ a *jealously* [=*closely*] guarded secret

jeal•ou•sy /ˈʤɛləsi/ *noun, pl* **-sies**
1 : an unhappy or angry feeling of wanting to have what someone else has [*noncount*] professional *jealousy* [=resentment of the success of someone who is in the same profession as you] [*count*] petty *jealousies* among political rivals
2 : an unhappy or angry feeling caused by the belief that someone you love (such as your husband or wife) likes or is liked by someone else [*noncount*] a marriage ruined by infidelity and *jealousy* ▪ He was driven crazy with *jealousy.* [*count*] He was unable to control his *jealousies.*

jeans /ˈʤiːnz/ *noun* [*plural*] : pants made of a strong cloth (called denim) ▪ He was wearing (a pair of) *jeans.* — see color picture on page C14

Jeep /ˈʤiːp/ *trademark* — used for a small truck that can be driven over very rough surfaces

jee•pers /ˈʤiːpɚz/ *interj, informal + old-fashioned* — used to express surprise ▪ *Jeepers,* it's cold out here!

jeer /ˈʤiɚ/ *verb* **jeers; jeered; jeer•ing** : to shout insulting words at someone : to laugh at or criticize someone in a loud and angry way [*no obj*] The crowd *jeered* (at him) when he struck out. ▪ He tried to ignore the *jeering* crowd. [*+ obj*] The crowd *jeered* him when he struck out. ▪ The prisoner was *jeered* by an angry mob.
– jeer *noun, pl* **jeers** [*count*] ▪ His appearance drew *jeers* from the crowd.

jeez *variant spelling of* GEEZ

Je•ho•vah /ʤɪˈhouvə/ *noun* [*singular*] — used as the name of God in the Old Testament of the Bible

Jehovah's Witness *noun, pl* **~ -nesses** [*count*] : a member of a religious group that believes that the world will end soon and that tries to get people to become members so they will be saved

je•june /ʤɪˈʤuːn/ *adj, formal*
1 : not interesting : BORING ▪ the novel's *jejune* plot
2 : too simple ▪ She made *jejune* remarks about life and art.

Je•kyll and Hyde /ˈʤɛkələnˈhaɪd/ *noun* [*singular*] : someone who is sometimes good and pleasant and sometimes very rude or bad ▪ He's a real *Jekyll and Hyde* who can become violent without warning. ▪ his *Jekyll and Hyde* tendencies ✧ This term comes from "The Strange Case of Dr. Jekyll and Mr. Hyde," a story by Robert Louis Stevenson. In the story, Dr. Jekyll is a scientist who creates a liquid that changes him from a good man to the evil Mr. Hyde when he drinks it.

jell /ˈʤɛl/ *verb* **jells; jelled; jell•ing** [*no obj*]
1 : to become clear and definite : GEL ▪ The idea *jelled.* ▪ Our plans are finally starting to *jell.* ▪ A few scenes in the movie don't *jell.* [=*work*]
2 : to change into a thick substance that is like jelly ▪ Boil the jam until it begins to *jell.*

Jell–O /ˈʤɛlou/ *trademark* — used for a fruit-flavored dessert made with gelatin

jel•ly /ˈʤɛli/ *noun, pl* **-lies**
1 : a sweet and soft food made by boiling sugar and fruit juice until it is thick [*count*] a selection of different *jellies* and jams [*noncount*] He spread some *jelly* on his toast. ▪ a jar of grape *jelly* ▪ a peanut butter and *jelly* sandwich ▪ a *jelly* doughnut [=a doughnut with jelly inside of it] — sometimes used figuratively ▪ One look from her reduces me to *jelly.* [=makes me feel very weak and nervous] ▪ Shock and fear turned my legs to *jelly.* [=made my legs feel very weak]
2 [*noncount*] *Brit* : a fruit-flavored dessert made with gelatin ✧ In the U.S., this kind of dessert is known by the trademark *Jell-O.*
3 [*noncount*] *old-fashioned* : a food made from meat juices and gelatin ▪ a meat glaze made with stock and *jelly*
4 : a substance that is soft and thick like jelly [*count*] liquid ointments and *jellies* [*noncount*] lubricating *jelly* — see also PETROLEUM JELLY
– jel•lied /ˈʤɛlid/ *adj* ▪ *jellied* candies **– jel•ly•like** /ˈʤɛliˌlaɪk/ *adj* ▪ a thick *jellylike* substance

jelly baby *noun, pl* **~ -bies** [*count*] *Brit* : a soft candy shaped like a baby and made with gelatin

jelly bean *noun, pl* **~ beans** [*count*] : a candy that is shaped like a bean and has a hard sugar shell with a soft center

jel·ly·fish /ˈʤɛli,fɪʃ/ *noun, pl* **jellyfish** [*count*] : a sea animal that has a very soft body and that can sting

jellyfish

jelly roll *noun, pl* ~ **rolls** [*count*] *US* : a thin sheet of cake that is spread with jelly and rolled up — called also (*Brit*) *Swiss roll*

[1]**jem·my** /ˈʤɛmi/ *noun, pl* **-mies** [*count*] *Brit* : [1]JIMMY

[2]**jemmy** *verb* **-mies; -mied; -my·ing** [+ *obj*] *Brit* : [2]JIMMY

je ne sais quoi /ʒənəˌseɪˈkwɑː/ *noun* [*singular*] *sometimes humorous* : a pleasant quality that is hard to describe ▪ Although the sculpture had flaws, it also had ***a certain je ne sais quoi*** that made it very appealing. ✧ In French the phrase *je ne sais quoi* means literally "I know not what."

jeop·ar·dize *also Brit* **jeop·ar·dise** /ˈʤɛpɚˌdaɪz/ *verb* **-diz·es; -dized; -diz·ing** [+ *obj*] : to put (something or someone) in danger ▪ The wrong decision could (seriously) *jeopardize* your career. ▪ His health has been *jeopardized* by poor nutrition.

jeop·ar·dy /ˈʤɛpɚdi/ *noun*

in jeopardy : in a situation in which someone or something is exposed to possible injury, loss, or evil : in danger ▪ He is responsible for placing innocent lives *in jeopardy*. ▪ The wrong decision could place your career *in* (serious) *jeopardy*. ▪ Public opinion puts this proposal *in* serious *jeopardy*.

– see also DOUBLE JEOPARDY

[1]**jerk** /ˈʤɚk/ *noun, pl* **jerks** [*count*]

1 *informal* : a stupid person or a person who is not well-liked or who treats other people badly ▪ That *jerk* can't do anything right. ▪ Most of the kids are nice, but some are *jerks*.

2 a : a quick pull or twist ▪ The dead branch came loose after a few *jerks*. ▪ He felt the *jerk* of the line as a fish took the bait. ▪ The door was stuck, but I ***gave it a jerk*** [=pulled on it very hard and very quickly] and it opened. **b** : a sudden sharp movement ▪ The car started with a *jerk*.

[2]**jerk** *verb* **jerks; jerked; jerk·ing**

1 [+ *obj*] : to push, pull, or twist (something) with a quick movement ▪ I *jerked* the door open. ▪ She *jerked* the phone out of my hand.

2 a : to move (something) with a sharp, quick motion [+ *obj*] He *jerked* his head in the direction of the door and said, "Let's go." [*no obj*] The car *jerked* into motion. **b** *always followed by an adverb, adjective, or preposition* : to cause (someone) to move suddenly [+ *obj*] He was *jerked* awake by the sound of a baby crying. — sometimes used figuratively ▪ She was *jerked* back to reality by the baby's crying. [*no obj*] He *jerked* awake when the baby started to cry.

jerk around [*phrasal verb*] ***jerk (someone) around*** *chiefly US, informal* : to be unfair or dishonest with (someone) : to lie to or cheat (someone) ▪ I felt like that salesman was trying to *jerk* me *around*. — often used as *(be/get) jerked around* ▪ I felt like I was *getting jerked around* by that salesman.

jerk off [*phrasal verb*] *informal + impolite, of a man* : MASTURBATE

jer·kin /ˈʤɚkən/ *noun, pl* **-kins** [*count*] : a type of short jacket that has no sleeves and that was worn in the past

jerk·wa·ter /ˈʤɚkˌwɑːtɚ/ *adj, always used before a noun, US, informal + disapproving* — used to describe a small town, village, etc., that is out in the country far from cities ▪ He lives in some *jerkwater* town in the middle of nowhere.

[1]**jer·ky** /ˈʤɚki/ *noun* [*noncount*] *US* : meat that has been cut into long strips and dried ▪ beef *jerky*

[2]**jerky** /ˈʤɚki/ *adj* **jerk·i·er; -est**

1 : marked by quick rough motions or sudden starts and stops ▪ He made *jerky* movements. ▪ The movie was *jerky* and hard to watch.

2 *informal* : foolish, stupid, or rude ▪ *jerky* behavior

– **jerk·i·ly** /ˈʤɚkəli/ *adv* ▪ The train moved *jerkily* into the station. – **jerk·i·ness** /ˈʤɚkinəs/ *noun* [*noncount*] ▪ the *jerkiness* of her movements ▪ I can't believe his *jerkiness*!

jer·ry–built /ˈʤeriˌbɪlt/ *adj, informal + disapproving* : built cheaply and quickly : not well-built ▪ *jerry-built* houses

jer·ry–rigged /ˈʤeriˌrɪgd/ *adj, chiefly US* : made in a quick or careless way : not built or designed well ▪ We'll have to replace the building's *jerry-rigged* heating system.

jer·sey /ˈʤɚzi/ *noun, pl* **-seys**

1 [*count*] **a** : a loose shirt worn by a member of a sports team as part of a uniform ▪ a football *jersey* **b** : a shirt made of knitted cloth

2 [*count*] *Brit* : SWEATER a

3 [*noncount*] : a soft knitted cloth ▪ The dress is made of cotton/wool *jersey*.

4 ***Jersey*** [*count*] : a type of small and light brown cow that produces rich milk ▪ We keep a herd of *Jerseys*. ▪ *Jersey* cows

Je·ru·sa·lem artichoke /ʤəˌruːsələm-/ *noun, pl* ~ **-chokes** [*count*] : the root of a plant that looks like a potato and is eaten as a vegetable

[1]**jest** /ˈʤɛst/ *noun, pl* **jests** *formal + old-fashioned* : something said or done to cause laughter : JOKE [*count*] It was a harmless *jest*. [*noncount*] I didn't mean to upset you; I only said it ***in jest***. [=I was only joking]

[2]**jest** *verb* **jests; jest·ed; jest·ing** [*no obj*] *formal + old-fashioned* : to say things that are meant to cause laughter : JOKE ▪ You voted for him? ***Surely you jest***. [=you must be joking]

jest·er /ˈʤɛstɚ/ *noun, pl* **-ers** [*count*] : a man who in the past was kept by a ruler to amuse people by acting silly and telling jokes ▪ the court *jester*

Je·su·it /ˈʤɛʒuwət, *Brit* ˈʤɛzjuət/ *noun, pl* **-its** [*count*] : a man who is a member of a religious group called the Roman Catholic Society of Jesus

Je·sus Christ /ˈʤiːzəsˈkraɪst/ *noun* [*singular*] : the man who Christians believe is the son of God and whose life, death, and resurrection as reported in the New Testament of the Bible are the basis of the Christian religion — called also *Christ, Jesus* ✧ *Jesus Christ, Christ,* and *Jesus* are commonly used as interjections to express surprise and anger. These uses are avoided in polite speech.

[1]**jet** /ˈʤɛt/ *noun, pl* **jets** [*count*]

1 : a fast airplane that has one or more jet engines ▪ a private/commercial/corporate *jet* — often used before another noun ▪ a *jet* airplane/plane ▪ a *jet* pilot — see also JUMBO JET

2 a : a very strong stream of liquid or gas that comes out through a narrow opening ▪ The telescope has photographed *jets* of gas shooting out from the distant star. **b** : a tube that contains and directs a very strong stream of liquid or gas ▪ One of the fountain's *jets* was blocked.

– compare [3]JET

[2]**jet** *verb* **jets; jet·ted; jet·ting**

1 : to travel by jet airplane [*no obj*] She *jetted* (off) from London to New York for a meeting. [+ *obj*] We *jetted* our representative from London to New York for the meeting.

2 : to come through a narrow opening with great force [*no obj*] Steam *jetted* from the kettle's spout. [+ *obj*] The geyser *jets* a tower of water into the air.

[3]**jet** *noun* [*noncount*] : a hard black stone that is often used for jewelry — compare [1]JET

jet black *noun* [*noncount*] : a very dark black color

– **jet–black** /ˈʤɛtˈblæk/ *adj* ▪ He had *jet-black* hair.

jet engine *noun, pl* ~ **-gines** [*count*] : an engine in which a very strong stream of heated air and gases shoots out from the rear of the engine and pushes the engine forward — see picture at AIRPLANE

jet lag *noun* [*noncount*] : a tired and unpleasant feeling that you sometimes get when you travel by airplane to a place that is far away ▪ I had bad *jet lag* after that last trip overseas.

– **jet–lagged** /ˈʤɛtˌlægd/ *adj* ▪ *jet-lagged* tourists

jet·lin·er /ˈʤɛtˌlaɪnɚ/ *noun, pl* **-ers** [*count*] *US* : a large jet airplane used for carrying passengers

jet–pro·pelled /ˈʤɛtprəˈpɛld/ *adj* : moved forward by a jet engine ▪ a *jet-propelled* missile

jet propulsion *noun* [*noncount*] : the use of a jet engine to create forward movement of an airplane, missile, etc.

jet·sam /ˈʤɛtsəm/ *noun* [*noncount*] : floating objects that are thrown into the water from a ship — usually used in the phrase ***flotsam and jetsam*** ▪ We walked along the *flotsam and jetsam* that had washed up onto the beach. — often used figuratively ▪ She was sorting through the *flotsam and jetsam* that had accumulated on her desk. — compare FLOTSAM

jet set *noun*

the jet set *somewhat old-fashioned* : wealthy people who often travel to different parts of the world ▪ It was a trend started by *the jet set*.

– **jet–set·ter** /ˈʤɛtˌsɛtɚ/ *noun, pl* **-ters** [*count*] ▪ a luxurious hotel that is popular among *jet-setters* – **jet–set·ting** /ˈʤɛtˌsɛtɪŋ/ *adj* ▪ *jet-setting* film stars

Jet Ski *trademark* — used for a small and fast vehicle that is used on water and carries one or two people

jet stream *noun, pl* ~ **streams** [*count*] *technical* : a strong current of fast winds high above the Earth's surface — usually singular ▪ unusual weather patterns caused by changes in the *jet stream*

jet·ti·son /ˈʤɛtəsən/ *verb* **-sons; -soned; -son·ing** [+ *obj*]
1 : to drop (something) from a moving ship, airplane, etc. ▪ The captain gave orders to *jettison* the cargo. ▪ They *jettisoned* the fuel and made an emergency landing.
2 : to get rid of (something) ▪ We should *jettison* these old computers and get new ones. **:** to reject (something, such as a plan or idea) ▪ They *jettisoned* plans for a vacation.

jet·ty /ˈʤɛti/ *noun, pl* **-ties** [*count*] **:** a long structure that is built out into water and used as a place to get on, get off, or tie up a boat

Jew /ˈʤu:/ *noun, pl* **Jews** [*count*] **:** someone whose religion is Judaism, who is descended from Jewish people, or who participates in the culture surrounding Judaism
– **Jew·ish** /ˈʤu:wɪʃ/ *adj* ▪ a *Jewish* temple ▪ Are you *Jewish*?
– **Jew·ish·ness** *noun* [*noncount*]

jew·el /ˈʤu:l/ *noun, pl* **-els** [*count*]
1 : a valuable stone (such as a ruby or diamond) that has been cut and polished ▪ That diamond is one of world's largest *jewels*.
2 : a piece of jewelry (such as a necklace or a bracelet) that is made of valuable metal and precious stones — usually plural ▪ She was dressed in an evening gown and *jewels*.
3 : someone or something that is highly valued or admired ▪ This painting is the *jewel* in our gallery. ▪ She's a *jewel*. ▪ The building is regarded as one of the *jewels* of modern architecture. ▪ He owns several successful businesses but this company is the ***jewel in the crown***. [=this company is the most valuable/important/admired] — see also CROWN JEWEL
4 : the part of a watch that is made of a crystal or a precious stone
the family jewels **1 :** jewelry that has been passed from one generation to another ▪ She inherited *the family jewels* after the death of her grandmother. **2** *informal + humorous* **:** a man's sexual organs
– **jew·eled** (*US*) *or Brit* **jew·elled** /ˈʤu:ld/ *adj* ▪ a *jeweled* sword [=a sword decorated with jewels] ▪ The guests were heavily *jeweled*. [=the guests were wearing a lot of jewelry]

jewel case *noun, pl* **~ cases** [*count*] **:** a clear plastic case in which a CD or DVD is stored — called also *jewel box*

jew·el·er (*US*) *or Brit* **jew·el·ler** /ˈʤu:lɚ/ *noun, pl* **-ers** [*count*] **:** a person who makes, repairs, or sells jewelry and watches

jew·el·ry (*US*) *or Brit* **jew·el·lery** /ˈʤu:lri/ *noun* [*noncount*] **:** decorative objects (such as rings, necklaces, and earrings) that people wear on their body ▪ silver and turquoise *jewelry* ▪ a store that sells *jewelry* ▪ *jewelry* stores — see color picture on page C11; see also COSTUME JEWELRY

Jew·ry /ˈʤu:ri/ *noun* [*noncount*] *formal* **:** Jewish people as a group ▪ American *Jewry*

[1]**jib** /ˈʤɪb/ *noun, pl* **jibs** [*count*]
1 : a small triangular sail near the front of a sailboat
2 *technical* **:** the long part of a crane that carries the weight of the object that the crane is lifting

[2]**jib** *verb* **jibs; jibbed; jib·bing** [*no obj*] *Brit, old-fashioned* **:** to hesitate or refuse to do or accept something **:** BALK — usually + *at* ▪ Investors *jibbed at* putting more money into the company.

[1]**jibe** /ˈʤaɪb/ *verb* **jibes; jibed; jib·ing** [*no obj*] *US, informal* **:** to agree *with* someone or something ▪ His story didn't *jibe with* the testimony of other witnesses. ▪ What he told me doesn't *jibe with* my experience. — compare [2]JIBE

[2]**jibe** *verb* **jibes; jibed; jibing** [*no obj*] **:** to cause a sailboat to change direction by swinging the sail to the opposite side of the boat — compare [1]JIBE

[3]**jibe** *variant spelling of* GIBE

jif·fy /ˈʤɪfi/ *noun* [*singular*] *informal* **:** a very brief time **:** MOMENT — usually used in the phrase ***in a jiffy*** ▪ I'll be there *in a jiffy*.

Jiffy bag *trademark, Brit* — used for a thick, padded mailing envelope

[1]**jig** /ˈʤɪg/ *noun, pl* **jigs** [*count*] **:** a type of lively dance ▪ She did/danced a little *jig*.; *also* **:** the music played for such a dance ▪ Hey, play us a *jig*!
the jig is up *US, informal + old-fashioned* — used to say that a dishonest plan or activity has been discovered and will not be allowed to continue ▪ *The jig is up*: where did you hide the stolen goods?

[2]**jig** *verb* **jigs; jigged; jig·ging**
1 : to move with quick sudden movements [+ *obj*] He *jigged* [=*jiggled*] his fishing line. [*no obj*] (*chiefly Brit*) The horses *jigged* around nervously.
2 [*no obj*] **:** to dance a jig ▪ We *jigged* to the fiddle music.

jig·ger /ˈʤɪgɚ/ *noun, pl* **-gers** [*count*] **:** a small cup or glass that is used to measure alcohol; *also* **:** the amount held in a jigger ▪ He poured a *jigger* of whiskey into the glass.

jig·gery–pok·ery /ˈʤɪgəriˈpoʊkəri/ *noun* [*noncount*] *Brit, informal* **:** dishonest or suspicious activity ▪ There's some *jiggery-pokery* [=*hanky-panky*] going on behind the scenes.

jig·gle /ˈʤɪgəl/ *verb* **jig·gles; jig·gled; jig·gling :** to move or cause (something) to move with quick, short movements up and down or side to side [+ *obj*] He *jiggled* the doorknob. ▪ Try to avoid *jiggling* the camera. [*no obj*] His belly *jiggled* like a bowlful of jelly.
– **jiggle** *noun, pl* **jiggles** [*count*] ▪ You have to give the doorknob a *jiggle* to open the door. ▪ It's hard to avoid a few *jiggles* when you're using a video camera.

jig·saw /ˈʤɪgˌsɑ:/ *noun, pl* **-saws** [*count*]
1 : a machine that has a narrow blade for cutting curved lines in thin pieces of wood, metal, plastic, etc.
2 *chiefly Brit* **:** JIGSAW PUZZLE

jigsaw puzzle *noun, pl* **~ puzzles** [*count*] **:** a puzzle made of many small pieces that are cut into various shapes and can be fit together to form a picture ▪ We spent many nights working on a *jigsaw puzzle* of Mount Everest. — often used figuratively ▪ Ecologists no longer view different species as independent, but instead see them as pieces of the same *jigsaw puzzle*. — called also (*chiefly Brit*) *jigsaw*

jigsaw puzzle

ji·had /ʤɪˈhɑ:d/ *noun, pl* **-hads** [*count*] **:** a war fought by Muslims to defend or spread their beliefs

jilt /ˈʤɪlt/ *verb* **jilts; jilt·ed; jilt·ing** [+ *obj*] **:** to end a romantic relationship with (someone) in a sudden and painful way ▪ She was crushed when he *jilted* her. — often used as *(be) jilted* ▪ She *was jilted* at the altar. [=the man who was supposed to marry her did not show up for the wedding] ▪ a *jilted* lover

Jim Crow /ˈʤɪmˈkroʊ/ *noun* [*noncount*] **:** the unfair treatment of black people in the past in the southern U.S. when laws were passed that did not give them the same rights as white people ▪ the era of *Jim Crow* ▪ *Jim Crow* laws

jim–dan·dy /ˈʤɪmˈdændi/ *adj, US, informal* **:** very fine or excellent ▪ We had a *jim-dandy* vacation.

jim·mies /ˈʤɪmiz/ *noun* [*plural*] *US* **:** small and thin pieces of candy often sprinkled on ice cream

[1]**jim·my** /ˈʤɪmi/ *noun, pl* **-mies** [*count*] *US* **:** a short metal bar used to force things open or as a lever ▪ The burglar used a *jimmy* to open the window. — called also (*Brit*) *jemmy*

[2]**jimmy** *verb* **-mies; -mied; -my·ing** [+ *obj*] *US* **:** to force (something, such as a lock, door, or window) open with a metal bar or a similar tool ▪ The burglar *jimmied* [=(*Brit*) *jemmied*] the window (open).

[1]**jin·gle** /ˈʤɪŋgəl/ *noun, pl* **jin·gles** [*count*]
1 : a light ringing sound that is made when metal objects hit each other ▪ I heard the *jingle* of bells.
2 : a short song that is easy to remember and that is used to help sell a product on television or radio ▪ an advertising *jingle*

[2]**jingle** *verb* **jingles; jin·gled; jin·gling :** to make or cause (something) to make a light ringing sound [*no obj*] Bells *jingled* in the distance. ▪ *jingling* bracelets/bells/coins ▪ a *jingling* sound [+ *obj*] She *jingled* the coins in her pocket.

jin·go·ism /ˈʤɪŋgoʊˌɪzəm/ *noun* [*noncount*] *disapproving* **:** the feelings and beliefs of people who think that their country is always right and who are in favor of aggressive acts against other countries ▪ When the war began many people were caught up in a wave of *jingoism*.
– **jin·go·is·tic** /ˌʤɪŋgoʊˈɪstɪk/ *adj* ▪ *jingoistic* attitudes

jin·ni /ˈʤi:ni/ *or* **jinn** /ˈʤɪn/ *also* **djinn** /ˈʤɪn/ *noun, pl* **jinn** *or* **jinns** *also* **djinns** [*count*] **:** GENIE

[1]**jinx** /ˈʤɪŋks/ *noun, pl* **jinx·es** [*count*] *informal* **:** someone or something that causes bad luck ▪ That guy is a *jinx*.; *also* **:** a state or period of bad luck caused by a jinx ▪ He felt like he'd finally broken the *jinx*. ▪ She threatened to put a *jinx* on him.

[2]**jinx** *verb* **jinxes; jinxed; jinx·ing** [+ *obj*] *informal* **:** to bring bad luck to (someone or something) ▪ I thought they were

going to win but I didn't say so because I didn't want to *jinx* them. ▪ His luck has been so bad he feels *jinxed*.

jit·ter·bug /ˈʤɪtəˌbʌg/ *noun* [*singular*] : a very lively type of dance from the 1940s
– **jitterbug** *verb* **-bugs**; **-bugged**; **-bug·ging** [*no obj*] ▪ Couples were *jitterbugging* on the dance floor.

jit·ters /ˈʤɪtəz/ *noun*
the jitters *informal* : a very nervous feeling ▪ I always get *the jitters* before I have to give a speech. = Having to give a speech gives me (a bad case of) *the jitters*.

jit·tery /ˈʤɪtəri/ *adj* [*more* ~; *most* ~] *informal* : very nervous ▪ I always get/feel *jittery* when I have to give a speech. ▪ The latest economic news has made some investors *jittery*.

[1]**jive** /ˈʤaɪv/ *noun, pl* **jives** *informal* + *somewhat old-fashioned*
1 [*noncount*] *US* **a** : informal language that includes many slang terms ▪ She grew up talking street *jive*. **b** : deceptive or foolish talk ▪ I'm tired of listening to your *jive*.
2 [*noncount*] : a type of fast lively music that was especially popular in the early part of the 20th century ▪ play some *jive*; *also* [*count*] : a dance performed to this type of music ▪ dancing a *jive*

[2]**jive** *verb* **jives**; **jived**; **jiv·ing** *informal* + *somewhat old-fashioned*
1 *US* : to say foolish or deceptive things to (someone) [+ *obj*] I know he's just *jiving* me. [*no obj*] Don't take him seriously—he's just *jiving*.
2 [*no obj*] : to dance to or play jive music ▪ Everyone was *jiving* to the beat.

Jnr *abbr, Brit* junior ▪ Dave Smith *Jnr*

job /ˈʤɑːb/ *noun, pl* **jobs** [*count*]
1 : the work that a person does regularly in order to earn money ▪ He took/got a *job* as a waiter. ▪ She has a high-paying *job* on Wall Street. ▪ She's trying to get/land/find a *job* in New York. ▪ The new factory will create thousands of *jobs*. ▪ They offered him the *job* but he turned it down. ▪ a part-time/full-time *job* ▪ a *job* interview/offer/description ▪ *job*-hunting ▪ *job*-hunters ▪ My teenage son is looking for a ***summer job***. [=a job for the summer only] ▪ If the restaurant closes, she'll ***lose her job***. = If the restaurant closes, she'll be ***out of a job***. [=she will no longer have a job] ▪ Although he plays music at night, he hasn't been able to give up his ***day job***. [=the regular job that he does during the day] ▪ You shouldn't blame her for what happened. She was ***just/only doing her job***. [=she was doing things that her job requires her to do] ▪ We wouldn't be having these problems if everyone had just ***done their job/jobs***. [=if everyone had properly done the work they were supposed to do]
2 : a duty, task, or function that someone or something has ▪ It was your *job* to mow the lawn. = You had the *job* of mowing the lawn. ▪ The blood's *job* is to carry oxygen to the different parts of the body. ▪ When I asked her to clean up the mess, she said, "That's not my *job*." [=I'm not supposed to do that] ▪ Construction of the bridge turned out to be a bigger *job* than they had expected. ▪ a small *job* ▪ It's a dirty *job*, but someone has to do it. ▪ The computer was processing a ***print job***. [=the computer was printing a document or file] ▪ The car needs a ***brake/valve job***. [=the car needs to have its brakes/valves repaired] ✧ ***Odd jobs*** are small tasks of different kinds that are not planned and do not happen regularly. ▪ He does *odd jobs* around the farm. ***synonyms*** see [1]TASK
3 — used to describe how well or badly something has been done ▪ Whoever planned the party ***did a good/great job***. [=that person planned the party very well] ▪ He ***did a bad job*** of explaining his reasons. [=he did not explain his reasons well] ▪ "I finished the project ahead of schedule." "***Good job***!" ✧ The phrase ***a good job*** is used in informal British English to refer to something fortunate. ▪ It's *a good job* I had my seat belt on! = I had my seat belt on—and *a good job*, too! [=it's good/lucky for me that I had my seat belt on] ✧ The phrase ***a bad job*** is used in informal British English to refer to something that is very difficult or impossible to do. ▪ I tried my best to persuade him, but in the end I ***gave it up as a bad job***. [=I stopped trying to do it because it could not be done]
4 : something that requires very great effort ▪ It was a real *job* to talk over all that noise.
5 *informal* : a thing of some kind ▪ I bought one of those little quilted *jobs* [=*items, numbers*] at the craft fair.
6 *informal* : a criminal act such as robbery ▪ They've finally caught the gang that pulled the bank *job*. [=the gang that robbed the bank] ▪ Police suspect that the bank robbery may have been an ***inside job***. [=that the bank robbery was done by or with the help of someone who works in the bank]
do a job on US, informal : to damage (something or someone) badly ▪ The collision really *did a job on* their car. ▪ Moving all that furniture *did a job on* my back.
do the job informal : to achieve a desired result ▪ The new system isn't working yet, but a few more adjustments ought to *do the job*. [=*do the trick*]
fall down on the job see [1]FALL
on the job **1** : while working on a job ▪ He was injured *on the job*. ▪ New employees are given *on-the-job* training. **2** *Brit slang* : having sex ▪ They were in the back room, *on the job*.
walk off the/your job see [1]WALK
— see also HATCHET JOB, NOSE JOB, PUT-UP JOB
– **job·less** /ˈʤɑːbləs/ *adj* ▪ The factory closing left 5,000 people *jobless*. – **job·less·ness** *noun* [*noncount*] ▪ *Joblessness* [=*unemployment*] is on the rise.

job action *noun, pl* ~ **-tions** [*count*] *US* : something (such as a strike or a slowing of work) done by workers to protest bad conditions, low wages, etc. ▪ The union has threatened a *job action* if wages are not increased. — called also (*Brit*) *industrial action*

job lot *noun, pl* ~ **lots** [*count*] *Brit* : a collection of goods that are being sold as a group ▪ The warehouse bought the pieces as a *job lot*.

job sharing *noun* [*noncount*] : a situation in which two people share the work, hours, and pay of one job ▪ *Job sharing* is becoming more common. ▪ a *job-sharing* arrangement

jock /ˈʤɑːk/ *noun, pl* **jocks** [*count*]
1 *chiefly US, informal* + *sometimes disapproving* : someone who is very involved in sports : ATHLETE ▪ She was a *jock* in high school and led her basketball team to the state championship. ▪ He's just a dumb *jock*.
2 *US, informal* : DISC JOCKEY — see also SHOCK JOCK

[1]**jock·ey** /ˈʤɑːki/ *noun, pl* **-eys** [*count*]
1 : someone who rides horses in races
2 *informal* : someone who operates or works with a specified vehicle, device, object, or material ▪ a bus *jockey* [=a bus driver] ▪ computer *jockeys* — see also DISC JOCKEY

[2]**jockey** *verb* **-eys**; **-eyed**; **-ey·ing**
1 [*no obj*] : to do something in an effort to get an advantage ▪ There was a lot of political *jockeying* at the fund-raiser. — often used in the phrase ***jockey for position*** ▪ Several companies are *jockeying for position* [=are trying to get a better position or situation] in the market.
2 [+ *obj*] *chiefly US* : to change the position of (something) by slow and careful movements ▪ The driver carefully *jockeyed* the truck into a narrow space in the crowded parking lot.

jock·strap /ˈʤɑːkˌstræp/ *noun, pl* **-straps** [*count*] : a piece of underwear worn by men and boys to protect their sexual organs while playing sports — called also (*chiefly US*) *athletic supporter*

jo·cose /ʤoʊˈkoʊs/ *adj* [*more* ~; *most* ~] *formal* + *literary* : very cheerful ▪ his *jocose* demeanor
– **jo·cose·ly** *adv*

joc·u·lar /ˈʤɑːkjələ/ *adj* [*more* ~; *most* ~] *formal*
1 : liking to tell jokes ▪ a *jocular* man who could make the most serious people smile
2 : said or done as a joke ▪ a *jocular* comment
– **joc·u·lar·i·ty** /ˌʤɑːkjəˈlerəti/ *noun* [*noncount*] – **joc·u·lar·ly** *adv*

jodh·purs /ˈʤɑːdpəz/ *noun* [*plural*] : tight pants that are worn for horseback riding ▪ a pair of *jodhpurs*

joe /ˈʤoʊ/ *noun, pl* **joes** *US, informal*
1 *or* **Joe** [*count*] : an ordinary man : GUY ▪ He's just an average/ordinary *Joe*.
2 [*singular*] : COFFEE — usually used in the phrase ***a cup of joe*** ▪ She starts the day with *a cup of joe*.

Joe Blow *noun, pl* ~ **Blows** [*count*] *US, informal* : an average or ordinary man — usually singular ▪ His movies have no appeal for the average *Joe Blow*. ▪ He's just some *Joe Blow* from off the streets. — called also (*Brit*) *Joe Bloggs*

jo·ey /ˈʤowi/ *noun, pl* **joeys** [*count*] : a baby kangaroo

[1]**jog** /ˈʤɑːg/ *verb* **jogs**; **jogged**; **jog·ging**
1 [*no obj*] : to run slowly especially for exercise ▪ She *jogs* three miles a day.
2 [+ *obj*] : to push or bump (someone or something) lightly ▪ She *jogged* [=(more commonly) *nudged*] him with her elbow.
3 [*no obj*] : to move up and down heavily with a short motion ▪ The bag *jogged* against her hip as she walked.
jog along [*phrasal verb*] : to continue in an ordinary or

steady way • Their marriage *jogged along* for several years without any major problems.

jog someone's memory : to cause or help someone to remember something • Maybe this photograph will *jog your memory.*

– jogging *noun* [*noncount*] • Her hobbies include gardening and *jogging.* • She ***goes jogging*** every day. • a ***jogging suit*** [=a set of clothes people wear when they jog]

²jog *noun, pl* **jogs** [*count*]
1 : a slow run done for exercise • Some people depend on a morning *jog* to give them energy. • We're going to go for a *jog* around the park.
2 : a light shake or push • She gave him a *jog* with her elbow.

jog·ger /ˈʤɑːgɚ/ *noun, pl* **-gers** [*count*] : someone who runs for exercise : someone who jogs • *joggers* out for their morning exercise

john /ˈʤɑːn/ *noun, pl* **johns** [*count*] *chiefly US, informal*
1 : a toilet or bathroom • Excuse me, I have to go to the *john.*
2 : a man who pays money to a prostitute for sex

John Bull /ˈʤɑːnˈbʊl/ *noun, old-fashioned*
1 [*noncount*] : the people or country of England
2 [*singular*] : a typical Englishman

John Doe /ˈʤɑːnˈdoʊ/ *noun, pl* **~ Does** [*count*] *US, law* — used as a name for a man whose true name is not known or is being kept secret; compare JANE DOE

John Han·cock /ˈʤɑːnˈhænˌkɑːk/ *noun, pl* **~ -cocks** [*count*] *US* : a person's signature • He put his *John Hancock* on the contract. [=he signed the contract]

john·ny /ˈʤɑːni/ *noun, pl* **john·nies** [*count*] *US* : a loose piece of clothing that is open at the back and that is worn by someone (such as a hospital patient) who is being examined, treated, etc., by a doctor

John·ny–come–late·ly /ˈʤɑːniˌkʌmˈleɪtli/ *noun, pl* **-lies** [*count*] *informal* : a person who has recently joined a group, started a new activity, etc. : NEWCOMER • When it comes to investing, she's no *Johnny-come-lately.*

joie de vi·vre /ˌʒwɑːdəˈviːvrə/ *noun* [*noncount*] *formal* : a feeling of happiness or excitement about life • She is admired for her energy and *joie de vivre.* ✧ *Joie de vivre* is a French phrase that means literally "joy of living."

join /ˈʤoɪn/ *verb* **joins; joined; join·ing**
1 a [+ *obj*] : to put or bring (two or more things) together • She *joined* [=*fastened*] the blocks of wood (together) with glue. : to connect (two or more things) • The islands are *joined* by a bridge. **b** : to come together with (something) [+ *obj*] where the river *joins* the sea [=where the river flows into the sea] • The roads/rivers *join* [=*meet*] each other near here. [*no obj*] the place where two roads/rivers *join* (together) • Atoms *join* (together) to make molecules. — often + *up* • The two paths eventually *join up* (with each other).
2 a [+ *obj*] : to go somewhere in order to be with (a person or group) • He insisted that I *join* them for lunch. • We're going out for lunch. Would you like to *join* us? • May I *join* you? • The magician asked for a volunteer from the audience to *join* him on stage. **b** : to do something with (a person or group) [+ *obj*] Everyone here *joins* me in congratulating you on a job well done! [*no obj*] All of us *join* (together) in congratulating you on a job well done! • Several companies have *joined* (together) to support this policy. • The singer started alone but soon the whole audience ***joined in.*** **c** : to become involved in or part of (something, such as an activity) [+ *obj*] I *joined* the line and waited patiently to buy a ticket. • Hundreds of people have *joined* the effort to save the building from demolition. • He agreed to *join* the debate. [*no obj*] — + *in* • Hundreds of people have *joined in* the effort to save the building. • She *joined in* the conversation/fun.
3 : to become a member of (a group or organization) [+ *obj*] She *joined* the band/club. • *Join* the Navy and see the world! [*no obj*] The Navy offers great career opportunities, so *join* [=*enlist*] today! — often + *up* • More than 100 people have *joined up.*

if you can't beat them, join them see ¹BEAT

join battle *formal* : to begin fighting : to engage in battle • troops *joining battle* against a hated enemy

join forces see ¹FORCE

join hands : to hold the hand of another person • The priest asked us all to *join hands* and bow our heads in prayer. — often used figuratively • We can accomplish great things if we all *join hands* and work together.

join (someone) in marriage/matrimony *formal* : to marry (someone) • a young couple *joined in marriage*

join the club see ¹CLUB

join the crowd see ²CROWD

join up [*phrasal verb*] : to meet each other at a particular place • We're planning to *join up* (with each other) and have a few drinks after the game.

join·er /ˈʤoɪnɚ/ *noun, pl* **-ers** [*count*]
1 *US* : a person who joins many organizations • He's not a *joiner.* He prefers to do things by himself.
2 *chiefly Brit* : a person whose job is to build things (such as door or window frames) by joining pieces of wood

join·ery /ˈʤoɪnəri/ *noun* [*noncount*] : the work done by a joiner (sense 2)

¹joint /ˈʤoɪnt/ *noun, pl* **joints**
1 [*count*] **a** : a point where two bones meet in the body • the elbow/knee/shoulder *joint* • She's been having pain in her muscles and *joints.* **b** : a place where two things or parts are joined • seal the *joints* of the pipes
2 [*count*] *informal* **a** : a particular place • People were running ***all over the joint.*** [=*everywhere*] **b** : a cheap bar or club • I can't believe we came to a (cheap) *joint* like this. **c** : an informal restaurant • a hamburger/pizza *joint*
3 [*count*] *informal* : a marijuana cigarette • smoking a *joint*
4 ***the joint*** *US slang* : PRISON • five years in *the joint*
5 [*count*] *chiefly Brit* : a large piece of meat for roasting • a *joint* of beef

out of joint **1** *of a bone* : not in the correct position : out of its socket • His shoulder kept slipping *out of joint.* **2** *informal* : not in agreement or order • My schedule has gotten a little *out of joint* [=*disorganized*] in the past few weeks. **3** *informal* ✧ If you have your ***nose out of joint,*** you are angry or annoyed. • We had to wait a while, but that wasn't any reason for him to get his *nose out of joint.*

stink up the joint *US, informal* : to perform or play very badly • This year the team is really *stinking up the joint.*

²joint *adj, always used before a noun*
1 : combining the work of two or more people or groups of people • It took a *joint* [=*united*] effort to get the job done. • a *joint* session of (both houses of) Congress
2 : done by or involving two or more people • a *joint* venture • *joint* research • filing a *joint* tax return • They had a *joint* account at the bank. • divorced parents who have *joint* custody of their child • (*Brit*) They came in *joint* third. [=they both finished in third place]
3 : doing something together • *joint* owners

– joint·ly *adv* • a study conducted *jointly* by scientists in two countries • *jointly* owned property

Joint Chiefs of Staff *noun* [*plural*] : a group made up of the leaders of the U.S. Army, Navy, Air Force, and Marines that advises the President on important military decisions

joint·ed /ˈʤoɪntəd/ *adj* : having joints that allow parts to move • a doll with *jointed* arms and legs — see also DOUBLE-JOINTED

joist /ˈʤoɪst/ *noun, pl* **joists** [*count*] : a strong, heavy board that supports a floor or ceiling

¹joke /ˈʤoʊk/ *noun, pl* **jokes** [*count*]
1 a : something said or done to cause laughter • She meant it as a *joke,* but many people took her seriously. • Is this your idea of a *joke?* [=do you think that what you are saying/doing is funny?] • They played a harmless *joke* on him. • They are always ***making jokes*** about his car. • He thought he could embarrass us, but now ***the joke is on him.*** [=he is the one who looks foolish] • He just can't ***take a joke.*** [=he does not like it when other people make jokes about him] **b** : a brief story with a surprising and funny ending • I heard a funny *joke* yesterday. • the punch line of a *joke* • She's always cracking/telling *jokes.* • I didn't get/understand the *joke.* • an ***inside joke*** [=a joke that is understood only by people with special knowledge about something] — see also IN-JOKE, PRACTICAL JOKE
2 *disapproving* : someone or something that is not worth taking seriously • That exam was a *joke.* • Their product became a *joke* in the industry. • He's in danger of becoming a national *joke.* • It's ***no joke*** to be lost in the woods. = Being lost in the woods is *no joke.* [=being lost in the woods is a serious situation]

²joke *verb* **jokes; joked; jok·ing** : to say things that are meant to cause laughter : to make jokes about someone or something [*no obj*] My friends would *joke* about the uniform I had to wear at work. • She *joked* about the possibility of losing her job. • I thought he was *joking* when he said he might quit, but it turned out that he really meant it. • Don't take it seriously: I was only *joking.* • She spent a few minutes *joking* with reporters after giving her speech. • "The report is

J

to be done by tomorrow." "***You're joking***." = "***You must be joking***." [=you must be kidding; what you say is very surprising or hard to believe] • It's ***no joking matter***. [=it is no joke; it is a serious matter] [+ *obj*] She *joked* that she could always get work as a truck driver if she lost her job.

joking aside *or Brit* ***joking apart*** — used to introduce a serious statement that follows a humorous statement • It looks like this is a job for Superman! But *joking aside*, this is a serious problem and we're going to need help.

– **jok·ing·ly** /ˈʤoʊkɪŋli/ *adv* [*more* ~; *most* ~] • She spoke *jokingly* about the possibility of losing her job.

jok·er /ˈʤoʊkɚ/ *noun, pl* **-ers** [*count*]
1 : a person who tells or makes many jokes • a constant *joker*
2 : an extra card used in some card games usually as a wild card • *Jokers* are wild in this game.
3 *informal* **:** an annoying, stupid, or offensive person • I can't believe I let that *joker* beat me. • Some *joker* hit our car.

joke·ster /ˈʤoʊkstɚ/ *noun, pl* **-sters** [*count*] **:** a person who tells or makes many jokes **:** JOKER • the family *jokester*

jok·ey /ˈʤoʊki/ *adj, informal* **:** tending or intended to make people laugh • a *jokey* movie • the *jokey* tone of his stories
– **jok·i·ness** /ˈʤoʊkinəs/ *noun* [*noncount*]

jol·lies /ˈʤɑːliz/ *noun*
get your jollies *US, informal + disapproving* **:** to get a feeling of enjoyment or excitement • She doesn't think much of people who *get their jollies* from watching violent movies. [=people who enjoy watching violent movies]

jol·li·ty /ˈʤɑːləti/ *noun* [*noncount*] *formal* **:** a happy and cheerful quality or state **:** the quality or state of being jolly • His *jollity* is infectious. • a scene of *jollity*

¹jol·ly /ˈʤɑːli/ *adj* **jol·li·er; -est** [*also more* ~; *most* ~]
1 : full of happiness and joy **:** happy and cheerful • Our boss was a very *jolly* man, always laughing. • *jolly* laughter/singing
2 *old-fashioned* **:** very pleasant or enjoyable • She had a *jolly* time at the party.

²jolly *adv, Brit, informal + old-fashioned* **:** very or extremely • a *jolly* good time/fellow/book • "I've finished my assignment." "*Jolly* good!" • She learned to be *jolly* careful in his presence.
jolly well *Brit, informal + old-fashioned* — used to emphasize anger, annoyance, or disapproval • I'm your father and you'll *jolly well* do as you're told!

¹jolt /ˈʤoʊlt/ *verb* **jolts; jolt·ed; jolt·ing**
1 a [+ *obj*] **:** to cause (something or someone) to move in a quick and sudden way • The explosion *jolted* the ship. • He was *jolted* forward when the bus stopped suddenly. • The loud bang *jolted* me awake. • The attack *jolted* the country into action. **b** [*no obj*] **:** to move with a quick and sudden motion • The car *jolted* [=*jerked*] forward when he let the clutch out too quickly.
2 [+ *obj*] **:** to surprise or shock (someone) • She *jolted* the medical world with her announcement.
– **jolting** *adj* [*more* ~; *most* ~] • a *jolting* ride • a *jolting* experience

²jolt *noun, pl* **jolts** [*count*]
1 : a sudden, rough movement • the initial *jolt* [=*shock*] of the earthquake • I sprang out of bed with a *jolt*. • The car stopped with a *jolt*.
2 : a sudden shock or surprise • I got/had quite a *jolt* when I heard the door slam. • The defeat was quite a *jolt* to the team. • a severe financial *jolt* • The stock market suffered a major *jolt* yesterday.
3 : a small but powerful amount of something • She needed a *jolt* of caffeine to start her day. • a *jolt* of electricity • The unexpected praise he received gave him a *jolt* of confidence.

¹jones /ˈʤoʊnz/ *noun* [*singular*] *US slang* **:** a very strong desire for something or to do something • She has a crazy *jones* [=*craving*] for fried chicken. • a basketball/writing *jones*

²jones *verb* **jones·es; jonesed; jones·ing** [*no obj*] *US slang* **:** to have a very strong desire *for* something or *to do* something — usually used as *(be) jonesing* • He *was jonesing for* a cigarette.

Jones·es /ˈʤoʊnzəz/ *noun*
keep up with the Joneses *informal + often disapproving* **:** to show that you are as good as other people by getting what they have and doing what they do • people trying to *keep up with the Joneses* by buying expensive cars and clothes that they can't afford

josh /ˈʤɑːʃ/ *verb* **josh·es; joshed; josh·ing** *informal* **:** to talk to someone in a friendly and joking way [*no obj*] Don't take him seriously. He's just *joshing*. [+ *obj*] He's just *joshing* [=*kidding*] you.

jos·tle /ˈʤɑːsəl/ *verb* **jos·tles; jos·tled; jos·tling :** to push against (someone) while moving forward in a crowd of people [+ *obj*] Everyone in the crowd was *jostling* each other trying to get a better view. [*no obj*] — often + *for* • Everyone in the crowd was *jostling for* room/space. — sometimes used figuratively • political candidates *jostling for* position as the election nears

¹jot /ˈʤɑːt/ *verb* **jots; jot·ted; jot·ting** [+ *obj*] **:** to write down (something) quickly • He paused to *jot* a few notes on a slip of paper. — usually + *down* • He *jotted down* her name and phone number.

²jot *noun* [*singular*] *informal + somewhat old-fashioned* **:** the smallest amount — usually used in negative statements • She has not changed a/one *jot* [=has not changed at all] since we last saw her. • It doesn't make a *jot* of difference.

jot·tings /ˈʤɑːtɪŋz/ *noun* [*plural*] **:** notes that are written down quickly • a story based on the *jottings* in his notebooks

joule /ˈʤuːl/ *noun, pl* **joules** [*count*] *physics* **:** a unit of work or energy

jour·nal /ˈʤɚnl/ *noun, pl* **-nals** [*count*]
1 : a book in which you write down your personal experiences and thoughts **:** DIARY • I've been keeping a *journal* for several years. • She records her dreams in a *journal*.
2 a : a newspaper — usually used in titles • the *Wall Street Journal* **b :** a magazine that reports on things of special interest to a particular group of people • an academic/scholarly *journal* • a medical *journal* — often used in titles • the *Journal of the American Medical Association*

jour·nal·ism /ˈʤɚnəˌlɪzəm/ *noun* [*noncount*] **:** the activity or job of collecting, writing, and editing news stories for newspapers, magazines, television, or radio • investigative/broadcast *journalism* • She plans to major in *journalism* when she goes to college. • bad/good/responsible *journalism*
– **jour·nal·ist** /ˈʤɚnəlɪst/ *noun, pl* **-ists** [*count*] • She is an investigative *journalist*. – **jour·nal·is·tic** /ˌʤɚnəˈlɪstɪk/ *adj* [*more* ~; *most* ~] • her *journalistic* career/experience • *journalistic* styles/standards/techniques – **jour·nal·is·ti·cal·ly** /ˌʤɚnəˈlɪstɪkli/ *adv*

¹jour·ney /ˈʤɚni/ *noun, pl* **-neys** [*count*] **:** an act of traveling from one place to another **:** TRIP • a long *journey* across the country • a *journey* by train/bus • She's on the last leg of a six-month *journey* through Europe. • We wished her a safe and pleasant *journey*. — often used figuratively • the *journey* from innocence to experience • a *journey* through time • a spiritual *journey*

²journey *verb* **-neys; -neyed; -ney·ing** [*no obj*] **:** to go on a journey **:** TRAVEL • They *journeyed* across Europe. • She was the first woman to *journey* into space.

jour·ney·man /ˈʤɚnimən/ *noun, pl* **-men** [*count*]
1 : a worker who learns a skill and then works for another person — often used before another noun • a *journeyman* carpenter
2 : a worker, performer, or athlete who is experienced and good but not excellent — often used before another noun • a *journeyman* musician • a *journeyman* baseball player

joust /ˈʤaʊst/ *verb* **jousts; joust·ed; joust·ing** [*no obj*] *of knights in the Middle Ages* **:** to fight on horseback with lances • The knights *jousted* against each other. — often used figuratively • The two teams *jousted* [=*competed*] for first place. • There was a lot of verbal *jousting* between the lawyers.
– **joust** *noun, pl* **jousts** [*count*] • a *joust* between two knights – **joust·er** *noun, pl* **-ers** [*count*] • an armored *jouster* • a skilled verbal *jouster*

Jove /ˈʤoʊv/ *noun*
by Jove *chiefly Brit, old-fashioned + sometimes humorous* — used to express surprise or agreement • *By Jove*, she's really done it! • *By Jove*, you're right!

jo·vi·al /ˈʤoʊvijəl/ *adj* [*more* ~; *most* ~] **:** full of happiness and joy **:** CHEERFUL • The audience was in a *jovial* mood. • He's a very *jovial* man.
– **jo·vi·al·i·ty** /ˌʤoʊviˈæləti/ *noun* [*noncount*] – **jo·vi·al·ly** *adv*

jowl /ˈʤawəl/ *noun, pl* **jowls** [*count*] **:** loose flesh on the cheeks, lower jaw, or throat — usually plural • a man with heavy *jowls* • a dog with big, floppy *jowls*
cheek by jowl see CHEEK
– **jowly** /ˈʤaʊli/ *adj* • a *jowly* face/man

joy /ˈʤoɪ/ *noun, pl* **joys**
1 [*noncount*] **:** a feeling of great happiness • Their sorrow turned to *joy*. • I can hardly express the *joy* I felt at seeing her again. • Seeing her again brought tears of *joy* to my eyes. • He found great *joy* in (doing) his work. • She answered the phone and, to her great *joy*, heard her son's voice on the line.

[=she felt very happy when she heard her son's voice] • They were ***shouting/jumping for joy***. [=they shouted/jumped because they were very happy] — see also *(little) bundle of joy* at [1]BUNDLE
2 [*count*] : a source or cause of great happiness : something or someone that gives joy to someone • The flowers are a *joy* to behold! • What a *joy* it was to see her again. • the *joy* of sailing • the *joys* of parenthood • Her son is her ***pride and joy***. [=her son makes her very proud and happy]
3 [*noncount*] *Brit, informal* : success in doing, finding, or getting something • "You've spent hours looking for it. Any *joy*? [=*luck*]" "No *joy* whatsoever, I'm afraid. I can't find it."

joy·ful /ˈʤoɪfəl/ *adj* [*more* ~; *most* ~] : feeling, causing, or showing great happiness : full of joy • a *joyful* family reunion • the children's *joyful* faces • *joyful* news • We were *joyful* at the news.
– **joy·ful·ly** *adv* • They greeted each other *joyfully*. – **joy·ful·ness** *noun* [*noncount*]

joy·less /ˈʤoɪləs/ *adj* [*more* ~; *most* ~] : not feeling, causing, or showing happiness : sad or unhappy • a *joyless* occasion/person/look
– **joy·less·ly** *adv* • He smiled *joylessly*. – **joy·less·ness** *noun* [*noncount*]

joy·ous /ˈʤojəs/ *adj* [*more* ~; *most* ~] : feeling, causing, or showing great happiness : JOYFUL • a *joyous* celebration • a *joyous* day • a mood of *joyous* anticipation
– **joy·ous·ly** *adv* – **joy·ous·ness** *noun* [*noncount*]

joy·ride /ˈʤoɪˌraɪd/ *noun, pl* **-rides** [*count*] : a fast car ride taken for pleasure; *especially* : a ride in a stolen car • Some teenager stole my car and took it for a *joyride*. — sometimes used figuratively • This movie is a wonderful *joyride*. [=is very exciting and enjoyable]
– **joy·rid·er** /ˈʤoɪˌraɪdɚ/ *noun, pl* **-ers** [*count*] – **joy·rid·ing** /ˈʤoɪˌraɪdɪŋ/ *noun* [*noncount*] • Some teenager went *joyriding* in my car.

joy·stick /ˈʤoɪˌstɪk/ *noun, pl* **-sticks** [*count*]
1 : an upright lever used to control an airplane — called also *stick*
2 : a lever used to control the movement of images on the screen in a computer or video game • This game works with either a mouse or *joystick*.

J.P. *abbr* justice of the peace

JPEG /ˈʤeɪˌpɛg/ *noun, pl* **JPEGs** *also* **JPEG's** [*noncount*] : a type of computer file used for storing images; *also* [*count*] : an image that is stored as this type of file • Most of the pictures are *JPEGs*. — often used before another noun • a *JPEG* file/image ◊ *JPEG* is an abbreviation of "Joint Photographic Experts Group."

Jr. *abbr* junior • John Smith, *Jr.*

ju·bi·lant /ˈʤuːbələnt/ *adj* [*more* ~; *most* ~] : feeling or expressing great joy : very happy • the *jubilant* winners • a *jubilant* celebration
– **ju·bi·lant·ly** *adv* • The fans celebrated *jubilantly*.

ju·bi·la·tion /ˌʤuːbəˈleɪʃən/ *noun* [*noncount*] : great happiness or joy • The team's victory was the cause of great *jubilation*. [=*rejoicing*] • the *jubilation* of the crowd

ju·bi·lee /ˈʤuːbəˌliː, ˌʤuːbəˈliː/ *noun, pl* **-lees** [*count*] : a special anniversary; *also* : a celebration at the time of such an anniversary • a silver/golden/diamond *jubilee*

Ju·da·ism /ˈʤuːdiˌɪzəm/ *noun* [*noncount*] : the religion developed among the ancient Hebrews that stresses belief in God and faithfulness to the laws of the Torah : the religion of the Jewish people
– **Ju·da·ic** /ʤuˈdejɪk/ *adj* • *Judaic* law/heritage/tradition

Ju·das /ˈʤuːdəs/ *noun, pl* **Ju·das·es** [*count*] : someone who betrays someone else : TRAITOR • He was called a *Judas* by the press.

jud·der /ˈʤʌdɚ/ *verb* **-ders**; **-dered**; **-der·ing** [*no obj*] *Brit* : to shake in a forceful way • The car *juddered* (and came) to a halt.
– **judder** *noun, pl* **-ders** [*count*] • The car gave a *judder* and came to a halt.

Ju·deo–Chris·tian /ʤuˌdejoʊˈkrɪsʧən/ *adj* : relating to both Judaism and Christianity • *Judeo-Christian* values/tradition

[1]**judge** /ˈʤʌʤ/ *verb* **judg·es**; **judged**; **judg·ing**
1 : to form an opinion about (something or someone) after careful thought [*+ obj*] You should not *judge* people by their appearance. • They *judged* her pie (as) the best. = They *judged* her pie to be the best. = They *judged* that her pie was the best. = Her pie was *judged* (to be) the best. • He was trying to *judge* the strength of his opponent. • It can be difficult to *judge* [=*estimate*] distances/sizes accurately. • We should do whatever we *judge* to be the right thing. [*no obj*] *Judging* from this schedule, we have a busy week ahead. [=this schedule indicates that we have a busy week ahead] • *Judging* by its smell, I'd say the milk is spoiled. = To *judge* from its smell, I'd say the milk is spoiled.
2 [*+ obj*] : to regard (someone) as either good or bad • Who are you to *judge* me? • He feels that they have *judged* him unfairly. • Don't *judge* her too severely/harshly.
3 [*+ obj*] *law* **a** : to make an official decision about (a legal case) • *judge* [=*try*] a case **b** : to decide about the guilt or innocence of someone • The jury will be asked to *judge* the defendant's guilt. • If you are accused of a crime you have the right to be *judged* by a jury of your peers.
4 [*+ obj*] : to decide the winner of (a competition) • *judge* a contest

[2]**judge** *noun, pl* **judges** [*count*]
1 a *law* : a person who has the power to make decisions on cases brought before a court of law • a federal *judge* • She's one of the strictest *judges* in the state. — often used as a title • The case is being heard by *Judge* Smith. **b** : a person who decides the winner in a contest or competition • He served as a *judge* at the baking contest. • a panel of *judges*
2 a : a person who makes a decision or judgment • "These problems don't concern you." "I'll be the *judge* of that!" [=I'll decide if they concern me; I am not interested in your opinion] • "I don't think we should trust her." "Let me be the *judge* of that." **b** : a person who is good, bad, etc., at making judgments • She is a good *judge* of character.

judge·ship /ˈʤʌʤˌʃɪp/ *noun, pl* **-ships** [*count*] *chiefly US, law* : the position of being a judge • She was appointed to a federal *judgeship*.

judg·ment *or chiefly Brit* **judge·ment** /ˈʤʌʤmənt/ *noun, pl* **-ments**
1 a [*count*] : an opinion or decision that is based on careful thought • We have to make a *judgment* about the value of their services. • In my *judgment* [=*opinion*], the stock has performed badly. = It is my *judgment* that the stock has performed badly. • The *judgment* of the editors is final. • I agreed to let him join us, even though it was ***against my better judgment***. [=even though I did not think it was the best thing to do] • a ***snap judgment*** [=a hasty decision or opinion] • ***value judgments*** [=opinions about the worth or value of something] **b** [*noncount*] : the act or process of forming an opinion or making a decision after careful thought : the act of judging something or someone • Don't rush to *judgment* without examining the evidence. • It would be premature to ***pass judgment on*** [=to state an opinion on] his place in history. • Don't *pass judgment on* me [=don't criticize me] until you know all the facts. • "Were his policies good or bad?" "I'll have to ***reserve/suspend judgment on*** that. It's too soon to know." — see also LAST JUDGMENT, VALUE JUDGMENT
2 [*noncount*] : the ability to make good decisions about what should be done • Use your own best *judgment*. • He showed bad *judgment*. = He showed a lack of *judgment*.
3 [*count*] *law* : a decision made by a court • The court granted/pronounced a *judgment* in favor of the plaintiffs. • the *judgment* of the court • I won a *judgment* against the bank.
4 [*count*] *formal* : something bad or unpleasant that is thought to be a punishment from God — usually singular • a divine *judgment* against sinners
sit in judgment : to say whether or not someone or something is morally good, proper, etc. • He has no right to *sit in judgment* on/of/over me. [=he has no right to judge me]

judg·ment·al *or chiefly Brit* **judge·ment·al** /ˌʤʌʤˈmɛntl/ *adj*
1 [*more* ~; *most* ~] *disapproving* : tending to judge people too quickly and critically • He's *judgmental* about everyone except himself. • You should try to avoid being so *judgmental*. • a very *judgmental* person
2 : of, relating to, or involving judgment • a *judgmental* error

judgment call *or chiefly Brit* **judgement call** *noun, pl* ~ **calls** [*count*] : a decision that is based on your opinion • The rules aren't clear in this case, so officials are required to make a *judgment call*.

Judgment Day *or chiefly Brit* **Judgement Day** *noun* [*noncount*] : the day at the end of the world when according to some religions all people will be judged by God

ju·di·cial /ʤuˈdɪʃəl/ *adj, always used before a noun*
1 a : of or relating to courts of law or judges • *judicial* power • the *judicial* system **b** : ordered or done by a court • a *judicial* decision/action

2 : responsible for dealing with all legal cases involving the government ▪ the ***judicial branch*** of government — compare EXECUTIVE, LEGISLATIVE
– **ju·di·cial·ly** *adv*
ju·di·cia·ry /ʤuˈdɪʃiˌeri, ʤuˈdɪʃəri/ *noun* [*noncount*] : the courts of law and judges in a country : the branch of government that includes courts of law and judges ▪ the federal *judiciary*
ju·di·cious /ʤuˈdɪʃəs/ *adj* [*more* ~; *most* ~] *formal* : having or showing good judgment : WISE ▪ *judicious* use of our resources ▪ *Judicious* planning now can prevent problems later. ▪ a *judicious* decision
– **ju·di·cious·ly** *adv* ▪ *judiciously* chosen examples – **ju·di·cious·ness** *noun* [*noncount*]
ju·do /ˈʤuːˌdoʊ/ *noun* [*noncount*] : a sport developed in Japan in which opponents attempt to throw or wrestle each other to the ground
jug /ˈʤʌg/ *noun, pl* **jugs** [*count*]
1 a *chiefly US* : a large, deep container with a narrow opening and a handle ▪ a *jug* of cider **b** *chiefly Brit* : ²PITCHER
2 : the amount held by a jug ▪ a *jug* of milk/wine
jug·ger·naut /ˈʤʌgɚˌnɑːt/ *noun, pl* **-nauts** [*count*]
1 : something (such as a force, campaign, or movement) that is extremely large and powerful and cannot be stopped ▪ an advertising/political *juggernaut*
2 *Brit* : a very large, heavy truck — called also *juggernaut lorry*
jug·gle /ˈʤʌgəl/ *verb* **jug·gles; jug·gled; jug·gling**
1 : to keep several objects in motion in the air at the same time by repeatedly throwing and catching them [*no obj*] He is learning to *juggle*. [+ *obj*] He *juggled* four balls at once.
2 [+ *obj*] : to do (several things) at the same time ▪ She somehow manages to *juggle* a dozen tasks at once. ▪ It can be hard to *juggle* family responsibilities and/with the demands of a full-time job. — see also *juggling act* at ¹ACT
3 [+ *obj*] : to make changes to (something) in order to achieve a desired result ▪ I'll have to *juggle* my schedule a bit to get this all to work out.
– **jug·gler** /ˈʤʌglɚ/ *noun, pl* **-glers** [*count*] ▪ a *juggler* at the circus
jug·u·lar /ˈʤʌgjəlɚ/ *noun, pl* **-lars** [*count*] : JUGULAR VEIN
go for the jugular informal : to attack or criticize an opponent in a very aggressive way ▪ He will very quickly *go for the jugular* in the debate.
jugular vein *noun, pl* ~ **veins** [*count*] : a large vein in the neck that takes blood from the head to the heart
¹**juice** /ˈʤuːs/ *noun, pl* **juic·es**
1 a : the liquid part that can be squeezed out of vegetables and fruits [*noncount*] a glass of apple/orange/carrot *juice* [*count*] a variety of fruit *juices* **b** : the liquid part of meat [*noncount*] the *juice* of a steak [*plural*] gravy made with real beef *juices*
2 [*noncount*] *informal* : something (such as electricity) that provides power ▪ Turn on the *juice*. ▪ His camera ran out of *juice* because he forgot to replace the battery.
3 [*count*] : the natural fluids in your stomach — usually plural ▪ digestive/gastric/stomach *juices*
4 [*plural*] *informal* : energy that gives you the ability to do something in a very effective way — used with *flow* ▪ He can be very tough to beat when he gets his competitive *juices flowing*. ▪ She came up with some great ideas when her creative *juices* started *flowing*.
stew in your own juice/juices see ²STEW
²**juice** *verb* **juices; juiced; juic·ing** [+ *obj*] : to remove juice from (a fruit or vegetable) ▪ *juice* a lemon/orange
juiced /ˈʤuːst/ *adj* [*more* ~; *most* ~] *US, informal* : very excited : full of energy ▪ The band's fans were *juiced* about the upcoming concert. — often + *up* ▪ He didn't realize just how *juiced up* his opponent would be.
juic·er /ˈʤuːsɚ/ *noun, pl* **-ers** [*count*] : a tool or machine for removing juice from fruit or vegetables ▪ a fruit/lemon *juicer*
juicy /ˈʤuːsi/ *adj* **juic·i·er; -est** [*also more* ~; *most* ~]
1 : containing a lot of juice ▪ The meat is tender and *juicy*. ▪ fresh, *juicy* oranges
2 *informal* : very interesting and exciting especially because of shocking or sexual elements ▪ a *juicy* scandal ▪ a *juicy* bit of news/gossip ▪ I want to know all the *juicy* details.
3 *informal* : involving or providing a large amount of money ▪ a *juicy* [=*fat*] contract ▪ She sued her former boss and won a *juicy* settlement in court.
– **juic·i·ness** /ˈʤuːsinəs/ *noun* [*noncount*]
ju·jit·su /ʤuˈʤɪtˌsuː/ *noun* [*noncount*] : a form of fighting without weapons that was developed in Japan : a Japanese martial art
juke /ˈʤuːk/ *verb* **jukes; juked; juk·ing** *US, sports, informal* : to make a false movement in order to deceive (an opponent) [+ *obj*] He *juked* a couple of defenders and scored. [*no obj*] She *juked* and weaved around the defense. ▪ He *juked* [=*faked*] left and went right.
juke·box /ˈʤuːkˌbɑːks/ *noun, pl* **-box·es** [*count*] : a machine that plays music when money is put into it

jukebox

juke joint *noun, pl* ~ **joints** [*count*] *US, informal* : a cheap bar or club that has a jukebox
Jul. *abbr* July
ju·lep /ˈʤuːləp/ *noun, pl* **-leps** [*count*] : a drink of bourbon, sugar, and mint served with crushed ice ▪ a mint *julep*
ju·li·enne /ˌʤuːliˈɛn/ *or* **ju·li·enned** /ˌʤuːliˈɛnd/ *adj* : cut into long, thin strips ▪ *julienne* carrots
– **julienne** *noun, pl* **-ennes** [*count*] ▪ a *julienne* of carrots
Ju·ly /ʤʊˈlaɪ/ *noun, pl* **-lys** : the seventh month of the year [*noncount*] in (early/middle/mid-/late) *July* ▪ early/late in *July* ▪ They arrived on *July* the first. = (*US*) They arrived on *July* first. = They arrived on the first of *July*. [*count*] Sales are up (for) this *July* in comparison with the previous two *Julys*. ▪ It happens every *July*. — abbr. *Jul*.; see also FOURTH OF JULY
¹**jum·ble** /ˈʤʌmbəl/ *verb* **jum·bles; jum·bled; jum·bling** [+ *obj*] : to cause (things) to be mixed together in a way that is not neat or orderly — often + *together* ▪ Earrings, bracelets, and necklaces were all *jumbled together* in the box. — often + *up* ▪ He *jumbled* the wires *up* when he moved the TV.
– **jumbled** *adj* ▪ *jumbled* thoughts
²**jumble** *noun, pl* **jumbles**
1 [*count*] : a group of things that are not arranged in a neat or orderly way ▪ The letters formed a meaningless *jumble*. ▪ a *jumble* of wires ▪ a *jumble* of hats and coats
2 [*noncount*] *Brit* : unwanted things (such as old clothes) that are being sold in an informal sale ▪ a bag/box of *jumble*
jumble sale *noun, pl* ~ **sales** [*count*] *Brit* : RUMMAGE SALE
jum·bo /ˈʤʌmboʊ/ *adj, always used before a noun* : very large ▪ The stadium has a *jumbo* TV screen. ▪ *jumbo* shrimp ▪ The soda is sold in small, medium, large, and *jumbo* sizes.
jumbo jet *noun, pl* ~ **jets** [*count*] : a very large airplane that can carry many passengers
¹**jump** /ˈʤʌmp/ *verb* **jumps; jumped; jump·ing**
1 a [*no obj*] : to move your body upward from the ground and often forward, backward, or sideways through the air by pushing with your legs ▪ The cat *jumped* [=*leaped*] (up) onto the table. ▪ Grasshoppers were *jumping* [=*hopping*] around in the field. ▪ The circus lion *jumped* through the hoop. ▪ The fans were ***jumping up and down*** with excitement. ▪ Everyone was ***jumping for joy*** when we found out that we had won an award. **b** [*no obj*] : to cause your body to drop or fall down from something by pushing with your legs ▪ The cat *jumped* down off/from the table. ▪ *jump* off a bridge **c** : to move forward through the air and over (something) [+ *obj*] The runner *jumped* a hurdle. ▪ The car *jumped* the curb. [*no obj*] — + *over* ▪ The runner *jumped over* a hurdle. ▪ The car *jumped over* the curb.
2 [*no obj*] **a** : to move quickly ▪ Everyone *jumped* into/in the pool. ▪ He *jumped* into/in his truck and drove away. ▪ She *jumped* up on [=quickly got up on] a chair and began to sing the national anthem. ▪ She *jumped* up [=she stood up quickly] and ran out the door. — often used figuratively ▪ The team *jumped* from last place to first place. ▪ If anyone criticizes her husband, she always ***jumps to his defense***. [=she always quickly defends him] ▪ They ***jumped into action***. [=acted immediately] **b** : to make a sudden movement because of surprise or shock ▪ She *jumped* when she heard a loud knock late at night. ▪ I almost ***jumped out of my skin*** when I heard her say my name. [=I was very surprised when I heard her say my name]
3 [*no obj*] : to start or go forward quickly ▪ She *jumped* to an early lead in the race. — sometimes + *off* ▪ She *jumped off* to a big lead.
4 [*no obj*] : to suddenly increase in value or amount ▪ The price of gasoline *jumped* (by) 10 percent in the spring. = Gasoline *jumped* in price by 10 percent in the spring.

5 [*no obj*] **a :** to go in a sudden and unexpected way ▪ She was always *jumping* from job to job. **b :** to suddenly go forward to a later point ▪ He *jumped* to the end of the chapter to find the answers. ▪ The movie *jumps* ahead/forward to when she was in college.

6 [*no obj*] **:** to be lively with activity ▪ The city really *jumps* on New Year's Eve. ▪ The bar/joint/place was *jumping*.

7 [+ *obj*] **:** to physically attack (a person) especially in a robbery ▪ He was *jumped* by a mugger while he was walking home from the store.

8 [*no obj*] **:** to move or behave in an energetic way especially to please another person ▪ When the boss walks in, everybody is supposed to *jump*.

9 [+ *obj*] *chiefly US* **:** to get onto (a moving train) ▪ *jump* a train

10 [+ *obj*] **:** to begin moving before (a signal to begin) ▪ The car ahead of me ***jumped the light***. [=started moving before the traffic light turned green]

11 : to move a piece in a board game so that it moves over another piece and lands on the next space [+ *obj*] She *jumped* three of my checkers in one move. [*no obj*] In this version of the game, *jumping* is not permitted. — sometimes + *over* ▪ She *jumped over* three of my checkers.

(go) jump in a/the lake see LAKE

jump all over *informal* **:** to become very angry at (someone) **:** to angrily criticize or shout at (someone) ▪ His mother *jumped all over* [=*jumped on*] him for wrecking the car.

jump at [*phrasal verb*] ***jump at (something)* :** to eagerly take (a chance, offer, etc.) ▪ She *jumped at* the chance/opportunity to show her boss what she could do. ▪ He *jumped at* the offer of a better job.

jump bail see [1]BAIL

jump down someone's throat see THROAT

jump in [*phrasal verb*] *informal* **:** to say something about a subject that another person is already talking about **:** to join a conversation ▪ *Jump in* if you have any questions.

jump off the page see [1]PAGE

jump on [*phrasal verb*] *informal* **1 *jump on (someone)* :** to become very angry at (someone) **:** to angrily criticize or shout at (someone) ▪ The teacher *jumped on* [=*jumped all over*] us for being late. ▪ The coach *jumped on* him for not playing hard enough. **2 *jump on (something)* a :** to strongly attack or criticize (something) ▪ She was quick to *jump on* her rival's poor record as governor. **b :** to get on (a train, bus, etc.) ▪ She *jumped on* [=*hopped*] a bus to Denver. ▪ He *jumped on* a plane and headed home.

jump out at [*phrasal verb*] ***jump out at (someone)* 1 :** to suddenly come at (someone) from a hiding place ▪ The hidden assailant *jumped out at* them. **2 :** to immediately get the attention of (someone) ▪ The sculpture *jumps out at* you when you enter the house. ▪ I checked for errors, but nothing *jumped out at* me. [=I did not notice any errors]

jump rope see [1]ROPE

jump ship see [1]SHIP

jump the gun see [1]GUN

jump the queue see [1]QUEUE

jump the track(s) (*US*) *or chiefly Brit* ***jump the rails*** *of a train* **:** to come off the track ▪ Dozens of people were injured when the train *jumped the track*.

jump through hoops *informal* **:** to do a complicated or annoying series of things in order to get or achieve something ▪ We had to *jump through* a lot of *hoops* to get a loan from the bank. ▪ It shouldn't be necessary to *jump through hoops* to get a computer to work properly.

jump to conclusions see CONCLUSION

jump to it *informal* **:** to begin doing something ▪ We don't have much time to finish this job, so we better *jump to it*.

[2]**jump** *noun, pl* **jumps**

1 [*count*] **:** an act of jumping ▪ He got over the fence with a ***running jump***. [=a jump made while running] — see also HIGH JUMP, LONG JUMP

2 [*singular*] **:** a sudden movement because of surprise or shock — usually used in the phrase ***give a jump*** ▪ He *gave a jump* [=*start*] when she entered the room.

3 [*count*] **a :** something to be jumped over ▪ The horse took/cleared the first *jump* easily but balked at the second. **b :** something (such as a ramp) that you ride over in order to jump through the air on a motorcycle, bicycle, etc. ▪ a motorcycle *jump* — see also SKI JUMP

4 [*count*] **:** a sudden increase ▪ a *jump* in the price of gasoline ▪ a *jump* in sales

a hop, skip, and (a) jump see [2]HOP

***get/have/gain a/the jump on* :** to get or have an early advantage over (someone) by acting quickly or doing something first ▪ The company came out with its software earlier than expected and *got the jump on* its competitors.

one jump ahead ◊ If you are/keep/stay *one jump ahead* of someone, you have or keep an advantage over someone by learning about or doing something new. ▪ The company has continued to be successful because it always *stays one jump ahead* of its competitors.

take a running jump *Brit, informal + impolite* — used to tell someone who angers or annoys you to go away ▪ She told him to (go) *take a running jump*. [=(*US*) *take a flying leap*]

jumped–up /ˌʤʌmptˈʌp/ *adj* [*more ~; most ~*] *Brit, disapproving* **:** having a too high opinion of your own importance ▪ She thinks that politicians are all just a bunch of *jumped-up* nobodies.

[1]**jump·er** /ˈʤʌmpɚ/ *noun, pl* **-ers** [*count*]

1 : a person or animal (such as a horse) that jumps ▪ a good *jumper*

2 *basketball* **:** JUMP SHOT

– compare [2]JUMPER

[2]**jumper** *noun, pl* **-ers** [*count*]

1 *US* **:** a type of dress that has no sleeves and that is usually worn with a blouse — called also *pinafore*

2 *Brit* **:** SWEATER, PULLOVER

– compare [1]JUMPER

jumper cables *noun* [*plural*] *US* **:** a pair of electrical cables that are used to start a car, truck, etc., when its battery is not working by connecting the battery to another source of power (such as another car's battery) **:** cables used to jump-start a vehicle

jumping bean *noun, pl* **~ beans** [*count*] **:** a seed that moves when a small insect moves inside it — called also *Mexican jumping bean*

jumping jack *noun, pl* **~ jacks** [*count*] *US* **:** an exercise in which a standing person jumps to a position with the legs and arms spread out and then jumps back to the original position ▪ We did a few *jumping jacks* to warm up.

jumping–off point *noun, pl* **~ points** [*count*] **:** a place or point from which something begins ▪ The essay provides a good *jumping-off point* [=*starting point*] for further discussions. ▪ a *jumping-off point* for a journey — called also *jumping-off place*

jump rope *noun, pl* **~ ropes** *US*

1 [*count*] **:** a rope used in exercise or a children's game that involves jumping over it when it is swung near the ground — called also (*Brit*) *skipping rope*

2 [*noncount*] **:** the game of jumping over a jump rope ▪ children playing *jump rope*

jump rope

jump shot *noun, pl* **~ shots** [*count*] **:** a basketball shot made while jumping ▪ make/sink/hit a *jump shot*

jump–start /ˈʤʌmpˈstɑɚt/ *verb* **-starts; -start·ed; -start ing** [+ *obj*]

1 : to start (a vehicle whose battery is not working) by connecting its battery to another source of power (such as the battery of another vehicle) ▪ I had to use his truck to *jump-start* my car.

2 a : to cause (something) to start quickly ▪ Advertising can *jump-start* a political campaign. ▪ Publishers often attempt to *jump-start* a new book with TV appearances by the author. **b :** to give new energy to (something) ▪ a plan to *jump-start* the economy

– jump–start *noun, pl* **-starts** [*count*] ▪ We had to give the car a *jump-start*. ▪ give the economy a *jump-start*

jump·suit /ˈʤʌmpˌsuːt/ *noun, pl* **-suits** [*count*] **:** a piece of clothing that consists of a blouse or shirt with attached pants or shorts

jumpy /ˈʤʌmpi/ *adj* **jump·i·er; -est** *informal* **:** very nervous **:** easily frightened ▪ trying to calm *jumpy* passengers

Jun. *abbr* June

junc·tion /ˈʤʌŋkʃən/ *noun, pl* **-tions** [*count*]

1 : a place where two things join ▪ a *junction* of nerves and muscle

2 a : a place where roads or railroad lines come together ▪ the *junction* of Route 12 and Route 87 ▪ a railroad *junction* **b** *Brit* **:** a road or ramp that you use when getting off a highway **:** EXIT

junc·ture /ˈʤʌŋktʃɚ/ *noun, pl* **-tures** [*count*]
1 : an important point in a process or activity ▪ Negotiations between the countries reached a critical *juncture*. ▪ At this *juncture* it looks like they are going to get a divorce.
2 : a place where things join : JUNCTION ▪ the *juncture* of two rivers

June /ˈʤu:n/ *noun, pl* **Junes** : the sixth month of the year [*noncount*] in (early/middle/mid-/late) *June* ▪ early/late in *June* ▪ They arrived on *June* the first. = (*US*) They arrived on *June* first. = They arrived on the first of *June*. [*count*] Sales are up (for) this *June* in comparison with the previous two *Junes*. ▪ It happens every *June*. — abbr. *Jun.*

jun·gle /ˈʤʌŋgəl/ *noun, pl* **jun·gles** [*count*]
1 : a tropical forest where plants and trees grow very thickly ▪ a dense *jungle* ▪ *jungle* wildlife
2 : a harsh or dangerous place or situation in which people struggle for survival or success ▪ the asphalt/concrete/urban *jungle* [=the city] ▪ life in the corporate *jungle* ▪ It's hard to succeed in the business world. It's a *jungle* out there.
3 : a confusing or complex mixture of things ▪ a *jungle* of alleys ▪ a *jungle* of environmental laws
the law of the jungle see LAW

jungle gym *noun, pl* ~ **gyms** [*count*] *US* : a structure of metal bars for children to climb on

[1]**ju·nior** /ˈʤu:njɚ/ *adj*
1 *not used before a noun, US* **a** : younger in age ▪ He is six years *junior* to me. = He is *junior* to me by six years. [=he is six years younger than I am] **b** — used chiefly in its abbreviated form *Jr.* to identify a son who has the same name as his father ▪ John Smith *Jr.* and John Smith Sr. — compare SENIOR
2 *always used before a noun* : lower in standing or rank ▪ She is a *junior* partner in the law firm. ▪ a *junior* army officer — compare SENIOR
3 *always used before a noun* : designed for or done by young people ▪ *junior* hockey/tennis

[2]**junior** *noun, pl* **-niors** [*count*]
1 : a person who is younger than another person ▪ He is six years my *junior*. [=he is six years younger than I am] — compare SENIOR
2 : a person who is of a lower rank than another person ▪ They are my *juniors* in rank. — compare SENIOR
3 a *US* : a student in the third of four years in a high school or college ▪ She's a *junior* at the state college. — often used before another noun ▪ the *junior* class ▪ the *junior* prom — compare FRESHMAN, SOPHOMORE, SENIOR **b** *Brit* : a student at a junior school
4 *US, informal* — used like a name for a male child or son ▪ They love to bring *junior* to the park. ▪ How did you do on the exam, *junior*?

junior college *noun, pl* ~ **-leges** [*count*] *US* : a school that has two years of studies similar to those in the first two years of a four-year college

junior high school *noun, pl* ~ **schools** [*count*] *US* : a school usually including the seventh, eighth, and sometimes ninth grades — called also *junior high*; compare HIGH SCHOOL, MIDDLE SCHOOL, SENIOR HIGH SCHOOL

junior school *noun, pl* ~ **schools** [*count*] *Brit* : a school for children aged 7 to 11

junior varsity *noun, pl* ~ **-ties** [*count, noncount*] *US* : a team whose members are less experienced and usually younger than members on a varsity team

ju·ni·per /ˈʤu:nəpɚ/ *noun, pl* **-pers** [*count, noncount*] : an evergreen shrub or tree that has tiny fruits that look like berries

[1]**junk** /ˈʤʌŋk/ *noun* [*noncount*]
1 a : old things that have been thrown away or that have little value ▪ a *junk* collector ▪ The yard was cluttered with *junk* like broken bicycles and old washing machines. **b** : something that is in very poor condition ▪ That car is *junk*. = That car is a piece of *junk*. **c** : material that has no real value or interest ▪ There's nothing but *junk* on TV tonight. ▪ movies that fill people's minds with *junk*
2 *slang* : HEROIN
– compare [2]JUNK

[2]**junk** *noun, pl* **junks** [*count*] : an Asian boat that is high in the front and has four-cornered sails — compare [1]JUNK

[3]**junk** *verb* **junks; junked; junk·ing** [+ *obj*] *informal* : to get rid of (something) because it is worthless, damaged, etc. ▪ We decided to *junk* our old computer and buy a new one. ▪ *junk* an old car — sometimes used figuratively ▪ They had to *junk* [=*scrap*] their vacation plans when their son got sick.

junk bond *noun, pl* ~ **bonds** [*count*] *business* : a type of bond that pays high interest but also has a high risk

junk e-mail *noun* [*noncount*] : SPAM

junk·er /ˈʤʌŋkɚ/ *noun, pl* **-ers** [*count*] *US, informal* : an old car, truck, etc., that is in very poor condition ▪ I can't believe he's still driving that old *junker*.

jun·ket /ˈʤʌŋkət/ *noun, pl* **-kets** [*count*] *chiefly US* : a trip or journey that is paid for by someone else: such as **a** : a trip made by a government official and paid for by the public ▪ The senator has been criticized for expensive *junkets* to foreign countries. **b** : a free trip by a member of the press to a place where something (such as a new movie) is being promoted ▪ a film's press *junket*

junk food *noun, pl* ~ **foods** *informal* : food that is not good for your health because it contains high amounts of fat or sugar [*noncount*] worrying about kids eating too much *junk food* [*count*] eating too many *junk foods*

junk·ie *also* **junky** /ˈʤʌŋki/ *noun, pl* **junk·ies** [*count*] *informal*
1 : a person who uses illegal drugs : a drug addict ▪ a heroin *junkie*
2 : a person who gets an unusual amount of pleasure from or has an unusual amount of interest in something ▪ a news *junkie* ▪ a political *junkie* [=a fan of politics] ▪ a sugar *junkie*

junk mail *noun* [*noncount*] : mail that is not wanted : mail that consists mostly of advertising ▪ bombarded with *junk mail*

[1]**junky** /ˈʤʌŋki/ *adj* **junk·i·er; -est** *chiefly US, informal* : of very poor quality ▪ *junky* furniture

[2]**junky** *variant spelling of* JUNKIE

junk·yard /ˈʤʌŋkˌjɑɚd/ *noun, pl* **-yards** [*count*] : a place where you can buy, sell, or leave junk ▪ The car was hauled off to the *junkyard*.

jun·ta /ˈhʊntə/ *noun, pl* **-tas** [*count*] : a military group controlling a government after taking control of it by force ▪ a military *junta*

Ju·pi·ter /ˈʤu:pətɚ/ *noun* [*singular*] : the planet that is fifth in order from the sun and that is the largest of the planets

ju·ris·dic·tion /ˌʤɚrəsˈdɪkʃən/ *noun, pl* **-tions**
1 [*noncount*] : the power or right to make judgments about the law, to arrest and punish criminals, etc. ▪ The court has *jurisdiction* over most criminal offenses. ▪ His attorney claimed the court lacked *jurisdiction* in this matter. ▪ The matter falls outside/within the *jurisdiction* of this court.
synonyms see [1]POWER
2 [*noncount*] : the power or right to govern an area ▪ territory under the *jurisdiction* of the federal government
3 [*count*] : an area within which a particular system of laws is used ▪ He was arrested in another *jurisdiction*.
– **ju·ris·dic·tion·al** /ˌʤɚrəsˈdɪkʃənl/ *adj*

ju·ris·pru·dence /ˌʤɚrəsˈpru:dəns/ *noun* [*noncount*] *formal* : the study of law ▪ a professor of *jurisprudence*

ju·rist /ˈʤɚrɪst/ *noun, pl* **-rists** [*count*] : a person who has a thorough knowledge of law; *especially* : [1]JUDGE 1

ju·ror /ˈʤɚrɚ/ *noun, pl* **-rors** [*count*] : a member of a jury

ju·ry /ˈʤɚri/ *noun, pl* **-ries** [*count*]
1 : a group of people who are members of the public and are chosen to make a decision in a legal case ▪ The *jury* failed to reach a verdict. ▪ The *jury* found the defendant guilty/innocent. = The *jury* returned a verdict of guilty/innocent. ▪ She was selected to serve/sit on a *jury*. ▪ (*US*) She was selected for ***jury duty***. = (*Brit*) She was selected for ***jury service***. ▪ I demand my right to a ***trial by jury***. = I demand my right to a ***jury trial***. [=a trial that is decided by a jury] — see also GRAND JURY, HUNG JURY
2 : a group of people who decide the winners in a contest ▪ The *jury* [=*judges*] found her pie to be the best.
jury is out *informal* ✧ If you say ***the jury is still out on*** something, you mean that something has not yet been decided or has not yet become clear. ▪ The *jury is still out on* whether the new company will succeed. [=no one knows yet whether the new company will succeed]

jury panel *noun, pl* ~ **-els** [*count*] *US* : [1]PANEL 1c

ju·ry–rig /ˈʤɚriˌrɪg/ *verb* **-rigs; -rigged; -rig·ging** [+ *obj*] *chiefly US* : to build or put together (a simple device or structure) using the materials that you have available ▪ He *jury-rigged* a new antenna out of coat hangers.
– **jury–rigged** *adj* ▪ a *jury-rigged* antenna

[1]**just** /ˈʤʌst/ *adj* [*more* ~; *most* ~] *formal*
1 a : agreeing with what is considered morally right or good

: FAIR • a *just* society • a *just* cause for war • a *just* decision **b : treating people in a way that is considered morally right** • a *just* man

2 a : reasonable or proper • The college treated the allegation with *just* seriousness. **b : deserved and appropriate** • They got their *just* punishment for the crime. • a *just* reward • We all want to see this criminal get his ***just deserts***. [=get the punishment that he deserves]

– just·ly *adv* • She is *justly* [=*properly*] admired for her charitable work. **– just·ness** /ˈʤʌstnəs/ *noun* [*noncount*] • the *justness* of their decision

²just *adv*

1 : to an exact degree or in an exact manner • You look *just* [=*exactly*] like your father. • The store has *just* the tool you need. • That's *just* what I expected. • You have to accept me *just* as I am. • This shirt fits *just* right. • She called him a liar and told him he was *just* like all the other men she'd met. • It's *just* like you to be jealous every time I speak to another woman. [=you're always jealous when I speak to another woman] — see also *just my luck* at ¹LUCK

2 a : very recently • The bell *just* rang. • He was *just* here a minute ago. • She had *just* returned when he entered. • She has *just* acted in her first play. = (*chiefly US*) She *just* acted in her first play. • I've *just* been trying to call you! = (*chiefly US*) I was *just* trying to call you! **b : at this or that exact moment or time** • I was *just* going to telephone you! • She's *just* finishing a letter, and she'll be with you shortly. **c — used to say that two or more events are happening at the same time or with very little time between them** • He confessed *just* before he died. • The phone rang *just* as/when we were leaving. • I came ***just as soon*** as I heard the news. **d — used to emphasize that a moment or time is not far from the present moment** • She'll be back in *just* a minute. [=she'll be back very soon] • I saw her here *just* yesterday.

3 a : by a small amount • I had *just* [=*barely*] enough time to eat breakfast before leaving. • I arrived *just* in time to see him win. • We could (only) *just* see the ship coming over the horizon. • The horse's time for the race was *just* short of the record. = The horse *just* missed breaking the record. • It should take us *just* [=*slightly*] under/over an hour to get there. **b : by a small distance** • She lives *just* west of here. • The bathroom is *just* down the hall. • *Just* [=*directly*] across from the bank is a hotel. • The restaurant is *just* around the corner. — see also *just around the corner* at ¹CORNER

4 a : nothing more than : ONLY • This is *just* [=*simply*] a note to say I love you. • He is *just* an assistant to the manager. • She was *just* a baby when her father went off to war. • Is it *just* a coincidence that I see him everywhere I go? • He has *just* two months left before his retirement. • "Will you have another drink?" "Well, perhaps *just* (the) one." • I don't know him well: I've met him *just* (the) once. [=I've met him only one time] • "Who is she?" "Oh, *just* somebody who works in the same office as me." • I love *just* you and nobody else but you. • She'll be away from her desk for *just* a few minutes. = She'll *just* be away from her desk for a few minutes. • They took a nice field and turned it into ***just another*** shopping mall. • He's *just another* guy trying to get rich without working too hard. **b — used to stress the simple truth of a description or statement** • We'd like to buy a new car. We *just* [=*simply*] don't have enough money. • Sometimes a person *just* wants to be left alone. • She *just* wanted to say goodbye. • You'll *just* have to be patient. • I'm sorry if I seem grouchy. I'm *just* tired. • The wedding was *just* wonderful. • I feel *just* great! • The kids want to camp in the backyard, ***just for fun***. [=simply to have fun] **c — used in polite requests** • Could I *just* borrow that pen for a minute? Thanks! • Would you *just* step this way, please, ladies and gentlemen. **d — used for emphasis when you give an order or make a suggestion** • Why don't we *just* forget the whole thing. • *Just* hold on a minute! Did you say you'd solved the problem?! • *Just* [=*simply*] tell him you don't feel like going out. • *Just* (you) wait until your father sees this mess, young lady! • Don't argue with me: *just* do it! • *Just* imagine how silly she'll feel when she realizes that she was wrong. • *Just* look at the size of that thing! • *Just* think how happy we could be. **e — used to describe what someone does instead of doing what is necessary or expected** • Don't *just* stand there: do something! • She *just* stood there watching as he walked away. • I can't *just* pretend nothing happened.

5 — used with words like *might* and *may* to refer to something that is possible • I know you don't expect him to succeed, but he might *just* surprise you. [=he might succeed] • It's a crazy idea, but it *just* might work! • You know, you *just* might be right about that.

6 *Brit, informal* **: INDEED** • Isn't the city hot, *just*!

just about **: almost or nearly** • It was *just about* time to leave. • The work is *just about* done. • That is *just about* the biggest horse I have ever seen. [=that is a very big horse] • That is *just about* the stupidest thing she has ever done.

just a minute/second/moment **1 — used to ask someone to wait or stop briefly** • *Just a second* and I will get that book for you. **2 — used to demand that someone stop or listen** • *Just a minute*, young lady! You can't park there!

just anyone **: any person at all** • I don't lend money to *just anyone*.

just as **: to an equal degree as** • Our house is *just as* nice as theirs. • This one is *just as* good as that one. • She performs *just as* well as he does. **: in the same way as** • *Just as* we hope to be forgiven, so we should forgive others. • *Just as* I thought/suspected, the door is locked. [=I thought that the door would be locked, and it is]

just as soon ✧ **If you would *just as soon* do something, you would prefer to do it.** • We asked him to come with us, but he said he'd *just as soon* stay home.

just as well ✧ **If it is *just as well* that something happens, then it is a good thing, even if it was not expected or intended.** • It's *just as well* she didn't get that job, since she will now be closer to home. • I really didn't want to stay home this weekend, but it's *just as well*. I have a lot to do.

just because see BECAUSE

just like that **: very suddenly** • The girl vanished *just like that*. • *Just like that* it started raining.

just now *or* ***just this minute/second*** **1 : a moment ago** • I saw him *just now*. • I was *just this minute* thinking about calling you. **2 : at this moment** • They are *just now* heading out the door.

just on *Brit, informal* **: EXACTLY** • It was *just on* midnight.

just so **: in a particular way** • They feel they have to dress *just so* to be popular. **: arranged in a very neat and tidy way** • Everything in her house has to be *just so* or she gets upset. [=everything has to be exactly as she likes it]

just the same see ²SAME

just the thing **: the best or perfect thing** • I have *just the thing* for your hair.

just yet **: right now — used in negative constructions to say that something is not done yet or true yet but will be soon** • I don't have the table finished *just yet*. • "Are you ready to leave?" "Not *just yet*."

not just **— used to say that one thing is true and that another thing is also true** • She's *not just* my friend, she's my lawyer.

jus·tice /ˈʤʌstəs/ *noun, pl* **-tic·es**

1 [*noncount*] **: the process or result of using laws to fairly judge and punish crimes and criminals** • They received *justice* in court. • the *justice* system • the U.S. Department of *Justice* • criminals attempting to escape *justice* • The role of the courts is to dispense *justice* fairly to everyone. • Many people do not believe that ***justice has been served/done*** in his case. [=that he has been given proper punishment or fair treatment by the legal system] • His supporters claim that he is an innocent man and that his conviction was a ***miscarriage of justice***. [=an error made in a court of law that results in an innocent person being punished or a guilty person being freed] ✧ **Someone who is *brought to justice* is arrested and punished for a crime in a court of law.** • The police couldn't *bring* the killer *to justice*. — see also POETIC JUSTICE

2 a [*count*] *US* **: a judge in a court of law** • She is a *justice* of the state supreme court. — see also CHIEF JUSTICE **b *Justice* — used as a title for a judge (such as a judge of the U.S. Supreme Court)** • *Justice* Marshall

3 [*noncount*] **a : the quality of being fair or just** • a sense of *justice* • I saw no *justice* in the court's decision. **b : fair treatment** • We should strive to achieve *justice* for all people.

do justice ✧ **To *do justice to something or someone* or to *do someone or something justice* is to treat or show something or someone in a way that is as good as it should be.** • Words could never *do justice to* her beauty. [=could not adequately describe her beauty] • The movie does not *do justice to* the book. = The movie does not *do* the book *justice*. [=the movie is not as good as the book] • a brief summary that does not *do justice to* [=does not adequately show] the complexity of this issue

J

obstruction of justice see OBSTRUCTION
pervert the course of justice see [1]PERVERT

justice of the peace *noun, pl* **justices of the peace** [*count*] : a local official who has the power to decide minor legal cases and in the U.S. to perform marriages — abbr. *J.P.*

jus·ti·fi·ca·tion /ˌʤʌstəfəˈkeɪʃən/ *noun, pl* **-tions** : an acceptable reason for doing something : something that justifies an action [*count*] He tried to present a *justification* for his behavior. • There is no possible *justification* for what she did. [*noncount*] His behavior is without *justification*. • He told lies ***in justification of*** his behavior. [=in order to make people think that his behavior was reasonable] • She noted ***with some justification*** that other people had experienced similar problems. [=it was not unreasonable of her to note that other people had experienced similar problems]

jus·ti·fy /ˈʤʌstəˌfaɪ/ *verb* **-fies; -fied; -fy·ing** [+ *obj*]
1 : to provide or be a good reason for (something) : to prove or show (something) to be just, right, or reasonable • He tried to *justify* his behavior by saying that he was being pressured unfairly by his boss. • The fact that we are at war does not *justify* treating innocent people as criminals. • It's hard to *justify* the cost of a new car right now. = It's hard to *justify* spending money on a new car right now. — see also *the end justifies the means* at [1]END
2 : to provide a good reason for the actions of (someone) • Why should I have to ***justify myself*** [=to provide an explanation for my actions] when it was their fault?
3 *technical* : to position (text) so that the edges form a straight line
– jus·ti·fi·able /ˈʤʌstəˌfajəbəl/ *adj* [*more ~; most ~*] • They felt *justifiable* pride in their son. • *justifiable* expenses **– jus·ti·fi·ably** /ˈʤʌstəˌfajəbli/ *adv* • were *justifiably* proud **– justified** *adj, not used before a noun* [*more ~; most ~*] • She was (perfectly/fully) *justified* in complaining to her boss. [=she had a good reason for complaining to her boss]

jut /ˈʤʌt/ *verb* **juts; jut·ted; jut·ting :** to stick out, up, or forward [*no obj*] mountains *jutting* into the sky — often + *out* • The peninsula *juts out* [=*projects*] into the bay. • The edge of the roof *juts out* a few feet. [+ *obj*] — usually + *out* • He *jutted out* his jaw in defiance.

jute /ˈʤuːt/ *noun* [*noncount*] : a natural fiber that is used for making rope and cloth

[1]**ju·ve·nile** /ˈʤuːvəˌnajəl/ *adj*
1 [*more ~; most ~*] *disapproving* : unpleasantly childish : IMMATURE • She criticized his *juvenile* behavior at the party. • *juvenile* pranks
2 *always used before a noun* **a :** relating to or meant for young people • *juvenile* fiction **b :** of or relating to young people who have committed crimes • the *juvenile* justice system • a *juvenile* court • a *juvenile* crime [=a crime committed by a young person]
3 : not yet fully grown • *juvenile* birds/animals

[2]**juvenile** *noun, pl* **-niles** [*count*]
1 : a young person : a person who is not yet old enough to be legally considered an adult • She works to keep *juveniles* away from drugs. • crimes committed by *juveniles*
2 : a young bird or animal

juvenile delinquent *noun, pl* **~ -quents** [*count*] : a young person who has committed a crime
– juvenile delinquency *noun* [*noncount*]

jux·ta·pose /ˈʤʌkstəˌpoʊz/ *verb* **-pos·es; -posed; -pos·ing** [+ *obj*] *formal* : to place (different things) together in order to create an interesting effect or to show how they are the same or different • a display that *juxtaposes* modern art with classical art
– jux·ta·po·si·tion /ˌʤʌkstəpəˈzɪʃən/ *noun, pl* **-tions** [*count, noncount*] • an interesting *juxtaposition* of colors

K

K

k *or* **K** /ˈkeɪ/ *noun, pl* **k's** *or* **ks** *or* **K's** *or* **Ks**
1 : the 11th letter of the English alphabet [*count*] There is one *k* in "book." [*noncount*] The word ends in *k*.
2 *pl* **K** [*count*] **a** *informal* : THOUSAND • She earned a salary of $30*K*. • The car costs $35*K*. **b** *computers* : KILOBYTE • The program uses 350*K* of disk space.
3 [*count*] *baseball, informal* : STRIKEOUT • The pitcher had more than 10 *Ks* in his last game.

K *abbr* **1** Kelvin • a temperature of 200 degrees *K* **2** kilometer • a 5*K* run **3** *or* **k** karat

kabob *variant spelling of* KEBAB

Ka·bu·ki /kəˈbuːki/ *noun* [*noncount*] : a traditional form of Japanese entertainment with singing and dancing

kaftan *variant spelling of* CAFTAN

kai·ser /ˈkaɪzɚ/ *noun, pl* **-sers** [*count*] : the title of the ruler of Germany from 1871 to 1918 • *Kaiser* Wilhelm

kale /ˈkeɪl/ *noun, pl* **kales** [*count, noncount*] : a type of cabbage that has wrinkled leaves — see color picture on page C4

ka·lei·do·scope /kəˈlaɪdəˌskoʊp/ *noun, pl* **-scopes**
1 [*count*] : a tube that has mirrors and loose pieces of colored glass or plastic inside at one end so that you see many different patterns when you turn the tube while looking in through the other end
2 [*singular*] **a :** a changing pattern or scene • The landscape was a *kaleidoscope* of changing colors. **b :** a mixture of many different things • a *kaleidoscope* of flavors
– ka·lei·do·scop·ic /kəˌlaɪdəˈskɑːpɪk/ *adj* • *kaleidoscopic* patterns/variety

ka·mi·ka·ze /ˌkɑːmɪˈkɑːzi, *Brit* ˌkæmɪˈkɑːzi/ *noun, pl* **-zes** [*count*] : one of a group of Japanese pilots in World War II who were assigned to crash their planes into their targets — usually used before another noun • a *kamikaze* pilot • a *kamikaze* attack/mission — often used figuratively • *kamikaze* drivers [=reckless drivers]

kan·ga·roo /ˌkæŋgəˈruː/ *noun, pl* **-roos** [*count*] : an Australian animal that moves by hopping on its powerful rear legs ✧ The female kangaroo has a pouch in which the young are carried.

kangaroo

kangaroo court *noun, pl* **~ courts** [*count*] : a court that uses unfair methods or is not a proper court of law

ka·put /kəˈpʊt/ *adj, not used before a noun, informal*
1 : no longer working • Our washing machine is *kaput*. [=*broken*] • Our washing machine was working perfectly, and then suddenly it ***went kaput***. [=it broke]
2 : no longer able to continue : completely ruined or defeated • His career is *kaput*. [=*finished, over*]

kar·a·o·ke /ˌkeriˈoʊki/ *noun* [*noncount*] : a form of entertainment in which a device plays the music of popular songs and people sing the words to the songs they choose • That bar has *karaoke* on Saturday night. — often used before another noun • a *karaoke* bar/club/machine • *karaoke* music

kar·at (*US*) *or chiefly Brit* **car·at** /ˈkerət/ *noun, pl* **-ats** [*count*] : a unit for measuring how pure a piece of gold is • She was wearing an 18 *karat* gold bracelet. • Pure gold is 24 *karats*. — abbr. *K* or *k*

ka·ra·te /kəˈrɑːti/ *noun* [*noncount*] : a form of fighting that was developed in Japan in which your feet and hands are used to kick and hit an opponent : a Japanese martial art — often used before another noun • *karate* chops/kicks

kar·ma /ˈkɑɚmə/ *noun* [*noncount*]
1 *often* **Karma :** the force created by a person's actions that is believed in Hinduism and Buddhism to determine what that person's next life will be like
2 *informal* : the force created by a person's actions that some people believe causes good or bad things to happen to that person • She believes that helping people produces good *karma*.

ka·ty·did /ˈkeɪtɪˌdɪd/ *noun, pl* **-dids** [*count*] *US* : a large green insect that looks like a large grasshopper

kay·ak /ˈkaɪˌæk/ *noun, pl* **-aks** [*count*] : a long narrow boat that is pointed at both ends and that is moved by a paddle with two blades — see picture at BOAT; compare CANOE

ka·zoo /kəˈzuː/ *noun, pl* **-zoos** [*count*] : a toy musical instrument that is shaped like a short tube and that produces a buzzing sound when you hum into the smaller end of the tube • play a *kazoo*

KB *abbr* kilobyte

KC *abbr, Brit* King's Counsel

ke·bab /kəˈbɑːb, *Brit* kəˈbæb/ *also chiefly US* **ka·bob** /kəˈbɑːb/ *noun, pl* **ke·babs** *also* **ka·bobs** [*count*] : a dish made by pushing a long, thin stick (called a skewer) through pieces of meat and vegetables and cooking them on a grill — called also *shish kebab*

[1]keel /ˈkiːl/ *noun, pl* **keels** [*count*] : a long piece of wood or metal along the center of the bottom of a boat — see picture at BOAT

on an even keel : strong and not likely to fail or get worse : in a stable condition • They struggled to keep the company *on an even keel* during its early years. • I'm trying to get back *on an even keel* [=to return to a normal life] now that the lawsuit is settled.

[2]keel *verb* **keels; keeled; keel·ing**

keel over [*phrasal verb*] *informal* : to fall down suddenly • He just *keeled over* and died. We found out later that he'd had a heart attack. • I almost *keeled over* with/in laughter.

[1]keen /ˈkiːn/ *adj* **keen·er; -est** [*also more ~; most ~*]

1 : having or showing an ability to think clearly and to understand what is not obvious or simple about something • a *keen* intellect/intelligence/mind • She's a very *keen* observer of the political world. • She made some *keen* [=*acute*] observations. • a *keen* wit

2 : very strong and sensitive : highly developed • The dog has a *keen* sense of smell. = The dog has a *keen* nose. • *keen* [=*acute*] eyesight/hearing • She had a *keen* awareness of what was happening. [=she knew exactly what was happening] • She has a ***keen ear*** for languages. [=she is able to easily learn and understand languages] • He has a ***keen eye*** for details. [=he is good at noticing details]

3 a : very excited about and interested in something • She's a *keen* tennis player. = She's *keen* about tennis. • He's a *keen* student of art history. = He has a *keen* interest in art history. **b** : feeling a strong and impatient desire *to do* something • He is *keen* [=*eager*] *to learn* more about art history.

4 : strong or intense • After his death, she felt a *keen* [=*profound*] sense of loss. • The two firms are in *keen* competition. • (*chiefly Brit*) a *keen* wind

5 *informal + old-fashioned* : very good : WONDERFUL • Gee, that's *keen*. ✧ This sense is now usually used in a playful or ironic way. — see also PEACHY KEEN

6 *literary* : having a sharp edge or point • a *keen* knife/sword

7 *Brit, of a price* : very low • They sell reliable products at very *keen* prices.

(as) keen as mustard *Brit* : very excited and interested : very enthusiastic • I gave him the job because he was willing to learn and seemed *as keen as mustard*.

keen on **1** : very excited about and interested in (something) • She's very *keen on* tennis. • I'm not *keen on* that idea. [=I don't like that idea] • (*Brit*) He's ***mad keen on*** golf. **2** *chiefly Brit* : interested in or attracted to (someone) • He's been very *keen on* her since they met at my party.

– keen·ly *adv* • They were *keenly* interested in how well I was doing. • a *keenly* felt change • The parents were *keenly* aware of the teacher's importance. **– keen·ness** /ˈkiːnnəs/ *noun* [*noncount*] The *keenness* of the saw made cutting the board easier. [*singular*] a *keenness* of sight

[2]keen *verb* **keens; keened; keen·ing** [*no obj*] *old-fashioned + literary* : to make a loud and long cry of sorrow • mourners *keening* at a funeral

[1]keep /ˈkiːp/ *verb* **keeps; kept** /ˈkɛpt/; **keep·ing**

1 [*+ obj*] : to continue having or holding (something) : to not return, lose, sell, give away, or throw away (something) • She's going to *keep* the money she found. • I can't decide whether to sell my old car or *keep* it for another year. • While the company laid off some employees, others had hopes of *keeping* their jobs. • The shirt will *keep* [=*retain*] its shape after many washings. • an actress who has *kept* her looks/beauty [=continued to be attractive/beautiful] as she has grown older • "The fare is $4." "Here's $5. ***Keep the change***." • He struggled to ***keep his cool/composure*** [=to remain calm; to not become upset or angry] • He vowed to ***keep his silence*** about what he had seen. [=to not tell anyone about what he had seen]

2 a [*linking verb*] : to continue in a specified state, condition, or position • I asked them to *keep* quiet. • *keep* still/warm • He vowed to *keep* silent about what he had seen. [=to not tell anyone about what he had seen] • She likes to *keep* [=*stay*] busy. • The program teaches kids how to *keep* safe near water. • Have you ***kept in touch*** with your college roommate? [=have you continued to talk to or write to your college roommate?] **b** [*+ obj*] : to cause (someone or something) to continue in a specified state, condition, or position • I tried to *keep* the children quiet during the ceremony. • The local newspaper *keeps* people informed about what's happening in town. • The article offers tips on how to *keep* kids safe near water. • The movie will *keep* you on the edge of your seat. • We need to *keep* costs under control. • This scarf will help *keep* you warm. • She *keeps* herself fit by jogging. • He *kept* his hands behind his back while we were talking. • *Keep* both hands on the steering wheel. • It was so cold inside that I *kept* my coat on. • I promise I'll *keep* your decision a secret. [=I will not tell anyone your decision] • *Keep* the mixture chilled until you are ready to serve it.

3 [*+ obj*] **a** : to cause or force (someone) to stay in a place • I won't *keep* you (here) much longer. • The doctors want to *keep* me in (the hospital) for further tests. • If you're in a hurry, don't let me *keep* you. • *keep* a prisoner in jail • She *kept* the children in the house during the storm. • There was nothing to *keep* me in the city. **b** : to cause (someone) to be late • You're late. ***What kept you?*** [=what delayed you?; why are you late?]

4 [*+ obj*] **a** : to do (something) continuously or again and again — *+ -ing verb* • The teacher asked them to be quiet, but they just *kept talking*. • The rain *kept falling* all afternoon. • The dog *keeps running* away. • *Keep walking/driving* until you come to a traffic light. — often *+ on* • The band's music just *keeps on getting* better (and better). • I'll never get this work done if you *keep on interrupting* me. **b** : to cause (someone or something) to do something continuously or again and again — *+ -ing verb* • She has a desire for success that *keeps* her *striving* to do better. • His boss *kept* him *waiting* [=forced him to wait] for over an hour. • They want to *keep* the company *growing*. — see also KEEP GOING (below)

5 [*+ obj*] **a** : to do what is required by (something, such as a promise) • She always *keeps* her promises/word. [=she always does what she promises to do; she always does what she says she will do] • He failed to *keep* his appointment. [=he did not go to his appointment; he missed his appointment] **b** : to not tell (a secret) • I can *keep* a secret. • a ***poorly kept*** secret [=a secret that has been told to many people] • a ***well-kept*** secret [=a secret that has not been told to people] **c** *somewhat formal* : to act properly in relation to (something) • He *keeps* [=*observes*] the Sabbath. • They *keep* kosher.

6 [*+ obj*] **a** : to store (something) in a specified place • They *keep* the ketchup in the refrigerator. • I *keep* my socks in a drawer. • The sheets are *kept* in the closet. • He *keeps* his wallet in his back pocket. **b** : to have or hold (something) for later use instead of using it now • We'll eat some of the cookies now and *keep* [=*save*] some for later. • I'll *keep* my news until later. [=I'll tell you my news later] • (*Brit*) Would you *keep* [=(*US*) *save*] a seat for me?

7 [*no obj*] *of food* : to continue to be in a good condition • Carrots and potatoes *keep* well. • The meat will *keep* in the freezer for several months. — sometimes used figuratively • I have something to tell you, but it will *keep*. [=I can tell you later]

8 [*+ obj*] *formal* : to protect (someone) • May the Lord bless you and *keep* you. — usually *+ from* • May the Lord *keep* you *from* harm.

9 [*+ obj*] : to produce (something, such as a journal or record) by putting information in a book, document, etc., over a period of time • She *kept* a diary/journal. • He *keeps* a detailed record of all his purchases. • She *keeps* a list of books for future reading.

10 [*+ obj*] **a** : to take care of (something) • *keep* [=*tend*] a garden • We *kept* chickens and goats when I was a child. **b** : to operate (something, such as a business) : MANAGE • They *keep* [=(more commonly) *run*] a bed-and-breakfast. • (*chiefly Brit*) *keep* a shop

11 [*+ obj*] *somewhat old-fashioned* **a** : to have (something) available for use • He *keeps* a car even though he lives in the city. **b** : to have a continuing sexual relationship with (someone who is not your husband or wife) • a married man

K

who *keeps* a mistress ▪ She never married but she *kept* a lover for years. ▪ a ***kept man/woman*** [=a man/woman who is kept as a lover by someone]

How are you keeping? *Brit* — used to ask if someone feels good, bad, happy, well, etc. ▪ *"How are you keeping* [=*how are you doing*], Jill?" "Oh, pretty well, thanks."

keep after [*phrasal verb*] **1** ***keep after (someone)*** *informal* **:** to tell (someone) again and again to do something ▪ My kids *kept after* me to quit smoking, so I finally did. ▪ I wasn't going to audition, but my friends *kept after* me. **2** ***keep (someone) after*** *US* **:** to require (a student) to stay at school after classes have ended ▪ The teacher *kept* him *after* (school) for misbehaving in class.

keep at [*phrasal verb*] **1** ***keep at it*** **:** to continue doing or trying to do something ▪ If you *keep at it* long enough you'll succeed. ▪ The project was difficult, but we *kept at it* and eventually it was done. **2** ***keep (someone) at it*** **:** to force or cause (someone) to continue doing something ▪ The coach *kept* us (hard) *at it* until late afternoon.

keep back [*phrasal verb*] **1 :** to not go near something ▪ The police asked the spectators to *keep back.* [=*stay back*] ▪ The guide told us to *keep back* from the edge of the cliff. **2** ***keep (someone) back*** or ***keep back (someone)*** **a :** to not allow (someone) to go near something ▪ The police *kept* the spectators *back.* **b** *US* **:** to not allow (a student) to advance to the next grade level — usually used as *(be) kept back* ▪ Students who fail the exam may *be kept back* a year. **c** *Brit* **:** to require (a student) to stay at school after classes have ended ▪ She was *kept back* [=*(US) kept after, kept after school*] for talking in class. **3** ***keep (something) back*** or ***keep back (something)*** **:** to not allow (something) to appear or be known ▪ He struggled to *keep back* his tears. [=he tried hard not to cry] ▪ The government *kept back* [=*withheld*] some crucial information from the media.

keep company [*phrasal verb*] **1** ***keep company with (someone)*** **:** to spend time with (someone) — usually used figuratively ▪ In her garden, roses *keep company with* lilies. **2** ***keep (someone) company*** **:** to spend time with (someone who would be alone if you were not there) ▪ I'll *keep you company* while you wait for the train.

keep down [*phrasal verb*] **1 :** to stay close to the ground or floor ▪ The soldiers were ordered to *keep down.* [=*stay down*] **2** ***keep (someone) down*** **:** to prevent (someone) from succeeding, winning, etc. ▪ You can't *keep* a good man *down.* [=you can't prevent a good or talented person from succeeding] **3** ***keep (something) down*** or ***keep down (something)*** **a :** to prevent (something) from increasing or rising ▪ The company is trying to *keep down* costs/expenses/prices. ▪ She watered the path to *keep* the dust *down.* **b :** to prevent (something) from coming up from your stomach and into your mouth again ▪ He was so ill that he could only *keep down* a small amount of food. **4** ***keep it down*** — used to ask someone to be quiet ▪ Please *keep it down* in there. I'm trying to study.

keep from [*phrasal verb*] **1** ***keep from (doing something)*** or ***keep (someone or something) from (doing something)*** **:** to not do or experience (something) **:** to prevent or stop (someone or something) from doing or experiencing (something) ▪ She found it hard to *keep from* laughing. [=she found it hard not to laugh] ▪ She's been trying to *keep* herself *from* eating too much candy. ▪ An umbrella will *keep* you *from* getting wet. ▪ It's difficult to *keep from* feeling worried about this situation. ▪ He was anxious to *keep* his son *from* getting into trouble. ▪ Her happy nature *kept* her *from* worrying. ▪ I don't want to *keep* you *from* (doing) your work. = I don't want to *keep* you *from* working. ▪ She tied the knot tightly to *keep* it *from* loosening. ▪ The company has taken steps to *keep* the building *from* being broken into again. ▪ It was hard to *keep from* [=*avoid*] confusing the twins. **2** ***keep (something) from (someone)*** **:** to not tell (something) to (someone) ▪ What information are you *keeping from* me? [=what information are you not telling me?] ▪ They think the government is *keeping* [=*withholding*] the truth *from* us.

keep going [*phrasal verb*] **1 :** to continue moving forward ▪ He walked right past me and just *kept going.* **2 :** to continue doing something ▪ I was ready to give up on the search, but they convinced me to *keep going.* [=to continue searching] **3** ***keep (someone) going*** **:** to make (someone) able to continue doing something at a difficult time ▪ I don't know what *keeps her going* after all these years. ▪ Their grandson is the only thing *keeping them going.* **4** ***keep (something) going*** **:** to cause (something) to continue to exist or function ▪ They tried everything they could think of to *keep* the business *going.* ▪ He *kept* the conversation *going.*

keep house see [1]HOUSE

keep in [*phrasal verb*] **1** ***keep (something) in*** **:** to not show or express (something, such as an emotion) ▪ You shouldn't *keep* your anger *in* all the time. **2** ***keep (someone) in (something)*** **:** to continue to provide (someone) with (something needed or wanted) ▪ It's very expensive *keeping* my children *in* clothes that fit. **3** ***keep in with (someone)*** *chiefly Brit* **:** to remain friendly with (someone) ▪ She's always *kept in with* the people with power.

keep off [*phrasal verb*] **1** ***keep off (something)*** or ***keep (someone or something) off (something)*** **:** to stop or prevent (someone or something) from being on (something) ▪ *Keep* [=*stay*] *off* the grass. [=do not walk on the grass] ▪ Please *keep* the dog *off* the sofa. **2** ***keep (weight) off*** **:** to continue to weigh a lower amount than you formerly weighed **:** to not regain weight that you have lost ▪ She has managed to *keep* (most of) the weight *off* for two years. ▪ Losing weight is not as hard as *keeping* it *off.* **3 a** ***keep off (something)*** **:** to not talk about (something) ▪ I think we'd better *keep off* [=*avoid*] the subject of the war. **b** ***keep (someone) off (something)*** **:** to prevent (someone) from talking about (something) ▪ We tried to *keep* them *off* (the subject of) the war.

keep on [*phrasal verb*] **1** *informal* **:** to continue happening, doing something, working, etc. ▪ The rain *kept on* [=*kept up*] throughout the day. ▪ He talked and talked. At one point I thought he would *keep on* all night. **2** ***keep (someone) on*** **:** to continue to have (someone) as an employee ▪ The chef was *kept on* even after the restaurant was sold. **3** ***keep on at (someone)*** *chiefly Brit, informal* **:** to say the same thing to (someone) again and again in a way that is annoying ▪ My parents *kept on at me* to go back to college.

keep out [*phrasal verb*] **1 :** to not enter a place ▪ The sign on the door said *"Keep out!"* **2** ***keep out of (something)*** **a :** to not enter (a place) ▪ We were told to *keep out of* his office. ▪ Please *keep* [=*stay*] *out of* the way. **b :** to not become involved in (something) ▪ This argument doesn't involve you, so you should just *keep* [=*stay*] *out of* it. **3** ***keep out (someone or something)*** or ***keep (someone or something) out (of a place)*** **:** to stop or prevent (someone or something) from entering (a place) ▪ The curtains help *keep out* the drafts. ▪ *Keep* the cat *out* of the bedroom.

keep pace with see [1]PACE

keep score see [1]SCORE

keep tabs on see [1]TAB

keep the faith see FAITH

keep time see [1]TIME

keep to [*phrasal verb*] **1** ***keep to (something)*** **a :** to stay in or on (something) **:** to not leave (something) ▪ He *kept to* the house most of the time. ▪ She *keeps to* the main roads when she travels. **b :** to not go beyond (something) ▪ He tried to *keep* [=*stick*] *to* his budget. **c :** to act or behave in the way required by (something) ▪ *keep to* [=*abide by, obey*] the rules of the game **d :** to not move away from or change (something) ▪ I wish you'd just *keep to* [=*stick to*] the point. ▪ They *kept to* their story. **2** ***keep to yourself*** **a** *or chiefly Brit* ***keep yourself to yourself*** **:** to stay apart from other people **:** to avoid other people ▪ She was a shy girl who *kept* pretty much *to herself.* **b** ***keep (something) to yourself*** **:** to keep (something) secret ▪ He knew what the facts were but *kept them to himself.* [=he did not tell anyone what the facts were] ▪ She likes to *keep things to herself.*

keep track see [1]TRACK

keep up [*phrasal verb*] **1 :** to go or make progress at the same rate as others **:** to stay even with others in a race, competition, etc. ▪ The leader began to run faster, and the other runners found it hard to *keep up.* — often + *with* ▪ The other runners struggled to *keep up with* the leader. ▪ He found it difficult to *keep up with* the rest of the class. **2 :** to continue to know the newest information about something ▪ There is so much happening in the world now that I find it hard to *keep up.* [=stay informed] ▪ I find it hard to *keep up* on/with the news. **3 :** to continue happening ▪ The rain *kept up* all night. ▪ The gunfire *kept up* for a long time. **4** ***keep up with (someone)*** *informal* **:** to continue to talk to or write to (someone) ▪ She still *keeps up with* [=*keeps in touch with*] her old friends from college. **5** ***keep (someone) up*** **:** to prevent (someone) from sleeping ▪ I hope our party didn't *keep* you *up* all night! **6** ***keep (something) up*** or ***keep up (something)*** **a :** to continue doing (something) ▪ *Keep up* the good work. ▪ *Keep* that *up* and you'll get into trouble! **b :** to prevent (something) from getting worse, weaker, etc. ▪ We need to *keep* standards *up*. ▪ *Keep* your spirits *up*! ▪ The house had been *kept up* [=*maintained*] nicely. ▪ You need to exercise more to *keep* your strength *up*. **c** ◊ If you ***keep up your end*** of something (such as a bargain or agreement) you do what you have promised or agreed to do. ▪ I'm never sure if she will *keep up her end* of the deal.

keep up appearances see APPEARANCE
keep up with the Joneses see JONESES
keep your chin up see CHIN
keep your distance see [1]DISTANCE
keep your head see [1]HEAD

[2]**keep** *noun, pl* **keeps** [*count*] **:** the strongest part of a castle built in the Middle Ages

for keeps *informal* **1 :** forever or permanently ▪ He moved back to the city *for keeps*. [=*for good*] **2 :** with the understanding that you may keep what you win ▪ playing marbles *for keeps*

your keep* :** the amount of money you need to pay for food, clothing, a place to live, etc. — used in the phrase ***earn your keep ▪ She's been living off her parents long enough. It's time for her to get a job and start *earning her keep*.

keep•er /ˈkiːpɚ/ *noun, pl* **-ers** [*count*]
1 a : a person whose job is to guard or take care of something or someone ▪ a lion *keeper* ▪ "... am I my brother's *keeper*?" —Genesis 4:9 (KJV) — see also DOORKEEPER, GAMEKEEPER, GATEKEEPER, SHOPKEEPER, STOREKEEPER, ZOOKEEPER **b** *Brit* **:** CURATOR
2 *US, informal* **:** something or someone that is worth keeping **:** something or someone that is good, valuable, etc. ▪ Hold on to that boyfriend of yours—he's a *keeper*!
3 : GOALKEEPER
4 *American football* **:** a play in which the quarterback runs with the ball ▪ The quarterback gained five yards on a *keeper*.
finders keepers (losers weepers) see FINDER

keep•ing /ˈkiːpɪŋ/ *noun*

in keeping with **1 a :** agreeing with or sharing important qualities with (something) ▪ The decorations in the house are *in* (perfect) *keeping with* her personality. ▪ The book is *in keeping with* novels of the time. [=it is like novels written around that same time] **b :** in a way that agrees with, obeys, or matches (something) ▪ *In keeping with* the overall design of the park, the playground will remain small. ▪ The new bus station offers wireless Internet access *in keeping with* the expectations of modern travelers.

in your keeping ◊ If someone or something is *in your keeping*, you are expected to protect or take care of that person or thing ▪ What happened to the money that had been left *in his keeping*? [=(more commonly) *in his care*]

***out of keeping with* :** not agreeing with or sharing important qualities with (something) ▪ Her comments revealed a nervousness that seemed *out of keeping with* her calm appearance. ▪ The modern décor was *out of keeping with* the church's architecture.

keep•sake /ˈkiːpˌseɪk/ *noun, pl* **-sakes** [*count*] **:** something that you keep to help you remember a person, place, or event **:** a memento or souvenir ▪ We were given books as *keepsakes* of the trip.

keg /ˈkɛg/ *noun, pl* **kegs** [*count*]
1 : a barrel for holding or serving something (such as beer) ▪ We bought a *keg* (of beer) for the party. — see also POWDER KEG
2 : the amount of something contained in a keg ▪ They drank an entire *keg* of beer.

keg•ger /ˈkɛgɚ/ *noun, pl* **-gers** [*count*] *US, informal* **:** a party at which people drink beer from a keg — called also *keg party*

kelp /ˈkɛlp/ *noun* [*noncount*] **:** a type of brown seaweed ▪ a bed of *kelp*

Kel•vin /ˈkɛlvən/ *adj, technical* **:** relating to or having a scale for measuring temperature on which the boiling point of water is at 373.1 degrees above zero and the freezing point is at 273.15 degrees above zero ▪ the *Kelvin* scale ▪ a temperature of 200 degrees *Kelvin* — abbr. *K*; compare CELSIUS, FAHRENHEIT

ken /ˈkɛn/ *noun*

***beyond someone's ken* :** not within the range of what someone knows or understands ▪ These changes occurred for reasons that are *beyond my ken*. [=reasons that I do not know or understand] ▪ miracles that are *beyond human ken* [=miracles that cannot be understood by human beings]

ken•nel /ˈkɛnl/ *noun, pl* **-nels** [*count*]
1 : a place where dogs are kept while their owners are away ▪ While I was on vacation my dog went to a *kennel*. — called also (*Brit*) *kennels*; compare CATTERY
2 : a container or very small building for a dog or cat to sleep or stay in

kept *past tense and past participle of* [1]KEEP

kerb, kerbside *Brit spelling of* [1]CURB 1, CURBSIDE

ker•chief /ˈkɚʧəf/ *noun, pl* **-chiefs** [*count*] **:** a square piece of cloth that is worn around your neck or as a covering for your head

ker•nel /ˈkɚnl/ *noun, pl* **-nels** [*count*]
1 a : the small, somewhat soft part inside a seed or nut **b :** a whole seed; *especially* **:** one of the yellow seeds that cover an ear of corn ▪ a *kernel* of corn — see color picture on page C4
2 : a very small amount of something ▪ There's not a *kernel* of truth in what they say. ▪ *kernels* of wisdom
3 : the origin or basis of something ▪ the *kernel* [=*germ*] of the idea for the book

ker•o•sene /ˈkerəˌsiːn/ *noun* [*noncount*] *chiefly US* **:** a type of oil that is burned as a fuel — often used before another noun ▪ a *kerosene* heater/lamp — called also (*Brit*) *paraffin*

ketch /ˈkɛʧ/ *noun, pl* **ketch•es** [*count*] **:** a type of sailboat that has two masts

ketch•up /ˈkɛʧəp/ *noun, pl* **-ups** [*count, noncount*] **:** a thick sauce made with tomatoes ▪ a bottle of *ketchup* ▪ She put *ketchup* on her hamburger. — called also *tomato ketchup*

ket•tle /ˈkɛtl/ *noun, pl* **ket•tles** [*count*] **:** a container used for heating or boiling liquid ▪ a soup *kettle*; *especially* **:** TEAKETTLE ▪ Put the *kettle* on (the stove) so we can have a cup of tea. ▪ The *kettle* is boiling. [=the water in the kettle is boiling] — see picture at KITCHEN

kettle of fish *informal* **1 :** a bad situation **:** MESS ▪ Well, this is a fine/nice/pretty *kettle of fish*. **2 :** something or someone that is being considered or dealt with ▪ I have experience in domestic law, but international law is another *kettle of fish*. [=*matter*]

ket•tle•drum /ˈkɛtlˌdrʌm/ *noun, pl* **-drums** [*count*] **:** a large drum that has a rounded bottom — see picture at PERCUSSION

[1]**key** /ˈkiː/ *noun, pl* **keys** [*count*]
1 a : a device that is used to open a lock or start an automobile ◊ The usual type of key is a small metal object that you insert into a narrow opening and turn. ▪ You need the *key* to get into the drawer. ▪ She turned the *key* and opened the door. ▪ house/car *keys* ▪ the ignition *key* of a car ▪ the *key* to the lock — often used figuratively ▪ That woman holds the *key* to his heart. — see also LATCHKEY, PASSKEY, SKELETON KEY **b :** a device that looks like a key and that is used to turn something ▪ a *key* for winding a clock
2 : something that is necessary in order to do or achieve something — usually singular ▪ If you want to improve your health, exercise is the *key*. — usually + *to* ▪ The *key to* hitting the ball well is following through on your stroke. ▪ Hard work is the *key to* success.
3 a : something that provides an explanation or solution — usually + *to* ▪ the *key to* a riddle **b :** a list of words or phrases that explain the meaning of symbols or abbreviations ▪ Use the *key* to decode the symbols. ▪ a pronunciation *key*
4 a : any one of the buttons of a computer or typewriter that you push with your fingers ▪ He tapped away at the *keys*, typing his letter. — see picture at COMPUTER; see also FUNCTION KEY, SHIFT KEY **b :** any one of the parts that you push with your fingers to play a piano or similar musical instrument ▪ She sat down at the piano and put her hands on the *keys*.
5 *music* **:** a system of musical tones based on a scale beginning on the note for which the system is named ▪ the *key* of C ▪ The symphony changes *key* from G major to E minor.
under lock and key see [2]LOCK
– compare [4]KEY

[2]**key** *adj* **:** extremely important ▪ He's a *key* player/person in the organization. ▪ The *key* question is "Can we afford it?" ▪ Underline *key* words and phrases as you read. ▪ Their votes were *key* in getting the bill passed.

[3]**key** *verb* **keys; keyed; key•ing** [+ *obj*]
1 : to enter (information) by using the keys of a computer, typewriter, etc. ▪ The changes to the manuscript are being *keyed* by the typist. — often + *in* ▪ In order to gain access to the network, you first have to *key in* [=*type in*] your name

K

and password. — often + *into* ▪ The cashier *keyed* each price *into* the cash register.

2 *US, informal* : to have the most important part in (something) ▪ Defense *keyed* the victory.

key to [*phrasal verb*] *chiefly US* **1** ***key (something) to (something or someone)*** : to make (something) suitable for (a particular use or type of person) ▪ I try to *key* my lectures *to* my audience. — often used as *(be) keyed to* ▪ The educational program *is keyed to* the needs of working women. **2** ***key (something) to (something)*** : to change (something) in a way that is closely related to (something else) — usually used as *(be) keyed to* ▪ The amount of money they receive *is keyed to* the rate of inflation. [=the amount increases or decreases if the rate of inflation increases or decreases] ▪ Diets *are keyed to* a person's lifestyle and weight-loss goal.

[4]**key** *noun, pl* **keys**

1 [*count*] : a low island or reef

2 ***the Keys*** : a group of small islands off the southern coast of Florida

– compare [1]KEY

[1]**key·board** /ˈkiːˌboɚd/ *noun, pl* **-boards** [*count*]

1 a : a row or set of keys that are pushed to play a musical instrument (such as a piano) — sometimes used before another noun ▪ The piano is a *keyboard* instrument. **b** : a musical instrument that is played by means of a keyboard like that of a piano and that produces sounds electronically ▪ She plays the *keyboard*. — often plural ▪ She plays *keyboards*.

2 : the set of keys that are used for a computer or typewriter — see picture at COMPUTER

keyboard instruments

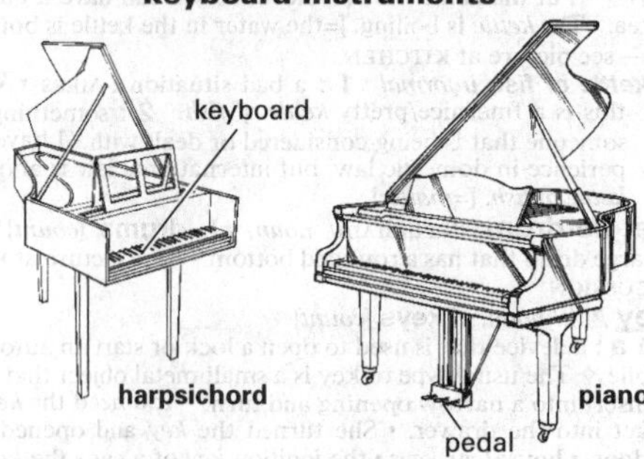

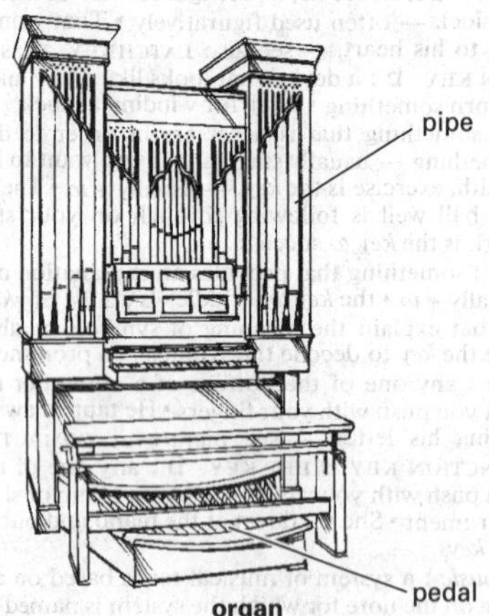

[2]**keyboard** *verb* **-boards; -board·ed; board·ing** : to enter (information) into a computer by using a keyboard [+ *obj*] *keyboard* [=*key*] a manuscript [*no obj*] learning how to *keyboard*

– key·board·er *noun, pl* **-ers** [*count*] **– keyboarding** *noun* [*noncount*] ▪ He is taking a class in *keyboarding*.

key·board·ist /ˈkiːˌboɚdɪst/ *noun, pl* **-ists** [*count*] : a musician who plays a keyboard (sense 1b)

key chain *noun, pl* ~ **chains** [*count*] : a device that is used to hold keys and that usually consists of a metal ring, a short chain, and a small decoration — called also *key ring*

keyed up *adj* [*more* ~; *most* ~] *informal* : excited or nervous ▪ The students were all *keyed up* for the test. ▪ I was too *keyed up* to sleep.

key·hole /ˈkiːˌhoul/ *noun, pl* **-holes** [*count*] : the opening in a lock into which a key is placed — see picture at DOOR

key lime *noun, pl* ~ **limes** [*count*] : a small lime that is grown especially in the Florida Keys ▪ ***key lime pie*** [=a sweet pie that is usually made with key limes]

key·note /ˈkiːˌnout/ *noun, pl* **-notes** [*count*] : the most important idea or part of something ▪ Humor is the *keynote* of the play.

keynote address *noun, pl* ~ **-dresses** [*count*] : the main speech given at a gathering (such as a political convention) ▪ Many of the convention guests left after the *keynote address*. — called also *keynote speech*

key·not·er /ˈkiːˌnoutɚ/ *noun, pl* **-ers** [*count*] : KEYNOTE SPEAKER

keynote speaker *noun, pl* ~ **-ers** [*count*] : a person who gives a keynote address ▪ Senator Williams was the *keynote speaker* at the convention. — called also *keynoter*

key·pad /ˈkiːˌpæd/ *noun, pl* **-pads** [*count*] : a set of keys or buttons for entering information into a calculator, telephone, etc. ▪ a numeric *keypad* [=a set of keys or buttons that have numbers on them] — see picture at TELEPHONE

key ring *noun, pl* ~ **rings** [*count*] : KEY CHAIN

key·stone /ˈkiːˌstoun/ *noun, pl* **-stones** [*count*]

1 : a large stone at the top of an arch that locks the other stones in place

2 : something on which other things depend for support ▪ Tourism is the city's economic *keystone*. ▪ the *keystone* of his faith

key·stroke /ˈkiːˌstrouk/ *noun, pl* **-strokes** [*count*] : the act of pushing down a key on a keyboard ▪ He deleted all of my work with a single *keystroke*.

key·word /ˈkiːˌwɚd/ *noun, pl* **-words** [*count*] : a word that is used to find information in a piece of writing, in a computer document, or on the Internet ▪ She typed the *keywords* "Medieval" and "medicine" into the search engine and pulled up a lot of results. ▪ a *keyword* search of the database

kg *abbr* kilogram

KGB *abbr* ✧ *KGB* is the abbreviation of the Russian name for the former Soviet organization responsible for national security and for collecting information about other countries or foreign groups. ▪ a member of the *KGB*

kha·ki /ˈkæki, ˈkɑːki/ *noun, pl* **-kis**

1 [*noncount*] : a yellowish-brown cloth ▪ a military uniform made of *khaki* — often used before another noun ▪ *khaki* pants

2 ***khakis*** [*plural*] : pants made of khaki ▪ a pair of *khakis*

3 [*noncount*] : a yellowish-brown color — see color picture on page C3

kHz *abbr* kilohertz

kib·butz /kɪˈbʊts/ *noun, pl* **kib·but·zim** /kɪˌbʊtˈsiːm/ [*count*] : a farm in Israel on which a group of people live and work together

ki·bitz /ˈkɪbəts/ *verb* **-bitz·es; -bitzed; -bitz·ing** *US, informal* **1** [*no obj*] : to talk to someone in a friendly and informal way : CHAT ▪ They sat around *kibitzing* about their children.

2 : to watch other people and make unwanted comments about what they are doing [*no obj*] My uncle likes to *kibitz* when I play poker with my cousins. [+ *obj*] He likes to *kibitz* our poker games.

– ki·bitz·er /ˈkɪbətsɚ/ *noun, pl* **-ers** [*count*] ▪ a *kibitzer* at a card game

ki·bosh /ˈkaɪˌbɑːʃ/ *noun*

put the kibosh on *informal* : to stop or end (something) : to prevent (something) from happening or continuing ▪ His mother *put the kibosh on* his smoking habit. [=his mother forced him to stop smoking]

[1]**kick** /ˈkɪk/ *verb* **kicks; kicked; kick·ing**

1 a [+ *obj*] : to hit (someone or something) with your foot ▪ The attacker *kicked* him in the stomach. ▪ She lost her temper and *kicked* over the box. ▪ He *kicked* the ball into the goal. ▪ She *kicked* the ball to me. ▪ The policeman *kicked* the door open. **b** : to move your leg or legs in the air or in water especially in a strong or forceful way [+ *obj*] The baby *kicked* his legs in the air. ▪ The swimming instructor reminded the children to *kick* their legs as they swam. [*no obj*] The baby *kicked* with pleasure. ▪ The boy ***kicked and screamed*** as his mother carried him out of the room. = The boy was car-

ried out of the room ***kicking and screaming.*** — often used figuratively ▪ They told him he needed a computer, but he had to be ***dragged kicking and screaming*** into the 21st century. [=he had to be forced to stop doing things the old way and use a computer]
2 [+ *obj*] *sports* **:** to score (a goal) by kicking a ball ▪ He *kicked* the winning field goal.
3 [+ *obj*] *informal* **:** to completely stop doing (something harmful to yourself) **:** to put an end to (a bad or dangerous habit) ▪ When he was 25, he *kicked* his cocaine habit and went back to school. ▪ I've been smoking for years, but this year I'm determined to ***kick the habit.***
4 [*no obj*] *informal* **:** to be full of life and energy — always used as *(be) kicking* ▪ He's almost 90 years old, but he's still *kicking.* ▪ The movement *is* still ***alive and kicking.***

kick around [*phrasal verb*] *informal* **1** ***kick around (a place) or kick around*** **:** to spend time in (a place) without having a goal or purpose **:** to wander around (a place) ▪ After graduation, he *kicked around* Boston for a while, trying to decide what to do next. = After graduation, he *kicked around* for a while, trying to decide what to do next. **2 :** to be lying somewhere within a general area or place ▪ I think I have a copy of that book *kicking around* [=lying around] somewhere in my house. **3 a :** to be considered or discussed in an informal way over a period of time ▪ These ideas have been *kicking around* for years. **b** ***kick around (something) or kick (something) around*** **:** to consider or talk about (ideas, plans, etc.) in an informal way ▪ We should have a meeting to *kick around* some ideas about possible new products. **4** ***kick (someone) around or kick around (someone)*** **:** to treat (someone) in a very bad or unfair way ▪ He gets *kicked around* by his older brother.

kick ass *US, informal + impolite* **1 :** to succeed or win in a very impressive way ▪ a lawyer who *kicks ass* in the courtroom ▪ Our team *kicked ass* in the soccer tournament. **2 :** to use force to achieve some purpose ▪ If they don't start answering my questions, I'm going to go over there and *kick* some *ass.* **3** ***kick someone's ass*** **a :** to attack and injure someone severely ▪ Some drunk threatened to *kick his ass.* ▪ He ***got his ass kicked*** by some drunk. **b :** to defeat someone easily or completely ▪ We *got our asses kicked* [=we lost badly] in the last game. — see also KICK-ASS

kick back [*phrasal verb*] *chiefly US, informal* **:** to relax and enjoy yourself ▪ After work, he likes to *kick back* and watch some TV. ▪ I spent the weekend just *kicking back.*

kick butt *US, informal + sometimes impolite* — used in the same ways as *kick ass* (above) ▪ Our team *kicked butt* in the soccer tournament. ▪ I'm going to go over there and *kick* some *butt.* ▪ Some drunk threatened to *kick his butt.*

kick in [*phrasal verb*] *informal* **1 :** to begin to work or to have an effect ▪ Once the heat *kicks in,* it will be a lot more comfortable in here. ▪ waiting for the new law to *kick in* **2** ***kick in (something) or kick (something) in*** *US* **:** to give (an amount of money) as your share **:** CONTRIBUTE ▪ We each *kicked in* a few dollars for her gift.

kick off [*phrasal verb*] **1 :** to start play in a game (such as American football or soccer) by kicking the ball ▪ Jones will *kick off* from the 30-yard line. — see also KICKOFF **2 a** ***kick off (something) or kick (something) off*** **:** to begin (something, such as a performance, an event, or a discussion) ▪ The chairman's speech will *kick off* the conference. **b :** to get started **:** BEGIN ▪ The conference *kicked off* with a speech by the chairman. ▪ The game *kicks off* at 1:00. **3** ***kick (someone) off (something)*** **:** to force (someone) to leave (a team or group) ▪ The coach threatened to *kick* him *off* the team if he continued to be late for practice. **4** ***kick off (your shoes) or kick (your shoes) off*** **:** to remove (your shoes) by making a kicking motion ▪ She *kicked off* her shoes and started to dance. **5** *informal* **:** to die ▪ I was so sick that I felt like I might *kick off* at any time.

kick out [*phrasal verb*] ***kick (someone) out or kick out (someone)*** **:** to force (someone) to leave a place, group, school, etc. ▪ He was/got *kicked out* [=*thrown out*] of the school when he was caught cheating again. ▪ They threatened to *kick* him *out* (of the bar) if he didn't stop annoying people. ▪ She *kicked* her husband *out* (of the house).

kick (someone) upstairs *informal* **:** to promote (someone) to a higher but less powerful or important position ▪ He was *kicked upstairs,* given a fancy title, and stripped of most of his power.

kick the bucket *informal + somewhat old-fashioned* **:** to die ▪ He inherited the house after his uncle *kicked the bucket.*

kick up [*phrasal verb*] **1** ***kick up (something) or kick (something) up*** **:** to cause (something) to rise upward ▪ The car sped away, *kicking up* dirt and gravel. **2** *informal* **a** ***kick up (something) or kick (something) up*** **:** to cause (something) to become stronger ▪ The praise *kicked up* her confidence. ▪ The intensity of the game got *kicked up* a notch when a fight broke out. **b :** to become stronger ▪ The wind suddenly *kicked up.* **3** ***kick up (something) or kick (something) up*** *informal* **:** to cause (something) to happen ▪ The high winds *kicked up* huge waves. ▪ The service in the restaurant wasn't very good, but we decided not to ***kick up a fuss/stink*** [=*complain*] about it.

kick up your heels *US, informal* **:** to relax and enjoy yourself **:** to have a good and lively time ▪ After exams were over, the students had a little time to *kick up their heels.*

kick yourself *informal* **:** to blame or criticize yourself for something you have done ▪ You've got to stop *kicking yourself.* It wasn't your fault that the project failed. ▪ He was *kicking himself* for having forgotten the meeting. ▪ He ***could have kicked himself*** [=he was very angry at himself] when he realized that he had forgotten the meeting.

²kick *noun, pl* **kicks** [*count*]
1 a : an act of hitting someone or something with your foot ▪ He gave me a *kick* in the leg. ▪ If you give the machine a little *kick,* it should start working again. **:** a sudden forceful movement with your foot ▪ a karate *kick* **b :** an act of hitting a ball with your foot ▪ a soccer *kick* ▪ a long *kick* in football — see also CORNER KICK, DROPKICK, FREE KICK, PENALTY KICK, PLACEKICK
2 a : a sudden forceful movement — usually singular ▪ I felt the *kick* of the engine when it started. ▪ The rifle has a powerful *kick.* **b** *informal* **:** a quality that produces a sudden powerful effect — usually singular ▪ The drink has a *kick* [=a strong effect from alcohol] to it. ▪ chili with a *kick* [=a very hot and spicy flavor]
3 *informal* **:** a feeling or source of pleasure ▪ She gets a *kick* out of watching old movies. [=she enjoys watching old movies] ▪ I got a *kick* out of seeing her again. = Seeing her again was a *kick.* ▪ We play ***for kicks*** [=for enjoyment], not for money. ▪ He ***gets his kicks*** from embarrassing his teammates. [=he enjoys embarrassing his teammates]
4 *informal* — used with *on* to say that someone is doing a lot of something for usually a brief period of time ▪ He's been *on* a health-food *kick* lately. [=he has been eating a lot of health food lately]
5 : an increase in speed at the end of the race ▪ a runner who has a strong ***finishing kick***

a kick in the teeth *informal* **:** something that is very shocking and disappointing ▪ Losing that game was *a* real *kick in the teeth.*

kick–ass /ˈkɪkˌæs/ *adj* [*more* ~; *most* ~] *chiefly US, informal + impolite*
1 : very tough and aggressive ▪ a *kick-ass* career woman who is determined to get to the top ▪ an executive with a *kick-ass* attitude/style
2 : very good or impressive ▪ a *kick-ass* stereo/movie/song — see also *kick ass* at ¹KICK

kick•back /ˈkɪkˌbæk/ *noun, pl* **-backs** [*count*] **:** an amount of money that is given to someone in return for providing help in a secret and dishonest business deal ▪ Several company executives were accused of accepting *kickbacks.*

kick•ball /ˈkɪkˌbɑːl/ *noun* [*noncount*] *US* **:** a game for children that is like baseball but that is played with a large rubber ball that is kicked instead of being hit with a bat

kick•box•ing /ˈkɪkˌbɑːksɪŋ/ *noun* [*noncount*] **:** a form of boxing in which fighters are allowed to kick each other with their bare feet

kick•er /ˈkɪkɚ/ *noun, pl* **-ers**
1 [*count*] **:** a person who kicks something; *especially* **:** a person who specializes in kicking the ball in a sport like American football
2 [*singular*] *US, informal* **:** a sudden and surprising occurrence, remark, etc. ▪ The real *kicker* came when the chairman announced that he was quitting.

kick•off /ˈkɪkˌɑːf/ *noun, pl* **-offs** [*count*]
1 : a kick that starts play in a game (such as American football or soccer) ▪ a long *kickoff* ▪ The *kickoff* (of the game) is at 1:00. [=the game begins at 1:00]
2 : the start of something ▪ At his campaign *kickoff,* the senator gave a passionate speech about combating poverty. ▪ His speech marked the *kickoff* of his campaign. — see also *kick off* at ¹KICK

kick•stand /ˈkɪkˌstænd/ *noun, pl* **-stands** [*count*] **:** a metal

K

bar on a bicycle or motorcycle that swings down to hold it in an upright position when it is not in use

kick–start /ˈkɪkˌstɑɚt/ *verb* **-starts; -start•ed; -start•ing** [+ *obj*]
1 : to start (a motorcycle) by pushing down on a lever with your foot
2 a : to cause (something) to start quickly ▪ Advertising can help to *kick-start* [=*jump-start*] a political campaign. **b :** to give new energy to (something) ▪ a plan to *kick-start* [=*jump-start*] the economy
– **kick–start** *noun, pl* **-starts** [*count*] ▪ a plan to give the economy a *kick-start*

[1]**kid** /ˈkɪd/ *noun, pl* **kids**
1 [*count*] *informal* **a :** a son or daughter : CHILD ▪ She has to leave early and pick up her *kids* at school. ▪ He has a wife and two *kids*. **b :** a young person ▪ I loved to play hopscotch when I was a *kid*. [=*child*] ▪ I wish I could do something to help that poor *kid*. ▪ I know he seems very mature, but he's really still just a *kid*. [=he's still very young] ▪ a bunch of college *kids* [=young people who are attending college] — sometimes used as a form of address ▪ Hey, *kid*! ▪ You'd better listen to me, *kid*, because I'm not going to say this twice.
2 a [*count*] **:** a young goat **b** [*noncount*] **:** a soft leather made from the skin of a young goat ▪ gloves made of *kid* ▪ *kid* leather
new kid on the block : someone who has recently joined a particular group ▪ I was the *new kid on the block*, having just been hired the week before.
– see also KID GLOVES

[2]**kid** *adj, always used before a noun, chiefly US, informal* **:** younger ▪ my *kid* brother/sister [=my brother/sister who is younger than I am]

[3]**kid** *verb* **kids; kid•ded; kid•ding** *informal*
1 : to speak to (someone) in a way that is not serious : to say things that are not true to (someone) in a joking way [+ *obj*] It's the truth. I wouldn't *kid* you about something so important. ▪ I'm not *kidding* you when I say that this is one of the best meals I've ever eaten. ▪ I panicked when he said the test was tomorrow, but then I realized he was just *kidding* me. ▪ The test is tomorrow? ***You must be kidding me***! ▪ "The test is tomorrow." "***Are you kidding me***?!" "***I kid you not***." [=I am not kidding you] [*no obj*] Don't be offended by what he said. He was just/only *kidding*. — often + *around* ▪ I'm not really angry—I'm just *kidding around*.
2 [+ *obj*] **:** to make fun of (someone) in a friendly way : TEASE ▪ We *kidded* her about her old car.
3 [+ *obj*] **:** to say (something) in a joking way ▪ "I might eat this whole pie by myself," she *kidded*. ▪ She *kidded* that she might eat the whole pie by herself.
kid yourself : to fail to admit the truth to yourself : to deceive yourself ▪ If you think he'll help us, you're just *kidding yourself*. ▪ "I think he'll help us if we ask him." "Don't *kid yourself*—he's only interested in his own problems."
no kidding *informal* **1** — used to emphasize the truth of a statement ▪ *No kidding*, the test is tomorrow. **2** — used to ask if a statement is really true ▪ "The test is tomorrow." "*No kidding*?" **3** — used to show that you are surprised by or interested in what has been said. ▪ "My brother got engaged last month." "*No kidding*! That's great news!" — often used in an ironic way in response to a statement that is regarded as very obvious ▪ "If we don't start going faster, we're not going to finish on time." "Gee, *no kidding*."
– **kid•der** *noun, pl* **-ders** [*count*] ▪ He's quite a *kidder*. [=he likes to kid around]

kid•die *also* **kid•dy** /ˈkɪdi/ *noun, pl* **-dies** [*count*] *informal* **:** a young child ▪ It's a scary movie that might not be appropriate for the *kiddies*. — often used before another noun ▪ a *kiddie* movie [=a movie intended for small children] ▪ a *kiddie* pool for the toddlers

kid•do /ˈkɪdoʊ/ *noun, chiefly US, informal* — used by an adult to speak to a young person ▪ Pay attention to me, *kiddo*, or you're going to get hurt!

kid gloves *noun*
with kid gloves : in a very gentle or careful way : with special care in order to avoid causing damage or offense ▪ He's very temperamental and needs to be treated *with kid gloves*. ▪ School reform is a sensitive issue, and many politicians treat it *with kid gloves*.
– **kid–glove** /ˈkɪdˈglʌv/ *adj, always used before a noun* ▪ Many politicians give the issue the ***kid-glove treatment***.

kid•nap /ˈkɪdˌnæp/ *verb* **-naps; -napped** *also US* **-naped; -nap•ping** *also US* **-nap•ing** [+ *obj*] **:** to take away (someone) by force usually in order to keep the person as a prisoner and demand money for returning the person ▪ She had been *kidnapped* (from her home).
– **kid•nap•per** *also US* **kid•nap•er** *noun, pl* **-nap•pers** *also US* **-nap•ers** [*count*] ▪ The *kidnapper* demanded one million dollars in ransom. – **kidnapping** *also US* **kidnaping** *noun* [*noncount*] He was found guilty of *kidnapping*. [*count*] There have been several recent *kidnappings*.

kid•ney /ˈkɪdni/ *noun, pl* **-neys** [*count*]
1 : either of two organs in your body that remove waste products from your blood and make urine ▪ a patient with a damaged *kidney* — often used before another noun ▪ *kidney* failure ▪ a *kidney* transplant — see picture at HUMAN
2 : an animal kidney used as food ▪ steak and *kidney* pie

kidney bean *noun, pl* **~ beans** [*count*] **:** a type of large and dark red bean

kidney stone *noun, pl* **~ stones** [*count*] *medical* **:** a hard object like a small stone that sometimes forms in a kidney and that can cause great pain

kid stuff *or* **kid's stuff** *noun* [*noncount*] *informal*
1 : something that is suited only for children ▪ toys and other *kid stuff*
2 : something that is very simple or easy ▪ It's time to cut out the *kid's stuff* and get down to business.

kike /ˈkaɪk/ *noun, pl* **kikes** [*count*] *informal + offensive* **:** a Jewish person ✧ The word *kike* is very offensive and should be avoided.

[1]**kill** /ˈkɪl/ *verb* **kills; killed; kill•ing**
1 : to cause the death of (a person, animal, or plant) : to end the life of (someone or something) [+ *obj*] This poison *kills* rats. ▪ The disease has *killed* thousands of people. ▪ Three people were *killed* in the accident. ▪ a chemical that *kills* weeds ▪ In despair he threatened to ***kill himself***. [=to commit suicide] ▪ If he keeps working this hard, he's going to *kill himself*. [=he's going to have health problems that cause his death] — often used figuratively ▪ My father will *kill* me [=he will be very angry] when he finds out that I dented the car. ▪ I'll finish this job ***if it kills me***! [=I am very determined to finish this job] ▪ ***It wouldn't kill you*** to help me clean up the kitchen. = ***Would it kill you*** to help me clean up the kitchen? [=you should help me clean up the kitchen] [*no obj*] Drunk driving *kills*. ▪ a disease that can *kill* ▪ I've never seen her so angry. ***If looks could kill***, I'd be dead right now. [=she looked at me in a very angry way] — often used figuratively ▪ I'd ***kill for*** hair like hers! [=I wish I had hair like hers]
2 [+ *obj*] **:** to cause the end of (something) ▪ If she enters the contest, it will *kill* [=*destroy*] our chances of winning. ▪ She took an aspirin to *kill* [=*stop*] her headache. ▪ taking drugs to *kill* the pain ▪ Despite protests, the mayor *killed* the program. ▪ The committee *killed* the bill. ▪ This delay has *killed* our chances of finishing the project on schedule. ▪ The editor decided to *kill* [=to not publish] the controversial news story.
3 [+ *obj*] *informal* **:** to turn (something) off with a switch ▪ She told him to *kill* the lights. ▪ He *killed* [=*shut off*] the engine and got out of the car.
4 [+ *obj*] *informal* **:** to spend (time) doing something while you are waiting ▪ We *killed* time by reading magazines. ▪ We have a couple of hours to *kill* before we board the plane.
5 [+ *obj*] *informal* **a :** to cause (someone) to feel extreme pain or to suffer ▪ My feet are *killing* me. [=my feet hurt very much] ▪ Working these long hours is *killing* me. **b :** to make (someone) nervous or unhappy ▪ I'm still waiting to hear if I got the job. The suspense is *killing* me. ▪ It really *kills* me to think of how much money I could have made if I had invested in that company.
6 [+ *obj*] *informal* **:** to amuse or entertain (someone) very much ▪ That guy *kills* me. [=I think he's very funny] ▪ His jokes always *kill* me. ▪ Her performance *killed* the audience. [=the audience loved her performance]
7 [+ *obj*] *informal* **:** to drink (something) completely ▪ He *killed* three beers in less than an hour.
dressed to kill see DRESSED
fit to kill see [1]FIT
kill off [*phrasal verb*] ***kill off (something) or kill (something) off*** **1 :** to kill all of (something) : to kill every one of (a group) ▪ Scientists aren't certain what *killed off* the dinosaurs. ▪ She *killed off* her relatives to get the inheritance. **2 :** to remove (something) completely : to get rid of (something) ▪ The company has become so successful that it has *killed off* the competition.
kill (someone) with kindness : to treat (someone) in a way that is too kind or helpful and that actually causes harm

kill the clock see [1]CLOCK

kill two birds with one stone : to achieve two things by doing a single action • We can *kill two birds with one stone* by dropping off the mail when we go the grocery store.

[2]**kill** *noun, pl* **kills** [*count*]

1 : an act of killing someone or something • The tiger has made several *kills* in this area. • The lion was ***moving in for the kill.*** [=was coming closer to another animal in order to kill it] — often used figuratively • Her political opponents believe that she can be defeated, and they are *moving in for the kill.*

2 : an animal that has been killed • The lion was devouring its *kill.* [=the animal that it had killed] — see also ROADKILL

[1]**kill·er** /ˈkɪlɚ/ *noun, pl* **-ers** [*count*]

1 : a person or thing that kills someone or something • The police finally captured the *killer.* [=*murderer*] • Heart disease is the leading *killer* of both men and women. • The chemical is used as a weed *killer.*

2 *informal* **:** something that is very difficult • That exam was a (real) *killer.* = That sure was a *killer* of an exam.

[2]**killer** *adj, always used before a noun, chiefly US*

1 : causing death or destruction • a *killer* tornado

2 *informal* **:** very impressive or appealing • She has a *killer* smile. [=a very attractive smile] • a *killer* résumé

3 *informal* **:** very difficult • a *killer* exam

killer app *noun, pl* **~ apps** [*count*] **:** an extremely valuable or useful computer program

killer bee *noun, pl* **~ bees** [*count*] **:** a dangerous type of bee that is originally from Africa

killer instinct *noun, pl* **~ -stincts** [*count*] **:** a very strong desire to succeed or win • Her *killer instincts* have helped her become one of the top tennis players in the world.

killer whale *noun, pl* **~ whales** [*count*] **:** a black-and-white whale that kills and eats other animals (such as seals) — called also *orca*

kill·ing /ˈkɪlɪŋ/ *noun, pl* **-ings** [*count*]

1 : an act of killing someone or something • The oil spill is responsible for the *killing* of thousands of birds. • A series of horrific *killings* [=*murders*] have made headlines across the nation. — see also MERCY KILLING

2 *informal* **:** a large amount of money — usually singular • He ***made a killing*** in the stock market.

kill·joy /ˈkɪlˌʤɔɪ/ *noun, pl* **-joys** [*count*] *disapproving* **:** a person who spoils other people's fun or enjoyment • I don't want to sound like a *killjoy*, but shouldn't we study tonight?

kiln /ˈkɪln/ *noun, pl* **kilns** [*count*] **:** an oven or furnace that is used for hardening, burning, or drying something (such as pottery)

ki·lo /ˈkiːloʊ/ *noun, pl* **-los** [*count*] **:** KILOGRAM

kilo- /ˈkɪlə/ *combining form* **:** thousand • *kilo*gram • *kilo*meter

ki·lo·byte /ˈkɪləˌbaɪt/ *noun, pl* **-bytes** [*count*] **:** a unit of computer information equal to 1,024 bytes — abbr. *KB*; compare GIGABYTE, MEGABYTE

ki·lo·gram /ˈkɪləˌgræm/ *noun, pl* **-grams** [*count*] **:** a unit of weight equal to 1,000 grams — abbr. *kg*

ki·lo·hertz /ˈkɪləˌhɚts/ *noun, pl* **-hertz** [*count*] *technical* **:** a unit of frequency equal to 1,000 hertz • a frequency of 80 *kilohertz* — abbr. *kHz*

kilo·li·ter (*US*) *or Brit* **ki·lo·li·tre** /ˈkɪləˌliːtɚ/ *noun, pl* **-ters** [*count*] **:** a unit for measuring the volume of a liquid or gas that is equal to 1,000 liters — abbr. *kl*

ki·lo·me·ter (*US*) *or Brit* **ki·lo·me·tre** /kəˈlɑːmətɚ, ˈkɪləˌmiːtɚ/ *noun, pl* **-ters** [*count*] **:** a unit of length equal to 1,000 meters — abbr. *km*

kilo·watt /ˈkɪləˌwɑːt/ *noun, pl* **-watts** [*count*] **:** a unit of electrical power equal to 1,000 watts — abbr. *kW*; compare MEGAWATT

kilowatt–hour *noun, pl* **-hours** [*count*] *technical* **:** a unit of work or energy equal to the amount produced by one kilowatt in one hour — abbr. *kWh*

kilt /ˈkɪlt/ *noun, pl* **kilts** [*count*]

1 : a type of skirt traditionally worn by men in Scotland — see color picture on page C16

2 : a woman's skirt that resembles a Scottish kilt

– kilt·ed /ˈkɪltəd/ *adj* • a *kilted* Scotsman

kil·ter /ˈkɪltɚ/ *noun*

out of kilter *or* ***off kilter*** — used to describe something that is not in the exactly right position or condition, is not working in the usual or proper way, etc. • Unexpected expenses threw the budget *out of kilter.* • Our schedule has been knocked *off kilter.* — see also OFF-KILTER

ki·mo·no /kəˈmoʊnoʊ/ *noun, pl* **-nos** [*count*] **:** a loose piece of clothing with wide sleeves that is traditionally worn on formal occasions in Japan — see color picture on page C16

kin /ˈkɪn/ *noun* [*plural*] *somewhat old-fashioned* **:** a person's relatives • They are her distant *kin.* • He and I are *kin.* [=we are related to each other] • Are you any ***kin to*** him? [=are you related to him?] • He's ***no kin to*** me. [=he is not related to me] — see also *next of kin* at [3]NEXT

kith and kin see KITH

[1]**kind** /ˈkaɪnd/ *noun, pl* **kinds** [*count*] **:** a group of people or things that belong together or have some shared quality **:** a particular type or variety of person or thing • hawks and other birds of that *kind* • "What *kind* of (a) car do you drive?" "The same *kind* you drive." • In this city, you'll find many *kinds* of people. • Most people prefer to be with their own *kind.* [=with people who are like them] • I like to try different *kinds* of food. • I know he would never lie to me because he's not that *kind* (of person). • She described the color as a *kind* of red. • I think he's an accountant, financial adviser, or something of that *kind.* • Did you honestly think that I'd agree to do this? What *kind* of fool do you think I am? [=do you think that I am a fool?] • Boston is ***my kind of*** (a) town. [=I like Boston]

all kinds of **1 :** a large number or variety of (things or people) **:** MANY • She reads *all kinds of* books. • He likes *all kinds of* sports. **2** *chiefly US, informal* **:** a large amount of (something) **:** plenty of (something) • There's no hurry. We have *all kinds of* time to get ready.

in kind **1 :** in a way that is equal or very similar to what someone else has done for you • If you help me, I promise to return the favor *in kind.* [=I promise to help you in the same way] **2** *business* **:** in goods or services rather than in money • payment *in kind* rather than in cash

kind of *informal* **:** to some small degree **:** SOMEWHAT • It's *kind of* cold in here. • I think he *kind of* likes me. • I'm *kind of* worried.

of a kind — used to say that people or things are the same or are very similar • John and his dad are ***two of a kind.*** [=they are very much alike]

of the kind **:** like the person or thing mentioned • I'd like to go to a movie or a concert, or ***something of the kind.*** [=something like that] — often used in negative statements • He said I hung up on him, but I never did ***anything of the kind.*** [=I never hung up on him] • This technology is completely new. I've never seen *anything of the kind* [=anything like it] before. • "He's really pretty arrogant, isn't he?" "He's ***nothing of the kind.*** [=he's not arrogant at all] He's a very friendly and helpful man." • This technology is completely new. *Nothing of the kind* [=nothing like it] has ever been seen before.

one of a kind **:** a person or thing that is not like any other person or thing • I don't know how we'll ever replace Mary after she retires. She's really *one of a kind.*

[2]**kind** *adj* **kind·er; -est**

1 : having or showing a gentle nature and a desire to help others **:** wanting and liking to do good things and to bring happiness to others • A *kind* old woman took the cat in and nursed it back to health. • It was very *kind* of you to show me the way. • Thank you for your *kind* words. • a *kind* smile — often + *to* • My uncle has always been very *kind to* me.

2 — used to say that something does not cause harm, is not harsh or unpleasant, etc.; usually + *to* • Old age has been very *kind to* her: she still looks great at 84. • a soap that is *kind to* your hands • The critics have not been *kind to* her latest novel. [=they have harshly criticized her latest novel]

3 — used to make a formal request • Would you ***be kind enough*** to show me the way? = Would you ***be so kind*** as to show me the way? [=would you please show me the way?]

kinda /ˈkaɪndə/ — used in writing to represent the sound of the phrase *kind of* when it is spoken quickly • It's *kinda* [=*kind of*] cold in here. [=it's somewhat cold in here] ✧ The pronunciation represented by *kinda* is common in informal speech. The written form should be avoided except when trying to represent or record such speech.

kin·der·gar·ten /ˈkɪndɚˌgɑɚtn̩/ *noun, pl* **-tens** [*count, noncount*] **:** a school or class for very young children ✧ In the U.S., children in kindergarten are usually about five years old. • My daughter is in *kindergarten* now; next fall she'll enter the first grade.

– kin·der·gart·ner /ˈkɪndɚˌgɑɚtnɚ/ *or* **kin·der·gar·ten·er** /ˈkɪndɚˌgɑɚtənɚ/ *noun, pl* **-gart·ners** *or* **-gar·ten·ers**

[count] US • All of the *kindergartners* [=children in kindergarten] drew pictures of their favorite animals.

kind·heart·ed /ˌkaɪndˈhɑɚtəd/ *adj* [*more* ~; *most* ~] : having or showing a kind and gentle nature • A *kindhearted* neighbor offered to help. • a *kindhearted* gesture
– **kind·heart·ed·ness** *noun* [*noncount*]

kin·dle /ˈkɪndl/ *verb* **kin·dles**; **kin·dled**; **kin·dling**
1 a [+ *obj*] : to cause (a fire) to start burning • using dry twigs to *kindle* a fire **b** [*no obj*] : to begin burning • waiting for the fire to *kindle*
2 [+ *obj*] : to cause the start of (something) • A trip to the museum when she was a child *kindled* her interest in art. • The incident *kindled* a new national debate.

kin·dling /ˈkɪndlɪŋ/ *noun* [*noncount*] : dry twigs, pieces of paper, etc., that burn easily and are used to start a fire • a pile of *kindling*

[1]**kind·ly** /ˈkaɪndli/ *adj* **kind·li·er**; **-est** [*also more* ~; *most* ~] : having or showing a gentle nature and a desire to help others : KIND • A *kindly* woman helped him find his way home. • a *kindly* smile
– **kind·li·ness** /ˈkaɪndlinəs/ *noun* [*noncount*]

[2]**kindly** *adv*
1 [*more* ~; *most* ~] : in a kind way • She always treats animals *kindly*. • They *kindly* offered to help us.
2 — used to make a formal request • Would you *kindly* [=*please*] pass the salt? — sometimes used in making a request that is caused by annoyance • Would you *kindly* turn down the music? I'm trying to read. • *Kindly* leave me alone.
look kindly on/upon : to approve of (something or someone) • Many people do not *look kindly on* the government's attempt to intervene in this matter. • He says that he will *look kindly on* any request you make.
take kindly to : to willingly accept or approve of (someone or something) — usually used in negative statements • He does not *take kindly to* criticism. [=he does not like to be criticized] • She does not *take kindly to* people who tell her what to do.

K

kind·ness /ˈkaɪndnəs/ *noun, pl* **-ness·es**
1 [*noncount*] : the quality or state of being kind • You should treat your elders with *kindness* and respect. = You should show *kindness* and respect to your elders. • They did it out of ***the kindness of their hearts***. [=they did it because they are kind people and not because they wanted something in return] — see also *the milk of human kindness* at [1]MILK
2 [*count*] : a kind act • We thanked her for her many *kindnesses*. • You would be doing me a great *kindness* if you agreed to help.
kill (someone) with kindness see [1]KILL

[1]**kin·dred** /ˈkɪndrəd/ *adj, always used before a noun, formal*
1 : alike or similar • philosophy, political theory, and *kindred* topics • I believe she and I are ***kindred spirits/souls***.
2 : closely related • *Kindred* tribes • German and English are *kindred* languages.

[2]**kindred** *noun* [*plural*] *old-fashioned* : a person's relatives • He went out to sea, and never saw his *kindred* again.

ki·net·ic /kəˈnɛtɪk/ *adj* : of or relating to the movement of physical objects • *kinetic* energy/theory • *kinetic* art [=art that has moving parts]

kin·folk /ˈkɪnˌfoʊk/ *noun* [*plural*] *old-fashioned* : a person's relatives : KIN • He settled in the North, but most of his *kinfolk* remained in the South.

king /ˈkɪŋ/ *noun, pl* **kings**
1 : a male ruler of a country who usually inherits his position and rules for life [*count*] dethrone a *king* • He pledged his loyalty to the *king* and queen. • the reign of *King* James [*noncount*] He was crowned *king*. • He became *king* at a young age.
2 a [*count*] : a boy or man who is highly respected and very successful or popular • an oil *king* • He's widely regarded as the *king* of soul music. **b** [*count*] : a boy or man who is awarded the highest honor for an event or contest • He was voted *king* of the prom. • the homecoming *king* **c** : something that is very powerful or that is considered better than all others [*count*] The lion is known as the *king* of the jungle. [*noncount*] It was a time when comedy was *king*. [=when comedy was the most important or popular form of entertainment]
3 [*count*] : the most important piece in the game of chess • She won the game by checkmating his *king*. — see picture at CHESS
4 [*count*] : a playing card that has a picture of a king and that is worth more than a queen • the *king* of hearts/spades/clubs/diamonds — see picture at PLAYING CARD
fit for a king see [1]FIT

king crab *noun, pl* ~ **crabs** [*count*] : a very large type of crab

king·dom /ˈkɪŋdəm/ *noun, pl* **-doms**
1 [*count*] : a country whose ruler is a king or queen • After Queen Mary I died, her half sister Elizabeth ruled the *kingdom*. • the *Kingdom* of Jordan — often used figuratively • He was one of the most successful planters in the cotton *kingdom*. • The office is his own private *kingdom*.
2 [*noncount*] : the spiritual world of which God is king • the *kingdom* of God/heaven
3 [*count*] : one of the three main divisions into which natural objects are classified • the animal/mineral/plant *kingdom*
to kingdom come *informal* : to a state of complete destruction • He took out his shotgun and threatened to blast/blow them all *to kingdom come*.

king·fish·er /ˈkɪŋˌfɪʃɚ/ *noun, pl* **-ers** [*count*] : a type of brightly colored bird that has a long, thin bill and that catches fish by diving into water

king·ly /ˈkɪŋli/ *adj* **king·li·er**; **-est**
1 : of or relating to a king • a symbol of *kingly* authority/power/rule
2 : typical of or suited for a king • a *kingly* feast • They paid a *kingly* price/fortune for their new house.

king·mak·er /ˈkɪŋˌmeɪkɚ/ *noun, pl* **-ers** [*count*] : a powerful person or group who influences decisions about who will become political candidates • the party's *kingmakers*

king·pin /ˈkɪŋˌpɪn/ *noun, pl* **-pins** [*count*] : a person who controls an organization or activity • *kingpins* of the movie industry • a mob *kingpin* [=a man who controls a gang of criminals] • a drug *kingpin* [=a man in charge of a large group of people who sell illegal drugs]

King's Counsel *noun, pl* ~ **-sels** [*count*] *Brit* : a barrister who is chosen to represent the British royal family in a court of law — used when Britain is ruled by a king; abbr. *KC*

king's evidence *noun*
turn king's evidence *Brit, law* — used with the same meaning as *turn queen's evidence* when Britain is ruled by a king; see QUEEN'S EVIDENCE

king·ship /ˈkɪŋˌʃɪp/ *noun* [*noncount*] : the position of a king • He has all the traits required for *kingship*.

king–size /ˈkɪŋˌsaɪz/ *or* **king–sized** /ˈkɪŋˌsaɪzd/ *adj*
1 : extremely large • a *king-size* sandwich • people with *king-sized* appetites
2 *US, of a bed* : having a size of 76 inches by 80 inches (about 1.9 by 2.0 meters) — compare FULL-SIZE, QUEEN-SIZE, TWIN-SIZE

king's ransom *noun* [*noncount*] *informal* : a very large amount of money • We paid a *king's ransom* for that car.

kink /ˈkɪŋk/ *noun, pl* **kinks** [*count*]
1 : a tight bend or curl in something (such as a rope or hose) — usually + *in* • There was a *kink in* the chain.
2 *chiefly US* : a pain especially in your neck or back that is caused by tight muscles — usually + *in* • I woke up on the bus with a *kink* [=*crick*] *in* my neck.
3 : a small problem or flaw — usually plural • We just installed a new computer program, and we're still ***working/ironing out the kinks***. [=trying to fix the problems]
4 : a strange or unusual part of someone's personality • Everyone's personality has a few *kinks*. [=*quirks*]
– **kink** *verb* **kinks**; **kinked**; **kink·ing** [+ *obj*] *Kink* the hose. [*no obj*] My hair *kinks* when it rains.

kinky /ˈkɪŋki/ *adj* **kink·i·er**; **-est**
1 *of hair* : having many tight bends or curls
2 *informal* : involving or liking unusual sexual behavior • *kinky* sex toys • a *kinky* fantasy • She says her boyfriend is a little *kinky*.
– **kink·i·ness** *noun* [*noncount*]

kins·folk /ˈkɪnzˌfoʊk/ *noun* [*plural*] *somewhat old-fashioned* : KINFOLK • returning home to her *kinsfolk*

kin·ship /ˈkɪnˌʃɪp/ *noun*
1 [*noncount*] : the state of being related to the people in your family • the bonds of *kinship*
2 : a feeling of being close or connected to other people [*singular*] He feels a strong *kinship* with other survivors of the war. [*noncount*] feelings of *kinship* between the team's players and their fans

kins·man /ˈkɪnzmən/ *noun, pl* **-men** /-mən/ [*count*] *formal* + *old-fashioned* : a male relative • honoring a dead *kinsman*

kins·wom·an /ˈkɪnzˌwʊmən/ *noun, pl* **-wom·en** /-ˌwɪmən/

[*count*] *formal + old-fashioned* : a female relative • writing a biography of his famous *kinswoman*

ki·osk /ˈkiːˌɑsk/ *noun, pl* **-osks** [*count*]
1 : a small store in a building or on the street where things (such as newspapers or candy) are sold • She sells souvenirs at a *kiosk* in the mall.
2 : a small structure that provides information and services on a computer screen • You can pick up your plane tickets at one of the airport's *kiosks*.

[1]**kip** /ˈkɪp/ *noun, Brit, informal* : [2]SLEEP [*noncount*] Try to get a bit of *kip*. [*singular*] She went home and had a *kip*. [=*nap*]

[2]**kip** *verb* **kips; kip·ped; kip·ping** [*no obj*] *Brit, informal* : [1]SLEEP • Can I *kip* here tonight? — often + *down* • We *kipped down* at a hotel.

kip·per /ˈkɪpɚ/ *noun, pl* **-pers** [*count*] *chiefly Brit* : a herring that has been preserved with salt and then smoked
– kip·pered /ˈkɪpɚd/ *adj* • a *kippered* herring

kirk /ˈkɚk/ *noun, pl* **kirks**
1 [*count*] *Scotland* : CHURCH
2 ***the Kirk*** : the national church of Scotland • an elder of *the Kirk*

kis·met /ˈkɪzˌmɛt/ *noun* [*noncount*] : a power that is believed to control what happens in the future : FATE • When we first met each other, we knew it must have been *kismet* (that brought us together).

[1]**kiss** /ˈkɪs/ *verb* **kiss·es; kissed; kiss·ing**
1 a : to touch (someone) with your lips as a greeting or as a way of showing love or sexual attraction [+ *obj*] He *kissed* her on the cheek. = He *kissed* her cheek. • They *kissed* each other passionately. • She *kissed* him good night/goodbye. [*no obj*] I'll never forget the night we first *kissed*. **b** [+ *obj*] : to touch (something) with your lips • When he got off the plane he knelt down and *kissed* the ground.
2 [+ *obj*] : to touch (something) gently or lightly • The tree's branches *kissed* the ground below.
kiss and make up *informal* : to become friendly again after a fight or disagreement • It's time for the mayor and the police chief to *kiss and make up*.
kiss and tell : to tell people about the private details of your romantic relationships • I never *kiss and tell*.
kiss ass *US, informal + impolite* **1** *or* ***kiss someone's ass*** *or Brit* ***kiss someone's arse*** : to be nice to people in order to make them like you or give something to you • He says he doesn't want a promotion if he has to *kiss ass* to get it. **2** ***kiss my ass*** — used to show that you are angry at someone • He told me to leave, and I told him he could *kiss my ass*!
kiss off [*phrasal verb*] *informal* **1** *impolite* — used in angry speech to tell someone to leave and stop bothering you • She told me to *kiss off* when I asked her to dance. **2** ***kiss (someone or something) off*** *or* ***kiss off (someone or something)*** : to reject or ignore (someone or something) in a casual or careless way • My boss *kissed off* my ideas for a new product. **3** ***kiss (something) off*** *or* ***kiss off (something)*** : to accept the fact that you have lost or will never get (something) • You can *kiss off* [=*give up on*] any hope of getting tickets to the game. — see also KISS-OFF
kiss (something) goodbye *informal* : to accept the fact that you have lost or will never get something • They can *kiss* their vacation plans *goodbye* now. [=their vacation plans are now ruined] • If you don't start working harder, you can *kiss* that promotion *goodbye*. [=you won't be getting that promotion]
kiss up to [*phrasal verb*] ***kiss up to (someone)*** *US, informal + disapproving* : to try to make (someone) like you • She is always *kissing up to* [=*sucking up to*] the boss.
– kiss·able /ˈkɪsəbəl/ *adj* [*more* ~; *most* ~] • soft, *kissable* lips

[2]**kiss** *noun, pl* **kisses** [*count*] : the act of kissing someone or something • He gave her a *kiss* on the cheek. • She greeted him with a hug and a *kiss*. • a tender/gentle/passionate *kiss* — see also FRENCH KISS
blow (someone) a kiss : to kiss the palm of your hand, put your hand flat in front of your mouth, and then blow on it toward (someone) • She *blew me a kiss* and waved goodbye.
throw (someone) a kiss : to kiss the palm of your hand and move your hand quickly away from your mouth in a waving motion toward (someone)

kiss–and–tell /ˈkɪsn̩dˈtɛl/ *adj, always used before a noun* : telling private details about romantic relationships • an actress who has written a *kiss-and-tell* book about the men she knew in her youth • a *kiss-and-tell* biography

kiss·er /ˈkɪsɚ/ *noun, pl* **-ers** [*count*]
1 : a person who kisses • He's a great *kisser*. [=he is very good at kissing]
2 *old-fashioned slang* : MOUTH • Punch him in the *kisser*.

kissing cousin *noun, pl* ~ **-ins** [*count*] *old-fashioned* : a person and especially a relative who you know well enough to kiss in a formal way when you meet — often used figuratively to describe two things that are similar or closely related • He says politics and show business are *kissing cousins*.

kiss of death *noun* [*singular*] : something that causes something to fail or be ruined — usually used with *the* • Bad reviews can be *the kiss of death* for a new movie.

kiss–off /ˈkɪsˌɑːf/ *noun, pl* **-offs** [*count*] *chiefly US, informal* : a quick and rude way of telling someone to go away • The song is a *kiss-off* to his ex-girlfriend. — see also *kiss off* at [1]KISS

kiss of life *noun*
the kiss of life *Brit* : MOUTH-TO-MOUTH RESUSCITATION

[1]**kit** /ˈkɪt/ *noun, pl* **kits**
1 [*count*] : a set of tools or supplies that a person uses for a particular purpose or activity • a makeup *kit* • shaving/sewing *kits* • an electrician's tool *kit* — see also DRUM KIT
2 [*count*] : a set of parts that are put together to build something • He built the shed from a *kit*. • We bought some goldfish and an aquarium ***starter kit***. [=a set of things needed to set up an aquarium]
3 [*count*] : a collection of written materials about a particular subject • a tourist information *kit* — see also PRESS KIT
4 [*noncount*] *Brit* : clothing or equipment used for a particular purpose • The team wore their new *kit*. • cricket/football/sports *kit*
first aid kit see FIRST AID
get/take your kit off *Brit, informal* : to take off your clothes • She agreed to *get her kit off* for the photos.
the whole (kit and) caboodle see CABOODLE

[2]**kit** *verb* **kits; kit·ted; kit·ting**
kit out/up [*phrasal verb*] ***kit out/up (someone or something)*** *or* ***kit (someone or something) out/up*** *Brit* : to give (someone or something) the clothing or equipment needed for a particular activity — usually used as *(be) kitted out/up* • The team *was kitted out* in new uniforms. • The room *was kitted out* with balloons and decorations for the party.

kitch·en /ˈkɪʧən/ *noun, pl* **-ens** [*count*] : a room in which food is cooked • She wants a house with a large *kitchen*. — often used before another noun • *kitchen* counters/cabinets/chairs • They sat down at the *kitchen* table. • When he goes on vacation he takes along ***everything but the kitchen sink***. [=an extremely large number of things] — see picture on next page; see also SOUP KITCHEN

kitch·en·ette /ˌkɪʧəˈnɛt/ *noun, pl* **-ettes** [*count*] : a small kitchen or a part of a room where food is cooked • a hotel room with a *kitchenette*

kitchen garden *noun, pl* ~ **-dens** [*count*] *chiefly Brit* : a garden where you grow fruits and vegetables for your own use

kitchen paper *noun* [*noncount*] *Brit* : soft paper that is used for cleaning, wiping up liquid, etc. • a roll of *kitchen paper* [=(US) *paper towels*] — called also *(Brit) kitchen roll, (Brit) kitchen towel*

kite /ˈkaɪt/ *noun, pl* **kites** [*count*]
1 : a toy that is made of a light frame covered with cloth, paper, or plastic and that is flown in the air at the end of a long string • The children were flying *kites*.
2 : a type of hawk that has long, narrow wings
as high as a kite *informal* : greatly affected by alcohol or drugs : very drunk or intoxicated • The driver was *as high as a kite*.
go fly a kite *US, informal + old-fashioned* — used to tell someone who is bothering you to go away • When I asked her what was wrong, she told me to *go fly a kite*.

kith /ˈkɪθ/ *noun*
kith and kin *old-fashioned* : friends and relatives • They invited all their *kith and kin* to their new home.

kitsch /ˈkɪʧ/ *noun* [*noncount*] : things (such as movies or works of art) that are of low quality and that many people find amusing and enjoyable • The restaurant is decorated with 1950s furniture and *kitsch* from old TV shows.
– kitschy /ˈkɪʧi/ *adj* **kitsch·i·er; -est** • *kitschy* horror films

kit·ten /ˈkɪtn̩/ *noun, pl* **-tens** [*count*] : a young cat
have kittens *Brit, informal* : to become very nervous or upset about something • They *had kittens* when they saw the mess we made.

K

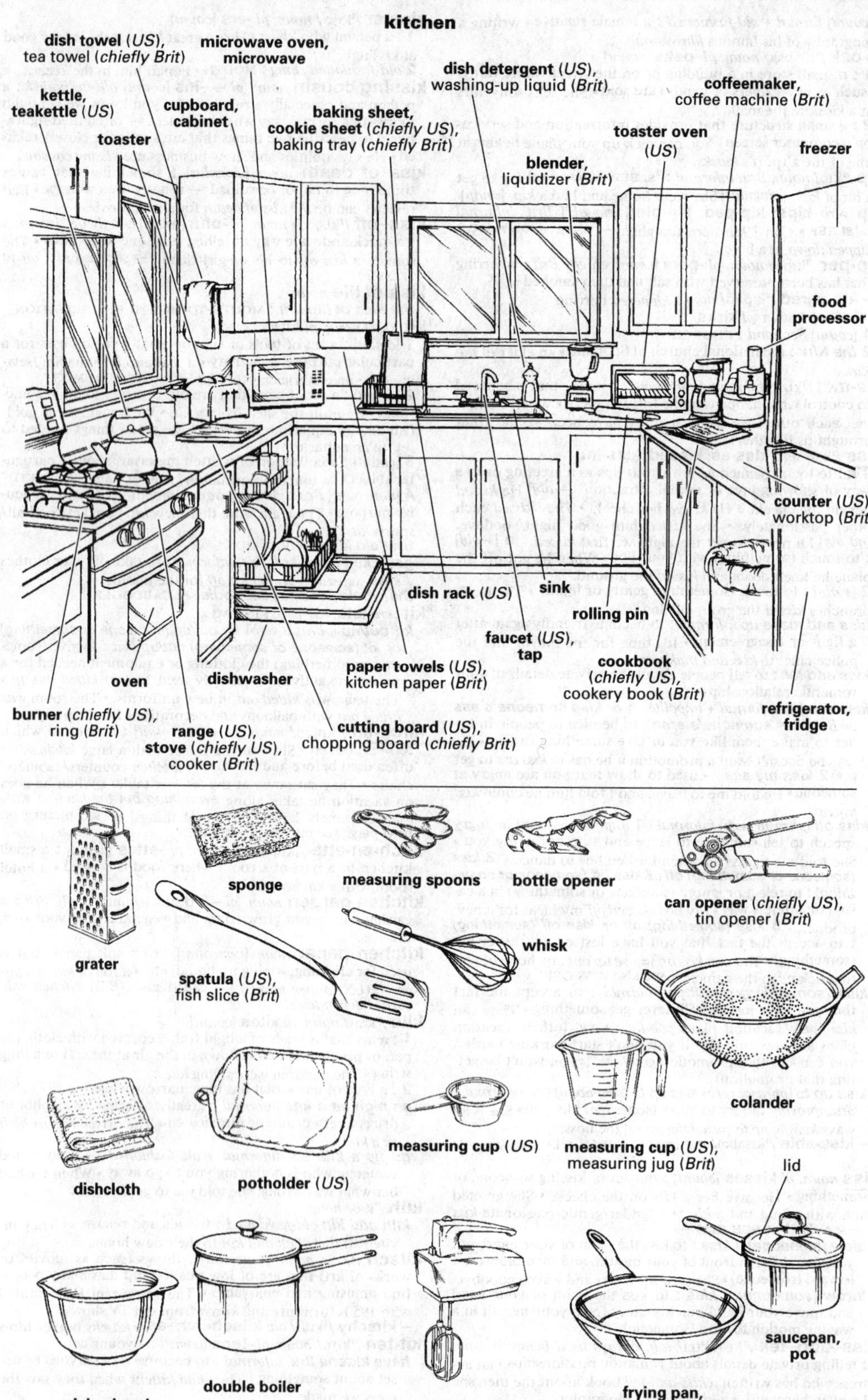
kitchen
dish towel (US), tea towel (chiefly Brit)
microwave oven, microwave
kettle, teakettle (US)
cupboard, cabinet
toaster
baking sheet, cookie sheet (chiefly US), baking tray (chiefly Brit)
dish detergent (US), washing-up liquid (Brit)
coffeemaker, coffee machine (Brit)
toaster oven (US)
blender, liquidizer (Brit)
freezer
food processor
counter (US), worktop (Brit)
dish rack (US)
sink
rolling pin
faucet (US), tap
cookbook (chiefly US), cookery book (Brit)
refrigerator, fridge
oven
dishwasher
paper towels (US), kitchen paper (Brit)
burner (chiefly US), ring (Brit)
range (US), stove (chiefly US), cooker (Brit)
cutting board (US), chopping board (chiefly Brit)
grater
sponge
measuring spoons
bottle opener
can opener (chiefly US), tin opener (Brit)
whisk
spatula (US), fish slice (Brit)
colander
dishcloth
potholder (US)
measuring cup (US)
measuring cup (US), measuring jug (Brit)
lid
saucepan, pot
mixing bowl
double boiler
mixer
frying pan, skillet (chiefly US)

kit•ten•ish /ˈkɪtn̩ɪʃ/ *adj [more ~; most ~]* **:** cute and playful in a way that attracts attention ▪ *kittenish* young women

kit•ty /ˈkɪti/ *noun, pl* **-ties** *[count]*
1 *informal* **:** a cat or kitten ▪ Come here, *kitty, kitty*.
2 : the amount of money that can be won in a card game and that is made up of all the bets added together
3 : an amount of money that has been collected from many people for some purpose ▪ She had a $10 million *kitty* for her campaign.

kit•ty–cor•ner /ˈkɪti,koɚnɚ/ *adv, US* — used to describe two things that are located across from each other on opposite corners ▪ The store is *kitty-corner* from the park.

ki•wi /ˈkiː,wiː/ *noun, pl* **-wis** *[count]*
1 *Kiwi informal* **:** a person who lives in or is from New Zealand
2 : a bird from New Zealand that cannot fly and that has a long bill
3 : KIWIFRUIT

ki•wi•fruit /ˈkiː,wiː,fruːt/ *noun, pl* **kiwifruit** *or* **kiwifruits** *[count, noncount]* **:** a small fruit that has green flesh, black seeds, and brown, hairy skin — see color picture on page C5

KJV *abbr* King James Version ✧ The King James Version is the version of the Christian Bible that is used for quotations in this dictionary.

KKK *abbr* Ku Klux Klan

kl *abbr* kiloliter

Klan /ˈklæn/ *noun*
the Klan **:** KU KLUX KLAN ▪ a member of *the Klan* ▪ a *Klan* rally

Klans•man /ˈklænzmən/ *noun, pl* **Klans•men** *[count]* **:** a member of the Ku Klux Klan

Klee•nex /ˈkliː,nɛks/ *trademark* — used for a paper tissue (sense 1)

klep•to•ma•nia /,klɛptəˈmeɪnijə/ *noun [noncount]* **:** a mental illness in which you have a strong desire to steal things
– klep•to•ma•ni•ac /,klɛptəˈmeɪni,æk/ *noun, pl* **-acs** *[count]*

kludge *or* **kluge** /ˈkluːʤ/ *noun, pl* **kludg•es** *or* **klug•es** *[count]* **:** an awkward or inferior computer system or program that is created quickly to solve a problem
– kludgy *also* **kludgey** /ˈkluːʤi/ *adj* **kludg•i•er; -est** ▪ a *kludgy* computer system

klutz /ˈklʌts/ *noun, pl* **klutz•es** *[count] chiefly US, informal* **:** a person who often drops things, falls down, etc. **:** a clumsy person ▪ I'm a complete *klutz* on the dance floor.
– klutzy /ˈklʌtsi/ *adj* **klutz•i•er; -est**

km *abbr* kilometer

knack /ˈnæk/ *noun [singular]* **:** an ability, talent, or special skill needed to do something — usually + *for* or *of* ▪ They have a *knack for* telling interesting stories. ▪ Once you get the *knack of* riding a bicycle [=once you learn how to ride a bicycle], you'll never lose it.

knack•ered /ˈnækɚd/ *adj [more ~; most ~] Brit, informal* **:** very tired or exhausted ▪ She was too *knackered* to join them for dinner.

knap•sack /ˈnæp,sæk/ *noun, pl* **-sacks** *[count] chiefly US* **:** BACKPACK

knave /ˈneɪv/ *noun, pl* **knaves** *[count] old-fashioned*
1 : a dishonest man ▪ fools and *knaves*
2 : a playing card that ranks below a queen and above a 10 **:** JACK ▪ the *knave* of hearts
– knav•ish /ˈneɪvɪʃ/ *adj [more ~; most ~]* ▪ a *knavish* trick

knead /ˈniːd/ *verb* **kneads; knead•ed; knead•ing** *[+ obj]*
1 : to prepare (dough) by pressing a mixture of flour, water, etc., with your hands ▪ *Knead* the dough until it is smooth.
2 : to press and squeeze (a person's muscles) with your hands ▪ He *kneaded* [=*massaged*] the muscles in my neck.

[1]**knee** /ˈniː/ *noun, pl* **knees** *[count]*
1 : the joint that bends at the middle of your leg ▪ I fell down and hurt my *knee*. ▪ She suffered a serious *knee* injury. ▪ His *knees* trembled/shook with fear. ▪ She ***dropped/fell/sank to her knees*** [=she knelt down] and begged for forgiveness. = She ***got down on her knees*** and begged for forgiveness. ▪ He ***got/went down on one knee*** and proposed to her. ▪ If you want to clean the floor properly, you have to ***get down on your (hands and) knees*** [=you have to kneel down on the floor] and start scrubbing. — see picture at HUMAN
2 : the upper part of your leg when you are sitting ▪ His little granddaughter sat ***on his knee***.
3 : the part that covers the knee on a pair of pants ▪ Her jeans had holes at the *knees*.
4 : a forceful hit with a bent knee ▪ She gave him a *knee* to the stomach. [=she kneed him in the stomach]
bring (someone) to his/her knees **:** to completely defeat or overwhelm (someone) ▪ The general vowed he would *bring* the enemy *to their knees*. — often used figuratively ▪ The increase in oil prices could *bring* the economy *to its knees*. [=it could greatly hurt the economy]
learn (something) at your mother's knee **:** to learn (something) when you are very young ▪ I learned to speak French *at my mother's knee*.
on bended knee/knees see [1]BEND
weak at/in the knees see WEAK
– see also BEE'S KNEES

[2]**knee** *verb* **knees; kneed; knee•ing** *[+ obj]* **:** to hit (a person) with your knee ▪ His attacker *kneed* him in the stomach.

[1]**knee•cap** /ˈniː,kæp/ *noun, pl* **-caps** *[count]* **:** a flat bone on the front of your knee — called also *patella*; see picture at HUMAN

[2]**kneecap** *verb* **-caps; -capped; -cap•ping** *[+ obj]* **:** to shoot or break the knee of (someone) as a form of attack or punishment ▪ They *kneecapped* one of the hostages.

knee–deep /ˈniːˈdiːp/ *adj*
1 : reaching as high as your knees ▪ The car was stuck in *knee-deep* snow.
2 : standing in something that reaches your knees — usually + *in* ▪ We were *knee-deep in* snow. — often used figuratively ▪ We were *knee-deep in* work. [=we were very busy]
– knee–deep *adv* ▪ We stood *knee-deep* in snow.

knee–high /ˈniːˈhaɪ/ *adj* **:** reaching as high as your knees ▪ *knee-high* boots ▪ The grass is *knee-high*. ▪ *(informal)* I haven't seen you since you were ***knee-high to a grasshopper***. [=since you were very young and small]

knee–jerk /ˈniː,ʤɚk/ *adj, always used before a noun [more ~; most ~]*
1 : occurring quickly and without thought ▪ It was a *knee-jerk* [=*automatic*] reaction.
2 *disapproving* **:** often reacting quickly and without thought ▪ He said that they were just a bunch of *knee-jerk* liberals.

kneel /ˈniːl/ *verb* **kneels; knelt** /ˈnɛlt/ *also chiefly US* **kneeled; kneel•ing** *[no obj]* **:** to move your body so that one or both of your knees are on the floor ▪ The prisoner was ordered to *kneel* (down) before the king. **:** to be in a position in which both of your knees are on the floor ▪ She was *kneeling* on the floor beside her child. ▪ He was *kneeling* in front of the altar and praying. — see picture at POSITION

knee–length /ˈniː,lɛŋkθ/ *adj, of clothing* **:** reaching the knees ▪ a *knee-length* skirt ▪ *knee-length* socks

knee–slap•per /ˈniː,slæpɚ/ *noun, pl* **-pers** *[count] US, informal* **:** a very funny joke or story ▪ That's a real *knee-slapper*.

knee sock *noun, pl* **~ socks** *[count] chiefly US* **:** a sock that reaches your knee — see color picture on page C13

knees–up /ˈniːz,ʌp/ *noun, pl* **-ups** *[count] Brit, informal* **:** a noisy party usually with dancing ▪ We had a *knees-up* to celebrate his retirement.

knell /ˈnɛl/ *noun, pl* **knells** *[count] literary* **:** a sound of a bell when it is rung slowly because someone has died ✧ A ***death knell*** is a sign or indication that something will fail or end soon. ▪ The mistake was the *death knell* for his campaign. ▪ Many people thought that the Internet would ***sound/ring/toll the death knell*** for newspapers. [=cause the end of newspapers]

knelt *past tense and past participle of* KNEEL

knew *past tense of* [1]KNOW

knick•er•bock•ers /ˈnɪkɚ,bɑːkɚz/ *noun [plural] Brit* **:** KNICKERS 1

knick•ers /ˈnɪkɚz/ *noun [plural]*
1 *US* **:** loose-fitting pants that reach just below the knee — called also *(Brit) knickerbockers*
2 *Brit* **:** PANTIES
get your knickers in a twist *Brit, informal* **:** to become upset about something that is not very important ▪ Don't *get your knickers in a twist*: I'll be ready in a minute!

knick•knack /ˈnɪk,næk/ *noun, pl* **-knacks** *[count]* **:** a small object used for decoration ▪ The shelves were filled with *knickknacks*.

[1]**knife** /ˈnaɪf/ *noun, pl* **knives** /ˈnaɪvz/ *[count]* **:** a usually sharp blade attached to a handle that is used for cutting or as a weapon ▪ Each dinner guest gets two forks, a *knife*, and a spoon. ▪ He pulled/drew a *knife* on me and threatened to stab me with it. — see picture at PLACE SETTING; see also BUT-

TER KNIFE, CARVING KNIFE, PALETTE KNIFE, PARING KNIFE, STEAK KNIFE, UTILITY KNIFE

like a (hot) knife through butter *informal* : very quickly and easily • The bill passed through the senate *like a hot knife through butter.*

the knives are out (for someone) — used to say that people are ready to blame or punish someone for something often in a way that is unfair • They lost yet another important game, and now the *knives are out* for their coach.

twist/turn the knife (in the wound) *informal* : to say or do things that cause more pain to someone who is already suffering • Any more cuts in government aid to these poor people will be *twisting the knife in the wound.*

under the knife *informal* : having a medical operation • I'm ***going under the knife*** [=having surgery] tomorrow.

²knife *verb* **knifes; knifed; knif·ing**
1 [+ *obj*] : to injure (someone) with a knife • He died after being *knifed* in the chest.
2 [*no obj*] : to move easily and quickly like a knife cutting through something • ships *knifing* through the waves

knife–edge /ˈnaɪfˌɛʤ/ *noun* [*singular*] : something that is very narrow or sharp • The path was a *knife-edge* on the side of a steep hill.

on a/the knife-edge : in a dangerous or important situation in which two very different results are possible • a region resting *on a knife-edge* after several wars • The election results hung *on a knife-edge.* • living *on the knife-edge* of poverty

knife·point /ˈnaɪfˌpoɪnt/ *noun*

at knifepoint — used to describe a situation in which someone is being threatened by a person with a knife • They were robbed *at knifepoint.* [=someone robbed them while threatening them with a knife]

¹knight /ˈnaɪt/ *noun, pl* **knights** [*count*]
1 : a soldier in the past who had a high social rank and who fought while riding a horse and usually wearing armor
2 : a man who is given a special honor and the title of *Sir* by the king or queen of England • He was made/dubbed a *knight.*
3 : a chess piece shaped like a horse's head — see picture at CHESS

knight in shining armor **1** : a man who behaves in a very brave way • The firefighter who rescued us was our *knight in shining armor.* **2** : a man who is the perfect romantic partner for a woman • She is still waiting for her *knight in shining armor.*

— see also WHITE KNIGHT

— **knight·ly** /ˈnaɪtli/ *adj* [*more* ~; *most* ~] • *knightly* adventures/quests

²knight *verb* **knights; knight·ed; knight·ing** [+ *obj*] : to give (a man) the rank of a knight • He is to be *knighted* by the Queen for his career as an actor.

knight–er·rant /ˈnaɪtˈerənt/ *noun, pl* **knights–errant** [*count*] : a knight who traveled in search of adventures in the Middle Ages

knight·hood /ˈnaɪtˌhʊd/ *noun, pl* **-hoods** : the rank or title of a knight [*count*] The Queen awarded a *knighthood* to the famous actor. [*noncount*] For their bravery, they were rewarded with *knighthood.*

¹knit /ˈnɪt/ *verb* **knits; knit** *or* **knit·ted; knit·ting**
1 : to make (a piece of clothing) from yarn or thread by using long needles or a special machine [+ *obj*] She *knit* a sweater for me. = She *knit/knitted* me a sweater. [*no obj*] He likes to *knit.*
2 [+ *obj*] **a** : to closely join or combine (things or people) • Her novels *knit* (together) science and fantasy. • a style that *knits* together material from many different sources **b** : to form (something) by bringing people or things together • a town *knit/knitted* together by farming — see also CLOSE-KNIT, TIGHT-KNIT
3 [*no obj*] *of a bone* : to grow together and heal after being broken • It will take some time for the broken bones to *knit (together).*

knit your brow/brows : to move your eyebrows together in a way that shows that you are thinking about something or are worried, angry, etc. • She *knit her brow* and asked what I was doing.

— **knit** *or* **knitted** *adj* • a red *knit* shirt • a *knitted* blouse • closely *knit* communities [=communities in which people care about each other very much] • a *knitted* cap — **knit·ter** *noun, pl* **-ters** [*count*] • She is a very talented *knitter.*

²knit *noun, pl* **knits** [*count*] : a piece of clothing that has been made by knitting • cotton *knits*

knitting *noun*
1 [*noncount*] : the action or process of knitting clothing • She enjoys *knitting.*
2 [*singular*] : materials that are being used by someone who is knitting • She keeps her *knitting* in the closet.

knitting needle *noun, pl* ~ **needles** [*count*] : one of two or more long, thin, usually metal or plastic sticks that are pointed at one end and used for knitting — see picture at SEWING

knit·wear /ˈnɪtˌweɚ/ *noun* [*noncount*] : knitted clothing • a few pieces of *knitwear*

knives *plural of* ¹KNIFE

knob /ˈnɑːb/ *noun, pl* **knobs** [*count*]
1 : a round switch on a television, radio, etc. • The left *knob* [=*dial*] controls the volume.
2 : a round handle on a door, drawer, etc. • The *knob* [=*doorknob*] is stuck and I can't open the door! • a carved walking stick with a silver *knob*
3 *chiefly Brit* : a small lump or piece of something • a *knob* of butter/coal
4 *Brit, informal + impolite* : PENIS

with knobs on *Brit, informal* : with extra things added • The movie is just an ordinary thriller *with knobs on.*

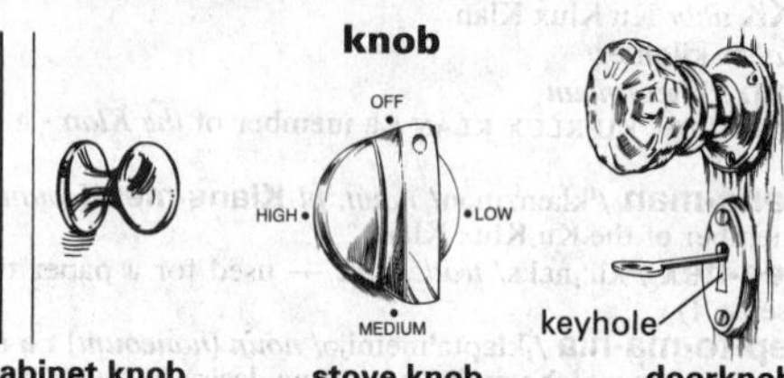

knob·bly /ˈnɑːbli/ *adj* **knob·bli·er; -est** *chiefly Brit* : KNOBBY • a *knobbly* mattress • *knobbly* knees

knob·by /ˈnɑːbi/ *adj* **knob·bi·er; -est** *chiefly US*
1 : covered with small bumps • *knobby* tires • a *knobby* mattress
2 : forming hard rounded lumps • *knobby* knees

¹knock /ˈnɑːk/ *verb* **knocks; knocked; knock·ing**
1 [*no obj*] : to hit something (such as a door) with the knuckles of your hand or with a hard object (such as a knocker) in order to get people's attention • I heard someone *knocking* (at the door). — usually + *on* • I *knocked on* the door but no one answered. • He *knocked on* the table to call the meeting to order. • Campaign workers have been ***knocking on doors*** throughout the neighborhood. [=have been going to each house or apartment in the neighborhood to talk with the people who live there] — sometimes used figuratively • a talented young singer who is ***knocking on the door of*** success [=who is very close to achieving success]
2 *always followed by an adverb, adjective, or preposition* [+ *obj*] : to hit (something or someone) in a forceful way • The ball *knocked* him on the chin. • *knock* one stick against another = *knock* two sticks together • She *knocked* the glass from his hand. • He *knocked* the baseball over the fence. • The ball hit him in the mouth and *knocked* out one of his teeth. • The wind *knocked* him backwards. • The wind almost *knocked* him off his feet. = The wind almost *knocked* him to the ground. [=the wind hit him so hard that he almost fell to the ground] • The collision *knocked* him unconscious/senseless. [=caused him to become unconscious] • The collision ***knocked him flying.*** [=sent him flying through the air]
3 *always followed by an adverb or preposition* : to touch or hit someone or something in a way that is not planned or intended [*no obj*] The dog *knocked* against the lamp. • My knee accidentally *knocked* against the table. • Skaters were *knocking* into each other all over the ice. • I kept *knocking* against him during the bumpy ride. = He and I kept *knocking* together during the bumpy ride. [+ *obj*] I accidentally *knocked* my knee against the table.
4 [+ *obj*] : to make (something, such as a hole) by hitting something • He used a hammer to *knock* a hole in the wall.
5 [+ *obj*] *informal* : to criticize (someone or something) • He's always *knocking* the government. • ***Don't knock it until you've tried it.*** [=wait until you try something before criticizing it]
6 [*no obj*] : to produce a repeated loud noise • The engine was *knocking.* • The pipes were *knocking.*

heart is knocking informal ✧ If your *heart is knocking* it is beating very hard, usually because you are nervous or excited. ▪ His *heart was knocking* in his chest.

knees are knocking informal ✧ If your *knees are knocking* they are shaking because you are nervous or afraid. ▪ Her *knees were knocking* in terror.

knock around** also Brit **knock about** [phrasal verb] informal* **1 a** ***knock around/about (a place) or knock around/about : to spend time in (a place) without having a goal or purpose : to wander around (a place) ▪ He spent the summer *knocking around* (in) Europe. **b** ***knock around/about with (someone) Brit*** : to spend time with (another person) ▪ She was *knocking around* [=*hanging around*] *with* her brother. **2 a** : to be considered or discussed in an informal way over a period of time ▪ These ideas have been *knocking around* [=*kicking around*] for years. **b** ***knock around (something) or knock (something) around*** : to consider or talk about (ideas, plans, etc.) in an informal way ▪ We *knocked* the plan *around* for a while before we came to an agreement. ▪ They *knocked around* several possible names for the new car. **3** ***knock (someone) around/about*** : to beat or hit (someone) badly or repeatedly ▪ The boy was getting *knocked around* by bullies. — often used figuratively ▪ I really got *knocked around* at the last staff meeting. **4** *chiefly Brit* : to be lying somewhere within a general area or place ▪ That jacket is *knocking about/around* here somewhere.

knock back informal **1** ***knock (something) back or knock back (something)*** : to drink or swallow (an alcoholic drink) quickly ▪ He stopped at a bar after work to *knock back* a few beers. **2** ***knock (someone) back*** : to cost (someone) a lot of money ▪ That car must have *knocked* you *back* quite a bit. [=you must have spent a lot of money on that car]

knock down** [phrasal verb]* **1** ***knock (someone or something) down or knock down (someone or something) **a** : to cause (someone or something) to fall to the ground ▪ He hit him on the chin and *knocked* him *down*. ▪ The storm *knocked down* [=*knocked over*] several big trees. ▪ Rowdy fans *knocked down* the fence. ▪ We're planning to *knock down* [=*remove, demolish*] a wall to create a bigger room. **b** *Brit* : to hit and injure or kill (a person or animal) with a vehicle ▪ She was *knocked down* [=*(Brit) knocked over*, *(US) hit*] by a car while crossing the street. **2** *informal* **a** ***knock (something) down or knock down (something)*** : to reduce or lower (a price, an amount, etc.) ▪ They *knocked down* the price of the house by 10 percent. ▪ He wanted $50 for it but I managed to *knock* the price *down* to $45. **b** ***knock (someone) down*** : to cause or persuade (someone) to reduce a price ▪ He wanted $50 for it but I managed to *knock* him *down* to $45. **3** ***knock down (an amount of money) US, informal*** : to receive (an amount of money) as income or salary ▪ He *knocks down* almost a million dollars a year. **4** ***knock down (a shot) or knock (a shot) down basketball*** : to succeed in making (a shot) especially from a long distance ▪ He was *knocking down* jump shots. **5** ***knock (something) down or knock down (something) chiefly US, informal*** : to say no to (an idea, plan, proposal, etc.) : REJECT ▪ His boss *knocked down* [=*shot down*] all of his ideas. **6** ***knock (something) down or knock down (something) US*** : to take (something) apart ▪ We *knocked* the bed *down* so it would fit in the truck.

knock heads US, informal **1** : to argue or disagree ▪ The two of them *knocked heads* soon after they started working together. **2** : to use angry or forceful methods to control or punish people ▪ I am going in there and *knock* some *heads* if they don't start behaving. — often + *together* ▪ I am going to go in there and *knock* their *heads together* if they don't start behaving.

knock in** [phrasal verb]* ***knock (a run or runner) in or knock in (a run or runner) baseball : to cause (a run or runner) to score ▪ He *knocked in* [=*batted in, drove in*] a run in the second inning with a double to left field.

knock off** [phrasal verb] informal* **1** ***knock off or knock (something) off or knock off (something) : to stop doing something (such as work) ▪ We are going to *knock off* for lunch in 10 minutes. ▪ The boss said we could *knock off* early today. = The boss said we could ***knock off work*** early today. — often used as a command to tell someone to stop doing something immediately ▪ *Knock off* your fighting right now! ▪ I told you two kids to ***knock it off***! **2** ***knock (something) off or knock off (something)*** **a** : to do or make (something) very quickly ▪ He *knocked off* 10 paintings in 4 days. ▪ We are planning to *knock* this project *off* in a weekend. **b** : to take (an amount) away from something ▪ He agreed to *knock off* 10 dollars from the price. [=to reduce the price by 10 dollars] ▪ This shortcut will *knock* at least 100 miles *off* the journey. **c** *US* : to steal money or things from (a bank or store) ▪ They *knocked off* [=*knocked over*] a jewelry store. **d** *chiefly Brit* : to steal (something) ▪ They *knocked off* a lot of valuable merchandise. **e** *US* : to make a cheaper copy of (something) ▪ Several other companies *knocked off* their dress design. — see also KNOCKOFF **3** ***knock (someone) off or knock off (someone)*** **a** : to kill (someone) ▪ He tried to *knock off* two men who owed him money. ▪ Did she really want to *knock* her husband *off*? **b** *US* : to defeat (someone) ▪ They *knocked off* the best team in the league.

knock on wood see [1]WOOD

knock out** [phrasal verb]* **1** ***knock (someone or something) out or knock out (someone or something) **a** : to make (a person or animal) unconscious ▪ The drug *knocked* him *out*. ▪ The force of the collision *knocked* him *out*. [=*knocked* him *cold*] ▪ He hit his head against the table when he fell and ***knocked himself out***. **b** *boxing* : to defeat (an opponent) with a punch that knocks the opponent down for a certain amount of time ▪ He was *knocked out* in the third round. — see also [1]KNOCKOUT 1 **c** : to defeat (an opponent) in a competition so that the opponent cannot continue ▪ My team was the favorite to win the championship, but we were *knocked out* (of the competition) in the third round. **d** *baseball* : to cause (a pitcher) to be removed from the game by getting many hits ▪ The starting pitcher was *knocked out* (of the game) in the fourth inning. **2** ***knock (something) out or knock out (something)*** **a** : to cause (something) to stop working ▪ Missiles *knocked out* the television station. ▪ The storm *knocked out* electricity across the state. **b** : to produce (something) very quickly ▪ a musical group that just keeps *knocking out* hit records **3** ***knock (yourself) out informal*** **a** : to make (yourself) very tired by doing work ▪ They *knocked* themselves *out* trying to build a garage. ▪ I *knocked* myself *out* [=I worked very hard] to get the job done on time. **b** *US* — used to tell someone to go ahead and do something ▪ "Do you mind if I use this exercise machine first?" "*Knock yourself out*." **4** ***knock (someone) out informal*** : to make a very strong and good impression on (someone) ▪ Her beauty just *knocks* me *out*. [=I think she is very beautiful] ▪ Everyone was *knocked out* by his suggestion. [=everyone liked his suggestion very much] — see also [1]KNOCKOUT 2

knock over** [phrasal verb]* **1** ***knock (someone or something) over or knock over (someone or something) **a** : to cause (someone or something) to fall to the ground ▪ The dog *knocked over* the lamp. ▪ The wind was so strong that it almost *knocked* her *over*. [=knocked her down] **b** *Brit* : to hit and injure or kill (a person or animal) with a vehicle ▪ The dog was *knocked over* [=*(Brit) knocked down*, *(US) hit*] by a car. **2** ***knock (someone) over or knock over (someone) informal*** : to greatly surprise or shock (someone) ▪ He was *knocked over* [=*overwhelmed*] by the news. ▪ When I found out I had won, ***you could have knocked me over with a feather***. [=I was extremely surprised or astonished] **3** ***knock (something) over or knock over (something) US, informal*** **a** : to steal money or things from (a bank or store) ▪ Three men *knocked over* [=*knocked off*] a bank. **b** : to steal (something) ▪ They *knocked over* a truckload of goods.

knock (someone) cold : to cause (someone) to become unconscious ▪ He *knocked* his opponent *cold* with one punch. ▪ She was *knocked cold* [=*knocked out*] by the collision.

knock (someone) dead informal : to make a very strong and good impression on (someone) ▪ Her performance really *knocked* the audience *dead*. [=the audience greatly enjoyed her performance] ▪ She told him to go out there on the stage and ***knock 'em dead***.

knock (someone) for a loop see [1]LOOP

knock (someone) for six see SIX

knock someone's head/block off informal : to hit someone very hard ▪ I'm so angry I'd like to *knock his block off*.

knock (someone) sideways Brit : to upset, confuse, or shock (someone) very much ▪ The news about his mother's accident really *knocked him sideways*.

knock some sense into see [1]SENSE

knock (something) on the head Brit, informal : to cause the end or failure of (something) ▪ The closing of the airport *knocked* our holiday plans *on the head*.

knock spots off see [1]SPOT
knock the (living) daylights out of see DAYLIGHT
knock the stuffing out of see STUFFING
knock together [*phrasal verb*] ***knock (something) together** or **knock together (something)*** : to make or build (something) in a quick or careless way • a rough table that was *knocked together* from old pieces of wood
knock up [*phrasal verb*] **1** ***knock (someone) up** or **knock up (someone)** informal* **a** *chiefly US, impolite* : to make (someone) pregnant • She got *knocked up*. [=she got pregnant] **b** *Brit* : to wake (someone) by knocking on a door • *knocked* him *up* at 6 a.m. **2** ***knock (something) up** or **knock up (something)** Brit* : to make or produce (something) quickly • *knock up* a quick meal
knock your socks off see [1]SOCK

[2]knock *noun, pl* **knocks**
1 [*count*] **a** : a hard, sharp hit • He gave him a *knock* on the head. **b** : the sound made by a hard hit • There was a loud *knock* at the door.
2 [*count*] *informal* : an experience that makes you less confident or successful for a period of time : a difficult or painful experience • She took some *knocks* early in her career. • Most performers have their share of *knocks* [=*setbacks*] on their way to stardom. — see also HARD KNOCKS (below)
3 [*count*] *informal* : a critical or negative comment • He likes praise but can't stand the *knocks*. — often used in U.S. English in the phrase ***the knock against*** • *The knock against* her is that she can't win the important matches. [=people say that she cannot win the important matches] • One of *the knocks against* television is that there are too many commercials.
4 : a loud noise produced by an engine when it is not working properly [*count*] We heard a *knock* in the engine. [*noncount*] a type of fuel that reduces engine *knock*
hard knocks : difficult or painful experiences that people have in their lives or careers • He has taken plenty of *hard knocks* in his life. • The ***school of hard knocks*** [=the difficult experiences in his life] taught him how to be tough.

knock·about /ˈnɑːkəˌbaʊt/ *adj, always used before a noun* : noisy or rough often in a silly or amusing way • *knockabout* humor • He lived a *knockabout* life in the city.

knock·back /ˈnɑːkˌbæk/ *noun, pl* **-backs** [*count*] *Brit, informal* : something (such as a criticism or refusal) that makes you less confident or successful • Everyone experiences a few *knockbacks* in their lives.

knock·down /ˈnɑːkˌdaʊn/ *adj, always used before a noun, chiefly Brit, informal, of a price* : greatly reduced from the original price : extremely low • Now's your chance to buy these items at *knockdown* prices!

knock–down, drag–out *or* **knock–down–drag–out** *adj, always used before a noun, US, informal* : very angry or violent • We had a *knock-down-drag-out* argument.

knock·er /ˈnɑːkɚ/ *noun, pl* **-ers**
1 [*count*] : a small metal device on a door that you move in order to make a knocking sound
2 ***knockers*** [*plural*] *informal + sometimes offensive* : a woman's breasts

knock–kneed /ˈnɑːkˈniːd/ *adj* [*more* ~; *most* ~] : having legs that curve inward at the knees • She is tall and *knock-kneed*.

knock·off /ˈnɑːkˌɑːf/ *noun, pl* **-offs** [*count*] : a cheap or inferior copy of something • That purse is a *knockoff*. — see also *knock off* at [1]KNOCK

knock–on effect *noun, pl* ~ **-fects** [*count*] *Brit* : something (such as a process, action, or event) that causes other things to happen : RIPPLE EFFECT • The drought is likely to have a *knock-on effect* throughout the whole economy.

[1]knock·out /ˈnɑːkˌaʊt/ *noun, pl* **-outs** [*count*]
1 : an occurrence in which a boxing match ends when a fighter has been knocked down by a punch and is unable to start fighting again before 10 seconds have passed • He won the match by a *knockout*. • He scored a *knockout* in the fourth round. — see also TECHNICAL KNOCKOUT
2 *informal* : a very attractive or appealing person or thing • She's a real *knockout* in that dress. — see also *knock out* at [1]KNOCK

[2]knockout *adj, always used before a noun*
1 : causing someone to become unconscious • a *knockout* punch/blow
2 *informal* : extremely attractive or appealing • a *knockout* actress/movie
3 *Brit, of a contest or competition* : designed so that winning teams or players continue to play and losing teams or players do not • The Wimbledon tennis tournament is a *knockout* competition.

knock–up *noun, pl* **-ups** [*count*] *Brit* : a time before a tennis game when players hit the ball to each other in order to practice

knoll /ˈnoʊl/ *noun, pl* **knolls** [*count*] : a small hill • a grassy *knoll*

[1]knot /ˈnɑːt/ *noun, pl* **knots** [*count*]
1 a : a part that forms when you tie a piece of rope, string, fabric, etc., to itself or to something else • She tied the rope in a *knot*. • He made/tied a *knot* in the rope. • untie a *knot* • loosen/tighten a *knot* — see also GRANNY KNOT, SLIPKNOT, SQUARE KNOT **b** : a part where something has become twisted or wrapped around itself • The electrical cord was tangled in *knots*. • She tried to untangle the *knots* [=*tangles*] in the child's hair. — often used figuratively • The project has been tied up in political and legal *knots* for years. [=nothing has happened with the project for years because of political and legal problems] — see also GORDIAN KNOT
2 : a painful or uncomfortable feeling of tightness in part of your body • a *knot* in a muscle • massaging the *knots* out of my back • I was so nervous that my stomach was ***in knots***. [=I had an unpleasant and tight feeling in my stomach]
3 : a dark round mark on a piece of wood that shows where a branch grew • a board full of *knots*
4 : a way of arranging long hair by twisting it into a round shape at the sides or back of the head • She pulled her hair into a *knot* [=*bun*] at the back of her neck.
5 : a group of people who are standing or sitting close together • A *knot* [=*cluster*] of people blocked the door.
6 : a unit of speed equal to one nautical mile per hour • Wind is from the north at 12 *knots*. • sailing at six *knots*
at a rate of knots see [1]RATE
***tie the knot** informal* : to get married • When are you two going to *tie the knot*?
tie yourself (up) in knots **1** : to cause problems for yourself because you are being too careful, trying too hard, etc. • The mayor *tied himself in knots* answering a touchy political question. [=he answered it in a confused or unclear way] **2** : to become very upset or worried • I don't know why they're *tying themselves in knots* over such a trivial problem.

[2]knot *verb* **knots; knot·ted; knot·ting**
1 [+ *obj*] : to tie a section of rope, string, fabric, etc., to itself or to something else so that a knot forms : to make a knot in (something) • He *knotted* his tie so that both ends would be the same length. • *knot* a string/rope; *also* : to connect (two or more parts or things) with a knot • *Knot* the threads together. • She *knotted* a sweater around her shoulders. [=tied the sleeves of the sweater together around her shoulders]
2 [*no obj*] : to develop a painful or uncomfortable feeling of tightness — often + *up* • My stomach *knotted* [=*tensed*] *up* as I waited for the interview.
3 [+ *obj*] *US, informal* : to make (the score of a game or contest) equal • He scored a goal that *knotted* [=*tied*] the score at 3 all.

knot·ted /ˈnɑːtəd/ *adj*
1 : having a knot or knots • a *knotted* rope/cord/string
2 : KNOTTY 1 • *knotted* pine
***get knotted** Brit slang* — used in speech as a rude way to tell someone to go away or to show that you are annoyed with someone

knot·ty /ˈnɑːti/ *adj* **knot·ti·er; -est**
1 *of wood* : having many dark round marks showing where branches grew : having many knots • *knotty* wood • *knotty* paneling • *knotty* pine
2 : difficult or complicated • a *knotty* problem/situation

[1]know /ˈnoʊ/ *verb, not used in progressive tenses* **knows; knew** /ˈnuː, *Brit* ˈnjuː/; **known** /ˈnoʊn/; **know·ing**
1 a : to have (information of some kind) in your mind [+ *obj*] He *knows* a lot about the history of the town. • Do you *know* the answer? • I don't *know* her name. • Do you *know* what time it is? • I don't *know* the words to that song. • They *knew* a good deal about the problem. • She *knows* the rules of the game. • He *knows* everything about horses. = He ***knows all/everything there is to know*** about horses. — often + *how, why, where*, etc. • Do you *know why* she left this suitcase here? • Do you *know where* she went? • No one *knows* (for sure) *how* long it will take the fix the problem. • He ***knows perfectly/full well*** *how* to do it. [*no obj*] If you want the answer, ask someone who *knows*. • "What is she doing?" "Be-

lieve me, ***you don't want to know.*** [=you would be shocked or upset to learn what she is doing] — **often +** ***about*** ▪ He *knows* (all) *about* horses. **b : to understand (something) : to have a clear and complete idea of (something)** [+ *obj*] I don't *know* much about art, but I *know* what I like. — **usually +** ***how, why, where,*** **etc.** ▪ Scientists don't yet *know why* this happens. ▪ I don't *know what* to do. ▪ I don't *know what* you want me to do. ▪ We had almost no money in those days. I don't *know how* we managed. ▪ I don't *know how* you could be so careless. ▪ You ***know perfectly/full well*** *what* I am trying to say. [*no obj*] "How could she do that?" "***How should/would I know?!***" [=I don't know, and you should not expect me to know] **c** [+ *obj*] **: to have learned (something, as a skill or a language)** ▪ She *knows* karate/CPR. ▪ He *knows* Spanish. — **often +** ***how*** ▪ Do you *know how* to type? ▪ I would go swimming with you, but I don't *know how* (to swim). [=I never learned to swim]

2 : to be aware of (something) : to realize (something) [+ *obj*] She *knows* that many people will not believe her. ▪ I *know* (that) this isn't easy for you, but you have to keep trying. ▪ As soon as I turned on the light I *knew* that something was missing. ▪ There was no way for me to *know* that he was your brother. = ***How was I to know*** that he was your brother? ▪ It's wrong and you ***know it!*** [=you are aware that it is wrong] ▪ "I'm sorry I threw out those bags." "It's okay: you ***couldn't have known*** that I needed them." = "It's okay: you ***had no way of knowing*** that I needed them." = (*Brit*) "It's okay: you ***weren't to know*** that I needed them." ▪ You ***ought to know by now*** that she is always late. ▪ It's impossible to *know* what will happen next. = There's ***no way of knowing*** what will happen next. = There's ***no knowing*** what will happen next. ▪ If you've never been to Venice, ***you don't know what you're missing.*** [=you would enjoy going to Venice very much] ▪ ***You know as well as I do*** that they expect us at 8:00. ▪ ***You don't know*** how happy I am to see you. [=I am extremely happy to see you] ▪ ***You'll never know*** what this means to me. = ***You can't know*** how much this means to me. [=this means a great deal to me] [*no obj*] ***As far as I know,*** they plan to arrive on Monday. [=I believe that they plan to arrive on Monday, but I am not sure] ▪ We're planning a party for George. ***As you know,*** he'll be leaving the company next month. — **often +** ***about*** **or** ***of*** ▪ I *knew about* the problem. [=I was aware of the problem] ▪ Does she *know about* the meeting? ▪ I don't *know of* any job openings right now. [=I am not aware of any job openings right now] ▪ I *know of* her as a poet but not as a novelist. [=I am familiar with her poetry but not with her novels] ▪ Do you *know of* a good lawyer? [=can you recommend a good lawyer?] ▪ "Does he have relatives nearby?" "***Not that I know of.***" [=I don't think he has any relatives nearby]

3 : to be certain of (something) [+ *obj*] Everyone else believes him, but I just *know* (that) he's lying. ▪ I don't *know* if I can trust her. [=I am not sure that I can trust her] ▪ It's hard to *know* exactly where the candidate stands on this issue. ▪ I *knew* he'd forget. ▪ I need to *know* if they are coming. ▪ "She says she's not coming." "***I knew it!***" [=I was sure that she wouldn't come] ▪ ***I knew it all along.*** [=I was always sure of it] [*no obj*] "They're coming." "Do you *know* [=are you certain], or are you just guessing?" = "Do you ***know for sure/certain,*** or are you just guessing?" ▪ He thinks he got the job but he doesn't *know for sure.*

4 [+ *obj*] **a : to have met and talked to (someone) : to be acquainted or familiar with (a person)** ▪ "Do you *know* Clara?" "Yes, we've met." ▪ "Do you *know* Clara?" "We've met but I wouldn't say that I really *know* her." [=I am not close to her; I don't know much about her] ▪ I've *known* him for years. He's one of my best friends. ▪ *Knowing* you, you'll be the first one there. [=because I know you so well, I expect you to be the first one there] ▪ She's the kindest person I *know.* ▪ ***To know him is to love him.*** [=the people who know him feel great affection for him] ▪ We just bought a house here last month, and we're still ***getting to know*** our neighbors. [=we're still meeting our neighbors; we're still becoming acquainted with our neighbors] **b : to have experience with (something) : to be acquainted or familiar with (something)** ▪ She *knows* the city very well. ▪ Do you *know* her painting/writing/work? ▪ Do you *know* any good restaurants in this area? ▪ We're still ***getting to know*** the neighborhood. ▪ The building ***as we know it*** [=as it exists now] is quite different from how it looked when it was first built. ▪ This is the end of the organization *as we know it.* [=the organization has changed and will never again be the same as it was] **c : to have experienced (something)** ▪ someone who *knows* grief well [=someone who has experienced a lot of grief] — **usually used as** ***known*** ▪ I've *known* failure and I've *known* success. [=I have failed and I have succeeded]

5 [+ *obj*] **a : to recognize (someone or something) : to identify (someone or something) accurately** ▪ "How will I *know* her?" "She'll be wearing a red sweater." ▪ I would *know* [=*recognize*] that voice anywhere. ▪ I *know* his face [=his face is familiar to me] but I don't remember his name. ▪ I feel like I *know* this house, but I've never been here before. ▪ I *know* many of the customers at the café by sight. [=I see them often enough that I recognize them] **b : to recognize the difference between two things : to be able to distinguish (one thing)** ***from*** **another** ▪ *know* right *from* wrong

6 [+ *obj*] **a : to be sure that (someone or something) has a particular quality, character, etc., because of your experiences with that person or thing — usually followed by** ***to*** **+** ***verb*** ▪ I've worked with him for many years, and I *know* him *to be* an honest man. ▪ I *know* the business *to be* legitimate. **b : to think of (someone or something) as having a particular quality, character, etc. — +** ***as*** ▪ His neighbors *knew* him *as* a quiet and friendly person, but the people he worked with saw a different side of him. — **often used as** ***(be) known as*** ▪ She *is known as* an expert in the field. [=people consider her an expert] **c — used to indicate the name that people know or use for someone or something; +** ***as*** ▪ Her neighbors *knew* her *as* Jill Brown, but her real name was Amy Smith. — **often used as** ***(be) known as*** ▪ Samuel L. Clemens *was* better/otherwise *known as* Mark Twain. [=most people called him Mark Twain] ▪ Beethoven's Third Symphony *is* widely *known as* the "Eroica." **d — used to say that someone or something has a particular quality, feature, ability, etc., that people know about; +** ***for*** ▪ Fans of the blues *know* the city *for* its live blues clubs. — **usually used as** ***(be) known for*** ▪ The restaurant *is known for* its desserts. [=the restaurant's desserts are popular, well-known, etc.] ▪ She *is known for* her ability to work quickly. = She *is known for* working quickly. ▪ He*'s known for* being late. [=he is often late] **e ✧ Someone who has been** ***known to be*** **or** ***known to do*** **something has been or done that thing in the past.** ▪ We've *known* him *to work* all night to meet a deadline. = He's been *known to work* all night to meet a deadline. ▪ I've never *known* her *to be* wrong. [=I do not know of any time when she has been wrong] ▪ He's been *known to do* this kind of thing before.

before you know it **: very quickly or soon** ▪ We'll be there *before you know it.* ▪ The game was over *before I knew it.*

better the devil you know than the devil you don't see DEVIL

don't I know it informal **— used to say that you agree with what has just been said** ▪ "It's freezing in here!" "*Don't I know it.*" [=I agree]

for all I know informal **— used to say that you have little or no knowledge of something** ▪ *For all I know,* he left last night. [=I don't know when he left; it's possible that he left last night] ▪ She may have already accepted another job, *for all we know.* [=we don't know what she has done; it's possible that she has already accepted another job]

God knows *or* ***goodness knows*** *or* ***heaven knows*** *or* ***Lord knows informal*** **1 — used to stress that something is not known** ▪ How long will the meeting last? *Heaven knows.* ▪ *God* (only) *knows* if the reports are true. **2 — used to make a statement more forceful** ▪ He finally got a raise. *Goodness knows* he deserved one. [=he certainly deserved one] ▪ She didn't win, but *Lord knows* she tried.

have known better days see [1]BETTER

I don't know **1 — used to say that you do not have the information someone is asking for** ▪ "What time does the library close?" "*I don't know.*" **2** ***informal*** **— used to express disagreement, doubt, or uncertainty** ▪ "I don't like that guy." "Oh, *I don't know,* he's not really so bad." ▪ "Which one is your favorite?" "Um, *I don't know,* maybe the red one." ▪ She thinks we should go now, but *I don't know.* [=I'm not sure] Maybe we should wait. **3 — used to say that you are uncertain** ***about*** **someone or something** ▪ ***I don't know about you*** [=you may think or feel differently than I do about this], but I'm leaving. ▪ "She said she'd be here by 5:00." "***I don't know about that.***" [=I'm not sure that will happen] ▪ ***I don't know about him***—he's hard to figure out.

if you must know **— used when you are answering a question that you do not want to answer because the information is personal, embarrassing, etc.** ▪ "How much did you pay for your car?" "Well, *if you must know,* it cost about

$20,000." ▪ "Why did you leave that job?" "*If you must know*, I was fired."

I'll have you know see HAVE

I know (it) **1** — used to express agreement ▪ "Hurry up, we're going to be late." "*I know*, but I can't find my shoe." ▪ "This place is such a mess." "*I know it.*" [=I agree] ▪ "I can't believe he lied." "*I know, I know.*" ▪ "The whole situation is just so stupid." "*I know.*" **2** — used to introduce a suggestion ▪ "What should we do tonight?" "*I know* [=I have an idea]—how about a movie?"

I wouldn't know — used to say that you have not experienced something ▪ "That restaurant has the best desserts!" "*I wouldn't know.* I've never been there."

know best *or* ***know what's best*** : to know or understand better than someone else what should be done ▪ I would take the highway myself, but you live here so you *know best.* ▪ I'll do whatever you say. You *know what's best.*

know better **1** : to be smart or sensible enough not to do something ▪ You walked home alone? Don't you *know better* (than that)? ▪ She'll ***know better than to*** trust them again. [=she will not trust them again] ▪ There's no excuse for his behavior. He's ***old enough to know better***. ▪ Don't blame him. He's just a child and he ***doesn't know (any) better***. [=he is too young, inexperienced, etc., to be expected to behave properly] **2** : to know or understand the truth about something ▪ She tried to tell me that it wasn't her fault, but I *know better.* [=I know that it really was her fault] **3** : to know or understand more than other people ▪ You can't tell him what to do. He always thinks that he *knows better.*

know different/otherwise : to know that something that people think or say is true is not really true ▪ She says she has no money but I *know otherwise.* [=I know that she does have money]

know from [*phrasal verb*] ***know from (someone or something)*** *US, informal* : to know anything about or care at all about (someone or something) — used in negative statements ▪ kids who don't *know from* sports

know no boundaries see BOUNDARY

know no bounds see [6]BOUND

know (something) backward and forward *or Brit* ***know (something) backwards*** *or* ***know (something) inside out*** *or US* ***know (something) inside and out*** *or* ***know (something) like the back of your hand*** : to know something completely ▪ He *knew the process backward and forward.* ▪ She *knows the business inside and out.* ▪ *I know this town like the back of my hand.*

know (something or someone) for what it/he/she is : to understand what something or someone truly is ▪ Now I *know them for what they are*—liars. ▪ before scientists *knew the disease for what it is*—a virus ▪ the friends who *know me for what I am* [=who truly know and understand me]

know (something) when you see it/one : to be able to recognize or identify something immediately ▪ She *knows a bargain when she sees it.* ▪ *I know a liar when I see one.* ▪ I'm not sure what I want but I'll *know it when I see it.*

know the drill see [1]DRILL

know the score see [1]SCORE

know what hit you — used in negative statements to say that something you did not expect surprised you very much ▪ I di*dn't know what hit me*—suddenly I just felt so dizzy. ▪ The company came out with an entirely new line of products last year, and their competitors *never knew what hit them.* [=their competitors were not prepared and were completely surprised]

know what it is *or* ***to know what it's like*** : to have experience with a situation, activity, or condition ▪ He *knows what it is to be* poor. [=he has been poor] ▪ They *know what it's like to* have no privacy.

know what you are talking about ✧ If *you know what you are talking about*, you deserve to be listened to because you have actual knowledge or experience with something and what you are saying is correct. ▪ Take her advice. She *knows what she's talking about.* ▪ "He said the movie is boring." "Don't listen to him. He ***doesn't know what he's talking about***." [=he is wrong]

know which side your bread is buttered on see [1]BREAD

know your own heart/mind : to be sure of what you want, like, think, etc. ▪ She's a woman who *knows her own mind.*

know yourself : to understand yourself fully : to understand your own emotions, desires, abilities, etc. ▪ I was so young then. I really didn't *know myself.*

know your stuff see [1]STUFF

know your way around ✧ If you *know your way around* a place or thing, you are very familiar with it or are good at using or operating it. ▪ He *knows his way around* Boston. ▪ She really *knows her way around* a sailboat. [=she knows how to sail; she is a very good sailor] ▪ They *know their way around* computers.

let (someone) know : to tell something to someone ▪ *Let me know* [=tell me] if you're going to the party. ▪ Please *let me know* if there's anything I can do to help. [=I would like to help; please tell me if you need help] ▪ He's not sure what time he'll arrive—he is going to *let us know.* ▪ She *let the staff know* her decision. [=she told the staff her decision]

let (something) be known *or* ***make (something) known*** *formal* : to tell people something ▪ He *let it be known* [=he announced] that he intends to run for mayor. ▪ She *made her decision known* to the staff. [=she told the staff her decision]

make yourself known *formal* : to introduce yourself : to cause people to know who you are ▪ The candidate *made herself known* to voters through an aggressive ad campaign. ▪ the movie in which the actor first *made himself known* to the world

might/should have known — used to say that you are not surprised to learn of something ▪ I *should have known* it would be too expensive. ▪ "She says she's going to be late." "I *might have known.*"

not know someone from Adam *informal* : to have never met with someone : to not know someone at all ▪ Why should she trust me? She *doesn't know me from Adam.*

not know the first thing about : to have little or no knowledge about (something or someone) ▪ I *don't know the first thing about* cooking/sports/children.

not know the meaning of (the word) see MEANING

not know your ass from your elbow (*chiefly US*) *or Brit* ***not know your arse from your elbow*** *informal + impolite* : to know nothing : to be stupid ▪ Don't take his word for it—he *doesn't know his ass from his elbow.*

what do you know *informal* **1** — used to express surprise ▪ She's an astronaut? Well, *what do you know!* ▪ "He's going to law school in the fall." "Well ***what do you know about that***?" [=I am surprised that he is going to law school] **2** — used to say that someone is wrong about something ▪ "She thinks I should take the job." "*What does she know*? You should do what you want."

wouldn't you know (it)? *informal* — used to say that something annoying that has happened is the kind of thing that often happens ▪ I was running late and—*wouldn't you know*?—I rushed off without my purse. ▪ "He's late again." "*Wouldn't you know it*?!"

you know *informal* **1** — used when you are trying to help someone remember something ▪ They live on the other side of town. *You know*—near the golf course. ▪ He was in our history class—*you know* [=*you remember*]—the tall blond guy in the front row. **2** — used for emphasis ▪ *You know*, we really have to go. ▪ It's cold outside, *you know.* ▪ *You know*, you really should write a novel. **3** — used when you are not sure of what to say or how to say it ▪ Would you like to, *you know*, go out sometime? ▪ We're planning to go shopping and, *you know*, just hang out.

you know something/what? *informal* **1** — used to emphasize the statement that comes after it ▪ *You know something*? I never trusted her. ▪ She lied to me again, but *you know what*? I really just don't care any more. **2** — used to get someone's attention ▪ Hey, *you know what*? I'm hungry.

you know what I mean *informal* — used to suggest that the hearer agrees with and understands what has been said or to ask if he or she does or not ▪ I grew up there, *you know what I mean*, so I know what it's like. ▪ He's kind of strange. Do *you know what I mean*? ▪ He's kind of strange, ***if you know what I mean***. — sometimes used in the shortened form ***know what I mean*** ▪ He's kind of strange—*know what I mean*?

you know what they say *informal* — used to introduce a common saying or a statement that expresses a common belief ▪ Keep trying, and you'll figure it out. *You know what they say*: if at first you don't succeed, try, try again.

you never know — used to say that it is impossible to be sure about what will happen ▪ *You never know*—you might win the lottery. ▪ *You never know* who will show up. ▪ *You never know* with her parties: anyone could show up.

[2]know *noun*

in the know : having knowledge about something : having information that most people do not have ▪ people who are *in the know* ▪ For those of you not *in the know*, Jane is the person who founded this organization.

know·able /ˈnowəbəl/ *adj* : able to be known ▪ information that is not easily *knowable*

know–all /ˈnoʊˌɑːl/ *noun, pl* **-alls** [*count*] *Brit, informal* : KNOW-IT-ALL

know–how /ˈnoʊˌhaʊ/ *noun* [*noncount*] : knowledge of how to do something well : EXPERTISE ▪ technical *know-how* ▪ Does he have the *know-how* to help us do this?

know·ing /ˈnowɪŋ/ *adj, always used before a noun* [*more* ~; *most* ~] : showing that you have special knowledge ▪ a *knowing* look/glance/smile ▪ She looked at us in a *knowing* way.

know·ing·ly /ˈnowɪŋli/ *adv* [*more* ~; *most* ~]
1 : in a way that shows that you have special knowledge : in a knowing way ▪ She looked at us *knowingly*. ▪ someone who can speak *knowingly* about investing
2 : with knowledge of what is being done ▪ Did he *knowingly* [=*deliberately, purposely*] withhold information?

know–it–all /ˈnowətˌɑːl/ *noun, pl* **-alls** [*count*] *informal* + *disapproving* : a person who talks and behaves like someone who knows everything ▪ My neighbor is a real *know-it-all*, always telling me what to do. — often used before another noun ▪ my *know-it-all* neighbor — called also *(Brit) know-all*

knowl·edge /ˈnɑːlɪʤ/ *noun*
1 : information, understanding, or skill that you get from experience or education [*noncount*] She has little/no/some *knowledge* of fashion/history/cooking. ▪ He has devoted himself to the pursuit of *knowledge*. ▪ a thirst/quest for *knowledge* [*singular*] a *knowledge* of carpentry ▪ She gained/acquired a thorough *knowledge* of local customs. ▪ I have a reading *knowledge* of French [=I can read French], but I can't speak it fluently.
2 [*noncount*] : awareness of something : the state of being aware of something ▪ He claimed to have no *knowledge* of the plan. = He denied all/any *knowledge* of the plan. ▪ Did you have any *knowledge* of her intentions? ▪ The decision was made ***without my knowledge***. [=I did not know about the decision]
common knowledge : something that many or most people know ▪ It's *common knowledge* that she plans to run for mayor.
public knowledge : something that people know because it has been reported in the news ▪ His legal problems are a matter of *public knowledge*.
safe/secure in the knowledge : feeling safe or secure because you know something specified ▪ They went on vacation, *safe in the knowledge* that the farm would be well cared for while they were away.
to someone's knowledge : according to what someone knows — usually used in negative statements ▪ "Did anyone arrive late?" "*Not to my knowledge*." ▪ No one arrived late *to my knowledge*. [=I am not aware that anyone arrived late, but it is possible that someone arrived late and I don't know about it]
to the best of my knowledge — used to say that you think a statement is true but that there may be something you do not know which makes it untrue ▪ *To the best of my knowledge* [=*as far as I know*], everyone arrived on time. ▪ I answered their questions *to the best of my knowledge*. [=I gave the best answers I could based on what I knew, but I might have answered differently if I had known something else]

knowl·edge·able /ˈnɑːlɪʤəbəl/ *adj* [*more* ~; *most* ~] : having information, understanding, or skill that comes from experience or education : having knowledge ▪ a *knowledgeable* person ▪ a *knowledgeable* observer ▪ He is very *knowledgeable* about chess. [=he knows a lot about chess]
– knowl·edge·ably /ˈnɑːlɪʤəbli/ *adv* ▪ She spoke *knowledgeably* on several topics.

[1]**known** *past participle of* [1]KNOW

[2]**known** /ˈnoʊn/ *adj*
1 *always used before a noun* **a** : generally accepted as something specified ▪ He's a *known* expert. ▪ That's a *known* fact! ▪ a *known* criminal **b** : included in the knowledge that all people considered as one group have ▪ There is no *known* cure for the disease. [=there is no cure that anyone knows about, although a cure may exist that has not yet been discovered] ▪ the earliest *known* use of a word [=the earliest use that anyone knows about]
2 : familiar to people — used with *little, widely*, etc. ▪ a widely *known* story [=a story that many people know] ▪ a little-*known* writer [=a writer that few people know about] — see also WELL-KNOWN

known quantity see QUANTITY

know–noth·ing /ˈnoʊˌnʌθɪŋ/ *noun, pl* **-ings** [*count*] : a person who lacks intelligence or knowledge : a stupid or ignorant person ▪ He regards his political rivals as a bunch of *know-nothings*. — often used before another noun ▪ a bunch of *know-nothing* politicians

[1]**knuck·le** /ˈnʌkəl/ *noun, pl* **knuck·les** [*count*]
1 : any one of the thick, bony parts (called joints) in your fingers ▪ She rapped her *knuckles* on the table. — see picture at HAND
2 : a piece of meat that includes a joint from the leg of an animal ▪ a pork *knuckle*
a rap on/over/across the knuckles see [1]RAP
rap (someone) on/over/across the knuckles see [2]RAP

[2]**knuckle** *verb* **knuck·les; knuck·led; knuck·ling**
knuckle down [*phrasal verb*] *informal* : to begin to work hard ▪ It's time to *knuckle down* and get to work. — often + *to* ▪ She *knuckled down to* the task.
knuckle under [*phrasal verb*] *informal* : to stop trying to fight or resist something : to agree to do or accept something that you have been resisting or opposing ▪ Despite the pressure, he refused to *knuckle under*. [=*give in*] — often + *to* ▪ He refused to *knuckle under to* anyone. ▪ He finally *knuckled under to* the pressure.

knuck·le·ball /ˈnʌkəlˌbɑːl/ *noun, pl* **-balls** [*count*] *baseball* : a pitch that is thrown with very little spin by holding the ball with the knuckles or fingertips — called also *knuckler*

knuck·le·head /ˈnʌkəlˌhɛd/ *noun, pl* **-heads** [*count*] *US, informal* : a stupid person : DUMMY ▪ Don't be such a *knucklehead*.

knuck·ler /ˈnʌkələ/ *noun, pl* **-lers** [*count*] *baseball* : KNUCKLEBALL

[1]**KO** /ˌkeɪˈoʊ/ *noun, pl* **KOs** [*count*] *boxing* : [1]KNOCKOUT ▪ He scored a *KO* in the second round.

[2]**KO** *verb* **KO's; KO'd** /ˌkeɪˈoʊd/; **KO'·ing** /ˌkeɪˈowɪŋ/ [+ *obj*] *boxing* : to knock (an opponent) out ▪ He was *KO'd* in the second round.

K

ko·ala /kəˈwɑːlə/ *noun, pl* **-al·as** [*count*] : an Australian animal that has thick gray fur, large hairy ears, sharp claws for climbing, and no tail — called also *koala bear*

koala

kohl /ˈkoʊl/ *noun* [*noncount*] : a type of makeup that is used to put a black or dark gray line or mark around the eyes ▪ eyes rimmed with *kohl*

kohl·ra·bi /koʊlˈrɑːbi/ *noun* [*count, noncount*] : a type of cabbage that has a large, round stem and that is eaten as a vegetable

kook /ˈkuːk/ *noun, pl* **kooks** [*count*] *informal* : a person whose ideas or actions are very strange or foolish ▪ a bunch of *kooks* dressed up in weird costumes ▪ a lovable *kook*
– kooky /ˈkuːki/ *adj* **kook·i·er; -est** ▪ another one of his *kooky* ideas ▪ a *kooky* outfit/person

kook·a·bur·ra /ˈkʊkəˌbərə/ *noun, pl* **-ras** [*count*] : a large Australian bird whose call is like loud laughter

Ko·ran *also* **Qur·an** *or* **Qur·'an** /kəˈræn, kəˈrɑːn/ *noun* [*singular*] : the book of sacred writings used in the Muslim religion
– Ko·ran·ic *also* **Qu·ran·ic** *or* **Qur·'an·ic** /kəˈrænɪk/ *adj*

Ko·re·an /kəˈriːjən/ *noun, pl* **-ans**
1 [*count*] : a person born, raised, or living in Korea : a person whose family is from Korea
2 [*noncount*] : the language of the Korean people
– Korean *adj* ▪ *Korean* culture/art/language ▪ the *Korean* people

ko·sher /ˈkoʊʃə/ *adj*
1 a : accepted by Jewish law as fit for eating or drinking ▪ *kosher* food ▪ *kosher* salt/pickles/meat/wine ▪ a family that ***keeps kosher*** [=a family that obeys Jewish laws about eating and drinking] **b** : selling or serving kosher food ▪ a *kosher* butcher ▪ a *kosher* restaurant
2 [*more* ~; *most* ~] *informal* : proper or acceptable : RIGHT ▪ Something about this deal is just not *kosher*.

kow·tow /ˈkaʊˌtaʊ/ *verb* **-tows; -towed; -tow·ing** [*no obj*] *informal* + *disapproving* : to agree too easily or eagerly to do what someone else wants you to do : to obey someone with power in a way that seems weak — usually + *to* ▪ She refused to *kowtow to* their demands.

kph *abbr* kilometers per hour

Kraut /ˈkraʊt/ *noun, pl* **Krauts** [*count*] *informal + offensive* : a German person

Krem·lin /ˈkrɛmlən/ *noun*
the Kremlin : the government of Russia and the former Soviet Union • an announcement from *the Kremlin*; *also* : the buildings of the Russian government in Moscow • We visited *the Kremlin* when we traveled to Russia.

krill /ˈkrɪl/ *noun* [*plural*] : very small creatures in the ocean that are the main food of some whales

kro·na /ˈkroʊnə/ *noun, pl* **kro·nor** /ˈkroʊˌnoɚ/ [*count*] : a basic unit of money that is used in Sweden and Iceland; *also* : a coin representing one krona

kro·ne /ˈkroʊnə/ *noun, pl* **kro·ner** /ˈkroʊnɚ/ [*count*] : a basic unit of money that is used in Denmark and Norway; *also* : a coin representing one krone

kryp·ton /ˈkrɪpˌtɑːn/ *noun* [*noncount*] : a chemical element that is a colorless gas and that is used especially in electric lights

KS *abbr* Kansas

ku·dos /ˈkuːˌdoʊz, *Brit* ˈkjuːˌdɒs/ *noun* [*noncount*] *informal* : praise or respect that you get because of something you have done or achieved • *Kudos* to everyone who helped. • The company has earned *kudos* for responding so quickly to customers' concerns.

Ku Klux Klan /ˈkuːˈklʌksˈklæn/ *noun*
the Ku Klux Klan : a secret organization in the U.S. that is made up of white people who are opposed to people of other races • a member of *the Ku Klux Klan* — abbr. *KKK*

kum·quat /ˈkʌmˌkwɑːt/ *noun, pl* **-quats** [*count*] : a fruit that looks like a small orange

kung fu /ˌkʌŋˈfuː/ *noun* [*noncount*] : a form of fighting without weapons that was developed in China : a Chinese martial art — often used before another noun • *kung fu* chops/kicks • a *kung fu* expert/master

Kurd /ˈkuɚd, ˈkɚd/ *noun, pl* **Kurds** [*count*] : a member of a group of people who live in a region that includes parts of Turkey, Iran, and Iraq
— **Kurd·ish** /ˈkuɚdɪʃ, ˈkɚdɪʃ/ *adj* • *Kurdish* people

kvetch /ˈkvɛtʃ/ *verb* **kvetch·es**; **kvetched**; **kvetch·ing** *chiefly US, informal* : to complain often or constantly [*no obj*] They're always *kvetching* about something. [+ *obj*] They're always *kvetching* (to us) that nothing is any good.
— **kvetch·er** *noun, pl* **-ers** [*count*]

kW *abbr* kilowatt

Kwan·zaa *also* **Kwan·za** /ˈkwɑːnzə/ *noun, pl* **-zaas** *also* **-zas** [*count, noncount*] : an African-American cultural festival held from December 26 to January 1

kWh *abbr* kilowatt-hour

KY *abbr* Kentucky

L

[1]l *or* **L** /ˈɛl/ *noun, pl* **l's** *or* **ls** *or* **L's** *or* **Ls** /ˈɛlz/
1 : the twelfth letter of the English alphabet [*count*] a word that starts with an *l* [*noncount*] a word that starts with *l*
2 [*count*] : the Roman numeral that means 50 • LV [=55]

[2]l *or* **L** *abbr* **1** large — usually used for a clothing size • The shirt comes in S, M, *L*, and XL. **2** left **3** length • The area of a rectangle is *L* x W. **4** line — used to refer to a line of poetry or of a play • act one, scene two, *l* 25 ✧ The abbreviation for "lines" is ***ll***. • *ll* 15–25 **5** liter • a 2 *L* bottle

la /ˈlɑː/ *noun* [*noncount*] *music* : the sixth note of a musical scale • do, re, mi, fa, sol, *la*, ti

LA *abbr* **1** Los Angeles **2** Louisiana

lab /ˈlæb/ *noun, pl* **labs** [*count*] *informal*
1 : LABORATORY • working in the *lab* • a chemistry/computer/crime *lab* — often used before another noun • a *lab* animal [=an animal used for experiments in a laboratory] • a *lab* coat [=a coat worn over the clothes for protection from spills and stains in a laboratory] • a *lab* report [=a written report of the results of work in a lab]
2 : a class period for laboratory work • I have (a) *lab* today.

[1]Lab /ˈlæb/ *noun, pl* **Labs** [*count*] *informal* : LABRADOR RETRIEVER • a black *Lab*

[2]Lab *abbr, Brit* Labour (Party) • Jane Smith MP (*Lab*)

[1]la·bel /ˈleɪbəl/ *noun, pl* **-bels** [*count*]
1 : a piece of paper, cloth, or similar material that is attached to something to identify or describe it • The name is prominently displayed on the *label*. • You should read the warning *label* before you take any medicine. • (*US*) a ***mailing label*** [=a piece of paper with a mailing address already printed on it]
2 : a word or phrase that describes or identifies something or someone • The word was given the *label* "obsolete." • Some people describe him as "selfish," but he doesn't deserve that *label*. • Once you give people *labels*, it's hard to see them as individuals.
3 : a company that produces musical recordings • a major/independent record *label* • The band has made records for/on/with several different *labels* in their career.
4 : a name shown on clothes that indicates the store, company, or person who sold, produced, or designed the clothes • a designer *label* • She always wears designer *label* jeans.

[2]label *verb* **-bels**; *US* **-beled** *or* **-belled**; *US* **-bel·ing** *or* **-bel·ling** [+ *obj*]
1 : to put a word or name on something to describe or identify it : to attach a label to (something) • Be sure to carefully *label* the switches so that you don't confuse them. • He *labels* his photographs with the date and place they were taken. — often used as *(be) labeled* • two switches, *labeled* "A" and "B"
2 : to name or describe (someone or something) in a specified way : to give a label to (someone or something) • Many people have unfairly *labeled* him (as) "selfish." — often used as *(be) labeled* • He *has been labeled* (as) a nuisance because of his past behavior. • words that *are labeled* "obsolete"

la·bia /ˈleɪbijə/ *noun* [*plural*] *technical* : the folds of skin at the outer part of a woman's sexual organs

la·bi·al /ˈleɪbijəl/ *adj, linguistics, of a sound* : produced by using one or both lips • the *labial* sounds /f/ and /p/
— **labial** *noun, pl* **-als** [*count*] • /f/ and /p/ are *labials*.

[1]la·bor (*US*) *or Brit* **la·bour** /ˈleɪbɚ/ *noun, pl* **-bors**
1 a : physical or mental effort : WORK [*noncount*] A day's *labor* should get the job done. • Getting the job done will require many hours of difficult *labor*. • menial/manual *labor* [*count*] He rested from his *labors*. ✧ A ***labor of love*** is a task that you do for enjoyment rather than pay. • Restoring the old car was a *labor of love* for him. ✧ When you ***enjoy the fruits of your labor/labors***, you enjoy the things that you have gained by working. • She worked hard for many years, but now she has retired and is able to *enjoy the fruits of her labor/labors*. **b** [*noncount*] : work for which someone is paid • The cost of repairing the car includes parts and *labor*.
2 [*noncount*] **a** : workers considered as a group • an area in which there is a shortage of cheap *labor* — often used before another noun • a *labor* dispute • The company sought to cut *labor* costs by increasing its efficiency. • The company has a history of poor ***labor relations*** [=the workers and the managers of the company have had many disputes] • the ***labor force*** [=the total number of people available for working] **b** : the organizations or officials that represent groups of workers • The proposed new law is opposed by ***organized labor***.
3 : the process by which a woman gives birth to a baby [*noncount*] She went ***into labor*** this morning. • She has been ***in labor*** for several hours. • She began to have/experience ***labor pains*** this morning. [*singular*] She had a difficult *labor*.
4 ***Labour*** [*singular*] *Brit, politics* : the Labour Party of the United Kingdom or another part of the Commonwealth of Nations • a proposal that is opposed by *Labour*

[2]labor (*US*) *or Brit* **la·bour** *verb* **-bors**; **-bored**; **-bor·ing** [*no obj*]
1 a : to do work • Workers *labored* in the vineyard. • He *labored* for several years as a miner. **b** : to work hard in order to achieve something • She has *labored* in vain to convince

them to accept her proposal. • Both sides continue to *labor* [=*struggle*] to find a solution. • We should honor those who *labored* so long to make the truth known.
2 : to move or proceed with effort • The truck *labored* up the hill. • I have been *laboring* through this book for months.
3 : to repeat or stress something too much or too often • She has a tendency to *labor* the obvious. • I don't want to ***labor*** [=*belabor*] ***the point***, but I think I should mention again that we are running out of time.
labor under a delusion/misapprehension/misconception ✧ If you continue to believe something that is not true, you are *laboring under a delusion/misapprehension/misconception*. • He still *labors under the delusion* that other people value his opinion.

lab•o•ra•to•ry /ˈlæbrəˌtori, *Brit* ləˈbɒrətri/ *noun, pl* **-ries** [*count*] **:** a room or building with special equipment for doing scientific experiments and tests • experiments conducted in a modern *laboratory* • a research *laboratory* — often used before another noun • *laboratory* experiments/research/studies/tests — see also LANGUAGE LABORATORY

labor camp *noun, pl* **~ camps** [*count*] **:** a place where prisoners are kept and forced to do hard physical labor

Labor Day *noun, pl* **~ Days** [*count, noncount*] **:** the first Monday in September celebrated in the U.S. as a holiday in honor of working people

la•bored (*US*) *or Brit* **la•boured** /ˈleɪbɚd/ *adj* [*more ~; most ~*]
1 : produced or done with great effort • The patient's symptoms included a rapid pulse and *labored* breathing.
2 : not having an easy or natural quality • The movie's dialogue seems very *labored*. • *labored* writing/speech

la•bor•er (*US*) *or Brit* **la•bour•er** /ˈleɪbərɚ/ *noun, pl* **-ers** [*count*] **:** a person who does hard physical work for money • a farm *laborer* • He has been working as a *laborer* on a construction project. — see also DAY LABORER

la•bor–in•ten•sive (*US*) *or Brit* **la•bour–in•ten•sive** /ˈleɪbərɪnˌtɛnsɪv/ *adj* [*more ~; most ~*] **:** requiring a lot of work or workers to produce • the *labor-intensive* task of weaving cloth • The manufacturing process is *labor-intensive* and expensive. — compare CAPITAL-INTENSIVE

la•bo•ri•ous /ləˈborijəs/ *adj* [*more ~; most ~*] **:** requiring a lot of time and effort • Removing mildew stains is a *laborious* [=*difficult, painstaking*] task. • a slow and *laborious* process/procedure
– la•bo•ri•ous•ly *adv* • They spent many hours *laboriously* polishing the silverware. **– la•bo•ri•ous•ness** *noun* [*noncount*]

la•bor–sav•ing (*US*) *or Brit* **la•bour–sav•ing** /ˈleɪbɚˌseɪvɪŋ/ *adj* **:** designed to make a job or task easier to do • a *labor-saving* device such as a dishwasher

labor union *noun, pl* **~ unions** [*count*] *US* **:** an organization of workers formed to protect the rights and interests of its members **:** UNION

Lab•ra•dor retriever /ˈlæbrəˌdoɚ-/ *noun, pl* **~ -ers** [*count*] **:** a medium to large short-haired dog that is black, yellow, or brown in color — called also *Lab, Labrador*; see picture at DOG

lab•y•rinth /ˈlæbəˌrɪnθ/ *noun, pl* **-rinths** [*count*]
1 : a place that has many confusing paths or passages **:** MAZE • an immense underground *labyrinth* • a complex *labyrinth* of tunnels and chambers
2 : something that is extremely complicated or difficult to understand • The cockpit was a *labyrinth* of instruments and controls. • a *labyrinth* of social customs and rules
– lab•y•rin•thine /ˌlæbəˈrɪnθən, *Brit* ˌlæbəˈrɪnˌθaɪn/ *adj* [*more ~; most ~*] • He found it difficult to follow the movie's *labyrinthine* [=*elaborate, intricate*] plot. • the *labyrinthine* halls of the palace

¹lace /ˈleɪs/ *noun, pl* **lac•es**
1 [*count*] **:** a cord or string used for tying or holding things together; *especially* **:** SHOELACE • I need new *laces* for these shoes.
2 [*noncount*] **:** a very thin and light cloth made with patterns of holes • She wore *lace* on her wedding gown. — often used before another noun • *lace* curtains/tablecloth • a white *lace* scarf

²lace *verb* **laced; lac•ing**
1 a [*+ obj*] **:** to pull a lace through the holes of (a shoe, boot, etc.) • She was *lacing* (up) her shoes. **b** [*no obj*] **:** to be tied or fastened with a lace • a dress that *laces* in the back **c** [*+ obj*] **:** INTERLACE, INTERTWINE • She *laced* her fingers (together) behind her head.
2 [*+ obj*] **a :** to add a small amount of a powerful substance (such as alcohol, a drug, or a poison) to (something, such as a drink) — usually *+ with* • Someone had *laced* the punch *with* brandy. • The pills had been *laced with* poison. **b :** to add something that gives flavor or interest to (something) — usually used as *(be) laced with* • a sauce *laced with* garlic [=a sauce that has had garlic added to it] • conversation *laced with* sarcasm • Her reports *were* often *laced with* witty humor.

lac•er•ate /ˈlæsəˌreɪt/ *verb* **-ates; -at•ed; -at•ing** [*+ obj*] **:** to cut or tear (someone's flesh) deeply or roughly • The broken glass *lacerated* his feet. • The patient's hand was severely *lacerated*. — sometimes used figuratively • Her cruel remarks *lacerated* his feelings.
– lacerating *adj* • his *lacerating* [=extremely harsh] attacks on his critics

lac•er•a•tion /ˌlæsəˈreɪʃən/ *noun, pl* **-tions**
1 [*count*] **:** a deep cut or tear of the flesh • She suffered *lacerations* on her legs.
2 [*noncount*] **:** the act of cutting or tearing flesh • The broken glass caused severe *laceration* of his feet.

lace–up /ˈleɪsˌʌp/ *noun, pl* **-ups** [*count*] **:** a shoe or boot that is fastened with laces • a pair of *lace-ups* — often used before another noun • *lace-up* boots/shoes

lach•ry•mose /ˈlækrəˌmoʊs/ *adj* [*more ~; most ~*] *formal + literary*
1 : tending to cause tears **:** MOURNFUL • a *lachrymose* drama
2 : tending to cry often **:** TEARFUL • a drama with a *lachrymose* hero

¹lack /ˈlæk/ *verb* **lacks; lacked; lack•ing :** to not have (something) [*+ obj*] His book *lacks* any coherent structure. • They *lack* a good strategy for winning the election. • This painting *lacks* any artistic value. **:** to not have enough of (something) • She has never been accused of *lacking* confidence. • *lack* money • Many of these people *lack* the basic necessities of life. [*no obj*] (*chiefly US*) — *+ for* • The area does not *lack for* good restaurants. [=the area has many good restaurants] • She does not *lack for* confidence.

²lack *noun* **:** the state or condition of not having any or enough of something **:** the state or condition of lacking something [*singular*] The problem is a *lack* of money. • a *lack* of experience • She has been suffering from a *lack* of sleep lately. [*noncount*] Her problem is *lack* of sleep. • There was ***no lack of*** interest in the proposal. [=there was much interest in the proposal] • His honesty, or ***lack thereof***, is the real problem. [=the real problem is his lack of honesty] • They called it a comet, ***for lack of*** a better term/word. [=because they could not think of a better term/word for it]

lack•a•dai•si•cal /ˌlækəˈdeɪzɪkəl/ *adj* [*more ~; most ~*] **:** feeling or showing a lack of interest or enthusiasm • a *lackadaisical* student • His teachers did not approve of his *lackadaisical* approach to homework.
– lack•a•dai•si•cal•ly /ˌlækəˈdeɪzɪkli/ *adv*

lack•ey /ˈlæki/ *noun, pl* **-eys** [*count*] *disapproving* **:** a person who is or acts like a weak servant of someone powerful • He was nothing but a spineless *lackey* of the establishment. • a celebrity surrounded by his *lackeys*

lack•ing /ˈlækɪŋ/ *adj*
1 : not having any or enough of something that is needed or wanted • Evidence that supports his claims is *lacking*. • Her performance was somehow *lacking*. — often *+ in* • This wine is *lacking in* any real flavor. [=this wine does not have any real flavor] • The applicant was completely/totally *lacking in* experience. • The case was found (to be) *lacking in* merit.
2 : needed, wanted, or expected but not present or available • There was something *lacking* [=*missing*] in her performance.

lack•lus•ter (*US*) *or Brit* **lack•lus•tre** /ˈlækˌlʌstɚ/ *adj* [*more ~; most ~*] **:** lacking excitement or interest • a *lackluster* [=*dull, mediocre*] performance • His writing can be *lackluster* [=*uninspired*] at times.

la•con•ic /ləˈkɑːnɪk/ *adj* [*more ~; most ~*] **:** using few words in speech or writing • a *laconic* reply/response • a *laconic* manner/style • *laconic* humor • He had a reputation for being *laconic*. ***synonyms*** see CONCISE
– la•con•i•cal•ly /ləˈkɑːnɪkli/ *adv*

lac•quer /ˈlækɚ/ *noun, pl* **-quers** [*count, noncount*] **:** a liquid that is spread on wood or metal and that dries to form a hard and shiny surface • Many coats of *lacquer* were applied to the table.
– lac•quered /ˈlækɚd/ *adj* • a *lacquered* table

la·crosse /lə'krɑːs/ *noun* [*noncount*] **:** an outdoor game in which players use long-handled sticks with nets for catching, throwing, and carrying the ball

lac·tate /'læk,teɪt/ *verb* **-tates; -tat·ed; -tat·ing** [*no obj*] *technical, of a woman or a female animal* **:** to produce milk ▪ *lactating* mothers
– lac·ta·tion /læk'teɪʃən/ *noun* [*noncount*]

lac·tic acid /'læktɪk-/ *noun* [*noncount*] *technical* **:** a chemical produced by the body in your muscles during exercise

lac·tose /'læk,toʊs/ *noun* [*noncount*] *chemistry* **:** a type of sugar that is present in milk ▪ people who are ***lactose intolerant*** [=unable to digest lactose]

la·cu·na /lə'kuːnə, *Brit* lə'kjuːnə/ *noun, pl* **-nae** /-,naɪ/ *or* **-nas** [*count*] *formal* **:** a gap or blank space in something **:** a missing part ▪ She found a *lacuna* in the historical record.

lacrosse

lacy /'leɪsi/ *adj* **lac·i·er; -est**
1 : made of lace ▪ a *lacy* veil/border
2 : resembling lace ▪ The flower's petals are *lacy* and delicate.

lad /'læd/ *noun, pl* **lads** [*count*] *informal*
1 *chiefly Brit* **:** a boy or young man ▪ a charming young *lad* ▪ Life was hard when I was a *lad*. ▪ Well, *lad*, I hope you won't make the same mistake again! ▪ He's a good *lad* at heart. — compare LASS
2 *Brit* **:** a man with whom you are friendly **:** FELLOW, CHAP ▪ They can't treat us like that, can they, *lads*?! ▪ He was out drinking with ***the lads*** [=(*US*) *the guys, the boys*] at the pub. ✧ In British English, a man who is ***a bit of a lad*** does things that are considered a bit wild, such as getting drunk and having sexual relations with many women. ▪ He was *a bit of a lad* until he settled down.

lad·der /'lædɚ/ *noun, pl* **-ders** [*count*]
1 : a device used for climbing that has two long pieces of wood, metal, or rope with a series of steps or rungs between them ▪ *climb* a ladder — see also STEPLADDER
2 : a series of steps or stages by which someone moves up to a higher or better position ▪ He was moving up the corporate *ladder*. ▪ climbing the social *ladder* ▪ She worked her way up from the lowest rung on the economic *ladder*.
3 *Brit* **:** a long hole in a stocking **:** RUN ▪ She got/had a *ladder* in her stocking.
– ladder *verb* **-ders; -dered; -der·ing** [*no obj*] *Brit* ▪ My stockings *laddered*. [+ *obj*] *laddered* tights

lad·die /'lædi/ *noun, pl* **-dies** [*count*] *chiefly Scotland, informal* **:** a young boy ▪ a wee *laddie* — compare LASSIE

lad·dish /'lædɪʃ/ *adj* [*more* ~; *most* ~] *Brit, informal* **:** having qualities or ways of behaving that are considered typical of young men ▪ a *laddish* actor ▪ *laddish* horseplay
– lad·dish·ness *noun* [*noncount*]

lad·en /'leɪdn̩/ *adj* [*more* ~; *most* ~] **:** loaded heavily with something **:** having or carrying a large amount of something ▪ a richly/heavily *laden* buffet table [=a buffet table on which there is a large amount of food] ▪ sugar-*laden* junk food — usually + *with* ▪ mules/trucks heavily *laden with* supplies ▪ branches *laden with* fruit ▪ airline passengers *laden with* luggage — often used figuratively ▪ The song is *laden with* meaning and feeling. [=the song has/carries a lot of meaning and feeling] ▪ His voice was heavily *laden with* sarcasm. [=his voice was very sarcastic]

la–di–da /,lɑ,di'dɑː/ *adj* [*more* ~; *most* ~] *informal* **:** acting or talking in a false and annoying way that is thought to be typical of rich and important people ▪ some *la-di-da* movie star ▪ talking with a *la-di-da* accent

la·dies /'leɪdiz/ *noun* [*singular*] *Brit, informal* **:** LADIES' ROOM — usually used with *the* ▪ Can you tell me where *the ladies* is, please? — compare GENTS

ladies' man *noun, pl* ~ **men** [*count*] *informal* **:** a man who enjoys being with and giving attention to women ▪ He considered himself a real *ladies' man*.

ladies' room *noun, pl* ~ **rooms** [*count*] *US* **:** a public bathroom for use by women and girls — called also (*US*) *women's room*, (*Brit*) *ladies*; compare MEN'S ROOM

¹la·dle /'leɪdl/ *noun, pl* **la·dles** [*count*] **:** a large and deep spoon with a long handle that is used for serving a liquid ▪ a soup *ladle*

²ladle *verb* **ladles; la·dled; la·dling** [+ *obj*] **:** to take up and carry (a liquid) by using a large spoon **:** to serve (a liquid) with a ladle ▪ The soup was *ladled* into the bowls. ▪ *ladling* the wine into cups — often + *out* ▪ volunteers *ladling out* soup to homeless people — sometimes used figuratively ▪ He's always *ladling out* unwanted advice to his friends.

la·dy /'leɪdi/ *noun, pl* **-dies** [*count*]
1 : a woman who behaves in a polite way ▪ Her mother was always telling her to act like a *lady*. ▪ She's a real *lady*.
2 : WOMAN ▪ He bumped into some *lady* walking to the bus stop. ▪ (*chiefly US, informal*) She's one feisty/sexy *lady*, I can tell you! ▪ He helped ***a little old lady*** cross the street. — used especially in polite speech or when speaking to a group of women ▪ The *lady* behind the counter will take your order. ▪ She told her little boy to say "thank you" to the nice *lady* for helping them. ▪ Would someone please get the/this *lady* a chair? ▪ Good evening, *ladies* and gentlemen! ▪ Please step this way, *ladies*. — sometimes used informally in U.S. English when speaking to one woman ▪ Hey, *lady*, you forgot your purse! [=(more commonly and politely) excuse me, ma'am, you forgot your purse] — sometimes used informally before another noun ▪ a *lady* doctor [=(more commonly and politely) a female/woman doctor] ✧ The phrase ***young lady*** is used in informal speech as a form of address for a girl or young woman. An angry parent speaking to a daughter, for example, might address her as *young lady*. ▪ Just where do you think you're going, *young lady*?! — see also BAG LADY, CLEANING LADY, DRAGON LADY, *lady luck* at ¹LUCK
3 : a woman of high social position ▪ the *ladies* of society
4 a *informal* **:** a man's girlfriend ▪ I've been wanting to meet his new *lady*. **b** *chiefly Brit, old-fashioned* **:** a man's wife ▪ What would you and your good *lady* like to drink?
5 ***Lady*** **:** a woman who is a member of the nobility — used as a title ▪ *Lady* Margaret
it ain't over until/till the fat lady sings *US, informal* — used to say that the final result of something (such as a sports contest) has not yet been decided and could still change ▪ We're losing, but remember: *it ain't over till the fat lady sings*. [=the game is not over; there is still a chance that we could win]
– see also FIRST LADY, LEADING LADY, OLD LADY

la·dy·bug /'leɪdi,bʌg/ *noun, pl* **-bugs** [*count*] *US* **:** a type of small flying insect that has a round red back with dark spots — called also (*Brit*) *la·dy·bird* /'leɪdi,bɚd/ see color picture on page C10

la·dy–in–wait·ing /'leɪdijɪn'weɪtɪŋ/ *noun, pl* **la·dies–in–wait·ing** [*count*] **:** a woman whose job is provide help to a queen or princess

la·dy–kill·er /'leɪdi'kɪlɚ/ *noun, pl* **-ers** [*count*] *informal* + *somewhat old-fashioned* **:** a man who is known for being very attractive to women and who has relations with many women ▪ He had a reputation as a real *lady-killer*.

la·dy·like /'leɪdi,laɪk/ *adj* [*more* ~; *most* ~] **:** polite and quiet in a way that has traditionally been considered suited to a woman ▪ *ladylike* behavior ▪ encouraging young women to be more *ladylike*

lady of the house *noun*
the lady of the house *somewhat old-fashioned* **:** the female family member who has the most responsibility for taking care of and making decisions about the household ▪ Is the *lady of the house* at home?

La·dy·ship /'leɪdi,ʃɪp/ *noun, pl* **-ships** [*count*] *chiefly Brit* — used in addressing or referring to a woman who is a member of the nobility ▪ *Her Ladyship* is not at home. ▪ Can I get *Your Ladyship* anything else?

¹lag /'læg/ *verb* **lags; lagged; lag·ging**
1 [*no obj*] **a :** to move more slowly than others **:** to fail to walk or move as quickly as others — usually + *behind* ▪ One of the hikers kept *lagging behind* the rest of the group. ▪ We had to stop and wait because someone was *lagging behind*. **b :** to be in a position that is behind others — usually + *behind* ▪ a politician who is *lagging behind* [=*trailing*] in the election campaign ▪ The company has *lagged behind* its competitors in developing new products.
2 [*no obj*] **:** to happen or develop more slowly than expected or wanted — usually + *behind* ▪ Production has continued to *lag* (far/well/way) *behind* schedule/demand.
– compare ³LAG

²lag *noun, pl* **lags** [*singular*] **:** a space of time between two events ▪ There is a *lag* of a day or two between the time you deposit a check and the time the funds are available for withdrawal. ▪ There is a slight *lag* between the time when the camera's shutter is pressed and the actual taking of the picture. ▪ Work on the project has resumed after a *lag* of several months. — called also *time lag*; see also JET LAG

³lag *verb* **lags; lagged; lagging** [+ *obj*] *Brit* : to cover (something, such as a pipe) with a special material (called lagging) that keeps it from losing or gaining heat ▪ Be sure to *lag* [=*insulate*] the pipe to prevent heat loss. — compare ¹LAG

la·ger /ˈlɑːgɚ/ *noun, pl* **-gers** [*count, noncount*] : a type of beer that is light in color and is aged at cool temperatures ▪ a pint of *lager*

lager lout *noun, pl* ~ **louts** [*count*] *Brit, informal* : a man who gets drunk and then behaves badly

lag·gard /ˈlægɚd/ *noun, pl* **-gards** [*count*] *somewhat old-fashioned* : a person or thing that does not go or move as quickly as others ▪ The company has been a *laggard* in developing new products.
– **laggard** *adj* [*more* ~; *most* ~] ▪ He was *laggard* [=*slow*] in payment of his debts.

lag·ging /ˈlægɪŋ/ *noun* [*noncount*] *Brit* : a special material that is used to cover something (such as a pipe) to keep it from losing or gaining heat

la·goon /ləˈguːn/ *noun, pl* **-goons** [*count*] : an area of sea water that is separated from the ocean by a reef or sandbar ▪ a tropical blue *lagoon*

laid *past tense and past participle of* ¹LAY

laid–back /ˈleɪdˈbæk/ *adj* [*more* ~; *most* ~] *informal* : relaxed and calm ▪ My boss is pretty *laid-back* about most things. ▪ a *laid-back* attitude ▪ He enjoyed the restaurant's *laid-back* style.

lain *past participle of* ¹LIE

lair /ˈleɚ/ *noun, pl* **lairs** [*count*]
1 : the place where a wild animal sleeps ▪ tracking the bear back to its *lair*
2 : a place where someone hides or where someone goes to be alone and to feel safe or comfortable ▪ the villain's *lair* ▪ She runs the project from her private *lair* in the suburbs.

laird /ˈleɚd/ *noun, pl* **lairds** [*count*] : a man who owns a large amount of land in Scotland

lairy /ˈleri/ *adj* **lair·i·er; -est** [*also more* ~; *most* ~] *Brit slang* : unpleasantly loud, confident, etc. ▪ When he drinks he gets a bit *lairy*.

¹lais·sez–faire /ˌlɛˌseɪˈfeɚ/ *noun* [*noncount*] *economics* : a policy that allows businesses to operate with very little interference from the government ▪ a strong advocate of *laissez-faire*

²laissez–faire *adj, always used before a noun* [*more* ~; *most* ~] *economics* : favoring a policy that allows businesses to operate with very little interference from the government ▪ *laissez-faire* capitalism/economics — often used figuratively ▪ She took a *laissez-faire* approach to managing her employees. [=she allowed her employees to do what they chose to do without much direction from her]

la·ity /ˈlejəti/ *noun* [*noncount*] : the people of a religion who are not priests, ministers, etc. ▪ a member of the *laity* ▪ The *laity* has/have played an important role in the history of the church. — compare CLERGY, LAYMAN, LAYWOMAN

lake /ˈleɪk/ *noun, pl* **lakes** [*count*] : a large area of water that is surrounded by land ▪ They own a cottage at/by/on the *lake*. ▪ the shores of the *lake* — often used in names ▪ *Lake* Michigan — see color picture on page C7
(go) jump in a/the lake *chiefly US, informal* — used as an angry way to tell someone to go away ▪ I was so mad at him that I told him to *go jump in a lake*.

lake·front /ˈleɪkˌfrʌnt/ *noun, pl* **-fronts** [*count*] *chiefly US* : the land beside a lake ▪ We went for a walk down at the *lakefront*. — often used before another noun ▪ *lakefront* property

lake·shore /ˈleɪkˌʃoɚ/ *noun, pl* **-shores** [*count*] : the shore of a lake ▪ Follow this path to the *lakeshore*.; *also* : LAKEFRONT ▪ *lakeshore* condominiums

lake·side /ˈleɪkˌsaɪd/ *noun, pl* **-sides** [*count*] : LAKEFRONT — usually used before another noun ▪ a *lakeside* home/cottage/community

la–la land /ˈlɑːˌlɑː-/ *noun* [*noncount*] *informal*
1 : the mental state of someone who is not aware of what is really happening — usually used in the phrase ***in la-la land*** ▪ I tried to talk to him, but he was off *in la-la land*. ▪ If that's what she thinks, she's living *in la-la land*. — called also (*Brit*) *cloud-cuckoo-land*
2 ***La-La Land*** — used as a nickname for Los Angeles, California ▪ stories about life in *La-La Land*

lam /ˈlæm/ *noun*
on the lam *US, informal* : trying to avoid being caught by the police ▪ two escaped convicts *on the lam* ✧ If you ***take it on the lam***, you try to escape. This expression is now used mainly to suggest or imitate the language of old movies about gangsters. ▪ She stole a lot of money from her employer and *took it on the lam*.

la·ma /ˈlɑːmə/ *noun, pl* **-mas** [*count*] : a Buddhist priest of Tibet or Mongolia

La·maze /ləˈmɑːz/ *adj, always used before a noun, medical* : of or relating to a method of preparing women to give birth to children without the use of drugs ▪ taking *Lamaze* classes ▪ the *Lamaze* method

¹lamb /ˈlæm/ *noun, pl* **lambs**
1 a [*count*] : a young sheep ▪ She's as gentle as a *lamb*. ▪ a sacrificial *lamb* — compare EWE, ¹RAM **b** [*noncount*] : the meat of a lamb ▪ leg/rack of *lamb* ▪ *lamb* chops
2 [*count*] *informal* : an innocent, weak, or gentle person ▪ You poor *lamb*.
like a lamb to the slaughter : in a very innocent way : without knowing that something bad will happen ▪ He walked into the meeting *like a lamb to the slaughter*.
mutton dressed as lamb see MUTTON

²lamb *verb* **lambs; lambed; lamb·ing** [*no obj*] *of a sheep* : to give birth to a lamb ▪ The ewes will *lamb* soon.

lam·baste *or* **lam·bast** /ˌlæmˈbeɪst, ˌlæmˈbæst/ *verb* **-bastes** *or* **-basts; -bast·ed; -bast·ing** [+ *obj*] : to criticize (someone or something) very harshly ▪ The coach *lambasted* the team for its poor play. ▪ They wrote several letters *lambasting* the new law.

lam·bent /ˈlæmbənt/ *adj, formal + literary*
1 : shining or glowing softly ▪ *lambent* flames ▪ *lambent* sunlight glinting off the waves
2 : having a light, appealing quality ▪ a writer known for her *lambent* wit

lamb·skin /ˈlæmˌskɪn/ *noun, pl* **-skins** [*count, noncount*] : the skin of a lamb ▪ gloves made of *lambskin* — often used before another noun ▪ *lambskin* gloves

lambs·wool /ˈlæmzˌwʊl/ *noun* [*noncount*] : soft wool from lambs — often used before another noun ▪ a *lambswool* sweater

lame /ˈleɪm/ *adj* **lam·er; -est** [*also more* ~; *most* ~]
1 : having an injured leg or foot that makes walking difficult or painful ▪ a *lame* horse ▪ The horse had gone *lame*, and it grew *lamer*. ▪ The accident left him *lame* for life.
2 *informal* : not strong, good, or effective : WEAK ▪ He offered a *lame* apology/defense/excuse for his actions. ▪ That joke was *lame*.
3 *US, informal* : not smart or impressive ▪ She's nice, but her boyfriend is really *lame*.
the lame : people who are lame ▪ providing care for the sick and *the lame*
– **lame·ly** *adv* ▪ He hobbled *lamely* down the path. ▪ He *lamely* listed his excuses. – **lame·ness** *noun* [*noncount*] ▪ a common cause of *lameness* in horses ▪ the *lameness* of his excuse

la·mé /lɑˈmeɪ/ *noun* [*noncount*] : shiny cloth that contains silver or gold threads

lame·brain /ˈleɪmˌbreɪn/ *noun, pl* **-brains** [*count*] *US, informal* : a stupid person ▪ Listen, *lamebrain*, we've had enough of your idiotic suggestions!
– **lamebrain** *or* **lame·brained** /ˈleɪmˌbreɪnd/ *adj, always used before a noun* ▪ *lamebrain* [=*stupid*] ideas ▪ The movie is a *lamebrained* comedy.

lame duck *noun, pl* ~ **ducks** [*count*]
1 *chiefly US* : an elected official whose time in an office or position will soon end ▪ The President was a *lame duck* during the end of his second term. — often used before another noun ▪ a *lame-duck* president
2 *chiefly Brit* : a person, company, etc., that is weak or unsuccessful and needs help

¹la·ment /ləˈmɛnt/ *verb* **-ments; -ment·ed; -ment·ing** *formal* : to express sorrow, regret, or unhappiness about something [*no obj*] She *lamented* over the loss of her best friend. ▪ (*chiefly US*) He was *lamenting* about rising gasoline prices. [+ *obj*] She *lamented* (the fact) that she had lost her best friend. = She *lamented* having lost her best friend. = She *lamented* the loss of her best friend. ▪ "I've lost my best friend!" she *lamented*. — see also LAMENTED

²lament *noun, pl* **-ments** [*count*] *formal* : an expression of sorrow; *especially* : a song or poem that expresses sorrow for someone who has died or something that is gone ▪ The poem is a *lament* for a lost love.

L

la·men·ta·ble /ləˈmɛntəbəl, ˈlæməntəbəl/ *adj* [*more* ~; *most* ~] *formal* : deserving to be criticized or regretted ▪ The region has a long and *lamentable* [=*regrettable*] history of ethnic fighting. ▪ a *lamentable* [=*unfortunate*] consequence of the war

– **la·men·ta·bly** /ləˈmɛntəbli, ˈlæməntəbli/ *adv* ▪ Funding for the project was *lamentably* low. ▪ *Lamentably*, they were unprepared for the disaster.

lam·en·ta·tion /ˌlæmənˈteɪʃən/ *noun, pl* **-tions** *formal* : an expression of great sorrow or deep sadness [*count*] bitter *lamentations* for the dead [*noncount*] words spoken in *lamentation* for the dead

la·ment·ed /ləˈmɛntəd/ *adj, always used before a noun* : deeply missed — used to refer to someone who has died ▪ her ***late lamented*** husband

[1]**lam·i·nate** /ˈlæməˌneɪt/ *verb* **-nates**; **-nat·ed**; **-nat·ing** [+ *obj*] : to cover (something) with a thin layer of clear plastic for protection ▪ *laminate* a photograph

[2]**lam·i·nate** /ˈlæmənət/ *noun, pl* **-nates** : a product made by pressing together thin layers of material [*noncount*] The kitchen counters are made of plastic *laminate*. [*count*] plastic *laminates*

lam·i·na·ted /ˈlæməˌneɪtəd/ *adj*

1 : made by pressing together thin layers of material ▪ *laminated* wood ▪ *laminated* kitchen counters

2 : covered with a thin layer of clear plastic for protection ▪ a *laminated* photograph

lamp /ˈlæmp/ *noun, pl* **lamps** [*count*]

1 : a device that produces light ▪ turn on/off the *lamp* ▪ a street *lamp* ▪ a table/desk *lamp* ▪ an ***oil lamp*** [=a device that produces light by burning oil] — see picture at LIVING ROOM; see also FLOOR LAMP

2 : LIGHT BULB

lamp·light /ˈlæmpˌlaɪt/ *noun* [*noncount*] : the light of a lamp ▪ We could see the glow of *lamplight* in the window.

[1]**lam·poon** /læmˈpuːn/ *verb* **-poons**; **-pooned**; **-poon·ing** [+ *obj*] : to publicly criticize (someone or something) in a way that causes laughter : to mock or make fun of (someone or something) ▪ The politician was *lampooned* in cartoons.

[2]**lampoon** *noun, pl* **-poons** [*count*] : a piece of writing, a cartoon, etc., that mocks or makes fun of a well-known person or thing ▪ He said such ridiculous things that he was often the target of *lampoons* in the press.

lamp·post /ˈlæmpˌpoʊst/ *noun, pl* **-posts** [*count*] : a post with an outdoor lamp on top

lamp·shade /ˈlæmpˌʃeɪd/ *noun, pl* **-shades** [*count*] : a cover that softens or directs the light of a lamp ▪ a silk/glass/paper *lampshade*

LAN /ˈlæn, ˌɛlˌeɪˈɛn/ *noun, pl* **LANs** [*count*] : LOCAL AREA NETWORK

[1]**lance** /ˈlæns, *Brit* ˈlɑːns/ *noun, pl* **lanc·es** [*count*] : a long, pointed weapon used in the past by knights riding on horses

[2]**lance** *verb* **lances**; **lanced**; **lanc·ing** [+ *obj*] *medical* : to cut (an infected area on a person's skin) with a sharp tool so that pus will flow out ▪ He had the boil/blister on his arm *lanced*.

lance corporal *noun, pl* ~ **-rals** [*count*] : a person in the U.S. Marines, the Royal Marines, or the British Army with a rank just below that of corporal

lan·cet /ˈlænsət, *Brit* ˈlɑːnsət/ *noun, pl* **-cets** [*count*] *medical* : a sharp tool used for cutting the skin

[1]**land** /ˈlænd/ *noun, pl* **lands**

1 [*noncount*] : the solid part of the surface of the Earth : an area of ground ▪ arid/fertile/flat *land* ▪ the *land* along the highway ▪ The *land* stretched as far as you could see. ▪ They cleared some *land* to grow crops. ▪ After two days of sailing, we were miles from *land*. ▪ They invaded the country by *land* and by sea. — often used before another noun ▪ *land* animals [=animals that live on land] ▪ a total *land* area of two miles ▪ a *land* battle/war [=a battle/war fought on the ground rather than at sea or in the air] — see also DRY LAND, LAY OF THE LAND, WETLAND

2 : an area of the earth's solid surface that is owned by someone [*noncount*] They own *land* in Alaska. ▪ They bought some *land* and built a house. ▪ a piece/plot of *land* [*plural*] His *lands* extend as far as the eye can see. — often used before another noun ▪ *land* development/ownership/prices

3 [*count*] : a country or nation ▪ He was the most powerful politician in the *land*. ▪ foreign *lands* ▪ the *lands* of/in the Far East ▪ He always remained loyal to his ***native land***. [=the country in which he was born] ▪ America, the ***land of opportunity*** — sometimes used figuratively ▪ in the *land* [=*realm*] of dreams ▪ a *land* of illusion — see also DREAMLAND, LA-LA LAND, NEVER-NEVER LAND, NO-MAN'S LAND, PROMISED LAND

4 ***the land*** : land in the countryside that is thought of as providing a simple and good way of living ▪ He wanted to move/get back to *the land*. ▪ people who are ***living off the land*** [=getting food by farming, hunting, etc.] ▪ farmers ***working the land*** [=planting and growing crops]

how the land lies *chiefly Brit* : the true facts about a situation ▪ Let's see *how the land lies* before we make any decisions. ▪ We don't know *how the land lies*.

in the land of the living *informal* : ALIVE ▪ I hadn't heard from him for years and was glad to find him still *in the land of the living*.

land of milk and honey : a place where there is plenty of food and money and life is very easy ▪ Many immigrants thought that America was a *land of milk and honey*.

live off/on the fat of the land see [2]FAT

[2]**land** *verb* **lands**; **land·ed**; **land·ing**

1 a [*no obj*] : to return to the ground or another surface after a flight ▪ The plane *landed* on the runway. ▪ We watched the seaplanes *landing* on the water. ▪ The bird *landed* in a tree. ▪ A butterfly *landed* on the flower. ▪ Our flight was scheduled to *land* in Pittsburgh at 4:00. ▪ It was raining heavily at the airport when we *landed*. ▪ The plane *landed* safely. **b** [+ *obj*] : to cause (an airplane, helicopter, etc.) to return to the ground or another surface after a flight ▪ The pilot was able to *land* the plane on the runway.

2 a [*no obj*] : to hit or come to a surface after falling or moving through the air ▪ I fell and *landed* on my shoulder. [=my shoulder hit the ground when I fell] ▪ He tripped and his plate *landed* on the floor. [=his plate fell to the floor] ▪ The golf ball *landed* in the trees. ▪ I could not see where the ball *landed*. ▪ The cat fell from the tree but *landed* on its feet. — sometimes used figuratively ▪ He lost his job but ***landed on his feet*** [=ended up in a good situation] when he was hired by another company just a few days later. **b** [+ *obj*] *sports* : to complete (a jump or other athletic movement) by landing on your feet ▪ The skater *landed* all her jumps. ▪ He *landed* his dismount from the parallel bars perfectly.

3 a [+ *obj*] : to cause (someone) to be in a specified place or situation ▪ The injury *landed* her in the hospital. ▪ His carelessness is going to *land* him in trouble. **b** [*no obj*] : to reach or come to a place or situation that was not planned or expected ▪ He *landed* (up) in jail. [=he ended up in jail] ▪ She took the wrong subway and *landed* on the other side of town. ▪ The team *landed* in first place. ▪ Another memo from the boss *landed* on my desk [=came to my desk] today.

4 [+ *obj*] : to succeed in getting (something) ▪ He *landed* the job. ▪ The salesman *landed* the order. ▪ She *landed* the lead part in the play.

5 a [+ *obj*] : to put (someone or something) onto the shore from a ship or boat ▪ The boat *landed* him close to the beach. ▪ The boat *landed* its cargo close to the beach. ▪ These craft are designed for *landing* troops and equipment. **b** [*no obj*] : to go onto the shore from a ship or boat ▪ The troops *landed* on the island. **c** [*no obj*] *of a ship or boat or its passengers* : to reach the shore ▪ Will the cruise ship *land* [=*arrive*] on schedule? ▪ The boat *landed* at dusk. ▪ There was nowhere for the boat to *land*.

6 [+ *obj*] : to catch and bring in (a fish) ▪ Farther down the stream he *landed* a trout.

7 [+ *obj*] : to hit someone with (a punch, blow, etc.) ▪ During the fight he never *landed* a punch.

land in your lap see [1]LAP

land with [*phrasal verb*] ***land (someone) with (something or someone)*** *Brit, informal* : to force (someone) to deal with (something or someone unpleasant) ▪ I always get *landed with* the washing-up.

land·ed /ˈlændəd/ *adj, always used before a noun*

1 : owning a large amount of land ▪ the *landed* gentry/aristocracy/class

2 : including a large amount of land ▪ a *landed* estate ▪ *landed* wealth

land·fall /ˈlændˌfɑːl/ *noun, pl* **-falls** [*count*] : the land that is first seen or reached after a journey by sea or air ▪ From the deck of the boat, we saw our first *landfall*. ▪ They ***made landfall*** [=they reached land] on the fourth day of their journey.

land·fill /ˈlændˌfɪl/ *noun, pl* **-fills**

1 [*noncount*] : a system in which waste materials are buried under the ground ▪ using *landfill* to dispose of trash

2 : an area where waste is buried under the ground [*count*]

waste buried in *landfills* [*noncount*] Part of the city was built on *landfill*.

land·form /ˈlænd,foəm/ *noun, pl* **-forms** [*count*] *geology* **:** a natural feature (such as a mountain or valley) of the Earth's surface • *landforms* created by glaciers

land·hold·er /ˈlænd,houldə/ *noun, pl* **-ers** [*count*] **:** a person who owns land **:** LANDOWNER • a large *landholder* [=a person who owns a large amount of land]

– **land·hold·ing** /ˈlænd,houldɪŋ/ *noun, pl* **-ings** [*count*] • a wealthy man with large *landholdings*

land·ing /ˈlændɪŋ/ *noun, pl* **-ings**

1 : an act of returning to the ground or another surface after a flight [*count*] The plane made a smooth/perfect *landing*. • The helicopter had to make an emergency *landing*. • The pilot was practicing takeoffs and *landings*. • a lunar/moon *landing* [=a landing on the moon] [*noncount*] *Landing* in high winds can be dangerous. • Our plane was cleared for *landing*. — often used before another noun • an airplane's *landing* lights • a *landing* zone/site — see also SOFT LANDING

2 [*count*] **:** a level area at the top of stairs or between two sets of stairs • We stopped to rest at the first floor *landing*.

3 [*count*] **:** a place where boats and ships load and unload passengers and cargo • I waited at the *landing* for the ferry.

4 [*count*] **:** a military action in which soldiers are brought by boat, airplane, helicopter, etc., to land at a place controlled by the enemy • troop *landings*

landing craft *noun, pl* ~ **craft** [*count*] **:** a boat or ship designed to bring soldiers and equipment to the shore

landing field *noun, pl* ~ **fields** [*count*] **:** a field where aircraft land and take off **:** AIRFIELD

landing gear *noun* [*noncount*] **:** the wheels and other parts of an aircraft that support its weight when it is on the ground — called also *undercarriage*

landing strip *noun, pl* ~ **strips** [*count*] **:** AIRSTRIP

land·la·dy /ˈlænd,leɪdi/ *noun, pl* **-dies** [*count*]

1 : a woman who owns a house, apartment, etc., and rents it to other people

2 : a woman who runs an inn, pub, or rooming house — compare LANDLORD

land·less /ˈlændləs/ *adj* **:** not owning any land • *landless* people

land·locked /ˈlænd,lɑːkt/ *adj* **:** surrounded by land • a *landlocked* country

land·lord /ˈlænd,loəd/ *noun, pl* **-lords** [*count*]

1 : a person who owns a house, apartment, etc., and rents it to other people — see also ABSENTEE LANDLORD

2 : a man who runs an inn, pub, or rooming house — compare LANDLADY

land·lub·ber /ˈlænd,lʌbə/ *noun, pl* **-bers** [*count*] *old-fashioned + humorous* **:** a person who knows very little or nothing about the sea or ships **:** a person who is not a sailor

land·mark /ˈlænd,mɑək/ *noun, pl* **-marks** [*count*]

1 a : an object or structure on land that is easy to see and recognize • The Golden Gate Bridge is a famous/familiar *landmark* in San Francisco. **b** *US* **:** a building or place that was important in history • The battlefield is a national historical *landmark*.

2 : a very important event or achievement • The moon landing is a *landmark* in space exploration. • The decision/ruling was a *landmark* in legal history. — often used before another noun • a *landmark* legal case • a *landmark* court decision • a *landmark* discovery

land·mass /ˈlænd,mæs/ *noun, pl* **-mass·es** [*count*] **:** a very large area of land (such as a continent) • continental *landmasses*

land mine *noun, pl* ~ **mines** [*count*] **:** a bomb that is buried in the ground and that explodes when someone steps on it or drives over it — sometimes used figuratively • an issue that is an emotional/political *land mine* [=an issue that could cause great emotional/political damage; an explosive issue]

land·own·er /ˈlænd,ounə/ *noun, pl* **-ers** [*count*] **:** a person who owns land • a large *landowner* [=a person who owns a large amount of land] • a wealthy *landowner*

– **land·own·ing** /ˈlænd,ounɪŋ/ *adj, always used before a noun* • *landowning* families

[1]**land·scape** /ˈlænd,skeɪp/ *noun, pl* **-scapes**

1 [*count*] **:** a picture that shows a natural scene of land or the countryside • She likes to paint *landscapes*. • a *landscape* painter/artist

2 [*count*] **:** an area of land that has a particular quality or appearance • The farm is set in a *landscape* of rolling hills. • He gazed out at the beautiful *landscape*. • a desert/rural/urban *landscape* — see color picture on page C7

3 [*count*] **:** a particular area of activity • The last several years have seen real changes in the political *landscape*. [=*scene*]

4 [*noncount*] **:** a way of printing a page so that the shorter sides are on the left and right and the longer sides are at the top and bottom — compare PORTRAIT

[2]**landscape** *verb* **-scapes; -scaped; -scap·ing** [+ *obj*] **:** to make changes to improve the appearance of (an area of land) • A professional *landscaped* the yard. • an area *landscaped* with flowering shrubs and trees • a beautifully *landscaped* campus

– **land·scap·er** *noun, pl* **-ers** [*count*] • He hired professional *landscapers* to plan a garden. – **landscaping** *noun* [*noncount*] • We admired the beautiful *landscaping* of the campus/yard. • a *landscaping* service

landscape architect *noun, pl* ~ **-tects** [*count*] **:** a person whose job is to plan and create large outdoor spaces such as gardens, parks, etc.

– **landscape architecture** *noun* [*noncount*]

landscape gardener *noun, pl* ~ **-ers** [*count*] **:** a person who designs and creates large gardens

– **landscape gardening** *noun* [*noncount*]

land·slide /ˈlænd,slaɪd/ *noun, pl* **-slides** [*count*]

1 : a large mass of rocks and earth that suddenly and quickly moves down the side of a mountain or hill • The earthquake triggered a *landslide*. • They were buried under the *landslide*.

2 : an election in which the winner gets a much greater number of votes than the loser • The presidential election turned out to be one of the biggest *landslides* in history. • a *landslide* victory • She won the election ***by/in a landslide***.

land·slip /ˈlænd,slɪp/ *noun, pl* **-slips** [*count*] *Brit* **:** LANDSLIDE 1

lane /ˈleɪn/ *noun, pl* **lanes** [*count*]

1 : a narrow road or path • a country *lane* — often used in the names of streets • Their house is on Maple *Lane*.

2 : a part of road that is marked by painted lines and that is for a single line of vehicles • traffic *lanes* • a highway with three *lanes* = a three-*lane* highway • The truck's driver kept ***changing lanes***. — see also BREAKDOWN LANE, FAST LANE, PASSING LANE, SLOW LANE

3 : a narrow part of a track or swimming pool that is used by a single runner or swimmer in a race • She moved to the outside *lane*.

4 : an ocean route used by ships • shipping *lanes*

5 : a long narrow surface that is used for bowling • a bowling *lane*

6 *US* **:** an area in a store (such as a supermarket) where customers form a line while waiting to pay for the things they are buying • Customers with fewer than 12 items can use the ***express lane***. [=the lane that lets people pay for their items more quickly than other lanes]

memory lane see MEMORY

lan·guage /ˈlæŋgwɪʤ/ *noun, pl* **-guag·es**

1 a [*noncount*] **:** the system of words or signs that people use to express thoughts and feelings to each other • spoken and written *language* • the origin of *language* — often used before another noun • *language* acquisition • *language* skills — see also BODY LANGUAGE **b** [*count*] **:** any one of the systems of human language that are used and understood by a particular group of people • the English *language* • How many *languages* do you speak? • a foreign *language* • French is her first/native *language*. • The book has been translated into several *languages*. • He's learning English as a second *language*. • After a few days in France, I realized that I didn't know the *language* [=I didn't know the French language] as well as I had thought. • a new word that has recently entered the *language* • a *language* instructor/teacher • foreign *language* classes • A ***language barrier*** existed between the two countries. [=people in the two countries did not understand each other because they spoke different languages] — see also SIGN LANGUAGE

2 [*noncount*] **:** words of a particular kind • the formal *language* of the report • the beauty of Shakespeare's *language* • She expressed her ideas using simple and clear *language*. • He is always careful in his use of *language*. • bad/foul/obscene/strong/vulgar *language* • You'd better ***watch your language*** [=be careful about the words you use] when you're talking to her.

3 [*noncount*] **:** the words and expressions used in a particular activity or by a particular group of people • the *language* of

L

diplomacy/lawyers ▪ legal/military *language*
4 [*count*] : a system of signs and symbols that is used to control a computer ▪ a programming *language*
5 [*count*] : a system of sounds or movements by which animals communicate with each other ▪ the *language* of bees/dolphins
speak/talk the same language : to understand each other well because of shared ideas and feelings ▪ She and I will never get along. We just don't *speak the same language*.

language arts *noun* [*plural*] *chiefly US* : school subjects (such as reading, spelling, and writing) that relate to using language

language laboratory *noun, pl* ~ **-ries** [*count*] : a room with equipment (such as computers or tape recorders) where people can listen to and practice speaking foreign languages — called also *language lab*

lan·guid /ˈlæŋgwəd/ *adj, formal + literary* : showing or having very little strength, energy, or activity ▪ a long, *languid* sigh ▪ They proceeded at a *languid* pace. ▪ It was a hot, *languid* summer day.
— **lan·guid·ly** *adv* ▪ He was leaning *languidly* against the wall. ▪ The river moved *languidly*.

lan·guish /ˈlæŋgwɪʃ/ *verb* **-guish·es; -guished; -guish·ing** [*no obj*] *formal + literary* : to continue for a long time without activity or progress in an unpleasant or unwanted situation — usually + *in* ▪ The bill *languished in* the Senate for months. ▪ She *languished in* obscurity for many years until the success of her novel made her famous. ▪ an innocent man who has been *languishing in* prison for years

lan·guor /ˈlæŋgɚ/ *noun, literary* : a state of feeling tired and relaxed [*noncount*] They enjoyed the *languor* brought on by a hot summer afternoon. [*singular*] They felt an indefinable *languor*.
— **lan·guor·ous** /ˈlæŋgərəs/ *adj* ▪ a long *languorous* afternoon — **lan·guor·ous·ly** *adv*

lank /ˈlæŋk/ *adj, of hair* : hanging straight down in an unattractive way ▪ a woman with long, *lank* hair

lanky /ˈlæŋki/ *adj* **lank·i·er; -est** [*also more* ~; *most* ~] : tall and thin with usually an awkward quality ▪ a *lanky* teenager ▪ a *lanky* fashion model

lan·o·lin /ˈlænələn/ *noun* [*noncount*] : an oily substance that comes from sheep's wool and that is used for making soaps and lotions

lan·tern /ˈlæntən/ *noun, pl* **-terns** [*count*] : a light that has usually a glass covering and that can be carried by a handle — see picture at CAMPING; see also MAGIC LANTERN

lan·tern–jawed /ˈlæntənˌʤɑːd/ *adj* — used to describe someone whose lower jaw sticks out beyond the upper jaw ▪ a tall *lantern-jawed* man

¹lap /ˈlæp/ *noun, pl* **laps** [*count*] : the area between the knees and the hips of a person who is sitting down ▪ A child was sitting on his *lap*. ▪ She held the baby in/on her *lap*. ▪ He kept his hands in/on his *lap*. ▪ The students rested the books in/on their *laps*.
drop/fall into your lap or ***land in your lap informal*** ✧ If something good *drops/falls into your lap* or *lands in your lap*, it comes to you suddenly in an unexpected way even though you did not try to get it. ▪ This wonderful new job just *fell into my lap* when I was least expecting it!
drop/dump (something) in/into/on your lap informal ✧ If something is *dropped/dumped in/into/on your lap*, it is given to you suddenly even though you did not want it or expect it. ▪ Another major problem was *dumped into her lap*.
in the lap of luxury : in a situation of great ease, comfort, and wealth ▪ She was reared *in the lap of luxury*.
in the lap of the gods *chiefly Brit* : not yet decided or certain ▪ The election is too close to call: the result is *in the lap of the gods*.
— compare ³LAP

²lap *verb* **laps; lapped; lap·ping** [+ *obj*]
1 : to cause (something) to partly cover something else — often + *over* ▪ *lap* one shingle *over* another
2 : to go past (another racer who is one or more laps behind you) ▪ When I *lapped* the runner who was in second place, I knew I'd have an easy victory.
— compare ⁴LAP

³lap *noun, pl* **laps** [*count*]
1 : an act of going completely around a track or over a course when you are running, swimming, etc. ▪ The race is 12 *laps* long. ▪ With one *lap* remaining, the race was still close. ▪ the last/final *lap* of the race ▪ (*US*) He was swimming/doing *laps* in the pool. [=he was swimming from one end of the pool to the other and then back again] ✧ The winner of a race often takes a ***victory lap*** (*US*) or ***lap of honour*** (*Brit*) by going around the track or over the course alone one more time as a way to celebrate.
2 : a part of a journey ▪ They were in the last *lap* [=*stage, leg*] of their trip home from Europe.
— compare ¹LAP

⁴lap *verb* **laps; lapped; lap·ping**
1 : to drink by licking with the tongue [*no obj*] The dog was *lapping* at the water in the puddle. [+ *obj*] The cat *lapped* the water in the dish. — often + *up* ▪ The dog *lapped up* the water in the puddle. — often used figuratively ▪ The crowd *lapped up* every word he said. [=the crowd eagerly listened to and accepted every word he said] ▪ He was making some outrageous claims, but the audience was really ***lapping it up***.
2 *of water* : to move repeatedly over or against something in gentle waves [*no obj*] The waves *lapped* at/against the shore. [+ *obj*] Waves gently *lapped* the shore.
— compare ²LAP
— **lapping** *noun* [*noncount*] ▪ the *lapping* of the waves

lap belt *noun, pl* ~ **belts** [*count*] : a seat belt that fastens across your lap

lap dancing *noun* [*noncount*] : an activity in which a performer (such as a dancer at a nightclub or strip club) makes sexual movements while sitting on the lap of a customer
— **lap dance** *noun, pl* ~ **dances** [*count*] — **lap dancer** *noun, pl* ~ **-ers** [*count*]

lap·dog /ˈlæpˌdɑːg/ *noun, pl* **-dogs** [*count*]
1 : a dog that is small enough to be held in a person's lap
2 : a weak person who is controlled by someone else ▪ His coworkers regarded him as the boss's *lap dog*.

la·pel /ləˈpɛl/ *noun, pl* **-pels** [*count*] : either one of the two folds of fabric that are below the collar on the front of a coat or jacket ▪ He wore a carnation in his *lapel*. — see color picture on page C15

la·pis la·zu·li /ˌlæpəsˈlæzəli, *Brit* ˌlæpəsˈlæzjʊli/ *noun* [*noncount*] : a deep blue stone that is used in jewelry — called also *lapis*; see color picture on page C11

¹lapse /ˈlæps/ *noun, pl* **laps·es** [*count*]
1 a : an occurrence in which you fail to think or act in the usual or proper way for a brief time and make a mistake ▪ He blamed the error on a minor mental *lapse*. ▪ As he grew older he began to have ***memory lapses***. [=times when he forgot things that he should have remembered] — often + *in* ▪ a *lapse in* decorum/civility/judgment ▪ a serious *lapse in* security — often + *of* ▪ She had a brief *lapse of* attention/concentration. **b** : an occurrence in which someone behaves badly for usually a short period of time ▪ moral *lapses* ▪ a politician who is being accused of ethical *lapses* [=accused of doing things that are not ethical] **c** : a change that results in worse behavior ▪ a *lapse* into bad habits
2 : a period of time between events — often + *of* ▪ He returned to college after a *lapse of* several years.
3 : the ending of something that happens when the payments necessary for it to continue are not made — often + *of* ▪ the *lapse of* an insurance policy ▪ the *lapse of* a magazine subscription

²lapse *verb* **lapses; lapsed; laps·ing** [*no obj*]
1 : to stop for usually a brief time ▪ After a few polite words the conversation *lapsed*. ▪ Her interest in politics *lapsed* while she was in medical school.
2 : to become no longer effective or valid ▪ She didn't pay the premium and her life insurance policy *lapsed*. ▪ He forgot to renew his driver's license, so it *lapsed*. ▪ She allowed the magazine subscription to *lapse*.
lapse into [*phrasal verb*] ***lapse into (something)*** **1** : to begin using or doing (something that should be avoided) for a short period of time ▪ He's a good writer, but he occasionally *lapses into* jargon. **2** : to begin to be in (a worse or less active state or condition) ▪ The crowd *lapsed into* silence. ▪ The patient *lapsed into* [=*slipped into*] a coma. ▪ He *lapsed into* unconsciousness. ▪ The society *lapsed into* decline.

lapsed *adj, always used before a noun*
1 : no longer believing or following the teachings of a religion ▪ a *lapsed* Catholic/Mormon
2 : no longer effective or valid ▪ a *lapsed* insurance policy

lap·top /ˈlæpˌtɑːp/ *noun, pl* **-tops** [*count*] : a small computer that is designed to be easily carried ▪ He uses a *laptop* for business when he travels. — called also *laptop computer*; compare DESKTOP

lar·ce·ny /ˈlɑəsəni/ *noun, pl* **-nies** *law* : the act of stealing something : THEFT [*noncount*] He was arrested and charged with *larceny*. [*count*] He has been accused of several *larcenies*. — see also GRAND LARCENY, PETIT LARCENY

– lar·ce·nous /ˈlɑɚsənəs/ *adj* ▪ a *larcenous* act

larch /ˈlɑɚʧ/ *noun, pl* **larch·es** [*count, noncount*] : a type of tree that is related to the pines and that drops its needles in the winter

laptop

¹lard /ˈlɑɚd/ *noun* [*noncount*] : a soft white substance that is made from the fat of pigs and used in cooking

²lard *verb* **lards; lard·ed; lard·ing** [+ *obj*] : to put pieces of fat onto or into (something) before cooking ▪ a roast *larded* with bacon

lard with [*phrasal verb*] ***lard (something) with (something)*** : to add a large amount of (something) to (something) ▪ He always *lards* his lectures *with* statistics. [=he always includes many statistics in his lectures] — often used as *(be) larded with* ▪ a novel *larded with* clichés ▪ Her comments *were larded with* phony sentiment.

lar·der /ˈlɑɚdɚ/ *noun, pl* **-ers** [*count*] : a small room or area where food is kept : PANTRY

¹large /ˈlɑɚʤ/ *adj* **larg·er; -est**

1 : great in size or amount : BIG ▪ a *large* room ▪ a *large* corporation ▪ a *large* glass of water ▪ It's the *largest* city in the state. ▪ It's the third *largest* city in the state. [=there are two other cities that are larger] ▪ These T-shirts are available in three sizes: small, medium, and *large*. ▪ Which city has the *largest* population? ▪ Her policies are supported by a *large* part/portion/percentage of the population. ▪ A *large* number of workers have filed complaints. ▪ She used to be thin, but she's gotten a bit *large* [=(less politely) *fat*] in recent years. ▪ He's a very *large* man. [=(usually) a tall and heavy man] ▪ He has a very *large* appetite.

2 : not limited in importance, range, etc. ▪ She's planning to play a *larger* [=more active] role in the negotiations. ▪ We need to take a/the *large* view of this issue. [=we need to look at this issue in a broad or general way]

(as) large as life see ¹LIFE

at large **1** : not having been captured ▪ The criminal is still *at large*. [=*free*] **2** : as a group : as a whole ▪ His statements do not reflect the beliefs of the public *at large*. [=the beliefs of most people] ▪ society *at large* **3** *US* : not having a specific subject ▪ a critic *at large* [=a critic who writes about many different things] **4** *US, politics* : representing a whole state or area rather than one of its parts — used in combination with a preceding noun ▪ a city councilor-*at-large*

bulk large see ³BULK

by and large see ²BY

in large part or ***in large measure*** : not entirely but mostly : LARGELY ▪ The success of the play was *in large part* due to the director. ▪ The economy is based *in large measure* [=*for the most part*] on farming.

larger than life **1** : bigger than the size of an actual person or thing ▪ The statue is *larger than life*. ▪ a *larger-than-life* image **2** *of a person* : having an unusually exciting, impressive, or appealing quality ▪ My grandmother was a remarkable woman who always seemed *larger than life* to me. ▪ a *larger-than-life* hero

live large see ¹LIVE

loom large see ¹LOOM

to a large extent see EXTENT

writ large see ²WRIT

– large·ness *noun* [*noncount*] ▪ the *largeness* of the dog ▪ the *largeness* of the population

²large *noun, pl* **larg·es** [*count*] : something that is sold in a large size : something that is bigger than others of the same kind ▪ These shirts are all *larges*. ▪ "What size ice-cream cones do you want?" "We'll take three *larges* and a small."

large intestine *noun, pl* **~ -tines** [*count*] : the end part of the intestine that is wider and shorter than the small intestine — see picture at HUMAN

large·ly /ˈlɑɚʤli/ *adv* [*more ~; most ~*] : not completely but mostly ▪ The story is *largely* true. ▪ He is *largely* responsible for the problem. ▪ The economy is based *largely* on farming.

large–scale *adj*

1 : involving many people or things ▪ Their equipment isn't suitable for *large-scale* production. [=it cannot be used to make things in large amounts]

2 : covering or involving a large area ▪ a *large-scale* network ▪ a *large-scale* map

lar·gesse *also* **lar·gess** /lɑɚˈʒɛs/ *noun* [*noncount*] *somewhat formal* : the act of giving away money or the quality of a person who gives away money ▪ He relied on the *largesse* of friends after he lost his job. ▪ a philanthropist known for his *largesse* [=*generosity*]; *also* : money that is given away ▪ projects depending on a flow of federal *largesse* [=money from the federal government]

larg·ish /ˈlɑɚʤɪʃ/ *adj* [*more ~; most ~*] : fairly large ▪ He has a *largish* nose.

¹lark /ˈlɑɚk/ *noun, pl* **larks** [*count*] : any one of several birds that usually have pleasant songs — see also MEADOWLARK, SKYLARK — compare ²LARK

²lark *noun, pl* **larks** *informal*

1 [*count*] : something done for enjoyment or adventure ▪ (*US*) She entered the race ***on/as a lark***. = (*chiefly Brit*) She entered the race ***for a lark***. [=she entered the race just as a way to have fun]

2 [*noncount*] *Brit* : activity of a specified kind : BUSINESS ▪ All this housework *lark* is harder than I thought!

– compare ¹LARK

³lark *verb* **larks; larked; lark·ing**

lark about or ***lark around*** [*phrasal verb*] *Brit informal* : to behave in a silly and enjoyable way ▪ The girls were *larking about* in the backyard.

lar·va /ˈlɑɚvə/ *noun, pl* **lar·vae** /ˈlɑɚˌviː/ [*count*] : a very young form of an insect that looks like a worm ▪ The *larva* of a butterfly is called a caterpillar.

– lar·val /ˈlɑɚvəl/ *adj* ▪ the *larval* stage of an insect

lar·yn·gi·tis /ˌlerənˈʤaɪtəs/ *noun* [*noncount*] *medical* : a disease in which your throat and larynx become sore so that it is difficult to talk

lar·ynx /ˈlerɪŋks/ *noun, pl* **la·ryn·ges** /ləˈrɪnˌʤiːz/ *or* **lar·ynx·es** [*count*] *medical* : the part of your throat that contains the vocal cords — called also *voice box*

la·sa·gna (*chiefly US*) *or chiefly Brit* **la·sa·gne** /ləˈzɑːnjə, *Brit* ləˈsænjə/ *noun, pl* **-gnas** [*count, noncount*] : a type of Italian food that has layers of flat noodles baked with a sauce usually of tomatoes, cheese, and meat — see picture at PASTA

las·civ·i·ous /ləˈsɪvijəs/ *adj* [*more ~; most ~*] *disapproving* : filled with or showing sexual desire ▪ *lascivious* acts/thoughts ▪ a *lascivious* young man ▪ He was arrested for ***lewd and lascivious*** behavior.

– las·civ·i·ous·ly *adv* **– las·civ·i·ous·ness** *noun* [*noncount*]

la·ser /ˈleɪzɚ/ *noun, pl* **-sers** [*count*] : a device that produces a narrow and powerful beam of light that has many special uses in medicine, industry, etc. ▪ doctors using a *laser* to perform delicate eye surgery — often used before another noun ▪ *laser* surgery ▪ *laser* technology

laser beam *noun, pl* **~ beams** [*count*] : the narrow beam of light produced by a laser

laser disc *noun, pl* **~ discs** [*count*] : OPTICAL DISK

laser printer *noun, pl* **~ -ers** [*count*] : a computer printer that prints an image formed by a laser beam — compare INK-JET PRINTER

¹lash /ˈlæʃ/ *verb* **lash·es; lashed; lash·ing**

1 : to hit (a person or animal) with a whip, stick, or something similar [+ *obj*] The sailor was *lashed* for disobeying the captain. [*no obj*] — + *at* ▪ The jockey *lashed* (away) *at* the horse with his whip.

2 : to hit (something) with force [+ *obj*] Rain *lashed* the side of the house. ▪ Waves *lashed* the shore. [*no obj*] — + *at* ▪ Waves *lashed at* the shore.

3 : to make a sudden and angry attack against (someone) [+ *obj*] The singer *lashed* her critics with angry words. [*no obj*] — + *at* ▪ The singer *lashed* back *at* her critics. — often used in the phrase ***lash out at*** ▪ He *lashed out at* the government for its failure to cut taxes. ▪ The cat suddenly *lashed out at* me when I tried to pet it.

4 [+ *obj*] : to cause (a group of people) to become angry or violent — + *into* ▪ He *lashed* [=*whipped*] the mob *into* a fury with his violent words.

5 *of an animal* : to move (the tail) from side to side in a forceful way [+ *obj*] The tiger *lashed* its tail. [*no obj*] The tiger's tail was *lashing* from side to side.

– compare ³LASH

²lash *noun, pl* **lashes**

1 a [*count*] **:** a hit with a whip ▪ They gave the sailor 50 *lashes* for disobeying orders. **b** ***the lash*** **:** the punishment of being hit with a whip ▪ The disobedient sailors were threatened with *the lash*. **c** [*count*] **:** the thin piece on the end of a whip **2** [*count*] **:** EYELASH — usually plural ▪ She has long and beautiful *lashes*.

3lash *verb* **lashes; lashed; lashing** [+ *obj*] **:** to tie (something) to an object with a rope, cord, or chain ▪ They *lashed* the canoe to the top of the car. ▪ He *lashed* the logs together to make a raft. ▪ Everything was *lashed* down securely so that it wouldn't blow away. — compare 1LASH

lash·ing /ˈlæʃɪŋ/ *noun, pl* **-ings**
1 [*singular*] **:** the act of hitting someone with a whip as a form of punishment ▪ They gave the sailor a *lashing*. — often used figuratively ▪ She gave him a *lashing* for being late. [=she shouted at him angrily for being late] — see also TONGUE-LASHING
2 ***lashings*** [*plural*] **:** ropes used for tying, wrapping, or connecting things ▪ a ship's *lashings*
3 ***lashings*** [*plural*] *Brit, informal* **:** a large amount of something ▪ She put *lashings of* butter on her muffin.

lass /ˈlæs/ *noun, pl* **lass·es** [*count*] *chiefly Brit, informal* **:** a girl or young woman ▪ a pretty Scottish *lass* — compare LAD

lass·ie /ˈlæsi/ *noun, pl* **-ies** [*count*] *chiefly Scotland, informal* **:** a young girl **:** LASS ▪ when she was just a wee *lassie* ▪ Don't cry, *lassie*. — compare LADDIE

las·si·tude /ˈlæsəˌtuːd, *Brit* ˈlæsəˌtjuːd/ *noun* [*noncount*] *formal + medical* **:** the condition of being tired **:** lack of physical or mental energy ▪ Symptoms of the disease include paleness and *lassitude*.

1las·so /ˈlæsoʊ, læˈsuː/ *noun, pl* **-sos** *or* **-soes** [*count*] **:** a rope with a loop that is used for catching animals (such as cattle or horses)

2lasso *verb* **-so** *or* **-soes; -soed; -so·ing** [+ *obj*] **:** to catch (an animal) with a lasso ▪ The cowboy *lassoed* the horse. — sometimes used figuratively ▪ an actor who has *lassoed* a major role [=an actor who has succeeded in getting a major role]

1last /ˈlæst, *Brit* ˈlɑːst/ *verb* **lasts; last·ed; last·ing**
1 a [*no obj*] **:** to continue in time ▪ How long does the movie *last*? ▪ The movie *lasts* (for) about two hours. [=the movie is about two hours long] ▪ The conference starts on Monday and it *lasts* until Friday. ▪ The game *lasted* (for) three hours. ▪ Don't worry, the storm won't/can't *last*. [=the storm will end soon] **b** [*no obj*] **:** to continue in good condition ▪ The car should *last* 10 years. ▪ I doubt that those boots will *last* (much longer). ▪ That bridge will *last* a long time. ▪ Our products are ***built to last*** **c** [*no obj*] **:** to continue to be available ▪ These oranges are on sale while they/supplies *last*. [=they are on sale until they have all been sold] **d :** to continue to be enough for the needs of someone [*no obj*] We have enough food to *last* (for) the rest of the week. [+ *obj*] We have enough food to *last* us (for) the rest of the week. ▪ That car should *last* you ten years. [=you should not have to get another car for ten years]
2 [*no obj*] **a :** to be able to continue in a particular situation or condition ▪ I am not sure he will *last* in his new job. ▪ Can you *last* a whole day without cigarettes? **b :** to continue to live ▪ My father is very ill. He may not *last* much longer. ▪ He may not *last* (through) the night. [=he may die before the night has ended] ▪ (*chiefly Brit*) He may not ***last out*** the night.
last the distance see 1DISTANCE

2last *adj*
1 a : coming after all others in time, order, or importance **:** FINAL ▪ He was the *last* one out of the building. ▪ She succeeded on her *last* attempt. ▪ These are the *last* two books in the series. ▪ He was sitting in the *last* [=*back*] row. ▪ We are going to the beach for the *last* week of the summer. ▪ The (very) *last* time we ever met was at a party. = (*Brit*) The *last* ever time we met was at a party. ▪ I'll have my revenge ***if it's the last thing I (ever) do*** [=I am determined to get my revenge] **b :** remaining after the rest are gone ▪ I am down to my *last* dollar. [=I have one dollar left] ▪ the *last* cookie in the jar ▪ She said she wouldn't marry him if he was the *last* man on earth.
2 : belonging to the final part of something ▪ He was tragically killed during the *last* days of the war. ▪ the *last* hours of her life = her *last* hours on earth
3 : most recent ▪ I haven't seen her recently. The *last* time we met was at a party. ▪ I liked her *last* [=*previous*] novel better than this new one. — used to identify a preceding period of time ▪ *Last* month we went to the museum. ▪ The weather was fine *last* week, but this week has been rainy, and next week is expected to be cold. ▪ He had trouble *last* semester in school. ▪ We saw them *last* week.
4 a : least likely ▪ You are the *last* person I would expect to see here. [=I never expected to see you here] ▪ That is the *last* place I would have looked for the ring. [=I would never have expected to find the ring there] **b :** least desirable ▪ Another bill to pay is the *last* thing I need right now! **c :** least important ▪ Right now work is the ***last thing on my mind*** [=I am not thinking about work at all right now]
every last — used as a more forceful way of saying *every* ▪ *Every last* soldier was captured. [=every soldier was captured] ▪ He ate *every last* cookie. [=he ate every cookie]
in the last analysis see ANALYSIS
last gasp **:** a final attempt or effort made at the very end ▪ This movie may be his *last gasp* as an actor. ▪ winter's *last gasp* [=the last bit of winter weather before spring] — see also LAST-GASP
last thing **:** after everything else ▪ Heat the vegetables *last thing* so that they don't get cold. **:** very late ▪ I'll be back *last thing* (on) Monday night.
on your/its last legs see 1LEG
the last laugh see 2LAUGH
the last moment see MOMENT
the last straw see STRAW
the last word see 1WORD
to the last man see 1MAN

3last *adv*
1 : after any others in time, order, or importance ▪ He spoke *last* at the meeting. ▪ My horse was/finished *last* in the race. ▪ My horse came in *last*. = (*chiefly Brit*) My horse came *last*. ▪ *Last* (of all) came the soldiers and tanks. ▪ She was first to arrive at the party and *last* to leave. **:** at the end ▪ The best part of the book ***comes last*** [=the best part of the book comes at the end] ◊ **In figurative use, something or someone that *comes last* is less important than other things or people.** ▪ His job was all he really cared about. His personal life always *came last* with him.
2 : most recently **:** on the most recent occasion ▪ I *last* saw him in the supermarket. ▪ They *last* went to the beach in June. ▪ This word was *last* used in the 17th century.
3 — used to introduce a final statement or subject ▪ *Last*, I'd like to talk about the company's future.
first and last see 2FIRST
last but not least — used to say that a final statement is not less important than previous statements ▪ The television is big, has an excellent picture, and *last but not least*, it's cheap. ▪ *Last but not least*, I would like to introduce our new vice president.

4last *pronoun*
1 ***the last*** **:** the last person or thing in a group or series ▪ He was *the last* in line. ▪ It was *the last* of many delays. ▪ She was *the last* to leave. ▪ *The last* of the tests was given today. ▪ This is the first time we've been here, but it definitely won't be *the last*! [=we will definitely come here again]
2 a ***the last*** **:** the last time someone is seen, something is mentioned, etc. ▪ I guess that is *the last* we will see of her. [=the last time we will see her] ▪ I hope that we have finally ***seen the last*** of them. [=I hope that we will not see them again] ▪ He knew he had not ***heard the last*** of his mistake. [=he knew that he would hear again about his mistake] ▪ Don't tell them about your mistake or you'll never ***hear the last of it*** [=they'll keep reminding you of it] **b :** a final action ▪ I've spoken my *last* on this subject. [=I've spoken for the last time on this subject; I will not be saying anything more on this subject] **c** *informal* — used to describe the most recent information you have about someone or something ▪ "Where's Hank these days?" "***(The) Last I heard***, he was living in New York." [=the most recent information I have heard is that he was living in New York] ▪ "Do you know where my keys are?" "***(The) Last I saw*** [=the last time I saw them], they were in the kitchen."
3 ***the last*** **a :** the end of something ▪ We stayed at the game till/until *the last*. [=until it ended] ▪ They fought hard to *the last*. **b :** the end of someone's life ▪ He was cheerful to *the last*. [=until he died]
4 a : the final thing or things that have been mentioned previously ▪ They had cats, dogs, and a horse. This *last* [=the horse] was kept in an old barn. **b :** the most recent one of something ▪ The week before *last* [=the week before last week] I saw him at a restaurant. ▪ the night before *last*
breathe your last *literary* **:** to die ▪ This is the room where

he *breathed his last.* [=where he breathed his last breath; where he died]

[5]**last** *noun*

at last *or* ***at long last*** : after a delay or long period of time • She was *at last* [=*finally*] reunited with her sister. • We're finished *at last.* • "We're finished." "*At last*!" • It appears that this problem will soon be solved, *at long last.*

last call *noun* [*noncount*] *US* : the time when the customers in a place where drinks are sold (such as a bar) are told that they can order one more drink before it closes • We stayed till *last call.* — called also (*Brit*) *last orders*

last–ditch /ˈlæstˈdɪʧ, *Brit* ˈlɑːstˈdɪʧ/ *adj, always used before a noun* : made as a final effort to keep something bad from happening • The troops made a desperate *last-ditch* effort to keep the town from being captured. • The negotiations were a *last-ditch* attempt to prevent a labor strike.

last–gasp /ˈlæstˈgæsp, *Brit* ˈlɑːstˈgɑːsp/ *adj, always used before a noun* : done or happening at the very end • The store changed its name in a *last-gasp* [=*last-ditch*] effort to attract customers. • (*chiefly Brit*) a *last-gasp* goal [=a goal scored at the very end of a game] — see also *last gasp* at [2]LAST

last hurrah *noun, pl* ~ **-rahs** [*count*] : a last effort, production, or appearance • The movie was his *last hurrah.* [=it was the last movie that he appeared in]

last•ing /ˈlæstɪŋ, *Brit* ˈlɑːstɪŋ/ *adj* [*more* ~; *most* ~] : existing or continuing for a long time • a book with *lasting* significance • The trip had a *lasting* effect on her.

— **last•ing•ly** *adv*

Last Judgment *noun*

the Last Judgment : the time when according to some religions all people will be judged by God : JUDGMENT DAY

last•ly /ˈlæstli, *Brit* ˈlɑːstli/ *adv* : at the end • He worked for the company as a manager, treasurer, vice president, and *lastly,* as president. — used to introduce the last things you are going to say • *Lastly,* I would like to discuss the company's future plans. — compare FIRSTLY

last minute *noun*

the last minute : the last possible time when something can be done • You shouldn't wait until *the last minute* before planning your retirement. • They were making changes to the show right up to *the last minute.*

— **last–minute** *adj, always used before a noun* • *last-minute* changes to the show • They won the game with a *last-minute* touchdown.

last name *noun, pl* ~ **names** [*count*] : the name that comes at the end of someone's full name • His first name is John and his *last name* is Smith. — compare SURNAME

last orders *noun* [*plural*] *Brit* : LAST CALL

last post *noun*

the last post *Brit* : TAPS

last rites *noun*

the last rites : a religious ceremony that is performed by a Catholic priest for someone who is dying • The priest administered *the last rites.*

[1]**latch** /ˈlæʧ/ *noun, pl* **latch•es** [*count*]

1 : a device that holds a door, gate, or window closed and that consists of a bar that falls into a holder when it is closed and that is lifted when it is open • He lifted the *latch* and opened the gate.

2 *chiefly Brit* : a type of door lock that can be opened from the inside by turning a lever or knob but can only be opened from the outside with a key • I heard her key turn/click in the *latch.*

on the latch *Brit, of a door* : closed but not locked • I left the front door *on the latch* so that she could get in.

[2]**latch** *verb* **latches; latched; latch•ing** [+ *obj*] : to close or fasten (something, such as a door) with a latch • *latch* the gate — compare [3]LATCH

[3]**latch** *verb* **latches; latched; latching**

latch on [*phrasal verb*] *informal* **1** *Brit* : to begin to understand something • What he was saying was complicated, so it took me a while to *latch on.* [=*catch on*] **2** ***latch on to (something) or latch onto (something)*** **a** : to grab and hold (something) • He *latched onto* her arm and wouldn't let go. — often used figuratively • The news media has *latched on to* the scandal. **b** : to begin using or doing (something) in an enthusiastic way • Many companies have *latched onto* [=*adopted*] the trend of using consultants. : to choose (something) in an enthusiastic way • He *latched onto* music as a way to relax. **3** ***latch on to (someone or something) or latch onto (someone or something)*** : to stay close to (someone or something) • Soon after she got to the party, some strange man *latched on to* her [=started talking to her] and wouldn't go away.

— compare [2]LATCH

latch•key /ˈlæʧˌkiː/ *noun, pl* **-keys** [*count*] : a key for opening an outside door

latchkey child *noun, pl* ~ **children** [*count*] : a young child who is alone at home after school because the child's parents are working — called also *latchkey kid*

[1]**late** /ˈleɪt/ *adj* **lat•er; -est**

1 : existing or happening near the end of a period of time • It happened in *late* spring. • His health problems began when he was in his *late* thirties. [=when he was about 38 or 39 years old] • The problems began in the *late* 1930s. [=in about 1938 or 1939] • a word first recorded in the *late* 17th century • It was *late* (in the evening) when we finally went to bed. — opposite EARLY; see also LATER

2 a : coming or happening after the usual, expected, or desired time • The train is (a half hour) *late.* • We had a *late* spring this year. • I'm sorry I'm *late.* • He made a *late* payment. = He was *late* with his payment. = He was *late* (in) paying. • Hurry up or we'll be *late* for school. • We arrived late because we ***got/had/made a late start.*** [=we started at a later time than we had meant to] • Their warning was ***too late*** to help him. — opposite EARLY **b** : doing something after the usual time or before others usually do • I've always been a *late* riser. • a *late* walker [=a child who learned to walk at a later age than most other children] — opposite EARLY

3 *always used before a noun* : living until recently : not now living • He made a donation to the school in memory of his *late* wife. • the *late* John Smith

born too late see BORN

it's getting late — used to say that time is passing and especially that evening or late evening is coming • *It's getting late* so we should probably go home.

late bloomer see BLOOMER

late in the day : after the expected or proper time • It's rather *late in the day* for an apology now, don't you think? [=it's late for an apology; you should have apologized sooner]

late night : a night when you stay awake until a late hour • We're tired today because we ***had a late night*** [=stayed up late] last night. — see also LATE-NIGHT

— **late•ness** *noun* [*noncount*] • the *lateness* of the hour • the *lateness* of the payment

[2]**late** *adv* **later; -est**

1 : at or near the end of a period of time or a process, activity, series, etc. • *Late* in the year he became ill. • It rained *late* in the day. • *Late* in his career he moved to the city. • a word first recorded *late* in the 17th century • They were trailing by a touchdown *late* in the fourth quarter. • The package should be arriving *late* next week. — opposite EARLY

2 : after the usual or expected time • She arrived at work (a half hour) *late.* • He sent in his job application *late.* • They arrived too *late* for breakfast. • I like getting up *late.* • The package arrived *late,* but ***better late than never!*** • She's been working *late.* • They stayed *late.* — opposite EARLY

as late as : as recently as — used in referring to a time that you think is surprisingly recent • The company is now in serious trouble, but it was reporting record profits *as late as* last year.

late of *formal* : having recently lived or worked in (a place, a company, etc.) • The company's new president is Mark Jones, *late of* Chicago.

of late *formal* : during a recent period • They have not seen him *of late.* [=*lately, recently*] • *Of late* she has been acting strangely.

late•com•er /ˈleɪtˌkʌmɚ/ *noun, pl* **-ers** [*count*]

1 : a person who arrives late • *Latecomers* had to park their cars far from the stadium.

2 : someone or something that has recently arrived or become involved in something : NEWCOMER — often + *to* • He's a *latecomer to* the trumpet. [=he started playing the trumpet recently] • The company is a *latecomer to* the video-game industry.

late•ly /ˈleɪtli/ *adv* : in the recent period of time : RECENTLY • He has been feeling better *lately.* • *Lately,* she has been worrying about her son.

late–night *adj, always used before a noun* : happening or appearing late at night • *late-night* television • *late-night* comedians

la•tent /ˈleɪtn̩t/ *adj* [*more* ~; *most* ~] — used to describe something (such as a disease) that exists but is not active or

L

cannot be seen ▪ a *latent* infection ▪ The house they bought had *latent* defects.

– **la·ten·cy** /ˈleɪtn̩si/ *noun* [*noncount*] ▪ The disease was in a period of *latency*. [=the disease was present but had not produced any noticeable symptoms] ▪ the *latency* period of a disease

¹lat·er /ˈleɪtɚ/ *adj, always used before a noun*

1 : happening near the end of a process, activity, series, life, etc. ▪ among the composer's *later* works ▪ The early sections of the book are quite different from the *later* sections. ▪ His *later* years were tranquil.

2 : coming or happening after a certain time or at a future time ▪ They met again on a *later* occasion.

²later *adv* **:** at a time in the future ▪ I'll talk to you again *later*. **:** at a time following an earlier time ▪ They *later* regretted the decision. ▪ She returned several weeks *later*. ▪ I saw him again *later* that morning. ▪ We'll need to know your decision ***no/not later than*** next week. [=we'll need to know your decision by next week] ✧ In informal spoken English, *later* is used especially by young people as a shortened form of the phrase ***(I'll) see you later*** to say goodbye to someone. ▪ *Later*, dudes!

***later on* :** at a time in the future or following an earlier time ▪ We'll talk about this subject some more *later on*. ▪ They regretted their decision *later on*.

sooner or later see SOON

¹lat·er·al /ˈlætərəl/ *adj* [*more ~; most ~*] **:** toward, on, or coming from the side ▪ a *lateral* view of the human body [=a view from the side] ▪ the *lateral* force of an earthquake

– **lat·er·al·ly** *adv* ▪ moved the eyeball *laterally* [=toward the side]

²lateral *noun, pl* **-als** [*count*] *American football* **:** a pass thrown to the side or backward — called also *lateral pass*

lateral thinking *noun* [*noncount*] *chiefly Brit* **:** a method for solving problems by making unusual or unexpected connections between ideas

– **lateral thinker** *noun, pl* **~ -ers** [*count*]

¹lat·est /ˈleɪtəst/ *adj, always used before a noun* **:** most recent ▪ She's interested in all the *latest* fashions. ▪ Have you heard the *latest* news (about it)? ▪ He is the *latest* person to announce his resignation.

²latest *noun* [*count*] **:** the last possible or acceptable time — usually used in the phrase ***at the latest*** ▪ The job will definitely be finished by next year *at the* (very) *latest*.

the latest *informal* **1 :** the most recent news or information about something ▪ Have you heard *the latest*? **2 :** the most recent or modern version of something — *+ in* ▪ The store carries *the latest in* home improvement products.

la·tex /ˈleɪˌtɛks/ *noun* [*noncount*] **:** a white fluid produced by certain plants that is used for making rubber; *also* **:** a similar material that is used for making various products (such as paint and glue) — often used before another noun ▪ *latex* paint ▪ *latex* gloves

lath /ˈlæθ, *Brit* ˈlɑːθ/ *noun, pl* **laths** [*count*] **:** a long and thin piece of wood that is used in walls and ceilings to support plaster, tiles, etc.

lathe /ˈleɪð/ *noun, pl* **lathes** [*count*] **:** a machine in which a piece of wood or metal is held and turned while being shaped by a sharp tool

¹lath·er /ˈlæðɚ, *Brit* ˈlɑːðə/ *noun*

1 : tiny bubbles formed from soap mixed with water [*noncount*] The soap and water formed a lot of *lather*. [*singular*] The soap and water formed a *lather*.

2 [*singular*] *informal* **:** a very upset, angry, or worried condition ▪ Her parents were ***in a lather*** [=were very upset] when she came home late. ▪ He ***worked himself into a lather*** [=he became very upset] thinking of his former wife and her new boyfriend. ▪ Don't ***get in a lather*** [=get upset] about something so unimportant.

²lather *verb* **-ers; -ered; -er·ing**

1 [*+ obj*] **:** to spread lather over (something) ▪ He *lathered* his face before shaving.

2 [*no obj*] **:** to form lather ▪ The soap *lathers* easily.

¹Lat·in /ˈlætn̩/ *noun, pl* **-ins**

1 [*noncount*] **:** the language of ancient Rome

2 [*count*] **:** a person born or living in Latin America or in a country (such as Spain or Italy) where a language that comes from Latin is spoken

²Latin *adj*

1 : based on, relating to, or written in Latin ▪ *Latin* grammar ▪ *Latin* poetry

2 : of or relating to the people of Central America and South America ▪ *Latin* music

3 : of or relating to the people of European countries (such as Spain and Italy) in which languages that come from Latin are spoken ▪ a *Latin* lover

La·ti·na /ləˈtiːnə/ *noun, pl* **-nas** [*count*] **:** a woman or girl who was born in or lives in South America, Central America, or Mexico or a woman or girl in the U.S. whose family is originally from South America, Central America, or Mexico — compare LATINO

– **Latina** *adj* ▪ a famous *Latina* singer

Latin–American *adj* **:** based in or relating to the American countries south of the U.S. where people speak Spanish and Portuguese ▪ a person of *Latin-American* origin ▪ *Latin-American* literature ▪ *Latin-American* leaders

La·ti·no /ləˈtiːnoʊ/ *noun, pl* **-nos** [*count*] **:** a person who was born or lives in South America, Central America, or Mexico or a person in the U.S. whose family is originally from South America, Central America, or Mexico ✧ The singular form *Latino* usually refers to a man. The plural form *Latinos* often refers to men and women as a group. — compare LATINA

– **Latino** *adj* ▪ *Latino* children

lat·i·tude /ˈlætəˌtuːd, *Brit* ˈlætəˌtjuːd/ *noun, pl* **-tudes**

1 a : distance north or south of the equator measured in degrees up to 90 degrees [*noncount*] a map of the world showing lines of *latitude* and longitude ▪ an island located at 40 degrees north *latitude* [=at a point 40 degrees north of the equator] [*count*] located at a *latitude* of 40 degrees north — compare LONGITUDE 1 **b** [*count*] **:** an imaginary line that circles the Earth at a particular latitude and that is parallel to the equator ▪ Madrid and New York City are on nearly the same *latitude*. ▪ islands located at different *latitudes* ▪ The star is only seen from the northern *latitudes*. [=the northern parts of the world] — compare LONGITUDE 2

2 [*noncount*] *somewhat formal* **:** freedom to choose how to act or what to do ▪ We weren't given much *latitude* in deciding how to do the job. ▪ The judge has wide/considerable *latitude* to reject evidence for the trial.

– **lat·i·tu·di·nal** /ˌlætəˈtuːdənəl, *Brit* ˌlætəˈtjuːdənəl/ *adj*

la·trine /ləˈtriːn/ *noun, pl* **-trines** [*count*] **:** an outdoor toilet that is usually a hole dug in the ground

lat·te /ˈlɑːˌteɪ, *Brit* ˈlæˌteɪ/ *noun, pl* **-tes** [*count*] **:** CAFFE LATTE

lat·ter /ˈlætɚ/ *adj, always used before a noun* **:** coming or happening near the end of a process, activity, series, life, etc. **:** LATER ▪ the *latter* stages of the process ▪ We'll go in the *latter* half of the year. ▪ In his *latter* years he became blind.

the latter **1 :** the second one of two things or people that have been mentioned ▪ Of these two options, the former is less expensive, while *the latter* is less risky. ▪ He has cars and trucks, and even though the former are easier to drive, *the latter* are more useful. **2 :** the last thing or person mentioned ▪ Of chicken, fish, and meat, I like *the latter* best. [=I like meat the best] **:** the thing or person that has just been mentioned ▪ The President—or, if *the latter* is too busy, the Vice President—will see you shortly. — compare *the former* at FORMER

lat·ter–day /ˈlætɚˌdeɪ/ *adj, always used before a noun* **:** regarded as a modern version of someone or something from the past ▪ He seems to think he's some sort of *latter-day* Moses who will lead us out of bondage.

lat·ter·ly /ˈlætəli/ *adv, chiefly Brit, formal*

1 : at a later time ▪ He devoted his time to painting, sculpture, and, *latterly*, to gardening.

2 : during a recent period ▪ His business has grown *latterly*. [=*lately*]

lat·tice /ˈlætəs/ *noun, pl* **-tic·es** [*count*] **:** a frame or structure made of crossed wood or metal strips

– **lat·ticed** /ˈlætəst/ *adj* ▪ a *latticed* door

lat·tice·work /ˈlætəsˌwɚk/ *noun, pl* **-works :** a frame or structure made of crossed wood or metal strips [*noncount*] the intricate *latticework* of the fence [*count*] intricate *latticeworks* — sometimes used figuratively ▪ gazing up at the sky through a *latticework* of branches

laud /ˈlɑːd/ *verb* **lauds; laud·ed; laud·ing** [*+ obj*] *somewhat formal* **:** to praise (someone or something) ▪ Many people *lauded* her efforts to help the poor. = Many people *lauded* her for her efforts to help the poor. ▪ He was much *lauded* as a successful businessman.

laud·able /ˈlɑːdəbəl/ *adj* [*more ~; most ~*] *somewhat formal* **:** deserving praise ▪ She has shown a *laudable* [=*praiseworthy, commendable*] devotion to her children. ▪ Improving the schools is a *laudable* goal.

– **laud·ably** /ˈlɑːdəbli/ *adv*

lau•da•to•ry /ˈlɑːdəˌtori, *Brit* ˈlɔːdətri/ *adj, formal* : expressing or containing praise ▪ a *laudatory* biography ▪ The play received mostly *laudatory* reviews.

[1]**laugh** /ˈlæf, *Brit* ˈlɑːf/ *verb* **laughs; laughed; laugh•ing**

1 [*no obj*] : to show that you are happy or that you think something is funny by smiling and making a sound from your throat ▪ What are you *laughing* about? ▪ The audience was *laughing* hysterically. ▪ I've never *laughed* so hard in my life. ▪ I couldn't stop *laughing* when I saw what he was wearing. ▪ I ***laughed out loud*** when I saw him. ▪ I ***burst out laughing***. [=I suddenly started laughing] ▪ He *laughed* so hard I thought he'd ***die laughing***. ▪ The movie was hilarious. We ***laughed our heads off***. ▪ I ***laughed until I cried***. [=I laughed so much that tears came out of my eyes] ▪ (*Brit*) She was ***laughing like a drain***. [=she was laughing very hard] ▪ I ***didn't know whether to laugh or cry*** [=I was surprised and shocked] when she told me she was getting married. ▪ It's ***no laughing matter*** when you lose your job. [=it's a serious and important thing that people should not joke about] — often + *at* ▪ She *laughed at* the joke. ▪ Why is everyone *laughing at* me?

2 [*no obj*] **a** : to think or say that someone or something is foolish and does not deserve serious attention or respect — usually + *at* ▪ People *laughed at* his predictions of disaster, but no one's *laughing* now. **b** : to not be bothered by something — + *at* ▪ Sitting inside their tent, they were able to *laugh at* the weather. ▪ He *laughed at* danger.

3 [+ *obj*] : to say (something) in an amused way ▪ "I've never seen anything so ridiculous," he *laughed*.

4 [+ *obj*] : to cause (someone) to go, move, etc., by laughing ▪ The audience *laughed* the singer off the stage. ▪ They *laughed* him out of town. ▪ He *laughed* himself sick. [=he made himself sick by laughing too much] ✧ Someone or something that is ***laughed out of court*** or (*US*) ***laughed out of town*** is regarded as very foolish and is not accepted or treated in a serious way. ▪ His theories were *laughed out of court*.

be laughing *Brit, informal* : to be in a very good situation with nothing to worry about ▪ If they can just close this important deal, they'll *be laughing*! [=they'll be on easy street]

don't make me laugh *informal* — used as a response to a statement that you think is very wrong or foolish ▪ "I could beat you at chess easily." "*Don't make me laugh*."

have to laugh ✧ If you say you *have to laugh* about something, you mean that it is amusing in a certain way, even if it is also unpleasant or foolish. ▪ I *had to laugh* when I found out that our luggage had been lost. What else could go wrong?

he who laughs last, laughs best *or* ***he laughs best that laughs last*** — used to say that even if you are not successful now you still succeed or win in the end

laugh all the way to the bank : to make a lot of money especially by doing something that other people thought was foolish or amusing ▪ People thought his invention was ridiculous, but now he's *laughing all the way to the bank*.

laughing hyena, laughing like a hyena see HYENA

laugh in someone's face : to laugh directly at someone in a way that shows disrespect ▪ When I asked for his help he *laughed in my face*.

laugh off [*phrasal verb*] ***laugh (something) off*** *or* ***laugh off (something)*** : to laugh about or make jokes about (something) in order to make people think it is not serious or important ▪ The candidate *laughed off* the question about his marriage. ▪ The injury was serious, but he *laughed* it *off*.

laugh on the other side of your face — used to say that a situation will change and someone will stop being happy or pleased ▪ You'll be *laughing on the other side of your face* when I've finished with you!

laugh up your sleeve : to be secretly happy about or amused by something (such as someone else's trouble) ▪ The mayor's critics were *laughing up their sleeves* when news of the scandal was first reported.

— **laugh•er** /ˈlæfɚ, *Brit* ˈlɑːfə/ *noun, pl* **-ers** [*count*]

[2]**laugh** *noun, pl* **laughs**

1 [*count*] : the act or sound of laughing ▪ He gave a loud *laugh*. ▪ a nervous *laugh* ▪ I kept telling jokes, but I couldn't ***get a laugh***. [=make people laugh] ▪ a joke that always ***gets a big laugh*** ▪ He'll do anything ***for a laugh***. [=to make people laugh] ▪ I thought her report was ***good for a laugh*** [=was amusing], but it didn't have much helpful information. ▪ She's always ***good for a laugh***. [=she always makes people laugh; she is a funny person] ▪ It seemed awful at the time, but we ***had a (good) laugh about it*** afterward. [=we laughed about it afterward]

2 *informal* **a** [*count*] : something that causes laughter : something funny or foolish ▪ The movie has a lot of *laughs*. ▪ You're going to be a movie star? That's a *laugh*. **b** [*singular*] *chiefly Brit* : a funny person ▪ He's a real *laugh*.

a barrel of laughs see [1]BARREL

a laugh a minute *informal* : someone or something that is very funny ▪ That guy is *a laugh a minute*. ▪ The movie is *a laugh a minute*.

for laughs *or chiefly Brit* ***for a laugh*** *informal* : for amusement ▪ The children were saying every word backward, just *for laughs*.

play for laughs see [1]PLAY

the last laugh ✧ If you ***have/get the last laugh***, you finally succeed or win after people laughed at or doubted you.

laugh•able /ˈlæfəbəl, *Brit* ˈlɑːfəbəl/ *adj* [*more* ~; *most* ~] : bad in a way that seems foolish or silly ▪ His attempt at skiing was *laughable*. ▪ The movie shows a *laughable* [=*pathetic*] ignorance of history.

— **laugh•ably** /ˈlæfəbli, *Brit* ˈlɑːfəbli/ *adv* ▪ a *laughably* small car

laughing gas *noun* [*noncount*] *informal* : NITROUS OXIDE

laugh•ing•ly /ˈlæfɪŋli, *Brit* ˈlɑːfɪŋli/ *adv* [*more* ~; *most* ~]

1 : with laughter : in an amused way ▪ He *laughingly* recalled his friends in college.

2 : in a way that is a joke or that you think is silly, foolish, etc. ▪ a painful and difficult time that some people now *laughingly* call "the good old days"

laugh•ing•stock /ˈlæfɪŋˌstɑːk, *Brit* ˈlɑːfɪŋˌstɒk/ *noun, pl* **-stocks** [*count*] : a person or thing that is regarded as very foolish or ridiculous ▪ The team has become the *laughingstock* of the league. ▪ The mayor became a *laughingstock*.

laugh lines *noun* [*plural*] *US* : wrinkles that appear next to the eyes and that are most noticeable when a person is smiling or laughing — called also (*Brit*) *laughter lines*

laugh•ter /ˈlæftɚ, *Brit* ˈlɑːftə/ *noun* [*noncount*] : the action or sound of laughing ▪ *Laughter* filled the air. ▪ peals/gales/shrieks of *laughter* ▪ The audience roared/shrieked/howled with *laughter*. ▪ The audience ***erupted in laughter***. = The audience ***burst into laughter***. [=the audience suddenly began laughing]

laugh track *noun, pl* ~ **tracks** [*count*] : recorded laughter that is heard during a television or radio program

[1]**launch** /ˈlɑːntʃ/ *verb* **launch•es; launched; launch•ing** [+ *obj*]

1 a : to send or shoot (something, such as a rocket) into the air or water or into outer space ▪ *launch* a rocket/missile/torpedo ▪ *launch* a satellite **b** : to put (a boat or ship) on the water ▪ *launch* a battleship/lifeboat **c** : to throw (something) forward in a forceful way ▪ *launch* [=*hurl*] a spear ▪ I was terrified when the ferocious animal suddenly ***launched itself*** at me. [=suddenly jumped at me]

2 a : to begin (something that requires much effort) ▪ The enemy *launched* an attack at sunrise. ▪ She's trying to *launch* a new career as a singer. ▪ *launch* a business ▪ *launch* an experiment ▪ The police have *launched* an investigation into his activities. **b** : to cause (a person or group) to start to be successful in a career, business, etc. ▪ He helped *launch* her in her career as a singer. **c** : to offer or sell (something) for the first time ▪ The company is expected to *launch* several new products next year. ▪ *launch* a Web site

3 *computers* : to cause (a program) to start operating ▪ You can *launch* the program by double-clicking on the icon.

launch into [*phrasal verb*] **1** ***launch into (something)*** : to suddenly begin doing or saying (something) in an energetic way ▪ He suddenly *launched into* a speech about taxes. **2** ***launch (yourself) into (something)*** : to become involved in (something) in an energetic way ▪ She *launched herself* enthusiastically *into* the campaign.

launch out [*phrasal verb*] : to begin doing something that is new and very different from what you have been doing ▪ It's time to *launch out* and expand my horizons. ▪ He left the company and *launched out* on his own.

— **launch•er** *noun, pl* **-ers** [*count*] ▪ a rocket *launcher*

[2]**launch** *noun, pl* **launches** [*count*] : an act of launching something: such as **a** : an act of shooting something (such as a rocket or missile) into the air or into outer space ▪ a rocket *launch* **b** : an act of beginning a major activity ▪ the *launch* of an attack ▪ the *launch* of a new business **c** : an act or occasion when something new (such as a new product) is first offered or announced ▪ the *launch* of a Web site ▪ a party to celebrate the *launch* of a new product/book = a ***launch party*** for a new product/book — compare [3]LAUNCH

[3]**launch** *noun, pl* **launches** [*count*] : a boat that carries pas-

sengers to the shore from a larger boat that is in a harbor — compare ²LAUNCH

launch·pad /ˈlɑːnʧˌpæd/ *noun, pl* **-pads** [*count*] **:** an area from which a rocket is launched — often used figuratively ▪ The program she hosted on local radio was the *launchpad* for her network career. [=it was the first step that led to her network career] — called also *launching pad*

laun·der /ˈlɑːndɚ/ *verb* **-ders; -dered; -der·ing** [+ *obj*]
1 : to make (clothes, towels, sheets, etc.) ready for use by washing, drying, and ironing them ▪ a freshly *laundered* shirt
2 : to put (money that you got by doing something illegal) into a business or bank account in order to hide where it really came from ▪ He used a phony business to *launder* money from drug dealing.
– laun·der·er /ˈlɑːndərɚ/ *noun, pl* **-ers** [*count*] ▪ a money *launderer* **– laundering** *noun* [*noncount*] ▪ He has been accused of ***money laundering***.

laun·der·ette /ˌlɑːndəˈrɛt/ *noun, pl* **-ettes** [*count*] *chiefly Brit* **:** a place that has machines to use for washing and drying clothes, towels, sheets, etc.

Laun·dro·mat /ˈlɑːndrəˌmæt/ *service mark* — used for a place that has machines for washing and drying clothes, towels, sheets, etc.

laun·dry /ˈlɑːndri/ *noun, pl* **-dries**
1 [*noncount*] **:** clothes, towels, sheets, etc., that need to be washed or that have been washed ▪ There's a pile of dirty *laundry* in the *laundry* basket. ▪ clean *laundry* ▪ a *laundry* bag ▪ I have to ***do the laundry*** today. [=to wash the dirty clothes, towels, etc.] — see also DIRTY LAUNDRY
2 [*count*] **:** a business or place where clothes, towels, sheets, etc., are washed and dried ▪ work at/in a *laundry* ▪ The patients' sheets are sent regularly to the hospital *laundry*.

laundry list *noun, pl* **~ lists** [*count*] *informal* **:** a long list of related things ▪ She described a *laundry list* of goals for the city's schools. ▪ He recited a *laundry list* of problems.

lau·re·ate /ˈlorijət/ *noun, pl* **-ates** [*count*]
1 : someone who has won an important prize or honor for achievement in an art or science ▪ a Nobel *laureate*
2 : POET LAUREATE

lau·rel /ˈlorəl/ *noun, pl* **-rels**
1 [*count, noncount*] **:** an evergreen tree or bush with shiny pointed leaves ▪ *laurel* leaves ▪ wearing a crown/wreath of *laurel* [=a crown/wreath made from laurel leaves that was awarded and worn around the head as a symbol of honor in ancient Greece]
2 ***laurels*** [*plural*] **:** honor or fame given for some achievement ▪ They enjoyed the *laurels* of their military victory. ▪ The player earned his *laurels* from years of hard work.
look to your laurels *chiefly Brit* **:** to work in order to keep your success or position ▪ If she performs this well in the championships, her rivals will have to *look to their laurels*.
rest/sit on your laurels **:** to be satisfied with past success and do nothing to achieve further success ▪ Although she won the championship, she isn't *resting on her laurels*. She is training hard to become even better next year.

la·va /ˈlɑːvə/ *noun* [*noncount*] **:** melted rock from a volcano ▪ a flow of molten *lava*

lav·a·to·ry /ˈlævəˌtori, *Brit* ˈlævətri/ *noun, pl* **-ries** [*count*]
1 *formal* **:** a room with a toilet and sink ✧ In U.S. English, *lavatory* is most often used for a room in an airplane. ▪ Smoking is not permitted in the airplane's *lavatory*. It may also be used for a room in other kinds of public places. ▪ the school's *lavatories* [=(more commonly) *restrooms*] In British English, *lavatory* is most often used for a room in a public place but may also be used for a room in a home.
2 *Brit* **:** TOILET 1
3 *US, technical* **:** a bathroom sink ▪ a wide choice of *lavatories* on sale at plumbing supply stores

lavatory paper *noun* [*noncount*] *Brit* **:** TOILET PAPER

lav·en·der /ˈlævəndɚ/ *noun, pl* **-ders**
1 a [*count, noncount*] **:** a plant with narrow leaves and small purple flowers that have a sweet smell **b** [*noncount*] **:** the dried leaves and flowers of the lavender plant used to make clothes and fabrics smell pleasant ▪ a small cloth bag filled with *lavender*
2 [*count, noncount*] **:** a pale purple color — see color picture on page C3

¹**lav·ish** /ˈlævɪʃ/ *adj* [*more ~; most ~*]
1 : giving or using a large amount of something ▪ *lavish* donors ▪ a cook who is known for her *lavish* use of spices [=a cook who uses a large amount of spices] ▪ a *lavish* display of flowers — often + *in* or *with* ▪ She is *lavish in* giving praise to her employees. [=she gives a lot of praise to her employees] ▪ a cook who is *lavish with* spices
2 : given in large amounts ▪ She has drawn/gained *lavish* praise [=a great amount of praise] for her charitable works. ▪ a *lavish* donation
3 : having a very rich and expensive quality ▪ a *lavish* home ▪ a *lavish* feast/party
– lav·ish·ly *adv* [*more ~; most ~*] ▪ a *lavishly* generous donor ▪ a *lavishly* [=*richly*] illustrated book **– lav·ish·ness** *noun* [*noncount*]

²**lavish** *verb* **-ish·es; -ished; -ish·ing**
lavish on/upon [*phrasal verb*] ***lavish (something) on/upon (someone)*** **:** to give a large amount of (something) to (someone) ▪ They *lavished* gifts *on* us. [=they gave us many gifts] ▪ They *lavished* attention *on* their children.
lavish with [*phrasal verb*] ***lavish (someone or something) with (something)*** **:** to give (someone or something) a large amount of (something) ▪ They *lavished* us *with* gifts. ▪ Everyone *lavished* the children *with* attention. ▪ The production was *lavished with* praise by the critics.

law /ˈlɑː/ *noun, pl* **laws**
1 [*noncount*] **a :** the whole system or set of rules made by the government of a town, state, country, etc. ▪ People who are supposed to obey the *law* also need to know their rights under the *law*. [=according to the law] ▪ The courts exist to uphold, interpret, and apply the *law*. ▪ state/federal *law* ▪ Stealing is ***against the law***. [=stealing is illegal] ▪ He denied that he had ***broken/violated the law***. [=that he had done anything illegal] ▪ You have to pay taxes. That's ***the law of the land***. [=the set of rules that exists in a certain place] ▪ The job of the police is to ***enforce the law***. [=make sure that people obey the law] ▪ He's interested in a career in ***law enforcement***. [=a career as a police officer] ▪ (*US*) *Law enforcement* officials [=police officials] in the area were alerted of the suspect's escape. — see also MARTIAL LAW **b :** a particular kind of law ▪ a lawyer who specializes in criminal/contract/immigration *law* — see also COMMON LAW
2 : a rule made by the government of a town, state, country, etc. [*count*] A *law* requires that schools provide a safe learning environment. = There is a *law* requiring schools to provide a safe learning environment. ▪ In our civics class we learned how a bill becomes a *law*. ▪ She has proposed a new *law* to protect people from being evicted unfairly. — often + *on* or *against* ▪ Congress passed several new *laws on* the environment. [=laws relating to the environment] ▪ a *law against* unfair eviction [=a law that makes unfair eviction illegal] ▪ We need stricter *laws against* discrimination. [*noncount*] Schools are required ***by law*** to provide a safe learning environment. ▪ The bill will ***become law*** at the beginning of the year. ▪ With the majority voting in favor, the bill has been ***passed into law***. [=the bill became a law] ▪ The bill was ***signed into law*** by the governor. [=the proposed law became officially active when the governor signed it]
3 ***the law*** **:** the people and organizations (such as the police and the courts) whose job is to find or punish people who do not obey laws ▪ They called in *the law* [=the police] to determine what should be done next. ▪ He's been in and out of trouble with *the law* for the last 10 years.
4 [*noncount*] **a :** the job of a lawyer : the legal profession ▪ She's been thinking about going into *law*. [=thinking about becoming a lawyer] ▪ a career in *law* ▪ The company hired a large ***law firm*** [=a group of lawyers who work together as a business] to handle the case. ▪ She ***practices law*** [=she works as a lawyer] with a firm in Boston. — see also ATTORNEY AT LAW **b :** the area of study that relates to laws and how they are used ▪ a professor of *law* ▪ studying *law* ▪ going to ***law school*** [=a school that trains you to become a lawyer]
5 : a religious rule [*count*] the body of Islamic *laws* [*noncount*] according to Jewish *law*
6 [*count*] **a :** a rule stating that something (such as an art or profession) should be done in a certain way ▪ the *laws* of poetry ▪ He teaches his students that balance is the ***first law of*** architecture. [=balance is the most important principle in architecture] **b** *Brit* **:** a rule in a sport or game ▪ the *laws* [=*rules*] of tennis
7 [*count*] **:** a statement that describes how something works in the natural world — often + *of* ▪ the *law of* gravity ▪ the *laws of* nature/physics ▪ Newton's *laws of* motion
above the law **:** not required to obey the law ▪ No one is *above the law*. [=everyone must obey the law] ▪ He complains that the new policy places corporations *above the law*. [=that the new policy allows corporations to do things that are not legal]

a law unto yourself ✧ People who are or think they are *a law unto themselves* act in a way that shows they do not care what kind of behavior other people think is acceptable. ▪ I've warned him that he can't keep behaving this way, but he won't listen. He seems to think that he's *a law unto himself.* [=that he can do whatever he wants to do]
go to law *Brit* : to ask a court of law to settle a dispute
law and order : a state or situation in which people obey the law : legal control and authority ▪ The police work to preserve *law and order.* ▪ a breakdown of *law and order*
lay down the law see *lay down* at [1]LAY
outside the law **1 :** not agreeing with the law ▪ actions that may have been *outside the law* [=*illegal*] **2 :** in an illegal way ▪ Investigators were unable to prove that the business was operating *outside the law.* [=*illegally*]
take the law into your own hands : to try to punish someone for breaking a law even though you do not have the right to do that ▪ Police are concerned that the victim's family may try to *take the law into their own hands.* [=may try to punish the criminal themselves instead of allowing the legal system to do it]
the law of averages : the idea or principle that something which can produce different results will produce those results in a regular or predictable way over a period of time ▪ I can't believe that team has lost 12 games in a row. The *law of averages* says that they should have won at least one game by now.
the law of the jungle — used to describe a situation in which people do whatever they want to or whatever is necessary to survive or succeed ▪ an industry governed by *the law of the jungle*
the long arm of the law see [1]ARM
within the law **1 :** agreeing with the law ▪ He says that everything he did was *within the law.* [=*legal*] **2 :** in a legal way ▪ With the organization under so much scrutiny, it is even more important that they work/operate *within the law.* [=*legally*]
your word is law ✧ If *your word is law,* other people must do what you say ▪ He'll listen to suggestions, but in the end, *his word is law.*

> ***synonyms*** LAW, RULE, REGULATION, STATUTE, and ORDINANCE are statements about what people are allowed to do. A LAW is made by a government, and people who live in the area controlled by that government must obey it. ▪ According to a state *law,* all drivers must pass a written test before they can be fully licensed. A RULE usually does not involve an official government. It typically describes what people are allowed to do in a game or in a particular place (such as a school). ▪ He explained the *rules* of football. ▪ The *rules* state clearly that smoking is prohibited on campus. A REGULATION is made by a government to protect people from being harmed. ▪ Safety *regulations* limit the number of hours an airline pilot can fly each month. STATUTE is a formal word for a law made by a government. ▪ The new *statute* requires that all passengers in a car wear seatbelts. In the U.S., an ORDINANCE is a law that is made by a local government and applies only to a limited area. ▪ The new city *ordinance* restricts parking on some streets.

law–abid·ing /ˈlɑːəˌbaɪdɪŋ/ *adj* : obeying the law : not doing anything that the law does not allow ▪ a *law-abiding* citizen

law·break·er /ˈlɑːˌbreɪkɚ/ *noun, pl* **-ers** [*count*] : a person who does something that is not legal : a person who breaks the law ▪ He admitted to being a *lawbreaker.*
– **law·break·ing** /ˈlɑːˌbreɪkɪŋ/ *noun* [*noncount*]

law court *noun, pl* ~ **courts** [*count*]
1 *US* : a court of law : COURT 1c ▪ a decision handed down by a *law court*
2 : a building or room where legal decisions are made : COURT 1b ▪ I have to appear in *law court* next week.

law·ful /ˈlɑːfəl/ *adj, formal*
1 : allowed by the law ▪ *lawful* conduct ▪ a *lawful* search of the property — opposite UNLAWFUL
2 : according to the law ▪ They went to court to determine the property's *lawful* [=*rightful, legal*] owner.
– **law·ful·ly** /ˈlɑːfəli/ *adv* ▪ Companies cannot *lawfully* [=*legally*] sell private medical information. ▪ In the wedding ceremony he was asked, "Do you take this woman to be your *lawfully* wedded wife?" [=do you accept this woman as your wife according to the law?] – **law·ful·ness** /ˈlɑːfəlnəs/ *noun* [*noncount*]

law·less /ˈlɑːləs/ *adj*
1 : having no laws ▪ the *lawless* society of the frontier
2 : not obeying the law ▪ a *lawless* mob
– **law·less·ness** *noun* [*noncount*]

law·mak·er /ˈlɑːˌmeɪkɚ/ *noun, pl* **-ers** [*count*] : someone who makes laws : LEGISLATOR
– **law·mak·ing** /ˈlɑːˌmeɪkɪŋ/ *noun* [*noncount*] ▪ the responsibilities of *lawmaking* — often used before another noun ▪ The legislature functions as the nation's *lawmaking* body.

law·man /ˈlɑːmən/ *noun, pl* **-men** /-mən/ [*count*] *US* : someone (such as a sheriff or marshal) whose job is to make sure that people obey the law ▪ Wyatt Earp was a famous American *lawman* of the Wild West.

lawn /ˈlɑːn/ *noun, pl* **lawns** : an area of ground (such as the ground around a house or in a garden or park) that is covered with short grass [*count*] We had a picnic on the *lawn* in front of the monument. ▪ a neighborhood with well-kept *lawns* ▪ He planned to ***mow the lawn*** [=cut the grass on his lawn] early Saturday morning. ▪ (*US*) We're having a ***lawn party*** [=an outdoor party on a lawn] to celebrate our daughter's graduation. [*noncount*] several acres of well-kept *lawn* — see picture at HOUSE

lawn bowling *noun* [*noncount*] *US* : a game in which wooden balls are rolled across an area of grass so that they stop as close as possible to a smaller ball — called also (*Brit*) *bowls*

lawn chair *noun, pl* ~ **chairs** [*count*] *US* : a light chair made to be used outside — called also (*Brit*) *garden chair*

lawn mower *noun, pl* ~ **-ers** [*count*] : a machine used for cutting the grass on lawns

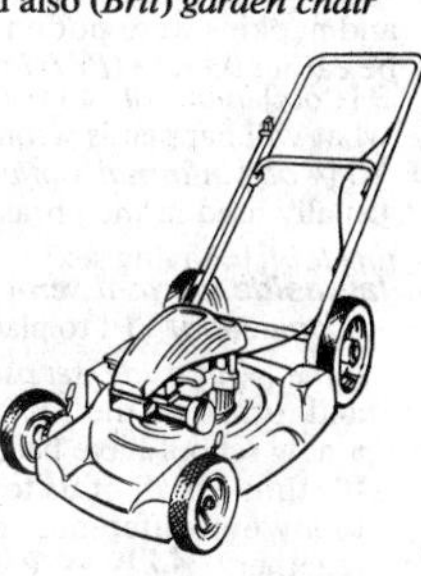
lawn mower

lawn tennis *noun* [*noncount*] : TENNIS

law·suit /ˈlɑːˌsuːt/ *noun, pl* **-suits** [*count*] : a process by which a court of law makes a decision to end a disagreement between people or organizations ▪ win/lose a *lawsuit* ▪ a complex *lawsuit* [=*suit*] that may take years to resolve ▪ When the newspaper refused to admit that the story was false, the actor ***filed/initiated a lawsuit*** against the publisher. [=the actor sued the publisher] ▪ They agreed to pay $100,000 to ***settle a lawsuit.*** [=to end a lawsuit before the court made a decision about it]

law·yer /ˈlɑːjɚ, ˈlojɚ/ *noun, pl* **-yers** [*count*] : a person whose job is to guide and assist people in matters relating to the law

lax /ˈlæks/ *adj* [*more* ~; *most* ~] *disapproving* : not careful enough : not strict enough ▪ *lax* regulations/policies ▪ Security has been *lax.* ▪ The university has been *lax* about/in enforcing these rules.
– **lax·ity** /ˈlæksəti/ *noun* [*noncount*] ▪ He wrote an essay condemning the moral *laxity* in society. – **lax·ly** *adv* ▪ laws *laxly* enforced – **lax·ness** *noun* [*noncount*] ▪ their *laxness* [=*laxity*] in enforcing these rules

lax·a·tive /ˈlæksətɪv/ *noun, pl* **-tives** *medical* : a medicine or food that makes it easier for solid waste to pass through the body [*count*] The doctor prescribed a *laxative.* [*noncount*] a dose of *laxative*
– **laxative** *adj* ▪ The herb has a mild *laxative* effect.

[1]**lay** /ˈleɪ/ *verb* **lays; laid** /ˈleɪd/; **lay·ing**
1 [+ *obj*] : to place (someone or something) down gently in a flat position ▪ *Lay* the fabric carefully on the table. ▪ He *laid* a gentle hand on her shoulder. ▪ She *laid* the baby in his crib for a nap. ▪ He says that he never ***laid a finger/hand on*** her. [=that he never touched her] — often + *down* ▪ He *laid* the newspaper *down* on the desk. ▪ She *laid* the baby down for his nap. — see also LAY DOWN (below)
2 [+ *obj*] **a :** to place (something) into position on or along a surface : to build or set (something) on or in the ground or another surface ▪ When will they *lay* the foundation for the addition? ▪ *lay* tracks for the new railroad ▪ *lay* pipe/cable/lines ▪ *laying* bricks — often + *down* ▪ *laying down* a new road/carpet — often used figuratively ▪ We are ***laying the groundwork/foundation*** [=providing conditions] for additional research. **b** *chiefly US* : to spread (something) over a surface ▪ *lay* plaster/paint ▪ *lay* wallpaper
3 [+ *obj*] : BURY 1a ▪ They *laid* him in his grave.

4 [*no obj*] *informal* : to be in a flat position on a surface : LIE ▪ The book was *laying* on the table. ✧ The use of *lay* to mean "lie" occurs commonly in informal speech but it is regarded as an error by many people.
5 [+ *obj*] **a** : to beat or strike (something) down with force ▪ The wheat was ***laid flat*** by the wind and rain. **b** : to change the condition of something in a specified way ▪ The mountainside has been ***laid bare*** by loggers. [=all the trees on the mountainside have been cut down by loggers] ▪ He *laid bare* his soul. = He *laid* his soul *bare*. [=he revealed his most private thoughts and feelings] ▪ He ***laid himself open*** to criticism [=he exposed himself to criticism] with his remarks.
6 *of a bird, insect, etc.* : to produce (an egg) outside of the body : to push (an egg) out of the body [+ *obj*] birds that typically *lay* only two eggs per year [*no obj*] old chickens that no longer *lay* — see also *lay an egg* at [1]EGG
7 [+ *obj*] — used like *make, place,* or *put* in various phrases ▪ She has ***laid plans*** [=she has made plans] to cut the staff down to just 15 people. ▪ Even the ***best-laid plans*** [=the most carefully made plans] sometimes go wrong. ▪ She ***lays great stress/emphasis*** on good manners. [=she stresses/emphasizes good manners very much] ▪ The author ***lays the blame/responsibility*** for the state of the environment squarely on the government. [=the author blames the government for the state of the environment]
8 [+ *obj*] : to make (something) ready : to prepare (something) ▪ *lay* a trap ▪ *lay* a fire in the fireplace ▪ (*Brit*) Places were *laid* (at the table) for three people. [=silverware, glasses, and napkins were put on the table for three people who will be eating there] ▪ (*Brit*) *lay* [=*set*] the table for a meal
9 [+ *obj*] *informal* : to risk losing (money) if your guess about what will happen is wrong : BET ▪ *lay* money on a race
10 [+ *obj*] *informal* + *offensive* : to have sex with someone — usually used in the phrase ***get laid*** ▪ All he cares about is *getting laid*. [=having sex]

lay aside [*phrasal verb*] ***lay (something) aside or lay aside (something)*** **1** : to place (something) to one side ▪ She *laid aside* [=*put aside, set aside*] the book she had been reading and turned on the TV. — often used figuratively ▪ Plans for a new school have been *laid aside*. [=*put aside, set aside*] ▪ It's time for all of us to *lay aside* old prejudices. ▪ We need to *lay* our differences *aside* so that we can learn to work together. **2** : to keep (something) for special or future use : to reserve or save (something) : to keep (something) for special or future use ▪ She has been able to *lay aside* [=*put aside*] a few dollars each week.

lay by [*phrasal verb*] ***lay (something) by or lay by (something)*** : to keep (something) for special or future use ▪ She has been able to *lay by* [=*lay aside*] a few dollars each week.

lay charges *Brit* : to accuse someone officially of doing something illegal ▪ Police are deciding whether to *lay charges* (against her).

lay claim to see [2]CLAIM

lay down [*phrasal verb*] **1** ***lay (something) down or lay down (something)*** **a** : to clearly state (a rule, standard, guideline, etc.) ▪ The company has *laid down* strict new safety standards. **b** : to stop using (something) ▪ At noon, we *laid down* the rakes and rested for a while. ▪ The strikers *laid down* their tools. **2** ***lay (a weapon) down or lay down (a weapon)*** : to put (a weapon) down and stop fighting ▪ The police ordered the criminals to *lay down* their weapons. **3** ***lay down your life*** *formal* : to give up your life for a good purpose : to die for a good cause ▪ heroes who *laid down their lives* to preserve our nation **4** ***lay down the law*** : to make a strong statement about what someone is or is not allowed to do ▪ The agreement *lays down the law* (to everyone) on what the group allows. ▪ When she came home after midnight, her father *laid down the law*: if she came home that late again, she would not be allowed to watch TV for a week. — see also [1]LAY 1 (above)

lay eyes on see [1]EYE

lay hold of see [2]HOLD

lay in [*phrasal verb*] ***lay (something) in or lay in (something)*** : to get and store (a supply of something) for future use ▪ They *laid in* [=*laid up*] canned goods for the winter.

lay into [*phrasal verb*] ***lay into (someone or something)*** *informal* : to angrily attack or criticize (someone or something) ▪ The coach really *laid into* us for playing so carelessly.

lay it on the line see [1]LINE

lay off [*phrasal verb*] **1** ***lay (someone) off or lay off (someone)*** : to stop employing (someone) because there is not enough work ▪ The company has had to *lay off* most of the staff. ▪ Costs have increased and many workers have been *laid off*. [=*let go*] — see also LAYOFF **2** ***lay off (something)*** *informal* : to stop doing, using, eating, or drinking (something) ▪ You should *lay off* the late nights. [=you should stop staying up so late] ▪ My doctor advised me to *lay off* caffeine. ▪ He's a much nicer person since he *laid off* the booze. [=since he stopped drinking alcohol] ▪ I need to *lay off* fatty foods and lose some weight. **3** ***lay off or lay off (someone)*** *informal* : to leave someone alone : to stop annoying someone ▪ I wish you'd just *lay off*! ▪ *Lay off* me! [=stop bothering me]

lay on [*phrasal verb*] **1** ***lay (something) on or lay on (something)*** **a** : to spread (something) over a surface ▪ Try to *lay* the grout *on* the surface evenly. — often used figuratively ▪ (*informal*) My parents have been *laying* a lot of guilt *on* me. [=have been saying things that make me feel guilty] ▪ (*informal*) If you have something to tell me, just *lay* it *on* me. [=just tell me] ▪ He *laid* the flattery *on* pretty heavily. ▪ She *laid on* a fake southern accent. [=she spoke with a southern accent although she doesn't usually speak that way] **b** *Brit* : to provide (something) for someone ▪ If a lot of people want to come, more coaches will be *laid on* for them. **2** ***lay it on (thick)*** *informal* : to speak in a way that is exaggerated and not sincere ▪ You should compliment her cooking but don't *lay it on too thick* or she'll know you don't mean it. ▪ He *laid it on* pretty heavily and pretended to be interested in what she said.

lay out [*phrasal verb*] **1** ***lay (something) out or lay out (something)*** **a** : to place (something) on a surface in a carefully arranged way ▪ The wires were *laid out* along the floor. ▪ Brochures were *laid out* on a table. ▪ She was *laying out* the cheese and crackers for the guests. **b** : to arrange (something) in a particular pattern or design ▪ The garden was *laid out* in a formal pattern. ▪ Much of Manhattan is *laid out* in the form of a grid. — see also LAYOUT **c** : to plan the details of (something) ▪ She's been hired to *lay out* [=*map out*] the election campaign. ▪ The work for tomorrow is all *laid out*. **d** : to explain the details of (something) ▪ He *laid out* the reasons for his decision. **e** *informal* : to spend (money) ▪ The city *laid out* millions of dollars for the new stadium. — see also OUTLAY **2** ***lay (someone's body) out or lay out (someone's body)*** : to prepare (someone's dead body) so that it can be seen by family and friends before it is buried ▪ They *laid* him *out* in a plain coffin. **3** ***lay (someone) out or lay out (someone)*** *informal* : to make (someone) unconscious : to knock (someone) out ▪ He *laid* his opponent *out* with a hard right to the jaw.

lay over [*phrasal verb*] *US* **1** : to make a stop in the middle of a journey ▪ Our flight to Italy *laid over* in Madrid for several hours. **2** ***lay (someone) over*** : to cause (someone) to stop in the middle of a journey — usually used as ***(be) laid over*** ▪ We *were laid over* in Madrid for several hours. — see also LAYOVER

lay siege to see SIEGE

lay (someone) to rest see [2]REST

lay to rest (something) or ***lay (something) to rest*** see [2]REST

lay up [*phrasal verb*] **1** ***lay (something) up or lay up (something)*** **a** *old-fashioned* : to store (something) ▪ *lay up* [=*lay in*] grain for the winter **b** : to take (something) out of active use or service ▪ We *laid up* the boat for the winter. **2** ***lay (someone) up or lay up (someone)*** : to cause (someone) to stay at home or in bed because of illness or injury ▪ The flu *laid him up* for two weeks. — usually used as ***(be) laid up*** ▪ He *was laid up* for six weeks with a bad back. ▪ He *was laid up* by the flu.

lay waste to : to cause very bad damage to (something) ▪ The fire *laid waste to* the land. [=the fire caused great destruction to the land]

lay your hands on see [1]HAND

the goose that lays the golden egg see [1]GOOSE

[2]**lay** *noun, pl* **lays** [*count*] *informal* + *offensive* : a person who is being described as a sexual partner ▪ a great *lay* ▪ an easy *lay* [=a person who is very willing to have sex] — see also LAY OF THE LAND

[3]**lay** *past tense of* [1]LIE

[4]**lay** *adj, always used before a noun*
1 : not trained in a certain profession : not having a lot of knowledge about a certain thing ▪ a science magazine written for the *lay* public ▪ *lay* and professional readers
2 : belonging to a religion but not officially a priest, minister, etc. ▪ *lay* preachers

lay·about /ˈlejəˌbaʊt/ *noun, pl* **-abouts** [*count*] *informal* : a lazy person ▪ an irresponsible *layabout* ▪ her *layabout* brother

lay·away /ˈlejəˌweɪ/ *noun* [*singular*] *US* **:** a way of buying something in which you do not receive the thing you are buying until you have paid the full price by making small payments over a period of time ▪ We bought the table and chairs ***on layaway***, so we won't have them until December. ▪ The store offers a ***layaway plan*** for large purchases.

lay–by /ˈleɪˌbaɪ/ *noun, pl* **-bys** [*count*] *Brit* **:** an area next to a road where vehicles can stop **:** TURNOUT

[1]**lay·er** /ˈlejɚ/ *noun, pl* **-ers** [*count*]

1 : an amount of something that is spread over an area ▪ Everything was covered by a thin *layer* of sand/dust. ▪ a *layer* of clouds — see also OZONE LAYER

2 : a covering piece of material or a part that lies over or under another ▪ The top *layer* of the rug is badly worn but the bottom *layer* is still OK. ▪ The cake has three *layers*. ▪ She glued together several *layers* of paper. ▪ He was wearing several *layers* of clothing. ▪ rocks that formed in *layers* from flows of lava ▪ (*US*) When the weather is cold you should ***dress in layers***. [=you should wear several pieces of clothing on top of one another] — often used figuratively ▪ His novels have many *layers* [=*levels*] of meaning. ▪ a dish that has many *layers* of flavor [=that has many different flavors]

3 : a bird that lays eggs ▪ Their hens were poor *layers*. [=their hens did not produce many eggs]

4 : a worker who lays something (such as bricks) ▪ a brick *layer*

[2]**layer** *verb* **-ers; -ered; -er·ing** [+ *obj*] **:** to form or arrange parts or pieces of something on top of each other **:** to form or arrange (something) in layers ▪ The next step in the recipe is to *layer* the pasta and the sauce in the pan. [=to place a layer of pasta in the pan, then a layer of sauce, then another layer of pasta, and so on] ▪ We *layered* the fruit with whipped cream and served it with cookies. ▪ He *layered* her hair. [=he cut her hair in sections that were different lengths] — often used as *(be) layered* ▪ pasta *layered* with sauce

layer cake *noun, pl* ~ **cakes** [*count*] *chiefly US* **:** a cake made of more than one layer

lay·ette /leɪˈɛt/ *noun, pl* **-ettes** [*count*] **:** a collection of basic clothing and other things needed for a new baby

lay·in /ˈleɪˌɪn/ *noun, pl* **-ins** [*count*] *US, basketball* **:** LAYUP ▪ an easy *layin*

lay·man /ˈleɪmən/ *noun, pl* **-men** /-mən/ [*count*]

1 : a person who is not a member of a particular profession ▪ For a *layman*, he knows a lot about the law. ▪ a medical journal written in language that is clear to the *layman* [=clear to someone who is not a medical professional] ▪ The process was explained to us in ***layman's terms***. [=in simple language that anyone can understand]

2 : a person who belongs to a religion but is not a priest, minister, etc. ▪ He's an important *layman* in his church. — compare LAITY

lay·off /ˈleɪˌɑːf/ *noun, pl* **-offs** [*count*]

1 : the act of ending the employment of a worker or group of workers ▪ The company announced the *layoff* of several hundred employees. ▪ More *layoffs* are expected at the factory later this year. — see also *lay off* at [1]LAY

2 : a period of time during which there is no activity ▪ The band finally has a new album after a three year *layoff*. ▪ a *layoff* of three years

lay of the land *noun*

the lay of the land *US* **:** the arrangement of the different parts in an area of land **:** where things are located in a place ▪ She knew the *lay of the land* from hiking through it daily. — often used figuratively ▪ It takes time for new employees to get *the lay of the land* [=to learn how things are done] in this department. — called also (*Brit*) *the lie of the land*

lay·out /ˈleɪˌaʊt/ *noun, pl* **-outs** [*count*] **:** the design or arrangement of something **:** the way something is laid out ▪ The *layout* of the apartment was good, but the kitchen was too small. ▪ She designed the page *layout* for the new magazine. — see also *lay out* at [1]LAY

lay·over /ˈleɪˌoʊvɚ/ *noun, pl* **-overs** [*count*] *US* **:** a period of time when you are not traveling in the middle of a journey **:** STOPOVER ▪ a two-hour *layover*

lay·per·son /ˈleɪˌpɚsn̩/ *noun, pl* **lay·per·sons** *or* **lay·peo·ple** /ˈleɪˌpiːpəl/ [*count*] **:** LAYMAN ▪ a meeting between clergy and *laypeople*

lay·up /ˈleɪˌʌp/ *noun, pl* **-ups** [*count*] *basketball* **:** a shot made from a position that is very close to the basket

lay·wom·an /ˈleɪˌwʊmən/ *noun, pl* **-wom·en** /-ˌwɪmən/ [*count*] **:** a woman who belongs to a religion but is not a member of the clergy ▪ a Catholic *laywoman* — compare LAITY

laze /ˈleɪz/ *verb* **laz·es; lazed; laz·ing** [*no obj*] **:** to spend time relaxing ▪ She's been *lazing* in the sun all afternoon. ▪ While he was sick, he just *lazed* around the house.

laze away [*phrasal verb*] ***laze (something) away*** *or* ***laze away (something)*** **:** to relax and do very little for (a period of time) ▪ She *lazed away* the afternoon lying in the sun.

la·zy /ˈleɪzi/ *adj* **la·zi·er; -est**

1 *disapproving* **:** not liking to work hard or to be active ▪ a *lazy* child who avoided household chores ▪ I should have done more work this weekend, but I was feeling *lazy*.

2 *always used before a noun* **:** not having much activity **:** causing people to feel that they do not want to be active ▪ a *lazy* summer day

3 *always used before a noun* **:** moving slowly ▪ a hawk flying in *lazy* circles ▪ a *lazy* river

– la·zi·ly /ˈleɪzəli/ *adv* ▪ The leaves floated *lazily* down the stream. **– la·zi·ness** /ˈleɪzinəs/ *noun* [*noncount*] ▪ Her parents blame her bad grades on *laziness*.

la·zy·bones /ˈleɪziˌboʊnz/ *noun, pl* **lazybones** [*count*] *informal* **:** a lazy person ▪ They're such *lazybones* they'll never get the work done on time. ▪ Don't be such a *lazybones*.

lazy Su·san /-ˈsuːzn̩/ *noun, pl* ~ **-sans** [*count*] *chiefly US* **:** a round tray that can be turned and that is used for serving food at a table

lb. *abbr, pl* **lbs.** pound ▪ a 5-*lb*. bag of flour [=a five-pound bag of flour, a bag of flour weighing five pounds] ▪ The baby weighed 8 *lbs*. at birth. ✧ The abbreviation *lb*. comes from Latin word "libra," which means "pound."

LCD /ˌɛlˌsiːˈdiː/ *noun, pl* **LCDs** [*count*] **:** a screen (such as a television screen or the screen on a watch) that works by passing a small amount of electricity through a special liquid ✧ *LCD* is an abbreviation of "liquid crystal display."

leach /ˈliːʧ/ *verb* **leach·es; leached; leach·ing** *technical*

1 [+ *obj*] **:** to remove (a chemical, a metal, etc.) from a substance by the action of a liquid passing through the substance ▪ Even a small amount of rain can *leach* the toxic material from the soil. **:** to release (a chemical, a metal, etc.) when a liquid passes through ▪ Certain kinds of treated wood can *leach* chemicals into the soil.

2 [*no obj*] *of a chemical, a metal, etc.* **:** to be removed from a substance by a liquid passing through the substance ▪ The chemical eventually *leaches* away from the soil.

[1]**lead** /ˈliːd/ *verb* **leads; led** /ˈlɛd/; **lead·ing**

1 a : to guide someone to a place especially by going in front [*no obj*] You *lead* and we'll follow right behind you. [+ *obj*] He *led* [=*took*] me into a room in the back of the house. ▪ You *lead* us and we'll follow right behind you. — often + *to* ▪ The teacher *led* the child by the hand *to* his seat. = The teacher took the child's hand and *led* him *to* his seat. ▪ Our hostess *led* us *to* the dinner table. — often used as *(be) led* ▪ The passengers *were led* onto/aboard the ship by the steward. ▪ The prisoner *was* ***led off*** to jail [=was taken to jail] in handcuffs. — often used figuratively ▪ I gradually *led* the interview around/back to the subject of his failed marriage. ▪ He says that he will follow the evidence wherever it *leads* (him). ▪ This *leads* me to my next point, which is that the building needs a new roof. ▪ The painting's composition ***leads the/your eye*** to the figures in the foreground. [=causes you to look at the figures in the foreground] **b** [+ *obj*] **:** to go or be at the front part of (something) ▪ The veterans will *lead* a parade down Main Street. ▪ *lead* a march

2 [*no obj*] **:** to lie or go in a specified direction ▪ The path *leads* uphill. ▪ This road doesn't *lead* to the village as we thought it did. ▪ a set of stairs that *leads* down to the basement ▪ There was a path *leading* (off) from the meadow into the woods. — often used figuratively ▪ She realized that their relationship would never *lead* to marriage. ▪ The investigation into the murder was ***leading nowhere***. [=the investigation was not solving the crime]

3 : to guide the actions of a person or group **:** to be in charge of a person, group, activity, etc. [*no obj*] We need to elect someone who can *lead*. ▪ bosses who ***lead by example*** [=who show employees how they should act by acting that way themselves] [+ *obj*] She *leads* her employees by setting a good example for them. ▪ She *led* a successful boycott of the store. ▪ *lead* an expedition ▪ A visiting professor will be *leading* the seminar. ▪ *lead* [=*direct*] an orchestra ▪ She *led* the children in a song. [=she sang a song and the children sang with her]

4 [+ *obj*] **:** to cause (a person, group, etc.) to do something or

L

to follow some course of action • Her interest in art *led* her into the field of art history. — usually followed by *to* or *to* + *verb* • His volunteer work in the hospital *led* him *to* a career in nursing. = His volunteer work in the hospital *led* [=*inspired*] him *to become* a nurse. • Her experience with cancer *led* her *to consider* writing a book on the subject. • The evidence *leads* me *to believe* [=makes me believe] that this disease is curable. • We've been *led to believe* that the labels on food items disclose all ingredients, but it's becoming clear that this is not the case. • I had been *led to expect* that someone would meet me at the airport, but no one came. • He *led me to understand* [=he told me or caused me to think] that the deadline was January 7.

5 : to be first, best, or ahead in a race or competition [*no obj*] the team that is currently *leading* in the pennant race • At the end of the fourth inning, the Red Sox *led* by two runs. [+ *obj*] *lead* a race • They *led* their opponents by 20 points at the end of the third quarter. • the team that is *leading* the league [=the team that is in first place] • a batter who *leads* the league in home runs [=who has hit more home runs than any other batter] • a runner who is ***leading the pack/field*** [=a runner who is ahead of the group of other runners] — often used figuratively • Their company ***leads the world*** [=is the most successful company in the world] in developing new technology to assist people with disabilities.

6 [+ *obj*] **: to go through (life) in a certain way : to have (a specified kind of life)** • They chose to *lead* [=*live*] a quiet life. • He *leads* a peaceful existence. • It turned out that he had been ***leading a double life*** [=deceiving people about his life, not telling the whole truth about his life] • He has always ***led a charmed life*** [=he has always been lucky] • She needs to ***lead her own life*** [=she needs to make her own decisions about her life]

7 : to begin play in a card game with (a certain card or kind of card) [+ *obj*] *lead* trumps • *led* a spade [*no obj*] *lead* with a spade

8 [*no obj*] **: to guide a dance partner through the steps of a dance** • I don't know this dance, so I'd prefer it if you *lead*.

9 [+ *obj*] *law* **: to ask (a witness) a question in a way that suggests what the answer should be : to ask (a witness) a leading question** • The judge ruled that the lawyer was *leading* the witness.

lead off [*phrasal verb*] ***lead off or lead (something) off or lead off (something)*** **1 : to start something (such as an activity or performance) in a specified way** • She *led off* [=*started, kicked off*] the presentation with a brief overview of the project. • She *led off* [=*began*] with a brief overview of the project. **2** *baseball* **: to be the first batter in an inning** • He *led off* with a walk. [=he was the first batter in his team's half of the inning and he was walked] • He *led off* the inning with a home run. — see also LEADOFF

lead on [*phrasal verb*] ***lead (someone) on*** **: to cause (someone) to wrongly continue believing or doing something** • She was devastated when she found out that he didn't really love her, and had only been *leading* her *on*. [=he had been leading her to believe that he loved her]

lead someone a merry chase (*US*) *or Brit* ***lead someone a (merry) dance*** *old-fashioned* **: to cause a series of troubles or worries for (someone)** • He *led me a merry chase* before I finally got him to agree to a meeting.

lead someone (around) by the nose see [1]NOSE

lead someone down/up the garden path *informal* **: to deceive someone : to cause someone to go, think, or proceed wrongly** • He believes the average consumer is being *led down the garden path* by the promises in advertisements.

lead the way **: to be the first person to go somewhere** • You *lead the way*, and we'll follow. — often used figuratively • Their company *led the way* in developing this technology. [=was the first to have success developing the technology]

lead to [*phrasal verb*] ***lead to (something)*** **: to result in (something)** • a course of study *leading to* a degree in agriculture • Her investigations ultimately *led to* the discovery of the missing documents. • His volunteer work in the hospital *led to* a career in nursing. = His volunteer work in the hospital *led to* him becoming a nurse. — see also [1]LEAD 1a, 4 (above)

lead up to [*phrasal verb*] ***lead up to (something)*** **1 : to occur in the time that comes before (something)** • Many voters were still undecided in the days *leading up to* [=*approaching*] the election. **2 : to come before and help to cause (something)** • There was a series of errors *leading up to* the accident. **3 : to come before and help to introduce (something)** • a chapter *leading up to* the main topic of the book • I had no idea what he was *leading up to* when he started talking about his father.

lead with [*phrasal verb*] ***lead with (something)*** **1 : to begin something (such as a story or speech) with (something specified)** • The newspaper story *led* [=*opened, began*] *with* a long report on the funeral. **2 : to begin a series of punches in boxing with (a punch thrown by a specified hand)** • The champion *led with* a left to the body, followed up quickly with a right to the jaw.

the blind leading the blind see [1]BLIND

[2]lead *noun, pl* **leads**

1 *the lead* **a : a position that is ahead of others** • They walked single file, with the oldest boy ***in the lead*** [=with the oldest boy at the front of the line] • You ***take the lead*** [=go first] and we'll follow right behind you. **b : a position that is ahead of others in a race or competition** • A runner from Kenya is ***in the lead*** in the race. [=is leading the race] • A runner from Kenya ***has/holds the lead*** • Her car has ***taken/gained the lead*** = Her car has ***gone to/into the lead*** • He was trailing in the polls last week, but now he has ***regained the lead*** — often used figuratively • Their company has *taken the lead* in developing this new technology.

2 [*count*] **: the amount or distance by which someone or something is ahead in a race or competition** — usually singular • Her car had a *lead* of 12 seconds over the next one. • They had a *lead* of 20 points. = They had a 20-point *lead*. • a narrow/slim *lead* • Our candidate has established a comfortable/commanding *lead* in the opinion polls.

3 [*count*] **: a piece of information that could help produce a desired result** • I'm a good salesman, but I need more *leads*. [=names of potential customers]; *especially* **: a piece of information that might help in solving a crime** • The police have no *leads* in the case. • Investigators are working on several *leads*.

4 [*count*] **a : the main role in a movie or play** • Her big break came when she got/played the *lead* in a major Hollywood movie. • He played the *lead* opposite Bette Davis [=he starred with Bette Davis] in two films. • She got the ***lead role***; *also* **: someone who plays the main role in movie or play** • She was the romantic *lead* in a major Hollywood movie. • Who will be the male/female *lead* in his next film? **b : the main performer in a group** • He ***sang/played lead*** [=sang/played as the main performer] in the band. — usually used before another noun • the *lead* singer/guitarist

5 [*count*] **a : the beginning part of a news story** • You should edit the *lead* so that it will grab the audience's attention. **b : the most important news story in a newspaper or broadcast** • The story of his arrest was the *lead* in newspapers across the country. • His arrest was the ***lead story*** [=the first and most important story] on the evening news.

6 [*count*] *baseball* **: a position taken by a runner at a distance from a base before a pitch is thrown** • The runner on first took a big *lead*. [=moved several steps toward second base] • The runner had a large *lead* off second base. [=stood several steps away from second base in the space between second and third base]

7 [*count*] *chiefly Brit* **:** [1]LEASH • train a dog to walk on a *lead*

8 [*count*] *chiefly Brit* **: a wire that carries electricity from a source to an electrical device (such as a lamp or radio) : an electrical cord**

follow someone's lead **: to do the same thing that someone else has done** • He *followed her lead* and voted in favor of the proposal.

— compare [3]LEAD

[3]lead /ˈlɛd/ *noun, pl* **leads**

1 [*noncount*] **: a heavy and soft metal that has a gray color** • a pipe made of *lead* — often used before another noun • a *lead* pipe • *lead* crystal [=glass made with lead in it] • *lead* poisoning [=poisoning from eating, drinking, or touching something with lead in it] • ***lead-free*** gasoline [=gasoline that does not contain lead]

2 : a thin stick of dark material used in pencils to make marks [*noncount*] a pencil with black *lead* • a *lead* pencil [*count*] pencils with broken *leads*

3 [*noncount*] *chiefly US, informal* **: bullets** • They shot him ***full of lead***

get the lead out *US, informal* **: to begin going or moving more quickly** • *Get the lead out*! If we don't leave in five minutes we'll be late for the movie!

go over/down like a lead balloon see [1]BALLOON

— compare [2]LEAD

lead·ed /ˈlɛdəd/ *adj*

1 : containing lead • *leaded* gasoline — opposite UNLEADED

2 : having pieces of glass separated by narrow pieces of lead ▪ *leaded* glass ▪ *leaded* windows ▪ (*Brit*) ***leaded lights*** [=windows with leaded glass]

lead·en /ˈlɛdn̩/ *adj, literary*
1 : having a dull gray color ▪ a *leaden* sky/sea
2 : feeling heavy and difficult to move ▪ walked with *leaden* feet
3 : not lively or exciting ▪ *leaden* [=*dull*] conversation

lead·er /ˈliːdɚ/ *noun, pl* **-ers** [*count*]
1 : someone or something that leads others: such as **a :** someone who guides other people ▪ He acted as our *leader* [=*guide*] on the climb. ▪ The tour *leader* suggested several restaurants in the area. **b :** someone or something that is ahead of others in a race or competition ▪ She was the *leader* for most of the race, but she eventually finished second. ▪ He is the league *leader* in home runs. [=he has the most home runs in the league] ▪ the ***leader board*** [=the list of players who are leading a golf tournament] **c :** a powerful person who controls or influences what other people do **:** a person who leads a group, organization, country, etc. ▪ The class focused on the great religious/political *leaders* of the last century. ▪ the *leader* of an army ▪ a gang *leader* ▪ a *leader* of the antiwar movement ▪ Some people are *leaders*, and some people are followers. ▪ He's a ***born/natural leader***. [=someone who has qualities that a good leader has] **d :** a person, group, or organization that is the best or most successful in some activity ▪ The company has become a *leader* in developing new technology. ▪ a market *leader* [=a product or company that is more successful than all competing products or companies]
2 a : a person who leads a musical group ▪ the *leader* of a popular big band of the 1930s; *specifically, US* **:** the conductor of an orchestra ▪ the orchestra *leader* **b** *Brit* **:** CONCERTMASTER
3 *Brit* **:** ²EDITORIAL ▪ *The Times* attacked the government in a *leader* today.
— see also LOSS LEADER
— **lead·er·less** *adj* ▪ a *leaderless* political movement

lead·er·ship /ˈliːdɚˌʃɪp/ *noun*
1 [*noncount*] **a :** a position as a leader of a group, organization, etc. ▪ She recently assumed (the) *leadership* of the company. **b :** the time when a person holds the position of leader ▪ The company has done very well ***under her leadership***. [=while she has been its leader]
2 [*noncount*] **:** the power or ability to lead other people ▪ a politician who lacks *leadership* ▪ What this country needs is the exercise of strong *leadership*! ▪ *leadership* skills
3 [*count*] **:** the leaders of a group, organization, or country ▪ The party *leadership* is uncertain about what to do next. = (*Brit*) The party *leadership* are uncertain about what to do next.

lead–in /ˈliːdˌɪn/ *noun, pl* **-ins** [*count*] **:** something that comes before and introduces something else ▪ The short animated movie is a good *lead-in* to the feature film.

lead·ing /ˈliːdɪŋ/ *adj, always used before a noun*
1 : having great importance, influence, or success ▪ a *leading* topic of conversation ▪ Their family played a *leading* part in the settlement of the town. ▪ the *leading* role in a major Hollywood movie ▪ a *leading* citizen of the town ▪ She's one of the *leading* authorities/experts on the stock market.
2 : most important **:** FOREMOST ▪ What is the *leading* [=*number one*] health problem for older women?

leading article *noun, pl* ~ **articles** [*count*] *Brit* **:** ²EDITORIAL

leading edge *noun, pl* ~ **edges**
1 [*count*] **:** the front edge of something that moves ▪ the *leading edge* of an airplane's wing ▪ the *leading edge* of a thunderstorm
2 [*singular*] **:** the most important or advanced area of activity in a particular field ▪ a company that is at/on the *leading edge* [=*cutting edge*] of new developments in technology

leading lady *noun, pl* ~ **-dies** [*count*] **:** an actress who plays the most important female role in a play or movie

leading light *noun, pl* ~ **lights** [*count*] **:** a person who is a very important member of a group, organization, or community ▪ He is one of the *leading lights* of the labor movement.

leading man *noun, pl* ~ **men** [*count*] **:** an actor who plays the most important male role in a play or movie

leading question *noun, pl* ~ **-tions** [*count*] **:** a question asked in a way that is intended to produce a desired answer ▪ The judge made it quite clear that the lawyers were not permitted to ask witnesses *leading questions*. ▪ The interviewer asked a lot of *leading questions* and was clearly biased.

lead·off /ˈliːdˌɑːf/ *adj, baseball* **:** batting first at the start of a game or an inning ▪ a *leadoff* hitter ▪ a batter ***hitting leadoff*** = a batter hitting in the *leadoff* position — see also *lead off* at ¹LEAD

lead time /ˈliːd-/ *noun* [*noncount*] **:** the time between the beginning of a process or project and the appearance of its results ▪ We will need at least six months *lead time* before production begins.

lead–up /ˈliːdˌʌp/ *noun* [*singular*] **:** something that comes before or prepares for something else ▪ the *lead-up* to the war/trial

¹leaf /ˈliːf/ *noun, pl* **leaves** /ˈliːvz/
1 : one of the flat and typically green parts of a plant that grow from a stem or twig [*count*] a maple *leaf* ▪ a tobacco *leaf* ▪ tea *leaves* ▪ I heard the rustle of the autumn *leaves*. ▪ a pile of dead *leaves* ▪ The trees drop their *leaves* in the fall, and new *leaves* grow again in the spring. [*noncount*] By the end of April, most trees are ***in leaf***. [=most trees have grown their new leaves] ▪ The trees have not yet ***come into leaf***. — see color picture on page C6
2 [*count*] **:** a sheet of paper in a book **:** PAGE — usually used figuratively ▪ I decided to ***take/borrow a leaf out of his book*** [=to do the same thing that he did] and invest some money in the stock market. — see also FLYLEAF, LOOSE-LEAF
3 [*count*] **:** a part that can be added to or removed from a table to change the size of its top surface
4 [*noncount*] **:** a very thin sheet of metal (such as gold or silver) that is used to decorate something ▪ silver *leaf*
turn over a new leaf **:** to start behaving or living in a different and better way ▪ I decided to *turn over a new leaf* and stop worrying so much. ▪ The program helps drug addicts to *turn over a new leaf* when they get out of jail.
— **leaf·less** /ˈliːfləs/ *adj* ▪ *leafless* trees — **leaf·like** /ˈliːfˌlaɪk/ *adj*

²leaf *verb* **leafs; leafed; leaf·ing**
leaf out [*phrasal verb*] *US, of a tree* **:** to produce leaves ▪ The tree will *leaf out* in the spring.
leaf through [*phrasal verb*] ***leaf through (something)*** **:** to turn the pages of (a book, a magazine, etc.) ▪ She was *leafing through* the magazine, looking at the pictures.

leafed /ˈliːft/ *adj* **:** having a specified kind or number of leaves **:** LEAVED — used in combination ▪ a silver-*leafed* plant ▪ a four-*leafed* clover

¹leaf·let /ˈliːflət/ *noun, pl* **-lets** [*count*] **:** a printed and often folded sheet of paper that is usually given to people for no cost ▪ Protesters were handing out *leaflets* condemning the government's environmental policies. ▪ an advertising *leaflet*

²leaflet *verb* **-let·ed; -let·ing :** to give leaflets to many people in (a place) [+ *obj*] They *leafleted* several neighborhoods. [*no obj*] We spent the morning *leafleting*.

leafy /ˈliːfi/ *adj* **leaf·i·er; -est**
1 : having many leaves or trees ▪ *leafy* woodlands ▪ *leafy* trees ▪ a *leafy* suburb [=a suburb in which there are many trees]
2 : consisting mostly of leaves ▪ *leafy* vegetables ▪ *leafy* greens

¹league /ˈliːg/ *noun, pl* **leagues** [*count*]
1 : a group of sports teams that play against each other ▪ a softball/bowling *league* ▪ the National Football *League* — often used figuratively ▪ I enjoy playing chess, but when I tried playing against George, I knew right away that I was ***out of my league***. [=I knew that he was much better than I was] ▪ According to one restaurant reviewer, the two chefs are ***not even in the same league***. [=one of the chefs is much better than the other] ▪ He's a pretty good writer, but he's ***not in the same league*** as she is. = He's a pretty good writer, but she's ***in a different league*** altogether. [=she is a much better writer than he is] ▪ When it comes to cooking, he's ***in a league of his own***. [=he is a much better cook than anyone else] — see also BIG LEAGUE, BUSH LEAGUE, IVY LEAGUE, LITTLE LEAGUE, MAJOR LEAGUES, MINOR LEAGUE
2 : a group or organization of nations or people united for a purpose ▪ the *League* of Nations ▪ joined the *League* of Voters ▪ The *league* has grown to include 12 member states.
in league (with) **:** working with someone especially to do something dishonest ▪ She denies that she is *in league with* [=*conspiring with*] corrupt officials. ▪ He suspects that they are *in league* together [=working with each other; working together] against him.
— compare ²LEAGUE

²league *noun, pl* **leagues** [*count*] **:** any one of several old units of distance from about 2.4 to 4.6 miles (3.9 to 7.4 kilometers) — compare ¹LEAGUE

L

leagu•er /ˈliːgɚ/ *noun, pl* **-ers** [*count*] : a person who belongs to a specified league ▪ a major/minor *leaguer* [=a player in baseball's major/minor leagues]

league table *noun, pl* ~ **tables** [*count*] *Brit* : a list of teams, schools, hospitals, etc. that shows them in order from best to worst

¹leak /ˈliːk/ *verb* **leaks; leaked; leak•ing**

1 a : to let something (such as a liquid or gas) in or out through a hole in a surface [*no obj*] The roof was *leaking*. [=rainwater was getting into the building through the roof] ▪ The boat *leaked* badly. [=a lot of water got into the boat through its bottom] ▪ That hose is *leaking*. [=water is coming out of the side of that hose] ▪ a *leaking* boat/roof [+ *obj*] The boat was *leaking* water. ▪ The cracked pipe *leaked* fumes into the room. **b** [*no obj*] *of a liquid, gas, etc.* : to come in or go out through a hole in a surface ▪ Fumes *leaked* through the crack in the pipe. ▪ Air *leaked* out of the tire. ▪ Water was *leaking* through a hole in the roof.

2 a [+ *obj*] : to give (secret information) to someone so that it becomes known to the public ▪ Someone *leaked* the story to the press. ▪ a *leaked* story **b** [*no obj*] : to become known to the public ▪ We can't let this information *leak*. [=*get out*] — usually + *out* ▪ Eventually, news of the accident *leaked out*. ▪ Details about the case started to *leak out*.

²leak *noun, pl* **leaks** [*count*]

1 a : a hole in a surface that lets something (such as a liquid or gas) pass in or out ▪ The boat had developed a bad *leak*. ▪ The landlord said he would fix the *leak* in the roof. ▪ One of the car's tires has a ***slow leak***. [=a small hole through which air escapes slowly] ▪ The pipe suddenly ***sprung a leak***. [=began to leak] **b** : an occurrence in which something (such as a liquid or gas) passes through a hole in a surface ▪ a gas/oil *leak* ▪ a slow *leak* of the chemical

2 : a situation in which people learn about information that is supposed to be secret ▪ When a reporter revealed classified information, the source of the *leak* was investigated. ▪ Security is high because of a fear of *leaks* before negotiations have been finished. ▪ a security *leak*

take a leak or *Brit* ***have a leak*** *informal + impolite* : to pass liquid from the body : URINATE

– leak•proof /ˈliːkˌpruːf/ *adj* ▪ a *leakproof* container

leak•age /ˈliːkɪʤ/ *noun, pl* **-ag•es**

1 a : an occurrence in which something (such as a liquid or gas) passes through a hole in a surface [*noncount*] Some of the water was lost from the containers because of *leakage*. [=because it leaked out] [*count*] trying to prevent accidental *leakages* **b** [*count*] : the amount that is lost when something leaks ▪ *Leakages* of about 30 percent were reported.

2 : an occurrence in which secret information becomes known [*noncount*] taking steps to prevent *leakage* of confidential information [*count*] *leakages* of confidential information

leaky /ˈliːki/ *adj* **leak•i•er; -est** : having a hole that allows something (such as a liquid or gas) to pass in or out : having a leak ▪ a *leaky* boat/pipe ▪ The roof was *leaky*.

¹lean /ˈliːn/ *verb* **leans; leaned** *or Brit* **leant** /ˈlɛnt/; **lean•ing**

1 a [*no obj*] : to bend or move from a straight position ▪ The tree *leans* to one side. ▪ He *leaned* back in his chair. ▪ They *leaned* over the table to smell the flowers. **b** [+ *obj*] : to cause (something) to bend or move from a straight position ▪ They *leaned* their heads back. ▪ He *leaned* his chair back.

2 a [*no obj*] : to rest *on* or *against* something or someone for support ▪ You can *lean on* me if you get tired. ▪ She stood *leaning on* her right leg. ▪ The ladder was *leaning against* the house. **b** [+ *obj*] : to cause (something) to rest *on* or *against* something ▪ He *leaned* the ladder *against* the house. ▪ The boy *leaned* his head *on* his mother's shoulder.

3 a — used to describe what someone wants to do, tends to do, or is likely to do ▪ She hasn't made a decision yet, and I don't know which way she's *leaning*. — often + *toward* ▪ She's *leaning toward* a career in medicine. [=she is probably going to choose a career in medicine] ▪ The mayor is *leaning toward* closing down the school. **b** — used to say that someone supports one group or set of beliefs more than another; often + *toward* ▪ an independent presidential candidate who *leans toward* the Democrats and their views **c** — used to say that something is more like one thing than another; often + *toward* ▪ Her new album *leans* more *toward* rock than country.

lean on [*phrasal verb*] **1** ***lean on (someone or something)*** : to depend on (someone or something) for support ▪ He *leaned on* his family during the crisis. ▪ She was someone you could *lean on*. **2** ***lean on (someone) informal*** : to force or try to force (someone) to do something especially by making threats : to put pressure on (someone) ▪ They were *leaning on* the governor to pass the law.

lean over backward see ¹BACKWARD

²lean *adj* **lean•er; lean•est** [*also more* ~; *most* ~]

1 : not having much fat on the body : physically thin, strong, and healthy ▪ She has a *lean*, athletic body. ▪ a *lean* racehorse

2 : containing little or no fat ▪ *lean* meat ▪ (*US*) *lean* ground beef

3 : not having or producing much money, food, etc. ▪ Those were *lean* years for the company. [=the company did not make much money in those years] ▪ a *lean* budget/profit/harvest

4 *usually approving* : not using a lot of something (such as words or money) ▪ He had a *lean* style of writing. [=his writing style did not use too many words] : not wasteful ▪ She ran a *lean* and efficient company. ▪ We wanted our business to be ***lean and mean***.

– lean•ness /ˈliːnnəs/ *noun* [*noncount*]

> ***synonyms*** LEAN, THIN, and SKINNY mean not having much fat on the body. LEAN suggests a lack of unnecessary fat and may also suggest the muscular body of an athlete. ▪ the strong *lean* legs of a runner THIN can describe a person whose lack of fat is unhealthy, but it also often describes a person who is considered attractive. ▪ a *thin* and sickly old man ▪ The room was full of beautiful *thin* women. SKINNY describes a person who has an extremely thin appearance and who may not be healthy or eat enough food. ▪ *skinny* children in poor countries ▪ *skinny* legs

lean•ing /ˈliːnɪŋ/ *noun, pl* **-ings** [*count*] : a preference for something or tendency to do something — often + *toward* ▪ Her *leaning* is *toward* a career in medicine. — often plural ▪ His political *leanings* are unknown. ▪ The two painters have similar artistic *leanings*.

lean–to /ˈliːnˌtuː/ *noun, pl* **-tos** [*count*] : a small and usually roughly made building that is built on the side of a larger building

¹leap /ˈliːp/ *verb* **leaps; leaped** /ˈliːpt, ˈlɛpt/ *or* **leapt** /ˈlɛpt, ˈliːpt/; **leap•ing**

1 a [*no obj*] : to jump from a surface ▪ The cat suddenly *leaped* into the air. ▪ Fish were *leaping* out of the water. ▪ He *leaped* off the bridge. ▪ The cat *leapt* down from (the top of) the table. ▪ The boys *leaped* over the stream. ▪ He made a *leaping* catch. [=he caught the ball as he jumped] **b** [+ *obj*] : to jump over (something) ▪ The horse *leaped* the stone wall.

2 [*no obj*] : to move quickly ▪ She *leapt* up [=she stood up quickly] and ran out the door. ▪ When the alarm went off, she *leapt* out of bed. ▪ The crowd ***leapt to its feet***. [=stood up quickly in excitement] — often used figuratively ▪ The team *leaped* from last place to first place. ▪ The conversation *leapt* from politics to religion. ▪ When other people accused her of being lazy, he ***leaped to her defense***. [=he quickly began to defend her] ▪ They ***leaped into action***. [=acted immediately]

3 [*no obj*] : to suddenly increase by a large amount ▪ The price of gasoline *leaped* (by) 10 percent.

leap at [*phrasal verb*] ***leap at (something)*** : to eagerly take (a chance, opportunity, etc.) ▪ She *leaped at* [=*jumped at*] the chance/opportunity to show her boss what she could do. ▪ He *leapt at* the offer of a better job.

leap off the page see ¹PAGE

leap out at [*phrasal verb*] ***leap out at (someone)*** **1** : to suddenly come at (someone) from a hiding place ▪ The hidden assailant *leaped* [=*jumped*] *out at* them. **2** : to immediately get the attention of (someone) ▪ The picture on the magazine's cover *leaps out at* you.

leap to conclusions see CONCLUSION

leap to mind see ¹MIND

look before you leap see ¹LOOK

your heart leaps see HEART

– leap•er /ˈliːpɚ/ *noun, pl* **-ers** [*count*]

²leap *noun, pl* **leaps**

1 [*count*] **a** : a long or high jump ▪ She made a graceful *leap* into the air. ▪ He ran and took ***a flying leap*** over the stream. **b** : the distance that a person or animal jumps ▪ He won the high jump with a *leap* of six feet.

2 [*count*] : a great and sudden change, increase, or improvement ▪ She made the difficult *leap* [=*transition*] from college to the workplace. ▪ the *leap* from childhood to adulthood ▪ a *leap* [=*jump*] in the cost of automobiles ▪ She has shown great *leaps* in ability. ▪ Technology has taken a great *leap* forward.

L

— see also QUANTUM LEAP

3 [*singular*] **:** a serious attempt to do or understand something new • an imaginative *leap* • It required a ***leap of the imagination*** to picture how the project would look when it was completed. ✧ A ***leap in the dark*** is something that is done without knowing anything about what the result might be. • He had no experience, so starting his own business was a real *leap in the dark*. ✧ A ***leap of faith*** is a decision to believe that something is true or possible even though other people may doubt it. • He has taken/made a *leap of faith* in starting his own business. • It takes/requires a *leap of faith* to believe that this project can succeed.

by/in leaps and bounds **:** very quickly and greatly • The company grew *by leaps and bounds*. • Their knowledge has increased *in leaps and bounds*.

take a flying leap *US, informal + impolite* — used to tell someone who angers or annoys you to go away • She told him to (go) *take a flying leap*. [=(*Brit*) *take a running jump*]

¹leap·frog /ˈliːpˌfrɑːg/ *noun* [*noncount*] **:** a children's game in which one player bends down so that another player can leap over the back of the first player • play *leapfrog*

²leapfrog *verb* **-frogs; -frogged; -frog·ging :** to move ahead of or beyond (someone or something) in a very quick and sudden way [+ *obj*] Skipping his last two years of high school, he *leapfrogged* his classmates and went to college. • This year's technologies are *leapfrogging* last year's designs. [*no obj*] — usually + *over* • She *leapfrogged over* her more experienced coworkers and became the company's president.

leap year *noun, pl* **~ years** [*count*] **:** a year of 366 days instead of 365 with February having 29 days instead of 28 ✧ A leap year occurs every four years. • The year 2004 was a *leap year*.

learn /ˈlən/ *verb* **learns; learned** *also chiefly Brit* **learnt** /ˈlənt/; **learn·ing**

1 : to gain knowledge or skill by studying, practicing, being taught, or experiencing something [*no obj*] People *learn* throughout their lives. • He is *learning* quickly. • I can't swim yet, but I'm *learning*. — often + *about* • We *learned about* the reasons for the war in our history class. — often + *from* • We all have the ability to *learn from* our mistakes. • She *learned from* experience that when grease catches on fire, you shouldn't put water on it. [+ *obj*] *learn* arithmetic • *learn* a trade • She's interested in *learning* French. • We had to *learn* the rules of the game. — often + *about* • She's been trying to *learn* more *about* our family history. — often *to + verb* • He never *learned* (how) *to dance/swim*. • I'm *learning to play* the guitar. • He *learned* how not *to offend* people. • You need to *learn* (how) *to take* care of your health.

2 [+ *obj*] **:** to cause (something) to be in your memory by studying it **:** MEMORIZE • I'm trying to *learn* my lines for the play. • We had to *learn* the names of the state capitals. • *learn* the alphabet

3 : to hear or be told (something) **:** to find out (something) [+ *obj*] She *learned* through/from a letter that her father had died. • I later *learned* that they had never called. • I was surprised when I *learned* (that) he wasn't coming. • We finally *learned* the truth about what had happened. [*no obj*] — + *of* • We were shocked to *learn of* her death. [=to find out about her death] • She first *learned of* the accident on Monday.

4 : to become able to understand (something) through experience [+ *obj*] *learn* the difference between right and wrong • He quickly *learned* what it means to be a father. • We *learned* that if we wanted a good job, we had to go to college. • I have *learned* that life isn't easy. • Someday you'll *learn* that money is not the most important thing in life. • He ***learned the hard way*** that crime doesn't pay. [=he found out by being punished for his crimes] — often followed by *to + verb* • It's important to *learn to respect* other people. • It's a bad situation, but we'll just have to ***learn to live with it***. [=we will have to accept it and deal with it] [*no obj*] Someday you'll *learn*. • Even after all his health problems, he's still eating and drinking too much. Some people never *learn*.

live and learn see ¹LIVE

– learn·able /ˈlənəbəl/ *adj* • *learnable* skills

learned *adj*

1 /ˈlənəd/ [*more ~; most ~*] *formal* **:** having or showing a lot of learning, education, or knowledge • a *learned* scholar • We had a *learned* discussion about politics. • a *learned* opinion • She has published articles in both *learned* [=*scholarly*] journals and popular magazines.

2 /ˈlənd/ — used to describe something that people get or have because of learning or experience • Speaking a language is a *learned* behavior. • a *learned* response

learn·er /ˈlənə/ *noun, pl* **-ers** [*count*]

1 : a person who learns • He is a fast *learner*. [=he learns fast] • slow *learners* **:** a person who is trying to gain knowledge or skill in something by studying, practicing, or being taught • an adult *learner* • an advanced *learner* • *learners* of English as a second language • a *learner's* dictionary

2 *Brit* **:** STUDENT DRIVER

learner driver *noun, pl* **~ -ers** [*count*] *Brit* **:** STUDENT DRIVER

learner's permit *noun, pl* **~ -mits** [*count*] *US* **:** a document that allows a person to learn how to drive a car • After you get your *learner's permit*, I'll let you drive my car. — called also (*Brit*) *provisional licence*

learn·ing /ˈlənɪŋ/ *noun* [*noncount*]

1 : the activity or process of gaining knowledge or skill by studying, practicing, being taught, or experiencing something **:** the activity of someone who learns • a computer program that makes *learning* fun • different methods of foreign language *learning* • The first year of college was a *learning* experience.

2 : knowledge or skill gained from learning • They were people of good education and considerable/great *learning*. • ***book learning*** [=knowledge gained from reading books]

learning curve *noun, pl* **~ curves** [*count*] **:** the rate at which someone learns something new **:** the course of progress made in learning something • The job has a very steep *learning curve*. [=there is a large amount that has to be learned quickly in order to do the job]

learning disability *noun, pl* **~ -ties** [*count*] **:** a condition that makes learning difficult • students with *learning disabilities* — called also (*chiefly Brit*) *learning difficulty*

– learning disabled *adj* • parents with *learning disabled* children

learnt *chiefly Brit past tense and past participle of* LEARN

¹lease /ˈliːs/ *noun, pl* **leas·es** [*count*] **:** a legal agreement that lets someone use a car, house, etc., for a period of time in return for payment • sign a *lease* • They took out a five-year *lease* on the house. • We hold *leases* on both of our cars. • The *lease* expires next month. = The *lease* runs out next month.

a new lease on life (*US*) *or Brit* ***a new lease of life*** **:** a chance to continue living or to become successful or popular again • This medicine gives patients *a new lease on life*. • After they made the movie, the book got *a new lease on life*. [=the book became newly popular] • The band has given this style of music *a new lease on life*.

²lease *verb* **leases; leased; leas·ing** [+ *obj*]

1 : to use (something) for a period of time in return for payment • She *leases* a red convertible. • I have *leased* this house for the last four years.

2 : to allow someone to use (something) for a period of time in return for payment • We *leased* the house to a young married couple.

¹leash /ˈliːʃ/ *noun, pl* **leash·es** [*count*] *chiefly US* **:** a long, thin piece of rope, chain, etc., that is used for holding a dog or other animal • put a dog on a *leash* • Dogs must be kept on a *leash* while in the park. • The dog saw a cat and was straining at its *leash* trying to get at it. — often used figuratively • The coach kept her players on a (short/tight) *leash* throughout the year. [=the coach closely watched and controlled the behavior of her players] • The kids were straining at the *leash* to get going. [=were very eager to get going] — called also (*chiefly Brit*) *lead*

²leash *verb* **leashes; leashed; leash·ing** [+ *obj*] **:** to put (a dog or other animal) on a leash • You need to *leash* your dog while in the park. • a *leashed* dog

¹least /ˈliːst/ *adj, superlative form of* ¹LITTLE **:** smallest in amount or degree • The *least* [=*slightest*] noise would startle her. • I try to spend the *least* (amount of) time possible in the kitchen. = I try to spend the *least* possible (amount of) time in the kitchen. • We finished without the *least* help from you. [=without any help from you] • She hasn't shown the *least* sign of remorse. [=she hasn't shown any remorse]

not (in) the least bit see ¹BIT

take/follow the path/line of least resistance see RESISTANCE

²least *noun*

the least **:** something of the lowest importance, strength, value, etc. • Any noise—even *the* (very) *least*—would startle her. — often + *of* • That's *the least of* my worries/problems. [=I have more important worries/problems to deal

L

with] ▪ We had many things to consider, not *the least of* which was the safety of our children. [=the safety of our children was very important]

at least **1 : not less than a specified amount, level, etc.** ▪ *At least* once a year, we visit our grandparents. ▪ We meet *at least* once a month. = We meet once a month *at least*. ▪ You must be *at least* 21 years of age to enter. ▪ He was *at least* six feet tall. ▪ He must have *at least* 300 CDs! **2 — used to say that something (such as a bad situation) could be or have been worse** ▪ The weather was cold, but *at least* it didn't rain. ▪ I was tired and hungry, but *at least* I was free. ▪ We don't have much money, but *at least* we still have each other. **3 — used to indicate the smallest or easiest thing that someone can or should do** ▪ Well, he could have *at least* apologized. **4 a — used to indicate that the truth of a statement might change or has changed** ▪ We're going to have a picnic, *at least* if it doesn't rain. ▪ I'm fine for now *at least*. [=I'm fine for now although I may not be fine later] ▪ He was unknown in the music world, *at least* until recently. **b — used to indicate that the truth of a previous statement is not certain** ▪ Her name is Sue, or *at least* I think it is. ▪ He is coming today. *At least* that's what he told me.

at the (very) least **— used to indicate the least thing that is true, acceptable, desirable, or certain to happen** ▪ He wanted to win the race, or *at the least*, to finish second. ▪ It is, *at the very least*, an interesting book. ▪ It will change your life or, *at the very least*, teach you something new. ▪ *At the very least*, she deserves to be heard.

not (in) the least **: not at all : not in any way or respect** ▪ It did *not* interest me *in the least*. [=it did not interest me at all] ▪ He did*n't* enjoy it *in the least*. ▪ That joke was *not in the least* funny. ▪ We were*n't in the least* tired. ▪ I'm *not the least* worried.

the least (someone) can do **: the smallest or easiest thing that someone can or should do** ▪ *The least he could do* is tell me what happened. ▪ There's no need to thank me for my help. Considering all the help you've given me in the past, it was *the least I could do*. [=I do not deserve to be thanked for the small thing I did]

to say the least **— used to emphasize a statement** ▪ She was not happy, *to say the least*. [=she was very unhappy] ▪ He is, *to say the least*, hopeful about the future. [=he is very hopeful about the future] ▪ *To say the least*, they were disappointed that their trip was canceled.

[3]**least** *adv, superlative form of* [2]LITTLE **: in or to the smallest degree** ▪ Who was the *least* at fault in the case? ▪ He asked me to help him when I *least* expected it. ▪ That was the *least* important of her reasons. ▪ That was the *least* interesting book I have ever read.

last but not least see [3]LAST

least of all **: especially not** ▪ No one, *least of all* the children, wanted to go home early.

not least *formal* **: especially or particularly** ▪ We had many things to consider, *not least* the safety of our children.

least common denominator *noun* [*noncount*] *US* **:** LOWEST COMMON DENOMINATOR

least·ways /ˈliːstˌweɪz/ *or* **least·wise** /ˈliːstˌwaɪz/ *adv, informal* **: at least** ▪ The weather was cold, but *leastways* it didn't rain. ▪ He was unknown in the music world, *leastwise* until recently.

leath·er /ˈlɛðɚ/ *noun* [*noncount*] **: animal skin that is chemically treated to preserve it and that is used in making clothes, shoes, furniture, etc. — see also** PATENT LEATHER

– leather *adj* ▪ a black *leather* jacket

leath·ery /ˈlɛðəri/ *adj* [*more ~; most ~*] **: looking or feeling like leather** ▪ The meat was dry and *leathery*. [=*tough*] ▪ the old farmer's *leathery*, brown skin

[1]**leave** /ˈliːv/ *verb* **leaves; left** /ˈlɛft/; **leav·ing**

1 a : to go away from (a place) [+ *obj*] What time will you *leave* the office? ▪ Don't *leave* home without your wallet. ▪ I *left* the party at seven o'clock. [*no obj*] We will *leave* at 10 o'clock. ▪ Are we *leaving* soon? ▪ She *left* quickly. ▪ They *left* by bus. ▪ The train *left* an hour ago but another will be arriving soon. **— often + *for*** ▪ We're *leaving for* the game in an hour. ▪ The train *left* from Paris *for* Barcelona an hour ago. **b** [+ *obj*] **: to go away from (a place) to live in a different place** ▪ They *left* the country for a new life in the city. ▪ He ***left town*** a month ago. ▪ He ***left home*** [=left his parent's house and lived somewhere else] after graduating from high school.

2 a [+ *obj*] **: to go away from (a person)** ▪ She *left* her friends and went home. ▪ We *left* him so that he could do his work. = We *left* him to his work. = He had work to do, so we *left* him to it. ▪ We *left* him doing his work. [=he was doing his work when we left him] **b : to stop living with and having a close personal relationship with (someone)** [+ *obj*] His mother *left* [=*abandoned, deserted*] him when he was very young. ▪ He *left* his wife and children. ▪ His wife *left* him for another man. [*no obj*] He hasn't been the same since his wife *left*.

3 a [+ *obj*] **: to give up or stop having (a job, position, etc.)** ▪ He *left* [=*quit*] his job and went back to school. ▪ a politician who will be *leaving* office next year **b : to stop attending, belonging to, or working for (a school, a group, an organization, etc.)** [+ *obj*] She *left* school and got a job. ▪ She *left* our team and joined another one. ▪ He has one more year before he *leaves* the army. ▪ He's going to be *leaving* the company soon and starting his own business. [*no obj*] You must give the company two weeks' notice before *leaving*. **c** [+ *obj*] **: to stop participating in (something, such as a game)** ▪ The starting quarterback had to *leave* the game because of an injury. ▪ When did she *leave* the meeting?

4 [+ *obj*] **a : to go away and allow or cause (something or someone) to remain** ▪ Please *leave* your books at home. ▪ You may *leave* your things in this room. **: to put or bring (something or someone) somewhere and go away** ▪ I *left* the groceries on the table. ▪ Please *leave* the package by the door. ▪ We *left* a turkey (roasting) in the oven. ▪ I *left* my brother at the airport. ▪ They *left* their dog in the car. **b ✧ If you *leave someone or something with someone*, you allow someone to keep and care for someone or something while you are away.** ▪ They went out to dinner and *left* their children (home) *with* a babysitter. ▪ We *left* our dog *with* the neighbors while we went on vacation. **c : to go away and forget or neglect to take (something)** ▪ He *left* [=*forgot*] his wallet at the restaurant. ▪ I *left* my homework in my car. ▪ Did you *leave* your key in the door again? **d : to go away permanently without taking (something or someone)** ▪ He *left* nothing in his old apartment. **— often + *behind*** ▪ They *left behind* everything they owned. ▪ We had to *leave* our family and friends *behind*. ▪ He *left* it all *behind*. [=took nothing with him] ▪ I wanted to ***leave the past behind***. [=forget about the past]

5 [+ *obj*] **: to put (something) in a place for another person to take or have** ▪ Did she *leave* a package for me? ▪ We *left* a good tip for our waitress. = We *left* our waitress a good tip. ▪ I *left* a message (for you) on your answering machine. ▪ He *left* his name and phone number.

6 [+ *obj*] **a : to allow someone else to deal with or do (something) — often + *with*** ▪ "It's a pretty complicated problem." "*Leave* it *with* me: I'll see what I can do." **— often + *for*** ▪ You don't have to wash the dishes. Just *leave* them *for* me. [=I will wash the dishes] **— often + *to*** ▪ *Leave* your computer problems *to* the experts. [=let the experts solve your computer problems] ▪ That kind of decision should be *left to* the parents. ▪ They *left* the decision (up) *to* me. ▪ She *left* it *to* the readers *to decide* the story's ending. ▪ I'll *leave* it (up) *to* you (*to decide*) whether or not we go to the movies. ▪ I'll *leave* you *to draw* your own conclusions. **— sometimes used figuratively** ▪ Whether or not we have a picnic will be *left* (up) *to* the weather. [=will be determined by the weather] **b ✧ In informal U.S. English, you can say *leave it to someone* (to do something), when someone has acted in a way that is typical or expected.** ▪ *Leave it to my mom* to make everyone feel comfortable. [=my mom always makes everyone feel comfortable] **c ✧ If people *leave you to do* something, they do not help you do it.** ▪ He *left me to find* my own way home. ▪ She was *left to finish* the job by herself. ▪ I'll *leave you to draw* your own conclusions. ▪ I was *left to fend* for myself.

7 [+ *obj*] **: to cause (something or someone) to be or remain in a specified condition or position** ▪ Years of pollution has *left* [=*made*] the water undrinkable. ▪ Their argument *left* him angry and confused. ▪ The accident *left* him paralyzed. ▪ Your kind words *leave* me speechless. ▪ I'll *leave* the door unlocked for you. ▪ She *left* the door/window open. ▪ Did you *leave* the lights on? ▪ Much was *left* undone. ▪ Let's just ***leave it at that***. [=let's not change it or discuss it further] **— often + *-ing verb*** ▪ They cut down the trees but *left* the rosebushes *standing*. ▪ It *left* them *wondering* when it would all end. **— often + *with*** ▪ I don't want to punish you, but your actions ***leave me (with) no/little choice***. [=your actions make it necessary for me to punish you] ▪ They were ***left with no option*** but to sell their car. [=they were forced to sell their car]

8 [+ *obj*] **a : to allow (something) to remain available or unused** ▪ He wanted to *leave* a way out for himself. = He wanted to *leave* himself a way out. ▪ Please *leave* space/room for another chair. ▪ Don't eat too much. You need to *leave* room for dessert. [=you need to leave enough room in your stom-

L

ach so that you can eat dessert] • That doesn't *leave* much room for discussion. **b** ✧ An amount that ***is left (over)*** or that you ***have left (over)*** is an amount that remains after the rest has been used or taken away. • There *is* only one piece of bread *left*. [=*remaining*] • After feeding 20 people, there *was* nothing *left* for me. • How much time do we *have left* before we can go home? • There *was* no one *left* in the city after the parade. • Do we *have* any pizza *left over* from last night? • We *have* many decorations *left over* from the party.

9 [+ *obj*] **:** to cause (something) to remain as a result, mark, or sign • The cut *left* an ugly scar. • The grape juice *left* a stain on the carpet. • The rain is *leaving* a thin layer of ice on the roads. • The thief was careful not to *leave* any clues. • We promise we won't *leave* a mess. • His visit *left* a lasting impression on our family. • The experience ***left a bad taste in my mouth***. [=the experience made me feel bad or disgusted]

10 [+ *obj*] **a :** to have (family members) living after your death • He *left* (behind) a widow and two children. • She *leaves* (behind) 7 children and 28 grandchildren. **b :** to give (something, such as money or property) to (someone) after your death • She *left* a fortune to her husband. • His parents *left* him a house and a small amount of money.

11 [+ *obj*] *mathematics* **:** to have (a number) as a remainder • Taking 7 from 10 *leaves* 3.

I must love you and leave you see ²LOVE

leave much to be desired see ¹DESIRE

leave no stone unturned see ¹STONE

leave off [*phrasal verb*] **1 :** to stop before finishing a story, conversation, etc. • Let's begin where we *left off*. • Where did we *leave off* in our conversation? **2 *leave off (doing something)*** *informal* **:** to stop (doing something) • They finally *left off* trying to reach an agreement.

leave out [*phrasal verb*] ***leave out (someone or something) or leave (someone or something) out*** **:** to not include or mention (someone or something) • The movie *leaves* a lot *out* of the story. • You *left out* the best part. • Did everyone get a piece of cake? I don't want to *leave* anyone *out*. • They always *leave* her *out* of the conversation. • He always ***feels left out*** when his friends talk about sports.

leave (someone) guessing see ¹GUESS

leave (someone) in the dust see ¹DUST

leave (someone) in the lurch see ³LURCH

leave (someone or something) alone **:** to not bother or touch (someone or something) • Please *leave* the baby *alone*. She needs to sleep. • Please *leave* the vase *alone*.

leave (someone or something) be **:** to not bother or touch (someone or something) • Please *leave* [=*let*] me *be*.

leave (someone or something) for dead see ¹DEAD

leave (someone) out in the cold see ²COLD

leave (something) to the imagination see IMAGINATION

leave well enough alone *or Brit* ***leave well alone*** **:** to stop changing something that is already good enough • He just doesn't know when to *leave well enough alone*.

leave you cold see ¹COLD

leave you to your own devices see DEVICE

left at the altar see ALTAR

take it or leave it see ¹TAKE

²leave *noun*

1 : a period of time when someone has special permission to be away from a job or from military service [*singular*] He took an unpaid *leave* from work. • The soldiers were given a two-month *leave* for the holidays. [*noncount*] 12 weeks of *leave* • He took a few months' *leave* to care for his sick mother. • The company granted her ***maternity leave***. [=time off to take care of a newborn child] • Our professor is ***on leave*** this semester. • She is *on leave* from her law firm. • a soldier *on* military *leave* — called also *leave of absence*; see also COMPASSIONATE LEAVE, FAMILY LEAVE, SHORE LEAVE, SICK LEAVE

2 [*noncount*] *formal* **:** permission to do something • I beg *leave* to differ with you, sir. • He was found guilty but was granted/given *leave* to appeal against the verdict. • The soldier was guilty of being absent without (official) *leave*.

take leave of someone *or* ***take your leave*** *formal* **:** to say goodbye to someone • It was late when they finally *took leave of* their friends and headed home. • After a few minutes of polite conversation, he *took his leave*.

take leave of your senses **:** to begin acting or thinking in a very foolish way • Have you *taken leave of your senses*?

without (so much as) a by your leave *old-fashioned* **:** without asking permission • He borrowed my car *without so much as a by your leave*!

leaved /ˈliːvd/ *adj* **:** having leaves of a particular kind or number — usually used in combination • This bush is red-*leaved* in autumn. • a broad-*leaved* tree

¹leav•en /ˈlɛvən/ *noun* [*noncount*]

1 : a substance (such as yeast) that makes dough rise and become light before it is baked — called also *leavening*

2 *literary* **:** something that makes a situation or mood less serious • a serious book that includes a few humorous stories as *leaven*

²leaven *verb* **-ens; -ened; -en•ing** [+ *obj*]

1 *formal* **:** to make (something) less serious and often more exciting • Her jokes *leavened* [=*lightened*] the meeting's mood. • He needs to *leaven* his speeches with more humor.

2 : to add leaven to (bread, dough, etc.) • using yeast to *leaven* the dough/bread • Some breads are *leavened* [=made with leaven] and some breads are unleavened.

leav•en•ing /ˈlɛvənɪŋ/ *noun* [*noncount*] **:** ¹LEAVEN 1

leave of absence *noun, pl* **leaves of absence**

1 [*noncount*] **:** permission to be away from a job for a period of time • He was granted/given *leave of absence*.

2 : a period of time when someone has special permission to be away from a job **:** LEAVE [*count*] He took two unpaid *leaves of absence*. [*noncount*] She has been ***on leave of absence*** for almost two years.

leaves *plural of* ¹LEAF

leave–tak•ing /ˈliːvˌteɪkɪŋ/ *noun, pl* **-ings** *formal* **:** an act of going away and saying goodbye [*count*] He announced his *leave-taking* [=*departure*] this morning. • The movie ended with an emotional *leave-taking*. [=*farewell*] [*noncount*] *Leave-taking* is always difficult for her.

leav•ings /ˈliːvɪŋz/ *noun* [*plural*] *old-fashioned* **:** things that remain after an activity is finished • the *leavings* [=*remnants*] of our dinner

lech•er /ˈlɛtʃɚ/ *noun, pl* **-ers** [*count*] *disapproving* **:** a man who shows an excessive or disgusting interest in sex • a dirty *lecher*

— lech•ery /ˈlɛtʃəri/ *noun* [*noncount*]

lech•er•ous /ˈlɛtʃərəs/ *adj* [*more* ~; *most* ~] *disapproving* **:** having or showing an excessive or disgusting interest in sex • a *lecherous* old man

lec•tern /ˈlɛktɚn/ *noun, pl* **-terns** [*count*] **:** a stand that holds a book, notes, etc., for someone who is reading, speaking, or teaching

¹lec•ture /ˈlɛktʃɚ/ *noun, pl* **-tures** [*count*]

1 : a talk or speech given to a group of people to teach them about a particular subject • a *lecture* about/on politics • She's planning to give/deliver a series of *lectures* on modern art. • Several hundred people are expected to attend the *lecture*.

2 : a talk that criticizes someone's behavior in an angry or serious way • I came home late and got a *lecture* from my parents. • I gave her a *lecture* about doing better in school.

²lecture *verb* **-tures; -tured; -tur•ing**

1 [*no obj*] **:** to give a talk or a series of talks to a group of people to teach them about a particular subject • She *lectures* (to undergraduates) on modern art at the local college. • She *lectures* in art at the local college.

2 [+ *obj*] **:** to talk to (someone) in an angry or serious way • They *lectured* their children about/on the importance of honesty. • I *lectured* her about doing better in school.

lec•tur•er /ˈlɛktʃərɚ/ *noun, pl* **-ers** [*count*]

1 : a person who gives a lecture • We had a guest *lecturer* in class today.

2 a *US* **:** someone who teaches at a college or university on a temporary basis **b** *Brit* **:** someone who teaches at a British college or university and ranks below a professor

lec•ture•ship /ˈlɛktʃɚˌʃɪp/ *noun, pl* **-ships** [*count*] *Brit* **:** a position as a lecturer at a British college or university • He was offered a *lectureship*. • She has a *lectureship* in chemistry.

led *past tense and past participle of* ¹LEAD

LED /ˌɛlˌiːˈdiː/ *noun, pl* **LEDs** [*count*] *technical* **:** a device that lights up and displays information when electricity passes through it ✧ LEDs are often used to show numbers and words on electronic devices such as digital clocks. *LED* is an abbreviation of "light-emitting diode."

ledge /ˈlɛʤ/ *noun, pl* **ledg•es** [*count*]

1 : a narrow, flat surface that sticks out from a wall • a window *ledge* • birds perched on the *ledge* of a building

2 : a flat rock surface that sticks out from a cliff • a *ledge* on the side of the mountain

led•ger /ˈlɛʤɚ/ *noun, pl* **-gers** [*count*] **:** a book that a company uses to record information about the money it has paid and received

lee /ˈliː/ *noun [singular]* **:** the side of something that is sheltered from the wind ▪ the *lee* of the ship ▪ on the *lee* (side) of the mountain — see also LEEWARD

leech /ˈliːʧ/ *noun, pl* **leech•es** *[count]*
1 : a type of worm that attaches itself to the skin of animals and sucks their blood
2 *disapproving* **:** a person who uses other people for personal gain ▪ a celebrity who is surrounded by *leeches* who only want his money

leech

leek /ˈliːk/ *noun, pl* **leeks** *[count]* **:** a vegetable that has long green leaves rising from a thick white base and that tastes like a mild onion — see color picture on page C4

leer /ˈliɚ/ *verb* **leers; leered; leer•ing** *[no obj]* **:** to look at someone in an evil or unpleasantly sexual way ▪ She complained that some disgusting man was *leering* at her. ▪ He gave her a *leering* look.
– leer *noun, pl* **leers** *[count]* ▪ a wicked/sinister *leer*

leery /ˈliri/ *adj [more ~; most ~]* **:** feeling or showing a lack of trust in someone or something ▪ a *leery* attitude ▪ She seemed a little *leery* [=*suspicious*] about/of the proposal. ▪ They were *leery* of their neighbors.

¹lee•ward /ˈliːwɚd, ˈluːwɚd/ *adj* **:** located on the side that is sheltered from the wind ▪ the *leeward* side of the island — compare WINDWARD

²leeward *noun [noncount]* **:** the side that is sheltered from the wind **:** the lee side ▪ We turned the boat to *leeward.* — compare WINDWARD

lee•way /ˈliːˌweɪ/ *noun [noncount]* **:** freedom to do something the way you want to do it ▪ They give/allow their students *leeway* to try new things. ▪ The new rules allow managers (to have) greater *leeway* in making decisions.
make up (the) leeway *Brit* **:** to get back into a good position or situation after you have fallen behind ▪ They're so far behind that they have little hope of *making up the leeway* on the leaders. [=of catching up with the leaders]

¹left /ˈlɛft/ *adj, always used before a noun*
1 a : located on the same side of your body as your heart ▪ He felt a pain in his *left* side. ▪ her *left* hand/leg **b :** done with your left hand ▪ He hit him with a *left* hook to the jaw. — opposite RIGHT
2 : located nearer to the left side of your body than to the right ▪ the *left* side of the street ▪ a chair's *left* arm ▪ taking a *left* turn
two left feet see ¹FOOT

²left *adv*
1 a : toward the left ▪ Please move *left.* ▪ She ran *left* and caught the ball. ▪ Taking one step *left,* he fell to the ground. **b :** toward the political Left ▪ a political party that has shifted *left* ▪ His political views are slightly ***left of center.*** [=are slightly liberal]
2 *US* **:** using the left hand ▪ He bats/throws *left.* [=*left-handed*] — opposite RIGHT
left and right *or Brit* ***left, right, and centre*** **:** in a very quick and uncontrolled way ▪ She has been spending money *left and right.* **:** in all directions ▪ He was calling out names *left and right.* ▪ The police were stopping cars *left and right.*

³left *noun, pl* **lefts**
1 *[noncount]* **:** a location closer to the left side of your body than to the right **:** the left side ▪ We read from *left* to right. — often used with *on* ▪ As you come down the street, my house will be *on* your/the *left.* — often used with *to* ▪ Move the picture a little *to* the *left.* ▪ The picture is ***to the left of*** the window.
2 *[count]* **:** a turn or movement toward the left ▪ Go to the next intersection and take a *left.* = (*US*) Go to the next intersection and make/hang a *left.* ▪ You'll take two *lefts* and then a right.
3 *[count]* **:** a punch made with the left hand ▪ He hit him with two quick *lefts* to the stomach followed by a right to the jaw.
4 a ***the Left*** **:** political groups who favor sharing money and property more equally among the members of a society **:** political groups who support liberal or socialist policies ▪ His nomination is opposed by *the* country's *Left.* ▪ The new law is disliked by *the Left.* ▪ Members of *the Left* have voiced their opinions on this matter. **b** ***the left*** **:** the position of people who support the beliefs and policies of the political Left ▪ The party has shifted to *the left.* [=has become more liberal] — compare RIGHT; see also *the far left* at ²FAR

⁴left *past tense and past participle of* ¹LEAVE

left field *noun [noncount]* **:** the part of a baseball outfield that is to the left when you are looking out from home plate ▪ a fly ball to (deep/shallow) *left field*; *also* **:** the position of the player defending left field ▪ He plays *left field.*
come out of left field *US, informal* **:** to be very surprising and unexpected ▪ That question *came out of left field.*
out in left field *US, informal* **:** very strange or unusual ▪ ideas that are *out in left field* ▪ Her position is way *out in left field.*
– left fielder *noun, pl* **~ -ers** *[count]* ▪ a good *left fielder*

left–hand /ˈlɛftˈhænd/ *adj, always used before a noun*
1 : located closer to your left hand **:** located on the left side ▪ Our building will be on the *left-hand* side. ▪ Please write your name on the upper *left-hand* corner of the page. ▪ Take a *left-hand* turn. — compare RIGHT-HAND
2 : made for the left hand ▪ a *left-hand* glove ▪ *left-hand* [=(more commonly) *left-handed*] tools — compare RIGHT-HAND

left–hand•ed /ˈlɛftˈhændəd/ *adj*
1 : using the left hand more easily than the right hand ▪ a *left-handed* person ▪ He is baseball's greatest *left-handed* pitcher. ▪ My sister is right-handed but I'm *left-handed.*
2 a : made for the left hand ▪ a *left-handed* glove ▪ She needs *left-handed* scissors. **b :** using or done with the left hand ▪ a *left-handed* catch/punch
3 : swinging from the left side of the body to the right side in sports like baseball and golf ▪ a *left-handed* batter/hitter
– left–handed *adv* ▪ She bats *left-handed.* **– left–hand•ed•ness** *noun [noncount]* ▪ They study *left-handedness* in children.

left–hand•er /ˈlɛftˈhændɚ/ *noun, pl* **-ers** *[count]* **:** a left-handed person; *especially* **:** a left-handed pitcher in baseball ▪ The team has eight right-handers and three *left-handers.*

left•ist /ˈlɛftɪst/ *noun, pl* **-ists** *[count]* **:** a person who belongs to or supports the political Left — compare RIGHTIST
– leftist *adj [more ~; most ~]* ▪ a *leftist* government ▪ *leftist* intellectuals

left•over /ˈlɛftˌoʊvɚ/ *noun, pl* **-overs**
1 ***leftovers*** *[plural]* **:** food that has not been finished at a meal and that is often served at another meal ▪ Are we having *leftovers* again?
2 *[count]* **:** a thing that remains after something is finished or ended ▪ The law is a *leftover* from earlier times.
– leftover *adj, always used before a noun* ▪ Do you have any *leftover* pizza from last night?

left•ward (*chiefly US*) /ˈlɛftwɚd/ *or chiefly Brit* **left•wards** /ˈlɛftwɚdz/ *adv* **:** toward the left ▪ Turn the boat *leftward.* ▪ She stepped *leftward* into the light. ▪ She has moved *leftward* in her political beliefs. — compare RIGHTWARD
– leftward *adj* ▪ a *leftward* turn

left wing *noun [singular]* **:** the part of a political group that consists of people who support liberal or socialist ideas and policies **:** the part of a political group that belongs to or supports the Left ▪ His nomination is supported by the party's *left wing* but opposed by the right wing.

left–wing /ˈlɛftˈwɪŋ/ *adj* **:** of, relating to, or belonging to the political Left **:** having or supporting ideas and policies that are associated with liberal or socialist groups ▪ *left-wing* politics/politicians
– left–wing•er /ˈlɛftˈwɪŋɚ/ *noun, pl* **-ers** *[count]* ▪ a policy opposed by *left-wingers*

lefty /ˈlɛfti/ *noun, pl* **left•ies** *[count] informal*
1 *chiefly US* **:** LEFT-HANDER ▪ Our starting pitcher is a *lefty.* — compare RIGHTY
2 *chiefly Brit, disapproving* **:** a person who supports liberal or socialist political policies **:** LEFTIST ▪ political *lefties* [=*left-wingers*]

¹leg /ˈlɛg/ *noun, pl* **legs**
1 *[count]* **:** one of the long body parts that are used especially for standing, walking, and running ▪ He sat on a chair with his *legs* crossed. ▪ He leaned against the wall with his *legs* spread so the police could search him. ▪ She broke her *leg* in a skiing accident. ▪ His *legs* gave way under him and he fell over. ▪ a wooden/artificial *leg* ▪ the dog's front/back/hind *legs* — see picture at HUMAN; see also PEG LEG, SEA LEGS
2 : an animal's leg when it is used as food *[count]* We had chicken *legs* for dinner. *[noncount]* Would you like some more *leg* of lamb?
3 *[count]* **:** any one of the long thin parts that support a table, chair, etc. ▪ the *legs* of a table ▪ a chair with a broken *leg*
4 *[count]* **:** the part of a pair of pants that covers the leg ▪ The *legs* of these jeans are too long. = These jeans are too long in the *leg(s).*

L

5 [*count*] **a** : a part of a journey or race ▪ She took the lead in the last *leg* of the race. ▪ The weather got worse on each *leg* of the trip. **b** : any one of several events or games that form a competition ▪ a horse that has won the first two *legs* of racing's Triple Crown

6 ***legs*** [*plural*] *US, informal* : lasting appeal or interest ▪ a news story with *legs*

a leg up *informal* **1** ***give someone a leg up*** **a** : to hold your hands together so that someone can step into them while climbing up onto something ▪ I don't think I can get on this horse without help. Can someone *give me a leg up*? **b** : to give someone an advantage over others ▪ These skills will *give you a leg up* in the job market. [=they will help you get a job] **2** ***have a leg up*** : to have an advantage over others ▪ The company *has a leg up* on the competition thanks to the recent publicity.

an arm and a leg see [1]ARM

break a leg *informal* — used in speech to wish good luck to someone (such as a performer)

get your leg over *Brit, informal + impolite, of a man* : to have sex with a woman

not have a leg to stand on : to have no support for what you think, say, or do ▪ He claims that the company cheated him, but without evidence of a written agreement, he *doesn't have a leg to stand on*.

on your/its last legs *informal* : very close to failure, exhaustion, or death ▪ The company is *on its last legs*. ▪ He was *on his last legs*, but he managed to finish the race. ▪ an old tree that is *on its last legs* [=that is dying and will not last much longer]

pull someone's leg *informal* : to make someone believe something that is not true as a joke : to trick or lie to someone in a playful way ▪ I panicked when he said the test was tomorrow, but then I realized he was just *pulling my leg*. ▪ When I got mad, she finally admitted that she was *pulling my leg*.

shake a leg *informal* : to go or move quickly ▪ You'd better *shake a leg* [=*hurry up*] if you don't want to be late for work. — often used as a command ▪ *Shake a leg*! You're going to be late!

stretch your legs *informal* : to stand up and walk especially after sitting for a long period of time

with your tail between your legs see [1]TAIL

[2]leg *verb* **legs; legged; leg·ging**

leg it *chiefly Brit, informal* : to run fast especially in order to get away from someone or something ▪ When they saw the police car, they *legged it*.

leg out [*phrasal verb*] ***leg out (a hit)*** *also* ***leg (a hit) out*** *baseball, informal* : to successfully complete (a hit) by running fast ▪ He hurt his knee while trying to *leg out* an infield hit. ▪ She *legged out* a triple.

leg·a·cy /ˈlɛgəsi/ *noun, pl* **-cies** [*count*]

1 : something (such as property or money) that is received from someone who has died ▪ She left us a *legacy* of a million dollars. ▪ a substantial *legacy*

2 : something that happened in the past or that comes from someone in the past ▪ He left his children a *legacy* of love and respect. ▪ The war left a *legacy of* pain and suffering. ▪ We discussed the country's *legacy* of slavery. [=the ways in which the country is still affected by slavery] ▪ Her artistic *legacy* lives on through her children.

le·gal /ˈliːgəl/ *adj*

1 a : of or relating to the law ▪ She has a lot of *legal* problems. ▪ *legal* books ▪ a *legal* adviser/representative ▪ a country's *legal* system [=the way that laws are made and controlled in a country] **b** : based on the law ▪ Do you know your *legal* rights? ▪ The amount of alcohol in his blood exceeded the *legal* limit. ▪ He plans on taking ***legal action*** against the company. [=he plans on having a court of law settle his argument with the company] ▪ ***legal proceedings*** [=actions taken to settle an argument in a court of law]

2 : allowed by the law or by the rules in a game ▪ What you did was not *legal*. ▪ "Is it *legal* to fish in this river?" "Yes, it's perfectly *legal*." ▪ The referee said it was a *legal* play. — opposite ILLEGAL

– le·gal·i·ty /lɪˈgæləti/ *noun, pl* **-ties** [*noncount*] They were unsure about the contract's *legality*. ▪ We questioned the *legality* [=*lawfulness*] of the testing. [*count*] We discussed the complex *legalities* involved in buying and selling a home.

– le·gal·ly /ˈliːgəli/ *adv* ▪ *Legally*, they cannot do that. ▪ The drug is *legally* bought and sold in many countries. ▪ This agreement is *legally* binding. ▪ He is *legally* blind. [=his vision is bad enough for him to be considered blind according to the law] ▪ He was *legally* drunk. [=he was drunk according to the law]

legal aid *noun* [*noncount*] : money provided by a special organization to pay legal fees for people who cannot pay them themselves

le·gal·ese /ˌliːgəˈliːz/ *noun* [*noncount*] *informal* : the language used by lawyers that is difficult for most people to understand : legal jargon ▪ I was confused by the *legalese* in the contract.

legal holiday *noun, pl* **~ -days** [*count*] *US* : a public holiday recognized by law — called also (*Brit*) *bank holiday*

le·gal·is·tic /ˌliːgəˈlɪstɪk/ *adj* [*more* ~; *most* ~] *disapproving* : too concerned with legal rules and details ▪ He has a narrow *legalistic* view of the controversy. ▪ The two sides in the dispute have been engaging in *legalistic* wrangling.

le·gal·ize *also Brit* **le·gal·ise** /ˈliːgəˌlaɪz/ *verb* **-iz·es; -ized; -iz·ing** [+ *obj*] : to make (something) legal ▪ They wanted to *legalize* gambling in their city. : to allow (something) by law ▪ The government has *legalized* the use of the new drug. — opposite CRIMINALIZE

– le·gal·i·za·tion *also Brit* **le·gal·i·sa·tion** /ˌliːgələˈzeɪʃən, *Brit* ˌliːgəˌlaɪˈzeɪʃən/ *noun* [*noncount*] ▪ the *legalization* of a drug

legal pad *noun, pl* **~ pads** [*count*] : a pad of yellow paper with lines on it for writing

legal tender *noun* [*noncount*] : money that the law allows people to use for paying debts ▪ Soon after France adopted the euro, the French franc ceased to be *legal tender*.

leg·ate /ˈlɛgət/ *noun, pl* **-ates** [*count*] : an official representative sent to a foreign country; *especially* : an official representative of the pope ▪ a papal *legate*

leg·a·tee /ˌlɛgəˈtiː/ *noun, pl* **-tees** [*count*] *law* : someone who receives money or property from a person who has died

le·ga·tion /lɪˈgeɪʃən/ *noun, pl* **-tions** [*count*] : a group of government officials sent to work in a foreign country; *also* : the building where such a group works

le·ga·to /lɪˈgɑːˌtoʊ/ *adv, music* : in a manner that is smooth and flowing ▪ singing/playing *legato* — compare STACCATO

– legato *adj* ▪ a *legato* musical passage

leg·end /ˈlɛʤənd/ *noun, pl* **-ends**

1 : a story from the past that is believed by many people but cannot be proved to be true [*count*] I don't believe the *legends* I've heard about this forest. ▪ the *legend* of a lost continent [*noncount*] ***According to legend***, the city was destroyed by a great flood in ancient times. = ***Legend has it*** that the city was destroyed by a great flood in ancient times. — see also URBAN LEGEND

2 [*count*] : a famous or important person who is known for doing something extremely well ▪ He has become a baseball *legend*. ▪ a guitar-playing *legend* ▪ She is ***a legend in her own time***. = She is ***a living legend***. [=she has become a legend while still living]

3 [*count*] **a** : a list that explains the symbols on a map **b** *formal* : the writing that appears on an object ▪ The gravestone bears the *legend* "Rest in Peace."

leg·end·ary /ˈlɛʤənˌderi, *Brit* ˈlɛʤəndri/ *adj*

1 *always used before a noun* : told about in a legend ▪ *legendary* tales ▪ *legendary* creatures from the sea

2 [*more* ~; *most* ~] : very famous or well-known ▪ He is the most *legendary* football player of his time. ▪ *legendary* musicians

leg·er·de·main /ˌlɛʤədəˈmeɪn/ *noun* [*noncount*] : skill in using your hands to perform magic tricks : SLEIGHT OF HAND — often used figuratively ▪ financial *legerdemain* [=*trickery*]

leg·ged /ˈlɛgəd/ *adj* : having legs of a specified type or number — usually used in combination with another adjective ▪ a four-*legged* animal ▪ a long-*legged* bird

leg·gings /ˈlɛgɪŋz/ *noun* [*plural*]

1 : pants for women that are made of a material that stretches to fit tightly around the legs — see color picture on page C13

2 : coverings for the legs that are usually made of cloth or leather and worn over pants

leg·gy /ˈlɛgi/ *adj* **leg·gi·er; -est**

1 : having long legs — used especially of a woman ▪ a *leggy* actress

2 *of a plant* : having very long stalks or stems ▪ The bush has gotten *leggy* and needs to be pruned.

leg·i·ble /ˈlɛʤəbəl/ *adj* [*more* ~; *most* ~] : capable of being read : clear enough to be read ▪ *legible* handwriting ▪ The

document is not *legible*. — opposite ILLEGIBLE
– leg·i·bil·i·ty /ˌlɛʤəˈbɪləti/ *noun [noncount]* **– leg·i·bly** /ˈlɛʤəbli/ *adv* ▪ He doesn't write *legibly* at all.

¹le·gion /ˈli:ʤən/ *noun, pl* **-gions** *[count]*
1 a : a large group of soldiers in ancient Rome ▪ a Roman *legion* **b :** a large group of soldiers : ARMY — used especially in names ▪ the French Foreign *Legion*
2 : a national organization for former soldiers — used in names ▪ the American *Legion* ▪ the Royal British *Legion*
3 : a very large number of people ▪ She has a *legion* [=*multitude*] of admirers/fans. ▪ *Legions* of people came to see him perform.

²legion *adj, not used before a noun* **:** very many or numerous ▪ Her admirers/fans are *legion*. [=she has a very large number of admirers/fans]

le·gion·ary /ˈli:ʤəˌneri, *Brit* ˈli:ʤənəri/ *noun, pl* **-ar·ies** *[count]* **:** a soldier who is a member of a legion
– legionary *adj, always used before a noun* ▪ *legionary* soldiers ▪ a Roman *legionary* camp

le·gion·naire /ˌli:ʤəˈneɚ/ *noun, pl* **-naires** *[count]* **:** a member of a legion (such as the French Foreign Legion, the Royal British Legion, or the American Legion)

Legionnaires' disease *also* **Legionnaire's disease** *noun [noncount]* **:** a serious disease of the lungs that is caused by bacteria

leg·is·late /ˈlɛʤəˌsleɪt/ *verb* **-lates; -lat·ed; -lat·ing**
1 : to make laws *[no obj]* The state *legislated* against hunting certain animals. [=the state created laws making it illegal to hunt certain animals] *[+ obj] legislate* a new law
2 *[+ obj]* **:** to control, create, or cause (something) by making laws ▪ They are attempting to *legislate* morality. ▪ the need to better *legislate* foreign trade ▪ trying to *legislate* changes in the current law

leg·is·la·tion /ˌlɛʤəˈsleɪʃən/ *noun [noncount]*
1 : a law or set of laws made by a government ▪ They passed new state *legislation* this week. ▪ Two new pieces of *legislation* are being considered. ▪ She introduced/proposed *legislation* for protecting the environment. ▪ More *legislation* is needed on this matter. ▪ Certain animals are protected under/by state *legislation*. ▪ The *legislation* was vetoed/repealed. ▪ anti-gun *legislation*
2 : the action or process of making laws ▪ One of the important functions of government is *legislation*.

leg·is·la·tive /ˈlɛʤəˌsleɪtɪv, *Brit* ˈlɛʤəslətɪv/ *adj, always used before a noun*
1 : having the power to make laws ▪ the state *legislative* body/assembly [=the group in a state government that makes laws] ▪ the *legislative* branch of the government — compare EXECUTIVE, JUDICIAL
2 : relating to the making of laws ▪ She is interested in the *legislative* process. ▪ *legislative* power
– leg·is·la·tive·ly *adv*

leg·is·la·tor /ˈlɛʤəˌsleɪˌtoɚ, ˈlɛʤəˌsleɪtɚ/ *noun, pl* **-tors** *[count]* **:** a person who makes laws : a member of a legislature ▪ Write to your state *legislator*. ▪ *Legislators* [=*lawmakers*] in both parties have supported the idea.

leg·is·la·ture /ˈlɛʤəˌsleɪʧɚ/ *noun, pl* **-tures** *[count]* **:** a group of people with the power to make or change laws ▪ Our *legislature* passed a law requiring people to wear safety belts. ▪ Each state has its own *legislature*. ▪ state *legislatures*

le·git /lɪˈʤɪt/ *adj, informal* **:** ¹LEGITIMATE ▪ What she's doing is perfectly *legit*. ▪ Is this deal *legit*? ▪ All I want is a *legit* chance to succeed.

¹le·git·i·mate /lɪˈʤɪtəmət/ *adj*
1 a : allowed according to rules or laws ▪ a *legitimate* [=*legal, lawful*] heir/government/business ▪ *legitimate* means for achieving success ▪ the *legitimate* use of firearms **b :** real, accepted, or official ▪ It's not clear that the letter is *legitimate* [=*genuine*]; it may be a forgery.
2 *[more ~; most ~]* **:** fair or reasonable ▪ We think her concern/excuse is *legitimate*. = We think she has a *legitimate* concern/excuse. ▪ There's no *legitimate* reason for prescribing this medication to a child. ▪ His claim is *legitimate*.
3 : born to a father and mother who are married ▪ *legitimate* children — opposite ILLEGITIMATE
– le·git·i·ma·cy /lɪˈʤɪtəməsi/ *noun [noncount]* ▪ Many question the *legitimacy* of the law. **– le·git·i·mate·ly** *adv* ▪ We earned the money *legitimately*. [=*legally*] ▪ He can *legitimately* [=*rightfully*] claim to be the best athlete in his class.

²le·git·i·mate /lɪˈʤɪtəˌmeɪt/ *verb* **-mates; -mat·ed; -mat·ing** *[+ obj] US* **:** to make (something or someone) legitimate: such as **a :** to make (something) real, accepted, or official ▪ slang words *legitimated* by usage **b :** to show that (something or someone) is fair or reasonable ▪ Her tendency to be secretive only serves to *legitimate* their suspicions.

le·git·i·ma·tize /lɪˈʤɪtəməˌtaɪz/ *verb* **-tiz·es; -tized; -tiz·ing** *[+ obj] chiefly US* **:** ²LEGITIMATE

le·git·i·mize /lɪˈʤɪtəˌmaɪz/ *also Brit* **le·git·i·mise** *verb* **-miz·es; -mized; -miz·ing** *[+ obj]* **:** ²LEGITIMATE

leg·less /ˈlɛgləs/ *adj*
1 : having no legs ▪ a *legless* lizard ▪ broken, *legless* chairs
2 *Brit slang* **:** extremely drunk ▪ get *legless* on lager

leg·room /ˈlɛgˌru:m/ *noun [noncount]* **:** space in which you can extend your legs when you are sitting ▪ I need a car with more *legroom*. ▪ airplane seats that offer little *legroom* — compare HEADROOM

leg·ume /ˈlɛˌgju:m/ *noun, pl* **-umes** *[count]* **:** a type of plant (such as a pea or a bean plant) with seeds that grow in long cases (called pods); *also* **:** these seeds eaten as food ▪ recipes that include *legumes* like lentils and chickpeas
– le·gu·mi·nous /lɪˈgju:mənəs/ *adj* ▪ *leguminous* plants

leg warmer *noun, pl* **~ -ers** *[count]* **:** a warm covering of usually soft cloth that you wear on your leg

leg·work /ˈlɛgˌwɚk/ *noun [noncount]* **:** the active physical work that is involved in doing something ▪ I wrote the article myself, but my assistant gathered the information and did most of the other *legwork*.

lei /ˈleɪ/ *noun, pl* **leis** *[count]* **:** a necklace of flowers that is given to a visitor in Hawaii

lei·sure /ˈli:ʒɚ, *Brit* ˈlɛʒə/ *noun [noncount]*
1 : time when you are not working : time when you can do whatever you want to do ▪ In his *leisure* [=*free time, spare time*], he paints and sculpts. ▪ I'd like to write more, but I simply don't have the *leisure* (to do it).
2 : enjoyable activities that you do when you are not working ▪ I don't have much time for *leisure*. ▪ She leads ***a life of leisure*** [=she does not have to work] ▪ a character described as ***a lady/man/gentleman of leisure*** [=a woman/man who does not work and who spends a lot of time doing things for pleasure] — often used before another noun ▪ *leisure* activities/pursuits ▪ Now that she's retired, she has more ***leisure time***. ▪ the ***leisure class*** [=people who do not have to work]
at leisure** or **at your leisure **1 :** in a way that is not hurried : in a slow and relaxed way ▪ We were able to study the menu *at leisure*. **2 :** when you have free time available ▪ You can look over the contract *at your leisure*.

lei·sured /ˈli:ʒɚd, *Brit* ˈlɛʒəd/ *adj, always used before a noun [more ~; most ~]*
1 : not having to work : having leisure ▪ the *leisured* class
2 : not hurried ▪ We set off at a *leisured* [=(more commonly) *leisurely*] pace.

lei·sure·ly /ˈli:ʒɚli, *Brit* ˈlɛʒəli/ *adj [more ~; most ~]* **:** not hurried : slow and relaxed ▪ They strolled along at a *leisurely* pace. ▪ proceeding in a *leisurely* fashion ▪ After a *leisurely* lunch, we went to see a movie.
– leisurely *adv* ▪ a restaurant where diners are allowed to eat *leisurely*

leisure suit *noun, pl* **~ suits** *[count]* **:** an informal suit that includes a jacket and matching pants

leit·mo·tiv *or* **leit·mo·tif** /ˈlaɪtmoʊˌti:f/ *noun, pl* **-tivs** *or* **-tifs** *[count]* **:** something (such as a short piece of music, an idea, or a phrase) that is repeated many times throughout an opera, book, story, etc. ▪ Troubled relationships are the *leitmotiv* of this novel.

lem·ming /ˈlɛmɪŋ/ *noun, pl* **-mings** *[count]* **:** a small animal that lives in northern areas of North America, Europe, and Asia ✧ Lemmings sometimes form large groups that move together. According to legend, these groups sometimes march into the sea, where large numbers of the lemmings drown. Because of this, people are sometimes said to be acting ***like lemmings*** when they do something that is harmful or stupid because other people are doing it.

lem·on /ˈlɛmən/ *noun, pl* **-ons**
1 *[count, noncount]* **:** a yellow citrus fruit that has a sour taste ▪ The recipe calls for the juice of two *lemons*. ▪ Garnish it with a slice of *lemon*. — often used before another noun ▪ *lemon* juice ▪ *lemon* trees ▪ a *lemon* grove — see color picture on page C5
2 *[noncount]* **:** a bright yellow color — called also *lemon yellow*; see color picture on page C2
3 *[count] chiefly US, informal* **:** a product that is not made well : a product that does not work the way it should ▪ Our new car is a *lemon*.

4 [*count*] *Brit, informal* : a stupid or silly person
– **lem·ony** /ˈlɛməni/ *adj* [*more* ~; *most* ~] • a *lemony* flavor • a *lemony* color

lem·on·ade /ˌlɛməˈneɪd/ *noun, pl* **-ades** [*count, noncount*]
1 : a drink made usually of lemon juice, sugar, and water
2 *Brit* : a sweet lemon-flavored drink that contains many bubbles : a lemon soda

lemon curd *noun* [*noncount*] : a sweet, soft food made with lemon juice, butter, sugar, and eggs

lemon law *noun, pl* ~ **laws** [*count*] *US* : a law that gives a person who buys a car that has a defect the right to return the car or to have the seller pay to have it fixed

lemon yellow *noun* [*noncount*] : LEMON 2

le·mur /ˈli:mɚ/ *noun, pl* **-murs** [*count*] : an animal that is related to monkeys and that lives in trees mostly in Madagascar

lend /ˈlɛnd/ *verb* **lends; lent** /ˈlɛnt/; **lend·ing**
1 a [+ *obj*] : to give (something) to (someone) to be used for a period of time and then returned • She often *lends* us books. = She often *lends* books to us. • Could you *lend* me your pen? [=could I borrow your pen?] • I *lent* our ladder to the neighbors. **b** : to give (money) to someone who agrees to pay it back in the future [+ *obj*] Can you *lend* me 50 cents? [=can I borrow 50 cents from you?] • The bank wouldn't *lend* us the money. [*no obj*] Many banks won't *lend* to people with bad credit.
2 [+ *obj*] : to make (something) available to (someone or something) • They offered to *lend* us their services. [=to provide us with their services] • They are glad to *lend* their support to worthy causes. • It's surprising that he would ***lend his name*** to such a venture. [=that he would allow his name to be associated with such a venture]
3 [+ *obj*] **a** : to add (something that is needed or wanted) to (something) • A bit of grated carrot *lends* some color to the dish. = A bit of grated carrot *lends* the dish some color. • A growing amount of evidence ***lends weight/credence/credibility*** to their theory. [=makes their theory seem true or correct] **b** : to provide (something that is needed or wanted) • She's always there to ***lend a (helping) hand.*** [=she's always there to help]
lend an ear see [1]EAR
lend itself to ✧ Something that *lends itself to* a purpose is good or suitable for that purpose. • Her voice *lends itself* well *to* (singing) opera. • The topics *lend themselves to* classroom discussion.
– **lend·er** *noun, pl* **-ers** [*count*] • banks and other *lenders* • borrowers and *lenders* — see also MONEYLENDER

lending library *noun, pl* ~ **-ries** [*count*] : a library that lends books to people who can take them home and then return them at a later time

length /ˈlɛŋθ/ *noun, pl* **lengths**
1 a : the distance from one end of something to the other end : a measurement of how long something is [*noncount*] "What is its *length*?" [=how long is it?] "It measures 10 inches in *length*." [=it is 10 inches long] • We walked the entire *length* of the beach. [=we walked from one end of the beach to the other] • The *length* of the table is six feet, and its width is three feet. [*count*] These pins are available in one- and two-inch *lengths*. • The adult animals reach a maximum *length* of two meters. — see also FOCAL LENGTH **b** [*noncount*] : the size or extent of a piece of writing • Your essay should be no more than 250 words in *length*. • five pages in *length* [=five pages long] • a book-*length* poem [=a very long poem; a poem that has the same number of pages as some books] **c** [*noncount*] : the quality or state of being long • Don't be put off by the book's *length*. [=(less commonly) *lengthiness*] • I was amazed by the *length* of the ape's arms. [=by how long the ape's arms were]
2 [*noncount*] : the amount of time something lasts • They want to extend the *length* of the school year. [=to make the school year longer; to lengthen the school year] • the *length* of a movie • If you're in town ***for any length of time*** [=for more than just a short time], be sure to see the museum.
3 [*count*] : the length of something used as a unit of measure • Our horse won the race by a *length*. [=by a distance equal to the length of one horse] • They were two car *lengths* behind us. • I managed to swim four *lengths* of the pool. [=to swim from one end of the pool to the other end four times] — see also *at arm's length* at [1]ARM
4 [*count*] : a piece of something that is long and thin or narrow • a *length* of pipe/chain/yarn
5 [*noncount*] : a measure of how far down on your body something (such as your hair or a piece of clothing) reaches • the *length* of a skirt • a waist-*length* jacket [=a jacket that reaches only to your waist] • chin-*length* hair — see also FLOOR-LENGTH, KNEE-LENGTH, SHOULDER-LENGTH
at length **1** : for a long time • We talked *at length* about the ceremony. • The speaker went on ***at considerable/great/some length.*** • No one was questioned ***at any length*** about it. [=no one was questioned for a long period of time] **2** : in a full or complete way • The topic will be treated *at length* in the next chapter. • The book doesn't discuss the topic ***at any length.*** [=the book only discusses the topic briefly] **3** *literary* : after a long time • *At length* [=*finally, in the end, at last*], we decided to return home.
go to any length *or* ***go to any/extreme/great (etc.) lengths*** : to make a great or extreme effort to do something • She'll *go to any length* to avoid doing work. = She'll *go to any lengths* to avoid doing work. • He *went to great lengths* to learn the truth.
the length and breadth of : through all parts of (a place) • I've been/traveled *the length and breadth of* the canyon, but I still haven't found the caves I'm looking for.

length·en /ˈlɛŋθən/ *verb* **-ens; -ened; -en·ing**
1 [*no obj*] : to become longer • The days *lengthened* with the approach of spring.
2 [+ *obj*] : to make (something) longer • Proper care will *lengthen* the life of the engine. • *lengthen* a pair of trousers — opposite SHORTEN

length·ways /ˈlɛŋθˌweɪz/ *adv, chiefly Brit* : LENGTHWISE
– **lengthways** *adj*

length·wise /ˈlɛŋθˌwaɪz/ *adv* : in the direction of the long side of something • Split the fruit *lengthwise* and discard the seeds. • a piece of paper folded *lengthwise*
– **lengthwise** *adj* • a *lengthwise* cut

lengthy /ˈlɛŋθi/ *adj* **length·i·er; -est** [*also more* ~; *most* ~]
1 : lasting for a long time • The process is both *lengthy* and costly. • We got involved in a *lengthy* [=*long*] discussion. • a series of *lengthy* delays • *Lengthier* trips require more planning.
2 : having many pages, items, etc. • a *lengthy* criminal record • *lengthy* [=*long*] lists
– **length·i·ly** /ˈlɛŋθəli/ *adv* • a *lengthily* titled book [=a book with a long title] • She complained loudly and *lengthily* [=*at length*] about the poor service. – **length·i·ness** /ˈlɛŋθinəs/ *noun* [*noncount*]

le·nient /ˈli:njənt/ *adj* [*more* ~; *most* ~] : allowing a lot of freedom and not punishing bad behavior in a strong way : not harsh, severe, or strict • a teacher who is *lenient* with students who have misbehaved • a *lenient* teacher • a *lenient* sentence/punishment/policy • Many people felt that the punishment was too *lenient*.
– **le·nien·cy** /ˈli:njənsi/ *also* **le·nience** /ˈli:njəns/ *noun* [*noncount*] • the *leniency* of the punishment – **le·nient·ly** *adv*

lens /ˈlɛnz/ *noun, pl* **lens·es** [*count*]
1 : a clear curved piece of glass or plastic that is used in eyeglasses, cameras, telescopes, etc., to make things look clearer, smaller, or bigger • glasses with thick *lenses* • a camera *lens* • Make sure the *lens* of the microscope is clean. — see picture at CAMERA; see also CONTACT LENS, FISH-EYE LENS, OBJECTIVE LENS, TELEPHOTO LENS, ZOOM LENS
2 : the clear part of the eye that focuses light to form clear images

lent *past tense and past participle of* LEND

Lent /ˈlɛnt/ *noun* [*noncount*] : a period of 40 days before Easter during which many Christians do not eat certain foods or do certain pleasurable activities as a way of remembering the suffering of Jesus Christ
– **Lent·en** /ˈlɛntn̩/ *adj, always used before a noun* • the *Lenten* season

len·til /ˈlɛntl̩/ *noun, pl* **-tils** [*count*] : a type of flat, round seed that is related to the pea and is eaten as a vegetable — often used before another noun • *lentil* soup

Leo /ˈli:ˌoʊ/ *noun, pl* **Leos**
1 [*noncount*] : the fifth sign of the zodiac that comes between Cancer and Virgo and has a lion as its symbol — see picture at ZODIAC
2 [*count*] : a person born under the sign of Leo : a person born between July 23rd and August 22nd • Are you a *Leo* or a Virgo?

le·o·nine /ˈli:jəˌnaɪn/ *adj* [*more* ~; *most* ~] *literary* : of, relating to, or resembling a lion • a *leonine* mane of hair • *leonine* strength

L

leop·ard /ˈlɛpəd/ *noun, pl* **-ards** [*count*] **:** a large brownish-yellow cat with black spots that lives in Asia and Africa — see picture at CAT

a leopard can't change its spots — used to say that people cannot change their basic personalities, habits, etc.

leop·ard·ess /ˈlɛpədəs/ *noun, pl* **-ess·es** [*count*] **:** a female leopard

le·o·tard /ˈli:jəˌtaəd/ *noun, pl* **-tards** [*count*] **:** a piece of clothing that fits tightly and covers the body except for the legs and sometimes the arms • Our aerobics instructor wore a bright red *leotard*. — often plural in U.S. English • She donned her *leotards* and headed off to ballet class. — see color picture on page C13

lep·er /ˈlɛpə/ *noun, pl* **-ers** [*count*]
1 : a person who has leprosy
2 : someone who is disliked and avoided by other people • After his arrest his former friends treated him like a (social) *leper*.

lep·re·chaun /ˈlɛprəˌkɑ:n/ *noun, pl* **-chauns** [*count*] **:** a creature in old Irish stories that looks like a very small man ✧ According to legend, if you catch a leprechaun he will show you where treasure is hidden.

lep·ro·sy /ˈlɛprəsi/ *noun* [*noncount*] *medical* **:** a serious disease that causes painful rough areas on the skin and that badly damages nerves and flesh
– leprous *adj*

les·bi·an /ˈlɛzbijən/ *noun, pl* **-ans** [*count*] **:** a woman who is sexually attracted to other women **:** a female homosexual • *lesbians* and gay men
– lesbian *adj, always used before a noun* • a *lesbian* relationship **– les·bi·an·ism** /ˈlɛzbijəˌnɪzəm/ *noun* [*noncount*]

le·sion /ˈli:ʒən/ *noun, pl* **-sions** [*count*] *medical* **:** an injured or diseased spot or area on or in the body • skin *lesions* • a brain *lesion*

[1]less /ˈlɛs/ *adj, comparative form of* [1]LITTLE **:** not so much **:** smaller in amount or number • We need *less* talk and more work! • She finished in *less* time than I did. • *Less* detail is sometimes better than more detail. • 8 times 2 is *less* than 6 times 3. • We made it there in *less* than six hours. • The whole procedure takes *less* than five minutes. • The illness affects *less* than one percent of the population.

no less — used to suggest that something is surprising or impressive • He insists on being driven to the airport, and in a limousine *no less*! [=it is surprising that he insists on being driven in a limousine] • She was contacted by the president, *no less*! • The plan was approved by *no less* (of) an authority than the president himself.

no less than **:** at least — used to suggest that a number or amount is surprisingly large • *No less than* half the students failed the test. • She has had *no less than* [=*no fewer than*] a dozen job offers.

> ***usage*** The adjectives *less* and *fewer* have similar meanings but are used in slightly different ways. *Fewer* is used with nouns that can be counted. • classrooms with *fewer* students • They have *fewer* than three children. *Less* is usually used with nouns that cannot be counted. • He makes *less* money than she does. • The new model uses *less* power. But *less* is also more likely than *fewer* to be used with count nouns that refer to distances and amounts of money. • an investment of *less* than $2,000 • It's *less* than 100 miles away. *Less* is also used in mathematical expressions and in certain phrases. • an angle of *less* than 180 degrees • Write it in 25 words or *less*. It is also used instead of *fewer* with other sorts of plural nouns, although many people still consider this use incorrect. • *Less* than 10 people showed up. = *Fewer* than 10 people showed up.

[2]less *adv, comparative form of* [2]LITTLE **:** not so much **:** to a smaller extent or degree • This test seemed much *less* difficult than the last one. • Which test is the *less* difficult of the two? • The test is no *less* difficult for being shorter. [=even though the test is shorter, it is not easier] • Do you have another one that's *less* expensive? • a *less* likely possibility • She visits much/far *less* often than she used to. • They're focusing more on quality and *less* on quantity. • I like this one (a little) *less* than the other. • Their band is *less* concerned with making music than with making money. • The cost is much/far *less* (of) a problem than we thought it would be.

in less than no time informal **:** very soon • If we get started now, we'll be finished *in less than no time*.

less and less **:** in a way that is gradually smaller, weaker, or less common • The medicine becomes *less and less* [=*decreasingly*] effective over time. • We see them *less and less* each year. = We see them *less and less* frequently/often each year.

less than **:** not completely or not at all • She was *less than* happy with the results. [=she was not entirely happy *or* she was unhappy] • He was *less than* honest in his replies. [=he was not completely honest *or* he was very dishonest]

more or less see [2]MORE

much less or chiefly Brit still less — used after a negative statement to say that something is even less likely or possible than the thing previously mentioned • I don't eat eggs, *much less* meat. • He can't run a mile, *much less* complete a marathon.

[3]less *pronoun*
1 : a smaller number or amount • We've learned to make do with *less*. [=to survive with less money, fewer possessions, etc.] • He's trying to save more and spend *less*. • I have *less* than you do. • I read much/far/even *less* of the second book than of the first. • I seem to save *less* each year. • We had exactly one day to get the job done—no more, no *less*. • *Less* is sometimes better than more. • Regarding his recent behavior, perhaps ***the less said, the better***. [=his recent behavior has been so bad that it is better to not say anything about it]
2 : something that is smaller or less important than another thing • You're lucky you didn't lose your job for swearing at your boss. People have been fired for *less* (than that).

could/couldn't care less see [2]CARE

less and less **:** an amount that becomes gradually smaller • I seem to save *less and less* each year. • We see *less and less* of them each year.

nothing less than see [2]NOTHING

think less of see [1]THINK

[4]less *prep* **:** after taking away or subtracting (something) • the regular price *less* [=*minus*] a discount • We earned two hundred dollars, *less* travel expenses.

-less /ləs/ *adj suffix*
1 : not having something specified **:** without something • child*less* • friend*less* • a cloud*less* sky • my first pain*less* day since leaving the hospital
2 a : never doing or becoming something specified • tire*less* workers [=workers who never become tired] • cease*less* noise [=noise that never ceases] **b :** not able to be acted on in a specified way • a daunt*less* hero [=a hero who cannot be daunted] • count*less* years [=too many years to be counted]

les·see /lɛˈsi:/ *noun, pl* **-sees** [*count*] *law* **:** a person who has an agreement that allows the use of a car, house, etc., for a period of time in exchange for a payment **:** a person who has a lease on something — compare LESSOR

less·en /ˈlɛsn̩/ *verb* **-ens; -ened; -en·ing :** to become less or to cause (something) to become less [*no obj*] The pain will *lessen* [=*decrease*] over time. [+ *obj*] Medication helps *lessen* the severity of the symptoms. • Taking a few simple precautions will *lessen* [=(more commonly) *reduce*] your risk of injury.

[1]less·er /ˈlɛsə/ *adj, always used before a noun*
1 : of smaller size • The winner will receive $100; *lesser* amounts will be given to three runners-up.
2 : of less strength, quality, or importance • A *lesser* man than he might have simply given up. • the artist's *lesser* works • She agreed to plead guilty to a *lesser* charge. — often used in the phrase ***to a lesser degree/extent*** • Traffic congestion is a problem in the city and, *to a lesser extent*, the suburbs. [=it is also a problem in the suburbs, but not as much of a problem as in the city]

lesser evil or lesser of two evils see [2]EVIL

[2]lesser *adv* **:** [2]LESS • *lesser*-known writers

les·son /ˈlɛsn̩/ *noun, pl* **-sons** [*count*]
1 a : an activity that you do in order to learn something • You can't go out to play until you've finished your *lessons*.; *also* **:** something that is taught • They studied the *lessons* [=*teachings*] of the great philosophers. **b :** a single class or part of a course of instruction • The book is divided into 12 *lessons*. • *Lesson* 1: Introduction • She took/gave piano *lessons* for years.
2 : something learned through experience • political leaders who have failed to learn the *lessons* of history • I've ***learned my lesson***—I'll never do that again! • We *learned our lesson* the hard way. [=we learned from an unpleasant experience] • I'm glad they got caught. That will ***teach them a lesson***! [=they will learn that they should not do that again] • ***Let that be a lesson to you***—if you don't take better care of your

toys they'll get broken! — see also OBJECT LESSON

3 : a part of the Bible read as part of a church service

les·sor /ˈlɛˌsoɚ/ *noun, pl* **-sors** [*count*] *law* **:** a person or company that leases property (such as a car or house) to someone — compare LESSEE

lest /ˈlɛst/ *conj, formal + literary*

1 : for fear that — used to say that you do not want something to happen • He was concerned *lest* anyone think that he was guilty. = (*chiefly Brit*) He was concerned *lest* [=*in case*] anyone should think he was guilty. [=he was concerned that people would think he was guilty; he did not want anyone to think he was guilty]

2 — used when you are saying something in order to prevent something from happening • And *lest* you think I'm joking, let me assure you that everything I've said is true. • She's a talented singer and, ***lest we forget***, a fine musician as well. [=we should not forget that she is also a fine musician]

[1]**let** /ˈlɛt/ *verb* **lets; let; let·ting**

1 [+ *obj*] **:** to allow or permit (someone or something) to do something • *Let* them go. • I'll be happy to help you if you'll *let* me (help you). • A break in the clouds *let* us see the summit. [=made it possible for us to see the summit] • Don't *let* this opportunity slip away! • *Let* me see the bruise. • I don't believe in *letting* children do whatever they want to do. = I don't believe that people should *let* children do whatever they want to do. • My philosophy is "***Live and let live.***" [=live your life as you choose and let other people do the same]

> ***usage*** *Let* is followed by a verb that has the form of the infinitive without *to*. • They *let* him *speak*. [=they allowed/permitted him *to speak*] *Let* is never used as *be let*; use *be allowed* or *be permitted* instead. • They *let* him speak. [=he *was allowed/permitted* by them to speak]

2 [+ *obj*] **a** — used in speech when you are making a polite offer to help someone • *Let* me help you with those packages. [=I would be happy to help you with those packages] • *Let* me do that for you. **b** — used to introduce a polite statement or request • *Let* me begin by saying how happy I am to see you here today. [=I want to begin by saying how happy I am to see you] • Please ***let me know*** [=tell me] what you decide. **c** *formal* — used to introduce a command • "The ambassadors have arrived, your Majesty." "*Let* them not wait a moment longer: *let* them enter at once." • *Let* there be music and laughter! — sometimes used figuratively in a way that is not formal • *Let* it rain all day—I don't care. **d** — used to express a warning • Just *let* her try to do it again! [=she will be in trouble if she tries to do it again]

3 a ✧ ***Let's*** and (more formally) ***let us*** are used to introduce statements that express a wish, request, suggestion, or command. • *Let's* [=*let us*] hope for the best. [=we should hope for the best] • *Let's* imagine what the world would be like with no war. • *Let's* suppose that he's right. What then? • *Let's* get out of here! • *Let us* all remember [=we should all remember] just how much we have to be thankful for. • I'm not calling her a liar. *Let's* just say that she tends to exaggerate the truth a little. • *Let's* see what's on the menu. = *Let's* have a look at the menu. • "*Let's* go, shall we?" [=shall we go?] "Yes, *let's*." • "*Let's* go." "No, *let's* not." • *Let's* not go. = (*Brit*) Don't *let's* go. = (*US, informal*) *Let's* don't go. **b** ✧ The phrase ***let's go*** is used in speech to tell someone to go or work faster. • Are you still getting dressed? *Let's go*! We need to leave in five minutes! **c** ✧ The phrase ***let us pray*** is used to introduce a prayer. • *Let us pray*. Dear God, we thank you for this day . . . **d** ✧ The phrases ***let's face it*** and ***let's be honest*** are used to say that something is true and cannot be denied. • *Let's face it*: we need more time. • *Let's be honest*, those two were never right for each other.

4 a [+ *obj*] **:** to allow someone to use (something) in return for payment **:** RENT • They have rooms ***to let***. [=rooms that people can rent to live in] **b** [*no obj*] *chiefly Brit* **:** to be rented or leased for a specified amount of money • The flat *lets* [=*rents*] for 350 pounds a month.

5 *always followed by an adverb or preposition* [+ *obj*] **:** to allow (someone or something) to go, pass by, etc. • *Let* me out! • She locked the door and refused to *let* him in. • The guard refused to *let* us through the gate. • *Let* me through/past! [=let me move through a group of people, past a barrier, etc.]

let alone* 1** — used to refer to something that is even less likely or possible than the thing previously mentioned • I can barely understand it, *let alone* explain it. **2** ***let (someone or something) alone **:** to not bother or touch (someone or something) • *Let* [=(more commonly) *leave*] your sister *alone*. • All I ask is to be *let alone*. [=(more commonly) *left alone*] • Would you please *let* it *alone*? • I never did learn to ***let well enough alone***. [=to leave well enough alone; to stop changing something that is already good enough]

let bygones be bygones see BYGONES

let down [*phrasal verb*] **1** ***let (someone) down*** **a :** to fail to give help or support to (someone who needs or expects it) **:** DISAPPOINT • I promised Mary that I'd help her, and I can't *let* her *down*. • It's my fault we lost the game. I *let* the team *down*. • He never *lets down* a friend in need. — sometimes used figuratively • His judgment *let* him *down*. [=his judgment was poor; he made a bad decision] **b :** to make (someone) unhappy or displeased by not being as good as expected • The end of the story really *let* me *down*. = I felt *let down* by the end of the story. [=the end of the story was disappointing] — see also LETDOWN **2** ✧ To ***let someone down easy/gently*** is to give someone unpleasant news in a gentle or kind way. • She tried to *let* him *down gently* when she told him he didn't get the job. • I knew I had to fire her, but I was trying to think of a way to *let* her *down easy*. **3** ***let (something) down*** or ***let down (something)*** **a :** to cause or allow (something) to move down gradually • *let* a bucket *down* into a well = *let down* a bucket into a well **b :** to make (a skirt, a pair of pants, etc.) longer • The pants were a little too short and needed to be *let down* a little. — see also *let your hair down* at HAIR

let fly or ***let fly with*** see [1]FLY

let go* 1** or ***let (something or someone) go or ***let go of (something or someone)*** or ***let go (something or someone)*** **:** to stop holding or gripping something or someone • I tried to take the ball from him, but he wouldn't *let go*. • She grabbed my hand and refused to *let go*. • He *let* the rope *go*. = He *let go of* the rope. = (less commonly) He *let go* the rope. — often used figuratively • When a child grows up and moves away from home, it can be hard for parents to *let go*. [=to allow the child to live independently; to not be too involved in the child's decisions, actions, etc.] • I know she disappointed you, but you need to *let* the past *go* and move on with your life. [=you need to stop caring or thinking about the past] • You need to *let go of* the past. • She felt she had been treated wrongly, and she wasn't willing to *let it go*. [=she wasn't willing to forget how she had been treated] • You're late. I'll *let it go* this time, but it had better not happen again. • The car is probably worth a lot more, but she agreed to *let it go* for five thousand dollars. [=she agreed to sell the car for five thousand dollars] **2** or ***let (yourself) go*** **:** to behave in a very free and open way • He really *lets go* when he's out partying with his friends. • She has a hard time relaxing and *letting herself go*. **3** ***let (someone) go*** **a :** to allow (someone who is being held as a slave, prisoner, etc.) to be free • They *let* the prisoner *go*. = The prisoner was *let go*. **b :** to officially make (someone) leave a job • The company *let* him *go* at the end of the month. = He was *let go* at the end of the month. **4** ***let (yourself) go*** **:** to fail to take care of (yourself) • I was very depressed back then and had really *let myself go*. [=I had stopped taking care of myself]

let it all hang out *informal* **:** to show your true feelings **:** to behave in a very free and open way • When I'm with my friends, I *let it all hang out*.

let loose see [1]LOOSE

let me see or ***let's see*** or ***let me think*** — used in speech by someone who is trying to remember something • *Let me see*, where did I put my keys? • *Let's see*, how long did it take last time? • What was the name of that restaurant? *Let me think*. Oh, that's right: "The High Street Café."

let off [*phrasal verb*] **1** ***let (someone) off*** or ***let off (someone)*** **:** to allow (someone) to get off a bus, an airplane, etc. • Could you *let* me *off* (the bus) at the next stop, please? • The bus stopped to *let off* a few passengers. **2** ***let (someone) off*** **:** to allow (someone who has been caught doing something wrong or illegal) to go without being punished • The police officer *let* her *off* with just a warning. • They *let* him *off* easy/easily/lightly, if you ask me. [=I do not think he was punished as severely as he could/should have been] — often used in the phrase ***let (someone) off the hook*** • If you ask me, they *let* him *off the hook* too easily. **3** ***let off (something)*** **:** to cause (something) to explode or to be released in a forceful way • *let off* [=*set off*] a firecracker • *let off* pressure — see also *let off (some) steam* at [1]STEAM

let on [*phrasal verb*] **1** ***let (someone) on*** or ***let on (someone)*** **:** to allow (someone) to get on a bus, an airplane, etc. • They *let* passengers with small children *on* (the airplane) first. ▪ The bus stopped to *let on* a few more passengers. **2** ***let on or let on (something) informal*** **:** to tell, admit, or show that you know something ▪ He knows a lot more than he *lets on*. ▪ Don't *let on* that I told you! ▪ She was unhappy, but she never *let on*. = She never *let on* to anyone that she was unhappy. [=she never showed or told anyone that she was unhappy] **3** *US, informal* **:** to pretend or seem ▪ She's not as happy as she *lets on*.

let out [*phrasal verb*] **1** ***let (something or someone) out or let out (something or someone)*** **:** to release (something or someone) ▪ She *let out* a scream. [=she screamed] ▪ They *let* the prisoner *out* (of prison) for the weekend. = The prisoner was *let out* for the weekend. ▪ *Let* the clutch *out* slowly. — see also LETOUT **2** ***let (something) out or let out (something)*** **:** to make (a shirt, a pair of pants, etc.) larger ▪ The skirt is too tight and needs to be *let out* a little. ▪ *let out* a pair of pants — opposite *take in* at [1]TAKE **3** *US, of a school* **:** to end a semester, year, or session ▪ School *lets out* in June.

let rip see [1]RIP

let sleeping dogs lie see [1]DOG

let (someone) have it *informal* **:** to attack, punish, or criticize (someone) in a violent or angry way ▪ When she found out what they'd been doing, she really *let* them *have it*.

let (someone) in on (something) **:** to allow (someone) to know (a secret) ▪ He said he'd *let* me *in on* a secret if I promised not to tell anyone else.

let (someone) know see [1]KNOW

let (someone or something) be **:** to not bother or touch (someone or something) ▪ Please *let* [=*leave*] *me be*.

let (something) be known see [1]KNOW

let (something) slip or let slip (something) see [1]SLIP

let the cat out of the bag see CAT

let the grass grow under your feet see [1]GRASS

let up [*phrasal verb*] **1 :** to stop or become slower ▪ Won't this rain ever *let up*? ▪ There's a lot of work still to be done. We can't *let up* now. — see also LETUP **2** ***let up on (someone)*** **:** to treat (someone) in a less harsh or demanding way ▪ The students might respond better if the teacher *let up on* [=*eased up on*] them a little. **3** ***let up on (something)*** **:** to apply less pressure to (something) ▪ I *let up on* [=*eased up on*] the gas pedal.

let (yourself) in for **:** to cause (yourself) to have or experience (something bad or unpleasant) ▪ She's *letting herself in for* a lot of trouble/criticism. ▪ When I agreed to help, I didn't know what I was *letting myself in for*. [=*getting myself into*]

[2]**let** *noun, pl* **lets** [*count*] *tennis* **:** a serve that is not accepted or allowed officially and must be done again ▪ The first serve was a *let*.

without let or hindrance *chiefly Brit, law* **:** without being interfered with ▪ They have the right to vote *without let or hindrance*. [=without anyone making it difficult or impossible for them to vote]

-let /lət/ *noun suffix* **:** small one ▪ book*let* [=a small book] ▪ drop*let* ▪ pig*let*

let·down /ˈlɛtˌdaʊn/ *noun, pl* **-downs** [*count*] **:** something that is not as good as it was expected to be ▪ The news was a *letdown*. [=*disappointment*] — see also *let down* at [1]LET

le·thal /ˈliːθəl/ *adj* [*more* ~; *most* ~] **:** causing or able to cause death ▪ *lethal* chemicals/weapons ▪ a potentially *lethal* dose of a drug ▪ He was sentenced to death by *lethal* injection. ▪ In rare instances, the disease can be *lethal*. [=(more commonly) *fatal*] — often used figuratively ▪ a pitcher with a *lethal* fastball [=a very powerful or effective fastball] ▪ a *lethal* [=very damaging] attack on her reputation ***synonyms*** see [1]DEADLY

— **le·thal·ly** *adv* ▪ *lethally* poisonous

le·thar·gic /ləˈθɑɚʤɪk/ *adj* [*more* ~; *most* ~] **:** feeling a lack of energy or a lack of interest in doing things ▪ The patient is weak and *lethargic*. — sometimes used figuratively ▪ a sluggish and *lethargic* economy

— **leth·ar·gic·al·ly** /ləˈθɑɚʤɪkli/ *adv* ▪ moving *lethargically*

leth·ar·gy /ˈlɛθɚʤi/ *noun* [*noncount*] **:** a lack of energy or a lack of interest in doing things **:** a lethargic feeling or state ▪ Symptoms of the disease include loss of appetite and *lethargy*. ▪ I snapped out of my *lethargy* and began cleaning the house. — sometimes used figuratively ▪ The stock market's recent *lethargy* is cause for concern.

let·out /ˈlɛtˌaʊt/ *noun, pl* **-outs** [*count*] *Brit, informal* **:** something (such as an excuse or a part of a contract) that makes it possible to avoid doing something ▪ Is there no *letout* I can use to get out of attending the meeting? — see also *let out* at [1]LET

let's /ˈlɛts/ — used as a contraction of *let us* ▪ *Let's* do our best.

[1]**let·ter** /ˈlɛtɚ/ *noun, pl* **-ters**

1 [*count*] **:** any one of the marks that are symbols for speech sounds in written language and that form an alphabet ▪ the *letter* "a" ▪ "F" is the sixth *letter* of the English alphabet. ▪ I wrote my name in capital *letters*.

2 [*count*] **:** a written or printed message to someone ▪ write/send/mail a business/love *letter* to someone ▪ *letters* to the editor ▪ They always answer the *letters* they get/receive from their fans. ▪ He asked them for a *letter* of recommendation/introduction. — see picture at MAIL; see also CHAIN LETTER, COVER LETTER, DEAD LETTER, FORM LETTER, NEWSLETTER, OPEN LETTER, POISON-PEN LETTER

3 ***letters*** [*plural*] *formal* **:** LITERATURE ▪ She's well-known in the field of English *letters*. — see also MAN OF LETTERS

4 [*singular*] **:** the exact meaning of something (such as a law) that is stated in writing ▪ They seem to be more concerned with obeying ***the letter of the law*** [=with doing exactly what the law says] than with understanding the spirit of the law.

5 [*count*] *US* **:** a large cloth letter that is the first letter of a school's name, that is awarded to a student for playing on a sports team, and that can be sewn onto a sweater or jacket ▪ He earned his *letter* in football.

by letter **:** by sending and receiving letters ▪ We communicated with each other *by letter*. ▪ a relationship that began *by letter*

to the letter **:** exactly or precisely ▪ obey the law *to the letter*

[2]**letter** *verb* **-ters; -tered; -ter·ing**

1 [+ *obj*] **:** to write or print letters on (something) **:** to mark (something) with letters — usually used as *(be) lettered* ▪ a sign *lettered* in bright red ▪ The sign *was* carefully *lettered* by hand. — often used in combination ▪ a hand-*lettered* sign

2 [*no obj*] *US* **:** to earn a school letter for playing on a sports team — usually + *in* ▪ He *lettered in* football.

letter bomb *noun, pl* ~ **bombs** [*count*] **:** a bomb that is mailed to someone in a letter or package and that explodes when the letter or package is opened — called also *(Brit) parcel bomb*

letter box *noun, pl* ~ **boxes** [*count*] *Brit* **:** MAILBOX

letter carrier *noun, pl* ~ **-ers** [*count*] *US* **:** a person who delivers mail

let·ter·head /ˈlɛtɚˌhɛd/ *noun, pl* **-heads** [*count*] **:** the name and address of an organization (such as a company) that is printed at the top of a piece of paper used for writing official letters ▪ We changed the design of our *letterhead*.; *also* [*noncount*] *US* **:** paper that has the name and address of an organization printed at the top ▪ They sent her a letter printed on company *letterhead*.

let·ter·ing /ˈlɛtərɪŋ/ *noun* [*noncount*] **:** letters written or printed on something ▪ I couldn't read the sign's *lettering*. ▪ a sign with gold *lettering*

letter opener *noun, pl* ~ **-ers** [*count*] **:** a device that has a sharp edge or part that is used to cut open envelopes — called also *(Brit) paper knife*

let·ter–per·fect /ˈlɛtɚˈpɚfɪkt/ *adj, US* **:** correct in every detail ▪ Her rendition of the song was *letter-perfect*.

let·tuce /ˈlɛtəs/ *noun, pl* **-tuces** [*count, noncount*] **:** a plant that has large leaves that are eaten especially in salads ▪ a head of *lettuce* ▪ iceberg/romaine *lettuce* ▪ I like a little *lettuce* and tomato on my sandwiches.

let·up /ˈlɛtˌʌp/ *noun* **:** a time during which something stops or slows down [*noncount*] It rained three days without *letup*. [=it rained continuously for three days] ▪ We worked without *letup*. [=we worked continuously] [*singular*] There's been a *letup* [=*break*] in the fighting. — see also *let up* at [1]LET

leu·ke·mia *or chiefly Brit* **leu·kae·mia** /luˈkiːmijə/ *noun* [*noncount*] *medical* **:** a very serious disease in which the body forms too many white blood cells

— **leu·ke·mic** *or chiefly Brit* **leu·kae·mic** /luˈkiːmɪk/ *adj* ▪ *leukemic* cells/patients

lev·ee /ˈlɛvi/ *noun, pl* **-ees** [*count*] *US* **:** a long wall of soil built along a river to prevent flooding

[1]**lev·el** /ˈlɛvəl/ *noun, pl* **-els**

1 a : a specific height [*noncount*] The pictures were hung on the wall at eye *level*. ▪ at street/ground *level* [*count*] The pictures were hung at different *levels*. — see also GROUND-LEVEL, SEA LEVEL **b** [*count*] **:** a part of a building that is at a specific height ▪ We were seated in the upper *level* [=*floor*] of the restaurant. — see also SPLIT-LEVEL

2 [*count*] **: an amount of something** • There was a high *level* of alcohol/lead in his blood. • a normal *level* of intelligence • Prices have risen to a new *level*. • He has shown a remarkable *level* of patience. [=he has been very patient] • They have demonstrated a high *level* of interest [=they have been very interested] in this proposal. • They checked the reservoir's water *level*. [=the amount of water in the reservoir]

3 [*count*] **: a position or rank in a scale : a position that is high or low when compared to others** • She rose to the *level* of manager. • She has reached a rare *level* of financial success. • These problems affect people at all *levels* of society. • Can this problem be dealt with at/on a national *level* or must it be addressed at/on an international *level*? — see also ENTRY-LEVEL, HIGH-LEVEL, LOW-LEVEL

4 [*count*] **: a way of thinking about, talking about, or dealing with something** • The argument appeals to me on a purely intellectual *level* but fails to reach me on a deeper emotional *level*. • I'm attracted to the job on many *levels*. • He studied the changes in the chemical at the molecular *level*. [=he studied the changes in the molecules of the chemical] • She has enjoyed great success in her professional life, but, ***on a*** (more) ***personal level***, this has been a very stressful time. [=this has been a very stressful time in her personal life]

5 [*count*] **: a device used to see when something is exactly flat — called also *spirit level*; see picture at** CARPENTRY

***descend/sink/stoop to someone's level* : to behave as badly as someone who has treated you wrongly** • Despite my opponent's personal attacks against me, I refuse to *stoop to his level*. [=I refuse to behave as badly as he has by attacking him personally]

on the level *informal* **: not false or dishonest** • Is this guy *on the level*? [=is this guy honest?]

²level *adj*

1 : having a flat or even surface • We pitched the tent on *level* ground. • a *level* floor/road • The recipe calls for a ***level teaspoon/tablespoon*** of sugar. [=an amount of sugar that fills a teaspoon/tablespoon exactly without going above its edges]

2 : not going up or down • an airplane in *level* flight • Interest rates have remained *level*.

3 a : having the same height as something else — usually + *with* • The water was *level with* my waist. • The window is *level with* the tops of the trees. **b : not in front of or behind something or someone else** • The boards are *level*. **— often + *with*** • They drew *level with* the rest of the runners. • Make sure that the ends of the boards are *level with* each other.

4 *chiefly Brit* **: having the same position, score, or rank :** EVEN • The teams are *level* (with each other) in the standings. • They trailed early in the game, but they drew *level* [=they tied the score] in the second half. **— compare** LEVEL-PEGGING

5 : steady and calm • She spoke in a *level* voice. • It's important to ***keep a level head*** [=to remain calm] when you're dealing with a dangerous situation like this one.

your level best* : your best effort at doing something** • He ***tried his level best to win the race. [=he tried as hard as he could to win the race] • She ***did her level best*** to please her mother. [=she tried very hard to please her mother]

³level *verb* **-els**; *US* **-eled** *or chiefly Brit* **-elled**; *US* **-el·ing** *or chiefly Brit* **-el·ling** [+ *obj*]

1 : to make (something) flat or level • They will *level* the field. • We need to *level* the garden before we plant anything.

2 : to knock (someone or something) down to the ground • The earthquake *leveled* the city. • He *leveled* his opponent with a right hook.

3 a : to point (a weapon) *at* someone • The robber *leveled* a gun *at* his head. **b : to direct (something, such as criticism) *at* or *against* someone** • They *leveled* a fraud charge *against* him. [=they charged him with fraud] • Several complaints have been *leveled at* the store. • Criticism has been *leveled against* the government for not responding to this crisis.

4 *chiefly Brit* **: to make (a score) equal :** TIE • He scored a goal that *leveled* the score at 3–3.

level off [*phrasal verb*] **1 : to stop going up or down** • The plane *leveled off* at 30,000 feet. • The road *levels off* just before the river. • Business at the restaurant is *leveling off*. **2 *level (something) off or level off (something)* : to make (something) flat or even** • They used a bulldozer *level off* the field.

level out [*phrasal verb*] **: to stop going up or down** • Divorce rates are *leveling out* for the first time in decades. • My moods have *leveled out*.

***level the playing field* : to make a situation fair for everyone** • He wants the government to *level the playing field* by breaking up large corporations so that smaller companies can compete. **— see also** LEVEL PLAYING FIELD

level with [*phrasal verb*] ***level with (someone)*** *informal* **: to speak honestly to (someone)** • He never *leveled with* his parents about the accident. • *Level with* me. Why did you do it?

level crossing *noun, pl* **~ -ings** [*count*] *Brit* **:** RAILROAD CROSSING

lev·el·er (*US*) *or chiefly Brit* **lev·el·ler** /ˈlɛvəlɚ/ *noun, pl* **-ers** [*count*] **: something that treats or affects all people the same way** • Death is the great *leveler*. [=death is the same for all people no matter how rich or powerful they may be]

lev·el·head·ed /ˌlɛvəlˈhɛdəd/ *adj* [*more ~; most ~*] **: having or showing an ability to think clearly and to make good decisions** • She is *levelheaded* about her chances for success as an actress. • a *levelheaded* assessment of the problem

— lev·el·head·ed·ness *noun* [*noncount*]

lev·el–peg·ging /ˌlɛvəlˈpɛgɪŋ/ *adj, Brit* **: even with one another in a contest or competition** • The candidates are *level-pegging* in all the opinion polls.

level playing field *noun* [*singular*] **: a state in which conditions in a competition or situation are fair for everyone** • He wants the government to break up large corporations so that there is a *level playing field* for smaller companies. **— see also *level the playing field* at** ³LEVEL

¹le·ver /ˈlɛvɚ, ˈliːvɚ/ *noun, pl* **-vers** [*count*]

1 : a strong bar that is used to lift and move something heavy

2 : a bar or rod that is used to operate or adjust something on a machine, vehicle, device, etc. • Pull the brake *lever*.

3 : something used to achieve a desired result • They used their money as a *lever* to gain political power.

²lever *verb* **-vers; -vered; -ver·ing** [+ *obj*] **: to lift or move (something) with a lever** • He *levered* the rock out of the hole. **— often used figuratively** • They tried unsuccessfully to *lever* him out of his job. [=to force him out of his job] • She *levered* her way into a position of political power.

le·ver·age /ˈlɛvərɪʤ, ˈliːvərɪʤ/ *noun* [*noncount*]

1 : influence or power used to achieve a desired result • The union's size gave it *leverage* in the labor contract negotiations. • The player's popularity has given him a great deal of *leverage* with the owners of the team.

2 : the increase in force gained by using a lever • I used the *leverage* of the bar and a wooden block to pry the rock out of the hole.

leverage *verb* **-ag·es; -aged; -ag·ing** [+ *obj*] *chiefly US* **: to use (something valuable) to achieve a desired result** • The company wants to *leverage* its brands more effectively.

leveraged buyout *noun, pl* **~ -outs** [*count*] *chiefly US* **: a business arrangement in which someone buys a company by borrowing money based on the value of the company that is being bought**

le·vi·a·than /lɪˈvajəθən/ *noun, pl* **-thans** [*count*] *literary* **: something that is very large and powerful :** GIANT • The factory is a towering *leviathan* in the middle of the town. • a *leviathan* corporation

Le·vi's /ˈliːˌvaɪz/ *trademark* **— used especially for blue jeans**

lev·i·tate /ˈlɛvəˌteɪt/ *verb* **-tates; -tat·ed; -tat·ing : to rise or make (something) rise into the air in a way that appears to be magical** [*no obj*] The woman *levitated* above the stage. [+ *obj*] The magician claimed he could *levitate* a car.

— lev·i·ta·tion /ˌlɛvəˈteɪʃən/ *noun* [*noncount*]

lev·i·ty /ˈlɛvəti/ *noun* [*noncount*] *somewhat formal*

1 : a lack of seriousness • She would not tolerate any *levity* [=*frivolity*] in the classroom.

2 : an amusing quality • They managed to find some *levity* in the situation.

¹levy /ˈlɛvi/ *noun, pl* **lev·ies** [*count*] **: an amount of money that must be paid and that is collected by a government or other authority** • The government imposed a *levy* [=*tax*] on gasoline.

²levy *verb* **levies; lev·ied; levy·ing** [+ *obj*] **: to use legal authority to demand and collect (a fine, a tax, etc.)** • They *levied* a tax on imports. • The government will *levy* a fine on the company.

lewd /ˈluːd/ *adj* [*more ~; most ~*] **: sexual in an offensive or rude way** • He made *lewd* remarks/comments to the woman at the bar. • *lewd* behavior • ***lewd and lascivious*** acts

— lewd·ly *adv* **— lewd·ness** *noun* [*noncount*] • He was arrested for public *lewdness*.

lex·i·cal /ˈlɛksɪkəl/ *adj* [*more ~; most ~*] *linguistics* **: relating**

to words or vocabulary • the *lexical* content of [=the words used in] a statement

lex·i·con /ˈlɛksəˌkɑːn, *Brit* ˈlɛksəkən/ *noun, pl* **-cons** [*count*]
1 : the words used in a language or by a person or group of people • a computer term that has entered the general *lexicon*
2 *somewhat formal* : DICTIONARY • a Latin *lexicon*

lg. *abbr* large

LH *abbr* left hand

li·a·bil·i·ty /ˌlajəˈbɪləti/ *noun, pl* **-ties**
1 [*noncount*] : the state of being legally responsible for something : the state of being liable for something • The company is trying to limit its *liability* in this case. • criminal *liability* [=the state of being responsible for a crime] • The judge cleared me of any/all *liability* for the accident. [=the judge said that I was not responsible for the accident]
2 [*count*] : something (such as the payment of money) for which a person or business is legally responsible • a tax *liability* [=taxes that will have to be paid] — usually plural • business assets and *liabilities* [=*debts*]
3 [*count*] : someone or something that causes problems • His small size was a *liability* (to him) as a football player. • This scandal has made the vice president a *liability* (for this administration).

li·a·ble /ˈlajəbəl/ *adj*
1 : legally responsible for something • If someone gets hurt on your property, you could be *liable*. • The amusement park was held *liable* in the boy's death. [=a court of law ruled that the amusement park was responsible for the boy's death] — usually + *for* • He is *liable for* his wife's debts. [=he is responsible for paying his wife's debts] • They are *liable for* any damage. [=they will be required to pay for any damage]
2 [*more* ~; *most* ~] : likely to be affected or harmed by something — + *to* • Her condition makes her *liable to* illness. • *liable to* injury
3 [*more* ~; *most* ~] : likely to do something — + *to* • You're *liable to* fall if you're not more careful. • It's *liable to* rain before we're done. • That guy's *liable to* say anything. [=he might say anything]

li·aise /liˈeɪz/ *verb* **-ais·es; -aised; -ais·ing** [*no obj*] *chiefly Brit* : to make it possible for two organizations or groups to work together and provide information to each other : to act as a liaison — usually + *with* or *between* • Administrators need to *liaise with* employees at the factory, and the personnel department needs to *liaise between* the administrators and the employees.

li·ai·son /ˈliːjəˌzɑːn, liˈeɪˌzɑːn/ *noun, pl* **-sons**
1 a [*count*] : a person who helps organizations or groups to work together and provide information to each other • She acts as a *liaison* between the police department and city schools. **b** : a relationship that allows different organizations or groups to work together and provide information to each other [*noncount*] Administrators need to maintain better/closer *liaison* with employees. [*singular*] Administrators need to establish a close *liaison* with employees.
2 [*count*] : a secret sexual relationship : AFFAIR • He regretted his *liaison* with a woman from the office. • sexual *liaisons*

li·ar /ˈlajɚ/ *noun, pl* **-ars** [*count*] : a person who tells lies • She called him a dirty *liar*.

lib /ˈlɪb/ *noun* [*noncount*] *informal* : LIBERATION • women's *lib*
— **lib·ber** /ˈlɪbɚ/ *noun, pl* **-bers** [*count*] • a women's *libber* [=a person who supports women's liberation]

li·ba·tion /laɪˈbeɪʃən/ *noun, pl* **-tions** [*count*]
1 *formal* : a liquid that is poured out to honor a god • They offered *libations* at the temple.
2 *humorous* : an alcoholic drink • We met for a *libation* after work.

Lib Dem /ˌlɪbˈdɛm/ *noun, pl* ~ **Dems** [*count*] *Brit, informal* : LIBERAL DEMOCRAT • Charles Kennedy MP (*Lib Dem*)

¹li·bel /ˈlaɪbəl/ *noun, pl* **-bels** : the act of publishing a false statement that causes people to have a bad opinion of someone [*noncount*] He sued the newspaper for *libel*. • The newspaper was found guilty of *libel*. [*count*] The newspaper's attorneys argued that the article was not a *libel*. — compare SLANDER

²libel *verb* **-bels**; *US* **-beled** *or chiefly Brit* **-belled**; *US* **-bel·ing** *or chiefly Brit* **-bel·ling** [+ *obj*] : to write and publish a false statement that causes people to have a bad opinion of (someone) • The jury found that the article *libeled* him.

li·bel·ous (*US*) *or chiefly Brit* **li·bel·lous** /ˈlaɪbələs/ *adj* : containing an untrue written statement that causes people to have a bad opinion of someone • a *libelous* magazine article

¹lib·er·al /ˈlɪbərəl, ˈlɪbrəl/ *adj*
1 a [*more* ~; *most* ~] : believing that government should be active in supporting social and political change : relating to or supporting political liberalism • a leading *liberal* thinker • *liberal* politicians/policies • She is a *liberal* Democrat who married a conservative Republican. — compare ¹CONSERVATIVE **b** *Liberal Brit* : of or belonging to the liberal political party in countries like Canada and the United Kingdom • *Liberal* voters/policies
2 [*more* ~; *most* ~] : not opposed to new ideas or ways of behaving that are not traditional or widely accepted • She has a *liberal* attitude toward sex. — compare ¹CONSERVATIVE
3 [*more* ~; *most* ~] **a** : generous to others : giving time, money, etc., freely to other people — often + *with* • She has always been *liberal with* her donations. **b** : very large in amount • He made a very *liberal* donation to the museum. • a cook who uses a *liberal* quantity of spices [=who uses a large amount of spices]
4 [*more* ~; *most* ~] : not strict or exact • a fairly *liberal* [=*loose*] interpretation of the law
5 *somewhat formal* : involving or relating to studies that are intended to give you general knowledge rather than to develop specific skills : relating to the liberal arts • He received a *liberal* education.
— **lib·er·al·ly** /ˈlɪbərəli, ˈlɪbrəli/ *adv* • The book is *liberally* sprinkled with humor. • She gave *liberally* to the charity.

²liberal *noun, pl* **-als** [*count*]
1 : a person who believes that government should be active in supporting social and political change : a person who is politically liberal • a policy that is supported both by *liberals* and conservatives in Congress — compare ²CONSERVATIVE
2 *Liberal Brit* : a member or supporter of a liberal political party in countries like the United Kingdom and Canada

liberal arts *noun* [*plural*] : areas of study (such as history, language, and literature) that are intended to give you general knowledge rather than to develop specific skills needed for a profession • the sciences and the *liberal arts* • She graduated from a *liberal arts* college in the Midwest.

Liberal Democrat *noun, pl* ~ **-crats** [*count*] : a member or supporter of a British political party that is known as the Liberal Democrats

lib·er·al·ism /ˈlɪbərəˌlɪzəm, ˈlɪbrəˌlɪzəm/ *noun* [*noncount*] *formal* : belief in the value of social and political change in order to achieve progress • political *liberalism* — compare CONSERVATISM

lib·er·al·i·ty /ˌlɪbəˈræləti/ *noun* [*noncount*] *formal* : a liberal quality or attitude: such as **a** : the quality of not being opposed to ideas or ways of behaving that are not traditional or widely accepted • They were shocked by the *liberality* of her views on sex. **b** : the quality of being generous : GENEROSITY • He treated his friends with remarkable *liberality*.

lib·er·al·ize *also Brit* **lib·er·al·ise** /ˈlɪbrəˌlaɪz/ *verb* **-iz·es; -ized; -iz·ing**
1 [+ *obj*] : to make (something) less strict or more liberal • The country began to *liberalize* its immigration policies. [=to make them less strict]
2 [*no obj*] : to become less strict or more liberal • The country's immigration policies have begun to *liberalize*.
— **lib·er·al·i·za·tion** *also Brit* **lib·er·al·i·sa·tion** /ˌlɪbrələˈzeɪʃən, *Brit* ˌlɪbrəˌlaɪˈzeɪʃən/ *noun* [*noncount*]

lib·er·ate /ˈlɪbəˌreɪt/ *verb* **-ates; -at·ed; -at·ing** [+ *obj*]
1 : to free (someone or something) from being controlled by another person, group, etc. • Rebels fought to *liberate* the country. • Soldiers *liberated* the hostages from their captors.
2 : to give freedom or more freedom to (someone) • Laptop computers could *liberate* workers from their desks.
3 *humorous* : to take or steal (something) • He was using materials that he had *liberated* from a construction site.
— **lib·er·a·tor** /ˈlɪbəˌreɪtɚ/ *noun, pl* **-tors** [*count*] • a *liberator* of slaves

liberated *adj* [*more* ~; *most* ~] : freed from or opposed to traditional social and sexual attitudes or ways of behaving • a *liberated* woman • a *liberated* marriage

liberating *adj* [*more* ~; *most* ~] : making you feel free • He found that changing jobs was very *liberating*. • a *liberating* discovery

lib·er·a·tion /ˌlɪbəˈreɪʃən/ *noun* [*noncount*]
1 : the act or process of freeing someone or something from another's control : the act of liberating someone or some-

thing • their *liberation* from slavery • The *liberation* of the city took weeks.

2 : the removal of traditional social or sexual rules, attitudes, etc. • women's *liberation* • sexual *liberation*

lib·er·tar·i·an /ˌlɪbɚˈterijən/ *noun, pl* **-ans** [*count*] **:** a person who believes that people should be allowed to do and say what they want without any interference from the government

– libertarian *adj* • *libertarian* theories **– lib·er·tar·i·an·ism** /ˌlɪbɚˈterijəˌnɪzəm/ *noun* [*noncount*]

lib·er·tine /ˈlɪbɚˌtiːn/ *noun, pl* **-tines** [*count*] *literary* **:** a person (especially a man) who leads an immoral life and is mainly interested in sexual pleasure • *libertines* of the royal court

– libertine *adj* [*more* ~; *most* ~] • *libertine* behavior

lib·er·ty /ˈlɪbɚti/ *noun, pl* **-ties**

1 [*noncount*] **:** the state or condition of people who are able to act and speak freely **:** FREEDOM • a nation that values *liberty* and democracy • soldiers willing to die in defense of *liberty*

2 [*noncount*] **:** the power to do or choose what you want to • They gave him the *liberty* to handle the problem himself.

3 [*count*] **:** a political right • hard-won *liberties* such as freedom of the press • personal *liberties*

at liberty *formal* **1 :** able to act or speak freely — followed by *to + verb* • You are *at liberty to go* or *stay*. • I am not *at liberty to say* if the rumor is true. **2 :** no longer held or kept as a prisoner • a former prisoner who is now *at liberty*

take liberties **1** *disapproving* **:** to make important changes to something — usually + *with* • I think the movie *takes* too many *liberties with* the original story. **2** *old-fashioned* **:** to be informal and friendly toward someone in a way that is not proper — usually + *with* • He was accused of *taking liberties with* several young women.

take the liberty of ♦ If you *take the liberty of* doing something, you do something without asking for permission to do it. • I *took the liberty of* making a reservation for us. • I *took the liberty of* telling them you weren't interested.

li·bid·i·nous /ləˈbɪdənəs/ *adj* [*more* ~; *most* ~] *formal* **:** feeling or relating to strong sexual desires • *libidinous* urges

li·bi·do /ləˈbiːdoʊ/ *noun, pl* **-dos** *technical* **:** a person's desire to have sex [*count*] They have healthy *libidos*. [*noncount*] Lack of *libido* may be a sign of depression.

Li·bra /ˈliːbrə/ *noun*

1 [*noncount*] **:** the seventh sign of the zodiac that comes between Virgo and Scorpio and has a pair of scales as its symbol — see picture at ZODIAC

2 [*count*] **:** a person born under the sign of Libra **:** a person born between September 22nd and October 23rd • I'm a *Libra*.

li·brar·i·an /laɪˈbrerijən/ *noun, pl* **-ans** [*count*] **:** a person who works in a library

li·brary /ˈlaɪˌbreri, *Brit* ˈlaɪbrəri/ *noun, pl* **-brar·ies** [*count*]

1 : a place where books, magazines, and other materials (such as videos and musical recordings) are available for people to use or borrow • I borrowed the book from the school *library*. • a public *library* • a *library* book/card — see also LENDING LIBRARY, REFERENCE LIBRARY

2 : a room in a person's house where books are kept

3 : a collection of similar things (such as books or recordings) • He has an impressive *library* of jazz records. • a *library* of computer programs

li·bret·tist /ləˈbretɪst/ *noun, pl* **-tists** [*count*] **:** a person who writes a libretto

li·bret·to /ləˈbretoʊ/ *noun, pl* **-tos** *or* **-ti** /-ti/ [*count*] *formal* **:** the words of an opera or musical

lice *plural of* [1]LOUSE 1

[1]li·cense (*US*) *or chiefly Brit* **li·cence** /ˈlaɪsn̩s/ *noun, pl* **-cens·es**

1 [*count*] **:** an official document, card, etc., that gives you permission to do, use, or have something • The restaurant's owner applied for a *license* to sell liquor. • a liquor *license* • a fishing *license* — often used to refer specifically to a driver's license • I have to renew my *license*. • She was arrested for driving without a *license*. • He lost his *license* after he was arrested for drunk driving. • He had to show his *license* to prove his age. — see also DRIVER'S LICENSE, MARRIAGE LICENSE

2 : freedom to act however you want to — followed by *to + verb* [*noncount*] His job as a reporter gives him *license to go* anywhere and ask anything. [*singular*] She regards her illness as a *license to treat* other people badly. [=she thinks that because she is ill she can treat other people badly]

3 [*noncount*] **:** the freedom of an artist, writer, etc., to change the way something is described or shown in order to produce a work of art • artistic/poetic/creative *license*

4 [*count*] **:** a document or agreement that allows a certain number of people to use a computer program • We have a *license* for 10 users.

a license to print money *sometimes disapproving* **:** a way of making a large amount of money very easily • He says that if the new law is passed it will give these companies *a license to print money*.

under license **:** in a business arrangement where one company gives official permission to another company to do or make something • The company makes computer chips *under license* from the original manufacturer.

[2]license *also Brit* **licence** *verb* **-censes; -censed; -censing** [+ *obj*]

1 : to give official permission to (someone or something) to do or use something **:** to give a license to (someone or something) • The restaurant has now been *licensed* to sell liquor.

2 : to give official permission for (something) • a new drug *licensed* by the government • The gun was not *licensed* to him. [=he did not have formal permission to own the gun]

3 : to allow the use of (a name, property, etc.) through a formal agreement • The company *licensed* its name to others.

licensed *adj*

1 : having official permission to have or do something **:** having a license • a *licensed* physician/teacher • a *licensed* driver/pilot

2 *chiefly Brit* **:** having official permission to sell liquor • a *licensed* hotel • *licensed* premises [=a place that has a license to sell liquor]

licensed practical nurse *noun, pl* ~ **nurses** [*count*] **:** a nurse who has completed a basic level of training and is licensed to provide routine care to sick people — abbr. *LPN*; compare REGISTERED NURSE

li·cens·ee /ˌlaɪsn̩ˈsiː/ *noun, pl* **-ees** [*count*] *business* **:** a person or company that has a license to have, make, do, or use something

license number *noun, pl* ~ **-bers** [*count*] *US* **:** the numbers and letters on a vehicle's license plate — called also (*Brit*) *registration number*

license plate *noun, pl* ~ **plates** [*count*] *US* **:** a metal plate on a vehicle that shows a series of numbers and letters that are used to identify the vehicle — called also (*chiefly Brit*) *number plate*; see picture at CAR

licensing law *noun, pl* ~ **laws** [*count*] *Brit* **:** a law that controls where and when alcoholic drinks may be sold — usually plural

li·cen·tious /laɪˈsenʃəs/ *adj* [*more* ~; *most* ~] *formal* **:** sexually immoral or offensive • *licentious* behavior

– li·cen·tious·ness *noun* [*noncount*]

lichee *variant spelling of* LYCHEE

li·chen /ˈlaɪkən/ *noun* [*noncount*] **:** a type of small plant that grows on rocks and walls

[1]lick /ˈlɪk/ *verb* **licks; licked; lick·ing**

1 : to pass the tongue over (a surface, an object, etc.) [+ *obj*] He *licked* the stamp before putting it on the envelope. • The dog *licked* my cheek. = The dog *licked* me on the cheek. [*no obj*] The dog *licked* at the plate.

2 [+ *obj*] **:** to take (something) into your mouth with your tongue • She *licked* the sauce off her finger. • The cat *licked* the milk off/from her paws.

3 : to lightly touch or go over (a surface) [+ *obj*] Flames were already *licking* the ceiling. [*no obj*] Flames were already *licking* at/against the ceiling.

4 [+ *obj*] *informal* **a :** to defeat (someone) in a fight or contest • He's pretty big, but I think I can *lick* him. **b :** to solve (a problem) • Engineers think they have *licked* the problem with the rocket engine.

lick someone's boots *informal* + *disapproving* **:** to treat someone powerful with too much respect in order to get approval • He's just the assistant to the manager, there's no need to *lick his boots*.

lick your lips **1 :** to pass your tongue over your lips • She *licked her lips* while she waited for the food to be served. **2** *or US* ***lick your chops*** **:** to feel or show excitement because something good is expected to happen • The players knew they would win and were *licking their chops* as they waited for the game to start.

lick your wounds **:** to recover from defeat or disappointment • He went home to *lick his wounds* after losing the election.

²lick *noun, pl* **licks** [*count*]

1 : the act of passing your tongue over something **:** the act of licking something • He gave the bowl a *lick*. [=he licked the bowl] • Could I have a *lick* of your ice cream?

2 *informal* **:** a small amount **:** BIT • It just needs a *lick* of paint. — often used in negative statements in U.S. English • She couldn't swim a *lick*. [=she couldn't swim at all] • He hasn't done a *lick* of work. [=he hasn't done any work] • She thinks he isn't worth a *lick*. [=she thinks he is worthless]

3 *informal* **:** a hard hit • a football player who has taken a lot of *licks* [=who has been hit hard many times] — often used figuratively in U.S. English • He said some pretty harsh things to her, but she got in a few *licks* herself. [=she also said some harsh things to him] • The movie has ***taken its licks*** from the critics. [=has been harshly reviewed by the critics]

4 *informal* **:** a very short part of a piece of music • guitar *licks*

a lick and a promise **1** *US* **:** a quick and careless attempt to do something • They gave the budget problems a *lick and a promise* and then moved on to the next issue. **2** *Brit* **:** the act of washing something quickly or carelessly • He gave the car *a lick and a promise*.

lick•e•ty–split /ˌlɪkətiˈsplɪt/ *adv, US, informal + old-fashioned* **:** very quickly • He ran out the door *lickety-split*.

lick•ing /ˈlɪkɪŋ/ *noun* [*singular*] *informal*

1 : a severe beating • His father threatened to give him a *licking* if he didn't stop misbehaving.

2 : a severe defeat • The team got/took a good *licking* [=was badly defeated] in the first game of the season. — often used figuratively • Many investors took a *licking* [=lost a lot of money] in the stock market last year.

lic•o•rice *or chiefly Brit* **li•quor•ice** /ˈlɪkərɪʃ/ *noun* [*noncount*] **:** a candy made from the dried root of a European plant

lid /ˈlɪd/ *noun, pl* **lids** [*count*]

1 : a cover on a box, can, jar, etc., that can be lifted or removed — see picture at KITCHEN

2 : EYELID

blow the lid off (*chiefly US*) *or chiefly Brit* ***lift the lid on*** **:** to reveal the truth about (something) • The investigation *blew the lid off* corruption in city hall.

flip your lid see ¹FLIP

keep a lid on **1 :** to keep (something secret) from being known • She tried to *keep a lid on* the news. **2 :** to control (something) **:** to keep (something) from becoming worse • The government has been unable to *keep a lid on* inflation.

put a lid on **1 :** to stop (something) from growing or becoming worse • These changes are intended to *put a lid on* rising medical costs. **2** *informal* **:** to stop doing or saying (something) • He angrily told them to *put a lid on* their complaints. [=to stop complaining] • I'm tired of listening to your complaints, so just ***put a lid on it***! [=*shut up*] **3** *or* ***put the lid on*** **:** to cause the end or failure of (something) • The government used the army to *put a lid on* [=*stop*] the rebellion. • The new official vowed that he would *put the lid on* violence once and for all. • (*chiefly Brit*) The rain has really *put the lid on* our holiday plans. [=has ruined our holiday plans]

lid•ded /ˈlɪdəd/ *adj* **:** having a lid or a particular kind of lid • a *lidded* container • He has heavy-*lidded* eyes. [=eyes with large/heavy eyelids or with eyelids that are almost closed]

li•do /ˈliːdoʊ/ *noun, pl* **lidos** [*count*] *Brit* **:** a public outdoor swimming pool or swimming area

¹lie /ˈlaɪ/ *verb* **lies; lay** /ˈleɪ/; **lain** /ˈleɪn/; **ly•ing** /ˈlajɪŋ/ [*no obj*]

1 *of a person or animal* **a :** to be in a flat position on a surface (such as a bed) • *Lie* still. • She *lay* asleep on the bed. • He *lay* dead on the floor. • The police found him *lying* unconscious in an alley. • All the dog did was just *lie* there. — see picture at POSITION **b :** to move from a standing or sitting position to a flat position on a surface • The doctor asked him to *lie* [=*lie down*] on the table. **c —** used to mark the place where a person is buried • Here *lies* John Smith. = Here *lies* the body of John Smith.

2 *of things* **:** to be in a flat position on a surface • snow *lying* on the ground • A note was *lying* on the table when he came home. • The leaves *lay* thick on the ground. • He placed a hand on her shoulder, where it *lay* [=*rested*] for a moment.

3 a : to be or remain in a specified state or condition • The city *lay* in ruins. • The book was *lying* open on the desk. • The factory continues to *lie* idle. • dishes *lying* dirty in the sink **b** *always followed by an adverb or a preposition* **:** to be in a specified direction • Our route *lay* to the west.

4 : to be located in a particular place • The village *lies* in a peaceful valley. • The river *lies* along the western edge of the mountains. • Ohio *lies* east of Indiana. = Ohio *lies* to the east of Indiana. • A ship was *lying* in the harbor. • The mountains *lay* between us and our goal. — often used figuratively • I don't know where the answer *lies*. [=I don't know where the answer can be found; I don't know what the answer is] • He doesn't know where his future *lies*. [=he doesn't know what he will do in the future] • The choice *lay* between fighting or surrendering. [=the choice was between fighting or surrendering] • There is no question about where her loyalties *lie*. [=about which person, group, etc., she is loyal to] • The problem *lies* in knowing what to do. • I don't know what to do, and ***therein lies the problem***. [=that is the problem]

5 *Brit* **:** to be at a specified level in a competition • They are *lying* third. = They are *lying* in third place. [=they are in third place]

how the land lies see ¹LAND

let sleeping dogs lie see ¹DOG

lie ahead **:** to be in the future • No one knows what *lies ahead* (of us). [=no one knows what will happen (to us) in the future]

lie around *or Brit* ***lie about*** [*phrasal verb*] **1 a :** to be lying in a disordered way • He always had a lot of clothes *lying around* his house. **b :** to be somewhere within a general area or place • I know that pen is *lying around* here somewhere. **2 :** to spend time resting in a lazy way • She spent the whole day just *lying around*. • My friends and I were *lying around* by the pool.

lie back [*phrasal verb*] **:** to lean backward from a sitting position to a flat position • The doctor asked him to *lie back* on the table.

lie behind [*phrasal verb*] ***lie behind (something)*** **:** to be the cause of (something) • Greed *lies behind* the higher prices.

lie down [*phrasal verb*] **1 :** to move from a standing or sitting position to a flat position on a surface • *Lie down* on the couch/bed. • I'm tired. I'm going to *lie down*. • The police ordered him to lay down his weapons and *lie down* on the ground. **2** ***lie down on the job*** **:** to fail to do your job **:** to neglect your responsibilities • He says pollution has been getting worse because government regulators have been *lying down on the job*. **3** ✧ To ***take something lying down*** is to accept something bad, such as an insult or unfair treatment, without trying to fight against it. • He vowed that he would not *take the court's decision lying down*. [=that he would fight against the court's decision]

lie in [*phrasal verb*] *Brit* **:** to stay in bed later than usual • She likes to *lie in* [=*sleep in*] on Saturdays.

lie in state see ¹STATE

lie in wait see ²WAIT

lie low **:** to try not to be noticed **:** to stay hidden or inactive in order to avoid being noticed or found • The prisoners had to *lie low* after their escape.

lie on/upon [*phrasal verb*] ***lie on/upon (someone or something)*** **:** to affect someone in a specified way • Sorrow *lay* heavily *on* him. [=he felt very sad] • Guilt *lies on* his conscience. [=he feels very guilty] • Her years *lie* lightly *upon* her. [=she seems younger than she is]

lie with [*phrasal verb*] **1** ***lie with (someone or something)*** *not used in the progressive tenses* — used to say who has the blame or responsibility for something • The blame *lies with* their mother for not watching them closely enough. • Responsibility for the accident *lies with* the company. **2** ***lie with (someone)*** *literary* **:** to have sex with (someone) • when he first *lay with* her

make your bed and lie in it see ¹BED

— compare ³LIE

²lie *noun, pl* **lies** [*count*] **:** the position in which something lies on the ground • a golf ball in a difficult *lie* — see also LIE OF THE LAND — compare ⁴LIE

³lie *verb* **lies; lied; ly•ing** [*no obj*]

1 : to say or write something that is not true in order to deceive someone **:** to tell a lie • I can't believe you *lied* to me. • He has been accused of *lying* about his military record. • She was *lying* when she told her parents that she had spent the afternoon studying. • She was ***lying through her teeth***. [=she was saying something completely untrue] • (*US, informal*) You can't trust that guy. He ***lies like a rug***. [=he lies constantly; he is dishonest]

2 : to indicate or suggest something that is not true or accurate • Statistics sometimes *lie*. [=do not accurately reflect the truth] • You may think that you still look young, but the mirror never *lies*. [=the mirror shows how you really look] – compare [1]LIE

[4]**lie** *noun, pl* **lies** [*count*] : something untrue that is said or written to deceive someone • She told a *lie* to her parents. • He has been accused of telling *lies* about his military record. • a bold/brazen/barefaced *lie* • a complete *lie* • The accusations are *lies*, all *lies*. • The claims he has made are nothing but a ***pack of lies***. • (*chiefly Brit*) He has woven a ***tissue of lies*** [=he has told many lies] about his military record. — see also WHITE LIE

give the lie to *formal* : to show that (something) is not true • Her success has *given the lie to* the notion that women cannot compete with men.

I tell a lie *Brit, informal* — used to correct something you have just said • I saw him just yesterday. No, *I tell a lie*. It was two days ago.

live a lie : to live in a false or deceptive way : to live in a way that does not show who you truly are or what your feelings truly are • Their friends thought that they had a happy marriage, but they were *living a lie*. [=their marriage was not happy] – compare [2]LIE

lie detector *noun, pl* ~ **-tors** [*count*] : a device used to measure the heart rate, breathing, etc., in order to find out if someone (such as a person suspected of a crime) is being honest • The murder suspect failed a *lie detector* test.

lie–down /ˈlaɪˌdaʊn/ *noun* [*singular*] *Brit* : a brief rest : NAP • They often have a *lie-down* in the afternoon. — see also *lie down* at [1]LIE

liege /ˈliːʤ/ *noun, pl* **lieg·es** [*count*] : a lord in the time of the Middle Ages

lie–in /ˈlaɪˌɪn/ *noun* [*singular*] *Brit, informal* : a time in the morning spent lying in bed instead of getting up • They had a nice long *lie-in* on the first morning of their holiday. — see also *lie in* at [1]LIE

lien /ˈliːn/ *noun, pl* **liens** [*count*] *law* : a legal claim that someone or something has on the property of another person until a debt has been paid back • The bank had a *lien* on our house. [=the bank had the right to take our house if we did not pay back the money we had borrowed to buy it]

lie of the land *noun* [*singular*] *Brit* : LAY OF THE LAND

lieu /ˈluː, *Brit* ˈljuː/ *noun*

in lieu of : in place of : instead of • *In lieu of* flowers, the family of the deceased has requested that donations be made to the church fund. • You can use your ATM card *in lieu of* cash.

lieut. *abbr* lieutenant

lieu·ten·ant /luˈtɛnənt, *Brit* lɛfˈtɛnənt/ *noun, pl* **-ants** [*count*]

1 : an officer in the army, navy, or air force with a fairly low rank • He was promoted to the rank of *lieutenant*. • Good morning, *Lieutenant* Smith. — abbr. *Lt.*; see also FIRST LIEUTENANT, SECOND LIEUTENANT

2 *US* : an officer in a fire or police department who has a rank below a captain

3 : an assistant to another, more powerful person : a person who represents and works for someone else • She has her best *lieutenants* working on a proposal. • one of the mobster's most loyal *lieutenants*

lieutenant colonel *noun, pl* ~ **-nels** [*count*] : a military officer who has a rank just below a colonel

lieutenant commander *noun, pl* ~ **-ers** [*count*] : an officer in the navy or coast guard who has a rank just below a commander

lieutenant general *noun, pl* ~ **-als** [*count*] : a military officer who has a rank just below a general

lieutenant governor *noun, pl* ~ **-nors** [*count*] : an elected official who is an assistant to the governor of a U.S. state

[1]**life** /ˈlaɪf/ *noun, pl* **lives** /ˈlaɪvz/

1 [*noncount*] : the ability to grow, change, etc., that separates plants and animals from things like water or rocks • He believes that God gives *life* to all creatures. • the miracle of *life* • eternal/everlasting *life*

2 a : the period of time when a person is alive [*noncount*] She knew what she wanted to do ***early in life***. [=when she was young] • He became famous relatively ***late in life***. [=at a relatively old age] • He became famous ***later in life***. = He became famous ***in later life***. [*count*] She was happy and healthy for most of her *life*. • The people in her family tend to have long/short *lives*. • I've known her all my *life*. • He is nearing the end of his *life*. • They spent their whole/entire *lives* in one town. = They lived in one town all their *lives*. • People can expect to change jobs several times in their *life/lives*. • They've been waiting their whole/entire *life/lives* for an opportunity like this. • This is the financial opportunity ***of his life***. [=*of his lifetime*; the best chance in his life to make money] **b** : the experience of being alive [*noncount*] What do you really want out of *life*? • He believes in living *life* to the fullest. [=in living a very full and rich life] • All this paperwork has made *life* much more difficult. • The details of everyday/ordinary *life* can be fascinating. • *life* in the city/country = city/country *life* • Sometimes *life* just isn't fair. • We can laugh at things in movies that would scare us in ***real life***. [=in a real situation; in actual existence] • Oh well, ***that's life***! [=bad things will happen, and you have to deal with them] • Despite the political upheaval, for most people ***life goes on*** as usual. [=the activities of life continue in the usual way] [*count*] What do you really want to do with your *life*? • Her children say that she has ruined their *lives*. • She talked about the men in her *life*. [=the men she has had a romantic or close relationship with during her life] • She has dedicated/devoted *her life* to helping other people. • All this paperwork has made my *life* much more difficult. • They're trying to ***get/put their lives back together***. [=to begin living in a normal way after suffering loss, hardship, etc.] • She was ***the love of my life***. [=the person I loved more than any other person at any time in my life] • I've never heard such a silly idea ***in all my life***! [=at any time] = Never ***in my life*** have I heard such a silly idea! • They're old enough to ***run/live their own lives***. [=to make their own decisions about how to live] • After all the problems they've had recently, they just want to ***get/move on with their lives***. [=to continue living their lives in the usual way] • I'm not surprised that I didn't get the job. That's ***the story of my life***. [=that's the way things usually or always happen in my life] — often used before another noun • She told us her ***life story***. [=she told us about many of the things that had happened to her in her life] • a lack of ***life experience*** [=experience and knowledge gained through living] ✧ If your ***life flashes/passes before your eyes*** or if your ***life flashes/passes before you***, many memories from different parts of your life quickly appear in your mind one after the other. • Her *life flashed before her eyes* when her car was about to crash.

3 [*count*] **a** : a specified part of a person's life • He talked about his *life* as an artist. • the social *lives* of college students • How's your love/sex *life*? • They had difficult home *lives* when they were children. • They are trying to keep their personal/private *lives* separate from their public *lives*. • the responsibilities of their family *life* **b** : a specified way or manner of living • He lived/led a *life* of crime. [=he was a criminal] • They have lived/led sheltered *lives*. • He is trying to make a better *life* for himself and his family. ✧ Your ***way of life*** is how you live your life. • a fisherman's *way of life* • Most people don't approve of my *way of life*. • a traditional *way of life*

4 [*count*] : the state or condition of being alive • They spared the horse's *life*. [=they did not kill the horse] • She feels that her *life* is in danger. = She ***fears for her life***. = She is ***in fear for her life***. [=she feels that she is in danger of being killed] • She ***risked her life*** [=she did something very dangerous that could have resulted in her death] to help him. • She ***gave/sacrificed her life*** [=she did something that resulted in her death] for her country. • He was ***running for his life***. [=he was running to escape from great danger] • He is ***fighting for his life***. [=he is very sick or injured and may die] • A would-be assassin ***made an attempt on the President's life***. [=tried to kill the President]

5 [*noncount*] : living things of a specified kind or in a specified place • There may be a great deal of animal/plant *life* still to be discovered in this region. • forest *life* • ocean *life* • Will we ever find intelligent *life* on other planets?

6 : the time when something exists or is useful or effective [*noncount*] battery *life* • the *life* of an insurance policy • They claim that using their product will extend the *life* of the car. • a warranty that is good for the *life* of the product [*count*] a product that extends the *lives* of the rugs/cars — see also HALF-LIFE, SHELF LIFE

7 [*noncount*] **a** : energy and spirit • eyes full of *life* • (*informal*) suck the *life* out of a room [=take all the fun and energy out of a group of people in a room] **b** : activity and movement • The streets were humming with *life*. [=the streets were filled with people and activity] • There were no signs of *life* in the deserted village.

8 [*count*] : a book that tells about the life of a person : BIOG-

RAPHY • She wrote a *life* of Napoleon. • Boswell's *Life of Johnson*

9 [*noncount*] : the punishment of being kept in a prison for the rest of your life : LIFE IMPRISONMENT • He was found guilty and sentenced to *life*. = (*informal*) He got *life*. = He was given *life*.

a dog's life see [1]DOG

a life of its own ✧ Something that ***takes on a life of its own*** becomes very large, important, or hard to control. • The project soon *took on a life of its own* and prevented us from getting any other work done. • The story *took on a life of its own* and began to appear on news broadcasts everywhere.

all walks of life *or* ***every walk of life*** see [2]WALK

a matter of life and death : something that is extremely important and often involves decisions that will determine whether someone lives or dies • Being prepared for severe weather can be *a matter of life and death*. — see also LIFE-AND-DEATH

a new lease on/of life see [1]LEASE

(as) big as life (*US*) *or chiefly Brit* ***(as) large as life*** *informal* : in person — used to describe the surprise of seeing someone • I never expected her to come to the party, but there she was, *as big as life*.

bet/stake your life on ✧ If you would *bet/stake your life on* something, you are very sure that it will happen. • "Will she keep her promise?" "I'd *bet/stake my life on* it!"

breathe (new) life into : to give new energy and excitement to (something) • She is credited with *breathing new life into* contemporary art. • The singer managed to *breathe life into* some tired old songs.

bring someone or something back to life : to cause someone or something that has died to begin living again • The story is about a mad scientist who tries to *bring* dead people *back to life*. — often used figuratively • They're trying to *bring* the restaurant *back to life* by introducing a new menu. • an old theory that is *being brought back to life*

bring something to life : to make something very interesting, appealing, or exciting • She *brings* history *to life* with her books.

come to life* 1** : to become very interesting, appealing, or exciting • The movie really *comes to life* when she appears on the screen. **2** *of a place* : to become filled with the energy and excitement of active people • Downtown *comes to life* each night when the clubs open. **3** *or* ***sputter/roar (etc.) to life *of a machine* : to begin working • The engine suddenly *roared to life*.

depart this life see DEPART

for dear life : very tightly or quickly because of fear or danger • He was hanging/holding on to the rope *for dear life*. • They were running *for dear life* to get away from the vicious dogs.

for life : for the whole of your life : for the rest of your life • They met in college and have remained friends *for life*. • He was sentenced to prison *for life*.

for the life of me *informal* : in any way at all — used to say that you are unable to remember or understand something • I couldn't *for the life of me* remember what her name was. • *For the life of me*, I can't think of any reasons why you wouldn't want a computer at home.

frighten/scare the life out of *informal* : to frighten (someone) very badly • You (nearly) *scared the life out of* me when you startled me like that!

from life *of a painting, drawing, etc.* : from looking at an actual person, object, etc. • drawings done *from life* rather than from photographs

get a life *informal* : to stop spending time doing or thinking about things that are not important or interesting : to begin to have a more interesting or exciting life • My girlfriend's parents are nice people, but all they do is watch TV all day. They need to *get a life*.

larger than life see [1]LARGE

lay down your life see *lay down* at [1]LAY

life depends on ✧ If your *life depends on* something, then you must do it. • His *life depends on* how he answers this question. • He was studying as if his *life depended on* it. — often used in negative statements • I wouldn't eat that food if my *life depended on* it. [=I would never eat it]

lose your life : to die • She nearly *lost her life* in a car accident. • Many *lives were lost*. [=many people died]

new life ✧ When something ***takes on (a) new life*** or when you ***give something new life*** or ***give new life to something***, it becomes more active, interesting, etc. • Plain old mashed potatoes *take on a new life* in this recipe. • Falling interest rates *gave new life to* the housing market.

not on your life *informal* — used as a very forceful way of saying "no" or "never" • Do the government's policies really help the average worker? *Not on your life.*

risk life and limb : to do something that is very dangerous • They *risked life and limb* to pull the child from the river.

save someone's life see [1]SAVE

spring into/to life see [2]SPRING

staff of life see [1]STAFF

such is life see [2]SUCH

take/claim someone's life : to cause someone's death • Two years ago he was diagnosed with the illness that eventually *took his life*. • The flood *claimed many lives*. [=caused the deaths of many people]

take your own life : to kill yourself • He threatened to *take his own life* [=*commit suicide*], but no one believed him.

the life of the party (*US*) *or chiefly Brit* ***the life and soul of the party*** : someone who is very lively and amusing at a party or other social gathering

the light of your life see [1]LIGHT

the next life *or* ***the life to come*** : a life that is believed by some people to come after death • He believed that he would see his family again in *the next life*.

the simple life see SIMPLE

to save your life see [1]SAVE

true to life see [1]TRUE

– see also FACT OF LIFE, GOOD LIFE, SLICE-OF-LIFE, STILL LIFE

[2]life *adj, always used before a noun*

1 : of or relating to life • the *life* force in all things

2 : done as long as a person lives : existing or lasting throughout a person's life • a *life* [=*lifelong*] member • my *life* savings [=all the money I have saved in my life] • He was given a *life* sentence in prison.

life–af·firm·ing /ˈlaɪfəˌfəmɪŋ/ *adj* [*more* ~; *most* ~] : indicating that life has value : positive and optimistic • Even though the heroine dies at the end, her struggle for a better world gives the movie a *life-affirming* message.

life–and–death *adj* : extremely important and serious especially because your survival or life may depend on success • They were engaged in a *life-and-death* struggle. • He plays every game like it's *life-and-death*. — see also *a matter of life and death* at [1]LIFE

life assurance *noun* [*noncount*] *Brit* : LIFE INSURANCE

life·blood /ˈlaɪfˈblʌd/ *noun* [*noncount*]

1 : the most important part of something : the part of something that provides its strength and energy • The town's *lifeblood* has always been its fishing industry. • The neighborhoods are the *lifeblood* of this city.

2 *literary* : a person's blood • the *lifeblood* that flows through his veins

life·boat /ˈlaɪfˌboʊt/ *noun, pl* **-boats** [*count*] : a boat used for saving people's lives; *especially* : a small boat that is carried on a ship and that is used for saving the lives of the passengers and crew if the ship sinks

life buoy *noun, pl* **~ buoys** [*count*] : a ring-shaped device that floats in water and that is used to keep a person from drowning

life cycle *noun, pl* **~ cycles** [*count*] *biology* : the series of stages through which a living thing passes from the beginning of its life until its death • the *life cycle* of a shark

life expectancy *noun, pl* **~ -cies** : the average number of years that a person or animal can expect to live [*noncount*] improvements in diet that have resulted in greater *life expectancy* for many people [*count*] calculating the *life expectancies* of different social groups — often used figuratively • What is the *life expectancy* of a new computer? [=how long can a new computer be expected to last or be useful?]

life form *noun, pl* **~ forms** [*count*] : a living thing of any kind • searching for alien *life forms* • higher *life forms* = more complex *life forms* • primitive/simple *life forms*

life–giv·ing /ˈlaɪfˌgɪvɪŋ/ *adj* [*more* ~; *most* ~] : giving or having power to create or support life : essential to life • the sun's *life-giving* energy

life·guard /ˈlaɪfˌgɑɚd/ *noun, pl* **-guards** [*count*] : a person whose job is to protect swimmers from drowning

life history *noun, pl* **~ -ries** [*count*] *biology* : the full range of changes, habits, and behaviors of a living thing over the course of its life • studying the *life history* of bears

life imprisonment *noun* [*noncount*] : the punishment of being kept in a prison for the rest of your life • The murderer was sentenced to *life imprisonment*.

life insurance *noun [noncount]* : a type of insurance that pays money to the family of someone who has died

life jacket *noun, pl* ~ **-ets** *[count]* : something that is worn over your upper body like a jacket or vest and that is designed to save you from drowning by holding you up when you are in water — called also *(US) life vest*

life·less /ˈlaɪfləs/ *adj [more ~; most ~]* : having no life: such as **a** : having no living things • a cold and *lifeless* landscape **b** : dead or appearing to be dead • a *lifeless* body **c** : lacking spirit, interest, or energy • The book's plot was *lifeless* and predictable.
– **life·less·ly** *adv* • His arms fell *lifelessly* to his sides. – **life·less·ness** *noun [noncount]*

life·like /ˈlaɪfˌlaɪk/ *adj [more ~; most ~]* : looking like a real person or thing • a very *lifelike* doll • The graphics in the video game are more *lifelike* than we imagined they would be. • a *lifelike* portrait

life jacket

life·line /ˈlaɪfˌlaɪn/ *noun, pl* **-lines** *[count]*
1 : something which provides help or support that is needed for success or survival • The river is the town's *lifeline*. • The new jobs were an economic *lifeline* for a city in need of help. • The radio was their *lifeline* to the outside world.
2 : a rope used for saving the life of someone (such as someone who has fallen into water) • They threw a *lifeline* to the man overboard.

life·long /ˈlaɪfˌlɑːŋ/ *adj, always used before a noun* : continuing or lasting through a person's life • He had a *lifelong* love of nature. • a *lifelong* friendship

life of Ri·ley /-ˈraɪli/ *noun*
the life of Riley informal + somewhat old-fashioned : a happy and comfortable life with few problems • He's been living/leading *the life of Riley*.

life–or–death *adj* : LIFE-AND-DEATH • a *life-or-death* struggle

life peer *noun, pl* ~ **peers** *[count]* : a British peer (sense 2) who has the title "Lord" or "Lady" for life but cannot pass it on to another person after death

life preserver *noun, pl* ~ **-ers** *[count] chiefly US* : a floating device that is designed to save you from drowning

lif·er /ˈlaɪfɚ/ *noun, pl* **-ers** *[count] informal*
1 *US* : a person who spends an entire career in the same job • He was a *lifer* at the factory. • an army *lifer*
2 : a criminal who has been sentenced to spend the rest of his or her life in prison • *lifers* seeking parole

life raft *noun, pl* ~ **rafts** *[count]* : a small rubber boat designed for saving the lives of people when a larger boat or ship sinks

life·sav·er /ˈlaɪfˌseɪvɚ/ *noun, pl* **-ers** *[count]*
1 : something that saves a person's life • a surgical procedure that has been a *lifesaver* for many people
2 : something or someone which provides help that is badly needed • This multipurpose tool can be a real *lifesaver* when something needs fixing. • Frozen dinners can be *lifesavers* for busy parents. • Thanks so much for offering to help. You're a real *lifesaver*!
3 *chiefly Australia* : LIFEGUARD

[1]**life·sav·ing** /ˈlaɪfˌseɪvɪŋ/ *adj, always used before a noun* : designed for or used in saving people's lives • a *lifesaving* surgical procedure

[2]**lifesaving** *noun [noncount]* : the skills needed to save the lives of people who are drowning • All lifeguards are trained in *lifesaving*.

life science *noun, pl* ~ **-ences** *[count]* : an area of science that deals with living things and life processes — usually plural • *life sciences* such as biology and medicine

life sentence *noun, pl* ~ **-tences** *[count]* : the punishment of being sent to prison for the rest of your life • He received a *life sentence* for his crimes.

life–size /ˈlaɪfˈsaɪz/ *also* **life–sized** /ˈlaɪfˈsaɪzd/ *adj* : having the same size as a real person or thing • a *life-size* image of a dog • a *life-size* model of a dinosaur • The statue was nearly twice *life-size*.

life span *noun, pl* ~ **spans** *[count]* : the amount of time that a person or animal actually lives • the average *life span* of house cats • increase/lengthen the human *life span* — often used figuratively • Recharging can extend the *life span* of a battery. • the *life span* of a building/appliance • the *life span* of a controversy

life·style /ˈlaɪfˌstajəl/ *noun, pl* **-styles** *[count]* : a particular way of living : the way a person lives or a group of people live • She envied the lavish *lifestyles* of wealthy people. • Eating right and exercising are essential to having/leading/living a healthy *lifestyle*.

life support *noun [noncount]*
1 *medical* : the equipment, material, and treatment needed to keep a very sick or hurt patient alive • He was removed from *life support*. • She was put/kept ***on life support***.
2 : the things that are needed to keep someone alive in a place (such as outer space) where life is usually not possible • equipment providing *life support* for astronauts
– **life–support** /ˈlaɪfsəˌpoɚt/ *adj, always used before a noun* • *life-support* equipment/machines • There was a problem with the submarine's *life-support* system.

life–sus·tain·ing /ˈlaɪfsəˌsteɪnɪŋ/ *adj* : helping someone or something to stay alive : supporting or extending life • *life-sustaining* medical treatment • The storm brought *life-sustaining* rain/water to the farms.

life's work *also US* **life·work** /ˈlaɪfˈwɚk/ *noun [noncount]* : the entire or main work of a person's life • She made photography her *life's work*.

life–threat·en·ing /ˈlaɪfˌθrɛtn̩ɪŋ/ *adj [more ~; most ~]* : capable of causing someone's death • a *life-threatening* disease/emergency • The injury wasn't *life-threatening*.

life·time /ˈlaɪfˌtaɪm/ *noun, pl* **-times** *[count]*
1 a : the time during which a person is alive • Four editions of the book were printed in his *lifetime*. [=during his life] • She has had a *lifetime* of hard work. [=she has worked hard all her life] • a *lifetime* spent traveling the world • I don't think it will happen in our *lifetime*. [=the time when we are alive] • She owns enough shoes to last (her) a *lifetime*. [=to last for the rest of her life] • the thrill ***of a lifetime*** [=a great thrill; the most exciting moment or event of a person's life] • This is the opportunity *of a lifetime*. = This sort of opportunity comes along ***once in a lifetime***. [=this is a very rare opportunity] — often used before another noun • He won a *lifetime* supply of ice cream. [=free ice cream for the rest of his life] • She was presented with a *lifetime* achievement award. [=an award for all the work she has done in her life] • a baseball player's *lifetime* batting average [=batting average measured over a baseball player's full career] **b** : a very long time • It would have taken me a *lifetime* to read all those books. • Childhood seems a *lifetime* ago now!
2 : the time during which something lasts or is useful • a chemical with a *lifetime* of only a few minutes • the *lifetime* of a planet/star/comet

life vest *noun, pl* ~ **vests** *[count] US* : LIFE JACKET

[1]**lift** /ˈlɪft/ *verb* **lifts; lift·ed; lift·ing**
1 a *[+ obj]* : to move (something or someone) to a higher position : RAISE • The paramedics *lifted* the stretcher into the ambulance. • *lift* a bucket of water • He *lifted* his foot from/off the gas pedal. • He *lifted* his pen from the paper. • She *lifted* her hands to the sky. • She *lifted* the child (up) onto her lap. • He *lifted* his head (up) and looked at us. • She *lifted* (up) the lid of the box. **b** *[no obj]* : to rise up from the ground or some other surface • The balloon *lifted* [=*rose*] into the sky.
2 *[+ obj]* : to move (someone or something) to a higher condition or position • The story *lifted* him to national recognition. • *lifting* people from poverty
3 ✧ If your ***spirits lift*** or your ***mood lifts*** or if something ***lifts your spirits/mood***, you become happier or less sad. • The beauty of the sunrise *lifted her spirits*. = Her *spirits lifted* when she saw the beauty of the sunrise.
4 ✧ When a ***weight/load/burden has been lifted from your shoulders/back***, you are able to stop worrying about some large problem or responsibility. • After I finally told my mother about my concerns, I felt as if a *weight had been lifted from my shoulders*. [=I felt very relieved]
5 *[+ obj]* : to increase the amount of (something) • The company has been trying to improve the quality of its products without *lifting* [=(more commonly) *raising*] prices.
6 *[+ obj]* : to make (your voice) louder • He barely *lifted* [=*raised*] his voice above a whisper. • The preacher told them to *lift* (up) their voices and sing.
7 *[+ obj] informal* **a** : to take (an idea, plan, etc.) *from* another source often in a way that is wrong • The plot of the movie was *lifted* [=*taken*] *from* real life. • an idea *lifted from* another novel **b** : to steal (something) • Somebody *lifted* her purse when she wasn't looking. **c** : to take (something) out

of a normal position or setting • *lift* a word out of context
8 [+ *obj*] **:** to stop or remove (something, such as a rule that prevents people from doing something) often for only a short time • *lift* a blockade • The city has temporarily *lifted* its ban on smoking in bars.
9 [*no obj*] *of fog, clouds, or smoke* **:** to move up and disappear so that it is possible to see • You can see the mountains when the clouds *lift.* • We were shocked by what we saw when the fog/smoke finally *lifted.* [=*cleared*]
10 [+ *obj*] **:** to move (someone or something) from one place to another in an aircraft **:** AIRLIFT • troops being *lifted* into enemy territory • supplies being *lifted* to remote areas
lift a finger see [1]FINGER
lift down [*phrasal verb*] ***lift (something) down also lift down (something)*** **:** to pick up (something) in order to move it to a lower position • I had to *lift* the box *down* from the top shelf to the floor.
lift off [*phrasal verb*] *of an airplane, rocket, etc.* **:** to rise up from the ground or another surface • planes *lifting off* from the runway • Thousands of spectators watched as the space shuttle *lifted off.* — see also LIFTOFF
lift weights **:** to exercise by lifting heavy objects (such as barbells) in order to become stronger • He has been *lifting weights* for exercise.
– lift•er *noun, pl* **-ers** [*count*] • a mechanical *lifter* — see also WEIGHT LIFTER

[2]lift *noun, pl* **lifts**
1 [*count*] **:** the act of raising or lifting something • a slight *lift* of his eyebrows
2 [*count*] **:** a free ride in a vehicle • Can I give you a *lift*? = Do you need a *lift*? • I need a *lift* to the bus station. • I got/hitched a *lift* [=(*US*) *ride*] home after the party.
3 [*count*] **a** *Brit* **:** ELEVATOR 1 • We took the *lift* to the fifth floor. **b :** SKI LIFT
4 [*singular*] **a :** a feeling of greater happiness • Her visit really gave me the *lift* I needed. [=made me feel better and happier] • The coach's speech gave the team a psychological *lift.* **b :** an improved state or condition • He claims that a tax cut will give the economy a *lift.* [=will improve the economy]
5 [*noncount*] *technical* **:** an upward force that makes it possible for aircraft to fly • a wing design that generates more *lift*

lift•off /ˈlɪftˌɑːf/ *noun, pl* **-offs :** the upward movement from the ground by a rocket, helicopter, or space vehicle as it begins flight [*noncount*] moments after *liftoff* • We have *liftoff*! [*count*] a series of successful *liftoffs* • Thousand of spectators gathered to watch the *liftoff* of the space shuttle. — see also *lift off* at [1]LIFT

lig•a•ment /ˈlɪgəmənt/ *noun, pl* **-ments** [*count*] **:** a tough piece of tissue in your body that holds bones together or keeps an organ in place • He sprained/tore *ligaments* in his knee. — compare TENDON

[1]light /ˈlaɪt/ *noun, pl* **lights**
1 [*noncount*] **:** the form of energy that makes it possible to see things **:** the brightness produced by the sun, by fire, a lamp, etc. • The *light* was bright/dazzling. • The landscape was bathed/awash in *light.* • a ray/shaft/beam of *light* • a source of *light* = a *light* source • a photograph taken in low/dim *light* • the *light* of the moon • a mixture of *light* and shadow • The windows let fresh air and *light* into the room. • a plant that grows best in direct/indirect *light* [=with light shining directly/indirectly on it] • ***natural light*** [=sunlight] • ***artificial light*** [=light produced by electric lamps] — sometimes used figuratively • He hates the harsh *light* of publicity.
2 [*count*] **a :** a source of light (such as an electric lamp) • turn/switch on/off the *light* • a fluorescent *light* • a *light* fixture [=a lamp that is permanently attached to a wall, ceiling, etc.] • a warning *light* • The *lights* suddenly went out. • The *lights* suddenly came on. • the twinkling *lights* of the city below • the bright *lights* of Broadway • a *light* switch [=a switch for turning lights on and off] • The *lights* are on, so there must be somebody at home. — see also NIGHTLIGHT **b :** a light on a vehicle • His car's battery died because he left his *lights* on.
3 [*singular*] **:** a way of showing or understanding something or someone • The situation looks less serious when looked at in a certain *light.* [=in a certain way] • I see things ***in a different light*** now. [=I see/understand things differently now] • The defendants were shown/depicted ***in a bad light*** [=in a way that made them seem bad] by the lawyer. • The news about his marital problems does not place/put him ***in a good light*** [=does not make him appear to be a good person] • She tried to explain her behavior ***in the best light*** possible. [=in a way that would make her appear as good as possible]
4 [*count*] **:** a light or set of lights used to control traffic **:** TRAFFIC LIGHT • Turn left at the next *light.* • The *light* was red. • We were waiting for the *light* to turn green.
5 [*singular*] *informal* **:** a flame for lighting a cigarette • I need a *light* for my cigarette. • Do you have a *light*? • I didn't have any matches, but a stranger gave me a *light.* [=lit my cigarette for me]
6 [*noncount*] *formal* **:** DAYLIGHT 1 • Things look different by ***the light of day.*** • We woke up ***at first light*** [=at dawn; at sunrise; when the sun came up] — see also SEE THE LIGHT OF DAY (below)
7 [*singular*] **:** a quality in a person's eyes that shows emotion • I saw the *light* of recognition in her eye.
8 ***lights*** [*plural*] **a :** light colors **:** colors that are more white than black • the composition of *lights* and darks in the painting/photograph **b :** light-colored clothes • Wash the *lights* and the darks separately.
according to your lights *formal* **:** according to your idea of what is right • You know my views on the matter; but of course you must act *according to your* (own) *lights.* [=you must be guided by your own opinions about what is right]
a light at the end of the tunnel **:** a reason to believe that a bad situation will end soon or that a long and difficult job will be finished soon • They are falling deeper into debt, and there is no *light at the end of the tunnel.* • The work on our house has been going on for months, but we're finally starting to see a *light at the end of the tunnel.*
bring (something) to light **:** to tell people about (something) **:** to make (something) known • Many new facts were *brought to light* during the investigation.
cast/shed/throw light on **:** to help to explain (something) **:** to make it possible to understand or know more about (something) • She is developing new theories that might *shed* some *light on* these unusual phenomena. • I hope my explanation *throws light on* their behavior.
come to light **:** to become known • Other details have *come to light* because of this investigation. • She was angry when it *came to light* that some people were being promoted unfairly.
hide your light under a bushel see BUSHEL
in someone's light **:** blocking the light that someone needs to see or read something • She asked him to move back a few steps because he was *in her light.*
in the cold light of day see [1]COLD
in the light of or *US* ***in light of*** **1 :** while thinking about (something that affects the way you see or understand things) • You should think about their advice *in light of* your own needs. • It is impossible to come to a conclusion *in the light of* the data we have here. • You should read the story *in light of* your own experiences. **2 :** because of (something) • It's a particularly important topic *in light of* recent events.
light dawns ✧ When people suddenly understand something that they had not understood before, ***(a/the) light dawns (on them).*** • When she saw the guilty look on her husband's face, a *light dawned,* and she knew he had been lying to her.
more heat than light see [1]HEAT
out like a light *informal* **1 :** ASLEEP • As soon as my head hit the pillow, I was *out like a light.* **2 :** UNCONSCIOUS • He took one punch to the jaw and was *out like a light.*
punch someone's lights out see [1]PUNCH
see the light *informal* **:** to suddenly understand or realize the truth of something • Many people doubted his theory, but most of them have now finally *seen the light.* [=most of them now realize that his theory is correct]
see the light of day **1 :** to be seen or used • our fine china, which hasn't *seen the light of day* in at least 10 years **2 :** to become publicly known • Important documents in this case have never *seen the light of day.* • Her theory first *saw the light of day* in a well-respected magazine.
set light to *chiefly Brit* **:** to cause (something) to begin burning • used a match to *set light to* [=*set fire to*] the paper
the light of your life **:** a person you love very much and who makes you happy • His daughter is *the light of his life.*
trip the light fantastic see [2]TRIP
– see also GREEN LIGHT, LEADING LIGHT, NORTHERN LIGHTS, SOUTHERN LIGHTS, *sweetness and light* at SWEETNESS

[2]light *adj* **light•er; -est**
1 : not dark or deep in color **:** PALE • *light* blue • She has a *light* complexion. • He has *light* [=*fair*] skin/hair.
2 a : having a lot of light **:** BRIGHT • a *light* and airy room **b**

: having the light of the day • We're planning to leave as soon as it's *light.* [=as soon as there is daylight] • We're hoping to arrive while it's still *light* out. [=to arrive before night has fallen] • In summer it ***gets light*** earlier and ***stays light*** later than in winter.
– compare ⁴LIGHT

³light *verb* **lights; light·ed** *or* **lit** /ˈlɪt/; **light·ing**
1 [+ *obj*] : to provide light for (something) • They used candles to *light* the room. = They *lighted/lit* the room with candles. • a dimly/poorly *lit* room • a brightly *lit* room • a well-*lighted* place • Our guide used a candle to ***light the way.*** [=to show the way that had to be followed]
2 a [+ *obj*] : to cause (something) to burn • *light* a match/candle • I *lit* (up) a cigarette for him. = I *lit* him a cigarette. — see also LIGHT UP 3 (below) **b** [*no obj*] : to begin to burn • waiting for the wood to *light*
light a fire under (someone) *US, informal* : to cause (someone) to move or work more quickly and effectively • I've never seen him work so hard. Someone must have *lit a fire under him.*
light into [*phrasal verb*] ***light into (someone)*** *US, informal* : to attack or criticize (someone) forcefully • He *lit into* his employees for their sloppy work. [=he criticized them very harshly] • She *lit into* her opponent and did not let up.
light on/upon [*phrasal verb*] ***light on/upon (something)*** : to find or see (something) by chance • Researchers have *lit upon* [=*found*] a solution. • His eye *lit on* a story in the newspaper.
light out [*phrasal verb*] *US, informal* : to leave in a hurry for someplace • He suddenly *lit out* for home.
light up [*phrasal verb*] **1 a** *of a light* : to become lit : to begin shining • All of the lights on the display suddenly *lit up.* — often used figuratively • His eyes/face *lit up* [=he looked very happy and pleased] when she walked in the room. **b** *informal, of a telephone* : to show a light indicating that someone is calling • When the DJ announced a contest, the phones *lit up.* [=the lights on the phones lit up because many people were calling] **2** ***light (something) up*** *or* ***light up (something)*** : to provide light for (something) : to fill (something) with light • *light up* a room = *light* a room *up* • Fireworks *lit up* the sky. — often used figuratively • A smile *lights up* her whole face. [=a smile makes her whole face look happy and radiant] • Her smile *lights up* the room. [=she has an extremely bright and attractive smile] **3** *informal* : to light a cigarette • I can't wait to *light up* [=smoke a cigarette] after work.

⁴light *adj* **lighter; -est**
1 a : not heavy : having little weight or less than usual weight • This suitcase is *light* enough for a child to carry. • The truck was carrying a *light* load. • "How heavy is it?" "Not very: it's actually quite *light.*" • It's very *light* in weight. = It's of very *light* weight. • This box is *lighter* than I thought it would be. • She would like to be a few pounds *lighter.* = She would like to be *lighter* by a few pounds. [=she would like to weigh less than she does by a few pounds] • Aluminum is a *light* metal. • lifting *light* weights • This box is ***as light as a feather.*** [=very light] **b** : small in size and weight • He has a *light* build.
2 a : less in amount or degree than usual • Only a *light* turnout is expected for the election. • Traffic was *light* this morning. • I have only a *light* course load this semester. • The stock market was slightly up today in *light* trading. • *light* rain/snow • She was wearing *light* makeup. • *light* perfume **b** : not strong or violent : MODERATE • a *light* breeze **c** : not great or large • The storm caused only *light* [=*slight*] damage. [=the storm did not cause much damage] • *light* competition • Casualties have so far been *light.* **d** : not difficult to accept or bear • a *light* responsibility : not harsh or severe • *light* punishment • He was given a surprisingly *light* sentence for his crimes. **e** : slight or minor in degree or effect • She has a *light* cold. • *light* discipline • These shrubs require only a little *light* pruning. — opposite HEAVY
3 : not involving a lot of physical effort • *light* lifting • doing a little *light* housework • *light* exercise/exertion • a *light* practice session • It's a big job, but ***many hands make light work*** [=if many people work on it, it will be easier to do] — opposite HEAVY
4 : not loud or forceful • *light* footsteps • a *light* tread • a *light* touch • just a *light* tap on the ball/shoulder — opposite HEAVY
5 : not important or serious : intended mainly for entertainment • doing some *light* reading — opposite HEAVY
6 : not dense and thick • He has a *light* beard. • a *light* growth of timber • an animal's *light* summer coat • *light* fog/smoke • *light* soil — opposite HEAVY
7 : made with thin cloth and not very warm • a *light* coat/blanket — opposite HEAVY
8 a : eating, drinking, or using a small amount of something • He's a *light* eater/smoker/drinker/user. • *light* alcohol consumption **b** : producing a small amount of something • a shrub that is a *light* bloomer [=a shrub that does not produce many flowers] **c** : not done often or in large amounts • *light* smoking — opposite HEAVY
9 a : not having a large amount of food : not making your stomach feel full • We ate a *light* lunch. • a *light* snack **b** : made with fewer calories or with less of some ingredient than usual • *light* beer **c** : not rich, dense, or thick • *light* cream • *light* syrup — opposite HEAVY
10 a : designed to carry a small load or few passengers • a *light* truck • a refueling point for ***light aircraft*** **b** : not as large and powerful as other weapons, machines, etc. • *light* artillery • *light* machinery **c** *of a group of soldiers* : having fewer and smaller weapons and less armor than other groups but able to move quickly • *light* infantry/cavalry
light on : having or using a small amount of (something) • a essay that is *light on* facts but heavy on speculation • She asked him to ***go light on*** the mustard. [=to not use a large amount of mustard]
light on your feet : capable of moving in a quick and graceful way • He's very *light on his feet* for such a big person.
light sleeper : someone who wakes up easily • She's a very *light sleeper.* The slightest noise will wake her.
make light of : to treat (something, such as a problem) in a joking way : to not be serious about (something important) • I don't mean to *make light of* this very serious issue. • He *made light of* his recent losses—but you could tell he was worried about them.
– compare ²LIGHT
– **light·ness** /ˈlaɪtnəs/ *noun* [*noncount*] • the *lightness* of the boxes • the *lightness* [=*delicacy, tenderness*] of her touch • the playful *lightness* of his manner • the *lightness* of her movements

⁵light *adv* **lighter; -est**
eat light *US* : to eat foods that will not cause you to gain weight • She is careful to *eat light* and exercise often.
travel light : to travel with little baggage • savvy vacationers who have learned to *travel light*

light bulb *noun, pl* **~ bulbs** [*count*] : a glass bulb or tube that produces light when it is supplied with electricity • change a *light bulb* that has burned out — called also *bulb*
a light bulb goes off/on *chiefly US, informal* ✧ When *a light bulb goes off/on* (*in your head*), you suddenly understand something or have a great idea. • After thinking about the problem for several days, a *light bulb went off in her head,* and she knew how to solve it.

¹light·en /ˈlaɪtn̩/ *verb* **-ens; -ened; -en·ing**
1 [+ *obj*] : to make (something) bright, light, or clear • She tried several dyes to *lighten* her hair. • He turned on a few lamps to *lighten* (up) the room.
2 [*no obj*] : to become bright, light, or clear • The sky *lightened* [=*brightened*] as the clouds began to move away but darkened again when the clouds returned.
– compare ²LIGHTEN
– **light·en·er** /ˈlaɪtn̩ɚ/ *noun, pl* **-ers** [*count*] • a hair/skin *lightener* [=a chemical or dye used to make a person's hair or skin less dark]

²lighten *verb* **-ens; -ened; -en·ing**
1 a [+ *obj*] : to make (something) less heavy, difficult, or severe • *lighten* a burden • Others helped out and *lightened* his load. • *lightening* her duties around the house **b** [*no obj*] : to become less heavy, difficult, or severe • His workload has *lightened* in recent weeks.
2 a [+ *obj*] : to make (something) less sad or serious • He told a few jokes in an attempt to *lighten* her mood. • *lighten* the atmosphere/conversation **b** [*no obj*] : to become less sad or serious • Her somber mood gradually *lightened* [=*brightened*] as the weather improved.
3 [*no obj*] : to become less forceful • The wind *lightened* a bit.
lighten up [*phrasal verb*] *informal* : to become more relaxed and informal : to stop being serious, worried, etc. • He really needs to *lighten up* and relax a little. — often used as a command • *Lighten up* (a bit) and enjoy yourself!
– compare ¹LIGHTEN

light·er /ˈlaɪtɚ/ *noun, pl* **-ers** [*count*] : a small device that produces a flame used for lighting something (such as a ciga-

L

rette) ▪ a cigarette *lighter* ▪ ***lighter fluid*** [=the liquid in a lighter that is its fuel]

lighter–than–air *adj* **:** able to float in the air ▪ a *lighter-than-air* balloon

light–fin·gered /ˈlaɪtˌfɪŋgɚd/ *adj* [*more* ~; *most* ~] **:** skillful at stealing things ▪ He discovered his wallet had been taken by some *light-fingered* thief.

light–foot·ed /ˈlaɪtˌfʊtəd/ *adj* [*more* ~; *most* ~] **:** able to move in a quick and graceful way ▪ a *light-footed* dancer

light–head·ed /ˈlaɪtˌhɛdəd/ *adj* [*more* ~; *most* ~] **:** unable to think and move in a normal way because of a weak and dizzy feeling ▪ I began to feel *light-headed* from lack of sleep. ▪ Standing up too quickly usually makes her *light-headed*.
– light–head·ed·ness *noun* [*noncount*] ▪ The patient complained of *light-headedness*. [=*dizziness*]

light·heart·ed /ˈlaɪtˌhɑɚtəd/ *adj* [*more* ~; *most* ~]
1 : having or showing a cheerful and happy nature ▪ a *lighthearted* mood ▪ a *lighthearted* young woman
2 : not serious ▪ a *lighthearted* comedy
– light·heart·ed·ly *adv* **– light·heart·ed·ness** *noun* [*noncount*]

light heavyweight *noun, pl* ~ **-weights** [*count*] **:** a fighter who is in a class of boxers with an upper weight limit of 175 pounds (79.5 kilograms) **:** a boxer who is heavier than a middleweight and lighter than a heavyweight

light·house /ˈlaɪtˌhaʊs/ *noun, pl* **-hous·es** [*count*] **:** a tower with a powerful light that is built on or near the shore to guide ships away from danger

light industry *noun* [*noncount*] **:** the production of small goods that will be sold to the people who use them rather than to another manufacturer — compare HEAVY INDUSTRY

light·ing /ˈlaɪtɪŋ/ *noun* [*noncount*]
1 a : light that is of a particular kind or that has a particular quality ▪ He prefers natural *lighting* for his photography. ▪ artificial *lighting* ▪ The *lighting* wasn't bright enough. ▪ The street *lighting* was so dim I got lost. **b :** the equipment used to provide light ▪ There was a problem with the *lighting*. ▪ a company that sells *lighting* equipment
2 : the use of light for a particular purpose in a movie, play, etc. ▪ He's in charge of the *lighting* for the show.

light·ly /ˈlaɪtli/ *adv* [*more* ~; *most* ~] **:** in a light manner: such as **a :** with little weight or force ▪ The rain fell *lightly* [=*softly*] on the roof. ▪ She touched his hand *lightly*. [=*gently*] ▪ The recipe says that you should beat the eggs *lightly*. [=*gently*] **b :** without care or concern **:** in a way that is not serious ▪ He talks *lightly* about the problems he's been having at work. ▪ This is a problem that should not be ***taken lightly***. [=this is a problem that should be treated seriously] **c :** in a quick and graceful way ▪ She moved *lightly* across the room. **d :** in a small amount **:** to a small degree or extent ▪ *lightly* [=*slightly*] salted/roasted peanuts ▪ *lightly* buttered toast ▪ These vegetables can be eaten either raw or *lightly* cooked. ▪ a *lightly* populated area ▪ Our troops were armed too *lightly* to take on the heavily armed invaders. **e :** in a way that is not as harsh or severe as it could or should be ▪ Considering the harm he did, he's ***gotten off lightly*** with only a warning. ▪ The judge ***let her off lightly*** with a short sentence.

light meter *noun, pl* ~ **meters** [*count*] **:** a small device used by photographers to measure the amount of light in an area

[1]light·ning /ˈlaɪtnɪŋ/ *noun* [*noncount*] **:** the flashes of light that are produced in the sky during a storm ▪ a bolt of *lightning* = a *lightning* bolt ▪ a flash of *lightning* ▪ The tree was hit/struck by *lightning*. = The tree was hit by a ***lightning strike***. — compare THUNDER; see also HEAT LIGHTNING
catch/capture lightning in a bottle *chiefly US* **:** to succeed in a way that is very lucky or unlikely ▪ He *caught lightning in a bottle* with the success of his very first book.
lightning never strikes (the same place) twice — used to say that a very unusual event is not likely to happen again to the same person or in the same place
like (greased) lightning *informal* **:** very quickly ▪ The news traveled across the country *like lightning*. ▪ moving *like greased lightning*

[2]lightning *adj, always used before a noun* **:** moving or done very quickly ▪ thoughts moving at *lightning* speed
– lightning *adv* — used in combination ▪ an athlete with *lightning*-quick reflexes ▪ making *lightning*-fast adjustments

lightning bug *noun, pl* ~ **bugs** [*count*] *US* **:** FIREFLY

lightning conductor *noun, pl* ~ **-tors** [*count*] *Brit* **:** LIGHTNING ROD 1

lightning rod *noun, pl* ~ **rods** [*count*] *US*
1 : a metal rod that is placed on a building and connected with the ground below to protect the building from being damaged by lightning
2 : someone or something that attracts criticism or gets blamed when things go wrong ▪ He has served well as his boss's *lightning rod*. [=he takes blame or criticism that might have been directed at his boss] — often + *for* ▪ He has long been a *lightning rod for* controversy/criticism. ▪ The company has become a *lightning rod for* the public's anger.

lightning strike *noun, pl* ~ **strikes** [*count*] *Brit* **:** a strike by workers that is done very suddenly

light pen *noun, pl* ~ **pens** [*count*] *computers* **:** a device shaped like a pen that senses light signals and is used to work with information on a computer screen ▪ writing/drawing with a *light pen*

light pollution *noun* [*noncount*] **:** light from cities, vehicles, etc., that makes it difficult to see things in the sky (such as stars) at night

light show *noun, pl* ~ **shows** [*count*] **:** a display of moving colored lights

lights–out /ˈlaɪtsˈaʊt/ *noun* [*noncount*] **:** a time when people

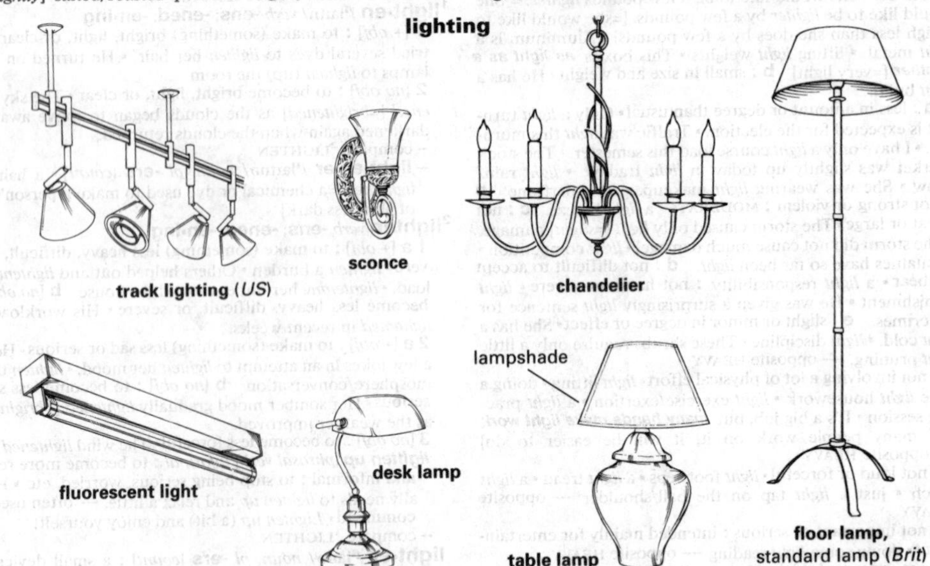

(such as soldiers, prisoners, or students) are required to turn out the lights and go to bed • *Lights-out* is at 10 p.m. • They have to be back before *lights-out*.

light·weight /ˈlaɪtˌweɪt/ *noun, pl* **-weights** [*count*]
1 : a fighter who is in a class of boxers weighing from 125 to 132 pounds (57 to 60 kilograms) — often used before another noun • a *lightweight* boxer • He won the *lightweight* title.
2 : someone or something that does not weigh as much as others — usually used before another noun • *lightweight* paper • *lightweight* cotton/wool/silk • a *lightweight* jacket
3 : someone or something that has little importance or power • The members of his staff were considered *lightweights*. • an intellectual *lightweight* — often used before another noun • He was dismissed as a *lightweight* artist. • They asked her several *lightweight* questions.

light–year /ˈlaɪtˌjiɚ/ *noun, pl* **-years**
1 [*count*] *technical* **:** a unit of distance equal to the distance that light travels in one year (about 5.88 trillion miles or 9.46 trillion kilometers) • a star about 10 *light-years* away
2 ***light-years*** [*plural*] **a** — used to say that someone or something is much better or more advanced than others • This new technology puts the company *light-years* ahead [=very far ahead] of its competitors. **b** — used to refer to a time that is or seems very far away • A cure for that disease is still probably *light-years* away.

lik·able *or* **like·able** /ˈlaɪkəbəl/ *adj* [*more* ~; *most* ~] **:** easy to like **:** having pleasant or appealing qualities • Detective Grant is the most *likeable* character in the novel. • She seems like a friendly, *likable* young woman.
– lik·abil·i·ty *or* **like·abil·i·ty** /ˌlaɪkəˈbɪləti/ *noun* [*noncount*]

[1]like /ˈlaɪk/ *verb* **likes; liked; lik·ing**
1 [+ *obj*] **a :** to enjoy (something) **:** to get pleasure from (something) • My son *likes* baseball. • He *likes* baseball, but he loves football. • Do you *like* Mexican food? • I *liked* the movie a lot more than I thought I would. • She *likes* (it) that I play the guitar. = She *likes* the fact that I play the guitar. • She *likes* it when I play the guitar. [=she enjoys hearing me play the guitar] • I *like* it very much. = I really *like* it. = (*chiefly Brit*) I quite *like* it. — often + *-ing verb* • I *like playing* the guitar. • He doesn't *like admitting* that he was wrong. — often followed by *to + verb* • I *like to play* the guitar. • He doesn't *like to admit* that he was wrong. **b :** to regard (something) in a favorable way • I don't *like* the idea of leaving my mother alone all week. [=I don't think that it would be a good idea to leave my mother alone all week] • I wouldn't *like* it if you got the wrong idea. = I wouldn't *like* you to get the wrong idea. = (*US*) I wouldn't *like* for you to get the wrong idea. [=I don't want you to get the wrong idea]
2 [+ *obj*] **:** to feel affection for (someone) **:** to enjoy being with (someone) • I don't know what it is about that guy, but I just don't *like* him. • I think she *likes* you. [=I think she is attracted to you] • They were political allies who truly/genuinely *liked* each other. • What is it that you *like* or dislike about him most? • a much-*liked*/well-*liked* colleague • She says she *likes* him as a friend but she's not attracted to him. • My boss was a tough guy, but I *liked* him for his honesty.
3 [+ *obj*] — used to ask about someone's feelings or opinion about something • So ***how do you like*** sailing now that you've tried it? [=do you like or dislike sailing?] • "*How do you like* this weather?" "I don't *like* it at all!" • "*How do you like* Mexican food?" "I love it!"
4 [+ *obj*] **a :** to want to have (something) — used with *would* to make a polite suggestion, offer, or request • Would you *like* another cup of coffee? • "Would anyone *like* a drink?" "Yes, I'd *like* one, please." • I'd *like* (a chance) to reply to the last speaker. **b :** to want or prefer *to do* something • Would you *like to go* sailing? [=do you want to go sailing?] • Despite everything, I (would) still *like to think* that people are basically good. **c** — used in various spoken phrases that typically express anger or surprise • She left without saying a word to me. ***How would you like it*** if someone ignored you that way? = *How would you like* being ignored that way? = *How would you like* to be ignored that way? [=don't you agree that it was wrong of her to ignore me that way?] • "So she just left without saying a word. ***How do you like that?***" "Incredible!" • (*Brit*) "You never listen!" "*I never listen? **I like that!***" [=that's not at all true/fair] • "You're an idiot!" "***How would you like*** a punch in the nose?!" [=I'm going to punch you in the nose if you keep talking to me that way] • "He thinks he can beat you." "***I'd (just) like to see him try!***" [=he can't beat me; he would lose if he tried to beat me]
5 [+ *obj*] **:** to choose or prefer to have (something) in a specified way or condition • "How do you *like* your steaks cooked?" "I *like* my steaks medium rare."
6 [*no obj*] **:** to make a choice about what to do, have, etc. • You can leave any time you *like*. • "What should we do now?" "Whatever you *like*!" [=whatever you want to do] • We can stay as long as you *like*. [=as long as you want to stay] • There are plenty of cookies, so take as many as you *like*.
7 [+ *obj*] **:** to do well in (certain conditions) • This plant *likes* dry soil. • My car does not *like* cold weather.
if you like **1 a** — used to say that you can do something if you want to do it • Have another drink, *if you like*. **b** — used to agree politely to a suggestion or request • "Could we stay a little longer?" "Yes, *if you like*." [=if that's what you want to do] **2** *chiefly Brit* — used to suggest a possible way of describing or thinking about something • The experience was, *if you like* [=*if you will*], a glimpse of the future.

[2]like *noun, pl* **likes** [*count*] **:** something that you like, approve of, or enjoy — usually plural • my *likes* and dislikes — compare [5]LIKE

[3]like *prep*
1 : similar to (something or someone) • The house looks *like* a barn. • Real life isn't at all *like* life in the movies. = Real life isn't at all *like* the movies. • It's *like* when we were kids. • She's not very (much) *like* her sister. • She's not at all *like* her sister. • The baby is/looks more *like* his mother than his father. • "Who is he *like*?" "He's not *like* anyone I've ever met before." • I know I used to be selfish, but I'm ***not like that*** any more. [=I'm not selfish any more] — used with *what* in phrases that ask about or refer to the qualities of a person or thing • "*What's* her new boyfriend *like*?" [=how would you describe her new boyfriend?] "He's very nice." • I don't know *what* the food is *like* in that restaurant. [=I don't know if the food is good or bad in that restaurant] • I thought he was nice, but then I found out *what* he's really *like*. [=I found out what kind of person he really is] • She knows *what* it's *like* to be lonely. = She knows *what* it feels *like* to be lonely.
2 : typical of (someone) • It's just *like* him to be late. [=he is often late] • It's not *like* her to be so selfish. [=she is not usually so selfish]
3 : comparable to or close to (something) • It costs ***something like*** five dollars. [=it costs about five dollars] • (*chiefly Brit*) That's ***nothing like*** [=*nowhere near, not nearly*] enough food! • I thought it would only take two or three minutes, but it ended up taking ***more like*** half an hour. [=it took about half an hour] • There's ***nothing like*** [=nothing better than] a mug of hot chocolate on a cold winter's night.
4 : in a way that is similar to (someone or something) • Quit acting *like* a fool. • She was screaming *like* a maniac. • We'll blow it up *like* a balloon. • He was laughing *like* a hyena.
5 — used to introduce an example or series of examples • They studied subjects *like* [=*such as*] physics (and chemistry).
it looks like rain — used to say that you think it is going to rain soon • I was going to play golf, but *it looks like rain*.
just like that see [2]JUST
like father, like son see [1]FATHER
like new see [1]NEW
like so **:** in the manner shown — used in speech when you are showing someone how to do something • The corner of the cloth should be folded down, *like so*.
like that **1 :** of that kind • I love books *like that*. **2 :** in that manner • Why does she talk *like that*?
like this **1 :** of this kind • I love weather *like this*. **2 :** in this manner • I hate it when it rains *like this*.
more like it *informal* — used to say that something is better or more pleasing • "I've done twice as much today as yesterday!" "Well, ***that's more like it***. Congratulations!" • It was a long and tiring day, but as the waiter brought me my dinner, I thought to myself, "Well, ***this is more like it***."

[4]like *adj* **:** having the same or similar qualities • All three sisters have *like* [=(more commonly) *similar*] dispositions.

[5]like *noun, pl* **likes** [*count*] **:** a person or thing that is similar to another person or thing • We may never see his *like* again. [=we may never see another person who is like him again] • It was a beautiful sunset. I've never seen the *like* before.; *also* **:** a group of similar people or things • He and his *like* [=*type*] tend to scare people away from the cause. • comparing *like* with *like* [=comparing similar people or things]
and the like **:** and others of a similar kind **:** and so forth • They told stories about ghosts and vampires *and the like*.
the likes of *also* ***the like of*** **1 :** such people as • She has read the complete works of many great writers, including *the likes of* Jane Austen and Robert Browning. **2** *disapproving* **:** such a person as • We have no use for *the likes of*

L

you. **3 : the kind or sort of** ▪ It was a beautiful sunset, *the likes of* which I've never seen before. [=I've never seen such a beautiful sunset before]
– compare ²LIKE

⁶like *adv*
as like as not *or* ***like as not*** **: PROBABLY** ▪ *Like as not* the crime will never be solved.

> ***usage*** **Like has many uses in informal speech, especially in the speech of young people. It is commonly used to emphasize a word or phrase.** ▪ He was, *like*, gorgeous. ▪ (*chiefly Brit*) He was gorgeous, *like*. **It is used in a way that shows you are not sure or confident about what you are saying.** ▪ I need to, *like*, borrow money. ▪ Her father is, *like*, a scientist or something. ▪ I think it costs, *like*, 20 dollars. **In very informal speech in U.S. English, it is used with the verb *be* to say what someone thinks, says, etc.** ▪ She was telling me what to do and I was *like* [=I was thinking], "Mind your own business." ▪ She was *like*, "Are you sure you want to do this?" and I was *like* "Yeah, why not?" [=she said, "Are you sure you want to do this?" and I said, "Yeah, why not?"] ▪ He's always criticizing everyone but it's *like*, "Who cares what he thinks?" [=he's always criticizing everyone but no one cares what he thinks]

⁷like *conj, informal*
1 a : the way it would be if ▪ The plane looked *like* [=*as if*] it would crash. ▪ It seemed *like* [=*as if*] he'd never been away. **b : the way someone would do if** ▪ She acts *like* [=*as if*] she's better than us.
2 : the same as : AS ▪ You sound just *like* [=*the way*] he does. ▪ Does it look *like* [=*the way, as*] it did when you began? ▪ Does it look now *like* (it did) before? [=does it look now as it did before?] ▪ Real life is not *like* [=*as, the way*] it is in the movies. ▪ Real life isn't at all *like* [=*the way*] the movies are. ▪ ***Like I said*** [=*as I said*] before, you've got to try harder.
3 : in the way or manner that ▪ I did it *like* [=*the way, just as*] you told me.
4 : such as ▪ a bag *like* a doctor carries [=a bag like the kind of bag that a doctor carries] ▪ The book tells you what to do when your car has trouble—*like* when it won't start. [=as, for example, when it won't start]

> ***usage*** **The use of *like* as a conjunction is regarded by some people as an error. It occurs mainly in speech and informal writing.**

-like /ˌlaɪk/ *adj combining form*
1 : similar to or resembling ▪ a large, ape*like* man
2 : like that or those of ▪ lady*like* steps ▪ child*like* innocence ▪ a home*like* atmosphere

likeable *variant spelling of* **LIKABLE**

like·li·hood /ˈlaɪkliˌhʊd/ *noun* **: the chance that something will happen** [*noncount*] A poor diet increases the *likelihood* of (developing) serious health problems. [=a poor diet makes it more likely that you will develop serious health problems] ▪ There is no *likelihood* of that happening. [=there is no chance of that happening] ▪ There is every *likelihood* that he will be reelected. [=he will almost certainly be reelected] ▪ ***In all likelihood*** it will rain tomorrow. [=it is very likely that it will rain tomorrow] [*singular*] There is a strong *likelihood* that he will be reelected.

¹like·ly /ˈlaɪkli/ *adj* **like·li·er; -est** [*or* *more* ~; *most* ~]
1 — used to indicate the chance that something will happen ▪ The car is *likely* to break down soon. = It's *likely* that the car will break down soon. [=there is a good chance that the car will break down soon] ▪ It is/seems highly/very *likely* that it will rain tomorrow. ▪ She doesn't seem *likely* to get the job. ▪ She may get the job, but it isn't *likely*. ▪ "Will she get the job?" "***Not likely***." [=she probably will not get the job] ▪ It's ***more than likely*** [=very probable] that this problem will occur again.
2 : seeming to be true : BELIEVABLE ▪ That seems to be the most *likely* explanation. ◇ The phrase ***a likely story*** is often used in an informal way to say that you do not believe what someone has said. ▪ He says he bought all that chocolate for his daughter, not himself. *A likely story*!
3 *always used before a noun* **: seeming to be right or suited for a purpose** ▪ This looks like a *likely* spot for a picnic. ▪ They regard him as a *likely* candidate for the job.
– like·li·ness *noun* [*noncount*]

²likely *adv* [*more* ~; *most* ~] **: without much doubt : PROBABLY** ▪ He'll very *likely* be late. ▪ It will ***most likely*** rain tomorrow. [=it will probably rain tomorrow] ▪ "Will it rain tomorrow?" "***Most likely***." ▪ She will ***more than likely*** not get the job. [=she will very probably not get the job]

> ***usage*** **In U.S. English, the adverb *likely* is often used by itself without *most, quite, very*, etc.** ▪ He will *likely* [=*probably*] be late. ▪ It will *likely* rain tomorrow. **This use of *likely* has sometimes been criticized, but it is very common. It does not occur in highly formal writing.**

like·ly–look·ing /ˈlaɪkliˈlʊkɪŋ/ *adj* **like·li·er–look·ing; like·li·est–look·ing** [*or* *more* ~; *most* ~] **: seeming to be right or suited for a purpose : LIKELY** ▪ This is a *likely-looking* spot for a picnic.

like–mind·ed /ˈlaɪkˈmaɪndəd/ *adj* **: having similar opinions and interests** ▪ He joined a local activists' group, hoping to meet *like-minded* people. [=people who shared his opinions]
– like–mind·ed·ness *noun* [*noncount*]

lik·en /ˈlaɪkən/ *verb* **-ens; -ened; -en·ing**
liken to [*phrasal verb*] ***liken (someone or something) to (someone or something)*** **: to describe (someone or something) as similar to (someone or something else)** ▪ Some critics have *likened* [=*compared*] his writing *to* Faulkner's. ▪ She *likened* her trip *to* a pilgrimage.

like·ness /ˈlaɪknəs/ *noun, pl* **-ness·es**
1 [*count*] **: a picture of a person : PORTRAIT** ▪ a stamp bearing the *likeness* of a president ▪ The painting is ***a good likeness*** of her. [=the painting looks very much like her]
2 : the quality or state of being alike or similar especially in appearance [*noncount*] People always remarked on his *likeness* [=*resemblance*] to his late father. ▪ There's some *likeness* between them. [*count*] There's an uncanny *likeness* between them. ▪ In comparing the two documents, researchers have noted some surprising *likenesses*. [=*similarities*]

like·wise /ˈlaɪkˌwaɪz/ *adv*
1 : in the same way ▪ All of your classmates have begun their projects, and you should do *likewise*. [=you should also begin your project]
2 : in addition : ALSO ▪ an acclaimed painter who is *likewise* a sculptor **— often used to introduce a statement that adds to and is related to a previous statement** ▪ They said that homelessness was increasing. *Likewise*, unemployment was up.
3 — used in informal speech to say that you share the feelings that someone else has just expressed ▪ "I'm pleased to meet you." "*Likewise*." [=I'm also pleased to meet you]

lik·ing /ˈlaɪkɪŋ/ *noun* [*singular*] **: the feeling of liking or enjoying something or someone** ▪ The colors are too bright ***for my liking***. [=I like colors that are less bright] **— usually + *for*** ▪ He has a (strong) *liking for* spicy foods. [=he likes spicy foods] ▪ She has a *liking for* loud music. ▪ She never showed any *liking for* him.
take a liking to **: to begin to like (someone or something)** ▪ He *took a liking to* his new neighbor. ▪ She *took an immediate liking to* sailing when she tried it for the first time.
to someone's liking **: appealing or enjoyable to someone** ▪ She reads poetry, but fiction is much more *to her liking*.

li·lac /ˈlaɪˌlæk, *Brit* ˈlaɪlək/ *noun, pl* **-lacs**
1 [*count*] **: a type of bush with purple or white flowers that bloom in the spring**
2 [*noncount*] **: a light purple color — see color picture on page C3**

lilt /ˈlɪlt/ *noun* [*singular*] **: the attractive quality of speech or music that rises and falls in a pleasing pattern** ▪ There was a charming *lilt* to her voice. ▪ a tune with a *lilt*
– lilt·ing /ˈlɪltɪŋ/ *adj* [*more* ~; *most* ~] ▪ a *lilting* melody ▪ a *lilting* voice ▪ the *lilting* rhythms of her speech **– lilt·ing·ly** *adv*

lily /ˈlɪli/ *noun, pl* **lil·ies** [*count*] **: a type of plant that has large white or colorful bell-shaped flowers;** *also* **: the flower — see color picture on page C6; see also WATER LILY**
gild the lily see **GILD**

lily–liv·ered /ˈlɪliˈlɪvəd/ *adj* [*more* ~; *most* ~] *informal* + *old-fashioned* **: lacking courage : COWARDLY** ▪ He considers his political enemies a bunch of *lily-livered* hypocrites.

lily of the valley *noun, pl* **lilies of the valley** [*count*] **: a small plant that produces small white flowers shaped like little bells**

lily pad *noun, pl* ~ **pads** [*count*] **: a large, floating leaf of a plant (called a water lily) that grows in the water of a pond or pool**

lily–white /ˈlɪliˈwaɪt/ *adj*
1 : very white ▪ a *lily-white* wedding dress ▪ *lily-white* skin
2 [*more* ~; *most* ~] **: completely without fault or blame**

: morally pure ▪ She's not as *lily-white* as you might think.
3 *chiefly US, disapproving* : consisting entirely or mostly of white people ▪ He grew up in a *lily-white* suburb in the Midwest. ▪ a TV show with a *lily-white* cast

li·ma bean /ˈlaɪmə-, *Brit* ˈliːmə-/ *noun, pl* **~ beans** [*count*] : a type of flat and pale green or white bean

limb /ˈlɪm/ *noun, pl* **limbs** [*count*]
1 : a leg or arm ▪ Many soldiers died in the battle, and many lost *limbs*. ▪ an artificial *limb* ▪ a dog with an injured *limb*
2 : a large branch of a tree ▪ They tied a rope to one of the *limbs* of the maple tree. — see color picture on page C6
out on a limb : in or into a risky or dangerous position or situation ▪ She went *out on a limb* to help you. [=she took a chance; she did something that meant she could be criticized or harmed in some way] ▪ If you try to oppose the boss yourself, you're likely to get caught *out on a limb*.
risk life and limb see [1]LIFE
tear (someone) limb from limb : to attack or kill (someone) in a very violent way ▪ The angry mob would have *torn him limb from limb* if the police hadn't protected him.
– limbed /ˈlɪmd/ *adj* — used in combination ▪ a strong-*limbed* young man [=a young man with strong arms and legs]

[1]**lim·ber** /ˈlɪmbɚ/ *adj* : bending easily : FLEXIBLE — used of people or their bodies ▪ a *limber* gymnast ▪ Yoga requires a *limber* body.

[2]**limber** *verb* **-bers; -bered; -ber·ing**
limber up [*phrasal verb*] : to prepare for physical activity by doing exercises so that your body can move and bend more easily ▪ She *limbered up* for a few minutes before starting to run. — sometimes used figuratively ▪ She *limbered up* for the election by learning the relevant statistics.

[1]**lim·bo** *or* **Lim·bo** /ˈlɪmboʊ/ *noun* [*singular*] *in the Roman Catholic religion* : a place where the souls of people who have not been baptized go after death
in limbo **1** : in a forgotten or ignored place, state, or situation ▪ orphaned children left *in limbo* in foster homes and institutions **2** : in an uncertain or undecided state or condition ▪ After graduating from college, he was *in limbo* for a while, trying to decide what to do next.
– compare [2]LIMBO

[2]**limbo** *noun* [*noncount*] : a dance or contest in which you have to bend backward and go under a bar which is lowered further after each time you go under it ▪ do/dance *the limbo* ▪ a *limbo* dancer — compare [1]LIMBO

[1]**lime** /ˈlaɪm/ *noun, pl* **limes**
1 : a small green fruit that is related to the lemon and orange and has a sour taste [*count*] The recipe calls for the juice of two *limes*. [*noncount*] a slice of *lime* — often used before another noun ▪ *lime* juice ▪ *lime* trees — see color picture on page C5
2 [*noncount*] : LIME GREEN
– compare [2]LIME, [3]LIME

[2]**lime** *noun* [*noncount*] : a white substance that is made by heating limestone or shells and that is used in various products (such as plaster and cement) and in farming ▪ He spread *lime* over the garden to make the soil less acidic. — compare [1]LIME, [3]LIME
– lime /ˈlaɪm/ *verb* **limes; limed; lim·ing** [+ *obj*] ▪ *lime* a garden [=spread lime on a garden]

[3]**lime** *noun, pl* **limes** [*count*] *chiefly Brit* : a type of European tree : LINDEN — compare [1]LIME, [2]LIME

lime green *noun* [*noncount*] : a bright, light yellowish-green color — see color picture on page C2
– lime–green *adj* ▪ wearing a *lime-green* shirt

lime·light /ˈlaɪm,laɪt/ *noun*
the limelight : public attention or notice thought of as a bright light that shines on someone ▪ She is a very private woman who never sought *the limelight*. [=who has never sought to be famous] ▪ She has shunned *the limelight*. ▪ When his new book caused an unexpected controversy, he was ***thrust into the limelight*** once again. [=he was given a lot of unwanted public attention] ▪ an actor who is used to being ***in the limelight*** ▪ He doesn't like having to ***share the limelight*** with other actors. ▪ He's always trying to ***grab/steal the limelight*** from other actors.

lim·er·ick /ˈlɪmərɪk/ *noun, pl* **-icks** [*count*] : a humorous rhyming poem of five lines

lime·stone /ˈlaɪm,stoʊn/ *noun* [*noncount*] : a type of white stone that is commonly used in building

lim·ey /ˈlaɪmi/ *noun, pl* **-eys** [*count*] *US, informal + old-fashioned* : a British person ✧ *Limey* can be an insulting word but it is now usually used in a joking way.

[1]**lim·it** /ˈlɪmət/ *noun, pl* **-its** [*count*]
1 : a point beyond which it is not possible to go ▪ He has reached the *limit* of his endurance. ▪ In training, she pushed her body to its physical *limits*. ▪ He tries to be creative within the *limits* of conventional journalism. ▪ Space travel tests the (outer) *limits* of human capabilities. ▪ It's important to exercise, but you need to ***know your limits***. [=you need to know how much you are able to do] ▪ I'm trying to be patient with him, but I've just about ***reached my limit***. [=reached the point where I can no longer be patient] ▪ ***There are limits*** to what I can put up with from him! ▪ ***There's no limit*** to what we can accomplish [=we can accomplish anything] if we work hard enough. ▪ There seems to be no *limit* to his enthusiasm. = His enthusiasm seems to ***know no limit(s)***.
2 : a point beyond which someone is not allowed to go ▪ Parents need to set *limits* for their children. = Parents need to set/place/impose *limits* on (the behavior of) their children. ▪ They must not go beyond these *limits*. = They must not exceed these *limits*.
3 : an amount or number that is the highest or lowest allowed ▪ Two drinks is my *limit*. [=I stop after having two drinks] ▪ When you take the test, you'll have a ***time limit***. [=you will have to complete the test within a certain amount of time] ▪ The lower ***age limit*** for voting is 18. [=you cannot vote unless you are at least 18 years old] — see also OFF-LIMITS, SPEED LIMIT
4 : an area or line that is at the outer edge of something — usually plural ▪ There are three high schools within the city *limits*. [=within the city] ▪ They ventured far beyond the *limits* of civilization. ▪ at the outer *limits* of the solar system
over the limit *Brit* : having more alcohol in the blood than is legally allowed for someone who is driving ▪ He was arrested for driving *over the limit*.
the limit *informal + old-fashioned* : a very annoying or upsetting person or thing ▪ He keeps forgetting his wife's birthday: he really is *the limit*! [=*too much*] ▪ He forgot his wife's birthday again. Isn't that *the limit*!
the sky's the limit — used to say that there are no limits and that anything is possible ▪ You can achieve anything if you really want to. *The sky's the limit*.
to the limit : to the greatest possible point : as much as possible ▪ Our resources have been stretched *to the limit*. [=we have used all of our resources] ▪ My schedule is filled *to the limit*. [=my schedule is completely filled]
within limits : without going beyond what is considered reasonable or allowable ▪ They told us that we could do whatever we liked, *within* (certain) *limits*.
without limit : without being controlled or stopped : without being limited ▪ allowing costs to increase *without limit*

[2]**limit** *verb* **-its; -it·ed; -it·ing** [+ *obj*]
1 : to stop or prevent an increase in (something) ▪ We need to find ways to *limit* expenses. : to keep (something) from becoming greater ▪ He tried to *limit* the damage to his reputation by blaming other people. ▪ A factor *limiting* our country's economic performance is its lack of resources. ▪ His political enemies have tried to *limit* [=*restrict*] his power.
2 : to prevent (something) from being larger, longer, more, etc. : to place a limit on the size or extent of (something) ▪ The hospital *limits* [=*restricts*] visits to 30 minutes. ▪ Our lack of money *limits* our options. — often used *(be) limited to* ▪ Visits *are limited to* 30 minutes. [=visits must not be longer than 30 minutes] ▪ The damage from the fire *was limited to* the rear of the building. [=only the rear of the building was damaged by the fire]
3 : to stop (someone) from having or doing more : to place a limit on (someone) ▪ Our lack of money *limits* [=*restricts*] us to fewer options. ▪ Because of our lack of money, we have to ***limit ourselves*** to fewer options. — often used as *(be) limited to* ▪ Guests *are limited to* visits of no longer than 30 minutes. ▪ We *are limited to* fewer options by our lack of money.

lim·i·ta·tion /,lɪməˈteɪʃən/ *noun, pl* **-tions**
1 [*noncount*] : the act of controlling the size or extent of something : the act of limiting something ▪ a law aimed at the *limitation* of federal power
2 [*count*] : something that controls how much of something is possible or allowed ▪ They have placed a *limitation* on the amount of time we have available. — often plural ▪ There are strict *limitations* on the uses of these funds. ▪ We'd like to include more material, but space *limitations* make that impossible.
3 [*count*] : something (such as a lack of ability or strength)

that controls what a person is able to do • He knows his *limitations.* • physical *limitations*
damage limitation see [1]DAMAGE

lim·it·ed /ˈlɪmətəd/ *adj* [*more* ~; *most* ~] : not high or great in number, amount, etc. • Only a *limited* number of students will be allowed in the class. • Our country has very *limited* resources. = Our country is very *limited* in its resources. • People with *limited* incomes are hit particularly hard by inflation. • The company has had *limited* success. • Her language skills are somewhat *limited.* [=are not very highly developed] • This offer is available for only a *limited* time. [=for only a short time]

limited edition *noun, pl* ~ **-tions** [*count*] : a special book, picture, medal, etc., for which only a small number of copies are produced and sold

lim·it·ing /ˈlɪmətɪŋ/ *adj* [*more* ~; *most* ~] : placing a limit on what is possible or allowed • A *limiting* factor on our country's economic performance is its lack of resources. • As a writer, I find the drama genre to be very *limiting.*

lim·it·less /ˈlɪmətləs/ *adj* : very great or large : having no limit • *limitless* possibilities • a seemingly *limitless* supply of material

limo /ˈlɪmoʊ/ *noun, pl* **lim·os** [*count*] *informal* : LIMOUSINE

lim·ou·sine /ˌlɪməˈziːn/ *noun, pl* **-sines** [*count*]
1 : a very large and comfortable car usually driven by a professional driver (called a chauffeur) • The bride and groom rode in a *limousine* from the church to the reception hall. — see picture at CAR
2 *chiefly US* : a vehicle (such as a bus or van) that carries passengers to and from an airport

[1]**limp** /ˈlɪmp/ *verb* **limps; limped; limp·ing** [*no obj*]
1 : to walk in a slow and awkward way because of an injury to a leg or foot • The injured player *limped* off the court. • The dog was *limping* slightly.
2 : to go or continue slowly or with difficulty • The damaged ship *limped* back to port. • The company has somehow managed to *limp* along despite the bad economy.

[2]**limp** *noun, pl* **limps** [*count*] : a slow and awkward way of walking caused by an injury to a leg or foot • We noticed that the dog was walking with a slight *limp.* • a noticeable/pronounced *limp*

[3]**limp** *adj* [*more* ~; *most* ~]
1 : having an unpleasantly soft or weak quality : not firm or stiff • He gave me a very *limp* handshake. • This plant isn't doing well—look how *limp* the leaves are. • Her hair hung *limp* around her shoulders. • I suddenly ***went limp*** and collapsed on the floor.
2 : feeling very tired • He was *limp* with fatigue.
— **limp·ly** *adv* • He let his hand hang *limply* off the couch. • Her hair hung *limply* around her shoulders. — **limp·ness** *noun* [*noncount*]

lim·pet /ˈlɪmpət/ *noun, pl* **-pets** [*count*] : a type of ocean animal that has a shell and that is able to attach itself to things (such as rocks) very tightly

lim·pid /ˈlɪmpəd/ *adj* [*more* ~; *most* ~] *literary*
1 : perfectly clear : TRANSPARENT • the *limpid* waters of the stream • *limpid* eyes
2 : clear and simple in style • *limpid* prose

linch·pin *also* **lynch·pin** /ˈlɪntʃˌpɪn/ *noun, pl* **-pins** [*count*] : a person or thing that holds something together : the most important part of a complex situation or system • This witness is the *linchpin* of the defense's case.

lin·den /ˈlɪndən/ *noun, pl* **-dens** [*count*] : a type of tree that has large heart-shaped leaves and yellowish flowers — called also (*chiefly Brit*) *lime*

[1]**line** /ˈlaɪn/ *noun, pl* **lines**
1 [*count*] **a** : a long narrow mark on a surface • I drew a straight *line* down the page to separate the two lists. • a curved *line* • Cut the paper along the dotted *line.* • a horizontal/vertical/diagonal *line* **b** : a mark on the ground that shows the edge of the playing area in a sport • a tennis serve that was over the *line* — see also FINISH LINE, FOUL LINE, GOAL LINE, STARTING LINE
2 [*count*] : an area or border that separates two places • property *lines* • After three hours on the road, they finally crossed the state *line.* • the town *line* — often used figuratively • They have overstepped the *line* of good taste. [=they have shown poor taste in their actions] • The community is divided along racial *lines.* [=people of different races do not like or agree with each other] • Their behavior has ***crossed the line.*** [=their behavior goes beyond what is acceptable] • There's sometimes only a very ***fine line*** [=a very small difference] between genius and madness. — see also BORDERLINE, DIVIDING LINE, INTERNATIONAL DATE LINE, POVERTY LINE
3 [*count*] **a** : a group of people or things that are next to each other in a row • The soldiers formed a *line.* = The soldiers got into a *line.* • Their yards were separated by a *line* of trees. **b** *US* : a group of people, vehicles, etc., that are in front of and behind each other in a row while they wait to move forward • The *line* [=(*chiefly Brit*) *queue*] of fans moved slowly toward the box office. • Everybody had to ***get in line*** and wait their turn. • The people were ***waiting/standing in line.*** ✧ In most areas of the U.S., it is usual to say that people are (waiting/standing) ***in line*** for something. • We waited *in line* for more than an hour to get tickets. In some areas, especially in and near New York City, ***on line*** is used instead. • We waited *on line* for more than an hour.
4 [*count*] : the outline of a figure, body, or surface — often plural • the car's sleek *lines* • the *lines* of a coat • a dress with figure-hugging *lines*
5 [*count*] : a long and thin rope, string, etc. • a fishing *line* • We hung the wet clothes on the *line.* [=*clothesline*]
6 [*count*] **a** : a pipe for carrying something (such as steam, water, or oil) • There was a break in the water *line.* — see also PIPELINE **b** : a wire or set of wires that carries electricity or a telephone signal • During the storm, several power *lines* were knocked down. • a telephone *line*
7 [*count*] : a telephone connection • I'm sorry, the *line* is busy/engaged. • The *line* suddenly went dead. • All of our *lines* are currently busy. Please hold. • There's a call for you on *line* 2. • Please ***hold the line.*** [=please do not hang up the phone] • Mr. Smith is ***on the line.*** [=Mr. Smith has called and is waiting to speak with you on the telephone] • The supervisor got *on the line* [=got on the phone] and explained the problem. • I wasn't able to get him *on the line.*
8 a [*count*] : a row of words, letters, numbers, or symbols written across a page • To save space, we'll cut out the last few *lines* of the article. • a *line* of poetry • making adjustments to *line* spacing [=to the amount of space between lines]; *also* : a space on a page where such a line could be placed • a blank *line* **b** **lines** [*plural*] : the words that an actor speaks in a play, movie, etc. • All of the actors should have their *lines* memorized by next Friday. • She fluffed some of her *lines* but delivered others well. **c** [*count*] : a short note or message • ***Drop me a line*** [=send me a brief message] while you're away. **d** [*count*] : a spoken or written comment • He always comes up with a funny/clever *line* to help people relax when the situation is tense. • He didn't really answer my question—he just handed/gave me some *line* about how hard it can be to deal with these issues. • a salesman with a smooth *line* [=a smooth way of talking] • (*US*) a guy with a clever ***pickup line*** = (*Brit*) a guy with a clever ***chat-up line*** [=a comment made by a man to start a conversation with a woman he is attracted to]
9 [*count*] : a wrinkle on a person's skin • the deep *lines* on his face • I noticed the fine *lines* around her eyes when she smiled. • a ***worry line*** [=a wrinkle on a person's face caused by worrying]
10 [*count*] : the path along which something moves or is directed • a bullet's *line* of flight • Some civilians got caught in the ***line of fire.*** [=they were in the place where bullets were being shot] • She was standing right in my ***line of sight/vision.*** [=she was standing right where I was looking]
11 [*count*] : a railroad track • The train was stopped because a tree had fallen across the *line.*
12 [*count*] : PRODUCTION LINE • They had to shut down the *line* when one of the machines broke down.
13 a [*singular*] : a series of similar things • This is just the latest in a long *line* of problems. **b** [*count*] : the people in a family : the series of people who are born in a family as years pass • She comes from a long *line* of farmers. [=there have been many farmers in her family in the past] • He claims that he is descended from a royal *line.*
14 [*count*] **a** : a way of behaving, thinking, etc. • He ***took a firm line*** with his son. [=he treated his son in a firm way] • I don't follow your ***line of reasoning.*** [=I don't understand the reasoning behind what you are saying] • The police are pursuing a new ***line of inquiry/investigation.*** • Our current method isn't working. We need to try a different ***line of attack.*** — see also HARD LINE **b** : an official or public position or opinion • He is a politician who has always adhered closely to the ***party line*** on just about everything. [=who has always supported the position taken by his political party]
15 [*count*] : an area of activity or interest • She got a job in the retail *line.* • That kind of thing isn't really in my *line.*

[=that kind of thing doesn't really interest me] • He's in a dangerous ***line of work.*** [=he has a dangerous job] • I don't know what ***line of business*** she's in. • a soldier/policeman/fireman who was killed ***in the line of duty*** [=was killed while doing his job]
16 [*count*] **:** the position of military forces who are facing the enemy • The enemy soldiers broke through the *line.* • a secret mission ***behind enemy lines*** [=a secret mission in an area controlled by the enemy] — see also FRONT LINE
17 [*count*] **:** a group of related products that are sold by one company • a *line* of clothing = a clothing *line* • The company is coming out with a new product *line.*
18 [*count*] **a :** a system used for moving people or things from one place to another • a bus *line* • a steamship *line* • military ***supply lines;*** *also* **:** a company that owns or controls such a system • He owns a trucking *line.* — see also AIRLINE **b :** a system that allows people to share information • We need to keep the ***lines of communication*** open.
19 ***lines*** [*plural*] — used in phrases like ***along the lines of*** to refer to something that is similar or close to the thing being mentioned • We need something *along the lines of* a small cart. = We need a small cart or something *along those/similar lines.* [=we need a small cart or something like that] • He said he was too busy to help, or something *along those lines.*
20 [*count*] *American football* **a :** LINE OF SCRIMMAGE **b :** the players who are positioned on the line of scrimmage • the defensive/offensive *line*
21 [*count*] **:** an amount of an illegal drug (such as cocaine) that is arranged in a thin line so that it can be breathed into the nose through a straw • a *line* of cocaine
along the line *informal* **:** during a process or series of events • He seems to have lost his interest in music somewhere *along the line.* [=at some time in the past]
cross the line see ²CROSS
down the line *informal* **:** in the future • If you don't finish school, you'll regret it *down the line.* • We'll have to correct these problems further *down the line.*
draw a/the line **1 :** to see or understand the difference *between* things • Where do you *draw the line between* what is good and bad art? • It is sometimes hard to *draw a line between* right and wrong. **2 :** to refuse to do or allow something **:** to set a limit — usually + *at* • We couldn't invite everyone so we *drew the line at* immediate family members only. • He helps me out a lot but *draws the line at* cleaning the bathroom.
fall in/into line see ¹FALL
get/have a line on *US, informal* **:** to get or have information about (someone or something that you are trying to find) • Have the police managed to *get a line on* any of the suspects? • She says she *has a line on* a new car.
hold the line **:** to not allow any more changes or increases — usually + *against* or *on* • We need to *hold the line against* further expansion into our territory. • The President has vowed to *hold the line on* tax increases. [=to not allow further tax increases] — see also ¹LINE 7 (above)
hook, line, and sinker see ¹HOOK
in line **1** — used to say that someone should get something or is likely to get something • He's *in line* for a promotion. = He's *in line* to get a promotion. [=he is going to be given a promotion] **2** — used to refer to a person or thing that follows or could follow another person or thing • The Vice President is ***first in line*** to succeed the President. **3 :** doing what other people want or expect **:** in a state of agreement or cooperation • He says he'll cooperate, but I don't know how much longer we can keep him *in line.* — see also ¹LINE 3b (above)
in line with **:** in agreement with • The new policy is *in line with* the plans that were discussed last year. • My thinking is *in line with* yours. [=my thinking agrees with yours] • The red one is more *in line with* what I had in mind. [=is more like what I had in mind]
into line **:** into a state of agreement or cooperation • It was difficult to get/bring everyone *into line.* [=to get everyone to agree]
lay it on the line *informal* **:** to speak very honestly and directly to someone • Let me *lay it on the line* (to/for you): if your work doesn't improve, you'll be fired.
on line **:** in or into operation • The new system will be coming *on line* next month. = The new system will be brought *on line* next month. [=the new system will begin working next month] — see also ¹LINE 3b (above), ONLINE
on the line **:** in danger of being lost or harmed **:** at risk • I have to finish this report by tomorrow. My job is *on the line.* [=I will lose my job if I don't finish this report by tomorrow] • The champ's title is *on the line* in this fight. [=he will lose the title if he loses the fight] • He put/laid his life *on the line* [=he risked his life] for his family.
out of line *informal* **:** beyond what is reasonable or allowable **:** not right or appropriate • Your behavior is *out of line.* • These prices are way *out of line* with what other stores are charging. • I can't believe that guy was so rude to you! He was really/way *out of line.* — see also *step out of line* at ²STEP
read between the lines see ¹READ
take/follow the line of least resistance see RESISTANCE
the end of the line see ¹END
toe the line see ²TOE
— see also BOTTOM LINE, STORY LINE

²line *verb* **lines; lined; lin·ing**
1 [+ *obj*] **:** to place or form a line along (something, such as a hallway, building, or street) • Students *lined* the hall, waiting to register for classes. • Shops *line* the street. = The street is *lined* with shops. [=there is a line of shops along the street] • a street *lined* with trees = a tree-*lined* street — see also LINED
2 *baseball* **:** to hit a line drive [*no obj*] He *lined* to center field. • He *lined* out to the shortstop. [=he hit a line drive that was caught by the shortstop for an out] [+ *obj*] She *lined* a single to left field. [=she hit a line drive into left field for a single]
line up [*phrasal verb*] **1 :** to form a line • The soldiers *lined up* for inspection. • (*US*) People *lined up* [=(*chiefly Brit*) *queued up*] at the theater waiting to buy tickets. **2** ***line (people or things) up or line up (people or things)*** **:** to put (people or things) into a line • The teacher *lined up* the children. • The soldiers were *lined up* for inspection. • The storekeeper carefully *lined up* the cans on the shelf. • (*US*) People were *lined up* [=(*chiefly Brit*) *queued up*] at the theater waiting to buy tickets. **3** ***line (things) up or line up (things)*** **:** to place (things) so that their edges form a straight line **:** ALIGN • *line up* (the edges of) two pieces of paper **4** ***line (something) up or line up (something)*** **:** to succeed in getting (something) • He has been trying to *line up* support for his proposal. • She managed to *line up* a summer job.
— compare ³LINE

³line *verb* **lines; lined; lin·ing** [+ *obj*] **:** to cover the inner surface of (something) • I *lined* the box with paper. • Tapestries *lined* the walls. • Her gloves were *lined* with fur. • Books *lined* the walls of the study. = The study was *lined* with books. — see also LINED, LINING
line your pockets *informal* **:** to take or get a lot of money by doing something illegal or dishonest • corrupt officials who have been *lining their pockets* at the public's expense [=have been stealing public money]
— compare ²LINE

lin·e·age /ˈlɪnijɪʤ/ *noun, pl* **-ag·es** [*count, noncount*] **:** the people who were in someone's family in past times • a person of unknown *lineage* [=*ancestry, descent*]

lin·e·al /ˈlɪnijəl/ *adj* **:** having a direct family relationship **:** related by a direct series of parents and children • He claims that he is a *lineal* descendent of a famous military hero. • a *lineal* ancestor
— **lin·e·al·ly** *adv*

lin·e·a·ments /ˈlɪnijəmənts/ *noun* [*plural*] *formal + literary* **:** the features of a person's body or face — sometimes used figuratively • the *lineaments* [=*features*] of his personality • describing the *lineaments* of the problem

lin·e·ar /ˈlɪnijɚ/ *adj*
1 [*more* ~; *most* ~] **a :** formed by lines **:** made up of lines • a *linear* design **b :** forming a line **:** STRAIGHT • a flat, almost *linear* horizon
2 : of or relating to the length of something • *linear* measurements
3 [*more* ~; *most* ~] **:** going from one thing to the next thing in a direct and logical way • a *linear* narrative • *linear* patterns of thought
— **lin·e·ar·i·ty** /ˌlɪniˈerəti/ *noun* [*noncount*] • the *linearity* of the narrative — **lin·e·ar·ly** *adv* • thinking *linearly*

line·back·er /ˈlaɪnˌbækɚ/ *noun, pl* **-ers** [*count*] *American football* **:** a player on the defending team whose usual position is a short distance in back of the line of scrimmage

lined /ˈlaɪnd/ *adj*
1 : marked with lines • a sheet of *lined* paper
2 : having many wrinkles • a deeply *lined* face • *lined* skin
3 *of clothing* **:** having a thin layer of different material on the

inner surface : having a lining • a *lined* jacket • a *lined* skirt

line dance *noun, pl* ~ **dances** [*count*] : a dance done by a group of people who stand next to each other in a line and who all perform the same movements
– **line dancer** *noun, pl* ~ **-ers** [*count*] – **line dancing** *noun* [*noncount*]

line drawing *noun, pl* ~ **-ings** [*count*] : a drawing made only with lines

line drive *noun, pl* ~ **drives** [*count*] *baseball* : a ball that is hit by the batter and goes in a nearly straight line not far above the ground • He hit a hard/soft *line drive* to the shortstop.

line–item veto *noun* [*singular*] *US* : a power that allows a president, governor, etc., to officially reject specific parts of a proposed bill without rejecting the entire bill

line•man /ˈlaɪnmən/ *noun, pl* **-men** /-mən/ [*count*]
1 *American football* : a player whose position is on the line of scrimmage • a defensive *lineman* • an offensive *lineman*
2 *US* : a person whose job is to set up and repair power lines or telephone lines

lin•en /ˈlɪnən/ *noun, pl* **-ens**
1 [*noncount*] : a smooth, strong cloth made from flax • a *linen* tablecloth
2 : tablecloths, sheets, etc., made of linen or a similar cloth [*noncount*] She washes the *linen* every week. • (*US*) a *linen* closet = (*Brit*) a *linen* cupboard [*plural*] *linens*, blankets, and towels — see also BED LINENS, TABLE LINEN

line of credit *noun, pl* **lines of credit** [*count*] : an amount of money that a person is allowed to borrow • a *line of credit* of up to $100,000 — called also *credit line*

line of scrimmage *noun* [*singular*] *American football* : an imaginary line that goes across the field at the place where the football is put before each play begins

[1]**lin•er** /ˈlaɪnɚ/ *noun, pl* **-ers** [*count*]
1 : a large ship used for carrying passengers • an ocean *liner* • I took a cruise on a luxury *liner*. • a cruise/passenger *liner*
2 *baseball* : LINE DRIVE • He hit a *liner* to the first baseman. — compare [2]LINER; see also AIRLINER, EYELINER

[2]**liner** *noun, pl* **-ers** [*count*] : something that covers the inner surface of another thing • the *liner* of a jacket • We had to replace the swimming pool *liner*. • The thermos has an aluminum *liner*. — compare [1]LINER

liner notes *noun* [*plural*] *chiefly US* : information about a record, CD, or tape that is printed on its cover or on a piece of paper placed inside its cover — called also (*Brit*) *sleeve notes*

lines•man /ˈlaɪnzmən/ *noun, pl* **-men** [*count*] : an official in a sport such as football, tennis, or hockey who decides if a ball, puck, or player has gone out of the proper playing area

line•up /ˈlaɪnˌʌp/ *noun, pl* **-ups** [*count*]
1 a : a list of the players who are playing in a game (such as baseball) • The manager has made some changes to the ***starting lineup***. [=the list of players who are playing when the game begins] **b** : the players on such a list • The team has a powerful *lineup*.
2 a : a group of people who are going to perform at an event • the show's star-studded *lineup* (of performers) **b** : a group of television programs that are shown one after another • tonight's *lineup* of shows • The networks all had different *lineups* for the new season.
3 *US* : a line of people who stand next to each other while someone tries to identify one of them as the person who has committed a crime • She was asked to pick her attacker out of a *lineup*. — called also (*Brit*) *identification parade*, (*Brit*) *identity parade*

-ling /lɪŋ/ *noun suffix*
1 : one connected with or having the quality of • nest*ling* • earth*ling* • weak*ling*
2 : young, small, or minor one • duck*ling*

lin•ger /ˈlɪŋgɚ/ *verb* **-gers; -gered; -ger•ing** [*no obj*]
1 : to stay somewhere beyond the usual or expected time • The tourists didn't *linger* very long. • She *lingered* at the art exhibit. • He *lingered* in bed and missed breakfast. • They *lingered* over coffee after dinner.
2 a : to continue to exist as time passes • The heat *lingered* long after the sun had gone down. • The smell of her perfume *lingered*. • The idea *lingered* in their minds. — often + *on* • His unhappiness/resentment *lingered on*. • The rain *lingered on* for days. **b** : to remain alive while becoming weaker — usually + *on* • He was very ill, but he *lingered on* for several more months.
– **lin•ger•er** /ˈlɪŋgərɚ/ *noun, pl* **-ers** [*count*] • After sunset there were a few *lingerers* on the beach. – **lin•ger•ing** /ˈlɪŋgərɪŋ/ *adj* • This latest evidence should remove any *lingering* doubts/questions about his innocence. • The company is still trying to recover from the *lingering* effects of the strike. • a long, *lingering* kiss • a last, *lingering* look • He suffered a long, *lingering* [=very slow] death. – **lin•ger•ing•ly** /ˈlɪŋgərɪŋli/ *adv*

lin•ge•rie /ˌlɑːnʤəˈreɪ, *Brit* ˈlænʒəri/ *noun* [*noncount*] : women's underwear and clothing that is worn in bed — often used before another noun • a *lingerie* shop • the *lingerie* department in a store

lin•go /ˈlɪŋgoʊ/ *noun, pl* **-goes** *informal*
1 [*count*] : a language • a foreign *lingo* • It can be hard to travel in a foreign country if you don't ***speak the lingo***.
2 : the special language used for a particular activity or by a particular group of people [*count*] — usually singular • Basketball has a distinct *lingo*. • He's starting to pick up the *lingo*. • She doesn't practice law anymore, but she can still *speak the lingo*. [*noncount*] The book has a lot of computer *lingo* that I don't understand.

lin•gua fran•ca /ˈlɪŋgwəˈfræŋkə/ *noun, pl* **lin•gua fran•cas** *or* **lin•guae fran•cae** /ˈlɪŋgwiˈfræŋki/ [*count*] : a language that is used among people who speak various different languages • English is used as a *lingua franca* among many airline pilots.

lin•gui•ne *or* **lin•gui•ni** /lɪŋˈgwiːni/ *noun* [*noncount*] : a type of pasta that is long, thin, and flat

lin•guist /ˈlɪŋgwɪst/ *noun, pl* **-guists** [*count*]
1 : a person who speaks several languages
2 : a person who studies linguistics

lin•guis•tic /lɪŋˈgwɪstɪk/ *adj* : of or relating to language or linguistics • *linguistic* differences/development • learning about *linguistic* theory
– **lin•guis•ti•cal•ly** /lɪŋˈgwɪstɪkli/ *adv*

lin•guis•tics /lɪŋˈgwɪstɪks/ *noun* [*noncount*] : the study of language and of the way languages work

lin•i•ment /ˈlɪnəmənt/ *noun, pl* **-ments** [*count, noncount*] : a liquid that is rubbed on your skin to relieve pain or stiffness in your muscles

lin•ing /ˈlaɪnɪŋ/ *noun, pl* **-ings** [*count*] : material that covers the inner surface of something • The coat had a soft *lining*. • gloves with silk *linings* • brake *linings* • the *lining* of the bladder/stomach • intestinal *lining* — see also SILVER LINING

[1]**link** /ˈlɪŋk/ *verb* **links; linked; link•ing**
1 a : to join or connect (two or more things, places, etc.) together [+ *obj*] A bridge *links* the island to the mainland. • The rooms are *linked* by hallways. • He drew a line *linking* New York and/with/to Los Angeles on the map. • She *linked* (up) the paper clips to form a chain. • The elderly couple ***linked arms*** [=kept their bent arms hooked together at the elbow] as they walked down the street. [*no obj*] The pipe *links* (up) to/with the main gas line. **b** : to connect (someone or something) to a system, network, etc. [+ *obj*] The network *links* several terminals. • The computer is *linked* with/to the fax machine. • providing equipment to *link* (up) students to the Internet [*no obj*] Guests can *link* (up) to the Internet from their hotel rooms.
2 a [+ *obj*] : to show or prove that a person or thing is related to or involved with something • The study *links* high cholesterol levels to/with an increased risk of heart attacks. • The police said that they have evidence *linking* him to these crimes. **b** ◊ A thing or person that ***is linked to/with*** something is connected or related to it in some way. • High cholesterol *is linked to* an increased risk of heart attacks. • He denied that his business partner *was* in any way *linked to* the theft. • Scientists have discovered a gene that *is linked to/with* [=*involved in*] the development of Alzheimer's disease. • Your raise *is linked to* your job performance. [=your raise is related to your job performance; the size of your raise is related to how well you do your job] • He argues that poverty *is* directly/indirectly *linked to/with* certain health problems. • My fate *is* inextricably *linked to* hers. = Our fates *are* inextricably *linked*.
3 : to cause (different groups, countries, etc.) to be joined together [+ *obj*] The marriage of their children has *linked* the two families. • These countries are *linked* in a loose confederation. [*no obj*] Her company recently *linked* (up) with three others to form a multinational association.

[2]**link** *noun, pl* **links** [*count*]
1 a : a relationship or connection between things • Their research shows a *link* between high cholesterol and an increased risk of heart attacks. [=shows that high cholesterol

causes an increased risk of heart attacks] ▪ Police have discovered/established a direct *link* between the two murders. **b :** a relationship between people, groups, nations, etc. ▪ The government has established/forged trade *links* with other countries. ▪ She felt a strong *link* with/to her ancestors.
2 a : something that allows movement from one place to another ▪ The bridge was the island's *link* to the mainland. ▪ There are plans to build a rail *link* from the airport to the city. **b :** something that allows two or more people or things to communicate with each other ▪ A radio was his only *link* to the outside world. ▪ a satellite/video *link* **c :** HYPERLINK ▪ His Web site includes *links* to other sites.
3 : a single part of a chain ▪ The chain broke at its weakest *link*. — often used figuratively ▪ an important *link* in the chain of events [=an important event in a series of related events] ▪ It is the ***weak link*** [=the least strong or successful part] in the company's line of products. ▪ the ***weakest link*** in a computer network [=the part of a computer network that is most likely to fail]
4 *US* **:** a long, narrow piece of sausage in a series of connected pieces; *also* **:** a small sausage that is long and narrow — see also CUFF LINK, LINKS, MISSING LINK

link•age /ˈlɪŋkɪʤ/ *noun, pl* **-ag•es**
1 : a connection or relationship between two or more things [*count*] *linkages* between population growth and disease [*noncount*] Some researchers doubt that there is any *linkage* between these phenomena. [=they doubt that these phenomena are connected or related]
2 [*count*] **:** a part that connects two or more things ▪ repairing a broken *linkage*

linking verb *noun, pl* ~ **verbs** [*count*] *grammar* **:** a verb (such as *appear, be, become, feel, grow,* or *seem*) that connects a subject with an adjective or noun that describes or identifies the subject ▪ "Look" in "you look happy" and "are" in "my favorite fruits are apples and oranges" are *linking verbs*. — compare ACTION VERB

links /ˈlɪŋks/ *noun, pl* **links** [*count*] **:** a golf course ▪ On Saturday morning, he's always out on the *links*.; *especially* **:** a golf course that is next to the ocean ▪ a seaside *links*

link•up /ˈlɪŋkˌʌp/ *noun, pl* **-ups**
1 [*count, noncount*] **:** the act of joining or connecting two things ▪ The maneuver will be done following (the) *linkup* of the two spacecraft.
2 [*count*] **:** a connection that allows two or more people or things to communicate with each other ▪ The interview will be broadcast nationally through a satellite *linkup*. ▪ A direct telephone *linkup* has been established.

lin•net /ˈlɪnət/ *noun, pl* **-nets** [*count*] **:** a small European bird that is a kind of finch

li•no /ˈlaɪnoʊ/ *noun* [*noncount*] *Brit, informal* **:** LINOLEUM

li•no•leum /ləˈnoʊlijəm/ *noun* [*noncount*] **:** a type of material that is produced in thin sheets, has a shiny surface, and is used to cover floors and counters

lin•seed /ˈlɪnˌsiːd/ *noun* [*noncount*] **:** the seed of the flax plant

linseed oil *noun* [*noncount*] **:** a yellowish oil from the seeds of the flax plant that is used in paint, printing ink, etc.

lint /ˈlɪnt/ *noun* [*noncount*]
1 *chiefly US* **:** tiny pieces of cloth or another soft material ▪ I always have *lint* in my pocket. ▪ The clothes dryer was clogged with *lint*.
2 *Brit* **:** a soft material that is used for covering and protecting cuts and wounds

lin•tel /ˈlɪntl̩/ *noun, pl* **-tels** [*count*] **:** a piece of wood or stone that lies across the top of a door or window and holds the weight of the structure above it

li•on /ˈlajən/ *noun, pl* **-ons** [*count*]
1 : a large wild cat that has golden brown fur and that lives mainly in Africa ▪ the roar of the *lion* ✧ The male lion has long, dark hair called a "mane" growing around its neck. — see picture at CAT; see also MOUNTAIN LION, SEA LION
2 : a very important, powerful, or successful person ▪ He was a literary *lion* among the writers of his time. ▪ a social *lion*

li•on•ess /ˈlajənəs/ *noun, pl* **-ess•es** [*count*] **:** a female lion

li•on•heart•ed /ˈlajənˌhɑɚtəd/ *adj* **:** very brave ▪ a *lion-hearted* hero

li•on•ize *also Brit* **li•on•ise** /ˈlajəˌnaɪz/ *verb* **-iz•es; -ized; -iz•ing** [+ *obj*] **:** to treat (someone) as a very important and famous person ▪ She was *lionized* everywhere after her novel won the Pulitzer Prize.
— **li•on•i•za•tion** *also Brit* **-i•sa•tion** /ˌlajənəˈzeɪʃən, *Brit* ˌlajəˌnaɪˈzeɪʃən/ *noun* [*noncount*]

lion's den *noun* [*singular*] **:** a place or situation in which someone must deal with an angry person or group of people ▪ He knew that he would be facing an angry crowd, but he entered the *lion's den* without hesitating.

lion's share *noun* [*noncount*] **:** the largest part of something ▪ He took the *lion's share* of the blame [=most of the blame] for the accident. ▪ She claimed the *lion's share* of the credit for the show's success.

lip /ˈlɪp/ *noun, pl* **lips**
1 [*count*] **:** either one of the two soft parts that surround the mouth ▪ the lower/upper *lip* ▪ thin/thick/full *lips* ▪ He had a cut on his *lip*. ▪ He kissed her (right) on the *lips*. ▪ She was nervously ***biting her lip***. ▪ She had ***a smile on her lips***. [=she was smiling] — see picture at MOUTH; see also *stiff upper lip* at [1]STIFF
2 [*count*] **:** the edge of a cut or hole ▪ the *lips* of a wound ▪ the *lip* of a crater
3 [*count*] **:** the edge of a container especially where it is slightly spread out ▪ the *lip* of a pitcher
4 [*noncount*] *informal* **:** rude speech in reply to someone who should be spoken to with respect ▪ Don't give me any of your *lip*! [=don't talk to me in that disrespectful way]
button your lip/lips see [2]BUTTON
fat lip see [1]FAT
lick your lips see [1]LICK
my lips are sealed *informal* — used to say that you will not tell secret information to anyone ▪ Your secret is safe with me: *my lips are sealed*.
on everyone's/everybody's lips *informal* **:** being said or discussed by many people ▪ The celebrity murder trial was *on everyone's lips*.
on the lips of *informal* **:** being said or discussed by (people) ▪ trendy words *on the lips of* talk show hosts ▪ a topic that is *on the lips of* many people
pass your lips see [1]PASS
read lips see [1]READ
smack your lips see [1]SMACK
zip your lip see [1]ZIP

lip•id /ˈlɪpəd/ *noun, pl* **-ids** [*count*] *technical* **:** any one of various substances that contain fat and that are important parts of living cells

li•po•suc•tion /ˈlaɪpəˌsʌkʃən/ *noun* [*noncount*] *medical* **:** a kind of surgery that removes fat from a person's body

lipped /ˈlɪpt/ *adj* **:** having lips of a specified type — used in combination with another adjective ▪ a thin-*lipped* man [=a man with thin lips] — see also TIGHT-LIPPED

lip•py /ˈlɪpi/ *adj* **lip•pi•er; -est** *informal* **:** speaking in a rude way that shows a lack of respect ▪ *lippy* kids ▪ Don't ***get lippy*** with me.

lip–read /ˈlɪpˌriːd/ *verb* **-reads; -read** /-ˌrɛd/; **-read•ing** /-ˌriːdɪŋ/ **:** to understand what people are saying by watching the movement of their lips [*no obj*] a deaf person who knows how to *lip-read* [=*read lips*] [+ *obj*] He was *lip-reading* the conversation.
— **lip–read•er** /ˈlɪpˌriːdɚ/ *noun, pl* **-ers** [*count*] ▪ a skillful *lip-reader* — **lip–reading** *noun* [*noncount*]

lip service *noun* [*noncount*] **:** support for someone or something that is expressed by someone in words but that is not shown in that person's actions ▪ She paid/gave/offered *lip service* to blue-collar workers, but she did nothing to help them. ▪ So far all we've gotten from him is *lip service*.

lip•stick /ˈlɪpˌstɪk/ *noun, pl* **-sticks** [*count, noncount*] **:** a type of makeup that is spread on the lips and that comes in the form of a stick ▪ She was wearing bright red *lipstick*. ▪ I put on some *lipstick*. — see picture at GROOMING

lip–synch *or* **lip–sync** /ˈlɪpˌsɪŋk/ *verb* **-synchs** *or* **-syncs; -synched** *or* **-synced; -synch•ing** *or* **-sync•ing :** to pretend to sing or say (recorded words) [+ *obj*] He *lip-synched* the song that was playing on the radio. [*no obj*] He *lip-synched* to the song. ▪ It was obvious that he was *lip-synching*.

liq•ue•fy *also* **liq•ui•fy** /ˈlɪkwəˌfaɪ/ *verb* **-fies; -fied; -fy•ing :** to cause (something) to become liquid [+ *obj*] The intense heat *liquefied* [=*melted*] the plastic. ▪ The vegetables were *liquefied* in a blender. [*no obj*] The plastic *liquefied* in the intense heat.

li•queur /lɪˈkɚ, *Brit* lɪˈkjʊə/ *noun, pl* **-queurs** [*count, noncount*] **:** a sweet, strong alcoholic drink that is usually flavored with fruits or spices and drunk in small glasses after a meal ▪ a bottle of orange *liqueur*

[1]**liq•uid** /ˈlɪkwəd/ *noun, pl* **-uids :** a substance that is able to flow freely **:** FLUID [*count*] Water and milk are *liquids*. ▪ His

diet was restricted to *liquids*. = He was on a ***liquid diet***. [*noncount*] a bottle of green *liquid*

²liquid *adj*
1 : capable of flowing freely like water : not a solid or a gas • Water and milk are *liquid* substances. • *liquid* mercury/detergent • The medicine is available in *liquid* form. • They offered us snacks and ***liquid refreshments***. [=*drinks*]
2 *literary* **a :** shining and clear • She had large *liquid* eyes. **b :** clear, smooth, and pleasant in sound • the *liquid* notes of a bird **c :** having or showing a smooth and easy style • the *liquid* grace of the dancer's movements
3 *business* **:** made up of money or easily changed into money • *liquid* assets • *liquid* funds/investments

liq·ui·date /ˈlɪkwəˌdeɪt/ *verb* **-dates; -dat·ed; -dat·ing**
1 *business* **a :** to sell (a business, property, etc.) especially to pay off debt [+ *obj*] The owners were ordered to *liquidate* the company and pay their creditors. • The company is *liquidating* its assets. • They *liquidated* the estate. [=they sold the property of the estate] [*no obj*] The owners were ordered to *liquidate*. **b** [+ *obj*] **:** to pay all the money owed for (a debt) • *liquidate* a debt/loan
2 [+ *obj*] *informal* **:** to destroy (something) or kill (someone) • The film is about a professional killer who's hired to *liquidate* a powerful businessman.
– liq·ui·da·tion /ˌlɪkwəˈdeɪʃən/ *noun, pl* **-tions** [*noncount*] raising money by the *liquidation* of assets • The company was forced ***into liquidation***. [*count*] inventory *liquidations* **– liq·ui·da·tor** /ˈlɪkwəˌdeɪtɚ/ *noun, pl* **-tors** [*count*]

liquid crystal display *noun, pl* **~ -plays** [*count*] **:** LCD

li·quid·i·ty /lɪˈkwɪdəti/ *noun* [*noncount*]
1 *business* **a :** the state of having things that can be easily changed into money • The company has progressively increased its *liquidity*. **b :** the quality of being easily changed into money • the *liquidity* of his investments
2 *technical* **:** the quality or state of being liquid

liq·uid·iz·er /ˈlɪkwəˌdaɪzɚ/ *noun, pl* **-ers** [*count*] *Brit* **:** BLENDER

liquify *variant spelling of* LIQUEFY

li·quor /ˈlɪkɚ/ *noun* **:** an alcoholic drink; *especially* **:** a strong alcoholic drink [*noncount*] Do you serve *liquor*? • He drinks beer and wine, but he doesn't drink any ***hard liquor***. [*count*] vodka, whiskey, and other *liquors* — often used before another noun • a *liquor* bottle/store • The restaurant has a *liquor* license. [=a license that allows it to sell liquor] — see also MALT LIQUOR
hold your liquor *informal* **:** to be able to drink alcoholic beverages without becoming too drunk • He can't *hold his liquor* at all.

liquorice *chiefly Brit spelling of* LICORICE

li·ra /ˈlirə/ *noun* [*count*]
1 *pl* ***li·re*** /ˈliˌreɪ/ *or* ***liras* :** a basic unit of money that was formerly used in Italy; *also* **:** a coin or bill representing one Italian lira
2 *pl* ***liras* :** the basic unit of money in Turkey; *also* **:** a coin or bill representing one Turkish lira

lisp /ˈlɪsp/ *noun* [*singular*] **:** a speech problem that causes someone to pronounce the letters "s" and "z" like "th" • He spoke with a *lisp*.
– lisp *verb* **lisps; lisped; lisp·ing** [*no obj*] a child who *lisps* [+ *obj*] He *lisped* (out) his reply. **– lisp·er** *noun, pl* **-ers** [*count*]

lis·some *or chiefly Brit* **lis·som** /ˈlɪsəm/ *adj* [*more* ~; *most* ~] **:** thin and graceful — usually used of women • a *lissome* fashion model

¹list /ˈlɪst/ *noun, pl* **lists** [*count*]
1 : a series of names, words, numbers, etc., that are usually written down with each new one appearing below the previous one • a long/short *list* of names • the first/last name on the *list* = the name at the top/bottom of the *list* • Make a *list* of the ingredients you need to bake the cake. • draw up a *list* • I wrote a *list* of the books I've most enjoyed. • a growing *list* of volunteers • a ***grocery list*** [=a list of groceries to be bought] • The restaurant has an extensive ***wine list***. [=a list of the wines that are available in a restaurant] • Her first novel was on the ***best-seller list*** for two months. [=the list of books that are selling the most copies] • We were included in the ***guest list***. [=the list of people who are invited to something, such as a party] • I have a long *list* of things to do. = I have a long ***to-do list***. • ***High on my list*** (of things to do) is getting the car fixed. • I like all of his books, but this one is ***at the top of the list***. [=this is the best one] — see also CHECKLIST, DEAN'S LIST, DISABLED LIST, HIT LIST, LAUNDRY LIST, MAILING LIST, SHOPPING LIST, SHORT LIST, WAITING LIST, WISH LIST
2 *US, informal* **:** LIST PRICE • The car sells for a *list* of $30,000.
— compare ⁴LIST

²list *verb* **lists; list·ed; list·ing**
1 [+ *obj*] **:** to make a list of (names, things, etc.) • He *listed* the required qualifications for the job. • *List* the ingredients that you need to bake the cake. • I *listed* my likes and dislikes.
2 [+ *obj*] **a :** to include (something) in a list • Her telephone number is *listed* [=*entered*] in the directory. **b :** to enter information about (someone or something) in a list • The hospital has *listed* him (as being) in fair condition. • The animal has been *listed* as endangered/threatened. • He *lists* himself as a political liberal. [=he says that he is a political liberal]
3 [*no obj*] *US* **:** to have a specified list price • The car *lists* at/for $30,000.
— compare ³LIST

³list *verb* **lists; listed; listing** [*no obj*] *of a ship* **:** to lean to one side • The ship was *listing* heavily to port/starboard. — compare ²LIST

⁴list *noun* [*singular*] **:** the condition of a ship that is leaning to one side • The ship had a heavy *list* to starboard. — compare ¹LIST

¹lis·ten /ˈlɪsn/ *verb* **lis·tens; lis·tened; lis·ten·ing** [*no obj*]
1 a : to pay attention to someone or something in order to hear what is being said, sung, played, etc. • I *listened* as hard as I could, but I couldn't hear a word of what he said over all that noise. • She *listened* with interest as he told her about his travels. — often + *to* • Everyone *listened* closely/carefully *to* the firefighter's instructions. • I enjoy *listening to* classical music. • He turned the radio on and *listened to* the news. **b** — used to tell a person to listen to what you are saying • *Listen*, no one is more concerned about this problem than I am. • Now *listen* (here), you can't keep treating people this way.
2 : to hear what someone has said and understand that it is serious, important, or true • She tried to warn him of the dangers, but he wouldn't *listen*. — often + *to* • Nobody *listened to* her warnings. • Her ideas are worth *listening to*. • I told him to be more careful, but he wouldn't *listen to* me. • You should *listen to* your father [=you should take your father's advice]: he knows what he's talking about. • The judge refused to *listen to* their pleas.
listen for *or Brit* ***listen out for*** [*phrasal verb*] ***listen for (something)*** *or Brit* ***listen out for (something)* :** to pay attention to sounds in order to hear (something expected) • We *listened for* (the sound of) his footsteps. • We saw lightning and *listened for* the thunder.
listen in [*phrasal verb*] **1 :** to listen to a radio broadcast • We'll have some interesting guests on tomorrow's show, so be sure to *listen in*. [=*tune in*] **2 :** to listen to a conversation without being part of it • They let me *listen in* when the plans were presented.; *especially* **:** to listen secretly to a private conversation : EAVESDROP — usually + *on* • Someone was *listening in on* our telephone conversation.
listen up [*phrasal verb*] *chiefly US, informal* **:** to listen closely to what is being said — usually used as a command • Everybody *listen up*! I have something to say.
– lis·ten·er /ˈlɪsnɚ/ *noun, pl* **-ers** [*count*] • She's a good *listener*. [=she is good at listening to other people and understanding what they are saying] • a radio program that has many *listeners*

²listen *noun* [*singular*] **:** the act of listening to something • Have a *listen* to this. [=listen to this]

lis·ten·a·ble /ˈlɪsnəbəl/ *adj* [*more* ~; *most* ~] **:** pleasant to listen to • He finds some of his son's music very *listenable*.

listening device *noun, pl* **~ -vices** [*count*] **:** a small hidden microphone that is used to secretly listen to and record people • The police planted/installed a *listening device* in the home of the suspected mobster. — called also *bug*

list·ing /ˈlɪstɪŋ/ *noun, pl* **-ings**
1 a [*count*] **:** a printed list — usually + *of* • The book includes a *listing of* local restaurants. **b *listings*** [*plural*] **:** a printed list of things that includes detailed information about them • The newspaper provides movie *listings*. [=information about where and when movies are being shown in theaters] • TV *listings* [=information about when and on what channel television programs will be shown] • job *listings*
2 [*count*] **:** something included in a list • The telephone *listing* is wrong. [=they listed the wrong telephone number]
3 [*count*] **:** the act of including something in a list or the state

of being included in a list • The company is seeking a *listing* on the stock exchange. [=the company wants to be listed on the stock exchange]

list·less /ˈlɪstləs/ *adj* [*more* ~; *most* ~] : lacking energy or spirit • The heat made everyone tired and *listless.* • The party was a *listless* affair. • a *listless* economy
– **list·less·ly** *adv* • The cat was lying *listlessly* on the bed.
– **list·less·ness** *noun* [*noncount*] Symptoms include depression and *listlessness.* [*singular*] He was filled with a *listlessness* he couldn't explain.

list price *noun, pl* ~ **prices** [*count*] : the price of a product that is shown in a catalog, advertisement, etc. • The car's *list price* was $30,000, but the actual selling price was less. • We were given a 10 percent discount off the *list price.*

List·serv /ˈlɪst,sɚv/ *trademark* — used for software that allows e-mail messages to be sent to and received from a list of subscribers

[1]**lit** /ˈlɪt/ *past tense and past participle of* [3]LIGHT

[2]**lit** *noun* [*noncount*] *informal* : LITERATURE • I signed up to take a course in American/English *lit.*

lit·a·ny /ˈlɪtni/ *noun, pl* **-nies** [*count*]
1 : a prayer in a Christian church service in which the people at the service respond to lines spoken by the person who is leading the service
2 : a long list of complaints, problems, etc. • He has a *litany* of grievances against his former employer. • The team blamed its losses on a *litany* of injuries.

litchi *variant spelling of* LYCHEE

lite /ˈlaɪt/ *adj, US* : containing fewer calories or less fat than usual : LIGHT • *lite* beer • *lite* salad dressing

li·ter (*US*) *or chiefly Brit* **li·tre** /ˈliːtɚ/ *noun, pl* **-ters** [*count*] : a metric unit for measuring the volume of a liquid or gas that is equal to 1.057 quarts • a *liter* of water

lit·er·a·cy /ˈlɪtərəsi/ *noun* [*noncount*]
1 : the ability to read and write • The program is intended to promote adult *literacy* among people who have had very little schooling. • Their goal is to achieve basic *literacy.* • *literacy* programs/skills/tests
2 : knowledge that relates to a specified subject • computer *literacy* [=knowledge of how to use a computer] • cultural *literacy* [=knowledge of the culture you live in]

lit·er·al /ˈlɪtərəl/ *adj*
1 : involving the ordinary or usual meaning of a word • I was using the word in its *literal* sense. • The *literal* meaning of "know your ropes" is "to know a lot about ropes," while figuratively it means "to know a lot about how to do something."
2 : giving the meaning of each individual word : EXACT • a *literal* translation of a book
3 : completely true and accurate : not exaggerated • The story he told was basically true, even if it wasn't the *literal* truth.
4 [*more* ~; *most* ~] — used to describe someone who understands words and statements only in the most basic and ordinary way and does not have much imagination • He was a very *literal* [=*literal-minded*] man.
– **lit·er·al·ness** /ˈlɪtərəlnəs/ *noun* [*noncount*]

lit·er·al·ly /ˈlɪtərəli/ *adv*
1 : in a literal way: such as **a** : in a way that uses the ordinary and usual meaning of a word • Many words can be used both *literally* and figuratively. • He took her comments *literally.* • He's a sailor who knows his ropes, *literally* and figuratively. **b** — used to stress that a statement or description is true and accurate even though it may be surprising • He was *literally* [=*truly, actually*] insane. • He was quite *literally* jumping up and down in his rage. • The party was attended by *literally* hundreds of people. **c** : with the meaning of each individual word given exactly • The term "Mardi Gras" *literally* means "Fat Tuesday" in French. **d** : in a completely accurate way • The story he told was basically true, even if it wasn't *literally* true.
2 *informal* — used in an exaggerated way to emphasize a statement or description that is not literally true or possible • The group *literally* poured out new ideas. [=the group produced many new ideas] • Steam was *literally* coming out of his ears. [=he was very angry] • She was *literally* beside herself with rage.

lit·er·al–mind·ed /ˈlɪtərəl,maɪndəd/ *adj* [*more* ~; *most* ~] : LITERAL 4 • a very *literal-minded* man
– **lit·er·al–mind·ed·ness** *noun* [*noncount*]

lit·er·ary /ˈlɪtə,reri, *Brit* ˈlɪtrəri/ *adj*
1 a : of or relating to literature • American *literary* culture/tradition • a *literary* magazine • Do his books have any *literary* merit? • Mystery fiction is only one of many *literary* forms. • *literary* criticism/theory **b** : used in literature • a *literary* word • an essay written in a very *literary* style • The author uses many *literary* devices in his work.
2 *always used before a noun* : having a lot of knowledge about literature : known for reading or writing books • a *literary* man
3 *always used before a noun* : relating to the writing and publishing of literature • He entered the *literary* world right out of college. • She hired a *literary* agent.

lit·er·ate /ˈlɪtərət/ *adj* [*more* ~; *most* ~]
1 : able to read and write • He was barely *literate.* • She is *literate* in both English and Spanish. • What percentage of the population is *literate?* — opposite ILLITERATE
2 : having or showing knowledge about a particular subject • The job requires you to be computer *literate.* • politically *literate* — opposite ILLITERATE
– **literate** *noun, pl* **-ates** [*count*] • computer *literates* [=people who know how to use computers]

li·te·ra·ti /,lɪtəˈrɑː,tiː/ *noun*
the literati : educated people who know about and are interested in literature • a new novelist who has been embraced by *the literati*

lit·er·a·ture /ˈlɪtərəʧɚ/ *noun, pl* **-tures**
1 : written works (such as poems, plays, and novels) that are considered to be very good and to have lasting importance [*noncount*] She took courses in history and *literature.* • Her education gave her an appreciation for great *literature.* • He's an expert in American/German *literature.* • the *literature* of the Renaissance [*count*] studies in different Asian *literatures*
2 [*noncount*] **a** : books, articles, etc., about a particular subject • medical/scientific *literature* • To be knowledgeable about the latest technology, you've got to keep abreast of the (relevant) *literature.* **b** : printed materials (such as booklets, leaflets, and brochures) that provide information about something • Can you send me some *literature* about your product? • promotional/sales *literature*

lithe /ˈlaɪð/ *adj* [*more* ~; *most* ~] : moving in an easy and graceful way • a *lithe,* muscular athlete • the *lithe* body of a dancer
– **lithe·ly** *adv* – **lithe·ness** *noun* [*noncount*]

lith·i·um /ˈlɪθijəm/ *noun* [*noncount*] : a soft silver-white element that is the lightest metal known

lith·o·graph /ˈlɪθə,græf, *Brit* ˈlɪθə,grɑːf/ *noun, pl* **-graphs** [*count*] : a picture made by lithography • a book of his finest *lithographs*

li·thog·ra·phy /lɪˈθɑːgrəfi/ *noun* [*noncount*] : a method of printing from a flat surface (such as a smooth stone or a metal plate) that has been prepared so that the ink will only stick to the design that will be printed
– **li·tho·gra·pher** /lɪˈθɑːgrəfɚ/ *noun, pl* **-phers** [*count*]
– **lith·o·graph·ic** /,lɪθəˈgræfɪk/ *adj* • the *lithographic* process • *lithographic* ink/printing – **litho·graph·i·cal·ly** /,lɪθəˈgræfɪkli/ *adv*

lit·i·gant /ˈlɪtɪgənt/ *noun, pl* **-gants** [*count*] *law* : a person who is involved in a lawsuit : someone who is suing another person or is being sued by another person

lit·i·gate /ˈlɪtə,geɪt/ *verb* **-gates**; **-gat·ed**; **-gat·ing** *law* : to make (something) the subject of a lawsuit : to cause (a case, an issue, etc.) to be decided and settled in a court of law [+ *obj*] They agree to *litigate* all disputes in this court. [*no obj*] The company's unwillingness to make a deal increased her desire to *litigate.*
– **lit·i·ga·tion** /,lɪtəˈgeɪʃən/ *noun* [*noncount*] • He is involved in *litigation* against the city. • The case is still ***in litigation.*** [=being decided in a court of law] – **lit·i·ga·tor** /ˈlɪtə,geɪtɚ/ *noun, pl* **-tors** [*count*] • She is a famous/successful *litigator.* [=*lawyer*]

li·ti·gious /ləˈtɪʤəs/ *adj* [*more* ~; *most* ~] *formal* : too ready or eager to sue someone or something in a court of law : tending or likely to engage in lawsuits • a very *litigious* group of people • this *litigious* age/society in which we live
– **li·ti·gious·ness** *noun* [*noncount*]

lit·mus paper /ˈlɪtməs-/ *noun* [*noncount*] *technical* : special paper that is used to test how much acid is in a solution ✧ Litmus paper turns red in acid solutions and blue in alkaline solutions.

litmus test *noun, pl* ~ **tests** [*count*] : something (such as an opinion about a political or moral issue) that is used to make a judgment about whether someone or something is acceptable • The party is using attitudes about gun control as a *litmus test* for political candidates. — compare ACID TEST

litre *Brit spelling of* LITER

[1]lit·ter /ˈlɪtɚ/ *noun, pl* **-ters**

1 a [*noncount*] **:** things that have been thrown away and that are lying on the ground in a public place • We decided to pick up the *litter* in the park. • roadside *litter* **b** [*singular*] **:** a messy pile or group of things • Her desk was covered with a *litter* of legal documents.

2 [*noncount*] **a :** dry material that is spread in a container and used as a toilet by animals (especially cats) while they are indoors • cat/kitty *litter* • (*chiefly US*) a ***litter box*** = (*Brit*) a ***litter tray*** [=a container holding litter for a cat] **b :** soft and dry material (such as straw) that is spread on the ground for some animals (such as horses) to sleep on

3 [*count*] **:** a group of young animals that are born at a single time • a *litter* of puppies/piglets • He was the runt of the *litter*. [=the smallest animal in the litter] — often used figuratively in the phrase ***the pick of the litter*** • Of all the cars on the market, this one is clearly *the pick of the litter*. [=the best one]

4 [*count*] **:** a covered bed that has long poles on the bottom and that was used in the past for carrying a very important person • The emperor was carried to the palace on a *litter*.

[2]litter *verb* **-ters; -tered; -ter·ing**

1 [+ *obj*] **:** to cover (a surface) with many things in an untidy way • Paper and popcorn *littered* the streets after the parade. • Leaves *littered* the forest floor. [=the forest floor was covered with leaves] • a desk *littered* with old letters and bills — often used figuratively • a landscape *littered* with ugly houses • Dirty words *litter* his vocabulary. [=his vocabulary includes many dirty words; he says a lot of dirty words] • The book is *littered* with errors. [=the book contains many errors]

2 [*no obj*] **:** to throw or leave trash on the ground in a public place • It is illegal to *litter*. • He had to pay a fine for *littering*.

— lit·ter·er /ˈlɪtərɚ/ *noun, pl* **-ers** [*count*] • *Litterers* are subject to a fine.

litter bin *noun, pl* **~ bins** [*count*] *Brit* **:** TRASH CAN

lit·ter·bug /ˈlɪtɚˌbʌg/ *noun, pl* **-bugs** [*count*] *informal* **:** a person who throws or leaves trash in a public place — called also (*Brit*) *litter lout*

[1]lit·tle /ˈlɪtl/ *adj* **less** /ˈlɛs/ *or* **less·er** /ˈlɛsɚ/ *also* **lit·tler** /ˈlɪtlɚ/; **least** /ˈliːst/ *also* **lit·tlest** /ˈlɪtləst/

1 a : small in size • She has *little* feet. • a *little* island/airplane • a *little* business • Our school is *little*. • a ***tiny little*** fish • This room is *littler* [=(more commonly) *smaller*] than that one. **b :** not tall **:** SHORT • a *little* man • a *littler* [=(more commonly) *smaller, shorter*] man **c :** small in amount • I have very *little* money, so I can't lend you any. • I have *less* money than I did before. • I got very *little* sleep last night. • There's *little* hope of a rescue now. • You have *little* choice but to pay attention. • The new version bears *little* resemblance to the original. • These programs have very/precious *little* chance of succeeding. • The help he offered us was ***too little, too late***. [=it was not as much help as we needed and it was offered too late to be helpful] • There has been ***little if any*** improvement. [=there has been almost no improvement] • These trinkets have ***little or no*** value. • There was ***no little*** sadness in his voice. [=there was a lot of sadness in his voice] **d :** not having many things or people included • We're having a *little* party this weekend. • a *little* group of people • a *little* village • her *little* hometown

2 : young or younger • I loved swimming when I was *little*. • a *little* boy/girl • He's very proud of his *little* boy/girl. [=of his young son/daughter] • How's your *little* one? [=your young(est) son or daughter] • my ***little brother/sister*** [=my brother/sister who is younger than I am]

3 *always used before a noun* **:** not lasting for a long time • I have to take a *little* break. • We sat down for a *little* chat. • We talked for a *little* while.

4 *always used before a noun* **:** not very important • There are a few *little* problems that still have to be dealt with. • He memorized every *little* detail of the scene. — sometimes used in an ironic way to describe something important • There's just one *little* problem we haven't discussed: the company is going bankrupt! • I need to talk to you about the *little* matter of the money you owe me.

5 *always used before a noun* **:** not easily seen, heard, etc. • He gave her a *little* smile. • She made a *little* wave with her hand. • She spoke in a quiet *little* voice.

6 *always used before a noun* **a —** used to refer to someone or something in an approving or friendly way • That's a nice *little* car you've got there. • You poor *little* thing. • Bless your *little* heart. **b —** used to refer to someone or something in a disapproving or critical way • He's a *little* jerk. • It was a mean *little* joke. • She has a dirty *little* secret.

7 *always used before a noun* **:** not open to new ideas • people with *little* [=*small, narrow*] minds

— lit·tle·ness /ˈlɪtlnəs/ *noun* [*noncount*] • the *littleness* of the room • the *littleness* of their minds

[2]little *adv* **less; least**

1 a : in a very small amount or degree • She works very *little* and sleeps even *less*. • Please speak ***as little as possible***. **b :** hardly at all **:** not very much • We had *little* more than we needed. • She cared *little* (about) what he thought. • His art is *little* known in this country. • a *little*-known fact • She *little* knew what fate had in store for her. = ***Little did she know*** what fate had in store for her.

2 : not very often • She travels *little*. [=she rarely travels]

little by little **:** by small steps or amounts **:** GRADUALLY • *Little by little*, he got better. • The protest gathered strength *little by little*. • I got to know them *little by little*.

little more than *or* ***little better than*** **:** not much more or better than (something) **:** only slightly more or better than (something) • They ate *little more than* ice cream and hot dogs all day.

[3]little *pronoun* **:** a small amount or quantity • There is *little* we can do to help. • *Little* is known about her life. • They say precious *little* [=they do not say much] about their job. • They understand *little* of what is going on. • His argument did *little* to change their minds. [=his argument did not change their minds]

a little **1 :** not much but some • I don't want much: I want just *a little* bit/piece. • There's *a little* brown sugar in these cookies. • I have *a little* money, so I may be able to lend you some. • They offered him ***a little something*** to drink before dinner. [=they offered him something to drink] • There was ***more than a little*** sadness [=there was much sadness] in his voice. **2 :** not much but somewhat or slightly • It bothered me *a little*. • His house is down the street *a little* further. • His house is down the street *a little*. = It's *a little* down the street. • I'm feeling *a little* better today. • Repairs will begin in *a little* [=*slightly*] more than a month. • He was ***not a little*** annoyed [=he was very annoyed] at the interruption. • Her vision of the future was ***more than a little*** upsetting. [=was very upsetting] **3 :** for a brief time • Please stay here with me *a little*. • We can walk *a little* and then catch a cab. **4 :** a small amount or quantity • There is only *a* very *little* at stake here. • They don't understand much but they do understand *a little*. • There's still some money in the bank, but only *a* very *little*. • They understand ***more than a little of*** what is going on. [=they understand much of what is going on] • Don't use too much of this. ***A little goes a long way***. [=a small amount will be enough]

a little bit **1 :** to some extent **:** SOMEWHAT • This one is *a little bit* bigger than that one. • It bothered me *a little bit*. **2** *chiefly US* **:** a short time • We talked for *a little bit*. **3 :** a small amount of something • The buffet had *a little bit* of everything. • We have *a little bit* of time left. • Oh, I'll have just *a little bit*, thanks.

as little as **—** used to suggest that a number or quantity is surprisingly small • I could be back in *as little as* five days.

little wonder see [1]WONDER

little bitty *adj, chiefly US, informal* **:** very small **:** TINY • She was living in a *little bitty* apartment.

Little Dipper *noun*

the Little Dipper *US* **:** a group of seven stars including the North Star in the northern sky that forms the shape of a dipper or ladle and that is smaller than the Big Dipper — compare BIG DIPPER

little finger *noun, pl* **~ -gers** [*count*] **:** the finger that is farthest from your thumb — called also (*chiefly US* + *Scotland*) *pinkie*; see picture at HAND

little guy *noun*

the little guy *chiefly US, informal* **:** LITTLE MAN

Little League *noun* [*singular*] *US* **:** a baseball league for boys and girls from 8 to 12 years old • a man who coaches *Little League* [=who coaches a team in Little League] • a *Little League* team/game/player/coach

— Little Leaguer *noun, pl* **~ -ers** [*count*] • His son is a *Little Leaguer*. [=a Little League player]

little man *noun*

the little man *chiefly US, informal* **:** an ordinary person who is not wealthy, famous, or powerful — used to refer to such people in general • a politician who portrays himself as a friend of *the little man* — called also *the little guy*

little people *noun* [*plural*]
1 : ordinary people who are not wealthy, famous, or powerful • I'd like to thank all the *little people* who made my success possible.
2 : people of unusually small size
3 : very small imaginary beings (especially leprechauns) with magical powers • a fairy tale about the *little people*

little toe *noun, pl* **~ toes** [*count*] **:** the smallest toe on the outside of your foot

little woman *noun*
the little woman *old-fashioned + humorous + sometimes offensive* — used to refer to a man's wife • He bought a bouquet of flowers for *the little woman.* [=for his wife]

lit•to•ral /ˈlɪtərəl/ *adj, technical* **:** of, relating to, or having a coast • *littoral* waters • a *littoral* country [=a country that has a coast]
– littoral *noun, pl* **-rals** [*count*] • the Atlantic *littoral* [=coastal region]

lit•ur•gy /ˈlɪtəʤi/ *noun, pl* **-gies :** a fixed set of ceremonies, words, etc., that are used during public worship in a religion [*count*] studying the *liturgies* of different religions [*noncount*] He was studying Christian *liturgy.*
– li•tur•gi•cal /ləˈtəʤɪkəl/ *adj, always used before a noun* • The church used Latin as the *liturgical* language. • the *liturgical* calendar [=a list of the important holy days in a religion]

liv•able *or chiefly Brit* **live•able** /ˈlɪvəbəl/ *adj* [*more ~; most ~*]
1 : suitable to live in **:** enjoyable to live in • a *livable* city • They described the house as very/barely *livable.*
2 *US* **:** making it possible to live or to have the things that people need to live properly • *livable* conditions • People need jobs that will pay them *livable* wages.
– liv•abil•i•ty *or chiefly Brit* **live•abil•i•ty** /ˌlɪvəˈbɪləti/ *noun* [*noncount*]

[1]**live** /ˈlɪv/ *verb* **lives; lived; liv•ing**
1 [*no obj*] **a :** to be alive • We learned about the people who *lived* during colonial times. • I wonder what it was like to *live* then. • She's one of the greatest writers who ever *lived.* • It was one of the largest animals that has ever *lived.* **b :** to continue to be alive • He *lived* to the age of 92. • He's very sick and he may not *live* much longer. • I hope to *live* (long enough) to see my grandchildren grow up. • I hope I *live* to see the day when you admit you've been wrong about me! • I'll remember that day ***for as long as I live.*** • She's ***living on borrowed time.*** [=she is continuing to live after she was expected to die, but she will probably die soon] • ***Long live*** the Queen/King! [=may the Queen/King live for many years]
2 [*no obj*] **a :** to have a home in a specified place • He *lives* next door to his parents. • We *lived in* the city/suburbs/country. • I *live* on Main St. [=my house is on Main St.] • It's a nice place to visit, but I wouldn't want to *live* there. • He's still *living* at home (with his parents). • animals *living* in zoos **b** *of a plant or animal* **:** to grow naturally in a specified place or area • Tigers don't *live* in Africa. [=there are no tigers in the wild in Africa] • We've been studying the plants and animals that *live* in this area.
3 : to spend your life in a certain way or condition [*no obj*] They *live* well/simply. • He likes to *live* dangerously. • They *lived* peacefully for many years. • animals *living* in captivity • We know very little about how people in these ancient cultures *lived.* • They all ***lived happily ever after.*** [=they all lived happily for the rest of their lives] • He is ***living within/beyond his means.*** [=he can/cannot afford the things that he buys or the way he lives] [*+ obj*] If she believes that, she's *living* a fantasy. [=she is not seeing or accepting reality] • They are *living* the American Dream. [=they are experiencing success in America]
4 [*no obj*] **:** to have an enjoyable and exciting life • Now that he's retired he just wants to ***live a little.*** [=to spend time doing enjoyable things] • ***You haven't lived*** until you've had a piece of my mom's apple pie! [=you would greatly enjoy my mom's apple pie]
5 [*+ obj*] **a :** to spend (your life or part of your life) in a specified way • They *lived* (the rest of) their lives in quiet retirement. • He had *lived* a childhood free from worry. • She *lived* her final years in seclusion. • He ***lived life to the full/fullest.*** [=he fully enjoyed his life] **b :** to have (a particular kind of life) • She wants to *live* [=*lead*] a more productive life. • They *live* a normal life. • They are *living* a life of luxury. • He made a lot of money in the stock market and he's been ***living the good life*** [=living the life of a wealthy person] ever since.
6 [*no obj*] **:** to continue to exist • The good that people do *lives* long after they are gone. • That day will always *live* in my memory. [=I will always remember that day]
7 [*no obj*] *chiefly Brit, informal* **:** to belong in a specified place **:** to be located or stored • "Where does this book *live?*" "It goes/belongs on the top shelf."

live a lie see [4]LIE
live and breathe see BREATHE
live and learn *or* ***you live and (you) learn*** *informal* — used to say that you have learned something from an experience that is surprising and usually unpleasant • I thought I could trust him, but I couldn't. Oh well, *you live and learn.*
live and let live **:** to let others live the way they want to • His philosophy was to *live and let live.*
live by [*phrasal verb*] **1** ***live by (something)*** **:** to agree with and follow (something, such as a set of beliefs) • He tried to *live by* his faith. • a principle I try to *live by* **2 a** ***live by (doing something)*** **:** to survive by (doing something) • They were an ancient people who *lived by* hunting and gathering. **b** ***live by your wits*** **:** to survive by doing clever and sometimes dishonest things • Out in the jungle, with no food or shelter, he had to *live by his wits.* • a young thief who *lives by her wits*
live down [*phrasal verb*] ***live down (something)*** *or* ***live (something) down*** **:** to stop being blamed or laughed at for (something, such as a foolish or embarrassing error) • He has a very bad reputation to *live down.* — often used in negative statements • I can't believe I forgot my wife's birthday! I'll never *live* this *down.*
live for [*phrasal verb*] ***live for (something)*** **1 :** to wait or hope for (something) very eagerly • I *live for* the day when we'll be together! **2 :** to think of (something) as the most important or enjoyable part of your life • She *lives for* her work. **:** to think of (something) as a reason for being alive • He's depressed and feels as if he has nothing left to *live for.*
live in [*phrasal verb*] *chiefly Brit* **:** to live in the place where you work **:** to live in another person's home • a maid who *lives in*
live in hope see [2]HOPE
live in sin *old-fashioned* **:** to live together and have sex without being married • His mother did not want him *living in sin* with his girlfriend.
live in the past **:** to think too much about something that happened in the past • You have to accept that he's gone and stop *living in the past.*
live it up *informal* **:** to do exciting and enjoyable things • He's been *living it up* out in California with his friends.
live large *US slang* **:** to live like a very wealthy and successful person • a star who is *living large*
live off [*phrasal verb*] ***live off (something or someone)*** **:** to use (someone or something) as a source of the money or other things you need to live • He has been *living off* his inheritance. • He has been *living off* his girlfriend. [=his girlfriend has been supporting him financially] • farmers who *live off* the land
live on [*phrasal verb*] **1 :** to continue to exist • His legend *lives on.* **2** ***live on (something)*** **a :** to have or use (an amount of money) to pay for the things that you need to live • You can't *live on* this salary. [=this salary does not provide enough money for food, shelter, etc.] **b :** to have (a particular food) as the only or main food that you eat • They *lived* mainly/mostly *on* fruits and berries.
live out [*phrasal verb*] **1** *Brit* **:** to live away from the place where you work • a servant who *lives out* **2** ***live out (something)*** *or* ***live (something) out*** **a :** to spend the rest of (your life) in a specified way • He *lived out* (the final years of) his life in quiet retirement. **b :** to do (the things you have dreamed of doing) • He has finally had the chance to *live out* his dreams/fantasies.
live through [*phrasal verb*] **1** ***live through (something)*** **:** to survive (an experience, a troubling time, etc.) **:** ENDURE • If I can *live through* this, I can *live through* anything. **2** ***live through (someone)*** *US, sometimes disapproving* **:** to enjoy the experiences and achievements of (another person) instead of your own experiences and achievements • She can't *live through* her daughter.
live together [*phrasal verb*] **:** to live with another person and have sex without being married • They *lived together* for several months before getting married.
live up to [*phrasal verb*] ***live up to (something)*** **1 :** to do what is required by (something) • She *lived up to* her promises. [=she kept her promises] **2 :** to be good enough for (something) • He has found it difficult to *live up to* his

L

name/reputation. [=to be as good/successful as people think he is or should be] • Their vacation didn't *live up to* their expectations. [=their vacation wasn't as good as they expected it to be]

live with [*phrasal verb*] **1 *live with (something)*** : to accept and deal with (something unpleasant) • You have to learn to *live with* [=*put up with*] other people's mistakes. • I don't agree with his decision, but I'll have to *live with* it. • Until we get a better answer, we will have to *live with* not knowing for sure. • Because there was no cure, he had to learn to *live with* the disease. **2 *live with (someone)*** : to live together and usually have sex with (someone) • She's been *living with* him since college.

²live /ˈlaɪv/ *adj*

1 a *always used before a noun* : having life : living or alive • They object to the use of *live* animals in scientific experiments. • a ***live birth*** [=a birth of a living child or animal] **b** *informal* : not imaginary : actually existing — used in the phrase ***real live*** • Everyone was excited about seeing a *real live* celebrity. [=an actual celebrity]

2 a : done in front of an audience : of or involving a play, concert, etc., that is performed in front of people • a nightclub with *live* music/entertainment • The group has just released a ***live album***. [=an album made by recording a performance before an audience] **b** : watching a performance as it happens • a television program filmed before a *live* (studio) audience **c** : broadcast while a performance, event, etc., is happening : not recorded earlier • a *live* television/radio program • She was nervous about being interviewed on *live* radio. • The network is providing *live* coverage of the debate.

3 : carrying an electric current : connected to electric power • Use caution when you are working near *live* electrical wires. • a *live* microphone — see also LIVE WIRE

4 *always used before a noun* **a** : carrying a charge and capable of exploding or being shot • a *live* bomb • *live* ammunition • We had thought the guns were loaded with blanks, but the soldiers were actually shooting *live* bullets. **b** : burning without a flame : GLOWING • *live* coals

5 : not yet decided or settled : still causing discussion, disagreement, or concern • a *live* issue • a *live* controversy

6 *US, sports* : still in play • The ball is *live* until it goes out of bounds.

7 *Brit, of yogurt* : containing living bacteria • We sell *live* yogurt.

³live /ˈlaɪv/ *adv* : during, from, or at the actual time that something (such as a performance or event) happens • The program was shown *live*. • We are broadcasting *live* from downtown. • Here he is—*live* in concert! • The album was recorded *live*.

go live : to begin operating or to become available for use • Our new Web site will be *going live* next month.

liveable *chiefly Brit spelling of* LIVABLE

live action *noun* [*noncount*] : a movie or scene in which actors and sets are used : a movie or scene that is not produced by animation • a combination of *live action* and animation

– live–ac·tion /ˈlaɪvˈækʃən/ *adj, always used before a noun* • a *live-action* scene/film/sequence

-lived /ˌlɪvd/ *combining form* : having a life of a specified length • long-*lived* • relatively short-*lived*

lived–in /ˈlɪvdˌɪn/ *adj* [*more* ~; *most* ~]

1 : having a comfortable and appealing appearance or quality that comes from being used for a long time • The room has a *lived-in* look to it. • a *lived-in* kitchen

2 : showing the effects of age • a *lived-in* voice • a *lived-in* face

live–in /ˈlɪvˌɪn/ *adj, always used before a noun*

1 : living in the place where you work • a *live-in* maid [=a maid who lives in the house where she works]

2 : living with someone else (especially a boyfriend or girlfriend) • a young woman and her *live-in* boyfriend [=her boyfriend who is living with her] • his *live-in* girlfriend

live·li·hood /ˈlaɪvliˌhʊd/ *noun, pl* **-hoods** : a way of earning money in order to live [*count*] Many fishermen believe that the new regulations threaten their *livelihoods*. [*noncount*] (*formal*) He claims he lost a source/means of *livelihood* when he was injured.

live·long /ˈlɪvˌlɑːŋ/ *adj*

(all) the livelong day *old-fashioned + humorous* : all day • I've been working *all the livelong day*.

live·ly /ˈlaɪvli/ *adj* **live·li·er; -est** [*also more* ~; *most* ~]

1 : very active and energetic • *lively* children • a very *lively* puppy • She has a very ***lively imagination***. [=she imagines many things]

2 : full of energy, excitement, or feeling • a very *lively* writing style • The book is *lively* and well written. • They had a *lively* debate/discussion. • She takes a ***lively interest*** in politics. [=she is very interested in politics]

3 : full of movement or activity • *lively* streets • a *lively* dance • A *lively* atmosphere keeps people coming back to the café. • Trading on the stock market today was rather *lively*. [=*active*]

step lively (*chiefly US*) *or chiefly Brit* ***look lively*** : to go or move quickly : HURRY • You'll have to *step lively* if you don't want to be late for work.

– live·li·ness *noun* [*noncount*] the *liveliness* of the children/discussion/dance [*singular*] There's a wonderful *liveliness* about him.

liv·en /ˈlaɪvən/ *verb* **-ens; -ened; -en·ing**

1 [+ *obj*] : to make (something) more lively, interesting, or exciting • He played some music to *liven* the atmosphere. — usually + *up* • She tried to *liven up* [=*enliven*] her speech with a few jokes. • He suggested that we *liven* things *up* with a friendly bet on the game.

2 [*no obj*] : to become more lively, interesting, or exciting — + *up* • The party really *livened up* after she arrived.

live oak /ˈlaɪv-/ *noun, pl* ~ **oaks** [*count*] : a large type of oak tree that grows in the southern U.S.

liv·er /ˈlɪvɚ/ *noun, pl* **-ers**

1 [*count*] : a large organ of the body that produces bile and cleans the blood — see picture at HUMAN

2 : the liver of an animal (such as a calf or a chicken) that is eaten as food [*noncount*] We had *liver* and onions for dinner. [*count*] sautéed chicken *livers*

liv·er·ied /ˈlɪvərid/ *adj, formal* : wearing a livery • a *liveried* servant/chauffeur

liv·er·wurst /ˈlɪvɚˌwɚst/ *noun* [*noncount*] *chiefly US* : a type of soft sausage made chiefly of cooked liver • a pound of *liverwurst* • a *liverwurst* sandwich — called also (*chiefly Brit*) *liver sausage*

liv·ery /ˈlɪvəri/ *noun, pl* **-eries**

1 [*noncount*] : the business of keeping vehicles that people can hire — usually used before another noun • *livery* service • a *livery* cab

2 *Brit* : the colors or designs that are used on a company's products, vehicles, etc. [*noncount*] aircraft *livery* • cars with similar *livery* [*count*] cars with similar *liveries*

3 : a special uniform worn by servants especially in the past [*noncount*] servants in blue *livery* [*count*] servants wearing *liveries*

lives *plural of* ¹LIFE

live·stock /ˈlaɪvˌstɑːk/ *noun* : farm animals (such as cows, horses, and pigs) that are kept, raised, and used by people [*plural*] a market where *livestock* are bought and sold [*noncount*] a market where *livestock* is bought and sold

live wire *noun, pl* ~ **wires** [*count*] *informal* : a very lively and energetic person • She's a real *live wire*.

liv·id /ˈlɪvəd/ *adj* [*more* ~; *most* ~]

1 : very angry : FURIOUS • My father was *livid* (with rage) when I came home three hours late.

2 *literary* : having a dark purplish color • a *livid* bruise

¹liv·ing /ˈlɪvɪŋ/ *adj*

1 : not dead : having life • I was taught to respect all *living* things. • *living* beings/creatures/animals/plants • His aunt is his closest *living* relative. • He's one of our greatest *living* authors. • She's a ***living legend***. [=a very famous and admired person who is still alive] • It was the first time I had ever seen a ***living, breathing*** bear in the wild.

2 *always used before a noun* : currently active or being used • a *living* faith • *living* cultures • a ***living language*** [=a language that is still being used and spoken by people]

3 *always used before a noun* : having the form of a person who is alive • He is the ***living embodiment*** of cheapness. [=he is very cheap] • I'm ***living proof*** that success is possible. [=my success shows that other people can succeed as well]

4 *always used before a noun* : of or relating to the place, conditions, or manner in which people live • He and his wife have an unusual ***living arrangement***; they work in different cities and only see each other on weekends. • They use their backyard as an outdoor ***living area***. • They're moving to a larger home because they need more ***living space***. • These poor children are being raised in terrible ***living conditions***. • He gave me a tour of his ***living quarters***. [=the rooms where he lives]

5 *informal* — used to emphasize a noun • You scared the *liv-*

ing daylights out of me! • They threatened to beat the *living* crap out of him.

in living color : in the bright colors of real life • a television program shown *in living color* — often used figuratively • His opinions are aired once a week *in living color.* [=on a television program]

in/within living memory : during a time that can be remembered by people who are still alive • These events occurred *within living memory*.

²living *noun, pl* **-ings**

1 [*count*] : a way of earning money : the money that someone needs to pay for housing, food, etc. — usually singular • His investments provide him with a good *living.* [=provide him with enough money to live well] • What do you do ***for a living***? [=what is your job?] • He struggled to ***scratch/eke out a living*** as a farmer. • He ***earned a/his living*** as a cook. = He ***made a living*** by working as a cook.

2 [*noncount*] : a way of living • the challenges of city *living* • outdoor *living* • healthy *living* • It's summertime, and the *living* is easy. — see also ASSISTED LIVING, COST OF LIVING, STANDARD OF LIVING

3 ***the living*** : people who are alive • *the living* and the dead • The world belongs to *the living.*

in the land of the living see ¹LAND

living room *noun, pl* **~ rooms** [*count*] : a room in a house for general family use — usually singular • He is watching TV in the *living room.*

living standard *noun, pl* **~ -dards** [*count*] : STANDARD OF LIVING — usually plural • trying to improve/raise *living standards* for poor people

living wage *noun* [*singular*] : an amount of money you are paid for a job that is large enough to provide you with the basic things (such as food and shelter) needed to live an acceptable life • He was barely earning a *living wage.*

living will *noun, pl* **~ wills** [*count*] *law* : a document in which you say what medical decisions should be made if you become too sick or injured to make those decisions ✧ A living will usually says that a very sick or injured person should be allowed to die if there is no real hope of recovery.

liz·ard /ˈlɪzəd/ *noun, pl* **-ards** [*count*] : a type of reptile that has four legs and a long body and tail

ll *abbr* lines • *ll* 15–25

'll — used as a contraction of *will* • That*'ll* be enough. • I don't know who*'ll* be there.

lla·ma /ˈlɑːmə/ *noun, pl* **-mas** [*count*] : a South American animal that has a long neck and thick fur and that is used for its wool and for carrying things

lo /ˈloʊ/ *interj, old-fashioned + literary* — used to call attention to something or to show wonder or surprise • *Lo,* the king approaches! • the adventures we have shared for *lo* these many years

lo and behold — used to express wonder or surprise; often used in a humorous or ironic way • She appeared on a magazine cover, and *lo and behold*, she began to get offers to star in movies. • We opened the door, and *lo and behold*, the delivery man had arrived.

¹load /ˈloʊd/ *noun, pl* **loads** [*count*]

1 a : something that is lifted and carried • He lifted the *load* onto his shoulders. • donkeys hauling/carrying large *loads* • She was carrying a heavy *load* of legal documents in her briefcase. • a light *load* **b** : an amount that can be carried at one time : an amount that fills something (such as a truck) • He picked up a *load* of firewood and carried it into the house. • The truck was carrying a full *load of* sand. • a ***load of laundry*** [=the amount of laundry that can fit into a washing machine] — often used in combination • an arm*load* of firewood • a truck*load* of sand • a boat*load* of tourists

2 *somewhat technical* : the weight that is carried or supported by something • Losing weight will lessen the *load* on your knees. • a *load*-bearing wall [=a wall that supports the weight of a building]

3 a : something that causes worry or sadness • His death is a heavy *load* to bear. • The good news has really ***taken a load off my mind***. [=has allowed me to stop worrying; has made me feel relieved] **b** : a difficult responsibility • There's a lot of work to be done, and you have to carry/bear your share of the *load.* [=you have to do your share of the work] • I wish there were some way I could help lift this *load* [=*weight, burden*] from his shoulders. • The company is trying to reduce its ***debt load***. [=the amount of money that it owes]

4 *informal* **a** : a large amount of something • They had a *load* of trouble. — usually plural • We had *loads* of fun. • The house has *loads* of room. • I have *loads* [=many things] to do today. **b** — used in phrases like ***a load of garbage, a load of trash, a load of hot air***, etc., to say that something is worthless • I think their ideas are a *load of garbage!*

living room

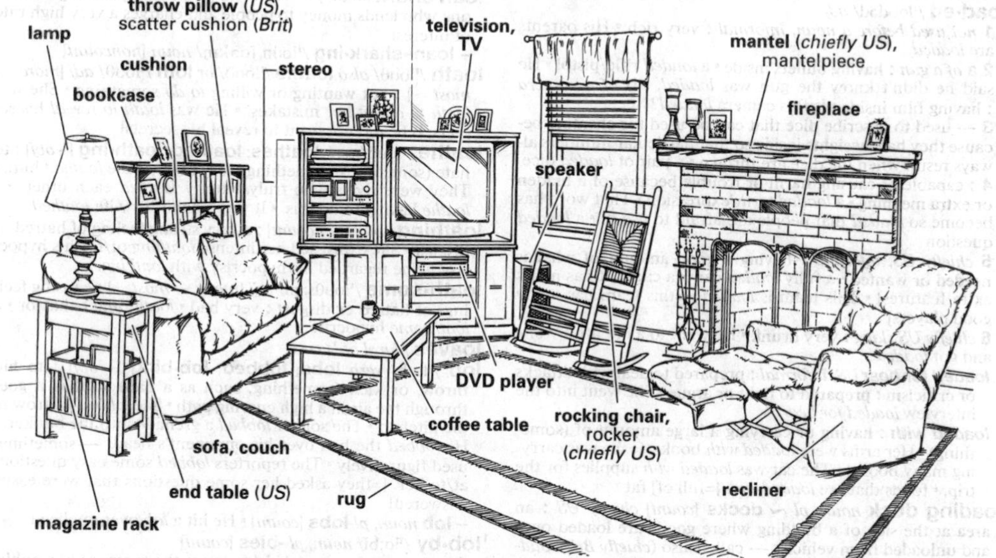

5 a : the amount of work done or expected to be done ▪ a full *load* of teaching work ▪ She's taking a full/heavy course *load* this semester. — see also CASELOAD, WORKLOAD **b** *technical* : the amount of work done by a machine ▪ the *load* on an engine **c** *technical* : the amount of power used by an electrical device or produced by a power source ▪ The electrical system failed because it couldn't handle the *load*.

get a load of *informal* : to look at (someone or something) ▪ *Get a load of* that car! ▪ You should *get a load of* his pants.

take a load off (your feet) *chiefly US, informal* : to sit down and relax ▪ You look tired. Come in and *take a load off*.

²load *verb* **loads; load·ed; load·ing**

1 a : to put an amount of something in or on (something) [+ *obj*] *load* a truck with packages ▪ We *loaded* (up) the car and drove off. ▪ Workers were *loading* and unloading the ships as they came into port. [*no obj*] We *loaded* up and drove off. **b** [+ *obj*] : to put (an amount of something) into or onto something ▪ *load* packages on/onto a truck ▪ We *loaded* our luggage in/into the car and drove off. ▪ Workers were *loading* cargo on/onto the ships. **c** [+ *obj*] : to supply (someone or something) *with* a large amount of something ▪ Mom *loaded* me (up) *with* supplies for the hike. ▪ She *loaded* the table *with* all kinds of delicious foods. ▪ My sister *loaded* [=*filled*] her plate *with* mashed potatoes and corn.

2 : to put something necessary into a machine or device so that it can be used [+ *obj*] *load* a camera with film = *load* film into a camera ▪ *load* a gun (with bullets) = *load* bullets into a gun ▪ *load* a tape into the VCR [*no obj*] The film didn't *load* properly.

3 a [+ *obj*] *of a boat, vehicle, etc.* : to be boarded by (passengers) ▪ The bus stopped to *load* a few more passengers. **b** [*no obj*] : to go onto something (such as a boat or vehicle) ▪ The passengers *loaded* on/onto the bus.

4 *computers* : to cause (a program, file, etc.) to begin being used or displayed by a computer [+ *obj*] *load* a program ▪ *load* a new Web page [*no obj*] The program takes less time to *load* than it used to. — see also DOWNLOAD, UPLOAD

5 [+ *obj*] *baseball* : to put runners on (first, second, and third base) ▪ He drew a walk to *load* the bases. ▪ The bases are *loaded*. [=there are runners on each of the bases]

load down with [*phrasal verb*] ***load (someone or something) down with (something)*** : to cause or force (someone or something) to accept or deal with (something difficult) — usually used as *(be) loaded down with* ▪ The company *is loaded down with* debt. [=is burdened with debt; has a large amount of debt] ▪ *I'm loaded down with* homework.

load the dice see ¹DICE

load up on [*phrasal verb*] ***load up on (something)*** *informal* **1 :** to drink or eat a large amount of (something) ▪ people *loading up on* fatty foods **2 :** to get a large amount of (something) ▪ investors who have been *loading up on* hot stocks

– load·er *noun, pl* **-ers** [*count*] ▪ a film *loader*

load·ed /ˈloʊdəd/ *adj*

1 *not used before a noun, informal* : very rich ▪ His parents are *loaded*.

2 a *of a gun* : having bullets inside ▪ a *loaded* rifle/pistol ▪ He said he didn't know the gun was *loaded*. **b** *of a camera* : having film inside ▪ Is this camera *loaded*?

3 — used to describe dice that can be used for cheating because they have weights inside so that particular numbers always result when the dice are thrown ▪ a pair of *loaded* dice

4 : capable of causing harm or trouble because of a hidden or extra meaning ▪ a *loaded* term/expression ▪ That word has become so *loaded* that people are afraid to use it. ▪ a *loaded* question

5 *chiefly US, informal* : having a good amount of what is needed or wanted ▪ a fully *loaded* car [=a car that has many extra features] ▪ This team is *loaded*. [=this team has many good players]

6 *chiefly US slang* : very drunk ▪ He went to a bar after work and got *loaded*.

loaded for bear *US, informal* : prepared to deal with attacks or criticism : prepared to fight or argue ▪ She went into the interview *loaded for bear*.

loaded with : having or carrying a large amount of (something) ▪ Her arms were *loaded with* books. [=she was carrying many books] ▪ The car was *loaded with* supplies for the trip. ▪ foods that are *loaded with* [=full of] fat

loading dock *noun, pl* **~ docks** [*count*] *chiefly US* : an area at the side of a building where goods are loaded onto and unloaded from vehicles — called also (*chiefly Brit*) *loading bay*

¹loaf /ˈloʊf/ *noun, pl* **loaves** /ˈloʊvz/

1 [*count*] : an amount of bread that has been baked in a long, round, or square shape ▪ slicing a *loaf* of bread

2 [*count, noncount*] : a dish made from foods (such as chopped meat, eggs, and seasoning) that are pressed together, shaped, and usually baked ▪ a salmon *loaf* — see also MEAT LOAF

²loaf *verb* **loafs; loafed; loaf·ing** [*no obj*] : to spend time relaxing instead of working ▪ I spent most of the weekend just *loafing* around the house. ▪ He has been accused of *loafing* on the job. [=he has been accused of not working when he should be working]

loaf·er /ˈloʊfɚ/ *noun, pl* **-ers** [*count*]

1 : a low shoe with no laces — usually plural ▪ He wore *loafers* with no socks. ▪ slipped on a pair of *loafers* — see picture at SHOE; see also PENNY LOAFER

2 : a person who does not work hard ▪ She's a lazy *loafer*.

loam /ˈloʊm/ *noun* [*noncount*] : a type of soil that is good for growing plants

– loamy /ˈloʊmi/ *adj* **loam·i·er; -est** ▪ *loamy* soil

¹loan /ˈloʊn/ *noun, pl* **loans**

1 [*count*] : an amount of money that is given to someone for a period of time with a promise that it will be paid back : an amount of money that is borrowed ▪ He took out a *loan* (from the bank) to pay for the car. ▪ He got a car *loan*. ▪ He'll need several more years to pay off/back the rest of the *loan*. ▪ She needed money, so she asked her friend for a *loan*. ▪ a ***student loan*** [=a loan that is used to pay for a student's education] ▪ a ***bank loan*** [=a loan that is made by a bank] ▪ a ***personal loan*** [=a loan that is made by a bank to someone for a personal need]

2 [*noncount*] *somewhat formal* : permission to use something for a period of time ▪ Can I have the *loan* of your car? [=(more commonly) can I borrow your car?]

on loan : borrowed from someone or something for a period of time ▪ This painting is *on loan* from the National Gallery. ▪ an actor *on loan* from another sitcom ▪ Some of the workers were *on loan* as temporary staff.

²loan *verb* **loans; loaned; loan·ing** [+ *obj*]

1 : to give (something) to (someone) for a period of time : LEND ▪ He *loaned* his car to me. = He *loaned* me his car. [=I borrowed his car] ▪ The National Gallery has been kind enough to *loan* this painting to our museum. — sometimes + *out* ▪ The National Gallery *loaned out* the painting to another museum.

2 *chiefly US* : to give (money) to (someone) who agrees to pay it back in the future : LEND ▪ His mother *loaned* him the money to buy a new car. ▪ Can you *loan* me $20?

loan·er /ˈloʊnɚ/ *noun, pl* **-ers** [*count*] *US* : something (such as a car) that is loaned to someone as a replacement for something that is being repaired ▪ The car he's driving is a *loaner*. His own car was damaged in an accident.

loan shark *noun, pl* **~ sharks** [*count*] *disapproving* : someone who lends money to people and charges a very high rate of interest

– loan–shark·ing /ˈloʊnˌʃɑɚkɪŋ/ *noun* [*noncount*]

loath /ˈloʊθ/ *also* **loathe** /ˈloʊð/ *or* **loth** /ˈloʊθ/ *adj* [*more ~; most ~*] : not wanting or willing *to do* something ▪ She was *loath to admit* her mistakes. ▪ He was *loath to reveal* his secrets. [=he did not want to reveal his secrets]

loathe /ˈloʊð/ *verb* **loathes; loathed; loath·ing** [+ *obj*] : to hate (someone or something) very much ▪ She *loathed* him. ▪ They were rivals who truly/bitterly *loathed* each other. ▪ I *loathe* having to do this. ▪ It was a habit his wife *loathed*.

loathing *noun* [*noncount*] : a very strong feeling of hatred or disgust ▪ She expressed her intense *loathing* of/for his hypocrisy. ▪ She regarded his hypocrisy with *loathing*.

loath·some /ˈloʊθsəm/ *adj* [*more ~; most ~*] : causing feelings of hatred or disgust : very bad ▪ *loathsome* behavior ▪ a *loathsome* hypocrite

loaves *plural of* ¹LOAF

lob /ˈlɑːb/ *verb* **lobs; lobbed; lob·bing** [+ *obj*] : to hit, throw, or kick (something, such as a ball) so that it goes through the air in a high curving path ▪ She *lobbed* a throw to the pitcher. ▪ The soldier *lobbed* a grenade into the bunker. ▪ He *lobbed* the ball over his opponent's head. — sometimes used figuratively ▪ The reporters *lobbed* some easy questions at/to her. [=they asked her some questions that were easily answered]

– lob *noun, pl* **lobs** [*count*] ▪ He hit a *lob* over my head.

¹lob·by /ˈlɑːbi/ *noun, pl* **-bies** [*count*]

1 : a large open area inside and near the entrance of a public building (such as a hotel or theater) ▪ a hotel *lobby* ▪ I'll meet you in the *lobby* after the show.

2 : an organized group of people who work together to influence government decisions that relate to a particular industry, issue, etc. ▪ the gun/tobacco *lobby* ▪ The proposed new law is supported/opposed by the oil *lobby*.

[2]lobby *verb* **-bies; -bied; -by·ing**

1 : to try to influence government officials to make decisions for or against something [*no obj*] an organization that has been *lobbying* for reform of the tax laws ▪ The health-care industry has *lobbied* against the proposal. [*+ obj*] an organization that has been *lobbying* Congress for reform of the tax laws — often followed by *to + verb* ▪ They were *lobbying* Congress *to reform* the tax laws.

2 : to try to get something you want by talking to the people who make decisions [*no obj*] She has begun *lobbying* for an interview. [=trying to get an interview] ▪ a player who has *lobbied* hard to be included in the team's starting lineup [*+ obj*] I *lobbied* our company for a new computer.

– lob·by·ist /ˈlɑːbijɪst/ *noun, pl* **-ists** [*count*] ▪ She was hired as a *lobbyist* for an oil company.

lobe /ˈloʊb/ *noun, pl* **lobes** [*count*]

1 : a curved or rounded part of something (such as a leaf or a part of the body) ▪ the frontal *lobe* of the brain

2 : EARLOBE

– lobed /ˈloʊbd/ *adj* ▪ deeply *lobed* leaves

lo·bot·o·my /loʊˈbɑːtəmi/ *noun, pl* **-mies** [*count*] *medical* **:** an operation in which part of the brain is cut in order to treat some mental disorders

– lo·bot·o·mize /loʊˈbɑːtəˌmaɪz/ *verb* **-miz·es; -mized; -miz·ing** [*+ obj*] ▪ The patient was *lobotomized*.

lob·ster /ˈlɑːbstɚ/ *noun, pl* **-sters**

1 [*count*] **:** an ocean animal that has a long body, a hard shell, and a pair of large claws and that is caught for food — see color picture on page C8

2 [*noncount*] **:** the meat of the lobster eaten as food ▪ I had *lobster* for dinner.

lobster pot *noun, pl* **~ pots** [*count*] **:** a trap for catching lobsters

[1]lo·cal /ˈloʊkəl/ *adj*

1 a : relating to or occurring in a particular area, city, or town ▪ *local* news ▪ a *local* custom ▪ Are you making a *local* (telephone) call or a long-distance one? ▪ a *local* newspaper ▪ *local* and state roads **b :** located or living nearby ▪ We had dinner at a *local* restaurant. ▪ The police have arrested a *local* man for the crime. ▪ This is a *local* shop for *local* people: we don't get many outsiders here.

2 *of a bus or train* **:** making all the stops on a route ▪ She took the *local* bus. — compare EXPRESS

3 : involving or affecting only a small area of the body ▪ a *local* infection ▪ *local* anesthesia

– lo·cal·ly *adv* ▪ *locally* grown corn ▪ The restaurant is known *locally* for its hamburgers. ▪ Do you live *locally*? [=in this area]

[2]local *noun, pl* **locals** [*count*]

1 : a person who lives in a particular area, city, or town **:** a local person — usually plural ▪ The restaurant is popular with (the) *locals*.

2 : a train or bus that makes all of the stops along its route — compare EXPRESS

3 *US* **:** a local part of a labor union ▪ He's the president of the union *local* at the factory.

4 *Brit, informal* **:** a pub that is near the place where you live **:** a local pub ▪ my mates down at the *local*

local area network *noun, pl* **~ -works** [*count*] *computers* **:** a network that allows the computers in a small area (such as an office) to share equipment (such as printers) and data — called also *LAN*

local authority *noun, pl* **~ -ties** [*count*] *Brit* **:** an organization that is in charge of the public services for a community

local color (*US*) *or Brit* **local colour** *noun* [*noncount*] **:** interesting information about a particular place and about the people who live there that is included in a story, movie, etc. ▪ a writer who uses *local color* in his stories

lo·cale /loʊˈkæl, *Brit* ləʊˈkɑːl/ *noun, pl* **-cales** [*count*] **:** the place where something happens ▪ They chose a tropical island as the *locale* for their wedding. **:** the place where a story happens in a movie, book, etc. ▪ the film's *locale* [=*setting*] ▪ the *locale* of the story

local government *noun, pl* **~ -ments** [*count, noncount*] **:** the government that controls and makes decisions for a local area (such as a town, city, or county)

lo·cal·i·ty /loʊˈkæləti/ *noun, pl* **-ties** [*count*] **:** a particular place or area ▪ The plant has only been found in one *locality*. ▪ a *locality* with high housing prices

lo·cal·ize *also Brit* **lo·cal·ise** /ˈloʊkəˌlaɪz/ *verb* **-iz·es; -ized; -iz·ing** [*+ obj*]

1 : to keep (something) within a limited area **:** to prevent the spread of (something) ▪ Doctors are trying to *localize* the infection by using antibiotics.

2 : to find or identify the location of (something) ▪ The computer technician was able to *localize* the fault quickly.

– lo·cal·i·za·tion *also Brit* **lo·cal·i·sa·tion** /ˌloʊkələˈzeɪʃən, *Brit* ˌləʊkəˌlaɪˈzeɪʃən/ *noun* [*noncount*]

localized *also Brit* **localised** *adj* [*more ~; most ~*] **:** occurring only within a small area ▪ The storm has caused *localized* flooding. ▪ a *localized* infection

local time *noun* [*noncount*] **:** the time in a particular part of the world ▪ We'll be arriving in New York at 10:45 *local time*. [=it will be 10:45 in New York when we arrive]

lo·cate /ˈloʊˌkeɪt, loʊˈkeɪt/ *verb* **-cates; -cat·ed; -cat·ing**

1 [*+ obj*] **:** to find the place or position of (something or someone) ▪ We tried to *locate* the border of the property. ▪ Can you *locate* your town on the map? ▪ The missing boy was *located* by police in the woods. ▪ The mechanic is still trying to *locate* the source of the problem. ▪ Reporters have been unable to *locate* the mayor for his comments.

2 a [*+ obj*] **:** to put (something or someone) in a particular place ▪ The company chose to *locate* its factory near the airport. ▪ The guard *located* [=*stationed, positioned*] himself by the back door. **b** [*no obj*] *US* **:** to make an area, city, etc., your home or the place where your business operates ▪ The company *located* near the airport. ▪ His parents *located* in Ohio. **c** ✧ Something or someone that ***is located*** in a specified place is in or at that place. ▪ The bathroom *is located* upstairs. ▪ The company's factory *is located* [=*situated*] near the airport. ▪ He was working in Chicago for many years, but he *is* currently *located* in New York. ▪ The restaurant *is* conveniently *located* just a few minutes from my house.

lo·ca·tion /loʊˈkeɪʃən/ *noun, pl* **-tions**

1 [*count*] **:** a place or position ▪ This is a lovely *location* for a house. ▪ The store has a new *location*. ▪ The company is moving its factory to a different *location*. ▪ Radar established the precise *location* of the aircraft.

2 : a place outside a studio where a movie is filmed [*count*] All of his movies feature lavish sets and exotic *locations*. [*noncount*] The picture was filmed ***on location*** in the desert.

3 [*noncount*] **:** the act of finding where something or someone is **:** the act of locating something or someone ▪ Fog made *location* of the harbor difficult.

loch /ˈlɑːk/ *noun, pl* **lochs** [*count*] *Scotland* **:** a lake or a part of the sea that is almost surrounded by land — used in names ▪ *Loch* Lomond ▪ *Loch* Ness

loci *plural of* LOCUS

[1]lock /ˈlɑːk/ *noun, pl* **locks**

1 [*count*] **:** a device that keeps something (such as a door, window, or box) from being opened and that is usually opened by using a key ▪ We had no key so we had to break the *lock* to open the door. ▪ The thief used a wire to pick the *lock*. — see also COMBINATION LOCK, PADLOCK

2 [*count*] **:** an area in a canal or river that has gates at each end which are opened and closed to control the level of the water in different sections of the canal or river as boats move through it

3 [*count*] **:** a method of holding someone so that the person being held cannot move ▪ a leg *lock* — see also HEADLOCK

4 *US, informal* **a** [*singular*] **:** complete control of something ▪ He appears to ***have a lock on*** the nomination for governor. [=he appears to be sure of getting the nomination for governor] ▪ He has been able to ***get a lock on*** the nomination. ▪ There seems to be no danger that the company will ***lose its lock on*** the industry. **b** [*count*] **:** someone or something that is certain to have or do something — usually singular ▪ He's a *lock* for the nomination. = He's a *lock* to get the nomination. [=he is certain to get the nomination] ▪ The team is a *lock* to win the championship. **c** [*count*] **:** something that is certain to happen — usually singular ▪ It looks like his nomination is a *lock*.

5 [*count, noncount*] *Brit* **:** the extent to which the front wheels of a vehicle can be turned ▪ a car ***on full lock*** [=a car with its wheels turned as far as possible]

lock, stock, and barrel **:** including everything **:** wholly or completely ▪ She gave her friend everything she owned, *lock, stock, and barrel*, and moved away. ▪ He insisted that

he be given control of the business, *lock, stock, and barrel.*
under lock and key : in a room, box, etc., that is locked • The jewels are kept *under lock and key.* • The prisoner is being kept/held *under lock and key.*
– compare ³LOCK

²lock *verb* **locks; locked; lock·ing**
1 a [+ *obj*] : to fasten (something) with a lock • They *locked* the door when they left and unlocked it when they returned. • She *locked* the bicycle to the railing with a chain. • The door was *locked.* **b** [+ *obj*] : to fasten the door, lid, etc., of (something) with a lock • He forgot to *lock* the car. • They *locked* the box (shut) with a padlock. • a *locked* room — often + *up* • She *locked up* the house. **c** [*no obj*] : to become fastened with a lock • The door *locked* behind him. [=after he went through it] • The car *locks* automatically when you start the engine.
2 a [*no obj*] : to become fixed in one position • The wheels/brakes *locked* and the car skidded off the road. • Their eyes *locked.* [=they looked directly at each other without looking away] **b** [+ *obj*] : to hold (someone or something) in a fixed position • He *locked* her in his arms. = He *locked* her in a tight/close embrace. [=he embraced her tightly/closely] • They were *locked* in each other's arms. • He *locked* his fingers around her wrist [=he gripped her wrist very tightly] and refused to let go. • She *locked* her hands around the steering wheel. • Protesters *locked* [=*linked*] arms across the forest road. • His ***eyes were locked on*** her as she walked across the room. [=he was looking at her and at nothing else] • Repeat the exercise, being careful not to ***lock your knees***. [=being careful not to hold your knees in a fully extended position] — often used figuratively • They were *locked* in a contract dispute. • two armies *locked* in a terrible struggle/fight • She was *locked* [=*trapped*] in a loveless marriage.
3 [+ *obj*] *computers* : to make (a file, database, etc.) impossible for others to open or change • *lock* a database • The file is *locked* for editing.
lock away [*phrasal verb*] **1 *lock (something) away or lock away (something)*** : to put (something) in a locked container, place, etc. • The jewelry was *locked away* [=*locked up*] in a cabinet. **2 *lock (someone) away or lock away (someone)*** : to put (someone) in a locked place (such as a prison) for a long period of time • *lock away* [=*lock up*] a criminal • The state *locked* their sister *away* in a psychiatric hospital. **3 *lock (yourself) away*** : to stay in a room or place by yourself for a long period of time • He *locked himself away* in his room while he studied. = He was *locked away* in his room while he studied.
lock horns : to disagree about how something should be done : to fight or argue • They've *locked horns* (with each other) over this issue a number of times.
lock in [*phrasal verb*] **1 *lock (someone or something) in*** : to put or keep (someone or something) in a locked place, room, etc. • She *locked* her brother *in* the bathroom. • They *locked* the jewels *in* a safe. • They threatened to *lock* him *in* jail. • They pushed him into the room and *locked* him *in.* **2 *lock (something) in or lock in (something)*** : to do something that makes you sure to get (something that could change, such as a good price, an interest rate, etc.) • If you sign the contract today, you can *lock in* this low interest rate before it goes any higher.
lock on/onto [*phrasal verb*] ***lock on/onto (something)*** : to use electronic methods to find (a target) • The pilot *locked onto* the ship and fired a missile. • The missile *locked on* the target.
lock out [*phrasal verb*] ***lock (someone) out or lock out (someone)*** **1** : to prevent (someone) from entering a place, car, etc., by locking it • I *locked* myself *out* accidentally. — often + *of* • She *locked* her husband *out of* the house. **2** : to prevent (workers) from going to work in order to force an agreement • The company has threatened to *lock out* its factory workers unless they agree to a new contract. — see also LOCKOUT
lock up [*phrasal verb*] **1** : to lock all of the doors of a building before leaving it • The last employee to leave the store at night has to *lock up.* **2 *lock (something) up or lock up (something)*** **a** : to put (something) in a locked container, room, etc. • The money is *locked up* [=*locked away*] in a safe. — sometimes used figuratively • Most of his money is *locked up* in real estate. [=most of his money is not easily available because it is invested in real estate] **b** *chiefly US* : to make control or achievement of (something) certain • The team has first place *locked up.* [=the team is certain of getting first place] • He was unable to *lock up* enough states to win the election. — see also ²LOCK 1b (above) **3 *lock (someone) up or lock up (someone)*** : to put (someone) in a locked place (such as a prison) for a long period of time • The police should *lock* him *up.* [=lock him away] — see also LOCKUP

³lock *noun, pl* **locks**
1 [*count*] : a small bunch of hair • She was nervously tugging on a *lock* of her hair. — see also FORELOCK
2 *locks* [*plural*] *literary + humorous* : a person's hair • I love her curly *locks.* [=her curly hair] • her long, flowing *locks* • golden *locks* — see also DREADLOCKS
– compare ¹LOCK

lock·er /ˈlɑːkɚ/ *noun, pl* **-ers** [*count*]
1 : a cupboard or cabinet that has a door which can be locked and that is used to store personal items (such as books, clothes, shoes, etc.) • a school *locker* — see also FOOTLOCKER
2 *US* : a cold room in which fresh or frozen foods are stored • a meat *locker*

locker room *noun, pl* **~ rooms** [*count*] : a room in a school, sports stadium, etc., for changing clothes and for storing clothes and equipment in lockers — called also (*Brit*) *changing room*

lock·er–room /ˈlɑːkɚˌruːm/ *adj, always used before a noun, chiefly US* : of, relating to, or suitable to a locker room • the *locker-room* entrance • *locker-room* language [=the kind of rough or rude language that is used by athletes in a locker room] • *locker-room* humor

lock·et /ˈlɑːkət/ *noun, pl* **-ets** [*count*] : a small case that is usually worn on a chain around a person's neck • She kept her husband's picture in her *locket.* — see color picture on page C11

lock·jaw /ˈlɑːkˌʤɑː/ *noun* [*noncount*] *informal* : TETANUS

lock·out /ˈlɑːkˌaʊt/ *noun, pl* **-outs** [*count*] : a situation in which an employer tries to force workers to accept certain conditions by refusing to let them come to work until those conditions are accepted — see also *lock out* at ²LOCK

lock·smith /ˈlɑːkˌsmɪθ/ *noun, pl* **-smiths** [*count*] : a person whose job is to make and repair locks

lock·step /ˈlɑːkˌstɛp/ *noun* [*noncount*] : a way of marching in which people follow each other very closely
in lockstep *chiefly US* : in a way that very closely matches someone or something else • Drug use and crime grew *in lockstep.* [=they grew at the same time and at the same rate] • He refused to ***march in lockstep with*** [=to conform with] others in the party.

lock·up /ˈlɑːkˌʌp/ *noun, pl* **-ups** [*count*]
1 : a place where prisoners are kept : JAIL • a police station *lockup* — see also *lock up* at ²LOCK
2 *Brit* : a garage (sense 1) that is rented out — called also *lockup garage*

lo·co /ˈloʊkoʊ/ *adj* [*more* ~; *most* ~] *chiefly US, informal* : CRAZY • The crowd went *loco* when she walked out on the stage. • He's not just weird, he's positively *loco.* — see also IN LOCO PARENTIS

lo·co·mo·tion /ˌloʊkəˈmoʊʃən/ *noun* [*noncount*] *technical* : the act or power of moving from place to place • studying the *locomotion* of spiders [=studying how spiders move] • Walking is one form of *locomotion.*

¹lo·co·mo·tive /ˌloʊkəˈmoʊtɪv/ *noun, pl* **-tives** [*count*] : the vehicle that produces the power that pulls a train

²locomotive *adj* [*more* ~; *most* ~] *technical* : of or relating to movement from place to place : of or relating to locomotion • the *locomotive* ability of spiders • *locomotive* power

lo·cum /ˈloʊkəm/ *noun, pl* **-cums** [*count*] *chiefly Brit* : someone (such as a priest or doctor) who does the work of another person who is away for a short time

lo·cus /ˈloʊkəs/ *noun, pl* **lo·ci** /ˈloʊˌsaɪ/ [*count*] *formal* : a central or main place where something happens or is found • The area became a *locus* of resistance to the government.

lo·cust /ˈloʊkəst/ *noun, pl* **-custs** [*count*] : a type of grasshopper that travels in very large groups and that can cause great destruction by eating crops • a swarm of *locusts*

lo·cu·tion /loʊˈkjuːʃən/ *noun, pl* **-tions** [*count*] *technical* : a particular way of using words : a word or phrase • We were taught to avoid certain *locutions* when speaking.

lode /ˈloʊd/ *noun, pl* **lodes** [*count*] : an amount of a mineral (such as gold or silver) that fills a crack or space in rock — often used figuratively • In her books she mines the seemingly endless *lode* of her personal experiences. — see also MOTHER LODE

lode·star /ˈloudˌstɑɚ/ *noun, pl* **-stars** [*count*] *formal* : something or someone that leads or guides a person or group of people • The idea of public service has been a *lodestar* for her throughout her life.

lode·stone /ˈloudˌstoun/ *noun, pl* **-stones** [*count*] : a magnetic rock — sometimes used figuratively • The city is a *lodestone* [=*magnet*] for aspiring actors and actresses.

¹lodge /ˈlɑːʤ/ *verb* **lodg·es; lodged; lodg·ing**
1 a [+ *obj*] : to provide (someone) with a place to stay for a short period of time • The workers were *lodged* in temporary camps. • The refugees needed to be *lodged* and fed. **b** [*no obj*] : to stay at a place for a short period of time • We *lodged* at the resort. — often + *with* • The guests *lodged with* their hosts overnight.
2 : to become stuck or fixed in a specified place or position [*no obj*] The bullet *lodged* in his brain. [+ *obj*] The bullet *lodged* itself in his brain. — often used as *(be) lodged* • The bullet *was lodged* in his brain. • A fish bone ***got/became lodged*** in her throat. — often used figuratively • a scene that *is lodged* in my memory [=a scene that I cannot forget]
3 [+ *obj*] : to present (something, such as a complaint) to someone so that it can be considered, dealt with, etc. : FILE • The group has *lodged* a grievance. — often + *against* • She *lodged* a complaint *against* her landlord in court. • He disputes the charges that have been *lodged against* him.
4 [+ *obj*] *chiefly Brit* : to place (something, such as money) *in* something or *with* someone so that it can be kept safe • The funds were *lodged in* an offshore account. • The funds were *lodged with* an offshore bank.

²lodge *noun, pl* **lodges** [*count*]
1 : a house or hotel in the country or mountains for people who are doing some outdoor activity • a hunting/ski *lodge*
2 : the place where a beaver lives • a beaver/beaver's *lodge*
3 a : a local group that is part of a larger organization • He's a member of a Masonic *lodge*. **b** : a meeting place for the members of such a group • an annual dinner at the *lodge*
4 a *chiefly Brit* : a small house used by a person who works on an estate • the gamekeeper's *lodge* **b** *Brit* : a shelter or room for the use of a worker (such as a gatekeeper, doorkeeper, or janitor) at a college • Ask for Professor Jones at the porter's *lodge*. **c** *Brit* : the official residence of the head of a college that is part of a British university and especially Cambridge University • the Master's *Lodge*

lodg·er /ˈlɑːʤɚ/ *noun, pl* **-ers** [*count*] : a person who rents a room in another person's house

lodging *noun, pl* **-ings** : a place where a person (such as a traveler) can stay for usually a short period of time : a place to sleep [*noncount*] There is gas, food, and *lodging* at the next highway exit. • (*Brit*) He worked in the kitchen in return for ***board and lodging***. [=(*US*) *room and board*] [*count*] — usually plural • luxury *lodgings* • It can be difficult to find inexpensive *lodgings* in the city. • He found *lodgings* with a family near the university.

lodging house *noun, pl* ~ **houses** [*count*] *chiefly Brit, old-fashioned* : a house with rooms that can be rented : ROOMING HOUSE

¹loft /ˈlɑːft/ *noun, pl* **lofts** [*count*]
1 : a room or space that is just below the roof of a building and that is often used to store things • The kids' bedroom has a *loft*.
2 : a high section of seats in a church or hall • the choir *loft*
3 *chiefly US* **a** : an upper floor of a warehouse or business building especially when it is not divided by walls **b** : an apartment made on the upper floor of a former warehouse or business building • He rents a converted *loft*.
4 : HAYLOFT

²loft *verb* **lofts; loft·ed; loft·ing** [+ *obj*] : to hit or throw (something, such as a ball) so that it rises high in the air • He *lofted* a home run into the stands. • The explosion *lofted* dust high into the air.

lofty /ˈlɑːfti/ *adj* **loft·i·er; -est** [*also more* ~; *most* ~]
1 *literary* : rising to a great height : very tall and impressive • *lofty* redwood trees • *lofty* buildings ***synonyms*** see ¹HIGH
2 : very high and good : deserving to be admired • He set *lofty* goals for himself as a teacher. • *lofty* ideals/standards
3 : showing the insulting attitude of people who think that they are better, smarter, or more important than other people • The professor spoke with a *lofty* [=*haughty*] air. • She showed a *lofty* disregard for their objections.
– loft·i·ly /ˈlɑːftəli/ *adv* • She *loftily* dismissed their objections. **– loft·i·ness** /ˈlɑːftinəs/ *noun* [*noncount*]

¹log /ˈlɑːg/ *noun, pl* **logs** [*count*]
1 a : a long, heavy section of a tree that has fallen or been cut down • a ***log cabin*** [=a cabin made from logs] **b** : a thick piece of wood • Throw another *log* on the fire.
2 a : the record of travel by a ship or airplane • the captain's *log* • keep a *log* **b** : a record of performance, events, or activities • The mechanic kept a *log* showing when repairs were done on the truck. • a computer *log*
as easy as falling off a log see ¹EASY
sleep like a log see ¹SLEEP
– compare ³LOG

²log *verb* **logs; logged; log·ging**
1 : to cut down trees in an area for wood [+ *obj*] Thousands of trees have been *logged* in this area. • The forest has been heavily *logged*. [*no obj*] The company has been *logging* in this area for many years.
2 [+ *obj*] : to make an official record of (something) • Part of his job is to *log* all deliveries. • *log* incoming phone calls
3 [+ *obj*] **a** : to do something for (a specified distance or time) • Truck drivers *log* thousands of miles every week. • She has only been flying for a few months, but she has already *logged* more than 80 hours. **b** *chiefly US* : to succeed in getting or achieving (something, such as a record of wins) • a pitcher who has *logged* more than a hundred victories
log off or log out [*phrasal verb*] *computers* : to end the connection of a computer to a network or system • Remember to *log off* when you're finished.
log on or log in [*phrasal verb*] *computers* : to start the connection of a computer to a network or system — often + *to* • *logged on to* the Internet • You need a password to *log in* (*to* the network).

³log *noun, pl* **logs** [*count*] : LOGARITHM — compare ¹LOG

lo·gan·ber·ry /ˈlougənˌberi, *Brit* ˈləugənbri/ *noun, pl* **-ries** [*count*] : a red berry that is sweet and juicy; *also* : the plant that loganberries grow on

log·a·rithm /ˈlɑːgəˌrɪðəm/ *noun, pl* **-rithms** [*count*] *mathematics* : a number that shows how many times a base number (such as ten) is multiplied by itself to produce a third number (such as 100)
– log·a·rith·mic /ˌlɑːgəˈrɪðmɪk/ *adj* **– log·a·rith·mi·cal·ly** /ˌlɑːgəˈrɪðmɪkli/ *adv*

log·book /ˈlɑːgˌbʊk/ *noun, pl* **-books** [*count*] : a written record of activity, events, or travel : LOG • a pilot's *logbook*

log·ger /ˈlɑːgɚ/ *noun, pl* **-gers** [*count*] : someone whose job is to cut down trees for wood

log·ger·heads /ˈlɑːgɚˌhɛdz/ *noun*
at loggerheads : in a state of strong disagreement • The two nations are *at loggerheads* (with each other) over agricultural issues.

log·gia /ˈlouʤijə/ *noun, pl* **-gias** [*count*] : an area on the side of a building that has a roof and that is open on one side

log·ic /ˈlɑːʤɪk/ *noun*
1 a : a proper or reasonable way of thinking about or understanding something [*noncount*] If you just use a little *logic*, you'll see I'm right. • the rules of *logic* • There's no *logic* in/to your reasoning. • I can't see the *logic* in always worrying about the future. = Where's the *logic* in always worrying about the future? • There's some *logic* to/in what he says. • She kept the dog, ***against all logic***, after it attacked her. [=her decision to keep the dog was not logical/sensible] • Her decision ***defies logic***. [=her decision makes no sense; her decision is not logical] [*singular*] There's a certain *logic* in/to what he says. **b** [*noncount*] : a particular way of thinking about something • I could not understand her *logic* in keeping the dog. [=I could not understand her reason for keeping the dog] • I fail to see your *logic*. = I fail to see the *logic* behind/of your reasoning. • faulty *logic*
2 [*noncount*] : the science that studies the formal processes used in thinking and reasoning • a professor of *logic* — see also FUZZY LOGIC
3 [*noncount*] : the way facts or events follow or relate to each other • The revolution proceeded according to its own *logic*. • the *logic* of the situation
4 [*noncount*] *technical* : the arrangement of circuits in a computer

log·i·cal /ˈlɑːʤɪkəl/ *adj*
1 [*more* ~; *most* ~] : agreeing with the rules of logic : sensible or reasonable • a *logical* argument/conclusion/decision • Since she helped us before, it's *logical* to assume that she'll help us again. • He seems to be a *logical* choice for the job. • She wasn't able to give me a *logical* explanation for her behavior. • a *logical* thinker
2 : of or relating to the formal processes used in thinking

and reasoning • *logical* principles/argumentation
– **log·i·cal·ly** /ˈlɑːʤɪkli/ *adv* • His argument doesn't proceed *logically.* • He couldn't explain his decision *logically.* • Since she helped us before, we can *logically* assume that she'll help us again.

lo·gi·cian /loʊˈʤɪʃən/ *noun, pl* **-cians** [*count*] : someone who is skilled or trained in the formal processes used in thinking and reasoning

lo·gis·tics /loʊˈʤɪstɪks/ *noun* [*plural*] : the things that must be done to plan and organize a complicated activity or event that involves many people • My mother was in charge of the *logistics* of our camping trip. • *Logistics* are the key to a successful military campaign. • the *logistics* of a political campaign — sometimes used with a singular verb • *Logistics* is the key to a successful military campaign.
– **lo·gis·tic** /loʊˈʤɪstɪk/ *or* **lo·gis·ti·cal** /loʊˈʤɪstɪkəl/ *adj* • The festival was a *logistical* nightmare. [=planning the details of the festival was extremely difficult]

log·jam /ˈlɑːgˌʤæm/ *noun, pl* **-jams** [*count*]
1 : a situation in which a large number of logs floating down a river become tangled with each other so that further movement is not possible
2 : a situation in which no progress seems possible • He was called in to try to ***break the logjam*** in the negotiations.

logo /ˈloʊgoʊ/ *noun, pl* **log·os** [*count*] : a symbol that is used to identify a company and that appears on its products • T-shirts with corporate *logos*

lo·gy /ˈloʊgi/ *adj* **lo·gi·er; -est** *US, informal* : not able to think or move normally because of being tired, sick, etc. • feeling *logy* [=*groggy*]

-logy *noun combining form*
1 : area of knowledge : theory : science • theo*logy* • bio*logy* • musico*logy* • psycho*logy*
2 : speech or writing • tri*logy*

loin /ˈlɔɪn/ *noun, pl* **loins**
1 a [*count*] : an area on the back of an animal's body near the tail • a horse's *loins* **b** [*count, noncount*] : meat from this area • pork *loin*
2 ***loins*** [*plural*] : the area of a person's body that includes the sexual organs • There was a towel wrapped around his *loins.* ✧ Your child or children can be referred to as ***the fruit of your loins***. A child can be described as ***springing/coming from the loins*** of his or her parents. These phrases are usually used in a humorous way.
gird (up) your loins : to prepare yourself for a fight or for some difficult task • The company is *girding its loins* for what could be a long strike.

loin·cloth /ˈlɔɪnˌklɑːθ/ *noun, pl* **-cloths** [*count*] : a piece of cloth worn to cover the sexual organs especially by men in very hot parts of the world

loi·ter /ˈlɔɪtɚ/ *verb* **-ters; -tered; -ter·ing** [*no obj*] : to remain in an area when you do not have a particular reason to be there • *Loitering* is prohibited outside the theaters. • There was a group of teenagers *loitering* (around) [=*hanging around*] in the parking lot.
– **loi·ter·er** /ˈlɔɪtərɚ/ *noun, pl* **-ers** [*count*]

LOL *abbr* laugh(ing) out loud — used on the Internet, in e-mail, etc., to indicate that something is considered very funny

loll /ˈlɑːl/ *verb, always followed by an adverb or preposition* **lolls; lolled; loll·ing** [*no obj*]
1 : to hang or bend loosely • a dog with its tongue *lolling* out • Her head was *lolling* to one side.
2 : to lie or sit in a relaxed or lazy manner • She was *lolling* by the pool. • He *lolled* about/around in his pajamas all day.

lol·li·pop *or* **lol·ly·pop** /ˈlɑːliˌpɑːp/ *noun, pl* **-pops** [*count*] : a round piece of hard candy on the end of a stick

lol·ly /ˈlɑːli/ *noun, pl* **lol·lies**
1 [*count*] **a** *chiefly Brit* : LOLLIPOP **b** *Brit* : ICE LOLLY
2 [*noncount*] *Brit, old-fashioned slang* : MONEY

lol·ly·gag /ˈlɑːliˌgæg/ *verb* **-gags; -gagged; -gag·ging** [*no obj*] *US, informal* : to spend time doing things that are not useful or serious : to fool around and waste time • He was kicked off the team for *lollygagging* during practice. • Stop *lollygagging* around/about and get to work!
– **lol·ly·gag·ger** *noun, pl* **-gers** [*count*]

lo mein /ˈloʊˈmeɪn/ *noun* [*noncount*] : a combination of soft noodles, vegetables, and usually meat or shrimp that is served in Chinese restaurants in the U.S. — compare CHOW MEIN

lone /ˈloʊn/ *adj, always used before a noun*
1 : standing, acting, or being alone • a *lone* traveler [=a traveler who is alone] • a *lone* gunman • He was the *lone* [=*only, sole*] official to vote against the plan. • a *lone* [=*solitary*] tree on the hill — see also LONE WOLF
2 *Brit* : not having a partner (such as a husband or wife) • a *lone* [=*single*] parent/father/mother

lone·ly /ˈloʊnli/ *adj* **lone·li·er; -est** [*also more ~; most ~*]
1 : sad from being apart from other people • He was/felt *lonely* without his wife and children. • a *lonely* old man • feeling *lonely* • She was a *lonely* child with few friends.
2 : causing sad feelings that come from being apart from other people • It was *lonely* living out in the country. • She spent too many *lonely* nights at home. • She had a *lonely* childhood. • It's ***lonely at the top***. [=powerful and successful people often have few friends]
3 : not visited by or traveled on by many people • a *lonely* spot in the woods • a *lonely* stretch of road
– **lone·li·ness** /ˈloʊnlinəs/ *noun* [*noncount*]

lonely hearts *adj, always used before a noun* : intended for lonely people who want to meet someone they can have a romantic or friendly relationship with • a *lonely hearts* club • the *lonely hearts* section of the newspaper

lon·er /ˈloʊnɚ/ *noun, pl* **-ers** [*count*] : a person who is often alone or who likes to be alone • The killer was a *loner* with no friends.

lone·some /ˈloʊnsəm/ *adj* [*more ~; most ~*] *chiefly US*
1 : sad from being apart from other people : LONELY • He was/felt *lonesome* for his family.
2 : causing sad feelings that come from being apart from other people : LONELY • The empty house seemed so *lonesome.*
3 : not visited by or traveled on by many people : LONELY • a *lonesome* highway • the *lonesome* frontier
(all) by your lonesome *informal* : without anyone else : entirely alone • He sat *by his lonesome* [=by himself] at the dinner table. • She made the cake *all by her lonesome.*

lone wolf *noun, pl* **~ wolves** [*count*] : someone who likes to act, live, or work alone : LONER • He had the reputation of being a *lone wolf* in high school.

[1]**long** /ˈlɑːŋ/ *adj* **lon·ger** /ˈlɑːŋgɚ/; **lon·gest** /ˈlɑːŋgəst/
1 a : extending a great distance from one end to the other end : not short • *long* hair • *long* legs • a *long* corridor • The bridge is the *longest* in the world. • We drove a *long* distance. • the *long/longer* side of the building • The pants are a little (too) *long* for me. [=they should be shorter in order to fit me] **b** : extending a specified distance : having a specified length • one meter *long* • The whale was 50 feet *long.* • "***How long*** was the race?" "The race was five miles *long.*"
2 a : lasting or continuing for a great amount of time • a *long* pause/wait • They've had a *long* and happy marriage. • She finds it hard to sit still for *long* periods of time. • It's a *long* movie. • The company has a *long* tradition of serving its customers well. • I've known them for ***a long time***. [=many years] • I haven't seen them for/in *a* (very) *long time.* = (*US*) I haven't seen them ***for the longest time***. • The changes took *a long time* to come. = The changes were ***long in coming***. [=the changes did not happen quickly] • It happened ***a long time ago***. [=far in the past; not at all recently] • The test should take an hour ***at the longest***. [=it should not be longer than an hour] • She is used to working ***long hours***. [=she often works for many hours at a time] • He has a very ***long memory***. [=he remembers things that happened far in the past] • someone with ***long experience*** in the UN [=someone who has been in the UN many years] • She gave him a ***long look***. [=she looked at him for many seconds] • It's been a ***long day***. [=a difficult day in which time seems to go by slowly] • We took Friday off and went to the coast for a ***long weekend***. [=a weekend with an extra day added to it] **b** : lasting or continuing for a specified amount of time • The movie is three hours *long.* [=it lasts three hours] • A day is 24 hours *long.* — see also DAYLONG, MONTHLONG, WEEKLONG
3 a : having many pages, items, etc. • a *long* book/essay/list • The team has had a *long* streak of wins. **b** : having a specified number of pages, items, etc. • The book is 300 pages *long.* • The team's winning streak is 12 games *long.*
4 *of clothing* : covering all or most of the arms or legs • a shirt with *long* sleeves • *long* pants • a *long* skirt
5 *sports* : going beyond the area of play • His second serve was *long,* so he lost the point.
6 *linguistics, of a vowel* — used to identify certain vowel sounds in English • *long* and short vowels • the *long* "a" in "make" • the *long* "e" in "sweet" • the *long* "i" in "ice" • the *long* "u" in "use" — compare [1]SHORT 8

7 *of someone's face* **:** showing sadness ▪ Why the ***long face***? [=you look sad; why are you sad?]

a long way **:** a great distance ▪ He grew up *a long way* from here. ▪ Their house is *a long way* (away) from here. — often used figuratively in various phrases ▪ We've done a lot of work, but we have ***a long way to go***. [=we still have a lot of work to do] ▪ These changes will ***go a long way toward/towards*** making the system more efficient. [=these changes will do a lot to make the system more efficient] ▪ The company has really ***come a long way*** [=the company has made a lot of progress] since/from its humble beginnings. ▪ These problems ***go back a long way***. [=these problems have existed for a long time] ▪ She and her business partner *go back a long way* (together). [=she and her business partner have known each other for a long time]

as long as someone's arm *informal* **:** very long **:** having many pages, items, etc. ▪ I had a list of things to do that was *as long as your/my arm*.

at long last see [5]LAST

how long is a piece of string see [1]STRING

long in the tooth see TOOTH

long on **:** having or providing a good amount of (something) ▪ He was *long on* criticism [=he said many critical things] but short on useful advice.

long time no see *informal* — used as a greeting for someone you have not seen for a long time ▪ Well hello there! *Long time no see!*

not by a long chalk see [1]CHALK

not long for this world see [1]WORLD

take the long view see [1]VIEW

the long arm of the law see [1]ARM

[2]long *adv* **longer; longest**

1 : for or during a long time **:** for many years, days, hours, etc. ▪ The extra food she brought did not last *long*. ▪ Will he be away (very) *long*? ▪ They'll have to wait a bit *longer*. ▪ The mall has *long* been a popular hangout for teenagers. ▪ They have *long* been devoted friends. ▪ It's been so *long* since we've seen each other. ▪ It's been much ***too long*** since we've seen each other. ▪ That meeting was way *too long*. ▪ She's been away ***so long***. [=for such a long time] ▪ We had to leave ***long before*** we were ready to go. ▪ ***Long live*** the King/Queen! [=may the King/Queen live for many years] — sometimes used in combination ▪ her ***long-awaited*** new novel ▪ a ***long-anticipated*** announcement

2 : for a specified period of time ▪ The children played all day *long*. [=throughout the day] ▪ We talked all night *long*. ▪ all summer/week *long*

3 : at a time far before or after a specified moment or event ▪ events that occurred ***long before*** the discovery of America ▪ He remembered that day ***long after*** it had faded from her memory. ▪ The book wasn't published until *long after* she had died. ▪ He went to bed at 10 o'clock. Not *long after/afterward*, the phone rang.

4 : for a great distance ▪ The quarterback threw the ball *long*.

as long as *or* ***so long as*** **1 :** SINCE ▪ *As long as* I'm here, we may as well begin. ▪ *As long as* you're up, would you mind getting me a drink? ▪ *So long as* you feel that way I'll leave. **2 :** IF ▪ I'll go with you *as long as* you'll drive. ▪ They can do anything they want, *so long as* they follow the rules. ▪ *As long as* she's allowed to go first, she's happy. **3 :** during the time that **:** WHILE ▪ The economy will remain strong *as long as* there are jobs to go around.

be long — used to ask how much time will be required or to say that something will take only a short amount of time or will happen soon ▪ "Will you *be long*?" "No, I'll be ready soon." ▪ I'm going out now, but I ***won't be long***. [=I will return soon] ▪ "Have you finished yet?" "No, but I *won't be long*." [=I will finish soon] ▪ "Will you ***be much longer***?" "No, I'm almost ready." ▪ We've been waiting since morning, but ***it won't be long now***. [=what we have been waiting for will happen/come soon] ▪ It ***can't be much longer*** before they give up. [=they will probably give up soon]

long ago **:** at a time in the distant past ▪ events that happened *long ago* ▪ The announcement was made ***not long ago***. [=the announcement was made recently] ▪ It wasn't so/very *long ago* that this place was empty field.

long gone **:** having ended, died, disappeared, etc., at a distant time in the past ▪ Those buildings are *long gone* now.

long since **:** at a time in the distant past **:** long ago ▪ questions that have *long since* been answered [=questions that were answered long ago] ▪ an animal that has *long since* disappeared from this region ▪ I *long since* gave up trying to change her mind.

no longer *or* ***not any longer*** — used to say that something that was once true or possible is not now true or possible ▪ They could wait *no longer*. = They couldn't wait *any longer*. [=it was not possible for them to continue waiting] ▪ I can *no longer* afford the car. [=I could afford the car at some time in the past but I cannot afford it now]

so long *informal* **:** [1]GOODBYE ▪ *So long* (for now)! Have a safe journey home! ▪ She said *so long* to her friends and family and headed off to college. — sometimes used figuratively ▪ the time of year when we say *so long* to winter coats [=when we stop wearing winter coats]

take long **:** to require a large amount of time ▪ It won't *take long* to make dinner. ▪ This is *taking longer* than I thought (it would).

[3]long *noun*

before long **:** in a short amount of time **:** SOON ▪ They said they would be finished *before long*. ▪ *Before long* the light rain had turned into a heavy downpour. ▪ We expect them to arrive *before long*. [=*before much longer*]

for long **:** for many years, days, hours, etc. **:** for a long time ▪ I haven't known him *for long*. ▪ Her life did not remain peaceful *for long*. ▪ He won't be away *for* (very) *long*. [=*for* (very) *much longer*] ▪ He didn't work here *for long*. ▪ She's been away ***for so long***. [=*for such a long time*]

the long and (the) short of it — used when making a statement that is brief and that tells someone only the most important parts of something ▪ I could give you a lot of reasons for my decision, but *the long and short of it* is that I just don't want to go.

[4]long *verb* **longs; longed; long·ing** [*no obj*] **:** to feel a strong desire or wish *for* something or *to do* something ▪ We all *long for* peace. = We all *long to live* in peace. ▪ I'm *longing for* the time when I will see you again. = I'm *longing to see* you again. = How I *long to see* you again! ▪ He began to feel that the ***longed-for*** day of her return would never come.

synonyms see YEARN

long. *abbr* longitude

long ball *noun, pl* **~ balls** [*count*] *baseball* **:** HOME RUN ▪ a pitcher who has given up a lot of *long balls* ▪ a batter known for hitting the *long ball* [=for hitting many home runs]

long·bow /ˈlɑːŋˌboʊ/ *noun, pl* **-bows** [*count*] **:** a large wooden weapon (called a bow) that shot arrows and was used for hunting and fighting in the past

long–dis·tance /ˈlɑːŋˈdɪstəns/ *adj*

1 *always used before a noun* **a :** going or covering a great distance ▪ *long-distance* trade routes ▪ *long-distance* travel ▪ *long-distance* roads ▪ a *long-distance* runner **b :** involving people who are far apart ▪ The two carried on a *long-distance* courtship/relationship/romance.

2 *of a telephone call* **:** connecting to a place that is far away ▪ She made several *long-distance* (phone/telephone) calls. ▪ Is this call *long-distance*? — opposite LOCAL

– long–distance *adv* ▪ She called her parents *long-distance*. [=she made a long-distance call to her parents]

– long distance *noun* [*noncount*] *chiefly US* ▪ You have to pay more for *long distance*. [=to make long-distance telephone calls]

long division *noun* [*noncount*] *mathematics* **:** a way of dividing one number by another number that involves several steps which are written out ▪ students learning to do *long division*

long–drawn–out *adj* [*more* ~; *most* ~] **:** continuing for a long time or for too long ▪ a *long-drawn-out* investigation ▪ The two sides have been engaged in *long-drawn-out* [=*protracted*] discussions.

lon·gev·i·ty /lɑnˈʤɛvəti/ *noun* [*noncount*]

1 a : long life **:** the fact of living for many years ▪ His *longevity* was remarkable considering he had been so sick when he was a child. ▪ The members of that family are famous for their *longevity*. [=for living to be very old] **b :** length of life ▪ Better medical treatment has led to greater *longevity*. ▪ a study of human *longevity*

2 : the length of time that something or someone lasts or continues ▪ The *longevity* of a car's tires depends on how the car is driven. ▪ She's a talented athlete, but many people have doubts about her *longevity*. [=about how long her athletic career will last] ▪ They're trying to increase the product's *longevity*.

long green *noun* [*noncount*] *US, old-fashioned slang* **:** MONEY ▪ was able to rustle up some *long green* in a hurry — often used with *the* ▪ The band was raking in *the long green*.

long·hair /ˈlɑːŋˌheɚ/ *noun, pl* **-hairs** [*count*]
1 *chiefly US, old-fashioned* : a person (such as a hippie) who has long hair • *Longhairs* crowded into the music festival.
2 : a cat that has long fur — compare SHORTHAIR
– **longhair** *adj, always used before a noun* • *longhair* cats

long–haired /ˈlɑːŋˈheɚd/ *adj* : having long fur or hair • *long-haired* cats • a beautiful *long-haired* girl

long·hand /ˈlɑːŋˌhænd/ *noun* [*noncount*] : writing that is done by using a pen or pencil rather than with a typewriter or computer • children learning (to do) *longhand* • She wrote the book in *longhand.* — compare SHORTHAND

long haul *noun* [*noncount*]
1 : a long journey or distance • Driving across the country would be a *long haul.*
2 *chiefly US* : a long period of time — usually used in the phrases ***for the long haul*** and ***over the long haul*** • It's going to be a tough project but we're in it *for the long haul.* [=we are prepared to work on the project until it is completed] • Will the company be able to succeed *over the long haul*?
– **long–haul** *adj, always used before a noun* • a *long-haul* flight

long·horn /ˈlɑːŋˌhoɚn/ *noun, pl* **-horns** [*count*] : a type of cow that has long horns • a herd of *longhorns* • a Texas *longhorn* — often used before another noun • a *longhorn* bull/steer • *longhorn* cattle

[1]**long·ing** /ˈlɑːŋɪŋ/ *noun, pl* **-ings** : a strong desire for something or someone [*noncount*] They looked with *longing* toward freedom. • She cast a look of *longing* at the shop window. [*count*] She never told anyone about her secret *longings.* — often + *for* • They were filled with a deep *longing for* peace. • He had/felt a *longing for* her. — often followed by *to* + *verb* • The refugees felt a deep *longing to return* home. • He had a *longing to be* with her.

[2]**longing** *adj, always used before a noun* : showing a strong desire for something or someone • She looked at the shop window with a *longing* gaze.
– **long·ing·ly** /ˈlɑːŋɪŋli/ *adv* • She gazed/looked *longingly* at the shop window.

long·ish /ˈlɑːŋɪʃ/ *adj* : somewhat long • She wore a *longish* coat/skirt. • He had *longish* black hair.

lon·gi·tude /ˈlɑːnʤəˌtuːd, *Brit* ˈlɒnʤəˌtjuːd/ *noun, pl* **-tudes**
1 : distance measured in degrees east or west from an imaginary line (called the prime meridian) that goes from the North Pole to the South Pole and that passes through Greenwich, England [*noncount*] a map of the world showing lines of latitude and *longitude* [*count*] calculating the *longitudes* of different places — compare LATITUDE 1a
2 [*count*] : an imaginary line that circles the Earth at a particular longitude • The regions are on roughly the same *longitude.* — compare LATITUDE 1b

lon·gi·tu·di·nal /ˌlɑːnʤəˈtuːdənəl, *Brit* ˌlɒnʤəˈtjuːdənəl/ *adj, always used before a noun*
1 : placed or going along the long side of something • The insect's body is black with yellow *longitudinal* stripes.
2 : of or relating to longitude • calculating the *longitudinal* position of a ship
3 : done by observing or examining a group of people or things over time to study how one or two particular things about them change • a *longitudinal* study of career aspirations among girls from 5 to 17
– **lon·gi·tu·di·nal·ly** *adv*

long johns /ˈlɑːŋˌʤɑːnz/ *noun* [*plural*] : underwear that covers your legs and that is worn in cold weather — called also (*US*) *long underwear;* see color picture on page C12

long jump *noun*
the long jump : an athletic event in which people compete by trying to jump as far as they can • He won a gold medal in *the long jump.* — sometimes used before another noun • a *long jump* competition • She set a *long jump* record at the meet. — called also (*US*) *the broad jump*
– **long jumper** *noun, pl* ~ **-ers** [*count*]

long–last·ing /ˈlɑːŋˈlæstɪŋ, *Brit* ˈlɒŋˈlɑːstɪŋ/ *adj* **long·er–last·ing; long·est–last·ing** [*or more* ~; *most* ~] : existing or continuing for a long time • a book that has *long-lasting* [=*lasting, enduring*] significance • The trip had a *long-lasting* effect on me.

long–life *adj, always used before a noun*
1 : made to last a long time • *long-life* batteries
2 *Brit* : having a substance added that allows something to remain fresh or good for a long time • *long-life* milk

long–lived /ˈlɑːŋˈlɪvd/ *adj* **long·er–lived; long·est–lived** [*or more* ~; *most* ~] : living or lasting for a long time • a *long-lived* woman, still vigorous in her 80s • The members of that family were all *long-lived.* • The redwood is a *long-lived* tree. • That fad was relatively/remarkably *long-lived.* — compare SHORT-LIVED

long–lost /ˈlɑːŋˈlɑːst/ *adj, always used before a noun* : lost a long time ago : not seen or found for many years • a *long-lost* masterpiece that has recently been rediscovered • He embraced his old friend like a *long-lost* brother.

long–play·ing record /ˈlɑːŋˈplejɪŋ-/ *noun, pl* ~ **-cords** [*count*] : LP

long–range /ˈlɑːŋˈreɪnʤ/ *adj, always used before a noun*
1 : able to travel or be used over great distances • *long-range* bombers/missiles/rockets/weapons • a *long-range* radio
2 : involving a long period of time • *long-range* planning • *long-range* [=*long-term*] goals/trends • a *long-range* forecast

long run *noun*
the long run : a long period of time after the beginning of something • Invest for *the long run* [=*the long term*], not to see what you can earn in a few months. • Your solution may cause more problems ***over the long run.*** — usually used in the phrase ***in the long run*** • It may be our best option *in the long run.* [=when a greater amount of time has passed] • This deal will cost you more *in the long run.* [=*in the long term*] — compare SHORT RUN
– **long–run** *adj, always used before a noun* • *long-run* benefits [=benefits that will exist or continue over a long period of time]

long·shore·man /ˈlɑːŋˌʃoɚmən/ *noun, pl* **-men** /-mən/ [*count*] *US* : a person whose job is to load and unload ships at a port — called also *stevedore,* (*US*) *dockworker,* (*Brit*) *docker*

long shot *noun, pl* ~ **shots** [*count*]
1 : an attempt or effort that is not likely to be successful • I hope to double my profits, but I know that's a *long shot.*
2 *chiefly US* : a person or thing that is not likely to win something (such as a contest or race) • The horse was a *long shot,* but we bet on him anyway. • She always bets on *long shots* at the racetrack. • a political *long shot*
by a long shot : by a great extent or degree : by far • It was the biggest problem we had—*by a long shot.*
not by a long shot : not at all • Our work isn't done yet, *not by a long shot.* [=we still have a lot more work to do]

long–sight·ed /ˈlɑːŋˌsaɪtəd/ *adj* [*more* ~; *most* ~] *Brit*
1 : FARSIGHTED 1 • He needs reading glasses because he is *long-sighted.*
2 : FARSIGHTED 2 • *long-sighted* planning for the future
– **long–sight·ed·ness** *noun* [*noncount*]

long–stand·ing /ˈlɑːŋˈstændɪŋ/ *adj* : lasting or existing for a long time • It was a *long-standing* tradition for them to camp in the mountains for a week during the summer. • Some *long-standing* problems are finally being corrected. • their *long-standing* relationship

long–suf·fer·ing /ˈlɑːŋˌsʌfərɪŋ/ *adj* : suffering for a long time without complaining : very patient during difficult times • his forgiving and *long-suffering* wife • When the Red Sox won the World Series, their *long-suffering* fans could finally celebrate.

long suit *noun* [*singular*] : something that a person does well : STRONG SUIT • Patience is not her *long suit.* [=she is not a patient person]

long term *noun*
the long term : a long period of time after the beginning of something • She is investing for *the long term.* [=*the long run*] • I think it's the better choice ***over the long term.*** — usually used in the phrase ***in the long term*** • an investment that should do well *in the long term* [=when a greater amount of time has passed] • These changes may improve profits now, but they are going to cost us money *in the long term.* [=*in the long run*] — compare SHORT TERM

long–term /ˈlɑːŋˈtɚm/ *adj* : lasting for, relating to, or involving a long period of time • The *long-term* effects of the medication are not known. • The company has a *long-term* plan/strategy for success. • His *long-term* memory is still okay, but his short-term memory is failing. [=he is still able to remember things that happened long ago but it is difficult for him to remember things that happened recently] • *long-term* care for the elderly • a *long-term* investment

long·time /ˈlɑːŋˈtaɪm/ *adj, always used before a noun* : having been something specified for many years • the *longtime* chairman of the committee • *longtime* residents of the neighborhood • her *longtime* boyfriend/editor/manager/partner • *longtime* rivals

lon·gueur /lɑŋˈgə/ *noun, pl* **-gueurs** [*count*] *literary* : a boring part of something (such as a book or play) — usually plural ▪ Though not without its *longueurs*, the opera came to life in the last act.

long underwear *noun* [*noncount*] *US* : LONG JOHNS

long–wind·ed /ˌlɑːŋˈwɪndəd/ *adj* : using too many words in speaking or writing ▪ The teacher was known for his *long-winded* explanations. ▪ a *long-winded* sermon/speech ▪ a *long-winded* speaker
– **long–wind·ed·ness** *noun* [*noncount*]

loo /ˈluː/ *noun, pl* **loos** [*count*] *Brit, informal* : TOILET

loo·fah /ˈluːfə/ *noun, pl* **-fahs** [*count*] : a rough sponge that is made from the dried fruit of a tropical plant and that people use to wash their bodies

[1]**look** /ˈlʊk/ *verb* **looks; looked; look·ing**
1 *always followed by an adverb or preposition* [*no obj*] : to direct your eyes in a particular direction ▪ He *looked* straight ahead and kept walking. ▪ When you take a walk, *look* around you. ▪ She smiled at me and then *looked* away. ▪ He *looked* back the way he had come. ▪ *Look* both ways before you cross the street. ▪ When I finally reached the top I was afraid to *look* down. ▪ She *looked* from one person to the next. ▪ *Look* in the mirror/box. ▪ They *looked* off into the distance. ▪ He was *looking* over his shoulder. — often + *at* ▪ She *looked* longingly *at* the photograph. ▪ "What are you *looking at*?" "I'm *looking at* this flower." ▪ *looking at* the stars through a telescope = *looking* through a telescope *at* the stars — see also LOOK AROUND (below), LOOK AT (below), *look over your shoulder* at [1]SHOULDER
2 a [*linking verb*] : to seem to be something especially because of appearance ▪ He *looks* angry. ▪ Her new haircut makes her *look* young/younger. ▪ That cake *looks* delicious. ▪ "How does the situation *look* (to you) now?" "It *looks* pretty bad/good." ▪ It *looks* dangerous/unlikely. ▪ a kind-*looking* woman = a woman who *looks* kind ▪ The child ***looked to be*** about seven years old. ▪ The once-famous star *looks to be* heading into obscurity. ▪ The year ahead *looks to be* a profitable one. [=it appears likely to be profitable; I/we expect it to be profitable] — often used in the phrases ***look as if, look as though***, and ***look like*** ▪ It *looks like* it will be hard work. ▪ It *looks like* it will rain/snow. = It *looks like* rain/snow. ▪ It *looks* to me *like* they're all the same. = It *looks like* they're all the same to me. = They *look like* they're all the same to me. ▪ It *looked as though* he was feeling ill. = He *looked as though* he was feeling ill. ▪ It *looks like* she's going to win the tournament again this year. = She *looks like* she's going to win the tournament again this year. = (*Brit*) She *looks like* winning the tournament again this year. [=she seems likely to win the tournament again this year] ▪ He *looks like* a nice man. = (*Brit*) He *looks* a nice man. [=he seems/appears to be a nice man] — see also LOOK LIKE (below) **b** [+ *obj*] : to have an appearance that is suitable for (something) ▪ She *looks* her age. [=her appearance shows her age] ▪ an actor who really *looks* the part [=whose appearance matches the appearance the character is supposed to have]
3 [*no obj*] : to try to find something or someone ▪ "I don't know where my keys are." "Try *looking* in the drawer." ▪ I've ***looked high and low***. = I've ***looked everywhere***. = I've ***looked all over***. ▪ "I still haven't found my keys." "Well, ***keep looking***." ▪ "I'm still trying to find my keys." "Well, ***look no further***—here they are." — see also LOOK FOR (below)
4 [*no obj*] : to pay attention by directing your eyes at something ▪ You can see many wonderful things in nature if you take the time to stop and *look*. ▪ The store clerk asked if I needed any help, but I told him I was ***just looking***. [=I was looking at the things being sold in the store but did not plan to buy anything specific]
5 [*no obj*] **a** — used to direct someone's attention to something or someone ▪ *Look*! Over there! Is that a hawk? ▪ *Look*! There he is! — often + *at* ▪ *Look at* those mountains. Have you ever seen anything so beautiful? ▪ Just ***look at the time***! I had no idea it was that late! — often used in phrases like ***look where, look what***, etc. ▪ *Look what* I found. ▪ *Look who's* here. ▪ *Look how* easy it is to do this. **b** — used in phrases like ***look where, look what***, etc., to warn someone or to express anger or disappointment ▪ *Look where* you're going. You almost walked into that pole. ▪ *Look what* you did! You broke it. ▪ Now *look what* you've done. It's broken. **c** — used to introduce a statement when you want someone to notice what you are saying ▪ *Look*, this just isn't going to work. ▪ ***Look here***, you need to start behaving more responsibly.
6 [+ *obj*] **a** : to want or try to do something — followed by *to + verb* ▪ a company *looking to become* a leader in the industry ▪ We're *looking to create* something new. **b** : to expect something — followed by *to + verb* ▪ We *look to have* a good year. = We are *looking to have* a good year.
7 [*no obj*] : to have a specified direction : to point or face in a specified direction ▪ The house *looks* east. ▪ The hotel *looks* toward the sea.

don't look now — used in speech before a statement to tell someone to be aware of something without looking ▪ *Don't look now*, but they're coming our way. ▪ *Don't look now*, but I think we're being followed.

look after [*phrasal verb*] ***look after (someone or something)*** : to take care of (someone or something) ▪ They hired a babysitter to *look after* the children. ▪ I can *look after* myself. ▪ He *looks after* his aging parents. ▪ They asked a friend to *look after* their house while they were away.

look a gift horse in the mouth see [1]HORSE

look ahead [*phrasal verb*] : to think about what will happen in the future ▪ The past year has been successful and, *looking ahead*, we expect to do even better in the coming months. — often + *to* ▪ *Looking ahead to* next year, we expect to be even more successful.

look around or *Brit* ***look round*** [*phrasal verb*] **1** ***look around/round*** or ***look around/round (a place)*** : to go through a place in order to see what is there : to explore a place ▪ We arrived early at the theater and spent a few minutes *looking around*. ▪ The kids *looked around* the shops while we unpacked. **2** ***look around/round for (something)*** : to search for (something) ▪ I *looked around for* my keys but I couldn't find them anywhere. ▪ He is *looking around for* a new car. — see also [1]LOOK 1 (above)

look at [*phrasal verb*] **1** ***look at (someone or something)*** **a** : to think about or consider (something or someone) ▪ Just *look at* how successful she's been. ▪ The company is *looking at* the possibility of moving to a larger office. ▪ I just haven't *looked at* him as (being) a potential roommate. ▪ The way I *look at* [=*see*] it, you're wrong. ▪ Some people are *looking at* her as a possible candidate for mayor. ▪ You can make changes in your life. Just *look at* Tim. [=consider that Tim has made changes to realize that you can also make changes] **b** : to examine or study (someone or something) ▪ You should have a doctor *look at* that bruise. ▪ I had the veterinarian *look at* my cat. **2** ***look at (something)*** **a** : to have (something bad or unpleasant) as a problem or possibility ▪ If you're found guilty, you could be *looking at* [=*facing*] five years in prison. **b** : to read (something or part of something) ▪ I haven't *looked at* [=*read*] the newspaper today. ▪ Did you *look at* that fax yet? — see also [1]LOOK 1, 5a (above)

look back [*phrasal verb*] : to think about something in the past ▪ *Looking back* to/at last season, I can see why they didn't win the pennant. ▪ I *look back* at/on that time with a lot of pride. [=I feel proud when I think about that time] ✧ If you make an important change in your life and ***never look back***, you never return to the way you had been before, and your life is very different from that time onward. ▪ After college, she moved to New York, got a job on Wall Street, and *never looked back*.

look before you leap : to think or learn about the possible bad results of an action before doing it ▪ If you're planning to invest in your friend's company, I advise you to *look before you leap*.

look daggers at see DAGGER

look down on [*phrasal verb*] ***look down on (someone or something)*** : to think of or treat (someone or something) as unimportant or not worthy of respect ▪ The family was *looked down on* for being different. ▪ The other children *looked down on* me because my parents were poor.

look down your nose at : to think of or treat (someone or something) as unimportant or not worthy of respect ▪ She *looked down her nose at* her neighbors. ▪ writers who *look down their noses at* popular culture

look for [*phrasal verb*] ***look for (something or someone)*** **1** : to try to find (someone or something) : to search for (someone or something) ▪ We had to wait while he *looked for* his keys. ▪ I've *looked* everywhere *for* my keys but I still can't find them. ▪ She's *looking for* a new job. ▪ *look for* a word in the dictionary ▪ The police continue to *look for* the escaped prisoners. ▪ His taste is—what's the word I'm *looking for*?—I know, "eclectic." — see also [1]LOOK 3 (above) **2** : to expect (something or someone) ▪ We're *looking for* better days in the future. ▪ Don't bother *looking for* me anytime too soon. — often followed by *to + verb* ▪ You can

L

look for me *to arrive* around noon. ▪ Economists are *looking for* the economy *to improve* in the next few months. **3** ***look for trouble informal*** : to act in a way that could cause violence or problems ▪ I could tell that he was *looking for trouble* as soon as he came in.

look forward to [*phrasal verb*] ***look forward to (something)*** : to expect (something) with pleasure ▪ They're *looking forward to* their vacation. ▪ He felt he had nothing to *look forward to* in his life. ▪ She's *looking forward to* meeting new friends.

look in on [*phrasal verb*] ***look in on (someone)*** : to make a brief social visit to (someone) ▪ I plan to *look in on* [=*drop in on, call on*] some old friends when I'm in town.

look into [*phrasal verb*] ***look into (something)*** : to try to get information about (something) ▪ Is there a problem? I could *look into* it. ▪ Investigators are *looking into* the cause of the accident.

look like : to have an appearance that is very similar to (someone or something) : to resemble (someone or something) ▪ You *look* just *like* your mother! [=you resemble your mother very closely] ▪ That powdered sugar *looks like* snow. — see also [1]LOOK 2a (above)

look like a million dollars/bucks see MILLION

look lively see LIVELY

look on/upon [*phrasal verb*] **1** ***look on*** : to watch something as it happens without becoming involved ▪ A crowd of people *looked on* [=*stood by*] helplessly as the house burned to the ground. **2** ***look on/upon (someone or something)*** : to think of or consider (someone or something) in a specified way — + *as* or *with* ▪ I've always *looked on* her *as* a friend. [=considered her to be a friend] ▪ They *looked on* reading *as* an escape from the troubles of life. ▪ He *looked upon* his son's accomplishments *with* pride.

look out [*phrasal verb*] **1** — used to tell someone to be aware of something dangerous ▪ *Look out* [=*watch out*]—one of the steps is missing! **2** ***look (something) out or look out (something) Brit*** : to succeed in finding (something) ▪ It may take me a while to *look out* [=*hunt down*] his phone number for you.

look out for [*phrasal verb*] **1** ***look out for (something)*** : to be aware of and try to avoid (something dangerous or unwanted) ▪ In the winter, drivers need to *look out for* icy patches on the roads. ▪ In buying a home, there are many potential problems (that) you should *look out for*. ▪ *Look out for* [=*watch out for*] that pothole! **2** ***look out for (someone or something)*** : to take care of or protect (someone or something) ▪ I can *look out for* myself. ▪ She is supposed to be *looking out for* our interests. ✧ If you ***look out for number one***, you only think about yourself and do what helps you most. ▪ We don't want a senator who's (only/always) *looking out for number one*.

look over [*phrasal verb*] ***look (something) over or look over (something)*** : to read or examine (something) usually in a quick or hurried way ▪ She *looked over* the plans on her way out of the office. ▪ He *looked over* his shopping list as he entered the store. ▪ *look* a proposal *over*

look sharp see [2]SHARP

look (someone) in the eye also look (someone) in the face : to look directly at (someone who is also looking at you) ▪ I wasn't afraid to *look him* (right) *in the eye* and tell him just what I thought of him!

look the other way : to ignore something that should be noticed or dealt with : to turn your attention away from something ▪ We can't just *look the other way* while these violations of basic human rights continue to occur. ▪ Residents of the neighborhood accuse police of *looking the other way* as drug dealers become more active there.

look through [*phrasal verb*] **1** ***look through (something)*** **a** : to read or briefly examine some of the pages of (a book, magazine, etc.) ▪ She was *looking* [=*leafing*] *through* a magazine as she waited in the doctor's office. ▪ *look through* the pages of a magazine **b** : to look at the different parts of (a collection or group of things) ▪ I *looked through* [=*went through*] all his letters. **2** ***look through (someone)*** : to pretend not to see or recognize (someone) in a rude or unfriendly way ▪ We used to be best friends but when she passed me on the street yesterday *she looked* (right/straight) *through me* without even saying hello!

look to [*phrasal verb*] **1** ***look to (something)*** : to think about or examine (something) : to direct your attention to (something) ▪ They *look to* the future with ever-increasing hope. — usually + *for* ▪ We can *look to* the past *for* help in figuring out how to deal with this problem. ▪ *look to* nature *for* inspiration **2** ***look to (someone)*** : to need (someone) to do something for or give something to you : to depend or rely on (someone) ▪ They *look to* me to fix the problem. ▪ Many parents *look to* their children to help them navigate the Internet. — often + *for* ▪ Many parents *look to* their children *for* help in navigating the Internet. ▪ She *looked to* her friends *for* help. ▪ They *look to* you *for* advice.

look up [*phrasal verb*] **1** : to get better : IMPROVE ▪ The economy is *looking up*. ▪ Things started to *look up* for me when I got the promotion. **2** ***look (something) up or look up (something)*** : to search for (something) in a reference book, on the Internet, etc. ▪ If you don't know what a word means, you should *look* it *up* (in the dictionary). ▪ *look up* a telephone number ▪ *look up* an article in the encyclopedia **3** ***look (someone) up or look up (someone)*** : to call or go to see (someone) when you are in the area where that person lives ▪ I told them to *look* me *up* if they came to town.

look up to [*phrasal verb*] ***look up to (someone)*** : to respect and admire (someone) ▪ I've always *looked up to* my older brother. ▪ The kids really *look up to* their coach.

Look what the cat dragged in! see CAT

look your best see [3]BEST

not much to look at informal : not physically attractive ▪ The restaurant *isn't much to look at*, but the food is good. ▪ The dog *isn't much to look at*, but he's a great hunting dog.

[2]look *noun, pl* **looks**

1 [*count*] : the act of looking at something — usually singular ▪ A quick *look* inside someone's refrigerator can tell you a lot about that person. ▪ Come on inside. ***Take a look*** around. ▪ She went inside the building to ***have a look*** around. ▪ I wanted to ***get a look*** inside the car's engine. — often + *at* ▪ Just *take/have a look at* this! ▪ It's our first chance to *get a look at* the new library. ▪ The witness wasn't able to describe the killer because she didn't ***get a good look at*** him. [=she didn't see him clearly] ▪ We ***took one look at*** the weather and decided to stay home. [=when we saw how bad the weather was we immediately decided to stay home]

2 [*count*] : the act of examining or considering something — usually singular ▪ movies that are worth a *look* [=movies that you should consider seeing because they are good, entertaining, etc.] — usually + *at* ▪ The report takes a close/revealing/hard *look at* the public school system. ▪ We need to take a closer *look at* these issues.

3 [*singular*] : the act of trying to find something or someone ▪ I don't think you left it here, but I'll take a *look* around for it. ▪ I took a quick *look*, but he wasn't there.

4 [*count*] : the emotions and feelings that can be seen in a person's face or eyes ▪ You should have seen the *look* [=*expression*] on her face! ▪ I'll never forget the *look* in her eyes. ▪ a *look* of jealousy/pride/remorse ▪ He gave me an angry/dirty *look*. ▪ They exchanged *looks* of love. [=they looked at each other lovingly] ▪ I've never seen her so angry. ***If looks could kill***, I'd be dead right now.

5 a [*count*] : a quality or characteristic that you can see when you look at something : the way that something looks ▪ The painting has an old-fashioned *look* to it. ▪ The building had the *look* [=*appearance*] of a fortress. ▪ a fabric that has the *look* of leather [=a fabric that has the same appearance as leather] ▪ Judging by/from the *look* of those clouds, we're going to get some rain. ▪ I ***don't like the look of*** those clouds. [=I don't like the way those clouds look; those clouds make me think that there will be a storm, it will rain or snow, etc.] ▪ The restaurant doesn't look very appealing, but ***looks can be deceiving/deceptive***. [=something can be very different from how it seems or appears to be] ▪ ***From the look of things***, that car won't last much longer. [=that car seems unlikely to last much longer] **b** ***looks*** [*plural*] : physical appearance ▪ Everyone says he's handsome, but I wasn't impressed by his *looks*.; *especially* : attractive physical appearance ▪ She's very pretty, but she's not going to get by just on her *looks*. ▪ He had boyish ***good looks***. ▪ She's worried about ***losing her looks*** [=becoming less attractive] as she grows older. **c** [*count*] : a style or fashion — usually singular ▪ a new *look* in women's fashion ▪ They wanted the right *look* for the company's new logo.

look–alike /ˈlʊkəˌlaɪk/ *noun, pl* **-alikes** [*count*] : someone or something that looks like another person or thing ▪ She and her cousin are *look-alikes*. [=they look like each other; they look very similar] ▪ a young actor who is a John Wayne *look-alike* [=a young actor who looks like John Wayne]

– **look–alike** *adj, always used before a noun* ▪ two *look-alike* cousins

look•er /ˈlʊkɚ/ *noun, pl* **-ers** [*count*] *informal* : a person (especially a woman) who is very attractive • His girlfriend's a real *looker*.

look·er–on /ˌlʊkɚˈɑːn/ *noun, pl* **look·ers–on** [*count*] : a person who watches something • The accident attracted a small group of *lookers-on*. [=(more commonly) *onlookers*]

look–in /ˈlʊkˌɪn/ *noun* [*singular*] *Brit* : a chance to succeed or be involved in something • She wanted to apply for the job, but they never let her ***get/have a look-in***.

looking glass *noun, pl* ~ **glasses** [*count*] *old-fashioned* : [1]MIRROR 1

look·out /ˈlʊkˌaʊt/ *noun, pl* **-outs** [*count*]
1 : a person who watches an area and warns others if there is danger • The troops posted a *lookout* for the night.
2 : a high place or structure from which you can see a wide area • The mountain road had several *lookouts* where you could enjoy the view. • a *lookout* tower
be someone's lookout *Brit, informal* — used to say that someone who makes a bad decision or does something foolish is responsible for the result and will have to deal with it alone • If he wants to spend all his money on expensive clothes, that's *his lookout*.
keep a lookout for : to watch for (something or someone) • The police officer walked through the neighborhood, *keeping a* (sharp) *lookout for* any suspicious activity.
on the lookout for : looking or searching for (something or someone) • An avid shopper, she was always *on the lookout for* sales. • The police are *on the lookout for* two men who escaped from custody yesterday.

look–see /ˈlʊkˈsiː/ *noun* [*singular*] *chiefly US, informal* : a quick act of looking at or examining something • They heard the house was for sale, so they drove over to have a *look-see*.

[1]**loom** /ˈluːm/ *verb* **looms**; **loomed**; **loom·ing** [*no obj*]
1 : to appear in a large, strange, or frightening form often in a sudden way • A ship *loomed* (up) out of the fog. • Storm clouds *loomed* on the horizon. : to appear in an impressively large or great form • The mountains *loom* above/over the valley.
2 : to be close to happening : to be about to happen — used especially of unpleasant or frightening things • A workers' strike is *looming*. • A battle is *looming* in Congress over the proposed budget cuts. • a *looming* battle/conflict/problem/storm • The deadline ***looms closer*** with each passing day.
loom large : to have great importance or influence • Rising tuition costs *loom large* in the minds of many parents. • She was a critic who *loomed large* in literary circles.

[2]**loom** *noun, pl* **looms** [*count*] : a frame or machine that is used to weave threads or yarns to produce cloth

loom

[1]**loon** /ˈluːn/ *noun, pl* **loons** [*count*] *informal* : a crazy person • That guy is a complete *loon*. — compare [2]LOON

[2]**loon** *noun, pl* **loons** [*count*] : a large bird that lives in the northern parts of the world and that eats fish and has a loud and strange cry — compare [1]LOON

loon·ie /ˈluːni/ *noun, pl* **-ies** [*count*] *Canada* : a coin that is worth one Canadian dollar

[1]**loo·ny** /ˈluːni/ *adj* **loo·ni·er**; **-est** *informal* : crazy or foolish • *loony* extremists • Every family includes someone who's a little *loony*.

[2]**loony** *noun, pl* **-nies** [*count*] *informal* : a crazy or foolish person • the *loonies* on that late-night television show

loony bin *noun, pl* ~ **bins** [*count*] *informal + offensive* : a hospital for people who are insane ✧ *Loony bin* is usually used in a joking way. • If you keep acting like that we'll have to send you off to the *loony bin*.

[1]**loop** /ˈluːp/ *noun, pl* **loops**
1 [*count*] **a** : a curved part or shape made when something long and thin (such as a rope or thread) bends so that it touches or crosses over itself • a closed *loop* of rope • a wire with a *loop* at the end • a *loop* of string/thread **b** : something that is shaped like a loop • They rowed along a *loop* in the river. • The road formed a *loop* around the pond. • letters formed with lots of *loops* **c** : a ring or curved piece used for holding something • a belt *loop*
2 [*count*] : an action in which an airplane flies in an upright circle perpendicular to the ground • The pilot did/performed a *loop*. — see also *loop the loop* at [2]LOOP
3 [*count*] : a piece of film or tape with the ends joined together so that the same pictures or sounds are repeated continuously; *also* : a recording that is repeated continuously • The computer-generated images are shown on a continuous *loop*.
4 [*count*] *computers* : a series of instructions that are repeated in a computer program until a specified condition is met
5 ***the loop*** : a group of people who know about or have influence or control over something — usually used in the phrases ***in the loop*** and ***out of the loop*** • She wants to stay *in the loop* as these changes are being considered. • He claims that he was kept *out of the loop* when the decision to sell the company was being made.
knock/throw (someone) for a loop *US, informal* : to cause (someone) to be very amazed, confused, or shocked • The news of her death really *knocked* me *for a loop*. • His parents were *thrown for a loop* when he quit college.
knock (something) for a loop *US, informal* : to damage or ruin (something) • The town's economy has been *knocked for a loop* by the factory's closing. • The news has *knocked* the stock market *for a loop*.

[2]**loop** *verb* **loops**; **looped**; **loop·ing**
1 : to form or cause (something) to form a loop [*no obj*] The road *loops* around the pond. • The necklace is long enough to *loop* twice around my neck. [+ *obj*] She *looped* a string around her finger. • He sat with his arms *looped* around his knees.
2 : to move or cause (something) to move in a high curving path [*no obj*] The ball *looped* over the shortstop's head into left field for a single. • The batter hit a *looping* single to left field. [+ *obj*] The batter *looped* a single to left field. • The quarterback *looped* a pass downfield.
loop the loop : to perform a loop in an airplane

looped /ˈluːpt/ *adj, US, informal* : drunk or intoxicated • I took one look at her and knew she was *looped*.

loop·hole /ˈluːpˌhoʊl/ *noun, pl* **-holes** [*count*] : an error in the way a law, rule, or contract is written that makes it possible for some people to legally avoid obeying it • She took advantage of a *loophole* in the tax law. • a tax *loophole* • His attorney has been hunting/searching for a *loophole* that would allow him to get out of the deal. • tried to close/plug a *loophole* in the new legislation

loopy /ˈluːpi/ *adj* **loop·i·er**; **-est**
1 : having many loops • *loopy* handwriting
2 *informal* : strange or silly • a *loopy* comedian • a *loopy* smile/grin • The movie has a certain *loopy* charm.

[1]**loose** /ˈluːs/ *adj* **loos·er**; **-est**
1 : not tightly fastened, attached, or held • a *loose* tooth • a *loose* thread • Some of the shingles on the roof were *loose*. • The rope was tied in a *loose* knot. • The nails had been pried *loose*. • Some of the shingles had ***come/worked loose***. • The boat *came loose* from its moorings and floated out into the harbor. • The ball ***popped loose*** from the shortstop's glove.
2 a : not pulled or stretched tight • a *loose* belt • *loose* reins on a horse • *loose* skin **b** *of clothing* : not fitting close to your body : not tight • She was wearing a *loose* dress/skirt. • a *loose* [=*baggy*] sweater
3 : not physically held or contained • The dog was wandering *loose* in the streets. • The lion had somehow gotten/broken *loose* [=*free*] from its cage. — see also LET LOOSE 1 (below)
4 a : not held together in a solid or tight mass • *loose* dirt • *loose* rocks • *loose* sandy soil **b** : not held together in a bundle, container, etc. • *loose* sheets of pages • *Loose* hairs stuck out from under his cap. • She let her hair hang down *loose*. • You can buy a bag of potatoes or some *loose* potatoes.
5 : not stiff or tense : flexible or relaxed • He walked with a *loose* stride. • *loose* muscles • I never relaxed that day; I just couldn't get *loose*. • Runners should warm up for a few minutes to get *loose*. • I tried to ***stay loose*** during the game, but I was too nervous. — see also HANG LOOSE (below)
6 : not closely joined or united • Ten advocacy groups from all parts of the country formed a *loose* alliance/association/coalition to present their shared interests to Congress.
7 a : not exact or precise • a very *loose* translation • a *loose* interpretation of the law • This book is only a novel in the *loose* sense of the word. [=the word "novel" does not usually refer to a book like this; many people would not consider the book a novel] **b** : not careful in speech : talking too freely • *Loose* [=*careless*] talk spread the rumor. • She has a ***loose tongue***. [=she talks too much about things that are private, secret, etc.]

8 *sports* : not controlled or held by any of the players in a game • a *loose* ball/puck
9 *old-fashioned* : not respectable sexually : not decent or moral • He was accused of *loose* conduct/behavior. • a *loose* woman • *loose* morals
10 *of solid waste from the body* : containing a larger than normal amount of fluid • *loose* stools; *also* : producing loose stools • *loose* bowels • *loose* bowel movements
all hell breaks loose see HELL
break loose see [1]BREAK
cut loose **1** *cut (someone) loose* : to stop supporting or employing (someone) • He worked here for a few years but he didn't do a good job, so we finally had to *cut* him *loose*. : to end an official relationship or agreement with (someone) • She's been *cut loose* from her contract. [=the company/organization with whom she had a contract to work has ended the contract] **2** *chiefly US, informal* : to act in a free and relaxed way after behaving in a way that is controlled • I enjoy *cutting loose* with friends on weekends.
hang loose *chiefly US, informal* : to remain calm and relaxed • Just *hang loose* for a minute. I'll be right back.
have a screw loose, have a loose screw see [1]SCREW
let loose **1** ***let (someone or something) loose*** *or* ***set/turn (someone or something) loose*** : to allow (someone or something) to move or go freely • He *let/set* the dogs *loose* in the courtyard. • cattle *let loose* to graze on the green fields — often used figuratively • It's the end of the school year, when schools *turn* students *loose* on our towns. • a director who's willing to *let* her actors *loose* to interpret their roles however they see fit • how to stop the violence that has been *let loose* [=*loosed*] on the city **2** : to produce (something, such as a cry) in a sudden and forceful way • The crowd *let loose* [=*let out*] an enormous groan when the pass was intercepted. • She *let loose* (with) a scream.
play fast and loose see [1]PLAY
– loose·ly *adv* • The clothes fit *loosely*. • The term is *loosely* used by most people. • The rider held the reins *loosely* as the horse slowed to a walk. • *loosely* affiliated/allied businesses • The company was *loosely* organized. • The movie is ***loosely based on*** the novel. [=it is based on the novel but many things are different in the movie] **– loose·ness** *noun* [*noncount*] • moral *looseness* • the *looseness* of the translation • the *looseness* of his clothing

[2]loose *adv* : in a way that does not fit close to your body • *loose*-fitting clothing

[3]loose *verb* **loos·es; loosed; loos·ing** [+ *obj*]
1 : to release or untie (an animal or person) • They *loosed* the dogs on the prowlers. [=they released the dogs so that they could catch, chase away, etc., the prowlers] — often used figuratively • riots that have *loosed* an epidemic of violence on the city
2 : to make (something) less tight : LOOSEN • He *loosed* his grip.
3 : to shoot or fire (something, such as an arrow or a bullet) • The soldiers *loosed* a volley of rifle fire.

[4]loose *noun*
on the loose : able to move freely : not controlled or held in a prison, cage, etc. — used especially to describe a dangerous person, animal, or group • The prisoner escaped and is still *on the loose*. • A killer is *on the loose*. • An angry mob was *on the loose*.

loose cannon *noun, pl* ~ **-nons** [*count*] : a person who cannot be controlled and who does or says things that cause problems, embarrassment, etc., for others • a politician who is regarded as a *loose cannon* by her colleagues

loose change *noun* [*noncount*] : coins that a person is carrying • He had a few dollars in *loose change* in his pockets.

loose end *noun, pl* ~ **ends** [*count*] : a part of something (such as a job or story) that has not been completed • We still have one more *loose end* to deal with before we're finished with the project. — usually plural • The project is almost complete, but we still have a few *loose ends* to tie up. • All the story's *loose ends* were wrapped up as the novel ended.
at loose ends (*US*) *or Brit* ***at a loose end*** : not knowing what to do : not having anything in particular to do • With everyone on vacation she was *at loose ends*. • Drop by if you find yourself *at loose ends* this weekend.

loose–joint·ed /ˈluːsˈʤoɪntəd/ *adj* [*more* ~; *most* ~] : able to move in a very free and relaxed way • a *loose-jointed* [=*flexible, loose-limbed*] dancer/gymnast

loose–leaf /ˈluːsˈliːf/ *adj* : designed so that sheets of paper can be added or removed by opening a locking device that holds the sheets of paper in place • a *loose-leaf* notebook/binder/folder

loose–limbed /ˈluːsˈlɪmd/ *adj* [*more* ~; *most* ~] : able to move in a very free and relaxed way • a *loose-limbed* [=*flexible, loose-jointed*] athlete

loos·en /ˈluːsn/ *verb* **-ens; -ened; -en·ing**
1 a [+ *obj*] : to make (something) less tight or firm : to make (something) loose or looser • He used a spade to *loosen* the soil. • She *loosened* the cake from the sides of the pan. • *loosen* a screw • After eating so much I had to *loosen* my belt. • When the meeting was over he *loosened* his tie. • She ***loosened her grip/hold*** on the rope. [=she began to hold the rope less tightly] — sometimes used figuratively • He has *loosened his grip/hold* on the company. **b** [*no obj*] : to become less tight or firm : to become loose or looser • One of the screws had *loosened* a bit and had to be tightened. • Her grip *loosened*.
2 : to become or to cause (something) to become less strict [+ *obj*] We want to *loosen* (up) the controls/restrictions that the law has imposed. • Each generation seems to *loosen* the established standards of behavior. [*no obj*] Standards of behavior seem to be *loosening* everywhere.
loosen someone's tongue : to cause someone to talk more freely : to cause someone to say things that would not usually be said • Drinking alcohol can *loosen your tongue*.
loosen up [*phrasal verb*] **1** : to make or become less tense : RELAX • He *loosens up* by exercising. • After a couple of drinks she had *loosened up* and was talking freely. • He seemed nervous and his friends kept telling him to *loosen up*. **2** ***loosen (someone or something) up*** *or* ***loosen up (someone or something)*** : to cause (someone or something) to relax • He exercises to *loosen up* his muscles. [=he exercises so that his muscles are not stiff] • I tried to *loosen her up* [=I tried to get her to relax and feel comfortable] by telling a few jokes.

loos·ey–goos·ey /ˌluːsiˈguːsi/ *adj* [*more* ~; *most* ~] *chiefly US, informal* : very loose or relaxed • a *loosey-goosey* attitude

[1]loot /ˈluːt/ *noun* [*noncount*]
1 : something that is stolen or taken by force • After raiding the town, the soldiers helped themselves to any *loot* that they could find. • The thieves got a lot of *loot* in the robbery.
2 *informal* : MONEY • He made a lot of *loot* selling cars.

[2]loot *verb* **loots; loot·ed; loot·ing** : to steal things from (a place, such as a store or house) during a war or after destruction has been caused by fire, rioting, etc. [+ *obj*] Rioters *looted* the stores. • The soldiers were *looting* every house that they came to. • The supplies had been *looted* [=*stolen*] from the warehouse. [*no obj*] Soldiers swept through the territory, *looting*, burning, and killing.
– loot·er *noun, pl* **-ers** [*count*] **– looting** *noun* [*noncount*] • There has been widespread *looting* throughout the city.

lop /ˈlɑːp/ *verb* **lops; lopped; lop·ping** [+ *obj*]
1 : to cut branches from (a tree, bush, etc.) • trees that have been heavily *lopped*
2 : to cut or cut off (something) • badly *lopped* hair — usually + *off* • *lop off* a dead branch • He accidentally *lopped off* [=*chopped off*] one of his fingers. — often used figuratively • She offered to *lop* $20 *off* the price. [=to reduce the price by $20] • They *lopped* several million dollars *off* the budget.

lope /ˈloʊp/ *verb* **lopes; loped; lop·ing** [*no obj*] : to run in a relaxed way with long strides • The horses *loped* easily across/over the fields. • He went *loping* up the hill. • The outfielder *loped* after the ball.
– lope *noun* [*singular*] • She ran with an easy *lope*. **– lop·ing** *adj* • She ran with a long *loping* gait. **– lo·ping·ly** *adv* • run/move *lopingly*

lop–eared /ˈlɑːpˌiɚd/ *adj* : having long ears that hang down • a *lop-eared* bunny/rabbit • a *lop-eared* dog

lop·pers /ˈlɑːpɚz/ *noun* [*plural*] : a garden tool used for cutting branches and twigs • a pair of *loppers*

lop·sid·ed /ˈlɑːpˌsaɪdəd/ *adj* [*more* ~; *most* ~]
1 : having one side that is lower or smaller than the other • The boat looked *lopsided*. • The house had a *lopsided* porch. • a *lopsided* grin/smile
2 : uneven or unequal • They won the game by a *lopsided* score of 25–3. • a *lopsided* vote of 99 to 1 • (*chiefly US*) He won a *lop-sided* victory in the recent election. [=he won the election very easily; he had many more votes than the other candidates]
– lop·sid·ed·ly *adv* **– lop·sid·ed·ness** *noun* [*noncount*]

L

lo·qua·cious /loʊˈkweɪʃəs/ *adj* **: liking to talk and talking smoothly and easily** ▪ a *loquacious* and glib politician ▪ the *loquacious* host of a radio talk show
— lo·qua·cious·ly *adv* **— lo·qua·cious·ness** *noun* [*noncount*] ▪ a politician known for her *loquaciousness* **— lo·quac·i·ty** /loʊˈkwæsəti/ *noun* [*noncount*] *formal* ▪ a politician known for her *loquacity*

¹lord /ˈloəd/ *noun, pl* **lords**
1 [*count*] **: a man who has power and authority: such as a : a man who ruled over a large area of land in the Middle Ages** ▪ a feudal *lord* **b : a very powerful criminal** ▪ a crime/drug/gang *lord* — see also SLUMLORD, WARLORD
2 ***Lord*** [*singular*] **a —** used as a name for God or Jesus Christ ▪ Ask the *Lord* for forgiveness. ▪ Praise the *Lord.* ▪ Oh *Lord,* hear our prayers. **b** ✧ ***Lord*** **is used informally by itself and in phrases to make a statement or question more forceful or to express surprise, anger, etc.** ▪ *Lord,* it's hot out today. ▪ ***Lord almighty***, is it that late already? ▪ ***Good Lord***, what have they done?! ▪ ***My Lord***, what were you thinking?! ▪ ***Oh my Lord!*** I can't believe it!
3 a [*count*] **: a man who is a member of the British nobility** ▪ He became a *lord* upon the death of his father. **b** [*noncount*] ***Lord*** — used as a title for certain British noblemen and male officials of high rank ▪ *Lord* Churchill ▪ Alfred, *Lord* Tennyson ▪ *Lord* Advocate — see also LORD MAYOR
4 ***the Lords*** *Brit* **:** HOUSE OF LORDS ▪ The government had the support of *the Lords.*
in the year of our Lord see YEAR
Lord help someone see ¹HELP
Lord knows see ¹KNOW
thank the Lord see THANK

²lord *verb* **lords; lord·ed; lord·ing**
lord it over someone **: to act in a way that shows you think you are better or more important than someone** ▪ She knows she's very smart and *lords it over* her younger brothers. ▪ He got the only A in the class and was *lording it over* his classmates.

lord·ly /ˈloədli/ *adj* **lord·li·er; -est** [*or more* ~; *most* ~]
1 a : having the qualities of a lord ▪ a *lordly* and dignified man **b : suitable for a lord : very large and impressive** ▪ a *lordly* estate
2 : having or showing a feeling of being better than other people ▪ *lordly* airs of superiority ▪ He regarded his neighbors with *lordly* disdain.

Lord Mayor *noun, pl* ~ **Mayors** [*count*] **: the title of the mayor of the City of London and of some other large cities in Britain and Ireland**

lord·ship /ˈloədˌʃɪp/ *noun, pl* **-ships** [*count*] *chiefly Brit*
1 ***Lordship*** — used as a title when addressing or referring to someone who has the title of lord (such as a member of the nobility, a judge, or a bishop); used with *his, your,* or *their* ▪ *His Lordship* is not at home. ▪ Can I get *your Lordship* anything else?
2 : the authority, power, or territory of a lord ▪ He inherited a *lordship.*

Lord's Prayer *noun*
the Lord's Prayer **: a prayer that Jesus Christ taught to his followers**

Lordy /ˈloədi/ *interj, informal* — used to make a statement or question more forceful or to express surprise ▪ *Lordy,* that girl can sing! ▪ *Lordy* it's hot today.

lore /ˈloə/ *noun* [*noncount*] **: traditional knowledge, beliefs, and stories that relate to a particular place, subject, or group** ▪ an event that has become part of local *lore* ▪ forest *lore* ▪ the *lore* of sailing — see also FOLKLORE

lor·ry /ˈlori/ *noun, pl* **-ries** [*count*] *Brit* **:** TRUCK

lose /ˈluːz/ *verb* **los·es; lost** /ˈlɑːst/; **los·ing**
1 [+ *obj*] **: to be unable to find (something or someone)** ▪ She's always *losing* her gloves. ▪ Don't *lose* your keys. ▪ Hold my hand: I don't want to *lose* you. ▪ The police *lost* him in the crowd. [=the police were no longer able to find/see him after he went into the crowd] ▪ The airline *lost* my luggage. [=my luggage did not arrive at the airport I flew into] ▪ He *lost* the fly ball in the sun. [=he was unable to see the fly ball because he was looking toward the sun] ▪ The letter was ***lost in the mail***. [=it was sent but never delivered to the person it was addressed to]
2 : to fail to win (a game, contest, etc.) [+ *obj*] *lose* a battle/game ▪ She *lost* her bid for reelection. [=she failed to win the election; she was not reelected] ▪ We *lost* the game by a score of 4–2. ▪ He *lost* his title in the rematch. ▪ She *lost* the lawsuit. ▪ The team *lost* three games but won the next four. [*no obj*] The team *lost* in the finals. ▪ an athlete known for *losing* with grace ▪ That horse always *loses.* ▪ He hates to *lose* when money is involved. ▪ How could she play that well and still *lose?* — often + *to* ▪ The Yankees *lost to* the Red Sox.
3 a [+ *obj*] **: to fail to keep or hold (something wanted or valued)** ▪ *lose* an advantage ▪ The country *lost* its independence 50 years ago. ▪ The mayor is *losing* power/influence/support. ▪ He is in danger of *losing* control of the company. ▪ She *lost* control of the car and skidded off the road. ▪ I was so angry that I *lost* control (of myself, of my temper) and yelled at them. ▪ She didn't *lose* her job but she *lost* access to all confidential company materials. ▪ The senator *lost* votes when he angered some of his supporters. ▪ The religious community was *losing* its younger members. ▪ He hasn't *lost* his sense of humor. ▪ They had *lost* all hope of winning the title. ▪ I don't want anything to eat. I've *lost* my appetite. [=I no longer feel hungry] ▪ She began to *lose* confidence in herself. [=to feel less confident] ▪ Try not to *lose* patience with the children. ▪ The accident victim was rapidly *losing* blood. ▪ I'm sorry I'm late. I ***lost track of*** the time. [=I failed to stay aware of the time; I did not realize that so much time had passed] ▪ She ***lost her balance*** [=failed to keep her weight spread equally] and fell. **b** ✧ **If you *have nothing (else/left) to lose*, you cannot make a situation worse by taking a risk. If you *have a lot to lose* or *have too much to lose*, you could make your situation much worse by taking a risk or doing something.** ▪ You might as well apply for the job. You have *nothing to lose* and everything to gain. ▪ Some of them are married and have young children—they *have a lot to lose.* ▪ I can't quit now. I *have too much to lose.* **c : to fail to earn or keep (money)** [+ *obj*] They *lost* all their money/savings in a poor investment. ▪ The company has been ***losing money*** for the past several years. [=it has been spending more money than it has been earning] [*no obj*] Investors *lost* heavily when the company's stock failed to meet expectations. **d** [+ *obj*] **: to have (something) taken from you or destroyed** ▪ We *lost* (electrical) power during the storm. ▪ He *lost* an arm in the war. [=one of his arms was destroyed or so badly injured that it had to be removed] ▪ They ***lost everything*** in the fire. [=all their possessions were destroyed in the fire] ▪ He yelled so much during the game that he ***lost his voice*** [=he was unable to speak] for two days. **e** [+ *obj*] **: to gradually have less of (something) as time passes** ▪ Many people who *lose* weight by dieting eventually gain the weight back. ▪ She has been *losing* strength in her legs. ▪ He was gradually *losing* his eyesight. ▪ He's *losing* his hair. [=becoming bald] ▪ The public seems to have *lost* interest in the case.
4 [+ *obj*] **: to cause (someone) to fail to win or keep (something) : to cause the loss of (something) for (someone)** ▪ One careless statement *lost* the election for her. = One careless statement *lost* her the election. [=she lost the election because of one careless statement]
5 a : to decrease in (something) [+ *obj*] The TV program has *lost* popularity [=become less popular] in recent years. ▪ The plane was *losing* altitude. ▪ What will you do if the company's stock *loses* value when you expect it to gain value? [*no obj*] What will you do if the stock *loses* when you expect it to gain? **b** [+ *obj*] **: to decrease in value by (a specified amount)** ▪ His retirement account *lost* three percent last quarter. **c** [*no obj*] **: to decrease in value when compared to something else** ▪ The dollar *lost* against the pound last week.
6 [+ *obj*] **a : to experience or suffer the death of (a relative, friend, etc.)** ▪ She *lost* her husband in the war. [=her husband was killed in the war] ▪ He *lost* his best friend to cancer. [=his best friend died of cancer] ▪ The country *lost* thousands of young men in/during the war. = Thousands of young men were *lost* [=*killed*] in/during the war. = Thousands of young men ***lost their lives*** in/during the war. ▪ She's very sick, and the doctors say they're afraid they're going to *lose* her. [=they're afraid that she is going to die] ▪ I was sad to hear that she ***lost the baby***. [=that her baby died before being born or soon after being born] ▪ a sailor who was ***lost at sea*** [=who died at sea] **b : to no longer have or be with (someone who leaves)** ▪ We'll be sorry to *lose* you when you leave for your new job. ▪ He begged his wife to forgive him and told her that he didn't want to *lose* her.
7 [+ *obj*] **: to fail to keep control of (something)** ▪ He ***lost his temper/cool/composure***. [=he became angry] ▪ She wondered if she was ***losing her mind/sanity***. [=becoming insane] ▪ He seems to be ***losing his nerve***. [=becoming afraid] — see also *lose your head* at ¹HEAD
8 [+ *obj*] **a : to fail to use (something, such as time) :** WASTE ▪ I don't want to *lose* this chance/opportunity. ▪ We *lost* (a

good bit of) *time* in that traffic jam. ▪ She ***lost no time*** in getting the project started. [=she got the project started immediately] ▪ We need to get started immediately. There's ***no time to lose.*** **b** *of a watch or clock* **: to show a time that is earlier than the correct time : to run slow by (an amount of time)** [+ *obj*] My old watch *loses* a minute every day. [*no obj*] a clock that *loses* less than any other clock yet invented
9 [+ *obj*] **: to explain something in a way that is not clear to (someone) : to confuse (someone)** ▪ I'm sorry. You've ***lost me.*** [=I don't understand what you're telling me] ▪ I understood the first part of the lecture, but when he started to talk about quantum physics he *lost me* completely. [=I was completely unable to understand what he was saying]
10 [+ *obj*] **: to succeed in getting away from (someone who is following or chasing you)** ▪ She tried to *lose* them by turning down a side street.
11 [+ *obj*] *informal* **: to get rid of (something unwanted)** ▪ I just can't seem to *lose* this cold. ▪ *Lose* the attitude, okay? [=stop having a bad attitude; stop being annoyed, uncooperative, etc.] ▪ You can *lose* [=*remove*] that sentence and the paragraph will sound better.
lose contact see [1]CONTACT
lose count see [2]COUNT
lose face see [1]FACE
lose ground see [1]GROUND
lose it *informal* **1 : to become insane** ▪ He was always a little strange, but now he's completely *lost it.* **2 : to start behaving in an uncontrolled way because you are angry or upset** ▪ I was so angry that I almost *lost it.*
lose out [*phrasal verb*] **: to fail to keep or get something valued or desired** ▪ Whoever benefits from the new government programs, the American taxpayer is bound to *lose out* in the end. — **often +** ***on*** **or** ***to*** ▪ If you don't invest with us, you'll be *losing out on* a great opportunity! [=you'll be missing/wasting a great opportunity] ▪ She *lost out to* a better-known actress for the lead role. [=she did not get the lead role because a better-known actress got it]
lose sleep over see [2]SLEEP
lose the plot see [1]PLOT
lose touch see [2]TOUCH
lose your bearings see BEARING
lose your grip see [2]GRIP
lose your head see [1]HEAD
lose your heart see HEART
lose your life see [1]LIFE
lose your lunch see [1]LUNCH
lose your marbles see MARBLE
lose yourself **: to give all of your attention or thought to something** ▪ He *lost himself* in his work. ▪ a musician who completely *loses herself* in the music
lose your shirt see SHIRT
lose your touch see [2]TOUCH
lose your way see [1]WAY
– los·able /ˈluːzəbəl/ *adj* ▪ a *losable* game **– los·ing** *adj* ▪ the *losing* candidate in the race [=the candidate who did not win; the candidate who lost] ▪ The team is on a *losing* streak. ▪ The team had a *losing* record/season.

los·er /ˈluːzɚ/ *noun, pl* **-ers** [*count*]
1 : someone or something that loses a game, contest, etc. ▪ She was a *loser* in the first round of the tournament. [=she lost in the first round of the tournament] ▪ The team had a reputation for being a *loser* year after year. ▪ The *loser* of the bet has to buy drinks for the winner. ▪ She's a ***good loser.*** [=she does not become upset or angry when she loses] ▪ He's a ***bad/poor loser.*** = (*US*) He's a ***sore loser.*** [=he becomes upset or angry when he loses]
2 : someone who is harmed or put in a worse position as the result of something ▪ Whoever benefits from the new government programs, the real *loser* will be the American taxpayer.
3 *informal + disapproving* **: a person who is not successful, attractive, etc.** ▪ She's a (total, complete) *loser.* ▪ That guy is a ***born loser.***
finders keepers (losers weepers) see FINDER

loss /ˈlɑːs/ *noun, pl* **loss·es**
1 a : failure to keep or to continue to have something [*noncount*] — **usually +** ***of*** ▪ the mayor's *loss of* support/influence ▪ Surgeons were unable to control the *loss of* blood in the victim. ▪ Symptoms include insomnia and *loss of* appetite. ▪ Both accidents were attributed to the drivers' *loss of* control. ▪ The recession has caused the *loss of* many jobs. ▪ The accident caused enormous ***loss of life.*** [=many people died in the accident] [*singular*] — **usually +** ***of*** ▪ a *loss of* innocence ▪ The victim died from a *loss of* blood to the brain. [*plural*] There have been heavy job *losses* because of the recession. [=many people have been laid off] **b** [*noncount*] **: the experience of having something taken from you or destroyed** ▪ The storm caused widespread *loss* of electricity. ▪ soldiers who have suffered the *loss* of a limb [=soldiers who have had an arm or leg destroyed or so badly injured that it had to be removed]
2 [*count*] **: money that is spent and that is more than the amount earned or received** ▪ The company's *losses* for the year were higher than expected. ▪ profits and *losses* ▪ They ***took a loss*** on the deal. [=the deal cost them money; they lost money on the deal] ▪ The business is operating ***at a loss.*** [=the business is spending more money than it is earning] ▪ They sold the property *at a* (considerable) *loss.* [=for less than they paid for it] — **see also** AT A LOSS **(below)**
3 : failure to win a game, contest, etc. [*noncount*] A careless error resulted in the *loss* of the game. [*count*] The team suffered a 3–2 *loss* in the last game. ▪ The team has an equal number of wins and *losses.* ▪ the party's *losses* in the recent election
4 a : a decrease in something or in the amount of something [*singular*] The plane experienced a *loss* of altitude. [*noncount*] We need to determine the *loss* in value due to the damage. ▪ The new windows reduce temperature *loss* by 15 percent. ▪ Don't be concerned about the *loss* of a few pounds. You're still a healthy weight. ▪ Side effects of the treatment include nausea and hair *loss.* ▪ memory/weight *loss* **b** [*singular*] **: a decrease in value by a specified amount** ▪ The stock market had a *loss* of four percent yesterday.
5 [*noncount*] **a : the death or a relative, friend, etc.** — **usually +** ***of*** ▪ She mourned the *loss of* her parents. ▪ the *loss of* a dear friend to cancer **b : the experience of having someone leave** — **usually +** ***of*** ▪ The company has had to deal with the *loss* [=*departure*] *of* several key employees. **c : a feeling of sadness that you have when someone dies, leaves, etc.** ▪ Their deaths left everyone with a great/deep ***sense of loss.*** ▪ The ***feeling of loss*** you experienced after your divorce is not uncommon.
6 [*singular*] **: something that causes harm, sadness, etc.,** ***to*** **a group or organization** ▪ Their deaths were a great *loss to* the community. ▪ His retirement was a real *loss to* the company.
7 [*singular*] **: something that is completely destroyed** ▪ After the flood, the crops were a total *loss.* ▪ No one was injured in the accident, but the car was a complete *loss.*
8 ***losses*** [*plural*] **: soldiers killed, wounded, or captured in battle** ▪ During the battle the allies suffered/sustained/took/experienced heavy *losses.*
9 [*count*] *American football* **: the distance the ball is moved away from the goal during a play** ▪ There was a gain of five yards on first down, but a *loss* of three yards on second down.
at a loss **: not able to decide what should be done or said** ▪ I don't know what to do. I'm *at a* (complete) *loss.* ▪ They were ***at a loss to explain*** [=they were unable to explain] why it took so long to correct the problem. — **see also** LOSS **2 (above)**
at a loss for words *chiefly US* **: unable to think of anything to say** ▪ I was so surprised to see her that I was *at a loss for words.* [=(*chiefly Brit*) *lost for words*]
cut your losses **: to stop an activity, business, etc., that is failing in order to prevent more losses or damage** ▪ With the economy continuing to do poorly, many investors have decided to *cut their losses* and sell their stocks.
it's your loss ✧ **People say that something** ***is your loss*** **when you choose not to do something that they think would help you or that you would enjoy.** ▪ If she doesn't want to come to the party, *it's her loss.*
throw (someone) for a loss **: to cause (someone) to be very amazed, confused, or shocked** ▪ Recent revelations have *thrown* me *for a loss.* [=(more commonly) *for a loop*]

loss adjuster *noun, pl* **~ -ers** [*count*] *Brit* **:** INSURANCE ADJUSTER

loss leader *noun, pl* **~ -ers** [*count*] *business* **: a product that is sold for less than it is worth in order to attract customers**

[1]**lost** *past participle of* LOSE

[2]**lost** /ˈlɑːst/ *adj*
1 : unable to be found ▪ He was looking for his *lost* keys. ▪ *lost* baggage/luggage ▪ Many have tried to find the ruins of the *lost* city. — **see also** LONG-LOST
2 : not knowing where you are or how to get to where you want to go : unable to find your way ▪ The child was *lost.* ▪ We took a wrong turn and got *lost.* ▪ a *lost* puppy ▪ Hold my hand. I don't want you to get *lost.*

3 a : no longer held, owned, or possessed ▪ He has been trying to recapture his *lost* youth. ▪ She's been lagging at the polls, but hopes to recover/recoup ***lost ground*** with tonight's debate. [=she hopes to gain again support she had lost] **b :** no longer known ▪ a *lost* civilization ▪ It's a *lost* art. ▪ The original music is *lost* to us forever. **c :** no longer available ▪ a *lost* opportunity/chance [=an opportunity that was not used] ▪ The strike has cost the company millions in *lost* sales/earnings/revenue. [=sales/earnings/revenue that the company would have had if the strike had not happened] ▪ We need to work faster to ***make up for lost time***. [=we need to work faster because we did not get enough of the work done before now]
4 a : not won ▪ a *lost* battle **:** not possible to win ▪ The game was irretrievably/hopelessly *lost* by the end of the first half. **b :** not capable of succeeding ▪ Finishing the project on time seemed like a ***lost cause***. [=finishing the project on time seemed impossible]
5 a *not used before a noun* [*more* ~; *most* ~] **:** lacking confidence and feeling unsure of what to do ▪ When she first moved to the city she felt a bit *lost* and out of her depth. ▪ I don't know how I ever managed without my computer: I'd be totally ***lost without*** it! ▪ I depend on her for everything. I'd be *lost without* her. **b :** very unhappy ▪ a ***lost soul*** [=a lonely and unhappy person]
6 *not used before a noun* **:** so interested in something that you do not notice other things ▪ When he's reading a book he's ***lost to the world***. — often + *in* ▪ He was *lost in* his book. ▪ She was ***lost in thought***. [=she was thinking about something and not noticing the people and things around her] ▪ He seems to be *lost in* a world of his own. ▪ *lost in* (a) reverie
get lost *informal* **:** to go away **:** LEAVE — used in speech as a rude or angry way to tell someone to go away; see also [2]LOST 2 (above)
give someone up for lost **:** to decide that someone cannot be helped or saved ▪ He was desperately ill, and most of the doctors had *given him up for lost*. [=most of the doctors said that he would die]
he who hesitates is lost see HESITATE
lost for words *chiefly Brit* **:** unable to think of anything to say ▪ I was so surprised to see her that I was *lost for words*. [=(*chiefly US*) *at a loss for words*]
lost in the shuffle see [2]SHUFFLE
lost on **:** not appreciated or understood by (someone) ▪ The jokes were *lost on* me. [=I didn't understand the jokes] ▪ The meaning of her remark wasn't *lost on* him. ▪ The message was *lost on* those for whom it was intended.
no love lost, very little love lost see [1]LOVE

lot /ˈlɑːt/ *noun, pl* **lots**
1 [*count*] **a** *chiefly US* **:** a small piece of land that is or could be used for buiding something or for some other purpose ▪ He bought the vacant/empty *lot* across the street. ▪ They own the house on the corner *lot*. ▪ a building *lot* — see also PARKING LOT **b :** the buildings and land that are owned by a company that makes movies and television programs ▪ We took a tour of the Universal *lot*.
2 [*count*] **:** a small object used to choose the person who will do or receive something ✧ When someone is ***chosen by lot*** or when people ***draw lots*** or (less commonly) ***cast lots*** to choose someone, each person in a group takes a small object or a piece of paper from a container. One of the objects or pieces of paper is different from the others, and the person who takes the different one is chosen. ▪ The winner was chosen *by lot*. ▪ We *drew lots* to determine the winner.
3 [*singular*] **:** a person's situation in life especially as decided by chance ▪ The organization has done much to improve the *lot* of underprivileged youth. ▪ Unhappy with her ***lot in life***, she moved to the city to start over. ***synonyms*** see DESTINY
4 *informal* **a** [*count*] *chiefly Brit* **:** all the members of a group of people — usually singular ▪ Do you know the *lot* [=*bunch, crowd*] that hang around the arcade? ▪ That *lot* will never amount to anything! They're a thoroughly bad *lot*. ▪ Pipe down, the (whole) *lot* of you. = Pipe down, ***you lot***. ✧ In British English, a person who is not liked is sometimes described as ***a bad lot***. ▪ He may be a bit wild, but he's not *a bad lot* once you get to know him. **b *the lot*** **:** all the things of a group ▪ They sell tuxedos, business suits, casual wear . . . *the lot*. ▪ This one's the best of *the lot*.
5 [*count*] **:** one or more things being sold as one item at an auction ▪ *Lot* 45 is a dining room set. — see also JOB LOT
a lot **1** *also (informal)* ***lots*** **:** a large amount ▪ She has done *a lot* to help other people. ▪ I'd give *a lot* to be able to write like that! ▪ I'm not asking for *a lot*. [=*much*] ▪ They must have paid *a lot* for that car. ▪ We did ***quite a lot*** this morning. ▪ We still have *a lot* to do. = We still have *lots* (*and lots*) to do. **2 :** very often ▪ Do they hike *a lot*? ▪ I've been seeing her *a lot* recently. **3** — used to say that you feel a particular emotion very strongly ▪ "Did you like the movie?" "Yes, I liked it *a lot*." [=very much] ▪ I miss her *a lot* since she went away. **4** *also (informal)* ***lots*** **:** to a large degree or extent **:** MUCH ▪ This is *a lot* nicer. [=this is much nicer] ▪ There's *a lot* more to it than I realized at first. [=it's more complicated than it looks] ▪ I'm feeling *lots* better. ▪ Thanks *a lot*. [=*very much*]
a lot of *also (informal)* ***lots of*** **:** a large number or amount of (things, people, etc.) ▪ *A lot of* people feel that way. ▪ There was *a lot of* space. = There was *lots of* space. ▪ We had *lots of* fun. ▪ You can enjoy yourself without spending *a lot of* money. ▪ It doesn't make *a* (whole) *lot of* difference. ▪ We don't have ***an awful lot of*** money/time. [=we don't have much money/time] ▪ (*informal*) I think their ideas are ***a lot of garbage/nonsense***. [=I think their ideas are very foolish] ▪ (*informal*) It doesn't make ***a whole lot of*** [=very much] difference. ▪ ***Not a lot of*** people [=not many people] know that. ▪ "I've brought an umbrella." "***A (fat) lot of good*** that will do [=that will not do any good] now that it's stopped raining!"
leave a lot to be desired see [1]DESIRE
throw in your lot with *or* ***cast your lot with*** **:** to join or become associated with a person, group, or thing that you hope will win or succeed ▪ During the American Civil War, my great-grandfather *threw in his lot with* the Confederacy/Union.

loth *variant spelling of* LOATH

lo·tion /ˈloʊʃən/ *noun, pl* **-tions** [*count, noncount*] **:** a liquid that is rubbed onto your skin or hair ▪ a bottle of suntan *lotion* ▪ styling *lotion*

lot·tery /ˈlɑːtəri/ *noun, pl* **-ter·ies**
1 [*count*] **:** a way of raising money for a government, charity, etc., in which many tickets are sold and a few of the tickets are chosen by chance to win prizes ▪ Which states have *lotteries*? ▪ a national *lottery* ▪ a *lottery* ticket ▪ She acted like she'd just ***won the lottery***. [=won a lottery run by a government] ▪ Do you ***play the lottery***? [=do you buy lottery tickets?]
2 : a system used to decide who will get or be given something by choosing names or numbers by chance [*count*] They held a *lottery* to determine who could get a green card. [*noncount*] Room assignments are determined ***by lottery***.
3 [*singular*] **:** an event or situation in which what happens is decided by luck or chance ▪ Life's a *lottery*, isn't it? It all depends on luck.

lo·tus /ˈloʊtəs/ *noun, pl* **-tus·es** [*count*] **:** a type of flowering plant that grows on the surface of water

loud /ˈlaʊd/ *adj* **loud·er; -est**
1 : making or causing a lot of noise **:** strong and noticeable in sound ▪ a *loud* noise/party ▪ *loud* music/laughter/applause ▪ She complained in a *loud* voice. ▪ "Is the television *loud* enough?" "It's too *loud*!" — opposite QUIET
2 a *of a person* **:** noisy in a way that bothers other people ▪ He's known for being *loud* and aggressive. **b :** expressing ideas or opinions in a very open and forceful way — + *in* ▪ He has been *loud in* (his) praise of their efforts. [=he has strongly praised their efforts] ▪ Her critics have been *loud in* (their) disapproval of her policies.
3 : very bright or too bright in color ▪ *loud* [=*gaudy, garish*] clothes/colors/jewelry
actions speak louder than words see ACTION
out loud **:** in a way that is loud enough to be clearly heard **:** ALOUD ▪ She doesn't like to read *out loud* [=*aloud*] in class.
– loud *adv, not used before a verb* ▪ Don't talk so *loud*! ▪ Say it *loud*. ▪ They complained ***loud and long*** about the decision. ▪ "Can you hear me now?" "***Loud and clear***." [=I can hear you very clearly] ▪ talking *loud* [=talking loudly, loudly talking] **– loud·ly** *adv* ▪ *loudly* singing ▪ complaining/protesting *loudly* **– loud·ness** *noun* [*noncount*] ▪ She complained about the *loudness* of the television.

loud·hail·er /ˌlaʊdˈheɪlɚ/ *noun, pl* **-ers** [*count*] *Brit* **:** BULLHORN

loud·mouth /ˈlaʊdˌmaʊθ/ *noun, pl* **-mouths** [*count*] *informal + disapproving* **:** a loud person **:** a person who talks too much and who says unpleasant or stupid things
– loud·mouthed /ˈlaʊdˌmaʊθt/ *adj* [*more* ~; *most* ~] ▪ a *loudmouthed* heckler

loud·speak·er /ˈlaʊdˌspiːkɚ/ *noun, pl* **-ers** [*count*] **:** a device that is used to make sound (such as music or a person's voice) louder and to send it out so that many people can hear it in a public space • He made an announcement ***over/on the loudspeaker***. = He made an announcement using the *loudspeaker*.

[1]lounge /ˈlaʊnʤ/ *verb* **loung·es; lounged; loung·ing** [*no obj*] : to sit or lie in a relaxed way • She was *lounging* on the sofa. • *lounging* in bed : to spend time resting or relaxing • He was *lounging* by the pool all afternoon. • *lounging* at the bar — often + *around* or (*Brit*) *about* • We spent our vacation just *lounging around* [=*relaxing*] on the beach.
– **loung·er** *noun, pl* **-ers** [*count*]

[2]lounge *noun, pl* **lounges**
1 [*count*] : a room with comfortable furniture for relaxing: such as **a** : a comfortable room where people can spend time while they are waiting in an airport or other public place • an airport *lounge* • the VIP *lounge* **b** : a comfortable room for relaxing in a public building (such as a hotel or school) • (*US*) the faculty/student *lounge* • The hotel has a television *lounge*. **c** *US* : COCKTAIL LOUNGE • We gathered in the hotel *lounge* for a couple of drinks. • a *lounge* act **d** *Brit* : LIVING ROOM
2 [*count*] *chiefly US* : a long chair or couch • She sat/reclined on the *lounge*.
3 [*singular*] : an act or period of relaxing • They had a long, leisurely *lounge* by the pool.

lounge chair *noun, pl* ~ **chairs** [*count*] *chiefly US* : CHAISE LONGUE

lounge suit *noun, pl* ~ **suits** [*count*] *Brit* : BUSINESS SUIT

[1]louse /ˈlaʊs/ *noun* [*count*]
1 *pl* ***lice*** /ˈlaɪs/ : a type of small insect that lives on the bodies of people or animals • a problem with ***head lice***
2 *pl* ***lous·es*** *informal* : a bad or cruel person • Her ex-husband is a real *louse*.

[2]louse *verb* **lous·es; loused; lous·ing**
louse up [*phrasal verb*] ***louse (something) up*** *or* ***louse up (something)*** *informal* : to do (something) badly • The waitress *loused up* [=*messed up*] our order. : to cause (something) to be ruined or spoiled • The weather really *loused up* our plans.

lousy /ˈlaʊzi/ *adj* **lous·i·er; -est**
1 *informal* **a** : bad or poor • She got *lousy* grades in high school. • I like the work, but the pay is *lousy*. • He was a *lousy* husband. : of poor quality : not good or skillful • They did a *lousy* job. • a *lousy* cook/driver • a *lousy* performance — often + *at* or *with* • He is *lousy* [=*terrible*] *at* sports/math/cooking. • She's *lousy with* kids. **b** : not well or healthy • We could see that she was ***feeling lousy***. [=*feeling ill*] • He drank too much and *felt lousy* the next morning. **c** : not happy or pleased • I ***feel lousy*** [=*sorry, bad*] about what happened. **d** : not pleasant • We've been having *lousy* [=*rotten*] weather. • It's a *lousy*, rainy day. **e** : not right or proper • That's a *lousy* way to treat a friend. **f** — used to make an angry statement or description more forceful • That *lousy* bastard!
2 : infested with lice (see [1]LOUSE 1)
lousy with *informal* : having too much or too many of (something) • Her family is *lousy with* money. [=her family is very rich] • That area is *lousy with* tourists.
– **lous·i·ness** /ˈlaʊzinəs/ *noun* [*noncount*]

lout /ˈlaʊt/ *noun, pl* **louts** [*count*] : a stupid, rude, or awkward man • a dumb/drunken *lout* — see also LAGER LOUT
– **lout·ish** /ˈlaʊtɪʃ/ *adj* [*more* ~; *most* ~] • a *loutish* thug
– **lout·ish·ly** *adv* • behaving *loutishly* – **lout·ish·ness** *noun* [*noncount*]

lou·ver (*US*) *or Brit* **lou·vre** /ˈluːvɚ/ *noun, pl* **-vers** [*count*]
1 : an opening in a door or window that has one or more slanted strips to allow air to flow in and out while keeping out rain and sun
2 : one of the slanted strips of a louver
– **lou·vered** (*US*) *or Brit* **lou·vred** /ˈluːvɚd/ *adj* • a *louvered* door/window

lov·able *also* **love·able** /ˈlʌvəbəl/ *adj* [*more* ~; *most* ~] : easy to love : having attractive or appealing qualities • a *lovable* clown • He has a bad temper, but he's still *lovable*.
– **lov·ably** *also* **love·ably** /ˈlʌvəbli/ *adv* • a *lovably* strange comedian

[1]love /ˈlʌv/ *noun*
1 [*noncount*] : a feeling of strong or constant affection for a person • motherly/maternal *love* • fatherly/paternal *love* • brotherly/sisterly *love* • Children need unconditional *love* from their parents. — often + *for* • No one could doubt her *love for* her family.
2 [*noncount*] : attraction that includes sexual desire : the strong affection felt by people who have a romantic relationship • a declaration of *love* • He was just a lonely man looking for *love*. • romantic *love* • unrequited *love* • After all these years, they're still very much ***in love*** (with each other). [=they still love each other] — often used before another noun • a *love* poem/song/letter • a *love* potion • a *love* scene/story — see also FREE LOVE, PUPPY LOVE ✧ When people begin to feel romantic love for each other, they ***fall in love***. • They *fell* (madly/passionately) *in love* (with each other). This phrase is also used figuratively. • She *fell in love* with sailing the first time she tried it. ✧ People are sometimes said to ***fall out of love*** when they stop loving each other. • It was sad to see how they gradually *fell out of love* (with each other) after they married. ✧ If people fall in love with each other when they first meet, it is called ***love at first sight***. This phrase is also used figuratively. • When he saw the house, it was *love at first sight*. [=he loved the house as soon as he saw it]
3 [*count*] : a person you love in a romantic way • a lost *love* • You never forget your ***first love***. [=the first person you loved in a romantic way] • He was her one ***true love***. = He was the ***love of her life***.
4 [*singular*] *chiefly Brit* **a** : a kind or helpful person : DEAR • Be a *love* and carry this inside for me, would you? **b** — used to address someone in a loving or friendly way • As long as you're up, (my) *love*, would you mind getting me a drink? • "How do I get to Trafalgar Square?" "Take the Number 24 bus, *love*."
5 [*noncount*] : an expression of love and affection • When you see them again, please ***give them my love***. • Mike and Meg ***send their love***, too. • The gift had a note saying "***With love from*** Meg & Mike." — used to express affection at the end of a written message • Thanks for everything. Hope to see you soon. *Love*, Mike • Be well, my darling, till we meet again! ***Love and kisses***, Meg
6 a [*singular*] : a feeling of great interest, affection, or enthusiasm for something — often + *for* or *of* • We all knew about his *love for* baseball. • She has a *love of* history. • a *love of* good food • "Do you sell your paintings?" "Oh no: I paint just ***for the love of it***." • She's ***in love with*** the idea of becoming an actress. **b** [*count*] : something about which a person feels great interest or enthusiasm • Baseball was his first *love*.
7 [*singular*] : a score of zero in tennis • The score was 40–*love*.
all's fair in love and war see [1]FAIR
for love or money *or chiefly Brit* ***for love nor money*** *informal* — used to give added force to a negative statement • We couldn't get him to go along *for love or money*. [=we failed completely in our attempt to get him to go along]
for the love of God *also* ***for the love of Mike/Pete*** *informal* — used to give added force to an angry statement • *For the love of God*, quiet down! I'm trying to get some sleep here!
labor of love see [1]LABOR
love is blind — used to say that people do not see the faults of the people that they love
make love : to have sex with someone • It was the first time they *made love* (to/with each other).
no love lost ✧ When there is ***no love lost*** or ***very little love lost*** between people, they dislike each other. • They were polite with each other, but it was clear that there was *no love lost* between them.
– **love·less** /ˈlʌvləs/ *adj* [*more* ~; *most* ~] • an unhappy *loveless* marriage

[2]love *verb* **loves; loved; lov·ing**
1 : to feel great affection for (someone) : to feel love for (someone) [+ *obj*] She obviously *loves* her family very much. • To know him is to *love* him. [=the people who know him feel great affection for him] [*no obj*] You have to *love* in order to be loved.
2 [+ *obj*] : to feel sexual or romantic love for (someone) • He swore that he *loved* her madly. • He *loves* her, but she doesn't *love* him back. [=she doesn't return his love] • She said she could never marry a man she didn't *love*.
3 [+ *obj*] **a** : to like or desire (something) very much : to take great pleasure in (something) • He *loves* good food. • a much-*loved* old song • I would *love* it if you came with us. = I would *love* you to come with us. = (*US*) I would *love* for you to come with us. [=I would be very happy if you came with us] — often followed by *to* + *verb* • I would *love to have* you come with us. • She *loved to play* the violin. • "Would you like to join us?" "Yes, I'd *love to* (*join you*)." — often + *-ing verb* • She *loved playing* the violin. **b** *informal* : to be very amused

by (something) • I just *love* it [=I find it very amusing] when politicians say that they don't care about polls. = I just *love* how politicians say that they don't care about polls.
4 [+ *obj*] : to do very well in (certain specified conditions) • This plant *loves* dry soil.
I must love you and leave you *Brit, informal* — used to say that you have to leave • I don't want to miss the last train, so I'm afraid *I must love you and leave you.*
loved one ✧ Your *loved ones* are the people you love, especially members of your family. • Many of her friends and *loved ones* visited her in the hospital.

love affair *noun, pl* **~ -fairs**
1 [*count*] : a romantic or sexual relationship especially between two people who are not married to each other • His wife discovered that he was having a *love affair* [=having an affair] with another woman. • Theirs was a great *love affair.* [=they were very much in love]
2 [*singular*] : a feeling of great interest in and enthusiasm for something — + *with* • The book describes America's *love affair with* baseball.

love•bird /ˈlʌvˌbɚd/ *noun, pl* **-birds**
1 [*count*] : a small usually gray or green bird that is a type of parrot
2 ***lovebirds*** [*plural*] *informal + humorous* : people who are lovers : people who have a romantic relationship • I think I'll leave you two *lovebirds* alone for a while.

love child *noun, pl* **~ children** [*count*] : a child whose father and mother are not married to each other when the child is born : an illegitimate child • the *love child* of a famous actor and one of his fans

love handles *noun* [*plural*] *informal* : areas of fat along the sides of a person's waist

love–hate /ˈlʌvˈheɪt/ *adj, always used before a noun* : feeling or showing a mixture of love and hate • She has a ***love-hate relationship*** with her ex-husband. [=she has strong feelings of both affection and hatred for her ex-husband]

love life *noun, pl* **~ lives** [*count*] : a person's romantic and sexual activities and relationships • At that time, he had virtually no *love life.* • She doesn't like to talk about her *love life.*

love•lorn /ˈlʌvˌloɚn/ *adj* [*more ~; most ~*] : unhappy because of love : feeling love for someone who does not feel the same way • a poem about a *lovelorn* [=*lovesick*] young suitor
the lovelorn : people who are unhappy because of love • Her newspaper column offers advice for *the lovelorn.*

¹love•ly /ˈlʌvli/ *adj* **love•li•er; -est**
1 : attractive or beautiful especially in a graceful way • She was wearing a *lovely* dress. • She looks simply *lovely* in that dress! = That dress looks simply *lovely* on her! • a *lovely* bouquet of flowers • The song has a *lovely* melody. ***synonyms*** see BEAUTIFUL
2 : very good or likable • He's a *lovely* man. [=he's a very good man]
3 : very pleasing : FINE • The hotel has a *lovely* view. • We enjoyed a *lovely* dinner. • a singer with a *lovely* voice • Their children have *lovely* manners. • How *lovely* of you to come! • It was *lovely* to have you here! • (*Brit*) Isn't the coffee ***lovely and*** hot! [=the coffee is pleasingly hot]
– love•li•ness *noun* [*noncount*] • the *loveliness* of the view

²lovely *noun, pl* **-lies** [*count*] *informal* : a beautiful woman : a lovely woman • A chorus line of young *lovelies* danced on the stage.

love•mak•ing /ˈlʌvˌmeɪkɪŋ/ *noun* [*noncount*] : sexual activity : the act of making love : SEXUAL INTERCOURSE

love nest *noun, pl* **~ nests** [*count*] *informal* : a place (such as an apartment) where people who are having a love affair meet each other secretly

lov•er /ˈlʌvɚ/ *noun, pl* **-ers** [*count*]
1 a : a partner in a romantic or sexual relationship — often plural • They were friends for many years before they became *lovers.* **b** : someone with whom a married person is having a love affair • His wife accused him of having a secret *lover.* • She left her husband and ran away with her *lover.*
2 : a person who loves something • a *lover* of music = a music *lover* • an art *lover*

lover boy *noun, pl* **~ boys** [*count*] *informal* : a man who is a woman's lover or who has sexual relations with many women • an actress and her *lover boy* • an aging *lover boy*

love seat *noun, pl* **~ seats** [*count*] *US* : a seat or sofa for two people

love•sick /ˈlʌvˌsɪk/ *adj* [*more ~; most ~*] : unhappy because of love : feeling weak, foolish, or unhappy because someone you love does not love you • The movie is a comedy about a *lovesick* [=*lovelorn*] teenager.
– love•sick•ness *noun* [*noncount*]

lovey /ˈlʌvi/ *noun, Brit, informal* — used to address a person in a loving or friendly way • As long as you're up, *lovey,* would you mind getting me a drink?

lovey–dovey /ˌlʌviˈdʌvi/ *adj* [*more ~; most ~*] *informal* : showing a lot of love or affection • a couple of *lovey-dovey* newlyweds • politicians who suddenly go/get all *lovey-dovey* after criticizing each other for years

lov•ing /ˈlʌvɪŋ/ *adj* [*more ~; most ~*]
1 : feeling or showing love : AFFECTIONATE • a *loving* home/family • a *loving* glance • a *loving* husband/wife
2 : very careful and thorough • The old house has undergone a *loving* restoration. • The landscape is described in *loving* [=*painstaking*] detail. • The house requires some ***tender loving care.*** [=the house needs many repairs]
– lov•ing•ly *adv* • He gazed at her *lovingly.* • The old house has been *lovingly* restored.

¹low /ˈloʊ/ *adj* **low•er; -est**
1 a : not rising or extending upward a great distance • *low* mountains/peaks • *low* hills • a *low* building — opposite HIGH **b** : extending or reaching upward less than other things of the same kind • *low* boots • a *low* fence • *low* [=*short*] grass — opposite HIGH **c** : not located far above the ground or another surface • *low* clouds/altitudes • The sun was *low* [=near the horizon] in the western sky. • The apartment has *low* ceilings. — opposite HIGH **d** *always used before a noun* : not rising above surrounding land • They have a home in the *low* country. • The houses are built on *low* ground. — opposite HIGH **e** : cut far down at the neck • a *low* dress • a dress with a *low* neckline [=a dress with a low-cut neckline]
2 a : less than usual in amount, number, or degree • They were traveling at a *low* (rate of) speed. • temperatures as *low* as 10 below zero • He's being treated for *low* blood pressure. • a *low* dose of medicine • She earns a *low* salary. • a *low*-income family • *low* heat/humidity/temperatures • *low* interest rates • *low* intelligence • Demand for his books has remained *low.* • a *low* price — opposite HIGH **b** : near or at the bottom of a range • Temperatures were in the *low* eighties. • Her salary is in the *low* 40s. [=her salary is between about $40,000 and $45,000] — opposite HIGH **c** : not having enough or the amount needed • Our supply of fuel is ***getting/running low.*** • The airplane was ***low on*** fuel. • We're getting/running *low on* coffee. **d** : having less than the usual or average amount of something — often used in combination • a *low-calorie* diet • *low-sodium* foods • a *low-risk* investment — see also LOW IN (below)
3 a : not favorable • He holds them in *low* regard/esteem. = He has a *low* opinion of them. [=he thinks poorly of them; he regards them unfavorably] • *low* hopes/expectations • Everyone was ***in low spirits*** [=*unhappy*] because of the rainy weather. — opposite HIGH **b** : sad or unhappy • She's been feeling pretty *low.* • a *low* mood **c** : not good : below a certain quality or standard • products of *low* quality • He got *low* marks/grades throughout college. • *low* morale • He has pretty *low* standards when it comes to choosing a hotel. • Our vacation ended ***on a low note*** [=it ended in an unpleasant way] when our flight was delayed. • The time we spent waiting at the airport was the ***low point*** [=the least enjoyable part] of our vacation. — opposite HIGH **d** : morally bad • a person of *low* character • *low* behavior • a *low* trick • *low* standards of conduct — opposite HIGH
4 : below others in power, importance, etc. • Losing weight is a *low* priority for him. = Losing weight is *low* on his list of priorities. • officials of *low* rank — see also LOWER, LOW-RANKING
5 a : not loud : SOFT • a *low* whisper • a *low* moan • They were speaking in *low* voices. [=they were speaking quietly] **b** : near the bottom of a range of sounds • a singer with a *low* [=*deep*] voice = a singer with a *low*-pitched voice : occurring near the bottom of the musical scale • a *low* note — opposite HIGH
6 a : not strong or forceful • *low* winds **b** : not bright • plants that grow well in *low* light **c** : not hot • The sauce is best when cooked slowly over *low* heat. • She uses the iron on a *low* setting when she is working with delicate fabrics.
7 : having qualities that do not appeal to intelligent people • a *low* style of writing • *low* humor • *low* art — opposite HIGH
8 *of a river, stream, etc.* : having less water than usual • The river is *low.* — opposite HIGH
low in : containing a small amount of (something) • Foods

L

that are *low in* sodium/fat/calories. • Her diet is *low in* fat/carbohydrates.

– **low·ness** *noun* [*noncount*]

[2]**low** *adv* **low·er; -est**

1 : at or to a low place or level • The village is nestled *low* in the foothills. • The plane circled *low* over the airport. • He aimed his punches *low*. • a *low*-flying airplane • I put the larger books *lower* down and the smaller books higher up.

2 a : in or to a low or poor condition • a family ***brought low*** by misfortune **b :** at a low rate • Don't value yourself too *low*. • a *low-paid* worker

3 : at a low price • buy *low* and sell high

4 : with a quiet voice : not loudly • speaking *low* [=*softly*]

high and low see [2]HIGH

lie low see [1]LIE

[3]**low** *noun, pl* **lows**

1 [*count*] **:** a low point or level • Prices are at an all-time/record *low*. • The dollar has fallen to a new *low* against the Euro. • Have the media reached/hit a new *low* in bad taste? • The *low* [=lowest temperature] last night was 25. • The forecast is for showers with *lows* in the 40s. • He talked about the ***highs and lows*** [=the good parts and bad parts] of his college years.

2 [*noncount*] *US* **:** a gear that is used for slow speeds in a vehicle • He shifted into *low*. — called also (*US*) *low gear*

3 [*count*] *weather* **:** an area of low atmospheric pressure • A strong *low* is expected to bring cloudy skies tomorrow.

[4]**low** *verb* **lows; lowed; low·ing** [*no obj*] *literary* **:** to make the low sound of a cow : MOO • *lowing* cattle

low·ball /ˈloʊˌbɑːl/ *verb* **-balls; -balled; -ball·ing** [+ *obj*] *US*

1 : to trick or deceive (someone) by saying that the price or cost of something is lower than it really is • It became clear that the contractor had *lowballed* us on the cost of materials.

2 : to give a very low or unfairly low offer to (someone) • Management *lowballed* him in contract negotiations.

low beam *noun, pl* ~ **beams** *US* **:** the setting of a vehicle's headlights that makes the least bright light [*noncount*] The car's headlights were on *low beam*. [*plural*] Turn on your *low beams*. — compare HIGH BEAM

low blow *noun, pl* ~ **blows** [*count*]

1 *boxing* **:** an illegal punch that hits a boxer below the waist

2 : an action or comment that is very hurtful and unfair • Firing her on her birthday was really a *low blow*.

low·brow /ˈloʊˌbraʊ/ *adj* [*more* ~; *most* ~] *often disapproving* **:** not interested in serious art, literature, ideas, etc. • The movie's humor is clearly meant for a *lowbrow* audience. **:** relating to or intended for people who are not interested in serious art, literature, ideas, etc. • *lowbrow* humor • a *lowbrow* comedy — compare HIGHBROW, MIDDLEBROW

– **lowbrow** *noun, pl* **-brows** [*count*] • Critics have dismissed him as a *lowbrow*.

low–carb *adj* **:** containing or having fewer carbohydrates than usual • *low-carb* foods • a *low-carb* diet

low–class *adj* **low·er–class; low·est–class** [*also more* ~; *most* ~] **:** LOWER-CLASS • a *low-class* neighborhood

low–cut *adj* [*more* ~; *most* ~] *of women's clothing* **:** having the opening around the neck shaped in a way that shows the top of the chest • She was wearing a *low-cut* dress/blouse.

low·down /ˈloʊˌdaʊn/ *noun*

the lowdown **:** important information or facts about something • Reporters are trying to ***get the lowdown on*** what caused the accident. [=trying to find out the truth about what caused the accident] • He ***gave me the lowdown about*** the company's vice president.

low–down /ˈloʊˌdaʊn/ *adj, always used before a noun* [*more* ~; *most* ~] *informal* **:** morally bad : dishonest and unfair • He's just a *low-down*, good-for-nothing liar!

low–end /ˈloʊˌɛnd/ *adj* **low·er–end; low·est–end** [*also more* ~; *most* ~] *US* **:** lower in price and quality than most others • This is a *low-end* [=*inexpensive*] camera without the extra features of more expensive models.

[1]**low·er** /ˈlowɚ/ *adj*

1 *always used before a noun* **a :** located below another or others of the same kind • her *lower* jaw/lip • his *lower* extremities/limbs [=his legs and feet] • the ship's upper and *lower* decks **b :** located toward the bottom part of something • The message appeared on the *lower* portion of the screen. • She felt a pain in her *lower* leg/back. [=the lower part of her leg/back] • the mountain's upper and *lower* slopes **c :** not high above the ground • The forecast is for strong winds at *lower* elevations.

2 : located toward the south • in the *lower* and higher latitudes • the *lower* and upper peninsulas

3 : below another or others in position, rank, or order • higher and *lower* courts

4 : less advanced or developed • higher and *lower* animals

[2]**low·er** /ˈlowɚ/ *verb* **-ers; -ered; -er·ing**

1 [+ *obj*] **:** to make (something or someone) lower: such as **a :** to cause (someone or something) to move to a lower position • He slowly *lowered* himself into the chair. • *lower* a flag • *lower* the window • The sailors *lowered* a life raft (down) to the people in the water. • She ***lowered her eyes***. [=she looked down] **b :** to reduce the loudness of (something) • Please *lower* your voice. [=please speak more quietly] **c :** to reduce the value or amount of (something) • Fuel prices have been *lowered* in recent weeks. • A combination of diet and exercise can help to *lower* your cholesterol.

2 [*no obj*] **:** to become lower : DECREASE • Prices have *lowered*. [=(more commonly) *fallen, gone down*] • The property has *lowered* [=*fallen*] in value.

lower the bar see [1]BAR

lower yourself **:** to do something that causes people to have less respect for you : to degrade yourself • I won't *lower myself* to respond to these accusations. [=I won't respond because I would be degrading myself if I did]

— compare [3]LOWER

– **lowering** *noun, pl* **-ings** [*count, noncount*] • a significant/slight *lowering* [=*reduction*] of cholesterol

[3]**low·er** /ˈlawɚ/ *verb* **-ers; -ered; -er·ing** [*no obj*] *literary, of the sky or clouds* **:** to become dark and threatening • Clouds *lowered* overhead. — compare [2]LOWER

– **lowering** *adj* • a gray, *lowering* sky

low·er·case /ˌlowɚˈkeɪs/ *adj* **:** having as its typical form a, b, c rather than A, B, C : not capital • *lowercase* letters — compare UPPERCASE

– **lowercase** *noun* [*noncount*] • letters written in *lowercase*

lower class *noun, pl* ~ **classes** [*count*] **:** a social class that is below the middle class and that has the lowest status in a society • a member of the *lower class/classes* — compare MIDDLE CLASS, UNDERCLASS, UPPER CLASS, WORKING CLASS

low·er–class /ˌlowɚˈklæs, *Brit* ˌləwəˈklɑːs/ *adj* **:** not fancy, wealthy, or expensive • a *lower-class* theater • *lower-class* families — compare HIGH-CLASS

lowest common denominator *noun* [*noncount*]

1 *mathematics* **:** the smallest number that can be divided exactly by all the numbers below the lines in a group of two or more fractions — called also (*US*) *least common denominator*

2 *disapproving* — used to say that the quality of something is poor because it is designed or intended to appeal to the largest possible number of people • The movie appeals to the *lowest common denominator*. • Television programming has sunk to the *lowest common denominator*.

low–fat *adj* **:** containing or having less fat than usual • a *low-fat* diet • *low-fat* dairy products

low gear *noun* [*noncount*] *US* **:** [3]LOW 2

low–grade /ˈloʊˈgreɪd/ *adj*

1 : of poor quality • *low-grade* food

2 : not very strong or severe • a *low-grade* fever

low–key /ˈloʊˈkiː/ *also* **low–keyed** /ˈloʊˈkiːd/ *adj* [*more* ~; *most* ~] **:** quiet and relaxed : not very forceful, emotional, or noticeable • a politician with a *low-key* style • The party was a *low-key* affair. • a *low-key* approach to management

low·land /ˈloʊlənd/ *noun, pl* **-lands** [*count*] **:** an area where the land is at, near, or below the level of the sea and where there are not usually mountains or large hills — usually plural • a village in the *lowlands* — compare HIGHLAND

– **lowland** *adj, always used before a noun* • a *lowland* region/village – **low·land·er** /ˈloʊləndɚ/ *noun, pl* **-ers** [*count*] • rivalries between highlanders and *lowlanders*

low–lev·el /ˈloʊˈlɛvəl/ *adj*

1 : of low importance or rank • The changes will mostly involve *low-level* jobs/workers.

2 : not strong : low in strength or degree • *low-level* lighting

low·life /ˈloʊˌlaɪf/ *noun, pl* **-lifes** [*count*] *US, informal* **:** a bad person : a person of low moral character • a cowardly *lowlife* • hanging around with a bunch of *lowlifes*

– **lowlife** *adj, always used before a noun* • a *lowlife* bum

low·light /ˈloʊˌlaɪt/ *noun, pl* **-lights** [*count*] *US* **:** something (such as an event or a detail) that is very unpleasant or dull : the worst part of something • That meal turned out to be one of the *lowlights* of our vacation. — compare HIGHLIGHT

low·ly /ˈlouli/ *adj* **low·li·er; -est :** low in rank, position, or importance : HUMBLE • He was working as a *lowly* clerk. • He resented his *lowly* status. • her *lowly* origins
– **low·li·ness** *noun* [*noncount*] • the *lowliness* of his status

low–ly·ing /ˈlouˈlajɪŋ/ *adj*
1 : not far above the level of the sea • *low-lying* land • *low-lying* hills
2 : close to the ground • *low-lying* clouds

low–pitched /ˈlouˈpɪtʃt/ *adj* **low·er–pitched; low·est–pitched** [*also more ~; most ~*] : making a low sound : LOW • The machine made a *low-pitched* hum. • They talked quietly in *low-pitched* voices.

low–rank·ing *adj, always used before a noun* **low·er–rank·ing; low·est–rank·ing :** having a low rank or position • *low-ranking* officials

low–rent /ˈlouˈrɛnt/ *adj, chiefly US, informal*
1 : not of good quality : cheaply made or done • a *low-rent* movie • They create *low-rent* [=*cheap, inexpensive*] versions of current fashions.
2 : low in moral character or social status • a *low-rent* thug

low–rise /ˈlouˈraɪz/ *adj*
1 *of a building* : not tall : having few floors or stories • a *low-rise* classroom building
2 : made up of low-rise buildings • a *low-rise* housing development

low–risk *adj*
1 : not likely to result in failure, harm, or injury : not having a lot of risk • *low-risk* investments
2 : less likely than others to get a particular disease, condition, or injury • *low-risk* patients

low season *noun* [*noncount*] : the time of year when a place is least busy or popular : OFF-SEASON

low–slung /ˈlouˌslʌŋ/ *adj* [*more ~; most ~*] : low and close to the ground or floor • She drives a *low-slung* convertible. • a *low-slung* sofa

low–spir·it·ed /ˈlouˈspirətəd/ *adj* [*more ~; most ~*] : feeling sad or depressed • I've never seen her looking so *low-spirited.*

low–tech /ˈlouˈtɛk/ *adj* [*more ~; most ~*] : not using new electronic devices and technology : technologically simple • *low-tech* industries • We found a *low-tech* solution to our problem. • The film's special effects were very *low-tech.*

low tide *noun, pl* **~ tides** [*count, noncount*] : the tide when the water is at its lowest point • You can walk across the sand bar at *low tide.* — compare HIGH TIDE

lox /ˈlɑːks/ *noun* [*noncount*] *chiefly US* : smoked salmon • bagels and *lox*

loy·al /ˈlojəl/ *adj* [*more ~; most ~*] : having or showing complete and constant support for someone or something : FAITHFUL • The team has many *loyal* fans. • a *loyal* customer/supporter • a *loyal* friend • She has provided the company with many years of *loyal* service. • fiercely/steadfastly *loyal* — often + *to* • She has remained/stayed *loyal to* her old friends. — opposite DISLOYAL
– **loy·al·ly** *adv* • has served *loyally* for many years

loy·al·ist /ˈlojəlɪst/ *noun, pl* **-ists** [*count*]
1 : a person who is loyal to a political cause, government, or leader • a group of ***party loyalists*** [=people who are loyal members of a political party]
2 : a person from Northern Ireland who believes that Northern Ireland should remain part of the United Kingdom — opposite REPUBLICAN

loy·al·ty /ˈlojəlti/ *noun, pl* **-ties**
1 [*noncount*] : the quality or state of being loyal • the *loyalty* of the team's fans — often + *to* • No one questions his *loyalty to* the cause.
2 [*count*] : a loyal feeling : a feeling of strong support for someone or something — usually plural • He was torn by conflicting/divided *loyalties.* • They shouldn't allow their decision to be influenced by political *loyalties.*
brand loyalty see [1]BRAND

loz·enge /ˈlɑːzn̩ʤ/ *noun, pl* **-eng·es** [*count*]
1 : a small candy that usually contains medicine • a throat/cough *lozenge*
2 : a shape that is formed by four equal straight lines and that has two opposite angles that are smaller than a right angle and two opposite angles that are larger than a right angle • a scarf decorated with a pattern of *lozenges* [=*diamonds*]

LP /ˌɛlˈpiː/ *noun, pl* **LP's** *or* **LPs** [*count*] : a phonograph record designed to be played at 33⅓ revolutions per minute — called also *long-playing record*

LPN /ˌɛlˌpiːˈɛn/ *noun, pl* **LPN's** *or* **LPNs** [*count*] *US* : LICENSED PRACTICAL NURSE

LSD /ˌɛlˌɛsˈdiː/ *noun* [*noncount*] : an illegal drug that causes people to see and hear things that do not really exist

Lt. *abbr* lieutenant

Ltd. *abbr* limited — used in business names • Roundy & Son *Ltd.*

lu·au /ˈluːˌaʊ/ *noun, pl* **-aus** [*count*] : a Hawaiian feast

lube /ˈluːb/ *noun, pl* **lubes** [*count*] *informal*
1 : the act of putting lubricant on the moving parts of a vehicle • He took his car to the garage for a *lube* and oil change. • a *lube* job
2 : LUBRICANT 1 • a high-quality *lube*

lu·bri·cant /ˈluːbrɪkənt/ *noun, pl* **-cants**
1 [*count, noncount*] : a substance (such as grease or oil) that causes something (such as a machine part) to be slippery and to move more smoothly • The car's axles need more *lubricant.*
2 [*count*] : something that makes it easier for people to work or talk with each other • using humor as a social *lubricant*

lu·bri·cate /ˈluːbrəˌkeɪt/ *verb* **-cates; -cat·ed; -cat·ing** [+ *obj*] : to make (something) smooth or slippery : to apply a lubricant to (something, such as a machine or a part of a machine) • *lubricate* a car engine • *lubricate* a hinge
– **lu·bri·ca·tion** /ˌluːbrəˈkeɪʃən/ *noun, pl* **-tions** [*noncount*] a hinge that needs *lubrication* [*count*] repeated *lubrications* of the engine

lu·cid /ˈluːsəd/ *adj* [*more ~; most ~*]
1 : very clear and easy to understand • a *lucid* explanation • *lucid* prose
2 : able to think clearly • The patient has remained *lucid* [=*clearheaded*] throughout his illness. • He is able to recognize his wife in his *lucid* moments.
– **lu·cid·i·ty** /luˈsɪdəti/ *noun* [*noncount*] • the *lucidity* of the explanation – **lu·cid·ly** *adv* • The problem was *lucidly* explained.

lu·cerne /luˈsən/ *noun* [*noncount*] *Brit* : ALFALFA

Lu·ci·fer /ˈluːsəfɚ/ *noun* [*singular*] — used as a name of the Devil

[1]**luck** /ˈlʌk/ *noun* [*noncount*]
1 : the things that happen to a person because of chance : the accidental way things happen without being planned • Our meeting happened by (pure) *luck.* [=*chance*] • Her business has been doing poorly, but she's hoping that her *luck* will change. [=she's hoping that she will begin to have success] • We had good/bad *luck* fishing. • He's been having nothing but bad/rotten/hard/tough/lousy *luck.* • He cursed his *luck.* ✧ When ***luck is on your side*** or ***luck is with you,*** your luck is good. When ***luck is against you,*** your luck is bad. • Our car broke down on the road, but *luck was on our side* and there was a garage nearby. • I arrived a little late and *luck was against me*: the last ticket had just been sold.
2 a : good fortune : good luck • He succeeded through hard work and a little *luck.* • We need a bit of *luck.* • If our *luck* holds [=if our luck continues to be good], we should be able to arrive on time. • Before her husband left for his job interview, she gave him a kiss ***for luck.*** [=so that he would have good luck] • I can't believe they gave the job to that guy. ***Some people/guys have all the luck.*** [=some people are very lucky] • The success of his first restaurant was just ***beginner's luck.*** [=he succeeded because he was lucky, as beginners sometimes are] • ***With (any) luck*** [=if we are lucky, if what we want to happen does happen] there'll still be some tickets left when we arrive. • By a ***stroke of luck,*** there were still a few tickets left when we arrived. **b :** success in doing or getting something • Have you had any *luck* [=*success*] (in) finding a new apartment? • "I've been looking for a new apartment." "Any *luck*?" "No, not yet." • I've had no *luck* in finding a new apartment. • He had no better *luck* than I did.

as luck would have it — used to say that something happened because of good or bad luck • Our car broke down on the road, but *as luck would have it* [=*as it turned out*], there was a garage nearby. • I arrived a little late and, *as luck would have it,* the last ticket had just been sold.

bad luck *or Brit* ***hard luck*** — used in speech to show sympathy for someone who has failed or has been disappointed • "I didn't get the job." "*Bad luck!*"

best of luck *informal* — used to say that you hope someone will succeed • We're sorry that you're leaving. *Best of luck* to you in your new job. — see also WISH SOMEONE (THE BEST OF) LUCK (below)

better luck next time — used to say that you hope someone will have more success in doing or trying something in the future • I'm sorry to hear that you didn't get the job. *Better luck next time.*

down on your luck ✧ When you are *down on your luck*, your luck is bad. • She's been *down on her luck* lately. [=she has been suffering through a difficult time lately]

good luck **1** — used to say that you hope someone will succeed • We're sorry that you're leaving. *Good luck* in your new job. **2** *informal* — used to say that you think what someone is trying to do is difficult or impossible • "I'm planning to ask for a raise." "Oh, really? Well, *good luck* (to you)." [=I think it is unlikely that you will get a raise]

in luck ✧ When you are *in luck*, something that you want to do is possible. • "Are there any tickets?" "You're *in luck*. We still have a few more left."

just my luck *informal* — used to say that bad or unpleasant things often happen to you because you are unlucky • The last ticket was sold a minute before I got there—*just my luck.*

Lady Luck *or* ***lady luck*** — used to refer to luck as if it were a woman • He blamed his problems on *lady luck*.

no such luck *informal* — used to say that you could not do or have something you wanted • We hoped we could still get tickets, but *no such luck*—they had all been sold.

out of luck ✧ When you are *out of luck*, something that you want to do is not possible. • We hoped we could still get tickets, but we were *out of luck*—they had all been sold.

push your luck *or* *US* ***press your luck*** ✧ If you are *pushing/pressing your luck*, you are taking more risks than you should or you are asking for more favors than you should. • "Can I have more time to finish the job?" "Don't *press/push your luck*. You've already been given extra time."

the luck of the draw — used to say that the result of something cannot be controlled and depends on chance • The weather may be good or bad that day—it all depends on *the luck of the draw*.

tough luck *informal* ✧ *Tough luck* can be used in speech to show sympathy for someone who has failed or has been disappointed, but it is more commonly used in an ironic way to show that you do not feel sympathy for someone. • "I need more time to finish the job." "*Tough luck*. You knew the job was supposed to be done by today."

try your luck ✧ To *try your luck* at something is to do something in the hope that you will succeed. • He's *trying his luck* at starting his own restaurant.

wish someone (the best of) luck : to say that you hope someone will have success • I *wish you (the best of) luck* in your new job. • I have a job interview this morning. *Wish me luck!*

– **luck·less** /ˈlʌkləs/ *adj* • a *luckless* loser

²luck *verb* **lucks; lucked; luck·ing**

luck into [*phrasal verb*] ***luck into (something)*** *US, informal* : to find or get (something) because of good luck • She *lucked into* a good job.

luck out [*phrasal verb*] *US, informal* : to have good luck • We arrived late but we *lucked out*—there were still a few tickets left.

luck·i·ly /ˈlʌkəli/ *adv* — used to say that something good or lucky has happened • *Luckily* [=*fortunately*] no one was hurt. [=it was lucky that no one was hurt]

lucky /ˈlʌki/ *adj* **luck·i·er; -est**

1 : having good luck : FORTUNATE • We're *lucky* that things turned out as well as they did. • You're *lucky* to have a choice. = You're *lucky* that you have a choice. • I feel *lucky* to be alive. • I count/consider myself *lucky* to know you. • Aren't you the *lucky* one! [=you are a lucky person] • "I managed to get a ticket!" "*Lucky* you! They were all sold out by the time I got there." • Tickets were available only for the *lucky* few. • The *lucky* winner will be given a brand new car. • I know you'll enjoy the show if you're *lucky* enough to get a ticket. • Congratulations on getting the job, you ***lucky dog/devil***. • (*chiefly US*) He's a ***lucky stiff***. [=he's very lucky] • He was always ***lucky in love***. [=he was always lucky in his romantic relationships]

2 : producing a good result by chance : resulting from good luck • He scored a goal on a *lucky* shot. • Their meeting was a *lucky* accident. • We got a *lucky* break. • It was a *lucky* coincidence that we were both there at the same time. • a *lucky* find/guess • It's *lucky* for us that the weather is so good. = We're *lucky* that the weather is so good. • a *lucky* coin/charm • This must be your ***lucky day***. [=a day when something good happens because of good luck] • You should ***thank your lucky stars*** [=you should be very grateful] that you have a friend like her.

get lucky **1** : to have good luck : to succeed because of good luck • We thought all the tickets might have already been sold, but we *got lucky*—there were still a few left when we arrived. **2** *informal* : to succeed in finding or getting someone to have sex with you • He's hoping to *get lucky* tonight.

third time lucky see ¹THIRD

lucky dip *noun, pl* **~ dips** [*count*] *Brit* : a game in which people reach into a container filled with small gifts without knowing what gift they will get — compare GRAB BAG

lu·cra·tive /ˈluːkrətɪv/ *adj* [*more ~; most ~*] : producing money or wealth : PROFITABLE • a *lucrative* job/investment • a *lucrative* career/contract • The business has proved to be highly *lucrative*.

– **lu·cra·tive·ly** *adv* • *lucratively* employed

lu·cre /ˈluːkɚ/ *noun* [*noncount*] *disapproving + often humorous* : money or profit • the lure of *lucre* — often used in the phrase ***filthy lucre*** • He compromised his art for the pursuit of *filthy lucre*.

lu·di·crous /ˈluːdəkrəs/ *adj* [*more ~; most ~*] : very foolish : RIDICULOUS • *ludicrous* ideas/thoughts • a *ludicrous* statement/suggestion • It's *ludicrous* [=*absurd*] to think that he can solve these problems himself.

– **lu·di·crous·ly** *adv* • a *ludicrously* improbable idea – **lu·di·crous·ness** *noun* [*noncount*]

¹lug /ˈlʌg/ *verb* **lugs; lugged; lug·ging** [+ *obj*] : to pull or carry (something) with great effort • She had to *lug* her suitcases out to the car by herself. • I was *lugging* a heavy camera around all day.

²lug *noun, pl* **lugs** [*count*]

1 : a part (such as a handle) that sticks out like an ear

2 *US, informal + humorous* : a large and awkward or stupid man • He's just a big *lug*. — often used in way that shows affection • It's great to see you again, you big *lug*.

3 *US* : LUG NUT

luge /ˈluːʒ/ *noun, pl* **lug·es** [*count*] : a small sled used for racing down an ice track

– **lug·er** /ˈluːʒɚ/ *noun, pl* **-ers** [*count*]

lug·gage /ˈlʌgɪʤ/ *noun* [*noncount*] : the bags and suitcases that a person carries when traveling : BAGGAGE • Passengers are limited to two items of carry-on *luggage*.

luggage rack *noun, pl* **~ racks** [*count*]

1 : a shelf for storing luggage on a train, bus, etc.

2 *US* : a frame on the roof of a car for carrying luggage — called also *roof rack*

lug nut *noun, pl* **~ nuts** [*count*] *US* : a heavy piece of metal that is screwed on to the bolts that hold a wheel on a vehicle

lu·gu·bri·ous /lʊˈguːbrijəs/ *adj* [*more ~; most ~*] *formal* : full of sadness or sorrow : very sad especially in an exaggerated or insincere way • a comic actor known for his *lugubrious* manner • wearing a *lugubrious* expression

– **lu·gu·bri·ous·ly** *adv* • sighing *lugubriously* – **lu·gu·bri·ous·ness** *noun* [*noncount*]

luke·warm /ˈluːkˈwoɚm/ *adj* [*more ~; most ~*]

1 : slightly warm • a *lukewarm* [=*tepid*] bath • I hate drinking *lukewarm* coffee.

2 : not enthusiastic : not having or showing energy or excitement • Our plan got a *lukewarm* reception. • The producer was *lukewarm* about her script.

– **luke·warm·ly** *adv* • They reacted/responded *lukewarmly* to our plan.

¹lull /ˈlʌl/ *verb* **lulls; lulled; lull·ing** [+ *obj*]

1 : to cause (someone) to fall asleep or become sleepy • The music *lulled* him to sleep. — often used as *(be) lulled* • He *was lulled* to sleep by her soothing voice. • *lulled* by the gentle rocking of the boat

2 : to cause (someone) to feel safe and relaxed instead of careful and alert — + *into* • He *lulls* you *into* believing his promises. [=he tricks you into believing his promises by making you feel that he can be trusted] — often used as *(be) lulled* • She *was lulled into* a false sense of security.

²lull *noun, pl* **lulls** [*count*] : a brief time when an action or activity stops — usually + *in* • There were several *lulls in* the conversation. • a *lull in* the fighting/action • a *lull in* the storm

lul·la·by /ˈlʌləˌbaɪ/ *noun, pl* **-bies** [*count*] : a song used to help a child fall asleep

lum·ba·go /ˌlʌmˈbeɪgoʊ/ *noun* [*noncount*] : pain in the lower back • experiencing an attack of *lumbago*

lum·bar /ˈlʌmbɚ/ *adj, always used before a noun, medical*

: relating to or lying near the lower back ▪ This seat provides good *lumbar* support. ▪ the *lumbar* region

[1]lum·ber /ˈlʌmbɚ/ *verb* **-bers; -bered; -ber·ing** [*no obj*] : to move in a slow or awkward way ▪ The parade *lumbers* through town once a year. ▪ We saw an elephant *lumbering* along the road. ▪ trucks *lumbering* [=*rumbling*] down the street ▪ an animal with a *lumbering* gait — sometimes used figuratively ▪ The economy continues to *lumber* along. ▪ a big, *lumbering* [=slow and awkward] bureaucracy — compare [3]LUMBER

[2]lumber *noun* [*noncount*]

1 *US* : wooden boards or logs that have been sawed and cut for use ▪ trees turned into *lumber* [=*timber*] ▪ He works for a *lumber* company. ▪ the *lumber* industry — see also LUMBERING

2 *Brit* : large objects that are no longer used or wanted ▪ had a clearout of all his old *lumber* and finally got rid of it

[3]lumber *verb* **-bers; -bered; -ber·ing**

lumber with [*phrasal verb*] ***lumber (someone) with (something)*** *Brit, informal* : to cause (someone) to have (something unwanted or unpleasant) ▪ His classmates *lumbered* him *with* [=saddled him with] an unfortunate nickname. — often used as *(be) lumbered with* ▪ He's *been lumbered with* an unfortunate nickname.

— compare [1]LUMBER

lum·ber·ing /ˈlʌmbərɪŋ/ *noun* [*noncount*] *US* : the activity or business of making lumber from logs ▪ There has been an increase in *lumbering* in this area. ▪ the *lumbering* industry

lum·ber·jack /ˈlʌmbɚˌʤæk/ *noun, pl* **-jacks** [*count*] : a person whose job is to cut down trees for wood : LOGGER

lumber room *noun, pl* **~ rooms** [*count*] *Brit* : a room for storing old pieces of furniture and other things that are not being used

lum·ber·yard /ˈlʌmbɚˌjɑɚd/ *noun, pl* **-yards** [*count*] *US* : a place where wooden boards are kept for sale ▪ He went to the *lumberyard* [=*(Brit) timber yard*] to buy wood.

lu·mi·nary /ˈluːməˌneri, *Brit* ˈluːmənəri/ *noun, pl* **-nar·ies** [*count*] : a very famous or successful person : CELEBRITY ▪ *luminaries* of the art world

lu·mi·nes·cence /ˌluːməˈnɛsn̩s/ *noun* [*noncount*] *technical* : the creation of light by processes that do not involve heat; *also* : the light created ▪ the *luminescence* of the watch

— **lu·mi·nes·cent** /ˌluːməˈnɛsn̩t/ *adj* [*more ~; most ~*] ▪ *luminescent* insects ▪ a *luminescent* watch dial

lu·mi·nous /ˈluːmənəs/ *adj* [*more ~; most ~*]

1 : producing or seeming to produce light : SHINING ▪ *luminous* stars/galaxies ▪ I saw the cat's *luminous* eyes in my car's headlights. ▪ a watch with a *luminous* dial — often used figuratively ▪ the *luminous* clarity of her writing ▪ a *luminous* essay

2 a : filled with light : brightly lit ▪ The room was *luminous* with sunlight. **b** : very bright in color ▪ a *luminous* blue

— **lu·mi·nos·i·ty** /ˌluːməˈnɑːsəti/ *noun* [*singular*] ▪ measuring a star's *luminosity* ▪ the *luminosity* of a typical galaxy

— **lu·mi·nous·ly** *adv* ▪ colors gleaming *luminously* in the sunlight ▪ a *luminously* clear writing style

[1]lump /ˈlʌmp/ *noun, pl* **lumps** [*count*]

1 : a small piece or mass of something ▪ a *lump* of coal ▪ turning a *lump* of clay into a beautiful pot ▪ He likes two *lumps* [=*cubes*] of sugar with his coffee.

2 : an area of swelling or growth on your body ▪ a cancerous *lump* ▪ He got a *lump* on his head after bumping into the doorway.

a lump in your throat : a tight feeling in your throat that you get when you are about to start crying or when you are trying not to cry ▪ The movie's final scene left me with a *lump in my throat*. = I got *a lump in my throat* when I watched the film's final scene.

take your lumps *or* ***take a lot of lumps*** *US, informal* : to be badly beaten or hurt ▪ He *took a lot of lumps* as a kid growing up in the city. — usually used figuratively ▪ Their first album *took its lumps* from the critics. [=it was harshly criticized] ▪ The team has *taken its lumps* [=it has lost many games] this year, but their play has improved recently.

[2]lump *verb* **lumps; lumped; lump·ing**

1 [+ *obj*] : to put (people or things) *together* or *in* the same group ▪ He made the mistake of *lumping* all their ideas *together* as foolish. ▪ She often gets *lumped in* with other modern artists even though her work is different from theirs.

2 [*no obj*] : to form lumps : to become lumpy ▪ You'll need to stir the mixture constantly to keep it from *lumping*.

lump it *informal* : to accept or allow something unpleasant or unwanted — usually used in the phrase ***like it or lump it*** ▪ *Like it or lump it*, the new law goes into effect today. [=it goes into effect whether you like it or not]

lump·ish /ˈlʌmpɪʃ/ *adj* [*more ~; most ~*] : heavy and dull or awkward ▪ a slow-witted, *lumpish* man

— **lump·ish·ness** *noun* [*noncount*]

lump sum *noun, pl* **~ sums** [*count*] : an amount of money that is paid at one time : a single sum of money ▪ The bonus is paid out in a *lump sum*. [=it is paid out all at once] ▪ a *lump-sum* payment

lumpy /ˈlʌmpi/ *adj* **lump·i·er; -est** : having lumps : full of lumps ▪ a *lumpy* mattress ▪ *lumpy* mashed potatoes

— **lump·i·ness** /ˈlʌmpinəs/ *noun* [*noncount*]

lu·na·cy /ˈluːnəsi/ *noun* [*noncount*]

1 a : extreme foolishness ▪ Quitting her job was an act of sheer/pure *lunacy*. [=*madness*] **b** : something that is very foolish ▪ Quitting her job was *lunacy*. ▪ It would be *lunacy* [=*madness*] to try driving home in this storm. ▪ His idea was considered total/sheer/complete *lunacy*.

2 *old-fashioned* : extreme mental illness : INSANITY

lu·nar /ˈluːnɚ/ *adj, always used before a noun* : of or relating to the moon ▪ a *lunar* rock ▪ the *lunar* surface ▪ a *lunar* eclipse ▪ a ***lunar month*** [=the time between one new moon and the next, one full moon and the next, etc.]

[1]lu·na·tic /ˈluːnəˌtɪk/ *noun, pl* **-tics** [*count*] *informal*

1 *old-fashioned + sometimes offensive* : an insane person ▪ a murderous *lunatic* ▪ He was raving like a *lunatic*.

2 *informal* : a person who behaves in a very foolish way ▪ I almost got into an accident with some *lunatic* on the highway. ▪ My boss is a complete *lunatic*. ▪ He was a *lunatic* out on the ski slopes. [=he was an extremely daring, reckless, or aggressive skier]

[2]lunatic *adj, always used before a noun*

1 a *old-fashioned + sometimes offensive* : designed for insane people ▪ a *lunatic* asylum **b** : not sane ▪ a *lunatic* [=*crazy*] genius

2 : wildly foolish ▪ He hatched a *lunatic* plot to overthrow the government. ▪ another of his *lunatic* ideas ▪ *lunatic* behavior ▪ a *lunatic* risk

lunatic fringe *noun* [*singular*] : the members of a political or social group or movement who have the most extreme or foolish ideas ▪ His nomination is opposed by the party's *lunatic fringe*.

[1]lunch /ˈlʌnʧ/ *noun, pl* **lunch·es** : a light meal eaten in the middle of the day [*count*] I like to eat/have a healthy *lunch* every day. ▪ a company *lunch* [=*luncheon*] ▪ We took a picnic *lunch* to the park. ▪ They've brought their own *lunches* with them. ▪ We discussed the idea over a ***working/business lunch***. [=a lunch during which people talk about business matters] [*noncount*] What's for *lunch*? ▪ I had/ate just a sandwich for *lunch*. ▪ Where do you want to go for *lunch*? = Where do you want to eat/have *lunch*? ▪ I bought her some *lunch*. ▪ She often sits alone at *lunch*. [=while eating lunch] ▪ We discussed the idea over *lunch*. [=during lunch; while eating lunch] ▪ I offered to take her ***out to lunch***. [=to take her to a restaurant for lunch] ▪ ***lunch hour*** [=the time when the people in a school or company eat lunch] ✧ When people ***do lunch*** they have lunch together. This is an informal phrase that is often associated with people in business. ▪ Let's *do lunch* sometime.

eat/have someone or something for lunch *or* ***eat someone's or something's lunch*** *US, informal* : to defeat someone or something very badly ▪ The big hardware chain was *eating* the local store's *lunch*. [=the big chain was taking a lot of business from the local store]

lose your lunch *US slang* : to throw up : VOMIT ▪ I felt like I was about to *lose my lunch*.

no free lunch ✧ The expression ***there is no free lunch*** or ***there is no such thing as a free lunch*** means that it is not possible to get something that is desired or valuable without having to pay for it in some way.

out to lunch *informal* : not aware of what is really happening : too strange or confused to notice or understand what is really happening ▪ That guy acts like he's *out to lunch*.

[2]lunch *verb* **lunches; lunched; lunch·ing** [*no obj*] : to eat lunch ▪ She often *lunches* in the park. ▪ We *lunched* on leftovers.

— **lunch·er** *noun, pl* **-ers** [*count*]

lunch box *noun, pl* **~ boxes** [*count*] : a box in which a lunch can be kept and carried to school, work, etc.

lunch break *noun, pl* **~ breaks** [*count*] : the time when people stop working or studying to have lunch : LUNCH

HOUR • Let's go out during our *lunch break*.

lunch counter *noun, pl* ~ **-ers** [*count*] *US*
1 : a long counter at which lunches are sold
2 : LUNCHEONETTE

lun·cheon /ˈlʌntʃən/ *noun, pl* **-cheons** [*count*] **:** a usually formal lunch that occurs as part of a meeting or for entertaining a guest • a company *luncheon* • a ladies' *luncheon*

lun·cheon·ette /ˌlʌntʃəˈnɛt/ *noun, pl* **-ettes** [*count*] *US* **:** a small restaurant where lunches are served

luncheon meat *noun, pl* ~ **meats** [*count, noncount*] **:** cooked meat (such as sliced meat or canned meat) that is usually eaten cold • sliced ham, turkey, and other *luncheon meats* — called also (*US*) *lunch meat*

lunch hour *noun, pl* ~ **hours** [*count*] **:** the time when people stop working or studying to have lunch • She likes to go for a walk during her *lunch hour*.

lunch·room /ˈlʌntʃˌruːm/ *noun, pl* **-rooms** [*count*] *US*
1 : a large room in a school or business where people eat lunch
2 : LUNCHEONETTE

lunch·time /ˈlʌntʃˌtaɪm/ *noun, pl* **-times :** the time in the middle of the day when people usually eat lunch [*noncount*] It was nearly *lunchtime* when we got there. [*count*] They enjoyed the *lunchtimes* they spent together.

lung /ˈlʌŋ/ *noun, pl* **lungs** [*count*] **:** either one of the two organs that people and animals use to breathe air • He filled his *lungs* with the clean. fresh air. • *lung* disease/cancer • She shouted ***at the top of her lungs*** [=she shouted as loudly as possible] — see picture at HUMAN

[1]lunge /ˈlʌndʒ/ *noun, pl* **lung·es** [*count*] **:** a sudden forward movement • He made a *lunge* at me with his knife. • He made a desperate *lunge* for the ball.

[2]lunge *verb* **lunges; lunged; lung·ing** [*no obj*] **:** to move or reach forward in a sudden, forceful way • He *lunged* at me with his knife. • She *lunged* across the table. • The crocodile *lunged* at its prey. • The dog *lunged* for his throat.

lu·pus /ˈluːpəs/ *noun* [*noncount*] *medical* **:** a disease that affects the nervous system, joints, and skin

[1]lurch /ˈlɚtʃ/ *verb* **lurch·es; lurched; lurch·ing** [*no obj*]
1 : to make a sudden sideways or forward motion • The boat *lurched* in the rough seas. • The bus *lurched* along/down the highway. • The jeep *lurched* to a stop.
2 : to move or walk in an awkward or unsteady way • She lost her balance and *lurched* into the counter. • He *lurched* to his feet. — often used figuratively • Investors worry as the economy *lurches* towards recession. • He always seems to be *lurching* from one crisis to another. • The movie *lurches* from one car chase scene to the next.

[2]lurch *noun, pl* **lurches** [*count*] **:** a sudden sideways or forward movement • You could feel the bumps and *lurches* as the bus moved down the highway. • The train gave a *lurch* as it left the station. = The train left the station with a *lurch*. — compare [3]LURCH

[3]lurch *noun*
leave (someone) in the lurch **:** to leave someone without help or protection when it is needed • His advisers *left him in the lurch* when he needed them the most.
— compare [2]LURCH

[1]lure /ˈluɚ/ *verb, always followed by an adverb or preposition* **lures; lured; lur·ing** [+ *obj*] **:** to cause or persuade (a person or an animal) to go somewhere or to do something by offering some pleasure or gain • advertisers trying to *lure* [=*attract*] a younger audience to their products • They *lured* the bear out of its den. • The suburbs are *luring* middle-class families away from the city. • The police *lured* him back to the scene of the crime. • Explorers were *lured* to the area by tales of a city of gold. • An attractive window display can help to *lure* shoppers into the store.

[2]lure *noun, pl* **lures** [*count*]
1 : an appealing or attractive quality — usually singular • Tourists are drawn to the area by the *lure* of the Arizona sunshine. • The birds find the *lure* of the feeder irresistible. • He was unable to resist the *lure* of easy money.
2 : a device used for attracting and catching animals, birds, or especially fish

lu·rid /ˈlɚrəd/ *adj* [*more* ~; *most* ~] *disapproving*
1 : causing shock or disgust **:** involving sex or violence in a way that is meant to be shocking • *lurid* [=*sensational*] tabloid headlines • a *lurid* front-page story • a *lurid* tale of violence and betrayal • the *lurid* [=*gruesome*] details of the crime
2 : shining or glowing with a bright and unpleasant color • a *lurid* neon sign • the *lurid* lighting of a nightclub • The light from the fire cast a *lurid* glow on everything.
— **lu·rid·ly** *adv* • *luridly* sensational headlines • a scene *luridly* lit by smoky sunlight — **lu·rid·ness** *noun* [*noncount*]

lurk /ˈlɚk/ *verb* **lurks; lurked; lurk·ing** [*no obj*]
1 : to be in a hidden place • The cat was *lurking* [=*hiding*] behind the sofa. **:** to wait in a secret or hidden place especially in order to do something wrong or harmful • She could tell there was someone out there *lurking* in the shadows. — often used figuratively • Trouble *lurks* around every corner. • There is tenderness that *lurks* underneath his tough appearance. • Who knows what evil *lurks* in the hearts of men? • The idea had been *lurking* in her mind for some time.
2 *computers* **:** to read messages written by other people on the Internet in a newsgroup, chat room, etc., without writing any messages yourself
— **lurk·er** *noun, pl* **-ers** [*count*]

lus·cious /ˈlʌʃəs/ *adj* [*more* ~; *most* ~]
1 : having a very appealing taste or smell **:** DELICIOUS • *luscious* fruits • chocolate cake with a *luscious* whipped cream topping • a *luscious* wine
2 a : richly appealing • a *luscious* [=*delightful*] singing voice **b** *informal* **:** very physically attractive • an incredibly *luscious* actress
— **lus·cious·ly** *adv* • a *lusciously* creamy cheesecake — **lus·cious·ness** *noun* [*noncount*]

[1]lush /ˈlʌʃ/ *adj* **lush·er; -est**
1 a : having a lot of full and healthy growth • *lush* grass • *lush* [=*luxuriant*] tropical vegetation • The frequent rainfall encourages the *lush* growth of trees, ferns, and shrubs. **b :** covered with healthy green plants • *lush* green fields/farms/pastures • She always wanted to live on a *lush* Caribbean island. • The hills are *lush* with deep, thick grass.
2 : having a pleasingly rich quality • a *lush* and fruity wine • *lush* color photos • the film's *lush* imagery • a *lush* carpet
— **lush·ly** *adv* • *lushly* planted gardens • a *lushly* [=*lavishly*] illustrated book — **lush·ness** *noun* [*noncount*] • the *lushness* of the surrounding countryside

[2]lush *noun, pl* **lush·es** [*count*] *informal* **:** a person who is often drunk **:** DRUNK • He's just an old *lush*.

[1]lust /ˈlʌst/ *noun, pl* **lusts**
1 : a strong feeling of sexual desire [*noncount*] He was consumed by *lust*. • He was motivated more by *lust* than love. [=more by the desire for sex than by affection] [*count*] satisfying their *lusts*
2 : a strong desire *for* something [*singular*] a *lust* [=*craving, desire*] *for* money/adventure • He was driven by a *lust for* power. • a ***lust for life*** [=a strong desire to live a full and rich life] [*noncount*] *Lust for* chocolate drew her into the candy store. — see also BLOODLUST

[2]lust *verb* **lusts; lust·ed; lust·ing** [*no obj*]
1 : to have a strong sexual desire for someone — usually + *after* • He *lusted after* the prettiest girl in the school. — sometimes + *for* • He had *lusted for* her for years.
2 : to have a strong desire for something — usually + *after* • She's been *lusting after* [=*craving*] that job for many months. — sometimes + *for* • investors *lusting for* profits — sometimes followed by *to* + *verb* • a general who *lusted to command*

lus·ter (*US*) *or Brit* **lus·tre** /ˈlʌstɚ/ *noun* [*singular*]
1 : the shiny quality of a surface that reflects light • the *luster* of polished metal • He polished the silverware for hours trying to restore its *luster*. • the *luster* of her eyes
2 : an appealing, exciting, or admired quality • The trip loses some of its *luster* [=it becomes less appealing or exciting] after you've done it several times. • The scandals have tarnished/dimmed his *luster*. [=damaged his reputation] • the *luster* [=*renown*] of the family's name
— **lus·ter·less** (*US*) *or Brit* **lus·tre·less** *adj* • dull *lusterless* eyes • *lusterless* silverware — **lus·trous** /ˈlʌstrəs/ *adj* [*more* ~; *most* ~] • *lustrous* silk • a *lustrous* [=*shining*] surface

lust·ful /ˈlʌstfəl/ *adj* [*more* ~; *most* ~] **:** feeling or showing strong sexual desire **:** feeling or showing lust • He looked at her with *lustful* eyes. • *lustful* feelings/dreams/thoughts
— **lust·ful·ly** /ˈlʌstfəli/ *adv* • gazing *lustfully* at one another

lusty /ˈlʌsti/ *adj* **lust·i·er; -est**
1 : full of strength and energy • a *lusty* shout/cry • *lusty* [=*powerful*] singing • working with *lusty* determination
2 : LUSTFUL • *lusty* teenagers
— **lust·i·ly** /ˈlʌstəli/ *adv* [*more* ~; *most* ~] • singing *lustily* • cheering/applauding *lustily* — **lust·i·ness** /ˈlʌstinəs/ *noun* [*noncount*]

lute /ˈluːt/ *noun, pl* **lutes** [*count*] : a musical instrument with strings that resembles a guitar and that was played especially in past centuries

Lu·ther·an /ˈluːθərən/ *noun, pl* **-ans** [*count*] : a member of one of the Protestant churches that follow the teachings of Martin Luther
– **Lutheran** *adj*

luv·vie /ˈlʌvi/ *noun, pl* **-vies** [*count*] *Brit, informal* : someone (such as an actor or actress) who is very friendly in a way that does not seem sincere

lux·u·ri·ant /ˌlʌgˈʒərijənt, *Brit* ˌlʌgˈzjuəriənt/ *adj* [*more* ~; *most* ~]
1 : having heavy and thick growth : LUSH ▪ a *luxuriant* gray beard ▪ *luxuriant* vegetation
2 : having an appealingly rich quality ▪ a *luxuriant* symphony ▪ *luxuriant* colors
– **lux·u·ri·ance** /ˌlʌgˈʒərijəns, *Brit* ˌlʌgˈzjuəriəns/ *noun* [*noncount*] ▪ the *luxuriance* of his beard – **lux·u·ri·ant·ly** *adv* ▪ a *luxuriantly* bearded man

lux·u·ri·ate /ˌlʌgˈʒəriˌeɪt, *Brit* ˌlʌgˈzjuəriˌeɪt/ *verb* **-ates; -at·ed; -at·ing** [*no obj*] : to enjoy something that is appealingly rich or relaxing — usually + *in* ▪ He spent the morning *luxuriating in* his bed. ▪ She *luxuriated in* the beauties of the natural world.

lux·u·ri·ous /ˌlʌgˈʒərijəs, *Brit* ˌlʌgˈzjuəriəs/ *adj* [*more* ~; *most* ~]
1 : very comfortable and expensive : richly appealing ▪ a *luxurious* apartment/restaurant ▪ one of the country's most *luxurious* resorts/hotels ▪ a *luxurious* fabric/fur
2 : feeling or showing a desire for expensive things ▪ a store that caters to the *luxurious* tastes of the rich
– **lux·u·ri·ous·ly** *adv* ▪ a *luxuriously* furnished/decorated apartment – **lux·u·ri·ous·ness** *noun* [*noncount*]

lux·u·ry /ˈlʌkʃəri/ *noun, pl* **-ries**
1 [*noncount*] : a condition or situation of great comfort, ease, and wealth ▪ living in *luxury* ▪ a symbol of *luxury* ▪ the height of *luxury* — often used before another noun ▪ a *luxury* apartment ▪ a *luxury* car/liner ▪ *luxury* goods/items
2 a [*count*] : something that is expensive and not necessary ▪ He spent a fortune on expensive wines and other *luxuries*. ▪ Right now a new car is a *luxury* that I can't afford. ▪ On my salary, I can afford few *luxuries*. **b** [*singular*] : something that is helpful or welcome and that is not usually or always available ▪ We were lucky to have the *luxury* of choosing from among several good options. ▪ We can't afford the *luxury* of waiting any longer.
in the lap of luxury see [1]LAP

luxury box *noun, pl* ~ **boxes** [*count*] *US* : an area with a roof and private seats near the top of a sports stadium

[1]**-ly** /li/ *adv suffix*
1 : in a (specified) manner ▪ sad*ly* ▪ jokingl*y* ▪ slow*ly*
2 a : in a (specified) period of time ▪ The paper is published week*ly*. **b** : to a (specified) degree or extent ▪ extreme*ly* good ▪ relative*ly* cheap ▪ partial*ly* true **c** : in a (specified) place in a series ▪ second*ly* ▪ last*ly*

[2]**-ly** *adj suffix*
1 : similar in appearance, manner, or nature to a (specified) person ▪ queen*ly* ▪ father*ly*
2 : characterized by regular occurrence in (specified) periods of time ▪ a week*ly* paper

ly·chee *or* **li·tchi** *also* **li·chee** /ˈliːˌtʃiː, *Brit* ˈlaɪˌtʃiː/ *noun, pl* **-chees** *or* **-tchis** [*count*] : the fruit of an Asian tree that has a hard outer covering and a seed surrounded by sweet flesh; *also* : the tree that produces this fruit

Ly·cra /ˈlaɪkrə/ *trademark* — used for a type of cloth that stretches

lye /ˈlaɪ/ *noun* [*noncount*] : a strong chemical that is used especially in making soap

lying *present participle of* LIE

ly·ing–in /ˌlajɪŋˈɪn/ *noun, pl* **lyings–in** *or* **lying–ins** [*count*] *old-fashioned* : the time when a woman lies in bed before, while, and after giving birth to a baby

Lyme disease /ˈlaɪm-/ *noun* [*noncount*] : a serious disease that is spread by the bite of a small insect (called a deer tick)

lymph /ˈlɪmf/ *noun* [*noncount*] *medical* : a pale fluid that contains white blood cells and that passes through channels in the body and helps to keep bodily tissues healthy
– **lym·phat·ic** /lɪmˈfætɪk/ *adj* ▪ *lymphatic* tissue ▪ the *lymphatic* system

lymph node *noun, pl* ~ **nodes** [*count*] *medical* : any one of many rounded masses of tissue in the body through which lymph passes to be filtered and cleaned

lynch /ˈlɪntʃ/ *verb* **lynch·es; lynched; lynch·ing** [+ *obj*] : to kill (someone) illegally as punishment for a crime ▪ The accused killer was *lynched* by an angry mob.

lynch mob *noun, pl* ~ **mobs** [*count*] : a crowd of people who lynch or try to lynch someone

lynchpin *variant spelling of* LINCHPIN

lynx /ˈlɪŋks/ *noun, pl* **lynx** *or* **lynx·es** [*count*] : a large wild cat of North America — see picture at CAT

lyre /ˈlajə/ *noun, pl* **lyres** [*count*] : a musical instrument with strings that was used especially in ancient Greece

[1]**lyr·ic** /ˈlirɪk/ *noun, pl* **-ics** [*count*]
1 : the words of a song ▪ a song with a beautiful *lyric* — usually plural ▪ a song with beautiful *lyrics* ▪ She knows the *lyrics* to all her favorite songs. ▪ The song's *lyrics* made no sense to her. ▪ Who wrote the *lyrics* for/to this song?
2 : a poem that expresses deep personal feelings in a way that is like a song : a lyric poem ▪ a poet admired for his *lyrics*

[2]**lyric** *adj* [*more* ~; *most* ~]
1 a : expressing deep feelings in a way that is like a song ▪ Greek *lyric* poetry **b** : writing lyric poetry ▪ a *lyric* poet
2 *always used before a noun, of an opera singer* : having a light and pure voice ▪ a *lyric* soprano

lyr·i·cal /ˈlirɪkəl/ *adj* [*more* ~; *most* ~] : having an artistically beautiful or expressive quality ▪ She is noted for her *lyrical* moviemaking style. ▪ a painter known for his *lyrical* landscapes ▪ a *lyrical* account of frontier life
wax lyrical *chiefly Brit, informal* : to talk about something in a very enthusiastic way ▪ He *waxed lyrical* about the time he spent living in southern France.
– **lyr·i·cal·ly** /ˈlirɪkli/ *adv*

lyr·i·cism /ˈlirəˌsɪzəm/ *noun* [*noncount*] : a quality that expresses deep feelings or emotions in a work of art : an artistically beautiful or expressive quality ▪ poetic *lyricism* ▪ music rich with *lyricism* ▪ the *lyricism* of his paintings

lyr·i·cist /ˈlirəsɪst/ *noun, pl* **-cists** [*count*] : a person who writes the words of a song : a writer of lyrics

M

[1]**m** *or* **M** /ˈɛm/ *noun, pl* **m's** *or* **ms** *or* **M's** *or* **Ms**
1 : the 13th letter of the English alphabet [*count*] a word that starts with an *m* [*noncount*] a word that starts with *m*
2 [*count*] : the Roman numeral that means 1,000 ▪ MM [=2,000]

[2]**m** *abbr* **1** male **2** married **3** meter **4** mile

M *abbr* **1** medium — usually used for a clothing size ▪ The shirt comes in S, *M*, L, and XL. **2** million

ma /ˈmɑː/ *noun, pl* **mas** [*count*] *informal* : a person's mother ▪ Her *ma* and pa both said she can't go. ▪ When's supper, *Ma*?

MA *abbr* **1** master of arts ▪ She has an *MA* in English. ▪ Laurence Smith, *MA* **2** Massachusetts

ma'am /ˈmæm/ *noun* [*noncount*]
1 *US* — used to politely speak to a woman who you do not know ▪ May I help you with your luggage, *ma'am*? [=*madam*]
2 *Brit* — used to speak to the Queen or to a woman of high rank in the police or military

mac *or* **mack** /ˈmæk/ *noun, pl* **macs** *or* **macks** [*count*] *Brit, informal* : MACKINTOSH

Mac /ˈmæk/ *noun* [*singular*] *US, informal* + *old-fashioned* + *sometimes impolite* — used to speak to a man who you do not know ▪ Hey, *Mac* [=*buddy*], could you move your car?

ma·ca·bre /məˈkɑːb, məˈkɑːbrə/ *adj* [*more* ~; *most* ~] : in-

M

volving death or violence in a way that is strange, frightening, or unpleasant ▪ a *macabre* story of murder and madness ▪ Police discovered a *macabre* scene inside the house.

mac·ad·am /məˈkædəm/ *noun* [*noncount*] **:** a road surface made with a dark material that contains small broken stones

mac·a·ro·ni /ˌmækəˈrouni/ *noun* [*noncount*] **:** a type of pasta in the shape of small curved tubes ▪ (*US*) ***macaroni and cheese*** = (*Brit*) ***macaroni cheese*** [=a dish of macaroni in a cheese sauce] — see picture at PASTA

mac·a·roon /ˌmækəˈruːn/ *noun, pl* **-roons** [*count*] **:** a cookie made of egg, sugar, and almonds or coconut

ma·caw /məˈkɑː/ *noun, pl* **-caws** [*count*] **:** a bird of South and Central America that has a long tail and bright colorful feathers

¹mace /ˈmeɪs/ *noun, pl* **mac·es** [*count*]
1 : a heavy club with many sharp points that was used as a weapon in the Middle Ages
2 : a decorated pole carried by an official in special ceremonies as a symbol of authority
– compare ²MACE

²mace *noun* [*noncount*] **:** a spice made from the dried covering of a type of seed (called a nutmeg) — compare ¹MACE

³mace *verb* **mac·es; maced; mac·ing** [+ *obj*] **:** to spray (a person) with Mace ▪ She *maced* the man who attacked her.

Mace /ˈmeɪs/ *trademark* — used for a liquid that stings the eyes and skin and that is used as a spray to defend against an attacker

Mach /ˈmɑːk, *Brit* ˈmæk/ *noun* [*noncount*] *technical* — used to indicate the high speed of something (such as an airplane) by comparing it to the speed of sound ▪ a jet flying at *Mach* 2 [=twice the speed of sound]

ma·chete /məˈʃɛti/ *noun, pl* **-chet·es** [*count*] **:** a large, heavy knife that is used for cutting plants and as a weapon

Ma·chi·a·vel·lian /ˌmækijəˈvɛlijən/ *adj* [*more* ~; *most* ~] **:** using clever lies and tricks in order to get or achieve something **:** clever and dishonest ▪ He relied on *Machiavellian* [=*devious*] tactics to get elected. ▪ a *Machiavellian* battle for control of the company
– **Machiavellian** *noun, pl* **-lians** [*count*] ▪ a political *Machiavellian*

mach·i·na·tions /ˌmækəˈneɪʃənz/ *noun* [*plural*] *formal* + *usually disapproving* **:** deceptive actions or methods that are used to get or achieve something ▪ His plans were defeated by the *machinations* of his enemies.

¹ma·chine /məˈʃiːn/ *noun, pl* **-chines** [*count*]
1 : a piece of equipment with moving parts that does work when it is given power from electricity, gasoline, etc. ▪ Shovels are tools; bulldozers are *machines*. ▪ Do you know how to operate/use/run this *machine*? ▪ The *machine* is working/running properly. ▪ The *machine* is broken. ▪ *machine*-sorted mail [=mail that is sorted by using a machine] ▪ a fax/copy/exercise *machine* ▪ a coffee/soda/ice/cash *machine* [=a machine from which you can get coffee/soda/ice/cash] — often used to refer informally to a specific type of machine ▪ Are there any new messages on the *machine*? [=on the answering machine] ▪ I have a load of laundry in the *machine*. [=in the washing machine] ▪ I'm having software problems on my *machine*. [=computer] — see also ANSWERING MACHINE, FLYING MACHINE, ROWING MACHINE, SEWING MACHINE, SLOT MACHINE, TIME MACHINE, VENDING MACHINE, VOTING MACHINE, WASHING MACHINE
2 *informal* **:** a vehicle (such as a car or motorcycle) ▪ He was bragging about his new *machine*.
3 a : a person or group that does something efficiently, quickly, or repeatedly like a machine ▪ The coach turned the team into a scoring *machine*. ▪ My younger brother is an eating *machine*. ▪ a publicity *machine* **b :** a powerful and well-organized group ▪ a politician who dared to challenge the local party *machine* ▪ a powerful war *machine* ▪ Their army is a ***well-oiled machine***.
by machine **:** with a machine ▪ The mail used to be sorted by hand but is sorted now *by machine*.
– **ma·chine·like** /məˈʃiːnˌlaɪk/ *adj* [*more* ~; *most* ~] ▪ He worked with *machinelike* efficiency.

²machine *verb* **-chines; -chined; -chin·ing** [+ *obj*] **:** to shape (something) by using a machine ▪ The parts of the engine have been precisely *machined*.

machine gun *noun, pl* ~ **guns** [*count*] **:** a gun that is able to shoot many bullets very quickly one after the other ▪ They heard the sound of *machine-gun* fire. — see picture at GUN
– **machine–gun** *verb* **-guns; -gunned; -gun·ning** [+ *obj*] ▪ The soldiers were *machine-gunned* from the air.
– **machine gunner** *noun, pl* ~ **-ners** [*count*]

ma·chine–gun /məˈʃiːnˌgʌn/ *adj, always used before a noun, informal* **:** very quick ▪ a comedian with a *machine-gun* [=*rapid-fire*] delivery

machine–readable *adj* **:** in a form that can be used and understood by a computer ▪ *machine-readable* data

ma·chin·ery /məˈʃiːnəri/ *noun* [*noncount*]
1 : machines of a particular kind or machines in general ▪ Some of the mill's *machinery* was damaged in the fire. ▪ a piece of farm *machinery*
2 : the working parts of a machine ▪ Something was clogging the *machinery*.
3 : an organization or system by which something is done ▪ the *machinery* of government ▪ The United Nations has set up *machinery* for mediation.

machine shop *noun, pl* ~ **shops** [*count*] **:** a place where metal parts are made and put together

machine tool *noun, pl* ~ **tools** [*count*] **:** a tool (such as a drill) that is powered by electricity and designed for shaping metal or wood

ma·chin·ist /məˈʃiːnɪst/ *noun, pl* **-ists** [*count*] **:** a person who makes, repairs, or operates machines ▪ He is a *machinist* at the factory.

ma·chis·mo /mɑˈtʃiːzmou, *Brit* məˈtʃɪzməu/ *noun* [*noncount*] *often disapproving* **:** an attitude, quality, or way of behaving that agrees with traditional ideas about men being very strong and aggressive ▪ athletes displaying their *machismo* ▪ a culture of *machismo*

ma·cho /ˈmɑːtʃou, *Brit* ˈmætʃəu/ *adj* [*more* ~; *most* ~] *often disapproving* **:** having or showing qualities (such as very noticeable strength and aggression) that agree with traditional ideas about what men are like **:** manly or masculine in a very noticeable or exaggerated way ▪ He thinks he's a real *macho* man. [=a very masculine man] ▪ the *macho* world of football

mack *variant spelling of* MAC

mack·er·el /ˈmækərəl/ *noun, pl* **-el** *or* **-els** [*count, noncount*] **:** a large fish that lives in the northern Atlantic Ocean and is often eaten as food — see color picture on page C8

mack·in·tosh /ˈmækənˌtɑːʃ/ *noun, pl* **-tosh·es** [*count*] *Brit, old-fashioned* **:** RAINCOAT — called also *mac*

mac·ra·mé /ˈmækrəˌmeɪ/ *noun* [*noncount*] **:** the art of tying knots in string to make decorative things ▪ Her hobbies include knitting and *macramé*.; *also* **:** things made in this way ▪ her collection of *macramé*

mac·ro /ˈmækrou/ *noun, pl* **-ros** [*count*] *computers* **:** a set of instructions that causes a computer to perform a series of tasks

mac·ro- /ˈmækrou/ *combining form* **:** large ▪ *macro*economics

mac·ro·bi·o·tic /ˌmækroubaɪˈɑːtɪk/ *adj* **:** consisting of mainly whole grains and vegetables ▪ a *macrobiotic* diet

mac·ro·cosm /ˈmækrəˌkɑːzəm/ *noun* [*singular*] **:** a large system (such as the entire universe) that contains many smaller systems — compare MICROCOSM

mac·ro·eco·nom·ics /ˌmækrouˌɛkəˈnɑːmɪks, ˌmækrouˌiːkəˈnɑːmɪks/ *noun* [*noncount*] **:** the study of the large economic systems of a country or region — compare MICROECONOMICS
– **mac·ro·eco·nom·ic** /ˌmækrouˌɛkəˈnɑːmɪk, ˌmækrouˌiːkəˈnɑːmɪk/ *adj*

mad /ˈmæd/ *adj* **mad·der; mad·dest**
1 *not used before a noun, chiefly US, informal* **:** very angry ▪ If you keep teasing that dog, you'll make/get him *mad*. ▪ She's *mad* at me. = (*less commonly*) She's *mad* with me. ▪ What are you so *mad* about? ▪ That guy makes me so *mad*! ▪ She was *mad* at me for being late. = She was *mad* that I was late. = She was *mad* about my being late. ▪ She was ***hopping mad***. [=extremely angry] — see also *fighting mad* at ¹FIGHT
2 a : having or showing severe mental illness **:** INSANE ▪ (*chiefly Brit*) The man in the park was clearly *mad*. ▪ a movie about a ***mad scientist*** ▪ He was ***stark raving mad***. [=completely insane] = (*Brit*) He was ***barking mad***. **b :** unable to think in a clear or sensible way ▪ He was *mad* [=*insane*] with jealousy/anger. ▪ (*chiefly Brit*) They must have been *mad* [=*crazy*] to buy that house. ▪ a power-*mad* prosecutor **c :** very foolish ▪ (*chiefly Brit*) He made a *mad* decision to drive home in the storm.
3 *chiefly Brit, informal* **:** liking someone or something very much **:** very fond of or enthusiastic about someone or something ▪ She's *mad* for a cute boy in her class. ▪ He's ***mad keen*** on sailing. — often + *about* ▪ She's *mad* [=*wild*] *about* danc-

M

ing. • He's *mad* [=*crazy*] *about* her.
4 *always used before a noun* : wild and uncontrolled • There was a *mad* [=*frantic*] rush when the store opened. • a *mad* scramble
drive (someone) mad **1** : to cause (someone) to become mentally ill • Years alone in the jungle had *driven* him *mad.* **2** : to annoy or bother (someone) very much. • That noise is *driving* me *mad!*
go mad **1** : to become mentally ill • Sometimes I think the whole world has *gone mad!* • He had *gone mad* after years alone in the jungle. **2** : to act in a way that is out of control : to act wildly • The crowd *went mad* [=*went crazy*] when the team won the championship.
like mad *informal* **1** : with a lot of energy and speed • We've been working *like mad* [=*like crazy*] to get done on time. **2** : very quickly • Cars were selling *like mad.* • He's been spending money *like mad.* **3** : very much • She started shivering *like mad.*
mad as a hatter see HATTER

mad•am /ˈmædəm/ *noun, pl* **-ams** [*count*]
1 *pl* **mes•dames** /meɪˈdɑːm, meɪˈdæm/ *formal* — used to politely speak to a woman who you do not know • Would *madam* care for a drink? = Would you care for a drink, *madam?*
2 *Madam* — used at the start of a formal letter to a woman whose name you do not know • Dear *Madam* • Dear Sir or *Madam*
3 *Madam* — used when you are speaking to a woman who has a high rank or position • *Madam* President • *Madam* Ambassador
4 : a woman who is in charge of a brothel
5 *Brit, informal + disapproving* : a girl who expects other people to do things for her • She was a bossy little *madam.*

ma•dame /məˈdæm, məˈdɑːm/ *noun, pl* **mes•dames** /meɪˈdɑːm, meɪˈdæm/ [*count*] — used like *Mrs.* as a title for a married Frenchwoman

mad•cap /ˈmædˌkæp/ *adj, usually used before a noun* [*more ~; most ~*] : very foolish or silly • a *madcap* scheme • a *madcap* [=*zany*] movie about a car race around the world • *madcap* antics

mad cow disease *noun* [*noncount*] : a fatal disease that affects the brain and nervous system of cattle

mad•den /ˈmædn̩/ *verb* **-dens; -dened; -den•ing** [+ *obj*] : to make (someone) angry — often used as *(be) maddened* • The general *was maddened* by the delays.

maddening *adj* [*more ~; most ~*] : very annoying • He has a *maddening* habit of interrupting other people. • She shows a *maddening* inability to control her children.
– mad•den•ing•ly /ˈmædn̩ɪŋli/ *adv* • a *maddeningly* difficult problem • *maddeningly* slow service

¹made *past tense and past participle of* ¹MAKE

²made /ˈmeɪd/ *adj*
1 *not used before a noun* **a** — used to say that someone has the right qualities *to be* or *to do* something • He was *made to be* an actor. = He was *made to act.* **b** — used to say that something has the right qualities *for* or *to do* something • She has a body *made for* running. • The furniture was *made to last.* [=the furniture will last a long time]
2 : built, formed, or shaped in a specified way • newly *made* tissue cells — often used in combination • American-*made* cars • machine-*made* rugs — see also HANDMADE, HOMEMADE, MAN-MADE, TAILOR-MADE
3 *informal* : certain of success • a ***made man*** • If this works, we'll all be ***made for life!*** [=we will have enough money to live well for the rest of our lives]
have it made *informal* : to be in a very good position or situation • My brother *has it made* with a good job, a beautiful wife, and a big house with a pool. • (*US*) She had to work hard for many years to achieve success, but now she ***has it made in the shade.***
made for each other *informal* : perfectly suited to each other • I'm not surprised that they have such a happy marriage. I always knew that they were *made for each other.*
made of money see MONEY
what you're made of ✧ If people want to find out *what you're made of,* they want to see if you have the necessary courage, skill, etc., to succeed. • Let's give him a chance and find out *what he's made of.*
– see also READY-MADE, SELF-MADE, UNMADE

ma•de•moi•selle /ˌmædmwəˈzɛl/ *noun, pl* **ma•de•moi•selles** /ˌmædmwəˈzɛlz/ *or* **mes•de•moi•selles** /ˌmeɪdmwəˈzɛl/ [*count*] — used like *Miss* as a title for a Frenchwoman who is not married

made–to–measure *adj* : made to fit a particular person or thing • a *made-to-measure* [=*custom-made*] suit • *made-to-measure* curtains

made–to–order *adj* : made to fit the needs or requirements of a particular person • *made-to-order* [=*custom-made*] shoes/furniture • a *made-to-order* meal

made–up /ˈmeɪdˈʌp/ *adj*
1 : created from the imagination : not true or real • a *made-up* [=*fictitious*] story/name
2 [*more ~; most ~*] : wearing makeup • *made-up* eyelids • She was nicely *made-up.*

mad•house /ˈmædˌhaʊs/ *noun, pl* **-hous•es** [*count*]
1 *old-fashioned + offensive* : a hospital for people who are mentally ill
2 *informal* : a place where there is a lot of excitement or confusion • The stadium was a *madhouse* when the team won the championship.

mad•ly /ˈmædli/ *adv*
1 : to an extreme or excessive degree • He told her that he loved her *madly.* • a *madly* ambitious businessman • She fell ***madly in love*** with him.
2 : in a mad or insane way • He pulled out a knife and started waving it around *madly.* [=*wildly*] • grinning *madly*

mad•man /ˈmædˌmæn/ *noun, pl* **-men** /-ˌmɛn/ [*count*]
1 : a man who has severe mental illness : an insane man • a celebrity being stalked by a *madman*
2 *informal* : a man who acts in a wild and uncontrolled way • He is a *madman* out on the ski slopes. [=he is an extremely daring or reckless skier] • He drives ***like a madman.*** [=he drives very recklessly]

mad•ness /ˈmædnəs/ *noun* [*noncount*]
1 : a state of severe mental illness • The king's *madness* [=*insanity*] was well-known. • He suffered a series of tragedies that nearly drove him to *madness.*
2 : behavior or thinking that is very foolish or dangerous • Her friends told her the idea was pure/sheer *madness,* but she went through with it anyway. • It was the height of *madness* for him to drive at such high speeds! — see also ***(a) method in/to your madness*** at METHOD

Ma•don•na /məˈdɑːnə/ *noun, pl* **-nas**
1 *the Madonna* : the Virgin Mary : the mother of Jesus Christ
2 [*count*] : a painting or statue of the Virgin Mary

mad•ri•gal /ˈmædrɪgəl/ *noun, pl* **-gals** [*count*] : a type of song for several singers without instruments that was popular in the 16th and 17th centuries

mad•wom•an /ˈmædˌwʊmən/ *noun, pl* **-wom•en** /-ˌwɪmən/ [*count*]
1 : a woman who has severe mental illness : an insane woman • a story about a *madwoman* locked up by her husband
2 *informal* : a woman who acts in a wild and uncontrolled way • She is a *madwoman* on the dance floor. • She drives ***like a madwoman.*** [=she drives recklessly]

mael•strom /ˈmeɪlstrəm/ *noun, pl* **-stroms** [*count*] *literary*
1 : a situation in which there are a lot of confused activities, emotions, etc. • She was caught in a *maelstrom* of emotions. • the *maelstrom* of war • a *maelstrom* of activity
2 : a dangerous area of water that moves very fast in a circle : WHIRLPOOL • The ship was drawn into the *maelstrom.*

mae•stro /ˈmaɪstroʊ/ *noun, pl* **mae•stros** *also* **mae•stri** /ˈmaɪˌstriː/ [*count*] : a man who is an expert at writing, conducting, or teaching music — often used as part of a title • The orchestra played under *Maestro* Bernstein. • Which tempo do you prefer, *Maestro?*

Ma•fia /ˈmɑːfijə, *Brit* ˈmæfiə/ *noun, pl* **-fias**
1 *the Mafia* **a** : a secret criminal organization in Italy **b** : a similar criminal organization in the U.S. • a member of *the Mafia* — often used as *Mafia* before another noun • a politician accused of having *Mafia* connections
2 *or* ***mafia*** [*count*] : a group of closely connected people who have great power or influence in a particular field or business • He's an important figure in the television *mafia.*

ma•fi•o•so /ˌmɑːfiˈoʊsoʊ, *Brit* ˌmæfiˈəʊsəʊ/ *noun, pl* **-si** /-si/ [*count*] : a member of the Mafia

mag•a•zine /ˈmægəˌziːn, ˌmægəˈziːn/ *noun, pl* **-zines** [*count*]
1 : a type of thin book with a paper cover that contains stories, essays, pictures, etc., and that is usually published every week or month • a literary/fashion *magazine* • a *magazine* rack • She subscribes to several gardening *magazines.*

M

2 : a radio or television program that discusses different topics
3 : a part of a gun that holds bullets
4 : a building or room where military supplies are stored

ma·gen·ta /mə'ʤɛntə/ *noun, pl* **-tas** [*count, noncount*] **:** a bright, deep purplish-red color — see color picture on page C3
– **magenta** *adj*

mag·got /'mægət/ *noun, pl* **-gots** [*count*] **:** an insect that looks like a small worm and that is a young form of a fly ▪ The rotten meat was infested with *maggots.*
– **mag·goty** /'mægəti/ *adj* [*more ~; most ~*] ▪ rotten *maggoty* meat

Ma·gi /'meɪˌʤaɪ/ *noun*
the Magi **:** the three wise men in the Bible who come from the East with gifts for the baby Jesus

[1]**mag·ic** /'mæʤɪk/ *noun* [*noncount*]
1 : a power that allows people (such as witches and wizards) to do impossible things by saying special words or performing special actions ▪ perform/work (feats of) *magic* ▪ children who believe in *magic* — see also BLACK MAGIC
2 : tricks that seem to be impossible and that are done by a performer to entertain people ▪ a book that explains how to do *magic*
3 : special power, influence, or skill ▪ Some doubted the company could ever get back its former *magic.* [=could ever succeed again as it had succeeded before] ▪ Both pitchers, though they are older, haven't lost their *magic.*
4 : a very pleasant, attractive, or exciting quality ▪ the *magic* of their singing ▪ They wanted to get the old *magic* back into their marriage.
by magic **:** by the power of magic ▪ a mop that gets rid of dirt as if *by magic*
like magic *informal* **:** in a very fast and impressive way ▪ Shapes changed *like magic* on the computer screen. ▪ a mop that works *like magic* [=that works extremely quickly or well]
work your magic **1 :** to do something very well ▪ the kitchen where a great cook *works her magic* **2 :** to have a desired good effect ▪ It may take a few hours for the medication to *work its magic.*

[2]**magic** *adj*
1 : having the power to make impossible things happen **:** having supernatural power ▪ a *magic* potion/spell that makes you able to fly ▪ a *magic* charm
2 : involving the skill of doing tricks that seem to be impossible ▪ *magic* tricks ▪ a *magic* show/act
3 : capable of producing good results very easily ▪ There is no *magic* solution to these problems. ▪ He claims to know the ***magic formula*** for financial success. [=he claims to know a simple and sure way to achieve financial success] ▪ She has a ***magic touch*** with animals. [=she is able to calm or control animals with unusual ease]
4 [*more ~; most ~*] **:** very pleasant or exciting ▪ It was a *magic* moment when they met. ▪ They spent a *magic* [=*magical*] evening together.

mag·i·cal /'mæʤɪkəl/ *adj*
1 : [2]MAGIC 1 ▪ a *magical* potion ▪ *magical* powers
2 [*more ~; most ~*] **:** very pleasant or exciting ▪ We had a *magical* time.
– **mag·i·cal·ly** /'mæʤɪkli/ *adv* ▪ The magician made the car *magically* appear. ▪ I can't *magically* make your problems go away.

magic bullet *noun, pl* **~ -lets** [*count*]
1 : a drug or treatment that cures a disease quickly and easily without producing bad effects
2 : something that solves a difficult problem easily ▪ There is no *magic bullet* to fix our educational system.

magic carpet *noun, pl* **~ -pets** [*count*] *in stories* **:** a carpet that can carry a person through the air

ma·gi·cian /mə'ʤɪʃən/ *noun, pl* **-cians** [*count*]
1 : a person who has the power to make impossible things happen **:** SORCERER
2 : a performer who does tricks that seem to be impossible ▪ The *magician* pulled a rabbit out of a hat.
3 : a person who has amazing skills ▪ She is a *magician* on the basketball court.

magic lantern *noun, pl* **~ -terns** [*count*] **:** a machine that was used in the past to show pictures on a wall or screen

Magic Marker *trademark* — used for a felt-tip pen

magic wand *noun, pl* **~ wands** [*count*] **:** a stick that is used to make magic things happen ▪ The magician waved his *magic wand* and pulled a rabbit out of the hat. — sometimes used figuratively ▪ The new law is not a *magic wand* that will solve all our problems.

mag·is·te·ri·al /ˌmæʤə'stirijəl/ *adj*
1 [*more ~; most ~*] *formal* **:** showing impressive knowledge about a subject ▪ His book is a *magisterial* [=*authoritative*] study of the artist.
2 [*more ~; most ~*] *formal* **:** having the confident quality of someone who expects to be obeyed by other people ▪ He spoke with a *magisterial* tone.
3 : of or relating to a magistrate ▪ *magisterial* duties
– **mag·is·te·ri·al·ly** /ˌmæʤə'stirijəli/ *adv*

mag·is·trate /'mæʤəˌstreɪt/ *noun, pl* **-trates** [*count*] **:** a local official who has some of the powers of a judge

mag·ma /'mægmə/ *noun* [*noncount*] *technical* **:** hot liquid rock below the surface of the Earth

mag·na cum lau·de /'mɑːgnəkʊm'laʊdə/ *adv, formal* **:** with great honor — used in the U.S. to indicate that a student has graduated from a college or university at the second highest of three special levels of achievement ▪ He graduated *magna cum laude.* — compare CUM LAUDE, SUMMA CUM LAUDE

mag·nan·i·mous /mæg'nænəməs/ *adj* [*more ~; most ~*] *formal* **:** having or showing a generous and kind nature ▪ The team was *magnanimous* in victory. [=the team treated its defeated opponents in a respectful and generous way] ▪ She was too *magnanimous* to resent all the things others had said to her. ▪ a *magnanimous* gesture
– **mag·na·nim·i·ty** /ˌmægnə'nɪməti/ *noun* [*noncount*] ▪ He had the *magnanimity* to forgive her for lying about him. ▪ The team showed *magnanimity* in victory. – **mag·nan·i·mous·ly** *adv*

mag·nate /'mægˌneɪt/ *noun, pl* **-nates** [*count*] **:** a person who has great wealth and power in a particular business or industry ▪ a railroad *magnate*

magnesia see MILK OF MAGNESIA

mag·ne·sium /mæg'niːzijəm/ *noun* [*noncount*] **:** a silver-white metallic element that produces a very bright white light when it burns

mag·net /'mægnət/ *noun, pl* **-nets** [*count*]
1 : a piece of material (such as iron or steel) that is able to attract certain metals ▪ (*US*) a ***refrigerator magnet*** [=a small object with a magnet attached to it that can stick to a refrigerator or other metal surface]
2 : something or someone that attracts people or things — often + *for* ▪ The town is a *magnet for* tourists in the summer months. ▪ a controversial politician who has become a *magnet for* criticism [=who attracts a great deal of criticism]

mag·net·ic /mæg'nɛtɪk/ *adj* [*more ~; most ~*]
1 : of or relating to a magnet or magnetism ▪ *magnetic* materials ▪ a strong/powerful *magnetic* field
2 : having great power to attract and hold the interest of other people ▪ a *magnetic* personality ▪ a *magnetic* performer
– **mag·net·i·cal·ly** /mæg'nɛtɪkli/ *adv* ▪ a *magnetically* charged particle ▪ a *magnetically* attractive personality

magnetic compass *noun, pl* **~ -pass·es** [*count*] **:** COMPASS 1

magnetic disk *noun, pl* **~ disks** [*count*] **:** DISC 2

magnetic north *noun* [*noncount*] **:** the direction or area to the north toward which the needle of a compass points — compare TRUE NORTH

magnetic pole *noun, pl* **~ poles** [*count*]
1 : an area near either the North or South Pole of the Earth toward which the needle of a compass points
2 : either one of the two ends of a magnet

magnetic resonance im·ag·ing /-'ɪmɪʤɪŋ/ *noun* [*noncount*] *medical* **:** a method used to produce images of the inside of a person's body by means of a strong magnetic field — called also *MRI*

magnetic tape *noun* [*noncount*] **:** a thin plastic tape that is coated with magnetic material on which information (such as sound or television images) may be stored

mag·ne·tism /'mægnəˌtɪzəm/ *noun* [*noncount*]
1 : the property of attracting certain metals **:** the attracting property of a magnet
2 : a quality that makes someone able to attract and hold the interest of other people ▪ Much of his success as a politician can be attributed to his personal *magnetism.* — see also *animal magnetism* at [2]ANIMAL

mag·ne·tize *also Brit* **mag·ne·tise** /'mægnəˌtaɪz/ *verb* **-tiz·es; -tized; -tiz·ing**

M

1 : to cause (something) to become magnetic ▪ *magnetize* a metal bar ▪ a highly *magnetized* particle
2 : to attract and hold the interest of (someone) ▪ Her performance *magnetized* the audience.
– **mag·ne·tiz·able** *also Brit* **mag·ne·tis·able** /ˈmægnəˌtaɪzəbəl/ *adj* – **mag·ne·ti·za·tion** *also Brit* **mag·ne·ti·sa·tion** /ˌmægnətəˈzeɪʃən, *Brit* ˌmægnəˌtaɪˈzeɪʃən/ *noun* [*noncount*]

magnet school *noun, pl* ~ **schools** [*count*] *chiefly US* : a school that has courses in special subjects (such as the arts or technology) and is designed to attract students from all parts of a community

mag·ni·fi·ca·tion /ˌmægnəfəˈkeɪʃən/ *noun, pl* **-tions**
1 [*noncount*] : the act of making something look larger than it is : the act of magnifying something ▪ *magnification* of an image
2 : the larger appearance of an object when it is seen through a microscope, telescope, etc. [*noncount*] We used a microscope to examine the cells under *magnification.* [*count*] At/Under higher *magnifications* the differences between the cells become clear. ▪ The telescope has a *magnification* of 30X. [=objects appear to be 30 times larger when viewed through the telescope]

mag·nif·i·cent /mægˈnɪfəsənt/ *adj* [*more* ~; *most* ~] : very beautiful or impressive : very great ▪ the *magnificent* cathedrals of Europe ▪ He gave a *magnificent* performance. ▪ The view was *magnificent.*
– **mag·nif·i·cence** /mægˈnɪfəsəns/ *noun* [*noncount*] ▪ We were awed by the splendor and *magnificence* of the palace.
– **mag·nif·i·cent·ly** *adv* ▪ a *magnificently* decorated palace ▪ He performed *magnificently.*

mag·ni·fy /ˈmægnəˌfaɪ/ *verb* **-fies; -fied; -fy·ing** [+ *obj*]
1 a : to make (something) greater ▪ The sound was *magnified* by the calm air. ▪ Their health problems have been *magnified* [=*worsened*] by unsanitary living conditions. ▪ Her successful handling of the crisis has *magnified* [=*increased, improved*] her chances to win reelection. **b** : to make (something) seem greater or more important than it is ▪ His failures have been *magnified* by the success of his friends. ▪ I don't want to *magnify* the importance of these problems.
2 : to make (something) appear larger ▪ The lens *magnified* the image 100 times. ▪ a *magnified* view of the image
– **mag·ni·fi·er** /ˈmægnəˌfajɚ/ *noun, pl* **-ers** [*count*]

magnifying glass *noun, pl* ~ **glasses** [*count*] : a specially shaped piece of glass that is attached to a handle and is used to make an object look larger than it is ▪ The jeweler examined the diamond with a *magnifying glass.*

mag·ni·tude /ˈmægnəˌtuːd, *Brit* ˈmægnəˌtjuːd/ *noun*
1 [*noncount*] : the size, extent, or importance of something ▪ The country's small army would be crushed in a war of such *magnitude.* [=in such a large war] ▪ At this point no one really knows the true/real *magnitude* [=*scale*] of the problem.
2 [*count, noncount*] *technical* **a** : a number that shows the brightness of a star **b** : a number that shows the power of an earthquake ▪ a *magnitude* 6.7 earthquake = an earthquake of *magnitude* 6.7

mag·no·lia /mægˈnoʊljə/ *noun, pl* **-lias** [*count*] : a tree or tall bush that has white, pink, yellow, or purple flowers

mag·num opus /ˈmægnəmˈoʊpəs/ *noun* [*singular*] : a great work : the greatest achievement of an artist or writer ▪ His last novel was his *magnum opus.*

mag·pie /ˈmægˌpaɪ/ *noun, pl* **-pies** [*count*]
1 : a noisy black-and-white bird
2 *chiefly Brit, informal* : a person who collects and keeps different things

ma·ha·ra·ja *or* **ma·ha·ra·jah** /ˌmɑːhəˈrɑːʤə/ *noun, pl* **-jas** *or* **-jahs** [*count*] : a Hindu prince

ma·ha·ra·ni *or* **ma·ha·ra·nee** /ˌmɑːhəˈrɑːni/ *noun, pl* **-nis** *or* **-nees** [*count*]
1 : the wife of a maharaja
2 : a Hindu princess

ma·hat·ma /məˈhɑːtmə, *Brit* məˈhætmə/ *noun, pl* **-mas** [*count*] : a person who is respected for being good, wise, and holy — used as a title of honor by Hindus ▪ *Mahatma* Gandhi

mah–jongg *or* **mah·jong** /ˌmɑːˈʒɑːŋ, ˌmɑːˈʤɑːŋ/ *noun* [*noncount*] : a Chinese game that four people play using small pieces of wood with symbols on them

ma·hog·a·ny /məˈhɑːgəni/ *noun, pl* **-nies**
1 [*noncount*] : a strong reddish-brown wood that is used especially for making furniture and that comes from several tropical trees; *also* [*count*] : a tree that produces this wood
2 [*noncount*] : a reddish-brown color — see color picture on page C3
– **mahogany** *adj*

maid /ˈmeɪd/ *noun, pl* **maids** [*count*]
1 : a female servant ▪ a lady's *maid*; *especially* : a woman or girl who does cleaning work in a house or hotel ▪ She hired a *maid* to do the cleaning. ▪ a hotel *maid*
2 *old-fashioned + literary* : a girl or woman who is not married : MAIDEN ▪ a young *maid* — see also OLD MAID

[1]**maid·en** /ˈmeɪdn̩/ *noun, pl* **-ens** [*count*] *old-fashioned + literary* : a young girl or woman who is not married ▪ a story about a courageous knight who rescues a fair *maiden* ▪ a *maiden* in distress — see also HANDMAIDEN

[2]**maiden** *adj, always used before a noun*
1 *of a woman, old-fashioned* : not married ▪ my ***maiden aunt***
2 : coming before all others : first or earliest ▪ the ship's *maiden* voyage ▪ the *maiden* issue of a new magazine ▪ a politician giving his *maiden* speech in the Senate

maid·en·hair /ˈmeɪdn̩ˌheɚ/ *noun* [*count, noncount*] : a type of fern that has thin stems and delicate leaves — called also *maidenhair fern*

maid·en·head /ˈmeɪdn̩ˌhɛd/ *noun, pl* **-heads** *old-fashioned*
1 [*noncount*] *of a woman* : the state of being a virgin
2 [*count*] : HYMEN

maiden name *noun, pl* ~ **names** [*count*] : a woman's family name before she is married ▪ After she divorced, she took back her *maiden name.*

maid of honor (*US*) *or Brit* **maid of honour** *noun, pl* **maids of honor** [*count*] *chiefly US* : an unmarried woman who is the main bridesmaid at a wedding ▪ She asked her sister to be her *maid of honor.* — compare MATRON OF HONOR

maid·ser·vant /ˈmeɪdˌsɚvənt/ *noun, pl* **-vants** *old-fashioned* : a female servant ▪ menservants and *maidservants*

[1]**mail** /ˈmeɪl/ *noun* [*noncount*] ✧ *Mail* is used in British English but it is much more common in U.S. English. The usual word in British English is *post.*
1 : the system used for sending letters and packages from one person to another ▪ They do business by *mail.* ▪ Don't bring the check to the office—send it through the *mail.* ▪ The check is in the *mail.* [=the check has been sent and will be delivered by mail] ▪ I hope the check hasn't gotten lost in the *mail.* ▪ interoffice *mail* — called also (*chiefly Brit*) *post*; see also AIRMAIL, DIRECT MAIL, REGISTERED MAIL, RETURN MAIL, SURFACE MAIL, VOICE MAIL
2 : letters or packages sent from one person to another ▪ Was the notice in today's *mail*? ▪ Did we get any *mail* today? ▪ Has the *mail* arrived yet? ▪ sorting through the *mail* ▪ There's a pile of *mail* on the table. ▪ collecting and delivering the *mail* ▪ reading the *mail* ▪ They got a lot of ***hate mail*** [=extremely angry letters, e-mail, etc.] from people who disagree with their policies. ▪ He has a job in the ***mail room***. [=the room in an office where mail is handled] — called also (*chiefly Brit*) *post*; see also FAN MAIL, JUNK MAIL, SNAIL MAIL
3 : [1]E-MAIL ▪ I need to check my computer to see if I've gotten any *mail* today.
the mails *chiefly US, law, formal* : the system used for sending letters, packages, etc. : a nation's postal system ▪ packages sent through *the mails* ▪ He was charged with using *the mails* to commit fraud.
– compare [3]MAIL

[2]**mail** *verb* **mails; mailed; mail·ing** [+ *obj*] *chiefly US* : to send (something, such as a letter or package) by mail ▪ Have you *mailed* (out) the invitations yet? [=(*chiefly Brit*) have you posted the invitations yet?] ▪ She *mailed* me a copy of her manuscript. = She *mailed* a copy of her manuscript to me.

[3]**mail** *noun* [*noncount*] : a kind of protective clothing (called armor) that is made of many small pieces or rings of metal which are linked together ▪ a coat of *mail* — see also CHAIN MAIL — compare [1]MAIL

mail·bag /ˈmeɪlˌbæg/ *noun, pl* **-bags** [*count*]
1 : a large bag used for sending letters and packages in a truck, airplane, etc.
2 *chiefly US* : a bag carried by a person who delivers the mail — called also (*Brit*) *postbag*

mail·box /ˈmeɪlˌbɑːks/ *noun, pl* **-box·es** [*count*] *chiefly US*
1 : a public box in which letters and packages are placed to be collected and sent out ▪ On the way to work, I dropped my letters in the corner *mailbox.* — called also (*Brit*) *letter box,* (*Brit*) *postbox*
2 : a private box on or near a house in which mail is placed when it is delivered ▪ She checked her *mailbox* daily, hoping

M

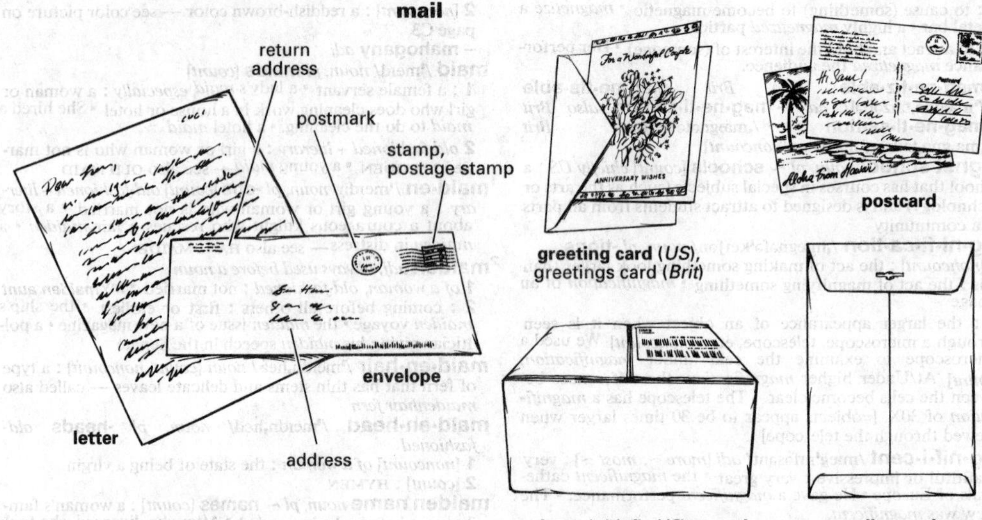

for a letter from her son. — called also (*Brit*) *letter box*; see picture at HOUSE

3 *computers* : a computer folder that holds e-mail • an electronic *mailbox*

mail carrier *noun, pl* ~ **-ers** [*count*] *US* : a person who delivers mail : LETTER CARRIER

mail drop *noun, pl* ~ **drops** [*count*] *US*

1 : a place or address where mail or messages can be left for someone

2 : a box in which mail can be placed

mail·er /ˈmeɪlɚ/ *noun, pl* **-ers** [*count*] *chiefly US*

1 : a person or organization that mails something • a letter *mailer*

2 : a container used for mailing something

3 : something (such as an advertisement) that is sent by mail

mail·ing /ˈmeɪlɪŋ/ *noun, pl* **-ings**

1 [*noncount*] : the act of mailing something • Get the check ready for *mailing* and take it to the post office.

2 [*count*] : something (such as a letter or an advertisement) that is mailed to many people at one time • mass *mailings* • The charity sent out several *mailings* to everyone on its mailing list. — called also (*Brit*) *mailshot*

mailing address *noun, pl* ~ **-dresses** [*count*] : an address to which mail can be sent • His *mailing address* [=*postal address*] is different from his home address.

mailing list *noun, pl* ~ **lists** [*count*]

1 : a list of names and addresses to which mail is sent • The charity sent out letters to everyone on its *mailing list*. • He asked the company to put him on their *mailing list* so that he could receive their catalog.

2 : a list of names and e-mail addresses to which e-mails are sent by people who are on the list • People subscribe to Internet *mailing lists* in order to exchange information about special subjects.

mail·man /ˈmeɪlˌmæn/ *noun, pl* **-men** /-ˌmɛn/ [*count*] *US* : a man who delivers mail : POSTMAN

mail order *noun, pl* ~ **-ders**

1 [*noncount*] : a method of buying products that are received by mail • You can purchase the books by *mail order*.

2 [*count*] : a product that is sent by mail to the person who bought it • The store sent out all its *mail orders* in time for the holiday.

— **mail–or·der** /ˈmeɪlˌoɚdɚ/ *adj, always used before a noun* • a *mail-order* catalog [=a catalog of products that can be ordered through the mail]

mail·shot /ˈmeɪlˌʃɑːt/ *noun, pl* **-shots** [*count*] *Brit* : MAILING 2

maim /ˈmeɪm/ *verb* **maims; maimed; maim·ing** [+ *obj*] : to injure (someone) very badly by violence • The bomb killed 16 people and *maimed* several others. • The accident left him (badly) *maimed* for life. — sometimes used figuratively • a career *maimed* by scandal

[1]**main** /ˈmeɪn/ *adj, always used before a noun* : most important : CHIEF, PRINCIPAL • the *main* idea/point • the *main* goal/purpose • Speed is the *main* advantage of this approach. • The company's *main* office is located in New York. • the novel's *main* character • driving down the *main* road/highway • the *main* gate/entrance • This dish can be served as a ***main course*** or appetizer. • And now for the ***main event*** of the evening!

— **main·ly** *adv* • The reviews have been *mainly* [=*mostly*] positive. • a plant found *mainly* [=*chiefly*] in coastal regions • I don't like the plan, *mainly* because I think it's too expensive. • The problems have been *mainly* minor ones. [=most of the problems have been minor ones] • They depend *mainly* on/upon fish for food.

[2]**main** *noun, pl* **mains**

1 [*count*] : the largest pipe in a system of connected pipes • a gas *main* • a water *main*

2 ***the mains*** *Brit* **a** : the system of pipes or wires for electricity, gas, or water • My radio runs either off batteries or off *the mains*. — often used as *mains* before another noun • We haven't had any *mains* water/electricity since the storm. **b** : the place where electricity, gas, or water enters a building or room • Turn off the water at *the mains*.

in the main : in general — used to say that a statement is true in most cases or at most times • The workers are *in the main* very capable. [=most of the workers are very capable] • The weather has *in the main* been quite good. [=has been quite good most of the time]

main clause *noun, pl* ~ **clauses** [*count*] *grammar* : a clause that could be used by itself as a simple sentence but that is part of a larger sentence — called also *independent clause*; compare COORDINATE CLAUSE, SUBORDINATE CLAUSE

main drag *noun, pl* ~ **drags** [*count*] *US, informal* : the main street in a town or city • A carload of teenagers were cruising down the *main drag*.

main·frame /ˈmeɪnˌfreɪm/ *noun, pl* **-frames** [*count*] : a large and very fast computer that can do many jobs at once

main·land /ˈmeɪnˌlænd/ *noun* [*singular*] : a large area of land that forms a country or a continent and that does not include islands — used with *the* • *the* Chinese *mainland* = *the mainland* of China • After spending a week on the tiny island, we were happy to return to *the mainland*. — often used before another noun • *mainland* China

[1]**main·line** /ˈmeɪnˌlaɪn/ *adj, chiefly US* : belonging to an established and widely accepted group or system • *mainline* [=*mainstream*] churches

[2]**mainline** *verb* **-lines; -lined; -lin·ing** *slang* : to inject (a drug) directly into a vein [+ *obj*] addicts *mainlining* heroin [*no obj*] His addiction grew worse when he began *mainlining*.

main line *noun, pl* ~ **lines** [*count*] : an important highway or railroad line

main man *noun, pl* ~ **men** [*count*] *US, informal*

1 : someone's best male friend • He's still her *main man*.

2 : the most important or admired man in a group • The team has many good players, but he is clearly the *main man*.

main•sail /ˈmeɪnˌseɪl, ˈmeɪnsəl/ *noun, pl* **-sails** [*count*] **:** the largest sail of a sailing ship

main•spring /ˈmeɪnˌsprɪŋ/ *noun, pl* **-springs** [*count*]

1 : the most important spring in a watch or clock

2 : the most important or powerful cause or part of something • Agriculture is the *mainspring* of their economy.

main squeeze *noun, pl* **~ squeezes** [*count*] *chiefly US slang* **:** someone's main girlfriend, boyfriend, or lover • She's my *main squeeze*.

main•stay /ˈmeɪnˌsteɪ/ *noun, pl* **-stays** [*count*] **:** a very important part of something • Fish is a *mainstay* of their diet. • a dietary *mainstay* **:** something or someone that provides support and makes it possible for something to exist or succeed • My mother has always been the *mainstay* of our family.

[1]main•stream /ˈmeɪnˌstriːm/ *noun*

the mainstream **:** the thoughts, beliefs, and choices that are accepted by the largest number of people • His ideas are well outside *the mainstream* of political opinion. = His ideas are well outside *the* political *mainstream*.

– mainstream *adj* [*more ~; most ~*] • *mainstream* medicine [=the type of medicine that is most widely practiced and accepted] • *mainstream* movies • Advertisers are trying to attract a more *mainstream* audience.

[2]main•stream /meɪnˈstriːm/ *verb* **-streams; -streamed; -stream•ing** [+ *obj*]

1 *chiefly US* **:** to place (a child with special educational needs) in regular school classes

2 : to cause (someone or something) to be included in or accepted by the group that includes most people • The poor should be *mainstreamed* into the private health-insurance system. • Ideas that were once controversial have now become *mainstreamed*.

main street *noun, pl* **~ streets**

1 [*count*] **:** the most important street of a U.S. town where there are many stores, banks, etc. — often used as a name • The restaurant is at 257 *Main Street*.

2 ***Main Street*** [*noncount*] *US* — used to refer to middle-class people in the U.S. who have traditional beliefs and values • What does *Main Street* think of this policy?

main•tain /meɪnˈteɪn/ *verb* **-tains; -tained; -tain•ing** [+ *obj*]

1 : to cause (something) to exist or continue without changing • They have always *maintained* high standards of professional conduct. • He has found it difficult to *maintain* a healthy weight. • *maintain* a good reputation • They barely had enough food to ***maintain life***. [=to make it possible for life to exist or continue]

2 : to keep (something) in good condition by making repairs, correcting problems, etc. • The company has done a poor job of *maintaining* its computer network. • It was obvious that the house had been poorly *maintained*.

3 : to continue having or doing (something) • She was finding it hard to *maintain* her balance. • She still *maintains* a close relationship with her college roommate. • It's difficult to *maintain* a correspondence when we're both so busy. • The pilot was struggling to *maintain* control of the aircraft. • The police say that they will do whatever is necessary to *maintain* law and order. • She continues to *maintain* her silence. [=she continues to say nothing] • He was struggling to ***maintain his cool/composure***. [=he was struggling not to become angry or upset]

4 : to say that (something) is true • He *maintains* that such decisions are best left to local authorities. • He continues to *maintain* his innocence. = He continues to *maintain* that he is innocent. • She *maintains* that my theory is flawed.

5 : to provide support for (someone or something) • He has a family to *maintain*.

main•te•nance /ˈmeɪntənəns/ *noun* [*noncount*]

1 : the act of maintaining something or someone: such as **a :** the act of keeping property or equipment in good condition by making repairs, correcting problems, etc. • The building has suffered from years of poor *maintenance*. • the costs of routine car *maintenance* — often used before another noun • a *maintenance* worker [=a worker whose job is to keep property or equipment in good condition] • a *maintenance* fee • She works in the company's *maintenance* department. **b :** the act of causing something to exist or continue without changing • *maintenance* of law and order **c :** the act of providing support for someone or something • money for the family's *maintenance*

2 *Brit* **:** CHILD SUPPORT

maize /ˈmeɪz/ *noun* [*noncount*] *Brit* **:** [1]CORN 1a

ma•jes•tic /məˈʤɛstɪk/ *adj* [*more ~; most ~*] **:** large and impressively beautiful • *majestic* mountains/trees • *majestic* phrases **– ma•jes•ti•cal•ly** /məˈʤɛstɪkli/ *adv* • mountains rising *majestically* above the surrounding hills

maj•es•ty /ˈmæʤəsti/ *noun, pl* **-ties**

1 [*noncount*] **:** a great and impressively beautiful quality • the *majesty* of the mountains

2 ***Majesty*** [*count*] — used as a title for a king, queen, emperor, or empress; used with *his, her, your,* or *their* • *Your Majesty* • *Her Majesty's* Government • *Their Majesties*

[1]ma•jor /ˈmeɪʤɚ/ *adj*

1 a : very important • a *major* poet/artist • He's one of the *major* figures in 19th-century U.S. history. • Researchers have announced a *major* advance/breakthrough in the treatment of cancer. • *major* American cities • a *major* event • a question of *major* [=*great*] importance • *major* rivers/roads • She played a *major* role in the negotiations. • a *major* earthquake • a writer's *major* works • No *major* changes are expected. • The problems do not appear to be (very) *major*. **b** ***always used before a noun*** **:** large in number, amount, or extent • The grant covered a *major* part of the cost. • Butter is one of the *major* ingredients in the recipe. • The movie turned out to be a *major* disappointment. [=the movie was very disappointing] • (*informal*) A car like that costs *major* money. [=a lot of money]

2 : very serious or bad • None of his health problems are *major*. • a *major* illness/disease • He suffered a *major* heart attack. • She's having *major* surgery. • *major* depression • a *major* accident

3 *music* **a** ***of a scale*** **:** having semitones between the third and fourth and the seventh and eighth notes • a *major* scale • the C-*major* scale [=the major scale that is in the key of C] **b :** based on a major scale • a *major* key — compare [1]MINOR 3

[2]major *noun, pl* **-jors** [*count*]

1 : a military officer in the army, air force, or marines who ranks above a captain • an Army *major* • *Major* Smith — see also SERGEANT MAJOR

2 *US* **a :** the main subject studied by a college or university student • He chose history as his *major* and French as his minor. • What was your *major* in college? — compare [2]MINOR 2 **b :** a student who has a specified main subject of study • In college, he was a history *major*. • a club for physics *majors*

the majors *US, informal* **:** the major leagues of baseball • As a boy, he dreamed of playing in *the majors*.

– see also DRUM MAJOR

[3]major *verb* **-jors; -jored; -jor•ing**

major in [*phrasal verb*] ***major in (something)*** *US, of a college or university student* **:** to have (a specified subject) as your main subject of study • In college, he *majored in* history and minored in French.

major on [*phrasal verb*] ***major on (something)*** *Brit* **:** to pay special attention to (something) • The carmaker *majors on* comfort in its new models.

ma•jor•do•mo /ˌmeɪʤɚˈdoʊmoʊ/ *noun, pl* **-mos** [*count*]

1 *old-fashioned* **:** the person who runs a large house

2 : someone who runs an organization or a project

ma•jor•ette /ˌmeɪʤəˈrɛt/ *noun, pl* **-ettes** [*count*] **:** a girl or woman who marches with a band and spins a baton — called also *drum majorette*

major general *noun, pl* **~ -als** [*count*] **:** a military officer of high rank in the army, air force, or marines

ma•jor•i•ty /məˈʤorəti/ *noun, pl* **-ties**

1 [*singular*] **:** a number that is greater than half of a total • Unfortunately, the *majority* of (the) students [=most of the students] in the class failed the test. • The policy is supported by the great/vast/overwhelming *majority* of (the) voters. • A clear *majority* of the voters support the policy.

2 a [*count*] **:** a number of votes that is more than half of the total number • They won by a *majority* of seven. [=the total number of votes they received was seven more than half of all the votes] • The proposal failed to win a *majority* in the Senate. [=the proposal was defeated because it was not voted for by more than half the senators] • The law will pass only if it is approved by at least a two-thirds *majority*. [=if two out of three voters approve it] **b** [*singular*] **:** the group or party that is the greater part of a large group • The Republicans/Democrats are currently the *majority* in the Senate. • Sup-

M

porters of the new law appear to be ***in the majority.*** [=there are more people who support the new law than who oppose it] — see also SILENT MAJORITY
3 [*noncount*] *law* **: the age at which a person is given the full rights of an adult** • The age of *majority* in the U.S. is 18. = The age when you reach your *majority* in the U.S. is 18. — compare MINORITY 4
– majority *adj, always used before a noun* • the *majority* opinion [=the opinion of most of the people] • a *majority* decision [=a decision supported by most of the people] • Republicans/Democrats are the *majority* party in the Senate.

majority leader *noun, pl* ~ **-ers** [*count*] **: the leader of the political party that has the most members in the U.S. Senate or House of Representatives** — compare MINORITY LEADER

majority rule *noun* [*noncount*] **: a political system in which the group that has the most members has the power to make decisions**

major leagues *noun*
the major leagues **: the two highest U.S. baseball leagues (the American League and the National League)** • He always dreamed of playing in *the major leagues.* [=(*US*) *the big leagues*] — sometimes used figuratively • She's moving up to *the major leagues* in the television industry. — compare MINOR LEAGUE
– major–league *adj* • *major-league* baseball • a *major-league* player — sometimes used figuratively • We've been experiencing some *major-league* problems. [=major problems, very serious problems] **– major leaguer** *noun, pl* ~ **-guers** [*count*] • He hopes to be a *major leaguer* [=(*US*) *big leaguer*] some day.

ma·jor·ly /ˈmeɪʤɚli/ *adv, informal* **: very or extremely** • She was *majorly* annoyed.

[1]**make** /ˈmeɪk/ *verb* **makes; made** /ˈmeɪd/; **mak·ing**
1 [+ *obj*] **a : to build, create, or produce (something) by work or effort** • *make* a box/chair/suit • *make* someone a dress = *make* a dress for someone • He works in a factory that *makes* jet engines. • She *made* the curtains herself. • He collected wood to *make* a fire. • She used cheese and a mixture of other ingredients to *make* a delicious sauce. — often followed by *with* to describe the things that are used to produce something • She *made* the sauce *with* cheese and other ingredients. — often followed by *of* to describe the material that forms something • The box is *made of* wood. [=it is a wood/wooden box; the material used to produce the box was wood] • The topping is *made* entirely *of* cheese. [=the topping consists entirely of cheese] — often followed by *from* to describe the source of a product • Cheese is *made from* milk. **b : to use (something) to create a product** — + *into* • She *made* the material *into* a dress. • She *made* a mixture of ingredients *into* a delicious sauce.
2 [+ *obj*] **: to cause (something) to exist, happen, or appear** • Someone was *making* a disturbance. • The car's engine has been *making* a strange noise lately. • The rock *made* a dent in the car's fender. • I'm not trying to *make* trouble. • The typist *made* a mistake. • I called the doctor's office to *make* an appointment. • They moved over and *made* room for her. • I want to *make* a good home for my children.
3 [+ *obj*] **: to create or write (something) in an official or legal way** • The government should *make* laws to protect poor people. • I don't *make* the rules; I just follow them. • You should *make* a will.
4 [+ *obj*] **: to produce, direct, or act in (something, such as a movie)** • a director who has *made* some classic films • That actor has *made* many films.
5 [+ *obj*] **: to cause (something or someone) to be changed in a specified way** • They adapted a Russian play and *made* the setting Dublin rather than Moscow. • We originally planned on a one-week vacation, but we decided to *make* it two weeks instead. • The experience *made* him a cynic. = The experience *made* a cynic (out) of him. = The experience *made* [=*changed, turned*] him into a cynic. • I'd like a hamburger. No, wait—*make* that a cheeseburger.
6 [+ *obj*] **: to cause (something or someone) to have a specified quality, feeling, etc.** • A good teacher *makes* learning enjoyable. • She *made* what she wanted clear to us. = She *made* (it) clear to us what she wanted. [=she said or showed clearly what she wanted] • He *made* it understood/known that he expected us to help. • The experience *made* him cynical. • Working in the garden *makes* me very tired. • It *makes* me sad to think that the summer is ending. • The photograph *makes* me seem/look fat. ✧ To ***make yourself useful*** means to do something useful. • Why don't you *make yourself useful* by washing the dishes? ✧ To ***make yourself heard/understood (etc.)*** means to do what is necessary to be sure that people hear you, understand you, etc. • The music was so loud that she could hardly *make herself heard.* • She doesn't speak French well, but she can *make herself understood.*
7 [+ *obj*] **: to cause (something) to be or become something** • A good teacher *makes* learning a pleasure. = A good teacher *makes* it a pleasure to learn. • Yes, you can leave work early today, but don't *make* it a habit. • The bright paint really *makes* the room come alive!
8 [+ *obj*] **a : to cause (someone) to do something** • He yelled at her and *made* her cry. • How can I *make* you understand that I love you?! **b : to force (someone) to do something** • We have to find a way to *make* them work faster. • They *made* me wait for an hour. • If he doesn't want to do it, we can't *make* him (do it). • They used threats to *make* her do it. = She was *made* to do it by the use of threats.
9 [+ *obj*] **: to give a particular job, title, status, etc., to (someone)** • They *made* him (the) Emperor. • They *made* her a member of their club. = She was *made* a member of their club.
10 [+ *obj*] **: to perform (a particular action)** • He *made* a bow. [=he bowed] • We *made* [=*took*] a detour to avoid traffic. • They *made* [=*got*] an early start. [=they started early] • I have to *make* a (telephone) call to my boss. [=I have to call/telephone my boss] • May I *make* a suggestion? [=may I suggest something?] • "*Make* love, not war!" shouted the demonstrators. • I'm not used to *making* [=*giving*] speeches. • They *made* a bet [=they bet] that she would win. • Don't *make* any sudden movements. • They *made* a contribution. [=they contributed] • We should *make* a distinction between them. • She *made* a promise to him. = She *made* him a promise. • He *made* note of her address. • Time is running out. You'll have to *make* a decision soon.
11 [+ *obj*] **: to form (a plan) in your mind** • Have you *made* any plans for your vacation?
12 [+ *obj*] **: to arrange the blankets and sheets on (a bed) so that the mattress is covered** • She always *makes* the bed after she gets up in the morning.
13 [+ *obj*] **: to prepare (food or drink)** • Let me *make* dinner for you. = Let me *make* you dinner. • Can I *make* you a drink? • I'll *make* the pasta if you *make* the salad. • She *made* a cake for her daughter's birthday.
14 a [*linking verb*] — **used to indicate a total** • That *makes* the third time you've said the same thing! • I've lost again! That *makes* $3 I owe you. • "I'm hungry." "***That makes two of us***" [=I'm hungry too] **b** [+ *obj*] **: to be equal to (an amount)** • Three plus two *make/makes* [=*equals, totals*] five. **c** [+ *obj*] **: to calculate (an amount, total, etc.)** • "What do you *make* the time?" [=what do you think the time is?] "(I *make* it) About half past three." • I *make* the distance back to camp about four miles. = I *make* it about four miles back to camp.
15 a [+ *obj*] **: to be used to produce (something)** • Rags *make* the best paper. **b** [*linking verb*] **: to be suited for use as (something)** • This new building would *make* [=*be*] a fine school. **c** [*linking verb*] **: to be or become (something)** • She and her boyfriend *make* [=*are*] a lovely couple. • She will *make* a fine judge one day. • She *made* [=*was*] a loving wife to him. = She *made* him a loving wife.
16 [+ *obj*] **: to arrive at (a place)** • The ship *made* port today.
17 [+ *obj*] **: to earn or gain (money, a profit, etc.)** • He *makes* $50,000 a year. • She *makes* a good salary. • Their products are so inexpensive I don't know how they *make* a profit. • She *made* $100 on the deal. = The deal *made* $100 for her. = The deal *made* her $100. • He ***makes a/his living*** by doing small jobs. • He ***made a/his fortune in*** the stock market.
18 [+ *obj*] **a : to be accepted as a member of (a group, team, etc.)** • She's finally *made* the team. **b : to appear on or in (a newspaper, a headline, etc.)** • The story of his accident *made* the front page of the paper. • The story *made* headlines all across the country. **c** *chiefly US* **: to be promoted to (a level or rank)** • My uncle is in the army. He *made* major last year.
19 [+ *obj*] *sports* **a : to succeed in doing (something that you attempt)** • I missed the first foul shot but *made* the second one. • He has to *make* this putt to win the tournament. — opposite MISS **b : to produce (a particular score)** • She *made* a 6 on the second hole. • He *made* a birdie/bogey.
20 [+ *obj*] **a : to not be too late for (something)** • They (just/barely) *made* the deadline. • We got to the station just in time to *make* the train. — opposite MISS **b : to reach or go to (a place)** • We *made* [=*reached*] Atlanta in just under two hours.

c : to succeed in reaching or going to (something) • The team *made* [=qualified for] the play-offs last year. • I don't know if I'll be able to *make* that meeting. — opposite MISS
21 [+ *obj*] : to act in a way that causes someone to be your friend, enemy, etc. • She *makes* friends easily. • He *made* a few enemies when he worked here.
22 [+ *obj*] : to cause the success of (someone or something) • This film could ***make or break*** her career. [=the success or failure of her career could depend on the success or failure of this film] — see also MAKE-OR-BREAK
23 [+ *obj*] : to cause (something) to be enjoyable, attractive, etc. • The bright paint really *makes* the room! • Meeting the star of the show really ***made our day***!
24 [*no obj*] *old-fashioned + literary* : to seem to begin an action • She *made* to go. = She *made* as if to go. [=she moved in a way that suggested she was going]

make a face see [1]FACE

make away with [*phrasal verb*] ***make away with (something)*** *literary* : to steal and take away (something) • Someone had *made away with* [=*made off with*] all the money.

make believe see BELIEVE

make do : to proceed or do what you can with the things that you have even though you do not have what you want • They didn't have much money but they somehow managed to *make do*. — often + *with* • If we can't get what we want, we'll just have to *make do with* what we've got. — often + *without* • If we don't have carrots for the soup, we'll just have to *make do without* them.

make eyes at see [1]EYE

make for [*phrasal verb*] ***make for (something)*** **1** : to go toward (a place) quickly • Everyone *made for* [=*headed for*] the exit as soon as the show was over. • After he left the office he *made* straight *for* home. **2** : to cause (something) to happen or to be more likely • Courtesy *makes for* safer driving.

make friends see FRIEND

make it **1** : to reach a particular place, goal, etc. • The ship *made it* to port. • You'll never *make it* that far. • The climbers finally *made it* to the top of the mountain. • Welcome to the party. I'm glad you could *make it*! = Welcome! I'm glad you could *make it* to the party! • The story *made it* to the front page. [=the story appeared on the front page] • She's finally *made it* onto the team. [=she finally was accepted on the team] • If we hurry, we can still *make it* home before dark. **2** : to not fail, die, etc. : SURVIVE • Many new businesses don't *make it* through their first year. • He's very sick. The doctor doesn't think he's going to *make it*. **3** : to become successful • It's tough to succeed in this business, but if you work hard I know you'll *make it* eventually. • He ***made it big*** [=became very successful] in real estate. **4** *chiefly US, informal* : to have sex • His girlfriend caught him *making it* with another girl.

make like *US, informal* **1** : to pretend to be (someone or something) • He *made like* a rooster and strutted across the stage. **2** : to act in a way that does not show your true feelings • He *made like* [=*acted like*] he didn't care.

make love see [1]LOVE

make merry see MERRY

make much of : to treat (something) as very important • In talking about his past, the book *makes much of* the influence of his brother. [=the book says that his brother's influence was very important] • She tends to *make* far too *much of* her problems. • You shouldn't *make* too *much of* what he said—he was only joking.

make nice see NICE

make of [*phrasal verb*] **1** ***make (something) of (something or someone)*** : to have or form an opinion about (something or someone) • What do you *make of* this? [=what is your opinion about this?] • I can't *make* anything *of* it at all. • I don't know what to *make of* her behavior. [=I don't understand her behavior] • He's a strange guy. I don't know quite what to *make of* him. **2** ***make (a day, night, etc.) of it*** : to continue with an enjoyable activity during all of (a day, night, etc.) • Since we're going out to dinner anyway, let's *make an evening of it* and go to a movie afterward. **3** ***make something of (yourself or your life)*** : to become successful • She has worked very hard to *make something of herself*. • He wants to *make something of his life*. [=to have a successful and productive life] **4** ***make something of it informal*** : to treat something as a reason for arguing or being angry — used in speech as an angry way of telling someone that you are prepared to fight or argue about something • Yes, I got home late last night. Do you want to *make something of it*? [=do you want to argue/fight about it?] — see also MAKE MUCH OF (above)

make off [*phrasal verb*] **1** *chiefly Brit* : to leave quickly especially in order to escape • After taking the money, the thieves *made off* toward the main highway. **2** ***make off with (something)*** : to take or steal (something) and go away • Someone broke into the office and *made off with* some valuable equipment.

make out [*phrasal verb*] **1** ***make (something) out*** or ***make out (something)*** : to write down the required information on (something, such as a check) • He *made out* a check for $100 to cover the cost of the repairs. • *make out* [=*fill out*] a form • The doctor will *make out* a prescription for you. = The doctor will *make* you *out* a prescription. • She *made out* a shopping list before going to the grocery store. **2** ***make (something) out*** or ***make out (something)*** **a** : to see and identify (something) • We could just *make out* a ship approaching through the fog. **b** : to hear and understand (something) • I couldn't quite *make out* what she said. **c** : to learn or understand (something) by studying, searching, etc. • I can't quite *make out* [=*tell*] whether he's drunk or sober. • We're still trying to *make out* [=*find out, figure out*] what really happened. **3** ***make (someone) out*** *informal* : to understand the behavior of (someone) — used in negative statements • I just *can't make* him *out* [=figure him out]—he's so contradictory. **4** ***make (someone or something) out*** : to describe (someone or something) in a specified and usually false way • The book *makes* them *out* to be criminals. • Don't *make* them *out* as worse than they are. • He's not as bad as he's *made out* (to be). = He's not as bad as people *make* him *out* (to be). **5** *informal* — used to ask about or describe the success or progress of someone or something • "How are you *making out* [=*doing, getting along*] in your new job?" "Just fine, thank you!" • "How did the team *make out* yesterday?" "They won." • (*US*) He ***made out like a bandit*** [=he made a lot of money] when he sold the company. **6** *chiefly US, informal* : to kiss and touch for a long time in a sexual way • She was *making out* [=(*old-fashioned*) *necking*] with her boyfriend.

make over [*phrasal verb*] **1** ***make (something or someone) over*** or ***make over (something or someone)*** : to change the appearance of (something or someone) • We *made* the whole house *over* so it looked more modern. — see also MAKEOVER **2** ***make (something) over*** or ***make over (something)*** : to give (property) to another person in an official or legal way • He *made* the ranch/shares *over* to his eldest son.

make up [*phrasal verb*] **1** ***make (something) up*** or ***make up (something)*** : to create or invent (a story, a lie, etc.) • He entertained the children by *making up* a funny story about a cat that lived on a sailboat. • He *made up* some excuse about having problems with his car, but no one believed him. • It never happened: you *made* it all *up*! • He didn't have a prepared speech. He just *made* it *up* as he went along. — see also MADE-UP **2** ***make (something) up*** or ***make up (something)*** **a** : to combine to produce (something) • Ten chapters *make up* this volume. = This volume is *made up* [=*composed*] of 10 chapters. **b** : to produce or create (something) by putting together different parts • They're going to *make up* a list of requirements for us. = They're going to *make* us *up* a list of requirements. **c** : to prepare (something) so that it is ready to be used • I'll *make up* a bed for you. = I'll *make* you *up* a bed. [=I'll prepare a bed for you to sleep in] **d** *Brit* : to supply (something) according to directions • *make up* [=(*US*) *fill*] a prescription **3** ***make (something) up*** or ***make up (something)*** : to provide an amount of time, money, etc., that is needed • The total cost of the repairs is $200. If you can pay half of that, I'll *make up* the rest. • I'll *make up* the difference. • I have to leave work early today, but I'll ***make up the time*** by working late tomorrow. **4** ***make up (someone or something)*** or ***make (someone or something) up*** **a** : to put makeup on (someone or someone's face) • She *made* herself *up* for the party. • Her face was heavily *made up*. [=there was a lot of makeup on her face] — see also MADE-UP **b** : to change the appearance of (someone or something) by using costumes, decorations, etc. • The actor was *made up* to look like George Washington. • The room was *made up* to look like a disco. **5** *informal* : to become friendly again after being angry • They quarreled but later *made up* (with each other). • He *made up* with his girlfriend. • (*chiefly Brit*) She's trying to ***make it up*** with him. **6** ***make up for (something)*** : to do or have something as a

M

way of correcting or improving (something else) • He wanted to *make up for* [=*atone for*] neglecting his children by spending more time with them. • She tried to *make up for* lost time by working extra hard. • What the movie lacks in plot it *makes up for* in special effects. **7** ***make up to (someone)*** *Brit, informal + disapproving* : to treat (someone) in a very friendly or helpful way in order to get something for yourself • an employee who's always *making up to* [=(*US, informal*) *sucking up to*] the boss **8** ***make it up to (someone)*** : to do something helpful or good for (someone you have hurt or treated wrongly) • He'd neglected his children and wanted to *make it up to* them by spending more time with them.

make up your mind see [1]MIND

make your way, make way see [1]WAY

— see also MADE

[2]**make** *noun, pl* **makes** [*count*] : a group of products that are all made by a particular company and given a particular name • The store sells computers in many different *makes* [=*brands*] and models. • "What *make* of car is that?" "I think it's a Ford."

on the make *informal + often disapproving* **1** : trying to get more money or power • He doesn't trust anyone in the movie business. He thinks that everyone in Hollywood is always *on the make*. **2** : trying to get sex • a beautiful woman who's often approached by guys *on the make*

make·able *or* **mak·able** /ˈmeɪkəbəl/ *adj* [*more ~; most ~*] *sports* : able to be made or likely to be made • a *makeable* putt • a *makable* field goal

[1]**make–be·lieve** /ˈmeɪkbəˌliːv/ *noun* [*noncount*] : things that are imagined or pretended to be true or real • He has been living in ***a world of make-believe***. [=he has been believing things that are not true; he has been living in a fantasy world] ✧ When children ***play make-believe***, they think of an imaginary world and pretend to live in it as people, animals, fairies, etc. — see also *make believe* at BELIEVE

[2]**make–believe** *adj, always used before a noun* : not real • The commercial showed a *make-believe* scientist in a white lab coat talking about the benefits of the product. • He has been living in a *make-believe* world.

make–or–break /ˈmeɪkɚˈbreɪk/ *adj, always used before a noun* : resulting in either definite success or definite failure • a *make-or-break* decision • The next year will be a *make-or-break* time for the company.

make·over /ˈmeɪkˌoʊvɚ/ *noun, pl* **-overs** [*count*] : the act or process of making changes to improve the appearance or effectiveness of someone or something • The actress had a complete *makeover* to turn her into a glamorous star. • They gave their advertising a total *makeover* to improve their corporate image. — see also *make over* at [1]MAKE

mak·er /ˈmeɪkɚ/ *noun, pl* **-ers**

1 [*count*] **a** : a person who makes something • a *maker* of action films — often used in combination • a film*maker* • a trouble*maker* • a glass*maker* • government policy-*makers* • a peace*maker* **b** : a company that makes a specified product • one of the nation's leading *makers* [=*manufacturers*] of fine cars • a *maker* of computer chips • computer *makers* — often used in combination • an auto*maker* **c** : a machine that makes something • an ice-cream *maker* • a pasta *maker* — often used in combination • a coffee*maker*

2 ***Maker*** [*singular*] : GOD • a hymn giving thanks to the *Maker* of all things

meet your maker *or* ***meet your Maker*** : to die • He says he's not afraid to *meet his maker*. — often used figuratively • My old car has finally gone to *meet its maker*.

make·shift /ˈmeɪkˌʃɪft/ *adj* : used as a usually rough and temporary replacement for something • A large box served as a *makeshift* table.

make·up /ˈmeɪkˌʌp/ *noun, pl* **-ups**

1 [*singular*] : the way in which something is put together or arranged — often + *of* • the *makeup of* the Earth's atmosphere • the ethnic *makeup of* the neighborhood • the *makeup* [=*layout*] *of* a printed page

2 [*singular*] : the physical, mental, and moral character of a person • His daring attitude toward risks is a major part of his *makeup*. • her psychological *makeup*

3 [*noncount*] **a** : substances (such as lipstick or powder) used to make someone's face look more attractive • She put on some *makeup* before the party. • She applied her *makeup* lightly/heavily. • wearing heavy/thick *makeup* • She's too young to wear *makeup*. • a *makeup* artist [=a person whose job is to put makeup on actors or models] **b** : materials (such as wigs or cosmetics) that are used to change the appearance of an actor • put on *makeup* for a play • I didn't recognize him when he was in his theatrical/stage *makeup*.

4 [*count*] *US* : a special test for a student who has missed or failed a previous test • He'll have to pass the *makeup* to graduate. — often used before another noun • a *makeup* exam/test/quiz — see also *make up* at [1]MAKE

mak·ing /ˈmeɪkɪŋ/ *noun, pl* **-ings**

1 [*noncount*] : the action or process of producing or making something • methods used in the *making* of wine — often used in combination • dress*making* • film*making* • government policy-*making*

2 [*noncount*] : something that causes someone to become better or more successful • His time in the army was ***the making of*** him. [=he became a better person because of his time in the army] • That movie was *the making of* her as an actress. [=that movie made her a well-known and successful actress]

3 ***makings*** [*plural*] **a** *US* : the people or things that are needed for making something • With beans, rice, cheese, and fresh salsa, you ***have (all) the makings of/for*** a delicious burrito. **b** : the qualities that are needed to become something • He ***has (all) the makings of*** a great quarterback. [=he has the talent needed to become a great quarterback]

in the making : in the process of being made • The film was three years *in the making*. [=it took three years to make the film] • She has a talent for spotting problems *in the making*. [=for spotting problems as they are beginning to develop] • We were watching ***history in the making***. [=we were watching an important historical event as it happened]

of your own making : caused by your own actions • The problem is entirely *of your own making*. [=the problem is entirely your own fault; you alone are responsible for the problem]

mal- *combining form* : bad or badly • *mal*practice • *mal*treatment • *mal*odorous

mal·ad·just·ed /ˌmæləˈʤʌstəd/ *adj* [*more ~; most ~*] : not able to deal with other people in a normal or healthy way • socially *maladjusted* people — opposite WELL-ADJUSTED

— **mal·ad·just·ment** /ˌmæləˈʤʌstmənt/ *noun* [*noncount*] • emotional *maladjustment*

mal·adroit /ˌmæləˈdroɪt/ *adj* [*more ~; most ~*] *formal* : very awkward : not skillful or adroit • The governor has been criticized for his *maladroit* handling of the budget crisis. • a socially *maladroit* teenager

— **mal·adroit·ly** *adv* — **mal·adroit·ness** *noun* [*noncount*]

mal·a·dy /ˈmælədi/ *noun, pl* **-dies** [*count*] *formal* : a disease or illness • The patient was suffering from a mysterious *malady* [=*ailment*] that the doctors were unable to identify. — often used figuratively • unemployment and other social *maladies*

mal·aise /məˈleɪz/ *noun*

1 *medical* : a slight or general feeling of not being healthy or happy [*noncount*] The symptoms include headache, *malaise*, and fatigue. [*singular*] An infected person will feel a general *malaise*. • a spiritual *malaise*

2 : a problem or condition that harms or weakens a group, society, etc. [*noncount*] postwar *malaise* [*singular*] The country's current economic problems are symptoms of a deeper *malaise*.

mal·a·prop·ism /ˈmæləˌprɑːpˌɪzəm/ *noun, pl* **-isms** [*count*] : an amusing error that occurs when a person mistakenly uses a word that sounds like another word but that has a very different meaning

ma·lar·ia /məˈlerijə/ *noun* [*noncount*] *medical* : a serious disease that causes chills and fever and that is passed from one person to another by the bite of mosquitoes

— **ma·lar·i·al** /məˈlerijəl/ *adj* • *malarial* fever

ma·lar·key /məˈlɑɚki/ *noun* [*noncount*] *informal* : foolish words or ideas : NONSENSE • He thinks everything politicians say is just a bunch of *malarkey*.

mal·con·tent /ˌmælkənˈtɛnt, *Brit* ˈmælkəntɛnt/ *noun, pl* **-tents** [*count*] *disapproving* : a person who is always or often unhappy or angry about something • He complained so much that he got a reputation for being a *malcontent*.

[1]**male** /ˈmeɪl/ *adj*

1 a : of or relating to the sex that cannot produce young or lay eggs • a *male* bird/mammal/insect • *male* athletes • a study of *male* [=*men's*] sexuality • There were more *male* than female students. **b** [*more ~; most ~*] : characteristic of boys or men • a *male* [=*masculine*] voice/name **c** : having members who are all boys or men • a *male* choir

2 *of a plant* : not producing fruit or seeds • a *male* holly

3 *technical* : having a part that fits into the hole in another part (called a female part) ▪ Most extension cords have a *male* plug on one end and a female plug on the other.

– **male·ness** *noun [noncount]*

[2]**male** *noun, pl* **males** *[count]*

1 : a man or a boy : a male person ▪ She attended a school where there were more *males* than females.

> ***usage*** The use of *male* to mean "man" or "boy" now occurs most commonly in scientific or technical language. ▪ According to the study, *males* scored about the same as females. ▪ The suspect was a white *male* aged about 30. In other contexts, it is often seen as a humorous or mildly insulting word. ▪ She referred to her husband's friends as "a bunch of clumsy *males*."

2 : a male animal ▪ The *male* of this species assists the female in feeding the young.

3 : a plant that does not produce seed or fruit : a male plant

male·fac·tor /ˈmæləˌfæktɚ/ *noun, pl* **-tors** *[count] formal* : someone who is guilty of a crime or offense : a person whose behavior is wrong or evil ▪ He favors harsh punishment for chronic *malefactors*. [=*criminals*]

ma·lev·o·lent /məˈlɛvələnt/ *adj [more ~; most ~] formal* : having or showing a desire to cause harm to another person ▪ Her reputation has been hurt by *malevolent* [=*malicious*] gossip. ▪ a *malevolent* demon ▪ a *malevolent* lie/smile

– **ma·lev·o·lence** /məˈlɛvələns/ *noun [noncount]* – **ma·lev·o·lent·ly** *adv*

mal·fea·sance /ˌmælˈfiːzn̩s/ *noun [noncount] law* : illegal or dishonest activity especially by a public official or a corporation ▪ The investigation has uncovered evidence of corporate *malfeasance*.

mal·for·ma·tion /ˌmælfoɚˈmeɪʃən/ *noun, pl* **-tions** *medical* : a condition in which part of the body does not have the normal or expected shape *[noncount]* The condition is marked by *malformation* of the spine. *[count]* She underwent surgery to correct a heart *malformation*.

mal·formed /ˌmælˈfoɚmd/ *adj, medical* : not having the normal or expected shape especially because of a problem in the way something has developed or grown : badly or improperly formed ▪ a *malformed* foot

mal·func·tion /ˌmælˈfʌŋkʃən/ *verb* **-tions; -tioned; -tion·ing** *[no obj]* : to fail to function or work properly ▪ A software problem is causing the system to *malfunction*.

– **malfunction** *noun, pl* **-tions** *[noncount]* The problem is causing *malfunction* of the system. *[count]* system *malfunctions*

mal·ice /ˈmæləs/ *noun [noncount]* : a desire to cause harm to another person ▪ an attack motivated by pure *malice* ▪ She claimed that her criticisms were without *malice*.

with malice aforethought *law* — used to describe a criminal act that was deliberately planned to cause harm to someone ▪ Murder is the killing of another person *with malice aforethought*.

ma·li·cious /məˈlɪʃəs/ *adj [more ~; most ~]* : having or showing a desire to cause harm to another person : having or showing malice ▪ a *malicious* liar ▪ *malicious* gossip ▪ a *malicious* distortion of the truth

– **ma·li·cious·ly** *adv* ▪ He claims his statements have been *maliciously* distorted. – **ma·li·cious·ness** *noun [noncount]*

[1]**ma·lign** /məˈlaɪn/ *verb* **-ligns; -ligned; -lign·ing** *[+ obj] formal* : to say bad things about (someone or something) publicly : to criticize (someone or something) harshly or unfairly ▪ Her supporters say she is being unfairly *maligned* in the press. ▪ I did not intend to *malign* [=*impugn*] his motives. ▪ They have given up their much-*maligned* [=widely criticized] attempt to reform tax policy.

[2]**malign** *adj [more ~; most ~] formal* : causing or intended to cause harm ▪ He has used his power for *malign* [=*malevolent*] purposes.

ma·lig·nan·cy /məˈlɪgnənsi/ *noun, pl* **-cies**

1 *[noncount] medical + formal* : a malignant quality or state ▪ the *malignancy* of the tumor

2 *[count] medical* : a tumor that is malignant ▪ The test revealed a *malignancy* in the patient's chest.

ma·lig·nant /məˈlɪgnənt/ *adj [more ~; most ~]*

1 *medical* : very serious and dangerous : tending or likely to grow and spread in a rapid and uncontrolled way that can cause death ▪ a *malignant* [=*cancerous*] tumor/growth ▪ a highly *malignant* form of cancer — opposite BENIGN

2 *formal* : very evil ▪ a powerful and *malignant* influence

– **ma·lig·nant·ly** *adv*

ma·lin·ger /məˈlɪŋgɚ/ *verb* **-gers; -gered; -ger·ing** *[no obj]* : to pretend to be sick or injured in order to avoid doing work ▪ His boss suspected him of *malingering* because of his frequent absences from work.

– **ma·lin·ger·er** /məˈlɪŋgərɚ/ *noun, pl* **-ers** *[count]*

mall /ˈmɑːl/ *noun, pl* **malls** *[count]*

1 : a large building or group of buildings containing stores of many different kinds and sizes ▪ They spent the afternoon shopping at the *mall*. — see also STRIP MALL

2 : a public area where people walk ▪ a pedestrian *mall*

mal·lard /ˈmæləd/ *noun, pl* **mallard** *or* **mal·lards** *[count]* : a very common kind of duck

mal·lea·ble /ˈmælijəbəl/ *adj [more ~; most ~]*

1 *technical* : capable of being stretched or bent into different shapes ▪ a *malleable* metal

2 *formal* : capable of being easily changed or influenced ▪ a *malleable* [=*flexible*] plan ▪ *malleable* young minds

– **mal·lea·bil·i·ty** /ˌmælijəˈbɪləti/ *noun [noncount]* ▪ the *malleability* of the metal

mal·let /ˈmælət/ *noun, pl* **-lets** *[count]*

1 : a hammer with a large usually wooden head

2 *sports* : a club used for hitting the ball in croquet or polo

mal·nour·ished /ˌmælˈnərɪʃt/ *adj [more ~; most ~]* : not eating enough food or not eating enough healthy food : poorly nourished ▪ *malnourished* children

mal·nu·tri·tion /ˌmælnuˈtrɪʃən, *Brit* ˌmælnjuˈtrɪʃən/ *noun [noncount]* : the unhealthy condition that results from not eating enough food or not eating enough healthy food : poor nutrition ▪ a program to help poor children suffering from *malnutrition*

mal·odor·ous /ˌmælˈoudərəs/ *adj [more ~; most ~] formal* : having a bad smell ▪ a *malodorous* [=*smelly*] mixture of chemicals

mal·prac·tice /ˌmælˈpræktəs/ *noun [noncount] law* : careless, wrong, or illegal actions by someone (such as a doctor) who is performing a professional duty ▪ a surgeon accused of *malpractice* ▪ Doctors need to have *malpractice* insurance to protect themselves against lawsuits.

malt /ˈmɑːlt/ *noun, pl* **malts**

1 *[noncount]* : grain and especially barley that is soaked in water and used in making alcoholic drinks (such as beer and whiskey)

2 *[count] US, informal* : MALTED MILK ▪ a chocolate *malt*

3 *[count, noncount]* : MALT WHISKEY

[1]**malt·ed** /ˈmɑːltəd/ *adj, always used before a noun* : changed into malt ▪ *malted* grain/barley

[2]**malted** *noun, pl* **-eds** *[count] US, informal* : MALTED MILK ▪ ordered a hot dog and a chocolate *malted*

malted milk *noun, pl* **~ milks** *[count, noncount] US* : a drink made by mixing a special powder of malted grains and dried milk into a liquid (such as milk) and usually adding ice cream and flavoring

malt liquor *noun, pl* **~ -quors** *[count, noncount] US* : a type of beer that has a high amount of alcohol

mal·treat /ˌmælˈtriːt/ *verb* **-treats; -treat·ed; -treat·ing** *[+ obj]* : to treat (someone) in a rough or cruel way ▪ He claims that he was *maltreated* [=(more commonly) *mistreated, abused*] by the prison guards.

– **mal·treat·ment** /ˌmælˈtriːtmənt/ *noun [noncount]*

malt whiskey *(US) or Brit* **malt whisky** *noun, pl* **~ -keys** *[count, noncount]* : whiskey made in Scotland from malted barley

mam /ˈmæm/ *noun, pl* **mams** *[count] Brit, informal* : a person's mother

ma·ma *or* **mam·ma** *also* **mom·ma** /ˈmɑːmə/ *noun, pl* **-mas** *[count] informal* : a person's mother — used especially by young children ▪ Where's *mama*? ▪ Read me a story, *Mama*! — compare PAPA

mama's boy *noun, pl* **~ boys** *[count] US, disapproving* : a boy or man who is seen as weak because he is controlled or protected too much by his mother

mam·bo /ˈmɑːmbou, *Brit* ˈmæmbəu/ *noun, pl* **-bos**

1 *[count]* : a lively dance originally from Cuba ▪ They learned to dance the *mambo*.

2 *[count, noncount]* : the music for the mambo ▪ The band played a *mambo*.

mam·mal /ˈmæməl/ *noun, pl* **-mals** *[count]* : a type of animal that feeds milk to its young and that usually has hair or fur covering most of its skin ▪ Human beings, dogs, and cats are all *mammals*.

M

– **mam·ma·li·an** /məˈmeılijən/ *adj, technical* ▪ characteristics of the *mammalian* brain ▪ *mammalian* species

mam·ma·ry /ˈmæməri/ *adj, technical* : of or relating to the breasts ▪ *mammary* cells

mammary gland *noun, pl* ~ **glands** [*count*] *technical* : a gland in a woman's breast or in a female animal that produces milk

mam·mo·gram /ˈmæməˌgræm/ *noun, pl* **-grams** [*count*] *medical* : a photograph of a woman's breasts made by X-rays ▪ She went to the hospital for her yearly *mammogram.*

– **mam·mog·ra·phy** /mæˈmɑːgrəfi/ *noun* [*noncount*]

[1]**mam·moth** /ˈmæməθ/ *noun, pl* **-moths** [*count*]

1 : a type of large, hairy elephant that lived in ancient times and that had very long tusks that curved upward

2 : something that is very large ▪ The little business she started by herself has now become a *mammoth* [=giant] in the industry.

mammoth

[2]**mammoth** *adj* [*more* ~; *most* ~] : very large ▪ a *mammoth* [=huge, gigantic] building ▪ Renovating the house is a *mammoth* undertaking.

[1]**man** /ˈmæn/ *noun, pl* **men** /ˈmɛn/

1 [*count*] : an adult male human being ▪ He was a shy boy, but he grew to be a strong and confident *man.* ▪ He's a grown *man* now. ▪ The movie is popular with *men* and women. ▪ He's a *man* of great talent. = He's a very talented *man.* ▪ a good/bad *man*

2 : a man or boy who shows the qualities (such as strength and courage) that men are traditionally supposed to have [*count*] Don't cry, little boy: ***be a man!*** ▪ A few years in the army will ***make a (real) man (out) of*** you! [*noncount*] Are you *man* enough to meet the challenge?

3 : a woman's husband or boyfriend [*count*] Who's the new *man* in her life? = Who's her new *man*? [*noncount*] I now pronounce you *man* [=*husband*] and wife. — see also OLD MAN

4 a [*count*] : an individual human being : PERSON ▪ Time waits for no *man.* [=for no one] ▪ the differences between *men* [=*people*] and beasts/animals ▪ He believes that all *men* are created equal. **b** [*noncount*] : the human race ▪ prehistoric *man* ▪ It's not a fit night out for *man* or/nor beast. [=for people or animals] ▪ the problems facing ***modern man*** [=the human race in modern times] ✧ Senses 4a and 4b are now sometimes avoided because they are considered sexist.

5 [*count*] — used when you are talking to a man ▪ (*chiefly US, informal*) Hey, *man,* how are you? ▪ (*old-fashioned*) Pull yourself together, *man!* ▪ Okay, *men,* let's go out there and win! ▪ (*US, informal*) Hey, ***my man!*** It's good to see you! ▪ (*chiefly Brit, old-fashioned*) ***My good man,*** can you tell me where the railroad station is?

6 [*count*] : a male worker who goes to people's homes ▪ The furnace *man* came to repair the heater.

7 men [*plural*] : a group of male workers, soldiers, etc. ▪ The *men* have threatened to go on strike. ▪ He led his *men* into battle against overwhelming odds.

8 [*count*] **a** : a man who does a particular kind of work ▪ a medical/military *man* **b** : a man who has a specified job or position or who belongs to a specified category of worker — used in combination ▪ a council*man* ▪ Has the mail*man* come yet? ▪ He's a shrewd business*man.* **c** : a man who works for or represents a particular person or organization ▪ our *man* in Washington ▪ He spoke with the president's *man.*

9 [*count*] *old-fashioned* : a male servant — usually singular ▪ My *man* will show you to your room.

10 [*count*] **a** *somewhat old-fashioned* : a male student or former student at a college or university ▪ He's a Harvard *man.* **b** : a man who comes from or lives in a specified town, city, etc. — used chiefly by journalists ▪ One of the accident victims has been identified as a Boston *man.*

11 [*count*] : a man who likes something very much or who is known for some activity or interest ▪ I'm strictly a vanilla ice cream *man.* [=I'm a man who likes vanilla ice cream]

12 [*singular*] **a** : a person who can do what is needed ▪ If you need someone to help organize the files, ***I'm/he's/she's your man!*** [=I'm/he's/she's the person you need for the job] **b** : the person someone (such as a police officer) is looking for ▪ He matches the description, but I don't think he's our *man.* ▪ a detective who always ***gets his man*** [=catches the criminal]

13 [*count*] : one of the pieces in a game like chess or checkers

a fine figure of a man see [1]FIGURE

as one man *old-fashioned, now usually used of a group of men* : as a group : all together ▪ The audience rose *as one man* [=everyone in the audience stood up] and cheered.

be/become your own man : to be or become a man who is not controlled by other people or who is able to support himself without the help of other people ▪ He left home and moved to the city to *become his own man.*

every man for himself — used to describe a situation in which people do not help each other and each person has to take care of himself or herself ▪ As soon as there was a crisis, it was *every man for himself.*

iron man see [2]IRON

man of action see ACTION

man of the hour see HOUR

man's best friend — used to refer to a dog or to dogs as a group ▪ She devotes her life to helping *man's best friend.*

poor man's see POOR

separate the men from the boys see [2]SEPARATE

the man *US, informal* **1** *or* ***the Man*** *somewhat old-fashioned* : the police ▪ He got in trouble with *the Man* and ended up in jail. **2** *or* ***the Man*** *also* ***The Man*** : the white people who are seen as having power in the U.S. : the white establishment ▪ He got a job working for *the Man.* **3** : a man who is admired or respected as a leader or as the best man in a particular field, sport, etc. ▪ The other players on the team all know that he's *the man.* ▪ You're *the man!* = (*very informal*) You *the man!* = (*very informal + humorous*) ***You da man!***

the man in the street *or Brit* ***the man on the Clapham omnibus*** : the ordinary and average person ▪ What does *the man in the street* think about it?

the odd man out see ODD

to a man — used to say that all the members in a group of men said, did, or thought the same thing ▪ He worried that some of his friends might object, but, *to a man,* they supported his decision. [=all of them supported his decision]

to the last man : until all the men in a group are killed, defeated, etc. ▪ They vowed to fight *to the last man.*

[2]**man** *interj, chiefly US, informal* — used to express excitement, surprise, etc. ▪ *Man,* what a game! ▪ Oh *man,* I can't believe she said that! ▪ *Man,* how much longer can this hot weather last?

[3]**man** *verb* **mans; manned; man·ning** [+ *obj*]

1 : to be the person who controls or is in charge of (something) ▪ He stocked shelves while I *manned* the cash register. ▪ We'll need someone to *man* the phones this evening. ▪ No one was *manning* the front desk.

2 : to place people at or on (something) to do work ▪ *man* the sails/lifeboats — see also MANNED

man–about–town /ˌmænəˌbaʊtˈtaʊn/ *noun* [*singular*] *somewhat old-fashioned* : a man who goes to many popular parties, clubs, etc.

man·a·cle /ˈmænıkəl/ *noun, pl* **-a·cles** [*count*] : either one of a set of two metal rings designed to lock around a person's wrists or ankles — usually plural ▪ The prisoner was led into the courtroom in *manacles.*

– **manacle** /ˈmænıkəl/ *verb* **-cles; -cled; -cling** [+ *obj*] ▪ The prisoner was *manacled* and led into the courtroom.

man·age /ˈmænıʤ/ *verb* **-ag·es; -aged; -ag·ing**

1 [+ *obj*] **a** : to have control of (something, such as a business, department, sports team, etc.) ▪ She *manages* [=*runs*] her family's bakery. ▪ The business is *managed* by the owner's daughter. ▪ The company is badly *managed.* ▪ When she *managed* the department, we never missed a deadline. **b** : to take care of and make decisions about (someone's time, money, etc.) ▪ He *manages* his own finances. ▪ You need to *manage* [=*use*] your time more wisely. **c** : to direct the professional career of (someone, such as an entertainer or athlete) ▪ an agency that *manages* entertainers — see also STAGE-MANAGE

2 [+ *obj*] **a** : to control the movements or actions of (something) ▪ She *manages* [=*handles*] her skis well. ▪ He is skillful in *managing* horses. : to keep (something) under your control ▪ He's not able to *manage* [=(more commonly) *control*] his emotions. ▪ This form of diabetes can be *managed* by diet. [=it can be controlled by eating a certain way] **b** : to

M

control the behavior of (a child, animal, etc.) ▪ She has difficulty *managing* [=*handling*] her young students.
3 [+ *obj*] **:** to use (something) carefully and without waste ▪ There's enough food if we *manage* it well. ▪ We need to do a better job of *managing* our natural resources.
4 a [*no obj*] **:** to be able to live or to do what is needed by using what you have even though you do not have much — often + *on* ▪ When he lost his job, we didn't know if we could *manage* [=*get by*] *on* just my salary. — often + *with* or *without* ▪ I wonder how they *manage with* so little income. ▪ We'll have to *manage with* just one car. ▪ This kind of plant can *manage* [=*survive*] *with* very little water. ▪ They'll have to *manage* [=*get by*] *without* presents this year. [=they'll have to accept that they are not getting presents this year] **b :** to succeed in doing (something) [+ *obj*] "We'll need to talk about this again. Can you *manage* a meeting next week?" ▪ With his ankle broken, he could only *manage* (taking) a few steps at a time. ▪ She wasn't feeling well, but she still *managed* a smile for the photographers. ▪ He's too weak to *manage* the stairs on his own. [=to go up/down the stairs on his own] — often followed by *to + verb* ▪ She never studies but always *manages to pass* her tests. ▪ He always *manages to win* somehow. ▪ Somehow, they've *managed to avoid* trouble. ▪ We were poor, but we still *managed to have* enough to eat. ▪ How'd they *manage to get away* with it? ▪ It was tough, but we *managed* not *to let* the secret out. ▪ Only a few passengers *managed to survive* the crash. ▪ These plants *manage to stay* alive with very little water. ▪ They couldn't get tickets, but we *managed to*. [*no obj*] I don't know how we ever *managed* without you. ▪ It's hard living alone, but somehow I *manage*. ▪ "Do you need help with that suitcase?" "No, thanks. I think I can *manage*."

man·age·able /ˈmænɪʤəbəl/ *adj* [*more* ~; *most* ~] **:** easy to control or deal with ▪ We bought smaller, more *manageable* suitcases. ▪ They divided the students into three *manageable* groups. ▪ *manageable* and unmanageable problems ▪ The conditioner makes your hair more *manageable*.
— **man·age·abil·i·ty** /ˌmænɪʤəˈbɪləti/ *noun* [*noncount*]

man·age·ment /ˈmænɪʤmənt/ *noun, pl* **-ments**
1 a [*noncount*] **:** the act or skill of controlling and making decisions about a business, department, sports team, etc. ▪ She's planning a career in (business) *management*. ▪ Business improved under the *management* of new owners. ▪ She's responsible for the day-to-day *management* [=*running*] of the hospital. ▪ a smart *management* decision ▪ We're using new *management* techniques/practices. **b :** the people who make decisions about a business, department, sports team, etc. [*noncount*] To save money, (the) *management* decided to reduce the size of the staff. ▪ *Management* and labor could not agree. ▪ He has a job in middle *management*. ▪ senior/top *management* ▪ (The) *Management* is planning to hire more workers. = (*Brit*) (The) *Management* are planning to hire more workers. ▪ The restaurant is now ***under new management***. [=is now controlled by different people] [*count*] The *managements* of several top corporations met yesterday.
2 [*noncount*] **:** the act or process of deciding how to use something ▪ He's extremely cautious when it comes to money *management*. [=he is careful about the way he uses money] ▪ time *management* ▪ a new system of water *management*
3 [*noncount*] **:** the act or process of controlling and dealing with something ▪ anger *management* ▪ crisis *management*

man·ag·er /ˈmænɪʤɚ/ *noun, pl* **-ers** [*count*]
1 : someone who is in charge of a business, department, etc. ▪ I'd like to speak to the *manager*, please. ▪ He was promoted to *manager* last year. ▪ a sales/bank/personnel *manager* ▪ The team's ***general manager*** acquired five new players for the upcoming season. — see also STAGE MANAGER
2 : someone who directs the training and performance of a sports team; *especially, US* **:** a person who directs a baseball team ▪ The *manager* decided to change pitchers in the eighth inning.
3 : someone who directs the professional career of an entertainer or athlete ▪ The actress recently fired her *manager*.
4 : someone who decides how to use something ▪ She's a bad *manager* of her time/money.

man·ag·er·ess /ˈmænɪʤərəs/ *noun, pl* **-ess·es** [*count*] *Brit* **:** a woman who is in charge of a business, shop, etc.

man·a·ge·ri·al /ˌmænəˈʤirijəl/ *adj*
1 : relating to the skill or process of controlling and making decisions about a business or organization ▪ They lack the *managerial* experience needed for the job. ▪ a change in (their) *managerial* practices
2 : of or relating to a manager or group of managers ▪ *managerial* positions ▪ a *managerial* team

managing director *noun, pl* ~ **-tors** [*count*] **:** someone who is in charge of a large company or organization

managing editor *noun, pl* ~ **-tors** [*count*] **:** an editor who is in charge of the editorial activities of a newspaper, magazine, etc.

man·a·tee /ˈmænəˌtiː/ *noun, pl* **-tees** [*count*] **:** a large animal that lives in warm waters and eats plants

man·da·rin /ˈmændərən/ *noun, pl* **-rins**
1 [*count*] **:** a small type of orange — called also *mandarin orange*
2 [*count*] **:** a public official in China in the past
3 ***Mandarin*** [*noncount*] **:** the official language of China

¹man·date /ˈmænˌdeɪt/ *noun, pl* **-dates** [*count*] *formal*
1 : an official order to do something ▪ Royal *mandates* must be obeyed. ▪ They carried out the governor's *mandate* to build more roads.
2 : the power to act that voters give to their elected leaders ▪ He won the election so convincingly that he believed he had been given a *mandate* for change/reform. — often followed by *to + verb* ▪ He believed he had been given a *mandate* (from the people) *to implement* his policies. ▪ There is no *mandate to raise* taxes.

²mandate *verb* **-dates; -dat·ed; -dat·ing** [+ *obj*] *chiefly US, formal*
1 : to officially demand or require (something) ▪ Ours was the first state to *mandate* [=*order*] the change. ▪ The law *mandates* that every car have seat belts. — often used as *(be) mandated* ▪ Drug tests have *been mandated* by the government. ▪ a *mandated* [=*required, mandatory*] drug test
2 : to officially give (someone) the power to do something ▪ He won the election so convincingly that he believed the people had *mandated* him to carry out his policies.

man·da·to·ry /ˈmændəˌtori, *Brit* ˈmændətri/ *adj* **:** required by a law or rule ▪ This meeting is *mandatory* for all employees. [=all employees must go to this meeting] ▪ The *mandatory* fine for littering is $200. [=everyone caught littering must pay $200] ▪ a *mandatory* retirement age [=an age at which workers are required to retire] ▪ a *mandatory* drug test

man·di·ble /ˈmændəbəl/ *noun, pl* **-di·bles** [*count*]
1 : JAWBONE
2 : either the upper or lower part of a bird's beak
3 : a part of an insect's mouth that looks like a jaw and is often used for biting things

man·do·lin /ˌmændəˈlɪn/ *noun, pl* **-lins** [*count*] **:** a small musical instrument that has a long neck, a body that is shaped like a pear, and usually four pairs of strings

mane /ˈmeɪn/ *noun, pl* **manes** [*count*]
1 : long, thick hair growing from the neck of a horse or around the neck of a lion — see picture at HORSE
2 *informal* **:** long, thick hair on a person's head ▪ an actor with a thick *mane* of silver hair

man–eat·er /ˈmænˌiːtɚ/ *noun, pl* **-ers** [*count*]
1 : an animal (such as a shark or a tiger) that kills and eats people
2 *humorous* **:** an attractive woman who has many lovers
— **man–eat·ing** /ˈmænˌiːtɪŋ/ *adj* ▪ *man-eating* tigers ▪ a *man-eating* shark

¹ma·neu·ver (*US*) or *Brit* **ma·noeu·vre** /məˈnuːvɚ/ *noun, pl* **-vers**
1 : a clever or skillful action or movement [*count*] With a quick *maneuver*, she avoided an accident. ▪ acrobats performing dangerous *maneuvers* ▪ Through a series of legal *maneuvers*, the defense lawyer kept her client out of jail. [*noncount*] The strict requirements left us very little ***room for maneuver***. [=opportunity to make changes or to do things differently in order to produce a better result]
2 a [*count*] **:** a planned movement of soldiers or ships ▪ He led his troops in a well-planned *maneuver*. **b** ***maneuvers*** [*plural*] **:** military activities that are done for training ▪ To prepare for war, the army is performing/conducting *maneuvers* off the coast. ▪ The army is ***on maneuvers***.

²maneuver (*US*) or *Brit* **manoeuvre** *verb* **-vers; -vered; -ver·ing**
1 *always followed by an adverb or preposition* **:** to move (something or someone) in a careful and usually skillful way [+ *obj*] She *maneuvered* her car into the tiny garage. ▪ It took seven people to *maneuver* the tiger out of its cage. ▪ We had a hard time *maneuvering* our furniture through the doorway. [*no obj*] The giant ships *maneuvered* into their docks. ▪ The vehicle easily *maneuvered* through rocky terrain. ▪ They held

M

hands while *maneuvering* through the crowd.

2 : to do something in an effort to get an advantage, get out of a difficult situation, etc. [*no obj*] The companies are *maneuvering* for position in the limited market. • The strict requirements left us very little ***room to maneuver*** [=opportunity to make changes or to do things differently in order to produce a better result] [+ *obj*] Somehow, she always manages to *maneuver* herself out of difficult situations. • He *maneuvered* his way into her heart. [=he did things to make her love him] — see also OUTMANEUVER

3 : to move (soldiers, ships, etc.) where they are needed for battle [+ *obj*] We *maneuvered* our troops to the south. [*no obj*] The opposing forces *maneuvered* quickly.

– maneuvering *noun, pl* **-ings** [*noncount*] It took a lot of legal *maneuvering* for the defense lawyer to keep her client out of jail. [*count*] political *maneuverings*

ma•neu•ver•able (*US*) *or Brit* **ma•noeu•vra•ble** /məˈnuːvərəbəl/ *adj* [*more* ~; *most* ~] **:** able to be moved quickly, easily, or in small spaces • The new ships are faster and more *maneuverable*. • a highly *maneuverable* airplane

– ma•neu•ver•abil•i•ty (*US*) *or Brit* **ma•noeu•vra•bil•i•ty** /məˌnuːvərəˈbɪləti/ *noun* [*noncount*] • They've improved the ship's speed and *maneuverability*.

man•ful•ly /ˈmænfəli/ *adv* **:** in a brave and strong way **:** in a manly way • He *manfully* accepted the challenge. • He walked *manfully* into the courtroom.

man•ga•nese /ˈmæŋgəˌniːz/ *noun* [*noncount*] **:** a grayish-white usually hard metal that breaks easily

mange /ˈmeɪnʤ/ *noun* [*noncount*] **:** a skin disease of animals (such as cats and dogs) and sometimes people that causes itching and loss of hair

man•ger /ˈmeɪnʤɚ/ *noun, pl* **-gers** [*count*] **:** an open box in which food for farm animals is placed

mange•tout /ˌmɑːnʒˈtuː/ *noun, pl* **mangetout** *or* **mange-touts** [*count*] *Brit* **:** SNOW PEA

[1]**man•gle** /ˈmæŋgəl/ *verb* **man•gles; man•gled; man•gling** [+ *obj*]

1 : to injure or damage (something or someone) severely by cutting, tearing, or crushing • His leg had been *mangled* by an explosion. • a *mangled* piece of metal

2 : to do (something) badly **:** to ruin (something) because of carelessness or a lack of skill • The newspaper *mangled* the story. [=it did not report the story correctly] • He *mangled* [=*botched*] the speech. • They *mangled* my favorite song!

[2]**mangle** *noun, pl* **mangles** [*count*] **:** an old-fashioned machine used to squeeze water out of wet clothes after they have been washed

man•go /ˈmæŋgoʊ/ *noun, pl* **man•goes** *also* **man•gos** [*count*] **:** a juicy tropical fruit that has firm yellow and red skin and a hard seed at its center — see color picture on page C5

man•grove /ˈmænˌgroʊv/ *noun, pl* **-groves** [*count*] **:** a tropical tree that has roots which grow from its branches and that grows in swamps or shallow salt water • a *mangrove* swamp

mangy /ˈmeɪnʤi/ *adj* **mang•i•er; -est**

1 *of an animal* **:** having a skin disease that causes itching and loss of hair **:** suffering from mange • a *mangy* dog

2 : having thin or bare spots • She finally threw out that *mangy* [=*shabby*] old rug. • a *mangy* beard

man•han•dle /ˈmænˌhændl̩/ *verb* **-han•dles; -han•dled; -han•dling** [+ *obj*]

1 : to move (something) by using rough force • They *manhandled* the heavy boxes onto the truck. • She *manhandled* the posts into place.

2 : to treat (someone) in a rough or physically harmful way • He was *manhandling* the boy. • He says he was *manhandled* by the police.

man•hole /ˈmænˌhoʊl/ *noun, pl* **-holes** [*count*] **:** a covered hole in a street that a person can go down into to do work under the street

man•hood /ˈmænˌhʊd/ *noun*

1 [*noncount*] **:** the qualities (such as strength and courage) that are expected in a man • He took the comment as a challenge to his *manhood*. • Boxing was a way for him to ***prove his manhood*** [=to prove that he was a strong/brave man]

2 [*noncount*] **:** the state or condition of being an adult man and no longer a boy • He grew from boyhood to *manhood* in a small southern town. • In his early *manhood* [=when he was a young man] he decided to become a doctor.

3 [*noncount*] **:** adult men • the *manhood* of a nation

4 [*singular*] *literary + humorous* **:** a man's penis • He wore no clothing except a cloth that hid his *manhood*.

man–hour /ˈmænˈawɚ/ *noun, pl* **-hours** [*count*] **:** an hour of work done by one worker • The job will take at least 300 *man-hours* and cost about $20 per *man-hour*.

man•hunt /ˈmænˌhʌnt/ *noun, pl* **-hunts** [*count*] **:** an organized search for a person and especially for a criminal • After several days of searching, the sheriff called off the *manhunt*. • The FBI launched a *manhunt* to find the kidnappers.

ma•nia /ˈmeɪnijə/ *noun, pl* **-nias**

1 : mental illness in which a person becomes very emotional or excited [*noncount*] She would typically experience a period of *mania* and then suddenly become deeply depressed. [*count*] patients affected by *manias*

2 : extreme enthusiasm for something that is usually shared by many people [*count*] — usually singular • The band was part of the early rock-and-roll *mania*. [=*craze*] • The city's sports *mania* is very well-known. — often + *for* • He had a *mania for* cleanliness. [*noncount*] The entire city has been gripped by baseball *mania*.

ma•ni•ac /ˈmeɪniˌæk/ *noun, pl* **-acs** [*count*]

1 : someone who is violent and mentally ill • The movie he rented was about a *maniac* [=*madman, lunatic*] who goes on a murderous rampage. • a homicidal *maniac*

2 *informal* **:** a person who behaves in a very wild way • He's a complete *maniac* when he's playing football. • She drives ***like a maniac*** [=she drives in a very reckless and dangerous way]

3 *informal* **:** a person who is extremely enthusiastic about something • His friends are all sports *maniacs*. [=*fanatics*] • a movie *maniac* [=*freak*]

– maniac *adj, always used before a noun* [*more* ~; *most* ~] • *maniac* killers/fans **– ma•ni•a•cal** /məˈnajəkəl/ *adj* [*more* ~; *most* ~] • a *maniacal* killer/fan • She let out a *maniacal* laugh. • *maniacal* sports fans **– ma•ni•a•cal•ly** /məˈnajəkli/ *adv* • laughing *maniacally*

man•ic /ˈmænɪk/ *adj* [*more* ~; *most* ~]

1 : having or relating to a mental illness that causes someone to become very excited or emotional • The patient has a *manic* personality. = The patient is *manic*. • a *manic* state/mood

2 : very excited, energetic, or emotional • a *manic* sense of humor • *manic* behavior/fans

– man•i•cal•ly /ˈmænɪkli/ *adv*

manic depression *noun* [*noncount*] **:** a mental illness in which a person experiences periods of strong excitement and happiness followed by periods of sadness and depression — called also *bipolar disorder, manic-depressive illness*

man•ic–de•press•ive /ˌmænɪkdɪˈprɛsɪv/ *noun, pl* **-ives** [*count*] **:** someone who is affected by manic depression • Her brother is a *manic-depressive*.

– manic–depressive *adj* • He takes medicine to control his *manic-depressive* behavior. • a *manic-depressive* patient

man•i•cot•ti /ˌmænəˈkɑːti/ *noun* [*noncount*] *US* **:** a type of pasta in the shape of tubes that are usually filled with meat or cheese and covered with tomato sauce

[1]**man•i•cure** /ˈmænəˌkjɚ/ *noun, pl* **-cures** [*count*] **:** a treatment to improve the appearance and health of the hands and fingernails • She gets a *manicure* every week or so. — compare PEDICURE

[2]**manicure** *verb* **-cures; -cured; -cur•ing** [+ *obj*]

1 : to give a beauty treatment to (someone's hands and fingernails) **:** to give a manicure to (someone's hands and fingernails) • She *manicured* her nails.

2 : to make (something, such as a lawn or a garden) look neat, smooth, and attractive • She spends her weekends working in her garden and *manicuring* her lawn.

– manicured *adj* • *manicured* hands • carefully *manicured* gardens • a well-*manicured* lawn

man•i•cur•ist /ˈmænəˌkjərɪst/ *noun, pl* **-ists** [*count*] **:** a person who does beauty treatments for the hands and fingernails **:** a person who gives manicures

[1]**man•i•fest** /ˈmænəˌfɛst/ *adj* [*more* ~; *most* ~] *formal*

1 : able to be seen **:** clearly shown or visible • Their sadness was *manifest* in their faces. • His love for literature is *manifest* in his large library. • There was *manifest* confusion in the streets.

2 : easy to understand or recognize • The truth was *manifest* [=(more commonly) *obvious*] to everyone but me. • a *manifest* injustice

– man•i•fest•ly *adv* • The decision was *manifestly* [=*clearly, obviously*] unjust.

[2]**manifest** *verb* **-fests; -fest•ed; -fest•ing** [+ *obj*] *formal* **:** to show (something) clearly • Both sides have *manifested* a

stubborn unwillingness to compromise. • Their religious beliefs are *manifested* in every aspect of their lives. • Love *manifests* [=*reveals*] itself in many different ways. [=love appears in many ways] • Her behavior problems began *manifesting* themselves soon after she left home.

man·i·fes·ta·tion /ˌmænəfəˈsteɪʃən/ *noun, pl* **-tions** [*count*] *formal*
1 : a sign that shows something clearly — usually + *of* • The first *manifestations of* her behavior problems occurred soon after she left home. • Her work with the poor was a *manifestation* [=*indication*] *of* her compassionate nature.
2 : one of the forms that something has when it appears or occurs • Hate in all its *manifestations* [=*forms*] is wrong.
3 : an occurrence in which the ghost or spirit of a dead person appears • ghostly *manifestations*

manifest destiny *or* **Manifest Destiny** *noun* [*noncount*] *formal* **:** a future event that is sure to happen **:** a destiny that can be clearly seen and that cannot be changed • They were living in a time when expansion to the Pacific was regarded by many people as the *Manifest Destiny* of the United States.

man·i·fes·to /ˌmænəˈfɛstoʊ/ *noun, pl* **-tos** *or* **-toes** [*count*] **:** a written statement that describes the policies, goals, and opinions of a person or group • The group's *manifesto* focused on helping the poor and stopping violence. • a political party's *manifesto*

[1]**man·i·fold** /ˈmænəˌfoʊld/ *adj, formal* **:** many and various • the country's *manifold* problems • The benefits of this approach are *manifold.*

[2]**manifold** *noun, pl* **-folds** [*count*] *technical* **:** a part of an engine that connects different pipes for moving fuel and air into the engine or for carrying gases away from the engine • an ***intake manifold*** [=a manifold that brings fuel and air into an engine] • an ***exhaust manifold*** — see picture at CAR

man·i·kin *also* **man·ni·kin** /ˈmænɪkən/ *noun, pl* **-kins** [*count*] **:** MANNEQUIN

ma·nila /məˈnɪlə/ *adj* **:** made of strong, light brown paper • a *manila* folder • *manila* envelopes

ma·nip·u·late /məˈnɪpjəˌleɪt/ *verb* **-lates; -lat·ed; -lat·ing** [+ *obj*]
1 a : to move or control (something) with your hands or by using a machine • *manipulate* a pencil • The baby is learning to *manipulate* blocks. • *manipulate* a computer mouse • The mechanical arms are *manipulated* by a computer. **b** *medical* **:** to move (muscles and bones) with your hands as a form of treatment • The doctor *manipulated* my back/spine.
2 : to use or change (numbers, information, etc.) in a skillful way or for a particular purpose • The program was designed to organize and *manipulate* large amounts of data. • He's always been good at *manipulating* numbers in his head. • As part of the experiment, students *manipulated* light and temperature to see how it affected the plants.
3 *usually disapproving* **a :** to deal with or control (someone or something) in a clever and usually unfair or selfish way • She knows how to *manipulate* her parents to get what she wants. • He felt that he had been *manipulated* by the people he trusted most. • The editorial was a blatant attempt to *manipulate* public opinion. **b :** to change (something) in an unfair or selfish way • He's accused of trying to *manipulate* the price of the stock. • The company *manipulated* its accounts to exaggerate its profits.
— ma·nip·u·la·tion /məˌnɪpjəˈleɪʃən/ *noun, pl* **-tions** [*count*] price *manipulations* [*noncount*] trying to control the election through blatant *manipulation* of public opinion • her shameless *manipulation* of her parents

ma·nip·u·la·tive /məˈnɪpjəˌleɪtɪv, məˈnɪpjələtɪv/ *adj* [*more ~; most ~*] *usually disapproving* **:** using or controlling other people in a clever and often unfair or selfish way • a clever and *manipulative* salesman • *manipulative* behavior

ma·nip·u·la·tor /məˈnɪpjəˌleɪtɚ/ *noun, pl* **-tors** [*count*] *often disapproving* **:** a person who uses or controls other people in a clever and often unfair or selfish way **:** a manipulative person • He said she was a clever political *manipulator.*

man·kind /ˈmænˈkaɪnd/ *noun* [*noncount*] **:** all people thought of as one group **:** HUMANKIND • All of *mankind* will benefit from this new technology. • We have seen the same pattern throughout the history of *mankind.* — compare WOMANKIND

man·ky /ˈmæŋki/ *adj* **man·ki·er; -est** *Brit, informal* **:** dirty and unattractive • a *manky* old dog • *manky* clothing

man·ly /ˈmænli/ *adj* **man·li·er; -est** [*also more ~; most ~*] **:** having or showing qualities (such as strength or courage) that are expected in a man • He wasn't *manly* enough to fight. • a *manly* competitor • He has a deep, *manly* voice.
— man·li·ness *noun* [*noncount*] • a test of his *manliness* [=*manhood*]

man–made /ˈmænˈmeɪd/ *adj* **:** made by people rather than by nature • The government flooded the valley to create a *man-made* lake. • She preferred wearing cotton to *man-made* [=*synthetic*] fabrics. • *man-made* building materials

man·na /ˈmænə/ *noun* [*noncount*]
1 : food which according to the Bible was supplied by a miracle to the Israelites after they escaped from Egypt
2 : something needed that is received unexpectedly • Your generous gift was ***manna from heaven***.

manned /ˈmænd/ *adj* **:** carrying or done by a person • *manned* spaceflight • a *manned* mission to the moon — opposite UNMANNED

man·ne·quin /ˈmænɪkən/ *noun, pl* **-quins** [*count*] **:** a figure shaped like a human body that is used for making or displaying clothes

man·ner /ˈmænɚ/ *noun, pl* **-ners**
1 [*singular*] *somewhat formal* **:** the way that something is done or happens • She has a very forceful *manner* of speaking. • I objected to the *manner* in which the decision was made. — often used after *in* • Continue stirring *in* this *manner* until the sauce thickens. • *In* this *manner*, we were able to save enough money for a new car. • *In* what *manner* was the data collected? [=how was the data collected?] • We worked *in* a quick *manner*. [=we worked quickly] • She taught her class *in* an informal *manner*. • He always begins his stories *in* the same *manner*. • We were allowed to spend the money *in* any *manner* we wanted.
2 a [*count*] **:** the way that a person normally behaves especially while with other people — usually singular • He had a gentle *manner* (about him). • He listened patiently to his children, as was his *manner*. • It was her energetic and friendly *manner* that got her the job. — see also BEDSIDE MANNER **b** *manners* [*plural*] **:** behavior while with other people • His children have excellent *manners*. [=his children behave very well] • It's ***bad manners*** [=it is impolite] to talk with your mouth full. **c** *manners* [*plural*] **:** knowledge of how to behave politely while with other people • Some people have no *manners*. • Someone should teach you some *manners*! • He ***forgot his manners*** and reached across the table for the salt. ✧ To ***remember/mind your manners*** is to behave in a polite and proper way. • "*Mind your manners*," Mom said sternly, "and thank your uncle for the nice gifts." — see also TABLE MANNERS
3 [*singular*] **:** an artistic style or method • He painted this picture in his early *manner*. — often used in the phrase ***in/after the manner of*** • She wrote *after the manner of* [=in the style of] her favorite poet. • This church was built *in the manner of* the English Gothic style.

all manner of **:** all kinds or sorts of (things or people) • The store sells *all manner of* musical instruments. • *All manner of* people come to the city.

in a manner of speaking — used to say that a statement is true or accurate in a certain way even if it is not literally or completely true • His retirement was, *in a manner of speaking*, the beginning of his real career. • After the storm destroyed their house, they were, *in a manner of speaking* [=*so to speak, as it were*], lost at sea. [=they felt lost and confused after their house was destroyed]

not by any manner of means see MEANS

to the manner born **:** suited to a particular position, role, or status in a way that seems very natural • He had never been on a boat before, but he walked along the deck as if *to the manner born.*

what manner of *old-fashioned + literary* **:** what kind or sort of • *What manner of* person could have committed such a crime? • *What manner of* woman is she to have done something like that?

man·nered /ˈmænɚd/ *adj*
1 : behaving in a certain way — used in combination • He was a mild-*mannered* [=*gentle*] man who rarely became angry. • well-*mannered* [=well-behaved] children
2 [*more ~; most ~*] *disapproving* **:** formal in a way that is intended to impress other people • He had a very *mannered* [=*unnatural*] way of speaking.

man·ner·ism /ˈmænəˌrɪzəm/ *noun, pl* **-isms** [*count*] **:** a person's particular way of talking or moving • The actor can mimic the President's *mannerisms* perfectly.

man·ner·ly /ˈmænɚli/ *adj* [*more ~; most ~*] *formal + literary* **:** behaving politely while with other people **:** showing good manners • When he was a child, he was quiet and *mannerly*. • a *mannerly* young man

man•nish /ˈmænɪʃ/ *adj* [*more* ~; *most* ~] : suitable for or typical of a man rather than a woman : not feminine • She was wearing a hat and *mannish* clothing. • She had a deep and rather *mannish* voice.
– **man•nish•ly** *adv* – **man•nish•ness** *noun* [*noncount*]

ma•no a ma•no /ˌmɑːnoʊɑˈmɑːnoʊ/ *adv* — used to describe a situation in which two people directly compete, fight, or argue with each other • They fought *mano a mano*. • Tomorrow night the candidates (will) ***go mano a mano*** [=compete against each other] in the first of two debates. ✧ *Mano a mano* comes from a Spanish phrase that means "hand to hand."

manoeuvre, manoeuvrable *Brit spellings of* MANEUVER, MANEUVERABLE

man of God *noun, pl* **men of God** [*count*] *formal* : a man who is a priest or minister

man of letters *noun, pl* **men of letters** [*count*] : a man who writes or who knows a lot about novels, poems, etc. : a literary man

man of straw *noun, pl* **men of straw** [*count*] *chiefly Brit* : STRAW MAN

man of the cloth *noun, pl* **men of the cloth** [*count*] *formal + old-fashioned* : a man who is a priest or minister

man of the house *noun*
the man of the house : the male family member who has the most responsibility for taking care of and making decisions about the household • When his father died, John became *the man of the house* even though he was only 18.

man of the people *noun*
a man of the people : a man (such as a politician) who understands and is liked by ordinary people

man of the world *noun, pl* **men of the world** [*count*] : a man who has had many experiences and who is not shocked by things that may be shocking to other people

man–of–war /ˌmænəvˈwoɚ/ *noun, pl* **men–of–war** /ˌmɛnəvˈwoɚ/ [*count*] : a ship that has many weapons and is used for war

man•or /ˈmænɚ/ *noun, pl* **-ors** [*count*]
1 : a large country house on a large piece of land
2 *Brit, informal* : the area or section of a city that a particular group of police officers are responsible for
to the manor born : born into a wealthy family that has a high social status
– **ma•no•ri•al** /məˈnorijəl/ *adj* • *manorial* landowners/estates

man•pow•er /ˈmænˌpawɚ/ *noun* [*noncount*] : the number of people who are available to work • Currently we are experiencing a shortage of *manpower*. • military *manpower*

man•qué /mɑnˈkeɪ, *Brit* ˈmɒŋkeɪ/ *adj, always used after a noun, formal* — used to describe what a person could or should have been but never was • He works as a cook but thinks of himself as a poet *manqué*. • an artist *manqué*

manse /ˈmæns/ *noun, pl* **mans•es** [*count*]
1 : the house of a minister
2 : a large and impressive house : MANSION

man•ser•vant /ˈmænˌsɚvənt/ *noun, pl* **menservants** [*count*] *old-fashioned* : a male servant • *menservants* and maidservants

man•sion /ˈmænʃən/ *noun, pl* **-sions** [*count*] : a large and impressive house : the large house of a wealthy person • a *mansion* with 10 bedrooms and an indoor swimming pool

man–sized /ˈmænˌsaɪzd/ *also* **man–size** /ˈmænˌsaɪz/ *adj* : large and suitable for or typical of a man • a *man-sized* sandwich • his *man-sized* appetite • a *man-size* effort • This is a *man-sized* job.

man•slaugh•ter /ˈmænˌslɑːtɚ/ *noun* [*noncount*] *law* : the crime of killing a person without intending to do so • She was convicted of *manslaughter* for driving while drunk and killing three people.

man's man *noun* [*singular*] : a man who is liked and admired by other men — compare LADIES' MAN

man•tel /ˈmæntl̩/ *noun, pl* **-tels** [*count*] *chiefly US* : the shelf above a fireplace — see picture at LIVING ROOM

man•tel•piece /ˈmæntl̩ˌpiːs/ *noun, pl* **-piec•es** [*count*]
1 : the shelf above a fireplace and the decorative pieces on the sides of the fireplace
2 : MANTEL

man•tis /ˈmæntəs/ *noun, pl* **man•tis•es** *or* **man•tes** /ˈmænˌtiːz/ [*count*] : PRAYING MANTIS

¹man•tle /ˈmæntl̩/ *noun, pl* **man•tles** [*count*]
1 : a loose piece of clothing without sleeves that was worn over other clothes especially in the past : CLOAK
2 *literary* : something that covers or surrounds something else — *+ of* • The ground was covered/cloaked in a *mantle of* leaves. • mountains blanketed/wrapped in a *mantle of* snow • A *mantle of* secrecy surrounded the family's past. [=the family's past was kept secret]
3 *formal* : the position of someone who has responsibility or authority • He ***took on the mantle of*** director. [=he took on the job of being the director] • She ***accepted/assumed the mantle of*** leadership.
4 *technical* : the middle layer of the Earth that is between the top crust and the inner core

²mantle *verb* **mantles; man•tled; man•tling** [+ *obj*] *formal + literary* : to cover or surround (something) — usually used as *(be) mantled* • The mountains *were mantled* with/in snow.

man–to–man /ˈmæntəˈmæn/ *adj*
1 *always used before a noun* : happening between two men — used to describe speech between men that is honest, open, and informal • We need to have a *man-to-man* talk. • a *man-to-man* discussion
2 *chiefly US, sports* : of or relating to a way of playing defense in football, basketball, etc., in which each player on the defense is supposed to stop a particular player on the offense • They were playing a *man-to-man* defense. • *man-to-man* coverage
– **man–to–man** *adv* • talking *man-to-man* • The defense was playing *man-to-man*.

man•tra /ˈmɑːntrə, *Brit* ˈmæntrə/ *noun, pl* **-tras** [*count*]
1 : a sound, word, or phrase that is repeated by someone who is praying or meditating
2 : a word or phrase that is repeated often or that expresses someone's basic beliefs • a businessman whose *mantra* is "bigger is better"

¹man•u•al /ˈmænjəwəl/ *adj, always used before a noun*
1 : doing or involving hard physical work • low-paid *manual* workers/laborers • She spent the summer doing *manual* labor on her uncle's farm.
2 : of or relating to using the hands • He has quite a bit of *manual* dexterity. [=skill and ease in using his hands] • *manual* skill
3 : operated or controlled with the hands or by a person • I can't drive her car because it has a ***manual transmission*** instead of an automatic transmission. [=it has a system for changing gears that has to be operated by the driver] : operated only with the hands and without electric power • He has a collection of old-fashioned *manual* typewriters.
– **man•u•al•ly** *adv* • *manually* operated machinery

²manual *noun, pl* **-als** [*count*]
1 : a small book that gives useful information about something : HANDBOOK • Here's the owner's *manual* of your new car. • The computer program comes with a user's *manual*. • We lost the instruction *manual* and couldn't put our bikes together. • Please refer to the training/employee *manual* if you have any questions about your job.
2 : a vehicle that has a system for changing gears that has to be operated by the driver : a car with a manual transmission • Is your car a *manual* or an automatic?

¹man•u•fac•ture /ˌmænjəˈfæktʃɚ/ *verb* **-tures; -tured; -tur•ing** [+ *obj*]
1 : to make (something) usually in large amounts by using machines • materials used in *manufacturing* cars/computers • a company that *manufactures* wool and cotton clothing
2 : to create (something, such as a false story or explanation) by using your imagination often in order to trick or deceive someone • He *manufactured* [=*fabricated, invented*] a story/lie/falsehood in order to get out of trouble.

²manufacture *noun* [*noncount*] : the process of making products especially with machines in factories • materials used in the *manufacture* of cars/computers • We're developing new methods of paper *manufacture*.

man•u•fac•tur•er /ˌmænjəˈfæktʃərɚ/ *noun, pl* **-ers** [*count*] : a company that makes a product • Follow the instructions recommended by the *manufacturer*. • They are one of the country's leading *manufacturers* of children's clothing. • car *manufacturers*

man•u•fac•tur•ing /ˌmænjəˈfæktʃərɪŋ/ *noun* [*noncount*] : the industry or business of making products especially with machines in factories • *Manufacturing* is central to the economy of the country. • They've created new jobs in *manufacturing*.

ma•nure /mə'nuɚ, *Brit* mə'njuə/ *noun, pl* **-nures** : solid waste from farm animals that is used to make soil better for growing plants [*noncount*] a bag of cow *manure* [*count*] fertilizers made from animal *manures*

man•u•script /'mænjə,skrɪpt/ *noun, pl* **-scripts** : the original copy of a play, book, piece of music, etc., before it has been printed [*count*] The library owns the author's original *manuscript*. ▪ a copy of the composer's *manuscript* [*noncount*] She read the book ***in manuscript***. [=she read the manuscript of the book]

¹many /'mɛni/ *adj* — used to refer to a large number of things or people ▪ She worked hard for *many* years. ▪ They were one of the *many, many* families that came to watch the parade. ▪ Gardening is one of her very *many* interests. ▪ They talked about the *many* benefits of learning English. ▪ You can never have too *many* friends. ▪ Some people will come, but ***many more*** people will not. ▪ A ***great/good many*** people [=very many people] did not survive. — often used in negative statements ▪ We don't have *many* choices. [=we have few choices] ▪ There weren't *many* people at the party.

as many — used to talk about or compare amounts ▪ She read *as many* books as she could. [=she read the largest number of books possible] ▪ She read three times *as many* books as he did. [=she read three times more books than he did] ▪ We saw three plays in *as many* days. [=we saw three plays in three days] ▪ She wrote five books in *as many* years.

how many — used to ask or talk about an amount ▪ *How many* people were there? ▪ I was surprised by *how many* people were there. ▪ ***How many times*** [=how often] do I have to tell you to lock the door?

²many *pronoun* : a large number of people or things ▪ Some people will come, but *many* [=many people] will not. ▪ The medicine has helped *many* with the disease. ▪ *Many* of his friends never went to college. ▪ I know some of the people here, but not (very) *many* of them. ▪ Far/All too *many* have died in this war. ▪ A lot of people have tried to climb the mountain, but a ***great/good many*** of them have failed. ▪ I wanted a dozen, but they didn't have ***that many***. = They didn't have ***as many as that***. [=they had fewer than a dozen]

as many as — used to suggest that a number or amount is surprisingly large ▪ She read *as many as* 60 books! ▪ *As many as* 60 students competed for the prize. ▪ They lost by *as many as* 20 points.

many a/an *formal + literary* — used with a singular noun to refer to a large number of things or people ▪ It remained a mystery for *many a* year. [=for many years] ▪ I've been there *many a* time. [=many times] ▪ *Many a* tale was told. [=many tales were told] ▪ *Many an* answer [=many answers] can be found in this book. ▪ *Many a* man has tried [=many men have tried] but few men have succeeded.

many's the *formal + literary* — used to say that something is common or has happened often ▪ *Many's the* day we have spent together. [=we have spent many days together] ▪ ***Many's the time*** I've been there. [=I've been there many times]

the many : the great majority of people ▪ policies that help the privileged few at the expense of *the many*

Mao•ri /'maʊri/ *noun, pl* **-ris**
1 [*count*] : a member of the original people living in New Zealand
2 [*noncount*] : the language of the Maori people
– Maori *adj* ▪ *Maori* culture

¹map /'mæp/ *noun, pl* **maps** [*count*]
1 : a picture or chart that shows the rivers, mountains, streets, etc., in a particular area ▪ a *map* of the country ▪ different *maps* of the world ▪ a road/street *map* [=a map showing the roads/streets of an area] ▪ "Can you find where we are on the *map*?" "Sorry: I'm no good at reading *maps*." ▪ "How do I get to the station?" "Here, let me draw you a *map*." — see also RELIEF MAP
2 : a picture or chart that shows the different parts of something ▪ a *map* of the brain

all over the map *US, informal* : not staying the same : characterized by frequent and extreme changes ▪ Prices have been *all over the map*.

put (something or someone) on the map : to make (a place, a person, etc.) famous or well-known ▪ The story has *put our little town on the map*. ▪ The success of his first album really *put him on the map* in the music industry.

²map *verb* **maps; mapped; map•ping** [+ *obj*]
1 : to make a map of (something) ▪ He *mapped* the stars. ▪ The coastline was *mapped* by early explorers.
2 *US* : to plan the details of (something) ▪ We *mapped* [=*mapped out*] a plan of action.

map onto [*phrasal verb*] ***map (something) onto (something)*** *technical* : to find or show the connections between two things or groups of things ▪ *map* brain functions *onto* brain structures

map out [*phrasal verb*] ***map (something) out or map out (something)*** : to plan the details of (something, such as a program or your future) ▪ We *mapped out* a plan of action. ▪ They *mapped* her campaign for governor all *out*. ▪ She has her future all *mapped out*.

ma•ple /'meɪpəl/ *noun, pl* **ma•ples**
1 [*count*] : a type of tree that grows in northern parts of the world and has hard wood often used in making furniture ▪ The *maple* leaf is an emblem of Canada. — called also *maple tree*
2 [*noncount*] : the wood of a maple tree ▪ a table made of *maple*

maple sugar *noun* [*noncount*] : a brown sugar made from the sap of maple trees

maple syrup *noun* [*noncount*] : a sweet, thick liquid made from the sap of maple trees ▪ pancakes served with butter and *maple syrup*

mar /'maɚ/ *verb* **mars; marred; mar•ring** [+ *obj*] : to ruin the beauty or perfection of (something) : to hurt or damage the good condition of (something) ▪ A large scar *marred* his face. ▪ Her acting *mars* an otherwise great movie. — often used as *(be) marred* ▪ The report *is marred* by numerous errors. ▪ a car *marred* by scratches

Mar. *abbr* March

ma•ra•ca /mə'rɑːkə, *Brit* mə'rækə/ *noun, pl* **-cas** [*count*] : a musical instrument with a handle and a round hollow top that is filled with beads, beans, etc., and is shaken to make noise — usually plural ▪ play the *maracas*

mar•a•schi•no /,merə'skiːnoʊ, merə'ʃiːnoʊ/ *noun, pl* **-nos**
1 [*count*] : a kind of sweet cherry that is used in desserts or alcoholic drinks — called also *maraschino cherry*
2 [*count, noncount*] : a sweet alcoholic drink made from cherry juice

¹mar•a•thon /'merə,θɑːn/ *noun, pl* **-thons** [*count*]
1 : a running race that is about 26 miles (42 kilometers) long ▪ He ran (in) a *marathon*.
2 a : something (such as an event or activity) that lasts an extremely long time or that requires great effort ▪ We watched a *marathon* of our favorite movies. ▪ a movie *marathon* ▪ a shopping *marathon* **b** : a contest in which people compete with each other to see who can do something for the longest amount of time ▪ a dance *marathon*

²marathon *adj, always used before a noun* : lasting an unusually long time ▪ Their *marathon* meeting lasted two full days. ▪ a *marathon* negotiating session

mar•a•thon•er /'merə,θɑːnɚ/ *noun, pl* **-ers** [*count*] : a runner who competes in a marathon

ma•raud•ing /mə'rɑːdɪŋ/ *adj, always used before a noun* : traveling from place to place to attack others ▪ *Marauding* soldiers wandered from town to town. ▪ a *marauding* band/gang of thieves ▪ *marauding* lions
– ma•raud•er /mə'rɑːdɚ/ *noun, pl* **-ers** [*count*] ▪ a band/gang of *marauders*

mar•ble /'maɚbəl/ *noun, pl* **mar•bles**
1 [*noncount*] : a kind of stone that is often polished and used in buildings and statues ▪ The statue is made of *marble*. ▪ a block of *marble* — often used before another noun ▪ the museum's polished *marble* floor/staircase ▪ a *marble* countertop
2 a [*count*] : a little glass ball used in some children's games ▪ I love to play with *marbles*. **b marbles** [*noncount*] : a children's game played with little glass balls ▪ Let's play *marbles*. = Let's play a game of *marbles*.

lose your marbles *informal + humorous* : to become insane ▪ When he started ranting about how the government was out to get him, I thought he'd *lost his marbles*. [=*gone crazy*] ▪ He hasn't completely *lost his marbles* yet.

mar•bled /'maɚbəld/ *adj*
1 : made from or decorated with marble ▪ The mansion has beautiful *marbled* columns. ▪ a *marbled* hall
2 : having markings or colors similar to marble ▪ *marbled* paper
3 *of meat* : having lines of fat mixed throughout ▪ *marbled* beef ▪ The meat was *marbled* with fat.

¹march /'maɚʧ/ *verb* **march•es; marched; march•ing**
1 [*no obj*] **a** : to walk with regular steps as a group : to walk

M

in the regular and organized way of soldiers • The band *marched* onto the field. • The soldiers were lined up and ordered to begin *marching*. • Hundreds of people *marched* in the parade. **b** *always followed by an adverb or preposition* : to go into, out of, or through a place as an army • The army *marched* south to cut off the enemy's retreat. • Enemy troops were ***marching on*** the city. [=they were coming toward the city to attack it]
2 [*no obj*] : to walk with a large group of people who are protesting or supporting something • We *marched* for/against new elections. • Demonstrators ***marched on*** City Hall to protest the war.
3 [*no obj*] : to walk somewhere quickly in a direct and forceful way • He *marched* angrily out the door. • I *marched* into the office and demanded an answer. • She *marched* right up to me and asked what was wrong.
4 [+ *obj*] : to cause or force (a person) to walk somewhere • They *marched* the prisoners through the streets of the city. • We *marched* the children off to bed. [=we made the children go to bed] — see also FROG-MARCH
march on [*phrasal verb*] : to go or continue onward • Time *marches on*. • Governments come and go, but civilization *marches on*.
– march·er /ˈmɑɚʧɚ/ *noun, pl* **-ers** [*count*] • There were hundreds of *marchers* in the parade. • protest *marchers*

²march *noun, pl* **marches**
1 [*count*] **a** : an act of walking together as an organized group : an act of marching • The soldiers were ordered to begin their *march*.; *especially* : an organized walk by a large group of people to support or protest something • a protest *march* • They led a *march* in support of affirmative action. **b** : the distance covered by marching for a specified period of time • The nearest town was a day's *march* away.
2 [*singular*] *somewhat formal* : forward movement or progress • the *march* of time/civilization • Time continues its *march* onward/forward.
3 [*count*] : a piece of music with a strong regular beat that is written to be played while people are marching • They played the general's favorite *march*.
on the march **1** : marching toward a place • Thousands of troops were *on the march*. **2** : going forward • Time is *on the march*.
steal a march on *chiefly Brit* : to get ahead of or win an advantage over (someone) in an unexpected and clever way • He *stole a march on* his competitors by being the first to put the product on the market.

March /ˈmɑɚʧ/ *noun, pl* **March·es** : the third month of the year [*noncount*] in (early/middle/mid-/late) *March* • early/late in *March* • We arrived on *March* the fourth. = (*US*) We arrived on *March* fourth. = We arrived on the fourth of *March*. [*count*] Sales are up (for) this *March*. • It happens every *March*. ✧ The saying ***March comes in like a lion and goes out like a lamb*** means that the month of March begins with bad weather and ends with good weather. — abbr. *Mar.*

marching band *noun, pl* ~ **bands** [*count*] : a group of musicians who play instruments while marching together at a parade or sports event

marching orders *noun* [*plural*]
1 *US* : orders that tell you what to do • The boss called a meeting and gave the new employees their *marching orders*.
2 *Brit* — used to say that someone has been ordered to leave a place, job, etc. • I was given my *marching orders*. = I got/received my *marching orders*. [=I was fired from my job]

Mar·di Gras /ˈmɑɚdiˌgrɑː/ *noun* : the Tuesday before the beginning of Lent that is often celebrated with parades and parties [*noncount*] We're going to New Orleans for *Mardi Gras*. [*singular*] It was a *Mardi Gras* to remember!

mare /ˈmeɚ/ *noun, pl* **mares** [*count*] : an adult female horse

mar·ga·rine /ˈmɑɚʤərən, *Brit* ˌmɑːʤəˈriːn/ *noun, pl* **-rines** [*count, noncount*] : a food that resembles butter and is made from vegetable oils • a stick of *margarine*

mar·ga·ri·ta /ˌmɑɚgəˈriːtə/ *noun, pl* **-tas** [*count*] : an alcoholic drink made of tequila, lime or lemon juice, and an orange-flavored liquor

marge /ˈmɑɚʤ/ *noun* [*noncount*] *Brit, informal* : MARGARINE

mar·gin /ˈmɑɚʤən/ *noun, pl* **-gins** [*count*]
1 : the part of a page that is above, below, or to the side of the printed part • Please write your name in the left/left-hand *margin* of the page. • a book with wide/narrow *margins*
2 : the place where something (such as a piece of land) stops : the edge of something • We'll meet at the *margin* [=(more commonly) *edge*] of the forest. • Mountains lie at the city's northern/southern *margins*. — often used figuratively in the phrase ***on the margins*** or (*US*) ***on the margin*** • We are trying to improve medical care for poor families living *on the margins* of society. [=poor families who are often forgotten or ignored by society] • The business has been operating *on the margins* of respectability. [=has been operating in a way that is not truly respectable]
3 : an extra amount of something (such as time or space) that can be used if it is needed • a safety *margin* ✧ If you have little or no ***margin for/of error***, it means that you need to be very careful not to make mistakes. If you have a greater *margin for/of error*, you can be less careful. • We want the design to offer users a generous *margin for error*. • The schedule allows us very little *margin for error*.
4 : a measurement of difference • The bullet missed his heart by a narrow/slim *margin*. [=the bullet narrowly missed his heart] • We lost the election by a one-vote *margin*. [=we lost the election by one vote] • She won by a *margin* of 3,000 votes. • He was the winner by a large/considerable *margin*. ✧ A ***margin of error*** is a number or percentage that shows how accurate a measurement is. • The poll indicates that the President is supported by 54 percent of the voters, with a *margin of error* of 3 percent. [=it is possible that as few as 51 percent or as many as 57 percent of the voters support the President] — see also PROFIT MARGIN

¹mar·gin·al /ˈmɑɚʤənl/ *adj*
1 a : not very important • a *marginal* problem **b** : very slight or small • There has been only a *marginal* improvement in her condition.
2 : not included in the main part of society or of a group • *marginal* voters
3 *chiefly US* : not very good • His reading and writing abilities are *marginal*. • She's a *marginal* athlete. • *marginal* living conditions
4 *always used before a noun* : written or printed in the margin of a page • *marginal* notes
5 *Brit* : able to be won or lost by changing only a few votes • At the next election the opposition parties will try to capture some *marginal* seats [=*marginals*] from the government.
6 *of land* : just able to produce enough crops to pay for the cost of producing those crops • farmers who must eke out a living on *marginal* land(s)

²marginal *noun, pl* **-als** [*count*] *Brit* : a political seat, position, etc., that is won or lost by only a few votes • How many *marginals* changed hands at the last election?

mar·gin·al·ize *also Brit* **mar·gin·al·ise** /ˈmɑɚʤənəˌlaɪz/ *verb* **-iz·es**; **-ized**; **-iz·ing** [+ *obj*] : to put or keep (someone) in a powerless or unimportant position within a society or group • We are protesting policies that *marginalize* women. [=that do not allow women to have important or powerful positions in a society] • The program helps people from *marginalized* groups/populations.
– mar·gin·al·i·za·tion *also Brit* **mar·gin·al·i·sa·tion** /ˌmɑɚʤənələˈzeɪʃən, *Brit* ˌmɑːʤənəˌlaɪˈzeɪʃən/ *noun* [*noncount*]

mar·gin·al·ly /ˈmɑɚʤənəli/ *adv*
1 : to a small extent or degree : SLIGHTLY • This book is *marginally* more interesting than the others. • Her plan was only *marginally* successful.
2 *US* : almost not : BARELY • He is only *marginally* qualified for the job.

ma·ri·a·chi /ˌmɑriˈɑːʧi, ˌmeriˈɑːʧi/ *noun* [*noncount*] *US* : a type of lively Mexican street music played by a band of trumpets and guitars — usually used before another noun • a *mariachi* band/musician

mari·gold /ˈmerəˌgoʊld/ *noun, pl* **-golds** [*count*] : a plant that is grown for its bright yellow or orange flowers

mar·i·jua·na /ˌmerəˈwɑːnə/ *noun* [*noncount*] : the dried leaves and flowers of the hemp plant that are smoked as a drug

ma·rim·ba /məˈrɪmbə/ *noun, pl* **-bas** [*count*] : a wooden musical instrument that is similar to a xylophone

ma·ri·na /məˈriːnə/ *noun, pl* **-nas** [*count*] : an area of water where privately owned boats (such as yachts) are kept

¹mar·i·nade /ˌmerəˈneɪd/ *noun, pl* **-nades** : a sauce in which meat or fish is soaked to add flavor or to make the meat or fish more tender [*noncount*] a bottle of *marinade* [*count*] a variety of spicy *marinades*

²marinade *verb* **-nades**; **-nad·ed**; **-nad·ing** [+ *obj*] : MARINATE

mar·i·nate /ˈmerəˌneɪt/ *verb* **-nates**; **-nat·ed**; **-nat·ing**

: to put meat or fish in a sauce for a period of time to add flavor or to make the meat or fish more tender : to soak in a marinade [+ *obj*] The recipe says that you should *marinate* the chicken overnight. [*no obj*] The chicken should be allowed to *marinate* overnight.

¹ma·rine /məˈriːn/ *adj, always used before a noun*
1 : of or relating to the sea or the plants and animals that live in the sea • *marine* life • *marine* animals such as dolphins and whales • a *marine* environment • ***marine biologists*** [=scientists who study life in the sea]
2 : of or relating to sailing on the sea or doing business (such as trading) by sea • a *marine* [=*nautical*] chart • *marine* [=(more commonly) *maritime*] law

²marine *or* **Marine** *noun, pl* **-rines** [*count*] : a member of the U.S. Marine Corps or the British Royal Marines • He is a former U.S. *Marine*. • The *marines* have landed. • the U.S. Army, Navy, Air Force, and *Marines* • *marine* barracks
the Marines : the part of a country's military forces that includes soldiers who serve on a ship or are closely associated with a naval force : the U.S. Marine Corps or the British Royal Marines • an officer in *the Marines*

Marine Corps *noun*
the Marine Corps : the part of the U.S. military that consists of soldiers who serve at sea and also on land

mar·i·ner /ˈmerənə/ *noun, pl* **-ners** [*count*] *old-fashioned + literary* : SAILOR

mar·i·o·nette /ˌmerijəˈnɛt/ *noun, pl* **-nettes** [*count*] : a puppet that is moved by pulling strings or wires that are attached to its body

marionette

mar·i·tal /ˈmerətl/ *adj, always used before a noun* : of or relating to marriage • They've been having *marital* problems/difficulties. • *marital* vows • They've enjoyed many years of ***marital bliss***. [=happiness in marriage]

marital status *noun* [*noncount*] : the state of being married or not married — used on official forms to ask if a person is married, single, divorced, or widowed • Please enter your *marital status*. • What is your *marital status*?

mar·i·time /ˈmerəˌtaɪm/ *adj*
1 : of or relating to sailing on the sea or doing business (such as trading) by sea • The country's *maritime* industry is an important part of its economy. • She's an expert in *maritime* law. • a *maritime* museum
2 : located near or next to the sea • *maritime* nations/provinces • the country's *maritime* region

mar·jo·ram /ˈmɑədʒərəm/ *noun* [*noncount*] : an herb that has a pleasant smell and is often used in cooking

¹mark /ˈmɑək/ *noun, pl* **marks**
1 [*count*] **a** : a small area on the surface of something that is dirty, damaged, etc. • a burn/scratch *mark* • The glass left a water *mark* on the wooden table. — see also BLACK MARK **b** : an area of something (such as an animal's fur or skin) that is a different color from the area around it • The cat has white fur with some black *marks* on its head and tail. — see also BIRTHMARK, STRAWBERRY MARK, STRETCH MARKS
2 [*count*] **a** : a written or printed shape or symbol • proofreading *marks* — see also PUNCTUATION MARK **b** : a symbol or shape on something that identifies it, shows its quality, etc. • The goldsmith's *mark* is stamped on the back. — see also LANDMARK, POSTMARK, TRADEMARK **c** : a cross made in place of a signature by someone who cannot read and write • We read him the document and he made his *mark* on it.
3 [*count*] : something that shows how someone feels about something : a sign or indication *of* something • He gave her the necklace as a *mark of* his esteem. • They left flowers on the grave as a *mark of* respect. • Those extra responsibilities he's giving you are a *mark of* confidence. [=they show that he has confidence in you]
4 [*count*] : a quality or trait that is typical of a particular type of person or thing — + *of* • Courtesy is the *mark* [=*hallmark, sign*] *of* a true gentleman. • A willingness to ask tough questions is the *mark of* a good journalist. • He thinks that indecisiveness is a *mark of* weakness. [=indecisiveness shows weakness]
5 [*count*] : a number or letter that indicates how a student has performed in a class or on a test : GRADE • I got a good/high/low *mark* in/for English. • I got a good/high/low *mark* on the spelling test. • She barely earned passing *marks* in her first year of college. • failing *marks* — often used figuratively • I'll give them ***high/top marks*** for honesty. [=they are very honest; I give them a lot of praise and credit for being honest] — see also FULL MARKS
6 [*singular*] : a specified point or level • We're at the halfway *mark* in the first period of play. • The population has topped the 1,000,000 *mark*. — see also HIGH-WATER MARK
7 [*count*] : something that is aimed at or shot at : TARGET • The arrow hit/missed/overshot the *mark*. • The bullet ***found its mark***. [=hit the target that was aimed for] — often used figuratively • Our fund-raising fell/was ***short of the mark***. [=we did not raise as much money as we needed]
8 [*count*] *US* : a person who is tricked into losing money or property • They proved to be easy *marks* for the swindler.
9 [*count*] : the line or place where a race starts • The runners were told to ***take their marks***. [=to get into position for the start of the race] • ***On your mark***, get set, go!
close to the mark *or* ***near the mark*** : fairly accurate : almost correct • Their estimate was pretty *close to the mark*.
leave/make a/your mark : to do something that causes you to be remembered : to create a lasting or strong impression • He worked at several jobs, but he didn't *make* much of *a mark* in any of them. • From the moment we saw her in action, we knew she would *make her mark* as a teacher. • Her kindness *left its mark* on her students.
miss its/the mark : to fail or be wrong • Their estimates completely *missed the mark*. [=were not accurate] • The ad campaign was supposed to appeal to young people but it *missed the mark*. — see also ¹MARK 7 (above)
off the mark *or* ***wide of the mark*** : not accurate or correct : not achieving the desired result • The results of the fund-raising were *wide of the mark*. • His efforts to console her were *off the mark*. [=his efforts to console her did not help]
quick/slow off the mark : quick or slow to act or to understand something • As soon as the opportunity arose, he was *quick off the mark* in exploiting it. • I was *slow off the mark* [=I did not act quickly] and missed my chance.
up to the mark : up to the usual standard of performance, quality, etc. : as good as usual — usually used in negative statements • I haven't been feeling *up to the mark* lately. • His work hasn't been *up to the mark*.
— compare ³MARK

²mark *verb* **marks; marked; mark·ing**
1 : to make or leave a visible mark on (something) [+ *obj*] Any little bit of dirt will *mark* that fabric. • Be careful not to *mark* the floor with your shoes. [*no obj*] a fabric that *marks* easily [=that easily becomes dirty or stained]
2 [+ *obj*] **a** : to write or make (a mark) • *mark* an accent on/over a letter • She *marked* an "X" on each box. **b** : to write a note about (something) • I have *marked* the event on my calendar. • *Mark* [=*jot*] down these names. **c** : to write or make a mark on (something) • She *marked* each box with an "X." • *Mark* that page.; *also* : to write on (something) in order to indicate what it is • The officials *marked* the document "Top Secret." = The officials *marked* the document as top secret. **d** : to write or put a mark around or near (something) so that it will be easily seen or noticed • I've *marked* several items on the first page. [=I've put marks next to several items on the first page]
3 [+ *obj*] **a** : to indicate (a location, such as a location on a map) with a mark or symbol • X *marks* the spot where the suspect was last seen. • I have *marked* (out) the best route on the map. **b** : to put something on or near (a particular place) in order to find it later • Use a bookmark to *mark* your place. • We put some tape on the floor to *mark* where the tables should go. **c** *of an animal* : to leave urine, feces, body oils, etc., in (a place) as a signal to other animals • The dog *marked* the base of the tree by urinating. • a tiger *marking* its territory
4 [+ *obj*] : to be a typical feature or quality of (someone or something) : CHARACTERIZE • the flamboyance that *marks* her style — often used as *(be) marked* • His artwork *is marked* by unusual uses of color. [=color is used in unusual ways in his artwork] • The adjective "paranoid" can be defined as "*marked* by paranoia."
5 [+ *obj*] : to have a permanent and usually bad effect on (someone or something) • Her time in prison *marked* her for life.
6 : to give a mark to (a student or a student's work) : GRADE [+ *obj*] Students will be *marked* on their reading ability. • She spent the evening *marking* the students' exams/papers. [*no obj*] She generally *marks* high/low. [=she generally gives high/low marks] — see also MARK DOWN (below)
7 [+ *obj*] **a** : to be or occur at (a particular time) • This year

marks her 10th year with the company. [=this is her 10th year with the company] **b :** to indicate the occurrence of (an important event or time) • Her death *marked* the end of an era. [=an era ended when she died] **c :** to celebrate (an important event or time) by doing something • We'll have a big party to *mark* our 50th anniversary.
8 [+ *obj*] **:** to show that (someone or something) is special or different in some way • Her very first book *marked* her as a great poet. [=showed that she was a great poet] • She was evidently *marked* [=*destined*] for greatness. — see also MARK OUT (below)
mark down [*phrasal verb*] **1** ***mark down or mark (someone or something) down or mark down (someone or something)*** **:** to give a lower mark to (someone or something) • *mark* a student *down* for not acknowledging his sources • Your paper was well-written, but I had to *mark* it *down* [=give it a lower grade] for being late. • Some teachers *mark down* for poor penmanship. **2** ***mark (something) down or mark down (something)*** **:** to give (something) a lower price • a product *marked down* from $15 to $13.75 • Everything has been *marked down* for the sale. — see also MARKDOWN
mark my words — used to tell someone to listen to and remember what you are saying • *Mark my words*: nothing good will come of this!
mark off [*phrasal verb*] ***mark (something) off or mark off (something)*** **:** to make (an area) separate with a line, fence, etc. • We *marked off* an area where people could wait.
mark out [*phrasal verb*] **1** ***mark (something) out or mark out (something)*** **:** to draw lines around (something) so that it can be clearly seen • He *marked out* his mining claim. **2** ***mark (something) out or mark out (something)*** **:** to plan the details of (a course of action) • She talked about the course the European Union has *marked out* [=*mapped out*] for itself. **3** ***mark (someone or something) out or mark out (someone or something) chiefly Brit*** **:** to show that (someone or something) is special or different in some way • Her very first book *marked* her *out* as a great poet. [=showed that she was a great poet] • She was *marked out* [=*destined, marked*] for greatness.
mark time **1 :** to move your feet up and down like someone who is marching but without moving forward • The soldiers *marked time* until ordered to advance. **2 :** to live without doing much while you wait for something to happen • I'm just *marking time* until I retire.
mark up [*phrasal verb*] **1** ***mark (something) up or mark up (something)*** **:** to make marks and write comments in or on (something) • *mark up* a manuscript **2** ***mark (something) up or mark up (something)*** **:** to give (something) a higher price • a product *marked up* from $15 to $15.99 • a product *marked up* by 10 percent — see also MARKUP
mark you *Brit, old-fashioned* — used in speech to give stress to a statement that you are making so that a preceding or following statement will not be misunderstood • I don't always agree with him. *Mark you*, [=*mind you*] I'm not criticizing him!
— see also MARKED

³mark *noun, pl* **marks** [*count*] **:** DEUTSCHE MARK — compare ¹MARK

mark•down /ˈmɑɚkˌdaʊn/ *noun, pl* **-downs** [*count*] **:** a reduction in price • a *markdown* of 10 percent = a 10 percent *markdown* — see also *mark down* at ²MARK

marked /ˈmɑɚkt/ *adj*
1 : having a mark or a particular kind of mark • a *marked* card [=a playing card that has a secret mark on its back so that someone can see what the card is without looking at its face] • All the streets are well-*marked*. [=all the streets have signs showing their names] • The bird's wings are *marked* with white. [=the bird has white marks on its wings]
2 *always used before a noun* [*more* ~; *most* ~] **:** very noticeable • He speaks with a *marked* accent. • There was a *marked* change in her attitude. • There's been a *marked* improvement in the weather. • His current friendly manner is ***in marked contrast to*** his usual behavior. [=is very different from his usual behavior]
a marked man/woman **1 :** someone who is famous or who gets a lot of attention • Winning the race made him *a marked man*. • As the front-runner, the candidate has become *a marked woman*. **2 :** someone who is not liked or trusted or who is in danger of being harmed • His unpopular ideas made him *a marked man* at work.
— mark•ed•ly /ˈmɑɚkədli/ *adv* • *markedly* different opinions • The town had changed *markedly*.

mark•er /ˈmɑɚkɚ/ *noun, pl* **-ers** [*count*]
1 : something (such as a sign or an object) that shows the location of something • a grave *marker*
2 : something that shows the presence or existence of something • a *marker* for/of cancer • A person's accent can be a *marker* of social class.
3 : a type of pen that makes wide lines — see picture at OFFICE; see also MAGIC MARKER

¹mar•ket /ˈmɑɚkət/ *noun, pl* **-kets**
1 [*count*] **a :** a place where products are bought and sold • a fish/meat/produce *market* • a street *market* • a country *market* — see also FLEA MARKET **b** *US* **:** a store where foods and often household items are sold **:** SUPERMARKET • I stopped at the *market* on the way home for some juice.
2 [*count*] **a :** an area (such as a country or part of a country) where a product or service can be sold • They are trying to develop foreign *markets* for American cotton. • The company sells mainly to the Southern *market*. • New *markets* are opening up all over the world. **b :** a particular type of people who might buy something • Advertisers are trying to appeal to the youth *market*. • targeting a more mature *market* • a reference work for the educational *market* — see also BLACK MARKET, BUYER'S MARKET, SELLER'S MARKET
3 [*singular*] **:** the amount of need and desire that people have for a product or service — used to describe how many people want to buy something; usually + *for* • There is a good/growing *market for* new homes. [=there are many people who want to buy new homes] • There is currently a poor/declining *market for* used cars. • They found a ready *market for* their products. [=they easily found many people who wanted to buy their products]
4 [*singular*] **:** the available supply of workers or jobs • the ***labor market*** [=the number of workers who are available to be hired] • the ***job market*** [=the number of jobs that are available for workers]
5 [*singular*] **:** the economic activity of buying and selling that causes prices to become higher or lower • He believes that housing prices should be determined by ***the market*** without government interference. • a ***market-driven*** industry/economy — see also FREE MARKET, SINGLE MARKET
6 [*count*] **:** the activity of buyers and sellers of a particular product • It's not clear how these changes may affect the software *market*.
7 [*singular*] **:** STOCK MARKET • The *market* was down today in heavy trading. • He enjoys ***playing the market***. [=actively buying and selling stocks in the hope of making a profit] — see also BEAR MARKET, BULL MARKET
in the market **:** looking for something in particular **:** interested in buying or finding something • He hasn't found a new job yet, but he is still *in the market*. [=he is still looking for a new job] — usually + *for* • She is *in the market for* a new house. [=she is looking for a new house to buy] • She's *in the market for* a husband.
on the market **:** available to be bought • Their house is still *on the market*. • The land just came *on the* (open) *market* last week. • The software will be *on the market* next month. • They've decided to ***put*** their house ***on the market***. [=they've decided to sell their house]
price (someone) out of the market see ²PRICE

²market *verb* **-kets; -ket•ed; -ket•ing** [+ *obj*]
1 : to do things that cause people to know about and want to buy (something) • The company has spent millions *marketing* the latest version of its software. • These products are being aggressively *marketed* to teenagers through television ads. — see also MARKETING
2 : to offer (something) for sale in a market **:** SELL • He *markets* his wares at craft shows.
— mar•ket•er *noun, pl* **-ers** [*count*] • a leading *marketer* of software • She is a *marketer* for a publishing company.

mar•ket•able /ˈmɑɚkətəbəl/ *adj* [*more* ~; *most* ~] **:** able to be sold **:** wanted by buyers or employers • a *marketable* product • an employee with highly/very *marketable* skills
— mar•ket•abil•i•ty /ˌmɑɚkətəˈbɪləti/ *noun* [*noncount*] • a product's potential *marketability*

market economy *noun, pl* ~ **-mies** [*count*] **:** an economic system in which prices are based on competition among private businesses and not controlled by a government

mar•ke•teer /ˌmɑɚkəˈtiɚ/ *noun, pl* **-teers** [*count*]
1 : a person or company that sells or promotes a product or service • software *marketeers* [=*marketers*]
2 : a person or company that is associated with a specified kind of market • a ***black marketeer*** [=a person who sells

things on the black market] ▪ a ***free marketeer*** [=a person who supports free markets]

market forces *noun [plural]* : the actions of buyers and sellers that cause the prices of goods and services to change without being controlled by the government : the economic forces of supply and demand ▪ The value of these commodities is determined by *market forces.*

market garden *noun, pl* ~ **-dens** *[count] Brit* : TRUCK FARM

– **market gardener** *noun, pl* ~ **-ers** *[count]*

mar·ket·ing /ˈmɑɚkətɪŋ/ *noun [noncount]* : the activities that are involved in making people aware of a company's products, making sure that the products are available to be bought, etc. ▪ The company will increase its budget for *marketing.* ▪ She has a job in *marketing.* ▪ She runs the company's *marketing* department.

mar·ket·place /ˈmɑɚkətˌpleɪs/ *noun, pl* **-plac·es**
1 *[singular]* : the economic system through which different companies compete with each other to sell their products ▪ Their products must compete in the *marketplace.* ▪ The company has struggled to survive in a rapidly changing *marketplace.*
2 *[count]* : a place in a town where markets are held

market price *noun [singular]* : the price at which a product can be sold at a particular time

market research *noun [noncount]* : research that is done to get information about what people want to buy, why they want to buy it, etc.

– **market researcher** *noun, pl* ~ **-ers** *[count]*

market share *noun, pl* ~ **shares** : the percentage that a company has of the total sales for a particular product or service *[noncount]* The company has gained/lost *market share* in the past year. *[count]* companies working to increase/improve their *market shares*

market value *noun, pl* ~ **-ues** : the price at which something can be sold : the price that buyers are willing to pay for something *[count]* When he tried to sell his car he found out that its *market value* was much lower than he had expected. *[noncount]* The house sold below *market value.*

mark·ing /ˈmɑɚkɪŋ/ *noun, pl* **-ings** *[count]*
1 : a mark, shape, or word that is written or drawn on something — usually plural ▪ road *markings* ▪ It was difficult to read the *markings* on the label.
2 : a mark or pattern of marks on the body of an animal — usually plural ▪ a black cat with white *markings*
3 : the act or process of giving a grade to a student's work ▪ the *marking* [=(US) *grading*] of students' papers
have (all) the markings of *chiefly US* : to have the qualities or features of (something) ▪ They have *all the markings of* a championship team. ▪ a movie that *has all the markings of* [=*has all the makings of*] a big hit

marks·man /ˈmɑɚksmən/ *noun, pl* **-men** /-mən/ *[count]* : a person (especially a man) who is skilled in shooting a gun at a target

marks·man·ship /ˈmɑɚksmənˌʃɪp/ *noun [noncount]* : skill in shooting guns

marks·wom·an /ˈmɑɚksˌwʊmən/ *noun, pl* **-wom·en** /-ˌwɪmən/ *[count]* : a woman who is skilled in shooting a gun at a target

mark·up /ˈmɑɚkˌʌp/ *noun, pl* **-ups** *[count]* : an amount added to the price of something : the difference between the cost of producing something and its selling price ▪ The retail *markup* on their products is 25 percent. ▪ selling used cars at high *markups* — see also *mark up* at [2]MARK

mar·lin /ˈmɑɚlən/ *noun, pl* **marlin** *or* **mar·lins** *[count]* : a large fish that lives in the sea and that people catch for sport — see color picture on page C8

mar·ma·lade /ˈmɑɚməˌleɪd/ *noun, pl* **-lades** *[count, noncount]* : a sweet jelly that contains pieces of fruit ▪ a jar of orange *marmalade*

mar·mo·set /ˈmɑɚməˌset, *Brit* ˈmɑːməˌzɛt/ *noun, pl* **-sets** *[count]* : a small monkey of South and Central America that has soft fur and a long tail

mar·mot /ˈmɑɚmət/ *noun, pl* **-mots** *[count]* : a small animal of America and Europe that has short legs and that lives in holes that it digs in the ground

[1]**ma·roon** /məˈruːn/ *noun [noncount]* : a dark red color — see color picture on page C3

– **maroon** *adj* ▪ a *maroon* fabric

[2]**maroon** *verb* **-roons; -rooned; -roon·ing** *[+ obj]* : to leave (someone) in a place (such as an island) that is difficult or impossible to get away from — usually used as *(be) marooned* ▪ The sailors *were marooned* [=*stranded*] on the island for six months. ▪ She *was marooned* [=*stuck*] at the office without a ride home.

marque /ˈmɑɚk/ *noun, pl* **marques** *[count]* : a group of products (such as sports cars) that are made by a particular company and given a particular name ▪ could finally afford a car of a fashionable *marque* [=*brand, make*]

[1]**mar·quee** /mɑɚˈkiː/ *noun, pl* **-quees** *[count]*
1 *US* **a** : a covered structure over the entrance to a building (such as a hotel or theater) **b** : a sign over the entrance to a theater that shows the name of the show, movie, play, etc., and the names of the main performers ▪ She dreamed of seeing her name on the theater *marquee.*
2 *Brit* : a large tent that is set up for an outdoor event (such as a party)

[2]**marquee** *adj, always used before a noun, US, informal* : very popular and well known ▪ The film features two *marquee* [=*big-name, star*] performers. ▪ *marquee* athletes/events

mar·quess /ˈmɑɚkwəs/ *noun, pl* **-quess·es** *[count]* : a British nobleman who has a rank that is below a duke and above an earl

mar·quis /ˈmɑɚkwəs/ *noun, pl* **-quis·es** *[count]* : MARQUESS

mar·riage /ˈmerɪʤ/ *noun, pl* **-riag·es**
1 a : the relationship that exists between a husband and a wife *[count]* It was his second *marriage.* ▪ They have a very happy *marriage.* ▪ Her first two *marriages* ended in divorce. *[noncount]* She has old-fashioned ideas about *marriage.* ▪ the institution of *marriage* ▪ He ***proposed marriage*** to his girlfriend. [=asked his girlfriend to marry him] ▪ couples living together before *marriage* ▪ They were ***joined in marriage*** [=they were married] last year. ▪ They are related ***by marriage.*** [=they are related because one of them is married to a family member of the other] — see also ARRANGED MARRIAGE, CIVIL MARRIAGE, MARRIAGE OF CONVENIENCE, MIXED MARRIAGE **b** : a similar relationship between people of the same sex *[count]* a same-sex *marriage* *[noncount]* opponents/supporters of same-sex *marriage* ▪ gay *marriage*
2 *[count]* : a ceremony in which two people are married to each other ▪ Many friends and relatives were present at their *marriage.* ▪ a priest who has performed many *marriages*
3 *[singular]* : a close union *of* or *between* two things ▪ a *marriage of* sweet and spicy flavors ▪ a *marriage of* science and art ▪ a *marriage between* form and function
marriage bed see [1]BED

mar·riage·able /ˈmerɪʤəbəl/ *adj* : able to marry or suitable for marriage ▪ a woman of *marriageable* age [=a woman who is old enough to marry]

marriage certificate *noun, pl* ~ **-cates** *[count]* : a legal document that shows that a marriage has taken place

marriage counseling *(US) or Brit* **marriage counselling** *noun [noncount] chiefly US* : help for married couples who have problems in their relationship ▪ They are going to *marriage counseling.* ▪ They need *marriage counseling.* — called also *(Brit) marriage guidance*

marriage license *noun, pl* ~ **-censes** *[count]* : a legal document that is needed for a marriage to occur

marriage of convenience *noun, pl* **marriages of convenience** *[count]* : a marriage made for social, political, or economic reasons and not for love — usually singular; often used figuratively ▪ The two companies have joined together in a *marriage of convenience.*

[1]**mar·ried** /ˈmerid/ *adj*
1 a : united in marriage ▪ a newly/recently *married* couple ▪ They are happily *married* with several children. ▪ They're planning to ***get married*** [=planning to marry] in October. **b** : having a husband or wife ▪ a *married* man/woman ▪ Is he *married?* — often + *to* ▪ He has been *married to* his wife for almost 50 years. = He and his wife have been *married to* each other for almost 50 years. **c** *always used before a noun* : of or relating to marriage ▪ He's enjoying *married* life.
2 : very involved with something (such as a job) — + *to* ▪ He's *married to* his work. [=he gives all of his attention to his work]

[2]**married** *noun, pl* **-rieds** *[count] informal* : a married person — usually plural ▪ Lots of young *marrieds* are moving into the neighborhood.

married name *noun, pl* ~ **names** *[count]* : a married woman's last name if she uses her husband's last name as her own ▪ She used to be Susan Brown, but her *married name* is Susan Wilson.

M

mar·row /ˈmeroʊ/ *noun, pl* **-rows**
1 [*noncount*] : a soft substance that fills the bones of people and animals — called also *bone marrow*
2 [*count, noncount*] *Brit* : a large, long vegetable with dark green skin
to the marrow : very much • We were frozen *to the marrow*. [=we were very cold] • The look in his eyes ***chilled me to the marrow*** [=made me feel very fearful]

mar·ry /ˈmeri/ *verb* **-ries; -ried; -ry·ing**
1 : to become the husband or wife of (someone) : to become joined with (someone) in marriage [+ *obj*] He *married* his college sweetheart. • *marrying* a doctor/lawyer • I asked her to *marry* me. • "Will you *marry* me?" "Yes, I will." [*no obj*] He hopes to *marry* [=*get married*] soon. • She *married* young. [=she was young when she married] • They *married* for love, not money.
2 [+ *obj*] : to perform a ceremony in which two people get married • The minister has *married* more than 100 couples. • They hope to have a priest *marry* them. • They were *married* by a justice of the peace.
3 [+ *obj*] : to find a husband or wife for (your child) — often + *to* • He *married* his daughter *to* his partner's son. — often + *off* • They *married* their son *off to* the daughter of a close friend. • trying to *marry* their children *off*
4 [+ *obj*] : to join or combine (two things) closely • The design *marries* traditional elements with/to/and modern methods.
marry into [*phrasal verb*] ***marry into (something)*** : to become a member of (something, such as a family, group, culture, etc.) by marrying someone • He *married into* a very wealthy family. [=his wife's family is very wealthy] • She *married into* the upper class.
marry money : to marry someone who is wealthy • My cousin hopes to *marry money*.

Mars /ˈmaɚz/ *noun* [*singular*] : the planet that is fourth in order from the sun

marsh /ˈmaɚʃ/ *noun, pl* **marsh·es** : an area of soft, wet land that has many grasses and other plants [*count*] wetlands and *marshes* [*noncount*] a wide expanse of *marsh* • *marsh* grasses
– marshy /ˈmaɚʃi/ *adj* **marsh·i·er; -est** [*also more* ~; *most* ~] • a wet *marshy* region/habitat • *marshy* ground

M

[1]**mar·shal** /ˈmaɚʃəl/ *noun, pl* **-shals** [*count*]
1 : an officer of the highest rank in some military forces — see also FIELD MARSHAL
2 *US* : a federal official who is responsible for doing the things that are ordered by a court of law, finding and capturing criminals, etc.
3 *US* : the head of a division of a police or fire department • a fire *marshal*
4 : person who arranges and directs ceremonies or parades • a parade *marshal* — see also GRAND MARSHAL

[2]**marshal** *verb* **-shals**; *US* **-shaled** *or chiefly Brit* **-shalled**; *US* **-shal·ing** *or chiefly Brit* **-shal·ling** [+ *obj*]
1 a : to arrange (a group of people, such as soldiers) in an orderly way • *marshal* the troops/forces **b** : to move or lead (a group of people) in a careful way • The teacher *marshaled* [=*ushered*] the children into the classroom.
2 : to arrange or prepare (something, such as your thoughts or ideas) in a clear, effective, or organized way • She carefully *marshaled* her thoughts before answering the question. • *marshal* an argument

marsh·land /ˈmaɚʃˌlænd/ *noun, pl* **-lands** : an area of soft and wet land : MARSH [*count*] living near a *marshland* [*noncount*] one hundred acres of *marshland*

marsh·mal·low /ˈmaɚʃˌmɛloʊ, *Brit* ˌmɑːʃˈmæləʊ/ *noun, pl* **-lows** [*count, noncount*] : a soft, white, sweet food made of sugar and eggs • We toasted *marshmallows* over the fire.

mar·su·pi·al /maɚˈsuːpijəl/ *noun, pl* **-als** [*count*] : a type of animal (such as a kangaroo or an opossum) that carries its babies in a pocket of skin on the mother's stomach
– marsupial *adj* • a *marsupial* species

mart /ˈmaɚt/ *noun, pl* **marts** [*count*] *chiefly US* : a place where things are bought and sold : MARKET • an antiques *mart*

mar·ten /ˈmaɚtn̩/ *noun, pl* **marten** *or* **mar·tens**
1 [*count*] : a small animal that is related to the weasel and has soft gray or brown fur
2 [*noncount*] : the fur of a marten

mar·tial /ˈmaɚʃəl/ *adj, always used before a noun* : of or relating to war or soldiers • *martial* music • *martial* [=*military*] discipline

martial art *noun, pl* ~ **arts** [*count*] : any one of several forms of fighting and self-defense (such as karate and judo) that are widely practiced as sports • He was trained in the *martial arts*.
– martial artist *noun, pl* ~ **-ists** [*count*]

martial law *noun* [*noncount*] : control of an area by military forces rather than by the police • The government has imposed/declared *martial law* throughout the city to stop the riots. • an area placed under *martial law*

[1]**Mar·tian** /ˈmaɚʃən/ *adj, always used before a noun* : of or relating to the planet Mars • the *Martian* landscape • the *Martian* day/year

[2]**Martian** *noun, pl* **-tians** [*count*] : an imaginary creature in books, movies, etc., that lives on or comes from the planet Mars

mar·tin /ˈmaɚtn̩/ *noun, pl* **-tins** [*count*] : a small bird that is related to the swallows

mar·ti·net /ˌmaɚtəˈnɛt/ *noun, pl* **-nets** [*count*] *formal* : a person who is very strict and demands obedience from others • The prison's warden was a cruel *martinet*.

mar·ti·ni /maɚˈtiːni/ *noun, pl* **-nis** [*count*] : an alcoholic drink made with gin and vermouth • He ordered a *martini*. • a *martini* glass • a dry *martini*; *also* : a similar drink made with vodka instead of gin • a vodka *martini*

[1]**mar·tyr** /ˈmaɚtɚ/ *noun, pl* **-tyrs** [*count*]
1 : a person who is killed or who suffers greatly for a religion, cause, etc. • the early Christian *martyrs* • They know that killing him will only make a *martyr* out of him. [=will make him someone who is admired as a hero for having suffered or died for a cause] — sometimes + *to* • He was a *martyr to* a noble cause. [=he died or suffered for a noble cause]
2 *disapproving* : a person who pretends to suffer or who exaggerates suffering in order to get praise or sympathy • He enjoys ***playing the martyr***. [=he enjoys acting like someone who deserves admiration or sympathy because of being badly treated]
3 : a person who suffers greatly from something (such as an illness) — + *to* • a *martyr to* rheumatism

[2]**martyr** *verb* **-tyrs; -tyred; -tyr·ing** [+ *obj*] : to kill (someone) for refusing to give up a belief or cause — usually used as *(be) martyred* • He *was martyred* for his religious beliefs.

mar·tyr·dom /ˈmaɚtɚdəm/ *noun, pl* **-doms** : the suffering and death of a martyr [*noncount*] He suffered *martyrdom* [=he was martyred] for his religious beliefs. [*count*] religious *martyrdoms*

[1]**mar·vel** /ˈmaɚvəl/ *noun, pl* **-vels** [*count*] : someone or something that is extremely good, skillful, etc. : a wonderful or marvelous person or thing • That boy is a *marvel*! [=*wonder*] • The bridge is a *marvel* of engineering. = The bridge is an engineering *marvel*. • architectural *marvels*

[2]**marvel** *verb* **-vels**; *US* **-veled** *or chiefly Brit* **-velled**; *US* **-vel·ing** *or chiefly Brit* **-vel·ling** : to feel great surprise, wonder, or admiration [*no obj*] — usually + *at* or *over* • The audience *marveled at* the magician's skill. • The doctors are *marveling over* her dramatic recovery. [+ *obj*] The doctors *marveled* that anyone could recover so quickly.

mar·vel·ous (*US*) *or chiefly Brit* **mar·vel·lous** /ˈmaɚvələs/ *adj* [*more* ~; *most* ~] : extremely good or enjoyable : WONDERFUL • We had a *marvelous* time at the party. • He has a *marvelous* way with children. • The weather was simply *marvelous*. • a *marvelous* writer/book/idea
– mar·vel·ous·ly (*US*) *or chiefly Brit* **mar·vel·lous·ly** *adv* • They all get along *marvelously*. • a *marvelously* entertaining book

Marx·ism /ˈmaɚkˌsɪzəm/ *noun* [*noncount*] : the political, economic, and social theories of Karl Marx including the belief that the struggle between social classes is a major force in history and that there should eventually be a society in which there are no classes
– Marx·ist /ˈmaɚksɪst/ *adj* • *Marxist* theory • a *Marxist* government **– Marxist** *noun, pl* **-ists** [*count*]

mar·zi·pan /ˈmaɚzəˌpæn/ *noun* [*noncount*] : a sweet food that is made with almonds, sugar, and eggs and that is often made into various shapes or used to cover cakes

mas·cara /mæˈskerə, *Brit* mæˈskɑːrə/ *noun, pl* **-caras** [*count, noncount*] : a type of makeup used for darkening and thickening eyelashes — see picture at GROOMING

mas·cot /ˈmæˌskɑːt/ *noun, pl* **-cots** [*count*] : a person, animal, or object used as a symbol to represent a group (such as a sports team) and to bring good luck • The team had a mountain lion as their *mascot*.

Color Art

Contents

Colors

A single color may be given different names by different people, and a single color name may be used for a range of colors that are similar to each other. These three pages show names that are commonly used for the colors shown.

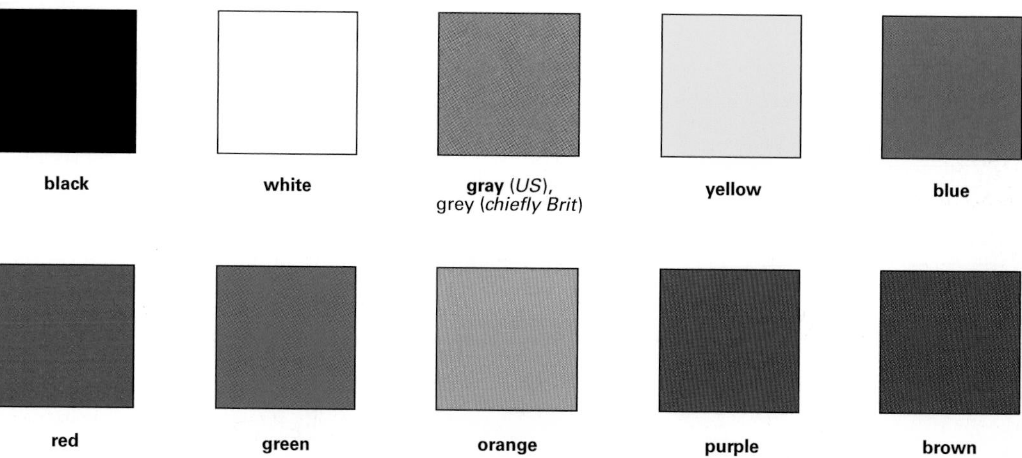

Colors

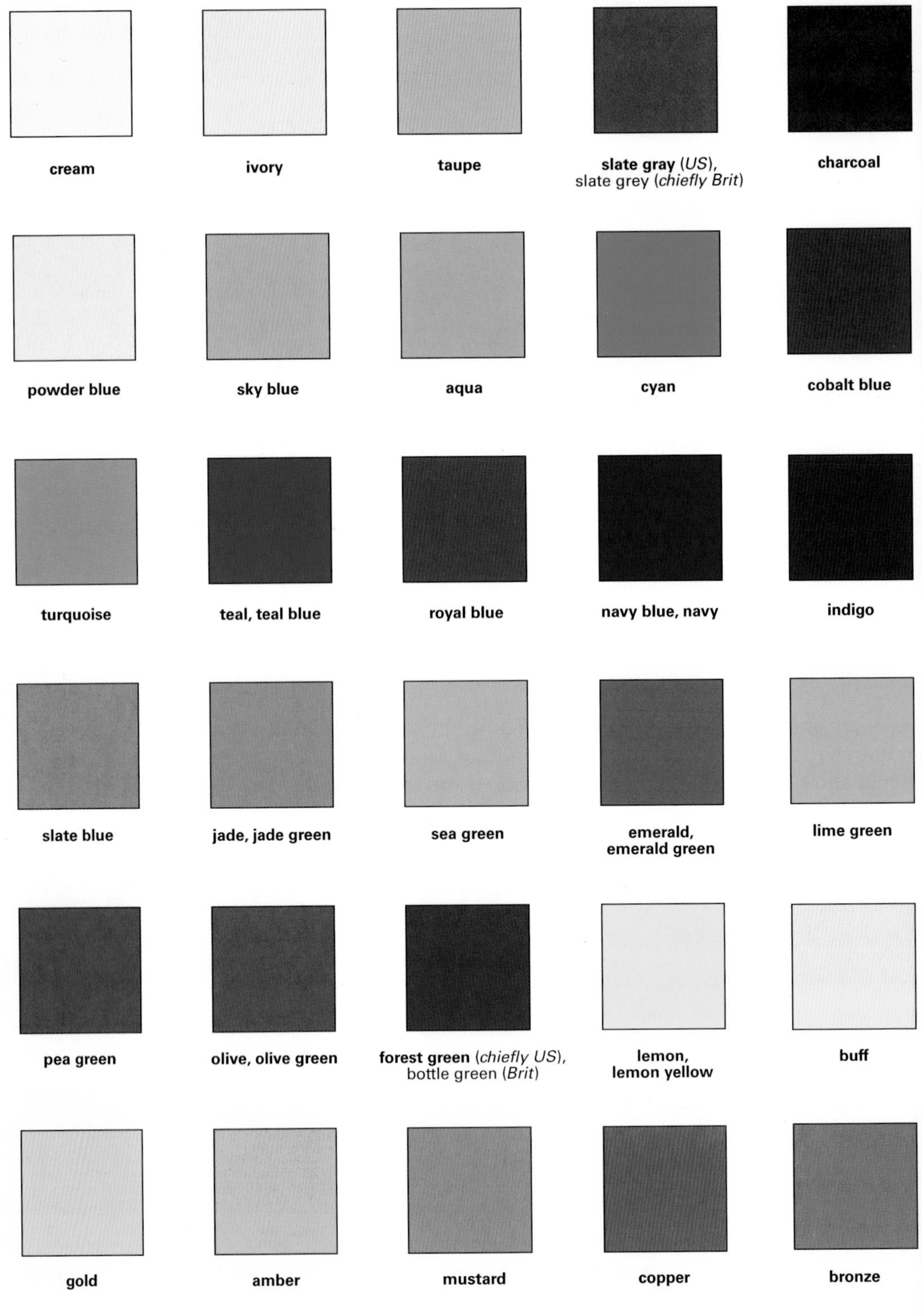

cream
ivory
taupe
slate gray (*US*), slate grey (*chiefly Brit*)
charcoal
powder blue
sky blue
aqua
cyan
cobalt blue
turquoise
teal, teal blue
royal blue
navy blue, navy
indigo
slate blue
jade, jade green
sea green
emerald, emerald green
lime green
pea green
olive, olive green
forest green (*chiefly US*), bottle green (*Brit*)
lemon, lemon yellow
buff
gold
amber
mustard
copper
bronze

Colors

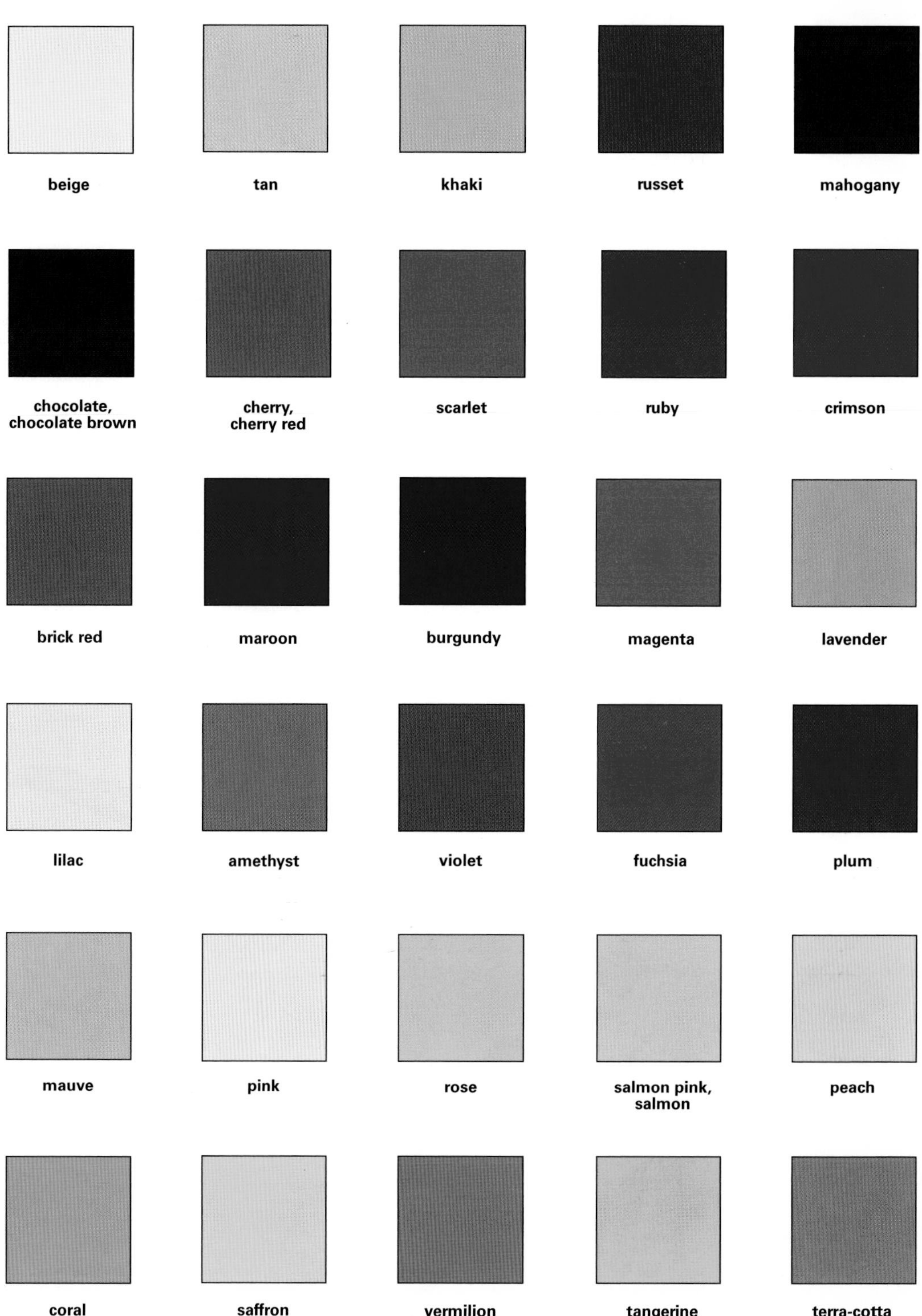
beige
tan
khaki
russet
mahogany
chocolate, chocolate brown
cherry, cherry red
scarlet
ruby
crimson
brick red
maroon
burgundy
magenta
lavender
lilac
amethyst
violet
fuchsia
plum
mauve
pink
rose
salmon pink, salmon
peach
coral
saffron
vermilion
tangerine
terra-cotta

Vegetables

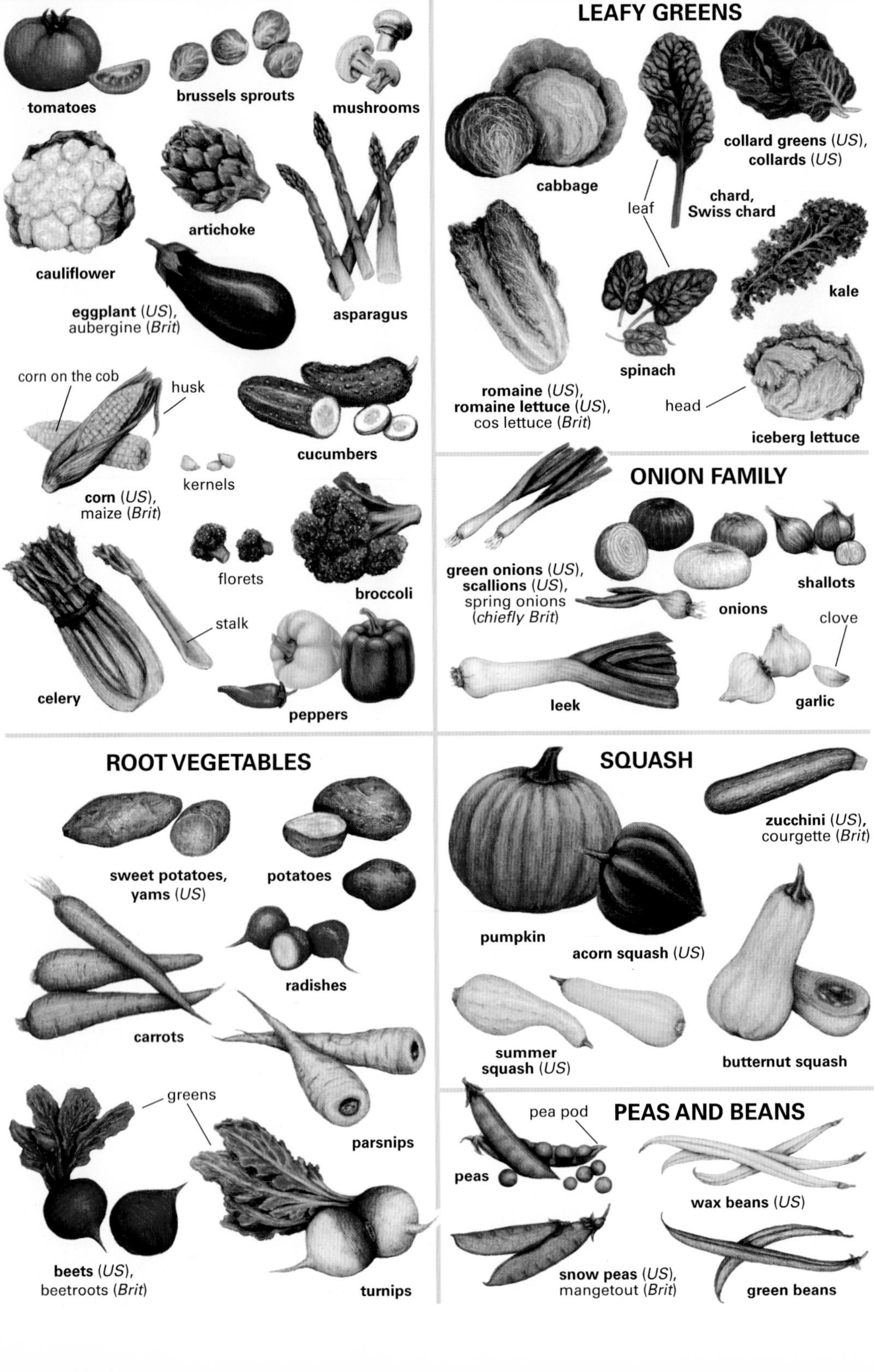

tomatoes

brussels sprouts

mushrooms

cauliflower

artichoke

asparagus

eggplant (*US*), aubergine (*Brit*)

corn on the cob

husk

cucumbers

kernels

corn (*US*), maize (*Brit*)

florets

broccoli

stalk

celery

peppers

LEAFY GREENS

cabbage

collard greens (*US*), **collards** (*US*)

leaf

chard, Swiss chard

kale

spinach

romaine (*US*), **romaine lettuce** (*US*), cos lettuce (*Brit*)

head

iceberg lettuce

ONION FAMILY

green onions (*US*), **scallions** (*US*), spring onions (*chiefly Brit*)

shallots

onions

clove

leek

garlic

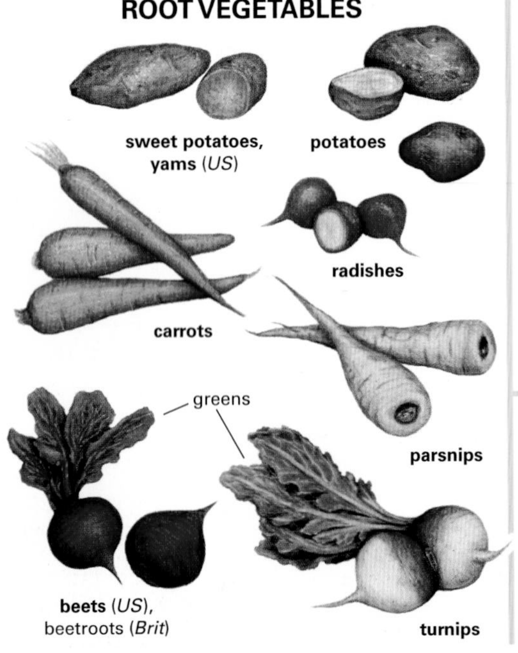

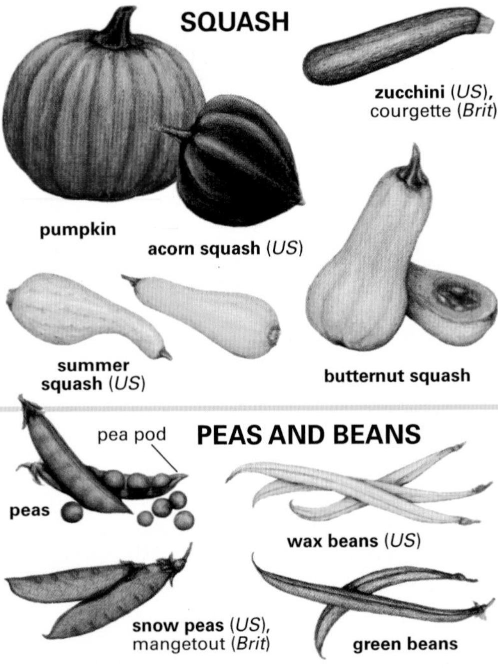

Fruits

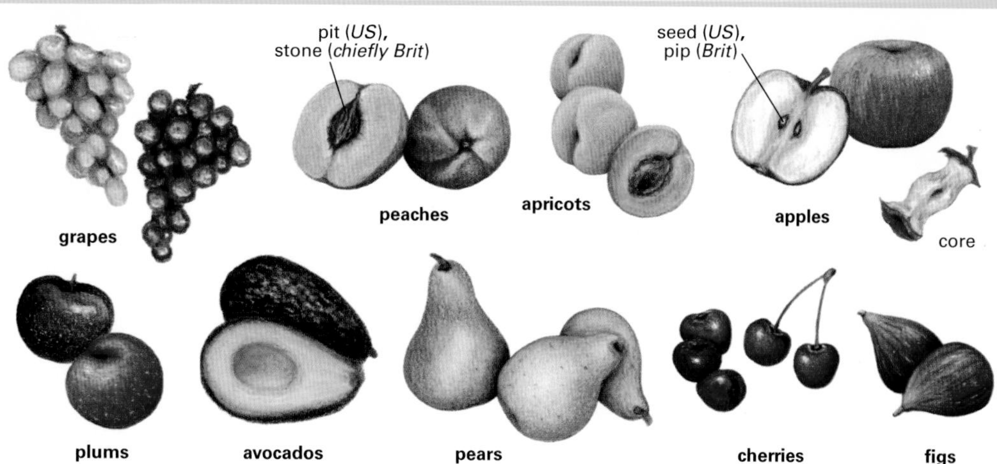

BERRIES

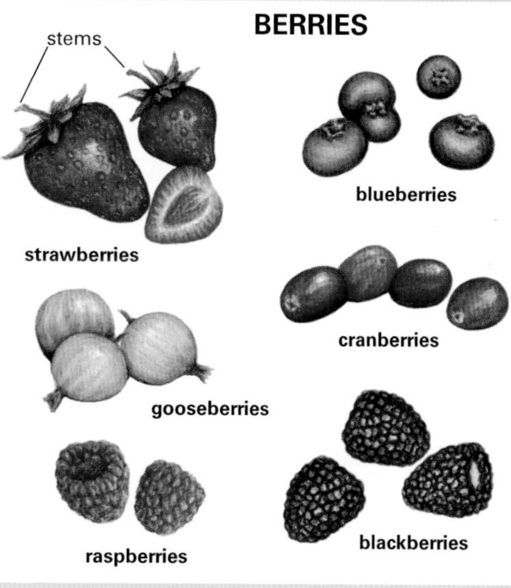

TROPICAL FRUIT

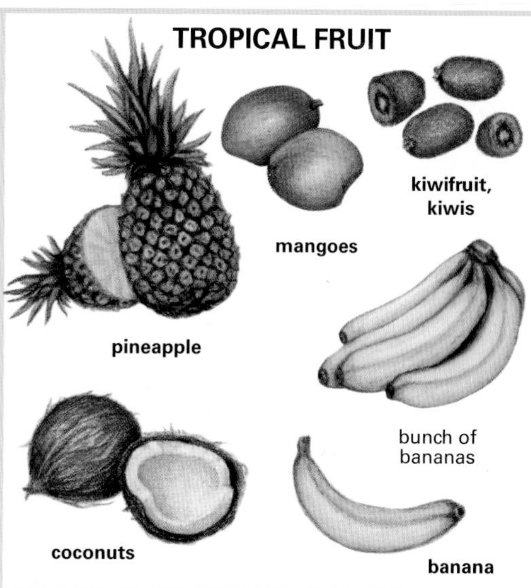

CITRUS FRUIT

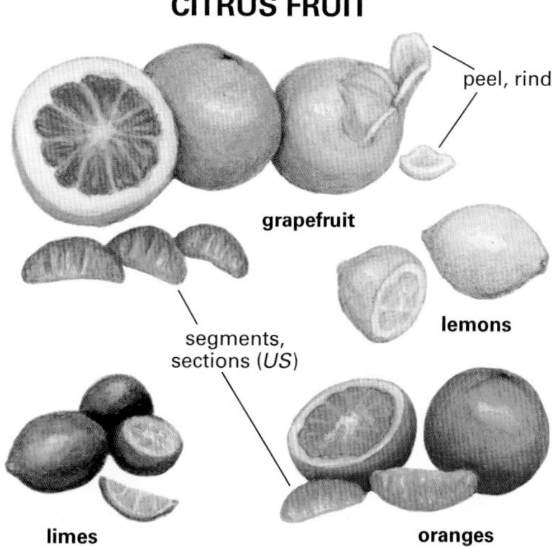

MELONS

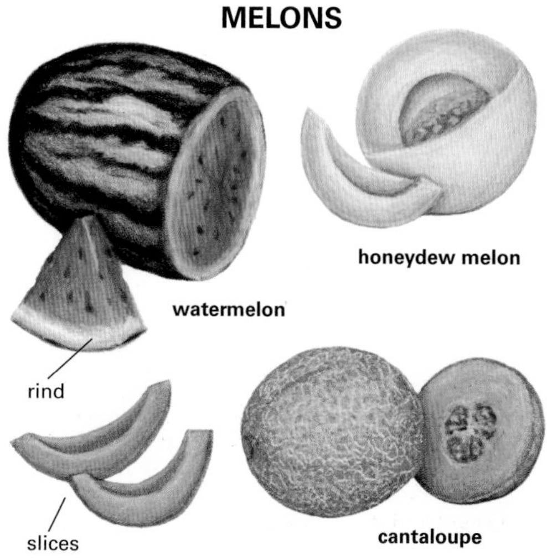

Plants

TREE

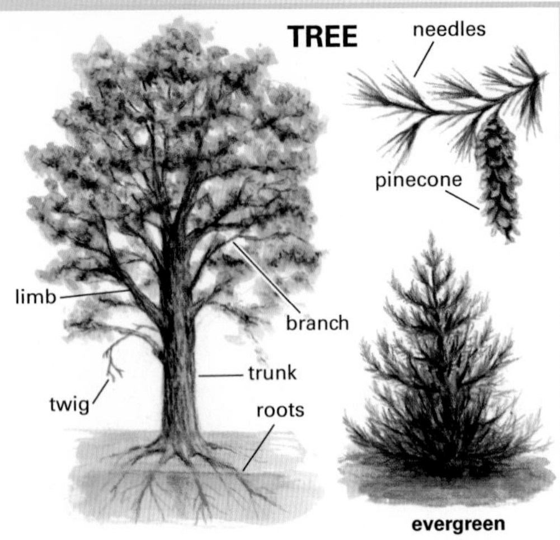
needles
pinecone
limb
branch
trunk
twig
roots
evergreen

YARD

ivy,
English ivy (*US*)
arbor
fence
birdbath
hedge
bush,
shrub
path
garden (*US*),
flower bed
lawn

FLOWERS

petal
vine
stem
leaf
thorn
geranium
irises
carnations
pansy
orchids
rose
daffodils
morning glories
bud
stalk,
stem
bulb
lily
tulips
poinsettia
chrysanthemums,
mums (*US*)
sunflower
hyacinth
fuchsias

HOUSEPLANTS

HERBS

bonsai
African violet
palm
philodendron
cactus
fern
basil
rosemary
cilantro (*US*),
coriander
(*chiefly Brit*)
dill,
dill weed (*US*)
thyme
sage
parsley
oregano
mint

Landscapes

mountain range
peak
mountain
valley
river
forest
bay
lake
peninsula
waterfall
cliff
field
island
mesa
plateau
butte
desert
dune, sand dune
horizon
the ocean,
the sea
beach
surf

Fish and Shellfish

FISH

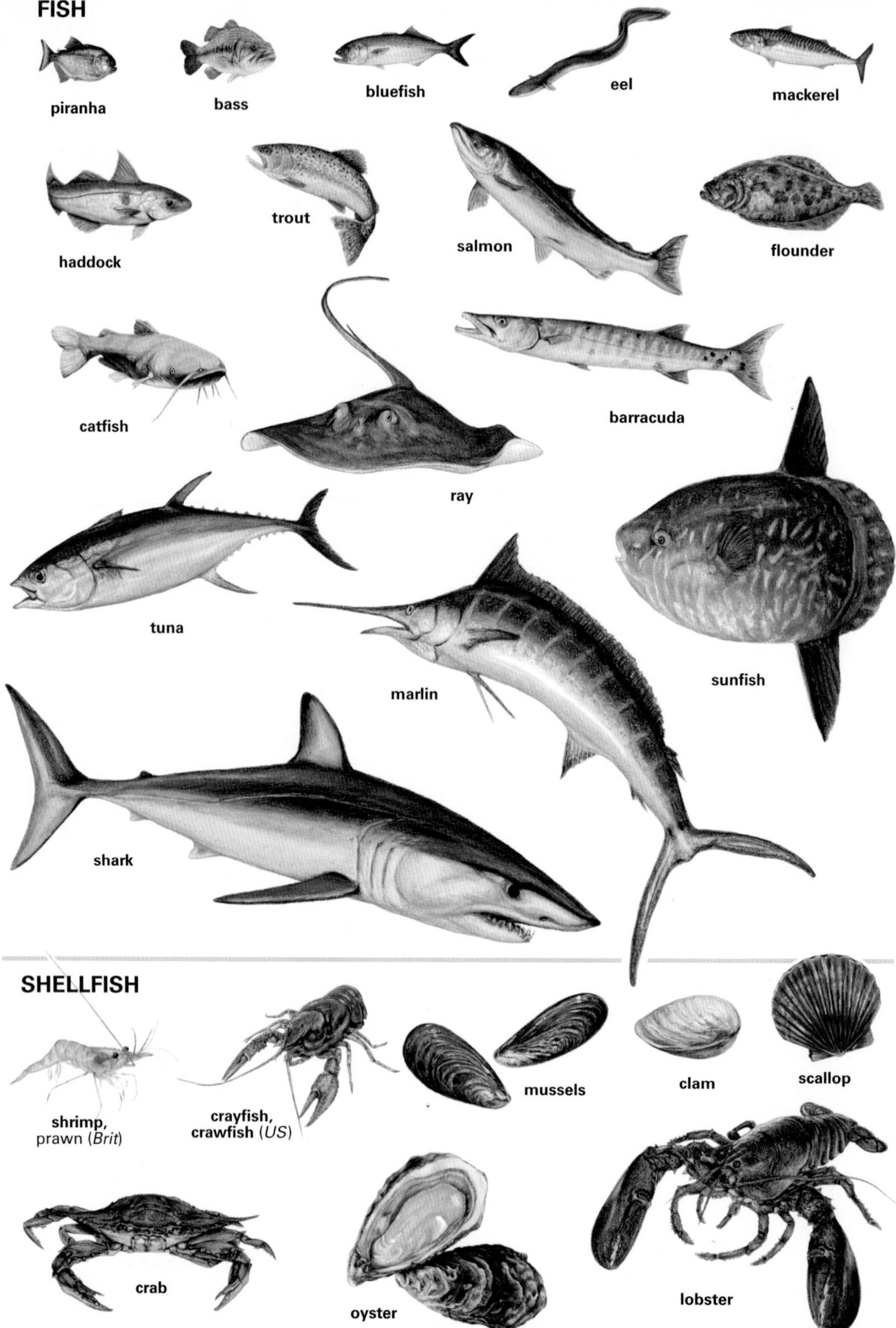

SHELLFISH

Birds

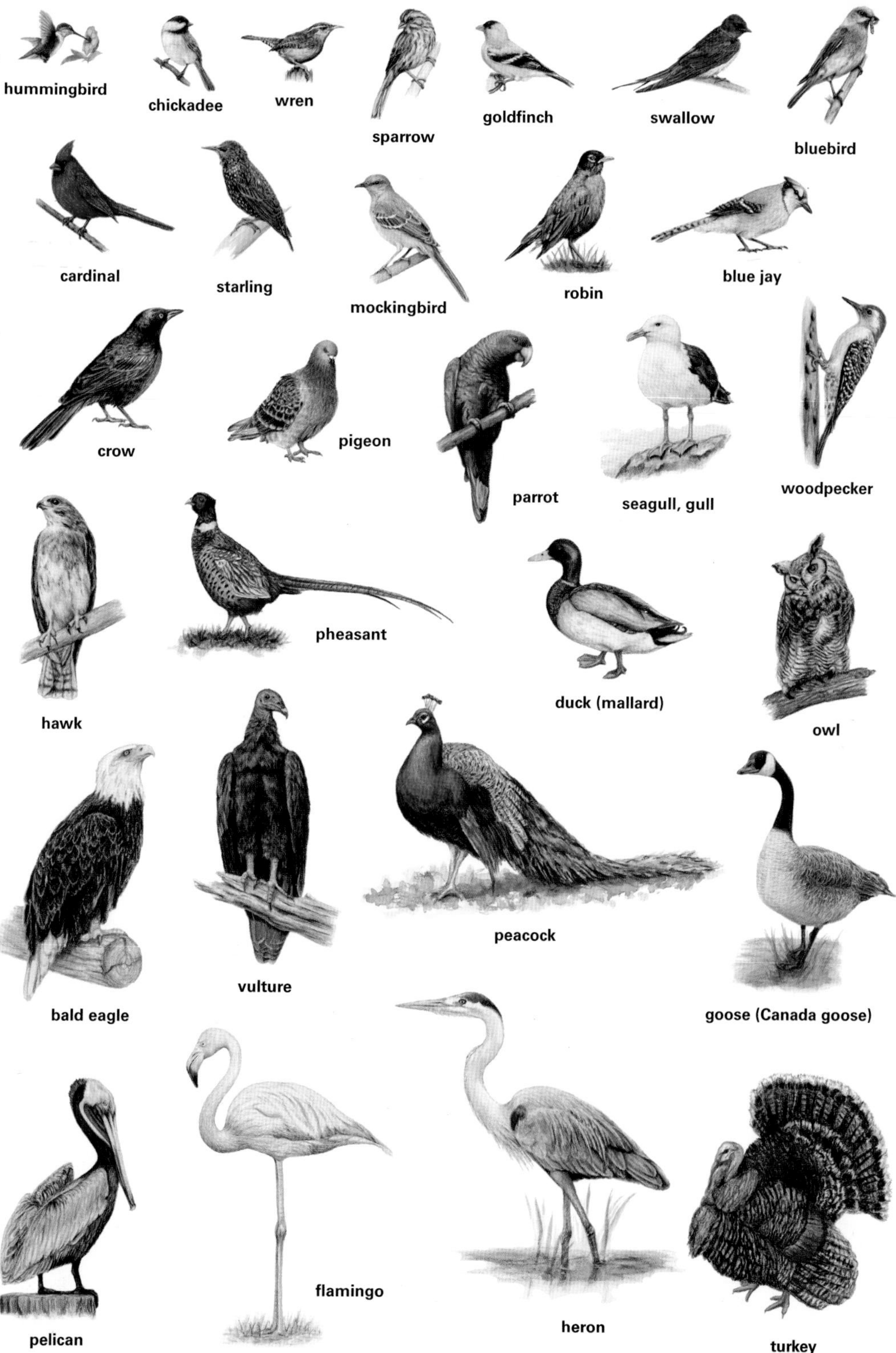
hummingbird
chickadee
wren
sparrow
goldfinch
swallow
bluebird
cardinal
starling
mockingbird
robin
blue jay
crow
pigeon
parrot
seagull, gull
woodpecker
hawk
pheasant
duck (mallard)
owl
bald eagle
vulture
peacock
goose (Canada goose)
pelican
flamingo
heron
turkey

Insects and Arachnids

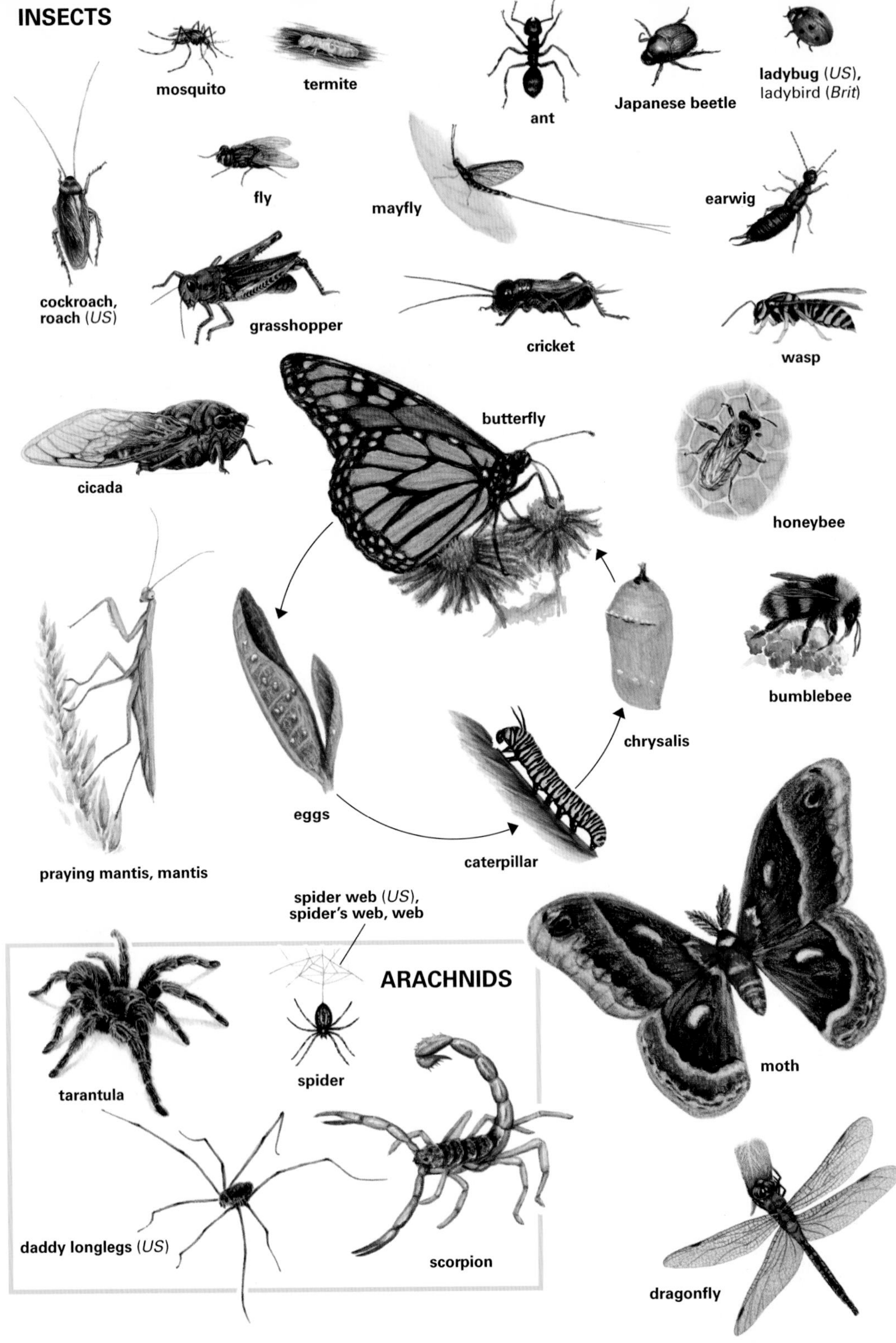
INSECTS
mosquito
termite
ant
Japanese beetle
ladybug (US),
ladybird (Brit)
cockroach,
roach (US)
fly
mayfly
earwig
grasshopper
cricket
wasp
cicada
butterfly
honeybee
praying mantis, mantis
eggs
caterpillar
chrysalis
bumblebee
moth
dragonfly
spider web (US),
spider's web, web
ARACHNIDS
tarantula
spider
daddy longlegs (US)
scorpion

Gems and Jewelry

amethyst **aquamarine** **diamond** **emerald** **garnet** **jade** **lapis lazuli, lapis**

onyx **opal** **peridot** **ruby** **sapphire** **topaz** **turquoise**

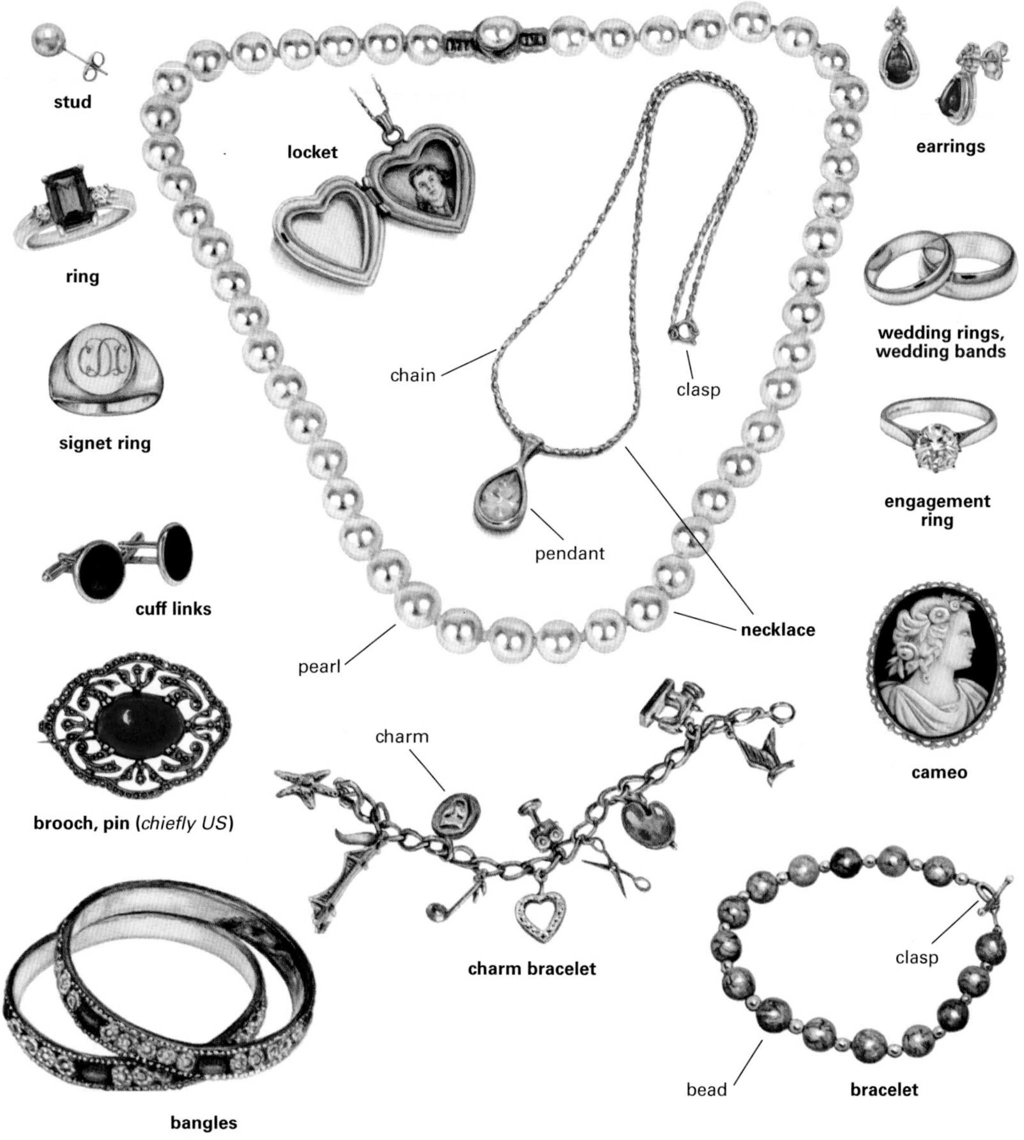

stud

locket

earrings

ring

wedding rings, wedding bands

chain

clasp

signet ring

engagement ring

pendant

cuff links

necklace

pearl

cameo

charm

brooch, pin (*chiefly US*)

charm bracelet

clasp

bead

bracelet

bangles

Patterns

solid

paisley

polka dots

floral

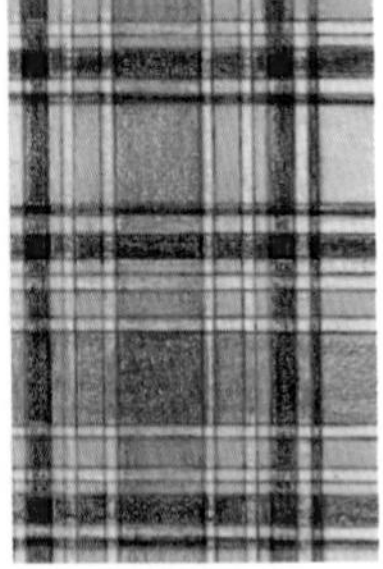
plaid

checked

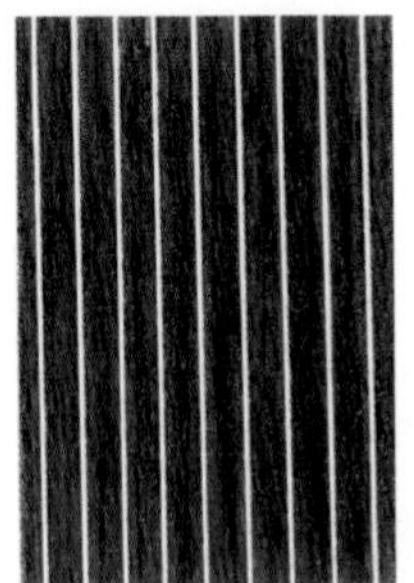
pinstripe

striped

Clothing

bathrobe,
robe (*chiefly US*)

nightgown,
nightdress (*Brit*)

pajamas (*US*),
pyjamas (*Brit*)

long johns,
long underwear (*US*)

Clothing

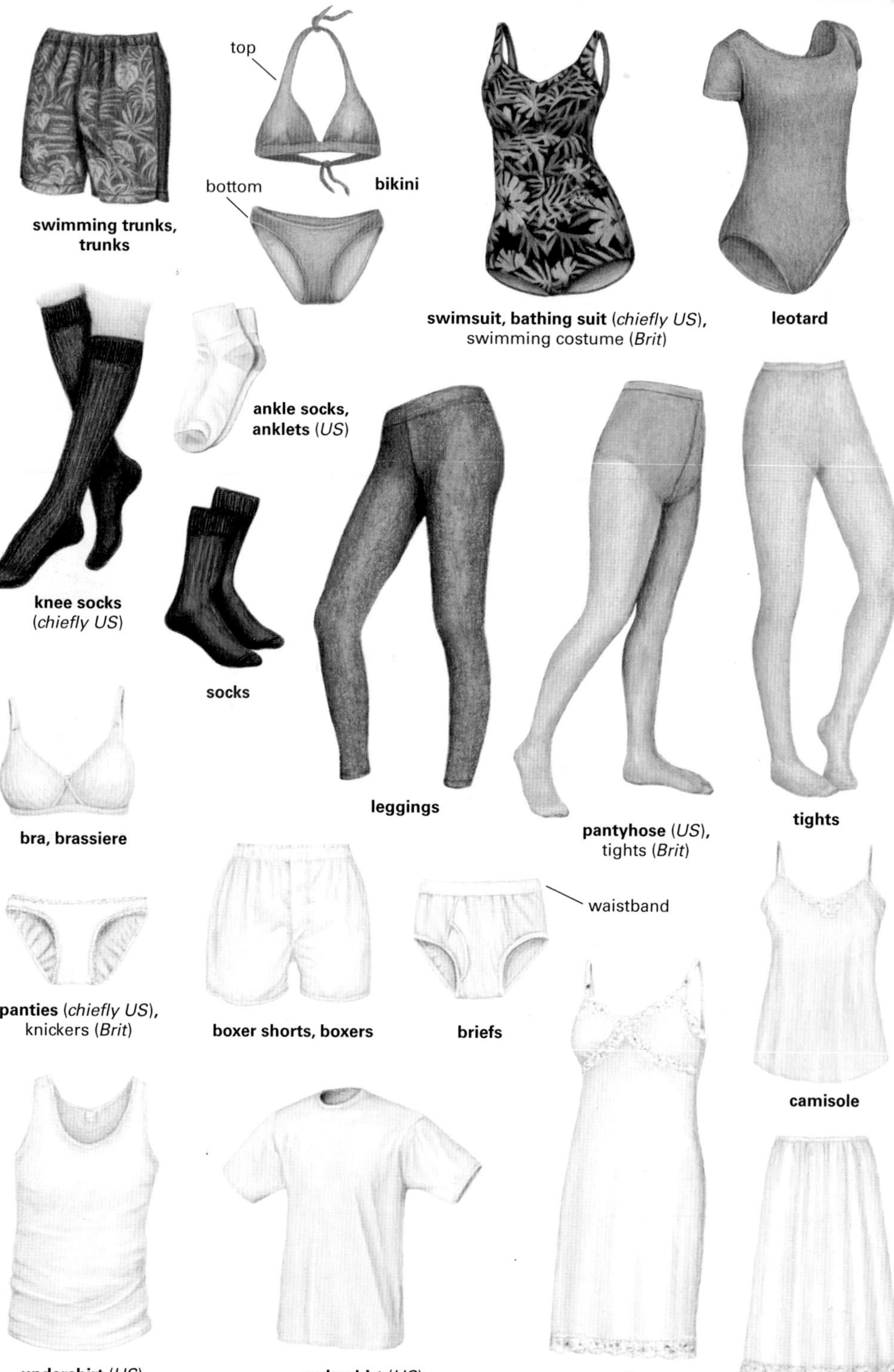
top
bottom
bikini
swimming trunks, trunks
swimsuit, bathing suit (chiefly US), swimming costume (Brit)
leotard
ankle socks, anklets (US)
knee socks (chiefly US)
socks
leggings
pantyhose (US), tights (Brit)
tights
bra, brassiere
waistband
panties (chiefly US), knickers (Brit)
boxer shorts, boxers
briefs
camisole
undershirt (US), vest (Brit)
undershirt (US), vest (Brit)
slip
half slip

collar
halter, halter top
blouse
tank top (*US*)
polo shirt
miniskirt, mini
shorts
skirt
capri pants, capris
necktie (*US*), tie
suspenders (*US*),
braces (*Brit*)
short-sleeved shirt
dress shirt (*US*)
cuff
sweatshirt
belt
T-shirt
sweatpants (*chiefly US*)
pants (*chiefly US*), trousers
jeans, blue jeans
overalls (*US*),
dungarees (*Brit*)

Clothing

cardigan, cardigan sweater (*US*)

suit

dress

evening gown, evening dress

turtleneck (*US*), polo neck (*Brit*)

sweater, pullover, jumper (*Brit*)

sport coat (*US*), **sports coat, sports jacket, sport jacket** (*US*)

jacket

raincoat

overcoat

parka

uniform

wedding dress, wedding gown

tuxedo (*chiefly US*), dinner suit (*Brit*)

kilt

muumuu

sarong

kimono

sari

[1]mas·cu·line /ˈmæskjələn/ *adj*
1 *[more ~; most ~]* **:** of, relating to, or suited to men or boys ▪ a *masculine* voice/perspective/name ▪ The living room is decorated in a more *masculine* style than the bedroom. ▪ She has a rather *masculine* [=*mannish*] voice/handshake. — compare [1]FEMININE
2 *grammar, in some languages* **:** of or belonging to the class of words (called a gender) that ordinarily includes most of the words referring to males ▪ a *masculine* noun ▪ "He" is a pronoun of the *masculine* gender. ▪ The *masculine* form of the Spanish adjective "linda" is "lindo." — compare [1]FEMININE, [1]NEUTER
– mas·cu·lin·i·ty /ˌmæskjəˈlɪnəti/ *noun [noncount]* ▪ traditional ideas about femininity and *masculinity*

[2]masculine *noun, pl* **-lines** *[count] grammar, in some languages* **:** a word or form of the masculine gender ▪ The *masculine* of the Spanish adjective "linda" is "lindo."

[1]mash /ˈmæʃ/ *verb* **mash·es; mashed; mash·ing** *[+ obj]* **:** to make (something, such as a type of food) into a soft mass by beating it or crushing it ▪ She *mashed* (up) the potatoes/carrots. ▪ *mashing* fruit for the baby ▪ She fed the baby some *mashed* carrots. ▪ For dinner we had steak with green beans and ***mashed potatoes***. [=potatoes that have been boiled and then mashed]

[2]mash *noun [noncount]*
1 : a wet mixture of crushed malt or grain that is used in making alcoholic drinks (such as beer and whiskey)
2 : a soft mixture of grains used as food for animals
3 *Brit, informal* **:** mashed potatoes ▪ bangers and *mash*

mash·er /ˈmæʃɚ/ *noun, pl* **-ers** *[count]* **:** a tool that is used for mashing food ▪ a potato *masher*

mash note *noun, pl* **~ notes** *[count] US, informal* **:** a note or letter that expresses love or affection for the person who receives it ▪ Her glowing review of his performance reads like a *mash note* from a lovesick fan.

[1]mask /ˈmæsk, *Brit* ˈmɑːsk/ *noun, pl* **masks** *[count]*
1 : a covering for your face or for part of your face: such as **a :** a covering used to hide or disguise your face ▪ a Halloween *mask* ▪ Everyone wore costumes and *masks* to the dance. ▪ The robbers wore *masks*. **b :** a covering used to protect your face or cover your mouth ▪ Doctors wear surgical *masks* in the operating room. ▪ a (baseball) catcher's *mask* — see picture at SCUBA DIVING; see also FACE MASK, GAS MASK, OXYGEN MASK, SKI MASK
2 : a way of appearing or behaving that is not true or real — usually singular ▪ Her anger and resentment were hidden behind a *mask* of friendship. [=she pretended to be friendly but was really angry and resentful]

mask

[2]mask *verb* **masks; masked; mask·ing** *[+ obj]*
1 : to hide (something) from sight ▪ The house was *masked* by trees.
2 : to keep (something) from being known or noticed ▪ She *masked* [=*hid*] her anger with a smile. ▪ They tried to *mask* their real purpose. ▪ She tried using perfume to *mask* the bad odor.

masked /ˈmæskt, *Brit* ˈmɑːskt/ *adj*
1 : wearing a mask ▪ The bank was held up by *masked* robbers. ▪ The dancers were *masked*.
2 *always used before a noun* **:** done by or involving people who wear masks ▪ a *masked* ball [=a formal party for dancing at which people wear masks] ▪ a *masked* dance

masking tape *noun [noncount]* **:** a type of tape that is sticky on one side and that has many different uses (such as to cover an area when you are painting near it)

mas·och·ism /ˈmæsəˌkɪzəm/ *noun [noncount]* **:** enjoyment of pain **:** pleasure that someone gets from being abused or hurt; *especially* **:** sexual enjoyment from being hurt or punished — compare SADISM
– mas·och·ist /ˈmæsəkɪst/ *noun, pl* **-ists** *[count]* ▪ sexual *masochists* **– mas·och·is·tic** /ˌmæsəˈkɪstɪk/ *adj* ▪ *masochistic* tendencies/behavior **– mas·och·is·ti·cal·ly** /ˌmæsəˈkɪstɪkli/ *adv*

ma·son /ˈmeɪsn̩/ *noun, pl* **-sons** *[count]*
1 : a skilled worker who builds or works with stone, brick, or concrete — see also STONEMASON
2 ***Mason*** **:** FREEMASON

Ma·son·ic /məˈsɑnɪk/ *adj* **:** of or relating to Freemasons or Freemasonry ▪ a *Masonic* temple

ma·son jar *or* **Ma·son jar** /ˈmeɪsn̩-/ *noun, pl* **~ jars** *[count] US* **:** a glass jar that has a wide opening and that is usually used in preserving fruits or vegetables

ma·son·ry /ˈmeɪsn̩ri/ *noun [noncount]*
1 : the stone, brick, or concrete used to build things ▪ a structure built of *masonry* ▪ blocks of *masonry* ▪ a *masonry* wall
2 : work done using stone, brick, or concrete **:** work done by a mason ▪ skillful *masonry*
3 ***Masonry*** **:** FREEMASONRY

masque /ˈmæsk, *Brit* ˈmɑːsk/ *noun, pl* **masques** *[count]* **:** a type of play that was performed in the 16th and 17th centuries by actors wearing masks

[1]mas·quer·ade /ˌmæskəˈreɪd/ *noun, pl* **-ades** *[count]*
1 : a party at which people wear masks and often costumes
2 : a way of appearing or behaving that is not true or real ▪ Their happy marriage was all just a *masquerade*. [=*charade*] ▪ She could not keep up the *masquerade* any longer.

[2]masquerade *verb* **-ades; -ad·ed; -ad·ing** *[no obj]* **:** to pretend to be someone or something else ▪ He was *masquerading* under a false name. — usually + *as* ▪ The movie is about a spy who *masquerades as* a salesman. ▪ a man *masquerading as* a woman
– mas·quer·ad·er *noun, pl* **-ers** *[count]*

[1]mass /ˈmæs/ *noun, pl* **mass·es**
1 *[count]* **:** a usually large amount of a substance that has no particular shape ▪ The slush froze into an icy *mass*. ▪ a cold air *mass* ▪ rock *masses* — often + *of* ▪ a *mass of* metal/clay/dough ▪ *masses of* floating ice — see also BODY MASS INDEX, CRITICAL MASS, LANDMASS
2 a *[count]* **:** a large number or amount *of* something ▪ The plant produces a (great/large/huge) *mass of* blossoms every spring. = The plant produces *masses of* blossoms every spring. ▪ a *mass of* data/information **b** *[count]* **:** a large number *of* people ▪ A great *mass of* voters turned out for the election. ▪ The team was greeted by a *mass* [=*crowd*] *of* fans. ▪ The war has forced *masses of* people to flee their homes. **c** ***masses*** *[plural] Brit, informal* **:** a large amount of something ▪ Don't worry: we've still got *masses* [=*lots*] of time.
3 ***the masses*** **:** the ordinary or common people ▪ His films are not intended to appeal to *the masses*. ▪ the needs of *the masses* ▪ a politician who is popular with *the masses* ▪ trying to reach *the masses*
4 *[noncount] physics* **:** the quantity of matter in something ▪ a star's *mass*
the mass of **:** the main part of (something) ▪ *The mass of* the iceberg [=the largest part of the iceberg] is below the surface of the water. ▪ His policies are supported by *the* (great/broad) *mass of* the people. [=by most of the people]

[2]mass *verb* **masses; massed; mass·ing :** to form or gather into a large group *[no obj]* A large crowd of demonstrators *massed* outside the courthouse. ▪ Clouds were *massing* on the horizon. *[+ obj]* The generals *massed* their troops.

[3]mass *adj, always used before a noun* **:** involving, affecting, or designed for many people ▪ *mass* demonstrations ▪ weapons of *mass* destruction ▪ *mass* murder ▪ a *mass* murderer ▪ *mass* hysteria ▪ Television is a *mass* medium. ▪ a *mass* market

Mass *noun, pl* **Mass·es**
1 : a Christian ceremony especially in the Roman Catholic Church in which people eat bread and drink wine representing the body and blood of Jesus Christ *[noncount]* They attend *Mass* every Sunday. ▪ a priest's duty to say/celebrate *Mass* *[count]* Sunday *Masses* are held at three different times.
2 *[count]* **:** music written for the parts of a Mass

[1]mas·sa·cre /ˈmæsɪkɚ/ *noun, pl* **-sa·cres**
1 : the violent killing of many people *[count]* a *massacre* of civilians ▪ bloody *massacres* *[noncount]* evidence of *massacre*
2 *[count] informal* **:** a game or competition in which one person or team easily defeats another ▪ The game turned out to be a complete *massacre*.

[2]massacre *verb* **-sa·cres; -sa·cred; -sa·cring** *[+ obj]*
1 : to violently kill (a group of people) **:** SLAUGHTER ▪ Hundreds have been *massacred* in the uprising.
2 *informal* **:** to easily defeat (someone or something) ▪ The other team really *massacred* us on Saturday.

3 : to do (something) very badly : to ruin (something) because of lack of skill ▪ He really *massacred* that song.

[1]**mas•sage** /məˈsɑːʒ, *Brit* ˈmæˌsɑːʒ/ *noun, pl* **-sag•es** : the action of rubbing or pressing someone's body in a way that helps muscles to relax or reduces pain in muscles and joints [*count*] She gave him a neck *massage*. ▪ a facial/foot *massage* [*noncount*] using *massage* to help relax ▪ a *massage* therapist ▪ *massage* therapy

[2]**massage** *verb* **-sages; -saged; -sag•ing** [+ *obj*]

1 : to rub or press (someone's body) in a way that helps muscles to relax or reduces pain in muscles and joints : to give a massage to (someone or a part of someone's body) ▪ She *massaged* his back. ▪ He *massaged* his forehead. ▪ She *massaged* her leg until the numbness was gone.

2 : to change (numbers, data, etc.) in a dishonest way in order to deceive people ▪ Researchers of the drug have been accused of *massaging* [=*manipulating*] the data to make it appear to be more effective than it really is.

massage someone's ego : to say things that make someone feel important and proud ▪ He gained the friendship of powerful politicians by *massaging their egos*.

massage parlor (*US*) *or Brit* **massage parlour** *noun, pl* ~ **-lors** [*count*]

1 : a place where people pay to be given a massage

2 : a place that is supposed to be for massages but where people pay to have sex

mas•seur /mæˈsɚ/ *noun, pl* **-seurs** [*count*] : a man whose job is to give massages

mas•seuse /mæˈsəz/ *noun, pl* **-seus•es** [*count*] : a woman whose job is to give massages

mas•sive /ˈmæsɪv/ *adj* [*more* ~; *most* ~]

1 : very large and heavy ▪ The fort had *massive* walls. ▪ *massive* furniture ▪ the dog's *massive* head/jaw ▪ stars more *massive* than the sun

2 a : large in amount or degree ▪ A *massive* effort will be required to clean up the debris. ▪ You can find a *massive* amount of information on the Internet. ▪ The stunt received *massive* publicity. ▪ a *massive* collection of baseball cards **b** : very severe ▪ a *massive* heart attack ▪ a *massive* stroke

– **mas•sive•ly** *adv* ▪ a *massively* built structure ▪ a *massively* popular actor [=an extremely popular actor] – **mas•sive•ness** *noun* [*noncount*] ▪ the castle's sheer *massiveness*

mass media *noun* [*plural*] : the radio stations, television stations, and newspapers through which information is communicated to the public ▪ an event that has attracted a lot of attention from the *mass media* ▪ the dissemination of news by *mass media* ▪ The *mass media* have ignored this important issue. — sometimes used with a singular verb ▪ The *mass media* has ignored this important issue.

mass noun *noun, pl* ~ **nouns** [*count*] *grammar* : NONCOUNT NOUN

mass–pro•duce /ˌmæsprəˈduːs, *Brit* ˌmæsprəˈdjuːs/ *verb* **-duc•es; -duced; -duc•ing** [+ *obj*] : to produce very large amounts of (something) usually by using machinery ▪ The company has begun *mass-producing* computer chips.

– **mass–produced** *adj* ▪ *mass-produced* foods/furniture – **mass production** *noun* [*noncount*] ▪ the *mass production* of computer chips

mass transit *noun* [*noncount*] *chiefly US* : the system that is used for moving large numbers of people on buses, trains, etc. ▪ The mayor is trying to encourage more commuters to use *mass transit* in order to alleviate traffic in the city. — called also *public transit*

mast /ˈmæst, *Brit* ˈmɑːst/ *noun, pl* **masts** [*count*]

1 : a long pole that supports the sails of a boat or ship — see picture at BOAT

2 : a tall pole that supports or holds something (such as a flag) — see also HALF-MAST

[1]**mas•ter** /ˈmæstɚ, *Brit* ˈmɑːstə/ *noun, pl* **-ters**

1 [*count*] : someone who has control or power over others: such as **a** : someone (especially a man) who has a servant or slave ▪ As a slave he was required to do his *master's* bidding without question. **b** : someone (especially a man) who owns a pet (such as a dog) ▪ The dog was always obedient to its *master*. **c** *formal* : the male head of a household ▪ the *master* and mistress of the house **d** : a man who is in charge of the people on a ship ▪ a ship's *master*

2 [*count*] : a person who has control of something — usually + *of* ▪ He was the *master of* his feelings. [=he was able to control his own feelings] ▪ She proved herself (to be) *master of* the situation. ▪ We are the *masters of* our own destiny.

3 [*count*] : a person who has become very skilled at doing something ▪ She is a *master* of her craft. ▪ a chess *master* ▪ a Dutch *master* [=one of the great Dutch painters of the past] — often + *at* ▪ He is a *master at* manipulating people. — see also GRAND MASTER, PAST MASTER

4 a [*count*] *old-fashioned* : a male teacher — see also HEADMASTER, SCHOOLMASTER **b** ***Master*** — used as a title for the male head of certain British colleges ▪ He was *Master* of Balliol.

5 [*count*] : a person who has received a master's degree ▪ a *master* of arts

6 [*count*] : an original version of something (such as a recording) from which copies can be made

7 ***Master*** *formal + old-fashioned* — used as a title for a boy who is too young to be called *Mister* ▪ *Master* Timothy

jack-of-all-trades, master of none see JACK-OF-ALL-TRADES

serve two masters see [1]SERVE

[2]**master** *adj, always used before a noun*

1 : highly skilled ▪ a *master* carpenter/electrician ▪ a *master* storyteller ▪ a *master* chef

2 : largest or most important ▪ the house's *master* bedroom/bathroom ▪ the network's *master* computer

3 — used to describe an original version from which other copies can be made ▪ a *master* tape recording ▪ the *master* copy

[3]**master** *verb* **-ters; -tered; -ter•ing** [+ *obj*]

1 : to succeed in controlling (something, such as an emotion) ▪ He *mastered* [=*overcame*] his fear. ▪ *master* a desire

2 : to learn (something) completely : to get the knowledge and skill that allows you to do, use, or understand (something) very well ▪ She *mastered* French in college. ▪ He is determined to *master* every aspect of the business.

mas•ter•ful /ˈmæstɚfəl, *Brit* ˈmɑːstəfəl/ *adj* [*more* ~; *most* ~]

1 : able to take control of people or situations ▪ a *masterful* commander ▪ His manner was *masterful* and abrupt.

2 : very skillful ▪ a *masterful* [=*masterly*] performance/translation ▪ a *masterful* work of art ▪ He did a *masterful* job of staying out of trouble.

– **mas•ter•ful•ly** *adv* ▪ The chairman walked *masterfully* into the meeting. ▪ The book was *masterfully* translated.

master key *noun, pl* ~ **keys** [*count*] : a key that can be used to open many locks (such as all the door locks in a building)

mas•ter•ly /ˈmæstɚli, *Brit* ˈmɑːstəli/ *adj* : showing great skill : very skillful ▪ He deserves congratulations for the *masterly* [=*masterful*] way in which he handled the crisis. ▪ a *masterly* performance ▪ She did a *masterly* job of organizing the conference.

[1]**mas•ter•mind** /ˈmæstɚˌmaɪnd, *Brit* ˈmɑːstəˌmaɪnd/ *noun, pl* **-minds** [*count*] : a person who plans and organizes something ▪ He is considered (to be) the *mastermind* of the team's winning strategy. ▪ a criminal *mastermind* ▪ the *mastermind* behind the terrorist plot

[2]**mastermind** *verb* **-minds; -mind•ed; -mind•ing** [+ *obj*] : to plan and organize (something) : to be the mastermind of (something) ▪ They *masterminded* a unique solution to the problem. ▪ He *masterminded* the bank robbery.

master of ceremonies *noun, pl* **masters of ceremonies** [*count*] : a person who introduces guests, speakers, or performers at a formal event ▪ The *master of ceremonies* introduced the guest of honor. — called also (*US*) *emcee, MC*

mas•ter•piece /ˈmæstɚˌpiːs, *Brit* ˈmɑːstəˌpiːs/ *noun, pl* **-piec•es** [*count*]

1 : a great book, painting, piece of music, movie, etc. ▪ a literary/cinematic *masterpiece* ▪ The painting was immediately recognized as a *masterpiece*; *also* : the best book, painting, piece of music, movie, etc., by a particular person ▪ Herman Melville's *masterpiece* was *Moby-Dick*.

2 : something done with great skill ▪ a *masterpiece* of planning ▪ Her study of apes is a *masterpiece*.

master plan *noun, pl* ~ **plans** [*count*] : a detailed plan for doing something that will require a lot of time and effort ▪ He has a *master plan* for becoming a millionaire.

master's *noun, pl* **master's** [*count*] *informal* : MASTER'S DEGREE ▪ She has a *master's* in biology.

master's degree *noun, pl* ~ **-grees** [*count*] : a degree that is given to a student by a college or university usually after one or two years of additional study following a bachelor's degree

mas•ter•work /ˈmæstɚˌwɚk, *Brit* ˈmɑːstəˌwəːk/ *noun, pl*

-works [*count*] : a great work of art : MASTERPIECE ▪ a musical *masterwork*

mas·tery /ˈmæstəri, ˈmɑːstəri/ *noun*
1 : knowledge and skill that allows you to do, use, or understand something very well : COMMAND — usually + *of* [*noncount*] We were impressed by her *mastery of* the subject. [*singular*] She achieved a complete *mastery of* French.
2 [*noncount*] **:** complete control of something ▪ He struggled to gain *mastery* of/over his fears.

mast·head /ˈmæstˌhɛd, *Brit* ˈmɑːstˌhɛd/ *noun, pl* **-heads** [*count*]
1 : the top of a ship's mast
2 : the name of a newspaper shown on the top of the first page

mas·ti·cate /ˈmæstəˌkeɪt/ *verb* **-cates; -cat·ed; -cat·ing** *technical* **:** to chew (food) [+ *obj*] The cows were *masticating* their food. [*no obj*] *masticating* cows
– mas·ti·ca·tion /ˌmæstəˈkeɪʃən/ *noun* [*noncount*]

mas·tiff /ˈmæstəf/ *noun, pl* **-tiffs** [*count*] **:** a type of large, powerful dog

mas·to·don /ˈmæstəˌdɑːn/ *noun, pl* **-dons** [*count*] **:** a type of animal that was related to the mammoth and that lived in ancient times

mas·tur·bate /ˈmæstəˌbeɪt/ *verb* **-bates; -bat·ed; -bat·ing** [*no obj*] **:** to touch or rub your own sexual organs for sexual pleasure
– mas·tur·ba·tion /ˌmæstəˈbeɪʃən/ *noun* [*noncount*]
– mas·tur·ba·to·ry /ˈmæstəbəˌtori, *Brit* ˌmæstəˈbeɪtəri/ *adj* ▪ *masturbatory* fantasies

mat /ˈmæt/ *noun, pl* **mats** [*count*]
1 a : a small piece of material used to cover the floor or ground ▪ Be sure to wipe your dirty feet on the *mat* [=*doormat*] before you enter the house. — see also BATH MAT, WELCOME MAT **b :** a small piece of material used to protect the surface of a table ▪ She set the hot plate on the *mat*. — see also PLACE MAT, TABLE MAT **c :** a thick pad that is used as a soft surface for some activities (such as wrestling, gymnastics, yoga, etc.)
2 : a thick mass of something that is stuck or twisted together — usually + *of* ▪ a thick *mat of* vegetation/hair
go to the mat *chiefly US, informal* **:** to make a lot of effort to do something : to try very hard at something ▪ They *went to the mat* to protect the program. ▪ She'll ***go to the mat for*** you. [=she will do everything she can to help you]

mat·a·dor /ˈmætəˌdoɚ/ *noun, pl* **-dors** [*count*] **:** the person who has the major part in a bullfight and who kills the bull

[1]match /ˈmætʃ/ *noun, pl* **match·es**
1 [*singular*] **:** someone or something that is equal to or as good as another person or thing ▪ He was ***no match for*** his opponent. [=his opponent was able to defeat him easily] ▪ He was ***more than a match for*** his opponent. [=he defeated his opponent easily] ▪ She knew after the first game that she had ***met her match***. [=knew that her opponent was as good as she was and could defeat her] ▪ a politician who has finally *met his match*
2 [*singular*] **a :** two people or things that are suited to each other ▪ The curtains and carpet are a good/perfect *match* (for each other). ▪ Deborah and Brad are/make a good *match*. ▪ Everyone thought that they were ***a match made in heaven***. [=two people perfectly suited to each other] **b :** someone or something that is suited to another person or thing — usually + *for* ▪ She found a sweater that was a nice *match for* her skirt. ▪ He was a good *match for* her because they shared the same interests.
3 [*count*] **:** a contest between two or more players or teams ▪ a soccer *match* [=*game*] ▪ a chess *match* ▪ He lost a close *match* against a tough opponent. ▪ a tennis/boxing *match* — sometimes used figuratively ▪ He got into a ***shouting match*** with his neighbor. = (*Brit*) He got into a ***slanging match*** with his neighbor. [=he and his neighbor were angrily shouting at each other] ▪ They got into a ***shoving match***. [=they were angrily shoving each other] — see also RETURN MATCH, *grudge match* at [1]GRUDGE
– compare [3]MATCH

[2]match *verb* **matches; matched; match·ing**
1 a : to be suited to (someone or something) : to go well with (someone or something) [+ *obj*] The curtains *match* the carpet perfectly. = The curtains and the carpet *match* each other perfectly. ▪ This color *matches* your skin tone. ▪ She was wearing a beautiful skirt, but her sweater didn't *match* it. ▪ The upbeat music *matched* her mood. [*no obj*] The curtains and carpet don't *match*. [=*go together*] ▪ Her skirt and sweater *matched* perfectly. ▪ Do these colors *match*? ▪ (*chiefly US*) a wine that *matches* (up) well with rich foods ▪ He's a large man with hands ***to match***. [=a large man with large hands] **b :** to have the same appearance, color, etc. [*no obj*] The pillows on the couch all *match*. ▪ Your socks don't *match*. [+ *obj*] Your socks don't *match* each other.
2 [+ *obj*] **:** to make or see a connection or relationship between (two people or things) ▪ The children *matched* (up) the names of the animals to the correct pictures. — often + *with* ▪ My mom is always trying to *match* me up *with* her friends' daughters. — see also *mix and match* at [1]MIX
3 : to be in agreement with (something) [+ *obj*] The description *matches* [=*fits*] him closely. ▪ His story doesn't *match* the facts. [*no obj*] Their stories didn't *match* (up). [=their stories didn't agree with each other] ▪ His story doesn't *match* (up) with the facts.
4 a : to be the equal of (something or someone) : to be as good as (something or someone) [+ *obj*] Nothing will ever *match* the sheer excitement of that game. = Nothing will ever *match* that game in/for sheer excitement. ▪ The movie didn't *match* our expectations. [=the movie was not as good as we expected it to be] ▪ Nobody can *match* him at golf. [=no one is as good as he is at playing golf] ▪ The car has a record of reliability that's hard to *match*. ▪ His talents are *matched* only by his ego. ▪ The company's growth has been *matched* by the increase in its political influence. ▪ I've never seen anything to *match* this spectacle. ▪ The two runners were *matching* each other stride for stride. ▪ It was a close game between two ***evenly matched*** teams. [=two teams that are equally good] [*no obj*] The concert didn't ***match up to*** [=*equal, meet*] our expectations. **b** [+ *obj*] **:** to provide, produce, or do something that is equal to (something else) ▪ We were unable to *match* their offer. ▪ The company will *match* employee contributions to the insurance plan. ▪ An anonymous donor has promised to *match* the first $10,000 donated to the charity. ▪ He could never hope to *match* his brother's success.
5 [+ *obj*] **:** to place (someone or something) in competition against another — often + *against* ▪ They were *matched against* each other in the first round of the play-offs. — often + *with* ▪ The game will *match* last year's champions *with* their leading rivals.
6 [+ *obj*] **:** to compare (something) with something else — usually + *against* ▪ The fingerprints were *matched against* those stored in the computer.
– matching *adj, always used before a noun* ▪ She was wearing a dark blue skirt with/and a *matching* sweater. ▪ *matching* colors

[3]match *noun, pl* **matches** [*count*] **:** a short, thin piece of wood or thick paper with a special tip that produces fire when it is scratched against something else ▪ light a *match* ▪ a book/box of *matches* — compare [1]MATCH

match·book /ˈmætʃˌbʊk/ *noun, pl* **-books** [*count*] **:** a small folder that contains rows of matches

match·box /ˈmætʃˌbɑːks/ *noun, pl* **-box·es** [*count*] **:** a small box for matches

match·less /ˈmætʃləs/ *adj* **:** having no equal : better than all others ▪ The museum has a *matchless* collection of paintings. ▪ *matchless* beauty

matchbook

match·mak·er /ˈmætʃˌmeɪkɚ/ *noun, pl* **-ers** [*count*] **:** a person who tries to bring two people together so that they will marry each other
– match·mak·ing /ˈmætʃˌmeɪkɪŋ/ *noun* [*noncount*]

match point *noun, pl* ~ **points**
1 : a situation in tennis in which one player or team can win the match by winning the next point [*count*] He won with an ace on his second *match point*. [*noncount*] He won with an ace on/at *match point*.
2 [*count*] **:** the final point that must be won to win a match in tennis — compare GAME POINT

match·stick /ˈmætʃˌstɪk/ *noun, pl* **-sticks** [*count*] **:** the wood or paper part of a match ▪ Cut the peppers into pieces the size of *matchsticks*.

[1]mate /ˈmeɪt/ *noun, pl* **mates**
1 [*count*] **:** a person who lives with you, works in the same place as you, etc. — usually used in combination with another noun ▪ We have been office *mates* for 10 years. [=we have worked together in the same office for 10 years] — see also CLASSMATE, FLATMATE, HOUSEMATE, PLAYMATE, ROOMMATE, RUNNING MATE, SCHOOLMATE, SEATMATE, SHIP-

MATE, SOUL MATE, STABLEMATE, TABLEMATE, TEAMMATE, WORKMATE
2 [*count*] **:** either one of a pair of animals that are breeding • One bird remains at the nest while its *mate* hunts for food.
3 [*count*] *chiefly US* **:** a person's husband, wife, or romantic or sexual partner • He was finding it difficult to find a *mate*. • an ideal *mate*
4 [*count*] *chiefly US, informal* **:** either one of a pair of objects • I can't find the *mate* to this glove.
5 [*count*] **:** an officer on a ship who has a rank below the captain • a first/second/third *mate*
6 [*count*] *chiefly Brit, informal* **:** a friend • Me and a couple of *mates* of mine went round to the pub. • She and I have been best *mates* for ages. — often used as a friendly way for one man to address another man • Got a light, *mate*?
7 [*count*] *chiefly Brit* **:** an assistant or helper • a plumber's *mate* • an electrician's *mate*
8 [*noncount*] **:** CHECKMATE

²mate *verb* **mates; mat·ed; mat·ing**
1 a [*no obj*] *of animals* **:** to have sexual activity in order to produce young • This species of bird *mates* in early spring. • The male *mated* with the female. = The male and the female *mated*. • a *mating* call/ritual • the ***mating season*** [=the time of year when an animal mates] • These birds ***mate for life***. [=they form pairs and stay together throughout their lives] **b** [+ *obj*] **:** to bring (animals) together so that they will breed and produce young • Researchers *mated* two different kinds of mice. • *mating* a male dog to/with a female
2 [+ *obj*] **:** to join or connect (things) together • The stereo sounds best when it is *mated* to/with high-quality speakers.

¹ma·te·ri·al /məˈtirijəl/ *noun, pl* **-als**
1 a : a substance from which something is made or can be made [*count*] building *materials* • paper, plastic, or other *materials* [*noncount*] small pieces of *material* • hard *material* like stone — see also RAW MATERIAL **b :** a substance that has a particular quality [*count*] a sticky *material* • explosive *materials* [*noncount*] genetic *material*
2 : something used in doing a particular activity [*count*] — usually plural • writing/reference *materials* [*noncount*] She was never without reading *material*.
3 [*noncount*] **:** cloth or fabric • The curtains required yards of expensive *material*.
4 [*noncount*] **:** information or ideas • He has been gathering *material* for a new biography. • The revised edition includes a large amount of new *material*. • The comedian gets his *material* from things that have happened to him.
5 [*noncount*] **:** a person who is suited to a particular position or job • Her boss regards her as executive *material*. [=as someone who would make a good executive] • My parents never felt that I was college *material*. [=that I was someone who should go to college]

²material *adj*
1 *always used before a noun* **a :** relating to or made of matter **:** PHYSICAL • the *material* world • *material* objects **b :** physical rather than spiritual or intellectual • He is concerned only with his own *material* comforts/needs. • *material* goods/possessions/rewards/wealth
2 *formal* **:** having real importance • The researchers included all data that was *material*. • *material* facts — often + *to* • The evidence is not *material* [=*relevant*] *to* the case. — opposite IMMATERIAL
— ma·te·ri·al·ly *adv* • The organization contributes *materially* to the efforts for peace. • a *materially* rich but spiritually poor culture

ma·te·ri·al·ism /məˈtirijəˌlɪzəm/ *noun* [*noncount*]
1 : a way of thinking that gives too much importance to material possessions rather than to spiritual or intellectual things • the *materialism* of modern society
2 *philosophy* **:** the belief that only material things exist
— ma·te·ri·al·ist /məˈtirijəlɪst/ *noun, pl* **-ists** [*count*] • a greedy *materialist* **— ma·te·ri·al·is·tic** /məˌtirijəˈlɪstɪk/ *adj* [*more* ~; *most* ~] • She is spoiled and very *materialistic*. • a *materialistic* culture/society

ma·te·ri·al·ize *also Brit* **ma·te·ri·al·ise** /məˈtirijəˌlaɪz/ *verb* **-iz·es; -ized; -iz·ing** [*no obj*]
1 : to become visible **:** to appear especially in a sudden or magical way • A waiter suddenly *materialized* beside our table. • Rain clouds *materialized* on the horizon.
2 : to begin to happen or exist **:** to occur or become real — usually used in negative statements • The bad weather we had worried about never *materialized*. • The money they promised us has so far failed to *materialize*.
— ma·te·ri·al·i·za·tion /məˌtirijələˈzeɪʃən, *Brit* məˌtɪəriəlaɪˈzeɪʃən/ *noun* [*noncount*]

ma·té·ri·el *or US* **ma·te·ri·el** /məˌtiriˈɛl/ *noun* [*noncount*] **:** equipment and supplies used by soldiers • weapons and other *matériel*

ma·ter·nal /məˈtənl/ *adj*
1 a : of or relating to a mother **:** MOTHERLY • *maternal* love • *maternal* feelings/instincts **b** *always used before a noun* **:** of or relating to a woman who is having a baby • Doctors are concerned about the effects of the drug on *maternal* health. • *maternal* smoking
2 *always used before a noun* **:** related through the mother • his *maternal* grandparents [=the parents of his mother] • a *maternal* aunt/uncle — compare PATERNAL
— ma·ter·nal·ly *adv* • She smiled at them *maternally*. • *maternally* inherited genes

¹ma·ter·ni·ty /məˈtənəti/ *noun* [*noncount*] **:** the state of being a mother **:** MOTHERHOOD — compare PATERNITY

²maternity *adj, always used before a noun*
1 : designed to be worn by a woman who is pregnant • *maternity* clothes • a *maternity* dress
2 : relating to the time when a woman gives birth to a baby • *maternity* pay • The company granted her ***maternity leave***. [=time off to take care of a newborn child]
3 — used to refer to an area in a hospital where women who are giving birth to babies are cared for • a *maternity* unit/ ward

¹mat·ey /ˈmeɪti/ *adj* **mat·i·er; -est** [*also more* ~; *most* ~] *Brit, informal* **:** FRIENDLY • a boss who is *matey* with his staff

²matey *noun* [*singular*] *Brit, informal + sometimes impolite* — used as a way for one man to address another man • Listen, *matey*, I'm not putting up with that anymore!

math /ˈmæθ/ *noun* [*noncount*] *US* **:** MATHEMATICS • She's always been good at *math*. [=(*Brit*) *maths*]

math·e·mat·i·cal /ˌmæθəˈmætɪkəl/ *adj*
1 : of, relating to, or involving mathematics • a *mathematical* problem/equation/formula • a *mathematical* genius
2 : very exact or complete • They recorded the changes with *mathematical* precision. • The results can be predicted with *mathematical* [=*absolute*] certainty.
3 : possible but very unlikely • The team has only a *mathematical* chance of making the play-offs.
— math·e·mat·i·cal·ly /ˌmæθəˈmætɪkli/ *adv* • *mathematically* precise • She solved the problem *mathematically*. • a *mathematically* inclined person

math·e·ma·ti·cian /ˌmæθəməˈtɪʃən/ *noun, pl* **-cians** [*count*] **:** a person who is an expert in mathematics

math·e·mat·ics /ˌmæθəˈmætɪks/ *noun* [*noncount*] **:** the science of numbers, quantities, and shapes and the relations between them • Algebra, arithmetic, calculus, geometry, and trigonometry are branches of *mathematics*. • She has a degree in *mathematics*. • a professor of *mathematics* • *Mathematics* is my favorite subject. — often used before another noun • a *mathematics* teacher • the *mathematics* department at the university

maths /ˈmæθs/ *noun* [*noncount*] *Brit* **:** MATHEMATICS • being tested in English and *maths* [=(*US*) *math*]

mat·i·nee *or* **mat·i·née** /ˌmætnˈeɪ, *Brit* ˈmætəˌneɪ/ *noun, pl* **-nees** *or* **-nées** [*count*] **:** a play, movie, etc., that is performed or shown in the afternoon

matinee idol *noun, pl* **~ idols** [*count*] *somewhat old-fashioned* **:** a handsome male actor who is popular with women

ma·tri·arch /ˈmeɪtriˌɑək/ *noun, pl* **-archs** [*count*] **:** a woman who controls a family, group, or government • Our grandmother was the family's *matriarch*. • The tribe's *matriarch* ruled for 20 years before her death. — compare PATRIARCH
— ma·tri·ar·chal /ˌmeɪtriˈɑəkəl/ *adj* • *matriarchal* societies [=societies that are controlled by women]

ma·tri·ar·chy /ˈmeɪtriˌɑəki/ *noun, pl* **-chies**
1 [*count*] **:** a family, group, or government controlled by a woman or a group of women • For 20 years, the country was ruled as a *matriarchy*. • ancient *matriarchies*
2 [*noncount*] **:** a social system in which family members are related to each other through their mothers • a region in which *matriarchy* is practiced — compare PATRIARCHY

matrices *plural of* MATRIX

ma·tri·cide /ˈmætrəˌsaɪd/ *noun, pl* **-cides** [*count*] **:** the act of murdering your own mother — compare FRATRICIDE, PATRICIDE

ma·tric·u·late /məˈtrɪkjəˌleɪt/ *verb* **-lates; -lat·ed; -lat-**

ing [*no obj*] *formal* **:** to become a student at a school and especially in a college or university • She *matriculated* in/at the college and began (to take) classes in the fall.
– ma·tric·u·la·tion /məˌtrɪkjəˈleɪʃən/ *noun* [*noncount*]

mat·ri·mo·nial /ˌmætrəˈmounijəl/ *adj, always used before a noun, formal* **:** of or relating to marriage • They took their *matrimonial* vows in the spring. [=they got married in the spring] • *matrimonial* [=(more commonly) *marital, marriage*] problems/troubles • *matrimonial* lawyers [=lawyers who specialize in marriage and divorce]

mat·ri·mo·ny /ˈmætrəˌmouni/ *noun* [*noncount*] *formal* **:** the joining together of a man and woman as husband and wife **:** MARRIAGE • two people joined in *matrimony* • They were united in (the bonds of) ***holy matrimony*** [=they were married in a religious ceremony] on the first of May.

ma·trix /ˈmeɪtrɪks/ *noun, pl* **-tri·ces** /-trəˌsiːz/ *also* **-trix·es** /-trɪksəz/ [*count*] *technical*
1 : something (such as a situation or a set of conditions) in which something else develops or forms • the complex social *matrix* in which people live their lives
2 : something shaped like a pattern of lines and spaces • The wires all crossed each other and formed a *matrix*.
3 : a container that can be filled with a material (such as very hot metal) to give the material a new shape **:** MOLD • a *matrix* used for making knives
4 : rock in which something hard (such as a diamond or a fossil) has been formed • pieces of light blue turquoise in a dark *matrix*
5 : the area on a human finger or toe from which the fingernail or toenail grows
6 *mathematics* **:** a set of numbers in which the numbers are listed in rows and columns and can be added or multiplied according to special rules
– see also DOT MATRIX

ma·tron /ˈmeɪtrən/ *noun, pl* **-trons** [*count*]
1 : an older married woman who usually has a high social position • society *matrons* who organize benefits for charity
2 *US* **:** a woman whose job is to be in charge of children or other women • the *matron* of a school for girls • a prison *matron*
3 *Brit, old-fashioned* **:** a female nurse who is in charge of the other nurses in a hospital

ma·tron·ly /ˈmeɪtrənli/ *adj* [*more ~; most ~*] **:** like or suitable for an older married woman • She feared she was becoming a *matronly* old woman. • She wore a *matronly* blue dress. ✧ *Matronly* is used as a polite way to describe a woman who is not young and is somewhat fat.

matron of honor (*US*) *or Brit* **matron of honour** *noun, pl* **matrons of honor** [*count*] **:** a married woman who is the main bridesmaid at a wedding • Her cousin was her *matron of honor*. — compare MAID OF HONOR

matte (*chiefly US*) *or chiefly Brit* **matt** /ˈmæt/ *adj* **:** having a surface that is not shiny • a *matte* fabric • a photograph with a *matte* finish • *matte* [=*dull*] black — opposite GLOSSY

mat·ted /ˈmætəd/ *adj* [*more ~; most ~*] **:** twisted together in an untidy way • *matted* hair • *matted* grass

¹mat·ter /ˈmætɚ/ *noun, pl* **-ters**
1 [*count*] **:** something that is being done, talked about, or thought about • He has a few personal *matters* to deal with. • Disagreement is one thing, but accusations of lying are a different *matter* altogether! • Thanks for bringing this *matter* to our attention. [=for telling us about this problem or issue] • That's ***a matter for*** a jury (to decide). • The schedule is ***a matter of some concern***. [=is something that we are worried about] • It's ***no easy/simple matter*** [=it's not easy] to find a decent place to live in this city. • This is ***no joking/laughing matter***. = This is a serious *matter*. • Getting the money to finance a project like this is ***no small matter***. [=is not an easy thing to do] — often used in an ironic way to refer to a difficult or important situation or problem • He wants to buy a new car, but first there's ***the little/small matter*** of getting enough money to pay for it. [=he can't buy a new car until he has enough money to pay for it]
2 *matters* [*plural*] **:** the situation or subject that is being discussed or dealt with • Let's not allow *matters* [=*things*] to get out of control. • She's an expert in legal/financial/money *matters*. = (*formal*) She's an expert in *matters* legal/financial. • It's best not to interfere in *matters* [=*affairs*] of the heart. • It didn't exactly ***help matters*** [=it didn't make the situation better] when he accused her of lying! • He laughed at her and then, ***to make matters worse***, he accused her of lying! [=it made the situation worse when he accused her of lying] • ***To (further) complicate matters***, they both have the same name. = ***To complicate matters further***, they both have the same name. [=the situation is more complicated because they both have the same name] • After months of waiting for something to happen, he decided to ***take matters into his own hands***. [=to do something himself instead of waiting for other people to do something]
3 [*noncount*] **a** *physics* **:** the thing that forms physical objects and occupies space • Can *matter* and energy be changed into each other? **b :** material of a particular kind • vegetable *matter* • organic/waste *matter* • printed/reading *matter* [=books, magazines, newspapers, etc.] — see also BACK MATTER, FRONT MATTER, GRAY MATTER, SUBJECT MATTER
4 *the matter* — used to ask if there is a problem or to say that there is or is not a problem • What's *the matter*? [=what's the problem?; what's wrong?] • "Is anything *the matter*?" [=is anything wrong?; is there a problem?] "No, nothing's *the matter*." — often + *with* • Nothing's *the matter with* me. I'm fine. • There's something *the matter with* the car. [=there's something wrong with the car; there's a problem with the car]

> ***usage*** The question "What's the matter?" is usually asked in a friendly way. • You look sad. *What's the matter*? [=what's wrong?] The question "What's the matter with you?" is usually asked in an unfriendly way by someone who is annoyed or angry. • You keep making stupid mistakes. *What's the matter with you*? [=what's wrong with you?; why do you keep making stupid mistakes?]

a matter of **1** — used to refer to a small amount • It cooks in *a matter of* (a few) minutes. [=it cooks in just a few minutes] • They quarreled over *a matter of* a mere couple of dollars. • The crisis was resolved in *a matter of* a few hours. • The ball was foul by *a matter of* inches. **2** — used to say that one thing results from or requires another • Learning to ride a bicycle is *a matter of* practice. [=learning to ride a bicycle requires practice] • His success was just *a matter of* being in the right place at the right time. [=he succeeded because he was in the right place at the right time] • It's only ***a matter of time*** before/until we catch him. [=we will catch him eventually] **3** — used to explain the reason for something • She insists on honesty ***as a matter of principle***. [=because she believes that honesty is morally right] • All requests for free tickets are turned down ***as a matter of policy***. [=because our policy requires it; because we have decided that that is what we should always do] **4** — used to say that something is based on opinion, taste, etc. • "He's doing a terrible job." "That's ***a matter of opinion***." [=that's not a definite fact; that's something that people have different opinions about] • Some people like seafood and some people don't. It's all just ***a matter of taste***. [=it is something that is based on personal taste] • Her plans for the election are still ***a matter of conjecture***. [=people are not sure about her plans for the election] **5** — used to say that something is important, interesting, etc. • The outcome of the trial is ***a matter of interest*** to many people. [=many people are interested in the outcome of the trial] • Resolving this problem quickly is ***a matter of (some) urgency/importance***. [=it is urgent/important to resolve this problem quickly] • I'd like to know how much it costs, just ***as a matter of interest***. [=because I am interested in knowing even though I do not need to know]

a matter of debate see ¹DEBATE

a matter of life and death see ¹LIFE

a matter of record **:** something that is known because it has been publicly said or reported in the past • His opposition to the plan is *a matter of record*.

as a matter of course — used to say that something will or should happen because it is natural, usual, or logical • You should take proper precautions *as a matter of course*. [=as part of your usual routine] • We went out to dinner on her birthday, and *as a matter of course* [=*of course, naturally*] we paid for her meal.

as a matter of fact see FACT

for that matter — used with a statement that adds to a previous statement • I haven't seen him for years—or her either, *for that matter*. [=I also haven't seen her for years]

mind over matter see ¹MIND

no matter **1** *informal* — used to say that something is not important • "I may be delayed for a few minutes." "*No matter*. [=it doesn't matter] We still have plenty of time." **2** — used with *what, how, when*, etc., to say that something does not, will not, or should not affect something else • I'm going to do it, *no matter what* you say. = *No matter what* you say, I'm going to do it. [=nothing you say will stop me from doing it] • He intends to buy that car *no matter how* much it costs. • Everyone is welcome here, *no matter where* they come from. • He wants to win, ***no matter what***. [=he wants to win so much that he will do anything to win] — see also *no matter how you slice it* at ²SLICE

the fact of the matter is — used to emphasize a statement that follows • She thinks she knows what she's talking about, but *the fact of the matter is*, she's wrong. • The budget is very tight this year. *The fact of the matter is*, we may have to lay off a few employees.

the truth of the matter — used to stress the truth of a statement • We may have to lay off a few employees this year. That's *the truth of the matter*. [=that's the truth] • *The truth of the matter is*, she was wrong and he was right.

²**matter** *verb, not used in progressive tenses* **-ters; -tered; -ter·ing** [*no obj*] : to be important • Our families and friends are the people who *matter* most to us. [=the people we care about most] • Her wealth doesn't *matter* to me. = It doesn't *matter* to me that she's rich. [=I don't care that she is rich] • It may not *matter* to you, but it *matters* a lot to me! • "Which would you prefer?" "Either one is fine. It really doesn't *matter* (to me)." • I don't care if you're a little late. All that *matters* is that you're safe. = The only thing that *matters* is that you're safe. = What *matters* is that you're safe. • "Why are you being so quiet?" "Does it *matter*?" "Of course it *matters*!" • ***What does it matter***? = It doesn't *matter*. [=it's not important; I don't care] • I see that she's late again. ***Not that it matters*** (to me). [=she's late again, but that's all right] — often + *that* • He acts as if it doesn't *matter that* he lied to us. — often + *how, who, what*, etc. • It doesn't *matter how* old you are. • It doesn't *matter what* I say to him. He just won't listen. • It doesn't *matter whether* we stay at home or go out.

mat·ter–of–fact /ˌmætərəˈfækt/ *adj* [*more* ~; *most* ~] : not showing emotion especially when talking about exciting or upsetting things • We were surprised by the *matter-of-fact* way he told us the terrible news. • Her voice had a *matter-of-fact* quality. • His tone was calm and *matter-of-fact*.
— **mat·ter–of–fact·ly** /ˌmætərəˈfæktli/ *adv* • She explained the problem *matter-of-factly*. — **mat·ter–of–fact·ness** /ˌmætərəvˈfæktnəs/ *noun* [*noncount*]

mat·ting /ˈmætɪŋ/ *noun* [*noncount*] : rough cloth used especially as floor covering • bamboo *matting*

mat·tress /ˈmætrəs/ *noun, pl* **-tress·es** [*count*] : a cloth case that is filled with material and used as a bed — see picture at BED

mat·u·ra·tion /ˌmætʃəˈreɪʃən/ *noun* [*noncount*] *formal* : the process of becoming mature : the process of developing in the body or mind • the early stages of *maturation* : the process of developing to a desired level • the *maturation* of wine/cheese • the *maturation* of his skills

¹**ma·ture** /məˈtuə, məˈtʃuə/ *adj* **ma·tur·er; -est** [*or more* ~; *most* ~]
1 : having or showing the mental and emotional qualities of an adult • We were surprised by how *mature* [=*adult*] she had become. • She's very *mature* for her age. • He has a *mature* outlook on life. • His parents didn't think he was *mature* enough to live on his own. — opposite IMMATURE
2 a : having a fully grown or developed body : grown to full size • The dog will stand three feet tall when (it has become) *mature*. [=when it has matured] • Their bodies were *mature*, but they still behaved like children. • *mature* [=*adult*] animals • *mature* trees/leaves • the dog's *mature* size [=the dog's size when it is fully grown] • ***sexually mature*** [=old enough or developed enough to produce a baby] — opposite IMMATURE **b** : having reached a final or desired state • a *mature* wine/cheese — opposite IMMATURE **c** : not young : middle-aged or older • airline discounts for *mature* travelers [=for senior citizens who travel; for old people who travel] • a man ***of mature years*** [=an older man]
3 a : based on careful thought • a *mature* plan • After/On *mature* reflection, he concluded that he had been mistaken. **b** : showing the highest level of skill that a person develops • an artist's *mature* work/style
4 *finance* : having reached the time when an amount of money (such as money for a government bond or an insurance policy) must be paid : due for payment • The bond becomes *mature* in 10 years.
— **ma·ture·ly** *adv* • They acted *maturely* and responsibly.

²**mature** *verb* **-tures; -tured; -tur·ing** [*no obj*] : to become mature: such as **a** : to become fully developed in the body and mind • Girls *mature* earlier than boys both physically and mentally. — often + *into* • He *matured into* a kind and intelligent young man. **b** : to continue developing to a desired level • Her talent is *maturing* slowly. • Wine and cheese *mature* with age. **c** *finance* : to become due for payment • The bond *matures* in 10 years.

mature student *noun, pl* ~ **-dents** [*count*] *Brit* : a student at a college or university who starts studying there at a later age than usual

ma·tu·ri·ty /məˈturəti, məˈtʃurəti/ *noun, pl* **-ties**
1 [*noncount*] : the condition of being mature: such as **a** : the state of being fully developed in the body or the mind • His behavior shows a lack of *maturity*. • He reached emotional *maturity* late in his life. • the *maturity* level of a child • full physical *maturity* **b** *finance* : the state of being due for payment • The bond will reach *maturity* in 10 years.
2 [*count*] *finance* : the amount of time that must pass before something (such as a bond) becomes due for payment • *Maturities* on these bonds can be as long as 10 years.

mat·zo *or* **mat·zoh** /ˈmɑːtsə/ *noun, pl* **mat·zoth** /ˈmɑːtˌsout/ *or* **mat·zos** *or* **mat·zohs** [*count, noncount*] : a dry, thin bread eaten especially by Jewish people at Passover — often used before another noun • a ***matzo ball*** [=a round dumpling made from matzo] • ***matzo meal*** [=flour made from ground matzo]

maud·lin /ˈmɑːdlən/ *adj* [*more* ~; *most* ~] : showing or expressing too much emotion especially in a foolish or annoying way • He became *maudlin* and started crying like a child. • a *maudlin* love story • *maudlin* poetry

maul /ˈmɑːl/ *verb* **mauls; mauled; maul·ing** [+ *obj*]
1 : to attack and injure (someone) in a way that cuts or tears skin : to attack (someone) and cause a bloody injury • The girl was *mauled* (to death) by a dog. • A bear killed one hiker and badly *mauled* the other. — often used figuratively • a movie that has been *mauled* by the critics • Many investors were badly *mauled* by the recession.
2 : to touch or handle (someone) in a rough sexual way • She was *mauled* [=*groped*] by some drunk as she left the bar.
— **mauling** *noun, pl* **-ings** [*count*] • The movie received a *mauling* from critics.

maun·der /ˈmɑːndə/ *verb* **-ders; -dered; -der·ing** [*no obj*] *Brit* : to talk for a long time in a boring way — often + *on* • I apologize for *maundering on* like this.

Maun·dy Thursday /ˈmɑːndi-/ *noun* [*singular*] *Christian religion* : the Thursday before Easter

mau·so·le·um /ˌmɑːsəˈliːjəm/ *noun, pl* **-le·ums** *also* **-lea** /-ˈliːjə/ [*count*] : a stone building with places for the dead bodies of several people or the body of an important person • a family *mausoleum*

mauve /ˈmɑːv, ˈmouv/ *noun, pl* **mauves** [*count, noncount*] : a light or medium purple color — see color picture on page C3
— **mauve** *adj*

ma·ven /ˈmeɪvən/ *noun, pl* **-vens** [*count*] *US* : a person who knows a lot about a particular subject : EXPERT • fashion/marketing *mavens* • a wine *maven*

mav·er·ick /ˈmævrɪk/ *noun, pl* **-icks** [*count*] : a person who refuses to follow the customs or rules of a group • He's always been a (bit of a) *maverick* in the world of fashion. • political *mavericks* [=*nonconformists*]
— **maverick** *adj, always used before a noun* • a *maverick* director/musician • *maverick* lawyers

maw /ˈmɑː/ *noun, pl* **maws** [*count*] *literary* : the mouth, jaws, or throat of an animal • the gaping *maw* of the tiger — often used figuratively • the dark *maw* of the cave • prisoners falling into the gaping *maw* of the criminal justice system

mawk·ish /ˈmɑːkɪʃ/ *adj* [*more* ~; *most* ~] : sad or romantic in a foolish or exaggerated way • a *mawkish* love story • *mawkish* poetry
— **mawk·ish·ly** *adv* • *mawkishly* romantic/sentimental
— **mawk·ish·ness** *noun* [*noncount*]

¹**max** /ˈmæks/ *noun* [*singular*] *chiefly US, informal* : the largest amount possible : MAXIMUM • The boat can hold a *max* of 20 people. • He bet the *max*. [=he bet the largest amount that he could]
to the max *informal* : as much as possible • The theater was filled *to the max*. [=it was completely filled] • She had three tests in one day and was stressed *to the max*. [=extremely stressed]

²**max** *adv, informal* : at the most : MAXIMUM • You'll need to wait two weeks *max*. [=you will not have to wait longer than

two weeks] ▪ The boat can hold 20 people *max.* [=it can hold no more than 20 people]

[3]**max** *verb* **max·es; maxed; max·ing**

max out *[phrasal verb] informal* **1 : to reach an upper limit : to come to the highest level possible** ▪ Most athletes *max out* before the age of 30. — **often +** ***at*** ▪ The car *maxed out at* 100 mph. [=the car could go no faster than 100 mph] ▪ Back in those days, teachers' salaries *maxed out at* $30,000 a year. **2** ***max (something) out*** *or* ***max out (something)*** **a : to spend all of the money that your credit card allows you to borrow : to use up all available credit on (a credit card)** ▪ She's *maxed out* three credit cards. **b : to use or fill (something) as much as possible : to push (something) to a limit or an extreme** ▪ The new increase in population has nearly *maxed out* the city's resources. [=has nearly used up all of the city's resources] ▪ The school is *maxed out* with students. [=the school does not have room for any more students] ▪ After years of competing, she has *maxed out* her potential as an ice-skater. ▪ Our schedule is *maxed out* [=is full] for this week.

max·im /ˈmæksəm/ *noun, pl* **-ims** *[count]* **: a well-known phrase that expresses a general truth about life or a rule about behavior** ▪ My mother's favorite *maxim* [=*saying*] was "Don't count your chickens before they hatch." [=don't assume that things will happen the way you expect them to happen]

max·i·mal /ˈmæksəməl/ *adj, technical* **: greatest or highest possible** ▪ a *maximal* heart rate
– max·i·mal·ly *adv*

max·i·mize *also Brit* **max·i·mise** /ˈmæksəˌmaɪz/ *verb* **-miz·es; -mized; -miz·ing** *[+ obj]*
1 : to increase (something) as much as possible : to increase (something) to a maximum ▪ The company is trying to *maximize* its profits. [=to make the most money possible]
2 : to use (something) in a way that will get the best result ▪ We planned out each day in order to *maximize* [=*make the most of*] our time on vacation. ▪ I rearranged the furniture to *maximize* the space in my small apartment. ▪ This program will teach you how to *maximize* your strengths while minimizing your weaknesses.
3 *computers* **: to make (a program's window) very large : to make (a program's window) fill the screen of a computer** — **opposite** MINIMIZE
– max·i·mi·za·tion *also Brit* **max·i·mi·sa·tion** /ˌmæksəməˈzeɪʃən, *Brit* ˌmæksəˌmaɪˈzeɪʃən/ *noun [noncount]* ▪ *maximization* of profits

[1]**max·i·mum** /ˈmæksəməm/ *noun, pl* **max·i·mums** *or technical* **max·i·ma** /-əmə/ *[count]* **: the highest number or amount that is possible or allowed** — **usually singular** ▪ Twenty years is the *maximum.* ▪ This security system gives you the *maximum* in protection. — **often +** ***of*** ▪ You may invite a *maximum of* 10 guests to the party. ▪ You may stay for a *maximum of* two weeks. ▪ She will serve a minimum of 10 and a *maximum of* 20 years in jail. — **opposite** MINIMUM

[2]**maximum** *adj, always used before a noun* **: greatest possible in amount or degree** ▪ He will receive the *maximum* (possible) punishment allowed by law. ▪ She took some *maximum-*strength medicine for her headache. ▪ The *maximum* number of points scored in one game is 100. ▪ shoes that are designed for *maximum* comfort ▪ What is the ***maximum occupancy*** of this room? [=what is the largest number of people who can legally be in this room at the same time?] ▪ a ***maximum security prison*** [=a prison that does as much as possible to keep prisoners from escaping and watches them very closely] — **opposite** MINIMUM

[3]**maximum** *adv* **: at the most** ▪ She will serve 20 years *maximum* in jail. [=she will not serve more than 20 years in jail]

may /ˈmeɪ/ *verb [modal verb]*
1 — used to indicate that something is possible or probable ▪ They *may* still succeed. ▪ Do you think they *may* [=*can, could, might*] still succeed? ▪ "Have they failed?" "They *may* have." = *(Brit)* "They *may* have done." [=it's possible that they failed] ▪ You *may* [=*might, could*] be right. ▪ If you work hard now, you *may* end up sitting in the boss's chair some day! ▪ What you see *may* (well/very well) surprise you. ▪ There *may* be some difficulties ahead. ▪ I think he *may* be trying to cheat us. ▪ It *may* possibly be true, mightn't it? [=(less formally) it could possibly be true, couldn't it?] ▪ *May* it not [=mightn't it, (less formally) couldn't it] after all turn out to be true? ▪ This vacation *may* [=*might*] not be so bad after all. ▪ When you're older, you *may* understand. ▪ We *may* go if they ask us, but then again we *may* not. ▪ As you ***may or may not*** have heard, we've won!
2 — used to say that one thing is true but something else is also true ▪ He *may* [=*might*] be slow, but he does very good work. = Slow though he *may* be, he (still) does very good work. [=although he's slow, he does very good work] ▪ It *may* [=*might*] be cold outside, but it's still a beautiful day. [=although it's cold outside, it's still a beautiful day] ▪ She *may* [=*might*] have been a great actress, but she was a terrible parent.
3 *formal* **— used to indicate that something is allowed** ▪ You *may* go now. [=you have permission to leave now] ▪ No one *may* enter without a ticket. ▪ The children *may* play wherever they choose. ▪ You *may* tell me your opinion, but I won't change my mind. — **compare** CAN **4b**
4 *formal* **— used to ask a question or make a request in a polite way** ▪ "*May* [=*might*] I borrow your pen?" "Of course you *may*!" ▪ "*May* I help you," asked the waiter, "or are you already being served?" ▪ *May* I ask who is calling? ▪ "*May* I leave a little early today?" "No, you *may* not." — **compare** CAN **4a**
5 *formal* **— used to express a wish** ▪ Long *may* the Queen reign! [=I hope the Queen will reign for a long time] ▪ *May* the best man win! ▪ *May* you have a long and happy life!
6 *formal* **— used to make a polite suggestion** ▪ You *may* [=*might*] want to think again and consider your options carefully. ▪ It *may* [=*might*] be wise to proceed cautiously.
7 *formal* **— used in various polite expressions with** ***I*** ▪ ***May I just say*** how pleased I am to be here. [=I would like to say how pleased I am to be here] ▪ ***If I may*** (interrupt you), would you please repeat the answer? ▪ I'd like to ask a question, *if I may.* ▪ This has been, ***if I may say so***, one of the happiest days of my life.
8 *formal + old-fashioned* **— used to indicate the reason for something or the purpose of something** ▪ We exercise so that we *may* [=*will*] be strong and healthy. [=we exercise in order to be strong and healthy] ▪ I work hard so that my family *may* [=*will*] not go hungry.
be that as it may *formal* **— used to introduce a statement that is somehow different from what has just been said** ▪ There has been some improvement in the economy in recent months, but, *be that as it may* [=*despite that, even so*], many people are still looking for work.
– see also ***come what may*** **at** [1]COME

May /ˈmeɪ/ *noun, pl* **Mays : the fifth month of the year** *[noncount]* in (early/middle/mid-/late) *May* ▪ early/late in *May* ▪ We arrived on *May* the fourth. = *(US)* We arrived on *May* fourth. = We arrived on the fourth of *May.* ▪ April showers bring *May* flowers. [=rain in April causes flowers to bloom in May] ▪ Shakespeare called it "the merry month of *May.*" *[count]* The last two *Mays* have been cold and rainy.

Ma·ya /ˈmajə/ *noun, pl* **Maya** *or* **Ma·yas** *[count]* **: a member of a group of people living mostly in southern Mexico and Guatemala**
– Ma·yan /ˈmajən/ *adj* ▪ *Mayan* culture ▪ the *Mayan* calendar

[1]**may·be** /ˈmeɪbi/ *adv* **: possibly but not certainly :** PERHAPS

> **Maybe is a more informal word than** ***perhaps.*** **It is used when you are talking about an action that has a chance of happening in the future.** ▪ *Maybe* we'll meet again. ▪ "Will you go to the party?" "I don't know. *Maybe.*" ▪ "Will you go?" "*Maybe, maybe* not." ▪ *Maybe* I'll go and *maybe* I won't. ▪ They're hoping that she'll *maybe* change her mind. = They're hoping that *maybe* she'll change her mind. ▪ You should hear from them soon, *maybe* even by next week. = *Maybe* you'll hear from them by next week. **It is also used to suggest something that is possibly correct, true, or proper.** ▪ *Maybe* we should just stay here and wait. ▪ *Maybe* it would be better if you left. ▪ There were *maybe* 10,000 fans at the game. ▪ I got three, *maybe* four hours [=about three or four hours] of sleep last night. ▪ *Maybe* it's time to stop fooling around. ▪ We waited an hour, *maybe* more. ▪ Did you ever think that ***maybe, just maybe***, it wasn't his fault? [=although it seems like it was his fault, did you ever consider the possibility that it wasn't?] **And** ***maybe*** **can be used to say that one thing is true but that something else is also true.** ▪ *Maybe* at first I didn't like her, but now she's one of my best friends. ▪ *Maybe* he's slow [=he may be slow], but he does very good work. ▪ Her accomplishments are impressive, *maybe*, but she's had a lot of help.

[2]**maybe** *noun, pl* **-bes** *[count]* **: something that is not known for certain** ▪ There are too many *maybes* [=*uncertainties*] about this project.

M

May·day /ˈmeɪˌdeɪ/ — a word used to call for help when an airplane or ship is in danger • The pilot shouted "*Mayday! Mayday!*" over the radio. — compare SOS

May Day /ˈmeɪˌdeɪ/ *noun* [*singular*] : May 1 celebrated in many countries as a spring festival and in some countries as a holiday in honor of working people

may·fly /ˈmeɪˌflaɪ/ *noun, pl* **-flies** [*count*] : a small flying insect that lives for only a short time — see color picture on page C10

may·hem /ˈmeɪˌhɛm/ *noun* [*noncount*] : actions that hurt people and destroy things : a scene or situation that involves a lot of violence • movies filled with murder and *mayhem* • committing *mayhem* • a criminal who escaped from prison and caused *mayhem* — often used figuratively • musical *mayhem* • There was *mayhem* [=a lot of excited activity] on the field after the winning goal was scored.

mayo /ˈmejoʊ/ *noun* [*noncount*] *informal* : MAYONNAISE • She ordered a turkey sandwich and told the waiter to ***hold the mayo***. [=to not include mayonnaise on the sandwich]

may·on·naise /ˈmejəˌneɪz/ *noun* [*noncount*]

1 : a thick, white sauce used especially in salads and on sandwiches and made chiefly of eggs, vegetable oil, and vinegar or lemon juice

2 *Brit* : a food made by mixing something (such as chopped eggs) with mayonnaise • ***egg mayonnaise*** [=(*US*) *egg salad*] • ***tuna mayonnaise*** [=(*US*) *tuna salad*]

may·or /ˈmejɚ/ *noun, pl* **-ors** [*count*]

1 : an official who is elected to be the head of the government of a city or town • the *mayor* of New York

2 : a British official who represents a city or borough at public events — see also LORD MAYOR

— **may·or·al** /ˈmejərəl/ *adj* • *mayoral* elections

may·or·al·ty /ˈmejərəlti/ *noun, pl* **-ties** *formal*

1 [*noncount*] : the time during which a person is mayor • During her *mayoralty*, the mayor greatly improved the city.

2 [*count*] : the job or position of being mayor • He won the *mayoralty* in the last two elections.

may·or·ess /ˈmejərəs, *Brit* ˈmɛərəs/ *noun, pl* **-ess·es** [*count*] *Brit*

1 : a woman who is a mayor

2 : the wife or official hostess of a mayor

may·pole *or* **May·pole** /ˈmeɪˌpoʊl/ *noun, pl* **-poles** [*count*] : a tall pole decorated with ribbons and flowers that forms a center for the spring festival held on May 1

M

maze /ˈmeɪz/ *noun, pl* **maz·es** [*count*]

1 : a complicated and confusing system of connected passages • The garden includes a *maze*. [=an area where there are tall walls or hedges on both sides of a path that keeps turning in different directions so that a person walking on the path cannot see where the path leads] • The experiment measured the time it took for a mouse to find its way through a *maze* to get its reward of cheese. • The school is a *maze* of classrooms. • I bought a book of *mazes*. [=a book of puzzles that are drawings which look like mazes]

2 : a confusing collection or mixture *of* things (such as rules) • a *maze of* rules and regulations

Mb *abbr* megabit

MB *abbr* **1** megabyte **2** *chiefly Brit* Bachelor of Medicine

M.B.A. *or* **MBA** *abbr* Master of Business Administration • He earned an *M.B.A.* from Harvard.

MC /ˌɛmˈsiː/ *noun, pl* **MC's** *or* **MCs** [*count*] : MASTER OF CEREMONIES

McCoy /məˈkoɪ/ *noun*

the real McCoy *also US* ***the McCoy*** *informal* : something or someone that is real or genuine : something or someone that is not a copy or imitation • Is that a fake gun, or is it *the real McCoy*? [=is it a real gun?] • These diamonds look like *the real McCoy*, but they could be fake. • To help her play the role of a lawyer, the actress studied with *the real McCoy*. [=with an actual lawyer] • Maybe he's *the McCoy*, and maybe he's not.

MD *abbr* **1** *or US* **M.D.** Doctor of Medicine **2** Maryland **3** *Brit* Managing Director

¹me /ˈmiː/ *pronoun, objective case of* I — used to refer to the speaker as the indirect object or direct object of a verb • She gave *me* a book. • They baked *me* a cake. • He sent *me* an e-mail. • They know *me* very well. • Can you help *me*? • She visited *me* in the hospital. — used to refer to the speaker as the object of a preposition • Are you talking to *me*? • Please come with *me*. • He talked with *me* for an hour.

> ***usage*** In ordinary speech *me* is used instead of *I* after the verb *to be*. • "Who's there?" "It's *me*." [="I am."] • Why is it always *me* who has to do the dirty work? [=why am I always the one who has to do the dirty work?] • This dress is pretty, but it's not really *me*. [=it doesn't look like the clothes I usually wear; it doesn't look right for me] *Me* is also used alone without a verb in spoken questions, answers, etc. • "Who's there?" "*Me*." • "Who did it?" "Not *me*!" • "Come here!" "Who? *Me*?" "Yes, you!" "Why *me*?" • "I'm hungry." "***Me too***." The expression *It is I* is extremely formal and old-fashioned and is unlikely to be used in speech except in a joking way. *Me* is also sometimes used in very informal speech in place of *I* if the subject of a sentence has two parts that are connected by *and*. • My brother and *me* went camping last weekend. = *Me* and my brother went camping last weekend. But in ordinary polite use, *I* is required in such sentences. • My brother and *I* went camping last weekend.

— see also *me either* at ⁴EITHER, *me neither* at ⁴EITHER

²me *chiefly Brit spelling of* MI

¹ME /ˌɛmˈiː/ *noun* [*noncount*] *Brit, medical* : CHRONIC FATIGUE SYNDROME ✧ *ME* is an abbreviation of "myalgic encephalomyelitis."

²ME *abbr* **1** Maine **2** *US* medical examiner

mea cul·pa /ˌmejəˈkʊlpə/ *noun, pl* **mea cul·pas** [*count*] : a statement in which you say that something is your fault • The mayor's public *mea culpa* didn't satisfy his critics. • (*humorous*) Okay, so maybe I misjudged you. *Mea culpa*!

mead /ˈmiːd/ *noun* [*noncount*] : an alcoholic drink made from honey

mead·ow /ˈmɛdoʊ/ *noun, pl* **-ows** [*count*] : a usually flat area of land that is covered with tall grass

mead·ow·lark /ˈmɛdoʊˌlaɚk/ *noun, pl* **-larks** [*count*] : a North American bird that has a brown back and a yellow breast

mea·ger (*US*) *or Brit* **mea·gre** /ˈmiːgɚ/ *adj* [*more ~; most ~*]

1 : very small or too small in amount • Every morning he eats a *meager* breakfast of toast and coffee. • We'll have to do the best we can with this year's *meager* harvest. • *meager* wages • She came to this country with a fairly *meager* English vocabulary, but she is learning more words every day.

2 : not having enough of something (such as money or food) for comfort or happiness • They suffered through several *meager* years at the beginning of their marriage. • Although she's now rich and famous, she remembers her *meager* beginnings as a child from a poor family.

— **mea·ger·ly** *adv* • They lived *meagerly* in order to save money. — **mea·ger·ness** *noun* [*noncount*]

> ***synonyms*** MEAGER, SCANTY, and SPARSE mean not having enough of what is normal, necessary, or wanted. MEAGER suggests a lack of good or necessary things. • They lived on a *meager* diet of rice and vegetables. • She earned a *meager* income of five dollars a day. SCANTY stresses that something is not large enough in size or amount. • She was wearing a *scanty* black dress. • We had a *scanty* supply of water. SPARSE suggests a small number of things or people that are far apart. • His hair had become white and *sparse*. • It's a large country with a *sparse* population.

¹meal /ˈmiːl/ *noun, pl* **meals** [*count*]

1 : the foods eaten or prepared for eating at one time • He eats/has three full *meals* a day. • Dad cooked/prepared/made a delicious *meal* of chicken and potatoes. • The waitress served our *meal*. • a three-course *meal* • This soup is ***a meal in itself***. [=all that is needed for a meal] — see also SQUARE MEAL

2 : a time or occasion when food is eaten : the act or time of eating a meal • Breakfast is her favorite *meal*. • the midday/evening *meal* • She makes us drink a glass of milk at every *meal*. • We went to Grandma's for a big holiday *meal*. • If you want to lose weight, don't eat between *meals*.

make a meal (out) of **1** : to eat (a particular food) as your meal without anything else • This bread is so good, I could *make a meal of* it. **2** *Brit, informal* : to do (something) in a way that makes it seem more important or difficult than it really is • It's not all that hard, you know! Don't *make a meal of* it!

— compare ²MEAL

²meal *noun* [*noncount*]

1 : a coarse flour made from ground seeds — see also CORNMEAL
2 : something that looks or feels like meal — see also BONEMEAL
– compare [1]MEAL

meals–on–wheels *noun* — used as the name of a service that delivers meals to the homes of old or sick people who are unable to prepare their own meals

meal ticket *noun, pl* ~ **-ets** [*count*]
1 *informal* **:** a person or thing that is depended on as a source of money, success, etc. ▪ a star player who is expected to be the team's *meal ticket* for many years ▪ An advanced degree was his *meal ticket*.
2 : a piece of paper that you can exchange for a meal ▪ We bought three *meal tickets* at the fair.

meal·time /ˈmiːlˌtaɪm/ *noun, pl* **-times :** the usual time when a meal is eaten [*noncount*] Take one pill at *mealtime*. [*count*] The two children have different *mealtimes*.

mealy /ˈmiːli/ *adj* **meal·i·er; -est :** feeling rough and dry in your mouth ▪ the *mealy* flesh of a pear ▪ a *mealy* potato
– meal·i·ness *noun* [*noncount*]

mealy·mouthed /ˈmiːliˌmaʊðd/ *adj* [*more* ~; *most* ~] *informal* **:** not willing to tell the truth in clear and simple language ▪ a *mealymouthed* politician

[1]**mean** /ˈmiːn/ *verb* **means; meant** /ˈmɛnt/; **mean·ing**
1 *not used in progressive tenses* [+ *obj*] **:** to have (a particular meaning) ▪ What does this word *mean* in English? = What is *meant* in English by this word? ▪ The word *meant* one thing in Shakespeare's day, but it *means* something else now. ▪ The abbreviation "U.S." *means* [=*stands for*] "United States." ▪ Red *means* "stop" and green *means* "go." ▪ Can you tell me what my dream *means*? ▪ "Bonjour" is a French word *meaning* "hello." = "Bonjour" is a French word that *means* "hello."
2 *not used in progressive tenses* [+ *obj*] **:** to want or intend to express (a particular idea or meaning) ▪ I *meant* what I said. [=I was sincere when I said it] ▪ What was *meant* by the poet? ▪ Don't distort what she *meant* by taking her words out of context. ▪ When she says the play was "interesting," she *means* (that) it wasn't very good. ▪ He's very ambitious, and I *mean* that as a compliment. ▪ It's a very easy question. Anyone, and I *mean* anyone, should be able to answer it. ▪ You hold it like this. **(Do you) See what I mean**? [=do you understand what I'm showing you?] ▪ She's not getting any thinner, **if you know/get what I mean**. ▪ "He can be a little difficult. **(Do you) Know what I mean**?" ▪ "He can be a little difficult." "**What/How do you mean**?" "**Meaning?**" [=what exactly do you mean when you say that?] ▪ "He can be a little difficult." "**I know what you mean**." [=I agree] ▪ "He can be a little difficult." "**What's that supposed to mean**?" [=I am surprised that you would say that; I don't agree with what you are saying]
3 [+ *obj*] **:** to have (something) in your mind as a purpose or goal ▪ Just what do you *mean* (by) coming into my room without knocking? [=what is your reason for coming into my room without knocking?] ▪ She says she didn't *mean* anything by what she did. ▪ She didn't *mean* (you) any harm. = She *meant* no harm (to you). [=she did not intend to cause any harm (to you)] ▪ I'm sorry if I hurt your feelings. I *meant* (you) no offense/disrespect. ▪ I don't trust him. He *means* no good. — often followed by *to* + *verb* ▪ He didn't *mean* [=*intend*] *to do* any harm. ▪ She *means to win*. ▪ I keep *meaning to visit* you—I just never seem to get around to it. ▪ He says he never *meant to hurt* her.
4 *not used in progressive tenses* **a :** to plan for or want (someone or something) to do or to be something [+ *obj*] — often + *as* ▪ His comment was *meant* [=*intended*] *as* a joke. — often followed by *to* + *verb* ▪ We *meant* her *to come* with us. ▪ She *meant* her remarks *to be* funny. ▪ "What you said hurt his feelings!" "Well, I *meant* it *to*!" [*no obj*] (*chiefly US*) — + *for* ▪ We *meant for* her to come with us. **b** [+ *obj*] **:** to want (something that you control, provide, or have made) to be used for a particular purpose or by a particular person — often + *for* ▪ I *meant* [=*intended*] the flowers *for* you, not for your sister. ▪ The book was *meant for* children, but it is popular with adults too. ▪ His criticism is *meant for* all of us. — often followed by *to* + *verb* ▪ They *meant* the book *to be* a present. — sometimes + *as* ▪ They *meant* the book *as* a present.
5 *not used in progressive tenses* [+ *obj*] **:** to make a statement to or about (someone) ▪ "Hey, you!" "I'm sorry: do you *mean* me?" [=are you talking to me?] ▪ "Some people here are too bossy!" "Do you *mean* me?" [=are you referring to me?]
6 *not used in progressive tenses* [+ *obj*] **a :** to indicate or show (something that is going to happen) ▪ Those clouds *mean* rain. = Those clouds *mean* (that) it's going to rain. ▪ When he gets that angry look in his eyes, you know it *means* trouble. [=you know that there will be trouble] **b :** to cause or result in (something) ▪ The bad weather could *mean* further delays. **c :** to involve or require (something) as a necessary part ▪ Becoming a concert pianist *means* practicing a lot. [=if you're going to become a concert pianist you have to practice a lot] ▪ I'll get the work done today even if it *means* staying late.
7 *not used in progressive tenses* [+ *obj*] — used to say or ask how important something is to someone; usually + *to* ▪ How much does your health *mean to* you? [=how important is your health to you?] ▪ It *means* a lot *to* me to know that you believe me. ▪ "I believe you." "Thank you. You don't know how much that *means to* me." ▪ Your good opinion *means* a great deal *to* me. ▪ He claims that money **means nothing to** him. [=that he does not care at all about money] ▪ Her words *meant nothing to* me. [=I did not care what she said] ▪ I thought our friendship **meant something to** you. [=I thought that you cared about our friendship] ▪ His wife **means everything to** him. = His wife **means the world to** him. [=he loves his wife very much]

I mean *informal* **1** — used to emphasize a statement ▪ He has to stop drinking. *I mean*, he's going to kill himself if he keeps it up. ▪ He throws, *I mean*, really hard! **2** — used to correct a previous statement ▪ We met in Toronto—*I mean* Montreal. **3** — used when you are unsure of what to say or how to say it ▪ I'm not mad. It's just that, *I mean*, I think you've been acting a little selfishly.

***know what it means* :** to understand what it is like to do or be something ▪ I *know what it means* to be poor. — usually used in negative statements ▪ You don't *know what it means* to be truly alone. — sometimes used in an exaggerated way to make a forceful statement ▪ I don't *know what it means* to surrender! [=I will never surrender]

mean business see BUSINESS

meant for (someone) *informal* **:** perfectly suited for (someone) ▪ You were *meant for* me and I was *meant for* you. ▪ I'm not surprised that they have such a happy marriage. I always knew that they were **meant for each other**. — see also [1]MEAN 4b (above)

meant to be/do something **1 :** intended to do or be something ▪ I was never *meant to* teach. ▪ They knew as soon as they met that they were *meant to* be together. ▪ I thought we could be friends, but I guess it just wasn't **meant to be**. [=it was not destined to happen] **2** *Brit* **:** supposed to be or do something ▪ The buses are *meant* [=*expected*] *to* arrive every 15 minutes. ▪ Brighton is *meant to* be very beautiful at this time of year. [=people say that Brighton is very beautiful at this time of year]

***mean well* :** to want to do good or helpful things **:** to have good intentions ▪ He *means well*, but he's not really helping anyone. — see also WELL-MEANING

[2]**mean** *adj* **mean·er; -est** [*also more* ~; *most* ~]
1 *somewhat informal* **a :** not kind to people **:** cruel or harsh ▪ My boss is a *mean* and nasty old man who treats everyone badly. ▪ the *mean* stepmother in the fairy tale ▪ Why are you being so *mean* to me? [=why are you treating me so harshly?] ▪ It was *mean* of them not to invite her to the party. ▪ Someone played a *mean* trick on her. ▪ He has a *mean* streak. **b** *chiefly US* **:** very dangerous **:** VICIOUS ▪ a *mean* dog
2 *chiefly Brit* **:** not liking to spend money **:** STINGY, CHEAP ▪ He's a *mean* man who never gives presents to anyone. ▪ He's very *mean* with his money.
3 *old-fashioned + literary* **:** of poor quality or status ▪ *mean* city streets ▪ living in *mean* circumstances
4 *chiefly US, informal* **:** excellent or impressive ▪ He plays a *mean* trumpet. = He's a *mean* trumpet player. [=he plays the trumpet very well] ▪ an athlete who describes himself as a **lean, mean** scoring machine ▪ We wanted our business to be **lean and mean**. [=to be efficient and successful]

no mean *informal* — used to say that something is good or impressive ▪ a tennis player of *no mean* ability [=a very good tennis player] ▪ Getting the project done on time will be **no mean feat**. [=will be a difficult and impressive accomplishment]
– compare [3]MEAN
– mean·ly /ˈmiːnli/ *adv* ▪ behaving/living *meanly* ▪ a *meanly* ambitious man **– mean·ness** /ˈmiːnnəs/ *noun* [*noncount*] ▪ the *meanness* of her character ▪ *meanness* of spirit

M

[3]**mean** *adj, always used before a noun* **: occurring exactly between the highest and lowest number : AVERAGE** ▪ the *mean* temperature — **compare** [2]**MEAN**

[4]**mean** *noun, pl* **means** *[count]*

1 : [1]**AVERAGE 1** ▪ Take all these temperatures and calculate/find their *mean*.

2 : a middle point between two things ▪ trying to find ***a golden mean*** between doing too little and doing too much

– see also MEANS

me·an·der /miˈændɚ/ *verb* **-ders; -dered; -der·ing** *[no obj]*

1 : to have a lot of curves instead of going in a straight or direct line : to follow a winding course ▪ The path *meanders* through the garden. ▪ a *meandering* stream

2 : to walk slowly without a specific goal, purpose, or direction ▪ We *meandered* around/through the village.

3 : to go from one topic to another without any clear direction ▪ The conversation *meandered* on for hours. ▪ He delivered a *meandering* [=*rambling*] speech about his early career.

– me·an·der *noun, pl* **-ders** *[count]* ▪ We went for a *meander* in the park.

mean·ie /ˈmiːni/ *noun, pl* **-ies** *[count] informal* **: a mean or unkind person — used especially by children** ▪ You're nothing but a big *meanie*!

mean·ing /ˈmiːnɪŋ/ *noun, pl* **-ings**

1 : the idea that is represented by a word, phrase, etc. *[count]* What is the precise/exact *meaning* of this word in English? ▪ Many words have developed more than one *meaning*. [=*sense*] ▪ an old word that has taken on a new *meaning* ▪ The word has both literal *meanings* and figurative *meanings*. *[noncount]* a word with various shades of *meaning*

2 a : the idea that a person wants to express by using words, signs, etc. *[count]* Don't distort her *meaning* by taking her words out of context. ▪ Do you get my *meaning*? = (*chiefly Brit*) Do you take my *meaning*? [=do you understand what I'm telling you?] ▪ I didn't understand the *meaning* of his remark/gesture. *[noncount]* a glance full of *meaning* [=a meaningful glance] **b : the idea that is expressed in a work of writing, art, etc.** *[count]* Literary critics disagree about the *meanings* of his poems. *[noncount]* a poem with subtle shades of *meaning*

3 *[noncount]* **a : the true purpose of something** ▪ What is the *meaning* of life? ▪ It's a story about the true *meaning* of Christmas. **b : a quality that gives something real value and importance** ▪ He began to feel that his life had lost its *meaning*. ▪ a life without *meaning* = a life devoid of *meaning* [=a meaningless life] ▪ Working with children has given her life new *meaning*. **c : the reason or explanation for something** ▪ What is the *meaning* of this intrusion?

know the meaning of (something) **: to understand (something) because you have experienced it** ▪ I *know the meaning of* loneliness. [=I know what it is like to be lonely] **— often used in negative statements** ▪ Those people don't *know the meaning of* hard work. **— often used in an exaggerated way to make a forceful statement** ▪ He doesn't *know the meaning of* fear. [=he is very brave] ▪ I'll never stop trying. I don't ***know the meaning of the word*** "failure." [=I am determined not to fail]

mean·ing·ful /ˈmiːnɪŋfəl/ *adj [more ~; most ~]*

1 : having a clear meaning ▪ The test did not produce any *meaningful* results.

2 : expressing an emotion or idea without words ▪ She looked at him in a *meaningful* way. ▪ a *meaningful* expression/glance/pause

3 : having real importance or value ▪ He wanted to feel that his job was *meaningful*. ▪ The trip turned out to be very *meaningful* for/to both of them. ▪ a *meaningful* relationship/discussion

– mean·ing·ful·ly *adv* ▪ She paused *meaningfully* before answering the question. **– mean·ing·ful·ness** *noun [noncount]*

mean·ing·less /ˈmiːnɪŋləs/ *adj [more ~; most ~]*

1 : having no meaning ▪ a *meaningless* phrase

2 : having no real importance or value ▪ He felt that his work was *meaningless*. ▪ The movie was filled with *meaningless* violence. ▪ Their offer to help us was just a *meaningless* [=*empty*] gesture.

– mean·ing·less·ly *adv* ▪ a *meaninglessly* violent movie **– mean·ing·less·ness** *noun [noncount]*

means /ˈmiːnz/ *noun, pl* **means**

1 *[count]* **: a way of doing something or of achieving a desired result** ▪ trains, buses, and other *means* of transportation ▪ a *means* of communication/expression ▪ using fingerprints as a *means* of identification ▪ "What's the best *means* of getting there?" "Public transportation." ▪ The property was obtained by illegal *means*. ▪ He vowed that he would succeed ***by any means necessary***. [=by doing whatever was needed] ▪ He would use all/any ***manner of means*** to succeed. ▪ For her, marrying a rich man was just ***a means to an end***. [=something done only to produce a desired result] All she really cared about was money. ▪ How can she survive when she has no visible ***means of support***? [=she has no apparent way to pay for the things that she needs to live] **— see also WAYS AND MEANS,** ***the end justifies the means*** **at** [1]**END**

2 *[plural]* **: the money that someone has : WEALTH** ▪ He has the *means* to give you everything you want. ▪ His *means* are enough to pay for college. ▪ a man/woman ***of means*** [=a wealthy man/woman] ▪ She is a woman ***of independent means***. [=she has enough money to support herself without help from others] ▪ He enjoys a style of living that is ***beyond the means*** of all but the wealthiest people. [=that only the wealthiest people can afford] ▪ She was ***living beyond her means***. [=she was spending more money than she could afford to spend] ▪ He began to save money when he finally learned to ***live within his means***. [=to spend money only on what he could afford]

by all means **: of course : CERTAINLY** ▪ "May I come in?" "*By all means*!" ▪ *By all means* feel free to get a second opinion.

by means of **: through the use of (something)** ▪ He got out of trouble *by means of* a clever trick.

by no means **or** ***not by any means*** **also** ***not by any manner of means*** **: in no way : not at all** ▪ It's *by no means* certain that he'll come. = It's *not* by *any means* certain that he'll come. ▪ This is *by no means* the first time we have had this problem. ▪ I was *not* happy about the arrangements *by any means*, but I agreed to do it. ▪ This issue has *not* been resolved yet *by any manner of means*.

mean–spir·it·ed /ˈmiːnˈspɪrətəd/ *adj [more ~; most ~]* **: feeling or showing a cruel desire to cause harm or pain** ▪ a *mean-spirited* person ▪ a *mean-spirited* book review

means test *noun, pl* **~ tests** *[count]* **: a process done to find out the amount of money a person has in order to see if that person qualifies for government assistance**

– means–test·ed /ˈmiːnzˈtɛstəd/ *adj* ▪ a *means-tested* program ▪ *means-tested* assistance/benefits [=assistance/benefits based on the results of a means test]

meant *past tense and past participle of* [1]**MEAN**

[1]**mean·time** /ˈmiːnˌtaɪm/ *noun*

for the meantime **: for the present time : until some time in the future** ▪ You should continue to take the medicine *for the meantime*. [=*for now*]

in the meantime **1 : during the time before something happens or before a specified period ends** ▪ He can come back to work when he's feeling better, but *in the meantime* he should be resting as much as possible. ▪ The project is scheduled for completion in three months, and there's a great deal of work to be done *in the meantime*. ▪ The new computers won't arrive until next week, but we can keep using the old ones *in the meantime*. **2 : while something else is being done or was being done** ▪ She spent four years studying for her law degree. *In the meantime*, she continued to work at the bank.

[2]**meantime** *adv, somewhat informal* **:** [1]**MEANWHILE** ▪ He can come back to work when he's feeling better. *Meantime*, he should be resting as much as possible.

[1]**mean·while** /ˈmiːnˌwajəl/ *adv* **: at or during the same time : in the meantime** ▪ You can set the table. *Meanwhile*, I'll start making dinner. ▪ She spent four years studying for her law degree. *Meanwhile*, she continued to work at the bank. ▪ He can come back to work when he's feeling better, but *meanwhile* he should be resting as much as possible.

[2]**meanwhile** *noun*

in the meanwhile **: at or during the same time : in the meantime** ▪ The new computers won't arrive until next week, but we can keep using the old ones *in the meanwhile*.

mea·sles /ˈmiːzəlz/ *noun [noncount]* **: a disease that causes a fever and red spots on the skin** ▪ He has (the) *measles*. ▪ get/catch the *measles* **— see also GERMAN MEASLES**

mea·sly /ˈmiːzli/ *adj* **mea·sli·er; -est** *informal + disapproving* **: very small or too small in size or amount** ▪ He left a *measly* [=*lousy*] dime for a tip. ▪ She complained about being given such a *measly* raise. ▪ All I want is a few *measly* minutes of your time.

M

mea•sur•able /ˈmɛʒərəbəl/ *adj* **:** large enough to be measured or noticed ▪ We haven't had a *measurable* amount of rain in the past several weeks. ▪ There has been a *measurable* [=*significant*] improvement in the company's performance.
– mea•sur•ably /ˈmɛʒərəbli/ *adv* ▪ His job performance has improved *measurably.*

¹mea•sure /ˈmɛʒɚ/ *noun, pl* **-sures**
1 : an amount or degree of something [*count*] She felt equal *measures* of hope and fear. — **usually singular** ▪ The province has gained a large *measure* of freedom. ▪ Their children want a greater *measure* of independence. [=they want more independence] ▪ The coating provides a *measure* of protection [=provides some protection] against corrosion. ▪ The proposal has been met with a *measure* [=a certain amount] of skepticism. ▪ The alarm system provides an added *measure* of security. [=provides more security] [*noncount*] The show mixes comedy and drama in equal *measure.* [=in equal amounts] ▪ He returned their hostility in full *measure.* [=he was as hostile toward them as they were toward him] ▪ The company's success is due in no small *measure* to her talents. [=its success is largely due to her talents] ▪ Their actions were motivated in large *measure* by a desire for revenge. ▪ An occasion like this calls for some *measure* of decorum.
2 [*count*] **a :** something (such as a cup or a ruler) that is used to measure things — **see also** TAPE MEASURE **b :** a unit used in measuring something ▪ The meter is a *measure* of length. ▪ The dictionary includes a table of weights and *measures.* — **see also** MADE-TO-MEASURE
3 [*count*] **:** an action planned or taken to achieve a desired result ▪ The legislature has passed a *measure* aimed at protecting consumers. ▪ The governor has proposed a number of cost-cutting *measures.* ▪ They were forced to resort to desperate/extreme *measures.* ▪ protective/punitive/preventive *measures* ▪ We need to ***take measures*** to protect ourselves.
4 [*count*] **:** a sign or indication *of* something — **usually singular** ▪ Wealth is not a *measure of* happiness. ▪ Her willingness to compromise is a *measure of* how much she's changed.
5 [*count*] **:** a way of judging something ▪ The company is a success by any *measure.* ▪ Are IQ tests the best *measure* of intelligence?
6 [*count*] *chiefly US, music* **:** a part of a line of written music that is between two vertical lines or the group of beats between these lines ▪ a brief clarinet solo in the third *measure* ▪ Can you hum a few *measures* [=*bars*] of that song?
beyond measure *formal* **:** to a very great degree ▪ an artist who is talented *beyond* (all) *measure* [=who is exceptionally talented] ▪ Her joy was *beyond measure.* [=she was very happy]
for good measure **:** as something added or extra ▪ He performed his most recent songs, and then threw in a couple of old ones *for good measure.*
have/take/get the measure of (someone) *or* ***have/take/get someone's measure*** *chiefly Brit* **:** to have or get a good understanding about what is needed to defeat or deal with (someone you are competing against) ▪ She failed to *take the measure of* her opponent. [=she failed to realize how good her opponent was]

²measure *verb* **-sures; -sured; -sur•ing**
1 [+ *obj*] **a :** to find out the size, length, or amount of (something) ▪ using a ruler to *measure* a piece of paper ▪ an instrument for *measuring* air pressure ▪ I *measured* [=*estimated*] the distance with my eye. ▪ mental abilities *measured* by IQ testing **b :** to find out the size of (someone) for clothing ▪ He's being *measured* for a new suit.
2 [+ *obj*] **:** to judge the importance, value, or extent of (something) ▪ It's difficult to *measure* [=*evaluate*] the importance of these events. ▪ His success cannot be *measured* solely on the basis of his popularity. — **often + *against*** ▪ Her accomplishments need to be *measured against* [=*compared with*] those of her predecessor.
3 [*linking verb*] **:** to have a specified size ▪ The cloth *measures* 3 meters. ▪ The room *measures* 15 feet wide by 30 feet long.
measure off [*phrasal verb*] ***measure off (something)*** *also* ***measure (something) off*** **:** to measure (something) and mark its edges or its beginning and ending ▪ They *measured off* a half-acre plot for the house lot. ▪ He *measured off* three yards of cloth.
measure out [*phrasal verb*] ***measure out (something)*** *also* ***measure (something) out*** **:** to measure and remove (something) from a larger amount ▪ She carefully *measured out* three cups of flour.
measure up [*phrasal verb*] **:** to be as good as expected or needed ▪ His early works were promising, but his recent films haven't *measured up.* [=his recent films haven't been as good as his early ones] — **often + *to*** ▪ His recent films haven't *measured up to* his earlier works. ▪ Her work didn't *measure up to* our expectations. [=was not as good as we expected it to be]
– mea•sur•er /ˈmɛʒərɚ/ *noun, pl* **-ers** [*count*]

mea•sured /ˈmɛʒɚd/ *adj* [*more* ~; *most* ~] **:** done with thought and care ▪ This crisis requires a *measured* response. ▪ She spoke in carefully *measured* tones.

mea•sure•less /ˈmɛʒɚləs/ *adj* **:** too great or large to be measured ▪ the *measureless* [=*immeasurable*] universe ▪ She seems to have *measureless* [=*boundless*] energy.

mea•sure•ment /ˈmɛʒɚmənt/ *noun, pl* **-ments**
1 [*noncount*] **:** the act or process of measuring something ▪ The test is for the *measurement* of a student's progress. ▪ Carpentry requires careful *measurement.* ▪ The instruments provide accurate *measurement* of atmospheric conditions.
2 [*count*] **:** a size, length, or amount known by measuring something ▪ The room's *measurements* are 30 by 15 feet. ▪ The instruments are used for taking *measurements* of atmospheric conditions. ▪ Accurate *measurements* are required in carpentry. ▪ The tailor took his *measurements,* and his waist *measurement* is 36 inches.

measuring cup *noun, pl* ~ **cups** [*count*] *US* **:** a cup that has markings for measuring ingredients when cooking; *also* **:** a cup that holds a particular amount of an ingredient used in cooking ▪ a set of *measuring cups* ranging from ¼ cup to 1 cup — **see picture at** KITCHEN; **compare** MEASURING JUG

measuring jug *noun, pl* ~ **jugs** [*count*] *Brit* **:** a cup that has markings for measuring liquids when cooking — **compare** MEASURING CUP

measuring tape *noun, pl* ~ **tapes** [*count*] **:** TAPE MEASURE

meat /ˈmiːt/ *noun, pl* **meats**
1 a [*noncount*] **:** the flesh of an animal used as food ▪ She doesn't eat *meat.* ▪ a piece/slice of *meat* ▪ raw *meat* ▪ (*US*) ground *meat* ▪ *meat* sauce [=sauce that contains meat] ✧ *Meat* often refers specifically to the flesh of mammals or birds instead of the flesh of fish. It can also sometimes refer only to the flesh of mammals. ▪ She eats fish but not *meat.* ▪ The soup can be made with *meat,* chicken, or fish. **b** [*count*] **:** a type of meat ▪ The restaurant serves a variety of *meats.* ▪ sandwich *meats* — **see also** DARK MEAT, LUNCHEON MEAT, WHITE MEAT
2 [*noncount*] **:** the part of something (such as a nut) that can be eaten ▪ coconut *meat*
3 [*noncount*] **:** the most important or interesting part *of* something ▪ The real *meat of* the book is found in its discussion of his economic plan.
4 [*noncount*] *US* **:** the thickest part *of* something (such as a baseball bat) ▪ He hit the ball right on the *meat of* the bat.
– **see also** DEAD MEAT

meat and potatoes *noun* [*noncount*] *US, informal* **:** the most basic or important part of something **:** MEAT ▪ Basic conservation is still the *meat and potatoes* of their environmental plan. ▪ the *meat and potatoes* of the contract/argument

meat–and–potatoes *adj, always used before a noun, chiefly US, informal*
1 : of, relating to, or preferring simple food (such as meat and potatoes) instead of fancy food ▪ a *meat-and-potatoes* diet ▪ The restaurant appeals to the *meat-and-potatoes* crowd. ▪ I'm a *meat-and-potatoes* guy.
2 : ordinary or simple ▪ *meat-and-potatoes* rock and roll

meat•ball /ˈmiːtˌbɑːl/ *noun, pl* **-balls** [*count*] **:** a small ball of chopped or ground meat ▪ spaghetti and *meatballs*

meat•head /ˈmiːtˌhɛd/ *noun, pl* **-heads** [*count*] *informal* **:** a stupid person ▪ Her brother's a real *meathead.*

meat loaf *noun, pl* ~ **loaves** *also* ~ **loafs** [*count, noncount*] **:** meat that is chopped in very small pieces, mixed with spices, chopped onions, eggs, etc., and baked in the form of a loaf ▪ a slice of *meat loaf*

meat market *noun, pl* ~ **-kets** [*count*]
1 : a place where meat is sold
2 *US, informal* **:** a place where people are judged only on the basis of their physical qualities (such as sexual attractiveness or athletic ability) ▪ That bar/club is a real *meat market.* ▪ The scouting camp is a *meat market* for pro football candidates.

meat•pack•ing /ˈmiːtˌpækɪŋ/ *noun* [*noncount*] *US* **:** the business of killing animals for meat and getting the meat ready to be sold — often used before another noun ▪ the *meatpacking* industry/business

meaty /ˈmiːti/ *adj* **meat·i·er; -est** [*also more ~; most ~*]
1 a : of, relating to, or resembling meat ▪ *meaty* flavors/aromas ▪ a *meaty* hunk of fish ▪ The mushrooms have a *meaty* texture. **b :** having or including a large amount of meat ▪ *meaty* bones ▪ a *meaty* diet/stew
2 : large and heavy or thick with flesh or muscles ▪ an athlete with *meaty* forearms/hands
3 : having a lot of interesting ideas or information ▪ a *meaty* novel ▪ an actor auditioning for a *meaty* role ▪ The *meatiest* part of the book is the historical background it gives.
– meat·i·ness *noun* [*noncount*] ▪ the *meatiness* of the stew

mec·ca /ˈmɛkə/ *noun, pl* **-cas**
1 *Mecca* [*singular*] **:** a city in Saudi Arabia that was the birthplace of Muhammad and is the holiest city of Islam
2 [*count*] **:** a place that attracts many people ▪ The valley is a *mecca* for wine lovers. ▪ The town has become a *mecca* for tourists. ▪ tourist *meccas*

me·chan·ic /mɪˈkænɪk/ *noun, pl* **-ics** [*count*] **:** a person who repairs machines (such as car engines) and keeps them running properly ▪ an automotive *mechanic* — see also MECHANICS

me·chan·i·cal /mɪˈkænɪkəl/ *adj*
1 a : of or relating to machinery ▪ The flight was delayed because of *mechanical* problems/difficulties. ▪ a *mechanical* failure/breakdown ▪ I was impressed by her *mechanical* know-how. ▪ He's a *mechanical* genius. [=he is a person who is very smart about machines] ▪ *mechanical* parts/components **b :** having or using machinery ▪ a *mechanical* toy/clock/device
2 [*more ~; most ~*] *disapproving* **:** happening or done without thought or without any effort to be different or interesting ▪ She gave a *mechanical* reply. ▪ Copying down the numbers is a boring and *mechanical* job. ▪ The actor gave a stiff and *mechanical* performance.

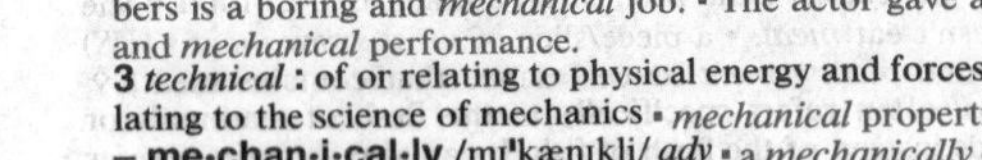

3 *technical* **:** of or relating to physical energy and forces **:** relating to the science of mechanics ▪ *mechanical* properties
– me·chan·i·cal·ly /mɪˈkænɪkli/ *adv* ▪ a *mechanically* complex apparatus ▪ He's not *mechanically* inclined. [=he is not knowledgeable about machinery]

mechanical drawing *noun, pl* **~ -ings** *US* **:** drawing done by using special instruments that allow you to draw a machine, building, etc., in a very precise and accurate way [*noncount*] She's taking a class in *mechanical drawing.* [*count*] a detailed series of *mechanical drawings*

mechanical engineering *noun* [*noncount*] **:** a type of engineering that is mainly concerned with the use of machines in industry
– mechanical engineer *noun, pl* **~ -neers** [*count*]

mechanical pencil *noun, pl* **~ -cils** [*count*] *US* **:** a pencil made of metal or plastic with a lead that is moved forward by a mechanical device — called also (*Brit*) *propelling pencil*

me·chan·ics /mɪˈkænɪks/ *noun*
1 [*noncount*] **:** a science that deals with physical energy and forces and their effect on objects — see also QUANTUM MECHANICS
2 [*plural*] **:** the details about how something works or is done ▪ the *mechanics* of running ▪ He still has a lot to learn about the *mechanics* of running a business.

mech·a·nism /ˈmɛkəˌnɪzəm/ *noun, pl* **-nisms** [*count*]
1 : a piece of machinery **:** a mechanical part or group of parts having a particular function ▪ The camera's shutter *mechanism* is broken. ▪ a timing/locking *mechanism*
2 : a process or system that is used to produce a particular result ▪ Scientists are studying the body's *mechanisms* for controlling weight. ▪ There is no *mechanism* in place for enforcing the new law. ▪ a legal *mechanism* to prevent lobbyists from exerting unfair influence
3 : a way of acting, thinking, or behaving that helps or protects a person in a specified way ▪ a coping/survival *mechanism* ▪ psychological *mechanisms* for dealing with a tragic loss — see also DEFENSE MECHANISM, ESCAPE MECHANISM

mech·a·nize *also Brit* **mech·a·nise** /ˈmɛkəˌnaɪz/ *verb* **-niz·es; -nized; -niz·ing** [*+ obj*] **:** to change (a process or an activity) so that it is done with machines instead of by people or animals ▪ an invention that helped to *mechanize* agriculture
– mech·a·ni·za·tion *also Brit* **mech·a·ni·sa·tion** /ˌmɛkənəˈzeɪʃən, *Brit* ˌmɛkəˌnaɪˈzeɪʃən/ *noun* [*noncount*] ▪ the *mechanization* of the industry **– mechanized** *also Brit* **mechanised** *adj* [*more ~; most ~*] ▪ a highly *mechanized* industry

¹med /ˈmɛd/ *adj, always used before a noun, chiefly US, informal* **:** ¹MEDICAL ▪ *med* school ▪ *med* students

²med *noun, pl* **meds** [*count*] *chiefly US, informal* **:** MEDICATION 1 — usually plural ▪ He stopped taking his *meds.*

³med *abbr* medium

Med *abbr* Mediterranean

MEd *abbr* master of education

¹med·al /ˈmɛdl̩/ *noun, pl* **-als** [*count*] **:** a piece of metal often in the form of a coin with designs and words in honor of a special event, a person, or an achievement ▪ He was awarded a *medal* for his heroism. — see also BRONZE MEDAL, GOLD MEDAL, MEDAL OF HONOR, SILVER MEDAL

medal

²medal *verb* **-als;** *US* **-aled** *or chiefly Brit* **-alled;** *US* **-al·ing** *or chiefly Brit* **-al·ling** [*no obj*] **:** to win a medal ▪ She *medaled* in figure skating in the Olympics.

med·al·ist (*US*) *or chiefly Brit* **med·al·list** /ˈmɛdl̩ɪst/ *noun, pl* **-ists** [*count*] **:** a person who receives or wins a medal ▪ an Olympic *medalist*

me·dal·lion /məˈdæljən/ *noun, pl* **-lions** [*count*]
1 : a large medal
2 : a decoration that is shaped like a large medal
3 : a small, round piece of food (such as meat) ▪ *medallions* of veal

Medal of Honor *noun, pl* **Medals of Honor** [*count*] **:** the highest U.S. military award that is given to someone for extreme bravery while in battle with an enemy

med·dle /ˈmɛdl̩/ *verb* **med·dles; med·dled; med·dling** [*no obj*]
1 : to become involved in the activities and concerns of other people when your involvement is not wanted **:** INTERFERE — usually + *in* ▪ He was always *meddling in* other people's personal lives. — sometimes + *with* ▪ They are *meddling with* things that don't concern them.
2 : to change or handle something in a way that is unwanted or harmful — + *with* ▪ Don't *meddle* with my stuff.
– med·dler /ˈmɛdlɚ/ *noun, pl* **med·dlers** [*count*] ▪ She thought she was being helpful, but her neighbors saw her as a *meddler.* **– meddling** *noun* [*noncount*] ▪ He was annoyed by his neighbor's *meddling.* **– meddling** *adj, always used before a noun* ▪ *meddling* neighbors

med·dle·some /ˈmɛdl̩səm/ *adj* [*more ~; most ~*] **:** interfering with the activities and concerns of other people in an unwanted or unwelcome way **:** inclined to meddle ▪ Her neighbors saw her as a *meddlesome* nuisance.

med·e·vac *also* **med·i·vac** /ˈmɛdəˌvæk/ *noun, pl* **-vacs** *US*
1 [*noncount*] **:** emergency removal of sick or injured people from an area especially by helicopter — usually used before another noun ▪ a *medevac* mission/team
2 [*count*] **:** a helicopter used to remove sick or injured people from an area ▪ The wounded soldiers were evacuated by *medevac* to the hospital. ▪ an Army *medevac*
– medevac *also* **medivac** *verb* **-vacs; -vaced** *or* **-vacked; -vac·ing** *or* **-vack·ing** [*+ obj*] ▪ The wounded soldiers were *medevaced* to the hospital.

¹media *plural of* ¹MEDIUM

²me·dia /ˈmiːdijə/ *noun* [*plural*]
1 : the radio stations, television stations, and newspapers through which information is communicated to the public **:** MASS MEDIA ▪ The event attracted a lot of attention from the *media.* = The event attracted a lot of *media* attention. ▪ the news *media* — sometimes used with a singular verb ▪ He feels that the *media* is ignoring this important issue.
2 *chiefly US* **:** people who work as news reporters, publishers, and broadcasters **:** members of the media ▪ The event attracted a lot of *media.* ▪ a large crowd of *media*

mediaeval *variant spelling of* MEDIEVAL

media event *noun, pl* **~ events** [*count*] **:** an event that attracts attention from the news media ▪ The President's visit to the school was a major *media event.*

¹me·di·an /ˈmiːdijən/ *noun, pl* **-ans** [*count*]
1 *mathematics* **:** the middle value in a series of values arranged from smallest to largest

2 *US* : MEDIAN STRIP

[2]**median** *adj, always used before a noun* : in the middle; *especially, mathematics* : having a value that is in the middle of a series of values arranged from smallest to largest • What is the *median* price of homes in this area?

median strip *noun, pl* ~ **strips** *[count]* *US* : a grassy or paved area that divides a highway so that traffic going in one direction is kept separate from traffic going in the opposite direction — called also *(US) median, (Brit) central reservation*

me·di·ate /ˈmiːdiˌeɪt/ *verb* **-ates; -at·ed; -at·ing**
1 a : to work with opposing sides in an argument or dispute in order to get an agreement *[no obj]* He has been appointed by the government to *mediate* (in the dispute) between the company and the striking workers. *[+ obj]* *(US)* • He has been appointed to *mediate* the dispute. **b** *[+ obj]* : to get (something, such as a settlement or agreement) by working with opposing sides in a dispute • He is attempting to *mediate* a settlement between the company and the striking workers. • Negotiators are trying to *mediate* a cease-fire.
2 *[+ obj] formal + technical* : to have an effect or influence in causing (something) to happen — usually used as *(be) mediated* • The study indicates that human aggression *is* partly *mediated* by biological factors.
– me·di·a·tion /ˌmiːdiˈeɪʃən/ *noun [noncount]* • *mediation* of the dispute **– me·di·a·tor** /ˈmiːdiˌeɪtɚ/ *noun, pl* **-tors** *[count]* • She has been appointed to act as a *mediator* [=*intermediary*] in the dispute.

med·ic /ˈmɛdɪk/ *noun, pl* **-ics** *[count]* : a person who does medical work: such as **a** *US* : a member of the military whose job is to provide emergency medical care to soldiers who have been wounded in battle **b** *Brit, informal* : a medical student or doctor

Med·ic·aid /ˈmɛdɪˌkeɪd/ *noun [singular]* *US* : a government program that provides money to people who are unable to pay for regular medical care • patients who are eligible for *Medicaid* — compare MEDICARE

[1]**med·i·cal** /ˈmɛdɪkəl/ *adj* : of or relating to the treatment of diseases and injuries : of or relating to medicine • *medical* care/advice/attention • high *medical* bills • *medical* problems/procedures • the *medical* profession • a *medical* breakthrough • *medical* school/students • He has a dangerous *medical* condition. • The report was published in a leading *medical* journal. • Her recovery was a *medical* miracle. • He opened his own *medical* practice. • an important advance in *medical* science • a ***medical center*** [=a place where people go for medical treatment]
– med·i·cal·ly /ˈmɛdɪkli/ *adv* • a *medically* necessary operation • a *medically* useful drug

[2]**medical** *noun, pl* **-cals** *[count]* *Brit* : a medical examination : PHYSICAL

medical examiner *noun, pl* ~ **-ers** *[count]* *US* : a public official who examines the bodies of dead people to find the cause of death

medical practitioner *noun, pl* ~ **-ers** *[count]* *formal* : [1]DOCTOR

Medi·care /ˈmɛdɪˌkeɚ/ *noun [singular]* *US* : a government program that provides medical care especially for old people • patients eligible for *Medicare* — compare MEDICAID

med·i·cate /ˈmɛdɪˌkeɪt/ *verb* **-cates; -cat·ed; -cat·ing** *[+ obj]* : to treat (a person or disease) with medicine and especially with drugs • *medicate* an illness • The patient had been heavily *medicated*.

med·i·cat·ed *adj* : containing a substance that kills germs and helps to keep your skin or hair healthy • *medicated* soap/shampoo • *medicated* foot powder

med·i·ca·tion /ˌmɛdɪˈkeɪʃən/ *noun, pl* **-tions**
1 : a substance used in treating disease or relieving pain : MEDICINE *[noncount]* She's taking *medication* for high blood pressure. = She's on *medication* for high blood pressure. *[count]* The company has developed a new allergy *medication*. • He stopped taking his *medications*.
2 *[noncount]* : the act or process of treating a person or disease with medicine • His condition requires *medication*. • Her illness has not responded to *medication*.

me·dic·i·nal /məˈdɪsənəl/ *adj* : used to prevent or cure disease or to relieve pain • a *medicinal* substance • *medicinal* herbs/plants • *medicinal* properties • This drug is to be used only for *medicinal* purposes.
– me·dic·i·nal·ly *adv* • a *medicinally* useful substance • The plant was once used *medicinally*.

med·i·cine /ˈmɛdəsən, *Brit* ˈmɛdsən/ *noun, pl* **-cines**
1 : a substance that is used in treating disease or relieving pain and that is usually in the form of a pill or a liquid *[count]* a cough *medicine* • herbal *medicines* • He forgot to take his *medicine*. *[noncount]* I took some *medicine*. • Did you look in the *medicine* cabinet/chest for a pain reliever?
2 *[noncount]* : the science that deals with preventing, curing, and treating diseases • Their research has led to many important advances in modern *medicine*. • She's interested in a career in *medicine*. • the practice/study of *medicine* • preventive *medicine* — see also INTERNAL MEDICINE, SOCIALIZED MEDICINE, SPORTS MEDICINE, WESTERN MEDICINE

a taste/dose of your own medicine *informal* : harsh or unpleasant treatment that is like the treatment you have given other people • The movie is about a playboy who gets *a taste of his own medicine* when the girl he falls in love with jilts him for another guy.

take your medicine *informal* : to accept something that is unpleasant because it is necessary and cannot be avoided • If he loses the case, he should just *take his medicine* and stop complaining.

medicine ball *noun, pl* ~ **balls** *[count]* : a heavy leather-covered ball that is used for exercises

medicine dropper *noun, pl* ~ **-pers** *[count]* : DROPPER

medicine man *noun, pl* ~ **men** *[count]* : a person in Native American cultures who is believed to have magic powers that can cure illnesses and keep away evil spirits

med·i·co /ˈmɛdɪˌkoʊ/ *noun, pl* **-cos** *[count]* *informal* : [1]DOCTOR • She proved the *medicos* wrong by recovering quickly from her injuries.

med·i·co·le·gal /ˌmɛdɪkoʊˈliːgəl/ *adj* : of or relating to both medicine and law • *medicolegal* problems

me·di·eval *also* **me·di·ae·val** /ˌmiːdiˈiːvəl, *Brit* ˌmɛdiˈiːvəl/ *adj [more ~; most ~]*
1 : of or relating to the Middle Ages : of or relating to the period of European history from about A.D. 500 to about 1500 • *medieval* music/history/warriors
2 *informal* : very old : too old to be useful or acceptable • They're using a computer system that seems positively *medieval* by today's standards.

me·di·o·cre /ˌmiːdiˈoʊkɚ/ *adj [more ~; most ~]* : not very good • The dinner was delicious, but the dessert was *mediocre*. • The carpenter did a *mediocre* job. • a *mediocre* wine • The critics dismissed him as a *mediocre* actor.

me·di·oc·ri·ty /ˌmiːdiˈɑːkrəti/ *noun, pl* **-ties**
1 *[noncount]* : the quality of something that is not very good : the quality or state of being mediocre • We were disappointed by the *mediocrity* of the wine.
2 *[count]* : a person who does not have the special ability to do something well • He thought that he was a brilliant artist himself and that all his fellow painters were just *mediocrities*.

med·i·tate /ˈmɛdəˌteɪt/ *verb* **-tates; -tat·ed; -tat·ing** *[no obj]* : to spend time in quiet thought for religious purposes or relaxation • He *meditates* for an hour every morning.

meditate on/upon *[phrasal verb]* ***meditate on/upon (something)*** : to think about (something) carefully • She *meditated on* whether or not to return to school. • He was *meditating upon* the meaning of life.

med·i·ta·tion /ˌmɛdəˈteɪʃən/ *noun, pl* **-tions**
1 : the act or process of spending time in quiet thought : the act or process of meditating *[noncount]* She spent the morning in *meditation*. • Daily *meditation* helps clear his mind. *[count]* his daily *meditations*
2 *[count] formal* : an expression of a person's thoughts on something — often + *on* or *upon* • The essay is a *meditation on* modern life. — often plural • She recently published her *meditations on* ethics.

med·i·ta·tive /ˈmɛdəˌteɪtɪv/ *adj [more ~; most ~]* : very thoughtful • a *meditative* student • I could see that she was in a *meditative* mood. : involving or allowing deep thought or meditation • *meditative* music
– med·i·ta·tive·ly *adv* • She gazed *meditatively* at him.

Med·i·ter·ra·nean /ˌmɛdətəˈreɪnijən/ *adj* : of or relating to the Mediterranean Sea or to the lands that surround it • a *Mediterranean* island/climate • *Mediterranean* cuisine

[1]**me·di·um** /ˈmiːdijəm/ *noun, pl* **me·di·ums** *or* **me·dia** /ˈmiːdijə/ *[count]*
1 *pl* ***mediums*** : something that is sold in a medium size : something that is the middle size when compared with things that are larger and smaller • I take a *medium*. • These shirts are all *mediums* and I take a large. • Make my French fries a *medium*.
2 *pl* ***usually media*** : a particular form or system of commu-

M

nication (such as newspapers, radio, or television) • an effective advertising *medium* = an effective *medium* for advertising — see also MEDIA
3 : the materials or methods used by an artist • Her preferred *medium* is sculpture. • The artist works in two *media/mediums*, pencil and watercolor.
4 : the thing by which or through which something is done • Money is a *medium* [=*means*] of exchange. • English is an important *medium* of international communication.
5 *pl* ***mediums*** **: a person who claims to be able to communicate with the spirits of dead people** • She visited a *medium* to try to talk to her dead son.
6 *formal* **: a surrounding condition or environment** • Ocean fish live in a *medium* of salt water.
happy medium **: a good choice or condition that avoids any extremes** • They are looking for a *happy medium*: a house that is not too big but that has lots of storage space. • The car's designers have found/struck a *happy medium* between affordability and luxury.

[2]medium *adj*
1 : in the middle of a range of possible sizes, amounts, etc. • These T-shirts are available in three sizes: small, *medium*, and large. • a person of *medium* build/height/weight • a *medium* blue [=a blue that is neither very light nor very dark]
2 *of meat* **: cooked to a point that is between rare and well-done** • How would you like your steak, sir: rare, *medium*, or well-done? ✧ **Meat that is *medium rare* is cooked to a point between rare and medium, while meat that is *medium well* is cooked to a point between medium and well-done.**
– medium *adv* • He likes his steak cooked *medium*.

medium–sized *or* **medium–size** *adj* **: neither large nor small** • a *medium-sized* pan • a *medium-size* car/house/city

medium–term *adj, always used before a noun* **: lasting for a period of time that is neither long nor short** • Our short-term prospects are grim and our *medium-term* prospects are uncertain, but our long-term prospects are good.

medivac *variant spelling of* MEDEVAC

med•ley /ˈmɛdli/ *noun, pl* **-leys** [*count*]
1 : a musical piece made up of parts of other musical works • a *medley* of show tunes
2 : a mixture of different people or things • a *medley* of sights/sounds/aromas
3 *sports* **: a race in swimming in which swimmers use a different stroke for each different part of the race** • the 400-meter *medley*

meek /ˈmiːk/ *adj* **meek•er; -est : having or showing a quiet and gentle nature : not wanting to fight or argue with other people** • a *meek* child dominated by his brothers • a *meek* reply • She may seem ***meek and mild*** but it is all an act.
– meek•ly *adv* • He asked *meekly* for help. **– meek•ness** *noun* [*noncount*]

[1]meet /ˈmiːt/ *verb* **meets; met** /ˈmɛt/; **meet•ing**
1 : to see and speak to (someone) for the first time : to be introduced to or become acquainted with (someone) [+ *obj*] He *met* his wife at work. • We *met* each other in college. • Did you *meet* anyone interesting at the party? • I'd like you to *meet* my good friend Bob. • I'm happy/glad/pleased to *meet* you. = (*informally*) Pleased to *meet* you. • It was nice *meeting* you. = It was a pleasure *meeting* you. = I'm happy/glad to have *met* you. [*no obj*] The couple *met* at a dance. • We *met* in college. • Have we *met*? You look familiar. • Actually, we've already *met*.
2 a : to come together in order to talk : to go to a place to be with someone else [*no obj*] They *met* for drinks after work. • We arranged to *meet* for lunch. • Let's *meet* at the park. • They *meet* together every week. • We are *meeting* downtown tomorrow. [+ *obj*] I arranged to *meet* her for lunch. • She said she'd *meet* me in/at the park. • I'm being *met* by a friend at the airport. • I'm planning to *meet* his plane at the airport. [=to be at the airport waiting for him when his plane arrives] **b** [*no obj*] **: to come together formally : to have a meeting** • The club *meets* every Wednesday night. **: to come together for a discussion** • We are *meeting* today to discuss the plans.
3 [+ *obj*] **a : to see (someone) by chance** • I *met* [=*ran into*] an old friend at the store. • I hope we'll *meet* again someday. **b : to come near (someone or something) as you are passing by** • We only *met* one other car on the road.
4 : to face each other in a game, competition, war, etc. [*no obj*] The teams *met* in the finals last year. • The candidates will *meet* for two debates. • Two great armies *met* on the battlefield that day. [+ *obj*] The Boston Red Sox will *meet* the New York Yankees in a three-game series this weekend. • The army was advancing to *meet* the enemy.
5 : to touch and join with or cross something else [+ *obj*] the point where the river *meets* the sea [*no obj*] the point where the river and the sea *meet* • His jacket does not *meet* in front. [=the two sides of his jacket do not touch in the front; his jacket is too small]
6 [+ *obj*] **a : to be equal to (something) : to match (something)** • The store promises to *meet* the price of any competitor. **b : to succeed in doing or providing (something)** • They *met* all our demands. [=they did everything that we demanded] • The restaurant didn't *meet* (our) expectations. [=it was not as good as we expected it to be] • They haven't yet *met* the requirements for entry. [=they have not done what they must do for entry] **c : to reach (something, such as a goal)** • They failed to *meet* their target/goals. • The students here are expected to *meet* very high standards. **: to succeed in doing what is required by (something)** • They *met* the challenge. • We somehow managed to *meet* the deadline. • The new policies are intended to help *meet* the growing demand for new housing. • The company was unable to *meet* its payroll. [=the company was unable to pay its employees when it was supposed to] • We have enough money to *meet* our needs. [=to pay for the things that we need] • We work very hard to *meet* the needs of our customers. [=to provide our customers with what they need]
7 [+ *obj*] **a : to experience or be affected by (something bad or unpleasant)** • They *met* defeat bravely. • They *met* trouble on the way home. • The proposal has *met* [=*encountered*] some opposition. [=there has been some opposition to the proposal] • This is the place where he *met* his death. [=where he was killed; where he died] • I hope they don't ***meet the fate*** of so many others in their situation. [=I hope the things that happen to others in their situation do not happen to them] **b : to deal with or face (something) directly** • She *met* his glance/gaze without looking away. [=she looked directly at him as he looked at her] ✧ **When two people's *eyes meet* they look directly at each other.** • Their *eyes met*. = His *eyes met* hers. = He *met her eyes*.
8 [+ *obj*] **: to be sensed by (the eyes, ears, etc.)** • We were shocked by the sight that *met* our eyes/gaze/view. [=we were shocked by what we saw] • A distant murmur *met* his ear/ears. [=he heard a distant murmur] • When they opened the door they were *met* by/with a shocking sight. [=they saw something shocking]
make ends meet see [1]END
meet (someone) halfway **: to reach an agreement with (someone) by giving up something that you want : to compromise with (someone)** • We can't comply with all your requests, but we can *meet you halfway*. • Can we at least *meet halfway* on this?
meet up with [*phrasal verb*] ***meet up with (someone)*** *informal* **: to come together with (someone) : to go to a place to be with (someone)** • I'll *meet up with* you later. [=I'll meet you later] • They *met up with* each other for drinks.
meet with [*phrasal verb*] **1 *meet with (someone)* : to come together with (someone) to talk about something : to have a meeting with (someone)** • We are *meeting with* the architect today to discuss the plans. • Can you *meet with* us later today? **2 *meet with (something)* : to have or experience (something)** • The proposal has *met with* (some) opposition. • We *met with* many adventures on our trip. • He *met with* a warm reception [=he was warmly received/welcomed] when he arrived. • When she didn't arrive on time, we were worried that she might have *met with* an accident. • Her ideas *met with* their approval. [=they approved her ideas]
meet your maker see MAKER
more than meets the eye see [1]EYE
– meet•er *noun, pl* **-ers** [*count*] • He's one of the company's *meeters* and greeters. [=a person who meets new people and welcomes them to a place]

[2]meet *noun, pl* **meets** [*count*]
1 *chiefly US* **: a large gathering of athletes for a sports competition** • a track/swim *meet* **— called also (*Brit*) *meeting*; see also SWAP MEET**
2 *Brit* **: an event or occasion when people come together to hunt foxes**

meet•ing /ˈmiːtɪŋ/ *noun, pl* **-ings**
1 a [*count*] **: a gathering of people for a particular purpose (such as to talk about business)** • The club's monthly *meeting* will be held next Monday evening. • She was too busy to attend the *meeting*. • Let's have/hold/call/convene a *meeting* to discuss these problems. • postpone/adjourn/close a business *meeting* • a committee/staff *meeting* • I wasn't able to talk to

him because he was ***in a meeting.*** **b :** a gathering of people for religious worship [*count*] a Quaker *meeting* ▪ a revival *meeting* ▪ a prayer *meeting* [*noncount*] (*US*) He attends Quaker *meeting.*

2 [*count*] **a :** a situation or occasion when two people see and talk to each other ▪ They started dating each other soon after their first *meeting.* ▪ Their friendship began with a chance *meeting* at a business convention. **b :** a situation or occasion when athletes or teams compete against each other ▪ Tonight's game will be their first *meeting* of the season. **c** *Brit* **:** [2]MEET 1 ▪ an athletics *meeting*

3 [*singular*] **:** the place where two things come together ▪ a town at the *meeting* of two rivers

a meeting of minds *or US* ***a meeting of the minds* :** an understanding or agreement between two people or groups ▪ The company and the union tried to come to *a meeting of the minds.* [=they tried to reach an agreement]

meet·ing·house /ˈmiːtɪŋˌhaʊs/ *noun, pl* **-hous·es** [*count*] **:** a building used for public gatherings and especially for Christian worship in the past

mega /ˈmɛgə/ *adj, informal*

1 : very large **:** VAST ▪ a *mega* electronics store

2 [*more ~; most ~*] **:** very popular, successful, or important ▪ an actor who has become a *mega* celebrity

mega- /mɛgə/ *combining form*

1 a : great **:** large ▪ a *mega*store **b** *informal* **:** extremely ▪ *mega*-rich

2 *technical* **:** million **:** multiplied by one million ▪ *mega*hertz ▪ *mega*byte

mega·bit /ˈmɛgəˌbɪt/ *noun, pl* **-bits** [*count*] *computers* **:** one million bits — abbr. *Mb*

mega·bucks /ˈmɛgəˌbʌks/ *noun* [*plural*] *informal* **:** an extremely large amount of money ▪ a star athlete who is earning *megabucks*

– mega·buck /ˈmɛgəˌbʌk/ *adj, always used before a noun* ▪ a *megabuck* movie [=a movie that cost a great amount of money to produce] ▪ an athlete with a *megabuck* contract

mega·byte /ˈmɛgəˌbaɪt/ *noun, pl* **-bytes** [*count*] *computers* **:** a unit of computer information equal to 1,048,576 bytes ▪ The CD has a storage capacity of 800 *megabytes.* — abbr. *MB*; compare GIGABYTE, KILOBYTE

mega·cor·po·ra·tion /ˌmɛgəˌkoəpəˈreɪʃən/ *noun, pl* **-tions** [*count*] **:** an extremely large and powerful corporation

mega·dose /ˈmɛgəˌdoʊs/ *noun, pl* **-dos·es** [*count*] *US* **:** a large amount of medicine, vitamins, etc. **:** a large dose ▪ He took *megadoses* of vitamin C.

mega·hertz /ˈmɛgəˌhəts/ *noun, pl* **-hertz** [*count*] *technical* **:** a unit of radio frequency equal to one million hertz — abbr. *MHz*

mega·hit /ˈmɛgəˌhɪt/ *noun, pl* **-hits** [*count*] *informal* **:** something (such as a movie) that is extremely successful ▪ His latest movie was a *megahit.*

mega·lith /ˈmɛgəˌlɪθ/ *noun, pl* **-liths** [*count*] **:** a very large stone used in ancient cultures as a monument or part of a building

– mega·lith·ic /ˌmɛgəˈlɪθɪk/ *adj* ▪ a *megalithic* tower/tomb/monument

meg·a·lo·ma·nia /ˌmɛgəloʊˈmeɪnijə/ *noun* [*noncount*] **:** a condition or mental illness that causes people to think that they have great or unlimited power or importance ▪ Their CEO has an arrogance that borders on *megalomania.*

meg·a·lo·ma·ni·ac /ˌmɛgəloʊˈmeɪniˌæk/ *noun, pl* **-acs** [*count*] **:** a person who believes that he or she has unlimited power or importance **:** a person who has megalomania ▪ Their CEO is a real *megalomaniac.*

– megalomaniac *adj* ▪ a *megalomaniac* artist **– meg·a·lo·ma·ni·a·cal** /ˌmɛgəloʊməˈnajəkəl/ *adj* ▪ *megalomaniacal* delusions ▪ a *megalomaniacal* politician

meg·a·lop·o·lis /ˌmɛgəˈlɑːpələs/ *noun, pl* **-lis·es** [*count*] *US*

1 : a very large city

2 : an area that includes a large city or several large cities

mega·phone /ˈmɛgəˌfoʊn/ *noun, pl* **-phones** [*count*] **:** a cone-shaped device used to make your voice louder when you speak through it — compare BULLHORN

mega·plex /ˈmɛgəˌplɛks/ *noun, pl* **-plexes** [*count*] *US* **:** a large building that contains many movie theaters — compare MULTIPLEX

mega·star /ˈmɛgəˌstɑə/ *noun, pl* **-stars** [*count*] *informal* **:** a very famous and successful performer (such as an actor or an athlete)

mega·store /ˈmɛgəˌstoə/ *noun, pl* **-stores** [*count*] **:** a very large store that sells many different products ▪ a discount *megastore* [=*superstore*]

mega·ton /ˈmɛgəˌtʌn/ *noun, pl* **-tons** [*count*] **:** an explosive force that is equal to one million tons of TNT ▪ an atomic explosion with a force of several *megatons*

mega·watt /ˈmɛgəˌwɑːt/ *noun, pl* **-watts** [*count*] **:** a unit of electrical power equal to one million watts ▪ 50 *megawatts* of electricity — compare KILOWATT

mein see CHOW MEIN, LO MEIN

meis·ter /ˈmaɪstə/ *noun, pl* **-ters** [*count*] *informal* **:** someone who knows a lot about something **:** someone who is an expert in something — usually used in combination ▪ a champion puzzle-*meister* ▪ a rap-*meister*

mel·a·mine /ˈmɛləˌmiːn/ *noun* [*noncount*] **:** a type of hard plastic that is used especially for covering other materials

mel·an·cho·lia /ˌmɛlənˈkoʊlijə/ *noun* [*noncount*] *old-fashioned + literary* **:** a feeling of sadness and depression

mel·an·chol·ic /ˌmɛlənˈkɑːlɪk/ *adj* [*more ~; most ~*] *old-fashioned + literary* **:** very sad **:** GLOOMY ▪ a *melancholic* outlook ▪ *melancholic* music

[1]**mel·an·choly** /ˈmɛlənˌkɑːli/ *noun* [*noncount*] *old-fashioned + literary* **:** a sad mood or feeling ▪ suffering from *melancholy* ▪ a time of *melancholy*

[2]**melancholy** *adj* [*more ~; most ~*] **:** feeling or showing sadness **:** very unhappy ▪ She was in a *melancholy* mood. ▪ He became quiet and *melancholy* as the hours slowly passed. ▪ *melancholy* [=*sad, depressing*] music/thoughts

mé·lange /meɪˈlɑːnʤ/ *noun, pl* **-lang·es** [*count*] **:** a mixture of different things ▪ a *mélange* of colors and shapes ▪ a *mélange* of architectural styles

mel·a·nin /ˈmɛlənən/ *noun* [*noncount*] **:** a dark brown or black substance that is a natural part of people's skin, hair, and eyes

mel·a·no·ma /ˌmɛləˈnoʊmə/ *noun, pl* **-mas** *also* **-ma·ta** /-mətə/ *medical* **:** a type of cancer or tumor that begins as a dark spot or area on the skin [*noncount*] She has *melanoma.* [*count*] a malignant *melanoma*

[1]**meld** /ˈmɛld/ *verb* **melds; meld·ed; meld·ing :** to blend or mix together [*no obj*] Cook the sauce slowly to let the flavors *meld* (together). [+ *obj*] Cook the sauce slowly to *meld* the flavors (together).

[2]**meld** *noun* [*singular*] *chiefly US* **:** a mixture of things ▪ a *meld* [=*blend*] of musical influences ▪ a *meld* of Jewish and Christian customs

me·lee /ˈmeɪˌleɪ, *Brit* ˈmɛˌleɪ/ *noun, pl* **-lees** [*count*] **:** a confused struggle or fight involving many people — usually singular ▪ They were seriously injured in the *melee.*

mel·lif·lu·ous /mɛˈlɪfləwəs/ *adj* [*more ~; most ~*] *formal* **:** having a smooth, flowing sound ▪ *mellifluous* speech ▪ a *mellifluous* voice

– mel·lif·lu·ous·ly *adv* ▪ She sang *mellifluously.*

[1]**mel·low** /ˈmɛloʊ/ *adj* **mel·low·er; -est** [*also more ~; most ~*]

1 : pleasantly rich, full, or soft **:** not harsh, bright, or irritating ▪ The painting captures the *mellow* light of a summer evening. ▪ *mellow* music ▪ a *mellow* golden color

2 : having a pleasing rich flavor that develops over time ▪ This wine is very *mellow.* ▪ a *mellow* cheese

3 a : very calm and relaxed ▪ He was in a *mellow* mood. ▪ She was a tough and demanding teacher, but she became *mellower* in her old age. ▪ He's a very *mellow* guy. ▪ a *mellow* crowd **b** *informal* **:** relaxed from drinking alcohol or using drugs ▪ After a couple of drinks we all started feeling pretty *mellow.*

[2]**mellow** *verb* **-lows; -lowed; -low·ing :** to become or to cause (someone or something) to become less harsh, irritating, nervous, etc. [*no obj*] She was a tough and demanding teacher, but she has *mellowed* in her old age. ▪ The wine needs time to *mellow.* [+ *obj*] She was a tough and demanding teacher, but old age has *mellowed* her. ▪ Time *mellowed* [=*softened*] their hard feelings.

mellow out [*phrasal verb*] *US, informal* **:** to become relaxed and calm ▪ She *mellowed out* as she grew older. **:** to calm down ▪ You're getting all upset over nothing. You need to *mellow out.*

– mel·low·ness *noun* [*noncount*]

me·lod·ic /məˈlɑːdɪk/ *adj*

1 : of or relating to melody ▪ the *melodic* flow of the music ▪ a pleasing *melodic* line/pattern

2 [*more ~; most ~*] **:** having a pleasant musical sound or

melody • a *melodic* tune • a *melodic* voice
– **me·lod·i·cal·ly** /məˈlɑːdɪkli/ *adv* • The birds were singing *melodically.*

me·lo·di·ous /məˈloudijəs/ *adj* [*more* ~; *most* ~] **:** having a pleasing melody • a *melodious* song **:** having or making a pleasant musical sound • a *melodious* sound/voice • *melodious* birds/instruments
– **me·lo·di·ous·ly** *adv* • singing *melodiously* – **me·lo·di·ous·ness** *noun* [*noncount*]

melo·dra·ma /ˈmɛləˌdrɑːmə/ *noun, pl* **-mas**
1 : drama in which many exciting events happen and the characters have very strong or exaggerated emotions [*noncount*] Critics dismissed his work as *melodrama.* • an actor with a talent for *melodrama* [*count*] She is starring in another *melodrama.*
2 : a situation or series of events in which people have very strong or exaggerated emotions [*count*] The trial turned into a *melodrama.* [*noncount*] a life full of *melodrama*

melo·dra·mat·ic /ˌmɛlədrəˈmætɪk/ *adj* [*more* ~; *most* ~] *often disapproving* **:** emotional in a way that is very extreme or exaggerated **:** extremely dramatic or emotional • a *melodramatic* movie/story/script • Oh, quit being so *melodramatic!* • *melodramatic* music
– **melo·dra·mat·i·cal·ly** /ˌmɛlədrəˈmætɪkli/ *adv* • She threw herself onto the bed *melodramatically* and sobbed.

melo·dra·mat·ics /ˌmɛlədrəˈmætɪks/ *noun* [*plural*] **:** extremely dramatic or emotional behavior **:** melodramatic behavior • He told the story without any *melodramatics.*

mel·o·dy /ˈmɛlədi/ *noun, pl* **-dies**
1 : a pleasing series of musical notes that form the main part of a song or piece of music [*count*] He wrote a piece that includes some beautiful/haunting *melodies.* [*noncount*] a composer known for his love of *melody*
2 [*count*] **:** a song or tune • He sang a few old-fashioned *melodies.*

mel·on /ˈmɛlən/ *noun, pl* **-ons** [*count, noncount*] **:** a large, round fruit that has a hard skin and sweet, juicy flesh — see also HONEYDEW MELON, WATERMELON

[1]**melt** /ˈmɛlt/ *verb* **melts; melt·ed; melt·ing**
1 : to change or to cause (something) to change from a solid to a liquid usually because of heat [*no obj*] The butter *melted* in the frying pan. • The snow is finally *melting.* [+ *obj*] She *melted* butter in the frying pan. • a tablespoon of *melted* butter • *melted* cheese
2 [*no obj*] **:** to gradually become less or go away **:** DISAPPEAR • Their determination *melted* in the face of opposition. — often + *away* • Her anger *melted away* when she saw that he was truly sorry. • As the sun rose the fog began to *melt away.*
3 : to begin to have feelings of love, kindness, sympathy, etc. [*no obj*] She *melted* at his kindly words. • Her heart *melted* with compassion. [+ *obj*] It would have ***melted your heart*** [=it would have filled you with compassion, sympathy, etc.] to see her lying in that hospital bed.
butter wouldn't melt in someone's mouth see [1]BUTTER
melt down [*phrasal verb*] **1 a** *of a nuclear reactor* **:** to heat up accidentally, melt, and release radiation • The reactor's core *melted down.* **b :** to experience a very fast collapse or failure • The stock market has *melted down.* — see also MELTDOWN **2** ***melt (something) down or melt down (something)*** **:** to melt (something) so that it can be used for another purpose • *melt down* a coin • The stolen gold has probably already been *melted down.*
melt into [*phrasal verb*] ***melt into (something)*** **:** to become difficult or impossible to see by changing into or becoming combined with (something else) • The colors in the painting *melt into* one another. • Her frown *melted into* a smile. • She *melted into* [=disappeared into] the crowd. • He seemed to *melt into* thin air. [=he seemed to disappear]
melt in your mouth ✧ Food that *melts in your mouth* is delicious and feels soft or becomes soft when you put it in your mouth. • chocolate candies that *melt in your mouth* • The fish practically *melts in your mouth.*

[2]**melt** *noun, pl* **melts** [*count*] *US* **:** a sandwich made with melted cheese • a tuna *melt*

melt·down /ˈmɛltˌdaun/ *noun, pl* **-downs**
1 : an accident in which the core of a nuclear reactor melts and releases radiation [*count*] a nuclear *meltdown* [*noncount*] fears that an accident could cause *meltdown*
2 a : a very fast collapse or failure [*count*] a stock market *meltdown* [*noncount*] a company experiencing financial *meltdown* **b** [*count*] *chiefly US, somewhat informal* **:** a very fast loss of emotional self-control • After a long day at the beach, our toddler had a major *meltdown* in the car on the way home. — see also *melt down* at [1]MELT

melt·ing /ˈmɛltɪŋ/ *adj* **:** having a quality that causes gentle feelings of love, sympathy, etc. • a love song's *melting* lyrics • She looked at him with *melting* eyes.
– **melt·ing·ly** *adv*

melting point *noun, pl* ~ **points** [*count, noncount*] **:** the temperature at which something melts • a metal's *melting point*

melting pot *noun, pl* ~ **pots** [*count*] **:** a place (such as a city or country) where different types of people live together and gradually create one community — usually singular • The city is a *melting pot* of different cultures. • the American *melting pot*
in the melting pot *Brit* **:** not yet certain or finally decided **:** still changing or likely to change • Our plans are still *in the melting pot.* • It looked like our team was winning, but then everything went back *in the melting pot.* [=the outcome became uncertain again]

mem·ber /ˈmɛmbɚ/ *noun, pl* **-bers** [*count*]
1 : someone or something that belongs to or is a part of a group or an organization • a club/committee/team *member* • family *members* • The club has 300 *members.* • She is a *member* of the House of Representatives. • She is a *member/Member* of Parliament. • a *member* of the audience • band/crew/gang *members* • This bird is a *member* of the finch family. • countries that are *members* of the United Nations — see also CHARTER MEMBER, FOUNDING MEMBER
2 *technical* **:** a part of a structure (such as a building or a bridge) • a horizontal *member* of a bridge • the roof's supporting *members*
3 a *old-fashioned* **:** a body part (such as an arm or a leg) • his lower *members* **b** — used as a polite way of saying *penis* • the male *member*

mem·ber·ship /ˈmɛmbɚˌʃɪp/ *noun, pl* **-ships**
1 : the state of belonging to or being a part of a group or an organization **:** the state of being a member [*noncount*] (*US*) He applied for *membership* in the club. = (*Brit*) He applied for *membership* of the club. [*count*] What is the cost of a one-year *membership?* • They renewed their *memberships.*
2 : all the people or things that belong to or are part of an organization or a group [*noncount*] *Membership* in the club doubled last year. • clubs that are hoping to increase their *membership* [*count*] The club has a large *membership.* • The *membership* has voted to accept the proposal. = (*Brit*) The *membership* have voted to accept the proposal. • clubs that are hoping to increase their *memberships*

mem·brane /ˈmɛmˌbreɪn/ *noun, pl* **-branes** [*count*] **:** a thin sheet or layer • The computer chip is covered by/with a plastic *membrane.* [=the computer chip is covered by/with a very thin sheet of plastic] ; *especially* **:** a thin sheet or layer of tissue that is part of a plant or an animal's body • a cell *membrane*
– **mem·bran·ous** /ˈmɛmbrənəs/ *adj, technical* • *membranous* tissue

me·men·to /məˈmɛntou/ *noun, pl* **-tos** *or* **-toes** [*count*] **:** something that is kept as a reminder of a person, place, or thing **:** SOUVENIR • a collection of photographs and *mementos* • It was a *memento* of our trip.

memo /ˈmɛmou/ *noun, pl* **mem·os** [*count*] **:** a usually brief written message from one person or department in an organization, company, etc., to another **:** MEMORANDUM • He sent a *memo* to the staff.

mem·oir /ˈmɛmˌwaɚ/ *noun, pl* **-oirs**
1 ***memoirs*** [*plural*] **:** a written account in which someone (such as a famous performer or politician) describes past experiences • a retired politician who is writing his *memoirs*
2 [*count*] **:** a written account of someone or something that is usually based on personal knowledge of the subject • He has written a *memoir* of his mother. • a *memoir* of Hollywood in the 1930s

mem·o·ra·bil·ia /ˌmɛmərəˈbɪlijə/ *noun* [*plural*] **:** objects or materials that are collected because they are related to a particular event, person, etc. **:** things collected as souvenirs • a display of sports/military *memorabilia* • She collects Beatles *memorabilia.*

mem·o·ra·ble /ˈmɛmərəbəl/ *adj* [*more* ~; *most* ~] **:** very good or interesting and worth remembering • a *memorable* vacation/experience • It was the most *memorable* line of the play. • She gave a *memorable* performance.
– **mem·o·ra·bly** /ˈmɛmərəbli/ *adv* • a *memorably* exciting event

mem·o·ran·dum /ˌmɛməˈrændəm/ *noun, pl* **-dums** *or* **-da** /-də/ [*count*]
1 : a usually brief written message or report from one person or department in a company or organization to another • The company president sent a *memorandum* [=(less formally) *memo*] to each employee.
2 *law* **:** an informal written record of an agreement that has not yet become official

¹me·mo·ri·al /məˈmorijəl/ *noun, pl* **-als** [*count*] **:** something (such as a monument or ceremony) that honors a person who has died or serves as a reminder of an event in which many people died • a war *memorial* — often + *to* • The new hospital is a fitting *memorial to* her.

²memorial *adj, always used before a noun* **:** created or done to honor a person who has died or to remind people of an event in which many people died • a *memorial* service/monument • a *memorial* scholarship fund

Memorial Day *noun, pl* ~ **Days** [*count, noncount*] **:** the last Monday in May that is a national holiday in the U.S. honoring members of the armed forces who died in wars

me·mo·ri·al·ize *also Brit* **me·mo·ri·al·ise** /məˈmorijəˌlaɪz/ *verb* **-iz·es; -ized; -iz·ing** [+ *obj*] *formal* **:** to do or create something that causes people to remember (a person, thing, or event) • an exciting period in history that has been *memorialized* in many popular books and movies

memoriam see IN MEMORIAM

mem·o·rize *also Brit* **mem·o·rise** /ˈmɛməˌraɪz/ *verb* **-riz·es; -rized; -riz·ing** [+ *obj*] **:** to learn (something) so well that you are able to remember it perfectly • He *memorized* the speech. • an actress *memorizing* her lines
– mem·o·ri·za·tion *also Brit* **mem·o·ri·sa·tion** /ˌmɛmərəˈzeɪʃən, *Brit* ˌmɛməˌraɪˈzeɪʃən/ *noun* [*noncount*]

mem·o·ry /ˈmɛməri/ *noun, pl* **-ries**
1 : the power or process of remembering what has been learned [*count*] He began to lose his *memory* as he grew older. • He has an excellent *memory* for faces. [=he is very good at remembering faces] • Those people have ***long memories.*** [=they remember things that happened long ago] • She has a ***short memory.*** [=she forgets things quickly] • Dad has a ***selective memory;*** he remembers the times he was right and forgets the times he was wrong. [*noncount*] They claim that these pills can improve (the) *memory.* • short-term/long-term *memory* • He committed the speech ***to memory.*** [=he memorized the speech] • ***If memory serves (me rightly/correctly),*** his name is John. [=if I remember accurately, his name is John] — see also PHOTOGRAPHIC MEMORY
2 a [*count*] **:** something that is remembered • We have pleasant *memories* of the trip. • trying to repress bitter/painful *memories* • childhood *memories* • His name evokes *memories* of a happier time. • That time is just a dim/faint *memory* to me now. **b** [*noncount*] **:** the things learned and kept in the mind • The happiness of those times is still vivid in my *memory.* • Her name has faded from *memory.* • I seem to have very little *memory* of that time in my life. • Her name has faded from my *memory.* [=I cannot remember her name] • That tragic day has become part of our collective *memory.* [=it is something that we all remember] • He has no *memory* of what happened. [=he does not remember what happened] • I can't remember exactly how much it costs. Could you ***refresh my memory?*** [=remind me] • The sudden shock ***jogged his memory*** and everything came flooding back into his mind.
3 [*count*] **:** the things that are remembered about a person who has died • Even though he is no longer with us, ***his memory lives on.*** [=we still remember him]
4 : the period of time that a person can remember [*count*] — usually singular • These events occurred within their *memory.* [=occurred during the time that they can remember] [*noncount*] These events occurred within ***living memory.*** • The harbor froze over for the first time ***in (modern/recent) memory.***
5 [*noncount*] *computers* **a :** capacity for storing information • a computer with 512MB of *memory* • The computer needs more *memory.* **b :** the part of a computer in which information is stored • information stored in *memory* — see also RANDOM-ACCESS MEMORY
from memory **:** without reading or looking at notes • She delivered the speech (entirely) *from memory.* • He played the entire piece *from memory.* • She can recite *from memory* the capitals of all the states of the U.S.
in memory of *or* ***in someone's memory*** **:** made or done to honor someone who has died • The monument is *in memory of* the soldiers who died in battle on this field. • He donated the painting *in his wife's memory.*
memory lane ✧ If you ***take a stroll/trip/walk (etc.) down memory lane,*** you think or talk about pleasant things from the past. • We *took a stroll down memory lane,* talking about our time at school together.

men *plural of* ¹MAN

¹men·ace /ˈmɛnəs/ *noun, pl* **-ac·es**
1 [*count*] **a :** a dangerous or possibly harmful person or thing — usually singular • Those dogs are a *menace.* — often + *to* • Those dogs are a *menace to* the neighborhood. • a criminal who is a *menace to* society **b :** someone who causes trouble or annoyance — usually singular • That kid is a *menace.*
2 [*noncount*] **:** a dangerous or threatening quality • There was an atmosphere of *menace* in the city. • She could hear the *menace* in his voice.
with menaces *Brit, law* **:** with threats **:** using threatening actions or language • They were accused of demanding money *with menaces.*

²menace *verb* **-aces; -aced; -ac·ing** [+ *obj*] *somewhat formal* **:** to threaten harm to (someone or something) — often used as *(be) menaced* • She *was menaced* by a man with a knife. • a country *menaced* by war
– menacing *adj* [*more* ~; *most* ~] • He gave her a *menacing* look. **– men·ac·ing·ly** /ˈmɛnəsɪŋli/ *adv* • He looked at her *menacingly.*

mé·nage à trois /meɪˈnɑːʒɑˈtrwɑː/ *noun, pl* **mé·nages à trois** /meɪˈnɑːʒɑˈtrwɑː/ [*count*] **:** an arrangement in which three people have sex with each other especially while living together

me·nag·er·ie /məˈnæʤəri/ *noun, pl* **-ies** [*count*] **:** a collection of animals kept especially to be shown to the public • a *menagerie* of rare creatures — sometimes used figuratively • The jail houses a *menagerie* of criminals.

¹mend /ˈmɛnd/ *verb* **mends; mend·ed; mend·ing**
1 [+ *obj*] **:** to make (something broken or damaged) usable again **:** to repair (something broken or damaged) • Dad's trying to *mend* [=*fix*] the roof. • The town needs to *mend* these roads. • Fishermen were *mending* their nets. • She spent the evening *mending* (the holes in) her socks. • *mending* a torn sleeve = *mending* a tear in a sleeve — often used figuratively • He's trying to *mend* his reputation. • We've *mended* our differences [=stopped arguing] and agreed on a plan.
2 : to heal or cure (a broken bone, a sad feeling, etc.) [+ *obj*] Surgery was needed to *mend* (the break in) the bone. • Only time can *mend* a broken heart. [=make someone stop being sad] [*no obj*] Her arm *mended* slowly after surgery. • His broken heart never completely *mended.*
mend fences *or* ***mend your fences*** **:** to improve or repair a relationship that has been damaged by an argument or disagreement • She *mended fences* with her father. • They are trying to *mend their fences.* • After the election, he spent a lot of time *mending* political *fences.*
mend your ways **:** to change or improve your behavior **:** to stop behaving badly • It's time (for you) to *mend your ways.* • She told her teenage son to start *mending his ways.*
– mend·er *noun, pl* **-ers** [*count*] • road *menders*

²mend *noun* [*singular*] **:** a place where something (such as a piece of clothing) has been repaired • You can hardly see the *mend* in the sleeve.
on the mend **:** becoming better after an illness or injury • Her broken leg is *on the mend.* • Her health is *on the mend.* **:** becoming better after a bad or poor period • The country's economy is *on the mend.* • They almost got a divorce, but now their marriage is *on the mend.*

men·da·cious /mɛnˈdeɪʃəs/ *adj* [*more* ~; *most* ~] *formal*
1 : not honest **:** likely to tell lies • a *mendacious* businessman
2 : based on lies • The newspaper story was *mendacious* and hurtful. • a *mendacious* political campaign
– men·da·cious·ly *adv* **– men·da·cious·ness** *noun* [*noncount*]

men·dac·i·ty /mɛnˈdæsəti/ *noun* [*noncount*] *formal* **:** lack of honesty **:** the condition of being mendacious • The people learned of their government's *mendacity* [=learned that their government had told lies] only after the war had ended.

men·di·cant /ˈmɛndɪkənt/ *noun, pl* **-cants** [*count*] *formal* **:** someone (such as a member of a religious group) who lives by asking people for money or food • wandering *mendicants*
– mendicant *adj* • *mendicant* friars • a *mendicant* monk

men·folk /ˈmɛnˌfoʊk/ *noun* [*plural*] *old-fashioned + humorous* **:** the men of a family, town, etc. • While the women pre-

M

pared dinner, the *menfolk* relaxed in the living room.

[1]**me·nial** /ˈmiːnijəl/ *adj* [*more* ~; *most* ~] — used to describe boring or unpleasant work that does not require special skill and usually does not pay much money ▪ a *menial* job ▪ She thought household chores were *menial* and unimportant. ▪ performing *menial* labor/tasks

[2]**menial** *noun, pl* **-nials** [*count*] *old-fashioned* : a person (such as a servant) who does boring or unpleasant work for little money : someone who does menial work ▪ low-paid *menials*

men·in·gi·tis /ˌmɛnənˈʤaɪtəs/ *noun* [*noncount*] *medical* : a serious and often deadly disease in which an outside layer of the brain or spinal cord becomes infected and swollen ▪ She was diagnosed with spinal *meningitis*.

Men·no·nite /ˈmɛnəˌnaɪt/ *noun, pl* **-nites** [*count*] : a person who belongs to a Christian religious group whose members live simply and wear plain clothing

men·o·pause /ˈmɛnəˌpɑːz/ *noun* [*noncount*] : the time in a woman's life when blood stops flowing from her body each month : the time when a woman stops menstruating ▪ (*US*) a woman going through *menopause* = (*Brit*) a woman going through ***the menopause*** ✧ Menopause usually occurs when a woman is near the age of 50.

– men·o·paus·al /ˌmɛnəˈpɑːzəl/ *adj* ▪ *menopausal* signs and symptoms ▪ *menopausal* women

me·no·rah /məˈnorə/ *noun, pl* **-rahs** [*count*] : an object that holds seven or nine candles and that is used in Jewish worship

menorah

men·ses /ˈmɛnˌsiːz/ *noun* [*plural*] *medical* : the flow of blood that comes from a woman's body each month

men's room *noun, pl* ~ **rooms** [*count*] *US* : a public bathroom for use by men and boys — called also (*Brit*) *gents*; compare LADIES' ROOM

men·stru·al /ˈmɛnstruwəl/ *adj* : of or relating to menstruation : of or relating to the flow of blood that comes from a woman's body each month ▪ *menstrual* pain ▪ *menstrual* blood ▪ the ***menstrual cycle*** [=the monthly series of changes that happen in the body of a woman who is menstruating]

menstrual period *noun, pl* ~ **-ods** [*count*] : the time when a woman menstruates each month ▪ She experiences pain during her *menstrual period*. — called also *period*

M

men·stru·ate /ˈmɛnstruˌeɪt/ *verb* **-ates; -at·ed; -at·ing** [*no obj*] *of a woman* : to have blood flow from your body as part of a process that happens each month ▪ She began *menstruating* at the age of 12.

– men·stru·a·tion /ˌmɛnstruˈeɪʃən/ *noun* [*noncount*]

mens·wear /ˈmɛnzˌweɚ/ *noun* [*noncount*] : clothes for men ▪ The store sells an extensive line of *menswear*. ▪ He works in the *menswear* department.

-ment /mənt/ *noun suffix*

1 : the action or process of doing something ▪ improve*ment* ▪ develop*ment*

2 : the product or result of an action ▪ entertain*ment*

3 : the state or condition caused by an action ▪ amaze*ment* ▪ fulfill*ment*

men·tal /ˈmɛntl̩/ *adj*

1 a : of or relating to the mind ▪ *mental* abilities ▪ She was worried about her son's *mental* and physical development. ▪ the *mental* state/condition of a criminal ▪ *mental* health **b** : existing or happening in the mind ▪ We had a *mental* image/picture of what we thought the house would look like. ▪ I've got a *mental* list of the things I need at the store. ▪ I'll make a *mental* note to see if we can reschedule the meeting. ▪ *mental* arithmetic [=arithmetic done in your mind without writing numbers or using a calculator]

2 *always used before a noun* **a** : relating to or affected by an illness of the mind ▪ She was beginning to show signs of *mental* illness. ▪ a *mental* disorder ▪ He suffered a *mental* breakdown. ▪ a *mental* patient **b** : caring for people with mental illnesses ▪ *mental* hospitals

3 *informal* : CRAZY ▪ She looked at me as if I had ***gone mental***. ▪ That guy is a complete ***mental case***. [=he is crazy]

– men·tal·ly *adv* ▪ *mentally* ill ▪ *mentally* competent ▪ *Mentally* I'm OK, but physically I'm a wreck!

mental age *noun, pl* ~ **ages** [*count*] *technical* : a measurement of a person's ability to think and understand that is expressed as the age at which an average person reaches the same level of ability ▪ a 40-year-old man with the *mental age* of 10

men·tal·i·ty /mɛnˈtæləti/ *noun, pl* **-ties** [*count*] : a particular way of thinking — usually singular ▪ You can only wonder about the *mentality* of someone who does such things. ▪ He criticizes filmmakers for their blockbuster *mentality*. [=for thinking only about making movies that could be blockbusters] ▪ a war *mentality* — see also BUNKER MENTALITY, SIEGE MENTALITY, VICTIM MENTALITY

menthe see CRÈME DE MENTHE

men·thol /ˈmɛnˌθɑːl/ *noun* [*noncount*] : an oil made from mint that has a strong smell and that is used in candies, cigarettes, and especially medicines for sore throats

– men·tho·lat·ed /ˈmɛnθəˌleɪtəd/ *adj* ▪ *mentholated* cigarettes [=cigarettes that contain menthol]

[1]**men·tion** /ˈmɛnʃən/ *verb* **-tions; -tioned; -tion·ing** [+ *obj*]

1 : to talk about, write about, or refer to (something or someone) especially in a brief way ▪ In her speech, she *mentioned* (the help of) her parents, husband, and fellow actors. ▪ She's never *mentioned* anything to me about her husband. ▪ I get nervous every time his name is *mentioned*. ▪ They *mentioned* him by name. ▪ I believe I *mentioned* the problem to you last week. ▪ Most history books don't even *mention* the event. ▪ As previously *mentioned*, his proposal has been widely criticized. ▪ He fails/neglects to *mention*, however, the seriousness of the crime. ▪ She *mentioned* that she would be out of the office the following day. ▪ She has helped me in ways ***too numerous to mention***. [=has helped me in very many ways] ▪ Her contributions were ***mentioned only in passing***. [=mentioned only in a way that was very brief] ▪ ***Now (that) you mention it***, I do remember seeing him before.

2 : to refer to or suggest (someone) *as* having a possible role or status ▪ He's being *mentioned as* a possible candidate. [=people are saying that he is a possible candidate]

don't mention it — used to answer someone who has just thanked you for something ▪ "Thank you so much for your help." "*Don't mention it.* It was the least I could do."

not to mention — used when referring to another thing that relates to what you have just said ▪ Our favorite Italian restaurant makes its own fresh bread and salad dressing, *not to mention* [=*in addition to*] a great spaghetti sauce. ▪ We were cold, wet, and hungry, *not to mention* [=*and also*] extremely tired.

[2]**mention** *noun, pl* **-tions** : a short statement about something or someone : an act of mentioning something or someone — usually singular [*count*] In her speech, she carefully avoided any *mention* of her costar. ▪ There was barely a *mention* of the plan's possible dangers. ▪ The mere *mention* of blood makes me ill. ▪ I get nervous at the *mention* of his name. ▪ Her contributions deserve a *mention*. [*noncount*] One other issue deserves special *mention*. ▪ Her contributions deserve some *mention*. = Her contributions are ***worthy of mention***. ▪ She ***made mention of*** [=she mentioned] their contributions. ▪ Most history books ***make no mention of*** the event. [=they say nothing about the event] — see also HONORABLE MENTION

[1]**men·tor** /ˈmɛnˌtoɚ/ *noun, pl* **-tors** [*count*] : someone who teaches or gives help and advice to a less experienced and often younger person ▪ After college, her professor became her close friend and *mentor*. ▪ He needed a *mentor* to teach him about the world of politics. ▪ We volunteer as *mentors* to/of disadvantaged children. ▪ young boys in need of *mentors*

[2]**mentor** *verb* **-tors; -tored; -tor·ing** [+ *obj*] : to teach or give advice or guidance to (someone, such as a less experienced person or a child) : to act as a mentor for (someone) ▪ The young intern was *mentored* by the country's top heart surgeon. ▪ Our program focuses on *mentoring* teenagers.

– mentoring *noun* [*noncount*] ▪ young boys in need of *mentoring*

menu /ˈmɛnˌjuː/ *noun, pl* **men·us** [*count*]

1 a : a list of the foods that may be ordered at a restaurant ▪ I'd like to see your lunch *menu*, please. ▪ What's good on the *menu* today? ▪ There are two chicken dishes under eight dollars listed on the *menu*. **b** : the foods that are served at a meal ▪ When you're planning a dinner party, the choice of (the/your) *menu* is very important.

2 : a list of things that you can choose from ▪ a *menu* of television programs; *especially, computers* : a list shown on a computer from which you make choices to control what the computer does ▪ You can save your work by choosing "Save" from the "File" *menu*. — see also DROP-DOWN MENU, PULL-DOWN MENU

[1]**me·ow** (*chiefly US*) *or Brit* **mi·aow** /miˈaʊ/ *noun, pl* **me·ows** [*count*] : the crying sound made by a cat

the cat's meow see CAT

²meow (*chiefly US*) *or Brit* **miaow** *verb* **meows; me·owed; me·ow·ing** [*no obj*] *of a cat* **: to make a crying sound** ▪ We could hear a cat *meowing* at the door.

mer·can·tile /ˈmɚkənˌtiːl, ˈmɚkənˌtajəl/ *adj, always used before a noun, formal* **: of or relating to the business of buying and selling products to earn money : of or relating to trade or merchants** ▪ *mercantile* policy ▪ a small *mercantile* [=*merchant*] town ▪ wealthy *mercantile* families

¹mer·ce·nary /ˈmɚsəˌneri, *Brit* ˈmɜːsənəri/ *noun, pl* **-nar·ies** [*count*] **: a soldier who is paid by a foreign country to fight in its army : a soldier who will fight for any group or country that hires him** ▪ an army of foreign *mercenaries*

²mercenary *adj*

1 *always used before a noun* **: hired to fight** ▪ *mercenary* armies ▪ a *mercenary* soldier

2 [*more ~; most ~*] *disapproving* **: caring only about making money** ▪ His motives in choosing a career were purely *mercenary*. ▪ a *mercenary* [=*greedy*] businesswoman

¹mer·chan·dise /ˈmɚtʃənˌdaɪz/ *noun* [*noncount*] *somewhat formal* **: goods that are bought and sold** ▪ We sell quality *merchandise*. ▪ The *merchandise* will arrive by truck at noon. ▪ He's developed his own brand of *merchandise*.

²merchandise *verb* **-dis·es; -dised; -dis·ing** [+ *obj*]

1 : to make the public aware of (a product being offered for sale) by using advertising and other methods ▪ *merchandising* women's shoes

2 : to present (someone) to the public like a product being offered for sale ▪ *merchandise* a movie star ▪ The political candidates are being *merchandised* to the public.

– mer·chan·dis·er *noun, pl* **-ers** [*count*] ▪ *Merchandisers* decorated their stores' windows for the holidays.

mer·chan·dis·ing /ˈmɚtʃənˌdaɪzɪŋ/ *noun* [*noncount*]

1 : the activity of trying to sell goods or services by advertising them or displaying them attractively ▪ She is the company's director of *merchandising*.

2 : the activity of selling products that are related to something (such as a television show, movie, or sports team) in order to make more money ▪ The film made a lot of money thanks to strong *merchandising*. ▪ Most of the movie's earnings came from *merchandising* and not ticket sales.

¹mer·chant /ˈmɚtʃənt/ *noun, pl* **-chants** [*count*]

1 *somewhat old-fashioned* **: someone who buys and sells goods especially in large amounts** ▪ a wine *merchant* [=*dealer*] ▪ *Merchants* traveled hundreds of miles to trade in the city. ▪ a family of wealthy *merchants*

2 *chiefly US or Scotland* **: the owner or manager of a store** ▪ The town's *merchants* closed their shops during the parade. ▪ Prizes were given by local *merchants*.

3 *informal* **: someone who is known for a particular quality, activity, etc.** ▪ He's a real ***speed merchant***. [=he runs very fast] ▪ ***doom merchants*** [=people who are always saying that bad things are going to happen]

²merchant *adj, always used before a noun* **: used for or involved in trading goods** ▪ *merchant* ships ▪ a society's *merchant* class ▪ a wealthy *merchant* family

mer·chant·able /ˈmɚtʃəntəbəl/ *adj, law* **: of good enough quality to be sold** ▪ *merchantable* wood

merchant bank *noun, pl* **~ banks** [*count*] *chiefly Brit* **: a bank for large companies that trade goods in other countries**

– merchant banker *noun, pl* **~ -ers** [*count*] **– merchant banking** *noun* [*noncount*]

merchant marine *noun* [*singular*] *chiefly US* **: all of a country's ships that are used for trading goods rather than for war;** *also* **: the people who work such ships** ▪ a member of the *merchant marine* — called also (*Brit*) *merchant navy*

merchant seaman *noun, pl* **~ -men** [*count*] **: a sailor who works on a ship involved in trading goods : a member of the merchant marine**

mer·ci·ful /ˈmɚsɪfəl/ *adj* [*more ~; most ~*]

1 : treating people with kindness and forgiveness : not cruel or harsh : having or showing mercy ▪ a *merciful* ruler ▪ a *merciful* god ▪ He became less *merciful* to his enemies. ▪ a *merciful* decision

2 : giving relief from suffering ▪ He died a quick and *merciful* death. ▪ The movie at last came to a *merciful* end. [=the movie was so bad that its ending was a relief]

mer·ci·ful·ly /ˈmɚsɪfəli/ *adv*

1 : in a kind or merciful way ▪ His crimes have been dealt with *mercifully*.

2 : in a good or lucky way ▪ He makes movies that are *mercifully* free of violence. [=it is good that his movies do not have much violence] ▪ The lecture was *mercifully* brief. [=I was glad that the lecture was so brief] ▪ *Mercifully*, the professor always makes our tests easy.

mer·ci·less /ˈmɚsɪləs/ *adj* [*more ~; most ~*] **: having or showing no mercy : very cruel or harsh** ▪ a *merciless* killer ▪ a *merciless* army ▪ the *merciless* killing of innocent people ▪ *merciless* honesty ▪ He has been *merciless* in his criticism of his opponent.

– mer·ci·less·ly *adv* ▪ *mercilessly* honest criticism ▪ the *mercilessly* hot sun

mer·cu·ri·al /mɚˈkjɚrijəl/ *adj* [*more ~; most ~*]

1 a : changing moods quickly and often — used to describe someone who often changes from being happy to being angry or upset in a quick and unexpected way ▪ a *mercurial* movie star ▪ She had a *mercurial* personality/disposition. ▪ *mercurial* behavior **b : changing often : very changeable** ▪ *mercurial* weather

2 : very lively and quick ▪ *mercurial* wit

mer·cu·ry /ˈmɚkjəri/ *noun*

1 [*noncount*] **a : a silver metal that is liquid at normal temperatures b : the mercury in a thermometer that shows the air's temperature** ▪ In the summer, the *mercury* can reach over 100 degrees Fahrenheit. ▪ By late afternoon, the *mercury* had dropped (to) below zero.

2 *Mercury* [*singular*] **: the planet that is closest to the sun**

mer·cy /ˈmɚsi/ *noun, pl* **-cies**

1 [*noncount*] **: kind or forgiving treatment of someone who could be treated harshly** ▪ He is a vicious criminal who deserves no *mercy*. ▪ She fell to her knees and asked/begged/pleaded for *mercy*. ▪ Have you no *mercy*? = Are you utterly without *mercy*? ▪ May God ***have mercy*** on us all. [=may God treat us all with kindness and forgiveness] ▪ He ***showed no mercy*** to his enemies. = He *showed* his enemies *no mercy*. [=he treated his enemies very harshly] ▪ The boss ***took mercy on*** us [=he treated us kindly] and let us go home early. ▪ a man ***of mercy*** [=a man who treats other people with kindness and forgiveness] ▪ The prisoner confessed his crimes and ***threw himself on the mercy of*** the court. [=the prisoner begged the court for mercy]

2 [*noncount*] **: kindness or help given to people who are in a very bad or desperate situation** ▪ an act of *mercy* ▪ They came on a ***mission/errand of mercy*** to provide food and medical care for starving children. ▪ a ***mercy mission***

3 [*count*] **: a good or lucky fact or situation** ▪ It's a *mercy* that the building was empty when the fire started. ▪ We should be ***grateful/thankful for small mercies***. [=even though bad things have happened to us, we should be grateful that our situation is not worse] ▪ Thank heaven *for small mercies*.

4 *old-fashioned + informal* **— used as an interjection to show surprise** ▪ *Mercy*! That wind is cold! ▪ I'm not hungry, but *mercy* [=*heavens, goodness*], that food sure does smell good! ▪ ***Mercy me***! That wind is cold.

at the mercy of *or* ***at someone's or something's mercy*** **: in a position or situation in which you can be harmed by (someone or something you cannot control)** ▪ With no way to control the ship, we were *at the mercy of* the sea. ▪ The people were *at the mercy of* the advancing army. = The army advanced, and the people were *at their mercy*. [=the people could do nothing to defend themselves from the army] ▪ Our plans were *at the mercy of* the weather.

to the mercy of *or* ***to the (tender) mercies of*** **: without any protection from (someone or something you cannot control)** ▪ He had to leave his boat *to the mercy of* the storm. ▪ As the army retreated, the people were left *to the mercies of* the advancing enemy.

mercy killing *noun, pl* **~ -ings : the killing of someone who is very sick or injured in order to prevent any further suffering** [*count*] Some called her death a *mercy killing*. [*noncount*] He is opposed to *mercy killing*. [=*euthanasia*]

mere /ˈmiɚ/ *adj, always used before a noun* **mer·est**

1 — used to say that something or someone is small, unimportant, etc. ▪ She was a *mere* child [=she was only a child] when her father died. ▪ His voice did not rise above a *mere* whisper. = His voice did not rise above the *merest* [=*slightest*] whisper. ▪ You can taste a *mere* hint of spice. = You can taste the *merest* hint of spice. ▪ The trip takes a *mere* two hours. [=the trip takes only two hours] ▪ You can own this car for a *mere* 20 dollars a week. ▪ These mysteries can't be solved by *mere* mortals like us.

2 — used to say that something small is important or has a big effect or influence ▪ The *mere* thought of going makes me nervous. ▪ The *mere* fact that he agreed to help us is a good sign. ▪ The *mere/merest* mention of his name makes her angry. ▪ He gets sick at the *merest* sight of blood.

mere·ly /ˈmiɚli/ *adv* : ONLY, JUST — used to say that someone or something is small, unimportant, etc. ▪ This is *merely* a minor delay. ▪ They were *merely* children when their father died. ▪ Was it *merely* a coincidence? ▪ It was *merely* a suggestion. — used to describe the only reason for something or the only effect of something ▪ She got the job *merely* because her father owns the company. [=the only reason she got the job was because her father owns the company] ▪ Your essay *merely* hints at the real problem. ▪ You shouldn't blame her. She was *merely* following orders. [=she was following orders and not doing anything more than that] ▪ I'm not criticizing you. I'm *merely* suggesting that we try a new approach.

not merely — used to say that one thing is true and that another thing is also true ▪ He was *not merely* a great baseball player, he was also a great person.

mer·e·tri·cious /ˌmerəˈtrɪʃəs/ *adj* [*more ~; most ~*] *formal + disapproving* : attractive in a cheap or false way ▪ *meretricious* beauty

merge /ˈmɚʤ/ *verb* **merg·es; merged; merg·ing**

1 a [+ *obj*] : to cause (two or more things, such as two companies) to come together and become one thing ▪ They planned to *merge* [=*combine, unite*] the two companies. ▪ Their music *merges* [=*blends, combines*] different styles from around the world. : to join or unite (one thing) *with* another ▪ To save the business, the owners decided to *merge* it *with* one of their competitors. **b** [*no obj*] : to become joined or united ▪ The two banks *merged* to form one large institution. ▪ Many small companies have been forced to *merge*. ▪ Three lanes of traffic all *merge* at this point. — often + *with* ▪ Many small companies have been forced to *merge with* other small companies. — often + *into* ▪ The two former rivals have *merged into* one large business. ▪ Three lanes of traffic *merge into* one.

2 [*no obj*] : to change into or become part of something else in a very gradual way ▪ Day slowly *merged* into night. ▪ Along the coast the mountains gradually *merge* with the shore. ▪ She *merged* into the crowd and disappeared.

merg·er /ˈmɚʤɚ/ *noun, pl* **-ers** [*count*] : the act or process of combining two or more businesses into one business ▪ The law firm announced its $50 million *merger* with one of its competitors. ▪ If the proposed *merger* of the two oil companies goes through, it would be bad for the economy.

me·rid·i·an /məˈrɪdijən/ *noun, pl* **-ans** [*count*] : any one of the lines that go from the North Pole to the South Pole on maps of the world — see also PRIME MERIDIAN

me·ringue /məˈræŋ/ *noun, pl* **-ringues** [*count, noncount*] : a light, sweet mixture of egg whites and sugar that is baked and used as a topping for pies and cakes ▪ a layer of *meringue* ▪ lemon *meringue* pie

[1]mer·it /ˈmerət/ *noun, pl* **-its**

1 [*count*] : a good quality or feature that deserves to be praised ▪ The great *merit* [=*advantage, strength*] of this plan is its simplicity. — usually plural ▪ The plan has many *merits*. ▪ It's difficult to judge the *merits* of her proposal. ▪ We were talking about the ***relative merits*** of running and walking as kinds of exercise. ▪ The five contestants will be judged ***on their own merits***. [=they will be judged by looking at their skills and their good and bad qualities] ▪ We should consider each idea *on its merits*. [=we should consider the good and bad things about each idea]

2 [*noncount*] *formal* : the quality of being good, important, or useful : value or worth ▪ His ideas have (some) *merit*. ▪ She saw *merit* in both of the arguments. ▪ Their idea is without *merit*. = Their idea has no *merit*. ▪ The study has no scientific *merit*. ▪ Hiring decisions are based entirely ***on merit***. [=people are hired because they have the skills to do the job well]

[2]merit *verb* **-its; -it·ed; -it·ing** [+ *obj*] : to deserve (something, such as attention or good treatment) by being important or good ▪ Both ideas *merit* further consideration. ▪ These issues *merit* special attention. ▪ His good work *merits* a raise. ▪ She did well enough to *merit* a second interview. ▪ The attention she received was not *merited*.

mer·i·to·ri·ous /ˌmerəˈtorijəs/ *adj* [*more ~; most ~*] *formal* : deserving honor or praise ▪ She was given an award for *meritorious* service. ▪ *meritorious* conduct ▪ a *meritorious* [=*praiseworthy*] achievement

mer·maid /ˈmɚˌmeɪd/ *noun, pl* **-maids** [*count*] : an imaginary sea creature that has a woman's head and body and a fish's tail instead of legs

mer·ri·ment /ˈmerɪmənt/ *noun* [*noncount*] : laughter and enjoyment ▪ a time of great joy and *merriment* ▪ Their house was always filled with *merriment*. ▪ My embarrassment was a cause/source of great *merriment* among my friends. [=my friends were very amused by my embarrassment]

mer·ry /ˈmeri/ *adj* **mer·ri·er; -est** *somewhat old-fashioned*

1 : very happy and cheerful : feeling or showing joy and happiness ▪ Let's eat, drink, and be *merry*! ▪ They sang a *merry* little song. ▪ a *merry* man ▪ *merry* laughter

2 : causing joy and happiness ▪ a very *merry* occasion

go on your merry way **1** *or* ***be on your merry way*** : to leave a place ▪ Soon I'll *be on my merry way*. [=soon I'll be leaving] **2** *often disapproving* : to continue doing what you have been doing ▪ She just *goes on her merry way*, loving men and then breaking their hearts.

lead (someone) a merry chase/dance see [1]LEAD

make merry *old-fashioned* : to have fun and enjoy yourself by eating, drinking, dancing, etc. ▪ They *made merry* throughout the night.

Merry Christmas — used to wish someone an enjoyable Christmas holiday ▪ *Merry Christmas* to you and your family. ▪ We wish you a *Merry Christmas* and a happy New Year!

the more the merrier — used to say that more people are welcome or invited to do something ▪ "Can I bring my friends to the party?" "Of course, *the more the merrier*!"

– mer·ri·ly /ˈmerəli/ *adv* ▪ laughing *merrily* **– mer·ri·ness** /ˈmerinəs/ *noun* [*noncount*] ▪ the *merriness* of the occasion

mer·ry–go–round /ˈmerigoʊˌraʊnd/ *noun, pl* **-rounds** [*count*]

1 : a large round platform that turns around in a circle and has seats and figures of animals (such as horses) on which children sit for a ride ▪ We rode the *merry-go-round* at the town fair. — called also (*US*) *carousel*, (*Brit*) *roundabout*

2 : a set or series of repeated activities that are quick, confusing, or difficult to leave ▪ a *merry-go-round* of parties ▪ She couldn't get off the legal *merry-go-round*.

merry-go-round

mer·ry·mak·ing /ˈmeriˌmeɪkɪŋ/ *noun* [*noncount*] : fun and enjoyment : joyful celebration that includes eating, drinking, singing, and dancing ▪ a night of *merrymaking*

– mer·ry·mak·er /ˈmeriˌmeɪkɚ/ *noun, pl* **-ers** [*count*] ▪ a crowd of *merrymakers*

me·sa /ˈmeɪsə/ *noun, pl* **-sas** [*count*] : a hill that has a flat top and steep sides and that is found in the southwestern U.S. — see color picture on page C7

mes·ca·line *also Brit* **mes·ca·lin** /ˈmeskələn/ *noun* [*noncount*] : a drug that comes from a cactus and that makes people see things that are not real

mes·clun /ˈmesklən/ *noun* [*noncount*] *US* : a mixture of young leaves from different plants (such as different types of lettuce) that is eaten as a salad

mesdames *plural of* MADAM 1, MADAME

mesdemoiselles *plural of* MADEMOISELLE

[1]mesh /ˈmeʃ/ *noun, pl* **mesh·es** : a material made from threads or wires with evenly spaced holes that allow air or water to pass through [*noncount*] We covered the blueberry bushes in nylon *mesh* to keep the birds from the fruit. ▪ wire *mesh* [*count*] a wire *mesh* — sometimes used figuratively ▪ She was caught in a *mesh* [=(more commonly) *web*] of her own lies.

[2]mesh *verb* **meshes; meshed; mesh·ing**

1 a [+ *obj*] : to cause (things) to fit together or work together successfully ▪ They *meshed* traditions from several cultures into one wedding ceremony. ▪ The book tries to *mesh* philosophy and/with humor. **b** [*no obj*] : to fit or work together successfully ▪ The two plans *mesh* well/nicely. — often + *with* ▪ The movie's score *meshes* well *with* its somber plot. ▪ He never *meshed with* the rest of the team.

2 [*no obj*] *of the parts of a machine* : to fit together and move together properly ▪ The gears weren't *meshing* properly.

mes·mer·ize *also Brit* **mes·mer·ise** /ˈmɛzməˌraɪz/ *verb* **-iz·es**; **-ized**; **-iz·ing** [+ *obj*] : to hold the attention of (someone) entirely : to interest or amaze (someone) so much that nothing else is seen or noticed — usually used as *(be) mesmerized* ▪ The crowd *was mesmerized* by the acrobats.
— **mesmerizing** *also Brit* **mesmerising** *adj* [*more* ~; *most* ~] ▪ a *mesmerizing* voice/performance/beat

mes·quite /məˈskiːt/ *noun, pl* **-quites** [*count*] : a tree or bush that grows in the southwestern U.S. and Mexico and that has a hard wood which is often used in grilling food because of the special flavor produced by its smoke; *also* [*noncount*] : the wood of the mesquite

¹mess /ˈmɛs/ *noun, pl* **mess·es**
1 a [*count*] : a very dirty or untidy state or condition — usually singular ▪ We found the papers in a *mess*. ▪ It took years to clean up the *mess* caused by the oil spill. ▪ She's the only cook in the family who never ***makes a mess*** of/in the kitchen. **b** [*singular*] : something or someone that looks very dirty or untidy ▪ The apartment was a *mess* when he left it. = He left the apartment a *mess*. ▪ He was a *mess* after gardening all day. ▪ My hair is a *mess*.
2 [*count*] **a** : a situation that is very complicated or difficult to deal with ▪ I don't know how the economy got to be (in) such a *mess*. ▪ Well, that's another fine *mess* you've gotten me into! ▪ How do we get ourselves into these *messes*? **b** : something that is not organized well or working correctly ▪ The school system is a *mess*. ▪ Things were a real *mess* for a while after she retired. ▪ My life is a complete *mess*.
3 [*singular*] *informal* **a** : someone who is very unhappy, confused, etc. ▪ She was a real *mess* for a while after her divorce. **b** *US* : someone who is showing a lot of emotion especially by crying ▪ He was a *mess* during his daughter's wedding ceremony.
4 [*count*] : the place where people in the military eat ▪ the officers' *mess* — called also *mess hall*
5 [*singular*] *US, informal* : a large amount of something — + *of* ▪ a *mess of* cash ▪ a *mess of* cabbage/greens/peas ▪ They're in a *mess of* trouble. [=a lot of trouble]
6 *informal* : solid waste from an animal [*count*] The puppy made a *mess* on the rug. [*noncount*] cleaning up dog *mess*
make a mess of : to ruin (something) or to make many mistakes in doing (something) ▪ The scandal *made a mess of* his political career. ▪ The weather *made a mess of* our plans. ▪ He *made a mess of* his speech.

²mess *verb* **messes**; **messed**; **mess·ing**
mess around *or Brit* ***mess about*** [*phrasal verb*] *informal* **1** : to spend time doing things that are not useful or serious : to waste time ▪ We just *messed around* [=*fooled around*] all afternoon. ▪ She spent the evening *messing around* on the computer. ▪ It's time we stopped *messing around* and got busy. **2** : to have sex with someone who is not your husband, wife, or regular partner ▪ His wife discovered that he was *messing around* [=*fooling around*] (on her). — often + *with* ▪ His wife discovered that he was *messing around with* his secretary. **3** ***mess (someone) around/about*** *Brit* : to cause problems or trouble for (someone) especially by making changes that are not expected ▪ I don't like being *messed about* this way! **4** ***mess around/about with (something)*** **a** : to use or do (something) in a way that is not very serious ▪ I'm not really a painter; I just like to *mess around with* paints. ▪ She spent the evening *messing around with* [=*fooling around with*] the computer. **b** : to handle or play with (something) in a careless or foolish way ▪ Stop *messing around* [=*fiddling around*] *with* the stereo.
mess up [*phrasal verb*] *informal* **1** : to make a mistake : to do something incorrectly ▪ About halfway into the recipe, I realized that I had *messed up*, and I had to start over. — often + *on* ▪ She's afraid she'll *mess up on* the test. ▪ I *messed up on* my first attempt. **2** ***mess (something) up*** *or* ***mess up (something)*** **a** : to make mistakes when you are doing or making (something) ▪ He *messed up* the speech. ▪ I *messed up* my first attempt and had to try again. **b** : to make (something) dirty or untidy : to make a mess of (something) ▪ Don't *mess up* my room. ▪ The wind *messed up* her hair. = Her hair got *messed up* in the wind. **c** : to damage or ruin (something) ▪ She's really *messed up* her life. ▪ His life has been *messed up* by his drug addiction. : to damage or change (something) so that it does not work properly ▪ I don't know what I did, but I somehow *messed up* the computer. ▪ My watch has been *messed up* [=has not worked properly] ever since I dropped it in the sink. ▪ The mountains *messed up* the cell phone signal. **3** ***mess (someone) up*** *or* ***mess up (someone)*** **a** *US* : to beat and injure (someone) ▪ He got *messed up* [=*roughed up, beaten up*] by a gang of bullies. ▪ They *messed* him *up* pretty badly. **b** : to make (someone) very upset and unhappy ▪ Breaking up with her boyfriend has really *messed* her *up*. ▪ She's been pretty *messed up* ever since she broke up with her boyfriend.
mess with [*phrasal verb*] *informal* **1** ***mess with (someone)*** : to cause trouble for (someone) : to deal with (someone) in a way that may cause anger or violence ▪ I wouldn't want to *mess with* him. ▪ You'd better not be *messing with* me. **2** ***mess with (something)*** **a** *chiefly US* : to deal with or be involved with (something that causes or that could cause trouble) ▪ The company doesn't want to *mess with* small distributors. ▪ He doesn't want to *mess with* cocaine anymore. **b** : to handle or play with (something) in a careless way : to mess around with (something) ▪ Don't *mess with* the camera. **3** ✧ In very informal English, something that ***messes with your mind/head*** causes you to feel confused. ▪ The movie *messes with your mind* and you don't find out what's going on until the end.

mes·sage /ˈmɛsɪʤ/ *noun, pl* **-sag·es**
1 [*count*] : a piece of information that is sent or given to someone ▪ an e-mail *message* ▪ deliver/send/receive a *message* ▪ Did you get my *message*? ▪ She has received *messages* of support/sympathy from hundreds of people. ▪ Were there any *messages* for me? = Did anyone ***leave a message*** for me? ▪ I *left a message* on her answering machine. ▪ He's not here right now. Can I ***take a message***? ▪ The computer displayed an ***error message***. [=a message indicating that an error has occurred] — see also TEXT MESSAGE
2 [*singular*] : an important idea that someone is trying to express in a book, movie, speech, etc. ▪ I liked the story but I didn't really agree with the book's *message*. ▪ He believed in the church's *message* of forgiveness. ▪ She hopes the speech will help her to get the party's *message* across. [=help her to tell people what the party believes or stands for]
get the message *informal* : to understand something that is not being said directly ▪ When they didn't return my phone calls, I finally *got the message*. [=I finally realized that they did not want to talk to me] ▪ He gave her an angry look, hoping she'd *get the message*.
mixed messages see MIXED
off message : saying things that do not agree with the official position of a political group or party ▪ A few Cabinet members seem *off message* on government policy.
on message : saying things that agree with the official position of a political group or party ▪ The President wants everyone to be/get back *on message* when giving interviews.

message board *noun, pl* ~ **boards** [*count*] : a public computer system on the Internet that allows people to read and leave messages for other users — called also *bulletin board*

mes·sag·ing /ˈmɛsɪʤɪŋ/ *noun* [*noncount*] : a system used for sending messages electronically ▪ an electronic *messaging* system/service ▪ wireless *messaging* — see also INSTANT MESSAGING

mes·sen·ger /ˈmɛsnʤɚ/ *noun, pl* **-gers** [*count*] : someone who delivers a message or does other small jobs that involve going somewhere ▪ Their company's *messenger* brought us the plans. = The company's plans were brought to us by *messenger*. ▪ They sent a *messenger* to pick up the package.
blame/shoot the messenger : to become angry at someone who has told you bad news

mess hall *noun, pl* ~ **halls** [*count*] : ¹MESS 4

mes·si·ah /məˈsajə/ *noun, pl* **-ahs**
1 ***the Messiah*** **a** *Judaism* : a king who will be sent by God to save the Jews **b** *Christianity* : Jesus Christ
2 [*count*] : a person who is expected to save people from a very bad situation ▪ They thought the new principal was the *messiah* the school had been hoping for. ▪ a political *messiah*

mes·si·an·ic /ˌmɛsiˈænɪk/ *adj*
1 : relating to or having the qualities of a messiah ▪ a *messianic* political leader
2 : supporting a social, political, or religious cause or set of beliefs with great enthusiasm and energy ▪ *messianic* zeal

Messrs. (*US*) *or Brit* **Messrs** /ˈmɛsɚz/ — used as a formal plural of *Mr.* ▪ *Messrs.* Lowry and Jones, Attorneys at Law

messy /ˈmɛsi/ *adj* **mess·i·er**; **-est**
1 : not clean or tidy ▪ a very *messy* room ▪ *messy* papers

M

2 : carelessly made or done **:** not careful or precise ▪ *messy* [=*sloppy*] thinking
3 : causing or involving a mess ▪ a *messy* pen ▪ Painting a room can be *messy* work. **:** likely to make something dirty or sticky ▪ Some kinds of glue are *messier* than others. ▪ *messy* hair gel ▪ a delicious but *messy* sandwich
4 : very unpleasant and complicated ▪ a *messy* divorce/scandal ▪ I heard all of the *messy* details of the lawsuit.
— **mess·i·ly** /ˈmɛsəli/ *adv* ▪ She splattered the paint *messily* [=*sloppily, carelessly*] on the wall. — **mess·i·ness** /ˈmɛsinəs/ *noun* [*noncount*]

met *past tense and past participle of* [1]MEET

meta- /mɛtə/ *prefix*
1 : change ▪ *meta*morphosis
2 : more than **:** beyond ▪ *meta*physics

me·tab·o·lism /məˈtæbəˌlɪzəm/ *noun, pl* **-lisms** *biology* **:** the chemical processes by which a plant or an animal uses food, water, etc., to grow and heal and to make energy [*count*] studying the *metabolisms* of various organisms ▪ Regular exercise can help to increase your *metabolism.* [=increase the rate at which your body turns food into energy] [*noncount*] protein *metabolism*
— **met·a·bol·ic** /ˌmɛtəˈbɑːlɪk/ *adj* ▪ *metabolic* rate ▪ a *metabolic* disorder — **met·a·bol·ic·al·ly** /ˌmɛtəˈbɑːlɪkli/ *adv*

me·tab·o·lize *also Brit* **me·tab·o·lise** /məˈtæbəˌlaɪz/ *verb* **-liz·es; -lized; -liz·ing** [+ *obj*] *biology* **:** to change (food) into a form that can be used by your body **:** to process and use (substances brought into your body) by metabolism ▪ *metabolizing* nutrients ▪ Food is *metabolized* by the body.

met·al /ˈmɛtl̩/ *noun, pl* **-als :** a substance (such as gold, tin, or copper) that usually has a shiny appearance, is a good conductor of electricity and heat, can be melted, and is usually capable of being shaped [*noncount*] scraps/strips/sheets/lumps/pieces of *metal* ▪ a mixture of various kinds of *metal* ▪ sculptors who work in *metal* and clay [*count*] a mixture of different *metals* ▪ Gold is a *metal.* — often used before another noun ▪ *metal* bowls ▪ a *metal* roof — see also HEAVY METAL, SHEET METAL, *precious metal* at PRECIOUS
put the pedal to the metal see [1]PEDAL

me·tal·lic /məˈtælɪk/ *adj*
1 [*more* ~; *most* ~] **:** resembling metal: such as **a :** shiny like metal ▪ a *metallic* blue color ▪ We chose a paint with a *metallic* luster. **b :** tasting like metal ▪ The medicine has a *metallic* taste.
2 : made of metal or containing metal ▪ *metallic* threads ▪ Silver is a *metallic* element.
3 [*more* ~; *most* ~] **:** having a harsh sound ▪ a *metallic* [=*grating*] voice ▪ the *metallic* screech of the car's brakes

met·al·lur·gy /ˈmɛtl̩ˌɚʤi, *Brit* məˈtæləʤi/ *noun* [*noncount*] **:** a science that deals with the nature and uses of metal ▪ studying *metallurgy*
— **met·al·lur·gi·cal** /ˌmɛtl̩ˈɚʤɪkəl/ *adj* ▪ *metallurgical* techniques — **met·al·lur·gist** /ˈmɛtl̩ˌɚʤɪst, *Brit* məˈtæləʤɪst/ *noun, pl* **-gists** [*count*] ▪ an expert *metallurgist*

met·al·work /ˈmɛtl̩ˌwɚk/ *noun* [*noncount*] **:** things that are made out of metal; *especially* **:** metal objects that are made in an artistic and skillful way ▪ fine *metalwork* ▪ a beautiful piece of *metalwork*

met·al·work·ing /ˈmɛtl̩ˌwɚkɪŋ/ *noun* [*noncount*] **:** the act or process of making things out of metal ▪ ancient *metalworking* techniques
— **met·al·work·er** /ˈmɛtl̩ˌwɚkɚ/ *noun, pl* **-ers** [*count*] ▪ a skillful *metalworker*

meta·mor·phose /ˌmɛtəˈmoɚˌfouz/ *verb* **-phos·es; -phosed; -phos·ing** [*no obj*] **:** to change in an important and obvious way into something that is very different **:** to undergo metamorphosis — usually + *into* ▪ This once-small company has *metamorphosed into* an industrial giant. ▪ She has *metamorphosed* from a shy schoolgirl *into* a self-confident young businesswoman. ▪ studying the process by which caterpillars *metamorphose into* butterflies

meta·mor·pho·sis /ˌmɛtəˈmoɚfəsəs/ *noun, pl* **-pho·ses** /-fəˌsiːz/
1 : a major change in the appearance or character of someone or something [*count*] We have watched her *metamorphosis* from a shy schoolgirl into a self-confident businesswoman. ▪ a company that has gone through a series of *metamorphoses* [*noncount*] The government has undergone political *metamorphosis* since his election.
2 *biology* **:** a major change in the form or structure of some animals or insects that happens as the animal or insect becomes an adult [*noncount*] the *metamorphosis* of tadpoles into frogs ▪ The class learned about how caterpillars undergo *metamorphosis* to become butterflies. [*count*] caterpillars undergoing *metamorphoses*

met·a·phor /ˈmɛtəˌfoɚ, *Brit* ˈmɛtəfə/ *noun, pl* **-phors**
1 : a word or phrase for one thing that is used to refer to another thing in order to show or suggest that they are similar [*count*] "He was drowning in paperwork" is a *metaphor* in which having to deal with a lot of paperwork is being compared to drowning in an ocean of water. ▪ Her poems include many imaginative *metaphors.* [*noncount*] a poet admired for her use of *metaphor* — compare SIMILE; see also MIXED METAPHOR
2 [*count*] **:** an object, activity, or idea that is used as a symbol of something else — often + ***for*** ▪ The author uses flight as a *metaphor for* freedom. ▪ The veil is a *metaphor for* [=*symbol of*] secrecy.
— **met·a·phor·i·cal** /ˌmɛtəˈforɪkəl/ *adj* ▪ a *metaphorical* description of children as plants growing in a garden ▪ In this class, we'll be taking a *metaphorical* journey through Russian literature of the 19th century. — **met·a·phor·i·cal·ly** /ˌmɛtəˈforɪkli/ *adv* ▪ speaking *metaphorically*

meta·phys·i·cal /ˌmɛtəˈfɪzɪkəl/ *adj*
1 : of, relating to, or based on metaphysics ▪ *metaphysical* philosophy ▪ *metaphysical* questions
2 : of or relating to things that are thought to exist but that cannot be seen ▪ a *metaphysical* world of spirits
— **meta·phys·i·cal·ly** /ˌmɛtəˈfɪzɪkli/ *adv*

meta·phys·ics /ˌmɛtəˈfɪzɪks/ *noun* [*noncount*] **:** the part of philosophy that is concerned with the basic causes and nature of things

mete /ˈmiːt/ *verb* **metes; met·ed; met·ing**
mete out [*phrasal verb*] ***mete (something) out or mete out (something)*** **:** to give (something) to the people who you decide should get it **:** to give out or distribute (something) ▪ We're trying to be fair in *meting out* rewards and punishments. — usually used to refer to something unpleasant (such as punishment) ▪ Huge fines were *meted out* as punishment. ▪ The king *meted out* justice as he saw fit.

me·te·or /ˈmiːtijɚ/ *noun, pl* **-ors** [*count*] **:** a piece of rock or metal that burns and glows brightly in the sky as it falls from outer space into the Earth's atmosphere ▪ a ***meteor shower*** [=a large number of meteors seen in a short time]

me·te·or·ic /ˌmiːtiˈorɪk/ *adj*
1 : very sudden or fast ▪ a *meteoric* rise to fame ▪ a *meteoric* ascent ▪ a *meteoric* fall
2 : marked by very quick success ▪ a *meteoric* career

me·te·or·ite /ˈmiːtijəˌraɪt/ *noun, pl* **-ites** [*count*] **:** a piece of rock or metal that has fallen to the ground from outer space **:** a meteor that reaches the surface of the Earth without burning up entirely

me·te·o·rol·o·gy /ˌmiːtijəˈrɑːləʤi/ *noun* [*noncount*] **:** a science that deals with the atmosphere and with weather
— **me·te·o·ro·log·i·cal** /ˌmiːtijərəˈlɑːʤɪkəl/ *adj* ▪ *meteorological* forecasts ▪ *meteorological* conditions — **me·te·o·rol·o·gist** /ˌmiːtiəˈrɑːləʤɪst/ *noun, pl* **-gists** [*count*] ▪ a storm forecast by *meteorologists*

[1]**me·ter** /ˈmiːtɚ/ *noun, pl* **-ters** [*count*]
1 : a device that measures and records the amount of something that has been used ▪ a gas *meter* ▪ a water *meter*
2 : PARKING METER ▪ He left the restaurant to ***feed the meter.*** [=to put more money in the parking meter]
— compare [2]METER, [3]METER

[2]**meter** (*US*) *or Brit* **me·tre** *noun, pl* **-ters** [*count*] **:** the basic metric unit of length equal to about 39.37 inches — compare [1]METER, [3]METER

[3]**meter** (*US*) *or Brit* **metre** *noun, pl* **-ters :** a way of arranging the sounds or beats in poetry **:** a particular rhythmic pattern in poetry [*count*] the poet's use of different *meters* [*noncount*] the poet's use of rhyme and *meter* — compare [1]METER, [2]METER

-meter *noun combining form* **:** device used to measure something ▪ baro*meter* ▪ thermo*meter*

meter maid *noun, pl* ~ **maids** [*count*] *chiefly US, somewhat old-fashioned* **:** a woman whose job is to find vehicles that are parked illegally

meth·a·done /ˈmɛθəˌdoun/ *noun* [*noncount*] **:** a drug that people take to help them stop taking heroin

meth·ane /ˈmɛˌθeɪn, *Brit* ˈmiːˌθeɪn/ *noun* [*noncount*] **:** a colorless gas that has no smell and that can be burned for fuel

meth·a·nol /ˈmɛθəˌnɑːl/ *noun* [*noncount*] *technical* **:** a poisonous alcohol that is used to keep liquids from freezing, as a fuel, etc. — called also *methyl alcohol*

M

me·thinks /mɪˈθɪŋks/ *verb* **me·thought** /mɪˈθɑːt/ *literary + humorous* : I think • It's going to rain, *methinks.* [=I think it's going to rain] • *Methought* [=I thought] I heard him calling.

meth·od /ˈmɛθəd/ *noun, pl* **-ods**

1 [*count*] : a way of doing something • He claims to have developed a new *method* for growing tomatoes. • Their teaching *method* tries to adapt lessons to each student. • We need to adopt more modern *methods* of doing things. — see also SCIENTIFIC METHOD

2 [*noncount*] *formal* : a careful or organized plan that controls the way something is done • The book lacks *method.* [=the book is not arranged in an orderly way]

(a) method in/to your madness ✧ If there is *method in your madness* or (*US*) *(a) method to your madness,* there are good reasons for your actions even though they may seem foolish or strange. • Though his staff is often confused by the way he runs the office, I've found that there's *method in his madness.*

me·thod·i·cal /məˈθɑːdɪkəl/ *adj* [*more ~; most ~*]

1 : done by using a careful and organized procedure • a *methodical* search • Their *methodical* review of the evidence exposed some problems with the study's findings.

2 : working in a very careful and organized way • She's a slow and *methodical* worker, and her drawings reflect the extra care she takes.

— **me·thod·i·cal·ly** /məˈθɑːdɪkli/ *adv* • They are *methodically* reviewing the evidence.

Meth·od·ist /ˈmɛθədɪst/ *adj* : of or relating to any one of several Christian churches that follow the teachings of John Wesley • He comes from a family of *Methodist* preachers. • a *Methodist* church

— **Meth·od·ism** /ˈmɛθəˌdɪzəm/ *noun* [*noncount*]

— **Methodist** *noun, pl* **-ists** [*count*]

meth·od·ol·o·gy /ˌmɛθəˈdɑːləʤi/ *noun, pl* **-gies** : a set of methods, rules, or ideas that are important in a science or art : a particular procedure or set of procedures [*count*] scientific theories and *methodologies* [*noncount*] He blamed the failure of their research on poor *methodology.*

methyl alcohol /ˈmɛθəl-/ *noun* [*noncount*] *technical* : METHANOL

me·tic·u·lous /məˈtɪkjələs/ *adj* [*more ~; most ~*] : very careful about doing something in an extremely accurate and exact way • He described the scene in *meticulous* detail. • She did *meticulous* work. • He keeps *meticulous* records. • He is *meticulous* about keeping accurate records. • She's a *meticulous* researcher.

— **me·tic·u·lous·ly** *adv* • It's a beautiful Victorian house, *meticulously* restored. • *meticulously* careful research

— **me·tic·u·lous·ness** /məˈtɪkjələsnəs/ *noun* [*noncount*]

mé·tier *also* **me·tier** /ˈmɛˌtjeɪ/ *noun, pl* **-tiers** [*count*] *formal* : something that a person does very well • After trying several careers, she found her true *métier* in computer science. • Public speaking is not my *métier.* [=*forte, strength*]

metre *Brit spelling of* [2]METER, [3]METER

met·ric /ˈmɛtrɪk/ *adj*

1 : of, relating to, or based on the metric system • The *metric* unit of energy is the "joule." • a *metric* wrench [=a wrench that is sized according to the metric system]

2 : METRICAL • *metric* patterns

met·ri·cal /ˈmɛtrɪkəl/ *adj* : of, relating to, or arranged in a rhythmic pattern of beats : of or relating poetic meter • *metrical* patterns

— **met·ri·cal·ly** /ˈmɛtrɪkli/ *adv*

metric system *noun*

the metric system : a system of weights and measures that is based on the meter and on the kilogram

metric ton *noun, pl* **~ tons** [*count*] : a unit of mass and weight equal to one million grams

[1]**met·ro** /ˈmɛtroʊ/ *noun, pl* **-ros** [*count*] : an underground railway system in some cities : SUBWAY • the Paris *Metro* • We took the *metro* to the museum. = We went by *metro* to the museum.

[2]**metro** *adj, always used before a noun, US, informal* : of or relating to a large city and sometimes to the area around it • The event was attended by people from all over the *metro* [=*metropolitan*] area.

met·ro·nome /ˈmɛtrəˌnoʊm/ *noun, pl* **-nomes** [*count*] : a device that makes a regular, repeated sound to show a musician how fast a piece of music should be played

— **met·ro·nom·ic** /ˌmɛtrəˈnɑːmɪk/ *adj*

me·trop·o·lis /məˈtrɑːpələs/ *noun, pl* **-lis·es** [*count*] : a very large or important city — usually singular • a bustling *metropolis*

met·ro·pol·i·tan /ˌmɛtrəˈpɑːlətən/ *adj* : of or relating to a large city and the surrounding cities and towns • the greater New York *metropolitan* area • This is one of the best seafood restaurants in *metropolitan* Los Angeles. • a *metropolitan* newspaper

met·tle /ˈmɛtl/ *noun* [*noncount*] : strength of spirit : ability to continue despite difficulties • He ***proved/showed his mettle*** [=he proved/showed how tough he is] as a fighter tonight. • The competition will ***test her mettle.***

on your mettle *chiefly Brit* : making an effort to do as well as possible • She'll have to be *on her mettle* [=at her best] to win this competition.

mew /ˈmjuː/ *noun, pl* **mews** [*count*] : MEOW • a cat's *mew*

— **mew** /ˈmjuː/ *verb* **mews; mewed; mew·ing** [*no obj*] • a *mewing* cat

mews /ˈmjuːz/ *noun, pl* **mews** [*count*] *chiefly Brit* : a street or area with buildings that were once horse stables but that have been made into houses • a house in an elegant *mews* • a ***mews house***

Mex·i·can /ˈmɛksɪkən/ *noun, pl* **-cans** [*count*]

1 : a person born, raised, or living in Mexico

2 : a person whose family is from Mexico

— **Mexican** *adj* • *Mexican* food/music • *Mexican* Spanish [=the Spanish spoken in Mexico]

Mexican jumping bean *noun, pl* **~ beans** [*count*] : JUMPING BEAN

Mexican wave *noun*

the Mexican wave *Brit* : [2]WAVE 7

mez·za·nine /ˈmɛzəˌniːn/ *noun, pl* **-nines** [*count*]

1 : a small floor that is between two main levels of a building and that is usually in the form of a balcony

2 *US* : the lowest balcony in a theater

mez·zo /ˈmɛtsoʊ/ *noun, pl* **-zos** [*count*] *music* : MEZZO-SOPRANO

mez·zo–so·pra·no /ˌmɛtsousəˈprænoʊ, ˌmɛtsousəˈprɑːnoʊ/ *noun, pl* **-nos** [*count*] *music* : a female singing voice that is higher than the contralto and lower than the soprano • a singer with a beautiful *mezzo-soprano*; *also* : a female singer with such a voice

MFA *abbr* master of fine arts

mfg. *abbr* manufacturing

mg *abbr* milligram

mgmt. *abbr* management

mgr. *abbr* manager

MHz *abbr* megahertz

mi *or chiefly Brit* **me** /ˈmiː/ *noun* [*noncount*] *music* : the third note of a musical scale • do, re, *mi,* fa, sol, la, ti

mi. *abbr* mile

MI *abbr* Michigan

MIA /ˌɛmˌaɪˈeɪ/ *noun, pl* **MIAs** [*count*] *chiefly US* : a soldier who was not found after a battle and who may or may not be dead : a soldier who is missing in action • The fate of most *MIAs* in the war is still not known.

miaow *Brit spelling of* MEOW

mi·as·ma /maɪˈæzmə/ *noun, pl* **-mas** [*count*] *formal + literary* : a heavy cloud of something unpleasant or unhealthy — usually singular • A *miasma* of smog settled over the city. • a *miasma* of smoke • a *miasma* of foul odors

mic /ˈmaɪk/ *noun, pl* **mics** [*count*] *US, informal* : MICROPHONE

mi·ca /ˈmaɪkə/ *noun* [*noncount*] : a mineral that separates easily into thin sheets

mice *plural of* MOUSE

mick·ey /ˈmɪki/ *noun, pl* **-eys** [*count*] *informal + old-fashioned* : a drink of alcohol to which a drug has been added to cause the person who drinks it to become unconscious • Someone tried to slip him a *mickey.* [=tried to knock him out by giving him a drugged drink]

take the mickey (out of someone) *Brit, informal* : to make fun of someone • Did you mean what you said about me or were you just *taking the mickey*? [=*kidding*] • We *took the mickey out of* her [=we teased her] about her new hairstyle.

Mickey Mouse *adj, informal + disapproving* : not deserving to be taken seriously : having little value or importance • He took a lot of *Mickey Mouse* [=very easy] courses when he was in college. • The company is just a *Mickey Mouse* operation.

micro- *combining form*

1 a : very small • *micro*film • *micro*computer **b** : making a sound louder or an image larger • *micro*phone • *micro*scope

2 : one millionth part of a (specified) unit ▪ *micro*second ▪ *micro*meter

mi·crobe /ˈmaɪˌkroʊb/ *noun, pl* **-crobes** [*count*] : an extremely small living thing that can only be seen with a microscope : MICROORGANISM ▪ a disease-causing *microbe*
– **mi·cro·bi·al** /maɪˈkroʊbijəl/ *adj* ▪ *microbial* life/growth/contamination

mi·cro·bi·ol·o·gy /ˌmaɪkroʊbaɪˈɑːləʤi/ *noun* [*noncount*] : a science that studies extremely small forms of life (such as bacteria and viruses) ▪ a degree in *microbiology*
– **mi·cro·bi·o·log·i·cal** /ˌmaɪkroʊˌbajəˈlɑːʤɪkəl/ *adj* ▪ *microbiological* contamination – **mi·cro·bi·ol·o·gist** /ˌmaɪkroʊbaɪˈɑːləʤɪst/ *noun, pl* **-gists** [*count*]

mi·cro·brew /ˈmaɪkroʊˌbruː/ *noun, pl* **-brews** [*count*] *chiefly US* : a beer made by a microbrewery ▪ The restaurant serves several locally produced *microbrews*.

mi·cro·brew·ery /ˌmaɪkroʊˈbruːwəri/ *noun, pl* **-er·ies** [*count*] *chiefly US* : a small brewery that makes beer in small amounts

mi·cro·chip /ˈmaɪkroʊˌʧɪp/ *noun, pl* **-chips** [*count*] *computers* : a group of tiny electronic circuits that work together on a very small piece of hard material (such as silicon) — called also *integrated circuit*

mi·cro·com·put·er /ˈmaɪkroʊkəmˌpjuːtɚ/ *noun, pl* **-ers** [*count*] : a small computer; *especially* : PERSONAL COMPUTER

mi·cro·cosm /ˈmaɪkrəˌkɑːzəm/ *noun, pl* **-cosms** [*count*] : something (such as a place or an event) that is seen as a small version of something much larger ▪ The village is a *microcosm* of the whole country. ▪ The game was a *microcosm* of the entire season. — compare MACROCOSM
in microcosm : in a greatly reduced size or form ▪ The model is designed to represent the town *in microcosm*.

mi·cro·eco·nom·ics /ˌmaɪkroʊˌɛkəˈnɑːmɪks, ˌmaɪkroʊˌiːkəˈnɑːmɪks/ *noun* [*noncount*] : the study of the economic decisions and actions of individual people, companies, etc. — compare MACROECONOMICS
– **microeconomic** *adj*

mi·cro·elec·tron·ics /ˌmaɪkrowɪˌlɛkˈtrɑːnɪks/ *noun, technical*
1 [*noncount*] : the design, production, or use of very small electronic devices and circuits ▪ a job in *microelectronics*
2 [*plural*] : very small electronic devices or circuits ▪ the manufacturing of *microelectronics*
– **mi·cro·elec·tron·ic** /ˌmaɪkrowɪˌlɛkˈtrɑːnɪk/ *adj* ▪ *microelectronic* chips/devices/technology

mi·cro·fiche /ˈmaɪkroʊˌfiːʃ/ *noun, pl* **-fiches** : a sheet of film that has very small photographs of the pages of a newspaper, magazine, etc., which are viewed by using a special machine : a sheet of microfilm [*noncount*] Every issue of the magazine is available on *microfiche*. [*count*] He looked at *microfiches* of old magazines.

mi·cro·film /ˈmaɪkrəˌfɪlm/ *noun, pl* **-films** : film on which very small photographs of the printed pages of a newspaper, magazine, etc., are stored [*noncount*] newspapers available on *microfilm* [*count*] studying newspaper *microfilms* from the early 1900s

mi·cro·man·age /ˌmaɪkroʊˈmænɪʤ/ *verb* **-ag·es; -aged; -ag·ing** [+ *obj*] *chiefly US* : to try to control or manage all the small parts of (something, such as an activity) in a way that is usually not wanted or that causes problems ▪ He *micromanaged* every detail of the budget.
– **mi·cro·man·age·ment** /ˌmaɪkroʊˈmænɪʤmənt/ *noun* [*noncount*] – **mi·cro·man·ag·er** /ˌmaɪkroʊˈmænɪʤɚ/ *noun, pl* **-ers** [*count*]

[1]**mi·crom·e·ter** /maɪˈkrɑːmətɚ/ *noun, pl* **-ters** [*count*] : a device used for measuring very small distances — compare [2]MICROMETER

[2]**mi·cro·me·ter** (*US*) *or Brit* **mi·cro·me·tre** /ˈmaɪkroʊˌmiːtɚ/ *noun, pl* **-ters** [*count*] : one millionth of a meter — compare [1]MICROMETER

mi·cron /ˈmaɪˌkrɑːn/ *noun, pl* **-crons** [*count*] : [2]MICROMETER

mi·cro·or·gan·ism /ˌmaɪkroʊˈoɚgəˌnɪzəm/ *noun, pl* **-isms** [*count*] *biology* : an extremely small living thing that can only be seen with a microscope

mi·cro·phone /ˈmaɪkrəˌfoʊn/ *noun, pl* **-phones** [*count*] : a device into which people speak or sing in order to record their voices or to make them sound louder — called also (*informal*) *mike*

mi·cro·pro·ces·sor /ˌmaɪkroʊˈprɑːˌsɛsɚ, *Brit* ˌmaɪkrəʊˈprəʊˌsesə/ *noun, pl* **-sors** [*count*] *computers* : the device in a computer that manages information and controls what the computer does

mi·cro·scope /ˈmaɪkrəˌskoʊp/ *noun, pl* **-scopes** [*count*] : a device used for producing a much larger view of very small objects so that they can be seen clearly ▪ Students viewed the crystals through/under/with a *microscope*. — see also ELECTRON MICROSCOPE
under a/the microscope : in a state of being watched very closely ▪ Celebrities can find it difficult (to be) living *under the microscope*. ▪ The business has recently been ***put under the microscope*** by federal investigators.

mi·cro·scop·ic /ˌmaɪkrəˈskɑːpɪk/ *adj*
1 a : able to be seen only through a microscope : extremely small ▪ At this point, the embryo is a *microscopic* clump of only 100 cells. ▪ There is a *microscopic* crack in the diamond. **b** : much smaller than what is usual, normal, or expected ▪ He has a *microscopic* attention span. ▪ He recorded every aspect of his trip in *microscopic* detail.
2 *always used before a noun* : done with a microscope ▪ a *microscopic* examination/analysis ▪ a *microscopic* study of plant tissues
– **mi·cro·scop·i·cal·ly** /ˌmaɪkrəˈskɑːpɪkli/ *adv* ▪ examined/studied the tissue *microscopically* ▪ a *microscopically* thin fiber

mi·cro·sec·ond /ˈmaɪkroʊˌsɛkənd/ *noun, pl* **-onds** [*count*]
1 : one millionth of a second
2 *informal* : a very short period of time ▪ She raised her hand a *microsecond* [=*second*] too late.

[1]**mi·cro·wave** /ˈmaɪkroʊˌweɪv/ *noun, pl* **-waves** [*count*]
1 : MICROWAVE OVEN ▪ The apartment came with a *microwave*. — often used before another noun ▪ *microwave* cooking [=cooking using a microwave oven] ▪ *microwave* [=*microwavable*] popcorn ▪ a *microwave* dinner
2 *physics* : a very short wave of electromagnetic energy ▪ antennas for detecting *microwaves* ▪ *microwave* radiation

[2]**microwave** *verb* **-waves; -waved; -wav·ing** [+ *obj*] : to cook or heat (food) in a microwave oven ▪ *microwave* a bowl of soup
– **mi·cro·wav·able** *or* **mi·cro·wave·able** /ˌmaɪkrəˈweɪvəbəl/ *adj* ▪ a *microwavable* pizza ▪ He heated up his soup in a *microwavable* bowl. [=a bowl that can be safely used in a microwave oven]

microwave oven *noun, pl* **~ ovens** [*count*] : an oven in which food is cooked or heated quickly by very short waves of electromagnetic energy — called also *microwave*; see picture at KITCHEN

mid /ˈmɪd/ *adj, always used before a noun* : in or near the middle of something ▪ He's in his *mid* [=*middle*] twenties. ▪ the *mid* to late 1700s — often used in combination ▪ the *mid*-18th century ▪ He's in his *mid*-twenties. ▪ We'll be there in *mid*-August. ▪ He cut me off in *mid*-sentence. ▪ The ship was adrift in *mid*-ocean.

mid·af·ter·noon /ˌmɪdˌæftɚˈnuːn, *Brit* ˌmɪdˌɑːftəˈnuːn/ *noun* [*noncount*] : the middle part of the afternoon ▪ We hope to make it home by *midafternoon*. — often used before another noun ▪ a *midafternoon* snack

mid·air /ˈmɪdˈeɚ/ *noun* [*noncount*] : a region in the air not close to the ground ▪ The two planes collided in *midair*. ▪ We watched birds catching insects in *midair*. — often used before another noun ▪ a *midair* collision

Mi·das touch /ˈmaɪdəs-/ *noun*
the Midas touch : the ability to make everything that you are involved with very successful ▪ an actor/businesswoman with *the Midas touch*

mid–Atlantic *also* **Mid–Atlantic** *adj, always used before a noun*
1 : of or relating to the region of the U.S. that includes all or some of the states between New York and South Carolina ▪ *mid-Atlantic* states/cities/beaches
2 : located in the middle of the Atlantic Ocean ▪ *mid-Atlantic* islands

mid·day /ˈmɪdˌdeɪ/ *noun* [*noncount*] : the middle of the day : NOON ▪ They arrived around *midday*. — often used before another noun ▪ the *midday* sun ▪ the ***midday meal*** [=*lunch*]

[1]**mid·dle** /ˈmɪdl/ *adj, always used before a noun*
1 : equally distant from the ends or sides : halfway between two points ▪ He walked down the *middle* [=*center*] aisle. ▪ during the century's *middle* decades ▪ High temperatures today should be in the *middle* 80s.
2 : in a state or place between two things or people ▪ He grew

up as the *middle* child in a family with three children. [=he was the child born before the youngest and after the oldest] • Franklin D. Roosevelt's *middle* initial stood for "Delano."

²middle *noun, pl* **mid·dles** *[count]*

1 : a middle part, point, or position • He parts his hair in the *middle*. [=*center*] • A good essay will have a clear beginning, *middle*, and end. • He stood exactly in the *middle* of the room. • She opened the book to the *middle* and began to read. • The car stopped in the *middle* of the road. • The house should be finished by the *middle* of next summer. • The beginning and ending of the movie were good, but the *middle* was pretty boring. • Slice the banana right ***down the middle***. [=slice it into two equal parts] • We split the cost *down the middle*. [=we split the cost equally]

2 : the middle part of a person's body : WAIST • She put her arms around his *middle*. • He tied the sash around his *middle*.

in the middle : in a difficult or unpleasant position • She hated conflict and did not want to be put *in the middle*. • He was ***caught in the middle*** of his parents' divorce. = He was *caught in the middle* when his parents got divorced.

in the middle of **1** : while (something) is happening or being done : during (something) • The protesters interrupted her *in the middle of* her speech. • He kept waking up *in the middle of* the night. • The movie was so bad we walked out right *in the middle of* it. **2** : in the process of (doing something) • I was *in the middle of* (eating) dinner [=I was eating dinner] when the phone rang.

in the middle of nowhere : in a place that is far away from other people, houses, or cities • We got lost *in the middle of nowhere*.

middle age *noun [noncount]* : the period in a person's life from about age 40 to about age 60 • as our generation approaches *middle age* • The patient was in late *middle age*. • He feared the approach of *middle age*.

– **mid·dle–aged** /ˌmɪdl̩ˈeɪʤd/ *adj* • health problems common in *middle-aged* men and women • a book loved by the young, the old, and ***the middle-aged*** [=*middle-aged people*]

Middle Ages *noun*

the Middle Ages : the period of European history from about A.D. 500 to about 1500

Middle America *noun [noncount]* : the usually traditional or conservative people of the middle class in the U.S. • a politician who understands the needs of *Middle America*

– **Middle American** *noun, pl* ~ **-cans** *[count]* – **middle–American** *also* **Middle–American** *adj* • a typical *middle-American* home • *Middle-American* values

Middle Atlantic *adj, usually used before a noun* : MID-ATLANTIC 1 • the *Middle Atlantic* region

– **Middle Atlantic** *noun [noncount]* • moderate winters in the *Middle Atlantic*

mid·dle·brow /ˈmɪdl̩ˌbraʊ/ *adj [more ~; most ~]* : interested in art, literature, etc., that is not very serious and that is easy to understand • This book appeals to *middlebrow* readers. : relating to or intended for people who are interested in art, literature, etc., that is not very serious and that is easy to understand • people with *middlebrow* tastes • a *middlebrow* magazine/movie — compare HIGHBROW, LOWBROW

middle C *noun, pl* ~ **Cs** *[count, noncount] music* : the musical note C that is close to the center of a piano's keyboard • the note above *middle* C

middle class *noun, pl* ~ **classes** *[count]* : the social class that is between the upper class and the lower class and that includes mainly business and professional people, government officials, and skilled workers — compare LOWER CLASS, UPPER CLASS

– **middle–class** *adj [more ~; most ~]* • traditional *middle-class* values • a typical *middle-class* family

middle distance *noun, pl* ~ **-tances**

1 ***the middle distance*** : the area in a scene or view that is neither very close nor very far away : an area between the foreground and the background • As I looked out over the water, a small boat appeared in *the middle distance*.

2 *[count]* : a racing distance that is neither short nor long and that is usually between 800 to 1,500 meters — often used as *middle-distance* before another noun • a *middle-distance* runner/race/event

middle ear *noun [singular]* : the middle part of the ear that is inside the eardrum • fluid in the *middle ear* • a *middle ear* infection

Middle East *noun*

the Middle East : the countries of northern Africa and southwestern Asia that are on or near the eastern edge of the Mediterranean Sea : the Near East — compare FAR EAST

– **Middle Eastern** *adj* • *Middle Eastern* culture/food – **Middle Easterner** *noun, pl* ~ **-ers** *[count]*

Middle English *noun [noncount]* : the English language between about 1100 and 1400 — compare OLD ENGLISH

middle finger *noun, pl* ~ **-gers** *[count]* : the long finger that is the middle one of the five fingers of the hand — see picture at HAND

middle ground *noun* : a position or set of opinions that is acceptable to many different people *[singular]* The judge of the case chose a *middle ground* between harshness and leniency. *[noncount]* Both sides in this debate need to do more to establish some *middle ground*.

mid·dle·man /ˈmɪdl̩ˌmæn/ *noun, pl* **-men** /-ˌmɛn/ *[count]*

1 : a person or company that buys goods from a producer and sells them to someone else • The Internet helps consumers save money by buying products directly from companies and eliminating/bypassing the *middleman*. • We've ***cut out the middleman*** and can reduce prices for our customers.

2 : a person who helps two people or groups to deal with and communicate with each other when they are not able or willing to do it themselves • He acted as the *middleman* in the talks between labor and management.

middle management *noun [noncount]* : the group of people in a company who are in charge of employees but are not involved in important decisions concerning the company • He was just promoted to *middle management*.

middle manager *noun, pl* ~ **-ers** *[count]* : a person who works in middle management

middle name *noun, pl* ~ **names**

1 *[count]* : a name between a person's first name and family name • President John F. Kennedy's *middle name* was "Fitzgerald."

2 *[singular] informal* : a word that accurately describes a person's qualities • Patience is her *middle name*. [=she is a very patient person]

middle–of–the–road *adj [more ~; most ~]* : supporting or following a course of action that is not extreme and that is acceptable to many different people • He took a *middle-of-the-road* approach to the problem. • *middle-of-the-road* [=*moderate*] voters/politicians

middle school *noun, pl* ~ **schools** *[count, noncount]*

1 *US* : a school for children that usually includes grades five to eight or six to eight — compare ELEMENTARY SCHOOL, HIGH SCHOOL, JUNIOR HIGH SCHOOL

2 *Brit* : a school for children between the ages of 8 and 12 or 9 and 13

mid·dle–sized /ˈmɪdl̩ˌsaɪzd/ *adj* : neither large nor small • a *middle-sized* [=*medium-sized*] business

mid·dle·weight /ˈmɪdl̩ˌweɪt/ *noun, pl* **-weights** *[count]* *sports* : a fighter who is in a class of boxers with an upper weight limit of 160 pounds (72 kilograms) : a boxer who is heavier than a lightweight and lighter than a heavyweight — often used before another noun • a *middleweight* boxer/champion • fighting for the *middleweight* title/crown

Middle West *noun*

the Middle West : the northern central part of the U.S. : the Midwest • the rich farmlands of *the Middle West*

– **Middle–Western** *adj* • *Middle-Western* states/cities/farms – **Middle–Western·er** *noun, pl* **-ers** *[count]*

mid·dling /ˈmɪdlɪŋ/ *adj* : of average size or quality • a *middling* profit • a *middling* performance • The food was ***fair to middling***. [=just average; not especially good]

Mid·east /ˌmɪdˈiːst/ *noun*

the Mideast *US* : the Middle East • a trip to *the Mideast*

– **Mid·east·ern** /ˌmɪdˈiːstən/ *adj*

mid·field /ˈmɪdˌfiːld/ *noun, pl* **-fields**

1 *[noncount]* : the area of a playing field in sports like American football and soccer that is in the middle between the two goals • The team captains shook hands at *midfield*. • The ball went out of bounds near *midfield*.

2 *[count]* : the players on a soccer team who normally play in the midfield • They have a talented *midfield* this year.

– **mid·field·er** /ˈmɪdˌfiːldə/ *noun, pl* **-ers** *[count]* • a talented *midfielder* [=a talented player who plays in the midfield]

midge /ˈmɪʤ/ *noun, pl* **midg·es** *[count]* : a very small flying insect that bites people and animals

¹midg·et /ˈmɪʤət/ *noun, pl* **-ets** *[count]* *often offensive* : a very small person

²midget *adj, always used before a noun* : very small : much

M

smaller than usual or normal ▪ a *midget* race car ▪ a *midget* submarine for two people

mid·land /ˈmɪdlənd/ *noun, pl* **-lands** [*count*] **:** the central region of a country — usually plural ▪ I left the *midlands* for the coast. ▪ Birmingham is the major city in ***the Midlands*** (of England).

mid·life /ˈmɪdˈlaɪf/ *noun* [*noncount*] **:** MIDDLE AGE ▪ changes that occur at *midlife*

midlife crisis *noun, pl* **~ crises** [*count*] **:** a time in middle age when a person feels a strong desire for change ▪ We knew he was going through a *midlife crisis* when he bought a new sports car.

mid·morn·ing /ˈmɪdˈmoənɪŋ/ *noun* [*noncount*] **:** the middle of the morning **:** the time around 10 a.m. ▪ I'm usually hungry by *midmorning*. — often used before another noun ▪ a *midmorning* snack

mid·night /ˈmɪdˌnaɪt/ *noun* [*noncount*] **:** the middle of the night **:** 12 o'clock at night ▪ Her parents wanted her home before *midnight*. ▪ The clock struck *midnight*. ▪ It was ***12 midnight*** when we arrived home. — often used before another noun ▪ a *midnight* snack ▪ at ***the midnight hour*** [=at midnight]
burn the midnight oil see [1]BURN

mid·point /ˈmɪdˌpoɪnt/ *noun, pl* **-points** [*count*] **:** a point at the middle of something ▪ The crowd begins to leave after the *midpoint* of the final period. ▪ The team is in last place at the *midpoint* of the season. **:** a point halfway between two ends ▪ the *midpoint* between her knee and ankle ▪ The train stopped to refuel at the *midpoint* between New York and Chicago. ▪ the *midpoint* of one side of the rectangle

mid·riff /ˈmɪˌdrɪf/ *noun, pl* **-riffs** [*count*] **:** the area around a person's middle **:** the front of a person's body between the chest and the waist ▪ She wore a skimpy outfit that showed her bare *midriff*.

mid·sea·son /ˈmɪdˈsiːzn̩/ *noun, pl* **-sons** [*count*] **:** the middle of a season (such as a season of games in a sport or a season of television programs) ▪ He was traded to a better team at *midseason*. ▪ The network added several new shows to its schedule at *midseason*. — often used before another noun ▪ a *midseason* slump ▪ The game show was a *midseason* replacement for a show that was canceled.

mid·sec·tion /ˈmɪdˌsekʃən/ *noun, pl* **-tions** [*count*] *chiefly US* **:** a middle section, part, or area ▪ Grassy plains used to cover large portions of America's *midsection*. ▪ the *midsection* of the boat/bridge; *especially* **:** the area around a person's middle ▪ He threw a hard punch to my *midsection*.

mid·ship·man /ˈmɪdˌʃɪpmən/ *noun, pl* **-men** /-mən/ [*count*]
1 : someone who is being trained to become an officer in the U.S. Navy
2 : an officer who is of the lowest rank in the British Navy

mid·size /ˈmɪdˌsaɪz/ *also* **mid·sized** /ˈmɪdˌsaɪzd/ *adj* **:** neither large nor small ▪ a *midsize* car ▪ The new service will appeal to large and *midsize* [=*medium-sized, middle-sized*] companies.

midst /ˈmɪdst/ *noun* [*noncount*]
1 a : the middle area or part of something ▪ The river passes through the *midst* of the city. ▪ a bustling city ***in the midst of*** the desert **b :** the period of time when something is happening or being done ▪ We are ***in the midst of*** a terrible war. ▪ They were *in the midst of* remodeling their house. ▪ The region is currently *in the midst of* a terrible drought. ▪ We never gave up hope *in the midst of* our troubles.
2 — used to say that someone is among the people in a group ▪ We sensed a traitor ***in our midst***. [=we sensed that one of the people in our group was a traitor] ▪ He stood *in their midst* [=he stood among them], waiting for a reply. ▪ strangers *in their midst*

mid·stream /ˈmɪdˈstriːm/ *noun*
in midstream **1 :** in the middle of a river or stream ▪ The boat struck a rock *in midstream*. **2 :** while in the process of doing something ▪ She began talking about the party but changed topics *in midstream*. ▪ The government stopped the project *in midstream*. — see also *change horses in midstream* at [1]HORSE

mid·sum·mer /ˈmɪdˈsʌmə/ *noun* [*noncount*] **:** the middle of summer ▪ The new product should be in stores by *midsummer*. — often used before another noun ▪ a hot *midsummer* night

mid·term /ˈmɪdˌtəm/ *noun, pl* **-terms** *US*
1 a [*count*] **:** an examination given at the middle of a school term ▪ The students will be busy taking *midterms* next week. ▪ a *midterm* exam **b** [*noncount*] **:** the middle of a school term ▪ He dropped the course before *midterm*.
2 [*noncount*] **:** the middle of a term of office ▪ assessing the President's performance at *midterm* — often used before another noun ▪ *midterm* Congressional elections [=elections that occur halfway through a President's term of office]

mid·town /ˈmɪdˌtaʊn/ *noun* [*noncount*] *chiefly US* **:** the part of a city or town between its downtown and uptown ▪ Rents in *midtown* are very expensive. — often used before another noun ▪ a *midtown* hotel/bar/restaurant ▪ *midtown* Manhattan

[1]**mid·way** /ˈmɪdˌweɪ/ *adv*
1 : in the middle between two places or points **:** at the halfway point ▪ We stopped for lunch about *midway* [=*halfway*] between New York and Philadelphia. ▪ You should begin reading at the paragraph that begins *midway* down the page.
2 : in the middle of an act, process, or period of time ▪ She was interrupted when she was *midway* [=*halfway*] through her presentation. ▪ They took the lead *midway* through the second period.
– **midway** *adj* ▪ at the *midway* point of our trip

[2]**midway** *noun, pl* **-ways** [*count*] *US* **:** an area at a fair, carnival, or amusement park for food stands, games, and rides ▪ We played every game on the *midway*.

mid·week /ˈmɪdˌwiːk/ *noun* [*noncount*] **:** the middle of the week ▪ She has to finish the report by *midweek*.
– **midweek** *adj, always used before a noun* ▪ a *midweek* deadline – **midweek** *adv* ▪ They'll be arriving *midweek*.

Mid·west /ˌmɪdˈwest/ *noun*
the Midwest **:** the northern central part of the U.S. **:** the Middle West ▪ the rich farmlands of *the Midwest* — often used before another noun ▪ my *Midwest* childhood ▪ *Midwest* cities
– **Mid·west·ern** /ˌmɪdˈwestən/ *adj* ▪ *Midwestern* states/cities/farms – **Mid·west·ern·er** /ˌmɪdˈwestənə/ *noun, pl* **-ers** [*count*]

mid·wife /ˈmɪdˌwaɪf/ *noun, pl* **-wives** /-ˌwaɪvz/ [*count*] **:** a person (usually a woman) who helps a woman when she is giving birth to a child ▪ a trained and certified *midwife*
– **mid·wife·ry** /ˌmɪdˈwɪfəri/ *noun* [*noncount*] ▪ She has been trained in *midwifery*. [=the work done by a midwife]

mid·win·ter /ˈmɪdˈwɪntə/ *noun* [*noncount*] **:** the middle of winter ▪ the heavy snows and frigid temperatures of *midwinter* — often used before another noun ▪ a cold *midwinter* day ▪ deep *midwinter* snows

mid·year /ˈmɪdˌjiə/ *noun* [*noncount*] **:** the middle of a year ▪ She expects to get a promotion at *midyear*. — often used before another noun ▪ *midyear* budget cuts ▪ a *midyear* performance review

mien /ˈmiːn/ *noun* [*singular*] *old-fashioned + literary* **:** a person's appearance or facial expression ▪ a kindly *mien* ▪ He has the *mien* of an ancient warrior.

miffed /ˈmɪft/ *adj* [*more ~; most ~*] *informal* **:** slightly angry or annoyed ▪ They were (a bit) *miffed* [=*upset*] about what they considered to be unfair treatment. ▪ She was *miffed* at them for not inviting her to the party.

[1]**might** /ˈmaɪt/ *verb* [*modal verb*]
1 — used to say that something is possible ▪ We *might* [=*may*] go if they ask us, but then again we *might* not. ▪ It *might* [=*could*] be true. ▪ *Might* it not be true? ▪ The test *might* include some questions about geography. ▪ There *might* be some difficulties ahead. ▪ She *might* get hundreds of responses to her survey. ▪ What you see *might* (well/very well) surprise you. ▪ I thought you *might* like this. ▪ She *might* have been the greatest actress of her generation. [=it's possible that she was the greatest actress of her generation] ▪ They *might* still succeed. ▪ I think he *might* be trying to cheat us. ▪ "Have they failed?" "They *might* have." = (*Brit*) "They *might* have done." ▪ If we hurry, we *might* get there before it rains. ▪ The movie *might* be better than you expect. ▪ Some people *might* have given up at that point, but not her. ▪ She's not as upset with them as *might* be expected. ▪ As you *might* or *might* not have heard, we've won! ▪ He *might* win and so *might* she.
2 — used to say that one thing is true but something else is also true ▪ He *might* [=*may*] be slow, but he does very good work. = Slow though he *might* be, he (still) does very good work. [=although he's slow, he does very good work] ▪ It *might* be cold outside, but it's still a nice day. ▪ She *might* have been a great actress, but she was a terrible parent.
3 — used to talk about a possible condition that does not or did not actually exist ▪ If you were older, you *might* understand. ▪ If she had been given a chance, she *might* have been a great actress.

4 *formal* **— used as the past tense of** *may* ▪ He asked if he *might* [=*could*] leave. [=he asked, "May I leave?"] ▪ He gave his life so that others *might* [=*could*] live.

5 a — used in speech to ask a question or make a request in a polite way ▪ *Might* [=*may*] I ask who is calling? [=who is calling?] ▪ "Do you think I *might* possibly borrow your pen?" "Of course you may!" **b — used to make a polite suggestion** ▪ You *might* [=*may*] want to consider leaving early. ▪ It *might* be wise to proceed cautiously. **c — used to politely say something about someone or something** ▪ ***Might I just say*** how pleased I am to be here. ▪ This has been, ***if I might say so***, one of the happiest days of my life. ▪ He is her husband and, ***I might add***, one of her biggest fans.

6 — used to say that you are annoyed by something that was or was not done ▪ You *might* [=*could*] at least apologize! ▪ If you weren't coming, you *might* (at least) have told me in advance!

7 — used to indicate what is or was expected ▪ You *might* [=*would*] think that he would be more grateful after all I've done for him. ▪ I *might* [=*should*] have known you wouldn't keep your promise!

8 — used in speech when asking a question about someone or something that surprises or annoys you ▪ "I have a request to make." "And what *might* that be?" [=what is your request?] ▪ And who *might* you be? [=who are you?]

²might *noun* [*noncount*] **: power to do something : force or strength** ▪ an impressive display of military *might* ▪ the legal *might* of the government ▪ He swung the bat ***with all his might***. [=he swung the bat as hard as he could]

might makes right** or **might is right **— used to say that people who have power are able to do what they want because no one can stop them**

might·i·ly /ˈmaɪtəli/ *adv*

1 : to a great degree : very much ▪ They contributed *mightily* to the cause. ▪ She struggled *mightily* to read his handwriting.

2 : with great force or strength ▪ The soldiers fought *mightily* before finally surrendering. ▪ He shouted *mightily*.

mightn't /ˈmaɪtn̩t/ **— used as a contraction of** *might not* ▪ People *mightn't* always agree with his decisions, but they do think he's fair.

might've /ˈmaɪtəv/ **— used as a contraction of** *might have* ▪ I think we *might've* had different goals. ▪ She did what any other smart person *might've* done in that situation.

¹mighty /ˈmaɪti/ *adj* **might·i·er; -est** [*also more ~; most ~*]

1 : having or showing great strength or power ▪ The barbarians faced a *mighty* army. ▪ the decline of a *mighty* empire ▪ the *mighty* Mississippi ▪ a *mighty* oak ▪ *mighty* deeds ▪ With a *mighty* leap, he jumped across the stream.

2 : very great ▪ A *mighty* famine devastated the land. ▪ It took a *mighty* effort to get everything done on time.

high and mighty see ¹HIGH

²mighty *adv, chiefly US, informal* **: to a great degree : VERY** ▪ Your father and I are *mighty* proud of you. ▪ That was a *mighty* tasty dinner. ▪ He made the offer *mighty* appealing. ▪ She has some *mighty* important decisions to make. ▪ It sure was *mighty* cold last night. ▪ We're *mighty* glad to be here.

mi·graine /ˈmaɪˌgreɪn, *Brit* ˈmiːˌgreɪn/ *noun, pl* **-graines : a very bad headache** [*count*] He suffers from *migraines*. ▪ a *migraine* headache/attack [*noncount*] He suffers from *migraine*.

mi·grant /ˈmaɪgrənt/ *noun, pl* **-grants** [*count*]

1 : a person who goes from one place to another especially to find work ▪ *migrants* in search of work on farms ▪ *migrant* (farm) workers **— compare** EMIGRANT, IMMIGRANT

2 : a bird or animal that moves from one area to another at different times of the year ▪ Not all birds are *migrants*. ▪ *migrant* birds

mi·grate /ˈmaɪˌgreɪt/ *verb* **-grates; -grat·ed; -grat·ing** [*no obj*]

1 : to move from one country or place to live or work in another ▪ He *migrates* from New York to Florida each winter. ▪ Thousands of workers *migrate* to this area each summer. **— compare** EMIGRATE, IMMIGRATE

2 *of a bird or animal* **: to move from one area to another at different times of the year** ▪ The whales *migrate* between their feeding ground in the north and their breeding ground in the Caribbean. ▪ They followed the *migrating* herds of buffalo across the plains. ▪ *migrating* birds

— mi·gra·tion /maɪˈgreɪʃən/ *noun, pl* **-tions** [*noncount*] an expert on bird *migration* [*count*] mass *migrations* of workers ▪ fall *migrations* to breeding grounds **— mi·gra·tion·al** /maɪˈgreɪʃənl/ *adj* ▪ *migrational* movements

mi·gra·to·ry /ˈmaɪgrəˌtori, *Brit* maɪˈgreɪtəri/ *adj* **: moving from one place to another at different times of the year : migrating regularly** ▪ *migratory* birds ▪ *migratory* [=(more commonly) *migrant*] workers

¹mike /ˈmaɪk/ *noun, pl* **mikes** [*count*] *informal* **:** MICROPHONE ▪ The announcer was wearing a *mike*.

²mike *verb* **mikes; miked; mik·ing** [+ *obj*] *informal* **: to put a microphone on (someone)** ▪ The announcer was *miked* (up) (for sound).

mil *or* **mill** /ˈmɪl/ *noun, pl* **mil** *or* **mill** [*count*] *US slang* **: a million dollars** ▪ He has a couple *mil* in the bank.

mild /ˈmajəld/ *adj* **mild·er; -est** [*more ~; most ~*]

1 : gentle in nature or behavior ▪ a *mild* young man ▪ He has a *mild* manner/disposition. ▪ He was a ***mild-mannered*** man who rarely became angry.

2 a : not strong in action or effect ▪ a *mild* drug/detergent ▪ *mild* [=*gentle*] soap **b : not strong or harsh in taste** ▪ *mild* flavors ▪ *mild* cheese **c : not strongly felt** ▪ He has only a *mild* [=*slight*] interest in politics. ▪ They had a *mild* disagreement.

3 a : not harsh or severe ▪ She has a *mild* case of the flu. ▪ a *mild* headache/fever ▪ *mild* pain ▪ He suffered a *mild* concussion/heart attack. ▪ a *mild* reprimand, not a stern one **b : not too hot or too cold : pleasantly warm** ▪ a *mild* [=*temperate*] climate ▪ a *mild* winter's day ▪ We've been having a very *mild* winter.

— mild·ly *adv* ▪ He's *mildly* [=*slightly, somewhat*] interested in politics. ▪ It's a *mildly* amusing comedy. ▪ He has been *mildly* criticized by a few former colleagues. ▪ She was upset, ***to put it mildly***. [=she was extremely upset] ▪ He is, *to put it mildly*, a demanding boss. [=he is a very demanding boss] **— mild·ness** *noun* [*noncount*] ▪ the *mildness* of the weather

mil·dew /ˈmɪlˌduː, *Brit* ˈmɪlˌdjuː/ *noun* [*noncount*] **: a usually white substance that grows on the surface of things in wet, warm conditions** ▪ The basement's damp walls were covered with *mildew*.

— mil·dewed /ˈmɪlˌduːd, *Brit* ˈmɪlˌdjuːd/ *adj* ▪ *mildewed* walls **— mil·dewy** /ˈmɪlˌduːwi, *Brit* ˈmɪlˌdjuːwi/ *adj* [*more ~; most ~*] ▪ a *mildewy* basement

mile /ˈmajəl/ *noun, pl* **miles**

1 [*count*] **: a unit of measurement equal to 5,280 feet (about 1,609 meters)** ▪ How many *miles* is it from here to New York? = How far is it from here to New York in *miles*? ▪ We passed *mile* after *mile* of beautiful scenery as we drove through the country. ▪ We traveled over *miles* of dirt road. ▪ He lives about a half (a) *mile* from here. ▪ The car was traveling at 70 *miles* per/an hour. **— often used figuratively** ▪ He won the election by a *mile*. [=he won the election by a very large margin] ▪ He missed the target by a *mile*. [=he completely missed the target] ▪ Her smile was a *mile* wide. ▪ You can see the stain (from) a *mile* away. = (*Brit*) You can see the stain a *mile* off. ▪ She was talking ***a mile a minute***. [=very fast] ▪ The twin's resemblance ***stood/stuck out a mile***. [=the resemblance was very obvious] **— see also** NAUTICAL MILE

2 miles [*plural*] **: a great distance** ▪ They walked for *miles*. ▪ There was no one (to be seen) for *miles* around. ▪ We were *miles* from home. ▪ We still have *miles* to go. ▪ The beach stretched on ***for miles and miles***. ▪ He lives by himself in a cabin ***miles from nowhere/anywhere***. [=very far from other people and places] **— often used figuratively** ▪ He was *miles* ahead of the other students in his class. ▪ Politically he's now *miles* away from his original position. ▪ She feels as if her sister is *miles* beyond her in education. ▪ They're still *miles* from an agreement. **— see also** MILES

3 [*singular*] **: a race that is a mile long** ▪ the first man to run a four-minute *mile* [=the first man to run a mile in less than four minutes]

go the extra mile **: to do more than you are required to do** ▪ She's always willing to *go the extra mile* to help a friend.

mile·age /ˈmaɪlɪʤ/ *noun* [*noncount*]

1 a : distance in miles ▪ What's the *mileage* from here to New York? [=how many miles is it from here to New York?] **b : distance traveled in miles by a vehicle** ▪ My old car has a lot of *mileage* on it. = My old car has racked up a lot of *mileage*. [=it has been driven for a large number of miles since it was new] ▪ a car with high/low *mileage* ▪ The car's rental rate includes unlimited *mileage*. [=the rate does not increase no matter how far the car is driven] ▪ The company pays me a ***mileage allowance*** [=an amount of money paid for every mile traveled] when I have to travel for work.

2 : the average number of miles a vehicle will travel on a gal-

M

lon of gasoline • My new car gets much better *mileage* than my old one did. • good/bad *mileage* • fuel/gas *mileage*

3 a : benefit or use over a period of time • The company has gotten a lot of *mileage* out of a simple idea. • The movie gets a lot of *mileage* out of an old story. **b :** useful ability • He's not the pitcher he once was, but he still has a lot of *mileage* left in him. [=he is still able to pitch well; his career as a pitcher is far from finished]

mile•om•e•ter *or* **mi•lom•e•ter** /maɪˈlɑːmətə/ *noun, pl* **-ters** [*count*] *Brit* **:** ODOMETER

mile•post /ˈmajəlˌpoʊst/ *noun, pl* **-posts** [*count*] *US*

1 : a post by the side of a road that shows the distance in miles to a specified place

2 : MILESTONE 2 • We've reached a new *milepost* in the field of genetic research.

mil•er /ˈmaɪlə/ *noun, pl* **-ers** [*count*] **:** a runner in a race that is a mile long

miles /ˈmajəlz/ *adv, chiefly Brit, informal* **:** very much • This one is *miles* worse/better than that one.

mile•stone /ˈmajəlˌstoʊn/ *noun, pl* **-stones** [*count*]

1 : a stone by the side of a road that shows the distance in miles to a specified place

2 : an important point in the progress or development of something **:** a very important event or advance — usually + *in* • The birth of their first child was a (major) *milestone in* their marriage. • The study marks an important *milestone in* our understanding of the disease.

mi•lieu /milˈjuː/ *noun, pl* **-lieus** *or* **-lieux** /milˈjuːz/ [*count*] *formal* **:** the physical or social setting in which people live or in which something happens or develops • He and his wife come from different cultural *milieus.* [=*backgrounds, environments*]

mil•i•tant /ˈmɪlətənt/ *adj* [*more* ~; *most* ~] **:** having or showing a desire or willingness to use strong, extreme, and sometimes forceful methods to achieve something • *militant* protesters • an angry and *militant* speech • *militant* foreign policy

– **mil•i•tan•cy** /ˈmɪlətənsi/ *noun* [*noncount*] • the *militancy* of the protesters – **militant** *noun, pl* **-tants** [*count*] • a protest by angry *militants* – **mil•i•tant•ly** *adv*

mil•i•ta•rism /ˈmɪlətəˌrɪzəm/ *noun* [*noncount*] **:** the opinions or actions of people who believe that a country should use military methods, forces, etc., to gain power and to achieve its goals • The administration has been criticized for the *militarism* of its foreign policy.

– **mil•i•ta•rist** /ˈmɪlətərɪst/ *adj* [*more* ~; *most* ~] • a *militarist* regime – **militarist** *noun, pl* **-rists** [*count*] • a government dominated by *militarists* – **mil•i•ta•ris•tic** /ˌmɪlətəˈrɪstɪk/ *adj* [*more* ~; *most* ~] • a *militaristic* foreign policy

mil•i•ta•rize *also Brit* **mil•i•ta•rise** /ˈmɪlətəˌraɪz/ *verb* **-rizes; -rized; -riz•ing** [+ *obj*]

1 : to put weapons and military forces in (an area) — usually used as *(be) militarized* • The area *is* now fully *militarized.* • a ***militarized zone*** — opposite DEMILITARIZE

2 : to give a military quality or character to (something) • *militarize* a country's foreign policy • an increasingly *militarized* society

– **mil•i•ta•ri•za•tion** *also Brit* **mil•i•ta•ri•sa•tion** /ˌmɪlətərəˈzeɪʃən, *Brit* ˌmɪləˌtaraɪˈzeɪʃən/ *noun* [*noncount*]

[1]mil•i•tary /ˈmɪləˌteri/ *adj*

1 a : of or relating to soldiers or the armed forces (such as the army, navy, marines, and air force) • *military* discipline/life • *military* glory • *military* aircraft/officers/history/personnel/operations • a *military* base/camp/hospital • He is being tried in a *military* court rather than in a civilian court. • He has had a long *military* career. • He tried to avoid *military* service. [=he tried to avoid becoming a member of the army, navy, etc.] **b :** of or relating to the army • *military* and naval affairs

2 : controlled or supported by armed forces • a *military* government/dictatorship/regime • a *military* coup

– **mil•i•tari•ly** /ˌmɪləˈterəli/ *adv* • a *militarily* superior force

[2]military *noun* [*plural*] **:** members of the armed forces **:** military people • There were many *military* present but only a few civilians.

the military **:** the armed forces • He has had a long career in *the military*. • The policy is opposed by *the military*. • *The military* oppose/opposes the policy. [=military leaders oppose the policy]

military police *noun* [*plural*] **:** an organized part of a military force (such as an army) that acts as the police for that force

– **military policeman** *noun, pl* ~ **-men** [*count*]

mil•i•tate /ˈmɪləˌteɪt/ *verb* **-tates; -tat•ed; -tat•ing**

militate against [*phrasal verb*] ***militate against (something)*** *formal* **:** to make (something) unlikely to happen **:** to prevent (something) from happening • His inexperience *militates against* his getting an early promotion. • factors *militating against* success

mi•li•tia /məˈlɪʃə/ *noun, pl* **-tias** [*count*] **:** a group of people who are not part of the armed forces of a country but are trained like soldiers

– **mi•li•tia•man** /məˈlɪʃəmən/ *noun, pl* **-men** /-mən/ [*count*]

[1]milk /ˈmɪlk/ *noun* [*noncount*]

1 : a white liquid produced by a woman to feed her baby or by female animals to feed their young • mother's/breast *milk* • cheese made from sheep's *milk*; *especially* **:** milk from cows or goats that is used as food by people • a glass of low-fat/whole *milk* • serving *milk* and cookies • pasteurized/homogenized *milk* • whole *milk* [=milk from which no fat has been removed] — see also CONDENSED MILK, EVAPORATED MILK, MALTED MILK, SKIM MILK

2 : a white liquid produced by a plant • coconut *milk*

cry over spilled/spilt milk see [1]CRY

land of milk and honey see [1]LAND

the milk of human kindness *literary* **:** kind feelings or behavior toward other people • He was filled with *the milk of human kindness.* [=he was filled with kindness; he was very kind]

[2]milk *verb* **milks; milked; milk•ing** [+ *obj*]

1 : to get milk from (an animal) • *milk* a cow

2 : to use (something or someone) in a way that helps you unfairly • They *milked* [=*exploited*] their advantage for all it was worth. • greedy landlords *milking* their tenants of all their money — see also *milk (someone or something) dry* at [1]DRY

– **milk•er** /ˈmɪlkə/ *noun, pl* **-ers** [*count*] • a mechanical *milker* [=a machine used for milking cows]

milk chocolate *noun* [*count, noncount*] **:** a kind of chocolate that is made with milk — compare DARK CHOCOLATE

milk float *noun, pl* ~ **floats** [*count*] *Brit* **:** a small electric vehicle used to deliver milk to people's homes

milk•maid /ˈmɪlkˌmeɪd/ *noun, pl* **-maids** [*count*] *old-fashioned* **:** DAIRYMAID

milk•man /ˈmɪlkˌmæn/ *noun, pl* **-men** /-ˌmen/ [*count*] **:** a man who sells or delivers milk

milk of mag•ne•sia /-mægˈniːʒə/ *noun* [*noncount*] **:** a thick, white liquid that contains magnesium and is used as a medicine for stomach problems (such as indigestion)

milk•shake /ˈmɪlkˌʃeɪk/ *noun, pl* **-shakes** [*count*] **:** a thick drink made of milk, a flavoring syrup, and often ice cream • a chocolate/vanilla *milkshake* — called also *shake*

milk•sop /ˈmɪlkˌsɑːp/ *noun, pl* **-sops** [*count*] *old-fashioned* **:** a weak boy or man

milk tooth *noun, pl* ~ **teeth** [*count*] **:** BABY TOOTH

milk•weed /ˈmɪlkˌwiːd/ *noun, pl* **-weeds** [*count, noncount*] **:** a type of North American plant that has white juice

milky /ˈmɪlki/ *adj* **milk•i•er; -est**

1 a : looking or tasting like milk • cheese with a light *milky* taste • *milky* (white) skin **b :** not clear • a *milky* [=*cloudy*] liquid • eyes covered by a *milky* glaze

2 : containing a large amount of milk • *milky* coffee

– **milk•i•ness** *noun* [*noncount*]

Milky Way *noun*

the Milky Way **1 :** a broad band of light that can be seen in the night sky and that is caused by the light of a very large number of faint stars **2 :** the galaxy in which we live that contains the stars that make up the Milky Way • Our solar system is in *the Milky Way* (galaxy).

[1]mill /ˈmɪl/ *noun, pl* **mills** [*count*]

1 a : a building with machinery for grinding grain into flour **b :** a machine for grinding grain

2 : a small machine for grinding or crushing pepper, coffee, etc. • a food/pepper *mill*

3 : a building in which a particular product is made **:** FACTORY • a paper/cotton/textile/lumber/steel *mill* • *mill* workers — see also SAWMILL

4 : something that is compared to a factory because it produces things in large numbers or in a mechanical way • Some critics have described the school as a diploma *mill.* [=a school where students can obtain diplomas very easily] • The rumor *mill* has been churning out stories about their marriage. [=there are many rumors about their marriage]

grist for/to your/the mill see GRIST

through the mill *chiefly Brit* : through a very difficult experience ▪ They've been (put) *through the mill* in the months since their father died.

[2]**mill** *verb* **mills; milled; mill·ing**
1 [+ *obj*] : to produce (something) in a mill especially by grinding, crushing, or cutting it ▪ *milled* wheat/lumber
2 [*no obj*] *of a group of people* : to walk around in a general area without any particular aim or purpose ▪ The crowd was *milling* outside the exit. — usually + *around* or (*chiefly Brit*) *about* ▪ People were just *milling around* while they waited.

[3]**mill** *variant spelling of* MIL

mil·len·ni·um /məˈlɛnijəm/ *noun, pl* **-nia** /-nijə/ *or* **-ni·ums** [*count*]
1 : a period of 1,000 years ▪ The book describes the changes that have occurred in the landscape over many *millennia*.
2 : a period of a thousand years counted from the beginning of the Christian era ▪ The year 2000 was celebrated as the beginning of the third *millennium*. ▪ We had a party to celebrate ***the millennium***. [=the beginning of the millennium]
– mil·len·ni·al /məˈlɛnijəl/ *adj* ▪ *millennial* celebrations

mill·er /ˈmɪlɚ/ *noun, pl* **-ers** [*count*] : a person who works in or is in charge of a flour mill

mil·let /ˈmɪlət/ *noun* [*noncount*] : a type of grass that is grown for its seeds which are used as food; *also* : the seeds of millet

milli- *combining form* : one thousandth part of something ▪ *milli*meter

mil·li·gram *also Brit* **mil·li·gramme** /ˈmɪləˌgræm/ *noun, pl* **-grams** [*count*] : a weight equal to 1/1000 gram

mil·li·li·ter (*US*) *or Brit* **mil·li·li·tre** /ˈmɪləˌli:tɚ/ *noun, pl* **-ters** [*count*] : a measure of capacity equal to 1/1000 liter

mil·li·me·ter (*US*) *or Brit* **mil·li·me·tre** /ˈmɪləˌmi:tɚ/ *noun, pl* **-ters** [*count*] : a length equal to 1/1000 meter

mil·li·ner /ˈmɪlənɚ/ *noun, pl* **-ners** [*count*] : a person who designs, makes, or sells women's hats

mil·li·nery /ˈmɪləˌneri/ *noun* [*noncount*]
1 : women's hats ▪ a shop that sells *millinery*
2 : the business of making or selling women's hats

mil·lion /ˈmɪljən/ *noun, pl* **mil·lions** *or* **million** [*count*]
1 : the number 1,000,000 ▪ a/one/two *million* (of them) ▪ a hundred *million* = 100 *million* ▪ several *million* (of them) = (less commonly) several *millions* (of them) ▪ hundreds of *millions* (of them) ▪ a *million* and one [=1,000,001] ▪ a *million* and a half = 1.5 *million* [=1,500,000] ▪ The company is worth *millions*. [=worth millions of dollars, pounds, euros, etc.] ▪ a *million* dollars
2 : a very large amount or number ▪ I've heard that excuse a *million* times before. [=many, many times before] — often plural ▪ The drug could save *millions* of lives. ▪ ***millions and millions*** of people
look/feel like a million dollars/bucks *informal* : to look/feel very good ▪ She *looks like a million bucks* since she lost all that weight.
never/not in a million years see YEAR
one in a million *informal* : a person or thing that is very unusual, special, or admired ▪ Thanks for all the help you've given me. You're *one in a million*.
thanks a million *informal* : thank you very much ▪ Hey, *thanks a million* for your help. ▪ (*humorous*) "I'll let you wash the dishes today." "*Thanks a million*."
– mil·lionth /ˈmɪljənθ/ *adj* ▪ our (one) *millionth* customer ▪ This is the *millionth* time I've seen this show. [=I have seen this show many times] **– millionth** *noun, pl* **-lionths** [*count*] ▪ one *millionth* [=one of a million equal parts] of a second

mil·lion·aire /ˌmɪljəˈneɚ/ *noun, pl* **-aires** [*count*] : a rich person who has at least a million dollars, pounds, etc.

mil·lion·air·ess /ˌmɪljəˈnerəs/ *noun, pl* **-ess·es** [*count*] : a rich woman who has at least a million dollars, pounds, etc. : a woman who is a millionaire

mil·li·pede /ˈmɪləˌpi:d/ *noun, pl* **-pedes** [*count*] : a small creature that is like an insect and that has a long, thin body with many legs

mil·li·sec·ond /ˈmɪləˌsɛkənd/ *noun, pl* **-onds** [*count*] : one thousandth of a second

mill·pond /ˈmɪlˌpɑ:nd/ *noun, pl* **-ponds** [*count*] : a pond that supplies water for running a mill

mill·stone /ˈmɪlˌstoun/ *noun, pl* **-stones** [*count*]
1 : either one of two large, round stones used for grinding grain in a mill
2 : a problem or responsibility that does not go away and that makes it difficult or impossible to do or achieve something ▪ College loans can quickly become a *millstone* for students. ▪ The scandal has become a political *millstone*. ▪ The scandal has been a ***millstone around her neck***.

milometer *variant spelling of* MILEOMETER

[1]**mime** /ˈmaɪm/ *noun, pl* **mimes**
1 [*noncount*] : a form of entertainment in which a performer plays a character or tells a story without words by using body movements and facial expressions ▪ an actor with a gift for *mime* ▪ a performance done in *mime*
2 [*count*] **a** : a performance done without speaking : a performance using mime **b** : a performer who uses mime ▪ an actor who is a talented *mime*

[2]**mime** *verb* **mimes; mimed; mim·ing** [+ *obj*] : to make the movements of someone who is doing (something) without actually doing it ▪ He *mimed* playing a guitar. ▪ She *mimed* picking up the phone and dialing a number. ▪ He *mimed* the words to the song. [=he moved his mouth like someone singing the song but he did not actually sing the words]

[1]**mim·ic** /ˈmɪmɪk/ *verb* **-ics; -icked; -ick·ing** [+ *obj*]
1 : to copy (someone or someone's behavior or speech) especially for humor ▪ He can *mimic* [=*imitate*] the way his father talks perfectly. ▪ He *mimicked* her accent. ▪ She has a talent for *mimicking* famous actresses.
2 : to create the appearance or effect of (something) ▪ software that can *mimic* [=*simulate*] human thought ▪ The lamp *mimics* natural sunlight.
3 : to naturally look like (something) ▪ a butterfly that *mimics* a leaf

[2]**mimic** *noun, pl* **-ics** [*count*] : a person who copies the behavior or speech of other people : a person who mimics other people ▪ She's a talented *mimic*.; *also* : an animal that naturally looks like something else

mim·ic·ry /ˈmɪmɪkri/ *noun* [*noncount*] : the activity or art of copying the behavior or speech of other people : the activity or art of mimicking other people ▪ a talent for *mimicry*

mi·mo·sa /məˈmousə/ *noun, pl* **-sas**
1 [*count, noncount*] : a tropical tree or shrub that has small white or pink flowers that are shaped like balls
2 [*count*] *US* : an alcoholic drink made with champagne and orange juice

min·a·ret /ˌmɪnəˈrɛt/ *noun, pl* **-rets** [*count*] : a tall, thin tower of a mosque with a balcony from which the people are called to prayer

[1]**mince** /ˈmɪns/ *verb* **minc·es; minced; minc·ing**
1 [+ *obj*] : to cut (food) into very small pieces ▪ The recipe says that you should *mince* the onions. ▪ *minced* parsley/carrots/garlic ▪ (*chiefly Brit*) *minced* beef [=(*US*) ground beef, hamburger]
2 *always followed by an adverb or preposition* [*no obj*] : to walk with quick, short steps in a way that does not seem natural and that is often meant to be funny ▪ The comedian *minced* across the stage. = The comedian walked with *mincing* steps across the stage.
not mince (your) words *or US* ***mince no words*** : to speak in a very direct and honest way without worrying that you may be offending someone ▪ He *doesn't mince words* about the proposed law, which he considers "unconstitutional" and "idiotic." ▪ She *minces no words* in stating her opinions.
– minc·ing·ly /ˈmɪnsɪŋli/ *adv* ▪ walked *mincingly* across the stage

[2]**mince** *noun* [*noncount*]
1 *Brit* : HAMBURGER 2 ▪ The recipe uses a pound of *mince*. [=(*US*) *ground beef*]; *also* : ground meat of a specified kind ▪ lamb *mince*
2 : MINCEMEAT 2 ▪ a *mince* pie

mince·meat /ˈmɪnsˌmi:t/ *noun* [*noncount*]
1 : meat that has been cut into very small pieces : minced meat
2 : a mixture of raisins, apples, spices, etc., that is used especially in pies ▪ *mincemeat* pie
make mincemeat out of *informal* : to destroy, ruin, or defeat (someone or something) in a very thorough and complete way ▪ Last year's champions have been *making mincemeat of* the competition again this year.

[1]**mind** /ˈmaɪnd/ *noun, pl* **minds**
1 : the part of a person that thinks, reasons, feels, and remembers [*count*] He read great literature to develop/cultivate his *mind*. ▪ It's important to keep your *mind* active as you grow older. ▪ He went for a walk to help clear his *mind*. ▪ the mysteries of the human *mind* ▪ My *mind* is always open to new ideas. ▪ You can't argue with him. His *mind* is closed. ▪

I can't concentrate: my *mind* is always wandering and I can't keep it focused on anything. ▪ Let me get this clear/straight in my *mind* [=let me understand this clearly]: are you saying that she was lying to me all along? ▪ I can't get that image out of my *mind*. = I can't stop seeing that image in my *mind*. = That image is stuck in my *mind*. ▪ The smell of pine sends my *mind* back to childhood. ▪ The sound of her voice jerked my *mind* back to the present. ▪ My *mind* tells me it can't work, but my heart tells me I want to try it. ▪ We must appeal to and win (over) the ***hearts and minds*** of the people. [=the emotions and the reasoning of the people] ▪ His ***conscious mind*** had forgotten the incident, but the memory of it was still buried somewhere in his ***subconscious/unconscious mind***. ▪ There's absolutely ***no doubt in my mind*** about his guilt. [=I am sure that he is guilty] ▪ I know you're disappointed by their decision, but you should just ***put that out of your mind*** [=stop thinking about that] and go back to work. ▪ I'll handle the schedule. Just *put it out of your mind*. [=don't think or worry about it] ▪ Is there something ***on your mind***? [=is there something troubling you?; are you worried or bothered about something?] ▪ Why don't you just say what's *on your mind*? [=why don't you just say what you are thinking?] ▪ I wish there were some way I could ***ease your (troubled) mind***. = I wish there were some way I could ***set/put your mind at ease/rest*** [=could make you stop worrying] ▪ These problems have been ***preying/weighing on his mind***. [=he has been worrying about these problems] ▪ The safety of the children should be ***foremost/uppermost in all our minds*** now. [=we should all be thinking most about the safety of the children now] ▪ The idea that we might lose was ***the furthest thing from my mind***. [=I never thought that we might lose] ▪ I have no intention of quitting my job. ***Nothing could be further from my mind***. ▪ She says that getting married again is ***the last thing on her mind*** right now. [=she is not thinking at all about getting married again] ▪ What was ***going/running through your mind*** [=what were you thinking] when you agreed to do this? ▪ His name ***slips/escapes my mind*** at the moment. [=I can't remember his name] ✧ **If something (such as an illness) is *all in your/the mind*, you are imagining it.** ▪ He thinks he's very ill, but it's *all in his mind*. ✧ **If *your mind is set on* something or you *have your mind set on* something, you are very determined to do or to get something.** ▪ *Her mind is set on* becoming a doctor. = She *has her mind set on* becoming a doctor. **[*noncount*]** It's important to be healthy in both body and *mind*. ▪ He's in a bad/good ***state of mind***. [=he's in a bad/good mood] ▪ Installing a security system in your home will give you greater ***peace of mind*** [=a feeling of being safe or protected] — **see also** FRAME OF MIND, PRESENCE OF MIND

2 **[*count*]** — **used to describe the way a person thinks or the intelligence of a person** ▪ She has a brilliant *mind*. ▪ He has an inquisitive/inquiring *mind*. ▪ He's an evil man with a warped/twisted *mind*. ▪ He's recognized as having one of the sharpest *minds* [=*intellects*] in this field.

3 — **used in phrases that describe someone as mentally ill or crazy** ▪ There's something wrong with him. He's ***not in his right mind*** [=he is mentally ill] ▪ No one *in their right mind* would try such a stunt. = Who *in their right mind* would try such a stunt? ▪ (*law*) She claims that her father was not ***of sound mind*** when he changed his will. = She claims her father was ***of unsound mind*** [=was not sane or rational] — **usually used informally in an exaggerated way** ▪ What a ridiculous idea! You must be ***out of your mind*** [=*crazy*] to believe that. ▪ I was (going) ***out of my mind with worry***. [=I was extremely worried] ▪ I feel like I'm ***losing my mind***. = I feel like I'm ***going out of my mind***. [=I feel like I'm going crazy] ▪ That noise is ***driving me out of my mind*** [=driving me crazy] ✧ **The phrase *out of your mind* is also used informally to make a statement stronger.** ▪ I was bored *out of my mind*. [=I was very bored] ▪ She was frightened *out of her mind*.

4 **[*count*]** : **a very intelligent person** ▪ Many of the world's greatest *minds* in physics will be attending the convention.

5 **[*noncount*]** : **a particular way of thinking about a situation** ▪ Everyone at the meeting was ***of like mind*** [=everyone agreed] about how to proceed. ▪ She is ***of the same mind*** as me. [=she agrees with me] ▪ We're all ***of one mind*** about him [=we all agree about him]: he's the one we want. ▪ ***To/In my mind***, that's wrong.

6 **[*noncount*]** : **attention that is given to a person or thing** ▪ Try to relax and ***take/get/keep your mind off*** your problems. [=stop thinking about your problems] ▪ I'm finding it hard to ***keep my mind on*** my work. [=to concentrate on my work] ▪ After finishing work on the remodeling project, she was able to ***turn her mind to*** [=direct her attention to; work on] other matters. ▪ ***Don't pay him any mind***. [=don't pay attention to him; ignore him] ▪ He kept talking but she ***paid him no mind***. ▪ You shouldn't ***pay any/much mind to*** what he says.

a meeting of (the) minds **see** MEETING

at/in the back of your mind **see** [1]BACK

blow someone's mind informal : **to strongly affect someone's mind with shock, confusion, etc. : to amaze or overwhelm someone's mind** ▪ The music really *blew my mind*. ▪ The thought of all she's accomplished at such a young age just *blows my mind*. — **see also** MIND-BLOWING

call/bring (something) to mind : **to cause (something) to be remembered or thought of** ▪ Seeing her again *brought to mind* the happy times we spent together in college.

change someone's mind : **to cause someone to change an opinion or decision** ▪ I tried to convince her, but I couldn't *change her mind*.

change your mind : **to change your decision or opinion about something** ▪ He wasn't going to come, but at the last minute he *changed his mind*. ▪ I tried to convince her, but she wouldn't *change her mind*.

come/spring/leap to mind : **to be remembered or thought of** ▪ What *comes to mind* when you hear his name? ▪ I didn't mean to offend you. I just said the first thing that ***came to/into my mind***.

concentrate the/your mind **see** [1]CONCENTRATE

cross someone's mind **see** [2]CROSS

enter your mind **see** ENTER

give someone a piece of your mind : **to speak to someone in an angry way** ▪ He stopped making so much noise after I went over there and *gave him a piece of my mind*.

have a good mind *or* ***have half a mind*** ✧ **If you *have a good mind* or *have half a mind* to do something, you have a feeling that you want to do it, especially because you are angry or annoyed, but you will probably not do it.** ▪ I *have a good mind* to go over there and tell him to be quiet. ▪ I *have half a mind* to tell her what I really think of her.

have a mind like a sieve **see** [1]SIEVE

have a mind of your own : **to have your own ideas and make your own choices about what should be done** ▪ Her parents want her to go to college, but she *has a mind of her own* and she insists on trying to become an actress. — **often used figuratively** ▪ I can't get the camera to work right. It seems to *have a mind of its own*.

have (someone or something) in mind : **to be thinking of (someone or something): such as a : to be thinking of choosing (someone) for a job, position, etc.** ▪ They *have you in mind* for the job. [=they are thinking of giving the job to you] **b : to be thinking of doing (something)** ▪ "I'd like to do something special for our anniversary." "What sort of thing did you *have in mind*?" ▪ He ***had it in mind*** [=*intended*] to leave the business to his daughter.

in mind : **in your thoughts** ▪ We designed this product with people like you *in mind*. [=we designed it for people like you] ▪ He went into the bar with trouble *in mind*. [=intending to cause trouble] ▪ Before you disregard his advice, ***keep/bear in mind*** [=*remember*] that he is regarded as one of the leading experts in this field. ▪ We have a limited amount of money to spend, and we need to *keep that in mind* [=think of that; consider that] while we're planning our vacation.

in your mind's eye **see** [1]EYE

know your own mind **see** [1]KNOW

make up your mind : **to make a decision about something** ▪ I can't *make up my mind* [=*decide*] where to take my vacation. ▪ He had *made up his mind* not to go. ▪ He's thinking about going, but he still hasn't *made up his mind* (about it). ▪ He's not going. ***His mind is made up***. [=he has made a decision and will not change it] ▪ I can't decide for you. You'll have to ***make up your own mind***.

mind over matter — **used to describe a situation in which someone is able to control a physical condition, problem, etc., by using the mind** ▪ His ability to keep going even when he is tired is a simple question of *mind over matter*.

of two minds *(US)* *or Brit* ***in two minds*** : **not decided or certain about something : having two opinions or ideas about something** ▪ I can't make up my mind where to take my vacation: I'm *of two minds* about where to go. ▪ I'm *of two minds* about (hiring) him: he seems well-qualified, but he doesn't have much experience.

open your mind **see** [2]OPEN

put (someone) in mind of (something) : **to cause (someone) to remember or think of (something)** ▪ What happened to you yesterday *puts me in mind of* [=reminds me of] what happened to me a year ago.

put/set your mind to (something) : to give your attention to (something) and try very hard to do it ▪ You'd be surprised at what you can accomplish when you *put your mind to* it. ▪ We can solve this problem if we *put our minds to* it.

read someone's mind : to know exactly what someone is thinking ▪ "I think we should go out to a movie tonight." "You *read my mind*. I was thinking the same thing." ▪ It's as if you could *read my mind*. ▪ He claims that he has the ability to ***read minds*** — see also MIND READER

speak your mind : to say what you think : to state your opinion ▪ If you don't agree with him, don't be afraid to *speak your mind*.

take a load/weight off your mind : to make you stop worrying about something ▪ Hearing that she's safe has really *taken a load off my mind*!

²mind *verb* **minds; minded; minding**

1 *not used in progressive tenses* : to be bothered by (something) : to object to or dislike (something) **[+ *obj*]** I *mind* it greatly [=it bothers me very much] when people are rude. ▪ I don't *mind* the rain. = I don't *mind* if it rains. [=the rain doesn't bother me] ▪ I don't *mind* making dinner. [=I am willing to make dinner; making dinner does not bother me] ▪ I wouldn't *mind* having a piece of pie myself. [=I would like to have a piece of pie too] **[*no obj*]** It was raining, but I didn't *mind*. ▪ Our flight was delayed—***not that I minded*** [=I was not bothered by it], since I was late getting to the airport myself. ▪ I'd like another cupcake, ***if you don't mind*** [=if it is all right with you]

2 [+ *obj*] : to care about or worry about (something or someone) ▪ They don't seem to *mind* where they sit. = They seem not to *mind* where they sit. ▪ I don't *mind* very much what happens. ▪ "Why is he so angry?" "Oh, ***don't mind him*** He's always complaining about something." ▪ *Don't mind me* [=don't worry about or pay attention to me]: I'll be all right.

3 [+ *obj*] **a** — used to make a polite request ▪ Do you *mind* me/my sitting here? [=would you be bothered if I sat here?] ▪ Do you *mind* if I smoke? = Would you *mind* if I smoked? ▪ Would you *mind* doing me a small favor? ▪ I'm tired. Would you *mind* leaving a little early? = Would you *mind* it if we left a little early? **b** — used in phrases with *if* when you have said something that might bother or upset someone ▪ How old are you, ***if you don't mind my/me asking***? [=may I ask how old you are?; would you be offended if I asked how old you are?] ▪ You look a bit old for this job, ***if you don't mind my/me saying so*** [=if I may say so] **c** — used in informal phrases with *I* ▪ "Would you like another cup of coffee?" "Thank you: ***I don't mind if I do***" [=yes, I'd like another cup] ▪ I was shocked by the news, ***I don't mind telling you*** [=I must say/admit that I was shocked by the news] ▪ ***I don't mind saying/admitting*** that I was very disappointed by her decision. **d** — used in informal phrases that show anger or annoyance ▪ "That old woman's a real pain!" "***Do you MIND***? That's my mother you're talking about!" ▪ "Let me help you with that." "I'll do it myself, ***if you don't mind***"

4 [+ *obj*] *US* : to do what you are told to do by (someone) : OBEY ▪ *Mind* your parents!

5 [+ *obj*] : to take care of (something or someone) : to watch or be in charge of (something or someone) ▪ Who's going to *mind* the office while you're away? ▪ Who's *minding* the children? — see also MIND THE STORE (below)

6 [+ *obj*] **a** : to be careful about (something) ▪ You'd better *mind* what you say. ▪ ***Mind your tongue/language*** [=stop saying offensive or improper things] ▪ His mother told him to ***mind his manners*** [=to behave in a polite and proper way] ▪ (*chiefly Brit*) *Mind* how you behave when we get there. — see also *mind your p's and q's* at ¹P **b** *chiefly Brit* — used to tell someone to be aware of something that could be a problem or danger ▪ The wind is very strong: *mind* your hat! ▪ *Mind* the broken glass! [=watch out for the broken glass] ▪ *Mind* the missing step! **c** *chiefly Brit* — used to tell someone to be sure to do something or to be careful to prevent something from happening ▪ *Mind* [=*make sure*] you've finished the project before he gets back! ▪ *Mind* he doesn't lose his ticket!

mind out [*phrasal verb*] *Brit* — used to tell someone to be careful ▪ *Mind out*—one of the steps is missing! ▪ There's a car coming! *Mind out*! [=*look out, watch out*]

mind the store (*US*) *or Brit* ***mind the shop*** : to be in charge of a place when the person who is usually in charge is not there ▪ Who's *minding the store* while the boss is away?

mind you informal — used in speech to give stress to a statement that you are making so that a preceding or following statement will not be misunderstood ▪ His advice wasn't very helpful. I'm not criticizing him, *mind you*. ▪ *Mind you*, I'm not criticizing him, but the truth is that his advice wasn't very helpful. — often used in British English without *you* ▪ His advice wasn't very helpful. I'm not criticizing him, *mind*!

mind your own business see BUSINESS

mind your step see ¹STEP

never mind **1** — used to tell someone not to worry about something ▪ *Never mind* your mistake: it wasn't serious. ▪ So you made a little mistake! *Never mind* (about that): it wasn't serious. ▪ Do you know where my keys are? Oh, *never mind*. Here they are. **2** — used to refer to something that is even less likely or possible than the thing previously mentioned ▪ I can barely understand it, *never mind* [=*let alone, much less*] explain it.

never you mind informal — used to tell someone that you will not be answering a question ▪ "Just how old are you anyway?" "*Never you mind*!"

mind–al·ter·ing /ˈmaɪndˌɑːltərɪŋ/ *adj* : causing changes to the mind or to behavior ▪ *mind-altering* drugs

mind–bend·ing /ˈmaɪndˌbɛndɪŋ/ *adj*

1 : causing changes to the mind or to behavior : MIND-ALTERING ▪ *mind-bending* drugs

2 [*more* ~; *most* ~] *informal* : very confusing, exciting, etc. : MIND-BLOWING ▪ a *mind-bending* experience ▪ *mind-bending* special effects

– mind–bend·ing·ly *adv*

mind–blow·ing /ˈmaɪndˌblowɪŋ/ *adj* [*more* ~; *most* ~] *informal* : very confusing, exciting, or shocking ▪ The power of her performance was positively *mind-blowing*. ▪ a *mind-blowing* [=*mind-boggling*] number of possibilities — see also *blow someone's mind* at ¹MIND

– mind–blow·ing·ly *adv*

mind–bog·gling /ˈmaɪndˌbɑːglɪŋ/ *adj* [*more* ~; *most* ~] *informal* : having a very powerful or overwhelming effect on the mind ▪ a *mind-boggling* [=*stunning*] performance : amazingly or confusingly large, great, etc. ▪ a *mind-boggling* array of options ▪ He received a *mind-boggling* $200 million in pay. ▪ The sheer vastness of space is *mind-boggling*.

– mind–bog·gling·ly *adv* ▪ *mind-bogglingly* large numbers

mind·ed /ˈmaɪndəd/ *adj*

1 a : having a particular kind of mind — used in combination ▪ narrow-*minded* ▪ open-*minded* ▪ closed-*minded* **b** : interested in or concerned about a particular subject — used in combination ▪ bargain-*minded* customers ▪ She's very health-*minded*. [=she is very concerned about doing things that promote good health]

2 *Brit, formal* : having a desire or intention *to do* something ▪ The government is *minded* [=*inclined, disposed*] *to grant* their request.

mind·er /ˈmaɪndɚ/ *noun, pl* **-ers** [*count*] *Brit, informal* : BODYGUARD ▪ The reporters were kept away by the celebrity's *minders*. — see also NETMINDER

mind·ful /ˈmaɪndfəl/ *adj* [*more* ~; *most* ~] : aware of something that may be important — often + *of* ▪ Investors should be *mindful of* current political trends. — often + *that* ▪ Investors should be *mindful that* political trends may influence the market.

– mind·ful·ly /ˈmaɪndfəli/ *adv* **– mind·ful·ness** *noun* [*noncount*]

mind·less /ˈmaɪndləs/ *adj*

1 a : having or showing no ability to think, feel, or respond ▪ a *mindless* killer ▪ a *mindless* bureaucracy **b** : showing no use of intelligence or thought ▪ *mindless* devotion to fashion ▪ The article was a *mindless* piece of nonsense. : having no purpose ▪ The movie has been criticized for its *mindless* violence. ▪ a *mindless* waste of time **c** : requiring very little attention or thought ▪ *mindless* activity/work

2 : not aware *of* something : not mindful *of* something ▪ He seemed to be completely *mindless of* the danger he was facing. ▪ She was *mindless of* her appearance.

– mind·less·ly *adv* ▪ a *mindlessly* violent movie **– mind·less·ness** *noun* [*noncount*]

mind–numb·ing /ˈmaɪndˌnʌmɪŋ/ *adj* [*more* ~; *most* ~] *informal* : very dull or boring ▪ *mind-numbing* work

– mind–numb·ing·ly *adv* ▪ *mind-numbingly* dull

mind reader *noun, pl* ~ **-ers** [*count*] : someone who is able to know another person's thoughts without being told what they are : someone who is able to read minds ▪ How was I

M

supposed to know what you were thinking? I'm no *mind reader.* • "I think we should eat out tonight." "You must be a *mind reader*: that's just what I was thinking myself!"

– mind reading *noun [noncount]*

mind–set /ˈmaɪndˌsɛt/ *noun, pl* **-sets** *[count]* **:** a particular way of thinking **:** a person's attitude or set of opinions about something • politicians trying to understand the *mind-set* of voters • a conservative/liberal *mind-set*

¹mine /ˈmaɪn/ *pronoun*

1 : that which belongs to me **:** my one **:** my ones • The book is *mine.* [=it is my book] • Those books are *mine.* [=those are my books] • *Mine* is the book on the left. [=my book is the one on the left] • His eyes are blue and *mine* are brown. • a former professor/friend ***of mine*** [=one of my former professors/friends]

2 *Brit, informal* **:** my home **:** my place • Let's go back to *mine* for a drink.

²mine *noun, pl* **mines** *[count]*

1 : a pit or tunnel from which minerals (such as coal, gold, diamonds, etc.) are taken — see also GOLD MINE, STRIP MINE

2 : a bomb that is placed in the ground or in water and that explodes when it is touched — see also LAND MINE

3 : a rich source of something (such as information) • He has proven to be a *mine* [=*gold mine*] of information. [=he has provided a large amount of information]

³mine *verb* **mines; mined; min•ing**

1 a : to dig a mine in order to find and take away coal, gold, diamonds, etc. — usually *+ for* *[no obj]* The area was soon filled with prospectors who were *mining for* gold. *[+ obj]* Prospectors *mined* the region *for* diamonds. **b** *[+ obj]* **:** to find and take away (coal, gold, diamonds, etc.) from a mine • Local people were hired to *mine* the gold.

2 *[+ obj]* **:** to search for something valuable in (something) — usually *+ for* • Police have been *mining* the tapes *for* information. [=they have been listening to the tapes in order to get information from them]

3 *[+ obj]* **:** to put mines (sense 2) in or under (something) • The enemy had *mined* the harbor. • The road was *mined.*

mine•field /ˈmaɪnˌfiːld/ *noun, pl* **-fields** *[count]*

1 : an area of land or water that contains mines (sense 2)

2 : something that has many dangers or risks • This issue is a political *minefield.*

min•er /ˈmaɪnɚ/ *noun, pl* **-ers** *[count]* **:** a person who works in a mine • coal/gold *miners*

min•er•al /ˈmɪnərəl/ *noun, pl* **-als** *[count]*

1 : a substance (such as quartz, coal, petroleum, salt, etc.) that is naturally formed under the ground

2 : a chemical substance (such as iron or zinc) that occurs naturally in certain foods and that is important for good health • an adequate supply of vitamins and *minerals*

min•er•al•o•gy /ˌmɪnəˈrɑːləʤi/ *noun [noncount]* **:** the scientific study of minerals

– min•er•al•og•i•cal /ˌmɪnərəˈlɑːʤɪkəl/ *adj* **– min•er•al•o•gist** /ˌmɪnəˈrɑːləʤɪst/ *noun, pl* **-gists** *[count]*

mineral water *noun, pl* **~ -ters** *[count, noncount]* **:** water that contains mineral salts and gases (such as carbon dioxide) • a glass of *mineral water*

min•e•stro•ne /ˌmɪnəˈstroʊni/ *noun [noncount]* **:** a thick Italian soup that is usually made with beans, vegetables, and pasta

mine•sweep•er /ˈmaɪnˌswiːpɚ/ *noun, pl* **-ers** *[count]* **:** a ship designed for removing or destroying mines

min•gle /ˈmɪŋgəl/ *verb* **min•gles; min•gled; min•gling**

1 : to combine or bring together two or more things *[+ obj]* The story *mingles* fact and/with fiction. *[no obj]* Several flavors *mingle* in the stew. • It's a story in which fact *mingles* with fiction.

2 *[no obj]* **:** to move around during a party, meeting, etc., and talk informally with different people • The host was too busy to *mingle* during the party. — often *+ with* • The speaker stayed to *mingle with* the audience after the lecture. — see also INTERMINGLE

min•gy /ˈmɪnʤi/ *adj* **min•gi•er; -est** *chiefly Brit, informal*

1 : not liking to spend money **:** STINGY • a *mingy* uncle

2 : not large enough • a *mingy* portion of food

– min•gi•ness *noun [noncount]*

mini /ˈmɪni/ *noun, pl* **minis** *[count]* **:** a very short skirt **:** MINISKIRT

mini- *combining form* **:** smaller or shorter than usual or normal **:** MINIATURE • *mini*bike • *mini*skirt

¹min•i•a•ture /ˈmɪnijəˌʧuɚ/ *adj, always used before a noun* **:** very small **:** TINY • a collection of *miniature* books • a *miniature* tea set • a *miniature* camera • The little boy looks like a *miniature* version of his father. • a *miniature* poodle [=a poodle that is bred to be smaller than normal; a poodle breed that is smaller than the normal breed]

²miniature *noun, pl* **-tures** *[count]* **:** a very small sculpture, portrait, or painting • She collects porcelain *miniatures.*

in miniature **:** in a very small form **:** on a very small scale • The model depicts the project *in miniature.* • The little boy looks like his father *in miniature.*

miniature golf *noun [noncount] US* **:** a golf game played with a putter on a small course that has various obstacles at each hole — called also *(US) minigolf, (Brit) crazy golf*

min•i•a•tur•ize *also Brit* **min•i•a•tur•ise** /ˈmɪnijəʧəˌraɪz/ *verb* **-iz•es; -ized; -iz•ing** *[+ obj]* **:** to design or make (something) in a very small size • Technology has made it possible to *miniaturize* electronic circuits. • a *miniaturized* radio

– min•i•a•tur•i•za•tion *also Brit* **min•i•a•tur•i•sa•tion** /ˌmɪnijəˌʧurəˈzeɪʃən/ *noun [noncount]*

mini•bar /ˈmɪniˌbɑɚ/ *noun, pl* **-bars** *[count]* **:** a small refrigerator in a hotel room that has drinks inside it for guests

mini•bike /ˈmɪniˌbaɪk/ *noun, pl* **-bikes** *[count] US* **:** a small motorcycle

mini•bus /ˈmɪniˌbʌs/ *noun, pl* **-bus•es** *[count]* **:** a small bus or van

mini•cab /ˈmɪniˌkæb/ *noun, pl* **-cabs** *[count] Brit* **:** a taxi that only picks up customers who call by telephone

mini•golf /ˈmɪniˌgɑːlf/ *noun [noncount] US* **:** MINIATURE GOLF

min•im /ˈmɪnəm/ *noun, pl* **-ims** *[count] Brit* **:** HALF NOTE

minima *plural of* ¹MINIMUM

min•i•mal /ˈmɪnəməl/ *adj [more ~; most ~]* **:** very small or slight in size or amount • The storm caused *minimal* damage. • The costs were *minimal.* • areas at *minimal* risk for flooding • They made the repairs with *minimal* disruption [=with the least possible disruption] to the schedule.

– min•i•mal•ly *adv* • a *minimally* adequate supply • a *minimally* useful tool

min•i•mal•ist /ˈmɪnəməlɪst/ *adj* **:** of, relating to, or following a style in art, literature, or music that is very simple and uses a small number of colors, parts, materials, etc. • *minimalist* art • a *minimalist* artist

– min•i•mal•ism /ˈmɪnəməˌlɪzəm/ *noun [noncount]* • a student of *minimalism* **– minimalist** *noun, pl* **-ists** *[count]* • artists who are *minimalists*

min•i•mize *or Brit* **min•i•mise** /ˈmɪnəˌmaɪz/ *verb* **-miz•es; -mized; -miz•ing** *[+ obj]*

1 : to make (something bad or not wanted) as small as possible • We need to *minimize* the chance of error. • The company will work to *minimize* costs.

2 : to treat or describe (something) as smaller or less important than it is • I don't want to *minimize* the contributions he has made to the company. • During the interview, she *minimized* her weaknesses and emphasized her strengths.

3 *computers* **:** to make (a program's window) change to a very small form that takes almost no room on a computer's screen • Please *minimize* all open windows. — opposite MAXIMIZE

– min•i•mi•za•tion *or Brit* **min•i•mi•sa•tion** /ˌmɪnəməˈzeɪʃən, *Brit* ˌmɪnəˌmaɪˈzeɪʃən/ *noun [noncount]*

¹min•i•mum /ˈmɪnəməm/ *noun, pl* **min•i•mums** *or technical* **min•i•ma** /ˈmɪnəmə/ *[count]* **:** the lowest number or amount that is possible or allowed — usually singular • Ten years is the *minimum* needed. = We'll need 10 years ***at a/the minimum.*** [=we'll need at least 10 years] • We need to keep expenses ***to a (bare) minimum.*** [=we need to keep expenses as low as possible] — often *+ of* • Refrigerate the dough for a *minimum of* two hours. [=for at least two hours] • She will serve a *minimum of* 10 years in jail. — opposite MAXIMUM

²minimum *adj, always used before a noun* **:** least or lowest possible in amount or degree • They made the repairs with *minimum* [=*minimal*] disruption to the schedule. • What are the *minimum* requirements for the job? • *minimum* height/weight • The *minimum* sentence for her crime is 10 years. • a ***minimum security prison*** [=a prison in which prisoners are allowed more freedom than in most other prisons because they are not considered dangerous or likely to escape] — opposite MAXIMUM

³minimum *adv* **:** at the least • She will serve 10 years *minimum.* [=the least amount of time she will serve is 10 years]

minimum wage *noun [singular]* **:** an amount of money

that is the least amount of money per hour that workers must be paid according to the law ▪ Congress will vote on a bill to raise the *minimum wage.*

min·ing /ˈmaɪnɪŋ/ *noun* [*noncount*] : the process or business of digging in mines to obtain minerals, metals, jewels, etc. ▪ He works in *mining.* ▪ the *mining* industry

min·ion /ˈmɪnjən/ *noun, pl* **-ions** [*count*] : someone who is not powerful or important and who obeys the orders of a powerful leader or boss ▪ one of the boss's *minions*

mini·se·ries /ˈmɪniˌsiriz/ *noun, pl* **miniseries** [*count*] : a story on television that is shown in two or more parts on different days

mini·skirt /ˈmɪniˌskɚt/ *noun, pl* **-skirts** [*count*] : a very short skirt — called also *mini*; see color picture on page C14

[1]**min·is·ter** /ˈmɪnəstɚ/ *noun, pl* **-ters** [*count*]
1 : a person whose job involves leading church services, performing religious ceremonies (such as marriages), and providing spiritual or religious guidance to other people : a member of the clergy in some Protestant churches
2 : an official who heads a government department or a major section of a department in some countries (such as Britain) ▪ (*Brit*) the *Minister* of Defence [=(*US*) the Secretary of Defense] — see also PRIME MINISTER
3 : a person who represents his or her own government while living in a foreign country

[2]**minister** *verb* **-ters; -tered; -ter·ing**
minister to [*phrasal verb*] ***minister to (someone or something)*** : to help or care for (someone or something) ▪ She devoted herself to *ministering to* the poor and sick. ▪ The nurse *ministered to* his wounds.

min·is·te·ri·al /ˌmɪnəˈstirijəl/ *adj, always used before a noun* : of or relating to a government minister ▪ She holds a *ministerial* office. ▪ *ministerial* meetings/duties ▪ They function in a *ministerial* capacity in the embassy.

min·is·tra·tions /ˌmɪnəˈstreɪʃənz/ *noun* [*plural*] *formal + humorous* : actions done to help someone ▪ She recovered quickly despite the *ministrations* of her doctor.

min·is·try /ˈmɪnəstri/ *noun, pl* **-tries**
1 a ***the ministry*** : religious leaders as a group : ministers as a group ▪ a member of *the ministry* **b :** the office, duties, or work of a religious minister [*count*] — usually singular ▪ His *ministry* is among the city's immigrants. [*noncount*] She learned a lot during her first year of *ministry.* ▪ When did he enter the *ministry*? [=when did he start doing religious work?; when did he become a minister?]
2 [*count*] **:** a government department or the building in which it is located ▪ (*Brit*) the *Ministry* of Defence [=(*US*) Department of Defense]

mini·van /ˈmɪniˌvæn/ *noun, pl* **-vans** [*count*] : a small van — called also (*Brit*) *people carrier,* (*Brit*) *people mover*; see picture at CAR

mink /ˈmɪŋk/ *noun, pl* **mink** *or* **minks**
1 [*count*] **:** a small animal that has a thin body and soft, dark brown fur
2 a [*noncount*] **:** the skin and fur of a mink used for making clothing ▪ a coat made of *mink* ▪ a *mink* coat
b [*count*] **:** a piece of clothing (such as a coat) made of mink ▪ women wearing expensive jewelry and *minks*

mink

min·now /ˈmɪnoʊ/ *noun, pl* **min·nows** *also* **minnow** [*count*] : a very small fish that is often used as bait to catch larger fish

[1]**mi·nor** /ˈmaɪnɚ/ *adj*
1 a : not very important or valuable ▪ a *minor* artist/author/celebrity ▪ Her role in the project was *minor.* ▪ a *minor* component/part ▪ I'm not worried about *minor* details. ▪ a *minor* news story ▪ *minor* characters ▪ Doctors described her recovery as a ***minor miracle.*** [=her health was very bad and doctors were not sure if she would recover] **b** *always used before a noun* : small in number, quantity, or extent ▪ The grant covered only a *minor* part of the cost.
2 : not very serious : not causing much trouble or damage ▪ a *minor* illness/injury/setback ▪ The delay will be *minor.* ▪ a very *minor* annoyance/accident ▪ a *minor* earthquake ▪ *minor* errors/mistakes ▪ He suffered a *minor* heart attack.
3 *music* **a :** having semitones between the second and third, the fifth and sixth, and sometimes the seventh and eighth notes in a scale ▪ a *minor* scale **b :** based on a minor scale ▪ a *minor* key — compare [1]MAJOR 3
4 *always used before a noun* : not yet old enough to have the rights of an adult ▪ He has *minor* children living in the house.

[2]**minor** *noun, pl* **-nors** [*count*]
1 : a person who is not yet old enough to have the rights of an adult ▪ families with children who are still *minors* ▪ The nightclub was shut down for selling alcohol to a *minor.*
2 *US* **:** a second subject studied by a college or university student in addition to a main subject ▪ She majored in chemistry with a *minor* in biology. — compare [2]MAJOR 2
the minors *US, informal* : the minor leagues of baseball ▪ He spent his entire career in *the minors.*

[3]**minor** *verb* **-nors; -nored; -nor·ing**
minor in [*phrasal verb*] ***minor in (something)*** *US* : to have (a specified second subject of study) in addition to your main subject ▪ In college, she majored in chemistry and *minored in* biology.

mi·nor·i·ty /məˈnorəti/ *noun, pl* **-ties**
1 [*singular*] **:** a number or amount that is less than half of a total ▪ The proposal is opposed by a *minority* of voters.
2 [*singular*] **:** the group that is the smaller part of a larger group ▪ The Republicans/Democrats are now the *minority* in the Senate. ▪ Opponents of the new law appear to be ***in the minority.*** [=there are fewer people who oppose the new law than who support it]
3 [*count*] **a :** a group of people who are different from the larger group in a country, area, etc., in some way (such as race or religion) ▪ the country's ethnic *minorities* ▪ The group is becoming an influential *minority* in the community. **b** *chiefly US* **:** a member of such a group — usually plural ▪ The college encouraged women and *minorities* to apply. ▪ The company is making an effort to hire more *minorities.*
4 [*noncount*] *law* **:** the time or period when a person is not yet old enough to have the full rights of an adult — compare MAJORITY 3
– minority *adj, always used before a noun* ▪ Republicans/Democrats are the *minority* party in the Senate. ▪ a *minority* group

minority leader *noun, pl* **~ -ers** [*count*] : the leader of the political party that has fewer members than the leading party in the U.S. Senate or House of Representatives ▪ the House/Senate *minority leader* — compare MAJORITY LEADER

minor league *noun, pl* **~ leagues** [*count*] : a professional baseball league that is not one of the major leagues — usually plural ▪ He spent many years in the *minor leagues* before being called up to the major leagues.; *also* : a league of lesser importance in another sport (such as hockey or football) — compare MAJOR LEAGUES
– minor–league *adj* ▪ *minor-league* baseball — sometimes used figuratively ▪ These problems are *minor-league.* [=these problems are not serious] **– minor lea·guer** *noun, pl* **~ -guers** [*count*] ▪ He was a *minor leaguer* before he was drafted into the majors. — sometimes used figuratively ▪ The police decided he was a *minor leaguer* in the drug trafficking world.

min·strel /ˈmɪnstrəl/ *noun, pl* **-strels** [*count*]
1 : a musical entertainer in the Middle Ages ▪ a wandering *minstrel*
2 *US* **:** a member of a group of entertainers who performed black American songs and jokes usually with blackened faces ▪ a *minstrel* show ✧ Minstrel shows were popular in the 19th and early 20th centuries.

[1]**mint** /ˈmɪnt/ *noun, pl* **mints**
1 [*noncount*] **:** an herb that has a strong pleasant smell and taste and that is used in medicine and food — see color picture on page C6
2 [*count*] **:** a piece of candy that tastes like mint
– compare [2]MINT
– minty /ˈmɪnti/ *adj* **mint·i·er; -est** ▪ a *minty* flavor

[2]**mint** *noun, pl* **mints**
1 [*count*] **:** a place where coins are made — usually used with *the* ▪ coins shipped directly from *the mint*
2 [*singular*] *informal* **:** a large amount of money ▪ He made a *mint* [=he earned a large sum of money] in real estate. ▪ Her family is worth a *mint.* [=is very wealthy]
in mint condition ✧ If something is *in mint condition,* it is in perfect condition, just as if it were new. ▪ He kept the car *in mint condition.*
– compare [1]MINT

[3]**mint** *verb* **mints; mint·ed; mint·ing** [+ *obj*] : to make (coins) out of metal ▪ coins that were *minted* before 1965 ▪ We *mint* coins out of copper.

min·u·et /ˌmɪnjəˈwɛt/ *noun, pl* **-ets** [*count*]
1 : a slow, graceful dance that was popular in the 17th and 18th centuries ▪ danced a *minuet*
2 : the music for a minuet ▪ The orchestra played a *minuet.*

[1]mi·nus /ˈmaɪnəs/ *prep*
1 — used to indicate that one number or amount is being subtracted from another ▪ 10 *minus* 5 equals/is 5. ▪ We earned 600 dollars *minus* travel expenses. [=the amount we earned was less than 600 dollars because we had to pay for travel expenses]
2 *informal* **:** not having (something) **:** WITHOUT ▪ He left the restaurant *minus* his hat. ▪ a fruit that looks like a peach, *minus* the fuzz ▪ The lower 48 states are all the United States *minus* Alaska and Hawaii. [=not counting or including Alaska and Hawaii]
plus or minus see [3]PLUS

[2]minus *noun, pl* **-nus·es** [*count*]
1 *informal* **:** a problem or disadvantage ▪ She decided that the pluses of owning a home outweighed the *minuses.* ▪ Some employers see a lack of experience as a real *minus.*
2 *mathematics* **:** MINUS SIGN ▪ Put the *minus* to the left of the number.

[3]minus *adj*
1 *always used before a noun* **:** having a value that is below zero **:** NEGATIVE ▪ a *minus* quantity ▪ *minus* 3 ▪ The temperature was *minus* 10. [=10 degrees below zero] **— opposite** [1]PLUS 1
2 — used following a grade (such as A, B, or C) to show that the work is slightly worse than the letter by itself would indicate ▪ I got a B *minus* on my English exam. ▪ The teacher said I could bring the C *minus* up to a C if I studied more. **— opposite** [1]PLUS 2
***on the minus side* —** used to describe the less appealing or attractive part of something ▪ *On the minus side,* the job doesn't pay well, but on the plus side, the work is easy.

mi·nus·cule /ˈmɪnəˌskjuːl/ *adj* **:** very small ▪ a *minuscule* [=*tiny*] house/apartment/garden

minus sign *noun, pl* **~ signs** [*count*] *mathematics* **:** the symbol – used to show that a number is being subtracted from another number or that a quantity is less than zero **— compare** PLUS SIGN

[1]min·ute /ˈmɪnət/ *noun, pl* **-utes**
1 [*count*] **a :** a unit of time equal to 60 seconds **:** one 60th of an hour ▪ Bake the cake for 25–30 *minutes.* ▪ We waited for several *minutes,* but no one came to the door. ▪ He can run a six-*minute* mile. [=he can run a mile in six minutes] **b :** a brief period of time **:** MOMENT ▪ I saw him a *minute* ago. ▪ Dinner will be ready in just a few *minutes.* ▪ One *minute* it was sunny, the next it was pouring rain. ▪ Could I have a *minute* of your time? = Do you have a *minute*? = Could I speak to you for a *minute*? [=could I speak to you briefly?] ▪ I'm coming, just give me a *minute.* [=wait for me] ▪ It was an excellent show. I enjoyed every *minute* of it. [=I enjoyed all of it] ▪ I'll explain that ***in a minute*** [=shortly, soon] **— see also** LAST MINUTE
2 [*count*] **:** the distance that can be traveled in a minute ▪ My house is just a few *minutes* from here.
3 ***minutes*** [*plural*] **:** an official record of what was said and done in a meeting ▪ The secretary read the *minutes* of the last meeting. ▪ The secretary took the *minutes* [=recorded in writing what happened] during the meeting.
4 [*count*] *technical* **:** one of 60 equal parts into which a degree can be divided for measuring angles ▪ 42 degrees and 30 *minutes*
a laugh a minute see [2]LAUGH
any minute ✧ If something could happen **(*at*) *any minute* (*now*)**, it could happen very soon. ▪ The bus should be here *any minute now.* ▪ I'm expecting a phone call *any minute.* ▪ Things could change *at any minute.* [=*at any moment*]
at/on a minute's notice see [1]NOTICE
from minute to minute *or* ***from one minute to the next*** *or* ***minute by minute* :** very quickly as time passes ▪ Things kept changing *from minute to minute.* [=*from moment to moment*]
hold/hang on a minute *or* ***wait/just a minute*** *informal* **1 —** used to tell someone to wait or to stop for a brief time ▪ "Aren't you finished yet?" "*Hold on a minute.* I'm almost done." ▪ *Hang on a minute*—I didn't hear you. Could you repeat what you said? **2 —** used to express surprise or disbelief ▪ Hey, *wait a minute*! That's not what you said yesterday!
just this minute see [2]JUST
***not for a/one minute* :** at no time **:** not at all **:** NEVER ▪ I did *not* believe her *for one minute.* = *Not for one minute* did I believe her. [=I never believed her]
***the minute* :** as soon as ▪ Please call me *the minute* you get home. ▪ I knew *the minute* (that) I saw it that I had to have this dress.
***this minute* :** right now **:** IMMEDIATELY ▪ Stop it *this minute*! ▪ I have to have the report *this minute.*
***to the minute* :** exactly or precisely ▪ The buses were on time *to the minute.* **— see also** UP-TO-THE-MINUTE
***within minutes* :** within a very short amount of time ▪ We called an ambulance and it arrived *within minutes.*

[2]mi·nute /maɪˈnuːt, *Brit* maɪˈnjuːt/ *adj* **mi·nut·er; -est** [*or more* ~; *most* ~]
1 : very small **:** TINY ▪ There were *minute* particles of dust in the air. ▪ The test detected *minute* amounts of contamination. ▪ The equipment is able to detect the *minutest* errors.
2 : very complete and precise ▪ She told him what happened in *minute* detail. ▪ a *minute* examination of the evidence
— mi·nute·ly *adv* ▪ a *minutely* detailed drawing ▪ studied the evidence *minutely*

minute hand *noun, pl* **~ hands** [*count*] **:** the long hand that marks the minutes on a watch or clock **— compare** HOUR HAND, SECOND HAND

min·ute·man /ˈmɪnətˌmæn/ *noun, pl* **-men** /-ˌmɛn/ [*count*] **:** a member of a group of men who fought on the side of the American colonies and who were ready to go quickly into battle during the American Revolution

mi·nu·ti·ae /məˈnuːʃiˌiː, *Brit* məˈnjuːʃiˌiː/ *noun* [*plural*] **:** small or minor details ▪ the *minutiae* of daily life ▪ He was bewildered by the contract's *minutiae.*

minx /ˈmɪŋks/ *noun, pl* **minx·es** [*count*] *old-fashioned* **:** a sexually attractive and playful woman who often causes trouble ▪ a clever little *minx*

mir·a·cle /ˈmirɪkəl/ *noun, pl* **-a·cles** [*count*]
1 : an unusual or wonderful event that is believed to be caused by the power of God ▪ a divine *miracle* ▪ She believed that God had given her the power to work/perform *miracles.* ▪ a *miracle* worker [=a person who is able to work/perform miracles]
2 : a very amazing or unusual event, thing, or achievement ▪ It would take a *miracle* for this team to win. ▪ The bridge is a *miracle* of engineering. = The bridge is an engineering *miracle.* ▪ the *miracle* of birth ▪ It's a (minor) *miracle* that he succeeded. ▪ the *miracle* of his recovery ▪ She worked *miracles* with those kids. [=she accomplished wonderful things with those kids] ▪ a ***miracle drug/cure*** [=a drug/cure that is extremely or amazingly effective] ▪ These days, thanks to ***the miracle of television,*** we can watch events happening on the other side of the world. ▪ ***By some miracle,*** I was on time for work every day this week. [=it is surprising/amazing that I was on time for work every day this week]

mi·rac·u·lous /məˈrækjələs/ *adj* [*more* ~; *most* ~] **:** very wonderful or amazing like a miracle ▪ He made a *miraculous* recovery after the accident. ▪ Her memory is nothing short of *miraculous.*
— mi·rac·u·lous·ly *adv* ▪ *Miraculously,* no one was hurt.

mi·rage /məˈrɑːʒ, *Brit* ˈmɪrɑːʒ/ *noun, pl* **-rag·es** [*count*]
1 : something (such as a pool of water in the middle of a desert) that is seen and appears to be real but that is not actually there
2 : something that you hope for or want but that is not possible or real ▪ A peaceful solution proved to be a *mirage.*

Mi·ran·da /məˈrændə/ *adj, always used before a noun, US, law* **:** of or relating to the legal rights of an arrested person to have an attorney and to refuse to answer questions ▪ ***Miranda rights*** ▪ The suspect was given a ***Miranda warning.*** [=was told about his Miranda rights]

mire /ˈmajɚ/ *noun* **:** thick and deep mud [*noncount*] The troops marched onward through the muck and the *mire.* **—** often used figuratively ▪ stuck in the *mire* of cynicism ▪ The economy is sinking deeper into the *mire.* [=the economy is bad and getting worse] ▪ His name/reputation has been ***dragged through the mire*** [=has been unfairly damaged or ruined] [*singular*] They found themselves in a *mire* of debt. [=they could not get out of debt]

mired /ˈmajɚd/ *adj, not used before a noun*
1 : stuck in a very difficult situation ▪ She was *mired* in work all weekend. ▪ He has been *mired* in controversy throughout his term in office. ▪ The company is *mired* in legal troubles.
2 : stuck in deep mud ▪ The car was *mired* in the muck.

[1]mir·ror /ˈmirɚ/ *noun, pl* **-rors** [*count*]

1 : a piece of glass that reflects images ▪ She saw her reflection in the *mirror.* = She looked at herself in the *mirror.* ▪ a bathroom *mirror* — see pictures at BATHROOM, CAR; see also REARVIEW MIRROR

2 : something that shows what another thing is like in a very clear and accurate way — usually singular ▪ Her art is a *mirror* of modern American culture.

— see also SMOKE AND MIRRORS

– **mir·rored** /ˈmirəd/ *adj* ▪ a *mirrored* wall [=a wall that has a mirror or mirrors on it] ▪ *mirrored* glass

²mirror *verb* **-rors; -rored; -ror·ing** [+ *obj*]

1 : to be very similar to (something) ▪ Her mood *mirrored* the gloomy weather. [=her mood was gloomy like the weather] **:** to show (something) in a very clear and accurate way ▪ Her art *mirrors* [=*reflects*] modern American culture.

2 : to show the image of (something) on a surface **:** REFLECT ▪ The building was *mirrored* in the lake.

mirror image *noun, pl* **~ -ages** [*count*]

1 : something that looks like something else but with its left and right sides reversed ▪ The left hand and the right hand are *mirror images* (of each other). = The left hand is the/a *mirror image* of the right hand. ▪ The left side of the building is a *mirror image* of the right.

2 : someone who looks like someone else ▪ He's the *mirror image* [=(more commonly) *spitting image*] of his father. [=he looks just like his father]

mirth /ˈmɚθ/ *noun* [*noncount*] *formal + literary* **:** happiness and laughter ▪ Her clumsy attempt to cut the cake was the cause of much *mirth.*

– **mirth·ful** /ˈmɚθfəl/ *adj* [*more ~; most ~*] ▪ He was in a *mirthful* mood.

mirth·less /ˈmɚθləs/ *adj* [*more ~; most ~*] *formal + literary* **:** showing or feeling no happiness or pleasure ▪ a *mirthless* smile/laugh

mis- /mɪs/ *prefix*

1 : badly **:** wrongly ▪ *mis*judge ▪ *mis*file ▪ *mis*behave

2 : bad **:** wrong ▪ *mis*understanding ▪ *mis*deed ▪ *mis*diagnosis

3 : opposite or lack of ▪ *mis*trust

mis·ad·ven·ture /ˌmɪsədˈvɛnʧɚ/ *noun, pl* **-tures** [*count*] **:** an unlucky event or occurrence **:** a bad experience or accident that is usually minor ▪ His vacation turned into a series of *misadventures.*

death by misadventure *Brit, law* **:** death caused by an accident ▪ a verdict of *death by misadventure*

mis·an·thrope /ˈmɪsn̩ˌθroʊp/ *noun, pl* **-thropes** [*count*] *formal* **:** a person who does not like other people

mis·an·thro·py /mɪsˈænθrəpi/ *noun* [*noncount*] *formal* **:** dislike or hatred of other people — compare PHILANTHROPY

– **mis·an·throp·ic** /ˌmɪsn̩ˈθrɑːpɪk/ *adj* [*more ~; most ~*] ▪ She became increasingly *misanthropic* in her old age.

mis·ap·ply /ˌmɪsəˈplaɪ/ *verb* **-plies; -plied; -ply·ing** [+ *obj*] **:** to use (something) incorrectly or in a way that was not intended ▪ a list of words that are often *misapplied* ▪ He has been accused of *misapplying* public funds.

– **mis·ap·pli·ca·tion** /mɪsˌæpləˈkeɪʃən/ *noun, pl* **-tions** [*count, noncount*] ▪ *misapplication* of public funds

mis·ap·pre·hen·sion /mɪsˌæprəˈhɛnʃən/ *noun, pl* **-sions** *formal* **:** an incorrect understanding of something **:** a wrong idea about something [*count*] He acted on/under the *misapprehension* that they would change their minds. [=he mistakenly thought that they would change their minds] [*noncount*] an error caused by *misapprehension* of the facts

labor under a misapprehension see ²LABOR

mis·ap·pro·pri·ate /ˌmɪsəˈproʊpriˌeɪt/ *verb* **-ates; -at·ed; -at·ing** [+ *obj*] *formal* **:** to take (something, such as money) dishonestly for your own use **:** to appropriate (something) wrongly ▪ They accused him of *misappropriating* town funds.

– **mis·ap·pro·pri·a·tion** /ˌmɪsəˌproʊpriˈeɪʃən/ *noun* [*noncount*] ▪ She was fired for the *misappropriation* of funds.

mis·be·got·ten /ˌmɪsbəˈgɑːtn/ *adj* [*more ~; most ~*] *formal* **:** badly planned or thought out ▪ He was sent on a *misbegotten* [=*misconceived*] diplomatic mission that was sure to fail.

mis·be·have /ˌmɪsbɪˈheɪv/ *verb* **-haves; -haved; -hav·ing** [*no obj*] **:** to behave badly ▪ The children *misbehaved* during dinner.

– **mis·be·hav·ior** (*US*) *or Brit* **mis·be·hav·iour** /ˌmɪsbɪˈheɪvjɚ/ *noun* [*noncount*] ▪ The children were punished for their *misbehavior.*

misc. *abbr* miscellaneous

mis·cal·cu·late /mɪsˈkælkjəˌleɪt/ *verb* **-lates; -lat·ed; -lat·ing**

1 : to make an error about the size or amount of something [+ *obj*] The waiter *miscalculated* our check. [*no obj*] Unless I *miscalculated,* we have about $500 left.

2 : to make an error in judging a situation [+ *obj*] She has clearly *miscalculated* the importance of her decision. [*no obj*] He realized that he had *miscalculated* in thinking that his proposal would be welcome.

– **mis·cal·cu·la·tion** /mɪsˌkælkjəˈleɪʃən/ *noun, pl* **-tions** [*count*] The waiter made a slight *miscalculation.* [*noncount*] The discrepancy could be caused by mistake or *miscalculation.*

mis·car·riage /mɪsˈkerɪʤ/ *noun, pl* **-riag·es**

1 *medical* **:** a condition in which a pregnancy ends too early and does not result in the birth of a live baby [*count*] She had a *miscarriage.* ▪ a woman who has suffered/had multiple *miscarriages* [*noncount*] a high risk of *miscarriage*

2 [*count*] *law* **:** an unjust legal decision — used in the phrase ***miscarriage of justice*** ▪ His conviction was a tragic/grave/gross *miscarriage of justice.*

mis·car·ry /ˌmɪsˈkeri/ *verb* **-ries; -ried; -ry·ing** [*no obj*]

1 *medical* **:** to have a miscarriage **:** to experience the early and unexpected end of a pregnancy ▪ She *miscarried* at 13 weeks. = She *miscarried* when she was 13 weeks pregnant.

2 *formal* **:** to go wrong **:** to fail to achieve the intended purpose ▪ The plan *miscarried.*

mis·cast /ˌmɪsˈkæst, *Brit* ˌmɪsˈkɑːst/ *verb* **-casts; -cast; -cast·ing** [+ *obj*]

1 : to give (an actor) a role for which the actor is not suited — usually used as *(be) miscast* ▪ He *was miscast* in that film.

2 : to make bad choices in selecting actors for (something, such as a play or movie) — usually used as *(be) miscast* ▪ The play *was miscast.*

mis·ce·ge·na·tion /mɪˌsɛʤəˈneɪʃən/ *noun* [*noncount*] *formal* **:** sexual relations or marriage between people of two different races (such as a white person and a black person)

mis·cel·la·neous /ˌmɪsəˈleɪnijəs/ *adj, always used before a noun* [*more ~; most ~*] **:** including many things of different kinds ▪ a *miscellaneous* collection of tools ▪ *miscellaneous* expenses/items

mis·cel·la·ny /ˈmɪsəˌleɪni, *Brit* mɪˈsɛləni/ *noun, pl* **-nies** [*count*] **:** a mixture or collection of different things ▪ a *miscellany* of old toys

mis·chance /ˌmɪsˈʧæns, *Brit* ˌmɪsˈʧɑːns/ *noun, pl* **-chanc·es** *formal*

1 [*noncount*] **:** bad luck ▪ two enemies brought together by *mischance*

2 [*count*] **:** something caused by bad luck **:** MISFORTUNE ▪ a series of *mischances*

mis·chief /ˈmɪsʧəf/ *noun* [*noncount*]

1 : behavior or activity that is annoying but that is not meant to cause serious harm or damage ▪ Those children are always up to some *mischief.* = Those children are always getting into *mischief.* ▪ engaging in *mischief* ▪ It's hard to keep him out of *mischief.*

2 : a playful desire to cause trouble ▪ There was (a hint of) *mischief* in his eyes/smile.

3 *somewhat formal* **:** harmful behavior ▪ criminal/malicious *mischief*

mis·chie·vous /ˈmɪsʧəvəs/ *adj* [*more ~; most ~*]

1 : causing or tending to cause annoyance or minor harm or damage ▪ a *mischievous* puppy/child

2 : showing a playful desire to cause trouble ▪ *mischievous* behavior ▪ a *mischievous* smile

3 : intended to harm someone or someone's reputation ▪ *mischievous* gossip ▪ a *mischievous* lie

– **mis·chie·vous·ly** *adv* ▪ She smiled *mischievously.* – **mis·chie·vous·ness** *noun* [*noncount*]

mis·con·ceived /ˌmɪskənˈsiːvd/ *adj* [*more ~; most ~*] **:** poorly planned or thought out **:** badly conceived ▪ a *misconceived* notion ▪ a *misconceived* attempt to fix the system

mis·con·cep·tion /ˌmɪskənˈsɛpʃən/ *noun, pl* **-tions** [*count*] **:** a wrong or mistaken idea ▪ a common/popular *misconception* ▪ I'd like to clear up a few *misconceptions* about the schedule.

labor under a misconception see ²LABOR

mis·con·duct /mɪsˈkɑːndəkt/ *noun* [*noncount*] **:** wrong behavior **:** behavior or activity that is illegal or morally wrong ▪ He was forced to defend himself against charges of sexual *misconduct.* ▪ There have been reports of *misconduct* by several employees.

mis·con·strue /ˌmɪskənˈstruː/ *verb* **-strues; -strued; -stru·ing** [+ *obj*] *formal* **:** to understand (something) incor-

M

rectly • My words were *misconstrued.* • They could *misconstrue* our intentions. — compare CONSTRUE

mis·count /mɪsˈkaʊnt/ *verb* **-counts; -count·ed; -count·ing : to count (something) incorrectly** [+ *obj*] They believe the votes were *miscounted.* [*no obj*] He had to start counting again when he realized that he had *miscounted.*

mis·cre·ant /ˈmɪskrijənt/ *noun, pl* **-ants** [*count*] *formal* **: a person who does something that is illegal or morally wrong** • He supports tough penalties against corporate *miscreants.*

mis·deed /ˌmɪsˈdiːd/ *noun, pl* **-deeds** [*count*] *formal* **: a morally wrong or illegal act** • She threatened to expose to the public the *misdeeds* he had committed.

mis·de·mean·or (*US*) *or Brit* **mis·de·mean·our** /ˌmɪsdɪˈmiːnɚ/ *noun, pl* **-ors** [*count*] *law* **: a crime that is not very serious : a crime that is less serious than a felony** • He was charged with (committing) a *misdemeanor.*

mis·di·ag·nose /mɪsˈdajɪgˌnous/ *verb* **-nos·es; -nosed; -nos·ing** [+ *obj*] **: to form an incorrect opinion about the cause of (a disease or problem) : to incorrectly diagnose (a disease or problem)** • Her condition was *misdiagnosed* by several doctors.

mis·di·ag·no·sis /mɪsˌdajɪgˈnousəs/ *noun, pl* **-no·ses** /mɪsˌdajɪgˈnouˌsiːz/ **: an incorrect conclusion about the cause of a disease or problem : an incorrect diagnosis** [*count*] The doctor made a *misdiagnosis.* • Following several *misdiagnoses,* we finally discovered what the problem really was. [*noncount*] Without proper testing, the potential for *misdiagnosis* is high.

mis·di·rect /ˌmɪsdəˈrɛkt/ *verb* **-rects; -rect·ed; -rect·ing** [+ *obj*]

1 : to use or direct (something) in a way that is not correct or appropriate • I feel that his criticism of the government is *misdirected.* [=that his criticism is not deserved or appropriate] • badly *misdirected* energy/efforts

2 a : to send (someone or something) to the wrong place • Their mail was *misdirected* to our address. **b : to give (someone) incorrect information** • If he tells you he's not interested, he's trying to *misdirect* you.

– mis·di·rec·tion /ˌmɪsdəˈrɛkʃən/ *noun* [*noncount*]

mi·ser /ˈmaɪzɚ/ *noun, pl* **-sers** [*count*] *disapproving* **: a person who hates to spend money : a very stingy person** • a mean-spirited old *miser*

mis·er·a·ble /ˈmɪzərəbəl/ *adj* [*more ~; most ~*]

1 a : very unhappy • He had a *miserable* childhood. • My boss is making my life thoroughly/utterly *miserable* with her constant demands and criticism. • He felt lonely and *miserable* after his divorce. **b : very sick or unwell** • She drank too much and felt *miserable* [=*wretched, rotten*] the next day.

2 : very severe or unpleasant • I've had a *miserable* cold for the past week. • We've been having *miserable* weather. = The weather has been *miserable.*

3 : very poor in condition or quality • He lived in a *miserable* little shack. • *miserable* [=*wretched*] living conditions

4 *always used before a noun* **: very bad** • He did a *miserable* job making the sign. [=he made the sign very poorly] • The business was a *miserable* failure. • Their trip turned out to be a *miserable* experience. • She has a *miserable* temper. • the *miserable* state of the economy

5 *always used before a noun* **: deserving to be hated** • Their boss is a rotten, *miserable* tyrant.

– mis·er·a·bly /ˈmɪzərəbli/ *adv* • The business failed *miserably.* • *miserably* poor/unhappy

mi·ser·ly /ˈmaɪzɚli/ *adj* [*more ~; most ~*] *disapproving*

1 : hating to spend money • The team's *miserly* [=*stingy, tight-fisted*] owner refused to pay for new equipment.

2 : very small or too small amount • He was given a *miserly* raise. • *miserly* wages

– mi·ser·li·ness *noun* [*noncount*] • the *miserliness* of the team's owner

mis·ery /ˈmɪzəri/ *noun, pl* **-er·ies**

1 [*noncount*] **: extreme suffering or unhappiness** • The war brought *misery* to thousands of refugees. • They were living in overcrowded slums in conditions of great *misery.* • a source of human *misery* • the joy and *misery* of life

2 a [*count*] **: something that causes extreme suffering or unhappiness — usually plural** • He tends to exaggerate the *miseries* of his childhood. • the joys and *miseries* of life **b** [*singular*] **: a very unhappy or painful time or experience** • The last years of her life were a *misery.* • My former boss made my life a *misery.* [=my former boss made my life miserable] ✧ When an injured or sick animal is ***put out of its misery,*** it is killed so that it no longer has to suffer. This phrase is sometimes used to refer to people as well. • patients who are in constant pain and want to be *put out of their misery* • (*humorous*) I know you're all anxious to hear the results, so let me *put you out of your misery.* [=let me end your suffering by telling you the results] • The champion finally *put him out of his misery* by knocking him out in the fifth round. [=the champion was beating him badly and finally ended the fight by knocking him out]

3 [*singular*] *Brit, informal* **: an unhappy person who complains often or constantly : MISERY GUTS** • Stop being such a *misery.*

misery guts *noun* [*singular*] *Brit, informal* **: an unhappy person who complains often or constantly** • Lighten up: don't be such an old *misery guts*! [=*sourpuss*]

mis·file /ˈmɪsˌfajəl/ *verb* **-files; -filed; -fil·ing** [+ *obj*] **: to put (a document) in the wrong place : to file (something) in the wrong place** • I found papers that had been *misfiled.*

mis·fire /ˌmɪsˈfajɚ/ *verb* **-fires; -fired; -fir·ing** [*no obj*]

1 *of an engine* **: to fail to work properly because the fuel mixture burns at the wrong time**

2 *of a gun* **: to fail to fire properly : to fail to shoot a bullet**

3 : to fail to have an intended effect : to fail to work properly • The plan/joke *misfired.* [=the plan/joke did not have the effect it was meant to have]

– misfire *noun, pl* **-fires** [*count*] • an engine *misfire* • The joke was an unfortunate *misfire.*

mis·fit /ˈmɪsˌfɪt/ *noun, pl* **-fits** [*count*] **: a person who is different from other people and who does not seem to belong in a particular group or situation** • a social *misfit*

mis·for·tune /ˌmɪsˈfoɚtʃən/ *noun, pl* **-tunes**

1 [*noncount*] **: bad luck** • a victim of economic *misfortune* • She endured her *misfortune* without complaint. • It was my *misfortune* to be chosen first. • It was the worst movie I've ever had the *misfortune* to see. = (*chiefly US*) It was the worst movie I've ever had the *misfortune* of seeing.

2 [*count*] **: an unlucky condition or event** • Her injury was a great *misfortune.* • He blamed the party's *misfortunes* on poor leadership.

mis·giv·ing /ˌmɪsˈgɪvɪŋ/ *noun, pl* **-ings : a feeling of doubt about something : a feeling that something might not be right or might not work as planned — often + *about*** [*count*] **— usually plural** • Many people have expressed (deep/serious/grave) *misgivings about* her qualifications for the job. • I felt some *misgivings about* his ability to do the job. [*noncount*] I felt some *misgiving about* his ability to do the job. • They regarded the plan with *misgiving.*

mis·guid·ed /ˌmɪsˈgaɪdəd/ *adj* [*more ~; most ~*]

1 : having wrong or improper goals or values • She's been getting a lot of bad advice from *misguided* friends.

2 : resulting from wrong or improper goals or values • He blames the crisis on the government's *misguided* economic policies. • a *misguided* attempt/effort to help • *misguided* ideas/notions

– mis·guid·ed·ly *adv* • *misguidedly* attempting to help

mis·han·dle /ˌmɪsˈhændl/ *verb* **-han·dles; -han·dled; -han·dling** [+ *obj*]

1 : to deal with or manage (something) badly or incorrectly • The police *mishandled* the investigation.

2 : to touch or treat (something) in a way that causes damage • *mishandle* a package • Apples are easily bruised when they are *mishandled.*

3 *sports* **: to fail to catch or hold (a ball) properly** • The shortstop *mishandled* the throw. • The quarterback fumbled when he *mishandled* the snap.

– mis·han·dling *noun* [*noncount*] • The police have been criticized for their *mishandling* of the investigation.

mis·hap /ˈmɪsˌhæp/ *noun, pl* **-haps**

1 : a small mistake or amount of bad luck [*count*] We experienced the usual *mishaps* of a family vacation. [*noncount*] The ceremony proceeded ***without mishap.***

2 [*count*] **: an unlucky accident or mistake** • The fire was a tragic *mishap* that could have been prevented.

mis·hear /ˌmɪsˈhiɚ/ *verb* **-hears; -heard** /-ˈhɚd/; **-hear·ing** [+ *obj*] **: to hear (a person who is speaking) incorrectly** • You *misheard* me. I said I was feeling anxious, not angry. **: to hear (something that is said) incorrectly** • I must have *misheard* the instructions. • I *misheard* "mother" as "mutter."

mis·hit /ˌmɪsˈhɪt/ *verb* **-hits; -hit; -hit·ting** [+ *obj*] *sports* **: to hit (something, such as a ball) incorrectly** • She made a bogey after *mishitting* her tee shot.

– mishit *noun, pl* **-hits** [*count*]

mish·mash /ˈmɪʃˌmæʃ/ *noun* [*singular*] *informal* **: a con-**

fused mixture of things — usually + *of* ▪ The collection is a *mishmash* [=*hodgepodge, jumble*] *of* different styles.

mis·in·form /ˌmɪsɪnˈfoɚm/ *verb* **-forms; -formed; -form·ing** [+ *obj*] **:** to give (someone) false or incorrect information ▪ The company is accused of *misinforming* its shareholders about last year's profits. ▪ I felt I had been *misinformed* about the risks involved. — see also MISINFORMED

mis·in·for·ma·tion /ˌmɪsˌɪnfɚˈmeɪʃən/ *noun* [*noncount*] **:** information that is not completely true or accurate ▪ a company accused of providing *misinformation* to its shareholders — compare DISINFORMATION

misinformed *adj* [*more* ~; *most* ~]
1 : not having accurate or completely accurate information about something ▪ The public is badly/sadly *misinformed* about the possible effects of the proposed law. ▪ questions from a *misinformed* reporter
2 : based on information that is not accurate or not completely accurate ▪ *misinformed* beliefs/choices

mis·in·ter·pret /ˌmɪsn̩ˈtɚprət/ *verb* **-prets; -pret·ed; -pret·ing** [+ *obj*] **:** to understand or explain (something) incorrectly **:** to interpret (something) incorrectly ▪ He claims that his statements have been *misinterpreted* by the media. ▪ Her silence should not be *misinterpreted* as consent.
— **mis·in·ter·pre·ta·tion** /ˌmɪsn̩ˌtɚprəˈteɪʃən/ *noun, pl* **-tions** [*count, noncount*] ▪ The rules should be written so that they are not subject to *misinterpretation*. [=so that they cannot be misunderstood]

mis·judge /ˌmɪsˈʤʌʤ/ *verb* **-judg·es; -judged; -judg·ing** [+ *obj*] **:** to judge (someone or something) incorrectly or unfairly: such as **a :** to have an unfair opinion about (someone) ▪ I can see that I've completely *misjudged* you. I apologize. **b :** to estimate (something, such as an amount, distance, etc.) incorrectly ▪ The outfielder *misjudged* the fly ball and it went over his head. ▪ The pilot *misjudged* the landing.
— **mis·judg·ment** *also chiefly Brit* **mis·judge·ment** /ˌmɪsˈʤʌʤmənt/ *noun, pl* **-ments** [*count, noncount*] ▪ tactical *misjudgments*

mis·lay /ˌmɪsˈleɪ/ *verb* **-lays; -laid** /ˌmɪsˈleɪd/; **-lay·ing** [+ *obj*] **:** to lose (something) for a short time by forgetting where you put it ▪ I *mislaid* [=*misplaced*] my car keys.

mis·lead /ˌmɪsˈliːd/ *verb* **-leads; -led** /ˌmɪsˈlɛd/; **-lead·ing** **:** to cause (someone) to believe something that is not true [+ *obj*] We believe that her comments were deliberately meant to *mislead* the public. ▪ Don't be *misled* [=*fooled*] by his friendly appearance—he's really a ruthless competitor. ▪ The early results *misled* us into thinking we would win the election easily. [*no obj*] We believe that her comments were deliberately meant to *mislead*.
— **mis·lead·ing** *adj* [*more* ~; *most* ~] ▪ The early results were very *misleading*. [=*deceptive*] ▪ deliberately *misleading* comments — **mis·lead·ing·ly** /ˌmɪsˈliːdɪŋli/ *adv* ▪ a *misleadingly* labeled product

mis·man·age /ˌmɪsˈmænɪʤ/ *verb* **-ag·es; -aged; -ag·ing** [+ *obj*] **:** to manage or control (something) badly ▪ *mismanage* a company
— **mis·man·age·ment** /ˌmɪsˈmænɪʤmənt/ *noun* [*noncount*] ▪ These problems are due to *mismanagement*.

[1]**mis·match** /ˈmɪsˌmæʧ/ *verb* **-match·es; -matched; -match·ing** [+ *obj*] **:** to put (people or things that are not suited to each other) together **:** to match (people or things) badly ▪ a designer who intentionally *mismatches* colors
— **mis·matched** *adj* ▪ wearing *mismatched* clothes ▪ They were married for three years, but they were badly *mismatched*. [=they were not suited to each other]

[2]**mismatch** *noun, pl* **-matches** [*count*] **:** a bad match: such as **a :** a situation in which two people or things that are not suited to each other are together ▪ a marital *mismatch* **b :** a situation in which two people or things are not balanced or equal to each other in some way ▪ a *mismatch* between supply and demand; *especially* **:** a game or contest in which one person, team, etc., is much better or stronger than the other ▪ The election turned out to be a *mismatch*.

mis·name /ˌmɪsˈneɪm/ *verb* **-names; -named; -nam·ing** [+ *obj*]
1 : to give (someone or something) a name that is not proper or appropriate ▪ They *misnamed* the airport when they called it "international." Almost all the arriving and departing flights are local.
2 : to give or show an incorrect name for (someone or something) ▪ The caption *misnamed* the person in the picture.

mis·no·mer /ˌmɪsˈnoʊmɚ/ *noun, pl* **-mers** [*count*] **:** a name that is wrong or not proper or appropriate ▪ "International Airport" is something of a *misnomer*, since almost all the arriving and departing flights are local.

mi·sog·y·nist /məˈsɑːʤənɪst/ *noun, pl* **-nists** [*count*] **:** a man who hates women — often used before another noun ▪ a *misogynist* joke ▪ their *misogynist* boss
— **mi·sog·y·ny** /məˈsɑːʤəni/ *noun* [*noncount*] ▪ lyrics that promote violence and *misogyny*

mis·place /ˌmɪsˈpleɪs/ *verb* **-plac·es; -placed; -plac·ing** [+ *obj*]
1 : to put (something) in the wrong place ▪ *misplace* a comma
2 : to lose (something) for a short time by forgetting where you put it **:** MISLAY ▪ He *misplaced* his keys.
3 : to direct (a feeling, such as trust or confidence) toward someone or something that does not deserve it ▪ She realized that her trust had been *misplaced*. [=she had trusted someone who did not deserve to be trusted]
— **misplaced** *adj* ▪ *misplaced* [=*unrealistic, inappropriate*] expectations ▪ His confidence in himself seems *misplaced*. ▪ *misplaced* loyalty/faith — **mis·place·ment** /ˌmɪsˈpleɪsmənt/ *noun* [*noncount*] ▪ the *misplacement* of trust

mis·play /ˈmɪsˌpleɪ/ *noun, pl* **-plays** [*count*] **:** a mistake made by a person who is playing a sport (such as baseball or tennis) ▪ a *misplay* [=*error*] by the shortstop
— **mis·play** /ˌmɪsˈpleɪ/ *verb* **-plays; -played; -play·ing** [+ *obj*] ▪ The shortstop *misplayed* the grounder. [=failed to catch it, stop it, etc.]

mis·print /ˈmɪsˌprɪnt/ *noun, pl* **-prints** [*count*] **:** a mistake (such as a spelling error) in something printed ▪ a book with many *misprints*

mis·pro·nounce /ˌmɪsprəˈnaʊns/ *verb* **-nounc·es; -nounced; -nounc·ing** [+ *obj*] **:** to pronounce (a word or name) incorrectly ▪ His name is often *mispronounced*.
— **mis·pro·nun·ci·a·tion** /ˌmɪsprəˌnʌnsiˈeɪʃən/ *noun, pl* **-tions** [*count, noncount*]

mis·quote /ˌmɪsˈkwoʊt/ *verb* **-quotes; -quot·ed; -quot·ing** [+ *obj*] **:** to report or repeat (something that someone has said or written) in a way that is not correct or accurate **:** to quote (someone) incorrectly ▪ *misquote* Shakespeare ▪ The mayor says that she was *misquoted* by the press.
— **mis·quo·ta·tion** /ˌmɪskwoʊˈteɪʃən/ *noun, pl* **-tions** [*count, noncount*] ▪ an article containing many *misquotations* — **misquote** *noun, pl* **-quotes** [*count*] ▪ an article containing many *misquotes*

mis·read /ˌmɪsˈriːd/ *verb* **-reads; -read** /-ˈrɛd/; **-read·ing** [+ *obj*]
1 : to read (something) incorrectly ▪ I guess I *misread* the instructions.
2 : to understand (something) incorrectly ▪ They have *misread* the lessons of the past. ▪ Politicians may have *misread* the mood of the public. ▪ I badly *misread* the situation.
— **mis·read·ing** *noun, pl* **-ings** [*count*] — usually singular ▪ a potentially dangerous *misreading* of the public mood

mis·rep·re·sent /ˌmɪsˌrɛprɪˈzɛnt/ *verb* **-sents; -sent·ed; -sent·ing** [+ *obj*] **:** to describe (someone or something) in a false way especially in order to deceive someone **:** to give someone a false idea about (something or someone) ▪ The company is accused of *misrepresenting* its earnings. ▪ He *misrepresented* himself as a writer. [=he claimed to be a writer but he wasn't one] ▪ The movie deliberately *misrepresents* the facts/truth about her life.
— **mis·rep·re·sen·ta·tion** /ˌmɪsˌrɛprɪˌzɛnˈteɪʃən/ *noun, pl* **-tions** [*count, noncount*] ▪ deliberate *misrepresentations* of the truth

mis·rule /ˌmɪsˈruːl/ *noun* [*noncount*] **:** bad government ▪ The people of that country have endured many years of *misrule*.

[1]**miss** /ˈmɪs/ *verb* **miss·es; missed; miss·ing**
1 : to fail to hit, catch, reach, or get (something) [+ *obj*] *miss* a target ▪ He swung and *missed* the ball completely. ▪ The shot *missed* the goal by inches. ▪ *miss* a putt ▪ They (just/barely) *missed* the deadline. ▪ The team *missed* the play-offs last year. [=the team failed to qualify for the play-offs] [*no obj*] The batter swung and *missed*. ▪ She took three shots and *missed* every time. ▪ The shot *missed* badly.
2 [+ *obj*] **a :** to fail to use (something, such as an opportunity) ▪ I would hate to *miss* this opportunity. ▪ She could have joined us, but she *missed* her chance. ▪ This opportunity is ***too good to miss***. [=so good that no one would want to fail to use it] **b :** to fail to do, take, make, or have (something) ▪ The driver was so distracted that he *missed* the turn. [=he failed to turn when he should have] ▪ They *missed* a payment on their car loan. ▪ *miss* a tackle ▪ She *missed* her medication.

▪ He was in such a hurry that he *missed* breakfast.
3 [+ *obj*] **: to be without (something) : to lack (something) — used in the phrase *be missing*** ▪ He *was missing* one of his front teeth. [=he did not have one of his front teeth; one of his front teeth was missing] ▪ The old house *is missing* some of its windows. **— see also** MISSING
4 [+ *obj*] **a : to fail to be present for (something)** ▪ She *missed* three days of school when she was sick. ▪ *miss* a class ▪ He hasn't *missed* a day's work in years. ▪ This is an event you won't want to *miss*. = This is an event that is ***not to be missed***. [=that you should experience] ▪ "Are you going to their wedding?" "Yes, I ***wouldn't miss it for the world***." [=I would not consider not going; I will definitely go] **b : to arrive too late for (something or someone)** ▪ He *missed* his train. ▪ I *missed* the flight/connection by only a few minutes. ▪ She was delayed in traffic and *missed* her appointment. ▪ You just *missed* him—he left five minutes ago.
5 [+ *obj*] **: to notice or feel the absence of (someone or something)** ▪ I'm so glad you're back. I've *missed* you. ▪ She left quietly, and it was a while before she was *missed*. [=before anyone noticed that she had left] ▪ We *miss* our old friends. [=we feel sad because we are not near our old friends] ▪ I *miss* being home at Christmas. [=I am sad not to be home at Christmas] ▪ You'll be (sorely/much) *missed* when you retire. ▪ He *misses* his wife terribly. ▪ I *miss* the old neighborhood. ▪ I didn't *miss* my bag [=I didn't notice that my bag was missing] until I got to the car.
6 [+ *obj*] **a : to fail to understand (something)** ▪ You *missed* the main point of the story. ▪ You're *missing* my point. ▪ Am I *missing* something? ▪ She doesn't *miss* a thing. [=she understands everything that is being said, that is happening, etc.] **b : to fail to hear or learn about (something)** ▪ Here's the latest news, in case you *missed* it. ▪ I'm sorry, but I *missed* the first part of what you said. **c : to fail to see or notice (something or someone)** ▪ It's a big white building on the corner—***you can't miss it***. [=it is impossible not to see/notice it] ▪ As the only woman in the race, she was hard to *miss*.
7 [+ *obj*] **: to avoid (something)** ▪ Her car skidded off the road and barely *missed* hitting a telephone pole. ▪ He just *missed* being seriously hurt. [=he was almost seriously hurt]
8 [*no obj*] **: to fail to succeed** ▪ With a cast like this, the movie ***can't miss***. [=it will definitely succeed]
9 [*no obj*] **:** MISFIRE 1 ▪ The engine *missed*.
miss a beat see [2]BEAT
miss its/the mark see [1]MARK
miss out [*phrasal verb*] **1 : to lose an opportunity : to be unable to have or enjoy something** ▪ It's too bad you weren't able to come with us. You really *missed out*. **— often + *on*** ▪ You really *missed out on* a good time. ▪ If you don't act now you could *miss out on* a great opportunity. **2 *miss out (someone or something) or miss (someone or something) out Brit* : to leave (someone or something) out :** OMIT ▪ You've *missed out* the most important fact!
miss the boat see [1]BOAT
miss the forest for the trees see TREE
never/not miss a trick see [1]TRICK

[2]**miss** *noun, pl* **misses** [*count*]
1 : a failure to hit something ▪ She hit the target five straight times without a *miss*. ▪ His first shot was a bad *miss*.
2 : a failure to reach a desired goal or result ▪ Her movies have been a mixture of hits and *misses*. [=some have been successful and some have not] **— see also** HIT-AND-MISS, NEAR MISS
***give (something) a miss chiefly Brit, informal* : to choose not to do (something) or go (somewhere)** ▪ I had so much else to do that I decided to *give the party a miss*.
— compare [3]MISS

[3]**miss** *noun, pl* **misses**
1 *Miss* a — used as a title before the name of an unmarried woman or girl ▪ *Miss* Jones **— compare** MRS., MS. **b — used as a title before the name of a married woman who does not use her husband's name** ▪ *Miss* Bette Davis **c — used as part of a title for a girl or young woman who has won a contest (such as a beauty contest) and who represents the place or thing indicated** ▪ *Miss* America **d *Brit* — used by children as a way to address a female teacher**
2 a — used as a polite way to address a girl or young woman ▪ Can I help you, *miss*? **b** [*count*] *old-fashioned* **: a girl or young woman** ▪ a talented young *miss*
3 *misses* [*plural*] *US* **: a clothing size for women of average height and weight — usually used before another noun** ▪ *misses* dresses
— compare [2]MISS

mis·shap·en /ˌmɪsˈʃeɪpən/ *adj* [*more* ~; *most* ~] **: badly shaped : having an ugly shape** ▪ a *misshapen* hand

mis·sile /ˈmɪsəl, *Brit* ˈmɪˌsaɪl/ *noun, pl* **-siles** [*count*] **: an object that is thrown, shot, or launched as a weapon** ▪ The protesters were arrested for throwing *missiles* [=rocks, bottles, etc.] at the police.; ***especially* : a rocket that explodes when it hits a distant target** ▪ a nuclear *missile* **— see also** BALLISTIC MISSILE, CRUISE MISSILE, GUIDED MISSILE, SURFACE-TO-AIR MISSILE, SURFACE-TO-SURFACE MISSILE

miss·ing /ˈmɪsɪŋ/ *adj*
1 : unable to be found : not in a usual or expected place ▪ My keys are *missing*. [=I can't find my keys] ▪ One of his front teeth is *missing*. [=he does not have one of his front teeth; he is missing one of his front teeth] ▪ a *missing* tooth ▪ *missing* children **— often + *from*** ▪ A few books are *missing from* the shelf. ▪ She discovered that some important papers were *missing from* her desk. **— sometimes used in the phrase *go missing*** ▪ My keys have *gone missing* again. [=I cannot find my keys again; my keys are missing again] ✧ **This phrase is more common in British English than in U.S. English.**
2 : needed or expected but not included ▪ The new director has provided the *missing* ingredient that was needed for the show's success. ▪ It's a good sauce, but there's something *missing*. [=it lacks something that would make it better] **— often + *from*** ▪ There was something *missing from* his life.
***missing in action* — used to say that a soldier cannot be found after a battle and might have been killed, captured, or wounded** ▪ soldiers who are *missing in action* and presumed dead

missing link *noun, pl* ~ **links**
1 [*count*] **: something that you do not have and that you need to complete a series or to solve a problem** ▪ Police are hopeful that the new evidence will provide the *missing links* needed to solve the crime.
2 *the missing link* : a kind of animal that was in some ways like an ape and in some ways like a human being and that is thought to have existed in the past but has not been discovered ▪ scientists searching for *the missing link*

missing person *noun, pl* ~ **-sons** [*count*] **: a person whose location is not known and whose absence has been reported to the police** ▪ Their teenage daughter has been officially listed as a *missing person* since she failed to return home after leaving school. ▪ They've filed a ***missing person report*** with the police. [=a document that officially reports that someone is missing]

mis·sion /ˈmɪʃən/ *noun, pl* **-sions** [*count*]
1 a : a task or job that someone is given to do ▪ Our *mission* was to recover the stolen plans. ▪ He was sent on a fact-finding *mission*. = He was sent on a *mission* to gather information. ▪ By patient negotiation she succeeded in her *mission* of averting a strike. ▪ go on a ***rescue mission*** [=go somewhere to rescue someone] ▪ The volunteers were on a ***mission of mercy*** to help victims of the disaster. [=the volunteers were sent to help the victims of the disaster] ▪ a ***mercy mission*** **b : a specific military or naval task** ▪ a reconnaissance *mission* ▪ a peacekeeping *mission* ▪ a combat/training *mission* **c : a flight by an aircraft or spacecraft to perform a specific task** ▪ a bombing *mission* ▪ a manned space *mission* ▪ a shuttle *mission* ▪ a *mission* to the moon **— see also** MISSION CONTROL
2 : a task that you consider to be a very important duty ▪ His *mission* is to help poor children. = He has made it his ***mission in life*** to help poor children. = He's a man ***with a mission*** to help poor children. ▪ She's ***on a mission*** to locate her lost sister. [=she is very determined to find her lost sister]
3 : a group of people sent to a foreign country for a specific reason (such as to have discussions or to provide training or assistance) ▪ a member of a trade *mission*
4 a : a group of people who are sent to a foreign country to do religious work : a group of missionaries ▪ a Catholic *mission* **b : a place or building where such work is done** ▪ touring a Spanish *mission* in California ▪ a *mission* church

[1]**mis·sion·ary** /ˈmɪʃəˌneri, *Brit* ˈmɪʃənri/ *noun, pl* **-ar·ies** [*count*] **: a person who is sent to a foreign country to do religious work (such as to convince people to join a religion or to help people who are sick, poor, etc.)** ▪ a Christian *missionary*

[2]**missionary** *adj, always used before a noun*
1 : of or relating to missionaries ▪ *missionary* work ▪ a *missionary* school
2 : very enthusiastic and eager about doing a job or support-

ing a cause • He spoke with ***missionary zeal*** about the project. [=he spoke with great enthusiasm about the project]

mission control *noun [noncount]* : the group of people on the ground who direct or control the flight of a spacecraft • The astronauts received a message from *mission control*.

mission statement *noun, pl* ~ **-ments** *[count]* : something that states the purpose or goal of a business or organization • The company's *mission statement* emphasizes its ongoing commitment to meeting the needs of the community.

missis *variant spelling of* MISSUS

mis·sive /ˈmɪsɪv/ *noun, pl* **-sives** *[count] formal + humorous* : a letter or other written message • a fund-raising *missive* • She received yet another lengthy *missive* from her father.

mis·spell /ˌmɪsˈspɛl/ *verb* **-spells; -spelled** *or chiefly Brit* **-spelt** /-ˈspɛlt/; **-spell·ing** *[+ obj]* : to spell (a word or name) incorrectly • The name of the town had been *misspelled* on the map.

– **mis·spell·ing** /ˌmɪsˈspɛlɪŋ/ *noun, pl* **-ings** *[count]* • The letter contains numerous *misspellings*.

mis·spend /ˌmɪsˈspɛnd/ *verb* **-spends; -spent** /-ˈspɛnt/; **-spend·ing** *[+ obj]* : to spend or use (something, such as time or money) in a way that is not legal, careful, or wise • Several government officials have been accused of *misspending* public money.

– **misspent** *adj* • *misspent* money • a *misspent* summer • He enjoys telling stories of his ***misspent youth***. [=of the time when he was young and doing things that are not considered wise or proper]

mis·state /ˌmɪsˈsteɪt/ *verb* **-states; -stated; -stating** *[+ obj]* : to state or report (something) incorrectly • The company *misstated* its profits. • An article in yesterday's paper *misstated* the name of the district attorney.

– **mis·state·ment** /ˌmɪsˈsteɪtmənt/ *noun, pl* **-ments** *[count, noncount]* • correcting a *misstatement*

mis·step /ˌmɪsˈstɛp/ *noun, pl* **-steps** *[count] chiefly US* : an action or decision that is a mistake • Their decision to relocate the company was a major *misstep*. • make a strategic *misstep* [=*blunder*]

mis·sus *also* **mis·sis** /ˈmɪsəz/ *noun, pl* **-sus·es** *also* **-sis·es** *[count]*

1 *informal + old-fashioned* : WIFE — usually singular • He had another argument with his *missus*. • How's the *missus*? — compare MISTER 2

2 *Brit, informal* — used to address a woman whose name is not known • Need a hand with your luggage, *missus*?

[1]mist /ˈmɪst/ *noun, pl* **mists**

1 : water in the form of very small drops floating in the air or falling as rain *[noncount]* We could barely see the shore through the *mist*. *[count]* The hills were veiled/shrouded in a fine *mist*.

2 *[count]* : a stream of liquid in the form of very small drops : a fine spray • an aerosol *mist*

3 *[count]* : something that makes understanding difficult • an issue clouded by *mists* of confusion

lost in the mists of time ✧ Something *lost in the mists of time* is forgotten because it happened long ago. • The origins of this ancient ritual are *lost in the mists of time*.

[2]mist *verb* **mists; mist·ed; mist·ing**

1 *[no obj]* **a** : to become covered with very small drops of water — usually + *up* • My glasses *misted* [=*fogged*] *up* when I came in from the cold. **b** *of a person's eyes* : to fill with tears • Her eyes *misted*. — usually + *over* or *up* • Her eyes *misted over* as she thought of her old friends.

2 *[+ obj]* **a** : to cover (something) with mist • a *misted* valley **b** : to spray (something) with very small drops of water • The plant should be *misted* regularly.

3 *[no obj]* : to rain very lightly • It was *misting* when we arrived. • a *misting* rain

[1]mis·take /məˈsteɪk/ *noun, pl* **-takes** *[count]* : something that is not correct : a wrong action, statement, or judgment : ERROR • It would be a *mistake* to assume that we can rely on their help. • There must be some *mistake*. • a stupid/careless *mistake* • a costly/serious/bad *mistake* • a deadly/fatal/tragic *mistake* • The manuscript contains numerous spelling *mistakes*. • There's a *mistake* in the schedule. • "When does the movie start?" "At 8:00. No, wait—***my mistake***—it starts at 8:30." • Don't worry about it. It was an ***honest mistake***. [=something that anyone could be wrong about] — often used with *make* • Everybody *makes mistakes* from time to time. • I *made* the *mistake* of believing her. — see also MAKE NO MISTAKE (below)

and no mistake *chiefly Brit, old-fashioned* — used to stress the truth or accuracy of a statement • She's the one I saw, *and no mistake*. [=she is definitely the person I saw]

by mistake : because of a mistake : without intending to • I got on the wrong train *by mistake*. [=*accidentally*]

make no mistake — used to stress the truth or accuracy of a statement • *Make no mistake* (about it), if we don't address these problems now, they will only get worse.

[2]mis·take *verb* **mis·takes; mis·took** /məˈstʊk/; **mis·tak·en** /məˈsteɪkən/; **mis·tak·ing** *[+ obj]*

1 : to understand (something or someone) incorrectly • They *mistook* my meaning.

2 : to make a wrong judgment about (something) • The army's leaders *mistook* the strength of the enemy. [=they did not realize how strong the enemy was] ✧ If you say ***there is no mistaking*** something, it is very clear or obvious. • She may be unconventional but *there's no mistaking* her ability to run the company. • *There was no mistaking* his determination. [=his determination was obvious]

3 : to identify (someone or something) incorrectly — usually + *for* • I *mistook* him *for* his brother. [=I thought that he was his brother]

mistaken *adj [more ~; most ~]* : not correct : incorrect or wrong • I may be *mistaken*, but I think we've met before. • If you think the job is finished, you are sadly/badly/sorely *mistaken*. • He ignored the law in the *mistaken* belief that he was immune from punishment. • If I'm not *mistaken*, the bus leaves at 7:00. • a *mistaken* assumption • Her arrest was ***a case of mistaken identity***. [=she was arrested because the police thought she was someone else] • a *mistaken* impression/interpretation

– **mis·tak·en·ly** *adv* • He *mistakenly* believed that he was immune from punishment.

mis·ter /ˈmɪstɚ/ *noun, pl* **-ters**

1 ***Mister*** — used sometimes in writing instead of *Mr.*

2 *[count] US, informal + old-fashioned* : HUSBAND — usually singular • She went off to the store while the/her *mister* [=her husband] stayed home. — compare MISSUS 1

3 *informal* — used in speech especially by children to address a man whose name is not known • Hey *mister*, do you want to buy a paper?

mis·time /ˌmɪsˈtaɪm/ *verb* **-times; -timed; -tim·ing** *[+ obj]* : to do or say (something) at the wrong time : to time (something) incorrectly • They *mistimed* their arrival. • a *mistimed* remark • The batter *mistimed* his swing.

mis·tle·toe /ˈmɪsəlˌtoʊ/ *noun [noncount]* : a plant with yellowish flowers and white berries that is traditionally used as a Christmas decoration ✧ Pieces of mistletoe are often hung from the ceiling or in a doorway at Christmastime. According to tradition, if you stand with someone under a piece of mistletoe, you are supposed to kiss that person.

mistook *past tense of* [2]MISTAKE

mis·treat /ˌmɪsˈtriːt/ *verb* **-treats; -treat·ed; -treat·ing** *[+ obj]* : to treat (someone or something) badly : ABUSE • They accuse him of *mistreating* his wife. • She claimed she had been *mistreated* by the police.

– **mis·treat·ment** /ˌmɪsˈtriːtmənt/ *noun [noncount]* • the *mistreatment* of prisoners

mis·tress /ˈmɪstrəs/ *noun, pl* **-tress·es** *[count]*

1 : a woman who has control or power over others: such as **a** : a woman who has a servant or slave • Servants were required to do the *mistress's* bidding without question. **b** : a woman who owns a pet (such as a dog) • The dog was always obedient to its master and *mistress*. **c** *formal* : the female head of a household • the master and *mistress* of the house — compare MASTER

2 : a woman who has control of something • She proved herself (to be) *mistress* of the situation.

3 : a woman who has a sexual relationship with a married man • a married man who has/keeps a *mistress* • His wife suspected that the woman she'd seen with him was his *mistress*.

4 a *chiefly Brit, old-fashioned* : a female teacher : SCHOOLMISTRESS — see also HEADMISTRESS **b** ***Mistress*** — used as a title for the female head of certain British colleges • She was *Mistress* of Girton (College).

5 ***Mistress*** *old-fashioned* — used as a title before the name of a woman • *Mistress* Jones

mistress of ceremonies *noun, pl* **mistresses of ceremonies** *[count]* : a woman who introduces guests, speakers, or performers at a formal event : a woman who is a master of ceremonies

mis·tri·al /ˈmɪsˌtrajəl/ *noun, pl* **-als** *[count] law* : a trial that is not valid because of an error or because the jury is unable to decide a verdict • The judge declared a *mistrial.*

[1]**mis·trust** /ˌmɪsˈtrʌst/ *noun* **:** lack of trust or confidence **:** a feeling that someone is not honest and cannot be trusted [*noncount*] She was very open about her *mistrust* [=*distrust*] of politicians. [*singular*] She has a strong *mistrust* of politicians.

– **mis·trust·ful** /ˌmɪsˈtrʌstfəl/ *adj* [*more* ~; *most* ~] — often + *of* • She is *mistrustful of* politicians. – **mis·trust·ful·ly** /ˌmɪsˈtrʌstfəli/ *adv*

[2]**mistrust** *verb* **-trusts; -trust·ed; -trust·ing** [+ *obj*] **:** to have no trust or confidence in (someone or something) **:** DISTRUST • She *mistrusts* politicians. • I was starting to *mistrust* my own judgment.

misty /ˈmɪsti/ *adj* **mist·i·er; -est**

1 : full of mist • a *misty* valley • *misty* weather

2 : not clearly seen or remembered • *misty* [=*vague, indistinct*] memories of the past

3 *informal* **:** TEARFUL • *misty* eyes • I ***get (all) misty*** [=I get tears in my eyes; I feel sentimental] when I hear that song.

– **mist·i·ly** /ˈmɪstəli/ *adv* • memories *mistily* remembered

– **mist·i·ness** /ˈmɪstinəs/ *noun* [*noncount*] • the *mistiness* of the weather

misty–eyed /ˈmɪstiˈaɪd/ *adj* [*more* ~; *most* ~]

1 : having tears in your eyes • He gets *misty-eyed* when he talks about that time.

2 : dreamy or sentimental • *misty-eyed* recollections

mis·un·der·stand /ˌmɪsˌʌndɚˈstænd/ *verb* **-stands; -stood** /-ˈstʊd/; **-stand·ing** [+ *obj*] **:** to fail to understand (someone or something) correctly • Don't *misunderstand* me—I'm not criticizing your decision. • You *misunderstood* my question. • He feels that the critics have completely *misunderstood* his movies. • She expressed herself in clear terms that no one could *misunderstand.*

misunderstanding *noun, pl* **-ings**

1 : a failure to understand something [*noncount*] The instructions are carefully written in order to avoid/prevent *misunderstanding.* [*count*] Her comments reflect a *misunderstanding* of the basic problem. • using clear language to avoid *misunderstandings*

2 [*count*] **:** a usually minor argument or disagreement • an unfortunate *misunderstanding* between old friends • We had our little *misunderstandings* in the past but we managed to clear them up long ago.

mis·un·der·stood /ˌmɪsˌʌndɚˈstʊd/ *adj* [*more* ~; *most* ~] **:** thought of incorrectly **:** not understood • a *misunderstood* genius • This is a common and often *misunderstood* problem. • He sees himself as a *misunderstood* victim of the media.

[1]**mis·use** /ˌmɪsˈjuːz/ *verb* **-us·es; -used; -us·ing** [+ *obj*]

1 : to use (something) incorrectly • She's charged with *misusing* company funds. • a word that is frequently *misused*

2 : to treat (someone) unfairly • He feels he has been *misused* [=(more commonly) *mistreated*] by the press.

– **mis·us·age** /ˌmɪsˈjuːsɪʤ/ *noun* [*noncount*] • *misusage* [=(more commonly) *misuse*] of company funds

[2]**mis·use** /ˌmɪsˈjuːs/ *noun, pl* **-us·es :** the act of using something in an illegal, improper, or unfair way **:** incorrect use [*noncount*] No refunds will be offered on products damaged by/through *misuse.* — usually + *of* • the *misuse of* words • She's charged with *misuse of* company funds. [*count*] — usually + *of* • a common *misuse of* a word • *misuses of* power

mite /ˈmaɪt/ *noun, pl* **mites** [*count*]

1 : a very small creature that often lives on plants, animals, and foods — see also DUST MITE

2 : a small person (such as a child) or thing • his *mite* of a daughter • a tiny *mite* of a woman • This little vacuum cleaner is a ***mighty mite*** [=something that is small but very strong or powerful]

3 *old-fashioned* **:** a very small amount • There could be a *mite* [=(more commonly) *bit*] of trouble.

a mite **:** to a small degree **:** somewhat or slightly • The box could stand to be *a mite* bigger. • The movie's plot is *a mite* [=*a bit, a little*] confusing. • This is *a mite* embarrassing.

[1]**mi·ter** (*US*) *or Brit* **mi·tre** /ˈmaɪtɚ/ *noun, pl* **-ters** [*count*]

1 : a high pointed hat worn by a bishop or abbot in church ceremonies

2 : MITER JOINT

[2]**miter** (*US*) *or Brit* **mitre** *verb* **-ters; -tered; -ter·ing** [+ *obj*] *technical* **:** to match or fit (boards) together in a miter joint • The corners of the frame were carefully *mitered.*

miter joint (*US*) *or Brit* **mitre joint** *noun, pl* ~ **joints** [*count*] **:** a joint or corner made by cutting the edges of two boards at an angle and fitting them together

mit·i·gate /ˈmɪtəˌgeɪt/ *verb* **-gates; -gat·ed; -gat·ing** [+ *obj*] *formal* **:** to make (something) less severe, harmful, or painful • Emergency funds are being provided to help *mitigate* the effects of the disaster. • *mitigate* a punishment • medicines used to *mitigate* a patient's suffering — see also UNMITIGATED

– **mit·i·ga·tion** /ˌmɪtəˈgeɪʃən/ *noun* [*noncount*] • the *mitigation* of suffering/punishment

mitigating *adj* — used to describe something (such as an unusual situation) that makes something (such as a crime or a mistake) seem less serious or deserving of blame; usually used in the phrase ***mitigating circumstances/factors*** • His sentence was reduced because of *mitigating circumstances.* [=*extenuating circumstances*]

mitt /ˈmɪt/ *noun, pl* **mitts** [*count*]

1 : MITTEN • children bundled up in hats and *mitts* — see also OVEN MITT

2 *baseball* **a :** a special type of heavy glove worn by the catcher • a catcher's *mitt* **b :** a special type of glove worn by the first baseman • a first baseman's *mitt*

3 *informal* **:** HAND • He can hold anything in those big *mitts* of his.

mit·ten /ˈmɪtn/ *noun, pl* **-tens** [*count*] **:** a covering for the hand that has a separate part for the thumb only — compare GLOVE

– **mit·tened** /ˈmɪtnd/ *adj* • a *mittened* hand [=a hand wearing a mitten]

[1]**mix** /ˈmɪks/ *verb* **mix·es; mixed; mix·ing**

1 a : to combine (two or more things) to make one thing that is the same throughout **:** to combine (two or more substances) to make a different substance [+ *obj*] *Mix* [=*blend*] flour and water (together) to make a paste. • To make frosting for the cake, *mix* powdered sugar with a little milk and vanilla. • You can make purple by *mixing* the colors red and blue. [*no obj*] Add the ingredients and *mix* [=*blend*] well. **b** [+ *obj*] **:** to add (something) to something else • *Mix* some water with the flour to make a paste. — often + *in* or *into* • I *mixed in* [=*added*] a little more sugar. • Slowly *mix* [=*stir*] *in* the rice. • *Mix* water *into* the flour to make a paste.

2 [*no obj*] **:** to be combined and become one thing that is the same throughout • Oil will not *mix* with water. = Oil and water don't *mix.* • Flour can *mix* [=*blend, combine*] with water to make a paste.

3 [+ *obj*] **:** to make or prepare (something, such as an alcoholic drink) by combining different things • Please *mix* a drink for me. = Please *mix* me a drink.

4 [+ *obj*] **:** to make (a recording of music) by electronically putting sounds together from more than one source • She *mixed* her own CD of dance music.

5 [+ *obj*] **:** to bring (different things) together • His novel *mixes* humor with drama. • Playing golf with clients is one way to ***mix business with pleasure*** [=to do something enjoyable that is related to your work]

6 [*no obj*] **:** to talk in a friendly way with different people and especially with strangers • She *mixes* well in social situations. • Our families ***don't mix*** [=don't get along] with each other.

7 [*no obj*] **:** to be able to be combined or put together in a way that has good results — used in negative statements • Drinking (alcohol) and driving *don't mix.* [=you should not drive after you have been drinking alcohol] • They claim that art and politics *do not mix.*

mix and match **:** to put different things (such as pieces of clothing) together in different ways • She's able to *mix and match* her sweaters with different skirts to create new outfits. • She buys clothing that she can *mix and match.*

mix it up (*US*) *or Brit* ***mix it informal*** **:** to fight or argue • The two boxers started *mixing it up.* • He loves to *mix it up* with his younger brothers.

mix up [*phrasal verb*] *informal* **1** ***mix (someone or something) up or mix up (someone or something)*** **:** to mistakenly think that (someone or something) is someone or something else • Those two women look so much alike—I always *mix* them *up.* [=I never know who is who] • He got the days *mixed up* [=*confused*] and thought the meeting was today. • I always *mix up* the times when my classes start. **2** ***mix (something) up or mix up (something)*** **:** to mistakenly put (something) in a place where something else should be • I accidentally *mixed up* the two files. [=I put each of the files in the place where the other one should have gone] — often + *with* • Did my homework get *mixed up with* your papers? **3** ***mix (someone) up or mix up (someone)*** **a :** to cause (someone) to be involved in a usually dangerous or improper activity or situation — usually used as *(be/get) mixed up in* ▪ He *got mixed up in* a plan to destroy the government. [=he became involved in a plan to destroy the government] **b :** to cause (someone) to become involved with a particular group of people and especially with people who cause trouble — usually used as *(be/get) mixed up with* ▪ She *was mixed up with* the wrong crowd. ▪ teenage boys *getting mixed up with* gangs — see also MIXED-UP, MIX-UP

²mix *noun, pl* **mixes**

1 : a dry mixture of ingredients that is sold in one package and used for making something (such as a type of food) [*count*] a cake *mix* ▪ a new brand of soup *mixes* [*noncount*] We bought two boxes of muffin *mix*. ▪ a bag of cement *mix* [=material that forms cement when you add water to it]

2 [*singular*] **:** a combination of different kinds of things **:** MIXTURE ▪ a snack *mix* containing pretzels, nuts, and raisins — often + *of* ▪ We worked on finding the right *mix of* food, music, and decorations for the wedding. ▪ They talked to each other in a *mix of* English and Spanish. ▪ an attractive *mix of* red, orange, and yellow flowers

mixed /ˈmɪkst/ *adj*

1 *always used before a noun* **:** made of different kinds of things mixed together or combined ▪ a can of *mixed* nuts ▪ bags of *mixed* candy ▪ We ate salads of *mixed* greens.

2 a : including or involving people of different races or religions ▪ They live in a *mixed* neighborhood. ▪ She's of *mixed* African and European ancestry. ▪ children of *mixed* race/races ▪ people of *mixed* racial origin/ancestry ▪ a racially *mixed* couple **b :** including or involving people of both sexes ▪ She went to a *mixed* school. [=a school for both boys and girls] ▪ a *mixed* chorus ▪ playing ***mixed doubles*** in tennis [=a game of doubles in which each team has a man and a woman] ✧ When people are ***in mixed company***, they are with both men and women. ▪ The women never spoke of sex or pregnancy *in mixed company*. [=when men were present]

3 : both good and bad, favorable and unfavorable, etc. ▪ The play received *mixed* reviews. = The play's reviews were *mixed*. [=some critics liked the play, while other critics did not] ▪ His decision got a *mixed* reaction from the family. ▪ The experiment got *mixed* results. ✧ When people have ***mixed emotions*** or ***mixed feelings*** about something, they have both good and bad thoughts or feelings about it. ▪ He had *mixed emotions* [=he was both happy and sad] about the end of his trip. ▪ I'm having *mixed feelings* about this class.

mixed messages/signals ✧ Someone gives *mixed messages* or *mixed signals* by showing a thought or feeling and then showing another very different thought or feeling. ▪ I don't know if he likes me; he keeps giving me *mixed messages*. ▪ She's sending *mixed signals* about her feelings.

mixed bag *noun* [*singular*]

1 : a collection of different kinds of things — often + *of* ▪ The movie has a *mixed bag of* characters. ▪ We're working with a *mixed bag of* old and new ideas.

2 : something that has both good and bad qualities or parts ▪ His performance was a *mixed bag*.

mixed blessing *noun, pl* **~ -ings** [*count*] **:** something that is good in some ways and bad in other ways ▪ He says that computers are a *mixed blessing* because sometimes they help and sometimes they create problems. ▪ Living next to your in-laws can be a *mixed blessing*.

mixed drink *noun, pl* **~ drinks** [*count*] **:** an alcoholic drink made with two or more ingredients ▪ a *mixed drink* of rum and soda

mixed economy *noun, pl* **~ -mies** [*count*] **:** an economy in which some companies are owned by the government and other companies are not

mixed marriage *noun, pl* **~ -riages :** marriage between two people of different races or religions [*count*] children of *mixed marriages* [*noncount*] a culture in which *mixed marriage* is rare

mixed metaphor *noun, pl* **~ -phors** [*count*] **:** a metaphor that combines different images or ideas in a way that is foolish or illogical ▪ "If we want to get ahead we'll have to iron out the remaining bottlenecks" is an example of a *mixed metaphor*.

mixed–up /ˈmɪkstˈʌp/ *adj* [*more ~; most ~*] *informal*

1 : confused and usually emotionally troubled **:** not capable of making good decisions about life ▪ They're just a bunch of crazy, *mixed-up* kids.

2 : confusing, difficult to understand, and filled with problems ▪ This is a crazy, *mixed-up* world we live in. ▪ He has *mixed-up* ideas about our past. — often written as two separate words when used following a verb ▪ She's a nice person, but her life is really *mixed up*. — see also *mix up* at ¹MIX

mix·er /ˈmɪksɚ/ *noun, pl* **-ers** [*count*]

1 : a machine used for mixing things ▪ a handheld *mixer* ▪ Using an electric *mixer*, blend the cake batter on medium (speed) for two minutes. ▪ a cement *mixer* [=a large machine that keeps cement wet and soft by turning until the cement is used] — see picture at KITCHEN

2 : a drink (such as soda) that does not contain alcohol and that is used in an alcoholic mixed drink ▪ Orange juice is her favorite *mixer*.

3 : someone who controls the recording of sounds (such as the words and music) that go with a movie or television show ▪ the sound *mixer*

4 ✧ A ***good mixer*** is someone who is comfortable in social situations and can talk easily with other people. A ***poor mixer*** is uncomfortable or awkward in social situations. ▪ For a politician, she was not a very *good mixer*. ▪ He was shy and a *poor mixer*.

5 *chiefly US* **:** a social gathering to help people in a group meet each other in a friendly and informal way ▪ an informal *mixer*

mixing bowl *noun, pl* **~ bowls** [*count*] **:** a large bowl used in cooking for mixing ingredients — see picture at KITCHEN

mix·ture /ˈmɪkstʃɚ/ *noun, pl* **-tures**

1 [*count*] **:** something made by combining two or more ingredients ▪ Stir the sugar and butter until the *mixture* is light and fluffy. ▪ Now add eggs to the *mixture*. ▪ Pour the cake *mixture* into a well-greased pan and bake. — often + *of* ▪ The chicken was marinated in a *mixture of* oil and spices. ▪ The horses were fed a *mixture of* grass and oats.

2 [*count*] **:** a combination of different things — + *of* ▪ The dog's coat is a *mixture of* yellow, brown, and black fur. ▪ We were feeling a *mixture of* fear and excitement. ▪ They talked to each other in a *mixture of* English and Spanish.

3 [*noncount*] **:** the act of mixing two or more things together — + *of* ▪ a society formed by the gradual *mixture of* different cultures

mix–up /ˈmɪksˌʌp/ *noun, pl* **-ups** [*count*] **:** a mistake caused by confusion about something ▪ Because of a *mix-up* [=*mistake, error*] at the hotel, we were overcharged for our stay. ▪ The *mix-ups* nearly cost him his job. ▪ I thought you were someone else. Sorry for the *mix-up*. [=*misunderstanding, confusion*] — see also *mix up* at ¹MIX

ml *abbr* milliliter

mm *abbr* millimeter

MN *abbr* Minnesota

mne·mon·ic /nɪˈmɑːnɪk/ *noun, pl* **-ics** [*count*] **:** something (such as a word, a sentence, or a song) that helps people remember something (such as a rule or a list of names) ▪ HOMES is used as a *mnemonic* for the names of the Great Lakes: *H*uron, *O*ntario, *M*ichigan, *E*rie, and *S*uperior.

– mnemonic *adj* ▪ a *mnemonic* device

mo /ˈmoʊ/ *noun* [*singular*] *chiefly Brit, informal* **:** a short time ▪ Hang on a *mo* [=*moment*]: who did you say you'd seen?

Mo. *abbr* Monday

¹MO /ˈɛmˈoʊ/ *noun, pl* **MOs** [*count*] **:** a usual way of performing a crime **:** MODUS OPERANDI ▪ two thieves with very different *MOs*

²MO *abbr* Missouri

¹moan /ˈmoʊn/ *verb* **moans; moaned; moan·ing**

1 [*no obj*] **:** to make a long, low sound because of pain, unhappiness, or physical pleasure ▪ The wounded soldier *moaned* in/with pain. ▪ The crowd *moaned* [=*groaned*] as the other team scored another goal. ▪ He *moaned* with pleasure as she rubbed his back.

2 a [*no obj*] **:** to express unhappiness about something **:** COMPLAIN ▪ We were all *moaning* about the cold, rainy weather. ▪ He's always *moaning* about his salary. ▪ The children were ***moaning and groaning*** all morning, but their mother would not let them go outside. ▪ I'm tired of all his *moaning and groaning* about his salary. **b** [+ *obj*] **:** to say (something) in a way that shows pain or unhappiness ▪ "But I don't want to go," *moaned* the boy. ▪ "Oh, my stomach hurts," she *moaned*. = She *moaned* that her stomach hurt.

3 [*no obj*] **:** to make a long, low sound ▪ The wind *moaned* in the trees.

– moan·er /ˈmoʊnɚ/ *noun, pl* **-ers** [*count*] ▪ He dismisses his critics as a bunch of *moaners*. [=people who are always unhappy or complaining about something]

²moan *noun, pl* **moans** [*count*]

1 : a long, low sound that someone makes because of pain,

M

unhappiness, or physical pleasure ▪ She let out a long, deep *moan*. ▪ a *moan* of despair/pleasure ▪ a low/feeble/weak *moan*

2 : a long, low sound ▪ the *moan* of the wind ▪ the *moan* of the car's engine

3 ***Brit, informal*** **: a complaint about something** ▪ He's always ***having a moan*** [=*complaining*] about his job.

moat /ˈmoʊt/ *noun, pl* **moats** [*count*] **: a deep, wide ditch that is usually filled with water and that goes around the walls of a place (such as a castle) to protect it from being attacked**

[1]mob /ˈmɑːb/ *noun, pl* **mobs**

1 [*count*] **: a large group or crowd of people who are angry or violent or difficult to control** ▪ The angry *mob* smashed store windows and attacked people on the streets. ▪ The police had to be called in to handle/disperse the growing/gathering *mob*. ▪ violent *mobs* — **see also** LYNCH MOB, MOB SCENE

2 [*count*] ***informal*** **: a large number of people — usually + *of*** ▪ On our walk, we were passed by a *mob of* bicycle riders. — **often plural** ▪ *Mobs of* teenagers filled the room. ▪ The team was greeted by *mobs of* excited fans.

3 ***the mob or the Mob informal*** **: a secret organized group of criminals** ▪ *The Mob* [=*the Mafia*] controlled most businesses in the city. ▪ He was jailed for his dealings with *the Mob*. — **often used as** *mob* **before another noun** ▪ Their family had *mob* [=*Mafia*] connections. ▪ a ***mob boss*** [=someone who controls part of an organized criminal group] — **see also** MOBSTER

4 ***the mob old-fashioned*** **: the people of a society who are poor and uneducated** ▪ politicians trying to keep *the mob* happy ✧ **This use of *the mob* is now usually considered insulting.**

[2]mob *verb* **mobs; mobbed; mob·bing** [+ *obj*]

1 ***of a group of people*** **: to move close to (someone) in an excited way : to crowd around (someone) in an aggressive, excited, or annoying way** ▪ The actor's fans *mobbed* him wherever he went. — **often used as** ***(be) mobbed*** ▪ The actor *was mobbed* by fans wherever he went. ▪ I walked into the room and *was* immediately *mobbed* by small children.

2 : to come together in (a place) with many other people ▪ Shoppers *mobbed* the stores during the holidays. — **often used as** ***(be) mobbed*** ▪ The stores *were mobbed* by/with customers.

– mobbed *adj* ▪ The stores were *mobbed* [=very crowded] today! ▪ *mobbed* airports

[1]mo·bile /ˈmoʊbəl, ˈmoʊˌbajəl/ *adj* [*more ~; most ~*]

1 a : able to move from one place to another ▪ the age at which most babies become *mobile* [=able to crawl or walk] ▪ The doctors say she will be *mobile* [=able to walk] again when her broken leg heals. **b : able to move with the use of vehicles (such as trucks and airplanes)** ▪ Their armies are now fully *mobile*. ▪ *mobile* fighting forces ▪ *mobile* troops

2 : able to be moved ▪ Computers have become more *mobile* [=*portable*] in recent years. ▪ *mobile* hospital equipment ▪ The news station has two *mobile* television units [=trucks or vans with television equipment] for reporting news directly from where events happen. ▪ a *mobile* kitchen that helps bring food to homeless people ▪ *mobile* health clinics ▪ a *mobile* crime laboratory

3 : able to move from one level of a society to another ▪ socially *mobile* workers — **see also** UPWARDLY MOBILE

[2]mo·bile /ˈmoʊˌbiːl, *Brit* ˈməʊbaɪl/ *noun, pl* **-biles** [*count*]

1 : a work of art or a decoration that is hung from above and that has attached shapes or figures that move easily in the air ▪ They hung a *mobile* over the baby's bed.

2 ***Brit, informal*** **:** CELL PHONE ▪ Even if I'm out of the office you can reach me on my *mobile*.

mobile home *noun, pl* **~ homes** [*count*] **: a house that is built in a factory and then moved to the place where people will live in it — compare** MOTOR HOME

mobile home

mobile library *noun, pl* **~ -braries** [*count*] ***Brit*** **:** BOOKMOBILE

mobile phone *noun, pl* **~ phones** [*count*] **:** CELL PHONE

mo·bil·i·ty /moʊˈbɪləti/ *noun* [*noncount*]

1 : the ability or tendency to move from one position or situation to another usually better one ▪ Social *mobility* is often affected by a person's birth, income, and education. ▪ The degree of economic *mobility* is different in different societies. ▪ the career *mobility* of women ▪ the geographic *mobility* of a country's workers [=the tendency of workers to move from one place to another]

2 : ability to move quickly and easily ▪ The army has improved its weapons and increased its *mobility* since the last war. ▪ He was a great football player known for his *mobility* on the field. ▪ She lost *mobility* in her left hand. ▪ elderly people with limited *mobility*

mo·bi·lize *also Brit* **mo·bi·lise** /ˈmoʊbəˌlaɪz/ *verb* **-liz·es; -lized; -liz·ing**

1 a [+ *obj*] **: to bring (people) together for action** ▪ The President *mobilized* [=*rallied*] his supporters. ▪ They couldn't *mobilize* enough support to pass the new law. **b** [*no obj*] **: to come together for action** ▪ Several groups have *mobilized* to oppose the proposed new law. ▪ They have the ability to *mobilize* quickly.

2 [+ *obj*] **: to make (soldiers, an army, etc.) ready for war** ▪ The government had to *mobilize* the army quickly. ▪ More than 10,000 troops were *mobilized* for war. ▪ *mobilizing* the nation's resources

– mo·bi·li·za·tion *also Brit* **mo·bi·li·sa·tion** /ˌmoʊbələˈzeɪʃən, *Brit* ˌməʊbəˌlaɪˈzeɪʃən/ *noun, pl* **-tions** [*count, noncount*] ▪ The army carried out a full-scale *mobilization*.

mob scene *noun, pl* **~ scenes** [*count*] ***US*** **: a place or situation where a crowd of people behave in a violent or uncontrolled way** ▪ The peaceful protest quickly turned into a *mob scene* as protesters began fighting the police.; ***also*** **: a very crowded place or situation** ▪ The store became a real *mob scene*.

mob·ster /ˈmɑːbstɚ/ *noun, pl* **-sters** [*count*] **: someone who is part of a secret organized group of criminals : a member of the Mob** ▪ a reputed *mobster*

moc·ca·sin /ˈmɑːkəsən/ *noun, pl* **-sins** [*count*] **: a flat shoe that is made of soft leather and is similar to a shoe originally worn by some Native Americans — see picture at** SHOE; **see also** WATER MOCCASIN

mo·cha /ˈmoʊkə, *Brit* ˈmɒkə/ *noun, pl* **-chas** [*count, noncount*] **: a drink that is a mixture of coffee and chocolate** ▪ a cup of *mocha*

[1]mock /ˈmɑːk/ *verb* **mocks; mocked; mock·ing** [+ *obj*]

1 : to laugh at or make fun of (someone or something) especially by copying an action or a way of behaving or speaking ▪ The boys *mocked* him for showing fear. ▪ They *mocked* his cries for help. [=they imitated his cries for help in an exaggerated way that was meant to ridicule him] ▪ Other children would *mock* her accent. [=would make fun of the way she spoke by copying it in an exaggerated way]

2 : to criticize and laugh at (someone or something) for being bad, worthless, or unimportant ▪ He *mocks* art only because he doesn't understand it. ▪ They continue to *mock* the idea of a new government. ▪ We are being *mocked* for our religious beliefs. ▪ You can *mock* me as much as you like, but I'm going to do it anyway.

– mock·er /ˈmɑːkɚ/ *noun, pl* **-ers** [*count*] ▪ *mockers* of poetry **– mocking** *adj* [*more ~; most ~*] ▪ *mocking* words ▪ a *mocking* crowd **– mock·ing·ly** /ˈmɑːkɪŋli/ *adv* ▪ They laughed at him *mockingly*.

[2]mock *adj, always used before a noun*

1 : not based on real or honest feelings ▪ "I'd love to go," he said with a *mock* [=*feigned, fake*] smile. ▪ We stared at him in *mock* surprise. ▪ *mock* anger

2 : done or performed to look like the real thing ▪ Two boys started a *mock* [=*simulated*] fight in the hallway. ▪ Every summer, our history club performs *mock* battles to relive our country's greatest war. ▪ a *mock* trial [=a fake legal trial used for education and practice] ▪ a *mock* election

[3]mock *noun, pl* **mocks** [*count*] ***Brit*** **: an exam that does not count and that is done to practice for a real exam : a mock exam — usually plural** ▪ He did so well on the *mocks* that I'm sure he'll pass the real ones.

mock·ery /ˈmɑːkəri/ *noun*

1 [*noncount*] **: behavior or speech that makes fun of someone or something in a hurtful way : mocking behavior or speech** ▪ The bright orange house was an object of *mockery* on our street. [=people mocked the house; people laughed at it and criticized it] • His kind of personality invites *mockery*. • the children's cruel *mockery* of each other

2 [*singular*] **: a bad or useless copy of something** • The judge's decisions are a *mockery* of real justice. [=the judge's decisions are very unjust] ◊ **If you *make a mockery of* something, you make it seem ridiculous or useless.** • The judge's decisions have *made a mockery of* the legal system. • He's *made a mockery of* our marriage.

mock·ing·bird /ˈmɑːkɪŋˌbɚd/ *noun, pl* **-birds** [*count*] **: a North American bird that sings loudly and copies the songs of other birds — see color picture on page C9**

mock turtleneck *noun, pl* ~ **-necks** [*count*] *US* **: a knit shirt or sweater with a high collar that goes all the way around your neck and that is not folded down — called also** (*chiefly Brit*) *turtleneck*

mock–up /ˈmɑːkˌʌp/ *noun, pl* **-ups** [*count*] **: a full-sized model of something (such as a boat or a car) that is used for studying, testing, or showing its features**

mod·al /ˈmoudl/ *noun, pl* **-als** [*count*] *grammar* **: MODAL VERB**

modal verb *noun, pl* ~ **verbs** [*count*] *grammar* **: a verb (such as *can, could, shall, should, ought to, will,* or *would*) that is usually used with another verb to express ideas such as possibility, necessity, and permission — called also *modal, modal auxiliary, modal auxiliary verb***

mod cons /ˌmɑːdˈkɑːnz/ *noun* [*plural*] *Brit, informal* **: the equipment and features that are found in a modern home and that make life easier and more comfortable** • Well, I see your new house has got all the *mod cons* you'd expect: a washing machine, a dishwasher, central heating . . . ◊ ***Mod cons* is taken from the phrase "modern conveniences."**

mode /ˈmoud/ *noun, pl* **modes** [*count*]

1 *formal* **a : a particular form or type *of* something (such as transportation or behavior)** • We're changing the factory's *mode* [=*method*] *of* operation in order to save money. • Technology has created new *modes of* communication. • different *modes of* thought • buses, trains, airplanes, and other ***modes of transportation*** **b : a particular way *of* doing something** • We're using a new *mode* [=*method*] *of* teaching. • a different *mode* [=*way*] *of* living • new *modes of* thinking

2 : the state in which a machine does a particular function • The VCR has two different recording *modes*. • When taking pictures indoors, put the camera in flash *mode*.

3 *informal* **: a specified way of thinking, feeling, or acting** • Let's get into work *mode*. [=let's get ready to work] • When I'm in my creative *mode* [=when I'm feeling creative], I can write for hours. • Reading helps me get into my relaxation *mode*. • He goes into attack *mode* [=he becomes very hostile and aggressive] whenever his decisions are questioned.

— see also À LA MODE

[1]mod·el /ˈmɑːdl/ *noun, pl* **-els** [*count*]

1 : a usually small copy of something • She's building a *model* of the Earth for science class. • *models* of famous buildings • a plastic *model* of the human heart • a ***scale model*** [=a small but exact copy] of a ship

2 : a particular type or version of a product (such as a car or computer) • We've improved on last year's *model*, making the car safer and easier to control. • He bought one of the old 1965 *models*. • We couldn't afford one of the fancy TVs and had to buy the standard *model*.

3 : a set of ideas and numbers that describe the past, present, or future state of something (such as an economy or a business) • a mathematical *model* • We've developed a computer *model* of the economy to predict what will happen in the future. • Companies are developing new business *models*.

4 a : something or someone that is a very good example *of* something • The city is now a *model of* safety and cleanliness. [=the city is now very safe and clean] • He is a *model of* politeness. [=he is very polite] • The country was the *model of* a peaceful nation for over 50 years. **b : something or someone that deserves to be copied by others** • The country's economy is a *model* for the rest of the world. • Her work has become a *model* to/for other writers. • These soldiers serve as *models* for their country. **— see also** ROLE MODEL

5 : someone who is paid to wear clothing, jewelry, etc., in photographs, fashion shows, etc., so that people will see and want to buy what is being worn • a fashion *model* • male *models* • She's a *model* turned actress. [=a model who later became an actress] **— see also** SUPERMODEL

6 : someone whose image is painted, photographed, etc., by an artist • The same *model* sat/posed for several of his paintings. • drawings of nude *models* • an artist's *model*

[2]model *adj, always used before a noun*

1 : deserving to be copied by others : very good or excellent • They're all *model* students. • He's a *model* husband. • Our university has a *model* program for training its athletes.

2 — used to describe something that is a small copy of something larger • a *model* airplane • He'll play with his *model* trains for hours.

[3]model *verb* **-els**; *US* **-eled** *or Brit* **-elled**; *US* **-el·ing** *or Brit* **-el·ling**

1 [+ *obj*] **: to design (something) so that it is similar to something else — + *on* or (*chiefly US*) *after*** • They *modeled* their educational system *on* the U.S. system. [=they used the U.S. system as a model when they created their educational system] • His best dish is closely *modeled on* his mother's recipe. [=is based on and very similar to his mother's recipe] • The church was *modeled after* an earlier French design.

2 [+ *obj*] **a : to make a small copy of (something) : to create a model of (something)** • The faces of the gods were *modeled* in white stone. **b : to make something by forming or shaping clay or some other material** • *modeling* [=*molding*] figures in/from clay = *modeling* clay into figures

3 : to wear clothing, jewelry, etc., in photographs, fashion shows, etc., so that people will see and want to buy what you are wearing [+ *obj*] They're *modeling* this year's new spring fashions. • She got a job *modeling* shoes for a catalog company. • a fashion model who has angered animal lovers by *modeling* fur coats [*no obj*] She *models* [=she works as a fashion model] for the world's most successful modeling agency.

4 [*no obj*] **: to be a model for an artist : to be painted or photographed by an artist** • She agreed to *model* for him and appeared in many of his most famous works.

model yourself on *or chiefly US* ***model yourself after*** **: to try to be like and to behave like (someone you admire)** • She *models herself on* the leaders that came before her. • Children often *model themselves after* their parents.

– mod·el·er (*US*) *or Brit* **mod·el·ler** /ˈmɑːdlɚ/ *noun, pl* **-ers** [*count*] • a ship *modeler* [=someone who makes small copies of ships]

mod·el·ing (*US*) *or Brit* **mod·el·ling** /ˈmɑːdlɪŋ/ *noun* [*noncount*]

1 : the work of a fashion model : the job of displaying things for sale usually by wearing them and being photographed • She hoped *modeling* would help start her acting career. **— often used before another noun** • a *modeling* agency • his *modeling* career

2 : the act or activity of making small copies of things (such as planes, trains, etc.) : the hobby of making models • ship *modeling*

3 : a process in which computers use a set of ideas and numbers to describe the past, present, or future state of something (such as an economy or a business) • Computer *modeling* helps scientists understand the Earth's weather systems. • economic *modeling*

mo·dem /ˈmoudəm/ *noun, pl* **-dems** [*count*] **: a device that changes the form of electric signals so that information can be sent through telephone lines from one computer to another computer** • a high-speed *modem*

[1]mod·er·ate /ˈmɑːdərət/ *adj*

1 a : average in size or amount : neither too much nor too little • Her doctor recommended *moderate* exercise. • There were *moderate* levels of chemicals in the lake. • drinking *moderate* amounts of coffee • Most of these medicines relieve mild to *moderate* pain. • a family of *moderate* income • a book of *moderate* length • a *moderate* distance **b : neither very good nor very bad** • The group met with only *moderate* success. • a writer of *moderate* talent

2 [*more* ~; *most* ~] **: not expensive : not too high in price** • The hotel offers comfortable rooms at *moderate* prices.

3 [*more* ~; *most* ~] **: having or expressing political beliefs that are neither very liberal nor very conservative** • Both *moderate* Democrats and *moderate* Republicans can agree on this new law. • She holds a *moderate* position on the subject of taxes. • The group is in need of more *moderate* voices. [=the group needs more members who do not express extreme ideas]

4 [*more* ~; *most* ~] **a : avoiding behavior that goes beyond what is normal, healthy, or acceptable** • a *moderate* eater [=a person who does not eat too much] • a *moderate* diet • He believes that *moderate* drinking is healthy. • a person of *moderate* habits **b : not showing strong emotions or excitement** • She expressed herself in *moderate* [=*calm, reasonable*] language.

M

[2]**mod•er•ate** /ˈmɑːdərət/ *noun, pl* **-ates** [*count*] **:** a person whose political ideas are not extreme **:** a person who has moderate opinions or is a member of a moderate political group ▪ *Moderates* from both political parties have agreed on an economic plan.

[3]**mod•er•ate** /ˈmɑːdəˌreɪt/ *verb* **-ates; -at•ed; -at•ing**
1 : to make (something) less harsh, strong, or severe or to become less harsh, strong, or severe [+ *obj*] The protesters have been unwilling to *moderate* their demands. [*no obj*] The wind *moderated* [=*lessened*] after the storm.
2 : to guide a discussion or direct a meeting that involves a group of people [*no obj*] She *moderates* at our office meetings. [+ *obj*] She *moderates* our discussions so that we don't argue or talk at the same time. ▪ *moderate* a debate

mod•er•ate•ly /ˈmɑːdərətli/ *adv*
1 : not completely or extremely **:** to a moderate degree or extent ▪ a *moderately* [=*fairly, rather, somewhat*] sweet wine ▪ a *moderately* hot day ▪ The medicine is only *moderately* effective against coughs. ▪ Cook the chicken over *moderately* high heat for three minutes.
2 [*more* ~; *most* ~] **:** in a way that is not too expensive **:** in a moderate way ▪ We tried to find a more *moderately* priced hotel. ▪ *moderately* priced wines

mod•er•a•tion /ˌmɑːdəˈreɪʃən/ *noun*
1 [*noncount*] **:** the quality or state of being reasonable and avoiding behavior, speech, etc., that is extreme or that goes beyond what is normal or acceptable ▪ She expressed her opinions with *moderation*. = She showed *moderation* in the expression of her opinions. [=she expressed her opinions moderately] ▪ The organization is encouraging *moderation* among the world's leaders. ▪ a diet of *moderation* [=a moderate diet] ▪ He has been a ***voice of moderation***. [=a person saying things that are reasonable and moderate]
2 : a decrease in something that is strong or severe — often + *in* [*singular*] The weather has been extremely hot, but the forecast calls for a slight *moderation in* temperatures over the next several days. [=temperatures will become slightly cooler] [*noncount*] We should be seeing some *moderation in* the growth of the economy.
in moderation **:** in a way that is reasonable and not excessive **:** in a moderate way ▪ She believes in doing things *in moderation*. ▪ Some people say that drinking alcohol *in moderation* can be good for you.

mod•er•a•tor /ˈmɑːdəˌreɪtɚ/ *noun, pl* **-tors** [*count*] **:** someone who leads a discussion in a group and tells each person when to speak **:** someone who moderates a meeting or discussion ▪ The *moderator* allowed audience members to ask the governor questions. ▪ She acts as the *moderator* in our office meetings.

[1]**mod•ern** /ˈmɑːdɚn/ *adj*
1 *always used before a noun* **a :** of or relating to the present time or the recent past **:** happening, existing, or developing at a time near the present time ▪ ancient and *modern* history ▪ He talked about the role of television in *modern* [=*contemporary*] politics. ▪ The country's *modern* [=*present*] government was formed over 100 years ago. ▪ The earthquake was one of the worst disasters in *modern* [=*recent*] times. ▪ Water pollution is a growing problem in the *modern* world. ▪ the *modern* American family [=the typical American family living today] ▪ He's known as the father of *modern* medicine. **b** *or* ***Modern*** **:** of or relating to the current or most recent period of a language ▪ The English that was spoken by William Shakespeare is very different from the *modern* English spoken today. ▪ She is learning *Modern* Greek.
2 [*more* ~; *most* ~] **:** based on or using the newest information, methods, or technology ▪ We'll need to have *modern* [=*up-to-date*] plumbing and wiring installed in the old house before we can move in. ▪ They live in one of the most *modern* cities in the world. ▪ *modern* methods of communication including e-mail and the Internet
3 [*more* ~; *most* ~] **:** of or relating to a style or way of thinking that is new and different ▪ She cut her long hair for a *modern* look. ▪ He made his old-fashioned apartment look more *modern* by changing the color of the walls and buying new furniture. ▪ Their latest movie is a *modern* version of a classic children's story. ▪ She has *modern* ideas about dating and marriage. — opposite OLD-FASHIONED
4 : of or relating to forms of art (such as dance, music, and architecture) in which the styles used are newer and very different from the older and more traditional styles ▪ She loves both ballet and *modern* dance. ▪ a combination of classical and *modern* architecture ▪ a museum of *modern* art
— **mod•ern•ness** /ˈmɑːdɚnnəs/ *noun* [*noncount*] ▪ the *modernness* of an artist's style

[2]**modern** *noun, pl* **-erns** [*count*] **:** a modern person: such as **a :** a person who has modern ideas, tastes, or attitudes — usually plural ▪ furniture designed for young *moderns* **b :** a modern artist or writer — usually plural ▪ comparing the art of the ancients and the *moderns*

mod•ern–day /ˈmɑːdɚnˈdeɪ/ *adj, always used before a noun* **:** existing today ▪ problems facing most *modern-day* families ▪ *modern-day* China — often used to indicate that someone or something of the present is similar to someone or something of the past ▪ The two lovers are a *modern-day* [=*latter-day*] Romeo and Juliet. ▪ He's been called a *modern-day* saint. ▪ the *modern-day* equivalent of slavery

mod•ern•ism /ˈmɑːdɚˌnɪzəm/ *noun* [*noncount*] **:** a style of art, architecture, literature, etc., that uses ideas and methods which are very different from those used in the past — compare POSTMODERNISM
— **mod•ern•ist** /ˈmɑːdɚnɪst/ *noun, pl* **-ists** [*count*] ▪ a leading *modernist* — **modernist** *adj* [*more* ~; *most* ~] ▪ a *modernist* painter — **mod•ern•is•tic** /ˌmɑːdɚˈnɪstɪk/ *adj* [*more* ~; *most* ~] ▪ a somewhat *modernistic* style

mo•der•ni•ty /məˈdɚnəti/ *noun* [*noncount*] *formal* **:** the quality of being modern ▪ the *modernity* of an artist's style **:** a modern way of living or thinking ▪ a traditional town that has resisted *modernity*

mod•ern•ize *also Brit* **mod•ern•ise** /ˈmɑːdɚˌnaɪz/ *verb* **-iz•es; -ized; -iz•ing**
1 [+ *obj*] **:** to make (something) modern and more suited to present styles or needs ▪ We're *modernizing* our kitchen with a new oven, refrigerator, and dishwasher. ▪ The country recently announced plans to begin *modernizing* its army. ▪ The school needs a building with *modernized* classrooms.
2 [*no obj*] **:** to become modern **:** to begin using the newest information, methods, or technology ▪ Older companies will need to *modernize* quickly if they are to survive in today's economy.
— **mod•ern•i•za•tion** *also Brit* **mod•ern•i•sa•tion** /ˌmɑːdɚnəˈzeɪʃən, *Brit* ˌmɒdəˌnaɪˈzeɪʃən/ *noun* [*noncount*] ▪ a company in need of *modernization*

mod•est /ˈmɑːdəst/ *adj* [*more* ~; *most* ~]
1 : not very large in size or amount ▪ Despite its *modest* [=somewhat small] size, the city has many things to offer tourists. ▪ They own a *modest* home near the beach. ▪ She enjoyed *modest* success with her singing career. ▪ He earns a *modest* income. ▪ We live on a *modest* budget. ▪ New cars are now available at relatively *modest* prices. ▪ He has only a *modest* amount of knowledge on the subject. ▪ It is a book of only *modest* importance.
2 *approving* **:** not too proud or confident about yourself or your abilities **:** not showing or feeling great or excessive pride ▪ She's very *modest* about her achievements. ▪ Don't be so *modest*. Your performance was wonderful! ▪ "I'm not a hero. I was just doing my job," he said in his characteristically *modest* way. ▪ He is unusually *modest* for a man who is so famous and successful. — opposite IMMODEST
3 a *of clothing* **:** not showing too much of a person's body ▪ She preferred wearing more *modest* swimsuits. ▪ In some countries, women must wear very *modest* clothing in public. **b :** shy about showing your body especially in a sexual way **:** preferring to wear modest clothing ▪ a *modest* young woman — opposite IMMODEST
— **mod•est•ly** *adv* ▪ Our business has been *modestly* successful. ▪ a *modestly* priced car ▪ a *modestly* dressed young woman ▪ She *modestly* refused to accept credit for the team's success.

mod•es•ty /ˈmɑːdəsti/ *noun* [*noncount*] **:** the quality of being modest: such as **a :** the quality of not being too proud or confident about yourself or your abilities ▪ She accepted the award with *modesty*. ▪ He is known for his *modesty*, an uncommon characteristic for a politician. ▪ There was no false *modesty* in her victory speech. ✧ The phrases ***in all modesty*** and (*US*) ***with all modesty*** are used to stress that a statement you are making about yourself is true even if it sounds like something said because of pride. ▪ *In all modesty*, I don't know anyone who could beat me at tennis. ▪ I'll admit *with all modesty* that I have had a very successful career. **b :** the quality of behaving and especially dressing in ways that do not attract sexual attention ▪ the young woman's *modesty* ▪ the *modesty* of her clothing

mo•di•cum /ˈmɑːdɪkəm/ *noun* [*singular*] *formal* **:** a small amount — + *of* ▪ The group had a *modicum of* success in the early 1990s. ▪ Anyone with even a *modicum of* intelligence would understand. ▪ He told a story that didn't have a *modicum of* truth to it.

mod·i·fi·ca·tion /ˌmɑːdəfəˈkeɪʃən/ *noun, pl* **-tions**

1 [*noncount*] **:** the act or process of changing parts of something **:** the act or process of modifying something ▪ The program can be used on all computers without *modification.* — often + *of* ▪ The bad weather required *modification of* our travel plans.

2 [*count*] **:** a change in something (such as a system or style) ▪ They passed the law with only a few minor/slight/small *modifications.* ▪ The weather required some major/minor *modifications* to our travel plans. — often + *of* or *to* ▪ A few *modifications of* the design might be necessary. ▪ We made some *modifications to* the original plan.

mod·i·fi·er /ˈmɑːdəˌfajɚ/ *noun, pl* **-ers** [*count*] *grammar* **:** a word (such as an adjective or adverb) or phrase that describes another word or group of words ▪ In "a red hat," the adjective "red" is a *modifier* describing the noun "hat." ▪ In "They were talking loudly," the adverb "loudly" is a *modifier* of the verb "talking."

mod·i·fy /ˈmɑːdəˌfaɪ/ *verb* **-fies; -fied; -fy·ing** [+ *obj*]

1 : to change some parts of (something) while not changing other parts ▪ We can help you *modify* an existing home or build a new one. ▪ He *modified* the recipe by using oil instead of butter. ▪ *modify* a plan ▪ She has *modified* her views on the matter. ▪ The design was *modified* to add another window. ▪ We played a *modified* version of our favorite game.

2 *grammar* **:** to limit or describe the meaning of (a word or group of words) ▪ Adjectives usually *modify* nouns, and adverbs usually *modify* verbs, adjectives, and other adverbs. ▪ In the phrase "a red hat," the adjective "red" *modifies* the noun "hat."

mod·ish /ˈmoʊdɪʃ/ *adj* [*more* ~; *most* ~] **:** fashionable or stylish in a modern way ▪ He wore a *modish* gray suit and hat. ▪ a *modish* writer

– mod·ish·ly *adv* ▪ a *modishly* dressed woman

mod·u·lar /ˈmɑːʤələ/ *adj* **:** having parts that can be connected or combined in different ways ▪ In many offices, desks are separated by *modular* walls that can be moved around. ▪ a factory that produces *modular* homes ▪ *modular* buildings ▪ (*chiefly Brit*) This is a *modular* course of three components, and students can take those three modules in any order.

mod·u·late /ˈmɑːʤəˌleɪt/ *verb* **-lates; -lat·ed; -lat·ing**

1 [+ *obj*] *formal* **:** to change the sound of (your voice) by making it quieter, higher, lower, etc. ▪ Please *modulate* [=*soften, tone down*] your voice. ▪ Because she doesn't *modulate* her voice, she sounds the same when she's excited as when she's sad.

2 [*no obj*] *music* **:** to move gradually from one key to another ▪ The music quickly *modulates* from its original key, changing the mood of the song.

3 [+ *obj*] **:** to change or adjust (something) so that it exists in a balanced or proper amount ▪ These organs *modulate* [=*regulate*] the amount of salt in the body.

– mod·u·la·tion /ˌmɑːʤəˈleɪʃən/ *noun, pl* **-tions** [*count, noncount*]

mod·ule /ˈmɑːˌʤuːl, *Brit* ˈmɒdjuːl/ *noun, pl* **-ules** [*count*]

1 : one of a set of parts that can be connected or combined to build or complete something ▪ factories that build engines, transmissions, brakes, and other *modules* for cars ▪ (*chiefly Brit*) This is a modular course of three components, and students can take those three *modules* in any order.

2 : a part of a computer or computer program that does a particular job ▪ special software *modules* ▪ a memory *module* for storing information

3 : a part of a space vehicle that can work alone ▪ the spacecraft's ***command module*** [=the main part of a spacecraft] ▪ a ***lunar module*** [=a space vehicle used to land on the moon]

mo·dus ope·ran·di /ˌmoʊdəsˌɑːpəˈrændi/ *noun* [*singular*] *formal* **:** a usual way of doing something; *especially* **:** the usual way that a particular criminal performs a crime ▪ the murderer's *modus operandi* ✧ *Modus operandi* is a Latin phrase that means "method of operation" in English. — called also *MO*

mo·dus vi·ven·di /ˌmoʊdəsvɪˈvɛndi/ *noun* [*singular*] *formal* **:** an arrangement that helps people, groups, or countries work together peacefully even though they do not agree with each other ▪ The two nations developed a *modus vivendi* in order to avoid war. ✧ *Modus vivendi* is a Latin phrase that means "manner of living" in English.

mog·gy *also* **mog·gie** /ˈmɑːgi/ *noun, pl* **-gies** [*count*] *Brit, informal* **:** CAT

¹mo·gul /ˈmoʊgəl/ *noun, pl* **-guls** [*count*] **:** a powerful and important person ▪ TV *moguls* ▪ advertising *moguls* ▪ a young Hollywood *mogul* — compare ²MOGUL

²mogul *noun, pl* **-guls** [*count*] **:** a bump or small hill on a ski slope — compare ¹MOGUL

mo·hair /ˈmoʊˌheɚ/ *noun* [*noncount*] **:** an expensive fabric or wool made from the long, soft hair of a goat from Asia ▪ a sweater made of *mohair* and silk — often used before another noun ▪ She wore her *mohair* hat and mittens.

Mo·hawk /ˈmoʊˌhɑːk/ *noun, pl* **-hawks** [*count*]

1 : a member of a Native American people of central New York state

2 *US* **:** a hairstyle in which the head is shaved except for a narrow strip of hair that goes down the center of the head — called also (*Brit*) *Mohican*

Mo·he·gan /moʊˈhiːgən/ *noun, pl* **-gans** [*count*] **:** MOHICAN 1b

Mo·hi·can /moʊˈhiːkən/ *noun, pl* **-cans** [*count*]

1 a : a member of a Native American people of northeastern New York State **b :** a member of a Native American people of southeastern Connecticut

2 *Brit* **:** MOHAWK 2

moist /ˈmoɪst/ *adj* **moist·er; -est** [*or more* ~; *most* ~]

1 : slightly or barely wet **:** not completely dry ▪ I love cookies when they are *moist* and chewy. ▪ The pork chops were tender and *moist.* ▪ a *moist* and spongy chocolate cake ▪ The plant grows best in direct sunlight and with rich, *moist* soil. ▪ She dabbed her *moist* eyes with a handkerchief.

2 : having a lot of moisture in the air **:** HUMID ▪ Fog is formed when warm *moist* air moves over a cold surface. ▪ *moist* tropical heat ▪ The eggs will hatch sooner in warm, *moist* conditions.

– moist·ness *noun* [*noncount*] the *moistness* of the air/cookies [*singular*] There is a *moistness* in the air today.

> ***synonyms*** MOIST, DAMP, and DANK mean somewhat wet. MOIST suggests a slight wetness that is usually pleasant or desirable. ▪ She wiped her face with a *moist* towel. DAMP suggests that the wetness of something makes it unpleasant to touch. ▪ His shirt was *damp* with sweat. DANK suggests a cold, unpleasant wetness that may be harmful to a person's health. ▪ He was kept prisoner in a cold, *dank* cell.

M

moist·en /ˈmoɪsn̩/ *verb* **-ens; -ened; -en·ing**

1 [+ *obj*] **:** to make (something) slightly wet **:** to make (something) moist ▪ Corn syrup can be used to *moisten* and flavor baked foods. ▪ The chemical reaction begins as soon as the powder is *moistened.*

2 [*no obj*] **:** to become slightly wet ▪ His eyes *moistened* [=his eyes became tearful] at the memory of their kindness.

mois·ture /ˈmoɪsʧɚ/ *noun* [*noncount*] **:** a small amount of a liquid (such as water) that makes something wet or moist ▪ These flowers grow best with *moisture* and shade. ▪ Wool socks will pull *moisture* away from your skin. ▪ The leaves absorb *moisture* from the air.

mois·tur·ize *also Brit* **mois·tur·ise** /ˈmoɪsʧəˌraɪz/ *verb* **-iz·es; -ized; -iz·ing** [+ *obj*] **:** to add moisture to (something, such as a person's skin) ▪ Use this cream to gently *moisturize* dry skin.

– mois·tur·iz·er *also Brit* **mois·tur·is·er** *noun, pl* **-ers** [*count, noncount*] ▪ She uses a *moisturizer* on her skin.

– mois·tur·iz·ing *also Brit* **mois·tur·is·ing** *adj* ▪ a *moisturizing* cream/lotion

mo·jo /ˈmoʊʤoʊ/ *noun, pl* **-jos** *chiefly US, informal* **:** a power that may seem magical and that allows someone to be very effective, successful, etc. [*noncount*] He's been suffering from incredibly bad *mojo* lately. ▪ The team has lost its *mojo.* [*count*] We need to get our *mojos* working again.

mo·lar /ˈmoʊlɚ/ *noun, pl* **-lars** [*count*] **:** a large tooth near the back of the jaw with a wide surface used especially for grinding food

mo·las·ses /məˈlæsəz/ *noun* [*noncount*] *chiefly US* **:** a thick, brown, sweet liquid that is made from raw sugar ▪ *molasses* cookies [=cookies made with molasses] — called also (*Brit*) *treacle*

slow as molasses *or* ***slower than molasses*** *US, informal* **:** very slow or slowly ▪ I used to be a fast runner, but now I'm *slow as molasses.* ▪ People have complained that the legislature is moving/working *slower than molasses.*

¹mold (*US*) *or Brit* **mould** /ˈmoʊld/ *noun, pl* **molds** [*count*]

1 a : a container that is used to give its shape to something that is poured or pressed into it • The candles are made in a *mold*. • The gelatin is poured into a *mold* and chilled until firm. **b :** something made in a mold • a large plaster *mold* of a foot

2 : a usual or typical example of something **:** a pattern or type of something that is an example to be followed • a movie in the classic/traditional/familiar *mold* of a Hollywood thriller • She does not ***fit (into/in) the mold*** of a typical college professor. [=she is not a typical college professor] • He is ***(cast) in the same mold*** as other troubled heroes. [=he resembles other troubled heroes]

break the mold **1 :** to do something in a completely new way • Voters are looking for a candidate who will *break the mold* and give them honest answers. **2** *informal* — used to describe a very unusual or admired person • He was the greatest man I ever knew. ***They broke the mold*** when they made that guy. [=there will never be another person like him]

– compare ³MOLD

²mold *(US) or Brit* **mould** *verb* **molds; mold·ed; mold·ing**

1 [+ *obj*] **a :** to form or press (something, such as wax, plastic, clay, or dough) into a particular shape • *mold* dough into loaves of bread **b :** to make (something) from a material that has been formed or pressed • *mold* loaves of bread • She gave her mother a tiny statue that she *molded* from clay. • The mountains were *molded* [=*formed, shaped*] by the glaciers over thousands of years.

2 [+ *obj*] **:** to make (something) by pouring or pressing material (such as wax or plastic) into a mold • The art class spent its time *molding* candles. • *mold* plastic toys • a *molded* plastic chair

3 [+ *obj*] **:** to create, influence, or affect the character of (someone or something) • She has dedicated her life to teaching and *molding* young children into responsible adults. • *molding* young minds • He took a struggling company and *molded* it into something special.

4 [*no obj*] **:** to fit *to* the shape of something • This new mattress pad will *mold to* your body [=it will change its shape to fit your body] when you sleep on it. • The fabric is thin and flexible and will *mold to* your shape.

– mold·er *(US) or Brit* **mould·er** /ˈmoʊldɚ/ *noun, pl* **-ers** [*count*] • He sees himself as a *molder* of world events. • a *molder* of young minds

³mold *(US) also Brit* **mould** *noun, pl* **molds :** a soft substance that grows on the surface of damp or rotting things [*noncount*] She's allergic to *mold*, cigarette smoke, and dust. • bread *mold* [=mold that grows on bread] [*count*] a slime *mold* [=a mold that is slimy] — compare ¹MOLD

mold·er *(US) or Brit* **mould·er** /ˈmoʊldɚ/ *verb* **-ers; -ered; -er·ing** [*no obj*] **:** to rot slowly especially from not being used **:** to decay slowly • An entire shipment of fruit is *moldering* (away) in the warehouse because of the strike. • *moldering* [=*decaying*] old books

mold·ing *(US) or Brit* **mould·ing** /ˈmoʊldɪŋ/ *noun, pl* **-ings** [*count, noncount*] **:** a strip of material (such as wood or metal) with some design or pattern that is used as a decoration on a wall, on the edge of a table, etc. • The house has beautiful *moldings* around its doors and windows.

moldy *(US) or Brit* **mouldy** /ˈmoʊldi/ *adj* **mold·i·er; -est**

1 : covered with mold • Her books became *moldy* after being left in a damp basement. • *moldy* bread/fruit

2 : resembling mold **:** tasting, smelling, or looking like mold • The wine had a slightly *moldy* aroma/flavor.

¹mole /ˈmoʊl/ *noun, pl* **moles** [*count*]

1 : a small animal with very small eyes and soft fur that digs tunnels in the ground and eats insects

2 : a spy who works inside an organization and gives secret information to another organization or country

– compare ²MOLE, ³MOLE

²mole *noun, pl* **moles** [*count*] **:** a small, brown spot on a person's skin • He has a *mole* on his cheek. — compare ¹MOLE, ³MOLE

³mo·le /ˈmoʊleɪ/ *noun, pl* **mo·les** [*count, noncount*] *chiefly US* **:** a spicy sauce used in Mexican cooking • chicken with *mole* (sauce) — compare ¹MOLE, ²MOLE

mol·e·cule /ˈmɑːlɪˌkjuːl/ *noun, pl* **-cules** [*count*]

1 : the smallest possible amount of a particular substance that has all the characteristics of that substance • a *molecule* of water/oxygen • sugar *molecules*

2 : a very small amount of something • There is not a *molecule* of evidence to support these charges.

– mo·lec·u·lar /məˈlɛkjəlɚ/ *adj* • *molecular* weight • *molecular* structure/movement • She studied *molecular* biology in college.

mole·hill /ˈmoʊlˌhɪl/ *noun, pl* **-hills** [*count*] **:** a small pile of dirt that is pushed up by a mole when it digs tunnels underground

make a mountain out of a molehill **:** to make something seem much more difficult or important than it really is • She thought that he was *making a mountain out of a molehill* by complaining about the placement of the silverware.

mole·skin /ˈmoʊlˌskɪn/ *noun* [*noncount*]

1 : the skin of the mole used as fur

2 : a soft cotton cloth • *moleskin* pants

mo·lest /məˈlɛst/ *verb* **-lests; -lest·ed; -lest·ing** [+ *obj*]

1 : to harm (someone) through sexual contact **:** to touch (someone) in a sexual and improper way • He was sent to jail for *molesting* children.

2 *old-fashioned* **:** to bother or annoy (someone or something) • It was illegal to *molest*, capture, or kill any of the animals in the park.

– mo·les·ta·tion /ˌmoʊˌlɛˈsteɪʃən/ *noun* [*noncount*] • child *molestation* • a victim of *molestation* **– mo·lest·er** /məˈlɛstɚ/ *noun, pl* **-ers** [*count*] • putting child *molesters* in jail

moll /ˈmɑːl/ *noun, pl* **molls** [*count*] *chiefly US, old-fashioned + informal* **:** a girlfriend of a criminal • a gangster's *moll* — called also *(chiefly US) gun moll*

mol·li·fy /ˈmɑːləˌfaɪ/ *verb* **-fies; -fied; -fy·ing** [+ *obj*] **:** to make (someone) less angry **:** to calm (someone) down • He tried to *mollify* his critics with an apology. • All attempts to *mollify* the extremists have failed. • The landlord fixed the heat, but the tenants still were not *mollified*.

mol·lusk *(US) or Brit* **mol·lusc** /ˈmɑːləsk/ *noun, pl* **-lusks** [*count*] *biology* **:** any one of a large group of animals (such as snails and clams) that have a soft body without a backbone and that usually live in a shell

mol·ly·cod·dle /ˈmɑːliˌkɑːdl/ *verb* **-cod·dles; -cod·dled; -cod·dling** [+ *obj*] **:** to treat (someone) with more kindness and attention than is appropriate **:** to treat (someone) too nicely or gently • You need to stop *mollycoddling* [=*babying, coddling*] that boy if you want him to succeed on his own. • The coach has been *mollycoddling* the team's star players.

Mo·lo·tov cocktail /ˈmɑːləˌtɑːf-/ *noun, pl* **~ -tails** [*count*] **:** a simple bomb made from a bottle filled with gasoline and stuffed with a piece of cloth that is lit just before the bottle is thrown — called also *(Brit) petrol bomb*

molt *(US) or Brit* **moult** /ˈmoʊlt/ *verb* **molts; molt·ed; molt·ing** [*no obj*] *biology* **:** to lose a covering of hair, feathers, etc., and replace it with new growth in the same place • Snakes *molt* as they grow, shedding the old skin and growing a larger new skin.

mol·ten /ˈmoʊltn̩/ *adj, always used before a noun* **:** melted by heat • *molten* metal/glass/lead • molten lava

mom /ˈmɑːm/ *noun, pl* **moms** [*count*] *US, informal* **:** a person's mother • My *mom* [=*(Brit) mum*] wants me to call when I get there. — often used as a form of address • *Mom*, do you know where I left my keys? — see also SOCCER MOM

mom–and–pop /ˈmɑːmənˈpɑːp/ *adj, always used before a noun, chiefly US* **:** owned and run by a married couple or by a small number of people • Big department stores can drive *mom-and-pop* shops/stores out of business. • a *mom-and-pop* business that grew to become a large corporation

mo·ment /ˈmoʊmənt/ *noun, pl* **-ments**

1 [*count*] **:** a very short period of time • The sunshine that was here a *moment* [=*minute, second*] ago is gone. • The sun was shining. *Moments* later, it began to rain. • It was a *moment* before she realized what had happened. • She stopped for a *moment* and peeked into the window. • It should only take a *moment* to fix the problem. • Do you have a (spare) *moment*? [=do you have some free time so we can talk to each other briefly?] • I'm very busy and I don't have a *moment* to spare. • The doctor arrived ***not a moment too soon***. [=the doctor arrived just in time to help] • I'll explain that ***in a moment***. [=shortly, soon] • The crowd observed a ***moment of silence*** [=a short period of silent thought or prayer] for those who died in the tragedy.

2 [*count*] **:** a particular time **:** a precise point in time • One *moment* it was sunny; the next it was pouring rain. • We enjoyed every *moment* of the play. [=we enjoyed all of the play] • The *moment* for us to act has arrived. • The *moment* is ripe for action. [=this is the right time for action] • War seemed unavoidable at that *moment* in history. • She knew exactly the right *moment* to ask for a raise. • We had an exciting va-

cation. There was ***never a dull moment***.
3 a [*noncount*] **:** the present time ▪ ***At the moment*** [=*right now, at the current time*] she is working on a novel. ▪ We aren't prepared ***at this moment*** [=*at this time, now*] to say what our plans are. ▪ ***As of this moment*** [=*as of now, right now*], there's nothing you can do. ✧ Something that is true ***for the moment*** is true now but might not be true for long. ▪ *For the moment*, it is the world's largest city. [=it is the world's largest city now, but that may not be true much longer] ▪ He's staying out of trouble *for the moment*. ▪ *For the moment*, at least, I had the room to myself. ✧ Someone or something that is ***of the moment*** is very popular at a particular time. ▪ the vacation destination *of the moment* [=the vacation destination that is now most popular] ▪ the man/woman *of the moment* [=the man/woman who is now very popular and admired] **b** [*count*] **:** a time of importance or success ▪ She took the time to relish her *moment* of triumph. ▪ He's not the best player on the team, but he ***has his moments***. [=he has times when he is extremely good, successful, etc.] ▪ It was a ***defining moment*** for him. ▪ It was a ***crowning moment*** in his presidency.

any moment ✧ If something could happen ***(at) any moment (now)***, it could happen very soon. ▪ He could lose his temper *at any moment*. ▪ The war could begin *at any moment*. ▪ She should be arriving *at any moment now*.

at/on a moment's notice see [1]NOTICE

from moment to moment or ***from one moment to the next*** or ***moment by moment*** **:** very quickly as time passes ▪ The weather kept changing *from one moment to the next*. = The weather kept changing *from moment to moment*. [=*from minute to minute*]

hold/hang on a moment or ***wait/just a moment*** *informal* — used to tell someone to wait or to stop for a brief time ▪ "Aren't you finished yet?" "*Hold on a moment*. I'm almost done." ▪ *Hang on a moment*—I don't understand.

moment of truth **:** the time when you have to do or decide something ▪ The *moment of truth* came early, when we had to decide whether to stay or go. ▪ It was her *moment of truth*, when she needed to show that she had the talent to succeed.

not for a/one moment **:** at no time **:** not at all ▪ I did *not* believe her *for one moment*. [=I never believed her]

of moment *formal* **:** having importance ▪ an event *of* great *moment* [=a very important event] ▪ There is no news *of* any *moment* to report.

on the spur of the moment see [1]SPUR

the last moment **:** the latest possible time **:** the last minute ▪ Our flight was canceled at *the last moment*. ▪ She finished her paper at *the last moment*. ▪ Many people wait until *the last* (possible) *moment* before shopping for Christmas presents.

the moment **:** as soon as ▪ *The moment* the cameras are turned off, he is able to relax. ▪ Everything stops *the moment* she walks in the room.

within moments **:** very quickly **:** within a very short amount of time ▪ *Within moments*, dozens of people had gathered.

mo·men·tari·ly /ˌmoʊmənˈterəli, *Brit* ˈməʊməntərəli/ *adv*
1 : for a short time **:** for a moment **:** BRIEFLY ▪ The pain eased *momentarily*. ▪ The wind let up *momentarily*, allowing us to start a campfire. ▪ He paused *momentarily* before finishing his speech.
2 *US* **:** very soon **:** at any moment ▪ We expect them to arrive *momentarily*. ▪ The pilot announced that the plane would be landing *momentarily*. [=*shortly*]

mo·men·tary /ˈmoʊmənˌteri, *Brit* ˈməʊməntəri/ *adj* **:** lasting a very short time **:** lasting only a moment ▪ There was a *momentary* [=*brief*] pause between songs. ▪ He experienced a *momentary* loss of consciousness.

mo·men·tous /moʊˈmɛntəs/ *adj* [*more* ~; *most* ~] **:** very important **:** having great or lasting importance ▪ My college graduation was a *momentous* day in my life. ▪ a *momentous* decision/event
– mo·men·tous·ly *adv* ▪ a *momentously* important decision

mo·men·tum /moʊˈmɛntəm/ *noun* [*noncount*]
1 a : the strength or force that something has when it is moving ▪ forward *momentum* ▪ The wagon ***gathered/gained momentum*** [=it moved faster] as it rolled down the hill. ▪ The wagon ***lost momentum*** [=it moved more slowly; it slowed down] as it rolled up the hill. **b :** the strength or force that allows something to continue or to grow stronger or faster as time passes ▪ The company has had a successful year and hopes to maintain its *momentum* by introducing new products. ▪ The campaign slowly *gained/gathered momentum*. [=the campaign slowly became more popular and successful] ▪ The movie *loses momentum* toward the end.
2 *physics* **:** the property that a moving object has due to its mass and its motion

mom·ma *variant spelling of* MAMA

mom·my /ˈmɑːmi/ *noun, pl* **-mies** [*count*] *chiefly US, informal* **:** a person's mother — used especially by children ▪ Where's my *mommy*? — often used as a form of address ▪ Can I go out to play, *mommy*?

Mon. *abbr* Monday

mon·arch /ˈmɑːˌnɑɚk/ *noun, pl* **-archs** [*count*] **:** a person (such as a king or queen) who rules a kingdom or empire ▪ a new history of French *monarchs* ▪ an absolute *monarch*

monarch butterfly *noun, pl* ~ **-flies** [*count*] **:** a large orange and black American butterfly

mo·nar·chi·cal /məˈnɑrkɪkəl/ *also* **mo·nar·chic** /məˈnɑɚkɪk/ *adj* **:** of or relating to a monarch or monarchy ▪ *monarchical* authority ▪ a *monarchical* government

mon·ar·chist /ˈmɑnɚkɪst/ *noun, pl* **-chists** [*count*] **:** a person who believes that a country should have a monarch (such as a king or queen) **:** a person who supports a monarch or monarchy ▪ Loyal *monarchists* fought for the king.
– monarchist *adj* ▪ *monarchist* loyalties/beliefs

mon·ar·chy /ˈmɑnɚki/ *noun, pl* **-chies**
1 [*count*] **:** a country that is ruled by a monarch (such as a king or queen)
2 [*count, noncount*] **:** a form of government in which a country is ruled by a monarch ▪ the French *monarchy* of the 18th century — see also CONSTITUTIONAL MONARCHY

mon·as·tery /ˈmɑːnəˌsteri, *Brit* ˈmɑːnəstri/ *noun, pl* **-teries** [*count*] **:** a place where monks live and work together ▪ a Catholic/Buddhist *monastery* — compare CONVENT

mo·nas·tic /məˈnæstɪk/ *adj* [*more* ~; *most* ~]
1 : of or relating to monks or monasteries ▪ a *monastic* community ▪ *monastic* life ▪ He founded a *monastic* order in Belgium.
2 : resembling or suggesting a monk or the life of a monk ▪ He shows a *monastic* dedication to his job. ▪ She studied for the test with *monastic* zeal. ▪ a quiet, *monastic* existence
– mo·nas·ti·cism /məˈnæstəˌsɪzəm/ *noun* [*noncount*] ▪ the history of Christian/Buddhist *monasticism*

Mon·day /ˈmʌnˌdeɪ/ *noun, pl* **-days :** the day of the week between Sunday and Tuesday [*count*] I had lunch with her last *Monday*. ▪ I'll be seeing her again next *Monday*. ▪ The class meets on *Mondays*. [=every Monday] ▪ My birthday falls on a *Monday* this year. ▪ (*Brit*) Next week I'll arrive on the *Monday* and leave on the Friday. [*noncount*] Next week I'll arrive on *Monday* and leave on Friday. ▪ The paper is due on *Monday*. = (*chiefly US*) The paper is due *Monday*. ▪ I will arrive on *Monday* morning. — abbr. *Mon.*
– Mondays *adv* ▪ He works late *Mondays*. [=he works late every Monday]

Monday–morning quarterback *noun, pl* ~ **-backs** [*count*] *US, disapproving* **:** a person who unfairly criticizes or questions the decisions and actions of other people after something has happened ▪ After the water main broke, the *Monday-morning quarterbacks* [=*second-guessers*] in the media criticized the city for not replacing the old pipes.

mon·e·tary /ˈmɑːnəˌteri, *Brit* ˈmʌnətri/ *adj*
1 : of or relating to money ▪ a crime committed for *monetary* gain
2 : of or relating to the money in a country's economy ▪ this administration's *monetary* policy ▪ Gold was once the basis of the U.S. *monetary* system.
– mon·e·tar·i·ly /ˌmɑːnəˈterəli, *Brit* ˈmʌnətrəli/ *adv* ▪ Many companies will benefit/gain *monetarily* from the decision.

mon·ey /ˈmʌni/ *noun, pl* **mon·ies** *or* **mon·eys** /ˈmʌniz/
1 [*noncount*] **:** something (such as coins or bills) used as a way to pay for goods and services and to pay people for their work ▪ Dinner cost a lot of *money* last night. = We were charged a lot of *money* for dinner last night. ▪ a sum of *money* ▪ That painting must be worth a lot of *money*. ▪ She's been making a lot of *money* in her new job. = (*informal*) She's been making big/good *money* in her new job. ▪ He earned some *money* last summer as a musician. ▪ We're trying to save enough *money* for a new car. ▪ The town is raising *money* for the elementary school. ▪ Friends would always ask her for *money*. ▪ It's an interesting idea, but there's no *money* in it: it'll never sell. ▪ The club ***made money*** [=earned money; made a profit] by selling advertisements in the newsletter. ▪

M

She knew she could *make money* [=earn a profit] on the deal. = She knew there was *money* to be *made* from/on the deal. • When they take a vacation, ***money is no object*** [=they are not concerned about the price of things] They always stay at the most expensive places. — see also BLOOD MONEY, FUNNY MONEY, HUSH MONEY, OLD MONEY, PAPER MONEY, POCKET MONEY, SEED MONEY, SOFT MONEY, SPENDING MONEY, *smart money* at [1]SMART
2 [*noncount*] **:** a person's wealth **:** the money that a person has • He made his *money* in the insurance business. • He lost his *money* on foolish investments. = He threw all his *money* away on foolish investments. • They decided to put all their *money* in the stock market. • We didn't have much *money* when I was growing up. • She ***comes from money.*** [=her family is rich] • She ***married into money.*** [=she married a wealthy man] — see also *marry money* at MARRY
3 ***monies*** *or* ***moneys*** [*plural*] *formal* **:** amounts of money • Most of the project is being paid for by federal *monies.* • All *monies* received will be deposited in a special account.
a run for your money see [2]RUN
for love or/nor money see [1]LOVE
for my money *informal* **:** in my opinion • This book is, *for my money*, her best novel yet. [=I think this is her best novel yet] • *For my money*, nothing beats a juicy peach on a hot summer day.
in the money **1** *US* **:** among the top three finishers in a race (such as a horse race) • Whatever horse I bet on, it never finishes *in the money.* **2** *informal* **:** having lots of money • They struggled for many years but now they're *in the money.*
made of money *informal* **:** having a lot of money **:** RICH • Do I look like I'm *made of money*? • Stop asking your father for a bigger allowance. He's not *made of money*, you know!
money for jam *or* ***money for old rope*** *Brit, informal* **:** money that is easily earned or gotten **:** easy money
money talks — used to say that money has a strong influence on people's actions and decisions • In politics, *money talks.* [=people and companies with a lot of money have a powerful influence in politics]
money to burn *informal* **:** a large amount of money to spend • expensive cars for people with *money to burn*
on the money *US, informal* **:** exactly right or accurate • His prediction that it would rain was (right) *on the money.*
put (your) money on **:** to bet on (something or someone) • Everyone there *put their money on* the underdog. — often used to say that you feel very sure that something is true, will happen, etc. • "Do you think he'll win?" "I'd *put money on* it." • It's going to rain tomorrow. I'd *put money on* it.
put your money where your mouth is *informal* **:** to give or spend money or take some action in order to do or support something that you have been talking about • It's time for the mayor to *put his money where his mouth is* and increase funding for schools.
throw money around **:** to spend money in a foolish or careless way • He really *throws* (his) *money around.*
throw money at **:** to try to solve (a problem) by spending a large amount of money on it without giving enough thought to exactly what should be done • The flaws in our school system will never be fixed as long as the government continues to just *throw money at* the problem.
time is money — used to say that a person's time is as valuable as money
your money's worth **:** as much as you deserve because of the money you paid or the effort you made • His new movie gives his fans *their money's worth.* [=his new movie is good and is worth the money that his fans pay to see it] • The people who showed up for the concert certainly ***got their money's worth*** • He insisted on staying until the end of the show so that he could *get his money's worth.*

mon•ey–back /ˈmʌniˈbæk/ *adj, always used before a noun* **:** allowing buyers to get their money back if the product breaks, does not work, or is not what the buyer wanted • All of their tools come with a *money-back* guarantee.

mon•ey•bags /ˈmʌniˌbægz/ *noun, pl* **moneybags** [*count*] *informal* **:** a very rich person • His campaign is being paid for by a local *moneybags.*

money box *noun, pl* ~ **boxes** [*count*] *chiefly Brit* **:** a box that has a narrow opening in the top and that is used for saving coins

mon•eyed *or* **mon•ied** /ˈmʌnid/ *adj, always used before a noun, formal* **:** having a lot of money **:** very rich • a member of the *moneyed* classes

mon•ey–grub•ber /ˈmʌniˌgrʌbɚ/ *noun, pl* **-bers** [*count*] *informal* **:** a person who cares too much about getting money • a selfish *money-grubber*
– mon•ey–grub•bing /ˈmʌniˌgrʌbɪŋ/ *adj* [*more* ~; *most* ~] • a bitter, *money-grubbing* old miser **– money–grubbing** *noun* [*noncount*]

mon•ey•lend•er /ˈmʌniˌlɛndɚ/ *noun, pl* **-ers** [*count*] **:** a person who lends money as a business • He was unable to repay his debts to the *moneylender.*

mon•ey–mak•er /ˈmʌniˌmeɪkɚ/ *noun, pl* **-ers** [*count*]
1 : something (such as a product) that earns a profit • The book eventually became a *money-maker* for its publisher. • This movie should be the biggest *money-maker* of the summer. — called also (*Brit*) *money-spinner*
2 : a person who earns or wins a large amount of money • He is one of the top *money-makers* in professional tennis.
– mon•ey–mak•ing /ˈmʌniˌmeɪkɪŋ/ *adj* • a film with *money-making* potential

mon•ey•man /ˈmʌniˌmæn/ *noun, pl* **-men** /-ˌmɛn/ [*count*] **:** a man who controls the use of large amounts of money — usually plural • a politician being bankrolled by a group of powerful *moneymen*

money order *noun, pl* ~ **-ders** [*count*] **:** a written order to pay a particular amount of money to a specified person or company ✧ A money order can be bought from a bank or post office and sent by mail like a check to make a payment to another person. • She mailed a *money order* to the company for the cost of the TV she bought. • Payments can be made by check or ***by money order.*** [=by using a money order] — called also (*Brit*) *postal order*

mon•ey–spin•ner /ˈmʌniˌspɪnɚ/ *noun, pl* **-ners** [*count*] *Brit, informal* **:** MONEY-MAKER 1
– mon•ey–spin•ning /ˈmʌniˌspɪnɪŋ/ *adj, Brit*

money supply *noun*
the money supply *business* **:** the total amount of money available for spending in a country's economy • an increase in *the money supply*

mon•goose /ˈmɑːnˌguːs/ *noun, pl* **-goos•es** [*count*] **:** a small and very fast animal from India that eats snakes and rodents

mongoose

mon•grel /ˈmɑːŋgrəl/ *noun, pl* **-grels** [*count*] **:** a dog with parents of different breeds • She owns several dogs, including a *mongrel* named Stella. — often used before another noun • a *mongrel* dog — sometimes used figuratively • The new house was a *mongrel*, with a mix of styles from different times and places.

monied *variant spelling of* MONEYED

monies *plural of* MONEY

mon•i•ker /ˈmɑːnɪkɚ/ *noun, pl* **-kers** [*count*] *informal* **:** a name or nickname • He earned the *moniker* "Gator" from his days wrestling alligators in Florida. • I think "Happy" is an appropriate *moniker* for someone who smiles so much.

[1]**mon•i•tor** /ˈmɑːnətɚ/ *noun, pl* **-tors** [*count*]
1 : a device that is used for showing, watching, or listening to something: such as **a :** a device that shows information or images on a screen • a computer *monitor* • a television *monitor* • They watched the press conference on a video *monitor* in a back room. — see pictures at CAMERA, COMPUTER **b :** a device that is used to listen to sounds being made in another room • We put a baby *monitor* in the nursery. **c :** a device that shows and records information about a condition or function of the body • a heart *monitor*
2 : a student who helps the teacher at a school • (*US*) He was chosen to be a ***hall monitor.*** [=a student who watches the hallways for bad behavior]
3 : a person who has the job of checking or watching some activity or behavior • U.N. weapons *monitors* and inspectors

[2]**monitor** *verb* **-tors; -tored; -tor•ing** [+ *obj*] **:** to watch, observe, listen to, or check (something) for a special purpose over a period of time • Nurses constantly *monitored* the patient's heart rate. • We're in a good position to *monitor* and respond to customer concerns. • She's been able to *monitor* [=*keep track of*] his progress. • Government agents have been *monitoring* the enemy's radio communications.

monk /ˈmʌŋk/ *noun, pl* **monks** [*count*] **:** a member of a religious community of men who usually promise to remain poor, unmarried, and separated from the rest of society • Catholic/Buddhist *monks* — compare NUN

– **monk·ish** /ˈmʌŋkɪʃ/ *adj* [*more* ~; *most* ~] ▪ a quiet *monkish* man ▪ a *monkish* way of life

[1]**mon·key** /ˈmʌŋki/ *noun, pl* **-keys** [*count*]
1 : a type of animal that is closely related to apes and humans and that has a long tail and usually lives in trees — see also RHESUS MONKEY
2 *chiefly Brit* **:** a person (especially a child) who causes trouble in a playful way ▪ He's quite a cheeky little *monkey*, isn't he?
a monkey on your back **:** a problem that you cannot easily get rid of or solve **:** a problem or situation that makes you unhappy and that lasts for a long time ▪ His drug addiction has been a *monkey on his back* for years. ▪ He finally ***got the monkey off his back*** and kicked his drug addiction. ▪ After many years of disappointment, she finally *got the monkey off her back* by winning the championship.
make a monkey out of *informal* **:** to cause (someone) to look very foolish **:** to make a fool out of (someone) ▪ I'm not going to let that salesman *make a monkey out of* me!
more fun than a barrel (full) of monkeys see [1]BARREL
not give a monkey's *Brit, informal* **:** to not care at all about something. ▪ *I don't give a monkey's* about their problems!
– see also GREASE MONKEY

[2]**monkey** *verb* **-keys; -keyed; -key·ing**
monkey around *or Brit* ***monkey about*** [*phrasal verb*] *informal* **1 :** to do things that are not useful or serious **:** to waste time ▪ We just *monkeyed around* [=*fooled around, messed around*] all afternoon. ▪ a young scientist *monkeying around* in the lab **2** ***monkey around/about with (something)*** *informal* **a :** to use or do (something) in a way that is not very serious ▪ He enjoys *monkeying around with* [=*fooling around with*] his car's engine. **b :** to handle or play with (something) in a careless or foolish way ▪ You shouldn't be *monkeying around with* dangerous chemicals.
monkey with [*phrasal verb*] ***monkey with (something)*** *informal* **:** to handle or play with (something) in a careless way **:** to monkey around with (something) ▪ I told you not to *monkey with* [=*fool with*] the lawn mower.

monkey bars *noun* [*plural*] *US* **:** a frame of bars that children can play on by climbing and by swinging from one bar to the next one in the way that monkeys in a tree swing from branch to branch

monkey business *noun* [*noncount*] *informal*
1 : playful tricks or jokes ▪ Our teacher warned us not to try any *monkey business* while she was out of the room.
2 : illegal or improper activity or behavior ▪ political *monkey business*

mon·key·shines /ˈmʌŋkiˌʃaɪnz/ *noun* [*plural*] *US, informal + old-fashioned* **:** playful tricks and jokes **:** MONKEY BUSINESS ▪ mischievous children engaging in *monkeyshines*

monkey wrench *noun, pl* ~ **wrenches** [*count*] **:** a wrench that can be adjusted to grip or turn things of different sizes — used in U.S. English to refer especially to a large, heavy wrench with a long, straight handle
throw/hurl/toss a monkey wrench into *US, informal* **:** to damage or change (something) in a way that ruins it or prevents it from working properly ▪ The storm *threw a monkey wrench into* their plans for a picnic. [=the storm ruined their plans for a picnic]

mono /ˈmɑːnoʊ/ *noun* [*noncount*]
1 *informal* **:** MONONUCLEOSIS
2 : a way of recording and playing back sound so that all the sound comes from one direction ▪ They recorded the album in *mono*. — compare STEREO
– **mono** *adj* ▪ a *mono* recording

mono- *combining form* **:** one **:** single ▪ *mono*plane ▪ *mono*lingual

mono·chro·mat·ic /ˌmɑːnəkroʊˈmætɪk/ *adj* **:** having or made up of one color or shades of one color ▪ It's a *monochromatic* room with a blue rug and blue furniture.

mono·chrome /ˈmɑːnəˌkroʊm/ *adj*
1 : having or made up of one color or shades of one color **:** MONOCHROMATIC ▪ a *monochrome* paint scheme ▪ *monochrome* colors
2 : using or showing only black and white and shades of gray ▪ a *monochrome* film/photograph — sometimes used figuratively ▪ a dull, *monochrome* existence

mon·o·cle /ˈmɑːnɪkəl/ *noun, pl* **mon·o·cles** [*count*] **:** a single round lens for one eye that helps people see and that is held in place by the muscles around the eye
– **mon·o·cled** /ˈmɑːnɪkəld/ *adj* ▪ a *monocled* professor [=a professor wearing a monocle]

mo·nog·a·my /məˈnɑːgəmi/ *noun* [*noncount*]
1 : the state or practice of being married to only one person at a time — compare POLYGAMY
2 : the state or practice of having only one sexual partner during a period of time ▪ young couples who practice *monogamy* ▪ *Monogamy* is common among birds.
– **mo·nog·a·mous** /məˈnɑːgəməs/ *adj* ▪ They've been in a *monogamous* relationship for many years. ▪ Many birds are *monogamous*.

mono·gram /ˈmɑːnəˌgræm/ *noun, pl* **-grams** [*count*] **:** a symbol that has the first letters of a person's first, middle, and last names and that is put on towels, blankets, clothes, etc., as a decoration or to show ownership
– **mono·grammed** /ˈmɑːnəˌgræmd/ *adj* ▪ *monogrammed* towels

monogram

mono·lin·gual /ˌmɑːnəˈlɪŋgwəl/ *adj*
1 : able to speak and understand only one language ▪ He regrets being *monolingual* and wishes he were bilingual.
2 : using or expressed in only one language ▪ a *monolingual* dictionary — compare BILINGUAL, MULTILINGUAL

mono·lith /ˈmɑːnəˌlɪθ/ *noun, pl* **-liths** [*count*]
1 a : a very large stone that is usually tall and narrow; *especially* **:** a stone that was put in position by people as a monument or for religious reasons ▪ an ancient *monolith* **b :** a very large building or other structure ▪ The new office building is a massive steel and concrete *monolith*.
2 *often disapproving* **:** a very large and powerful organization that acts as a single unit ▪ The media *monolith* owns a number of networks. ▪ a global *monolith*
– **mono·lith·ic** /ˌmɑːnəˈlɪθɪk/ *adj* ▪ a large, *monolithic* building ▪ a *monolithic* organization

mono·logue *also US* **mono·log** /ˈmɑːnəˌlɑːg/ *noun, pl* **-logues** *also US* **-logs** [*count*]
1 : a long speech given by a character in a story, movie, play, etc., or by a performer (such as a comedian) ▪ The play begins with the main character's *monologue*. ▪ The comedian is famous for his *monologue* about winning the lottery.
2 : a long speech made by one person that prevents anyone else from talking ▪ I stifled a yawn as she launched into a *monologue* about how she is going to become a famous star.

mono·nu·cle·o·sis /ˌmɑːnəˌnuːkliˈoʊsəs, *Brit* ˌmɒnəˌnjuːkliˈəʊsəs/ *noun* [*noncount*] *medical* **:** a disease that makes people very tired and weak for a long time — called also (*Brit*) *glandular fever*, (*informal*) *mono*

mono·plane /ˈmɑːnəˌpleɪn/ *noun, pl* **-planes** [*count*] **:** an airplane with one set of wings — compare BIPLANE ✧ Most modern airplanes are monoplanes.

mo·nop·o·lize *also Brit* **mo·nop·o·lise** /məˈnɑːpəˌlaɪz/ *verb* **-liz·es; -lized; -liz·ing** [+ *obj*] **:** to take over and control (something or someone) completely ▪ He's always *monopolizing* the conversation. ▪ The company has *monopolized* the market for computer operating systems. ▪ The demands of the job have been *monopolizing* my time. [=using up all my time] **:** to use (something) in a way that prevents others from using it ▪ One group *monopolized* the camping area, taking almost all of the campsites.
– **mo·nop·o·list** /məˈnɑːpəlɪst/ *noun, pl* **-lists** [*count*] ▪ a powerful *monopolist* [=a person or company that has or controls a monopoly] – **mo·nop·o·li·za·tion** *also Brit* **mo·nop·o·li·sa·tion** /məˌnɑːpələˈzeɪʃən, *Brit* məˌnɒpəˌlaɪˈzeɪʃən/ *noun* [*noncount*]

mo·nop·o·ly /məˈnɑːpəli/ *noun, pl* **-lies**
1 [*count*] **a :** complete control of the entire supply of goods or of a service in a certain area or market ▪ The company has gained/acquired a (virtual/near) *monopoly* of/on/over the logging industry in this area. **b :** a large company that has a monopoly ▪ The government passed laws intended to break up *monopolies*.
2 [*singular*] **:** complete ownership or control of something — usually + *on* or (*chiefly Brit*) *of* ▪ He seems to think he has a *monopoly on* the truth. [=to think that he is the only person who knows what is true]
– **mo·nop·o·lis·tic** /məˌnɑːpəˈlɪstɪk/ *adj* ▪ *monopolistic* business practices

mono·rail /ˈmɑːnəˌreɪl/ *noun, pl* **-rails :** a type of railroad that uses a single track which is usually high off the ground [*count*] *Monorails* connect different parts of the park. [*noncount*] traveling by *monorail*, *also* [*count*] **:** a vehicle that

M

travels on a monorail • The passengers boarded the *monorail.*

mono·so·di·um glu·ta·mate /ˌmɑːnəˌsoudijəmˈgluːtəˌmeɪt/ *noun [noncount]* : a kind of salt used for seasoning foods — called also *MSG*

mono·syl·la·ble /ˈmɑːnəˌsɪləbəl/ *noun, pl* **-la·bles** *[count]* : a word that has only one syllable • He answered all their questions with *monosyllables* like "yes" and "no."

mono·syl·lab·ic /ˌmɑːnəsəˈlæbɪk/ *adj*
1 : having only one syllable • a *monosyllabic* word/reply : made up of words that have only one syllable • a *monosyllabic* conversation
2 : saying very little or responding with one-syllable words • The movie star was *monosyllabic* with newspaper reporters.

mono·the·ism /ˈmɑːnəˌθiːˌɪzəm/ *noun [noncount]* : the belief that there is only one God
– mono·the·ist /ˈmɑnəˌθiːjɪst/ *noun, pl* **-ists** *[count]*
– mono·the·is·tic /ˌmɑːnəˌθiˈɪstɪk/ *adj* • a *monotheistic* religion

mono·tone /ˈmɑːnəˌtoun/ *noun [singular]* : a way of talking or singing without raising or lowering the sound of your voice • She read the story in a dull *monotone.* • He sang in a soft, low *monotone.* • She spoke in a *monotone* voice.

mo·not·o·nous /məˈnɑːtnəs/ *adj [more ~; most ~]* — used to describe something that is boring because it is always the same • a *monotonous* task • Students complained that the meals were *monotonous.* • She spoke in a *monotonous* voice.
– mo·not·o·nous·ly *adv* • The teacher droned on *monotonously.*

mo·not·o·ny /məˈnɑːtni/ *noun [noncount]* : a lack of change that makes something boring : a monotonous quality • She hated the *monotony* of the job. • The brief storm was a relief from the *monotony* of the hot summer afternoon.

mono·un·sat·u·rat·ed /ˌmɑːnouˌʌnˈsætʃəreɪtəd/ *adj, technical* — used to describe a type of oil or fat that is found in foods such as olives and almonds and that is better for your health than saturated fats and trans fats • *monounsaturated* fats • *monounsaturated* oils such as olive, peanut, and canola oils — compare POLYUNSATURATED, SATURATED, UNSATURATED

monoxide see CARBON MONOXIDE

mon·si·gnor /mɑnˈsiːnjə/ *noun, pl* **mon·si·gnors** *or* **mon·si·gno·ri** /ˌmɑːnˌsiːnˈjori/ *[count]* : a Roman Catholic priest of high rank • bishops and *monsignors* • *Monsignor* Donsuso

mon·soon /mɑnˈsuːn/ *noun, pl* **-soons** *[count]*
1 : a wind in the Indian Ocean and southern Asia that brings heavy rains in the summer
2 a : the rainy season that occurs in southern Asia in the summer • the beginning of the *monsoon* (season) **b** : the rain that falls during this season • floods caused by summer *monsoons* — sometimes used in an exaggerated way to refer to a heavy rainstorm • The game was played in a *monsoon.*

¹mon·ster /ˈmɑːnstə/ *noun, pl* **-sters** *[count]*
1 : a strange or horrible imaginary creature • mythical *monsters* • a sea *monster* • a *monster* movie [=a movie about monsters]
2 *informal* : something that is extremely or unusually large • That car is a *monster.* • It's a *monster* of a house. [=a very large house]
3 : a powerful person or thing that cannot be controlled and that causes many problems • Inflation has become an economic *monster.*
4 a : an extremely cruel or evil person • His father was a *monster* who punished his children for no reason. • You don't want to work for that *monster.* **b** : a person (such as a child) who behaves very badly • My nephew is a little *monster.*
— see also GREEN-EYED MONSTER

²monster *adj, always used before a noun, informal* : very popular and successful • The movie turned out to be a *monster* hit. • a *monster* band

mon·stros·i·ty /mɑnˈstrɑːsəti/ *noun, pl* **-ties** *[count]* : something (such as a building) that is very large and ugly • Did you see the new mall? It's a *monstrosity.*

mon·strous /ˈmɑːnstrəs/ *adj [more ~; most ~]*
1 : extremely or unusually large : GIGANTIC • a *monstrous* billboard
2 : very wrong or unfair • It was *monstrous* of him to keep the truth from them all those years. • a *monstrous* injustice
3 : very ugly, cruel, or vicious • a *monstrous* crime/criminal • *monstrous* depravity
– mon·strous·ly *adv* • a *monstrously* large billboard

mon·tage /mɑnˈtɑːʒ/ *noun, pl* **-tag·es**
1 : a work of art that is made up of several different kinds of things (such as strips of newspaper, pictures, or pieces of wood) *[count]* a photographic *montage* *[noncount]* a photographer who often uses *montage* in her pictures
2 *[count]* : a mixture of different things — usually *+ of* • a *montage of* emotions/sounds/images

Mon·te·rey jack /ˈmɑːntəˌreɪˈdʒæk/ *noun [noncount] US* : a mild kind of cheese

month /ˈmʌnθ/ *noun, pl* **months**
1 *[count]* : any one of the 12 parts into which the year is divided • July is my favorite *month.* • It was hard to keep warm in the cabin during the winter *months.* • the merry *month* of May • The payments are due (on) the third of the *month.* [=on the third day of every month] • We visit them twice a *month.* [=two times every month] • I saw her last *month* and I'll see her again next *month.* • The price changes ***from month to month.*** = The price changes each/every *month.* • The price sometimes changes dramatically ***from one month to the next.*** • His health has been getting better ***month by month.*** = His health has been getting better ***with each passing month.*** [=his health has been getting better in a gradual and steady way as months have passed] • These problems have continued ***month after month.*** [=for several or many months]
2 *[count]* : a period of time that lasts about four weeks or 30 days • The baby is four *months* old. [=a four-*month*-old baby] • a pregnant woman who is in her eighth *month* = a woman who has been pregnant for eight *months* • He was gone for a *month.* • She was back to work a *month* after the accident. • I'll be seeing her again in a *month.* = I'll be seeing her again a *month* from now. = I'll be seeing her again in ***a month's time.***
3 months *[plural]* : a long period of time that is less than a year • He's been gone for *months.* • I haven't talked to her in *months.*
a month of Sundays *informal* : an extremely long time • I haven't talked to her in *a month of Sundays.*
of the month : chosen for special honors or attention during a particular month • He's been chosen as the employee *of the month* four times this year! [=chosen as the employee who is honored in a particular month for doing excellent work] • the book *of the month* — see also *flavor of the month* at ¹FLAVOR

month·long /ˈmʌnθˈlɑːŋ/ *adj* : lasting an entire month • a *monthlong* vacation

¹month·ly /ˈmʌnθli/ *adj*
1 : happening, done, or made every month • The *monthly* meeting is today. • The regional manager visits the office on a *monthly* basis.
2 : published once every month • She writes a *monthly* column for the magazine. • a *monthly* magazine/newsletter
3 : of or relating to one month • *monthly* payments • her *monthly* salary [=the salary she receives every month] • a *monthly* fee • the *monthly* total of traffic accidents
– monthly *adv* • The magazine is published *monthly.* • Water the plant when the soil feels dry and feed it *monthly.* [=once every month]

²monthly *noun, pl* **-lies** *[count]* : a magazine that is published once every month • He reads one of the travel *monthlies.*

mon·u·ment /ˈmɑːnjəmənt/ *noun, pl* **-ments** *[count]*
1 a : a building, statue, etc., that honors a person or event • They have erected a *monument* in his honor. — often *+ to* • The statue serves as a *monument to* those who have served in the armed forces. **b** : a building or place that is important because of when it was built or because of something in history that happened there • ancient *monuments* **c** : NATIONAL MONUMENT
2 : an example of something — *+ to* • The fashions of that era are a *monument to* bad taste. [=they are a perfect example of bad taste] • His life is a *monument to* what people can endure and overcome.

mon·u·men·tal /ˌmɑːnjəˈmɛntl/ *adj*
1 : very important • a *monumental* discovery/achievement
2 : very great or extreme • It's more than a mistake; it's a case of *monumental* stupidity. • the *monumental* complexity of the issue • Repairing the damage will be a *monumental* task/job.
3 *always used before a noun* : of or relating to a monument • The class was about modern *monumental* architecture.
– mon·u·men·tal·ly *adv* • *monumentally* stupid/important

moo /ˈmuː/ *noun, pl* **moos** *[count]* : the sound made by a cow

– **moo** *verb* **moos; mooed; moo·ing** [*no obj*] ▪ We heard the cows *mooing* in the field.

mooch /ˈmuːʧ/ *verb* **mooch·es; mooched; mooch·ing** *US, informal + disapproving* **: to ask for and get things from other people without paying for them or doing anything for them** [+ *obj*] He's always *mooching* [=*bumming*] cigarettes. — **often + *off*** ▪ She's been *mooching* money *off* everyone she knows. [*no obj*] — **usually + *off*** ▪ He's always *mooching off* his friends. ▪ He *mooched off* his parents for a few years [=he lived with his parents and didn't do any work] and then found a job and moved to the city.

mooch around/about [*phrasal verb*] *Brit, informal* **: to walk around with no particular purpose** ▪ I've just been *mooching about* all afternoon. ▪ We *mooched around* at some antique stores and then went to a café.

[1]**mood** /ˈmuːd/ *noun, pl* **moods**

1 [*count*] **: the way someone feels : a person's emotional state** ▪ He's been in a good *mood* all week. [=he's been happy and pleasant all week] ▪ Watching the news has put me in a bad *mood*. [=has made me unhappy and depressed] ▪ The kids are in a silly *mood* today. ▪ The good news lifted/lightened her *mood*. ▪ The bad news darkened/depressed her *mood*. ▪ She is a woman of many *moods*. Let's hope she's in one of her cheerful *moods* today. ▪ She may join us later. It depends on what kind of *mood* she's in. ▪ He's in one of his *moods*. [=he's in a bad mood] ▪ Quit teasing him. He's obviously ***in no mood*** for joking. ▪ It's a gorgeous day, and I'm *in no mood* to clean the house. ▪ It's hard to relate to someone who has such wild/extreme ***mood swings***. [=someone whose mood changes very quickly] ▪ (*medical*) ***mood disorders*** such as severe depression or anxiety

2 [*singular*] **: an attitude or feeling shared by many people** ▪ The *mood* of the country/city was grim.

3 [*count*] **: a quality that creates a particular feeling** ▪ She turned down the lights and lit a candle to create a more romantic *mood*. [=*atmosphere*]

in the mood **: feeling a desire *for* (something) or *to do* something** ▪ I'm *in the mood for* sushi. ▪ She was *in the mood for* love. ▪ He's a great pianist and goes to the jazz club whenever he's *in the mood to play*. ▪ I'm sorry. I'm just not *in the mood to talk*. [=I do not want to talk to anyone right now] ▪ "Would you like to see a movie?" "No, I'm not *in the mood* (*to see* a movie)."

the mood takes you ◊ When *the mood takes you*, you have the feeling of wanting to do something. ▪ She can be very sociable when/if *the mood takes her*.

– compare [2]MOOD

[2]**mood** *noun, pl* **moods** [*count*] *grammar* **: a set of forms of a verb that show whether the action or state expressed by the verb is thought of as a fact, a command, or a wish or possibility** ▪ In "I walked to school," the verb "walked" is in the indicative *mood*. ▪ the imperative/subjunctive *mood* — compare [1]MOOD

mood music *noun* [*noncount*] **: music that is meant to create a relaxed or romantic feeling** ▪ He lit some candles and put on some *mood music*.

moody /ˈmuːdi/ *adj* **mood·i·er; -est** [*also more* ~; *most* ~]

1 a : often unhappy or unfriendly ▪ *moody* teenagers ▪ I don't know why I get so *moody* sometimes. **b : having moods that change often** ▪ She's a *moody* woman—she can be happy one minute and angry the next.

2 : creating a certain mood or feeling ▪ The room's *moody* lighting suggested mystery and romance. ▪ a *moody* painting/ballad/film

– **mood·i·ly** /ˈmuːdəli/ *adv* ▪ He stared *moodily* out the window. ▪ a *moodily* lit room – **mood·i·ness** /ˈmuːdinəs/ *noun* [*noncount*] ▪ Her *moodiness* makes her hard to get along with.

moo·la *or* **moo·lah** /ˈmuːˌlɑː/ *noun* [*noncount*] *US slang* **: MONEY** ▪ They're making major/much *moola*. [=a lot of money]

[1]**moon** /ˈmuːn/ *noun, pl* **moons**

1 *the moon or the Moon* : the large round object that circles the Earth and that shines at night by reflecting light from the sun ▪ The telescope makes the craters on the surface of the *moon* incredibly clear. ▪ The *moon* isn't out tonight. = There's no *moon* tonight. [=the moon cannot be seen tonight] ▪ the first *moon* [=*lunar*] landing [=the first time people landed a spacecraft on the moon] ▪ the orbit of the *Moon* around the Earth — see also BLUE MOON, FULL MOON, HALF-MOON, HARVEST MOON, NEW MOON

2 [*count*] **: a large round object like the moon that circles around a planet other than the Earth** ▪ Europa and Io are both *moons* of Jupiter. ▪ a planet orbited by one *moon*

ask for the moon *or Brit* ***cry for the moon*** *informal* **: to ask for something that is very difficult or impossible to get** ▪ The striking workers say they just want to be paid what they're worth. They're not *asking for the moon*.

many moons *informal* **: a very long time** ▪ I visited my old school yesterday for the first time in *many moons*. ▪ But that was all *many moons* ago.

over the moon *informal* **: very happy or pleased about something** ▪ She's *over the moon* at being chosen for the award.

promise (someone) the moon see [2]PROMISE

reach/shoot for the moon **: to try to do or get something that is very difficult to do or get** ▪ an ambitious businessman who is always *shooting for the moon*

– **moon·less** /ˈmuːnləs/ *adj* ▪ a *moonless* night [=a night during which the moon cannot be seen]

[2]**moon** *verb* **moons; mooned; moon·ing** *informal* **: to bend over and show your bare buttocks to someone as a rude joke or insult** [+ *obj*] One of the boys *mooned* the crowd. [*no obj*] One of the boys *mooned* at the crowd.

moon around/about [*phrasal verb*] *Brit, informal* **: to move around slowly because you are unhappy** ▪ I was feeling depressed and just *mooned about* [=*moped around*] all day.

moon over *also US* ***moon after*** [*phrasal verb*] ***moon over/after (something or someone)*** **: to spend too much time thinking about or looking at (someone or something that you admire or want very much)** ▪ All the girls in the class are *mooning over* the handsome new teacher. ▪ fans *mooning after* movie stars

moon·beam /ˈmuːnˌbiːm/ *noun, pl* **-beams** [*count*] **: a ray of light from the moon : a beam of moonlight** ▪ *Moonbeams* shone through the leaves of the trees.

[1]**moon·light** /ˈmuːnˌlaɪt/ *noun* [*noncount*] **: the light of the moon** ▪ A figure appeared in the *moonlight*. ▪ a *moonlight* cruise down the river = a cruise down the river by *moonlight*

do a moonlight flit *Brit, informal* **: to leave a place secretly during the night especially to avoid paying money that you owe**

[2]**moonlight** *verb* **-lights; -light·ed; -light·ing** [*no obj*] **: to work at a second job in addition to your regular job** ▪ She is a secretary who *moonlights* as a waitress on weekends.

– **moon·light·er** *noun, pl* **-ers** [*count*]

moon·lit /ˈmuːnˌlɪt/ *adj* **: lighted by the moon** ▪ a *moonlit* night/landscape/room

moon·roof /ˈmuːnˌruːf/ *noun, pl* **-roofs** [*count*] *chiefly US* **: a part of a roof of a car or truck that is made of glass and that can be opened to let air in** — compare SUNROOF

moon·scape /ˈmuːnˌskeɪp/ *noun, pl* **-scapes**

1 [*singular*] **: the way the surface of the moon looks**

2 [*count*] **: a dry and empty place that looks like the surface of the moon** ▪ The valley is a desolate *moonscape*.

moon·shine /ˈmuːnˌʃaɪn/ *noun* [*noncount*] *informal*

1 *chiefly US* **: a kind of alcohol that people make illegally** ▪ a jug of *moonshine*

2 *Brit* **: foolish or untrue words : NONSENSE** ▪ Everything they said was just a load of *moonshine*.

– **moon·shin·er** /ˈmuːnˌʃaɪnɚ/ *noun, pl* **-ers** [*count*] ▪ an old *moonshiner* [=a person who makes moonshine]

moon·struck /ˈmuːnˌstrʌk/ *adj* **: silly, foolish, or crazy especially because you are in love** ▪ a celebrity mobbed by *moonstruck* teenage girls

moony /ˈmuːni/ *adj* **moon·i·er; -est** *chiefly US, informal* **: full of romantic feelings : MOONSTRUCK** ▪ *moony* teenagers

[1]**moor** /ˈmuɚ/ *noun, pl* **moors** [*count*] **: a broad area of open land that is not good for farming — used especially to refer to land in Great Britain; usually plural** ▪ We watched the sun setting over the *moors*.

[2]**moor** *verb* **moors; moored; moor·ing : to hold (a boat or ship) in place with ropes or cables or with an anchor** [+ *obj*] We found a harbor and *moored* the boat there for the night. ▪ The boat was *moored* alongside the dock. [*no obj*] We need to find a place to *moor* for the night.

Moor /ˈmuɚ/ *noun, pl* **Moors** [*count*] **: a member of a group of North African Arab people who ruled parts of Spain from the eighth century until 1492**

– **Moor·ish** /ˈmurɪʃ/ *adj* ▪ *Moorish* architecture ▪ a *Moorish* instrument

moor·ing /ˈmurɪŋ/ *noun, pl* **-ings**

1 [*count*] **: a place where a boat or ship can be anchored or moored** ▪ We found a temporary *mooring* in the harbor. —

M

often plural • We'll be renting private *moorings* there for the summer.
2 moorings [*plural*] **:** the anchors, ropes, and cables that are used to hold a boat or ship in place • The wind was strong enough to tear the boat from its *moorings*. • secure the *moorings*

moor·land /ˈmuɚlənd/ *noun, pl* **-lands :** land that consists of moors [*noncount*] an area of open *moorland* [*count*] We hiked across the *moorlands*.

moose /ˈmu:s/ *noun, pl* **moose** [*count*] **:** a large animal with very large, flat antlers that lives in forests in the northern part of America, Europe, and Asia — see picture at DEER

[1]**moot** /ˈmu:t/ *adj*
1 : not certain **:** argued about but not possible for people to prove • He says that they should have foreseen the accident, but that point is *moot*. [=*debatable*]
2 *US* **:** not worth talking about **:** no longer important or worth discussing • The court ruled that the issue is now *moot* because the people involved in the dispute have died. • I think they were wrong, but the point is *moot*. Their decision has been made and it can't be changed now.

[2]**moot** *verb* **moots; moot·ed; moot·ing** [+ *obj*] *formal* **:** to introduce (an idea, subject, etc.) for discussion — usually used as *(be) mooted* • The idea has *been mooted* in Congress, and it should be a topic of discussion for some time.

[1]**mop** /ˈmɑ:p/ *noun, pl* **mops** [*count*]
1 : a tool for cleaning floors that has a bundle of cloth or yarn or a sponge attached to a long handle
2 : a large amount of tangled or untidy hair on a person's head • a *mop* of hair

mop

[2]**mop** *verb* **mops; mopped; mop·ping**
1 : to clean (a floor) with a mop [+ *obj*] The kitchen (floor) needs to be *mopped*. [*no obj*] I'm almost done *mopping*.
2 [+ *obj*] **a :** to wipe (something that is wet) • He *mopped* his brow (dry) with a handkerchief. **b :** to wipe (a liquid) from something • He *mopped* the sweat from/off his brow.
mop up [*phrasal verb*] **1** ***mop (something) up or mop up (something)*** **:** to remove (a liquid) from a surface by using a mop, towel, etc. • It will only take a moment to *mop up* the spill. • She used the thick bread to *mop up* the last of her soup. — sometimes used figuratively • The movie *mopped up* all the awards. **2** ***mop up or mop (something) up or mop up (something)*** *informal* **:** to do the final things that are needed to complete a job or task • I'm almost done with the project. I just need a little more time to *mop up*. • Just let me *mop up* [=*finish*] a few things and I'll be done. • The battle has been won. The focus is now on *mopping up* small pockets of resistance. — see also MOP-UP

mope /ˈmoup/ *verb* **mopes; moped; mop·ing** [*no obj*] *disapproving*
1 : to behave in a way that shows you are unhappy and depressed • Like a little child, he often *moped* when he didn't get what he wanted.
2 : to move around slowly because you are unhappy — often + *around* or (*Brit*) *about* • I was feeling depressed and just *moped around* all day. • I spent hours just *moping around* the house.

mo·ped /ˈmouˌpɛd/ *noun, pl* **-peds** [*count*] **:** a small motorcycle that can be pedaled like a bicycle — see picture at MOTORCYCLE

mop·pet /ˈmɑ:pət/ *noun, pl* **-pets** [*count*] *informal* **:** a young person **:** CHILD

mop–up /ˈmɑ:pˌʌp/ *noun* [*singular*] *informal* **:** the actions that complete a job or task after the more difficult parts have been done • The project is almost done. All that's left is the *mop-up*. — often used before another noun • *mop-up* duty • the *mop-up* phase of operations — see also *mop up* at [2]MOP

[1]**mor·al** /ˈmorəl/ *adj*
1 *always used before a noun* **a :** concerning or relating to what is right and wrong in human behavior • The church takes a strong stand on a number of *moral* [=*ethical*] issues. • The author avoids making *moral* judgments. • *moral* arguments • Each story teaches an important *moral* lesson. **b :** based on what you think is right and good • He felt that he had a *moral* obligation/responsibility/duty to help the poor. • He's a man with strong *moral* convictions. [=a man who believes strongly that some things are right and others are wrong] • We're confident she has the *moral* fiber/fortitude to make the right decision.
2 a [*more* ~; *most* ~] **:** considered right and good by most people **:** agreeing with a standard of right behavior • *moral* conduct • Their behavior was not *moral*. • a *moral* young man [=a young man who tries to behave in a moral way] — compare AMORAL, IMMORAL **b :** able to choose between right and wrong behavior • Animals are not *moral* creatures and are not responsible for their actions.
moral authority ✧ A person, group, or organization that has *moral authority* is trusted to do what is right. • The scandal has undermined the government's *moral authority*.
moral support ✧ Someone who gives you *moral support* helps you by supporting or encouraging you rather than by giving you money or practical help. • She counted on her sisters for *moral support*.
moral victory ✧ If you achieve a *moral victory* you do not win anything but you achieve something that is important and good. • Although they lost, the minority claimed the vote as a *moral victory* since they had won the support of so many former opponents.

[2]**moral** *noun, pl* **-als**
1 [*count*] **:** a lesson that is learned from a story or an experience • The *moral* of the story is to be satisfied with what you have. • the movie's *moral* • The *moral* here is: pay attention to the warning lights in your car.
2 morals [*plural*] **:** proper ideas and beliefs about how to behave in a way that is considered right and good by most people • No one questions her *morals*. [=no one doubts that she is a good person who tries to behave in a moral way] • Socrates was accused of corrupting the *morals* of the youth of Athens. • He has no *morals*. [=he is not a good or honest person] • The author points to recent cases of fraud as evidence of the lack of *morals* in the business world. • a person with/of ***loose morals*** [=a person whose behavior and especially whose sexual behavior is considered morally wrong by some people]

mo·rale /məˈræl/ *noun* [*noncount*] **:** the feelings of enthusiasm and loyalty that a person or group has about a task or job • The company has been struggling and employee *morale* is low. [=employees do not feel happy or enthusiastic about their work] • The team is playing well and their *morale* is high. • The President's speech boosted/raised/improved the *morale* of the troops.

mor·al·ist /ˈmorəlɪst/ *noun, pl* **-ists** [*count*] *usually disapproving* **:** a person who has strong feelings and opinions about what is right and who tries to control the moral behavior of other people

mor·al·is·tic /ˌmorəˈlɪstɪk/ *adj* [*more* ~; *most* ~] *disapproving* **:** having or showing strong opinions about what is right behavior and what is wrong behavior • While a *moralistic* speech won't convince kids not to try drugs, a story about people affected by drugs might. • a *moralistic* tone/attitude

mo·ral·i·ty /məˈræləti/ *noun, pl* **-ties**
1 : beliefs about what is right behavior and what is wrong behavior [*noncount*] the changing cultural *morality* • The group is calling for a return to traditional *morality*. • Christian *morality* [*count*] two groups with clashing *moralities*
2 [*noncount*] **:** the degree to which something is right and good **:** the moral goodness or badness of something • The decision may be legally justified, but I question its *morality*. — usually + *of* • We discussed the *morality of* telling lies to protect someone.

mor·al·ize *also Brit* **mor·al·ise** /ˈmorəˌlaɪz/ *verb* **-iz·es; -ized; -iz·ing** [*no obj*] *usually disapproving* **:** to express beliefs about what is good behavior and what is bad behavior • an essay *moralizing* about the evils of alcohol • *moralizing* judgments/statements
– mor·al·iz·er *also Brit* **mor·al·is·er** *noun, pl* **-ers** [*count*]

mor·al·ly /ˈmorəli/ *adv* **:** according to what is considered right and good by most people • a *morally* good person • She behaved in a way that was *morally* wrong/right. • She felt *morally* obligated to help. • He acted *morally*. [=in a moral way] • She seems to think she's *morally* superior to the rest of us. • His behavior cannot be *morally* justified.

mo·rass /məˈræs/ *noun, pl* **-rass·es** [*count*] **:** an area of soft, wet ground **:** a marsh or swamp — usually singular • a *morass* of muck — usually used figuratively to refer to a complicated or unpleasant situation that is difficult to get out of or to move through • a legal *morass* • trying to find our way through a *morass* of city traffic

mor·a·to·ri·um /ˌmorəˈtorijəm/ *noun, pl* **-to·ri·ums** *or* **-to·ria** /-ˈtorijə/ [*count*] **: a time when a particular activity is not allowed** • The treaty calls for a nuclear testing *moratorium.* — often + *on* • a *moratorium on* nuclear testing • City officials declared a *moratorium on* building more houses in that part of the city.

mor·bid /ˈmoɚbəd/ *adj* [*more ~; most ~*]

1 : relating to unpleasant subjects (such as death) • She has a *morbid* interest in funerals. • He has a *morbid* sense of humor. • a *morbid* fascination with death • wanting to learn about a celebrity's downfall out of *morbid* curiosity

2 *technical* **: not healthy or normal** • suffering from a *morbid* condition • *morbid* obesity • The child has a *morbid* fear/horror of snakes.

– mor·bid·ly *adv* • She was *morbidly* fascinated with death. • *morbidly* obese

mor·dant /ˈmoɚdn̩t/ *adj* [*more ~; most ~*] *formal* **: expressing harsh criticism especially in a way that is funny** • a writer famous for her *mordant* humor/wit

– mor·dant·ly *adv* • *mordantly* funny/witty novels

[1]more /ˈmoɚ/ *adj*

1 : greater in amount, number, or size • I felt *more* pain after the procedure, not less. • The new engine has even *more* power. • You like *more* sugar in your tea than I do. • He had done *more* harm than he had intended. • ***More and more*** people [=an increasingly large number of people] are using e-mail these days. • The company has ***more than*** [=*over*] 2,000 employees. [=the number of employees is greater than 2,000] • Choose ***no/not more than*** three options. [=choose three options or fewer]

2 : extra or additional • I bought *more* apples. • The series will have five *more* episodes. • The company hired a few *more* employees. • I offered him some *more* coffee. • One *more* thing and then I'm leaving. • Can you say that one *more* time? • She wants *more* money.

[2]more *adv*

1 : to a greater degree or extent • The shot hurt *more* than I expected. • This cake is pretty good, but I'd like it (even) *more* if it had chocolate frosting. • It happens *more* often than it used to. • The building looks *more* like a museum than a library. • *more* active/important • *more* actively/importantly • The players grew *more* intense as the game went on. • She wanted a *more* sporty car. [=a sportier car] • To me, there's nothing *more* exciting than playing football. • She *more* closely resembles her aunt than her mother. • He struggled to find a *more* comfortable position. • a *more* complex explanation • It's the same product—they've done nothing *more* than change the label. • It's getting ***more and more*** difficult [=increasingly difficult] to distinguish fake diamonds from real ones. • The fact that they'd written the play themselves made it ***all the more*** impressive. [=made it even more impressive]

2 : more often or for a longer period of time • You need to help (out) with the housework *more.* = You need to help (out) *more* with the housework. • She's a better piano player than I am because she practices *more* (than I do). • You need to work on it (some) *more.*

3 : in addition • wait one day *more* • a couple of times *more* • What *more* could you ask for?

4 — used to say that one way of describing a person or thing is better or more accurate than another • She is *more* an acquaintance than a friend. = She's an acquaintance *more* than she is a friend.

more like it see [3]LIKE

more or less **1 : not completely but to a great degree** • The clothes are *more or less* [=*mostly*] dry. • The problem is *more or less* [=(*informal*) *pretty much*] fixed now. • They were *more or less* willing. • The building remains *more or less* [=*essentially*] intact. • The business has remained *more or less* [=*fairly, reasonably*] successful. **2 — used to indicate that a number, amount, time, etc., is not exact or certain** • The garden contains five acres, *more or less.* [=about/approximately five acres] • It should take you 20 minutes, *more or less.* [=it should take you about/approximately 20 minutes] • I divided it into six *more or less* equal parts. [=into six approximately equal parts]

more than **: to a great degree : VERY, EXTREMELY** • Please call me anytime. I'm *more than* happy to help (out) in any way I can. ✧ **A clause that includes *more than* is often followed by another clause that gives more information or limits the first clause in some way.** • I am *more than* happy to help you, but I'd appreciate being asked politely. • You are *more than* [=*entirely*] welcome to stay for dinner, but we aren't having anything special.

more than a little **: to a great degree : VERY, EXTREMELY** • He was *more than a little* surprised by her decision.

once more see [1]ONCE

what's more see [1]WHAT

[3]more *pronoun* **: a greater number or amount** • *More* [=more people] were found as the search continued. • We're waiting until *more* [=more information] is known. • I need to spend less and save *more.* • You have *more* than everyone else. • I'm too full to eat (any) *more.* • If these estimates are correct, we'll need much/far/even *more.* • It costs a little *more* but it's worth it. • People are often willing to pay *more* for a better product. • We got *more* than we expected. • (We'll have) *More* on the weather later. • We need 22 boxes—no *more,* no less. • ***More and more*** of them [=an increasingly large number of them] are willing to try. • People expect *more and more* from their computers. • We've been hearing *more and more* about this issue in recent months.

little more than see [2]LITTLE

more of **— used to say that one way of describing a person or thing is better or more accurate than another** • It's *more of* a guess than an estimate. • No, I wouldn't call the color red—it's *more of* a maroon.

more's the pity see [1]PITY

more than meets the eye see [1]EYE

the more the merrier see MERRY

more·over /moɚˈoʊvɚ/ *adv, somewhat formal* **: in addition to what has been said** • It probably wouldn't work. *Moreover* [=*furthermore, besides, in addition*], it would be very expensive to try it. • The cameras will deter potential criminals. *Moreover*, they will help police a great deal when a crime actually is committed.

mo·res /ˈmoɚˌeɪz/ *noun* [*plural*] **: the customs, values, and behaviors that are accepted by a particular group, culture, etc.** • social *mores* • society's changing *mores* • current cultural/sexual *mores*

morgue /ˈmoɚg/ *noun, pl* **morgues** [*count*]

1 : a place where the bodies of dead people are kept until they are buried or cremated • the city *morgue* • a hospital *morgue* **— often used figuratively or in the phrase *like a morgue* to describe a place that is very quiet and sad** • The locker room was a *morgue* after the team lost yet another game. • The locker room was *like a morgue.* **— called also (*chiefly Brit*) *mortuary***

2 *US* **: a place in the editorial offices of a newspaper, magazine, etc., where old articles and other documents are kept** • old news stories found in a newspaper *morgue*

mor·i·bund /ˈmorəˌbʌnd/ *adj, formal*

1 : no longer active or effective : close to failure • an actor who is trying to revive his *moribund* career • a *moribund* economy/industry • The peace talks are *moribund.*

2 : very sick : close to death • The patient was *moribund.* • *moribund* [=*dying*] trees

Mor·mon /ˈmoɚmən/ *noun, pl* **-mons** [*count*] **: a member of a Christian church that was founded by Joseph Smith in the U.S. in 1830 : a member of the Church of Jesus Christ of Latter-day Saints**

– Mormon *adj* • a *Mormon* church **– Mor·mon·ism** /ˈmoɚməˌnɪzəm/ *noun* [*noncount*]

morn /ˈmoɚn/ *noun, pl* **morns** *literary* **: MORNING** [*count*] a frosty winter *morn* • early in the *morn* [*noncount*] from *morn* to night

morn·ing /ˈmoɚnɪŋ/ *noun, pl* **-ings**

1 a : the early part of the day : the time of day from sunrise until noon [*count*] She liked to get things done early in the *morning.* • I worked in the yard for part of the *morning.* • I saw him this *morning*, and I'll be meeting with him again tomorrow *morning.* • We have a meeting scheduled for 10 o'clock Wednesday *morning.* • On Sunday *mornings* I like to relax and read the newspaper. • She arrived on the *morning* of March 18. • the *morning* after a storm • that night and the next/following *morning* = that night and ***the morning after*** • I'll talk to you again ***in the morning.*** [=I'll talk to you again early tomorrow] [*noncount*] It was early/late *morning* when I woke. • We sat around drinking coffee all *morning.* • We won't find out until *morning.* • (*literary*) *Morning* has broken. [=the sun has risen; it is dawn] **— often used before another noun** • the *morning* sun/light • my *morning* (cup of) coffee [=the coffee I drink every morning] • My brother is a night

M

owl/person, but I'm a ***morning person***. [=a person who likes the early part of the day; a person who has the most energy in the morning] **b** *[noncount]* **: the part of the day between midnight and noon** ▪ The party continued into the wee/small hours of the *morning*. [=after midnight] ▪ The phone rang at 2 o'clock in the *morning*. [=at 2 a.m.]
2 — used informally to say hello to someone in the morning ▪ *Morning*. [=*good morning*] How are you today?
morning, noon, and night **: during all times of the day : all the time** ▪ The system is operating *morning, noon, and night*. ▪ We've been working *morning, noon, and night* [=many hours each day] to get the project finished on time. **— see also MORNINGS**

morning–after pill *noun, pl* **~ pills** *[count]* **: a pill that a woman takes after having sex so that she will not become pregnant**

morning coat *noun, pl* **~ coats** *[count]* **: a type of formal black coat worn by men with some suits** ▪ The groom wore a *morning coat*.

morning glory *noun, pl* **~ -ries** *[count]* **: a plant that has many brightly colored flowers that open in the morning — see color picture on page C6**

morn·ings /ˈmoɚnɪŋz/ *adv* **: in the morning** ▪ She works *mornings* in the kitchen of a small local restaurant. ▪ *Mornings*, I like to weed the garden.

morning sickness *noun [noncount]* **: a feeling of sickness that a pregnant woman may feel especially early in the morning : a feeling of nausea caused by pregnancy**

morning star *noun*
the morning star **: the planet Venus when it can be seen in the eastern sky in the early morning — compare EVENING STAR**

mo·ron /ˈmoɚˌɑːn/ *noun, pl* **-rons** *[count] informal* **: a very stupid or foolish person : IDIOT** ▪ They were acting like a bunch of *morons*. ▪ I can't believe I did something so stupid. I feel like a complete *moron*. ▪ an utter *moron*
– mo·ron·ic /məˈrɑːnɪk/ *adj [more ~; most ~]* ▪ That's the most *moronic* thing I've ever heard. ▪ *moronic* behavior ▪ *moronic* humor **– mo·ron·i·cal·ly** /məˈrɑːnɪkli/ *adv* ▪ They were behaving *moronically*.

mo·rose /məˈrous/ *adj [more ~; most ~]*
1 *of a person* **: very serious, unhappy, and quiet** ▪ He became *morose* and withdrawn and would not talk to anyone.
2 : very sad or unhappy ▪ *morose* song lyrics ▪ *morose* thoughts
– mo·rose·ly *adv* ▪ gazing/staring *morosely* at the sad scene ▪ "I lost," she said *morosely*. **– mo·rose·ness** *noun [noncount]*

morph /ˈmoɚf/ *verb* **morphs; morphed; morph·ing**
1 *of an image on a screen* **: to gradually change into a different image** *[no obj]* The picture of a dog *morphed* into a picture of a cat. *[+ obj]* Using the new software, we *morphed* a picture of a dog into a picture of a cat.
2 : to change gradually and completely from one thing into another thing usually in a way that is surprising or that seems magical *[no obj]* a quiet college student who has *morphed* into a glamorous actress *[+ obj]* He is trying to *morph* himself into a different person.

mor·pheme /ˈmoɚˌfiːm/ *noun, pl* **-phemes** *[count] linguistics* **: a word or a part of a word that has a meaning and that contains no smaller part that has a meaning** ▪ The word "pins" contains two *morphemes*: "pin" and the plural suffix "-s."
– mor·phe·mic /moɚˈfiːmɪk/ *adj*

mor·phine /ˈmoɚˌfiːn/ *noun [noncount]* **: a powerful drug made from opium that is used to reduce pain** ▪ a shot/dose of *morphine*

mor·phol·o·gy /moɚˈfɑːləʤi/ *noun, pl* **-gies**
1 *[noncount] linguistics* **: the study and description of how words are formed in language**
2 *biology* **a** *[noncount]* **: the study of the form and structure of animals and plants b : the form and structure of a plant or animal or any of its parts** *[noncount]* plants with unusual *morphology* *[count]* plants with unusual *morphologies*
– mor·pho·log·i·cal /ˌmoɚfəˈlɑːʤɪkəl/ *adj*

mor·row /ˈmɑrou/ *noun, pl* **-rows** *old-fashioned + literary*
1 : MORNING *[noncount]* "Good-night, good-night! parting is such sweet sorrow / That I shall say good-night till it be *morrow*." —Shakespeare, *Romeo and Juliet* *[count]* "Many ***good morrows*** to my noble lord!" —Shakespeare, *Richard III*
2 ***the morrow*** **: the next day** ▪ We don't know what *the morrow* may bring. [=we don't know what may happen in the future] ▪ We expect them to arrive ***on the morrow***. [=*tomorrow*]

Morse code /ˈmoɚs-/ *noun [noncount]* **: a system of sending messages that uses long and short sounds, flashes of light, or marks to represent letters and numbers**

mor·sel /ˈmoɚsəl/ *noun, pl* **-sels** *[count]* **: a small piece of food** ▪ tender *morsels* of beef ▪ bite-size *morsels* ▪ She ate every *morsel*. ▪ a tasty/delicious *morsel* **— often used figuratively** ▪ a juicy *morsel* of gossip

[1]**mor·tal** /ˈmoɚtl̩/ *adj*
1 : certain to die ▪ Every living creature is *mortal*. **— opposite [1]IMMORTAL**
2 a : causing death : FATAL ▪ He suffered a *mortal* wound in the battle. ▪ a *mortal* injury/blow **— often used figuratively** ▪ She claims that the proposed law would deal/strike a *mortal* blow to many small businesses. [=would cause many small businesses to fail] ***synonyms*** **see [1]DEADLY b : possibly causing death** ▪ facing *mortal* danger ▪ two gladiators locked in ***mortal combat*** [=a fight that will result in the death of the loser; a fight to the death] **c : relating to or connected with death** ▪ *mortal* agony **— see also *mortal remains* at REMAINS**
3 *always used before a noun* **: very great or severe** ▪ She lived in *mortal* fear/terror/dread of being betrayed. [=she was very afraid of being betrayed]
mortal enemy also mortal foe/rival **: someone you hate very much and for a long time** ▪ They've been *mortal enemies* for many years.
– mor·tal·ly /ˈmoɚtl̩i/ *adv* ▪ He was *mortally* [=*fatally*] wounded in the battle. ▪ She is *mortally* [=(more commonly) *terminally*] ill with cancer. ▪ I'm *mortally* [=*extremely*] afraid of snakes.

[2]**mortal** *noun, pl* **-tals** *[count]* **: a human being** ▪ stories about gods interfering in the lives of *mortals* ▪ the troubles that come to ordinary *mortals* **— often used humorously** ▪ He's a big star now. He doesn't waste his time talking to mere/lesser *mortals* [=*people*] like you and me. **— compare [2]IMMORTAL**

mor·tal·i·ty /moɚˈtæləti/ *noun, pl* **-ties**
1 *[noncount]* **: the quality or state of being a person or thing that is alive and therefore certain to die : the quality or state of being mortal** ▪ The news of her cousin's death reminded her of her own *mortality*. [=reminded her that she would also die some day] **— opposite IMMORTALITY**
2 : the death of a person, animal, etc. *[count]* cancer *mortalities* [=deaths caused by cancer] *[noncount]* a leading cause of *mortality*
3 *[noncount]* **: the number of deaths that occur in a particular time or place** ▪ a decrease in cancer *mortality* [=a decrease in the number of people dying from cancer] ▪ The government is trying to reduce ***infant mortality***. = The government is trying to reduce the ***mortality rate*** among infants. [=trying to reduce the number of infants who die each year]

mortal sin *noun, pl* **~ sins** *[count] in the Roman Catholic Church* **: a sin (such as murder) that will result in punishment that lasts forever unless the person who has sinned sincerely confesses to God and asks to be forgiven** ▪ commit a *mortal sin* **— compare VENIAL SIN**

mor·tar /ˈmoɚtɚ/ *noun, pl* **-tars**
1 *[count]* **: a heavy, deep bowl in which seeds, spices, etc., are pounded or crushed with a heavy tool (called a pestle)**
2 *[count]* **: a military weapon used to fire shells (sense 5a) high into the air at a low speed** ▪ fire/shoot a *mortar* **— often used before another noun** ▪ The soldiers came under *mortar* fire. ▪ a *mortar* attack
3 *[noncount]* **: a wet substance that is spread between bricks or stones and that holds them together when it hardens** ▪ seal the joints with *mortar* **— see also BRICK-AND-MORTAR, *bricks and mortar* at [1]BRICK**
– mortar *verb* **-tars; -tared; -tar·ing** *[+ obj]* ▪ a building *mortared* with mud ▪ bricks *mortared* together

mor·tar·board /ˈmoɚtɚˌboɚd/ *noun, pl* **-boards** *[count]* **: a hat with a flat square top that is worn for special ceremonies at some schools** ▪ The students donned robes and *mortarboards* for graduation.

[1]**mort·gage** /ˈmoɚgɪʤ/ *noun, pl* **-gag·es** *[count]* **: a legal agreement in which a person borrows money to buy property (such as a house) and pays back the money over a period of years** ▪ He will have to take out a *mortgage* in order to buy the house. ▪ a 30-year *mortgage* ▪ a $50,000 *mortgage* ▪ They hope to pay off the *mortgage* on their home soon. **— often used before another noun** ▪ a *mortgage* agreement/banker/lender/loan ▪ *Mortgage* rates are down. **— see also REVERSE MORTGAGE**

²mortgage *verb* **-gages; -gaged; -gag·ing** [+ *obj*] **:** to give someone a legal claim on (property that you own) in exchange for money that you will pay back over a period of years ▪ She *mortgaged* her house in order to buy the restaurant.

mortgage the/your future *chiefly US, disapproving* **:** to borrow a large amount of money that will have to be paid back in the future or to do something that may cause problems for you in the future ▪ The city has *mortgaged its future* to pay for the new stadium. ▪ Some critics say that she has *mortgaged her political future* on a program that is likely to fail.

mort·gag·ee /ˌmoɚgɪˈʤiː/ *noun, pl* **-ees** [*count*] *law* **:** a person or organization (such as a bank) that lends money to someone for buying property

mort·gag·or /ˌmoɚgɪˈʤoɚ/ *also* **mort·gag·er** /ˈmoɚgɪʤɚ/ *noun, pl* **-ors** *also* **-ers** [*count*] *law* **:** a person who borrows money for buying property **:** a person who takes out a mortgage in order to buy property

mor·ti·cian /moɚˈtɪʃən/ *noun, pl* **-cians** [*count*] *US, formal* **:** a person whose job is to prepare dead people to be buried and to arrange and manage funerals **:** UNDERTAKER

mor·ti·fy /ˈmoɚtəˌfaɪ/ *verb* **-fies; -fied; -fy·ing** [+ *obj*] **:** to cause (someone) to feel very embarrassed and foolish ▪ Her behavior *mortified* her parents. = Her parents were *mortified* by her behavior. ▪ It *mortified* me to have to admit that I'd never actually read the book.

– mor·ti·fi·ca·tion /ˌmoɚtəfəˈkeɪʃən/ *noun* [*noncount*] ▪ He was filled with *mortification* when he realized his mistake. ▪ Imagine my *mortification* when I realized who she was! **– mortified** *adj* [*more* ~; *most* ~] ▪ I was completely *mortified* when I realized who she was. **– mortifying** *adj* [*more* ~; *most* ~] ▪ a completely *mortifying* experience **– mor·ti·fy·ing·ly** *adv* ▪ a *mortifyingly* stupid mistake

mortis see RIGOR MORTIS

mor·tise *also Brit* **mor·tice** /ˈmoɚtəs/ *noun, pl* **-tis·es** [*count*] *technical* **:** a hole that is cut in a piece of wood or other material so that another piece (called a tenon) will fit into it to form a connection

mortise lock *or Brit* **mortice lock** *noun, pl* ~ **locks** [*count*] *chiefly Brit* **:** DEAD BOLT

¹mor·tu·ary /ˈmoɚʧəˌweri, *Brit* ˈmɔːʧuəri/ *noun, pl* **-ar·ies** [*count*]

1 *US* **:** FUNERAL HOME

2 *chiefly Brit* **:** MORGUE 1 ▪ a hospital *mortuary*

²mortuary *adj, always used before a noun, formal* **:** of or relating to death or burial ▪ *mortuary* ceremonies/customs/rituals

mo·sa·ic /moʊˈzejɪk/ *noun, pl* **-ics**

mosaic

1 : a decoration on a surface made by pressing small pieces of colored glass or stone into a soft material that then hardens to make pictures or patterns [*count*] a church decorated with old *mosaics* [*noncount*] a picture done in *mosaic* — often used before another noun ▪ a *mosaic* floor ▪ *mosaic* glass/tiles

2 [*count*] **:** something made up of different things that together form a pattern — usually singular ▪ a complex *mosaic* of islands ▪ the country's ethnic/political/religious/social *mosaic*

mo·sey /ˈmoʊzi/ *verb* **mo·seys; mo·seyed; mo·sey·ing** [*no obj*] *US, informal* **:** to walk or move in a slow and relaxed way ▪ I think I'll *mosey* (on) over to the post office and see if the mail has come in yet. ▪ He *moseyed* up to the bar.

mosey along [*phrasal verb*] *informal* **:** to go away **:** LEAVE ▪ I'm finished here, so I'll just *mosey along* now.

mosh /ˈmɑːʃ/ *verb* **mosh·es; moshed; mosh·ing** [*no obj*] *informal* **:** to dance in a wild and rough way near the stage at a rock concert

– mosh·er *noun, pl* **-ers** [*count*]

mosh pit *noun, pl* ~ **pits** [*count*] *informal* **:** an area in front of a stage at a rock concert where people dance in a wild and rough way

Mos·lem /ˈmɑːzləm/ *variant spelling of* MUSLIM ✧ The spelling *Moslem* is old-fashioned and is sometimes considered offensive. It should be avoided.

mosque /ˈmɑːsk/ *noun, pl* **mosques** [*count*] **:** a building that is used for Muslim religious services

mos·qui·to /məˈskiːtoʊ/ *noun, pl* **-toes** *also* **-tos** [*count*] **:** a small flying insect that bites the skin of people and animals and sucks their blood ▪ a swarm of *mosquitoes* ▪ the bite of a *mosquito* = a *mosquito* bite ✧ Mosquitoes sometimes spread serious diseases like malaria. — see color picture on page C10

mosquito net *noun, pl* ~ **nets** [*count*] **:** a net that is placed over something (such as a bed) in order to keep out mosquitoes

moss /ˈmɑːs/ *noun, pl* **moss·es :** a type of green plant that has very small leaves and no flowers and that grows on rocks, bark, or wet ground [*noncount*] *Moss* covered the fallen logs. [*count*] ferns and *mosses* — see also PEAT MOSS, SPANISH MOSS

– moss·like /ˈmɑːsˌlaɪk/ *adj* **– mossy** /ˈmɑːsi/ *adj* **moss·i·er; -est** ▪ a *mossy* roof [=a roof covered with moss] ▪ *mossy* rocks/stones

¹most /ˈmoʊst/ *adj*

1 : almost all **:** the majority of — usually used before a plural noun ▪ *Most* people believe this. ▪ *Most* eligible voters went to the polls. ▪ I'm afraid of *most* dogs, but not this one. ▪ I like *most* foods.

2 : greatest in amount or degree ▪ Choosing a color took the *most* time. ▪ That family owned the *most* land. ▪ Unfortunately the negative aspects of our schools get the *most* attention.

for the most part **1 :** almost all or almost completely ▪ Menu items are, *for the most part*, under $5. [=almost all the menu items cost less than $5] ▪ We wanted to keep it simple, and I think we were successful *for the most part*. **2** — used to describe a condition or situation that usually exists or is true ▪ Streets fill with people during the festival, but *for the most part* [=*usually, most of the time*] it's a quiet, sleepy town.

²most *adv*

1 : in or to the greatest degree ▪ Of all the gifts he received that day, the book pleased him *most*. ▪ What matters *most* to you? ▪ The island is the *most* southern in the chain. ▪ You'll benefit *most* from the exercises if you do them every day. ▪ *most* active/important ▪ *most* actively/importantly ▪ It's the *most* challenging job she has ever had. ▪ the *most* beautiful woman there ▪ Even the *most* careful of us make mistakes. ▪ the *most* common/popular kind ▪ The report shows the intersections at which accidents are *most* likely to occur. ▪ the *most* widely used treatment

2 *somewhat formal* **:** to a great extent **:** VERY ▪ He is a *most* careful driver. ▪ Their argument was *most* persuasive.

– compare ⁵MOST

³most *noun*

at most *or* ***at the most*** **:** not more than a specified amount, level, etc. ▪ It took an hour *at most*. [=it took no more than an hour; it took an hour or less than an hour] ▪ She only worked here for a month or two *at the most*. ▪ It costs, *at most*, only a few dollars. ▪ This is worth $10 *at most*.

make the most of **:** to use (something) in a way that will get the best result ▪ She was determined to *make the most of* the opportunity.

the most **:** something of the greatest importance, strength, value, etc. ▪ *The most* I can give you is $10. [=I can give you $10, but I can't give you more than $10] ▪ Is that *the most* you can do? ▪ You'll need to make wise investments if you want get *the most* out of your money. ▪ A second chance is *the most* we can hope for now. ▪ He tries hard, but that's *the most* [=*all*] we can say for him. [=the best thing we can say about him is that he tries hard]

⁴most *pronoun*

1 : the largest number of people or things ▪ Some people kept working, but *most* became discouraged and quit. ▪ Some of the chairs were broken but *most* were in good condition. ▪ *Most* (of the people) who were present voted in favor of the proposal. ▪ *Most* of them will appreciate the offer. ▪ She was more fragile than *most*.

2 : the largest part of something ▪ *Most* of it is hidden from view. ▪ They spent *most* of the decade overseas.

⁵most *adv, US, informal* **:** very nearly **:** ALMOST — usually used with the adjectives *all, every*, and *any*; the pronouns *all, everyone, everything, everybody, anyone, anything*, and *anybody*; and the adverbs *everywhere, anywhere*, and *always* ▪ The cost of *most everything* is higher. ▪ *Most anyone* can go. ▪ *most everywhere* in the country ▪ We'll be arriving *most any* time now. ▪ They *most always* skip lunch. — compare ²MOST

-most /moʊst/ *adj suffix* **:** in or to the greatest degree **:** MOST ▪ inner*most* ▪ outer*most* ▪ top*most*

M

most·ly /ˈmoustli/ *adv*
1 — used to say that a statement you are making is true or correct at most times or that it describes a usual situation or condition ▪ He gets around *mostly* [=*mainly, chiefly*] by car. [=he usually uses a car to get around] ▪ "What did you do this weekend?" "I worked in the yard, *mostly*." [=I spent most of my time working in the yard] ▪ I concentrated *mostly* [=*mainly*] on getting good grades when I was in college.
2 : almost all or almost completely ▪ The story was *mostly* accurate. [=most of the story was accurate] ▪ The people at the concert were *mostly* older people. [=most of the people were older people]

MOT /ˌɛmˌouˈtiː/ *noun, pl* **MOTs** *or* **MOT's** [*count*] *Brit* : an official test of all cars and other vehicles in Britain that are more than three years old to make sure that they are safe to drive — called also *MOT test*

mote /ˈmout/ *noun, pl* **motes** [*count*] *old-fashioned* : a very small piece of dust, dirt, etc. ▪ a *mote* [=*speck*] of dust ▪ dust *motes*

mo·tel /mouˈtɛl/ *noun, pl* **-tels** [*count*] : a place that is next to a road and that has rooms for people to stay in especially when they are traveling by car ✧ The rooms of a motel are usually reached directly from an outdoor parking lot.

moth /ˈmɑːθ/ *noun, pl* **moths** /ˈmɑðz/ [*count*] : a kind of insect that is similar to a butterfly but that flies mostly at night and is usually less colorful — see color picture on page C10; see also GYPSY MOTH ✧ Some types of small moths eat holes in clothing.

[1]**moth·ball** /ˈmɑːθˌbɑːl/ *noun, pl* **-balls**
1 [*count*] : a small ball that contains a strong-smelling chemical and that is used to keep moths away from stored clothing
2 ***mothballs*** [*plural*] — used in phrases like ***in/into mothballs*** and ***out of mothballs*** to describe something that is stored without being used for a long time ▪ Many ships in the navy's fleet were put *in mothballs* after the war. ▪ a computer system that has gone *into mothballs* ▪ The old ship is being taken *out of mothballs*. — sometimes used to describe a person (such as a performer) who has not been seen for a long time ▪ an old comedian who is being brought *out of mothballs* to star in a new television show

[2]**mothball** *verb* **-balls; -balled; -ball·ing** [+ *obj*] : to stop using (something) while keeping it to be possibly used in the future ▪ Many navy ships were *mothballed* after the war.

moth–eat·en /ˈmɑːθˌiːtn̩/ *adj* [*more* ~; *most* ~] : having holes caused by moths : eaten into by moths ▪ a *moth-eaten* sweater/sofa — often used figuratively ▪ a *moth-eaten* [=*outdated, antiquated*] computer system

[1]**moth·er** /ˈmʌðɚ/ *noun, pl* **-ers**
1 [*count*] : a female parent ▪ She became a *mother* when she was in her 20s. ▪ She's the *mother* of three small children. ▪ She has been like a *mother* to me. ▪ Our dog is the *mother* of all those puppies. ▪ She has always been close to her *mother*. ▪ an ***expectant mother*** [=a woman who is pregnant] ▪ She is a ***single mother*** [=a mother who does not have a husband or partner] — see also BIRTH MOTHER, GRANDMOTHER, QUEEN MOTHER, STEPMOTHER, SURROGATE MOTHER
2 [*count*] : a woman who is thought of as being like a mother ▪ She was a *mother* to me after my own mother died. — see also DEN MOTHER
3 a [*count*] : a woman who invents or begins something — usually singular ▪ She is regarded as the *mother* of an entire industry. ▪ the *mother* of an important social movement **b** [*singular*] : a cause or origin of something ▪ Some say that scandal is the *mother* of reform.
4 [*count*] : MOTHER SUPERIOR — used especially as a title or as a form of address ▪ *Mother* Teresa ▪ Thank you, *Mother*.
5 [*singular*] *informal* — used to say that something is larger, better, worse, etc., than all other things of the same kind ▪ It has been described as ***the mother of all*** construction projects. [=an extremely large construction project]
6 [*count*] *US, offensive* : MOTHERFUCKER ▪ That guy is one mean *mother*.
learn (something) at your mother's knee see [1]KNEE
necessity is the mother of invention — used to say that new ways to do things are found or created when there is a strong and special need for them
– moth·er·hood /ˈmʌðɚˌhʊd/ *noun* [*noncount*] ▪ She is looking forward to marriage and *motherhood*. **– moth·er·less** /ˈmʌðɚləs/ *adj* ▪ Her death left three *motherless* children. ▪ a *motherless* calf

[2]**mother** *verb* **-ers; -ered; -er·ing** [+ *obj*]
1 : to give birth to (a child) ▪ She *mothered* two sons but no daughters.
2 : to be or act as mother to (someone) : to care for or protect (someone) like a mother ▪ He says he's old enough to care for himself and he doesn't want to be *mothered*. [=he doesn't want to be cared for as if he were a child]
– moth·er·ing /ˈmʌðərɪŋ/ *noun* [*noncount*] ▪ a sensitive child who needs careful *mothering* **– mothering** *adj* ▪ her *mothering* [=*maternal*] abilities/instincts

moth·er·board /ˈmʌðɚˌboɚd/ *noun, pl* **-boards** [*count*] : the main circuit board of a computer

mother country *noun, pl* ~ **-tries** [*count*]
1 : the country where people who live in a colony or former colony came from — usually singular; usually used with *the* ▪ The colonies rebelled against *the mother country*.
2 : the country where you were born or where your family came from : MOTHERLAND — usually singular ▪ Her books have sold better abroad than in her *mother country*. — often used with *the* ▪ an immigrant's nostalgia for *the mother country*

Mother Earth *noun* [*singular*] — used to refer to the planet Earth as a woman or a goddess ▪ to respect/worship *Mother Earth* ▪ We must protect the resources of *Mother Earth*.

mother figure *noun, pl* ~ **-ures** [*count*] : an older woman who is respected and admired like a mother ▪ Camp counselors are *mother figures* to many of the girls at the camp.

moth·er·fuck·er /ˈmʌðɚˌfʌkɚ/ *noun, pl* **-ers** [*count*] *chiefly US, offensive*
1 : an annoying person or thing ▪ a stupid *motherfucker*
2 : a person or thing that is impressive in some way ▪ He's a strong *motherfucker*. ✧ This is one of the most offensive words in U.S. English and should be avoided.

moth·er·fuck·ing /ˈmʌðɚˌfʌkɪŋ/ *adj, always used before a noun, chiefly US, offensive* — used to make an angry statement more forceful ▪ a *motherfucking* jerk ✧ This is one of the most offensive words in U.S. English and should be avoided.

mother hen *noun, pl* ~ **hens** [*count*] : a person who worries about, cares for, or watches over other people in a way that is annoying or unwanted ▪ a football coach who fusses over his players like a *mother hen*

Mothering Sunday *noun, pl* ~ **-days** [*count, noncount*] *Brit, old-fashioned* : MOTHER'S DAY

moth·er–in–law /ˈmʌðərənˌlɑː/ *noun, pl* **moth·ers–in–law** /ˈmʌðɚzənˌlɑː/ [*count*] : the mother of your husband or wife

mother–in–law apartment *noun, pl* ~ **-ments** [*count*] *US* : IN-LAW APARTMENT

moth·er·land /ˈmʌðɚˌlænd/ *noun* [*count*] : the country where you were born or where your family came from — usually singular ▪ Although she had lived in America for many years, she still spoke the language of her *motherland*. — often used with *the* ▪ The whole family wanted to return to *the motherland*. ✧ *Motherland* can refer to any country, but it is often associated especially with Russia. — compare FATHERLAND

mother lode *noun, pl* ~ **lodes** [*count*] *chiefly US* : the place where the largest amount of gold, silver, etc., in a particular area can be found — usually singular ▪ a gold miner who struck/hit the *mother lode* [=who found the place containing the largest amount of gold] — often used figuratively ▪ The library's collection of old newspapers has proven to be a *mother lode* of information about the town's early history.

moth·er·ly /ˈmʌðɚli/ *adj* [*more* ~; *most* ~] : of a mother ▪ She took her *motherly* duties very seriously. ▪ *motherly* [=*maternal*] instincts : resembling a mother ▪ a *motherly* nurse : showing the affection or concern of a mother ▪ *motherly* advice

Mother Nature *noun* [*singular*] — used to refer to the natural world as if it were a woman ▪ the forces of *Mother Nature* ▪ an athlete whose talents are a gift from *Mother Nature*

moth·er–of–pearl /ˌmʌðərəvˈpɚl/ *noun* [*noncount*] : a hard, shiny, and smooth substance that is on the insides of the shells of some shellfish (such as mussels) and that is used to decorate objects (such as buttons)

Mother's Day *noun, pl* ~ **Days** [*count, noncount*] : the second Sunday in May in the U.S. and the fourth Sunday in Lent in Britain treated as a special day for honoring mothers

mother ship *noun, pl* ~ **ships** [*count*] : a large ship or spaceship that sends out boats or smaller spaceships to explore, do scientific research, etc.

M

Mother Superior *noun, pl* ~ **-ors** [*count*] : a woman who is the head of a convent • the watchful eye of the *Mother Superior* — often used as a form of address • Good morning, *Mother Superior*. — called also *Reverend Mother*

mother tongue *noun, pl* ~ **tongues** [*count*] : the language that a person learns to speak first • He speaks English fluently but his *mother tongue* [=*native language, first language*] is Chinese.

mo·tif /moʊˈtiːf/ *noun, pl* **-tifs** [*count*]
1 : something (such as an important idea or subject) that is repeated throughout a book, story, etc.
2 : a single or repeated design or pattern • The wallpaper has a flower *motif*.

¹mo·tion /ˈmoʊʃən/ *noun, pl* **-tions**
1 a : an act or process of moving : MOVEMENT [*noncount*] All *motion* stopped. • She has a simple golf swing with no/little wasted *motion*. [*count*] a rocking/smooth/steady *motion* • planetary *motions* • the rhythmic *motions* of the waves — see also SLOW MOTION **b** [*count*] : a movement of your body or of a part of your body • He caught the ball and flipped it back to me in one fluid *motion*. • She made a *motion* [=*gesture*] to her assistant. • The wax should be applied using a circular *motion*. • He made hand *motions* to get our attention.
2 [*count*] **a** : a formal suggestion or proposal that is made at a meeting for something to be done • She made a *motion* calling for the repeal of the law. • Her *motion* was voted on. • She made a *motion* that the meeting (should) be adjourned. = She made a *motion* to adjourn (the meeting). **b** *law* : a formal request made to a court of law or judge for something to be done or happen • His lawyer filed a *motion* for a mistrial. • Her lawyer has filed a *motion* that the case (should) be dismissed. • The judge denied a *motion* to delay the hearing.
3 [*count*] *Brit, medical* **a** : an act of passing solid waste from the body : a bowel movement **b** : the solid waste that is passed from the body
go through the motions : to do something without making much effort to do it well • He claimed that he was looking for a job, but he was really just *going through the motions*.
in motion **1** : moving • She's a very busy person who's constantly *in motion*. • He likes taking photographs of people *in motion*. **2** ◇ When something, such as a plan or process, is ***in motion*** or has been ***set in motion*** or ***put in/into motion***, it has begun and is proceeding. • They will be taking steps to *set/put* the divorce proceedings *in motion*. [=to begin the divorce proceedings] • The plan has been *put into motion*.
poetry in motion see POETRY

²motion *verb* **-tions; -tioned; -tion·ing** : to make a movement of your hand, head, etc., that tells someone to move or act in a certain way [+ *obj*] They *motioned* me to come forward. = They *motioned* me forward. • The guard *motioned* us through the gate. [*no obj*] She *motioned* to her assistant. • He *motioned* (to me) with one hand while opening the door with the other. • She *motioned* at the empty chair beside her and told me to sit down.

mo·tion·less /ˈmoʊʃənləs/ *adj* : not moving • He stood there absolutely *motionless*, waiting for her to speak.

motion picture *noun, pl* ~ **-tures** [*count*] *US* : MOVIE, FILM • He was given a starring role in a major *motion picture*. • the *motion-picture* industry

motion sickness *noun* [*noncount*] : a feeling of sickness caused by the motion of a car, airplane, boat, etc. — called also (*Brit*) *travel sickness*

mo·ti·vate /ˈmoʊtəˌveɪt/ *verb* **-vates; -vat·ed; -vat·ing** [+ *obj*]
1 : to give (someone) a reason for doing something • No one knows what *motivated* him to act in such a violent way. • The company has used a number of methods to *motivate* its employees (to work harder). — often used as (*be*) *motivated* • She said that she *was motivated* by a desire to help children.
2 : to be a reason for (something) • He denied that political pressures had *motivated* his decision. = He denied that his decision was politically *motivated*. [=done for political reasons] • a racially *motivated* crime
– motivated *adj* [*more* ~; *most* ~] • a highly *motivated* employee [=an employee who is eager to do work and who wants to be successful] **– mo·ti·va·tor** /ˈmoʊtəˌveɪtɚ/ *noun, pl* **-tors** [*count*] • The fear of failure can be a powerful *motivator*.

mo·ti·va·tion /ˌmoʊtəˈveɪʃən/ *noun, pl* **-tions**
1 [*noncount*] **a** : the act or process of giving someone a reason for doing something : the act or process of motivating someone • Some students need *motivation* to help them through school. **b** : the condition of being eager to act or work : the condition of being motivated • employees who lack *motivation*
2 : a force or influence that causes someone to do something [*noncount*] His behavior seemed to be without *motivation*. = There seemed to be no *motivation* [=*reason, motive*] for his behavior. [*count*] Many people have questioned her *motivations* in choosing to run for office at this time.
– mo·ti·va·tion·al /ˌmoʊtəˈveɪʃənl/ *adj* • a *motivational* speech [=a speech that is intended to motivate people]

¹mo·tive /ˈmoʊtɪv/ *noun, pl* **-tives** [*count*] : a reason for doing something • Their *motive* in running away was to avoid being punished. • I think he's guilty of the crime. He had the *motive*, the means, and the opportunity. • She denied that her offer to help was based on selfish *motives*. • hidden/ulterior *motives* • making decisions based on the ***profit motive*** [=the desire to make a profit] — often + *for* • No one knows the main/real/underlying *motive for* his behavior.
– mo·tive·less /ˈmoʊtɪvləs/ *adj*

²motive *adj, always used before a noun, technical* : of, relating to, or causing motion • *motive* power

mot·ley /ˈmɑːtli/ *adj* [*more* ~; *most* ~] *usually disapproving* : made up of many different people or things • a *motley* collection of junk • a *motley* crew/group of musicians

mo·to·cross /ˈmoʊtoʊˌkrɑːs/ *noun* [*noncount*] : the sport of racing motorcycles over a rough course with many hills, sharp turns, etc.

¹mo·tor /ˈmoʊtɚ/ *noun, pl* **-tors** [*count*]
1 : a machine that produces motion or power for doing work • a gasoline *motor* [=*engine*] • electric *motors* — see also OUTBOARD MOTOR
2 *chiefly Brit, informal + old-fashioned* : CAR
– mo·tor·less /ˈmoʊtɚləs/ *adj* • a *motorless* lawn mower • a *motorless* boat

²motor *adj, always used before a noun*
1 a : of, relating to, used in, or involving a vehicle that is powered by a motor (such as a car or motorcycle) • a *motor* mechanic/trip/accident • *motor* fuel/oil • *motor* racing/sports **b** : having a motor • a *motor* [=*motorized*] cart
2 *technical* : of or relating to the part of the nervous system that controls the movement of muscles • *motor* nerves/activities • *motor* areas of the brain • a *motor* reaction

³motor *verb, always followed by an adverb or preposition* **-tors; -tored; -tor·ing** [*no obj*]
1 : to travel in a car : DRIVE • We spent the afternoon *motoring* through the countryside.
2 *of a car, truck, etc.* : to move in a specified manner or direction : DRIVE • The car *motored* slowly up the hill.

mo·tor·bike /ˈmoʊtɚˌbaɪk/ *noun, pl* **-bikes** [*count*]
1 *US* : a small motorcycle
2 *Brit* : ¹MOTORCYCLE

mo·tor·boat /ˈmoʊtɚˌboʊt/ *noun, pl* **-boats** [*count*] : a boat with a motor — see picture at BOAT

mo·tor·cade /ˈmoʊtɚˌkeɪd/ *noun, pl* **-cades** [*count*] : a group or line of cars or other vehicles that travel together • a presidential *motorcade* [=a line of vehicles that includes a car carrying the President]

mo·tor·car /ˈmoʊtɚˌkaɚ/ *noun, pl* **-cars** [*count*] *old-fashioned* : CAR • driving an antique *motorcar*

motor court *noun, pl* ~ **courts** [*count*] *US* : MOTEL — used chiefly in the names of motels • We stayed overnight at the Pleasant Valley *Motor Court*.

¹mo·tor·cy·cle /ˈmoʊtɚˌsaɪkəl/ *noun, pl* **-cy·cles** [*count*] : a vehicle with two wheels that is powered by a motor and that can carry one or two people • ride (on) a *motorcycle* • a *motorcycle* race/accident — see picture on the next page

²motorcycle *verb* **-cy·cles; -cy·cled; -cy·cling** [*no obj*] : to ride on a motorcycle • He spent his vacation *motorcycling* across the country.
– mo·tor·cy·clist /ˈmoʊtɚˌsaɪkəlɪst/ *noun, pl* **-clists** [*count*] • a law requiring *motorcyclists* to wear helmets

motor home *noun, pl* ~ **homes** [*count*] : a type of vehicle that people can live and sleep in when they are traveling — compare MOBILE HOME

motoring *adj, always used before a noun, chiefly Brit* : involving or relating to cars or driving • a *motoring* accident/offense

motor inn *noun, pl* ~ **inns** [*count*] *US* : MOTEL; *especially* : a large motel — used chiefly in the names of motels • We stayed at the South Bridge *Motor Inn*.

M

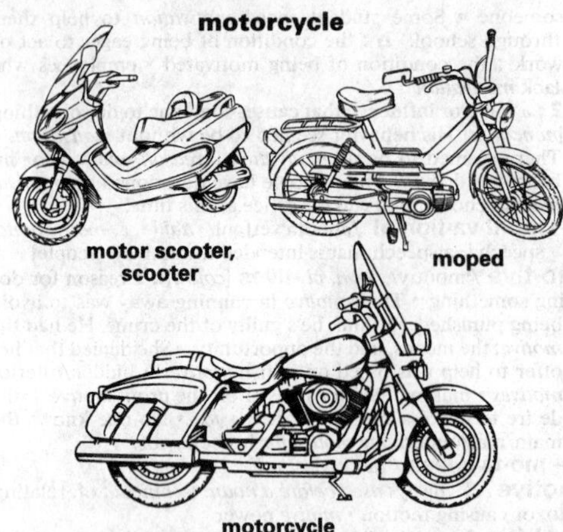

mo·tor·ist /ˈmoutərɪst/ *noun, pl* **-ists** [*count*] : a person who drives a car ▪ When our car broke down, we were helped by a passing *motorist.* ▪ an uninsured *motorist*

mo·tor·ized *also Brit* **mo·tor·ised** /ˈmoutəˌraɪzd/ *adj*
1 : having a motor ▪ *motorized* vehicles ▪ a *motorized* bicycle/wheelchair
2 : using motorized vehicles ▪ *motorized* troops

mo·tor·man /ˈmoutəmən/ *noun, pl* **-men** /-mən/ [*count*] : a man whose job is to drive a subway train or a streetcar

mo·tor·mouth /ˈmoutəˌmauθ/ *noun, pl* **-mouths** [*count*] *informal* : a person who talks too much

motor pool *noun, pl* **~ pools** [*count*] : a group of vehicles that are available for use

motor scooter *noun, pl* **~ -ers** [*count*] : a small vehicle with two wheels that is powered by a motor and that has a low seat and a flat area for resting your feet — called also *scooter*; see picture at MOTORCYCLE

motor vehicle *noun, pl* **~ -hi·cles** [*count*] : a vehicle (such as a car, truck, or motorcycle) that is powered by a motor ▪ You can register your car at the Registry of *Motor Vehicles.*

mo·tor·way /ˈmoutəˌweɪ/ *noun, pl* **-ways** [*count*] *Brit* : a large highway : EXPRESSWAY

mot·tled /ˈmɑːtl̩d/ *adj* [*more ~; most ~*] : marked with colored spots or areas ▪ a tree with *mottled* leaves ▪ *mottled* skin ▪ a fabric *mottled* with green and yellow

mot·to /ˈmɑːtou/ *noun, pl* **mot·toes** *also* **mot·tos** [*count*] : a short sentence or phrase that expresses a rule guiding the behavior of a particular person or group ▪ "Hope for the best and prepare for the worst" is my *motto.* ▪ The Boy Scout *motto* is "Be prepared."

mould *Brit spelling of* MOLD

moulder *Brit spelling of* MOLDER

moulding *Brit spelling of* MOLDING

mouldy *Brit spelling of* MOLDY

moult *Brit spelling of* MOLT

¹mound /ˈmaund/ *noun, pl* **mounds** [*count*]
1 : a small hill or pile of dirt or stones ▪ the burial *mounds* of an ancient people
2 : the slightly raised area of ground on which a baseball pitcher stands ▪ the pitcher's/pitching *mound*
3 : a heap or pile *of* something ▪ a *mound of* dirty laundry ▪ a *mound of* snow ▪ a *mound of* mashed potatoes — sometimes used figuratively ▪ We have a *mound of* work to do. [=we have a lot of work to do] ▪ an athlete who has earned *mounds of* money [=a large amount of money]

²mound *verb* **mounds; mound·ed; mound·ing** [+ *obj*] *chiefly US*
1 : to make a pile with or of (something) ▪ He *mounded* the food onto his plate. ▪ The snow was *mounded* (up) on both sides of the road. [=there was a pile of snow on both sides of the road]
2 : to cover (something) *with* a pile of something ▪ His plate was *mounded with* food. [=there was a pile of food on his plate] ▪ a desk *mounded with* books and papers

¹mount /ˈmaunt/ *verb* **mounts; mount·ed; mount·ing**
1 [+ *obj*] : to go or climb up (something) ▪ *mount* a ladder ▪ *mount* the stairs : to climb up onto (something) ▪ *mount* a platform
2 [*no obj*] : to increase in amount ▪ Their troubles have continued to *mount.* ▪ The pressure *mounted* as the crisis continued. ▪ Costs can *mount* (up) very quickly.
3 : to seat yourself on a horse, bicycle, etc. [+ *obj*] The cowboy *mounted* his horse and then quickly dismounted. ▪ She *mounted* her bicycle and rode away. [*no obj*] The cowboy *mounted* (up) and rode off.
4 [+ *obj*] : to attach (something) to something for support or use ▪ The jeweler *mounted* the pearl in a ring. ▪ She *mounted* the photograph to a piece of cardboard. — often + *on* ▪ The airplane's engines are *mounted on* the wings. [=are attached to the wings] ▪ He *mounted* a rack *on* the roof of his car. ▪ The speakers were *mounted on* the walls. ▪ He *mounted* a specimen *on* a slide for examination with a microscope.
5 [+ *obj*] : to organize and do (something that usually requires the effort of many people) ▪ *mount* an assault/attack ▪ The police have *mounted* a nationwide search for the killer. ▪ She is expected to *mount* a serious challenge in the coming election. ▪ The museum is *mounting* an exhibition of his paintings.
6 [+ *obj*] *of a male animal* : to climb onto (a female animal) in order to have sex
– mounting *adj* ▪ The company is faced with *mounting* [=*increasing*] costs. ▪ *mounting* debts/tension/frustration

²mount *noun, pl* **mounts** [*count*]
1 : something onto which something else is or can be attached ▪ a lens *mount* [=the part of a camera where a lens is attached]
2 *old-fashioned + literary* : a horse that is being ridden by a person ▪ The cowboy got down slowly from his *mount.*
— compare ³MOUNT

³mount *noun, pl* **mounts** [*count*] : MOUNTAIN — used chiefly in names ▪ *Mount* Everest — compare ²MOUNT

moun·tain /ˈmauntn̩/ *noun, pl* **-tains** [*count*]
1 : an area of land that rises very high above the land around it and that is higher than a hill ▪ She watched the sun set behind the *mountains.* ▪ the Rocky *Mountains* ▪ He climbed the *mountain.* ▪ a cabin in the *mountains* ▪ They both like *mountain* climbing. ▪ *mountain* scenery ▪ a *mountain* range/lake ▪ a *mountain* man [=a man who lives in the mountains] — see color picture on page C7
2 : a very large amount *of* something ▪ We've received a *mountain of* mail. ▪ *mountains of* data
make a mountain out of a molehill see MOLEHILL

mountain ash *noun, pl* **~ ashes** [*count*] : a small tree that produces red berries — called also (*Brit*) *rowan*

mountain bike *noun, pl* **~ bikes** [*count*] : a type of bicycle that has a strong frame, thick tires, and straight handlebars and that is used for riding over rough ground
– mountain biker *noun, pl* **~ -ers** [*count*] **– mountain biking** *noun* [*noncount*] ▪ He enjoys *mountain biking.*

moun·tain·eer /ˌmauntəˈniə/ *noun, pl* **-eers** [*count*] : a person who climbs mountains : a mountain climber
– moun·tain·eer·ing /ˌmauntəˈnirɪŋ/ *noun* [*noncount*] ▪ the sport of *mountaineering*

mountain goat *noun, pl* **~ goats** [*count*] : an animal that has horns and a thick white coat and that lives in the mountains of western North America

mountain laurel *noun, pl* **~ -rels** [*count*] : a North American evergreen tree or bush that has shiny leaves and pink or white flowers

mountain lion *noun, pl* **~ -ons** [*count*] : COUGAR

moun·tain·ous /ˈmauntənəs/ *adj* [*more ~; most ~*]
1 : having many mountains ▪ *mountainous* terrain/country/land ▪ a *mountainous* area/region
2 : extremely large : HUGE ▪ *mountainous* costs ▪ *mountainous* waves

moun·tain·side /ˈmauntn̩ˌsaɪd/ *noun, pl* **-sides** [*count*] : the side of a mountain ▪ a steep *mountainside*

moun·tain·top /ˈmauntn̩ˌtɑːp/ *noun, pl* **-tops** [*count*] : the top of a mountain ▪ a snowy *mountaintop*

moun·te·bank /ˈmauntɪˌbæŋk/ *noun, pl* **-banks** [*count*] *old-fashioned + literary* : a dishonest person : a person who tricks and cheats other people ▪ a gang of swindlers and *mountebanks*

mounted *adj, usually used before a noun* : having a horse or horses for riding ▪ *mounted* infantry/troops ▪ a *mounted* policeman

Mount·ie /ˈmaunti/ *noun, pl* **-ies** [*count*] : a member of the Royal Canadian Mounted Police

mount·ing /ˈmauntɪŋ/ *noun, pl* **-ings** [*count*] : something on which something else is or can be attached ▪ a *mounting* for an engine • a *mounting* for a diamond

mourn /ˈmoɚn/ *verb* **mourns; mourned; mourn·ing**
1 : to feel or show great sadness because someone has died [*no obj*] When he dies, people throughout the world will *mourn.* [=*grieve*] — often + *for* • Thousands *mourned for* him. [+ *obj*] She is still *mourning* her husband, who died last year. • Thousands of people *mourned* his death/passing. • She was *mourned* by everyone who knew her.
2 : to feel or show great sadness or unhappiness about (something) [+ *obj*] She *mourned* the loss of her youth. • He still *mourns* the fact that he never went to college. [*no obj*] — usually + *for* • She *mourned for* her lost youth.

mourn·er /ˈmoɚnɚ/ *noun, pl* **-ers** [*count*] **:** a person who mourns for someone who has died; *especially* **:** a person who goes to someone's funeral • His funeral services attracted hundreds of *mourners.*

mourn·ful /ˈmoɚnfəl/ *adj* [*more* ~; *most* ~] **:** full of sorrow **:** very sad • a *mournful* face • *mournful* eyes • a *mournful* song/occasion
– mourn·ful·ly /ˈmoɚnfəli/ *adv* • He spoke *mournfully.*
– mourn·ful·ness *noun* [*noncount*]

mourn·ing /ˈmoɚnɪŋ/ *noun* [*noncount*]
1 : the act of mourning for someone who has died • a day of national *mourning* • She is still ***in mourning*** for her dead husband. • The whole town was *in mourning.* • She ***went into mourning*** for her dead husband. [=she began to mourn for her dead husband]
2 : great sadness felt because someone has died • a period of deep *mourning*
3 : black clothing that is worn to show that you are mourning for someone who has died • His widow was dressed in *mourning.*

mouse /ˈmaʊs/ *noun, pl* **mice** /ˈmaɪs/ [*count*]
1 : a very small animal that has a pointed nose and a long, thin tail • The house was infested with *mice* and rats. • a ***field mouse*** [=a type of mouse that lives in fields] • a ***house mouse*** [=a type of mouse that lives in people's houses] — sometimes used figuratively to refer to a weak, frightened, or quiet person • Stand up for your rights! What are you—a man or a *mouse*?! — see picture at RODENT
2 *pl also* **mous·es :** a small device that is connected to a computer and that you move with your hand to control the movement of a pointer on the computer screen • He moved the *mouse* to click on the icon. • (*US*) a ***mouse pad*** = (*Brit*) a ***mouse mat*** [=a small pad that a computer's mouse rests on] — see picture at COMPUTER
– see also CAT AND MOUSE

mous·er /ˈmaʊsɚ/ *noun, pl* **-ers** [*count*] **:** a cat that is good at catching mice

mouse·trap /ˈmaʊsˌtræp/ *noun, pl* **-traps** [*count*] **:** a small trap for catching mice

mousetrap

mous·sa·ka /muˈsɑːkə/ *noun, pl* **-kas** [*count, noncount*] **:** a Greek dish of ground meat (such as lamb or beef) and sliced eggplant

mousse /ˈmuːs/ *noun, pl* **mouss·es** [*count, noncount*]
1 : a cold and sweet food made with whipped cream or egg whites and usually fruit or chocolate • chocolate *mousse* • a lemon *mousse*
2 : a foamy substance that is used in styling a person's hair • a jar of styling/hair *mousse*

moustache *chiefly Brit spelling of* MUSTACHE

moustachio *chiefly Brit spelling of* MUSTACHIO

mousy *also* **mous·ey** /ˈmaʊsi/ *adj* **mous·i·er; -est**
1 : shy and quiet • The movie is a fantasy about a *mousy* housewife who is transformed into a glamorous star.
2 *of hair* **:** dull brown in color • *mousy* [=*drab*] brown hair

¹mouth /ˈmaʊθ/ *noun, pl* **mouths** /ˈmaʊðz/
1 : the opening through which food passes into the body **:** the part of the face that includes the lips and the opening behind them [*count*] He kissed her on the *mouth.* • He threatened to punch me in the *mouth.* • She stood there with her *mouth* agape/open. • I burned the roof of my *mouth.* • They told him to keep his *mouth* closed when chewing and not to talk with his *mouth* full. • He wiped his *mouth* with a napkin after eating. • She regretted saying it as soon as the words were out of her *mouth.* • The smell of the food made my *mouth* water. • The candy melts in your *mouth.* • He says something stupid ***every time he opens his mouth.*** [=every time he speaks] • The experience ***left a bad taste in my mouth.*** [=the experience left me feeling bad or disgusted] [*noncount*] The medication is taken ***by mouth.***

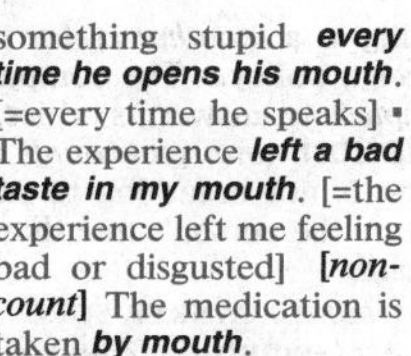

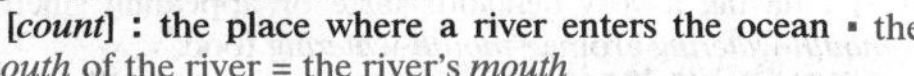

2 [*count*] **:** an opening in something — usually + *of* • the *mouth of* a cave/bottle — see also GOAL MOUTH
3 [*count*] **:** the place where a river enters the ocean • the *mouth* of the river = the river's *mouth*
4 [*singular*] *informal* **:** an unpleasant or offensive way of talking • That guy has quite a *mouth* on him. • He has a loud *mouth.* • He cursed and his mother angrily told him to ***watch his mouth.*** [=to not use offensive language] — see also BIG MOUTH, LOUDMOUTH, SMART-MOUTH
all mouth (and no trousers/action) *Brit, informal* — used to describe someone who talks a lot about doing something but never actually does it
born with a silver spoon in your mouth see BORN
butter wouldn't melt in someone's mouth see ¹BUTTER
by word of mouth see ¹WORD
down in the mouth **:** unhappy or depressed • I was surprised to see her looking so *down in the mouth.*
foam at the mouth see ²FOAM
from the horse's mouth see ¹HORSE
froth at the mouth see ²FROTH
hand to mouth see ¹HAND
heart in your mouth see HEART
keep your mouth shut **1 :** to not say anything • When he starts talking about politics, I just *keep my mouth shut.* **2 :** to not talk about something (such as a secret) • She told me to *keep my mouth shut* about the news. [=she told me not to tell anyone about the news] • I never tell him anything important because he doesn't know how to *keep his mouth shut.* [=he tells other people what he has been told]
look a gift horse in the mouth see ¹HORSE
melt in your mouth see ¹MELT
mouth to feed **:** a person (such as a child) who needs to be fed • They can't afford another child. They already have too many (hungry) *mouths to feed.*
put words in/into someone's mouth see ¹WORD
put your foot in your mouth see ¹FOOT
put your money where your mouth is see MONEY
run your mouth see ¹RUN
shoot your mouth off see ¹SHOOT
shut your mouth see ¹SHUT
take the words right out of someone's mouth see ¹WORD

²mouth /ˈmaʊð/ *verb* **mouths; mouthed; mouth·ing** [+ *obj*]
1 : to say or repeat (something) without really meaning it or understanding it • She was just *mouthing* the usual meaningless platitudes about the need for reform.
2 : to form (words) with your lips without speaking • The librarian *mouthed* "quiet." • silently *mouthing* the words to a song
mouth off [*phrasal verb*] *informal* **:** to talk in a loud, unpleasant, or rude way • He got in trouble again for *mouthing off* to his teacher. • She's always *mouthing off* about how much better she could run the company herself.

-mouthed /ˌmaʊðd/ *adj* **:** having a mouth of a specified type — usually used in combination with another adjective • a large-*mouthed* jar • big-*mouthed* • loud*mouthed*

mouth·ful /ˈmaʊθˌfʊl/ *noun, pl* **-fuls**
1 [*count*] **:** as much as a mouth will hold • a *mouthful* of food/water • It was a delicious meal. We enjoyed every *mouthful.*
2 [*singular*] *informal* **a :** a word, name, or phrase that is very long or difficult to say • His last name is a real *mouthful.* **b** *US* **:** something said that has a lot of meaning or importance • You ***said a mouthful!*** [=I agree with what you said; you said something that was entirely correct and that was worth saying]

mouth organ *noun, pl* **~ -gans** [*count*] **:** HARMONICA

mouth·piece /ˈmaʊθˌpiːs/ *noun, pl* **-piec·es** [*count*]
1 : a part of something that is placed between or near your lips • the *mouthpiece* of a trumpet/telephone
2 : someone who speaks for another person or for a group

M

or organization • He's been acting as a *mouthpiece* for the government on questions of foreign policy. • The company has hired an attorney as a *mouthpiece* to answer its critics.

mouth–to–mouth resuscitation *noun* [*noncount*] : a method of helping a person who is not breathing to start breathing again by blowing air into the person's mouth and lungs — called also *mouth-to-mouth*

mouth ulcer *noun, pl* ~ **-cers** [*count*] : CANKER SORE

mouth•wash /ˈmaʊθˌwɑːʃ/ *noun, pl* **-wash•es** [*count, noncount*] : a liquid that is used to clean your mouth and teeth and to make your breath smell better

mouth–wa•ter•ing /ˈmaʊθˌwɑːtərɪŋ/ *adj* [*more* ~; *most* ~] : having a very delicious taste or appealing smell • a *mouth-watering* aroma • *mouth-watering* food
– mouth–wa•ter•ing•ly *adv* • food that smells *mouth-wateringly* good

mouthy /ˈmaʊθi/ *adj* **mouth•i•er; -est** *informal* : talking too much and often in an unpleasant or rude way • a *mouthy* show-off

mov•able *also* **move•able** /ˈmuːvəbəl/ *adj*
1 : able to be moved • a *movable* antenna/partition • *movable* property — opposite IMMOVABLE
2 : happening on a different date each year • Thanksgiving is a *movable* holiday. • Easter is a ***movable feast***. [=a religious festival that occurs on a different date each year]

[1]**move** /ˈmuːv/ *verb* **moves; moved; mov•ing**
1 a [+ *obj*] : to cause (something or someone) to go from one place or position to another • He *moved* the chair closer to the table. • It may be necessary to *move* the patient to intensive care. • The breeze *moved* the branches of the trees. • The knife had sunk deeply into the wood and couldn't be *moved*. [=*budged*] **b** [*no obj*] : to go from one place or position to another • The boat *moved* [=*rocked*] slowly from side to side as the wind rose. • The branches *moved* gently in the breeze.
2 a : to cause (your body or a part of your body) to go from one position to another [+ *obj*] She was unable to *move* her legs. • Nobody ***moved a muscle***. [=nobody moved at all; everyone was very still] [*no obj*] The dancers *moved* gracefully. • Nobody *moved*. • She was so frightened that she could hardly *move*. • I *moved* over so that she could sit next to me. **b** [*no obj*] : to go or walk from one place to another • We *moved* into the shade. • The police were *moving* through the crowd telling people to *move* toward the exit. • People were *moving* (about/around) freely. • We could hear someone *moving* around upstairs. • *move* along • They *moved* closer to each other and spoke in whispers.
3 [+ *obj*] **a** : to cause (something) to go to a specified place or to proceed in a specified way • The records show that she *moved* large amounts of money to a foreign bank account. • He lacks enough support to *move* his proposals through the legislature. **b** : to cause (something) to happen at a different time • The meeting has been *moved* [=*changed*] to this afternoon.
4 *always followed by an adverb or preposition* : to go to a different and usually higher position [*no obj*] The team has *moved* into second place. • She has been steadily *moving* up the corporate ladder. • Congratulations on your promotion. It's nice to see how you're ***moving up in the world***. [+ *obj*] A win will *move* the team into second place.
5 a : to go to a different place to live [*no obj*] We've had to *move* twice in the past year. • He didn't like small towns and decided to *move* to the city. • We're planning to *move* into a new apartment. • He *moved* (away) with his family to California. [+ *obj*] He *moved* his family to California. • (*Brit*) We've had to ***move house*** twice in the past year. **b** : to go to a different place to work or do business [*no obj*] The company is *moving* from New York to Chicago. [+ *obj*] The company is *moving* its offices from New York to Chicago. — see also MOVING 3
6 [+ *obj*] **a** : to affect the feelings of (someone) : to cause (someone) to feel an emotion and especially sadness or sympathy • The sad story of his childhood *moved* us deeply. • I was greatly *moved* by his story/kindness. • He's not easily ***moved to*** anger. [=he does not become angry easily] • His story ***moved us to tears***. [=it affected us so strongly that we cried] — see also MOVING 2 **b** : to cause (someone) to act or think in a specified way — followed by *to* + *verb* • The report *moved* [=*persuaded*] me *to change* my mind. • His arguments *moved* them *to reconsider* the plan. • I felt *moved* [=*compelled*] *to speak*. **c** : to cause (someone) to feel or think in a different way • We were unable to *move* him from his convictions. • He would not be *moved*.
7 [*no obj*] : to take action : ACT • We need to *move* quickly to close this deal. • He was waiting for the right time to *move* against his enemies. • She hasn't yet *moved* on their recommendations. • We must *move* [=*proceed*] very carefully to avoid offending them.
8 a : to formally make a suggestion or proposal at a meeting [*no obj*] — + *for* • She *moved for* an adjournment. [+ *obj*] She *moved* to adjourn the meeting. = She *moved* that the meeting be adjourned. **b** [*no obj*] *law* : to make a formal request to a court of law or judge for something to be done or happen — + *for* • His lawyer *moved for* a mistrial. • The plaintiff *moved for* a retrial.
9 *always followed by an adverb or preposition* [*no obj*] : to make progress • The plot of the novel *moves* [=*develops*] slowly. • They're *moving* closer to making a decision.
10 *informal* : SELL [+ *obj*] a store that *moves* a lot of merchandise [*no obj*] The products have been *moving* slowly.
11 [*no obj*] *informal* : to go fast • When the police car passed us it was really *moving*.
12 [*no obj*] : to spend time with a particular group of people or at a particular level of society • She *moves* in high circles. [=she is friendly with wealthy and powerful people] • She and her sister *move* in very different circles. [=they are friendly with very different groups of people]
13 [*no obj*] *informal* : to leave a place • It was getting late and I thought it was time to be *moving*. [=*going*]
14 : to cause a piece in a game (such as chess or checkers) to go from one place to another [+ *obj*] He *moved* a pawn. [*no obj*] It's your turn to *move*.
as/when the spirit moves you see [1]SPIRIT
get moving *informal* : to start moving or going quickly • We need to *get moving* [=*hurry*] or we'll miss the show.
move ahead/along **1** : to make progress • The project is finally starting to *move ahead*. **2** : to go on to something else • Let's *move along* [=*move on*] to the next item.
move heaven and earth : to work very hard to do something • He vowed that he would *move heaven and earth* to finish the project on schedule.
move in [*phrasal verb*] **1** : to start living in a house, apartment, etc. • I remember when our neighbors first *moved in*. • He's planning to *move in* with his girlfriend. **2** ***move in on (someone or something)*** : to move closer or nearer to (someone or something that you are trying to reach, get, etc.) • The police *moved in on* [=*closed in on*] the wanted criminal. • The police *moved in on* the criminal's hideout. • The lion was *moving in on* its prey. — often used figuratively • Our competitors are trying to *move in on* our territory. [=trying to get control of our territory] • He was trying to *move in on* my girlfriend. [=trying to take my girlfriend from me]
move it *US, informal* : to start moving or going quickly • We'd better *move it* if we don't want to be late.
move on [*phrasal verb*] : to go on to a different place, subject, activity, etc. • Let's put that issue aside and *move on*. • We should *move on* [=*move ahead*] to the next item on the list. • After 10 years working for one company, she felt it was time to *move on* to a new job.
move out [*phrasal verb*] : to leave your house, apartment, etc., and go to live somewhere else • He was 20 when he *moved out* of his parents' house. • Her lease ends next month, so she'll have to *move out* (of her apartment) soon.

[2]**move** *noun, pl* **moves** [*count*]
1 : an act of moving your body or a part of your body : MOVEMENT • fancy dance *moves* • He made a sudden *move* that scared away the squirrel. • an athlete who has some good *moves* • No one made a *move* toward the exits. [=no one moved toward the exits] • The policeman warned him not to make any false *moves*. • He was afraid to make a *move*.
2 : an action • The police are watching his every *move*. = The police are watching every *move* he makes. [=the police are watching everything he does] • No one is sure what his next *move* will be. • He was waiting for her to ***make the first move***. [=to act first]
3 : the act of moving to a different place • He's preparing for his *move* to California.
4 : something done to achieve a desired result or goal • Starting her own business was a risky/bold *move*. • In a *move* to attract new customers, the company has decided to devote more money to advertising. • a smart/wise *move* • a good ***career move*** [=something done to help a person's career]
5 : an act of moving a piece in a game (such as chess or checkers) • the opening *moves* in a game of chess • It's your *move*. [=*turn*]

M

***get a move on** informal* : to start moving or going quickly ▪ We'd better *get a move on* if we don't want to be late.
***make a move** Brit, informal* : to leave a place ▪ It's been a lovely evening, but it's time we were *making a move*.
on the move **1** : moving or going from place to place ▪ As a young man, he was always *on the move*. **2** : making progress ▪ After a slow start, the project is finally *on the move*. ▪ a civilization *on the move*
***put the moves on** US, informal* : to do or say things in an effort to start a sexual relationship with someone ▪ He accused me of trying to *put the moves on* his girlfriend.

move·ment /ˈmuːvmənt/ *noun, pl* **-ments**
1 a : the act or process of moving people or things from one place or position to another [*noncount*] He developed an efficient system for *movement* of raw materials to the factory. [*count*] troop *movements* **b** : the act of moving from one place or position to another [*noncount*] increased cell *movement* [*count*] studying the *movements* of the planets **c** : the act of moving your body or a part of your body [*noncount*] We wore loose clothes to allow for easier *movement*. ▪ freedom of *movement* [*count*] the graceful *movements* of a dancer ▪ careful and precise *movements* ▪ muscle/hand/eye *movements*
2 ***movements*** [*plural*] : a person's actions or activities ▪ The police have been keeping a careful record of his *movements*.
3 [*count*] **a** : a series of organized activities in which many people work together to do or achieve something ▪ She started a *movement* [=*campaign*] for political reform. ▪ There's a *movement* afoot to rename the town. ▪ a book about the history of the civil rights *movement* **b** : the group of people who are involved in such a movement ▪ They joined the anti-war/peace/feminist *movement*.
4 a : a noticeable change in the way people behave or think [*noncount*] There has been a *movement* back to more therapeutic treatments of mental disorders in recent years. [*count*] There has been some *movement* to more therapeutic treatments. **b** : a noticeable change in a situation [*noncount*] There hasn't been any *movement* in the negotiations. [=the negotations have not progressed] [*count*] There has been a *movement* [=*tendency*] toward lower prices in the housing market recently. [=prices have been going lower in the housing market recently]
5 [*count*] *music* : a main section of a longer piece of music ▪ the first *movement* of the symphony
6 [*count*] *medical* : an act of passing solid waste from the body — called also *bowel movement*

mov·er /ˈmuːvɚ/ *noun, pl* **-ers** [*count*]
1 : someone or something that moves in a certain way ▪ a slow/fast *mover*
2 : a machine that moves people or things from one place to another ▪ an ***earth mover*** [=a machine that is used to move large amounts of soil] — see also PEOPLE MOVER
3 *US* : a person or company that moves furniture and other possessions from one home or place of business to another ▪ a furniture *mover* [=(*Brit*) *remover*]
movers and shakers : people who are active or powerful in some field ▪ the *movers and shakers* of the computer industry ▪ political *movers and shakers*

mov·ie /ˈmuːvi/ *noun, pl* **-ies** *chiefly US*
1 [*count*] : a recording of moving images that tells a story and that people watch on a screen or television ▪ He's making a *movie* [=*film, motion picture*] about growing up in a small town. ▪ a Hollywood *movie* ▪ We went to (see) a *movie* after dinner. ▪ Do you want to rent a *movie* [=rent a video or DVD] tonight? ▪ an action *movie* ▪ a horror *movie* — often used before another noun ▪ a *movie* star/producer/director ▪ a *movie* camera/studio ▪ the *movie* business/industry ▪ a *movie* critic/review ▪ a *movie* house/theater — see also HOME MOVIE
2 ***the movies*** **a** : a showing of a movie in a theater ▪ We are ***going to the movies*** tonight. [=we are going to see a movie tonight]; *also* : a movie theater ▪ What's (playing/showing) ***at the movies***? **b** : the business of making movies : the film industry ▪ He wants to work in *the movies*. ▪ a career in *the movies*

mov·ie·go·er /ˈmuːviˌgowɚ/ *noun, pl* **-ers** [*count*] *chiefly US* : a person who goes to a theater to watch movies

mov·ie·mak·er /ˈmuːviˌmeɪkɚ/ *noun, pl* **-ers** [*count*] *chiefly US* : a person who makes movies : FILMMAKER
– mov·ie·mak·ing /ˈmuːviˌmeɪkɪŋ/ *noun* [*noncount*] ▪ a talent for *moviemaking*

moving *adj*
1 : changing place or position ▪ a *moving* target ▪ the machine's *moving* parts
2 [*more ~; most ~*] : having a strong emotional effect : causing feelings of sadness or sympathy ▪ a *moving* story of a faithful dog ▪ The tribute was very *moving*. [=*touching*] ▪ He gave a *moving* speech at the memorial service.
3 *always used before a noun* : relating to the activity or process of moving to a different place to live or work ▪ *moving* expenses
moving force/spirit : someone or something that causes something to happen ▪ one of modern sculpture's *moving spirits* ▪ He has been the *moving force/spirit* behind the project from the beginning.
– mov·ing·ly *adv* ▪ He spoke *movingly* at the memorial service.

moving picture *noun, pl* **~ -tures** [*count*] *old-fashioned* : MOVIE

moving staircase *noun, pl* **~ -cases** [*count*] *old-fashioned* : ESCALATOR

moving van *noun, pl* **~ vans** [*count*] *US* : a large vehicle in which furniture and other things are moved from one home or building to another — called also (*Brit*) *removal van*

[1]**mow** /ˈmoʊ/ *verb* **mows**; **mowed**; **mowed** *or* **mown** /ˈmoʊn/; **mow·ing** [+ *obj*] : to cut (something, such as grass) with a machine or a blade ▪ *mow* the grass ▪ *mow* hay ▪ ***mow the lawn*** [=cut the grass that grows on the lawn]
mow down [*phrasal verb*] ***mow (someone) down** or **mow down (someone)** informal* : to kill or knock down (a person or many people) in a sudden and violent way ▪ The soldiers were *mowed down* by machine guns. ▪ The car *mowed down* four pedestrians.
– mow·er /ˈmowɚ/ *noun, pl* **-ers** [*count*]

[2]**mow** *noun, pl* **mows** [*count*] *informal* : an act of mowing something (such as a lawn) ▪ The lawn needs a *mow*. [=needs to be mowed]

mox·ie /ˈmɑːksi/ *noun* [*noncount*] *US, informal + old-fashioned*
1 : the ability to be active : ENERGY ▪ full of *moxie* [=*pep*]
2 : courage or determination ▪ He showed a lot of *moxie* in questioning the policy.

moz·za·rel·la /ˌmɑːtsəˈrɛlə/ *noun* [*noncount*] : a soft Italian cheese that has a mild flavor

MP /ˈɛmˈpiː/ *noun, pl* **MPs** [*count*]
1 : a member of the military police
2 *Brit* : an elected member of Parliament

mpg *abbr* miles per gallon ▪ a car that gets 30 *mpg*

mph *abbr* miles per hour ▪ a car traveling 60 *mph*

MP3 /ˌɛmˌpiːˈθriː/ *noun, pl* **MP3s**
1 [*noncount*] : a computer format for creating sound files (such as songs) that are much smaller than standard sound files — often used before another noun ▪ *MP3* files ▪ an ***MP3 player*** [=a device that stores and plays songs in the MP3 format]
2 [*count*] : a computer file (such as a song) in the MP3 format ▪ downloading *MP3s* off the Internet

Mr. (*US*) *or Brit* **Mr** /ˈmɪstɚ/ *noun*
1 a — used as a title before the name of a man ▪ *Mr.* Doe ▪ How are you, *Mr.* Jones? ▪ *Mr.* John Doe — compare MISTER; see also MESSRS. **b** — used as a title when speaking to a man who has an honored position or office ▪ "It's an honor to meet you, *Mr.* President/Chairman."
2 a — used as part of a title for a man who has won a contest ▪ *Mr.* Universe **b** — used to refer to a man who is very successful and famous for a particular activity (such as a sport) or who has a particular quality ▪ He came to be known as *Mr.* Baseball. ▪ She thinks her boyfriend is *Mr.* Wonderful. [=she thinks her boyfriend is wonderful]

Mr. Big (*US*) *or Brit* **Mr Big** *noun* [*singular*] *informal* : a very powerful or important man; *especially* : the leader of a group of criminals

MRI /ˌɛmˌɑɚˈaɪ/ *noun, pl* **MRIs** *medical*
1 [*noncount*] : MAGNETIC RESONANCE IMAGING ▪ an *MRI* machine/scanner
2 [*count*] : a procedure in which magnetic resonance imaging is used ▪ He had an *MRI* (done) on his knee.

Mr. Nice Guy (*US*) *or Brit* **Mr Nice Guy** *noun* [*singular*] *informal* : a man who treats people kindly : a nice man — used chiefly in the phrase ***no more Mr. Nice Guy*** ▪ I'm tired of the way they treat me. From now on, *no more Mr. Nice Guy*! [=I'm not going to be nice to them from now on]

Mr. Right (*US*) *or Brit* **Mr Right** *noun* [*singular*] *informal* : a man who would be the best husband for a particular woman

M

• She's still looking for *Mr. Right*. [=the perfect man for her to marry]

Mrs. *(US) or Brit* **Mrs** /ˈmɪsəz/ *noun*
1 a — used as a title for a married woman • *Mrs.* Smith • *Mrs.* Jane Smith • *Mrs.* Robert Smith [=the wife of Robert Smith] — compare MISS, MS. **b** — used as a title when speaking to a married woman who holds an honored position or office • "It's an honor to meet you, *Mrs.* [=(more commonly) *Madam*] President/Chairman."
2 a — used as part of a title for a married woman who has won a contest • *Mrs.* America **b** — used to refer to a married woman who is very successful and famous for a particular activity (such as a sport) or who has a particular quality • She has come to be known as *Mrs.* Golf. • He thinks his wife is *Mrs.* Wonderful. [=he thinks his wife is wonderful]

Ms. *(US) or Brit* **Ms** /ˈmɪz/ *noun* — used as a title before a woman's name instead of *Miss* or *Mrs.* • *Ms.* Smith • *Ms.* Jane Smith ✧ *Ms.* can be used whether or not a woman is married. — compare MISS, MRS.

MS *abbr* **1** Mississippi **2** multiple sclerosis

MSG /ˌɛmˌɛsˈʤiː/ *noun* [*noncount*] : MONOSODIUM GLUTAMATE

MT *abbr* **1** Montana **2** mountain time

[1]**much** /ˈmʌʧ/ *adj* : large in amount or extent : not little • *Much* research [=a lot of research] was carried out. • Fixing the problem will require *much* effort. [=a lot of effort] • The project is taking ***too much*** time. [=is taking more time than it should] • I can't believe that we spent ***so much*** money. [=such a large amount of money] — often used in questions and in negative statements • How *much* money do you have? • Was there *much* food at the party? • He doesn't know *much* French. • There wasn't *much* more that we could do. • It doesn't cost *much* money. • There isn't *much* difference between them. • The clerk wasn't *much* help. [=was not very helpful] • There wasn't *much* doubt about who would win.
a bit much see [1]BIT
never so much as see NEVER
so much — used for emphasis • The house burned like *so much* paper. [=it burned as if it were made of paper] • The explanation sounded like *so much* nonsense. [=it sounded like a lot of nonsense]
too much **1** : too difficult to accept or deal with • Working two jobs was *too much* (for him). **2** *informal* : very unusual in either an enjoyable or annoying way • I can't believe the way he talks. That guy is *too much*. • We laughed so hard. It was just *too much*.

[2]**much** *adv*
1 a : to a great degree or extent • I'm feeling *much* better. • *much* happier/prettier/wealthier • The new car is *much* better on gas mileage. • They both talk ***too much***. • Thank you ***so/very much*** for your help. **b** : VERY, EXTREMELY • He is *much* interested in the project. • They were *much* pleased by the compliment. • some *much*-needed repairs • a *much*-deserved vacation • He's ***not much good at*** golf. [=he plays golf badly; he is not a good golfer] **c** : FREQUENTLY, OFTEN • She doesn't visit her family *much*. • Do you travel *much*? **d** : by a long time • He didn't arrive *much* before noon. [=he didn't arrive until almost noon]
2 : very nearly • The town still looks *much* [=*essentially*] the way it did years ago. • The town looks *much* the same. • We came to *much* the same conclusion. • We left the house *much* as we found it.
as much : the same • I helped her through the divorce—I know she would do *as much* for me. [=I know that she would help me if I were going through a divorce] • He likes baseball but he likes hockey just *as much*. • "Where is he?" "He's still at home." "***I thought as much***." [=I thought so; that is what I thought]
as much as **1** — used to say that two things are equal in amount or degree • He likes hockey *as much as* he likes basketball. [=he likes hockey and basketball equally] **2** : ALMOST — used to say that someone came very close to doing something • He *as much as* admitted his guilt.
much as : ALTHOUGH • She knew the truth, *much as* [=*even though*] she wanted to deny it.
much less see [2]LESS
pretty much see [2]PRETTY
so much as see [1]SO
so much the better see [3]BETTER
very much — used for emphasis • She is *very much* [=*entirely, decidedly*] in control of the situation. • The company is still *very much* an important part of the community.

[3]**much** *pronoun*
1 : a large amount • *Much* that was said is false. • We all learned *much* [=*a lot*] from this experience. • He gave away *much* of what he owned. • Not *much* is known about his childhood. • She did *much* to improve the city. • Do you see *much* of your family? [=do you see your family often?] • She's trying to do ***too much***. [=trying to do more than she should]
2 : something that is important or impressive — used in negative statements • There was some food there, but it ***wasn't much***. [=there was not much food] • The evidence didn't ***amount to much***. [=there was not much evidence] • Her contributions didn't ***add up to much***. [=her contributions were not important] • Before the renovations, the house was ***not much to look at***. [=was not attractive]
as much as — used to say that an amount is as large as another amount • She earns *as much as* he does.
make much of see [1]MAKE
not much of a — used to say that someone or something is not very good • He's *not much of* a cook. [=he's not a very good cook] • It *wasn't much of* a vacation.
not much on : not known for, good at, or interested in (something) • He's *not much on* looks. [=he is not very attractive] • She's *not much on* studying. [=she does not like to study]
not think much of see [1]THINK
so much see [1]SO

[1]**muck** /ˈmʌk/ *noun* [*noncount*] *informal*
1 : wet dirt or mud • Clean that *muck* off your shoes.
2 *chiefly Brit* : solid waste from farm animals : MANURE
3 *informal* : something that is disgusting • How can they expect us to eat this *muck*? [=*garbage, junk*]
make a muck of something *Brit, informal* : to do something badly or with many mistakes • He's *made a muck of* things.
– mucky /ˈmʌki/ *adj* **muck·i·er; -est** • *mucky* shoes

[2]**muck** *verb* **mucks; mucked; muck·ing**
muck about/around [*phrasal verb*] *Brit, informal* **1** : to spend time doing things that are not useful or serious : to waste time • We just *mucked about* [=*messed around*] all afternoon. **2** ***muck about/around with (something)*** : to use or do (something) in a way that is not very serious • She spent the evening *mucking around with* [=*fooling around with*] the computer. **3** ***muck (someone) about/around*** : to be unfair or dishonest with (someone) : to lie to or cheat (someone) • I want them to stop *mucking* me *around*. • He's tired of being *mucked about*. [=(US) *jerked around*]
muck in [*phrasal verb*] *Brit, informal* : to help out especially by doing work • *muck in* [=*pitch in*] with the hard work
muck out [*phrasal verb*] ***muck (something) out*** *or* ***muck out (something)*** *informal* : to clean (the place where a farm animal lives) : to remove animal waste and dirty hay, sawdust, etc., from (a place, such as a barn) • We went to the barn to *muck out* [=*clean out*] the stalls.
muck up [*phrasal verb*] ***muck (something) up*** *or* ***muck up (something)*** *chiefly Brit, informal* **1** : to make (something) dirty • Take those dirty shoes off before you *muck up* the floor. **2** : to spoil or ruin (something) : to make mistakes in doing or making (something) • He *mucked up* [=*messed up*] the speech. = He *mucked* the speech *up*. • I *mucked up* my first attempt and had to try again.

muck·rak·er /ˈmʌkˌreɪkɚ/ *noun, pl* **-ers** [*count*] : someone (such as a reporter) who tries to find embarrassing or shocking information about famous people
– muck·rak·ing /ˈmʌkˌreɪkɪŋ/ *noun* [*noncount*] • a journalist accused of *muckraking* **– muckraking** *adj* • a *muckraking* journalist

mu·cous membrane /ˈmjuːkəs-/ *noun, pl* **~ -branes** [*count*] : a thin, wet layer of skin that is inside some parts of the body (such as the nose and throat) and that produces mucus

mu·cus /ˈmjuːkəs/ *noun* [*noncount*] : a thick liquid that is produced in some parts of the body (such as the nose and throat)

mud /ˈmʌd/ *noun* [*noncount*] : soft, wet dirt • He tracked *mud* into the house. • His shoes were covered with *mud*. = His shoes were caked in/with *mud*. • The car was stuck in the *mud*.
as clear as mud *informal* : very difficult to understand : not clear at all • The explanation was *as clear as mud*.
drag someone's name through the mud see [1]DRAG
sling/throw mud *chiefly US* : to publicly say false or bad

things about someone (such as a political opponent) in order to harm that person's reputation • The candidates started *slinging mud* (at each other) early in the campaign. — see also MUDSLINGING

your name is mud *informal* ✧ If *your name is mud* people do not like or trust you. • The scandal ruined his reputation and now *his name is mud*.

[1]**mud·dle** /ˈmʌdl̩/ *verb* **mud·dles; mud·dled; mud·dling** [+ *obj*]

1 : to cause confusion in (someone or someone's mind) — often used as *(be) muddled* • a mind *muddled* by too much advice

2 : to mix up (something) in a confused way • *muddle* the household accounts • I always get their names *muddled* (up) [=*mixed up*] in my mind.

muddle along [*phrasal verb*] *informal* **:** to think, act, or proceed in a confused way or without a plan • She *muddled along* for a few years before going to college.

muddle through [*phrasal verb*] *informal* **:** to do something without doing it very well or easily • I had a hard time with the class, but somehow I *muddled through*. [=*got by*] • We won't have much money but we'll *muddle through* [=*manage*] somehow.

– muddled *adj* [*more ~; most ~*] • a *muddled* story • The instructions were so *muddled* [=*confused, confusing*] that we couldn't follow them.

[2]**muddle** *noun* [*singular*]

1 a : a state of confusion or disorder • Her thoughts were ***in a muddle***. [=she was very confused] • His papers were *in a muddle*. • (*chiefly Brit*) They ***got in/into a muddle*** over the train schedule. **b :** a situation or mistake caused by confusion • There's been a bit of a *muddle* [=*mix-up*] about the plan.

2 : a confused mess • His mind was a *muddle*. **:** a disordered mixture • a *muddle* of documents

[1]**mud·dy** /ˈmʌdi/ *adj* **mud·di·er; -est**

1 : filled or covered with mud • a *muddy* pond • His shoes were *muddy*.

2 : similar to mud • a *muddy* color • *muddy* coffee

3 : not clear or bright **:** dull or cloudy • a *muddy* complexion • The recording sounded *muddy*.

4 : unclear in thought or meaning • *muddy* thinking • The facts in the case are *muddy*.

[2]**muddy** *verb* **-dies; -died; -dy·ing** [+ *obj*] **:** to make (something) muddy: such as **a :** to cover (something) with mud • His shoes were *muddied*. • The flooding *muddied* the roads. **b :** to make (a color) cloudy or dull • She *muddied* the color by adding some brown. **c :** to cause (something) to become unclear or confused • *muddying* the line between fact and fiction • The debate further *muddied* the issues.

muddy the waters **:** to make something more complicated or difficult to understand • The latest study *muddies the waters* by suggesting an alternate explanation.

mud flap *noun, pl* **~ flaps** [*count*] **:** a sheet of thin material that hangs behind a wheel of a vehicle and that stops mud and water from hitting the vehicle or other vehicles

mud·guard /ˈmʌdˌgɑɚd/ *noun, pl* **-guards** [*count*]

1 *US* **:** MUD FLAP

2 *Brit* **:** FENDER 2

mud·room /ˈmʌdˌruːm/ *noun, pl* **-rooms** [*count*] *US* **:** a room at an entrance to a house where people can leave wet or dirty shoes and clothing

mud·slide /ˈmʌdˌslaɪd/ *noun, pl* **-slides** [*count*] **:** a large mass of wet earth that suddenly and quickly moves down the side of a mountain or hill • The heavy rain triggered a *mudslide*.

mud·sling·ing /ˈmʌdˌslɪŋɪŋ/ *noun* [*noncount*] **:** the act or practice of publicly saying false or bad things about someone (such as a political opponent) in order to harm that person's reputation • a campaign marred by *mudslinging* on both sides

– mud·sling·er /ˈmʌdˌslɪŋɚ/ *noun, pl* **-ers** [*count*] • a political *mudslinger*

[1]**muff** /ˈmʌf/ *noun, pl* **muffs** [*count*] **:** a warm covering for your hands that is shaped like a tube with open ends in which both hands may be placed — see also EARMUFF

[2]**muff** *verb* **muffs; muffed; muff·ing** [+ *obj*] *informal* **:** to make a mistake in doing or handling (something) **:** BOTCH • She *muffed* the speech. • He *muffed* his chance for a promotion. • The outfielder *muffed* an easy catch.

muf·fin /ˈmʌfən/ *noun, pl* **-fins** [*count*]

1 : a small bread or cake that is usually eaten at breakfast • a blueberry/bran/corn *muffin* — see picture at BAKING

2 *Brit* **:** ENGLISH MUFFIN

muf·fle /ˈmʌfəl/ *verb* **muf·fles; muf·fled; muf·fling** [+ *obj*]

1 : to make (a sound) quieter • They tried to *muffle* the noise. **:** to decrease the noise made by (something) • *muffle* [=*suppress*] a cough • I could hear their *muffled* voices from the next room. • a *muffled* cough

2 *chiefly Brit* **:** to wrap or cover (someone or something) in clothing or cloth for warmth or protection • She was *muffled* (up) in a huge overcoat.

muf·fler /ˈmʌflɚ/ *noun, pl* **-flers** [*count*]

1 *US* **:** a device that is attached to the engine of a vehicle to make it quieter — called also (*Brit*) *silencer*; see picture at CAR

2 : a piece of cloth worn around your neck to keep it warm **:** SCARF

[1]**mug** /ˈmʌg/ *noun, pl* **mugs** [*count*]

1 a : a large drinking cup with a handle • a collection of coffee *mugs* • a beer *mug* **b :** the liquid that is contained in a mug • He drank a *mug* of coffee.

2 *slang* **:** the face or mouth of a person • his ugly *mug*

3 *Brit, informal* **:** a foolish person who is easily tricked **:** PATSY • They're taking you for a *mug*. • Drinking and driving is ***a mug's game***. [=something that only a foolish person would do]

mug

[2]**mug** *verb* **mugs; mugged; mug·ging**

1 [+ *obj*] **:** to attack and rob (someone) • He was *mugged* (when he was) walking home from work.

2 [*no obj*] *chiefly US* **:** to act or pose in a silly way or make silly facial expressions especially to attract attention or when being photographed — usually + *for* • She was *mugging for* the camera. • *mugging for* the crowd

mug up [*phrasal verb*] ***mug up*** or ***mug (something) up*** or ***mug up (something)*** or ***mug up on (something)*** *Brit, informal* **:** to study or try to learn a lot of information quickly for a test, exam, etc. • He's going to *mug up* for the exam. • She had better *mug up* before she interviews him. • He *mugged up on* his French for the trip.

mug·ger /ˈmʌgɚ/ *noun, pl* **-gers** [*count*] **:** a person who attacks and robs another person **:** a criminal who mugs someone • The police arrested the *mugger*.

mugging *noun, pl* **-gings :** the act of attacking and robbing someone **:** the act of mugging someone [*count*] There have been several *muggings* in the park recently. [*noncount*] The park has had an increased rate of *mugging* recently.

mug·gins /ˈmʌgənz/ *noun* [*singular*] *Brit, informal* **:** a foolish person who is easily tricked — usually used to refer to yourself • He left early and *muggins* here was left to finish the job.

mug·gy /ˈmʌgi/ *adj* **mug·gi·er; -est :** unpleasantly warm and humid • a *muggy* day in August • It's very *muggy* out today. • *muggy* weather

mug shot *noun, pl* **~ shots** [*count*] **:** a photograph of someone's face; *especially* **:** a photograph taken by the police of someone who has been arrested

mu·lat·to /məˈlætoʊ, məˈlɑːtoʊ/ *noun, pl* **-toes** *or* **-tos** [*count*] *old-fashioned + often offensive* **:** a person with one black and one white parent

mul·ber·ry /ˈmʌlˌberi, *Brit* ˈmʌlbəri/ *noun, pl* **-ries** [*count*]

1 : a type of tree that has purple berries that can be eaten — called also *mulberry tree*

2 : a berry from a mulberry tree

[1]**mulch** /ˈmʌltʃ/ *noun, pl* **mulch·es** [*count, noncount*] **:** a material (such as straw, leaves, or small pieces of wood) that is spread over the ground in a garden to protect the plants or help them grow and to stop weeds from growing • She spread some *mulch* around the plants.

[2]**mulch** *verb* **mulches; mulched; mulch·ing** [+ *obj*] **:** to cover (the ground, a garden, etc.) with mulch • She *mulched* the flower beds.

mule /ˈmjuːl/ *noun, pl* **mules** [*count*]

1 : an animal that has a horse and a donkey as parents

2 : a woman's shoe that is open at the heel • wearing a pair of *mules*

3 *slang* **:** someone who secretly brings illegal drugs into a country

mul·ish /ˈmjuːlɪʃ/ *adj* [*more ~; most ~*] **:** refusing to do what other people want or to change your opinion or the way you do something **:** very stubborn • She approached the job with

M

mulish determination. • a *mulish* insistence on doing things his own way

mull /ˈmʌl/ *verb* **mulls; mulled; mull·ing** [+ *obj*] **: to think about (something) slowly and carefully : PONDER** • The company is *mulling* the offer. — usually + *over* • *mull over* an idea • It's a fine offer, but we need time to *mull* it *over*.

mulled /ˈmʌld/ *adj* **: mixed with sugar and spices and served warm** • *mulled* wine/cider

mul·let /ˈmələt/ *noun*

1 *pl* **mullet** *or* **mul·lets** [*count, noncount*] **: a type of fish that lives in the ocean and is often eaten as food**

2 *pl* **mullets** [*count*] **: a hairstyle in which the hair is short on the top and sides and long in the back**

mul·lion /ˈmʌljən/ *noun, pl* **-lions** [*count*] **: an upright piece of wood, stone, metal, etc., that separates two windows**

– mul·lioned /ˈmʌljənd/ *adj* • *mullioned* windows

multi- *combining form*

1 a : many : much • *multi*colored **b : more than two** • *mul*tinational • *multi*racial

2 : many times over • *multi*millionaire

mul·ti·col·ored (*US*) *or Brit* **mul·ti·col·oured** /ˈmʌltiˌkʌlɚd/ *adj* **: having, made up of, or including many colors** • *multicolored* balloons/ribbons

mul·ti·cul·tur·al /ˌmʌltiˈkʌlʧərəl/ *adj* [*more* ~; *most* ~] **: relating to or including many different cultures** • a *multicultural* society

– mul·ti·cul·tur·al·ism /ˌmʌltiˈkʌlʧərəlɪzəm/ *noun* [*noncount*]

mul·ti·dis·ci·plin·ary /ˌmʌltiˈdɪsəpləˌneri, *Brit* ˌmʌltiˈdɪsəplənəri/ *adj* **: involving two or more subject areas** • a *multidisciplinary* class taught jointly by a history teacher and an English teacher

mul·ti·eth·nic /ˌmʌltiˈɛθnɪk/ *adj* **: relating to or including people from many ethnic groups** • a *multiethnic* country

mul·ti·fac·et·ed /ˌmʌltiˈfæsətəd/ *adj* [*more* ~; *most* ~] **: having many different parts : having many facets** • a *multifaceted* approach to health care

mul·ti·far·i·ous /ˌmʌltəˈferijəs/ *adj* [*more* ~; *most* ~] *formal* **: of many and various kinds** • *multifarious* [=*diverse*] activities

mul·ti·func·tion·al /ˌmʌltiˈfʌŋkʃənəl/ *adj* **: having many uses or functions : MULTIPURPOSE** • a *multifunctional* tool

M

mul·ti·lat·er·al /ˌmʌltiˈlætərəl/ *adj* **: involving more than two groups or countires** • a *multilateral* treaty/agreement — compare BILATERAL, TRILATERAL, UNILATERAL

mul·ti·lay·ered /ˌmʌltiˈlejɚd/ *adj* **: having or involving three or more layers or levels** • a *multilayered* cake • The novel's plot is *multilayered*. • a *multilayered* political system

mul·ti·lin·gual /ˌmʌltiˈlɪŋgwəl/ *adj*

1 : able to speak and understand several languages • *multilingual* students

2 : using or expressed in several languages • *multilingual* instructions • a *multilingual* dictionary • *multilingual* countries — compare BILINGUAL, MONOLINGUAL

mul·ti·me·dia /ˌmʌltiˈmiːdijə/ *adj, always used before a noun* **: using or involving several forms of communication or expression** • a *multimedia* exhibit of photographs, films, and music

mul·ti·mil·lion /ˌmʌltiˈmɪljən/ *adj, always used before a noun* **: involving two or more million : costing or worth millions of dollars or pounds — often used in combination** • a *multimillion*-dollar home

mul·ti·mil·lion·aire /ˌmʌltiˌmɪljəˈneɚ/ *noun, pl* **-aires** [*count*] **: a very wealthy person : a person who has property or money worth millions of dollars or pounds**

[1]**mul·ti·na·tion·al** /ˌmʌltiˈnæʃənəl/ *adj*

1 : of, relating to, or involving more than two nations • a *multinational* alliance/force

2 : working in several countries • a *multinational* corporation

[2]**multinational** *noun, pl* **-als** [*count*] **: a company that works in several countries : a multinational corporation**

mul·ti·par·ty /ˌmʌltiˈpɑɚti/ *adj* **: of or involving more than one political party** • *multiparty* elections • *multiparty* democracy

[1]**mul·ti·ple** /ˈmʌltəpəl/ *adj, always used before a noun*

1 : more than one : MANY, NUMEROUS • She made *multiple* copies of the report. • a person of *multiple* achievements • He suffered *multiple* injuries in the accident. • a ***multiple birth*** [=the birth of more than one baby at a time; a birth of twins, triplets, etc.]

2 : shared by many people • *multiple* ownership [=ownership by more than one person]

[2]**multiple** *noun, pl* **-ti·ples** [*count*]

1 *mathematics* **: a number that can be produced by multiplying a smaller number** • 35 is a *multiple of* 7. • 12 is a *multiple* of 6.

2 *Brit* **: CHAIN STORE**

multiple–choice *adj*

1 : having several answers from which one is to be chosen • a *multiple-choice* question

2 : made up of multiple-choice questions • a *multiple-choice* test • The exam will be *multiple-choice*.

multiple sclerosis *noun* [*noncount*] *medical* **: a disease of the nervous system that causes the gradual loss of muscle control** — abbr. *MS*

mul·ti·plex /ˈmʌltəˌplɛks/ *noun, pl* **-plex·es** [*count*] **: a building that contains several movie theaters** — called also *multiplex cinema*

mul·ti·pli·ca·tion /ˌmʌltəpləˈkeɪʃən/ *noun*

1 [*noncount*] *mathematics* **: the process of adding a number to itself a certain number of times : the act or process of multiplying numbers** • Students are learning *multiplication* and division.

2 : an increase in the number or amount of something [*noncount*] a disease causing uncontrolled *multiplication* of cells [*singular*] an uncontrolled *multiplication* of cells

multiplication sign *noun, pl* ~ **signs** [*count*] *mathematics* **: a symbol (such as "x") that is used to show that two numbers are to be multiplied — usually singular**

multiplication table *noun, pl* ~ **tables** [*count*] *mathematics* **: a list that shows the results of multiplying certain numbers (such as 1 through 12) by each other — called also** *times table*

mul·ti·plic·i·ty /ˌmʌltəˈplɪsəti/ *noun* [*singular*] *formal* **: a very large number — +** ***of*** • a *multiplicity of* colors/ideas/styles

mul·ti·ply /ˈmʌltəˌplaɪ/ *verb* **-plies; -plied; -ply·ing**

1 a [*no obj*] **: to increase greatly in number or amount : to become much more numerous** • Complaints about the new procedure soon *multiplied*. • Her responsibilities *multiplied* when she was promoted. **b** [+ *obj*] **: to cause (something) to increase greatly in number or amount** • Her responsibilities were *multiplied* by the promotion.

2 [*no obj*] **: to increase in number by reproducing** • The bacteria *multiply* rapidly in warm, moist conditions.

3 *mathematics* **: to add a number to itself a certain number of times** [+ *obj*] If you *multiply* 5 by 2 you get 10. = If you *multiply* 5 and 2 (together) you get 10. = 5 *multiplied* by 2 equals 10. [*no obj*] The teacher taught the children how to add, subtract, *multiply*, and divide. — compare DIVIDE

mul·ti·pur·pose /ˌmʌltiˈpɚpəs/ *adj* **: having more than one use or purpose** • *multipurpose* furniture • a *multipurpose* room/tool

mul·ti·ra·cial /ˌmʌltiˈreɪʃəl/ *adj* **: relating to or including more than one race of people** • a *multiracial* society • His family is *multiracial*.

mul·ti·sto·ry (*US*) *or Brit* **mul·ti·sto·rey** /ˌmʌltiˈstori/ *adj, of a building* **: having many stories** • a *multistory* apartment building • (*Brit*) a ***multistorey car park*** [=a parking garage with more than one level]

mul·ti·task·ing /ˈmʌltiˌtæskɪŋ, *Brit* ˈmʌltiˌtɑːskɪŋ/ *noun* [*noncount*] **: the ability to do several things at the same time** • The job requires someone who is good at *multitasking*.

mul·ti·tude /ˈmʌltəˌtuːd, *Brit* ˈmʌltəˌtjuːd/ *noun, pl* **-tudes** [*count*]

1 : a great number of things or people • A vast *multitude* [=a great crowd of people] waited to hear the news. — often + *of* • A *multitude of* complaints reached the office. • a *multitude of* choices • Some new paint on an old house can ***cover/hide a multitude of sins*** [=can hide many problems or faults]

2 ***the multitude*** **: ordinary or common people as a group** • a candidate trying to appeal to *the multitude* — often plural • His films are not intended to appeal to *the multitudes*. [=*masses*]

mul·ti·tu·di·nous /ˌmʌltəˈtuːdnəs, *Brit* ˌmʌltəˈtjuːdənəs/ *adj, formal* **: very many** • *multitudinous* questions/concerns • Their lives have changed in *multitudinous* ways.

mul·ti·us·er /ˈmʌltiˌjuːzɚ/ *adj, always used before a noun, computers* **: able to be used by more than one person at a time** • *multiuser* software • a *multiuser* computer system

mul·ti·vi·ta·min /ˌmʌltiˈvaɪtəmən, *Brit* ˌmʌltɪˈvɪtəmən/

noun, pl **-mins** [count] : a pill that contains many vitamins

mul·ti·vol·ume /ˌmʌltiˈvɑːlˌjuːm/ *adj, always used before a noun* : published as two or more books : having more than one volume • a *multivolume* biography/encyclopedia

¹mum /ˈmʌm/ *adj, informal* : not talking about something • I'd like to know how much they paid, but they've been *mum* on that subject. • She told him to ***keep/stay mum*** about the project. [=she told him not to tell anyone about the project]

mum's the word *informal* — used to say that some information is being kept secret or should be kept secret • We want her birthday party to be a surprise, so *mum's the word.* [=don't tell her about the party]

²mum *noun, pl* **mums** [count] *US* : CHRYSANTHEMUM

³mum *noun, pl* **mums** [count] *Brit, informal* : MOTHER, MOM

¹mum·ble /ˈmʌmbəl/ *verb* **mum·bles; mum·bled; mum·bling** : to say (something) quietly in an unclear way that makes it difficult for people to know what you said [+ *obj*] He *mumbled* something and then left. • He *mumbled* "Goodbye" and then left. [*no obj*] I can't understand you when you *mumble.* • a *mumbling* response

— **mum·bler** /ˈmʌmbələ/ *noun, pl* **-blers** [count]

— **mumbling** *noun, pl* **-blings** [count, noncount] • There were *mumblings* [=*rumblings*] (of discontent) about the decision. [=people complained quietly to each other about the decision]

²mumble *noun* [singular] : a way of speaking that is not clear enough to be understood • He answered in his usual *mumble.* • She spoke in a *mumble.*

mum·bo jum·bo /ˌmʌmboʊˈʤʌmboʊ/ *noun* [noncount] *informal* : confusing or meaningless words or activity : NONSENSE • We were confused by all the legal *mumbo jumbo.* • His explanation was just a lot of *mumbo jumbo.*

mum·mi·fy /ˈmʌmɪˌfaɪ/ *verb* **-fies; -fied; -fy·ing**

1 [+ *obj*] : to preserve (a dead body) by treating it with oils and wrapping it in strips of cloth • learning how ancient Egyptians *mummified* their dead

2 : to become very dry and wrinkled [*no obj*] a body that *mummified* in the desert heat [+ *obj*] a body that was *mummified* by the desert heat

— **mummified** *adj* • a *mummified* body

¹mum·my /ˈmʌmi/ *noun, pl* **-mies** [count] : a dead body of a person or animal prepared for burial in the manner of the ancient Egyptians by treating it with oils and wrapping it in strips of cloth

²mummy *noun, pl* **-mies** [count] *Brit, informal* : MOTHER, MOMMY — used especially by children • Where's my *mummy*?

mumps /ˈmʌmps/ *noun* [noncount] *medical* : a disease that causes fever and swelling in the lower part of the cheek • *Mumps* is usually a childhood illness. • She got (the) *mumps.*

munch /ˈmʌntʃ/ *verb* **munch·es; munched; munch·ing** : to chew or eat (something) especially in a noisy way [+ *obj*] We *munched* [=*snacked on*] popcorn during the movie. • cattle *munching* grass [*no obj*] — + *on* • We *munched on* popcorn during the movie.

munch·ies /ˈmʌntʃiz/ *noun, informal*

1 [plural] *US* : light foods that are eaten as a snack • *Munchies* are served at the bar.

2 ***the munchies*** : a feeling of hunger • I have a serious case of *the munchies.* [=I'm very hungry] • I always get/have *the munchies* when I'm watching TV. = Watching TV always gives me *the munchies.*

munch·kin /ˈmʌntʃˌkɪn/ *noun, pl* **-kins** [count] *US, informal* : a child or small person • "What's wrong, *munchkin*?" she asked the toddler. ✧ The original Munchkins were a race of small people in the book *The Wonderful Wizard of Oz* (1900) by L. Frank Baum. The 1939 movie *The Wizard of Oz* was based on this book.

mun·dane /ˌmʌnˈdeɪn/ *adj* [more ~; most ~]

1 : dull and ordinary • *mundane* chores, like washing dishes • They lead a pretty *mundane* life.

2 : relating to ordinary life on earth rather than to spiritual things • prayer and meditation helped her put her *mundane* worries aside

mung bean /ˈmʌŋ-/ *noun, pl* **~ beans** [count] : a small, round bean often used to grow bean sprouts

mu·nic·i·pal /mjʊˈnɪsəpəl/ *adj, always used before a noun* : of or relating to the government of a city or town • *municipal* government • a *municipal* building/library/election

mu·nic·i·pal·i·ty /mjʊˌnɪsəˈpæləti/ *noun, pl* **-ties** [count] : a city or town that has its own government to deal with local problems • laws that have been enacted by many states and *municipalities*; *also, chiefly Brit* : the group of people who run such a government • locally elected *municipalities*

mu·nif·i·cent /mjʊˈnɪfəsənt/ *adj* [more ~; most ~] *formal* : very generous • a *munificent* gift/donation • a *munificent* benefactor

— **mu·nif·i·cence** /mjʊˈnɪfəsəns/ *noun* [noncount] • the *munificence* of their donation

mu·ni·tions /mjʊˈnɪʃənz/ *noun* [plural] : military supplies and equipment; *especially* : military weapons • rockets and other *munitions* • unexploded *munitions* • a *munitions* factory

mu·ral /ˈmjərəl/ *noun, pl* **-rals** [count] : a usually large painting that is done directly on the surface of a wall

¹mur·der /ˈmədə/ *noun, pl* **-ders**

1 : the crime of deliberately killing a person [noncount] He was found guilty of (committing) *murder.* • She was accused/convicted of *murder.* • She was charged with *murder.* [=she was officially accused of the crime of murder] • the mass *murder* of civilians in wartime [count] a string of unsolved *murders* — often used before another noun • the *murder* weapon • a *murder* suspect/victim/case • *murder* mysteries [=mystery stories about murder]

2 [noncount] *informal* : something that is very difficult or unpleasant • That test was *murder.* [=it was very difficult] • Traffic is *murder* this time of day. ✧ To ***be murder on*** something is to cause pain or harm to it. • Carrying the luggage *was murder on* my back. • These shoes *are murder on* my feet.

get away with murder : to murder someone without being captured or punished • a vicious killer who nearly *got away with murder* — usually used figuratively to describe someone who does something very bad or wrong without being criticized or punished • The company had been *getting away with murder* for years before the scandal broke.

scream bloody/blue murder see ¹SCREAM

²murder *verb* **-ders; -dered; -der·ing** [+ *obj*]

1 : to kill (a person) in a deliberate and unlawful way : to commit the murder of (someone) • He was arrested and accused of *murdering* his wife. • His wife was found *murdered.* • a dictator who is responsible for *murdering* thousands of innocent people — sometimes used figuratively • My father will *murder* me [=he will be very angry] when he finds out that I dented the car.

2 *informal* **a** : to spoil or ruin (something) • a writer who *murders* [=*butchers*] the English language : to perform (something) very badly • The band *murdered* that song. **b** : to defeat (an opponent) very badly • He got *murdered* [=*slaughtered*] in the opening round by last year's winner.

— **mur·der·er** /ˈmədərə/ *noun, pl* **-ers** [count] • a convicted *murderer* • a **mass murderer** [=a person who has killed many people] — **mur·der·ess** /ˈmədərəs/ *noun, pl* **-ess·es** [count] *old-fashioned* • an infamous *murderess* [=a woman who commits murder]

mur·der·ous /ˈmədərəs/ *adj* [more ~; most ~]

1 : very violent or deadly • *murderous* machine-gun fire • a *murderous* dictator/attack • a *murderous* regime

2 a : very angry • a *murderous* glance **b** : very harsh or severe • I can't stand this *murderous* heat. • The lead runner set a *murderous* pace.

— **mur·der·ous·ly** *adv* • a *murderously* intolerant regime • *murderously* hot weather • a *murderously* angry glance

murk /ˈmək/ *noun* [noncount] : darkness or fog that is hard to see through • A figure emerged from the *murk.* [=*gloom*]; *also* : dark or dirty water • We could not see the bottom of the lake through the *murk.*

murky /ˈməki/ *adj* **murk·i·er; -est**

1 a : very dark or foggy • *murky* skies • She peered into one of the church's *murky* chapels. **b** *of a liquid* : not clear : CLOUDY • the lake's *murky* water

2 a : not clearly expressed or understood • He offered a *murky* [=*vague*] explanation. • Her employment history is somewhat *murky.* [=*unclear*] **b** : involving dishonest or illegal activities that are not clearly known • a politician with a *murky* past

— **murk·i·ly** /ˈməkəli/ *adv* — **murk·i·ness** /ˈməkinəs/ *noun* [noncount] • the *murkiness* of the water

¹mur·mur /ˈməmə/ *noun, pl* **-murs**

1 [count] **a** : a low sound made when many people are speaking • a *murmur* of voices • the *murmur* of the crowd **b** : a quiet expression of an opinion or feeling • The suggestion brought *murmurs* of disapproval. • a *murmur* of agreement/protest • *murmurs* of recognition • They accepted the deci-

M

sion ***without a murmur*** (of protest/complaint). [=they accepted the decision without protesting/complaining at all] **c : speech or a way of speaking that is quiet and soft** • He spoke in a *murmur*. • They spoke to each other in *murmurs*.
2 [*singular*] **: a low, quiet, and continuous sound** • a *murmur* of bees • the *murmur* of the waves along the shore
3 [*count*] *medical* **: an unusual heart sound that may indicate a problem with the heart's function or structure — usually singular** • Her doctor detected a (heart) *murmur* during a routine physical exam.

²murmur *verb* **-murs; -mured; -mur·ing**
1 [+ *obj*] **: to say (something) in a quiet and soft voice** • He *murmured* something about having to get home. • "Thank you," she *murmured* as she left the room.
2 [*no obj*] **: to make a low, continuous sound** • The breeze *murmured* in the pines. • the *murmuring* breeze
– murmuring *noun, pl* **-ings** [*count, noncount*] • We could hear the *murmuring* of the bees. • *Murmurings* (of disapproval) were heard [=people complained quietly] when the decision was announced.

Mur·phy bed /ˈmɚfi-/ *noun, pl* **~ beds** [*count*] *US* **: a bed with a frame that can be folded into a space in a wall**

Mur·phy's Law /ˈmɚfiz-/ *noun* [*noncount*] **— used to refer to the humorous statement that if it is possible for something to go wrong then it will go wrong — called also** (*Brit*) *Sod's Law*

¹mus·cle /ˈmʌsəl/ *noun, pl* **mus·cles**
1 : a body tissue that can contract and produce movement [*count*] the *muscles* of the arm • stomach *muscles* • flex a *muscle* • relax a *muscle* • an athlete with bulging/rippling *muscles* • He pulled/tore/strained a *muscle* playing tennis. • She has a strained *muscle* in her back. • Wait here and ***don't move a muscle.*** [=don't move at all] [*noncount*] She started lifting weights to build *muscle*. **— often used before another noun** • *muscle* fiber(s)/tissue • *muscle* spasms • an athlete practicing to develop ***muscle memory*** [=the ability to repeat a bodily movement exactly] • a ***muscle relaxant*** [=a drug that relaxes muscles]
2 [*noncount*] **a : physical strength** • She doesn't have the *muscle* to lift something so heavy. • To clean that floor you have to ***put some muscle into*** it. [=you have to make a forceful effort] **b : power and influence** • He lacks the political *muscle* [=*clout*] to get the policy changed.
flex your muscles see **¹FLEX**

²muscle *verb* **muscles; mus·cled; mus·cling**
1 [+ *obj*] **: to move (something) by using physical strength and force** • They *muscled* the heavy boxes onto the truck. • They *muscled* the furniture up the stairs. **— often used figuratively** • She was *muscled* [=*forced*] out of office by political opponents. • He helped *muscle* the bill through Congress.
2 : to move forward by using physical force [*no obj*] He *muscled* through the crowd. • They *muscled* into line behind us. [+ *obj*] He ***muscled his way*** through the crowd. [=he moved ahead by pushing and forcing people to move out of the way]
muscle in [*phrasal verb*] **: to use force or influence in a way that is wrong or unwanted in order to become involved in something for selfish reasons — usually + *on*** • His competitors have tried to *muscle in on* his business.

mus·cle–bound /ˈmʌsəlˌbaʊnd/ *adj* [*more ~; most ~*] **: having large muscles that do not move and stretch easily** • a *muscle-bound* athlete **— sometimes used figuratively** • a *muscle-bound* [=*rigid, inflexible*] organization

muscle car *noun, pl* **~ cars** [*count*] *US, informal* **: an American-made two-door sports car with a powerful engine**

mus·cled /ˈmʌsəld/ *adj* **: having large muscles or muscles of a specified kind** • his *muscled* [=*muscular*] back • hard-*muscled* arms • a lightly *muscled* runner [=a runner with fairly small muscles]

mus·cle·man /ˈmʌsəlˌmæn/ *noun, pl* **-men** /-ˌmɛn/ [*count*] **: a strong man with large muscles** • *musclemen* and bodybuilders working out in the gym

Mus·co·vite /ˈmʌskəˌvaɪt/ *noun, pl* **-vites** [*count*] **: a person who lives in or comes from Moscow**
– Muscovite *adj*

mus·cu·lar /ˈmʌskjəlɚ/ *adj*
1 : of or relating to muscles • *muscular* strength/weakness • a *muscular* injury
2 [*more ~; most ~*] **: having large and strong muscles** • a *muscular* athlete • He has a *muscular* physique. • His legs are very *muscular*.
– mus·cu·lar·i·ty /ˌmʌskjəˈlerəti/ *noun* [*noncount*]

muscular dys·tro·phy /-ˈdɪstrəfi/ *noun* [*noncount*] *medical* **: a serious disease that causes increasing weakness of muscles**

mus·cu·la·ture /ˈmʌskjələˌʧuɚ/ *noun* [*noncount*] *formal* **: the muscles of the body or of one of its parts** • human *musculature* • facial *musculature* • an athlete with well-developed *musculature*

¹muse /ˈmjuːz/ *verb* **mus·es; mused; mus·ing**
1 [*no obj*] **: to think about something carefully or thoroughly — usually + *about, on, over,* or *upon*** • She *mused on* the possibility of changing jobs. • *musing about/over* what might have been
2 [+ *obj*] **: to think or say (something) in a thoughtful way** • I could sell the house, she *mused*, but then where would I go?
– musing *noun, pl* **-ings** [*count*] He recorded his *musings* [=*thoughts*] in his diary. [*noncount*] Her *musing* was interrupted by the arrival of her friend. **– mus·ing·ly** /ˈmjuːzɪŋli/ *adv* • "I could sell the house," she said *musingly*, "but then where would I go?"

²muse *noun, pl* **muses** [*count*]
1 : a person who causes someone else to have ideas about creating a work of art : a person who inspires an artist, writer, etc. • The writer lost his *muse* when his wife left him.
2 *Muse* : any one of the nine sister goddesses of song and poetry and the arts and sciences in Greek mythology

mu·se·um /mjʊˈziːjəm/ *noun, pl* **-ums** [*count*] **: a building in which interesting and valuable things (such as paintings and sculptures or scientific or historical objects) are collected and shown to the public** • an art *museum* • a history *museum* • a *museum* of natural history

museum piece *noun, pl* **~ pieces** [*count*]
1 : a valuable object that is in a museum or that is suitable for a museum
2 : something or someone that is very old or old-fashioned • That old computer will soon be a *museum piece*.

¹mush /ˈmʌʃ/ *noun*
1 : a soft and wet mass of material (such as food) [*noncount*] The rotting apples turned into/to *mush*. **— sometimes used figuratively** • I was so tired my brain ***turned into/to mush***. [=I was too tired to think well] [*singular*] a *mush* of rotting apples
2 [*noncount*] *US* **: a soft food made by boiling cornmeal in water or milk** • a bowl of *mush*
3 /ˈmʊʃ/ [*noncount*] *informal + disapproving* **: a story or part of a story in a book, movie, etc., that is too romantic or sentimental** • a movie full of *mush*

²mush *interj* **— used as a command to tell dogs to start pulling a sled**

¹mush·room /ˈmʌʃˌruːm/ *noun, pl* **-rooms** [*count*] **: a fungus that is shaped like an umbrella** • wild *mushrooms*; ***especially* : one that can be eaten** • cut up some *mushrooms* for the salad **— often used before another noun** • *mushroom* soup • a ***mushroom cap*** [=the top part of a mushroom] **— compare** TOADSTOOL; **see also** BUTTON MUSHROOM

mushroom

²mushroom *verb* **-rooms; -roomed; -room·ing** [*no obj*]
1 : to increase or develop very quickly • The population has *mushroomed* [=*shot up*] over the past 10 years. = The town has *mushroomed* in population over the past 10 years. • Interest in local history is suddenly *mushrooming*. • Her hobby *mushroomed* into a thriving business.
2 : to collect wild mushrooms • He goes *mushrooming* in the spring every year.

mushroom cloud *noun, pl* **~ clouds** [*count*] **: a large cloud that forms after an explosion; *especially* : a cloud that is caused by the explosion of a nuclear weapon**

mushy /ˈmʌʃi/ *adj* **mush·i·er; -est**
1 : soft and wet • The rotting apples turned *mushy*. [=the rotting apples turned to mush]
2 *informal + disapproving* **: too romantic or sentimental** • a *mushy* movie/novel

mu·sic /ˈmjuːzɪk/ *noun* [*noncount*]
1 : sounds that are sung by voices or played on musical instruments • listening to live/recorded *music* • This is one of my favorite pieces of *music*. • performing *music* in front of an audience • dancing to the *music* of a big band • They are writing/composing *music* for a new album. • a song with *music* by George Gershwin and words/lyrics by Ira Gershwin •

classical/popular *music* • They like to ***make music*** [=play or sing music] with friends. • The play/poem was ***set to music.*** [=music was written to go with the words of the play/poem] • ***background music*** [=music played while something else is happening] — often used before another noun • the *music* industry • a ***music video*** [=a video recording of a performance of popular music] — see also CHAMBER MUSIC, COUNTRY MUSIC, FOLK MUSIC, SOUL MUSIC

2 : written or printed symbols showing how music should be played or sung • He is learning to read *music.* • a ***music stand*** [=a holder on which printed music is placed so that a musician can see it while playing or singing] — see also SHEET MUSIC

3 : the art or skill of creating or performing music • She studied *music* in college. • *music* theory

4 : a pleasant sound • the *music* of a brook • Her words were ***music to my ears.*** [=I was very happy to hear what she said]

face the music see ²FACE

¹mu·si·cal /ˈmjuːzɪkəl/ *adj*

1 *always used before a noun* **: of or relating to music** • the film's *musical* score • *musical* notes • a ***musical instrument*** [=a device (such as a violin, piano, or flute) used to make music]

2 [*more ~; most ~*] **: having the pleasing qualities of music** • She has a very *musical* voice.

3 [*more ~; most ~*] **: enjoying music : having a talent for playing music** • a *musical* family

4 *always used before a noun* **: having music and songs as a main feature : telling a story with songs** • a *musical* film/play

– mu·si·cal·i·ty /ˌmjuːzɪˈkæləti/ *noun* [*noncount*] • the *musicality* [=musical quality] of the performance • a dancer who shows great *musicality* [=musical talent] **– mu·si·cal·ly** /ˈmjuːzɪkli/ *adv* • a *musically* talented child • a *musically* complex symphony • expressing her feelings *musically* [=through music]

²musical *noun, pl* **-cals** [*count*] **: a movie or play that tells a story with songs and often dancing** • a Broadway *musical* — called also *musical comedy*

musical box *noun, pl* **~ boxes** [*count*] *Brit* **:** MUSIC BOX

musical chairs *noun* [*noncount*]

1 : a children's game in which players walk around a row of chairs while music plays and try to sit down when the music stops ✧ In musical chairs the number of chairs is always one less than the number of players, and the player who is not fast enough to find a chair when the music stops has to leave the game.

2 : a situation in which many changes happen in a way that is confusing or harmful • The changes in the administration amounted to a game of *musical chairs.*

musical comedy *noun, pl* **~ -dies** [*count*] **:** ²MUSICAL

music box *noun, pl* **~ boxes** [*count*] **: a box that contains a device which plays a tune when the box is open** — called also *(Brit) musical box*

music hall *noun, pl* **~ halls** [*count*] **: a theater in which popular entertainers performed in the late 19th and early 20th centuries** — often used before another noun • a *music-hall* performer • *music-hall* dancers/comedians; *also* [*noncount*] *chiefly Brit* **: the type of entertainment that was performed in such a theater :** VAUDEVILLE

mu·si·cian /mjuˈzɪʃən/ *noun, pl* **-cians** [*count*] **: a person who writes, sings, or plays music** • She's a very talented *musician.* • a rock/jazz/classical *musician*

mu·si·cian·ship /mjuˈzɪʃənˌʃɪp/ *noun* [*noncount*] **: the skill of performing or writing music** • The critics praised her *musicianship.*

mu·si·col·o·gy /ˌmjuːzɪˈkɑːləʤi/ *noun* [*noncount*] **: the study of music as an area of knowledge or as a field of research** • a professor of *musicology*

– mu·si·col·o·gist /ˌmjuːzɪˈkɑːləʤɪst/ *noun, pl* **-gists** [*count*]

musk /ˈmʌsk/ *noun* [*noncount*] **: a strong-smelling substance used in perfume**

– musky /ˈmʌski/ *adj* **musk·i·er; -est** • a *musky* scent/odor • a *musky* perfume

mus·ket /ˈmʌskət/ *noun, pl* **-kets** [*count*] **: a type of long gun that was used by soldiers before the invention of the rifle**

mus·ke·teer /ˌmʌskəˈtiɚ/ *noun, pl* **-teers** [*count*] **: a soldier who has a musket**

musk·rat /ˈmʌskˌræt/ *noun, pl* **muskrat** *or* **musk·rats** [*count*] **: a North American animal that lives in or near water** — see picture at RODENT

Mus·lim /ˈmʌzləm/ *noun, pl* **Mus·lims** [*count*] **: a person whose religion is Islam : a follower of Islam**

– Muslim *adj* • the *Muslim* faith

mus·lin /ˈmʌzlən/ *noun* [*noncount*] **: a thin and loosely woven cotton cloth** • curtains of white *muslin*

muss /ˈmʌs/ *verb* **muss·es; mussed; muss·ing** [*+ obj*] *US, informal* **: to make (something, such as clothing or hair) messy or untidy** • His suit was/got *mussed* when he got out of the car. — often + *up* • The wind *mussed up* my hair.

mus·sel /ˈmʌsəl/ *noun, pl* **-sels** [*count*] **: a type of shellfish that has a long dark shell** — see color picture on page C8

¹must /ˈmʌst/ *verb* [*modal verb*]

1 a *somewhat formal in US English* **— used to say that something is required or necessary** • You *must* stop. [=you have to stop; I command you to stop] • I told him what he *must* do. [=what he had to do] • One *must* eat to live. • You *must* follow the rules. • We *must* [=*have to, need to*] correct these problems soon or the project will fail. • I *must* remember to stop at the store. • "*Must* you go?" [=do you have to go?] "Yes, I'm afraid I really *must.*" • "*Must* you go?" "No, I don't have to." • If you *must* go, at least wait until the storm is over. • It *must* be noted, however, that the company was already in financial difficulties. • We *must* keep/bear in mind that she didn't have any previous experience. = It *must* be borne in mind that she didn't have any previous experience. **✧ Note the difference in meaning between *must not* and *not have to.*** • You *must not* do it. [=it is necessary that you do not do it; I command you not to do it] • You *don't have to* do it. [=it is not necessary for you to do it] **b — used to say that something is required by a rule or law** • All passengers *must* exit at the next stop. • Students *must* have completed Sociology 101 before they can take Sociology 102.

2 *somewhat formal in US English* **— used to say that someone should do something** • You *must* [=*ought to, should, have to*] read this book. It's fantastic! • You *must* come visit us soon. [=we would like to have you come visit us soon] • You really *must* see the doctor about that cough. [=I urge you to see the doctor; I really think you need to see the doctor]

3 — used to say that something is very likely • It *must* be almost dinner time. • She *must* think I'm a fool. • It *must* have been the coffee that kept me awake. • He *must* have been the most gifted student at the school. [=I think he was the most gifted student] • He *must* have a lot of money to live the way he does. • The bus *must* be coming soon. • You haven't eaten all day. You *must* be hungry. • You're going to wear that? You *must* be joking! • You *must* have been very worried. • You *must* be thrilled about the new baby. • If he really was there, I *must* have seen him, but I don't remember seeing him. • There *must* be some mistake.

4 — used in various phrases to emphasize a statement • ***I must say,*** I was surprised to hear from him. • She's a talented actress, *I must say.* • She's a talented actress, ***you must admit.*** • ***I must admit,*** I expected better results. • ***I must warn you,*** this will not be easy. • ***I must confess,*** I haven't actually read the book yet.

5 *somewhat formal in US English* **— used in questions that express annoyance or anger** • *Must* you be so unreasonable? [=do you have to be so unreasonable?] • Why *must* it always rain on the weekend? [=why does it always have to rain on the weekend?]

if you must **— used to say that you will allow someone to do something even though you do not approve of it** • You can smoke *if you must,* but please do it outdoors.

if you must know see ¹KNOW

²must *noun, pl* **musts** [*count*] **: something that is or seems to be required or necessary — usually singular** • If you're going to hike this trail, sturdy shoes are a *must.* • Regular exercise is a *must* [=is very important; is strongly recommended] as you grow older.

mus·tache *(US) or chiefly Brit* **mous·tache** /ˈmʌˌstæʃ, *Brit* məˈstɑːʃ/ *noun, pl* **-tach·es** [*count*] **: hair growing on a man's upper lip** • He used a small pair of scissors to trim his *mustache.* • He decided to grow a *mustache.* • The actor was wearing a false/fake *mustache.* — see picture at BEARD

– mus·tached *(US) or chiefly Brit* **mous·tached** /ˈmʌˌstæʃt, *Brit* məˈstɑːʃt/ *adj* • a *mustached* man [=a man who has a mustache]

mus·ta·chio *(US) or chiefly Brit* **mous·ta·chio** /məˈstæʃiˌoʊ, *Brit* məˈstɑːʃiˌoʊ/ *noun, pl* **-chios** [*count*] *old-fashioned* **: a large mustache**

– mus·ta·chioed *(US) or chiefly Brit* **mous·ta·chioed** /məˈstæʃiˌoʊd, *Brit* məˈstɑːʃiˌoʊd/ *adj* • a *mustachioed* villain in a melodrama

mus·tang /ˈmʌˌstæŋ/ *noun, pl* **-tangs** [*count*] **:** a small and strong wild horse of western North America

mus·tard /ˈmʌstɚd/ *noun, pl* **-tards** [*count, noncount*]
1 : a thick and spicy yellow or brownish-yellow sauce that is usually eaten with meat ▪ Would you like some *mustard* on your hot dog?
2 : a plant with yellow flowers, leaves that can be used for food, and seeds that are used in making mustard
3 : a brownish-yellow color — see color picture on page C2
(as) keen as mustard see [1]KEEN
cut the mustard *informal* **:** to be good enough to succeed or to do what is needed ▪ She tried to join the soccer team, but she couldn't *cut the mustard.* ▪ Now that we have computers, typewriters just don't *cut the mustard* anymore.

mustard gas *noun* [*noncount*] **:** a poison gas used as a weapon in a war

[1]**mus·ter** /ˈmʌstɚ/ *verb* **-ters; -tered; -ter·ing**
1 [+ *obj*] **:** to work hard to find or get (courage, support, etc.) ▪ They pushed the car with all the strength they could *muster.* ▪ He finally *mustered* (up) the courage to ask her on a date. ▪ The country's leaders have been trying to *muster* (up) support for the war. ▪ They *mustered* (up) the 20 votes needed to pass the law.
2 : to gather together (a group of people, soldiers, etc.) especially for battle or war [+ *obj*] *muster* an army [*no obj*] The soldiers *mustered* [=*gathered*] in the center of town.

[2]**muster** *noun, pl* **-ters** [*count*] **:** a formal military gathering to examine or test soldiers ▪ a *muster* of soldiers
pass muster **:** to be judged as acceptable or good enough ▪ These excuses will not *pass muster.* [=they are not acceptable] ▪ His cooking could *pass muster* in an expensive French restaurant.

must–have /ˈmʌstˌhæv/ *noun, pl* **-haves** [*count*] *chiefly US, informal* **:** something that is necessary to have or get ▪ The newest version of the software is a *must-have.*
– must–have *adj, always used before a noun* ▪ *must-have* software ▪ a *must-have* accessory

mustn't /ˈmʌsn̩t/ — used as a contraction of *must not* ▪ We *mustn't* forget the lessons that history has taught us. ▪ You *mustn't* say such things.

must–see /ˈmʌstˈsiː/ *noun, pl* **-sees** [*count*] *chiefly US, informal* **:** something that must or should be seen ▪ His latest movie is a *must-see.*
– must–see *adj, always used before a noun* ▪ a *must-see* movie

must've /ˈmʌstəv/ — used as a contraction of *must have* ▪ He *must've* left already.

musty /ˈmʌsti/ *adj* **must·i·er; -est :** having a bad smell because of wetness, old age, or lack of fresh air ▪ *musty* old books ▪ a dark and *musty* basement
– must·i·ness /ˈmʌstinəs/ *noun* [*noncount*]

mu·ta·ble /ˈmjuːtəbəl/ *adj* [*more* ~; *most* ~] *formal* **:** able or likely to change often ▪ *mutable* opinions ▪ the government's *mutable* economic policies — opposite IMMUTABLE
– mu·ta·bil·i·ty /ˌmjuːtəˈbɪləti/ *noun* [*noncount*] ▪ the *mutability* of the government's policies

mu·tant /ˈmjuːtn̩t/ *noun, pl* **-tants** [*count*] *biology* **:** a plant or animal that is different from other plants or animals of the same kind because of a change in the structure of its genes **:** something produced by genetic mutation
– mutant *adj, always used before a noun* ▪ a *mutant* fish

mu·tate /ˈmjuːˌteɪt/ *verb* **-tates; -tat·ed; -tat·ing**
1 *biology* **a** [+ *obj*] **:** to cause (a gene) to change and create an unusual characteristic in a plant or animal **:** to cause mutation in (a gene) ▪ a disease that *mutates* genes in humans ▪ a group of *mutated* genes **b** [*no obj*] **:** to change and cause an unusual characteristic to develop in a plant or animal ▪ The cells *mutated.*
2 [*no obj*] **:** to change *into* something very different ▪ Over time, her feelings *mutated* from hatred *into* love. ▪ opera singers *mutating into* pop stars

mu·ta·tion /mjuˈteɪʃən/ *noun, pl* **-tions**
1 *biology* **:** a change in the genes of a plant or animal that causes physical characteristics that are different from what is normal [*noncount*] The cat's short tail is the result of *mutation.* [*count*] The condition is caused by a genetic *mutation.* ▪ The cat's short tail is the result of a *mutation.* ▪ *mutations* in mice
2 [*count*] **:** a new form of something that has changed ▪ The building is a *mutation* of the original design.
– mu·ta·tion·al /mjuˈteɪʃənl/ *adj* ▪ a *mutational* change

[1]**mute** /ˈmjuːt/ *adj*
1 : not able or willing to speak ▪ The defendant stood *mute* [=*silent*] during questioning. ▪ She knew the answer, but she decided to remain *mute.* [=*silent*] ▪ We just sat there, *mute* [=*speechless*], unable to explain what happened. ▪ The scientists have been *mute* [=they have not said anything] about the results of the tests. ▪ *mute* witnesses
2 : felt or expressed without the use of words ▪ They hugged each other in *mute* sympathy. ▪ I could see a *mute* plea for help in his eyes.
– mute·ly *adv* ▪ They waited *mutely* [=*silently, quietly*] for an answer. ▪ We stood staring *mutely* at the sky.

[2]**mute** *noun, pl* **mutes** [*count*]
1 *sometimes offensive* **:** a person who cannot speak
2 : a device on a musical instrument (such as a trumpet) that makes its sound much softer

[3]**mute** *verb* **mutes; mut·ed; mut·ing** [+ *obj*]
1 a : to make (a sound) softer or quieter ▪ They covered their ears to *mute* [=*muffle*] the sound of the guns. ▪ We *muted* our voices. **b :** to make (something, such as a television) silent ▪ He used the remote control to *mute* the TV.
2 : to make (something) softer or less harsh ▪ The loud colors in this room need to be *muted.* ▪ He *muted* his criticism of the president. [=he expressed his criticism less harshly]

mut·ed /ˈmjuːtəd/ *adj* [*more* ~; *most* ~]
1 : soft in color **:** not bright ▪ We painted our house a *muted* [=*dull*] blue. ▪ The artist chose colors that are dark and *muted.* ▪ *muted* lighting
2 : soft or quiet in sound **:** quieter than usual ▪ the *muted* sound of a distant trumpet ▪ *muted* voices
3 : not done or expressed in a strong, forceful, or excited way ▪ a *muted* political discussion ▪ The government chose a more *muted* response to the threat. ▪ Their proposal has drawn a *muted* reaction from most observers.

mu·ti·late /ˈmjuːtəˌleɪt/ *verb* **-lates; -lat·ed; -lat·ing** [+ *obj*]
1 : to cause severe damage to (the body of a person or animal) ▪ traps that *mutilate* animals — usually used as *(be) mutilated* ▪ Her arm *was mutilated* in a car accident. ▪ the *mutilated* body of a murder victim
2 : to ruin the beauty of (something) **:** to severely damage or spoil (something) ▪ a painting *mutilated* by vandals ▪ *mutilated* books
– mu·ti·la·tion /ˌmjuːtəˈleɪʃən/ *noun, pl* **-tions** [*noncount*] a victim of *mutilation* [*count*] facial *mutilations*

mu·ti·neer /ˌmjuːtəˈniɚ/ *noun, pl* **-neers** [*count*] **:** a person who is involved in a mutiny

mu·ti·nous /ˈmjuːtənəs/ *adj*
1 : involved in a mutiny ▪ *mutinous* sailors
2 [*more* ~; *most* ~] **:** feeling or showing a desire not to do what someone has told or ordered you to do ▪ Several *mutinous* [=*rebellious*] party members threatened to defect to the opposition.

mu·ti·ny /ˈmjuːtəni/ *noun, pl* **-nies** [*count*] **:** a situation in which a group of people (such as sailors or soldiers) refuse to obey orders and try to take control away from the person who commands them ▪ The *mutiny* was led by the ship's cook. ▪ The sailors staged a *mutiny* and took control of the ship.
– mutiny *verb* **-nies; -nied; -ny·ing** [*no obj*] ▪ The crew was threatening to *mutiny.*

mutt /ˈmʌt/ *noun, pl* **mutts** [*count*] *informal* **:** a dog with parents of different breeds **:** MONGREL — sometimes used in a disapproving way to refer to a dog of any kind ▪ a mangy *mutt*

mut·ter /ˈmʌtɚ/ *verb* **-ters; -tered; -ter·ing**
1 : to speak quietly so that it is difficult for other people to hear what you say [+ *obj*] She angrily *muttered* something about her bad luck. ▪ He *muttered* an apology. ▪ a *muttered* comment [*no obj*] She sat practicing her speech, *muttering* to herself.
2 [*no obj*] **:** to complain in a quiet or indirect way ▪ Some employees are *muttering* about the changes in the pension plan.
– mutter *noun, pl* **-ters** [*count*] ▪ She answered with/in a *mutter.* **– muttering** *noun, pl* **-ings** [*noncount*] There has been some *muttering* among the employees. [*count*] We've been hearing *mutterings* from some employees about the changes in the pension plan.

mut·ton /ˈmʌtn̩/ *noun* [*noncount*] **:** the meat of an adult sheep used as food ▪ a meal of *mutton* and potatoes ▪ a leg/shoulder of *mutton*
mutton dressed as lamb *Brit, informal + disapproving* **:** a woman who tries to make herself look younger by wearing clothes designed for young people

mut·ton·chops /ˈmʌtn̩ˌtʃɑːps/ *noun [plural]* **:** hair that covers the sides of a man's face but not his chin — called also *muttonchop whiskers, (US) muttonchop sideburns*

mu·tu·al /ˈmjuːtʃəwəl/ *adj*
1 : shared between two or more people or groups ▪ *Mutual* love and respect was the key to their successful marriage. ▪ The partnership was based on *mutual* admiration and understanding. ▪ *mutual* trust ▪ countries relying on *mutual* support during difficult times ✧ If a feeling ***is mutual,*** then two people or groups feel the same way about each other. ▪ Her fans love her, and the feeling *is mutual*. [=and she loves her fans] ▪ Their attraction *was mutual*. [=they were both attracted to each other] ▪ "I'm pleased to meet you." "The feeling *is mutual*!" [=I'm also pleased to meet you]
2 *always used before a noun* **:** shared by two or more people or groups ▪ They met through a *mutual* friend. [=a person who was a friend of both of them] ▪ our *mutual* hobby of car racing ▪ The two countries have several *mutual* [=*joint*] interests. ▪ It was a *mutual* effort. ▪ We had a *mutual* agreement not to tell our secret.
– mu·tu·al·i·ty /ˌmjuːtʃəˈwæləti/ *noun [noncount] formal* ▪ *mutuality* of interest

mutual fund *noun, pl* **~ funds** *[count] US* **:** a type of investment in which the money of many people is used to buy stock from many different companies ▪ She invested her money in a *mutual fund*. — called also *(Brit) unit trust*

mu·tu·al·ly /ˈmjuːtʃəwəli/ *adv* **:** in an equal way for each person or group involved ▪ We hope that these changes will be *mutually* beneficial. ▪ a *mutually* rewarding relationship ▪ *mutually* dependent countries [=countries that are equally dependent on each other] ▪ They loved and respected each other *mutually*.

mutually exclusive *adj* **:** related in such a way that each thing makes the other thing impossible **:** not able to be true at the same time or to exist together ▪ War and peace are *mutually exclusive*. [=war and peace cannot exist at the same time] ▪ *mutually exclusive* events — often used after *not* to describe things that can exist together or at the same time ▪ In a marriage, love and conflict are *not mutually exclusive*. [=both love and conflict can exist in a marriage at the same time]

muu·muu /ˈmuːˌmuː/ *noun, pl* **-muus** *[count]* **:** a Hawaiian dress that is usually long, loose-fitting, and decorated with bright colors — see color picture on page C16

Mu·zak /ˈmjuːˌzæk/ *trademark* — used for recorded music that is played in public buildings or rooms (such as stores or offices)

[1]muz·zle /ˈmʌzəl/ *noun, pl* **muz·zles** *[count]*
1 : the usually long nose and mouth of an animal (such as a dog, horse, or pig) **:** SNOUT — see picture at HORSE
2 : a covering for the mouth of a dog that stops it from biting people
3 : the hole at the end of a gun where the bullet comes out — see picture at GUN

[2]muzzle *verb* **muz·zles; muz·zled; muz·zling** *[+ obj]*
1 : to put a muzzle on (a dog) **:** to place a covering on (the mouth of a dog) to stop biting ▪ a dangerous dog that should be *muzzled*
2 : to prevent (a person or group) from speaking or writing in a free or normal way ▪ attempts by the government to *muzzle* the press ▪ The company has tried to *muzzle* its employees by forbidding them to speak to the press.

muz·zy /ˈmʌzi/ *adj* **muzz·i·er; -est** *Brit, informal*
1 : confused or unclear in the mind especially after drinking alcohol ▪ He stopped drinking when his head started getting *muzzy*. ▪ The medicine made her feel *muzzy* [=*dazed, groggy*] and tired.
2 : not clear or exact ▪ The story gets *muzzy* [=*(US) fuzzy*] in the middle of the book. ▪ *muzzy* conclusions ▪ *muzzy* [=*fuzzy, blurry*] photographs
– muz·zi·ly /ˈmʌzəli/ *adv* **– muz·zi·ness** /ˈmʌzinəs/ *noun [noncount]*

my /ˈmaɪ/ *adj, possessive form of* I
1 *always used before a noun* **:** relating to or belonging to me ▪ Welcome to *my* home. ▪ I enjoy *my* job very much. ▪ *My* favorite TV show was on last night. ▪ *My* name is John. ▪ When I woke up this morning, *my* head ached and *my* throat was sore. ▪ *My* wife and I both love to dance. **:** made or done by me ▪ I always keep *my* promises. ▪ It was *my* fault that we lost the game.
2 *always used before a noun* — used to express affection for someone you are talking to ▪ How are you, *my* friend? ▪ Come with me, *my* love. ▪ Sleep well, *my* child.
3 *informal* — used by itself and in phrases to express surprise, excitement, or fear ▪ Oh *my*, what a wonderful gift! ▪ Oh, ***my goodness***. What happened to you? ▪ Oh ***my lord***, look at the time! ▪ ***My God***, you must be joking!

my·al·gic en·ceph·a·lo·my·eli·tis /maɪˈældʒɪkɪnˌsɛfəloʊˌmajəˈlaɪtəs/ *noun [noncount] Brit, medical* **:** CHRONIC FATIGUE SYNDROME

my·nah *or* **my·na** /ˈmaɪnə/ *noun, pl* **-nahs** *or* **-nas** *[count]* **:** a black bird from Asia that is often kept as a pet and trained to copy the sounds of words — called also *mynah bird*

my·o·pia /maɪˈoupijə/ *noun [noncount] medical* **:** a condition of the eye that makes it difficult to see objects that are far away **:** NEARSIGHTEDNESS ▪ She wears eyeglasses to correct her *myopia*. — often used figuratively ▪ cultural *myopia* [=an inability to see what is good in other cultures] ▪ religious and moral *myopia*

my·o·pic /maɪˈɑːpɪk/ *adj [more ~; most ~]*
1 *medical* **:** not able to clearly see objects that are far away **:** affected with myopia **:** NEARSIGHTED ▪ *myopic* vision
2 *disapproving* **:** only thinking or caring about things that are happening now or that relate to a particular group rather than things that are in the future or that relate to many people ▪ *myopic* politicians ▪ He has criticized the government's *myopic* [=*shortsighted*] diplomatic policies. ▪ a *myopic* view of the world

[1]myr·i·ad /ˈmirijəd/ *noun, pl* **-ads** *[count] somewhat formal* **:** a very large number *of* things ▪ The car comes in a *myriad of* colors. [=in many colors] ▪ There are a *myriad of* possibilities. — often plural ▪ *myriads of* stars/insects

[2]myriad *adj, somewhat formal* **:** very many ▪ The old system's problems were *myriad*. — usually used before a noun ▪ *myriad* problems ▪ Today we remember the *myriad* ways she helped others in her lifetime.

myrrh /ˈmɚ/ *noun [noncount]* **:** a sticky brown substance that comes from trees, that has a sweet smell, and that is used in products that give the air or people's bodies a pleasing smell

myr·tle /ˈmɚtl̩/ *noun, pl* **myr·tles** *[count]* **:** a type of small tree that has sweet-smelling white or pink flowers and black berries

my·self /maɪˈsɛlf/ *pronoun*
1 : the person who is speaking or writing: **a** — used as the object of a verb or preposition to refer to yourself after you have already been mentioned ▪ I accidentally cut *myself* while cooking. ▪ I'm going to get *myself* a new car. ▪ I bought *myself* a new suit. ▪ I consider *myself* to be a pretty good swimmer. ▪ I had to ask *myself* if this was what I truly wanted. ▪ I reminded *myself* that this is just a game. ▪ I told a bad joke and made *myself* look foolish. ▪ I am proud of *myself* for finishing college. ▪ I could no longer keep the secret to *myself*. ▪ I'm doing this for *myself*. [=for my own benefit] ▪ I said to *myself*, "Here's a man who knows what he's doing." ▪ I had the house (all) ***to myself***. [=I was alone in the house] ▪ I wanted to see it ***for myself***. [=to see it rather than have someone tell me about it, describe it to me, etc.] **b** — used for emphasis to refer again to yourself after you have already been mentioned ▪ I told him so *myself*. ▪ If you won't go, then I'll go *myself*. ▪ I *myself* have never been to Italy. ▪ I *myself* have experienced the same thing.
2 : my normal or healthy self ▪ I was nervous and uncomfortable and just didn't feel (like) *myself*. ▪ I'm not feeling (like) *myself* today. I think I may be coming down with a cold. ▪ I'm not *myself* today. I just don't feel right. ▪ I find it hard to ***be myself*** [=to relax and behave in my usual way] when I'm with people I don't know well.
by myself **1 :** without any help from other people ▪ I can't do it (all) *by myself*. ▪ It's hard to believe that I started this company *by myself* 20 years ago. **2 :** with nobody else **:** ALONE ▪ I went to movies *by myself*. ▪ I had to play in my room (all) *by myself*.

mys·te·ri·ous /mɪˈstirijəs/ *adj [more ~; most ~]* **:** strange, unknown, or difficult to understand ▪ the *mysterious* ways of nature ▪ We heard a *mysterious* noise outside our tent. ▪ He died under *mysterious* circumstances. ▪ A *mysterious* illness has been spreading through the city. ▪ There's something *mysterious* about that old woman. ▪ Her behavior was very *mysterious*. ✧ *Mysterious* people are often interesting because many things are not known about them. ▪ A *mysterious* stranger came to our door. ▪ the movie's handsome and *mysterious* main character

M

be mysterious : to talk or behave in a way that makes other people feel that you must have a secret • What are you *being so mysterious* about?
– mys·te·ri·ous·ly *adv* • He died *mysteriously* at the age of 32. • She smiled *mysteriously*.

mys·tery /ˈmɪstəri/ *noun, pl* **-ter·ies**
1 [*count*] **: something that is not known** • Where they went is a *mystery*. [=no one knows where they went] • The girl's name remains a *mystery*. **: something that is difficult to understand or explain** • The *mystery* surrounding/of her disappearance has never been solved. • His success is something of a *mystery*. = His success is a bit of a *mystery*. • The cause of the disease remains a *mystery* to scientists. • I don't know how he did it. It's a *mystery* to me!
2 [*noncount*] **: the quality of being difficult to understand or explain : the quality of being mysterious** • The experiment is cloaked/shrouded/veiled in *mystery*. • There is an air of *mystery* surrounding her. = She is a woman of *mystery*. • There's no *mystery* (to/as to/about) why we're here. = It's no *mystery* why we're here. [=we know why we are here]
3 [*count*] **: a religious event or idea that cannot be fully understood or explained** • the *mystery* of creation
4 [*count*] **: a book, play, or movie that describes a crime and the process of solving it** • She has written many adventure novels and murder *mysteries*. **— often used before another noun** • *mystery* novels/stories • She's a *mystery* writer.
5 [*count*] **: someone or something whose identity has been kept secret especially in order to create interest or excitement — usually used before another noun** • We'll reveal the identity of today's *mystery* guest after these commercials. • You'll find a *mystery* prize in each box.

mystery play *noun, pl* **~ plays** [*count*] **: a religious play in the Middle Ages based on a story from the Bible (such as the creation of the world or the birth of Jesus Christ)**

¹mys·tic /ˈmɪstɪk/ *noun, pl* **-tics** [*count*] **: a person who tries to gain religious or spiritual knowledge through prayer and deep thought : someone who practices mysticism**

²mystic *adj* [*more ~; most ~*] **: MYSTICAL** • She had a *mystic* vision while praying. • a *mystic* journey

mys·ti·cal /ˈmɪstɪkəl/ *adj*
1 [*more ~; most ~*] **: having a spiritual meaning that is difficult to see or understand** • He has a *mystical* [*mystic*] union/relationship with God. • She says that the symbol has *mystical* powers. • the deep, almost *mystical* quality of her poetry
2 : of or relating to mystics or mysticism : resulting from prayer or deep thought • a *mystical* experience • a *mystical* journey in search of God • *mystical* knowledge of the spirit world
– mys·ti·cal·ly /ˈmɪstɪkli/ *adv* • *mystically* united with God

mys·ti·cism /ˈmɪstəˌsɪzəm/ *noun* [*noncount*] **: a religious practice based on the belief that knowledge of spiritual truth can be gained by praying or thinking deeply** • Jewish, Christian, and Islamic *mysticism* • a student of Eastern *mysticism*

mys·ti·fy /ˈmɪstəˌfaɪ/ *verb* **-fies; -fied; -fy·ing** [+ *obj*] **: to confuse (someone) completely** • The cause of the disease *mystified* doctors for many years. • Her strange behavior has *mystified* [=*baffled*] her friends and family. • I was thoroughly *mystified* by his reaction. [=I could not understand his reaction] • The magician has been *mystifying* his audiences for years with his amazing tricks.
– mys·ti·fi·ca·tion /ˌmɪstəfəˈkeɪʃən/ *noun* [*noncount*]
– mystifying *adj* [*more ~; most ~*] • her *mystifying* behavior **– mys·ti·fy·ing·ly** *adv*

mys·tique /mɪˈstiːk/ *noun* [*singular*] **: a special quality that makes a person or thing interesting or exciting** • There's a certain *mystique* to/about people who fight fires. • No one has been able to copy the legendary singer's *mystique*. • the *mystique* of mountain climbing

myth /ˈmɪθ/ *noun, pl* **myths**
1 : an idea or story that is believed by many people but that is not true [*count*] It's an enduring/persistent *myth* that money brings happiness. • The book dispels/refutes/debunks many *myths* about early American history. [=shows that many beliefs about early American history are wrong] • I don't believe the *myths* and legends about/surrounding this forest. [*noncount*] Contrary to popular *myth*, no monster lives in this lake.
2 a [*count*] **: a story that was told in an ancient culture to explain a practice, belief, or natural occurrence** • creation *myths* [=stories about how people and the world were first created] **b** [*noncount*] **: such stories as a group** • a student of Greek *myth* [=*mythology*]

myth·ic /ˈmɪθɪk/ *adj*
1 : of or relating to a myth • a *mythic* story **: described in a myth** • a *mythic* [=(more commonly) *mythical*] hero
2 : suitable to a myth : very famous or important • He's reached the end of a *mythic* [=*legendary*] career. • She's one of the *mythic* figures in ice-skating. • His fame has grown to ***mythic proportions***.

myth·i·cal /ˈmɪθɪkəl/ *adj*
1 : based on or described in a myth • Hercules was a *mythical* hero who was half man and half god. • gods fighting in a *mythical* battle in the sky • a *mythical* beast/creature
2 : existing only in the imagination : IMAGINARY • The sportswriters picked a *mythical* all-star team. • The benefits of the new policy proved to be *mythical*.
– myth·i·cal·ly /ˈmɪθɪkli/ *adv* • *mythically* heroic characters of the past

my·thol·o·gize *also Brit* **my·thol·o·gise** /mɪˈθɑːləˌʤaɪz/ *verb* **-giz·es; -gized; -giz·ing** [+ *obj*] **: to talk about or describe (someone or something) as a subject that deserves to be told about in a myth or legend : to make (someone or something) seem great or heroic** • a politician who has been *mythologized* by his supporters • *mythologize* the past

my·thol·o·gy /mɪˈθɑːləʤi/ *noun, pl* **-gies**
1 : the myths of a particular group or culture [*noncount*] We have been studying ancient Greek *mythology*. [*count*] We compared the two cultures' *mythologies*.
2 : ideas that are believed by many people but that are not true [*noncount*] Contrary to popular *mythology* [=*myth*], he did not actually discover the cause of the disease by himself. [*singular*] There is a popular *mythology* that he discovered the cause of the disease by himself.
– myth·o·log·i·cal /ˌmɪθəˈlɑːʤɪkəl/ *adj* • *mythological* heroes • a *mythological* story

N

¹n *or* **N** /ˈɛn/ *noun, pl* **n's** *or* **ns** *or* **N's** *or* **Ns** /ˈɛnz/
1 : the 14th letter of the English alphabet [*count*] a word that starts with an *n* [*noncount*] a word that starts with *n*
2 [*noncount*] *mathematics* **: a number that is part of an equation and that has a value that is not stated** • What is the value of *n* in the equation 5n + 2 = 37?

²n *abbr* noun

'n' *also* **'n** /ən, n̩/ *conj* **: AND** • rock *'n'* roll

N *abbr* north, northern

NA *abbr* **1** North America **2** not applicable — often written as *N/A* **3** not available — often written as *N/A*

NAACP *abbr* National Association for the Advancement of Colored People ✧ The *NAACP* is an American organization that works to protect the rights of African-Americans.

naan *also* **nan** /ˈnɑːn/ *noun* [*count, noncount*] **: an Indian bread that is round, flat, and soft**

nab /ˈnæb/ *verb* **nabs; nabbed; nab·bing** [+ *obj*] *informal*
1 : to catch and stop or arrest (someone) • The police *nabbed* [=(more formally) *apprehended*] the two men in their hideout. • *nabbing* criminals • The boss *nabbed* [=*caught*] me at the coffee machine and asked me to stay late.
2 : to take or get (something) quickly and often in a way that is clever or rude • I was thinking about *nabbing* [=*grabbing, snatching*] that last piece of pizza. • We *nabbed* seats in the front row of the theater.

na·bob /ˈneɪˌbɑːb/ *noun, pl* **-bobs** [*count*] *informal* **: a very rich or important person** • corporate *nabobs*

N

na·chos /ˈnɑːˌʧoʊz/ *noun* [*plural*] **:** tortilla chips that are covered with warm melted cheese and often with hot peppers, beans, salsa, etc.

na·da /ˈnɑːdə/ *noun* [*noncount*] *informal* **:** [1]NOTHING 1 ▪ It won't cost you anything—zero, nothing, *nada*.

na·dir /ˈneɪˌdiɚ/ *noun* [*singular*] *formal* **:** the worst or lowest point of something ▪ The relationship between the two countries reached a/its *nadir* in the 1920s. — opposite ZENITH

naff /ˈnæf/ *adj* **naff·er; -est** [*also more ~; most ~*] *Brit slang* **:** of low quality especially in a way that shows a lack of style or taste ▪ The film was a bit *naff*.

[1]**nag** /ˈnæg/ *verb* **nags; nagged; nag·ging**
1 a : to annoy (someone) by often complaining about his or her behavior, appearance, etc. [+ *obj*] — + *about* ▪ My wife *nags* me *about* my busy work schedule. ▪ Mom's always *nagging* me *about* my hair. [*no obj*] All you ever do is *nag*. **b :** to annoy (someone) with repeated questions, requests, or orders [+ *obj*] My parents are always *nagging* me to clean my room. ▪ He kept *nagging* her until she agreed to see the movie. [*no obj*] Quit *nagging*! I already said I'm not going.
2 : to cause (someone) to feel annoyed or worried for a long period of time [+ *obj*] She's still *nagged* [=*bothered*] by the thought that she could have done better. [*no obj*] — often + *at* ▪ The problem has been *nagging at* me for weeks.
– nagging /ˈnægɪŋ/ *adj, always used before a noun* [*more ~; most ~*] ▪ A few *nagging* questions/problems remain. ▪ I have this *nagging* doubt/feeling/fear/suspicion that our troubles aren't over yet. ▪ a *nagging* headache/cough/pain ▪ *nagging* injuries that just won't heal

[2]**nag** *noun, pl* **nags** [*count*] *informal* **:** a person who nags or complains too often ▪ His wife's an awful *nag*. — compare [3]NAG

[3]**nag** *noun, pl* **nags** [*count*] **:** a horse that is old and usually in bad condition — compare [2]NAG

nah /ˈnæ, ˈnæə, ˈnɑː/ *adv, informal* **:** [1]NO ◇ *Nah* is used in very informal spoken English. ▪ "Do you want to come with us?" "*Nah*, I've got too much work to do."

[1]**nail** /ˈneɪl/ *noun, pl* **nails** [*count*]
1 : a long, thin piece of metal that is sharp at one end and flat at the other end and that is used chiefly to attach things to wood ▪ a hammer and some *nails* — see picture at CARPENTRY; compare [1]SCREW 1
2 : the hard covering at the end of a finger or toe **:** a fingernail or toenail ▪ I get my *nails* done at the beauty salon every other week. ▪ a pair of *nail* clippers — see also HANGNAIL
a nail in the/someone's coffin **:** something that makes it more likely that someone or something will fail, be destroyed, etc. ▪ Every mistake is one more *nail in the coffin* of his professional baseball career. ▪ The lawyers put another *nail in her coffin* today.
(as) hard/tough as nails *of a person* **:** very tough ▪ When she's negotiating a contract, she can be *as tough as nails*.
hit the nail on the head see [1]HIT
tooth and nail see TOOTH

[2]**nail** *verb* **nails; nailed; nail·ing** [+ *obj*]
1 *always followed by an adverb, adjective, or preposition* **:** to attach (something) with a nail ▪ *Nail* the picture to the wall. ▪ *nailing* [=*hammering*] the boards together ▪ All the doors were *nailed* shut. ▪ The desks and chairs had been *nailed* (down) to the floor.
2 *informal* **a :** to catch (someone) doing something illegal or wrong ▪ He got *nailed* by his parents while trying to sneak out of the house. **b :** to arrest or punish (someone) for doing something that is illegal or wrong ▪ He got *nailed* for not paying his taxes. ▪ The FBI has *nailed* the hackers.
3 *informal* **:** to hit (someone or something) forcefully ▪ Someone *nailed* [=*whacked*] him on the head with a rock.
4 *US, informal* **:** to make or do (something) in a perfect or impressive way ▪ She *nailed* a three-point shot in the final seconds of the game. ▪ You really *nailed* that song. It sounded great!
nail down [*phrasal verb*] ***nail (something) down or nail down (something)*** **1 :** to make (something, such as a victory) certain to happen ▪ They need to score another touchdown to *nail down* the victory. **2 :** to find out or identify (something) exactly ▪ Her doctors haven't yet been able to *nail down* a diagnosis. ▪ They're trying to *nail down* the cause of our network problems. **3 :** to make (something) definite or final ▪ *nail down* a decision

nail–bit·er /ˈneɪlˌbaɪtɚ/ *noun* [*singular*] **:** something (such as a game or movie) that causes people to feel nervous because the ending is not known until the final moment ▪ This election's going to be a real *nail-biter*.
– nail–bit·ing /ˈneɪlˌbaɪtɪŋ/ *adj* ▪ The election is heading for a *nail-biting* finish.

nail file *noun, pl* **~ files** [*count*] **:** a small, flat piece of metal or cardboard that has a rough surface and that is used for shaping your fingernails — see picture at GROOMING

nail polish *noun* [*noncount*] **:** a liquid that is used to paint fingernails and toenails ▪ red *nail polish* ▪ *nail polish* remover — called also (*Brit*) *nail varnish*; see picture at GROOMING

na·ive *or* **na·ïve** /nɑˈiːv, naɪˈiːv/ *adj* [*more ~; most ~*] **:** having or showing a lack of experience or knowledge **:** innocent or simple ▪ a *naive* belief that all people are good ▪ a *naive* view of the world ▪ She asked a lot of *naive* questions. ▪ He's politically *naive*. = He's *naive* about the nature of politics. ▪ I was young and *naive* at the time, and I didn't think anything bad could happen to me. ▪ The plan seems a little *naive*. ▪ If you're *naive* enough to believe him, you'll believe anyone. ▪ We're not *naive* to the fact [=we're not unaware of the fact] that there are problems with the system.
– na·ive·ly *or* **na·ïve·ly** *adv* ▪ I *naively* believed that we could fix the problem. **– na·ïve·té** *also* **na·ive·te** *or* **na·ive·té** /nɑˌiːvˈteɪ, naɪˌiːvˈteɪ/ *noun* [*noncount*] ▪ political *naïveté* **– na·ive·ty** *also* **na·ïve·ty** /nɑˈiːvəti, naɪˈiːvəti/ *noun* [*noncount*] *chiefly Brit* ▪ political *naïvety*

na·ked /ˈneɪkəd/ *adj*
1 [*more ~; most ~*] **:** not wearing any clothes **:** not covered by clothing ▪ a *naked* [=*nude*] man ▪ the *naked* human body ▪ her *naked* [=(more commonly) *bare*] shoulders ▪ He was *naked* from the waist up. ▪ The prisoners were stripped *naked*. [=all of their clothes were taken off] ▪ She was ***half naked*** [=partly dressed] when the doorbell rang. ▪ He's ***stark naked***. [=he's completely naked]
2 : not having a usual covering ▪ The trees are still *naked* [=(more commonly) *bare*], but their leaves will return soon. ▪ a *naked* [=*uncovered*] lightbulb
3 : not having any decorations ▪ the room's *naked* [=*bare, plain*] walls
4 *always used before a noun* **a :** not hidden or changed in any way **:** stated in a very clear and direct way ▪ These are the *naked* facts of the case. ▪ Tell me everything. I want ***the naked truth***. [=the complete truth, the whole story] **b :** completely obvious ▪ an act of *naked* aggression
5 *always used before a noun* **:** without the use of a telescope, microscope, etc. ▪ distant stars and planets that cannot be seen with ***the naked eye*** ▪ Though extremely small, this insect is visible to *the naked eye*.
– na·ked·ly *adv* ▪ She's the most *nakedly* ambitious person I know. **– na·ked·ness** *noun* [*noncount*] ▪ The actor was uncomfortable with his *nakedness*. [=the fact that he was naked]

nam·by–pam·by /ˌnæmbiˈpæmbi/ *adj* [*more ~; most ~*] *informal + disapproving* **:** too weak or gentle **:** not strong or strict enough ▪ *namby-pamby* politicians ▪ *namby-pamby* treatment of criminals

[1]**name** /ˈneɪm/ *noun, pl* **names** [*count*]
1 : a word or phrase that refers to or that can refer to a specific person ▪ "What's his (first) *name*?" "His *name* is Jacob." ▪ I took my husband's (last) *name* when we got married. ▪ Please write/sign your *name* on this line. ▪ State your *name* and occupation. ▪ I refused to give/tell them my *name*. ▪ She has one of the most famous *names* [=she is one of the most famous people] in show business. ▪ Can you give me the *name* of a good dentist? [=do you know a good dentist that I could use?] ▪ Mark Twain's real *name* was Samuel Clemens. ▪ She registered at the hotel under/using a false/assumed *name*. ▪ Samuel Clemens wrote under the *name* (of) Mark Twain. ▪ My ***full name*** is Susan Elaine Smith. ▪ Her name is Susan, but she goes ***by the name (of)*** Sue. [=people call her Sue] ▪ Do you know a man ***by the name of*** [=do you know a man named] James Smith? ▪ She now owns several restaurants that ***bear her name***. [=that are named after her] ▪ Can I ***put your name down*** for a donation? [=can I write down your name on the list of people who are giving a donation?; would you like to make a donation?] — see also CHRISTIAN NAME, FAMILY NAME, FIRST NAME, FORENAME, GIVEN NAME, LAST NAME, MAIDEN NAME, MARRIED NAME, MIDDLE NAME, NICKNAME, PEN NAME, PET NAME, STAGE NAME, SURNAME
2 a : a word or phrase that refers to a specific place or thing ▪ We had to memorize the *names* of all the countries in Africa. ▪ "What's your dog's *name*?" "His *name* is Sandy." ▪ What was the *name* [=*title*] of that movie we saw last night? ▪ This

N

is his song "Loving You" from the album of the same *name*. • The ship's *name* was "Titanic." • The band ***takes/gets its name from*** [=it is named after] its hometown. • The company ***gives/lends its name*** to one of the biggest golf tournaments in the country. [=the golf tournament is named after the company] **b :** a word or phrase that refers to a type or group of things • Psychologists have a *name* for this kind of behavior. • Is there a *name* for the part of the leg behind the knee? • The cougar is also known by the *names* "puma" and "mountain lion." • The plant's ***botanical/scientific name*** is *Chrysanthemum leucanthemum*, but we know it by its ***common name*** "daisy." • ***True to their name***, killer bees have been known to kill people. = ***As their name implies/suggests***, killer bees really do kill. = Killer bees really ***live up to their name***. = Killer bees are known to kill people, ***hence the name***. — see also BRAND NAME, CODE NAME, PLACE NAME, PROPER NAME, TRADE NAME

3 : the general opinion that most people have about someone or something • A few dishonest players have given the sport a ***bad name***. [=they have made people think badly about the sport] • I won't let you ruin our family's ***good name***. [=good reputation] • He's still trying to ***clear his name***. [=to prove that he is not guilty of a crime]

4 : a famous person or thing • He's one of the biggest *names* in music. • Our agency has represented some of the most famous *names* in the business. • The following year, she took the role that would make her a ***household name***. [=a very well-known person] — see also BIG NAME, NAME-DROPPING, NO-NAME

5 : a word or phrase that is used to describe and insult someone • a bad/dirty *name* — usually plural • Sticks and stones may break my bones but *names* will never hurt me! • "You're such a stupid jerk!" "Hey, don't ***call me names***!" • A bully at school was *calling her names*. — see also NAME-CALLING

by name **:** using a name **:** by saying the name of someone or something • He never mentioned her *by name* [=he never said her name], but we all knew who he was talking about. • The victim was able to identify his attacker *by name*. [=he knew the name of the person who attacked him] • We've had people come in to the store and ask for it *by name*.

drag someone's name through the mud see [1]DRAG

in all/everything but name **:** not in an official way but in every other way • Military governors ruled the country *in all but name* for many years. • Their marriage was over *in all but name* five years ago.

in name only *also* ***in name*** — used to describe a person or thing that does not have the qualities that its name suggests • For many years, the Emperor was the ruler *in name only*. = The Emperor ruled *in name* but not in fact. • She's my boss *in name only*. We're really more like partners. • a friend *in name only*

in someone's/something's name *or* ***in the name of someone/something*** **1 a** — used to say that something officially or legally belongs to a specified person • We both own the house, but the car is *in my name*. • The business is registered *in her husband's name* for tax purposes. **b** — used to say that something has or uses the name of a specified person • Our reservation at the restaurant is *in my name*. **2** — used to say that something is done with the authority of a specified person or thing • The leader refused to allow such violent acts to be done *in his name*. • Stop *in the name of* the law! **3** — used to say that something is given as the official reason for doing something • These laws were passed *in the name of* national security. • They're tearing down historic buildings *in the name of* progress!

know (someone) by name **1 :** to know a person well enough to know the person's name • She *knows* all of her customers *by name*. • I took her to a restaurant where the owner *knows* me *by name*. • The police *know* him *by name*. **2 :** to know a person's name only • He said he only *knew* her *by name* and didn't know much more about her.

make your name *or* ***make a name for yourself*** **:** to become well-known or famous • She *made her name* in politics as a powerful public speaker. • He has *made* quite *a name for himself* as a golfer. • She is *making a name for herself* in the art world.

put a name to (someone or something) **:** to think of and say the name of (someone or something) • Can you *put a name to* the face in this photograph? • I couldn't *put a name to* the emotion I was feeling.

take someone's name in vain see VAIN

the name of the game *informal* **:** the basic goal or purpose of an activity • When all is said and done, in business, profit is *the name of the game*. • *The name of the game* was winning by any means necessary.

to your name **:** belonging to you • I haven't a dollar/dime/penny *to my name*. [=I have no money] • She has more than 20 novels *to her name*. [=she has written more than 20 novels] • a band with three hit songs *to their name*

under someone's/something's name *or* ***under the name (of) someone/something*** **1** — used to say that something officially or legally belongs to a specified person • We both own the house, but the car is *under my name*. • The business is registered *under her husband's name* for tax purposes. **2** — used to say that something has or uses the name of a specified person • We have dinner reservations *under the name of* Jones.

with someone's name on it *informal* **:** intended for someone • There's a piece of cake over there *with your name on it*. [=you should go get that piece of cake] • He told me he had a bullet *with my name on it*. [=he was going to shoot me]

your name is mud see MUD

[2]**name** *verb* **names; named; nam·ing** [+ *obj*]

1 : to give a name to (someone or something) • "What are you going to *name* your new dog?" "I think I'll *name* him Sandy." • The aptly *named* HMS "Victorious" helped the British Royal Navy win an important victory. • A man *named* James Smith is on the phone. • We *named* our daughter "Mary" in honor of her grandmother. • Alzheimer's disease was ***named after*** Dr. Alois Alzheimer. = (*US*) It was ***named for*** Dr. Alois Alzheimer.

2 : to say the name of (someone or something) • Can you *name* the person who attacked you? • All of the authors *named* above were influenced by his work. • "How many of the 50 states of the U.S. can you *name*?" "Well, there's New York, Connecticut, and Massachusetts, ***to name (but/just/only) a few***."

3 : to choose (someone) to be (something) • The company president *named* [=*appointed*] his son (as) his successor. • She was *named* to replace him as the company's vice president. • She has been *named* (as) the winner of the competition. • The magazine *named* him (as) the best artist of the year.

4 : to decide on or choose (something) • NASA has not yet *named* [=*set*] the date for the shuttle launch. • We've decided to get married, but we haven't *named* the day (of the wedding) yet.

name names **:** to say the names of people who were involved in something • He said he knew who did it, but he wouldn't *name names*.

name your price **:** to say how much you want to pay for something or how much you want to sell something for • Customers can *name their price*. • People selling homes on the beach can basically *name their price*. [=they can sell their homes for any amount of money they want]

you name it *informal* **:** anything you could say or think of • *You name it*, we sell it! • I like all kinds of music: rock, blues, reggae, classical—*you name it*!

[3]**name** *adj, always used before a noun, chiefly US* **:** having a well-known name and good reputation • We got a couple of *name* [=*big-name*] bands for the show. • books by *name* authors • *name* players

name brand *noun, pl* **~ brands** [*count*] **:** a product that is made by a well-known company • clothing stores that sell *name brands* at low prices — compare BRAND NAME, STORE BRAND

– name–brand *adj, always used before a noun* • *name-brand* clothing

name–call·ing /ˈneɪmˌkɑːlɪŋ/ *noun* [*noncount*] **:** the act of using offensive names to insult someone • "That man is an arrogant, immoral fool!" "I understand your anger, but *name-calling* won't get you anywhere." • Don't resort to *name-calling*. Let's talk about the real issues.

name–drop·ping /ˈneɪmˌdrɑːpɪŋ/ *noun* [*noncount*] **:** the act of trying to impress someone by saying the names of well-known people that you know or have met • There's an excessive amount of *name-dropping* in his autobiography.

– name–drop /ˈneɪmˌdrɑːp/ *verb* **-drops; -dropped; -drop·ping** [*no obj*] • He kept *name-dropping* [=*dropping names*] but no one was impressed. **– name–drop·per** /ˈneɪmˌdrɑːpɚ/ *noun, pl* **-pers** [*count*]

name·less /ˈneɪmləs/ *adj*

1 : having a name that is not known or told • the *nameless* [=*anonymous, unknown*] author of the editorial • She left the

hotel with a *nameless* man in a black jacket. ▪ a *nameless* informant ▪ The source for my story prefers to remain *nameless.* ▪ A top government official, ***who shall remain nameless***, has expressed concern about the decision.
2 : not having a name ▪ a *nameless* [=*unnamed*] stream in the woods ▪ a *nameless* baby
3 : not marked with a name ▪ The men were buried there in *nameless* graves.
4 a : not able to be identified by name ▪ There was a strange, *nameless* odor coming from the basement. ▪ *nameless* fears and worries **b :** too bad to talk about ▪ the *nameless* horrors of war

name·ly /ˈneɪmli/ *adv* — used when giving exact information about something you have already mentioned ▪ They brought lunch, *namely* sandwiches, chips, and soda. ▪ The disease can be prevented, *namely* by exercising, eating right, and not smoking. ▪ I have a question; *namely*, should we sell the property or not? ▪ She made a suggestion, *namely* that the student not be admitted.

name·plate /ˈneɪmˌpleɪt/ *noun, pl* **-plates** [*count*] **:** a metal or plastic sign that is attached to a door or wall and that shows the name of the person, group, or company that lives or works there

name·sake /ˈneɪmˌseɪk/ *noun, pl* **-sakes** [*count*] **:** someone or something that has the same name as another person or thing ▪ How much did President George Bush influence his son and *namesake* George W. Bush?

name tag *noun, pl* **~ tags** [*count*] **:** a piece of paper, cloth, plastic, or metal that has a person's name written on it and that is attached to the person's clothing ▪ She handed out *name tags* for people to wear at the conference. ▪ I didn't notice the supervisor's *name tag* on his uniform.

[1]**nan** /ˈnæn/ *noun, pl* **nans** [*count*] *Brit* **:** NANA

[2]**nan** *variant spelling of* NAAN

nana *also Brit* **nan·na** /ˈnænə/ *noun, pl* **nan·as** [*count*] **:** GRANDMOTHER — used especially by young children ▪ Are we going to visit *nana* today?

nan·ny /ˈnæni/ *noun, pl* **-nies** [*count*]
1 : a woman who is paid to care for a young child usually in the child's home ▪ When I was growing up, I had a *nanny.*
2 *Brit* **:** GRANDMOTHER

nanny goat *noun, pl* **~ goats** [*count*] **:** a female goat — compare BILLY GOAT

nano- *combining form, technical* **:** one billionth part of something ▪ *nano*second

nano·sec·ond /ˈnænəˌsɛkənd/ *noun, pl* **-onds** [*count*]
1 *technical* **:** one billionth of a second ▪ It happens in less than a *nanosecond.*
2 : a very short time

nano·tech·nol·o·gy /ˌnænoʊtɛkˈnɑːləʤi/ *noun* [*noncount*] *technical* **:** the science of working with atoms and molecules to build devices (such as robots) that are extremely small

[1]**nap** /ˈnæp/ *noun, pl* **naps** [*count*] **:** a short period of sleep especially during the day ▪ She awoke from her *nap* rested and refreshed. ▪ You look like you could use a *nap.* ▪ He put the baby down for a *nap.* ▪ Grandma ***takes a nap*** every afternoon. — compare [3]NAP

[2]**nap** *verb* **naps; napped; nap·ping** [*no obj*]
1 : to sleep for a short period of time especially during the day ▪ He's *napping* [=*dozing*] on the couch.
2 : to be in a state in which you are not prepared to deal with something because you were not paying attention ▪ The goalie had to be *napping* when that ball got by him. ▪ When the problem appeared again, the government was ***caught napping.*** [=the government was not prepared to deal with it]

[3]**nap** *noun, pl* **naps** [*count*] **:** a soft layer of threads on the surface of a piece of cloth, a carpet, etc. — compare [1]NAP

na·palm /ˈneɪˌpɑːm/ *noun* [*noncount*] **:** a thick substance that contains gasoline and that is used in bombs that cause a destructive fire over a wide area

nape /ˈneɪp/ *noun* [*singular*] **:** the back of the neck ▪ Her hair was tied back at the *nape* of her neck.

nap·kin /ˈnæpkən/ *noun, pl* **-kins** [*count*] **:** a small piece of cloth or paper used during a meal to clean your lips and fingers and to protect your clothes — called also (*Brit*) *serviette*; see picture at PLACE SETTING; see also SANITARY NAPKIN

[1]**nap·py** /ˈnæpi/ *adj* **nap·pi·er; -est** *US, informal, of hair* **:** having many tight bends or curls ▪ short *nappy* [=*kinky*] hair

[2]**nappy** *noun, pl* **-pies** [*count*] *Brit* **:** [1]DIAPER

nappy rash *noun* [*noncount*] *Brit* **:** DIAPER RASH

narc *also* **nark** /ˈnɑɚk/ *noun, pl* **narcs** *also* **narks** [*count*] *US, informal* **:** a person (such as a government agent) who tries to catch criminals who buy and sell illegal drugs

nar·cis·sis·tic /ˌnɑɚsəˈsɪstɪk/ *adj* [*more ~; most ~*] *formal + disapproving* **:** loving and admiring yourself and especially your appearance too much ▪ a *narcissistic* young actor
– nar·cis·sism /ˈnɑɚsəˌsɪzəm/ *noun* [*noncount*] ▪ the actor's *narcissism*

nar·cis·sus /nɑɚˈsɪsəs/ *noun, pl* **nar·cis·si** /nɑɚˈsɪˌsaɪ/ *or* **narcissus** *or* **nar·cis·sus·es** [*count*] **:** DAFFODIL

nar·co·lep·sy /ˈnɑɚkəˌlɛpsi/ *noun* [*noncount*] *medical* **:** a medical condition in which someone suddenly falls into a deep sleep while talking, working, etc.

nar·cot·ic /nɑɚˈkɑːtɪk/ *noun, pl* **-ics** [*count*]
1 : a drug (such as cocaine, heroin, or marijuana) that affects the brain and that is usually dangerous and illegal ▪ an addictive *narcotic* — often plural ▪ He was arrested for selling *narcotics.* ▪ *narcotics* agents/detectives ▪ *narcotics* dealers/traffickers [=people who sell narcotics]
2 *medical* **:** a drug that is given to people in small amounts to make them sleep or feel less pain ▪ a mild *narcotic*
– narcotic *adj* ▪ *narcotic* addiction ▪ *narcotic* drugs ▪ The drug has a mild *narcotic* effect. [=the drug makes you feel slightly sleepy]

nar·rate /ˈneɚˌeɪt, *Brit* nəˈreɪt/ *verb* **-rates; -rat·ed; -rat·ing** [+ *obj*]
1 : to tell (a story) ▪ The author *narrates* her story in great detail.
2 : to say the words that are heard as part of (a movie, television show, etc.) and that describe what is being seen **:** to do the narration for (something) ▪ Who *narrated* that film? ▪ a documentary *narrated* by a famous actor
– nar·ra·tor /ˈneɚˌeɪtɚ, *Brit* nəˈreɪtə/ *noun, pl* **-tors** [*count*] ▪ The *narrator* of the story is a ten-year-old child.

nar·ra·tion /næˈreɪʃən/ *noun, pl* **-tions**
1 *somewhat formal* **:** the act or process of telling a story or describing what happens [*noncount*] the *narration* of events ▪ The novel uses first-person *narration.* [*count*] first-person *narrations*
2 : words that are heard as part of a movie, television show, etc., and that describe what is being seen [*noncount*] They got a famous actor to do the *narration* for the documentary. [*count*] an actor who does *narrations* for documentaries

[1]**nar·ra·tive** /ˈnerətɪv/ *noun, pl* **-tives** [*count*] *formal* **:** a story that is told or written ▪ He is writing a detailed *narrative* of his life on the island. ▪ People have questioned the accuracy of his *narrative.* ▪ fictional *narratives*

[2]**narrative** *adj, always used before a noun*
1 : of or relating to the process of telling a story ▪ her *narrative* style/technique [=the way she tells a story]
2 : having the form of a story ▪ a *narrative* poem

[1]**nar·row** /ˈneroʊ/ *adj* **nar·row·er; -est** [*also more ~; most ~*]
1 : long and not wide **:** small from one side to the other side ▪ a long, *narrow* table ▪ *narrow* hallways/passageways ▪ The city's ancient streets are too *narrow* for buses. ▪ The sofa isn't *narrow* enough [=it is too wide] to fit through the door. ▪ a *narrow* path ▪ We crossed at the *narrowest* part of the river. ▪ His shoulders are very *narrow.* — opposite BROAD, WIDE
2 : including or involving a small number of things or people **:** limited in range or amount ▪ within the *narrow* limits allowed by law ▪ They offer a *narrow* range/choice of flavors: chocolate, strawberry, and vanilla. ▪ the study's *narrow* focus on 30-year-old men ▪ The study was *narrow* in scope. ▪ a *narrow* view/perspective of politics — opposite BROAD, WIDE
3 : almost not successful **:** very close to failure ▪ a *narrow* escape/victory **:** almost not enough for success ▪ They won by a *narrow* [=*close, small*] margin.
the straight and narrow see [3]STRAIGHT
– nar·row·ness *noun* [*noncount*]

[2]**narrow** *verb* **-rows; -rowed; -row·ing**
1 a [+ *obj*] **:** to make (something) less wide ▪ She *narrowed* her eyes and stared at me. = She stared at me through *narrowed* [=partly closed] eyes. ▪ The path was *narrowed* by overgrowth. **b** [*no obj*] **:** to become less wide ▪ His eyes *narrowed* as he focused on the words in front of him. ▪ The vase *narrows* at its top.
2 a [+ *obj*] **:** to make (something) smaller in amount or range ▪ The field has been *narrowed* [=*reduced*] from eight to two candidates. ▪ We've been able to *narrow* [=*limit*] the search to a three-mile area. ▪ *narrowing* the range of options ▪ You'll

N

need to *narrow* the focus of your paper to one central idea. — often + *down* ▪ The choices have been *narrowed down* to two. ▪ To *narrow down* its pool of applicants, the school made its admission requirements stricter. **b** [*no obj*] **: to become smaller in amount or range** ▪ The gap between their salaries was beginning to *narrow*.

– narrowing *noun, pl* **-ings** [*count*] — usually singular ▪ a *narrowing* of the blood vessels

nar·row·ly /ˈneroʊli/ *adv* [*more ~; most ~*]

1 : by a very small number, amount, or distance ▪ The bullet *narrowly* missed his heart. [=the bullet did not hit his heart, but it almost did] ▪ We *narrowly* [=*barely*] escaped with our lives. ▪ The team *narrowly* won the last game of the season.

2 : in a way that does not include or involve many things or people ▪ While the organization defines the term "family" very *narrowly*, many people have a rather liberal idea of what it means to be a family. ▪ The study *narrowly* focuses on 30-year-old men.

nar·row–mind·ed /ˈneroʊˈmaɪndəd/ *adj* [*more ~; most ~*] **: not willing to accept opinions, beliefs, or behaviors that are unusual or different from your own** ▪ Her mother was *narrow-minded* about religion. ▪ a *narrow-minded* view of racial issues

– nar·row–mind·ed·ness *noun* [*noncount*]

nar·rows /ˈneroʊz/ *noun* [*plural*] **: a narrow passage that connects two areas of water** ▪ He skillfully sailed the ship through the *narrows*.

nary /ˈneri/ *adj* **: not one** — used in the phrases ***nary a*** or ***nary an*** ▪ They survived the accident with *nary a* scratch. [=without a single scratch] ▪ *Nary a* word was spoken.

NASA /ˈnæsə/ *abbr* National Aeronautics and Space Administration ✧ **NASA is a U.S. government organization that is responsible for space travel and research.**

na·sal /ˈneɪzəl/ *adj*

1 *always used before a noun* **: of or relating to the nose** ▪ a bottle of *nasal* spray ▪ medicine for *nasal* congestion ▪ *nasal* passages

2 a *always used before a noun* **: produced by pushing air out through the nose when you speak** ▪ the *nasal* consonants /m/ and /n/ ▪ the *nasal* vowels in French ▪ *nasal* sounds **b : producing nasal sounds** ▪ Her voice is harsh and *nasal*.

– na·sal·ly *adv* ▪ She sung/spoke *nasally*.

NASCAR /ˈnæsˌkɑɚ/ *abbr, US* National Association for Stock Car Auto Racing

na·scent /ˈnæsn̩t/ *adj, formal* **: beginning to exist : recently formed or developed** ▪ *nascent* democratic governments ▪ a *nascent* technology ▪ The actress is now focusing on her *nascent* singing career.

nas·tur·tium /nəˈstɚʃəm/ *noun, pl* **-tiums** [*count*] **: a plant with circular leaves and yellow, orange, or red flowers that are sometimes eaten**

nas·ty /ˈnæsti, *Brit* ˈnɑːsti/ *adj* **nas·ti·er; -est** [*also more ~; most ~*]

1 : very unpleasant to see, smell, taste, etc. ▪ She has a *nasty* habit of biting her fingernails. ▪ The food looks *nasty*. ▪ The medicine left a *nasty* taste in my mouth. ▪ a *nasty*-tasting medicine

2 : indecent and offensive ▪ a violent movie with a lot of *nasty* [=*bad, dirty*] language

3 : unpleasant and unkind ▪ That was a *nasty* [=*cruel, mean*] trick! ▪ That *nasty* old man yelled at me just for stepping on his lawn! ▪ He sent a *nasty* letter/e-mail to the company. ▪ She's got quite a *nasty* temper/disposition. ▪ He said lots of downright *nasty* things about her. ▪ She called him a few *nasty* names and left.

4 : very bad or unpleasant ▪ *nasty* weather/storms ▪ It's rainy and *nasty* outside. ▪ I've got a really *nasty* problem. ▪ He's in for a *nasty* surprise when he gets home. ▪ He just went through a *nasty* divorce. ▪ a *nasty* legal battle ▪ Their relationship ***got/turned nasty*** soon after they were married.

5 : very serious or severe ▪ You've got a *nasty* cut on your head. ▪ a *nasty* wound **: causing much damage** ▪ She had a *nasty* fall on the ice. ▪ He took a *nasty* spill while riding his bike.

– nas·ti·ly /ˈnæstəli, *Brit* ˈnɑːstəli/ *adv* ▪ He spoke *nastily* about his ex-girlfriend. **– nas·ti·ness** /ˈnæstinəs, *Brit* ˈnɑːstinəs/ *noun* [*noncount*]

natch /ˈnætʃ/ *adv, informal* **: as you would expect : NATURALLY** ▪ He bought the most expensive car he could find, *natch*.

na·tion /ˈneɪʃən/ *noun, pl* **-tions**

1 a [*count*] **: a large area of land that is controlled by its own government : COUNTRY** ▪ It's one of the richest/poorest *nations* in the world. ▪ the largest state/province in the *nation* ▪ industrialized/developing *nations* ▪ the United *Nations* **b *the nation* : the people who live in a nation** ▪ The President will speak to *the nation* tonight. ▪ *The* entire *nation* is celebrating the victory.

2 *Nation* [*count*] **: a tribe of Native Americans or a group of Native American tribes that share the same history, traditions, or language** ▪ the Cheyenne Indian *Nation* ▪ the Navajo *Nation*

[1]**na·tion·al** /ˈnæʃənl/ *adj*

1 : of or relating to an entire nation or country ▪ local and *national* governments ▪ *national* politics ▪ the *national* economy ▪ *national* security/defense ▪ the country's *national* flag/symbol ▪ She won the *national* championship/title last year. ▪ His test scores were higher than the *national* average. ▪ They were *national* heroes. ▪ Doing well in the Olympics is a matter of *national* pride. ▪ Baseball is called America's *national* pastime. ▪ The game was shown on *national* television.

2 *always used before a noun* **: owned and controlled or operated by a national government** ▪ Arlington *National* Cemetery in Washington, D.C. ▪ the *National* Museum of Art ▪ a *national* bank/forest

– na·tion·al·ly /ˈnæʃənəli/ *adv* ▪ a *nationally* televised game ▪ The movie opens *nationally* [=in theaters throughout the nation] this weekend. ▪ She ranks high *nationally* in her math and science scores. ▪ The university is known *nationally* and internationally for its writing program.

[2]**national** *noun, pl* **-als**

1 [*count*] *formal* **: a person who is a citizen of a country** ▪ She's a Mexican *national* now working in the United States. ▪ foreign *nationals*

2 *nationals* [*plural*] **: competitions in which people or teams from all areas of a country compete** ▪ The U.S. *Nationals* will be held in New York City this year.

national anthem *noun, pl* **~ -thems** [*count*] **: a song that praises a particular country and that is officially accepted as the country's song** ✧ ***National anthems* are often played or sung at special events.**

national debt *noun, pl* **~ debts** [*count*] **: the total amount of money that the government of a country owes to companies, countries, etc.**

National Guard *noun* [*singular*] **: a military group that is organized in each U.S. state but given money and supplies by the national government and that can be used by the state or the country**

National Health Service *noun*

***the National Health Service* : the public system of medical care in Britain that is paid for by taxes**

National Insurance *noun* [*noncount*] **: a British insurance system that workers and their employers contribute to regularly and which gives money to people who are retired, ill, or unemployed**

na·tion·al·ism /ˈnæʃənəˌlɪzəm/ *noun* [*noncount*]

1 : a feeling that people have of being loyal to and proud of their country often with the belief that it is better and more important than other countries ▪ The war was caused by *nationalism* and greed. — compare PATRIOTISM

2 : a desire by a large group of people (such as people who share the same culture, history, language, etc.) to form a separate and independent nation of their own ▪ Scottish *nationalism*

[1]**na·tion·al·ist** /ˈnæʃənəlɪst/ *noun, pl* **-ists** [*count*]

1 : a supporter of or believer in nationalism ▪ German/American/Russian *nationalists*

2 *or* ***Nationalist*** **: a member of a political group that wants to form a separate and independent nation** ▪ Irish *Nationalists*

[2]**nationalist** *adj, always used before a noun*

1 : of or relating to nationalism ▪ *nationalist* beliefs/ideologies/sentiments

2 *or* ***Nationalist*** **: of or relating to a political group that wants to form a separate and independent nation** ▪ The country's *Nationalist* Party won the election.

na·tion·al·is·tic /ˌnæʃənəˈlɪstɪk/ *adj* [*more ~; most ~*] **: relating to or showing a belief that your country is better and more important than other countries** ▪ the political party's *nationalistic* ideology ▪ *nationalistic* election speeches

na·tion·al·i·ty /ˌnæʃəˈnæləti/ *noun, pl* **-ties**

1 [*count*] **: a group of people who share the same history, traditions, and language, and who usually live together in a particular country** ▪ The country is home to five *nationalities*

and seven languages. • people of all races and *nationalities*
2 *formal* **: the fact or status of being a member or citizen of a particular nation** [*noncount*] She's American, but her parents are of Japanese *nationality*. • He has held French *nationality* for the past 20 years. [*count*] The university has students of over 50 *nationalities*.

na·tion·al·ize /ˈnæʃənəˌlaɪz/ *also Brit* **na·tion·al·ise** *verb* **-iz·es; -ized; -iz·ing** [+ *obj*] **: to cause (something) to be under the control of a national government** • The government *nationalized* the health-care system in the mid-1950s. • *nationalizing* the country's oil supply — opposite PRIVATIZE, (*Brit*) DENATIONALIZE
– **na·tion·al·i·za·tion** *also Brit* **na·tion·al·i·sa·tion** /ˌnæʃənələˈzeɪʃən, *Brit* ˌnæʃənəˌlaɪˈzeɪʃən/ *noun* [*noncount*] • the *nationalization* of health care

National League *noun*
the National League **: one of the two major leagues in professional U.S. baseball** — compare AMERICAN LEAGUE

national monument *noun, pl* ~ **-ments** [*count*] **: a place (such as an old building or an area of land) that is owned and protected by a national government because of its natural beauty or its importance to history or science** • the Statue of Liberty *National Monument*

national park *noun, pl* ~ **parks** [*count*] **: an area of land that is owned and protected by a national government because of its natural beauty or its importance to history or science** • Yellowstone *National Park*

na·tion·hood /ˈneɪʃənˌhʊd/ *noun* [*noncount*] **: the state of being an independent nation** • the early days of U.S. *nationhood* • The colonists showed a strong desire for *nationhood*.

na·tion–state /ˈneɪʃənˈsteɪt/ *noun, pl* **-states** [*count*] **: a form of political organization in which a group of people who share the same history, traditions, or language live in a particular area under one government**

na·tion·wide /ˌneɪʃənˈwaɪd/ *adj* **: including or involving all parts of a nation or country** • The murders attracted *nationwide* attention.
– **nationwide** *adv* • The company has opened several stores *nationwide*.

¹na·tive /ˈneɪtɪv/ *adj*
1 *always used before a noun* **a : born in a particular place** • I'm a *native* New Yorker. [=I was born in New York] • people who are *native* to France **b — used to refer to the place where a person was born and raised** • He's a hero in his *native* country. • After 30 years, I am finally returning to my *native* land.
2 a *always used before a noun* **: belonging to a person since birth or childhood** • She speaks English, but it's not her *native* [=*first*] language/tongue. — see also NATIVE SPEAKER
b : existing naturally as an ability, quality, etc., that someone has • She has a *native* ability to learn quickly. • his *native* wit
3 a : produced, living, or existing naturally in a particular region • *native* [=*indigenous*] birds and animals • The island is home to several *native* species of trees. — often + *to* • birds that are *native to* the continent **b — used to refer to the place or type of place where a plant or animal normally or naturally lives** • Increasing pollution is endangering the plant's *native* habitat.
4 *always used before a noun* **: of or relating to a group of people who were living in an area (such as North America or Africa) when a new group of usually European people arrived** • *native* societies • *native* art/traditions • *native* inhabitants/peoples
go native **: to start to behave or live like the local people** • After a few weeks, she was comfortable enough to *go native* and wear shorts to work.

²native *noun, pl* **-tives** [*count*]
1 : a person who was born or raised in a particular place • She's a *native* of France who moved to the United States when she was 15. • I'm a California *native*. • He wishes he could speak Spanish like a *native*.
2 : a person from a group of people who were living in an area (such as South America or Africa) when Europeans first arrived ✧ This sense of *native* was commonly used in the past but is now often considered offensive.
3 : a kind of plant or animal that originally grew or lived in a particular place • The plant is a *native* of Central and South America.

Native American *noun, pl* ~ **-cans** [*count*] **: a member of any of the first groups of people living in North America or South America;** *especially* **: a member of one of these groups from the U.S.**

> ***usage*** *Native American* is the term that is now most often used for people whose ancestors lived in North and South America before the arrival of Europeans in 1492. The term *American Indian* is also often used, but it is offensive to some people. The term *Indian* by itself is also still used but is now often considered offensive and should usually be avoided.

– **Native American** *adj* • *Native American* tribes • their *Native American* ancestors • She's part *Native American*.

native speaker *noun, pl* ~ **-ers** [*count*] **: a person who learned to speak the language of the place where they were born as a child rather than learning it as a foreign language** • She's a *native speaker* of Swahili. • That kind of mistake is rarely made by *native speakers*.

Na·tiv·i·ty /nəˈtɪvəti/ *noun*
the Nativity **: the birth of Jesus** • a painting of *the Nativity*
– **Nativity** *or* **nativity** *adj, always used before a noun* • the *nativity* stories in the Bible • a ***Nativity scene*** [=a picture or a set of statues representing the birth of Jesus]

natl. *or* **nat'l** *abbr* national

NATO /ˈneɪtoʊ/ *abbr* North Atlantic Treaty Organization ✧ NATO is an organization of countries that have agreed to provide military support to each other. It includes many European countries as well as the U.S. and Canada.

nat·ter /ˈnætɚ/ *verb* **-ters; -tered; -ter·ing** [*no obj*] *chiefly Brit* **: to talk about unimportant things for a long time** • If you ask about his grandchildren, he'll *natter* on about them for hours. • She *nattered* about herself through our entire meal.
– **natter** *noun* [*singular*] *Brit* • We had a nice *natter* [=*chat*] on the phone.

nat·ty /ˈnæti/ *adj* **nat·ti·er; -est** *informal* **: very neat and clean** • a soldier in his *natty* blue uniform • He's quite a *natty* dresser.
– **nat·ti·ly** /ˈnætəli/ *adv* • a *nattily* dressed man

¹nat·u·ral /ˈnætʃərəl/ *adj*
1 a : existing in nature and not made or caused by people : coming from nature • *natural* silk • furniture made of *natural* materials • The river forms a *natural* boundary between the two countries. • That's not his *natural* hair color. [=he dyes his hair] • a *natural* lake [=a lake that is not man-made] • She prefers to use *natural* light [=light from the sun] when taking photographs. • a country rich in ***natural resources*** [=a country that has many valuable plants, animals, minerals, etc.] • learning more about the ***natural world*** [=animals, plants, etc.] **b : not having any extra substances or chemicals added : not containing anything artificial** • *natural* soap/yogurt • ***natural foods*** like whole grain bread and fresh vegetables • Our bakery uses ***all-natural*** ingredients. [=ingredients that are from nature and not artificial]
2 : usual or expected : NORMAL • Gray hair is one of the *natural* consequences of getting older. • a *natural* increase in the population • the *natural* course of the disease • It's perfectly/only *natural* to feel nervous before a test. • He died of ***natural causes***. [=he died because he was ill or old and not by being killed in an accident, battle, etc.] — see also NATURAL CHILDBIRTH
3 *always used before a noun* **— used to describe a quality, ability, etc., that a person or animal is born with and does not have to learn** • The science class will encourage his *natural* curiosity. • She has a *natural* talent for art. • He has a *natural* ability to make people feel comfortable. • She's a *natural* athlete/leader. [=she has natural abilities that make her a good athlete/leader]
4 ✧ To ***be/act/look natural*** is to be normal and relaxed in the way you behave and look. • I'm going to take your picture but don't pose—*look natural*. • Try to *be/act natural*.
5 *always used before a noun* **a : related by blood** • his *natural* mother [=the woman who gave birth to him] • She was adopted immediately after she was born and never knew her *natural* [=(more commonly) *birth*] parents. **b** *old-fashioned* **: born to parents who are not married to each other : ILLEGITIMATE** • a *natural* son/daughter
6 *of a choice, decision, etc.* **: logical and reasonable** • We considered our options, and this car was the *natural* choice. [=the choice that made the most sense] • He is the *natural* choice to succeed his father as company president. • They made the *natural* decision to keep trying.
7 *always used before a noun, formal* **: based on a sense of what is right and wrong** • ***natural justice/law***
8 *music* **: neither a sharp nor flat** • B *natural* • F *natural*

– **nat·u·ral·ness** /ˈnætʃərəlnəs/ *noun* [*noncount*] ▪ his *naturalness* as an actor ▪ the *naturalness* of his acting

²natural *noun, pl* **-rals** [*count*]

1 a : someone who is good at doing something from the first time it is done **:** someone who has a natural ability to do something — usually singular ▪ She loved rock climbing from the start. She's a *natural*. — often + *at* ▪ He's a *natural at* (playing) the piano. ▪ a *natural at* golf **b :** someone or something that is suited for a particular job, purpose, etc. — usually singular; usually + *for* ▪ He is a *natural for* the job. ▪ The bread's texture makes it a *natural for* eating with stew.

2 a : a musical note that is neither sharp nor flat **b :** a written symbol ♮ that is placed before a musical note to show that it is neither sharp nor flat

natural–born *adj, always used before a noun* **:** able to do something well immediately or from the very first time ▪ She's a *natural-born* artist/leader. [=she has natural abilities that make her a good artist/leader]

natural childbirth *noun* [*noncount*] **:** a method of giving birth to a baby in which the mother chooses not to use drugs to reduce pain or to make the birth happen more quickly

natural disaster *noun, pl* **~ -ters** [*count*] **:** a sudden and terrible event in nature (such as a hurricane, tornado, or flood) that usually results in serious damage and many deaths

natural gas *noun* [*noncount*] **:** gas that is taken from under the ground and used as fuel ▪ a house heated by *natural gas*

natural history *noun* [*noncount*] **:** the study of plants, animals, and sometimes ancient human civilizations ▪ the *natural history* of bees ▪ We went to the *Natural History* Museum.

nat·u·ral·ism /ˈnætʃərəˌlɪzəm/ *noun* [*noncount*] **:** a style of art or literature that shows people and things as they actually are

¹nat·u·ral·ist /ˈnætʃərəlɪst/ *noun, pl* **-ists** [*count*] **:** a person who studies plants and animals as they live in nature ▪ a world-renowned *naturalist*

²naturalist *adj* **:** NATURALISTIC 2 ▪ a *naturalist* painting/painter

nat·u·ral·is·tic /ˌnætʃərəˈlɪstɪk/ *adj* [*more* ~; *most* ~]

1 : looking like what appears in nature **:** not looking artificial or man-made ▪ The zoo strives to create *naturalistic* settings for the animals.

2 : using naturalism in art or literature **:** showing people or things as they really are ▪ *naturalistic* writing/paintings

nat·u·ral·ize *also Brit* **nat·u·ral·ise** /ˈnætʃərəˌlaɪz/ *verb* **-iz·es; -ized; -iz·ing**

1 [+ *obj*] **:** to allow (someone who was born in a different country) to become a new citizen ▪ The government refused to *naturalize* them without documentation. ▪ *naturalized* citizens of the U.S.

2 : to cause (a plant or animal from another place) to begin to grow and live in a new area [+ *obj*] Several Asian fish have become *naturalized* in these lakes. ▪ Before you *naturalize* bulbs in your lawn, fertilize well. [*no obj*] These daisies *naturalize* well in the Pacific Northwest.

– **nat·u·ral·i·za·tion** *also Brit* **nat·u·ral·i·sa·tion** /ˌnætʃərələˈzeɪʃən, *Brit* ˌnætʃərəˌlaɪˈzeɪʃən/ *noun* [*noncount*] ▪ immigrants seeking *naturalization* ▪ the *naturalization* of new plants in the river basin

nat·u·ral·ly /ˈnætʃərəli/ *adv*

1 — used to describe something that happens or exists by itself without being controlled or changed by someone ▪ Her hair curls *naturally*. ▪ a *naturally* sweet tea ▪ A number of important vitamins are found *naturally* in dark green vegetables like spinach. ▪ Pearls are produced *naturally* by oysters. ▪ He is *naturally* blond. ▪ Their friendship developed *naturally* over time.

2 — used to say that something is expected or normal ▪ *Naturally*, some mistakes were made. ▪ When he heard the comment, he was *naturally* [=*of course*] a little offended. ▪ *Naturally* you'll want rooms for the night. ▪ "Did you visit her while you were there?" "*Naturally*." [=*of course; yes*]

3 : because of a quality or skill that a person or animal is born with ▪ She's *naturally* competitive. ▪ He's *naturally* able to make people feel comfortable. ▪ Cats are said to be *naturally* curious.

4 : in a way that is relaxed and normal ▪ It's hard to speak/act *naturally* when you're nervous.

5 : in a way that makes sense **:** in a logical and reasonable way ▪ Her conclusions follow *naturally* from the theory. ▪ Questions about the journalist's sources arise *naturally* from such a controversial report. ▪ When I saw that there were no lights on in the house, I *naturally* assumed you were asleep.

come naturally ✧ If something *comes naturally* to you, you are able to do or learn it easily. ▪ Musical talent *comes naturally* to that family. ▪ Memorizing important dates in history *came naturally* to him [=was easy for him] in school.

natural science *noun, pl* **~ -ences :** a science (such as physics, chemistry, or biology) that studies the physical and natural world or the events that happen in nature [*count*] He is interested in the *natural sciences*. [*noncount*] a new approach to *natural science*

natural selection *noun* [*noncount*] **:** the process by which plants and animals that can adapt to changes in their environment are able to survive and reproduce while those that cannot adapt do not survive

natural wastage *noun* [*noncount*] *Brit* **:** ATTRITION 1

na·ture /ˈneɪtʃɚ/ *noun, pl* **-tures**

1 *also* **Nature** [*noncount*] **a :** the physical world and everything in it (such as plants, animals, mountains, oceans, stars, etc.) that is not made by people ▪ the beauty of *nature* ▪ She is a real *nature* lover. = She really loves *nature*. [=she loves to spend time outdoors] ▪ He devoted himself to the study of *nature*. ▪ That is a color not found in *nature*. ▪ *nature* photography ▪ *nature* conservation **b :** the natural forces that control what happens in the world ▪ the forces of *nature* ▪ Hunger is *nature's* way of telling you to eat. ▪ Gravity is one of the basic ***laws of nature***. — see also CALL OF NATURE, FREAK OF NATURE, MOTHER NATURE

2 : the way that a person or animal behaves **:** the character or personality of a person or animal [*count*] She has a competitive *nature*. [=she is competitive] ▪ The differences in their *natures* was easy to see. ▪ an animal with a gentle *nature* [=a gentle animal] [*noncount*] The children took advantage of the teacher's good *nature*. [=the teacher's kindness] ▪ She's very competitive ***by nature***. — see also GOOD-NATURED, HUMAN NATURE, ILL-NATURED, SECOND NATURE

3 : a basic quality that something has [*count*] — usually singular; often + *of* ▪ the *nature of* steel ▪ What is the true *nature of* democracy? ▪ Because of the fragile *nature of* the manuscripts [=because the manuscripts are fragile], the museum keeps them behind glass. [*noncount*] Her writing is humorous ***in nature***. [=her writing has humorous qualities]

4 [*singular*] **:** a particular kind of thing ▪ What is the *nature* of your problem? [=what kind of problem do you have?] ▪ papers of a confidential *nature* [=papers that are confidential] ▪ His medical condition is not of a serious *nature*. [=is not serious] ▪ You'll need to bring a toothbrush, soap, and things ***of that nature***. [=other similar things]

get/go back to nature *also* ***return to nature*** **:** to spend time living in a simple way without modern machines, electricity, etc. ▪ They went on a camping trip to *get back to nature*.

let nature take its course **:** to allow something to happen without trying to control it ▪ The injury should heal within a few weeks if you just *let nature take its course*.

nature reserve *noun, pl* **~ -serves** [*count*] **:** an area where animals and plants are protected and that has few buildings or homes — called also (*US*) *nature preserve*

nature trail *noun, pl* **~ trails** [*count*] **:** a path through a forest, field, mountain range, etc., that is used for hiking and seeing plants and animals

na·tur·ism /ˈneɪtʃəˌrɪzəm/ *noun* [*noncount*] *Brit* **:** NUDISM

na·tur·ist /ˈneɪtʃərɪst/ *noun, pl* **-ists** [*count*] *Brit* **:** NUDIST

na·tu·rop·a·thy /ˌneɪtʃəˈrɑːpəθi/ *noun* [*noncount*] **:** the treatment of illness by using diet, herbs, exercises, etc., without using standard drugs or surgery

– **na·tu·ro·path** /ˈneɪtʃərəˌpæθ/ *noun, pl* **-paths** [*count*] ▪ She has been trained as a *naturopath*. – **na·tu·ro·path·ic** /ˌneɪtʃərəˈpæθɪk/ *adj* [*more* ~; *most* ~] ▪ a *naturopathic* treatment

naught (*chiefly US*) *or chiefly Brit* **nought** /ˈnɑːt/ *pronoun, old-fashioned* **:** ¹NOTHING ▪ All our efforts ***came to naught***. = (*US*) All our efforts ***went for naught***. [=we did not succeed in doing what we were trying to do] ▪ (*chiefly US*) It was ***all for naught***. [=it was all for nothing]

naugh·ty /ˈnɑːti/ *adj* **naugh·ti·er; -est**

1 : behaving badly — used especially to describe a child who does not behave properly or obey a parent, teacher, etc. ▪ a *naughty* [=*bad*] boy/girl ▪ Were you *naughty* today at school or did you obey the teacher? — sometimes used humorously to describe an adult who does something slightly wrong or improper ▪ I was *naughty* and cheated on my diet.

2 *informal* **:** relating to or suggesting sex in usually a playful way ▪ She gave him a *naughty* smile. ▪ No *naughty* [=*dirty*]

jokes in front of the children, please! ▪ a *naughty* outfit
– **naugh·ti·ly** /ˈnɑːtəli/ *adv* ▪ She smiled *naughtily*.
– **naugh·ti·ness** /ˈnɑːtinəs/ *noun [noncount]* ▪ Oh, you'll be punished for your *naughtiness*!

nau·sea /ˈnɑːzijə/ *noun [noncount]* : the feeling you have in your stomach when you think you are going to vomit ▪ Some people experience *nausea* when flying. ▪ A feeling/wave of *nausea* suddenly came over me.

nau·se·ate /ˈnɑːziˌeɪt/ *verb* **-ates; -at·ed; -at·ing** *[+ obj]*
1 : to cause (someone) to feel like vomiting ▪ The smell of gasoline *nauseates* me.
2 : to cause (someone) to feel disgusted ▪ It *nauseated* him to see the way the animals were treated.
– **nauseated** *adj* ▪ He was feeling weak and *nauseated*.

nauseating *adj [more ~; most ~]*
1 : causing you to feel like you are going to vomit ▪ the *nauseating* smell of rotting garbage
2 : causing disgust ▪ The way the animals were treated was *nauseating*. ▪ It was *nauseating* to see the two of them act like lovesick teenagers.
– **nau·se·at·ing·ly** *adv* ▪ His letter to her was *nauseatingly* sweet.

nau·seous /ˈnɑːʃəs, ˈnɑːzijəs/ *adj [more ~; most ~]*
1 : feeling like you are about to vomit ▪ The smell of gasoline makes me *nauseous*. ▪ I began to feel *nauseous*.
2 : causing you to feel like you are going to vomit ▪ the *nauseous* [=(more commonly) *nauseating*] smell of rotting garbage
3 : causing disgust ▪ the *nauseous* [=(more commonly) *nauseating*] spectacle of politicians blaming each other

nau·ti·cal /ˈnɑːtɪkəl/ *adj* : relating to ships and sailing ▪ a dictionary of *nautical* terms ▪ *nautical* charts

nautical mile *noun, pl* ~ **miles** *[count]* : a unit of distance equal to 1,852 meters or 1.15 miles that is used for sea and air travel

Na·va·jo /ˈnævəˌhoʊ/ *noun, pl* **Navajo** *or* **Na·va·jos**
1 *[count]* : a member of a Native American people originally from New Mexico and Arizona
2 *[noncount]* : the language of the Navajo people

na·val /ˈneɪvəl/ *adj, always used before a noun* : of or relating to a country's navy ▪ *naval* base/history/officer

nave /ˈneɪv/ *noun, pl* **naves** *[count]* : the long center part of a church where people sit

na·vel /ˈneɪvəl/ *noun, pl* **-vels** *[count]* : the small, hollow or raised area in the middle of your stomach — called also *belly button*; see picture at HUMAN

navel–gaz·ing /ˈneɪvəlˈgeɪzɪŋ/ *noun [noncount] somewhat humorous* : the activity of thinking too much or too deeply about yourself, your experiences, your feelings, etc. ▪ I think she's a good writer, but her essays are full of *navel-gazing*.

navel orange *noun, pl* ~ **-anges** *[count]* : a kind of orange that does not have seeds

nav·i·ga·ble /ˈnævɪgəbəl/ *adj* : deep and wide enough for boats and ships to travel on or through : capable of being navigated ▪ a *navigable* river ▪ The marsh was *navigable* only by canoe. — sometimes used figuratively ▪ This Web site is well-organized and easily *navigable*. [=it is easy to get from one Web page to another within that Web site] ▪ The legal system is not easily *navigable*. [=it is difficult to understand the legal system]
– **nav·i·ga·bil·i·ty** /ˌnævɪgəˈbɪləti/ *noun [noncount]* ▪ We are unsure about the *navigability* of the river.

nav·i·gate /ˈnævəˌgeɪt/ *verb* **-gates; -gat·ed; -gat·ing**
1 : to find the way to get to a place when you are traveling in a ship, airplane, car, etc. *[no obj]* For thousands of years, sailors *navigated* by the stars. ▪ How about if you drive and I *navigate*? *[+ obj]* I'd need a map to *navigate* the city. — often used figuratively ▪ We have had to carefully *navigate* (our way) through a maze of rules and regulations.
2 a : to sail on, over, or through an area of water *[+ obj]* Only flat-bottomed boats can safely *navigate* the canal. *[no obj]* He has learned to *navigate* in rough waters. **b** : to travel on, over, or through (an area or place) *[+ obj]* The downtown area is easily *navigated* on foot. ▪ She has trouble *navigating* the stairs with her crutches. *[no obj]* It took us 10 minutes to *navigate* through the parking lot to the exit.
3 *[+ obj]* : to control the direction of (something, such as a ship or airplane) : STEER ▪ The captain *navigated* the ship. ▪ He has had experience *navigating* airplanes through storms. — often used figuratively ▪ She has carefully *navigated* the company through some difficult times.
4 *computers* : to go to different places on the Internet or on a particular Web site in order to find what you want *[+ obj]* You *navigate* this site by clicking on the pictures. ▪ There are a number of browsers that can be used to *navigate* the Web/Internet. *[no obj]* A fast connection makes it easier to *navigate* on the Internet.

nav·i·ga·tion /ˌnævəˈgeɪʃən/ *noun [noncount]*
1 : the act, activity, or process of finding the way to get to a place when you are traveling in a ship, airplane, car, etc. ▪ If you're going to be a good sailor/pilot, you need to master *navigation*. ▪ *navigation* by satellite ▪ I don't mind driving if you're willing to do the *navigation*. ▪ Our new car has an onboard *navigation* system.
2 : the act of moving in a boat or ship over an area of water ▪ *Navigation* becomes more difficult further upriver.
3 *computers* : the act of going to different places on the Internet or on a particular Web site in order to find what you want ▪ There are back and forward buttons for easier browser *navigation*.
– **nav·i·ga·tion·al** /ˌnævəˈgeɪʃənl/ *adj, always used before a noun* ▪ The car is equipped with a *navigational* system.

nav·i·ga·tor /ˈnævəˌgeɪtɚ/ *noun, pl* **-tors** *[count]*
1 : a person who finds out how to get to a place : a person who navigates a ship, an airplane, etc. ▪ The crew includes a copilot and a *navigator*. ▪ Would you be willing to act as *navigator* while I drive?
2 : a device (such as a computer) that is used to plan or find the route to a place ▪ The ship is equipped with a satellite *navigator*.

nav·vy /ˈnævi/ *noun, pl* **-vies** *[count] Brit* : a worker who does very hard physical labor

na·vy /ˈneɪvi/ *noun, pl* **-vies**
1 *[count]* : the part of a country's military forces that fights at sea using ships, submarines, airplanes, etc. ▪ A similar submarine is used by several foreign *navies*. ▪ a career in the *navy* — usually capitalized when a specific navy is being referred to ▪ the Russian *Navy* ▪ He plans to join the *Navy*.
2 *[noncount]* : NAVY BLUE ▪ The shirt comes in black, white, and *navy*. ▪ a *navy* sweater

navy bean *noun, pl* ~ **beans** *[count] US* : a type of white bean — called also *(Brit) haricot bean*

navy blue *noun [noncount]* : a very dark blue ▪ I ordered the same jacket in *navy blue*. — called also *navy*; see color picture on page C2
– **navy blue** *adj* ▪ a *navy blue* dress

[1]nay /ˈneɪ/ *adv*
1 *old-fashioned + literary* — used to correct what you have said by replacing a word with one that is more accurate or appropriate ▪ The letter made her happy—*nay*, ecstatic. [=it did not just make her happy, it made her ecstatic]
2 *old-fashioned* : [1]NO ▪ *Nay*, I do not wish to go. ▪ I dare not say him *nay*. [=I dare not say no to him]

[2]nay *noun, pl* **nays** *[count] formal* : a no vote ▪ We have 6 *nays* [=6 votes of "no"] and 12 yeas, so the measure passes. — compare [2]AYE, [2]YEA

nay·say·er /ˈneɪˌsejɚ/ *noun, pl* **-ers** *[count] formal* : a person who says something will not work or is not possible : a person who denies, refuses, or opposes something ▪ There are always *naysayers* who say it can't be done.

Na·zi /ˈnɑːtsi/ *noun, pl* **-zis** *[count]*
1 : a member of a German political party that controlled Germany from 1933 to 1945 under Adolf Hitler
2 *disapproving* : an evil person who wants to use power to control and harm other people especially because of their race, religion, etc. ▪ a gang of racist *Nazis* — see also NEO-NAZI
– **Nazi** *adj* ▪ *Nazi* ideology – **Na·zism** /ˈnɑːtˌsɪzəm/ *noun [noncount]*

NB *also* **N.B.** *abbr* please note — used in writing to tell the reader that something is important ▪ *NB*: applications will not be accepted after May 5. ✧ The abbreviation *NB* comes from the Latin phrase "nota bene," which means "mark well."

NBA *abbr, US* National Basketball Association ✧ The NBA is the major professional basketball league in the U.S.

NBC *abbr, US* National Broadcasting Company ✧ NBC is one of the major television networks in the U.S.

NC *abbr* North Carolina

NCAA *abbr, US* National Collegiate Athletic Association ✧ The NCAA is an organization that organizes athletic activities for many U.S. colleges and universities.

NCO /ˌɛnˌsiːˈoʊ/ *noun, pl* **NCOs** *[count]* : NONCOMISSIONED OFFICER

NC–17 /ˈɛnˈsiːˌsɛvənˈtiːn/ — used as a special mark to indicate that no one who is 17 years old or younger may see a particular movie in a movie theater ▪ The movie is rated *NC-17*. — compare G, PG, PG-13, R, X

ND *abbr* North Dakota

-nd — used in writing after the number 2 for the word *second* ▪ He's in 2*nd* [=*second*] grade. ▪ She came in 42*nd* in the race.

NE *abbr* **1** Nebraska **2** New England **3** northeast

Ne·an·der·thal /niˈændɚˌtɑːl/ *noun, pl* **-thals** [*count*]
1 : a type of early human being that existed very long ago in Europe — called also *Neanderthal man*
2 *informal* + *disapproving* **a :** a man who is stupid and rude ▪ I can't believe I was married to that *Neanderthal* for three years. **b :** a person who has very old-fashioned ideas and who does not like change ▪ Some *Neanderthals* continue to resist the education reform bill.

Ne·a·pol·i·tan ice cream /ˌniːjəˈpɑːlətən-/ *noun* [*noncount*] **:** ice cream with three different flavors (such as strawberry, vanilla, and chocolate) that are arranged in layers

[1]**near** /ˈniɚ/ *adv* **near·er; -est**
1 : close to someone or something in distance ▪ I hope that dog doesn't come any *nearer* (to me). ▪ Be sure to have a fire extinguisher ***near at hand***. [=close enough to reach easily] — often used figuratively ▪ We're getting *nearer* to the truth. ▪ We came very *near* to canceling the trip. [=we almost canceled the trip] ▪ Her new book is good, but it doesn't even come *near* to her first book. [=it is not nearly as good as her first book]
2 : not far away in time ▪ The end of the long winter is *near*. [=it will happen soon] ▪ He became more nervous as the day of the wedding ***drew near***. [=*approached*; got closer]
3 : almost or nearly ▪ The plant was *near* dead when I got it. ▪ a *near* perfect score ▪ The job is (damn/damned/darn) *near* impossible. — see also *nowhere near* at [1]NOWHERE
as near as damn it or ***as near as dammit*** *Brit, informal* — used to say that something is so close to being correct or true that it can be regarded as correct or true ▪ The hotel room will cost 300 pounds, *as near as damn it*. ▪ She's the best player in the world or *as near as dammit*.
(as) near as I can tell/figure *US, informal* **:** based on what I know ▪ *As near as I can tell*, we'll arrive by six o'clock.
from far and near, from near and far see [1]FAR

[2]**near** *prep* **:** close to (something or someone) ▪ I left the box *near* the door. ▪ The cat won't go *near* fire. ▪ She stood *near* me. ▪ There are several beaches *near* here. ▪ She came home *near* midnight. ▪ We feared he was *near* death.

[3]**near** *adj* **nearer; -est**
1 : located a short distance away **:** CLOSE ▪ The *nearest* grocery store is three blocks away. ▪ The airport is quite *near*. [=*nearby*]
2 : not far away in time ▪ Summer is getting *nearer*. ▪ I hope to visit in the *near* future. [=I hope to visit soon]
3 *always used before a noun* **a** — used to refer to the side, end, etc., that is closer ▪ There is a fishing camp on the far side of the lake, but nothing on the *near* side. **b** *Brit, of a car* **:** LEFT-HAND ▪ The *near* side headlight is out. — compare OFF; see also NEARSIDE
4 *always used before a noun* **:** almost happening ▪ The ceremony was a *near* disaster. [=was nearly a disaster] ▪ After a *near* win [=after nearly winning] in the first competition, he is ready to try again. ▪ (*Brit*) Our team won the match, but it was a very ***near thing***. [=we almost lost the match] — see also NEAR MISS
5 *always used before a noun* **a :** close to being something ▪ Her victory is a *near* certainty. [=it is nearly certain that she will win] ▪ a *near* miracle ▪ celebrities and *near* celebrities [=people who are almost celebrities] **b** ***nearest*** **:** most similar ▪ The lake was the *nearest* thing to an ocean [=the thing most like an ocean] that she had ever seen.
6 : coming after someone or something **:** in the position or rank after someone or something ▪ He finished the race ahead of his *nearest* rival by only a few feet.
7 *always used before a noun* **:** closely related ▪ These two kinds of plants are *near* relatives. ▪ Only ***near relations*** [=sisters, brothers, parents, etc.] were invited to the wedding.
near and dear **:** very close in relationship ▪ friends who are *near and dear* ▪ my ***nearest and dearest*** friend
too near for comfort see [1]COMFORT
to the nearest — used to indicate the number of pounds, dollars, etc., that is closest to a slightly higher or lower number or amount ▪ What is the weight of your baggage *to the nearest* pound? ▪ $13.75 rounded up *to the nearest* dollar is $14.
— **near·ness** *noun* [*noncount*] ▪ He missed her *nearness*. [=*closeness*] ▪ the *nearness* of the storm

[4]**near** *verb* **nears; neared; near·ing :** to come closer in space or time to someone or something **:** APPROACH [*no obj*] As the date of the performance *neared*, we grew more and more anxious. ▪ He always cheers up when baseball season *nears*. [+ *obj*] The airplane began to descend as it *neared* the island. ▪ He must be *nearing* 80 years of age. ▪ The negotiators were *nearing* a decision. ▪ The project is ***nearing completion***. [=is almost finished]

near·by /niɚˈbaɪ/ *adj* **:** not far away **:** located at a short distance from someone or something ▪ a *nearby* village/river ▪ I spoke with a *nearby* policeman about the accident. ▪ He works at the *nearby* university.
— **nearby** *adv* ▪ They live *nearby*. ▪ The children played *nearby* at the park.

near–death experience *noun, pl* ~ **-ences** [*count*] **:** an occurrence in which a person comes very close to dying and has memories of a spiritual experience (such as meeting dead friends and family members or seeing a white light) during the time when death was near

Near East *noun*
the Near East **:** MIDDLE EAST

near·ly /ˈniɚli/ *adv* **:** not completely **:** almost but not quite ▪ I see her *nearly* every day. ▪ We very *nearly* missed the plane. [=we came very close to missing the plane] ▪ I *nearly* won. ▪ I am *nearly* finished. ▪ We lived there for *nearly* two years. ▪ *Nearly* 100 people attended. ▪ *Nearly* all of us got sick that weekend.
not nearly **:** much less than **:** not at all ▪ There's *not nearly* enough flour for a cake here. ▪ It's *not nearly* as late as I thought it was.

near miss *noun, pl* ~ **miss·es** [*count*]
1 : an attempt that is almost successful ▪ After years of *near misses*, the team has finally won a championship.
2 : an accident that is just barely avoided ▪ There have been two *near misses* [=*close calls*] at that airport recently.
3 : a bomb that misses its target but still causes damage

near·side /ˈniɚˌsaɪd/ *adj, Brit* **:** on the left side **:** LEFT-HAND ▪ The car's *nearside* headlight is out. ▪ the *nearside* lane
the nearside **:** the left-hand side ▪ The car was hit on *the nearside*.— compare OFFSIDE

near·sight·ed /ˈniɚˌsaɪtəd/ *adj, chiefly US* **:** unable to see things that are far away **:** able to see things that are close more clearly than things that are far away ▪ He needs glasses because he's *nearsighted*. [=(*chiefly Brit*) *shortsighted*] — compare FARSIGHTED
— **near·sight·ed·ness** /ˈniɚˌsaɪtədnəs/ *noun* [*noncount*]

neat /ˈniːt/ *adj* **neat·er; -est**
1 : not messy **:** clean and orderly ▪ He keeps his apartment *neat* and clean. ▪ *neat* handwriting ▪ The store is always busy but they manage to keep the shelves stocked and *neat*. ▪ a nice *neat* pile of magazines ▪ Try to be a little *neater* [=try not to make such a mess] the next time you bake cookies. ▪ Fold the paper to make a *neat* edge.
2 : liking to keep things very clean and orderly ▪ His two roommates are both pretty *neat* people. [=they both like to have things cleaned up and put away] ▪ a *neat* man who always wore a suit
3 a : simple and clever ▪ a *neat* trick ▪ He's got a *neat* way of memorizing information. ▪ There is, unfortunately, no *neat* solution to the problem. **b** *US, informal* **:** pleasant, fun, or interesting ▪ I think it's a *neat* idea [=a good idea] to invite the new neighbors to the cookout. ▪ She's a *neat* person who has traveled a lot.
4 *of alcoholic drinks* **:** not mixed with anything **:** made without ice or water added ▪ I like my bourbon/whiskey *neat*. [=(*US*) *straight*]
— **neat·ly** *adv* ▪ The books were stacked *neatly* in the corner. ▪ *neatly* arranged plates ▪ The children were dressed *neatly* for the ceremony. — **neat·ness** *noun* [*noncount*] ▪ I was amazed by the *neatness* of the room.

neat·en /ˈniːtn̩/ *verb* **-ens; -ened; -en·ing :** to make (something) orderly or neat **:** to clean up (something) [+ *obj*] I am trying to *neaten* my desk. — often + *up* ▪ I didn't have a chance to *neaten up* the house before the guests arrived. [*no obj*] — + *up* ▪ *Neaten up* before you leave.

neat freak *noun, pl* ~ **freaks** [*count*] *US, informal* **:** a person who always wants things to be very orderly and clean ▪ My first college roommate was a real *neat freak*.

'neath /ˈniːθ/ *prep, literary* : BENEATH ▪ We slumbered *'neath* the starry sky.

neb·u·la /ˈnɛbjələ/ *noun, pl* **-lae** /-ˌliː/ *also* **-las** [*count*] *astronomy*

1 : a cloud of gas or dust in space that can sometimes be seen at night

2 : a group of stars that are very far away and look like a bright cloud at night

– neb·u·lar /ˈnɛbjələ/ *adj* ▪ *nebular* gases

neb·u·lous /ˈnɛbjələs/ *adj, formal* : not clear : difficult to see, understand, describe, etc. ▪ These philosophical concepts can be *nebulous.* ▪ She gave a *nebulous* [=*vague*] answer to the question.

nec·es·sar·i·ly /ˌnɛsəˈserəli/ *adv, formal* — used to say that something is necessary and cannot be changed or avoided ▪ This endeavor *necessarily* involves some risk.

not necessarily : possibly but not certainly — used to say that something is not definitely true ▪ Seats in the front row are *not necessarily* the best. ▪ "We're going to lose this game." "*Not necessarily.*" [=maybe not]

¹nec·es·sary /ˈnɛsəˌseri, *Brit* ˈnɛsəsri/ *adj*

1 [*more ~; most ~*] **:** so important that you must do it or have it : absolutely needed ▪ Is it really/absolutely *necessary* for me to have surgery? ▪ The threat of a thunderstorm made it *necessary* to cancel the picnic. ▪ It's not *necessary* to wear a tie. ▪ Food is *necessary* for life. ▪ We had all the *necessary* ingredients. ▪ Apply another coat of paint ***if necessary.*** [=if it is needed] ▪ Take as much time ***as necessary.*** [=as much time as you need] ▪ She took the medicine only ***when absolutely necessary.*** ▪ a ***medically necessary*** procedure

2 *always used before a noun, formal* **:** unable to be changed or avoided ▪ Higher prices are a ***necessary consequence*** of the company's new services. ▪ There is no ***necessary connection*** between what is legal and what is moral. [=what is legal does not always have to be moral and what is moral does not always have to be legal]

necessary evil see ²EVIL

²necessary *noun, pl* **-sar·ies**

1 ***necessaries*** [*plural*] **:** things (such as food, a place to live, and clothing) that you must have : necessary things ▪ We need the *necessaries* [=(more commonly) *necessities*] of life (to survive).

2 ***the necessary*** *Brit, informal* **:** whatever is needed for some purpose ▪ I'll ***do the necessary*** [=do whatever is necessary] to get the job done.

ne·ces·si·tate /nɪˈsɛsəˌteɪt/ *verb* **-tates; -tat·ed; -tat·ing** [+ *obj*] *formal* **:** to make (something) necessary ▪ New safety regulations *necessitated* adding a railing to the stairs.

ne·ces·si·ty /nɪˈsɛsəti/ *noun, pl* **-ties**

1 [*count*] **:** something that you must have or do : something that is necessary ▪ Sunscreen is an absolute *necessity* for the beach. ▪ food, clothes, and other basic *necessities* ▪ Getting plenty of rest is a *necessity.* ▪ Without a car, living close to work is a *necessity.* ▪ All we took with us on our hiking trip were the bare *necessities.* ▪ Many families cannot even afford the basic/bare ***necessities of life*** [=things that a person must have in order to survive]

2 [*noncount*] *formal* **:** the quality of being necessary — usually + *of* or *for* ▪ She talked about the *necessity of* having the right training. [=she said that having the right training is necessary] ▪ He questioned the *necessity for* the change. [=he questioned whether the change was necessary]

by necessity *or* ***out of necessity*** : because of conditions that cannot be changed ▪ The process is *by necessity* a slow one. [=the process is necessarily slow; the slowness of the process cannot be avoided] ▪ He works two jobs *out of necessity.* [=because it is necessary]

make a virtue (out) of necessity see VIRTUE

necessity is the mother of invention see ¹MOTHER

of necessity *formal* — used to say that something must happen or must be the way it is ▪ Further changes to the company will occur *of necessity.*

¹neck /ˈnɛk/ *noun, pl* **necks** [*count*]

1 : the part of the body between the head and the shoulders ▪ She craned/stretched her *neck* to see what was going on. ▪ A giraffe is an animal with a very long *neck.* ▪ He broke his *neck* in the accident. ▪ Stop jumping on the bed. You're going to ***break your neck*** [=you're going to hurt yourself] — see picture at HUMAN

2 : the part of a piece of clothing that fits around your neck ▪ He likes T-shirts with round *necks.* — see also CREW NECK, POLO NECK, SCOOP NECK, TURTLENECK, V-NECK

3 : a long and narrow part of something : a part that is shaped like a neck ▪ He grabbed the *neck* of the bottle. ▪ a *neck* of land [=a narrow stretch of land] ▪ a guitar's *neck*

breathe down someone's neck see BREATHE

dead from the neck up see ¹DEAD

get it in the neck *Brit, informal* : to be severely punished or criticized ▪ He really *got it in the neck* for not finishing the job on time.

neck and neck : extremely close together in a race or contest ▪ The two candidates for president were *neck and neck* in the election. ▪ The two horses were running *neck and neck* to the finish line.

neck of the woods *informal* : the place or area where someone lives ▪ He's from my *neck of the woods.* [=he's from the area where I live] ▪ How is the weather in your *neck of the woods?*

risk your neck : to do something that puts you in danger of serious injury or death ▪ I would never *risk my neck* on a sport like skydiving. ▪ News reporters often *risk their necks* by working in war zones.

save someone's neck see ¹SAVE

stick your neck out : to do or say something you think is important even though it may have bad results ▪ He's not afraid to *stick his neck out* to help people he thinks are being mistreated. ▪ I respect my boss because she will *stick her neck out* against unfair policies.

up to your neck in : deeply involved in or affected by (something) ▪ She's *up to her neck in* work. [=she's very busy] ▪ He's *up to his neck in* debt.

wring someone's neck see WRING

²neck *verb* **necks; necked; neck·ing** [*no obj*] *old-fashioned + informal* **:** to kiss for a long time in a sexual way ▪ The young lovers *necked* on the park bench. ▪ They were *necking* in the corner of the room.

neck–deep *adj*

1 : reaching as high as your neck ▪ She stood in *neck-deep* water.

2 : standing in something that reaches to your neck — usually + *in* ▪ She was *neck-deep in* water. — often used figuratively ▪ We were *neck-deep in* work. [=we were very busy]

– neck–deep *adv* ▪ She stood *neck-deep* in the water.

necked /ˈnɛkt/ *adj* **:** having a neck of a specified kind — used in combination with another adjective ▪ a round-*necked* T-shirt ▪ a long-*necked* bottle

neck·er·chief /ˈnɛkɚʧəf/ *noun, pl* **-chiefs** *also* **-chieves** /-ʧəfs/ [*count*] **:** a square piece of cloth that is worn folded around your neck

neck·lace /ˈnɛkləs/ *noun, pl* **-lac·es** [*count*] **:** a piece of jewelry that is worn around your neck ▪ a gold/diamond/pearl *necklace* — see color picture on page C11

neck·line /ˈnɛkˌlaɪn/ *noun, pl* **-lines** [*count*] **:** the shape of the opening of a piece of woman's clothing around the neck ▪ The dress has a square/round *neckline.* ▪ a low/plunging *neckline* [=a neckline that leaves the top part of your chest uncovered]

neck·tie /ˈnɛkˌtaɪ/ *noun, pl* **-ties** [*count*] *US* **:** a long piece of cloth that is worn by men around the neck and under a collar and that is tied in front with a knot at the top — called also *tie*; see color picture on page C14; compare BOLO TIE, BOW TIE, CRAVAT

nec·ro·man·cy /ˈnɛkrəˌmænsi/ *noun* [*noncount*] *literary*

1 : the practice of talking to the spirits of dead people

2 : the use of magic powers especially for evil purposes ▪ The town accused her of witchcraft and *necromancy.*

– nec·ro·man·cer /ˈnɛkrəˌmænsɚ/ *noun, pl* **-cers** [*count*] *literary*

nec·ro·phil·ia /ˌnɛkrəˈfɪlijə/ *noun* [*noncount*] **:** sexual feelings or activities that involve dead bodies

– nec·ro·phil·i·ac /ˌnɛkrəˈfɪliˌæk/ *noun, pl* **-acs** [*count*]

ne·crop·o·lis /nəˈkrɑːpələs/ *noun, pl* **-lis·es** [*count*] *formal* **:** a large cemetery especially of an ancient city ▪ Archaeologists uncovered a *necropolis* of ancient Rome.

nec·tar /ˈnɛktɚ/ *noun* [*noncount*]

1 *literary* **:** the drink that the Greek and Roman gods drank

2 : a thick juice made from a particular fruit ▪ apricot/mango *nectar*

3 : a sweet liquid produced by plants and used by bees in making honey

nec·tar·ine /ˌnɛktəˈriːn, *Brit* ˈnɛktəˌriːn/ *noun, pl* **-ines** [*count*] **:** a sweet fruit that is like a peach but that has smooth skin

née *or* **nee** /ˈneɪ/ *adj* — used after a married woman's name to identify the family name that she had when she was born ▪ Mrs. Jane Doe, *née* Smith

[1]**need** /ˈniːd/ *verb* **needs; need·ed; need·ing**

1 [+ *obj*] **:** to be in a condition or situation in which you must have (something) **:** to require (something) ▪ Do you *need* help? ▪ I *need* some advice. What do you think of this dress? ▪ I just *need* a couple of minutes to get ready. ▪ Most babies *need* at least 12 hours of sleep a day. ▪ We badly *need* a vacation. ▪ a badly *needed* vacation = a much-*needed* vacation ▪ Further research is urgently *needed* if we are to find a cure. ▪ Another delay is ***the last thing I need***! ▪ Men? ***Who needs them***?! I certainly don't. — often used of things ▪ This plant *needs* lots of sunlight. ▪ The soup *needs* some salt. [=this soup does not have enough salt] ▪ They're buying a house that *needs* a lot of work. [=that is in poor condition] ▪ This problem *needs* your attention. [=you should give your attention to this problem]

2 [+ *obj*] **a** — used to say that some action is necessary ▪ I've got a lot of laundry that *needs* washing. — usually followed by *to + verb* ▪ I've got a lot of laundry that *needs to be* washed. ▪ We *need to hurry* or we'll miss the bus. ▪ A lot of work *needs to be* done to the house. ▪ You don't *need to* [=*have to*] *answer* that if you don't want to. ▪ "Should we lock the car doors?" "No, I don't think we *need to*." **b** — used to say that it is important and necessary for someone to do something; followed by *to + verb* ▪ I *need* you *to tell* me the truth. [=you have to tell me the truth] ▪ We *need* you *to be* well-rested for the game tomorrow. ▪ We *need* you *to answer* a few questions.

3 [*modal verb*] — used to say that something is necessary ▪ All you *need* do is ask. [=all you need to do is ask] ▪ You *need* only look at her [=it is only necessary for you to look at her] to understand why I fell in love. — usually used in negative statements and in questions for which the answer is assumed by the speaker to be "no" ▪ You *needn't* leave if you don't want to. [=you don't have to leave if you don't want to] ▪ You *need not* answer these questions. [=you don't have to answer these questions] ▪ I told him he *needn't* worry. ▪ Nothing bad happened. You *need* not have worried. ▪ *Need* I point out that your father disagrees? ✧ The modal verb *need* is used especially in British English. In U.S. English, it is commonly used in phrases like ***need not apply*** and ***need I say more***. ▪ High school dropouts *need not apply*. [=they should not apply because they will not get the job] ▪ The movie was a complete waste of time. *Need I say more*? [=that is all I need to say]

need no introduction see INTRODUCTION

[2]**need** *noun, pl* **needs**

1 : a situation in which someone or something must do or have something [*noncount*] You can always call me at home if the *need* arises. ▪ These new methods reduce the *need* to use harmful chemicals on crops. [*singular*] We find that there is still a *need for* further discussion. ▪ There is a great/desperate/pressing *need for* change. — see also *a crying need* at CRYING

2 [*count*] **:** something that a person must have ▪ Our experienced staff will go out of their way to meet/satisfy/fulfill your every *need*. **:** something that is needed in order to live or succeed or be happy — usually plural ▪ She struggles to meet the daily *needs* of her children. ▪ the basic *needs* of every human being ▪ This ought to be enough money to cover/meet your immediate *needs*. ▪ economic/financial *needs* ▪ The house is large enough for the family's *needs*. — see also SPECIAL NEEDS

3 [*count*] **:** a strong feeling that you must have or do something ▪ He has trouble expressing his emotional *needs*. ▪ I felt a *need* to take control of the situation. ▪ a *need* to be loved ▪ She has an overwhelming *need* to be liked and respected. ▪ I don't feel the *need* to defend my decision. ▪ drivers who feel the *need* for speed [=who want to drive fast]

4 [*noncount*] **:** a situation in which people do not have things that they need ▪ They helped us ***in our hour of need***. [=when we most needed help] ▪ We can always count on them to help us ***in times of need***. [=when we need help] ▪ a charity that raises money for women and children ***in need*** [=who are poor] — see also *a friend in need is a friend indeed* at FRIEND

if need be **:** if something becomes necessary ▪ You can always call me at home *if need be*. ▪ We'll leave without them *if need be*. [=if we have to]

in need of — used to say that someone or something needs to have something ▪ The program is *in* desperate/dire/urgent *need of* financial support. ▪ More important things were *in need of* her attention. ▪ The trucks are *in* constant *need of* repair.

no need — used to say that something is not necessary ▪ "I'll get someone to help you." "*No need*. I can do it myself." — often followed by *to + verb* ▪ There's no *need to get* excited. ▪ There's no *need to apologize*. ▪ There's no *need to shout*. I can hear you. — often + *for* ▪ There's no *need for* him *to apologize*. ▪ There's no need *for* you *to shout*. = There's no *need for* shouting. ▪ There's no *need for* that kind of behavior. ▪ The doctor says that there's no *need for* surgery.

need·ful /ˈniːdfəl/ *adj* [*more* ~; *most* ~]

1 *formal + somewhat old-fashioned* **:** needed or necessary ▪ What's most *needful* now is patience.

2 *chiefly US* **:** in a state of needing something **:** NEEDY ▪ *needful* children — sometimes + *of* ▪ They are *needful of* protection. [=they need protection]

— need·ful·ness *noun* [*noncount*]

[1]**nee·dle** /ˈniːdl̩/ *noun, pl* **nee·dles** [*count*]

1 a : a small, very thin object that is used in sewing and that has a sharp point at one end and a hole for thread ▪ I need a *needle* and thread to sew the button on your shirt. — see picture at SEWING **b :** one of the two long, thin sticks that are used in knitting and that are pointed at one end **c :** a very thin, pointed steel tube that is pushed through the skin so that something (such as a drug) can be put into your body or so that blood or other fluids can be taken from it ▪ a hypodermic *needle* **d :** a very thin tube used with a pump to put air into a ball (such as a basketball or football)

2 : a long, thin object that moves to point to something (such as a measurement or direction) ▪ The *needle* on the scale points to 9 grams. ▪ The compass *needle* points north.

3 : a leaf that is shaped like a very thin stick ▪ pine *needles* — see color picture on page C6

4 : a very small piece of metal that touches a record and produces sound when the record is played ▪ the *needle* of a record player

a needle in a haystack informal **:** someone or something that is very hard to find ▪ Searching for your earring at the park will be like looking for *a needle in a haystack*. ▪ Bumping into an old friend in New York City is like finding a *needle in a haystack*.

— see also PINS AND NEEDLES

— nee·dle·like /ˈniːdl̩ˌlaɪk/ *adj* [*more* ~; *most* ~]

[2]**needle** *verb* **needles; nee·dled; nee·dling** [+ *obj*] *informal* **:** to criticize and laugh at (someone) in either a friendly or an unkind way **:** TEASE ▪ His classmates *needled* him about his new haircut.

nee·dle·point /ˈniːdl̩ˌpoɪnt/ *noun* [*noncount*]

1 : designs made by covering a piece of cloth with small stitches ▪ She sold her *needlepoint* at the arts and crafts fair.

2 : the activity or art of making needlepoint ▪ Her hobbies include knitting and *needlepoint*.

— needlepoint *adj, always used before a noun* ▪ *needlepoint* pillows/classes

need·less /ˈniːdləs/ *adj* [*more* ~; *most* ~] **:** not needed or necessary — used to describe something bad that did not have to happen ▪ *needless* [=*unnecessary*] waste ▪ *needless* human suffering ▪ a *needless* death

needless to say — used to say that the statement you are making is obvious ▪ The two candidates were equally popular. *Needless to say* [=*of course, obviously*], the election was very close.

— need·less·ly *adv* ▪ *needlessly* [=*unnecessarily*] complicated instructions **— need·less·ness** *noun* [*noncount*] ▪ the *needlessness* of his death

nee·dle·work /ˈniːdl̩ˌwɚk/ *noun* [*noncount*]

1 : things that are made by hand with a needle and thread ▪ She showed us a sample of her *needlework*.

2 : the activity or art of making needlework ▪ She still enjoys doing *needlework*.

needn't /ˈniːdn̩t/ — used as a contraction of *need not* ▪ You *needn't* worry about me. I'll be fine.

needy /ˈniːdi/ *adj* **need·i·er; -est** [*also more* ~; *most* ~]

1 : not having enough money, food, etc., to live properly **:** POOR ▪ *needy* families

2 : needing a lot of attention, affection, or emotional support ▪ As a child, she was extremely *needy* and had no self-confidence. ▪ emotionally *needy* adults

the needy **:** poor people ▪ Our church collected food for *the needy*.

— need·i·ness *noun* [*noncount*] ▪ emotional *neediness*

ne'er /ˈneɚ/ *adv, literary* **:** NEVER

ne'er–do–well /ˈneɚduˌwɛl/ *noun, pl* **-wells** [*count*] *old-fashioned* **:** a lazy and worthless person ▪ a *ne'er-do-well* who

hangs out at bars [=a person who goes to bars instead of working hard]
– ne'er–do–well *adj* • She was abandoned by her *ne'er-do-well* [=*good-for-nothing*] father.

ne·far·i·ous /nɪˈferijəs/ *adj* [*more ~; most ~*] *formal* : evil or immoral • *nefarious* criminal activities • a *nefarious* scheme to cheat people out of their money

neg. *abbr* negative

ne·gate /nɪˈgeɪt/ *verb* **-gates; -gat·ed; -gat·ing** [+ *obj*] *formal*
1 : to cause (something) to not be effective • Alcohol *negates* the effects of the medicine. [=alcohol prevents the medicine from working] • The fact that she lied about her work experience *negated* the contract.
2 *grammar* : to make (a word or phrase) negative • a verb that is *negated* by "not"
– ne·ga·tion /nɪˈgeɪʃən/ *noun, pl* **-tions** *formal* [*count*] — usually singular • The jury's verdict was a *negation* of justice. [=the jury's verdict was unjust] [*noncount*] actions done in *negation* of the rules

¹neg·a·tive /ˈnɛgətɪv/ *adj*
1 [*more ~; most ~*] : harmful or bad : not wanted • Car exhaust has a *negative* effect/impact on the environment. • the *negative* effects of the drug • We had a very *negative* [=*unpleasant*] experience at the restaurant. — opposite POSITIVE
2 [*more ~; most ~*] : thinking about the bad qualities of someone or something : thinking that a bad result will happen : not hopeful or optimistic • She has a *negative* attitude about the new plan. [=she only thinks about the things that can go wrong with the new plan] • Why do you have such a *negative* outlook on the merger? [=why do you think the merger won't work?] • "I know we're going to lose." "Don't be so *negative*." [=*pessimistic*] — opposite POSITIVE
3 a : expressing dislike or disapproval • The reviews were mostly *negative*. [=*unfavorable*] • The feedback about the new product was all *negative*. • There are no *negative* feelings between us. [=we do not dislike each other] — opposite POSITIVE **b** : showing or talking about the bad qualities of someone or something • The senator is running a *negative* campaign. [=a campaign that criticizes the other candidate instead of saying what good things the senator wants to do] • *negative* advertising [=advertising that criticizes competitors]
4 [*more ~; most ~*] : expressing denial or refusal • a *negative* reply/answer [=a reply of "no"] • *negative* words like "no" and "not" • "I didn't hear anything" is a *negative* phrase/construction/statement. — opposite AFFIRMATIVE
5 a *mathematics* : less than zero • My checking account has a *negative* balance. • -2 is a *negative* number. — opposite POSITIVE **b** : less than the amount of money spent or invested • We got a *negative* return on the investment. [=we lost money on the investment] — opposite POSITIVE
6 *technical* **a** : containing or producing electricity that is charged by an electron • a *negative* charge/current — opposite POSITIVE **b** : having more electrons than protons • a *negative* particle — opposite POSITIVE
7 : not showing the presence of a particular germ, condition, or substance • a *negative* HIV test • Her pregnancy test was *negative*. [=her test showed that she was not pregnant] — opposite POSITIVE
– neg·a·tive·ly *adv* • a *negatively* charged particle • The patient reacted *negatively* to the new drug. [=the patient had harmful side effects from the drug] • Customers responded *negatively* to the new product. [=customers did not like the new product]

²negative *noun, pl* **-tives** [*count*]
1 : something that is harmful or bad • One of the *negatives* [=*drawbacks*] of the house is that it's on a busy street. • Since the positives outweigh the *negatives*, I'm going to take the job. [=there are more good things about the job than bad things] — opposite POSITIVE
2 : a word or statement that means "no" or that expresses a denial or refusal • "No" and "not" are *negatives*. — see also DOUBLE NEGATIVE
3 : an image on film that is used to make a printed photograph and that has light areas where the photograph will be dark and dark areas where the photograph will be light; *also* : the film that has such an image • Can I have the *negatives* to make copies of the photos? — compare POSITIVE
4 : the result from a test that shows that a particular germ, condition, or substance is not present • There is a high rate of ***false negatives*** for this test. [=this test often incorrectly indicates that something is not present when it really is] — opposite POSITIVE

in the negative *formal* : with a reply that means "no" • She answered (the question) *in the negative*. [=she answered "no"] — compare *in the affirmative* at ²AFFIRMATIVE

negative equity *noun* [*noncount*] : a situation in which the amount of money that a person owes for something (such as a house or a car) is less than its worth

neg·a·tiv·i·ty /ˌnɛgəˈtɪvəti/ *noun* [*noncount*] : an attitude in which someone considers only the bad qualities of someone or something • Her *negativity* about society began to depress me. • There is a lot of *negativity* about the new boss.

¹ne·glect /nɪˈglɛkt/ *verb* **-glects; -glect·ed; -glect·ing** [+ *obj*]
1 : to fail to take care of or to give attention to (someone or something) • The building has been *neglected* for years. • She *neglects* her child. • The city has *neglected* the teacher shortage for too long.
2 : to fail to do (something) • The prison guard *neglected* his duty. — often followed by *to + verb* • He *neglected to mention* that he was fired. • He *neglected to sign* the check.

²neglect *noun* [*noncount*]
1 : lack of attention or care that someone or something needs • The park was overgrown and littered from years of *neglect*. • The parents were charged with child *neglect*. — often + *of* • the city's *neglect of* the homeless • He was dismissed for *neglect of* duty. [=for not doing his duty]
2 : the condition of not being taken care of • The house is in a state of *neglect*.

neglected *adj* [*more ~; most ~*] : not given enough attention or care • *neglected* children • a sadly *neglected* garden • His wife felt *neglected*. [=she felt unhappy because she wanted him to pay more attention to her]

ne·glect·ful /nɪˈglɛktfəl/ *adj* [*more ~; most ~*] : not giving enough care or attention to someone or something • *neglectful* parents — often + *of* • She is *neglectful of* her appearance/responsibilities. • He is *neglectful of* what other people might think. [=he does not care about what other people might think]

neg·li·gee /ˌnɛgləˈʒeɪ/ *noun, pl* **-li·gees** [*count*] : a long piece of clothing made of a thin material (such as silk) that is worn in bed by women

neg·li·gence /ˈnɛglɪʤəns/ *noun* [*noncount*] *formal* : failure to take the care that a responsible person usually takes : lack of normal care or attention • Medical *negligence* may be the cause of death. [=the patient's death may have happened because the doctor did not do something that should have been done] • The company was charged with *negligence* in the manufacturing of the defective tires.

neg·li·gent /ˈnɛglɪʤənt/ *adj* [*more ~; most ~*] : failing to take proper or normal care of something or someone • The fire was started by a *negligent* smoker. • *negligent* parents • He was *negligent* in not reporting the accident to the police. • She was *negligent* about sending a thank-you note. [=she neglected to send a thank-you note]
– neg·li·gent·ly *adv* • The defendant drove *negligently* and hit a pedestrian.

neg·li·gi·ble /ˈnɛglɪʤəbəl/ *adj* [*more ~; most ~*] : very small or unimportant • A *negligible* amount of damage was done to the vehicle. • The price difference was *negligible*.
– neg·li·gi·bly /ˈnɛglɪʤəbli/ *adv* • The difference between the prices was *negligibly* small.

ne·go·tia·ble /nɪˈgoʊʃijəbəl/ *adj*
1 : able to be discussed and changed before an agreement or decision is made • The terms of the contract are *negotiable*. • The price was not *negotiable*.
2 : able to be successfully traveled over • a rough but *negotiable* road
3 *finance* : able to be passed from one person to another in return for something of equal value • *negotiable* bonds/securities

ne·go·ti·ate /nɪˈgoʊʃiˌeɪt/ *verb* **-ates; -at·ed; -at·ing**
1 a : to discuss something formally in order to make an agreement [*no obj*] The customer wanted to *negotiate* over/about the price. • She has good *negotiating* skills. — often + *with* or *for* • The team is *negotiating with* the player's agent. • Teachers are *negotiating for* higher salaries. [+ *obj*] She is *negotiating* a higher salary. [=she is trying to get a higher salary by negotiating] **b** [+ *obj*] : to agree on (something) by formally discussing it • We *negotiated* a fair price/contract.
2 [+ *obj*] : to get over, through, or around (something) successfully • The driver carefully *negotiated* the winding road.

negotiating table *noun*
the negotiating table — used to say that people are having

N

formal discussions in order to reach an agreement • The two sides in this dispute have returned to *the negotiating table.* [=they have begun to have discussions again] • They came to an agreement at *the negotiating table.* [=they came to an agreement after their discussions]

ne·go·ti·a·tion /nɪˌgoʊʃiˈeɪʃən/ *noun, pl* **-tions :** a formal discussion between people who are trying to reach an agreement **:** an act of negotiating [*count*] We need a *negotiation* between the townspeople and mayor over the site of the new library. — usually plural • The buyer and seller are continuing *negotiations* on the sale price and repairs to the house. • *Negotiations* between the two governments have failed to produce an agreement. • *Negotiations* with the protesters began today. [*noncount*] She is skilled at *negotiation.* • The college president was against any *negotiation* with the students. • The contract is ***under negotiation***. [=the details of the contract are being discussed] • The price is ***open to negotiation***. [=the price has not been finally decided and can be discussed] • The team is ***in negotiation*** with the player. [=the team is discussing the details of a contract with the player]

ne·go·ti·a·tor /nɪˈgoʊʃiˌeɪtɚ/ *noun, pl* **-tors** [*count*] **:** a person who is involved in formal financial or political discussions in order to try to reach an agreement • a skilled trade/labor *negotiator*

Ne·gro /ˈniːgroʊ/ *noun, pl* **-groes** [*count*] *old-fashioned + sometimes offensive* **:** a person who has dark skin and who belongs to a race of people who are originally from Africa
– **Negro** *adj, sometimes offensive*

neigh /ˈneɪ/ *verb* **neighs; neighed; neigh·ing** [*no obj*] *of a horse* **:** to make a loud, long sound • We heard the horses *neighing* in the stable. — compare WHINNY
– **neigh** *noun, pl* **neighs** [*count*] • We heard a distant *neigh.*

neigh·bor (*US*) *or Brit* **neigh·bour** /ˈneɪbɚ/ *noun, pl* **-bors** [*count*]
1 : a person who lives next to or near another person • We invited our friends and *neighbors.* • our ***next-door neighbors*** [=the people who live in the house next to us]
2 : a person or thing that is next to or near another • Please pass your paper to your *neighbor.* [=the person sitting next to you] • Canada is a *neighbor* of the U.S. • Venus is Earth's nearest *neighbor.*

neigh·bor·hood (*US*) *or Brit* **neigh·bour·hood** /ˈneɪbɚˌhʊd/ *noun, pl* **-hoods**
1 [*count*] **:** a section of a town or city • They bought a house in a beautiful/quiet *neighborhood.* — often used before another noun • the *neighborhood* school/park/children
2 [*noncount*] **:** the people who live near each other • The whole *neighborhood* heard about it.
in the neighborhood **:** in the area that is close to something • Is there a grocery store *in the neighborhood*? [=is there a grocery store close by?] • We might as well pay them a visit while we're *in the neighborhood.*
in the neighborhood of **1 :** close to (a place) • An earthquake was reported somewhere *in the neighborhood of* southern California. **2 :** close to or around (an amount) **:** ABOUT • The album sold *in the neighborhood of* 1,000 copies. • A house like this costs somewhere *in the neighborhood of* $200,000.

neighborhood watch (*US*) *or Brit* **neighbourhood watch** *noun* [*noncount*] **:** an organization of neighbors who pay special attention to each other's houses in order to prevent crime — often used before another noun • a *neighborhood watch* group/program

neigh·bor·ing (*US*) *or Brit* **neigh·bour·ing** /ˈneɪbərɪŋ/ *adj, always used before a noun* **:** near or next to something or someone • *neighboring* cities/countries • a *neighboring* building • people from (the) *neighboring* tribes

neigh·bor·ly (*US*) *or Brit* **neigh·bour·ly** /ˈneɪbɚli/ *adj* [*more ~; most ~*] **:** helpful and friendly • It was very *neighborly* [=*kind*] of you to help. • the importance of *neighborly* [=*friendly*] relations between countries • She was friendly in a *neighborly* way.
– **neigh·bor·li·ness** *noun* [*noncount*]

[1]**nei·ther** /ˈniːðɚ, ˈnaɪðɚ/ *adj* **:** not one or the other of two people or things • *Neither* answer is correct. [=both answers are wrong] • "Which answer is correct?" "*Neither* one." • *Neither* sweater fits her.

[2]**neither** *pronoun* **:** not the one and not the other of two people or things • *Neither* (of the two answers) is correct. • "Which one do you want?" "*Neither,* thanks." • *Neither* of them dances well. • There are two flashlights, *neither* of which works.

> ***usage*** According to the rules of grammar, the pronoun *neither* is singular and requires a singular verb. • *Neither* is correct. However, in informal writing and speech, a plural verb is common when *neither* is followed by *of.* • *Neither of* the answers is/are correct. • *Neither of* them know/knows my friend.

[3]**neither** *conj*
1 — used with *nor* to indicate two or more people, things, actions, etc., about which something is not true • *Neither* my wife *nor* I can attend the party. • *Neither* wood *nor* plastic conducts heat like metal does. • I *neither* know *nor* care. • I'm *neither* happy *nor* sad. • She eats *neither* meat *nor* cheese. [=(more commonly) she does not eat meat or cheese] ✧ When *neither* and *nor* are used to join two subjects, the verb should agree with the subject that is closer to it. • *Neither* my father *nor* I am going to the meeting.
2 : also not — used after a negative statement • "I don't believe his story." "*Neither* do I." [=I also do not believe his story] • They didn't believe his story, and *neither* did I. • I did not believe his story, but *neither* did I believe hers.
me neither see [4]EITHER
neither here nor there see [1]HERE

nem·e·sis /ˈnɛməsəs/ *noun, pl* **-ses** /-ˌsiːz/ [*count*] **:** an opponent or enemy that is very difficult to defeat • He will be playing his old *nemesis* for the championship.

neo- *prefix* **:** a new and different form of something that existed in the past (such as a theory, style, language, or philosophy) • *neo*-Darwinism • *neo*-Gothic • *neo*-Latin • *neo*classical

neo·clas·si·cal /ˌniːjoʊˈklæsɪkəl/ *also* **neo·clas·sic** /ˌniːjoʊˈklæsɪk/ *adj* **:** relating to a style of art or architecture like the ones found in ancient Greece or Rome • a building designed in a *neoclassical* style • The museum will be exhibiting paintings from the *neoclassical* movement.
– **neo·clas·si·cism** /ˌniːjoʊˈklæsəˌsɪzəm/ *noun* [*noncount*] • a painter who practiced *neoclassicism* in the late 18th century – **neo·clas·si·cist** /ˌniːjoʊˈklæsəsɪst/ *noun, pl* **-cists** [*count*]

Neo·lith·ic /ˌniːjəˈlɪθɪk/ *adj* **:** of or relating to the time during the Stone Age when people used stone tools and began to grow crops, raise animals, and live together in large groups but did not read or write • *Neolithic* man/tribes/cave painters • the *Neolithic* age/period — compare PALEOLITHIC

ne·ol·o·gism /niˈɑːləˌʤɪzəm/ *noun, pl* **-gisms** [*count*] **:** a new word or expression or a new meaning of a word • scientific *neologisms* [=new scientific words]

[1]**ne·on** /ˈniːˌɑːn/ *noun* [*noncount*] **:** a type of gas that is used in brightly colored electric signs and lights

[2]**neon** *adj, always used before a noun*
1 : using neon • flashing *neon* lights/signs
2 : extremely bright • *neon* yellow/green

neo·na·tal /ˌniːjoʊˈneɪtl/ *adj, medical* **:** of, relating to, or taking care of babies in the first month after their birth • a *neonatal* intensive care unit • *neonatal* diseases

neo–Na·zi /ˌniːjoʊˈnɑːtsi/ *noun, pl* **-zis** [*count*] **:** a person who belongs to a group that believes in the ideas and policies of Hitler's Nazis and that sometimes commits violent acts
– **neo–Nazi** *adj*

neo·phyte /ˈniːjəˌfaɪt/ *noun, pl* **-phytes** [*count*] *formal*
1 : a person who has just started learning or doing something **:** BEGINNER • a *neophyte* on computers • a political *neophyte* [=a person just starting in politics] — often used before another noun • a *neophyte* journalist
2 : a person who has recently joined a religious group

neph·ew /ˈnɛfju/ *noun, pl* **-ews** [*count*] **:** a son of your brother or sister — compare NIECE

nep·o·tism /ˈnɛpəˌtɪzəm/ *noun* [*noncount*] *disapproving* **:** the unfair practice by a powerful person of giving jobs and other favors to relatives • *Nepotism* has hurt the company.

Nep·tune /ˈnɛpˌtuːn, *Brit* ˈnɛpˌtjuːn/ *noun* [*singular*] **:** the planet that is eighth in order from the sun

nerd /ˈnɚd/ *noun, pl* **nerds** [*count*] *informal + usually disapproving*
1 : a person who behaves awkwardly around other people and usually has unstylish clothes, hair, etc. • He dresses like a *nerd.*
2 : a person who is very interested in technical subjects, computers, etc. • My brother is a computer *nerd.* [=*geek*] • a grammar *nerd*
– **nerd·i·ness** /ˈnɚdinəs/ *noun* [*noncount*] • She was embarrassed by her sister's *nerdiness.* – **nerd·ish** /ˈnɚdɪʃ/ *adj*

N

[*more* ~; *most* ~] ▪ a *nerdish* teenager – **nerdy** /ˈnɚdi/ *adj* **nerd·i·er; -est** [*also more* ~; *most* ~] ▪ She wears *nerdy* glasses. ▪ He plays a *nerdy* scientist in the movie.

nerve /ˈnɚv/ *noun, pl* **nerves**

1 [*count*] **: one of the many thin parts that control movement and feeling by carrying messages between the brain and other parts of the body** ▪ The optic *nerve* in the eye allows you to see. ▪ a condition affecting the *nerves* in her arm

2 [*noncount*] **: courage that allows you to do something that is dangerous, difficult, or frightening** ▪ It takes a lot of *nerve* to start a new career. ▪ He found/summoned the *nerve* to stand up to his boss. ▪ I was going to ask her to the dance, but I lost my *nerve*.

3 [*singular, noncount*] **: the rude attitude of someone who says or does things that make other people angry or upset** ▪ You have a lot of *nerve* to talk to me that way. ▪ I can't believe she had the *nerve* to call me a liar. ▪ "After making the mess, he didn't even offer to help clean it up." "What (a) *nerve*!"

4 ***nerves*** [*plural*] **: feelings of being worried or nervous** ▪ The groom was overcome by *nerves* before his wedding. ▪ The singer still suffers from *nerves* before a performance. ▪ Her ***nerves were on edge*** [=she was nervous] before her exam. ▪ I need a drink to ***steady/calm my nerves***. [=*relax*]

a bag/bundle of nerves *informal* **: an extremely nervous person** ▪ He was *a bundle of nerves* before his speech.

get on someone's nerves **: to become extremely annoying to someone** ▪ That car alarm is *getting on my nerves*.

hit/strike/touch a nerve **: to make someone feel angry, upset, embarrassed, etc.** ▪ Something she said to him must have *hit/struck/touched a nerve*. I've never seen him so angry. ▪ His controversial column might have *hit a* (raw/sensitive) *nerve* with some readers.

nerves of steel **: an impressive ability to remain calm in dangerous or difficult situations** ▪ It takes *nerves of steel* to work in such a high-pressure job.

war of nerves **: a situation in which people do or say things to make other people feel afraid or nervous about what will happen** ▪ The company and the union are engaged in a *war of nerves*, with each side threatening the other.

nerve cell *noun, pl* ~ **cells** [*count*] **:** NEURON

nerve center (*US*) *or Brit* **nerve centre** *noun, pl* ~ **-ters** [*count*] **: a place from which the activities of an organization, system, etc., are controlled** ▪ the economic *nerve center* of a nation

nerve gas *noun* [*noncount*] **: a poisonous gas that is used as a weapon in war**

nerve–rack·ing *or* **nerve–wrack·ing** /ˈnɚvˌrækɪŋ/ *adj* [*more* ~; *most* ~] **: causing a person to feel very nervous** ▪ The job interview was a *nerve-racking* experience. ▪ She endured a *nerve-racking* wait for her test scores.

ner·vous /ˈnɚvəs/ *adj*

1 [*more* ~; *most* ~] **a : having or showing feelings of being worried and afraid about what might happen** ▪ She is/feels *nervous* about her job interview. ▪ All this waiting is making me *nervous*. ▪ He gave a *nervous* glance at the clock. ▪ a *nervous* smile ▪ Before the wedding the bride's father was a ***nervous wreck***. [=he was extremely nervous] **b : often or easily becoming worried and afraid about what might happen** ▪ His *nervous* mother is always worrying that something terrible will happen to him. ▪ He has a *nervous* disposition. **c : causing someone to feel worried and afraid : making someone nervous** ▪ It was a very *nervous* situation.

2 *always used before a noun* **: of or relating to the nerves in your body** ▪ *nervous* tissue ▪ She suffers from a *nervous* disorder/condition. **: caused by or affected by nerves** ▪ He walked around with a *nervous* twitch. ▪ He had a *nervous* habit of pulling at his hair. ▪ The boy has a lot of *nervous* energy.

– **ner·vous·ly** *adv* ▪ Dad paced *nervously* around the waiting room. – **ner·vous·ness** *noun* [*noncount*] ▪ The student showed no sign of *nervousness*.

nervous breakdown *noun, pl* ~ **-downs** [*count*] **: a sudden failure of mental health that makes someone unable to live normally** ▪ She had/suffered a *nervous breakdown* shortly after her sister's death. ▪ He is on the verge of a *nervous breakdown*.

nervous Nel·lie *or* **nervous Nel·ly** /-ˈnɛli/ *or* **Nervous Nellie** *or* **Nervous Nelly** *noun, pl* ~ **Nel·lies** [*count*] *US, informal* **: a very fearful or nervous person** ▪ My sister is a real *nervous Nellie* when it comes to flying.

nervous system *noun, pl* ~ **-tems** [*count*] **: the system of nerves in your body that sends messages for controlling movement and feeling between the brain and the other parts of the body** — see also CENTRAL NERVOUS SYSTEM

nervy /ˈnɚvi/ *adj* **nerv·i·er; -est** [*also more* ~; *most* ~] *informal*

1 *US, approving* **: having or showing courage or confidence** ▪ a *nervy* performance in the play-offs ▪ a *nervy* film director who's not afraid to take risks

2 *US, disapproving* **— used to describe someone who says or does rude or shocking things that make other people angry or upset** ▪ She was *nervy* enough to criticize the food we served her. [=she had the nerve to criticize the food we served her]

3 *Brit* **: feeling unpleasantly nervous or excited : not calm** ▪ The passengers were restless and *nervy* after the long flight. ▪ Too much coffee makes me *nervy*.

-ness /nəs/ *noun combining form* **: state : condition : quality** ▪ good*ness* ▪ friendli*ness* ▪ sick*ness* ▪ fresh*ness*

[1]**nest** /ˈnɛst/ *noun, pl* **nests** [*count*]

1 a : the place where a bird lays its eggs and takes care of its young ▪ The bird built a *nest* out of small twigs. ▪ If you look closely, you can see a *nest* in that tree. **b : a place where an animal or insect lives and usually lays eggs or takes care of its young** ▪ a *nest* of hornets ▪ a turtle/squirrel *nest* — see also HORNET'S NEST

2 : a home where people live ▪ They lived in a cozy little *nest* in the suburbs. ▪ Their children will soon be ready to ***leave/flee the nest***. [=their children will soon be ready to move away from home] — see also LOVE NEST

3 : a group of objects that are made in different sizes that fit inside each other ▪ a *nest* of boxes/tables

feather your (own) nest see [2]FEATHER

[2]**nest** *verb* **nests; nest·ed; nest·ing** [*no obj*]

1 : to build or live in a nest ▪ Robins *nested* in the tree. ▪ This area is a *nesting* ground/place/site for seagulls. [=this is a place where seagulls build nests and raise their young] ▪ She studied the *nesting* habits of the turtle.

2 : to fit inside each other ▪ The set of four chairs can *nest* into one stack. ▪ The smaller bowl is designed to *nest* inside the larger one.

– **nest·er** /ˈnɛstɚ/ *noun, pl* **-ters** [*count*] ▪ These birds are cliff *nesters*. — see also EMPTY NESTER

nest egg *noun, pl* ~ **eggs** [*count*] **: an amount of money that is saved over a usually long period of time to pay for something in the future** ▪ They built up a *nest egg* for their son's college education.

nes·tle /ˈnɛsəl/ *verb, always followed by an adverb or preposition* **nes·tles; nes·tled; nes·tling**

1 [*no obj*] **: to lie comfortably close to or against someone or something** ▪ The puppy *nestled* (up) against the sleeping boy.

2 [+ *obj*] **: to place (something) close to, next to, or within something** ▪ He *nestled* his head against his mother's shoulder. ▪ She carefully *nestled* the hamster into its cage. — often used as *(be) nestled* ▪ The vacation resort *was nestled* among the hills. ▪ Campsites *were nestled* along the river. ▪ His wife's head *was nestled* against his chest.

3 [*no obj*] **: to land or settle softly into something** ▪ The fly ball *nestled* into the outfielder's glove.

nest·ling /ˈnɛstlɪŋ/ *noun, pl* **-lings** [*count*] **: a young bird that is not yet able to fly away from the nest**

[1]**net** /ˈnɛt/ *noun, pl* **nets**

1 a [*count*] **: a device that is used for catching or holding things or for keeping things out of a space and that is made of pieces of string, rope, wire, etc., woven together with spaces in between** ▪ He caught a fish in the *net*. ▪ a butterfly *net* — often used figuratively ▪ They were caught in a *net* [=*web*] of deception. — see picture at FISHING; see also MOSQUITO NET, SAFETY NET **b** [*noncount*] **: the material used to make nets : NETTING** ▪ *net* curtains

2 [*count*] *sports* **a : a net that is hung across the middle of a playing area in some games (such as tennis, badminton, or volleyball)** ▪ The ball barely went over the *net*. **b : a net that is attached to a frame and that is used as the goal in some games (such as soccer, hockey, or basketball)** ▪ He shot the puck into the *net*. ▪ The ball swished through the *net*.

3 ***the Net*** **: the Internet** ▪ She likes to surf *the Net*. [=*the Web*] ▪ doing business on *the Net*

cast/spread your net wide **: to try many different things so that you will have the best chance of finding what you want** ▪ Companies are *casting their nets wide* in search of young, talented employees.

slip/fall through the net **: to fail to be noticed or included with others** ▪ There are plenty of talented players who *slip*

through the net and never get to play professionally.
– compare ⁵NET

²**net** *verb* **nets; net·ted; net·ting** [+ *obj*]
1 : to catch (something) in a net • We *netted* nine fish during the trip. — often used figuratively • The escaped convict was *netted* by police.
2 *sports* **a :** to hit (a ball) into the net during a game (such as tennis) • She *netted* her first two serves. **b :** to score (a goal or point) by hitting, kicking, or shooting a ball or puck into a net • He *netted* two goals in his first game. • She *netted* 15 points in the first half.
– compare ⁴NET

³**net** *also Brit* **nett** *adj, always used before a noun*
1 — used to describe the amount or value of something after all costs and expenses have been taken away • They determined the *net* value of the estate. • The company suffered a decline in *net* profit for the third quarter. • a billionaire's *net* worth — compare ¹GROSS
2 — used to describe the weight of something without its packaging or container • the *net* weight of the shipment
3 : after everything is completed • The ***net result/outcome/effect*** of the new bridge will be fewer traffic jams.

⁴**net** *verb* **nets; netted; netting** [+ *obj*]
1 : to gain or receive (an amount) as a profit • We *netted* $50 on the sale. — compare ⁴GROSS
2 : to produce or get (something) as the result of an effort • The investigation *netted* no clues. • The running back *netted* 20 yards on his first run.
– compare ²NET

⁵**net** *noun, pl* **nets** [*count*] **:** an amount that is left over after all costs and expenses have been taken away **:** a net amount • The *net* is significantly lower than we had anticipated. — compare ⁵GROSS — compare ¹NET

net·ball /ˈnɛtˌbɑːl/ *noun* [*noncount*] **:** a sport played chiefly in Britain that is similar to basketball and has two teams of seven players each ✧ Netball is usually played by women and girls.

neth·er /ˈnɛðɚ/ *adj, always used before a noun, literary or humorous* **:** located toward the bottom or more distant part of something **:** LOWER • Snakes nested in the *nether* reaches of the cave. [=snakes nested deep in the cave] • His shorts fell down and exposed his ***nether parts/regions***. [=his genitals and buttocks]

neth·er·world /ˈnɛðɚˌwɚld/ *noun, pl* **-worlds**
1 ***the netherworld*** *literary* **:** the world of the dead **:** HELL
2 [*count*] **:** a place unknown to most people where secret and often illegal things are done — usually singular • The book describes the author's journey into the *netherworld* of drug dealers. • a criminal *netherworld*

net·i·quette /ˈnɛtɪkət/ *noun* [*noncount*] *informal* **:** rules about the proper and polite way to communicate with other people when you are using the Internet • Writing an e-mail message in all capital letters is considered a breach/violation of *netiquette* because it looks like you are shouting. • the rules of *netiquette*

net·i·zen /ˈnɛtəzən/ *noun, pl* **-zens** [*count*] **:** a person who actively uses the Internet especially in a proper and responsible way

net·mind·er /ˈnɛtˌmaɪndɚ/ *noun, pl* **-ers** [*count*] **:** GOALKEEPER

nett *Brit spelling of* ³NET

netting *noun* [*noncount*] **:** material consisting of pieces of string, rope, wire, etc., that are woven together with open spaces left in between **:** material that is used to make nets • He put up wire *netting* around the garden.

¹**net·tle** /ˈnɛtl̩/ *verb* **net·tles; net·tled; net·tling** [+ *obj*] **:** to make (someone) angry • The mayor's recent actions have *nettled* some members of the community. • It *nettles* him that his younger coworker got a promotion before he did.

²**nettle** *noun, pl* **nettles** [*count*] **:** a tall plant that has leaves with hairs that sting you if you touch them
grasp the nettle *Brit* **:** to deal with an unpleasant situation without delay • He decided to *grasp the nettle* and try to solve the problem himself.

¹**net·work** /ˈnɛtˌwɚk/ *noun, pl* **-works** [*count*]
1 a : a system of lines, wires, etc., that are connected to each other • a telephone/rail *network* — often + *of* • a *network of* blood vessels **b :** a system of computers and other devices (such as printers) that are connected to each other • He hooked up his computer to the *network*.
2 : a group of people or organizations that are closely connected and that work with each other • a volunteer *network* — often + *of* • a *network of* political allies
3 : a group of radio or television stations that usually broadcast the same programs • The show is getting good ratings for the *network*. • a *network* news program

²**network** *verb* **-works; -worked; -work·ing**
1 [+ *obj*] **:** to connect (computers) in a way that allows information and equipment to be shared • The computers are *networked* to one main server.
2 [*no obj*] **:** to talk with people whose jobs are similar to yours especially for business opportunities or advice • She spent the day *networking* with other executives.
– **networking** *noun* [*noncount*] • He did some *networking* at the conference. • She attributes her success to *networking*.

neu·ral /ˈnɚrəl, *Brit* ˈnjuərəl/ *adj, medical* **:** of, relating to, or involving a nerve or the nervous system • She suffers from a *neural* disorder. • *neural* activity/impulses • the brain's *neural* pathways

neu·ral·gia /nʊˈrælʤə, *Brit* njʊˈrælʤə/ *noun* [*noncount*] *medical* **:** a sharp pain that is felt along the length of a nerve
– **neu·ral·gic** /nʊˈrælʤɪk, *Brit* njʊˈrælʤɪk/ *adj* • *neuralgic* pain

neu·rol·o·gy /nʊˈrɑːləʤi, *Brit* njʊˈrɒləʤi/ *noun* [*noncount*] *medical* **:** the scientific study of the nervous system and the diseases that affect it
– **neu·ro·log·i·cal** /ˌnurəˈlɑːʤɪkəl, *Brit* ˌnjʊrəˈlɒʤɪkəl/ *or chiefly US* **neu·ro·log·ic** /ˌnɚrəˈlɑːʤɪk, *Brit* ˌnjʊrəˈlɒʤɪk/ *adj* • a *neurological* disorder – **neu·rol·o·gist** /nʊˈrɑːləʤɪst, *Brit* njʊˈrɒləʤɪst/ *noun, pl* **-gists** [*count*]

neu·ro·mus·cu·lar /ˌnɚroʊˈmʌskjəlɚ, *Brit* ˌnjʊrəʊˈmʌskjələ/ *adj, medical* **:** relating to both nerves and muscles • a *neuromuscular* disease

neu·ron /ˈnɚˌɑːn ˈnjʊərɒn/ *also Brit* **neu·rone** /ˈnɚˌoʊn, *Brit* ˈnjʊərəʊn/ *noun, pl* **-rons** [*count*] *medical* **:** a cell that carries messages between the brain and other parts of the body and that is the basic unit of the nervous system **:** NERVE CELL

neu·ro·sci·ence /ˌnɚroʊˈsajəns, *Brit* ˌnjʊərəʊˈsajəns/ *noun* [*noncount*] **:** the scientific study of nerves and especially of how nerves affect learning and behavior

neu·ro·sis /nʊˈroʊsəs, *Brit* njʊˈrəʊsəs/ *noun, pl* **-ses** /-ˌsiːz/ [*count, noncount*] *medical* **:** an emotional illness in which a person experiences strong feelings of fear or worry • The patient is clearly suffering from (a) *neurosis*.

¹**neu·rot·ic** /nʊˈrɑːtɪk, *Brit* njʊˈrɒtɪk/ *adj* [*more* ~; *most* ~]
1 *medical* **:** having or suggesting neurosis • The psychiatrist diagnosed the patient as *neurotic*. • *neurotic* symptoms
2 : often or always fearful or worried about something **:** tending to worry in a way that is not healthy or reasonable • My *neurotic* mother scolded me for staying out 10 minutes past curfew. • He is *neurotic* about his job. • a *neurotic* personality
– **neu·rot·i·cal·ly** /nʊˈrɑːtɪkli, *Brit* njʊˈrɒtɪkli/ *adv* • He was *neurotically* obsessed with keeping his clothes neat.

²**neurotic** *noun, pl* **-ics** [*count*]
1 *medical* **:** a person who has a neurosis • He was diagnosed as a *neurotic*.
2 : a person who is always fearful or worried about something • He is a *neurotic* about keeping his clothes neat.

neu·ro·trans·mit·ter /ˌnɚroʊˌtrænsˈmɪtɚ, *Brit* ˌnjʊərəʊˌtrænsˈmɪtə/ *noun, pl* **-ters** [*count*] *medical* **:** a substance in the body that carries a signal from one nerve cell to another

¹**neu·ter** /ˈnuːtɚ, *Brit* ˈnjuːtə/ *adj, grammar, in some languages* **:** of or belonging to the class of words (called a gender) that ordinarily includes most of the words referring to things that are neither masculine nor feminine • The pronoun "it" is *neuter*. • a *neuter* noun

²**neuter** *verb* **-ters; -tered; -ter·ing** [+ *obj*]
1 : to remove the sex organs from (an animal) • She had her dog *neutered* by the veterinarian. ✧ *Neuter* usually refers to the action of removing the sex organs from a male animal, while *spay* usually refers to the action of removing the sex organs from a female animal.
2 *disapproving* **:** to make (something) much less powerful or effective • The bill was *neutered* by the changes made by the legislature.

¹**neu·tral** /ˈnuːtrəl, *Brit* ˈnjuːtrəl/ *adj*
1 [*more* ~; *most* ~] **a :** not supporting either side of an argument, fight, war, etc. • *neutral* countries • He ***remained/stayed neutral*** while his brothers argued. **b :** not supporting one political view over another • She tries to be a fair and *neutral* journalist. • a *neutral* magazine
2 : not connected with either side involved in a war, contest,

etc. • The battle took place in *neutral* waters. • The duel will be held on *neutral* ground. • *neutral* territory

3 [*more* ~; *most* ~] **:** not expressing strong opinions or feelings • The report was written in *neutral* language. • "Why did you do that?" he asked in a *neutral* tone of voice.

4 : not bright or strong in color **:** able to go easily with other colors • They decorated the room in *neutral* tones/colors. • a *neutral* gray • *neutral* fabrics

5 *technical* **:** neither an acid nor a base • a *neutral* compound • a chemical with a *neutral* pH

6 *technical* **:** not having an electrical charge • a *neutral* molecule

– neu·tral·ly *adv* • The judge must try to view the dispute *neutrally*. • *neutrally* charged atoms

[2]**neutral** *noun, pl* **-trals**

1 [*count*] **:** a color that is not bright or strong **:** a neutral color — usually plural • She painted the room in *neutrals*.

2 [*noncount*] **:** the position of the gears in a car, truck, etc., when they do not touch each other and power from the engine does not move the wheels • He put/left the car ***in neutral***.

3 [*count*] **:** a person, country, etc., that does not support either side of an argument, fight, war, etc. • Their sister remained a *neutral* in the dispute. • The two countries were *neutrals* while their neighbors were at war.

neu·tral·i·ty /nuˈtræləti, *Brit* njuˈtræləti/ *noun* [*noncount*] **:** the quality or state of not supporting either side in an argument, fight, war, etc. **:** the quality or state of being neutral • The country adopted an official policy of *neutrality*. • The newspaper is known for its political *neutrality*.

neu·tral·ize *also Brit* **neu·tral·ise** /ˈnuːtrəˌlaɪz, *Brit* ˈnjuːtrəˌlaɪz/ *verb* **-iz·es; -ized; -iz·ing** [+ *obj*]

1 : to stop (someone or something) from being effective or harmful • The soldiers tried to *neutralize* the attack by dividing the invading army.

2 *technical* **:** to cause (a chemical) to be neither an acid nor a base • This medicine *neutralizes* stomach acids.

3 : to make (something, such as a country or area) neutral during a war • The lands between the warring countries were *neutralized*.

– neu·tral·i·za·tion *also Brit* **neu·tral·i·sa·tion** /ˌnuːtrələˈzeɪʃən, *Brit* ˌnjuːtrəˌlaɪˈzeɪʃən/ *noun* [*noncount*]

neutral zone *noun*

the neutral zone **:** the middle part of an ice hockey rink that is between the two zones defended by the teams

neu·tri·no /nuˈtriːnoʊ, *Brit* njuˈtriːnəʊ/ *noun, pl* **-nos** [*count*] *physics* **:** a particle that is smaller than an atom and that has no electrical charge

neu·tron /ˈnuːˌtrɑːn, *Brit* ˈnjuːˌtrɒn/ *noun, pl* **-trons** [*count*] *physics* **:** a very small particle of matter that has no electrical charge and is part of the nucleus of all atoms except hydrogen atoms

neutron bomb *noun, pl* ~ **bombs** [*count*] **:** a nuclear bomb that releases very large amounts of radiation

nev·er /ˈnɛvɚ/ *adv*

1 : not ever **:** not at any time • I will *never* shop at that store again. • I have *never* seen that happen before. • That man has *never* heard of you. • We will *never* forget what we saw. • You *never* know what you'll find at a flea market. • I *never* meant to hurt you. • She *never* really said that. • There is *never* enough time to finish our work. • *Never* in my whole life have I been so offended! • A resume without a cover letter ***will never do*** [=will never be considered acceptable] • ***Never again*** will I buy a car from that dealer. = I will *never again* buy a car from that dealer. • I gave him my business for years and ***never for one moment*** did I suspect that he was a criminal. — opposite ALWAYS

2 *chiefly Brit* **a** — used to express surprise, doubt, or disbelief • "He's won the lottery." "*Never!*" • "They're getting married." "***Well, I never!*** [=I am very surprised or shocked to hear that they're getting married]" **b** — used to say that you did not do something • "You stole my CD." "Me? *Never.*"

never ever see EVER

never fear — used to tell someone not to worry or be afraid • *Never fear*, I think I have a solution.

never mind, never you mind see [2]MIND

never say die see [1]DIE

never say never — used to say that you should not say that you will never do something because you might change your mind later • "Would you ever go there again?" "Well, (I'll) *never say never*, but I'm certainly not planning to go there anytime soon!"

never so much as — used to say that someone did not do something that was expected or should have been done • She *never so much as* thanked me [=she did not even thank me] for my help.

never the wiser see [1]WISE

never–ending *adj* **:** having or seeming to have no end **:** ENDLESS • Keeping the house clean is a *never-ending* chore. • the *never-ending* fight against poverty

nev·er·more /ˌnɛvɚˈmoɚ/ *adv, literary* **:** not happening again **:** never again • *Nevermore* shall I call you a friend. [=I shall never call you a friend again; I no longer consider you to be a friend of mine]

nev·er–nev·er land /ˌnɛvɚˈnɛvɚ-/ *noun, pl* ~ **lands** [*count*] **:** an imaginary place without problems • He daydreamed of a *never-never land* where people never had to go to work.

nev·er·the·less /ˌnɛvɚðəˈlɛs/ *adv* **:** in spite of what has just been said • I had lost a lot of money in the poker game; *nevertheless* [=*however*], I decided to continue playing. • Her date was a bit of a slob, but she had fun *nevertheless*. • It was a predictable, but *nevertheless* funny, story.

[1]**new** /ˈnuː, *Brit* ˈnjuː/ *adj* **new·er; -est**

1 a : not old **:** recently born, built, or created • They visited the *new* library. • She was looking for the *new* [=most recent] issue of the magazine. • I saw their *new* baby for the first time. • They planted *new* trees on the campus. • a *new* kind of music **b :** not used by anyone else previously • She couldn't afford a *new* car, so she bought a used one. • He bought the car *new*. • shiny *new* shoes • This watch is *new*. — see also BRAND-NEW

2 a : recently bought, rented, etc. • She is eager to see his *new* apartment/house/dog. **b :** having recently become someone's relative, friend, employee, etc. • This is my *new* stepsister. • the young man and his *new* wife • Come meet our *newest* [=most recently hired] employee. • I made a *new* friend today. **c :** recently added to an existing group, organization, etc. • There was a *new* kid in school today. • The union voted in 10 *new* members. • The company created a *new* department to run its Web site. — often + *to* • She is *new to* this school. • Don't worry about it. You are still *new to* the job.

3 : replacing someone or something that came before • The team has a *new* coach. • Have you met his *new* girlfriend? • He starts his *new* job on Monday. • I like your *new* haircut. • The tree is growing *new* leaves. • Waiter, could I please have a *new* fork? This one is dirty.

4 : recently discovered or learned about **:** not known or experienced before • Scientists discovered a *new* comet. • a *new* species of fish • The promotion gave her a *new* sense of optimism. • This drug gives *new* hope to patients. • This is a *new* experience for me. — often + *to* • This kind of work is still *new to* me. [=I have been doing this kind of work for only a short time]

5 — used to describe a time, period, etc., that is beginning again and that is different from what came before • A *new* day has begun. • We are looking forward to the *new* year. • A *new* semester starts in the fall. • After college, he moved to the city to begin ***a new life***. [=a time in a person's life that is different in some important way from what came before]

6 : healthier or more energetic • I felt like a *new* man/woman after my vacation.

(as) good as new or like new **:** in very good condition **:** like something that has recently been made • He painted the bicycle, and now it's *as good as new*. • Once the jewelry has been cleaned, it'll be *like new*.

new arrival see ARRIVAL

new kid on the block see [1]KID

pastures new see [1]PASTURE

the new **:** new things • The band played a good mix of the old and *the new*.

turn over a new leaf see [1]LEAF

what else is new? see [2]ELSE

what's new? *US, informal* — used as a friendly greeting • Hey man, *what's new?*

– new·ness *noun* [*noncount*] • The couple admired the shiny *newness* of their remodeled kitchen.

[2]**new** *adv* **:** newly or recently — usually used in combination • *new*-laid cement

New Age *noun* [*noncount*]

1 : of or relating to ways of thinking and living that are similar to those of older cultures and that have been accepted in recent times by a group of people in place of the usual be-

N

liefs and methods of modern society • the *New Age* movement • a *New Age* bookstore • *New Age* spirituality

2 — used to describe a type of instrumental music that is usually soft and relaxing • He likes to listen to *New Age* music. • a *New Age* composer

– New Age *noun [noncount]* • He likes to listen to *New Age*. • the beginning of the *New Age* [=the New Age movement] **– New Ager** /-ˈeɪʤɚ/ *noun, pl* **~ -ers** *[count]* • She's a *New Ager* who writes spiritual self-help books. **– New Agey** /-ˈeɪʤi/ *adj [more ~; most ~]* • His apartment has a *New Agey* atmosphere.

new·bie /ˈnu:bi, *Brit* ˈnju:bi/ *noun, pl* **-bies** *[count] chiefly US, informal* : a person who has recently started a particular activity • She is a *newbie* on the Internet. = She's an Internet *newbie*. • He is a *newbie* to local politics. • a *newbie* [=*beginner*] chess player

[1]new·born /ˈnu:ˌboɚn, *Brit* ˈnju:ˌbɔ:n/ *adj, always used before a noun* : recently born • a *newborn* baby/calf

[2]newborn *noun, pl* **newborn** *or* **new·borns** *[count]* : a person or animal that has recently been born : a newborn person or animal • a mother goat and all of her *newborn*

New·burg *or* **New·burgh** /ˈnu:ˌbɚg, *Brit* ˈnju:ˌbə:g/ *adj, used after a noun* : served with a sauce that is made of cream, butter, sherry, and egg yolks • lobster/shrimp *Newburg*

new·com·er /ˈnu:ˌkʌmɚ, *Brit* ˈnju:ˌkʌmə/ *noun, pl* **-ers** *[count]*

1 : a person who has recently arrived somewhere or who has recently started a new activity — often + *to* • She is a *newcomer to* the city. • My father is a relative *newcomer to* the world of computers.

2 : something new that has recently been added or created — often + *to* • The word "chat room" is a relative *newcomer to* the English language. • Our company is a *newcomer to* this market.

new·fan·gled /ˈnu:ˈfæŋgəld, *Brit* ˈnju:ˈfæŋgəld/ *adj, always used before a noun* : recently invented or developed and hard to understand • His grandson owns all of the latest *newfangled* electronics. • *newfangled* gadgets • the *newfangled* speech used by teenagers

new·found /ˈnu:ˈfaʊnd, *Brit* ˈnju:ˈfaʊnd/ *adj, always used before a noun* : recently discovered, acquired, or achieved : newly found or gotten • He is enjoying his *newfound* freedom. • a *newfound* friend • *newfound* fame

new·ly /ˈnu:li, *Brit* ˈnju:li/ *adv* : a short time ago : RECENTLY • They are a *newly* married couple. • That is a *newly* acquired habit. • Here is where we keep the *newly* arrived merchandise. • a *newly* discovered galaxy • The room is *newly* painted.

new·ly·wed /ˈnu:liˌwed ˈnju:liˌwed/ *noun, pl* **-weds** *[count]* : a person who has recently married • They took pictures of the happy *newlyweds*. • a *newlywed* hotel suite [=a hotel suite for couples on their honeymoon]

new moon *noun, pl* **~ moons** *[count]* : the moon when it is completely dark — compare FULL MOON, HALF-MOON

news /ˈnu:z, *Brit* ˈnju:z/ *noun*

1 *[noncount]* : new information or a report about something that has happened recently • Do you have any *news* to report? • I have some good *news*, and I have some bad *news*. • Have you heard the good *news*? She's going to have a baby! • What's the big/latest *news*? • It was late summer when ***news of*** his death arrived. [=when we learned that he had died] • We tried to ***break the news*** [=tell the bad news] to her gently. • "The concert has been canceled." "Well, that ***is news to me***." [=I didn't know that; no one told me that] • Lower ticket prices ***are good news for*** [=make things easier for] sports fans. • We haven't heard from his teacher lately, but ***no news is good news***. [=if he was doing badly, his teacher would have told us]

2 *[noncount]* **a** : information that is reported in a newspaper, magazine, television news program, etc. • local/international *news* • The company has been ***in the news*** recently. • and now this ***late-breaking news*** [=the most recent news of the day] • ***front-page news*** [=important news that could be reported on the front page of a newspaper] — often used before another noun • TV *news* reporters • *news* stories/reports • the *news* media • a ***slow news day*** [=a day with little news to report] **b** *informal* : someone or something that is exciting and in the news • She's big *news* here in the city. • That band is ***old news***. = The band is ***yesterday's news***. [=that band isn't new or exciting anymore]

3 *the news* : a television news program • We saw it on *the* evening/nightly *news*. • *The* local *news* is on at 5:30.

have news for someone — used when you are making a definite and forceful statement that someone does not expect, know about, or agree with • "You think you're going to win? Well, *I've got news for you*: you're not." • People tell me that my business will never succeed. Well, I *have news for them*. I'm going to make a profit by the end of the year.

— see also BAD NEWS

news agency *noun, pl* **~ -cies** *[count]* : an organization that collects and gives news to newspapers, magazines, television news programs, and radio stations — called also *press agency*

news·agent /ˈnu:zˌeɪʤənt, *Brit* ˈnju:zˌeɪʤənt/ *noun, pl* **-agents** *[count] chiefly Brit* : a person or shop that sells newspapers, magazines, and often paperback books

news·boy /ˈnu:zˌboɪ ˈnju:zˌboɪ/ *noun, pl* **-boys** *[count] chiefly US, old-fashioned* : a boy who sells or delivers newspapers

news·cast /ˈnu:zˌkæst, *Brit* ˈnju:zˌkɑ:st/ *noun, pl* **-casts** *[count] chiefly US* : a radio or television program that reports the news • the nightly TV *newscast*

news·cast·er /ˈnu:zˌkæstɚ, *Brit* ˈnju:zˌkɑ:stə/ *noun, pl* **-ers** *[count] chiefly US* : a person who reports and sometimes discusses the news on a radio or television show — called also *(Brit) newsreader*

news conference *noun, pl* **~ -ences** *[count]* : PRESS CONFERENCE • The President will hold a *news conference* later today.

news flash *noun, pl* **~ flash·es** *[count]* : a report on an important piece of news that is given in the middle of another television or radio show — often used ironically when you are saying something that is not new or surprising • *News flash*! Your brother's late again!

news·group /ˈnu:zˌgrup, *Brit* ˈnju:zˌgru:p/ *noun, pl* **-groups** *[count]* : a place on the Internet where people can talk about a particular subject by reading and leaving messages • I posted a message to a gardening *newsgroup*.

news·let·ter /ˈnu:zˌlɛtɚ, *Brit* ˈnju:zˌlɛtə/ *noun, pl* **-ters** *[count]* : a short written report that tells about the recent activities of an organization and that is sent to members of the organization • the club's monthly *newsletter*

news·man /ˈnu:zmən, *Brit* ˈnju:zmən/ *noun, pl* **-men** /-mən/ *[count]* : a person (usually a man) who gathers, reports, or comments on the news

news·pa·per /ˈnu:zˌpeɪpɚ, *Brit* ˈnju:zˌpeɪpə/ *noun, pl* **-pers**

1 *[count]* : a set of large sheets of paper that have news stories, information about local events, advertisements, etc., and that are folded together and sold every day or every week • He likes to stay home and read the Sunday *newspaper*. [=*paper*] • a daily/weekly *newspaper* — often used before another noun • *newspaper* headlines/articles/columns/clippings • a *newspaper* reporter/editor/columnist

2 *[noncount]* : the paper on which a newspaper is printed • He used some *newspaper* to get the fire started.

3 *[count]* : a company that publishes a newspaper • She worked for the *newspaper* for 20 years.

news·pa·per·man /ˈnu:zˌpeɪpɚˌmæn, *Brit* ˈnju:zˌpeɪpəˌmæn/ *noun, pl* **-men** /-ˌmɛn/ *[count]* : a person (usually a man) who works as a reporter for a newspaper

news·pa·per·wom·an /ˈnu:zˌpeɪpɚˌwʊmən, *Brit* ˈnju:zˌpeɪpəˌwʊmən/ *noun, pl* **-wom·en** /-ˌwɪmən/ *[count]* : a woman who works as a reporter for a newspaper

new·speak *or* **New·speak** /ˈnu:ˌspi:k, *Brit* ˈnju:ˌspi:k/ *noun [noncount] disapproving* : speech or writing that uses words in a way that changes their meaning especially to persuade people to think a certain way • political *newspeak*

news·per·son /ˈnu:zˌpɚsn̩, *Brit* ˈnju:zˌpə:sn/ *noun, pl* **-peo·ple** *[count]* : a person who gathers, reports, or comments on the news : REPORTER

news·print /ˈnu:zˌprɪnt, *Brit* ˈnju:zˌprɪnt/ *noun [noncount]* : the thin paper that is used for newspapers

news·read·er /ˈnu:zˌri:dɚ, *Brit* ˈnju:zˌri:də/ *noun, pl* **-ers** *[count] Brit* : NEWSCASTER

news·reel /ˈnu:zˌri:l, *Brit* ˈnju:zˌri:l/ *noun, pl* **-reels** *[count]* : a short film that reported the news and that was shown in theaters in the past • old *newsreels* from World War II

news·room /ˈnu:zˌru:m, *Brit* ˈnju:zˌru:m/ *noun, pl* **-rooms** *[count]* : an office where the news is prepared for a newspaper or a television or radio program

news·stand /ˈnu:zˌstænd, *Brit* ˈnju:zˌstænd/ *noun, pl* **-stands** *[count]* : a place (such as a small outdoor store) where newspapers and magazines are sold

news·wom·an /ˈnu:zˌwʊmən, *Brit* ˈnju:zˌwʊmən/ *noun, pl*

-wom•en /-ˌwɪmən/ *[count]* : a woman who gathers, reports, or comments on the news

news•wor•thy /ˈnuːzˌwəði, *Brit* ˈnjuːzˌwəːði/ *adj [more ~; most ~]* : interesting or important enough to report as news ▪ a *newsworthy* story

newsy /ˈnuːzi, *Brit* ˈnjuːzi/ *adj* **news•i•er; -est** *[also more ~; most ~] informal* : containing or full of a lot of news ▪ I got a long *newsy* letter from her. ▪ a *newsy* magazine

newt /ˈnuːt, *Brit* ˈnjuːt/ *noun, pl* **newts** *[count]* : a small animal that lives mostly in water and that has four short legs, a long, low body and tail, and soft, wet skin ▪ a bright orange *newt*

New Testament *noun*
the New Testament : the second part of the Christian Bible that describes the life of Jesus Christ and the lessons that he taught — compare OLD TESTAMENT

new wave *noun, pl* **~ waves**
1 *[count]* : a movement in which a group of people introduce new styles or ideas in art, music, politics, etc. — usually singular; often + *of* ▪ a *new wave of* feminism
2 ***New Wave*** *[noncount]* : a style of rock music that was popular especially in the 1970s and 1980s, has a strong beat, and uses many electronic instruments (such as keyboards) ▪ people who listened to punk, *New Wave*, or disco
3 *[noncount]* : a modern style of art, film, or fashion that tries to be very different or unusual often in a shocking way — often used before another noun ▪ *new wave* design/films

New World *noun*
the New World : North, Central, and South America, especially in the past ▪ Columbus reached *the New World* in 1492. — compare OLD WORLD

New Year *noun*
1 *or chiefly US* ***New Year's*** *[noncount]* : the first day of the year celebrated as a holiday; *especially* : NEW YEAR'S DAY ▪ Happy *New Year*! ▪ *(chiefly US)* a *New Year's* party = *(Brit)* a *New Year* party ▪ *(US)* the week between Christmas and *New Year's* = *(Brit)* the week between Christmas and *New Year*
2 *or* ***new year*** *[singular]* : the year that is about to start or that has just started — usually used with *the* ▪ They will welcome/greet *the New Year* with festivities. ▪ It's sure to be the best film of *the new year*. ▪ We stayed up past midnight on New Year's Eve to ***see the new year in***. [=to see the beginning of the new year] ▪ the ***Chinese New Year*** [=the new year according to the Chinese calendar] ▪ the ***Jewish New Year*** [=*Rosh Hashanah*]

New Year's Day *noun, pl* **~ Days** *[count, noncount]* : January 1 celebrated as a holiday : the first day of the year

New Year's Eve *noun, pl* **~ Eves** *[count, noncount]* : December 31 : the last day of the year; *especially* : the evening of December 31

New York minute *noun [singular] US, informal* : a very short amount of time ▪ He was down the stairs ***in a New York minute***. [=*in an instant; in a flash*]

[1]**next** /ˈnɛkst/ *adj*
1 : coming after this one : coming after the one that just came, happened, etc. ▪ the *next* day [=the day that comes after this day] ▪ Please turn to the *next* [=*following*] page. ▪ I'll see you *next* Monday. ▪ Are you coming this Thursday or *next* Thursday? [=are you coming on Thursday of this week or Thursday of next week?] ▪ *Next* year's party will be even better. ▪ For the *next* two years [=two years after this point], she did nothing but eat, sleep, and study. ▪ the very *next* thing that happened ▪ Can I help the *next* person in line? Who's *next*? ▪ We could hear people talking in the *next* room. ▪ At the *next* set of lights, turn left. ▪ *Next* stop, Los Angeles. ▪ I need the *next* size up. ▪ The *next* time we will see each other will be on our wedding day. ▪ ***Next time***, please remember to bring your books to class. ▪ ***in the next life*** [=in the afterlife; in the life that we may have after death] ▪ I slipped, and ***the next thing I knew*** [=right after that happened], I was lying face up on the ground.
2 : any other ▪ He said he's as willing to do it ***as the next man***. [=he's as willing as anyone else would be] ▪ She knew the answer as well ***as the next person***.
next to : almost but not quite ▪ It's *next to* [=*nearly, practically*] impossible to drive in this snow. ▪ You ate *next to* nothing at dinner. Aren't you hungry? ▪ We were ***next to last*** in line. [=there was one person or group behind us] ▪ He finished *next to last* in the race. ▪ the *next to last* day of our vacation [=the day immediately before the last day of our vacation]

[2]**next** *adv*
1 : in the time or place that follows or comes directly after someone or something : after this ▪ Open this present *next*. ▪ There's a small grocery store in town. The *next* closest store is 20 miles away. [=not including the store in town, the closest store is 20 miles away] ▪ What happens *next*? ▪ *Next*, I need to ask you a few questions about your family. ▪ You're up *next*. [=it's your turn]
2 : at the first time after this ▪ when we *next* see each other = when we see each other *next* = *(formal)* when *next* we see each other
next best see [1]BEST
next to **1** : at the side of (someone or something) ▪ I stood right *next to* [=*beside*] her. ▪ The house *next to* ours is for sale. ▪ He sat *next to* his grandmother. **2** : following or coming immediately after (someone or something) ▪ *Next to* [=*after, besides*] math, science was my worst subject in school. ▪ It's the most important news story *next to* the war. **3** : in comparison with (someone or something) ▪ *Next to* you, I'm wealthy.

[3]**next** *pronoun [noncount]* : a person or thing that immediately follows another person or thing : someone or something that is next ▪ Her first novel was good, but I hope her *next* will be even better. ▪ We'll meet the week ***after next***. [=we will meet on a day that is in the week after next week; we'll meet in about two weeks] — usually used with *the* ▪ We went from one store to *the next* looking for the new CD. ▪ She finished one project and began working on *the next*. ▪ Who will be *the next* to leave the company? ▪ All she does ***from one day to the next*** is complain. [=she complains all the time] ▪ I was ***the next to last*** person [=not the last person, but the person before the last person] in line.
next of kin : the person or people most closely related to you : your closest living relative or relatives (such as your husband, wife, child, parent, sister, or brother) ▪ We notified his *next of kin* of his death.

next door *adv*
1 a : in the next house, apartment, room, etc. ▪ The people (who live) *next door* own a very large dog. ▪ We've lived ***next door to*** [=*next to*] each other for the past 30 years. ▪ He/She seemed like ***the boy/girl next door***. [=like a wholesome young man/woman from a middle-class family] **b** : next to your or someone else's house, apartment, room, etc. ▪ He bought the house *next door*. ▪ I'll be staying in the room *next door*. ▪ Go *next door* [=to the house/apartment next door] and ask for a cup of sugar, please.
2 : in a place that is very close to something else ▪ Canada is right *next door* to the U.S.

next–door /ˈnɛkstˈdoə/ *adj, always used before a noun*
1 : living in the next house, apartment, room, etc. ▪ We've been ***next-door neighbors*** for the past 30 years.
2 : next to your or someone else's house, apartment, room, etc. ▪ the *next-door* house

nex•us /ˈnɛksəs/ *noun [singular] formal* : a relationship or connection between people or things — often + *between* or *of* ▪ the *nexus between* teachers and students ▪ the *nexus between* drugs, guns, and crime ▪ a *nexus of* money and politics

NFC *abbr, US* National Football Conference ✧ The *NFC* and the AFC make up the NFL.

NFL *abbr, US* National Football League ✧ The NFL is the major professional (American) football league in the U.S.

NGO *abbr* nongovernmental organization

NH *abbr* New Hampshire

NHL *abbr, US* National Hockey League ✧ The NHL is the major professional league for ice hockey in the U.S. and Canada.

ni•a•cin /ˈnajəsən/ *noun [noncount] technical* : a type of natural substance (called a vitamin) that is found in certain foods and that helps your body to be healthy

nib /ˈnɪb/ *noun, pl* **nibs** *[count]* : the pointed metal tip of a pen

[1]**nib•ble** /ˈnɪbəl/ *verb* **nib•bles; nib•bled; nib•bling**
1 : to eat slowly or with small bites *[+ obj]* We *nibbled* cheese and crackers. *[no obj]* We *nibbled* on some cheese and crackers before dinner. — often + *at* ▪ She felt a fish *nibble at* the end of her fishing line. ▪ Insects *nibbled at* the tree's leaves. — sometimes used figuratively ▪ He *nibbled* at the idea of changing careers [=he thought briefly about changing careers], but decided against it in the end.
2 *[+ obj]* : to bite (something) very gently ▪ He *nibbled* her ear.
nibble (away) at *[phrasal verb]* ***nibble (away) at (something)***

: to make (something) disappear or go away very slowly • Police have been *nibbling (away) at* crime in the city for years. [=police have been very slowly reducing the amount of crime in the city]

²nibble *noun, pl* **nib•bles**

1 [*count*] : a small bite • He felt a *nibble* on his fishing line. — often + *of* • May I have a *nibble of* your sandwich?

2 [*count*] : an expression of interest in something • We've gotten a couple of *nibbles* on our house [=a couple of people have said that they were thinking about buying our house], but nobody has made a serious offer for it yet.

3 ***nibbles*** [*plural*] *informal* : small things to eat before a meal or at a party : snacks or appetizers • They served some delicious *nibbles* before dinner.

ni•cad *or* **Ni•Cad** /ˈnaɪˌkæd/ *noun, pl* **-cads** [*count*] *technical* : a battery that contains the metals nickel and cadmium and that you can refill with electricity and use again

nice /ˈnaɪs/ *adj* **nic•er; -est**

1 : giving pleasure or joy : good and enjoyable • I hope you all had a *nice* time. • What a *nice* [=*pleasant*] surprise! • It's so *nice* to see you again. • It's *nice* to be back home. • It's *nice* to know that you're all right. • It would be *nice* to try something different. • We had a very *nice* dinner. • It's supposed to be a *nice* day tomorrow. = The weather should be *nice* tomorrow. • (*US*) Thank you. ***Have a nice day***! [=goodbye] • "Hello, my name is Sara." "It's ***nice to meet you***, Sara." • It's ***nice to see you***, Luis. How have you been? — often used with another adjective for emphasis • a *nice* clear sky [=a sky that is nice because it is clear] • *nice* green grass • The hotel has *nice* big rooms. • a *nice* fresh salad • some *nice* hot soup • The soup is *nice* and hot. • Make sure your room's *nice* and clean. • The library is always *nice* and quiet.

2 : attractive or of good quality • *nice* restaurants • a *nice* car/house • She wears the *nicest* clothes. • She looks *nice*. [=she is attractive] • He looks *nice* in his new suit. • It's a ***nice idea*** [=the idea is a good one], but I don't think it'll work.

3 : kind, polite, and friendly • She is a really *nice* person. • He's such a *nice* young man. • He said some very *nice* things about you. • It's *nice* of you to call. • Try to be *nice* to each other, okay? • That wasn't a very *nice* thing to do. • How *nice* of you to remember my birthday! • As they say, "*Nice* guys finish last." [=you must act in a selfish way if you want to win a competition] — see also MR. NICE GUY

4 : acting in a way that is correct according to social or moral rules : proper and well-behaved • What's a *nice* girl like you doing in a place like this? • They have such *nice* children.

5 : done very well • That was a *nice* [=*great, outstanding*] shot! • *Nice* work! • They've done a *nice* job fixing up the house. — sometimes used in an ironic way to say that something was not good or not done well • What a *nice* mess we've made of things! • *Nice* try, but you're not going to trick me this time. • You crashed her car? Oh, ***nice going***. [=that was a stupid thing to do]

6 *formal* : involving a small difference : difficult to notice or recognize • There is a *nice* distinction between those two words.

make nice *US, informal* : to behave in a polite or friendly way toward other people even though you do not have kind or polite feelings towards them • It's time to forget about the past and *make nice*.

nice and easy *informal* : in a way that is slow, careful, gentle, or easy • The pilot brought the plane down *nice and easy*. • She hit the ball *nice and easy*. [=without a lot of force] • They broke him in *nice and easy*. [=*gently*]

– nice•ness *noun* [*noncount*]

nice–looking *adj* : pleasant to look at : ATTRACTIVE • She's a *nice-looking* young lady.

nice•ly /ˈnaɪsli/ *adv* [*more* ~; *most* ~] : in a pleasant or correct way : WELL • a *nicely* dressed older man • a very *nicely* written essay • Good work. *Nicely* done. • The project seems to be moving along *nicely*. • I think her idea will fit *nicely* into/with our original plans. • "I only have this screwdriver." "Thanks. It will ***do nicely***." [=it is suitable for what I want to do] • Her new book is *doing nicely* in the bookstores. [=is selling well; is a success] • He lives in New York City and ***is doing nicely for himself***. [=is earning a lot of money]

nice•ty /ˈnaɪsəti/ *noun, pl* **-ties** [*count*] : a small detail and especially one that is a part of polite or proper behavior — usually plural • Our grandmother taught us the *niceties* of table manners. • social/legal *niceties* • the *niceties* of English grammar

niche /ˈnɪtʃ, ˈniːʃ/ *noun, pl* **nich•es** [*count*]

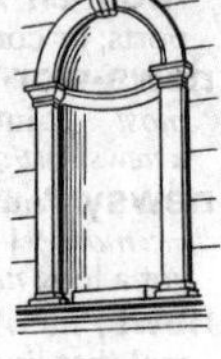
niche

1 : a job, activity, etc., that is very suitable for someone • I found a *niche* for myself after high school. • She finally found her *niche* as a teacher.

2 : the situation in which a business's products or services can succeed by being sold to a particular kind or group of people — usually singular • They're still trying to find their *niche* in the market/industry. • This product ***fills a niche*** in the market. = This product *fills a* market *niche*. [=provides something that certain kinds of people want to buy] — often used before another noun • Teenage girls are our *niche* market. [=are the people we can sell our products to] • *niche* products/publications [=products/publications that appeal to a particular kind or group of people]

3 *technical* : an environment that has all the things that a particular plant or animal needs in order to live • the species that fill an environmental/ecological *niche*

4 : a curved space in a wall that is designed to hold a statue, vase, etc.

¹nick /ˈnɪk/ *noun, pl* **nicks**

1 [*count*] **a** : a small broken area that appears on something after something else hits or cuts it • There is a *nick* [=*chip*] in the cup. • There are a couple of *nicks* on the painting. **b** : a small cut on your skin • His face was covered with *nicks* and cuts after shaving.

2 ***the nick*** *Brit slang* : a prison or police station • She spent a night in *the nick*.

3 [*noncount*] *Brit, informal* : the condition that someone or something is in • I watched the team practice, and all the players looked ***in good nick***. [=*in good shape*] • an economy ***in bad nick***

in the nick of time *informal* : just before the last moment when something can be changed or something bad will happen • He decided to go just *in the nick of time*. • The ambulance arrived *in the nick of time*.

²nick *verb* **nicks; nicked; nick•ing** [+ *obj*]

1 a : to cut or damage a small part of the surface of (something) : to put a nick in (something) • Something *nicked* [=*chipped*] the painting. **b** : to make a small cut on (someone) • He *nicked* himself shaving. • He was *nicked* on the shoulder by a bullet.

2 *Brit slang* **a** : to catch and arrest (someone) • She was *nicked* for the theft. **b** : to steal (something) • I *nicked* a couple of cars when I was younger.

nick•el /ˈnɪkəl/ *noun, pl* **-els**

1 [*noncount*] : a hard silver-white metal

2 [*count*] : a U.S. or Canadian coin that is worth five cents

¹nick•el–and–dime /ˌnɪkələnˈdaɪm/ *adj, always used before a noun, US, informal*

1 : involving, making, or spending a small amount of money • *nickel-and-dime* charges/fees • *nickel-and-dime* tax increases • *nickel-and-dime* customers/tourists

2 : not very important • *nickel-and-dime* [=*small-time*] businesses • *nickel-and-dime* candidates

²nickel–and–dime *verb* **nick•els–and–dimes** *or* **nick•el–and–dimes; nick•eled–and–dimed** *or* **nick•el–and–dimed; nickel•ing–and–dim•ing** *or* **nick•el–and–dim•ing** [+ *obj*] *US, informal* + *disapproving* : to make (someone) pay many small amounts of money over a long period of time • Customers are being *nickeled-and-dimed* by the cell phone company. [=customers are being charged extra small fees by the cell phone company that will add up to a lot of money over time] • You should buy a new car before this one *nickle-and-dimes* you to death. [=before you need to pay for a lot of repairs on this one]

¹nick•name /ˈnɪkˌneɪm/ *noun, pl* **-names** [*count*] : a name (such as "Moose" or "Lady Bird") that is different from your real name but is what your family, friends, etc., call you when they are talking to you or about you • His mother gave him the *nickname* "Winky" when he was a baby. • Earvin "Magic" Johnson got his *nickname* from the way he handled a basketball.

²nickname *verb* **-names; -named; -nam•ing** [+ *obj*] : to give (someone) a name that is not that person's real name : to give a nickname to (someone) • She *nicknamed* him "Winky."

nic•o•tine /ˈnɪkəˌtiːn/ *noun* [*noncount*] : a poisonous substance in tobacco that makes it difficult for people to stop smoking cigarettes

niece /ˈniːs/ *noun, pl* **niec·es** [*count*] **:** a daughter of your brother or sister ▪ If he's my uncle, then I'm his *niece.* — compare NEPHEW

nif·ty /ˈnɪfti/ *adj* **nif·ti·er; -est** *informal + somewhat old-fashioned* **:** very good, useful, or attractive ▪ a *nifty* pair of shoes ▪ This *nifty* little machine can do just about anything.

nig·gard·ly /ˈnɪgɚdli/ *adj* [*more ~; most ~*] *formal + disapproving*
1 : hating to spend money ▪ The story is about a *niggardly* [=*stingy, miserly*] old man who learns to share what he has with others.
2 : very small in amount ▪ a *niggardly* allowance/wage

nig·ger /ˈnɪgɚ/ *noun, pl* **-gers** [*count*] *offensive* **:** a black person ✧ This is one of the most offensive words in English. Do not use this word.

[1]**nig·gle** /ˈnɪgəl/ *verb* **nig·gles; nig·gled; nig·gling** *Brit*
1 : to worry or annoy (someone) [*+ obj*] She had been *niggled* by worry her entire life. ▪ It really *niggles* [=*bothers, bugs*] me that she didn't call. [*no obj*] — often *+ at* ▪ One question continued to *niggle* [=*nag*] *at* him.
2 [*no obj*] **:** to argue or make criticisms about something that is not important ▪ He's always *niggling* over small details.

[2]**niggle** *noun, pl* **nig·gles** [*count*] *chiefly Brit*
1 : a slight feeling of something (such as doubt) ▪ a *niggle of* doubt
2 : a slight pain ▪ I've had a knee *niggle* for the past few days. ▪ He has a bit of a *niggle* in his back.
3 : a small criticism or complaint ▪ I have a few minor *niggles* about the performance.

nig·gling /ˈnɪgəlɪŋ/ *adj, always used before a noun* **:** causing you to feel a slight pain or to be worried or annoyed for a long time ▪ *niggling* [=*nagging*] injuries that just won't heal ▪ a *niggling* doubt

nigh /ˈnaɪ/ *adv, old-fashioned + literary*
1 : close in time or place **:** NEAR ▪ The snow is melting. Spring is *nigh.* ▪ Morning was drawing *nigh.* [=it was almost morning] ▪ The end is *nigh.*
2 : almost or nearly ▪ It would be *nigh* impossible to fix it. ▪ a *nigh* perfect evening — often *+ on, onto,* or *unto* ▪ We've lived here for *nigh on* 40 years. [=almost 40 years] ▪ *nigh onto* a century — see also WELL-NIGH

[1]**night** /ˈnaɪt/ *noun, pl* **nights**
1 : the time of darkness between one day and the next **:** the part of the day when no light from the sun can be seen and most people and animals sleep [*noncount*] Who are you calling at this time of *night*? ▪ It's eleven o'clock ***at night.*** ▪ She and her husband both work *at night* and sleep during the day. ▪ The store's open ***all night.*** ▪ They were up ***all night long*** playing video games. ▪ People keep coming back ***night after night.*** [=every night for a period of time] [*count*] Let's stop for the *night* and get a hotel. ▪ a cold, rainy *night* in the city ▪ Where were you (on) the *night* of June 20th? ▪ The room costs $100 a/per *night.* = The room costs $100 for one *night.* ▪ I stayed up late five *nights* in a row. ▪ We were woken up ***in the middle of the night*** by a loud crash. = (less commonly) We were woken up ***in the dead of night*** by a loud crash. ▪ Did you have a ***good night's sleep***? [=did you sleep well during the night?] ▪ ***Last night,*** I had the strangest dream. ▪ I had a ***late night*** [=I stayed up very late] last night. ▪ Let's ***call it an early night.*** = Let's ***make an early night of it.*** [=let's go home or go to bed early tonight] ▪ Let's ***call it a night.*** [=let's go home or go to bed now] ▪ She'll have to ***spend/stay the night*** in the hospital. [=she will have to sleep overnight in the hospital] ▪ He *spent* many sleepless *nights* worrying about his children. [=he lay awake at night worrying about his children] ▪ *Spend* six *nights* and seven days on a tropical island in the Caribbean! ▪ He ***spent the night with*** [=had sex with and slept with] her. ▪ They decided to ***spend the night together.*** [=they decided to have sex and sleep together]
2 [*noncount*] **:** the darkness that occurs during the nighttime ▪ They walked out into the *night.* ▪ Her eyes were as black/dark as (the) *night.* ▪ animals that hunt ***by night*** [=in darkness] ▪ When ***night fell*** [=when the sky became dark for the night; at nightfall], we walked back to our car.
3 [*count*] **:** the final part of the day that is usually after work, school, etc., and before you go to bed **:** the early part of the night **:** EVENING ▪ They go bowling every Tuesday *night.* ▪ Friday *nights,* we play cards with the neighbors. ▪ What did you have for dinner last *night*? ▪ He planned a *night* of dinner and dancing. ▪ We've planned a ***night out.*** [=an evening that you spend outside of your home doing something fun]
4 [*count*] **a :** an evening or night that has a special event ▪ Poetry *night* [=the night when people read poetry aloud] at the café is every Saturday at eight o'clock. ▪ Wednesday night is our family *night.* [=the night that our family does things together] ▪ Tuesday night is ***ladies' night*** at the ballpark/bar. [=on Tuesday evening, women get a special benefit at the ballpark/bar, such as paying only half price for something] ▪ Tomorrow is the play's ***opening night.*** [=the play will be performed in front of an audience for the first time tomorrow night] **b :** the part of a special day that occurs during the nighttime ▪ Christmas *night* ▪ They spent their wedding *night* in a hotel. — compare EVE 2
day and night *or* ***night and day*** see DAY
night night *or* ***nighty night*** — used by a child or when speaking to a child as a way of saying "good night" ▪ "*Night night,* dear." "*Nighty night,* Mommy."
the still of the night see [4]STILL
— see also ALL-NIGHT, FLY-BY-NIGHT, GOOD NIGHT, ONE-NIGHT STAND

[2]**night** *adj, always used before a noun*
1 : of or relating to the night ▪ the *night* sky ▪ the cool *night* air ▪ during the *night* hours
2 : for use at night ▪ a *night* lamp ▪ an animal with excellent ***night vision*** [=ability to see in the dark]
3 a : happening at night ▪ He is taking a *night* flight. ▪ a *night* game/class [=a game/class in the evening] **b :** active, working, or operating at night ▪ a *night* manager at the supermarket ▪ This is the last *night* bus/train. ▪ I am a ***night person.*** [=a person who likes the night; a person who has the most energy at night]

night·cap /ˈnaɪtˌkæp/ *noun, pl* **-caps** [*count*]
1 : a drink that you have just before you go to bed at night and that usually has alcohol in it
2 : a cloth cap that people used to wear in bed in the past

night·clothes /ˈnaɪtˌkloʊðz, ˈnaɪtˌkloʊz/ *noun* [*plural*] *old-fashioned* **:** clothes that people wear in bed

night·club /ˈnaɪtˌklʌb/ *noun, pl* **-clubs** [*count*] **:** a place that is open at night, has music, dancing, or a show, and usually serves alcoholic drinks and food ▪ He's performed his comedy show in *nightclubs* [=*clubs*] across the country.

night crawler *noun, pl* **~ -ers** [*count*] *US* **:** EARTHWORM

night depository *noun, pl* **~ -to·ries** [*count*] *US* **:** a special box built into the side of a bank that allows a customer to put money, valuable things, etc., in a safe place when the bank is closed — called also (*Brit*) *night safe*

night·dress /ˈnaɪtˌdrɛs/ *noun, pl* **-dress·es** [*count*] *Brit* **:** NIGHTGOWN

night·fall /ˈnaɪtˌfɑːl/ *noun* [*noncount*] **:** the time of day when the sky gets dark **:** the time when night begins ▪ When *nightfall* came, we were still waiting for the electricity to come back on. ▪ We should be back by/before *nightfall.* [=*dark*]

night·gown /ˈnaɪtˌgaʊn/ *noun, pl* **-gowns** [*count*] **:** a loose dress that is worn in bed especially by women and girls — see color picture on page C12

night·ie /ˈnaɪti/ *noun, pl* **-ies** [*count*] *informal* **:** NIGHTGOWN; *especially, US* **:** a sexy and often short nightgown that is worn by women

night·in·gale /ˈnaɪtn̩ˌgeɪl/ *noun, pl* **-gales** [*count*] **:** a small brown European bird that sings a beautiful song especially at night

night·life /ˈnaɪtˌlaɪf/ *noun* [*noncount*] **:** social activities and forms of entertainment that are available at night in bars, nightclubs, etc. ▪ The city is famous for its *nightlife.*

night·light /ˈnaɪtˌlaɪt/ *noun, pl* **-lights** [*count*] **:** a small light that is on during the night ▪ We keep a *nightlight* on in the baby's room.

[1]**night·ly** /ˈnaɪtli/ *adj* **:** happening or done every night ▪ There were *nightly* attacks on the city. ▪ a *nightly* event ▪ the *nightly* news ▪ These clubs provide *nightly* entertainment. ▪ She asked me about it ***on a nightly basis.*** [=every night]

[2]**nightly** *adv* **:** every night ▪ She performs at the club *nightly.* ▪ The restaurant serves dinner *nightly.*

night·mare /ˈnaɪtˌmeɚ/ *noun, pl* **-mares** [*count*]
1 : a dream that frightens a sleeping person **:** a very bad dream ▪ Mommy, I had a really scary *nightmare.* ▪ She had a recurring *nightmare* [=she had the same bad dream many times] about losing her job.
2 : a very bad or frightening experience or situation ▪ The party was a complete *nightmare.* ▪ a *nightmare* situation/scenario ▪ Losing a child is every parent's ***worst nightmare.*** [=the thing every parent fears most]
— night·mar·ish /ˈnaɪtˌmerɪʃ/ *adj* [*more ~; most ~*] ▪ a *nightmarish* experience

night owl *noun, pl* ~ **owls** [*count*] *informal* **: a person who enjoys staying up late at night**

nights /ˈnaɪts/ *adv, chiefly US* **: at night : during the nighttime** ▪ He works *nights* and weekends. ▪ *Nights*, we usually watch TV. — **compare** DAYS

night safe *noun, pl* ~ **safes** [*count*] *Brit* **:** NIGHT DEPOSITORY

night school *noun* [*noncount*] **: high school or college classes that are taught at night for people who work during the day** ▪ You could go to *night school* and earn a degree.

night shift *noun, pl* ~ **shifts** [*count*]
1 : a period of time during the night (such as from 11 p.m. to 7 a.m.) in which a person is scheduled to work — usually singular ▪ He works the *night shift* [=(*US*) *graveyard shift*] and sleeps during the day.
2 : a group of people who work during the night shift — usually singular ▪ The *night shift* is starting to arrive.

night·shirt /ˈnaɪtˌʃɚt/ *noun, pl* **-shirts** [*count*] **: a long, loose shirt that you wear in bed**

night·spot /ˈnaɪtˌspɑːt/ *noun, pl* **-spots** [*count*] **:** NIGHTCLUB

night·stand /ˈnaɪtˌstænd/ *noun, pl* **-stands** [*count*] *US* **: a small table that is next to a bed — called also** *night table*

night·stick /ˈnaɪtˌstɪk/ *noun, pl* **-sticks** [*count*] *US* **: a heavy stick that is carried by police officers and is used as a weapon — called also** *baton,* (*US*) *billy club,* (*Brit*) *truncheon*

night·time /ˈnaɪtˌtaɪm/ *noun* [*noncount*] **: the time of darkness between one day and the next : the time of day when no light from the sun can be seen** ▪ It's not safe to go out at *nighttime*. [=(more commonly) *night*] ▪ The animal hunts in the *nighttime*. **— often used before another noun** ▪ *nighttime* temperatures ▪ a *nighttime* attack

night watchman *noun, pl* ~ **-men** [*count*] **: a person whose job is to watch and guard property at night**

NIH *abbr* National Institutes of Health ✧ In the U.S., the National Institutes of Health is a branch of government that pays doctors and scientists to do medical research.

ni·hil·ism /ˈnajəˌlɪzəm/ *noun* [*noncount*] *formal*
1 : the belief that traditional morals, ideas, beliefs, etc., have no worth or value
2 : the belief that a society's political and social institutions are so bad that they should be destroyed
– ni·hil·ist /ˈnajəlɪst/ *noun, pl* **-ists** [*count*] **– ni·hil·is·tic** /ˌnajəˈlɪstɪk/ *adj* [*more* ~; *most* ~] ▪ a *nihilistic* vision of the world ▪ *nihilistic* people

N

-nik /-ˌnɪk/ *noun suffix, informal* + *often disapproving* **: a person connected to an activity, an organization, a movement, etc.** ▪ a peace*nik* [=a person who is opposed to war] ▪ (*US*) a neat*nik* [=a very neat person]

nil /ˈnɪl/ *noun* [*noncount*]
1 : none at all : ZERO ▪ The chances of that happening are practically/almost *nil*. [=*nothing*]
2 *Brit* **: a score of zero** ▪ They took a 2 to *nil* lead in the second half of the game.

nim·ble /ˈnɪmbəl/ *adj* **nim·bler; nim·blest** [*or more* ~; *most* ~]
1 : able to move quickly, easily, and lightly ▪ a *nimble* [=*agile*] dancer ▪ the pianist's *nimble* fingers
2 : able to learn and understand things quickly and easily ▪ a *nimble* [=*quick, clever*] mind
– nim·bly /ˈnɪmbli/ *adv* ▪ She ran *nimbly* up the stairs.

nim·bus /ˈnɪmbəs/ *noun, pl* **-bus·es** [*count*] *formal* + *literary* **: a circle of light :** HALO

NIMBY /ˈnɪmbi/ *adj, always used before a noun* **— used to describe the attitude and actions of people who try to prevent something (such as a prison or a shelter for homeless people) from being built near the place where they live** ✧ *NIMBY* comes from the phrase "*n*ot *i*n *m*y *b*ack *y*ard." ▪ News about toxic leaks from old landfills has resulted in the *NIMBY* syndrome. [=nobody wants a new landfill built nearby, because landfills in other places have poisoned people] ▪ *NIMBY* issues/pressures

NIMH *abbr* National Institute of Mental Health ✧ In the U.S., the National Institute of Mental Health supplies money for research about mental illness.

nim·rod /ˈnɪmˌrɑːd/ *noun, pl* **-rods** [*count*] *US slang*
1 : a foolish or stupid person ▪ Don't be such a *nimrod*.
2 : a person who hunts wild animals : HUNTER

nin·com·poop /ˈnɪnkəmˌpuːp/ *noun, pl* **-poops** [*count*] *informal* **: a foolish or stupid person** ▪ The people running that company are a bunch of *nincompoops*!

nine /ˈnaɪn/ *noun, pl* **nines**
1 [*count*] **: the number 9**
2 [*count*] **: the ninth in a set or series** ▪ The next card was the *nine* of diamonds. ▪ She wears a size *nine*.
3 [*noncount*] **: nine o'clock** ▪ "What time is it?" "It's *nine*." ▪ He woke up at *nine* this morning. ▪ a ***nine-to-five job*** [=a job that you work during regular business hours usually in an office]
4 [*count*] **: the first or last nine holes of an 18-hole golf course — usually singular** ▪ She didn't play well on the ***front nine*** [=on holes 1 through 9], but she was one under par on the ***back nine***. [=on holes 10 through 18]
on cloud nine see [1]CLOUD
the whole nine yards see [2]YARD
to the nines **: in a very fancy or impressive way** ▪ He was dressed *to the nines*.
– nine *adj* ▪ It took us *nine* hours to get there. **– nine** *pronoun* ▪ I would like *nine* (of them), please. ▪ *Nine* out of 10 [=90 percent of] doctors agree that this treatment works.

nine days' wonder *or* **nine day wonder** *noun* [*singular*] *chiefly Brit, somewhat old-fashioned* **: something (such as a news story) that people talk about a lot but only for a short time** ▪ She left her husband and ran away with a younger man. It was a *nine days' wonder*.

nine·teen /naɪnˈtiːn/ *noun, pl* **-teens** [*count*] **: the number 19**
– nineteen *adj* ▪ *nineteen* hours **– nineteen** *pronoun* ▪ She bought *nineteen* (of them). **– nine·teenth** /naɪnˈtiːnθ/ *noun, pl* **-teenths** [*count*] ▪ The book is due back on the *nineteenth* (of the month). ▪ one *nineteenth* of the total cost **– nineteenth** *adj* ▪ He was the country's *nineteenth* president. ▪ I was the *nineteenth* person to cross the finish line. ▪ (*humorous*) the ***nineteenth hole*** [=the bar at a golf course where players drink after playing a round of 18 holes of golf] **– nineteenth** *adv* ▪ She finished *nineteenth* in the race. ▪ the country's *nineteenth* largest state

nine·ty /ˈnaɪnti/ *noun, pl* **-ties**
1 [*count*] **: the number 90**
2 ***nine·ties*** [*plural*] **a : the numbers ranging from 90 to 99** ▪ temperatures in the *nineties* ▪ It was priced in the low *nineties*. [=its price was about $91,000–$93,000] **b : a set of years ending in digits ranging from 90 to 99** ▪ I studied there in the *nineties*. [=between 1990–1999] ▪ During the *nineties*, he was going to college and working part-time. ▪ He lived into his *nineties*. [=he was over ninety years old when he died]
– nine·ti·eth /ˈnaɪntijəθ/ *noun, pl* **-eths** [*count*] ▪ one *ninetieth* of the total cost **– ninetieth** *adj* ▪ her *ninetieth* birthday **– ninety** *adj* ▪ *ninety* dollars **– ninety** *pronoun* ▪ We spent thirty dollars and had *ninety* left.

nin·ja /ˈnɪnʤə/ *noun, pl* **ninja** *also* **nin·jas** [*count*] **: a fighter who is trained in the Japanese martial arts**

nin·ny /ˈnɪni/ *noun, pl* **-nies** [*count*] *informal* + *somewhat old-fashioned* **: a foolish or stupid person**

[1]**ninth** /ˈnaɪnθ/ *noun, pl* **ninths**
1 [*singular*] **: the number nine in a series** ▪ We'll be leaving on the *ninth*. [=the ninth day of the month] ▪ He hit a home run in the *ninth*. [=the ninth inning of a baseball game]
2 [*count*] **: one of nine equal parts of something** ▪ She owned one *ninth* of the company.

[2]**ninth** *adj* **: occupying the number nine position in a series** ▪ on the *ninth* day ▪ the book's *ninth* edition ▪ She's in (the) *ninth* grade at school.
– ninth *adv* ▪ He finished *ninth* in the race. ▪ the country's *ninth* largest city

[1]**nip** /ˈnɪp/ *verb* **nips; nipped; nip·ping**
1 : to bite or pinch (someone or something) lightly [+ *obj*] The dog *nipped* my ankles. [*no obj*] — + *at* ▪ The dog *nipped at* my ankles.
2 [+ *obj*] *US, sports* **: to defeat (someone or something) by a small amount** ▪ The New York Mets *nipped* the Atlanta Braves 1–0.
3 *always followed by an adverb or preposition* [*no obj*] *chiefly Brit, informal* **: to go to a place quickly or for a short period of time** ▪ I had to *nip* back to my place. ▪ He *nipped* in ahead of me in line. ▪ He *nipped* into the store to buy milk.
4 : to harm or hurt (something) with cold [+ *obj*] An early frost *nipped* the crops. ▪ The cold wind was *nipping* my nose. [*no obj*] — + *at* ▪ The cold wind *nipped at* my nose.
nip off [*phrasal verb*] ***nip off (something) or nip (something) off*** **: to remove (something) by squeezing it tightly between your fingers or the parts of a tool** ▪ He *nipped off* the bud

with his fingers. ▪ She *nipped* the dead branches *off* with her clippers.

***nip (something) in the bud** informal* : to stop (something) immediately so that it does not become a worse problem ▪ Inflation will only get worse if the government doesn't do something right now to *nip it in the bud*.

²nip *noun, pl* **nips**

1 [*singular*] : a feeling of cold ▪ I could feel the *nip* [=*coldness*] in the air.

2 [*count*] : a light bite or pinch ▪ The dog ***gave me a nip*** on the leg.

– compare ³NIP

³nip *noun, pl* **nips** [*count*]

1 *informal* : a small amount of liquor ▪ a *nip* of whiskey ▪ He ***takes a nip*** now and then.

2 : a very small bottle of liquor

– compare ²NIP

nip and tuck *adj, US, of a race or other competition* : so close that the lead changes quickly and very often from one person or team to another ▪ The race was *nip and tuck* for a while.

– **nip and tuck** *adv* ▪ The candidates were running *nip and tuck* early in the campaign.

nip·per /ˈnɪpɚ/ *noun, pl* **-pers**

1 ***nippers*** [*plural*] : a device or tool that is used for cutting something ▪ She used the *nippers* to prune the bush.

2 [*count*] *chiefly Brit, informal* : a small child ▪ when I was just a *nipper*

nip·ple /ˈnɪpəl/ *noun, pl* **nip·ples** [*count*]

1 : either one of the two small, round parts on a person's chest that are darker in color than the area around them — see picture at HUMAN

2 *US* : a rubber or plastic device that is attached to a bottle and that has a small opening from which a baby can suck milk — called also (*Brit*) *teat*

nip·py /ˈnɪpi/ *adj* **nip·pi·er; -est** *informal*

1 : somewhat cold : CHILLY ▪ a *nippy* morning

2 *Brit* : able to move quickly : FAST ▪ a *nippy* car

nir·va·na /niɚˈvɑːnə, nəˈvɑːnə/ *noun, pl* **-nas**

1 [*noncount*] : the state of perfect happiness and peace in Buddhism where there is release from all forms of suffering

2 : a state or place of great happiness and peace [*count*] — usually singular ▪ The island is a *nirvana* for divers. [*noncount*] Spending the afternoon at the museum was her idea of *nirvana*. [=*paradise, heaven*]

nit /ˈnɪt/ *noun, pl* **nits** [*count*] *Brit, informal* : a stupid or silly person : NITWIT

nit·pick·ing /ˈnɪtˌpɪkɪŋ/ *noun* [*noncount*] *informal + disapproving* : the act of arguing about details that are not important or criticizing small mistakes that are not important ▪ She was tired of all the *nitpicking* and wanted to get on with the project.

– **nit·pick·er** /ˈnɪtˌpɪkɚ/ *noun, pl* **-ers** [*count*] ▪ *Nitpickers* might question his choice of words, but his point was worth making.

ni·trate /ˈnaɪˌtreɪt/ *noun, pl* **-trates** [*count, noncount*] : a chemical compound that contains oxygen and nitrogen and that is used in fertilizer

ni·tric acid /ˈnaɪtrɪk-/ *noun* [*noncount*] : a strong acid that contains nitrogen and that is used in making fertilizers, explosives, etc.

ni·tro·gen /ˈnaɪtrədʒən/ *noun* [*noncount*] : a chemical that has no color or smell and that makes up a large part of the atmosphere

ni·tro·glyc·er·in *or* **ni·tro·glyc·er·ine** /ˌnaɪtrəˈglɪsərən/ *noun* [*noncount*] : a liquid that is used in making explosives and in medicine

ni·trous oxide /ˈnaɪtrəs-/ *noun* [*noncount*] : a gas that is used by dentists to keep patients from feeling pain — called also *laughing gas*

nit·ty–grit·ty /ˈnɪtiˌgrɪti/ *noun*

the nitty-gritty** informal* : the most important and basic facts or details about something ▪ He deals with *the nitty-gritty* of running the department. ▪ We finally ***got down to the nitty-gritty of the problem. ▪ Let's *get down to the nitty-gritty* and find out what happened.

nit·wit /ˈnɪtˌwɪt/ *noun, pl* **-wits** [*count*] *informal* : a stupid or silly person ▪ Don't be such a *nitwit*.

¹nix /ˈnɪks/ *verb* **nix·es; nixed; nix·ing** [+ *obj*] *US, informal* : to refuse to accept or allow (something) : to say no to (something, such as a suggestion or plan) ▪ We quickly *nixed* [=*rejected*] his idea.

²nix *adv, US, informal + somewhat old-fashioned* : ¹NO — used to show that you disagree with or will not allow something; often + *on* ▪ They put a *nix on* our plan. [=they rejected our plan]

NJ *abbr* New Jersey

NM *abbr* New Mexico

NNE *abbr* north-northeast

NNW *abbr* north-northwest

¹no /ˈnoʊ/ *adv*

1 a — used to give a negative answer or reply to a question, request, or offer ▪ "Are you going?" "*No*, I am not going." ▪ *No*, you can't have any more candy. ▪ "Did you hear something?" "*No*." ▪ "Do you need a ride?" "*No*, thank you. My wife is picking me up." ▪ He wanted to stay longer but I had to say *no*. ▪ I told him that I couldn't come to the party, but he ***wouldn't take no for an answer***. [=he insisted that I come to the party] **b** : in a way that shows a negative response ▪ She shook her head *no*.

2 — used to introduce a statement that corrects an earlier statement ▪ *No*, that's not the way it happened. ▪ I saw him yesterday—*no*, the day before. ▪ It's big, *no*, it's gigantic. ▪ She has the right, *no*, the duty, to continue her studies.

3 : in no degree or amount : not at all — used in comparisons ▪ The hotel was *no* better than I expected it to be. ▪ You are *no* worse off now than you were before. ▪ He works *no* more than 30 hours per week. ▪ Your experience was *no* different from mine.

4 — used before an adjective to indicate a meaning that is the opposite of the adjective's meaning ▪ He made it clear in *no* uncertain terms [=he made it very clear] that he did not approve of the decision. ▪ It is a matter of *no* small importance. [=it is a matter of much importance]

5 — used to show surprise, doubt, or disbelief ▪ Oh, *no*. Not again. ▪ *No*—you don't say? ▪ *No*, that's impossible. ▪ *No*, you couldn't have been the one responsible.

6 — used to express agreement with a negative statement ▪ "She shouldn't work so hard." "*No*, she really shouldn't."

7 — used to tell someone not to do something ▪ *No*, don't touch that switch.

²no *adj, always used before a noun*

1 : not any ▪ She said she had *no* money. ▪ I wanted *no* part of the plan. ▪ They showed *no* concern for my feelings. ▪ people with little or *no* experience with computers ▪ There is *no* parking [=parking is not allowed] on this street. ▪ The sign says "*No* smoking." [=smoking is not allowed] ▪ There's *no* disputing [=it is not possible to dispute] the decision.

2 — used to say that someone or something is not the kind of person or thing being described ▪ He's *no* expert [=he's not an expert] in American history. ▪ She's *no* fool. ▪ This is *no* simple matter. [=this is not a simple matter]

³no *noun, pl* **noes** *or* **nos**

1 [*count*] : a negative answer : an answer of no — usually singular ▪ I asked for the day off and received a *no* in reply.

2 a [*count*] : a vote of no ▪ There were 110 ayes and only 16 *noes*. **b** [*plural*] : people who are voting no ▪ The *noes* raised their hands.

No. *or* **no.** *abbr* **1** number ▪ He lives at *No*. 35 Main Street. **2** north, northern

no–account *adj, always used before a noun, US, informal + disapproving* : having no worth or value : WORTHLESS ▪ I don't trust her or her lazy, *no-account* husband.

– **no–account** *noun, pl* **-counts** [*count*] ▪ Her husband is a lazy *no-account*.

nob /ˈnɑːb/ *noun, pl* **nobs** [*count*] *chiefly Brit, informal + old-fashioned* : a person who is wealthy or belongs to the upper class ▪ She threw a party and invited all the local *nobs*.

nob·ble /ˈnɑːbəl/ *verb* **nob·bles; nob·bled; nob·bling** [+ *obj*] *Brit, informal*

1 : to give a drug to (a horse) to keep it from winning a race ▪ We found out later that the horse had been *nobbled*, which explained its poor performance.

2 : to cause or force (someone) to do something that you want by offering money, making threats, etc. ▪ She was trying to *nobble* the jury. ▪ *nobble* a witness

3 : to succeed in getting or catching (something or someone) ▪ I was about to leave when I was *nobbled* [=*nabbed*] by a man asking for directions.

No·bel Prize /noʊˈbɛl-/ *noun, pl* ~ **Prizes** [*count*] : one of six annual prizes that are awarded to people for important work in the fields of literature, physics, chemistry, medicine, and economics and for helping to bring about peace in the

N

world • He won the *Nobel Prize* for economics. • the *Nobel Peace Prize* — called also *Nobel*

no·bil·i·ty /noʊˈbɪləti/ *noun*

1 [*noncount*] : the quality or state of being noble in character or quality • the *nobility* of his character • I admire her *nobility*. • They have shown great courage and *nobility* of purpose.

2 ***the nobility*** : the group of people who are members of the highest social class in some countries • a member of *the nobility* [=*aristocracy*]

[1]**no·ble** /ˈnoʊbəl/ *adj* **no·bler; no·blest** [*also more* ~; *most* ~]

1 : having, showing, or coming from personal qualities that people admire (such as honesty, generosity, courage, etc.) • He was a man of *noble* character. • It was *noble* of her to come forward with this information. • a *noble* ideal/ambition/cause/purpose

2 *always used before a noun* : of, relating to, or belonging to the highest social class : of, relating to, or belonging to the nobility • She married a man of *noble* [=*aristocratic*] birth/rank. • his *noble* ancestry • the *noble* class

3 : impressive in size or appearance • a *noble* cathedral

4 *technical* : not chemically affected by other substances (such as oxygen) • Platinum is a *noble* metal. • Helium is a *noble* gas.

— no·bly /ˈnoʊbli/ *adv* • He worked *nobly* in support of their efforts.

[2]**noble** *noun, pl* **no·bles** [*count*] : a person who is a member of the nobility

no·ble·man /ˈnoʊblmən/ *noun, pl* **-men** /-mən/ [*count*] : a man who is a member of the nobility

no·blesse oblige /noʊˌblɛsəˈbliːʒ/ *noun* [*noncount*] *formal* : the idea that people who have high social rank or wealth should be helpful and generous to people of lower rank or to people who are poor • He was raised to have a strong sense of *noblesse oblige*.

no·ble·wom·an /ˈnoʊbəlˌwʊmən/ *noun, pl* **-wom·en** /-ˌwɪmən/ [*count*] : a woman who is a member of the nobility

[1]**no·body** /ˈnoʊbədi/ *pronoun* : no person : NO ONE • There's *nobody* here. • *Nobody* could answer my question. • I guess I'll have to volunteer because it's clear ***nobody else*** will.

nobody's business see BUSINESS

nobody's fool see [1]FOOL

[2]**nobody** *noun, pl* **-bod·ies** [*count*] : someone who is not important or has no influence • He was a *nobody* in high school.

no–brain·er /ˈnoʊˈbreɪnɚ/ *noun, pl* **-ers** [*count*] *informal* : a decision or choice that is very easy to make and requires very little thought • The offer of a full scholarship made his choice of colleges a *no-brainer*.

noc·tur·nal /nɑkˈtənl/ *adj*

1 : active mainly during the night • *nocturnal* animals — opposite DIURNAL

2 *formal* : happening at night • a *nocturnal* journey

noc·turne /ˈnɑːkˌtən/ *noun, pl* **-turnes** [*count*] : a piece of music especially for the piano that has a soft and somewhat sad melody

[1]**nod** /ˈnɑːd/ *verb* **nods; nod·ded; nod·ding**

1 a : to move your head up and down as a way of answering "yes" or of showing agreement, understanding, or approval [*no obj*] She *nodded* when I asked her if she was ready. • He *nodded* in agreement. [+ *obj*] He *nodded* agreement/approval. • I asked her if she could hear me, and she ***nodded her head***. **b** : to move your head up and down as a signal to someone or as a way of saying hello or goodbye to someone [*no obj*] — often + *to* • The guard *nodded to* us as we walked in. • He *nodded to* his assistant to start the slide show. — often + *at* • She *nodded at* us as she walked past. [+ *obj*] She *nodded* hello.

2 *always followed by an adverb or preposition* [*no obj*] : to slightly move your head in a specified direction • "The bathroom is around the corner," he said, *nodding* to the left. • She *nodded* toward the dirty dishes and said she would get to them later.

3 [*no obj*] : to move up and down • The tulips *nodded* [=*bobbed, swayed*] in the breeze.

nod off [*phrasal verb*] *informal* : to fall asleep • I *nodded off* during his speech.

[2]**nod** *noun, pl* **nods**

1 [*count*] : a movement of your head up and down especially as a way of answering "yes" or of showing agreement, understanding, or approval : an act of nodding • He ***gave me a nod*** [=he nodded at me] as he walked by.

2 [*singular*] *somewhat informal* : something done to show that someone or something has been chosen, approved, etc. • He received/got the party's *nod* as candidate for governor. [=the party chose him as candidate for governor] • She deserves at least a *nod* [=she deserves at least some recognition] for her management of the project. • We're waiting to ***get the nod*** [=to get approval] from the city to start the project. • She finally ***gave us the nod*** on the plans. [=she finally approved our plans]

on the nod *Brit, informal* : by general agreement and without discussion • The proposal went through *on the nod*.

nodding *adj, always used before a noun* : bending downward or forward • a plant with *nodding* [=*drooping*] flowers

a nodding acquaintance : a small amount of knowledge about someone or something • We only have a *nodding acquaintance* with each other. [=we only know each other slightly] • I only have a *nodding acquaintance* with Greek history. [=I know only a little about Greek history]

node /ˈnoʊd/ *noun, pl* **nodes** [*count*] *technical*

1 : a small lump or mass of tissue in your body; *especially* : LYMPH NODE

2 : the small round part on the stem of a plant where a leaf grows

3 : a place where lines in a network cross or meet • a network *node*

— nod·al /ˈnoʊdl/ *adj, always used before a noun* • *nodal* tissue • a *nodal* point

nod·ule /ˈnɑːʤul, *Brit* ˈnɒdjul/ *noun, pl* **nod·ules** [*count*] *technical* : a small lump on a part of the body or on the root of a plant • The examination revealed a *nodule* on his lung. • root *nodules*

No·el /noʊˈɛl/ *noun* [*noncount*] : Christmas or the Christmas season ✧ *Noel* is especially used in Christmas greetings and Christmas songs.

noes *plural of* [3]NO

no–fault *adj, always used before a noun, chiefly US*

1 — used to describe a type of insurance in which someone involved in a car accident is paid a certain amount of money for damages without the need to decide who caused the accident • *no-fault* insurance • a *no-fault* policy/claim

2 *law* — used to describe a type of divorce in which neither the husband nor the wife is blamed for the end of the marriage • a *no-fault* divorce

no–fly zone *noun, pl* ~ **zones** [*count*] *technical* : an area where military airplanes are not allowed to fly during a conflict or war

no–frills *adj, always used before a noun* : offering or providing only the most important or basic things : not fancy or luxurious • We flew with a *no-frills* airline. • The restaurant offers *no-frills* dining.

nog·gin /ˈnɑːgən/ *noun, pl* **-gins** [*count*] *informal* : a person's head • He fell and got a bump on his *noggin*. • ***Use your noggin***. [=*think*; use your head]

no–go area *noun, pl* ~ **areas** [*count*] *chiefly Brit* : an area that is dangerous or where people are not allowed to go • He reported from one of the city's *no-go areas*. — often used figuratively • Religion is a *no-go area* when you talk with her.

[1]**no–good** *adj, always used before a noun, informal* : having no worth, use, or chance of success • Look at what that *no-good* idiot has done. • I don't trust that lying *no-good* brother of hers.

[2]**no–good** *noun, pl* **-goods** [*count*] *US, informal* : a bad or useless person • Stay away from those *no-goods*.

no–hit *adj, always used before a noun, baseball* — used to describe a game or inning in which a pitcher does not allow the batters from the other team to get a base hit • He pitched a *no-hit* game today. • After seven *no-hit* innings, he gave up a home run in the eighth.

no–hit·ter /ˌnoʊˈhɪtɚ/ *noun, pl* **-ters** [*count*] *baseball* : a game in which a pitcher does not allow the batters from the other team to get a base hit • He pitched a *no-hitter*.

no–holds–barred /ˌnoʊˌhoʊldzˈbaɚd/ *adj* : free from the usual limits or rules • a *no-holds-barred* interview with the senator • a *no-holds-barred* contest

no–hop·er /ˈnoʊˈhoʊpɚ/ *noun, pl* **-ers** [*count*] *chiefly Brit, informal* : someone or something that has no chance of success • a team of *no-hopers*

noise /ˈnɔɪz/ *noun, pl* **nois·es**

1 a [*noncount*] : a loud or unpleasant sound • I couldn't hear him over all the *noise*. • That's not music. To me it's a bunch of *noise*. • The furnace makes a lot of *noise* when it comes on. • We closed the windows to block out the traffic *noise*. •

The landlord has been getting complaints from the tenants about *noise*. **b :** a sound that someone or something makes [*count*] There were *noises* coming from the basement. • The sink was making a gurgling *noise*. • Do you hear that rattling/buzzing/banging *noise*? [*noncount*] The machine hardly makes any *noise*. — see also BACKGROUND NOISE, WHITE NOISE

2 [*noncount*] **a** *technical* **:** unwanted electronic signals that harm the quality of something (such as a radio or television broadcast or a digital photograph) **b :** information that is not useful or important and that makes it more difficult to find the information that you want or need • The initial data included a lot of *noise* that had to be weeded out.

make noise **1 :** to talk about something — often used to suggest that the things being said are not sincere or effective • Congress has been *making* (a lot of) *noise* about lowering taxes, but no one expects it to happen. **2 :** to complain about something • People have been *making* (a lot of) *noise* about the price increases.

make noises **1 :** to talk about something in usually an indirect way — usually + *about* • She started *making noises about* running for office. [=she started saying things that showed she was thinking about running for office] • Her parents are *making noises about* wanting a grandchild. • The government has been *making* some encouraging *noises about* the possibility of a tax cut. **2 :** to make statements of a specified kind • The company has been ***making soothing/reassuring noises*** to calm the fears of investors. — often used to suggest that the things being said are not sincere or effective • Politicians are ***making (all) the right noises*** about improving the schools, but they don't want to spend any money to do it.

– see also BIG NOISE

– **noise·less** /ˈnoɪzləs/ *adj* • The machine is almost *noiseless*. • *noiseless* footsteps – **noise·less·ly** *adv* • He slipped into the room *noiselessly*.

noise·mak·er /ˈnoɪzˌmeɪkɚ/ *noun, pl* **-ers** [*count*] *US* **:** a device (such as a horn) that is used to make noise at parties • All the guests had *noisemakers* and party hats.

noise pollution *noun* [*noncount*] **:** loud or unpleasant noise that is caused by automobiles, airplanes, etc., and that is harmful or annoying to the people who can hear it • The airport has made changes to decrease *noise pollution*.

noi·some /ˈnoɪsəm/ *adj* [*more ~; most ~*] *formal + literary* **:** very unpleasant or disgusting • a *noisome* [=*sickening*] odor

noisy /ˈnoɪzi/ *adj* **nois·i·er; -est** [*also more ~; most ~*]

1 : making a lot of loud or unpleasant noise • The playground was filled with *noisy* children. • His lawnmower is very *noisy*. • a *noisy* crowd

2 : full of loud or unpleasant noise • a *noisy* street/restaurant/office

– **nois·i·ly** /ˈnoɪzəli/ *adv* • The dog barked *noisily*.

no·mad /ˈnoʊˌmæd/ *noun, pl* **-mads** [*count*] **:** a member of a group of people who move from place to place instead of living in one place all the time • a tribe of *nomads* • He lived like a *nomad* for a few years after college, never holding a job in one place for very long.

– **no·mad·ic** /noʊˈmædɪk/ *adj* [*more ~; most ~*] • *nomadic* tribes • He has a very *nomadic* lifestyle. [=he is always moving to different places]

no–man's–land /ˈnoʊˌmænzˌlænd/ *noun* [*singular*] **:** an area of land between two countries or armies that is not controlled by anyone — often used figuratively • His music lies in the *no-man's-land* between jazz and rock. • The downtown area was a *no-man's-land* of abandoned buildings and decay.

nom de plume /ˌnɑːmdɪˈpluːm/ *noun, pl* **noms de plume** /ˌnɑːmzdɪˈpluːm/ [*count*] *formal* **:** a name used by a writer instead of the writer's real name **:** PEN NAME • He wrote under a *nom de plume*.

no·men·cla·ture /ˈnoʊmənˌkleɪtʃɚ, *Brit* nəʊˈmɛŋklətʃə/ *noun, pl* **-tures** *formal* **:** a system of names for things especially in science [*noncount*] botanical *nomenclature* [*count*] the *nomenclatures of* zoology and chemistry

nom·i·nal /ˈnɑːmənl/ *adj, formal*

1 : existing as something in name only **:** not actual or real • He was the *nominal* head of the party. [=he was called the head of the party but he did not actually run the party] • Her title of vice president had been *nominal* only.

2 : very small in amount • a *nominal* price/charge • They charge a *nominal* fee for the service. • His involvement was *nominal*.

– **nom·i·nal·ly** *adv* • He was *nominally* in charge of the project.

nom·i·nate /ˈnɑːməˌneɪt/ *verb* **-nates; -nat·ed; -nat·ing** [+ *obj*]

1 a : to formally choose (someone) as a candidate for a job, position, office, etc. • We expect the party to *nominate* him for president. • The President *nominated* her for Attorney General. — often used as *(be) nominated* • She *was nominated* for a second term. **b :** to choose (someone) for a job, position, office, etc. • The chairman can *nominate* [=*name, appoint*] three members to the committee. • Someone has to tell her the truth—I *nominate* you. — often used as *(be) nominated* • He *was nominated* to the Supreme Court. • She *was nominated* by the chairman.

2 : to choose (someone or something) as a candidate for receiving an honor or award • We *nominated* her for player of the year. — often used as *(be) nominated* • He *was nominated* for an Academy Award for his role in the film. • She *was nominated* as Best Actress three times in her career.

nom·i·na·tion /ˌnɑːməˈneɪʃən/ *noun, pl* **-tions**

1 a [*count*] **:** the act of formally choosing someone as a candidate for a job, position, office, etc. • We expect him to get the Democratic *nomination*. **b :** the act of choosing someone for a job, position, office, etc. [*count*] The Senate has to approve his *nomination*. [=*choice*] [*noncount*] Membership is by *nomination* only.

2 [*count*] **a :** the act of choosing someone or something as a candidate for receiving an honor or award • The novel earned a *nomination* for the National Book Award. • The film received five Academy Award *nominations*. **b :** someone or something that has been chosen as a candidate for receiving an honor or award • The *nominations* for the Academy Awards have been announced.

nom·i·na·tive /ˈnɑːmənətɪv/ *noun* [*noncount*] *grammar* **:** the form of a noun, pronoun, or adjective when it is the subject of a verb • "He" in "He sees her" is in the *nominative*. — compare ACCUSATIVE

– **nominative** *adj* • the *nominative* case

nom·i·nee /ˌnɑːməˈniː/ *noun, pl* **-nees** [*count*] **:** someone or something that has been chosen as a candidate for a job, position, office, honor, award, etc. **:** someone or something that has been nominated • He is expected to be the Democratic *nominee*. • There's been a lot of controversy about the *nominee* to the Supreme Court. — often + *for* • She is one of the *nominees for* Best Actress. • the President's *nominee for* Attorney General

non- /nɑn/ *prefix* **:** not • *non*fatal • *non*fiction • *non*profit • *non*-native English speakers • a *non*religious holiday

no·na·ge·nar·i·an /ˌnoʊnədʒəˈnerijən/ *noun, pl* **-ans** [*count*] **:** a person who is between 90 and 99 years old

non·ag·gres·sion /ˌnɑːnəˈgrɛʃən/ *noun* [*noncount*] **:** a situation in which countries promise that they will not attack each other • a policy of *nonaggression* • The countries have signed a ***nonaggression treaty/pact***. [=a formal agreement between countries to not attack each other]

non·al·co·hol·ic /ˌnɑːnˌælkəˈhɑːlɪk/ *adj* — used to describe a drink that does not contain any alcohol • *nonalcoholic* drinks/beer

non·aligned /ˌnɑːnəˈlaɪnd/ *adj* **:** not having made an official agreement to receive support from and give support to one extremely powerful country (such as the U.S. or the U.S.S.R.) rather than another • *nonaligned* countries

– **non·align·ment** /ˌnɑːnəˈlaɪnmənt/ *noun* [*noncount*] • a policy of *nonalignment* [=*neutrality*]

no–name /ˈnoʊˌneɪm/ *adj, always used before a noun, chiefly US*

1 : having a name that most people do not know **:** not well-known • She often buys cheap, *no-name* products.

2 : having players, members, etc., whose names are not by most people • a *no-name* baseball team

– **no–name** *noun, pl* **-names** [*count*] • He was surprised that a team full of *no-names* won the championship.

non·ap·pear·ance /ˌnɑːnəˈpirəns/ *noun, pl* **-anc·es** [*count, noncount*] *somewhat formal* **:** failure to be at a place where you are expected to be • His fans were disappointed by his *nonappearance* at the concert.

non·at·ten·dance /ˌnɑːnəˈtɛndəns/ *noun* [*noncount*] **:** failure to be at a place or event where you are expected to be • The school district worked on ways to lower the rate of *nonattendance* among its students.

non·be·liev·er /ˌnɑːnbəˈliːvɚ/ *noun, pl* **-ers** [*count*] **:** a person who does not believe in something (such as a religious belief or a scientific idea about how something happens or

N

could happen) ▪ a memorial service that is suitable for both believers and *nonbelievers* ▪ They're trying to convince the *nonbelievers*.

non·bind·ing /nɑnˈbaɪndɪŋ/ *adj, law* **: not officially requiring that you do something : not able to be enforced by law** ▪ We entered/signed a ***nonbinding agreement*** to buy our competitor. [=we agreed to buy our competitor, but we did not make a legal and official promise to buy it]

non·bi·o·log·i·cal /nɑnˌbajəˈlɑːʤɪkəl/ *adj*
1 : not coming from or related to things that are alive ▪ rocks, minerals, and other *nonbiological* things
2 : related through adoption rather than birth ▪ *nonbiological* parents and siblings

[1]**nonce** /ˈnɑːns/ *noun*
for the nonce *somewhat formal* **: for now : for the moment** ▪ The team is called "the Lions," at least *for the nonce*.

[2]**nonce** *adj, always used before a noun* **: used or made only once or for a special occasion** ▪ a *nonce* word/term

non·cha·lant /ˌnɑːnʃəˈlɑːnt/ *adj* [*more* ~; *most* ~] **: relaxed and calm in a way that shows that you do not care or are not worried about anything** ▪ He was surprisingly *nonchalant* about winning the award. ▪ She faced the crowd with the *nonchalant* ease of an experienced speaker. ▪ The team may have been somewhat *nonchalant* at the beginning of the season, but they now know that they need to work hard.
– non·cha·lance /ˌnɑːnʃəˈlɑːns/ *noun* [*noncount*] ▪ She faced the crowd with the *nonchalance* of an experienced speaker. ▪ His *nonchalance* about winning the award is a little surprising. **– non·cha·lant·ly** *adv*

non·cit·i·zen /nɑnˈsɪtəzən/ *noun, pl* **-zens** [*count*] *chiefly US* **: a person who lives in a country and is not a legal citizen of it** ▪ Voting rights do not apply to *noncitizens*. [=*aliens*]

non·com /ˈnɑːnˌkɑːm/ *noun, pl* **-coms** [*count*] *US* **:** NONCOMMISSIONED OFFICER

non·com·ba·tant /ˌnɑːnkəmˈbætn̩t/ *noun, pl* **-tants** [*count*]
1 : a person (such as a military chaplain or doctor) who is in the army, navy, etc., but does not fight
2 : a person who is not in the army, navy, etc. : CIVILIAN

non·com·mer·cial /ˌnɑːnkəˈmɚʃəl/ *adj*
1 a : not used for earning money ▪ *noncommercial* properties ▪ The worksheets are free for anyone to use for *noncommercial* purposes. **b : not made or operated for the purpose of earning money** ▪ a *noncommercial* theater ▪ *noncommercial* art
2 : without advertisements : not paid for by advertisers ▪ *noncommercial* radio/television

N

non·com·mis·sioned officer /ˌnɑːnkəˈmɪʃənd-/ *noun, pl* ~ **-cers** [*count*] **: an officer (such as a sergeant or corporal) who has a low rank in the army, air force, or marine corps — called also** *NCO, noncom*

non·com·mit·tal /ˌnɑːnkəˈmɪtl̩/ *adj* [*more* ~; *most* ~] **: not telling or showing what you think about something** ▪ She would only give *noncommittal* answers about her plans. ▪ The president remained *noncommittal*, saying only that all options would be considered. **— often +** ***about*** ▪ He was *noncommittal about* how the money would be spent.
– non·com·mit·tal·ly *adv* ▪ "We'll have to wait and see," she replied *noncommittally*.

non·com·mu·nist /nɑnˈkɑːmjənɪst/ *adj* **: not having or supporting communism as a political and economic system** ▪ *noncommunist* nations/parties

non·com·pet·i·tive /ˌnɑːnkəmˈpɛtətɪv/ *adj, chiefly US*
1 a : not very interested in winning or being more successful than other people ▪ He's a pretty *noncompetitive* guy, especially compared to his brothers. **b : not involved in official competitions, contests, etc.** ▪ Once a week, he plays hockey in a *noncompetitive* league.
2 : not good enough to compete with others ▪ The school was unable to hire good teachers because it was paying *noncompetitive* wages/salaries.
3 : not having or allowing competition ▪ The report describes dozens of ***noncompetitive contracts*** [=contracts that were unfairly given to a company without seeing if another company would do the job for less money] that the state has illegally given out in the past five years.
– non·com·pet·i·tive·ly *adv* **– non·com·pet·i·tive·ness** *noun* [*noncount*]

non·com·pli·ance /ˌnɑːnkəmˈplajəns/ *noun* [*noncount*] *chiefly US, formal* **: the condition of not having or doing something that is officially required** ▪ The town has increased the fine for *noncompliance* (with the law) to $100. ▪ When the law goes into effect next month, every school found to be ***in noncompliance*** will be fined $1,000 per day.
– non·com·pli·ant /ˌnɑːnkəmˈplajənt/ *adj* [*more* ~; *most* ~] ▪ a *noncompliant* prisoner/patient ▪ *noncompliant* software ▪ Schools that are *noncompliant* will be fined.

non·con·form·ist /ˌnɑːnkənˈfoɚmɪst/ *noun, pl* **-ists** [*count*] **: a person who does not behave the way most people behave : someone who does not conform** ▪ He was a *nonconformist* in college but now wears a three-piece suit to work every day. ▪ They were stubborn *nonconformists* who chose to be arrested instead of obeying the laws. **— opposite** CONFORMIST
– nonconformist *adj* ▪ *nonconformist* behavior ▪ *nonconformist* [=*unorthodox*] views

non·con·for·mi·ty /ˌnɑːnkənˈfoɚməti/ *noun* [*noncount*] **: failure or refusal to behave the way most people behave : failure or refusal to conform** ▪ As a teenager, he was embarrassed by his parents' *nonconformity*.

non·con·fron·ta·tion·al /nɑnˌkɑːnfrənˈteɪʃənl/ *adj* **: not likely to make people angry or upset** ▪ She wanted to talk to them about their behavior in a *nonconfrontational* way. **: tending to avoid arguments and conflict with other people** ▪ He has a mild, *nonconfrontational* nature.

non·con·sen·su·al /ˌnɑːnkənˈsɛnʃəwəl/ *adj* **: not agreed to by one or more of the people involved** ▪ *nonconsensual* sex

non·con·trib·u·to·ry /ˌnɑːnkənˈtrɪbjəˌtori, *Brit* ˌnɒnkənˈtrɪbjətri/ *adj* **: paid for completely by an employer : not requiring payments from the workers** ▪ The company offered both a contributory and a *noncontributory* plan for workers' pensions.

non·con·tro·ver·sial /nɑnˌkɑːntrəˈvɚʃəl/ *adj* **: not causing a lot of discussion, disagreement, or argument : not likely to cause controversy** ▪ a relatively *noncontroversial* issue

non·co·op·er·a·tion /ˌnɑːnkoʊˌɑːpəˈreɪʃən/ *noun* [*noncount*] **: failure or refusal to do what someone has told or asked you to do : lack of cooperation** ▪ They adopted a strategy of *noncooperation* until they were treated fairly.

non·count noun /ˈnɑːnˈkaʊnt-/ *noun, pl* ~ **nouns** [*count*] *grammar* **: a noun (such as "sand" or "butter") that refers to something that cannot be counted ✧ Noncount nouns do not have a plural form and are not used with the indefinite articles** ***a*** **and** ***an***. **— called also** ***mass noun***; **compare** COUNT NOUN

non·cred·it /ˈnɑːnˈkrɛdət/ *adj, always used before a noun, US* **: not able to be counted as one of the courses that you must take to get a degree from a college or university : not taken for credit (sense 7b)** ▪ a *noncredit* course/class

non·cus·to·di·al /ˌnɑːnkəˈstoudijəl/ *adj, always used before a noun, law*
1 : not living with your child or having the responsibility of caring for your child after a divorce, legal separation, etc. : not having custody ▪ a *noncustodial* parent
2 ***non-custodial*** *Brit* **: involving punishment that does not require a criminal to spend time in prison** ▪ The judge favors *non-custodial* sentences/punishments for most first offenses.

non·dairy /nɑnˈderi/ *adj* **: not containing or made with milk** ▪ *nondairy* whipped topping ▪ *nondairy* creamer

non·de·nom·i·na·tion·al /ˌnɑːndɪˌnɑːməˈneɪʃənl/ *adj* **: made for or used by people who belong to different religious groups : not restricted to a single denomination** ▪ a *nondenominational* church/congregation/service

non·de·script /ˌnɑːndɪˈskrɪpt/ *adj* [*more* ~; *most* ~] **: not easily described : having no special or interesting qualities, parts, etc. : typical and uninteresting** ▪ I work in one of the *nondescript* office buildings downtown. ▪ Their performance was disappointingly *nondescript*.

[1]**none** /ˈnʌn/ *pronoun* **: not any of a group of people or things : no amount or part of something** ▪ *None* of this was necessary. ▪ Why are all the guests standing in the kitchen and *none* sitting in the living room? ▪ Half a piece is better than *none*. ▪ The frozen yogurt tastes like ice cream but has *none* of the fat (that ice cream has). ▪ Though the languages are related they share almost/virtually *none* of the same vocabulary. ▪ *None* of it is finished yet. ▪ "Can I have some soup?" "I'm afraid there's *none* left." [=there is no more soup; no soup remains] ▪ *None* of the birds was/were singing. ▪ Of all the competitions, *none* is/are more important than this one. = Of all the competitions, there is/are *none* as important as this one. ▪ To cut back on cholesterol my doctor said I should eat less meat or ***none at all***. ▪ "You have no doubts?" "***None whatsoever***." ▪ This is ***none of your affair/business***. [=you should not interfere in this situation; it is not proper for you

to say, do, or ask anything about this]

have none of **: to refuse to accept, allow, or be influenced by (a particular behavior) : to not allow someone to do (something)** • I will *have none of* that kind of talk in my house. • The group petitioned to have the votes counted again, but the government would *have none of* that. • They begged their mother to take them out for ice cream, but she was ***having none of it.***

none but *somewhat formal* **: no person or kind of person except : ONLY** • a sport for *none but* the most brave • It was a request that *none but* the most coldhearted (person) could refuse.

none other than **— used to show that you are surprised or impressed by the person or thing you are about to mention** • It turns out I was sitting next to *none other than* the founder of the magazine. • *None other than* my favorite actor was cast in the lead role.

none the less **: NONETHELESS**

second to none **: better than all others of the same kind** • His cakes are *second to none.* [=the cakes he makes are better than all other cakes] • The city's public transportation system is *second to none.*

[2]**none** *adv*

none the **— used in phrases with adjectives like** ***worse, better,*** **etc., to say that someone or something is not any worse, better, etc., than before; often + *for*** • We had to change our plans, but we were *none the worse for* it in the end. • She's been traveling constantly for the past several weeks, but she seems to be ***none the worse for wear.*** • The restaurant replaced the lobster with crab and the customers were ***none the wiser.*** [=customers who ate the crab did not know that it was not lobster; customers thought they were eating lobster]

none too **: not at all** • He was *none too* happy [=not happy at all] about the situation. • She was *none too* pleased. • The firefighters reached the burning house ***none too soon.*** [=they reached it just in time to prevent something bad from happening]

non·en·ti·ty /nɑnˈɛntəti/ *noun, pl* **-ties** *[count]* **: a person who is not famous or important** • She quickly went from being a *nonentity* [=*nobody*] to being one of the most famous women in the country.

[1]**non·es·sen·tial** /ˌnɑːnɪˈsɛnʃəl/ *adj* **: not completely necessary : not essential** • All *nonessential* personnel had to be laid off. • Please avoid all *nonessential* uses of water.

[2]**nonessential** *noun, pl* **-tials** *[count]* **: something that is not completely necessary : something that is not essential — usually plural** • She puts aside money in her monthly budget for *nonessentials* like haircuts and vacations.

none·the·less /ˌnʌnðəˈlɛs/ *adv, somewhat formal* **: in spite of what has just been said : NEVERTHELESS** • There's no doubt the city is changing for the better. *Nonetheless* [=*however*], no one has been too surprised by the recent violence. • The hike was difficult, but fun *nonetheless.* [=the hike was fun even though it was difficult]

non·event /ˈnɑːnɪˌvɛnt/ *noun, pl* **-events** *[count] informal* **: an event that is much less interesting or important than it was expected to be — usually singular** • To their surprise, her resignation was a *nonevent.* • The town expected protests, but the smoking ban actually turned out to be a *nonevent.*

non·ex·ec·u·tive *(chiefly US) or chiefly Brit* **non–ex·ec·u·tive** /ˌnɑːnɪgˈzɛkjətɪv/ *adj, always used before a noun, business* **: allowed to give advice but not allowed to make important decisions** • She will remain with the company as *nonexecutive* chairman after she retires. • *nonexecutive* director

non·ex·is·tent /ˌnɑːnɪgˈzɪstənt/ *adj* **: not present or real : not existing** • Programs to protect endangered animals are virtually/practically/almost/essentially *nonexistent* in that country. • These days the disease is rare or *nonexistent* in most places. • You are living in fear of a *nonexistent* threat.

– non·ex·is·tence /ˌnɑːnɪgˈzɪstəns/ *noun [noncount]* • a debate over the existence or *nonexistence* of God

non·fat /ˈnɑːnˈfæt/ *adj* **: having no fat : with the fat removed** • *nonfat* milk

non·fa·tal /ˈnɑːnˈfeɪtl/ *adj* **: not causing death : not fatal** • There has been an increase in the number of *nonfatal* shootings in the city.

non·fic·tion /ˈnɑːnˈfɪkʃən/ *noun [noncount]* **: writing that is about facts or real events : all writing that is not fiction** • He reads a lot of *nonfiction.* **— often used before another noun** • *nonfiction* books/works • History books are in the library's *nonfiction* section.

non·fi·nite /ˈnɑːnˈfaɪˌnaɪt/ *adj, grammar* **: not showing differences in tense, grammatical person, or number : not finite** • "Be" in "I'm going to be a teacher when I grow up" is a *nonfinite* verb. • "Standing" is one of the verb's *nonfinite* forms.

non·flam·ma·ble /ˈnɑːnˈflæməbəl/ *adj* **: not burning or not burning easily : not easily set on fire** • *nonflammable* fabric

non·gov·ern·men·tal /nɑnˌgʌvənˈmɛntl/ *also* **non·gov·ern·ment** /nɑnˈgʌvənmənt/ *adj, always used before a noun* **: not belonging to or controlled by a government** • Many *nongovernmental* charities are run by religious groups. • We turned to an environmentalist ***nongovernmental organization*** [=*NGO*] for advice on responsible waste disposal.

non·hu·man /nɑnˈhjuːmən/ *adj* **: not a man, woman, or child : not a human being** • *nonhuman* primates/animals **— compare INHUMAN, SUBHUMAN**

non·in·ter·ven·tion /ˌnɑːnˌɪntəˈvɛnʃən/ *noun [noncount]* **: refusal to become involved in another country's business, problems, etc.** • The country has adopted a policy of *nonintervention.*

– non·in·ter·ven·tion·ist /ˌnɑːnˌɪntəˈvɛnʃənɪst/ *adj* • a strict *noninterventionist* policy

non·in·va·sive /ˌnɑːnɪnˈveɪsɪv/ *adj, medical* **: done without cutting the body or putting something into the body** • *noninvasive* techniques of measuring brain activity

non·is·sue /ˈnɑːnˈɪʃu/ *noun, pl* **-issues** *[count]* **: an issue that is not important : something that people are not concerned about — usually singular** • She's very good at her job. Her disability is a *nonissue.* • The fact that one of the candidates is an immigrant is a *nonissue.* [=people do not care that the candidate is an immigrant]

non·judg·men·tal *or chiefly Brit* **non·judge·men·tal** /ˌnɑːnˌʤʌʤˈmɛntl/ *adj [more ~; most ~]* **: tending not to judge other people harshly or unfairly : not too critical of other people** • A good friend is *nonjudgmental.* • *nonjudgmental* people

non·mem·ber /ˈnɑːnˈmɛmbə/ *noun, pl* **-bers** *[count]* **: someone who is not a member of a particular organization** • Entry to the museum costs $10 for *nonmembers.*

non–na·tive /nɑnˈneɪtɪv/ *adj* **: not native: such as a** *of an animal or plant* **: living or growing in a place that is not the region where it naturally lives and grows** • Irrigation allows *non-native* plants to grow in the desert. • *Non-native* species of insects are having devastating effects on local crops. **b : not born or raised in the place where a particular language is spoken** • The college has English classes for *non-native* speakers. [=people who are not native speakers of English]

– non–native *noun, pl* **-tives** *[count]* • I was surprised at how well people in that country treated me, a *non-native.* • classes for *non-natives*

non–ne·go·tia·ble /ˌnɑːnnɪˈgoʊʃijəbəl/ *adj*

1 : not allowed to be discussed and possibly changed • The school must meet several *non-negotiable* requirements to be eligible for the funding. • a *non-negotiable* contract • Her parents simply said, "You must finish high school. It's *non-negotiable.*"

2 *finance, of a check* **: able to be exchanged for money only by the person whose name is on it**

no–no /ˈnoʊˌnoʊ/ *noun, pl* **no–no's** *or* **no–nos** *[count] informal*

1 : something that people are not supposed to do because it is not proper, safe, fashionable, etc. • Forgetting to introduce your guests to one another is a big *no-no* when hosting a party. • Sharing prescription medication with other people is a definite *no-no.* • fashion *no-no's*

2 *baseball* **: NO-HITTER**

no–nonsense *adj [more ~; most ~]* **: very serious about doing things in a direct and efficient way without any foolishness or nonsense** • I want to wear something that will make me look like a *no-nonsense* professional. • a doctor who is very *no-nonsense* • a *no-nonsense* attitude

[1]**non·pa·reil** /ˌnɑːnpəˈrɛl/ *adj, formal* **: better than any other : having no equal** • That bakery's cakes are *nonpareil.* [=*incomparable, unparalleled*] • He was the teacher *nonpareil* [=the best teacher] at his school.

[2]**nonpareil** *noun, pl* **-reils**

1 *[singular] formal* **: someone or something that is better than any other** • Elvis was the *nonpareil* of early American rock and roll.

2 *[count] US* **: a candy that is a small, flat, round piece of chocolate covered with tiny balls made of sugar**

non·par·ti·san /ˈnɑːnˈpɑətəzən/ *adj* **: not supporting one**

N

political party or group over another : not partisan ▪ It's a nonprofit, *nonpartisan* organization dedicated to preserving our national parks.

non·pay·ment /ˈnɑːnˈpeɪmənt/ *noun* [*noncount*] *formal* : failure to pay money that you owe for rent, taxes, etc. — often + *of* ▪ Their electricity was turned off for *nonpayment of* bills. [=because they did not pay their electricity bills]

non·per·ish·able /nɑnˈpɛrɪʃəbəl/ *adj* : able to be stored for a long time before being eaten or used ▪ *nonperishable* food items

– nonperishable *noun, pl* **-ables** [*count*] — usually plural ▪ The students collected *nonperishables* to give to the poor.

non·plussed *also US* **non·plused** /ˌnɑːnˈplʌst/ *adj, not used before a noun* [*more ~; most ~*] *formal* : so surprised or confused by something that you do not know what to say, think, or do : PERPLEXED ▪ He was *nonplussed* by his daughter's confession that she had stolen the CD. ▪ She looked slightly *nonplussed* at first but composed herself quickly.

non·po·lit·i·cal /ˌnɑːnpəˈlɪtɪkəl/ *adj* [*more ~; most ~*] : not political : not influenced by or interested in political issues ▪ The organization is *nonpolitical*. [=*apolitical*] ▪ a *nonpolitical* speech/magazine ▪ *nonpolitical* motives/issues

non·prac·tic·ing /ˌnɑːnˈpræktɪsɪŋ/ *adj, always used before a noun* : not regularly doing the things that are associated with your religion, the profession you were trained in, etc. ▪ a *nonpracticing* Catholic/lawyer

non·pre·scrip·tion /ˌnɑːnprɪˈskrɪpʃən/ *adj, always used before a noun* : possible to buy without an official written order from a doctor : possible to buy without a prescription ▪ a *nonprescription* [=*over-the-counter*] pain reliever

non·prof·it /ˈnɑːnˈprɑːfət/ *adj* : not existing or done for the purpose of making a profit ▪ a *nonprofit* group/agency that provides care to recovering drug addicts ▪ Schools don't pay sales tax on supplies because they have *nonprofit* status. ✧ A nonprofit organization uses whatever money it earns or raises to run the organization and to do the work of the organization. Nonprofit organizations usually do work that helps people or supports something valued by many people in a society (such as art or education).

– nonprofit *noun, pl* **-its** [*count*] ▪ She works for a local *nonprofit* that provides care to recovering drug addicts.

non–profit–making *adj, Brit* : NONPROFIT ▪ a *non-profit-making* organization

non·pro·lif·er·a·tion /ˌnɑːnprəˌlɪfəˈreɪʃən/ *noun* [*noncount*] : the act of stopping the production of nuclear and chemical weapons or of limiting the number of nuclear and chemical weapons in the world ▪ a conference to discuss nuclear *nonproliferation* ▪ a *nonproliferation* treaty

non·re·fund·able /ˌnɑːnrɪˈfʌndəbəl/ *adj*

1 *of something you buy* : not allowed to be returned in exchange for the money you paid ▪ The tickets are *nonrefundable* unless the show is canceled.

2 *of a payment* : not to be returned ▪ A *nonrefundable* deposit [=a deposit of money that will not be returned to you] is required when you place an order.

non·re·new·able /ˌnɑːnrɪˈnuːwəbəl/ *adj*

1 : not able to grow again or be made again : not able to be replaced by nature ▪ Scientists are looking for new sources of fuel to replace our dependence on *nonrenewable* resources such as oil.

2 : not continued or repeated after a period of time has ended ▪ a *nonrenewable* contract/lease ▪ a *nonrenewable* college scholarship

non·res·i·dent /ˈnɑːnˈrɛzədənt/ *noun, pl* **-dents** [*count*]

1 : a person who does not live in a particular town, city, state, or country : a person who is not a resident ▪ *Nonresidents* need to fill out special paperwork to get a library card. ▪ This parking lot is closed to *nonresidents*.

2 ***non-resident*** *Brit* : a person who is not staying in a particular hotel ▪ The hotel dining room is open to *non-residents* for dinner.

– nonresident *adj* ▪ For her U.S. income taxes, she is considered a ***nonresident alien***. [=a person who is born in another country and is not considered a permanent resident of the U.S.]

non·res·i·den·tial /nɑnˌrɛzəˈdɛnʃəl/ *adj*

1 : not made for people to live in ▪ The company installs security systems in *nonresidential* buildings. ▪ The bottom floor of the building is for *nonresidential* use and the top two floors have apartments.

2 ***non-residential*** *Brit, of an activity, class, etc.* : not including or providing a place for people to live ▪ a *non-residential* course ▪ *non-residential* summer school

non·re·stric·tive /ˌnɑːnrɪˈstrɪktɪv/ *adj*

1 : not limiting or controlling something ▪ It's a *nonrestrictive* diet that stresses eating smaller portions rather than not eating certain foods. ▪ You'll be moving around a lot, so wear ***nonrestrictive clothing***. [=clothes that do not make it difficult to move freely]

2 *grammar, of a word or group of words* : describing or giving more information about a person or thing but not needed to understand which person or thing is meant ▪ In the sentence "My brother, who works at a restaurant, just got his first car," "who works at a restaurant" is a ***nonrestrictive clause***. — compare RESTRICTIVE

non·re·turn·able /ˌnɑːnrɪˈtɚnəbəl/ *adj*

1 : not allowed to be returned to a store for money or something of similar value ▪ Clothing bought during the sale is *nonreturnable*. [=you cannot bring it back to the store in exchange for the money you paid for it] ▪ *nonreturnable* bottles/cans

2 : not to be returned ▪ a *nonreturnable* [=*nonrefundable*] deposit

non·sci·en·tif·ic /nɑnˌsajənˈtɪfɪk/ *adj*

1 : not based on scientific methods or principles ▪ a *nonscientific* [=*unscientific*] survey/poll/study

2 : not trained in science ▪ A *nonscientific* reader may be unfamiliar with some of the terms in the article.

non·sense /ˈnɑːnˌsɛns/ *noun* [*noncount*]

1 : words or ideas that are foolish or untrue ▪ I don't know why you believe that *nonsense* about certain numbers being unlucky. ▪ The stories she told about him are sheer/utter/complete/absolute *nonsense*. [=the stories are completely false] ▪ He says he was attacked by a frog? *Nonsense*. [=I do not believe that he was attacked by a frog] ▪ She thinks that astrology is *nonsense*. ▪ The rumors are a lot of *nonsense*. [=they are not true] ▪ Don't listen to him. He's ***talking nonsense***.

2 : behavior that is silly, annoying, or unkind ▪ He was not in the mood to put up with any *nonsense* from his little brother. ▪ If they start pushing each other or some such *nonsense*, send them to their rooms. ▪ She doesn't ***take any nonsense*** from anyone. — see also NO-NONSENSE

3 : language that has no meaning ▪ Many of the words in the poem are *nonsense*. ▪ I understood so few of the words they were using that the conversation sounded like *nonsense* to me. — often used before another noun ▪ When he didn't know the words, he sang along using *nonsense* syllables. ▪ Her stories are full of *nonsense* words that kids have fun trying to say. ▪ *nonsense* verse/poems/rhyme [=silly poetry that often uses words that are not real words]

make (a) nonsense of *Brit* : to cause (something) to no longer be effective : to take away the value or usefulness of (something) ▪ The lack of guards *makes a nonsense of* the security checkpoint.

non·sen·si·cal /ˌnɑːnˈsɛnsɪkəl/ *adj* : very foolish or silly ▪ a *nonsensical* argument ▪ It would be *nonsensical* to accept the lower paying job.

non se·qui·tur /ˈnɑːnˈsɛkwətɚ/ *noun, pl* **~ -turs** [*count*] : a statement that is not connected in a logical or clear way to anything said before it ▪ We were talking about the new restaurant when she threw in some *non sequitur* about her dog. ✧ *Non sequitur* is a Latin phrase that literally means "it does not follow."

non·sex·ist /nɑnˈsɛksɪst/ *adj* : not sexist : treating men and women equally and fairly ▪ *nonsexist* language

non·skid /ˈnɑːnˈskɪd/ *adj* : made to prevent slipping or skidding : not allowing something to slide ▪ shoes with *nonskid* soles ▪ a *nonskid* surface

non·slip /ˈnɑːnˈslɪp/ *adj* : made to prevent slipping : not allowing something to slide ▪ shoes with *nonslip* soles ▪ a *nonslip* handle

non·smok·er /ˌnɑːnˈsmoʊkɚ/ *noun, pl* **-ers** [*count*] : a person who does not smoke

non·smok·ing /nɑnˈsmoʊkɪŋ/ *adj*

1 — used to describe a place where people are not allowed to smoke ▪ Let's sit in the restaurant's *nonsmoking* section. ▪ The bar is *nonsmoking*. [=people are not allowed to smoke in the bar]

2 *always used before a noun, of a person* : not having the habit of smoking ▪ I'm looking for a *nonsmoking* roommate. [=a roommate who does not smoke]

non·spe·cif·ic /ˌnɑːnspɪˈsɪfɪk/ *adj*

1 *medical* : not clearly having one specific cause ▪ *nonspecif-*

ic pain/inflammation ▪ a patient complaining of *nonspecific* symptoms

2 : not clearly understood or described : lacking specific details ▪ a *nonspecific* [=*general*] threat ▪ What little information we have is *nonspecific.*

non·stan·dard /ˌnɑːnˈstændəd/ *adj*

1 : not accepted or used by most of the educated speakers and writers of a language ▪ *nonstandard* dialects ▪ a *nonstandard* word

2 : not the usual size or kind ▪ He works *nonstandard* hours so that he can pick his kids up from school. ▪ a *nonstandard*-sized bottle/card ▪ *nonstandard* fuels — opposite STANDARD; compare SUBSTANDARD

non·start·er /ˌnɑːnˈstɑɚtɚ/ *noun, pl* **-ers** [*count*]

1 *informal* **:** someone or something that will not be effective or successful — usually singular ▪ Tax reform appears to be a *nonstarter* this year. ▪ As a candidate, he's a *nonstarter.* [=he has no chance to succeed as a candidate] ▪ She acknowledges that the proposal may be a political *nonstarter.*

2 *US, sports* **:** a player who is not chosen to play at the beginning of games : a player who is not one of the starters on a team ▪ She's the leading scorer among the team's *nonstarters.*

non·stick /ˈnɑːnˈstɪk/ *adj* **:** allowing easy removal of cooked food ▪ There is a *nonstick* coating on the pan. ▪ a *nonstick* skillet/spray

non·stop /ˈnɑːnˈstɑːp/ *adj*

1 : done or made without stopping ▪ a *nonstop* [=*direct*] flight ▪ The airline has *nonstop* service between Boston and Seattle. [=it has planes that regularly fly between Boston and Seattle without stopping]

2 : not stopping ▪ The festival is five days of *nonstop* [=*continuous*] music. ▪ The action in the movie is *nonstop.* [=very exciting things happen throughout the movie]

– nonstop *adv* ▪ The plane is capable of flying *nonstop* between New York and Beijing. ▪ They danced *nonstop* until the club closed. ▪ The baby cried *nonstop* [=*continuously*] for hours. ▪ She drove 15 hours *nonstop.*

non·tax·able /nɑnˈtæksəbəl/ *adj* **:** not taxed ▪ *nontaxable* income

non·threat·en·ing /nɑnˈθrɛtnɪŋ/ *adj* **:** not likely to cause someone to be afraid or worried : not threatening ▪ It's best to approach the dog in a calm, *nonthreatening* way.

non·tox·ic /nɑnˈtɑːksɪk/ *adj* **:** not poisonous ▪ The school uses only *nontoxic* paint. ▪ The chemicals are relatively *nontoxic* but should be kept away from children and animals.

non·tra·di·tion·al /ˌnɑːntrəˈdɪʃənl/ *adj* **:** different from what is typical or usual ▪ He has a very *nontraditional* approach to teaching. ▪ The college encourages ***nontraditional students*** [=students who are older than the typical age of college students] to apply. ▪ children growing up in ***nontraditional families*** [=families that are not made up of one mother, one father, and a child or children]

non–trans·fer·able /ˌnɑːntrænsˈfɚrəbəl/ *adj* **:** not able to be given to or used by another person ▪ The plane tickets are nonrefundable and *non-transferable.*

non·union /ˈnɑːnˈjuːnjən/ *adj*

1 : not belonging to a labor union ▪ *nonunion* employees/workers ▪ They are cutting costs by using *nonunion* labor.

2 : not accepting labor unions ▪ *nonunion* employers : not having employees who are members of a labor union ▪ It's a *nonunion* construction firm.

non–union·ized *also Brit* **non–union·ised** /nɑnˈjuːnjəˌnaɪzd/ *adj* **:** NONUNION ▪ *non-unionized* employees ▪ a *non-unionized* company

non·ver·bal /ˈnɑːnˈvɚbəl/ *adj*

1 : not involving or using words ▪ Facial expressions are very important for *nonverbal* communication.

2 : not able to speak ▪ a *nonverbal* child

– non·ver·bal·ly *adv* ▪ People communicate a lot of information *nonverbally.*

non·vi·o·lence /ˈnɑːnˈvajələns/ *noun* [*noncount*] **:** the practice of refusing to respond to anything (such as unfair or violent acts by a government) with violence ▪ The group promotes *nonviolence.* ▪ Demonstration organizers are urging *nonviolence.*

non·vi·o·lent /ˈnɑːnˈvajələnt/ *adj* **:** not using or involving violence ▪ He argued that *nonviolent* drug offenders should receive shorter sentences. ▪ a *nonviolent* [=*peaceful*] protest against the war

– non·vi·o·lent·ly *adv* ▪ The group marched *nonviolently* to the courthouse to protest the decision.

non–West·ern /ˈnɑːnˈwɛstɚn/ *adj, always used before a noun* **:** of or relating to the part of the world that does not include the countries of western Europe and North America ▪ *non-Western* countries ▪ the *non-Western* world ▪ *non-Western* art/culture

non·white /ˈnɑːnˈwaɪt/ *noun, pl* **-whites** [*count*] **:** a person who is not a member of the white race : a person who does not have the light-colored skin of people whose ancestors were European ▪ The program is even less popular among *nonwhites.*

– nonwhite *adj* ▪ The city just elected its first *nonwhite* mayor. ▪ About half the students are *nonwhite.*

¹noo·dle /ˈnuːdl/ *noun, pl* **noo·dles** [*count*] **:** a thin strip of dough that is made from flour, water, and eggs and that is cooked in boiling liquid ▪ Chinese/egg *noodles* ▪ chicken *noodle* soup [=soup made with chicken and noodles]

²noodle *verb* **noodles; noo·dled; noo·dling** [*no obj*] *US, informal*

1 : to play a musical instrument in an informal way without playing a particular piece of music ▪ He was just *noodling* around on the guitar.

2 : to think about something in a way that is not very serious ▪ It's a thought I've been *noodling* around with for some time.

noog·ie /ˈnʊgi/ *noun, pl* **-ies** [*count*] *US, informal* **:** the act of rubbing your knuckles on a person's head to cause annoyance or slight pain ▪ The boys gave each other *noogies.*

nook /ˈnʊk/ *noun, pl* **nooks** [*count*]

1 : a small space or corner that is inside something ▪ an old house full of ***nooks and crannies***

2 : a part of a room (such as a corner) that is used for a specific purpose ▪ a breakfast *nook* ▪ a cozy *nook* perfect for reading

3 *literary* **:** a quiet place that is sheltered by a tree, rock, etc. ▪ We found a shady *nook* under an old oak tree.

every nook and cranny **:** every part or place ▪ We searched *every nook and cranny.* [=we searched everywhere] ▪ He knows *every nook and cranny* of that engine.

nooky *or* **nook·ie** /ˈnʊki/ *noun* [*noncount*] *slang* **:** the act of having sex ▪ guys looking for a little *nookie*

noon /ˈnuːn/ *noun* [*noncount*] **:** the middle of the day : 12 o'clock in the daytime ▪ Meet me at/around *noon.* ▪ half past *noon* ▪ The party will take place from *noon* to 4 p.m. ▪ He showed up at precisely 12 *noon.* — often used before another noun ▪ the *noon* meal/hour ▪ the hot *noon* sun — see also HIGH NOON

morning, noon, and night see MORNING

noon·day /ˈnuːnˌdeɪ/ *noun* [*noncount*] *literary* **:** the middle of the day : MIDDAY — usually used before another noun ▪ the heat of the *noonday* sun

no one *pronoun* **:** no person : NOBODY ▪ We called, but *no one* answered. ▪ *No one* has ever done this before. ▪ There's *no one* else here. ▪ *No one* knows her better than I do. ▪ The news came as a surprise to *no one.* [=nobody was surprised by the news]

noon·time /ˈnuːnˌtaɪm/ *noun* [*noncount*] **:** NOON ▪ The traffic gets heavy around/at *noontime.* — often used before another noun ▪ the *noontime* meal/sun

noose /ˈnuːs/ *noun, pl* **noos·es** [*count*] **:** a large loop at the end of a rope that gets smaller when you pull the rope and that is used to hang people, to capture animals, etc. ▪ the hangman's *noose*

tighten the noose **:** to make a situation more difficult for someone ▪ The new tougher penalties will *tighten the noose* on traffic offenders. ▪ They *tightened the noose* around the enemy by cutting the supply lines.

nope /ˈnoʊp/ *adv, informal* **:** ¹NO ▪ "Have you finished the book yet?" "Nope." — compare YEP

nor /ˈnoɚ/ *conj*

1 — used after *neither* to show something is also not true, possible, allowed, etc. ▪ It's neither good *nor* bad. ▪ I neither know *nor* care what they think. ▪ Neither you *nor* I *nor* anyone else will tell him. ▪ His problems are neither my business *nor* yours. ✧ When *neither* and *nor* are used to join two subjects, the verb should agree with the subject that is closer to it. ▪ *Neither* my mother *nor* I am going there today. — see also *neither here nor there* at ¹HERE

2 — used after a negative statement to introduce a related negative word or statement ▪ She's not the best student in her class, (but) *nor* is she the worst. ▪ He didn't quit his job, *nor* was he fired. ▪ He is not going to the meeting (and) *nor* am I. ▪ (*formal*) "I don't know her." "*Nor* do I." [=neither do I; I don't know her either]

N

Nor·dic /ˈnoədɪk/ *adj* : of or relating to Sweden, Norway, Denmark, and sometimes Finland and Iceland, or to the people who live there ▪ the *Nordic* countries ▪ *Nordic* languages ▪ She looks very *Nordic*. [=she has the skin, hair, and eye color of a person who lives in Scandinavia]

nor'easter *variant spelling of* NORTHEASTER 2

norm /ˈnoəm/ *noun, pl* **norms**

1 ***norms*** [*plural*] : standards of proper or acceptable behavior ▪ social/cultural *norms*

2 ***the norm*** : an average level of development or achievement ▪ She scored well above/below *the norm* in math.

3 ***the norm*** : something (such as a behavior or way of doing something) that is usual or expected ▪ Smaller families have become *the norm*. ▪ Women used to stay at home to take care of the children, but that's no longer *the norm*.

[1]**nor·mal** /ˈnoəməl/ *adj* [*more ~; most ~*]

1 : usual or ordinary : not strange ▪ a *normal* day ▪ He had a *normal* childhood. ▪ These little setbacks are a *normal* part of life. ▪ Our *normal* [=*regular*] business hours are from nine to five. ▪ a potato twice as big as *normal* size ▪ Despite her illness, she was able to lead a *normal* life. ▪ ***Under/In normal circumstances*** [=*normally, usually*], this wouldn't be a problem.

2 : mentally and physically healthy ▪ They had a *normal*, healthy baby. ▪ *Normal* people don't react that way. ▪ It's (perfectly) *normal* to feel that way. ▪ After being very ill, he is finally back to ***his normal self*** [=he is feeling better]

– **nor·mal·ly** *adv* ▪ The drug is *normally* used for depression. ▪ Rainfall amounts are higher than would *normally* be expected. ▪ *Normally*, I would say no, but this time I'll make an exception. ▪ The dog is not behaving *normally*.

[2]**normal** *noun* [*noncount*] : the usual or expected state, level, amount, etc. ▪ Your blood pressure is higher than *normal*. ▪ Let's hope everything returns to *normal* soon. ▪ I'm glad that things are back to *normal*. ▪ Oil prices are above/below *normal*.

nor·mal·cy /ˈnoəməlsi/ *noun* [*noncount*] *chiefly US* : a normal condition or situation : NORMALITY ▪ Let's hope for an end to the war and a return to *normalcy*.

nor·mal·i·ty /noəˈmæləti/ *noun* [*noncount*] : a condition or situation in which things happen in the normal or expected way ▪ I'm trying to maintain a sense/semblance of *normality*.

nor·mal·ize *also Brit* **nor·mal·ise** /ˈnoəməˌlaɪz/ *verb* **-iz·es; -ized; -iz·ing** *formal* : to bring (someone or something) back to a usual or expected state or condition [+ *obj*] The drug *normalizes* heart/liver function. ▪ The talks are aimed at *normalizing* relations between the countries. [*no obj*] It took years for the political situation in the country to *normalize*.

– **nor·mal·i·za·tion** *also Brit* **nor·mal·i·sa·tion** /ˌnoəmələˈzeɪʃən, *Brit* ˌnɔːməˌlaɪˈzeɪʃən/ *noun* [*noncount*]

Nor·man /ˈnoəmən/ *noun, pl* **-mans** [*count*]

1 : one of the people from northern Europe and France who conquered England in 1066

2 : a person born, raised, or living in Normandy

– **Norman** *adj, always used before a noun* ▪ the *Norman* conquest [=the time when Normans conquered England in 1066] ▪ *Norman* architecture

nor·ma·tive /ˈnoəmətɪv/ *adj, formal* : based on what is considered to be the usual or correct way of doing something ▪ *normative* rules of ethics ▪ *normative* tests/grammar

Norse /ˈnoəs/ *noun*

1 [*noncount*] : the language of ancient Norway, Sweden, Denmark, and Iceland

2 ***the Norse*** : the people of ancient Norway, Sweden, Denmark, or Iceland ▪ *The Norse* arrived in the ninth century.

– **Norse** *adj, always used before a noun* ▪ *Norse* mythology ▪ the *Norse* sagas

[1]**north** /ˈnoəθ/ *noun*

1 [*noncount*] : the direction that is to your left when you are facing the rising sun : the direction that is the opposite of south ▪ The nearest town is 20 miles to the *north* (of here). ▪ The wind is coming from the *north*. ▪ Which way is *north*? — see also MAGNETIC NORTH, TRUE NORTH

2 ***the north*** *or* ***the North*** : regions or countries north of a certain point ▪ The birds migrate from *the North*.; *especially* : the northern part of the U.S. ▪ Parts of *the North* were hit hard by the storm. ▪ I grew up in *the North*. ▪ The American Civil War was between *the North* and the South.

[2]**north** *adj*

1 : located in or toward the north ▪ the *north* entrance/coast ▪ *North* America

2 : coming from the north ▪ a *north* wind

[3]**north** *adv* : to or toward the north ▪ Turn *north* onto Elm Street. ▪ It's a few miles *north* of here. ▪ The bird is found as far *north* as Canada.

up north informal : in or to the northern part of a country or region ▪ She spent a few years *up north*. ▪ We'll be heading *up north* for the summer. — compare ***down south*** at [3]SOUTH

north·bound /ˈnoəθˌbaʊnd/ *adj* : going or heading north ▪ a *northbound* train ▪ The *northbound* lanes are closed.

[1]**north·east** /noəθˈiːst/ *noun*

1 [*noncount*] : the direction between north and east

2 ***the northeast*** *or* ***the Northeast*** : the northeastern part of a country or region ▪ A mountain range is in *the northeast* of the country.; *especially* : the northeastern part of the U.S. ▪ Parts of *the Northeast* were hit hard by the storm. ▪ I grew up in *the Northeast*.

[2]**northeast** *adj*

1 : located in or toward the northeast ▪ *northeast* India ▪ My office is in the *northeast* corner of the building.

2 : coming from the northeast ▪ a *northeast* wind

[3]**northeast** *adv* : to or toward the northeast ▪ It's a few miles *northeast* of here. ▪ We left the city and headed *northeast*.

north·east·er /noəθˈiːstə/ *noun, pl* **-ers** [*count*]

1 : a strong wind that blows from the northeast

2 *or* ***nor'·east·er*** /noəˈiːstə/ : a storm with winds that blow from the northeast

north·east·er·ly /noəθˈiːstəli/ *adj*

1 : located in or moving toward the northeast ▪ They sailed in a *northeasterly* direction.

2 : blowing from the northeast ▪ *northeasterly* winds

north·east·ern /noəθˈiːstən/ *adj*

1 : located in or toward the northeast ▪ the *northeastern* corner of the state

2 : of or relating to the northeast ▪ a *northeastern* bird

north·east·ern·er *or* **North·east·ern·er** /noəθˈiːstənə/ *noun, pl* **-ers** [*count*] : a person born, raised, or living in the northeast; *especially* : a person born, raised, or living in the northeastern U.S.

north·east·ward /noəθˈiːstwəd/ *also chiefly Brit* **north·east·wards** /noəˈiːstwədz/ *adv* : toward the northeast ▪ The storm is moving *northeastward*.

– **northeastward** *adj* ▪ The storm will follow a *northeastward* course.

north·er·ly /ˈnoəðəli/ *adj* [*more ~; most ~*]

1 : located in or moving toward the north ▪ the more *northerly* latitudes ▪ We sailed in a *northerly* direction.

2 : blowing from the north ▪ *northerly* winds

– **northerly** *adv* ▪ The storm is headed *northerly*. ▪ We sailed *northerly* around the island.

north·ern /ˈnoəðən/ *adj*

1 [*more ~; most ~*] : located in or toward the north ▪ *northern* Europe ▪ the *northern* part of the state

2 : of or relating to the north ▪ a *northern* species ▪ *northern* winters/cities

north·ern·er *or* **Northerner** /ˈnoəðənə/ *noun, pl* **-ers** [*count*] : a person born, raised, or living in the north; *especially* : a person born, raised, or living in the northern U.S. — compare SOUTHERNER

Northern Lights *noun*

the Northern Lights : large areas of green, red, blue, or yellow light that sometimes appear in the night sky in far northern regions — called also *aurora borealis*

north·ern·most /ˈnoəðənˌmoʊst/ *adj* : furthest to the north ▪ the *northernmost* tip of the island

North Pole *noun*

the North Pole : the most northern point on the surface of the earth

North Star *noun*

the North Star : a bright star that can be seen in the sky in northern parts of the world when you look directly toward the north — called also *the Pole Star*

north·ward /ˈnoəθwəd/ *also chiefly Brit* **north·wards** /ˈnoəθwədz/ *adv* : toward the north ▪ The storm is moving *northward*.

– **northward** *adj* ▪ a *northward* advance/retreat

[1]**north·west** /noəθˈwest/ *noun*

1 [*noncount*] : the direction between north and west

2 ***the northwest*** *or* ***the Northwest*** : the northwestern part of a country or region ▪ A mountain range is in *the northwest* of the country.; *especially* : the northwestern part of the U.S. ▪ We traveled throughout *the Northwest*. ▪ ***the Pacific North-***

N

west [=the northwestern part of the U.S. near the Pacific coast]

²northwest *adj*
1 : located in the northwest ▪ *northwest* China ▪ the *northwest* corner of the building
2 : blowing from the northwest ▪ a *northwest* wind

³northwest *adv* **:** to or toward the northwest ▪ It's about 80 miles *northwest* of here. ▪ I headed *northwest* on Route 1.

north·west·er·ly /noəθˈwɛstəli/ *adj*
1 : located in or moving toward the northwest ▪ The storm is headed in a *northwesterly* direction.
2 : blowing from the northwest ▪ *northwesterly* winds
– northwesterly *adv* ▪ We sailed *northwesterly*.

north·west·ern /noəθˈwɛstən/ *adj*
1 : in, toward, or from the northwest ▪ the *northwestern* corner of the state
2 : of or relating to the northwest ▪ a *northwestern* bird

north·west·ern·er *or* **North·west·ern·er** /noəθˈwɛstənə/ *noun, pl* **-ers** [*count*] **:** a person born, raised, or living in the northwest; *especially* **:** a person born, raised, or living in the northwestern U.S.

north·west·ward /noəθˈwɛstwəd/ *also chiefly Brit* **north·west·wards** /noəθˈwɛstwədz/ *adv* **:** toward the northwest ▪ The storm is moving *northwestward*.
– northwestward *adj* ▪ The storm will follow a *northwestward* course.

Nor·we·gian /noəˈwi:ʤən/ *noun, pl* **-gians**
1 [*count*] **:** a person born, raised, or living in Norway
2 [*noncount*] **:** the language of Norway
– Norwegian *adj* ▪ the *Norwegian* government ▪ She lives in the U.S., but she's *Norwegian*.

nos *plural of* ³NO

nos. *abbr* numbers

¹nose /ˈnoʊz/ *noun, pl* **nos·es**
1 [*count*] **:** the part of the face or head through which a person or animal smells and breathes ▪ The ball hit me right on/in the *nose*. ▪ You need to wipe/blow your *nose*. ▪ Stop picking your *nose*. ▪ I have a runny/stuffy *nose*. ▪ the long *nose* of the anteater ▪ He got some water up his *nose*. ▪ She wrinkled her *nose* in disgust. — see picture at FACE
2 [*singular*] **:** the ability to smell things **:** the sense of smell ▪ That dog has a good *nose*. — often used figuratively ▪ He is a good reporter with a ***nose for*** news. [=he's a reporter who is good at finding news] ▪ a baseball scout with a *nose for* talent [=a scout who is good at finding new talent]
3 : the front end or part of something [*count*] — usually singular ▪ the *nose* of an airplane [*noncount*] The whale measures 40 feet from *nose* to tail. ▪ (*Brit*) The cars were ***nose to tail*** [=(*US*) *bumper-to-bumper*] on the highway today. — see picture at AIRPLANE
4 [*singular*] *of wine* **:** a particular smell ▪ The wine has a lovely *nose*. [=*bouquet*]
as plain as the nose on your face informal **:** very clear or obvious ▪ The solution is *as plain as the nose on your face*.
by a nose ✧ If an animal wins a race *by a nose*, it wins by a very short distance. ▪ Secretariat won the race *by a nose*!
cut off your nose to spite your face **:** to do something that is meant to harm someone else but that also harms you ▪ You can refuse to talk to her if you like, but you're just *cutting off your nose to spite your face*.
follow your nose see FOLLOW
get up someone's nose Brit, informal **:** to annoy or irritate (someone) ▪ His jokes are really beginning to *get up my nose*. [=(*US*) *get on my nerves*]
have your nose in ✧ If you *have your nose in* a book, magazine, newspaper, etc., you are reading it. ▪ It seems like she always *has her nose in* a book [=she's always reading a book] whenever I see her.
hold your nose **:** to hold your nostrils together so that you cannot smell something ▪ The smell was so bad that we had to *hold our noses*.
keep your nose clean **:** to stay out of trouble by behaving well ▪ He is a former criminal who has *kept his nose clean* since he got out of prison.
keep your nose out of **:** to avoid becoming involved in (someone else's situation, problem, etc.) ▪ It's not your problem, so *keep your nose out of* it.
lead someone (around) by the nose informal **:** to completely control a person ▪ I'm amazed that he lets them *lead him around by the nose* like that.
look down your nose at see ¹LOOK
nose in the air ✧ If you have your *nose in the air*, you behave in a way that shows you think you are better than other people. ▪ She walks around with her *nose in the air* like she's some big shot.
nose to the grindstone see GRINDSTONE
no skin off my nose see ¹SKIN
on the nose informal **:** very accurate **:** done very accurately ▪ You hit it *on the nose*. [=you are exactly right] ▪ Her prediction was right *on the nose*.
pay through the nose informal **:** to pay a very high price ▪ I found the perfect dress, but I *paid through the nose* for it.
powder your nose see ²POWDER
rub someone's nose in see ¹RUB
stick/poke your nose in/into **:** to get involved in or want information about (something that does not concern you) ▪ He's always *poking his nose into* other people's business.
thumb your nose at see ²THUMB
turn up your nose *or* ***turn your nose up*** **:** to refuse to take or accept something because it is not good enough ▪ I offered the cat some food, but it *turned up its nose* and walked away. — usually + *at* ▪ They *turned up their nose at* our offer. [=they rejected our offer]
under your nose — used to describe something that you fail to see or notice even though you should ▪ I don't know why you couldn't find it—it's right here *under your nose*. ▪ They were embezzling funds ***right under his nose***. ▪ The answer was *right under our noses* [=the answer was very obvious] the whole time.

²nose *verb* **noses; nosed; nos·ing**
1 [+ *obj*] **:** to push or move (something) with the nose ▪ The horse *nosed* my hand. ▪ Some animal must have *nosed* the lid off the garbage can. ▪ The dog *nosed* the door open.
2 *always followed by an adverb or preposition* [*no obj*] *of an animal* **:** to search for or find something by smelling ▪ The dogs were *nosing* around in the garbage.
3 *always followed by an adverb or preposition* **:** to move forward slowly or carefully [*no obj*] The boat *nosed* around the bend. [+ *obj*] I *nosed* my car into the parking space. ▪ The car *nosed* its way into the street.
nose around *also Brit* ***nose about*** [*phrasal verb*] ***nose around/about*** *or* ***nose around/about (something)*** **:** to search for something (such as private or hidden information) in usually a quiet or secret way ▪ She caught him *nosing around* in her papers/office. ▪ The police *nosed around* the property for a while, but they didn't find anything.
nose out [*phrasal verb*] ***nose (someone or something) out*** *or* ***nose out (someone or something)*** **1 :** to defeat (someone or something) by a small amount in a race or other competition ▪ My horse was/got *nosed out* at the finish line. ▪ The home team barely *nosed out* the visitors. **2 :** to find (information) by careful searching ▪ The detective *nosed out* some interesting information on the suspect.

nose bag *noun, pl* ~ **bags** [*count*] *Brit* **:** FEEDBAG

¹nose·bleed /ˈnoʊzˌbli:d/ *noun, pl* **-bleeds** [*count*] **:** a condition in which you are bleeding from your nose ▪ I had/got a *nosebleed*. ▪ She often suffers from *nosebleeds*.

²nosebleed *adj, always used before a noun, US, informal* **:** very high ▪ We had seats in the *nosebleed* section of the stadium.

nose cone *noun, pl* ~ **cones** [*count*] **:** the pointed front end of an aircraft, rocket, missile, etc.

nosed /ˈnoʊzd/ *adj* **:** having a nose of a specified kind — used in combination with another adjective ▪ a long-*nosed* rodent ▪ a snub-*nosed* little girl — see also HARD-NOSED

nose·dive /ˈnoʊzˌdaɪv/ *noun, pl* **-dives** [*count*]
1 : a sudden sharp drop made by an airplane with its front end pointing toward the ground ▪ The plane went ***into a nosedive***.
2 : a sudden sharp drop in price, value, condition, etc. ▪ The stock market took a *nosedive*.

nose–dive /ˈnoʊzˌdaɪv/ *verb* **-dives; -dived; -div·ing** [*no obj*]
1 *somewhat informal* **:** to drop suddenly or sharply ▪ As demand fell, prices *nosedived*.
2 *of an aircraft* **:** to drop suddenly with the front end pointing toward the ground

nose·gay /ˈnoʊzˌgeɪ/ *noun, pl* **-gays** [*count*] *old-fashioned* **:** a small bouquet of flowers

nose·guard /ˈnoʊzˌgaəd/ *noun, pl* **-guards** [*count*] *American football* **:** a defensive player who plays in a position that is directly opposite the offensive center — called also *nose tackle*

nose job *noun, pl* ~ **jobs** [*count*] *informal* **:** a medical oper-

N

ation on your nose to improve its appearance ▪ an actor who has had a *nose job*

nose ring *noun, pl* **~ rings** [*count*]
1 : a piece of jewelry worn in your nose ▪ She had a *nose ring.*
2 : a ring put through an animal's nose to control it

nose tackle *noun, pl* **~ tackles** [*count*] *American football* **:** NOSEGUARD

nosey *variant spelling of* NOSY

[1]**nosh** /ˈnɑːʃ/ *verb* **nosh·es; noshed; nosh·ing** [*no obj*] *informal* **:** to eat food — usually + *on* ▪ We *noshed on* chips.

[2]**nosh** *noun, pl* **nosh·es** *informal*
1 [*count*] *US* **:** a light meal **:** SNACK ▪ I'll just have a quick *nosh* before we go.
2 *Brit* **a** [*noncount*] **:** FOOD ▪ have some *nosh* **b** [*count*] **:** a serving of food **:** MEAL ▪ have a *nosh*

no–show /ˈnoʊˌʃoʊ/ *noun, pl* **-shows** [*count*] **:** someone who is expected to be somewhere but does not arrive or appear ▪ There were a lot of *no-shows* at the game. ▪ My sister made it to the party, but my brother was a *no-show.*

nosh–up /ˈnɑːʃˌʌp/ *noun, pl* **-ups** [*count*] *Brit, informal* **:** a very large meal

no–smoking *adj* — used to describe a place where people are not allowed to smoke ▪ This is a *no-smoking* [=(more commonly) *nonsmoking*] section.

nos·tal·gia /nɑˈstælʤə/ *noun* [*noncount*] **:** pleasure and sadness that is caused by remembering something from the past and wishing that you could experience it again ▪ A wave of *nostalgia* swept over me when I saw my childhood home. ▪ He was filled with *nostalgia* for his college days.
– nos·tal·gic /nɑˈstælʤɪk/ *adj* [*more ~; most ~*] ▪ *nostalgic* memories ▪ Seeing pictures of my old friends made me feel very *nostalgic.* ▪ They remained *nostalgic* about the good old days. **– nos·tal·gi·cal·ly** /nɑˈstælʤɪkli/ *adv* ▪ She spoke *nostalgically* about her childhood on the farm.

nos·tril /ˈnɑːstrəl/ *noun, pl* **-trils** [*count*] **:** one of the two openings of the nose ▪ My left *nostril* is stuffed up. ▪ She left in a rage, her *nostrils* flaring. — see picture at FACE

nos·trum /ˈnɑːstrəm/ *noun, pl* **-trums** [*count*]
1 *formal* **:** a suggested solution for a problem that will probably not succeed ▪ politicians repeating all the usual *nostrums* about the economy
2 *old-fashioned* **:** something that is used for treating illness, pain, etc., but that is not an accepted and effective medicine ▪ using garlic as a *nostrum* to prevent disease

nosy *also* **nos·ey** /ˈnoʊzi/ *adj* **nos·i·er; -est** [*also more ~; most ~*] *informal + disapproving* **:** wanting to know about other people's lives, problems, etc. ▪ *nosy* reporters/neighbors ▪ Don't be so *nosy!*

nosy par·ker /-ˈpɑɚkɚ/ *noun, pl* **~ -ers** [*count*] *chiefly Brit, informal + disapproving* **:** a person who is too interested in what other people are doing **:** a nosy person

not /ˈnɑːt/ *adv*
1 a — used to form the negative of modal verbs (such as "should" and "could") and auxiliary verbs (such as "do" and "have") ▪ He would/could *not* stay. ▪ We have *not* spoken with them. ▪ It may *not* be fast, but it's reliable. ▪ That kind of behavior should *not* be allowed. ▪ He did *not* seem to care. **b** — used before a verb or clause to make it negative or give it an opposite meaning ▪ They gave us the option of *not* attending. ▪ She told me *not* to do it. ▪ You are *not* to go there without permission. ▪ He seemed *not* to care. ▪ It's odd, but ***that's not to say*** [=that does not mean] that it's bad. — see also ***not to mention*** at [1]MENTION
2 a — used with a word or phrase to make it negative or give it an opposite meaning ▪ The books are *not* here. ▪ No, that's *not* what I said. ▪ That's *not* funny! ▪ That is *not* necessarily true. ▪ You're *not* always right. ▪ You are *not* the only one who is worried. ▪ She is *not* (at all/very) pleased/happy. ▪ I'm *not* happy or sad, just bored. ▪ It is *not* as easy as it seems. ▪ Things are *not* going well. ▪ He is *not* guilty. ▪ He lives *not* far from here. ▪ "Are we there yet?" "*Not* quite." ▪ "Is there any left?" "*Not* much." ▪ It is ***not just/only/merely*** [=more than just] a novel; it is a literary classic. ▪ ***Not many*** [=*few*] people showed up. — see also *not a few* at [1]FEW **b** — used with a negative word to make a positive statement ▪ Their request is *not* unreasonable. [=their request is reasonable] ▪ His experience is *not* unusual. [=others have had similar experiences] ▪ "What do you think of the food?" "It's *not* bad." [=it's pretty good] **c** *informal + humorous* — used humorously at the end of a positive statement to show that you really meant the opposite ▪ That's very interesting—*not!* [=that's not interesting]
3 : less or fewer than ▪ He was standing *not* six feet away from me. ▪ The bullet passed *not* five inches from my head! ▪ *Not* all of us agree. [=some of us do not agree] ▪ *Not* everybody finds her work interesting. [=some people find her work boring]
4 — used to refer to a possible situation, condition, etc., that is different from or opposite to another situation, condition, etc. ▪ The planet is sometimes hard to see and sometimes *not.* [=and sometimes easy to see] ▪ It works in theory if *not* in practice. [=even if it doesn't work in practice] — often used in the phrase ***or not*** ▪ Believe it *or not* [=whether you believe me or don't believe me], we were there just last week. ▪ Ready *or not,* here I come! ▪ Like it *or not,* you'll do as he says. [=you'll do as he says whether you like or don't like it]
5 — used to give a negative answer to a question ▪ "Do you think they forgot?" "I hope *not.*" ▪ "Should we go?" "I'd rather *not.*" ▪ "Do you think it's true?" "Probably/Certainly *not.*" ▪ "Do you mind?" "***Not at all.***"
as like as not *or* ***like as not*** see [6]LIKE
more often than not **:** happening more than half the time ▪ He wins *more often than not.* [=he wins more than he loses] ▪ *More often than not,* I stay home instead of going out.
not a/one **:** no thing or person ▪ There was *not one* available taxi to be found. [=no taxis were available] ▪ *Not a/one* single person showed up. [=no one showed up] ▪ *Not a* word came out of her mouth.
not that — used to say that something said before is not important ▪ I tried to help, *not that* it mattered. [=but it did not matter] ▪ I saw him with some other woman, *not that* I care. [=but I don't care]

[1]**no·ta·ble** /ˈnoʊtəbəl/ *adj* [*more ~; most ~*]
1 : unusual and worth noticing **:** REMARKABLE ▪ a *notable* example/improvement ▪ There are a few *notable* exceptions.
2 : very successful or respected ▪ a *notable* author

[2]**notable** *noun, pl* **no·ta·bles** [*count*] **:** a famous or important person ▪ The guest list included such *notables* as the President and First Lady. ▪ They introduced her to all the local *notables.*

no·ta·bly /ˈnoʊtəbli/ *adv* [*more ~; most ~*]
1 : in a way that attracts or deserves attention ▪ Several senior executives were *notably* absent from the proceedings. ▪ The film's plot was *notably* lacking.
2 : especially or particularly ▪ Some patients, (most) *notably* the elderly and the very young, have greater risks.

no·ta·rize *also Brit* **no·ta·rise** /ˈnoʊtəˌraɪz/ *verb* **-riz·es; -rized; -riz·ing** [*+ obj*] *law* **:** to sign (a document) as a notary public

no·ta·ry public /ˈnoʊtəriˈpʌblɪk/ *noun, pl* **no·ta·ries public** *or* **notary pub·lics** [*count*] *law* **:** a person who has the authority to act as an official witness when legal documents are signed — called also *notary*

no·ta·tion /noʊˈteɪʃən/ *noun, pl* **-tions** *technical* **:** a system of marks, signs, figures, or characters that is used to represent information [*noncount*] musical/scientific *notation* [*count*] a mathematical *notation* for computer programming

[1]**notch** /ˈnɑːʧ/ *noun, pl* **notch·es** [*count*]
1 : a small cut that is shaped like a V and that is made on an edge or a surface ▪ Cut small *notches* at the corners of the fabric. ▪ The tool has a *notch* for prying out nails.
2 *US* **:** a narrow passage between mountains ▪ The town is on the other side of the *notch.*
3 : a slightly higher or lower level in a series of levels that measure something ▪ Turn the radio up/down a *notch.* [=up/down slightly] ▪ They turned the volume up several *notches.* ▪ This product is a *notch* [=*step*] above its competitors in quality and price. — see also TOP-NOTCH

[2]**notch** *verb* **notches; notched; notch·ing** [*+ obj*]
1 : to make a small cut in (something, such as wood) **:** to make a notch in (something) ▪ *Notch* the ends so that they fit together.
2 *informal* **:** to achieve or get (something) ▪ He *notched* his fifth victory this year. — often + *up* ▪ The team *notched up* another win in yesterday's game.
– notched /ˈnɑːʧt/ *adj* ▪ a jacket with a *notched* collar [=a collar that has a notch in it] ▪ a *notched* edge [=an edge with many notches in it]

[1]**note** /ˈnoʊt/ *noun, pl* **notes**
1 a [*count*] **:** a short piece of writing that is used to help someone remember something ▪ She wrote a *note* to remind herself about the appointment. ▪ I left you a *note* on the kitchen table. ▪ making/writing *notes* in the margins of a book ▪ She jotted down a few *notes* during the interview. ▪ I'll

make a ***mental note*** [=I'll try to remember] to reschedule the meeting. **b** ***notes*** [*plural*] **:** an informal written record of things that are said and done ▪ After class, I usually study my *notes* and read the next chapter. ▪ I can't come to class today. Would you mind ***taking notes*** for me? ▪ His secretary *took notes* during our meeting.

2 [*count*] **a :** a short piece of writing that gives you information **:** a brief comment or explanation ▪ Please include a brief *note* about where the picture was taken. ▪ He writes in the program *notes* that the play was inspired by his own childhood. ▪ The dictionary includes many ***usage notes***. [=short explanations about how a word or phrase is used] ▪ One ***final note***: tickets will be available at the door the night of the concert. — see also LINER NOTES **b :** a comment or added piece of information that is separate from the main writing of a book ▪ For further details, see the *notes* to Chapter 3. — see also FOOTNOTE

3 [*count*] **:** a short and usually informal letter ▪ Remember to send a thank-you *note* to the host of the party. ▪ This is just a brief *note* to say how much I enjoyed your party. ▪ Drop me a *note* while you're away. ▪ I have a handwritten *note* here from the governor. ▪ If you are out sick for more than one week, you will need a *note* from your doctor. ▪ The girl's kidnappers left a ***ransom note***. — see also MASH NOTE

4 [*count*] *music* **a :** a specific musical tone ▪ musical *notes* ▪ That *note*'s a B not a C. ▪ Despite a few wrong *notes*, the pianist gave a generally good performance. **b :** a written symbol that is used to show what note should be played and how long it should last — see also EIGHTH NOTE, HALF NOTE, QUARTER NOTE, SIXTEENTH NOTE, WHOLE NOTE

5 [*singular*] **:** a characteristic or quality that expresses a mood or feeling ▪ I detected a *note* of sadness in his voice. — often used after *on* ▪ Let's try to end our conversation *on* a lighter/happier *note*. ▪ If I may end *on* a personal *note*, I'd like to wish my father a happy 85th birthday! ▪ The party ended ***on a high note***. [=the party ended pleasantly or well] ▪ Their relationship ended ***on a sour note***. [=ended unpleasantly] — often used with *hit, strike* or *sound* ▪ The movie *hits* just the right *note* with young audiences. ▪ Her judgment rarely *strikes* a wrong *note*. ▪ In her chapter about rising oil prices, she *sounds* a cautionary *note*. ▪ Most reviewers loved the show, but one critic *struck* a discordant *note*, finding it "clichéd" and "predictable."

6 [*count*] *Brit* **:** BILL ▪ a ten-pound *note*

compare notes see [1]COMPARE

of note **:** important and deserving to be noticed or remembered ▪ American writers *of note* include Herman Melville, Mark Twain, and Emily Dickinson. ▪ historical events *of note*

take note **:** to notice or give special attention to someone or something ▪ She has been extremely successful in her own country, and now the rest of the world is beginning to *take note*. ▪ She *took note* of the exact time.

[2]**note** *verb* **notes; not·ed; not·ing** [+ *obj*] *formal*

1 : to notice or pay attention to (something) ▪ You may have *noted* my late arrival. ▪ The thing to *note* here is that people are suffering. ▪ It's interesting to *note* how quickly things have changed. ▪ Their objections were ***duly noted***. — often + *that* ▪ Please *note that* the office will close today at noon. ▪ *Note that* I have enclosed full payment with this letter.

2 : to say or write (something) ▪ As one official *noted*, the situation has begun to get out of control. ▪ As *noted* above/earlier/previously, most people survive the disease. ▪ "They've asked us to leave," he *noted* with amusement. — often + *that* ▪ She said she was unaware of the problem and *noted that* everything was fine when she went home that night. ▪ It should be *noted*, however, *that* no one was injured in the accident. ▪ It's ***worth noting that*** he gave no reason for his decision.

note down [*phrasal verb*] ***note (something) down or note down (something)*** **:** to write down (a piece of information that you want to remember) ▪ Let me *note down* your telephone number. ▪ The police officer *noted down* the names of all the people present during the incident.

note·book /ˈnoʊtˌbʊk/ *noun, pl* **-books** [*count*]

1 : a book with blank pages that is used for writing notes ▪ Take out your *notebook* and write down some of your ideas. ▪ She kept a *notebook* for her poetry.

2 : a small computer that is designed to be easily carried — called also *notebook computer*

not·ed /ˈnoʊtəd/ *adj* [*more ~; most ~*] **:** famous or well-known ▪ She is a *noted* scholar specializing in Latin-American literature. — often + *for* ▪ The city is *noted for* its many restaurants and nightclubs. ▪ a judge *noted for* her fairness and intelligence

note·pad /ˈnoʊtˌpæd/ *noun, pl* **-pads** [*count*] **:** sheets of paper that are attached at one end and used for writing notes **:** PAD ▪ I wrote down her number on my *notepad*. — see picture at OFFICE

note·pa·per /ˈnoʊtˌpeɪpɚ/ *noun* [*noncount*] **:** paper that is suitable for writing notes and letters

note·wor·thy /ˈnoʊtˌwɚði/ *adj* [*more ~; most ~*] **:** important or interesting enough to be noticed **:** deserving attention **:** NOTABLE ▪ He gave several *noteworthy* performances during his short career. ▪ Nothing *noteworthy* happened that evening. ▪ Her art is *noteworthy* for its great quality and beauty. ▪ a *noteworthy* feat/achievement

— **note·wor·thi·ness** /ˈnoʊtˌwɚðinəs/ *noun* [*noncount*]

not–for–profit *adj, chiefly US* **:** not existing or done for the purpose of making a profit **:** NONPROFIT ▪ a *not-for-profit* organization

noth·er *or* **'noth·er** /ˈnʌðɚ/ *adj*

whole nother *US, informal* **:** completely different ▪ That's a *whole nother* story/issue. [=that's a whole other story/issue; that's a story/issue that is completely different from the one we have been talking about] ▪ He has taken his performance to a *whole nother* level. [=to a completely different and much higher level]

[1]**noth·ing** /ˈnʌθɪŋ/ *pronoun*

1 : not anything **:** not a thing ▪ There's *nothing* in my hands. ▪ She knows *nothing* of/about our plans. ▪ You have *nothing* to worry about. ▪ "What are you doing?" "*Nothing* (much)." ▪ There's *nothing* fun to do around here. ▪ I have *nothing* against them. [=I do not dislike or resent them] ▪ We'll accept *nothing* less than a full refund. [=we will only accept a full refund] ▪ It costs *nothing* for the first month. [=you do not have to pay anything for the first month] ▪ The phone call was *nothing* more than a sales pitch. [=it was just a sales pitch and not anything else] ▪ They live on practically *nothing*. [=no money] ▪ This has ***nothing to do with*** you. [=it does not involve you in any way] ▪ There's ***nothing else*** [=no more] to say. ▪ ***If nothing else***, you should send him a card. [=you should at least send him a card] ▪ I've had ***next to nothing*** to eat. [=I have had very little to eat] ▪ He could ***make nothing of*** the coded message. [=he could not understand the coded message at all] ▪ We discussed plans for a new project, but ***nothing came of*** them. [=we did not do anything about what we discussed] ▪ He ***left nothing to*** chance. [=he planned for every possibility] ▪ The food ***leaves nothing to be desired***. [=the food is excellent] ▪ Their children ***lack/want for nothing***. [=their children have everything they need] ▪ Why should they help? There's ***nothing in it for them***. [=they will not gain anything for themselves by helping] ▪ It looks like ***nothing so much as*** a big stick. [=it looks very much like a big stick] ▪ Those kids are ***nothing but*** trouble. [=they are always causing trouble] ▪ He is ***nothing if not*** persistent. [=he is extremely persistent] ▪ "I'm quitting school." "You'll do ***nothing of the sort***!" [=you will not do that; I will not allow you to do that] ▪ She'll ***stop at nothing*** [=she will do anything] to get what she wants. ▪ She finished up ***in nothing flat***. [=in no time at all; very quickly] — see also GOOD-FOR-NOTHING

2 : someone or something that has no interest, value, or importance ▪ Money is *nothing* to them. [=they do not care at all about money] ▪ You think that's bad? It's *nothing* compared to what I went through. ▪ Don't get all upset over *nothing*. ▪ "Thanks for your help." "It was *nothing*." [=it was no trouble] ▪ Your opinion means *nothing* to me. ▪ "Are you hurt?" "Don't worry. It's *nothing*." ▪ All our work came to *nothing*. = All our work resulted in *nothing*. ▪ He's *nothing* to me now. [=I don't care about him at all now]

double or nothing see [3]DOUBLE

have nothing on see HAVE

here goes nothing see [1]HERE

nothing daunted see DAUNT

nothing doing *informal* — used as a forceful way of saying "no" to a question or suggestion ▪ He asked her to lend him the money, but she said *nothing doing*. [=she said that she would definitely not lend him the money] ▪ "Why don't you try it?" "*Nothing doing*." [=no way; definitely not]

nothing else for it *or Brit* ***nothing for it*** *old-fashioned* — used to say that something must be done because there is no other choice ▪ By the time we discovered the mistake, there was *nothing else for it* but to start over. ▪ We don't want to sell the house, but there is *nothing else for it* (but to sell).

N

nothing in/to ✧ If you say that there is *nothing in/to* something, you mean that it is not true at all. ▪ There's *nothing to* the story/claim. ▪ There is *nothing in* the rumor.

nothing like **1** — used to say that something is very enjoyable or satisfying ▪ There's *nothing like* a cool swim on a hot day. **2** *Brit, informal* : not nearly ▪ The report is *nothing like* thorough enough.

nothing to it — used to say that something is very easy to do ▪ There's really *nothing to it* once you know how.

on a hiding to nothing see ²HIDING

to say nothing of see ¹SAY

²nothing *adv* : not at all : in no way ▪ She is *nothing* like her sister. ▪ It's *nothing* close to finished.

nothing less than **1** — used to give emphasis to a description ▪ The idea is *nothing less than* revolutionary. [=the idea is revolutionary] **2** — used to say that something is the least that a situation, person, etc., requires or will accept ▪ He demands *nothing less than* the best service. [=he demands the best service] ▪ I want *nothing less than* a full refund! ▪ This job requires *nothing less than* our best effort.

nothing short of — used to give emphasis to a description ▪ His recovery was *nothing short of* miraculous. [=his recovery was miraculous] ▪ That treatment is *nothing short of* torture!

³nothing *noun, pl* **-things**

1 [*noncount*] : empty space ▪ It appeared out of *nothing*. ▪ The UFO hovered for a while, then vanished into *nothing*.

2 [*noncount*] : the number 0 : ZERO ▪ (*chiefly US*) The score is two (to) *nothing*. ▪ (*Brit*) She is five foot *nothing* [=she is exactly five feet tall] without her shoes on.

3 : someone or something that has little or no worth, importance, or influence [*count*] I knew her back when she was a *nothing*. [=*nobody*] [*noncount*] My children are important to me—I'm *nothing* without them. ▪ Today was a *nothing* day. [=nothing interesting or important happened today]

for nothing **1** : without reason ▪ It's not *for nothing* that they put her in charge. ▪ We did all that work *for nothing*. [=we did all that work when we did not need to] **2** : at no charge : for free ▪ He gave it to me *for nothing*. ▪ You can't get something *for nothing*.

sweet nothings : loving and romantic words ▪ He whispered *sweet nothings* in her ear.

noth·ing·ness /ˈnʌθɪŋnəs/ *noun* [*noncount*]

1 : empty space ▪ He was staring into *nothingness*.

2 : the state of being no longer seen, heard, or felt : NONEXISTENCE ▪ The sound faded into *nothingness*. ▪ philosophers who feel that when we die, we pass into *nothingness* [=we no longer exist]

¹no·tice /ˈnoʊtəs/ *noun, pl* **-tic·es**

1 [*noncount*] **a** : information that tells you or warns you about something that is going to happen ▪ Please give us enough *notice* to prepare for your arrival. ▪ They gave no advance *notice* that they were moving. [=they did not tell anyone that they were moving before they did it] ▪ Terms of the agreement are subject to change ***without notice***. [=terms of the agreement may be changed without telling you before they are changed] ▪ The beach is closed ***until further notice***. [=until there is an announcement saying that it is open] ▪ I received ***written notice*** that my bank account will be credited. [=I received a letter telling me that my bank account will be credited] ▪ The senator ***served notice*** [=made it known] that he will be opposing the new regulations. ▪ With the success of her first film, she *served notice* [=*showed*] that she is a serious and talented director. **b** : a statement telling someone that an agreement, job, etc., will end soon ▪ She gave her landlord *notice* (that she is moving next month). ▪ I gave (my employer) two weeks' *notice*. [=I told my employer that I would be quitting my job in two weeks] ▪ My boss gave me two weeks' *notice*. [=my boss told me that I would be losing my job in two weeks]

2 [*noncount*] : attention that people give to someone or something ▪ Her red dress attracted *notice*. [=her red dress made people look at her; people noticed her red dress] ▪ The band first ***came to public notice*** in 1991. [=the public first heard about the band in 1991] ▪ The error ***escaped my notice***. [=I did not notice the error] ▪ ***Take no notice*** of them. [=ignore them] ▪ No one ***took much notice*** of her [=no one paid much attention to her] at the party. ▪ The team has been playing better recently, and people are starting to ***(sit up and) take notice***. [=are starting to notice and give attention to the team's improved play] ▪ He ***brought the problem to my notice***. [=he brought the problem to my attention; he told me about the problem]

3 [*count*] : a written or printed statement that gives information ▪ *Notices* were sent to parents about the school trip. ▪ The *notice* [=*sign*] said, "BEACH CLOSED." ▪ Did you see the *notice* about the meeting? ▪ Newspapers print *notices* of marriages and deaths.

4 [*count*] : a short piece of writing that gives an opinion about a play, book, etc. ▪ The play received good *notices*. [=*reviews*]

at a moment's/minute's notice or *US* ***on a moment's/minute's notice*** or ***at short notice*** or *US* ***on short notice*** : immediately after you have been told about something ▪ They're prepared to help us *at/on a moment's notice*. [=as soon as we tell them that we need their help] ▪ They can be ready to go *at/on a moment's notice*. ▪ She had to leave on a business trip *at/on* (very) *short notice*.

on notice *formal* : warned or told about something ▪ The police are *on notice* to have more security at the concert. [=the police have been warned to have more security at the concert] ▪ She ***put us on notice*** [=she told us in a very definite and forceful way] that she would not be available for interviews until after the trial.

²notice *verb* **-tices; -ticed; -tic·ing** [+ *obj*] : to become aware of (something or someone) by seeing, hearing, etc. ▪ He *noticed* his friend sitting at the next table. = He *noticed* that his friend was sitting at the next table. ▪ She *noticed* a smell of gas. ▪ You didn't *notice* that I got my hair cut. ▪ She *noticed* me leaving the meeting early. ▪ The police *noticed* [=*observed*] a connection between the murders. ▪ I *noticed* an error in the book. ▪ The problem was first *noticed* several days ago. ▪ I ***couldn't help noticing*** the spot on his tie. = I ***couldn't help but notice*** the spot on his tie. [=I saw the spot even though I wasn't trying to look for it]

get noticed : to get attention that you want from other people ▪ You'll *get noticed* in that new sports car. = That new sports car will *get* you *noticed*. ▪ a young actor who's trying to *get noticed* ▪ The band *got noticed* by a record producer. [=a record producer showed interest in the band]

no·tice·able /ˈnoʊtəsəbəl/ *adj* [*more* ~; *most* ~] : able to be easily seen or noticed ▪ The spot on your shirt is very *noticeable*. ▪ There has been a *noticeable* improvement in her behavior. ▪ a *noticeable* change/difference in the weather ▪ It was *noticeable* that they were not prepared to give the presentation.

— **no·tice·ably** /ˈnoʊtəsəbli/ *adv* ▪ The sound got *noticeably* louder. ▪ Test scores were *noticeably* higher the next year.

no·tice·board /ˈnoʊtəsˌboəd/ *noun, pl* **-boards** [*count*] *Brit* : BULLETIN BOARD 1

no·ti·fi·able /ˌnoʊtəˈfajəbəl/ *adj, formal* : required by law to be reported to the government or to the proper officials ▪ a *notifiable* disease

no·ti·fi·ca·tion /ˌnoʊtəfəˈkeɪʃən/ *noun, pl* **-tions** : something that gives official information to someone : the act of notifying someone [*noncount*] I was given no *notification* that you received my payment. [*count*] You will be sent a written *notification*.

no·ti·fy /ˈnoʊtəˌfaɪ/ *verb* **-fies; -fied; -fy·ing** [+ *obj*] : to tell (someone) officially about something ▪ She *notified* [=*informed*] the police about the accident. ▪ Customers were *notified* of the changes in the company. ▪ I was *notified* that I did not get the job.

no·tion /ˈnoʊʃən/ *noun, pl* **-tions**

1 [*count*] : an idea or opinion ▪ He has some pretty strange *notions*. ▪ I only have a (slight) *notion* of the poem's meaning. ▪ She had a vague *notion* about what happened. ▪ They have different *notions* [=*conceptions*] of right and wrong. ▪ The study disproves any *notion* that dolphins are not intelligent.

2 [*count*] : an idea about doing something : a sudden wish or desire ▪ She had a *notion* to try skydiving.

3 ***notions*** [*plural*] *US* : small useful things (such as pins, thread, buttons) that are used for sewing ▪ a sewing shop that sells fabrics, books, tools, and *notions*

no·tion·al /ˈnoʊʃənl/ *adj* : existing as an idea rather than as something real ▪ The *notional* earnings of the company were close to the actual ones.

— **no·tion·al·ly** *adv*

no·to·ri·ety /ˌnoʊtəˈrajəti/ *noun* : the condition of being famous or well-known especially for something bad : the state of being notorious [*noncount*] He achieved instant fame and *notoriety* with the release of his film. ▪ She gained *notoriety* when nude photographs of her appeared in a magazine. [*singular*] His comment about the President has given him a *notoriety* that he enjoys very much.

no·to·ri·ous /noʊˈtorijəs/ *adj* [*more* ~; *most* ~] **:** well-known or famous especially for something bad ▪ The coach is *notorious* for his violent outbursts. ▪ *notorious* [=*infamous*] cases of animal cruelty
— **no·to·ri·ous·ly** *adv* ▪ The weather is *notoriously* difficult to predict.

[1]**not·with·stand·ing** /ˌnɑːtwɪθˈstændɪŋ/ *prep, formal* **:** without being prevented by (something) **:** DESPITE — used to say that something happens or is true even though there is something that might prevent it from happening or being true ▪ *Notwithstanding* their youth and inexperience, the team won the championship. — often used after its object ▪ The law was passed, our objections *notwithstanding*. [=the law was passed despite our objections]

[2]**notwithstanding** *adv, formal* **:** in spite of what has just been said **:** NEVERTHELESS ▪ Although there are some who oppose the plan, we will go through with it *notwithstanding*.

nou·gat /ˈnuːgət, *Brit* ˈnuːˌgɑː/ *noun* [*noncount*] **:** a sweet candy that usually contains nuts or pieces of fruit

[1]**nought** /ˈnɑːt/ *noun, pl* **noughts** [*count, noncount*] *Brit* **:** the number 0 **:** ZERO ▪ One million is a 1 with six *noughts* after it.

[2]**nought** *chiefly Brit spelling of* NAUGHT

noughts and crosses *noun* [*noncount*] *Brit* **:** TIC-TAC-TOE

noun /ˈnaʊn/ *noun, pl* **nouns** [*count*] **:** a word that is the name of something (such as a person, animal, place, thing, quality, idea, or action) and is typically used in a sentence as subject or object of a verb or as object of a preposition — see also COMMON NOUN, COUNT NOUN, NONCOUNT NOUN, PROPER NOUN

noun phrase *noun, pl* ~ **phrases** [*count*] **:** a group of words that acts like a noun in a sentence ▪ In the sentence "I found the owner of the dog," "the owner of the dog" is a *noun phrase*.

nour·ish /ˈnərɪʃ/ *verb* **-ish·es; -ished; -ish·ing** [+ *obj*]
1 : to provide (someone or something) with food and other things that are needed to live, be healthy, etc. ▪ Plants are *nourished* [=*fed*] by rain and soil. ▪ Vitamins are added to the shampoo to *nourish* the hair. ▪ a well-*nourished* baby
2 : to cause (something) to develop or grow stronger ▪ a friendship *nourished* by trust ▪ Her parents *nourished* [=*supported*] her musical talent.

nour·ish·ing /ˈnərɪʃɪŋ/ *adj* [*more* ~; *most* ~] **:** providing the things that are needed for health, growth, etc. **:** giving nourishment ▪ This cereal is more *nourishing* [=*nutritious*] than that one. — often used figuratively ▪ The sermon was spiritually *nourishing*. [=*enriching*]

nour·ish·ment /ˈnərɪʃmənt/ *noun* [*noncount*] **:** food and other things that are needed for health, growth, etc. ▪ These children are suffering because they lack proper/adequate *nourishment*. ▪ Soil provides *nourishment* to plants. — often used figuratively ▪ intellectual *nourishment* ▪ emotional/spiritual *nourishment*

nous /ˈnaʊs/ *noun* [*noncount*] *Brit, informal* **:** the intelligence and ability to make good judgments and decisions ▪ At least he had the foresight and *nous* [=*common sense*] to sell his stocks when he did.

nou·veau riche /ˌnuːvoʊˈriːʃ/ *noun, pl* **nou·veaux rich·es** /ˌnuːvoʊˈriːʃ/ [*count*] *disapproving* **:** a person who has recently become rich and who likes to spend a lot of money
— **nouveau riche** *adj* ▪ Our *nouveau riche* neighbors just bought some expensive but tacky furniture.

nou·velle cuisine /nuˈvɛl-/ *noun* [*noncount*] **:** a modern style of cooking in which light, healthy food is prepared and served in an attractive way

Nov. *abbr* November

no·va /ˈnoʊvə/ *noun, pl* **no·vas** *or* **no·vae** /ˈnoʊvi/ [*count*] *astronomy* **:** a star that suddenly increases greatly in brightness and then within a few months or years becomes less bright again — see also SUPERNOVA

[1]**nov·el** /ˈnɑːvəl/ *noun, pl* **-els** [*count*] **:** a long written story usually about imaginary characters and events ▪ write/publish/read a *novel* ▪ a detective/romance/science-fiction *novel*

[2]**novel** *adj* [*more* ~; *most* ~] **:** new and different from what has been known before ▪ a *novel* idea ▪ She has suggested a *novel* approach to the problem. ▪ Handheld computers are *novel* devices.

nov·el·ist /ˈnɑːvəlɪst/ *noun, pl* **-ists** [*count*] **:** a person who writes novels

no·vel·la /noʊˈvɛlə/ *noun, pl* **-las** [*count*] **:** a short novel **:** a story that is longer than a short story but shorter than a novel

nov·el·ty /ˈnɑːvəlti/ *noun, pl* **-ties**
1 [*noncount*] **:** the quality or state of being new, different, and interesting ▪ The toy's *novelty* soon wore off. [=the toy became uninteresting in a short time] ▪ the *novelty* of space exploration
2 [*count*] **a :** something that is new or unusual **:** something novel ▪ Electric-powered cars are still *novelties*. ▪ Eating shark meat is a *novelty* to many people. **b :** something unusual and entertaining that is popular for a short period of time — usually used before another noun ▪ *novelty* songs ▪ The band was a ***novelty act*** that had two hits and then disappeared.
3 [*count*] **:** a small and unusual decoration or toy ▪ *Novelties* filled the shelves. — often used before another noun ▪ a *novelty* shop/item

No·vem·ber /noʊˈvɛmbɚ/ *noun, pl* **-bers :** the 11th month of the year [*noncount*] in (early/middle/mid-/late) *November* ▪ early/late in *November* ▪ We arrived on *November* the fourth. = (*US*) We arrived on *November* fourth. = We arrived on the fourth of *November*. [*count*] Sales are up (for) this *November* in comparison with the previous two *Novembers*. ▪ It happens every *November*. — abbr. *Nov.*

nov·ice /ˈnɑːvəs/ *noun, pl* **nov·ic·es** [*count*]
1 : a person who has just started learning or doing something ▪ He's a *novice* in cooking. ▪ a *novice* [=*beginner*] at skiing ▪ a book for the *novice* chess player
2 : a new member of a religious group who is preparing to become a nun or a monk

no·vi·tiate /noʊˈvɪʃət/ *noun, pl* **-tiates** [*count*] **:** the time when a person is a religious novice

no·vo·caine /ˈnoʊvəˌkeɪn/ *noun* [*noncount*] *medicine* **:** a drug that causes part of your body to feel no pain and that is used especially by dentists

[1]**now** /ˈnaʊ/ *adv*
1 : at the present time ▪ We were having trouble before, but everything's okay *now*. ▪ I'm feeling much better *now*, thank you. ▪ I love you *now* and I'll love you forever. ▪ *Now*'s the time for action. ▪ "And *now*," he said, "all we have to do is wait." ▪ "Can we talk?" "Not *now*. I'm really busy." ▪ The room is *now* used as a home office. = They *now* use the room as a home office. ▪ He knows *now* that he was wrong. ▪ Police have *now* identified the man who they believe stole the car. ▪ Scientists *now* believe that the bones belong to a different species of reptile. ▪ the *now* famous photograph of an American sailor kissing his young wife ▪ I wish I knew then what I know *now*. ▪ This is the only chance you'll ever get. ***It's now or never***. — often used to show that you are annoyed about something ▪ *Now* you tell me?! I needed to know that yesterday! ▪ You tracked dirt everywhere! *Now* I have to spend all day cleaning again! ▪ "I know you've explained a lot—but can I ask just one more question?" "What *now*?" = "What is it *now*?" = "*Now* what?" ▪ OK: I'll do it your way. Are you happy *now*?
2 : in the next moment **:** very soon ▪ I have to leave *now*. [=*right now, right away, immediately*] ▪ It's time to go home *now*. ▪ If I don't do it *now*, I'll forget to do it later. ▪ They'll be back any minute *now*! ▪ Any day *now*, he'll be walking through that door. ▪ *Now* which way do we go? ▪ What do I do *now*? ▪ What *now*? = *Now* what? [=what next?]
3 : in the present situation ▪ He'll never believe me *now*! ▪ If you can't stand the heat *now*, you certainly won't be able to stand it in the summer.
4 : at the time referred to in the past ▪ Her parents arrived home the next day. *Now* the trouble really began. ▪ I next met her again a few years later. She was *now* 30 years old and working for a law firm.
5 : for an amount of time until the present time ▪ It's been several years *now* since I last saw her. [=I haven't seen her for several years] — often used with *for* ▪ We've lived here *for* a long time *now*. = We've lived here *for* some time *now*. ▪ She has been teaching *for* 20 years *now*. = She has been teaching *now for* 20 years.
6 — used to make a command or request or to express criticism or disapproval ▪ Hurry up, *now*, class started three minutes ago. ▪ *Now*, Billy, that's no way to talk to your mother! ▪ *Now* you be sure to write, you hear? ▪ Well, *now*, what is this I hear about you going back to school? ▪ Come *now*. You know that's not true. = (*chiefly US*) Come on, *now*. You know that's not true. ▪ *Now*, which one of you kids broke the window? ▪ *Now*, you listen to me. ▪ *Now* see here!

7 — used to introduce an important idea or to show a change in subject ▪ *Now,* I'd like to call your attention to the statue in the middle of the room. ▪ "What's the meaning of life?" "*Now* that's what I call a really important question!" ▪ *Now* that was a great song! ▪ *Now* where was I? Oh yes, I was telling you about my Uncle Harry. ▪ *Now* you've done it! ▪ *Now* don't get too excited. ▪ *Now* who could that be? ▪ ***Now then,*** what shall we do next? ✧ The phrase ***now for*** is often used to introduce a different idea or activity. ▪ That was an easy question. *Now for* something a bit more challenging. ▪ *Now for* today's top news stories.

8 *literary* : at one moment : SOMETIMES ▪ *now* one and *now* another ▪ She was *now* laughing, *now* crying.

even now see ²EVEN

(every) now and then *also* ***(every) now and again*** : not often but sometimes ▪ We still see each other *(every) now and then.* ▪ *Now and then* she would come in to check on me. ▪ The silence in the house was broken *now and again* by the ringing of the telephone.

just now see ²JUST

now, now **1** — used to tell someone not to be worried or unhappy ▪ *Now, now,* don't cry. Everything will be all right. You'll see! **2** — used to express criticism or disapproval ▪ *Now, now.* There's no need to use that kind of language.

now you're talking see ¹TALK

right now see ²RIGHT

²**now** *conj* : since something is true : because of the fact that something happened ▪ *Now* you mention it, I am kind of hungry. — usually + *that* ▪ *Now that* you mention it, I am kind of hungry. ▪ *Now that* we're all here, let's start the meeting. = Let's start the meeting *now that* everyone's here.

³**now** *noun [singular]* : the present time or moment ▪ A lot of things can happen between *now* and then. ▪ ***By now,*** you must have heard the news. = You must have heard the news *by now.* ▪ The kids are supposed to be in bed *by now.* ▪ That's enough ***for now,*** but we may need some more later. ▪ Things are fine *for now.* ▪ Fifty years ***from now*** you'll be telling your grandchildren about this day. ▪ She's due back a week *from now.* ▪ We'll be here *from now* until November. ▪ I promise, ***from now on*** [=from this moment and forever into the future], I'll always tell you the truth. ▪ *From now on,* no one can use my car without my permission. ▪ ***Until now,*** doctors had no idea what caused the disease. = ***Up to now,*** they didn't know what caused it. — see also *here and now* at ¹HERE

now·a·days /ˈnawəˌdeɪz/ *adv* : at the present time ▪ People don't wear hats much *nowadays.* ▪ *Nowadays* [=these days], many people need two jobs in order to make ends meet.

N

¹**no·where** /ˈnoʊˌweə/ *adv* : not in or at any place ▪ I have *nowhere* to go/sit/live. ▪ These facts are *nowhere* stated (in the book). ▪ *Nowhere* is there more of a population problem than in this city. ▪ The book is ***nowhere to be found.*** = The book is ***nowhere to be seen.*** = The book is ***nowhere in sight.***

get nowhere **1** *or* ***go nowhere*** : to have no success at all in doing something : to make no progress ▪ I have *gotten nowhere* with my research. [=my research has been completely unsuccessful] ▪ The research is *going nowhere.* ▪ We're ***getting/going nowhere fast.*** **2** ***get (someone) nowhere*** : to not help (someone) at all : to not make a situation any better for (someone) ▪ Arguing will *get us nowhere.* [=arguing will not help our situation]

nowhere near *informal* : not at all : not nearly ▪ Their house is *nowhere near* as nice as yours. ▪ That is *nowhere near* enough water. ▪ The house is *nowhere near* finished.

²**nowhere** *noun [noncount]* : no place — used figuratively ▪ They live ***miles from nowhere.*** [=they live in a place that is very far from other people] ▪ We got lost ***in the middle of nowhere.*** [=in a place far away from other people, houses, etc.]

from nowhere *or* ***out of nowhere*** — used to say that someone or something comes, appears, happens, etc., in a sudden and unexpected way ▪ The car came *out of nowhere*! ▪ Suddenly, *out of nowhere,* she offered me the job. ▪ Starting *from nowhere* [=with nothing], he built a very successful business. ▪ The horse came *from nowhere* to win the race. ▪ She rose to fame *out of nowhere.* ▪ ***From out of nowhere*** he asked her if she was having an affair.

no–win /ˈnoʊˈwɪn/ *adj, always used before a noun* — used to describe something (such as a situation) that cannot have a good result no matter what you do ▪ We're in a *no-win* situation. ▪ a *no-win* war ▪ She's stuck in a *no-win* job.

nowt /ˈnaʊt/ *noun [noncount] Brit, informal* : NOTHING ▪ There's *nowt* like it. ▪ He said *nowt.* ✧ *Nowt* is used in northern England.

nox·ious /ˈnɑːkʃəs/ *adj [more ~; most ~] formal* : harmful to living things : TOXIC ▪ *noxious* fumes/waste

noz·zle /ˈnɑːzəl/ *noun, pl* **noz·zles** *[count]* : a short tube that is put on the end of a hose or pipe to control the way a liquid or gas flows out

nr *abbr, Brit* near

NRA *abbr* National Rifle Association ✧ The NRA is an organization that is active in supporting the rights of U.S. citizens to own guns.

NS *abbr* Nova Scotia

NSW *abbr* New South Wales

NT *abbr* **1** New Testament **2** Northern Territory **3** Northwest Territories

nth /ˈɛnθ/ *adj* — used to refer to an unknown number in a series of numbers ▪ I told him for the *nth* time that I would not support him. [=I told him again that I would not support him, as I have told him many times before]

to the nth degree : extremely : as much as possible ▪ He is dedicated *to the nth degree.* [=he is extremely dedicated]

nu·ance /ˈnuːˌɑːns, *Brit* ˈnjuːˌɑːns/ *noun, pl* **-anc·es** : a very small difference in color, tone, meaning, etc. *[count] nuances* [=*shades*] of color/meaning ▪ He listened to the subtle *nuances* in the song. *[noncount]* a poem of little depth and *nuance*

– nu·anced /ˈnuːˌɑːnst, *Brit* ˈnjuːˌɑːnst/ *adj [more ~; most ~]* ▪ a complex and *nuanced* poem/story/painting

nub /ˈnʌb/ *noun, pl* **nubs** *[count]* : a small piece or end ▪ The dog chewed his bone down to a *nub.* : a small part that sticks out ▪ The shoes have little *nubs* on the bottom that prevent you from slipping.

the nub : the main part or point of something ▪ *the nub* of the story/problem/matter/argument

nu·bile /ˈnuːˌbajəl, *Brit* ˈnjuːˌbajəl/ *adj [more ~; most ~]* : sexually attractive — used of a young woman ▪ a *nubile* young starlet

nu·cle·ar /ˈnuːklijə, *Brit* ˈnjuːklijə/ *adj, always used before a noun* **1 a** : of, relating to, producing, or using energy that is created when the nuclei of atoms are split apart or joined together ▪ *nuclear* [=*atomic*] weapons/bombs ▪ a *nuclear* (power) plant ▪ *nuclear* fuel ▪ *nuclear* waste [=waste materials that are created when nuclear energy is produced] **b** : having or involving nuclear weapons ▪ the *nuclear* [=*atomic*] age ▪ a *nuclear* war/attack ▪ *nuclear* powers [=countries that have nuclear weapons]

2 : of or relating to the nucleus of an atom ▪ *nuclear* [=*atomic*] physics/fission/fusion

nuclear energy *noun [noncount] physics* : energy that is created by splitting apart the nuclei of atoms — called also *atomic energy, nuclear power*

nuclear family *noun, pl* **~ -lies** *[count]* : the part of a family that includes only the father, mother, and children — compare EXTENDED FAMILY

nuclear fission *noun [noncount]* : FISSION 1

nuclear–free *adj* : not having or allowing nuclear energy, weapons, or materials ▪ a *nuclear-free* zone/area

nuclear fusion *noun [noncount]* : FUSION 2

nuclear power *noun [noncount] physics* : NUCLEAR ENERGY

nuclear reaction *noun, pl* **~ -tions** *[count] physics* : REACTION 5b

nuclear reactor *noun, pl* **~ -tors** *[count] physics* : REACTOR

nu·cle·ic acid /nʊˈkliːjɪk-/ *noun, pl* **~ acids** *[count] technical* : any of various acids (such as DNA or RNA) that are found in living cells

nu·cle·us /ˈnuːklijəs/ *noun, pl* **nu·clei** /ˈnuːkliˌaɪ/ *also* **nu·cle·us·es** *[count]*

1 *biology* : the central part of most cells that contains genetic material and is enclosed in a membrane

2 *physics* : the central part of an atom that is made up of protons and neutrons

3 : a central or most important part of something — usually + *of* ▪ players who are the *nucleus* [=*core*] *of* the team

¹**nude** /ˈnuːd, *Brit* ˈnjuːd/ *adj*

1 : having no clothes on : NAKED ▪ The artists sketched the *nude* model.

2 : of or involving people who have no clothes on ▪ a *nude* movie scene ▪ a *nude* beach [=a beach where people wear no clothes] ▪ He took *nude* photos of her. [=he took photos of her when she was not wearing clothes]

3 : having the color of a white person's skin ▪ *nude* pantyhose

– **nude** *adv* ▪ She posed *nude* for the magazine.

[2]**nude** *noun, pl* **nudes** [*count*] : a painting, sculpture, etc., that shows a nude person ▪ the *nudes* of Greek sculpture

in the nude : without any clothes on ▪ He stood there *in the nude.*

nudge /ˈnʌʤ/ *verb* **nudg·es; nudged; nudg·ing**

1 [+ *obj*] **a** : to touch or push (someone or something) gently ▪ I *nudged* the plate closer to him. ▪ The guard *nudged* the prisoner forward. ▪ The dog *nudged* the ball with his nose. ▪ We *nudged* our way (through the crowd) to the exit. **b** : to push (someone) gently with your elbow in order to get that person's attention ▪ He *nudged* me and pointed to the deer.

2 [+ *obj*] : to encourage (someone) to do something ▪ He was *nudged* (by his parents) towards a career in law. ▪ The salesman *nudged* her into testing out the car.

3 a [+ *obj*] : to come close to (a particular level or amount) ▪ Album sales are *nudging* the one million mark. **b** *always followed by an adverb or preposition* [*no obj*] : to move slightly to a different level or amount ▪ The price of gold has *nudged* a little higher.

– **nudge** *noun, pl* **nudges** [*count*] ▪ He gave me a *nudge* in the ribs.

nud·ism /ˈnuːˌdɪzəm, *Brit* ˈnjuːˌdɪzəm/ *noun* [*noncount*] : the practice of not wearing any clothes especially in private places (such as camps or beaches) that are separated from public areas — called also (*Brit*) *naturism*

nud·ist /ˈnuːdɪst, *Brit* ˈnjuːdɪst/ *noun, pl* **-ists** [*count*] : a person who practices nudism — called also (*Brit*) *naturist*

– **nudist** *adj* ▪ a *nudist* colony/resort

nu·di·ty /ˈnuːdəti, *Brit* ˈnjuːdəti/ *noun* [*noncount*] : the state of having no clothes on : the condition of being nude ▪ The movie has scenes of *nudity.*

nug·get /ˈnʌgət/ *noun, pl* **-gets** [*count*]

1 : a solid lump of a valuable metal (such as gold) ▪ gold *nuggets*

2 : a small, usually round piece of food ▪ chicken *nuggets*

3 : a piece of valuable information ▪ *nuggets* of wisdom/advice/information

nui·sance /ˈnuːsn̩s, *Brit* ˈnjuːsn̩s/ *noun, pl* **-sanc·es** [*count*] : a person, thing, or situation that is annoying or that causes trouble or problems — usually singular ▪ The sticky clay was a *nuisance* to work with. [=was difficult to work with] ▪ My allergies are a *nuisance* in the springtime. ▪ Filling out all the paperwork was a *nuisance.* ▪ I'm sorry to be such a *nuisance* [=I'm sorry to bother you], but I need your help again. ▪ He ***made a nuisance of himself*** [=he behaved in an annoying way] ▪ (*law*) The landfill was declared a ***public nuisance***.

[1]**nuke** /ˈnuːk, *Brit* ˈnjuːk/ *noun, pl* **nukes** [*count*] *informal* : a nuclear weapon

[2]**nuke** *verb* **nukes; nuked; nuk·ing** [+ *obj*] *informal*

1 : to attack or destroy (something) with a nuclear weapon

2 : to heat or cook (food) in a microwave oven : MICROWAVE ▪ *nuke* a pizza

null /ˈnʌl/ *adj, law* : having no legal power ▪ The contract was declared *null.* [=*invalid*] — often used in the phrase ***null and void*** ▪ The law was declared *null and void.*

nul·li·fy /ˈnʌləˌfaɪ/ *verb* **-fies; -fied; -fy·ing** [+ *obj*]

1 : to make (something) legally null ▪ The law has been *nullified* by the U.S. Supreme Court.

2 : to cause (something) to lose its value or to have no effect ▪ The penalty *nullified* the goal. ▪ Drinking coffee does not *nullify* [=*negate*] the effects of alcohol.

num. *abbr* numeral

[1]**numb** /ˈnʌm/ *adj* [*more* ~; *most* ~]

1 : unable to feel anything in a particular part of your body because of cold, injury, etc. ▪ The side of my face was still *numb* an hour after the surgery. ▪ I had a *numb* feeling in my toes. ▪ It was so cold that my fingers ***went numb***. ▪ A stroke can cause one side of your body to *go numb.*

2 : unable to think, feel, or react normally because of something that shocks or upsets you ▪ Her son had died and she just felt *numb.* ▪ He stood there *numb* with fear/rage.

– **numb·ly** *adv* ▪ They moved *numbly* through their routine.

– **numb·ness** *noun* [*noncount*] A stroke can cause *numbness* in one side of your body. [*singular*] The patient was complaining of a *numbness* in her fingers.

[2]**numb** *verb* **numbs; numbed; numb·ing** [+ *obj*]

1 : to cause (a part of the body) to be unable to feel anything ▪ The injection will *numb* the area to be operated on. ▪ The cold wind *numbed* my face.

2 : to make (someone) unable to think, feel, or react normally ▪ She was *numbed* by the news of her son's death.

– **numbing** *adj* [*more* ~; *most* ~] ▪ the *numbing* cold ▪ We had to sit through a *numbing* [=very boring] lecture. — see also MIND-NUMBING – **numb·ing·ly** *adv* ▪ a *numbingly* cold wind ▪ These tasks are *numbingly* repetitive.

[1]**num·ber** /ˈnʌmbɚ/ *noun, pl* **-bers**

1 [*count*] : a word or symbol (such as "five" or "16") that represents a specific amount or quantity ▪ the *number* seven ▪ He wrote down two *numbers* [=*numerals*]: 3 and 9. ▪ the *numbers* and letters on a license plate ▪ a three-digit *number* like 429 ▪ Think of a *number* between one and one hundred. ▪ The *number* 7¾ is greater than the *number* 7.25. ▪ 2, 4, 6, and 8 are ***even numbers***; 1, 3, 5, and 7 are ***odd numbers***. ▪ Let's say I have $100 to spend—that's a nice, ***round number***. [=a number that is easily multiplied, divided, etc., and especially a number that ends in zero] — see also CARDINAL NUMBER, ORDINAL NUMBER, PRIME NUMBER, WHOLE NUMBER

2 [*count*] **a** : a number or a set of numbers and other symbols that is used to identify a person or thing ▪ a student's ID/identification *number* ▪ Never give out your credit card *number* to anyone over the phone. ▪ What's the account *number* on your electricity bill? ▪ The page *numbers* are on the top corner of each page. ▪ Today's winning lottery *numbers* are 17, 8, and 46. ▪ I'm waiting for the *number* 3 bus. ▪ Flight *number* 101 from Los Angeles to London is now boarding at Gate *number* 36. ▪ What's the answer to question *number* 6? ▪ My daughter's the pitcher, *number* 21. — abbr. *No.* or *no.*; see also REGISTRATION NUMBER, SERIAL NUMBER, SOCIAL SECURITY NUMBER **b** : a person who is identified by a number and not treated in a personal or friendly way ▪ We get to know each of our customers and make sure that they don't feel like they're just a *number.* ▪ a large university where the students are just *numbers* **c** : PHONE NUMBER ▪ What's your work/office/daytime *number*? ▪ My home *number* is (413) 555-2917. ▪ Call our toll-free *number.* ▪ Did you get her *number*? = Did she give you her *number*? ▪ Well, you've got my *number.* Give me a call sometime. ▪ "May I speak with Sara, please?" "I'm sorry. You must have the ***wrong number***." — see also 800 NUMBER

3 a : the total amount of people or things [*count*] Fish were once plentiful in this river, but they have since declined ***in numbers***. [=there are now fewer fish than there once were] ▪ New houses are being built ***in record numbers***. [=more new houses are being built now than ever before] — often + *of* ▪ Were you surprised by the *number of* people who came to the party? ▪ More should be done to decrease the *number of* violent crimes in the city. ▪ Large *numbers of* people have left. [=many people have left] ▪ Serious side effects were observed in a small *number of* patients. [=a few patients had serious side effects] ▪ A ***good number of*** college students [=many college students] have entered the competition. ▪ There are ***a number of*** [=*several*] different options to choose from. ▪ Some students have already been absent on *a number of* occasions. ▪ The dish can be prepared in ***any number of*** ways. [=many different ways] ▪ Residents have left the city for *any number of* reasons. [*noncount*] They have declined ***in number***. [=there are not as many of them as there were before] ▪ The protesters were few *in number,* but they were very loud. **b** ***numbers*** [*plural*] : a large group of people or things ▪ There's ***safety/strength in numbers***. [=people are safer/stronger when they are together in a group] ▪ They won the battle through sheer ***weight of numbers***. [=they won because there were so many of them]

4 [*count*] **a** — used to indicate the position of someone or something in a numbered list or series ▪ You're *number* 7 on the waiting list. ▪ Now serving *number* 28. — abbr. *No.* or *no.* **b** : the version of a magazine, newspaper, etc., that is published at a particular time ▪ The article is in volume 36, *number* 2 of this journal. ▪ (*Brit*) the June *number* [=(*US*) *issue*] of the magazine — abbr. *No.* or *no.*

5 [*singular*] *formal* : a group of people ▪ One of their *number* [=one of them] went missing.

6 [*count*] : a song or dance that is usually performed as part of a concert or performance ▪ For his final *number* he sang "Heartbreak Hotel." ▪ The actors broke into a song and dance *number.*

7 [*count*] *informal* : someone or something that is attractive or desirable ▪ She wore a cute little black *number* [=a small attractive black dress] to the dance. ▪ I just bought a new car: a fast, blue *number.* ▪ I'm going to ask that hot *number* [=attractive girl or woman] over there if she'll dance with me.

8 ***numbers*** [*plural*] : numbers that show amounts of money that are spent, earned, or needed • We won't be able to stay in business with *numbers* like these! • I'm afraid the *numbers* just don't make your idea a profitable option. • I don't know if we can afford it. I have to look at the *numbers*. • I ***ran the numbers*** [=determined the amount of money to be spent, earned, etc.], and I just don't think we can afford it. • When we sat down to ***crunch the numbers*** [=to calculate exactly how much money is available, needed, etc.] we realized that we couldn't afford a new car.

9 *numbers* [*plural*] *chiefly US* **a : numbers that show how many people are listening to or watching a particular radio or television program** • The network looked at the show's *numbers* and decided to cancel it. **b : numbers that show how a person (such as an athlete) has performed in the past** • Her *numbers* [=*statistics, stats*] make her the team's most valuable player. • I don't remember all of his *numbers*, but I know he made 63 home runs last year.

10 *numbers* [*plural*] *US* **: a gambling game in which people bet on which numbers will be chosen each day** • playing the *numbers* **— often used before another noun** • an illegal *numbers* game • the *numbers* racket

11 [*noncount*] *grammar* **: the quality of a word form that shows whether the word is singular or plural** • A verb and its subject must agree ***in number***. [=if the subject is the singular, the verb must be singular; if the subject is plural, the verb must be plural]

bad/good (etc.) with numbers **:** bad, good, etc., at using numbers (such as for adding, subtracting, multiplying, and dividing) • What's 43 times 12? Oh, I don't know—I'm *bad/lousy with numbers*. [=I am bad at mathematics] • Ask her to do the books, she's *good with numbers*.

beyond number *formal + literary* **: too many to count** • a paradise inhabited by animal species *beyond number* • The stars are *beyond number*.

by numbers *or US* ***by the numbers*** **: in a way that follows the rules or instructions but that is not interesting or original** • Dancing *by the numbers* isn't good enough. You have to really feel the music.

do a number on *informal* **: to have a very bad effect on (someone or something) : to hurt or damage (someone or something)** • This heavy backpack is *doing a number on* my back. • The scandal really *did a number on* his career.

have someone's number *informal* **: to be able to deal with or defeat someone easily especially because you know or understand that person so well** • She thinks she's *got my number*, but I'm going to prove her wrong.

without number *formal* **: too many to count** • This area has been inhabited for years *without number*. [=for very many years]

your number is up ✧ If *your number is up*, you are about to suffer or die. • You never know when *your number is up*. [=when you will die]

[2]number *verb* **-bers; -bered; -ber·ing**

1 [+ *obj*] **: to give a number to (someone or something in a series) : to label or identify (people or things in a series) with a number** • She *numbers* and arranges the photographs according to when they were taken. • For the quiz, take out a sheet of paper and *number* it from one to ten. [=write the numbers one through ten down the side of the paper] • Each print is signed and *numbered* by the artist. • The team's coach bought all the players *numbered* jerseys.

2 — used to indicate a total amount [*linking verb*] The population now *numbers* about 400,000. [=the population is now about 400,000] • In that year, European settlers in the area *numbered* nearly 15,000. • Though his years *number* only 45 [=though he is only 45 years old], he looks like an old man. [*no obj*] The animal, which once *numbered* in the millions, is now extinct.

3 *somewhat formal* **: to include (someone or something) as part of a larger group — + *among* or *with*** [+ *obj*] She *numbers among* her friends three Nobel Prize winners. = She *numbers* three Nobel Prize winners *among* her friends. [=three of her friends are Nobel Prize winners] • He *numbers* her *with* the other great poets of the time. **— usually used as *(be) numbered*** • John Keats *is numbered* [=*ranked*] *among* the greatest English poets. • I am proud to *be numbered among* those who have served our country. [*no obj*] She *numbers among* the best. [=she is one of the best]

days are numbered **— used to say that someone or something will die, fail, or end soon.** • The doctors have told me that my *days are numbered*. [=I will die soon]. • He knew that his *days* as the team's coach *were numbered*. [=that he was going to be fired from his job as the team's coach soon] • The *days* of large gas-guzzling cars *are numbered*. [=people will not be making/buying large gas-guzzling cars for much longer]

number cruncher /-ˈkrʌntʃɚ/ *noun, pl* **~ -ers** [*count*] **: a person who collects and studies information in the form of numbers** • The *number crunchers* in Washington are expecting a budget surplus by the fall. • the company's *number crunchers*

— number crunching *noun* [*noncount*] • doing some *number crunching*

num·ber·less /ˈnʌmbɚləs/ *adj, literary* **: too many to count** • the *numberless* [=*countless*] stars in the sky

[1]number one *or* **No. 1** *noun* [*noncount*]

1 a : a person, thing, or position that is highest in rank : the most important person or thing in a group of people or things • Who's *number one* in this office? • Getting the car fixed is *number one* on my list of priorities. • I'll tell you why we can't go on a vacation: *number one*, we can't afford it, and number two, we'll miss my sister's party. • Two of their songs have gone to *number one* [=the highest rank] on the pop charts. **b : the most successful person or thing in a group of people or things** • Her movie is currently *number one* at the box office. • When the goal was scored, the fans started to chant, "We're *number one*, we're *number one*."

2 : your own happiness, health, or success : YOURSELF • I've been taking care of other people for too long. It's time for me to take care of *number one*. • If you don't ***look out for number one*** [=if you don't take care of yourself], who will?

3 *informal* **: liquid waste from the body : URINE — used mainly by children or when speaking to children; compare NUMBER TWO**

[2]number one *or* **No. 1** *adj* **: highest in rank or importance** • Heart disease is the country's *number one* [=*leading*] killer of women. • My *number one* [=*main*] concern is getting my car fixed. • The book is the company's *number one* seller. • Rule *number one* is don't get caught! • He's ***public enemy number one***: the nation's most wanted criminal.

number plate *noun, pl* **~ plates** [*count*] *chiefly Brit* **: LICENSE PLATE**

number sign *noun, pl* **~ signs** [*count*] *US* **: [3]POUND**

Number Ten *or* **Number 10** *noun* [*singular*] *Brit*

1 : the place in London where the British Prime Minister lives

2 : the British government

number two *noun* [*noncount*] *informal* **: solid waste from the body — used mainly by children or when speaking to children; compare NUMBER ONE 3**

numb·skull *also* **num·skull** /ˈnʌmˌskʌl/ *noun, pl* **-skulls** [*count*] *informal* **: a stupid or foolish person** • Why did you do that? How can you be such a *numbskull*?

nu·mer·al /ˈnuːmərəl, *Brit* ˈnjuːmərəl/ *noun, pl* **-als** [*count*] **: a symbol (such as 1, 2, or 3) that represents a number — see also ARABIC NUMERAL, ROMAN NUMERAL**

nu·mer·a·tor /ˈnuːməˌreɪtɚ, *Brit* ˈnjuːməˌreɪtə/ *noun, pl* **-tors** [*count*] *mathematics* **: the number in a fraction that is above the line and that is divided by the number below the line** • The *numerator* in the fraction ⅗ is 3. **— compare DENOMINATOR**

nu·mer·ic /nʊˈmerɪk, *Brit* njʊˈmerɪk/ *adj* **: of or relating to numbers** • a *numeric* code/system • a *numeric* keypad

nu·mer·i·cal /nʊˈmerɪkəl, *Brit* njʊˈmerɪkəl/ *adj* **: of or relating to numbers or a system of numbers** • The files are organized according to a *numerical* system. • a *numerical* code • The files are in *numerical* order.

— nu·mer·i·cal·ly /nʊˈmerɪkli, *Brit* njʊˈmerɪkli/ *adv* • The files are organized *numerically*.

nu·me·ro uno /ˈnuːməroʊˈuːnoʊ/ *noun* [*noncount*] *US, informal* **: [1]NUMBER ONE 1** • The company is *numero uno* in computer technology.

nu·mer·ous /ˈnuːmərəs, *Brit* ˈnjuːmərəs/ *adj* [*more ~; most ~*] *somewhat formal* **: existing in large numbers** • They had *numerous* [=*many*] friends. • She decided to leave for *numerous* reasons. • The birds are becoming more *numerous* in this area. • The people I'd like to thank are ***too numerous to mention/list***. [=there are so many of them that I can't mention all their names]

nu·mi·nous /ˈnuːmənəs, *Brit* ˈnjuːmənəs/ *adj* [*more ~; most ~*] *formal + literary* **: having a mysterious, holy, or spiritual quality** • Her poetry is filled with a *numinous* beauty.

nu·mis·mat·ics /ˌnuːməzˈmætɪks, *Brit* ˌnjuːməzˈmætɪks/

noun [*noncount*] : the study or act of collecting of coins, paper money, and medals
– **nu·mis·mat·ic** /ˌnuːməzˈmætɪk, *Brit* ˌnjuːməzˈmætɪk/ *adj* ▪ a *numismatic* error – **nu·mis·ma·tist** /nuˈmɪzmətɪst, *Brit* njuˈmɪzmətɪst/ *noun, pl* **-tists** [*count*]

numskull *variant spelling of* NUMBSKULL

nun /ˈnʌn/ *noun, pl* **nuns** [*count*] : a woman who is a member of a religious community and who usually promises to remain poor, unmarried, and separate from the rest of society in order to serve God — compare MONK

nun·cio /ˈnʌnsijoʊ/ *noun, pl* **-ci·os** [*count*] : a person who is the Pope's representative in a foreign country

nun·nery /ˈnʌnəri/ *noun, pl* **-ner·ies** [*count*] *literary* + *old-fashioned* : a place where nuns live : CONVENT

nup·tial /ˈnʌpʃəl/ *adj, always used before a noun, formal* : of or relating to marriage or a wedding ceremony ▪ *nuptial* vows

nup·tials /ˈnʌpʃəlz/ *noun* [*plural*] *formal* : a wedding or wedding ceremony ▪ He was to attend the *nuptials* of his sister. ▪ The *nuptials* will take place in the nearby church.

[1]**nurse** /ˈnɚs/ *noun, pl* **nurs·es** [*count*]
1 : a person who is trained to care for sick or injured people and who usually works in a hospital or doctor's office ▪ The *nurse* will take your blood pressure before the doctor sees you. ▪ *Nurse*, may I have some water? — see also CHARGE NURSE, LICENSED PRACTICAL NURSE, REGISTERED NURSE
2 *old-fashioned* : a woman who is paid to take care of a young child usually in the child's home — see also WET NURSE

[2]**nurse** *verb* **nurses; nursed; nurs·ing**
1 [+ *obj*] : to take care of or help (someone who is sick or injured) ▪ The staff *nursed* me back to health. [=the staff took care of me until I was healthy again] ▪ She is *nursing* her son through his illness.
2 [+ *obj*] : to give special care or attention to (something) : to try to keep (something) from failing ▪ The couple *nursed* the business through hard times. ▪ He *nursed* the farm back to productivity. ▪ The team *nursed* a 1–0 lead until the last inning. ▪ The player is still out *nursing* an ankle injury. = The player is still out *nursing* her ankle. [=the player is caring for her injured ankle so that it will not get worse]
3 a [+ *obj*] : to feed (a baby or young animal) with milk from the mother's body ▪ She *nursed* [=*breast-fed, suckled*] her baby for several months. ▪ The dog *nursed* her puppies. **b** [*no obj*] *of a baby or young animal* : to take milk from the mother's body ▪ The baby *nursed* for several months. ▪ The puppies *nursed* for eight weeks.
4 [+ *obj*] : to hold (something, such as an idea or a strong feeling) in your mind for a long time ▪ He is not one to *nurse* a grievance/grudge. ▪ She *nursed* a secret desire to move to the city.
5 [+ *obj*] : to drink (something) very slowly over a long period of time ▪ He *nursed* his glass of wine.

nurse·maid /ˈnɚsˌmeɪd/ *noun, pl* **-maids** [*count*] *old-fashioned* : a girl or woman whose job is to take care of children

nurse–mid·wife /nɚsˈmɪdˌwaɪf/ *noun, pl* **-wives** [*count*] : a nurse who is also a midwife and who delivers babies and cares for the mother and baby before and after the baby's birth

nurse prac·ti·tion·er /nɚsprækˈtɪʃənɚ/ *noun, pl* ~ **-ers** [*count*] : a nurse who is trained to do some of the things a doctor does (such as give physical exams or order certain medical tests)

nurs·ery /ˈnɚsəri/ *noun, pl* **-er·ies**
1 [*count*] **a** *US* : the room where a baby sleeps ▪ She still needs to decorate the *nursery* before the baby comes. **b** : the room in a hospital where new babies are kept and cared for by nurses **c** *old-fashioned* : a room where children sleep, play, and are sometimes taught
2 [*count*] **a** : a place where plants (such as trees or shrubs) are grown and sold ▪ We get our flowers from a local *nursery*. **b** : a place where some young animals (such as fish) are grown ▪ salmon *nurseries*
3 *Brit* **a** [*count*] : a place where children are cared for during the day while their parents are working ▪ She dropped her daughter off at the (day) *nursery*. [=(*US*) day care center] **b** [*count, noncount*] : NURSERY SCHOOL

nurs·ery·man /ˈnɚsərimən/ *noun, pl* **-men** /-mən/ [*count*] : a person who owns or works in a place where plants are grown and sold

nursery rhyme *noun, pl* ~ **rhymes** [*count*] : a short poem or song for children

nursery school *noun, pl* ~ **schools** [*count, noncount*] : a school for very young children : PRESCHOOL

nursery slope *noun, pl* ~ **slopes** [*count*] *Brit* : BUNNY SLOPE

nurse's aide *noun, pl* ~ **aides** [*count*] *US* : a person whose job is to help nurses to take care of patients

nursing *noun* [*noncount*] : the job of taking care of people who are sick, injured, or old ▪ She has been employed in *nursing* for several years now. ▪ *Nursing* is difficult work. ▪ He went to ***nursing school***. [=a school that trains people to be nurses]

nursing home *noun, pl* ~ **homes** [*count*] : a place where people who are old or who are unable to take care of themselves can live and be taken care of

nur·tur·ance /ˈnɚʧərəns/ *noun* [*noncount*] *formal* : the love, care, and attention that you give to someone or something ▪ maternal *nurturance*

[1]**nur·ture** /ˈnɚʧɚ/ *verb* **-tures; -tured; -tur·ing** [+ *obj*]
1 : to help (something or someone) to grow, develop, or succeed ▪ Teachers should *nurture* their students' creativity. ▪ a professor who *nurtures* any student who shows true interest in history
2 : to take care of (someone or something that is growing or developing) by providing food, protection, a place to live, etc. ▪ The study looks at the ways parents *nurture* their children. ▪ You have to carefully *nurture* the vines if you want them to produce good grapes.
3 : to hold (something, such as an idea or a strong feeling) in your mind for a long time ▪ She *nurtured* a secret ambition to be a singer. ▪ *nurture* a dream/grudge
– **nur·tur·er** /ˈnɚʧərɚ/ *noun, pl* **-ers** [*count*] ▪ a *nurturer* of the weak ▪ She tends to be the *nurturer* in the family.

[2]**nurture** *noun* [*noncount*] *formal* : the care and attention given to someone or something that is growing or developing ▪ Members of the family helped in the *nurture* of the baby. ▪ Is our character affected more by nature or by *nurture*? [=by the way we are treated and taught to behave when we are young]

nut /ˈnʌt/ *noun, pl* **nuts**
1 [*count*] **a** : a small dry fruit with a hard shell that grows on trees, bushes, etc. ▪ The squirrel cracked/opened the *nut* and ate the meat inside. ▪ walnuts, almonds, peanuts, and other *nuts* — see picture on next page **b** : the inside part of a nut that is used as food ▪ The squirrel sat and ate the *nut*. ▪ Are you allergic to *nuts*? ▪ a bowl of *nuts* and raisins
2 [*count*] : a piece of metal that has a hole through it so that it can be screwed onto a bolt or screw — see picture at CARPENTRY; see also LUG NUT, WING NUT
3 [*count*] *informal* **a** : a crazy or strange person ▪ That guy is a real *nut*. **b** : a person who is very interested in or enthusiastic about something ▪ She's a real baseball/car/health/movie/travel *nut*.
4 ***nuts*** [*plural*] *informal* + *impolite* : a man's testicles ▪ He got kicked in the *nuts*.
a hard/tough nut (to crack) : a person or thing that is difficult to deal with, understand, or influence ▪ The team's defense is *a tough nut to crack*. ▪ The problem is *a hard nut to crack*. ▪ He's *a tough nut*, but I think I can get him to agree to the contract.
nuts and bolts : the basic parts or details of an activity, job, etc. ▪ She's still learning the *nuts and bolts* of the business. ▪ Tell me what the *nuts and bolts* of the plan involve.
soup to nuts see [1]SOUP
– **nut·like** /ˈnʌtˌlaɪk/ *adj* [*more* ~; *most* ~] ▪ The cake had a *nutlike* [=*nutty*] taste. n

nut–brown /ˈnʌtˈbraʊn/ *adj* : medium brown or dark brown in color ▪ *nut-brown* hair

nut·case /ˈnʌtˌkeɪs/ *noun, pl* **-cas·es** [*count*] *informal* : a crazy or very strange person ▪ He's a total/complete *nutcase*.

nut·crack·er /ˈnʌtˌkrækɚ/ *noun, pl* **-ers** [*count*] : a tool or device that is used to open the shells of nuts

nut·hatch /ˈnʌtˌhæʧ/ *noun, pl* **-hatch·es** [*count*] : a small bird with a narrow beak and short tail

nut·house /ˈnʌtˌhaʊs/ *noun, pl* **-hous·es** [*count*] *US, informal* + *old-fashioned* : a hospital for people who are mentally ill — usually used figuratively ▪ This office is a *nuthouse*. [=a place where there is a lot of confusion, disorganization, etc.]

nut·meg /ˈnʌtˌmɛg/ *noun* [*noncount*] : a spice made from the hard seed of a tropical tree and used in cooking and baking

nu·tra·ceu·ti·cal /ˌnuːtrəˈsuːtɪkəl, *Brit* ˌnjuːtrəˈsjuːtɪkəl/ *noun, pl* **-cals** [*count*] *technical* : a specially treated food, vi-

N

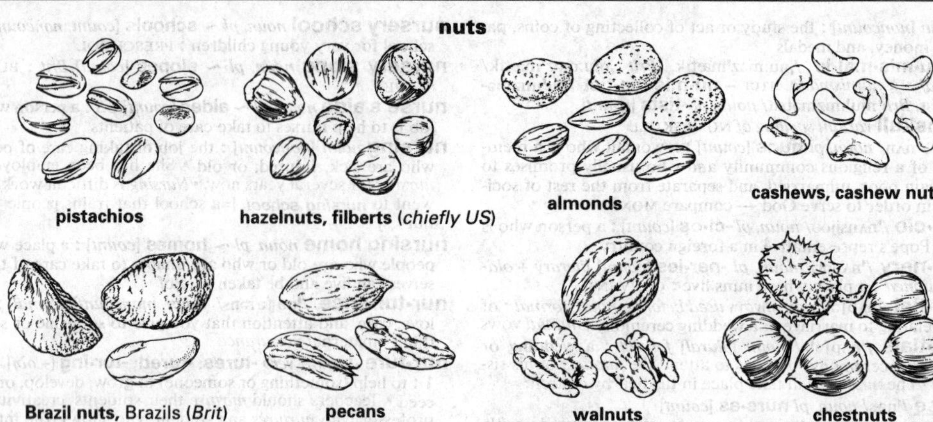

tamin, mineral, herb, etc., that you eat or drink in order to improve your health

nu·tri·ent /ˈnuːtrijənt, *Brit* ˈnjuːtrijənt/ *noun, pl* **-ents** [*count*] *technical* **:** a substance that plants, animals, and people need to live and grow • Fruits and vegetables have important *nutrients.* • The soil is low in *nutrients.* • You need more *nutrients* in your diet.

– **nutrient** *adj, always used before a noun* • the *nutrient* composition of different foods • The disease is caused by *nutrient* deficiencies.

nu·tri·tion /nʊˈtrɪʃən, *Brit* njʊˈtrɪʃən/ *noun* [*noncount*] **:** the process of eating the right kind of food so you can grow properly and be healthy • The speaker discussed diet and *nutrition* with the class. • good *nutrition* and proper exercise

– **nu·tri·tion·al** /nʊˈtrɪʃənəl, *Brit* njʊˈtrɪʃənəl/ *adj* [*more ~; most ~*] • a *nutritional* supplement [=a vitamin, herb, etc., that you take in order to help your body be healthy] • the *nutritional* value of fruits and vegetables – **nu·tri·tion·al·ly** *adv* • a *nutritionally* complete meal

nu·tri·tion·ist /nʊˈtrɪʃənɪst, *Brit* njʊˈtrɪʃənɪst/ *noun, pl* **-ists** [*count*] **:** a person whose job is to give advice on how food affects your health

nu·tri·tious /nʊˈtrɪʃəs, *Brit* njʊˈtrɪʃəs/ *adj* [*more ~; most ~*] **:** having substances that a person or animal needs to be healthy and grow properly **:** promoting good health and growth • highly *nutritious* salad greens • The food was both *nutritious* and delicious.

nu·tri·tive /ˈnuːtrətɪv, *Brit* ˈnjuːtrətɪv/ *adj, always used before a noun, technical* **:** of or relating to nutrition • the *nutritive* value of certain grains

[1]**nuts** /ˈnʌts/ *adj, not used before a noun* [*more ~; most ~*] *informal*

1 : CRAZY • They looked at me like I was *nuts.* • She's going to ***drive me nuts*** [=make me crazy; make me go insane] with her jealousy.

2 a : very enthusiastic about or interested in something — often + *about* • He was *nuts* [=*crazy*] *about* baseball. **b :** feeling affection or love for someone or something — often + *for* or *about* • She is *nuts for* children and animals. [=she loves children and animals] • He's *nuts about* her. [=he's deeply in love with her]

go nuts **1 :** to become mentally ill **:** to become insane • She *went nuts* [=*went crazy*] and started to believe that everyone was trying to kill her. **2 :** to act in a way that is wild or out of control because of strong emotion • The crowd *went nuts* when the team won the championship. • When Dad sees you broke the window, he's going to *go nuts.*

[2]**nuts** *interj, US, informal + old-fashioned* — used to express anger, disappointment, etc. • Aw *nuts!* I broke my glasses!

nut·shell /ˈnʌtˌʃɛl/ *noun, pl* **-shells** [*count*] **:** the hard outer shell of a nut

in a nutshell **:** very briefly • And that, *in a nutshell,* is what happened. • ***To put it in a nutshell,*** the party was a disaster.

nut·ter /ˈnʌtə/ *noun, pl* **-ters** [*count*] *Brit, informal* **:** a crazy or strange person **:** NUT • He's a complete *nutter.*

nut·ty /ˈnʌti/ *adj* **nut·ti·er; -est**

1 a : tasting or smelling like nuts • candy with a *nutty* taste • a *nutty* coffee **b :** containing nuts • a *nutty* candy bar

2 *informal* **a :** silly, strange, or foolish • What a *nutty* idea. • He's got some *nutty* [=*weird*] friends. **b :** mentally ill • Her aunt's a little *nutty.* [=*crazy*]

– **nut·ti·ness** *noun* [*noncount*] • I noticed some *nuttiness* in the coffee's taste. • the sheer *nuttiness* of the idea

nuz·zle /ˈnʌzəl/ *verb* **nuz·zles; nuz·zled; nuz·zling :** to gently push or rub your nose or face against (someone or something) to show affection [+ *obj*] She *nuzzled* his neck. • The dog *nuzzled* my leg. [*no obj*] The dog *nuzzled* (up) against my leg. • He *nuzzled* into her neck.

NV *abbr* Nevada

NW *abbr* northwest, northwestern

NWT *abbr* Northwest Territories

NY *abbr* New York

NYC *abbr* New York City

ny·lon /ˈnaɪˌlɑːn/ *noun, pl* **-lons**

1 [*noncount*] **:** a strong material that is made from a chemical process and that is used for making clothes, ropes, and other products • The rope is made of *nylon.* — often used before another noun • a *nylon* rope

2 *nylons* [*plural*] **:** clothing for women made of nylon that fits closely over the feet and legs and goes up to the waist • a pair of *nylons* [=*pantyhose, stockings*]

nymph /ˈnɪmf/ *noun, pl* **nymphs** [*count*]

1 *in stories* **:** a spirit in the shape of a young woman who lives in mountains, forests, meadows, and water

2 *technical* **:** a young insect that has almost the same form as the adult

nym·phet /nɪmˈfɛt/ *noun, pl* **-phets** [*count*] **:** a sexually attractive girl

nym·pho /ˈnɪmfoʊ/ *noun, pl* **-phos** [*count*] *informal* **:** NYMPHOMANIAC

nym·pho·ma·ni·ac /ˌnɪmfəˈmeɪniˌæk/ *noun, pl* **-acs** [*count*] **:** a woman who has an unusually strong desire to have sex very often

– **nym·pho·ma·ni·a** /ˌnɪmfəˈmeɪnijə/ *noun* [*noncount*] *somewhat technical* • a patient affected with *nymphomania*

NZ *abbr* New Zealand

O

o *or* **O** /ˈoʊ/ *noun, pl* **o's** *or* **os** *or* **O's** *or* **Os** /ˈoʊz/
1 : the 15th letter of the English alphabet *[count]* a word that starts with an *o* *[noncount]* a word that starts with *o*
2 *[count]* **:** the number zero — used in speech when referring to numbers ▪ I live in apartment number three *o* two. [=302]
3 *[count]* — used as a mark at the end of a letter, an e-mail, etc., to represent a hug ▪ XO, Mom

o' *also* **o** /ˈoʊ/ *prep* **:** [1]OF — used in some words and informally in some phrases ▪ jack-*o'*-lantern ▪ a cup *o'* tea

O *variant spelling of* [1]OH

oaf /ˈoʊf/ *noun, pl* **oafs** *[count]* **:** a stupid or awkward person — usually used for a man ▪ Get out of the way, you big *oaf*!
– oaf·ish /ˈoʊfɪʃ/ *adj [more ~; most ~]* ▪ an *oafish* bore **– oaf·ish·ly** *adv* **– oaf·ish·ness** *noun [noncount]*

oak /ˈoʊk/ *noun, pl* **oaks** *or* **oak**
1 *[count]* **:** a type of tree that grows in northern parts of the world and that produces acorns ▪ Tall *oaks* line the street. — called also *oak tree*; see also POISON OAK
2 *[noncount]* **:** the wood of an oak tree ▪ The table is solid *oak*. ▪ *oak* floors/chairs ▪ The cabinets are made of *oak*.
– oak·en /ˈoʊkən/ *adj, always used before a noun* ▪ *oaken* [=(more commonly) *oak*] floors/chairs

OAP /ˌoʊˌeɪˈpiː/ *noun, pl* **OAPs** *[count] Brit, old-fashioned* **:** a person who is old enough to receive a government pension ▪ reduced prices for *OAPs* [=*senior citizens*] ✧ *OAP* is an abbreviation for "old-age pensioner."

oar /ˈoɚ/ *noun, pl* **oars** *[count]* **:** a long pole that is flat and wide at one end and that is used for rowing and steering a boat ✧ Oars are usually used in pairs with one oar on each side of the boat. ▪ She gripped the *oars* and began rowing the boat to shore. — see picture at BOAT; compare PADDLE
get/put/stick your oar in *Brit, informal* **:** to give people your opinion when they do not want it

oar·lock /ˈoɚˌlɑːk/ *noun, pl* **-locks** *[count]* **:** a part that holds an oar in place on either side of a boat — called also *(Brit) rowlock*

oars·man /ˈoɚzmən/ *noun, pl* **-men** /-mən/ *[count]* **:** a person who rows a boat especially as a member of a racing team — called also *rower*

oars·wom·an /ˈoɚzˌwʊmən/ *noun, pl* **-wom·en** /-ˌwɪmən/ *[count]* **:** a woman who rows a boat especially as a member of a racing team — called also *rower*

oa·sis /oʊˈeɪsəs/ *noun, pl* **oa·ses** /oʊˈeɪˌsiːz/ *[count]*
1 : an area in a desert where there is water and plants ▪ a desert *oasis*
2 a : a pleasant place that is surrounded by something unpleasant ▪ The small park is a welcome *oasis* amid the city's many factories. ▪ an *oasis* of quiet **b :** a time or experience that is pleasant and restful ▪ Our brief trip to the beach was a much-needed *oasis* in a summer of hard work.

oat /ˈoʊt/ *noun, pl* **oats**
1 *[noncount]* **:** a kind of grain that is widely grown — often used before another noun ▪ *oat* bran/flour
2 oats *[plural]* **:** the seeds of the oat plant used as feed for farm animals and in foods (such as bread and oatmeal) for people
feel your oats *US, informal* **:** to feel new confidence and energy ▪ He's really been *feeling his oats* since he was given that promotion.
sow your (wild) oats see [1]SOW

oath /ˈoʊθ/ *noun, pl* **oaths** /ˈoʊðz/ *[count]*
1 : a formal and serious promise to tell the truth or to do something ▪ They were required to take/swear an *oath* of loyalty. [=promise formally to remain loyal] ▪ an *oath* to defend the nation ▪ an ***oath of office*** [=an official promise by a person who has been elected to a public office to fulfill the duties of the office according to the law]
2 *old-fashioned* **:** an offensive or rude word that is used to express anger, frustration, surprise, etc. ▪ He uttered an *oath* and walked away.
under oath *also* ***on oath*** *law* **:** having made a formal promise to tell the truth in a court of law ▪ In a U.S. court of law, a witness must swear *under oath* to tell "the truth, the whole truth, and nothing but the truth." ▪ He said in testimony given *under oath* that he was not there the night of the crime.

oat·meal /ˈoʊtˌmiːl/ *noun [noncount]*
1 : oats that have been ground into flour or flattened into flakes ▪ grinding oats into *oatmeal* — often used before another noun ▪ *oatmeal* cookies
2 *US* **:** a hot breakfast food that is made from oats ▪ a bowl of *oatmeal* — called also *(Brit) porridge*

ob·du·rate /ˈɑːbdərət, *Brit* ˈɒbdjərət/ *adj [more ~; most ~] formal* **:** refusing to do what other people want **:** not willing to change your opinion or the way you do something **:** STUBBORN ▪ He is known for his *obdurate* determination. ▪ Officials at the hospital were *obdurate*. [=*adamant*] The patient could have no visitors.
– ob·du·ra·cy /ˈɑːbdərəsi, *Brit* ˈɒbdjərəsi/ *noun [noncount]* ▪ Her *obduracy* angered them. **– ob·du·rate·ly** *adv*

obe·di·ent /oʊˈbiːdijənt/ *adj [more ~; most ~]* **:** willing to do what someone tells you to do or to follow a law, rule, etc. **:** willing to obey ▪ *obedient* to the law ▪ an *obedient* child/dog — opposite DISOBEDIENT
– obe·di·ence /oʊˈbiːdijəns/ *noun [noncount]* ▪ blind/unquestioning *obedience* ▪ Students are expected to act ***in obedience to*** the rules of the school. [=are expected to obey the rules of the school] ▪ He's been taking his dog to *obedience* classes/school/training. **– obe·di·ent·ly** *adv* ▪ The children stood *obediently* in line.

obei·sance /oʊˈbiːsn̩s/ *noun, pl* **-sanc·es** *formal*
1 *[count]* **:** a movement of your body (such as bowing) that shows respect for someone or something ▪ making *obeisances* to the king [=bowing to the king]
2 *[noncount]* **:** respect for someone or something ▪ They ***paid obeisance*** to him. [=they showed or expressed great respect for him]

obe·lisk /ˈɑːbəˌlɪsk/ *noun, pl* **-lisks** *[count]* **:** a tall, four-sided stone column that becomes narrower toward the top and that ends in a point

obese /oʊˈbiːs/ *adj [more ~; most ~]* **:** very fat **:** fat in a way that is unhealthy ▪ providing medical treatment for *obese* patients
– obe·si·ty /oʊˈbiːsəti/ *noun [noncount]* ▪ the problem of *obesity* in children

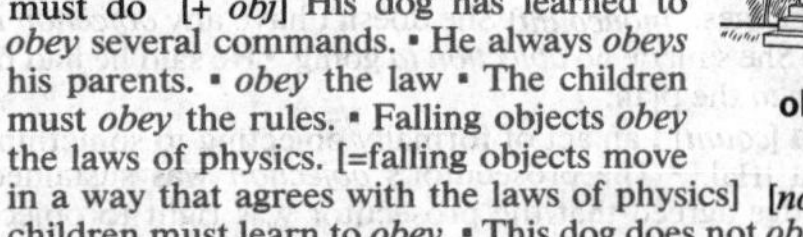
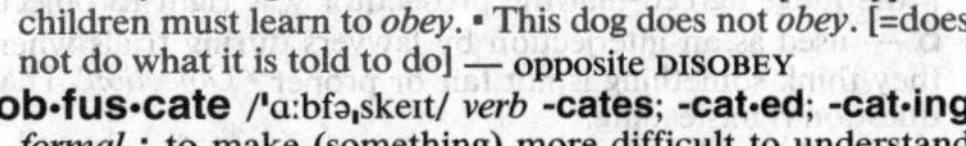
obelisk

obey /oʊˈbeɪ/ *verb* **obeys; obeyed; obey·ing :** to do what someone tells you to do or what a rule, law, etc., says you must do *[+ obj]* His dog has learned to *obey* several commands. ▪ He always *obeys* his parents. ▪ *obey* the law ▪ The children must *obey* the rules. ▪ Falling objects *obey* the laws of physics. [=falling objects move in a way that agrees with the laws of physics] *[no obj]* The children must learn to *obey*. ▪ This dog does not *obey*. [=does not do what it is told to do] — opposite DISOBEY

ob·fus·cate /ˈɑːbfəˌskeɪt/ *verb* **-cates; -cat·ed; -cat·ing** *formal* **:** to make (something) more difficult to understand *[+ obj]* Politicians keep *obfuscating* the issues. *[no obj]* Their explanations only serve to *obfuscate* and confuse.
– ob·fus·ca·tion /ˌɑːbfəˈskeɪʃən/ *noun [noncount]*

ob–gyn /ˌoʊˌbiːˌʤiːˌwaɪˈɛn/ *noun, pl* **ob–gyns** *[count] US, medical* **:** a doctor who deals with the birth of children and with diseases that affect the reproductive system of women ▪ She has an appointment with her *ob-gyn* tomorrow. ▪ an *ob-gyn* practice/specialist ✧ *Ob-gyn* comes from shortened forms of the words "obstetrician" and "gynecologist."

OB–GYN *abbr* obstetrics-gynecology

obit /oʊˈbɪt, *Brit* ˈɒbɪt/ *noun, pl* **obits** *[count] informal* **:** OBITUARY

obit·u·ary /oʊˈbɪʧəˌweri, *Brit* əˈbɪʧuəri/ *noun, pl* **-ar·ies** *[count]* **:** an article in a newspaper about the life of someone who has died recently ▪ I read/saw her *obituary* in the newspaper. ▪ an *obituary* writer/notice — sometimes used figuratively ▪ The company is not doing well, but it's too soon to write an/its *obituary*. [=too soon to think that the company will fail]

obj *abbr* object

[1]**ob·ject** /ˈɑːbʤɪkt/ *noun, pl* **-jects**

1 [*count*] **: a thing that you can see and touch and that is not alive** ▪ There were three *objects* in the box: a comb, a pen, and a button. ▪ an ***inanimate object*** [=a thing that is not alive, such as a rock, a chair, a book, etc.]

2 [*count*] **a : someone or something that makes you feel a specified emotion — + *of*** ▪ The book's lead character is both an *object of* desire and an *object of* pity. [=the lead character is both desired and pitied by other characters in the book] ▪ She is the *object of* his affection. **b : someone or something that your attention or interest is directed toward — often + *of*** ▪ The *object of* study in her research is the human brain. — see also SEX OBJECT

3 [*singular*] **: the goal or aim of a plan or action : the reason or purpose for an activity** ▪ His *object* is to determine how much the business will cost to operate. **— usually + *of*** ▪ The *object of* the game is to score the most points.

4 [*count*] *grammar* **: a noun, noun phrase, or pronoun that receives the action of a verb or completes the meaning of a preposition — compare** SUBJECT; **see also** DIRECT OBJECT, INDIRECT OBJECT

no object **— used to say that something is not important or worth worrying about** ▪ When they take a vacation, ***money is no object***. [=they don't worry about how much something costs] They always stay at the most expensive places. ▪ If *cost was/were no object* [=if cost did not matter; if we had enough money] we'd buy a new car instead of fixing the old one.

[2]**ob·ject** /əbˈʤɛkt/ *verb* **-jects; -ject·ed; -ject·ing**

1 [*no obj*] **: to disagree with something or oppose something** ▪ No one *objected* when the paintings were removed. ▪ (*law*) "Your honor, I *object*. That question is misleading." **— often + *to*** ▪ A number of people *objected to* the proposed changes. ▪ Many people *object to* [=do not like] the amount of violence on television.

2 [+ *obj*] **: to say (something that explains why you oppose something or disagree)** ▪ "We can't buy the chair," he *objected*. "It won't fit in the car." **— often + *that*** ▪ He *objected that* the chair was too big to fit in the car.

— ob·jec·tor /əbˈʤɛktɚ/ *noun, pl* **-tors** [*count*] — see also CONSCIENTIOUS OBJECTOR

ob·jec·ti·fy /əbˈʤɛktəˌfaɪ/ *verb* **-fies; -fied; -fy·ing** [+ *obj*] *disapproving* **: to treat (someone) as an object rather than as a person** ▪ She says beauty pageants *objectify* women.

— ob·jec·ti·fi·ca·tion /əbˌʤɛktəfəˈkeɪʃən/ *noun* [*noncount*] ▪ the *objectification* of women

ob·jec·tion /əbˈʤɛkʃən/ *noun, pl* **-tions**

1 : a reason for disagreeing with or opposing something : a reason for objecting [*count*] My main *objection* is that some people will have to pay more than others. **— often + *to*** ▪ His main *objection to* buying the car is that it's too expensive. ▪ People have raised/voiced a number of *objections to* the proposed changes. [*noncount*] She doesn't have any *objection to* going. = She's made no *objection to* going. ▪ He said he had no *objection to* the plan.

2 *law* **a** [*count*] **: an act of formally objecting to something during a trial.** ▪ The prosecutor's *objection* was sustained. [=the judge agreed that the prosecutor was right to object] **b — used as an interjection by lawyers during trials when they think something is not fair or proper** ▪ *Objection*! That question is misleading.

ob·jec·tion·able /əbˈʤɛkʃənəbəl/ *adj* [*more* ~; *most* ~] **: not good or right** ▪ Some people find the taste of the water *objectionable* [=*unpleasant*], but I think it's fine. **: causing people to be offended** ▪ He won't allow his children to watch television shows with *objectionable* [=*offensive*] language.

— ob·jec·tion·ably /əbˈʤɛkʃənəbli/ *adv* ▪ behaving *objectionably*

[1]**ob·jec·tive** /əbˈʤɛktɪv/ *adj*

1 [*more* ~; *most* ~] **: based on facts rather than feelings or opinions** ▪ We need someone outside the company to give us an *objective* analysis. ▪ Scientists must be *objective*. **: not influenced by feelings** ▪ It's hard to be *objective* [=*fair, unbiased*] about my own family. **— opposite** SUBJECTIVE

2 *philosophy* **: existing outside of the mind : existing in the real world** ▪ *objective* reality

3 *grammar* **: relating to nouns, noun phrases, or pronouns that are the objects of verbs or prepositions** ▪ The pronoun "her" is in the *objective* [=*accusative*] case in the sentence "I saw her." **— compare** SUBJECTIVE

— ob·jec·tive·ly *adv* ▪ Scientists must look at facts *objectively*. ▪ It's hard to think *objectively* about your own family.

— ob·jec·tiv·i·ty /ˌɑːbˌʤɛkˈtɪvəti/ *noun* [*noncount*] ▪ The passionate tone of the article made me question the author's *objectivity*.

[2]**objective** *noun, pl* **-tives**

1 [*count*] **: something you are trying to do or achieve : a goal or purpose** ▪ The main/primary *objective* of the class is to teach basic typing skills. ▪ She's expanding the business with the *objective* of improving efficiency. ▪ We've set specific *objectives* for each day.

2 [*count*] **:** OBJECTIVE LENS

3 [*noncount*] *grammar* **:** ACCUSATIVE

objective lens *noun, pl* ~ **lenses** [*count*] *technical* **: a lens or system of lenses in a microscope, telescope, etc., that forms an image of an object — called also *objective***

object lesson *noun, pl* ~ **-sons** [*count*] **: an example from real life that teaches a lesson or explains something** ▪ His life story is an *object lesson* in how not to run a business.

ob·jet d'art /ˌɑːbˌʒeɪˈdaɚ/ *noun, pl* **ob·jets d'art** /ˌɑːbˌʒeɪˈdaɚ/ [*count*] **: a small object that is valued because it is beautiful or interesting : an object that has artistic value** ▪ The house is decorated with *objets d'art* from around the world. **— called also *objet***

ob·li·gate /ˈɑːbləˌgeɪt/ *verb* **-gates; -gat·ed; -gat·ing** [+ *obj*] **: to make (a person or organization) do something because the law requires it or because it is the right thing to do** ▪ The contract *obligates* the firm to complete the work in six weeks. **— usually used as *(be) obligated*** ▪ You *are* legally *obligated* to repay the loan. = You *are obligated* by law to repay the loan. ▪ I feel *obligated* to return his call.

ob·li·ga·tion /ˌɑːbləˈgeɪʃən/ *noun, pl* **-tions**

1 : something that you must do because of a law, rule, promise, etc. [*count*] The firm must fulfill its *obligations* under the contract. = The firm must fulfill its contractual *obligations*. ▪ legal/financial/constitutional *obligations* ▪ Both landlord and tenant should know their rights and *obligations*. [=*responsibilities*] [*noncount*] You can try the machine for free ***without obligation***. [=without being required to buy it or to do anything else] ▪ You are ***not under any obligation*** to stay. [=you are not required to stay] ▪ You're ***under no*** (legal) ***obligation*** to return the money. [=there is no law that requires you to return the money; you do not have to return the money]

2 : something that you must do because it is morally right [*count*] family/social *obligations* ▪ She believes that all people have a moral *obligation* to defend human rights. ▪ He argues that people in a community have certain *obligations* to each other. ▪ She failed to fulfill her *obligations* as a parent. [*noncount*] We visited them out of a ***sense of obligation***. [=a feeling that it was the right thing to do]

oblig·a·to·ry /əˈblɪgəˌtori, *Brit* əˈblɪgətri/ *adj*

1 *formal* **: required by a law or rule** ▪ *obligatory* [=*mandatory*] military service ▪ The training is *obligatory* for all personnel.

2 *always used before a noun, humorous* **: always or often included as a familiar and expected part of something** ▪ This action movie includes the *obligatory* chase scenes.

oblige /əˈblaɪʤ/ *verb* **oblig·es; obliged; oblig·ing**

1 [+ *obj*] **: to force or require (someone or something) to do something because of a law or rule or because it is necessary** ▪ The law *obliges* the government to release certain documents to the public. ▪ Her job *obliges* her to work overtime and on weekends. **— usually used as *(be) obliged*** ▪ The government *is obliged* [=*required, obligated*] by law to release certain documents to the public.

2 : to do something that someone has asked you to do : to do a favor for (someone) [+ *obj*] She's always ready to *oblige* her friends. [*no obj*] "Thank you for your help." "I'm happy/glad to *oblige*." ▪ They asked for food and he *obliged* with soup and sandwiches.

— see also NOBLESSE OBLIGE

obliged *adj, not used before a noun, old-fashioned* **: very grateful :** THANKFUL ▪ I'd be much *obliged* if you'd hold the door for me. ▪ We felt *obliged* [=*indebted*] to them for all their help. ▪ You've been so helpful. We are much *obliged*. [=we are very grateful; we thank you very much]

obliging *adj* [*more* ~; *most* ~] **: willing to help : helpful in a friendly way** ▪ An *obliging* passerby helped her with her packages.

— oblig·ing·ly *adv* ▪ A passerby *obligingly* helped her with her packages.

[1]**oblique** /oʊˈbliːk/ *adj* [*more* ~; *most* ~]

1 : not direct : not stated directly ▪ She made only *oblique*

O

[=*indirect*] references to the scandal in her speech.

2 *of a line* **:** having a slanting direction or position **:** neither perpendicular nor parallel ▪ The short lines of the letter "k" are *oblique* lines.

– oblique·ly *adv* ▪ She referred to the scandal *obliquely* in her speech. **– oblique·ness** *noun* [*noncount*] ▪ The poem's *obliqueness* is what interests me.

[2]**oblique** *noun, pl* **obliques** [*count*] *Brit* **:** [2]SLASH 4

oblique angle *noun, pl* **~ angles** [*count*] *mathematics* **:** an angle that is not 90 degrees **:** an acute or obtuse angle ▪ The dancer held his leg at an *oblique* angle to his body.

oblit·er·ate /əˈblɪtəˌreɪt/ *verb* **-ates; -at·ed; -at·ing** [+ *obj*] **:** to destroy (something) completely so that nothing is left ▪ The tide eventually *obliterated* [=*wiped out*] all evidence of our sand castles. — often used as *(be) obliterated* ▪ The garden *was obliterated* in the hurricane.

– oblit·er·a·tion /əˌblɪtəˈreɪʃən/ *noun* [*noncount*]

obliv·i·on /əˈblɪvijən/ *noun* [*noncount*]

1 : the state of something that is not remembered, used, or thought about any more ▪ The technology is destined/headed for *oblivion*. ▪ The names of the people who lived here long ago have faded/drifted into *oblivion*. ▪ His theories have faded into scientific *oblivion*. ▪ Her work was rescued from *oblivion* when it was rediscovered in the early 1900s.

2 : the state of being unconscious or unaware **:** the state of not knowing what is going on around you ▪ After being awake for three days straight, he longed for the *oblivion* of sleep. ▪ She drank herself into *oblivion*.

3 : the state of being destroyed ▪ The little village was bulldozed into *oblivion* to make way for the airport.

obliv·i·ous /əˈblɪvijəs/ *adj* [*more ~; most ~*] **:** not conscious or aware of someone or something ▪ We called out to them, but they remained *oblivious*. [=they did not notice us] — usually + *of* or *to* ▪ He was completely *oblivious of* [=*unaware of*] the fact that he'd offended them. ▪ She kept dancing, *oblivious to* everyone around her.

– obliv·i·ous·ly *adv* **– obliv·i·ous·ness** *noun* [*noncount*]

ob·long /ˈɑːˌblɑːŋ/ *adj*

1 *US* **:** longer in one direction than in the other direction ▪ an *oblong* [=*oval*] loop ▪ the plant's *oblong* leaves

2 *chiefly Brit* **:** having four straight sides that meet at right angles and having two opposite sides that are short and two opposite sides that are long ▪ an *oblong* [=*rectangular*] block of wood

– oblong *noun, pl* **-longs** [*count*] ▪ Draw an *oblong*.

ob·lo·quy /ˈɑːbləkwi/ *noun* [*noncount*] *formal*

1 : harsh or critical statements about someone ▪ a victim of hatred and *obloquy*

2 : the condition of someone who lost the respect of other people ▪ For years they endured the *obloquy* [=*shame*] that follows scandal.

ob·nox·ious /ɑbˈnɑːkʃəs/ *adj* [*more ~; most ~*] **:** unpleasant in a way that makes people feel offended, annoyed, or disgusted ▪ He said some really *obnoxious* things about his ex-girlfriend at the party. ▪ Some teenagers were being loud and *obnoxious*. ▪ an *obnoxious* smell

– ob·nox·ious·ly *adv* ▪ *obnoxiously* loud music **– ob·nox·ious·ness** *noun* [*noncount*]

oboe /ˈoʊboʊ/ *noun, pl* **oboes** [*count*] **:** a musical instrument that is shaped like a tube and that is played by blowing into a small, thin piece at the top of the tube — see picture at WOODWIND

– obo·ist /ˈoʊbowɪst/ *noun, pl* **-ists** [*count*] ▪ He's an *oboist* in the city's orchestra.

ob·scene /ɑbˈsiːn/ *adj* [*more ~; most ~*]

1 a : relating to sex in an indecent or offensive way ▪ The book is filled with *obscene* [=*(informal) dirty*] pictures. ▪ He was accused of making *obscene* phone calls. **b :** very offensive in usually a shocking way ▪ *obscene* lyrics/language ▪ He made an *obscene* gesture at the driver who cut him off.

2 : so large an amount or size as to be very shocking or unfair ▪ The company's executives earn *obscene* salaries. ▪ He spends an *obscene* amount of money on clothes.

3 : morally disturbing or upsetting ▪ What an *obscene* [=*disgusting*] waste of money!

– ob·scene·ly *adv* ▪ *obscenely* wealthy/rich

ob·scen·i·ty /ɑbˈsɛnəti/ *noun, pl* **-ties**

1 [*noncount*] **:** the quality or state of being obscene ▪ He was arrested for *obscenity*. = He was arrested on *obscenity* charges.

2 [*noncount*] **:** obscene words or actions ▪ The author uses *obscenity* to make a point about the culture.

3 [*count*] **:** an offensive word **:** SWEARWORD — usually plural ▪ People were shouting/screaming/yelling *obscenities* at one another. ▪ The song's lyrics are full of *obscenities*.

ob·scu·ran·tism /ɑbˈskjərənˌtɪzəm/ *noun* [*noncount*] *formal* **:** the practice of keeping knowledge or understanding about something from people **:** the policy of not letting people know something ▪ secrecy and political *obscurantism*

– ob·scu·rant·ist /ɑbˈskjərəntɪst/ *adj* ▪ *obscurantist* art

[1]**ob·scure** /ɑbˈskjə/ *adj* [*more ~; most ~*]

1 : not well-known **:** not known to most people ▪ *obscure* books/titles ▪ a little antique shop in an *obscure* [=*out-of-the-way*] corner of the city

2 a : difficult to understand **:** likely to be understood by only a few people ▪ The movie is full of *obscure* references that only pop culture enthusiasts will understand. **b :** difficult or impossible to know completely and with certainty ▪ The origins of the language are *obscure*.

– ob·scure·ly *adv* ▪ an *obscurely* titled book

> ***synonyms*** OBSCURE, VAGUE, and AMBIGUOUS mean not clearly understandable. OBSCURE often suggests a meaning that cannot be easily understood because it has not been clearly expressed or because special knowledge is needed. ▪ an *obscure* poem VAGUE suggests something that cannot be described clearly. ▪ She felt a *vague* sense of obligation. It can also describe something that is difficult to understand because it is not specific. ▪ *vague* instructions AMBIGUOUS describes language that can be understood in more than one way. ▪ an *ambiguous* statement

[2]**obscure** *verb* **-scures; -scured; -scur·ing** [+ *obj*]

1 : to make (something) difficult to understand or know **:** to make (something) obscure ▪ The true history has been *obscured* by legends about what happened. ▪ They accused the company of trying to *obscure* the fact that the product poses a health risk.

2 : to hide or cover (something) **:** to be in front of (something) so that it cannot be seen ▪ Low clouds *obscured* the mountains. = The mountains were *obscured* by low clouds. ▪ Her view of the game was *obscured* [=*blocked*] by a post.

ob·scu·ri·ty /ɑbˈskjərəti/ *noun, pl* **-ties**

1 [*noncount*] **:** the state of being unknown or forgotten ▪ In recent years, the tradition has emerged from *obscurity*. ▪ He has been living in relative *obscurity* in a small town in the mountains. ▪ After a promising first novel, she faded/sank into *obscurity*.

2 a [*count*] **:** something that is difficult to understand — usually plural ▪ The essay is full of *obscurities*. **b** [*noncount*] **:** the quality of being difficult to understand ▪ A good writer avoids *obscurity* of language. [=does not use words people are not likely to understand]

ob·se·quies /ˈɑːbsəkwiz/ *noun* [*plural*] *formal* **:** the acts that make up a funeral ceremony ▪ solemn *obsequies*

ob·se·qui·ous /əbˈsiːkwijəs/ *adj* [*more ~; most ~*] *disapproving* **:** too eager to help or obey someone important ▪ She's constantly followed by *obsequious* assistants who will do anything she tells them to.

– ob·se·qui·ous·ly *adv* ▪ smiling *obsequiously* [=smiling in a way that shows that you are obsequious] **– ob·se·qui·ous·ness** *noun* [*noncount*]

ob·serv·able /əbˈzəvəbəl/ *adj* **:** possible to see or notice **:** able to be observed ▪ The trend is *observable* [=*noticeable, perceptible*] all over the country. ▪ the size of the *observable* universe

– ob·serv·ably /əbˈzəvəbli/ *adv* ▪ *observably* different

ob·ser·vance /əbˈzəvəns/ *noun, pl* **-vanc·es**

1 [*noncount*] **:** the practice of following a custom, rule, law, etc. ▪ Sabbath *observance* — often + *of* ▪ strict *observance of* the law/ban/rule ▪ The office will be closed in *observance of* the holiday.

2 [*count*] **:** an act that is part of a ceremony or ritual ▪ a special holiday *observance* — usually plural ▪ religious/ritual *observances*

ob·ser·vant /əbˈzəvənt/ *adj* [*more ~; most ~*]

1 : good at watching and listening **:** good at noticing what is going on around you ▪ A particularly *observant* child, he noticed even the slightest changes in the classroom. ▪ Good reporters are keenly *observant* of everything around them.

2 : careful to follow religious teachings or customs ▪ an *observant* Jew/Muslim = a Jew/Muslim who is *observant* of Jewish/Islamic law ▪ The family is strictly *observant*.

[1]**ob·ser·va·tion** /ˌɑːbsəˈveɪʃən/ *noun, pl* **-tions**

1 [*count*] **:** a statement about something you have noticed **:** a

comment or remark • I'm not criticizing that kind of clothing. I'm just making an *observation* about the style. • Her constant *observations* about the weather bored me. ***synonyms*** see [1]REMARK
2 a [*noncount*] : the act of careful watching and listening : the activity of paying close attention to someone or something in order to get information • These facts are based on close *observation* of the birds in the wild. • Children learn by *observation*. • The author's excellent ***powers of observation*** [=ability to notice and pay close attention to things] are evident in the book's detailed descriptions. • The plants seem to have recovered from the disease, but they are still ***under observation*** [=someone is watching them carefully] • He has been *under* government *observation* [=the government has been watching him carefully] for six months. • They're keeping him at the hospital ***for observation*** [=so that doctors can watch him carefully] for another few days. **b** [*count*] : something you notice by watching and listening • *Observations* made using the telescope have led to new theories. • Some interesting *observations* came from the study. • scientific *observations* **c** [*count*] : a written or spoken report or description of something that you have noticed or studied • He recorded his *observations* in a notebook.
3 [*noncount*] : the act of doing what is required by a custom, rule, law, etc. : OBSERVANCE — usually + *of* • *observation of* the law
– ob·ser·va·tion·al /ˌɑːbsɚˈveɪʃənl/ *adj* • *observational* data/skills

[2]**observation** *adj, always used before a noun* : designed to be used while watching people or things • *observation* airplanes/helicopters • an *observation* deck/platform/post/tower

ob·ser·va·to·ry /əbˈzɚvəˌtori, *Brit* əbˈzəːvətri/ *noun, pl* **-ries** [*count*] : a special building for studying stars, planets, weather, etc. : a building from which scientists study and watch the sky • the McDonald *Observatory*

ob·serve /əbˈzɚv/ *verb* **-serves; -served; -serv·ing**
1 : to watch and sometimes also listen to (someone or something) carefully [+ *obj*] The class will be *observing* the movements of fish. • The patient must be *observed* constantly. • Children learn by *observing* their parents and others. • The story is a ***closely/well observed*** [=very realistic] portrait of the city. [*no obj*] The new teacher will give the lesson today and the principal will *observe*.
2 [+ *obj*] : to see and notice (someone or something) • We *observed* a large flock of birds heading north. • He *observed* two children playing with marbles on the street corner. • She *observed* that every man in the room had removed his hat. • Few cases of the disease have been *observed* in humans.
3 [+ *obj*] : to make a comment about something you notice • "The paint," she *observed* [=*remarked, said*], "is already starting to peel." • Looking around at the shuttered houses, he *observed* [=*commented*] that the island was entirely different in the winter.
4 [+ *obj*] : to do what a custom, rule, law, etc., says you should do • The game will continue only when both teams agree to *observe* [=*follow*] the rules. • *observing* [=*keeping*] the Sabbath
5 [+ *obj*] : to celebrate (a holiday) or honor (a person or event) • We'll *observe* Independence Day at home this year. • They *observed* a moment of silence to remember their loved ones.

ob·serv·er /əbˈzɚvɚ/ *noun, pl* **-ers** [*count*]
1 : a person who sees and notices someone or something • According to one *observer*, the event was poorly organized. • The star is not visible to an *observer* without a telescope. • Even a ***casual observer*** [=even someone who is not looking carefully] can tell that the building is in need of repair.
2 : a person who pays close attention to something and is considered to be an expert on that thing • According to one military *observer*, this change comes after years of planning. • *Observers* say the economy is improving.
3 : a person who is present at something (such as a meeting) in order to watch and listen to what happens • The class has an *observer* today, so please be on your best behavior.
4 — used in the names of newspapers and magazines • the Raleigh News and *Observer* • the London *Observer*

ob·sess /əbˈsɛs/ *verb* **-sess·es; -sessed; -sess·ing**
1 [+ *obj*] : to be the only person or thing that someone thinks or talks about • The war *obsesses* him—he talks about nothing else. — usually used as *(be) obsessed* • He *is obsessed* by the war. • She *was obsessed* with her weight. [=she thought about her weight all the time] • She became more and more *obsessed* with the project.
2 [*no obj*] *informal* : to think and talk about someone or something too much • You need to stop *obsessing* and just deal with the problem. — usually + *about* or *over* • I'm trying to *obsess* less *about* my weight. • He's always *obsessing over* money.

ob·ses·sion /ɑbˈsɛʃən/ *noun, pl* **-sions**
1 : a state in which someone thinks about someone or something constantly or frequently especially in a way that is not normal [*count*] He was fascinated by the actress and tracking her every move had become an *obsession*. • She has an *obsession* about cleanliness. • the object of her *obsession* [=the thing that she is obsessed about] • The restaurant's menu is evidence of the chef's lifelong *obsession* with international cuisines. [=the chef's lifelong interest in international cuisines] [*noncount*] Her concern about cleanliness approaches the level of *obsession*. • He's concerned about money to the ***point of obsession*** [=he is very/too concerned about money]
2 [*count*] **a** : someone or something that a person thinks about constantly or frequently • Cleanliness is her *obsession*. = Cleanliness is an *obsession* with her. • Money has become an *obsession* for him. **b** : an activity that someone is very interested in or spends a lot of time doing • Stamp collecting has become an *obsession* with/for me. [=I have become obsessed with collecting stamps]
– ob·ses·sion·al /ɑbˈsɛʃənl/ *adj* [*more* ~; *most* ~] • *obsessional* [=(more commonly) *obsessive*] thinking

[1]**ob·ses·sive** /ɑbˈsɛsɪv/ *adj* [*more* ~; *most* ~] : thinking about something or someone too much or in a way that is not normal : having an obsession • Many dancers are *obsessive* about their weight. • He is an *obsessive* workaholic who never stops thinking about his job. : showing or relating to an obsession • an *obsessive* interest in space travel • The new therapy is supposed to help people control their *obsessive* thoughts. • *obsessive* attention to detail
– ob·ses·sive·ly *adv* • She works *obsessively*, often for weeks at a time. • talking *obsessively* about food **– ob·ses·sive·ness** *noun* [*noncount*]

[2]**obsessive** *noun, pl* **-sives** [*count*] *psychology* : a person who thinks about something too much or in a way that is not normal : someone who is obsessed

obsessive–compulsive *adj, psychology* : relating to or having a mental illness that involves repeating actions or thinking about certain things too much • *obsessive-compulsive* behavior • a patient with *obsessive-compulsive* disorder • an *obsessive-compulsive* person/patient = a person/patient who is *obsessive-compulsive*
– obsessive–compulsive *noun, pl* **-sives** [*count*] • treatment for *obsessive-compulsives* [=people who have obsessive-compulsive disorder]

ob·sid·i·an /əbˈsɪdijən/ *noun* [*noncount*] : a dark natural glass that forms when lava cools

ob·so·les·cence /ˌɑːbsəˈlɛsn̩s/ *noun* [*noncount*] : the condition of no longer being used or useful : the condition of being obsolete • the *obsolescence* of the old technology • Once a useful tool, slide rules have fallen into *obsolescence*. • ***built-in/planned obsolescence*** [=the practice of making or designing something (such as a car) in such a way that it will only be usable for a short time so that people will have to buy another one]

ob·so·les·cent /ˌɑːbsəˈlɛsn̩t/ *adj* : no longer useful : becoming obsolete • *obsolescent* machinery/computers

ob·so·lete /ˌɑːbsəˈliːt/ *adj*
1 : no longer used because something newer exists • *obsolete* [=*outdated*] computers • The system was made/rendered *obsolete* by their invention. : replaced by something newer • *obsolete* mills and factories
2 : no longer used by anyone • an *obsolete* word

ob·sta·cle /ˈɑːbstɪkəl/ *noun, pl* **-sta·cles** [*count*]
1 : something that makes it difficult to do something • He overcame the *obstacles* of poverty and neglect. • They must overcome a number of *obstacles* before the restaurant can be opened. • Lack of experience is a major *obstacle* for her opponent. • an *obstacle* to learning/progress
2 : an object that you have to go around or over : something that blocks your path • She swerved to avoid an *obstacle* in the road.

obstacle course *noun, pl* ~ **courses** [*count*]
1 : a series of objects that people or animals in a race have to jump or climb over, go around, go under, etc.

2 : a training area for soldiers that is filled with objects (such as hurdles, ditches, walls, etc.) that the soldiers have to jump or climb over, go around, go under, etc. — called also (*Brit*) *assault course*

3 : a series of problems, events, or requirements that make it difficult to do something • We finally made it through the bureaucratic *obstacle course* and got our visas.

obstacle race *noun, pl* ~ **races** [*count*] *chiefly Brit* : a race through an obstacle course

ob•ste•tri•cian /ˌɑːbstəˈtrɪʃən/ *noun, pl* **-cians** [*count*] *medical* : a doctor who specializes in obstetrics — compare OB-GYN

ob•stet•rics /əbˈstɛtrɪks/ *noun* [*noncount*] *medical* : a branch of medicine that deals with the birth of children and with the care of women before, during, and after they give birth to children — compare GYNECOLOGY

– **ob•stet•ric** /əbˈstɛtrɪk/ *or US* **ob•stet•ri•cal** /əbˈstɛtrɪkəl/ *adj* • *obstetric* patients/treatment • *obstetrical* care

ob•sti•nate /ˈɑːbstənət/ *adj* [*more* ~; *most* ~]

1 : refusing to change your behavior or your ideas : STUBBORN • his *obstinate* refusal to obey • an *obstinate* little boy • her *obstinate* behavior • My parents remain as *obstinate* as ever.

2 : difficult to deal with, remove, etc. : STUBBORN • an *obstinate* stain • a very *obstinate* problem

– **ob•sti•na•cy** /ˈɑːbstənəsi/ *noun* [*noncount*] – **ob•sti•nate•ly** *adv* • people who cling *obstinately* to the past • He *obstinately* refused to obey.

ob•strep•er•ous /əbˈstrɛpərəs/ *adj* [*more* ~; *most* ~] *formal* : difficult to control and often noisy • a room full of *obstreperous* children • *obstreperous* [=*unruly*] teenagers

ob•struct /əbˈstrʌkt/ *verb* **-structs**; **-struct•ed**; **-struct•ing** [+ *obj*] *somewhat formal*

1 : to block (something, such as a pipe or street) so that things cannot move through easily • A large tree *obstructed* the road. • A piece of food *obstructed* his airway and caused him to stop breathing.

2 : to slow or block the movement, progress, or action of (something or someone) • Several issues have *obstructed* [=*hindered, impeded*] efforts to bring peace to the region. • She was charged with *obstructing* police/investigators. • She was charged with ***obstructing justice*** by lying to investigators.

3 : to be in front of (something) : to make (something) difficult to see • His neighbors built a wall that *obstructed* [=*blocked*] his view of the ocean.

ob•struc•tion /əbˈstrʌkʃən/ *noun, pl* **-tions**

1 [*count*] : something that blocks something else and makes it difficult for things to move through • They are removing trees and other *obstructions* from the path. • There were *obstructions* [=*blockages*] in his blood vessels.

2 : the condition of being blocked so that things cannot move through easily [*noncount*] cases of intestinal *obstruction* in children [*count*] She died from an *obstruction* of the airway.

3 [*noncount*] : the act of making it difficult for something to happen or move forward • He is on trial for the *obstruction* of a criminal investigation. ✧ ***Obstruction of justice*** is the crime of trying to stop police from learning the truth about something. • He is being charged with *obstruction of justice* for lying to investigators.

ob•struc•tion•ism /əbˈstrʌkʃəˌnɪzəm/ *noun* [*noncount*] *formal* : things that are done to stop or delay the progress of a legal or political process • They accused the other political party of *obstructionism*.

– **ob•struc•tion•ist** /əbˈstrʌkʃənɪst/ *noun, pl* **-ists** [*count*] • stubborn *obstructionists* – **obstructionist** *adj* • *obstructionist* practices

ob•struc•tive /əbˈstrʌktɪv/ *adj* [*more* ~; *most* ~] : trying to cause problems in order to stop or delay something • *obstructive* public officials • deliberately *obstructive* tactics

ob•tain /əbˈteɪn/ *verb* **-tains**; **-tained**; **-tain•ing**

1 [+ *obj*] *somewhat formal* : to gain or get (something) usually by effort • The information may be difficult to *obtain*. • We *obtained* a copy of the original letter. • They've *obtained* [=*acquired*] the necessary permission to enter.

2 *not used in progressive tenses* [*no obj*] *formal* : to continue to be accepted or in use • These ideas no longer *obtain* for our generation.

– **ob•tain•able** /əbˈteɪnəbəl/ *adj, formal* • The drug is legally *obtainable* in this country.

ob•trude /əbˈtruːd/ *verb* **-trudes**; **-trud•ed**; **-trud•ing** *formal* : to become involved with something or to become noticeable in an unpleasant or annoying way [*no obj*] She didn't want to *obtrude* [=*intrude*] on/upon their conversation. • The historical details in the movie do not *obtrude*—they enhance the story by making it more realistic. [+ *obj*] He was confident at first, but then doubts began to *obtrude* themselves. [=he began to have doubts]

ob•tru•sive /əbˈtruːsɪv/ *adj* [*more* ~; *most* ~]

1 : tending to bother people by appearing where you are not welcome or invited • The waiter was attentive without being *obtrusive*.

2 : noticeable in an unpleasant or annoying way • We used less *obtrusive* colors in the bedrooms. • *obtrusive* advertising

– **ob•tru•sive•ly** *adv* • an *obtrusively* large building

ob•tuse /ɑbˈtuːs, *Brit* ɒbˈtjuːs/ *adj* [*more* ~; *most* ~]

1 *formal* : stupid or unintelligent : not able to think clearly or to understand what is obvious or simple • He is too *obtuse* to take a hint. • an incredibly *obtuse* person

2 *mathematics* : not ending in a sharp point : measuring between 90 degrees and 180 degrees • an *obtuse* angle — compare ACUTE 6

– **ob•tuse•ness** *noun* [*noncount*] • We laughed at her *obtuseness*.

ob•verse /ɑbˈvəs/ *noun* [*singular*] *formal* : something that is the opposite of something else : OPPOSITE • joy and its *obverse*, sadness • We thought they would be pleased with our decision. We have learned, however, that the *obverse* is true.

ob•vi•ate /ˈɑːbviˌeɪt/ *verb* **-ates**; **-at•ed**; **-at•ing** [+ *obj*] *formal* : to make (something) no longer necessary • The new medical treatment *obviates* the need for surgery.: to prevent or avoid (something) • The new treatment *obviates* many of the risks associated with surgery.

ob•vi•ous /ˈɑːbvijəs/ *adj* [*more* ~; *most* ~]

1 : easy to see or notice • Her doctor immediately noticed the *obvious* signs of the disease. • She saw only the most *obvious* differences.

2 : easy for the mind to understand or recognize • It was *obvious* that things weren't working out. • Her reasons for leaving were *obvious*. = It's *obvious* why she left. • The answer seems *obvious* enough to me. • The problem was immediately *obvious* to everyone in the room. • He was the *obvious* candidate/choice for president. • The *obvious* question is: how did he become so successful? • For *obvious* reasons, I would not like to reveal my name.

the obvious : something that is obvious • You are stating *the obvious*. Tell me something I don't already know. • Try to look beyond *the obvious*.

– **ob•vi•ous•ness** *noun* [*noncount*] • the *obviousness* of his answer

ob•vious•ly /ˈɑːbvijəsli/ *adv*

1 [*more* ~; *most* ~] : in a way that is easy to see, understand, or recognize • She *obviously* enjoys her work. • Their answer was *obviously* wrong. • That's *obviously* not her real name.

2 — used to emphasize that you are talking about something that is easy to see, understand, or recognize • *Obviously*, something is wrong. • *Obviously*, that's not her real name.

¹oc•ca•sion /əˈkeɪʒən/ *noun, pl* **-sions**

1 [*count*] : a special event or time • birthdays, anniversaries, and other special *occasions* • They marked/celebrated the *occasion* with their families. • She wrote a song especially for the *occasion*. • Roses are the perfect flower for any *occasion*. • formal *occasions* • a memorable/historic *occasion* • ***On the occasion of*** their 25th wedding anniversary, they took a vacation to Paris.

2 [*count*] *somewhat formal* : a particular time when something happens • This would mark the first *occasion* [=*time*] that the club accepted new members.— often used after *on* • We usually meet at noon, but *on* this particular *occasion*, we met at two o'clock. • I heard him speak *on* more than one *occasion*. = I heard him speak *on* several *occasions*.

3 *somewhat formal* : a chance or opportunity : a situation that allows something to happen — usually followed by *to* + *verb* [*noncount*] We had *occasion to watch* her perform last summer. • The boys never had *occasion to meet* each other. [*singular*] She never found an *occasion to suggest* her ideas. • He took/used the *occasion to make* an announcement.

4 [*singular*] *somewhat formal* : a reason to do something — often + *for* • The team's win was an *occasion for* celebration.

on occasion : sometimes but not often : from time to time • *On occasion* [=*occasionally*], we'll drive out to the beach and watch the sunset. • I have *on occasion* tried to help him

O

with his homework. • These machines are still used *on occasion* today.
rise to the occasion see [1]RISE

[2]**occasion** *verb* **-sions; -sioned; -sion•ing** [+ *obj*] *formal* **:** to cause (something) • The program has *occasioned* [=*brought about*] much discussion about violence on television. — often used as *(be) occasioned* • Her trip back home *was occasioned* by her mother's recent death.

oc•ca•sion•al /əˈkeɪʒənl/ *adj, always used before a noun*
1 : happening or done sometimes but not often **:** not happening or done in a regular or frequent way • She receives *occasional* phone calls from her mother. • There will be *occasional* showers during the morning. • She makes *occasional* appearances on television. = She appears on the *occasional* television show. • Most mornings, we'll see deer or the *occasional* bear walking past our house. • He tells an *occasional* joke to keep his students interested. • I need to take *occasional* breaks from work. • Sure, I drink an *occasional* glass of wine from time to time.
2 : sometimes doing a particular job or activity • She's an *occasional* lecturer at the university. • an *occasional* actor • *occasional* smokers [=people who smoke occasionally]

oc•ca•sion•al•ly /əˈkeɪʒənəli/ *adv* **:** sometimes but not often • *Occasionally*, we see deer in the field. = We *occasionally* see deer in the field. • *Occasionally*, things don't go as planned. • Cook on medium heat, stirring *occasionally*, for about 10 minutes. • ***Very occasionally*** [=*rarely*], she will have a glass of wine.

Oc•ci•dent /ˈɑːksədənt/ *noun*
the Occident *formal + literary* **:** the western areas of the world; *especially* **:** Europe and America • The crew set sail for *the Occident*. — compare ORIENT

occult /əˈkʌlt/ *adj, always used before a noun* **:** of or relating to supernatural powers or practices • *occult* practices such as magic and fortune-telling • the *occult* sciences/arts • He began to believe he had *occult* powers.
the occult **:** supernatural powers or practices and the things (such as gods, ghosts, and magic) that are connected with them • He's a student of *the occult*. • religion, mythology, and *the occult*

oc•cult•ism /əˈkʌlˌtɪzəm/ *noun* [*noncount*] **:** the belief in or study of supernatural powers
– oc•cult•ist /əˈkʌltɪst/ *noun, pl* **-ists** [*count*]

oc•cu•pan•cy /ˈɑːkjəpənsi/ *noun* [*noncount*]
1 : the act of living or staying in a particular place • This building is unsafe for human *occupancy*. [=people cannot live here]
2 : the number of people who are in a particular building or room at one time • The sign above the auditorium door says, "Maximum *occupancy*: 500 persons." • hotel rates for ***double occupancy*** [=two people staying in a room]

oc•cu•pant /ˈɑːkjəpənt/ *noun, pl* **-pants** [*count*]
1 : a person who is using or living in a particular building, apartment, or room • The apartment's previous *occupant* was a painter. • the building's *occupants*
2 : a person who is in a room, vehicle, etc., at a particular time • Both of the car's *occupants* were injured.

oc•cu•pa•tion /ˌɑːkjəˈpeɪʃən/ *noun, pl* **-tions**
1 [*count*] **:** the work that a person does **:** a person's job or profession • He is thinking about changing *occupations* and becoming a police officer. • "What's your *occupation*?" "I'm a stay-at-home mom." • She listed her *occupation* as "writer" on the form. [=she wrote "writer" on the part of the form that asked what she did for work]
2 [*count*] **:** an activity that a person spends time doing • His favorite *occupation* [=*pastime*] is playing chess. • Swimming was their main *occupation* at summer camp.
3 [*noncount*] **:** the activity of living in or using a particular place • Some evidence of human *occupation* was found in these caves. • The offices are ready for *occupation*.
4 [*noncount*] **:** a situation in which the military of a foreign government goes into an area or country and takes control of it • *occupation* of a foreign country • people living under *occupation* • The novel tells about life during the *occupation*.

oc•cu•pa•tion•al /ˌɑːkjəˈpeɪʃənl/ *adj, always used before a noun* **:** of or relating to a person's job or occupation • The program offered free *occupational* training to the poor. • *occupational* safety and health • Hand injuries are an ***occupational hazard*** for typists. [=typists are likely to have hand injuries because of the work they do]
– oc•cu•pa•tion•al•ly *adv* • He was *occupationally* exposed to radiation.

occupational therapy *noun* [*noncount*] *medical* **:** treatment that helps people who have physical or mental problems learn to do the activities of daily life
– occupational therapist *noun, pl* **~ -pists** [*count*]

occupied *adj*
1 *not used before a noun* [*more ~; most ~*] *somewhat formal* **:** busy doing something • The governor is *occupied* at the moment. May I take a message? • She keeps herself *occupied* with volunteer work.
2 *somewhat formal* **:** being used by someone • This chair is *occupied* [=(less formally) *taken*], but I believe those chairs are free/available. • His free time is *occupied* with his wife and children.
3 : controlled by foreign soldiers or a foreign government • We live in an *occupied* country. = Our country is *occupied* by a foreign government. • an *occupied* territory

oc•cu•pi•er /ˈɑːkjəˌpajə/ *noun, pl* **-ers** [*count*]
1 : a soldier in an army that has taken control of a foreign place — usually plural • The foreign *occupiers* were beginning to lose control of the area.
2 *Brit* **:** a person who is using or living in a particular building, apartment, room, etc. **:** OCCUPANT • the current *occupiers* of the flat

oc•cu•py /ˈɑːkjəˌpaɪ/ *verb* **-pies; -pied; -py•ing** [+ *obj*]
1 *somewhat formal* **:** to live in (a house, apartment, etc.) • They have *occupied* the apartment for three years. • She *occupies* the house that her grandfather built 50 years ago. • They own another house that they *occupy* only three months out of the year. • They *occupy* the room next to ours.
2 a : to fill or be in (a place or space) • Someone was *occupying* [=sitting in] my place at the table. • This region was once almost completely *occupied* by forests. • Their house *occupies* a beautiful spot next to the ocean. — sometimes used figuratively • That family trip *occupies* [=*has*] a special place in my memory. **b :** to fill or use (an amount of time) • Studying *occupies* nearly all of my time on the weekends. [=I spend nearly all of my time studying] • Much of our time is *occupied* by answering questions from our customers.
3 : to make (someone, someone's mind, etc.) busy • During the long train ride, they *occupied* [=*busied*] themselves with card games. • These questions have continued to *occupy* her mind. • Reading *occupied* me for most of the summer. = I *occupied* myself with reading for most of the summer.
4 : to take and keep control of (a town, foreign country, etc.) by using military power • Enemy troops *occupied* the town. • The army is *occupying* half of the country.
5 *somewhat formal* **:** to have (a job or position) • She now *occupies* the highest position in the country's government. • *occupying* a position of power

oc•cur /əˈkɚ/ *verb* **-curs; -curred; -cur•ring** [*no obj*]
1 *somewhat formal* **:** to happen • The event is scheduled to *occur* at noon tomorrow. • No one was ready for what was about to *occur*. • There's a chance that a similar event will *occur* in the future. • The disease tends to *occur* in children under the age of five.
2 *formal* **:** to appear or exist **:** to be found • The plant *occurs* naturally throughout South America. • a naturally *occurring* compound/chemical/substance
occur to [*phrasal verb*] ***occur to (someone)*** **:** to be thought of by (someone) • An idea just *occurred to* me. [=I just had an idea] • It suddenly *occurred to* me that there was a simpler way to deal with the problem. • Did it ever *occur to* you [=did you ever think] that maybe you were wrong? • It never *occurred to* me to ask. [=I never thought of asking]

oc•cur•rence /əˈkərəns/ *noun, pl* **-renc•es**
1 [*count*] **:** something that happens • Getting headaches has become a common/frequent/everyday *occurrence* for her. • a rare/unusual *occurrence* • the recent *occurrences* of the disease • Lightning is a natural *occurrence*.
2 [*noncount*] **:** the fact of happening or occurring — usually *+ of* • We were trying to prevent the *occurrence of* further problems. [=trying to prevent further problems from occurring] • The *occurrence of* theft in the locker room has stopped. • The *occurrence of* the disease is low. [=the disease does not occur commonly]

OCD *abbr* obsessive-compulsive disorder

ocean /ˈoʊʃən/ *noun, pl* **oceans**
1 [*noncount*] **:** the salt water that covers much of the Earth's surface • We've sailed across hundreds of miles of *ocean*. — often used with *the* • They lived near *the ocean*. [=*the sea*] • He had never seen *the ocean* before. • There's a storm moving in from *the ocean*. • The ship quickly sank to the bottom

of *the ocean*. ▪ the deepest parts of *the ocean* — often used before another noun ▪ the *ocean* floor/bottom/surface ▪ the salty *ocean* air ▪ *ocean* fish ▪ an *ocean* voyage/liner — see color picture on page C8

2 *or* ***Ocean*** [*count*] **: one of the five large areas of salt water that cover much of the Earth's surface** ▪ the Atlantic *Ocean* ▪ the Pacific and Indian *oceans* ▪ the Arctic/Antarctic *Ocean*

3 [*count*] *informal* **: a very large number or amount** ***of*** **something** ▪ an *ocean* of sadness — often plural ▪ *oceans* of time [=lots of time]

a drop in the ocean see ¹DROP

– oce·an·ic /ˌoʊʃiˈænɪk/ *adj, technical* ▪ *oceanic* birds/islands/waters

ocean·front /ˈoʊʃənˌfrʌnt/ *noun, pl* **-fronts** [*count*] *chiefly US* **: the land that is next to the ocean** ▪ They built a house on the *oceanfront*. — often used before another noun ▪ an *oceanfront* home/hotel/restaurant

ocean·go·ing /ˈoʊʃənˌgowɪŋ/ *adj, always used before a noun* **: made for traveling on or across the ocean** ▪ *oceangoing* ships

ocean·og·ra·phy /ˌoʊʃəˈnɑːgrəfi/ *noun* [*noncount*] **: a science that studies the ocean** ▪ a professor of *oceanography*

– ocean·og·ra·pher /ˌoʊʃəˈnɑːgrəfɚ/ *noun, pl* **-phers** [*count*] **– ocean·o·graph·ic** /ˌoʊʃənəˈgræfɪk/ *adj* ▪ an *oceanographic* research

oce·lot /ˈɑːsəˌlɑːt/ *noun, pl* **-lots** [*count*] **: a wildcat that lives mainly in Central and South America and that has light brown fur with black spots and stripes**

ochre *or US* **ocher** /ˈoʊkɚ/ *noun* [*noncount*]

1 : a type of red or yellow dirt that is used to make colored paints

2 : the color of ochre and especially of yellow ochre

o'·clock /əˈklɑːk/ *adv* **: according to the clock — used when the time is a specific hour** ▪ It's three *o'clock* in the afternoon. [=it's three p.m.] ▪ She was 10 minutes late for her 8 *o'clock* appointment. ▪ Be here at nine *o'clock*, not at nine fifteen.

Oct. *abbr* October

oc·ta·gon /ˈɑːktəˌgɑːn/ *noun, pl* **-gons** [*count*] *mathematics* **: a flat shape that has eight sides and eight angles** — see picture at GEOMETRY

– oc·tag·o·nal /ɑkˈtægənl/ *adj* ▪ a large *octagonal* table

oc·tane /ˈɑːkˌteɪn/ *noun* [*noncount*] **: a chemical in petroleum that is used to rate the quality of different kinds of gasoline** ▪ an *octane* rating of 90 — see also HIGH-OCTANE

oc·tave /ˈɑːktɪv/ *noun, pl* **-taves** [*count*] *music* **: the difference in sound between the first and eighth note on a musical scale** ▪ He sang the song an *octave* lower. ▪ The two tones are (spaced) an *octave* apart.

oc·tet /ɑkˈtɛt/ *noun, pl* **-tets** [*count*]

1 : a song or piece of music performed by eight singers or musicians

2 : a group of eight singers or musicians who perform an octet

Oc·to·ber /ɑkˈtoʊbɚ/ *noun, pl* **-bers : the 10th month of the year** [*noncount*] She started her job in early/mid-/late *October*. ▪ He started early/late in *October*. ▪ They were married on *October* the eighteenth. = They were married on the eighteenth of *October*. = (*US*) They were married on *October* eighteenth. [*count*] This will be our last *October* in New England. ▪ Sales are up for this *October*. ▪ The event happens every *October*. — abbr. *Oct.*

oc·to·ge·nar·i·an /ˌɑːktədʒəˈnerijən/ *noun, pl* **-ans** [*count*] **: a person who is between 80 and 89 years old**

oc·to·pus /ˈɑːktəˌpʊs/ *noun, pl* **-pus·es** *or* **-pi** /-ˌpaɪ/

1 [*count*] **: a sea animal that has a soft body and eight long arms**

2 [*noncount*] **: the flesh of an octopus used as food**

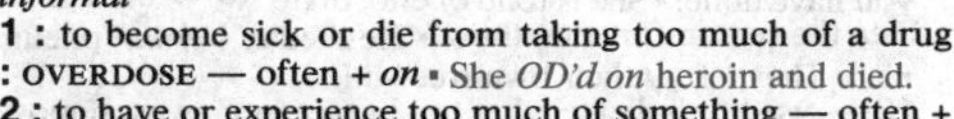

octopus

oc·u·lar /ˈɑːkjəlɚ/ *adj, technical* **: of or relating to the eye** ▪ *ocular* muscles/surgery

OD /ˌoʊˈdiː/ *verb* **OD's; OD'd** *or* **ODed; OD'·ing** [*no obj*] *informal*

1 : to become sick or die from taking too much of a drug : OVERDOSE — often + *on* ▪ She *OD'd on* heroin and died.

2 : to have or experience too much of something — often + *on* ▪ I *OD'd on* video games during my vacation.

odd /ˈɑːd/ *adj*

1 ***odd·er; -est*** [*also more ~; most ~*] **: strange or unusual : different from what is normal or expected** ▪ He has some *odd* [=*peculiar, weird*] habits. ▪ She had an *odd* look on her face. ▪ People would call at *odd* hours during the night. ▪ She's got a really *odd* sense of humor. ▪ Some rather *odd* people used to live in this house. ▪ There was something *odd* about his story. ▪ It's *odd* that nobody told me about this before. ▪ That's *odd*. He was here a minute ago. ▪ That is one of the *oddest* creatures I have ever seen. ▪ What an ***odd-looking*** animal. ▪ They made quite an ***odd couple***. [=they were very different from each other] ▪ He's an ***odd duck***. = (*Brit*) He's an ***odd fish***. [=he's a very strange person]

2 *always used before a noun* **: happening in a way that is not planned or regular** ▪ She kept a stack of magazines that she would read at *odd* moments. ▪ During the summer, he would do ***odd jobs*** for his neighbors to earn extra money.

3 *always used before a noun* **: of different kinds or types** ▪ I stopped by the grocery store to pick up a few *odd* [=*miscellaneous*] things. ▪ They were selling an *odd* assortment of candy and jewelry. ▪ a few *odd* [=*random*] bits of information

4 *always used before a noun* **: not matched or paired with another thing or person** ▪ I folded all the laundry and had one *odd* sock left. ▪ an *odd* shoe ▪ The students got into groups of two, and the *odd* student worked with the teacher.

5 a : not able to be divided into two equal whole numbers ▪ The numbers 1, 3, 5, and 7 are *odd*, while 2, 4, 6, and 8 are even. ▪ *odd* and even numbers ▪ There's an *odd* number of chairs. **b : marked by an odd number** ▪ There's a picture on every *odd* page of the book. ▪ Please do the *odd*-numbered problems on page 20 of your textbook. ▪ The *odd*-numbered houses are on the left side of the street.

6 *informal* **: a little more than a particular number — used in combination with a number** ▪ The book's only 100-*odd* pages long. [=only slightly more than 100 pages long] ▪ I'd guess that he's 40 *odd* years old. ▪ 30-*odd* years ago

the odd man/one out **: the person or thing that is different from the other members of a group** ▪ It looks like he's *the odd one out* on this particular issue. [=he has a different opinion than everyone else] ▪ All my college friends have gotten married. I'm *the odd man out*.

– odd·ness *noun* [*noncount*] ▪ the *oddness* [=*oddity, strangeness*] of the situation

odd·ball /ˈɑːdˌbɑːl/ *noun, pl* **-balls** [*count*] *informal* **: a person who behaves in strange or unusual ways** ▪ He used to be a real *oddball* back in high school.

– oddball *adj, always used before a noun* ▪ The film's *oddball* characters are hilarious. ▪ *oddball* behavior

odd·i·ty /ˈɑːdəti/ *noun, pl* **-ties**

1 [*count*] **: a strange or unusual person or thing** ▪ Her shyness makes her a bit of an *oddity* in the business world. ▪ The zoo has such *oddities* as anteaters and platypuses.

2 [*noncount*] **: the quality or state of being strange or unusual** ▪ the *oddity* [=*oddness, strangeness*] of the situation

odd·ly /ˈɑːdli/ *adv*

1 [*more ~; most ~*] **: in a strange or unusual way** ▪ the house's *oddly* shaped roof ▪ She had never been there before, but the place seemed *oddly* [=*strangely*] familiar to her. ▪ Their lives had been *oddly* similar.

2 — used to say that something is strange, odd, or surprising ▪ He felt, *oddly*, that he had been happier before becoming famous. ▪ It was cold and rainy, but ***oddly enough***, everyone seemed to be enjoying themselves.

odd·ments /ˈɑːdmənts/ *noun* [*plural*] **: different kinds of things that are usually small and unimportant : ODDS AND ENDS** ▪ The car has plenty of room for storing *oddments*.

odds /ˈɑːdz/ *noun* [*plural*]

1 : the possibility that something will happen : the chance that one thing will happen instead of a different thing ▪ She wanted to improve her *odds* [=*chances*] of winning. ▪ They believe that surgery may increase his *odds* of survival. [=may make it more likely that he will survive] ▪ There's a chance it could rain, but *odds* are that it'll be sunny tomorrow. [=it is more likely to be sunny than rainy tomorrow] ▪ The team has made some major improvements, but they still face ***long odds***. [=they still are not likely to win] — often used with *the* ▪ *The odds* are good that he'll survive. [=he is likely to survive] ▪ What are *the odds* of winning? ▪ What are *the odds* that they'll be there on time? ▪ Smoking increases *the odds* of getting lung cancer. ▪ *The odds* are in our favor. [=it is likely that we will succeed] ▪ She knew that *the odds* were against her. [=she knew that she was not likely to succeed] ▪ It could rain tomorrow, but *the odds* are against it. [=it probably will not

rain] ▪ *The odds* are in favor of a major storm this weekend. [=a major storm is likely this weekend]
2 : conditions that make it difficult for something to happen ▪ They fought against great/heavy/impossible/overwhelming *odds* and won. ▪ He was able to do it, ***against all odds***. [=even though it was very difficult and unlikely] — often used with *the* ▪ They defied/overcame *the odds*. ▪ ***Despite/against the odds***, she has survived breast cancer. ▪ I tried to ***beat the odds***. [=to succeed even though I was not likely to succeed]
3 : two numbers that show how much a person can win by betting a certain amount of money ▪ I bet $1,000 at 4–1 *odds*. If the horse I bet on wins, I will walk away with $4,000. ▪ winning at *odds* of 6–1
at odds : not agreeing with each other : in a state of disagreement ▪ The parents and teachers are still *at odds* (about/over what to teach the students). — often + *with* ▪ The two groups have long been *at odds with* each other. ▪ He was completely *at odds* [=he completely disagreed] *with* the way the problem was being handled. ▪ The results of the study are *at odds with* our previous findings.
make no odds *Brit, informal* — used to say that a choice is not important ▪ It *makes no odds* [=*makes no difference*] to me when we leave.
odds are in favor see [1]FAVOR
over the odds *Brit, informal* : more than the usual or expected amount ▪ We had to ***pay over the odds*** to get good seats for the concert.
what's the odds? *Brit, informal* — used to say that something is not likely to have an effect or make a difference ▪ He'll do it anyway, so *what's the odds* [=*what's the use*] of telling him not to?

odds and ends *noun [plural] informal* : different kinds of things that are usually small and unimportant ▪ There are still a few *odds and ends* that need to be done before the party tomorrow. ▪ The box is full of *odds and ends*. — called also (*Brit, informal*) *odds and sods*

odds–on /ˈɑːdzˈɑːn/ *adj* : having a very good chance to win : believed to be likely to win ▪ They're the *odds-on* favorite to win the championship. = They are *odds-on* to win the championship.

ode /ˈoʊd/ *noun, pl* **odes** [*count*] : a poem in which a person expresses a strong feeling of love or respect for someone or something ▪ This poem is titled, "An *Ode* to My Mother."

odi·ous /ˈoʊdijəs/ *adj* [*more* ~; *most* ~] *formal* : causing hatred or strong dislike ▪ It was one of the most *odious* crimes of recent history. ▪ an *odious* criminal

odom·e·ter /oʊˈdɑːmətɚ/ *noun, pl* **-ters** [*count*] *chiefly US* : a device in a car, truck, etc., that measures the distance that the vehicle has traveled — called also (*Brit*) *mileometer*; see picture at CAR; compare SPEEDOMETER, TACHOMETER

odor (*US*) *or Brit* **odour** /ˈoʊdɚ/ *noun, pl* **odors** : a particular smell [*count*] The cheese has a strong *odor*. ▪ a fishy *odor* [*noncount*] This deodorant prevents bad *odor* from occurring. — see also BODY ODOR
– **odor·less** (*US*) *or Brit* **odour·less** /ˈoʊdɚləs/ *adj* ▪ a colorless and *odorless* gas

odor·ous /ˈoʊdərəs/ *adj* [*more* ~; *most* ~] *technical + formal* : having a strong smell ▪ an *odorous* gas ▪ *Odorous* cheeses need to be tightly wrapped.

od·ys·sey /ˈɑːdəsi/ *noun, pl* **-seys** [*count*]
1 *literary* : a long journey full of adventures
2 : a series of experiences that give knowledge or understanding to someone ▪ The story is about the emotional *odyssey* experienced by a teenage girl. ▪ the spiritual *odyssey* of the deeply religious

oe·di·pal *or* **Oe·di·pal** /ˈɛdəpəl, *Brit* ˈiːdəpəl/ *adj, psychology* : of, relating to, or resulting from an Oedipus complex ▪ *oedipal* fantasies/myths ▪ an *oedipal* relationship

Oe·di·pus complex /ˈɛdəpəs-, *Brit* ˈiːdəpəs-/ *noun* [*singular*] *psychology* : a sexual desire that a child feels toward the parent of the opposite sex along with jealous feelings toward the parent of the same sex

[1]**o'er** /ˈoɚ/ *adv, literary* : [1]OVER ▪ when the night is *o'er*

[2]**o'er** /ˈoɚ/ *prep, literary* : [2]OVER ▪ *o'er* hill and dale

oesophagus *Brit spelling of* ESOPHAGUS

oestrogen *Brit spelling of* ESTROGEN

oeu·vre /ˈuvrə, *Brit* ˈɜːvrə/ *noun, pl* **-vres** [*count*] *formal* : all the works that a writer, an artist, or a composer has created — usually singular ▪ Her *oeuvre* consists mostly of landscapes.

of /ˈʌv, əv, *Brit* ˈɒv, əv, ə/ *prep*
1 : belonging to, relating to, or connected with (someone or something) ▪ He is a coworker *of* mine. ▪ I threw out that old shirt *of* yours. ▪ She's a friend *of* my mother's. ▪ He had the support *of* his family to help him. ▪ the plays *of* William Shakespeare ▪ What is the name *of* the band? ▪ We admired the courage *of* the young woman. ▪ the President *of* the United States ▪ the Queen *of* England ▪ What is the total cost *of* the repairs? ▪ The value *of* the antique is high. ▪ the responsibility/duty *of* parents ▪ the work *of* the artist ▪ the behavior *of* the child ▪ the actions *of* the President ▪ the results *of* the experiment ▪ The score *of* the game is tied. ▪ The product *of* 2 times 2 is 4. ▪ I can't stand the sight *of* it. [=I can't stand seeing it] ▪ the color *of* the dress ▪ the social issues *of* the time ▪ the greatest invention *of* the 20th century ▪ She was voted (Most Outstanding) Woman *of* the Year. ▪ the top *of* the mountain ▪ The leg *of* the table is loose. ▪ a masterpiece *of* modern fiction ▪ the fourth *of* July [=the fourth day in the month of July] ▪ We are having a party on the day *of* graduation. ▪ Where were you at the time *of* the murder? ▪ She told a story *of* [=*about*] her travels in Italy. ▪ The news/announcement *of* our victory was greeted with delight. ▪ He dreams *of* becoming rich and famous. ▪ He was neglectful *of* his duties.
2 — used to indicate that someone or something belongs to a group of people or things ▪ He is one *of* my friends. ▪ This is page one *of* two (pages). ▪ Many/Most *of* the students will be going on the field trip. ▪ The four *of* us enjoyed ourselves at the party. ▪ members *of* the team ▪ *Of* (all) my friends, you are the only one I really trust. ▪ She is the older/younger *of* my two sisters. ▪ He has written two novels, ***of which*** the first is the best. = He has written two novels, the first *of which* is the best.
3 : living or occurring in (a specified country, city, town, etc.) ▪ the people *of* Puerto Rico ▪ a fish *of* the western Atlantic ▪ a plant *of* the tropics
4 : showing (someone or something) ▪ a painting *of* a mother holding her child ▪ a picture *of* my house
5 — used to indicate the thing that is being referred to ▪ the country *of* Ireland ▪ the city *of* Rome ▪ the month *of* August ▪ the crime *of* murder ▪ a good piece *of* advice ▪ 1758 is the year *of* Noah Webster's birth. ▪ a difference *of* $5 ▪ The savings account has an interest rate *of* 5 percent. ▪ The arrangement includes several kinds *of* flowers. = The arrangement includes flowers *of* several kinds.
6 : involving or dealing with (something) ▪ a test *of* basic skills ▪ the Department *of* Agriculture
7 — used to indicate what something is made from or includes ▪ a throne *of* gold = a throne made (out) *of* gold ▪ a bar *of* chocolate ▪ a flock *of* sheep ▪ a herd *of* cattle ▪ a small group *of* people
8 — used to indicate what an amount, number, etc., refers to ▪ We got a large amount *of* rain. ▪ A small number *of* people were at the concert. ▪ a pound *of* sliced cheese ▪ two acres *of* land ▪ two lumps *of* sugar ▪ a big piece *of* cake ▪ a pair *of* scissors ▪ a hot cup *of* coffee = a cup *of* hot coffee ▪ hundreds *of* dollars ▪ eight hours *of* sleep ▪ He is 40 years *of* age. [=he is 40 years old]
9 — used to indicate a quality or characteristic that someone or something has ▪ a man *of* noble birth ▪ He is *of* Polish descent. ▪ a boy *of* 12 (years of age) ▪ a woman *of* [=*with*] great wealth ▪ She is the girl *of* his dreams. [=she has all the qualities that he is attracted to] ▪ She recently lost her husband *of* 30 years. [=her husband who she was married to for 30 years before he died] ▪ a matter *of* no importance ▪ The house is *of* his own design. ▪ The trash smells *of* fish.
10 — used to indicate the location of something ▪ The cabins are north *of* the lake. ▪ The arrow went wide *of* the target. [=the arrow missed the target] ▪ The dart landed to the left/right *of* the bull's-eye. ▪ The shark passed within five feet *of* me.
11 a — used to indicate the subject of an action ▪ the arrival *of* guests ▪ the departure *of* the ship ▪ the landing *of* the airplane **b** — used to indicate the object of an action ▪ the evaluation *of* students ▪ the destruction *of* property ▪ The police conducted an investigation *of* the crime. ▪ She asked a favor *of* [=*from*] me. ▪ Can you think *of* his name? ▪ I thought *of* calling you. **c** — used to indicate the cause of a specified feeling or opinion ▪ He has a love *of* [=*for*] nature. ▪ He has a fear *of* spiders. ▪ I'm so proud *of* you. = I'm so proud *of* what you have done. ▪ She is fond *of* chocolate. **d** — used to indicate the reason for something ▪ He died *of* [=*from*] pneumonia. ▪ They left *of* their own free will.
12 — used to indicate what has been taken away, removed, or given away ▪ She was robbed *of* her fortune. ▪ The con man cheated him (out) *of* his money. ▪ He was stripped *of* all

his titles. • The cats helped rid the barn *of* rats. • He gave generously *of* his time. [=he gave his time generously]
13 — **used to indicate that someone has behaved in a specified way** • It was very kind/nice *of* you to say that. [=you were very kind/nice to say that]
14 *US* — **used to indicate that there is a specified amount of time left before the next hour begins** • It's a quarter *of* [=*to, before*] ten. [=9:45] • 10 (minutes) *of* 10 [=9:50]
15 *old-fashioned* — **used to indicate the time when something happens or happened** • You can often see him walking in the park *of* an afternoon. • He died *of* [=*on*] a Monday.
as of see ²AS
of a *US, informal* — **used to indicate that someone or something is a particular type of person or thing** • her idiot *of a* husband [=her idiot/idiotic husband] • Some fool *of a* policeman had arrested the wrong man! • It is not that much *of a* problem. [=it is not a big problem] • It wasn't that difficult *of a* shot. [=it was not a difficult shot] • It wasn't that big *of a* deal. • How big *of a* piece do you want?
of all (the) see ¹ALL
of course see ¹COURSE

OF *abbr* outfield

¹off /ˈɑːf/ *adv*
1 a : away from a place • The dog ran *off*. • The car sped *off*. • She put on her jacket and *off* she went. • We get *off* at the next bus stop. [=we exit the bus at the next stop] **b : away from a main road, path, etc.** • The car turned *off* onto a side street.
2 : at a distance in time or space • Football season is not far *off*. [=football season will start soon] • The completion of the new office building is still a long way *off*. [=it will be a long time before the new office building is finished]
3 — **used to describe something that moves or is moved so that it is no longer on something or attached to something** • She set the ball on the table and it rolled *off*. • His hat fell *off*. • He twisted *off* the cap. • The handle on the pan broke *off*. • She took *off* her coat.
4 : into sleep • I dozed *off* in the chair. • He closed his eyes and drifted *off* (to sleep).
5 a — **used to describe stopping something** • Shut *off* the water. • Shut *off* the engine. • Turn the TV *off*. **b** — **used to describe getting something into a desired condition especially by removing something** • I need to smooth *off* the corners of the bookshelf. • I dusted *off* the shelves. • She wiped the counter *off*. **c** — **used to describe finishing something** • We paid *off* all our debts. • Can you finish *off* the pizza? There are only two slices left.
6 : away from regular work • I took the day *off* (from work). • At noon, workers take time *off* for lunch. • I have weekends *off*. [=I do not go to work on the weekends]
off and on or on and off **: starting, stopping, and starting again : not constant or steady over a period of time** • It rained *off and on* all day. • The fighting continued *off and on* throughout the years. • She worked here *on and off* for several years. • They've had an *on-and-off* relationship.

²off *prep*
1 — **used to indicate separation, distance, or removal from someone or something** • She cut a slice *off* the loaf. • The ball bounced *off* the wall. • She stepped *off* the train and looked around. • There are many paths *off* the main trail around the mountain. • There is a bathroom *off* the kitchen. • The shop is just *off* the main street. • He had his wallet stolen *off* him. • Keep *off* the grass. • Get your feet *off* the table. • The boat was two miles *off* the coast. • The discussion got/moved *off* the original subject. • My favorite dish has been taken *off* the menu. • I'll take your name *off* the list. • She wore the gown *off* the shoulder.
2 : on money, food, energy, etc., supplied by (someone or something) • She is still living *off* her parents. • The family lives *off* welfare. • They live *off* the land. • They make their living *off* tourism. • The machine runs *off* [=*on*] diesel fuel.
3 — **used to indicate something that someone is no longer doing or using** • She has recently gone *off* smoking. • He is *off* his diet. • The officers were *off* duty. • I took a day *off* work. • He has been *off* liquor for three years.
4 — **used to indicate the object of an action** • I borrowed a dollar *off* [=*from*] him. • I bought a CD *off* him. [=he sold a CD to me]
5 — **used to indicate the source or cause of something** • He spent all the money he made *off* [=*from*] gambling.
6 : below the usual standard or level of (something) • (*chiefly US*) He is *off* his game. [=he is not playing as well as he usually does] • The DVDs are being offered at 15 percent *off* the regular price. • I asked him to knock $100 *off* the price.
off of *chiefly US, informal* **:** OFF • She fell *off of* the swing. • farmers who live *off of* the land • He is *off of* his diet. • We ate *off of* paper plates. • 15 percent *off of* the regular price

³off *adj*
1 *not used before a noun* **: not attached to or covering something : not on** • The lid is *off*.
2 a *not used before a noun* **: not operating, functioning, or flowing** • The radio is *off*. • The electricity/water is *off*. **b : in a position that stops the flow of electricity, water, etc.** • The switch is *off*. • The lever is in the *off* position.
3 : away from home or work • He is *off* playing golf. • She is *off* on a trip/vacation. • He's *off* today. • They enjoy hiking and biking on their *off* days. [=the days when they are not working] • She is *off* [=*out*] sick today.
4 *not used before a noun* **: not happening** • The deal/game that was on is now *off*. [=has been canceled] • In case of a tie, all bets are *off*.
5 *not used before a noun, chiefly US* **: not correct :** WRONG • I must be *off* in my calculations. • These numbers are *off*. • Your guess is ***way off***!
6 *always used before a noun* **: very small in degree :** SLIGHT • There is an ***off chance*** that you will win.
7 *always used before a noun* **: not as busy or active as other periods of time** • an *off* time of year • We vacation during the ***off season***.
8 *not used before a noun* **: not completely sane** • The poor fellow is a little *off* (in the head).
9 *not used before a noun* — **used to ask about or describe someone's situation or condition** • Are you better or worse *off* financially than you were a year ago? • The other accident victims are much worse *off* than she is. [=her injuries are not as bad as theirs] • (*chiefly Brit*) We're comfortably *off*. • (*chiefly Brit*) How are you *off* for money? [=how are you for money?; do you need money?] — see also BETTER OFF, WELL-OFF
10 *not used before a noun, chiefly US* **: below the usual price or value** • Stocks are *off* [=*down*] today. • The DVDs are 15 percent *off*.
11 *chiefly US* **: not as good as usual** • My golf game is *off* today. [=I am not playing golf as well as I usually do] • I am having an *off* day.
12 *not used before a noun, Brit* **: not being served : no longer on the menu** • Sorry, love, the steak-and-kidney pie is *off*.
13 *not used before a noun, chiefly Brit* **: no longer fresh :** SPOILED • The milk has gone *off*. = The milk is *off*.
14 *not used before a noun, Brit, informal* **: not polite or friendly** • His manners were a bit *off*, don't you think? • She felt he was being *off* with her.
be off **: to leave : to start going, running, etc.** • I must *be off* [=I must leave now] if I want to make the next bus. • And the runners *are off*. [=the runners have started running] • They're *off* and running!

⁴off *verb* **offs; offed; off·ing** [+ *obj*] *US slang* **: to kill or murder (someone)** • The movie is about a gangster who gets power by *offing* his rivals.

⁵off *noun*
the off *Brit* **1 : the beginning of a race** **2 : the very beginning** • Right ***from the off*** [=(*US*) *from the get-go*], I knew she was against me.

off–air *adj, always used before a noun* **: occurring when a radio or television program is not being recorded** • an *off-air* conversation

of·fal /ˈɑːfəl/ *noun* [*noncount*] **: the organs (such as the liver or kidney) of an animal that are used for food** • beef *offal*

off·beat /ˈɑːfˌbiːt/ *adj* [*more ~; most ~*] *informal* **: different from the ordinary, usual, or expected** • She has an *offbeat* sense of humor. • He often plays *offbeat* characters in his films. • an *offbeat* approach to teaching • The performance was refreshingly *offbeat*.

off–brand /ˈɑːfˌbrænd/ *adj* **: not sold or made under a particular brand name** • *off-brand* sneakers/soda/cereal/cigarettes

off–Broadway *or* **Off–Broadway** *adj* **: relating to theater in New York City that involves productions that are smaller and often less conventional than typical Broadway productions** • an *off-Broadway* production/show/play
– off–Broadway *or* **Off–Broadway** *adv* • The play opened *off-Broadway*. • He performed *off-Broadway* for years.

off–center (*US*) *or Brit* **off–centre** *adj* [*more ~; most ~*]

1 *not used before a noun* **: not exactly in the center of something** ▪ The mirror over the sink is a little bit *off-center*. ▪ The title is slightly *off-center* on the page.
2 : different or unusual ▪ He has an *off-center* sense of humor.
– off–center (*US*) *or Brit* **off–centre** *adv* ▪ He hung the picture *off-center*.

off–col•or (*US*) *or Brit* **off–col•our** /ˈɑːfˈkʌlɚ/ *or US* **off–col•ored** *or Brit* **off–col•oured** /ˈɑːfˈkʌlɚd/ *adj* [*more ~; most ~*]
1 *not used before a noun* **: feeling somewhat ill : not quite well** ▪ He has been *off-color* for a few days.
2 *chiefly US* **: not socially acceptable : indecent or improper** ▪ We were shocked by his *off-color* [=*rude, offensive*] remarks. ▪ an *off-color* joke

off•cut /ˈɑːfˌkʌt/ *noun, pl* **-cuts** [*count*] *chiefly Brit* **: a piece of wood, cloth, etc., that remains after a larger piece is removed**

off–duty *adj* **: free from the responsibilities of your job : not working at a particular time** ▪ an *off-duty* cop

of•fend /əˈfɛnd/ *verb* **-fends; -fend•ed; -fend•ing**
1 : to cause (a person or group) to feel hurt, angry, or upset by something said or done [*+ obj*] His comments about minority groups *offended* many of us. ▪ She had carefully worded her comments so as not to *offend* anyone. ▪ It *offends* me that you would make such a remark. ▪ Don't worry. I wasn't *offended*. ▪ I felt a little *offended* by their lack of respect. ▪ Some people are *offended* by the song's lyrics. ▪ I'm sorry, I didn't mean to *offend* you. [*no obj*] I'm sorry, I didn't mean to *offend*.
2 [*+ obj*] **: to be unpleasant to (someone or something)** ▪ The billboard ***offends the eye***. [=the billboard is not attractive]
3 [*no obj*] *formal* **: to do wrong : to be against what people believe is acceptable or proper — often + *against*** ▪ Her actions *offended against* our sensibilities.
4 [*no obj*] *formal* **: to commit a crime** ▪ Is he likely to *offend* again after his release from prison?

of•fend•er /əˈfɛndɚ/ *noun, pl* **-ers** [*count*]
1 : a person who commits a crime ▪ a ***repeat offender*** [=someone who has committed a crime more than once] ▪ She recently prosecuted a ***sex/sexual offender***. [=someone who commits sex crimes] **— see also** FIRST OFFENDER
2 : someone or something that does something harmful or wrong ▪ The factory is one of the worst *offenders* in terms of air and water pollution.

offending *adj, always used before a noun*
1 *often humorous* **: causing difficulty, discomfort, or harm** ▪ He took off his shoe and removed the *offending* pebble. [=the pebble that was making it uncomfortable to walk]
2 [*more ~; most ~*] **: causing disapproval** ▪ We agreed to omit the *offending* word from the passage.
3 : guilty of doing something wrong ▪ The *offending* driver was given a ticket for speeding.

of•fense (*US*) *or Brit* **of•fence** /əˈfɛns/ *noun, pl* **-fens•es**
1 a [*noncount*] **: something that causes a person to be hurt, angry, or upset** ▪ She didn't mean to ***give/cause offense***. [=to offend anyone] ▪ I ***mean no offense*** [=I do not want to offend anyone], but isn't there someone more qualified for the job? ▪ ***No offense*** [=I do not want to offend you when I say this], but I think you are mistaken. **b** [*count*] **: something that is wrong or improper — often + *to*** ▪ His actions are an *offense to* public morals. **— often + *against*** ▪ Such language is an *offense against* common decency.
2 [*count*] **: a criminal act** ▪ He was found guilty and fined $250 for each *offense*. ▪ Penalties for a first *offense* range from fines to jail time. ▪ a capital/federal/criminal *offense* ▪ serious/minor *offenses*
3 /ˈɑːˌfɛns/ *US, sports* **a : the group of players on a team who try to score points or goals against an opponent** [*count*] Our team has the best *offense* in the league. ▪ a talented *offense* ▪ The quarterback directs the *offense*. [*noncount*] She began the season ***on offense*** [=playing on the part of the team that tries to score points or goals], but her coach later put her on defense. **b** [*noncount*] **: the way that players on a team try to score points or goals against an opponent** ▪ The team needs some work on its *offense*. ▪ The team plays good *offense*. **— compare** DEFENSE 6
take offense **: to become angry or upset by something that another person has said or done : to be offended by something** ▪ He *took offense* when I suggested exchanging the gift. **— often + *at*** ▪ She *takes offense at* any criticism.

[1]**of•fen•sive** /əˈfɛnsɪv/ *adj*
1 [*more ~; most ~*] **: causing someone to feel hurt, angry, or upset : rude or insulting** ▪ He made some *offensive* remarks. ▪ *offensive* words/terms **— often + *to*** ▪ The song lyrics are *offensive to* women. [=women are offended by the song lyrics] ▪ His behavior is *offensive to* many people. **— opposite** INOFFENSIVE
2 [*more ~; most ~*] **: very unpleasant** ▪ An *offensive* odor was coming from the basement.
3 *always used before a noun, sports* **: of or relating to the way that players try to score against an opponent in a game or contest** ▪ an *offensive* position/strategy ▪ an *offensive* lineman/player **— compare** [1]DEFENSIVE 3
4 *always used before a noun* **: relating to or designed for attacking an enemy** ▪ The troops will take *offensive* action against the enemy. ▪ We studied their *offensive* maneuvers and anticipated the attack. ▪ *offensive* weapons **— compare** [1]DEFENSIVE 1
– of•fen•sive•ly *adv* ▪ *Offensively*, the team is strong. **– of•fen•sive•ness** *noun* [*noncount*] ▪ the *offensiveness* of his remarks

[2]**offensive** *noun, pl* **-sives** [*count*] **: a large military attack — usually singular** ▪ They plan to launch an air *offensive* before sending in ground troops. ▪ a ground *offensive* **— often used figuratively** ▪ Union leaders have mounted an *offensive* against the company's proposal to limit health benefits. **— see also** COUNTEROFFENSIVE
on the offensive **: in or into a situation or position in which you attack or fight against someone or something** ▪ The soldiers are *on the offensive*. ▪ She ***went on the offensive*** to fight the charges against her. ▪ The team was on the defensive in the early part of the game but they *went on the offensive* in the second half.
take the offensive **: to begin to attack or fight against someone or something** ▪ Opponents of the development project *took the offensive* and defeated the land sale.

[1]**of•fer** /ˈɑːfɚ/ *verb* **-fers; -fered; -fer•ing**
1 a [*+ obj*] **: to give someone the opportunity to accept or take (something)** ▪ We'd like to *offer* the job to you. = We'd like to *offer* you the job. ▪ I was *offered* a position at a bank, but I turned it down. ▪ She *offered* [=she said that she would pay] $250,000 for the house. ▪ The victims were *offered* money as compensation for their injuries. ▪ I *offered* her my hand/arm [=I held out my hand/arm for her to grasp], and she took it. ▪ I *offered* my assistance. ▪ If I may, I'd like to *offer* you a bit of advice. **b : to say that you are willing *to do* something** [*+ obj*] One of his neighbors *offered to mow* his lawn. ▪ A woman stopped and *offered to help* us. [*no obj*] We don't need any help, but thank you for *offering*.
2 [*+ obj*] **: to make (something) available : to provide or supply (something)** ▪ They *offer* [=*sell*] a wide range of products/services at reasonable prices. ▪ A few of my teachers *offer* [=*give*] extra help after class. ▪ They *offer* their customers a choice between soup or salad. ▪ The car *offers* [=*has*] a wide range of safety features. ▪ Living in a large city *offers* a number of advantages. ▪ They serve the best food this town has to *offer*. [=the best food in the town] ▪ This city has so much to *offer*. [=there are many good and interesting things to do and see in this city] ▪ She has a great deal to *offer*. [=she has many talents, abilities, good qualities, etc.] **— often + *up*** ▪ The restaurant *offers up* a completely new menu every season.
3 [*+ obj*] **: to say or express (something) as an idea to be thought about or considered** ▪ I'd like to *offer* a couple of comments/remarks/observations on the points you've raised. ▪ I really don't know enough about it to *offer* an opinion. ▪ She *offers* [=*proposes, suggests*] another possible explanation in her book. ▪ The film *offers* a unique perspective on the issue. **— often + *up*** ▪ Would anyone else like to *offer up* a suggestion?
4 [*+ obj*] **: to say or give (something, such as a prayer or a sacrifice) as a form of religious worship** ▪ Let us bow our heads and *offer* a prayer of thanks. ▪ *offer* a sacrifice **— often + *up*** ▪ *offering up* prayers to the saints
offer resistance **: to try to resist or fight** ▪ The people *offered* no *resistance* when the enemy entered the town.

[2]**offer** *noun, pl* **-fers** [*count*]
1 : the act of giving someone the opportunity to accept something : the act of offering something ▪ I don't really need any help, but I appreciate the *offer*. [=thanks for offering to help] ▪ After considering several job *offers*, she accepted a position with a local bank. ▪ He turned down an *offer* to run the company. ▪ Take advantage of our 30-day trial *offer*. [=try our product free for 30 days] ▪ She received an *offer* of marriage. [=someone proposed marriage to her]

2 : an amount of money that someone is willing to pay for something ▪ I'll pay $500. That's my final/best *offer.* [=I won't pay more] ▪ We accepted/rejected their *offer.* ▪ We decided to hold out for a better *offer.* ▪ They ***made an offer*** on our house. [=they said that they would pay a specified amount of money for our house] ▪ "How much do you want for the bike?" "I don't know. *Make* me *an offer.*" — see also TENDER OFFER
3 : an opportunity to buy something at a price that is lower than the usual price ▪ This ***special offer*** is good only while supplies last.
on offer *chiefly Brit* **:** available to be bought especially at low prices **:** on sale ▪ The store has a wide range of cameras *on offer* at reasonable prices. ▪ Eggs are *on offer* [=(*chiefly US*) *on special*] this week.

of·fer·ing /ˈɑːfərɪŋ/ *noun, pl* **-ings** [*count*]
1 a : something that is given to God or a god as a part of religious worship ▪ ceremonial/sacrificial *offerings* **b :** an act of giving a religious offering ▪ Each household must ***make*** daily ***offerings*** to the gods. — see also PEACE OFFERING
2 : something that is available for sale or use ▪ The company is trying to generate interest in its new *offerings.* ▪ the café's tasty dessert *offerings* — see also INITIAL PUBLIC OFFERING

of·fer·to·ry /ˈɑːfəˌtori, *Brit* ˈɒfətri/ *noun, pl* **-ries** [*count*]
1 *or* ***Offertory*** **a :** the offering of bread and wine to God as part of the Communion ceremony during a Christian church service **b :** a verse from a psalm that is said or sung at the beginning of the Offertory
2 a : the part of a Christian church service during which offerings of money are collected **b :** the music played or sung during an offertory

[1]**off·hand** /ˈɑːfˈhænd/ *adv* **:** without previous thought or preparation ▪ I couldn't give them the figures *offhand.* ▪ Do you happen to know, *offhand,* when he'll be back?

[2]**offhand** *also* **off·hand·ed** /ˈɑːfˈhændəd/ *adj* [*more* ~; *most* ~]
1 : done or made without previous thought or preparation ▪ It was just an *offhand* remark. ▪ *offhand* excuses
2 : casual or informal ▪ She spoke in an *offhand* manner.
– off·hand·ed·ly *adv* ▪ I *offhandedly* asked where he worked.

of·fice /ˈɑːfəs/ *noun, pl* **-fic·es**
1 [*count*] **a :** a building or room in which people work at desks doing business or professional activities ▪ She works at/in our Chicago *office.* ▪ Are you going to the *office* today? ▪ The company's ***main/home office*** [=the company's most important office] is in San Francisco. — often used before another noun ▪ A new *office* building [=a building with offices] is being built on Main Street. ▪ *office* equipment/supplies ▪ Our company is having an *office* party [=a party for the people who work at the office] next week. ▪ The company is renting *office* space downtown. ▪ *office* workers/staff — see picture on the next page **b :** a room with a desk where a particular person works ▪ The supervisor held an informal meeting in his *office.* ▪ Her *office* is on the top floor near the elevator. ▪ He misbehaved in class and was sent to the principal's *office.* ▪ We use the extra bedroom in our house as an *office.* **c** *chiefly US* **:** a building or room where a doctor, lawyer, etc., works and meets with patients or clients ▪ We stopped by the lawyer's *office* to pick up some documents. ▪ the doctor's *office* [=(*Brit*) *surgery*] — see also BOX OFFICE, OVAL OFFICE, TICKET OFFICE
2 : the job or position of someone who has authority especially in the government [*noncount*] He has been in *office* for a decade. ▪ He was voted out of *office.* ▪ He won the election and will ***take office*** at the beginning of the year. ▪ She has decided to ***leave office*** after two successful terms. ▪ She plans to ***run for office*** [=campaign to be elected to an office] again. ▪ U.S. senators are elected to a ***term of office*** of six years. [*count*] She has held several public *offices.*
3 [*count*] **:** a department of a company, organization, government, or school. ▪ She went to the unemployment *office.* ▪ Where is the registrar's *office* on campus? ▪ the U.S. Patent *Office* — see also FOREIGN OFFICE, HOME OFFICE, POST OFFICE, REGISTER OFFICE, REGISTRY OFFICE
good offices *formal* **:** help from someone who has power or authority ▪ I got the interview ***through the good offices of*** a former classmate.

office boy *noun, pl* ~ **boys** [*count*] *old-fashioned* **:** a boy or man employed to do simple jobs in an office

office girl *noun, pl* ~ **girls** [*count*] *old-fashioned* **:** a girl or woman employed to do simple jobs in an office

of·fice·hold·er /ˈɑːfəsˌhoʊldɚ/ *noun, pl* **-ers** [*count*] **:** a person who has an official job or position especially in the government ▪ the city's/state's *officeholders*

office hours *noun* [*plural*]
1 : the time during the day when people work in an office ▪ Our *office hours* are 8:30 to 4:00 Monday through Friday.
2 *US* **:** the time during the day when a teacher is available to meet with students in his or her office ▪ She has *office hours* Monday and Wednesday mornings from 9:00 to 11:00.
3 *US* **:** a time during the day when people can see a doctor or dentist — called also (*Brit*) *surgery*

of·fi·cer /ˈɑːfəsɚ/ *noun, pl* **-cers** [*count*]
1 : a member of a police force **:** POLICE OFFICER — often used as a title ▪ *Officer* Ruiz responded to the call. — see also PROBATION OFFICER
2 : a person who has an important position in a company, organization, or government ▪ The bank's *officers* [=*executives*] will meet next week. — see also CHIEF EXECUTIVE OFFICER, RETURNING OFFICER
3 : a person who has a position of authority or command in the military ▪ an *officer* in the navy = a naval *officer* — see also COMMANDING OFFICER, PETTY OFFICER, STAFF OFFICER

[1]**of·fi·cial** /əˈfɪʃəl/ *adj*
1 *always used before a noun* **:** of or relating to the job or work of someone in a position of authority ▪ *official* responsibilities ▪ She was accused of destroying *official* documents. ▪ Her illness did not prevent her from performing her *official* duties. ▪ The Vice President is on an *official* trip/visit.
2 a — used to describe something that is said in a public way by someone in a position of authority ▪ We're still waiting for an *official* announcement of his resignation. ▪ It's *official.* His resignation has been accepted. ▪ The *official* explanation is that he hurt himself accidentally, but many people suspect that he was injured in a fight. **b** — used to describe something that is done in a public and often formal way ▪ The museum's *official* opening will be next month. ▪ an *official* ceremony
3 *always used before a noun* **:** proper for or used by someone who has a position of authority ▪ We extended an *official* greeting to the ambassador. ▪ the mayor's *official* residence
4 *always used before a noun* **:** having authority ▪ *Official* sources have confirmed the rumor. **:** having authority to perform a service or duty ▪ He attended the funeral as the president's *official* representative. ▪ the *official* government of the 13 colonies
5 : permitted, accepted, or approved by the government or by a person or organization that has authority ▪ What is your country's *official* language? ▪ an *official* major-league baseball ▪ The change in the policy should soon be *official.*
– of·fi·cial·ly *adv* ▪ The museum *officially* opens next month. ▪ The company's name was *officially* changed in 1982. ▪ She *officially* entered the race for mayor.

[2]**official** *noun, pl* **-cials** [*count*]
1 : a person who has a position of authority in a company, organization, or government **:** a person who holds an office ▪ She interviewed a senior *official* from the previous administration. ▪ public/government/city *officials* ▪ A company *official* responded to our request.
2 : a person (such as a referee or umpire) who makes sure that players are following the rules of a game ▪ a football *official*

of·fi·cial·dom /əˈfɪʃəldəm/ *noun* [*noncount*] *formal + often disapproving* **:** the people in an organization or government who are in positions of authority ▪ church *officialdom*

of·fi·cial·ese /əˌfɪʃəˈliːz/ *noun* [*noncount*] *usually disapproving + formal* **:** the language used in official documents that is difficult for most people to understand ▪ The documents were full of confusing *officialese.*

of·fi·ci·ate /əˈfɪʃiˌeɪt/ *verb* **-ates; -at·ed; -at·ing**
1 *formal* **:** to perform the official duties of a ceremony [*no obj*] — usually + *at* ▪ Our parish priest *officiated at* our wedding. ▪ The mayor *officiated at* the opening of the new public library. [+ *obj*] The bishop *officiated* the memorial Mass.
2 *sports* **:** to be a referee, umpire, or judge at a game, tournament, etc. [*no obj*] — usually + *at* ▪ She *officiated at* the tennis match. [+ *obj*] Two referees *officiated* the hockey game.

of·fi·cious /əˈfɪʃəs/ *adj* [*more* ~; *most* ~] *disapproving* — used to describe an annoying person who tries to tell other people what to do in a way that is not wanted or needed ▪ After the boss told his workers what to do, his *officious* assistant stepped in to supervise.

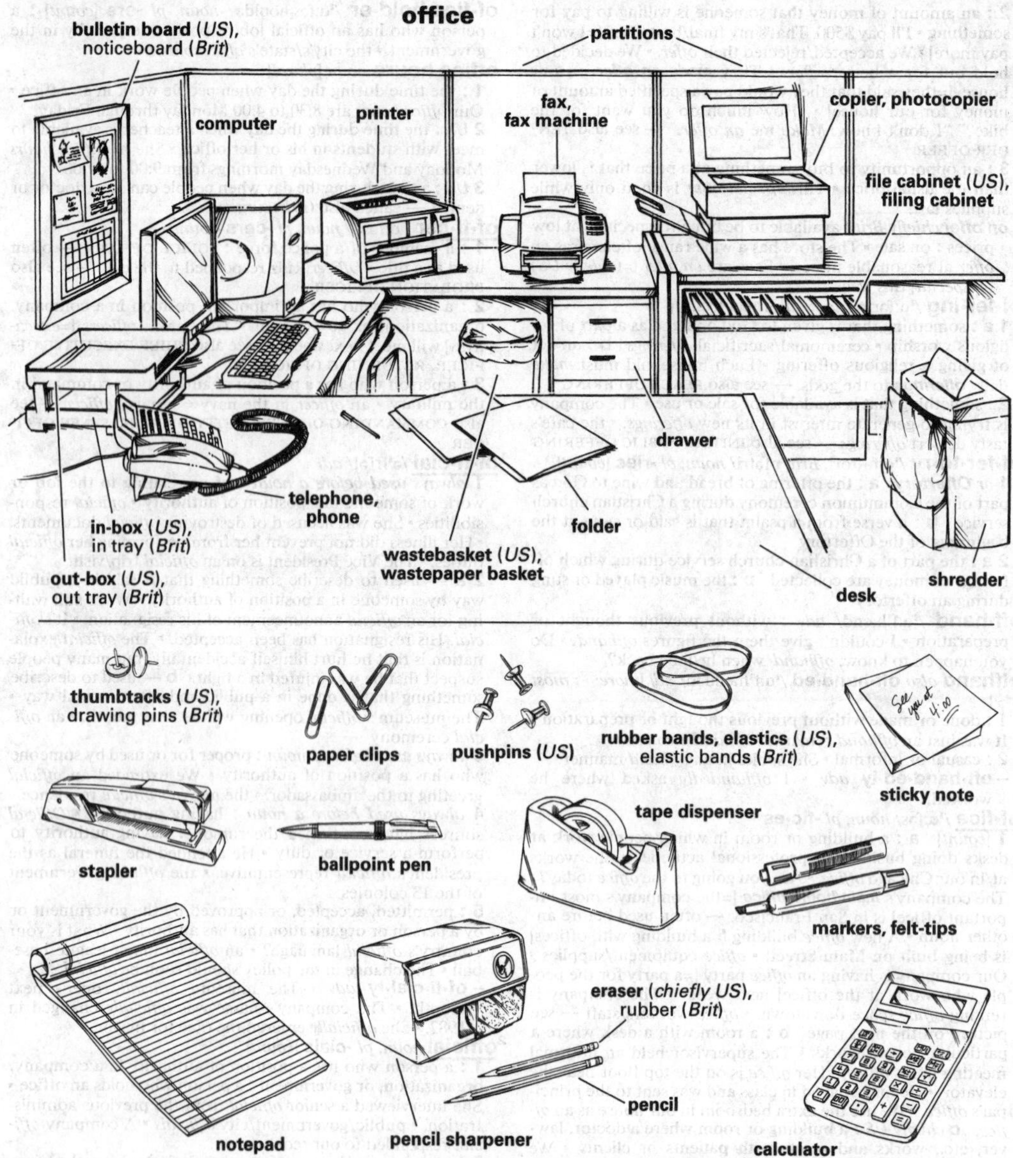

— **of·fi·cious·ly** *adv* ▪ He *officiously* shouted orders at the workers.

off·ing /ˈɑːfɪŋ/ *noun*
in the offing : likely to happen soon ▪ A promotion might be *in the offing* for him. ▪ Some big changes are *in the offing*.

off–key /ˈɑːfˈkiː/ *adj [more ~; most ~]* : not in tune : above or below the proper pitch ▪ Some of the notes were slightly *off-key*.
— **off–key** *adv* ▪ He sang *off-key*.

off–kil·ter /ˈɑːfˈkɪltɚ/ *adj [more ~; most ~]*
1 : not perfectly balanced or even ▪ The stairs are a little *off-kilter*.
2 : different from the ordinary, usual, or expected ▪ Her novels are full of *off-kilter* characters in odd situations.

off–licence *noun, pl* **-cences** [*count*] *Brit* : a store that sells alcoholic drinks

off–lim·its /ˈɑːfˈlɪməts/ *adj, not used before a noun*
1 — used to say that people are not allowed to enter a place or use something ▪ The basement and garage will be *off-limits* during the renovations. ▪ The historical documents have been placed *off-limits*. — often + *to* ▪ Certain areas in the museum are currently *off-limits to* visitors.
2 — used to say that people are not allowed to talk about something ▪ The subject of sex was *off-limits* in her family.

off–line /ˈɑːfˈlaɪn/ *adj*
1 : not connected to a computer, a computer network, or the Internet ▪ The system will be *off-line* for about an hour this afternoon. ▪ The printer is *off-line*.
2 : not done on a computer network or the Internet ▪ *off-line* activities/storage
— **off–line** *adv* ▪ I'm working *off-line* today because the network has been slow. — opposite ONLINE

off–load /ˌɑːfˈloud/ *verb* **-loads; -load·ed; -load·ing** [+ *obj*]
1 : to remove (something) from a truck, ship, etc. ▪ Workers *off-loaded* [=(more commonly) *unloaded*] the equipment from the trailer. ▪ I'll *off-load* the truck at the warehouse.
2 : to give away or sell (something unwanted) to someone : to get rid of (something) ▪ He *off-loaded* part of his baseball card collection. ▪ She tried to *off-load* some of her stock before prices fell.

off–peak /ˈɑːfˈpiːk/ *adj* : less busy or active than other times

: not peak ▪ What are the telephone rates during *off-peak* hours? ▪ They always vacation during *off-peak* periods.

off–put·ting /ˈɑːfˌpʊtɪŋ/ *adj* [*more* ~; *most* ~] : not pleasing or likable : causing you to feel dislike of someone or something ▪ He has an *off-putting* [=*unfriendly*] manner. ▪ The restaurant's décor was strangely *off-putting*. ▪ The wording of the memo was very *off-putting*.

– **off–put·ting·ly** *adv* ▪ His manner is *off-puttingly* formal.

off–ramp /ˈɑːfˌræmp/ *noun, pl* **-ramps** [*count*] *US* : a short road that is used to gradually slow down after leaving a highway — called also (*Brit*) *slip road*; compare ON-RAMP

off–road /ˈɑːfˈroʊd/ *adj, always used before a noun*

1 : designed to be used on trails or dirt roads ▪ *Off-road* vehicles are prohibited on the beach.

2 : involving or used by off-road vehicles ▪ *off-road* racing/trails

off·screen /ˈɑːfˈskriːn/ *adv*

1 : not happening or present in the scene that is being shown on a television or movie screen ▪ In one scene you could see the shadow of someone *offscreen*. ▪ Strange sounds were heard *offscreen*.

2 *of an actor* : in private life ▪ *Offscreen*, she is nothing like the character she plays on TV.

– **off·screen** *adj* ▪ The characters had an *offscreen* argument. ▪ There were rumors of an *offscreen* romance between her and the leading man.

off–sea·son /ˈɑːfˌsiːzən/ *noun, pl* **-sons** [*count*]

1 : a period of time when travel to a particular place is less popular and prices are usually lower ▪ They always travel during the *off-season* to take advantage of low prices. ▪ *off-season* rates/travel

2 *sports* : a period of time when official games, tournaments, etc., are not being played ▪ During the *off-season*, he had surgery on his shoulder. ▪ He was brought to the team in an *off-season* trade.

– **off–season** *adv* ▪ They like to travel *off-season*.

off·set /ˈɑːfˌsɛt/ *verb* **-sets; -set; -set·ting** [+ *obj*] : to cancel or reduce the effect of (something) : to create an equal balance between two things ▪ Gains in one area *offset* losses in another. ▪ The limited storage space in the house is *offset* by the large garage.

off·shoot /ˈɑːfˌʃuːt/ *noun, pl* **-shoots** [*count*]

1 : something (such as a business) that develops from something larger ▪ The business started as an *offshoot* of an established fashion design company.

2 : a branch that grows on one of the main stems of a plant

off·shore /ˈɑːfˈʃoɚ/ *adj*

1 : moving away from the shore toward the water ▪ an *offshore* breeze

2 : located in the ocean away from the shore ▪ We sailed to an *offshore* island. ▪ He works on an *offshore* oil rig.

3 : located in a foreign country ▪ They opened an *offshore* bank account. ▪ He traced the money to an *offshore* investment company.

– **offshore** *adv* ▪ An oil company is drilling *offshore*. ▪ The ships are anchored about a mile *offshore*. ▪ A light breeze was blowing *offshore*.

off·side /ˈɑːfˈsaɪd/ *adj*

1 *sports* : in a position in a game (such as football or hockey) on the opponent's part of the field where you are not allowed to be : not onside ▪ The play was stopped because the center was *offside*.

2 *Brit* : on the right side : RIGHT-HAND ▪ the car's *offside* mirror/headlight — compare NEARSIDE

the offside *Brit* : the right-hand side ▪ The car was damaged on *the offside*.

– **offside** *adv*

off–site /ˈɑːfˈsaɪt/ *adv* : away from the place of a business or activity ▪ Printing of our dictionary is done *off-site*. — opposite ON-SITE

– **off–site** *adj* ▪ *Off-site* parking is available at the airport.

off–speed /ˈɑːfˈspiːd/ *adj, baseball, of a pitch* : slower than usual or expected ▪ He has trouble hitting *off-speed* pitches.

off·spring /ˈɑːfˌsprɪŋ/ *noun, pl* **offspring** [*count*]

1 : a person's child ▪ The disease can be transmitted from parent to *offspring*. ▪ The show is about two couples and the adventures of their rebellious *offspring*.

2 : the young of an animal or plant ▪ The colt is the *offspring* of two racing champions.

off·stage /ˈɑːfˈsteɪʤ/ *adv*

1 : on the part of the stage that the audience cannot see : behind or to the side of the stage ▪ She waited *offstage* for her cue. ▪ We heard a loud crash *offstage*. — compare BACKSTAGE, ONSTAGE

2 *of a performer* : in private life ▪ *Offstage*, the actress is very down-to-earth.

3 : in a place that is away from public view : behind the scenes ▪ Much of the important work of the conference was done *offstage*.

– **offstage** *adj* ▪ Their *offstage* relationship ended soon after the play closed.

off–street *adj, always used before a noun* : not on a public road ▪ *Off-street* parking is available for residents.

off–the–cuff *adj* : not prepared in advance : done without planning or preparation ▪ He made some *off-the-cuff* remarks during his presentation which drew laughter. — see also *off the cuff* at [1]CUFF

off–the–peg *adj, chiefly Brit* : OFF-THE-RACK

off–the–rack *adj, US* — used to describe clothes that you can buy in a store in different sizes that are not made to fit a particular person ▪ an *off-the-rack* suit — see also *off the rack* at [1]RACK

off–the–record *adj* — used to describe statements that are made to a reporter but that are not supposed to be included in a story, newspaper report, etc. ▪ The reporter used *off-the-record* comments in the story that should not have been made public. — see also *off the record* at [1]RECORD

off–the–shelf *adj* : available for sale from a store's supply of goods : not specially designed or custom-made ▪ They used mostly *off-the-shelf* stereo components for the media room. ▪ *off-the-shelf* software

off–the–wall *adj* [*more* ~; *most* ~] *informal* : very unusual or strange ▪ She has an *off-the-wall* sense of humor. ▪ Some of his ideas are really *off-the-wall*.

off–white /ˈɑːfˈwaɪt/ *noun* [*noncount*] : a yellowish or grayish white ▪ They painted the walls in *off-white*.

– **off–white** *adj* ▪ an *off-white* shirt

off year *noun, pl* ~ **years** [*count*]

1 : a year in which activity or production is lower than usual ▪ It has been an *off year* for auto sales.

2 *US, politics* : a year in which no major elections are held

oft /ˈɑːft/ *adv, literary* : OFTEN — often used in combination with a past participle ▪ an *oft*-repeated story ▪ an *oft*-quoted statement

of·ten /ˈɑːfən/ *adv* **of·ten·er; -est** [*or more* ~; *most* ~] : many times : on many occasions : FREQUENTLY ▪ They go out to dinner fairly *often*. ▪ How *often* do you call your mother? ▪ The condition *often* returns even after treatment with antibiotics. ▪ I *often* take a walk during my lunch break. ▪ He travels more *often* than I do. ▪ The disease is diagnosed most *often* in children. ▪ They seem to be getting into arguments more and more *often*. ▪ *Often*, she works late. ▪ It's not *often* that I get to enjoy a day off. ▪ Water the plants *often* enough to keep the soil moist. ▪ We hear from her ***every so often***. [=*occasionally, once in a while*] ▪ ***More often than not*** [=*typically, usually*], he forgets his hat. ▪ She arrived home from work late, ***as often as not***. [=very often] ▪ We see this problem ***all too often***. [=too commonly]

of·ten·times /ˈɑːfənˌtaɪmz/ *adv, US* : OFTEN ▪ *Oftentimes*, he is the only man in the aerobics class.

ogle /ˈoʊgəl/ *verb* **ogles; ogled; ogling** [+ *obj*]

1 *usually disapproving* : to look at (someone) in a way that shows sexual attraction ▪ He sat at the bar, *ogling* several women.

2 : to look at (something) in a way that suggests strong interest or desire ▪ He *ogled* the new cars on the lot. ▪ I was *ogling* the dessert menu before my meal even arrived.

ogre /ˈoʊgɚ/ *noun, pl* **ogres** [*count*]

1 : an ugly giant in children's stories that eats people

2 : someone or something that is very frightening, cruel, or difficult to deal with ▪ The book portrays their father as an *ogre* who mistreated them. ▪ the *ogre* of inflation

[1]**oh** /ˈoʊ/ *interj*

1 — used to express surprise, happiness, disappointment, or sadness ▪ *Oh*, it's so windy out here! ▪ *Oh*, I'm so sorry to hear that. ▪ ***Oh no***! I forgot my purse.

2 — used in response to a physical sensation (such as pain) ▪ *Oh*, that hurt. ▪ *Oh*, that does taste good.

3 *also* **O** — used to address someone directly ▪ *Oh* sir, you forgot your change. ▪ *Oh*, waiter! We'd like the bill, please ▪ Bless us, *O* Lord.

4 — used for emphasis when responding to a question or statement or when making a statement ▪ "Have you ever been to Venice?" "*Oh*, yes. It's one of my favorite cities." ▪

"He's planning to change jobs." "*Oh*? Really?" • *Oh* all right. If you insist. • *Oh* for some time to relax and read a book! [=I wish I had some time to relax and read a book]

5 — used to show that something is understood • "I'm going to the dentist now." "*Oh*, okay. I'll see you later." • "But I won't be available on Monday." "*Oh*, I see. My mistake."

6 — used during a pause in speaking • Their house is about, *oh*, I'd say four miles from here.

[2]**oh** /ˈoʊ/ *noun, pl* **ohs** [*count*] *US* — used to show the way the number 0 is often pronounced • The number is three, *oh*, nine. [=309]

OH *abbr* Ohio

ohm /ˈoʊm/ *noun, pl* **ohms** [*count*] *technical* **:** a unit for measuring electrical resistance

oi /ˈoɪ/ *interj, Brit, informal* — used to get the attention of someone or to express disapproval • *Oi*, what are you doing with my car! • *Oi!*—get away from there!

oik /ˈoɪk/ *noun, pl* **oiks** [*count*] *Brit slang* **:** a person who is very rude or stupid

[1]**oil** /ˈojəl/ *noun, pl* **oils**

1 [*noncount*] **a :** a thick, black liquid that comes from the ground and that is used in making various products (such as gasoline) • The price of crude *oil* is expected to rise. • drilling for *oil* — often used before another noun • *oil* prices/companies/wells/refineries • the *oil* industry • The world's *oil* supplies/reserves are diminishing. **b :** a type of oil that is used as a fuel to produce heat or light • We heat our house with *oil*. • heating *oil* • an *oil* lamp **c :** a type of oil that makes the different parts in an engine, machine, etc., run smoothly • I asked the mechanic to check the *oil*. [=to make sure that there was enough oil to make the car engine run smoothly] • A little bit of *oil* will help lubricate the chain.

2 [*count, noncount*] **:** a liquid substance that comes from a plant or animal, that contains fat, and that is used in cooking • Add a little *oil* to the pan and stir-fry the onions. • The dressing is made with *oil*, vinegar, and a pinch of herbs. — see also CASTOR OIL, COCONUT OIL, COD-LIVER OIL, CORN OIL, ESSENTIAL OIL, LINSEED OIL, OLIVE OIL, PALM OIL

3 [*count, noncount*] **:** a smooth substance that is used on the skin, hair, or body to make it soft or healthy • scented bath *oils*

4 a ***oils*** [*plural*] **:** oil paints • He works mostly ***in oils*** [=he mostly uses oil paints] **b** [*count*] **:** an oil painting • The exhibit includes *oils* and watercolors. • an *oil* on canvas

a/the squeaky wheel gets the oil see [1]WHEEL

burn the midnight oil see [1]BURN

[2]**oil** *verb* **oils; oiled; oil·ing** [+ *obj*] **:** to put oil in or on (something) • He *oiled* the bearings of the machine.

oil·can /ˈojəlˌkæn/ *noun, pl* **-cans** [*count*] **:** a can for holding oil; *especially* **:** a can with a long thin part through which oil comes out slowly

oil·cloth /ˈojəlˌklɑːθ/ *noun* [*noncount*] **:** cloth that is treated with oil so that it does not let water in and that is used especially to cover tables and shelves

oiled /ˈojəld/ *adj* **:** treated or covered with oil • Place the vegetables in the *oiled* pan. • *oiled* paper — see also WELL-OILED

oil field *noun, pl* ~ **fields** [*count*] **:** an area where there is a lot of oil and where special equipment has been set up to remove it from the ground

oil·man /ˈojəlmən/ *noun, pl* **-men** /-mən/ [*count*] **:** a person (usually a man) who owns or works for an oil company

oil paint *noun, pl* ~ **paints** [*count, noncount*] **:** paint that contains oil

oil painting *noun, pl* ~ **-ings**

1 [*noncount*] **:** the art of painting with oil paints • He studied *oil painting* in college.

2 [*count*] **:** a picture that is painted with oil paints • A large *oil painting* hangs above the mantel.

no oil painting *Brit, informal* **:** not physically attractive • His new girlfriend is *no oil painting*.

oil pan *noun, pl* ~ **pans** [*count*] *chiefly US* **:** the lower part of an engine that holds the oil — called also (*Brit*) *sump*

oil rig *noun, pl* ~ **rigs** [*count*] **:** a structure above an oil well on land or in the sea that has special equipment attached to it for drilling and removing oil from the ground — called also *oil platform*

oil·seed rape /ˈojəlˌsiːd-/ *noun* [*noncount*] *chiefly Brit* **:** [3]RAPE

oil·skin /ˈojəlˌskɪn/ *noun, pl* **-skins**

1 [*noncount*] **:** cloth that is treated with oil so that it does not let water in and that is used to make clothing

2 [*count*] **:** a raincoat that is made of oilskin

3 ***oilskins*** [*plural*] **:** a coat and pants that are made of oilskin and that are worn to keep dry • fishermen dressed in *oilskins*

oil slick *noun, pl* ~ **slicks** [*count*] **:** a thin layer of oil that is floating on the surface of the ocean, a lake, etc.

oil tanker *noun, pl* ~ **-ers** [*count*] **:** a large ship that carries oil

oil well *noun, pl* ~ **wells** [*count*] **:** a hole that has been drilled into the ground through which oil can be removed

oily /ˈoili/ *adj* **oil·i·er; -est** [*also more ~; most ~*]

1 : having the smooth or greasy quality of oil • The liquid has an *oily* feel.

2 a : covered or soaked with oil • a pile of *oily* rags **b :** containing or producing a large amount of oil • Her skin/hair is *oily*. • an *oily* fish • The salad dressing was very *oily*.

— oil·i·ness *noun* [*noncount*] • The skin cleanser helps reduce *oiliness*.

oink /ˈoɪŋk/ *noun, pl* **oinks** [*count*] **:** the sound made by a hog or pig

— oink *verb* **oinks; oinked; oink·ing** [*no obj*] • an *oinking* pig

oint·ment /ˈoɪntmənt/ *noun, pl* **-ments** [*count, noncount*] **:** a smooth substance that is rubbed on the skin to help heal a wound or to reduce pain or discomfort • You should put some *ointment* on that cut.

fly in the ointment see [3]FLY

OJ *abbr, US* orange juice

[1]**OK** *or* **okay** /oʊˈkeɪ/ *adv, informal*

1 a — used to ask for or express agreement, approval, or understanding • "I'm going to stay here, *OK*?" "Yes, that's fine." • "Let's eat out tonight." "*OK*. Where do you want to go?" • "Can we rent a video tonight?" "*OK*." • "I'll be there in a minute, *okay*?" **b** — used for emphasis at the beginning of a statement • *Okay* everybody, it's time to go now. • "Hurry up!" "*Okay, okay*, I'm almost ready." • *OK*, so I was wrong. I'm sorry.

2 : fairly well **:** well enough • "How did you do at the interview?" "I think I did *okay*." • He's doing *OK* in math.

[2]**OK** *or* **okay** *adj, informal*

1 : fairly good **:** not very good or very bad • She's an *OK* [=*fair*] player. • He's *okay* [=he is not bad] at math, but he really likes history. • The movie was just *OK*.

2 : acceptable or agreeable • Is it *OK* if I take tomorrow off? • Is she *OK* with the schedule change? • It's *okay* by me if you want to stay longer. • Is my dress *OK*? • It may be *OK* to do that sort of thing at home, but it isn't *OK* here.

3 *not used before a noun* **a :** not ill, hurt, unhappy, etc. • "Are you feeling *OK*? [=*well*]" "Yes, I'm fine." **b :** not marked by problems, danger, etc. • Don't worry. Everything will be *OK*. [=*all right*] • "I'm so sorry that I'm late." "It's/That's *OK*. We still have plenty of time." • "Are you *OK* for money?" "Yes, I have enough."

4 : likable, good, or honest • He seems like an *okay* [=*decent*] guy.

[3]**OK** *or* **okay** *verb* **OK's** *or* **okays; OK'd** *or* **okayed; OK'·ing** *or* **okay·ing** [+ *obj*] *informal* **:** to approve (something) **:** to say or decide that (something) will be allowed • The boss needs to *OK* this before we place the order. • Who *OK'd* your request?

[4]**OK** *or* **okay** *noun* [*singular*] *informal* **:** approval or permission • We need her *OK* on this before we place the order. • The boss gave his *okay*.

[5]**OK** *abbr* Oklahoma

okey·doke /ˌoʊkiˈdoʊk/ *or* **okey·do·key** /ˌoʊkiˈdoʊki/ *adv, informal*

1 — used to express agreement or approval • "I'll be there in a minute." "*Okeydoke*."

2 — used for emphasis at the beginning of a statement • "*Okeydoke* kids, it's time to clean up now."

okra /ˈoʊkrə/ *noun* [*noncount*] **:** a tall plant whose pods are eaten as a vegetable and are used in soups and stews; *also* **:** the pods of this plant

okra

[1]**old** /ˈoʊld/ *adj* **old·er; -est**

1 a : having lived for many years **:** not young • He's an *old* man now. • a little *old* lady • She was helping an *old* [=(more politely) *elderly*] woman cross the street. **b** — used to talk about or

O

ask about a person's age • He looks *old* for his age. [=he looks older than he really is] • She's *older* than she looks. [=she has a young appearance] • He's dating an *older* woman. [=a woman who is older than he is] • I wasn't *old* enough [=I was too young] to vote in the last election. • "How *old* is your daughter?" "She's almost six." • Their *oldest* [=*eldest*] child is 18 years *old*. • My sister's three years *older* than me. • She lived to the ***ripe old age*** of 85. • He joked that he was ***as old as the hills***. [=very old] **c : having a specified age** • He's 30 years *old*. • a nine-month-*old* baby

2 a : having existed or been in use for a long time : not new • We rented an *old* black-and-white movie. • *old* newspapers/magazines • a beautiful *old* house • There's an *old* saying that good fences make good neighbors. • an *old* family tradition • a new approach to an *old* problem • She wore a T-shirt and an *old* pair of jeans. • I wish you would stop wearing that dirty *old* hat! • The hotel was *old* and dingy. • the *oldest* known civilization in the region **b : having existed for a specified amount of time** • The house we live in is 50 years *old*. • a 400-year-*old* castle

3 *always used before a noun* **a : belonging to, used by, or known by someone in the past** • We went back to visit our *old* neighborhood. • I met one of my *old* [=*former*] professors at the library. • one of his *old* cars • I made a lot less money at my *old* job. • That's their *old* number. The new number is 555-4397. • She is now just a shadow of her *old* self. [=she is not the person she was in the past] **b — used to say that someone or something has been your friend, enemy, etc., for a long time** • I had lunch with an *old* friend of mine. [=a friend I have known for a very long time] • They're *old* enemies. • Spaghetti is an *old* favorite in our home.

4 *always used before a noun* **: done or experienced many times** • Do we have to go through that *old* routine again? • Grandpa tells the ***same old*** stories over and over again. • When she brought up the *same old* argument, I just stopped listening.

5 *informal* **— used for emphasis after adjectives like *big*, *good*, etc.** • We had a big *old* party in her honor. • You poor *old* thing. You must be exhausted! • ***Good old*** Joe. He's always helping people in need.

any old *informal* **— used to describe someone or something that is not special or specific** • I don't care where I sleep. *Any old* couch will do. • She won't drink *any old* tea; it has to be her favorite kind. • You'll have to park *any old* way [=any way] you can. • Give me beer over champagne ***any old day*** (of the week).

chip off the old block see [1]CHIP

for old times' sake see [1]SAKE

old boy/chap/man/etc. *Brit, old-fashioned* **— used to address a man** • Don't worry, *old chap*, it'll be all right. — see also OLD BOY

— see also GOOD OLD BOY

> ***synonyms*** OLD, ANCIENT, ANTIQUE, and ARCHAIC describe things that existed or were used in the past. OLD is the most common and general of these words and can refer to either the recent past or to the distant past. • This is one of my *old* sweaters. • The neighborhood has many *old* houses that were built more than 200 years ago. ANCIENT refers to things that happened or existed in the very distant past and that may or may not exist today. • an *ancient* custom • the *ancient* pyramids of Egypt ANTIQUE refers to things, such as toys, machines, and pieces of furniture, that have been kept from the past and that are often valuable. • She collects *antique* furniture. ARCHAIC refers to things, such as words or ways of behaving, that belong to a much earlier time and that are no longer used. • The play used *archaic* language to convey a sense of the past. • an *archaic* tradition

[2]old *noun, pl* **olds**

1 [*count*] **: a person who has a specified age — used in combination** • The game is suitable for six-year-*olds*. [=for children who are six years old] • Their 11-month-*old* has just learned how to walk. • 30-year-*olds*

2 ***old*** [*plural*] **: old people** • Young and *old* alike will enjoy the movie. — often used with ***the*** • *The old* [=(more commonly) *the elderly*] and the sick were helped first.

of old *formal + literary* **: in the past : in a time that was long ago** • in (the) days *of old* • (*Brit*) She's a friend who ***knows me of old***. [=has known me for a long time]

old age *noun* [*noncount*] **: the fact of being old** • She died of *old age*. **: the time of life when a person is old** • He's getting sweeter in his *old age*.

– old–age *adj, always used before a noun* • an *old-age* home • (*Brit*) He is eligible to receive an *old-age* pension.

old boy *noun, pl* **~ boys** [*count*]

1 *or* ***Old Boy*** *chiefly Brit* **: a person who went to a respected or well-known private school for boys** • an *Old Boys'* reunion — compare OLD GIRL

2 *chiefly Brit, informal* **: an old man** • The *old boy* had some trouble getting up the stairs.

old boy network *also* ***old boys' network*** *usually disapproving* **: an informal system in which wealthy men with the same social and educational background help each other** • He got his job through the *old boy network*.

— see also GOOD OLD BOY

old country *noun*

the old country **: the country where a person was born or lived before moving to a new country** • They left *the old country* more than 30 years ago. • This music reminds me of *the old country*.

olde /ˈould/ **— used as a variant spelling of "old" in the names of places, in advertisements, etc.** • Ye *Olde* Pub • merry *olde* England

old•en /ˈouldən/ *adj, always used before a noun* **: of or relating to a time in the distant past** • What was life like in the *olden* days? • stories of *olden* times

Old English *noun* [*noncount*] **: the English language before 1100** • *Old English* is very different from modern English. — called also *Anglo-Saxon*; compare MIDDLE ENGLISH

old–fash•ioned /ˈouldˈfæʃənd/ *adj* [*more ~; most ~*]

1 : of or relating to the past: such as a : no longer used or accepted : replaced by something more recent • an *old-fashioned* word • His views on the role of women in society are terribly *old-fashioned*. • Her clothes are so plain and *old-fashioned*. **b : typical of the past in a pleasing or desirable way** • *old-fashioned* courtesy and good manners • an *old-fashioned* love story • I feel like listening to some good *old-fashioned* rock 'n' roll. • She worked hard and became successful ***the old-fashioned way***.

2 *of a person* **: using or preferring traditions or ideas from the past** • She was an *old-fashioned* girl from a small town. • I'm rather *old-fashioned* when it comes to dating. — opposite MODERN

old girl *noun, pl* **~ girls** [*count*] *chiefly Brit*

1 *or* ***Old Girl*** **: a woman who went to a respected or well-known private school for girls** • an *Old Girls'* reunion — compare OLD BOY

2 *informal* **: an old woman** • The *old girl* had some trouble getting up the stairs.

Old Glory *noun* [*noncount*] **: the flag of the United States**

old–growth *adj, always used before a noun* **: of or relating to forests that have been growing for a long time** • *old-growth* forests • *old-growth* trees • *old-growth* timber

old guard *noun*

the old guard **: the usually older members of an organization (such as a political party) who do not want or like change** • She's not popular with *the old guard*. • (*US*) *The old guard* is stronger than ever. = (*Brit*) *The old guard* are stronger than ever.

old hand *noun, pl* **~ hands** [*count*] **: a person who has a lot of experience doing something** • He's an *old hand* at working on cars.

old hat *adj, not used before a noun* [*more ~; most ~*] **: seen or done many times and no longer interesting** • I suppose my favorite joke's a bit *old hat* by now. • Making hit movies is *old hat* for/to him.

old•ie /ˈouldi/ *noun, pl* **-ies** [*count*] *informal* **: someone or something that is not new** • This recipe's an *oldie* and a favorite in my family. • an *oldie* but goodie • (*Brit*) He's one of the *oldies* [=(*US*) *old-timers*] on the soccer team. — see also GOLDEN OLDIE

old lady *noun, pl* **~ -dies** [*count*] *informal*

1 : someone's wife or girlfriend • He cheated on his *old lady*.

2 : someone's mother • My *old lady* says I have to be home by eight.

old–line /ˈouldˈlaɪn/ *adj, always used before a noun* [*more ~; most ~*] *US*

1 a : having a good reputation because of the high quality of a service, product, etc., that has been provided for many years • We made sure he used an *old-line* law firm. • *old-line* wine producers **b : powerful and important in a society for a long time** • *old-line* Virginia families

2 : supporting traditional policies or practices : not encouraging or liking change within an organization • His more *old-*

O

line colleagues expressed their concern with the changes. • an *old-line* Democrat

old maid *noun, pl* ~ **maids** [*count*] *old-fashioned + disapproving* : a woman who has never been married and who is no longer young • In my generation, you were considered an *old maid* at 25.

old man *noun, pl* ~ **men** [*count*] *informal*
1 : someone's husband or boyfriend • I've been with my *old man* for 12 years now.
2 : someone's father • I used to work with your *old man*.

old master *or* **Old Master** *noun, pl* ~ **-ters** [*count*]
1 : a famous and highly skilled artist; *especially* : a famous painter of the 16th, 17th, or early 18th century • He is now recognized as one of the *Old Masters* of the Dutch school.
2 : a work of art created by an Old Master • their collection of *old masters*

old money *noun* [*noncount*] : people whose families have been rich for a long time • He comes from *old money*.
– **old money** *adj* • an *old money* family/neighborhood

Old Nick /ˈoʊldˈnɪk/ *noun, chiefly Brit, old-fashioned* — used as a name of the devil

old salt *noun, pl* ~ **salts** [*count*] *informal* : someone who has sailed for many years • An *old salt* told me tales about life in the navy.

old–school *adj* [*more* ~; *most* ~] *informal*
1 : typical of an earlier style or form • I mostly listen to *old-school* rap and hip-hop. • *old-school* comedians : based on a way of doing things that was common in the past • *old-school* [=*traditional*] values • *old-school* medicine
2 : using or supporting traditional practices • We had an *old-school* coach who made us run two miles every day.

old school *noun*
the old school : the people who support traditional policies and practices • a politician of *the old school*

old•ster /ˈoʊldstɚ/ *noun, pl* **-sters** [*count*] *informal* : an old person • active and lively *oldsters*

old–style *adj, always used before a noun* : typical of the past often in a pleasing way • I love the *old-style* elegance of those black-and-white movies. • *old-style* entertainment • *old-style* politicians

Old Testament *noun*
the Old Testament : the first part of the Christian Bible that tells about the Jews, their history, and God's words to them in the time before Jesus Christ was born — compare NEW TESTAMENT

old–time /ˈoʊldˈtaɪm/ *adj, always used before a noun*
1 : of a kind or style that was typical of the past • *old-time* songs • an *old-time* movie star • *old-time* religion • *old-time* liberalism
2 *US* : having been something specified for a long time : LONGTIME • They're *old-time* residents of the neighborhood. • an *old-time* rivalry

old–tim•er /ˈoʊldˈtaɪmɚ/ *noun, pl* **-ers** [*count*]
1 : a person who has a lot of experience : someone who has been a member of a company or organization for a long time • I've asked some of the *old-timers* to help train new workers.
2 *US* : an old person • It's good for *old-timers* like me to have young people around. • Only a few *old-timers* still speak the language. • How are you feeling today, *old-timer*?

old–timey /ˈoʊldˈtaɪmi/ *adj* [*more* ~; *most* ~] *US, informal* : of a kind or style that was popular in the past • There's an *old-timey* feel to their music. • *old-timey* folk music

old wives' tale *noun, pl* ~ **tales** [*count*] *disapproving* : a common belief about something that is not based on facts and that is usually false • Frogs won't give you warts. That's just an *old wives' tale*. • the *old wives' tale* about the full moon causing people to act crazy — compare SUPERSTITION

Old World *noun*
the Old World : Africa, Asia, and especially Europe • The animal is found throughout *the Old World*. — compare NEW WORLD

old–world /ˈoʊldˈwɚld/ *adj, always used before a noun* : old-fashioned or traditional in a way that pleasantly reminds you of the past • I like the restaurant's *old-world* elegance/charm.

ole /ˈoʊl/ — used to represent a very informal way of saying "old" • a big *ole* tractor • We had a fine *ole* time.

ole•an•der /ˈoʊliˌændɚ/ *noun, pl* **-ders** [*count, noncount*] : a bush with long, narrow leaves and white, pink, or yellow flowers

O level *noun, pl* **O levels** [*count*] *Brit* : a basic test in a particular subject taken by students in England, Wales, and Northern Ireland usually at the age of 18 — called also *Ordinary level*; compare A LEVEL, S LEVEL

ol•fac•to•ry /ɑlˈfæktəri/ *adj, technical* : of, relating to, or connected with the sense of smell • an *olfactory* stimulus

ol•i•garch /ˈɑːləˌgɑɚk/ *noun, pl* **-garchs** [*count*] *somewhat formal* : a person who belongs to a small group of people who govern or control a country, business, etc.

oli•gar•chy /ˈɑːləˌgɑɚki/ *noun, pl* **-chies**
1 [*count*] **a** : a country, business, etc., that is controlled by a small group of people • Their nation is an *oligarchy*. **b** : the people that control a country, business, etc. • An *oligarchy* rules their nation.
2 [*noncount*] : government or control by a small group of people • The corporation is ruled by *oligarchy*.

ol•ive /ˈɑːlɪv/ *noun, pl* **-ives**
1 [*count*] **a** : a small, egg-shaped black or green fruit that is used as food or for making oil • a sauce made with chopped *olives* **b** : a tree on which olives grow — called also *olive tree*
2 [*noncount*] : a yellowish-green color • Does the suit come in *olive*? — called also *olive green*; see color picture on page C2
– **olive** *adj* • She has *olive* skin. [=her skin has a yellowish-green tone to it] • He has an *olive* complexion.

olive branch *noun, pl* ~ **branch•es** [*count*] : something that is said or done to make peace or to show that you want peace : a symbol of peace • The winner ***extended/offered an olive branch*** to his opponent by calling him a great player.

olive drab *noun* [*noncount*] *chiefly US* : a grayish-green color • a shirt in *olive drab*; *also* : clothing of this color • The soldiers were dressed in *olive drab*.

olive green *noun* [*noncount*] : OLIVE 2

olive oil *noun, pl* ~ **oils** [*count, noncount*] : a yellow to yellowish-green oil that is made from olives and used in cooking • a teaspoon of *olive oil*

olive tree *noun, pl* ~ **trees** [*count*] : OLIVE 1b

Olym•pi•ad /əˈlɪmpiˌæd/ *noun, pl* **-ads** [*count*] : an occasion when the modern Olympics are held • the games of the 24th *Olympiad*

[1]**Olym•pi•an** /əˈlɪmpijən/ *noun, pl* **-ans** [*count*] : an athlete who competes in the Olympics • modern *Olympians*

[2]**Olympian** *adj, always used before a noun, formal* : like that of a god : very impressive, powerful, etc. • the *Olympian* heights of his disdain • an *Olympian* effort

Olym•pic /əˈlɪmpɪk/ *adj, always used before a noun* : of or relating to the Olympics • the U.S. *Olympic* team • She won an *Olympic* medal in diving. • an *Olympic* athlete

Olym•pics /əˈlɪmpɪks/ *noun*
the Olympics : a series of international athletic contests held in a different country once every four years — called also (*formal*) *the Olympic Games*

om•buds•man /ˈɑːmˌbudzmən/ *noun, pl* **-men** /-mən/ [*count*] : a person (such as a government official or an employee) who investigates complaints and tries to deal with problems fairly • The insurance company's *ombudsman* was able to resolve the problem. • The town's *ombudsman* said he would look into charges of corruption.

ome•ga /oʊˈmeɪgə, *Brit* ˈəʊmɪgə/ *noun, pl* **-gas** [*count*] : the 24th and last letter of the Greek alphabet — Ω or ω; see also ALPHA AND OMEGA

omega–3 /oʊˈmeɪgəˈθriː, *Brit* ˈəʊmɪgəˈθriː/ *noun, pl* **omega–3s** [*count, noncount*] : a type of fat that is good for your heart and is found in fish, green leafy vegetables, and some nuts — called also *omega-3 fatty acid*

om•e•let *or* **om•e•lette** /ˈɑːmlət/ *noun, pl* **-lets** *or* **-lettes** [*count*] : a dish made from eggs that are mixed together, cooked without stirring, and served folded in half often with a filling of cheese, vegetables, or meat

omen /ˈoʊmən/ *noun, pl* **omens** [*count*] : something that is believed to be a sign or warning of something that will happen in the future • a bad *omen* • They regarded the win as a good *omen* for the team. • *omens* of things to come

om•i•nous /ˈɑːmənəs/ *adj* [*more* ~; *most* ~] : suggesting that something bad is going to happen in the future • *ominous* clouds • an *ominous* threat of war • He spoke in *ominous* tones.
– **om•i•nous•ly** *adv* • A threat of war loomed *ominously*. • The sky was *ominously* dark.

omis•sion /oʊˈmɪʃən/ *noun, pl* **-sions**
1 [*count*] : something that has not been included or done

: something that has been omitted • There are a few *omissions* in the list/book.
2 [*noncount*] **a : the act of not including or doing something — often + *of*** • I believe that the *omission of* my name was intentional. **b : the state of being not included in something — often + *from*** • I am surprised by her *omission from* the team.

omit /oʊˈmɪt/ *verb* **omits; omit·ted; omit·ting** [+ *obj*]
1 : to leave out (someone or something) : to not include (someone or something) • Please don't *omit* any details. — often + *from* • They *omitted* your name *from* the list. • You can *omit* the salt *from* the recipe. • He has been *omitted from* the pool of candidates.
2 *formal* **: to fail to do (something) — followed by *to* + *verb*** • I *omitted* [=(more commonly) *neglected*] *to mention* that it was my fault. • They *omitted to tell* us the directions.

omni- *combining form* **: all : in all ways, places, etc. : without limits** • *omni*potent • *omni*present

[1]om·ni·bus /ˈɑːmnɪbəs/ *noun, pl* **-bus·es** [*count*] *old-fashioned* **: [1]BUS**

[2]omnibus *adj, always used before a noun, US* **: of, relating to, or including many things** • an *omnibus* edition of his more popular stories • an *omnibus* legislative bill

om·nip·o·tent /ɑmˈnɪpətənt/ *adj, formal* **: having complete or unlimited power : ALL-POWERFUL** • *omnipotent* gods • an *omnipotent* ruler/state
– **om·nip·o·tence** /ɑmˈnɪpətəns/ *noun* [*noncount*] • divine *omnipotence* • the *omnipotence* of God

om·ni·pres·ent /ˌɑːmnɪˈpreznt/ *adj, formal* **: present in all places at all times** • The problem is *omnipresent* and unavoidable.
– **om·ni·pres·ence** /ˌɑːmnɪˈprezns/ *noun* [*noncount*] • the *omnipresence* of poverty

om·ni·scient /ɑmˈnɪʃənt/ *adj, formal* **: knowing everything : having unlimited understanding or knowledge** • an *omniscient* deity • The novel has an *omniscient* narrator. [=a narrator who knows what all the characters are doing and thinking]
– **om·ni·science** /ɑmˈnɪʃəns/ *noun* [*noncount*] • the belief in divine *omniscience*

om·ni·vore /ˈɑːmnɪˌvoɚ/ *noun, pl* **-vores** [*count*] *technical* **: an animal that eats both plants and other animals — sometimes used to refer to people** • I'm an *omnivore*—I'll eat anything.

om·niv·o·rous /ɑmˈnɪvərəs/ *adj* [*more* ~; *most* ~]
1 : eating both plants and animals • *omnivorous* animals
2 : eager to learn about many different things • She is an *omnivorous* reader. • a child with *omnivorous* curiosity

[1]on /ˈɑːn/ *prep*
1 a : touching and being supported by the top surface of (something) • The book is (lying) *on* the table. • There is a lot of frosting *on* the cake. **b : to a position that is supported by (something)** • You can get *on* [=*onto*] the horse as soon as we've put the saddle *on* it. • I climbed out *on* [=*onto*] the roof. **c — used to indicate the part or object by which someone or something is supported** • How long can you stand *on* one foot? • He stood *on* the stool. • He was *on* his hands and knees looking for her earring.
2 — used to say that something is attached to something • He hung the painting *on* the wall. • Apples hung *on* the branches.
3 — used to indicate where someone or something is hit or touched • I bumped my head *on* a low branch. • He slapped me *on* the hand. • She kissed him *on* the cheek.
4 a — used to indicate the surface or part where something is seen or located • There are marks *on* the wall. • I have a cut *on* my finger. **b — used to say that something (such as jewelry) is being worn by someone** • the ring *on* her finger
5 : near or close to (something or someone) • a village *on* [=*by*] the sea
6 — used to indicate the location or position of something or someone • Our house is *on* the left. • There is a garden *on* the side of the house. • We saw cows and chickens *on* the farm. • He lives *on* Main Street. • *on* page 102 in/of the book • Which side is it *on*?
7 — used to indicate the time when something happened or will happen • We met *on* July 24th. • *On* my way home [=while I was going home], I saw a car accident. • (*formal*) *On* the morning of July 24th, the suspect left his house at 8:15 a.m. • I would like the report ***on or before*** July 24th. • The TV station gives news ***every hour on the hour***. [=at 6:00, 7:00, 8:00, etc.] • The project was finished ***on schedule/time***. [=when it was supposed to be finished]
8 : immediately after (something) • What was your first reaction *on* hearing the news? [=when you heard the news] • You'll be required to pay *on* delivery of the package. [=when the package is delivered]
9 — used to indicate the subject of something • a book *on* [=*about*] North American birds • a discussion *on* current events • Let's reflect *on* [=*upon*] the poem for a moment. • a test *on* parts of speech
10 a — used to indicate the device or instrument that is used to do something • He played a couple songs *on* the piano. • He cut his foot *on* a piece of broken glass. **b — used to say that someone is using a telephone, computer, etc.** • They talked *on* the phone for hours. • She was *on* the phone when I went to her office. • He has been *on* the computer all night. **c — used to describe the device, system, etc., that is used for seeing something, hearing something, etc.** • It's the best show *on* television. • I heard that song *on* the radio. • the display *on* the computer screen • a Web site *on* the Internet • I have the movie *on* DVD.
11 — used to indicate a source of something (such as money, food, information, or energy) • She lives *on* a small salary. • The family lives *on* welfare. • They make their living *on* [=*off*] tourism. • They profited *on* [=*from*] the sale of the house. • The animal feeds *on* insects. • I lived *on* cereal [=I ate a lot of cereal regularly] in my college years. • The machine runs *on* diesel fuel. • The story is based *on* fact.
12 — used to indicate the vehicle or animal by which someone or something is moved from one place to another • I sometimes go to work *on* a bus. [=I sometimes take a bus to get to work] • Have you ever ridden *on* a horse?
13 — used to say that you have something in your possession at a particular time • I only have $10 *on* me. • He had a knife *on* him.
14 — used to indicate the state of something • The house is *on* fire! • House sales are ***on the rise***. [=are rising] • All shoes are ***on sale***.
15 — used to indicate an activity that someone did or is now doing • She did well *on* the exam/test. • The band is currently *on* tour. • He is off/away *on* a trip/vacation. • She is *on* a diet. • The officers are *on* duty.
16 — used to indicate something (such as a medicine or drug) that a person or animal is using • He used to be *on* drugs, but he's off them now. • (*informal*) What (drugs) is she *on*? • They put the dog *on* antibiotics.
17 — used to indicate the person or thing that is responsible for something • The drinks are *on* me. [=I will pay for the drinks] • They blamed it *on* me. [=they said it was my fault]
18 a — used to indicate the person or thing that something is directed toward • The deadline was creeping up *on* us. [=the deadline was getting closer] • an attack *on* religion • He is working *on* [=*at*] his skiing. • They are still working *on* the problem. • They made a down payment *on* the house. • He pulled a gun *on* me. • He turned his back *on* her and walked away. • a ban *on* smoking • Her eyes were *on* the road. [=she was watching the road] **b — used to say that someone has been affected by something** • The crops died *on* them. • Her husband walked out *on* her.
19 — used after an adjective to indicate the thing that a statement relates to • I am short *on* cash. [=I don't have much cash] • Opinions are divided *on* this issue. • (*Brit*) Sales are up *on* last year's but down *on* those of previous years.
20 : as stated or shown by (someone or something) • I have it *on* good authority [=a trustworthy person has told me] that the company will be relocating. • (*Brit*) *On* [=*according to*] these estimates, we'll be out of debt soon.
21 — used to indicate that someone or something is included as part of a team, list, etc. • She served *on* the jury/committee/board. • He is *on* the team. • That dish is no longer *on* the menu. • His name was *on* the list.
22 — used to say that someone or something has an advantage • She has three inches in height *on* me. [=she is three inches taller than I am] • The team has a 3-game lead *on* last year's champions. • She is very talented but ***has nothing on*** [=has no advantage over] her brother who is an even better singer.
23 *chiefly US* **— used to say that someone is playing or performing well** • He is *on* his game. [=he is playing very well]

on about *Brit, informal + disapproving* **: talking about** • I haven't a clue what you're *on about*! • She is always *on about* the importance of exercise.

on at *Brit, informal* **1 : asking (someone) for something repeatedly and in a way that is annoying** • She is always *on at* him for money. **2 : asking or telling (someone) to do something repeatedly and in a way that is annoying** ▪ Mummy's always *on at* me about cleaning up my room!

on it **: actively dealing with a problem, job, etc.** ▪ "We need to get this paperwork done." "Don't worry; ***I'm on it.***" [=I am taking care of it]

²on *adv*

1 a — used to indicate that something is attached to, covering, or supported by something else ▪ Put the lid *on.* ▪ I'll steady the horse while you get *on.* ▪ She put *on* her glasses to read the letter. ▪ Keep the tablecloth *on.* **b — used to describe something that is being worn by someone** ▪ He put *on* his coat and went outside. ▪ You can keep your shoes *on.* ▪ What did he have *on*? [=what was he wearing?] ▪ He had *on* a black shirt and jeans.

2 — used to indicate movement forward ▪ The car stopped and then drove *on.* ▪ We traveled *on* to the next town. ▪ The boys went *on* home.

3 a — used to indicate that an activity, event, or condition continues ▪ The argument went *on* for weeks. ▪ He worked *on* without a break. ▪ Please read *on* for information about our products. ▪ The teams played *on* in the snow. ▪ She rambled *on* (and *on*) about her lazy husband. ▪ ***From now on*** [=from this point in time forward], be sure to double-check your answers. ▪ ***From here on (out)***, things should get easier. = ***From this point on***, things should get easier. **b : in an advanced state** ▪ We're far/well *on* with/in our project. **c : at a more advanced time : at a later time** ▪ I'll come by to help you later *on.*

4 : from one person or thing to another ▪ Pass the word/note *on.* ▪ The tradition has been passed/handed *on* [=*down*] through the years. ▪ Let's move/go *on* to the next point.

5 a — used to indicate that something is operating, flowing, etc. ▪ He switched the light *on* to read. ▪ The lights came *on.* ▪ Turn the water/TV *on.* **b — used to indicate that something is being heated, prepared, etc.** ▪ I'll put the kettle/tea/coffee *on* (to boil). [=I will put the kettle/tea/coffee on the stove to make it warmer] ▪ I've got coffee *on*, if you're interested.

6 : in or into a train, bus, etc. ▪ She got *on* at the last station.

on and off see ¹OFF

³on *adj*

1 ***not used before a noun*** **: attached to or covering something** ▪ The lid is *on* tight.

2 ***not used before a noun*** **: performing or speaking in public** ▪ The band will be *on* in 10 minutes. ▪ Mr. President, you are *on* in two minutes. [=you will be giving your speech in two minutes]

3 ***not used before a noun*** **: working at a job** ▪ He is *on* tomorrow from 6 a.m to 6 p.m.

4 a ***not used before a noun*** **: operating or flowing** ▪ The radio/water/electricity is *on.* **b : in a position that starts the flow of electricity, water, etc.** ▪ The switch is *on.* ▪ The lever is in the *on* position.

5 ***not used before a noun*** **a : taking place or happening** ▪ The deal/game is *on.* ▪ (*Brit*) We do not have anything *on* [=*planned*] this weekend. **b : doing something as planned** ▪ Are we still *on* for dinner tomorrow? [=are we still having dinner tomorrow, as we planned to do?]

6 ***not used before a noun*** **: being broadcast on television or radio** ▪ The show is *on* at 8 p.m. ▪ The game is *on* tonight. ▪ My favorite show is *on.*

7 ***not used before a noun, chiefly US*** **— used to say that you are able to do something well at a particular time** ▪ My golf game was off yesterday, but it/I was *on* today. [=I played well today]

not on ***Brit, informal*** **1 : not acceptable or proper** ▪ Cheating old ladies out of their savings just ***isn't on.*** [=is not acceptable] **2 : not possible** ▪ I'm afraid that scheme's just *not on.*

you're on ***informal*** **— used to say that you accept a bet or challenge** ▪ "I bet I can run faster than you can." "OK, *you're on.*"

on–again, off–again *adj, chiefly US* **: happening or existing at some times and not at other times** ▪ *on-again, off-again* fads ▪ She has been his *on-again, off-again* girlfriend for the past several years. [=she has been his girlfriend at certain times and not been his girlfriend at other times during the past several years]

on–air *adj* **: appearing, used, or done on a radio or television broadcast** ▪ an *on-air* telephone call ▪ our live, *on-air* fundraiser

on·board /ˈɑːnˈboɚd/ *adj, always used before a noun* **: carried or happening on a vehicle** ▪ The car comes with an *onboard* computer. ▪ *onboard* electronics/systems

¹once /ˈwʌns/ *adv*

1 : one time only ▪ I will repeat the question *once.* ▪ We try to get together (at least) *once* every month. ▪ The play was performed ***only once.*** ▪ He had ridden a horse *only once* (before). ▪ We go to the movies ***once or twice*** a month. [=we go to the movies a few times a month] ▪ I've only seen her *once or twice.* [=I have only seen her a few times]

2 : at any one time : EVER ▪ She didn't *once* thank me. ▪ He didn't look at me *once.*

3 : at some time in the past ▪ It was *once* done that way. ▪ A river *once* flowed through this canyon. ▪ It was *once* a booming mining town. ▪ Their music was *once* very popular. **— sometimes used in combination** ▪ a *once*-successful actor ▪ a *once*-popular restaurant

once again/more **: for another time : one more time : AGAIN** ▪ Let me explain the problem *once again.* ▪ *Once again*, you've ignored my instructions. ▪ Could I hear the question *once more*?

once and for all **: now and for the last time** ▪ Let's settle this problem *once and for all.* ▪ Winning its fourth straight championship game, the team proved *once and for all* that they are the best. ▪ I'm asking you *once and for all.* ▪ Please, *once and for all*, stop worrying.

once bitten, twice shy see ¹BITE

once in a blue moon see BLUE MOON

once in a while **: sometimes but not often : OCCASIONALLY** ▪ We spend most of our time at home and go out *once in a while.* ▪ ***Every once in a while***, we have wine with dinner.

once upon a time **: at some time in the past** ▪ He was a famous actor *once upon a time.* ✧ ***Once upon a time*** **is the traditional way to begin a fairy tale.** ▪ *Once upon a time*, there was a beautiful princess named Snow White.

²once *noun* [*noncount*] **: one single time** ▪ I have tried Indian food more than *once.* ▪ Please be on time ***just this once.*** ▪ ***For once*** you seem to know what I'm talking about.

at once **1 : at the same time** ▪ two people talking *at once* ▪ The book is *at once* [=*both*] funny and sad. ▪ She had several projects going on ***all at once.*** **2 : right away : without delay : IMMEDIATELY** ▪ We need to leave *at once.* ▪ You can call the office and get advice *at once.*

³once *conj* **: at the moment when : as soon as** ▪ Things got better *once* he found a job. = *Once* he found a job, things got better. ▪ *Once* she spoke, I recognized her.

once–over /ˌwʌnsˈoʊvɚ/ *noun* [*singular*] **: a quick look or examination** ▪ The paper got a *once-over* before he turned it in. ▪ I saw him ***giving me a/the once-over.*** [=I saw him looking at me]

on·col·o·gy /ɑnˈkɑːləʤi/ *noun* [*noncount*] *medical* **: the study and treatment of cancer and tumors**

— on·col·o·gist /ɑnˈkɑːləʤɪst/ *noun, pl* **-gists** [*count*] ▪ He is studying to be an *oncologist.*

on·com·ing /ˈɑːnˌkʌmɪŋ/ *adj, always used before a noun* **: coming closer to you : coming toward you** ▪ an *oncoming* car ▪ the *oncoming* traffic

on–demand *adj, always used before a noun* **: available when needed or wanted** ▪ My cable company offers *on-demand* service/movies. **— see also** *on demand* at ¹DEMAND

¹one /ˈwʌn/ *noun, pl* **ones**

1 [*count*] **: the number 1** ▪ *one*, two, three, four, . . .

2 [*count*] *US* **: a one-dollar bill** ▪ I don't have any *ones.* Can you break a five?

3 [*noncount*] **: one o'clock** ▪ I'll be there at *one.*

4 [*count*] **: the first in a set or series** ▪ On day *one* of his diet, he cut out sweets. ▪ She wears a size *one.*

as one ***formal*** **1 : at the same time : all together** ▪ They rose *as one* and cheered her. **2 : in agreement with each other** ▪ We are *as one* on this issue.

at one with **1 : in a peaceful state as a part of something else** ▪ I feel *at one with* nature. [=I feel very closely connected to nature] **2** ***formal*** **: in a state of agreement with another person** ▪ I am *at one with* you on this issue.

for one **: as an example** ▪ I, *for one*, disagree. [=I disagree] ▪ There were many spelling mistakes in the essay. "There" for "their," *for one.*

in one **: combined in a single thing** ▪ a dictionary and thesaurus ***(all) in one*** ▪ a DVD and VCR player *in one*

the odd one out see ¹ODD

²one *pronoun*

1 : that person or thing ▪ "I'll have an iced tea, please." "I'll have *one*, too." ▪ Their dog died, but they plan to get another *one*. ▪ "You should wear the blue *one*." "The *one* with the stripes?" "No, the other *one*." ▪ I'd like to see the ring next to that *one*. ▪ Which *one* did you like better? ▪ He is the *one* who called the police. ▪ Have you heard ***the one about*** [=the joke about] the priest and the rabbi? ▪ That's one possible answer—but not the ***only one***. ▪ He had ***one too many*** at the bar last night. [=he had too many alcoholic drinks at the bar] ✧ This sense of *one* can be used in the plural form *ones*. ▪ The *ones* on the team who are most successful practice every day. ▪ Those batteries are the *ones* that still work.

2 : someone or something that is a part of a particular group — + *of* ▪ I met *one of* your friends at the party. ▪ She is *one of* the best players on the team. ▪ *One of* the puppies has a brown patch around its eye. ▪ He'll come back ***one of these days***. [=*someday*] ▪ Don't worry—he's ***one of us***. [=he is part of our group and can be trusted]

3 a *somewhat formal* **:** people in general : any person ▪ *One* never knows [=(more commonly) you never know] what the weather will be. ▪ It is now possible to buy just about anything from the privacy of *one's* [=(more commonly) *your*] own home. **b** *Brit, old-fashioned* **:** I or we ▪ I would like to read more, but *one* doesn't have the time.

one after another see ²ANOTHER

one and all *old-fashioned* **:** EVERYONE ▪ Merry Christmas to *one and all*.

one by one **:** separately in a series ▪ The performers took the stage *one by one*.

one in a million see MILLION

there's one born every minute see BORN

— see also NO ONE

³one *adj*

1 *always used before a noun* **:** having the value of 1 ▪ There is *one* minute left in the game. ▪ I have a few *one*-dollar bills in my purse. ▪ She is *one* year old.

2 *always used before a noun* — used to refer to a single person or thing ▪ There is *one* cookie left. ▪ Let's take it *one* day at a time. [=let's not think or plan too far ahead] ▪ My *one* [=*only, sole*] concern is for your safety. ▪ We need to keep all the tools in *one* [=the same] place. ▪ He was the *one* (and only) person she wanted to marry. ▪ He caught the ball *one*-handed. ▪ a *one*-parent [=single-parent] family ▪ There is ***only/just one*** more thing to do. ▪ I could not solve ***one or two*** [=*a few*] problems on the test. ▪ ***Not one*** person knew the answer. [=no one knew the answer]

3 a — used before a noun to indicate that someone or something is part of a group of similar people or things ▪ She is *one* singer who I would like to see in concert. ▪ early *one* morning ▪ The Grand Canyon is *one* place I'd like to visit. ▪ That's *one* possible solution. ▪ I don't like being around him. ***For one thing***, he smokes. ▪ The ***one thing*** I hate most is being lied to. ▪ ***It's one thing*** to understand the problem, but another thing to actually fix it. **b** *chiefly US, informal* — used to emphasize a description ▪ She is *one* tough lady. [=she's a tough lady] ▪ That is *one* ugly dog. ▪ That was *one* great party.

4 *always used before a noun* **:** not known exactly **:** SOME ▪ I'll see you again *one* day soon. ▪ He'll come back *one* day. ▪ At *one* time or another/other, the building was a school.

5 — used to indicate that two or more people or things are actually the same person or are the same kind of thing ▪ The writer and her main character are *one*. ▪ "Puma" and "cougar" are different names for *one* animal. ▪ The writer and her main character are ***one and the same***.

6 *formal* — used before a name to indicate that you do not know the person specified ▪ *One* Ms. Jones called this morning. [=a woman named Ms. Jones called this morning]

7 *not used before a noun* **:** in agreement with each other ▪ You and I are *one* on this issue.

the one and only — used before the name of a famous person to say that there is no one else like that person ▪ *the one and only* Elvis Presley

one another *pronoun* **:** each of two or more people, animals, etc., who are doing something together or in relationship to the other or others in the group ▪ We shared our thoughts with *one another*. [=*each other*]

one–armed bandit /ˈwʌnˈɑɚmd-/ *noun, pl* ~ **-dits** [*count*] *informal* **:** SLOT MACHINE

one–dimensional *adj, disapproving* **:** simple and uninteresting ▪ The novel's characters were *one-dimensional*.

one–hand•ed /ˈwʌnˈhændəd/ *adj* **:** done using only one hand ▪ a *one-handed* catch

— **one–handed** *adv* ▪ She caught the ball *one-handed*.

one–hit wonder *noun, pl* ~ **-ders** [*count*] **:** a performer, group, etc., that is popular or successful only once for a brief time ▪ She was a *one-hit wonder*. [=she had only one hit song, movie, etc.]

one–horse /ˈwʌnˈhoɚs/ *adj, always used before a noun*

1 *informal* **:** small and dull ▪ He grew up in a little ***one-horse town***.

2 : pulled by one horse ▪ a *one-horse* wagon/buggy

one–lin•er /ˌwʌnˈlaɪnɚ/ *noun, pl* **-ers** [*count*] **:** a very short joke or funny remark

one–man *adj, always used before a noun*

1 : done, performed, or controlled by one person ▪ a *one-man* job/show/play/business ▪ This is strictly a *one-man* operation.

2 : designed for one person ▪ a *one-man* kayak/tent

one–man band *noun, pl* ~ **bands** [*count*]

1 : a musician who plays several instruments at the same time

2 : a person who is responsible for or does several tasks alone ▪ Our receptionist is a *one-man band*.

one•ness /ˈwʌnnəs/ *noun* [*singular*] **:** the state of being completely united with or a part of someone or something — usually + *with* ▪ I felt a sense of *oneness with* nature. ▪ a feeling of spiritual *oneness with* others

one–night stand *noun, pl* ~ **stands** [*count*]

1 : a situation in which you have sex with someone once and you do not continue in a relationship afterwards ▪ I really hope this wasn't just a *one-night stand*.; *also* **:** one of the people involved in this situation ▪ She was a *one-night stand*. I haven't seen her since.

2 : a performance of a play, concert, etc., that is given only once in a particular place

one–note /ˈwʌnˈnoʊt/ *adj, always used before a noun* **:** boring because it does not change ▪ Critics disliked his *one-note* performance as the movie's villain.

one–off /ˌwʌnˈɑːf/ *adj, always used before a noun, chiefly Brit* **:** done or happening only once ▪ *one-off* gigs/events ▪ a *one-off* cost/payment

— **one–off** *noun, pl* **-offs** [*count*] ▪ The event is a *one-off*.

one–on–one /ˌwʌnɑnˈwʌn/ *adj* **:** involving two people who are dealing with or competing against each other directly ▪ a *one-on-one* meeting/discussion ▪ a *one-on-one* defense/competition ▪ *one-on-one* tutoring

— **one–on–one** *adv* ▪ I'd like to talk with you *one-on-one*. ▪ They will compete *one-on-one* for the championship.

one–piece *adj, always used before a noun* **:** consisting of a single piece ▪ a *one-piece* bathing suit

— **one–piece** *noun, pl* **-pieces** [*count*] ▪ She prefers *one-pieces* to bikinis.

oner•ous /ˈɑːnərəs/ *adj* [*more* ~; *most* ~] *formal* **:** difficult and unpleasant to do or deal with ▪ an *onerous* chore/duty/task ▪ The government imposed *onerous* taxes on imports.

one•self /ˌwʌnˈsɛlf/ *pronoun, formal*

1 — used as the object of a verb or preposition when *one* is the stated subject or is understood to be the subject ▪ One can easily teach *oneself* how to sew. ▪ It is not wrong to congratulate *oneself*. ▪ when one discovers how different others are from *oneself* ▪ One usually associates with people of the same age as *oneself*. ▪ It is important to have good feelings about *oneself*.

2 — used for emphasis to refer again to the subject when *one* is the subject ▪ If one does not have the information *oneself*, one can ask others.

one–shot /ˈwʌnˌʃɑːt/ *adj, always used before a noun, chiefly US, informal* **:** done or happening only once ▪ a *one-shot* tax cut ▪ a *one-shot* offer/deal

— **one–shot** *noun, pl* **-shots** [*count*] ▪ These tax cuts are strictly *one-shots*.

one–sid•ed /ˈwʌnˈsaɪdəd/ *adj*

1 *disapproving* **:** showing only one opinion or point of view ▪ Their interpretation of the study's results seems *one-sided*. ▪ His book presents a somewhat *one-sided* [=*biased*] view of the issue.

2 : led or controlled by one of the two people or groups involved ▪ Our conversation was very *one-sided*: Mom talked, and I listened. ▪ The game has been *one-sided* so far with the home team winning six to nothing.

— **one–sid•ed•ness** *noun* [*noncount*] ▪ The *one-sidedness* of the game made it very boring.

one–stop /ˈwʌnˈstɑːp/ *adj, always used before a noun* **:** providing or offering many different types of goods or services at one location ▪ a *one-stop* shop for office furniture and supplies ▪ *one-stop* shopping

one·time /ˈwʌnˈtaɪm/ *adj, always used before a noun*
1 : having been someone or something specified in the past **:** FORMER ▪ a *onetime* actor now turned singer
2 : done or happening only once ▪ a *onetime* offer/deal

one–to–one /ˌwʌntəˈwʌn/ *adj*
1 : involving two people who are dealing with each other directly ▪ We had a *one-to-one* meeting.
2 *formal* **:** perfectly matching one thing in a group to another thing in another group ▪ There was a *one-to-one* correspondence between the number of times the bell rang and the number of times the dog barked.
– one–to–one *adv* ▪ a mentor who advises *one-to-one* and in groups

one–track *adj, always used before a noun* **:** continuously thinking about only one particular subject ▪ You've got ***a one-track mind.***

one–trick pony *noun, pl* ~ **ponies** [*count*] *chiefly US, informal*
1 : someone or something that is skilled in only one area ▪ As a knitter, I'm a *one-trick pony*: I can only knit scarves.
2 : someone or something that has success only once ▪ a musician who was a *one-trick pony* and then faded away

one–two /ˈwʌnˈtuː/ *noun* [*singular*] **:** a combination of two quick punches in boxing ▪ He knocked him out with the old *one-two* (punch/combo). — often used figuratively to describe two bad things that happen very close together or at the same time ▪ Yesterday's earthquakes dealt the city a ***one-two punch.***

one up *adj, not used before a noun, informal* **:** having an advantage over someone **:** in a position that is better than someone else's position — usually + *on* ▪ He's a good artist, which puts him *one up on* most of his classmates. ▪ You're *one up on* me.

one–up /ˌwʌnˈʌp/ *verb* **-ups; -upped; -up·ping** [+ *obj*] *US, informal* **:** to get an advantage over (someone) ▪ They're always trying to *one-up* each other by buying the latest gadgets.

one–up·man·ship /ˌwʌnˈʌpmənˌʃɪp/ *noun* [*noncount*] **:** behavior in which someone tries to get an advantage by doing, saying, or having better things than someone else ▪ a round of verbal *one-upmanship*

one–way *adj*
1 a : moving in or allowing movement in only one direction ▪ *one-way* traffic ▪ a *one-way* street/valve ▪ This street is just *one-way.* — compare TWO-WAY, THREE-WAY **b** *US* **:** allowing travel to a place but not back from the place ▪ a *one-way* [=(*Brit*) *single*] ticket/fare/trip — compare ROUND TRIP
2 : able to receive signals but not to send signals ▪ a *one-way* radio — compare TWO-WAY
3 : controlled by one of the two people who are involved ▪ a *one-way* [=*one-sided*] conversation ▪ a *one-way* relationship — compare TWO-WAY, THREE-WAY

one–way mirror *noun, pl* ~ **-rors** [*count*] **:** a piece of glass that is a mirror on one side but that you can see through like a window from the other side — called also *two-way mirror*

one–woman *adj, always used before a noun* **:** done, performed, or controlled by one woman ▪ a *one-woman* job/show/play/business

on·go·ing /ˈɑːnˌgowɪŋ/ *adj* **:** continuing to exist, happen, or progress **:** continuing without reaching an end ▪ The investigation is *ongoing.* ▪ the *ongoing* events at the school ▪ *ongoing* efforts/research to find a cure for the disease ▪ an *ongoing* problem ▪ There is an *ongoing* debate over the issue.

on·ion /ˈʌnjən/ *noun, pl* **-ions :** a round vegetable that is usually white, yellow, or red and has a strong smell and taste [*count*] The recipe calls for chopped *onions.* ▪ He is growing *onions* in the garden this year. [*noncount*] The recipe calls for chopped *onion.* — see color picture on page C4; see also GREEN ONION

onion ring *noun, pl* ~ **rings** [*count*] **:** a ring of sliced onion that is covered with batter or bread crumbs and fried

on·line /ˈɑːnˌlaɪn/ *adj*
1 : connected to a computer, a computer network, or the Internet ▪ an *online* printer ▪ The city libraries are all *online.*
2 : done over the Internet ▪ He likes to engage in *online* chats/discussions. ▪ *online* shopping/banking ▪ the company's *online* sales — opposite OFF-LINE
– online *adv* ▪ people who shop/chat *online* ▪ I went *online* to do a search for information about new cars. ▪ She spends a lot of her free time *online.*

on·look·er /ˈɑːnˌlʊkɚ/ *noun, pl* **-ers** [*count*] **:** a person who watches an activity or event without being involved in it ▪ Curious *onlookers* watched the ceremony. ▪ An *onlooker* noticed the disturbance. ▪ A crowd of *onlookers* gathered at the fire.

¹on·ly /ˈounli/ *adj, always used before a noun* **:** alone in a class or category **:** existing with no other or others of the same kind — usually used with *the* or a possessive (such as *my, her, its, their, John's,* etc.) ▪ He's *the only* [=*one*] man I've ever loved. ▪ They were *the only* people to survive the crash. ▪ You're not *the only* one who's worried about the future. [=other people are also worried about the future] ▪ You're *the only* person I trust. ▪ my *only* true friend ▪ He was her *only* brother. ▪ What a shame, your party is on *the only* day I can't come! ▪ Mondays are Kim's *only* days off from work. ▪ This is *the only* cleaning product you'll ever need! ▪ Keeping you safe is our *only* [=*sole*] concern. ▪ That was *the only* reason I didn't take the job. ▪ *The only* way out is through that window. ▪ It's *the only* possible answer. = It's *the only* answer possible. ▪ *The only* thing left for us to do is wait. [=there is nothing else we can do but wait] ▪ (informally) I can probably come Friday. ***The only thing*** [=the one problem] is that my car is in the shop. ▪ It's ***the first and only*** drug of its kind. — see also ONLY CHILD, *the one and only* at ³ONE
***one of the only* :** one of very few **:** one in a small class or category ▪ That was *one of the only* times I ever saw my father cry. ▪ This is *one of the only* places in the world where the plant is found.
the only — used to emphasize that a particular person or thing should be the one chosen; usually + *for* ▪ This is *the only* book *for* serious collectors. ▪ She's *the only* person *for* the job.

²only *adv*
1 a : no more than ▪ They lost *only* [=*just, merely*] one game this season. ▪ I've met him *only* once. = I've *only* met him once. ▪ She had been there *only* twice in her life. ▪ We have *only* five minutes to get there. = We *only* have five minutes to get there. ▪ There are *only* two more weeks until summer vacation. ▪ It's *only* a matter of time before someone gets hurt. ▪ Do you really have to leave? It's *only* eight o'clock. ▪ He was *only* a baby when his father died. ▪ Leave her alone. She's *only* a kid. ▪ The building is *only* about 10 years old. ▪ She plays several instruments including the guitar, violin, and piano, to name *only* [=*but*] a few. ▪ It was quiet in the room, but *only* for a moment. ▪ She is *only* partly/partially to blame. **b :** nothing other than — used to indicate that a single thing was done, is needed, is possible, etc. ▪ I asked him a question, but he *only* smiled in response. ▪ I'm happy to help. You *only* have/need to ask. = (more formally) You have *only* to ask. = (more formally) You need *only* ask. [=I will gladly help you if you ask me to] ▪ We can *only* guess/imagine/wonder [=we cannot know] what they will do next. ▪ One can *only* hope for the best. [=there is nothing to do but hope for the best] **c** — used for emphasis ▪ ***I only wish*** [=I wish very much] you'd told me sooner. ▪ I ***only hope*** that the mistake will be corrected soon. ▪ It's ***only natural*** [=it's normal/reasonable] (that) you would feel that way. — sometimes used in the phrase ***only just*** ▪ We *only just* missed the bus. [=we missed it by a very small amount of time; we almost caught the bus] ▪ Our trip had *only just* begun.
2 : excluding all others ▪ The club is for women *only.* ▪ The sign on the door says "Employees *Only.*" ▪ *Only* employees can use that door. **:** nobody or nothing except ▪ I love *only* you and no one else. ▪ She said *only* that she knew him. [=she said nothing other than that she knew him] ▪ The storm destroyed the house leaving *only* a pile of rubble. ▪ That sound can mean *only* one thing. = That sound can *only* mean one thing. ▪ *Only* the strongest will survive. ▪ *Only* the best fabric will do. [=I want nothing except the best fabric] ▪ The restaurant serves *only* vegetarian cuisine. ▪ For reasons known *only* to her/herself, she sold her house and left town.
3 a : in no time, place, or situation except the one specified ▪ Violence should be used *only* as a last resort. = Violence should *only* be used as a last resort. ▪ It should be used *only* when (it's) absolutely necessary. ▪ *Only* then did I realize that I had made a mistake. ▪ The animal is found *only* on the continent of Australia. ▪ *Only* in America can such things happen! [=such things cannot happen anywhere but in America] ▪ The drug is available *only* by prescription. = The drug is available by prescription *only.* ▪ I'll go ***only if*** he goes with me. = (more strongly) I'll go ***if and only if*** he goes with me. ▪ We made the change ***only after*** careful consideration of the consequences. **b :** for no other reason than ▪ I came here

O

only because she asked me to. ▪ *only* for the sake of argument **4 :** nothing more important or serious than ▪ It was *only* [=*just, merely*] a minor accident. No one got hurt. ▪ I'm fine. It's *only* a scratch. ▪ "Who was that on the phone?" "Oh, it was *only* a salesperson." ▪ I didn't hit him. I *only* touched him! ▪ She didn't mean to insult you. She was *only* joking! ▪ They were *only* following orders.

5 — used to emphasize that something happened recently ▪ It happened *only* [=*just*] last week. ▪ I saw her here *only* a moment ago. ▪ *Only* in the last few years have we come to understand the condition. ▪ It seems like *only* yesterday that you were a baby.

6 a — used to say that something has or will have a particular and usually bad result ▪ You shouldn't eat that. It will *only* make you sick. ▪ The large number of people who came to help *only* added to the confusion. **b** — used to indicate something bad or surprising that happens after something else; followed by *to + verb* ▪ They won the battle, *only to lose* the war. [=they won the battle but lost the war] ▪ I ran to the station *only to find* (that) I had missed the train.

for your eyes only see [1]EYE

if only see [1]IF

in name only see [1]NAME

not only — used to say that both of two related statements are true ▪ *Not only* did they win, they won by a landslide. ▪ The killing of these animals is *not only* illegal, it's also immoral. ▪ The game is *not only* lots of fun, it's educational too! ▪ Photographs are *not only* permitted, they are encouraged. ▪ I'm concerned ***not only*** for myself, ***but*** for my children (as well). ▪ She had the nerve to accuse me of lying. And *not only* that, *but* she refused to apologize! ▪ The festivals take place ***not only*** in the city ***but also*** in the surrounding rural areas.

only have eyes for see [1]EYE

***only too* :** very or completely ▪ He knew *only too* well [=he knew very well] what it meant to go to war. ▪ They were *only too* ready to give up and go home.

second only to see [1]SECOND

[3]**only** *conj, informal* **:** BUT, HOWEVER ▪ I'd love to sing along, *only* I don't know the words. ▪ They did have a radio, *only* it was broken. ▪ We wanted to buy that painting, *only* it was far too expensive.

only child *noun, pl* ~ **children** [*count*] **:** a person who never had a brother or sister ▪ I was an *only child.* ▪ As an *only child,* it was her duty to take care of her aging parents.

on–off *adj, always used before a noun*

1 : used to turn something on and off ▪ an *on-off* switch

2 : relating to something that is sometimes on and sometimes off ▪ an *on-off* pattern

on•o•mato•poe•ia /ˌɑːnəˌmɑːtəˈpiːjə, ˌɑːnəˌmætəˈpiːjə/ *noun* [*noncount*] *technical* **:** the creation of words that imitate natural sounds ▪ *Buzz* and *hiss* are examples of *onomatopoeia.*

– **on•o•mato•poe•ic** /ˌɑːnəˌmɑːtəˈpiːjɪk, ˌɑːnəˌmætəˈpiːjɪk/ *or* **on•o•mato•po•et•ic** /ˌɑːnəˌmɑːtəpoʊˈɛtɪk, ˌɑːnəˌmætəpoʊˈɛtɪk/ *adj* ▪ *onomatopoetic* words

on–ramp /ˈɑːnˌræmp/ *noun, pl* **-ramps** [*count*] *US* **:** a short road that is used for driving onto a highway — called also (*Brit*) *slip road*; compare OFF-RAMP

on•rush /ˈɑːnˌrʌʃ/ *noun* [*singular*]

1 : a strong, fast movement forward — usually + *of* ▪ an *onrush of* water/traffic

2 : a sudden development or appearance of something — usually + *of* ▪ the *onrush of* new technologies ▪ an *onrush of* tears/memories

– **on•rush•ing** /ˈɑːnˌrʌʃɪŋ/ *adj, always used before a noun* ▪ an *onrushing* train/tide ▪ *onrushing* events

on–screen /ˈɑːnˈskriːn/ *adv*

1 : in a movie or television program ▪ They play newlyweds *on-screen,* but in real life they've been married 10 years.

2 : on a computer, television, or movie screen ▪ The images appear *on-screen.* ▪ Edit the text *on-screen.* ▪ She's only *on-screen* for a few seconds in this movie.

– **on–screen** *adj* ▪ the *on-screen* action (of the movie) ▪ the actor's *on-screen* family ▪ an *on-screen* display

on•set /ˈɑːnˌsɛt/ *noun* [*singular*] **:** the beginning of something ▪ the disease's sudden *onset* — usually + *of* ▪ the *onset of* winter ▪ the *onset of* the disease/war

on•shore /ˈɑːnˌʃoɚ/ *adj*

1 : moving from an ocean, lake, etc., toward land ▪ *onshore* winds

2 : on land ▪ an *onshore* oil field

– **on•shore** /ˈɑːnˈʃoɚ/ *adv* ▪ The winds are blowing *onshore.*

on•side /ˈɑːnˈsaɪd/ *adv, sports* **:** in a position in which you are allowed to play or receive the ball or puck **:** not offside ▪ He stepped back *onside.*

– **onside** *adj* ▪ He was *onside.* ▪ (*American football*) an ***onside kick*** [=a kick that goes only a short distance so that the team making the kick can try to get the ball instead of having it go to the other team]

on–site /ˈɑːnˈsaɪt/ *adv* **:** at the place where a business or activity happens ▪ Production is all done *on-site.*

– **on–site** *adj, always used before a noun* ▪ *on-site* parking

on•slaught /ˈɑːnˌslɑːt/ *noun, pl* **-slaughts** [*count*] **:** a violent attack ▪ an *onslaught* by the enemy — often used figuratively ▪ The article recommends several things you can do to prevent the *onslaught* of the disease. ▪ Employers are expecting an *onslaught* of recent college graduates [=a very large number of recent college graduates] looking for jobs.

on•stage /ˈɑːnˈsteɪʤ/ *adv* **:** on or onto a stage and in front of an audience ▪ She walked *onstage.* ▪ go *onstage*

– **onstage** *adj* ▪ a great *onstage* performance

on–the–job *adj, always used before a noun* **:** received, learned, or done while working at a job ▪ *on-the-job* training/experience/accidents

on•to /ˈɑːntʊ/ *prep*

1 : to a position that is on (something, such as a surface, area, or object) ▪ We climbed *onto* the building's roof. ▪ The book fell *onto* the floor. ▪ The water spilled *onto* the floor. ▪ The cowboy leaped *onto* his horse. ▪ Transfer the data *onto* a disk. ▪ Turn left *onto* Third Street at the traffic light. — often used figuratively ▪ Don't try to shift the blame *onto* me. [=don't try to blame me instead of the person who should be blamed]

2 : in a direction that allows you to get to or see (something) ▪ The door opens *onto* a balcony. [=when you go through the door you are on a balcony] ▪ The dining hall opens *onto* a courtyard. [=you can enter the courtyard from the dining hall] ▪ The bedroom window looks (out) *onto* the bay.

3 a — used to say that someone knows about what someone is doing or has done ▪ The police are *onto* them. [=the police know what they did or are doing] **b** — used to say that someone is becoming aware of or is finding something ▪ Scientists believe they are *onto* something big. [=scientists believe they are close to making an important discovery] ▪ When the crowd responded to the show so positively, we realized we were ***onto something.*** [=we had done/discovered something important, special, etc.]

4 *chiefly Brit* **:** in the process of talking to (someone) usually to tell or ask something ▪ My parents are *onto* me again about getting a job.

onus /ˈoʊnəs/ *noun* [*singular*] *formal* **:** the responsibility for something — usually used with *the* ▪ *The onus* is on parents to teach their children not to use drugs.

[1]**on•ward** (*chiefly US*) /ˈɑːnwɚd/ *or chiefly Brit* **on•wards** /ˈɑːnwɚdz/ *adv* **:** to or toward what is ahead in space or time ▪ The troops kept moving *onward.* [=*forward*] ▪ They have lived in that house from 1983 *onward.*

onward and upward *or* ***onwards and upwards* :** toward a better condition or higher level ▪ Technology has been steadily moving *onward and upward.* ▪ He is moving *onward and upward* in his business career.

[2]**onward** *adj, always used before a noun* **:** moving toward the future or toward a more advanced state or condition ▪ the *onward* [=*forward*] march of time

on•yx /ˈɑːnɪks/ *noun* [*noncount*] **:** a kind of stone that has straight lines of usually white and black or white and brown and that is used especially in jewelry — see color picture on page C11

oo•dles /ˈuːdlz/ *noun* [*plural*] *informal* **:** a large amount of something ▪ She has *oodles* of money.

[1]**ooh** /ˈuː/ *interj* — used to express pleasure, surprise, or both pleasure and surprise ▪ *Ooh,* that feels good. ▪ *Ooh,* those flowers are beautiful!

[2]**ooh** *verb* **oohs; oohed; ooh•ing** [*no obj*] *informal* **:** to express pleasure, surprise, or both pleasure and surprise — used in the phrase ***ooh and aah*** ▪ Everyone in the crowd was *oohing and aahing* at/over the fireworks.

– **ooh** *noun, pl* **oohs** [*count*] ▪ ***Oohs and aahs*** could be heard from the crowd.

oomph /ˈʊmf/ *noun* [*noncount*] *informal*

1 : a quality that makes something attractive or appealing ▪ This sauce needs more *oomph.* [=*kick*] ▪ The plot of the story lacks *oomph.*

O

2 : **power or energy** ▪ His argument lacks *oomph*. ▪ The truck doesn't have the *oomph* to haul the boat.

oops /ˈups/ *interj* — **used to express surprise or distress or to say in a mild way that you are sorry about having done or said something wrong** ▪ *Oops* [=*whoops, woops*], I spilled a little milk. ▪ *Oops*, I didn't mean to do that.

¹ooze /ˈuːz/ *verb* **ooz·es; oozed; ooz·ing**
1 a [*no obj*] **: to flow out slowly** ▪ Sap *oozed* from the tree. ▪ Juice *oozed* out of the plum. ▪ The cut on her finger was *oozing* with blood. **b** [+ *obj*] **: to have (something) flow out slowly** ▪ The tree was *oozing* sap. ▪ The cut on her finger was *oozing* blood.
2 : to show (a quality, emotion, etc.) very clearly or strongly [+ *obj*] She *oozes* confidence. [=she has a lot of confidence] [*no obj*] — **usually + *with*** ▪ His letter *oozed with* sympathy.

²ooze *noun* [*singular*] **: a slow flow of something (such as blood)** ▪ A bandage will stop the *ooze* from that cut. — **compare ³OOZE**

³ooze *noun* [*noncount*] **: soft mud or slime (such as on the bottom of a lake)** ▪ The turtle buried itself in the *ooze*. — **compare ²OOZE**

¹op /ˈɑːp/ *noun, pl* **ops** [*count*]
1 *Brit, informal* **: a medical operation** ▪ I have my *op* tomorrow. — **see also POST-OP, PRE-OP**
2 *chiefly US* **: a set of planned actions for a particular purpose — usually plural** ▪ military *ops* [=*operations*]

²op *abbr* **1 operation; operative; operator 2 opportunity 3 opus**

opac·i·ty /oʊˈpæsəti/ *noun* [*noncount*]
1 : the quality of a material that does not allow light to pass through it : the quality of being opaque ▪ the *opacity* of the glass
2 *formal* **: the quality of being difficult to understand or explain** ▪ Critics have noted the *opacity* of her writing style.

opal /ˈoʊpəl/ *noun, pl* **opals** [*count, noncount*] **: a white or clear stone that reflects changing colors and that is used in jewelry — see color picture on page C11**

opaque /oʊˈpeɪk/ *adj* [*more ~; most ~*]
1 : not letting light through : not transparent ▪ *opaque* glass ▪ the *opaque* water of the muddy river
2 : difficult to understand or explain ▪ *opaque* writing/theories

op–art /ˈɑːpˌɑɚt/ *noun* [*noncount*] **: paintings, drawings, etc., made up of lines and shapes that are repeated and often placed in such a way that they look as though they are moving**

OPEC /ˈoʊˌpɛk/ *abbr* **Organization of Petroleum Exporting Countries**

O

op–ed /ˈɑːpˈɛd/ *noun, pl* **-eds** [*count*] *US* **: an essay in a newspaper or magazine that gives the opinion of the writer and that is written by someone who is not employed by the newspaper or magazine** ▪ She wrote an *op-ed* for the Wall Street Journal. — **usually used before another noun** ▪ an *op-ed* article/piece/writer

¹open /ˈoʊpən/ *adj* **open·er; open·est** [*or* **more ~; most ~**]
1 : not closed: such as a : not covering an opening ▪ an *open* gate/window ▪ The door suddenly swung/flew *open*. ▪ You left the blinds ***wide open***. **b : having an opening that is not covered** ▪ an *open* doorway ▪ an *open* box/container ▪ The meat was roasted over an *open* fire. ▪ I was so tired that I couldn't keep my eyes *open*. ▪ Don't chew with your mouth *open*. ▪ *open* cuts/wounds [=cuts/wounds not covered by skin] ▪ staring with her eyes/mouth ***wide open***
2 : not sealed or locked ▪ *open* bottles of wine ▪ There's already an *open* jar of pickles in the refrigerator. ▪ an *open* envelope ▪ Go on in. The house/door is *open*. [=it is not locked]
3 : allowing movement or travel : not blocked ▪ They kept the road *open* throughout the winter. ▪ an *open* passageway
4 : able to be entered and used by customers, visitors, etc. ▪ The new store is now *open* for business! ▪ The store is *open* from 9 a.m. to 10 p.m. on Saturdays. ▪ The library will not be *open* on Labor Day. ▪ The diner is *open* daily [=it is open every day] for breakfast. ▪ It's hard to find an *open* restaurant this time of night. ▪ We fought to keep the school *open*—but it closed anyway.
5 : having parts that are spread apart instead of folded together or attached ▪ an *open* umbrella ▪ Several of the pink roses are *open* this morning. ▪ The book was left *open* at/to page 42. ▪ Your zipper is *open*. ▪ His shirt was *open* [=was not buttoned] at the neck/collar. ▪ your *open* hands ▪ She ran toward me with her arms ***wide open***. [=with her arms held away from her body so that she could embrace me] ▪ They'll welcome you ***with open arms***. [=in a very kind and friendly way]
6 a : not containing or surrounded by walls, fences, buildings, etc. ▪ the ***wide open*** spaces of the American West ▪ fish caught in the ***open ocean*** [=an area of ocean that is far from land] ▪ He hung his clothes out to dry in ***the open air***. [=outside] ▪ traveling on ***the open road*** [=on roads that are away from cities and towns] ▪ Miles and miles of ***open country*** [=land with few buildings] lie beyond the town. **b** ***of a building or room*** **: having few walls** ▪ The house has an *open* floor plan. ▪ a bright, *open* kitchen
7 a : including or allowing a particular group of people — usually + *to* ▪ The contest is *open to* children between the ages of 8 and 13. ▪ The beach is *open to* residents only. ▪ The university library is also *open to* the public. ▪ The after-school program is *open to* anyone who needs extra academic help. **b : including or allowing all people** ▪ a meeting that allowed for *open* debate on the issue ▪ The town soccer program will hold *open* registration [=a time when people can register to participate] from now until September 21. ▪ an *open* golf tournament [=a golf tournament for both amateur and professional players]
8 a : available to be used ▪ I haven't decided to take the job yet. I'm keeping my options *open*. ▪ He gave us an ***open invitation*** to come and visit. [=he said we could visit any time we wanted] ▪ Leaving your car running with the keys inside is an *open invitation* to thieves. — **often + *to*** ▪ It's the only course *open to* us. ▪ Few career paths were *open to* women then. **b** ***of a job, position, etc.*** **: not yet taken : available for someone to take or fill** ▪ The job/position is still *open*. [=*vacant*] ▪ She's running for one of two *open* seats on the committee.
9 : happening or done in public so that people can participate or know what is being said or done ▪ The committee is holding *open* hearings on the issue. ▪ *open* sessions/meetings ▪ He testified in ***open court***. [=in a court that anyone is allowed to attend]
10 : not hidden or secret ▪ He is now facing *open* [=*undisguised, overt*] hostility from members of his own political party. ▪ They're in *open* disagreement about what should be done next. ▪ She speaks of the government with *open* disdain. ▪ his *open* affection for his wife ▪ *open* warfare
11 : expressing thoughts and feelings in a direct and honest way ▪ Be *open* [=*candid, frank*] with each other about your feelings. ▪ She encourages *open* communication between family members. ▪ an *open* discussion about religion
12 : willing to listen to or accept different ideas or opinions ▪ a free and *open* society ▪ We have one of the best systems in the country, but we're always ***open to suggestions***. ▪ I know it's different, but try to keep an ***open mind***. ▪ She spoke to them with an *open mind* and an ***open heart***.
13 a : not having ended : not yet finished or decided ▪ The case remains *open* to this day. [=it has not been solved] ▪ We can't talk about the case. It's still an ***open investigation***. [=the police are still investigating the case] ▪ The mayoral race is still ***wide open***. [=any of the candidates could still win] **b : allowing further comments or discussion** ▪ It's still an *open* question whether or not you may go. ▪ The question is still *open*. ▪ "Should we set a date for the next meeting?" "No, let's leave it *open* for now." ▪ The issue is not ***open for discussion***. [=we will not discuss the issue] — **see also *open to debate* at ¹DEBATE**
14 : able to be criticized, harmed, doubted, etc. — usually + *to* ▪ He lays/makes himself *open* [=*subject, liable*] *to* criticism with his foolish remarks. ▪ She argues that the current law is *open to* abuse [=the law can be abused] and should be changed. ▪ It's *open to* doubt whether she will run for governor. ▪ The author's exact meaning is *open to* question. [=no one knows exactly what the author means]
15 *sports* **: not blocked or guarded by players from the other team** ▪ She threw the ball to an *open* teammate. ▪ I'm *open*! Pass me the ball!
16 *computers* **— used to describe a file, document, etc., that is being used** ▪ You should close any *open* programs/documents before you reboot your computer.
17 — used to describe a microphone that is turned on ▪ He didn't realize that the microphone was *open*. ▪ Her comments were heard over an *open* microphone.
18 *of fabric* **: having large openings or spaces between threads** ▪ an *open* mesh/texture fabric ▪ an *open* weave wool sweater
keep your eyes open **see ¹EYE**
with your/both eyes open **see ¹EYE**

²open *verb* **opens; opened; open·ing**

1 a [+ *obj*] **: to move (a door, window, etc.) so that an opening is no longer covered** • This door is hard to *open.* • "*Open* the door!" shouted the police officer. • Would you mind if I *opened* a window? • Let's *open* (up) the curtains and let in some sunlight. **b** [*no obj*] **: to move and no longer cover an opening** • The car door *opened* and a beautiful woman stepped out. • The door *opened* and closed so quietly that I didn't notice he had come in the room. • This drawer is stuck. It just won't *open*! ✧ **The opposite of *open* is *close* in every sense except sense 10.**
2 [+ *obj*] **: to cause (something) to no longer be covered, sealed, or blocked** • It's time to *open* (up) your birthday presents! • *open* a can/box/jar • She comes home, turns on the TV, and starts *opening* her mail. • The janitor *opens* the building [=unlocks the doors of the building] at 7 o'clock. • The city only *opened* (up) this street to cars five years ago.
3 : to separate the parts or edges of something [+ *obj*] *Open* (up) your books to page 27. • She *opened* her eyes and smiled at me. • I *opened* my umbrella and stepped out into the rain. • "*Open* your mouth wide for me," said the dentist. • You haven't *opened* your mouth [=you have not said anything] since you've been here. [*no obj*] "*Open* wide," said the dentist. • His eyes *opened* slowly. • I can't get this suitcase to *open.* • The roses are starting to *open* (up).
4 : to make a hole or opening in (something) [+ *obj*] The surgery requires *opening* (up) the patient's chest. [*no obj*] ***The heavens opened*** [=it began to rain] and the rain poured down. = *The heavens opened up* and the rain poured down.
5 : to allow (a park, road, etc.) to be used [+ *obj*] The town *opened* the road again 10 days after the flood. • They've finally *opened* the bridge (up) to traffic again. [=allowed cars to use the bridge again] [*no obj*] The park *opens* every morning at dawn.
6 a : to begin the regular services or activities of (a business, school, etc.) [+ *obj*] We'll be *opening* (up) the café an hour early tomorrow morning. [*no obj*] The café will be *opening* (up) an hour early tomorrow morning. • What time does the library *open*? • The store *opens* at 9 a.m. on Saturdays. **b : to begin the activities or services of (a business, school, etc.) for the first time** [+ *obj*] I've always dreamed of *opening* (up) a restaurant. • a newly *opened* elementary school [*no obj*] They're building a drugstore, which is scheduled to *open* in May. • We *opened* for business in 1955. • The play *opens* [=begins being performed] next week. • The film/movie *opens* [=begins being shown in movie theaters] nationwide later this month.
7 : to begin (something) [+ *obj*] The police have *opened* an inquiry/investigation into the matter. = The police have *opened* (up) an inquiry/investigation into the matter. • We plan to *open* negotiations with the other side. • a way of *opening* debate/discussion on the issue • Let's *open* the bidding for this beautiful painting at $2,000. • Her most famous poem *opens* the new collection. [=it is the first poem in the new collection] • He always *opens* his speeches with a joke. • It's traditional to *open* baseball games with the national anthem. • She *opened* the meeting by thanking everyone for coming. [*no obj*] The song *opens* with a single voice singing a haunting melody. • The novel *opens* (up) with a description of a small apartment. • He always *opens* with a joke.
8 [+ *obj*] **: to begin keeping money in (an account at a bank)** • I *opened* (up) a new savings account at a different bank.
9 [+ *obj*] ***computers*** **: to begin to use (a file, document, or program) on a computer** • *opening* (up) a new document/file • *Open* the program by double-clicking on the icon.
10 *always followed by an adverb or preposition* [*no obj*] **: to allow movement or passage through a doorway or other opening** • The hallway *opens* (up) into a large family room. • A porch *opens* off the kitchen. = The kitchen *opens* onto a porch. **— often + *out*** • Their bedroom *opens out* onto the backyard.
11 [*no obj*] **: to have a specified price or be at a specified level at the beginning of the day** • The stock *opened* at $19 a share and closed at $22. • Stocks *opened* weak but closed strong.

***open doors for* : to give special opportunities to (someone)** • Being the daughter of the famous actor *opened doors for* her in Hollywood.

open fire* : to begin shooting** • A man *opened fire* in a crowded mall. • The soldiers ***opened fire on [=began shooting at] enemy troops.

open for [*phrasal verb*] ***open for (someone or something)*** **: to perform before (the main performer at a concert, show, etc.)** • One of my favorite comedians is *opening for* the band on their current tour.

open out [*phrasal verb*] *Brit* **: to become less shy and speak more freely** • He began to *open out* [=*open up*] about an hour into our date. — see also [2]OPEN 10 (above)

open someone's eyes see [1]EYE

open the door* or *open the way* : to make (something) easier or more likely to happen — often + *for* or *to • Her success *opened the door for* thousands of young women who wanted to play sports. • The court ruling *opened the way for* similar cases. • His experiences in the army *opened the door to* a career in politics. • It has *opened the way to* real progress.

open to [*phrasal verb*] **1 *open (something) to (someone or something)* : to allow (a particular group of people) to enter, use, or participate in (something)** • He *opens* his home *to* anyone who needs a place to stay. • This year, we've *opened* the contest *to* all children under the age of 16. • They decided to *open* the meeting *to* the general public. **2 *open (someone or something) to (something)* : to cause or allow (someone or something) to be affected by (something bad, such as criticism)** • Their actions have *opened* the government *to* charges of corruption. • By being secretive about her past, she *opens* herself (up) *to* political attacks. [=she makes herself open to political attacks]

open up [*phrasal verb*] **1 : to become less shy and speak more freely** • She tried to get the patient to *open up* to her about his problems. • He finally began *opening up* to her. **2 : to begin shooting** • The ships *opened up* with heavy gunfire. • The enemy *opened up* [=*opened fire*] on us with automatic rifles. **3 — used to demand that someone who is inside a room, building, etc., let you in** • This is the police! *Open up*! **4 *open up* or *open up (something)* or *open (something) up* a : to become or cause (something) to become available or possible** • It seemed that the whole world was *opening up* for me. [=it seemed that anything was possible] • Once he had his degree, many new opportunities *opened up* for him. • This discovery *opens up* the possibility of new research. • The government *opened up* the land for settlement. • People *opened up* their homes to those affected by the tragedy. [=they invited those affected by the tragedy to stay in their homes] **b : to become or cause (something) to become wider or less crowded** • At the bottom of the hill, the forest/landscape *opens up* to reveal a beautiful valley. • It looks like the road/traffic *opens up* ahead. • a drug that *opens up* the blood vessels **c : to develop or cause (something) to develop** • A wide gap in the polls has *opened up* between the two candidates. • The team won after *opening up* a 20-point lead in the game. • This *opens up* an important question: why did it happen?

open your bowels see BOWEL

open your doors see DOOR

open your heart* : to behave in a kind and generous way** • We were asked to *open our hearts* and our wallets. [=we were asked to be generous and give money] **— often + *to • Please, *open your hearts to* these poor people. They desperately need your help.

open your mind* : to become able to understand different ideas or ways of thinking** • She encourages her students to *open their minds* and try to see things from new perspectives. **— often + *to • Traveling in Africa *opened my mind to* a completely different way of life. • *Open your mind to* the possibility that you both may be right.

— open·able /ˈoupənəbəl/ *adj* • an *openable* window

[3]**open** *noun, pl* **opens**
1 [*count*] **: a competition (such as a major golf tournament or tennis tournament) that allows both professionals and amateurs to participate — usually used in names** • She lost at Wimbledon but won the French *Open.* • a golfer who has played in several U.S. *Opens*
2 *the open* a : an area or place without walls, barriers, etc. : an area or place that is not covered or enclosed — used in the phrase *(out) in/into the open* • We slept *out in the open* with nothing above us but the stars. • We would look for deer feeding *in the open* [=away from the forest] at dusk. • food left *out in the open* [=uncovered and not put away] **b : a situation in which something (such as a feeling) is no longer hidden or kept secret — used in the phrase *(out) in/into the open*** • Her true feelings were finally *in the open.* • He rarely fought his political battles *in the open.* [=he usually fought them in a secretive way] • Let's get everything *out in the open.* You've been lying to me, haven't you?

open admission *noun* [*noncount*] *US* **:** OPEN ENROLLMENT

O

open adoption *noun, pl* ~ **-tions** [*count*] *chiefly US* : an adoption in which the people who become the legal parents of a child meet the child's biological parents

open–air *adj* : located outside rather than inside a building ▪ We visited an *open-air* [=*outdoor*] market in the center of the city. ▪ *open-air* restaurants

open–and–shut *adj* : able to be settled or decided very quickly and easily ▪ Her first assignment as a lawyer was an ***open-and-shut case*** involving a drunk driver.

open bar *noun, pl* ~ **bars** [*count*] *US* : a counter at a party or other gathering where alcoholic drinks are served for free ▪ They had a buffet and an *open bar* at the reception.

open·cast /ˈoʊpənˌkæst, *Brit* ˈəʊpənˌkɑːst/ *adj, Brit* : involving the removal of the surface of a large area of land to get at coal or other material that is near to the surface ▪ an *opencast* mine

open day *noun, pl* ~ **days** [*count*] *Brit* : OPEN HOUSE 1

open–door *adj*
1 : allowing all people to enter or participate ▪ *open-door* meetings ▪ an *open-door* immigration policy
2 : allowing people to talk directly with the people who control a business, organization, etc. ▪ an *open-door* environment ▪ The school has an ***open-door policy*** with parents.

open–end·ed /ˌoʊpənˈɛndəd/ *adj*
1 : able to change : not ending in a certain way or on a certain date ▪ "Our military presence in the region," he said, "should not be *open-ended*." ▪ *open-ended* plans
2 : allowing people to talk in a way that is not planned or controlled ▪ an *open-ended* conversation/discussion ▪ You have to ask ***open-ended questions*** if you don't want people to answer simply "yes" or "no."

open enrollment *noun* [*noncount*] *chiefly US*
1 : a policy or process by which parents may send their children to a different public school than the one in their own community ▪ Many voters support *open enrollment*. ▪ the city's *open enrollment* policy — called also *open admission*
2 : a period of time during which you can join something as a member or participant : a period of time during which you can enroll in something ▪ Employees can sign up for new benefits during *open enrollment*. ▪ an *open enrollment* period

open·er /ˈoʊpənɚ/ *noun, pl* **-ers** [*count*]
1 : a tool, device, or machine that is used to open something ▪ a bottle *opener* ▪ a garage door *opener* — see also CAN OPENER, EYE-OPENER, LETTER OPENER
2 : the first game, performance, etc., in a series ▪ This game will be the season *opener* [=the first game of the season] for both teams. ▪ The album's *opener* is a slow love song. ▪ the meal's delicious *opener* [=*starter*]
for openers *informal* : as the first thing to be thought about or said : to begin with ▪ She began by asking what we'd done with her money. And that was just *for openers*! ▪ (*chiefly US*) "What didn't you like about my poem?" "Well, *for openers* [=*for starters*], I hated the title."

open–eyed /ˌoʊpənˈaɪd/ *adj* : having eyes that are open or wide open ▪ They stared at her with *open-eyed* wonder. — sometimes used figuratively to describe dealing with, showing, or understanding something in a clear and honest way ▪ The film is an *open-eyed* look at the costs of war.
– **open–eyed** *adv* ▪ lying *open-eyed* in the dark

open–faced sandwich *also* **open–face sandwich** *noun, pl* ~ **-es** [*count*] *US* : a piece of bread that is covered with meat, cheese, etc. : a sandwich made with no bread on top — called also (*Brit*) *open sandwich*

open·hand·ed /ˌoʊpənˈhændəd/ *adj* [*more* ~; *most* ~]
1 : having or showing the quality of being very generous ▪ *openhanded* hospitality ▪ Of all our contributors, she was the most *openhanded*. [=*generous*]
2 : done with the hand held open ▪ an *openhanded* slap

open–heart *adj, always used before a noun, medical* : done by stopping the heart from beating for a period of time, opening the heart, and repairing damage ▪ *open-heart* surgery ▪ *open-heart* procedures/operations

open–hearted *adj* [*more* ~; *most* ~] : kind and generous ▪ an *open-hearted* young woman

open house *noun, pl* ~ **houses**
1 [*count*] *US* : an event in which an organization (such as a school or company) invites the public to visit in order to see the things that happen there ▪ Westside High School will host an *open house* from 3 to 7 p.m. today, and all parents are invited to attend. ▪ colleges holding *open houses* for prospective students — called also (*Brit*) *open day*
2 [*count*] *US* : an event in which anyone who is interested in buying a particular house, apartment, etc., is invited to go inside and look at it ▪ We held an *open house* last week in the hopes that someone would offer to buy our house.
3 *chiefly Brit* : a home or other place in which guests or visitors are welcome [*noncount*] They ***kept open house***, and in the evenings neighbors would stop by to talk or play music. [*singular*] They always *kept* an *open house* for visitors.

¹open·ing /ˈoʊpənɪŋ/ *noun, pl* **-ings**
1 [*count*] : a hole or empty space that you can go through ▪ the *opening* of a cave ▪ They squeezed through a narrow *opening* between the fence and an oak tree. ▪ The enemy's troops poured through an *opening* in our defenses.
2 [*count*] : the first part of something : BEGINNING — usually singular ▪ We missed the *opening* of her speech. ▪ He injured himself two weeks after the *opening* of the season. ▪ the *opening* of the school year ▪ The story has a clever *opening*.
3 [*count*] : the first time that something happens ▪ We attended the *opening* [=the first performance] of the play. ▪ We went to the play's *opening*.
4 [*count*] : an event that is held in order to announce that something (such as a new store or public building) is ready to accept customers or visitors ▪ Come help us celebrate the official *opening* of the library. ▪ the *opening* of a new art exhibit — see also GRAND OPENING
5 [*count*] : a job or position that is available ▪ We do have an *opening* for someone with your qualifications and experience. ▪ We don't currently have any *openings*. ▪ a job *opening*
6 [*count*] : a chance or opportunity to do or say something ▪ She was waiting for an *opening* to tell her story. ▪ I saw an *opening* and went for it.
7 [*noncount*] : the act of causing something to open or of becoming open ▪ It has been 10 years since the *opening* of the café. ▪ the *opening* of a bank account ▪ the *opening* of the area for mining ▪ the *opening* of diplomatic relations between the two countries ▪ the *opening* (up) of the land to settlers

²opening *adj, always used before a noun*
1 : first or beginning ▪ It's the *opening* day of the fishing season. ▪ the *opening* lines of the poem ▪ the *opening* ceremonies of the Olympic Games ▪ In her ***opening statement***, she told the jury that her client was not guilty.
2 — used to describe the time when something is performed or shown for the first time ▪ The movie made 10 million dollars in its *opening* weekend. ▪ the play's ***opening night***

opening hours *noun* [*plural*] *chiefly Brit* : the time during which a business or organization is open for customers or visitors ▪ The store's *opening hours* [=*business hours*] are 9 a.m. to 6 p.m.

open letter *noun, pl* ~ **-ters** [*count*] : a letter that is published in a newspaper but that is addressed to a well-known person or to an organization ▪ In an *open letter* to the company, a citizens' group implored company executives to reconsider their decision to close the factory.

open·ly /ˈoʊpənli/ *adv* [*more* ~; *most* ~] : in a direct and honest way : without hiding feelings or opinions ▪ He *openly* acknowledged/admitted his mistake. ▪ She spoke *openly* about her failed marriage. ▪ Please feel free to express your opinions *openly*. ▪ The governor has been *openly* critical of the President. ▪ an *openly* gay politician [=a politician who does not hide the fact that he or she is gay]

open market *noun* [*singular*] : an economic market in which prices are based on competition among private businesses and not controlled by a government : FREE MARKET ▪ How much is it worth ***on the open market***? ▪ bought/sold/traded *on the open market*

open marriage *noun, pl* ~ **-riages** [*count*] : a marriage in which both people agree to allow each other to have sex with other people

open mike *noun, pl* ~ **mikes** [*count*] : an event in which anyone may use a microphone to sing, read poetry, tell jokes, etc., for an audience ▪ There's an *open mike* tonight at my favorite café. ▪ an *open mike* night

open–mind·ed /ˌoʊpənˈmaɪndəd/ *adj* [*more* ~; *most* ~] : willing to consider different ideas or opinions ▪ Try to be *open-minded* about the changes. ▪ He's one of the most *open-minded* people I've ever met. — opposite CLOSED-MINDED
– **open–mind·ed·ness** *noun* [*noncount*]

open·mouthed /ˌoʊpənˈmaʊðd/ *adj* [*more* ~; *most* ~] : having your mouth open usually because you are shocked or surprised ▪ I stood there *openmouthed*, unable to believe what I was seeing.

open–necked *adj, of a shirt* : having the top button unfastened ▪ wearing jeans and an *open-necked* shirt

open·ness /ˈoʊpənnəs/ *noun* [*noncount*]
1 : the fact of not hiding your opinions, feelings, etc. • She has been criticized for her lack of *openness* with the public.
2 : the quality of being willing to consider different ideas or opinions • An *openness* to new ideas is essential in our work. • *openness* of mind
3 : the state of not being surrounded or covered • the *openness* of the desert/plains

open–pit *adj, US* **:** involving the removal of the surface of a large area of land to get at a mineral or other material that is near to the surface • an *open-pit* mine • *open-pit* mining

open–plan *adj, chiefly Brit* **:** having or consisting of a large room that is not divided into smaller rooms or areas • an *open-plan* office

open prison *noun, pl* ~ **-sons** [*count*] *Brit* **:** a prison in which prisoners are allowed more freedom than in other prisons **:** a minimum security prison

open sandwich *noun, pl* ~ **-es** [*count*] *Brit* **:** OPEN-FACED SANDWICH

open season *noun* [*noncount*]
1 : a time of year when it is legal to kill certain fish or animals • *open season* for deer/bear
2 : a time when someone or something is being attacked or criticized by many people — often + *on* • It's always *open season on* politicians!

open secret *noun, pl* ~ **-crets** [*count*] **:** something that many people know about but that is supposed to be a secret • It's an *open secret* that he's been cheating on his wife.

open sesame *noun* [*singular*] **:** something that allows a person or thing to do or enter something successfully and easily • Perfect test scores are an *open sesame* to the best schools. ✧ *Open sesame* comes from the story *Ali Baba and the Forty Thieves*, in which Ali Baba uses the magical command "open sesame" to open the door of the thieves' cave.

open–toed *adj, of a shoe* **:** not covering the toes or the tips of the toes • *open-toed* shoes/sandals

open verdict *noun, pl* ~ **-dicts** [*count*] *Brit, law* **:** an official statement or decision saying that a crime has been committed but not naming a criminal or saying that there has been a death but not naming the cause of death

open·work /ˈoʊpənˌwɚk/ *noun* [*noncount*] **:** decoration that consists of designs made with openings or holes • a potter who decorates her vases with *openwork*
— **openwork** *adj, always used before a noun* • *openwork* carvings/patterns • *openwork* fabrics such as lace

[1]**op·era** /ˈɑːpərə/ *noun, pl* **-eras**
1 [*noncount*] **:** a kind of performance in which actors sing all or most of the words of a play with music performed by an orchestra • He is studying *opera*. • French *opera* — often used before another noun • an *opera* singer • *opera* fans — see also GRAND OPERA
2 : a show in which opera is performed [*count*] I am going to an *opera* tonight. • my favorite *operas* [*noncount*] I enjoy going to ***the opera***. [=going to opera performances]
3 [*count*] **:** a group of actors who perform operas together — often used in names • the New York City *Opera*
— see also SOAP OPERA
— **op·er·at·ic** /ˌɑːpəˈrætɪk/ *adj* [*more* ~; *most* ~] • an *operatic* singer/voice

[2]**opera** *plural of* OPUS

op·er·a·ble /ˈɑːpərəbəl/ *adj*
1 *formal* **:** able to be used **:** capable of operating or of being operated • The subway system will be fully *operable* [=*functional, operational*] by next month. • The radio is *operable* without the car running. — opposite INOPERABLE 2
2 *medical* **:** able to be corrected or removed by surgery • an *operable* cancer — opposite INOPERABLE 1

opera glasses *noun* [*plural*] **:** small binoculars that are designed to be used in a theater

op·era·go·er /ˈɑːpərəˌgowɚ/ *noun, pl* **-ers** [*count*] **:** a person who frequently goes to operas

opera house *noun, pl* ~ **houses** [*count*] **:** a theater where operas are performed

op·er·ate /ˈɑːpəˌreɪt/ *verb* **-ates; -at·ed; -at·ing**
1 [*no obj*] **:** to function or behave in a proper or particular way • They hope to have the windmill *operating* again tomorrow. • The camera also *operates* underwater. • The machine can *operate* at high speeds. • We need someone who *operates* [=*performs*] well under pressure. • The drug *operates* [=(more commonly) *works*] quickly.
2 [+ *obj*] **:** to use and control (something) • instructions for *operating* the new microwave oven • a license to *operate* a motor vehicle • *operate* machinery — sometimes used in combination • a coin-*operated* washing machine [=a washing machine that you must put coins into in order to use] • voice-*operated* computer systems
3 a [+ *obj*] **:** to have control of (something, such as a business, department, program, etc.) • *operating* [=*managing, running*] a business • The café is owned and *operated* by a young couple. • The organization *operates* a recycling program. **b** [*no obj*] **:** to function as a business, group, etc. • It's the only casino *operating* in the state. • The mill has been *operating* [=(more commonly) *in operation*] for 100 years. • The company *operates* from Chicago. • soldiers *operating* overseas • a militant group *operating* against the government
4 [*no obj*] *medical* **:** to perform surgery • The doctors needed to *operate* immediately. — often + *on* • *operate on* a tumor/patient

operating *adj, always used before a noun* **:** of or relating to the operation of something: such as **a :** relating to the way a machine, vehicle, device, etc., functions or is used and controlled • *operating* speed/conditions/controls **b :** relating to the way a business, department, program, etc., functions or is controlled • *operating* costs/expenses

operating room *noun, pl* ~ **rooms** [*count*] *US* **:** a room in a hospital where operations are done — called also (*Brit*) *operating theatre*

operating system *noun, pl* ~ **-tems** [*count*] *computers* **:** the main program in a computer that controls the way the computer works and makes it possible for other programs to function

operating table *noun, pl* ~ **tables** [*count*] **:** a special table in an operating room that a person lies on while having an operation

operating theatre *noun, pl* ~ **-atres** [*count*] *Brit* **:** OPERATING ROOM

op·er·a·tion /ˌɑːpəˈreɪʃən/ *noun, pl* **-tions**
1 [*count*] **:** a process in which a doctor cuts into someone's body in order to repair or remove a damaged or diseased part • She is recovering from a major heart *operation*. [=she is recovering from major heart surgery] • a minor/routine *operation* • organ transplant *operations*
2 [*count*] **a :** a usually small business or organization • The family runs a small farming *operation*. • The company is a billion-dollar *operation*. **b :** an activity of a business or organization — usually plural • a company's banking *operations* • An independent company has been hired to review the hospital's *operations*.
3 [*noncount*] **:** the state of functioning or being used — used with *in* or *into* • The system is now *in operation*. • The mill has been *in operation* for over 100 years. • Safety goggles must be worn while the machine is *in operation*. [=*in use*] • The dam will go *into operation* next month.
4 [*noncount*] **:** the way something functions or is used • The camera's design allows for easy *operation*. • the quiet *operation* of the printer
5 [*count*] **:** a set of planned actions for a particular purpose • The city has launched an *operation* to clean up the neighborhood. • Ten arrests were made in an undercover *operation*. • a rescue *operation* • The military *operation* gave them control of the city. • peacekeeping *operations*
6 [*count*] **:** a single action performed by a computer • The computer can perform millions of *operations* per second.
7 [*noncount*] **:** the act of using and controlling something • He was arrested for unlicensed *operation* of a motor vehicle.
8 [*count*] *mathematics* **:** a mathematical process (such as addition or multiplication) that is used for getting one number or set of numbers from others according to a rule

op·er·a·tion·al /ˌɑːpəˈreɪʃənl/ *adj*
1 : ready for use **:** able to be used • The new airport should be fully *operational* by next year. • The computer network is now *operational*.
2 *always used before a noun* **:** of or relating to the operation of a business or machine • *operational* costs/performance

[1]**op·er·a·tive** /ˈɑːpərətɪv/ *adj*
1 : ready for use **:** capable of being used • The factory must pass inspection before it becomes *operative*. • The telephone system is now fully *operative*. — opposite INOPERATIVE
2 : most important • If I go, I will bring a salad. "If," however, is the ***operative word***, since I am not sure that I can go.

[2]**operative** *noun, pl* **-tives** [*count*]
1 *chiefly US* **:** a person who does secret work for a govern-

O

ment or political organization • political *operatives* [=spies] • CIA/FBI *operatives* [=agents]
2 : a person who does work that involves using tools, operating machinery, etc. • factory *operatives* • a skilled *operative*

op·er·a·tor /ˈɑːpəˌreɪtɚ/ *noun, pl* **-tors** [*count*]
1 : a person who uses and controls something (such as a machine, device, or business) : someone who operates something • a computer/crane *operator* • the *operator* of an automobile • the *operator* of a nuclear power plant
2 : a person whose job is to help to connect telephone calls : a person who is in charge of a telephone switchboard • Call the *operator* for the phone number. • *Operator*, please connect me with extension 123.
3 : a person who is able to easily achieve things especially by persuading people or by being dishonest • She's quite an *operator*—no one else could have gotten them all to agree to the project. • a smooth *operator*

op·er·et·ta /ˌɑːpəˈrɛtə/ *noun, pl* **-tas** [*count*] **:** a usually short and funny opera that includes dancing

oph·thal·mic /ɑfˈθælmɪk/ *adj, medical* **:** of or relating to the eye • *ophthalmic* surgery/surgeons

ophthalmic optician *noun, pl* ~ **-cian** [*count*] *Brit* **:** OPTOMETRIST

oph·thal·mol·o·gist /ˌɑːfθəlˈmɑːləʤɪst/ *noun, pl* **-gists** [*count*] *medical* **:** a doctor who studies and treats problems and diseases of the eye — compare OPTICIAN, OPTOMETRIST

oph·thal·mol·o·gy /ˌɑːfθəlˈmɑːləʤi/ *noun* [*noncount*] *medical* **:** the study of the structure, functions, and diseases of the eye

opi·ate /ˈoʊpijət/ *noun, pl* **-ates** [*count*]
1 : a drug (such as morphine or codeine) that is made from opium and that is used to reduce pain or cause sleep
2 *disapproving* **:** something that causes people to ignore problems and to relax instead of doing things that need to be done • Many see television as an *opiate* of/for the masses.

opine /oʊˈpaɪn/ *verb* **opines; opined; opin·ing** *formal* **:** to express an opinion about something [+ *obj*] Many people *opine* that the content of Web pages should be better regulated. [*no obj*] You can *opine* about/on any subject you like.

opin·ion /əˈpɪnjən/ *noun, pl* **-ions**
1 : a belief, judgment, or way of thinking about something : what someone thinks about a particular thing [*count*] Why ask (for) my *opinion* if you have already decided? • I value your *opinion*. [=I respect the way you think about things] • We asked for their *opinions* about/on the new stadium. • ***In my opinion***, it's the best car on the market. • Most of the people surveyed have a ***high/low opinion of*** the organization. [=most of the people surveyed think that the organization is good/bad] • She has enough knowledge of the system to offer an ***informed opinion*** [=an opinion based on information] of why it isn't working. • The meeting will give residents a chance to listen to some ***expert opinions***. [=opinions of experts] [*noncount*] The owner of the store is often there to offer customers *expert opinion*. [=an expert's opinion] • Which one is better is a ***matter of opinion***. [=people have different opinions about which one is better] • I'm glad that we can have a ***difference of opinion*** [=we can disagree] and still be friends. • The ***general opinion*** is that the players are paid too much. [=most people think that the players are paid too much] • The company has been unsuccessful in its efforts to sway/change ***public opinion***. [=to change what most people think] • ***Contrary to popular opinion*** [=despite what many people think], fame does not always bring happiness.
2 [*count*] **:** advice from someone with special knowledge : advice from an expert • We're still seeking ***medical opinions*** [=advice from doctors] on the cause of the pain. • My doctor says I need surgery, but I'm going to get a ***second opinion***. [=advice from a second doctor to make sure advice from the first doctor is correct]
3 [*count*] *technical* **:** a formal statement by a judge, court, etc., explaining the reasons a decision was made according to laws or rules • The article discusses two recent Supreme Court *opinions*.
be of the opinion **:** to have a specifed opinion or belief • They *are of the opinion* [=they think/believe] that the accident was caused by faulty wiring.
the court of public/world opinion see [1]COURT

opin·ion·at·ed /əˈpɪnjəˌneɪtɪd/ *adj* [*more* ~; *most* ~] *often disapproving* **:** expressing strong beliefs or judgments about something : having or showing strong opinions • an articulate and *opinionated* critic • People don't expect such *opinionated* commentary in what is supposed to a news article.

opinion maker *noun, pl* ~ **-ers** [*count*] **:** a person whose opinion influences the opinions of many other people — usually plural • bloggers, journalists, and other *opinion makers*

opinion poll *noun, pl* ~ **polls** [*count*] **:** an activity in which many people are asked the same questions in order to find out what most people think about something • An *opinion poll* showed that he was favored to win the election.

opi·um /ˈoʊpijəm/ *noun* [*noncount*] **:** a powerful illegal drug that is made from a type of poppy

opos·sum /əˈpɑːsəm/ *noun, pl* **-sums** *also* **-sum** [*count*] **:** a somewhat small white or gray animal that is usually active at night and that lives in North and South America and in Australia — called also *possum*

opossum

opp *or* **opp.** *abbr* opposite

op·po·nent /əˈpoʊnənt/ *noun, pl* **-nents** [*count*]
1 : a person, team, group, etc., that is competing against another in a contest • She is a formidable *opponent* in the race for senator. • The team's *opponents* have not lost a game this season. • He knocked out his *opponent* in the third round.
2 : a person, group, etc., that is against something (such as an action, law, or system) : someone or something that does not want something to exist, be done, etc. — often + *of* • *opponents of* the war • *opponents of* building a new baseball stadium • *opponents of* abortion/slavery/communism — opposite PROPONENT

op·por·tune /ˌɑːpɚˈtuːn, *Brit* ˈɒpətjuːn/ *adj* [*more* ~; *most* ~]
1 : suitable or right for a particular situation • She was waiting for an *opportune* [=appropriate] moment to ask for money. • There isn't a more *opportune* time to invest in the stock market. — opposite INOPPORTUNE
2 : done or happening at the right time • The book's publication is *opportune*. [=timely] — opposite INOPPORTUNE

op·por·tun·ist /ˌɑːpɚˈtuːnɪst, *Brit* ˌɒpəˈtjuːnɪst/ *noun, pl* **-ists** [*count*] *disapproving* **:** someone who tries to get an advantage or something valuable from a situation without thinking about what is fair or right • Most burglars are *opportunists*. • a political *opportunist* who changed his health-care plan to win the election
— op·por·tun·ism /ˌɑːpɚˈtuːˌnɪzəm, *Brit* ˌɒpəˈtjuːˌnɪzəm/ *noun* [*noncount*] • The release of the movie so soon after the scandal is shameless *opportunism*. **— op·por·tu·nis·tic** /ˌɑːpɚtuˈnɪstɪk, *Brit* ˌɒpətjuˈnɪstɪk/ *adj* [*more* ~; *most* ~] • an *opportunistic* merger/investment/politician

op·por·tu·ni·ty /ˌɑːpɚˈtuːnəti, *Brit* ˌɒpəˈtjuːnəti/ *noun, pl* **-ties :** an amount of time or a situation in which something can be done : CHANCE [*count*] You'll have an/the *opportunity* to ask questions after the presentation. • There were many missed *opportunities* (to score) throughout the game. • When the *opportunity* came for her to prove that she could do the job, she was ready. • I had the rare/unique *opportunity* of speaking to the president. • Studying abroad provides a great *opportunity* to learn a foreign language. • This sort of *opportunity* comes along once in a lifetime. = This is a once-in-a-lifetime *opportunity*. • There are fewer job/employment *opportunities* this year for graduates. • This is a ***golden opportunity***. [=an excellent chance to do or get something] • I would like to ***take this opportunity*** to thank everyone who helped me with this book. • He was given ***every opportunity*** to prove that he was trustworthy. • The dog ran away ***at every opportunity***. [=whenever it was able to] • Please call us ***at your earliest opportunity***. [=please call us as soon as you can] • We will correct the error ***at the first opportunity***. [=as soon as we are able to] [*noncount*] There is plenty of *opportunity* for advancement within the company. • The contract provides us with a two-year ***window of opportunity***. [=two years to do something that we want to do] • the ***land of opportunity*** [=a place where there are many opportunities; a place where people have many chances to succeed, achieve things, etc.] • You need to be ready ***when opportunity knocks***. [=when you get the chance to do something you want to do]
equal opportunity employer (*US*) *or Brit* ***equal opportuni-***

ties employer : an employer who does not discriminate against people because of their race, religion, etc.

op·pos·able /əˈpoʊzəbəl/ *adj, technical* : able to be placed against one or more of the other fingers or toes on the same hand or foot ▪ Humans have an ***opposable thumb***.

op·pose /əˈpoʊz/ *verb* **-pos·es; -posed; -pos·ing** [+ *obj*]
1 : to disagree with or disapprove of (something or someone) ▪ The governor *opposes* the death penalty. ▪ The change is *opposed* by many of the town's business leaders. ▪ The group *opposes* the mayor and is trying to find a candidate to run against her. ▪ You've *opposed* every suggestion I've made.
2 a : to compete against (someone) : to be an opponent of (someone) ▪ He met the man who will *oppose* him in the next election. ▪ These two teams *opposed* each other in last year's playoffs. **b** : to try to stop or defeat (something) ▪ We're hoping we can get more senators to *oppose* the legislation.

opposed /əˈpoʊzd/ *adj, not used before a noun*
1 [*more* ~; *most* ~] : not agreeing with or approving of something or someone ▪ Many voters approve of the plan, but some are *opposed*. [=some are against it] — usually + *to* ▪ He is *opposed to* the new law. [=he opposes the new law] ▪ She is often *opposed to* the governor on budget issues.
2 : completely different ▪ Their political philosophies are ***diametrically opposed*** (to each other).
as opposed to — used to refer to something that is different from what has just been mentioned ▪ The car gets 30 miles per gallon, *as opposed to* [=*unlike*] last year's model, which got only 25. ▪ They use fresh fish, *as opposed to* [=*instead of*] fish that has been frozen. ▪ I'd say she is a good player, *as opposed to* [=*rather than*] a great one. ▪ Try to see it as an opportunity to learn something, *as opposed to* a setback.

opposing *adj, always used before a noun*
1 : fighting or competing against another person or group ▪ The crowd booed the *opposing* team. ▪ members of the *opposing* political party : fighting or competing against each other ▪ *opposing* teams/armies
2 : completely different ▪ *opposing* viewpoints ▪ He and his wife have *opposing* opinions on the issue.
3 : opposite in direction or position ▪ The trains were moving in *opposing* directions. [=the trains were moving away from each other] ▪ The boxers sat in *opposing* corners of the ring.

[1]**op·po·site** /ˈɑːpəzət/ *adj*
1 : located at the other end, side, or corner of something : located across from something ▪ The two boys lived on *opposite* sides of the street. ▪ the *opposite* bank of the river ▪ Fold the bottom right corner of the paper over to the *opposite* corner. ▪ She switched her ring to the *opposite* hand. [=she took her ring off the finger of one hand and put it on a finger of the other hand] ▪ The text refers to an illustration on the *opposite* page. [=on the page that faces it]
2 : completely different ▪ The two scientists had the same information but reached *opposite* conclusions. ▪ They represent *opposite* sides of the issue. ▪ They ran in *opposite* directions. ▪ Some herbs help you sleep while others have the *opposite* effect. [=other herbs keep you awake] ▪ Her music is ***at the opposite end of the spectrum/continuum*** from the music her mother made. ▪ Once serving only small portions at high prices, the restaurant has gone to the ***opposite extreme*** under the new owners. [=the restaurant now serves large amounts of food for low prices]
the opposite side of the coin see [1]COIN

[2]**opposite** *adv* : on the other side of someone or something : across from someone or something ▪ I sat down and he sat *opposite*. — usually + *to* ▪ He lives *opposite to* me. ▪ Put one leg forward, and then lift the arm that is *opposite to* the forward leg. [=lift your right arm if your left leg is forward; lift your left arm if your right leg is forward]

[3]**opposite** *noun, pl* **-sites** [*count*]
1 : someone or something that is completely different from someone or something else ▪ We thought the job might be difficult, but it was quite the *opposite*. [=it was easy] ▪ He said that the disease is becoming more common, but really the *opposite* is true. [=the disease is not becoming more common; it is becoming less common] ▪ My two sisters are polar/complete/exact *opposites* (of each other)—one is very friendly while the other is very shy.
2 : a word with a meaning that is completely different from the meaning of another word : ANTONYM ▪ "Wet" is the *opposite* of "dry." ▪ The terms "black" and "white" are *opposites*.
opposites attract — used to say that people who are very different from each other are often attracted to each other

[4]**opposite** *prep*
1 : on the other side of (something or someone) : across from (something or someone) ▪ He sat *opposite* me. ▪ She lives in the house *opposite* ours. ▪ The school is *opposite* a park. ▪ I played *opposite* the best player in the league.
2 *of an actor* : in a play, movie, etc., with (another actor) ▪ She stars/plays *opposite* Clint Eastwood in her latest movie.

opposite number *noun, pl* ~ **-bers** [*count*] : someone who has the same job or position as you but in a different company, organization, etc. : COUNTERPART

opposite sex *noun*
the opposite sex : the people who are not the same sex as you : the other sex ▪ people of *the opposite sex* — used by men to refer to women or by women to refer to men ▪ He's never been comfortable around (members of) *the opposite sex*. [=never been comfortable around women]

op·po·si·tion /ˌɑːpəˈzɪʃən/ *noun, pl* **-tions**
1 [*noncount*] : actions or opinions that show that you disagree with or disapprove of someone or something ▪ They're going ahead with the plans despite strong/fierce *opposition* from residents. ▪ The nominee faces strong *opposition* in the Senate. ▪ The proposed change has met with *opposition* from the town's business leaders. — often + *to* ▪ He expressed his *opposition to* the new law.
2 [*noncount*] : action that is done to stop or defeat someone or something ▪ Rebels have so far offered little *opposition* to advancing troops.
3 ***the opposition*** **a** : a person or group that you are trying to defeat or succeed against : a person or group that you are competing with ▪ Each candidate is focused on raising more money than *the opposition*. ▪ The coach advised her team not to underestimate *the opposition*. **b** *or* ***the Opposition*** : a political party that is trying to replace the political party in power ▪ *The opposition* is likely to win (in) the upcoming elections. ▪ The leader of *the Opposition* criticized the prime minister for his comments. — often used before another noun ▪ He's a member of the country's *opposition* party.
4 [*noncount*] *formal* : the state or relationship of two things that are completely different from each other ▪ Her article looks at the *opposition* between science and religion.
in opposition to **1** : in a way that is against someone or something ▪ He spoke *in opposition to* the new law. ▪ Her theories stand *in opposition to* traditional beliefs. **2** : in a way that shows how two things are different or disagree ▪ two words that can be defined *in opposition to* each other
– op·po·si·tion·al /ˌɑːpəˈzɪʃənl̩/ *adj* [*more* ~; *most* ~] *formal* ▪ *oppositional* groups/behavior

op·press /əˈprɛs/ *verb* **-press·es; -pressed; -press·ing** [+ *obj*]
1 : to treat (a person or group of people) in a cruel or unfair way ▪ The country has long been *oppressed* by a ruthless dictator. ▪ They condemned attempts by the government to *oppress* its citizens. ▪ people who have traditionally been *oppressed* by society ▪ *oppressed* minorities/people
2 : to make (someone) feel sad or worried for a long period of time — usually used as *(be) oppressed* ▪ He *was oppressed* by a sense of failure. ▪ The family *was oppressed* by grief.
the oppressed : people who are oppressed ▪ freedom for *the oppressed*
– op·pres·sion /əˈprɛʃən/ *noun* [*noncount*] ▪ the *oppression* of women in the workplace ▪ the fight against political *oppression* in the world **– op·pres·sor** /əˈprɛsɚ/ *noun, pl* **-sors** [*count*] ▪ They remain at the mercy of their *oppressors*.

op·pres·sive /əˈprɛsɪv/ *adj* [*more* ~; *most* ~]
1 : very cruel or unfair ▪ The country is ruled by an *oppressive* regime. ▪ I think these laws are *oppressive*.
2 : very unpleasant or uncomfortable ▪ This region suffers from *oppressive* heat in the summer months. ▪ The situation was extremely tense; no one said a word, and the silence was *oppressive*. ▪ an *oppressive* work environment
– op·pres·sive·ly *adv* ▪ It was an *oppressively* humid day. ▪ an *oppressively* dull office

op·pro·bri·um /əˈproʊbrijəm/ *noun* [*noncount*] *formal* : very strong disapproval or criticism of a person or thing especially by a large number of people ▪ They're going ahead with the plan despite public *opprobrium*. ▪ a group of critics who use "romanticism" as a ***term of opprobrium*** [=a word that is used to show disapproval]

opt /ˈɑːpt/ *verb* **opts; opt·ed; opt·ing** [*no obj*] : to choose one thing instead of another — often + *for* ▪ He usually or-

O

ders strawberry ice cream but *opted for* chocolate this time. — often followed by *to + verb* ▪ She was offered a job but *opted to go* to college instead. ▪ We *opted* not *to buy* the extra insurance.

opt in [*phrasal verb*] : to choose to do or be involved in something ▪ The company offered a new health insurance plan so that more workers would *opt in.*

opt out [*phrasal verb*] : to choose not to do or be involved in something ▪ Most employees participated in the pension plan, but a few *opted out.* — often + *of* ▪ A few employees *opted out of* the pension plan. — see also OPT-OUT

op·tic /ˈɑːptɪk/ *adj, always used before a noun, technical* : of or relating to the eyes ▪ the *optic* nerve ▪ *optic* surgery

op·ti·cal /ˈɑːptɪkəl/ *adj, technical*

1 : used to help a person see ▪ The company manufactures microscopes, telescopes, and other *optical* instruments.

2 : relating to or using light ▪ an *optical* laser

3 : involving the use of devices that get information for a computer by identifying patterns of light ▪ an *optical* scanner ▪ *optical* character recognition

– op·ti·cal·ly /ˈɑːptɪkli/ *adv* ▪ The page was *optically* scanned.

optical disk *noun, pl* **~ disks** [*count*] : a computer disk on which information is recorded in a way that can be read by a laser

optical fiber (*US*) *or Brit* **optical fibre** *noun, pl* **~ -bers** [*count*] *technical* : a long, thin, glass or plastic thread that carries information in the form of light : a fiber-optic thread

optical illusion *noun, pl* **~ -sions** [*count*] : something that looks different from what it is : something that you seem to see but that is not really there ▪ The closer building looks larger than the farther one, but it's just an *optical illusion.* The two buildings are actually the same size.

op·ti·cian /ɑpˈtɪʃən/ *noun, pl* **-cians** [*count*] : a person whose job is to sell eyeglasses and contact lenses, to make sure that they fit correctly, and sometimes to make eyeglasses — compare OPHTHALMOLOGIST, OPTOMETRIST

op·tics /ˈɑːptɪks/ *noun* [*noncount*] : the science that studies light and the way it affects and is affected by other things — see also FIBER OPTICS

op·ti·mal /ˈɑːptəməl/ *adj, formal* : best or most effective : OPTIMUM ▪ He keeps his engine tuned for *optimal* performance. ▪ Under *optimal* conditions, these plants grow quite tall. ▪ *optimal* health — see also SUBOPTIMAL

– op·ti·mal·ly *adv* ▪ Her plants were *optimally* placed to receive the greatest amount of light.

op·ti·mism /ˈɑːptəˌmɪzəm/ *noun* [*noncount*] : a feeling or belief that good things will happen in the future : a feeling or belief that what you hope for will happen ▪ Both of them expressed *optimism* about the future of the town. ▪ The early sales reports are cause/reason/grounds for *optimism.* ▪ Most of us reacted to the news with cautious/guarded *optimism.* [=a feeling that something good may happen but will not definitely happen] ▪ There is growing *optimism* that the problem can be corrected. ▪ He maintains a sense of *optimism,* despite all that has happened. — opposite PESSIMISM

op·ti·mist /ˈɑːptəmɪst/ *noun, pl* **-mists** [*count*] : a person who usually expects good things to happen ▪ You have to be a bit of an *optimist* to start a business. ▪ Somehow he remained an *optimist* despite all that had happened to him. — opposite PESSIMIST

op·ti·mis·tic /ˌɑːptəˈmɪstɪk/ *adj* [*more ~; most ~*] : having or showing hope for the future : expecting good things to happen : HOPEFUL ▪ Both of them were *optimistic* about the future of the town. ▪ He has an *optimistic* view of the company's future. ▪ People are increasingly *optimistic* that the problem can be corrected. ▪ Somehow he remained *optimistic* despite all that had happened to him. — opposite PESSIMISTIC

– op·ti·mis·ti·cal·ly /ˌɑːptəˈmɪstɪkli/ *adv* ▪ Both of them spoke *optimistically* about the future of the town.

op·ti·mize *also Brit* **op·ti·mise** /ˈɑːptəˌmaɪz/ *verb* **-miz·es; -mized; -miz·ing** [*+ obj*] *formal* : to make (something) as good or as effective as possible ▪ The new system will *optimize* the efficiency with which water is used. ▪ efforts to *optimize* service/performance — often used as *(be) optimized* ▪ The car's design *is optimized* for speed. [=the car has been specially made to go as fast as possible]

¹op·ti·mum /ˈɑːptəməm/ *noun, pl* **-ma** /-mə/ *also* **-mums** [*count*] *formal* : the amount or degree of something that is best or most effective ▪ The substances were mixed in various proportions until an *optimum* was reached.

²optimum *adj, always used before a noun, formal* : best or most effective : OPTIMAL ▪ They made *optimum* use of limited funds. ▪ We were not working under *optimum* conditions. ▪ For *optimum* results, allow the paint to dry overnight.

op·tion /ˈɑːpʃən/ *noun, pl* **-tions** [*count*]

1 : the opportunity or ability to choose something or to choose between two or more things ▪ You have the *option* of staying home or coming with us. ▪ He has the *option* to cancel the deal. ▪ Given the *option* [=*choice*], I'd rather stay home tonight. ▪ I'll probably take the job, but I'm ***leaving/keeping my options open*** [=waiting to decide; not making a final decision yet] for now.

2 : something that can be chosen : a choice or possibility ▪ For us, quitting is not an *option.* [=we cannot quit] ▪ You must accept the contract. There are no other *options.* [=*alternatives*] ▪ We have a wide range of *options* available to us. ▪ Menu *options* at the café include soups, salads, and sandwiches. ▪ Select an *option* from the drop-down menu. ▪ Filing taxes online is an *option* for people with Internet access. ▪ I had no *option* but to start over. ▪ A good/better *option* is to do the work yourself. ▪ The scandal ***left him no option*** but to resign. [=forced him to resign]

3 : a right to buy or sell something for a specified price during a specified period of time ▪ Employees will each be granted/given *options* to buy 1,000 shares of company stock. ▪ The *option* must be exercised within five years. ▪ The company has ***taken an option*** on some land nearby. [=it has obtained the right to buy the land at a particular price] ▪ The ad is for a condo to rent with an ***option to buy.*** [=a condo that you can choose to eventually buy for a specified price] — see also STOCK OPTION

4 : an extra part or feature that you can pay to have in addition to the regular features that come with something you are buying ▪ A sunroof was one of the *options* that you could get with the car.

5 *Brit* : a class that is not required in a particular course of study : ELECTIVE ▪ I took an *option* in history last year.

op·tion·al /ˈɑːpʃənl/ *adj* : available as a choice but not required ▪ Jackets are required at the restaurant, but ties are *optional.* ▪ Many *optional* features are available on this car. ▪ Registration is *optional,* not mandatory.

op·tom·e·trist /ɑpˈtɑːmətrɪst/ *noun, pl* **-trists** [*count*] : a person whose job is to examine people's eyes to find out if they need eyeglasses or medical treatment — called also (*Brit*) *ophthalmic optician;* compare OPHTHALMOLOGIST, OPTICIAN

op·tom·e·try /ɑpˈtɑːmətri/ *noun* [*noncount*] : the profession of examining people's eyes to find out if they need eyeglasses or medical treatment

opt–out *noun, pl* **-outs** [*count*] : an opportunity to choose not to do or take part in something ▪ The school will offer an *opt-out* for students whose parents object to the program. ▪ There is an *opt-out* clause in the contract. — see also *opt out* at OPT

op·u·lent /ˈɑːpjələnt/ *adj* [*more ~; most ~*]

1 : very comfortable and expensive : LUXURIOUS ▪ *opulent* new homes ▪ *opulent* furnishings ▪ the *opulent* [=*affluent*] lifestyle of wealthy people

2 : very wealthy ▪ an *opulent* widow

– op·u·lence /ˈɑːpjələns/ *noun* [*noncount*]

opus /ˈoʊpəs/ *noun, pl* **op·era** /ˈoʊpərə/ *also* **opus·es** /ˈoʊpəsəz/ [*count*]

1 : a piece of music written by a major composer — usually singular; usually followed by a number (called an *opus number*) that indicates when a piece of music was written in the list of works written by the same composer ▪ The concert began with Beethoven's *Opus* 27.

2 *formal* : an important work done by a writer, painter, etc. — usually singular ▪ the author's latest *opus* — see also MAGNUM OPUS

or /ˈoɚ, ɚ/ *conj*

1 — used to introduce another choice or possibility ▪ You can have coffee *or* tea. ▪ Would you like beer, wine, *or* something else? ▪ He must be her brother—*or* is he? [=maybe he is not her brother] ▪ I'll call (either) today *or* tomorrow. ▪ (*somewhat informal*) I didn't mean to annoy you ***or anything.*** ▪ (*somewhat informal*) Can I get you a cup of coffee ***or something***?

2 — used in negative statements to introduce something else that is also true ▪ We couldn't stop *or* even slow down the whole time. [=we could not stop and we could not slow down] ▪ They have no food *or* water. [=they do not have food and they do not have water]

3 — used to say what will happen if a specified thing is not done ▪ Finish your dinner *or* you won't get any dessert. [=if you do not finish your dinner, then you will not get any dessert] ▪ Be at the station by 5 o'clock *or* you will miss the bus.
4 — used to introduce another number or amount that is possibly the correct one ▪ It's been two *or* three years since I've seen her. ▪ The package should arrive in five *or* six days. ▪ We waited for an hour ***or more***.
5 — used to introduce the reason why something said previously is true ▪ He must be hiding something *or* he wouldn't be lying. [=he would not lie if he were not hiding something; the fact that he is lying means that he must be hiding something]
6 a — used to introduce a word or phrase that defines or explains what another word or phrase means ▪ Botany, *or* the science of plants, is a fascinating subject. = The science of plants, *or* botany, is a fascinating subject. ▪ This pan is used for sautéing, *or* frying, the vegetables. **b** — used to introduce a word or phrase that corrects or states more precisely something you have just said ▪ We got here quickly—*or* more quickly than last time, anyway. = We got here quickly—***or at least*** more quickly than last time. ▪ The building is 500, ***or to be precise***, 502 years old. ▪ She breeds rabbits, ***or rather*** hares.
or else see [1]ELSE
or so see [2]SO

OR *abbr* **1** Oregon **2** operating room

-or /ɚ/ *noun suffix* **:** a person or thing that does a specified action ▪ elevat*or* ▪ translat*or*

or·a·cle /ˈorəkəl/ *noun, pl* **-a·cles** [*count*]
1 *in ancient Greece* **a :** a person (such as a priestess) through whom a god was believed to speak ▪ consulting an *oracle* **b :** the place (such as a shrine) where people went to ask questions of an oracle **c :** an answer or message given by an oracle
2 : a person who has a lot of knowledge about something and whose opinions and advice are highly valued ▪ I met her long before she had become the *oracle* of pop culture.
– orac·u·lar /oˈrækjəlɚ/ *adj, formal* ▪ The students admired the old professor's *oracular* wisdom. ▪ an *oracular* pronouncement

[1]**oral** /ˈorəl/ *adj*
1 : of or relating to the mouth ▪ She practices good *oral* hygiene by brushing her teeth at least twice a day. ▪ *oral* cancer/surgery ▪ an *oral* surgeon
2 — used to describe a medicine that you eat or swallow ▪ They gave him *oral* doses of the antibiotic. ▪ an *oral* contraceptive
3 : spoken rather than written ▪ As part of her *oral* examination, she had to recite the names of all the presidents. ▪ *oral* [=*verbal*] communication skills
– oral·ly *adv* ▪ The vaccine was given to the patient *orally*. ▪ The information was communicated *orally*.

[2]**oral** *noun, pl* **orals** [*count*] **:** a test in which you answer questions by speaking rather than by writing **:** an oral examination — usually plural ▪ He's preparing for his *orals*.

oral history *noun, pl* **~ -ries**
1 [*noncount*] **:** recorded information about the past that you get from talking to people about their experiences, families, etc.
2 [*count*] **:** a book, article, etc., that is based on oral history ▪ I'm reading an *oral history* of the Great Depression.
– oral historian *noun, pl* **~ -ans** [*count*]

oral sex *noun* [*noncount*] **:** sexual activity that involves stimulating someone's genitals with the tongue or mouth

or·ange /ˈɑrɪnʤ, ˈorɪnʤ/ *noun, pl* **-ang·es** [*count, noncount*]
1 : a citrus fruit that is round and that has an orange skin ▪ He peeled the *orange*. ▪ a slice of *orange* — often used before another noun ▪ an *orange* tree/grove/peel ▪ I drink a glass of ***orange juice*** [=juice from an orange] every morning. — see color picture on page C5; see also BLOOD ORANGE
2 : a color between red and yellow that is like the color of fire and carrots — see color picture on page C1
compare apples and/to/with oranges see [1]COMPARE
– orange *adj* ▪ an *orange* flame ▪ He was wearing an *orange* shirt. **– or·ang·ish** /ˈɑrɪnʤɪʃ, ˈorɪnʤɪʃ/ *adj* ▪ the cat's *orangish* fur

orang·u·tan /əˈræŋəˌtæn/ *noun, pl* **-tans** [*count*] **:** a large ape that has very long arms and reddish-brown hair — see picture at APE

ora·tion /əˈreɪʃən/ *noun, pl* **-tions** [*count*] *formal* **:** a formal speech ▪ She made/gave/delivered an *oration* on the value of art in society. ▪ funeral *orations*

or·a·tor /ˈorətɚ/ *noun, pl* **-tors** [*count*] *formal* **:** a person who makes speeches and is very good at making them

or·a·tor·i·cal /ˌorəˈtorɪkəl/ *adj* [*more* ~; *most* ~] *formal* **:** of or relating to the skill or activity of giving speeches **:** of or relating to oratory ▪ *oratorical* skills/techniques

or·a·to·rio /ˌorəˈtorijou/ *noun, pl* **-ri·os** [*count*] **:** a large piece of music for a group of singers and musicians that is usually about a religious subject

[1]**or·a·to·ry** /ˈorəˌtori, *Brit* ˈɒrətri/ *noun* [*noncount*] *formal* **:** the art or skill of speaking to groups of people in a way that is effective ▪ She is a master of *oratory*. ▪ The President's inauguration speech was a fine demonstration of political *oratory*. — compare [2]ORATORY

[2]**oratory** *noun, pl* **-ries** [*count*] **:** a room or building where people can pray privately — compare [1]ORATORY

orb /ˈoɚb/ *noun, pl* **orbs** [*count*]
1 *literary* **:** something (such as a planet, the sun, or the moon) that is shaped like a ball ▪ The moon was a silvery *orb*.
2 : a gold ball with a cross on top that is carried by a king or queen on formal occasions as a symbol of power and justice — compare SCEPTER

[1]**or·bit** /ˈoɚbət/ *noun, pl* **-bits**
1 a : the curved path that something (such as a moon or satellite) follows as it goes around something else (such as a planet) [*count*] the *orbit* of the Moon around the Earth ▪ the *orbit* of the Earth around the Sun ▪ an electron's *orbit* around the nucleus of an atom [*noncount*] The satellite was put/launched into *orbit*. ▪ The satellite remains in *orbit*. **b** [*count*] **:** one complete movement along this path ▪ The space shuttle has completed its second *orbit*.
2 [*singular*] **:** the area over which or throughout which someone or something has power ▪ These territories remained ***within the orbit of*** the empire for hundreds of years.

[2]**orbit** *verb* **-bits; -bit·ed; -bit·ing :** to travel around (something, such as a planet or moon) in a curved path **:** to make an orbit around (something) [+ *obj*] The Moon *orbits* the Earth. [*no obj*] The satellites *orbit* at different heights/altitudes. ▪ The Moon *orbits* around the Earth.

[1]**or·bit·al** /ˈoɚbətl/ *adj, always used before a noun*
1 : relating to an orbit ▪ the planet's *orbital* motion
2 *Brit, of a road* **:** built around a city ▪ Take the *orbital* road/route/motorway around London.

[2]**orbital** *noun, pl* **-als** [*count*] *Brit* **:** a highway that goes around a city **:** BELTWAY

or·bit·er /ˈoɚbətɚ/ *noun, pl* **-ers** [*count*] **:** a vehicle or device that travels around a planet or moon in space ▪ a lunar *orbiter*

or·ca /ˈoɚkə/ *noun, pl* **-cas** [*count*] **:** KILLER WHALE

or·chard /ˈoɚʧɚd/ *noun, pl* **-chards** [*count*] **:** a place where people grow fruit trees ▪ an apple *orchard*

or·ches·tra /ˈoɚkəstrə/ *noun, pl* **-tras**
1 [*count*] **:** a group of musicians who play usually classical music together and who are led by a conductor ▪ He plays violin in the school *orchestra*. — compare BAND; see also CHAMBER ORCHESTRA, SYMPHONY ORCHESTRA
2 ***the orchestra*** *US* **:** a group of seats in a theater that are close to the stage ▪ Our seats were in *the orchestra* (section). [=(*Brit*) *the stalls*]
– or·ches·tral /oɚˈkɛstrəl/ *adj* ▪ *orchestral* players/music

or·ches·trate /ˈoɚkəˌstreɪt/ *verb* **-trates; -trat·ed; -trat·ing** [+ *obj*]
1 : to write or change (a piece of music) so that it can be

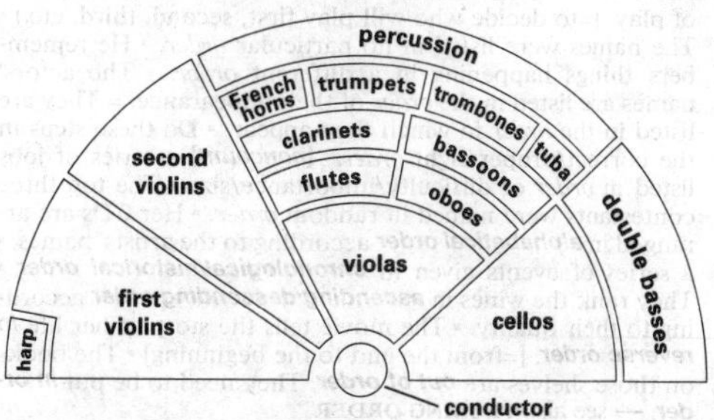

O

played by an orchestra • He recently *orchestrated* a musical. **2 : to organize or plan (something that is complicated)** • She *orchestrated* the entire event. • It's still unclear who was responsible for *orchestrating* the attack. • A strike was *orchestrated* by union members. • a ***carefully orchestrated*** campaign/plot

– or·ches·tra·tion /ˌoɚkəˈstreɪʃən/ *noun, pl* **-tions** [*count, noncount*] • the *orchestration* of the music/attack

or·chid /ˈoɚkəd/ *noun, pl* **-chids**

1 [*count*] **: a plant with flowers that are brightly colored and that have unusual shapes — see color picture on page C6**

2 [*noncount*] **: a light purple color**

or·dain /oɚˈdeɪn/ *verb* **-dains; -dained; -dain·ing** [+ *obj*]

1 : to officially make (someone) a minister, priest, rabbi, etc. • He was *ordained* (as) a priest. • She is an *ordained* minister.

2 *formal* **: to officially establish or order (something)** • We the people . . . do *ordain* and establish this constitution . . . —*U.S. Constitution* (1787) • The process was *ordained* by law. **— sometimes used figuratively** • It's futile to try to avoid what destiny has *ordained*.

or·deal /oɚˈdiːl/ *noun, pl* **-deals** [*count*] **: an experience that is very unpleasant or difficult — usually singular** • Being trapped in the elevator was a harrowing *ordeal* for the shoppers. • the *ordeal* of cancer treatment • I need to find a way to make traveling less of an *ordeal*.

[1]**or·der** /ˈoɚdɚ/ *noun, pl* **-ders**

1 : a statement made by a person with authority that tells someone to do something : an instruction or direction that must be obeyed [*count*] The captain was barking out *orders* [=*commands*] to the crew. • That's an *order*, not a request! • Failing to comply with an *order* will result in the loss of your job. • She received an *order* to appear in court. • They can't close down the school without an *order* from the governor's office. • The mayor gave/issued an *order* to evacuate the city. • It's not his fault. He was only following/obeying *orders*. • I'm not taking *orders* from you! You're not my boss. • She left the hospital against her doctor's *orders*. [=her doctor told her not to leave, but she left anyway] • The soldiers were ***under (strict) orders*** to shoot anything that moved. [*noncount*] The city was evacuated ***by order of*** the mayor. **— see also** CEASE AND DESIST ORDER, COURT ORDER, EXECUTIVE ORDER, GAG ORDER, MARCHING ORDERS, MONEY ORDER, RESTRAINING ORDER, STANDING ORDER, TALL ORDER

2 a : a specific request asking a company to supply goods or products to a customer [*count*] The store received an *order* for 200 roses this morning. • They had trouble filling large customer *orders*. • I placed a book *order* [=an order for a book] yesterday. • I'd like to cancel my *order*. • We offer free shipping on *orders* over 50 dollars. [*noncount*] We don't have that CD in the store right now, but we do have it ***on order***. [=we have ordered it but it has not yet been delivered] • The book is ***on (special) order*** from the publisher. • Dresses in larger sizes are available ***by special order***. **— see also** BACK ORDER, MAIL ORDER, PURCHASE ORDER **b** [*count*] **: a product or a group of products that someone has requested from a company** • We shipped your *order* last Thursday.

3 [*count*] **a : a request for food or drinks made at a restaurant** • The waiter still hasn't come to take our *order*. • May I take your *order*? • Please wait in this line to place your *order*. **b : the food and drinks that someone has requested at a restaurant** • Your *order* will be ready any minute now. • Is this *order* for here or to go? [=do you want to eat in this restaurant or take the food somewhere else?] **c : an amount of food that is served at a restaurant** • I'd like a large *order* of French fries, please. • I'd like a hamburger with a ***side order*** of fries. [=I'd like an order of fries with my hamburger]

4 : the particular way that things or events are organized in a list or series [*singular*] Roll the dice to determine the *order* of play. [=to decide who will play first, second, third, etc.] • The names were listed in no particular *order*. • He remembers things happening in a different *order*. • The actors' names are listed in the *order* of their appearance. = They are listed in the *order* in which they appear. • Do these steps in the correct/proper/right *order*. [*noncount*] a series of jobs listed in *order* of difficulty/importance/size • The top three contestants were named in random *order*. • Her CDs are arranged in ***alphabetical order*** according to the artists' names. • a series of events given in ***chronological/historical order*** • They rank the wines in ***ascending/descending order*** according to their quality. • The movie tells the story of her life ***in reverse order***. [=from the end to the beginning] • The books on those shelves are ***out of order***. They need to be put ***in order***. **— see also** PECKING ORDER

5 [*noncount*] **a : an organized and proper state or condition** • Two weeks after the disaster, he has managed to bring *order* out of (the) chaos. • Hundreds of families are struggling to get/put their lives back ***in order*** after the earthquake. • Get your passport *in order* before you leave for your trip. • All her documents were *in order*. • She makes sure the organization's finances are ***in good order***. • Drivers must keep their trucks clean and ***in (good) working order***. [=working properly] **— opposite** DISORDER **b : the state in which people behave properly, follow rules or laws, and respect authority** • Our leaders must restore *order* to the city. • the loss of public *order* • Some teachers have trouble maintaining *order* in the classroom. • a lack of *order* and discipline • "*Order, order* in the court!" the judge shouted at the unruly men.

6 [*singular*] **: a social or political system : the way that a society is organized or controlled** • These young activists dared to challenge the established social *order*. • calling for the end of the old *order* • a new world *order* • They seem to have accepted poverty as part of the ***natural order of things***.

7 [*singular*] **: a level of quality or excellence** • a teacher of the first/highest *order* [=an excellent teacher] • Their customer service is of a higher *order* than that of their competitors.

8 [*count*] *chiefly Brit* **: a social class — usually plural** • servants and other members of ***the lower orders***

9 [*count*] *biology* **: a group of related plants or animals that is larger than a family** • humans, apes, and other members of the *order* Primates

10 [*count*] **: a large organization of people who have similar jobs or interests and who give help to other members** • the Masonic *Order* • the Fraternal *Order* of Police

11 [*count*] **: a religious organization whose members usually live together and promise to follow special rules and traditions** • joining a religious/monastic *order* • an *order* of Catholic missionaries **— see also** HOLY ORDERS

12 [*count*] **: a group of people who have been given an honor or reward by a country's ruler** • The Queen made him a Member of the *Order* of the British Empire.

call (something) to order **: to say that (something, such as a meeting or court session) should begin** • She *called* the meeting *to order* at 8:15. • His lawyer arrived 10 minutes before court was *called to order*.

house in order see [1]HOUSE

in apple-pie order see APPLE PIE

in order **: appropriate or desirable** • After finishing that three-year project, I decided that a vacation was *in order*. • An apology is *in order*, I believe. **— see also** [1]ORDER 4 (above), [1]ORDER 5a (above)

in order for **: to make it possible for someone or something** *to be* **or** *to do* **something** • *In order for* companies *to be* successful, they have to sell their products at competitive prices. • We all have to work together *in order for* us *to win*. = We can win, but *in order for* that *to happen*, we all have to work together. • They were told that *in order for* them *to keep* their jobs, they would have to accept a cut in pay.

in order that *formal* **— used to say the reason for something** • These soldiers gave their lives *in order that* [=*so that*] we may live in a safer and more peaceful world.

in order to **: to make it possible for something to happen** • *In order to* succeed, companies have to sell their products at competitive prices. • People come here *in order to* give their children a better life. • She has to work two jobs *in order to* [=so that she can] support her family. • I checked my bags twice *in order to* make sure that I had everything.

in short order see [1]SHORT

law and order see LAW

on the order of (*chiefly US*) **or** *Brit* ***in/of the order of*** **: around or about (a specified number)** • The government has spent *on the order of* [=*approximately*] ten million dollars on the project. • He receives something *on the order of* 100 e-mails a day.

out of order **1 : not working properly : not able to be used** • The elevator's *out of order* [=*broken*] again. We'll have to take the stairs. • The sign on the coffee machine says "*out of order*." **2 : not following the formal rules of a meeting, court session, etc.** • At the last town council meeting, her proposal was ruled *out of order* by the mayor. • The mayor ruled her *out of order*. **3** *Brit, informal* **: beyond what is reasonable or allowable : not right or appropriate** • Your behavior was completely *out of order*. [=*out of line*] • His comments were *out of order*. **— see also** [1]ORDER 4 (above)

to order **: in response to a specific order or request** • Everything in this restaurant is cooked *to order*. **— see also** MADE-TO-ORDER

O

– or·der·less /ˈoədələs/ *adj* ▪ a lawless and *orderless* society

²order *verb* **-ders; -dered; -der·ing**
1 [+ *obj*] **a :** to use your authority to tell someone to do something **:** to give an order to someone ▪ They *ordered* everyone out of the house. ▪ The soldiers were *ordered* back to the base. ▪ "Stop! Drop your weapon!" *ordered* the officer. — usually followed by *to + verb* ▪ The police officer *ordered* him *to stop* and drop his weapon. ▪ The soldiers were *ordered to return* to the base. ▪ Everyone on the ship was *ordered to put* on their life jackets. ▪ I *order* you *to leave* this instant! **b :** to say that (something) must be done ▪ The court threw out the conviction and *ordered* a new trial. ▪ The judge *ordered* that the charges be dismissed. ▪ He was accused of *ordering* the murder of his wife.
2 : to place an order for (something): such as **a :** to request (something) from a company [+ *obj*] I *ordered* the books from the company's Web site. ▪ The shirt you *ordered* should arrive in the mail in a couple of days. [*no obj*] To *order*, call the number at the bottom of your screen. ▪ *Order* now and receive a free gift! **b :** to request (food or drinks) from a restaurant [+ *obj*] I'd like to *order* a large cheese pizza. ▪ She sat down at the bar and *ordered* a drink. ▪ Would you like me to *order* you a drink? = Would you like me to *order* a drink for you? ▪ I had the fish and he *ordered* the steak. ▪ Do you know what you're going to *order*? [*no obj*] "Are you ready to *order*?" the waiter asked. ▪ We've already *ordered*.
3 [+ *obj*] **:** to organize (things) in a particular list or series **:** to put things in a particular order or position ▪ The books are *ordered* [=*arranged*] alphabetically by author. — see also RE-ORDER
just what the doctor ordered see ¹DOCTOR
order around *or chiefly Brit* ***order about*** [*phrasal verb*] ***order (someone) around/about*** **:** to give orders to (someone) **:** to tell (someone) what to do ▪ He was tired of being *ordered* [=*bossed*] *around* by his parents and teachers. ▪ You can't just come in here and start *ordering* people *around*.
– or·der·able /ˈoədərəbəl/ *adj* ▪ an *orderable* book **– or·der·er** /ˈoədərə/ *noun, pl* **-ers** [*count*]

order book *noun, pl* **~ books** [*count*] **:** a book that shows the number of orders that a company has received from its customers — often used figuratively ▪ The company is starting the year with a full *order book*. [=it has many orders for its products]

or·dered /ˈoədəd/ *adj* [*more ~; most ~*] **:** carefully organized or controlled ▪ an *ordered* sequence of events ▪ He leads an *ordered* [=*well-ordered, orderly*] life in the suburbs. — opposite DISORDERED

order form *noun, pl* **~ forms** [*count*] **:** a form that customers can use to order products from a company

¹or·der·ly /ˈoədəli/ *adj* [*more ~; most ~*]
1 : arranged or organized in a logical or regular way ▪ Try to keep your desk neat and *orderly*. [=*tidy*] ▪ an *orderly* arrangement of pictures ▪ She sorted the information into *orderly* categories.
2 : peaceful or well-behaved ▪ Outside the theater, an *orderly* line of people waited to buy tickets. ▪ an *orderly* crowd of protesters ▪ Please exit the building ***in an orderly fashion***. — opposite DISORDERLY
– or·der·li·ness /ˈoədəlinəs/ *noun* [*noncount*]

²orderly *noun, pl* **-lies** [*count*]
1 : a person who works in a hospital and does various jobs (such as moving patients or cleaning)
2 : a soldier who performs various services (such as carrying messages) for a superior officer

order of business *noun* [*singular*] **:** a job that must be done or an issue that must be discussed ▪ The first *order of business* at the committee meeting was the budget.

order of magnitude *noun, pl* **orders of magnitude** [*count*] **:** a range of numbers or sizes that goes from a particular number or size to 10 times larger or 10 times smaller ▪ These molecules are several *orders of magnitude* smaller than a grain of sand. ▪ Donations to the organization increased by an *order of magnitude* [=they became 10 times greater] after the earthquake. — often used figuratively ▪ two problems of the same *order of magnitude* [=two problems that are equally important]

order of the day *noun*
the order of the day **:** a characteristic or activity that is common during a particular period of time or in a particular situation ▪ Change was very much *the order of the day* in that time in our country's history. ▪ Wasteful government spending seems to be *the order of the day*. ▪ At the resort's outdoor café, bathing suits and sandals are *the order of the day*. [=they are popular and appropriate]

order paper *noun, pl* **~ -pers** [*count*] *Brit* **:** a list of the subjects that will be discussed in Parliament on a particular day ▪ The issue did not appear on the *order paper* as expected. ▪ parliamentary *order papers*

or·di·nal number /ˈoədənəl-/ *noun, pl* **~ -bers** [*count*] **:** a number (such as first, fifth, or 22nd) that is used to show the position of someone or something in a series — compare CARDINAL NUMBER

or·di·nance /ˈoədənəns/ *noun, pl* **-nanc·es** *US* **:** a law or regulation made by a city or town government [*count*] The town has passed a zoning *ordinance* limiting construction. [*noncount*] (*formal*) Gambling is prohibited by local *ordinance*. ***synonyms*** see LAW

or·di·nar·i·ly /ˌoədəˈnerəli, *Brit* ˈɔːdənrəli/ *adv* — used to describe the way things are normally or usually done ▪ *Ordinarily*, we don't accept this as a valid form of identification, but we'll accept it this time. ▪ It *ordinarily* [=*usually*] takes two people to operate the machine. ▪ She's not *ordinarily* in on Wednesdays, but she's here today.

¹or·di·nary /ˈoədəˌneri, *Brit* ˈɔːdənri/ *adj* [*more ~; most ~*]
1 *always used before a noun* **:** normal or usual **:** not unusual, different, or special ▪ Today was just another *ordinary* [=*routine*] day at work. ▪ They've had the *ordinary* problems associated with starting a new business. ▪ the *ordinary* [=*regular*] language/speech we use every day ▪ My wife thought our guide was strange, but he seemed perfectly *ordinary* to me. ▪ *ordinary* people [=people who are not famous, rich, etc.] ▪ It was ***no ordinary*** day. [=it was a special or unusual day]
2 *disapproving* **:** neither very good nor very bad **:** not very impressive ▪ The quality of her work has been pretty *ordinary*. [=*average*] ▪ The meal was *ordinary* and uninspired.
in the ordinary way *Brit* **:** in the normal or usual way **:** as something is always done ▪ They had their morning coffee *in the ordinary way*, reading the paper and not speaking until they were finished.
– or·di·nar·i·ness /ˈoədəˌnerinəs/ *noun* [*noncount*] ▪ the *ordinariness* of daily life

²ordinary *noun*
out of the ordinary **:** unusual, different, or strange **:** not what is considered to be normal ▪ What happened is nothing *out of the ordinary*. ▪ They didn't do anything that was *out of the ordinary*. ▪ Her taste is a bit *out of the ordinary*.

Ordinary level *noun, pl* **~ -els** [*count*] *Brit* **:** O LEVEL

or·di·na·tion /ˌoədəˈneɪʃən/ *noun, pl* **-tions :** the official act or process of making someone a priest, minister, etc. [*noncount*] He is a candidate for *ordination*. [*count*] After his *ordination*, he will be assigned to a local parish.

ord·nance /ˈoədnəns/ *noun* [*noncount*] *technical*
1 : military supplies including weapons, ammunition, armor, vehicles, etc. ▪ The field was full of unexploded *ordnance*. [=bombs that had not exploded] ▪ an *ordnance* facility
2 : large, heavy guns on wheels **:** ARTILLERY ▪ The company was outfitted with 50-millimeter *ordnance*. ▪ a military *ordnance* company

or·dure /ˈoədʒə/ *noun* [*noncount*] *chiefly Brit, formal* **:** solid waste matter that is released from the body **:** EXCREMENT

ore /ˈoə/ *noun, pl* **ores :** rocks, earth, etc., from which a valuable metal can be taken [*noncount*] The mine is an important producer of iron *ore*. [*count*] The company extracts metals from *ores*.

oreg·a·no /əˈrɛgənoʊ/ *noun* [*noncount*] **:** an herb that has green leaves with a sweet smell which are used in cooking ▪ The recipe calls for a tablespoon of chopped *oregano*. — see color picture on page C6

or·gan /ˈoəgən/ *noun, pl* **-gans** [*count*]
1 a : a part of the body (such as the heart or liver) that has a particular function ▪ internal *organs* ▪ vital *organs* ▪ an *organ* transplant/donor — see also SENSE ORGAN **b** — used as a polite way of saying *penis* ▪ the male *organ*
2 a : a musical instrument that has a keyboard and pipes of different lengths and that makes sound by pushing air through the pipes — called also *pipe organ*; see picture at KEYBOARD **b :** an electronic musical instrument that has a keyboard and makes sounds like those of an organ — see also BARREL ORGAN, MOUTH ORGAN
3 *formal* **:** a group or organization that has a special function within a larger organization ▪ the legislative *organ* of our government
4 *formal* **:** a newspaper, magazine, etc., that is published by a

particular group and that gives the news and opinions of that group ▪ The magazine functions as the official *organ* of the tobacco industry. ▪ a ***house organ*** [=a publication that expresses the opinions of a business or group]

or·gan–grind·er /ˈoɚgən͵graɪndɚ/ *noun, pl* **-ers** [*count*] **:** a musician who plays a barrel organ in a public place for money

or·gan·ic /oɚˈgænɪk/ *adj*

1 a *of food* **:** grown or made without the use of artificial chemicals ▪ *organic* vegetables ▪ Is this broccoli ***certified organic***? [=has the government said that it was grown without the use of artificial chemicals?] **b :** not using artificial chemicals ▪ *organic* farming/methods ▪ She's an *organic* gardener.

2 : of, relating to, or obtained from living things ▪ *organic* materials/matter/substances ▪ *organic* fertilizers — opposite INORGANIC

3 [*more ~; most ~*] **a :** having different parts that work together well ▪ He thinks of the city not as a collection of different neighborhoods but as an *organic* whole. **b :** forming an important part of something ▪ This neighborhood is an *organic* part of the city.

4 [*more ~; most ~*] **:** happening or developing in a slow and natural way ▪ The company has gone through a period of steady *organic* growth in recent years.

5 [*more ~; most ~*] *somewhat formal* **:** having a curving form similar to the shapes found in nature ▪ I like the *organic* lines of his architecture. ▪ His architecture is very *organic*.

6 *medical* **:** of or relating to the organs of the body ▪ an *organic* disease ▪ *organic* illness

– or·gan·i·cal·ly /oɚˈgænɪkli/ *adv* ▪ This farm specializes in *organically* grown food. ▪ Her opinions grew *organically* from her observations.

organic chemistry *noun* [*noncount*] **:** a branch of chemistry that is concerned with carbon and especially carbon compounds which are found in living things — compare INORGANIC CHEMISTRY

or·gan·ism /ˈoɚgə͵nɪzəm/ *noun, pl* **-isms** [*count*]

1 : an individual living thing ▪ a microscopic *organism* ▪ A human being is a complex *organism*. — see also MICROORGANISM

2 : a system with many parts that depend on each other and work together — usually singular ▪ He thinks of the city as a complex social/political/economic *organism*.

or·gan·ist /ˈoɚgənɪst/ *noun, pl* **-ists** [*count*] *music* **:** a person who plays an organ ▪ a church *organist*

or·ga·ni·za·tion *also Brit* **or·ga·ni·sa·tion** /͵oɚgənəˈzeɪʃən, *Brit* ͵ɔːgə͵naɪˈzeɪʃən/ *noun, pl* **-tions**

1 [*count*] **:** a company, business, club, etc., that is formed for a particular purpose ▪ She is the leader of an international *organization* devoted to the protection of natural resources. ▪ religious *organizations* ▪ a charitable *organization*

2 [*noncount*] **a :** the act or process of putting the different parts of something in a certain order so that they can be found or used easily ▪ He has been working on the *organization* of his notes into an outline. **b :** the act or process of planning and arranging the different parts of an event or activity ▪ She is responsible for the *organization* of the party.

3 [*noncount*] **:** the way in which the different parts of something (such as a company) are arranged ▪ The new president plans to make changes to the company's *organization*.

4 [*noncount*] **:** the quality of being arranged in a way that is sensible and useful ▪ You have a lot of good ideas in this paper, but there's no *organization* to your thoughts.

– or·ga·ni·za·tion·al *also Brit* **or·ga·ni·sa·tion·al** /͵oɚgənəˈzeɪʃənl, *Brit* ͵ɔːgə͵naɪˈzeɪʃənl/ *adj* ▪ She has strong *organizational* skills. [=she is very skillful at arranging things in a sensible and useful way] ▪ an ***organizational chart*** [=a chart that shows how all of the jobs in a large company relate to each other]

or·ga·nize *also Brit* **or·ga·nise** /ˈoɚgə͵naɪz/ *verb* **-niz·es; -nized; -niz·ing**

1 [+ *obj*] **:** to arrange and plan (an event or activity) ▪ They hired a professional to help *organize* their wedding. ▪ We are *organizing* a fund-raiser.

2 : to arrange or order things so that they can be found or used easily and quickly **:** to put things into a particular arrangement or order [+ *obj*] His office is a mess. He needs someone to help him *organize* his work/papers. ▪ She took a moment to *organize* [=*collect*] her thoughts before she responded. ▪ The book is *organized* around a central theme. [=the action, plot, characters, etc., of the book are guided by a central theme] ▪ I spent some time *organizing* my closet last weekend. [*no obj*] You need to learn to *organize* better.

3 a : to gather (people) into a group that will work on something together [+ *obj*] She *organized* people to work for social justice. ▪ The players were *organized* into separate teams. [*no obj*] He encouraged them to *organize* for social justice. **b :** to form a labor union [*no obj*] The company has tried to prevent the workers from *organizing*. [+ *obj*] He tried to *organize* [=*unionize*] the workers in the factory.

– or·ga·niz·er *also Brit* **or·ga·nis·er** /ˈoɚgə͵naɪzɚ/ *noun, pl* **-ers** [*count*] ▪ an events *organizer* ▪ She's a skillful *organizer*. ▪ a labor/union/political *organizer*

organized *also Brit* **organised** *adj*

1 a : arranged into a formal group with leaders and with rules for doing or planning things ▪ *organized* baseball [=the sport of baseball and its teams, members, leaders, and rules] ▪ *organized* religion [=religion that has large numbers of followers and a set of rules that must be followed] ▪ ***organized crime*** [=a large group of professional criminals who work as part of a powerful and secret organization] **b :** arranged into or belonging to a labor union ▪ *organized* mine workers ▪ ***organized labor*** [=labor unions as a group]

2 [*more ~; most ~*] **:** arranged or planned in a particular way ▪ They ran a well-*organized* political campaign. ▪ a poorly *organized* meeting

3 [*more ~; most ~*] **a :** having things arranged in a neat and effective way ▪ an *organized* office ▪ His office is a mess. He needs to ***get organized***. [=he needs to organize his office] **b :** able to keep things arranged in a neat or effective way ▪ She's a very *organized* person. — opposite DISORGANIZED

or·gasm /ˈoɚ͵gæzəm/ *noun, pl* **-gasms :** the point during sexual activity when sexual pleasure is strongest [*noncount*] achieve/experience/reach *orgasm* [*count*] have an *orgasm*

or·gas·mic /oɚˈgæzmɪk/ *adj*

1 *always used before a noun* **:** of or relating to an orgasm ▪ *orgasmic* dysfunction

2 : very exciting or enjoyable ▪ White-water rafting was an *orgasmic* experience.

or·gy /ˈoɚʤi/ *noun, pl* **-gies** [*count*]

1 : a wild party and especially one in which many people have sex together ▪ a drunken *orgy*

2 : something that is done too much and in a wild way ▪ an eating *orgy* — often + *of* ▪ The troops took part in an *orgy of* destruction. ▪ an *orgy of* violence and crime

ori·ent /ˈori͵ɛnt/ *verb* **-ents; -ent·ed; -ent·ing** [+ *obj*]

1 : to change or create (something, such as a book or a film) so that it appeals to a particular group of people or is suitable for a particular group of people — often + *to* or *toward* ▪ They are planning to *orient* the movie *toward* teenagers. [=to make the movie interesting to teenagers] ▪ The authors *oriented* the text *to/toward* high-school students. = The text is *oriented toward* high-school students.

2 : to direct (someone) toward a goal ▪ The program is intended to *orient* students toward a career in medicine.

3 : to place (something) in a particular position or direction ▪ *Orient* the map so that north is at the top. ▪ The house is *oriented* so that it faces west.

4 : to help (someone) become familiar with a new situation, place, etc. ▪ The guide is intended to *orient* travelers (to their surroundings). ▪ The hikers stopped to ***orient themselves*** [=to find out where they were] by looking at their map. ▪ She needs time to *orient herself* to her new job. [=to become familiar with her new job] — compare DISORIENT

Ori·ent /ˈorijənt/ *noun*

the Orient *old-fashioned* **:** the countries of eastern Asia ▪ a plant that grows in *the Orient* ▪ We're planning a trip to *the Orient*. — compare OCCIDENT

ori·en·tal *or* **Ori·en·tal** /͵oriˈɛntl/ *adj, old-fashioned* **:** of, relating to, or from Asia and especially eastern Asia ▪ I like *oriental* food. ▪ *oriental* art ✧ The adjective *Oriental* is now often considered offensive when it is used to describe a person. The adjective *Asian* should be used instead.

Oriental *noun, pl* **-tals** [*count*] *old-fashioned* + *offensive* **:** a person from eastern Asia

ori·en·tal·ist /͵oriˈɛntəlɪst/ *noun, pl* **-ists** [*count*] *somewhat old-fashioned* **:** a person who studies Asian countries, languages, etc.

Oriental rug *noun, pl* **~ rugs** [*count*] **:** a rug or carpet that is made in central or southern Asia and that usually has very fancy designs on it

ori·en·tate /ˈorijən͵teɪt/ *verb* **-tates; -tat·ed; -tat·ing** [+ *obj*] *chiefly Brit* **:** ORIENT ▪ a program that helps to *orientate* new students • She needs to ***orientate herself*** to her new job.

orientated *adj, chiefly Brit* : ORIENTED

ori·en·ta·tion /ˌorijənˈteɪʃən/ *noun, pl* **-tions**

1 [*count, noncount*] **a** : a person's feelings, interests, and beliefs • his political/religious/spiritual *orientation* **b** : SEXUAL ORIENTATION • patients identifying themselves as homosexual or bisexual in *orientation* • He makes no secret of his *orientation*.

2 : a main interest, quality, or goal [*count*] The organization has a decidedly conservative *orientation*. [*noncount*] Her later works were more introspective in *orientation*.

3 : the process of giving people training and information about a new job, situation, etc. [*noncount*] These materials are used for the *orientation* of new employees. • an *orientation* meeting/session • The weekend before the semester begins is the ***freshman orientation*** period. [=the time when new students start to become familiar with a college] [*count*] New students need to go through a short *orientation* before they begin classes.

4 [*count*] : the position or direction of something • They had to adjust the antenna's *orientation* in order to receive a clear signal. • The valley has a north-south *orientation*. [=the valley runs from north to south]

oriented *adj*

1 : interested in a particular thing, activity, etc. • politically *oriented* journalists [=journalists who are interested in politics] • The audience was academically *oriented*.

2 : designed to appeal to a certain kind of people • We went to a family-*oriented* amusement park. [=an amusement park designed to appeal to families]

ori·en·teer·ing /ˌorijənˈtirɪŋ/ *noun* [*noncount*] : a sport in which people use a map and a compass to travel along a route they do not know as quickly as possible

or·i·fice /ˈorəfəs/ *noun, pl* **-fic·es** [*count*] *formal* : a hole or opening and especially one in your body (such as your mouth, ear, nostril, etc.) • a bodily *orifice*

ori·ga·mi /ˌorəˈgɑːmi/ *noun* [*noncount*] : the Japanese art of folding paper into shapes that look like birds, animals, etc.

or·i·gin /ˈorəʤən/ *noun, pl* **-gins**

1 : the point or place where something begins or is created : the source or cause of something [*count*] The *origin* of this custom/tradition is not known. = The *origins* of this custom/tradition are not known. [=no one knows how this custom/tradition started] • What is the *origin* [=*etymology*] of that word? • The school ***had its origin*** [=the school was created] with a large gift from a donor. • The story *had its origin* [=*originated*] in the 19th century. [*noncount*] The English word "rendezvous" is French ***in origin***. [=the English word comes from French] • The infection was bacterial *in origin*. [=the infection was caused by bacteria] • The wine is named for its ***place of origin***. [=the place where it was made/created] • The game is ***of recent origin***. [=the game was created recently] • a disease ***of unknown origin*** [=a disease whose origin is not known]

2 : the place, social situation, or type of family that a person comes from [*noncount*] She is of French *origin*. [=*ancestry*] • What is his ***country of origin***? [=what country does he come from?] [*count*] Her ethnic *origins* are French. • He comes from ***humble origins***. [=he comes from a family that did not have high social status or much money]

[1]**orig·i·nal** /əˈrɪʤənl/ *adj*

1 *always used before a noun* : happening or existing first or at the beginning • Their *original* idea was to fix their old car, but they decided to buy a new one instead. • The word's *original* meaning was very different from its current meaning. • That piece of furniture is still in its *original* condition. [=the furniture is in the same condition it was in when we first bought it] • We were the *original* [=*first*] owners of that van.

2 *always used before a noun* : made or produced first : not a copy, translation, etc. • I gave her a copy and kept the *original* document myself. • The book has been translated into English from the *original* Spanish.

3 [*more* ~; *most* ~] **a** : not like others : new, different, and appealing • The concept is very *original*. • The car has a highly *original* design. **b** : able to think of or make new and creative things • She has a very *original* and creative mind. • He is admired as an *original* American composer.

[2]**original** *noun, pl* **-nals**

1 [*count*] : a document, film, painting, etc., which is created by someone and from which a copy or translation is made • I gave her a copy of the report and kept the *original*. • This isn't a reprint, it's an *original*.

2 [*singular*] : a person who is different from other people in an appealing or interesting way • Compared to other actresses of her generation, she is a true *original*.

in the original : in the language used by the original writer • We read Homer *in the original*, not in translation. [=we read the original words that Homer wrote in ancient Greek]

orig·i·nal·i·ty /əˌrɪʤəˈnæləti/ *noun* [*noncount*] : the quality of being new and different in a good and appealing way • Critics have praised the movie's startling *originality*. • I was amazed by the *originality* of her ideas. • an artist of great *originality* [=*creativity*]

orig·i·nal·ly /əˈrɪʤənli/ *adv*

1 : in the beginning : when something first happened or began • That van *originally* belonged to us. • The building was *originally* a school. • They *originally* planned to fix their old car, but they decided to buy a new one instead. • *Originally*, the word had a very different meaning from its current meaning. • a New Yorker who is *originally* from Mexico

2 [*more* ~; *most* ~] : in a new, fresh, or original way • She has shown an ability to think *originally* about ways to improve the company.

original sin *noun* [*noncount*] : the belief taught in Christianity that people will naturally do bad or evil things

orig·i·nate /əˈrɪʤəˌneɪt/ *verb* **-nates; -nat·ed; -nat·ing**

1 [*no obj*] : to begin to exist : to be produced or created • No one knows when or where the idea (first) *originated*. • These stories *originated* during earlier times. • The book *originated* as/from a series of lectures. • The sound seemed to *originate* from outside the room. • The custom is believed to have *originated* in the western U.S. • That idea did not ***originate with*** him. [=he was not the first person to have that idea]

2 [+ *obj*] : to cause (something) to exist : to produce or create (something) • He did not *originate* the idea. • The policy was *originated* by the previous administration.

– orig·i·na·tor /əˈrɪʤəˌneɪtɚ/ *noun, pl* **-tors** [*count*]

ori·ole /ˈoriˌoʊl/ *noun, pl* **-oles** [*count*]

1 : a colorful North American bird that has an orange or yellow body with black wings

2 : a European bird ✧ The male European oriole has a bright yellow body and black wings.

Ori·on /əˈrajən/ *noun* [*noncount*] : a group of stars in the sky that looks like a hunter with a line of three bright stars for a belt ✧ This group of stars is named for a famous hunter in stories from Greek mythology.

[1]**or·na·ment** /ˈoɚnəmənt/ *noun, pl* **-ments**

1 [*count*] : a small, fancy object that is put on something else to make it more attractive • She wore a hair *ornament*. • (*US*) the ***hood ornament*** on a car [=a small metal figure on the front edge of a car's hood] • ***Christmas ornaments*** [=small balls, figures, etc., that are hung on a Christmas tree for decoration]

2 [*noncount*] *formal* : a way to make something look more attractive and less plain • A satin bow was used for *ornament*. [=*decoration*] • The columns are there purely as *ornament*—they have no structural function.

[2]**ornament** *verb* **-ments; -ment·ed; -ment·ing** [+ *obj*] *formal* : to make (something) more attractive by adding small objects to it : DECORATE • flower patterns used to *ornament* boxes — usually used as *(be) ornamented* • a dress *ornamented* with pearls • elaborately/highly *ornamented* ceilings

[1]**or·na·men·tal** /ˌoɚnəˈmɛntl/ *adj* : used to make something more attractive : used for decoration • *ornamental* vases • The garden has many *ornamental* shrubs. • The columns are purely *ornamental*. [=*decorative*]

– or·na·men·tal·ly *adv*

[2]**ornamental** *noun, pl* **-tals** [*count*] *chiefly US* : a plant that is grown for its beauty rather than for its fruit, wood, etc. : an ornamental plant • The garden has many beautiful *ornamentals*.

or·na·men·ta·tion /ˌoɚnəmənˈteɪʃən/ *noun* [*noncount*] *somewhat formal* : something that is added to make something else more attractive • A bright ribbon was used for *ornamentation*. • a ballroom with elaborate *ornamentation*

or·nate /oɚˈneɪt/ *adj* [*more* ~; *most* ~]

1 : covered with decorations : covered with fancy patterns and shapes • *ornate* silver candlesticks • She doesn't like *ornate* jewelry. — opposite PLAIN

2 : using many fancy words • an *ornate* writing style • *ornate* prose

– or·nate·ly *adv* • *ornately* carved staircases **– or·nate·ness** *noun* [*noncount*]

O

or·nery /ˈoɚnəri/ *adj* **or·neri·er; -est** [*or more ~; most ~*] *US, informal + often humorous*
1 : easily annoyed or angered • I'm getting more and more *ornery* in my old age.
2 : difficult to deal with or control • an *ornery* mule
– **or·neri·ness** *noun* [*noncount*] • She has a reputation for *orneriness*. [=people know that she gets annoyed easily]

or·ni·thol·o·gy /ˌoɚnəˈθɑːləʤi/ *noun* [*noncount*] : a branch of science that deals with the study of birds
– **or·ni·tho·log·i·cal** /ˌoɚnəθəˈlɑːʤɪkəl/ *adj* – **or·ni·thol·o·gist** /ˌoɚnəˈθɑːləʤɪst/ *noun, pl* **-gists** [*count*]

[1]**or·phan** /ˈoɚfən/ *noun, pl* **-phans** [*count*] : a child whose parents are dead • He was left an *orphan* [=he became an orphan] when his parents died in a car accident. — sometimes used of animals • The baby raccoon were *orphans*.
– **orphan** *adj, always used before a noun* • an *orphan* boy/girl

[2]**orphan** *verb* **-phans; -phaned; -phan·ing** [+ *obj*] : to cause (a child) to become an orphan — usually used as *(be) orphaned* • He *was orphaned* as a young boy when his parents died in a car accident. • Thousands of children *were orphaned* by the war. — sometimes used of animals • *orphaned* puppies — sometimes used figuratively • The second volume of the two-volume set *was orphaned* when we lost the first volume.

or·phan·age /ˈoɚfənɪʤ/ *noun, pl* **-ag·es** [*count*] : a place where children whose parents have died can live and be cared for : a home for orphans • After the death of his parents, he was raised in an *orphanage*.

or·tho·don·tia /ˌoɚθəˈdɑːnʃijə/ *noun* [*noncount*] *US, technical* : treatment and devices used on teeth to make them grow straight • We took out a loan to pay for our son's *orthodontia*.

or·tho·don·tics /ˌoɚθəˈdɑːntɪks/ *noun* [*noncount*] : a branch of dentistry that deals with helping teeth to grow straight
– **or·tho·don·tic** /ˌoɚθəˈdɑːntɪk/ *adj* • He underwent *orthodontic* treatment. • an *orthodontic* device – **or·tho·don·tist** /ˌoɚθəˈdɑːntɪst/ *noun, pl* **-tists** [*count*] • The *orthodontist* put braces on my teeth.

or·tho·dox /ˈoɚθəˌdɑːks/ *adj*
1 [*more ~; most ~*] : accepted as true or correct by most people : supporting or believing what most people think is true : CONVENTIONAL • He took an *orthodox* approach to the problem. • *orthodox* thinking • *orthodox* political views • She believes in the benefits of both *orthodox* medicine and alternative medicine. — opposite UNORTHODOX
2 a *or* ***Orthodox*** : accepting and closely following the traditional beliefs and customs of a religion • *Orthodox* Jews • He is a very *orthodox* Muslim. **b** ***Orthodox*** : of or relating to the Orthodox Church • I attend an Eastern *Orthodox* church. • My grandmother is Russian *Orthodox*.

O

Orthodox Church *noun*
the Orthodox Church : a branch of the Christian church that has members mainly in the area from eastern Europe to eastern Africa • *the* Eastern *Orthodox Church* • *the* Russian/Greek/Ethiopian *Orthodox Church*

or·tho·doxy /ˈoɚθəˌdɑːksi/ *noun, pl* **-dox·ies** *formal*
1 : a belief or a way of thinking that is accepted as true or correct [*noncount*] I was surprised by the *orthodoxy* of her political views. [*count*] He rejected the *orthodoxies* of the scientific establishment.
2 ***Orthodoxy*** [*noncount*] : the beliefs, practices, and institution of the Orthodox Church

or·thog·ra·phy /oɚˈθɑːgrəfi/ *noun* [*noncount*] *technical* : the way in which the words of a language are spelled • the rules of English *orthography* [=*spelling*]
– **or·tho·graph·ic** /ˌoɚθəˈgræfɪk/ *adj, always used before a noun* • *orthographic* reforms

or·tho·pe·dic (*chiefly US*) *also chiefly Brit* **or·tho·pae·dic** /ˌoɚθəˈpiːdɪk/ *adj, medical*
1 : used in the treatment of illnesses and injuries that affect bones and muscles • *orthopedic* medicine • an *orthopedic* surgeon • She was wearing *orthopedic* shoes.
2 : affecting bones or muscles • *orthopedic* injuries

or·tho·pe·dics (*chiefly US*) *also chiefly Brit* **or·tho·pae·dics** /ˌoɚθəˈpiːdɪks/ *noun* [*noncount*] *medical* : a branch of medicine that tries to prevent and correct problems that affect bones and muscles
– **or·tho·pe·dist** (*chiefly US*) *also chiefly Brit* **or·tho·pae·dist** /ˌoɚθəˈpiːdɪst/ *noun, pl* **-dists** [*count*]

[1]**-ory** *noun suffix* : a place for • observat*ory* • reformat*ory*

[2]**-ory** *adj suffix* : of, relating to, or doing • regulat*ory* [=regulating] • explanat*ory* [=explaining]

OS *abbr, computers* operating system

Os·car /ˈɑːskɚ/ *trademark* — used for a small statue that is awarded by part of the American film industry to the best actors, movies, directors, etc., of the year

os·cil·late /ˈɑːsəˌleɪt/ *verb* **-lates; -lat·ed; -lat·ing** [*no obj*]
1 : to move in one direction and then back again many times • The fan was *oscillating*. [=was turning to the right, then to the left, then to the right, etc.] • Stock prices have continued to *oscillate*. [=to go up and down] • an *oscillating* fan
2 *formal* : to keep changing from one belief, feeling, condition, etc., to an opposite one — usually + *between* • The mood of voters has *oscillated between* optimism and pessimism. • The weather *oscillated between* brutal cold and searing heat.
3 *technical* : to change in strength or direction regularly • an *oscillating* electric current • *oscillating* radio waves • stars that *oscillate* in brightness [=that get brighter, then fainter, then brighter, etc.]

os·cil·la·tion /ˌɑːsəˈleɪʃən/ *noun, pl* **-tions**
1 : the act of regularly moving from one position to another and back to the original position [*noncount*] the continued *oscillation* of the fan [*count*] the fan's *oscillations*
2 *somewhat formal* : a frequent change from one state, position, or amount to another [*noncount*] the continual *oscillation* [=(more commonly) *fluctuation*] of stock prices [*count*] price/temperature *oscillations*
3 *somewhat formal* : the act of changing from one belief, feeling, etc., to an opposite one — usually + *between* [*noncount*] There has been *oscillation between* optimism and pessimism among voters. [*count*] His friends were alarmed by his *oscillations* [=(less formally) *swings*] *between* hope and despair.
4 [*count*] *technical* : a single movement from one position or state to another • Each *oscillation* of the pendulum represents one second.

os·mo·sis /ɑzˈmousəs/ *noun* [*noncount*]
1 *biology* : the process that causes a liquid (especially water) to pass through the wall of a living cell
2 : an ability to learn and understand things gradually without much effort • She seems to learn foreign languages by/through *osmosis*.

os·prey /ˈɑːspri, ˈɑːˌspreɪ/ *noun, pl* **-preys** [*count*] : a large bird that eats fish

os·si·fy /ˈɑːsəˌfaɪ/ *verb* **-fies; -fied; -fy·ing**
1 *formal + disapproving* : to become or to cause something to become unable to change [*no obj*] Her opinions have *ossified*. [+ *obj*] an *ossified* social hierarchy • *ossified* ideologies
2 *technical* : to become or to cause something to become hard like bone [*no obj*] The cartilage will *ossify*, becoming bone. [+ *obj*] a disease that *ossifies* the joints
– **os·si·fi·ca·tion** /ˌɑːsəfəˈkeɪʃən/ *noun* [*noncount*] • intellectual *ossification* • *ossification* of the cartilage

os·ten·si·ble /ɑˈstɛnsəbəl/ *adj, always used before a noun* : seeming or said to be true or real but very possibly not true or real • The *ostensible* reason for his visit was to see an old friend. [=he said the reason was to see an old friend, but the real reason may have been something different] • The *ostensible* [=*apparent*] purpose of the article is to encourage young adults to vote.
– **os·ten·si·bly** /ɑˈstɛnsəbli/ *adv* • The story is *ostensibly* fiction, but some of the events are based on real life. • *Ostensibly*, the reason for his visit was to see an old friend.

os·ten·ta·tion /ˌɑːstənˈteɪʃən/ *noun* [*noncount*] *disapproving* : an unnecessary display of wealth, knowledge, etc., that is done to attract attention, admiration, or envy • The actress avoids *ostentation*. She owns a small house and drives an inexpensive car. • She dressed stylishly without *ostentation*. [=she dressed in a way that was simple yet attractive] • He writes simply and clearly and without *ostentation*.

os·ten·ta·tious /ˌɑːstənˈteɪʃəs/ *adj* [*more ~; most ~*] *disapproving* : displaying wealth, knowledge, etc., in a way that is meant to attract attention, admiration, or envy • the *ostentatious* [=very large and expensive] summer homes of the rich • the *ostentatious* [=*pretentious*] use of foreign phrases in conversation • an *ostentatious* display of knowledge
– **os·ten·ta·tious·ly** *adv* • He dresses *ostentatiously*. • Her ring had an *ostentatiously* large diamond.

os·teo·ar·thri·tis /ˌɑːstijowɑɚˈθraɪtəs/ *noun* [*noncount*] *medical* : a disease that causes the joints to become very painful and stiff

os·te·op·a·thy /ˌɑːstiˈɑːpəθi/ *noun* [*noncount*] *medical* **:** a method of treating people who are sick or in pain by pushing and moving bones and muscles
— **os·teo·path** /ˈɑːstijəˌpæθ/ *noun, pl* **-paths** [*count*] ▪ He is a trained *osteopath*. — **os·teo·path·ic** /ˌɑːstijəˈpæθɪk/ *adj* ▪ *osteopathic* treatment — **os·teo·path·i·cal·ly** /ˌɑːstijəˈpæθɪkli/ *adv*

os·te·o·po·ro·sis /ˌɑːstijoʊpəˈroʊsəs/ *noun* [*noncount*] *medical* **:** a condition in which the bones become weak and break easily

os·tra·cize *also Brit* **os·tra·cise** /ˈɑːstrəˌsaɪz/ *verb* **-ciz·es; -cized; -ciz·ing** [+ *obj*] **:** to not allow (someone) to be included in a group **:** to exclude (someone) from a group ▪ She was *ostracized* from/by the scientific community for many years because of her radical political beliefs. ▪ The other girls *ostracized* her because of the way she dressed.
— **os·tra·cism** /ˈɑːstrəˌsɪzəm/ *noun* [*noncount*] ▪ She suffered years of *ostracism* from the scientific community.

os·trich /ˈɑːstrɪʧ/ *noun, pl* **-trich·es** [*count*] **:** a very large African bird that runs very fast but cannot fly

ostrich

OT *abbr* **1** occupational therapist; occupational therapy **2** ***O.T.*** Old Testament **3** ***O.T.*** *US* overtime ▪ He scored a goal in *O.T.* to win the game.

OTC *abbr* over-the-counter

[1]**oth·er** /ˈʌðɚ/ *adj, always used before a noun* **1** — used to refer to the one person or thing that remains or that has not been mentioned ▪ What's in your *other* hand? ▪ "Is this the ear that hurts?" "No, it's my *other* ear." ▪ My *other* son is a doctor. ▪ Their *other* car is a lot smaller than this one. ▪ I didn't like this novel as much as the *other* one. ▪ Do you want the *other* half of my bagel? — see also OTHER HALF
2 — used to refer to all the members of a group except the person or thing that has already been mentioned ▪ "Is this the last copy?" "Yes, all the *other* copies have been sold." ▪ She was taller than the *other* girls in her class. [=she was taller than the rest of the girls in her class] ▪ One of her daughters lives in Texas and her two *other* daughters live in California. ▪ This car got better gas mileage than the *other* ones we tested.
3 : in addition to the person or thing that has already been mentioned ▪ Does anyone have any *other* [=*additional, more*] ideas? ▪ These and *other* issues will be discussed at the next meeting. ▪ The driver's wife and two *other* passengers were injured in the accident. ▪ Leaders from China, Russia, and 14 *other* countries attended the conference. ▪ The study found, ***among other things*** [=in addition to things that are not specifically mentioned], that men and women are equally at risk for the disease. ▪ There's ***one other*** [=one more] person I'd like you to meet.
4 : different or separate from the person or thing that has already been mentioned ▪ Some people believe it while *other* people don't. ▪ "Parents should teach their children to respect *other* people's property," she said. ▪ Gas prices are even higher in *other* parts of the country. ▪ We are asking people to donate money or to help in *other* ways. ▪ The main road is closed, so you'll need to find ***some other*** [=*another*] way to get there. ▪ I'm afraid we'll have to finish this meeting *some other* time. ▪ ***Any other*** day but tomorrow would be okay. ▪ There weren't *any other* children for us to play with. ▪ It was horrible. There's really ***no other*** way to describe it. ▪ It's a problem that's affecting this town and ***every other*** one [=all the towns] in the state.
5 — used to refer to the place that is furthest away from the speaker or to the direction that is opposite to an original direction ▪ We live near the school, but his house is on the *other* [=*opposite*] side of town. ▪ I was sitting at the *other* end of the room. ▪ She turned around and started walking in the *other* direction. ▪ We should have gone the *other* way.
6 : opposite or completely different ▪ Some days he doesn't eat anything, while other days he goes to the *other* extreme and eats everything in the refrigerator. ▪ We ate dinner and then watched the movie, but we should have done it ***the other way around*** [=we should have watched the movie first]
every other — used to indicate how often a repeated activity happens or is done ▪ I run *every other* day. [=I run one day, then the next day I do not run, then the day after that I run, etc.] ▪ The contest is held *every other* year. [=every two years]
in other words see [1]WORD
look the other way see [1]LOOK
none other than see [1]NONE
on the other hand see [1]HAND
other than **1 :** not including (something or someone) ▪ We're open every day *other than* [=*except, except for*] Sunday. ▪ I saw a movie, but ***other than that***, I didn't do much last weekend. **2 a : different from (something)** ▪ Could we have something *other than* cereal [=something that is not cereal] for breakfast? ▪ We never saw him drink anything *other than* beer. [=we only saw him drink beer] ▪ Do you have this sweater in any color *other than* red? ▪ She said nothing about the case *other than* that her client would not be found guilty. **b : in a different way from a specified way** ▪ She's never spoken *other than* kindly of him. [=she has only spoken about him in a kind way] **3 :** EXCEPT — used to introduce a statement that indicates the only person or thing that is not included in or referred to by a previous statement ▪ Take no orders *other than* from me. ▪ No one may enter *other than* by special permission. ▪ You can't get there *other than* by boat.
the other day/night/evening (etc.) **:** on a day/night/evening (etc.) in the recent past ▪ I talked to him just *the other day*. [=a few days ago] ▪ *The other morning*, I saw a deer on our lawn.

[2]**other** *pronoun*
1 a : a different or additional person or thing ▪ This car is ***like no other***! [=this is a very special car] ▪ The storms came ***one right after the other***. [=they happened very close together] ▪ I love you and ***no other***. [=no one else] — see also EACH OTHER, SIGNIFICANT OTHER **b** ***others*** **: different or additional people or things** ▪ These issues and *others* will be discussed at the next meeting. ▪ She and two *others* were injured in the accident. ▪ Some medicines work better than *others*. ▪ Some (people) believe it while *others* don't. ▪ Be kind to *others*. ▪ One student stood out above all *others*.
2 a ***the other*** **: the person or thing that remains or that has not been shown or mentioned yet** ▪ She ate one half of the bagel and gave me *the other*. ▪ I held on with one hand and waved with *the other*. ▪ Each of them looked at *the other*. = They each looked at *the other*. [=they looked at each other] ▪ You can have (either) ***one or the other***—but not both. **b** ***the others*** **: all the members of a group except the person or thing that has already been mentioned** ▪ He got a drink of water while *the others* continued playing. ▪ This is the last copy. All *the others* have been sold. ▪ This car got better gas mileage than *the others* we tested.
3 ***the other*** **: an opposite place or thing** ▪ We moved from one side of town to *the other*. ▪ She sat at one end of the table while I sat at *the other*. ▪ The weather can go from one extreme to *the other*. [=the weather can change very suddenly]
4 — used in phrases like ***something or other*** or ***somehow or other*** when the specific details about something are not important or have been forgotten ▪ He said he had to go buy *something or other* at the grocery store. ▪ *Somehow or other*, we managed to get all of the boxes into the car. ▪ ***For some reason or other***, they wouldn't let her in the building. ▪ Everyone has felt that way ***at some time or other*** in their lives.
in one ear and out the other see [1]EAR

other half *noun* [*singular*]
1 : a group of people who are not like you because they are either very rich or very poor — used in the phrase ***how the other half lives*** ▪ They won a million dollars and, for a few years, got to see *how the other half lives*. [=how rich people live]
2 *chiefly Brit, old-fashioned + humorous* **: a person's wife or husband :** BETTER HALF ▪ I don't believe we have anything planned for that night, but let me check with my *other half*.

oth·er·ness /ˈʌðɚnəs/ *noun* [*noncount*] *literary* **: the quality of being different or unusual** ▪ As an American growing up in Africa, I always felt a sense of *otherness*. ▪ the *otherness* of their small religious community

[1]**otherwise** /ˈʌðɚˌwaɪz/ *adv*
1 : in a different way or manner ▪ All of the books had been burned or *otherwise* destroyed. ▪ The women talked in the living room while the men were *otherwise* occupied. ▪ Art allows us to express things that we would not be able to express *otherwise*. ▪ All shows begin at 7:00 unless *otherwise* noted. [=unless there is a note indicating that a show begins at a different time] ▪ employees who are sick or *otherwise* un-

O

available [=unavailable for some other reason] • France's King Louis XIV, ***otherwise known as*** [=*also known as*] the Sun King, died in 1715 at the age of 77.

2 : if something did not happen, was not true, etc. • Thank you for reminding me; I might have missed the meeting *otherwise*. [=if you did not remind me] • Something must be wrong; *otherwise*, he would have called. • The new computer program allows us to do in seconds what would *otherwise* [=without the computer program] take us days to accomplish. • The test helps identify problems that might *otherwise* go unnoticed/undetected.

3 : in all ways except the one mentioned • One of the boys has a freckle on his cheek. *Otherwise*, the twins are nearly identical. • I didn't like the ending, but *otherwise* it was a very good book. • It rained in the morning; *otherwise*, it was a beautiful day. = It rained in the morning, but it was a beautiful day *otherwise*.

4 : if not : or else • Finish your dinner. *Otherwise* [=if you don't finish your dinner], you won't get any dessert. • I hope we haven't missed the last train; *otherwise* [=if we have missed the train], we'll have to get a taxi.

5 — used to indicate that something different from the thing mentioned is suggested, shown, done, etc. • He claims to be innocent, but the evidence suggests *otherwise*. [=the evidence suggests that he is not innocent] • While some people think it is true, our research proves *otherwise*. [=our research proves it is false] • Although her political rivals would have us believe *otherwise*, she would be an excellent President. • You know what happened, so don't try to pretend *otherwise*. [=that you don't know what happened]

and/or otherwise — used to refer to something that is different from something already mentioned • The company has been having problems, financial *and otherwise* [=the company has been having financial problems and other kinds of problems], for several years. • They couldn't afford a house, small *or otherwise*. [=or any other kind of house] • Intentionally *or otherwise*, they never told her about the party.

[2]**otherwise** *adj* : not the same : DIFFERENT • If conditions were *otherwise*, I wouldn't be so worried.

other woman *noun*

the other woman : a woman who is having a sexual relationship with a man who is married to someone else • She was *the other woman* who broke up their marriage.

oth·er·world·ly /ˌʌðɚˈwɚdli/ *adj* [*more* ~; *most* ~] : suggesting a world that is different from the world we know : seeming to belong to or come from another world • *otherworldly* creatures from the deep sea • the *otherworldly* [=*ethereal*] beauty of the landscape • *otherworldly* music

— **oth·er·world·li·ness** *noun* [*noncount*] • the *otherworldliness* of the landscape

OTT /ˌoʊˌtiːˈtiː/ *adj* [*more* ~; *most* ~] *Brit, informal* : beyond what is expected, usual, normal, or appropriate • an *OTT* performance • His reaction was a bit *OTT*. ✧ *OTT* is an abbreviation of the phrase "over the top."

ot·ter /ˈɑːtɚ/ *noun, pl* **otter** *or* **ot·ters** [*count*] : an animal that has dark brown fur and webbed feet with claws and that eats fish

otter

ot·to·man /ˈɑːtəmən/ *noun, pl* **-mans** [*count*]

1 *US* : a low piece of furniture that has a soft top and that you can put your feet on when you are sitting : a soft footstool — called also (*Brit*) *pouf*

2 : a long seat with no back that has a soft top and that typically has space inside where things can be stored

ouch /ˈaʊʧ/ *interj* — used to express sudden pain • *Ouch*! That hurt!

ought /ˈɑːt/ *verb* [*modal verb*] ✧ *Ought* is almost always followed by *to* and the infinitive form of a verb. The phrase ***ought to*** has the same meaning as *should* and is used in the same ways, but it is less common and somewhat more formal. The negative forms ***ought not*** and ***oughtn't*** are often used without a following *to*.

1 — used to indicate what is expected • They *ought to* be here by now. • You *ought to* be able to read this book. • There *ought to* be a gas station on the way. • He *ought to* have known better. • If my math is correct, the result *ought to* be zero. • He *ought to* have enough money for the trip. • She *ought to* be ashamed of herself. • It *ought not* (*to*) make any difference. [=(more commonly) it shouldn't make any difference]

2 — used to say or suggest what should be done • You *ought to* get some rest. • That leak *ought to* be fixed. • You *ought to* do your homework. • We *ought to* go now. • We *ought to* get together some time soon. • You *ought to* apologize. • Children *ought not* [=*should not*] run near the pool.

oughtn't /ˈɑːtn̩t/ — used as a contraction of *ought not* • It *oughtn't* (to) make any difference.

Oui·ja /ˈwiːʤə/ *trademark* — used for a board that has the alphabet and other signs on it and that some people believe can be used to communicate with the spirits of dead people

ounce /ˈaʊns/ *noun, pl* **ounc·es**

1 [*count*] : a unit of weight equal to 1/16 pound (about 28 grams)

2 [*count*] : FLUID OUNCE

3 [*singular*] *informal* : a very small amount of something • If you had an *ounce* of common sense, you wouldn't try it. • He doesn't have an *ounce* of decency. • She doesn't have an *ounce* of fat on her body. [=she is very thin] • That story doesn't have an *ounce* of truth in it. [=that story is completely untrue]

our /ˈawɚ, ɑɚ/ *adj, always used before a noun, possessive form of* WE : relating to or belonging to us • *our* house/dog/country • We bumped *our* heads. • We are defending *our* rights. • *our* family/parents/relatives • Rare wines are *our* specialty. [=we specialize in rare wines] : made or done by us • We were criticized for *our* actions/misbehavior. • We kept *our* promise. • He was angry because of *our* being late. [=he was angry because we were late]

Our Father *noun, pl* ~ **-thers**

1 ***the Our Father*** : LORD'S PRAYER

2 [*count*] : an act of saying the Lord's Prayer • She knelt down and said an *Our Father*.

ours /ˈawɚz, ɑɚz/ *pronoun* : that which belongs to or is connected with us : our one : our ones • That house is *ours*. [=that is our house] • Those books are *ours*. [=those are our books] • *Ours* is the house on the left. [=our house is the one on the left] • Their house is brown and *ours* is gray. • He is a friend ***of ours***. [=he is our friend]

our·selves /ˌawɚˈsɛlvz, ɑɚˈsɛlvz/ *pronoun*

1 : those same ones that we are: **a** — used as the object of a verb or preposition to refer to a group that includes you after that group has already been mentioned • We consider *ourselves* lucky. • We can see *ourselves* being parents someday. • We kept the money for *ourselves*. • We made fools (out) of *ourselves*. [=we made ourselves look foolish] • We have the house to *ourselves* this weekend. [=we are the only ones staying in the house this weekend] • We want to see it ***for ourselves***. [=we wanted to see it rather than have someone tell us about it, describe it to us, etc.] **b** — used for emphasis to refer again to a group that includes you after that group has already been mentioned • We *ourselves* do not agree. • We did it *ourselves*. • We told them *ourselves* that we would help. • We were young once *ourselves*. [=we are old now but were once young]

2 : our normal or healthy selves • We are tired and just not *ourselves*. • We were sick, but we are back to *ourselves* today.

by ourselves **1 :** without any help from other people • We did it (all) *by ourselves*. **2 :** with nobody else except us • We went to the movies *by ourselves*. • We both live *by ourselves*. [=*alone*]

-ous /əs/ *adj suffix* : full of : having a large amount of • danger*ous* [=full of danger] • poison*ous* [=having or containing poison] • mountain*ous* [=having many mountains] : having the quality of • courage*ous* [=having courage] • glamor*ous* [=having glamour]

oust /ˈaʊst/ *verb* **ousts; oust·ed; oust·ing** [+ *obj*]

1 : to cause or force (someone or something) to leave a position of power, a competition, etc. • The rebels *ousted* the dictator from power. — often used as *(be) ousted* • He *was ousted* as chairman. • The team *was ousted* from the tournament in the first round of the play-offs.

2 : to take the place of (someone or something) • Large national banks are *ousting* local banks in many communities.

oust·er /ˈaʊstɚ/ *noun* [*singular*] *US* : the act of removing someone or something from a position of power or authority • The news reported the *ouster* of the dictator. • the dictator's *ouster* by the rebels

[1]**out** /ˈaʊt/ *adv*

1 : in a direction away from the inside or center of something • He went *out* to the garden. • He looked *out* at the snow. • She poured the tea *out.* • The girl stuck her tongue *out.* • His shirttail was hanging *out.* • He pulled *out* the cork (from the bottle). • I heard a noise in the bushes and *out* jumped a cat!

2 : in or to a place outside of something (such as a building, room, etc.) • He waited *out* in the hall. • I cleaned my car inside and *out.* • A car pulled up and two men got *out.* • She is *out* [=*outside*] playing with her friends. • She took the dog *out* [=*outdoors*] for a walk. • He grabbed his coat and *out* he went. • It is raining/sunny *out* today.

3 a : away from home or work • They went *out* on a date. • We dine *out* once a week. • We went *out* for/to lunch. • Are you going to ***ask her out***? [=ask her to go on a date with you] **b : away from a place** • They flew *out* yesterday. • Did you ship *out* the packages yet? • The house is *out* in the country. • I was just ***on my way out*** [=I was just leaving] when the phone rang. **c : away from the shore** • The ship sailed *out* to sea. • The tide is going *out.* • They rowed *out* to the ship. • She swam about 100 yards *out.*

4 — used to indicate that something is not in the usual or proper place • You left *out* a comma here. • She threw *out* her shoulder. • He knocked a tooth *out.*

5 : from among a group of things • She picked *out* a shirt to wear.

6 : in or into the control or possession of another person • She is always willing to lend *out* money to friends. • The library book I want is still *out.* [=someone else has borrowed the library book] • Please don't let my secret *out.* [=don't tell anyone my secret] • They passed *out* free samples.

7 a : to a state in which something has been used or removed completely • Their food supply ran *out.* • I couldn't get the stain *out.* [=I could not remove the stain] **b : to a state in which something is completed** • Please fill *out* this form. • She worked *out* the math problem by herself.

8 : in the position of someone who is not involved or participating in something • Count me *out.* [=do not include me in your plans] • "Do you want to dance?" "Sorry, but I think I'd better sit this one *out.*" • "Do you want to go shopping?" "No, I'm *out.*" [=I don't want to go]

9 : in the position of someone who is no longer in a political office or job • They voted him *out* by an overwhelming margin. • Some people want the President *out.*

10 : to the full or a great extent • He was all decked *out* in a new suit. • She stretched *out* on the couch. • The horse was tired *out.*

11 : in a way that can be clearly heard or understood • He spoke *out* against the proposed tax. • She read *out* [=*aloud*] the names on the list. • He cried *out* in pain.

12 *baseball* **: no longer batting or on a base because of a play made by the other team** • He threw/tagged the runner *out.* • She flied/grounded *out.* • It's the bottom of the ninth inning with two men *out.* • The runner/batter was (called) *out.*

13 : no longer operating, burning, etc. • The electricity/fire is *out.* • He landed the plane with one engine *out.* • The wind blew the candle *out.*

14 : at an end • We should be finished before the day is *out.* [=*done*]

15 : no longer in fashion • That style of dress is definitely *out.*

16 : trying to achieve or do something • He was ***out to*** [=*determined to*] get revenge. = He was ***out for*** revenge. • She was *out for* a good time. [=she wanted to have a good time] — see also *out for blood* at BLOOD

17 : available to the public • The band's new CD is not *out* yet.

18 : not possible : not to be considered • That choice was *out* as far as we were concerned.

19 : able to be seen • The sun is *out.* • There is a full moon *out* tonight. • The roses are not *out* [=*blooming*] yet.

20 : in or into a state of being asleep or unconscious • He was *out* as soon as his head hit the pillow. • She was ***out cold*** — see also *out for the count* at ²COUNT

21 : not correct • She was *out* [=*off*] in her calculations by $25.

22 : having less than an earlier amount • He went gambling and was $100 *out* at the end of the night. = He was *out* $100 at the end of the night.

23 : no longer in jail or prison • He will be *out* (of prison) in two months.

24 : known publicly as a homosexual • He's been *out* for a long time now.

25 *sports* **: not in the area in which a game is played : OUT-OF-BOUNDS** • Her last serve was *out.*

26 — used to indicate that a radio message is complete and no reply is expected • Message received, Mission Control. Over and *out.*

odd man/one out see ODD

out and about **:** going to different places • She is always *out and about,* doing one thing or another.

out back see ¹BACK

out front see ¹FRONT

out loud see LOUD

out of **1 — used to show the direction or movement of a person or thing from the inside to the outside of something** • She walked *out of* the room. • Take your hands *out of* your pockets. • We've decided to move *out of* the country/state/city. • Don't get *out of* your chair/seat. • It's time to get *out of* bed. • They're flying *out of* Washington [=they're leaving Washington] this afternoon. **2 — used to say that a person or thing is not or no longer at a particular place** • She's *out of* [=away from] the office at the moment. • He just got *out of* the hospital. • He just got *out of* prison/jail yesterday. • She's fresh *out of* college. [=she has recently graduated from college] • She's been *out of* town for two days. • Let's get *out of* here. [=let's leave] • Move! Get *out of* the way! • His case was settled ***out of court*** [=settled without a trial or a decision by a judge] • an ***out-of-court*** settlement — see also *out of here* at ¹HERE **3 — used to say that a person or thing is not or no longer in a particular state or situation** • They woke him up *out of* a deep sleep. • Try to stay *out of* trouble at school, okay? • Our favorite store's going *out of* business. • We're not *out of* danger yet. [=we're still not safe] • He came *out of* retirement to play one more season. • He got kicked *out of* the game for playing too rough. • Disco dancing went *out of* fashion in the early 1980s. • *out of* style • All of the pictures are *out of* focus. • I think your guitar is *out of* tune. • She's *out of* her league. [=she can't compete well in this situation] • Has anything *out of* the ordinary [=anything unusual] happened? • a book that is ***out of print*** = an ***out-of-print*** book [=a book that is no longer being printed] **4 — used to say that a person or thing is beyond the range or limits of something** • Try to stay *out of* the sun. • We went inside to get *out of* the rain. • Keep all medicines *out of* (the) reach of children. [=keep medicines in a place where children cannot reach them] • The train was soon *out of* sight. [=it was too far away for people to see it] • You know the old saying, "*out of* sight, *out of* mind." If you don't see it, you won't think about it. • It's *out of* our hands now. We can't control what happens anymore. • The situation has gotten completely *out of* hand. = Things are *out of* control. **5 — used to say that a person or thing is not in the usual or expected condition** • If you're *out of* shape [=if you're not in shape], start exercising slowly. • I hadn't skated in five years, and I was really *out of* practice. • That big table seems *out of* place in their tiny kitchen. **6 a — used to say what something is made from** • She wore a necklace made *out of* gold and diamonds. • a boat built *out of* small trees and rope • Let's try to make the best *out of* a bad situation. **b — used to say where a person or thing comes from** • I got the idea *out of* [=*from*] the book. • He had to pay for it *out of* his own pocket. • That meeting was a complete waste of time. I got nothing *out of* it. **7 — used to say where an activity takes place** • He runs his business *out of* [=*from*] his home. **8 — used to say what causes something** • Most people watched the show *out of* curiosity. [=because they were curious] • *Out of* concern for her children, she decided to move to a safer neighborhood. • They became soldiers *out of* a sense of duty and honor. **9 — used to say that a person or thing no longer has something** • "Are we *out of* milk?" "Yes, I finished it this morning." • The store's *out of* bread. • The car's almost *out of* gas. • I'm *out of* breath. • I ran *out of* time and didn't get to finish the test. • She's been *out of* [=*without*] a job for two months now. **10 — used to compare a small number to a larger number in order to say how many people or things are selected, do something, etc.** • Only one *out of* four of our tomato plants survived. • Nine *out of* 10 dentists prefer this toothpaste. • The disease occurs in one *out of* a thousand people. • *Out of* a group of 20 students, only 10 passed the test. • She scored 49 *out of* a possible 50 points.

out of it *informal* **1 : in a state in which you are not thinking clearly** • I had just woken up and was still pretty much *out of it.* **2 : not part of an activity, group, or fashion** • I felt completely *out of it* at the club.

out of nowhere see NOWHERE

O

out on your ear see [1]EAR
out there see [1]THERE
out to lunch see [1]LUNCH
out with it *informal* — used to tell someone to say something that they do not want to say or that they are having difficulty saying • OK, *out with it*. Tell us what she said.

[2]**out** *prep, chiefly US*
1 — used to indicate that a person or animal is looking at something that is outside of a building, room, etc. • She looked *out* [=*out of*] the window.
2 — used to indicate that a person or animal is moving from the inside of a building, room, etc., to the outside • He ran *out* [=*out of*] the door.

[3]**out** *verb* **outs; out·ed; out·ing**
1 [+ *obj*] **a** : to tell people that (someone) is a homosexual • a gay actor who was *outed* in a magazine article **b** : to tell people that (someone) is or does a particular thing • He is threatening to *out* other players who have used steroids.
2 [*no obj*] : to become publicly known • The truth will *out*. • Murder will *out*.

[4]**out** *noun, pl* **outs**
1 [*count*] *baseball* : the act of causing a player to be out or the situation that exists when a player has been put out • The play resulted in an *out*. • With two *outs* in the bottom of the ninth inning, he hit a home run to win the game.
2 [*singular*] : a way of avoiding an embarrassing or difficult situation • I think she was just using her mother's illness as an *out*. [=*excuse*] • He changed the wording of the contract to give/leave himself an *out*.
on the outs *US, informal* : in an unfriendly or bad relationship : no longer friendly or together • There's a rumor that she and her husband are *on the outs*. — often + *with* • She is *on the outs with* her husband.
— see also INS AND OUTS

out- /ˌaʊt/ *prefix* : in a manner that is greater, better, or more than something else • *out*number • *out*grow • *out*run • *out*maneuver • *out*play

out·age /ˈaʊtɪʤ/ *noun, pl* **-ag·es** [*count*] *US* : a period of time when there is no electricity in a building or area • The power *outage* left us in the dark for five hours. [=we did not have electrical power for five hours] — called also (*Brit*) *power cut*

out–and–out /ˌaʊtnˈaʊt/ *adj, always used before a noun* — used to emphasize a description • He's an *out-and-out* liar. • He told an *out-and-out* lie.

out·back /ˈaʊtˈbæk/ *noun*
the outback : the part of Australia that is far from cities and where few people live

out·bid /ˈaʊtˈbɪd/ *verb* **-bids; -bid; -bid·ding** [+ *obj*] : to offer to pay a higher price than (someone) for something especially at an auction : to make a higher bid than (someone) • He *outbid* me for the painting I wanted. • She tried to buy the antique vase but was *outbid*.

out·board /ˈaʊtˌboɚd/ *adj, technical* : located on or toward the outside of a vehicle (such as an airplane or ship) • an *outboard* engine — compare INBOARD
— **outboard** *adv*

outboard motor *noun, pl* ~ **-tors** [*count*] : a small engine that is attached to the back of a small boat — see picture at BOAT

out·bound /ˈaʊtˌbaʊnd/ *adj* : traveling away from a place : outward bound • The airline has canceled all *outbound* flights. • The bridge is closed to *outbound* traffic. [=the bridge is closed to traffic going away from a city or town] — opposite INBOUND

out–box /ˈaʊtˌbɑːks/ *noun, pl* **-box·es** [*count*]
1 *US* : a box or other container on a desk in which letters, notes, etc., that are being sent from the desk are placed — called also (*Brit*) *out tray*; see picture at OFFICE; compare INBOX
2 *computers* : a computer folder that holds e-mail messages you have not yet sent

out·break /ˈaʊtˌbreɪk/ *noun, pl* **-breaks** [*count*] : a sudden start or increase of fighting or disease • a cholera *outbreak* — often + *of* • an *outbreak of* violence/war • They are preparing for an *outbreak of* the virus.

out·build·ing /ˈaʊtˌbɪldɪŋ/ *noun, pl* **-ings** [*count*] : a small building that is separated from a main building

out·burst /ˈaʊtˌbɚst/ *noun, pl* **-bursts** [*count*]
1 : a sudden expression of strong feeling • an *outburst* of anger/kindness • He later apologized for his *outburst* (of anger). • an angry *outburst*
2 : a sudden increase in activity • an *outburst* of violence/creativity/rumors

out·cast /ˈaʊtˌkæst, *Brit* ˈaʊtˌkɑːst/ *noun, pl* **-casts** [*count*] : someone who is not accepted by other people • She felt like a social *outcast*.

out·class /ˌaʊtˈklæs, *Brit* ˌaʊtˈklɑːs/ *verb* **-class·es; -classed; -class·ing** [+ *obj*] : to be or do much better than (someone or something) • The new model *outclasses* all past models. • She *outclassed* everyone else in the dance competition. — often used as *(be) outclassed* • She *was outclassed* in the tennis tournament. [=other people played better than she did]

out·come /ˈaʊtˌkʌm/ *noun, pl* **-comes** [*count*] : something that happens as a result of an activity or process : RESULT • the *outcome* of the election/game • We are still awaiting the final *outcome* of the trial. • There are two possible *outcomes*.

out·cry /ˈaʊtˌkraɪ/ *noun, pl* **-cries** : an expression of strong anger or disapproval by many people : a reaction showing that people are angry or unhappy about something [*count*] There was a public *outcry* over his comments. [=many people objected publicly to his comments] • They were surprised by the *outcry* against the casino proposal. [*noncount*] There was a lot of public *outcry* over his racial comments.

out·dat·ed /ˌaʊtˈdeɪtəd/ *adj* [*more* ~; *most* ~] : no longer useful or acceptable : not modern or current • *outdated* [=*out-of-date*] computers/technology • *outdated* laws/information • *outdated* fashions

out·dis·tance /ˌaʊtˈdɪstəns/ *verb* **-tanc·es; -tanced; -tanc·ing** [+ *obj*] : to go far ahead of or beyond (someone or something) • She easily *outdistanced* the other runners. • This television *outdistances* all others in the number of sales.

out·do /ˌaʊtˈduː/ *verb* **-does** /-ˈdʌz/; **-did** /-ˈdɪd/; **-done** /-ˈdʌn/; **-do·ing** /-ˈduːwɪŋ/ [+ *obj*] : to do better than (someone or something) : to be more successful than (someone or something) • Smaller companies often *outdo* larger ones in customer service. • My sister always tried to *outdo* me in school. • She's a great cook, but she really ***outdid herself*** this time. The meal was wonderful. [=it was the best meal she ever made] • She scored 20 points in the first game. ***Not to be outdone***, I scored 30 points myself in the second game.

out·door /ˈaʊtˌdoɚ/ *adj, always used before a noun* : done, used, or located outside a building • *outdoor* sports/activities • *outdoor* clothing • an *outdoor* concert/theater/track — compare INDOOR

[1]**out·doors** /ˌaʊtˈdoɚz/ *adv* : outside a building : not inside a building • The game is meant to be played *outdoors*. • He worked *outdoors* all afternoon. • I went *outdoors* for some fresh air. — compare INDOORS

[2]**outdoors** *noun*
the outdoors : the natural world : the places outside where you can enjoy nature • We went for a walk to enjoy *the outdoors*. • They love *the outdoors*. • Every summer they go camping to enjoy ***the great outdoors***.

out·doors·man /ˌaʊtˈdoɚzmən/ *noun, pl* **-men** /-mən/ [*count*] : a man who likes outdoor activities

out·doors·wom·an /ˌaʊtˈdoɚzˌwʊmən/ *noun, pl* **-women** /-ˌwɪmən/ [*count*] : a woman who likes outdoor activities

out·doorsy /ˌaʊtˈdoɚzi/ *adj* [*more* ~; *most* ~] *informal* : enjoying outdoor activities • an *outdoorsy* couple

out·er /ˈaʊtɚ/ *adj, always used before a noun*
1 : located on or toward the outside of something : not on or at the inside or center of something • the city's *outer* limits • the planet's *outer* ring • the *outer* edges of the roof • The package's *outer* covering was damaged. • I removed the *outer* skin of the onion. — opposite INNER
2 : of or relating to a person's body or physical appearance rather than to a person's mind or spirit • Her inner turmoil was masked by an *outer* calm.

outer ear *noun, pl* ~ **ears** [*count*] *biology* : the part of the ear that can be seen on the outside of your head — compare INNER EAR

out·er·most /ˈaʊtɚˌmoʊst/ *adj, always used before a noun* : farthest from the center of something • The arrow hit the *outermost* ring on the target. • the *outermost* planet in our solar system — opposite INNERMOST

outer space *noun* [*noncount*] : the region beyond the Earth's atmosphere in which there are stars and planets • a satellite in *outer space* • Is there life in *outer space*?

out·er·wear /ˈaʊtɚˌweɚ/ *noun* [*noncount*] : clothes (such as sweaters, coats, or jackets) that you wear over other clothing

O

especially for warmth when you are outside

out·field /ˈaʊtˌfiːld/ *noun, pl* **-fields** [*count*]

1 a : the part of a baseball field that includes the area beyond the infield and between the foul lines ▪ He threw the ball to home plate from the *outfield*. **b :** the part of a cricket field that is away from the wickets

2 : the players who are positioned in the outfield ▪ The team has one of the best *outfields* in the league. — compare INFIELD

– out·field·er /ˈaʊtˌfiːldɚ/ *noun, pl* **-ers** [*count*] *US* ▪ a young *outfielder* [=a baseball player who plays in the outfield]

[1]**out·fit** /ˈaʊtˌfɪt/ *noun, pl* **-fits** [*count*]

1 : a set of clothes that are worn together ▪ She bought a new *outfit* for the party. ▪ a cowboy/ski *outfit*

2 : a group of people working together in the same activity ▪ He works for a publishing *outfit*. [=*organization*] ▪ My *outfit* [=military unit] was stationed in Iraq during the war.

[2]**outfit** *verb* **-fits; -fit·ted; -fit·ting** [+ *obj*] **:** to provide (someone or something) with equipment or clothes especially for a special purpose ▪ The company *outfitted* us with food and supplies. — often used as *(be) outfitted* ▪ The car *was outfitted* [=*equipped*] with a new stereo system.

out·fit·ter /ˈaʊtˌfɪtɚ/ *noun, pl* **-ters** [*count*]

1 *US* **:** a business that provides equipment, supplies, and often trained guides for activities such as hunting, hiking, etc. ▪ Hunters say it's the best *outfitter* in the state.; *also* **:** a guide who works for such a business ▪ Our *outfitter* showed us where the deer feed.

2 *Brit, old-fashioned* **:** a person or business that sells men's clothing

out·flank /ˌaʊtˈflæŋk/ *verb* **-flanks; -flanked; -flank·ing** [+ *obj*]

1 : to move around the side of (something, such as an opposing force) to attack from behind ▪ The army *outflanked* the enemy.

2 : to gain an advantage over (someone or something) ▪ trying to *outflank* the competition

out·flow /ˈaʊtˌfloʊ/ *noun, pl* **-flows :** an outward flow or movement of something [*count*] The campaign has seen a massive *outflow* [=the campaign has spent a lot] of funds/money/cash in recent months. ▪ We joined the *outflow* of fans from the stadium after the game. [*noncount*] The vents provide improved *outflow* of air/water. — opposite INFLOW

out·fox /ˌaʊtˈfɑːks/ *verb* **-fox·es; -foxed; -fox·ing** [+ *obj*] **:** to defeat or trick (someone) by being more intelligent or clever ▪ He *outfoxed* [=*outsmarted, outwitted*] the police and escaped.

out·go·ing /ˈaʊtˌgowɪŋ/ *adj*

1 [*more* ~; *most* ~] — used to describe someone who is friendly and likes being with and talking to other people ▪ His *outgoing* personality made him very popular in school. ▪ an *outgoing* [=*extroverted*] person

2 : going away **:** leaving a place ▪ *outgoing* [=*departing*] ships ▪ *Outgoing* mail goes in this box. ▪ *outgoing* messages/calls/letters/e-mails — opposite INCOMING

3 : leaving a particular position ▪ the *outgoing* president — opposite INCOMING

out·go·ings /ˈaʊtˌgowɪŋz/ *noun* [*plural*] *Brit* **:** the money that is spent on something ▪ monthly *outgoings* [=*costs, expenses*]

out·grow /ˌaʊtˈgroʊ/ *verb* **-grows; -grew** /-ˈgruː/; **-grown** /-ˈgroʊn/; **-grow·ing** [+ *obj*]

1 : to grow too large for (someone or something) ▪ Kids *outgrow* their clothes so quickly. ▪ The plant has *outgrown* my garden. ▪ Our business is *outgrowing* its small office building.

2 : to stop doing (something) because you are older and more mature ▪ Her bad behavior is just a phase. I'm sure she'll *outgrow* it. [=grow out of it]

3 : to stop being interested in or involved with (something or someone) because you have changed as you have grown older ▪ She's *outgrown* most of her toys. ▪ I realized that I had *outgrown* my old high school friends.

4 : to grow faster than (something) ▪ populations *outgrowing* their food supplies

out·growth /ˈaʊtˌgroʊθ/ *noun, pl* **-growths** [*count*]

1 : something that develops or results from something else — often + *of* ▪ Traffic jams are often an *outgrowth* [=*consequence, product*] *of* poor urban planning. ▪ a natural *outgrowth of* our research

2 *technical* **:** something that grows out of something else ▪ an *outgrowth* of bone

out·gun /ˌaʊtˈgʌn/ *verb* **-guns; -gunned; -gun·ning** [+ *obj*] **:** to have more military weapons and power than (someone or something) — often used as *(be) outgunned* ▪ We *were outgunned* (by the enemy). — often used figuratively ▪ The defending champions *were outgunned* last night 36–10.

out·house /ˈaʊtˌhaʊs/ *noun, pl* **-hous·es** [*count*]

1 *US* **:** a small outdoor building that is used as a toilet

2 *Brit* **:** a small building (such as a shed) that is separated from a main building

out·ing /ˈaʊtɪŋ/ *noun, pl* **-ings** [*count*]

1 : a brief trip that people take for fun usually as a group ▪ We went on a backpacking *outing*. ▪ a family/school *outing* — often + *to* ▪ She took the children on an *outing to* the zoo.

2 : a time when an athlete (such as a baseball pitcher) competes in a game or contest ▪ The pitcher has struggled in his last three *outings*. [=the last three times he has pitched in a game] ▪ He had a good/bad *outing*. [=he played well/poorly]

3 a : an act of telling the public that a person is homosexual when that person does not want the public to know ▪ the *outing* of a famous actor by gay activists **b :** an act of telling people that a person has a certain job, identity, etc., that was supposed to be kept secret ▪ the *outing* of a secret agent

out·land·ish /ˌaʊtˈlændɪʃ/ *adj* [*more* ~; *most* ~] **:** very strange or unusual **:** extremely different from what is normal or expected ▪ She fills her books with *outlandish* characters. ▪ The actress wore an *outlandish* dress to the awards ceremony. ▪ an *outlandish* story

– out·land·ish·ly *adv* ▪ He was *outlandishly* dressed.

out·last /ˌaʊtˈlæst, *Brit* ˌaʊtˈlɑːst/ *verb* **-lasts; -last·ed; -last·ing** [+ *obj*] **:** to last longer than (someone or something) **:** to continue to exist, be active, etc., longer than (someone or something) ▪ We watched him *outlast* his opponent in one of the greatest boxing matches of all time. ▪ The policies he has established will *outlast* his presidency.

[1]**out·law** /ˈaʊtˌlɑː/ *noun, pl* **-laws** [*count*] **:** a person who has broken the law and who is hiding or running away to avoid punishment ▪ Billy the Kid was one of the most famous *outlaws* of America's early history. ▪ a gang of *outlaws*

[2]**outlaw** *verb* **-laws; -lawed; -law·ing** [+ *obj*] **:** to make (something) illegal ▪ That type of gun was *outlawed* last year. ▪ The government passed a bill *outlawing* the hiring of children under the age of 12.

out·lay /ˈaʊtˌleɪ/ *noun, pl* **-lays** *formal* **:** an amount of money that is spent [*count*] The initial *outlay* for the program will be 2.4 million dollars. ▪ an *outlay* of $2,000 ▪ large cash *outlays* [*noncount*] Maintaining a horse requires considerable *outlay*.

out·let /ˈaʊtˌlɛt/ *noun, pl* **-lets** [*count*]

1 : something that people use to express their emotions or talents ▪ emotional/artistic *outlets* — often + *for* ▪ She used poetry as an *outlet for* her sadness. ▪ They needed a healthy *outlet for* their anger. ▪ an *outlet for* his talents

2 : a store that sells products made usually by one company and often at reduced prices ▪ designer clothing *outlets* ▪ a discount furniture *outlet* ▪ retail *outlets* ▪ *outlet* stores

3 : a television, radio, or publishing company ▪ media/news *outlets* ▪ a cable TV *outlet*

4 *US* **:** a device in a wall into which an electric cord can be plugged in order to provide electricity for a lamp, television, etc. ▪ electrical *outlets* ▪ a wall *outlet* — called also *socket*, *(Brit) point*, *(Brit) power point*

5 : a place or opening through which something can go out ▪ an *outlet* for the air to escape ▪ the river's *outlet* to the sea

[1]**out·line** /ˈaʊtˌlaɪn/ *noun, pl* **-lines**

1 a [*count*] **:** a drawing or picture that shows only the shape of an object — often + *of* ▪ An *outline of* his face showed his high forehead, long nose, and small chin. ▪ *Outlines of* animals were carved into the cave's walls. **b** [*noncount*] **:** a style of drawing in which only the outer edges of an object are shown ▪ The pictures were drawn ***in outline*** and then filled in with color.

2 [*count*] **:** a line that is drawn around the edges of something ▪ The leaves etched into the vase have a gold *outline*.

3 : a written list or description of only the most important parts of an essay, speech, plan, etc. [*count*] Organize your essay by writing an *outline* in which you state your main idea followed by your supporting points. ▪ a plot *outline* ▪ a brief *outline* of American history [*noncount*] Her speech was written ***in outline*** on note cards.

[2]**outline** *verb* **-lines; -lined; -lin·ing** [+ *obj*]

1 : to draw a line around the edges of (something) — usually

used as *(be) outlined* ▪ The leaves on the vase *are outlined* in gold. ▪ the *outlined* areas on the map — sometimes used figuratively ▪ The mountain *was outlined* against the setting sun.
2 : to list or describe only the most important parts of (an essay, speech, plan, etc.) : to give an outline of (something) ▪ The President *outlined* his agenda for the next term. ▪ The book *outlines* the major events of the country's history. ▪ All players must follow the rules *outlined* above.

out·live /ˌaʊtˈlɪv/ *verb* **-lives; -lived; -liv·ing** [+ *obj*]
1 : to live longer than (someone) ▪ No mother wants to *outlive* her children. ▪ He *outlived* his wife by 10 years.
2 : to continue to exist longer than (something) : to outlast (something) ▪ The law has ***outlived its usefulness.*** [=the law still exists, but it is no longer useful]

out·look /ˈaʊtˌlʊk/ *noun, pl* **-looks**
1 : the way that a person thinks about things [*count*] The students all seemed to have the same *outlook.* ▪ the *outlook* of the 1990s [=the general attitude of people living in the 1990s] ▪ her political *outlook* — often + *on* ▪ The book totally changed my *outlook on* politics. ▪ They had very different *outlooks on* the world. ▪ a positive/optimistic ***outlook on life*** [*noncount*] Despite our differences ***in outlook,*** we got along together very well.
2 [*count*] **:** a set of conditions that will probably exist in the future : the future of someone or something — usually singular ▪ the country's economic *outlook* — often + *for* ▪ The *outlook for* the company is hopeful. ▪ The *outlook for* tomorrow is scattered showers and temperatures in the 70s.
3 [*count*] **:** a place where you can look out over a wide area ▪ scenic *outlooks* along the highway; *also* **:** a view from such a place ▪ a beautiful *outlook*

out·ly·ing /ˈaʊtˌlajɪŋ/ *adj, always used before a noun* **:** far away from the center of a place ▪ the *outlying* areas of the city ▪ the country's *outlying* islands

out·ma·neu·ver (*US*) *or Brit* **out·ma·noeu·vre** /ˌaʊtməˈnuːvɚ/ *verb* **-vers; -vered; -ver·ing** [+ *obj*] **:** to use cleverness or skill to gain an advantage over (someone) ▪ She *outmaneuvered* her political opponents. ▪ He *outmaneuvered* the cars in front of him and won the race.

out·mod·ed /ˌaʊtˈmoʊdəd/ *adj* [*more* ~; *most* ~] **:** no longer useful or acceptable : not modern or current ▪ The army was using *outmoded* [=*old-fashioned, antiquated*] weapons from the 1950s. ▪ *outmoded* technology ▪ *outmoded* beliefs

out·num·ber /ˌaʊtˈnʌmbɚ/ *verb* **-bers; -bered; -ber·ing** [+ *obj*] **:** to be more than (someone or something) in number ▪ With 20 girls and 10 boys in the class, girls *outnumber* boys by 2 to 1. ▪ Their wins *outnumber* their losses. [=they have more wins than losses] ▪ The few men in the audience were greatly *outnumbered* by the women. [=there were many more women than men in the audience]

O

out–of–body experience *noun, pl* **~ -ences** [*count*] **:** an experience in which you have a feeling of being separated from your body and in which you can look at yourself and other people from the outside

out–of–bounds /ˌaʊtəvˈbaʊndz/ *adj* **:** outside the area in which a game is played ▪ The catch was *out-of-bounds.* — see also *out of bounds* at ⁶BOUND

out–of–date /ˌaʊtəvˈdeɪt/ *adj* [*more* ~; *most* ~] **:** no longer useful or acceptable : not modern or current ▪ *out-of-date* [=*outdated*] ideas ▪ an *out-of-date* history book

out of doors *adv* **:** outside rather than inside a building ▪ The play was performed *out of doors.* [=*outdoors, outside*]

out–of–pock·et /ˌaʊtəvˈpɑːkət/ *adj* **:** paid for with your own money rather than with money from another source (such as the company you work for or an insurance company) ▪ *out-of-pocket* medical expenses ▪ You can be reimbursed for *out-of-pocket* expenses when you are on a business trip.
– out of pocket *adv* ▪ She paid *out of pocket* for the prescription. — see also *out of pocket* at ²POCKET

out–of–the–way /ˌaʊtəðəˈweɪ/ *adj* [*more* ~; *most* ~] **:** located far from other places that are well-known ▪ We had dinner at this little *out-of-the-way* place. ▪ *out-of-the-way* restaurants

out–of–town *adj, always used before a noun*
1 : coming from or going to another town or city ▪ *out-of-town* mail ▪ *out-of-town* visitors
2 : happening in another town or city ▪ The band has an *out-of-town* show tomorrow night.
3 *Brit* **:** located away from the center of a town ▪ *out-of-town* shopping centers

out–of–town·er /ˌaʊtəvˈtaʊnɚ/ *noun, pl* **-ers** [*count*] **:** someone who is from another town or city ▪ The convention attracts a lot of *out-of-towners* to the city.

out–of–work *adj* **:** not having a job ▪ *out-of-work* [=*unemployed*] actors and actresses

out·pace /ˌaʊtˈpeɪs/ *verb* **-pac·es; -paced; -pac·ing** [+ *obj*] **:** to go or grow faster than (something) ▪ Population growth has continued to *outpace* [=*surpass*] job growth for the last several decades. ▪ The demand for the product has *outpaced* [=*exceeded*] the company's ability to produce it.

out·pa·tient /ˈaʊtˌpeɪʃənt/ *noun, pl* **-tients** [*count*] **:** a person who goes to a doctor's office or hospital for treatment but who does not spend the night there — often used before another noun ▪ *outpatient* surgery [=surgery that does not require patients to stay in the hospital] ▪ *outpatient* care/treatment — compare INPATIENT

out·per·form /ˌaʊtpɚˈfoɚm/ *verb* **-forms; -formed; -form·ing** [+ *obj*] **:** to do or perform better than (someone or something) ▪ The car consistently *outperforms* all other vehicles in its class. ▪ *outperforming* the competition

out·place·ment /ˌaʊtˈpleɪsmənt/ *noun* [*noncount*] **:** the activity or process of helping workers find new jobs when they are no longer wanted or needed — usually used before another noun ▪ *outplacement* services ▪ an *outplacement* program/firm

out·play /ˌaʊtˈpleɪ/ *verb* **-plays; -played; -play·ing** [+ *obj*] **:** to play better than (a person or team) ▪ They *outplayed* the visiting team in the last half of the game.

out·point /ˌaʊtˈpɔɪnt/ *verb* **-points; -point·ed; -point·ing** [+ *obj*] **:** to win more points than (an opponent) in a boxing match

out·post /ˈaʊtˌpoʊst/ *noun, pl* **-posts** [*count*]
1 : a large military camp that is in another country or that is far from a country's center of activity ▪ an American *outpost* in Africa ▪ The city was established as a military *outpost* in the 1800s.
2 : a small town in a place that is far away from other towns or cities ▪ a remote *outpost* of the old British Empire

out·pour·ing /ˈaʊtˌporɪŋ/ *noun, pl* **-ings** [*count*]
1 : an act of expressing an emotion or feeling in a very powerful way — often + *of* ▪ There was an *outpouring of* support for the president. [=many people expressed strong support for the president] ▪ an *outpouring of* love and affection ▪ *outpourings of* emotion
2 : a large amount of something that is given or received in a short period of time — often + *of* ▪ They received an *outpouring of* money for their charity.

¹out·put /ˈaʊtˌpʊt/ *noun, pl* **-puts**
1 : the amount of something that is produced by a person or thing [*noncount*] The country's yearly agricultural *output* [=*production*] has increased in recent years. ▪ the daily *output* of each worker [=the amount that each worker produces in a day] ▪ the author's literary *output* [*count*] stars with large energy *outputs*
2 *technical* **a :** something (such as power, energy, or information) that is produced by a machine or system [*noncount*] The computer's *output* is shown on this screen. [*count*] *outputs* of up to 400 watts **b** [*count*] **:** the place at which information, power, etc., comes out of a machine or system ▪ the television's video and audio *outputs* — compare INPUT

²output *verb* **-puts; -put·ted** *or* **-put; -put·ting** [+ *obj*] **:** to produce and send out (something, such as information) ▪ Computers *output* data very quickly. — compare INPUT

¹out·rage /ˈaʊtˌreɪʤ/ *noun, pl* **-rag·es**
1 [*noncount*] **:** extreme anger : a strong feeling of unhappiness because of something bad, hurtful, or morally wrong ▪ Many people expressed *outrage* at the court's decision. ▪ Public *outrage* over the scandal was great. ▪ moral *outrage*
2 [*count*] **:** something that hurts people or is morally wrong ▪ The rule is an *outrage* against women. ▪ This is an *outrage*! I won't allow this kind of behavior to continue.

²outrage *verb* **-rages; -raged; -rag·ing** [+ *obj*] **:** to make (someone) very angry ▪ His comments *outraged* nearly everyone in the room. — often used as *(be) outraged* ▪ Many people *were outraged* at the court's decision. ▪ Parents *were outraged* by the teacher's actions.

out·ra·geous /aʊtˈreɪʤəs/ *adj* [*more* ~; *most* ~]
1 : very bad or wrong in a way that causes anger : too bad to be accepted or allowed ▪ They will be punished for their *outrageous* behavior/conduct. ▪ This is *outrageous*! I will not put up with such treatment. ▪ *outrageous* prices
2 : very strange or unusual : surprising or shocking ▪ She's known for her wild hairdos and *outrageous* costumes. ▪ At

first it seemed like an *outrageous* idea, but then we realized that it wasn't so crazy after all. • The article makes some *outrageous* claims about her personal life.

– **out·ra·geous·ly** *adv* • a pair of *outrageously* expensive earrings – **out·ra·geous·ness** *noun [noncount]*

out·rank /ˌaʊtˈræŋk/ *verb* **-ranks**; **-ranked**; **-rank·ing** [+ *obj*]

1 : to have a higher rank or position than (someone) • A general *outranks* a colonel.

2 : to be more important than (someone or something) • The only topic to *outrank* the economy this week was the war.

ou·tré /uˈtreɪ, *Brit* ˈuːtreɪ/ *adj [more ~; most ~] formal* : very strange, unusual, or shocking : BIZARRE • His art is a bit too *outré* for most people to enjoy.

out·reach /ˌaʊtˈriːtʃ/ *noun [noncount]* : the activity or process of bringing information or services to people • He is responsible for the campaign's *outreach* to college students. • She was hired to do community *outreach* [=to do helpful things in the community] for the company. — often used before another noun • They set up an *outreach* center for children in the inner city. • community *outreach* programs/workers

out·rid·er /ˈaʊtˌraɪdɚ/ *noun, pl* **-ers** *[count]* : a person (such as a police officer) who rides a horse or motorcycle next to or in front of a vehicle that is carrying an important person as a form of protection

out·rig·ger /ˈaʊtˌrɪgɚ/ *noun, pl* **-gers** *[count]*

1 : a structure that is attached to the side of a boat or canoe to keep it from turning over in the water

2 : a boat or canoe that has an outrigger

[1]**out·right** /ˌaʊtˈraɪt/ *adv*

1 : in a full and complete way • They rejected the idea *outright*. [=*altogether, completely*] • She won the competition *outright*. • The painting is now owned *outright* by the museum.

2 : quickly and completely : not gradually • Those who were not killed *outright* [=*immediately*] later died of hunger. • Their house was destroyed *outright* by the fire.

3 : in one payment of money • I bought the car *outright*.

4 : in a direct and open way that does not hide anything • Some people laughed *outright* when he told us his idea.

[2]**out·right** /ˈaʊtˌraɪt/ *adj, always used before a noun*

1 : complete and total — used to make a statement more forceful • Your room is an *outright* mess! • That's an *outright* lie!

2 : not limited in any way : done, made, or given in a complete way • They passed an *outright* ban on guns. [=all guns were completely banned] • an *outright* gift • I was surprised by their *outright* rejection of the idea.

out·run /ˌaʊtˈrʌn/ *verb* **-runs**; **-ran** /-ˈræn/; **-run**; **-run·ning** [+ *obj*]

1 : to run or move faster than (someone or something) • The rabbit had no chance of *outrunning* the dogs. • His motorcycle could *outrun* any car on the road.

2 : to be or become more or greater than (something) • The demand for the product has quickly *outrun* [=*exceeded, outpaced*] the company's ability to produce it.

out·sell /ˌaʊtˈsɛl/ *verb* **-sells**; **-sold** /-ˈsoʊld/; **-sell·ing** [+ *obj*]

1 : to be sold more than (something) • Diet sodas are now beginning to *outsell* regular sodas in the supermarkets.

2 : to sell more than (another person, store, etc.) • We've been *outselling* our competitors for the past five years.

out·set /ˈaʊtˌsɛt/ *noun [singular]* : the start or beginning of something • There have been problems with the project ***from the outset***. • ***From its very outset***, the company has produced the highest quality products. • He made it clear ***at the outset*** that he is not going to quit his job. • She set high goals for herself *at the outset* of her career.

out·shine /ˌaʊtˈʃaɪn/ *verb* **-shines**; **-shone** /-ˈʃoʊn, *Brit* -ˈʃɒn/ *or* **-shined**; **-shin·ing** [+ *obj*] : to do better than (someone or something) : to earn more respect or attention than (someone or something) • They're determined to *outshine* [=*outdo, outperform*] their competition. • She *outshines* all the other actors in the film.

[1]**out·side** /ˌaʊtˈsaɪd, ˈaʊtˌsaɪd/ *noun, pl* **-sides**

1 ***the outside*** : an area around or near something (such as a building) • The house looks nice from *the outside*.

2 *[count]* : an outer side, edge, or surface of something — usually singular • The door can be locked from the inside or *outside*. — often + *of* • The *outside of* the building needs painting.

at the outside : at the most : at the greatest amount or limit • The crowd numbered 10,000 *at the outside*. • It took him an hour *at the outside* to finish. • It costs, *at the outside*, $20.

on the outside **1** : on the outer side, edge, or surface of something • The number 22 car tried to pass the leader *on the outside* (of the track). **2** *baseball* : on the side of home plate farthest from the batter • The next pitch was a fastball *on the outside*. **3** — used to describe someone's appearance • I might seem calm *on the outside*, but I'm actually really nervous. **4** : not in prison • He looked forward to life *on the outside* again.

[2]**outside** *adj*

1 : located on or near an outer side, edge, or surface of something • an *outside* wall/corner/door • the *outside* edge of the foot • (*baseball*) He struck out on an *outside* pitch.

2 *always used before a noun* **a** : located in or near the area around a building and not inside it • She turned on the *outside* light to see what was making the noise. **b** : involving people who are not in the same building, group, or organization as you • The phone will not let you make *outside* calls. • an *outside* (telephone) line [=a telephone that allows you to talk to people who are not in the same building as you] • The company hired an *outside* consultant. — see also *outside world* at [1]WORLD

3 *always used before a noun* : not involving your regular job or duties • a businessman with few *outside* interests besides golf • There were *outside* influences that affected his decision to retire early.

4 *always used before a noun* : barely possible : very unlikely • We still have an *outside* [=*small, slight*] chance of winning.

[3]**outside** *adv*

1 a : in or to a place that is near but separate from another place • He waited *outside* [=*out*] in the hall. **b** : in or to a place that is in the area around or near a building and not inside it : OUTDOORS • The children love playing *outside*. • It's raining *outside*. • It's nice *outside*, with not a cloud in the sky. • She took the dog *outside*. [=*out*] • He ran *outside* to see what the noise was about. • He looked *outside* at the snow.

2 : on the outer side, edge, or surface of something • The candy was hard *outside* but chewy inside. • The car seemed in good condition *outside*.

[4]**outside** *prep*

1 : in a place that is near but separate from (something) • We waited *outside* the store. • He kept his hands *outside* his pockets. • There was a dog barking *outside* the house.

2 : beyond the limits or borders of (something) • activities *outside* the law [=unlawful activities] • She finished the race five seconds *outside* the record. • We live *outside* the city. • I have never traveled *outside* the U.S. before.

3 : not belonging to (a group or organization) • No one *outside* the group knew of their plans. • He hired consultants (from) *outside* the company.

4 : apart from (someone or something) : EXCEPT, BESIDES • Nobody knew *outside* [=(more commonly) *outside of*] a few close friends.

outside of *chiefly US* : OUTSIDE • We waited *outside of* the store. • We live *outside of* the city. • people *outside of* the group • Nobody knew *outside of* a few close friends.

think outside the box see [1]BOX

out·sid·er /ˌaʊtˈsaɪdɚ, ˈaʊtˌsaɪdɚ/ *noun, pl* **-ers** *[count]*

1 : a person who does not belong to or is not accepted as part of a particular group or organization • To *outsiders*, the ritual may seem strange. • She felt like an *outsider* in her new school. — opposite INSIDER

2 *chiefly Brit* : a person or animal that is not expected to win a race or competition • An *outsider* defeated the champion! • She was a ***rank/complete outsider*** who managed to win.

out·size /ˈaʊtˌsaɪz/ *also* **out·sized** /ˈaʊtˌsaɪzd/ *adj* : very large in size • *outsize* boots • *outsized* cars and trucks

out·skirts /ˈaʊtˌskɚts/ *noun [plural]* : the parts of a city or town that are far from the center • We live ***on the outskirts of*** town.

out·smart /ˌaʊtˈsmaɚt/ *verb* **-smarts**; **-smart·ed**; **-smart·ing** [+ *obj*] : to defeat or trick (someone) by being more intelligent or clever • He *outsmarted* [=*outwitted*] his attackers and escaped unharmed. • The government must gather large amounts of information in order to *outsmart* its enemies.

out·source /ˈaʊtˌsoɚs/ *verb* **-sourc·es**; **-sourced**; **-sourc·ing** [+ *obj*] : to send away (some of a company's work) to be done by people outside the company • The company *outsources* many of its jobs to less developed countries. • The work was *outsourced* to a factory in China.

– **outsourcing** *noun [noncount]*

out·spend /ˌaʊtˈspɛnd/ *verb* **-spends; -spent; -spend·ing** [+ *obj*] **: to spend more money than (someone or something)** • He has *outspent* the other candidates in the election by millions of dollars.

out·spo·ken /ˌaʊtˈspoʊkən/ *adj* [*more* ~; *most* ~] **: talking in a free and honest way about your opinions** • She has been an *outspoken* advocate/supporter of women's rights throughout her life. • an *outspoken* and controversial radio host • My father was an *outspoken* critic of the war. = He was *outspoken* in his criticism of the war. • She's very *outspoken* about political issues.

– out·spo·ken·ly *adv* • She is *outspokenly* liberal/conservative in her views. **– out·spo·ken·ness** /aʊtˈspoʊkənnəs/ *noun* [*noncount*]

out·spread /ˌaʊtˈsprɛd/ *adj* **: spread out completely : stretched out from the sides** • a bird gliding through the air on *outspread* [=*outstretched*] wings

out·stand·ing /aʊtˈstændɪŋ/ *adj*

1 [*more* ~; *most* ~] **: extremely good or excellent** • Tonight we will honor the school's most *outstanding* students/teachers/athletes/performers. • You did an *outstanding* job on the project. • the *outstanding* quality of your work • a wine that is *outstanding* in quality • As a president, he was *outstanding* in many ways. • Her novels are *outstanding* for their complex characters and interesting plots. • The painting is an *outstanding* example of the artist's style.

2 [*more* ~; *most* ~] **: easy to notice especially because of being important or very good** • There are some *outstanding* [=*conspicuous*] exceptions to this rule. • *Outstanding* among the menu items were the tomato soup and the swordfish.

3 : not yet paid • *outstanding* [=*unpaid*] bills • She had several *outstanding* parking tickets in her car. • He left a balance of 50 dollars *outstanding* on his account.

4 : continuing to exist • It remains one of the long *outstanding* [=*unresolved*] problems in mathematics. • There are several *outstanding* issues between the two countries.

– out·stand·ing·ly *adv* [*more* ~; *most* ~] • an *outstandingly* fine example of his work • He played *outstandingly*.

out·stay /ˌaʊtˈsteɪ/ *verb* **-stays; -stayed; -stay·ing**

outstay your welcome see [4]WELCOME

out·stretched /ˌaʊtˈstrɛʧt/ *adj* **: stretched out or extended from the sides** • She ran toward him with *outstretched* [=*open*, *outspread*] arms.

out·strip /ˌaʊtˈstrɪp/ *verb* **-strips; -stripped; -strip·ping** [+ *obj*]

1 : to be or become better, greater, or larger than (someone or something) • Their achievements far *outstrip* [=*excel*, *surpass*] our own. • The new hotel *outstrips* all other hotels in the area in size and luxury. • Demand continues to *outstrip* [=*exceed*] supply.

2 : to do better than (someone or something) • She *outstripped* [=*outdid*] all of her competitors.

3 : to go faster than (someone or something) • The fullback *outstripped* the defenders and scored a touchdown.

out·ta /ˈaʊtə/ **— used in writing to represent the sound of the phrase *out of* when it is spoken quickly** • Get *outta* my way! • I'm *outta* here in half an hour. [=I'm leaving in half an hour] ✧ **The pronunciation represented by *outta* is common in informal speech. The written form should be avoided except when trying to represent or record such speech.**

out·take /ˈaʊtˌteɪk/ *noun, pl* **-takes** [*count*]

1 : a scene that is not used in the final version of a movie or television show

2 : a song that is not used for a music album • a collection of the band's old *outtakes*

out–there /ˈaʊtˈðeə/ *adj* [*more* ~; *most* ~] *US, informal* **: very strange or unusual : out of the ordinary** • *out-there* hairstyles • Most of his ideas were really *out-there*.

out tray *noun, pl* ~ **trays** [*count*] *Brit* **:** OUT-BOX

out·vote /ˌaʊtˈvoʊt/ *verb* **-votes; -vot·ed; -vot·ing** [+ *obj*] **: to defeat (a person or idea) by winning a larger number of votes** • I didn't like the idea, but I was *outvoted* by the rest of the group.

[1]**out·ward** /ˈaʊtwəd/ *adj, always used before a noun*

1 : of or relating to the way that someone or something looks or seems on the outside • Despite her *outward* [=*apparent*] calm, she was extremely nervous about the interview. • They showed no *outward* signs of fear, but they must have been afraid. • She was waiting for some *outward* expression of his love. • To/By/From ***all outward appearances***, their marriage was quite normal.

2 : able to be seen • He has great *outward* [=*physical*] beauty, but is he beautiful on the inside? [=is he a good person?] • There was no *outward* [=*visible*] evidence that the parents abused the child. • *outward* symptoms of the disease

3 : moving or directed away from something • The *outward* migration of people from the city has hurt the city's economy greatly. • He made a slight *outward* movement with his right hand. **— opposite** INWARD

[2]**outward** (*chiefly US*) *or chiefly Brit* **out·wards** /ˈaʊtwədz/ *adv*

1 : toward the outside of something : away from a center • The window faces *outward* toward the street. • Stand with your heels together, toes pointing *outward*. • air flowing *outwards* from the lungs **— opposite** INWARD

2 : away from yourself • She turns her students' attention *outward* [=away from their own lives] by making them aware of different cultures. • The country has become more ***outward looking*** [=thinking about other people or places] in its economic policies.

out·ward·ly /ˈaʊtwədli/ *adv* **: on the outside** • The two brothers may be *outwardly* similar, but their personalities couldn't be more different. **: in a way that can be seen** • Though extremely nervous, she was able to remain *outwardly* calm during the interview. • an *outwardly* friendly person • *Outwardly*, their marriage seemed quite normal. **— opposite** INWARDLY

out·weigh /ˌaʊtˈweɪ/ *verb* **-weighs; -weighed; -weigh·ing** [+ *obj*] **: to be greater than (someone or something) in weight, value, or importance** • She *outweighs* her sister by 10 pounds. • The advantages far *outweigh* [=*exceed*] the disadvantages. • This issue *outweighs* all others in importance.

out·wit /ˌaʊtˈwɪt/ *verb* **-wits; -wit·ted; -wit·ting** [+ *obj*] **: to defeat or trick (someone) by being more intelligent or clever :** OUTSMART • The fox managed to *outwit* the hunter by hiding in a tree. • They thought they had *outwitted* the new teacher.

out·work·er /ˈaʊtˌwəkə/ *noun, pl* **-ers** [*count*] *Brit* **: a person who does work for a business, company, etc., at home**

out·worn /ˌaʊtˈwoən/ *adj* **: no longer useful or acceptable : not modern or current :** OUTDATED • an *outworn* set of beliefs

ouzo /ˈuːzoʊ/ *noun* [*noncount*] **: a strong, clear liquor from Greece**

ova *plural of* OVUM

[1]**oval** /ˈoʊvəl/ *adj* **: having the shape of an egg : shaped like a circle that is longer than it is wide** • an *oval* mirror • *oval* leaves

[2]**oval** *noun, pl* **ovals** [*count*] **: something that has the shape of an egg** • The racetrack is an *oval*.

Oval Office *noun*

the Oval Office **: the office of the U.S. President in the White House**

ovar·i·an /oʊˈverijən/ *adj* **: of or relating to an ovary** • *ovarian* cancer

ova·ry /ˈoʊvəri/ *noun, pl* **-ries** [*count*]

1 : one of usually two organs in women and female animals that produce eggs and female hormones

2 : the part of a flower where seeds are formed — see picture at FLOWER

ova·tion /oʊˈveɪʃən/ *noun, pl* **-tions** [*count*] **: an occurrence in which a group of people at a play, speech, sporting event, etc., show enthusiastic approval or appreciation by clapping their hands together over and over** • They gave her a long *ovation*. [=they applauded her for a long time] • He was welcomed by/with a warm *ovation* when he came out onto the stage. **— see also** STANDING OVATION

ov·en /ˈʌvən/ *noun, pl* **-ens** [*count*] **: a piece of cooking equipment that is used for baking or roasting food** • Preheat the *oven* to 350 degrees. • Please take the pizza out of the *oven*. • brick *ovens* • *oven* roasted potatoes **— see picture at** KITCHEN; **see also** CONVECTION OVEN, DUTCH OVEN, MICROWAVE OVEN, TOASTER OVEN

have a bun in the oven see BUN

like an oven *informal* **: very hot** • Open the window. It's *like an oven* in here.

oven mitt *noun, pl* ~ **mitts** [*count*] *chiefly US* **: a mitten that is made out of a thick material and used for taking hot dishes out of an oven — called also** (*Brit*) ***oven glove***

oven·proof /ˈʌvənˌpruːf/ *adj* **: able to be used in an oven** • *ovenproof* dishes

oven–ready *adj, always used before a noun* **: able to be**

cooked in an oven with no additional preparation • an *oven-ready* chicken

[1]over /ˈoʊvɚ/ *adv*

1 : in an upward and forward direction across something • The wall's too high for us to climb *over.* • We came to a stream and jumped *over.* • Throw the ball *over.*

2 a : downward from an upright position • She leaned *over* and kissed him. • I hurt my back bending *over* [=*down*] to pick up my child. **b : downward to a flat or horizontal position** • She knocked *over* the lamp. • He tripped and fell *over.* [=*down*] • A couple of trees fell *over* during the storm.

3 : so that the bottom or opposite side is on top • The baby rolled *over* onto his stomach. • Turn/Flip your cards *over.*

4 a : from one place to another place • We sent *over* a card and a basket of fruit. • The teacher called the three girls *over.* • Come *over* here. I need to talk to you. • I'm flying *over* to London this afternoon. • He ran *over* to his neighbor's house to see what was going on. • Let's head *over* to the cafeteria. • I'll be right *over.* • Could you move *over* a little, please? I need some more space. • Do you want to come *over* to my place? **b : to your home** • I invited some friends *over* for dinner. • They're nice. Why don't you ask them *over* some time? **c : in a particular place** • Their house is two streets *over* (from here). • They're building a new library *over* by the high school. • Who's that man *over* by the door? • It's summer now *over* in Australia. • I grew up in the next town *over.* [=the town that is next to this town]

5 : from one person or group to another • And now *over* to our foreign correspondent for the news from abroad. • It's mine! Hand it *over!* • They turned *over* the stolen money to the police. **— often used figuratively** • After years of supporting the Democrats, she suddenly went *over* to the Republican side. • He's gone *over* to the opposition.

6 : more than an expected or stated amount or number • The show ran a minute *over.* = The show ran *over* by a minute. • The condition is most common in women 65 ***and over.*** • Children eight *and over* [=children who are eight years old and older] may participate in the contest. • At this restaurant, parties of six ***or over*** will have a 20 percent gratuity added to their bill.

7 : remaining and not used • We ate the turkey that was left *over* from Thanksgiving Day dinner. • Most of the money would be spent on fixing the house with some left *over* for emergencies.

8 : during or throughout a period of time : until a later time (such as the next day) • Do you have enough money to tide you *over?* • Feel free to stay *over* [=*overnight*] if you don't want to drive home tonight. • Mom, can I sleep *over* [=can I spend the night] at Carrie's house?

9 : so as to cover the entire surface of something • The sky had clouded *over* [=it had become covered with clouds], and it was beginning to rain. • The empty house's windows had been boarded *over* several years ago. • He's become famous the world *over.* [=throughout the world]

10 a : in a complete and thorough way • I'll have to talk the matter *over* with my wife. • She's still thinking it *over.* **b : from the beginning to the end** • Read it *over* [=*through*] and let me know what you think.

11 a *chiefly US* **: one more time : AGAIN** • You've done it wrong. Do it *over.* • Let's start *over* (again) from the beginning. • He lost the computer file and had to do his assignment *over.* **b — used to say how many times something is done or repeated** • I had to read the poem ***twice over*** [=two times] before I understood its meaning. **c — used to say that something is done or happens repeatedly** • She became a millionaire many times *over.* [=she earned many millions of dollars] • I remind him ***over and over*** (again) not to leave the door open. • Say the lines *over and over* until you have memorized them.

12 — used when talking on a radio to show that a message is complete • "We are ready for takeoff instructions. *Over.*"

all over see **[2]ALL**

over (and done) with **: finished or completed** • Don't worry. The operation will be *over with* before you know it. • I'd like to get this *over with* as soon as possible. • No one wants to be here, so let's just get this meeting *over with.* • I'm just glad to have the test *over and done with.* • The past is *over and done with.*

[2]over *prep*

1 : from, to, or at a place that is higher than (someone or something) : ABOVE • The sun's coming up *over* the mountain. • She looked at him *over* the top of her glasses. • He stood *over* me [=he stood near me while I was sitting, kneeling, etc.] and asked what I was doing. • Their balcony looks out *over* the city. • He looked *over* the fence. • A plane was flying low *over* the trees. • The meat was cooked *over* an open fire.

2 : on top of (something) • Someone hit him *over* [=*on*] the head with a rock. • She slung the bag *over* her shoulder. • They served grilled chicken breast *over* [=*on*] a bed of rice. **: so as to cover (something)** • His hat was pulled low *over* his eyes.

3 : beyond and down from (something) • Throw the rocks *over* the side of the boat. • He fell *over* the cliff's edge. • She knocked the glass *over* the edge of the table.

4 a : from one side to the other side of (something or someone) • We've just crossed *over* the border into Canada. • walking *over* [=*across*] a bridge • Excuse me, I need to reach *over* you to get the salt. • Tomato vines grew up and *over* the fence. **b : upward and across (something)** • We both jumped *over* the stream. • They couldn't climb *over* the wall, so they dug a hole under/underneath it. **c : on the other side of (something)** • Our house is just *over* that hill.

5 : in the direction of (something) • Hey, look *over* there! • We're *over* here! • those trees *over* yonder

6 : more than (a specified number or amount) • I've been waiting for *over* an hour. • We haven't seen each other in *over* a year. • The condition is most common in women *over* 65. • It was really hot yesterday. It must have been *over* 100 degrees. • They had *over* 300 people at their wedding. • That car costs ***well over*** [=much more than] $50,000.

7 — used to say that a person or thing is better than (someone or something else) • The new model has several advantages *over* the old one. • This is a big improvement *over* our last apartment. • I would choose you *over* any other woman in the world. • She now has a two-minute lead *over* [=she is two minutes ahead of] the other runners. • When it comes to creative thinking, humans ***have it over*** [=are better than] computers. = When it comes to creative thinking, humans have the advantage *over* computers.

8 : in a position of power and authority that allows a person or thing to control (someone or something) • We must respect those *over* us. • The vice president presides *over* every meeting. • She should be given more authority *over* her staff. • We have no control *over* the situation. • countries that hold power *over* their neighbors • In this case, federal law takes precedence *over* state law.

9 a : so as to cover the surface of (something) • A strange expression came *over* his face. • People were boarding *over* their windows in preparation for the storm. **b : in every part of (a place)** • These trees once flourished *over* [=*throughout*] much of North America.

10 : throughout or during (a particular amount of time) • I'll think about it *over* the weekend and give you my answer on Monday. • He has accomplished many remarkable things *over* the course of his career. • The festival is spread (out) *over* three days. • happening/occurring/developing *over* a period of 20 years • *Over* the past 25 years, she has been a valuable asset to our company. • I've come to understand him better *over* the years. • ***Over time,*** the paper begins to turn yellow and brittle.

11 : by using (a radio, television, computer, etc.) • I heard it *over* [=*on*] the radio. • We spoke *over* the phone just yesterday. • sending messages *over* the Internet • The game was broadcast *over* the air/airwaves. [=on television or the radio]

12 : because of (someone or something) • Don't get angry *over* [=*about*] something so silly. • He got into trouble *over* a comment about his wife's mother. • She was crying *over* her old boyfriend. • Afterwards, we laughed *over* the incident.

13 : concerning or regarding (something) • There is still some controversy *over* [=*about*] the use of the drug. • a dispute *over* the land • the debate *over* assisted suicide

14 — used to describe something that is done while some activity (such as a meal) is taking place • I plan to meet with my advisers *over* lunch. [=while we eat lunch together] • We sat *over* our wine [=drinking our wine] and talked.

15 : finished with (something) : past or beyond (something) • I think we're *over* the worst of it. Things should get better from now on. • After she got *over* the initial surprise of being tricked, she started getting angry. • He's upset now, but he'll ***get over it*** [=he will stop being upset about it] soon.

16 : without being stopped or prevented by (something) : DESPITE • She spoke to the police *over* the objections of her lawyer. • *Over* the protests of several members, the committee passed the bill.

17 : without including or considering (someone or some-

thing) ▪ You can skip *over* that paragraph. ▪ I agree with what you've said, but you passed *over* an important point.

18 : more loudly and clearly than (another sound) ▪ The players couldn't hear their coach *over* [=*above*] the roar of the crowd. ▪ talking/shouting *over* the noise of the engines

all over see ²ALL

over against — used to describe things that are being compared or that are somehow opposed to each other ▪ comparing the results of one method *over against* another

over and above : in addition to (something) : along with (something) ▪ *Over and above* the fact that I don't like cats, I am allergic to them. ▪ We each received a bonus *over and above* our regular paychecks.

³over *adj, not used before a noun* : having reached the end : FINISHED ▪ When is this class *over*? ▪ And before we knew it, the storm was *over*. ▪ Those days are *over*. ▪ When it's *over*, it's *over*. You don't get a second chance. ▪ It's *over* between them. [=their relationship has ended]

over easy *not used before a noun, US, of eggs* : fried on one side then turned and fried for a short time on the other side ▪ He ordered two eggs *over easy*.

over- /ˌouvɚ/ *prefix*

1 a : too much or too great ▪ *over*confident ▪ *over*crowded ▪ *over*qualified ▪ *over*ripe **b :** so as to be better or beyond ▪ *over*achieve ▪ *over*take

2 : very or extremely ▪ *over*joyed

3 : above ▪ *over*coat ▪ *over*hang

4 : forward and often downward ▪ *over*bite ▪ *over*board

over·abun·dance /ˌouvɚrəˈbʌndəns/ *noun, pl* **-danc·es** [*count*] *chiefly US* : an amount that is too much — often + *of* ▪ There is an *overabundance of* lead in the water.

over·achiev·er /ˌouvɚrəˈʧi:vɚ/ *noun, pl* **-ers** [*count*] : someone who has much more success than is normal or expected especially at a young age ▪ She is an *overachiever* who plans to attend a top college. — opposite UNDERACHIEVER

– over·achieve /ˌouvɚrəˈʧi:v/ *verb* **-achieves; -achieved; -achiev·ing** [*no obj*] ▪ The team *overachieved* last year and won the title. ▪ an *overachieving* student

over·act /ˌouvɚˈækt/ *verb* **-acts; -act·ed; -act·ing** [*no obj*] *disapproving* : to show too much emotion when you are acting in a play, movie, etc. ▪ His tendency to *overact* made his performance less realistic.

over·ac·tive /ˌouvɚˈæktɪv/ *adj* [*more* ~; *most* ~] : too active especially in a way that produces a bad result ▪ She has an *overactive* bladder. ▪ His crazy ideas are products of an *overactive* imagination.

– over·ac·tiv·i·ty /ˌouvɚrækˈtɪvəti/ *noun* [*noncount*] ▪ This condition is caused by *overactivity* of the thyroid gland.

¹over·age /ˌouvɚˈeɪʤ/ *adj* : of an age that is greater than what is normal or allowed ▪ The college has many *overage* students. ▪ The players were banned from the league for being *overage*. — opposite UNDERAGE

²over·age /ˈouvərɪʤ/ *noun, pl* **-ag·es** [*count*] : an amount by which something (such as a payment) is too much ▪ They paid me back the *overage*. ▪ She kept track of the cost *overages*.

¹over·all /ˌouvɚˈɑ:l/ *adv*

1 : with everyone or everything included ▪ He scored highest *overall*. ▪ She figured out what it would cost *overall*. [=*altogether*]

2 : as a whole : in general ▪ He made a few mistakes but did well *overall*. ▪ *Overall*, the project was successful.

²over·all /ˌouvɚˈɑ:l/ *adj, always used before a noun*

1 : including everyone or everything ▪ your *overall* score after two rounds ▪ What is the *overall* [=*total*] cost?

2 : viewed as a whole or in general ▪ His mistake didn't change my *overall* impression of him. ▪ Your *overall* health is sound. ▪ She likes the *overall* quality of the product. ▪ The scratch didn't affect the car's *overall* appearance.

³over·all /ˈouvɚˌɑ:l/ *noun, pl* **-alls**

1 *overalls* [*plural*] *US* : a pair of pants with an extra piece attached that covers the chest and has straps that go over the shoulders ▪ wearing (a pair of) *overalls* — called also (*Brit*) *dungarees*; see color picture on page C14

2 [*count*] *Brit* : a loose coat that is worn over clothes so that they do not get dirty : SMOCK

3 *overalls* [*plural*] *Brit* : a piece of clothing that is worn over other clothes to protect them ▪ The mechanic was dressed in (a pair of) *overalls*. [=(*US*) *coveralls*]

over·arch·ing /ˌouvɚˈɑɚʧɪŋ/ *adj, formal* : including or influencing every part of something ▪ the book's *overarching* theme ▪ Computer downtime is an *overarching* problem in all departments.

over·arm /ˈouvɚˌɑɚm/ *adj, Brit* : OVERHAND ▪ He made an *overarm* throw.

– overarm *adv, Brit* ▪ He threw the ball *overarm*.

over·awe /ˌouvɚˈɑ:/ *verb* **-awes; -awed; -aw·ing** [+ *obj*] : to make (someone) unable to think, speak, or behave normally because of a strong feeling of respect and fear — usually used as (*be*) *overawed* ▪ She has competed in the finals before, so she won't *be overawed* by the experience.

over·bal·ance /ˌouvɚˈbæləns/ *verb* **-anc·es; -anced; -anc·ing** *Brit* : to lose your balance [*no obj*] He *overbalanced* and fell off the stool. [+ *obj*] She tried to reach the vase but *overbalanced* herself and fell off the stool.

over·bear·ing /ˌouvɚˈberɪŋ/ *adj* [*more* ~; *most* ~] *disapproving* : often trying to control the behavior of other people in an annoying or unwanted way ▪ He had to deal with his *overbearing* mother. ▪ Her husband's *overbearing* manner made her miserable.

over·bite /ˈouvɚˌbaɪt/ *noun, pl* **-bites** [*count*] : a condition in which your upper teeth are too far in front of your lower teeth ▪ He has a severe *overbite*.

over·blown /ˌouvɚˈbloun/ *adj* [*more* ~; *most* ~] *disapproving* : made to seem very important, intelligent, or great especially in order to impress people ▪ *overblown* [=*pretentious*] claims/rhetoric ▪ The problem is *overblown*. [=it has been exaggerated; it is not as bad as people say it is]

over·board /ˈouvɚˌboɚd/ *adv* : over the side of a ship into the water ▪ He threw/tossed the fish *overboard*. ▪ The boy fell *overboard* and almost drowned. ▪ One of the sailors fell into the water, and someone shouted "***Man overboard***!" — sometimes used figuratively ▪ The managers had to throw the plan *overboard* [=had to abandon the plan] because it was too expensive.

go overboard *informal* : to do something in a way that is excessive or extreme : to do too much of something ▪ Don't *go overboard* on/with the spices. [=do not add too many spices] ▪ She *went overboard* with the decorations.

over·book /ˌouvɚˈbʊk/ *verb* **-books; -booked; -book·ing** : to allow too many people to buy tickets or to reserve seats, tables, rooms, etc. [*no obj*] The hotel/restaurant *overbooked*. [+ *obj*] The flight was *overbooked*, and I got bumped off. ▪ The airline *overbooked* the flight. ▪ The doctor's office called and said that they *overbooked* the appointments for today. — compare DOUBLE-BOOK

over·bur·den /ˌouvɚˈbɚdən/ *verb* **-dens; -dened; -den·ing** [+ *obj*] : to give (someone or something) too much work, worry, etc. : to burden (someone or something) too much ▪ She *overburdened* me with work/guilt. ▪ Why *overburden* yourself when people are offering to help? — often used as (*be*) *overburdened* ▪ He *was overburdened* by work. ▪ The Web site *was overburdened* with a high amount of traffic.

over·ca·pac·i·ty /ˌouvɚkəˈpæsəti/ *noun, technical* : a situation in which an industry, company, etc., has or produces more of something than it is able to sell or use [*noncount*] problems with *overcapacity* [*singular*] The airlines are lowering their prices because of an *overcapacity* of seats.

over·cast /ˈouvɚˌkæst, *Brit* ˈəʊvəˌkɑ:st/ *adj* [*more* ~; *most* ~] : covered with clouds ▪ The sky was *overcast*. : darkened by clouds ▪ It was an *overcast* morning. ▪ They worked in *overcast* conditions.

over·charge /ˌouvɚˈʧɑɚʤ/ *verb* **-charg·es; -charged; -charg·ing**

1 : to charge too much for something : to make someone pay too much money for something [*no obj*] He *overcharges* for car repairs. [+ *obj*] He *overcharges* his customers for car repairs. ▪ The store *overcharged* me for my skirt. ▪ The customer was *overcharged* (by) $10. — opposite UNDERCHARGE

2 [+ *obj*] : to give too much of an electric charge to (a battery) ▪ I *overcharged* the battery.

over·coat /ˈouvɚˌkout/ *noun, pl* **-coats** [*count*] : a long coat that is worn to keep a person warm during cold weather — see color picture on page C15

over·come /ˌouvɚˈkʌm/ *verb* **-comes; -came** /-ˈkeɪm/; **-come; -com·ing** [+ *obj*]

1 : to defeat (someone or something) ▪ After a tough battle, they *overcame* the enemy.

2 : to successfully deal with or gain control of (something difficult) ▪ a story about *overcoming* adversity ▪ She *overcame* a leg injury and is back running again. ▪ He *overcame* [=*conquered*] his fear of heights and climbed the ladder.

3 : to affect (someone) very strongly or severely — usually used as *(be) overcome* ▪ The people trapped in the burning building *were overcome* by the heat and smoke. ▪ The family *was overcome* [=*overwhelmed*] by grief.

over·com·pen·sate /ˌoʊvɚˈkɑːmpənˌseɪt/ *verb* **-sates; -sat·ed; -sat·ing** [*no obj*] : to try to make up for something that is lacking or bad by doing too much of something else ▪ He *overcompensated* for his lateness by showing up two hours early the next day. ▪ She *overcompensated* for her bad skin by wearing too much makeup.

over·com·pli·cate /ˌoʊvɚˈkɑːmpləˌkeɪt/ *verb* **-cates; -cat·ed; -cat·ing** [+ *obj*] : to make (something) too difficult to understand ▪ Don't *overcomplicate* the recipe.
– **overcomplicated** *adj* ▪ These instructions are *overcomplicated.* [=are too complicated]

over·con·fi·dent /ˌoʊvɚˈkɑːnfədənt/ *adj* : having too much confidence about something ▪ He was *overconfident* about passing the test and didn't study for it.

over·cook /ˌoʊvɚˈkʊk/ *verb* **-cooks; -cooked; -cook·ing** [+ *obj*] : to cook (food) for too long ▪ She always *overcooks* steak. — usually used as *(be) overcooked* ▪ My hamburger was *overcooked.* [=*overdone*] ▪ *overcooked* chicken — opposite UNDERCOOK

over·crowd·ed /ˌoʊvɚˈkraʊdəd/ *adj* [*more* ~; *most* ~] : filled with too many people or things ▪ The prison is very *overcrowded.* ▪ They are forced to live in *overcrowded* conditions. ▪ This train feels a bit *overcrowded.* ▪ *overcrowded* schools and hospitals

over·crowd·ing /ˌoʊvɚˈkraʊdɪŋ/ *noun* [*noncount*] : a situation in which there are too many people or things in one place ▪ They need to reduce *overcrowding* in the prison.

over·do /ˌoʊvɚˈduː/ *verb* **-does** /-ˈdʌz/; **-did** /-ˈdɪd/; **-done** /-ˈdʌn/; **-do·ing** [+ *obj*]
1 : to do too much of (something) : to do (something) in an excessive or extreme way ▪ You should exercise every day, but don't *overdo it.* ▪ The acting in that play was badly *overdone.*
2 : to use too much of (something) ▪ Don't *overdo* the salt in this recipe. ▪ I think you might have *overdone* it with the decorations. [=used too many decorations] ▪ Love is a theme that is *overdone* [=used too often] in the movies.
3 : to cook (food) for too long ▪ The cook *overdid* the hamburgers. ▪ My steak was slightly *overdone.* [=*overcooked*] ▪ an *overdone* steak

[1]over·dose /ˈoʊvɚˌdoʊs/ *noun, pl* **-dos·es** [*count*]
1 : an amount of a drug or medicine that is too much and usually dangerous ▪ She died from a cocaine *overdose.* — often + *of* ▪ He ***took/had an overdose of*** pills.
2 : an amount of something that is too much ▪ a sugar *overdose* — often + *of* ▪ An *overdose of* horror movies gave him nightmares.

[2]over·dose /ˌoʊvɚˈdoʊs/ *verb* **-dos·es; -dosed; -dos·ing** [*no obj*] : to take too much of a drug or medicine : to take an overdose of a drug or medicine — usually + *on* ▪ She *overdosed on* tranquilizers and fell into a coma. — sometimes used figuratively ▪ She *overdosed on* romance novels over the summer.

over·draft /ˈoʊvɚˌdræft, *Brit* ˈəʊvəˌdrɑːft/ *noun, pl* **-drafts** [*count*] : an amount of money that is spent by someone using a bank account that is more than the amount available in the account : an amount that is overdrawn from an account

over·draw /ˌoʊvɚˈdrɑː/ *verb* **-draws; -drew** /-ˈdruː/; **-drawn** /-ˈdrɑːn/; **-draw·ing** [+ *obj*] : to withdraw more money from (an account) than is available ▪ She *overdrew* her account by $100.
– **overdrawn** *adj* ▪ Your account is *overdrawn.* ▪ an *overdrawn* account ▪ Customers must pay a fee for being *overdrawn* on their accounts.

over·dress /ˌoʊvɚˈdrɛs/ *verb* **-dress·es; -dressed; -dress·ing** [*no obj*] : to dress in clothes that are too fancy, formal, or warm for an occasion ▪ He *overdressed* for such a casual party. — opposite UNDERDRESS
– **overdressed** *adj* [*more* ~; *most* ~] ▪ He was *overdressed* for the party. ▪ I was *overdressed* for the weather.

over·drive /ˈoʊvɚˌdraɪv/ *noun* [*noncount*]
1 : a gear in an automobile that allows it to be driven at higher speeds ▪ He put/shifted the car into *overdrive.*
2 : a state of great activity especially in order to achieve something ▪ His acting career is in *overdrive.* ▪ The reporters went into *overdrive* to finish their stories on time.

over·due /ˌoʊvɚˈduː, *Brit* ˌəʊvəˈdjuː/ *adj*
1 : not paid at an expected or required time ▪ She reminded him that the rent was *overdue.* ▪ He has many *overdue* bills.
2 : not appearing or presented by a stated, expected, or required time ▪ The train is 10 minutes *overdue.* ▪ Her baby is *overdue* by one week. [=her baby has not been born yet and it is a week since its birth was expected] ▪ an *overdue* library book
3 — used to say that something should have happened or been done before now ▪ His promotion is long *overdue.* = He is long *overdue* for a promotion. [=he should have been given a promotion by now] ▪ Repairs on that building are long *overdue.*

over·ea·ger /ˌoʊvɚˈiːgɚ/ *adj, chiefly US* : too eager ▪ He seemed *overeager* to pin the blame on someone. ▪ an *overeager* opponent

over·eat /ˌoʊvɚˈiːt/ *verb* **-eats; -ate** /-ˈeɪt/; **-eat·en** /-ˈiːtn̩/; **-eat·ing** [*no obj*] : to eat more than is needed or more than is healthy : to eat too much ▪ When I'm tired or stressed, I tend to *overeat.*
– **overeating** *noun* [*noncount*] ▪ *Overeating* is unhealthy.

over·em·pha·size *also Brit* **over·em·pha·sise** /ˌoʊvɚˈɛmfəˌsaɪz/ *verb* **-siz·es; -sized; -siz·ing** [+ *obj*] : to treat (something) with more importance than is needed or proper : to emphasize (something) too strongly ▪ The teacher tends to *overemphasize* the value of tests. ▪ The importance of a healthy diet cannot be *overemphasized.* [=a healthy diet is extremely important]
– **over·em·pha·sis** /ˌoʊvɚˈɛmfəsəs/ *noun* [*singular*] The article has/puts an *overemphasis* on the role of the news media in politics. [*noncount*] There has been some *overemphasis* on testing.

over·es·ti·mate /ˌoʊvɚˈɛstəˌmeɪt/ *verb* **-mates; -mat·ed; -mat·ing** [+ *obj*]
1 : to estimate (something) as being greater than the actual size, quantity, or number ▪ I *overestimated* the number of chairs we would need for the party. [=I thought we would need more chairs than we actually did] ▪ We *overestimated* the value of the coins.
2 : to think of (someone or something) as being greater in ability, influence, or value than that person or thing actually is ▪ She *overestimated* his ability to do the job. ▪ The importance of a good education cannot be *overestimated.* [=a good education is very important] — opposite UNDERESTIMATE
– **over·es·ti·mate** /ˌoʊvɚˈɛstəmət/ *noun, pl* **-mates** [*count*] ▪ Cost *overestimates* in the budget left us with extra money in the end. – **over·es·ti·ma·tion** /ˌoʊvɚˌɛstəˈmeɪʃən/ *noun, pl* **-tions** [*count, noncount*]

over·ex·cited /ˌoʊvɚrɪkˈsaɪtəd/ *adj* : too excited ▪ The children got *overexcited* and couldn't get to sleep.

over·ex·pose /ˌoʊvɚrɪkˈspoʊz/ *verb* **-pos·es; -posed; -pos·ing** [+ *obj*]
1 : to leave (something) without covering or protection for too long ▪ It is harmful to *overexpose* your skin to the sun's rays.
2 : to let too much light fall on (film in a camera) when you are taking a photograph ▪ He *overexposed* the picture/film. ▪ a badly *overexposed* picture/image
3 : to give too much public attention or notice to (someone or something) ▪ He has been *overexposed* by/in the media. ▪ an *overexposed* celebrity
– **over·ex·po·sure** /ˌoʊvɚrɪkˈspoʊʒɚ/ *noun* [*noncount*] ▪ *overexposure* of the skin ▪ The photograph was ruined by *overexposure.* ▪ a celebrity whose career has been harmed by *overexposure*

over·ex·tend /ˌoʊvɚrɪkˈstɛnd/ *verb* **-tends; -tend·ed; -tend·ing** [+ *obj*] : to extend or stretch (something) too far ▪ He *overextended* a muscle in his arm. ▪ She *overextended* her back.
overextend yourself **1** : to try to do too much ▪ Don't *overextend yourself* or else you'll burn out. **2** : to spend more money than you can afford to spend ▪ Young people with credit cards often *overextend themselves.*
– **overextended** *adj* ▪ people who are financially *overextended*

over·feed /ˌoʊvɚˈfiːd/ *verb* **-feeds; -fed** /-ˈfɛd/; **-feed·ing** [+ *obj*] : to give too much food to (someone or something) ▪ Don't *overfeed* the animals.

over·fill /ˌoʊvɚˈfɪl/ *verb* **-fills; -filled; -fill·ing** [+ *obj*] : to fill a container with too much of something ▪ He *overfilled* the pail and the water spilled out. ▪ an *overfilled* trash can

over·fish /ˌoʊvɚˈfɪʃ/ *verb* **-fish·es; -fished; -fish·ing** [+ *obj*] : to catch too many fish so that there are not enough remaining — often used as *(be) overfished* ▪ The lake has *been*

O

overfished by both commercial and sport fishermen.
– **overfishing** *noun* [*noncount*] ▪ Several species were nearly wiped out by *overfishing*.

[1]**over·flow** /ˌoʊvɚˈfloʊ/ *verb* **-flows; -flowed; -flow·ing**
1 : to flow over the edge or top of (something) [+ *obj*] The river *overflowed* its banks. [*no obj*] The creek *overflows* every spring. ▪ The water in the tub *overflowed*. — often used figuratively ▪ The large crowd filled the room and *overflowed* into the lobby.
2 [+ *obj*] **:** to fill or cover (something) completely ▪ Books and papers *overflowed* his desk. ▪ The paragraph *overflowed* the page.
3 [*no obj*] **:** to be completely filled with something **:** to be so filled that there is not enough room for anything or anyone more ▪ *overflowing* trash cans — often + *with* ▪ His desk was *overflowing with* papers. ▪ The hotels are all ***filled/full to overflowing with*** tourists. — often used figuratively ▪ Her heart was *overflowing with* joy.

[2]**over·flow** /ˈoʊvɚˌfloʊ/ *noun, pl* **-flows** [*count*]
1 : an act of flowing over the edge or top of something — usually singular; often + *of* ▪ The rescuers put up sandbags to stop the *overflow of* the river.
2 a : the amount of something that flows over the edge or top of something else — usually singular ▪ The *overflow* from the river flooded the field. **b :** the number of people or things that goes over a limit — usually singular; often + *of* ▪ The police tried to control the *overflow of* traffic. ▪ The company hired more people to handle the *overflow of* phone calls. — sometimes used before another noun ▪ The band played to an *overflow* crowd. [=a crowd larger than a place is meant to hold]
3 : a pipe or container for liquid that overflows from something else

over·fly /ˌoʊvɚˈflaɪ/ *verb* **-flies; -flew** /-ˈfluː/; **-flown** /-ˈfloʊn/; **-fly·ing** [+ *obj*] **:** to fly over (a place) ▪ The jets *overflew* the stadium.

over·ground /ˈoʊvɚˌgraʊnd/ *adv, Brit* **:** on or above the ground ▪ These trains all run *overground*.
– **overground** *adj, always used before a noun* ▪ an *overground* train [=(*US*) an aboveground train]

over·grow /ˌoʊvɚˈgroʊ/ *verb* **-grows; -grew** /-ˈgruː/; **-grown** /-ˈgroʊn/; **-grow·ing** [+ *obj*] **:** to grow in an uncontrolled way and completely cover or fill (something) ▪ The weeds have *overgrown* the garden.
– **over·growth** /ˈoʊvɚˌgroʊθ/ *noun* [*noncount*] ▪ He cut down the *overgrowth*. ▪ Prune the branches to prevent *overgrowth*.

overgrown *adj*
1 : covered with plants that have grown in an uncontrolled way ▪ The garden is *overgrown* with weeds. ▪ an *overgrown* path
2 : grown to a size that is unusually or too large ▪ an *overgrown* plant ▪ an *overgrown* ego ▪ He acts like an *overgrown* child.

over·hand /ˈoʊvɚˌhænd/ *adj, US* **:** made with the hand brought forward and down from above the shoulder ▪ an *overhand* [=(*Brit*) overarm] pitch/throw ▪ an *overhand* tennis stroke — compare UNDERHAND
– **overhand** *adv* ▪ I can pitch *overhand* or underhand.

[1]**over·hang** /ˈoʊvɚˌhæŋ/ *verb* **-hangs; -hung** /-ˌhʌŋ/; **-hang·ing** [+ *obj*] **:** to stick out beyond or hang over (something) ▪ A cliff *overhangs* the trail. ▪ The patio was *overhung* by a canopy. ▪ The path was *overhung* with willow trees.
– **overhanging** *adj* ▪ an *overhanging* cliff ▪ The path was shaded by *overhanging* branches.

[2]**overhang** *noun, pl* **-hangs** [*count*]
1 : a part that sticks out or hangs over something ▪ The *overhang* of the roof cast a shadow on the ground.
2 : the amount by which something hangs over something else ▪ a five-foot *overhang*

over·haul /ˌoʊvɚˈhɑːl/ *verb* **-hauls; -hauled; -haul·ing** [+ *obj*]
1 : to look at every part of (something) and repair or replace the parts that do not work ▪ The mechanic *overhauled* the car's engine.
2 : to change (something) completely in order to improve it ▪ They had to *overhaul* their original plans. ▪ Lawmakers are *overhauling* the welfare program.
– **over·haul** /ˈoʊvɚˌhɑːl/ *noun, pl* **-hauls** [*count*] ▪ The engine underwent a complete *overhaul*. ▪ Lawmakers are attempting a major *overhaul* of the welfare program.

[1]**over·head** /ˌoʊvɚˈhɛd/ *adv* **:** above someone's head **:** in the sky or space above someone ▪ Geese were flying *overhead*. ▪ A chandelier hung directly *overhead*. ▪ People were making noise in the balcony *overhead*.
– **over·head** /ˈoʊvɚˌhɛd/ *adj* ▪ *overhead* branches. ▪ *overhead* lights/wires

[2]**over·head** /ˈoʊvɚˌhɛd/ *noun* [*noncount*] *US* **:** costs for rent, heat, electricity, etc., that a business must pay and that are not related to what the business sells ▪ Her company has very little *overhead*. ▪ *overhead* costs — called also (*Brit*) *overheads*

overhead projector *noun, pl* **~ -tors** [*count*] **:** a device that shows information or pictures on a wall or screen by shining a light through a sheet with the information or pictures on it

overhead projector

over·hear /ˌoʊvɚˈhiɚ/ *verb* **-hears; -heard** /-ˈhɚd/; **-hear·ing :** to hear (something that was said to another person) by accident [+ *obj*] She *overheard* what her boss said to his secretary. ▪ I *overheard* a rumor about you. ▪ We *overheard* their discussion of the project. = We *overheard* them discussing the project. ▪ They were *overheard* discussing the project. [*no obj*] I couldn't help but *overhear*. = I couldn't help *overhearing*. [=I couldn't avoid hearing what was said]

over·heat /ˌoʊvɚˈhiːt/ *verb* **-heats; -heat·ed; -heat·ing**
1 [*no obj*] **:** to become too hot ▪ The car's engine *overheated*.
2 [+ *obj*] **:** to cause (something) to become too hot ▪ I *overheated* the food in the microwave. ▪ Be careful not to *overheat* the engine.

over·heat·ed /ˌoʊvɚˈhiːtəd/ *adj*
1 : too hot ▪ She worked in a stuffy, *overheated* office.
2 : too excited or emotional ▪ an *overheated* imagination/argument ▪ The discussion was getting *overheated*.
3 *of a market or economy* **:** having too much activity, growth, etc. ▪ The market for new houses is *overheated*. ▪ an *overheated* economy

over·joyed /ˌoʊvɚˈʤoɪd/ *adj* [*more* ~; *most* ~] **:** filled with great joy **:** very happy ▪ She was *overjoyed* to see her sister again. ▪ They weren't *overjoyed* at the idea of working together. ▪ I'm *overjoyed* that you can come to my party.

over·kill /ˈoʊvɚˌkɪl/ *noun* [*noncount*] *disapproving* **:** something that is much larger, greater, etc., than what is needed for a particular purpose ▪ Yes, we need a new car, but this huge truck seems like *overkill*. ▪ The incident got blown out of proportion because of media *overkill*. [=the media gave it much more attention than it deserved]

over·land /ˈoʊvɚˌlænd/ *adv* **:** on or across land instead of over water ▪ We traveled *overland* by horse to the mountains.
– **overland** *adj* ▪ They made an *overland* journey. ▪ an *overland* trade route

over·lap /ˌoʊvɚˈlæp/ *verb* **-laps; -lapped; -lap·ping**
1 : to lie over the edge of (something) **:** to cover part of the edge of (something) [+ *obj*] The roof shingles *overlap* each other. [*no obj*] The roof shingles *overlap*. ▪ The petals of the flower *overlap*. = The flower has *overlapping* petals.
2 : to happen at the same time as something else [*no obj*] — often + *with* ▪ Baseball season *overlaps with* football season in September. [+ *obj*] Baseball season *overlaps* football season in September.
3 : to have parts that are the same as parts of something else [*no obj*] Some of their duties *overlap*. = They have/share *overlapping* duties. — often + *with* ▪ Some of the material in the course *overlaps with* what I was taught in another course. [+ *obj*] Some of your duties *overlap* his.
– **over·lap** /ˈoʊvɚˌlæp/ *noun, pl* **-laps** [*count*] The map shows an *overlap* in the regions controlled by the two tribes. [*noncount*] There is some *overlap* between the two courses. [=the courses cover some of the same material]

[1]**over·lay** /ˌoʊvɚˈleɪ/ *verb* **-lays; -laid** /-ˈleɪd/; **-lay·ing** [+ *obj*] **:** to cover (something) with a layer of another material — often + *with* ▪ She *overlaid* the photograph *with* a piece of glass. ▪ The tabletop is *overlaid with* marble. — often used figuratively ▪ Her song was *overlaid with* sad lyrics and melodic vocals.

[2]**over·lay** /ˈoʊvɚˌleɪ/ *noun, pl* **-lays**
1 : material that covers the complete surface or part of the surface of something and that changes its appearance [*noncount*] a silver ring with gold *overlay* [*count*] The wooden ta-

ble has a marble *overlay*. — often used figuratively • Her voice had an *overlay* of sadness. [=there was a sad quality in her voice]

2 [*count*] **:** a transparent sheet with information or pictures on it that is placed on top of another sheet to change what is being shown

over·leaf /ˈoʊvɚˌli:f/ *adv, chiefly Brit* **:** on the other side of the page • You can find the answers *overleaf.*

over·lie /ˌoʊvɚˈlaɪ/ *verb* **-lies; -lay** /-ˈleɪ/; **-lain** /-ˈleɪn/; **-ly·ing** [+ *obj*] *formal* **:** to lie over or on (something) • Sand *overlies* the clay.

– overlying *adj* • the *overlying* layers of rock

over·load /ˌoʊvɚˈloʊd/ *verb* **-loads; -load·ed; -load·ing** [+ *obj*]

1 : to put too great a load on or in (something) • Don't *overload* the washing machine. — often + *with* • The truck was *overloaded with* wood. — often used figuratively • He *overloaded* his essay *with* facts and figures.

2 : to give too much work to (someone) — often + *with* • My boss is *overloading* me *with* extra work.

3 : to cause (something, such as an electrical circuit) to be used for too many things at the same time • That outlet is *overloaded* and could start a fire. • an *overloaded* circuit

– over·load /ˈoʊvɚˌloʊd/ *noun, pl* **-loads** [*count*] The barge had an *overload* of cargo. • Fires can start from circuit *overloads*. [*noncount*] I'm suffering from advertising *overload*. [=I have been seeing too many advertisements; I am sick of advertisements] • information *overload*

over·long /ˌoʊvɚˈlɑ:ŋ/ *adj* **:** longer than usual or necessary **:** too long • an *overlong* essay • The movie/meeting was *overlong.*

over·look /ˌoʊvɚˈlʊk/ *verb* **-looks; -looked; -look·ing** [+ *obj*]

1 a : to fail to see or notice (something) • The detective *overlooked* an important clue. **b :** to pay no attention to (something) • She learned to *overlook* [=*ignore*] her boyfriend's minor faults. • Such a crime should not be *overlooked.*

2 : to not consider (someone) for a job, position, promotion, etc. • The quarterback was *overlooked* by other teams. — often + *for* • I was *overlooked for* a promotion.

3 a : to rise above (something) • the mountains that *overlook* the village **b :** to have a view looking down at (something) • We rented a suite that *overlooks* the lake.

over·lord /ˈoʊvɚˌloɚd/ *noun, pl* **-lords** [*count*] **:** a person who has power over a large number of people • He is the *overlord* of the underground gambling industry. • a colonial *overlord*

over·ly /ˈoʊvɚli/ *adv* **:** to an excessive degree **:** TOO • These directions are *overly* complex. • She's *overly* sensitive to criticism. • They didn't seem *overly* concerned about the problem.

over·matched /ˌoʊvɚˈmætʃt/ *adj* **:** fighting or competing against a much stronger opponent • The boxer was badly *overmatched.* • They wiped out the *overmatched* rebel army.

over·much /ˌoʊvɚˈmʌtʃ/ *adv* **:** too much or very much — usually used in negative statements • Her comments didn't bother me *overmuch.*

¹over·night /ˌoʊvɚˈnaɪt/ *adv*

1 : for or during the entire night • He stayed *overnight* and went home the next day. • Let the paint dry *overnight.*

2 : very quickly or suddenly • The novel made her famous *overnight.*

²overnight *adj*

1 : happening, traveling, or staying during the night • They went on an *overnight* bus trip. • an *overnight* train • *Overnight* guests are not allowed in the dormitory.

2 : happening very quickly or suddenly • The show was an *overnight* success.

overnight bag *noun, pl* **~ bags** [*count*] **:** a bag for carrying the clothes and other things that you take for an overnight trip

over·night·er /ˌoʊvɚˈnaɪtɚ/ *noun, pl* **-ers** [*count*]

1 a : an overnight trip • He is on an *overnighter*. **b :** OVERNIGHT BAG • You should pack an *overnighter.*

2 : a person who stays somewhere overnight • *Overnighters* will appreciate the area's fine hotels.

over·op·ti·mis·tic /ˌoʊvɚˌɑ:ptəˈmɪstɪk/ *adj, disapproving* **:** expecting something to be much better in the future **:** too optimistic • He is *overoptimistic* about his future success.

over·pass /ˈoʊvɚˌpæs, *Brit* ˈəʊvəˌpɑ:s/ *noun, pl* **-pass·es** [*count*] *US* **:** a bridge that allows a road or railroad to cross over another • Boys stood beneath the highway *overpass.* • Traffic was stalled on the *overpass.* — called also (*Brit*) *flyover*; compare UNDERPASS

over·pay /ˌoʊvɚˈpeɪ/ *verb* **-pays; -paid** /-ˈpeɪd/; **-pay·ing**

1 : to pay too much for something [*no obj*] He *overpaid* for his car. [+ *obj*] I accidentally *overpaid* the plumber.

2 [+ *obj*] *disapproving* **:** to pay (someone) more money for a job than is deserved • She is *overpaid* for the work she does. • The company tends to *overpay* upper management. • *overpaid* baseball players — opposite UNDERPAY

– over·pay·ment /ˌoʊvɚˈpeɪmənt/ *noun, pl* **-ments** [*count, noncount*]

over·play /ˌoʊvɚˈpleɪ/ *verb* **-plays; -played; -play·ing** [+ *obj*]

1 : to give too much attention to (something) **:** to make (something) seem more important than it really is • The network news *overplayed* the story just to get good ratings. — opposite UNDERPLAY

2 *disapproving* **:** to show too much emotion when acting in a play, movie, etc. • He *overplayed* the death scene.

overplay your hand also overplay your cards **:** to make a mistake because you believe that your position is stronger or better than it really is • The union *overplayed its hand* by demanding too much, causing the company to withdraw what would have been its best offer.

over·pop·u·la·tion /ˌoʊvɚˌpɑ:pjəˈleɪʃən/ *noun* [*noncount*] **:** a situation in which too many people or animals live in a certain area • He is studying the problem of deer *overpopulation.* • world *overpopulation*

– over·pop·u·lat·ed /ˌoʊvɚˈpɑ:pjəˌleɪtəd/ *adj* • the shortage of housing in *overpopulated* cities

over·pow·er /ˌoʊvɚˈpawɚ/ *verb* **-ers; -ered; -er·ing** [+ *obj*]

1 : to defeat or gain control of (someone or something) by using force • She was able to *overpower* her attacker. • The police *overpowered* the man and handcuffed him. • The troops were *overpowered* by the stronger enemy forces.

2 : to affect (someone) very strongly or severely • The smell *overpowered* [=*overwhelmed*] us. • We were *overpowered* [=*overcome*] by hunger/grief.

3 : to have more strength, force, or effect than (someone or something) • His personality *overpowers* everyone else's. • The delicate taste of the wine was *overpowered* by the spiciness of the food.

overpowering *adj* [*more ~; most ~*] **:** very strong or powerful • an *overpowering* smell • an *overpowering* fastball • He has an *overpowering* personality. • I felt an *overpowering* urge to tell him what I really thought of him.

over·price /ˌoʊvɚˈpraɪs/ *verb* **-pric·es; -priced; -pric·ing** [+ *obj*] **:** to give a price that is too high to (something) **:** to price (something) too high • The store was guilty of *overpricing* its goods. • Everything in the store is grossly *overpriced.* • *overpriced* jewelry

over·print /ˌoʊvɚˈprɪnt/ *verb* **-prints; -print·ed; -print·ing** [+ *obj*] **:** to add something to (a picture, document, etc.) by printing — usually + *with* • They *overprinted* the photo *with* red lettering. • The money is *overprinted with* pictures of the queen.

over·pro·duc·tion /ˌoʊvɚprəˈdʌkʃən/ *noun* [*noncount*] **:** the act of producing more of something than is needed or wanted • The *overproduction* of oil caused the fuel companies to lower their prices. • Heartburn can be caused by the *overproduction* of stomach acid.

over·pro·tec·tive /ˌoʊvɚprəˈtɛktɪv/ *adj* **:** trying too hard to protect someone (such as a child) from danger • His *overprotective* mother won't let him go out after dark. • He is *overprotective* of his little sister.

over·qual·i·fied /ˌoʊvɚˈkwɑ:ləˌfaɪd/ *adj* **:** having more experience, knowledge, or training than is needed • They didn't hire her because she was *overqualified* for the job.

over·rate /ˈoʊvɚˌreɪt/ *verb* **-rates; -rat·ed; -rat·ing** [+ *obj*] **:** to rate, value, or praise (someone or something) too highly • The coach tends to *overrate* the players on his own team.

– overrated *adj* [*more ~; most ~*] • (*disapproving*) That movie was disappointing and highly/very *overrated.*

over·reach /ˌoʊvɚˈri:tʃ/ *verb* **-reach·es; -reached; -reach·ing :** to try to do something that is beyond your ability to do [*no obj*] She *overreaches* in her latest book, and her argument is not convincing. [+ *obj*] The company ***overreached itself*** and ran out of money after one year.

over·re·act /ˌoʊvɚriˈækt/ *verb* **-acts; -act·ed; -act·ing** [*no obj*] **:** to respond to something with an emotion that is too strong or an action that is unnecessary **:** to react to

O

something too strongly • My mother *overreacted* when she learned that I had been in an accident. • The news media always *overreacts* to any kind of scandal. • He *overreacted* to his bad grades by quitting school.

– **over·re·ac·tion** /ˌoʊvəriˈækʃən/ *noun, pl* **-tions** [*count, noncount*] • His angry response was an *overreaction*.

over·ride /ˌoʊvəˈraɪd/ *verb* **-rides**; **-rode** /-ˈroʊd/; **-rid·den** /-ˈrɪdn̩/; **-rid·ing** [+ *obj*]

1 : to make (something) no longer valid • Congress *overrode* the President's veto. • These new rules *override* the old ones.

2 : to have more importance or influence than (something) • Don't let anger *override* common sense.

3 : to stop an action that is done automatically by using a special command • You must enter a code to *override* the alarm. • She *overrode* the default settings on her computer.

overriding *adj, always used before a noun* **:** more important than anything else • We have one *overriding* concern. • The weather is the *overriding* factor in deciding whether to cancel the picnic.

over·ripe /oʊvəˈraɪp/ *adj*

1 : grown or aged past the point of ripeness and beginning to decay **:** too ripe • *overripe* fruit/cheese

2 a : not new or young • an *overripe* [=*aging*] rock star **b :** not fresh or original • *overripe* [=*trite*] prose

over·rule /oʊvəˈru:l/ *verb* **-rules**; **-ruled**; **-rul·ing** [+ *obj*] **:** to decide that (something or someone) is wrong **:** to rule against (something or someone) • The judge *overruled* the objection/attorney. • His conviction was *overruled* by the supreme court. — sometimes used figuratively • We sometimes let our hearts *overrule* our sense of reason.

[1]**over·run** /ˌoʊvəˈrʌn/ *verb* **-runs**; **-ran** /-ˈræn/; **-run**; **-run·ning** [+ *obj*]

1 : to enter and be present in (a place) in large numbers • The tank divisions *overran* the countryside. • The city was being *overrun* by enemy troops. • Rats *overran* the ship. • In the summer, the town is *overrun* with/by tourists. [=is filled with tourists]

2 : to run or go beyond or past (something) • The runner *overran* [=ran past] third base. • The plane *overran* the runway. • The stream has *overrun* [=*overflowed*] its banks. • His speech *overran* the time allowed.

3 : to spread over or throughout (something) • Weeds *overran* the garden. = The garden was *overrun* with/by weeds. • Crime *overran* the neighborhood.

[2]**over·run** /ˈoʊvəˌrʌn/ *noun, pl* **-runs** [*count*] **:** an amount of money that is spent and that is more than the expected or planned amount • cost/budget *overruns*

over·seas /ˌoʊvəˈsi:z/ *adv* **:** in or to a foreign country that is across a sea or ocean • I lived *overseas* [=*abroad*] for a time. • The troops were sent *overseas*.

– **over·seas** /ˈoʊvəˌsi:z/ *adj* • *overseas* flights/markets

over·see /ˌoʊvəˈsi:/ *verb* **-sees**; **-saw** /-ˈsɑ:/; **-seen** /-ˈsi:n/; **-see·ing** [+ *obj*] **:** to watch and direct (an activity, a group of workers, etc.) in order to be sure that a job is done correctly **:** SUPERVISE • He was hired to *oversee* design and construction of the new facility.

over·seer /ˈoʊvəˌsi:jə/ *noun, pl* **-seers** [*count*] **:** a person who watches and directs the work of other people in order to be sure that a job is done correctly • She was named *overseer* [=*supervisor*] of new product development. • government/industry *overseers* • (*US*) a plantation/slave *overseer* [=the person who was in charge of the slaves on a plantation]

over·sell /ˌoʊvəˈsɛl/ *verb* **-sells**; **-sold** /-ˈsoʊld/; **-sell·ing** [+ *obj*]

1 : to accept payment or reservations for more rooms, seats, tickets, etc., than you have available • Hotels routinely *oversell* their rooms, expecting a small percentage of no-shows. • The concert was *oversold*. [=more tickets were sold than there were seats] • an *oversold* [=*overbooked*] flight

2 : to praise (something or someone) too much • Don't *oversell* yourself in the job interview. • The salesman *oversold* the features on the new model.

over·sen·si·tive /ˌoʊvəˈsɛnsətɪv/ *adj* **:** too sensitive: such as **a :** too easily upset or offended • *Oversensitive* readers might be unhappy with some parts of the book. • students who are *oversensitive* to criticism **b :** acting or reacting too quickly • a car with *oversensitive* brakes

over·sexed /ˌoʊvəˈsɛkst/ *adj* **:** having more interest in sex than is usual • a movie about *oversexed* college students

over·shad·ow /ˌoʊvəˈʃædoʊ/ *verb* **-ows**; **-owed**; **-ow·ing** [+ *obj*]

1 : to cause (something or someone) to seem less important or impressive when compared to something or someone else • The pitcher's outstanding performance should not *overshadow* the achievements of the rest of the team. — often used as *(be) overshadowed* • She felt *overshadowed* by the success of her brother.

2 : to make (something) less enjoyable because of sadness, fear, or worry — often used as *(be) overshadowed* • Their lives *are overshadowed* by the constant threat of earthquakes. • Recent peace efforts have *been overshadowed* by violence.

3 : to cast a shadow over (something) • a house *overshadowed* by tall trees [=a house with tall trees next to it]

over·shoe /ˈoʊvəˌʃu:/ *noun, pl* **-shoes** [*count*] **:** a rubber shoe worn over another shoe in bad weather

over·shoot /ˌoʊvəˈʃu:t/ *verb* **-shoots**; **-shot** /-ˈʃɑ:t/; **-shoot·ing** [+ *obj*] **:** to go over or beyond (something) • The plane *overshot* the runway. • He *overshot* the target. • We're afraid that costs may *overshoot* [=*exceed*] projections. • Sometimes we *overshoot* our time limits.

over·sight /ˈoʊvəˌsaɪt/ *noun, pl* **-sights**

1 [*count*] **:** a mistake made because someone forgets or fails to notice something • The fact that you didn't get an invitation is surely just an *oversight*. • The error was a simple *oversight*.

2 [*noncount*] **:** the act or job of directing work that is being done • The new manager was given *oversight* of the project. • a congressional *oversight* committee [=a congressional committee that oversees something]

over·sim·pli·fy /ˌoʊvəˈsɪmpləˌfaɪ/ *verb* **-fies**; **-fied**; **-fy·ing :** to describe (something) in a way that does not include all the facts and details and that causes misunderstanding [+ *obj*] The article *oversimplifies* the problem. • She tends to *oversimplify* things. [*no obj*] We must resist the temptation to *oversimplify*.

– **over·sim·pli·fi·ca·tion** /ˌoʊvəˌsɪmpləfəˈkeɪʃən/ *noun, pl* **-tions** [*count, noncount*]

over·size /ˌoʊvəˈsaɪz/ *or* **over·sized** /ˌoʊvəˈsaɪzd/ *adj* **:** larger than the normal size **:** very large • an *oversize* package

over·sleep /ˌoʊvəˈsli:p/ *verb* **-sleeps**; **-slept** /-ˈslɛpt/; **-sleep·ing** [*no obj*] **:** to sleep past the time when you planned to get up • Be sure to set your alarm clock so that you don't *oversleep*.

over·spend /ˌoʊvəˈspɛnd/ *verb* **-spends**; **-spent** /-ˈspɛnt/; **-spend·ing :** to spend more than the planned or proper amount of money [*no obj*] The studio clearly *overspent* on marketing, and the movie was still a flop. [+ *obj*] We try not to *overspend* our budget. [=to spend more than our budget allows]

– **overspend** *noun, pl* **-spends** [*count*] *Brit* • The government *overspend* on administrative costs hit record levels.

over·spill /ˈoʊvəˌspɪl/ *noun, Brit* **:** the movement of people from crowded cities to less crowded areas [*singular*] an *overspill* into nearby towns [*noncount*] a new town built to absorb London's *overspill*

over·staffed /ˌoʊvəˈstæft, *Brit* ˌəʊvəˈstɑ:ft/ *adj* **:** having more workers than is necessary • The store is *overstaffed* and will probably begin to lay off some workers.

over·state /ˌoʊvəˈsteɪt/ *verb* **-states**; **-stat·ed**; **-stat·ing** [+ *obj*] **:** to say that (something) is larger or greater than it really is • The company *overstated* revenue [=the company reported more revenue than it actually earned] for the past year. • It would be *overstating* the case to say that it was a matter of life or death. • It would be difficult to *overstate* the damage done by the storm. [=the storm did a great amount of damage] • The importance of tomorrow's test ***cannot be overstated***. [=tomorrow's test is very important]

– **over·state·ment** /ˌoʊvəˈsteɪtmənt/ *noun, pl* **-ments** [*count*] an *overstatement* of profits • It's not an *overstatement* to say that he'll eat anything. [*noncount*] He is often given to *overstatement*.

over·stay /ˌoʊvəˈsteɪ/ *verb* **-stays**; **-stayed**; **-stay·ing** [+ *obj*] **:** to stay longer than you are expected or allowed to stay • She was guilty of *overstaying* a student visa. • Don't ***overstay your welcome***. [=do not stay longer than you should]

over·step /ˌoʊvəˈstɛp/ *verb* **-steps**; **-stepped**; **-step·ping** [+ *obj*] **:** to go beyond what is proper or allowed by (something) • The judges *overstepped* their authority. [=the judges did something that they are not allowed to do] • He ***overstepped the bounds/limits*** of good taste. [=he did something that was not proper] • She warned us not to ***overstep the mark/line***. [=do something that is not proper or allowed]

over·stim·u·late /ˌoʊvɚˈstɪmjəˌleɪt/ *verb* **-lates; -lat·ed; -lat·ing** [+ *obj*] **:** to cause (someone or something) to become too active or excited **:** to stimulate (someone or something) too much • antibodies that *overstimulate* the thyroid • an *overstimulated* child

– over·stim·u·la·tion /ˌoʊvɚˌstɪmjəˈleɪʃən/ *noun* [*noncount*]

over·stock /ˌoʊvɚˈstɑːk/ *verb* **-stocks; -stocked; -stock·ing** [+ *obj*] **:** to cause (something) to have a larger amount of something than is needed or wanted — often used as *(be) overstocked* • The stores *are overstocked* with toys around Christmas. • The pond *is overstocked* with fish. • an *overstocked* refrigerator/warehouse

– over·stock /ˈoʊvɚˌstɑːk/ *noun* [*noncount*] • At the end of the season, the *overstock* is sold off at a discount.

over·stretch /ˌoʊvɚˈstrɛʧ/ *verb* **-stretch·es; -stretched; -stretch·ing** [+ *obj*]

1 : to stretch (something) too far or too much • Take care not to *overstretch* his sweater. • *overstretch* a muscle

2 *chiefly Brit* **:** to try to do too much with (something) • Don't *overstretch* your resources. **:** to try to make (someone) do too much • an *overstretched* serving staff • Home buyers should not financially ***overstretch themselves***. [=not spend more money than they can afford to spend]

over·stuffed /ˌoʊvɚˈstʌft/ *adj*

1 : completely full or too full • *overstuffed* plastic bags • pockets *overstuffed* with cash

2 *of furniture* **:** having a large amount of soft padding **:** very soft and comfortable • an *overstuffed* armchair

over·sub·scribed /ˌoʊvɚsəbˈskraɪbd/ *adj* — used to describe a situation in which something is wanted by many people but there are not enough copies, rooms, etc., for everyone • an *oversubscribed* stock issue • an *oversubscribed* course/school

over·sup·ply /ˈoʊvɚsəˌplaɪ/ *noun, pl* **-plies** [*count*] **:** an amount of something that is more than is needed or wanted • An *oversupply* of office space drove down rent prices. • There is a global *oversupply* of sugar.

overt /oʊˈvɚt/ *adj* [*more* ~; *most* ~] **:** easily seen **:** not secret or hidden **:** OBVIOUS • *overt* hostility — opposite COVERT

– overt·ly *adv* • an *overtly* religious reference

over·take /ˌoʊvɚˈteɪk/ *verb* **-takes; -took** /-ˈtʊk/; **-tak·en** /-ˈteɪkən/; **-tak·ing**

1 a [+ *obj*] **:** to move up to and past (someone or something that is in front of you) by moving faster • The car *overtook* [=*passed*] the leader of the race on the turn. • She *overtook* the other runners and went on to win the race. — often used figuratively • All of the other candidates hope to *overtake* the front-runner by election day. • Obesity may soon *overtake* smoking as the leading cause of preventable deaths. • Frank has *overtaken* his father in height. [=Frank is now taller than his father] **b** [*no obj*] *Brit* **:** to go past another vehicle that is moving more slowly in the same direction • Never *overtake* [=(*US*) *pass*] on a curve. • The sign says "No *Overtaking*."

2 [+ *obj*] **:** to happen to or affect (someone) in a sudden and unexpected way • The pain *overtook* him. • Seasickness can *overtake* passengers when the ship encounters a storm. • Sleep had *overtaken* them. • I could feel the impulse to buy it *overtaking* [=*seizing*] me.

overtaken by events **:** forced to be changed because of something that has suddenly and unexpectedly happened • The original date for the meeting was *overtaken by events* and had to be changed.

over·tax /ˌoʊvɚˈtæks/ *verb* **-tax·es; -taxed; -tax·ing** [+ *obj*]

1 : to make (someone or something) do more than that person or thing is able to do or should do **:** to make heavy demands on (someone or something) • New housing development in the town will *overtax* sewer and drinking water systems. • We are afraid the trip might *overtax* his health/strength. • The children *overtaxed* her patience. • The hospital's *overtaxed* emergency room needs more doctors.

2 : to make (people) pay too much in taxes • He claims that the city has been *overtaxing* its residents for years.

over–the–counter *adj, always used before a noun*

1 : available for purchase without a special note (called a prescription) from a doctor • an *over-the-counter* medication • *over-the-counter* drugs — abbr. *OTC*; see also *over the counter* at ¹COUNTER

2 *US, business* **:** not traded on an organized stock exchange • an *over-the-counter* stock

over–the–top *adj* [*more* ~; *most* ~] *informal* **:** going beyond what is expected, usual, normal, or appropriate **:** excessive or exaggerated • an *over-the-top* performance — see also *over the top* at ¹TOP

over·throw /ˌoʊvɚˈθroʊ/ *verb* **-throws; -threw** /-ˈθruː/; **-thrown** /-ˈθroʊn/; **-throw·ing** [+ *obj*]

1 : to remove (someone or something) from power especially by force • *overthrow* a government • The dictator was *overthrown*.

2 *US, sports* **:** to throw a ball over or past (someone) • He *overthrew* the first baseman. = He *overthrew* first base. • The quarterback *overthrew* his receiver.

– over·throw /ˈoʊvɚˌθroʊ/ *noun, pl* **-throws** [*count, noncount*]

over·time /ˈoʊvɚˌtaɪm/ *noun* [*noncount*]

1 a : time spent working at your job that is in addition to your normal working hours • I worked two hours of *overtime* last week. • He was doing a lot of *overtime* to save for his vacation. **b :** the money paid for work that is done in addition to your normal working hours • How much did you earn last month in *overtime*? • *overtime* pay

2 : extra time added to a game when the score is tied at the end of the normal playing time • The game went ***into overtime***. • They lost the game ***in overtime***. — often used before another noun • an *overtime* win/period/game

– overtime *adv* • He has been working *overtime*. — often used figuratively • Her imagination was ***working overtime***. [=her imagination was extremely active] • He's been *working overtime* [=working very hard] around the house to please his wife.

over·tired /ˌoʊvɚˈtajɚd/ *adj* **:** extremely tired • I've been feeling *overtired* and stressed out.

over·tone /ˈoʊvɚˌtoʊn/ *noun, pl* **-tones** [*count*]

1 : an idea or quality that is suggested without being said directly • Their words carried an *overtone* [=*hint, suggestion*] of menace. • racist/political *overtones*

2 : a very small amount of something • The wine has *overtones* of fruitiness. [=hints of the taste of fruit]

3 *music* **:** a higher tone that is part of the sound of a musical note

over·ture /ˈoʊvɚʧɚ/ *noun, pl* **-tures** [*count*]

1 : a piece of music played at the start of an opera, a musical play, etc.

2 : something that is offered or suggested with the hope that it will start a relationship, lead to an agreement, etc. • The government has made a significant peace *overture* by opening the door to negotiation. • He was making (romantic/sexual) *overtures* to her during dinner. • The company's board rejected *overtures* [=*offers*] for a merger.

3 : the first part of an event **:** the beginning of something • Experts feared that the tremor was an *overture* [=*prelude*] to a major earthquake.

over·turn /ˌoʊvɚˈtɚn/ *verb* **-turns; -turned; -turn·ing**

1 a [+ *obj*] **:** to turn (something) over • The dog *overturned* the bowl. **b** [*no obj*] **:** to turn over • The truck went off the road and *overturned* several times.

2 [+ *obj*] **:** to decide that (a ruling, decision, etc.) is wrong and change it **:** REVERSE • The court *overturned* his conviction.

¹over·use /ˌoʊvɚˈjuːz/ *verb* **-us·es; -used; -us·ing** [+ *obj*] **:** to use (something) too much or too often • Try not to *overuse* the medication. • an *overused* phrase

²over·use /ˌoʊvɚˈjuːs/ *noun* [*noncount*] **:** too much use • the *overuse* of antibiotics • The couch sagged from *overuse*.

over·val·ue /ˌoʊvɚˈvælju/ *verb* **-val·ues; -val·ued; -val·u·ing** [+ *obj*]

1 : to place too high a value on (something) • Is property in this part of town *overvalued*? [=priced too high]

2 : to give too much importance to (something) • He *overvalues* the opinions of his friends.

over·view /ˈoʊvɚˌvjuː/ *noun, pl* **-views** [*count*] **:** a general explanation or description of something **:** SUMMARY • I was asked to give an *overview* of the company's sales figures. • This book provides a broad/general *overview* of American history.

over·ween·ing /ˌoʊvɚˈwiːnɪŋ/ *adj, formal + disapproving*

1 : too confident or proud • speeches by *overweening* politicians

2 : too great **:** excessive and unpleasant • *overweening* ambition/pride

over·weight /ˌoʊvɚˈweɪt/ *adj* [*more* ~; *most* ~] **:** weighing more than the normal or expected amount **:** too heavy • He's

O

only slightly *overweight*. • He looked to be at least 20 pounds *overweight*. • an *overweight* package

over·whelm /ˌouvəˈwɛlm/ *verb* **-whelms; -whelmed; -whelm·ing** [+ *obj*]
1 : to affect (someone) very strongly • Grief *overwhelmed* her. = She was *overwhelmed* by grief. [=she felt grief so strongly that she was unable to think or act in a normal way] • Her neighbor's kindness *overwhelmed* her. [=moved her deeply]
2 : to cause (someone) to have too many things to deal with • The many requests for assistance *overwhelmed* them. = They were *overwhelmed* by the many requests for assistance. [=they could not respond to the many requests for assistance because there were too many] • Don't *overwhelm* him with facts. • They were *overwhelmed* with work.
3 : to defeat (someone or something) completely • The city was *overwhelmed* by the invading army. • She was *overwhelmed* at the polls. [=she was badly defeated in the election]
4 : to cover over (something) completely with water • The boat was *overwhelmed* [=*engulfed*] by a huge wave.

over·whelm·ing /ˌouvəˈwɛlmɪŋ/ *adj* [*more* ~; *most* ~]
1 : very great in number, effect, or force • The response was *overwhelming*. • *overwhelming* [=very strong] evidence/support • an *overwhelming* majority/success
2 — used to describe something that is so confusing, difficult, etc., that you feel unable to do it • She found the job *overwhelming* at first.
– over·whelm·ing·ly *adv* • The town voted *overwhelmingly* for the new library. • an *overwhelmingly* difficult task

over·win·ter /ˌouvəˈwɪntə/ *verb* **-ters; -tered; -ter·ing** [*no obj*] **: to spend or survive the winter** • The geese will *overwinter* in a warmer climate.

over·work /ˌouvəˈwək/ *verb* **-works; -worked; -work·ing**
1 : to work too hard [*no obj*] The whole crew seemed exhausted, probably from *overworking*. [+ *obj*] The captain routinely *overworked* the crew.
2 [+ *obj*] **: to use (something) too much or too often** • He *overworks* the melody in the song. • *overwork* a phrase
3 [+ *obj*] **: to work on (something) too much** • She *overworked* the painting. • If you *overwork* the dough, the bread will be tough.
– overwork *noun* [*noncount*] • They were exhausted from *overwork*. **– overworked** *adj* • He says that he's *overworked* and underpaid. • She always looks tired and *overworked*. • an *overworked* phrase/expression

over·write /ˌouvəˈraɪt/ *verb* **-writes; -wrote** /-ˈrout/; **-writ·ten** /-ˈrɪtn̩/; **-writ·ing**
1 [+ *obj*] **: to replace information in (a computer file) with new information** • *overwrite* the existing file
2 : to write in a way that is too detailed or complicated [*no obj*] The author has a tendency to *overwrite*. [+ *obj*] — usually used as ***(be) overwritten*** • The novel *was overwritten* and dull.

over·wrought /ˌouvəˈrɑːt/ *adj* [*more* ~; *most* ~] **: very excited or upset** • The witness became *overwrought* as she described the crime. • an *overwrought* performance

over·zeal·ous /ˌouvəˈzɛləs/ *adj* [*more* ~; *most* ~] **: too eager or enthusiastic : too zealous** • *overzealous* fans • *overzealous* enforcement of the rules
– over·zeal·ous·ly *adv* **– over·zeal·ous·ness** *noun* [*noncount*]

ovi·duct /ˈouvəˌdʌkt/ *noun, pl* **-ducts** [*count*] *biology* **: a tube through which eggs pass from the ovary of a female animal**

ovoid /ˈouˌvoɪd/ *adj, formal* **: shaped like an egg** • an *ovoid* leaf

ovu·late /ˈɑːvjəˌleɪt/ *verb* **-lates; -lat·ed; -lat·ing** [*no obj*] *biology, of a woman or a female animal* **: to produce eggs within the body**
– ovu·la·tion /ˌɑːvjəˈleɪʃən/ *noun* [*noncount*]

ovum /ˈouvəm/ *noun, pl* **ova** /ˈouvə/ [*count*] *biology* **: [1]EGG 3**

ow /ˈau/ *interj* **— used to express sudden pain** • *Ow*! That hurts!

owe /ˈou/ *verb* **owes; owed; ow·ing**
1 : to need to pay or repay money to a person, bank, business, etc. [+ *obj*] I still *owe* money on the car. [=I have not yet paid back all the money I borrowed to buy the car] • We *owe* no income tax. • He *owes* me $5. • Don't I *owe* money to you? = Don't I *owe* you money? • I *owe* the bank a lot of money. • Additional payments are *owed* on the mortgage. • How much is *owed*? = What is the amount *owed*? • How much do I *owe* (you) for this? [*no obj*] I still *owe* on the car.
2 [+ *obj*] **a : to need to do or give something to someone who has done something for you or given something to you** • I *owe* you a drink/favor. • I *owe* you my thanks. • (*informal*) What do you mean you won't help? You *owe* me! • She still *owes* me for all the times I've helped her out. • Thanks for your help. I ***owe you one***. [=I will give you help when you need it] **b — used to say that something should be done for or given to someone** • You *owe* me an explanation. • I *owe* you an apology. • The senator is *owed* a degree of respect. [=the senator deserves some respect] • We ***owe it to*** the veterans to build a memorial. [=we should build a memorial to honor and thank the veterans] • You ***owe it to yourself*** to have fun. [=you deserve to let yourself have fun] • He *owes it to himself* to travel while he still can.
3 [+ *obj*] **— used to indicate the person or thing that made something possible** • She *owes* her family for her success. [=her family enabled her to become successful] **— often + *to*** • I *owe* my success *to* my teachers. [=my teachers deserve credit for my success] • She *owes* her success *to* hard work. [=she has succeeded because of hard work] • He *owes* his wealth *to* his father. • He *owes* his fame *to* several movies. [=he is famous because he was in several movies] • His success *owes* more *to* luck than skill. [=is more because of luck than skill] • I *owe* my life *to* the surgeon's skill. [=the surgeon's skill saved my life] • We *owe* our understanding of gravity *to* Newton.
owe a debt of gratitude/thanks to someone see DEBT

owing *adj, not used before a noun, Brit* **: due to be paid** • Do you have any bills *owing*? [=any bills that you have not yet paid]

owing to *prep* **: because of (something)** • The ambassador was absent *owing to* [=*due to*] illness. • She walks with a limp *owing to* a childhood injury.

owl /ˈawəl/ *noun, pl* **owls** [*count*] **: a bird that usually hunts at night and that has a large head and eyes, a powerful hooked beak, and strong claws — see color picture on page C9; see also** BARN OWL, NIGHT OWL, SCREECH OWL

owl·et /ˈaulət/ *noun, pl* **-ets** [*count*] **: a young or small owl**

owl·ish /ˈaulɪʃ/ *adj* **: resembling or suggesting an owl** • an *owlish* face • *owlish* eyes/glasses **— often used to describe a person who wears round glasses and seems serious and intelligent**

[1]own /ˈoun/ *adj, always used before a noun*
1 — used to say that something belongs or relates to a particular person or thing and to no other; always used after a possessive (such as "my," "your," or "their") • We each had our *own* book. • The star of the show needs his *own* private dressing room. • Each of the houses is beautiful in its *own* way. • His novel is based on his *own* personal experiences. • "In my *own* experience," she said, "I have found that women are better workers than men." • My father built this boat with his *own* (two) hands. • I've got my *own* problems; I don't have time to listen to yours. • She had her *own* reasons for not wanting to go. • Mind your *own* business! This has nothing to do with you! • I don't like punishing you, but it's for your *own* good. • It's your *own* fault that you failed the test. You should have studied more. • He's too old for her. Why doesn't she date someone her *own* age? [=someone who is the same age as her] • I now have my ***very own*** office!
2 — used to stress the fact that a person does or makes something without the help of other people; always used after a possessive • She's always dreamed of starting her *own* business. • They built their *own* home. • I'm going out tonight, so you'll have to cook your *own* dinner. • He acted as his *own* lawyer during the trial.

[2]own *pronoun* **: something or someone that belongs or relates to a particular person or thing and to no other — always used after a possessive (such as "my," "your," "their," or "Joe's")** • The teacher gave out books so that each of us had our *own*. • Do you want to share a bag of popcorn, or should we each get our *own*? • He loves children and would like one of his *own* someday. • We've got problems of our *own*. • I have a few ideas of my *own*. • The Senator's views are entirely his *own* and do not represent those of his party. • The band has a style ***all its own*** [=no other band has the same style] • I don't need much—just a little place to ***call my own*** [=just a little place that belongs only to me] • The apartment isn't much, but she's ***made it her own*** [=she has changed it to suit her; she has personalized it] • ***Through no fault of their own***

these children are forced to live in poverty. ▪ When you're a little older, you can have a bike of your ***very own***

come into your own see [1]COME

get your own back see *get back* at GET

hold your own see [1]HOLD

on your own **1 :** without being helped by anyone or anything ▪ He's still too weak to stand *on his own.* ▪ No one had to tell me; I found out *on my own.* ▪ The rash went away *on its own* after a few days. ▪ Keys don't just disappear *on their own.* You must have left them somewhere. ▪ I came up with the idea ***all on my own*** **2 a :** without anyone or anything else **:** ALONE ▪ She lived *on her own* for a few years before getting married. **b :** in a state or condition in which there is nobody to help you ▪ If you mess up, you're *on your own.* ▪ They can't survive *on their own* in the wilderness.

to each his own or each to his own see [2]EACH

[3]**own** *verb* **owns; owned; own·ing**

1 *not used in progressive tenses* [+ *obj*] **:** to have (something) as property **:** to legally possess (something) ▪ We hope to someday *own* our own home. ▪ She drives a red truck that was originally *owned* by her grandfather. ▪ He *owns* the rights to the band's music. ▪ a publicly/privately *owned* company ▪ The couple ***owns and operates*** the business. ▪ (*disapproving*) He walks/struts around here ***like he owns the place*** [=like someone who has the right to tell other people what to do]

2 *old-fashioned* **:** to admit that something is true [+ *obj*] After everyone else denied any responsibility, he *owned* that he was at fault. [*no obj*] — usually + *to* ▪ He would not *own to* the mistake. [=he would not admit the mistake]

own up [*phrasal verb*] **:** to admit that you have done a usually bad thing **:** to confess to something ▪ I know he broke the window, but so far, he hasn't *owned up.* — usually + *to* ▪ I'm waiting for him to *own up to* it.

own–brand *adj, Brit* **:** STORE-BRAND

own·er /ˈounɚ/ *noun, pl* **-ers** [*count*] **:** a person or group that owns something ▪ Who's the *owner* of that car? [=who owns that car?; whose car is that?] ▪ The restaurant's previous *owner* was unable to make a profit. ▪ Congratulations! You are now the ***proud owner*** of a brand-new car! ▪ The stolen jewelry was found and returned to its ***rightful owner*** — often used in combination ▪ dog-*owners* and cat-*owners* — see also HOMEOWNER, LANDOWNER

– own·er·less *adj* ▪ *ownerless* pets

owner–occupied *adj* **:** lived in by the owner ▪ *owner-occupied* apartments

– owner–occupier *noun, pl* **-ers** [*count*] *chiefly Brit* ▪ renters and *owner-occupiers*

own·er·ship /ˈounɚˌʃɪp/ *noun* [*noncount*] **:** the state or fact of owning something ▪ Home *ownership* is on the rise in this country. [=an increasing number of people own their own homes in this country] ▪ The restaurant is now under new *ownership.* [=different people now own the restaurant] ▪ The company is under private *ownership.*

own goal *noun, pl* **~ goals** [*count*]

1 *chiefly Brit* **:** a goal in soccer, hockey, etc., that a player accidentally scores against his or her own team ▪ We lost the game when one of our players scored an *own goal* for the other team.

2 *Brit* **:** something that you do because you think it will help you but that actually hurts you ▪ The workers scored an *own goal* by demanding such high wages that no one could afford to employ them.

own–label *adj, Brit* **:** STORE-BRAND

ox /ˈɑːks/ *noun, pl* **ox·en** /ˈɑːksən/ *also* **ox** [*count*]

1 : a bull that has had its sex organs removed

2 : a cow or bull

ox·bow /ˈɑːksˌbou/ *noun, pl* **-bows** [*count*] *US* **:** a place where a river curves in the shape of a U

Ox·bridge /ˈɑːksˌbrɪʤ/ *adj, always used before a noun, Brit* **:** of or relating to Oxford and Cambridge Universities ▪ *Oxbridge* graduates — compare REDBRICK

– Oxbridge *noun* [*noncount*] ▪ graduates of *Oxbridge*

ox·cart /ˈɑːksˌkɑɚt/ *noun, pl* **-carts** [*count*] **:** a cart pulled by oxen

ox·ford /ˈɑːksfɚd/ *noun, pl* **-fords**

1 [*count*] *chiefly US* **:** a low shoe usually made of leather and fastened with laces ▪ a pair of *oxfords*

2 a [*noncount*] **:** soft, strong cotton usually used for making shirts **b** [*count*] *US* **:** a shirt made of oxford ▪ a button-down *oxford* ▪ a blue *oxford* shirt

ox·ide /ˈɑːkˌsaɪd/ *noun, pl* **-ides** [*count, noncount*] *chemistry* **:** a compound of oxygen and another substance ▪ iron *oxide*

ox·i·dize /ˈɑːksəˌdaɪz/ *also Brit* **ox·i·dise** *verb* **-diz·es; -dized; -diz·ing** [*no obj*] **:** to become combined with oxygen ▪ The paint *oxidizes* and discolors rapidly.

– ox·i·da·tion /ˌɑːksəˈdeɪʃən/ *noun* [*noncount*]

ox·y·gen /ˈɑːksɪʤən/ *noun* [*noncount*] **:** a chemical that is found in the air, that has no color, taste, or smell, and that is necessary for life ▪ breathing pure *oxygen* — often used before another noun ▪ an *oxygen* tank ▪ The doctors monitored *oxygen* levels in her blood.

ox·y·gen·ate /ˈɑːksɪʤəˌneɪt/ *verb* **-ates; -at·ed; -at·ing** [+ *obj*] *technical* **:** to add oxygen to (something) ▪ *oxygenate* the blood

– ox·y·gen·a·tion /ˌɑːksɪʤəˈneɪʃən/ *noun* [*noncount*]

oxygen mask *noun, pl* **~ masks** [*count*] **:** a mask worn over your nose and mouth so that you can breathe oxygen from a storage tank

oxygen tent *noun, pl* **~ tents** [*count*] **:** a piece of medical equipment that surrounds the body or head of a patient like a small, clear tent and that is filled with flowing oxygen

ox·y·mo·ron /ˌɑːksɪˈmoɚˌɑːn/ *noun, pl* **-rons** [*count*] **:** a combination of words that have opposite or very different meanings ▪ The phrase "cruel kindness" is an *oxymoron.*

– ox·y·mo·ron·ic /ˌɑːksɪməˈrɑːnɪk/ *adj* ▪ an *oxymoronic* statement/concept

oys·ter /ˈoɪstɚ/ *noun, pl* **-ters** [*count*] **:** a type of shellfish that has a rough shell with two parts and that is eaten both cooked and raw — see color picture on page C8

the world is your oyster informal ✧ If *the world is your oyster,* your life is good and you have the ability to do whatever you want to do. ▪ We were young and happy, and *the world was our oyster.*

oyster bed *noun, pl* **~ beds** [*count*] **:** a place in the ocean where oysters grow

oyster cracker *noun, pl* **~ -ers** [*count*] *US* **:** a small salted cracker that is usually round

oysters Rocke·fel·ler /-ˈrɑːkɪˌfɛlɚ/ *noun* [*plural*] *US* **:** cooked oysters that are covered with various toppings (such as spinach) and a buttery sauce and served on their shells

oz. *abbr, US* ounce; ounces

Oz /ˈɑːz/ *noun* [*noncount*] *Brit, informal* — used as a name for Australia

ozone /ˈouˌzoun/ *noun* [*noncount*]

1 : a form of oxygen that is found in a layer high in the earth's atmosphere ▪ Scientists are concerned about *ozone* depletion. ▪ an ***ozone-friendly*** product [=a product that will not reduce the ozone in the upper atmosphere]

2 *chiefly Brit, informal* **:** fresh healthy air especially near the sea ▪ A light breeze filled the rooms of our seaside cottage with *ozone.*

ozone hole *noun, pl* **~ holes** [*count*] **:** an area of the ozone layer where there is very little ozone

ozone layer *noun* [*noncount*] **:** a layer of ozone in the upper atmosphere that prevents dangerous radiation from the Sun from reaching the surface of the Earth

P

[1]p *or* **P** /ˈpiː/ *noun, pl* **p's** *or* **ps** *or* **P's** *or* **Ps** /ˈpiːz/ **:** the 16th letter of the English alphabet [*count*] a word that starts with a *p* [*noncount*] a word that starts with *p*
mind your p's and q's** also US **watch your p's and q's **:** to be careful about behaving in a polite or proper way • We knew to *mind our p's and q's* around our aunt.

[2]p *abbr* **1** *or* **p.** page • *p.* 46 ✧ The abbreviation for "pages" is *pp.* • *pp.* 46–48 **2** per • m*p*h [=miles per hour] **3** *Brit* pence; penny • That costs 40*p*.

pa /ˈpɑː/ *noun, pl* **pas** [*count*] *informal + old-fashioned* **:** a person's father • my ma and *pa* • *Pa*, can I go out?

p.a. *abbr, chiefly Brit* per annum

[1]PA *abbr* Pennsylvania

[2]PA /ˌpiːˈeɪ/ *noun, pl* **PAs** [*count*]
1 : a machine with a microphone and speakers used for making announcements in a public place — usually used with *the* • The name of the raffle winner was announced over *the PA*. — called also *PA system, public address system*
2 *US* **:** PHYSICIAN'S ASSISTANT

PAC /ˈpæk/ *noun, pl* **PACs** [*count*] *US* **:** POLITICAL ACTION COMMITTEE

[1]pace /ˈpeɪs/ *noun, pl* **pac·es**
1 [*singular*] **a :** the speed at which someone or something moves • He can run at a decent *pace*. [=he can run fairly fast] • We walked at a leisurely *pace* along the shore. • I told the kids to ***pick/step up the pace***. [=go faster] • He rode his bike up the hill ***at a snail's pace***. [=very slowly] • We encourage you to hike the trail ***at your own pace***. [=at a speed that suits you and lets you be comfortable] **b :** the speed at which something happens • The *pace* of the story was slow. • His new album is selling at a blistering/breakneck/dizzying *pace*. • Despite quickly advancing medical technology, the *pace* [=(more commonly) *rate*] of change in her field remained slow and steady. • She liked the fast ***pace of life*** in the city. [=she liked the fast way things happened in the city] — see also CHANGE OF PACE
2 [*count*] **:** a single step or the length of a single step — usually plural • The tree is about 30 *paces* from the front door. • The dog walked a few *paces* behind us.
go through your paces **:** to do something in order to show others how well you do it • The athletes *went through their paces* as the coaches looked on. • a show horse *going through its paces* for the judges
keep pace with **:** to go or make progress at the same speed as (someone or something else) • Our production can't *keep pace with* [=*keep up with*] the orders coming in. • The law has not *kept pace with* technology. [=the law has not changed fast enough to reflect changes in technology] • She struggles to *keep pace with* her classmates.
***off the pace** US* **:** behind in a race, competition, etc. • The winner finished in 4 minutes, 30 seconds, and the next runner was three seconds *off the pace*. [=finished three seconds later] • The other runners were way *off the pace*.
put someone or something through his/her/its paces **:** to test what someone or something can do • We brought home three different computers and *put them through their paces*.
set the pace **:** to be the one that is at the front in a race and that controls how fast the other racers have to go • As our fastest runner, he usually *sets the pace* for the rest of the team. — often used figuratively • The company's advanced equipment *sets the pace* for the recording industry. — see also PACESETTER

[2]pace *verb* **paces; paced; pac·ing**
1 : to walk back and forth across the same space again and again especially because you are nervous [+ *obj*] He *paced* the floor/room. [*no obj*] When she gets nervous she *paces* back and forth. • He was *pacing* and muttering to himself.
2 [+ *obj*] **:** to control or set the speed of (someone or something) • She *paced* the other runners for the first half of the race. • Advertisements are *paced* so that they are shown more often during peak sales seasons. — see also OUTPACE
pace off [*phrasal verb*] ***pace (something) off** or **pace off (something)*** **:** to measure (something) by walking and counting the number of steps you take • The new garden is 25 feet long. I *paced* it *off*. • *Pace off* 20 feet.
pace yourself **:** to do something at a speed that is steady and that allows you to continue without becoming too tired • If you don't *pace yourself*, you'll wear yourself out. • He quickly learned he would need to *pace himself* so he could get all of his work done.
– paced *adj* • a moderately *paced* stroll • a frenetically *paced* comedy • a well-*paced* meal • fast-*paced* music
– pacing *noun* [*noncount*] • Her continuous *pacing* was making me anxious. • The *pacing* of the movie was all wrong. [=the events in the movie happened too quickly or slowly]

pace·mak·er /ˈpeɪsˌmeɪkɚ/ *noun, pl* **-ers** [*count*]
1 *medical* **:** a small electrical machine put inside a person to make the heart beat evenly
2 *Brit* **:** PACESETTER

pace·set·ter /ˈpeɪsˌsɛtɚ/ *noun, pl* **-ters** [*count*] *US* **:** a person who runs ahead of the other runners in a race in order to set a pace — often used figuratively • The company has continued to be the industry's *pacesetter*.

pachy·derm /ˈpækɪˌdɚm/ *noun, pl* **-derms** [*count*] **:** a type of animal that has hooves and thick skin; *especially* **:** ELEPHANT

pa·cif·ic /pəˈsɪfɪk/ *adj*
1 ***Pacific*** **:** of, relating to, bordering on, or near the Pacific Ocean • a *Pacific* nation • fishing in *Pacific* waters
2 [*more ~; most ~*] *literary* **a :** calm and peaceful • a *pacific* setting **b :** loving peace : not wanting war or conflict • a *pacific* people

Pacific Rim *noun*
the Pacific Rim **:** a group of countries that are in or next to the Pacific Ocean — used especially of Asian countries on the Pacific Ocean • His family immigrated from *the Pacific Rim*.

pac·i·fi·er /ˈpæsəˌfajɚ/ *noun, pl* **-ers** [*count*] *US* **:** a rubber object shaped like a nipple for babies to suck or bite on — called also *(Brit) dummy*

pac·i·fism /ˈpæsəˌfɪzəm/ *noun* [*noncount*] **:** the belief that it is wrong to use war or violence to settle disputes

pac·i·fist /ˈpæsəfɪst/ *noun, pl* **-fists** [*count*] **:** someone who believes that war and violence are wrong and who refuses to participate in or support a war • A group of *pacifists* were protesting the war.
– pacifist *adj, always used before a noun* • He did not enter the army because of his *pacifist* beliefs/ideals.

pac·i·fy /ˈpæsəˌfaɪ/ *verb* **-fies; -fied; -fy·ing** [+ *obj*]
1 : to cause (someone who is angry or upset) to become calm or quiet • *pacify* [=*soothe*] a crying child • She resigned from her position to *pacify* her accusers.
2 : to cause or force (a country, a violent group of people, etc.) to become peaceful • Their efforts to *pacify* the nation by force failed. • trying to *pacify* a mob of protesters
– pac·i·fi·ca·tion /ˌpæsəfəˈkeɪʃən/ *noun* [*noncount*] • Many died in the years before *pacification*.

[1]pack /ˈpæk/ *noun, pl* **packs** [*count*]
1 : a bag or bundle of objects that is carried on a person's or animal's back • He took a map and a bottle of water out of his *pack*. • hikers carrying heavy *packs* up a mountain • They loaded the *packs* onto the horses. — see also BACKPACK, FANNY PACK
2 *chiefly US* **a :** a small paper or cardboard package in which small things are sold • a *pack* [=(*Brit*) *packet*] of gum/cigarettes/needles • The entire *pack* of crayons spilled on the floor. • Cigarettes typically come in *packs* of 20. **b :** the amount contained in one pack • He smokes two *packs* (of cigarettes) a day. — see also SIX-PACK
3 *Brit* **:** PACKET 2b • You'll receive your informational *pack* upon arrival.
4 : a complete set of playing cards **:** DECK • Take a card from the top and put it in the middle of the *pack*.
5 : a group of similar people or things • A *pack* of reporters were following them wherever they went. • *packs* of teenagers/lawyers/thieves • The information he gave us was just a ***pack of lies***. [=all lies] • One writer ***stands out from the pack***. [=one writer is different from the others] • She's not content to simply ***follow the pack***. [=to do what everyone else does]
6 : a large number of people who are grouped together dur-

P

ing a race or competition — usually singular • In the last few seconds, she broke/drew/pulled away from the *pack* and won the race. • The company is trying to stay ahead of the *pack*. [=ahead of their competitors]
7 : a group of usually wild animals that hunt together • a wolf *pack* • a *pack* of wild dogs • animals that hunt in *packs*
8 a : an organized group of Cub Scouts • Cub Scout *Pack* No. 5398 **b** *chiefly Brit* : an organized group of Brownies • a Brownie *pack* [=(*US*) *troop*]
9 : a thick, wet substance that is put on the skin as a beauty treatment • an herbal face *pack* • mud *packs*
10 : a folded cloth that is pressed against a part of the body to reduce pain or stop bleeding from an injury • a cold *pack* [=*compress*] — see also ICE PACK

²pack *verb* **packs; packed; pack·ing**
1 a [+ *obj*] : to put (something) into a bag, suitcase, etc., so that you can take it with you • Don't forget to *pack* your toothbrush. • Be sure to *pack* your bathing suit and a towel. • I've *packed* a picnic lunch for us. • *Pack* your things/gear. We're leaving tonight. **b** : to put things into (a bag, box, etc.) [+ *obj*] We *packed* our bags the night before our trip. • Have you *packed* your suitcase yet? • My bags are *packed*, and I'm ready to go. • *packing* and unpacking boxes [*no obj*] I spent the evening *packing* for my trip. • She *packed* [=*packed up*] and left. • We had only one week to *pack* and move out of our apartment. — see also PACKED 4
2 [+ *obj*] : to put (something) into a box or other container so that it can be moved, stored, or protected • We've *packed* [=*boxed*] (up) all our books. [=we've put all our books into boxes] — often + *in* or *into* • They *pack* the meat *in* dry ice before shipping it. • They *packed* the statue *into* a crate.
3 a [+ *obj*] : to fill (a place) with as many people as possible • Over 25,000 people will *pack* the stadium for tonight's concert. • a famous comedian who *packs* clubs in every city : to fill a place completely with (people) — often + *into* • Concert organizers *pack* hundreds of people *into* tiny nightclubs. **b** *always followed by a preposition* [*no obj*] : to gather close together as a group • Her fans *pack* into theaters to hear her sing. • We all *packed* into the car. • The entire family *packs* around a small table for dinner.
4 [+ *obj*] : to put a large amount of something into (something) • directors who *pack* their movies full of violence — often + *with* • They *pack* their magazine *with* lots of helpful decorating ideas. • The van had been *packed with* explosives. — see also PACKED 2
5 [+ *obj*] : to make (dirt, snow, etc.) more firm or solid by pressing down on it • *Pack* the soil firmly around the roots of the plant. • Other skiers had already *packed* the snow down. — see also PACKED 1
6 [+ *obj*] *US* : to unfairly control the kinds of people or things that are in (a group, list, etc.) in order to get the result you want • They *packed* the meeting with their supporters. • *packing* juries with people of a particular race
7 [+ *obj*] *somewhat informal* : to have or be able to produce (something powerful) • The storm is *packing* hurricane-force winds. • an engine that *packs* a lot of power [=an engine that is very powerful]
8 *US, informal* : to wear or carry (a weapon) [+ *obj*] They might be *packing* guns/pistols/weapons. • She's ***packing heat***. [=she's carrying a gun] [*no obj*] We don't know if he's *packing* or not.
pack a punch/wallop *informal* : to be very forceful or effective • Careful—these hot peppers really *pack a punch*. [=they are very hot and spicy] • Unlike her last album, her new release *packs a wallop*. [=it is forceful and energetic]
pack away [*phrasal verb*] ***pack (something) away or pack away (something)*** : to put (something) in a safe place to be used at a later time • It's time to *pack away* your winter clothes and get ready for summer. • Her grandmother's dolls had been *packed away* in the attic for many years.
pack in [*phrasal verb*] **1** *Brit, informal* : to stop or quit • I have no intention of *packing in* just yet. **2 a** ***pack in (someone or something) or pack (someone or something) in*** : to cause (someone or something) to fit into a small space • My suitcase was full, but I managed to *pack in* one more sweater. • There must have been a hundred people in that room. They *packed* us *in* like sardines! — see also ²PACK 2 (above) **b** ***pack in (people) or pack (people) in*** : to cause (large groups of people) to come to a show or performance • His show still *packs in* (the) crowds/audiences. [=large crowds/audiences still go to his show] • *packing in* fans of all ages • The movie has been ***packing them in*** at theaters across the country. **3** ***pack in (something)*** **a** *US, informal* : to stop using (something) forever • She isn't *packing in* her skis [=she is not giving up skiing] just yet. • I decided to *pack in* my paintbrushes and go to business school. **b** *Brit, informal* : to give up doing (something) • He *packed in* [=*quit*] his job and became a farmer. • They might *pack in* [=*stop, give up*] the project altogether. **4** ***pack it in*** *informal* : to stop doing a job or an activity : QUIT • Do you think we should *pack it in* or keep going? • They were ready to *pack it in* for the day.
pack in/into [*phrasal verb*] ***pack (something) in/into (something)*** : to put (a large amount of something) into (something) • She *packs* a lot of information *in* her short essays.
pack off [*phrasal verb*] ***pack (someone) off*** : to send (someone) away to a different place — usually + *to* • Despite his protests, his mom *packed* him *off to* bed. [=sent him to bed] • parents *packing* their kids *off to* college
pack on the pounds or pack on five/ten/fifteen (etc.) pounds *chiefly US, informal* : to gain weight or a certain amount of weight • Americans are continuing to *pack on the pounds*. • He hopes to *pack on 20 pounds* of muscle before the competition.
pack out [*phrasal verb*] ***pack out (a place)*** *Brit* : to cause (a place) to be filled with people • The band still *packs out* stadiums throughout the world. : to fill (a place) • Over 600 people *packed out* the theatre.
pack up [*phrasal verb*] **1** ***pack up or pack up (something) or pack (something) up*** **a** : to gather things together so that you can take them with you • He *packed up* and left town. • You may take a few minutes to *pack up* your things, but then you must leave. • You should *pack up* your tools at the end of the day. **b** *Brit, informal* : to stop or quit : to give up doing (something) • She *packs up* when things become difficult. • She *packed up* her teaching job after five years. **2** *Brit, informal* : to stop working properly • The lift has *packed up*, so you'll have to take the stairs to her flat.
pack your bags : to leave a place • I told him to shape up or he could *pack his bags*. • He said goodbye and *packed his bags* for Denmark.
send (someone or something) packing see SEND
– pack·able /ˈpækəbəl/ *adj* [*more* ~; *most* ~] • *packable* clothing

¹pack·age /ˈpækɪʤ/ *noun, pl* **-ag·es** [*count*]
1 *chiefly US* : a box or large envelope that is sent or delivered usually through the mail or by another delivery service • The mail carrier left the *package* [=*parcel*] on the front steps. — see picture at MAIL
2 *US* **a** : a wrapper or container that covers or holds something • All ingredients are listed right on the *package*. **b** : something that comes in a container • You'll need a 12-ounce *package* [=(*Brit*) *packet*] of chocolate chips for the cookies. • She ate the whole *package* of crackers for lunch.
3 a : a group of related things that are sold together for a single price • The hotel, airfare, and museum fees were all part of our vacation *package*. • a software *package* [=a group of computer programs that are sold together] **b** : a group of related things that go together • My new job offers a great benefits *package*. [=my new job offers great benefits] • The financial aid *packages* we'll be awarding this year are smaller than we had hoped they would be. • (*informal*) If you let her move in with you, living with her cat is all ***part of the package***. [=it is part of the situation that you will have to accept]
good things come in small packages — used to say that people or things do not have to be large to be good

²package *verb* **-ages; -aged; -ag·ing** [+ *obj*]
1 : to put (something) in a package in order to sell it or send it somewhere • *Package* the books carefully. — often used as *(be) packaged* • The china needs to *be packaged* properly.
2 : to show or present (something or someone) in a particular way — often used as *(be) packaged* • If the issue *is* not *packaged* correctly, it will not get voters to come to the polls.
– packaged *adj* • individually *packaged* food • *packaged* goods [=things that are sold in packages]

package deal *noun, pl* ~ **deals** [*count*]
1 : PACKAGE TOUR
2 : a group of people or things which must be accepted together • They presented their proposals to the committee as a *package deal*.

package store *noun, pl* ~ **stores** [*count*] *US* : a store that sells alcoholic beverages : a liquor store

package tour *noun, pl* ~ **tours** [*count*] : a group of services related to travel or vacations that are sold together for one price • They got the bus tour, hotel room, and plane ticket as

P

a *package tour.* — called also *package deal,* (*Brit*) *package holiday*

packaging *noun* [*noncount*]
1 a : material used to enclose or contain something ▪ The frozen spinach can be heated up right in its original *packaging.* ▪ The colorful *packaging* of many candy bars attracts the eyes of children. **b :** the act or process of putting something in a package or container ▪ *packaging* and shipping services
2 : the way something or someone is presented in order to be more attractive or appealing ▪ the *packaging* of a political candidate

pack animal *noun, pl* ~ **-mals** [*count*] **:** an animal (such as a horse or donkey) that is used for carrying packs

packed /ˈpækt/ *adj*
1 : pressed together so there is very little space between the parts or pieces ▪ *packed* snow/dirt/earth ▪ Add one cup of firmly *packed* brown sugar. ▪ ½ cup loosely *packed* fresh parsley — see also VACUUM-PACKED
2 : filled with a large amount of something ▪ Oranges are ***packed full of*** vitamin C. — usually + *with* ▪ The magazine is *packed with* lots of ideas for decorating your home. ▪ a novel *packed with* romance and suspense ▪ The garage is *packed with* junk. ▪ a room *packed* to the brim/ceiling/rafters/roof *with* books — see also ACTION-PACKED, JAM-PACKED
3 a : full of people **:** filled with as many people as possible ▪ a *packed* auditorium ▪ The stadium was *packed* (full) with sports fans. = It was *packed* to capacity/bursting/overflowing. ▪ The theater is always *packed* when he performs there. **b** *of a crowd of people* **:** large enough to fill a space or place ▪ bands playing to *packed* audiences/crowds
4 — used to say that you have finished putting things into bags, boxes, etc. ▪ We're (all) *packed* and ready to go. [=we have packed everything we need and are ready to go]
packed out *Brit, informal* **:** filled with as many people as possible ▪ The theatre is always *packed out* (with fans) when he performs there.

packed lunch *noun, pl* ~ **lunch·es** [*count*] *chiefly Brit* **:** BAG LUNCH

pack·er /ˈpækɚ/ *noun, pl* **-ers** [*count*] **:** a person or company that prepares and packages products and sends them to people or stores ▪ She worked as a *packer* for a candy company. ▪ meat *packers*

pack·et /ˈpækət/ *noun, pl* **-ets**
1 [*count*] **a** *US* **:** a small, thin package ▪ I got two *packets* of broccoli seeds to plant this summer. ▪ He puts two *packets* of sugar in his coffee. ▪ Could you get me another *packet* of ketchup? — called also (*Brit*) *sachet* **b** *Brit* **:** a package in which something is sold and bought ▪ a *packet* [=(*US*) *box*] of crackers ▪ a *packet* [=(*US*) *pack*] of cigarettes
2 [*count*] **a** *US* **:** a group of things that have been gathered together for a particular purpose and usually put into a container (such as a folder or a large envelope) ▪ Your information *packet* includes a map and a schedule of all the events at the conference. ▪ The senator's comments are included in his ***press packet*** [=papers that give reporters official statements from public figures] **b** *chiefly Brit* **:** a small, thin package sent through the mail or delivered to a person ▪ I received the *packet* of legal papers today.
3 [*count*] *computers* **:** an amount of information that is sent as a single unit from one computer to another over a network or the Internet
4 [*singular*] *Brit, informal* **:** a large amount of money ▪ The furniture wasn't expensive but we spent a *packet* on shipping charges.

pack·horse /ˈpækˌhoɚs/ *noun, pl* **-hors·es** [*count*] **:** a horse used for carrying things

pack ice *noun* [*noncount*] **:** a very large sheet of ice floating in the sea that is made from smaller pieces that have frozen together

¹pack·ing /ˈpækɪŋ/ *noun* [*noncount*]
1 : the act or process of putting things into bags or boxes ▪ We finished all our *packing* yesterday.
2 : material that is used to hold or protect things so that they can be moved or sent somewhere ▪ I used some old newspapers for *packing.* ▪ (*Brit*) For mail-order purchases, add £2.50 to the price to cover ***postage and packing***

²packing *adj, always used before a noun*
1 : used to hold or protect things so that they can be moved or sent somewhere ▪ *packing* materials ▪ a *packing* case/box/crate
2 : doing the job of preparing and wrapping products and sending them to people or stores ▪ a *packing* plant/factory/house

pack rat *noun, pl* ~ **rats** [*count*] *US, informal* **:** a person who collects or keeps things that are not needed ▪ I'm a terrible *pack rat.* I never throw anything away.

pact /ˈpækt/ *noun, pl* **pacts** [*count*] **:** a formal agreement between two countries, people, or groups especially to help each other or to stop fighting ▪ We supported a peace/free-trade/nonaggression *pact* between the two countries. ▪ They made a *pact* to go to the gym together three times a week. — see also SUICIDE PACT

pacy /ˈpeɪsi/ *adj* **pac·i·er; -est** *Brit, informal* **:** moving quickly **:** having a fast pace ▪ He's a small but *pacy* player. ▪ The movie is a *pacy* thriller.

¹pad /ˈpæd/ *noun, pl* **pads** [*count*]
1 a : an object that is thin, flat, and usually soft ▪ He sits with a foam *pad* behind him to help support his lower back. ▪ The doctor put a gauze *pad* over the wound. ▪ She lay in bed with a ***heating pad*** [=an electric mat that heats up and is held against the body to reduce pain] ▪ a ***mattress pad*** [=a covering that goes under a sheet on a bed to protect the mattress] ▪ She had trouble finding a suit jacket without ***shoulder pads*** [=small pads used to shape the shoulders of a shirt, dress, or jacket] ▪ You need to replace your car's ***brake pads*** [=the part of the brakes that are pressed on the wheel when you stop or slow down the car] — see also INK PAD **b** *sports* **:** a covering for a specific part of the body that is worn to protect that part from injury — usually plural ▪ The football players wore their helmets and shoulder and hip *pads* to practice today. ▪ She wears elbow and knee *pads* when she goes skating. **c :** SANITARY NAPKIN **d :** a usually rough piece of material used in cleaning ▪ a scouring *pad*
2 : a set of paper sheets for writing or drawing that are glued or fastened at one edge ▪ They keep a *pad* and pencil by the phone. ▪ a ***sketch pad*** [=a notebook or pad of blank paper for drawing] — see also NOTEPAD, SCRATCH PAD
3 : the soft part on the bottom of the foot of a dog, cat, etc.
4 *informal + old-fashioned or humorous* **:** the place where someone lives — usually singular ▪ She lent me the keys to her *pad* while she was away. ▪ He held many wild parties in his ***bachelor pad***
5 : a flat area on the ground where helicopters can take off or land ▪ The town has no airport but there is a landing *pad* near the hospital. — see also LAUNCHPAD
6 : LILY PAD
– see also KEYPAD

²pad *verb* **pads; pad·ded; pad·ding** [+ *obj*]
1 : to cover or fill (something) with soft material especially to protect it or make it more comfortable ▪ He *padded* the inside of the box with cloth and crumpled newspaper. ▪ She used a cushion to *pad* the bench.
2 : to make (something) larger, longer, or more attractive by adding things that are unnecessary, unimportant, or false ▪ She *padded* (out) her speech with quotes from local citizens. ▪ He hoped that by *padding* his résumé his lack of experience would be overlooked.
3 *US* **:** to dishonestly add more charges to (a bill) in order to collect more money than is owed ▪ He *padded* the bill he sent to the company for his consulting work.
– compare ³PAD

³pad *verb, always followed by an adverb or preposition* **pads; pad·ded; pad·ding** [*no obj*] **:** to move with quiet steps ▪ She *padded* around/about (the house) all day in her pajamas. ▪ The dog *padded* into the bedroom. — compare ²PAD

padded *adj* **:** filled or covered with soft material ▪ a *padded* envelope ▪ The boxers are wearing thickly/heavily *padded* gloves. ▪ a *padded* bra ▪ The chairs have *padded* seats.

padded cell *noun, pl* ~ **cells** [*count*] **:** a room in a mental hospital that has soft walls so that patients cannot hurt themselves

padding *noun* [*noncount*]
1 : soft material used to cover a hard surface in order to make it more comfortable ▪ the *padding* on the seat of the chairs ▪ These shoes have extra *padding* in the heel.
2 : unnecessary words used to make a speech or a piece of writing longer ▪ If you remove the *padding* from his speech you can see that he offers no new ideas.

¹pad·dle /ˈpædl/ *noun, pl* **pad·dles** [*count*]
1 : a long, usually wooden pole that has a wide, flat part at the end and is used to move and steer a small boat (such as a canoe) — see picture at BOAT; compare OAR
2 *US* **:** an object with a short handle and a wide, flat part that

is used to hit the ball in various games (such as table tennis) **3 :** any one of various tools or devices that are wide, flat, and thin • Use the mixer's *paddle* attachment to mix the dough. • The potter used a *paddle* to shape the clay.

up the creek without a paddle see CREEK

²pad·dle *verb* **paddles; pad·dled; pad·dling**

1 : to move a boat forward through water with a paddle [*no obj*] We *paddled* across the lake in our canoe this morning. [+ *obj*] We *paddled* our canoe across the lake this morning. • Get in the boat and I'll *paddle* you to shore.

2 [*no obj*] **:** to swim by moving your hands and feet in short quick motions • The dog *paddled* across the lake. — see also DOG-PADDLE

3 [+ *obj*] *US* **:** to beat or hit (someone or something) with a flat piece of wood • In those days many people believed it was okay to *paddle* children. • (*informal*) If you don't get in here, I'm going to *paddle* your behind.

– compare ³PADDLE

³paddle *verb* **paddles; paddled; paddling** [*no obj*] *Brit* **:** to walk or play in shallow water for pleasure • They took off their sandals and *paddled* [=(*US*) *waded*] at the edge of the pond. — compare ²PADDLE

– paddle *noun* [*singular*] • The children ***went for a paddle*** before lunch.

pad·dle·boat /ˈpædl̩ˌbout/ *noun, pl* **-boats** [*count*]

1 *US* **:** a small boat with paddle wheels that you turn by moving pedals with your feet like someone riding a bicycle — called also *pedal boat,* (*Brit*) *pedalo*

2 : a large, old-fashioned boat that moves along the water using a large paddle wheel usually turned by steam power

paddle wheel *noun, pl* **~ wheels** [*count*] **:** a wheel that moves through water as it turns and has a series of paddles around its outer edge

paddling pool *noun, pl* **~ pools** [*count*] *Brit* **:** WADING POOL

pad·dock /ˈpædək/ *noun, pl* **-docks** [*count*]

1 : a small field where animals (such as horses) are kept

2 : an enclosed area at a race track where horses, dogs, etc., are kept before a race

pad·dy /ˈpædi/ *noun, pl* **-dies** [*count*] **:** a wet field where rice is grown • rice *paddies*

paddy wagon *noun, pl* **~ -ons** [*count*] *US, informal* **:** PATROL WAGON

pad·lock /ˈpædˌlɑːk/ *noun, pl* **-locks** [*count*] **:** a strong lock with a curved bar that connects to the main part of the lock and holds together two parts of something (such as a chain or a gate)

– padlock *verb* **-locks; -locked; -lock·ing** [+ *obj*] She *padlocked* the garage door. • The front gate was *padlocked.*

padlock

pa·dre /ˈpɑːdreɪ/ *noun, pl* **-dres** [*count*] *informal*

1 : a Christian priest

2 : a Christian clergyman who works in the military

pad thai *or* **pad Thai** /ˈpɑːdˈtaɪ/ *noun* [*noncount*] *chiefly US* **:** a Thai dish of rice noodles that are stir-fried with other ingredients (such as seafood, chicken, egg, or bean sprouts)

pae·an /ˈpiːjən/ *noun, pl* **-ans** [*count*] *literary* **:** a song of joy, praise, or victory

paediatric, paediatrician, paediatrics *chiefly Brit spellings of* PEDIATRIC, PEDIATRICIAN, PEDIATRICS

paedophile *Brit spelling of* PEDOPHILE

pa·el·la /pɑˈejə/ *noun* [*noncount*] **:** a Spanish dish of rice, meat, seafood, vegetables, and spices

pa·gan *also* **Pagan** /ˈpeɪgən/ *noun, pl* **-gans** [*count*]

1 : a person who worships many gods or goddesses or the earth or nature **:** a person whose religion is paganism

2 *old-fashioned + often offensive* **:** a person who is not religious or whose religion is not Christianity, Judaism, or Islam

– pagan *adj* • *pagan* religions

pa·gan·ism /ˈpeɪgəˌnɪzəm/ *noun* [*noncount*]

1 : the state of being pagan • the *paganism* of early Rome

2 *also* ***Paganism*** **:** a religion that has many gods or goddesses, considers the earth holy, and does not have a central authority • He is a practitioner of *Paganism.*

¹page /ˈpeɪʤ/ *noun, pl* **pag·es** [*count*]

1 a : one side of a sheet of paper especially in a book, magazine, etc. • The book is 237 *pages* long. • The article continues on *page* 12. • a three-*page* article • See the chart on the following/facing/opposite/next *page.* • They ran the story on the front *page* of the newspaper. • a ***blank page*** [=a sheet of paper that does not have anything written on it] • It was thrilling to finally see her poetry ***on the printed page.*** [=in a book, magazine, etc.] • The computer will automatically put a ***page number*** at the bottom of each *page.* — abbr. *p*; see also FRONT-PAGE, TITLE PAGE **b :** the material printed or written on a page • Read the second *page* out loud. • The event described in these *pages* is nothing like what I remember. • the ***sports/financial/business pages*** [=the part of the newspaper that has sports, financial information, business news, etc.] **c :** a sheet of paper in a book, magazine, etc. • He ripped a *page* out of the phone book. — see also WHITE PAGES, YELLOW PAGES

2 : one section of a Web site that is found at a single address • You'll find that information on the "Contact Us" *page.* — see also HOME PAGE, WEB PAGE

3 *literary* **:** an important event or period in history • His accomplishments hold a special place in the ***pages of history.***

borrow/take a page from someone *or* ***borrow/take a page from someone's book*** *US* **:** to do the same thing that someone else has done • You may want to *borrow/take a page from his book* and study harder for your finals.

jump/leap off the page *of writing, a picture, etc.* **:** to be very noticeable, interesting, exciting, etc. • The characters are so real that they *leap off the page.*

on the same page *chiefly US, informal* **:** agreeing about something (such as how things should be done) • Try to get employees and clients *on the same page.* • Make sure everyone is *on the same page* before you give your final answer.

– compare ⁴PAGE

²page *verb* **pages; paged; pag·ing**

page through [*phrasal verb*] ***page through (something)*** **:** to turn the pages of (a book, magazine, etc.) especially in a quick, steady manner • He *paged through* the magazine looking for the article.

– compare ³PAGE

³page *verb* **pages; paged; paging** [+ *obj*]

1 : to call the name of (someone) in a public place usually over a speaker in order to find that person, deliver a message, etc. • You can *page* the manager if you need help.

2 : to send a message to (someone) by using a special device (called a pager or beeper) • *Page* the doctor in case of an emergency. • I'm going to switch to a new *paging* service.

– compare ²PAGE

⁴page *noun, pl* **pages** [*count*]

1 *US* **:** a student who works as an assistant for a member of Congress

2 a : a young man or boy in the Middle Ages who trained to be a knight by serving a knight **b :** a young man or boy who worked as a servant for an important person in the Middle Ages

3 *Brit* **:** BELLHOP

– compare ¹PAGE

pag·eant /ˈpæʤənt/ *noun, pl* **-eants** [*count*]

1 *US* **:** BEAUTY CONTEST • She entered a (beauty) *pageant.* • They disagreed with the *pageant* judges.

2 : a play or performance made of scenes from a historical event or a legend • Their church puts on an annual Christmas *pageant.* — sometimes used figuratively • The museum celebrates the rich *pageant* of the town's history. [=celebrates all the interesting things that have happened in the town's history]

pag·eant·ry /ˈpæʤəntri/ *noun* [*noncount*] **:** the use of special clothing, traditions, and ceremonies as part of a special event or celebration • I like the tradition and *pageantry* that come with graduations.

page·boy /ˈpeɪʤˌbɔɪ/ *noun, pl* **-boys** [*count*]

1 : a woman's haircut in which straight shoulder-length hair is curled under at the ends

2 ***page boy*** *Brit* **:** a boy who follows or stands with the bride in a wedding

3 *Brit* **:** BELLHOP

pag·er /ˈpeɪʤɚ/ *noun, pl* **-ers** [*count*] **:** a small electronic device that beeps or vibrates and shows a telephone number for the person carrying the device to call — called also (*chiefly US*) *beeper,* (*Brit*) *bleeper*

page–turn·er /ˈpeɪʤˌtɚnɚ/ *noun, pl* **-ers** [*count*] **:** a book, story, etc., that is difficult to stop reading because it is so interesting • His last novel was a real *page-turner.*

P

pag·i·na·tion /ˌpæʤəˈneɪʃən/ *noun* [*noncount*] *technical*
1 : the act or process of putting numbers on the pages of a book, document, etc. • computerized *pagination*
2 : the page numbers on a book, document, etc. • Is the *pagination* correct?
– pag·i·nate /ˈpæʤəˌneɪt/ *verb* **-nates; -nat·ed; -nat·ing** [+ *obj*] • The program automatically *paginated* the document.

pa·go·da /pəˈgoʊdə/ *noun, pl* **-das** [*count*] **:** a type of tall building in eastern Asia that has many floors with roofs that stick out on each floor and curve up

pagoda

[1]paid /ˈpeɪd/ *past tense and past participle of* [1]PAY

[2]paid *adj*
1 a : receiving money for work • She is one of the few *paid* public officials in a town run mostly by volunteers. **b** — used to indicate if someone receives low or high pay for work • He got a job as a highly *paid* consultant. • She is very well *paid*. • low-*paid* workers
2 *chiefly US* **:** having been paid for • a *paid* political announcement • a *paid* advertisement
3 : including payment of normal wages, salary, etc. • I get two weeks of *paid* vacation [=time off during which you receive your normal pay] at my new job. • She was given a *paid* day off to deal with some personal matters.
put paid to *chiefly Brit, informal* **:** to end or stop (something) **:** to put an end to (something) • The pressure of work *put paid to* his holiday plans!

pail /ˈpeɪl/ *noun, pl* **pails** [*count*] *chiefly US*
1 : a round container that is open at the top and usually has a handle • a garbage *pail* • A plastic beach *pail* was lying on the sand. • Fill up that *pail* [=*bucket*] with water.
2 : the amount held by a pail • She poured a *pail* of water on the campfire.

pail·ful /ˈpeɪlˌfʊl/ *noun, pl* **-fuls** [*count*] *chiefly US* **:** the amount held by a pail • a *pailful* of water

[1]pain /ˈpeɪn/ *noun, pl* **pains**
1 : the physical feeling caused by disease, injury, or something that hurts the body [*noncount*] The medication may upset your stomach but if you experience acute abdominal *pain* call your doctor. • I've had chronic back *pain* since the accident. • It was obvious that she was ***in pain***. [=feeling pain] • Each patient has a different ***pain threshold***. [=ability to tolerate pain] • The medicine provides 12 hours of ***pain relief***. • For a week after surgery she took prescription ***pain medication/relievers***. [=*painkillers*] [*count*] I feel a dull/sharp *pain* if I touch the bruise. — see also *aches and pains* at [2]ACHE
2 : mental or emotional suffering **:** sadness caused by some emotional or mental problem [*noncount*] They didn't want to cause him *pain*. [=they didn't want to upset or hurt him] • the *pain* of a difficult childhood [*count*] It is a story about the joys and *pains* of life. — see also GROWING PAINS
3 [*singular*] *informal* **:** someone or something that causes trouble or makes you feel annoyed or angry • Rush hour traffic is such a *pain*. • This orange is a *pain* to peel. • Our neighbor can be such a *pain*. [=*nuisance*] — often used in phrases like ***pain in the neck*** or (*impolite*) ***pain in the ass*** • My little sister can be a (real/royal) *pain in the neck*.
be at pains **:** to try hard *to do* something • They *were at pains to distance* themselves from the scandal.
feel no pain see [1]FEEL
go to great pains *or* ***take (great) pains*** **:** to be careful in doing something **:** to try hard to do something — followed by *to* + *verb* • We *went to great pains* not *to offend* anyone. • He *took great pains to explain* the situation to us.
no gain without pain see [2]GAIN
no pain, no gain see [2]GAIN
on/under pain of *formal* **:** at the risk of being given (a particular form of punishment) • She was ordered to remain silent *under pain of* imprisonment. • He cannot return to the country ***on pain of death***. [=he will be killed if he returns to the country]

[2]pain *verb* **pains; pained; pain·ing** [+ *obj*] *formal* **:** to cause (someone) to feel emotional pain **:** to make (someone) upset, sad, worried, etc. • He was deeply *pained* [=*hurt*] by your words. • As much as it *pains* me to admit it, she was right.

pained /ˈpeɪnd/ *adj* **:** appearing upset, sad, worried, etc. • She wore/had a *pained* expression on her face. • He truly looked *pained* when he heard the news.

pain·ful /ˈpeɪnfəl/ *adj* [*more* ~; *most* ~]
1 : causing pain to your body • I got a *painful* sunburn. • a *painful* skin condition • His ankle is swollen and ***painful to the touch***. [=his ankle hurts if he touches it]
2 : causing emotional pain • We can't ignore our country's *painful* history of slavery. • His questions brought up a lot of *painful* memories. • It was *painful* to watch.

pain·ful·ly /ˈpeɪnfəli/ *adv* [*more* ~; *most* ~]
1 : very or extremely — used especially to describe something that is bad, unpleasant, or upsetting • They made it *painfully* obvious/clear that we were not welcome. [=they made it very clear in a way that was rude or upsetting that we were not welcome] • After the injury she was *painfully* aware that her career in tennis would be over. • New developments have been *painfully* slow. • She is *painfully* shy.
2 : in a way that causes pain • After her tooth was pulled, her jaw was *painfully* swollen.
3 : in a way that requires a lot of effort • He labored *painfully* over his work.

pain·kill·er /ˈpeɪnˌkɪlɚ/ *noun, pl* **-ers** [*count*] **:** a drug that decreases or removes pain that you feel in your body • I took some over-the-counter *painkillers* for my headache.
– pain·kill·ing /ˈpeɪnˌkɪlɪŋ/ *adj, always used before a noun* • *painkilling* drugs

pain·less /ˈpeɪnləs/ *adj* [*more* ~; *most* ~] **:** not causing or marked by pain: such as **a :** not causing pain to the body • a *painless* medical procedure **b :** not upsetting, disturbing, or difficult • Buying my new car was a surprisingly *painless* experience. • We had a relatively *painless* breakup.
– pain·less·ly *adv* • We'll try to get through this as quickly and *painlessly* as possible.

pains·tak·ing /ˈpeɪnˌsteɪkɪŋ/ *adj* [*more* ~; *most* ~] **:** showing or done with great care and effort • The book describes the election process in *painstaking* detail. • *painstaking* work/research
– pains·tak·ing·ly *adv* • The old house was *painstakingly* restored to its original splendor. • She *painstakingly* researched all of her articles.

[1]paint /ˈpeɪnt/ *noun, pl* **paints**
1 : a liquid that dries to form a thin colored layer when it is spread on a surface [*noncount*] Apply *paint* to the canvas in a series of short strokes. • I need more blue *paint*. • The old walls are coated with several layers of *paint*. • a can of latex/acrylic *paint* • The house needs a fresh/second ***coat of paint***. • ***face paint*** [=colorful makeup for drawing pictures on children's faces] [*count*] The store sells many different *paints*. • a box of *paints* [=different types of paint that are used by an artist to paint pictures and that are usually sold in a dry form or in tubes] • ***finger paints*** [=paints that children spread onto paper with their hands] — see also GREASEPAINT, OIL PAINT, SPRAY PAINT
2 [*singular*] **:** a layer of dried paint on a surface • Did you chip the *paint*? • The car's *paint* is cracking. — called also (*Brit*) *paintwork*

[2]paint *verb* **paints; paint·ed; paint·ing**
1 [+ *obj*] **:** to cover (something) with paint **:** to put paint on (something) • I need to *paint* the bookcase. • We're going to *paint* the room yellow. • The classroom wall was *painted* with clouds and rainbows.
2 : to make (a picture or design) by using paints [+ *obj*] He *painted* that portrait of his wife. • She *painted* the landscape on a square canvas. • The store carries ***hand-painted*** tiles. [=tiles that have pictures or designs on them that were painted by a person and not by a machine] [*no obj*] She *paints* well. • I like to draw and my sister likes to *paint*. • The beauty of the world inspires me to *paint*. • He *paints* mostly in oils. — compare DRAW
3 [+ *obj*] **:** to describe (someone or something) in a particular way • The study *paints* a bleak/grim picture of the effects of pollution on animal life. • Opponents *paint* a picture of the president as corrupt and irresponsible. = Opponents *paint* the president as corrupt and irresponsible.
4 [+ *obj*] **:** to put makeup on (a part of the body) • She *painted* her nails with pink nail polish. • She put on eye shadow and *painted* her lips with red lipstick.
paint over [*phrasal verb*] ***paint over (something)*** **:** to cover (something) with a layer of paint • They *painted over* the graffiti.
paint the town (red) *informal* **:** to go out drinking, dancing, etc., to have a good time

paint·ball /ˈpeɪntˌbɑːl/ *noun* [*noncount*] **:** a game in which

P

two teams use special guns to shoot balls filled with paint at each other

paint·brush /ˈpeɪntˌbrʌʃ/ *noun, pl* **-brush·es** [*count*] : a brush used for putting paint on a surface

paint·er /ˈpeɪntɚ/ *noun, pl* **-ers** [*count*]
1 : a person whose job it is to paint walls, houses, etc. • The *painters* were unable to work in the rain.
2 : an artist who paints pictures • He became famous as an abstract/landscape/Impressionist *painter*. • She was a *painter* of still lifes.

paint·er·ly /ˈpeɪntɚli/ *adj*
1 : typical of painters • He has a *painterly* eye. • a *painterly* sensibility
2 [*more* ~; *most* ~] **:** suggesting a painting : made in a way that reminds you of a painting • a *painterly* picture of the sea • *painterly* brushstrokes

paint·ing /ˈpeɪntɪŋ/ *noun, pl* **-ings**
1 [*count*] **:** a picture that is painted : a picture made by putting paint on a canvas, board, etc. • They hung the *painting* in the living room. • The woman in that *painting* is my grandmother. • We went to see ancient ***cave paintings*** [=pictures painted on the wall of a cave] in Spain. — see also OIL PAINTING 2
2 [*noncount*] **:** the art or act of making pictures using paint • I like *painting* more than sculpture. • He is studying abstract/Chinese/watercolor *painting*. • She wants to devote all her time to *painting*. — see also OIL PAINTING 1
3 [*noncount*] **:** the activity of painting houses, walls, etc. • The room is ready for *painting*.

paint thinner *noun, pl* ~ **-ners** [*count, noncount*] : a liquid that is mixed with paint to make it easier to spread

paint·work /ˈpeɪntˌwɚk/ *noun* [*noncount*] *Brit* : [1]PAINT 2

[1]**pair** /ˈpeɚ/ *noun, pl* **pairs** *or* **pair** [*count*]
1 : two things that are the same and are meant to be used together • a *pair* of gloves • a *pair* of shoes/socks • He blushed when he saw all three *pairs* of eyes watching him. • She won with a *pair* of aces. • I can't do everything at once—I've only got ***one pair of hands***. [=I am only one person] • It will take ***two pairs of hands*** [=two people] to move this rock.
2 : a thing that has two parts which are joined • a *pair* of scissors • a *pair* of pants/underwear • I got my first *pair* of glasses when I was eight.
3 : two people who are related in some way or who do something together • His two closest friends lived in the city and the *pair* of them visited him often. • The dance is usually performed by a male and female *pair*. • Those two kids make quite a *pair*.
4 : two animals that mate together • To avoid competition, breeding/mating *pairs* stay away from other male chimpanzees. • A *pair* of parrots can raise one chick each year.
in pairs : in a group of two people or things • The teacher let the students work *in pairs* on the assignment. • They walked down the aisle *in pairs*.

[2]**pair** *verb* **pairs; paired; pair·ing** [+ *obj*] : to put (two people or things) together • The teacher *paired* students with partners for the assignment. — often used as *(be) paired* • We met when we *were paired* to work together on the project. • The suit *is paired* with black shoes for a sophisticated look. • The fish *was paired* with a white wine.
pair off [*phrasal verb*] **1 :** to join together in a romantic relationship • He hated being single while his friends were *pairing off* and having kids. **2** ***pair off*** *or* ***pair (someone or something) off*** *or* ***pair off (someone or something)*** : to join with someone or something else to form a group of two • People *paired off* for the next dance. • She *paired* the students *off*. = She *paired off* the students.
pair up [*phrasal verb*] ***pair up*** *or* ***pair (someone or something) up*** *or* ***pair up (someone or something)*** : to join together or to cause (two people or things) to join together for a purpose, job, etc. • The two organizations *paired up* to educate the public about the threat of global warming. • They *paired* me *up* with a new partner for the last game. • The program *pairs up* volunteers with children who need help learning to read.

pairing *noun, pl* **-ings** [*count*]
1 : the action of putting two things or people into a group • The play was a successful *pairing* of strong acting and an interesting script. • People were surprised by the *pairing* of candidates for president and vice president.
2 : two things or people that work together with a single purpose • The menu suggested many food and wine *pairings*.

pais·ley /ˈpeɪzli/ *adj* : covered in a pattern made up of colorful curved shapes • a *paisley* tie • The wallpaper is a *paisley* print. — see color picture on page C12
— **paisley** *noun, pl* **-leys** [*count, noncount*] • The fabric comes in *paisley*.

pa·ja·mas (*US*) *or Brit* **py·ja·mas** /pəˈʤɑːməz/ *noun* [*plural*]
1 : clothing that people wear in bed or while relaxing at home • silk *pajamas* • Put on your *pajamas* [=*pj's*] and get ready for bed. — see color picture on page C12
2 : loose pants that are worn in some parts of Asia and the Middle East
the cat's pajamas see CAT
— **pa·ja·ma** (*US*) *or Brit* **py·ja·ma** /pəˈʤɑːmə/ *adj, always used before a noun* • The boys slept in only their *pajama* bottoms. • She is having a ***pajama party*** [=a party for children who spend the night at the house of a friend] to celebrate her 10th birthday.

pak choi *Brit spelling of* BOK CHOY

Paki /ˈpæki/ *noun, pl* **Pakis** [*count*] *Brit, informal + offensive* : a person from Pakistan ✧ The word *Paki* is very offensive and should be avoided.

[1]**pal** /ˈpæl/ *noun, pl* **pals** *informal*
1 [*count*] **:** a close friend • We've been *pals* since we were kids. • He and a *pal* [=*buddy*] started the business 15 years ago. • Come on—be a *pal* and lend me the money. • a ***gal pal*** [=a girl/woman who is a friend] — see also PEN PAL
2 — used to address a man in an angry or annoyed way • Listen, *pal*, I've had just about enough of your advice. • Wait a minute, *pal*. You're trying to trick me.

[2]**pal** *verb* **pals; palled; pal·ling**
pal around with [*phrasal verb*] *informal* ***pal around with (someone)*** *chiefly US* : to spend time with (someone) as a friend • She's been *palling around with* a girl she met at school.
pal up [*phrasal verb*] *chiefly Brit, informal* : to become friends with someone • They *palled up* when they were neighbors long ago. • He *pals up* with anyone who can help his career.

[1]**pal·ace** /ˈpæləs/ *noun, pl* **-ac·es** [*count*]
1 : the official home of a king, queen, president, etc. • the royal/imperial/presidential *palace* • Buckingham *Palace*
2 : a very large and impressive house : MANSION
3 *old-fashioned* **:** a large and fancy public building • The town's old movie *palace* has been torn down. — often used in the names of buildings • the Crystal *Palace* • the *Palace* Hotel
4 ***the Palace*** *chiefly Brit* : the people who live in a palace; *especially* : the British royal family • The prime minister left to inform *the Palace* in person.

[2]**palace** *adj, always used before a noun*
1 : of or relating to a palace • a *palace* guard/official
2 : of, relating to, or involving people in the government • *palace* politics • a *palace* revolution/coup

palaeolithic, palaeontology *Brit spellings of* PALEOLITHIC, PALEONTOLOGY

pal·at·able /ˈpælətəbəl/ *adj* [*more* ~; *most* ~] *somewhat formal*
1 : having a pleasant or agreeable taste • *palatable* food • a less than *palatable* beer
2 : pleasant or acceptable to someone — usually + *to* • The play has been rewritten in an attempt to make it more *palatable to* modern audiences. • Traveling by train is a *palatable* alternative *to* driving.
— **pal·at·abil·i·ty** /ˌpælətəˈbɪləti/ *noun* [*noncount*]

pal·a·tal /ˈpælətl/ *adj, linguistics, of a speech sound* : made by placing the tongue so that it is near or touching the top surface (called the palate) of your mouth • The first sound in the English word "jar" is a *palatal* sound.
— **palatal** *noun, pl* **-tals** [*count*] • English/German *palatals*

pal·ate /ˈpælət/ *noun, pl* **-ates** [*count*]
1 : the top part of the inside of your mouth : the roof of your mouth — see also CLEFT PALATE
2 : the sense of taste • The restaurant serves Korean food adapted for the American *palate*. • She's been working hard on a menu that will please the *palates* of all her guests. • Sorbet is sometimes served between courses to ***cleanse the palate***. [=to clean and refresh your mouth between different parts of a meal]

pa·la·tial /pəˈleɪʃəl/ *adj* [*more* ~; *most* ~] : very large and impressive : like a palace • a *palatial* home

pa·la·ver /pəˈlævɚ, *Brit* pəˈlɑːvə/ *noun, informal*
1 [*noncount*] *chiefly US* : talk that is not important or mean-

P

ingful : NONSENSE • Enough of this *palaver*. We have a lot to discuss.

2 [*singular*] *chiefly Brit* : excitement and activity caused by something that is not important • What a *palaver* [=*fuss*] over nothing!

[1]**pale** /ˈpeɪl/ *adj* **pal·er; pal·est** [*also more* ~; *most* ~]

1 : light in color • the *pale* wood of the table • The walls were painted a *pale* blue. — opposite DEEP

2 : having a skin color that is closer to white than is usual or normal • She has a *pale* complexion. • His *pale* [=*fair*] skin burns easily. • Her illness had left her *pale* and weak. • She grew/became *pale* with fright. • Are you feeling well? You look *pale*.

3 *of light* : not bright or intense : DIM • the *pale* light of dawn

4 : not as good as something else • He was once a great athlete, but now he's just a *pale* version of his younger self. • The remake of the movie was a ***pale imitation*** of the original.

– **pale·ness** /ˈpeɪlnəs/ *noun* [*noncount*]

[2]**pale** *verb* **pales; paled; pal·ing** [*no obj*]

1 : to lose color : to become pale • His face *paled* (in fear) when he saw her walk through the door. • The bright blue walls had *paled* over time.

2 : to appear less important, good, serious, etc., when compared with something else • His accomplishments *pale* beside those of his father. • Once you've tasted the local apples, all others ***pale by comparison***. [=all others seem less good] • The afternoon meal ***paled in comparison to/with*** [=was not nearly as good as] the feast they had later. • Last year's losses ***pale by comparison with*** this year's. • (*chiefly Brit*) Your financial debt ***pales into insignificance*** [=seems much smaller] when you compare it with mine.

[3]**pale** *noun*

beyond the pale : offensive or unacceptable • conduct that was *beyond the pale*

pale ale *noun, pl* ~ **ales** [*count, noncount*] : a type of ale that has a pale color and a somewhat bitter taste

Pa·leo·lith·ic (*chiefly US*) *or Brit* **Pal·aeo·lith·ic** /ˌpeɪlijəˈlɪθɪk, *Brit* ˌpæliəˈlɪθɪk/ *adj* : of or relating to the time during the early Stone Age when people made rough tools and weapons out of stone • *Paleolithic* artifacts/tools/hunters • the *Paleolithic* age/period — compare NEOLITHIC

pa·le·on·tol·o·gy (*chiefly US*) *or Brit* **pal·ae·on·tol·o·gy** /ˌpeɪliˌɑːnˈtɑːləʤi, *Brit* ˌpælianˈtɒləʤi/ *noun* [*noncount*] : the science that deals with the fossils of animals and plants that lived very long ago especially in the time of dinosaurs

– **pa·le·on·tol·o·gist** (*chiefly US*) *or Brit* **pal·ae·on·tol·o·gist** /ˌpeɪliˌɑːnˈtɑːləʤɪst, *Brit* ˌpæliˌɒnˈtɒləʤɪst/ *noun, pl* **-gists** [*count*]

pal·ette /ˈpælət/ *noun, pl* **-ettes** [*count*]

1 : a thin board that has a hole for the thumb at one end and that is used by a painter to mix colors while painting

2 : the range of colors used by someone — usually singular • The designer's *palette* consists mainly of earth tones. • The *palette* for this season's fashions is full of pastels.

palette knife *noun, pl* ~ **knives** [*count*]

1 : a knife that has a blade which bends easily and that is used by painters to mix colors and apply paint

2 *Brit* : SPATULA 2

pal·i·mo·ny /ˈpæləˌmouni/ *noun* [*noncount*] *chiefly US* : money that a court orders one person to pay to his or her former partner after they have stopped living together

pa·limp·sest /ˈpæləmpˌsɛst/ *noun, pl* **-sests** [*count*]

1 *technical* : a very old document on which the original writing has been erased and replaced with new writing

2 *formal* : something that has changed over time and shows evidence of that change • The ancient city is an architectural *palimpsest*. • a *palimpsest* of memories

pal·in·drome /ˈpælənˌdroum/ *noun, pl* **-dromes** [*count*] : a word, phrase, or number that reads the same backward or forward • The word "dad" and the number "1881" are *palindromes*.

paling *noun, pl* **-ings** [*count*] *chiefly Brit* : a piece of wood that is one of the upright pieces of a fence

pal·i·sade /ˌpæləˈseɪd/ *noun, pl* **-sades**

1 [*count*] : a high fence made of pointed stakes that was used in the past to protect a building or area

2 ***palisades*** [*plural*] *US* : a line of steep cliffs especially along a river or ocean

[1]**pall** /ˈpɑːl/ *noun, pl* **palls** [*count*] *formal*

1 : something (such as a cloud of smoke) that covers a place and makes it dark — usually singular • A *pall* of smoke hung over the village after the fire. — often used figuratively • a *pall* of grief • The sad news cast a *pall* on/over the school.

2 : a heavy cloth that is used for covering a coffin, hearse, or tomb

[2]**pall** *verb* **palls; palled; pall·ing** [*no obj*] *formal*

1 : to become dull : to no longer be enjoyable or interesting • He found that his retirement hobbies *palled* after a couple of years.

2 : to lessen or fade • His interest in politics has *palled* over the years. • The excitement of the party quickly began to *pall*. [=*dwindle*]

pall·bear·er /ˈpɑːlˌberə/ *noun, pl* **-ers** [*count*] : a person who helps to carry the coffin at a funeral

pal·let /ˈpælət/ *noun, pl* **-lets** [*count*]

1 : a wooden or metal platform that is used to support heavy things while they are being stored or moved • The computers are packed in boxes and then stacked on *pallets* until they're ready to be shipped.

pallet

2 **a** : a cloth bag that is filled with straw and used as a bed **b** : a small, hard bed

pal·li·ate /ˈpæliˌeɪt/ *verb* **-ates; -at·ed; -at·ing** [+ *obj*] *formal* : to make the effects of (something, such as an illness) less painful, harmful, or harsh • treatments that can *palliate* the painful symptoms of the disease

– **pal·li·a·tion** /ˌpæliˈeɪʃən/ *noun* [*noncount*] • *palliation* of pain

pal·li·a·tive /ˈpæliˌeɪtɪv, *Brit* ˈpæliətɪv/ *noun, pl* **-tives** [*count*]

1 *medical* : something that reduces the effects or symptoms of a medical condition without curing it • The disease has no cure, but a number of *palliatives* exist. • Travel is like a *palliative* against depression for him.

2 *formal* : something that is intended to make a bad situation seem better but that does not really improve the situation • symbolic *palliatives* for inner-city troubles

– **palliative** *adj* • *palliative* care/treatment

pal·lid /ˈpæləd/ *adj* [*more* ~; *most* ~] *formal*

1 : very pale in a way that suggests poor health • the patient's *pallid* face

2 : dull and uninteresting • a *pallid* performance • The movie is a *pallid* version of the classic novel.

pal·lor /ˈpælə/ *noun* [*singular*] *formal* : paleness especially of the face that is caused by illness • The boy's sickly *pallor* concerned his mother even though he had no fever.

pal·ly /ˈpæli/ *adj, not used before a noun* [*more* ~; *most* ~] *chiefly Brit, informal* : very friendly • He got very *pally* [=*chummy*] with the manager. • We've been *pally* for years.

[1]**palm** /ˈpɑːm/ *noun, pl* **palms** [*count*] : the inside part of the hand between the wrist and the fingers • He placed a coin in the child's outstretched *palm*. • The kitten was small enough to fit in the *palm* of my hand. • He claimed that he could ***read my palm***. [=look at the lines on the palm of my hand and tell me what was going to happen to me in the future] — see picture at HAND

grease the palm of see [2]GREASE

have someone in the palm of your hand : to have control or influence over someone : to be able to control someone easily • She *has* her boss *in the palm of her hand*.

– compare [2]PALM

[2]**palm** *noun, pl* **palms** [*count*]

1 **a** : a kind of tree that grows in tropical regions and has a straight, tall trunk and many large leaves at the top of the trunk — called also *palm tree* **b** : a bush or large plant that is related to the palm and can be grown indoors — see color picture on page C6

2 : the leaf of a palm especially when it is carried as a symbol of victory or in celebration of something • People were waving *palms* in the streets.

– compare [1]PALM

[3]**palm** *verb* **palms; palmed; palm·ing** [+ *obj*]

1 : to hide (something) in the palm of your hand • The store's owner had seen one of the girls *palm* a lipstick before heading for the door. • To do the card trick, you have to learn to *palm* one of the cards.

2 **a** *basketball* : to hold (a basketball) in an illegal way for a moment while you are dribbling • He was called for *palming* the ball. **b** *soccer* : to knock (the ball) away from the goal with your hands • The kick was *palmed* away by the goalkeeper.

palm off [*phrasal verb*] *informal* **1** ***palm (something) off*** or ***palm off (something)*** **a** : to sell (something) for more than it is worth by being dishonest about it • The antique dealer had tried to *palm* the painting *off* as an original. • He'll *palm* [=*pawn*] the car *off* on/onto some unsuspecting fool if he can. **b** : to get someone to accept or do (something) • He tried to *palm off* science fiction as truth. • She's good at *palming off* her household chores on her little sister. **2** ***palm yourself off as (someone)*** : to pretend to be (someone you are not) • He *palmed* [=*passed*] *himself off as* a lawyer.

palm·ist·ry /ˈpɑːməstri/ *noun* [*noncount*] : the art or activity of looking at the lines on the palms of people's hands and telling them what will happen to them in the future
– **palm·ist** /ˈpɑːmɪst/ *noun, pl* **-ists** [*count*]

palm oil *noun* [*noncount*] : oil that is obtained from the fruit of some palm trees and used in cooking and in making soap and other products

Palm Sunday *noun* [*noncount*] : the Christian holiday celebrated on the Sunday before Easter

palm·top /ˈpɑːmˌtɑːp/ *noun, pl* **-tops** [*count*] : a computer that is small enough to be held in the palm of your hand

palm tree *noun, pl* **~ trees** [*count*] : [2]PALM 1a

pal·o·mi·no /ˌpæləˈmiːnoʊ/ *noun, pl* **-nos** [*count*] : a horse that is light golden or cream in color and that has a cream or white mane and tail

pal·pa·ble /ˈpælpəbəl/ *adj* [*more ~; most ~*] *formal* : obvious and noticeable • I felt a *palpable* sense of relief. • The attraction between them was *palpable*. • There was a *palpable* excitement in the air as the town prepared for the festival.
– **pal·pa·bly** /ˈpælpəbli/ *adv* • the *palpably* real danger

pal·pate /ˈpælˌpeɪt/ *verb* **-pates; -pat·ed; -pat·ing** [+ *obj*] *medical* : to examine (part of the body) by touching it • The doctor *palpated* his ribs to see if there was any tenderness.
– **pal·pa·tion** /pælˈpeɪʃən/ *noun* [*noncount*]

pal·pi·tate /ˈpælpəˌteɪt/ *verb* [*no obj*] *of the heart* : to beat quickly and strongly and often in a way that is not regular because of excitement, nervousness, etc. • My heart began to *palpitate* when I was announced as the winner.
– **pal·pi·ta·tion** /ˌpælpəˈteɪʃən/ *noun, pl* **-tions** [*count*] *medical* — usually plural • Symptoms include dizziness and (heart) *palpitations*. • I was under so much stress that I developed *palpitations*. [=my heart began to palpitate]

[1]**pal·sy** /ˈpɑːlzi/ *noun* [*noncount*] *medical* : a medical condition that causes your body or part of your body to shake uncontrollably • facial *palsy* — see also CEREBRAL PALSY
– **pal·sied** /ˈpɑːlzid/ *adj*

[2]**palsy** /ˈpælzi/ *adj* **palsi·er; -est** *informal* : PALSY-WALSY

palsy–walsy /ˌpælziˈwælzi/ *adj* [*more ~; most ~*] *informal* : friendly in a way that is not proper or sincere • I don't think the boss should be getting *palsy-walsy* with her employees.

pal·try /ˈpɑːltri/ *adj* **pal·tri·er; -est** [*also more ~; most ~*] *formal*
1 : very small or too small in amount • They're offering a *paltry* [=*meager*] salary for the position. • Sales have increased by a *paltry* [=*measly*] two percent.
2 : having little meaning, importance, or worth • a *paltry* excuse • *paltry* work

pam·pas /ˈpæmpəz/ *noun*
the pampas : large, flat, grassy areas of land in South America • cattle roaming *the pampas*

pamp·er /ˈpæmpɚ/ *verb* **-pers; -pered; -per·ing** [+ *obj*] : to treat (someone or something) very well : to give (someone or something) a lot of attention and care • They really *pamper* their guests at that hotel. • She *pampered* herself with a day at the spa. • He was *pampered* all his life and doesn't know how to function in the real world.
– **pampered** *adj* [*more ~; most ~*] • a *pampered* pet • the *pampered* life of the wealthy

pam·phlet /ˈpæmflət/ *noun, pl* **-phlets** [*count*] : a small, thin book with no cover or only a paper cover that has information about a particular subject

pam·phle·teer /ˌpæmfləˈtiɚ/ *noun, pl* **-teers** [*count*] : a person who writes pamphlets usually to support a cause or to criticize someone or something

[1]**pan** /ˈpæn/ *noun, pl* **pans** [*count*]
1 a : a usually shallow and open metal container that has a handle and that is used for cooking or baking • The rice is in a *pan* on the stove. • Spread the batter evenly in the *pan* [=(*Brit*) *tin*] and bake for 40 minutes. • a cake/loaf/roasting *pan* — see also FRYING PAN, SAUCEPAN **b** : a container that is like a cooking pan that is used for holding something — see also BEDPAN, DUSTPAN
2 *Brit* : [1]BOWL 2a • a toilet *pan*
3 : STEEL DRUM
down the pan *Brit, informal* **1** — used to describe something that is being wasted or lost • It's just money *down the pan*. [=(*US*) *down the drain*] • All my hard work ***went down the pan***. **2** — used to describe something that is getting much worse • The business is ***going down the pan***. [=(*US*) *going down the drain*]
flash in the pan see [2]FLASH

[2]**pan** *verb* **pans; panned; pan·ning** : to move (a movie, video, or television camera) across a scene or along with someone or something that is moving [+ *obj*] He *panned* the camera over the seats of the stadium. • The camera *panned* the seats of the stadium. [*no obj*] The director/camera *panned* past the pile of shoes to the bare feet of the playing children. — compare [3]PAN

[3]**pan** *verb* **pans; panned; pan·ning**
1 [+ *obj*] *informal* : to criticize (a book, movie, play, etc.) severely • The newspaper's movie critic *panned* the film. — often used as *(be) panned* • The book *was panned* by the critics.
2 : to wash pieces of earth or stones with water in a special kind of pan in order to find pieces of gold or other metals [*no obj*] — usually + *for* • The gold mine is no longer in use, but visitors to the mine can still *pan for* gold. [+ *obj*] We heard reports of people *panning* gold upriver.
pan out [*phrasal verb*] **1** : to develop or happen • We'll have to see how things *pan out*. [=*turn out*] **2** : to have the end or result that you want : to succeed or turn out well • If things don't *pan out* [=*work out*] here, I'll move back to the city. • Her plans never *panned out*. • He applied for a number of jobs and is hoping that one of them will *pan out*. [=hoping that he will get one of the jobs]
— compare [2]PAN

pan- *prefix*
1 : all or completely • *pan*orama
2 : involving all of a specified group • *Pan*-American • *pan*demic

pan·a·cea /ˌpænəˈsiːjə/ *noun, pl* **-ce·as** [*count*] *somewhat formal* : something that will make everything about a situation better • The law will improve the lives of local farmers, but it is no *panacea*. • An increase in tuition won't be a *panacea* [=*cure-all*] for the college's financial problems.

pa·nache /pəˈnæʃ/ *noun* [*noncount*] : lots of energy and style • She played the role of hostess with great *panache*.

pan·a·ma hat *or* **Pan·a·ma hat** /ˈpænəˌmɑː-/ *noun, pl* **~ hats** [*count*] : a light hat with a broad brim that is made from straw — called also *panama*; see picture at HAT

Pan–Amer·i·can /ˌpænəˈmerɪkən/ *adj* : of, relating to, or involving the countries of North and South America • the *Pan-American* highway

pan·cake /ˈpænˌkeɪk/ *noun, pl* **-cakes** [*count*]
1 : a thin, flat, round cake that is made by cooking batter on both sides in a frying pan or on a hot surface (called a griddle) • We had blueberry *pancakes* and sausage for breakfast. — see also POTATO PANCAKE
2 : thick makeup worn especially by actors • She wore sequins, false eyelashes, and *pancake* onstage. — called also *pancake makeup*
(as) flat as a pancake see [1]FLAT

Pancake Day *noun* [*noncount*] *Brit* : SHROVE TUESDAY

pan·cet·ta /pænˈtʃetə/ *noun* [*noncount*] : a kind of Italian bacon

pan·cre·as /ˈpæŋkrijəs/ *noun, pl* **-as·es** [*count*] : a large gland of the body that is near the stomach and that produces insulin and other substances that help the body digest food — see picture at HUMAN
– **pan·cre·at·ic** /ˌpæŋkriˈætɪk/ *adj* • *pancreatic* cancer/tissue

pan·da /ˈpændə/ *noun, pl* **-das** [*count*]
1 : a large animal with black-and-white fur that looks like a bear, lives in China, and eats mostly bamboo shoots — called also *giant panda, panda bear*
2 : RED PANDA

panda

panda car *noun, pl* **~ cars** [*count*] *Brit, informal* : a small police car

P

pan·dem·ic /pænˈdɛmɪk/ *noun, pl* **-ics** [*count*] *medical* : an occurrence in which a disease spreads very quickly and affects a large number of people over a wide area or throughout the world • The 1918 flu *pandemic* claimed millions of lives. • the AIDS *pandemic*
– **pandemic** *adj* • a *pandemic* virus/disease • *pandemic* malaria

pan·de·mo·ni·um /ˌpændəˈmounijəm/ *noun* [*noncount*] : a situation in which a crowd of people act in a wild, uncontrolled, or violent way because they are afraid, excited, or confused • The announcement that the concert was canceled was met with *pandemonium*. • *Pandemonium* erupted in the courtroom when the verdict was announced.

pan·der /ˈpændɚ/ *verb* **-ders**; **-dered**; **-der·ing** [*no obj*] *disapproving* : to do or provide what someone wants or demands even though it is not proper, good, or reasonable — usually + *to* • The film *panders to* the popular taste for violence in entertainment.

Pan·do·ra's box /pænˈdorəz-/ *noun* [*singular*] : a source of many troubles : something that will lead to many problems • Her parents are understandably afraid of ***opening a Pandora's box*** [=causing many worries and problems] if they buy her a car.

pane /ˈpeɪn/ *noun, pl* **panes** [*count*] : a sheet of glass in a window or door • a *pane* of glass — see picture at WINDOW

pan·e·gy·ric /ˌpænəˈʤirɪk/ *noun, pl* **-rics** [*count*] *formal* : something (such as a speech or a piece of writing) that praises someone or something — often + *to* • The film is a *panegyric to* old-fashioned virtues.

[1]**pan·el** /ˈpænl/ *noun, pl* **-els** [*count*]
1 a : a group of people who answer questions, give advice or opinions about something, or take part in a discussion for an audience • The university is hosting a *panel* on free speech. • Tonight's show features a *panel* of famous chefs. • Three of the members ***on the panel*** are doctors. • a ***panel discussion*** on (the topic of) education **b** : a group of people with special knowledge, skill, or experience who give advice or make decisions • The advisory *panel* has recommended that the drug be approved. • A *panel* of judges selected the book for this year's award. **c** *US* : a group of people who are chosen to be jurors : JURY — called also *jury panel*
2 a : one of the flat pieces that make up a door, wall, or ceiling • The room was visible through the door's glass *panel*. • One of the ceiling *panels* needs to be replaced. **b** : a piece of cloth that makes up part of something sewn together • Each of the skirt's five *panels* is a different color. • Sew the two *panels* together to form a tablecloth. **c** : a piece of metal or plastic that forms part of the outside surface of a vehicle • Aside from a dent in one of the side *panels* the car is in good shape.
3 : a flat surface where the controls of a vehicle, machine, etc., are located • the control *panel* • The last number you called is listed on the phone's display *panel*. — see also INSTRUMENT PANEL
— see also SOLAR PANEL

[2]**panel** *verb* **-els**; *US* **-eled** *or Brit* **-elled**; *US* **-el·ing** *or Brit* **-el·ling** [+ *obj*] : to cover (a wall, ceiling, etc.) with flat pieces of wood, glass, etc. • We *paneled* the living room with oak. • The walls were *paneled* in oak.
– **paneled** *adj* • The bedroom had dark *paneled* walls and large windows. • a heavy *paneled* door

paneling (*US*) *or Brit* **panelling** *noun* [*noncount*] : square or rectangular pieces of wood that are joined together to cover a wall or ceiling • The dining room had dark *paneling*.

pan·el·ist /ˈpænlɪst/ *noun, pl* **-ists** [*count*] : a person who is a part of a group of people who answer questions, give advice or opinions, etc. : a person who is a member of a panel

panel truck *noun, pl* ~ **trucks** [*count*] *US* : a small truck or van with a fully enclosed body that is often used to deliver goods

pan–fry /ˈpænˌfraɪ/ *verb* **-fries**; **-fried**; **-fry·ing** [+ *obj*] : to cook (food) in a frying pan with a small amount of fat • *pan-fried* fish

pang /ˈpæŋ/ *noun, pl* **pangs** [*count*] : a sudden, strong feeling of physical or emotional pain • hunger *pangs* — often + *of* • She felt a *pang of* guilt for not offering to help.

[1]**pan·han·dle** /ˈpænˌhændl/ *noun, pl* **-handles** [*count*] *US* : a part of a land area (such as a state) that is narrow and sticks out from a larger area • the *panhandle* of Florida = the Florida *Panhandle* • The Texas *Panhandle* is the northernmost part of the state. • the Oklahoma *Panhandle*

[2]**panhandle** *verb* **-handles**; **-han·dled**; **-han·dling** [*no obj*] *chiefly US* : to ask strangers for money in a public place (such as on a sidewalk) • He *panhandled* for his bus fare. • There is a law against *panhandling* in the subway.
– **pan·han·dler** /ˈpænˌhændlɚ/ *noun, pl* **-dlers** [*count*]

[1]**pan·ic** /ˈpænɪk/ *noun, pl* **-ics**
1 : a state or feeling of extreme fear that makes someone unable to act or think normally [*singular*] He was in a *panic* when he realized how late he was. • There's no reason to get into a *panic*. [*noncount*] The villagers fled in *panic* from the approaching army. • The crowd was in a ***state of panic***. • She has ***panic attacks*** whenever she has to speak in public. • (*medical*) He was diagnosed with ***panic disorder***. [=an illness that causes someone to have frequent panic attacks]
2 [*count*] : a situation that causes many people to become afraid and to rush to do something — usually singular • The recent *panic* over/about unsafe drinking water resulted in a shortage of bottled water in the stores.
– **pan·icky** /ˈpænɪki/ *adj* [*more* ~; *most* ~] • He got *panicky* when he realized how late he was.

[2]**panic** *verb* **-ics**; **-icked**; **-ick·ing**
1 [*no obj*] : to be overcome with extreme fear : to be affected by panic • If something goes wrong, don't *panic*.
2 [+ *obj*] : to cause (a person or animal) to feel extreme fear : to cause (a person or animal) to feel panic • The deer, *panicked* by the headlights, ran in front of the car.

panic button *noun, pl* ~ **-tons** [*count*] : a button in a bank, store, etc., that a person can press to call for help during an emergency (such as a robbery)
push/hit/press the panic button : to become extremely afraid or nervous when something bad happens or might happen • Medical officials says there is no need to *push the panic button* over two isolated cases of the disease.

pan·ic–strick·en /ˈpænɪkˌstrɪkən/ *adj* [*more* ~; *most* ~] : too frightened to think or act normally : overcome with panic • The *panic-stricken* horses crashed through the door of the burning barn.

pan·nier /ˈpænjɚ/ *noun, pl* **-niers** [*count*] *chiefly Brit* : SADDLEBAG

pan·o·ply /ˈpænəpli/ *noun, pl* **-plies** [*count*] *formal* : a group or collection that is impressive because it is so big or because it includes so many different kinds of people or things — usually singular • A *panoply* of drugs [=a wide array of drugs] is now available to treat depression. • the full *panoply* of American literature

pan·o·ra·ma /ˌpænəˈræmə, *Brit* ˌpænəˈrɑːmə/ *noun, pl* **-mas** [*count*]
1 : a full and wide view of something — usually singular • You can see a *panorama* of the entire bay from here.
2 a : a way of showing or telling something that includes a lot of information and covers many topics : a thorough presentation of a subject — usually singular • The book presents a *panorama* [=*overview*] of immigration in America. **b** : a group that includes many different people or things : a wide selection — usually singular • a *panorama* of cultures
– **pan·o·ram·ic** /ˌpænəˈræmɪk/ *adj* • a *panoramic* view of the city • a *panoramic* photograph of the Grand Canyon

pan·pipe /ˈpænˌpaɪp/ *noun, pl* **-pipes** [*count*] : a musical instrument that is made up of several short pipes of different lengths and that is played by blowing air across the top • play the *panpipe* — often plural especially in British English • play the *panpipes*

pan·sy /ˈpænzi/ *noun, pl* **-sies** [*count*]
1 : a small plant that is grown in gardens and has colorful flowers with five petals; *also* : its flower — see color picture on page C6
2 *informal + old-fashioned* **a** : a weak man or boy who is easily frightened **b** *offensive* : a male homosexual

pant /ˈpænt/ *verb* **pants**; **pant·ed**; **pant·ing**
1 a [*no obj*] : to breathe hard and quickly • Dogs *pant* when they are hot. • The hikers were *panting* by the time they reached the top of the hill. • They *panted* up the hill. [=they were panting as they went up the hill] • The patient was ***panting for breath***. [=breathing heavily] — sometimes used figuratively • The engine was *panting* noisily as it stood on the tracks. • The car *panted* up the hill. **b** [+ *obj*] : to say (something) while you are breathing quickly and heavily • "I've run far enough," he *panted*. [=*gasped*]
2 [*no obj*] *informal* : to wish for or want something very eagerly — often + *for* or *after* • Fans are *panting for* the writer's next book. • We knew she was *panting after* the starring role in the play. [=she wanted the starring role very much] — of-

ten followed by *to + verb* ▪ The crowd was *panting to hear* the outcome.
— see also PANTS

pan·ta·loons /ˌpæntəˈluːnz/ *noun* [*plural*] *old-fashioned* : pants with wide legs that become narrow at the bottom ▪ a clown in brightly colored *pantaloons*

pan·the·on /ˈpænθiˌɑːn/ *noun, pl* **-ons** [*count*]
1 : the gods of a particular country or group of people ▪ the Greek and Roman *pantheons*
2 *somewhat formal* : a group of people who are famous or important — often + *of* ▪ He occupies a place in the *pantheon of* great American writers. [=he is one of the great American writers]
3 : a temple that is built to honor all the gods of a particular country or group of people

pan·ther /ˈpænθɚ/ *noun, pl* **pan·thers** *also* **panther** [*count*]
1 : a large, black wildcat
2 *US* : COUGAR

pant·ies /ˈpæntiz/ *noun* [*plural*] *chiefly US* : a piece of girl's or woman's underwear that covers the area between the waist and the top of the legs — called also *(Brit) knickers*; see color picture on page C13

pan·to /ˈpæntoʊ/ *noun, pl* **-tos** [*count, noncount*] *Brit, informal* : [1]PANTOMIME ▪ a Christmas *panto*

[1]**pan·to·mime** /ˈpæntəˌmaɪm/ *noun, pl* **-mimes**
1 a [*noncount*] : a way of expressing information or telling a story without words by using body movements and facial expressions ▪ In the game of charades, one player uses *pantomime* to represent a word or phrase that the other players have to try to guess. **b** : a performance in which a story is told without words by using body movements and facial expressions [*count*] We saw *pantomimes* at the fair. [*noncount*] a ballet that is part dance and part *pantomime*
2 [*count*] *Brit* : a play for children performed during the Christmas season that is based on a fairy tale and includes singing and dancing

[2]**pantomime** *verb* **-mimes; -mimed; -mim·ing** [+ *obj*] : to make the movements of someone who is doing something without actually doing it : MIME ▪ He *pantomimed* someone talking on the phone.

pan·try /ˈpæntri/ *noun, pl* **-tries** [*count*] : a small room in a house in which food is stored

pants /ˈpænts/ *noun* [*plural*]
1 *chiefly US* : a piece of clothing that covers your body from the waist to the ankle and has a separate part for each leg ▪ a pair of *pants* [=*trousers*] ▪ short/long *pants* ▪ a *pants* leg — sometimes used in the singular form ***pant*** especially before another noun and in clothing catalogs ▪ a *pant* leg ▪ a classic khaki *pant* = (more commonly) classic khaki *pants* — see color picture on page C14
2 *Brit* : UNDERPANTS 1
ants in your pants see ANT
by the seat of your pants see [1]SEAT
keep your pants on *US, informal* — used to tell someone to be patient ▪ "Aren't you ready to leave yet?" "*Keep your pants on*! I'll be ready in a minute."
the pants off *informal* — used for emphasis after words like *charm, scare, frighten, bore,* and *beat* ▪ He can *charm the pants off* anybody. [=he is very charming] ▪ She *scared the pants off* us [=she scared us very badly] when she phoned at 3 a.m. ▪ The meeting *bored the pants off* me. ▪ The home team *beat the pants off* the visiting team last night.
wear the pants see [1]WEAR
with your pants down *US, informal* : in an embarrassing or unprepared position ▪ The clinic now maintains an adequate supply of vaccine so that it won't be ***caught with its pants down*** if there is a flu outbreak two years in a row.

pant·suit /ˈpæntˌsuːt/ *noun, pl* **-suits** [*count*] *US* : a woman's suit consisting of a jacket and pants that are made of the same material — called also *(US) pants suit, (Brit) trouser suit*

panty·hose /ˈpæntiˌhoʊz/ *noun* [*plural*] *US* : clothing for women made of thin material that fits closely over the feet and legs and goes up to the waist ▪ a pair of *pantyhose* — called also *(Brit) tights*; see color picture on page C13

panty line *noun, pl* ~ **lines** [*count*] : the edge of a woman's panties especially when it can be seen through her clothing as a long, thin line ▪ a visible *panty line*

panty liner *noun, pl* ~ **ers** [*count*] : a very thin pad that is worn inside a woman's panties in order to protect them from stains

pap /ˈpæp/ *noun* [*noncount*] *informal* : books, television programs, etc., that are worthless or dull ▪ That show is better than most of the *pap* on TV. ▪ Why do you read that *pap*?

pa·pa *also US* **pop·pa** /ˈpɑːpə/ *noun, pl* **-pas** [*count*] *informal + somewhat old-fashioned* : a person's father — used especially by young children ▪ Where's *papa*? ▪ Good morning, *Papa*! — compare MAMA

pa·pa·cy /ˈpeɪpəsi/ *noun, pl* **-cies**
1 ***the papacy*** : the office or position of the pope ▪ He was selected by the cardinals for *the papacy*.
2 [*count*] : the time when a particular pope is in power — usually singular ▪ during the *papacy* of John Paul II

pa·pal /ˈpeɪpəl/ *adj, always used before a noun* : of or relating to the pope or the government of the Roman Catholic Church ▪ a *papal* decree/visit ▪ *papal* authority

papal infallibility *noun* [*noncount*] : the Roman Catholic belief that the pope cannot be wrong when using his official position of power to give instructions about Christian faith or morals

pa·pa·raz·zo /ˌpɑːpəˈrɑːtsoʊ, *Brit* ˌpæpəˈrætsoʊ/ *noun, pl* **pa·pa·raz·zi** /ˌpɑːpəˈrɑːtsi, *Brit* ˌpæpəˈrætsi/ [*count*] : a photographer who follows famous people in order to take their pictures and then sells the pictures to newspapers or magazines — usually plural ▪ a movie star surrounded by a swarm of *paparazzi*

pa·pa·ya /pəˈpajə/ *noun, pl* **-yas** [*count, noncount*] : a yellowish-green fruit with black seeds that grows on a tropical tree

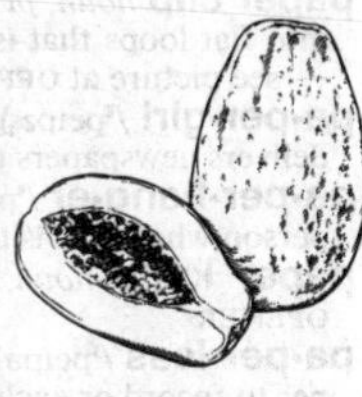
papaya

[1]**pa·per** /ˈpeɪpɚ/ *noun, pl* **-pers**
1 [*noncount*] : the material that is used in the form of thin sheets for writing or printing on, wrapping things, etc. ▪ We'll need pens, glue, and some *paper*. ▪ Be sure to print/write the letter on good *paper*. ▪ She wrapped the present in pretty *paper* [=*wrapping paper*] and put a bow on the top. ▪ a sheet of *paper* ▪ He scribbled the number on a scrap of *paper*. ▪ a crumpled/torn piece of *paper* ▪ a pad of *paper* — see also GRAPH PAPER, SCRAP PAPER, SILVER PAPER, TISSUE PAPER, TOILET PAPER, WAX PAPER, WRITING PAPER
2 a [*count*] : a sheet of paper with information written or printed on it — usually plural ▪ A pile of *papers* blew off the desk. ▪ She has possession of the writer's personal *papers*. **b** ***papers*** [*plural*] : official documents that give information about something or that are used as proof of something ▪ The border guards asked to see my *papers*. ▪ divorce *papers* ▪ legal *papers* — see also WALKING PAPERS, WORKING PAPERS
3 [*count*] **a** : a piece of writing usually on an academic or official subject ▪ They published a landmark *paper* in 1995. ▪ She presented a *paper* [=she delivered a speech about a written work] at the conference. ▪ a scientific *paper* ▪ a government *paper* — see also POSITION PAPER **b** *US* : a piece of writing that is done for a course at a school ▪ He handed in a *paper* [=*essay*] about the nesting habits of birds. ▪ The teacher was busy grading *papers*. — see also TERM PAPER **c** *Brit* : an exam or test in which students write answers to written questions ▪ She did well on her history *paper*.
4 [*count*] : NEWSPAPER ▪ a news story in the local *paper* ▪ the morning *paper* ▪ Did you hear what the *papers* are saying/reporting? ▪ It was the sort of thing you read about in the *papers*. — see also FUNNY PAPERS
5 [*count, noncount*] : paper that is used to cover or decorate the walls of a room : WALLPAPER ▪ She picked a light green *paper* for the living room.
on paper **1** : in a written form : in writing ▪ He finally put his ideas *on paper*. [=he finally wrote down his ideas] **2** — used to say that something seems to be true or likely when you read or hear what is known about it but that the real situation may be different ▪ The other team looked better *on paper*, but we beat them anyway. ▪ *On paper*, the procedure is relatively simple.
push paper(s) *informal* : to do boring or unimportant work in an office ▪ She wanted to be a pilot, but instead she ended up *pushing papers* in a government job. — see also PAPER PUSHER
put/set pen to paper see [1]PEN

[2]**paper** *adj*
1 : made of paper ▪ a *paper* bag ▪ *paper* cups/plates [=cups/plates made of thick paper and usually designed to be used

P

once and then thrown away] ▪ The cups/plates were *paper*.

2 *always used before a noun* **: of or relating to paper** ▪ *paper* manufacturers ▪ a *paper* mill [=a mill/factory where paper is made]

3 *always used before a noun* **: existing or shown on paper or in documents but not real** ▪ Their accounts showed lots of *paper* profits, but they went bankrupt anyway. ▪ *paper* losses

³paper *verb* **-pers; -pered; -per·ing** [+ *obj*] **: to cover (something, such as a wall) with paper** ▪ *paper* [=*wallpaper*] the bedroom

paper over [*phrasal verb*] ***paper (something) over*** *or* ***paper over (something)*** **: to hide (something bad, such as differences or problems)** ▪ They *papered over* their disagreements [=they pretended that they did not disagree] in order to convince the investors to put up the money. ▪ (*chiefly Brit*) We have to acknowledge these problems. We can't just ***paper over the cracks***

pa·per·back /ˈpeɪpɚˌbæk/ *noun, pl* **-backs : a book that has a thick paper cover** [*count*] The store sells both *paperbacks* and hardcovers. [*noncount*] The book is sold only ***in paperback*** — compare HARDCOVER, SOFTCOVER

— **paperback** *adj* ▪ a *paperback* novel/edition

pa·per·boy /ˈpeɪpɚˌboɪ/ *noun, pl* **-boys** [*count*] **: a boy who delivers newspapers to people's houses**

paper clip *noun, pl* **~ clips** [*count*] **: a piece of wire bent into flat loops that is used to hold sheets of paper together** — see picture at OFFICE

pa·per·girl /ˈpeɪpɚˌgɚl/ *noun, pl* **-girls** [*count*] **: a girl who delivers newspapers to people's houses**

pa·per·hang·er /ˈpeɪpɚˌhæŋɚ/ *noun, pl* **-ers** [*count*] *US* **: a person whose job is to put up wallpaper**

paper knife *noun, pl* **~ knives** [*count*] *Brit* **:** LETTER OPENER

pa·per·less /ˈpeɪpɚləs/ *adj* **: using computers instead of paper to record or exchange information** ▪ a *paperless* office ▪ a *paperless* business transaction

paper money *noun* [*noncount*] **: money that is made of paper : money in the form of bills instead of coins**

paper pusher *noun, pl* **~ -ers** [*count*] *chiefly US, informal + disapproving* **: someone who does boring or unimportant work in an office** — called also (*US*) *pencil pusher,* (*Brit*) *pen pusher*

pa·per–thin /ˈpeɪpɚˌθɪn/ *adj* **: very thin** ▪ *paper-thin* slices of roast beef ▪ The walls are *paper-thin*.

paper tiger *noun, pl* **~ -gers** [*count*] **: someone or something that appears powerful or dangerous but is not** ▪ The new laws are just *paper tigers* without any method of enforcement.

paper towel *noun, pl* **~ -els : a sheet of soft and thick paper that can soak up liquid and that is used for drying your hands, cleaning up spills, etc.** [*count*] She used a *paper towel* to wipe off the counter. ▪ (*US*) a roll of *paper towels* [=(*Brit*) a roll of kitchen paper] [*noncount*] (*US*) a piece of *paper towel* [=(*Brit*) *kitchen paper*]

paper trail *noun, pl* **~ trails** [*count*] *chiefly US* **: documents (such as financial records or memos) that make it possible for someone at a later time to know what was done, discussed, etc.** ▪ They covered up the fraud and were careful not to leave a *paper trail*.

pa·per·weight /ˈpeɪpɚˌweɪt/ *noun, pl* **-weights** [*count*] **: a small, heavy object that is used to hold down loose papers on a surface**

pa·per·work /ˈpeɪpɚˌwɚk/ *noun* [*noncount*]

1 : routine work that involves writing letters, reports, etc. ▪ He spent most of the morning doing (his) *paperwork*. ▪ administrative *paperwork*

2 : the official documents that are needed for something to happen or be done ▪ She failed to file the *paperwork* on time. ▪ The lawyer had us fill in the *paperwork* for the mortgage.

pa·pery /ˈpeɪpəri/ *adj* [*more ~; most ~*] **: very thin or dry like paper** ▪ a berry with *papery* skin ▪ the *papery* wing of a moth

pa·pier–mâ·ché /ˌpeɪpɚməˈʃeɪ, *Brit* ˌpæpjeɪˈmæʃeɪ/ *noun* [*noncount*] **: a material that is made of paper mixed with water, glue, and other substances and that hardens as it dries** ▪ She made a mask out of *papier-mâché*. — often used before another noun ▪ a large *papier-mâché* sculpture

pap·py /ˈpæpi/ *noun, pl* **-pies** [*count*] *US, informal* **: a person's father :** PAPA — used chiefly in the southern and east central part of the U.S.

pa·pri·ka /pəˈpriːkə/ *noun* [*noncount*] **: a red powder that is made from sweet peppers and used as a spice for food** ▪ tomato sauce made with garlic, *paprika*, and pepper

Pap smear /ˈpæpˈsmiɚ/ *noun, pl* **~ smears** [*count*] *US, medical* **: a test for the early detection of cancer of the uterus and cervix** ▪ She has a *Pap smear* done every year. — called also (*US*) *Pap test,* (*Brit*) *cervical smear,* (*Brit*) *smear test*

pa·py·rus /pəˈpaɪrəs/ *noun, pl* **pa·py·ri** /pəˈpaɪri/ *or* **pa·py·rus·es**

1 [*noncount*] **: a tall plant that is like grass and that grows in marshes especially in Egypt**

2 a [*noncount*] **: paper made from papyrus that was used in ancient times** ▪ an ancient text written on *papyrus* ▪ a roll/scroll of *papyrus* ▪ a *papyrus* scroll **b** [*count*] **: a piece of paper made from papyrus that has writing on it** ▪ He discovered a *papyrus* in the ruins. per made from papyrus that has writing on it ▪ He discovered a *papyrus* in the ruins.

par /ˈpaɚ/ *noun, pl* **pars**

1 : the number of strokes a good golfer is expected to take to finish a golf hole or course [*noncount*] He made/scored *par* on the ninth hole. ▪ She finished the 18th hole three strokes under/over *par*. ▪ The 18th hole is a *par* 5. [=par for the 18th hole is five strokes] ▪ a *par*-5 hole [*count*] He made/scored a *par* on the ninth hole. ▪ She made/scored nine *pars* in a row.

2 [*noncount*] *business* **: the value of a stock or bond that is printed on the paper of the stock or bond itself or that is decided upon when the stock or bond is issued** ▪ That stock is trading (at) 16 percent above/below *par*. — called also *par value*

above par **: better than normal or expected : very good** ▪ The performance was *above par*.

below par *also* ***under par*** **: worse than expected : not very good :** BAD ▪ Our meal was *below par*. [=*subpar*] ▪ I'm feeling a little *below par*.

on (a) par with **: at the same level or standard as (someone or something else)** ▪ The new version of the software is *on a par with* the old one. [=is as good as the old one] ▪ His new book is *on par with* his best sellers.

par for the course *disapproving* **: normal or typical : not unusual or unexpected** ▪ His son's bad behavior is just *par for the course*. [=his son often/always behaves badly] ▪ It's *par for the course* that she's late to the meeting.

up to par **: good enough : as good as expected or wanted** ▪ She was checking to see if his work was *up to par*. — usually used in negative statements ▪ His course work is *not up to par*. [=not as good as it should be] ▪ She's not feeling *up to par*. [=she is not feeling well; her health is not good]

para. *abbr* paragraph

¹para- *prefix*

1 : beyond or outside of ▪ *para*normal

2 : helping highly trained professionals by doing tasks that require less training ▪ *para*medic ▪ *para*legal

²para- *combining form* **: parachute** ▪ *para*trooper ▪ *para*sailing

par·a·ble /ˈperəbəl/ *noun, pl* **-ables** [*count*] **: a short story that teaches a moral or spiritual lesson** ▪ He told the children a *parable* about the importance of forgiveness.; *especially* **: one of the stories told by Jesus Christ and recorded in the Bible** ▪ the *parable* of the Good Samaritan

pa·rab·o·la /pəˈræbələ/ *noun, pl* **-las** [*count*] *technical* **: a curve that is shaped like the path of something that is thrown forward and high in the air and falls back to the ground** — sometimes used figuratively ▪ a biography that follows the *parabola* of the actress's career [=a biography that shows the rise and fall of the actress's career]

— **par·a·bol·ic** /ˌperəˈbɑːlɪk/ *adj* ▪ a *parabolic* curve

para·cet·a·mol /ˌperəˈsiːtəˌmɑːl/ *noun* [*noncount*] *Brit* **:** ACETOMINOPHEN

¹para·chute /ˈperəˌʃuːt/ *noun, pl* **-chutes** [*count*] **: a piece of equipment usually made of cloth that is fastened to people or things and that allows them to fall slowly and land safely after they have jumped or been dropped from an aircraft** ▪ The pilot was wearing a *parachute*. ▪ The supplies were dropped by *parachute*. — often used before another noun ▪ a *parachute* jump/drop — see also GOLDEN PARACHUTE

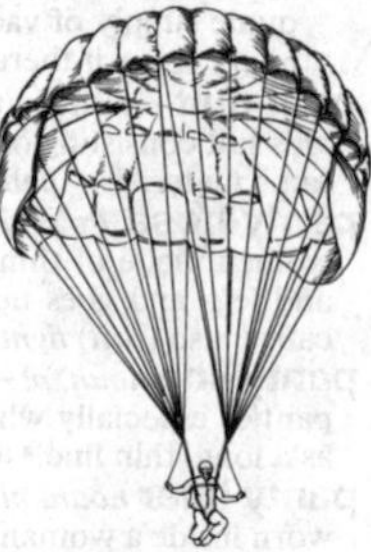

parachute

²parachute *verb, always followed*

by an adverb or preposition **-chutes; -chut·ed; -chut·ing**
1 [*no obj*] **: to jump from an aircraft using a parachute** • The soldiers *parachuted* in and quickly hid their gear. • New troops *parachuted* into enemy territory.
2 [+ *obj*] **: to drop (someone or something) from an aircraft using a parachute** • We will *parachute* supplies in after you arrive. • New troops were *parachuted* into enemy territory.

para·chut·ist /ˈperəˌʃuːtɪst/ *noun, pl* **-ists** [*count*] **: a person who jumps from an aircraft and uses a parachute to land**

[1]**pa·rade** /pəˈreɪd/ *noun, pl* **-rades** [*count*]
1 : a public celebration of a special day or event that usually includes many people and groups moving down a street by marching or riding in cars or on special vehicles (called floats) • the annual Thanksgiving Day *parade* • After the team won the championship, the city threw/had a *parade* for them. • The town will put on a *parade*. • The marching band lined up for the homecoming *parade*. • the *parade* route
2 : a military ceremony in which soldiers march or stand in lines so that they can be examined by officers or other important people
3 : a long series of people or things that come one after the other — usually singular; usually + *of* • We had a *parade of* visitors this morning. [=we had many visitors this morning] • The prosecution called a *parade of* witnesses to the stand. • We watched a *parade of* cars go by our house on the way to the stadium for the game.
4 *Brit* **: a street with a row of small shops** • a shopping *parade*
***on parade* 1 : shown or displayed especially in a way that attracts attention or notice** • Her new diamond engagement ring was *on parade* for all her friends to stare at. • Television executives learned that violent shows attract more viewers, and pretty soon it was violence *on parade* all day long. **2 : marching or standing in a military parade** • The general carefully watched the soldiers *on parade*. • a military honor guard *on parade*
rain on someone's parade see [2]RAIN

[2]**parade** *verb* **-rades; -rad·ed; -rad·ing**
1 *always followed by an adverb or preposition* [*no obj*] **: to walk or march together in public especially as a way of celebrating or protesting something** • The team and its fans *paraded* down the street. • Protesters *paraded* in front of City Hall.
2 *always followed by an adverb or preposition* [*no obj*] **: to walk in a way that attracts attention** • The models *paraded* up and down the runway. • She *paraded* around on the beach in her bikini.
3 [+ *obj*] **: to force (someone) to walk or march in public** • The victors *paraded* the prisoners through the streets.
4 *of soldiers* **: to march in lines in order to be examined by officers or other important people** [*no obj*] The soldiers *paraded* past the generals. [+ *obj*] The soldiers were *paraded* past the generals.
5 *always followed by an adverb or preposition* [+ *obj*] **: to show or present (someone or something) proudly or in a way that attracts attention** • They don't like having their personal problems *paraded* in print for everyone to see.
6 *disapproving* **: to be falsely presented as something good — + *as*** [*no obj*] The book is just propaganda *parading as* literature. [+ *obj*] **— usually used as *(be) paraded*** • lies *being paraded as* the truth

parade ground *noun, pl* **~ grounds** [*count*] **: a place where parades begin or happen** • a military *parade ground* **— often plural** • Meet me at the *parade grounds* after the fireworks.

par·a·digm /ˈperəˌdaɪm/ *noun, pl* **-digms** [*count*] *formal*
1 : a model or pattern for something that may be copied • Her recent book provides us with a new *paradigm* for modern biography.
2 : a theory or a group of ideas about how something should be done, made, or thought about • the Freudian *paradigm* of psychoanalysis • a new study that challenges the current evolutionary *paradigm*
– par·a·dig·mat·ic /ˌperədɪgˈmætɪk/ *adj* [*more ~; most ~*] • a *paradigmatic* example

paradigm shift *noun, pl* **~ shifts** [*count*] *formal* **: an important change that happens when the usual way of thinking about or doing something is replaced by a new and different way** • This discovery will bring about a *paradigm shift* in our understanding of evolution. [=will cause people to understand evolution in a completely new way]

par·a·dise /ˈperəˌdaɪs/ *noun, pl* **-dis·es**
1 a [*count*] **: a very beautiful, pleasant, or peaceful place that seems to be perfect** • a rural *paradise* • tropical *paradises* • Their marriage was very happy at first, but now there's ***trouble in paradise***. **b** [*singular*] **: a place that is perfect for a particular activity or for a person who enjoys that activity** • a marsh that is a birdwatcher's *paradise* • This shop is an antique collecting *paradise*! **c** [*noncount*] **: a state of complete happiness** • When I'm with you, I'm ***in paradise***. [=I'm very happy] — see also FOOL'S PARADISE
2 *or* ***Paradise*** [*noncount*] **a : a place where in some religions good people are believed to go after they die : HEAVEN b : the place where Adam and Eve first lived according to the Bible : EDEN**
– see also BIRD OF PARADISE

par·a·dox /ˈperəˌdɑːks/ *noun, pl* **-dox·es**
1 [*count*] **a : something (such as a situation) that is made up of two opposite things and that seems impossible but is actually true or possible** • It is a *paradox* that computers need maintenance so often, since they are meant to save people time. **b : someone who does two things that seem to be opposite to each other or who has qualities that are opposite** • As an actor, he's a *paradox*—he loves being in the public eye but also deeply values and protects his privacy.
2 a [*count*] **: a statement that seems to say two opposite things but that may be true b** [*noncount*] **: the use of such statements in writing or speech** • a novel full of *paradox*
– par·a·dox·i·cal /ˌperəˈdɑːksɪkəl/ *adj* [*more ~; most ~*] • the *paradoxical* theory that global warming will lead to the next Ice Age **– par·a·dox·i·cal·ly** /ˌperəˈdɑːksɪkli/ *adv*

par·af·fin /ˈperəfən/ *noun* [*noncount*]
1 : a soft, waxy substance that is usually made from petroleum or coal and is used in candles and other products — called also *paraffin wax*
2 *Brit* **: KEROSENE** • a *paraffin* lamp

para·glid·ing /ˈperəˌglaɪdɪŋ/ *noun* [*noncount*] **: a sport in which a person jumps from a high place (such as a cliff or an airplane) and uses a special kind of parachute to float down to the ground**
– para·glide /ˈperəˌglaɪd/ *verb* **-glides; -glid·ed; -glid·ing** [*no obj*] • He *paraglided* down from the cliff. • She likes to ***go paragliding***. **– para·glid·er** /ˈperəˌglaɪdɚ/ *noun, pl* **-ers** [*count*]

par·a·gon /ˈperəˌgɑːn, *Brit* ˈpærəgən/ *noun, pl* **-gons** [*count*] *formal* **: a person or thing that is perfect or excellent in some way and should be considered a model or example to be copied** • He's no moral *paragon*. **— often + *of*** • The company is a *paragon of* modern manufacturing techniques. • He is a ***paragon of virtue***. [=he is a very virtuous person]

para·graph /ˈperəˌgræf, *Brit* ˈpærəˌgrɑːf/ *noun, pl* **-graphs** [*count*] **: a part of a piece of writing that usually deals with one subject, that begins on a new line, and that is made up of one or more sentences** • In the second *paragraph* from the bottom, you've misspelled "their" as "thier." • Please refer to section 2, *paragraph* 4 for the appropriate information. • The two introductory *paragraphs* were written by the editor.

par·a·keet /ˈperəˌkiːt/ *noun, pl* **-keets** [*count*] **: a small, brightly colored tropical bird that has a long tail and that is often kept as a pet**

para·le·gal /ˈperəˌliːgəl/ *noun, pl* **-gals** [*count*] *US* **: a person who is trained to help a lawyer by doing research, office work, etc.**
– para·le·gal /ˌperəˈliːgəl/ *adj, always used before a noun* • *paralegal* studies

[1]**par·al·lel** /ˈperəˌlɛl/ *adj*
1 — used to describe lines, paths, etc., that are the same distance apart along their whole length and do not touch at any point • *parallel* train tracks • A square is made of two sets of *parallel* lines. • The corn is planted in *parallel* rows. • The lines are *parallel* to each other. • The row of trees is *parallel* with the road. **— compare PERPENDICULAR**
2 : very similar and often happening at the same time • the *parallel* careers of the two movie stars • These two sentences are *parallel* in structure. • Notice the *parallel* development/evolution of the two technologies.
3 *computers* **: designed for a computer system in which very small pieces of information are sent over separate wires at the same time** • a *parallel* cable/connection/port/printer **— compare [1]SERIAL 4**
– parallel *adv* • The sidewalk runs *parallel* to/with the street.

[2]**parallel** *noun, pl* **-lels**
1 a [*count*] **: a way in which things are similar : a shared quality or characteristic** • These myths have some striking/

obvious *parallels* with myths found in cultures around the world. • There are many ***parallels between*** the stories. • The essay ***draws parallels between*** the lives of the two presidents. [=describes ways in which the lives of the two presidents were similar] **b** [*noncount*] **:** something that is equal or similar — usually used in negative statements • This period of growth has ***no parallel*** [=there has never been a similar period of growth] in the history of the region. • a masterpiece ***without parallel*** [=better than all others] in the history of art • As an insult, it was *without parallel.* [=worse or more effective than all others]

2 [*count*] **:** any one of the imaginary circles on the surface of the Earth that are parallel to the equator and that are shown as lines on maps • Most of the United States is south of the 49th *parallel.* — compare MERIDIAN

in parallel (with) **:** at the same time and in a way that is related or connected • Prices are rising *in parallel with* increasing fuel costs. • The two systems work *in parallel.*

³parallel *verb* **-lels; -leled; -lel·ing** [+ *obj*]

1 : to be similar or equal to (something) • Their test results *parallel* our own. • Nothing *parallels* that experience. [=that experience is unlike any other experience; it is unique]

2 : to happen at the same time as (something) and in a way that is related or connected • Rising prices *parallel* increasing fuel costs. • Spending is *paralleled* by an increase in the number of loans given.

3 : to be parallel to (something) **:** to go or extend in the same direction as (something) • The highway *parallels* the river.

parallel bars *noun* [*plural*] *sports* **:** a pair of long bars on posts that are parallel to each other and are used in gymnastics — compare UNEVEN BARS

par·al·lel·ism /ˈperəˌlɛˌlɪzəm/ *noun, pl* **-isms** *formal* **:** the fact of being similar in development or form [*noncount*] There is some degree of *parallelism* between the lives of the two women. [*count*] There is a certain *parallelism* in the development of the two technologies.

par·al·lel·o·gram /ˌperəˈlɛləˌgræm/ *noun, pl* **-grams** [*count*] *geometry* **:** a four-sided shape made up of two pairs of straight parallel lines that are equal in length • Rectangles, squares, and rhombuses are all *parallelograms.*

parallel park *verb* **~ parks; ~ parked; ~ park·ing :** to park a car, truck, etc., so that the long side of the vehicle is parallel to the side of the road [*no obj*] I still have to learn how to *parallel park.* [+ *obj*] *parallel park* a car

– parallel parking *noun* [*noncount*]

pa·ral·y·sis /pəˈræləsəs/ *noun*

1 *medical* **:** a condition in which you are unable to move or feel all or part of your body [*noncount*] The disease causes *paralysis.* • *paralysis* of the legs • partial/temporary *paralysis* [*singular*] The disease causes a *paralysis* of the legs.

2 *formal* **:** a state of being unable to function, act, or move [*noncount*] The whole country is in a state of *paralysis.* • They are trying to end the political *paralysis* that has been gripping the country. [*singular*] a *paralysis* of fear [=an inability to function, act, or move that is caused by fear]

¹par·a·lyt·ic /ˌperəˈlɪtɪk/ *adj*

1 *always used before a noun, medical* **:** affected with or causing paralysis • *paralytic* patients [=patients who are unable to move or feel all or part of their bodies] • a *paralytic* drug/stroke/disease [=a drug/stroke/disease that causes paralysis]

2 *Brit, informal* **:** very drunk • a group of *paralytic* drunks

²paralytic *noun, pl* **-ics** [*count*] *medical* **:** a person who is paralyzed • treatment for *paralytics*

par·a·lyze (*US*) *or Brit* **par·a·lyse** /ˈperəˌlaɪz/ *verb* **-lyz·es; -lyzed; -lyz·ing** [+ *obj*]

1 : to make (a person or animal) unable to move or feel all or part of the body • The snake's venom *paralyzed* the mouse. • The accident *paralyzed* him from the neck down. [=the accident caused him to lose the ability to move or feel his body below his neck]

2 : to make (someone or something) unable to function, act, or move • The air strikes have *paralyzed* the city's transportation system. • The company was *paralyzed* by debt.

– paralyzed *adj* • The accident left him *paralyzed* from the neck down. • I was practically *paralyzed* with fear/embarrassment. [=unable to function, act, or move because I was so afraid/embarrassed] **– paralyzing** *adj* • the snake's *paralyzing* venom • a *paralyzing* fear

para·med·ic /perəˈmɛdɪk/ *noun, pl* **-ics** [*count*] **:** a person whose job is to provide emergency medical care to sick or injured people who are being taken to a hospital • She's training to be a *paramedic.*

– paramedic *adj, always used before a noun* • *paramedic* training

pa·ram·e·ter /pəˈræmətɚ/ *noun, pl* **-ters** [*count*] **:** a rule or limit that controls what something is or how something should be done — usually plural • First we need to ***set/define the parameters*** of the project. • The investigation stayed ***within the parameters*** set by the court.

¹para·mil·i·tary /ˌperəˈmɪləˌteri, *Brit* ˌpærəˈmɪlətri/ *adj, always used before a noun* **:** of or relating to a group that is not an official army but that operates and is organized like an army • *paramilitary* militias • Government forces have been attacked by heavily armed *paramilitary* groups in several villages. • *paramilitary* training • a *paramilitary* police force

²paramilitary *noun, pl* **-tar·ies** [*count*] **:** a member of a paramilitary group — usually plural • Forces encountered heavily armed *paramilitaries.*

par·a·mount /ˈperəˌmaʊnt/ *adj* [*more* ~; *most* ~] **:** very important **:** of highest rank or importance • Safety is of *paramount* importance. = Safety is *paramount.* • Unemployment was the *paramount* [=*chief, main*] issue in the election.

par·amour /ˈperəˌmuɚ/ *noun, pl* **-amours** [*count*] *literary* **:** a person with whom someone is having a romantic or sexual relationship and especially a secret or improper relationship • Her husband found a love letter from her *paramour.* [=*lover*]

para·noia /ˌperəˈnojə/ *noun* [*noncount*]

1 *medical* **:** a serious mental illness that causes you to falsely believe that other people are trying to harm you • She was diagnosed with delusional *paranoia.*

2 : an unreasonable feeling that people are trying to harm you, do not like you, etc. • I had to admit that my fears were just *paranoia.*

¹para·noid /ˈperəˌnoɪd/ *adj*

1 *medical* **:** of, relating to, or suffering from a mental illness that causes you to falsely believe that people are trying to harm you • *paranoid* behavior/schizophrenia • a *paranoid* mental patient

2 [*more* ~; *most* ~] **:** having or showing an unreasonable feeling that people are trying to harm you, do not like you, etc. **:** feeling or showing paranoia • I guess I was just being *paranoid.* • She's a little *paranoid* about her job. • It's nothing more than a *paranoid* fantasy.

²paranoid *noun, pl* **-noids** [*count*] *medical* **:** a person who has paranoia • a new treatment for *paranoids*

para·nor·mal /ˌperəˈnoɚməl/ *adj* **:** very strange and not able to be explained by what scientists know about nature and the world • Some believe she had *paranormal* [=*supernatural*] powers. • *paranormal* phenomena

the paranormal **:** strange events, abilities, etc., that cannot be explained by what is known about nature and the world • I've always been fascinated by *the paranormal.*

par·a·pet /ˈperəpət/ *noun, pl* **-pets** [*count*] **:** a low wall at the edge of a platform, roof, or bridge • The invaders fired arrows over the castle's *parapet.*

put/stick/raise your head above the parapet *Brit, informal* **:** to do or say something you think is important even though it may have bad results • I'll *put my head above the parapet* to defend him.

par·a·pher·na·lia /ˌperəfəˈneɪljə/ *noun* [*noncount*] **:** objects that are used to do a particular activity **:** objects of a particular kind • hockey *paraphernalia* [=*equipment*] • Drug *paraphernalia* was found in his car.

¹para·phrase /ˈperəˌfreɪz/ *verb* **-phras·es; -phrased; -phras·ing :** to say (something that someone else has said or written) using different words [+ *obj*] He *paraphrased* the quote. • She frequently *paraphrases* (the words of) famous authors in her lectures. [*no obj*] I'm *paraphrasing,* but he did say something like that.

²paraphrase *noun, pl* **-phrases** [*count*] **:** a statement that says something that another person has said or written in a different way • This is just a *paraphrase* of what he said, not an exact quote.

para·ple·gia /ˌperəˈpliːʤijə/ *noun* [*noncount*] *medical* **:** a condition in which you are permanently unable to move or feel your legs and the lower half of your body because of injury or illness

para·ple·gic /ˌperəˈpliːʤɪk/ *noun, pl* **-gics** [*count*] *medical* **:** a person who is permanently unable to move or feel the legs or lower half of the body because of injury or illness • Although she is a *paraplegic,* she is an accomplished athlete. — compare QUADRIPLEGIC

– **paraplegic** *adj, always used before a noun* • a *paraplegic* war veteran

para·pro·fes·sion·al /ˌperəprəˈfɛʃənl/ *noun, pl* **-als** [*count*] *US* : a person whose job is to help a professional person (such as a teacher) • There is at least one *paraprofessional* in each classroom.
– **paraprofessional** *adj, always used before a noun* • *paraprofessional* training

para·psy·chol·o·gy /ˌperəˌsaɪˈkɑːləʤi/ *noun* [*noncount*] : the scientific study of events that cannot be explained by what scientists know about nature and the world

para·sail·ing /ˈperəˌseɪlɪŋ/ *noun* [*noncount*] : a sport or activity in which you are pulled behind a motorboat while wearing a parachute so that you sail through the air • They went *parasailing* while they were on vacation.

par·a·site /ˈperəˌsaɪt/ *noun, pl* **-sites** [*count*]
1 : an animal or plant that lives in or on another animal or plant and gets food or protection from it • Many diseases are caused by *parasites*. — compare [1]HOST 3
2 *disapproving* : a person or thing that takes something from someone or something else and does not do anything to earn it or deserve it • She's a *parasite* who only stays with him for the money. • These new companies are *parasites* feeding off the success of those who spent the last decade establishing the industry.

par·a·sit·ic /ˌperəˈsɪtɪk/ *adj*
1 *of an animal or plant* : living in or on another animal or plant and getting food or protection from it • *parasitic* plants/mites/worms
2 *always used before a noun* : caused by a parasite • a *parasitic* disease/infection
3 *disapproving* : getting food, money, etc., from other people without doing anything to earn it or deserve it • her lazy, *parasitic* brother

para·sol /ˈperəˌsɑːl/ *noun, pl* **-sols** [*count*] : a light umbrella that you use to protect yourself from the sun

para·troop·er /ˈperəˌtruːpɚ/ *noun, pl* **-ers** [*count*] : a member of a group of soldiers who are trained to jump out of airplanes using a parachute

para·troops /ˈperəˌtruːps/ *noun* [*plural*] : a group of soldiers who are trained to jump out of airplanes using a parachute : a group of paratroopers
– **para·troop** /ˈperəˌtruːp/ *adj, always used before a noun* • a *paratroop* unit

par·boil /ˈpɑɚˌbojəl/ *verb* **-boils; -boiled; -boil·ing** [+ *obj*] : to boil (a piece of food) for a short time often before cooking it fully in another way • *Parboil* the potatoes before you roast them.

[1]**par·cel** /ˈpɑɚsəl/ *noun, pl* **-cels** [*count*]
1 : a section or area of land • Several 10-acre *parcels* (of land) are available. • a *parcel* of real estate
2 : a box or large envelope that is usually given, sent, or delivered to a person • The *parcel* [=(*chiefly US*) *package*] was shipped today. • She was carrying several brown paper *parcels*. [=boxes wrapped in heavy brown paper] — see picture at MAIL
part and parcel of see [1]PART

[2]**parcel** *verb* **parcels;** *US* **par·celed** *or Brit* **par·celled;** *US* **par·cel·ing** *or Brit* **par·cel·ling**
parcel off [*phrasal verb*] ***parcel (something) off or parcel off (something)*** : to divide (something, such as land) into separate, smaller parts especially in order to sell it • The property was eventually *parceled off* and sold in pieces.
parcel out [*phrasal verb*] ***parcel (something) out or parcel out (something)*** : to divide or share (something) among different people, groups, etc. • The money was *parceled out* [=*distributed*] to local charities. • They plan to *parcel* the tickets *out* in a lottery. • We need to stop *parceling out* the blame for this problem and start working on a solution.
parcel up [*phrasal verb*] ***parcel (something) up or parcel up (something)*** *Brit* : to wrap (something) or put (something) into a box in order to mail it to someone • The paintings have all been *parcelled up*.

parcel bomb *noun, pl* **~ bombs** [*count*] *Brit* : LETTER BOMB

parcel post *noun* [*noncount*] : a service that people in the U.S. can use to mail packages • Do you want to send this (by) *parcel post*?

parch /ˈpɑɚʧ/ *verb* **parch·es; parched; parch·ing** [+ *obj*] *formal* : to make (something) very dry • The hot desert sun had *parched* the land.

parched /ˈpɑɚʧt/ *adj* [*more ~; most ~*]
1 : very dry especially because of hot weather and no rain • *parched* land
2 *somewhat informal* : very thirsty • Could I have some water? I'm *parched*.

Par·chee·si /pɑɚˈʧiːzi/ *trademark* — used for a game in which players try to be the first to move all of their pieces all the way around a board

parch·ment /ˈpɑɚʧmənt/ *noun, pl* **-ments**
1 a [*noncount*] : paper made from the skin of a sheep or goat • Ancient people wrote on *parchment*. **b** [*count*] : a document written on parchment • a *parchment* dating back to ancient times
2 [*noncount*] : strong and thick paper; *especially, chiefly US* : strong, tough paper that is used by cooks • Line the pan with a sheet of *parchment*. — called also *parchment paper*

[1]**par·don** /ˈpɑɚdn/ *verb* **par·dons; par·doned; par·don·ing** [+ *obj*]
1 : to officially say that someone who is guilty of a crime will be allowed to go free and will not be punished • *pardon* a criminal
2 : to say that someone should not be blamed for thinking, doing, or saying something — usually used as *(be) pardoned for* • Voters can/should/could *be pardoned for* thinking this election would be different.
3 : to officially say that a person, country, etc., does not have to pay (a debt) • The group wants the debt of the world's poorest countries to be *pardoned*. [=*forgiven*]
4 — used to be polite in asking questions or saying things that could be considered rude • *Pardon* my ignorance, but what does "naiveté" mean? • *Pardon* my asking, but is that your natural hair color? • *Pardon* my saying so, but you look tired today. = You look tired today, if you'll *pardon* my saying so. • *Pardon* me for asking, but how old are you?
pardon me **1** — used as a polite way of starting to say something when you are interrupting someone, trying to get someone's attention, or disagreeing with someone • *Pardon me*, but can I speak to you privately for a moment? • *Pardon me*, (but) you dropped this envelope. • *Pardon me*, but I believe you've made a mistake. **2** *also* ***pardon*** — used as a polite apology for a minor fault or offense (such as laughing, coughing, or bumping into someone) • Oh, *pardon me*. I didn't see you standing there. • *Pardon*—I didn't mean to bump you. **3** *also* ***pardon*** — used as a polite way of asking someone to repeat something spoken • *Pardon me*? I didn't hear you. • "Are you ready to go?" "*Pardon*?" "I asked if you were ready to go."
pardon my French *informal + humorous* — used to apologize for using offensive language • Everything he said is bullshit. *Pardon my French*.
pardon the expression see EXPRESSION

[2]**pardon** *noun, pl* **-dons** [*count*]
1 : an act of officially saying that someone who was judged to be guilty of a crime will be allowed to go free and will not be punished • The governor granted him a *pardon*. • She received a ***presidential/royal pardon***. [=a pardon from a president or a king or queen]
2 *formal* : forgiveness for something • He asked/begged my *pardon* for taking so much of my time. — see also *beg your pardon* at BEG

par·don·able /ˈpɑɚdṇəbəl/ *adj* [*more ~; most ~*] : able to be forgiven : not so bad that it cannot be forgiven or excused • It was a *pardonable* mistake/error.

pare /ˈpeɚ/ *verb* **pares; pared; par·ing** [+ *obj*]
1 : to carefully cut off the outside or the ends of (something) • *pare* an apple • She was *paring* [=(more commonly) *trimming*] her fingernails. — often + *away* • *Pare away* any brown spots on the avocado. — see also PARING KNIFE
2 : to make (something) smaller : to reduce (something) in size, amount, or number • The company has to find a way to *pare* expenses. • The budget has been ***pared to the bone***. [=reduced as much as possible] — often + *down* • The book was *pared down* to 200 pages. • The company has to *pare down* the office staff. • The *pared-down* staff was forced to work longer hours.

par·ent /ˈperənt/ *noun, pl* **-ents** [*count*]
1 a : a person who is a father or mother : a person who has a child • My *parents* live in New York. • They recently became *parents*. = They're new *parents*. • The form must be signed by a *parent* or guardian of the child. • A few of us are ***single parents***. [=parents who live with a child or children and no husband, wife, or partner] • my ***adoptive parents*** [=the people who adopted me] • The organization helps people who were

adopted find their ***birth/biological parents***. [=their natural parents] • They'd like to become ***foster parents***. [=people who volunteer to care for a child who is not their biological child] — compare GRANDPARENT, STEPPARENT **b :** an animal or plant that produces a young animal or plant • The *parent* brings food to the chicks. • the *parent* bird • The new plant will have characteristics of both *parent* plants.

2 a : something out of which another thing has developed — usually used before another noun • Latin is the *parent* language of several languages, including Italian, Spanish, and French. **b :** a company or organization that owns and controls a smaller company or organization • the hospital's corporate *parent* = the corporate *parent* of the hospital — often used before another noun • a *parent* bank/company/corporation/firm

– pa•ren•tal /pəˈrɛntl/ *adj, always used before a noun* • *parental* responsibility/consent

par•ent•age /ˈperəntɪʤ/ *noun [noncount] formal* **:** a person's parents — used especially to describe the origins or social status of someone's parents • She was born in Japan, but (is) of African *parentage*. [=*descent*] • a person of noble/wealthy *parentage* [=*birth, ancestry*]

pa•ren•the•sis /pəˈrɛnθəsəs/ *noun, pl* **-the•ses** /-θəˌsiːz/ *[count]* **:** one of a pair of marks ( ) that are used around a word, phrase, sentence, number, etc. — usually plural • The plant's common name is followed by its Latin name *in parentheses*. — called also *(Brit) bracket*

par•en•thet•i•cal /ˌperənˈθɛtɪkəl/ *adj* **:** included or added to give information which is not directly related to the main subject that is being discussed • *parenthetical* remarks/references • He explained the process thoroughly, including *parenthetical* comments about his own experiences with it. • a *parenthetical* note [=a note that is shown in parentheses]

– par•en•thet•i•cal•ly /ˌperənˈθɛtɪkli/ *adv* • The author notes *parenthetically* that these meetings were not public.

par•ent•hood /ˈperəntˌhʊd/ *noun [noncount]* **:** the state of being a mother or a father • the joys of *parenthood*

par•ent•ing /ˈperəntɪŋ/ *noun [noncount]* **:** the process of taking care of children until they are old enough to take care of themselves **:** the things that parents do to raise a child • They share the responsibilities of *parenting*. — often used before another noun • *parenting* skills/issues

parent–in–law *noun, pl* **parents–in–law** *[count]* **:** a parent of your husband or wife **:** IN-LAW

Parent–Teacher Association *noun, pl* ~ **-tions** *[count]* **:** a local organization of teachers and parents who work together to improve schools and to help students — abbr. *PTA*

Parent–Teacher Organization *noun, pl* ~ **-tions** *[count] US* **:** PARENT-TEACHER ASSOCIATION — abbr. *PTO*

par ex•cel•lence /ˈpɑrˌɛksəˈlɑːns, *Brit* ˌpɑːrˈɛksəˌlɑːns/ *adj, always used after a noun, formal* **:** better than all others • a chef *par excellence* [=an excellent chef]

par•fait /pɑəˈfeɪt/ *noun, pl* **-faits** *[count, noncount] US* **:** a cold dessert made usually of layers of ice cream, fruit, and syrup with whipped cream on top

pa•ri•ah /pəˈrajə/ *noun, pl* **-ahs** *[count]* **:** a person who is hated and rejected by other people • He's a talented player but his angry outbursts have made him a *pariah* in the sport of baseball. • a social *pariah*

paring knife *noun, pl* ~ **knives** *[count]* **:** a small knife with a short blade used especially for cutting fruit and vegetables

par•ings /ˈperɪŋz/ *noun [plural]* **:** thin pieces that have been cut from something • fingernail/cheese *parings*

par•ish /ˈperɪʃ/ *noun, pl* **-ish•es** *[count]*

1 a : an area that has its own local church and priest or minister • The *parish* will be getting a new priest soon. **b :** the group of people who go to the church in a particular area • The *parish* has grown significantly in the last three years.

2 a *US* **:** an area in Louisiana that is like a county **b** *Brit* **:** a small area that has its own local government

– parish *adj, always used before a noun* • a *parish* priest/minister • the *parish* church • He was elected to the *parish* council.

pa•rish•io•ner /pəˈrɪʃənɚ/ *noun, pl* **-ners** *[count]* **:** a person who goes to a particular local church **:** a person who belongs to a parish • the *parishioners* of First Baptist Church

parish–pump *adj, always used before a noun, Brit, old-fashioned + disapproving* **:** only important or interesting to people in a small area • All the articles are about *parish-pump* politics.

par•i•ty /ˈperəti/ *noun [noncount] formal* **:** the state of being equal • the struggle for gender/racial/social *parity* [=(more commonly) *equality*] • Women have fought for *parity* with men in the workplace. • The two currencies are approaching *parity* for the first time in decades. [=they are coming close to having the same value] • Currently, there is ***rough parity*** in the number of students entering and graduating from the school system. [=the number of students entering and graduating from the school system is about the same]

¹park /ˈpɑək/ *noun, pl* **parks**

1 *[count]* **a :** a piece of public land in or near a city that is kept free of houses and other buildings and can be used for pleasure and exercise • We went for a walk in the *park*. • New York City's Central *Park* • He was sitting on a *park* bench. [=a bench in a park] • the city's *park/parks* department **b :** a large area of public land kept in its natural state to protect plants and animals • The nation's *parks* are a popular destination for tourists. • Yellowstone (National) *Park* • Many *parks* have campsites. — see also NATIONAL PARK, STATE PARK

2 *[count] sports* **a :** a field or stadium where a sport (especially baseball) is played • a baseball *park* • He hit the ball out of the *park*. • Fenway *Park* in Boston — see also BALLPARK **b** *Brit* **:** a soccer or rugby field • a rugby game in Eden *Park* • She's the best player ***on the park***. [=in the game]

3 *[count]* **:** an area that is designed for a specified use • a new ***office park*** [=an area with several buildings that are full of offices; an area for office buildings] • the town's only ***mobile home park*** [=an area for people to live in mobile homes] — see also AMUSEMENT PARK, CAR PARK, INDUSTRIAL PARK, THEME PARK, TRAILER PARK, WATER PARK

4 *[noncount] US* **:** a condition in which the gears of a vehicle are in a position that prevents the vehicle from moving • The car must be in *park* before you can turn the engine off. • She pulled over and ***put the car in park***.

walk in the park see ²WALK

²park *verb* **parks; parked; park•ing**

1 a : to leave a car, truck, motorcycle, etc., in a particular place *[no obj]* I couldn't find anywhere to *park*. • I *parked* on the street. *[+ obj]* I *parked* the car on the street. • My car is *parked* behind your truck. = I'm *parked* behind your truck. • a *parked* car — see also DOUBLE-PARK, PARALLEL PARK **b** *[no obj] of a car, truck, etc.* **:** to be left in a particular place by a driver • Cars are only allowed to *park* on the right side of this street. • The bus *parked* behind the museum.

2 *[+ obj] informal* **a :** to temporarily leave (something) in a particular place • *Park* your bags in the hallway. **b :** to leave (something) in a particular place for a long time or what seems like a long time • She *parked* the money in a savings account and forgot about it for several years.

park yourself *informal* **:** to sit in a particular place especially for a long time • The kids *parked themselves* in front of the TV. • *Park yourself* in that chair and wait.

par•ka /ˈpɑəkə/ *noun, pl* **-kas** *[count]* **:** a very warm jacket with a hood — see color picture on page C15

park and ride *noun [noncount]* **:** a system in which you drive to a place where you can leave your car and get on a bus or train that will take you the rest of the way to where you are going

parking *noun [noncount]*

1 : the act of leaving a car, truck, motorcycle, etc., in a particular place • There is no *parking* in this area. [=you are not allowed to park in this area] • It's always difficult to find a ***parking place/space/spot*** [=a place to park your car, truck, etc.] in this neighborhood.

2 : space in which vehicles can be parked • The restaurant has very little *parking*, so we'll have to park on the street. • They have plenty of free *parking*.

parking brake *noun, pl* ~ **brakes** *[count] US* **:** a piece of equipment in a car, truck, etc., that prevents the vehicle from moving when it is parked or stops the vehicle if the main brakes fail

parking garage *noun, pl* ~ **garages** *[count] US* **:** a building in which people usually pay to park their cars, trucks, etc. — called also *(Brit) car park*

parking light *noun, pl* ~ **lights** *[count] US* **:** either one of two small lights that are on the front of a vehicle next to the headlights — called also *(Brit) sidelight*; see picture at CAR

parking lot *noun, pl* ~ **lots** *[count] US* **:** an area outside a building for parking cars, trucks, etc. • the school/hospital/mall *parking lot* — called also *(Brit) car park*

parking meter *noun, pl* ~ **-ters** *[count]* **:** a machine near a parking place on the side of a road that you put coins into in order to legally park there — see picture at STREET

parking ticket *noun, pl* ~ **-ets** [*count*] : a piece of paper that officially tells you that you have parked your car, truck, etc., illegally or for too long and will have to pay a fine

Par·kin·son's disease /ˈpɑɚkənsənz-/ *noun* [*noncount*] *medical* : a disease that affects the nervous system and causes people's muscles to become weak and their arms and legs to shake — called also *Parkinson's*

park–keeper *noun, pl* **-ers** [*count*] *Brit* : a person who takes care of a park

park·land /ˈpɑɚkˌlænd/ *noun, pl* **-lands** : land with trees, bushes, etc., that is or could be used as a park [*noncount*] an area of beautiful *parkland* [*count*] beautiful *parklands*

park ranger *noun, pl* ~ **-ers** [*count*] : RANGER 1b

park·way /ˈpɑɚkˌweɪ/ *noun, pl* **-ways** [*count*] *US* : a wide road with trees and grass along the sides and often in the middle

par·lance /ˈpɑɚləns/ *noun* [*noncount*] *formal* : language used by a particular group of people • In military *parlance*, "bug out" means "to retreat." [=for people in the military, "bug out" means "to retreat"] • The book introduced many readers to terms that are now ***in common parlance***. [=used by many people in ordinary conversation]

par·lay /ˈpɑɚˌleɪ, *Brit* ˈpɑːli/ *verb* **-lays; -layed; -lay·ing** [+ *obj*] *US* : to use or develop (something) to get something else that has greater value — + *into* • He hoped to *parlay* his basketball skills *into* a college scholarship. • She *parlayed* $5,000 and years of hard work *into* a multimillion-dollar company.

Do not confuse *parlay* with *parley*.

par·ley /ˈpɑɚli/ *verb* **-leys; -leyed; -ley·ing** [*no obj*] *old-fashioned* : to talk with an enemy or someone you disagree with especially in order to end a conflict — usually + *with* • The government refused to *parley with* the rebels.

Do not confuse *parley* with *parlay*.

– parley *noun, pl* **-leys** [*count*] *old-fashioned* • a secret *parley*

par·lia·ment /ˈpɑɚləmənt/ *noun, pl* **-ments**

1 a : the group of people who are responsible for making the laws in some kinds of government [*count*] The *parliament* has authority over the armed forces. • the *parliaments* of Russia and Canada = the Russian and Canadian *parliaments* [*noncount*] laws made by *parliament* **b *Parliament*** [*noncount*] : a particular parliament; *especially* : the parliament of the United Kingdom that includes the House of Commons and the House of Lords • The issue was debated in *Parliament*. • a member of *Parliament* — see also HUNG PARLIAMENT

2 [*count*] : the period of time during which a parliament is working • The law was passed in the present *parliament*.

par·lia·men·tar·i·an /ˌpɑɚləˌmɛnˈterijən/ *noun, pl* **-ans** [*count*] : a member of a parliament; *especially* : a member who knows a lot about the way things are done in a parliament

par·lia·men·ta·ry /ˌpɑɚləˈmɛntri/ *adj, always used before a noun* : relating to or including a parliament • a *parliamentary* democracy/government • *parliamentary* elections/candidates

par·lor (*US*) *or Brit* **par·lour** /ˈpɑɚlɚ/ *noun, pl* **-lors** [*count*]

1 : a store or business that sells a specified kind of food or service • an ice-cream *parlor* • a pizza *parlor* • a beauty/funeral/tattoo *parlor* — see also MASSAGE PARLOR

2 *old-fashioned* : a room in a house or apartment that is used for conversation or for spending time with guests • We sat in the ***front parlor*** [=a parlor in the front of a house/apartment] and had a nice visit.

parlor game (*US*) *or Brit* **parlour game** *noun, pl* ~ **games** [*count*] *somewhat old-fashioned* : a game (such as a board game, card game, or guessing game) that you play inside your home

par·lous /ˈpɑɚləs/ *adj, formal* : full of danger or risk : PERILOUS • The company is in a *parlous* financial situation. • He talked about the *parlous* state of the country.

Par·me·san /ˈpɑɚməˌzɑːn, *Brit* ˌpɑːməˈzæn/ *noun* [*noncount*] : a hard Italian cheese — called also *Parmesan cheese*

pa·ro·chi·al /pəˈroʊkijəl/ *adj*

1 *always used before a noun* : of or relating to a church parish and the area around it • our pastor and other *parochial* leaders

2 [*more* ~; *most* ~] *formal* + *usually disapproving* : limited to only the things that affect your local area • voters worried about their own *parochial* concerns • a small town with a *parochial* [=*narrow-minded, small-minded*] point of view

– pa·ro·chi·al·ism /pəˈroʊkijəˌlɪzəm/ *noun* [*noncount*] • the *parochialism* of their views

parochial school *noun, pl* ~ **schools** [*count*] *US* : a private school that is run by a church parish

par·o·dist /ˈperədɪst/ *noun, pl* **-ists** [*count*] : a person who writes parodies

[1]**par·o·dy** /ˈperədi/ *noun, pl* **-dies**

1 : a piece of writing, music, etc., that imitates the style of someone or something else in an amusing way [*count*] a political *parody* • He has a talent for writing *parodies*. — often + *of* • The book was written as a *parody of* Henry James's style. • a *parody of* a soap opera [*noncount*] a writer with a talent for *parody*

2 [*count*] *disapproving* : a bad or unfair example of something — often + *of* • The trial was a *parody of* justice. [=the trial was very unfair]

[2]**parody** *verb* **-dies; -died; -dy·ing** [+ *obj*] : to imitate (someone or something) in an amusing way • It was easy to *parody* the book's fancy language. • She *parodied* her brother's poetry.

[1]**pa·role** /pəˈroʊl/ *noun* [*noncount*] : permission given to a prisoner to leave prison before the end of a sentence usually as a reward for behaving well • The prisoner will be eligible for *parole* after three years. • He was given a life sentence without (the possibility of) *parole*. • He was granted/denied *parole*. • a *parole* hearing • She robbed a bank while out ***on parole***. • The prisoner was released *on parole*.

[2]**parole** *verb* **-roles; -roled; -rol·ing** [+ *obj*] : to release (a prisoner) on parole — usually used as *(be) paroled* • He *was paroled* after three years.

pa·rol·ee /pəˌroʊˈliː/ *noun, pl* **-ees** [*count*] : a prisoner who is released on parole

par·ox·ysm /ˈperəkˌsɪzəm/ *noun, pl* **-ysms** [*count*]

1 *medical* : a sudden attack or increase of symptoms of a disease (such as pain, coughing, shaking, etc.) that often occurs again and again — usually + *of* • *paroxysms of* pain/coughing

2 *formal* : a sudden strong feeling or expression of emotion that cannot be controlled • a *paroxysm of* rage • He went into *paroxysms* of laughter.

par·quet /ˈpɑɚˌkeɪ/ *noun* [*noncount*] : a surface (such as a floor) made of small pieces of wood that fit together to form a pattern — often used before another noun • a *parquet* floor

[1]**par·rot** /ˈperət/ *noun, pl* **-rots** [*count*] : a bright-colored tropical bird that has a curved bill and the ability to imitate speech — see color picture on page C9

[2]**parrot** *verb* **-rots; -rot·ed; -rot·ing** [+ *obj*] *disapproving* : to repeat (something, such as words, ideas, etc.) without understanding the meaning • Some of the students were just *parroting* what the teacher said.

parrot–fashion *adv, Brit* : without understanding what something means • The student recited the speech *parrot-fashion* and could not answer any questions about it.

par·ry /ˈperi/ *verb* **-ries; -ried; -ry·ing**

1 : to defend yourself by turning or pushing aside (a punch, a weapon, etc.) [+ *obj*] *parry* [=*deflect*] a blow • He *parried* the thrust of his opponent's sword. [*no obj*] He *parried* and then threw a punch.

2 [+ *obj*] : to avoid giving a direct answer to (a question) by being skillful or clever • She cleverly *parried* the reporters' questions.

– parry *noun, pl* **-ries** [*count*]

parse /ˈpɑɚs, *Brit* ˈpɑːz/ *verb* **pars·es; parsed; pars·ing** [+ *obj*]

1 *grammar* : to divide (a sentence) into grammatical parts and identify the parts and their relations to each other • Students were asked to *parse* the sentence.

2 : to study (something) by looking at its parts closely : ANALYZE • Economists *parsed* the census data.

par·si·mo·ni·ous /ˌpɑɚsəˈmounijəs/ *adj* [*more* ~; *most* ~] *formal* : very unwilling to spend money • The company is *parsimonious* [=*stingy*] with employee benefits. • a *parsimonious* [=*thrifty*] shopper

– par·si·mo·ni·ous·ly *adv*

par·si·mo·ny /ˈpɑɚsəˌmouni/ *noun* [*noncount*] *formal* : the quality of being very unwilling to spend money • The charity was surprised by the *parsimony* of some larger corporations.

pars·ley /ˈpɑɚsli/ *noun* [*noncount*] : a plant with small green

P

leaves that are used to season or decorate food — see color picture on page C6

pars•nip /ˈpɑɚsnəp/ *noun, pl* **-nips** [*count, noncount*] : a vegetable that is the long white root of a plant related to the carrot — see color picture on page C4

par•son /ˈpɑɚsn̩/ *noun, pl* **-sons** [*count*] *old-fashioned*
1 : a minister who is in charge of a parish
2 : a member of the clergy and especially a Protestant pastor

par•son•age /ˈpɑɚsənɪʤ/ *noun, pl* **-ag•es** [*count*] : the house in which a parson lives

[1]part /ˈpɑɚt/ *noun, pl* **parts**
1 [*count*] **a** : one of the pieces, sections, qualities, etc., that make or form something • The entire book is good, but the best *part* is the ending. • I don't remember him saying that. I must have missed that *part.* — often + *of* • This is the best *part of* the movie. • He's from the western *part of* the state. • The disease is increasingly common in this *part of* the world. • the early/latter *part of* this century • Music is an important/major/essential *part of* my life. It's very much a *part of* me. • It's the *part of* the job he enjoys the least. • a natural *part of* growing up • A *part of* me wants to stay, but another *part of* me wants to go. • That was not a *part of* our original agreement. • She left out that *part of* the story. • Some *parts of* your speech were excellent. = Your speech was excellent ***in parts.*** • Babies spend ***a good part of*** [=a large amount of] the day sleeping. — see also BEAUTY PART, PART OF SPEECH, PRINCIPAL PARTS **b** : one of the pieces that are put together to form a machine • The mechanic had to order the *part* from the manufacturer. • an auto *parts* warehouse • The *parts* of a radio include the speaker, dials, and antenna. • Do you have any spare/replacement *parts* for this model of car? • the moving *parts* of the machine **c** : one of the pieces or areas of the body of a plant or animal • *parts* of the human body • My favorite *part* of the chicken is the drumstick. • body *parts* • a diagram labeling the different *parts* of the flower — see also PRIVATE PARTS
2 [*noncount*] : some but not all of something — + *of* • We spent *part of* the day at the beach. • The river forms *part of* the border between the two countries. • The numbers tell only *part of* the story. • Instead of being *part of* the solution, they became *part of* the problem. • Sure it's messy, but that's *part of* the fun/appeal. • Homelessness is *part of* a larger problem facing this country. • The program is *part of* a larger effort to help the world's children.
3 : a person who is a member of a group or who is included in an activity — usually + *of* [*noncount*] Come join us and be *part of* a winning team. • She wanted to be *part of* the action. [*count*] They considered her (to be) a *part of* the family. • He was an important *part of* the team's win. [=he did a lot to help the team to win]
4 [*count*] : one of the sections into which a book, play, television show, etc., is divided • *Part* one of the miniseries airs next Monday. • The first and second *parts* of Goethe's *Faust* are divided into acts. • Shakespeare's *Henry VI, Parts* I, II, and III
5 [*count*] : the character played by an actor in a play, movie, etc. • He got/landed the *part* of Romeo in his high school play. • They said she was wrong for the *part* because she was too tall. = They said she was too tall to play the *part.* • He has a small/bit *part* in the movie. — often used figuratively • In his cowboy hat and boots, he certainly ***looked the part*** [=he looked like a cowboy] • Now that he's rich he certainly ***acts the part*** [=behaves like a rich person] • If you want people at work to believe that you're a professional, you have to ***dress the part*** • I've ***played the part*** of (the) devoted wife and mother, and now I want to do something more with my life. • He was *playing the part* of (the) gracious host.
6 [*count*] : an influence in producing a result or causing something — usually + *in* • My father's *part in* my upbringing was minimal. [=my father was not very involved in my upbringing] • She talked about television's *part in* modern elections. • Did alcohol ***play a part in*** the car accident? = Did alcohol ***have a part in*** causing the accident? [=was alcohol involved in the accident?] • Your family's finances *play a* big/major/significant *part in* determining how much financial aid you will receive for college. • We all ***have a part to play in*** the future of this company. • Parents *have a* big/important/significant *part to play in* the habits of their children. • So far, she has ***had no part in*** planning the event. [=she has not been involved in planning the event] • He stated that politics ***played no part in*** his decision. • When her father became ill, she began to ***take an active part in*** running her family's farm. • They *took an active part in* the antiwar movement. — see also TAKE PART (below)
7 [*count*] : the notes that are sung by a particular singer or played on a particular instrument in a piece of music that is written for more than one voice or instrument • I'm usually a soprano, but I was told to sing the alto *part* for this song. • The song's flute *part* is especially beautiful. • singing in four-*part* harmony
8 ***parts*** [*plural*] *somewhat old-fashioned* : a general area with no exact limits or boundaries • I can tell from your accent that you're not from around ***these parts*** [=not from around here] • Tornadoes are pretty rare in *these parts.* • She graduated from high school and left for ***parts unknown*** [=a place that isn't known]
9 [*count*] *US* : the line where a person's hair is separated and combed to opposite sides of the head • a *part* down the middle of her head • a side *part* • He combs his hair back without a *part.* — called also (*Brit*) *parting*; see picture at HAIR
10 [*count*] : an amount that is equal to another amount • Mix one *part* sugar with two *parts* flour. • The movie is one *part* action and one *part* comedy. = The movie is equal *parts* action and comedy.

do your part : to do what you are responsible for doing or are able to do • I've *done my part*, and now it's time for him to do his. • Please *do your part* by donating what you can to the organization.

for someone's part : in someone's opinion • She doesn't trust him, but *for my part* [=as for me; in my opinion], I think he's a nice guy. • *For his part*, the Senator believes that the proposal will benefit American companies.

for the most part see [1]MOST

in good/great/large part : not entirely but mostly • The success of our company depends, *in good part*, on the condition of the economy. • I believe that their actions were motivated *in great part* [=*largely*] by a desire for revenge.

in no small part : to a great degree : largely or mostly • The team's success is due *in no small part* to the hard work of its players.

in part : to some extent : partially or partly • Thanks *in part* to her performance in that movie role, she became one of the most popular actresses in Hollywood. • The project failed *in part* because of a lack of funds. • The city's problems are due, at least *in part*, to its geographical location.

of parts : having many talents or skills • a man/woman *of* (many) *parts*

on someone's part or ***on the part of someone*** : by or from someone • It took a lot of hard work *on* everyone's *part* [=done by everyone] to finish the project on time. • It was a good effort *on the part of* all the students. [=all the students made a good effort] • There is a lot of sympathy for the accused woman *on the part of* the public. [=the public feels a lot of sympathy for her]

part and parcel of : a basic and necessary part of (something) • Stress was *part and parcel of* the job.

sum of its parts see [1]SUM

take part : to be involved in something : to participate in something • The event was a great success, and I would like to thank everyone who *took part.* • The entire family *takes part* in cleaning the house. • They refused to *take part* in the discussion. • He swore that he ***took no part*** [=was not involved] in the group's illegal activities. — see also [1]PART 6 (above)

take someone's part *chiefly Brit* : to show support for someone in an argument, disagreement, etc. • The public has *taken the accused woman's part* [=*taken her side, sided with her*] because of her young age.

take something in good part *Brit, old-fashioned* : to not become too angry or upset about something : to not object too much to something • I was nervous when I had to tell him that he was wrong, but fortunately he *took it in good part* and we stayed friends.

the best/better/greater part of something : more than half of something : most of something • It took us *the better part of* a week to finish the job. • We've been waiting for *the better part of* an hour. • They live here for *the greater part of* the year.

want no part of/in something : to refuse to be involved in something • She said that she didn't agree with what they were doing and *wanted no part of* it. • I *want no part of* this scheme. • He *wanted no part in* discussing the issue.

[2]part *verb* **parts; part•ed; part•ing**
1 : to separate into two or more parts that move away from each other [*no obj*] The crowd *parted* to let the president

through. • The rain stopped and the clouds *parted.* • The big red curtains *parted* to reveal a new car! [+ *obj*] The Bible tells the story of how God *parted* the Red Sea. • She closed her eyes and *parted* her lips. • Her lips were *parted.*

2 [+ *obj*] **:** to separate (the hair on a person's head) into two parts on each side of a line by using a comb • She *parts* her hair on the side. • His dark hair was *parted* down/in the middle.

3 *formal* **a** [*no obj*] **:** to leave each other • The two lovers *parted* at dawn. • Tomorrow we shall *part* and, I fear, never see each other again. **:** to go or move away *from* someone • She couldn't bear the thought of *parting from* her family. **b** [+ *obj*] **:** to cause (someone) to be separated *from* someone — usually used as *(be) parted* • She couldn't bear to *be parted from* her family.

4 [*no obj*] *somewhat formal* **:** to end a relationship • The band *parted* after 10 successful years of performing together. • We *parted* on friendly terms. • The couple *parted* [=*separated*] in the summer of 2005. — often + *from* • By that time, he had already *parted from* his first wife.

part company *formal* **1 :** to end a relationship • There are rumors that the football team and its coach have *parted company.* — often + *with* • I *parted company with* my business partners after a dispute about finances. **2 :** to leave each other • Much has happened since we *parted company.* • The two friends *parted company* in the parking lot and drove home separately. **3 :** to disagree with someone about something • The president and I *part company* on some important issues. — often + *with* • I don't believe in the death penalty, so I'm afraid I must *part company with* you there. [=I do not agree with you about that]

part ways *chiefly US* **1 :** to end a relationship • The band *parted ways* after releasing their third album. — often + *with* • She has since *parted ways with* the organization. **2 :** to leave each other • We said our goodbyes and *parted ways.* **3 :** to disagree with someone about something • We *part ways* on that issue.

part with [*phrasal verb*] ***part with (something)*** **:** to give up possession or control of (something) • He hated to *part with* that old car. • *parting with* a large amount of money

³part *adv* **:** somewhat but not completely **:** to some extent or in some degree • The story is *part* science and *part* fiction. • She's *part* French and *part* Italian. [=some of her relatives or ancestors are from France and some are from Italy] • His statement is only *part* [=*partially, partly*] right. [=only part of his statement is right] • The Chimera is a monster in Greek mythology that is *part* lion, *part* goat, and *part* serpent.

⁴part *adj, always used before a noun* **:** not complete or total • The claim is a *part* truth—there is more to the story than they are telling you. • She's the executive chef and ***part owner*** of the restaurant. [=she and other people own the restaurant as partners] • (*Brit*) You can trade in your old car as ***part payment*** for a new one.

par·take /pɑɚˈteɪk/ *verb* **-takes; -took** /-ˈtʊk/; **-tak·en** /-ˈteɪkən/; **-tak·ing** [*no obj*] *formal*

1 a : to have a share or part of something along with others • There was food available, but he chose not to *partake.* [=he chose not to eat any of the food] — usually + *of* • Music lovers *partook of* the rich offerings of the music festival. • He had *partaken of* too much dinner and was now stuffed. **b :** to join with others *in* doing something **:** to take part *in* something • Let us all *partake in* [=(more commonly) join in] this celebration.

2 : to have some of the qualities *of* something • a story that *partakes of* the nature of poetry

– par·tak·er *noun, pl* **-ers** [*count*] • *partakers* of the feast • *partakers* in the ceremony

par·tial /ˈpɑɚʃəl/ *adj*

1 : not complete or total • These plants prefer full sun or *partial* shade. • The *partial* ban on immigration has been lifted. • His latest play was deemed only a *partial* success by the critics. • a *partial* eclipse of the sun • He wears a *partial* denture. • She suggested a *partial* solution to the problem.

2 [*more ~; most ~*] **:** tending to treat one person, group, or thing better than another • The competition's judges take great care not to seem *partial.* [=*biased*] • A referee must not be *partial* toward either team. — opposite IMPARTIAL

partial to **:** liking something or someone very much and usually more than other things or people • I like all the food here, but I'm particularly *partial to* the fried chicken. • She says she's *partial to* tall men with dark hair. • I'm not *partial to* red wine. [=I do not like red wine]

par·tial·i·ty /ˌpɑɚʃiˈæləti/ *noun, formal*

1 [*noncount*] **:** an unfair tendency to treat one person, group, or thing better than another • Judges must not show *partiality* [=*bias*] during the competition.

2 [*singular*] **:** a tendency to like something or someone — often + *to* • I don't understand his *partiality to* modern art. [=I don't understand why he likes modern art] — often + *for* • She has a *partiality for* tall men with dark hair.

par·tial·ly /ˈpɑɚʃəli/ *adv* **:** somewhat but not completely **:** to some extent or in some degree **:** PARTLY • I guess I'm *partially* responsible for what happened. • He only *partially* explained his reason for leaving. • The building was *partially* destroyed in the fire.

par·tic·i·pant /pɑɚˈtɪsəpənt/ *noun, pl* **-pants** [*count*] **:** a person who is involved in an activity or event **:** a person who participates in an activity or event — often + *in* • All the *participants in* the cooking contest received a free cookbook. • They were active *participants in* the project.

par·tic·i·pate /pɑɚˈtɪsəˌpeɪt/ *verb* **-pates; -pat·ed; -pat·ing** [*no obj*] **:** to be involved with others in doing something **:** to take part in an activity or event with others • Most people joined the game, but a few chose not to *participate.* — often + *in* • If you don't *participate in* the planning of the trip, you can't complain about what we plan. • He never *participated in* sports in high school. • *Participating* employees [=employees who have chosen to join] can contribute up to 14 percent of their wages to the retirement plan. • Look for these specials at a *participating* store [=a store that participates in an advertised sale or promotion] near you.

– par·tic·i·pa·tion /pɑɚˌtɪsəˈpeɪʃən/ *noun* [*noncount*] • He noted a lack of *participation* by the people who would benefit the most. • The show had a lot of audience *participation.* — often + *in* • He is known for his active *participation in* community affairs. • the *participation* of women *in* politics • *Participation in* the retirement plan is voluntary.

par·tic·i·pa·to·ry /pɑɚˈtɪsəpəˌtori, *Brit* pɑˌtɪsəˈpeɪtri/ *adj, formal* **:** providing the opportunity for people to be involved in deciding how something is done • *participatory* democracy/management

par·ti·ci·ple /ˈpɑɚtəˌsɪpəl/ *noun, pl* **-ciples** [*count*] *grammar* **:** a form of a verb that is used to indicate a past or present action and that can also be used like an adjective • In the phrases "the finishing touches" and "the finished product," "finishing" and "finished" are *participles* formed from the verb "finish." — see also PAST PARTICIPLE, PRESENT PARTICIPLE

– par·ti·cip·i·al /ˌpɑɚtəˈsɪpijəl/ *adj* • a *participial* phrase

par·ti·cle /ˈpɑɚtɪkəl/ *noun, pl* **-ticles** [*count*]

1 a : a very small piece of something • fine *particles* of sand • food *particles* **b :** a very small amount of something • There is ***not a particle of*** evidence to support their claim. • There is *not a particle of* truth in what he said.

2 *physics* **:** any one of the very small parts of matter (such as a molecule, atom, or electron) • subatomic *particles*

3 *grammar* **:** an adverb or preposition that when combined with a verb creates a phrasal verb • The phrasal verb "look up" consists of the verb "look" and the adverbial *particle* "up."

par·ti·cle·board /ˈpɑɚtɪkəlˌboɚd/ *noun* [*noncount*] **:** a type of board made by gluing together very small pieces of wood — called also *chipboard;* compare FIBERBOARD

¹par·tic·u·lar /pɚˈtɪkjəlɚ/ *adj*

1 — used to indicate that one specific person or thing is being referred to and no others • Is there one *particular* [=*specific*] brand you prefer? • I asked for that *particular* seat because it's the one my father used to sit in. • Some lawyers are limited to one *particular* area of law. • Their names are listed in no *particular* order. • He quit his job for no *particular* reason. • I have nothing/something *particular* planned for this evening. • Are you looking for anything *particular*? [=(more commonly) *in particular*]

2 *always used before a noun* **:** special or more than usual • The computer program will be of *particular* interest to teachers. • Pay *particular* attention to the poet's choice of words.

3 [*more ~; most ~*] **:** having very definite opinions about what is good or acceptable • You're more *particular* than I am when it comes to (choosing) a restaurant. • Our teacher is very *particular* when it comes to punctuation. — usually + *about* • Grandma is very *particular* [=*choosy, picky*] *about* the kind of olive oil she uses. • She's *particular about* her clothes.

4 [*more ~; most ~*] *somewhat formal* **:** including many details • He gave us a very *particular* account of his trip. • a more *particular* description

²**particular** *noun, pl* **-lars** [*count*] : a specific detail or piece of information • They wanted to know the facts down to every *particular*. — usually plural • Just give us a brief report; you can fill us in on the *particulars* later. • (*Brit*) The teacher asked the students to write down their *particulars* [=personal facts, such as their names and addresses] on a sheet of paper. • (*US, law*) The court ordered the state to file a ***bill of particulars*** [=a detailed list of the charges or claims made in a legal case]

in particular **1** : special or unusual • "What are you doing?" "Nothing *in particular*." • Are you looking for anything *in particular*? [=*specific*] • I have something *in particular* that I would like to discuss. • I made the cookies for ***no one in particular.*** [=I did not make the cookies for any particular person] **2** : PARTICULARLY — used to indicate someone or something that deserves special mention • The whole family, but Mom *in particular* [=*especially*], loves to ski. • Heavy rains, in the central valley *in particular*, have driven up the price of lettuce. • He's a brilliant pianist known for his recordings of Bach, *in particular* his recording of the Goldberg Variations.

par·tic·u·lar·i·ty /pəˌtɪkjəˈlerəti/ *noun, pl* **-ties** *formal*

1 [*count*] : a small detail • The actors studied all of the *particularities* of the script.

2 : a quality or feature that makes a person or thing different from others [*count*] the special *particularities* of the South • The *particularities* of the job take some time to get used to. [*noncount*] The critic's review stressed the *particularity* [=*uniqueness*] of each work of art in the collection.

3 [*noncount*] : careful attention to detail • She described the scene with great *particularity*.

par·tic·u·lar·ize *also Brit* **par·tic·u·lar·ise** /pəˈtɪkjələˌraɪz/ *verb* **-iz·es; -ized; -iz·ing** *formal* : to give specific details or examples of (something) [+ *obj*] My lawyer advised me to *particularize* all my complaints against my landlord. [*no obj*] He said he had been treated rudely, then went on to *particularize*.

par·tic·u·lar·ly /pəˈtɪkjələli/ *adv*

1 : more than usually : VERY, EXTREMELY • It has been a *particularly* [=*especially*] dry summer. • Pay *particularly* close attention to the second paragraph.

2 — used to indicate someone or something that deserves special mention • I liked all the food, *particularly* [=*especially*] the dessert. • He's good at all his subjects and he's *particularly* good at math. • I am *particularly* pleased that you agreed to take the job. • The tools were useful, *particularly* the knife. [=the tools were useful, and the knife was the most useful of all; the knife, in particular, was useful]

not particularly : only a little : not very or not very much • He is *not particularly* good at math. • I did *not particularly* like the movie. [=I only liked the movie a little] • "Did you like the movie?" "No, *not particularly*."

¹**part·ing** /ˈpɑɚtɪŋ/ *noun, pl* **-ings**

1 : a time or occurrence when people leave each other [*count*] I feared the morning, for I knew that our *parting* would be difficult. • a bitter/sad/tearful *parting* [*noncount*] On *parting*, he took my hand and promised to return. • "Good-night, good-night! *Parting* is such sweet sorrow . . ." —Shakespeare, *Romeo and Juliet*

2 [*count*] : the act of separating something into two or more parts • the *parting* of the Red Sea

3 [*count*] *Brit* : the line where a person's hair is separated : PART • a middle/side *parting*

parting of the ways : a point at which two people or groups decide to end a relationship • She and her political party came to a *parting of the ways* over the war. • These disagreements eventually led to the *parting of the ways* between the two organizations.

²**parting** *adj, always used before a noun* : given, taken, or done when leaving someone • a *parting* gift/kiss/glance • His *parting* words to me were "Be patient." • As her ***parting shot,*** she said that the other candidate simply did not understand the needs of the city's citizens.

¹**par·ti·san** /ˈpɑɚtəzən, *Brit* ˌpɑːtəˈzæn/ *noun, pl* **-sans** [*count*]

1 : a person who strongly supports a particular leader, group, or cause • a *partisan* [=*supporter*] of affirmative action • political *partisans* who only see one side of the problem

2 : a member of a military group that fights against soldiers who have taken control of its country

— **par·ti·san·ship** /ˈpɑɚtəzənˌʃɪp, *Brit* ˌpɑːtəˈzænʃɪp/ *noun* [*noncount*] • The mayor was accused of *partisanship* in his decisions.

²**partisan** *adj* [*more* ~; *most* ~] *often disapproving* : strongly supporting one leader, group, or cause over another • *partisan* interests/loyalties/politics • She is highly/fiercely *partisan*. — compare BIPARTISAN, NONPARTISAN

¹**par·ti·tion** /pɑɚˈtɪʃən/ *noun, pl* **-tions**

1 [*count*] : a wall or screen that separates one area from another • A thin *partition* separates the two rooms in the cabin. • Folding *partitions* separate the different banquet halls in the building. • The bank teller sat behind a glass *partition*. — see picture at OFFICE

2 [*noncount*] : the division of a country into separate political units • the *partition* of former Yugoslavia • the *partition* of Korea into North and South Korea

²**partition** *verb* **-tions; -tioned; -tion·ing** [+ *obj*]

1 *formal* : to divide (something) into parts or shares • It was necessary to *partition* the work to be done to make the job easier to accomplish. • The room is *partitioned* into four sections.

2 : to divide (a country) into two or more parts having separate political status • After the war, the country was *partitioned*.

partition off [*phrasal verb*] ***partition (something) off*** *or* ***partition off (something)*** : to separate (an area or part of a room) by using a wall, screen, etc. • The storage area was *partitioned off* from the rest of the basement.

part·ly /ˈpɑɚtli/ *adv* : somewhat but not completely : to some extent or in some degree • We're both *partly* [=*partially*] to blame for what happened. • The project failed *partly* because of a lack of funds. • What you say is only *partly* true. • *partly* cloudy skies

¹**part·ner** /ˈpɑɚtnɚ/ *noun, pl* **-ners** [*count*]

1 : someone's husband or wife or the person someone has sexual relations with • His *partner*, his wife of 20 years, was shocked to hear about his accident. • marital/sexual/same-sex *partners* — see also DOMESTIC PARTNER

2 : one of two or more people, businesses, etc., that work together or do business together • They are *partners* in the real estate business. • law *partners* • Singapore's most important trading *partner* is Indonesia. • She was a senior *partner* at the Wall Street firm. — see also SILENT PARTNER, *partner in crime* at CRIME

3 : someone who participates in an activity or game with another person • We were each assigned a *partner* for the project. • a golf/tennis/dance *partner* — see also SPARRING PARTNER

²**partner** *verb* **-ners; -nered; -ner·ing** : to be or become a partner : to join *with* someone or something as a partner [*no obj*] The sporting goods store *partnered with* the newspaper to sponsor the road race. • She *partnered with* her sister, and they opened a candy shop together. [+ *obj*] The teacher *partnered* [=*paired*] me *with* Susan for the project. — usually used as *(be) partnered* • I *was partnered with* her in the tournament. [=we were partners in the tournament]

part·ner·ship /ˈpɑɚtnɚˌʃɪp/ *noun, pl* **-ships**

1 [*noncount*] : the state of being partners • two people joined ***in partnership*** • scientists working *in partnership* with each other • The company is developing a new car *in partnership* with leading auto manufacturers in Japan. • The two companies have gone/entered ***into partnership*** (with each other).

2 [*count*] : a relationship between partners • Their marriage is a *partnership* that has remained strong despite family illness. • The singing duo has maintained a successful *partnership* for 20 years. • a notable *partnership* between two experienced scientists in the field

3 [*count*] : a business that is owned by partners • He joined the *partnership* last year.

part of speech *noun, pl* **parts of speech** [*count*] : a class of words (such as adjectives, adverbs, nouns, verbs, etc.) that are identified according to the kinds of ideas they express and the way they work in a sentence • What *part of speech* is the word "lovely?"

par·tridge /ˈpɑɚtrɪʤ/ *noun, pl* **partridge** *or* **par·tridg·es** [*count*] : a brown bird with a round body and short tail that is often hunted for food and sport

part–time /ˈpɑɚtˈtaɪm/ *adj* : working or involving fewer hours than is considered normal or standard • *part-time* employees/students • a *part-time* job — compare FULL-TIME

— **part–time** *adv* • She works *part-time* at the office. • I go to college *part-time*. — **part–tim·er** /ˈpɑɚtˌtaɪmɚ/ *noun, pl*

-ers [*count*] ▪ Some of the employees are full-timers, but most of them are *part-timers*.

part·way /ˈpɑɚtˈweɪ/ *adv* **: at a distance or time that is between two points** ▪ I was *partway* to school when I realized I had forgotten my book. ▪ *Partway* down the mountain, he sprained his ankle. ▪ The team got a new coach *partway* through the season. ▪ They met up with some friends *partway* through the trip.

[1]**par·ty** /ˈpɑɚti/ *noun, pl* **-ties** [*count*]
1 : a social event in which entertainment, food, and drinks are provided ▪ We are having/giving/throwing a *party*. ▪ a high school dance *party* ▪ Were you invited to her *party*? ▪ Our New Year's Eve *party* was a huge success. ▪ a dinner *party* ▪ a birthday/costume/farewell *party* **— often used before another noun** ▪ a *party* hat/dress ▪ *party* decorations/games ▪ Get in the *party* spirit. ▪ I'm not in a *party* mood. **— see also** BLOCK PARTY, COCKTAIL PARTY, DRINKS PARTY, HEN PARTY, HOUSE PARTY, SLUMBER PARTY, STAG PARTY, TAILGATE PARTY, TEA PARTY
2 : an organization of people who have similar political beliefs and ideas and who work to have their members elected to positions in the government ▪ political *parties* with opposing agendas ▪ the Democratic/Republican *Party* ▪ The senator is loyal to his *party*. ▪ the ruling *party* [=the party that is in power] ▪ *party* members/policy ▪ the *party* leader
3 *law* **: a person who is involved in a legal case or contract** ▪ the two *parties* in the marriage contract ▪ the guilty *party* ▪ The *parties* in the lawsuit reached a settlement. **— see also** THIRD PARTY
4 *formal* **: someone or something that is involved in an activity** ▪ The principal of the school was urged to be a *party* [=*participant*] in the educational council. ▪ Interested *parties* are asked to contact their local representative. **— often + *to*** ▪ a *party to* the international coalition aimed at fighting hunger ▪ He refused to be a *party to* [=he refused to take part in] the gambling ring.
5 : a group of people who do something together ▪ a mountain-climbing *party* ▪ a rescue/search *party* **— often + *of*** ▪ a *party of* travelers from Great Britain ▪ He made a reservation at the restaurant for a *party of* four. [=for a group of four people] ▪ A *party of* teenagers is in charge of the neighborhood cleanup.
the life (and soul) of the party see [1]LIFE

[2]**party** *verb* **-ties; -tied; -ty·ing** [*no obj*] *informal* **: to have a party or be involved in a party : to spend enjoyable time eating, drinking, dancing, etc., with a group of people** ▪ He spent the weekend *partying* with his friends. ▪ We *partied* all night.
– partying *noun* [*noncount*] ▪ His parents told him to stop his *partying* and start studying more.

party animal *noun, pl* **~ -mals** [*count*] *informal* **: a person who enjoys going to parties and drinking a lot of alcohol and behaving in a loud and wild way**

par·ty·er /ˈpɑɚtijɚ/ *noun, pl* **-ers** [*count*]
1 : a person who goes to a party
2 *informal* **: a person who enjoys going to parties** ▪ He was a big *partyer* in college.

party favor *noun, pl* **~ -vors** [*count*] *US* **: a small gift that is given to people at a party — usually plural** ▪ All the children received *party favors*.

par·ty·go·er /ˈpɑɚtiˌgowɚ/ *noun, pl* **-ers** [*count*] **: a person who goes to a party**

party line *noun, pl* **~ lines** [*count*] **: the official policy or opinion of a political party or other organization that members are expected to support** ▪ Congress ***voted along party lines*** [=members of each party voted in the expected way] on the new education bill.

party politics *noun* [*plural*] *often disapproving* **: political activities, decisions, etc., that relate to or support a particular political party** ▪ *Party politics* played a large role in determining who would be chosen for the position. ▪ They shouldn't allow their votes to be influenced by *party politics*.

party poop·er /-ˈpuːpɚ/ *noun, pl* **~ -ers** [*count*] *chiefly US, informal* **: a person who spoils the fun for other people** ▪ Don't be such a *party pooper*!

par value *noun, pl* **~ -ues** [*count*] **:** PAR 2

par·ve·nu /ˈpɑɚvəˌnuː, *Brit* ˈpɑːvəˌnjuː/ *noun, pl* **-nus** [*count*] *formal + disapproving* **: a person from usually a low social position who has recently or suddenly become wealthy, powerful, or successful but who is not accepted by other wealthy, powerful, and successful people**

pash·mi·na /pəʃˈmiːnə/ *noun, pl* **-nas**
1 [*noncount*] **: a kind of fine, soft wool from Asia**
2 [*count*] **: a long piece of clothing made from pashmina and worn around a woman's neck**

[1]**pass** /ˈpæs, *Brit* ˈpɑːs/ *verb* **pass·es; passed; pass·ing**
1 a : to move past someone or something [*no obj*] The boat was too tall to *pass* beneath/under the bridge. ▪ A flock of geese were *passing* overhead. ▪ Stand here and don't let anyone *pass*. [=move past you] **— often + *by*** ▪ They *pass by* the library on their way to school. ▪ I was just *passing by* and thought I'd stop and say hello. [+ *obj*] They *pass* the library every morning on their way to school. ▪ The ships *passed* each other in the night. ▪ We *passed* each other in the hallway without looking up. **— often + *by*** ▪ She was hoping he would stop and talk to her, but he *passed* her *by*. **b : to move past someone or something that is moving more slowly in the same direction** [*no obj*] (*US*) "Is it safe to *pass*?" [=(*Brit*) *overtake*] "No, there's a car coming in the other lane." [+ *obj*] She *passed* two other runners just before the finish line. ▪ He *passed* the slower cars on the highway.
2 *always followed by an adverb or preposition* **a** [*no obj*] **: to move or go into or through a particular place** ▪ The drug *passes* quickly into the bloodstream. ▪ In a solar eclipse, the moon *passes* between the sun and the Earth. ▪ The airplane *passed* out of sight. **— often + *through*** ▪ Fear and panic *passed through* the crowd. ▪ A river *passes through* the middle of the city. ▪ Millions of tourists *pass through* the museum every year. ▪ The paper *passes through* the fax machine and comes out the other end. ▪ The bullet *passed through* his shoulder. ▪ We *passed through* Texas on our way to Mexico. ▪ We're just ***passing through***. [=staying here for a very short time] **b** [+ *obj*] **: to cause (something) to move or go in a specified way** ▪ *Pass* the end of the string through the loop. ▪ He *passed* the rope around the pole.
3 [+ *obj*] **: to give (something) to someone using your hands** ▪ She *passed* the baby back to his mother. ▪ Would you please *pass* the salt? ▪ *Pass* [=*hand*] me the butter, please. ▪ They started *passing* around pictures of their trip. ▪ Take one sheet and *pass* the rest down/on/along. [=take one sheet and give the rest to the next person] ▪ Can you *pass* that screwdriver over to me?
4 *sports* **: to throw, hit, or kick a ball or puck to a teammate** [+ *obj*] *Pass* me the ball! = *Pass* the ball to me! [*no obj*] She *passed* to her teammate who then scored a goal.
5 [+ *obj*] **a : to cause someone to have or be affected by (something that you have had or been affected by)** ▪ The disease was *passed* from mother to child. = She *passed* the disease to her child. **— often + *on*** ▪ She contracted the disease and *passed* it *on* to her child. ▪ Gas prices have risen, forcing companies to *pass* the cost *on* to the consumer. ▪ We lowered our costs and are now able to *pass on* the savings to our customers. **— sometimes + *along*** ▪ We're *passing* the savings *along* to our customers. **b : to give (information) to another person — often + *on*** ▪ Doctors need to *pass* this information *on* to their patients. ▪ Everyone's invited to the party. ***Pass it on***! [=tell people that everyone is invited] **— often + *along*** ▪ They quickly *passed* the word *along* that the meeting was postponed. ▪ He told me about it, and now I'm *passing* it *along* to you.
6 [*no obj*] **a : to go from one person to another person** ▪ The rumor quickly *passed* [=*spread*] from person to person. ▪ The book *passed* from hand to hand. **b : to be given to someone especially according to a law, rule, etc.** ▪ The throne *passed* to the king's son. ▪ Ownership *passes* to the buyer upon payment in full. ▪ After her death, the house ***passed into the hands of*** her granddaughter. [=her granddaughter became the owner of the house]
7 *of time* **a** [*no obj*] **: to go by** ▪ Several months *passed* before I received a reply. ▪ He became sleepy as the time *passed*. ▪ The days *pass* quickly when you're on vacation. ▪ Another day *passed* without any news about the whereabouts of their missing son. **b** [+ *obj*] **: to let (time or a period of time) go by especially while you are doing something enjoyable** ▪ He *passes* [=*spends*] his days reading and taking walks around the neighborhood. ▪ They *passed* the evening playing cards. ▪ We played games to ***pass the time*** on the bus. ▪ I walked over to my neighbor's house to ***pass the time of day***. [=to have a friendly and informal conversation]
8 [*no obj*] **a : to happen or take place** ▪ The meeting *passed* without incident. ▪ He hoped that his mistake would ***pass unnoticed***. [=not be noticed by anyone] **— often + *between*** ▪ A meaningful glance *passed between* them. [=they glanced at each other in a meaningful way] ▪ It's hard to believe that they're still friends after everything that's *passed between* them. **b : to end or go away** ▪ She couldn't let the moment

P

pass (away) without saying something. ▪ This crisis will soon *pass*. [=will soon be over] ▪ A storm had just *passed*. ▪ They waited until it was clear that the danger had *passed*. ▪ They were happy once, but that time has *passed*. [=that time is over] ▪ The era of the traveling salesman has ***passed into history***. [=traveling salesmen no longer exist]
9 [*no obj*] **:** to be done, said, etc., without producing a response ▪ I disagreed with what he said, but I let it *pass*. [=I did not say anything in response to his remark] ▪ She let his remark *pass* without comment.
10 [*no obj*] **a :** to not take, accept, or use something that is offered to you ▪ Thanks for the offer, but I'll *pass*. — often + *on* ▪ He *passed on* the cake. [=he did not eat any cake] ▪ I think I'll *pass on* going with you. **b :** to decide not to do something at a particular point in a game (such as a card game) when it is your turn ▪ "I bid three of hearts." "I *pass*."
11 a : to complete (a test, class, etc.) successfully [+ *obj*] He failed his driver's test the first time he took it, but he *passed* it the second time. ▪ I almost didn't *pass* my French class this semester. [*no obj*] "How did you do on the test?" "I *passed*!" **b** [+ *obj*] **:** to decide that (someone) has passed an examination or course of study ▪ The teacher said she couldn't *pass* me because I failed all of my tests.
12 a [+ *obj*] **:** to officially approve (a law, bill, etc.) ▪ Congress *passed* a law banning the sale of automatic rifles. ▪ The measure was *passed* by both the House and the Senate. ▪ We've been trying to get this legislation *passed* for several months now. **b** *chiefly US* **:** to become approved by (a legislature) [+ *obj*] The measure *passed* both the House and the Senate. ▪ The bill *passed* the House but was defeated/rejected by the Senate. [*no obj*] The proposal *passed* (into law). ▪ The bill failed to *pass* in the Senate.
13 [+ *obj*] *formal* **:** to say or state (something) especially in an official way ▪ Before ***passing sentence*** [=announcing the punishment], the judge commented on the seriousness of the crime. ▪ The court is now ready to ***pass judgment***. ▪ It would be premature to ***pass judgment on*** [=to state an opinion on] his place in history. ▪ Don't *pass judgment on* me [=don't criticize me] until you know all the facts.
14 [+ *obj*] **:** to go beyond (a number or amount) — usually used with *mark* ▪ It's an extremely successful movie that has just *passed* [=*exceeded, surpassed*] the $100 million *mark*. [=it has earned more than $100 million] ▪ I've *passed* the half-century *mark*. [=I am over 50 years old]
15 [*no obj*] **:** to change from one state or form to another ▪ The water *passes* from a liquid to a gas. ▪ *passing* through the different stages of human development
16 [*no obj*] **:** to be good enough **:** to be adequate ▪ The work isn't perfect, but it ***will pass***. [=*will do*]
17 [+ *obj*] **:** to illegally use (checks, bills, etc., with no real value) as money ▪ They were charged with *passing* bad checks. ▪ He was trying to *pass* counterfeit money.
18 [+ *obj*] **:** to have (something) come out from your body ▪ He had been *passing* blood in his urine. [=blood had been appearing in his urine] ▪ *pass* a kidney stone — see also *pass gas* at [1]GAS, *pass water* at [1]WATER
19 [*no obj*] **:** to die — used as a polite way to avoid saying the word "die" ▪ I'm sorry, but your grandfather has *passed*. — see also PASS AWAY, PASS ON (below)
come to pass see [1]COME
pass as [*phrasal verb*] **1** ***pass as (someone or something)*** **:** to cause people to believe that you are (someone or something that you are not) ▪ He thought that growing a mustache would help him *pass as* an adult. ▪ Your mom could *pass as* your sister! **2** ***pass as (something)*** **:** to be accepted or regarded as (something) ▪ the ancient practices that once *passed as* [=*passed for*] science
pass away [*phrasal verb*] **:** to die — used as a polite way to avoid saying the word "die" ▪ Her father *passed away*.
pass by [*phrasal verb*] ***pass (someone) by*** **:** to happen without being noticed or acted upon by (someone) ▪ Don't let this opportunity *pass* (you) *by*! ▪ I realized that I was letting life *pass* me *by*. — see also [1]PASS 1a (above)
pass down [*phrasal verb*] ***pass (something) down*** *or* ***pass down (something)*** **:** to give (something) to a younger person especially within the same family ▪ She will *pass down* her diamond ring to her niece. ▪ It's a family recipe *passed down* [=*handed down*] from my great-grandmother. ▪ The painting is a family heirloom that has been *passed down* through the generations.
pass for [*phrasal verb*] ***pass for (something)*** **:** to be accepted or regarded as (something) ▪ I can't believe the garbage that's *passing for* [=*passing as*] art these days. ▪ the tasteless soup that was supposed to *pass for* our dinner ▪ What *passes for* entertainment around here?
pass in [*phrasal verb*] ***pass (something) in*** *or* ***pass in (something)*** **:** to give (something) to a person who will review it ▪ Students should *pass* their papers *in* before they leave. ▪ He *passed in* [=*handed in*] his test.
pass muster see [2]MUSTER
pass off [*phrasal verb*] **1** ***pass (someone or something) off as (someone or something)*** *or* ***pass off (someone or something) as (someone or something)*** **:** to cause people to wrongly believe that someone or something is someone or something else ▪ amateurs *passing* themselves *off as* professionals ▪ He managed to *pass* himself *off as* the son of the famous actor. ▪ She *passed* the poem *off as* her own. ▪ They tried to *pass* it *off as* an original painting, but I suspected it was a copy. ▪ a cheap piece of glass *passed off as* a diamond **2** *Brit* **:** to happen or take place in a particular way ▪ The event *passed off* [=*went off*] with no major incidents. ▪ The evening *passed off* quietly.
pass on [*phrasal verb*] **:** to die — used as a polite way to avoid saying the word "die" ▪ Her parents have *passed on*.
pass out [*phrasal verb*] **1 :** to fall asleep or become unconscious ▪ They both *passed out* in front of the TV. ▪ I felt like I was going to *pass out* from exhaustion. ▪ He drank until he *passed out*. ▪ Someone was *passed out* on the floor. [=someone was lying unconscious on the floor] **2** ***pass out (something)*** *or* ***pass (something) out*** **:** to give (something) to several or many people ▪ They *passed out* [=*handed out, distributed*] copies of the newsletter. ▪ The teacher hasn't finished *passing out* the tests yet. ▪ She *passed out* flyers at the grocery store.
pass over [*phrasal verb*] **1** ***pass over (someone)*** *or* ***pass (someone) over*** **:** to not choose (someone) for a job, position, etc. ▪ When it came time to select the recipient of the award, the committee once again *passed* him *over*. [=the committee did not give him an award] ▪ The quarterback was *passed over* by other teams. — often + ***for*** ▪ She was *passed over for* another promotion. **2** ***pass over (something)*** *or* ***pass (something) over*** **:** to leave out (something) ▪ *passing over* [=*skipping*] the more boring parts of the book **:** to not discuss or deal with (something) ▪ Let's *pass over* the technical details and get straight to the parts that really interest you.
pass the buck see [1]BUCK
pass the hat see HAT
pass the torch see [1]TORCH
pass up [*phrasal verb*] ***pass up (something)*** *or* ***pass (something) up*** **:** to not take or accept (something that is offered to you) ▪ We couldn't afford to *pass up* her offer. ▪ Her offer was too good to *pass up*.
pass your lips **1** *of words* **:** to come out of your mouth **:** to be spoken ▪ The word "quit" has never *passed her lips*. [=she has never said the word "quit"] **2** *of food or drink* **:** to go into your mouth **:** to be eaten or drunk ▪ He refused to let alcohol *pass his lips*. [=he never drank alcohol]

[2]**pass** *noun, pl* **passes** [*count*]
1 *sports* **:** an act of throwing, hitting, or kicking a ball or puck to a teammate ▪ throwing/making/completing a perfect *pass* to a teammate ▪ a forward *pass* ▪ He caught a 20-yard *pass* from Johnson. ▪ The quarterback threw two touchdown *passes* in the first half of the game. — see also BOUNCE PASS, SCREEN PASS, SHOVEL PASS
2 : a card or ticket which shows that you are allowed to enter or leave a particular place or to ride a vehicle ▪ a one-day/weekend/season *pass* to the amusement park ▪ Each new student will be given a ***bus pass***. [=a ticket that permits you to ride the bus] ▪ We won ***backstage passes*** [=cards that allow you to go behind the stage] for tonight's concert. ▪ (*US*) You have to get a ***hall pass*** [=a card that shows you have permission to be out of class during class time] from the teacher. — see also BOARDING PASS
3 : a single, complete set of actions that are done together as a stage in a process ▪ The machine is able to print on both sides in a single *pass*. ▪ I did another *pass* to check for any spelling mistakes in my essay. ▪ The error was discovered in the next *pass* through the data.
4 : an act of moving over a place ▪ The planes made several *passes* over the area. ▪ The pilot spotted the missing group on a second *pass*.
5 *chiefly Brit* **:** a grade which shows that you have passed a test or class ▪ I got a *pass* in my History class. ▪ The required ***pass mark*** was 75 percent.
make a pass at **:** to do or say something that clearly shows

P

you want to begin a romantic or sexual relationship with (someone) • He *made a pass at* his wife's friend.
– compare ³PASS

³pass *noun, pl* **passes**
1 [*count*] **:** a low place in a mountain range where a road or path goes through • a mountain *pass* = a *pass* through the mountains
2 [*singular*] *somewhat formal* **:** a usually bad situation or condition • We had come to a very strange *pass.* • What brought them to such a sorry *pass*?
– compare ²PASS

pass•able /ˈpæsəbəl, *Brit* ˈpɑːsəbəl/ *adj*
1 : capable of being passed, crossed, or traveled on • The main road is *passable* but most others are still covered with snow. • The river is *passable* during the summer months.
2 : good enough **:** adequate or satisfactory • He did a *passable* job with the assignment. • She plays *passable* golf but prefers tennis. • His Italian is *passable.*
– pass•ably /ˈpæsəbli, *Brit* ˈpɑːsəbli/ *adv* • She speaks French *passably.* • He gets along *passably* (well) with his in-laws.

pas•sage /ˈpæsɪʤ/ *noun, pl* **-sag•es**
1 [*count*] **:** a long, narrow space that connects one place to another • They escaped through a secret underground *passage.* [=*passageway*] • (*Brit*) Her office is at the end of the *passage.* [=*hallway*]
2 [*count*] **:** a narrow space that people or things can move through • We squeezed through a narrow *passage* between the rocks. • Special ships clear *passages* through the ice. • The medicine makes breathing easier by opening nasal *passages.*
3 : an act of moving or passing from one place or state to another [*noncount*] They controlled the *passage* of goods through their territory. • He guaranteed us safe *passage.* [=he promised that we could safely travel through the area] • the *passage* of food through the digestive system • the *passage* of air into and out of the lungs • the *passage* from life to death • the *passage* of the seasons • He left after the *passage* of a few hours. • With ***the passage of time***, the number of children suffering with the disease has decreased dramatically. [*singular*] a child's *passage* into adulthood — see also RITE OF PASSAGE
4 [*count*] **a :** a usually short section of a book, poem, speech, etc. • He quoted a *passage* from the Bible. • The book's main theme is reflected in the following *passage.* • long descriptive *passages* **b :** a usually short section of a piece of music • complex musical *passages*
5 : an act of officially approving a bill, law, etc. [*noncount*] The *passage* [=*enactment*] of this law will save lives. • the *passage* of the 25th Amendment to the U.S. Constitution • government leaders who are determined to get *passage* of their bills [*singular*] a bill's *passage* into law
6 *old-fashioned* **a** [*count*] **:** a voyage or journey usually on a boat • a long ocean *passage* **b** [*noncount*] **:** the right to travel on a boat, airplane, etc. • They booked *passage* on a ship/train bound for Mexico.

pas•sage•way /ˈpæsɪʤˌweɪ/ *noun, pl* **-ways** [*count*] **:** a long, narrow space that connects one place to another • An underground *passageway* [=*corridor*] connects the two buildings.

pass•book /ˈpæsˌbʊk, *Brit* ˈpɑːsˌbʊk/ *noun, pl* **-books** [*count*] **:** BANKBOOK

pas•sé /pæˈseɪ, *Brit* ˈpɑːˌseɪ/ *adj* **:** no longer fashionable or popular • That style of music is now considered *passé.*

pas•sel /ˈpæsəl/ *noun, pl* **-sels** [*count*] *US, informal* **:** a large number or group of people or things — usually singular • A *passel* of children waited in the hall. • a *passel* of problems

pas•sen•ger /ˈpæsṇʤɚ/ *noun, pl* **-gers** [*count*]
1 : a person who is traveling from one place to another in a car, bus, train, ship, airplane, etc., and who is not driving or working on it • There were two *passengers* in the car in addition to the driver. — often used before another noun • a *passenger* train/ship [=a train/ship that carries passengers]
2 *Brit* **:** a person in a group who does not do as much work as others • There's no room for *passengers* on this project; everybody must do his share of the work.

passenger car *noun, pl* **~ cars** [*count*] *US* **:** a railroad car that carries passengers — called also (*Brit*) *carriage*

passenger seat *noun, pl* **~ seats** [*count*] **:** the front seat of a vehicle (such as a car) where a passenger sits

pass•er /ˈpæsɚ, *Brit* ˈpɑːsə/ *noun, pl* **-ers** [*count*] **:** someone or something that passes something • a *passer* of bad checks; *especially* **:** a player who passes a ball or puck to a teammate in a sport • a quarterback who is an excellent *passer*

pass•er•by /ˌpæsɚˈbaɪ, *Brit* ˌpɑːsəˈbaɪ/ *noun, pl* **pass•ers•by** /ˌpæsɚzˈbaɪ, *Brit* ˌpɑːsəzˈbaɪ/ [*count*] **:** a person who walks by something on a street or road • A *passerby* saw the accident and stopped to help. • *Passersby* were asked if they were registered to vote.

pass–fail /ˈpæsˈfeɪl, *Brit* ˈpɑːsˈfeɪl/ *adj, US* **:** using a system of grading in which the grades "pass" and "fail" are used instead of traditional grades like "A," "B," and "C" • a *pass-fail* class/test

¹pass•ing /ˈpæsɪŋ, *Brit* ˈpɑːsɪŋ/ *noun* [*noncount*]
1 : the act of moving toward and beyond something — usually + *of* • I could hear the *passing of* a distant train. [=I could hear a distant train passing]
2 — used to talk about the movement of time; usually + *of* • They celebrate the *passing of* each season. • She grew stronger with the *passing of* each year. • We lament the *passing of* an era. • Only ***the passing of time*** will help her deal with this tragedy.
3 *formal* **:** a person's death • After her husband's *passing*, she moved to a smaller house. • We all mourned his *passing.*
4 : the act of officially approving a bill, law, etc. • the *passing* [=*passage*] of the bill through Congress
in passing **:** in a brief way while discussing something else • She mentioned *in passing* that she was studying law. • The report notes the incident only *in passing.*

²passing *adj, always used before a noun*
1 : moving past someone or something • Someone called out from a *passing* car. • She sells flowers to *passing* motorists. • a *passing* ship/airplane/train
2 — used to talk about time that is going past • I love you more with each *passing* day. • with every *passing* year
3 : lasting for only a short time • Let's hope that these shoes are just a *passing* fad. • a *passing* phase in childhood
4 : done or made quickly • He made a few *passing* [=*cursory*] remarks about his work at the hospital. • We gave the restaurant a *passing* [=*quick*] glance before moving on. • She never gave the matter more than a *passing* thought. • Her assistants get only a *passing* mention at the end of the article.
5 : not very strong or thorough **:** SLIGHT • She has only a *passing* acquaintance with the subject. • I admit that I have only a *passing* interest in sports. • You can see a *passing* resemblance between him and his father.
6 : showing that you completed a test or class in an acceptable way • She completed the class with a ***passing grade/mark*** of 65 percent.
7 *sports* **:** relating to the skill of throwing, hitting, or kicking a ball or puck to a teammate • shooting and *passing* skills • The football team needs to improve its ***passing game.*** [=its ability to pass the ball]

passing lane *noun, pl* **~ lanes** [*count*] *US* **:** a part of a road or highway that drivers use to pass other vehicles

pas•sion /ˈpæʃən/ *noun, pl* **-sions**
1 a : a strong feeling of enthusiasm or excitement for something or about doing something [*count*] Everyone could see the *passion* in his approach to the work. • a controversy that has stirred *passions* in Congress [*noncount*] Her performance is full of *passion* and originality. • She spoke with *passion* about preserving the building. **b :** a strong feeling (such as anger) that causes you to act in a dangerous way [*noncount*] The crime was committed in a fit of *passion.* • a crime of *passion* [*count*] destructive *passions*
2 : a strong sexual or romantic feeling for someone [*noncount*] — often + *for* • He had never felt such *passion* [=*love, devotion*] *for* anyone but her. [*count*] sexual *passions*
3 [*count*] **a :** something that you enjoy or love doing very much • Music/golf/writing has always been his *passion.* **b :** a strong feeling of love *for* something • She developed a *passion for* opera. • a student with a *passion for* literature
4 ***the Passion*** **:** the sufferings of Jesus Christ between the night of the Last Supper and his death • *the Passion* of Christ
with a passion *informal* — used to say that you strongly dislike someone or something • I hate him *with a passion.*
– pas•sion•less /ˈpæʃənləs/ *adj* • a *passionless* marriage/performance/speech

pas•sion•ate /ˈpæʃənət/ *adj* [*more ~; most ~*]
1 : having, showing, or expressing strong emotions or beliefs • a *passionate* coach/performance • He gave a *passionate* speech on tax reform. • She has a *passionate* interest in animal rights. • She is *passionate* about art/music/sports. • We were moved by his *passionate* plea for forgiveness.
2 : expressing or relating to strong sexual or romantic feel-

P

ings • a long, *passionate* kiss • a *passionate* love affair
– **pas·sion·ate·ly** *adv* • She spoke *passionately* about animal rights. • They kissed *passionately*. • They were *passionately* opposed to the war.

pas·sion·flow·er /ˈpæʃən̩flawɚ/ *noun, pl* **-ers** [*count*] **:** a tall plant with large flowers and berries that are often eaten as fruit

passion fruit *noun, pl* **passion fruit** *or* **passion fruits** [*count*] **:** a small round fruit that has many seeds and is often used to make juice

passion play *or* **Passion play** *noun, pl* ~ **plays** [*count*] **:** a play about the suffering and death of Jesus Christ

pas·sive /ˈpæsɪv/ *adj*
1 [*more ~; most ~*] — used to describe someone who allows things to happen or who accepts what other people do or decide without trying to change anything • His *passive* acceptance of the decision surprised us. • In her books, women are often portrayed in *passive* roles.
2 *grammar* **a** *of a verb or voice* **:** showing that the subject of a sentence is acted on or affected by the verb • "Hits" in "She hits the ball" is active, while "hit" in "The ball was hit" is *passive*. • In "He was hit by the ball," "hit" is a *passive* verb. ✧ The ***passive voice*** is a way of writing or speaking that uses passive verbs. • The sentence "The house was destroyed by the tornado" is written in the *passive voice*. — compare ACTIVE **b :** containing a passive verb form • a *passive* sentence
– **pas·sive·ly** *adv* • He waited *passively* for me to decide.
– **pas·siv·i·ty** /pæˈsɪvəti/ *noun* [*noncount*] • She was angered by the *passivity* of her coworkers.

passive resistance *noun* [*noncount*] **:** a way of opposing the government without using violence especially by refusing to obey laws

passive smoking *noun* [*noncount*] **:** the breathing in of cigarette smoke from people who are smoking nearby

pass·key /ˈpæs̩kiː, *Brit* ˈpɑːs̩kiː/ *noun, pl* **-keys** [*count*] **:** a key that opens many locks **:** MASTER KEY

Pass·over /ˈpæs̩oʊvɚ, *Brit* ˈpɑːs̩əʊvə/ *noun* [*noncount*] **:** a Jewish holiday in March or April that celebrates the freeing of the Jews from slavery in Egypt

pass·port /ˈpæs̩poɚt, *Brit* ˈpɑːs̩pɔːt/ *noun, pl* **-ports** [*count*]
1 : an official document issued by the government of a country that identifies someone as a citizen of that country and that is usually necessary when entering or leaving a country
2 : something that allows a person to achieve something — + *to* • Education can be a *passport to* a successful future.

pass·word /ˈpæs̩wɚd, *Brit* ˈpɑːs̩wɜːd/ *noun, pl* **-words** [*count*]
1 : a secret word or phrase that a person must know before being given permission to enter a place
2 : a secret series of numbers or letters that allows you to use a computer system • You need to enter your *password* to check your e-mail.

P

[1]**past** /ˈpæst, *Brit* ˈpɑːst/ *adj*
1 *always used before a noun* **:** having existed in a time before the present **:** from, done, or used in an earlier time • The museum displays artifacts from *past* [=*earlier*] civilizations. • She was hired based on her ***past experience*** in sales.
2 *always used before a noun* — used to refer to a time that has gone by recently • He has worked there for the *past* few months. • I spoke with him this *past* [=*last*] weekend.
3 *always used before a noun* — used to say what someone or something was in the past • She is a *past* [=*former*] president of the club. • Several *past* employees were interviewed for the story. • *past* champions
4 — used to describe something that ended or was completed in the past • The time is *past* for apologies. • In winters *past*, we have had much more snow. = In *past* winters, we have had much more snow.

[2]**past** *prep*
1 : at the farther side of (something) **:** beyond (a particular place) • The office is two blocks *past* the intersection. • Turn left just *past* the stairs.
2 : up to and beyond (a person or place) • We drove *past* the house. • I must have walked right *past* her. • He looked *past* me to the next customer.
3 : later than (a time) • We need to leave by half *past* two. [=2:30] • It was *past* [=*after*, (*Brit*) *gone*] five o'clock by the time we got home. • It's *past* his bedtime. • The bill is ***past due***. [=it is late; it should have been paid before now]
4 a : older than (an age) • Now that he is *past* 60, he's thinking about retiring. **b :** beyond the age for (something) • She is *past* playing with dolls.
5 : beyond or no longer at (a particular point) • The milk is *past* its expiration date. • The daffodils are *past* blooming. • They tried marriage counseling, but they were already *past* the point of reconciling. • The house is a mess, but she is *past* caring. [=she doesn't care] • As a singer, he is ***past his prime***. [=he is no longer as good at singing as he once was]
I wouldn't put it past (someone) — used to say that you would not be surprised if someone did something bad • *I wouldn't put it past him* to lie. • I don't know if she ever cheated on an exam, but *I wouldn't put it past her*.
past it *Brit, informal* **:** too old to do something or to be useful • At the age of 45, he is *past it* as a football player.

[3]**past** *noun, pl* **pasts**
1 [*noncount*] **:** an earlier time **:** the time before the present • *Past*, present, and future are all linked together. — usually used with *the* • happy memories of *the past* • ***In the past***, there was a company luncheon every month. • Try not to worry about it anymore. It's *in the past*. • She wants to forget about *the past*. = She wants to ***put the past behind her***. • The disease is mostly ***a thing of the past***. [=something that no longer exists] • She had some financial problems, but that is ***all in the past***. [=she has no financial problems now] — see also ***live in the past*** at [1]LIVE
2 [*count*] **:** the events of a person's life, of a place, etc., before the present time — usually singular • Do you know anything about her *past*? • His *past* caught up with him when a former coworker recognized him. • He has an interesting *past*. • The city's *past* is full of interesting events. • We learned about the building's *past* as a textile factory.
3 ***the past*** *grammar* **:** PAST TENSE • *The past* of "walk" is "walked."
blast from the past see [1]BLAST

[4]**past** *adv* **:** to and beyond a certain point or time • He drove *past* [=*by*] slowly so we could look at the house. • A deer ran *past*. • Several weeks went *past* before we heard from her.

pas·ta /ˈpɑːstə, *Brit* ˈpæstə/ *noun, pl* **-tas :** a food made from a mixture of flour, water, and sometimes eggs that is formed into different shapes (such as thin strips, tubes, or shells) and usually boiled [*noncount*] They ordered *pasta* with meat sauce. • *pasta* salad/sauce [*count*] Breads and *pastas* are high in carbohydrates.

pasta

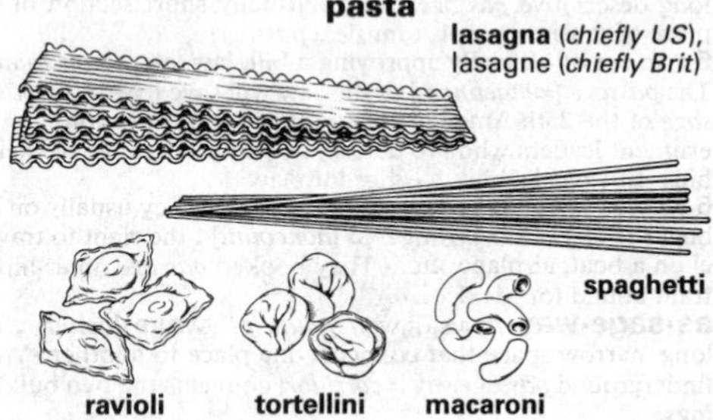

[1]**paste** /ˈpeɪst/ *noun*
1 [*singular*] **:** a soft, wet mixture of usually a powder and a liquid • Stir the flour and water to a *paste*. — see also TOOTHPASTE
2 [*noncount*] **:** a type of glue that is used to make things stick together • The children used *paste* and construction paper to make Mother's Day cards. • wallpaper *paste*
3 a [*noncount*] **:** a soft, smooth food that is made by grinding something (such as tomatoes or nuts) into very small pieces • canned tomato *paste* • a cake with an almond *paste* filling • anchovy/bean *paste* **b** [*singular*] **:** a type of dough made with flour and butter that is used in baking • Stir the ingredients to form a *paste*.
4 [*noncount*] **:** a type of glass that is used to make artificial gems • The necklace contains real gems and *paste*.

[2]**paste** *verb* **pastes; past·ed; past·ing** [+ *obj*]
1 : to stick (something) to or onto something by using paste • I *pasted* the edges of the paper together. • He cut out the newspaper article and *pasted* it into a scrapbook.
2 : to put (something cut or copied from a computer document) into another part of the document or into another document • After you select the text with your mouse, you can cut it and then *paste* it at the beginning of the paragraph.

• You can ***cut and paste*** the picture into your file. — see also CUT-AND-PASTE
– compare ³PASTE

³**paste** *verb* **pastes; pasted; pasting** [+ *obj*] *informal* : to beat or defeat (someone or something) very badly • They got *pasted* 10–0. — compare ²PASTE
– **past·ing** /ˈpeɪstɪŋ/ *noun, pl* **-ings** [*count*] — usually singular • They got/took a real *pasting* from the opposition.

pas·tel /pæˈstɛl, *Brit* ˈpæstl̩/ *noun, pl* **-tels**
1 a : a type of chalk made from a powdery substance that is used for drawing and comes in many different colors [*count*] — usually plural • She asked for a box of *pastels* for her birthday. • The artist works mostly ***in pastels***. [=the materials the artist uses are mostly pastels] [*noncount*] a drawing/portrait done in *pastel* = a *pastel* drawing/portrait **b :** a drawing that is done using pastels • She has a collection of *pastels*.
2 [*count*] **:** a pale or light color • She prefers a *pastel* like light yellow. • a *pastel* sweater • The room is painted in a *pastel* shade of blue. — usually plural • She wears a lot of *pastels*.

pas·teur·i·za·tion *also Brit* **pas·teur·i·sa·tion** /ˌpæstʃərəˈzeɪʃən, *Brit* ˌpɑːstʃəˌraɪˈzeɪʃən/ *noun* [*noncount*] **:** a process in which a liquid (such as milk or cream) is heated to a temperature that kills harmful germs and then cooled quickly
– **pas·teur·ize** *also Brit* **pas·teur·ise** /ˈpæstʃəˌraɪz, *Brit* ˈpɑːstʃəˌraɪz/ *verb* **-iz·es; -ized; -iz·ing** [+ *obj*] • Dairy products are often *pasteurized*. • *pasteurized* milk/cream

pas·tiche /pæˈstiːʃ/ *noun, pl* **-tich·es**
1 : something (such as a piece of writing, music, etc.) that imitates the style of someone or something else [*count*] His earlier building designs were *pastiches* based on classical forms. [*noncount*] With this work she goes beyond *pastiche*.
2 [*count*] **a :** a piece of writing, music, etc., that is made up of selections from different works • The research paper was essentially a *pastiche* made up of passages from different sources. **b :** a mixture of different things • The house is decorated in a *pastiche* of Asian styles.

pas·time /ˈpæsˌtaɪm, *Brit* ˈpɑːsˌtaɪm/ *noun, pl* **-times** [*count*] **:** an activity that you enjoy doing during your free time • Her favorite *pastime* [=*hobby*] is gardening. • Baseball has been a national *pastime* for years.

past master *noun, pl* ~ **-ters** [*count*] **:** a person who has done something many times before and has become very skilled at doing it **:** EXPERT • He's a *past master* at finding ways to get out of trouble. • They are *past masters* of the art of propaganda.

pas·tor /ˈpæstɚ, *Brit* ˈpɑːstə/ *noun, pl* **-tors** [*count*] **:** a minister or priest in charge of a church or parish • We have a new *pastor* at our church.

pas·to·ral /ˈpæstərəl, *Brit* ˈpɑːstərəl/ *adj*
1 : of or relating to the countryside or to the lives of people who live in the country • The house is situated in a charming *pastoral* setting. • Her favorite painting in the collection is a *pastoral* landscape. • *pastoral* scenes • a *pastoral* poem
2 : of or relating to the spiritual care or guidance of people who are members of a religious group • The bishop outlined the church's views in a *pastoral* letter. • *pastoral* counseling
3 : of or relating to the pastor of a church • *pastoral* duties/responsibilities

past participle *noun, pl* ~ **-ciples** [*count*] *grammar* **:** the form of the verb that is used with "have" in perfect tenses and with "be" in passive constructions • The verbs "thrown" in "the ball has been thrown" and "raised" in "many hands were raised" are *past participles*.

past perfect *noun*
the past perfect *grammar* **:** the form of the verb that is used in referring to an action that was completed by a particular time in the past ✧ The *past perfect* in English is formed by using *had* and the past participle of a verb, as in "She had visited there once before."

pas·tra·mi /pəˈstrɑːmi/ *noun* [*noncount*] **:** highly seasoned smoked beef that is usually eaten in sandwiches • hot *pastrami* on rye • He ordered a *pastrami* sandwich.

past·ry /ˈpeɪstri/ *noun, pl* **-ries**
1 [*noncount*] **:** dough that is used to make pies and other baked goods • He worked on the filling while I prepared the *pastry*. • a *pastry* shell — see also PUFF PASTRY
2 [*count*] **:** a small, baked food made from pastry • She had a *pastry* and coffee for breakfast. • a *pastry* shop — see also DANISH PASTRY

past tense *noun, pl* ~ **tenses** [*count*] *grammar* **:** a verb tense that is used to refer to the past

¹**pas·ture** /ˈpæstʃɚ, *Brit* ˈpɑːstʃə/ *noun, pl* **-tures :** a large area of land where animals feed on the grass [*count*] The horses were grazing in the *pasture*. [*noncount*] Most of their land is *pasture*. • She put/sent/turned the sheep ***out to pasture***. [=she brought the sheep to a pasture to eat the grass]
greener pastures or Brit pastures new **:** a new and better place or situation • He left for *greener pastures* after working here for 10 years. • She is looking for *pastures new*.
put (someone) out to pasture **:** to force (someone) to leave a job because of old age • I'm not ready to be *put out to pasture* yet. — sometimes used of things • I *put* my old computer *out to pasture*. [=got rid of my old computer]

²**pasture** *verb* **-tures; -tured; -tur·ing** [+ *obj*] **:** to put (an animal) in a pasture to feed on the grass • The horses are *pastured* on several acres of land.

pas·ture·land /ˈpæstʃɚˌlænd, *Brit* ˈpɑːstʃəˌlænd/ *noun, pl* **-lands** [*count, noncount*] **:** a large area of land where animals feed on the grass • The area between the mountains is mostly *pastureland*.

¹**pasty** /ˈpeɪsti/ *adj* **past·i·er; -est**
1 : resembling paste • The mixture has a *pasty* consistency.
2 : pale and unhealthy in appearance • She has a *pasty* complexion. • You look a little *pasty*. Are you feeling OK?

²**pas·ty** /ˈpæsti/ *noun, pl* **pas·ties** [*count*] *chiefly Brit* **:** a small pie that usually contains meat — see also CORNISH PASTY

pasty–faced /ˈpeɪstiˌfeɪst/ *adj, informal + often disapproving* **:** having a face that looks pale and unhealthy • I don't know what she sees in that *pasty-faced* loser.

PA system /ˌpiːˈeɪ-/ *noun, pl* ~ **-tems** [*count*] **:** ²PA 1

¹**pat** /ˈpæt/ *verb* **pats; pat·ted; pat·ting** [+ *obj*]
1 : to lightly touch (someone or something) with your hand usually several times in order to show affection or approval or to provide comfort • The child gently *patted* the dog's head. • He *patted* my knee and told me everything would be fine. — often + *on* • He *patted* me *on* my knee.
2 a : to flatten, smooth, or shape (something) by lightly pressing on it with your hand • He *patted* his hair down. • She *patted* the dough into a square. **b :** to lightly press (something) several times until it is dry • He *patted* the lettuce dry with a paper towel.
pat down [*phrasal verb*] ***pat (someone) down or pat down (someone)*** *US* **:** to move your hands over (someone) in order to search for something (such as a weapon) that may be hidden in clothing • The police *patted* the suspect *down* at the scene.
pat (someone) on the back **:** to praise or give credit to (someone) for doing good work • They deserve to be *patted on the back* for the way they've handled this problem. • You should *pat yourselves on the back* for doing such a great job.

²**pat** *noun, pl* **pats** [*count*]
1 : an act of lightly touching someone or something with your hand to show affection or approval • The teacher smiled and gave the boy a *pat* on the head. [=the teacher patted the boy on the head] • She gave the dog a quick *pat*.
2 : a small, flat, usually square piece of something (such as butter) • a *pat* of butter
a pat on the back *informal* **:** a show of praise or approval • You all deserve *a pat on the back* [=you all deserve to be praised] for making this possible. • You did a great job, so give yourself *a pat on the back*.

³**pat** *adv* **:** learned completely or perfectly • (*US*) She has her lines ***down pat***. • (*Brit*) He had his story ***off pat***.
stand pat *US* **:** to refuse to change your opinion or decision • Despite our objections, they are going to *stand pat* with their decision.

⁴**pat** *adj, disapproving* **:** said or done without any real thought or effort to be truthful or original • a *pat* response • The movie's *pat* ending was a disappointment. • His explanation was too *pat* to be believable.

pat–a–cake *variant spelling of* PATTY-CAKE

¹**patch** /ˈpætʃ/ *noun, pl* **patch·es** [*count*]
1 : a piece of material that is used to cover a hole in something or to provide extra protection to an area • His pants have *patches* on the knees. • a jacket with brown *patches* on the elbows • He put a *patch* over the hole in the tire tube.
2 a : a piece of material that is worn over your eye because of injury or for medical reasons **b :** a piece of material that contains a drug and that is worn on your skin to allow the drug to slowly enter your body over a long period of time • She wears a nicotine *patch* to help her quit smoking.

3 : a small spot or area that is different from the surrounding area • There were icy *patches* [=areas of ice] on the road. • Fog *patches* made driving difficult. • He is developing a bald *patch* on the back of his head. • The cat has black *patches* on its forehead and tail. • The chair's original paint is still visible ***in patches*** [=in spots] — often + *of* • I could see a *patch of* blue sky through the clouds. • There are *patches of* weeds all over the lawn.
4 : a small area of land where a particular fruit or vegetable grows • a pumpkin/strawberry *patch*
5 : a period of time • He's going through a bad/difficult/rough *patch* [=*spell*] right now.
6 *US* **:** a piece of cloth with words or pictures that is sewn on clothing as a decoration or as part of a uniform : BADGE
7 *computers* **:** a program that corrects or updates an existing program • a software *patch*
8 *Brit, informal* **:** an area that someone knows well, works or lives in, or comes from • He knows everything that happens in/on his *patch*.
be not a patch on *Brit, informal* **:** to be much less good, appealing, impressive, etc., than (someone or something) • The new chairman *isn't a patch on* his predecessor.

[2]patch *verb* **patches; patched; patch·ing** [+ *obj*]
1 : to cover a hole in (something) with a piece of material • She *patched* (the hole in) the blanket. • The fence needs to be *patched*. • He *patched* (up) the roof.
2 : to connect (a person, telephone call, etc.) to a communication system especially for a short period of time • They *patched* him into the conference call. — often + *through* • The operator *patched* the call/caller *through*.
patch together [*phrasal verb*] ***patch (something) together*** *or* ***patch together (something)*** **:** to put (something) together usually in a quick or careless way • She *patched* a meal *together* from what was in the cupboard. • They quickly *patched together* a new plan.
patch up [*phrasal verb*] **1** ***patch (something) up*** *or* ***patch up (something)*** **:** to deal with (a problem, disagreement, etc.) in order to improve or repair a relationship • They finally *patched up* [=*settled*] their differences. • He is going to try to ***patch things up*** with his girlfriend. **2** ***patch (something or someone) up*** *or* ***patch up (something or someone)*** **:** to give quick and usually temporary medical treatment to (someone or something) • The doctor *patched* him *up*, so he's going to be as good as new. • She *patched up* his wounded arm. — see also [2]PATCH 1 (above)

patch·ou·li /ˈpætʃəli, pəˈtʃuːli/ *noun* [*noncount*] **:** a perfume that is made from the oil of a southeast Asian plant

patch·work /ˈpætʃˌwɚk/ *noun*
1 [*singular*] **:** something that is made up of different things • The valley is a *patchwork* of family farms. • A *patchwork* of laws prevent the land from being developed. • a *patchwork* system of laws
2 [*noncount*] **:** pieces of cloth of different colors and shapes that are sewn together in a pattern • a *patchwork* quilt/bedspread

patchy /ˈpætʃi/ *adj* **patch·i·er; -est** [*also more* ~; *most* ~]
1 : having some parts that are good and some that are bad • The lawn is kind of *patchy* this year. • a *patchy* performance
2 : existing or seen in some areas but not others • *Patchy* fog made driving difficult.
3 : not thorough or complete enough to be useful • His knowledge of the language is *patchy*. • She has only a *patchy* understanding of his condition.

pate /ˈpeɪt/ *noun, pl* **pates** [*count*] *somewhat old-fashioned* **:** the top of a person's head • his bald *pate*

pâ·té *also* **pa·te** /pɑˈteɪ, *Brit* ˈpæteɪ/ *noun, pl* **-tés** *also* **-tes** [*count, noncount*] **:** liver or meat that has been chopped into very small pieces and that is usually spread on bread or crackers • liver *pâté*

pa·tel·la /pəˈtɛlə/ *noun, pl* **-lae** /-li/ *or* **-las** [*count*] *technical* **:** KNEECAP — see picture at HUMAN

[1]pat·ent *adj, always used before a noun*
1 /ˈpætn̩t, *Brit* ˈpeɪtn̩t/ **:** of, relating to, or concerned with patents • a *patent* law/lawyer • The company settled a *patent* dispute last year. • the licensing of *patent* rights • a *patent* application • They were sued for *patent* infringement. • a *patent* holder/owner
2 /ˈpeɪtn̩t/ *formal* **:** obvious or clear • His explanation turned out to be a *patent* lie. • She acted with *patent* disregard for the rules.
– pat·ent·ly *adv* • It is *patently* obvious that she is overqualified for the job.

[2]pat·ent /ˈpætn̩t, *Brit* ˈpeɪtn̩t/ *noun, pl* **-ents :** an official document that gives a person or company the right to be the only one that makes or sells a product for a certain period of time [*count*] — often + *on* • The company holds the/a *patent on* the product. • They want to ***take out a patent on*** [=obtain a patent for] the process. — often + *for* • She applied for *patents for* several of her inventions. [*noncount*] The product is protected by *patent*.

[3]pat·ent /ˈpætn̩t, *Brit* ˈpeɪtn̩t/ *verb* **-ents; -ent·ed; -ent·ing** [+ *obj*] **:** to get a patent for (something) • They *patented* their invention. • The product was *patented* by its inventor. • a *patented* process/drug

pat·ent leather /ˈpætn̩t-, *Brit* ˈpeɪtn̩t-/ *noun* [*noncount*] **:** a type of leather that has a hard and shiny surface • shoes made of *patent leather = patent-leather* shoes

pa·ter·fa·mil·i·as /ˌpætɚfəˈmɪlijəs, *Brit* ˌpeɪtəfəˈmɪliˌæs/ *noun, pl* **pa·tres·fa·mil·i·as** /ˌpeɪˌtriːzfəˈmɪlijəs, *Brit* ˌpeɪˌtriːzfəˈmɪliˌæs/ [*count*] *formal* **:** a man who is the head of a family

pa·ter·nal /pəˈtɚnl/ *adj*
1 : of or relating to a father • He did not neglect his *paternal* responsibilities after the divorce. • He offered them some *paternal* [=*fatherly*] advice.
2 *always used before a noun* **:** related through the father • his *paternal* grandparents [=the parents of his father] • a *paternal* aunt/uncle — compare MATERNAL
– pa·ter·nal·ly *adv* • He smiled at them *paternally*. • *paternally* inherited genes

pa·ter·nal·ism /pəˈtɚnəˌlɪzəm/ *noun* [*noncount*] *usually disapproving* **:** the attitude or actions of a person, organization, etc., that protects people and gives them what they need but does not give them any responsibility or freedom of choice
– pa·ter·nal·ist /pəˈtɚnəlɪst/ *or* **pa·ter·nal·is·tic** /pəˌtɚnəˈlɪstɪk/ *adj* • They resent the boss's *paternalistic* attitude.

[1]pa·ter·ni·ty /pəˈtɚnəti/ *noun* [*noncount*] *formal* **:** the state or fact of being the father of a particular child • He acknowledged *paternity* of her child. [=he admitted that he was the father of her child] • The child's *paternity* was in question. [=people questioned who the child's father was] — compare MATERNITY

[2]paternity *adj, always used before a noun*
1 : relating to the time when a father's child is born • *paternity* rights • Will he be able to take ***paternity leave***? [=time off to take care of a newborn child]
2 : done to prove that a man is the father of a particular child • a *paternity* suit • *paternity* (DNA) tests/testing

path /ˈpæθ, *Brit* ˈpɑːθ/ *noun, pl* **paths** /ˈpæðz, *Brit* ˈpɑːðz/ [*count*]
1 a : a track that is made by people or animals walking over the ground • We followed a winding *path* through the woods. • a steep mountain *path* • The *path* led down the hill. **b :** a track that is specially made for people to walk or ride on • a bike *path* • a paved *path* — see also BRIDLE PATH
2 : the area in front of someone or something that is moving • The car skidded into the *path* of an oncoming truck. • The fire destroyed everything in its *path*. • The cars moved aside to clear a *path* for the ambulance. • He tried to leave but one of the guards blocked his *path*. — see also FLIGHT PATH
3 : a way of living or proceeding that leads to something • the *path* to peace/success • They are heading down a dangerous *path* that could lead to war. • Their older children all became doctors, but their youngest son chose/followed a different (career) *path*. — see also *primrose path* at PRIMROSE
beat a path see [1]BEAT
cross paths see [2]CROSS
lead someone down/up the garden path see [1]LEAD
off the beaten path see BEATEN
take/follow the path of least resistance see RESISTANCE

pa·thet·ic /pəˈθɛtɪk/ *adj* [*more* ~; *most* ~]
1 : causing feelings of sadness and sympathy • I could hear her *pathetic* [=*pitiful*] cries for help. • The blind, old dog was a *pathetic* sight.
2 *informal + disapproving* **:** very bad, poor, weak, etc. • The team was pretty bad last year, but this year they're downright *pathetic*. • The story he told was a *pathetic* attempt to cover up a lie. • a *pathetic* excuse • His car is a *pathetic* piece of junk.
– pa·thet·i·cal·ly /pəˈθɛtɪkli/ *adv* • The child cried *pathetically*.

path·find·er /ˈpæθˌfaɪndɚ, *Brit* ˈpɑːθˌfaɪndə/ *noun, pl* **-ers** [*count*]
1 : a person who goes ahead of a group and finds the best way to travel through an unknown area
2 : a person or group that is the first to do something and that makes it possible for others to do the same thing **:** TRAILBLAZER ▪ a *pathfinder* of the fashion world ▪ technological *pathfinders*

path·o·gen /ˈpæθəʤən/ *noun, pl* **-gens** [*count*] *medical* **:** something (such as a type of bacteria or a virus) that causes disease ▪ a deadly *pathogen*
– path·o·gen·ic /ˌpæθəˈʤɛnɪk/ *adj* [*more* ~; *most* ~] ▪ *pathogenic* bacteria

path·o·log·i·cal /ˌpæθəˈlɑːʤɪkəl/ *also US* **path·o·log·ic** /ˌpæθəˈlɑːʤɪk/ *adj*
1 : extreme in a way that is not normal or that shows an illness or mental problem ▪ He is a *pathological* liar/gambler. ▪ She has a *pathological* fear of heights.
2 *medical* **:** relating to or caused by disease ▪ a *pathological* condition ▪ *pathological* changes in the body
3 *technical* **:** of or relating to the study of diseases **:** relating to pathology ▪ a *pathological* study ▪ *pathological* research/findings
– path·o·log·i·cal·ly /ˌpæθəˈlɑːʤɪkli/ *adv* ▪ a *pathologically* greedy person

pa·thol·o·gist /pəˈθɑːləʤɪst/ *noun, pl* **-gists** [*count*] *medical* **:** a doctor who specializes in pathology; *especially* **:** a doctor who examines bodies to find out the cause of death

pa·thol·o·gy /pəˈθɑːləʤi/ *noun* [*noncount*] *technical*
1 : the study of diseases and of the changes that they cause ▪ a professor of *pathology* ▪ plant *pathology*
2 : changes in a person, an animal, or a plant that are caused by disease ▪ the *pathology* of lung diseases

pa·thos /ˈpeɪˌθɑːs/ *noun* [*noncount*] *literary* **:** a quality that causes people to feel sympathy and sadness ▪ Our knowledge of his tragic end adds an element of *pathos* to the story of his early success.

path·way /ˈpæθˌweɪ, *Brit* ˈpɑːθˌweɪ/ *noun, pl* **-ways** [*count*] **:** PATH ▪ We walked along a winding *pathway*. ▪ a *pathway* to success ▪ (*technical*) a ***neural pathway*** [=a series of connected nerves along which electrical impulses travel in the body]

pa·tience /ˈpeɪʃəns/ *noun* [*noncount*]
1 : the quality of being patient: such as **a :** the ability to wait for a long time without becoming annoyed or upset ▪ I don't have the *patience* to wait in line for hours just to buy a ticket. ▪ Investors need to have *patience*. The economy will improve soon. ▪ "Aren't you finished yet?" "Have *patience* (with me). I'll be done soon." ▪ Those people have been waiting for hours, and they're starting to ***run out of patience***. = They're starting to ***lose patience***. ▪ After 10 long weeks, ***his patience was rewarded***. [=he got what he wanted after waiting 10 weeks for it] **b :** the ability to remain calm and not become annoyed when dealing with problems or with difficult people ▪ She treated her students with great *patience* and humor. ▪ I don't have (much) *patience* for that kind of behavior. = I have little/no *patience* for that kind of behavior. [=I am not willing to accept that kind of behavior] ▪ The team continues to play poorly, and many fans are starting to ***lose patience*** (with them). [=many fans are starting to become angry or upset about the team] ▪ She has ***the patience of a saint***. [=she is a very patient person] ▪ All these mistakes of yours are ***trying my patience***. [=I am starting to get upset because you have made so many mistakes] **c :** the ability to give attention to something for a long time without becoming bored or losing interest ▪ I don't have the *patience* to do crossword puzzles.
2 *Brit* **:** SOLITAIRE 1

¹pa·tient /ˈpeɪʃənt/ *adj* [*more* ~; *most* ~]
1 : able to remain calm and not become annoyed when waiting for a long time or when dealing with problems or difficult people ▪ I hate having to stand in long lines. I'm just not very *patient*. ▪ The teacher treated her students in a *patient* and understanding way. ▪ "Aren't you finished yet?" "Be *patient*. I'll be done soon." — often + *with* ▪ The teacher was *patient with* her students. — opposite IMPATIENT
2 : done in a careful way over a long period of time without hurrying ▪ Proofreading requires *patient* attention to detail. ▪ They put in years of *patient* labor/work on the project.
– pa·tient·ly *adv* ▪ He *patiently* waited for his turn. ▪ The teacher *patiently* explained the new material.

²patient *noun, pl* **-tients** [*count*] **:** a person who receives medical care or treatment ▪ Several *patients* were waiting to see the doctor/dentist. ▪ hospital/cancer *patients* — see also INPATIENT, OUTPATIENT

pa·ti·na /pəˈtiːnə/ *noun, pl* **-nas** [*count*]
1 : a thin usually green layer that forms naturally on the metals copper and bronze when they are exposed to the air for a long time
2 : a shiny or dark surface that forms naturally on something (such as wood or leather) that is used for a long time — usually singular ▪ the beautiful *patina* of this antique table
3 : a thin layer — usually singular ▪ The kitchen counter was covered with a *patina* of grease. — often used figuratively ▪ a criminal who has been given a *patina* of respectability by his friendship with well-known businessmen

pa·tio /ˈpætiˌoʊ/ *noun, pl* **-ti·os** [*count*] **:** a flat area of ground that is covered with a hard material (such as bricks or concrete), is usually behind a house, and is used for sitting and relaxing ▪ Let's have dinner on the *patio*. [=at a table on the patio] ▪ a ***patio door*** [=a sliding glass door that opens to a patio, deck, etc.]

pa·tis·se·rie /pəˈtɪsəri/ *noun, pl* **-ries**
1 [*count*] **:** a shop that sells cakes, cookies, etc. **:** a pastry shop
2 [*noncount*] **:** the things that are sold in a patisserie ▪ a delicious selection of French *patisserie*

pa·tois /ˈpæˌtwɑː/ *noun, pl* **pa·tois** /ˈpæˌtwɑːz/ [*count*] **:** a form of a language that is spoken only in a particular area and that is different from the main form of the same language ▪ the local *patois* [=*dialect*]

patresfamilias *plural of* PATERFAMILIAS

pa·tri·arch /ˈpeɪtriˌɑɚk/ *noun, pl* **-archs** [*count*]
1 : a man who controls a family, group, or government ▪ Our grandfather was the family's *patriarch*. ▪ The tribe's *patriarch* ruled for 20 years before his death. — compare MATRIARCH
2 : an official (called a bishop) of very high rank in the Orthodox Church
– pa·tri·ar·chal /ˌpeɪtriˈɑɚkəl/ *adj* ▪ *patriarchal* cultures/societies [=cultures/societies that are controlled by men]

pa·tri·ar·chy /ˈpeɪtriˌɑɚki/ *noun, pl* **-chies**
1 [*count*] **:** a family, group, or government controlled by a man or a group of men ▪ For 20 years, the country was ruled as a *patriarchy*. ▪ ancient *patriarchies*
2 [*noncount*] **:** a social system in which family members are related to each other through their fathers ▪ a region in which *patriarchy* is practiced — compare MATRIARCHY

pa·tri·cian /pəˈtrɪʃən/ *noun, pl* **-cians** [*count*] *formal* **:** a person who is a member of the highest social class **:** ARISTOCRAT
– patrician *adj* ▪ *patrician* families

pat·ri·cide /ˈpætrəˌsaɪd/ *noun, pl* **-cides** [*count*] **:** the act of murdering your own father — compare FRATRICIDE, MATRICIDE

pat·ri·mo·ny /ˈpætrəˌmoʊni/ *noun* [*singular*] *formal*
1 : property that you receive from your father when he dies **:** INHERITANCE
2 : things that are from the past **:** HERITAGE ▪ These historic landmarks are an important part of our cultural *patrimony*.

pa·tri·ot /ˈpeɪtrijət, *Brit* ˈpætrijət/ *noun, pl* **-ots** [*count*] **:** a person who loves and strongly supports or fights for his or her country ▪ He was a great *patriot* who devoted his life to serving his country.

pa·tri·ot·ic /ˌpeɪtriˈɑːtɪk, *Brit* ˌpætriˈɒtɪk/ *adj* [*more* ~; *most* ~] **:** having or showing great love and support for your country **:** having or showing patriotism ▪ *patriotic* songs/speeches ▪ A *patriotic* fervor swept the country.
– pa·tri·ot·i·cal·ly /ˌpeɪtriˈɑːtɪkli, *Brit* ˌpætriˈɒtɪkli/ *adv*

pa·tri·o·tism /ˈpeɪtrijəˌtɪzəm, *Brit* ˈpætrijəˌtɪzəm/ *noun* **:** love that people feel for their country [*noncount*] You may not agree with him politically, but no one can question his *patriotism*. [*singular*] They supported the war with a fierce *patriotism*. — compare NATIONALISM

¹pa·trol /pəˈtroʊl/ *noun, pl* **-trols**
1 : the act of walking or going around or through an area, building, etc., in order to make sure that it is safe **:** the act of patrolling an area [*count*] The guard makes a *patrol* of the building every hour. [*noncount*] Soldiers are ***on patrol*** along the border. ▪ a ***patrol officer***
2 [*count*] **:** a group of people, vehicles, etc., that go through an area to make sure that it is safe **:** a group that patrols an area ▪ Army *patrols* combed the area. ▪ the highway *patrol* ▪ the U.S. Border *Patrol* ▪ a ***foot patrol*** [=a group that patrols by walking] ▪ the ***ski patrol*** [=a group that patrols an area on skis]

P

[2]**patrol** *verb* **-trols; -trolled; -trol·ling** : to walk or go around or through (an area, building, etc.) especially in order to make sure that it is safe [+ *obj*] The squad had orders to *patrol* the area. ▪ The border is *patrolled* by the army. ▪ Police *patrol* the streets. [*no obj*] They *patrolled* on foot.
– **pa·trol·ler** *noun, pl* **-lers** [*count*]

patrol car *noun, pl* ~ **cars** [*count*] : a car that is used by the police to patrol an area

pa·trol·man /pəˈtroʊlmən/ *noun, pl* **-men** [*count*]
1 *US* : a police officer who patrols an area
2 *Brit* : a person who works for an organized group of car owners and who goes to help if one of the owners' cars stops working when it is being driven

patrol wagon *noun, pl* ~ **-ons** [*count*] *US* : a truck that is used by the police to carry prisoners — called also (*US, informal*) *paddy wagon*

pa·tron /ˈpeɪtrən/ *noun, pl* **-trons** [*count*]
1 : a person who gives money and support to an artist, organization, etc. ▪ She is a well-known *patron* of the arts. ▪ a *patron* of musicians/poets
2 *somewhat formal* : a person who buys the goods or uses the services of a business, library, etc. ▪ A number of *patrons* [=*customers*] were waiting for tables at the restaurant. ▪ library *patrons*

pa·tron·age /ˈpætrənɪʤ/ *noun* [*noncount*]
1 : money and support that is given to an artist, organization, etc. ▪ The college relied on the *patronage* of its wealthy graduates to expand its funds. ▪ They thanked her for her *patronage* of the new hospital.
2 *chiefly US, somewhat formal* : support that is given to a business, library, etc., by buying its goods or using its services ▪ The city should do more to encourage *patronage* of local businesses. ▪ The new library is expected to have heavy *patronage*. [=many people are expected to use the new library]
3 *often disapproving* : the power to give jobs or provide other help to people as a reward for their support ▪ a system of political *patronage*

pa·tron·ess /ˈpeɪtrənəs/ *noun, pl* **-ess·es** [*count*] : a woman who gives money and support to an artist, organization, etc. : a female patron ▪ a *patroness* of the arts

pa·tron·ize *also Brit* **pa·tron·ise** /ˈpeɪtrəˌnaɪz, *Brit* ˈpætrəˌnaɪz/ *verb* **-iz·es; -ized; -iz·ing**
1 [+ *obj*] : to give money or support to (someone or something) ▪ The family *patronizes* the arts/symphony.
2 *disapproving* : to talk to (someone) in a way that shows that you believe you are more intelligent or better than other people [+ *obj*] He hated being *patronized* and pitied by those who didn't believe his story. [*no obj*] "I'm sure you did your best even though you failed." "Please don't *patronize*."
3 [+ *obj*] *somewhat formal* : to be a frequent or regular customer or user of (a place) ▪ It's a popular department store *patronized* by many people. [=many people shop at the store] ▪ I *patronize* the library regularly.

patronizing *adj* [*more* ~; *most* ~] *disapproving* : showing that you believe you are more intelligent or better than other people ▪ She spoke to us in a *patronizing* [=*condescending*] tone. ▪ a *patronizing* smile
– **pa·tron·iz·ing·ly** *adv*

patron saint *noun, pl* ~ **saints** [*count*]
1 : a saint who is believed to protect a particular place or type of person ▪ St. David is the *patron saint* of Wales. ▪ St. Christopher is the *patron saint* of travelers.
2 : a person who is known or admired as a leader or example ▪ The success of her books has made her the *patron saint* of a new literary movement.

pat·sy /ˈpætsi/ *noun, pl* **-sies** [*count*] *chiefly US, informal* : a foolish person who is easily tricked or cheated ▪ They treated us like a bunch of *patsies*.

[1]**pat·ter** /ˈpætɚ/ *noun* [*singular*] : fast, continuous talk that is used to sell something or to entertain people ▪ sales *patter* ▪ The band leader kept up a running *patter* between songs. — compare [2]PATTER

[2]**patter** *noun* [*singular*] : a quick series of light sounds or beats often + *of* ▪ I heard the *patter of* little feet as the children ran down the hall. ▪ the *patter of* rain against/on the windows — see also PITTER-PATTER — compare [1]PATTER
– **patter** *verb, always followed by an adverb or preposition* **-ters; -tered; -ter·ing** [*no obj*] ▪ Their feet *pattered down* the hall. ▪ The rain was *pattering on* the roof.

[1]**pat·tern** /ˈpætɚn/ *noun, pl* **-terns** [*count*]
1 : a repeated form or design especially that is used to decorate something ▪ The dishes have a floral *pattern* around the rim. ▪ The fabric comes in different colors and *patterns*. ▪ The rug is decorated with a geometric *pattern*. ▪ The shadows made a *pattern* of lines on the ground. — see color picture on page C12
2 a : the regular and repeated way in which something happens or is done ▪ They are studying behavior *patterns* among high-school students. ▪ Analysts are noticing different spending *patterns* by consumers. ▪ The trees followed a characteristic *pattern* of growth. ▪ Your symptoms ***fit the pattern*** of diabetes. [=your symptoms are the same as the symptoms of diabetes] ▪ His daily routine followed a ***set pattern***. [=it was always the same] ▪ The book ***set the pattern*** [=created an example which is followed by others] for detective fiction. **b** : something that happens in a regular and repeated way ▪ We have to find a way to break the *pattern* of violence. [=to make the violence stop]
3 : a shape or model that is used as guide for making something ▪ a ***dress pattern*** [=a large piece of paper that is used as a guide for cutting the cloth to make a dress]
– see also HOLDING PATTERN

[2]**pattern** *verb* **-terns; -terned; -tern·ing** [+ *obj*]
1 : to make or design (something) so that it is similar to something else of the same type — usually used as (*be*) *patterned* + *on* or (*US*) *after* ▪ Her garden ***is patterned on*** [=*modeled on*] one she saw on her travels. ▪ The new program ***is patterned after*** an earlier one.
2 : to decorate or mark (something) with a design : to form a pattern on (something) ▪ Animals tracks *patterned* the mud.
pattern yourself on *or US* ***pattern yourself after*** : to try to be like and to behave like (someone you admire) ▪ When he started his own business, he *patterned himself after* [=*modeled himself after*] his father. [=he tried to do the things that his father would do]

pat·terned /ˈpætɚnd/ *adj* : having a design that is repeated many times : decorated with a pattern ▪ *patterned* fabrics/rugs/wallpaper

pat·tern·ing /ˈpætɚnɪŋ/ *noun* [*noncount*] : the designs or patterns that appear on something ▪ The wallpaper is decorated with floral *patterning*.

pat·ty *also* **pat·tie** /ˈpæti/ *noun, pl* **pat·ties** [*count*]
1 *chiefly US* : a small, flat cake of chopped food ▪ hamburger/beef/chicken *patties*
2 *US* : a soft, flat candy ▪ a peppermint *patty*

pat·ty–cake (*US*) /ˈpætiˌkeɪk/ *also* **pat–a–cake** /ˈpætəˌkeɪk/ *noun* [*noncount*] : a children's game in which two people lightly hit their hands together while singing a short poem (called a nursery rhyme) ▪ Let's do/play *patty-cake*.

pau·ci·ty /ˈpɑːsəti/ *noun* [*singular*] *formal* : a small amount *of* something : an amount that is less than what is needed or wanted ▪ There was a relative *paucity* [=*lack*] *of* detail in the report. ▪ a *paucity* [=*dearth*] *of* evidence

paunch /ˈpɑːnʧ/ *noun, pl* **paunch·es** [*count*] : a belly that sticks out especially on a man : a fat stomach ▪ He sat with his hands folded over his *paunch*. ▪ He used to be very thin but now he has a slight *paunch*.
– **paunchy** /ˈpɑːnʧi/ *adj* **paunch·i·er; -est** [*also more* ~; *most* ~] ▪ a *paunchy* middle-aged man

pau·per /ˈpɑːpɚ/ *noun, pl* **-pers** [*count*] *old-fashioned* : a very poor person who has no money to pay for food, clothing, etc.

[1]**pause** /ˈpɑːz/ *noun, pl* **paus·es**
1 : a temporary stop : a period of time in which something is stopped before it is started again [*count*] There was a brief/long *pause* in the conversation. ▪ After a *pause* the teacher continued the lesson. [*noncount*] He talked for over an hour ***without pause***. [=without pausing or stopping]
2 [*noncount*] : a control that you use when you want to stop a recorded song, movie, etc., for a short time ▪ He hit *pause* on the player and explained the significance of the song's lyrics. ▪ Please hit the ***pause button*** on the remote control.
3 [*count*] *music* : the sign 𝄐 that is placed over or under a musical note, rest, etc., to show that it should be held longer than usual
give (someone) pause *also* ***give (someone) pause for thought*** : to cause (someone) to stop and think about something carefully or to have doubts about something ▪ I was going to ask her for help, but the look on her face *gave me pause*. [=made me hesitate] ▪ The latest economic news has *given investors pause for thought*.

[2]**pause** *verb* **pauses; paused; paus·ing**
1 [*no obj*] : to stop doing something for a short time before

doing it again • She *paused* for a few seconds before crossing the street. • We *paused* briefly to look at the scenery. • He talked for over an hour without *pausing*.
2 [+ *obj*] : to cause (a recorded song, movie, etc.) to stop for a short time by pushing a button on a device • He picked up the remote control and *paused* the movie.

pave /ˈpeɪv/ *verb* **paves; paved; pav·ing** [+ *obj*] : to cover (something) with a material (such as stone, tar, or concrete) that forms a hard, level surface for walking, driving, etc. • The crew was *paving* the road. • Some of the roads were *paved* over. • The driveway is *paved* with concrete. • a *paved* highway/road • It was said that this country was so rich, the streets were ***paved with/in gold***.
pave over [*phrasal verb*] ***pave over (something)*** *or* ***pave (something) over*** *disapproving* : to cover (an area) with roads, parking lots, buildings, etc. • All this beautiful farmland will be *paved over*.
pave the way for (something or someone) : to make it easier for something to happen or for someone to do something • The discovery *paves the way for* the development of effective new treatments.

pave·ment /ˈpeɪvmənt/ *noun, pl* **-ments**
1 [*noncount*] *US* : the hard surface of a road, driveway, etc. • He stopped the car just off the *pavement*. • The summer heat rose off the *pavement*.
2 [*count*] *Brit* : SIDEWALK
hit the pavement see [1]HIT
pavement café see CAFÉ
pound the pavement see [4]POUND

pa·vil·ion /pəˈvɪljən/ *noun, pl* **-ions** [*count*]
1 : a building in a park or garden that usually has open sides and is used for parties, concerts, or other events
2 : a temporary building that is used at public events and exhibitions • The World's Fair had numerous *pavilions*.
3 *US* : a large building that is used for sports or public events
4 *Brit* : a building that is next to a sports field and used by players and people watching the game

paving *noun* [*noncount*]
1 : material (such as stone, tar, or concrete) that is used to form the hard surface of a road, driveway, etc. • The driveway was covered with concrete/brick *paving*.
2 : the hard surface of a road, driveway, etc. : PAVEMENT • They had to break up the *paving* to lay a new gas line.

paving stone *noun, pl* **~ stones** [*count*] : a flat stone or brick used to make a hard surface to walk on outdoors

[1]**paw** /ˈpɑː/ *noun, pl* **paws** [*count*]
1 : the foot of an animal that has claws • The dog injured his *paw*. • a cat's *paw*
2 *informal + disapproving* : a person's hand • Keep your dirty *paws* off me! [=don't touch me]

[2]**paw** *verb* **paws; pawed; paw·ing**
1 *of an animal* : to touch or hit (someone or something) with a paw or foot [+ *obj*] The bull was *pawing* the dirt/ground. [*no obj*] — usually + *at* • The dog *pawed at* the door.
2 [+ *obj*] : to touch (someone or something) in a rough or sexual way • The celebrity couple was *pawed* by a mob of adoring fans. • She claims that her boss got drunk and tried to *paw* her at the company Christmas party.
3 *always followed by an adverb or preposition* [*no obj*] : to search by using your hands in an awkward or careless way • A crowd of customers was *pawing* over the remaining sales items. • She *pawed* through her purse to find her cell phone.

[1]**pawn** /ˈpɑːn/ *noun, pl* **pawns** [*count*]
1 : one of the eight small pieces that have the least value in the game of chess — see picture at CHESS
2 : a person or group that does not have much power and that is controlled by a more powerful person or group — usually + *in* • He became a *pawn in* the power struggle.

[2]**pawn** *verb* **pawns; pawned; pawn·ing** [+ *obj*] : to give (something that you own) to a pawnbroker in exchange for money • She was forced to *pawn* her diamond ring.
pawn off [*phrasal verb*] ***pawn (something) off*** *or* ***pawn off (something)*** *US, informal* **1** : to sell (something) for more than it is worth by being dishonest about it • He'll *pawn* [=*palm*] the car *off* on/onto some unsuspecting fool if he can. • I *pawned off* my old computer on him. **2** : to get someone to accept or do (something) • He tried to *pawn off* science fiction as truth.

pawn·bro·ker /ˈpɑːnˌbroʊkɚ/ *noun, pl* **-kers** [*count*] : a person who lends money to people in exchange for personal property that can be sold if the money is not returned within a certain time • He was desperate for money so he hocked his watch to a *pawnbroker*.

pawn·shop /ˈpɑːnˌʃɑːp/ *noun, pl* **-shops** [*count*] : a pawnbroker's shop

paw·paw /pəˈpɑː, ˈpɑːˌpɑː/ *noun, pl* **-paws** [*count, noncount*] *chiefly Brit* : PAPAYA

[1]**pay** /ˈpeɪ/ *verb* **pays; paid** /ˈpeɪd/; **pay·ing**
1 a [*no obj*] : to give money for goods or services • I already *paid* last week. • Where do we *pay* to get in? • Do we have to *pay* to park here? • They left the restaurant without *paying*. • Should I *pay* in dollars or pesos? • We're trying to attract more ***paying customers*** [=customers that buy things from our company] through our Web site. • ***paying passengers*** • After their children left for college, they began opening their home to ***paying guests***. [=people who give you money to live in your house with you for a short time] — often + *for* • He offered to *pay for* our dinner. • How will you be *paying for* your purchase: (in) cash, (by) check, or (with a) credit card? • "That cheap camera I bought is broken already." "Well, ***you get what you pay for***." [=a thing that can be bought for a very low price probably isn't very good] **b** [+ *obj*] : to give money to (someone) for goods or services • I'll *pay* the taxi driver. • Has anyone *paid* her yet? • We get *paid* on Fridays. • The workers get *paid* well. = The workers are well-*paid*. — often followed by *to + verb* • They're going to *pay* a crew *to paint* the house. • ***You couldn't pay me*** *to jump* out of an airplane! [=I would never jump out of an airplane, even if you gave me a lot of money] — sometimes + *in* • "Did he give you a check?" "No, he *paid* me *in* cash." • When he mowed her lawn, she *paid* him *in* cookies. [=she gave him cookies for mowing her lawn] **c** [+ *obj*] : to give (something, such as an amount of money) for goods or services • I *paid* $200 to him yesterday. = I *paid* him $200 yesterday. • These workers are *paid* extremely low wages by their employers. • She *pays* 15 percent (of her earnings) to her agent. • I *paid* a lot of money for this car. • How much are you willing to *pay*? • They *paid* over $300,000 for their house. • They *paid* a high price [=a lot of money] for that painting. • I couldn't afford to ***pay cash***, so I put it on my credit card. • We ***paid good money*** [=we gave a large amount of money] to see this show, and we want our money's worth! **d** — used to say how much someone earns for doing a job [*no obj*] My job doesn't *pay* very well. [=I don't earn much money from my job] • It's difficult work that *pays* relatively poorly. • high-*paying* jobs [+ *obj*] The job *pays* $150,000 a year.
2 [+ *obj*] : to give the money that you owe for (something) • I can't afford to *pay* my rent. • *paying* taxes/fines/penalties • Use the company's financing plan and *pay* no interest for a full year. • Has this bill been *paid*? • The receipt shows that their bill has been ***paid in full***. [=all of the money they owed has been paid]
3 : to have a good or helpful result : to be worth the expense or effort to do something [*no obj*] Hard work always *pays* [=*pays off*] in the long run. • ***Crime doesn't pay***. [=you get more trouble than benefit from committing a crime] — often followed by *to + verb* • ***It pays*** [=it is worth the effort] *to study* your notes after every class. • When the roads are icy, *it pays to drive* slowly. • *It pays to advertise.* [+ *obj*] ***It pays*** stores *to be* open on the weekends. [=stores benefit from being open on the weekends] • Spending a lot of money on advertising has ***paid dividends*** for our company. [=has given our company extra advantages or benefits] • Our efforts are finally *paying dividends*. [=we are finally getting the results we want from our efforts]
4 [+ *obj*] : to give (a percentage of money) as the profit from an investment or business • The investment *paid* eight percent last year. • a savings account *paying* four percent interest
5 a [*no obj*] : to deal with the bad result of something that you did : to be punished for doing something • If you offend him, he will make you *pay*. — often + *for* • I'll make you *pay for* what you've done to me! • You'll *pay for* this! • She ***paid dearly*** *for* her mistakes. [=she suffered a lot as a result of her mistakes] • He thinks that the people who committed these terrible crimes should ***pay with their lives***. [=should be killed] **b** [+ *obj*] : to give, lose, or suffer (something) as a punishment for or result of something else • We all felt that 25 years in prison was a ***high/small price to pay*** for his crimes. ✧ If you ***pay a/the price*** or ***pay a heavy/high/steep (etc.) price*** or (*Brit*) ***pay the penalty*** for something, you experience the bad effects or results of that thing. • I knew the consequences of what I was about to do, but I was willing to *pay the price*. • Famous people always *pay a price* for their

P

fame. ▪ She *paid a heavy price* for telling the truth. ▪ Someone has to *pay the penalty* for these mistakes.

6 [+ *obj*] — used in various phrases that describe giving your attention to what is being done or said ▪ Are you ***paying attention***? [=are you listening and trying to understand?] ▪ Remember to ***pay close attention*** to the instructions. ▪ He's just teasing you. ***Don't pay any attention*** to him. = ***Pay no attention*** to him. [=don't be upset by what he is saying] ▪ He kept talking but she ***paid him no mind***. [=she didn't listen to what he said] ▪ ***Pay heed*** to what he says. [=listen to what he says]

7 [+ *obj*] — used to describe saying or doing something that expresses respect, admiration, etc., for someone ▪ She ***paid me a compliment***. [=she said something nice about me] ▪ We gather here today to ***pay tribute/homage to*** [=to honor and praise] a great woman.

hell to pay *or* ***the devil to pay*** — used to say that if a specific thing happens, something else that is very bad will be the result or someone will get very upset ▪ We knew that if anyone caught us cheating there would be *hell to pay*. [=we would be severely punished] ▪ There'll be *the devil to pay* if we don't finish on time.

pay a call/visit : to go somewhere to visit someone ▪ She ***paid me a visit*** [=she came to visit me] while I was in the hospital. = She ***paid a call on me*** while I was in the hospital.

pay back [*phrasal verb*] **1** ***pay back (something)*** *or* ***pay (something) back*** : to return (an amount of money) that someone allowed you to borrow ▪ She has to *pay back* the $100 she borrowed. ▪ He said that he'll *pay* the money *back* tomorrow. ▪ *paying back* a loan **2** ***pay (someone) back*** *or* ***pay back (someone)*** **a** : to give (someone) the amount of money that you borrowed ▪ I'll *pay* you *back* when I get the money. ▪ I lent him money and he never *paid* me *back*. ▪ I have to *pay back* my sister for that loan. **b** : to punish or hurt (someone who did something bad to you) ▪ I wanted to *pay* him *back* [=*get back at him*; make him suffer] for all the pain he caused me. ▪ He's finally getting *paid back* for all the trouble he caused. — see also PAYBACK **c** : to do something good for (someone who did something good for you) ▪ How can I *pay* you *back* for all your help?

pay court to see [1]COURT

pay for itself ✧ If you buy something that *pays for itself*, the amount of money you save by using the product for a period of time is more than the amount of money you spent when you bought the product. ▪ You save so much on heating costs with our high-quality windows that the windows will *pay for themselves* within five years!

pay in [*phrasal verb*] ***pay in (something)*** *or* ***pay (something) in*** *Brit* : to put (money) in an account : DEPOSIT ▪ I went to the bank to *pay in* a cheque. ▪ *paying* a cheque *in* an account

pay into [*phrasal verb*] ***pay into (something)*** *chiefly US* : to put money into (a fund or account) ▪ Each month she *pays into* an account that can be used for medical expenses.

pay off [*phrasal verb*] **1** : to produce a result that you want ▪ It's great to see that all of our hard work has finally *paid off*. **2** ***pay off (something)*** *or* ***pay (something) off*** : to give all of the money that you owe for (something that you pay for over a period of time) ▪ It will take us 30 years to *pay off* our mortgage, but then the house will be ours. ▪ If I won the money, I'd use it to *pay off* all my credit cards. ▪ *paying off* your debts ▪ She finally got her car *paid off*. [=she finally paid all the money she had borrowed to buy her car] **3** ***pay off (someone)*** *or* ***pay (someone) off*** **a** : to give money to (someone) in order to make that person do something illegal or dishonest for you or to convince that person not to talk about something ▪ He tried to *pay off* [=*bribe*] a police officer. ▪ The company was accused of *paying off* its employees to keep them from talking about its illegal activities. **b** *Brit* : to stop employing (someone) after paying all of the money that was owed to that person ▪ They *paid off* all their workers and then closed the factory. — see also PAYOFF

pay out [*phrasal verb*] ***pay out (something)*** *or* ***pay (something) out*** **1** : to give (an amount of money) to someone usually over a period of time ▪ The government has *paid out* [=*disbursed*] millions of dollars in foreign aid. ▪ The prize money will be *paid out* (to the winner) over the course of five years. — see also PAYOUT **2** : to allow (a rope or chain) to become loose and move through your hands ▪ We lowered the anchor and continued to *pay out* several more feet of rope.

pay the piper see PIPER

pay through the nose see [1]NOSE

pay up [*phrasal verb*] *somewhat informal* **1** : to pay what you owe : to pay what is due ▪ We *paid up* and left. ▪ He decided to *pay up* after they threatened to take him to court for the money. **2** ✧ If you ***are paid up***, you have given all of the money that you owe until a specific date. ▪ You*'re* (all) *paid up* through June. [=you do not have to pay any more money until after June]

pay your dues see [2]DUE

pay your (own) way : to use your own money to pay for the things you need or do ▪ She got a part-time job in order to *pay her way* through college. ▪ Students must *pay their own way* if they choose to participate in the trip. ▪ I wanted to buy him dinner, but he insisted on *paying his own way*.

pay your respects *formal* : to visit or speak with someone in a polite way as a sign of respect ▪ I went up to her after the meeting and *paid my respects*. ▪ We ***paid our last respects*** at his funeral. [=we went to his funeral as a sign of respect]

put paid to *Brit, informal* : to cause (something) to end : to stop (something) ▪ The storm *put paid to* his attempt to sail around the world. ▪ They hope to *put paid to* the argument once and for all.

– see also [2]PAID

[2]pay *noun* [*noncount*] : money received in exchange for work : money paid to someone for doing work ▪ receiving higher/better/lower *pay* ▪ The work is hard, but the *pay* is good. [=you earn a lot of money by doing the work] ▪ She spent a week's *pay* [=the amount of money she earns in one week] in just one night. ▪ He has been suspended without *pay* pending the results of the investigation. ▪ "Women," she said, "should receive equal *pay* for equal work." [=they should be paid the same amount of money as men who perform the same job] ▪ When he works on the weekends, he collects ***overtime pay***. [=an increased rate of money earned for working more than the usual number of hours in one week] ▪ The company owes her $500 in ***back pay***. [=money that is owed to a worker from an earlier time] ▪ ***severance pay*** [=money given to workers when a company ends their jobs] ▪ The workers are demanding an increase in their ***rate of pay***. = The workers are demanding an increase in their ***pay rate***. [=the amount of money they are paid per hour, week, etc.] ▪ Each ***pay period*** begins on the first of the month. ▪ (*US*) He asked for a ***pay raise*** = (*Brit*) He asked for a ***pay rise***. ▪ Workers received a $4,000 ***pay increase***. ▪ I took a significant ***pay cut*** when I took this job, but I think it was worth it. — see also BASE PAY, CO-PAY, SICK PAY, TAKE-HOME PAY

in the pay of someone : working usually in a secret way for a person or organization ▪ He was accused of being *in the pay of* gangsters.

pay·able /ˈpejəbəl/ *adj, always used after a noun* : possible or necessary to pay ▪ She charges her patients $3,000, *payable* in installments. ▪ The bill was *payable* [=*due*] on the first of February. ▪ The plan defines the maximum amount *payable* [=that will be paid] by the insurance company. ▪ (*business*) ***accounts payable*** [=the amounts of money that you owe to people or other businesses] — often + *to* ▪ benefits *payable to* the insured ✧ If a check is ***made payable to*** someone, the name of that person or business is written on the check. ▪ All checks should be *made payable to* the university. ▪ *Make* your check *payable to* "Therapy Associates Inc."

pay–as–you–go *adj* — used to describe a system of payment in which bills are paid when they are due or goods and services are paid for when they are bought ▪ The city adopted a *pay-as-you-go* policy to avoid future debt. ▪ I use a *pay-as-you-go* plan for my cell phone.

pay·back /ˈpeɪˌbæk/ *noun, pl* **-backs**

1 [*noncount*] : punishment for something that was done in the past ▪ This is *payback* [=this is my revenge] for all the pain you've caused me. ▪ They beat our team last year, so we've got to beat them this year as *payback*. ▪ You've ruined my life, and now it's ***payback time***. [=now I'm going to hurt you because you hurt me] — see also *pay back* at [1]PAY

2 [*count*] : an amount of money that you receive after investing in something and that is equal to or greater than the amount of money that you originally invested — usually singular ▪ The investment has yielded a big *payback* for the company. — sometimes used figuratively ▪ While these cars are expensive, there's a significant *payback* in terms of safety. [=the safety of the cars make them worth their high cost]

3 [*count*] : the amount of time that passes before invested money is returned or before money that is owed is paid — usually singular ▪ a five-year *payback* ▪ The ***payback period*** is expected to be less than six months on this investment. ▪ The loan calls for a two-year *payback period*.

pay–cable *noun* [*noncount*] *chiefly US* : pay-TV that is sent through a cable television system — often used before another noun • a *pay-cable* channel/network

pay·check (*US*) /ˈpeɪˌʧɛk/ *or Brit* **pay cheque** /ˈpeɪˌʧɛk/ *noun, pl* **-checks** [*count*]

1 : a check that is used to pay an employee for his or her work • I went to the office to pick up my *paycheck*. • a big *paycheck* [=a paycheck for a large amount of money] • (*US*) We are ***living paycheck to paycheck*** [=we spend all of the money from one paycheck before we receive the next paycheck] and have no money left over for savings.

2 *chiefly US* : the money that you regularly earn : a wage or salary • Your weekly *paycheck* will be almost $600 after taxes. • When I was in college, I earned my first ***steady paycheck*** [=I was earning money regularly for the first time] as a waitress.

pay·day /ˈpeɪˌdeɪ/ *noun* : the day when you are regularly paid your wages [*noncount*] *Payday* is every other Friday. [=the company pays its employees every two weeks on a Friday] • Next Friday is *payday*. [*count*] Is this Friday a *payday*?

pay dirt *noun*

hit/strike pay dirt *chiefly US, informal* : to do, find, or get something that results in money or success • The band *hit pay dirt* [=had a big success] with their first single. • The police *struck pay dirt* when a witness came forward with new information.

PAYE /ˌpiːˌeɪˌwaɪˈiː/ *noun* [*noncount*] *Brit* : WITHHOLDING TAX ✧ *PAYE* is an abbreviation of the words "pay as you earn."

pay·ee /peɪˈiː/ *noun, pl* **-ees** [*count*] *technical* : a person or organization that receives money : a person or organization that is paid • The *payee* must endorse the back of the check. • a *payee* bank

pay envelope *noun, pl* ~ **-lopes** [*count*] *US*

1 : an envelope that contains your wages

2 : the money that you regularly earn : a wage or salary • Workers will be expecting bigger/fatter *pay envelopes* [=(more commonly) *paychecks*] next year. — called also (*Brit*) *pay packet*

pay·er /ˈpejɚ/ *also* **pay·or** /peɪˈoɚ/ *noun, pl* **-ers** *also* **-ors** [*count*] : a person, organization, etc., that pays or is responsible for paying something • He is a regular bill *payer*. [=he pays his bills when they are due] • a single-*payer* health-care system [=a system in which the government pays for everyone's health care] — see also TAXPAYER

paying–in slip *noun, pl* ~ **slips** [*count*] *Brit* : DEPOSIT SLIP

pay·load /ˈpeɪˌloud/ *noun, pl* **-loads** [*count*]

1 a : the amount of goods or material that is carried by a vehicle (such as a truck) • a heavy *payload* • truckers delivering their *payloads* **b** : the things (such as passengers or bombs) that are carried by an aircraft or spacecraft

2 : the weight of a payload • The truck is carrying a *payload* of 2,580 pounds.

3 : the power of the explosive material in a bomb or missile

pay·mas·ter /ˈpeɪˌmæstɚ, *Brit* ˈpeɪˌmɑːstə/ *noun, pl* **-ters** [*count*]

1 : a person whose job is paying salaries or wages • She worked as the company's *paymaster* for 22 years.

2 *usually disapproving* : a person, country, etc., that pays people and controls their actions • a *paymaster* of/to terrorists

pay·ment /ˈpeɪmənt/ *noun, pl* **-ments**

1 [*noncount*] **a** : the act of giving money for something : the act of paying • *Payment* is due on the first of every month. • Prompt *payment* of your bill ensures that you will not have to pay any additional fees. • We require *payment* in advance for all goods purchased. • an online/electronic *payment* system • a *payment* plan to reduce your debt • He was released from prison ***on payment of*** [=after paying] a $5,000 fine. • cash, credit cards, and other ***methods of payment*** • I had the bank ***stop payment on*** the check. = I had a ***stop payment*** (order) put on the check. [=I told the bank not to take money from my account to pay for the check] **b** : something that is given to someone in exchange for something else • He accepted the tickets as *payment* (for his services). • We bought them dinner ***in payment*** [=as a way of paying them] for all their help.

2 [*count*] : an amount of money that is paid for something • Our records show that we received a *payment* of $215.36 in May. • Buy this product for three easy *payments* of only $19.95! • low monthly *payments* • It took me five years to pay off the car, but I never missed a *payment*. • ***making payments*** on a loan • Their family is struggling to ***meet the payments on*** their house. = They're struggling to keep up (with) their ***mortgage payments***. • The credit card company just increased the penalty on ***late payments***. • She wrote the first three chapters of her book and received an ***advance payment*** from the publisher. • ***cash payments*** from donors • ***interest payments*** on a loan — see also BALANCE OF PAYMENTS, BALLOON PAYMENT, DOWN PAYMENT

pay·off /ˈpeɪˌɑːf/ *noun, pl* **-offs**

1 : a good result : the advantage or benefit that is gained from doing something [*count*] You'll have to work hard but there'll be a big/large *payoff* in the end. • We expected more of a *payoff* for all our hard work. • What's the *payoff*? [*noncount*] We made a lot of sacrifices with little *payoff*.

2 [*count*] : something valuable (such as money) that you give to someone for doing something and especially for doing something illegal or dishonest : BRIBE • Several city officials have been accused of receiving *payoffs* from the company.

3 [*count*] *Brit* : money that a company gives to a worker who is being forced to leave a job • He lost his factory job but received a *payoff* and a pension. — see also *pay off* at [1]PAY

pay·o·la /peɪˈoulə/ *noun* [*noncount*] *chiefly US, informal*

1 : money that is paid to someone for illegally helping to sell or advertise a product • These radio disc jockeys accepted *payola* to play particular songs.

2 : the illegal practice of giving or receiving payola • *payola* in the music industry • a *payola* scandal

payor *variant spelling of* PAYER

pay·out /ˈpeɪˌaut/ *noun, pl* **-outs** [*count*] : a usually large amount of money that is given to someone • Each year, the government spends millions of dollars in *payouts* [=*disbursements*] to corporate farms. • a large insurance *payout* — see also *pay out* at [1]PAY

pay packet *noun, pl* ~ **-ets** [*count*] *Brit* : PAY ENVELOPE • her weekly/monthly *pay packet*

pay–per–view *noun* [*noncount*] : cable television channels that charge a fee for each show you watch • We're watching a boxing match on *pay-per-view* tonight. — often used before another noun • *pay-per-view* movies

pay phone *noun, pl* ~ **phones** [*count*] : a public telephone that you can use if you put coins into it or use a calling card to pay for your call — see picture at TELEPHONE

pay·roll /ˈpeɪˌroul/ *noun, pl* **-rolls** [*count*]

1 : a list of the people who work for a company and the amount of money that the company has agreed to pay them • They cut him from their *payroll*. — often used before another noun • She's in charge of the company's *payroll* department. [=the department that is responsible for paying employees] • ***payroll deductions*** [=money that you earn but is not included in the pay you receive because it is used to pay your taxes, insurance costs, etc.] — often used in the phrase ***on the payroll*** • Her company has over 3,000 employees *on the payroll*. • He's currently *on the payroll* of a small law firm.

2 : the total amount of money that a company pays to all of its employees • He's the manager of a baseball team with a $50 million *payroll*. • Businesses are keeping their *payrolls* low by embracing new technologies.

P

payroll tax *noun, pl* ~ **taxes** [*count*]

1 : a tax that is paid by a company and that is based on the amount of money that the company spends paying all of its employees

2 : WITHHOLDING TAX

pay stub *noun, pl* ~ **stubs** [*count*] *US* : a piece of paper that is given to an employee with each paycheck and that shows the amount of money that the employee earned and the amount that was removed for taxes, insurance costs, etc. • Keep your *pay stubs* for your financial records. — called also (*Brit*) *pay slip*

pay–TV *noun* [*noncount*] : television channels that you must order and pay for • a movie on *pay-TV* • subscribers to *pay-TV* channels/networks — called also *pay television*; compare PAY-CABLE

PB&J *abbr* peanut butter and jelly

PBS *abbr* Public Broadcasting Service ✧ PBS is an organization that produces educational television programs that are shown without commercials in a network of stations throughout the U.S.

[1]**PC** /ˌpiːˈsiː/ *noun, pl* **PCs** *or* **PC's** [*count*] : PERSONAL COMPUTER

²PC *abbr* **1** Peace Corps **2** politically correct; political correctness **3** *Brit* police constable

PCP *abbr, US* primary care physician; primary care provider

pct *abbr* percent; percentage

pd *abbr* paid

PD *abbr, US* police department

PDA /ˌpiːˌdiːˈeɪ/ *noun, pl* **PDAs** [*count*] **:** a small electronic device that is used for storing and organizing information (such as phone numbers, addresses, appointments, and notes) ✧ *PDA* is an abbreviation of "personal digital assistant."

PDQ *or* **pdq** *or* **p.d.q.** /ˌpiːˌdiːˈkjuː/ *adv, informal* **:** as quickly as possible **:** immediately ▪ We need to hire someone *PDQ*. ✧ *PDQ* is an abbreviation of the phrase "pretty damned quick."

P.E. (*US*) *or* **PE** *abbr* physical education

pea /ˈpiː/ *noun, pl* **peas** [*count*] **:** a small, round, green seed that is eaten as a vegetable and that is formed in a seed case (called a pod) of a climbing plant; *also* **:** a plant that produces peas ▪ We're growing tomatoes and *peas* in our garden this year. — see color picture on page C4; see also BLACK-EYED PEA, CHICKPEA, SNAP PEA, SNOW PEA, SUGAR SNAP PEA, SWEET PEA

two peas in a pod — used to say that two people or things are very similar to each other ▪ My brother and I are *two peas in a pod*. We both like the same things.

peace /ˈpiːs/ *noun*

1 a : a state in which there is no war or fighting [*noncount*] After many years of war, people on both sides were longing for *peace*. ▪ We said a prayer for world *peace*. ▪ They have lived ***in peace*** [=*peacefully*] for many years. ▪ We grew up in a time when the nation was prosperous and ***at peace***. [=not fighting a war] ▪ The United Nations has sent troops to the area to try to ***keep (the) peace***. [*singular*] a lasting *peace* ▪ The two countries have maintained an ***uneasy peace***. [=a state in which fighting could start at any time] **b** [*singular*] **:** an agreement to end a war ▪ He tried to negotiate a *peace* between the warring countries. ▪ After many years of war, the two countries have finally ***made peace*** (with each other). — often used before another noun ▪ a *peace* agreement/accord/treaty ▪ a *peace* initiative/conference ▪ *peace* talks ▪ the ***peace process*** [=the steps that are taken by countries or groups that are trying to end a war] **c** [*singular*] **:** a period of time when there is no war or fighting ▪ There was a *peace* of 50 years before war broke out again.

2 [*noncount*] **a :** a quiet and calm state ▪ I just want a few moments of *peace*. = I just want a little ***peace and quiet***. ▪ Why won't they leave him ***in peace***? [=why won't they stop bothering him?] **b :** a safe and calm state in a public place ▪ ***Peace and order*** were finally restored in the town. ▪ He was arrested for ***a breach of the peace***. = He was arrested for ***disturbing the peace***. [=for behaving in a loud or violent way in a public place] — see also JUSTICE OF THE PEACE

3 : a state in which a person is not bothered by thoughts or feelings of doubt, guilt, worry, etc. [*singular*] After years of therapy, he has finally achieved an inner *peace*. [*noncount*] He is searching for inner *peace*. ▪ She has found *peace* (within herself). ▪ Insurance can provide you with ***peace of mind***. ▪ The problem was settled and his mind was ***at peace***. ▪ They are ***at peace with*** each other. ▪ She's *at peace with* their decision. [=she has accepted their decision] ▪ May our dearly departed friend ***rest in peace***. [=we hope our friend who has died will have peace after death]

4 [*noncount*] **:** a state in which people do not argue or cause trouble ▪ There will never be *peace* between those families. ▪ She wants to go, and we won't have any *peace* until we agree to let her do what she wants.

hold your peace see ¹HOLD

make your peace with ✧ If you *make your peace with* someone, you end an argument or disagreement that you had with that person. ▪ He wanted to *make his peace with* his father before he died.

sue for peace see SUE

peace·able /ˈpiːsəbəl/ *adj* [*more ~; most ~*]

1 : not liking or wanting to fight or argue ▪ They are a *peaceable* [=*peaceful*], good-natured people. ▪ He has a *peaceable* nature.

2 : not involving violence or fighting ▪ The crowd dispersed in a *peaceable* manner.

– peace·ably /ˈpiːsəbli/ *adv* ▪ As neighbors, they had lived *peaceably* for many years.

Peace Corps *noun*

the Peace Corps **:** a U.S. organization that trains and sends people who work without pay to help poor people in other countries

peace dividend *noun, pl* **~ -dends** [*count*] **:** money that a government originally planned to spend on its military that becomes available for other things when a situation changes (such as when a war ends) — usually singular

peace·ful /ˈpiːsfəl/ *adj* [*more ~; most ~*]

1 : quiet and calm **:** without noise, excitement, etc. ▪ a *peaceful* countryside ▪ The park is so *peaceful* and quiet.

2 : not fighting a war ▪ *peaceful* nations

3 : not involving violence or force ▪ a *peaceful* rally/demonstration/protest ▪ They settled the conflict by *peaceful* means. ▪ We need to find a *peaceful* alternative to war.

4 : not liking or wanting to fight **:** preferring peace ▪ They are a *peaceful* [=*peaceable*] people.

– peace·ful·ly *adv* ▪ She slept *peacefully*. ▪ The nations managed to coexist *peacefully*. ▪ He lived *peacefully* among the villagers. **– peace·ful·ness** *noun* [*noncount*]

peace·keep·er /ˈpiːsˌkiːpɚ/ *noun, pl* **-ers** [*count*] **:** someone (such as a soldier) who helps to prevent or stop fighting between countries or groups ▪ *Peacekeepers* were sent in to stop the violence.

– peace·keep·ing /ˈpiːsˌkiːpɪŋ/ *adj, always used before a noun* ▪ a *peacekeeping* force/mission ▪ *peacekeeping* operations/troops

peace·mak·er /ˈpiːsˌmeɪkɚ/ *noun, pl* **-ers** [*count*] **:** a person who helps to prevent or stop an argument, a fight, or a war ▪ She acted as *peacemaker* in the dispute.

– peace·mak·ing /ˈpiːsˌmeɪkɪŋ/ *adj, always used before a noun* [*noncount*] ▪ *peacemaking* efforts/activities ▪ He was sent on a *peacemaking* trip. **– peacemaking** *noun* [*noncount*] ▪ Our attempts at *peacemaking* have failed.

peace offering *noun, pl* **~ -ings** [*count*] **:** a gift that is given as a way of apologizing or making peace ▪ After our last argument, I sent her flowers as a *peace offering*.

peace officer *noun, pl* **~ -ers** [*count*] *US, law* **:** a police officer or similar official ▪ He was arrested for assaulting a *peace officer*.

peace pipe *noun, pl* **~ pipes** [*count*] **:** a pipe that is smoked by Native Americans in a special ceremony as a sign of peace

peace sign *noun, pl* **~ signs** [*count*]

1 : a sign that you make by holding your hand up with the palm facing away from you and with only the two fingers that are closest to your thumb pointing upward in the shape of a V ✧ This gesture was popular especially in the late 1960s. It is used either as a peaceful greeting or to show that you want peace rather than war. — usually singular ▪ He flashed a *peace sign* at us as we drove by.

2 : PEACE SYMBOL

peace symbol *noun, pl* **~ -bols** [*count*] **:** the symbol ☮ that is used to say that peace is wanted instead of war

peace·time /ˈpiːsˌtaɪm/ *noun* [*noncount*] **:** a period of time during which a country is not fighting a war ▪ The size of the army was reduced during/in *peacetime*. — often used before another noun ▪ the *peacetime* army/economy — opposite WARTIME

peach /ˈpiːtʃ/ *noun, pl* **peach·es**

1 [*count*] **:** a round, sweet fruit that has white or yellow flesh, soft yellow or pink skin, and a large, hard seed at the center ▪ a ripe, juicy *peach* — see color picture on page C5

2 [*noncount*] **:** a yellowish-pink color — see color picture on page C3

3 [*singular*] *informal + old-fashioned* **:** a person or thing that is liked or admired very much ▪ He's a real *peach*. = He's a *peach* of a guy. [=he's a great guy]

peaches and cream **1** — used to describe someone who has smooth and pale skin with light pink cheeks ▪ She has a ***peaches and cream complexion***. **2** *chiefly US, informal* **:** a situation, process, etc., that has no trouble or problems ▪ He promised her that if she married him, life would be *peaches and cream*. ▪ We've managed to finish the job, but it hasn't been all *peaches and cream*.

peachy /ˈpiːtʃi/ *adj* **peach·i·er; -est** [*also more ~; most ~*]

1 : like a peach ▪ a *peachy* pink color ▪ a *peachy* flavor

2 *chiefly US, informal* **:** very good **:** fine or excellent ▪ That's just *peachy* with me. ▪ For the first few months of their marriage, everything was *peachy*. — often used in an ironic way to describe something that is bad, unpleasant, etc. ▪ "It's starting to rain." "Oh, that's just *peachy*! What are we going to do now?"

P

peachy keen *adj, chiefly US, informal* : very good : fine or excellent ▪ She acts as if everything in her life is *peachy keen* [=*peachy*], but I don't think she's really happy.

pea·cock /ˈpiːˌkɑːk/ *noun, pl* **-cocks** [*count*] : a large male bird that has a very long bright blue and green tail that it can lift up and spread apart like a fan — see color picture on page C9

pea green *noun* [*noncount*] : a yellowish-green color — see color picture on page C2

¹peak /ˈpiːk/ *noun, pl* **peaks** [*count*]
1 a : the pointed top of a mountain ▪ a line of rocky *peaks* **b** : a tall mountain with a pointed or narrow top ▪ Pikes *Peak* in Colorado — see color picture on page C7 **c** : something that looks like a pointed top of a mountain ▪ the *peak* of the roof ▪ The recipe says to beat the cream until it forms soft/stiff *peaks*.
2 : the highest level or degree of excellence, quantity, activity, etc. ▪ His cooking is the *peak* of perfection. [=is excellent] ▪ a singer at the *peak* [=*height*] of her popularity ▪ The team was at its *peak* [=played best] in the 1980s. ▪ At her *peak* she was writing a new novel every year. ▪ Violence reached a *peak* just before the election. ▪ The graph shows that murders in the city declined from a *peak* of 173 in 2004. ▪ There are ***peaks and valleys*** [=very high and very low levels] in electricity usage during the summer.
3 *chiefly Brit* : the front part of a cap or hat that shades the eyes : VISOR

²peak *adj, always used before a noun*
1 : at the highest point or level ▪ He is in *peak* [=*top, excellent*] physical condition. ▪ *peak* [=best possible] engine performance ▪ The factory has been running at *peak* capacity for the past year.
2 : filled with the most activity ▪ Phone calls cost more during *peak* calling hours. [=the time period when most calls are made] ▪ the *peak* season for fishing ▪ *peak* [=*prime*] television viewing time — opposite OFF-PEAK

³peak *verb* **peaks; peaked; peak·ing** [*no obj*] : to reach the highest level ▪ Electricity usage *peaks* during the summer. ▪ The singer's popularity *peaked* years ago. [=he is not as popular now] ▪ The stock price *peaked* several months ago at 30 dollars per share.

¹peaked /ˈpiːkt/ *adj* : having a peak ▪ a *peaked* [=*pointed*] roof ▪ (*chiefly Brit*) a *peaked* cap — compare ²PEAKED

²peak·ed /ˈpiːkəd/ *adj, US, informal* : pale and sick ▪ She looks a bit *peaked* today. — compare ¹PEAKED

peaky /ˈpiːki/ *adj, Brit, informal* : pale and sick : PEAKED ▪ He's looking a bit *peaky*.

peal /ˈpiːl/ *noun, pl* **peals** [*count*]
1 : the loud ringing of bells ▪ the *peal* of wedding bells
2 : a loud sound or series of sounds ▪ *peals* of laughter ▪ a *peal* of thunder
– peal *verb* **peals; pealed; peal·ing** [*no obj*] ▪ Bells *pealed* as the wedding ceremony ended.

pea·nut /ˈpiːˌnʌt/ *noun, pl* **-nuts**
1 [*count*] : a nut with a thin shell that grows under the ground and that can be eaten ▪ roasted *peanuts* — often used before another noun ▪ *peanut* oil — called also (*Brit*) *groundnut*
2 peanuts [*plural*] *informal* : a very small amount of money ▪ Five billion dollars is *peanuts* compared to what the government spends each year. ▪ He works all day for *peanuts*.

peanut

peanut butter *noun* [*noncount*] : a creamy food made from peanuts ▪ a jar of *peanut butter* ▪ a *peanut butter* and jelly sandwich

pear /ˈpeɚ/ *noun, pl* **pears** [*count*] : a sweet fruit that is narrow near the stem and rounded at the other end and that grows on a tree; *also* : the tree that this fruit grows on — see color picture on page C5; see also PRICKLY PEAR

pearl /ˈpɚl/ *noun, pl* **pearls**
1 [*count*] : a hard, shiny, white ball that is formed inside the shell of an oyster and that is often used as jewelry ▪ She wore a string of *pearls*. ▪ a *pearl* necklace ▪ *pearl* earrings — see color picture on page C11
2 [*noncount*] : MOTHER-OF-PEARL
3 [*count*] : something that is shaped like a pearl ▪ *Pearls* of dew glistened on the grass. ▪ *pearl* onions
4 [*count*] : someone or something that is very good or admired ▪ She was a *pearl* among swine. ▪ The island is a cultural *pearl* of the Pacific.
cast/throw pearls before swine : to give or offer something valuable to someone who does not understand its value
pearls of wisdom : wise words or statements ▪ He offered some *pearls of wisdom* [=good advice] about raising children. ▪ (*humorous*) A crowd of reporters gathered around the coach after the game to hear him dispense his usual *pearls of wisdom*.

pearly /ˈpɚli/ *adj* : having the shiny, white color of pearls ▪ Her teeth were *pearly* white. ▪ (*informal*) Don't forget to brush your ***pearly whites***. [=*teeth*]

Pearly Gates *noun*
the Pearly Gates *informal + humorous* : a pair of gates thought of as the place through which people enter heaven when they die

pear–shaped /ˈpeɚˌʃeɪpt/ *adj* : shaped like a pear ▪ a *pear-shaped* fruit ▪ She has a *pear-shaped* figure. [=she has wide hips and thighs and a small chest]
go pear-shaped *Brit, informal* : to go wrong ▪ She was in debt, and when she lost her job it all *went pear-shaped*.

peas·ant /ˈpɛznt/ *noun, pl* **-ants** [*count*]
1 : a poor farmer or farm worker who has low social status — used especially to refer to poor people who lived in Europe in the past or to poor people who live in some countries around the world today ▪ This land was farmed for centuries by *peasants*. — often used before another noun ▪ *peasant* farmers ▪ a *peasant* community/girl ▪ *peasant* food [=good food that is made with simple ingredients and that is not fancy]
2 *disapproving* : a person who is not educated and has low social status ▪ They treated us like a bunch of *peasants*.

peas·ant·ry /ˈpɛzn̩tri/ *noun*
the peasantry : all the peasants living in an area or country ▪ He tried to organize *the peasantry* for a revolt. ▪ *the* Russian *peasantry*

pease pudding /ˈpiːz-/ *noun* [*noncount*] *Brit* : a soft food made by boiling dried peas

pea soup *noun* [*noncount*]
1 : a thick soup made of boiled dried peas
2 *informal* — used to describe heavy and thick fog ▪ fog as thick as *pea soup* = *pea-soup* fog

pea–soup·er /ˌpiːˈsuːpɚ/ *noun, pl* **-ers** [*count*] *Brit, old-fashioned + informal* : a very heavy and thick fog ▪ The fog was very bad—a real *pea-souper*.

peat /ˈpiːt/ *noun* [*noncount*] : a dark material made of decaying plants that is burned for heat or added to garden soil
– peaty /ˈpiːti/ *adj* **peat·i·er; -est** ▪ *peaty* ground

peat moss *noun* [*noncount*] *chiefly US* : a type of moss that usually grows on wet land and that is used by gardeners as a fertilizer, for growing plants in pots, etc. — called also *sphagnum, sphagnum moss*

peb·ble /ˈpɛbəl/ *noun, pl* **peb·bles** [*count*] : a small, round stone; *especially* : one that has been made smooth by the movement of water ▪ *pebbles* in the stream
– peb·bly /ˈpɛbəli/ *adj* ▪ a *pebbly* beach [=a beach with many pebbles]

pe·can /pɪˈkɑːn, ˈpiːˌkæn, *Brit* pɪˈkæn, ˈpiːkən/ *noun, pl* **-cans** [*count*] : a nut that grows on a tall tree in the United States and Mexico and that can be eaten ▪ *pecan* pie — see picture at NUT

pec·ca·dil·lo /ˌpɛkəˈdɪloʊ/ *noun, pl* **-loes** *or* **-los** [*count*] : a small mistake or fault that is not regarded as very bad or serious ▪ a politician's sexual *peccadillos*

¹peck /ˈpɛk/ *verb* **pecks; pecked; peck·ing**
1 *of a bird* **a** : to strike sharply at something with the beak [*no obj*] — + *at* ▪ A crow *pecked at* the lawn, hunting for bugs. [+ *obj*] The hen *pecked* my finger. **b** [+ *obj*] : to make (something) by pecking with the beak ▪ The woodpecker *pecked* a hole in the tree.
2 [+ *obj*] : to kiss (someone) lightly and quickly ▪ He *pecked* his wife on the cheek as he headed out the door.
peck at [*phrasal verb*] ***peck at (something)*** : to take small bites of (food) ▪ Her son *pecked at* his food and said he wasn't hungry.
– see also HUNT-AND-PECK

²peck *noun, pl* **pecks** [*count*]
1 : the act of pecking something : a quick, sharp strike with the beak ▪ The bird took a *peck* at the corn. [=the bird pecked the corn]
2 *informal* : a quick kiss ▪ She gave her son a *peck* on the cheek.
– compare ³PECK

P

[3]**peck** *noun, pl* **pecks** [*count*] **:** a unit for measuring an amount of fruit, vegetables, or grain that is equal to about 8.8 liters in the U.S. and about 9.1 liters in the U.K. — compare [2]PECK

peck·er /ˈpɛkɚ/ *noun, pl* **-ers** [*count*] *US, informal + offensive* **:** PENIS

keep your pecker up *Brit, informal* **:** to stay happy or hopeful

pecking order *noun, pl* **~ -ders** [*count*] **:** the way in which people or things in a group or organization are placed in a series of levels with different importance or status ▪ As an assistant manager, he was pretty low in the company's *pecking order*. ▪ the *pecking order* of Washington politics

peck·ish /ˈpɛkɪʃ/ *adj* [*more ~; most ~*] *informal*
1 *chiefly Brit* **:** slightly hungry ▪ If you're feeling *peckish*, there's some cheese in the fridge.
2 *US* **:** irritated or annoyed ▪ a *peckish* tone of voice

pecs /ˈpɛks/ *noun* [*plural*] *informal* **:** PECTORALS ▪ a bodybuilder with great *pecs*

pec·tin /ˈpɛktən/ *noun* [*noncount*] **:** a substance in some fruits that makes fruit jellies thick when the fruit is cooked

pec·to·ral /ˈpɛktərəl/ *adj, technical* **:** relating to or located on the chest ▪ *pectoral* muscles

pec·to·rals /ˈpɛktərəlz/ *noun* [*plural*] **:** the muscles of the chest — called also (*informal*) *pecs*

pe·cu·liar /pɪˈkjuːljɚ/ *adj* [*more ~; most ~*]
1 : not usual or normal **:** STRANGE ▪ It seems *peculiar* that he would leave town and not tell anybody. ▪ The dog's *peculiar* behavior worried them. ▪ She got a *peculiar* feeling when the phone rang. ▪ She had a *peculiar* expression on her face.
2 *not used before a noun, Brit, informal* **:** not well **:** somewhat ill ▪ He's feeling *peculiar*.
peculiar to **:** of, relating to, or found in (only one person, thing, or place) ▪ a custom *peculiar to* America [=a custom that is found only in America]
— pe·cu·liar·ly *adv* ▪ The movie has a *peculiarly* [=*distinctively, uniquely, particularly*] American quality. ▪ He's been behaving *peculiarly*. [=(more commonly) *strangely, oddly*]

pe·cu·liar·i·ty /pɪˌkjuːlˈjerəti/ *noun, pl* **-ties**
1 [*noncount*] **:** the quality or state of being unusual or peculiar ▪ the *peculiarity* of his appearance
2 [*count*] **:** something that is unusual or peculiar in a person or thing ▪ It is a *peculiarity* of the house that there is no front door. ▪ her *peculiarities* as a writer ▪ Scientists tried to explain some *peculiarities* in the results of the experiment.

pe·cu·ni·ary /pɪˈkjuːniˌeri, *Brit* pɪˈkjuːnri/ *adj, formal* **:** relating to or in the form of money ▪ the hope of *pecuniary* [=(more commonly) *financial*] reward ▪ *pecuniary* losses

ped·a·gog·i·cal /ˌpɛdəˈgɑːʤɪkəl/ *also* **ped·a·gog·ic** /ˌpɛdəˈgɑːʤɪk/ *adj, formal* **:** of or relating to teachers or education ▪ *pedagogical* methods/practices
— ped·a·gog·i·cal·ly /ˌpɛdəˈgɑːʤɪkli/ *adv*

ped·a·gogue /ˈpɛdəˌgɑːg/ *noun, pl* **-gogues** [*count*] *formal + old-fashioned* **:** TEACHER

ped·a·go·gy /ˈpɛdəgoʊʤi/ *noun* [*noncount*] *formal* **:** the art, science, or profession of teaching

[1]**ped·al** /ˈpɛdl/ *noun, pl* **-als** [*count*]
1 : a flat piece of metal, rubber, etc., that you push with your foot to make a machine move, work, or stop ▪ a bike's *pedals* ▪ a car's ***gas/brake pedal*** — see picture at BICYCLE
2 : a lever on a piano, organ, etc., that you push with your foot to make or change a sound
put the pedal to the metal *US, informal* **1 :** to drive very fast **2 :** to work very quickly ▪ We are going to have to *put the pedal to the metal* if we want to finish on time.

[2]**pedal** *verb* **-als;** *US* **-aled** *or Brit* **-alled;** *US* **-al·ing** *or Brit* **-al·ling**
1 : to push the pedals of (something, such as a bicycle) [+ *obj*] *pedal* a bike [*no obj*] He was *pedaling* as fast as he could.
2 *always followed by an adverb or preposition* [*no obj*] **:** to ride a bicycle to a particular place ▪ He *pedaled* down to the store.

pedal boat *noun, pl* **~ boats** [*count*] **:** PADDLEBOAT 1

ped·a·lo /ˈpɛdəˌloʊ/ *noun, pl* **-los** [*count*] *Brit* **:** PADDLEBOAT 1

pedal pushers *noun* [*plural*] *old-fashioned* **:** girls' or women's pants that go down to a part of the leg that is a short distance below the knee

pedal steel *noun, pl* **~ steels** [*count*] **:** a musical instrument that has strings which are plucked while being pressed with a movable steel bar and a pedal that can change the pitch of the strings — called also *pedal steel guitar, steel guitar*

ped·ant /ˈpɛdn̩t/ *noun, pl* **-ants** [*count*] *disapproving* **:** a person who annoys other people by correcting small errors and giving too much attention to minor details ▪ a dull *pedant*
— pe·dan·tic /pɪˈdæntɪk/ *adj* [*more ~; most ~*] ▪ a *pedantic* teacher ▪ a *pedantic* insistence on following the rules exactly **— pe·dan·ti·cal·ly** /pɪˈdæntɪkli/ *adv* **— ped·ant·ry** /ˈpɛdn̩tri/ *noun* [*noncount*] ▪ His instructions were precise to the point of *pedantry*.

ped·dle /ˈpɛdl/ *verb* **ped·dles; ped·dled; ped·dling** [+ *obj*]
1 : to sell (something) usually in small amounts and often by traveling to different places ▪ They *peddled* fruits and vegetables out of their truck on the side of the road. ▪ She now ***peddles her wares*** [=sells her products] on the Internet.
2 : to try to get people to accept or believe (something) ▪ He *peddled* his idea for a new movie to every executive in Hollywood. ▪ The mayor's aides tried to *peddle* his innocence to reporters. ▪ *peddling* gossip

ped·dler /ˈpɛdlɚ/ *noun, pl* **-dlers** [*count*]
1 *US* **:** someone who sells things in small amounts often by traveling to different places **:** a person who peddles something ▪ a poor street *peddler* [=(*Brit*) *pedlar*] ▪ a *fruit* peddler
2 : a person who sells illegal drugs ▪ The police are trying to get drug *peddlers* off the streets. = (*Brit*) The police are trying to get *peddlers* off the street.

ped·es·tal /ˈpɛdəstl/ *noun, pl* **-tals** [*count*]
1 : the base of a column or other tall object ▪ the *pedestal of* a vase/lamp/statue
2 — used to describe the position of someone who is admired, successful, etc. ▪ Her boyfriend ***put/placed her on a pedestal.*** [=thought of her as a perfect person with no faults] ▪ He wanted a career as an actor, but he didn't want to be *put on a pedestal*. [=to be treated like a big star] ▪ They're trying to ***knock the champions off their pedestal.*** [=to defeat the champions]

pedestal

[1]**pe·des·tri·an** /pəˈdɛstrijən/ *noun, pl* **-ans** [*count*] **:** a person who is walking in a city, along a road, etc. ▪ The car slid off the road and almost hit a group of *pedestrians*.

[2]**pedestrian** *adj*
1 [*more ~; most ~*] **:** not interesting or unusual **:** ORDINARY ▪ He lived a *pedestrian* life, working at the paper mill and living in his trailer. ▪ *pedestrian* concerns like paying the bills and getting the kids to school on time
2 *always used before a noun* **:** relating to or designed for people who are walking ▪ This area has a lot of *pedestrian* traffic. [=there are a lot of pedestrians in this area] ▪ a *pedestrian* mall

pedestrian crossing *noun, pl* **~ -ings** [*count*] *formal* **:** CROSSWALK

pe·des·tri·an·ise /pəˈdɛstrijəˌnaɪz/ *verb* **-is·es; -ised; -is·ing** [+ *obj*] *Brit* **:** to change (an area, street, etc.) so that no vehicles are allowed ▪ the city's *pedestrianised* shopping district

pe·di·at·ric (*US*) *or Brit* **pae·di·at·ric** /ˌpiːdiˈætrɪk/ *adj, always used before a noun, medical* **:** of or relating to the medical care or illnesses of children ▪ *pediatric* treatment ▪ a *pediatric* surgeon

pe·di·a·tri·cian (*US*) *or Brit* **pae·di·a·tri·cian** /ˌpiːdijəˈtrɪʃən/ *noun, pl* **-cians** [*count*] **:** a doctor who treats babies and children

pe·di·at·rics (*US*) *or Brit* **pae·di·at·rics** /ˌpiːdiˈætrɪks/ *noun* [*noncount*] *medical* **:** a branch of medicine that deals with the development, care, and diseases of babies and children ▪ a doctor who specializes in *pediatrics*

ped·i·cure /ˈpɛdɪˌkjɚ/ *noun, pl* **-cures** [*count*] **:** a treatment to improve the appearance and health of the feet or toenails ▪ She's getting a *pedicure* tomorrow. — compare MANICURE

ped·i·gree /ˈpɛdəˌgriː/ *noun, pl* **-grees**
1 : the history of the family members in a person's or animal's past especially when it is good or impressive [*count*] That horse has an impressive *pedigree*. ▪ Her husband has a noble/aristocratic *pedigree*. [=the people in his family were noble/aristocratic] ▪ What is the dog's *pedigree*? [*noncount*] The puppy came with papers proving its *pedigree*.
2 : the origin and history of something especially when it is good or impressive [*count*] a painting's *pedigree* ▪ Democracy is an idea with a *pedigree* stretching back to ancient

Greece. ▪ The company has an excellent *pedigree* with over a century in the business. [*noncount*] She wants to go to a school with *pedigree*. [=a school that has a long and impressive history]

– **ped·i·greed** /ˈpɛdəˌgriːd/ *or* **pedigree** *adj* ▪ a *pedigreed* horse/school/family

ped·i·ment /ˈpɛdəmənt/ *noun, pl* **-ments** [*count*] : a triangular area on the face of a building below the roof, above an entrance, etc.

ped·lar /ˈpɛdlɚ/ *noun, pl* **-lars** [*count*] *Brit* : PEDDLER 1

pe·dom·e·ter /pɪˈdɑːmətɚ/ *noun, pl* **-ters** [*count*] : a device that measures the distance a person travels by walking

pe·do·phile (*US*) *or Brit* **pae·do·phile** /ˈpɛdəˌfajəl, *Brit* ˈpiːdəˌfajəl/ *noun, pl* **-philes** [*count*] : a person who has a sexual interest in children

pe·do·phil·ia (*US*) *or Brit* **pae·do·phil·ia** /ˌpɛdəˈfɪlijə, *Brit* ˌpiːdəˈfɪlijə/ *noun* [*noncount*] : sexual feelings or activities that involve children

pee /ˈpiː/ *noun, informal*

1 [*noncount*] : URINE

2 [*singular*] : an act of passing urine from the body ▪ Does she have to ***take a pee***? = (*Brit*) Does she have to ***have a pee***? = (*Brit*) Does she have to ***go for a pee***?

– **pee** *verb* **pees; peed; pee·ing** [*no obj*] ▪ The dog *peed* [=*urinated*] on the floor.

peek /ˈpiːk/ *verb* **peeks; peeked; peek·ing** [*no obj*]

1 a : to look at someone or something secretly especially from a hidden place ▪ A little girl *peeked* around the corner of the chair at him. ▪ She *peeked* [=*peered*] through a hole in the fence. ▪ Close your eyes, and no *peeking*! **b :** to look at something briefly ▪ She *peeked* ahead to the next chapter to see what happened next. ▪ He allowed some of his friends to *peek* at his next painting.

2 : to show slightly : to be slightly visible — usually *+ out* ▪ Her slip *peeked out* from beneath her skirt. [=a small part of her slip could be seen beneath her skirt]

– **peek** *noun, pl* **peeks** [*count*] ▪ Take another *peek* at the cake in the oven to see if it's done. ▪ They tried to ***sneak a peek*** at the actors getting ready behind the curtain. ▪ We saw a ***sneak peek*** [=a brief showing] of the movie that will be released next month.

peek·a·boo /ˈpiːkəˌbuː/ *noun* [*noncount*] : a game played with a baby in which you cover and then uncover your face and say "Peekaboo!" ▪ play *peekaboo* — called also (*Brit*) *peepbo*

[1]**peel** /ˈpiːl/ *verb* **peels; peeled; peel·ing**

1 [*+ obj*] : to remove the skin from (a fruit, vegetable, etc.) ▪ *peel* an apple ▪ *peel* the cucumbers

2 *always followed by an adverb or preposition* [*+ obj*] : to remove (a covering, shell, etc.) from something ▪ They *peeled* back the sheet to display the new sculpture. — often *+ from* ▪ An animal had *peeled* the bark *from* the tree. ▪ We had to *peel* the wallpaper *from* the wall. — often *+ off* ▪ (*informal*) Guests *peeled off* [=*took off*] their wet coats by the door. ▪ They *peeled* the old wallpaper *off*.

3 [*no obj*] **a :** to come off in pieces ▪ The paint is *peeling* (off). ▪ She got sunburned and the skin on her back is *peeling* (off). **b :** to lose an outer layer of skin, bark, etc. ▪ She got sunburned and her back is *peeling*.

keep your eyes peeled see [1]EYE

peel off [*phrasal verb*] *informal* : to turn and go away from something quickly ▪ One of the jets *peeled off* from the formation and headed back.

peel out [*phrasal verb*] *US, informal* : to speed away from a place in a car, on a motorcycle, etc. ▪ Dirt and gravel flew as he *peeled out* into the street.

– **peel·er** *noun, pl* **-ers** [*count*] ▪ a potato/vegetable *peeler*

[2]**peel** *noun, pl* **peels** [*count*] : the skin of a fruit ▪ a banana *peel* ▪ an orange *peel* — see color picture on page C5

[1]**peep** /ˈpiːp/ *noun, pl* **peeps**

1 [*count*] : a quick, high sound that is made by a young bird or that is like the sound made by a young bird ▪ the *peep* of a chick

2 [*singular*] *informal* : a word or sound ▪ I don't want to hear a single *peep* out of you. ▪ We didn't hear a *peep* coming from his office. ▪ They accepted her decision with hardly a *peep* of protest.

– see also PEEPS

[2]**peep** *verb* **peeps; peeped; peep·ing** [*no obj*] : to make a quick, high sound : to make a peep ▪ I heard a chick *peep*. ▪ a *peeping* sound — compare [3]PEEP

[3]**peep** *verb* **peeps; peeped; peeping**

1 *always followed by an adverb or preposition* [*no obj*] : to look very quickly at someone or something ▪ I'll just *peep* [=*peek*] in the room to see if the baby is sleeping. ▪ He *peeped* [=*peered*] through a hole in the fence.

2 *always followed by an adverb or preposition* [*no obj*] : to show slightly : to be slightly visible ▪ Early spring flowers were *peeping* through the snow.

3 [*+ obj*] *slang* : to look at or see (someone or something) ▪ We *peeped* [=*saw*] him at the restaurant. ▪ *Peep* this [=check this out]—I've got two tickets for the show.

– compare [2]PEEP

peep·bo /ˈpiːpˌbou/ *noun* [*noncount*] *Brit* : PEEKABOO

peep·er /ˈpiːpɚ/ *noun, pl* **-ers** [*count*] : a type of small American frog that makes a peeping sound — called also *spring peeper*

peep·hole /ˈpiːpˌhoul/ *noun, pl* **-holes** [*count*] : a hole that is used to look through something (such as a door) to the other side

peeping Tom *noun, pl* **~ Toms** [*count*] : a person who secretly looks into other people's windows to see them naked

peeps /ˈpiːps/ *noun* [*plural*] *US slang* : people and especially the people who are your friends ▪ just me and my *peeps*

peep show *noun, pl* **~ shows** [*count*] : a show in which someone looks into a box, room, etc., through a small hole or window and sees pictures or a performance usually involving sex

[1]**peer** /ˈpiɚ/ *noun, pl* **peers** [*count*]

1 : a person who belongs to the same age group or social group as someone else ▪ his academic *peers* [=people in the same grade or level of school] ▪ He was respected and admired by his *peers*. ▪ teenagers spending time with their ***peer groups*** ▪ (*chiefly US, law*) You have the right to be tried by ***a jury of your peers***. [=a jury whose members are from the same community as you]

2 : a member of the British nobility — see also LIFE PEER

[2]**peer** *verb, always followed by an adverb or preposition* **peers; peered; peer·ing** [*no obj*] : to look closely or carefully especially because something or someone is difficult to see ▪ She *peered* into the dark closet looking for her missing shoe. ▪ He *peered* down the well. ▪ An animal *peered* out from the woods next to their camp. ▪ He *peered* over the fence.

peer·age /ˈpirɪʤ/ *noun, pl* **-ages** *formal*

1 ***the peerage*** : the people who are members of the British nobility : the people who are peers

2 [*count*] : the rank of a British peer ▪ He was given the *peerage* after years of devoted service to the community.

peer·ess /ˈpirəs/ *noun, pl* **-ess·es** [*count*]

1 : a woman who is a member of the British nobility

2 : the wife or widow of a peer (sense 2)

peer·less /ˈpiɚləs/ *adj* : having no equal : better than all others ▪ As an athlete he is *peerless*.

peer pressure *noun* [*noncount*] : a feeling that you must do the same things as other people of your age and social group in order to be liked or respected by them ▪ She started drinking in high school because of *peer pressure*.

peer review *noun* [*noncount*] : a process by which a scholarly work (such as a paper or a research proposal) is checked by a group of experts in the same field to make sure it meets the necessary standards before it is published or accepted

peeve /ˈpiːv/ *noun, pl* **peeves** [*count*] : something that annoys someone ▪ One of her *peeves* is people who are always late. — see also PET PEEVE

peeved /ˈpiːvd/ *adj* [*more ~; most ~*] *informal* : angry or annoyed ▪ He's *peeved* at me because I borrowed his car without asking. ▪ Her boss was *peeved* by/about the mistakes she made with the customer's order. ▪ I'm feeling pretty *peeved*.

pee·vish /ˈpiːvɪʃ/ *adj* [*more ~; most ~*] : feeling or showing irritation ▪ a *peevish* frown ▪ *peevish* patients in the doctor's waiting room

– **pee·vish·ly** *adv* ▪ "I didn't do anything wrong," he answered *peevishly*. – **pee·vish·ness** *noun* [*noncount*]

[1]**peg** /ˈpɛg/ *noun, pl* **pegs** [*count*]

1 : a small piece of wood, metal, or other material that is used to hold or fasten things or to hang things on ▪ Her coat hung on a *peg* by the door. ▪ a ***tent peg*** [=a pointed piece of wood or metal that is pushed into the ground to hold the corners of a tent in position]

2 : a wooden piece in a musical instrument (such as a violin) that is turned to tighten or loosen a string ▪ a ***tuning peg***

3 *Brit* : CLOTHESPIN

a peg to hang something on *Brit* : something (such as a

P

fact or issue) that is used as support or a reason for something said or done • He used the incident as *a peg to hang* his theory *on.*

a square peg in a round hole **:** someone who does not fit in a particular place or situation • She felt like *a square peg in a round hole* at the new school until she made some new friends.

off the peg Brit **:** in a store where clothes are sold in different sizes that are not made to fit a particular person • He bought that suit *off the peg.* [=(*US*) *off the rack*] — see also OFF-THE-PEG

take/knock/bring someone down a peg **:** to make (someone) feel less important or proud • He was *taken down a peg* when an even better player joined the team. • She needs to be *taken down a peg.* [=*humbled*]

[2]**peg** *verb* **pegs; pegged; peg·ging** [+ *obj*]

1 a : to fasten (something) with pegs • Is the tent *pegged* down all the way? • (*Brit*) She was outside *pegging* the laundry to the clothesline. **b :** to put a peg into (something) • He *pegged* the boards.

2 a : to keep (something, such as a price) at a particular level or rate • *peg* the price of wheat at its current level **b :** to link (something) to another amount or value • The foreign currency is *pegged* to the U.S. dollar. [=its value changes when the U.S. dollar's value does] • His bonus is *pegged* to how many sales he makes each year for the company.

3 *informal* **:** to think of or identify (someone) as a certain kind of person • The salesman ***had me pegged*** [=understood what kind of person I am] in a matter of minutes. — usually + *as* • She *pegged* him right away *as* a nice guy. — sometimes + *for* • She had him *pegged for* a liar.

4 *US, informal* **:** [1]THROW • He *pegged* the ball to first base.

peg away [*phrasal verb*] *chiefly Brit, informal* **:** to work hard — usually + *at* • He sat there *pegging away at* his homework.

peg out [*phrasal verb*] *Brit, informal* **:** to die • He doesn't want to *peg out* because of somebody else's mistakes.

peg leg *noun, pl* **~ legs** [*count*] *old-fashioned + informal* **:** an artificial leg usually made of wood and attached at the knee

pe·jo·ra·tive /pɪˈʤorətɪv/ *adj* [*more ~; most ~*] *formal* **:** insulting to someone or something **:** expressing criticism • a *pejorative* term • a word with *pejorative* connotations

– pejorative *noun, pl* **-tives** [*count*] • a word that is used as a *pejorative* [=an insulting word] **– pe·jo·ra·tive·ly** *adv* • The word is often used *pejoratively.*

Pe·king·ese *or* **Pe·kin·ese** /ˌpiːkəˈniːz/ *noun, pl* **Pekingese** *or* **Pekinese** [*count*] **:** a small dog with a flat face and long, soft fur

pe·lag·ic /pəˈlæʤɪk/ *adj, technical* **:** relating to or living in the sea far from the shore • *pelagic* fish/birds/waters

pel·i·can /ˈpɛlɪkən/ *noun, pl* **-cans** [*count*] **:** a large ocean bird that has a large bag that is part of its lower bill for catching and holding fish — see color picture on page C9

pelican crossing *noun, pl* **~ -ings** [*count*] *Brit* **:** a place where a person can stop traffic in order to cross the road by pressing a button that controls the traffic lights

pel·let /ˈpɛlət/ *noun, pl* **-lets** [*count*]

1 : a small, hard ball of food, medicine, etc. • food *pellets* for rabbits = rabbit *pellets*

2 : a small metal object that is shot from a gun • shotgun *pellets* • a ***pellet gun*** [=a special gun that is designed to shoot pellets]

pell–mell /ˌpɛlˈmɛl/ *adv* **:** in a confused and hurried way • a car racing *pell-mell* through the streets

– pell–mell *adj* • the *pell-mell* pace of modern life

pel·lu·cid /pəˈluːsəd/ *adj* [*more ~; most ~*] *literary* **:** very clear • *pellucid* water • *pellucid* prose

pel·met /ˈpɛlmət/ *noun, pl* **-mets** [*count*] *Brit* **:** VALANCE 1

pel·o·ton /ˈpɛləˌtɑːn/ *noun, pl* **-tons** [*count*] **:** the main group of riders in a bicycle race • He broke away from the *peloton* and sprinted into the lead.

[1]**pelt** /ˈpɛlt/ *verb* **pelts; pelt·ed; pelt·ing**

1 [+ *obj*] **:** to repeatedly hit (someone or something) with things thrown from a distance • Rioters *pelted* the police. — often + *with* • The boys *pelted* the building *with* rocks.

2 [+ *obj*] **:** to hit against (something) repeatedly • Rain *pelted* the windowpanes. • the *pelting* rain

3 *always followed by an adverb or preposition* [*no obj*] **:** to move very quickly • The children came *pelting* down the street. • We were *pelting* along.

[2]**pelt** *noun, pl* **pelts** [*count*] **:** the skin of a dead animal especially with its hair, wool, or fur still on it • a lion's *pelt*

pel·vic /ˈpɛlvɪk/ *adj* **:** relating to or located in or near the pelvis • *pelvic* bones • a *pelvic* exam [=an examination of the pelvis and the organs in it]

pel·vis /ˈpɛlvəs/ *noun, pl* **-vis·es** [*count*] **:** the wide curved bones between the spine and the leg bones — see picture at HUMAN

[1]**pen** /ˈpɛn/ *noun, pl* **pens :** a writing instrument that uses ink [*count*] She signed her name with a *pen.* [*noncount*] She signed her name ***in pen.*** — compare PENCIL

put/set pen to paper **:** to write or begin to write something • She thought about writing a novel for several years before she finally *put pen to paper.*

– compare [3]PEN, [5]PEN

[2]**pen** *verb* **pens; penned; pen·ning** [+ *obj*] **:** to write (something) • *pen* a letter • She *penned* a novel. • a poem *penned* by Shakespeare — compare [4]PEN

[3]**pen** *noun, pl* **pens** [*count*] **:** a small enclosed area for farm animals • a sheep *pen* — compare [1]PEN, [5]PEN

[4]**pen** *verb* **pens; penned; pen·ning** [+ *obj*] **:** to put or keep (a person or animal) in an enclosed area — usually used as *(be) penned* • They *were penned* behind a wooden fence. • cattle *penned* in the barn

pen in/up [*phrasal verb*] ***pen (someone or something) in/up*** **:** to put or keep (a person or animal) in an enclosed area **:** to prevent (someone or something) from moving beyond a particular area — usually used as *(be) penned in/up* • Several dogs *were penned up* [=*penned*] behind the house. • The men *were penned up* [=*trapped*] on the ship for months. — often used figuratively • She felt *penned in* by their relationship.

– compare [2]PEN

[5]**pen** *noun*

the pen US, informal **:** PRISON • He was sent to *the pen* [=the penitentiary] for armed robbery.

– compare [1]PEN, [3]PEN

pe·nal /ˈpiːnl/ *adj*

1 *always used before a noun* **:** relating to or used for punishment • *penal* laws • a ***penal institution*** [=*prison*] • a ***penal colony*** [=a place where prisoners are sent to live]

2 *Brit* **:** very severe • *penal* interest rates

penal code *noun, pl* **~ codes** [*count*] *law* **:** a set of laws relating to crimes and the punishments for those crimes

pe·nal·ize *also Brit* **pe·nal·ise** /ˈpiːnəˌlaɪz/ *verb* **-iz·es; -ized; -iz·ing** [+ *obj*]

1 : to punish (someone or something) for breaking a rule or a law • The company was *penalized* for not paying taxes. • The hockey player was *penalized* for holding.

2 : to give (someone) an unfair disadvantage • This law would unfairly *penalize* immigrants.

pen·al·ty /ˈpɛnlti/ *noun, pl* **-ties**

1 : punishment for breaking a rule or law [*count*] The company was given/assessed a severe/stiff *penalty* for the violation. • They allowed him to pay back the money without a *penalty.* [*noncount*] They allowed him to pay back the money without *penalty.* — see also DEATH PENALTY

2 [*count*] **:** a disadvantage or difficulty you experience • Lack of privacy is one of the *penalties* you pay for fame.

3 [*count*] **:** a punishment or disadvantage given to a team or player for breaking a rule in a game • The hockey player was given/assessed a *penalty* for holding.

pay the penalty see [1]PAY

penalty box *noun, pl* **~ boxes** [*count*] **:** the area beside an ice hockey rink where a player who has been given a penalty sits for a certain amount of time

penalty kick *noun, pl* **~ kicks** [*count*] **:** a kick in soccer or rugby that a player makes when the other team has broken a rule

penalty shot *noun, pl* **~ shots** [*count*] **:** a shot in hockey that a player makes when the other team has broken a rule

pen·ance /ˈpɛnəns/ *noun* **:** something that you do or are given to do in order to show that you are sad or sorry about doing something wrong [*noncount*] She did/performed (an act of) *penance* for her sins. [*singular*] He did charitable work as a *penance.*

pence *Brit plural of* PENNY

pen·chant /ˈpɛntʃənt/ *noun, pl* **-chants** [*count*] **:** a strong liking for something or a strong tendency to behave in a certain way — usually + *for* • He has a *penchant for* asking stupid questions. [=he asks a lot of stupid questions] • Her *penchant for* mathematics helped her to become an engineer.

[1]**pen·cil** /ˈpɛnsəl/ *noun, pl* **-cils** : an instrument used for writing and drawing that has a hard outer part and a black or colored center part [*count*] Use a *pencil* instead of a pen so you can erase your mistakes. [*noncount*] Write your answers ***in pencil.*** [=using a pencil] — often used before another noun • a *pencil* sketch • a ***pencil sharpener*** [=a device used to make the tip of a pencil sharp so that it can be used for writing] • a ***pencil case*** [=a small box for holding pencils and other small items, such as erasers] — see picture at OFFICE; compare PEN

[2]**pencil** *verb, pl* **-cils**; *US* **-ciled** *or Brit* **-cilled**; *US* **-cil·ing** *or Brit* **-cil·ling** [+ *obj*] : to draw or write (something) with a pencil • He *penciled* some notes on a piece of paper.

pencil in [*phrasal verb*] ***pencil (someone or something) in*** *or* ***pencil in (someone or something)*** : to put (someone or something that may be changed later) on a schedule, list, etc. • Would you like me to *pencil* you *in* [=to schedule you] for Thursday morning at 11? — sometimes used figuratively • He was *penciled in* as the director's replacement.

pencil pusher *noun, pl* ~ **-ers** [*count*] *US, informal* : PAPER PUSHER

pen·dant /ˈpɛndənt/ *noun, pl* **-dants** [*count*] : a piece of jewelry that hangs on a chain or a cord which is worn around your neck — see color picture on page C11

pen·dent *or* **pen·dant** /ˈpɛndənt/ *adj, formal* : hanging down from above • a *pendent* light fixture

[1]**pend·ing** /ˈpɛndɪŋ/ *prep, formal* : while waiting for (something) • He is being held in jail *pending* trial. • She received a four-year sentence and is currently out on bail *pending* appeal.

[2]**pending** *adj, formal*

1 : not yet decided or acted on • bills *pending* in Congress • a *pending* visa application • The results of the investigation are *pending.* • There are lawsuits *pending* against the company.

2 : happening or likely to happen soon • the company's *pending* [=*impending*] move to a new location

pen·du·lous /ˈpɛnʤələs/ *adj* [*more* ~; *most* ~] *formal + literary* : hanging down and swinging freely • *pendulous* silver earrings

– **pen·du·lous·ly** *adv* • blossoms dangling *pendulously* from the branches

pen·du·lum /ˈpɛnʤələm/ *noun, pl* **-lums** [*count*] : a stick with a weight at the bottom that swings back and forth inside a clock — often used figuratively • The fashion *pendulum* swung from silver jewelry to gold and back again. [=silver jewelry was popular for a while, then gold became popular, and then silver became popular again]

pen·e·tra·ble /ˈpɛnətrəbəl/ *adj* [*more* ~; *most* ~] : allowing someone or something to pass through or enter : able to be penetrated • an easily *penetrable* border

– **pen·e·tra·bil·i·ty** /ˌpɛnətrəˈbɪləti/ *noun* [*noncount*]

pen·e·trate /ˈpɛnəˌtreɪt/ *verb* **-trates**; **-trat·ed**; **-trat·ing**

1 : to go through or into something [+ *obj*] These bullets can *penetrate* armor. • radiation *penetrating* the Earth's atmosphere [*no obj*] The bullet failed to *penetrate.* • The heat *penetrated* through the wall. • The roots of these plants have been known to *penetrate* to a depth of more than 15 feet.

2 [+ *obj*] : to see or show the way through (something) • Our eyes were unable to *penetrate* the darkness. [=we were unable to see through the darkness] • My car's headlights couldn't *penetrate* the dense fog. • They were unable to ***penetrate his disguise.*** [=to see or realize who he really was behind his disguise]

3 [+ *obj*] : to succeed in becoming part of (an organization, a community, etc.) • The movie is about foreign agents who *penetrate* [=*infiltrate*] the CIA. • The company is trying to *penetrate* [=sell its products in] the U.S. market.

4 [+ *obj*] : to succeed in understanding or finding (something) • scientists trying to *penetrate* the secrets hidden in our genes • attempting to *penetrate* the mysteries of human nature

5 : to be understood or noticed by someone [+ *obj*] The truth had not yet *penetrated* my consciousness. [=I had not yet realized the truth] [*no obj*] The truth had not yet *penetrated.*

6 [+ *obj*] *of a man* : to put the penis into the vagina or the anus of (another person) during sex

penetrating *adj* [*more* ~; *most* ~]

1 a : able to understand something clearly and fully • She is one of our most *penetrating* and provocative critical thinkers. • a *penetrating* mind **b** : helping people to understand something clearly and fully • an author famous for her *penetrating* social commentary • a *penetrating* account of what really happened during the crisis

2 : spreading out deeply or widely • *penetrating* cold • flowers that give off a *penetrating* perfume

3 *of sounds* : loud and clear and sometimes unpleasant • a deep, *penetrating* voice • a baby's *penetrating* wail

4 ✧ People who have ***penetrating eyes*** or a ***penetrating gaze/stare/look*** make you feel uncomfortable by looking at you in a way that makes you feel that they know what you are thinking. • She transfixed me with a *penetrating gaze.*

– **pen·e·trat·ing·ly** *adv* • a *penetratingly* sweet aroma

pen·e·tra·tion /ˌpɛnəˈtreɪʃən/ *noun, pl* **-tions**

1 : the act of going through or into something : the act of penetrating something [*noncount*] Cuts in the skin could permit the *penetration* of bacteria into the body. • the *penetration* of the CIA by foreign agents • the *penetration* of the U.S. market by a foreign company [*count*] multiple *penetrations* into enemy territory

2 [*noncount*] *formal* : an ability to understand things clearly and fully • a writer who analyzes the underlying causes of the recession with great *penetration*

pen·e·tra·tive /ˈpɛnəˌtreɪtɪv, *Brit* ˈpɛnətrətɪv/ *adj*

1 — used to describe sexual activity in which a man puts his penis into another person's vagina or anus • *penetrative* sex

2 [*more* ~; *most* ~] *formal* : able to enter or go through something • *penetrative* ammunition

3 [*more* ~; *most* ~] *formal* : having or showing an ability to understand things clearly and fully • *penetrative* insights

pen friend *noun, pl* ~ **friends** [*count*] *Brit* : PEN PAL

pen·guin /ˈpɛŋgwən/ *noun, pl* **-guins** [*count*] : a black-and-white bird that cannot fly, that uses its wings for swimming, and that lives in or near the Antarctic

penguin

pen·i·cil·lin /ˌpɛnəˈsɪlən/ *noun* [*noncount*] : a medicine that is used to kill harmful bacteria

pe·nile /ˈpiːˌnajəl/ *adj, always used before a noun, formal* : of or relating to the penis • *penile* dysfunction

pen·in·su·la /pəˈnɪnsələ, *Brit* pəˈnɪnsjələ/ *noun, pl* **-las** [*count*] : a piece of land that is almost entirely surrounded by water and is attached to a larger land area • They built their house on a narrow *peninsula.* • the Yucatan *Peninsula* — see color picture on page C7

– **pen·in·su·lar** /pəˈnɪnsələ, *Brit* pəˈnɪnsjələ/ *adj, formal* • the culture of *peninsular* Spain

pe·nis /ˈpiːnəs/ *noun, pl* **-nis·es** [*count*] : the part of the body of men and male animals that is used for sex and through which urine leaves the body

pen·i·tence /ˈpɛnətəns/ *noun* [*noncount*] *formal* : a feeling of deep sadness because you have done something wrong • Forgiveness requires *penitence.*

[1]**pen·i·tent** /ˈpɛnətənt/ *adj* [*more* ~; *most* ~] *formal* : feeling or showing sorrow and regret because you have done something wrong • a *penitent* [=(more commonly) *repentant*] sinner • a *penitent* gesture

[2]**penitent** *noun, pl* **-tents** [*count*] *formal* : a person who is sorry for doing something wrong and asks for forgiveness : a penitent person • *penitents* seeking God's forgiveness

pen·i·ten·tial /ˌpɛnəˈtɛnʃəl/ *adj, formal* : relating to the feeling of being sorry for doing something wrong : relating to penitence or penance • *penitential* prayers • a *penitential* journey/pilgrimage

pen·i·ten·tia·ry /ˌpɛnəˈtɛnʃəri/ *noun, pl* **-ries** [*count*] *US* : PRISON — often used in the names of prisons • Colorado State *Penitentiary* ***synonyms*** see [1]JAIL

pen·knife /ˈpɛnˌnaɪf/ *noun, pl* **-knives** [*count*] : a small knife with a folding blade : POCKETKNIFE

pen·light /ˈpɛnˌlaɪt/ *noun, pl* **-lights** [*count*] : a small flashlight that looks like a pen

pen·man·ship /ˈpɛnmənˌʃɪp/ *noun* [*noncount*] *formal*

1 : the art or practice of writing by hand • My third grade teacher thought it was important for us to learn *penmanship.*

2 : the quality or style of someone's handwriting • Your poor *penmanship* [=*handwriting*] makes it hard to read your work.

pen name *noun, pl* ~ **names** [*count*] : a name used by a writer instead of the writer's real name • Samuel L. Clemens is better known by his *pen name* "Mark Twain."

pen·nant /ˈpɛnənt/ *noun, pl* **-nants** [*count*]

P

1 : a long, thin, pointed flag • *pennants* waving atop the tower
2 *baseball* : the prize that is awarded to the champions of the American League and the National League each year • The Red Sox won the American League *pennant* in 2004.

pen·ni·less /ˈpɛnɪləs/ *adj* : having no money : very poor • a *penniless* vagrant • She was unemployed and *penniless.*

Penn·syl·va·nia Dutch /ˌpɛnsəlˈveɪnjə-/ *noun* [*noncount*]
1 : a group of people originally from Germany who settled in Pennsylvania in the 18th century
2 : a form of German spoken by the Pennsylvania Dutch

pen·ny /ˈpɛni/ *noun, pl US* **pen·nies** /ˈpɛniz/ *or Brit* **pence** /ˈpɛns/ [*count*]
1 **a** *pl* ***pennies*** : a coin or a unit of money equal to 1/100 of a dollar : CENT **b** *pl* ***pence*** : a coin or a unit of money equal to 1/100 of a British pound — abbr. *p* **c** *pl* ***pence*** : a British coin used before 1971 that was equal to 1/12 of a shilling — abbr. *p*
2 **a** : a small amount of money • We got the car for just *pennies.* [=it didn't cost very much] • When you're trying to save money, ***every penny helps/counts.*** [=even a small amount of money is important] • Our vacation was expensive, but it was ***worth every penny.*** [=it was worth the entire amount that we paid for it] • (*chiefly Brit*) He was trying to ***earn/turn an honest penny.*** [=earn money for honest hard work] **b** : the least amount of money • I didn't have a *penny* (to my name). [=I did not have any money at all]
(a) penny for your thoughts — used to ask what someone is thinking about • "*A penny for your thoughts*?" "Oh, I'm just thinking about what I want to do over the weekend."
a penny saved ✧ The saying ***a penny saved (is a penny earned)*** means that it is important to save your money. • Well, you know what they say about *a penny saved.*
a pretty penny : a large amount of money • That will cost *a pretty penny.* [=that will be very expensive]
in for a penny, in for a pound *Brit* — used to say that you should finish what you have started to do even though it may be difficult or expensive • "If you want to quit, I'll understand." "No, I'm sure we can do this. *In for a penny, in for a pound.*"
not a penny less/more : no less or no more than a certain amount of money • I'll do the job for 100 dollars and *not a penny less.* [=I won't do the job unless I am paid at least 100 dollars] • I'll pay you 100 dollars and *not a penny more.* [=I'll pay you 100 dollars, but I won't pay you any more than that]
pinch pennies see [1]PINCH
ten a penny see TEN
the penny drops *Brit, informal* — used to say that someone finally understands something after not understanding it for a time • I had to explain it to him three times, but finally *the penny dropped.* [=he understood the explanation]

penny–ante *adj, US, informal + disapproving* : not important, valuable, or impressive : SMALL-TIME • a *penny-ante* operation • *penny-ante* politics

penny arcade *noun, pl* ~ **-cades** [*count*] *US* : ARCADE 3

penny candy *noun* [*noncount*] *US* : candy that costs only a few pennies for each piece • bags of *penny candy*

penny loafer *noun, pl* ~ **-ers** [*count*] *chiefly US* : a shoe without laces that has a strap with a slit that a penny can fit into on the top of the shoe

pen·ny–pinch·ing /ˈpɛniˌpɪntʃɪŋ/ *adj* : not wanting to spend a lot of money : very careful or too careful about spending money • a *penny-pinching* shopper
– **pen·ny–pinch·er** /ˈpɛniˌpɪntʃɚ/ *noun, pl* **-ers** [*count*] • Her roommate was a real *penny-pincher.*

pen·ny–wise /ˈpɛniˌwaɪz/ *adj*
penny-wise and/but pound-foolish : careful about small amounts of money but not about large amounts — used especially to describe something that is done to save a small amount of money now but that will cost a large amount of money in the future • The administration's plans to cut funding are *penny-wise and pound-foolish.*

pen pal *noun, pl* ~ **pals** [*count*] : a person (such as someone in a foreign country) who you exchange letters with even though you have never met — called also (*Brit*) *pen friend*

pen pusher *noun, pl* ~ **pushers** [*count*] *Brit, informal* : PAPER PUSHER

[1]**pen·sion** /ˈpɛnʃən/ *noun, pl* **-sions** [*count*] : an amount of money that a company or the government pays to a person who is old or sick and no longer works • Her *pension* arrives in the mail every month. • collect/receive a *pension* • retired people living on/off their *pensions* • a job with ***pension benefits*** [=a job that pays a pension after a number of years of employment] • a ***pension fund*** [=money that a company invests in order to earn money to pay pensions]

[2]**pension** *verb* **-sions; -sioned; -sion·ing**
pension off [*phrasal verb*] ***pension (someone) off*** *or* ***pension off (someone)*** *chiefly Brit* : to allow or force (an employee) to leave a job and accept a pension • She was *pensioned off* after 35 years with the company. [=she was forced to retire after 35 years with the company]

pen·sion·able /ˈpɛnʃənəbəl/ *adj, always used before a noun, chiefly Brit* : allowing someone to receive a pension • The factory offered *pensionable* employment. [=a job that includes pension benefits] • Her husband had reached *pensionable* age. [=her husband was old enough to qualify for a pension]

pen·sion·er /ˈpɛnʃənɚ/ *noun, pl* **-ers** [*count*] *chiefly Brit* : a person who receives or lives on a pension; *especially* : a person who receives a government pension • an ***old-age pensioner*** — compare OAP

pension plan *noun, pl* ~ **plans** [*count*] : an arrangement made with an employer to pay money to an employee after retirement • I work for this company because they have a good *pension plan.* — called also (*Brit*) *pension scheme*

pen·sive /ˈpɛnsɪv/ *adj* [*more* ~; *most* ~] : quietly sad or thoughtful • The child sat by himself, looking *pensive.* • a *pensive* young poet • a *pensive* mood/expression/sigh
– **pen·sive·ly** *adv* • She stared *pensively* out the window.
– **pen·sive·ness** *noun* [*noncount*]

pen·ta·gon /ˈpɛntəˌgɑːn/ *noun, pl* **-gons**
1 [*count*] *mathematics* : a flat shape that has five sides and five corners — see picture at GEOMETRY
2 ***the Pentagon*** **a** : the building in Washington, D.C., that is the headquarters of the U.S. Department of Defense • The general attended a meeting at *the Pentagon.* • *Pentagon* officials **b** : the leaders of the U.S. military • There was disagreement between the President and *the Pentagon* over the new military budget.
– **pen·tag·o·nal** /pɛnˈtægənl/ *adj, mathematics* • a *pentagonal* shape

pent·a·gram /ˈpɛntəˌgræm/ *noun, pl* **-grams** [*count*] : a shape that is like a star with five points formed by five straight lines and that is often used as a magic or religious symbol

pen·tam·e·ter /pɛnˈtæmətɚ/ *noun* [*noncount*] *technical* : a rhythm in poetry that has five stressed syllables in each line • a poem written in iambic *pentameter*

pen·tath·lon /pɛnˈtæθlən/ *noun, pl* **-lons** [*count*] : a sports contest for men that consists of five different events • the winner of the Olympic *pentathlon*
– **pen·tath·lete** /pɛnˈtæθˌliːt/ *noun, pl* **-letes** [*count*] • Olympic *pentathletes*

Pen·te·cost /ˈpɛntɪˌkɑːst/ *noun* [*noncount*] : a Christian holiday on the seventh Sunday after Easter that celebrates the appearance of the Holy Spirit to the apostles — called also (*Brit*) *Whit Sunday*

Pen·te·cos·tal /ˌpɛntɪˈkɑːstl/ *adj* : of, relating to, or belonging to a Christian group that emphasizes the power of the Holy Spirit and the authority of the Bible • a *Pentecostal* church • *Pentecostal* beliefs • She's *Pentecostal.*

pent·house /ˈpɛntˌhaʊs/ *noun, pl* **-hous·es** [*count*] : an apartment on the top floor or roof of a building • a luxurious *penthouse* — often used before another noun • a *penthouse* suite/apartment

pent–up *adj* : held or kept inside : not released • The children were full of *pent-up* energy after the long car ride. • *pent-up* anger/frustration/enthusiasm/excitement

pen·ul·ti·mate /pɪˈnʌltəmət/ *adj, always used before a noun, formal* : occurring immediately before the last one : next to the last • the *penultimate* chapter of the book [=the chapter that comes before the last chapter] • the *penultimate* syllable of the word

pe·nu·ri·ous /pəˈnɚrijəs, *Brit* pəˈnjʊərijəs/ *adj* [*more* ~; *most* ~] *formal* : very poor • *penurious* peasants • The *penurious* school system had to lay off several teachers.

pen·u·ry /ˈpɛnjəri/ *noun* [*noncount*] *formal* : the state of being very poor : extreme poverty • struggling with *penury* • living in *penury*

pe·on /ˈpiːˌɑːn/ *noun, pl* **-ons** [*count*]
1 *US* : a person who does hard or boring work for very little

money : a person who is not very important in a society or organization • The new policy changes affect the whole department, from the manager down to the office *peons.* [=the lowest paid workers in the office] • "Those rich politicians don't care about *peons* like us," she complained.

2 : a poor farm worker especially in Latin America

pe·o·ny /ˈpiːjəni/ *noun, pl* **-nies** [*count*] : a type of plant that has large round red, pink, or white flowers; *also* : the flower

[1]peo·ple /ˈpiːpəl/ *noun*

1 [*plural*] **a :** individual human beings ✧ This sense of *people* is the plural of *person.* • We met all sorts of *people* on the trip. • rich/poor *people* • The neighbors are nice *people.* • The *people* next door own a dog. **b :** human beings as a group : all or most people • He doesn't care what *people* think of him. [=he doesn't care what anyone thinks of him] • *People* can be really cruel sometimes. • *People* think the coach should be fired. • She tends to annoy *people.* • *People* say it's impossible, but I'm still going to try.

2 [*plural*] : a group of people who share a quality, interest, etc. • a book for young *people* • the American *people* • The environmental *people* [=the people who are interested in protecting the environment] are against the town's plan to build more houses along the river. • city *people* [=people who live in cities] — often used in compounds • business*people* [=people whose jobs involve business] • sales*people*

3 *pl* **peoples** [*count*] : a group of people who make up a race, tribe, nation, etc. • a *people* who migrated across the Bering Strait • the native *peoples* of Mexico • *peoples* of Asia

4 a ***the people*** : the ordinary people in a country who do not have special power or privileges • She is well-liked as a senator because she listens to *the people.* • *the* common *people* • He is a ***man of the people.*** [=he is someone who understands or is like ordinary people] **b** ***the People*** *US, law* — used to refer to the government of the U.S. or of a particular state in the name of a legal case • *The People* vs. John Doe

5 [*plural*] : people who are related to or connected with someone: such as **a** *literary* : people who are ruled or governed by someone • The queen was loved by her *people.* **b** *somewhat old-fashioned* : family members : people you are related to • She is visiting her *people* [=*folks, family*] in Texas. • Where are your *people* from? **c :** the people who work for you or your company, organization, etc. • Our *people* are working hard to restore electricity to the city.

good people *US, informal + old-fashioned* : an honest, helpful, or morally good person • I like him; he's *good people.*

of all people — used to emphasize that a specified person is the person you most or least expect to do or know something • You, *of all people,* should know the answer to this. [=I expect you to know the answer to this] • My best friend, *of all people,* betrayed me. [=I was very surprised that my best friend betrayed me]

[2]people *verb* **peo·ples; peo·pled; peo·pling** [+ *obj*] *formal*

1 *of people* : to live or be in (a place) — usually used as *(be) peopled* • The town *is peopled* [=*inhabited*] almost entirely by factory workers. • a campus *peopled* with students from around the world

2 : to put people in (something, such as a story) — usually used as *(be) peopled* • The story *is peopled* with odd characters. [=the characters in the story are odd]

people carrier *noun, pl* ~ **-ers** [*count*] *Brit* : MINIVAN

people mover *noun, pl* ~ **-ers** [*count*]

1 *US* : a vehicle or moving surface that is used to take groups of people from one place to another • The airport has a *people mover* to bring passengers to the far terminals.

2 *Brit* : MINIVAN

people person *noun* [*singular*] : someone who enjoys being with or talking to other people • The company is looking for a *people person* to join their customer service staff.

people skills *noun* [*plural*] : the ability to work with or talk to other people in an effective and friendly way • Good *people skills* are important in customer service.

[1]pep /ˈpɛp/ *noun* [*noncount*] *somewhat old-fashioned* : energy or enthusiasm • The young teacher was full of *pep.*

[2]pep *verb* **peps; pepped; pep·ping**

pep up [*phrasal verb*] *informal* **1 :** to become more lively or active • The economy has started to *pep up* in recent months. **2** ***pep (someone or something) up or pep up (someone or something)*** : to cause (someone or something) to become more lively or active • To *pep up* [=*improve, increase*] sales, the company is offering a free trial subscription for one month. • The coach tried to *pep* the team *up.*

[1]pep·per /ˈpɛpɚ/ *noun, pl* **-pers**

1 [*noncount*] : a food seasoning that is made by grinding the dried berries of an Indian plant along with their hard, black covers : BLACK PEPPER • Please pass the salt and *pepper.* • freshly ground *pepper* — see also CAYENNE PEPPER, SALT-AND-PEPPER, WHITE PEPPER

2 [*count*] : a hollow vegetable that is usually red, green, or yellow and that is eaten raw or cooked • The steak was served with *peppers* and onions. • Be careful handling hot *peppers.* — see color picture on page C4; see also BELL PEPPER, GREEN PEPPER, RED PEPPER, SWEET PEPPER

[2]pepper *verb* **peppers; pep·pered; pep·per·ing** [+ *obj*] : to add pepper to (food) • You need to *pepper* the stew more.

pepper with [*phrasal verb*] **1** ***pepper (someone or something) with (something)*** : to hit (someone) repeatedly with your fists or with objects • The boxer *peppered* his opponent *with* punches. • The goalie was *peppered with* shots. — often used figuratively • The reporters *peppered* her *with* questions. [=the reporters asked her a lot of questions] **2** ***pepper (something) with (something)*** **a :** to put a small amount of (something) on many different parts of (a surface) — usually used as *(be) peppered with* • His face *is peppered with* freckles. [=he has freckles on many different parts of his face] **b :** to put something in many places in (a story, speech, etc.) • She *peppered* the report *with* statistics.

pep·per·corn /ˈpɛpɚˌkoɚn/ *noun, pl* **-corns** [*count*] : a dried berry from an Indian plant that is ground to make pepper

pep·per·mint /ˈpɛpɚˌmɪnt/ *noun, pl* **-mints**

1 [*noncount*] : a plant that produces an oil that is used especially to flavor candies

2 [*count*] : a candy flavored with peppermint

pep·per·o·ni /ˌpɛpəˈrouni/ *noun* [*noncount*] : a spicy sausage that is usually eaten on pizza

pepper shaker *noun, pl* ~ **-ers** [*count*] *US* : a small container with holes on top that is used to put small amounts of pepper on food — called also *(Brit) pepper pot*

pepper spray *noun, pl* ~ **sprays** [*count, noncount*] : a substance made from a chemical found in peppers that causes temporary blindness and pain to the nose, throat, and skin when it is sprayed on someone • The police used *pepper spray* to bring the suspect under control.

pep·pery /ˈpɛpəri/ *adj* [*more* ~; *most* ~]

1 : containing pepper or having the qualities of pepper • a *peppery* soup/salad • a *peppery* flavor/smell

2 : having a lively, aggressive, or somewhat shocking quality • She's a *peppery,* outspoken woman. • *peppery* language

pep pill *noun, pl* ~ **pills** [*count*] *informal* : a pill that contains a drug which makes you happier or gives you more energy for a short period of time

pep·py /ˈpɛpi/ *adj* **pep·pi·er; -est** [*also more* ~; *most* ~] *chiefly US, somewhat old-fashioned*

1 : full of energy or enthusiasm • At 75 years old, he is as *peppy* as ever. • a group of *peppy* cheerleaders • The song was a *peppy* little dance number.

2 : able to move fast • a *peppy* [=*zippy*] little car

pep rally *noun, pl* ~ **rallies** [*count*] *US* : an event before a school sports event that is meant to get students and fans excited and to encourage the team to win • The school held a *pep rally* in the gym before the football game.; *also* : a similar event in which speakers try to get a group of people excited and enthusiastic about something • The mayor gave an inspiring speech at the party's *pep rally.*

pep talk *noun, pl* ~ **talks** [*count*] *informal* : a short speech that is given to encourage someone to work harder, to feel more confident and enthusiastic, etc. • The coach gave the team a *pep talk* before the game. • She needs a *pep talk.*

pep·tic ulcer /ˈpɛptɪk-/ *noun, pl* ~ **-cers** [*count*] *medical* : a painful sore inside the stomach or another part of the digestive system

per /ˈpɚ/ *prep*

1 : for each • The pay is $12 *per* hour. [=for every hour you work, you will be paid $12] • The tickets are $25 *per* person. [=each ticket costs $25] • The speed limit is 35 miles *per* hour. • The car gets 32 miles *per* gallon. • He averages 15 points *per* game.

2 *somewhat formal* : as directed by or stated in : ACCORDING TO • *Per* your advice, I accepted their offer. • The work was done ***as per*** [=*according to*] your instructions. • ***As per usual*** [=*as usual*], I paid for our meal. [=I paid for our meal, which is what I usually do]

P

per·am·bu·la·tor /pəˈræmbjəˌleɪtɚ/ *noun, pl* **-tors** [*count*] *Brit* : STROLLER

per an·num /pɚˈænəm/ *adv, somewhat formal* : in or for each year • She earns $60,000 *per annum.* [=(more commonly) *per year, annually*] — abbr. *p.a.*

per cap·i·ta /pɚˈkæpətə/ *adv* : by or for each person • What is the average income *per capita* in the state? [=what is the average income for people in the state?; how much money does each person in the state earn on average?]
– **per capita** *adj* • The state's average *per capita* income is $35,000.

per·ceive /pɚˈsiːv/ *verb* **-ceives; -ceived; -ceiv·ing** [+ *obj*]
1 *formal* : to notice or become aware of (something) • I *perceived* [=*noticed*] that she had been crying. • The detective *perceived* [=*saw*] a change in the suspect's attitude.
2 : to think of (someone or something) as being something stated • She *perceived* herself as an independent woman. = She *perceived* herself to be an independent woman. — often used as *(be) perceived* • He *is perceived* as one of the best players in baseball.
– **perceived** *adj* • a *perceived* threat [=something that is thought of as being a threat]

per·cent (*US*) *or Brit* **per cent** /pɚˈsɛnt/ *noun, pl US* **percent** *or Brit* **per cent**
1 [*count*] : one part in a hundred : an amount that is equal to one one-hundredth of something • The value has increased half a *percent.* • several *percent* — usually used with a number • Thirty *percent* [=3⁄10] of the class failed the test. • Water covers more than 70 *percent* of the Earth's surface.
2 [*singular*] : a part of a whole : PORTION • A large *percent* [=(more commonly) *percentage*] of their profits comes from online sales.
– **percent** (*US*) *or Brit* **per cent** *adv* • Gas prices rose 15 *percent.* [=15%] • I'm 99.9 *percent* sure that I am right. [=I am almost completely sure that I am right] • I agree with her ***100 percent.*** [=I agree with her completely] • He feels *100 percent* better. [=he feels completely healthy again]
– **percent** (*US*) *or Brit* **per cent** *adj* • I received a five *percent* [=5%] increase in my salary.

per·cent·age /pɚˈsɛntɪʤ/ *noun, pl* **-ag·es**
1 [*count*] : a number or rate that is expressed as a certain number of parts of something divided into 100 parts • If a goalie saves 96 out of 100 shots, his save *percentage* is 96 percent. • The *percentages* of women completing high school and college were 95 percent and 52 percent, respectively. • Interest rates fell two ***percentage points.*** [=interest rates fell two percent]
2 [*singular*] : a part of a whole : PORTION • What *percentage* of your income do you spend on rent? • A large *percentage* of students passed the test. [=most of the students passed the test]
3 [*count*] : a part or share of the profit earned when something is sold — usually singular • He gets a *percentage* for every car he sells.
no percentage informal — used to say that something should not be done because there is no chance that it will produce a good result • There's *no percentage* in arguing with them. They'll never change their minds.

per·cen·tile /pɚˈsɛnˌtajəl/ *noun, pl* **-tiles** [*count*] : one of 100 equal parts that a group of people can be divided into in order to rank them • She scored in the 95th *percentile* in math. [=she got a higher score in math than 95 percent of her classmates] • His height and weight are in the 80th *percentile* for boys his age.

per·cep·ti·ble /pɚˈsɛptəbəl/ *adj* [*more ~; most ~*] : able to be seen or noticed : able to be perceived • The sound was barely *perceptible.* • There was a *perceptible* change in the audience's mood.
– **per·cep·ti·bly** /pɚˈsɛptəbli/ *adv* • The size has not changed *perceptibly* in three months. • It is *perceptibly* [=*noticeably*] cooler this evening.

per·cep·tion /pɚˈsɛpʃən/ *noun, pl* **-tions**
1 a [*count*] : the way you think about or understand someone or something — often + *of* • People's *perceptions of* this town have changed radically. • the public/public's *perception of* nuclear power — see also SELF-PERCEPTION **b** [*noncount*] *somewhat formal* : the ability to understand or notice something easily • She shows remarkable *perception.*
2 [*noncount*] *somewhat formal* : the way that you notice or understand something using one of your senses • visual/spatial *perception* — see also DEPTH PERCEPTION, EXTRASENSORY PERCEPTION

per·cep·tive /pɚˈsɛptɪv/ *adj* [*more ~; most ~*] : having or showing an ability to understand or notice something easily or quickly • a *perceptive* analysis/observation/comment • He is a very *perceptive* young man.
– **per·cep·tive·ly** *adv* • As one critic *perceptively* observes, the city itself is perhaps the most important character in the novel. – **per·cep·tive·ness** *noun* [*noncount*]

[1]**perch** /ˈpɚʧ/ *verb* **perch·es; perched; perch·ing**
1 [*no obj*] : to sit on or be on something high or on something from which it is easy to fall — usually + *on* • Birds often *perch on* the ledge outside my window. • People *perched on* the railing to get a better view. • Their house *perches on* a rocky cliff.
2 [+ *obj*] : to put (someone or something) on something high or on something from which it is easy to fall • People ***perched themselves*** on the railing [=people sat on the railing] to get a better view. — usually used as *(be) perched* • He stood there in his coat, a small hat *perched* on/atop his head. • A bird *was perched* on the telephone wire. • Their house *is perched* on a rocky cliff. • The castle *is perched* high in/among the hills of Scotland.

[2]**perch** *noun, pl* **perches** [*count*]
1 : something (such as a tree branch) that a bird sits on • The bird flew down from its *perch.*
2 : a high seat or location • The lifeguard watches the swimmers from her *perch.*
– compare [3]PERCH

[3]**perch** *noun, pl* **perch** *or* **perches** [*count, noncount*] : a fish that lives in rivers and streams and that is eaten as food — compare [2]PERCH

per·chance /pɚˈʧæns, *Brit* pəˈʧɑːns/ *adv, old-fashioned + literary* : maybe but not definitely : PERHAPS • "To sleep: *perchance* to dream . . . " —Shakespeare, *Hamlet*

per·co·late /ˈpɚkəˌleɪt/ *verb* **-lates; -lat·ed; -lat·ing**
1 [*no obj*] : to pass slowly through something that has many small holes in it • The water *percolates* [=*filters, seeps*] through the sand. • Sunlight *percolated* down through the trees.
2 [*no obj*] : to spread slowly • Rumors *percolated* throughout the town.
3 : to make (coffee) in a special pot (called a percolator) [+ *obj*] There is nothing like *percolating* coffee over an open campfire. [*no obj*] Coffee was *percolating* on the stove.
4 [*no obj*] **a** : to continue for a long time without obvious activity • The feud *percolated* [=*simmered*] for decades. **b** : to develop slowly • Ideas are always *percolating* [=*simmering*] in my mind.

per·co·la·tor /ˈpɚkəˌleɪtɚ/ *noun, pl* **-tors** [*count*] : a covered pot that has a narrow tube in the center and that is used for making coffee

per·cus·sion /pɚˈkʌʃən/ *noun* [*noncount*] : musical instruments (such as drums, cymbals, or xylophones) that you play by hitting or shaking • He plays *percussion* for the band. • The marimba is a *percussion* instrument. • The song features Tito Puente ***on percussion.*** [=Tito Puente plays percussion instruments for the song] • The ***percussion section*** [=the group of musicians who play percussion instruments in a band or orchestra] did a great job.

per·cus·sion·ist /pɚˈkʌʃənɪst/ *noun, pl* **-ists** [*count*] : a person who plays a percussion instrument

per·cus·sive /pɚˈkʌsɪv/ *adj* [*more ~; most ~*] : of or relating to a percussion instrument or to the sounds that a percussion instrument makes • The song had a punchy, *percussive* rhythm. • The language uses a lot of *percussive* sounds. [=sharp, short sounds that are similar to the sounds some percussion instruments make]

[1]**per di·em** /pɚˈdiːjəm/ *adv, formal* : for each day : per day • Employees will be given $20 *per diem* for expenses.
– **per diem** *adj, always used before a noun* • a *per diem* allowance

[2]**per diem** *noun, pl* **~ -ems** [*count*] *US* : an amount of money given to someone for daily expenses (such as food or fuel) • He received a $30 *per diem* for food.

per·di·tion /pɚˈdɪʃən/ *noun* [*noncount*] *old-fashioned* : the state of being in hell forever as punishment after death : DAMNATION • sinners condemned to eternal *perdition* — usually used figuratively • It's this kind of selfishness that leads down the ***road/path to perdition.*** [=that is very dangerous or harmful]

per·e·grine falcon /ˈperəgrən-/ *noun, pl* **~ -cons** [*count*]

P

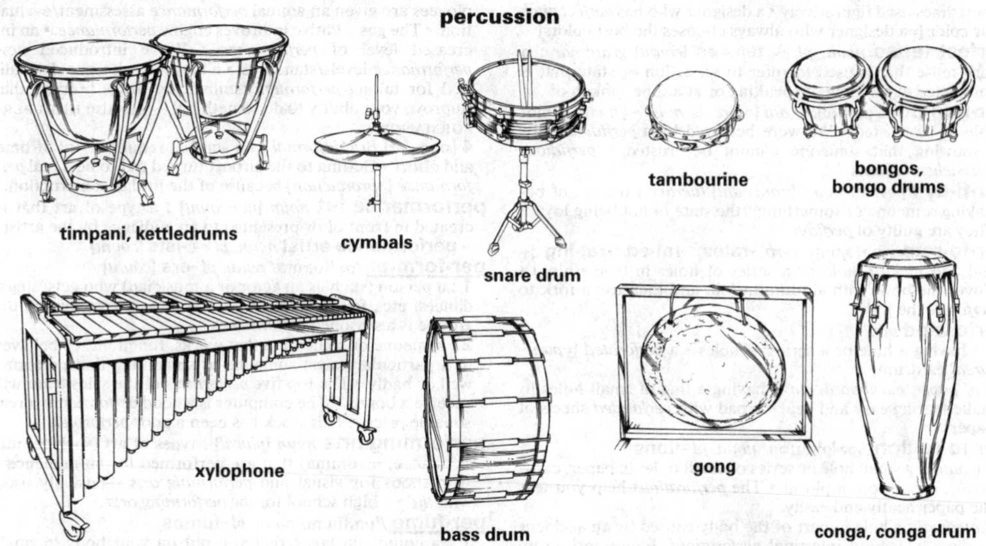

: a type of hawk that can fly very fast and is sometimes trained to hunt — called also *peregrine*

pe·remp·to·ry /pəˈrɛmptəri/ *adj* [*more ~; most ~*] *formal*
1 — used to describe an order, command, etc., that you must obey without any questions or excuses ▪ a *peremptory* order/instruction from the court
2 *disapproving* : having or showing the insulting attitude of people who think that they should be obeyed without question : ARROGANT ▪ Her *peremptory* tone/attitude angered me.
– pe·remp·to·ri·ly /pəˈrɛmptərəli/ *adv*

[1]**pe·ren·ni·al** /pəˈrɛnijəl/ *adj*
1 *of a plant* : living for several years or for many years : having a life cycle that is more than two years long ▪ a *perennial* plant ▪ This variety of oregano is *perennial.* — compare [1]ANNUAL, [1]BIENNIAL
2 a : existing or continuing in the same way for a long time ▪ Hot dogs are a *perennial* favorite at barbecues. [=people always like to eat hot dogs at barbecues] **b** : happening again and again ▪ Flooding is a *perennial* problem for people living by the river.
– pe·ren·ni·al·ly *adv* ▪ a *perennially* popular restaurant

[2]**perennial** *noun, pl* **-als** [*count*] : a plant that lives for several years or for many years : a perennial plant ▪ Her garden is full of *perennials.* — compare [2]ANNUAL, [2]BIENNIAL

[1]**per·fect** /ˈpɚfɪkt/ *adj*
1 [*more ~; most ~*] **a** : having no mistakes or flaws ▪ a *perfect* [=*flawless*] diamond ▪ Your teeth are *perfect.* ▪ The car is in *perfect* [=*mint*] condition. ▪ The performance was *perfect.* ▪ I'm not *perfect* [=I make mistakes], but at least I can admit when I'm wrong. ▪ He thought he had committed the ***perfect crime*** [=a crime that is done so carefully that the criminal will never be caught] ▪ Yes, you made a mistake, but it's okay; ***nobody's perfect*** [=everyone makes mistakes] ▪ Students who have ***perfect attendance*** [=who have been present at every class] will get 10 extra points. ▪ If you want to be a good writer, you should write every day. Remember, ***practice makes perfect*** [=you become better at something if you practice it often] — see also PICTURE-PERFECT **b** : completely correct or accurate ▪ She spoke *perfect* English. ▪ He drew a *perfect* circle. ▪ a *perfect* replica **c** : having all the qualities you want in that kind of person, situation, etc. ▪ She's a *perfect* baby. She hardly cries and she sleeps through the night. ▪ His behavior is a *perfect* example of what not to do. ▪ In a ***perfect world*** [=in the best possible situation], there would be no need for weapons.
2 [*more ~; most ~*] : exactly right for a particular purpose, situation, or person ▪ This is a *perfect* time/place/day to have a wedding. ▪ Going to the museum was a *perfect* way to spend a rainy day. ▪ "Is that a big enough piece of pie?" "Yes, it's *perfect*, thanks." ▪ You have ***perfect timing*** [=your timing is exactly right; you are present, ready, etc., at exactly the right time] I just took dinner out of the oven. — often + *for* ▪ I found the *perfect* [=*ideal*] gift *for* you. ▪ They are a *perfect* match *for* each other. ▪ That picture is *perfect for* this room. ▪ The weather was *perfect for* a day at the beach.
3 *always used before a noun* : complete and total — used for emphasis ▪ a *perfect* stranger/fool/angel/gentleman ▪ You have a *perfect* right to be angry. ▪ My cat and dog live together in *perfect* harmony.

[2]**per·fect** /pəˈfɛkt/ *verb* **-fects; -fect·ed; -fect·ing** [+ *obj*] : to make (something good) perfect or better ▪ He needs to *perfect* [=*refine*] his reading skills over the summer. ▪ Scientists are still *perfecting* [=*improving*] the treatment.

[3]**per·fect** /ˈpɚfɪkt/ *noun*
the perfect *grammar* : PERFECT TENSE ▪ a verb that is in *the perfect* — see also FUTURE PERFECT, PAST PERFECT, PRESENT PERFECT

perfect game *noun, pl* **~ games** [*count*] *baseball* : a game in which a pitcher does not allow the batters from the other team to get a base hit or to get to first base in any other way

per·fec·tion /pəˈfɛkʃən/ *noun, pl* **-tions**
1 : the state or condition of being perfect [*noncount*] The coach expects *perfection* from his players. [=expects the players to make no mistakes] [*singular*] She has achieved a rare *perfection* in her playing. ▪ a *perfection* of form
2 [*noncount*] : the act of making something perfect or better : the act of perfecting something — + *of* ▪ the *perfection of* surgical techniques ▪ She is working on the *perfection of* her art.
3 [*noncount*] : something that cannot be improved : something that is perfect ▪ The meal was sheer *perfection.* [=the meal was perfect] ▪ His poetry is pure *perfection.*
to perfection : in a way or to a degree that is exactly right ▪ The steak was cooked *to perfection.* [=was perfectly cooked]

per·fec·tion·ist /pəˈfɛkʃənɪst/ *noun, pl* **-ists** [*count*] : a person who wants things to be done perfectly or who tries to do things perfectly ▪ I'm a bit of a *perfectionist*, which makes it difficult for me to finish things sometimes.
– per·fec·tion·ism /pəˈfɛkʃəˌnɪzəm/ *noun* [*noncount*] ▪ *Perfectionism* can make it difficult for people to finish things—they keep wanting to improve them.

per·fect·ly /ˈpɚfɪktli/ *adv*
1 : in every way : COMPLETELY — used for emphasis ▪ I was *perfectly* willing to help. ▪ They are throwing out a *perfectly* good sofa. ▪ It is *perfectly* normal/natural to feel nervous. ▪ You know *perfectly* well what I mean. [=you know exactly what I mean] ▪ To be *perfectly* honest, I don't want to go. ▪ You are *perfectly* capable of doing it yourself. ▪ The bridge is *perfectly* safe.
2 [*more ~; most ~*] : without errors, mistakes, or flaws : in a perfect way ▪ She sang *perfectly.* [=she sang without making a mistake] ▪ The dress fits *perfectly.* [=the dress is the right size] ▪ The steak was *perfectly* cooked. ▪ a *perfectly* formed rose

perfect pitch *noun* [*noncount*] *music* : the ability to correctly name any musical note that you hear or to sing any musical note correctly without help ▪ He has *perfect pitch.* —

P

sometimes used figuratively ▪ a designer who has *perfect pitch* for color [=a designer who always chooses the best colors]

perfect tense *noun, pl* ~ **tens·es** [*count*] *grammar* : a verb tense that is used to refer to an action or state that is completed at the time of speaking or at a time spoken of

per·fid·i·ous /pɚˈfɪdijəs/ *adj* [*more* ~; *most* ~] *literary* : not able to be trusted ▪ We were betrayed by a *perfidious* ally. : showing that someone cannot be trusted ▪ *perfidious* [=*treacherous*] acts

per·fi·dy /ˈpɚfədi/ *noun* [*noncount*] *literary* : the act of betraying someone or something : the state of not being loyal ▪ They are guilty of *perfidy*.

per·fo·rate /ˈpɚfəˌreɪt/ *verb* **-rates**; **-rat·ed**; **-rat·ing** [+ *obj*] : to make a hole or a series of holes in (something) ▪ Cover the bowl with aluminum foil, and then use a fork to *perforate* the foil.

perforated *adj*
1 : having a hole or a series of holes ▪ a *perforated* [=*punctured*] eardrum
2 *of paper, cardboard, etc.* : having a line of small holes to make tearing easy and neat ▪ a pad with *perforated* sheets of paper

per·fo·ra·tion /ˌpɚfəˈreɪʃən/ *noun, pl* **-tions**
1 [*count*] : a small hole or series of small holes in paper, cardboard, etc. — often plural ▪ The *perforations* help you tear the paper neatly and easily.
2 *medical* : a hole in part of the body caused by an accident or disease [*count*] intestinal *perforations* [*noncount*] an infection that can cause *perforation* of the intestine

per·force /pɚˈfoɚs/ *adv, formal + literary* — used to say that something is necessary or must be done ▪ They must *perforce* obey the law.

per·form /pɚˈfoɚm/ *verb* **-forms**; **-formed**; **-form·ing**
1 [+ *obj*] : to do an action or activity that usually requires training or skill ▪ The doctor had to *perform* surgery immediately. ▪ A team of six scientists *performed* [=*carried out*] the experiment. ▪ He has been unable to *perform* [=*complete, fulfill*] his duties since the accident. ▪ The magician *performed* some amazing tricks. ▪ The gymnasts *performed* their routines perfectly. ▪ You are required to *perform* 50 hours of community service. ▪ The wedding (ceremony) was *performed* by a justice of the peace. = A justice of the peace *performed* the wedding (ceremony). ▪ You can't expect me to ***perform miracles***. [=to do something that is impossible]
2 : to entertain an audience by singing, acting, etc. [*no obj*] The band will be *performing* on the main stage. ▪ She's a wonderful singer who loves to *perform* before a live audience. [+ *obj*] The band will *perform* songs from their new album. ▪ The class *performed* the play for the school. ▪ He *performed* [=*acted*] the part/role of Othello. [=he played Othello; he said the words and did the actions of the character Othello]
3 [*no obj*] — used to describe how effective or successful someone or something is ▪ The stock market is *performing* well/badly. ▪ The engine/computer was *performing* poorly. ▪ I *perform* best under pressure.

per·for·mance /pɚˈfoɚməns/ *noun, pl* **-manc·es**
1 [*count*] **a** : an activity (such as singing a song or acting in a play) that a person or group does to entertain an audience ▪ This evening's *performance* will start at 8 o'clock. ▪ The hall is usually used for orchestra *performances*. — sometimes used figuratively ▪ That tearful apology was quite a *performance*—I almost believed you really were sorry. **b** : the way an actor performs a part in a play, movie, etc. ▪ The critics loved her *performance* as the villain. ▪ She gave a brilliant *performance* as the villain. [=she played the role of the villain brilliantly]
2 *somewhat formal* : the act of doing a job, an activity, etc. [*noncount*] the *performance* of procedures/activities/duties [*singular*] Event planners hope to avoid a ***repeat performance*** of last year's problems. [=hope that last year's problems will not happen again this year]
3 : how well someone or something functions, works, etc. : how well someone or something performs [*count*] A supervisor will evaluate each employee's *performance*. ▪ employees with strong job *performances* ▪ a student's academic *performance* ▪ The team's *performance* last night was poor. [=the team performed/played poorly last night] ▪ This car had the best overall *performance*. [=this car functioned better than all the other cars] ▪ How has the company's stock *performance* been? [=has the value of the company's stock been increasing/decreasing?] [*noncount*] She was fired for poor job *performance*. [=she was fired for doing her job badly] ▪ Employees are given an annual *performance* assessment/evaluation. ▪ The gas additive improves engine *performance*. ▪ an increased level of *performance* ▪ We've introduced new *performance* levels/standards. ▪ a bicyclist who was disqualified for taking *performance*-enhancing drugs [=drugs that improve your ability to do something] — see also HIGH PERFORMANCE
4 [*singular*] *Brit, informal* : an act that requires a lot of time and effort ▪ Getting to the airport turned out to be a real *performance* [=*production*] because of the bridge construction.

performance art *noun* [*noncount*] : a type of art that is created in front of or presented to an audience by the artist
— **performance artist** *noun, pl* ~ **-ists** [*count*]

per·form·er /pɚˈfoɚmɚ/ *noun, pl* **-ers** [*count*]
1 : a person (such as an actor or a musician) who acts, sings, dances, etc., for an audience ▪ The new actress joining the troupe is a seasoned *performer*.
2 : someone or something that works, functions, or behaves in a particular way : someone or something that performs well or badly ▪ The top five *performers* of the sales team will receive a bonus. ▪ The computer is a good *performer* at a reasonable price. ▪ This stock has been a poor *performer*.

performing arts *noun* [*plural*] : types of art (such as music, dance, or drama) that are performed for an audience ▪ workshops for visual and *performing arts* — usually used with *the* ▪ a high school for *the performing arts*

¹per·fume /ˈpɚˌfjuːm/ *noun, pl* **-fumes**
1 : a liquid substance that you put on your body in small amounts in order to smell pleasant [*noncount*] Are you wearing *perfume*? ▪ a bottle of *perfume* [*count*] She smelled the different *perfumes* at the store.
2 [*count*] : a pleasant smell ▪ The *perfume* [=*fragrance, scent*] of lilies filled the room.

²per·fume /pɚˈfjuːm/ *verb* **-fumes**; **-fumed**; **-fum·ing** [+ *obj*]
1 *literary* : to fill or cover (something) with a pleasant smell ▪ Roses *perfumed* the air. ▪ The meal included a delicate fish *perfumed* with butter and herbs.
2 *somewhat formal* : to put perfume in or on (something) ▪ a time when it was common for men to *perfume* their hair
— **per·fumed** *adj* ▪ *perfumed* soap/paper

per·func·to·ry /pɚˈfʌŋktəri/ *adj* [*more* ~; *most* ~] *formal* — used to describe something that is done without energy or enthusiasm because of habit or because it is expected ▪ a *perfunctory* smile/nod/salute ▪ He made/issued a *perfunctory* statement supporting the mayor.
— **per·func·to·ri·ly** /pɚˈfʌŋktərəli/ *adv* ▪ She smiled/nodded *perfunctorily*.

per·haps /pɚˈhæps/ *adv* : possibly but not certainly : MAYBE

> *Perhaps* is a more formal word than *maybe*. It is used when you are talking about an action that might happen in the future. ▪ *Perhaps* we'll meet again. ▪ "Will you come with us?" "I don't know. *Perhaps*." ▪ "Will you come with us?" "*Perhaps, perhaps* not." ▪ "*Perhaps* I'll come with you and *perhaps* I won't." ▪ They're hoping that she'll *perhaps* change her mind. = They're hoping that *perhaps* she'll change her mind. ▪ You should hear from them soon, *perhaps* even by next week. = *Perhaps* you'll hear from them by next week. It is also used to suggest something that is possibly correct, true, or proper. ▪ *Perhaps* we should just stay here and wait. ▪ *Perhaps* it would be better if you left. ▪ There were *perhaps* 10,000 people at the event. ▪ The shed is 20, *perhaps* 25, feet long. ▪ We waited an hour, *perhaps* more. ▪ *Perhaps* it's time to think about your future. And *perhaps* can be used to say that one thing is true but that something else is also true. ▪ *Perhaps* it's not as great as her first book, but it's still worth reading. ▪ The instructions are still confusing, *perhaps*, but they're much better than they were before.

per·i·dot /ˈperəˌdɑːt/ *noun, pl* **-dots** [*count, noncount*] : a clear, yellowish-green stone that is used in jewelry — see color picture on page C11

peri·gee /ˈperəˌʤiː/ *noun* [*singular*] *technical* : the point in outer space where an object traveling around the Earth (such as a satellite or the moon) is closest to the Earth — compare APOGEE

per·il /ˈperəl/ *noun, pl* **-ils** *somewhat formal + literary*
1 [*noncount*] : the possibility that you will be hurt or killed or that something unpleasant or bad will happen : DANGER ▪ People are unaware of the *peril* these miners face each day.

— usually used in the phrase ***in peril*** ▪ They put their lives *in peril*. [=*in jeopardy*] ▪ The species is *in peril* [=(more commonly) *in danger*] of dying out. ▪ His career is *in peril*.
2 [*count*] : something that is likely to cause injury, pain, harm, or loss : DANGER ▪ She described global warming as "a growing *peril*." — usually plural ▪ the *perils* of childbirth ▪ They faced many *perils* in their journey through the region.
at your (own) peril — used to say that if you do something you should be aware that it is dangerous and that you could be harmed, injured, punished, etc. ▪ No lifeguard is on duty: swim *at your own peril*. [=*at your own risk*] ▪ Restaurants that ignore the smoking ban do so *at their peril*.

per·il·ous /ˈperələs/ *adj* [*more* ~; *most* ~] *somewhat formal* + *literary* : full of danger : DANGEROUS ▪ a *perilous* journey across the mountains ▪ The climb was *perilous*.
— **per·il·ous·ly** *adv* ▪ He leaned *perilously* over the edge of the boat. ▪ She came ***perilously close to*** drowning. [=she almost drowned] ▪ The company was *perilously close to* bankruptcy.

pe·rim·e·ter /pəˈrɪmətɚ/ *noun, pl* **-ters**
1 [*count*] **a** : the outside edge of an area or surface — often + *of* ▪ The soldiers defended the *perimeter of* the camp. ▪ They put up a fence around the *perimeter of* the yard. **b** : the total length of the lines that form a shape — often + *of* ▪ The *perimeter of* the rectangle is 24 inches.
2 ***the perimeter*** *basketball* : the area on a basketball court that is not close to the basket ▪ He scored from *the perimeter*.

peri·na·tal /ˌperəˈneɪtl̩/ *adj, medical* : happening during or around the time of birth ▪ The doctor took steps to prevent *perinatal* infection. ▪ *perinatal* death

[1]**pe·ri·od** /ˈpirijəd/ *noun, pl* **-ods** [*count*]
1 : a length of time during which a series of events or an action takes place or is completed ▪ We have had two power failures in a five-month *period*. ▪ The *period* between Christmas and New Year's Eve is a very busy one for us. — often + *of* ▪ Two snowstorms hit the area in a *period of* one week. ▪ There was a brief *period of* silence. ▪ The country is in a *period of* economic growth. ▪ Scattered showers are expected with a few *periods of* sunshine. ▪ We didn't speak for a long ***period of time***. — see also COOLING-OFF PERIOD
2 : a length of time that is very important in the history of the world, a nation, etc. ▪ We are studying our country's colonial *period*.
3 : a time that is very important in the life of a person ▪ Picasso's Blue *Period* ▪ Children go through many changes during the *period* of adolescence.
4 a : one of the parts that a school day is divided into ▪ I have algebra class during third *period*. **b** : one of the parts that the playing time of a game (such as hockey) is divided into ▪ He scored a goal in the first *period*. ▪ The score was tied after two *periods*.
5 *US* **a** : a point . used to show the end of a sentence or an abbreviation — called also (*Brit*) *full stop* **b** — used in speech to emphasize that a decision, command, or opinion has been made and will not be changed ▪ You are not leaving this house, *period*. ▪ I don't want to talk to her again, *period*.
6 : MENSTRUAL PERIOD

[2]**period** /ˈpirijəd/ *adj, always used before a noun* : of, relating to, or typical of a particular time in history ▪ *period* costumes/furniture ▪ a *period* play

pe·ri·od·ic /ˌpiriˈɑːdɪk/ *adj, always used before a noun* : happening regularly over a period of time ▪ He takes the car in for *periodic* oil changes. ▪ She makes *periodic* [=*regular*] payments to the bank.
— **pe·ri·od·i·cal·ly** /ˌpiriˈɑːdɪkli/ *adv* ▪ The directory is updated *periodically*.

pe·ri·od·i·cal /ˌpiriˈɑdɪkəl/ *noun, pl* **-cals** [*count*] : a magazine that is published every week, month, etc. ▪ She writes for a monthly *periodical*. ▪ The library has a large collection of scholarly *periodicals*.

periodic table *noun* [*singular*] *chemistry* : a list that shows the chemical elements arranged according to their properties

period piece *noun, pl* ~ **pieces** [*count*] : something (such as a play, a movie, or a piece of furniture) that is from, set in, or typical of a particular time in history

peri·pa·tet·ic /ˌperəpəˈtɛtɪk/ *adj, formal* : going from place to place usually as part of your job ▪ She worked as a *peripatetic* journalist for most of her life. ▪ He had a *peripatetic* career as a salesman.

[1]**pe·riph·er·al** /pəˈrɪfərəl/ *adj*
1 [*more* ~; *most* ~] *formal* : not relating to the main or most important part ▪ If we focus too much on *peripheral* issues, we will lose sight of the goal. — often + *to* ▪ His role in the negotiations was *peripheral to* the outcome. [=his role in the negotiations was not important in deciding the outcome]
2 *computers* : connected to a computer but not an essential part of it ▪ *peripheral* devices/equipment such as modems and scanners
3 : of or relating to the area that is to the side of the area you are looking at ▪ He saw in his ***peripheral vision*** that a car was trying to pass him.
4 *medical* : of or relating to the part of the nervous system that is separate from the brain and spinal cord ▪ *peripheral* nerves ▪ the ***peripheral nervous system***
— **pe·riph·er·al·ly** *adv* ▪ He was only *peripherally* involved in the sale of the house. [=he played a small part in the sale of the house]

[2]**peripheral** *noun, pl* **-als** [*count*] *computers* : a piece of equipment (such as a printer, speaker, etc.) that is connected to a computer but is not an essential part of it ▪ computer *peripherals*

pe·riph·ery /pəˈrɪfəri/ *noun, pl* **-er·ies** [*count*] *formal* : the outside edge of an area : the area that surrounds a place or thing — often + *of* ▪ A fence was built around the *periphery of* the site. ▪ The factory is located on the *periphery of* the city. — often used figuratively ▪ the *periphery of* society ▪ There was little we could do as we watched the case unfold from the *periphery*. [=we were not actively involved so there was little we could do]

peri·scope /ˈperəˌskoup/ *noun, pl* **-scopes** [*count*] : a long tube that contains lenses and mirrors and that is used to look over or around something and especially by a person in a submarine to see above the surface of the water

per·ish /ˈperɪʃ/ *verb* **-ish·es; -ished; -ish·ing** [*no obj*]
1 *formal* + *literary* : to die or be killed ▪ Two people *perished* in the fire. ▪ The sailors *perished* at sea.
2 *formal* : to disappear or be destroyed : to cease to exist ▪ The civilization *perished* after 500 years. ▪ Many ancient languages have *perished* over time.
3 *Brit* : to slowly break apart by a natural process ▪ The rubber will *perish* with age.
perish the thought — used to say that you hope that something does not happen or to say that something will not happen ▪ Who would take over as goalie if, *perish the thought*, he got injured? ▪ What? Me help him out? *Perish the thought*.

per·ish·able /ˈperɪʃəbəl/ *adj* [*more* ~; *most* ~] : likely to spoil or decay quickly : not likely to stay fresh for a long time if not eaten or used ▪ *perishable* foods

per·ish·ables /ˈperɪʃəbəlz/ *noun* [*plural*] : foods that are perishable ▪ You should store *perishables* in the refrigerator.

perished *adj, not used before a noun, Brit, informal* : very cold ▪ We were all *perished*.

perishing *adj, Brit, informal*
1 : very cold ▪ It is *perishing* out here. ▪ Why don't we light a fire? I am *perishing*. ▪ a ***perishing cold*** day
2 *old-fashioned* : very annoying ▪ a *perishing* nuisance

peri·to·ni·tis /ˌperətəˈnaɪtəs/ *noun* [*noncount*] *medical* : a serious condition in which the covering of the stomach, intestines, and nearby organs becomes swollen and infected

per·i·win·kle /ˈperɪˌwɪŋkəl/ *noun, pl* **-win·kles**
1 [*count*] : a plant with blue or white flowers that spreads along the ground
2 [*count, noncount*] : a light purplish blue color — called also *periwinkle blue*
3 [*count*] : a small snail that lives in the sea and that can be eaten

per·jure /ˈpɚdʒɚ/ *verb* **-jures; -jured; -jur·ing**
perjure yourself *law* : to tell a lie in a court of law after promising to tell the truth : to commit perjury ▪ He *perjured himself* before the court by giving a false testimony.
— **per·jur·er** /ˈpɚdʒərɚ/ *noun, pl* **-ers** [*count*]

per·ju·ry /ˈpɚdʒəri/ *noun* [*noncount*] *law* : the crime of telling a lie in a court of law after promising to tell the truth ▪ He was found guilty of *perjury*.

[1]**perk** /ˈpɚk/ *verb* **perks; perked; perk·ing**
perk up [*phrasal verb*] *informal* **1 a** : to become more lively or cheerful ▪ We *perked up* when we heard the good news. **b** ***perk (someone) up or perk up (someone)*** : to make (someone) more lively or cheerful ▪ The good news *perked* everyone *up*. **2** ***perk (something) up or perk up (some-***

P

thing) : to make (something) fresher or more appealing • The new paint job really *perked up* the room. **3** *chiefly US* **a** ***perk (ears) up or perk up (ears) of an animal*** : to lift (the ears) in a quick or alert way • The dog heard its name and *perked up* its ears. — sometimes used without *up* • The dog *perked* its ears. — often used figuratively of a person • I *perked up* my ears [=I began to listen closely] when I heard his name mentioned. **b** *of ears* : to be lifted in a quick and alert way • The dog's ears *perked up*. — often used figuratively of a person • My ears *perked up* [=I began to listen closely] when she said she knew my brother.

– compare ²PERK

²perk *verb* **perks; perked; perk·ing** *[no obj] chiefly US, informal* : PERCOLATE 3 • Start the coffee *perking*. — compare ¹PERK

³perk *noun, pl* **perks** *[count]*

1 : something extra that someone receives in addition to regular pay for doing a job — usually plural • The job came with several *perks*, including use of a company car.

2 : a good thing that you have or get because of your situation — usually plural • One of the *perks* of being a celebrity is that people often want to give you things.

perky /ˈpɚki/ *adj* **perk·i·er; -est** *[also more ~; most ~] informal* : lively in manner or appearance • a *perky* teenager • He hasn't been his *perky* self lately. • She drove around in a *perky* little car.

– **perk·i·ness** *noun [noncount]*

¹perm /ˈpɚm/ *noun, pl* **perms** *[count]* : a process in which someone's hair is curled and treated with chemicals so that it remains curly for a long time • She got a *perm* last week.

²perm *verb* **perms; permed; perm·ing** *[+ obj]* : to make (hair) curly for a long time by using chemicals : to give a perm to (hair) • She got her hair *permed* at the salon.

per·ma·frost /ˈpɚməˌfrɑːst/ *noun [noncount] technical* : a layer of soil that is always frozen in very cold regions of the world

¹per·ma·nent /ˈpɚmənənt/ *adj [more ~; most ~]* : lasting or continuing for a very long time or forever : not temporary or changing • She made a *permanent* home in this country. • Prolonged exposure to the sun can cause *permanent* skin damage. • The museum's *permanent* collection includes works of art from the 18th century. • The transcripts will serve as a *permanent* record of the proceedings.

– **per·ma·nence** /ˈpɚmənəns/ *noun [noncount]* • the *permanence* of the written word – **per·ma·nen·cy** /ˈpɚmənənsi/ *noun [noncount]* – **per·ma·nent·ly** *adv* • He was *permanently* banned from the store.

²permanent *noun, pl* **-nents** *[count] US, old-fashioned* : ¹PERM

per·me·able /ˈpɚmijəbəl/ *adj [more ~; most ~] technical* : allowing liquids or gases to pass through • The cell has a *permeable* membrane. • *permeable* limestone

– **per·me·abil·i·ty** /ˌpɚmijəˈbɪləti/ *noun [noncount]* • They tested the *permeability* of the fabric.

per·me·ate /ˈpɚmiˌeɪt/ *verb* **-ates; -at·ed; -at·ing** *formal* : to pass or spread through (something) *[+ obj]* The water *permeated* the sand. • The smell of baking bread *permeated* the kitchen. • A feeling of anxiety *permeated* the office as we rushed to meet the deadline. *[no obj]* The rain *permeated* through/into the soil.

per·mis·si·ble /pɚˈmɪsəbəl/ *adj, formal* : allowed or permitted by laws or rules • *permissible* levels of noise — often + *to* • It is not *permissible* for students *to* wear hats in school. — opposite IMPERMISSIBLE

per·mis·sion /pɚˈmɪʃən/ *noun [noncount]* : the right or ability to do something that is given by someone who has the power to decide if it will be allowed or permitted • They got/received *permission* from the city to build an apartment complex. • The teacher gave me her *permission* to go home early. • He asked (for) my *permission* to paint his room. • You have my *permission*.

per·mis·sive /pɚˈmɪsɪv/ *adj [more ~; most ~] often disapproving* : giving people a lot of freedom or too much freedom to do what they want to do • *permissive* parents • a *permissive* society • Some states have more *permissive* laws than others.

– **per·mis·sive·ness** *noun [noncount]* • He sometimes takes advantage of the *permissiveness* of his parents.

¹per·mit /pɚˈmɪt/ *verb* **-mits; -mit·ted; -mit·ting**

1 *[+ obj]* **a** : to allow (something) to happen : to give permission for (something) • The judge *permitted* the release of the prisoner. • Smoking is not *permitted* in the building. • When we arrived at customs we realized we had more than the *permitted* number of items. **b** : to allow (someone) to do or have something • He *permitted* himself one more cookie. — often followed by *to + verb* • Her parents will not *permit* them *to marry*. • He was not *permitted to serve* on the jury. • *(formal) Permit* me *to offer* my congratulations on your victory. [=I would like to congratulate you on your victory]

2 : to make something possible *[no obj]* If time *permits* [=if there is enough time left], we can go out to eat later. • The picnic will be held at the park, ***weather permitting***. [=if the weather is good enough to allow it] *[+ obj]* The new ramp *permits* easier access to the highway.

²per·mit /ˈpɚˌmɪt/ *noun, pl* **-mits** *[count]* : an official document that shows that a person is allowed to do or have something • He got a fishing/work *permit*. • The city will issue the *permit*. • You cannot park here without a *permit*. • A *permit* is required to own a gun. — see also LEARNER'S PERMIT

per·mu·ta·tion /ˌpɚmjuˈteɪʃən/ *noun, pl* **-tions** *[count] formal* : one of the many different ways or forms in which something exists or can be arranged — usually plural • Computer technology, in all of its *permutations*, is here to stay. • Early *permutations* of the design look nothing like the final result. • I have heard various *permutations* of this theory.

per·ni·cious /pɚˈnɪʃəs/ *adj [more ~; most ~] formal* : causing great harm or damage often in a way that is not easily seen or noticed • More *pernicious* still has been the acceptance of the author's controversial ideas by the general public. • the *pernicious* effects of jealousy • She thinks television has a *pernicious* influence on our children.

– **per·ni·cious·ly** *adv*

per·nick·e·ty /pəˈnɪkəti/ *adj [more ~; most ~] Brit, informal + disapproving* : PERSNICKETY

per·ora·tion /ˌperəˈreɪʃən/ *noun, pl* **-tions** *[count] formal*

1 : the last part of a speech

2 *disapproving* : a long and dull speech • We sat through a lengthy *peroration* on the evils of the government's policies.

per·ox·ide /pəˈrɑːkˌsaɪd/ *noun [noncount]* : a chemical that is used chiefly to kill bacteria or to make hair lighter in color — see also HYDROGEN PEROXIDE

perp /ˈpɚp/ *noun, pl* **perps** *[count] US slang* : a person who commits a crime or does something wrong • The victim wasn't able to identify the *perp*. [=*perpetrator*]

per·pen·dic·u·lar /ˌpɚpənˈdɪkjələ/ *adj* : going straight up or to the side at a 90 degree angle from another line or surface • a *perpendicular* line • She lives on the street that is *perpendicular* to mine. • a *perpendicular* cliff [=a cliff that goes straight up] — compare PARALLEL

– **per·pen·dic·u·lar·ly** *adv* • The two cars were parked *perpendicularly* to each other.

per·pe·trate /ˈpɚpəˌtreɪt/ *verb* **-trates; -trat·ed; -trat·ing** *[+ obj] formal* : to do (something that is illegal or wrong) • The men were planning to *perpetrate* a robbery. • The attack was *perpetrated* by a street gang. • He vowed revenge for the crime *perpetrated* on his family.

– **per·pe·tra·tion** /ˌpɚpəˈtreɪʃən/ *noun [noncount]* – **per·pe·tra·tor** /ˈpɚpəˌtreɪtɚ/ *noun, pl* **-tors** *[count]* • The police caught the *perpetrators* who robbed the bank.

per·pet·u·al /pɚˈpɛʧəwəl/ *adj*

1 : continuing forever or for a very long time without stopping • The region is in a state of *perpetual* war. • He seems to have a *perpetual* grin on his face. • *(humorous)* the *perpetual* student/bachelor

2 : happening all the time or very often • Lack of government funding has been a *perpetual* [=*constant*] problem for the organization. • the *perpetual* demands of parenthood

– **per·pet·u·al·ly** *adv* • The two civilizations were *perpetually* at war.

per·pet·u·ate /pɚˈpɛʧəˌweɪt/ *verb* **-ates; -at·ed; -at·ing** *[+ obj] formal* : to cause (something that should be stopped, such as a mistaken idea or a bad situation) to continue • He *perpetuates* the myth that his house is haunted. • Fears about an epidemic are being *perpetuated* by the media.

– **per·pet·u·a·tion** /pɚˌpɛʧəˈweɪʃən/ *noun [noncount]* • The *perpetuation* of these lies will not help our cause.

per·pe·tu·ity /ˌpɚpəˈtuːwəti, *Brit* ˌpɜːpəˈtjuːwəti/ *noun [noncount] formal* : the state of continuing forever or for a very long time • The land will be passed on from generation to generation ***in perpetuity***. [=*forever*]

per·plex /pɚˈplɛks/ *verb* **-plex·es; -plexed; -plex·ing** *[+ obj]* : to confuse (someone) very much • Her attitude *perplexes* me. = I am *perplexed* by her attitude. • Questions about the meaning of life have always *perplexed* humankind.

per·plexed /pɚˈplɛkst/ *adj* [*more* ~; *most* ~] **:** unable to understand something clearly or to think clearly **:** CONFUSED ▪ He gave her a *perplexed* look. ▪ The explanation left me thoroughly *perplexed*.
– **per·plexed·ly** /pɚˈplɛksədli/ *adv* ▪ The boy stared *perplexedly* at the chalkboard.

perplexing *adj* [*more* ~; *most* ~] **:** difficult to understand **:** CONFUSING ▪ *perplexing* questions/problems ▪ His sudden change of attitude is very *perplexing*.

per·plex·i·ty /pɚˈplɛksəti/ *noun, pl* **-ties**
1 [*noncount*] **:** the state of being very confused because something is difficult to understand ▪ There was a look of *perplexity* on his face. ▪ He stared at her in *perplexity*.
2 [*count*] **:** something that is confusing and difficult to understand ▪ We will never solve all of the *perplexities* of life.

per·qui·site /ˈpɚkwəzət/ *noun, pl* **-sites** [*count*] *formal* **:** ³PERK ▪ Use of the company's jet is a *perquisite* of the job.

per·ry /ˈperi/ *noun, pl* **-ries** [*count, noncount*] *Brit* **:** an alcoholic drink made from pears

per se /pɚˈseɪ/ *adv, formal* **:** by, of, or in itself — used to indicate that something is being considered by itself and not along with other things ▪ She feels that there is nothing wrong with gambling *per se*, but she thinks that it should be done in moderation.

per·se·cute /ˈpɚsɪˌkjuːt/ *verb* **-cutes; -cut·ed; -cut·ing** [+ *obj*]
1 : to treat (someone) cruelly or unfairly especially because of race or religious or political beliefs ▪ The country's leaders relentlessly *persecuted* those who fought against the regime. ▪ They were *persecuted* for their beliefs. ▪ a *persecuted* minority/people
2 : to constantly annoy or bother (someone) ▪ He complained about being *persecuted* [=*harassed*] by the media.
– **per·se·cu·tion** /ˌpɚsɪˈkjuːʃən/ *noun* [*noncount*] They were victims of religious *persecution*. ▪ He was forced to flee the country to avoid *persecution*. [*count*] the *persecutions* of ethnic minorities – **per·se·cu·tor** /ˈpɚsɪˌkjuːtɚ/ *noun, pl* **-tors** [*count*]

per·se·ver·ance /ˌpɚsəˈvirəns/ *noun* [*noncount*] **:** the quality that allows someone to continue trying to do something even though it is difficult ▪ His *perseverance* was rewarded: after many rejections, he finally found a job. ▪ *Perseverance* is required to perfect just about any skill.

per·se·vere /ˌpɚsəˈviɚ/ *verb* **-veres; -vered; -ver·ing** [*no obj*] **:** to continue doing something or trying to do something even though it is difficult ▪ She *persevered* in her studies and graduated near the top of her class. ▪ Even though he was tired, he *persevered* and finished the race.
– **persevering** *adj* [*more* ~; *most* ~] ▪ If you are *persevering*, I am convinced you will find a job. ▪ a very determined and *persevering* young woman

Per·sian cat /ˈpɚʒən-, *Brit* ˈpɜːʃən-/ *noun, pl* ~ **cats** [*count*] **:** a type of cat that has a round head and long, soft fur

per·sim·mon /pɚˈsɪmən/ *noun, pl* **-mons** [*count*] **:** a small, round, orange fruit

per·sist /pɚˈsɪst/ *verb* **-sists; -sist·ed; -sist·ing** [*no obj*]
1 : to continue to do something or to try to do something even though it is difficult or other people want you to stop ▪ She had turned him down for a date before, but he *persisted* and asked her again. ▪ The reporter *persisted* with his questioning. ▪ If you *persist* with this behavior, you will be punished. ▪ Must you *persist* in making that noise?
2 : to continue to occur or exist beyond the usual, expected, or normal time ▪ If the pain *persists*, see a doctor. ▪ Doubts about the defendant's story have *persisted* for some time now. ▪ Rumors *persist* that they are dating.

per·sis·tence /pɚˈsɪstəns/ *noun* [*noncount*]
1 : the quality that allows someone to continue doing something or trying to do something even though it is difficult or opposed by other people ▪ He admired her dogged *persistence* in pursuing the job. ▪ His *persistence* in asking for a raise was finally rewarded. ▪ She has shown a lot of *persistence*.
2 : the state of occurring or existing beyond the usual, expected, or normal time — usually + *of* ▪ The *persistence of* the rash worried him.

per·sis·tent /pɚˈsɪstənt/ *adj* [*more* ~; *most* ~]
1 : continuing to do something or to try to do something even though it is difficult or other people want you to stop ▪ We were nagged by a *persistent* salesman. ▪ He is one of the government's most *persistent* critics. ▪ She has been *persistent* in pursuing the job.
2 : continuing beyond the usual, expected, or normal time **:** not stopping or going away ▪ He has been fighting a *persistent* cold/infection. ▪ Flooding has been a *persistent* problem in the area this year. ▪ *Persistent* rumors that the business is for sale have alarmed the staff.
– **per·sis·tent·ly** *adv* ▪ He has *persistently* denied the charges.

persistent vegetative state *noun* [*singular*] *medical* **:** an unconscious state that is the result of severe brain damage and that can last for a very long time

per·snick·e·ty /pɚˈsnɪkəti/ *adj* [*more* ~; *most* ~] *US, informal + disapproving* **:** giving a lot of attention to details that are minor or not important ▪ a *persnickety* teacher ▪ The editor is *persnickety* [=(*Brit*) *pernickety*] about comma usage.

per·son /ˈpɚsn̩/ *noun, pl* **people** *or* **per·sons** [*count*] ✧ The plural of *person* is usually *people* except in formal or legal contexts, where the plural is often *persons*.
1 a : a human being ▪ She is a very nice/shy/interesting *person*. ▪ I saw a *person* standing on the dock. ▪ Any *person* who wants a refund must have a receipt. ▪ Most *people* here are quite friendly. ▪ The tickets are $25 per *person*. ▪ The *person* at the front desk will be able to help you. ▪ The tax break is only applicable to *persons* in a high income bracket. ▪ I like her ***as a person***, but she is not a very good writer. ▪ The disease is easily transmitted from ***person to person***. — sometimes used in compounds to avoid using *man* or *woman* ▪ a spokes*person* ▪ sales*people* — see also MISSING PERSON **b :** a person who likes or enjoys something specified ▪ Our new friends are real party *people*. [=our new friends like parties] ▪ I'm just not a city *person*. [=I do not like the city very much] ▪ She's always been a cat *person*. [=she likes cats a lot] — see also PEOPLE PERSON
2 *pl* ***persons*** *law* **:** the body or clothing of a person especially when considered as a place to hide things ▪ He was arrested for having a gun ***on his person*** without a permit. [=he was arrested for carrying a gun without having a gun permit] ▪ The dogs discovered that the men were hiding drugs ***about their persons***.
in person — used to say that a person is actually present at a place ▪ The president appeared *in person* at the ceremony. ▪ They met *in person* after speaking on the phone. ▪ You will need to sign for the package *in person*.
in the person of *formal* — used to say that someone is the person who does something, provides something, etc. ▪ Relief during the blackout arrived *in the person of* my brother, who brought flashlights and candles.
– see also FIRST PERSON, SECOND PERSON, THIRD PERSON

per·so·na /pɚˈsounə/ *noun, pl* **per·so·nae** /pɚˈsouni/ *or* **per·so·nas** [*count*] **:** the way you behave, talk, etc., with other people that causes them to see you as a particular kind of person **:** the image or personality that a person presents to other people ▪ His public *persona* is that of a strong, determined leader, but in private life he's very insecure. ▪ The band takes on a whole new *persona* when they perform live. — see also DRAMATIS PERSONAE, PERSONA NON GRATA

per·son·able /ˈpɚsənəbəl/ *adj* [*more* ~; *most* ~] **:** friendly or pleasant in manner **:** easy to get along with ▪ The hostess was very *personable*. ▪ He is a *personable* young man.

per·son·age /ˈpɚsənɪʤ/ *noun, pl* **-ag·es** [*count*] *formal* **:** an important or famous person ▪ The premiere was attended by no less a *personage* than the president himself.

per·son·al /ˈpɚsənəl/ *adj*
1 *always used before a noun* **a :** belonging or relating to a particular person ▪ *personal* property/belongings ▪ This is just my *personal* opinion/preference. ▪ I can only tell you what I know from *personal* experience. ▪ He added his own *personal* touches to the recipe. ▪ We don't accept *personal* checks. ▪ He is a *personal* friend of mine. ▪ She is always concerned about her *personal* appearance. ▪ We provide each of our customers with *personal* service. ▪ Golf is a *personal* interest of mine. **b :** made or designed to be used by one person ▪ a *personal* stereo **c —** used to describe someone whose job involves working for or helping a particular person ▪ She has her own *personal* chauffeur. ▪ the director's *personal* assistant ▪ a *personal* trainer
2 a [*more* ~; *most* ~] **:** relating to a person's private feelings, thoughts, problems, etc. ▪ May I ask you a *personal* question? ▪ That information is very *personal*, and you have no business asking about it. **b :** relating to the parts of your life that do not involve your work or job ▪ He doesn't speak much about his *personal* life. ▪ The company car is not for *personal* use. ▪ I had to leave work early because I had some

P

personal matters/problems/issues to take care of. • Is the letter *personal* or about business? • a *personal* phone call **c** — used to describe the feelings of two people who know and deal with each other • We have a close *personal* relationship. • He is a good boss, but I don't get along with him on a *personal* level.

3 [*more* ~; *most* ~] **:** relating to a particular person's character, appearance, opinions, etc., in a way that is offensive or hurtful • His speech included some *personal* remarks about me that I found offensive. • He took her comment as a *personal* insult. • It's ***nothing personal*** [=I don't mean to offend you], but I'd rather not talk to you about it. • *Nothing personal*, but why are you still friends with him? • Let's not ***get personal*** here.

4 *always used before a noun* **:** done by a particular person instead of by someone else who is working or acting for that person • The mayor made a *personal* appearance at the ceremony. • I shall give the matter my (own) *personal* attention.

5 *always used before a noun* **:** relating to a person's physical body or health • It's important to practice good *personal* hygiene. • *personal* care products

personal ad *noun, pl* ~ **ads** [*count*] **:** a short message in a special section of a newspaper, magazine, etc., that is written by someone who is interested in forming a friendly or romantic relationship with someone else

personal column *noun*

the personal column *Brit* **:** PERSONALS

personal computer *noun, pl* ~ **-ers** [*count*] **:** a small computer designed for use by one person at home or in an office — called also *PC*

personal digital assistant *noun, pl* ~ **-tants** [*count*] **:** PDA

personal foul *noun, pl* ~ **fouls** [*count*] *basketball* **:** a foul that involves physical contact with an opponent — compare TECHNICAL FOUL

per·son·al·i·ty /ˌpɚsəˈnæləti/ *noun, pl* **-ties**

1 : the set of emotional qualities, ways of behaving, etc., that makes a person different from other people [*count*] He has a very pleasant/strong *personality*. • We all have different *personalities*. • There was a ***clash of personalities*** [=a disagreement between people with different personalities] in the office. [*noncount*] The psychiatrist considered behavior as well as *personality* before prescribing a treatment. — often used before another noun • *personality* disorders/traits — see also SPLIT PERSONALITY

2 a [*noncount*] **:** attractive qualities (such as energy, friendliness, and humor) that make a person interesting or pleasant to be with • He has lots of *personality*. **b :** attractive qualities that make something unusual or interesting • He wants to buy a car that has *personality*. • The city lacks *personality*.

3 [*count*] **a :** a person who is famous • She has met many television *personalities*. • a sports/radio *personality* **b :** a person who is unusual or different from other people in a noticeable way • He was an influential *personality* in genetic engineering.

cult of personality *or* ***personality cult*** **:** a situation in which a public figure (such as a political leader) is deliberately presented to the people of a country as a great person who should be admired and loved

per·son·al·ize *also Brit* **per·son·al·ise** /ˈpɚsənəˌlaɪz/ *verb* **-iz·es; -ized; -iz·ing** [+ *obj*]

1 : to mark (something) in a way that shows it belongs to a particular person — usually used as *(be) personalized* • The stationery *was personalized* with her initials.

2 : to change or design (something) for a particular person — usually used as *(be) personalized* • The computer program can *be personalized* to fit your needs.

– personalized *also Brit* **personalised** *adj* • The children have *personalized* towels with their names sewn in. • You can receive *personalized* service at the salon. • a *personalized* license plate

per·son·al·ly /ˈpɚsənəli/ *adv*

1 — used to say that something was done or will be done by a particular person and not by someone else • He said he would attend to the matter *personally*. • I *personally* approved the changes. • She *personally* replied to my letter.

2 — used to say that someone knows a person or thing from personal experience and not because of someone else • "Do you know him *personally*?" "No, but my friend does."

3 : in a way that involves a particular person and no one else • You will be held *personally* responsible for any losses or damages. • The player was *personally* criticized by his coach. • He blamed me *personally* for causing the problem. • I was *personally* offended by the article.

4 : in a way that relates to a particular person and is offensive or hurtful • He didn't mean it *personally*. • Don't take my comments *personally*.

5 — used to say what your opinion is • *Personally*, I liked the first version more. = I *personally* liked the first version more.

6 : in a way that involves someone's personal life rather than someone's work or job • I knew him both *personally* and professionally.

personal pronoun *noun, pl* ~ **-nouns** [*count*] *grammar* **:** a pronoun (such as *I, you, they*, or *it*) that is used to refer to a specific person or thing

per·son·als /ˈpɚsənəlz/ *noun*

the personals *US* **:** a special section of a newspaper, magazine, etc., where people can place short personal messages (called personal ads) — called also (*Brit*) *the personal column*

personal space *noun* [*noncount*] **:** the amount of space between you and another person that makes you feel comfortable being near that person • You are invading my *personal space*.

per·so·na non gra·ta /pɚˌsounəˌnɑːnˈgrɑːtə/ *noun* [*noncount*] **:** someone who is not accepted or welcome by other people • His shocking book about the movie industry has made him *persona non grata* in Hollywood.

per·son·i·fi·ca·tion /pɚˌsɑːnəfəˈkeɪʃən/ *noun, pl* **-tions**

1 [*count*] **a :** a person who has a lot of a particular quality and who is the perfect example of someone who has that quality — often + *of* • Your father is the *personification of* kindness and generosity. [=he is very kind and generous] • He is the *personification of* evil. **b :** an imaginary person that represents a thing or idea — often + *of* • Uncle Sam is the *personification of* the U.S. government.

2 : the practice of representing a thing or idea as a person in art, literature, etc. [*noncount*] the use of *personification* in a story [*count*] a *personification* of justice as a woman with her eyes covered

per·son·i·fy /pɚˈsɑːnəˌfaɪ/ *verb* **-fies; -fied; -fy·ing** [+ *obj*]

1 : to have a lot of (a particular quality) **:** to be the perfect example of a person who has (a quality) • She *personifies* kindness. = She is kindness *personified*. [=she is a very kind person]

2 : to think of or represent (a thing or idea) as a person or as having human qualities or powers • The ancient Greeks *personified* the forces of nature as gods and goddesses. • Justice is *personified* as a woman with her eyes covered.

per·son·nel /ˌpɚsəˈnɛl/ *noun, pl* **personnel**

1 [*plural*] **:** the people who work for a particular company or organization • Over 10,000 military *personnel* were stationed in the country. • They've reduced the number of *personnel* working on the project. • medical/security/administrative *personnel*

2 [*noncount*] **:** a department within a company or organization that deals with the people who work for it **:** HUMAN RESOURCES • Talk to *personnel* if you have any questions about your health insurance. • She's the director of *personnel*. — often used before another noun • the *personnel* director/manager/department

personnel carrier *noun, pl* ~ **-ers** [*count*] **:** a vehicle with thick, strong walls that is used for transporting military workers and their equipment • armored *personnel carriers*

person–to–person *adj* **:** involving two people or going directly from one person to another person • *person-to-person* communication • *person-to-person* meetings • a *person-to-person* phone call

– person–to–person *adv* • The reporter talked *person-to-person* with the hostage.

per·spec·tive /pɚˈspɛktɪv/ *noun, pl* **-tives**

1 : a way of thinking about and understanding something (such as a particular issue or life in general) [*count*] He helped us see the problem from a new *perspective*. [=*angle, point of view*] • The story is told from the *perspective* of a teenage boy in the 1940s. • marriage as seen from a male/female *perspective* • From an economic *perspective*, the policy has some merit. • a critique of the war from a historical *perspective* — often + *on* • My grandmother has a surprisingly modern *perspective* [=*outlook*] *on* life. • They had totally different *perspectives on* the war. [*noncount*] He had a complete ***change of perspective*** after his illness.

2 [*noncount*] **a :** a condition in which a person knows which things are important and does not worry or think

P

about unimportant things • He had lost all ***sense of perspective*** and believed that his life was ruined. — often used after *in* or *into* • She helped him put his life *in* proper *perspective*. • Seeing how difficult their lives are has really put my problems *into perspective*. **b** : the ability to understand which things are truly important and which things are not • Try to keep/maintain your *perspective* and not get too worried about it. • I was trying to gain some *perspective* on the things that I learned in college. [=I was deciding which things were important and which things were not]
3 [*count*] : the angle or direction that a person uses to look at an object • She drew the building from several different *perspectives*. • From this *perspective*, the city looks peaceful.
4 [*noncount*] : a way of showing depth or distance in a painting or drawing by making the objects that are far away smaller and making the objects that are closer to the viewer larger • I admire her use of *perspective* in her paintings. • a drawing done in *perspective* = a *perspective* drawing

Per·spex /ˈpɚˌspɛks/ *trademark, Brit* — used for a type of clear plastic

per·spi·ca·cious /ˌpɚspəˈkeɪʃəs/ *adj* [*more* ~; *most* ~] *formal* : having or showing an ability to notice and understand things that are difficult or not obvious • She considers herself a *perspicacious* [=*shrewd, astute*] judge of character. • The critic made some *perspicacious* [=*insightful*] observations about the film.
— **per·spi·ca·cious·ly** *adv* — **per·spi·cac·i·ty** /ˌpɚspəˈkæsəti/ *noun* [*noncount*] • her intellectual *perspicacity*

per·spi·ra·tion /ˌpɚspəˈreɪʃən/ *noun* [*noncount*] *somewhat formal*
1 : the clear liquid that forms on your skin when you are hot or nervous : SWEAT • She wiped the *perspiration* from her forehead.
2 : the act or process of perspiring • Drink plenty of water to replace the liquid lost by *perspiration*. [=*sweating*]

per·spire /pɚˈspajɚ/ *verb* **-spires; -spired; -spir·ing** [*no obj*] *somewhat formal* : to produce a clear liquid from your skin when you are hot or nervous : SWEAT • I was nervous and could feel myself start to *perspire*. • She ran two miles and wasn't even *perspiring*.

per·suade /pɚˈsweɪd/ *verb* **-suades; -suad·ed; -suad·ing** [+ *obj*]
1 : to cause (someone) to do something by asking, arguing, or giving reasons • He *persuaded* his friend to go back to school. • She couldn't be *persuaded* to go. • He would not let himself be *persuaded* into buying the more expensive stereo. • I am not easily *persuaded*. — compare DISSUADE
2 : to cause (someone) to believe something : CONVINCE • They *persuaded* us that we were wrong. • He *persuaded* himself that he had made the right choice.

per·sua·sion /pɚˈsweɪʒən/ *noun, pl* **-sions**
1 [*noncount*] : the act of causing people to do or believe something : the act or activity of persuading people • It would take a lot of *persuasion* to get him to agree to such an offer. • Most kids don't need much *persuasion* to use computers. • Many voters are still open to *persuasion*. [=many voters can still be persuaded to change their opinions] • She used her ***powers of persuasion*** [=her ability to persuade people] to convince them to buy the house.
2 [*count*] *formal* : a particular type of belief or way of thinking • an individual's religious/moral *persuasion* • people of all different *persuasions* — sometimes used humorously to refer to a particular type of person or thing • artists of the female/feminine *persuasion* [=artists who are women]

per·sua·sive /pɚˈsweɪsɪv/ *adj* [*more* ~; *most* ~] : able to cause people to do or believe something : able to persuade people • We weren't shown any *persuasive* evidence that he had committed the crime. • a very *persuasive* [=*convincing*] argument • a *persuasive* salesman
— **per·sua·sive·ly** *adv* • She argues *persuasively* that the drug should be legal. — **per·sua·sive·ness** *noun* [*noncount*]

pert /ˈpɚt/ *adj* [*more* ~; *most* ~]
1 : having or showing confidence and a lack of respect or seriousness especially in an amusing or appealing way — used especially to describe girls or young women • a lively and *pert* young actress • He laughed at the girl's *pert* answer.
2 : small and attractive • a *pert* little hat • a *pert* bottom/nose
— **pert·ly** *adv* • She winked at him *pertly* and smiled.

per·tain /pɚˈteɪn/ *verb* **-tains; -tained; -tain·ing** [*no obj*] *formal* : to relate *to* someone or something : to have a connection *to* a person or thing • The law *pertains* [=*applies*] only *to* people who were born in this country. • The questions *pertained to* [=the questions were about] the role of religion in society. • books *pertaining to* the country's history

per·ti·nent /ˈpɚtənənt/ *adj* [*more* ~; *most* ~] *formal* : relating to the thing that is being thought about or discussed : RELEVANT • a *pertinent* question • His comments weren't *pertinent* (to the discussion).
— **per·ti·nence** /ˈpɚtənəns/ *noun* [*noncount*] • the *pertinence* [=*relevance*] of the question — **per·ti·nent·ly** *adv*

per·turb /pɚˈtɚb/ *verb* **-turbs; -turbed; -turb·ing** [+ *obj*] : to cause (someone) to be worried or upset • It *perturbed* him that his son was thinking about leaving school.
— **perturbed** *adj* [*more* ~; *most* ~] • She was so *perturbed* that she forgot to say goodbye. • *perturbed* behavior • He looked very *perturbed* when he heard the news.

per·tur·ba·tion /ˌpɚtɚˈbeɪʃən/ *noun, pl* **-tions**
1 *technical* : a change in the normal state or regular movement of something [*count*] a *perturbation* in the planet's orbit [*noncount*] gravitational *perturbation*
2 [*noncount*] *formal* : the state of being worried or upset • mental/emotional *perturbation*

per·tus·sis /pɚˈtʌsəs/ *noun* [*noncount*] *medical* : WHOOPING COUGH

pe·ruse /pəˈruːz/ *verb* **-rus·es; -rused; -rus·ing** [+ *obj*] *formal*
1 : to look at or read (something) in an informal or relaxed way • Would you like something to drink while you *peruse* [=*look over*] the menu? • He *perused* the newspaper over breakfast.
2 : to examine or read (something) in a very careful way • She *perused* [=*studied*] the lists closely.
— **pe·rus·al** /pəˈruːzəl/ *noun, pl* **-als** [*count*] — usually singular • a quick *perusal* of the menu • Here is the list of guests for your *perusal*. [*noncount*] This book deserves careful *perusal*.

perv /ˈpɚv/ *noun, pl* **pervs** [*count*] *slang* : PERVERT

per·vade /pɚˈveɪd/ *verb* **-vades; -vad·ed; -vad·ing** [+ *obj*] *formal* : to spread through all parts of (something) • A sense of excitement *pervaded* the room. [=everyone in the room felt excited] : to exist in every part of (something) • A feeling of great sadness *pervades* the film. • Art and music *pervade* every aspect of their lives.

per·va·sive /pɚˈveɪsɪv/ *adj* [*more* ~; *most* ~] : existing in every part of something : spreading to all parts of something • a *pervasive* odor • the *pervasive* nature of the problem • television's *pervasive* influence on our culture
— **per·va·sive·ly** *adv* — **per·va·sive·ness** *noun* [*noncount*]

per·verse /pɚˈvɚs/ *adj* [*more* ~; *most* ~] : wrong or different in a way that others feel is strange or offensive • their *perverse* cruelty to animals • She has a *perverse* fascination with death. • He seems to take *perverse* pleasure/delight in making things as difficult as possible. • His friends all enjoy his *perverse* sense of humor. • Is this some kind of *perverse* joke? • *perverse* [=*perverted*] sexual desires
— **per·verse·ly** *adv* • The movie was *perversely* amusing.

per·ver·sion /pɚˈvɚʒən/ *noun, pl* **-sions**
1 : sexual behavior that people think is not normal or natural [*count*] sexual *perversions* [*noncount*] sexual *perversion*
2 a [*count*] : something that improperly changes something good • *perversions* of the truth • The judge's decision was a *perversion* of justice. [=was very unjust] **b** [*noncount*] : the process of improperly changing something that is good • They fought against *perversion* of the health-care system.

per·ver·si·ty /pɚˈvɚsəti/ *noun, pl* **-ties**
1 [*noncount*] : the quality of being wrong or different in a strange or offensive way : a perverse quality • The sheer *perversity* of her actions is shocking. • sexual *perversity* [=*perversion*] • acting out of stubborn *perversity* [=a feeling of not wanting to do what other people want or expect]
2 [*count*] : something that is wrong or perverse • sexual *perversities* — often + *of* • It is one of the many *perversities of* the system.

[1]**per·vert** /pɚˈvɚt/ *verb* **-verts; -vert·ed; -vert·ing** [+ *obj*]
1 : to change (something good) so that it is no longer what it was or should be • people who *pervert* their religion to support violence • They *perverted* the truth to help further their careers.
2 : to cause (a person or a person's mind) to become immoral or not normal • movies that *pervert* the minds of young people by glorifying violence
pervert justice *or* ***pervert the course of justice*** *Brit* : to

try to stop the police from learning the facts about a criminal case ▪ She was convicted of *perverting justice* [=(US) *obstructing justice*] for lying to the police.

[2]**per·vert** /ˈpɚˌvɚt/ *noun, pl* **-verts** [*count*] : a person whose sexual behavior is considered not normal or acceptable

per·vert·ed /pɚˈvɚtəd/ *adj* [*more* ~; *most* ~]
1 : having or showing sexual desires that are considered not normal or acceptable ▪ *perverted* minds ▪ *perverted* criminals ▪ *perverted* behavior
2 : not considered normal or acceptable : PERVERSE ▪ *perverted* logic ▪ He took a *perverted* pleasure/delight in watching them suffer.

pe·se·ta /pəˈseɪtə/ *noun, pl* **-tas** [*count*] : the basic unit of money of Spain until 2002

pes·ky /ˈpɛski/ *adj* **pes·ki·er**; **-est** *US, informal* : making someone annoyed or irritated ▪ I've been trying to get rid of this *pesky* cold for weeks. ▪ *pesky* insects ▪ *pesky* reporters

pe·so /ˈpeɪsoʊ/ *noun, pl* **pe·sos** [*count*] : the basic unit of money of several Latin-American countries and the Philippines; *also* : a coin or bill representing one peso

pes·si·mism /ˈpɛsəˌmɪzəm/ *noun* [*noncount*] : a feeling or belief that bad things will happen in the future : a feeling or belief that what you hope for will not happen ▪ She has expressed *pessimism* over the outcome of the trial. [=she thinks the outcome will be bad] ▪ Although the economy shows signs of improving, a sense of *pessimism* remains. ▪ He expressed his *pessimism* about politics and politicians. [=his belief that politics and politicians are generally bad] — opposite OPTIMISM

pes·si·mist /ˈpɛsəmɪst/ *noun, pl* **-mists** [*count*] : a person who usually expects bad things to happen ▪ Stop being such a *pessimist*. Not everything is wrong with the world. — opposite OPTIMIST

pes·si·mis·tic /ˌpɛsəˈmɪstɪk/ *adj* [*more* ~; *most* ~] : having or showing a lack of hope for the future : expecting bad things to happen ▪ I'm *pessimistic* about our chances of winning. [=I don't think we'll win] ▪ Most doctors were *pessimistic* that a cure could be found. ▪ The film gives a very *pessimistic* view of human nature. ▪ He has an extremely negative and *pessimistic* attitude. — opposite OPTIMISTIC
– **pes·si·mis·ti·cal·ly** /ˌpɛsəˈmɪstɪkli/ *adv* ▪ He spoke *pessimistically* about the country's future.

pest /ˈpɛst/ *noun, pl* **pests** [*count*]
1 : an animal or insect that causes problems for people especially by damaging crops ▪ These insects/birds are *pests* for farmers. ▪ agricultural/garden *pests* ▪ mice and other household *pests* — often used before another noun ▪ *pest* control/management
2 *informal* : a person who bothers or annoys other people ▪ You're being a real *pest*. Would you leave us alone, please?

pes·ter /ˈpɛstɚ/ *verb* **-ters -tered; -ter·ing** [+ *obj*] : to annoy or bother (someone) in a repeated way ▪ His mother's always *pestering* [=*harassing*] him (with questions) about his love life. ▪ Leave me alone! Stop *pestering* me!

pes·ti·cide /ˈpɛstəˌsaɪd/ *noun, pl* **-cides** [*count, noncount*] : a chemical that is used to kill animals or insects that damage plants or crops

pes·ti·lence /ˈpɛstələns/ *noun, pl* **-lenc·es** *literary* : a disease that causes many people to die [*noncount*] After years of war and *pestilence*, few people remained in the city. [*count*] — usually singular ▪ a deadly *pestilence*

pes·tle /ˈpɛsəl/ *noun, pl* **pestles** [*count*] : a hard tool with a rounded end that is used for pounding or crushing substances (such as medicines) in a deep bowl (called a mortar)

pes·to /ˈpɛstoʊ/ *noun* [*noncount*] : an Italian sauce that is made especially of fresh basil, garlic, oil, and grated cheese ▪ Top the bread with *pesto*.

[1]**pet** /ˈpɛt/ *noun, pl* **pets** [*count*]
1 : an animal (such as a dog, cat, bird, or fish) that people keep mainly for pleasure ▪ He caught a snake and kept it as a *pet* for several years. ▪ No *pets* (are) allowed. ▪ An orange cat named Alex was our first ***family pet*** [=a pet kept by a family] — often used before another noun ▪ *pet* food ▪ a *pet* store ▪ a *pet* dog/cat
2 *Brit* — used to address someone in a loving or friendly way ▪ What's the matter, *pet*? [=*darling*]
– see also TEACHER'S PET

[2]**pet** *adj, always used before a noun* : very interesting or important to a particular person ▪ The mayor's *pet* project has been the construction of a new high school. ▪ I have my own *pet* [=*favorite*] theory about that. ▪ a politician's *pet* causes/issues

[3]**pet** *verb* **pets; pet·ted; pet·ting**
1 [+ *obj*] : to touch (a cat, dog, child, etc.) with your hand in a loving or friendly way ▪ My dog loves to be *petted*.
2 [*no obj*] *informal* : to kiss and touch someone in a sexual way ▪ There was some ***heavy petting*** going on at the party.

pet·al /ˈpɛtl̩/ *noun, pl* **-als** [*count*] : one of the soft, colorful parts of a flower ▪ rose *petals* ▪ flowers with pink and white *petals* — see picture at FLOWER

pe·tard /pəˈtaɚd/ *noun*
hoist by/on/with your own petard : hurt by something that you have done or planned yourself : harmed by your own trick or scheme ▪ a politican who has been *hoist by his own petard*

pe·ter /ˈpiːtɚ/ *verb* **-ters; -tered; -ter·ing**
peter out [*phrasal verb*] *informal* : to gradually become smaller, weaker, or less before stopping or ending ▪ Their romantic relationship *petered out* after the summer. ▪ Interest in the sport is beginning to *peter out*.

pet hate *noun, pl* ~ **hates** [*count*] *Brit* : PET PEEVE

pe·tit bour·geois /pəˈtiːbuɚʒˈwɑː/ *noun, pl* **petit bour·geois** [*count*] *often disapproving* : a member of the petite bourgeoisie — called also *petty bourgeois*

pe·tite /pəˈtiːt/ *adj* [*more* ~; *most* ~] : having a small and thin body — usually used to describe a woman or girl ▪ She's *petite* and has short black hair. ▪ a *petite* young woman ▪ clothes in *petite* sizes [=sizes that fit petite women]

petite bourgeoisie *noun*
the petite bourgeoisie : a social class that is between the middle class and the lower class : the lower middle class ▪ a member of *the petite bourgeoisie* — called also *the petty bourgeoisie*

pe·tit four /ˌpɛtiˈfoɚ/ *noun, pl* **pe·tits fours** *or* **petit fours** /ˌpɛtiˈfoɚz/ [*count*] : a very small cake that is decorated with frosting

[1]**pe·ti·tion** /pəˈtɪʃən/ *noun, pl* **-tions** [*count*]
1 : a written document that many people sign to show that they want a person or organization to do or change something ▪ They collected 2,000 signatures on a *petition* demanding that women be allowed to join the club. ▪ Would you like to sign our *petition*?
2 a : a formal written request made to an official person or organization ▪ We presented a *petition* to the legislature to change the law. **b** *law* : a formal written request to have a legal case decided by a court ▪ She filed a *petition* for divorce. ▪ They've denied your *petition*. [=the court will not hear your case]
3 *formal* : a prayer or request to God or to a very powerful person or group ▪ We ask you to hear our *petition*.

[2]**petition** *verb* **-tions; -tioned; -tion·ing** : to ask (a person, group, or organization) for something in a formal way [+ *obj*] The organization *petitioned* the government to investigate the issue. ▪ All people had the right to *petition* the king for help. [*no obj*] She *petitioned* to join their club. — often + *for* ▪ The students *petitioned for* permission to wear hats in school.

pe·ti·tion·er /pəˈtɪʃənɚ/ *noun, pl* **-ers** [*count*]
1 : a person who creates a petition or signs a petition in order to change or ask for something ▪ We have the signatures of over 300 *petitioners*.
2 *law* : a person who asks to have a legal case decided by a court ▪ The *petitioner* is trying to have the Supreme Court overrule the decision.

pet·it larceny /ˈpɛti-/ *noun* [*noncount*] *US, law* : the crime of stealing something that does not have a high value — called also *petit theft, petty larceny, petty theft*; compare GRAND LARCENY

pet·it theft /ˈpɛti-/ *noun* [*noncount*] *US, law* : PETIT LARCENY

pet name *noun, pl* ~ **names** [*count*] : a name that a person uses for someone to show love or affection ▪ His *pet name* for her is "Sweet Pea."

pet peeve *noun, pl* ~ **peeves** [*count*] *US* : something that annoys or bothers a person very much ▪ One of my biggest *pet peeves* is people driving too slowly on the highway. — called also (*Brit*) *pet hate*

pe·trel /ˈpɛtrəl/ *noun, pl* **-trels** [*count*] : a bird that has long wings and usually dark feathers and that lives mainly on the ocean

Pe·tri dish /ˈpiːtri-/ *noun, pl* ~ **dishes** [*count*] : a small, shallow dish that has a loose cover and that is is used in scientific experiments especially for growing bacteria

petrified *adj*
1 : very afraid or frightened of something : unable to move or act because you are afraid ▪ "Are you afraid?" "I'm not just afraid, I'm *petrified.*" ▪ We were *petrified* with fear.
2 — used to describe something (such as wood) that has slowly changed into stone or a substance like stone over a very long period of time ▪ *petrified* wood ▪ the *petrified* bones of a fish ▪ a *petrified* forest

pet·ri·fy /ˈpɛtrəˌfaɪ/ *verb* **-fies; -fied; -fy·ing**
1 [+ *obj*] **:** to make (someone) very afraid ▪ It *petrifies* [=*terrifies*] me to think of how close we came to dying.
2 *technical* **:** to slowly change (something, such as wood) into stone or a substance like stone over a very long period of time [+ *obj*] the processes that *petrify* wood [*no obj*] The dead tree *petrified* into stone.

pet·ro·chem·i·cal /ˌpɛtroʊˈkɛmɪkəl/ *noun, pl* **-cals** [*count*] *technical* **:** a chemical that is made from petroleum or natural gas

pet·rol /ˈpɛtrəl/ *noun* [*noncount*] *Brit* **:** GASOLINE

petrol bomb *noun, pl* **~ bombs** [*count*] *Brit* **:** MOLOTOV COCKTAIL

pe·tro·leum /pəˈtroʊlijəm/ *noun* [*noncount*] **:** a kind of oil that comes from below the ground and that is the source of gasoline and other products

petroleum jelly *noun* [*noncount*] **:** an oily substance that is made from petroleum, has no taste or odor, and is used especially in products that are rubbed on the skin to help heal a wound, reduce pain, etc.

petrol station *noun, pl* **~ -tions** [*count*] *Brit* **:** GAS STATION

pet·ti·coat /ˈpɛtiˌkoʊt/ *noun, pl* **-coats** [*count*] **:** a skirt that a woman or girl wears under a dress or outer skirt

pet·ti·fog·ging /ˈpɛtiˌfɑːgɪŋ/ *adj, old-fashioned* **:** worrying too much about details that are minor or not important ▪ *pettifogging* lawyers

petting zoo *noun, pl* **~ zoos** [*count*] *US* **:** a collection of animals that children can touch and feed

pet·ty /ˈpɛti/ *adj* **pet·ti·er; -est** [*also more ~; most ~*]
1 a : not very important or serious ▪ Let's not waste time arguing over *petty* [=*trivial*] details. ▪ *petty* [=*minor*] crimes ▪ a *petty* official [=an official who is not important and has little power] **b :** relating to things that are not very important or serious ▪ a *petty* argument about grammar ▪ *petty* jealousy **c :** committing crimes that are not very serious ▪ *petty* criminals/thieves/crooks
2 : treating people harshly and unfairly because of things that are not very important ▪ a small-minded, *petty* person ▪ My behavior was *petty* and stupid. I apologize.
– **pet·ti·ness** /ˈpɛtinəs/ *noun* [*noncount*] ▪ the *pettiness* of their concerns

petty bourgeois *noun, pl* **petty bourgeois** [*count*] **:** PETIT BOURGEOIS

petty bourgeoisie *noun* [*noncount*] **:** PETIT BOURGEOISIE

petty cash *noun* [*noncount*] **:** a small amount of money that is kept in an office in order to pay for small items

petty larceny *noun* [*noncount*] **:** PETIT LARCENY

petty officer *noun, pl* **~ -cers** [*count*] **:** an officer with a low rank in the Navy or U.S. Coast Guard

petty theft *noun* [*noncount*] **:** PETIT LARCENY

pet·u·lant /ˈpɛtʃələnt/ *adj* [*more ~; most ~*] *disapproving* **:** having or showing the attitude of people who become angry and annoyed when they do not get what they want ▪ a *petulant* child ▪ Her tone was *petulant* and angry.
– **pet·u·lance** /ˈpɛtʃələns/ *noun* [*noncount*] – **pet·u·lant·ly** *adv*

pe·tu·nia /pɪˈtuːnjə/ *noun, pl* **-nias** [*count*] **:** a plant that has colorful flowers which are shaped like funnels

pew /ˈpjuː/ *noun, pl* **pews** [*count*] **:** one of the benches that are placed in rows in a church

pew·ter /ˈpjuːtɚ/ *noun* [*noncount*] **:** a dull gray metal that is a mixture of tin and usually lead ▪ cups made of *pewter* = *pewter* cups

PG /ˈpiːˈʤiː/ — used as a special mark to indicate that people of all ages may see a particular movie but that parents may want to watch the movie with their children ▪ This movie is rated *PG*. Parental guidance is suggested. — compare G, NC-17, PG-13, R, X

pg. *abbr* page ▪ *pg.* 26

PGA *abbr* Professional Golfers' Association

PGCE *abbr, Brit* Postgraduate Certificate of Education

PG-13 /ˈpiːˈʤiːθəˈtiːn/ — used as a special mark to indicate that people of all ages may see a particular movie but that parents may want to watch the movie with their children especially when their children are younger than 13 years old; compare G, NC-17, PG, R, X

pH /ˈpiːˈeɪtʃ/ *noun* [*singular*] *technical* **:** a number between 0 and 14 that indicates if a chemical is an acid or a base ✧ A chemical with a pH lower than 7 is an acid, and a chemical with a pH higher than 7 is a base. ▪ You should test the *pH* of the soil in your garden.

PH *abbr* pinch hitter

pha·lanx /ˈfeɪˌlæŋks, *Brit* ˈfæˌlæŋks/ *noun, pl* **-lanx·es** [*count*] *formal* **:** a large group of people, animals, or things often placed close together ▪ A solid *phalanx* of armed guards stood in front of the castle. ▪ She had to go through a *phalanx* of television cameras.

phal·lic /ˈfælɪk/ *adj* [*more ~; most ~*] **:** of, relating to, or resembling a penis ▪ The poem is filled with *phallic* imagery. ▪ an ancient Greek ***phallic symbol*** representing fertility

phal·lus /ˈfæləs/ *noun, pl* **phal·li** /ˈfæˌlaɪ/ *or* **phal·lus·es** [*count*]
1 : an image or representation of a penis
2 : PENIS

phan·tasm /ˈfænˌtæzəm/ *noun, pl* **-tasms** [*count*] *literary* **:** something that exists only in a person's mind ▪ the *phantasm* of equality ▪ a ghostly *phantasm*

phan·tas·ma·go·ria /fænˌtæzməˈgorijə/ *noun, pl* **-rias** [*count*] *literary* **:** a confusing or strange scene that is like a dream because it is always changing in an odd way ▪ He saw a *phantasmagoria* of shadowy creatures through the fog.
– **phan·tas·ma·gor·ic** /fænˌtæzməˈgorɪk/ *or* **phan·tas·ma·gor·i·cal** /fænˌtæzməˈgorɪkəl/ *adj* ▪ a *phantasmagoric* scene

[1]**phan·tom** /ˈfæntəm/ *noun, pl* **-toms** [*count*]
1 : the soul of a dead person thought of as living in an unseen world or as appearing to living people : GHOST ▪ The book is about the *phantoms* that are said to haunt the nation's cemeteries.
2 : something that is not real and exists only in a person's mind ▪ The crisis is merely a *phantom* made up by the media.
3 : something that is hard to see or achieve — often + *of* ▪ He spent years chasing the *phantoms of* fame and fortune.

[2]**phantom** *adj, always used before a noun*
1 : coming from or associated with the world of ghosts ▪ People claim to have seen a *phantom* ship floating on the lake.
2 a : not real or true or not based on something real or true ▪ A number of ballots from *phantom* voters had to be thrown out. ▪ *phantom* fears **b :** not real but felt or experienced as something real ▪ *phantom* illnesses ▪ a ***phantom pregnancy*** [=a medical condition in which a woman believes that she is pregnant and can appear to be pregnant when she is not pregnant]

pha·raoh *or* **Pharaoh** /ˈferoʊ/ *noun, pl* **-raohs** [*count*] **:** a ruler of ancient Egypt

Phar·i·see /ˈferəˌsiː/ *noun, pl* **-sees** [*count*] **:** a member of an ancient Jewish group that followed Jewish religious laws and teachings very strictly

[1]**phar·ma·ceu·ti·cal** /ˌfɑɚməˈsuːtɪkəl/ *adj, always used before a noun* **:** of or relating to the production and sale of drugs and medicine ▪ a *pharmaceutical* company ▪ lobbyists from the *pharmaceutical* industry

[2]**pharmaceutical** *noun, pl* **-cals** [*count*] *technical* **:** a drug or medicine — usually plural ▪ The company manufactures *pharmaceuticals.*

phar·ma·cist /ˈfɑɚməsɪst/ *noun, pl* **-cists** [*count*] **:** a person whose job is to prepare and sell the drugs and medicines that a doctor prescribes for patients ▪ He is trained as a *pharmacist.* [=(*US*) *druggist,* (*Brit*) *chemist*]

phar·ma·col·o·gy /ˌfɑɚməˈkɑːləʤi/ *noun* [*noncount*] *technical*
1 : the scientific study of drugs and how they are used in medicine
2 : a drug's qualities and effects ▪ We don't have a complete understanding of the new drug's *pharmacology* yet.
– **phar·ma·col·o·gist** /ˌfɑɚməˈkɑːləʤɪst/ *noun, pl* **-gists** [*count*] – **phar·ma·co·log·i·cal** /ˌfɑɚməkəˈlɑːʤɪkəl/ *also* **phar·ma·co·log·ic** /ˌfɑɚməkəˈlɑːʤɪk/ *adj, always used before a noun* ▪ the *pharmacological* treatment of depression [=the treatment of depression using drugs] ▪ *pharmacologic* effects – **phar·ma·co·log·i·cal·ly** /ˌfɑɚməkəˈlɑːʤɪkli/ *adv* ▪ The two drugs are *pharmacologically* similar.

P

phar·ma·co·pe·ia (*chiefly US*) *or chiefly Brit* **phar·ma·co·poe·ia** /ˌfɑɚməkəˈpiːjə/ *noun, pl* **-ias** [*count*] *technical*
1 : a collection or supply of drugs ▪ The new discovery added another drug to the global *pharmacopeia*.
2 : an official book that describes drugs and how to use them as medicine

phar·ma·cy /ˈfɑɚməsi/ *noun, pl* **-cies**
1 [*count*] **a :** a store or part of a store in which drugs and medicines are prepared and sold ▪ There's a *pharmacy* in our grocery store now. **b :** a place in a hospital where drugs and medicines are prepared and given out : DISPENSARY
2 [*noncount*] **:** the practice and profession of preparing drugs and medicines ▪ She's studying *pharmacy* at the university.

phar·ynx /ˈferɪŋks/ *noun, pl* **phar·yng·es** /fəˈrɪnˌʤiz/ *or* **phar·ynx·es** [*count*] *medical* **:** the part inside your mouth where the passages of the nose connect to your mouth and throat

[1]**phase** /ˈfeɪz/ *noun, pl* **phas·es**
1 [*count*] **:** a part or step in a process : one part in a series of related events or actions ▪ The project will be done in three *phases*. ▪ He's in the final *phase* of treatment now. ▪ The building project marks a new *phase* in the town's development. ▪ These poems are from an early *phase* [=*stage*] in her career.
2 [*count*] **:** a short period of time during which a person behaves in a particular way or likes a particular thing ▪ He has been throwing tantrums a lot, but the doctor says it's just a *phase*. ▪ She's going through a punk *phase* right now. [=she likes punk music and fashion at this point in her life]
3 [*count*] **:** the shape of the part of the moon that is visible at different times during a month ▪ a calendar based on the *phases* of the moon
4 [*noncount*] *Brit* **:** the state in which things work together with each other — used in the phrases ***in phase*** or ***out of phase*** ▪ Make sure the machine's wheels are moving *in phase* with each other. ▪ The sound on this movie is *out of phase*. [=the sound does not match the images of the movie] ▪ He seems to be *out of phase* [=(*US*) *out of step*] with the rest of the team.

[2]**phase** *verb* **phases; phased; phas·ing**
phase in [*phrasal verb*] ***phase (something) in or phase in (something)*** **:** to start to use or do (something) gradually over a period of time : to introduce (something) slowly ▪ The country is *phasing in* new paper currency. ▪ The tax cut will be *phased in* over the next three years. ▪ The law will *phase* tax cuts *in* over a period of two years.
phase out [*phrasal verb*] ***phase (something) out or phase out (something)*** **:** to stop using, making, or doing (something) gradually over a period of time ▪ The company is *phasing* its old equipment *out*. ▪ The airplane is being *phased out* in favor of a new design. — see also PHASEOUT

phased *adj* **:** done gradually in steps and according to a plan ▪ The government has announced the *phased* closure of a number of military bases. ▪ a *phased* withdrawal of troops

phase·out /ˈfeɪzˌaʊt/ *noun, pl* **-outs** [*count*] *US* **:** the act of stopping something gradually over a period of time in a planned series of steps or phases — usually singular ▪ The restaurant will continue its *phaseout* of many unhealthy menu items over the next two years. — see also *phase out* at [2]PHASE

phat /ˈfæt/ *adj* **phat·ter; -est** *US slang* **:** very attractive or appealing ▪ That song has a *phat* beat. ▪ That car is *phat*!

PhD /ˌpiːˌeɪʧˈdiː/ *noun, pl* **PhDs** [*count*]
1 : the highest degree given by a university or college ▪ He got his *PhD* [=*doctorate*] from Harvard. ▪ She has two *PhDs*. [=doctoral degrees] ▪ a *PhD* candidate [=a person who is trying to get a PhD]
2 : a person who has a PhD ▪ We're not hiring new *PhDs* at this point. ▪ Sheila Jones, *PhD* ✧ *PhD* is an abbreviation of "doctor of philosophy."

pheas·ant /ˈfɛzn̩t/ *noun, pl* **pheasant** *or* **pheas·ants**
1 [*count*] **:** a large bird that has a long tail and is often hunted for food or sport ✧ The male pheasant is brightly colored and the female is mostly brown. — see color picture on page C9
2 [*noncount*] **:** the meat of the pheasant eaten as food

phe·nom /ˈfiːˌnɑːm/ *noun, pl* **-noms** [*count*] *US, informal* **:** a person who is very good at doing something (such as a sport) ▪ a football/baseball *phenom* [=(more formally) *phenomenon*]

phenomena *plural of* PHENOMENON

phe·nom·e·nal /fɪˈnɑːmənl/ *adj* [*more* ~; *most* ~] **:** very good or great : unusual in a way that is very impressive ▪ The book was a *phenomenal* [=*huge*] success. ▪ Her performance was *phenomenal*. [=*amazing*]

phe·nom·e·nal·ly /fiˈnɑːmənl̩i/ *adv*
1 : in a very great or impressive way ▪ It's a *phenomenally* [=*hugely*] successful book.
2 : very or extremely : to an unusually high degree ▪ The speech was *phenomenally* boring.

phe·nom·e·non /fiˈnɑːməˌnɑːn/ *noun* [*count*]
1 *pl* ***-e·na*** /-ənə/ **:** something (such as an interesting fact or event) that can be observed and studied and that typically is unusual or difficult to understand or explain fully ▪ natural *phenomena* like lightning and earthquakes ▪ the *phenomenon* of love
2 *pl* ***-e·nons*** **:** someone or something that is very impressive or popular especially because of an unusual ability or quality ▪ the greatest literary *phenomenon* of the decade ▪ He's a football/baseball *phenomenon*. ▪ The movie eventually became a cultural *phenomenon*.

pher·o·mone /ˈferəˌmoun/ *noun, pl* **-mones** [*count*] *biology* **:** a chemical substance that an animal or insect produces in order to attract other animals or insects and especially a mate

phew /ˈfjuː/ *interj* — used to show that you are relieved, tired, hot, or disgusted ▪ *Phew*! I thought we were going to miss the bus! ▪ *Phew*! What a long day it's been! ▪ *Phew*! It's hot in here. ▪ *Phew*! What's that smell?

phi·al /ˈfajəl/ *noun, pl* **-als** [*count*] *Brit* **:** VIAL

Phi Be·ta Kap·pa /ˌfaɪˌbeɪtəˈkæpə/ *noun, pl* ~ **-pas**
1 [*noncount*] **:** a special society for students who do excellent academic work at a college or university in the U.S. ▪ He belongs to *Phi Beta Kappa*. ▪ He made *Phi Beta Kappa* his sophomore year. ▪ She graduated *Phi Beta Kappa*. [=when she graduated, she was a member of Phi Beta Kappa]
2 [*count*] **:** a person who is a member of Phi Beta Kappa ▪ He's a *Phi Beta Kappa*.

phi·lan·der·er /fəˈlændərɚ/ *noun, pl* **-ers** [*count*] *old-fashioned + disapproving* **:** a man who has sexual relations with many women and especially with women who are not his wife
— **phi·lan·der·ing** /fɪˈlændərɪŋ/ *adj, always used before a noun* ▪ a *philandering* husband — **philandering** *noun* [*noncount*] ▪ She refused to tolerate his *philandering*.

phi·lan·thro·pist /fəˈlænθrəpɪst/ *noun, pl* **-ists** [*count*] **:** a wealthy person who gives money and time to help make life better for other people ▪ wealthy *philanthropists*

phi·lan·thro·py /fəˈlænθrəpi/ *noun* [*noncount*] **:** the practice of giving money and time to help make life better for other people ▪ The family's *philanthropy* made it possible to build the public library. — compare MISANTHROPY
— **phil·an·throp·ic** /ˌfɪlənˈθrɑːpɪk/ *adj* ▪ She started a *philanthropic* [=*charitable*] foundation. ▪ He is involved in various *philanthropic* activities.

phi·lat·e·list /fəˈlætəlɪst/ *noun, pl* **-lists** [*count*] *technical* **:** a person who studies or collects postage stamps

phi·lat·e·ly /fəˈlætəli/ *noun* [*noncount*] *technical* **:** the study or collection of postage stamps ▪ She has enjoyed *philately* [=(more commonly) *stamp collecting*] since she was a child.
— **phil·a·tel·ic** /ˌfɪləˈtɛlɪk/ *adj* ▪ a *philatelic* society

-phile /ˌfajəl/ *noun combining form* **:** someone who likes something very much ▪ Franco*phile* [=a person who likes France or French culture] ▪ techno*phile* — compare -PHOBE

Phil·har·mon·ic /ˌfɪləˈmɑːnɪk/ *noun, pl* **-ics** [*count*] **:** SYMPHONY ORCHESTRA — usually used in the names of orchestras ▪ the New York *Philharmonic*

-phil·ia /ˈfɪlijə/ *noun combining form*
1 : a strong feeling of love or admiration for something ▪ Anglo*philia* [=a love of England] — compare -PHOBIA
2 : a feeling of unusual or abnormal sexual desire for someone or something ▪ pedo*philia* [=adult sexual desire for children]

phi·lis·tine *or* **Phi·lis·tine** /ˈfɪləˌstiːn, *Brit* ˈfɪləˌstaɪn/ *noun, pl* **-tines** [*count*] *formal + disapproving* **:** a person who does not understand or care about art or culture ▪ They're just a bunch of *philistines* who don't care if the city's orchestra goes bankrupt.
— **philistine** *adj* ▪ a *philistine* public concerned only with celebrities — **phi·lis·tin·ism** /ˈfɪləstəˌnɪzəm/ *noun* [*noncount*]

Phil·lips screw /ˈfɪləps-/ *noun, pl* ~ **screws** [*count*] **:** a type of screw that has a slot in its top that looks like a cross — called also *Phillips-head screw*

P

Phillips screwdriver *noun, pl* ~ **-ers** [*count*] : a screwdriver that is designed to be used with a Phillips screw — called also *Phillips-head screwdriver*

philo·den·dron /ˌfɪləˈdɛndrən/ *noun, pl* **-drons** [*count*] : a kind of plant with attractive leaves that people often grow indoors — see color picture on page C6

phi·lol·o·gy /fəˈlɑːləʤi/ *noun* [*noncount*] *somewhat old-fashioned + technical* : the study of language; *especially* : the study of how languages or words develop — compare LINGUISTICS

— **phil·o·log·i·cal** /ˌfɪləˈlɑːʤɪkəl/ *adj* ▪ *philological* evidence — **phi·lol·o·gist** /fəˈlɑːləʤɪst/ *noun, pl* **-gists** [*count*]

phi·los·o·pher /fəˈlɑːsəfə/ *noun, pl* **-phers** [*count*] : a person who studies ideas about knowledge, truth, the nature and meaning of life, etc. : a person who studies philosophy ▪ the Greek *philosopher* Plato

philosopher's stone *noun* [*singular*] : an imaginary substance that people in the past believed had the power to change other metals into gold

philo·soph·i·cal /ˌfɪləˈsɑːfɪkəl/ *also* **philo·soph·ic** /ˌfɪləˈsɑːfɪk/ *adj*

1 : of, relating to, or based on philosophy ▪ They got into a *philosophical* debate about what it means for something to be "natural." ▪ Chinese *philosophical* texts

2 [*more* ~; *most* ~] : having a calm attitude toward a difficult or unpleasant situation ▪ He's trying to be *philosophical* about their decision since he knows he can't change it.

— **philo·soph·i·cal·ly** /ˌfɪləˈsɑːfɪkli/ *adv* ▪ She's *philosophically* opposed to capital punishment. ▪ He accepted their decision *philosophically*.

phi·los·o·phize *also Brit* **phi·los·o·phise** /fəˈlɑːsəˌfaɪz/ *verb* **-phiz·es**; **-phized**; **-phiz·ing** [*no obj*] : to talk about something in a serious way for a long time — often + *about* or *on* ▪ We had to listen to him *philosophizing about* art again. ▪ She was *philosophizing on* the meaning of life.

phi·los·o·phy /fəˈlɑːsəfi/ *noun, pl* **-phies**

1 a [*noncount*] : the study of ideas about knowledge, truth, the nature and meaning of life, etc. ▪ a professor of *philosophy* ▪ Her degree is in *philosophy* and religion. — often used before another noun ▪ a *philosophy* book/class/professor **b** [*count*] : a particular set of ideas about knowledge, truth, the nature and meaning of life, etc. ▪ The group eventually split over conflicting political *philosophies*. — often + *of* ▪ the *philosophy of* Plato

2 [*count*] : a set of ideas about how to do something or how to live ▪ Her main cooking *philosophy* is to use only fresh ingredients. ▪ My *philosophy* is to live and let live. [=let other people live the way they want to] ▪ His ***philosophy of life*** [=his way of living] is to treat people as he would like to be treated.

phlegm /ˈflɛm/ *noun* [*noncount*]

1 : a thick, yellowish liquid that is produced in the nose and throat especially when a person has a cold

2 *literary* : calmness in a difficult or unpleasant situation ▪ He displayed remarkable *phlegm* in very dangerous conditions.

— **phlegmy** /ˈflɛmi/ *adj* ▪ a *phlegmy* cough

phleg·mat·ic /flɛgˈmætɪk/ *adj* [*more* ~; *most* ~] *literary* : not easily upset, excited, or angered ▪ our *phlegmatic* leader ▪ She was *phlegmatic* [=*calm*] even during the most difficult moments of the crisis.

phlox /ˈflɑːks/ *noun, pl* **phlox** *or* **phlox·es** [*count, noncount*] : a tall plant that has groups of white, pink, or purple flowers

-phobe /ˌfoʊb/ *noun combining form* : a person who dislikes or is afraid of something or someone ▪ techno*phobe* [=a person who is afraid of technology] ▪ arachno*phobe* [=a person who is afraid of spiders] — compare -PHILE

pho·bia /ˈfoʊbijə/ *noun, pl* **-bias** [*count*] : an extremely strong dislike or fear of someone or something ▪ His fear of crowds eventually developed into a *phobia*.

-pho·bia /ˈfoʊbijə/ *noun combining form* : an extremely strong dislike or fear of someone or something ▪ xeno*phobia* [=fear and hatred of foreign people and things] — compare -PHILIA

pho·bic /ˈfoʊbɪk/ *adj* [*more* ~; *most* ~] : of, relating to, or having an extremely strong fear or dislike of someone or something ▪ She is *phobic* about heights.

— **phobic** *noun, pl* **-bics** [*count*] ▪ social *phobics* [=people who are very nervous and afraid in social situations]

-phobic /ˈfoʊbɪk/ *adj combining form* : having an extremely strong dislike or fear of someone or something ▪ claustro*phobic* [=afraid of being in closed or narrow spaces]

phoe·nix /ˈfiːnɪks/ *noun, pl* **-nix·es** [*count*] : a magical bird in ancient stories that lives for 500 years before it burns itself to death and then is born again from its ashes — sometimes used figuratively ▪ The arts scene in this city is a *phoenix* rising from the ashes and is more vibrant than ever before.

phon- *or* **phono-** *combining form* : connected with sound, voice, or speech ▪ *phon*ology [=the study of speech sounds] ▪ *phono*graph [=a kind of machine that plays recorded sounds]

¹phone /ˈfoʊn/ *noun, pl* **phones**

1 : TELEPHONE: such as **a** [*noncount*] : a system that uses wires and radio signals to send people's voices over long distances ▪ We spoke by *phone* earlier. ▪ The voice on the other end of the *phone* [=*line*] was familiar, but I couldn't place it. ▪ a *phone* bill/company/conversation ▪ I just have to make a quick ***phone call*** before we leave. ▪ You can order ***over the phone*** [=by calling on the telephone] **b** [*count*] : a device that is connected to a telephone system and that you use to listen or speak to someone who is somewhere else ▪ The *phone* has been ringing all morning! ▪ He slammed the *phone* [=*receiver*] down and stormed out of the room. ▪ Our new *phone* is cordless. ▪ I left the *phone* off the hook. — see pictures at OFFICE, TELEPHONE; see also CELL PHONE, MOBILE PHONE, PAY PHONE, WIRELESS PHONE

2 phones [*plural*] : HEADPHONES

on the phone **1** : using a telephone to talk to someone ▪ Can you see who's at the door? I'm *on the phone*. ▪ I was *on the phone* with my sister until late last night. **2** *Brit* : connected to a telephone system ▪ How many households aren't *on the phone*?

²phone *verb* **phones**; **phoned**; **phon·ing** : to speak or try to speak to (someone) over a telephone system : TELEPHONE [+ *obj*] She *phoned* [=*called*] them already. — often + *up* in British English ▪ I *phoned* her *up* earlier today. [*no obj*] Someone from the newspaper will be *phoning* with a few questions. — often + *up* in British English ▪ She said she would be *phoning up* later.

phone in [*phrasal verb*] **1 a** : to make a telephone call to a place (such as the place where you work) ▪ Our boss is on a business trip but she will *phone in* [=*call in*] periodically. ▪ She ***phoned in sick*** [=*called in sick*] yesterday. [=she telephoned the place where she works to say that she was sick and would not be coming to work] **b** : to make a telephone call to a radio or television program ▪ Thousands of people *phoned in* to make a donation. ▪ People *phoned in* [=*called in*] (to the show) from all over the country. — see also PHONE-IN **2** ***phone (something) in*** *or* ***phone in (something)*** : to deliver (something, such as a message) by making a telephone call ▪ He only *phoned in* the pizza order a little while ago, so it's probably not ready yet.

-phone /ˌfoʊn/ *noun combining form*

1 : sound ▪ homo*phones* [=words that sound the same but are spelled differently and have different meanings] — often used in the names of musical instruments and devices that relate to sound ▪ saxo*phone* ▪ micro*phone*

2 : a speaker of a specified language ▪ Franco*phone* [=a person who speaks French]

phone book *noun, pl* ~ **books** [*count*] : a book that lists the names, addresses, and phone numbers of the people and businesses in a certain area — called also *directory, phone directory, telephone book, telephone directory*

phone booth *noun, pl* ~ **booths** [*count*] *US* : a very small room or enclosed structure with a public telephone in it — called also *telephone booth,* (*Brit*) *phone box,* (*Brit*) *telephone box*

phone card *noun, pl* ~ **cards** [*count*] : CALLING CARD 1

phone–in /ˈfoʊnˌɪn/ *noun, pl* **-ins** [*count*] *chiefly Brit* : CALL-IN — see also *phone in* 1b at ²PHONE

pho·neme /ˈfoʊˌniːm/ *noun, pl* **-nemes** [*count*] *linguistics* : the smallest unit of speech that can be used to make one word different from another word ▪ The sounds represented by "c" and "b" are different *phonemes*, as in the words "cat" and "bat."

— **pho·ne·mic** /fəˈniːmɪk/ *adj* ▪ *phonemic* analysis — **pho·ne·mi·cal·ly** /fəˈniːmɪkli/ *adv* ▪ *phonemically* distinct

phone number *noun, pl* ~ **-bers** [*count*] : a number that you dial on a telephone to reach a particular person, business, etc. ▪ What's your *phone number*? ▪ I don't have her new *phone number*. — called also *number, telephone number*

phone sex *noun* [*noncount*] : a conversation held over the telephone in which people describe sex acts to one another for sexual pleasure

phone tag *noun [noncount] US, informal* : TELEPHONE TAG ▪ "Have you talked to your sister about the party yet?" "No, we've been ***playing phone tag*** all week."

phone tapping *noun [noncount] Brit* : WIRETAPPING

pho·net·ic /fəˈnɛtɪk/ *adj, linguistics*

1 : of or relating to spoken language, speech sounds, or the science of phonetics ▪ the *phonetic* units of a language

2 : representing each speech sound with a single symbol ▪ a *phonetic* transcription ▪ This dictionary uses the International *Phonetic* Alphabet.

3 [*more* ~; *most* ~] : using a system of written symbols that represent speech sounds in a way that is very close to how they actually sound ▪ Spanish is a more *phonetic* language than English.

– **pho·net·i·cal·ly** /fəˈnɛtɪkli/ *adv* ▪ He is able to spell words *phonetically*.

pho·net·ics /fəˈnɛtɪks/ *noun [noncount] linguistics* : the study of speech sounds

– **pho·ne·ti·cian** /ˌfoʊnəˈtɪʃən/ *noun, pl* **-cians** *[count]*

phoney *chiefly Brit spelling of* PHONY

pho·nic /ˈfɑːnɪk/ *adj, always used before a noun, linguistics* : of or relating to speech sounds or phonics ▪ the *phonic* [=(more commonly) *phonetic*] elements of a word

phon·ics /ˈfɑːnɪks/ *noun [noncount]* : a method of teaching people to read and pronounce words by learning the sounds of letters, letter groups, and syllables

phono- *variant spelling of* PHON-

pho·no·graph /ˈfoʊnəˌgræf, *Brit* ˈfəʊnəˌgrɑːf/ *noun, pl* **-graphs** *[count] old-fashioned* : RECORD PLAYER

pho·nol·o·gy /fəˈnɑːləʤi/ *noun [noncount] linguistics* : the study of the speech sounds used in a language ▪ a professor of *phonology* ▪ He's studying Japanese *phonology*.

– **pho·no·log·i·cal** /ˌfoʊnəˈlɑːʤɪkəl/ *adj, always used before a noun* ▪ We will compare the *phonological* features of the two languages. – **pho·no·log·i·cal·ly** /ˌfoʊnəˈlɑːʤɪkli/ *adv* ▪ *phonologically* similar languages – **pho·nol·o·gist** /fəˈnɑːləʤɪst/ *noun, pl* **-gists** *[count]*

[1]**pho·ny** *(US) or chiefly Brit* **pho·ney** /ˈfoʊni/ *adj* **pho·ni·er; -est** *informal*

1 : not true, real, or genuine : intended to make someone think something that is not true ▪ He gave a *phony* name to the police. = The name he gave the police was *phony*. ▪ a *phony* [=(more commonly) *counterfeit*] $100 bill ▪ She's been talking in a *phony* [=*fake*] Irish accent all day.

2 *of a person* : not honest or sincere : saying things that are meant to deceive people ▪ *phony* politicians

– **pho·ni·ness** *noun [noncount]* ▪ I recognized the *phoniness* of her accent.

[2]**phony** *(US) or chiefly Brit* **phoney** *noun, pl* **pho·nies** *[count] informal*

1 : a person who pretends to be someone else or to have feelings or abilities that he or she does not really have : a person who is not sincere ▪ According to him, politics is full of *phonies*. ▪ I don't think she ever meant to help us. What a *phony*!

2 : something that is not real or genuine ▪ The painting is a *phony*. [=*fake*]

phoo·ey /ˈfuːwi/ *interj, chiefly US, informal + humorous* — used to express disbelief, disappointment, or a strong dislike for something ▪ You say it was a mistake? *Phooey*!

phos·phate /ˈfɑːsˌfeɪt/ *noun, pl* **-phates** *[count, noncount] chemistry* : a salt or compound that has phosphorus in it and that is used especially in products (called fertilizers) that help plants grow

phos·pho·res·cent /ˌfɑːsfəˈrɛsn̩t/ *adj, technical* : of or relating to a type of light that glows softly in the dark and that does not produce heat ▪ a *phosphorescent* glow

– **phos·pho·res·cence** /ˌfɑːsfəˈrɛsn̩s/ *noun [noncount] technical* ▪ Some sea creatures exhibit *phosphorescence*.

phos·pho·rus /ˈfɑːsfərəs/ *noun [noncount] chemistry* : a poisonous chemical element that glows in the dark and burns when it is touched by air

– **phos·phor·ic** /fɑsˈforɪk/ *adj* ▪ *phosphoric* acid [=a type of acid that contains phosphorus]

phot- *or* **photo-** *combining form*

1 : related to light ▪ *photon* ▪ *photo*graphy

2 : relating to photography ▪ *photo*copy ▪ *photo*journalism

pho·to /ˈfoʊtoʊ/ *noun, pl* **-tos** *[count]* : PHOTOGRAPH ▪ black-and-white *photos* ▪ We gave them a framed family *photo* for their anniversary. ▪ You aren't allowed to take *photos* inside the theater. ▪ The magazine published a ***photo spread*** [=photographs printed together usually on a number of pages] of scenes from the play. ▪ All of my baby pictures are in one ***photo album***. [=a book that holds photographs]

photo booth *noun, pl* ~ **booths** *[count]* : a small room that one or two people can go into to have their photograph taken by putting money into a slot

pho·to·call /ˈfoʊtoʊˌkɑːl/ *noun, pl* **-calls** *[count] Brit* : PHOTO SHOOT

pho·to·cell /ˈfoʊtəˌsɛl/ *noun, pl* **-cells** *[count] technical* : PHOTOELECTRIC CELL

pho·to·copi·er /ˈfoʊtəˌkɑːpijɚ/ *noun, pl* **-ers** *[count]* : COPIER

pho·to·copy /ˈfoʊtəˌkɑːpi/ *noun, pl* **-cop·ies** *[count]* : a paper copy of a document, picture, etc., that is made with a special machine (called a copier or photocopier) ▪ She made a *photocopy* of the letter.

– **photocopy** *verb* **-copies; -cop·ied; -copy·ing** *[+ obj]* She asked her assistant to *photocopy* the letter and send it to all of her clients. ▪ He gave me a bunch of *photocopied* articles to use in my research. *[no obj]* His job includes answering the phones, filing, and *photocopying*.

photocopy machine *or* **photocopying machine** *noun, pl* ~ **-chines** *[count]* : COPIER

pho·to·elec·tric /ˌfoʊtowɪˈlɛktrɪk/ *adj, technical* : involving, relating to, or using an electric current that is controlled by light

photoelectric cell *noun, pl* ~ **cells** *[count] technical* : an electronic device that converts changes in light into changes in an electric current — called also *photocell*

photo finish *noun [singular]* : a finish in a race in which the racers are so close that the judges have to look at a photograph of the racers crossing the finish line to see who has won

pho·to·ge·nic /ˈfoʊtəˈʤɛnɪk/ *adj [more ~; most ~]* : tending to look good in photographs ▪ She's a very *photogenic* child. ▪ This is the city's most *photogenic* park. — compare TELEGENIC

[1]**pho·to·graph** /ˈfoʊtəˌgræf, *Brit* ˈfəʊtəˌgrɑːf/ *noun, pl* **-graphs** *[count]* : a picture made by a camera ▪ The man's *photograph* was on the front page of the paper. = A *photograph* of the man was on the front page of the paper. ▪ I always take a lot of *photographs* when I travel. ▪ a digital *photograph* ▪ The exhibit included videos as well as ***still photographs***. [=ordinary photographs that are not videos, movies, etc.]— called also *photo*

[2]**photograph** *verb* **-graphs; -graphed; -graph·ing**

1 *[+ obj]* : to take a photograph of (someone or something) ▪ He *photographed* the women sitting on the bench. ▪ She was *photographed* in the studio.

2 *[no obj]* : to appear in photographs ▪ He *photographs* well. [=he looks good in photographs; he is photogenic]

pho·tog·ra·pher /fəˈtɑːgrəfɚ/ *noun, pl* **-phers** *[count]* : a person who takes photographs especially as a job ▪ He worked for the magazine as a fashion *photographer*.

pho·to·graph·ic /ˌfoʊtəˈgræfɪk/ *adj* : relating to or used to make photographs ▪ *photographic* film/paper ▪ the *photographic* process ▪ *photographic* images of the galaxy

– **pho·to·graph·i·cal·ly** /ˌfoʊtəˈgræfɪkli/ *adv* ▪ I reduced the images *photographically*.

photographic memory *noun, pl* ~ **-ries** *[count]* : an unusual ability to remember things completely and exactly as they were seen, read, etc. — usually singular ▪ He is a good detective because he has a *photographic memory*.

pho·tog·ra·phy /fəˈtɑːgrəfi/ *noun [noncount]* : the art, process, or job of taking pictures with a camera ▪ He studied both film and still *photography*. ▪ Landscape *photography* is her hobby. ▪ The art museum is showing a *photography* exhibit. [=an exhibit of photographs] ▪ the ***director of photography*** [=the person who is in charge of filming for a movie]

pho·to·jour·nal·ism /ˌfoʊtoʊˈʤɚnəˌlɪzəm/ *noun [noncount]* : the job or activity of using photographs to report news stories in magazines or newspapers

– **pho·to·jour·nal·ist** /ˌfoʊtoʊˈʤɚnəlɪst/ *noun, pl* **-ists** *[count]*

pho·ton /ˈfoʊˌtɑːn/ *noun, pl* **-tons** *[count] physics* : a tiny particle of light or electromagnetic radiation

photo opportunity *noun, pl* ~ **-ties** *[count]* : a situation in which a famous person (such as a politician) can be photographed while doing something good or impressive that is meant to be seen in a favorable way by the public ▪ The mayor's visit to the hospital was a good *photo opportunity*. — called also *photo op*

pho·to·sen·si·tive /ˌfoutouˈsɛnsətɪv/ *adj* [*more* ~; *most* ~] *technical* : reacting to light by changing color, creating electricity, etc. • paper with a *photosensitive* coating
– **pho·to·sen·si·tiv·i·ty** /ˌfoutouˌsɛnsəˈtɪvəti/ *noun* [*noncount*]

photo shoot *noun, pl* ~ **shoots** [*count*] : an occasion when a professional photographer takes pictures of someone famous for use in a magazine or for some other purpose • The magazine used only two of the pictures from the *photo shoot.* — called also *photo session, shoot, (Brit) photocall*

pho·to·syn·the·sis /ˌfoutouˈsɪnθəsəs/ *noun* [*noncount*] *biology* : the process by which a green plant turns water and carbon dioxide into food when the plant is exposed to light

phras·al /ˈfreɪzəl/ *adj, grammar* : of, relating to, or consisting of a phrase or phrases • *phrasal* categories • a *phrasal* unit

phrasal verb *noun, pl* ~ **verbs** [*count*] *grammar* : a group of words that functions as a verb and is made up of a verb and a preposition, an adverb, or both • "Take off" and "look down on" are *phrasal verbs.*

[1]**phrase** /ˈfreɪz/ *noun, pl* **phras·es** [*count*]
1 : a group of two or more words that express a single idea but do not usually form a complete sentence • Answer the questions in complete sentences, not *phrases.* • She used the *phrase* "I strongly believe" too many times in her speech. • Underline the key words or *phrases* in the paragraph. • an adverbial/adjectival *phrase* — see also NOUN PHRASE, PREPOSITIONAL PHRASE
2 : a brief expression that is commonly used • To borrow a *phrase* from my mother, I spend too much time "watching the boob tube" and not enough time outside. • a famous *phrase* — see also CATCHPHRASE, *to coin a phrase* at [2]COIN, *turn of phrase* at [2]TURN
3 *music* : a short section of a longer piece of music • musical *phrases*

[2]**phrase** *verb* **phrases; phrased; phras·ing** [+ *obj*]
1 : to say (something) in a particular way • He *phrased* his version of the story in a way that made him look good. • The question was awkwardly *phrased.*
2 : to perform (a piece of music) with the notes grouped together in a particular way • The singer *phrased* the music beautifully.

phrase book *noun, pl* ~ **books** [*count*] : a book for travelers that contains common phrases and expressions of a foreign language with their translations

phrase·ol·o·gy /ˌfreɪziˈɑːləʤi/ *noun* [*noncount*] *formal* : the way that a particular person or group uses words • legal *phraseology*

phrasing *noun* [*noncount*]
1 : the way something is expressed in words : the particular words or the order of words that are used to express something • The *phrasing* of the instructions was confusing.
2 *music* : the act of grouping notes together in a particular way • a singer known for her elegant/fluid/artful *phrasing*

phut /ˈfʌt/
go phut *Brit, informal* : to stop working • The television *went phut* this morning.

phyl·lo *also* **filo** /ˈfiːlou/ *noun* [*noncount*] : very thin dough that is used in pastries — called also *phyllo dough, phyllo pastry*

phy·lum /ˈfaɪləm/ *noun, pl* **phy·la** /ˈfaɪlə/ [*count*] *biology* : a large group of related animals or plants

phys ed /ˈfɪzˈɛd/ *noun* [*noncount*] *chiefly US, somewhat informal* : PHYSICAL EDUCATION

physi- *or* **physio-** *combining form*
1 : related to nature • *physio*logy
2 : physical • *physio*therapy

[1]**phys·i·cal** /ˈfɪzɪkəl/ *adj*
1 : relating to the body of a person instead of the mind • *physical* abuse • The program is designed to address both *physical* and emotional health. • No *physical* contact with other players is allowed in the game. • He has an unusual *physical* appearance. • He is ***in good physical condition***. [=he is strong and healthy; he is in good shape] • ***physical fitness*** [=good health and strength that you get through exercise]
2 : existing in a form that you can touch or see • *physical* objects • the *physical* environment/world • There was no *physical* evidence of the crime.
3 [*more* ~; *most* ~] : involving or related to sex • *physical* attraction • Their relationship was purely *physical.*
4 [*more* ~; *most* ~] **a** : involving or having a lot of movement or activity • *physical* comedy [=comedy in which people hit each other, fall down, etc.] • He's a very *physical* comedian. **b** : involving or having very violent and forceful activity • Ice hockey is a very *physical* sport. • It was a very *physical* hockey game. • He's one of the team's most *physical* players.
5 a : of or relating to the laws of nature • Scientists used the space station to study *physical* phenomena in a weightless environment. **b** *always used before a noun* : of or relating to the study of physics • *physical* forces
6 [*more* ~; *most* ~] : tending to express love or affection by touching other people • She is a very *physical* person.
– **phys·i·cal·i·ty** /ˌfɪzəˈkæləti/ *noun* [*noncount*] • a comedian known for his *physicality*

[2]**physical** *noun, pl* **-cals** [*count*] : a medical examination to see if a person's body is healthy • Her doctor performed a routine *physical.* [=*checkup*] • an annual *physical* — called also *physical examination*

physical education *noun* [*noncount*] : sports and exercise taught in schools • He teaches *physical education* at the high school. — abbr. *P.E.* — called also (*chiefly US, somewhat informal*) *phys ed*

phys·i·cal·ly /ˈfɪzɪkli/ *adv*
1 : related to or involving the body or physical form • I don't think I am *physically* able to climb all the way to the top. • The doctor could find nothing *physically* wrong with him. • Her sister is *physically* disabled. • The buildings were designed to resemble one another *physically.* • a *physically* attractive person
2 — used to say what can truly happen or be done by physical effort • It is *physically* impossible for me to get everything done and still go to sleep on time. • She did everything *physically* possible to make us happy.

physical science *noun, pl* ~ **-ences** [*count*] : an area of science that deals with materials that are not alive and the ways in which nonliving things work — usually plural • *physical sciences* such as physics, chemistry, and astronomy — compare LIFE SCIENCE

physical therapist *noun, pl* ~ **-pists** [*count*] *US, medical* : a person whose job is to give people physical therapy — abbr. *PT* — called also (*Brit*) *physiotherapist,* (*Brit, informal*) *physio*

physical therapy *noun* [*noncount*] *US, medical* : the treatment of a disease or an injury of the muscles or joints with massage, exercises, heat, etc. — abbr. *PT* — called also (*Brit*) *physiotherapy,* (*Brit, informal*) *physio*

phy·si·cian /fəˈzɪʃən/ *noun, pl* **-cians** [*count*] *chiefly US, somewhat formal* : a medical doctor; *especially* : a medical doctor who is not a surgeon

physician assistant *noun, pl* ~ **-tants** [*count*] *US* : PHYSICIAN'S ASSISTANT

physician–assisted suicide *noun* [*noncount*] *chiefly US* : suicide that is done with the help of a doctor — compare ASSISTED SUICIDE

physician's assistant *noun, pl* ~ **-tants** [*count*] *US* : a person who provides basic medical care and who usually works with a doctor — called also (*US*) *PA,* (*US*) *physician assistant*

phys·i·cist /ˈfɪzəsɪst/ *noun, pl* **-cists** [*count*] : a scientist who studies or is a specialist in physics

phys·ics /ˈfɪzɪks/ *noun* [*noncount*] : a science that deals with matter and energy and the way they act on each other in heat, light, electricity, and sound • high-energy/nuclear/modern/particle *physics* • laws of *physics* — see also ASTROPHYSICS, GEOPHYSICS

phys·io /ˈfɪzijou/ *noun, pl* **phys·ios** *Brit, informal*
1 [*noncount*] : PHYSICAL THERAPY
2 [*count*] : PHYSICAL THERAPIST

physio- *variant spelling of* PHYSI-

phys·i·og·no·my /ˌfɪziˈɑːgnəmi/ *noun, pl* **-mies** [*count*] *formal* : the appearance of a person's face : a person's facial features • He and his son have the same distinctive *physiognomy.*

phys·i·ol·o·gy /ˌfɪziˈɑːləʤi/ *noun* [*noncount*]
1 : a science that deals with the ways that living things function • She took a course in anatomy and *physiology.*
2 : the ways that living things or any of their parts function • human *physiology* • the *physiology* of diseased plants
– **phys·i·o·log·i·cal** /ˌfɪzijəˈlɑːʤɪkəl/ *also chiefly US* **phys·i·o·log·ic** /ˌfɪzijəˈlɑːʤɪk/ *adj* • *physiological* changes/processes • a normal *physiological* response to cold temperatures – **phys·i·o·log·i·cal·ly** /ˌfɪzijəˈlɑːʤɪkli/ *adv* – **phys·i·ol·o·gist** /ˌfɪziˈɑːləʤɪst/ *noun, pl* **-gists** [*count*] • She's a trained *physiologist.*

P

phys·io·ther·a·pist /ˌfɪzijoʊˈθerəpɪst/ *noun, pl* **-pists** [*count*] *Brit* : PHYSICAL THERAPIST

phys·io·ther·a·py /ˌfɪzijoʊˈθerəpi/ *noun* [*noncount*] *Brit* : PHYSICAL THERAPY

phy·sique /fəˈziːk/ *noun, pl* **-siques** [*count*] : the size and shape of a person's body : BUILD — usually singular • He has the *physique* of a trained athlete. • a dancer's *physique*

pi /ˈpaɪ/ *noun* [*noncount*] *geometry* : the number that results when the circumference of a circle is divided by its diameter and that is approximately 3.1416; *also* : the symbol π used for this number

PI *abbr* private investigator • Joe Smith, *PI*

pi·a·nis·si·mo /ˌpijəˈnɪsəmoʊ/ *adv, music* : very softly • The first section is meant to be sung *pianissimo*.
– **pianissimo** *adj* • *pianissimo* notes

pi·a·nist /piˈænɪst, ˈpiːjənɪst/ *noun, pl* **-nists** [*count*] : a person who plays the piano • a concert/classical/jazz *pianist*

[1]**pi·ano** /piˈænoʊ/ *noun, pl* **-an·os** [*count*] : a large musical instrument with a keyboard that you play by pressing black and white keys and that produces sound when small hammers inside the piano hit steel wires • Do you play the *piano*? • a concerto that is played on the *piano* = a *piano* concerto • a *piano* player [=*pianist*] • He takes *piano* lessons on Wednesdays. — see picture at KEYBOARD; compare HARPSICHORD; see also GRAND PIANO, UPRIGHT PIANO

[2]**piano** /piˈɑːnoʊ/ *adv, music* : quietly or softly
– **piano** *adj* • a *piano* passage

piano bar *noun, pl* **~ bars** [*count*] : a bar where there is a piano player who plays music to entertain the customers

pi·ano·forte /piˈænəˌfoət, *Brit* piˌænəʊˈfɔːti/ *noun, pl* **-fortes** [*count*] *old-fashioned* : [1]PIANO

pi·az·za /piˈɑːtsə/ *noun, pl* **-zas** [*count*] : an open public area in a town or city (especially in Italy) that is usually surrounded by buildings

pic /ˈpɪk/ *noun, pl* **pics** *or* **pix** /ˈpɪks/ [*count*] *informal*
1 : [1]PHOTOGRAPH • She showed me her vacation *pics*.
2 : MOVIE • an exciting action *pic*

pi·ca·resque /ˌpɪkəˈrɛsk/ *adj* : telling a story about the adventures of a usually playful and dishonest character • a *picaresque* novel

pic·a·yune /ˌpɪkiˈjuːn/ *adj* [*more* ~; *most* ~] *US, informal* : not very valuable or important • They argued over the most *picayune* details.

pic·co·lo /ˈpɪkəˌloʊ/ *noun, pl* **-los** [*count*] : a musical instrument that looks like a small flute and plays very high notes — see picture at WOODWIND

[1]**pick** /ˈpɪk/ *verb* **picks; picked; pick·ing** [+ *obj*]
1 : to choose or select (someone or something) from a group • *Pick* a card—any card. • They *picked* a name out of a hat. • The winners will be *picked* by lottery. • She was *picked* to replace the retiring CEO. • Who do you think he will *pick* as/for his running mate? • He *picked* the blue tie to wear to the interview. • He *picked* the right/wrong answer. • They both *picked* New York to win the World Series. [=they both said that they thought the New York team would win the World Series] — see also CHERRY-PICK
2 : to remove (a fruit, flower, etc.) from a plant especially by using your hand • She *picked* a flower for her mother. • I *picked* some carrots and a few tomatoes. • They sell freshly *picked* fruits and vegetables. • Our grapes are *picked* by hand. — see also HANDPICK
3 a : to remove unwanted material from (something) by using your finger, a small tool, etc. • It's considered impolite to ***pick your nose*** in public. • He was sitting at the table, ***picking his teeth*** with a toothpick. **b** *always followed by an adverb or preposition* : to remove (something) from something by using your fingers • *Pick* the meat from/off the bones. • She *picked* all the pepperoni off (of) the pizza.
4 *chiefly US* : to play (a guitar, banjo, etc.) by pulling the strings with your fingers or with a pick : PLUCK • She was strumming and *picking* her guitar.

bone to pick see [1]BONE

pick a fight/quarrel : to deliberately start a fight with someone • Never *pick a fight* you can't win. • She sometimes *picked fights* with other girls at school.

pick a lock : to open a lock by using something that is not the key • He used a knife to *pick the lock* on the front door.

pick and choose : to choose only the best or most appropriate things or people • As one of Hollywood's most successful actors, he's now in a position to carefully *pick and choose* his roles. • The newspaper *picks and chooses* which stories to report. • With so many candidates, we can afford to *pick and choose*. [=we can afford to take our time and only choose the best candidate]

pick apart [*phrasal verb*] ***pick (someone or something) apart*** *or* ***pick apart (someone or something)*** *chiefly US* : to say all of the things that are bad or wrong about (someone or something) : to criticize (a person or thing) in a very detailed and usually unkind way • You can expect political analysts to *pick apart* the governor's speech. • The film's critics *picked* his performance *apart*.

pick at [*phrasal verb*] **1** ***pick at (something)*** **a** : to eat small amounts of (food) very slowly usually because you do not want to eat • She *picked at* a salad while I ate my steak. **b** : to pull on (something) with your fingertips or your fingernails often because you are nervous • She *picked at* the buttons on her jacket while waiting for her interview. • He was *picking at* his shoelaces. **2** ***pick at (someone or something)*** : to criticize (someone or something) especially for small mistakes • They're constantly arguing and *picking at* each other.

pick off [*phrasal verb*] **1** ***pick off (someone or something)*** *or* ***pick (someone or something) off*** : to aim at and shoot (someone or something) • The hunters hid by the stream and waited to *pick off* deer as they passed. • A sniper was *picking off* soldiers from the top of the building. **2** ***pick off (someone)*** *or* ***pick (someone) off*** *baseball* : to cause (a player who is standing close to a base) to be tagged out by making a quick throw • The runner on second base was *picked off* by the catcher. • The pitcher almost *picked* her *off* with a quick throw to first base. — see also PICKOFF

pick on [*phrasal verb*] ***pick on (someone)*** **1** : to laugh at or make fun of (someone) in an unkind way • Kids used to *pick on* me for wearing old worn-out clothes. • He used to get *picked on* by the other kids at the bus stop. • Why is she always *picking on* me? • Hey, why don't you *pick on* someone your own size? **2** : to unfairly criticize (one person or group) when others also deserve to be criticized • It's unfair to *pick on* teachers for the problems in our schools when politicians are equally to blame.

pick out [*phrasal verb*] **1** ***pick (something) out*** *or* ***pick out (something)*** **a** : to choose or select (the best or most appropriate person or thing) from a group • It took him an hour to *pick out* [=*pick*] what to wear. • They let their two-year-old daughter *pick out* her own clothes. • I've *picked out* the perfect spot for our picnic. • *picking out* a gift for a friend **b** : to play (a song, melody, etc.) by playing each note separately • She sat *picking out* a tune on the piano. **2** ***pick (someone or something) out*** *or* ***pick out (someone or something)*** : to see and identify (someone or something) • His red hair makes it easy to *pick* him *out* of/in a crowd. • The police had a witness *pick* the suspect *out* of a lineup. • I could *pick out* the pattern against the background. • No one was able to *pick out* the originals from the copies.

pick over [*phrasal verb*] ***pick over (something)*** *or* ***pick (something) over*** : to look at (a group of objects or an amount of material) in order to choose the best ones or to remove pieces you do not want • They *picked over* the strawberries and threw away the green ones. • *Pick over* the fish to remove any bones. • The applications were thoroughly *picked over* and only the best applicants were given interviews.

pick pockets *or* ***pick someone's pocket*** : to steal money or objects from someone's pockets or purse • One of the boys distracted her while the other *picked her pocket*. • She survived on the streets by shoplifting and *picking pockets*. — see also PICKPOCKET

pick (someone or something) to pieces/shreds : to study and criticize all of the parts of (someone or something) • The media *picked* his personal life *to pieces*. • Her ideas were *picked to shreds* by her coworkers.

pick someone's brain/brains see [1]BRAIN

pick (something) clean : to remove all the material that covers something • The birds *picked* the bones *clean*. = The bones were *picked clean* by the birds.

pick up [*phrasal verb*] **1** ***pick (someone or something) up*** *or* ***pick up (someone or something)*** **a** : to lift (someone or something) from the ground or a low surface • Would you *pick* that pencil *up* for me, please? • She *picked* the book *up* off/from the ground by its cover. • He bent to *pick up* his hat. • *Pick up* the ball! • They *picked up* their guitars and started to play. • She always *picks up* her baby when he cries. **b** : to go somewhere in order to get and bring back (someone or something) • I have to *pick up* my kids at school. = I have to *pick* them *up* from school. • Have you *picked up* the car from the repair shop yet? • He *picked up* his dry cleaning. • They'll hold our tickets but we have to *pick* them *up* an hour before the show. **c** : to let or put (people or things) into or onto a car, bus, ship, etc. • She had a taxi *pick* her *up* at the airport and take her to the hotel. • Have you ever *picked up* a hitchhiker? • The ship will be *picking up* more cargo at the next port. **2 a** ***pick up*** *or* ***pick (something) up*** *or* ***pick up (something)*** *chiefly US* : to make an area clean and organized by removing trash and putting things in the proper places • We have just enough time to *pick up* [=*clean up*] and wash our hands before dinner. • The children worked together to *pick up* the toys. • *Pick up* that mess! • You may go outside after you *pick* your room *up*. • Everyone needs to help *pick up* the kitchen after dinner. • We spent the morning *picking up* the yard after the storm. **b** ***pick up after (someone)*** : to clean the mess created by (someone) • You have to *pick up after* yourself if you make a mess. • His mother still *picks up after* him. **3** : to answer a telephone • I called your house, but no one *picked up*. • She got to the phone just before the answering machine *picked up*. **4** : to become busy usually after a period of little activity : to improve or increase in activity • Sales slowed down after the winter holidays, but we're expecting things to *pick up* again this summer. • Business really *picked up* last month. • The economy/market seems to be *picking up*. **5 a** : to increase in speed or strength • The wind will *pick up* later this afternoon. • The movie starts out slowly, but the pace *picks up* when the two main characters meet for the first time. **b** ***pick up speed/momentum (etc.)*** : to begin to have more speed/momentum (etc.) • The cyclists quickly *picked up speed* [=gained speed; began to go faster] as they headed down the mountain. • His campaign has begun to *pick up momentum*. • The idea began to ***pick up steam*** [=become more popular] around the turn of the century. **c** ***pick up the pace*** : to go faster • If we want to finish on time, we're going to have to *pick up the pace*. **6 a** : to begin again after a temporary stop • The discussion *picked up* this morning at the point where we had stopped yesterday. • After being separated for three years, they ***picked up (right) where they left off***. **b** ***pick (something) up*** *or* ***pick up (something)*** : to start (something) again after a temporary stop • We'll *pick up* this discussion tomorrow. **7** ***pick (something) up*** *or* ***pick up (something)*** **a** : to buy or get (something) • Have you *picked up* a copy of her new CD yet? • On Tuesdays, he *picks up* dinner at our favorite restaurant and brings it home. • She stopped to *pick up* a few groceries at the supermarket. **b** : to earn or gain (something) • She'll likely *pick up* an award for her performance in the film. • The team *picked up* [=*gained*] a few yards on the last play. • They've finally *picked up* their first victory of the season. **c** : to become aware of (something, such as a story) and begin to write about it, work on it, etc. • Few people had heard about this problem until the press *picked up* [=*took up*] the story. **d** : to learn (something) usually in an informal way • I *picked up* a few French phrases on my trip to Paris. • He seems to *pick* foreign languages *up* very easily. • She uses a style of singing she *picked up* from listening to jazz music. • He's been *picking up* some bad habits from his friends. **e** : to become sick with (an illness) from someone or something • I think I *picked up* [=*caught*] a cold from someone at work. **f** : to be able to see, hear, or smell (something) • This radio lets me *pick up* stations from other countries. • The planes were *picked up* [=*detected*] by radar. • telescopes *picking up* the faint glow of distant stars • The dogs *picked up* the scent and started to bark. : to become aware of (something) • He learned that he could *pick up* cues from his partner if he paid close attention. • They studied the evidence and managed to *pick up* some clues. **8** ***pick (someone) up*** *or* ***pick up (someone)*** **a** : to meet and begin a usually brief sexual relationship with (someone) • She used to go to bars to *pick up* men. • He *picked* her *up* at a club. **b** *of the police* : to use the power of the law to take and keep (someone, such as a criminal) • The cops *picked up* the suspect at a local bar. • The police *picked* him *up* [=arrested him] for trespassing/robbery/murder. • The police *picked* him *up* for questioning. [=they brought him to the police station in order to ask him questions] **c** : to make (someone) feel more energetic and lively • I drank some coffee hoping that it would *pick* me *up* a little. — see also PICK-ME-UP **d** *sports* : to get (a player) from another team or from some other source • The team *picked up* three new players in the draft. • They *picked* him *up* from a rival team. **e** *sports* : to begin to guard (a player from the opposite team) during a game • Your job is to *pick up* an opposing player and block him. **9** ***pick yourself up*** **a** : to stand up again after falling • I fell to the ground but *picked myself up* and continued running. **b** : to recover from a difficult situation • After his divorce, he *picked himself up* and started looking for love again. **10** ***pick up and leave/go*** : to leave suddenly with your possessions • I couldn't just *pick up and leave/go* without saying goodbye. **11** ***pick up the tab/bill/check*** : to pay the money that is owed for something • When she stays at expensive hotels during business trips, her company *picks up the tab*. • They always offer to *pick up the check* when we go out to dinner with them. **12** ***pick up the pieces*** : to try to make a situation better after something bad has happened • After her business went bankrupt, she *picked up the pieces* and started again. • They created the problem, and now they expect us to *pick up the pieces*. — see also *pick up the cudgels for* at [1]CUDGEL, *pick up the gauntlet* at [2]GAUNTLET, *pick up the slack* at [2]SLACK, *pick up the threads* at [1]THREAD

pick up on [*phrasal verb*] **1** ***pick up on (something)*** **a** : to notice or become aware of (something) • He didn't *pick up on* the hint. • I seemed to be the only one who *picked up on* the mistake. • The reader soon *picks up on* the fact that the story's main character is crazy. • She was nervous, but no one *picked up on* it. **b** : to take (something, such as an idea) from another person or group and use it or continue to develop it yourself • The media has recently begun to *pick up on* this issue. • The fashion world *picked up on* this trend after she wore that dress to the award show. • The other students quickly *picked up on* [=*adopted*] the expression. **c** : to continue talking about (a statement, subject, etc.) • I'd like to *pick up on* your last comment. • She began the class by *picking up on* a point she made earlier. **2** ***pick up (someone) on (something)*** *or* ***pick (someone) up on (something)*** *Brit* : to question (someone) about (something said or done) • I'd like to *pick up* the last speaker *on* one of the points she made. • When he said that whales were fish, I felt I had to *pick* him *up on* it. [=to challenge him on it]

pick your way *always followed by an adverb or preposition* : to walk very slowly while carefully choosing where to put your feet • The horses slowly *pick their way* across the rocky ground. • We *picked our way* down the muddy path.

[2]pick *noun, pl* **picks**

1 [*singular*] : the ability to choose the person or thing that you want • If you get there early enough, you'll ***have your pick*** of seats. • All of these restaurants are good. ***Take your pick***. [=choose any of them] • The girls got to choose their partners, and she got (the) ***first pick***. [=she was able to choose her partner first]

2 [*count*] : someone or something that is chosen • My *picks* [=choices] are the roasted duck and the chocolate cake. — usually singular • Who is your *pick* to win? [=who do you think will win?] • The team made him the second *pick* [=the second person who was chosen] in the 1998 draft. • She was their ***number one pick***. = She was their ***first pick***. [=she was the person they wanted most] • Here is our ***top pick for*** this year's wine list.

3 [*singular*] : the best part of something or the best thing or things in a group — used in the phrase ***the pick of*** • It was surely *the pick of* this year's films. [=it was the best film this year] • I read many books this summer, and that was ***the pick of the bunch***. [=the best of the bunch/group] • There are many good cars on the market now, but this one is clearly ***the pick of the litter***. [=the best one]

— compare [3]PICK

[3]pick *noun, pl* **picks** [*count*]

1 : a large tool that has a long handle and a heavy metal bar that is pointed at one or both ends and that is used for breaking rocks or digging in hard ground — see also ICE PICK, TOOTHPICK

2 : a small, thin piece of plastic or metal that is used to play a guitar or similar instrument — called also *plectrum*

— compare [2]PICK

pick–and–mix *or* **pick'n'mix** *adj, Brit* : having a mixture of different things that you can choose • The shop offers a *pick-and-mix* assortment of new and used items. • a *pick'n'mix* approach to the problem

pick•ax (*US*) *or chiefly Brit* **pick•axe** /ˈpɪkˌæks/ *noun, pl* **-axes** [*count*] : [3]PICK 1

picked /ˈpɪkt/ *adj* : carefully chosen • a *picked* [=(more commonly) *handpicked*] group/team/force of soldiers

P

pick·er /ˈpɪkɚ/ *noun, pl* **-ers** [*count*] : a person or machine that picks crops • fruit/orange/strawberry *pickers* • a cotton *picker*

pick·er·el /ˈpɪkərəl/ *noun, pl* **pickerel** [*count*] : a small North American fish that lives in rivers and streams

[1]**pick·et** /ˈpɪkət/ *noun, pl* **-ets** [*count*]
1 : a stick or post that is pointed at the end so that it can be put into the ground • a house surrounded by a white ***picket fence***
2 a : a person or group of people who are standing or marching near a place to protest something • *Pickets* marched in front of the company headquarters. • The strikers held ***picket signs*** painted with angry slogans. **b** *Brit* **:** a protest or strike involving pickets • The students were barred from holding a *picket* outside the company's headquarters.
3 : a soldier or a group of soldiers whose duty is to guard something (such as a camp)

[2]**picket** *verb* **-ets; -et·ed; -et·ing**
1 : to stand or march in a public place in order to protest something or to prevent other workers from going to work during a strike [*no obj*] Workers *picketed* outside the grocery store. [+ *obj*] The union is *picketing* the factory.
2 [+ *obj*] **:** to guard (something, such as a road or camp) with a group of soldiers

pick·et·er /ˈpɪkətɚ/ *noun, pl* **-ers** [*count*] *US* **:** a person who stands or marches in front of a business, a government building, etc., as a form of protest — usually plural • *Picketers* crowded the sidewalk in front of the clinic.

picket line *noun, pl* **~ lines** [*count*] **:** a line or group of people who are refusing to go to work until their employer agrees to certain demands • She joined her coworkers on the *picket line*. • The other employees refused to ***cross the picket line***. [=to work while other workers were picketing]

picking *noun* [*noncount*] **:** the activity of removing fruits from a plant for use • Berry *picking* is a favorite summer activity. • We're going apple *picking*.

pick·ings /ˈpɪkɪŋz, ˈpɪkənz/ *noun* [*plural*] *informal* **:** opportunities for getting the things you want or need • I try to go to yard sales early to get the best *pickings*. • It was ***slim pickings*** [=there were very few good things to choose from] at this year's show. • thieves looking for ***easy pickings*** • (*chiefly Brit*) ***rich pickings***

[1]**pick·le** /ˈpɪkəl/ *noun, pl* **pick·les**
1 [*count*] *chiefly US* **:** a cucumber that is preserved in salt water or vinegar — see also DILL PICKLE
2 [*noncount*] *Brit* **:** a thick, cold sauce made of chopped vegetables preserved in vinegar
3 [*singular*] *informal* **:** an unpleasant or difficult situation — usually used in the phrase ***in a pickle*** • We were *in a pickle* when we missed our deadline.

[2]**pickle** *verb* **pickles; pick·led; pick·ling** [+ *obj*] **:** to preserve (food) with salt water or vinegar • They *pickled* the cabbage.

pickled *adj*
1 : preserved with salt water or vinegar • *pickled* ginger • The herring is *pickled*.
2 *not used before a noun, informal* **:** very drunk or intoxicated • He got *pickled* at the office party.

pick–me–up /ˈpɪkmiˌʌp/ *noun, pl* **-ups** [*count*] **:** something (such as a drink) that makes you feel better and more lively • Coffee is my usual morning *pick-me-up*. • I could really use a *pick-me-up* after the day I just had.

pick'n'mix *variant spelling of* PICK-AND-MIX

pick·off /ˈpɪkˌɑːf/ *noun, pl* **-offs** [*count*] *US, baseball* **:** a play in which a runner who is close to a base is tagged out when the pitcher or catcher quickly throws the ball to that base • He made a *pickoff* throw to third base. — see also *pick off* at [1]PICK

pick·pock·et /ˈpɪkˌpɑːkət/ *noun, pl* **-ets** [*count*] **:** a thief who steals money and other things from people's pockets and purses — see also *pick pockets* at [1]PICK

[1]**pick·up** /ˈpɪkˌʌp/ *noun, pl* **-ups**
1 [*count*] **:** a small truck that has an open back with low sides — called also *pickup truck*; see picture at TRUCK
2 : the act of going somewhere to get a person or thing that you will then take to another place [*noncount*] The fee pays for garbage/trash *pickup*. • Is this order for *pickup* or delivery? [=do you want to come and get the order yourself, or do you want us to deliver the order to you?] • Your pizza will be ready for *pickup* [=you can pick up your pizza] in 20 minutes. [*count*] The school bus was late for its afternoon *pickup*. • The truck is scheduled to make a *pickup* today.
3 [*count*] **:** an increase in activity — usually + *in* • They saw a *pickup in* business during the last quarter. • Several of our stores have reported a *pickup in* orders. • a *pickup in* consumer spending
4 [*noncount*] *US* **:** the ability of a vehicle to increase speed quickly • The car corners well and has good *pickup*. [=(more formally) *acceleration*]
5 [*count*] **:** a person you meet and have a usually brief sexual relationship with • He looked for *pickups* in singles bars.
6 [*count*] **:** a device on a musical instrument (such as an electric guitar) that makes sounds louder by changing them into electrical signals • a guitar *pickup*
7 [*count*] *sports* **:** a player who becomes part of a team after being obtained from another team • He joined the team as a free agent *pickup* last summer.

[2]**pickup** *adj, always used before a noun, US*
1 : organized informally with people who are available or nearby at the time • He plays with *pickup* bands at nightclubs. • a *pickup* football game • playing *pickup* basketball
2 : of or relating to the act of trying to meet strangers in order to have brief sexual relationships with them • What's the *pickup* scene like in this city? • He tried using one of his ***pickup lines*** [=a comment used to start a conversation with someone you are attracted to] on her, but it didn't work.

picky /ˈpɪki/ *adj* **pick·i·er; -est :** very careful or too careful about choosing or accepting things **:** hard to please • He's a *picky* [=*fussy*] eater. • She's very *picky* [=*choosy*] about what brands of shoes she'll wear.

[1]**pic·nic** /ˈpɪknɪk/ *noun, pl* **-nics** [*count*]
1 a : a meal that is eaten outdoors especially during a trip away from home • We decided to have a *picnic* on the beach. • We ate our *picnic* by the lake. **b :** a trip or party that includes a meal eaten outdoors • This weekend I have a family *picnic* [=a picnic with family members] to go to. • The annual school/company *picnic* is this weekend. ✧ If you ***go on a picnic***, you go somewhere to have a picnic • Let's *go on a picnic* today.
2 *informal* **:** something that is pleasant or easy • This winter is a *picnic* compared with last year's. — often used in negative statements • Breaking a leg is no *picnic*. [=breaking a leg is not a pleasant experience] • Being president isn't exactly a *picnic*. [=being president is not easy]

[2]**picnic** *verb* **-nics; -nicked; -nick·ing** [*no obj*] **:** to eat a meal outdoors especially during a trip away from home **:** to have a picnic • We *picnicked* in the park.
– pic·nick·er *noun, pl* **-ers** [*count*] • The park was full of *picnickers*.

pic·to·ri·al /pɪkˈtorijəl/ *adj, always used before a noun*
1 : of or relating to painting or drawing • *pictorial* art
2 : having or using pictures • *pictorial* magazines • a *pictorial* message • a *pictorial* record of the trip
– pic·to·ri·al·ly *adv*

[1]**pic·ture** /ˈpɪkʧɚ/ *noun, pl* **-tures**
1 [*count*] **:** a painting, drawing, or photograph of someone or something • I hung the *picture* on the wall. • The book has a lot of *pictures*. • Draw a *picture* of your house. • We looked at family *pictures*. [=*photos*] • We took *pictures* [=*photographs*] of the wedding. • a ***picture frame*** [=a frame for holding a picture]
2 [*count*] **:** an idea of how something or someone looks, of what something is like, etc. — usually singular • I have a mental *picture* of what he looks like. • The book gives us a *picture* of life in a small village. • I don't yet have a full *picture* of what's going on. • After your explanation, I have a better/clearer *picture* of what to expect. • (*informal*) You've said enough. I ***get the picture***. [=I understand; I get the idea]
3 [*noncount*] **:** a general situation • The staff looked at the financial *picture* of the company. • The overall economic *picture* is improving. • Marriage never ***entered the picture*** [=was never considered] until now. • After a brief separation, her boyfriend is back ***in the picture***. [=she is dating him again] • With last year's winner ***out of the picture*** [=no longer in the competition], she has a good chance of winning. — see also BIG PICTURE
4 [*count*] **:** an image on the screen of a television set • The *picture* is fuzzy.
5 a [*count*] **:** a movie or film • "Casablanca" won the award for Best *Picture* in 1943. **b *the pictures*** *old-fashioned* **:** a showing of a movie in a theater • I took my girlfriend to *the pictures*. [=(*US*) *the movies*] **c pictures** [*plural*] **:** the movies or movie industry • He wants to work ***in pictures***.
6 [*noncount*] **a :** someone or something that looks exactly

P

like someone or something else ▪ He is ***the picture of*** his father. [=he looks just like his father] **b :** a perfect example of something ▪ She is *the picture of* health. [=she looks very healthy]

a picture is worth a thousand words see [1]WORTH

(as) pretty as a picture see [1]PRETTY

keep someone in the picture or put someone in the picture *chiefly Brit* **:** to give someone the information that is needed to understand something ▪ Teachers meet regularly with parents to *keep them in the picture* about their child's progress. ▪ I'll *put you in the picture* as soon as a final decision has been made.

paint/draw a picture of **:** to create an idea or understanding of something or someone through words, facts, etc. ▪ The author *paints a* disturbing *picture of* life in the camp. ▪ These statistics *paint a* clear *picture of* how the population is aging.

[2]**picture** *verb* **-tures; -tured; -tur•ing** [+ *obj*]

1 : to have a thought, understanding, or idea about (something or someone) **:** IMAGINE ▪ I can still *picture* the house I grew up in. ▪ I can't *picture* changing jobs at this point in my life. ▪ *Picture* what it would be like if you didn't own a car. ▪ Can you *picture* him as a teacher?

2 : to show or represent (someone or something) in a painting, drawing, or photograph — usually used as *(be) pictured* ▪ She *is pictured* here with her sister.

3 : to describe (something or someone) in a particular way — + *as*; usually used as *(be) pictured* ▪ She *is pictured* [=*portrayed*] *as* being very businesslike.

picture book *noun, pl* **~ books** [*count*] **:** a book that has many pictures and is usually for children

picture–book *adj, always used before a noun* **:** very pretty or charming **:** like a picture in a picture book ▪ *picture-book* scenery

picture card *noun, pl* **~ cards** [*count*] *Brit* **:** FACE CARD

picture–perfect *adj* [*more ~; most ~*] *US* **:** having an appearance or quality that is exactly right **:** completely perfect ▪ The pilot made a *picture-perfect* landing. ▪ The bride looked *picture-perfect*. [=the bride looked beautiful]

picture postcard *noun, pl* **~ -cards** [*count*] *old-fashioned* **:** a postcard with a photograph or picture on one side

picture–postcard *adj, always used before a noun* **:** very pretty or charming **:** like a picture on a picture postcard ▪ a *picture-postcard* village

pic•tur•esque /ˌpɪkʧəˈrɛsk/ *adj* [*more ~; most ~*]

1 : very pretty or charming **:** like a painted picture ▪ a *picturesque* village/setting ▪ The view of the mountains was very *picturesque*.

2 : telling about something in a way that makes it very easy to imagine **:** causing someone to have a very clear mental picture of something ▪ He gave a *picturesque* [=*vivid*] account of his travels.

picture tube *noun, pl* **~ tubes** [*count*] **:** CATHODE-RAY TUBE

picture window *noun, pl* **~ -dows** [*count*] **:** a large window that is made from a single piece of glass — see picture at WINDOW

pid•dle /ˈpɪdl̩/ *verb* **pid•dles; pid•dled; pid•dling** [*no obj*] *informal* **:** URINATE ▪ The dog *piddled* [=*peed*] on the rug.

piddle around [*phrasal verb*] *chiefly US, informal* **:** to waste time doing something that is not important or useful ▪ We should stop *piddling around* and get busy.

piddle away [*phrasal verb*] ***piddle (something) away or piddle away (something)*** *chiefly US, informal* **:** to waste (something, such as time, money, an opportunity, etc.) ▪ We *piddled* the whole morning *away* doing nothing. ▪ He *piddled away* his entire paycheck.

pid•dling /ˈpɪdlən/ *adj, always used before a noun, informal + disapproving* **:** small or unimportant ▪ He was paid a *piddling* amount of money. ▪ *piddling* details

pid•dly /ˈpɪdli/ *adj, always used before a noun, informal + disapproving* **:** PIDDLING ▪ I don't want to argue about *piddly* details.

pid•gin /ˈpɪʤən/ *noun, pl* **-gins** [*count, noncount*] **:** a language that is formed from a mixture of several languages when speakers of different languages need to talk to each other — often used before another noun ▪ linguists studying *pidgin* languages around the world ▪ He spoke to me in ***Pidgin English***. [=English mixed with words from other languages]

pie /ˈpaɪ/ *noun, pl* **pies :** a food that consists of a pastry crust that is filled with fruit, meat, etc. [*count*] The bakery sells *pies* and cakes. [*noncount*] Would you like a piece/slice of apple *pie*? ▪ I would like some *pie*. ▪ a *pie* plate [=a dish used for holding a pie] — see picture at BAKING; see also BOSTON CREAM PIE, POTPIE, SHEPHERD'S PIE

a piece/slice/share of the pie **:** a portion of a particular amount of money ▪ The state needs to give public schools a larger *piece of the pie*. [=the state needs to give public schools more funds] ▪ He's the best player on the team and he wants a bigger *slice of the pie*. [=he wants more money]

(as) easy as pie see [1]EASY

eat humble pie see EAT

have a finger in a/the pie see [1]FINGER

— see also COW PIE, CUTIE-PIE, PIE CHART, PIE IN THE SKY, SWEETIE PIE

pie•bald /ˈpaɪˌbɑːld/ *adj, always used before a noun* **:** spotted with two different colors (especially black and white) ▪ a *piebald* horse

[1]**piece** /ˈpiːs/ *noun, pl* **piec•es**

1 [*count*] **a :** an amount that is cut or separated from a larger section of something ▪ Divide the pie into six equal *pieces*. ▪ The cheese was cut into small *pieces* and arranged on a silver platter. — often + *of* ▪ I need a few more *pieces of* tape. ▪ a long *piece of* string ▪ a *piece of* wood/metal/plastic/leather/cloth ▪ a *piece of* steak/chicken/fish ▪ a *piece* [=*slice*] *of* pizza/bread/cake — see also PIECE OF CAKE **b :** an amount of something considered separately from the rest — + *of* ▪ She bought a small *piece of* land/property in the country.

2 [*count*] **:** a small often broken part of something ▪ *pieces* [=*fragments*] of broken glass ▪ You have a *piece* of lettuce stuck between your teeth. ▪ Her broken bicycle lay ***in pieces*** by the side of the road. ▪ I watched her rip the letter ***to/into pieces*** and throw it away. ▪ The old bridge was ***blown to pieces*** [=*blown apart*] during the war.

3 [*count*] **:** one of the parts that form a complete thing when they are put together ▪ There are 12 *pieces* in this stainless steel knife set. ▪ a jigsaw puzzle with 500 *pieces* ▪ We're missing one *piece* of the puzzle. ▪ They built up the stone wall one *piece* at a time. = They built up the stone wall ***piece by piece***. ▪ I took apart the engine *piece by piece* and put it back together again. ▪ (*Brit*) The rifle ***comes to pieces*** [=it separates into parts] for easy storage. ▪ (*Brit*) They ***took*** the bed ***to pieces*** [=they took apart the bed] and moved it out of the room. — often used in combination ▪ a three-*piece* suit ▪ one-*piece* bathing suits ▪ a five-*piece* band

4 [*singular*] **:** a part of someone or something that is shared with other people **:** PORTION — + *of* ▪ a *piece of* the jackpot ▪ They went there to claim a *piece of* the American dream for themselves. ▪ The town is growing fast, and these construction companies want a *piece of* the new housing market. ▪ Once she became famous, everyone wanted ***a piece of her***. = Everyone wanted a *piece of* her time. [=everyone wanted her to do things for them] — see also ***a piece of the action*** at ACTION, ***a piece of the pie*** at PIE

5 [*count*] **:** one of a particular type of thing — + *of* ▪ Please take out a *piece* [=*sheet*] *of* paper and write your name on the top. ▪ I packed three *pieces of* fruit: two apples and a banana. ▪ a *piece of* candy/chalk ▪ We had several new *pieces of* furniture delivered to our home. ▪ You got two *pieces of* mail today. ▪ a *piece of* clothing ▪ an expensive *piece of* jewelry/luggage/equipment ▪ His last car was ***a piece of junk***. [=it was worthless or of poor quality] — see also CONVERSATION PIECE, PIECE OF WORK

6 [*count*] **:** an example or amount of something — usually singular; + *of* ▪ May I offer you a *piece* [=*bit*] *of* advice? [=may I offer you some advice?] ▪ I just heard a wonderful *piece of* news! ▪ a new *piece of* information/evidence ▪ an important *piece of* legislation ▪ a silly *piece of* nonsense ▪ That's a really nice *piece of* work you've done there! ▪ an impressive *piece of* acting ▪ a famous *piece* [=*work*] *of* art/literature/music

7 [*count*] **a :** a work of art, music, drama, or literature ▪ The statue *David* is one of Michelangelo's most famous *pieces*. ▪ a *piece* painted by Pablo Picasso ▪ Next, we will be performing a *piece* by J. S. Bach. ▪ a piano *piece* = a *piece* (written) for piano ▪ They performed a short dramatic *piece* written for the king's birthday. — see also MUSEUM PIECE, PERIOD PIECE, SET PIECE **b :** an article in a newspaper or magazine or one of the parts of a television or radio news program ▪ He has written several *pieces* for the magazine. ▪ The newspaper printed her ***opinion piece*** [=an article that expresses someone's beliefs or views] criticizing the president. — often + *about* or *on* ▪ Did you see that *piece about/on* the earthquake survivors? — see also PUFF PIECE

8 [*count*] **:** one of the small movable objects in a game like

chess or checkers • Move your *piece* [=*man*] forward three spaces. • capturing an opponent's *pieces*
9 [*count*] **a** : a coin that has a specified value • a 50-cent *piece* • a 10-pence *piece* **b** : a coin that is made of a specified metal • 30 gold *pieces*
10 [*count*] : GUN • (*chiefly US, informal*) He reached into his pocket and pulled out a *piece*. [=*handgun*] • ***artillery pieces*** [=large guns that shoot over long distances] from the First World War
11 [*singular*] *US, informal* : an amount of distance that is not specified • Their house is a fair *piece* from here. [=is a fairly long way away from here] • It's down the road a *piece*.
bits and pieces see [1]BIT
fall to pieces **1** : to break into parts • The old map *fell to pieces* [=*came apart, fell apart*] in my hands. **2** : to become ruined or destroyed • His life *fell to pieces* after his divorce. **3** : to become unable to control your emotions • She *falls to pieces* [=*breaks down*] when she tries to talk about the accident. • When he heard the bad news, he just *fell to pieces*. [=he started to cry]
give someone a piece of your mind see [1]MIND
go to pieces : to become unable to behave normally because you are very nervous or upset • He tends to *go to pieces* [=*break down*] under pressure. • I *go* (all) *to pieces* if I have to talk in front of a large group of people.
in one piece : without being hurt or damaged • It was a difficult trip, but we all made it home *in one piece*. [=*safe and sound*] • All our furniture arrived *in one piece*.
of a piece **1** : having similar qualities or characteristics : matching each other or belonging together • She believes that the two crimes are *of a piece*. [=are very similar] • We chose these 12 songs for the album because they were ***all of a piece***. **2** : in agreement or harmony *with* something • This new theory is very much *of a piece* [=(more commonly) *consistent*] *with* their earlier work.
pick (someone or something) to pieces see [1]PICK
pick up the pieces see *pick up* at [1]PICK
say your piece : to say what you want to say : to express your opinions or ideas • You will all be given a chance to *say your piece* [=*speak your mind*] at the meeting tonight. • You've *said your piece*, now please let me respond.
tear (someone or something) to pieces see [1]TEAR
to pieces *informal* : to a very great degree : very much • We're thrilled *to pieces* [=*to bits*] that you've decided to stay! • She loves him *to pieces*. — see also [1]PIECE 2, 3 (above)

[2]**piece** *verb* **pieces; pieced; piec·ing**
piece together [*phrasal verb*] ***piece (something) together*** *or* ***piece together (something)*** : to make (something) by bringing together various parts or pieces • She *pieced* the quilt *together* from scraps of old cloth. • Watching the movie was like *piecing together* [=*putting together*] a jigsaw puzzle. : to bring together (various parts or pieces) to form one complete thing • The police had to *piece together* reports from several witnesses to get an accurate account of what happened. • *piecing together* the clues/evidence

pièce de ré·sis·tance /pi,ɛsdərə,zi:ˈstɑ:ns/ *noun, pl* **pièces de ré·sis·tance** /pi,ɛsdərə,zi:ˈstɑ:ns/ [*count*] : the best or most important thing or event • The *pièce de résistance* of the whole concert was when the two bands came onstage to perform together. • The waiter suggested we try the restaurant's *pièce de résistance*: the chocolate soufflé.

piece·meal /ˈpi:sˈmi:l/ *adj* [*more* ~; *most* ~] : done or made in a gradual way in a series of separate steps • They've done *piecemeal* repairs in the past, but the bridge now needs major reconstruction. • Some people want the changes to be made all at once, but I think we should take a more *piecemeal* approach.
– **piecemeal** *adv* • Our parents started selling off the family farm *piecemeal* [=*gradually, piece by piece*] several years ago, and now there are only five acres left.

piece of cake *noun* [*singular*] *informal* : something that is easy to do • "How was the test?" "The essay portion was hard, but the rest was a *piece of cake*." [=*cinch, breeze*]

piece of work *noun, pl* **pieces of work** [*count*] *chiefly US, informal* + *often disapproving* : someone who is difficult to understand : a complicated or strange person • She's a *piece of work*, isn't she? • Man, that guy's a real *piece of work*.
a nasty piece of work *chiefly Brit* : an unkind or unpleasant person • Her boyfriend is *a nasty piece of work*.

piece·work /ˈpi:s,wɚk/ *noun* [*noncount*] : work in which you are paid for each thing you make or do and not for the amount of time you work • doing *piecework* in a factory — often used before another noun • *piecework* rates/earnings
– **piece·work·er** /ˈpi:s,wɚkɚ/ *noun, pl* **-ers** [*count*]

pie chart *noun, pl* ~ **charts** [*count*] : a chart consisting of a circle that is divided into parts to show the size of the different amounts that are a part of a whole amount

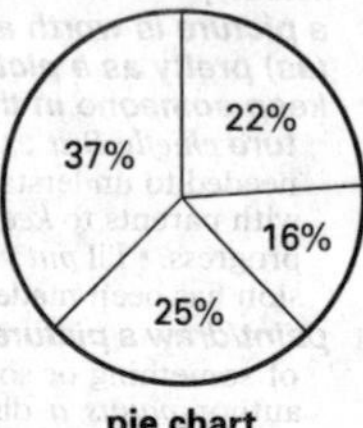

pie chart

pie·crust /ˈpaɪ,krʌst/ *noun, pl* **-crusts** [*count*] : the outer part of a pie

pie hole *noun, pl* ~ **holes** [*count*] *US slang* : someone's mouth • teenagers shoving pizza down their *pie holes* • ***Shut your pie hole***! [=*shut up*; stop talking]

pie in the sky *noun* [*noncount*] : something good that someone says will happen but that seems impossible or unlikely : a very unlikely or unrealistic goal, plan, etc. • His plan to reduce the national debt seems like *pie in the sky*.
– **pie–in–the–sky** *adj* • Voters did not believe his *pie-in-the-sky* promises.

pier /ˈpiɚ/ *noun, pl* **piers** [*count*] : a structure that goes out from a shore into the water ✧ Piers are typically used as a place for ships to load and unload people or things or as a place where people can walk. • The ferry leaves from *pier* 4. • People were fishing off the *pier*. • Couples walked on/along the *pier*.

pierce /ˈpiɚs/ *verb* **pierc·es; pierced; pierc·ing**
1 : to make a hole in or through (something) [+ *obj*] The needle *pierced* her skin. • The bullet *pierced* his lung. • She had her ears *pierced*. = She *pierced* her ears. [=she had holes made in her ears so that she could wear earrings] [*no obj*] The needle *pierced* into her skin. • The bullet *pierced* through his lung.
2 : to go through or into (something) in a forceful or noticeable way [+ *obj*] A scream *pierced* the silence. • The fog was *pierced* by a dim light. [=a dim light could be seen through the fog] [*no obj*] — often + *through* • The flashlight *pierced through* the darkness. • A scream *pierced through* the air. • The troops *pierced through* the enemy's defenses.

pierced *adj*
1 *of a body part* : having a hole that was made so that a piece of jewelry can be worn through it • She has *pierced* ears. • a *pierced* nose/navel
2 : having holes made in one or more parts of your body so you can wear jewelry in them • a tattooed and *pierced* musician

[1]**piercing** *noun, pl* **-ings**
1 [*noncount*] : the act or practice of decorating your body with jewelry or other objects that are attached directly to your skin • There's a small shop in town where they do tattooing and ***body piercing***.
2 [*count*] : a hole through part of the body where a piece of jewelry can be attached • She got another ear *piercing*.

[2]**piercing** *adj* [*more* ~; *most* ~]
1 : seeming to have the power to see a person's thoughts or feelings • She looked at me with *piercing* eyes, and I was suddenly frightened that she knew what I had done. • I tried to avoid his *piercing* stare.
2 : very loud and high-pitched • a *piercing* scream/voice
3 : having a strong affect on someone : felt in a very noticeable way • She felt a *piercing* sadness when she heard the news.
4 : very cold • a *piercing* wind
– **pierc·ing·ly** *adv* • My father looked *piercingly* at me. • It is *piercingly* cold outside.

pi·e·ty /ˈpajəti/ *noun* [*noncount*] : devotion to God : the quality or state of being pious • He was admired for his extreme *piety*. • an act of *piety*

pif·fle /ˈpɪfəl/ *noun* [*noncount*] *informal* + *old-fashioned* : words or ideas that are false or silly : NONSENSE • His story is complete *piffle*.

pif·fling /ˈpɪfəlɪŋ/ *adj, chiefly Brit, informal* + *disapproving* : small and unimportant • a *piffling* [=*piddling*] amount of money

[1]**pig** /ˈpɪg/ *noun, pl* **pigs**
1 [*count*] : an animal that has a fat body with short legs, a small tail, and a wide nose and that is raised on a farm or lives in the wild — compare HOG, PIGLET, SOW; see also GUINEA PIG, POTBELLIED PIG

P

2 [*count*] *informal + disapproving* **a :** someone who eats a lot of food especially at one time • The kids eat like *pigs*. [=the kids eat a lot] • I ***made a pig of myself*** at dinner. [=I ate too much at dinner] **b :** someone who selfishly wants or takes more than other people • a greedy *pig* **c :** someone who is unpleasant or offensive • Don't be a *pig*. Say "excuse me" after you burp. • They live like *pigs*. [=they live in a dirty environment] • He is a sexist *pig*. = He is a ***male chauvinist pig***. [=he is a man who thinks women are not equal to men]

pig

3 [*count*] *slang, offensive* **:** POLICE OFFICER

4 [*singular*] *Brit, informal* **:** something that is very difficult or unpleasant — + *of* • I had ***a pig of a*** day at work. [=I had a very difficult day at work]

a pig in a poke *old-fashioned* **:** something usually of poor quality that someone tries to persuade you to buy or accept when you do not know much about it • If you buy a used car without testing it, you're buying *a pig in a poke*.

in a pig's eye see [1]EYE

make a pig's ear (out) of *Brit, informal* **:** to do or manage something badly • He has *made a pig's ear of* his reelection campaign.

pig in the middle see [1]PIGGY

pigs might fly *Brit, informal* — said as a response to something that seems unlikely to happen • "This time I think he'll ask me to marry him!" "Yeah, and *pigs might fly*."

when pigs fly *US, informal* — used to say that you think that something will never happen • The train station will be renovated *when pigs fly*. [=it will never be renovated]

[2]**pig** *verb* **pigs; pigged; pig·ging**

pig out [*phrasal verb*] *informal* **:** to eat a lot of food at one time • I *pigged out* at the picnic. — often + *on* • The boys *pigged out on* pizza.

pi·geon /ˈpɪʤən/ *noun, pl* **-geons** [*count*] **:** a gray bird that is common in cities and that has a fat body and short legs — see color picture on page C9; see also CLAY PIGEON, HOMING PIGEON, STOOL PIGEON

[1]**pi·geon·hole** /ˈpɪʤənˌhoul/ *verb* **-holes; -holed; -hol·ing** [+ *obj*] *disapproving* **:** to unfairly think of or describe (someone or something) as belonging to a particular group, having only a particular skill, etc. • She likes to perform different types of music because she doesn't want to be *pigeonholed*. — often + *as* • She doesn't want to be *pigeonholed as* a jazz musician.

[2]**pigeonhole** *noun, pl* **-holes** [*count*]

1 *chiefly Brit* **:** a small open space in a desk, cabinet, or wall for keeping letters or papers

2 *disapproving* — used to say that someone or something is being unfairly thought of or described as belonging to a particular group, having only a particular skill, etc. • He's a talented actor who doesn't want to be ***put in a pigeonhole***. [=doesn't want to be pigeonholed]

pi·geon–toed /ˈpɪʤənˌtoud/ *adj* [*more* ~; *most* ~] **:** having feet that are turned toward each other so that the toes do not point straight ahead • The child is *pigeon-toed*.

pig·gery /ˈpɪgəri/ *noun, pl* **-ger·ies** [*count*] *chiefly Brit* **:** a place where pigs are kept or raised

pig·gish /ˈpɪgɪʃ/ *adj* [*more* ~; *most* ~] *chiefly US, informal + disapproving* **:** greedy, offensive, or unpleasant • a *piggish* demand for more money • He has a *piggish* attitude toward women.

— pig·gish·ly *adv*

[1]**pig·gy** /ˈpɪgi/ *noun, pl* **-gies** [*count*] *informal* **:** a pig ✧ *Piggy* is used especially by children or when talking to children. • Hey, look at the little *piggy*!

piggy in the middle *also* ***pig in the middle*** *Brit, informal* **:** someone who is brought into an argument between two people or groups • They're arguing again, and I'm *piggy in the middle*.

[2]**piggy** *adj* [*more* ~; *most* ~] *informal + disapproving* **:** PIGGISH • *piggy* behavior

[1]**pig·gy·back** /ˈpɪgiˌbæk/ *noun, pl* **-backs** [*count*] **:** the act of carrying someone on your back or shoulders • Her father gave her a *piggyback*. = Her father gave her a ***piggyback ride***. [=her father carried her on his back]

— piggyback *adv* • a child being carried *piggyback*

[2]**piggyback** *verb* **-backs; -backed; -back·ing :** to be carried by or connected to something else or to cause (something) to be carried by or connected to something else — usually used figuratively [*no obj*] Other companies are trying to *piggyback* on our success. [=trying to use our success to help themselves] [+ *obj*] The legislation is being *piggybacked* on another bill. [=is being added to another bill so that they will both be passed together]

piggy bank *noun, pl* ~ **banks** [*count*] **:** a container that is often shaped like a pig with a narrow opening in the top and that is used for saving coins

pig·head·ed /ˈpɪgˌhɛdəd/ *adj* [*more* ~; *most* ~] *disapproving* **:** refusing to do what other people want or to change your opinion or the way you do something **:** very stubborn • He was too *pigheaded* to listen to my suggestion.

— pig·head·ed·ness *noun* [*noncount*]

pig in a blanket *noun, pl* **pigs in a blanket** *or* **pigs in blankets** [*count*] *US* **:** a small hot dog that is served in a wrapping of baked dough

pig Latin *noun* [*noncount*] *chiefly US* **:** a playful way of speaking English in which the sound at the beginning of a word is moved to the end and the sound "ay" is added • "Oseclay the oorday" is *pig Latin* for "close the door."

pig·let /ˈpɪglət/ *noun, pl* **-lets** [*count*] **:** a baby pig

pig·ment /ˈpɪgmənt/ *noun, pl* **-ments**

1 : a natural substance that gives color to animals and plants [*count*] Chlorophyll is a group of green *pigments*. • Melanin is a *pigment* that gives color to skin and fur. [*noncount*] Albinos lack normal skin *pigment*.

2 : a substance that gives color to something else [*count*] *Pigments* are used to give color to paint, ink, and plastic. [*noncount*] Red *pigment* is mixed into the ink.

— pig·ment·ed /ˈpɪgˌmɛntəd/ *adj* • dark *pigmented* skin • *pigmented* paints

pig·men·ta·tion /ˌpɪgmənˈteɪʃən/ *noun* [*noncount*] **:** the natural coloring of people, animals, or plants • dark skin *pigmentation*

pigmy *variant spelling of* PYGMY

pig·pen /ˈpɪgˌpɛn/ *noun, pl* **-pens** [*count*] *US*

1 : PIGSTY 1

2 : PIGSTY 2 • Their house is a real *pigpen*.

pig·skin /ˈpɪgˌskɪn/ *noun, pl* **-skins**

1 [*noncount*] **:** leather made from the skin of a pig • The collar is made of *pigskin*. — often used before another noun • a *pigskin* jacket

2 [*count*] *US, informal* **:** the ball used in American football • We threw the *pigskin* [=*football*] around.

pig·sty /ˈpɪgˌstaɪ/ *noun, pl* **-sties** [*count*]

1 : a place where pigs are kept — called also (*US*) *pigpen, sty*

2 *informal* **:** a dirty or messy place • His room was a *pigsty*. — called also (*US*) *pigpen, sty*

pig·tails /ˈpɪgˌteɪlz/ *noun* [*plural*] **:** hair tied in two ponytails or braids with one on each side of the head • I want to wear *pigtails*, but my mom tells me that they're for little girls. • She wore her hair ***in pigtails***. — see picture at HAIR

— pig·tailed /ˈpɪgˌteɪld/ *adj, always used before a noun* • a *pigtailed* little girl

[1]**pike** /ˈpaɪk/ *noun, pl* **pike** *or* **pikes** [*count*] **:** a large fish that lives in rivers and lakes and that has a long body and sharp teeth — compare [2]PIKE, [3]PIKE

[2]**pike** *noun, pl* **pikes** [*count*] *US, informal* **:** a road that people must pay to use **:** TURNPIKE — usually used with *the* • There might be a lot of traffic on *the pike*.

down the pike *US, informal* **1 :** in the future • Today's technology is only a hint at what's *down the pike*. [=down the road] **2 *come down the pike* :** to happen or appear • He is the greatest boxer to *come down the pike* [=*come along*] in years. • A chance like this doesn't *come down the pike* every day.

— compare [1]PIKE, [3]PIKE

[3]**pike** *noun, pl* **pikes** [*count*] **:** a long wooden pole with a steel point that was used in the past as a weapon — compare [1]PIKE, [2]PIKE

pi·laf /pɪˈlɑːf, ˈpiːˌlɑːf, *Brit* ˈpiːˌlæf/ *noun, pl* **pi·lafs** [*count, noncount*] **:** a dish that is made of seasoned rice and vegetables and often meat • a vegetable *pilaf* • a serving of ***rice pilaf*** — called also (*chiefly Brit*) *pilau*

pi·las·ter /pɪˈlæstɚ/ *noun, pl* **-ters** [*count*] **:** a rectangular column that is attached to a wall and that is used for decoration or support

Pi·la·tes /pəˈlɑːtiz/ *noun* [*noncount*] **:** a system of exercises that are often done with special equipment

pi·lau /pəˈloʊ, *Brit* ˈpiːˌlaʊ/ *noun, pl* **-laus** [*count, noncount*] *chiefly Brit* : PILAF

¹pile /ˈpajəl/ *noun, pl* **piles** [*count*]
1 : a group of things that are put one on top of another • He put the magazines into a neat *pile*. • She raked the leaves into *piles*. • Take a card from the *pile*. — often + *of* • a *pile of* wood • a *pile of* clothes
2 *informal* **a :** a very large amount of something • She had *piles* of work to do. • He makes a *pile* of money. **b :** a large amount of money • He made his *pile* and then retired. • He made a *pile* in the stock market.
at the bottom of the pile **:** in a low or very unimportant position • He is *at the bottom of the pile* but should get a promotion soon. • The team finished the season *at the bottom of the pile*.
at the top of the pile **:** in a high or very important position • With this promotion, he will be *at the top of the pile*. • The team finished the season *at the top of the pile*.
– compare ³PILE, ⁴PILE

²pile *verb* **piles; piled; pil·ing**
1 [+ *obj*] **:** to put (something) in a pile • The campers *piled* [=*stacked*] wood for the fire. • The books were *piled* [=*heaped*] high on the table. — often + *up* • The teacher neatly *piled up* the students' papers.
2 [+ *obj*] **:** to put a large amount of things on or in (something) — + *with* • He *piled* his plate *with* potatoes. • The chair was *piled with* clothes. [=there was a pile of clothes on the chair]
3 [+ *obj*] **:** to put (things or people) inside or on top of something in a quick and careless way — + *into* or *onto* • I *piled* all my clothes *into* one suitcase. • We *piled* the kids *into* the van. • He *piled* potatoes *onto* his plate.
4 [*no obj*] *of a group of people, animals, etc.* **:** to enter or get on something (such as a building or vehicle) quickly — + *into* or *onto* • The kids *piled* [=*crowded*] *into* the van. • People *piled into* the theater. • We *piled onto* the sofa.
pile in [*phrasal verb*] *of a group of people, animals, etc.* **:** to move into a place or vehicle quickly • She parked the van and we all *piled in*.
pile on [*phrasal verb*] **1** ***pile on (something)*** **:** to put a large amount of (something) on something or someone • He *piled on* the gravy. • The teacher punished the class by *piling on* more work. [=the teacher punished the class by giving them more work] • Her parents *piled on* the pressure to do well in school. [=her parents put a lot of pressure on her to do well in school] ✧ If you ***pile on the pounds***, you gain a lot of weight. **2** *US, informal* **:** to join other people in criticizing something or someone in usually an unfair way • After the first few negative reviews, all the other critics started *piling on*.
pile out [*phrasal verb*] *of a group of people, animals, etc.* **:** to move out of a place or a vehicle quickly • She parked the van, and the kids *piled out*. • The crowd *piled out* of the theater.
pile up [*phrasal verb*] **:** to increase in amount or number to a total that is difficult to manage • Work *piled up* while she was on vacation. • The bills are *piling up*. • Traffic *piled up* because of the accident. • Snow *piled up* on the cars. — see also PILEUP

³pile *noun* **:** a soft surface of short threads on a rug, carpet, etc. [*singular*] The rug has a thick *pile*. [*noncount*] It's a yellow rug with shaggy *pile*. — compare ³NAP — compare ¹PILE, ⁴PILE

⁴pile *noun, pl* **piles** [*count*] **:** a long stake or pointed post that is pushed into the ground to support something (such as a building) — compare ¹PILE, ³PILE

pile driver *noun, pl* **~ -ers** [*count*]
1 : a machine used for hammering posts into the ground
2 *Brit, informal* **:** a very hard kick or hit • He hit a *pile driver* into the net from 20 yards out.

piles *noun* [*plural*] *medical* **:** a swollen mass of veins located at or near the anus • He has *piles*. [=*hemorrhoids*]

pile·up /ˈpajəlˌʌp/ *noun, pl* **-ups** [*count*]
1 : an accident in which several or many vehicles crash into each other • A five-car *pileup* slowed traffic.
2 : a large amount of something that has increased gradually over a period of time • a *pileup* of debt — see also *pile up* at ²PILE

pil·fer /ˈpɪlfɚ/ *verb* **-fers; -fered; -fer·ing :** to steal things that are not very valuable or to steal a small amount of something [*no obj*] He was caught *pilfering*. [+ *obj*] She *pilfered* stamps and paper from work.

pil·grim /ˈpɪlgrəm/ *noun, pl* **-grims** [*count*]
1 : someone who travels to a holy place • Thousands of Muslim *pilgrims* traveled to Mecca.
2 ***Pilgrim*** **:** one of the people who traveled by boat from England and created the first permanent settlement in New England at Plymouth in 1620

pil·grim·age /ˈpɪlgrəmɪʤ/ *noun, pl* **-ag·es**
1 : a journey to a holy place [*count*] He made a *pilgrimage* to Mecca. [*noncount*] The tradition of *pilgrimage* is important in Islam.
2 : a journey to a special or unusual place [*count*] The family went on a *pilgrimage* to historical battlefields. [*noncount*] The poet's grave site has become a place of *pilgrimage*.

¹pill /ˈpɪl/ *noun, pl* **pills** [*count*]
1 a : a small, rounded object that you swallow and that contains medicine, vitamins, etc. • She took a *pill* for her headache. • The drug is available as a *pill* or a liquid. • diet *pills* — see also PEP PILL, POISON PILL, SLEEPING PILL, SUGAR PILL **b** ***the pill*** **:** a pill that a woman takes so that she will not become pregnant **:** a contraceptive in pill form • She is ***on the pill***. [=she is taking birth control pills regularly] — see also MORNING-AFTER PILL
2 *US, informal* **:** an annoying person — usually singular • Don't be such a *pill*.
(a) bitter pill (to swallow) see ¹BITTER
sugar/sweeten the pill **:** to make an unpleasant thing less difficult to accept or deal with • Faster service may *sugar the pill* of higher fees.

²pill *verb* **pills; pilled; pill·ing** [*no obj*] *of a sweater, fabric, etc.* **:** to begin to have small balls of fiber on the surface usually after having been worn or used many times • Wool sweaters may *pill* after you wash them.

pil·lage /ˈpɪlɪʤ/ *verb* **-lag·es; -laged; -lag·ing :** to take things from (a place, such as a city or town) by force especially during a war **:** to loot or plunder (a place) [+ *obj*] The enemy *pillaged* the town. • The town was *pillaged* and burned. [*no obj*] barbarians known for looting and *pillaging*
– **pillage** *noun* [*noncount*] • The town suffered *pillage* and destruction. – **pil·lag·er** *noun, pl* **-ers** [*count*] • The museum's artwork was stolen by *pillagers*.

pil·lar /ˈpɪlɚ/ *noun, pl* **-lars** [*count*]
1 : a large post that helps to hold up something (such as a roof)
2 : someone who is an important member of a group — + *of* • He is a *pillar of* the church/community. • a *pillar of* society
3 : a basic fact, idea, or principle of something — + *of* • a central *pillar of* the theory • one of the five *pillars of* Islam • The right to vote is a *pillar of* democracy.
4 : something that rises into the air in a tall, thin shape • *Pillars* of smoke rose from the factory. • a *pillar* of rock
from pillar to post *chiefly Brit* **:** from one place or one situation to another • His book has been passed *from pillar to post*, but no one wants to publish it. • He has been running *from pillar to post* his whole life.
pillar of strength **:** someone or something that gives support or help during difficult times • My husband was my/a *pillar of strength* during my mother's illness. • Religion was his *pillar of strength* after his wife died.

pill·box /ˈpɪlˌbɑːks/ *noun, pl* **-box·es** [*count*]
1 : a small box for holding pills
2 : a small, low shelter for machine guns and other weapons
3 : a small, round hat without a brim

pil·lion /ˈpɪljən/ *noun* [*singular*] *chiefly Brit* **:** a seat for a passenger on a motorcycle — often used before another noun • a *pillion* passenger/seat
– **pillion** *adv, chiefly Brit* • He rode *pillion*. [=on a pillion]

pil·lock /ˈpɪlək/ *noun, pl* **-locks** [*count*] *Brit slang* **:** a stupid person • He was acting like a total *pillock*.

¹pil·lo·ry /ˈpɪləri/ *verb* **-ries; -ried; -ry·ing** [+ *obj*] **:** to publicly criticize (someone) in a very harsh way • The press *pilloried* the judge for her decision. — often used as *(be) pilloried* • The mayor *was pilloried* by the press for his comments.

²pillory *noun, pl* **-ries** [*count*] **:** a device that was used in the past for punishing someone in public and that consists of a wooden frame with holes in which the head and hands can be locked

pil·low /ˈpɪloʊ/ *noun, pl* **-lows** [*count*] **:** a bag filled with soft material that is used as a cushion usually for the head of a person who is lying down — see picture at BED

pil·low·case /ˈpɪloʊˌkeɪs/ *noun, pl* **-cas·es** [*count*] **:** a removable covering for a pillow — called also *pillowslip*; see picture at BED

pil·low·slip /ˈpɪloʊˌslɪp/ *noun, pl* **-slips** [*count*] : PILLOWCASE

pillow talk *noun* [*noncount*] *informal* : a conversation between lovers in bed

[1]**pi·lot** /ˈpaɪlət/ *noun, pl* **-lots** [*count*]
1 : a person who flies an airplane, helicopter, etc. ▪ an airline *pilot* ▪ a fighter/bomber *pilot* — see also AUTOPILOT, BUSH PILOT, COPILOT, TEST PILOT
2 : a person who steers or guides a ship into and out of a port or in dangerous waters
3 : a single television show that is made as a test to see if a television series based on the show would be popular and successful
4 : PILOT LIGHT
– pi·lot·less /ˈpaɪlətləs/ *adj* ▪ *pilotless* aircraft/planes

[2]**pilot** *verb* **-lots; -lot·ed; -lot·ing** [+ *obj*]
1 : to fly (an airplane, spacecraft, etc.) ▪ He is learning how to *pilot* a helicopter.
2 : to steer or guide (a ship) ▪ He skillfully *piloted* the ship into port during the storm. — often used figuratively ▪ The education bill was *piloted* through the House and Senate. ▪ The hostess *piloted* us to our table. ▪ a skillful manager who has *piloted* his team to the playoffs

[3]**pilot** *adj, always used before a noun* : done as a test to see if a larger program, study, etc., should be done ▪ The group conducted a *pilot* program/project/study. ▪ a *pilot* episode

pilot light *noun, pl* ~ **lights** [*count*] : a small flame that is always burning in a gas stove, burner, etc., and that is used to light a larger flame

pilot officer *noun, pl* ~ **-cers** [*count*] : an officer of low rank in the British Air Force

pil·sner *or* **pil·sen·er** /ˈpɪlsnɚ/ *noun, pl* **-sners** *or* **-seners** [*count, noncount*] : a light beer with a strong flavor of hops

pi·men·to /pəˈmɛntoʊ/ *noun, pl* **-tos** *or* **-to** [*count*] : PIMIENTO

pi·mien·to /pəmˈjɛntoʊ/ *noun, pl* **-tos** [*count*] : a type of small, mildly sweet pepper

[1]**pimp** /ˈpɪmp/ *noun, pl* **pimps** [*count*] : a man who makes money illegally by getting customers for prostitutes

[2]**pimp** *verb* **pimps; pimped; pimp·ing** [*no obj*] : to get customers for prostitutes : to work as a pimp — often + *for* ▪ He *pimps for* three women.

pim·ple /ˈpɪmpəl/ *noun, pl* **pimples** [*count*] : a small, red, swollen spot on the skin ▪ a teenager who has *pimples* [=*acne*]
– pim·pled /ˈpɪmpəld/ *adj* [*more* ~; *most* ~] ▪ a *pimpled* face **– pim·ply** /ˈpɪmpəli/ *adj* **pim·pli·er; -est** [*also more* ~; *most* ~] ▪ *pimply* skin ▪ a *pimply* teenager

[1]**pin** /ˈpɪn/ *noun, pl* **pins**
1 [*count*] : a thin, pointed piece of stiff wire with a rounded head at one end that is used especially for fastening pieces of cloth — see picture at SEWING; see also BOBBY PIN, CLOTHESPIN, DRAWING PIN, HAIRPIN, SAFETY PIN
2 [*count*] **a** : a thin, pointed piece of stiff wire with a decoration at one end — see also HATPIN **b** *chiefly US* : BROOCH **c** : a small usually circular object that has writing and often a picture on it and that has a pin on the back so that it can be fastened to clothing, bags, etc. ▪ He handed out *pins* with the peace sign on them. ▪ political campaign *pins*
3 [*count*] **a** : a thin piece of wood, metal, or plastic that is used for holding things together or for hanging one thing from another **b** : a long, thin piece of metal that is used to fasten together the ends of broken bone
4 [*count*] *Brit* : one of the metal pieces that stick out from an electric plug and fit into a socket : PRONG ▪ a three-*pin* plug
5 [*count*] : a thin piece of metal that is removed to trigger the explosion of a small bomb (called a grenade) ▪ pull the *pin*
6 [*count*] *golf* : a long stick with a flag at the top that shows where the hole is on a green ▪ The ball landed near the *pin*.
7 [*count*] *bowling* : one of the usually white standing pieces that are knocked down with the ball — see also TENPIN
8 ***pins*** [*plural*] *informal* : the legs of a person or animal ▪ They were knocked right off their *pins* by the heavy winds.
you could hear a pin drop — used to say that it was so quiet that the smallest noise could be heard ▪ After he announced that he was leaving, *you could hear a pin drop* in the office.

[2]**pin** *verb, always followed by an adverb or preposition* **pins; pinned; pin·ning** [+ *obj*]
1 : to fasten or attach (something) with a pin ▪ She *pinned* a rose to her dress. ▪ The general *pinned* the medal on the soldier. ▪ She *pinned* up/back her hair. ▪ He *pinned* a sign on the wall.
2 : to prevent or stop (someone or something) from moving by holding or pressing firmly against something ▪ The passengers were *pinned* under the wreckage. ▪ The guards *pinned* his arms to his sides. ▪ She was *pinned* against the side of the car. ▪ The police officers *pinned* the suspect down (on the ground). — sometimes used figuratively ▪ The soldiers were *pinned* down by enemy fire. [=the soldiers were unable to move because they were being shot at by the enemy]
pin down [*phrasal verb*] **1** ***pin (someone) down*** : to cause or force (someone) to make a definite statement or decision about something ▪ Reporters tried to *pin* him *down* on the specific changes he wants to make to the tax laws. ▪ He talked in a general way, but they couldn't *pin* him *down* to specifics. **2** ***pin down (something)*** *or* ***pin (something) down*** : to find out (something) with certainty ▪ Can you *pin down* when the change occurred? ▪ I'm trying to *pin down* [=*identify*] the source of the problem.
pin on [*phrasal verb*] **1** ***pin (something) on (someone)*** : to say that (something) was done or caused by (someone) ▪ The police *pinned* the robbery *on* the night watchman. ▪ He always manages to *pin* [=*fasten*] the blame *on* someone else. **2** ***pin (all) your hopes on (something)*** : to hope very much that (something) will help you or allow you to succeed ▪ Many cancer patients are *pinning their hopes on* a new drug that is now being developed. ▪ You shouldn't *pin all your hopes on* getting the job.

PIN /ˈpɪn/ *abbr* personal identification number ✧ A personal identification number is a secret number that is used to get money from a bank account through a machine, to get personal information on a Web site, etc.

pi·ña co·la·da /ˈpiːnjəkoʊˈlɑːdə/ *noun, pl* ~ **-das** [*count*] : a drink that is made of rum, coconut juice, and pineapple juice mixed with ice

pin·a·fore /ˈpɪnəˌfoɚ/ *noun, pl* **-fores** [*count*] : [2]JUMPER 1

pi·ña·ta *or* **pi·na·ta** /pinˈjɑːtə/ *noun, pl* **-tas** [*count*] : a decorated container filled with candies, fruits, and gifts that is hung up at parties or celebrations and hit with a stick by children until it is broken and the things inside it fall out

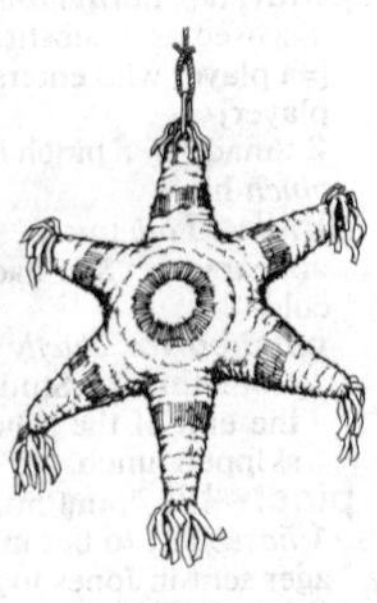
piñata

pin·ball /ˈpɪnˌbɑːl/ *noun* [*noncount*] : a game played on a special machine in which a ball scores points by hitting targets while rolling down a slanting surface and the player tries to control the ball with a set of levers ▪ We spent hours playing *pinball*. ▪ a *pinball* machine

pince–nez /ˌpænsˈneɪ/ *noun, pl* **pince–nez** /ˌpænsˈneɪz/ [*count*] : a pair of old-fashioned eyeglasses that do not have pieces that fit over the ears and that are worn by being clipped onto the nose

pin·cer /ˈpɪnsɚ/ *noun, pl* **-cers**
1 ***pincers*** [*plural*] : a small tool that is used for holding or gripping small objects ▪ He used (a pair of) *pincers* to remove the nail.
2 [*count*] : a claw of a lobster or crab and some insects

pincer movement *noun, pl* ~ **-ments** [*count*] : a military attack by two groups of soldiers that approach an enemy position from two different directions at the same time

[1]**pinch** /ˈpɪntʃ/ *verb* **pinch·es; pinched; pinch·ing**
1 [+ *obj*] **a** : to squeeze (someone's skin) between your thumb and finger often in a painful way ▪ My little brother is always trying to *pinch* me. ▪ He *pinched* her cheeks and told her how cute she was. — often used figuratively ▪ It was all so beautiful ***I had to pinch myself*** [=I had to remind myself that it was real] to be sure I wasn't dreaming. ▪ ***Pinch me.*** [=I can't believe this is happening] **b** : to squeeze or press (something) together with your thumb and finger ▪ *Pinch* together the edges of the dough. ▪ He *pinched* the top of his nose to stop the bleeding and leaned forward. **c** : to remove (part of a plant) by squeezing with your thumb and finger ▪ He *pinched* off/out the top of the shoots. ▪ She *pinched* back the new growth.
2 : to press against or squeeze (a part of the body) in a painful way [+ *obj*] These new shoes are *pinching* my toes. ▪ I *pinched* my fingers in the door. ▪ He had a ***pinched nerve*** [=a nerve pressed against a bone in the neck in a painful way] in

P

his neck. [*no obj*] These shoes *pinch.*

3 [*no obj*] : to be very careful about spending money : to spend as little money as possible • By ***pinching and scraping***, she managed to save enough money to buy a new car. — see also PINCH PENNIES (below)

4 [+ *obj*] *chiefly Brit, informal* : to steal (something) • Someone *pinched* her purse. • The material was *pinched* [=*lifted*] from another book.

5 [+ *obj*] *informal* + *old-fashioned* : to arrest (someone) — often + *for* • He was *pinched for* speeding.

6 [+ *obj*] *chiefly US, informal* **a** : to cause financial problems for (someone or something) • Many people are now being/feeling *pinched* [=*squeezed*] by high gasoline prices. • The recession is ***pinching the pocketbooks*** of many people. **b** : to reduce or limit (something) in a way that causes problems • The trade embargo drove up prices and *pinched* supplies.

pinch pennies *informal* : to be very careful about spending money : to spend as little money as possible • He *pinched pennies* to live on his small paycheck.

²pinch *noun, pl* **pinches** [*count*]

1 : the act of pinching someone or something — usually singular • He gave me a *pinch* on the cheek. [=he pinched my cheek]

2 : the amount of something that can be held between your finger and thumb — often + *of* • Add a *pinch of* salt to the soup. • He took a *pinch of* snuff.

feel the pinch : to experience the problems caused by not having enough money or by paying higher costs • The family began to *feel the pinch* after the mother lost her job. • We are starting to *feel the pinch* of high fuel costs.

in a pinch (*US*) *or Brit* ***at a pinch*** : in a bad situation when help is needed • I can help out *in a pinch* if you need a babysitter. • *In a pinch*, you can substitute another ingredient in the recipe. • She can be resourceful *in a pinch*. [=in an emergency]

take (something) with a pinch of salt see ¹SALT

³pinch *adj, always used before a noun, US, baseball*

1 : used as a substitute for another player • a *pinch* runner [=a player who enters a game as a runner in place of another player]

2 : made by a pinch hitter • A *pinch* homer won the game. • a *pinch* hit

pinched *adj* [*more* ~; *most* ~] : having a thin and unhealthy appearance • She had *pinched* cheeks. • a face *pinched* with cold

pinched for *chiefly US, informal* : not having enough of (something) • Students are especially *pinched for* time at the end of the school year. • *Pinched for* cash/money, he skipped lunch.

pinch–hit /ˈpɪntʃˈhɪt/ *verb* **-hits; -hit; -hit·ting** [*no obj*] *US*

1 *baseball* : to bat in the place of another player • The manager sent in Jones to *pinch-hit* for the pitcher.

2 *informal* : to act or serve in place of another person : SUBSTITUTE • The President wasn't able to attend the ceremony, so the Vice President was there to *pinch-hit* for him.

– pinch hitter *noun, pl* ~ **-ters** [*count*]

pin·cush·ion /ˈpɪnˌkʊʃən/ *noun, pl* **-ions** [*count*] : a small bag filled with a soft material that pins and needles can be pushed into when they are not being used — see picture at SEWING

¹pine /ˈpaɪn/ *noun, pl* **pines** *or* **pine**

1 [*count*] : a tree that has long, thin needles instead of leaves and that stays green throughout the year — called also *pine tree*

2 [*noncount*] : the wood of a pine tree that is often used to make furniture

– pine *adj* • *pine* trees/needles/forests/floors • The box is *pine*. **– pin·ey** *also* **piny** /ˈpaɪni/ *adj, chiefly US* • a *piney* aroma • a *piney* forest [=a forest with many pine trees]

²pine *verb* **pines; pined; pin·ing** [*no obj*] : to become thin and weak because of sadness or loss — usually + *away* • Since his wife left him, he spends his days alone, *pining away*.

synonyms see YEARN

pine after [*phrasal verb*] ***pine after (someone or something)*** *US* : to want or desire (someone or something) very much • teenage girls *pining after* rock stars

pine for [*phrasal verb*] ***pine for (someone or something)*** : to feel very sad because you want (something) or because you are not with (someone) • She was *pining for* the old days. • He's *pining for* his college sweetheart. • At this time of year, most people are *pining for* [=longing for] the return of spring.

pine·ap·ple /ˈpaɪˌnæpəl/ *noun, pl* **-apples** [*count, noncount*] : a large fruit that grows on a tropical tree and that has thick skin and very sweet, juicy, yellow flesh • a can of chopped *pineapple* • *pineapple* juice — see color picture on page C5

pine·cone /ˈpaɪnˌkoʊn/ *noun, pl* **-cones** [*count*] : a hard and dry part that is the fruit of a pine tree and contains many seeds — see color picture on page C6

pine nut *noun, pl* ~ **nuts** [*count*] : the seed of some pine trees that is used as food — usually plural • The recipe calls for ¼ cup of *pine nuts*. — called also (*Brit*) *pine kernel*

pinecone

ping /ˈpɪŋ/ *verb* **pings; pinged; ping·ing** [*no obj*]

1 : to make the high, sharp sound of a small, hard object bouncing off metal or glass • The engine in my car keeps *pinging*. [=(*Brit*) *pinking*]

2 : to bounce off something with a sharp, high sound • Pebbles *pinged* off the car.

– ping *noun, pl* **pings** [*count*]

Ping–Pong /ˈpɪŋˌpɑːŋ/ *trademark* — used for table tennis

pin·head /ˈpɪnˌhɛd/ *noun, pl* **-heads** [*count*]

1 : the rounded end of a pin • The insect is the size of a *pinhead*.

2 *US, informal* : a stupid or foolish person • Her boss is a real *pinhead*.

pin·head·ed /ˈpɪnˌhɛdəd/ *adj* [*more* ~; *most* ~] *US, informal* : stupid or foolish • her *pinheaded* boss/decision

pin·hole /ˈpɪnˌhoʊl/ *noun, pl* **-holes** [*count*] : a very small hole made by a pin or in some other way • The water was leaking through a *pinhole* in the pipe. • *pinhole* leaks

¹pin·ion /ˈpɪnjən/ *verb* **-ions; -ioned; -ion·ing** [+ *obj*] : to tie up (someone's arms or legs) very tightly • They *pinioned* his arms behind his back.

²pinion *noun, pl* **-ions** [*count*] *technical* : a small gear in a machine • a car with rack and *pinion* steering

¹pink /ˈpɪŋk/ *noun, pl* **pinks**

1 [*count, noncount*] : a pale red color : a color that is a mixture of red and white — see color picture on page C3; see also SHOCKING PINK

2 [*count*] : a plant with narrow leaves and colorful flowers

in the pink *informal* + *old-fashioned* : in very good health • Regular exercise helped to keep her *in the pink* (of good health).

– pink·ish /ˈpɪŋkɪʃ/ *adj* • a *pinkish* rose/color **– pink·ness** *noun* [*noncount*]

²pink *adj* : of the color pink • *pink* roses • Her dress is pale/salmon *pink*.

tickled pink see TICKLE

³pink *verb* **pinks; pinked; pink·ing** [*no obj*] *Brit* : PING 1

pink–collar *adj, chiefly US* : traditionally held by women • *pink-collar* jobs — compare BLUE-COLLAR, WHITE-COLLAR

pink·eye /ˈpɪŋkˌaɪ/ *noun* [*noncount*] *chiefly US, medical* : CONJUNCTIVITIS

pin·kie *or* **pin·ky** /ˈpɪŋki/ *noun, pl* **-kies** [*count*] *chiefly US* + *Scotland, informal* : LITTLE FINGER • She cut her left *pinkie*. • a *pinkie* ring

pinking shears *noun* [*plural*] : scissors with special blades that make an edge with many sharp points when they cut cloth

pinko /ˈpɪŋkoʊ/ *noun, pl* **pink·os** [*count*] *informal*

1 *US, disapproving* : a person who is a communist or socialist or who supports the ideas of communists and socialists

2 *Brit* : a person whose political or economic opinions are slightly liberal or radical

pink slip *noun, pl* ~ **slips** [*count*] *chiefly US, informal* : a notice that is given to a worker by an employer saying that the worker's job is ending • Thousands of factory workers have been ***given the pink slip*** [=have been laid off; have lost their jobs] in recent months. = Thousands of workers have ***gotten the pink slip***.

– pink–slip *verb* **-slips; -slipped; -slip·ping** [+ *obj*] — usually used as (*be/get*) *pink-slipped* • Thousands of factory workers have *been/gotten pink-slipped* in recent months.

pin money *noun* [*noncount*] *old-fashioned* : money that is used for small expenses • She had a babysitting job to earn *pin money*.

pin·na·cle /ˈpɪnɪkəl/ *noun, pl* **-na·cles** [*count*]

1 : a high mountain top • a lofty *pinnacle*

2 : the best or most important part of something : the point of greatest success or achievement — usually singular • His career reached its *pinnacle* when he won the championship. — often + *of* • Winning the championship was the *pinnacle of* his career. • She stands at the *pinnacle of* the fashion industry. • She has achieved/reached the *pinnacle of* success.

3 : a tower on the roof of a building that comes to a narrow point at the top

pin·ny /ˈpɪni/ *noun, pl* **-nies** [*count*] *Brit, informal* : PINAFORE

pi·noch·le /ˈpiːˌnʌkəl/ *noun* [*noncount*] : a card game played with a special deck of 48 cards

Pinot Blanc /ˈpiːnoʊˈblɑːŋk/ *noun, pl* ~ **Blancs** [*count, noncount*] : a dry white wine originally from France

Pinot Gri·gio /ˈpiːnoʊˈgriːʤijoʊ/ *noun, pl* ~ **-gios** [*count, noncount*] : a dry white wine originally from Italy

Pinot Noir /ˈpiːnoʊˈnwɑɚ/ *noun, pl* ~ **Noirs** [*count, noncount*] : a dry red wine originally from France

¹pin·point /ˈpɪnˌpoɪnt/ *noun, pl* **-points** [*count*] : a very small point or dot — often + *of* • a *pinpoint of* light

²pinpoint *adj, always used before a noun* : very exact or precise • The pitcher showed *pinpoint* control of his fastball. • *pinpoint* accuracy/precision

³pinpoint *verb* **-points; -point·ed; -point·ing** [+ *obj*]

1 : to find out (something) with certainty • They were finally able to *pinpoint* the cause of the fire.

2 : to find or locate the exact position of (something) • He *pinpointed* the city on the map. • Rescuers were able to *pinpoint* where the lost girl was. • The military uses computer imaging to *pinpoint* targets.

pin·prick /ˈpɪnˌprɪk/ *noun, pl* **-pricks** [*count*]

1 : a small hole that is made by a pin or other sharp tool : PINHOLE

2 : a very small point or dot — often + *of* • a *pinprick* [=*pinpoint*] *of* light

3 : a slight but sharp pain caused by a pin or needle • He felt a *pinprick* in his leg. — often used figuratively • I felt a *pinprick* of jealousy when I saw them together.

pins and needles *noun* [*noncount*] : the unpleasant tingling feeling in a part of your body (such as your arm or leg) as it becomes numb or recovers from being numb

on pins and needles *US* : feeling very nervous and unsure about what will happen • Everyone was *on pins and needles* waiting to hear the jury's verdict.

pin·stripe /ˈpɪnˌstraɪp/ *noun, pl* **-stripes**

1 [*count*] : a thin vertical stripe on cloth • a dark suit with white *pinstripes* — often used before another noun • a *pinstripe* pattern/shirt/suit — see color picture on page C12

2 ***pinstripes*** [*plural*] : a suit with pinstripes • a man dressed in *pinstripes*

– pin–striped /ˈpɪnˌstraɪpt/ *adj* • a *pin-striped* suit

pint /ˈpaɪnt/ *noun, pl* **pints** [*count*]

1 *US* : a unit for measuring liquids that is equal to 0.473 liters

2 *Brit* : a unit for measuring liquids that is equal to 0.568 liters

3 a : a container that holds a pint of something • The ice cream comes in *pints*. **b** *chiefly Brit* : a pint of beer • I'd like another *pint*, please. • We'll all ***go for a pint*** after work.

pin·to /ˈpɪntoʊ/ *noun, pl* **-tos** [*count*] *US* : a horse or pony that has patches of white and another color

pinto bean *noun, pl* ~ **beans** [*count*] : a type of small bean that is grown for food

pint–sized /ˈpaɪntˌsaɪzd/ *or* **pint–size** /ˈpaɪntˌsaɪz/ *adj, informal* : very small • *pint-sized* children • a *pint-sized* actress • The restaurant serves *pint-sized* portions.

pin·up /ˈpɪnˌʌp/ *noun, pl* **-ups** [*count*]

1 : a photograph of an attractive person (such as an actress or model) that is hung or pinned on a wall

2 : a person who appears in or is attractive enough to appear in a pinup • He is dating a glamorous *pinup*.

– pinup *adj, always used before a noun* • a *pinup* calendar

pin·wheel /ˈpɪnˌwiːl/ *noun, pl* **-wheels** [*count*] *US*

1 : a toy that has a set of thin blades that are arranged like a fan on the end of a stick and that spin like a wheel when air is blown on them — called also (*Brit*) *windmill*

2 : a type of firework that spins like a wheel — called also (*Brit*) *Catherine wheel*

¹pi·o·neer /ˌpajəˈniɚ/ *noun, pl* **-neers** [*count*]

1 : a person who helps create or develop new ideas, methods, etc. — often + *in* • They were *pioneers in* the field of American medicine. • She was a *pioneer in* the development of new cancer treatments. — often + *of* • a *pioneer of* digital technology

2 : someone who is one of the first people to move to and live in a new area • the *pioneers* who settled in the American West in the 19th century

– pioneer *adj, always used before a noun* • *pioneer* surgeons • the *pioneer* days of the old West

²pioneer *verb* **-neers; -neered; -neer·ing** : to help create or develop (new ideas, methods, etc.) : to be a pioneer in the development of (something) [+ *obj*] a painter who *pioneered* a new art form • The new method of cancer treatment was *pioneered* by an international team of researchers. • He helped *pioneer* a new route to the West. [*no obj*] He *pioneered* in the development of airplanes.

pioneering *adj* : using new and better ideas for the first time • *pioneering* studies • a *pioneering* experiment • He played a *pioneering* role in the development of online business models.

pi·ous /ˈpajəs/ *adj*

1 [*more* ~; *most* ~] : deeply religious : devoted to a particular religion • *pious* [=*devout*] churchgoing people • They lived a quiet, *pious* life.

2 *disapproving* : falsely appearing to be good or moral • I'm tired of hearing politicians making *pious* pronouncements about their devotion to the people.

pious hope/wish : something that is hoped for but will probably not happen • His speech contained no practical solutions, just the *pious hope* that the war would end soon.

– pi·ous·ly *adv*

¹pip /ˈpɪp/ *noun, pl* **pips** [*count*] *US*

1 : one of the dots on dice or dominoes that show their value

2 : a design on a playing card that shows the suit and value — compare ²PIP

²pip *noun, pl* **pips** [*count*]

1 *chiefly Brit* : a small, hard seed of some fruits • orange/apple *pips* [=(*US*) *seeds*]

2 *informal + old-fashioned* : a person or thing that is liked or admired very much • It's a *pip* of an idea. • She's a *pip*!

3 *Brit* : a short, high sound : BEEP

— compare ¹PIP

³pip *verb* **pips; pipped; pip·ping** [+ *obj*] *Brit, informal* : to defeat (someone or something) by a small amount in a race or other competition • The horse *pipped* his rival at the wire. • The team was ***pipped at/to the post*** by its longtime rival.

¹pipe /ˈpaɪp/ *noun, pl* **pipes**

1 [*count*] : a long, hollow tube for carrying water, steam, gas, etc. • water/sewer *pipes* • copper/lead *pipes* — see picture at PLUMBING; see also DRAINPIPE, HOSEPIPE, STOVEPIPE, TAILPIPE, WINDPIPE

pipe

2 [*count*] : a tube with a small bowl at one end that is used for smoking tobacco • He smokes a *pipe*. • He lit the *pipe*. — see also PEACE PIPE, WATER PIPE

3 a [*count*] : a musical instrument that is in the shape of a tube, has holes along the top, and is played by blowing — see also PANPIPE **b** [*count*] : any one of the large tubes of an organ that produce sound when air goes through them **c** ***pipes*** [*plural*] : BAGPIPE **d** ***pipes*** [*plural*] *US, informal* : a singer's voice • He has the *pipes* to sing on Broadway. • a singer with a fine set of *pipes*

put/stick that in your pipe and smoke it *informal* — used to tell someone that they must accept what you say is true even though they might not like it or agree with you • "It's a stupid movie." "Oh really? Well it was just nominated for an Oscar, so *put/stick that in your pipe and smoke it*!"

²pipe *verb* **pipes; piped; pip·ing**

1 [+ *obj*] : to carry or move (something, such as water or oil) in a pipe — often used as *(be) piped* • Water *is piped* into the cabin from an underground stream.

2 [+ *obj*] : to send (music or recorded sound) from one place to another through an electrical connection — usually used as *(be) piped* • Music *is piped* into every store in the mall.

3 a [*no obj*] : to play a pipe or the bagpipes • The pipers *piped* while the drummers drummed. **b** [+ *obj*] : to play (a tune or song) on a pipe or the bagpipes • The musician *piped* a tune.

4 [+ *obj*] : to decorate a cake, cookie, etc., with a line of (something, such as cream or frosting) by using a special bag or tube • I *piped* the frosting around the edge of the cake.

P

***pipe down** [phrasal verb] informal* **:** to become quiet **:** to stop talking ▪ The teacher told the students to *pipe down.* [=*quiet down*]

***pipe up** [phrasal verb] informal* **:** to start talking **:** to say something ▪ After being quiet for almost an hour, he suddenly *piped up* [=*spoke up*] to ask where we were going.

pipe cleaner *noun, pl* **~ -ers** *[count]* **:** a piece of wire that is covered with soft cloth and used to clean the inside of a tobacco pipe

pipe dream *noun, pl* **~ dreams** *[count]* **:** a hope, wish, or dream that is impossible to achieve or not practical ▪ His plan for starting his own business was just a *pipe dream.*

pipe fitter *noun, pl* **~ -ters** *[count]* **:** a person whose job is to install and repair pipes that carry water, gas, etc.

pipe·line /ˈpaɪpˌlaɪn/ *noun, pl* **-lines**

1 *[count]* **:** a line of connected pipes that are used for carrying liquids and gases over a long distance ▪ a natural gas *pipeline* — sometimes used figuratively ▪ a weapons *pipeline* ▪ a news *pipeline* from the mayor's office

2 ***the pipeline*** **:** the system for developing and producing something ▪ the next wave of products to ***come down the pipeline*** [=to be produced] ▪ Newer treatments for the disease are ***in the pipeline*** [=are being developed] ▪ He's a film producer with several projects *in the pipeline.* [=in the works]

pipe organ *noun, pl* **~ -gans** *[count]* **:** ORGAN 2a

pip·er /ˈpaɪpɚ/ *noun, pl* **-ers** *[count]* **:** a person who plays a pipe or the bagpipes

pay the piper** informal* **1 :** to pay the cost of something ▪ We have to do what they say because they're the ones who are *paying the piper.* ▪ You know what they say: ***he who pays the piper calls the tune [=the person who pays for something controls how it is done] **2** *chiefly US* **:** to pay money or suffer in some way because of something you have done ▪ They have mismanaged the company for years, and now they have to *pay the piper.*

pi·pette /paɪˈpɛt, *Brit* pɪˈpɛt/ *noun, pl* **-pettes** *[count] technical* **:** a narrow glass tube used for measuring liquid or for moving small amounts of liquid from one place to another

[1]**pip·ing** /ˈpaɪpɪŋ/ *noun [noncount]*

1 : pipes that carry water, gas, etc. ▪ There's a problem with the *piping* in the building. ▪ kitchen/bathroom *piping*

2 : the music of a pipe or pipes

3 : a narrow tube of cloth that is used to decorate clothes, furniture, etc. ▪ a sofa trimmed with blue *piping* ▪ a uniform with yellow *piping* down the pants

[2]**piping** *adj* **:** having a high-pitched sound or tone ▪ the *piping* voices of small children

piping hot *adj, of food or drink* **:** very hot ▪ The coffee was served *piping hot.* ▪ *piping hot* soup

pip·squeak /ˈpɪpˌskwiːk/ *noun, pl* **-squeaks** *[count] informal* **:** a person who is very small or unimportant ▪ He's just a *pipsqueak* compared to his teammates.

P

pi·quant /ˈpiːkənt/ *adj [more ~; most ~] formal*

1 : having a pleasant, spicy taste ▪ *piquant* vegetables seasoned with pepper ▪ He served the fish with a *piquant* sauce.

2 : interesting and exciting ▪ a *piquant* bit of gossip

— pi·quan·cy /ˈpiːkənsi/ *noun [noncount]* ▪ The pepper added *piquancy* to the sauce. **— pi·quant·ly** *adv*

[1]**pique** /ˈpiːk/ *noun [noncount] formal* **:** a sudden feeling of annoyance or anger when someone has offended you ▪ After a moment of *pique,* the senator responded calmly to his accusers. ▪ He slammed the door ***in a fit of pique.***

[2]**pique** *verb* **piques; piqued; piqu·ing** *[+ obj]*

1 *chiefly US* **:** to cause (curiosity or interest) ▪ The package *piqued* [=*sparked, aroused*] my curiosity. ▪ Brightly colored objects *pique* a baby's interest.

2 *chiefly Brit* **:** to make (someone) annoyed or angry — usually used as *(be) piqued* ▪ I *was piqued* by his rudeness.

pi·ra·cy /ˈpaɪrəsi/ *noun [noncount]*

1 : the act of attacking and stealing from a ship at sea ▪ *piracy* on the high seas

2 a : the act of illegally copying someone's product or invention without permission ▪ software/music/video *piracy* **b :** the act of illegally making television or radio broadcasts ▪ radio *piracy*

pi·ra·nha /pəˈrɑːnə/ *noun, pl* **-nhas** *[count]* **:** a small South American fish that has sharp teeth and that eats the flesh of animals — see color picture on page C8

[1]**pi·rate** /ˈpaɪrət/ *noun, pl* **-rates** *[count]*

1 : someone who attacks and steals from a ship at sea ▪ the famous *pirate* Jean Lafitte — often used before another noun ▪ a *pirate* ship/costume/captain/movie

2 a : someone who illegally copies a product or invention without permission ▪ A software *pirate* made bootleg copies of the computer program. — often used before another noun ▪ *pirate* videotapes/CDs/software ▪ *pirate* translations **b :** a person or organization that illegally makes television or radio broadcasts — usually used before another noun ▪ *pirate* radio

— pi·rat·i·cal /pəˈrætɪkəl/ *adj* ▪ *piratical* activity

[2]**pirate** *verb* **-rates; -rat·ed; -rat·ing** *[+ obj]* **:** to illegally copy (something) without permission ▪ He was accused of *pirating* their invention.

— pirated *adj* ▪ *pirated* videotapes/software/recordings

pir·ou·ette /ˌpirəˈwɛt/ *noun, pl* **-ettes** *[count]* **:** a full turn on the front of one foot in ballet ▪ the elegant *pirouettes* of the prima ballerina

— pirouette *verb* **-ettes; -ett·ed; -ett·ing** *[no obj]* ▪ Twelve dancers *pirouetted* across the stage.

Pi·sces /ˈpaɪˌsiːz/ *noun, pl* **Pisces**

1 *[noncount]* **:** the 12th sign of the zodiac that comes between Aquarius and Aries and is symbolized by a pair of fish — see picture at ZODIAC

2 *[count]* **:** a person born under the sign of Pisces **:** a person born between February 19 and March 20 ▪ He was born on March first, so he's a *Pisces.*

[1]**piss** /ˈpɪs/ *verb* **piss·es; pissed; piss·ing** *informal + impolite*

1 *[no obj]* **:** URINATE ▪ I have to *piss.*

2 *[+ obj]* **:** to urinate in or on (something) ▪ He *pissed* [=*wet*] the bed. ▪ I was so scared I almost *pissed* my pants.

***not have a pot to piss in** informal + impolite* **:** to have no money or possessions ▪ I had just moved to the city and *didn't have a pot to piss in.*

***piss about/around** [phrasal verb] Brit, informal + impolite*

1 : to spend time doing things that are not useful or serious **:** to waste time ▪ She didn't come all this way just to *piss about.* ▪ Don't *piss around* with your health—see a doctor! ▪ It's time we stopped *pissing about* [=*fooling around*] and got busy. **2** ***piss (someone) about/around*** **:** to be unfair or dishonest with (someone) ▪ The sales clerk is *pissing* us *around* [=*(US) jerking us around*]—he keeps saying he'll help us, but we've been waiting for 20 minutes!

***piss and moan** US, informal + impolite* **:** to complain in a constant or annoying way ▪ He's always *pissing and moaning* about having to pay taxes.

piss away** [phrasal verb]* ***piss (something) away or piss away (something) *US, informal + impolite* **:** to foolishly waste (something, such as money, talent, opportunities, etc.) ▪ He *pissed* a fortune *away* on gambling and drinking.

***piss down** [phrasal verb] Brit, informal + impolite* **:** to rain hard ▪ Let's go, mate. It's going to *piss down* any minute.

***piss like a racehorse** US, informal + impolite* **:** to urinate a large amount

piss off** [phrasal verb]* **1** *Brit, informal + impolite* **:** to go away ▪ Why don't you *piss off*? [=*(US) buzz off*] **2** ***piss (someone) off or piss off (someone) *informal + impolite* **:** to make (someone) very angry or annoyed ▪ Her superior attitude really *pisses* me *off.*

***piss yourself (laughing)** Brit, informal + impolite* **:** to laugh very hard ▪ We *pissed ourselves laughing* during the movie.

[2]**piss** *noun, informal + impolite*

1 *[noncount]* **:** URINE

2 *[singular]* **:** an act of urinating ▪ He says he has to ***take a piss.*** = *(Brit)* He says he has to ***have a piss.***

***on the piss** Brit, informal + impolite* **:** drinking heavily at a pub or bar ▪ He's had a big night out *on the piss.*

***piss and vinegar** US, informal + impolite* **:** strength and energy ▪ We were full of *piss and vinegar* back then.

***take the piss out of** Brit, informal + impolite* **:** to make fun of or laugh at (someone or something) ▪ He *took the piss out of* me about my tattoo.

pissed /ˈpɪst/ *adj [more ~; most ~]*

1 *or* ***pissed off*** *chiefly US, informal + impolite* **:** very angry or annoyed at someone ▪ She is *pissed* at her boyfriend for not calling her. ▪ I got really *pissed* when she said that! ▪ Aren't you *pissed off* [=*ticked off*] that your team lost?

2 *Brit slang* **:** very drunk or intoxicated ▪ They went to the pub and got completely *pissed.*

piss–poor /ˈpɪsˌpuɚ/ *adj, US, informal + impolite* **:** very bad **:** extremely poor ▪ He did a *piss-poor* job.

pis·ta·chio /pəˈstæʃijoʊ/ *noun, pl* **-chios** *[count]* **:** a small green nut — often used before another noun • *pistachio* ice cream — see picture at NUT

piste /ˈpiːst/ *noun, pl* **pistes** [*count*] *chiefly Brit* : a downhill ski trail

pis·til /ˈpɪstl/ *noun, pl* **-tils** [*count*] *botany* : the long central part of a flower that extends from the ovary — see picture at FLOWER

pis·tol /ˈpɪstl/ *noun, pl* **-tols** [*count*]
1 : a small gun made to be aimed and fired with one hand — see picture at GUN; see also WATER PISTOL
2 *US, informal* : a person who has a lot of energy and spirit — usually singular • That guy's a real *pistol*.

pistol–whip *verb* **-whips; -whipped; -whip·ping** [+ *obj*] : to hit (someone) many times with a pistol • He was *pistol-whipped* to the ground by a prison guard.

pis·ton /ˈpɪstən/ *noun, pl* **-tons** [*count*] : a part of an engine that moves up and down inside a tube and that causes other parts of the engine to move — see picture at ENGINE

[1]**pit** /ˈpɪt/ *noun, pl* **pits**
1 [*count*] : a hole in the ground usually made by digging • The explorers discovered a burial *pit* containing human bones. • The impact of the meteor created a huge *pit*. [=*crater*] • The hikers dug a *pit* for the fire.
2 [*count*] **a** : a large, deep hole in the ground from which stones or minerals are dug out • a gravel/chalk/tar *pit* — see also SANDPIT **b** *chiefly Brit* : a coal mine
3 [*count*] : something that uses up or holds a very large amount of money, food, information, etc. • My house is such a ***money pit***—I'm always paying for repairs on it! • My brother's stomach is a ***bottomless pit*** [=my brother eats constantly] • The Internet is a *bottomless pit* of information. [=the Internet contains a great amount of information]
4 [*count*] : an area separated from and often placed below the areas next to it: such as **a** : an outdoor area where food is cooked • a barbecue *pit* **b** *US* : an area where particular investments are traded • the oil futures *pit* of the New York Mercantile Exchange **c** : an area where animals are brought to fight **d** : the space in a theater where an orchestra plays • The conductor walked down into the (orchestra) *pit* and stood at the podium. **e** : an area of dirt or grass used for playing certain games • a horseshoe *pit* **f** : MOSH PIT **g** : an area beside a racetrack used for servicing cars during a race — usually plural • The driver stopped in the *pits* to refuel. — see also PIT STOP
5 [*count*] : a small hole or dent on the surface of something • The car's door was covered with *pits* and scratches. • The boy had *pits* [=*pockmarks*] on his face.
6 a [*count*] : a very bad or unpleasant place or situation — usually + *of* • The downtown area is a *pit of* depression/despair/hopelessness. **b** ***the pits informal*** : something that is very bad or unpleasant • You caught the flu on your birthday? That's *the pits*! [=that is awful] • This rainy weather is *the* absolute *pits*. [=I hate this rainy weather] • I usually like her movies, but her most recent one is really *the pits*! [=her most recent one is terrible]
7 [*count*] *informal* : ARMPIT
the pit of your/the stomach : the part of a person's stomach where strong feelings of nervousness, excitement, etc., can be felt • She felt a flutter in *the pit of her stomach* when he walked through the door.
— compare [3]PIT

[2]**pit** *verb* **pits; pit·ted; pit·ting**
1 [+ *obj*] : to make small holes or dents in (something) • A hailstorm badly *pitted* the car's roof. — see also PITTED 2
2 [*no obj*] *car racing* : to make a pit stop • The driver was forced to *pit* because of engine problems.
pit against [*phrasal verb*] ***pit (someone or something) against (someone or something)*** : to cause (someone or something) to fight or compete against (another person or thing) • Tonight's game will *pit* Smith *against* Johnson for the championship. [=Smith will be playing against Johnson for the championship in tonight's game] • The team will be *pitted against* [=will be playing against] last year's champion in the finals. • The game requires you to ***pit your wits against*** the computer. [=to use your wits to try to defeat the computer]
— compare [4]PIT

[3]**pit** *noun, pl* **pits** [*count*] *US* : the hard middle part of a fruit : STONE • peach/cherry/olive *pits* — see color picture on page C5 — compare [1]PIT

[4]**pit** *verb* **pits; pit·ted; pit·ting** [+ *obj*] *chiefly US* : to remove the pit from (a piece of fruit) • He *pitted* the plum and cut it into pieces. — see also PITTED 1 — compare [2]PIT

pi·ta (*US*) *or Brit* **pit·ta** /ˈpiːtə, *Brit* ˈpɪtə/ *noun, pl* **-tas** [*count, noncount*] : a type of thin, flat bread that can be separated to form a pocket for holding food — called also (*US*) *pita bread*, (*Brit*) *pitta bread*; see picture at BAKING

pit–a–pat /ˌpɪtɪˈpæt/ *noun* [*singular*] : PITTER-PATTER — often + *of* • the *pit-a-pat of* the raindrops on the roof
– pit–a–pat *adv* • Her heart went *pit-a-pat* [=her heart beat rapidly with excitement] when he walked into the room.

pit boss *noun, pl* **~ bosses** [*count*] *chiefly US* : a person whose job is to supervise the gambling that is done in a casino

pit bull *noun, pl* **~ bulls** [*count*] : a type of dog that is known for its strength and its ability to fight — called also *pit bull terrier*

[1]**pitch** /ˈpɪʧ/ *noun, pl* **pitch·es**
1 : the highness or lowness of a sound [*count*] instruments with different *pitches* • Her voice has a high *pitch*. • The *pitch* of the engine suddenly changed from a low to a high squeal. [*noncount*] He noticed the change of *pitch* in the sound of the engine. • You were a little ***off pitch*** [=too high or too low] on that last note. • His singing was perfectly ***on pitch*** — see also PERFECT PITCH
2 [*count*] *baseball* : an act of throwing a baseball to a batter or the ball that is thrown to a batter • His third *pitch* was a fastball down the middle of the plate. • The batter was hit by an inside *pitch*. [=a ball that is thrown close to the batter] • She fouled off the first *pitch*. — see also WILD PITCH
3 [*count*] : things that are said by someone (such as a salesman) in order to make someone want to buy, do, or accept something • The salesman started making/delivering his *pitch* as soon as he saw us looking at the car. • an advertising *pitch* — see also SALES PITCH
4 [*singular*] : a state of intense feeling • Tensions between the two groups have risen to a high/feverish *pitch*. [=have become very intense] • They brought the audience to such a *pitch* of excitement that you could no longer hear the music. — see also FEVER PITCH
5 [*count*] : the amount or degree of slope on a roof or other surface • All the houses have roofs with steep *pitches* to prevent the buildup of snow.
6 [*noncount*] : up and down movement of a ship or airplane • The water was choppy that day, and the continual *pitch* of the boat made everyone seasick. • Flaps on the airplane's wings are used to control *pitch*.
7 [*count*] *Brit* : an area that is used for playing sports : PLAYING FIELD • Fans ran onto the *pitch* at the end of the match. • a rugby/cricket *pitch*
8 [*count*] *Brit* : an outdoor area where someone performs or sells things
9 [*count*] *golf* : PITCH SHOT
— compare [3]PITCH

[2]**pitch** *verb* **pitch·es; pitched; pitch·ing**
1 [+ *obj*] : to throw or toss (something) • Passersby on the street *pitched* coins into her open guitar case as she played. • They were *pitching* horseshoes. • She *pitched* the empty box into the garbage. • (*American football*) The quarterback *pitched* the ball underhanded to the halfback.
2 *baseball* **a** : to throw a baseball to a batter : to throw a pitch [+ *obj*] He *pitched* me a curveball. • a perfectly *pitched* ball [=a pitch that is thrown perfectly] • The batter was hit by a *pitched* ball. [=by a pitch] [*no obj*] Will you *pitch* to me so I can practice my swing? • They've worked on improving their *pitching* and hitting since last season. • He hurt his *pitching* arm/shoulder/hand. [=the arm/shoulder/hand that he uses to pitch baseballs] • the team's *pitching* coach/staff **b** : to play baseball as a pitcher [+ *obj*] She *pitched* the first three innings. • In his last game of the year, he *pitched* a no-hitter/shutout against the school's rival team. [*no obj*] He *pitched* in the major leagues for several years. • She *pitched* well/great yesterday.
3 [+ *obj*] : to talk about or describe (something) in a favorable way so that people will want to buy it, accept it, etc. • She can now be seen *pitching* [=*plugging*] cleaning products on television. • It's one of the many products their company *pitches*. • commercials *pitching* toys to children • The drug has been *pitched* as a treatment for many ailments. — often + *to* • I've been thinking about *pitching* the idea *to* my boss. • She *pitched* the story *to* her editor. • They *pitched* the TV show *to* several different networks before they found one that wanted to produce it.
4 [+ *obj*] **a** : to cause (a sound, your voice, etc.) to be high

P

or low • He sometimes *pitches* his voice lower to make himself sound older. • differently *pitched* sounds — see also HIGH-PITCHED, LOW-PITCHED **b** : to cause (a song, an instrument, etc.) to be in a particular musical key • a tune *pitched* in the key of C • differently *pitched* instruments
5 *always followed by an adverb or preposition* [+ *obj*] **a** : to make or design (something) for people at a particular level • They *pitched* the test at a fifth-grade reading level. • The lesson was originally *pitched* to younger students. [=it was designed/intended for younger students] **b** : to cause (something) to be at a particular level • Try not to *pitch* your hopes/ambitions too high.
6 *always followed by an adverb or preposition* [*no obj*] *of a surface* : to slope downward • The road *pitches* steeply down the side of the mountain. — see also PITCHED
7 *always followed by an adverb or preposition* [*no obj*] : to fall or move suddenly in a particular direction • He lost his balance and *pitched* forward onto the ground. • The boat was *pitching* up and down in the rough waters. • The nose of the airplane suddenly *pitched* downward.
8 a *golf* : to hit a golf ball so that it goes very high in the air and rolls very little after hitting the ground [*no obj*] She *pitched* onto the green from a patch of tall grass. • a ***pitching wedge*** [=a type of golf club used for pitching] [+ *obj*] She *pitched* the ball up on to the green. **b** [+ *obj*] *cricket* : to cause (the ball) to bounce on the ground before reaching a batsman **c** [*no obj*] *of a ball* : to bounce on the ground • Her shot landed short of the green and *pitched* into a bunker.
9 [+ *obj*] : to set up (a tent or camp) • We decided to *pitch* our tents there for the night. • We *pitched* camp by the river.
pitch a fit/tantrum *US, informal* : to become very upset and angry in a loud and uncontrolled way • He *pitched* [=*threw*] *a fit* when she said she was going to be late again. • My three-year-old *pitched* one of her temper *tantrums* when we tried to leave the party early.
pitch in [*phrasal verb*] ***pitch in or pitch in (something)*** *informal* : to do something or give something (such as money) to help a person, group, or cause • Everyone has to *pitch in* [=*chip in, contribute*] if we're going to finish this project on time. • They all *pitched in* to help. • People in the town have been *pitching in* to pay the family's medical bills. • I *pitched in* [=*contributed*] a couple of bucks to help pay for his birthday cake.
pitch into [*phrasal verb*] ***pitch into (someone)*** *chiefly Brit, informal* : to attack or criticize (someone) forcefully • He said his mother would *pitch into* him when he got home.
pitch up [*phrasal verb*] *Brit, informal* : to appear or arrive at a place • Several hundred fans *pitched up* [=*showed up*] at the hotel to welcome the team.

[3]**pitch** *noun* [*noncount*]
1 : a thick, black, sticky substance that is used on roofs, boats, etc., to keep out water • ships sealed/coated with *pitch* • The night sky was ***as black/dark as pitch***. [=extremely black/dark]
2 : a sticky substance that is produced by some trees (such as pines trees) • pine *pitch*
– compare [1]PITCH

pitch–black /ˈpɪʧˈblæk/ *adj* : very dark or black • It's already *pitch-black* outside. • *pitch-black* hair

pitch–dark /ˈpɪʧˈdɑɚk/ *adj* : very dark • It's *pitch-dark* outside.

pitched /ˈpɪʧt/ *adj* : not flat : having a slope • a *pitched* roof

pitched battle *noun, pl* ~ **battles** [*count*]
1 : a major battle that is fought by large groups of soldiers
2 : a long argument or fight between people who have become very angry or emotional • She has been in a *pitched battle* with her ex-husband over custody of their children.

[1]**pitch·er** /ˈpɪʧɚ/ *noun, pl* **-ers** [*count*] : the player who throws the ball to the batter in baseball — see also RELIEF PITCHER — compare [2]PITCHER

[2]**pitcher** *noun, pl* **-ers** [*count*] *US*
1 : a container with a lip and handle that is used for holding and pouring out liquids • a *pitcher* of beer — called also (*Brit*) *jug*; see picture at PLACE SETTING
2 : the amount held by a pitcher • We drank a *pitcher* of water.
3 *Brit* : JUG
– compare [1]PITCHER

[1]**pitch·fork** /ˈpɪʧˌfoɚk/ *noun, pl* **-forks** [*count*] : a tool that has two or three long, thin metal bars on a long handle and that is used for lifting hay

[2]**pitchfork** *verb* **-forks; -forked; -fork·ing** [+ *obj*]
1 : to lift and throw (something) with a pitchfork • The farmer *pitchforked* the hay onto the truck.
2 *Brit, informal* : to force (someone) into a situation or position suddenly or without preparation — usually used as *(be) pitchforked* • He *was pitchforked* into the job.

pitchfork

pitch·man /ˈpɪʧmən/ *noun, pl* **-men** /-mən/ [*count*] *US* : a man whose job is to talk about something (such as a product) in order to persuade people to buy or accept it • a former star athlete who now works as a *pitchman* on TV

pitch·out /ˈpɪʧˌaʊt/ *noun, pl* **-outs** [*count*] *baseball* : a pitch that is deliberately thrown far from the batter so that the catcher can catch the ball and throw it quickly to a base to try to put out a runner

pitch–per·fect /ˈpɪʧˈpɚfɪkt/ *adj* : having exactly the right tone or style • a *pitch-perfect* performance

pitch shot *noun, pl* ~ **shots** [*count*] *golf* : a high shot that is made from an area near the green • She hit a *pitch shot* onto the green. — called also *pitch*

pitch·wom·an /ˈpɪʧˌwʊmən/ *noun, pl* **-wom·en** /-ˌwɪmən/ [*count*] *US* : a woman whose job is to talk about something (such as a product) in order to persuade people to buy or accept it • a celebrity *pitchwoman*

pit·e·ous /ˈpɪtijəs/ *adj* [*more* ~; *most* ~] *literary* : deserving or causing feelings of sympathy or pity • a *piteous* tale • The child cried out in a *piteous* voice.
– **pit·e·ous·ly** *adv*

pit·fall /ˈpɪtˌfɑːl/ *noun, pl* **-falls** [*count*] : a danger or problem that is hidden or not obvious at first — usually plural; often + *of* • I warned him about the (hidden) *pitfalls of* online dating.

pith /ˈpɪθ/ *noun* [*noncount*]
1 : the white covering that is found under the skin of oranges, lemons, etc.
2 : the most important part of something — often + *of* • the *pith of* the matter

pit·head /ˈpɪtˌhɛd/ *noun, pl* **-heads** [*count*] *chiefly Brit* : the top of a coal mine and the area and buildings around it

pith helmet *noun, pl* ~ **-mets** [*count*] : a light, hard hat that is worn for protection from the sun in hot countries

pithy /ˈpɪθi/ *adj* **pith·i·er; -est** [*also more* ~; *most* ~]
1 : using few words in a clever and effective way • The critic gave the film a *pithy* review. • The book is filled with *pithy* sayings about love and loss. • a *pithy* little Mother's Day card ***synonyms*** see CONCISE
2 : resembling or having a lot of pith • a white, *pithy* substance
– **pith·i·ly** /ˈpɪθəli/ *adv*

piti·able /ˈpɪtijəbəl/ *adj* [*more* ~; *most* ~] *formal* : deserving pity or sympathy : PITIFUL • a *pitiable* orphan
– **piti·ably** /ˈpɪtijəbli/ *adv*

piti·ful /ˈpɪtɪfəl/ *adj* [*more* ~; *most* ~]
1 : deserving or causing feelings of pity or sympathy • a *pitiful* lost dog • the child's *pitiful* cries
2 : causing feelings of dislike or disgust by not being enough or not being good enough • a *pitiful* [=very small] amount of money • a *pitiful* excuse • She made a *pitiful* attempt to complete her work.
– **piti·ful·ly** *adv* • a *pitifully* sad story • a *pitifully* small amount of money

piti·less /ˈpɪtɪləs/ *adj* [*more* ~; *most* ~]
1 : very cruel : having or showing no pity • a *pitiless* [=*merciless*] ruler/critic • The soldiers were *pitiless* toward their enemy.
2 : very harsh or severe • the *pitiless* desert heat • a *pitiless* storm
– **piti·less·ly** *adv* • *pitilessly* cruel

pi·ton /ˈpiːˌtɑːn/ *noun, pl* **-tons** [*count*] : a pointed piece of metal used in rock climbing that is hammered into a crack in the rock in order to hold the rope which is attached to the climber

pit stop *noun, pl* ~ **stops** [*count*]
1 : a stop for fuel and minor repairs during a car race
2 *US, informal* **a** : a short stop during a journey for rest, food, or to use a bathroom • We made a *pit stop* for some food before getting back on the highway. **b** : a place for

P

making such a stop • This little town is an ideal *pit stop* between the two cities.

pitta *Brit spelling of* PITA

pit·tance /ˈpɪtn̩s/ *noun, pl* **-tanc·es** [*count*] **:** a very small amount of money — usually singular • For all her work, she only made a *pittance.* • He bought the car for a *pittance.*

pitted *adj*
1 *of a fruit* **:** with the pit removed • *pitted* olives/dates
2 [*more ~; most ~*] **:** having many small holes or dents **:** having many pits • the *pitted* surface of the bowl • a man with *pitted* and scarred cheeks

pit·ter–pat·ter /ˈpɪtɚˌpætɚ/ *noun* [*singular*] **:** a quick series of light sounds — often *+ of* • the *pitter-patter of* little feet • the *pitter-patter* of the rain
– pit·ter–pat·ter /ˌpɪtɚˈpætɚ/ *adv* • His feet went *pitter-patter* up the stairs.

pitting *noun* [*noncount*] **:** small holes or dents on a surface • The car's paint showed some *pitting* from flying gravel. • Her face had some minor *pitting* from the chicken pox.

pi·tu·i·tary /pəˈtu:wəˌteri, *Brit* pəˈtju:wətri/ *noun, pl* **-taries** [*count*] *medical* **:** a small organ in the brain that produces hormones and influences growth and development — called also *pituitary gland*

¹pity /ˈpɪti/ *noun*
1 [*noncount*] **:** a strong feeling of sadness or sympathy for someone or something • She has had a hard life and deserves your *pity.* • I felt deep *pity* for the lost dog.
2 [*singular*] **:** something that causes sadness or disappointment • It's a *pity* [=*shame*] you can't go. = *Pity* (that) you can't go. [=I'm sorry that you can't go] • I'll be out of town on that day—a (great) *pity,* since I'd love to see you. • He didn't live to see his daughter grow up, and that's a *pity.*
more's the pity **:** UNFORTUNATELY — used to say that something is disappointing • "Did you get to see her before she left?" "No, *more's the pity.*" [=I regret that I didn't get to see her]
take pity on **:** to feel pity for (a person or animal) and do something to help • I *took pity on* the stray cat and fed him.

²pity *verb* **pit·ies; pit·ied; pity·ing** [*+ obj*] **:** to feel pity for (someone or something) **:** to feel sorry for (someone or something) • I *pity* anyone who has to work at that place.

pitying *adj* [*more ~; most ~*] **:** showing or expressing pity for someone or something • a *pitying* look/smile

¹piv·ot /ˈpɪvət/ *noun, pl* **-ots**
1 [*count*] **:** a pin or shaft on which a mechanical part turns
2 [*count*] **:** the action of turning around a point **:** the action of pivoting — usually singular • The quarterback made a quick *pivot* [=*turn*] and threw the ball to the running back.
3 [*count*] **:** a person or thing that is central or important to someone or something else — usually singular • Their children had become the *pivot* around which their life turned.
4 [*noncount*] *basketball* **:** a position in which a player on offense faces away from the basket to pass to or assist other teammates trying to score • Their center is a strong player ***in the pivot***.

²pivot *verb* **-ots; -ot·ed; -ot·ing** [*no obj*] **:** to turn on or around a central point • The dancers *pivoted* on their toes and changed direction. • The door hinge *pivots* around the pin. • The quarterback *pivoted* and threw the ball to the running back.
pivot on/around [*phrasal verb*] ***pivot on/around (something)*** **:** to be based on (something) • Our vacation plans will *pivot around* how much money we can save. • The book's plot *pivots on* the main character's need for revenge.

piv·ot·al /ˈpɪvətl/ *adj* [*more ~; most ~*] **:** very important • She is at a *pivotal* point in her career. • a *pivotal* [=*critical*] moment/decision

piv·ot·man /ˈpɪvətˌmæn/ *noun, pl* **-men** /-ˌmɛn/ [*count*] *basketball* **:** a player who plays in the pivot **:** the center on a team

pix *plural of* PIC

pix·el /ˈpɪksəl/ *noun, pl* **-els** [*count*] **:** any one of the very small dots that together form the picture on a television screen, computer monitor, etc.

pix·e·lat·ed *also* **pix·i·lat·ed** /ˈpɪksəˌleɪtəd/ *adj, of an image on a computer or television screen* **:** made up of a small number of large pixels that produce a picture which is not clear or sharp • a heavily *pixelated* image

pix·ie *also* **pixy** /ˈpɪksi/ *noun, pl* **pix·ies** [*count*] **:** an imaginary creature that looks like a small person and has magical powers

piz·za /ˈpi:tsə/ *noun, pl* **-zas :** a food made from flat, usually round bread that is topped with usually tomato sauce and cheese and often with meat or vegetables [*count*] We ordered a *pizza* for supper. [*noncount*] I ordered *pizza* for supper. • a slice of pepperoni/cheese *pizza* — called also *pizza pie*

piz·zazz *or* **pi·zazz** /pəˈzæz/ *noun* [*noncount*] *informal* **:** a quality or style that is exciting and interesting • The young actress has a lot of *pizzazz.* • The song has plenty of *pizzazz.*

piz·ze·ria /ˌpi:tsəˈri:jə/ *noun, pl* **-rias** [*count*] **:** a restaurant where mainly pizzas are served

piz·zi·ca·to /ˌpɪtsɪˈkɑ:toʊ/ *adv* — used as a direction in music to indicate that notes should be played by plucking the strings of a violin, viola, cello, etc., with the fingers instead of by using a bow • The section should be played *pizzicato.*
– pizzicato *adj* • a *pizzicato* solo

pj's /ˈpi:ˌʤeɪz/ *noun* [*plural*] *informal* **:** PAJAMAS

pkg. *abbr* package

pkt *abbr* packet

pkwy *abbr* parkway

pl. *abbr* **1** place **2** plural

plac·ard /ˈplækəd/ *noun, pl* **-ards** [*count*] **:** a large notice or sign put up in a public place or carried by people • The *placard* on the door says that the church was built in the late 1600s. • protesters carrying *placards*

pla·cate /ˈpleɪˌkeɪt, *Brit* pləˈkeɪt/ *verb* **-cates; -cat·ed; -cat·ing** [*+ obj*] *formal* **:** to cause (someone) to feel less angry about something • The administration *placated* protesters by agreeing to consider their demands. • The angry customer was not *placated* by the clerk's apology.

¹place /ˈpleɪs/ *noun, pl* **plac·es**
1 [*count*] **:** a specific area or region of the world **:** a particular city, country, etc. • Please state your *place* of birth and your current *place* of residence. [=where you were born and where you live now] • New York City is a nice *place* to visit, but I wouldn't want to live there. • I've heard it's a good *place* to raise children. • *places* like Africa and South America • traveling to distant/exotic/faraway/remote *places* • the hottest *place* on earth
2 [*count*] **:** a building or area that is used for a particular purpose • churches and other *places* of worship • a *place* of learning/business • You should plan to meet him in a public *place.* • a local gathering/meeting *place* • Muslim holy *places* • ancient burial *places* • We had dinner at a great little Italian *place* [=*restaurant*] downtown. • He tried several *places* [=*stores*], but no one sold the ingredients he needed. • You've come to the right *place.* I have just what you need. • This bar is ***the place to be*** [=it is where many people go and where exciting things happen] on Saturday nights.
3 [*count*] **a :** a building, part of a building, or area that is used for shelter • They gave him a *place* to stay for the night. **b :** a house, apartment, etc., where a person lives **:** HOME • We're going to need a bigger *place* once the baby is born. • He's looking to buy a *place* in the country. • Shall we go to my *place* or yours? • our summer *place*
4 [*count*] **:** a particular space or area • This looks like a good *place* [=*location, spot*] to stop and rest. • It's nice to have the whole family together in one *place.* • Keep your jewelry and other valuables in a safe *place.* • The map is torn in (some) *places.* [=some parts of the map are torn] • The bone in her leg broke in two *places.* • Try looking for the phrase in another *place* in the dictionary. • A person can only be in one *place* at one time. • The guards/chairs were not in their proper *places.* • Wires carry the information ***from place to place***. = They carry it ***from one place to another***. • Success is sometimes just a matter of being in ***the right place at the right time***. • You were just unlucky; you happened to be at ***the wrong place at the wrong time***. — sometimes used figuratively • She keeps a special *place* in her heart for mistreated animals. • When I left the army, I was in a very strange *place* mentally. [=I was in a very strange mental state] — see also HIDING PLACE, RESTING PLACE
5 [*count*] **:** a particular point that you reach in a discussion, book, etc. — usually singular • This seems like a good *place* to end our discussion for today. • He used the receipt to keep/mark his *place* in the book he was reading. • She dropped the magazine on the floor and ***lost her place***.
6 [*count*] **:** an available seat, space, or amount of room • There's no *place* to sit down. • I found a *place* to put my things. • They didn't have a good *place* for the painting in their apartment. • If you get to the theater before me, could you save me a *place*? • "Excuse me, is this *place* taken?" "Yes,

I'm saving it for my friend." • She said she couldn't see the stage and asked if he would change/trade/swap/switch *places* with her. • During the ceremony, he was given a ***place of honor*** [=a seat for someone who is being honored] next to the president's wife. • We'll have to ***make a place*** [=make a space available; make room] for our guests. • We *made a place* for you at the dinner table.

7 [*count*] **: a particular position in a line especially of people or vehicles** • I had to use the bathroom, but I didn't want to lose my *place* in line. • Would you save/hold our *places* (in line), please?

8 [*count*] **: a particular position during or at the end of a race or competition — usually singular** • The runner from the U.S. is currently in third *place*. • Their horse finished in last *place*. • The two teams are tied for second *place*. • "Who took first *place*?" "First *place* went to the red team."

9 [*count*] **a : a position in a group, course, organization, school, etc.** • They offered her a *place* [=*job*] on their staff. • He started getting bad grades and lost his *place* on the basketball team. [=he was no longer allowed to be on the team] • She was guaranteed a *place* in the college. • There are two *places* still open in the course/class. • He has friends ***in high places*** [=friends who have power and influence] **— often used figuratively** • Her courage during the war earned her a *place* in history. [=she is remembered as an important person in history because of her courage during the war] • She has an important *place* in the community. [=she is an important part of the community] • He occupies a prominent *place* among the great musicians of our time. **b : the proper position of someone in a group or society** • The queen's servants must know their *place* and act accordingly. [=they must act like servants] • It's not my *place* [=it is not appropriate for me] to punish other people's children. • It was not his *place* to make the final decision.

10 a [*singular*] **: an appropriate situation or setting** • There's a time and a *place* for everything. • This is neither the time nor the *place* to talk about money. **b** [*count*] **: a particular situation or set of conditions** • Call me if you ever find yourself in a tight *place*. • Anyone in her *place* [=*position*] would have done the same thing. • I love my life and wouldn't ***change/trade/swap/switch places*** with anyone in the world!

11 [*count*] *mathematics* **: the position of a digit in a number** • In the number 316, the digit 1 is in the tens *place*. • Move the decimal point two *places* to the right. • a number with three ***decimal places*** [=a number with three digits that follow the decimal point; a number like 2.345 or .678] • In the number 2.468, the 4 is in the first *decimal place*.

12 — used in the names of streets • He lives at 313 Jackson *Place*.

all over the place *informal* **1 : in many different areas or locations : EVERYWHERE** • New houses are springing up *all over the place* in that part of the country. • The kids left their toys *all over the place*. • Bullets were flying *all over the place*. **2 : not organized in a logical way** • Your essay lacks organization; your ideas are *all over the place*.

between a rock and a hard place see [2]ROCK

fall into place see [1]FALL

give place to (something) *formal* **: to be replaced by (something)** • Confidence *gave place to* [=(more commonly) *gave way to*] fear. • Further down the street, tall office buildings *give place to* rows of tidy houses.

go places **: to become successful** • She has enough ambition to really *go places*. • The band is clearly *going places*.

keep (someone) in his/her place **: to prevent (someone) from achieving a higher social status** • Such social rules were used to *keep* women *in their place*.

in place **1 : in the proper position** • He makes sure that every hair on his head is *in place* before leaving the house. • Tape held/kept the photo *in place*. • The house's walls are *in place*, but nothing else has been done. • With all the performers *in place*, we were ready to rehearse. **2 : in the state of being used or active** • The new computer system should be *in place* by next Monday. • These changes were already *in place* when the new president took office. • Plans are *in place* for the upcoming hurricane season. **3** *US* **: in the same location without moving forward or backward.** • To warm up before swimming practice, we run *in place* [=(*Brit*) *on the spot*] for five minutes.

in place of (someone or something) *or* ***in someone's or something's place*** **: as a substitute or replacement for someone or something** • Use milk *in place of* [=*instead of*] water for creamier hot chocolate. • *In place of* butter, olive oil was served with the bread. • The prince ruled the kingdom *in place of* his father. = The prince ruled the kingdom *in* his father's *place*. • She couldn't attend the meeting, so she sent her secretary *in* her *place*.

***in the first place* — used at the end of a sentence to indicate what was true or what should have been done at the beginning of a situation** • We should never have gone there *in the first place*. [=*to begin with*] • I didn't care much for the job *in the first place*.

***in the first/second place* — used when listing the most important parts of something or the most important reasons for something** • I'm not going to tell you because, *in the first place*, it's none of your business, and *in the second place*, you would tell everyone else.

into place **1 : into the proper position** • She lowered her glasses then pushed them back *into place*. **2 : into the state of being used or active** • The curfew was ***put into place*** [=was established] by the town's mayor. • The plan will be *put into place* over the course of several months.

***no place for* — used to say that someone or something does not belong in a particular place, situation, etc.** • This party is *no place for* children. [=children should not be allowed at this party] • There is *no place for* racism in our society.

***of all places* — used to say that it is unusual or surprising that something happened in or is true about a particular place** • She met her future husband in a grocery store, *of all places*.

out of place **1 : not in the correct location or position** • Nothing in the room was *out of place*. **2 : not in a typical or appropriate situation or setting** • Their modern style home seems oddly *out of place* among the town's old farmhouses. • She wouldn't look *out of place* on the cover of a fashion magazine. • I feel a bit *out of place* [=I feel like I don't belong] with my wife's family. • The law seems particularly *out of place* in today's society.

place in the sun see [1]SUN

pride of place see [1]PRIDE

put someone in his/her place ✧ **Someone who *puts you in your place* shows you that you are not better than other people and should not be acting in such a confident and proud way.** • He told her to stop talking, but she quickly *put him in his place*.

take place **: to happen** • The wedding is set to *take place* this July. • Negotiations are now *taking place* between the two governments. • He didn't understand what had just *taken place*. • Where does the story ***take place***? [=where is the story set?]

take someone's or something's place *or* ***take the place of (someone or something)*** **: to replace someone or something** • Who will *take the king's place* when he dies? • We solved the original problem, but now a new one has *taken its place*. • I was too busy to attend the meeting, so I had my secretary *take my place*. • Who will *take the place of* the current pope? • Televisions began to *take the place of* radios in most families' homes.

take your place **1 : to go to the location where you are supposed to sit, stand, etc.** • The goalie *took her place* on the field. • The actors *take their places* on the stage and the curtain rises. • (*chiefly Brit*) Ladies and gentlemen, please *take your places*. [=(*US*) *take your seats*] The play is about to begin. **2 : to be thought of or considered as sharing a particular rank or status with others** • He has *taken his place* among/alongside/beside/with history's most brutal dictators. • The film will surely *take its place* among the greatest films of all time. [=will be recognized as one of the greatest films of all time] • The hurricane will *take its place* in history as one of this country's worst natural disasters.

[2]**place** *verb* **places; placed; plac•ing**

1 [+ *obj*] **: to put (something or someone) in a particular place or position** • Please *place* [=*set, lay*] the book on my desk. • She *placed* [=*rested*] her hand on his shoulder. • The box was *placed* at the center of the room. • You can really see the similarities when you *place* the two pictures side by side. • Her name was *placed* on the list. • The husbands and wives were *placed* in separate groups. • New flowers had been *placed* [=*positioned*] around the edges of the garden. • They were *placed* next to each other in line.

2 [+ *obj*] **: to put (someone or something) in a particular state, condition, or situation** • Working with sick people *places* him at risk for infection. • By not accepting the prosecutor's deal, he *places* his future in the hands of the jury. • We're *placing* you under arrest. • He was released from jail and *placed* on probation.

3 [+ *obj*] **a — used to say that something is thought of as**

important, valuable, etc.; + *on* or *upon* ▪ They *place* great importance *on* both work and family. [=they believe that both work and family are important] ▪ She talked about the high value that her parents *place on* education. ▪ Some parents *place* a lot of emphasis *on* winning, but we just want our children to have fun playing sports. **b — used to say who or what you believe should be trusted, blamed, etc.** ▪ We have no choice but to *place* our faith in the legal system. [=to trust the legal system] ▪ Too many children in this country are overweight, and I *place* most of the blame on a lack of exercise. [=I blame the problem on a lack of exercise] ▪ Their plan *places* heavy reliance [=their plan relies heavily] upon cooperation from others.

4 [+ *obj*] **: to cause or require someone or something to deal with (a demand, burden, etc.) — + *on* or *upon*** ▪ The growing population is *placing* increasing demands *on* our schools. [=it is causing our schools to deal with increasing demands] ▪ The financial burden of the program is ultimately *placed upon* the taxpayers. [=the taxpayers have to pay for the program] ▪ He managed to get a lot done, considering the time constraints that were *placed on* him. ▪ restrictions *placed upon* a person's freedom

5 [+ *obj*] **a : to perform the actions that are required for (something)** ▪ He *placed* a collect (phone) call to his wife. ▪ ***Place your bets.*** **b : to give (an order) to someone** ▪ The company *placed* an order (with the manufacturer) for an additional 100 units. ▪ "Are you ready to *place* your order?" asked the waiter. **c : to cause (something, such as an advertisement) to appear somewhere** ▪ We tried selling our house by *placing* an ad in the newspaper.

6 [+ *obj*] **: to find an appropriate place for (someone) to live, work, or learn** ▪ The agency helps *place* unemployed workers. ▪ The child was removed from the home and *placed* in the care of relatives. ▪ The children were *placed* with a foster family. ▪ In high school, she was *placed* in advanced math and science classes.

7 [+ *obj*] **: to show or prove the location of (someone or something) at a particular time** ▪ The evidence *places* you at the scene of the crime. ▪ Investigators were able to *place* him at several of these meetings. ▪ The company's records *place* three of their trucks in the area that day.

8 [+ *obj*] **: to remember where you saw (someone or someone's face) in the past** ▪ The man looked familiar but she couldn't quite *place* him. ▪ It wasn't until later that I *placed* her face: she was my ninth grade English teacher, Ms. Lee.

9 a [*no obj*] *US* **: to end a race or competition in a particular position** ▪ He *placed* fifth in last year's race. ▪ The team *placed* second overall. ▪ The first three participants to *place* in each event will receive medals. **b** *Brit* ✧ **Someone who *is placed* first, second, (etc.) in a race or competition has finished in that position.** ▪ He *was placed* fifth in last year's race. ▪ The team *was placed* second overall.

10 [+ *obj*] **: to give (someone or something) a particular rank in a series or category** ▪ Tolstoy's *War and Peace* is often *placed* [=*ranked, rated*] among the greatest masterpieces of world literature. ▪ Among the most serious problems facing the world, global warming is often *placed* first. ▪ The administration *places* [=*puts, sets*] improving the country's health-care system high on their list of priorities.

pla·ce·bo /plə'siːboʊ/ *noun, pl* **-bos** [*count*] *medicine* **: a pill or substance that is given to a patient like a drug but that has no physical effect on the patient** ✧ **Patients who have been given a placebo that they think is a real drug may feel better because they believe that they are getting actual medicine. The improvement that they experience in their health is called the *placebo effect*. Placebos are also used in tests to compare the effect of a real drug with a substance that does not have any physical effect.**

place·kick /'pleɪsˌkɪk/ *noun, pl* **-kicks** [*count*] **: a kick that is made in sports like American football and rugby when the ball has been put on the ground or is being held on the ground**

— place·kick·er /'pleɪsˌkɪkɚ/ *noun, pl* **-ers** [*count*] *chiefly US*

place mat *noun, pl* **~ mats** [*count*] **: a small, often rectangular mat on which a set of dishes, knives, forks, etc., for one person are placed at a table — see picture at** PLACE SETTING

place·ment /'pleɪsmənt/ *noun, pl* **-ments**

1 : the act of putting something in a particular place [*noncount*] the strategic *placement* of products at the entrance of a store ▪ the *placement* of microphones around the room [*count*] The director tried several different camera *placements* for the scene.

2 [*noncount*] **: the act of finding an appropriate place for someone to live, work, or learn** ▪ The agency has overseen the *placement* of hundreds of children in loving homes. ▪ the *placement* of unemployed workers **— often used before another noun** ▪ We give all applicants *placement* tests to determine their level of proficiency. ▪ job *placement* programs

place name *noun, pl* **~ names** [*count*] **: the name of a city, town, lake, country, etc.** ▪ Many of the area's *place names* come from Native American languages.

pla·cen·ta /plə'sɛntə/ *noun, pl* **-tas** [*count*] *medical* **: the organ in mammals that forms inside the mother's uterus, nourishes the unborn baby, and is pushed out of the mother after the birth of the baby**

— pla·cen·tal /plə'sɛntl/ *adj, always used before a noun* ▪ *placental* blood ▪ the *placental* membrane

place setting *noun, pl* **~ -tings** [*count*] **: a set of dishes, knives, forks, etc., that are put on a table for one person** ▪ Please lay another *place setting* for our guest.

plac·id /'plæsəd/ *adj* [*more ~; most ~*]

1 : not easily upset or excited ▪ a person with a sunny, *placid* disposition

2 : not moving much : calm and steady ▪ the *placid* surface of the lake

— pla·cid·i·ty /plə'sɪdəti/ *noun* [*noncount*] ▪ the *placidity* of the quiet morning **— plac·id·ly** *adv*

plac·ing /'pleɪsɪŋ/ *noun, pl* **-ings** [*count*] *Brit* **:** RANKING

P

place setting

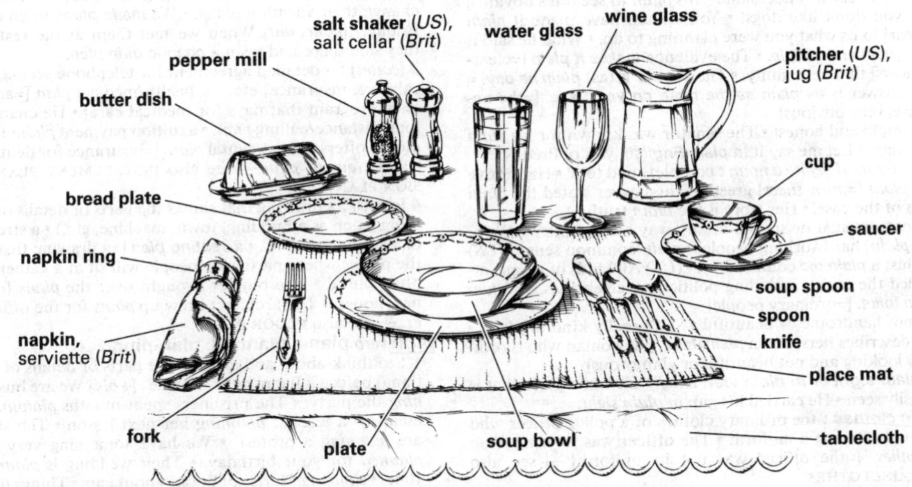

pla·gia·rism /ˈpleɪʤəˌrɪzəm/ *noun* [*noncount*] **:** the act of using another person's words or ideas without giving credit to that person **:** the act of plagiarizing something • The student has been accused of *plagiarism*.
– pla·gia·rist /ˈpleɪʤərɪst/ *noun, pl* **-rists** [*count*] • The student is accused of being a *plagiarist*.

pla·gia·rize *also Brit* **pla·gia·rise** /ˈpleɪʤəˌraɪz/ *verb* **-riz·es; -rized; -riz·ing :** to use the words or ideas of another person as if they were your own words or ideas [+ *obj*] He *plagiarized* a classmate's report. [*no obj*] She *plagiarized* from an article she read on the Internet.

[1]**plague** /ˈpleɪg/ *noun, pl* **plagues**
1 [*count*] *old-fashioned* **:** a large number of harmful or annoying things • The country was hit by a *plague* of natural disasters that year. • a *plague of* locusts • There has been a *plague of* bank robberies in the area.
2 a : a disease that causes death and that spreads quickly to a large number of people [*count*] a *plague* that swept through the tribe in the 1600s [*noncount*] a time of *plague*
b [*noncount*] **:** BUBONIC PLAGUE • an outbreak of (the) *plague*
avoid (someone or something) like the plague *informal* **:** to stay away as much as possible from (someone or something) • I *avoid* my weird neighbor *like the plague*.

[2]**plague** *verb* **plagues; plagued; plagu·ing** [+ *obj*]
1 : to cause constant or repeated trouble, illness, etc., for (someone or something) • parasites that *plague* deer • Computer viruses *plague* Internet users. • Crime *plagues* the inner city. • Drought and wildfires continue to *plague* the area. — often used as *(be) plagued* • The new plane has *been plagued* by/with mechanical problems. [=has had many mechanical problems] • an athlete *plagued* by knee injuries
2 : to cause constant worry or distress to (someone) — usually used as *(be) plagued* • He *is plagued* by a sense of guilt. • She *is plagued* by fear of another terrorist attack. • I *was plagued* with doubts about my decision.

plaice /ˈpleɪs/ *noun, pl* **plaice** [*count, noncount*] **:** a fish that has a flat body and that is eaten as food

plaid /ˈplæd/ *noun, pl* **plaids**
1 [*noncount*] **:** a pattern on cloth of stripes with different widths that cross each other to form squares — often used before another noun • a *plaid* pattern • a *plaid* shirt — see color picture on page C12
2 ***plaids*** [*plural*] *US* **:** clothes with plaid patterns • She likes to wear *plaids*.
3 [*count*] **:** a woolen cloth with a plaid pattern that is worn over the shoulder as part of the Scottish national costume

[1]**plain** /ˈpleɪn/ *adj* **plain·er; -est** [*also more ~; most ~*]
1 : having no pattern or decoration • Her dress was *plain*. • a *plain* fabric • It was a *plain* room with no curtains. • She was wearing *plain* black shoes. • He printed the picture on *plain* paper.
2 : not having any added or extra things • a glass of *plain* [=*pure*] water • a piece of *plain* chicken • *plain* yogurt • You don't have to call me Mr. Johnson—just *plain* Fred will be fine. • (*Brit*) The recipe calls for 250 grams of ***plain flour***. [=(*US*) all-purpose flour]
3 : easy to see or understand • It's *plain* to see [=it's obvious] that you don't like dogs. • You should have made it *plain* [=*clear*] to us what you were planning to do. • What he said is a lie, ***plain and simple***. • The evidence ***makes it plain*** [=clearly shows] that he is guilty. • The answer is (as) ***plain as day***. = The answer is ***as plain as the nose on your face***. [=the answer is very obvious]
4 : simple and honest • The senator was known for his *plain* speaking. • Let me say it in ***plain English***: you're fired.
5 *always used before a noun* **:** complete and total • His motive was *plain* [=*pure, sheer*] greed. • The lawyer stated the *plain* facts of the case. • Her story is the *plain* truth.
6 : not unusual or special in any way **:** ORDINARY • We're just *plain*, hardworking people. • *plain* common sense • (*US*) I'm just a ***plain old*** country boy. • (*US*) All kinds of people attended the event, including politicians, celebrities, and ***just plain folks***. [=ordinary people]
7 : not handsome or beautiful • She's really kind of *plain*. • She describes herself as a ***plain Jane***. [=a woman who is ordinary looking and not beautiful or glamorous]
in plain sight or ***in plain view*** *chiefly US* **:** in a place that is easily seen • He carried his gun *in plain sight*.
plain clothes **:** the ordinary clothes of a police officer who is not wearing a uniform • The officer was wearing *plain clothes*. [=the officer was not in uniform] — see also PLAINCLOTHES
plain sailing see SAILING
– plain·ly *adv* • The camp is for kids who like sports, which he *plainly* [=*obviously, definitely*] does. • The star was *plainly* [=*clearly*] visible in the sky toward the north. • The book states quite *plainly* [=*openly, simply*] that he was part of the plot. • She always dresses *plainly*. **– plain·ness** *noun* [*noncount*] • the *plainness* of her clothes

[2]**plain** *noun, pl* **plains** [*count*] **:** a large area of flat land without trees • the Spanish *plain* • the Great *Plains* of the United States

[3]**plain** *adv, informal* **:** truly or completely • Her answer was misleading, if not *plain* dishonest. — used to make a statement or description more forceful • She *plain* forgot to call me. • You are ***just plain*** wrong.

plain chocolate *noun* [*noncount*] *Brit* **:** DARK CHOCOLATE

plain·clothes /ˈpleɪnˈkloʊz/ *adj, always used before a noun* **:** dressed in ordinary clothes and not a uniform while on duty • a *plainclothes* police officer — see also *plain clothes* at [1]PLAIN

plain·clothes·man /ˈpleɪnˈkloʊzmən/ *noun, pl* **-men** /-mən/ [*count*] **:** a police officer who does not wear a uniform while on duty

plain·spo·ken /ˈpleɪnˈspoʊkən/ *adj* [*more ~; most ~*] **:** expressing opinions, ideas, beliefs, etc., in a simple and honest way • a *plainspoken* man • *plainspoken* eloquence

plain·tiff /ˈpleɪntəf/ *noun, pl* **-tiffs** [*count*] *law* **:** a person who sues another person or accuses another person of a crime in a court of law — compare DEFENDANT

plain·tive /ˈpleɪntɪv/ *adj* [*more ~; most ~*] *formal* **:** expressing suffering or sadness **:** having a sad sound • a *plaintive* [=*mournful, sorrowful*] sigh • We could hear the *plaintive* cry of a wounded animal in the woods.
– plain·tive·ly *adv*

plain–vanilla *adj, chiefly US, informal* **:** not having any special features or qualities • We bought the *plain-vanilla* CD player. [=the most basic model]

[1]**plait** /ˈpleɪt, *Brit* ˈplæt/ *verb* **plaits; plait·ed; plait·ing** [+ *obj*] *chiefly Brit* **:** to twist together three pieces of (hair, rope, etc.) **:** BRAID • My mum taught me how to *plait* my own hair.

[2]**plait** *noun, pl* **plaits** [*count*] *chiefly Brit* **:** an arrangement of hair made by weaving three sections together **:** BRAID • She wore her hair in *plaits*.

[1]**plan** /ˈplæn/ *noun, pl* **plans**
1 : a set of actions that have been thought of as a way to do or achieve something [*count*] the President's economic *plan* • the army's *plan* of attack • We need to agree on a ***plan of action***. — often + *for* • The partners created a business *plan for* their new store. • The city has a ten-year *plan for* fixing the city's roads. [*noncount*] Not everything at the show went ***according to plan***. [=the way it was supposed to] — see also GAME PLAN, MASTER PLAN
2 : something that a person intends to do [*count*] Our *plan* was to have the guests park on the street, not the lawn. — often plural • We would love to have dinner at your house Friday night, but we already have *plans*. [=we are already planning/expecting to do something else] • They didn't want to change their vacation *plans*. • We ***made plans*** to go out this Friday. [*noncount*] When we met them at the restaurant, they said there had been a ***change of/in plan***.
3 [*count*] **:** a detailed agreement for telephone service, medical care, insurance, etc. • a health/medical *plan* [=an insurance program that pays for medical care] • He changed his long-distance/calling *plan*. • a tuition payment *plan* • Her employer offers a great dental *plan*. [=insurance for dental care] • a retirement *plan* — see also INSTALLMENT PLAN, PENSION PLAN
4 [*count*] **:** a drawing that shows the parts or details of something (such as a building, town, machine, etc.) • a street *plan* of Washington, D.C. • a ***seating plan*** [=a drawing that shows the places where particular people will sit at a gathering] — often plural • The builder brought over the *plans* for their new house. • The architect drew up *plans* for the office tower. — see also FLOOR PLAN

[2]**plan** *verb* **plans; planned; plan·ning**
1 : to think about and arrange the parts or details of (something) before it happens or is made [+ *obj*] We are busy *planning* the party. • The prisoners spent months *planning* their escape. • a teacher *planning* her next lesson • The students are *planning* a protest. • We have something very special *planned* for your birthday. • Their wedding is *planned* for June. • a *planned* series of books about cars • Things don't al-

ways **go as planned**. — sometimes + *out* ▪ That crash was no accident. They had the whole thing *planned out* to get insurance money. ▪ They *planned* the whole thing *out*. ▪ You should first *plan out* your essay. [*no obj*] Always remember to **plan ahead**.

2 a : to intend or expect to do (something) [+ *obj*] — followed by *to + verb* ▪ She *plans to move out* and get a divorce. ▪ Please let us know if you *plan to attend*. [*no obj*] — followed by *on + -ing verb* ▪ We don't *plan on going* anywhere tonight. ▪ They *plan on coming* to the party. **b** [*no obj*] **:** to expect something to happen — + *for* or *on* ▪ They didn't *plan for* [=*anticipate*] such a long wait at the restaurant. ▪ She didn't *plan on* such cold weather.

[1]plane /ˈpleɪn/ *noun, pl* **planes**

1 : a vehicle that has wings and an engine and can carry people or things in the air **:** AIRPLANE [*count*] a cargo *plane* [*noncount*] We will be traveling to Rome by *plane*. — often used before another noun ▪ a *plane* crash/ride

2 [*count*] *geometry* **:** a flat or level surface that extends outward like a sheet ▪ a horizontal *plane*

3 [*count*] **:** a level of thought, existence, or development ▪ He uses meditation to reach a higher spiritual *plane*. ▪ I don't consider the two writers' stories as being on the same *plane*.

[2]plane *verb* **planes; planed; plan·ing** [+ *obj*] **:** to make (a piece of wood) smooth or level by cutting off thin pieces with a special tool (called a plane) ▪ He had to *plane* the edge of the door so it would close better.

[3]plane *noun, pl* **planes** [*count*] **:** a sharp tool that is pushed along a piece of wood to smooth or shape the surface — see picture at CARPENTRY

plane·load /ˈpleɪnˌloud/ *noun, pl* **-loads** [*count*] **:** an amount or number of people or things that will fill an airplane ▪ a *planeload* of troops

plan·er /ˈpleɪnɚ/ *noun, pl* **-ers** [*count*] **:** an electric tool that is used for smoothing the surface of a board

plan·et /ˈplænət/ *noun, pl* **-ets**

1 [*count*] **:** a large, round object in space (such as the Earth) that travels around a star (such as the sun)

2 ***the planet*** **:** the planet Earth ▪ We must help preserve *the planet*. = We must help preserve *the planet's* environment.

3 — used in informal phrases to say that someone is not aware of what is really happening or has ideas that are not realistic or practical ▪ You think they'll help us? Are you ***(living) on another planet***? ▪ ***What planet are you living on***? ▪ She looked at me as if I were ***someone from another planet***.

plan·e·tar·i·um /ˌplænəˈterijəm/ *noun, pl* **-i·ums** *or* **-ia** /-ijə/ [*count*] **:** a building or room in which images of stars, planets, etc., are shown on a high, curved ceiling

plan·e·tary /ˈplænəˌteri, *Brit* ˈplænətri/ *adj, always used before a noun, technical* **:** of or relating to planets ▪ a *planetary* system ▪ *planetary* motion/orbit

plan·gent /ˈplænʤənt/ *adj* [*more* ~; *most* ~] *formal + literary, of a sound* **:** loud, deep, and often sad ▪ a *plangent* tone/chord ▪ a *plangent* cry

plank /ˈplæŋk/ *noun, pl* **planks** [*count*]

1 : a long, thick board that is used especially in building something

2 *formal* **:** one of the official beliefs and goals of an organization (such as a political party) ▪ Before the convention, there was debate over the foreign policy and economic *planks*. — compare PLATFORM

walk the plank see [1]WALK

plank·ing /ˈplæŋkɪŋ/ *noun* [*noncount*] **:** heavy boards that are used to build something ▪ deck *planking*

plank·ton /ˈplæŋktən/ *noun* [*noncount*] **:** the very small animal and plant life in an ocean, lake, etc. ▪ fish that feed mainly on *plankton*

plan·ner /ˈplænɚ/ *noun, pl* **-ners** [*count*]

1 : a person who plans things; *especially* **:** a person whose job is to plan things for other people ▪ They hired a wedding *planner*. ▪ financial *planners*

2 : a person whose job is to plan the growth and development of a town or city ▪ City *planners* refused to approve a proposed shopping center.

planning *noun* [*noncount*] **:** the act or process of making a plan to achieve or do something ▪ financial/city/business *planning* ▪ Careful *planning* made the party a success.

[1]plant /ˈplænt/ *noun, pl* **plants** [*count*]

1 : a living thing that grows in the ground, usually has leaves or flowers, and needs sun and water to survive ▪ a cotton *plant* ▪ *plant* and animal life — see also HOUSEPLANT, POT PLANT

2 a : a building or factory where something is made ▪ an auto *plant* ▪ an ice-cream *plant* — see also POWER PLANT **b** *US* **:** the land, buildings, and equipment of an organization ▪ the college's ***physical plant***

3 a : something that is put in a place to trick or confuse people ▪ He claimed police left the glove at the crime scene as a *plant*. [=as false evidence to make it look like he committed the crime] **b :** a person who is put in a place as a spy or for a secret purpose ▪ The gangsters never suspected that he was a police *plant*.

– plant·like /ˈplæntˌlaɪk/ *adj* [*more* ~; *most* ~] ▪ *plantlike* organisms

[2]plant *verb* **plants; plant·ed; plant·ing** [+ *obj*]

1 a : to put (a seed, flower, or plant) in the ground to grow ▪ He *planted* the seeds. ▪ I *planted* corn this year. **b :** to fill (an area) *with* seeds, flowers, or plants ▪ I *planted* the border *with* roses. ▪ a field *planted with* corn

2 a : to put or place (something) in the ground ▪ She *planted* stakes in the garden to hold the vines. **b :** to put or place (something or yourself) firmly or forcefully on a surface or in a particular position ▪ He *planted* a punch on the other boxer's nose. [=he punched the other boxer's nose] ▪ She *planted* a big kiss on his cheek. [=she gave him a big kiss on his cheek] ▪ I firmly *planted* my feet and refused to move. ▪ He *planted* himself in front of the TV and stayed there.

3 a : to put (someone or something) in a place secretly ▪ Terrorists *planted* a bomb in the bus station. ▪ She claims that the police *planted* the drugs in her car. ▪ The police officers were accused of *planting* evidence at the scene. [=placing objects at the scene to make someone seem guilty of a crime] ▪ He was a spy *planted* in the office by a rival company. **b :** to cause (a story, rumor, etc.) to be reported or talked about usually for some secret purpose ▪ Someone *planted* a rumor saying that he had died. ▪ They *planted* a story in the press about her mental problems.

4 : to cause (an idea, feeling, etc.) to be in someone's mind ▪ She *planted* the first seeds of doubt in my mind. ▪ The story *planted* the idea of starting my own business in my mind. [=the story made me think of starting my own business]

[1]plan·tain /ˈplæntn̩/ *noun, pl* **-tains** [*count, noncount*] **:** a greenish fruit that comes from a kind of banana plant and is eaten after it has been cooked ▪ a fried *plantain* — compare [2]PLANTAIN

[2]plantain *noun, pl* **-tains** [*count*] **:** a common weed with leaves that grow near the ground and small greenish flowers — compare [1]PLANTAIN

plan·ta·tion /plænˈteɪʃən/ *noun, pl* **-tions** [*count*]

1 : a large area of land especially in a hot part of the world where crops (such as cotton) are grown ▪ a southern *plantation* ✧ Because slaves worked on cotton plantations in the southern U.S. in the past, the word *plantation* is often associated with the history of slavery in the U.S. ▪ He compared the situation of black college basketball players to the *plantation*. [=compared the college basketball system to slavery]

2 : a group of trees that have been planted together ▪ a *plantation* of pines

plant·er /ˈplæntɚ/ *noun, pl* **-ers** [*count*]

1 : a container in which plants are grown ▪ She bought a *planter* to put on their deck. ▪ a hanging *planter*

2 : a person who owns a plantation ▪ a wealthy South American *planter*

3 : a machine that plants seeds in the ground

plaque /ˈplæk/ *noun, pl* **plaques**

1 [*count*] **:** a flat, thin piece of metal or wood with writing on it that is used especially as a reminder of something (such as a historic event or an achievement) ▪ A bronze *plaque* marked the city's oldest building. ▪ They gave him a *plaque* in honor of his 30 years of service.

2 a [*noncount*] **:** a thin coating that forms on teeth and contains bacteria ▪ Brushing your teeth prevents the buildup of *plaque*. **b** [*count*] *medical* **:** a change in brain tissue that occurs in Alzheimer's disease ▪ The scientists are studying the way the *plaques* form. **c** [*noncount*] *medical* **:** a harmful material that can form in arteries and be a cause of heart disease

plas·ma /ˈplæzmə/ *noun, pl* **-mas**

1 [*noncount*] *medical* **:** the watery part of blood that contains blood cells

2 [*noncount*] *technical* **:** a substance that is similar to a gas but that can carry electricity ▪ the *plasma* that makes up a star

3 a [*noncount*] **:** a type of visual display for computers, televisions, etc., that uses plasma with electrical charges between two sheets of glass and that produces pictures that are very clear and bright — usually used before another noun • a *plasma* screen/TV **b** [*count*] : a television with a plasma screen • Our new TV is a 50-inch *plasma*.

[1]**plas•ter** /ˈplæstɚ, *Brit* ˈplɑːstə/ *noun, pl* **-ters**
1 [*noncount*] **a :** a wet substance that hardens when it becomes dry and that is used to make smooth walls and ceilings — often used before another noun • *plaster* walls **b :** PLASTER OF PARIS
2 [*count*] *Brit* **:** a piece of material that is put on the skin over a small wound
in plaster *Brit* **:** in a hard covering that protects a broken bone and allows it to heal : in a plaster cast • Her arm is *in plaster*.

[2]**plaster** *verb* **-ters; -tered; -ter•ing** [+ *obj*]
1 a : to cover (a surface) with plaster • We *plastered* and sanded the walls before painting them. **b :** to cover (a surface or area) *with* something • They *plastered* the walls *with* posters. — usually used as *(be) plastered* • The walls *were plastered with* posters. • The Web page *is plastered with* ads.
2 : to put (something, such as a poster or sign) *on* a surface • Someone had *plastered* a political poster *on* the wall. — often used figuratively • He had a silly smile *plastered on* his face. [=he was smiling in a silly way]
3 : to make (something) lie flat against or stick to something • His clothes were *plastered* to his body from the rain. • He *plastered* his hair down/back with gel.
plaster over [*phrasal verb*] ***plaster over (something) or plaster (something) over*** **:** to cover (something) with plaster • We *plastered over* the holes and cracks in the wall.

plas•ter•board /ˈplæstɚˌboɚd, *Brit* ˈplɑːstəˌbɔːd/ *noun* [*noncount*] **:** building material that is used for making walls and ceilings and that is made of large sheets of plaster covered with thick paper : DRYWALL

plaster cast *noun, pl* **~ casts** [*count*]
1 : [2]CAST 2 • She had a *plaster cast* on her leg.
2 : a copy of something made of plaster of paris • The mask was made from a *plaster cast* of his face.

plastered *adj, not used before a noun* [*more ~; most ~*] *informal* **:** very drunk • I got/was totally *plastered* at the party.

plas•ter•er /ˈplæstərɚ, *Brit* ˈplɑːstərə/ *noun, pl* **-ers** [*count*] **:** a person whose job is to put plaster on walls and ceilings

plaster of par•is *or* **plaster of Paris** /-ˈperəs/ *noun* [*noncount*] **:** a white powder that is mixed with water to form a paste which hardens quickly and which is used for making decorations, plaster casts, etc.

[1]**plas•tic** /ˈplæstɪk/ *noun, pl* **-tics**
1 : a light, strong substance that can be made into different shapes and that is used for making many common products [*noncount*] The toy was made of *plastic*. [*count*] a company that manufactures *plastics*
2 [*noncount*] *informal* **:** a credit card when used for payment • She used *plastic* to pay for her new computer.

[2]**plastic** *adj*
1 : made or consisting of plastic • *plastic* dishes/toys • a *plastic* bag/bottle/bin/container • a *plastic* bullet [=a bullet made of plastic that is used by the police, military, etc., to stop violent people without killing them] — see also PLASTIC WRAP
2 [*more ~; most ~*] *informal* **:** not real or sincere • a politician with a *plastic* [=*fake*] smile
3 *technical* **:** capable of being made into different shapes • *plastic* clay

plastic explosive *noun, pl* **~ -sives** [*count, noncount*] **:** an explosive that is made of a soft substance like clay that can be formed into different shapes • a bomb made with *plastic explosives*

Plas•ti•cine /ˈplæstəˌsiːn/ *trademark* — used for a soft material that is like clay and that is used especially by children for making models of people, animals, etc.

plas•tic•i•ty /plæˈstɪsəti/ *noun* [*noncount*] *technical* **:** the quality of being able to be made into different shapes • the *plasticity* of clay

plastic surgeon *noun, pl* **~ -geons** [*count*] **:** a doctor who performs plastic surgery

plastic surgery *noun* [*noncount*] **:** surgery that improves or repairs the form or appearance of body parts • He needed *plastic surgery* on his face after the car accident.

plastic wrap *noun* [*noncount*] *US* **:** thin, clear plastic that is used to wrap food or to cover containers that have food in them — called also (*Brit*) *cling film*

[1]**plate** /ˈpleɪt/ *noun, pl* **plates**
1 [*count*] **a :** a flat and usually round dish that is used for eating or serving food • *plates*, bowls, and cups • a paper *plate* • fancy dinner/salad/bread/dessert *plates* • a large serving *plate* [=*platter*] • pie *plates* [=plates used to hold pies] — see picture at PLACE SETTING **b :** the food that is served on a plate • a *plate* of cheese and crackers • a fruit/vegetable/meat *plate* [=a plate filled with different fruits/vegetables/meats] • I ate a salad and a *plate* of spaghetti.
2 [*count*] **:** a thin, flat piece of metal • A shiny metal *plate* was screwed to the door. • He had a steel *plate* put in his shoulder after the accident. • a *plate* of armor — see also BREASTPLATE, NAMEPLATE
3 [*count*] **:** LICENSE PLATE — usually plural • a car with New York *plates*
4 [*count*] **:** one of the usually flat, hard pieces that cover the body of some animals • a dinosaur covered in bony *plates*
5 [*singular*] **:** a dish or small container used in some churches to collect money • They passed around the *plate* during services. • the collection *plate*
6 ***the plate*** *baseball* **:** HOME PLATE • The runner was tagged out at *the plate*. — see also STEP UP TO THE PLATE (below)
7 [*count*] *geology* **:** one of the very large sections of the Earth's surface that are believed to move and cause earthquakes where they touch each other — see also PLATE TECTONICS
8 [*noncount*] **a :** metal that is covered with a thin layer of gold or silver • gold/silver *plate* **b :** objects (such as dishes, knives, forks, etc.) that are covered with a thin layer of gold or silver • The dishes were solid silver, not *plate*.
9 [*count*] **:** a special page in a book that has pictures on it • The book is 500 pages long and contains over 50 color *plates*. — see also BOOKPLATE
10 [*count*] **:** a surface of metal, plastic, or wood that is used in printing words or pictures on paper • printing *plates*
11 [*count*] **:** a sheet of glass or plastic that is treated with a special chemical and used in photography • photographic *plates*
12 [*count*] **:** the part of a set of false teeth that attaches to the mouth • the upper/lower *plate* of a set of dentures
clean your plate see [2]CLEAN
on a plate *informal* **:** in a way that requires no effort : as a gift • He was handed the job *on a plate*. [=he was given the job without having to do anything to earn it] • The victory was handed to us *on a plate*.
on your plate *informal* — used to refer to the things that a person has to do or deal with at one time • She has a lot *on her plate* right now. [=she has a lot of things that she has to deal with right now] • I've got enough *on my plate* to keep me busy this summer.
step up to the plate *baseball* **:** to move into position next to home plate in order to bat — often used figuratively in U.S. English • He finally *stepped up to the plate* [=he finally took action] and asked her to marry him. • If you want this promotion, you're going to have to *step up to the plate*. [=you will have to improve your work performance to show that you deserve the promotion]
– see also FASHION PLATE

[2]**plate** *verb* **plates; plat•ed; plat•ing** [+ *obj*]
1 : to add a layer of metal to the outside of (something) — usually used as *(be) plated* • The tin cups *were plated* with silver.
2 *baseball* **:** to cause (a run or a runner) to score • His second hit *plated* [=*drove in*] two runs.

[1]**pla•teau** /plæˈtoʊ/ *noun, pl* **pla•teaus** *also* **pla•teaux** /plæˈtoʊz/ [*count*]
1 : a large flat area of land that is higher than other areas of land that surround it • a *plateau* covering hundreds of miles • the Colorado *Plateau* — see color picture on page C7
2 : a period when something does not increase or advance any further • After several years of rapid growth, the company is now at a *plateau*. [=it has stopped growing] • The price of gas seems to have reached a *plateau*.

[2]**plateau** *verb* **-teaus; -teaued; -teau•ing** [*no obj*] **:** to stop growing or increasing : to reach a plateau • Sales of computers have *plateaued* in recent years.

plate•ful /ˈpleɪtˌfʊl/ *noun, pl* **-fuls** [*count*] **:** the amount of food that fills a plate • two *platefuls* of salad

plate glass *noun* [*noncount*] **:** large sheets of very clear and thick glass — often used before another noun • *plate glass* windows

plate•let /ˈpleɪtlət/ *noun, pl* **-lets** [*count*] **:** a small, round, thin blood cell that helps blood to stop flowing from a cut by becoming thick and sticky — called also *blood platelet*

plate tectonics *noun* [*noncount*] *geology* **:** a scientific theory that the Earth's surface is made of very large sections that move very slowly; *also* **:** the movements of the large sections that form the Earth's surface • earthquakes caused by *plate tectonics*

plat•form /ˈplætˌfoɚm/ *noun, pl* **-forms** [*count*]
1 a : a flat surface that is raised higher than the floor or ground and that people stand on when performing or speaking • a raised wooden *platform* • He stepped up onto the *platform* and looked out into the audience. **b :** a flat area next to railroad tracks where people wait for a train or subway • She stepped off the train onto the *platform*. • Our train is boarding on *platform* 6. **c :** a usually raised structure that has a flat surface where people or machines do work • a viewing/observation *platform* • oil drilling *platforms*
2 : the official beliefs and goals of a political party or candidate • political *platforms* • the Republican/Democratic *platform* • The party adopted a new *platform*. • She was elected on a *platform* of peace. [=people elected her because she promised to work for peace] — compare PLANK
3 : something that allows someone to tell a large number of people about an idea, product, etc. • The company plans to use the show as a *platform* to launch the new soft drink.
4 : a shoe with a very thick sole — usually plural • In the 1970s, we all wore *platforms* and bell-bottom pants. — called also *platform shoe*
5 *computers* **:** a program or set of programs that controls the way a computer works and runs other programs **:** OPERATING SYSTEM • The program can be run on various PC *platforms*.

plat•ing /ˈpleɪtɪŋ/ *noun* [*noncount*]
1 : a thin layer of metal that has been added to the outside of something • spoons covered in silver *plating*
2 : a layer of wide, thin pieces of metal • armor *plating*

plat•i•num /ˈplætnəm/ *noun* [*noncount*] **:** a heavy, silver-colored metal that is difficult to melt and that is used especially in expensive jewelry

platinum blonde *or* **platinum blond** *noun, pl* **~ blondes** *or* **~ blonds** [*count*] **:** a person who has very light blonde hair • She dyed her hair and now she's a *platinum blonde*.
– platinum blonde *or* **platinum blond** *adj* • *platinum blonde* supermodels

platinum record *noun, pl* **~ -cords** [*count*] **:** an award that is given to a singer or musical group for selling at least one million copies of a record — compare GOLD RECORD

plat•i•tude /ˈplætəˌtuːd, *Brit* ˈplætəˌtjuːd/ *noun, pl* **-tudes** [*count*] *disapproving* **:** a statement that expresses an idea that is not new • His speech was filled with familiar *platitudes* about the value of hard work and dedication.
– plat•i•tu•di•nous /ˌplætəˈtuːdnəs, *Brit* ˌplætəˈtjuːdnəs/ *adj* [*more* ~; *most* ~] *formal* • *platitudinous* remarks

pla•ton•ic /pləˈtɑːnɪk/ *adj* **:** of, relating to, or having a close relationship in which there is no romance or sex • They had a *platonic* friendship, not a romantic one. • Our relationship was strictly *platonic*. • *platonic* love

pla•toon /pləˈtuːn/ *noun, pl* **-toons** [*count*]
1 : a group of soldiers that includes two or more squads usually led by one lieutenant • a *platoon* of soldiers
2 : a group of people who are doing something together • *platoons* of waiters

plat•ter /ˈplætɚ/ *noun, pl* **-ters** [*count*]
1 a : a large plate that is used for serving food and especially meat • a silver *platter* **b :** the food that is served on a platter • large *platters* of hot turkey and ham • a *platter* [=*plate*] of cheese and crackers
2 : a meal in a restaurant that has a particular type of food • The chicken *platter* comes with fries and coleslaw. • She ordered the seafood *platter*.
on a (silver) platter **:** in a way that requires no effort **:** as a gift • He has had everything handed/given to him *on a silver platter*. [=he has not had to work for the things that he has; he is very lucky and has been given everything he has]

platy•pus /ˈplætɪpəs/ *noun, pl* **-pus•es** [*count*] **:** a small animal from Australia that has a bill like the bill of a duck, webbed feet, and a wide flat tail — called also *duck-billed platypus*

plau•dits /ˈplɑːdəts/ *noun* [*plural*] *formal* **:** strong approval • The book received the *plaudits* [=*acclaim, praise*] of the critics. • He has earned/won *plaudits* for his work abroad.

plau•si•ble /ˈplɑːzəbəl/ *adj* [*more* ~; *most* ~] **:** possibly true **:** believable or realistic • a *plausible* [=*possible*] conclusion • a *plausible* excuse • I thought her explanation was perfectly/entirely/completely *plausible*. [=I believed her explanation] — opposite IMPLAUSIBLE
– plau•si•bil•i•ty /ˌplɑːzəˈbɪləti/ *noun* [*noncount*] **– plau•si•bly** /ˈplɑːzəbli/ *adv* • She *plausibly* [=*believably*] argued that she was innocent. • Any of those things could *plausibly* happen.

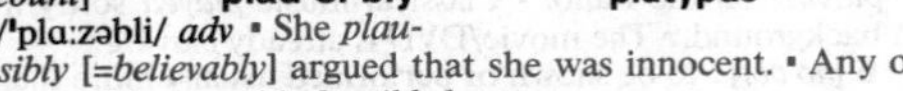
platypus

¹play /ˈpleɪ/ *verb* **plays; played; play•ing**
1 : to do activities for fun or enjoyment [*no obj*] The children were *playing* in the yard. • Can Sara come out and *play*? • He *played* by himself in his room. — often + *with* • She's outside *playing with* her friends. • You already have lots of toys to *play with*. • a baby *playing with* his toes [+ *obj*] ♦ If children ***play teacher/school (etc.)***, they play by pretending to be adults. • She likes to *play teacher/doctor* with her sisters. — see also *play house* at ¹HOUSE
2 a : to participate in (a game or sport) [+ *obj*] Did you *play* any sports in high school? • She *plays* soccer. • Do you want to *play* (a game of) cards/poker? • No one dares to *play* chess with/against him. • It's not whether you win or lose (that's important), it's how you *play* the game. • The children were *playing* hide-and-seek. [*no obj*] I have a chess set. Do you want to *play*? • It's your turn to *play*. • She hurt her wrist but decided to continue *playing*. • He *played* in every major tournament this year. • He's always dreamed of *playing* on a professional hockey team. — often + *for* • We never *play for* money. • I'm on a basketball team at school, but I also ***play for fun*** with my friends. ♦ If you ***play for*** a particular team, you are a member of that team. • Babe Ruth *played for* the Yankees. • He used to *play for* Boston but got traded to New York. **b :** to compete against (someone) in a game [+ *obj*] The Yankees are *playing* the Red Sox tonight at Yankee Stadium. • No one dares to *play* him at chess. • When Tom and I are finished with this game, you can *play* the winner. [*no obj*] The Yankees and the Red Sox are *playing* at Yankee Stadium. • She has *played* against some of the best tennis players in the world. ♦ If you ***play (someone) for (something)***, you play a game in which the winner will be able to take or keep something. • "Is that the last can of soda?" "Yeah, I'll *play* you *for* it." **c** [+ *obj*] **:** to have (a particular position on a sports team) • He dreamed about *playing* quarterback in the National Football League. • She *played* center field in their last game. • He *plays* third base. • What position does he *play*? **d** [+ *obj*] **:** to allow (someone) to play during a game especially in a particular position • Her coach didn't *play* her in yesterday's game. • They decided to *play* him at first base. **e** [+ *obj*] **:** to place (a playing card) on the table during your turn in a card game • I *played* the ace of hearts. — often used figuratively • lawyers who *play* the race card to defend their clients [=who say that their clients were treated unfairly because of their race] — see also *play your cards close to the chest/vest* at ¹CARD, *play your cards right* at ¹CARD **f** [+ *obj*] **:** to move (a piece) during your turn in a chess game • He *played* his rook/bishop/queen for the win. **g** [+ *obj*] **:** to hit, kick, throw, or catch (a ball, puck, etc.) • You have to *play* the ball where it lies. • He *played* a wedge shot to the green. • He *played* a great shot to his opponent's forehand. • The shortstop *played* the ball perfectly.
3 [+ *obj*] **a :** to bet money on (something) • I used to gamble a lot. Mostly, I *played* the races/horses/slots. • She only *plays* the lottery when there's a large jackpot. **b :** to invest money in (the stock market) in order to try to earn money • You can lose a lot of money *playing* the (stock) market.
4 a : to perform music on (an instrument) [+ *obj*] She's been *playing* the violin since she was 10 years old. • Where did you learn to *play* the piano? • He can *play* guitar and drums. [*no obj*] He *played* while she sang. • Would you *play* for us? • He *plays* in a band. **b** [*no obj*] *of an instrument* **:** to produce music • I could hear a guitar *playing* in the distance. **c** [+ *obj*] **:** to perform (a song, a piece of music, etc.) on an instrument • Would you *play* something for us? • The band *played* their new hit song. • The conductor had us *play* the piece again from the beginning. • The band *played* a waltz. • She started her career *playing* country music. **d** [+ *obj*] **:** to perform music written by (a particular composer) • The orchestra will be *playing* Mozart tonight. **e :** to perform mu-

P

sic in (a particular place) [+ *obj*] It was her dream to *play* Carnegie Hall. ▪ She prefers *playing* small concert halls rather than big stadiums. ▪ The band has been *playing* bars and nightclubs. [*no obj*] We mostly *play* in bars and nightclubs.
5 : to cause (a song, a piece of music, a movie, etc.) to be heard or seen [+ *obj*] You kids are *playing* your music too loud. ▪ The radio station *plays* mostly hip-hop and R&B. ▪ Who decides which songs get *played* on the radio? ▪ We're waiting for you to *play* the movie. ▪ I asked him to *play* the album/CD/DVD for me. [*no obj*] Our favorite song was *playing* on the radio. ▪ Classical music *played* softly in the background. ▪ The movie/DVD is already *playing*.
6 [*no obj*] **:** to be shown or performed usually more than one time ▪ The film is now *playing* [=is now being shown] in theaters across the country. ▪ What's *playing* at the theater/movies? ▪ The show has been *playing* to full/packed houses.
7 a [+ *obj*] **:** to act the part of (a particular character) in a film, play, etc. ▪ He *played* the lead role in *Hamlet*. ▪ Her character is being *played* by a relatively unknown actress. ▪ She's not a doctor, but she *plays* one on TV. — often used figuratively ▪ My wife never disciplines the children. She gets to *play* the good guy while I have to *play* the bad guy. [=I have to discipline the children] ▪ I survived a terrible tragedy, but I don't want to *play* the victim. [=I don't want to act like a victim] — often used with *part* or *role* ▪ Luck *played* an important *part* in their success. [=a lot of their success was because of luck] ▪ The essay discusses the *role* that television *plays* in modern society. [=the effect that television has on modern society] ▪ He's been ***playing the part/role*** of the jealous husband. [=he has been acting like a jealous husband] ▪ We all ***have a part/role to play*** in the future of this company. [=we all will be involved in an important way in the future of this company] — see also ROLE-PLAY **b** [*no obj*] **:** to pretend that you have a particular quality or are in a particular condition ▪ Don't *play* [=*act*] all innocent with me! ▪ She tried to teach her dog to ***play dead***. [=to lie on its back and pretend to be dead] ▪ If anyone asks you about it, ***play dumb***. [=act like you do not know anything about it]
8 : to act or behave in a particular way [*no obj*] It's a very competitive business, and not everyone *plays* fair. = Not everyone *plays* by the rules. ▪ If you *play* smart [=if you make good decisions], you should be able to graduate in four years. [+ *obj*] She didn't want to seem too eager, so she decided to ***play it cool***. [=to act calm] ▪ If you ***play it smart***, you should be able to graduate in four years. ▪ I decided to ***play it safe*** [=to be careful and avoid risk or danger] and leave early so that I would be sure to arrive on time. — see also *play by ear* at [1]EAR
9 [*no obj*] **:** to do or say things in a joking way ▪ Don't take it so seriously. He was just *playing*. [=*kidding*, *joking*] — often + *around* ▪ I was just *playing around*. I didn't really mean it. ▪ Stop *playing around* and talk to me seriously for a moment.
10 [+ *obj*] **:** to do (something) to someone in order to amuse yourself or others ▪ He's known for *playing* pranks, so I wouldn't trust him if I were you. — usually + *on* ▪ Let's *play* a joke *on* her. ▪ The students got in trouble for *playing* a trick *on* their teacher. ▪ I can't believe what I'm seeing. My eyes must be *playing* tricks *on* me.
11 [+ *obj*] *informal* **:** to use or control (someone or something) in a clever and unfair way ▪ I'm never going to let anyone *play* me again. ▪ She *played* you like a fool. — often + *for* ▪ She realized too late that she had been *played for* a fool. ▪ They had been *playing* the guy *for* a sucker all along.
12 [+ *obj*] **:** to base a decision or action on (something) ▪ Sometimes you just have to *play* your luck [=to take a chance] and hope that everything turns out okay. ▪ The coach was *playing* the odds that his pitcher would get through the inning without giving up a run. ▪ Criminal investigators need to *play* [=to act on] their hunches.
13 [*no obj*] *US* **:** to be accepted or received in a particular way ▪ The script looked good on paper but didn't *play* well on Broadway. — often + *with* ▪ His idea did not *play* well *with* the committee. [=the committee did not like his idea]
14 [*no obj*] **:** to move in a lively and irregular way ▪ A knowing smile *played* on/about her lips. ▪ We watched the moonlight *playing* on the water.

play along [*phrasal verb*] **:** to agree to do or accept what other people want ▪ They wanted me to cooperate with them, but I refused to *play along*. [=*go along*] ▪ If I pretend to be sick, will you *play along* and tell everyone that I had to go to the doctor? — often + *with* ▪ I refused to *play along with* them. ▪ Will you *play along with* my plan?

play around *also Brit* ***play about*** [*phrasal verb*] **1 :** to have sex with someone who is not your husband, wife, or regular partner ▪ He's not the kind of guy who *plays around*. [=*fools around*, *messes around*] — often + *on* ▪ She's been *playing around on* her husband. — often + *with* ▪ She's been *playing around with* one of her coworkers. **2 :** to deal with or treat something in a careless way ▪ When it comes to protecting his family, he doesn't *play around*. [=*fool around*, *mess around*] — often + *with* ▪ You can't *play around with* diabetes; it's a very serious disease. **3 :** to use or do something in a way that is not very serious ▪ It's time to stop *playing around* [=*fooling around*] and get busy. — often + *on* ▪ I spent the evening *playing around on* the piano/computer/Internet. — often + *with* ▪ I'm not really a painter; I just like to *play around with* paints. **4** ***play around with (something)*** **:** to move or change (something) or to think about (something) in different ways often in order to find out what would work best ▪ I see you've been *playing around with* the living room furniture again. ▪ The supervisor *played around with* our work schedules this week. ▪ We *played around with* the idea for a while but eventually realized that it just wouldn't work. — see also [1]PLAY 9 (above)

play at [*phrasal verb*] ***play at (something)*** **1 :** to do (something) in a way that is not serious ▪ They were only *playing at* trying to fix the problem. **2** *chiefly Brit* **:** to play by pretending to be (someone or something) ▪ (*Brit*) She liked to *play at* doctors and nurses as a child. — often used in the phrase ***play at being (something)*** ▪ boys *playing at being* soldiers **3** *Brit* — used to say in an annoyed way that you do not know the reason for someone's behavior ▪ What is he *playing at*? ▪ I have no idea what he was *playing at*.

play back [*phrasal verb*] ***play back (something)*** *or* ***play (something) back*** **:** to cause (recorded sounds or pictures) to be heard or seen ▪ The machine allows you to record and *play back* sounds. ▪ We finished recording our first take and *played it back* to hear how it sounded. ▪ He *played* the tape *back* to/for us. — see also PLAYBACK

play ball see [1]BALL

play down [*phrasal verb*] ***play down (something)*** *or* ***play (something) down*** **:** to make (something) seem smaller or less important ▪ She *played down* [=*downplayed*] her role in the research. ▪ It was a significant mistake though our CEO tried to *play* it *down*.

play fast and loose **:** to behave in a clever and dishonest way — usually + *with* ▪ He was accused of *playing fast and loose with* the truth. [=of being dishonest] ▪ reporters *playing fast and loose with* the facts

play for laughs *or* ***play (something) for laughs*** **:** to act in a funny way that makes people laugh ▪ She's fantastic in serious roles, but she also knows how to *play for laughs*. ▪ Most performers would have taken a serious tone during the scene, but he decided to *play* it *for laughs*.

play for time **:** to try to make something happen later instead of sooner **:** to try to delay something ▪ They're just *playing for time*, hoping that the situation will resolve itself.

play games see [1]GAME

play God *usually disapproving* **:** to make decisions that have a very powerful and important effect on other people's lives ▪ lawyers who *play God* with people's lives

play hard to get **:** to pretend that you are not interested in having a romantic or sexual relationship with someone in order to make that person more attracted to you ▪ She's been *playing hard to get*, but I can tell that she likes me.

play into [*phrasal verb*] ***play into (something)*** **:** to help support (something, such as an idea) ▪ This new evidence *plays into* their theory quite nicely. ▪ Her methods *play into* the stereotype that lawyers are dishonest.

play into someone's hands *or* ***play into the hands of someone*** **:** to do something that you do not realize will hurt you and help someone else ▪ You're only *playing into their hands* by making such ridiculous accusations.

play off [*phrasal verb*] **1** *chiefly Brit* **:** to participate in a game that decides a winner from people or teams that had the same results in an earlier game **:** to play in a play-off ▪ The two teams *played off* for third place. — see also PLAY-OFF **2** ***play off (someone or something)*** *US* **:** to react to (someone or something) in a pleasing way **:** to combine with (someone or something) in a way that makes each part better ▪ In this scene, the two actors *play off* each other extremely well. ▪ The sweetness of the wine *plays off* the sharp flavor of the cheese. **3** ***play (someone or something) off against (someone or something)*** **:** to cause two people or groups to fight or compete with each other in a way that helps you • They have been *playing* him *off against* his old enemies. [=causing him to fight with his old enemies] • He *played* one side *off against* the other.

play on** also **play upon** [phrasal verb]* ***play on/upon (something) : to make people do what you want by using (their emotions, fears, concerns, etc.) in an unfair way • The company *plays on* [=*takes advantage of*] the concerns of parents in order to sell their products. • Politicians often win votes by *playing on* [=*exploiting*] people's emotions.

play out** [phrasal verb]* **1 a** : to happen or occur in usually a gradual way • Let's wait and see how things *play out.* [=*take place, develop*] • The consequences of the error will *play out* for several years to come. • Their personal tragedy was being *played out* in public. **b *play out (something)* or *play (something) out : to make (something) happen • She got to *play out* [=*realize*] her fantasy of being on TV. • We watch professional athletes *play out* [=*act out, live out*] our dreams on the field. • This scene ***plays itself out*** [=*happens*] daily in every large city in this country. **2 *play out (something) or play (something) out*** : to finish (something) • Her coach let her *play out* the rest of the season but said she wouldn't be allowed on the team next year. • We'll stop the game after we *play out* this hand. • *playing out* dangerous experiments • That style of music had ***played itself out*** [=stopped being current or popular] and the record companies wanted something new. — see also PLAYED-OUT

play the field : to have romantic or sexual relationships with more than one person at a time : to date more than one person • He wanted to *play the field* a bit before he got married and settled down.

play the fool see [1]FOOL

play to** [phrasal verb]* **1 *play to (someone or something) : to behave or perform in a particular way for (someone or something) in order to get approval or attention • He didn't mean what he was saying. He was just ***playing to the crowd***. • He loves publicity and ***plays to the cameras*** every chance he gets. **2 *play to (something)*** : to make use of (something) • a film that *plays to* stereotypes of housewives • In his latest album, he once again *plays to* his strengths as a classical musician.

play to the gallery see GALLERY

play up** [phrasal verb]* **1 *play up (something) or play (something) up **a** : to talk about or treat (something) in a way that gives it special importance : to emphasize or stress (something) • During the interview, try to play down your weaknesses and *play up* your strengths. **b** : to make (something) seem bigger or more important • It was only a small achievement though our CEO tried to *play* it *up*. **2 *play up or play (someone) up Brit*** : to cause problems or pain • The children have been *playing up* [=*misbehaving, acting up*] again. • The camera started *playing up* [=*acting up*] after I dropped it. • Whenever it rains, my arthritis starts *playing up*. [=*acting up*] • My back has been *playing* me *up* again.

play with** [phrasal verb]* ***play with (something) **1** : to move or handle (something) with your hands or fingers often without thinking • She *played with* her hair while she talked on the phone. • Stop *playing with* your food and eat. **2** : to handle, change, or deal with (something) in a careless way • I *played* [=*fiddled, messed*] *with* the radio for a while but couldn't get it to work. • It's important to teach your children not to *play with* guns/fire/matches. • Don't *play with* [=*play around with*] my heart/emotions. • You have to take this seriously. You're *playing with* people's lives! • They're *playing with* other people's money. **3** : to think about (something) briefly and not very seriously • Management has been *playing with* [=*toying with*] the idea of moving to a different building. • I *played with* the idea of moving to Chicago but ended up staying in New York.

play with fire : to do something that is risky or dangerous • People who use drugs are *playing with fire*.

play with words/language : to use words that sound similar or that have several different meanings especially in a clever or funny way • a writer who enjoys *playing with words*

play with yourself : to touch your own sex organs for sexual pleasure : MASTURBATE

[2]play *noun, pl* **plays**

1 *[count]* : a piece of writing that tells a story through the actions and words of characters and that is performed on a stage • The *play* is based on a real-life event. • He wrote, directed, and starred in the *play*. • *plays* by Shakespeare • His fifth grade class is ***putting on a play*** about the first Thanksgiving. • I've gone to all of my daughter's ***school plays***. • She's currently adapting a ***stage play*** [=a play that is written to be performed on a stage] for the big screen. — see also MYSTERY PLAY, PASSION PLAY, SCREENPLAY

2 *[noncount]* : activities that are done especially by children for fun or enjoyment • The book discusses the role of *play* in a child's development. • imaginative *play* • As the saying goes, "All work and no *play* makes Jack a dull boy." • a safe *play* area • the sounds of children ***at play*** [=the sounds of children playing] — see also CHILD'S PLAY

3 a *[noncount]* : the action that happens during a game • Please, no talking during *play*. • Rain held up *play* for an hour. • The chess match finally ended after three hours of *play*. • The two golfers were tied at the start of *play* yesterday. • We were surprised with/by the other team's level/quality of *play*. **b** : the time when a person playing a game is supposed to do something *[count]* It's your *play*. [=(more commonly) *turn*] *[noncount]* Roll the dice to determine the order of *play*. [=to decide who plays first, second, etc.]

4 *[count] US* : a particular action or set of actions that happens during a game: such as **a** *American football* : a planned attempt to move the ball forward or to stop an opponent from moving the ball forward • The quarterback called out the *play* to his teammates. • He ran 50 yards on that last *play*. • running/passing *plays* • a defensive/offensive *play* **b** *baseball* : an action that is done to try to get a player out • He was called safe on a close *play* at first base. — often used with *make* • The shortstop *made* a great *play* to end the inning. • She had a chance to catch the ball, but she failed to *make* the *play*. — see also DOUBLE PLAY, TRIPLE PLAY **c** : the act of moving a piece in a game like chess or checkers • the first/opening *play* [=*move*] of the game

5 *[noncount]* : the state of being active or having an effect • the *play* of market forces • She promotes the free *play* of ideas in her classroom. • Several issues are ***at play*** [=are involved] in determining the price of gasoline. • The students' creativity was ***brought/called/put into play*** on this last assignment. [=the students had to use their creativity] • Two important factors ***come into play***. [=are involved]

6 *[noncount]* **a** : time when a musical recording is played by a radio station : AIRPLAY • The song has been getting heavy radio *play*. [=radio stations have been playing the song frequently] **b** *US* : attention in newspapers, on television, etc. • The story has so far received little *play* in the press. [=has not gotten much attention in the press]

7 *[count]* : a humorous or clever way of using a word or phrase so that more than one meaning is suggested — + *on* • The title of the article makes a *play on* the prime minister's last name. • a *play on* the word's original meaning • a clever ***play on words*** [=*pun*] — see also WORDPLAY

8 *[noncount]* **a** : a function of a machine that causes recorded sounds or pictures to be heard or seen • Press "*Play*" to start the movie. **b** : time when a machine is being used to hear or see recorded sounds or pictures • The CD player's batteries only provided three to four hours of *play*.

9 *[singular]* : the irregular or lively movement *of* something • Look at the dazzling *play of* colors in this diamond. • a *play of* shadow and light

10 *[noncount]* : loose and free movement of something (such as part of a machine) • There's too much *play* in the car's steering wheel.

***in/into play** of a ball* : in or into the area where players must stay in sports • She tried to keep the ball *in play*, but it bounced out of bounds. • He put the ball back *into play*.

make a play for : to try to get (someone or something) • He *made a play for* her. [=he tried to start a romantic or sexual relationship with her] • She *made a play for* the job, but she didn't get it.

***out of play** of a ball* : outside the area where players must stay in sports • The ball is *out of play* [=*dead*] if it crosses these lines.

— see also FAIR PLAY, FOUL PLAY, POWER PLAY

play·able /ˈplejəbəl/ *adj*

1 : capable of being played • The ball was out-of-bounds and no longer *playable*. • Many older computer games aren't *playable* on the new system. • The violin they found in the attic was old but still *playable*.

2 *[more ~; most ~]* : suitable for being played on • The field was muddy but *playable*. • Changes have been made to make the golf course more *playable*.

play·act·ing /ˈpleɪˌæktɪŋ/ *noun [noncount]* : behavior that is not honest or sincere • The company was losing money,

P

but all of the *playacting* had people believing that it was doing well.

play–action pass *noun, pl* **~ passes** [*count*] *American football* : a play in which the quarterback pretends to hand the ball to a runner before passing it to another player

play·back /ˈpleɪˌbæk/ *noun, pl* **-backs**

1 [*noncount*] : the act of causing recorded sounds or pictures to be heard or seen again • devices used for the *playback* of audio/video recordings = *playback* devices

2 [*count*] : a recording that is heard or seen again : a recording that is played back • The band listened to a *playback* of their first recording. — see also *play back* at ¹PLAY

play·bill /ˈpleɪˌbɪl/ *noun, pl* **-bills** [*count*] : a poster or piece of paper that advertises a play

play·book /ˈpleɪˌbʊk/ *noun, pl* **-books** [*count*] *American football* : a book that contains descriptions of the different offensive and defensive plays that are used by a team • He studied the new plays in the team's *playbook*. — often used figuratively in U.S. English • They began to fight the war using the enemy's *playbook*. • The competition beat us using a play straight from our own *playbook*.

play·boy /ˈpleɪˌbɔɪ/ *noun, pl* **-boys** [*count*] : a man who spends most of his time doing things that give him pleasure • She was dating a rich American *playboy* who was seeing two other women at the same time.

play–by–play /ˈpleɪˌbaɪˌpleɪ/ *noun, pl* **-plays** *US* : a description of a game that is given while the game is being played [*count*] I listened to a *play-by-play* of the game. [*noncount*] a broadcaster who does *play-by-play*

– play–by–play *adj, always used before a noun* • a *play-by-play* announcer/commentator/account — sometimes used figuratively • He gave the jury a *play-by-play* analysis of the videotape.

play·date /ˈpleɪˌdeɪt/ *noun, pl* **-dates** [*count*] *chiefly US* : a time that parents arrange for their young children to play together • She has a *playdate* with a friend from kindergarten.

played–out *adj* [*more ~; most ~*] : no longer current, popular, or effective • *played-out* ideas — see also *play out* at ¹PLAY

play·er /ˈplejɚ/ *noun, pl* **-ers** [*count*]

1 : a person who plays a sport or game • She's one of the team's best *players*. • a star baseball *player* • professional poker *players* — see also TEAM PLAYER

2 : a person who performs music usually on a particular instrument • The band's lead guitar *player* hurt his hand and couldn't play. • Piano *players* are called pianists.

3 : a machine that causes recorded sounds or pictures to be heard or seen • a record/DVD/CD *player*

4 : a person who participates in a usually competitive field or activity • She is a key/major/top *player* in genetics research. • one of the industry's inside *players*

5 *old-fashioned* : an actor or actress • a traveling band of *players* • Even the movie's ***bit players*** [=people who perform very small roles] are excellent.

6 *US slang* : a person and especially a man who has sexual relationships with more than one person at the same time • That guy's a *player*.

player piano *noun, pl* **~ -nos** [*count*] : a piano that is played by a machine inside the piano

play·ful /ˈpleɪfəl/ *adj* [*more ~; most ~*]

1 : happy and full of energy : eager to play • She's an old dog, but she's still very *playful*. • *playful* kittens

2 : showing that you are having fun and not being serious • He had a *playful* expression on his face. • a *playful* tone of voice • You're certainly in a *playful* mood! • She gave him a light *playful* slap on the knee.

– play·ful·ly *adv* **– play·ful·ness** *noun* [*noncount*]

play·girl /ˈpleɪˌgɚl/ *noun, pl* **-girls** [*count*] : a woman who spends most of her time doing things that give her pleasure • He's dating a rich, beautiful *playgirl*.

play·go·er /ˈpleɪˌgowɚ/ *noun, pl* **-ers** [*count*] : a person who often goes to plays or who is at a particular play : THEATERGOER

play·ground /ˈpleɪˌgraʊnd/ *noun, pl* **-grounds** [*count*]

1 : an outdoor area where children can play that usually includes special equipment (such as swings and slides)

2 : a place where people go to do enjoyable things • The island was a *playground* of the rich and famous until the 1950s. • These mountains are a *playground* for hikers, skiers, and nature lovers.

play·group /ˈpleɪˌgruːp/ *noun, pl* **-groups** [*count*]

1 *US* : an organized group of young children and their parents that meet regularly so the children can play together

2 *Brit* : a school where children younger than five years old go to play and learn — called also (*chiefly Brit*) *play school*

play·house /ˈpleɪˌhaʊs/ *noun, pl* **-hous·es** [*count*]

1 : THEATER — usually used in names • the Provincetown *Playhouse* in New York City

2 : a small house for children to play in — called also (*Brit*) *Wendy house*

playing card *noun, pl* **~ cards** [*count*] : ¹CARD 1a

playing field *noun, pl* **~ fields** [*count*] : an area that is used for playing some sports; *especially* : the part of a field that is officially marked as the place where the action of a game happens — see also LEVEL PLAYING FIELD

level the playing field see ³LEVEL

play·list /ˈpleɪˌlɪst/ *noun, pl* **-lists** [*count*] : a list of songs to be played especially by a radio station • Most of the city's DJs have added the song to their *playlists*.

play·mak·er /ˈpleɪˌmeɪkɚ/ *noun, pl* **-ers** [*count*] : a skillful player in sports like basketball, soccer, and hockey who makes plays that help a team to score during games

play·mate /ˈpleɪˌmeɪt/ *noun, pl* **-mates** [*count*] : a friend with whom a child plays • She was my *playmate* and best friend. • He wasn't allowed to join his *playmates* outside.

P

playground

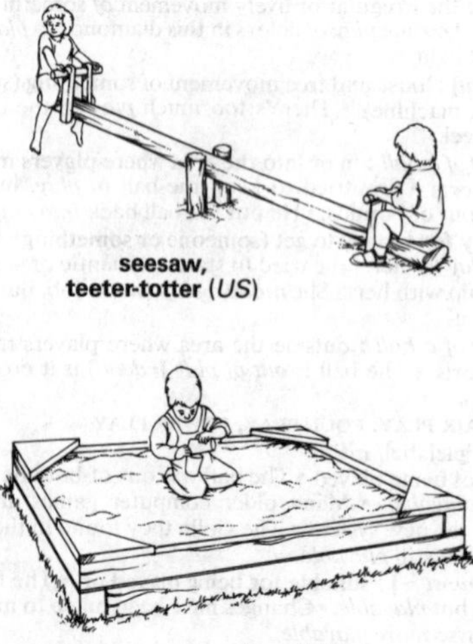

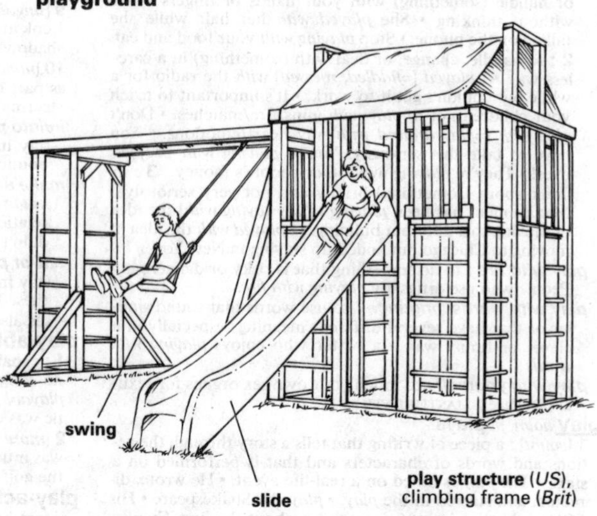

playing cards

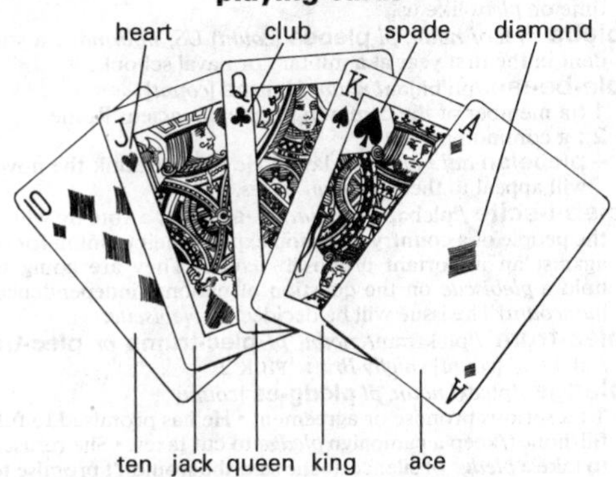

play–off /ˈpleɪˌɑːf/ *noun, pl* **-offs** [*count*]
1 *US* **:** a series of games that is played after the end of the regular season in order to decide which player or team is the champion — usually plural ▪ The teams will once again face each other in the *play-offs.*
2 : a game or series of games that is played to decide the winner when people or teams are tied ▪ We tied the first day, but I beat her the next day in a *play-off.* ▪ an 18-hole *play-off* — see also *play off* at ¹PLAY

play·pen /ˈpleɪˌpɛn/ *noun, pl* **-pens** [*count*] **:** a structure with high sides that provides an enclosed area in which a baby or young child can play — called also (*US*) *play yard*

play·room /ˈpleɪˌruːm/ *noun, pl* **-rooms** [*count*] **:** a room for children to play in ▪ Their basement has a *playroom.*

play school *noun, pl* ~ **schools** [*count*] *chiefly Brit* **:** PLAYGROUP 2

play structure *noun, pl* ~ **-tures** [*count*] *US* **:** a structure that is designed for children to climb on for fun and that often includes a slide — called also (*Brit*) *climbing frame*; see picture at PLAYGROUND

play·thing /ˈpleɪˌθɪŋ/ *noun, pl* **-things** [*count*]
1 : a toy ▪ a child's *plaything* ▪ VCRs were once the expensive, high-tech *playthings* of the rich.
2 : a person or thing that you treat in a careless way and use for your own amusement or advantage ▪ We mustn't let the environment become the *plaything* of oil companies. ▪ The emperor used people as his *playthings.*

play·time /ˈpleɪˌtaɪm/ *noun* [*noncount*]
1 : a time to play and have fun ▪ She has a little *playtime* in the morning before she goes to school. ▪ This isn't *playtime*; get to work!
2 *Brit* **:** RECESS ▪ The children have *playtime* after lunch.

play·wright /ˈpleɪˌraɪt/ *noun, pl* **-wrights** [*count*] **:** a person who writes plays **:** DRAMATIST

play·writ·ing *also US* **play·wright·ing** /ˈpleɪˌraɪtɪŋ/ *noun* [*noncount*] **:** the activity of writing plays ▪ He gave classes in *playwriting* and poetry. ▪ a *playwriting* course

play yard *noun, pl* ~ **yards** [*count*] *US* **:** PLAYPEN

pla·za /ˈplɑːzə/ *noun, pl* **-zas** [*count*]
1 : an open public area that is usually near city buildings and that often has trees and bushes and places to sit, walk, and shop ▪ They put his statue in the town's *plaza.*
2 *chiefly US* **:** SHOPPING CENTER
3 *US* **a :** an area on or next to a highway having restaurants, gas stations, restrooms, etc. ▪ a rest/information/service *plaza* **b :** a place where you stop to pay money before going onto a highway — called also *toll plaza*

plea /ˈpliː/ *noun, pl* **pleas** [*count*]
1 : a serious and emotional request for something ▪ We are making a *plea* to all companies to stop polluting the environment. — often + *for* ▪ No one heard his *pleas for* help. ▪ the prisoner's passionate/desperate/fervent *plea for* mercy
2 *law* **a :** a statement in which a person who has been accused of a crime says in court that he or she is guilty or not guilty of the crime ▪ The defendant entered a *plea* of not guilty. ▪ a guilty *plea* **b :** a statement in which a person says that he or she is guilty of a particular crime **:** a plea of guilty ▪ She and her lawyers accepted a lesser *plea* [=they said that she was guilty of a less serious crime] of manslaughter. **c :** a reason or excuse for committing a crime ▪ He murdered his wife and got off on an ***insanity plea***. [=the court said that he was not guilty because he was insane]
cop a plea see ²COP

plea bargaining *noun* [*noncount*] **:** a process in which a person who is accused of a crime is allowed to say that he or she is guilty of a less serious crime in order to be given a less severe punishment ▪ As a result of *plea bargaining*, he would not be sentenced to death.
– plea bargain *noun, pl* ~ **-gains** [*count*] ▪ She could confess and be granted a *plea bargain.* ▪ He refused to accept a *plea bargain.* **– plea–bargain** *verb* **-gains; -gained; -gaining** [*no obj*] ▪ He *plea-bargained* to avoid spending time in jail.

plead /ˈpliːd/ *verb* **pleads; plead·ed** /ˈpliːdəd/ *or* **pled** /ˈplɛd/; **plead·ing**
1 [*no obj*] **:** to ask for something in a serious and emotional way ▪ He begged and *pleaded*, but she would not change her mind. — often + *for* ▪ She *pleaded* [=*begged*] *for* forgiveness and got her job back. ▪ *pleading for* help/mercy — often + *with* ▪ He *pleaded with* the judge not to send him to jail.
2 [+ *obj*] **:** to try to prove (a case) in a court of law ▪ She couldn't afford a lawyer to *plead* her case.
3 [*no obj*] **:** to say in court that you are either guilty or not guilty of a crime **:** to make a plea ▪ "How do you *plead*?" asked the judge. ▪ "We *plead* guilty, Your Honor." ▪ He *pled* not guilty by reason of insanity. [=he said in court that he was not responsible for the crime because he was insane] ▪ He agreed to *plead* to a lesser charge of manslaughter.
4 [+ *obj*] **:** to give (something) as a reason or excuse for something ▪ He *pleaded* that he didn't have enough money to pay his bill. ▪ On that particular issue, I will have to ***plead ignorance***. [=to say that I do not know anything about it]
5 : to argue in support of (a cause) [+ *obj*] They went to *plead* their cause to the governor. [*no obj*] We will *plead* on your behalf.
plead the Fifth see ¹FIFTH

pleading *noun, pl* **-ings**
1 : the act of asking for something in a serious and emotional way [*noncount*] I'm tired of their begging and *pleading.* [*count*] Despite our *pleadings* to be allowed to leave, they kept us there for several more hours.
2 [*count*] *law* **:** one of the formal, usually written statements made by the two sides of a legal case in a court of law

plead·ing·ly /ˈpliːdɪŋli/ *adv* [*more* ~; *most* ~] **:** in a way that shows that someone wants something very much ▪ He looked up at me *pleadingly.*

pleas·ant /ˈplɛznt/ *adj* **pleas·ant·er; -est** [*or more* ~; *most* ~]
1 : causing a feeling of happiness or pleasure ▪ the *pleasant* smell of cookies baking in the oven ▪ We had a *pleasant* conversation. ▪ Our evening together was *pleasant* but not very exciting. ▪ Have a *pleasant* day/afternoon/evening. ▪ I didn't know you were coming. What a ***pleasant surprise***!
2 : friendly and likable ▪ Their new teacher seems *pleasant* enough. ▪ a very *pleasant* young man
– pleas·ant·ly *adv* ▪ She smiled at him *pleasantly.* ▪ We were *pleasantly* surprised to see her there. **– pleas·ant·ness** *noun* [*noncount*]

pleas·ant·ry /ˈplɛzntri/ *noun, pl* **-ries** [*count*] *formal* **:** something (such as a greeting) that people say in order to be polite — usually plural ▪ After exchanging *pleasantries*, she brought me into her office to discuss the project.

¹please /ˈpliːz/ *adv*
1 a — used to ask for something in a polite way ▪ *Please* come in. ▪ *Please* bring your books with you to every class. ▪ Pass the salt, *please.* = Would you *please* pass the salt. ▪ I'll have a glass of red wine, *please.* ▪ *Please* don't leave the door open. ▪ Next, *please*! = Will the next person *please* come forward? **b** — used to show that a request is serious or important ▪ *Please*, God, help us. ▪ I beg you. *Please*, don't leave me here alone. ▪ Will everyone *please* be quiet and listen?
2 — used as a polite way of saying yes ▪ "Would you like some tea?" "*Please.*" ▪ "How about a piece of cake?" "Yes, *please.*"
3 *informal* — used to show that you do not agree with or believe something that was said ▪ Oh, *please.* You can't be serious! That makes no sense!

²please *verb* **pleas·es; pleased; pleas·ing**
1 : to make (someone) happy or satisfied [+ *obj*] He joined the football team to *please* his father. ▪ She enjoys *pleasing* others. ▪ Her parents were *pleased* by her decision. ▪ It *pleases* me to know that you liked the gift. ▪ They're very hard/easy to *please.* ▪ You can't *please* everyone. [*no obj*] — used in the

phrase *to please* ▪ She's always been eager *to please*. ▪ restaurants that aim *to please* ▪ All of their desserts are sure *to please*. [=everyone will like them] — opposite DISPLEASE

2 [*no obj*] **:** to make a choice about what to do, have, etc. ▪ Since he no longer lives with his parents, he's able to come and go as he *pleases*. [=to come and go whenever he wants to] ▪ There's no hurry. Stay as long as you *please*. [=as long as you want to stay] ▪ I can do whatever I *please*. [=*like*] ▪ You can ***do as you please***. [=you can do whatever you want/choose to do]

as you please *Brit, informal* — used to make a statement more forceful especially when describing behavior that is surprising ▪ She walked right in, bold *as you please*. [=in a very bold way]

if you please *old-fashioned + formal* **1** — used to make a polite request ▪ Follow me, *if you please*, and I'll show you to the garden. **2** — used to express your surprise or annoyance about something ▪ He insulted her, and then, *if you please* [=if you would believe it], asked for her help.

please yourself — used to say that you can do what you want to do ▪ "I'm going to skip the party tonight." "OK, *please yourself*." [=*suit yourself*]

pleased *adj* [*more* ~; *most* ~] **:** happy or satisfied ▪ We're all *pleased* that you came. ▪ My father was ***none too pleased*** [=not pleased at all; very angry or unhappy] when he found out that my brother had wrecked the car. — often + *with* ▪ I'm *pleased with* the grade I got in the class. ▪ You look rather *pleased with* yourself. — often followed by *to* + *verb* ▪ We are *pleased to announce* that the school has hired a new teacher. ▪ You'll be *pleased to learn* that you're getting a raise. ▪ "This is my friend, Jane." "(I'm) ***Pleased to meet you.***"

(as) pleased as punch *informal* **:** very happy or satisfied ▪ We were *pleased as punch* that he decided to visit.

pleas·ing *adj* [*more* ~; *most* ~] **:** good in a way that gives pleasure or enjoyment **:** attractive or appealing ▪ the *pleasing* [=*pleasant*] smell of freshly baked bread ▪ *pleasing* sounds/sights ▪ He wanted his kitchen to be both functional and aesthetically *pleasing*.

– pleas·ing·ly *adv* ▪ The meal was *pleasingly* simple.

plea·sur·able /ˈplɛʒərəbəl/ *adj* [*more* ~; *most* ~] *somewhat formal* **:** causing a feeling of pleasure or enjoyment ▪ She has *pleasurable* [=*pleasant*] memories of her childhood. ▪ a *pleasurable* activity/experience

– plea·sur·ably /ˈplɛʒərəbli/ *adv* ▪ walking *pleasurably* along the beach

plea·sure /ˈplɛʒɚ/ *noun, pl* **-sures**

1 [*noncount*] **a :** a feeling of happiness, enjoyment, or satisfaction **:** a pleasant or pleasing feeling ▪ I paint for the sheer/pure *pleasure* of it. ▪ intense physical/sexual *pleasure* ▪ He smiled with *pleasure*. ▪ She gets *pleasure* from helping others. [=she enjoys helping others] ▪ She ***takes pleasure in*** [=*enjoys*] her work. ▪ His grandparents *took* great/special *pleasure in* seeing him graduate from college. **b :** activity that is done for enjoyment ▪ Is this trip for business or *pleasure*?

2 [*count*] **:** something or someone that causes a feeling of happiness, enjoyment, or satisfaction ▪ It's been a *pleasure* working with you. = You were a *pleasure* to work with. [=I enjoyed working with you] ▪ It would be my *pleasure* to help. [=I would be glad to help] ▪ It is a special *pleasure* for me to be here with you today. ▪ Now I can enjoy the ***simple pleasures*** of life, like spending time with my family. ▪ "Thanks for your help." "(It was) ***My pleasure.***" [=I was happy to help] ▪ Dark chocolate is a ***guilty pleasure*** of mine. [=something that I enjoy even though it causes guilty feelings]

at someone's pleasure *or* ***at the pleasure of someone*** — used to say that something is done or can be done because someone wants it to be done ▪ The building can be converted to condominiums *at* the owner's *pleasure*. ▪ I serve *at the pleasure of* the president, and I will continue to serve as long as the president wants me to.

what's your pleasure? *informal* — used to ask what drink someone would like to be served

with pleasure — used to say that you are happy to do something for someone ▪ "Would you deliver a message for me?" "Yes, *with pleasure*."

pleat /ˈpliːt/ *noun, pl* **pleats** [*count*] **:** a fold in cloth that is made by folding the material onto itself ▪ Her skirt has *pleats* at the waist. — see color picture on page C16

– pleat·ed /ˈpliːtəd/ *adj* ▪ a *pleated* skirt [=a skirt that has pleats]

pleb /ˈplɛb/ *noun, pl* **plebs** [*count*] *chiefly Brit, informal + disapproving* **:** an ordinary person who has low social status — usually plural ▪ They think they're too important to waste time on *plebs* like us.

plebe /ˈpliːb/ *noun, pl* **plebes** [*count*] *US, informal* **:** a student in the first year at a military or naval school

ple·be·ian /plɪˈbiːjən/ *noun, pl* **-ians** [*count*]

1 : a member of the common people of ancient Rome

2 : a common person

– plebeian *adj* ▪ *plebeian* laws ▪ He doesn't think the novel will appeal to their *plebeian* tastes.

pleb·i·scite /ˈplɛbəˌsaɪt/ *noun, pl* **-scites :** a vote by which the people of a country or region express their opinion for or against an important proposal [*count*] They are going to hold a *plebiscite* on the question of national independence. [*noncount*] The issue will be decided by *plebiscite*.

plec·trum /ˈplɛktrəm/ *noun, pl* **plec·trums** *or* **plec·tra** /ˈplɛktrə/ [*count*] *chiefly Brit* **:** [3]PICK 2

[1]pledge /ˈplɛʤ/ *noun, pl* **pledg·es** [*count*]

1 : a serious promise or agreement ▪ He has promised to fulfill/honor/keep a campaign *pledge* to cut taxes. ▪ She refused to take a *pledge* of silence. [=she said she wouldn't promise to stay silent]

2 : a promise to give money ▪ To make a *pledge* or donation, please call the charity's office. ▪ The company has made a *pledge* of over $3,000.

3 : something that you leave with another person as a way to show that you will keep your promise ▪ He left his car as a *pledge* that he would return with the money.

4 *US* **:** a person who has promised to join a college fraternity or sorority but who has not been officially accepted into the group ▪ Our sorority usually accepts 10 *pledges* each year.

the Pledge of Allegiance *US* **:** a formal promise of loyalty to the United States that groups of people say together ▪ The children recited *the Pledge of Allegiance*.

[2]pledge *verb* **pledges; pledged; pledg·ing**

1 [+ *obj*] **:** to formally promise to give or do (something) ▪ Her family *pledged* $100,000 toward the construction of a new school. ▪ He called to *pledge* money to the charity. ▪ We've all *pledged* (our) loyalty/support/allegiance to the organization. ▪ Every morning, we *pledge* allegiance to the flag. ▪ teenagers who have *pledged* not to start smoking ▪ During his campaign, he *pledged* that he would not raise taxes.

2 [+ *obj*] **:** to cause (someone) to formally promise something ▪ She *pledged* herself to silence. [=she promised that she would not say anything] ▪ The chefs are *pledged* to keep the restaurant's special recipe a secret.

3 [+ *obj*] **:** to give (something) as a way to show that you will keep your promise to someone ▪ He *pledged* his paintings as collateral/security for a loan.

4 *US* **:** to promise to join (a college fraternity or sorority) [+ *obj*] She *pledged* the sorority as a freshman. [*no obj*] A few of his friends *pledged* to/with fraternities.

ple·na·ry /ˈpliːnəri/ *adj, always used before a noun, formal*

1 : attended by all the people who have the right to attend ▪ A *plenary* meeting of the 500 members was held last summer. ▪ *plenary* sessions of the legislature

2 : complete in every way ▪ the *plenary* [=*absolute*] power of the federal government

pleni·po·ten·tia·ry /ˌplɛnəpəˈtɛnʃəri/ *noun, pl* **-ries** [*count*] *technical* **:** a person (such as a diplomat) who has complete power to do business for a government

– plenipotentiary *adj* ▪ *plenipotentiary* powers

plen·i·tude /ˈplɛnəˌtuːd, *Brit* ˈplɛnəˌtjuːd/ *noun, formal*

1 [*singular*] **:** a large number or amount of something ▪ She has gathered a *plenitude* of information on the topic. ▪ a *plenitude* of choices

2 [*noncount*] **:** the state of being full or complete ▪ a life of happiness and *plenitude* [=a life in which there is plenty of food, money, etc.]

plen·te·ous /ˈplɛntijəs/ *adj* [*more* ~; *most* ~] *formal + literary* **:** existing in large amounts **:** plentiful or abundant ▪ a *plenteous* [=*copious*] harvest

plen·ti·ful /ˈplɛntɪfəl/ *adj* [*more* ~; *most* ~]

1 : present in large amounts ▪ When I was a teenager, jobs were *plentiful* [=there were plenty of jobs] and the economy was strong. ▪ Gasoline won't always be cheap and *plentiful*. ▪ Space is *plentiful* enough for several homes. ▪ *plentiful* amounts of rain ▪ Natural gas is a *plentiful* resource. ▪ Doctors and nurses are now ***in plentiful supply***. = There is now a *plentiful* supply of doctors and nurses.

2 : containing or giving large amounts of something ▪ These vegetables are a *plentiful* source of vitamins. ▪ *plentiful* [=*fruitful*] land

– plen·ti·ful·ly *adv* • fruit growing *plentifully* on the trees

> ***synonyms*** PLENTIFUL, ABUNDANT, and AMPLE mean more than enough but not too much. PLENTIFUL suggests a large or rich supply of something. • We moved to the city where jobs are more *plentiful*. • a *plentiful* supply of fruits and vegetables • Oranges are *plentiful* this summer. ABUNDANT suggests a very large supply that is far greater than what is necessary. • an *abundant* crop of corn • The fish are becoming increasingly *abundant*. AMPLE suggests an amount that may not be very large but that is more than enough in a specific situation. • The deer had *ample* food to last the winter. • There is *ample* evidence to prove that he is guilty of the crime.

[1]plen·ty /ˈplɛnti/ *pronoun* [*noncount*] : a large number or amount of something : a number or amount of something that is enough for a particular purpose • "Would you like more pie?" "No, thanks. I've had *plenty*." • There's *plenty* [=*enough*] for everyone. — often + *of* • He has *plenty of* room to work. • There will be *plenty of* time to relax later. • Remember to drink *plenty of* water before and after you exercise. • He'll be in *plenty of* trouble when he gets home. — often followed by *to* + *verb* • There's *plenty to see* and do in the city. • Your family has *plenty to be* thankful for. • We always have *plenty to talk* about.

[2]plenty *noun* [*noncount*] *formal* : the state of having enough of the things that make life good and easy • They thought of America as the land of *plenty*. • Businesses tend to give more to charity in times of *plenty*. [=when they have more money] • a season of *plenty*

in plenty — used to say that something is present or exists in large amounts • She has the qualities of patience and courage *in plenty*. [=she has plenty of patience and courage]

[3]plenty *adv, informal* : to a great degree : more than enough • We're *plenty* [=*very*] busy with the work we have already. • It's *plenty* cold outside. • There's *plenty* more where that came from. • The car is *plenty* large enough to fit six people.

pleth·o·ra /ˈplɛθərə/ *noun* [*singular*] *formal* : a very large amount or number : an amount that is much greater than what is necessary • A *plethora* of books have been written on the subject. • a *plethora* of information

pleu·ri·sy /ˈplərəsi/ *noun* [*noncount*] *medical* : a serious and painful disease of the lungs

Plex·i·glas /ˈplɛksɪˌglæs/ *trademark* — used for sheets of strong, clear plastic

plex·us /ˈplɛksəs/ *noun* see SOLAR PLEXUS

pli·able /ˈplajəbəl/ *adj* [*more* ~; *most* ~]

1 : able to bend, fold, or twist easily : FLEXIBLE • Because the leather is *pliable*, it's easy to work with.

2 : too easily influenced or controlled by other people • She sometimes takes advantage of her *pliable* parents. • His principles are *pliable*.

– pli·abil·i·ty /ˌplajəˈbɪləti/ *noun* [*noncount*] • the *pliability* of the leather

pli·ant /ˈplajənt/ *adj* [*more* ~; *most* ~]

1 a : able to bend without breaking : FLEXIBLE • a *pliant* [=(more commonly) *pliable*] material **b** : able to move freely • the dancer's *pliant* body

2 : too easily influenced or controlled by other people • a *pliant* Congress that will do whatever the President wants • a *pliant* wife/husband

– pli·an·cy /ˈplajənsi/ *noun* [*noncount*]

pli·ers /ˈplajəz/ *noun* [*plural*] : a tool that is used for holding small objects or for bending and cutting wire • No toolbox is complete without (a pair of) *pliers*. — see picture at CARPENTRY

[1]plight /ˈplaɪt/ *noun, pl* **plights** [*count*] : a very bad or difficult situation — usually singular • The recent cut in funding will only contribute to the hospital's financial *plight*. • the *plight* of the unemployed/homeless

[2]plight *verb* **plights; plight·ed; plight·ing**

plight your troth *old-fashioned* : to promise to marry someone • the garden where the lovers *plighted their troth*

plim·soll /ˈplɪmsəl/ *noun, pl* **-solls** [*count*] *Brit* : a light sports shoe that is made of strong cloth and has a rubber bottom

plinth /ˈplɪnθ/ *noun, pl* **plinths** [*count*] : a block of stone or wood that is used as the base for a pillar, statue, etc.

plod /ˈplɑːd/ *verb, always followed by an adverb or preposition* **plods; plod·ded; plod·ding**

1 : to walk slowly and usually heavily : TRUDGE [*no obj*] We *plodded* through mud that came up past our ankles. • I could hear my roommate *plodding* up the steps to our apartment. [+ *obj*] We *plodded* our way across the muddy field.

2 [+ *obj*] : to progress or develop slowly • He *plodded* through his work. • The day was *plodding* along.

– plod *noun* [*singular*] • The pace had slowed to a *plod*.

– plod·der /ˈplɑːdə/ *noun, pl* **-ders** [*count*] • a steady *plodder* **– plodding** *adj, always used before a noun* • the movie's *plodding* pace • The book was written in *plodding* prose. **– plod·ding·ly** *adv* • *ploddingly* dull prose

[1]plonk /ˈplɑːŋk/ *noun* [*noncount*] *chiefly Brit, informal* : cheap wine that is not of good quality

[2]plonk *verb* **plonks; plonked; plonk·ing** [+ *obj*] *Brit, informal* : to drop or place (something or someone) in a forceful and often careless way : PLUNK • He *plonked* the suitcase onto the bench.

plonk down [*phrasal verb*] ***plonk down or plonk yourself down*** *Brit, informal* : to sit or lie down suddenly in a careless way • He *plonked down* [=(*chiefly US*) *plunked down*] beside me. • She *plonked herself down* on the sofa.

plonk·er /ˈplɑːŋkə/ *noun, pl* **-ers** [*count*] *Brit, informal* : a stupid person • He was acting like a complete/total *plonker*.

[1]plop /ˈplɑːp/ *verb, always followed by an adverb or preposition* **plops; plopped; plop·ping** *informal*

1 [*no obj*] : to fall, drop, or move with a sound like something dropping into liquid • The stone *plopped* into the river. • An ice cube *plopped* noisily into the glass.

2 [+ *obj*] : to drop (something) into a liquid so that it makes a splashing sound • I filled the glass with water and *plopped* a few ice cubes into it.

3 : to sit or lie down in a heavy or careless way : to allow your body to drop heavily or carelessly [*no obj*] She *plopped* onto the couch. • They *plopped* down on the floor. [+ *obj*] He *plopped* himself down in the chair.

4 [+ *obj*] : to drop or place (something or someone) in a heavy or careless way : PLUNK • He *plopped* the tray down. • The article warns parents against *plopping* their toddlers in front of the TV for hours on end.

plop down [*phrasal verb*] ***plop down (money) or plop (money) down*** *US, informal* : to pay or spend (money) • I can't afford to just *plop down* [=*plunk down*] $30 for a T-shirt.

[2]plop *noun, pl* **plops** [*count*] : the sound made when something (such as a small object) drops into liquid — usually singular • The rock landed in the water with a *plop*.

plo·sive /ˈploʊsɪv/ *noun, pl* **-sives** [*count*] *linguistics* : [2]STOP 6

[1]plot /ˈplɑːt/ *noun, pl* **plots**

1 [*count*] **a** : an area of land that has been measured and is considered as a unit • The *plots* are selling for $15,000 per acre. • They just bought a 12-acre ***plot of land***. **b** : a usually small piece of land that is used for a particular purpose • a garden *plot* • He bought a ***burial plot*** in the local cemetery. [=a small area of land where his body will be buried when he dies]

2 : a series of events that form the story in a novel, movie, etc. [*count*] The book's *plot* revolves around a woman who is searching for her missing sister. • The movie has a weak/strong *plot*. • As the *plot* unfolds [=as the story continues; as things happen in the novel, movie, etc.], we learn more about the hero's family. [*noncount*] The movie lacks *plot* [=nothing interesting happens in the movie], but it's a fascinating character study. • He is a master of *plot* [=he is very good at thinking of interesting stories], but his characters are not realistic. — see also SUBPLOT

3 [*count*] : a secret plan to do something that is usually illegal or harmful • Police uncovered a *plot* to assassinate the prime minister. • The prime minister was the target of an assassination *plot*. • *plots* against the government • They ***hatched a plot*** [=made a plan] to steal the famous painting.

lose the plot *Brit, informal* : to become confused or crazy • She was so nervous she thought she was going to *lose the plot*. [=*lose it*]

the plot thickens ♦ When *the plot thickens* in a novel, movie, etc., the story becomes more complicated or interesting. • *The plot thickens* when the audience learns that the missing woman used to work for the FBI. The phrase is also used in a usually humorous way to talk about things that happen in real life. • So you've worked with him before? Ah, *the plot thickens*.

[2]plot *verb* **plots; plot·ted; plot·ting**

1 a : to plan secretly to do something usually illegal or harmful [+ *obj*] They *plotted* to steal the painting. • She spent her years in prison *plotting* her revenge. • He *plotted* his es-

P

cape. • They are accused of *plotting* the assassination of the prime minister. = They are accused of *plotting* to assassinate the prime minister. [*no obj*] — usually + *against* • He feared the other prisoners were *plotting against* him. **b** [+ *obj*] : to plan (something) • We've been *plotting* growth strategies for the company. • She carefully *plotted* her career path.

2 [+ *obj*] : to mark (something, such as a location or path) on a map, graph, chart, etc. • They've *plotted* the locations where the trees will be planted. • Have you *plotted* the route for your trip yet? • Students *plotted* soil temperatures on a graph throughout the school year. — often + *out* • The investigators *plotted out* the airplane's route.

3 [+ *obj*] : to create a plot for (a novel, movie, etc.) — usually used as *(be) plotted* • Her latest book *is* a brilliantly *plotted* novel [=a novel with a brilliant plot] about the war.

plot·line /ˈplɑːtˌlaɪn/ *noun, pl* **-lines** [*count*] : the things that happen in a book, movie, etc. : PLOT • the movie's main *plotline*

plot·ter /ˈplɑːtɚ/ *noun, pl* **-ters** [*count*]

1 : a person who secretly plans to do something illegal or harmful : someone who plots something • The police caught the *plotters* of the bank heist.

2 : a computer program or device that creates a graph or chart from information

Plough /ˈplaʊ/ *noun*

the Plough Brit : BIG DIPPER

plough, ploughshare *Brit spelling of* PLOW, PLOWSHARE

plo·ver /ˈplʌvɚ/ *noun, pl* **plover** *or* **plo·vers** [*count*] : a type of bird that has a short beak and that lives near the sea

¹plow (*US*) *or Brit* **plough** /ˈplaʊ/ *noun, pl* **plows** [*count*]

1 : a piece of farm equipment that is used to dig into and turn over soil especially to prepare the soil for planting

2 : SNOWPLOW

under the plow *of land* : used for growing crops • The amount of local land *under the plow* is decreasing.

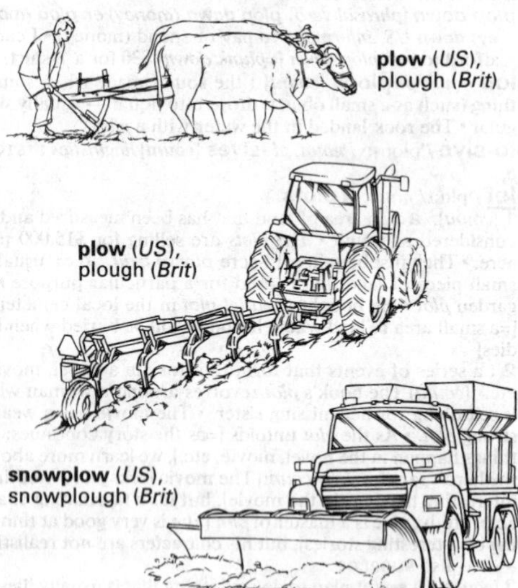

²plow (*US*) *or Brit* **plough** *verb* **plows; plowed; plow·ing**

1 [+ *obj*] : to dig into or break up (dirt, soil, land, etc.) with a plow • The soil was freshly *plowed*. • They used oxen to *plow* the field. • *Plow* the weeds back into the soil. [=use a plow to bury the weeds]

2 *chiefly US* : to use a snowplow to remove snow from a road, parking lot, etc. [+ *obj*] My street hasn't been *plowed* yet. • We hired someone to *plow* the snow from our driveway. [*no obj*] The town won't start *plowing* until the storm is almost over.

3 : to move through, over, or across (something) in a forceful and steady way [+ *obj*] a ship/whale *plowing* the ocean • They continued to *plow* their way through the tall grass. [*no obj*] — followed by an adverb or preposition • A series of damaging storms *plowed* across the state last fall. • We *plowed* through the crowd.

4 *always followed by an adverb or preposition* [*no obj*] : to do something difficult in a slow or steady way • She spent several hours *plowing* through the paperwork on her desk.

plough a furrow see ¹FURROW

plow ahead [*phrasal verb*] : to continue to do something without being stopped by problems or opposition • The city is *plowing ahead* with plans to demolish the building.

plow into [*phrasal verb*] **1** ***plow into (someone or something)*** : to crash into (someone or something) usually at a high speed • The car *plowed into* the guardrail. **2** ***plow (money, profits, etc.) into (something)*** : to invest (money, profits, etc.) in (something) : to put (money) into (something) • The company *plowed* millions of dollars *into* research. — often + *back* • For the first 10 years, the profits were all *plowed back into* the company.

plow on [*phrasal verb*] : to continue doing something that is slow and difficult • I was discouraged, but I *plowed on*.

plow·share (*US*) *or Brit* **plough·share** /ˈplaʊˌʃeɚ/ *noun, pl* **-shares** [*count*] : the part of a plow that digs into the soil

beat/turn swords into plowshares see SWORD

ploy /ˈplɔɪ/ *noun, pl* **ploys** [*count*] : a clever trick or plan that is used to get someone to do something or to gain an advantage over someone • Her story about being sick is only a *ploy* to get you to give her money. • a ***marketing ploy*** [=something that people who are selling a product use to make people want to buy the product]

¹pluck /ˈplʌk/ *verb* **plucks; plucked; pluck·ing**

1 [+ *obj*] : to pull (something) quickly to remove it • My sister *plucked* a white hair from my head. • The hunter *plucked* the bird's feathers. • *plucking* petals off/from a flower • *pluck* [=*pick*] a lemon from the tree

2 [+ *obj*] : to remove some or all of the feathers or hairs from (something) • They *plucked* a chicken. • She *plucks* her eyebrows. [=she regularly removes some of the hairs in her eyebrows to make her eyebrows have a particular shape]

3 *always followed by an adverb or preposition* [+ *obj*] **a** : to take (someone or something) away from a place or situation suddenly or by force • Firefighters *plucked* the child from the top floor of the burning building. • He'd been *plucked* from obscurity and thrust into the national spotlight. • a cat that was *plucked* off the city's streets last winter **b** : to select or take (something) usually from a group, container, or place • We *plucked* [=*chose*] passages at random from the book and read them aloud. • He *plucked* a stone out of the river.

4 a : to pull and release (a string on a musical instrument) with your fingers in order to make a sound [+ *obj*] *pluck* a guitar string [*no obj*] *pluck* on a guitar string **b** : to play (a guitar, banjo, etc.) by pulling and releasing the strings with your fingers [+ *obj*] She was softly *plucking* a banjo. [*no obj*] *plucking* on/at a banjo

pluck at [*phrasal verb*] ***pluck at (something)*** : to pull part of (something) with your fingers especially more than once • He nervously *plucked at* the blanket.

pluck up (the) courage ✧ If you *pluck up (the) courage* to do something, you become brave enough to do it. • He finally *plucked up the courage* to ask her out on a date.

²pluck *noun* [*noncount*] *old-fashioned + informal* : a quality that makes you continue trying to do or achieve something that is difficult : courage and determination • It takes *pluck* to do what she did. • She showed *pluck* in getting up on stage.

plucky /ˈplʌki/ *adj* **pluck·i·er; -est** [*also more* ~; *most* ~] *informal* : having or showing a lot of courage or determination • a *plucky* young man

¹plug /ˈplʌg/ *noun, pl* **plugs** [*count*]

1 a : a part at the end of an electric cord that has two or three metal pins that connect the cord to a source of electricity • the lamp's *plug* • The only way to turn the machine off is to ***pull the plug***. [=remove the plug from the outlet] — see also PULL THE PLUG (below) **b** : a part at the end of a wire or cable that is used to connect machines or devices • a microphone *plug* **c** *chiefly Brit* : OUTLET 4

2 : a thing that is used to close a hole in a container or object • I put the *plug* [=*stopper*] in the drain and let the sink/bathtub fill with water. • a ***drain plug***

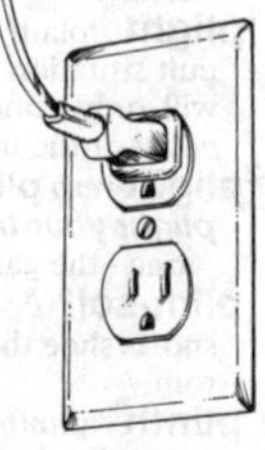
plug

3 : a thing that is used to fill a hole or empty area • a wooden *plug* • We replanted the area with *plugs* of grass. [=bunches of grass plants] — see also EARPLUG

4 : a piece of tobacco used for chewing • He put a *plug* of tobacco in his mouth.
5 : SPARK PLUG
6 : something that is said on the radio, on television, etc., in order to create interest in something (such as a book, movie, or restaurant) — often + *for* • I heard a *plug for* that café on the radio. • He ***gave a plug for*** [=talked about] his new film during the interview. • She ***put in a plug for*** the band's new album on her radio program.
pull the plug *informal* **1 :** to turn off the machine that is keeping a very sick or injured person alive and allow that person to die • Only his wife can decide to *pull the plug.* **2 :** to allow or cause something to end by stopping the money or support that is needed for it — usually + *on* • At the end of the season, the network is *pulling the plug on* the show. • They may *pull the plug on* the tutoring program.

²plug *verb* **plugs; plugged; plug·ging** [+ *obj*]
1 : to fill or cover (a hole, space, etc.) with something • We were able to *plug* the hole with cement. • Leaves and dirt were *plugging* [=*blocking*] the storm drain.— often + *up* • He *plugged up* the spaces between the stones with mud. • The drain was *plugged up*. [=*clogged, blocked*]— often used figuratively • The company needs to *plug* the holes/gaps in its security system.
2 : to praise (something, such as a book, movie, or restaurant) publicly in a way that makes people want to buy it, see it, etc. **:** to advertise (something) by talking about it especially on the radio or television • One of the DJs on the local radio station has been *plugging* the band's new album.
3 *US, informal + old-fashioned* **:** to shoot (someone) with a gun • He *plugged* him right in the chest.
plug away [*phrasal verb*] *informal* **:** to continue doing something even though it is difficult or boring — often + *at* • She kept *plugging away at* her homework.
plug in [*phrasal verb*] ***plug (something) in*** *or* ***plug in (something)*** **1 :** to connect (something, such as a lamp or television) to an electrical source or to another device by using a plug • Don't *plug* the stereo *in* yet. • He *plugged in* the lamp. • The microphone isn't *plugged in.* **2 :** to put (information, such as a word or number) in something • The form has spaces where you just *plug in* [=*insert*] your name and address.— see also PLUG-IN
plug into [*phrasal verb*] **1** ***plug into (something)*** *or* ***plug (something) into (something)*** **:** to become connected or to cause (something) to become connected to an electrical source or another device • The heater *plugs into* the dashboard of your car. • *Plug* the heater *into* the dashboard of the car. • I'm trying to figure out how to *plug* the scanner *into* my computer. — sometimes used figuratively • The company has *plugged into* the international market. [=the company has become connected to the international market; the company has begun to do business in the international market] • His friends are *plugged into* the city's music scene. [=his friends are actively involved in the city's music scene] **2** ***plug (something) into (something)*** **:** to put (information, such as a word or number) into something • The computer program will take data from these sources and automatically *plug* it *into* the equation.

plug and play *noun* [*noncount*] *computers* **:** a feature of a computer system that makes it possible for the computer to use a device as soon as it is connected to the computer
– plug–and–play *adj* • *plug-and-play* software

plug·hole /ˈplʌgˌhoʊl/ *noun, pl* **-holes** [*count*] *Brit* **:** ²DRAIN 1
down the plughole *informal* **1** — used to describe something that is being wasted or lost • All my hard work ***went down the plughole***. [=*went down the drain*] • You're ***pouring your money down the plughole***. [=you're wasting your money] **2** — used to describe something that is getting much worse • The business is ***going down the plughole***.

plug–in /ˈplʌgˌɪn/ *noun, pl* **-ins** [*count*] *computers* **:** a small piece of software that adds a feature to a larger program or makes a program work better • a (Web) browser *plug-in* • *plug-in* software

plum /ˈplʌm/ *noun, pl* **plums**
1 [*count*] **:** a round, juicy fruit that has red or purple skin, sweet yellow flesh, and a hard seed at the center • a bowl of peaches and *plums* • Dried *plums* are also called "prunes." • *plum* sauce • *plum* trees— see color picture on page C5
2 [*count*] *somewhat informal* **:** something that many people want or think is very good • That deal is a real *plum* for the contractor.— usually used before another noun • It's a *plum* job. • How did she get such a *plum* role in the play?
3 [*noncount*] **:** a dark reddish-purple color — see color picture on page C3

plum·age /ˈplʌmɪʤ/ *noun* [*noncount*] **:** the feathers that cover the body of a bird • The peacock has colorful *plumage.*

¹plumb /ˈplʌm/ *adv*
1 *technical* **:** exactly straight down or up **:** in a perfectly vertical position • He set the board *plumb.*
2 *US, informal + old-fashioned* **:** to a complete degree **:** COMPLETELY • I *plumb* forgot about the party. • We were *plumb* [=*totally*] exhausted after the game.
3 *informal* **:** EXACTLY, DIRECTLY • The island is located *plumb* [=*right*] in the middle of the lake.

²plumb *adj* [*more* ~; *most* ~] *technical* **:** exactly vertical **:** standing perfectly straight and not leaning in any way • The carpenter made sure that the wall was *plumb*. • The chimney is ***out of plumb***. = The chimney is ***off plumb***. [=not straight upright; leaning to one side]

³plumb *verb* **plumbs; plumbed; plumb·ing** [+ *obj*]
1 a *literary* **:** to examine (something) in a careful and complete way in order to understand it • The book *plumbs* the complexities of human relationships. • a scientist who spent her life *plumbing* the minds of criminals • The play ***plumbs the depths of*** human nature. **b :** to experience or reach (something) • someone who has ***plumbed the depths of*** loss/pain [=who has experienced a lot of loss/pain] • The company's stocks ***plumbed new depths*** [=reached their lowest value] this week.
2 *US* **a :** to install pipes for sinks, toilets, etc., in (a building or room) • The plumber is almost finished *plumbing* the apartment. • The new house has been wired and *plumbed.* **b :** to connect (something, such as a sink) to a water supply • All the bathroom fixtures have been *plumbed.*
plumb in [*phrasal verb*] *chiefly Brit* ***plumb (something) in*** *or* ***plumb in (something)*** **:** to connect (something) to a water supply • I *plumbed in* the washing machine.

plumb bob *noun, pl* ~ **bobs** [*count*] *US*
1 : a usually small, heavy object that is used to make a string or rope hang straight **:** the heavy object that is part of a plumb line — called also *bob*
2 : PLUMB LINE

plumb·er /ˈplʌmɚ/ *noun, pl* **-ers** [*count*] **:** a person whose job is to install or repair sinks, toilets, water pipes, etc.

plumber's snake *noun, pl* ~ **snakes** [*count*] **:** ¹SNAKE 3

plumb·ing /ˈplʌmɪŋ/ *noun* [*noncount*]
1 : a system of pipes that carries water through a building • The house has old *plumbing.* • The cottage has electricity but no ***indoor plumbing***. [=the cottage does not have a toilet or sink; there are no pipes that supply clean water to the cottage] • a store that sells ***plumbing fixtures*** [=sinks, toilets, faucets, etc.]

plumbing

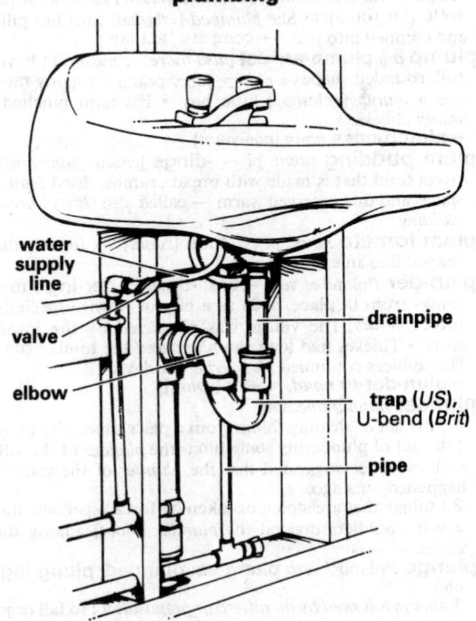

P

2 : the work of a plumber : the job of installing and repairing sinks, toilets, water pipes, etc.

plumb line *noun, pl* ~ **lines** [*count*] : a tool that consists of a small, heavy object attached to a string or rope and that is used especially to see if something (such as a wall) is perfectly vertical — called also (*US*) *plumb bob*

plume /ˈpluːm/ *noun, pl* **plumes** [*count*]
1 : a feather or group of feathers on a bird ▪ the peacock's colorful *plumes*
2 : a decoration made of feathers or something similar ▪ a hat with bright ostrich *plumes*
3 : something (such as smoke, steam, or water) that rises into the air in a tall, thin shape ▪ A *plume* [=*column*] of smoke rose from the chimney.
– see also NOM DE PLUME
– plumed /ˈpluːmd/ *adj* ▪ The knights wore *plumed* helmets. ▪ a white-*plumed* bird

plum·met /ˈplʌmət/ *verb* **-mets; -met·ed; -met·ing** [*no obj*]
1 *always followed by an adverb or preposition* **:** to fall suddenly straight down especially from a very high place ▪ The acrobat *plummeted* into the net. ▪ The car *plummeted* to the bottom of the canyon. ▪ The satellite *plummeted* into/toward the ocean.
2 : to fall or drop suddenly in amount, value, etc. : PLUNGE ▪ Stock prices *plummeted* 40 percent during the scandal. ▪ The TV show has *plummeted* in the ratings. ▪ Temperatures are expected to *plummet* this weekend. ▪ The town's population *plummets* when the students leave for the summer.

plum·my /ˈplʌmi/ *adj* **plum·mi·er; -est** [*also more* ~; *most* ~]
1 : like a plum in color, taste, or smell ▪ the wine's ripe, *plummy* flavors
2 *often disapproving, of a person's voice* **:** full and formal often in a way that sounds too proper and not natural ▪ his *plummy* British accent
3 *informal* **:** wanted by many people : very good and desirable ▪ a *plummy* job [=a good job that people want to have]

¹plump /ˈplʌmp/ *verb* **plumps; plumped; plump·ing :** to sit, fall, or lie down in a sudden, awkward, or relaxed way : PLOP [*no obj*] He came home and *plumped* [=*flopped*] down on the couch. [+ *obj*] She *plumped* her bags onto the bench.
plump for [*phrasal verb*] ***plump for (someone or something)*** *informal* **1** *US* **:** to express support for (someone or something) ▪ The President *plumped for* the incumbent candidate in the election. **2** *Brit* **:** to choose (someone or something) after thinking carefully ▪ I finally *plumped for* the blue dress.
– compare ²PLUMP

²plump *verb* **plumps; plumped; plumping** [+ *obj*] **:** to shake or hit (something, such as a pillow) to make it fuller, softer, or rounder ▪ She *plumped* [=*fluffed*] (up) her pillows and climbed into bed. — compare ¹PLUMP

³plump *adj* **plump·er; -est** [*also more* ~; *most* ~] **:** having a full, rounded shape ▪ a *plump*, juicy peach : slightly fat ▪ He was a *plump* [=*chubby*] little boy. ▪ His aunt pinched his *plump* cheeks.
– plump·ness *noun* [*noncount*]

plum pudding *noun, pl* ~ **-dings** [*count, noncount*] **:** a sweet food that is made with bread crumbs, dried fruit, and spices and that is served warm — called also (*Brit*) *Christmas pudding*

plum tomato *noun, pl* ~ **-toes** [*count*] **:** a tomato that is shaped like an egg

¹plun·der /ˈplʌndɚ/ *verb* **-ders; -dered; -der·ing :** to steal things from (a place, such as a city or town) especially by force [+ *obj*] The village was *plundered* by the invading army. ▪ Thieves had long ago *plundered* the tomb. [*no obj*] The soldiers continued *plundering* for days.
– plun·der·er *noun, pl* **-ers** [*count*]

²plunder *noun* [*noncount*]
1 : the act of stealing things from a place especially by force : the act of plundering something ▪ the *plunder* of the village ▪ All evidence suggested that the *plunder* of the tomb had happened long ago.
2 : things that are stolen or taken by force especially during a war ▪ Soldiers divided the *plunder* [=*loot*] among themselves.

¹plunge /ˈplʌnʤ/ *verb* **plung·es; plunged; plung·ing** [*no obj*]
1 *always followed by an adverb or preposition* **:** to fall or jump suddenly from a high place ▪ Her car *plunged* off a bridge. ▪ He *plunged* [=*dove*] into the pool. ▪ The rocket *plunged* [=*plummeted*] toward the Earth. ▪ The parachute failed to open, and the jumper ***plunged to her death*** [=died from her fall]
2 : to fall or drop suddenly in amount, value, etc. : PLUMMET ▪ The stock market *plunged* yesterday. ▪ The President's approval rating has *plunged* to 20 percent. ▪ The moose population has *plunged* in recent years.
3 *always followed by an adverb or preposition* **:** to have a steep slope or drop downward ▪ The rocky cliffs *plunge* into the swirling rapids below. ▪ The road *plunges* down the mountain.
plunge in/into [*phrasal verb*] **1** ***plunge (something) in or plunge (something) into (something)*** **:** to push (something) into (something) quickly and forcefully ▪ The nurse grabbed his arm and *plunged* the needle *in*. ▪ He *plunged* the knife *into* the cake. ▪ I *plunged* the sponge *into* the bucket of water. ▪ He *plunged* his hands *into* his pockets. **2** ***plunge in or plunge into (something)*** **:** to start doing (something) with enthusiasm and energy ▪ It was a big project, so we all just had to *plunge in* [=*dive in*] and get started. ▪ She *plunged* (right) *into* the assignment. **3 a** ***plunge into (something)*** **:** to suddenly begin to be in (a particular and usually bad condition or situation) ▪ He *plunged into* a severe depression. **b** ***plunge (someone or something) into (something)*** **:** to cause (someone or something) to suddenly be in (a particular condition or situation) ▪ A series of bad management decisions had *plunged* the company *into* debt. ▪ The author *plunges* his readers *into* a world of fantasy. ▪ The museum was recently *plunged into* scandal when it was learned that some of its art had been sold on the black market. ▪ The city was ***plunged into darkness*** [=the city suddenly became dark]

²plunge *noun, pl* **plunges** [*count*]
1 : a sudden fall or jump usually from a high place ▪ Amazingly, the cat survived its *plunge* from the building's roof.
2 : a sudden quick fall in amount, value, etc. ▪ Market analysts predicted a price *plunge*. ▪ The store experienced a sharp *plunge* in sales.
3 : the act of suddenly beginning to be in a particular condition or situation — usually + *into* ▪ his *plunge into* severe depression ▪ A series of bad management decisions are responsible for the company's *plunge into* debt.
take the plunge *informal* **:** to do something after thinking about it especially for a long time ▪ We've been thinking of buying a new car, and yesterday we finally *took the plunge*. [=we bought a new car] ▪ They're talking about marriage, but they don't know if they're ready to *take the plunge*.

plung·er /ˈplʌnʤɚ/ *noun, pl* **-ers** [*count*]
1 : a tool made of a stick with a rubber cup on the end that is used to clear a blocked pipe in a toilet or sink — see picture at BATHROOM
2 : a part that moves up and down usually inside a tube or cylinder (such as a syringe) to push something out

plunk /ˈplʌŋk/ *verb* **plunks; plunked; plunk·ing** *informal*
1 *chiefly US* **:** to pull or hit a string or key on a musical instrument with your fingers especially in a way that makes a brief, somewhat harsh sound [+ *obj*] You've been *plunking* that banjo all afternoon! ▪ She *plunked* out a little tune on the piano. [*no obj*] *plunking* away on a guitar
2 [+ *obj*] *US* **:** to hit (someone or something) especially with a ball ▪ The pitcher *plunked* the first two batters of the game.
3 *always followed by an adverb or preposition* [+ *obj*] *chiefly US* **:** to drop or place (something or someone) in a forceful and often careless way : PLOP ▪ He *plunked* [=(*Brit*) *plonked*] the suitcase onto the bench. ▪ She *plunked* a mug of coffee on the counter. — often used figuratively ▪ He was *plunked* down into a job he wasn't qualified to do.
plunk down [*phrasal verb*] *informal* **1** ***plunk down (money) or plunk (money) down US*** **:** to pay or spend (money) ▪ He just *plunked down* $25,000 for a new car. **2** ***plunk down or plunk yourself down chiefly US*** **:** to sit or lie down suddenly in a careless way ▪ He *plunked down* [=(*Brit*) *plonked down*] beside me. ▪ She *plunked herself down* on the sofa.

plu·per·fect /ˌpluːˈpɚfɪkt/ *noun* [*noncount*] *grammar* **:** PAST PERFECT

¹plu·ral /ˈplɚrəl/ *adj*
1 *grammar* **:** relating to a form of a word that refers to more than one person or thing ▪ The word "trees" is a *plural* noun. ▪ The *plural* form of the word "child" is "children." ▪ a *plural* verb such as "are" or "were" rather than a singular verb such

as "is" or "was" — compare SINGULAR

2 *formal* **a :** relating to or made up of more than one kind or group • Our country is a *plural* society. [=it includes people of different social classes, religions, races, etc.] **b :** relating to or made up of more than one person or thing • the practice of ***plural marriage*** [=a marriage in which there is more than one husband or wife]

²plural *noun, pl* **-rals** [*count*] **:** a form of a word that is used to refer to more than one person or thing • English *plurals* usually end in an "s." — usually used with *the* • *The plural* of (the word) "child" is "children." • "Books" is *the plural* of "book." • "Children" is ***in the plural***. — abbr. *pl.*

plu·ral·ism /ˈplərəˌlɪzəm/ *noun* [*noncount*] *formal*

1 : a situation in which people of different social classes, religions, races, etc., are together in a society but continue to have their different traditions and interests • He spoke of the benefits of cultural/religious *pluralism*.

2 : the belief that people of different social classes, religions, races, etc., should live together in a society • She's a champion of *pluralism*.

– **plu·ral·ist** /ˈplərəlɪst/ *noun, pl* **-ists** [*count*] – **pluralist** *or* **plu·ral·is·tic** /ˌplərəˈlɪstɪk/ *adj* [*more* ~; *most* ~] • a *pluralistic* society

plu·ral·i·ty /plʊˈrælәti/ *noun, pl* **-ties**

1 [*count*] *formal* **:** a usually large number of things — usually singular; usually + *of* • The researchers studied a *plurality of* approaches.

2 [*count*] *chiefly US, technical* **:** a number of votes that is more than the number of votes for any other candidate or party but that is not more than half of the total number of votes — usually singular • Her party won by receiving a *plurality* of the vote. • He was elected with a *plurality*, not a majority. — compare MAJORITY

3 [*noncount*] *grammar* **:** the state of being plural • The verb "are" indicates the *plurality* of the subject. [=the verb "are" shows that the subject is plural]

¹plus /ˈplʌs/ *adj*

1 *always used before a noun* **:** having a value that is above zero **:** POSITIVE • The temperature was *plus* 10 degrees. [=10 degrees above zero] — opposite ³MINUS 1

2 — used after a letter grade (such as A, B, or C) to show that the work is slightly better than the letter by itself would indicate • He got a C *plus* in history. — opposite ³MINUS 2

3 — used after a number to indicate a range greater than that number • The concert is an 18-*plus* show. [=a show for people who are 18 years old or older] • This stadium seats 20,000-*plus* people. [=more than 20,000 people]

on the plus side — used to describe the more appealing or attractive part of something • On the minus side, the job doesn't pay very well, but *on the plus side*, the hours are very convenient.

²plus *noun, pl* **plus·es** [*count*]

1 *informal* **:** something that is useful or helpful • The apartment isn't perfect, but the fact that it has new appliances is a *plus*. • The state college's low tuition is only one of its *pluses*. [=*advantages, benefits*] • The job doesn't pay well, but the convenient hours are a definite *plus*. — opposite ²MINUS 1

2 *mathematics* **:** PLUS SIGN

³plus *prep*

1 — used to indicate that one number or amount is being added to another • 4 *plus* 5 equals/is 9 • The cost is $10 *plus* $2 for shipping.

2 : and also **:** as well as • The hotel has two restaurants, *plus* a bar and a swimming pool.

plus or minus — used to indicate that a value, number, or amount may be above or below a certain number • It should take a month, *plus or minus* a few days.

⁴plus *conj, informal* **:** in addition **:** AND • He works a full-time job during the day, *plus* he goes to school at night. • I enjoy gardening, *plus* it's good exercise.

¹plush /ˈplʌʃ/ *adj* **plush·er; -est** [*also more* ~; *most* ~]

1 a : made of a thick, soft fabric • *plush* carpeting/toys **b :** thick and soft • *plush* fabric

2 : very fancy and usually expensive **:** LUXURIOUS • a *plush* apartment/office/suite • The hotel accommodations were *plush*.

²plush *noun* [*noncount*] **:** a thick, soft fabric

plus sign *noun, pl* ~ **signs** [*count*] **:** the symbol + used to show that a number is being added to another number or that a quantity is greater than zero — compare MINUS SIGN

plus size *noun, pl* ~ **sizes** [*count*] *chiefly US* **:** a clothing size made for large women • The store sells *plus sizes*.

– **plus–size** *adj* • *plus-size* clothing/women • the *plus-size* department/market

Plu·to /ˈpluːtoʊ/ *noun* [*singular*] **:** the object in our solar system that in the past was thought to be the planet farthest from the sun but that is no longer considered to be a planet

plu·toc·ra·cy /pluˈtɑːkrəsi/ *noun, pl* **-cies**

1 a [*noncount*] **:** government by the richest people • a trend toward *plutocracy* **b** [*count*] **:** a country that is ruled by the richest people • If only the wealthy can afford to run for public office, are we more a *plutocracy* than a democracy?

2 [*count*] **:** a group of very rich people who have a lot of power • corporate greed and America's growing *plutocracy*

plu·to·crat /ˈpluːtəˌkræt/ *noun, pl* **-crats** [*count*] *often disapproving* **:** a person who has power because of great wealth

– **plu·to·crat·ic** /ˌpluːtəˈkrætɪk/ *adj* • a *plutocratic* society

plu·to·ni·um /pluˈtoʊnijəm/ *noun* [*noncount*] **:** a radioactive element that is used to make nuclear energy and nuclear weapons

¹ply /ˈplaɪ/ *verb* **plies; plied; ply·ing** *formal*

1 [+ *obj*] **a :** to work at (a job, activity, etc.) • The carpenter *plies* his art/craft in his workshop. • Wood-carvers were ***plying their trade*** [=doing their work] in the town square. • a street where many artists ***ply their wares*** [=sell their goods] on the sidewalk **b** *old-fashioned* **:** to use (something, such as a tool) with care and skill • She makes a living as a writer, busily *plying* her pen each day.

2 *always followed by an adverb or preposition, of a bus, ship, airplane, etc.* **:** to go along the same route regularly **:** to travel on a particular road, way, etc., regularly [*no obj*] Barges *plied* back and forth along the canal. • Two ferries *ply* between the island and mainland in the summer months. [+ *obj*] Trucks *ply* the highway between the two cities. • ships *plying* the country's northern coast

ply for hire/business/trade *Brit* **:** to try to get customers or business • Taxis *ply for hire/business* outside the train station. • The company is *plying for trade* in America.

ply with [*phrasal verb*] ***ply (someone) with (something)*** **:** to offer or give (something) to (someone) repeatedly or constantly • Someone who is *plying* you *with* gifts [=giving you many gifts] probably wants something in return. • Waiters *plied* guests *with* wine and hors d'oeuvres. • He *plied* me *with* questions. [=he asked me many questions]

²ply *noun, pl* **plies** [*count*] **:** one of the layers, folds, or strands that make something (such as yarn or plywood) • a single *ply* of fabric — usually used in combination • four-*ply* yarn [=yarn made up of four strands] • two-*ply* paper towels

ply·wood /ˈplaɪˌwʊd/ *noun* [*noncount*] **:** a strong board that is made by gluing together thin sheets of wood • a floor made of *plywood* = a *plywood* floor

p.m. *or* **PM** *or Brit* **pm** *abbr* in the afternoon or evening — used with numbers to show the time of day • She went to bed at 10 *p.m.* • He works every day from 8:00 a.m. to/until 4:30 *p.m.* • Lunch will be served at ***12 p.m.*** [=*noon*; one hour after 11 a.m.] ✧ The abbreviation *p.m.* stands for the Latin phrase *post meridiem*, which means "after noon." — compare A.M.

PM *abbr* prime minister

PMS /ˌpiːˌɛmˈɛs/ *noun* [*noncount*] *US* **:** PREMENSTRUAL SYNDROME

PMT /ˌpiːˌɛmˈtiː/ *noun* [*noncount*] *Brit* **:** PREMENSTRUAL SYNDROME

pneu·mat·ic /nʊˈmætɪk, *Brit* njuˈmætɪk/ *adj*

1 *technical* **a :** using air pressure to move or work • a *pneumatic* hammer **b :** filled with air • *pneumatic* tires

2 *US, informal, of a woman* **:** having a body with full, pleasing curves • The movie stars a *pneumatic* blonde.

pneumatic drill *noun, pl* ~ **drills** [*count*] **:** JACKHAMMER

pneu·mo·nia /nʊˈmoʊnjə, *Brit* njuˈməʊnjə/ *noun* [*noncount*] *medical* **:** a serious disease that affects the lungs and makes it difficult to breathe • He caught/contracted *pneumonia* over the winter. • Her father died from/of ***double pneumonia***. [=pneumonia in both lungs]

P.O. *abbr* **1** post office **2** postal order

¹poach /ˈpoʊʧ/ *verb* **poach·es; poached; poach·ing** [+ *obj*]

1 : to cook (something) in a small amount of liquid that is almost boiling • The vegetables were *poached* in chicken broth.

2 : to cook (an egg without its shell) in boiling water or in a small cup over boiling water • *poach* an egg

– compare ²POACH

– **poached** *adj* • We had *poached* eggs for breakfast. • *poached* salmon/oysters

P

²poach *verb* **poaches; poached; poaching**
1 : to hunt or fish illegally **:** to catch or kill an animal illegally [*+ obj*] Elephants are often *poached* for their ivory tusks. [*no obj*] The state fines anyone who is caught *poaching*.
2 [*+ obj*] **:** to take (something, such as an idea, or someone, such as an employee or customer) from someone else illegally or unfairly • She was accused of *poaching* [=*plagiarizing*] the material for her essay from a Web site. • Her former company accused her of *poaching* clients.
poach on someone's territory/turf **:** to do something that someone else should do **:** to interfere in an area that another person usually controls • You can't keep other candidates from *poaching on your turf*. [=from trying to get voters who usually vote for you or your party to vote for them]
— compare ¹POACH
— **poach·er** *noun, pl* **-ers** [*count*] • *Poachers* are responsible for the declining rhinoceros population in this area.
— **poaching** *noun* [*noncount*] • a heavy fine for *poaching*

P.O. Box *noun, pl* ~ **Boxes** [*count*] **:** a box at a post office where you can have mail delivered — used in mailing addresses • Write to *P.O. Box* 100, New York, New York.

po'·boy /ˈpoʊˌbɔɪ/ *noun, pl* **-boys** [*count*] *US* **:** SUBMARINE SANDWICH — used especially to refer to a type of submarine sandwich that is served in Louisiana

pock /ˈpɑːk/ *verb* **pocks; pocked; pock·ing** [*+ obj*] **:** to make holes in or marks on (something) • one of the many craters that *pock* the moon's surface
— **pocked** *adj* • the moon's *pocked* surface • a bullet-*pocked* wall [=a wall that bullets have pocked] • The road was *pocked* with potholes. • a face *pocked* with scars

¹pock·et /ˈpɑːkət/ *noun, pl* **-ets** [*count*]
1 : a usually small cloth bag that is sewn into a piece of clothing, a larger bag, etc., and that is open at the top or side so that you can put things into it • He keeps his gloves in his coat *pocket*. • She was standing there with her hands in her *pockets*. • a hip/breast/shirt *pocket* • I have a hole in my *pocket*. • Her *pocket* was full of change/coins. • The security guard asked us to ***empty our pockets*** [=to take out everything in our pockets] — see color picture on page C15
2 : the amount of money that someone has available to spend • We're looking for investors with *pockets* that are deep enough to pay for the project. [=investors with enough money to pay for the project] • There are items in our store that ***suit every pocket*** [=that everyone can afford to buy] • The governor paid for the event ***out of his own pocket*** [=with his own money rather than the state's money] • The mayor diverted city funds ***into his own pockets*** [=he took money that belonged to the city] — see also DEEP POCKETS
3 : a small bag or container that is attached to something and used to hold things • There are *pockets* on the back of each car seat. • The tickets are in the zippered *pocket* on the front of the suitcase.
4 : a small area or group that is different from the larger area or group it is in or near — usually *+ of* • Military forces have encountered a few *pockets of* resistance.
5 *pool and billiards* **:** a bag or cup that you hit the ball into at the corner or side of a pool table or billiard table • He knocked the ball into the corner/side *pocket*.
6 : AIR POCKET
be/live in each other's pockets *Brit, informal* **:** to be too close to someone or spend too much time with someone
in someone's pocket *or* ***in the pocket of someone*** *disapproving* **:** under someone's control or influence • The judge in the case was *in the senator's pocket*. [=was controlled by the senator] • researchers/scientists who are *in the pocket of* pharmaceutical companies
in your pocket *informal* ✧ If you have something *in your pocket*, you are certain to win or get it. • The interview went really well. I thought I had the job *in my pocket*. • She knew that she had the game/match *in her pocket*. [=she knew she would win the game]
line your pockets see ³LINE
out of pocket *chiefly Brit, informal* **:** having less money because of something that has happened • The lawsuit has left company shareholders $30 million *out of pocket*. — see also OUT-OF-POCKET
pick pockets see ¹PICK

²pocket *verb* **-ets; -et·ed; -et·ing** [*+ obj*]
1 : to put (something) in a pocket • He *pocketed* the change.
2 a : to take or keep (something that does not belong to you) • The chairman was fired for *pocketing* funds. • It turned out that they had *pocketed* [=*stolen*] most of the money that was supposed to go to victims of the fire. • The saleswoman had overcharged them and *pocketed* the difference. **b :** to earn or win (something, such as money) • a professional golfer who *pocketed* more than four million dollars in winnings
3 *US* **:** to ignore (an emotion or feeling) • I had to *pocket* my pride and ask for some help.
4 *pool and billiards* **:** to hit (a ball) into a pocket of a pool table or billiard table • She *pocketed* the eight ball.

³pocket *adj, always used before a noun*
1 : small enough to fit in a pocket • a *pocket* calculator/dictionary
2 : carried in a pocket • *pocket* change • a *pocket* watch/handkerchief

pocket billiards *noun* [*noncount*] **:** ³POOL 2

pock·et·book /ˈpɑːkətˌbʊk/ *noun, pl* **-books** [*count*]
1 *US, somewhat old-fashioned* **:** a bag usually with handles and pockets that is used by women to carry money and personal belongings **:** PURSE, HANDBAG
2 *US* **:** the amount of money that someone has available to spend **:** someone's ability to pay for things • The restaurant has meals priced to ***suit every pocketbook*** [=it has meals that everyone can afford] • People ***vote their pocketbooks*** [=people vote according to how a candidate or issue will affect their financial situation]
3 *Brit* **:** NOTEBOOK 1

pock·et·ful /ˈpɑːkətˌfʊl/ *noun, pl* **pock·et·fuls** *or* **pock·ets·ful** /ˈpɑːkətsˌfʊl/ [*count*] **:** an amount of something that can be carried in a pocket • He carried a *pocketful* of money.

pock·et·knife /ˈpɑːkətˌnaɪf/ *noun, pl* **-knives** [*count*] **:** a small knife that has one or more blades that fold into the handle — called also *jackknife, penknife*

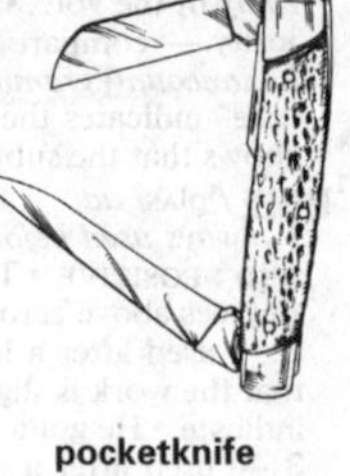
pocketknife

pocket money *noun* [*noncount*]
1 : a small amount of extra money • She mowed lawns in the summers to earn *pocket money*. [=*spending money*]
2 *Brit* **:** money that is regularly given to children by their parents **:** money that children are given as an allowance

pock·et–size /ˈpɑːkətˌsaɪz/ *also* **pock·et–sized** /ˈpɑːkətˌsaɪzd/ *adj* **:** small enough to be carried in a pocket • a *pocket-size* dictionary

pocket veto *noun, pl* ~ **-toes** [*count*] *US* **:** a method that the President can use to prevent a bill from becoming a law by not signing the bill before the session of Congress ends

pock·mark /ˈpɑːkˌmɑɚk/ *noun, pl* **-marks** [*count*]
1 : a mark or scar on the skin that is usually caused by a disease (such as chicken pox or acne)
2 : a hole in or mark on something • The bullets left *pockmarks* in the wall.
— **pockmarked** /ˈpɑːkˌmɑɚkt/ *adj* • A severe case of the chicken pox had left her badly *pockmarked*. • The car was *pockmarked* [=*pocked*] with rust.

¹pod /ˈpɑːd/ *noun, pl* **pods** [*count*]
1 : a long, thin part of some plants that has seeds inside • pea *pods* • a seed *pod* • Carob seeds grow in edible *pods*.
2 : a long, narrow area that is under the wings or body of an airplane and that is used to hold something (such as fuel or a jet engine)
3 : a part of a spacecraft that can be separated from the main part
4 : a case that contains the eggs of certain insects (such as grasshoppers)
two peas in a pod see PEA
— compare ²POD

²pod *noun, pl* **pods** [*count*] **:** a group of ocean animals (such as whales) that are swimming together • *pods* of whales/dolphins — compare ¹POD

PO'd /ˌpiːˈoʊd/ *adj* [*more* ~; *most* ~] *US, informal* **:** very angry or annoyed at someone or something • He was/got really *PO'd* [=(*impolite*) *pissed off*] when his date didn't show up.

podgy /ˈpɑːʤi/ *adj* **podg·i·er; -est** [*also more* ~; *most* ~] *Brit, informal* **:** PUDGY

po·di·a·trist /poʊˈdajətrɪst/ *noun, pl* **-trists** [*count*] *chiefly US* **:** a doctor who treats injuries and diseases of the foot — called also (*chiefly Brit*) *chiropodist*
— **po·di·a·try** /poʊˈdajətri/ *noun* [*noncount*]

po·di·um /ˈpoʊdijəm/ *noun, pl* **-ums** [*count*]
1 : a raised platform for a speaker, performer, or the leader of an orchestra
2 *US* **:** a stand with a slanted surface that holds a book, notes, etc., for someone who is reading, speaking, or teaching **:** LECTERN

Po·dunk *also* **po·dunk** /ˈpoʊˌdʌŋk/ *noun* [*singular*] *US, informal* **:** a small, unimportant town ▪ folks who move to the big city from *Podunk* ▪ a *Podunk* town

po·em /ˈpowəm/ *noun, pl* **-ems** [*count*] **:** a piece of writing that usually has figurative language and that is written in separate lines that often have a repeated rhythm and sometimes rhyme ▪ a love/epic *poem* ▪ He wrote a *poem* about his parents.

po·et /ˈpowət/ *noun, pl* **-ets** [*count*] **:** a person who writes poems

po·et·ess /ˈpowətəs/ *noun, pl* **-ess·es** [*count*] *old-fashioned* **:** a girl or woman who writes poems

po·et·ic /poʊˈɛtɪk/ *also* **po·et·i·cal** /poʊˈɛtɪkəl/ *adj* [*more* ~; *most* ~]
1 : of, relating to, or characteristic of poets or poetry ▪ *poetic* words ▪ *poetic* meter
2 : having a beautiful or graceful quality ▪ *poetic* language
– po·et·i·cal·ly /poʊˈɛtɪkli/ *adv* ▪ a *poetically* written description of the forest

poetic justice *noun* [*noncount*] **:** a result or occurrence that seems proper because someone who has done bad things to other people is being harmed or punished ▪ After the way he treated his staff, it was *poetic justice* that he lost his job.

poet laureate *noun, pl* **poets laureate** *or* **poet laureates** [*count*] **:** a poet who is honored by being chosen for an official position by a ruler or government

po·et·ry /ˈpowətri/ *noun* [*noncount*]
1 : the writings of a poet **:** poems ▪ I read the poem in a collection of modern *poetry*. ▪ She's published two books of lyric *poetry* and a novel. ▪ He found it easiest to express himself in the language of *poetry*. ▪ He reads/writes *poetry*. ▪ The bookstore holds a ***poetry reading*** [=an event in which people read poems that they have written aloud for a group] every Thursday night.
2 : something that is very beautiful or graceful ▪ Her dancing is pure *poetry*.
poetry in motion **:** someone or something that moves in a way that is very graceful or beautiful ▪ He is *poetry in motion* when he catches and throws the ball.

po–faced /ˈpoʊˌfeɪst/ *adj* [*more* ~; *most* ~] *Brit, informal*
1 : having a serious expression on the face ▪ a *po-faced* police officer
2 : too serious ▪ the writer's *po-faced* [=*humorless*] style

po·go stick /ˈpoʊgoʊ-/ *noun, pl* ~ **sticks** [*count*] **:** a toy that children use for bouncing up and down which consists of a pole with handles at the top, a strong spring at the bottom, and two pieces near the bottom to stand on

po·grom /pəˈgrɑːm, *Brit* ˈpɒgrəm/ *noun, pl* **-groms** [*count*] **:** the organized killing of many helpless people usually because of their race or religion

poi·gnant /ˈpɔɪnjənt/ *adj* [*more* ~; *most* ~] **:** causing a strong feeling of sadness ▪ a *poignant* moment ▪ The photograph was a *poignant* reminder of her childhood.
– poi·gnan·cy /ˈpɔɪnjənsi/ *noun* [*noncount*] ▪ The anniversary of the flood has a special *poignancy* in the town that suffered the most damage. **– poi·gnant·ly** *adv*

poin·set·tia /pɔɪnˈsɛtijə/ *noun, pl* **-tias** [*count*] **:** a plant with large red, pink, or white leaves that look like petals — see color picture on page C6 ✧ Poinsettias are tropical plants but are often grown indoors in pots. Red poinsettias are especially popular at Christmastime.

[1]**point** /ˈpɔɪnt/ *noun, pl* **points**
1 a [*count*] **:** an idea that you try to make other people accept or understand ▪ She showed us several graphs to illustrate the *point* she was making. ▪ I see your *point*, but I don't think everyone will agree. ▪ There's no use in arguing the *point*. ▪ He made a very good *point* about the need for change. ▪ Let me make one final *point*. ▪ That's the *point* I've been trying to make. ▪ "What's your *point*?" "Actually, I have two *points*." ▪ My *point* is simply that we must do something to help the homeless. ▪ That's my *point* exactly. ▪ Maybe there's a better way to ***get your point across***. [=to make people understand what you are saying] ▪ He's willing to do almost anything to ***prove a point***. [=to show that he is right about something] ▪ If you want to ***stretch a point*** [=exaggerate slightly], you could say that he is handsome. ▪ "If we leave now, we won't make it back in time." "That's a ***good point***." ▪ "You have to help them." "***Point taken***. [=I understand what you are saying] I'll do what I can." ▪ I don't want to ***labor/belabor the point*** [=repeat myself too many times], but I think I should mention again that we are running out of time. **b** [*count*] **:** a particular detail of an idea or argument ▪ There are two critical/crucial/key *points* that I would like to discuss. ▪ There are several weak *points* in their theory. **c *the point*** **:** the main or most important idea of something that is said or written ▪ It took several paragraphs for her to ***come/get to the point*** of her argument. ▪ If you drive while drunk, you could lose your license, but even ***more to the point*** [=more importantly], you could kill someone. — see also TO THE POINT (below)
2 : a reason for doing something **:** PURPOSE [*singular*] Is there a *point* to/for all of this paperwork? — often + *of* ▪ What's the *point of* having [=why have] a swimming pool if you never use it? — often + *in* ▪ I saw no *point in* continuing the discussion. ▪ There's no *point in* getting upset. [=there is no reason to get upset] [*noncount*] There's not much *point in* making rules if no one's going to follow them.
3 [*count*] **:** an individual detail or part of something ▪ The only *point* at issue is when the meeting should be held. ▪ Carefully consider each *point* in the witness's testimony. ▪ We debated the ***fine/finer points*** of the law. ▪ The main ***point of contention*** [=the main thing that people are arguing over] is who owns the rights to the land. — see also RALLYING POINT, SELLING POINT, STICKING POINT, TALKING POINT
4 [*count*] **:** a particular position, location, or place ▪ We met at a *point* halfway between the two cities. ▪ The sun reaches its highest *point* in the sky at noon. ▪ the country's northernmost *point* ▪ distant *points* in the solar system ▪ Change trains here for all *points* south. ▪ The break occurred at a weak *point* in the bone. ▪ She showed us the old capital building and other ***points of interest***. ▪ Ellis Island in Manhattan was the ***point of entry*** of many American immigrants. [=the place where many immigrants entered the U.S.] ▪ The package's ***point of origin*** [=the place from where the package was sent] was somewhere in the U.S.
5 [*count*] **:** a particular time or a particular stage in the development of something — usually singular ▪ At no *point* (in time) did the defendant ask for a lawyer. ▪ By this *point* in the conversation, I was beginning to lose my patience. ▪ I imagine the change will take place at some *point* in the next year or so. ▪ We are approaching the cutoff *point* of the negotiations. ▪ At that time, she enjoyed more success than at any other *point* in her career. ▪ That was the high/low *point* of her career. ▪ At this *point* in my life, I can't afford to take any risks. = I'm at a *point* in my life where I can't afford to take any risks. ▪ It got to the *point* where we could no longer ignore his behavior. ▪ The game had gone past the *point* of being fun. [=the game had stopped being fun] ▪ We walked all day and were beyond the *point* of exhaustion. ▪ The temperature will rise to 33 degrees Fahrenheit, ***at which point*** the ice will begin to melt. ▪ It's the natural ***starting point*** for a discussion on how to help the homeless. ▪ ***There comes a point*** in a man's life when he has to think seriously about his future. ▪ ***From that point on*** [=beginning at that time], I took my studies more seriously. ▪ ***From this point on***, any further changes must be approved by your supervisor. ▪ ***Up to that point*** it had been a successful meeting. ▪ The animals were hunted ***to the point of*** extinction. [=the animals were hunted until they were extinct] ▪ She was ***at the point of*** leaving [=she was just about to leave] when he asked her to dance. ▪ The police are ***on the point of*** solving the case. [=the police have almost solved the case] — see also BREAKING POINT, POINT OF NO RETURN, TURNING POINT
6 [*count*] **a :** a unit of measurement ▪ Her blood pressure had risen 16 *points* since her last checkup. ▪ Support for the President dropped three *points* [=*percent*] after the incident. ▪ She is currently 10 *points* behind the leading candidate in the polls. ▪ Interest rates have risen about two ***percentage points***. [=interest rates rose about two percent] — see also BOILING POINT, DEW POINT, FLASH POINT, FREEZING POINT, MELTING POINT **b :** a unit that is used to score a game or contest ▪ We won (the game) by three *points*. ▪ They scored 13 *points* in the first quarter. ▪ She has to win this *point* in order to win the match. ▪ She lost a *point* for falling off the balance beam. ▪ A touchdown is worth six *points*. ▪ He beat his opponent ***on points***. [=by winning more points than his opponent] — see also EXTRA POINT, GAME POINT, MATCH POINT, SET POINT
7 *points* [*plural*] *informal* **:** praise, credit, or approval for do-

P

ing something good or helpful • She washed the car in order to score *points* [=*brownie points*] with her father. • He's not too smart, but he gets *points* for effort. [=he should be given credit for the effort he makes]

8 [*count*] : the usually sharp end of something (such as a sword, needle, or pencil) • the sharp *point* [=*tip*] of the needle • She sharpened the pencil down ***to a point***. • The alligator's tail tapers *to a point*.

9 [*count*] : a small dot • We see the stars and planets as tiny *points* of light. • a line drawn between two *points*

10 [*count*] : DECIMAL POINT — used especially in speech to say a number that includes a decimal point • The number 9.5 is read aloud as "nine *point* five." • He had a temperature of one hundred and four *point* two. [=104.2] • You're listening to ninety-three *point* nine [=93.9] FM.

11 [*count*] : any one of the 32 marks on a compass that are used for showing directions • The *point* SSW is between the *points* S and SW. • The ***cardinal points*** [=the four main directions] are North, South, East, and West.

12 [*count*] : a piece of land that sticks out into a lake, ocean, etc. • The light was coming from the lighthouse on the *point*. — sometimes used in names • Montauk *Point* is at the eastern tip of Long Island.

13 [*count*] *Brit* : OUTLET 4

14 [*count*] : a unit that measures the size of letters typed on a computer or printed in a published work • Your essays should be double-spaced and written in 12-*point* type.

beside the point see BESIDE

from point A to point B see [1]A

in point of *formal* : when considering (a particular quality) : with regard to (something) • The two painters differ greatly *in point of* skill. [=the level of their skill is very different] • Some people think that all fat is unhealthy to eat when, ***in point of fact*** [=in truth, in actuality], some types of fat are good for you.

make a point ✧ If you ***make a point of*** doing something or ***make it a point*** to do something, you give your attention to it so that you are sure that it happens. • She *makes a point of* treating her employees fairly. = She *makes it a point to* treat her employees fairly.

not to put too fine a point on it see [1]FINE

on point *US* : relating very well to the subject that is being discussed : accurate and appropriate • His criticisms about the war were very much *on point*. • Her message is (right) *on point*.

to the point : relating to the thing that is being thought about or discussed • Please keep your questions brief and *to the point*. — see also [1]POINT 1c (above)

up to a point — used to indicate that a statement is partly but not completely true • I understand his feelings *up to a point*. [=*to some extent*] • Competition is good but only *up to a* certain *point*.

— see also CASE IN POINT, EXCLAMATION POINT, PRICE POINT

[2]**point** *verb* **points; point·ed; point·ing**

1 : to show someone where to look by moving your finger or an object held in your hand in a particular direction [*no obj*] "It's not polite to *point*," she said. • When I asked the child where his mother was, he *pointed* in the direction of the house. • *Pointing* with his cane, the old man asked, "Whose dog is that?" — often + *at* • It's not polite to *point at* people. • All the kids were *pointing* and laughing *at* me. • She *pointed at* the map on the wall. • "It's time to leave," he said *pointing at* his watch. — often + *to* • She *pointed to* me and asked me to stand up. — often + *toward* • He *pointed toward* the door. [+ *obj*] She *pointed* her finger *at* the door. — see also FINGER-POINTING

2 [+ *obj*] : to cause the front or tip of (something) to be turned toward someone or something • *Point* [=*aim*] the flashlight into the hole. • They *pointed* their microphones in my direction. — often + *at* • She *pointed* her camera *at* us. • A gun was *pointed at* his head.

3 *always followed by an adverb or preposition* [*no obj*] : to have the end or tip extended, aimed, or turned in a specified direction • We can leave when the minute hand *points* to 12. • Stand with your arms at your sides and your hands *pointing* downward. • The ship was *pointing* into the wind.

4 *computers* : to use a mouse or other device to move the pointer on a computer screen to a particular object or place [+ *obj*] Just *point* the arrow on the icon and click. [*no obj*] Just *point* and click.

5 [+ *obj*] : to show (someone) which direction to travel in order to reach a particular place : to direct (someone) toward something • She *pointed* him to the school's library. • Could you *point* me in the direction of the train station? • If you just *point* me in the general direction, I think I can find it.

6 [+ *obj*] : to give a sharp end to (something) • He was *pointing* [=(more commonly) *sharpening*] a stick with a knife.

7 [+ *obj*] : to repair (a wall, chimney, etc.) by putting new cement or other material between the bricks or stones • The wall needs to be *pointed*.

point an accusing finger at, point a/the finger at see [1]FINGER

point out [*phrasal verb*] **1** ***point out (someone or something) or point (someone or something) out*** : to direct someone's attention to (someone or something) by pointing • He *pointed* his girlfriend *out* in the crowd. • Could you *point out* the restrooms, please. • We asked her to *point out* (to us) her country on the map. • He *pointed out* the houses of famous people as we drove by. • He *pointed out* the way to the restrooms. **2** ***point out (something) or point (something) out*** : to talk about or mention (something that you think is important) • Let me *point out* [=*mention*] a few things before we switch topics. • He was quick to *point* our mistake *out*. • He *pointed out* the benefits/importance of daily exercise. • As she likes to *point out*, she distrusted him from the beginning. • I would like to *point out* that no one is perfect. • He *pointed out* that there are several advantages to owning your own home.

point the way : to show the way to go in order to get somewhere • She *pointed the way* to the exit. — often used figuratively • We led good lives, and we must thank our parents for *pointing the way*. • Their work *pointed the way* for future scientific research.

point to [*phrasal verb*] ***point to (something)*** : to mention or refer to (something) as a way of supporting an argument or claim • The prosecution is unable to *point to* anything that proves its case. • I can *point to* several past accomplishments that show that I can perform the job well.

point to/toward [*phrasal verb*] ***point to/toward (someone or something)*** : to show that something is true or probably true • All the evidence *points to* him as the murderer. [=all the evidence indicates that he is the murderer] • Her symptoms *point to* diabetes. [=her symptoms suggest that she has diabetes] • Everything *points to* a bright future for their company. • The results from these tests *point toward* a different conclusion.

point up [*phrasal verb*] ***point up (something) or point (something) up*** *formal* : to bring attention to (something) : to highlight or emphasize (something) • The speaker *pointed up* the importance of improving public education. • The destruction caused by the earthquake *points up* the need for improvements in construction standards.

point your toes : to bend your foot down so that the top of it and the front of your leg form a straight line • She forgot to *point her toes* when she dove into the water.

point–and–click *adj, computers* : used by pointing to images on a computer screen and pressing a mouse or other device • *point-and-click* links • a *point-and-click* interface

point–and–shoot *adj, of a camera* : having simple controls that do not need to be changed by the user and that make it possible to take pictures easily • *point-and-shoot* cameras/camcorders

point–blank /ˈpoɪntˈblæŋk/ *adv*

1 : from a very close distance • The victim was shot *point-blank* in the head.

2 : in a direct and open way that does not hide anything • He told me *point-blank* [=*bluntly, outright*] that he didn't believe me. • I asked her *point-blank* what she wanted. • She refused him *point-blank*.

– **point–blank** *adj* • a *point–blank* question/refusal • a *point-blank* shot to the goal • The shots were taken at/from *point-blank* range.

pointe *also* **pointes** /ˈpwænt/ *noun* [*noncount*] : a ballet position in which the dancer stands on the ends of the toes • a ballerina on *pointe*

point·ed /ˈpoɪntəd/ *adj* [*more* ~; *most* ~]

1 a : ending in a point • a sharply *pointed* pencil • the long *pointed* [=*pointy*] leaves of a willow tree • *pointed* rocks • He had a mustache and a short *pointed* beard. **b** : having a particular number of points — used in combination • a six-*pointed* star

2 : clearly directed toward a particular person or group • *pointed* remarks/criticism • He made a *pointed* reference to his mother-in-law.

3 : very easy to see or notice • She reacted to the news with *pointed* indifference.

– **point·ed·ness** *noun [noncount]* • the *pointedness* of their remarks

point·ed·ly /ˈpɔɪntədli/ *adv [more ~; most ~]* : in a way that is very easy to see or notice • He *pointedly* ignored the question. • She *pointedly* refused to go to their party.

point·er /ˈpɔɪntɚ/ *noun, pl* **-ers** *[count]*

1 : a useful suggestion about how to do or understand something better • She got some *pointers* [=*hints, tips*] about the use of commas. • Let me give you a few *pointers* on managing a successful business.

2 *Brit* : a sign that shows the condition or existence of something : INDICATOR • The latest data gives a *pointer* to the economy's overall growth. • This may be a *pointer* to a very serious problem.

3 : a thin stick that a person uses to show people where to look on a screen, map, etc.

4 *computers* : a small object (such as an arrow or cursor) that is moved on a computer screen by a mouse and that is used to make selections or change where work is being done

5 : a large dog that has long ears and short hair and that is trained to work with hunters by finding and pointing toward hunted animals with its head and body

point guard *noun, pl* **~ guards** *[count] basketball* : a player who is one of the two guards on a team and is the one most responsible for leading the team when it has the ball and is trying to score

poin·til·lism /ˈpɔɪntəˌlɪzəm/ *noun [noncount]* : a style of painting in which a picture is formed from small dots of color

– **poin·til·list** /ˈpɔɪntəlɪst/ *adj* • a *pointillist* painting

– **pointillist** *noun, pl* **-ists** *[count]*

point·ing /ˈpɔɪntɪŋ/ *noun [noncount]* : the material that is used to fill the cracks between the bricks of a wall, chimney, etc.

point·less /ˈpɔɪntləs/ *adj [more ~; most ~]* : having no meaning, purpose, or effect • He made a few more *pointless* [=*meaningless, senseless*] remarks. • a *pointless* exercise • It would be *pointless* for us to continue the investigation. • It's *pointless* [=*useless*] to argue with her. • a *pointless* killing

– **point·less·ly** *adv* • Her answer was *pointlessly* complicated. – **point·less·ness** *noun [noncount]*

point man *noun, pl* **~ men** *[count] chiefly US* : the main person who speaks for or supports someone or something • He's the President's *point man* on national defense.

point of departure *noun, pl* **points of departure** *[count]* : a starting point in a discussion, project, etc. • The study will be a *point of departure* [=*jumping-off point*] for future research.

point of honor *noun, pl* **points of honor** *[count]* : something that you do because you believe it is the right and honorable thing to do • My father considers it a *point of honor* to finish any project he starts.

point of no return *noun [singular]* : the time when it becomes no longer possible for you to make a different decision or to return to an earlier place or state • If you've signed the contract, you've already reached the *point of no return*.

point of order *noun, pl* **points of order** *[count] formal* : a question or statement about the way things should be done at a meeting, debate, etc. • The senator raised a *point of order* demanding that debate be allowed to continue.

point of reference *noun, pl* **points of reference** *[count]* : something that is used to judge or understand something else • The professor used the study as a *point of reference* for evaluating and discussing other theories.

point of view *noun, pl* **points of view** *[count]* : a way of looking at or thinking about something : VIEWPOINT • Even if you disagree with her, you should try to see things from her *point of view*. [=*perspective*] • They considered/approached the problem from opposite *points of view*. • From a strictly financial *point of view*, selling the house makes sense.

point person *noun, pl* **~ people** *[count] chiefly US* : POINT MAN

point spread *noun, pl* **~ spreads** *[count] US, sports* : the number of points by which a team is expected to win in a particular game

pointy /ˈpɔɪnti/ *adj* **point·i·er; -est** *[also more ~; most ~] informal* : having a somewhat sharp end : ending in a point • a *pointy* nose • *pointy* shoes = shoes with *pointy* toes

[1]**poise** /ˈpɔɪz/ *noun [noncount]*

1 : a calm, confident manner • She kept her *poise* even when under attack. • He behaved with *poise* and dignity.

2 : a graceful way of walking, moving, standing, etc. • Strength and flexibility are important for good *poise* and posture. • a dancer of great *poise* and grace

[2]**poise** *verb, always followed by an adverb or preposition* **pois·es; poised; pois·ing** *[+ obj]* : to hold (something) in a balanced and steady position • She *poised* her pencil above the paper and waited for the signal to begin writing.

poised *adj*

1 *not used before a noun* : not moving but ready to move • The actors were *poised* on the stage, ready for the curtain to come up. • She held the pencil *poised* over/above the paper.

2 *not used before a noun* : ready or prepared for something • The company is *poised* for success. • She seemed *poised* to take on the leadership of the country. • He is now *poised* to become the next big star in country music.

3 *not used before a noun* : in a state, place, or situation that is *between* two different or opposite things • a city *poised between* the mountains and the sea • a group of people *poised between* hope and fear

4 *[more ~; most ~]* : having or showing a calm, confident manner • a very *poised* young woman

[1]**poi·son** /ˈpɔɪzn̩/ *noun, pl* **-sons**

1 : a substance that can cause people or animals to die or to become very sick if it gets into their bodies especially by being swallowed *[noncount]* a jar of rat *poison* • The killer gave her victims food laced with *poison*. • suck *poison* from a snake bite • The villain in the play dies by drinking a vial of *poison*. *[count]* deadly *poisons*

2 : something (such as an idea, emotion, or situation) that is very harmful or unpleasant *[noncount]* Jealousy is relationship *poison*. [=jealousy can destroy a relationship] • Hiring a carpenter is expensive and doing it yourself is slow. ***Pick/Choose your poison***. [=neither choice is good but you have to choose one] *[count]* Poverty is a *poison* to society.

– ***what's your poison?*** *informal + old-fashioned* — used to ask what kind of alcoholic drink someone wants to be served

[2]**poison** *verb* **-sons; -soned; -son·ing** *[+ obj]*

1 a : to cause (a person or animal) to die or to become very sick with poison • How did the murderer *poison* the victim? • Hundreds were *poisoned* from drinking the contaminated water. • He was *poisoned* with cyanide. **b** : to put a harmful or deadly substance in or on (something) • The factory *poisoned* the air with its fumes. • Illegal dumping of waste is *poisoning* the stream and killing fish. • The food was *poisoned*.

2 : to change (something) in a very harmful or unpleasant way • He *poisoned* their minds with hatred for her. • They let the disagreement *poison* [=*destroy*] their friendship. • His angry outburst *poisoned* the atmosphere of the party. • She was working in a hostile environment *poisoned* by sexist jokes. ***poisoned chalice*** see CHALICE

– **poi·son·er** /ˈpɔɪzn̩nɚ/ *noun, pl* **-ers** *[count]*

– **poisoning** *noun, pl* **-ings** *[noncount]* alcohol/lead *poisoning* [=illness caused by having too much alcohol/lead in your body] • carbon monoxide *poisoning* *[count]* *poisonings* caused by bacteria — see also BLOOD POISONING, FOOD POISONING

poison gas *noun [noncount]* : gas that can cause a person to die or to become very sick : poisonous gas

poison ivy *noun [noncount]*

1 : a common plant in the central and eastern U.S. that has leaves which cause a very itchy and painful rash on your skin if you touch them

2 : the rash that is caused by poison ivy • I got/have *poison ivy* all over my arm.

poison oak *noun [noncount]*

1 : a common bush in the western U.S. that causes a very itchy and painful rash on your skin if you touch it

2 : POISON IVY

poi·son·ous /ˈpɔɪzn̩nəs/ *adj [more ~; most ~]*

1 a : causing sickness or death by entering or touching the body : containing poison • *poisonous* mushrooms • The leaves of the plant are *poisonous*. [=*toxic*] • Chocolate is *poisonous* to dogs. **b** : capable of putting poison into another animal's body by biting it • This species of spider is extremely *poisonous*. • *poisonous* snakes

2 : very harmful or unpleasant • *poisonous* rumors • He was in a particularly *poisonous* [=*nasty*] mood last night.

– **poi·son·ous·ly** *adv*

poison–pen letter *noun, pl* **~ -ters** *[count]* : a very harsh

P

or critical letter written to someone and usually not signed ▪ The mayor received some *poison-pen letters* after he fired several city employees.

poison pill *noun, pl* ~ **pills** [*count*] *business* : something that a company does to make itself less valuable or appealing in order to avoid being bought by another company — often used before another noun ▪ a *poison pill* defense/plan

poison su•mac /-ˈʃuːˌmæk/ *noun* [*noncount*] : a common bush in the eastern U.S. and Canada that causes a very itchy and painful rash on your skin if you touch it

¹poke /ˈpoʊk/ *verb* **pokes; poked; pok•ing**

1 a : to push your finger or something thin or pointed into or at someone or something [+ *obj*] He *poked* a stick at the snake. = He *poked* the snake with a stick. ▪ He *poked* [=*jabbed*] me in the ribs. ▪ I accidentally *poked* my finger right through the old fabric. ▪ Throwing pencils is not allowed because someone's eye could get *poked* out. [*no obj*] — often + *at* ▪ She *poked at* the sand with her toes. **b** [+ *obj*] : to make (a hole) in something by pushing something sharp or pointed through or into it — usually + *in* ▪ As a practical joke, she *poked* holes *in* the bottom of some of the paper cups. ▪ He used a fork to *poke* holes *in* the potatoes.

2 : to stick out so that a part can be seen [*no obj*] — often + *out* ▪ Your toe is *poking out* through the hole in your sock. — often + *through* ▪ You can see the seedlings beginning to *poke through* the soil. ▪ After days of rain, sunshine finally *poked through* the clouds. [+ *obj*] — often + *out* ▪ She *poked* her head *out* the window and yelled down to us.

poke along [*phrasal verb*] *US, informal* : to move along very slowly ▪ They were just *poking along* towards home. ▪ The car *poked along* down the street.

poke around *or Brit* ***poke about*** [*phrasal verb*] ***poke around/about*** *or* ***poke around/about (something)*** *informal* : to look around or search through something ▪ The police found him *poking around* (in) the deserted house. ▪ He *poked around* in his closet for something to wear to the party. ▪ She's in the kitchen *poking around* for something to eat. — often used figuratively ▪ I don't want you *poking around* in my personal life.

poke fun at see ¹FUN

poke your nose in/into see ¹NOSE

²poke *noun, pl* **pokes** [*count*]

1 : a quick push with your finger or with something thin or pointed — usually singular ▪ She gave my arm a quick *poke* [=*jab*] to tell me it was my turn.

2 *US, informal* : a usually minor criticism or insult that is directed toward a particular person or group — usually singular ▪ She thanked everyone in her speech but she couldn't resist ***taking a poke at*** the people who said the movie would never succeed.

a pig in a poke see ¹PIG

¹po•ker /ˈpoʊkɚ/ *noun* [*noncount*] : a card game in which players bet money on the value of their cards — compare ²POKER

²pok•er /ˈpoʊkɚ/ *noun, pl* **-ers** [*count*] : a metal rod for moving coal or wood in a fire — compare ¹POKER

poker face *noun, pl* ~ **faces** [*count*] : an expression on your face that does not show your thoughts or feelings — usually singular ▪ She maintained her *poker face* even after she heard the bad news.

– po•ker–faced /ˈpoʊkɚˌfeɪst/ *adj* ▪ Her usually *poker-faced* boss gave her a big smile when he told her she was being promoted.

po•key /ˈpoʊki/ *noun*

the pokey *US slang, old-fashioned* : PRISON ▪ He spent six months in *the pokey*.

poky *or* **pok•ey** /ˈpoʊki/ *adj* **pokier; -est** *informal*

1 *US* : very slow ▪ a *poky* old car ▪ Stop being so *poky*.

2 *Brit, of a room or building* : small and uncomfortable ▪ a *poky* little room

pol /ˈpɑːl/ *noun, pl* **pols** [*count*] *US, informal* : POLITICIAN ▪ Many of the city's residents have criticized local *pols* for their decision to close the public library.

Po•lack /ˈpoʊˌlɑːk/ *noun, pl* **-lacks** [*count*] *US, informal + offensive* : a Polish person ✧ The word *Polack* is very offensive and should be avoided.

po•lar /ˈpoʊlɚ/ *adj, always used before a noun*

1 : of or relating to the North or South Pole or the region around it ▪ *polar* ice caps

2 : completely different or opposite ▪ They took *polar* positions on the issue. ▪ She and I are good friends even though we're ***polar opposites***.

3 *technical* : relating to one or both of the poles of a magnet

polar bear *noun, pl* ~ **bears** [*count*] : a large white bear that lives near the North Pole — see picture at BEAR

po•lar•i•ty /poʊˈlerəti/ *noun, pl* **-ties** [*count, noncount*]

1 *formal* : a state in which two ideas, opinions, etc., are completely opposite or very different from each other ▪ There is (a) considerable *polarity* of opinion on this issue. [=there are two sides with completely different opinions on this issue]

2 *physics* : the condition of having positive and negative charges and especially magnetic or electrical poles

po•lar•ize *also Brit* **po•lar•ise** /ˈpoʊləˌraɪz/ *verb* **-iz•es; -ized; -iz•ing**

1 : to cause (people, opinions, etc.) to separate into opposing groups [+ *obj*] The war has *polarized* the nation. [*no obj*] The current debate *polarizes* along lines of class and race.

2 [+ *obj*] *physics* : to cause (something, such as light waves) to vibrate in a particular pattern ▪ a filter that *polarizes* light = a *polarizing* filter

3 [+ *obj*] *physics* : to cause (something) to have positive and negative charges : to give polarity to (something) ▪ *polarize* atoms ▪ *polarize* a magnet

– po•lar•i•za•tion *also Brit* **po•lar•i•sa•tion** /ˌpoʊlərəˈzeɪʃən, *Brit* ˌpəʊləˌraɪˈzeɪʃən/ *noun* [*noncount*]

Po•lar•oid /ˈpoʊləˌroɪd/ *trademark* — used for a material that is used chiefly in eyeglasses to prevent glare and for a camera that produces developed pictures

¹pole /ˈpoʊl/ *noun, pl* **poles** [*count*] : a long, straight piece of wood, metal, etc., that is often placed in the ground so that it stands straight up ▪ They have a couple of bird feeders hanging from a *pole* in the backyard. ▪ A *pole* was blocking their view of the field. ▪ He connected the *poles* of the tent. ▪ a fishing *pole* [=*rod*] ▪ I ***wouldn't touch it with a 10-foot pole.*** [=I do not want to get near it; I do not want to discuss it or be involved with it at all] — see also FLAGPOLE, MAYPOLE, TELEGRAPH POLE, TELEPHONE POLE, TOTEM POLE

up the pole *Brit, informal* : CRAZY ▪ The pressure of his job nearly drove him *up the pole*.

— compare ³POLE

²pole *verb* **poles; poled; pol•ing** [+ *obj*] : to move (a boat) by using a pole to push against the bottom of a river, lake, etc. ▪ *pole* a boat

³pole *noun, pl* **poles** [*count*]

1 : either end of the imaginary line around which something (such as the earth) turns — see also NORTH POLE, SOUTH POLE

2 *technical* **a** : either one of the two ends of a magnet **b** : the positive point or the negative point on a battery

3 : either one of two opposite positions, situations, etc. ▪ When it comes to politics, we're on opposite *poles*. ▪ They were on opposite *poles* of the argument.

poles apart : as far apart or as different as possible ▪ Though they were generally *poles apart* politically, they did agree on this one issue.

— compare ¹POLE

Pole /ˈpoʊl/ *noun, pl* **Poles** [*count*] : a Polish person

pole•ax (*US*) *or Brit* **pole•axe** /ˈpoʊlˌæks/ *verb* **-ax•es; -axed; -ax•ing** [+ *obj*] : to hit and knock down (someone) ▪ He went down as if he'd been *poleaxed*. — often used figuratively ▪ I was *poleaxed* [=shocked and stunned] by the horrible news. ▪ The department has been *poleaxed* by cutbacks.

pole bean *noun, pl* ~ **beans** [*count*] *US* : a bean plant that grows up a pole, fence, etc.; *also* : the bean that grows on this plant

pole•cat /ˈpoʊlˌkæt/ *noun, pl* **-cats** [*count*]

1 : a European animal that has dark brown fur and a long thin body and that gives off a bad smell to defend itself

2 *US, informal* : SKUNK

po•lem•ic /pəˈlɛmɪk/ *noun, pl* **-ics** *formal*

1 [*count*] : a strong written or spoken attack against someone else's opinions, beliefs, practices, etc. ▪ Her book is a fierce *polemic* against the inequalities in our society.

2 ***polemics*** [*plural*] : the art or practice of using language to defend or harshly criticize something or someone ▪ They managed to discuss the issues without resorting to *polemics*.

– po•lem•i•cal /pəˈlɛmɪkəl/ *also* **po•lem•ic** /pəˈlɛmɪk/ *adj* [*more* ~; *most* ~] ▪ *polemical* writing ▪ I don't like the book's *polemical* tone. **– po•lem•i•cal•ly** /pəˈlɛmɪkli/ *adv*

po•lem•i•cist /pəˈlɛməsɪst/ *noun, pl* **-cists** [*count*] : a person who is good at making forceful arguments in speech or writing ▪ She has a reputation as a fierce *polemicist*.

pole position *noun, pl* ~ **-tions** [*count, noncount*] : the front position at the start of a car race ▪ He won the *pole po-*

sition by having the fastest qualifying time.

Pole Star *noun*
the Pole Star : NORTH STAR

pole vault *noun*
the pole vault : an athletic event in which people compete by using a pole to jump over a bar that is high above the ground
– **pole–vault** *verb* **-vaults; -vault•ed; -vault•ing** [*no obj*]
– **pole–vault•er** *noun, pl* **-ers**

pole vault

[1]**po•lice** /pəˈliːs/ *noun* [*plural*] : the people or the department of people who enforce laws, investigate crimes, and make arrests ▪ (The) *Police* blocked the street to clear a path for the parade. ▪ *Police* arrested a man whom they identified as the murderer. ▪ In case of emergency, call the *police*. [=(*US*) the police department] ▪ I was pulled over by the state *police* [=by state police officers] for speeding. ▪ the ***chief of police*** [=the chief of the police department] — often used before another noun ▪ He applied for a job with the New York *Police* Department. ▪ They were arrested for interfering with a *police* investigation. ▪ According to the *police* report the thieves broke in around midnight. ▪ The mayor attempted to cover up what was a clear case of *police* brutality. [=physical abuse by police officers] ▪ the *police* academy/chief ▪ He is in *police* custody. [=he is being held by the police] — see also MILITARY POLICE, SECRET POLICE
help the police with their inquiries see INQUIRY

[2]**police** *verb* **-lic•es; -liced; -lic•ing** [+ *obj*]
1 : to control and keep order in (an area) by the use of police or military forces ▪ The officers *police* the streets for reckless drivers. ▪ The coast is *policed* by the military.
2 : to control (something) by making sure that rules and regulations are being followed ▪ The international agency *polices* the development of atomic energy facilities.
– **policing** /pəˈliːsɪŋ/ *noun* [*noncount*] ▪ Community *policing* has helped cut down on crime in the neighborhood. ▪ The industry is operating without adequate *policing*.

police car *noun, pl* ~ **cars** [*count*] : a car used by police officers — called also (*US*) *cruiser*, (*US*) *police cruiser*, *squad car*

police constable *noun, pl* ~ **-stables** [*count*] *chiefly Brit* : a police officer of the lowest rank — abbr. *PC* — called also *constable*

police dog *noun, pl* ~ **dogs** [*count*] : a dog that is trained to help police find criminals and illegal drugs

police force *noun, pl* ~ **forces** [*count*] : the police organization in a particular area ▪ He joined the local *police force*.

po•lice•man /pəˈliːsmən/ *noun, pl* **-men** /-mən/ [*count*] : a man who is a police officer

police officer *noun, pl* ~ **-cers** [*count*] : a person whose job is to enforce laws, investigate crimes, and make arrests : a member of the police

police state *noun, pl* ~ **states** [*count*] : a country in which the activities of the people are strictly controlled by the government with the help of a police force

police station *noun, pl* ~ **-tions** [*count*] : a place where local police officers work ▪ They brought him down to the *police station* for questioning. — called also *station house*

po•lice•wom•an /pəˈliːsˌwʊmən/ *noun, pl* **-wom•en** /-ˌwɪmən/ [*count*] : a woman who is a police officer

[1]**pol•i•cy** /ˈpɑːləsi/ *noun, pl* **-cies**
1 : an officially accepted set of rules or ideas about what should be done [*count*] Ask the cashier what the store's return *policy* is. ▪ They voted to adopt/pursue more liberal trade *policies*. [*noncount*] Each employee is given a handbook on company *policy*. ▪ American ***foreign policy***
2 : an idea or belief that guides the way you live or behave [*count*] — usually singular ▪ I make it a *policy* not to lend my friends money. [=I don't lend my friends money] [*noncount*] I don't lend my friends money as a matter of *policy*.
honesty is the best policy see HONESTY
— compare [2]POLICY

[2]**policy** *noun, pl* **-cies** [*count*] : a document that contains the agreement that an insurance company and a person have made ▪ Property damage caused by fire is not covered under this *policy*. — compare [1]POLICY

pol•i•cy•hold•er /ˈpɑːləsiˌhoʊldɚ/ *noun, pl* **-ers** [*count*] : a person who owns an insurance policy

po•lio /ˈpoʊlijoʊ/ *noun* [*noncount*] *medical* : a serious disease that affects the nerves of the spine and often makes a person permanently unable to move particular muscles — called also *infantile paralysis, poliomyelitis*

po•lio•my•eli•tis /ˌpoʊlijoʊˌmajəˈlaɪtəs/ *noun* [*noncount*] *medical* : POLIO

[1]**pol•ish** /ˈpɑːlɪʃ/ *verb* **-ish•es; -ished; -ish•ing** [+ *obj*]
1 : to make (something) smooth and shiny by rubbing it ▪ He *polished* his shoes. ▪ She *polished* the silverware.
2 : to improve (something) : to make (something) better than it was before ▪ He spent the summer *polishing* his math skills. — often + *up* ▪ Your essay needs to be *polished up*. = You need to *polish up* your essay. ▪ They *polished up* [=practiced singing/playing] some old songs for the performance.
3 : to put nail polish on (a fingernail or toenail) ▪ I *polished* her fingernails for her. [=I painted her nails with nail polish]
polish off [*phrasal verb*] **1** ***polish (something) off or polish off (something) informal*** : to finish (something) completely ▪ We *polished off* the whole pie. ▪ He had *polished off* the book before bed. **2** ***polish (someone or something) off or polish off (someone or something)*** : to defeat (someone or something) in a contest, game, etc. ▪ They *polished off* the visiting team, 6–0.
– **pol•ish•er** *noun, pl* **-ers** [*count*] ▪ a floor *polisher* [=a piece of equipment that is used to make a floor smooth and shiny] ▪ She worked as a diamond *polisher*. — see also APPLE POLISHER

[2]**polish** *noun, pl* **-ishes**
1 : a substance that is rubbed on a surface to make it smooth and shiny [*noncount*] I need more shoe/furniture *polish*. [*count*] Did you use a wax *polish* on the table or an oil-based one? — see also NAIL POLISH
2 [*singular*] : a smooth and shiny surface ▪ Buff the floor ***to a polish***. [=until it has a smooth and shiny surface] ▪ The stone ***takes a high polish***. [=the stone can become very shiny when it is polished]
3 [*noncount*] **a** : good quality or style that comes from practice or effort ▪ The movie has the *polish* we've come to expect from that director. ▪ His performance lacked *polish*. **b** *somewhat old-fashioned* : good manners ▪ He's rude and lacks *polish*.
4 [*singular*] : the act of polishing something ▪ She gave the statue a quick *polish*. — see also SPIT AND POLISH

Pol•ish /ˈpoʊlɪʃ/ *noun*
1 [*noncount*] : the language of Poland ▪ Do you speak *Polish*?
2 ***the Polish*** : the people of Poland ▪ a tradition of *the Polish* [=*Poles*]
– **Polish** *adj* ▪ She is *Polish*. ▪ *Polish* food/traditions

polished *adj*
1 : made smooth and shiny by polishing ▪ *polished* silver/granite ▪ brightly *polished* fingernails
2 [*more* ~; *most* ~] : very impressive or skillful ▪ This is a highly/very *polished* piece of writing. ▪ The dancers gave a *polished* [=*excellent*] performance. ▪ She is a *polished* actress.
3 [*more* ~; *most* ~] *somewhat old-fashioned* : very polite : having good manners ▪ a *polished* gentleman

po•lit•bu•ro /ˈpɑːlətˌbjɚroʊ/ *noun, pl* **-ros** [*count*] : the main group of people in a Communist government who make decisions about policy

po•lite /pəˈlaɪt/ *adj* **po•lit•er; -est** [*or more* ~; *most* ~]
1 : having or showing good manners or respect for other people ▪ Your children are very *polite*. [=they behave well with other people] ▪ It was *polite* of him to hold the door for them. ▪ Please be *polite* to the guests. ▪ It isn't *polite* to interrupt people when they're talking. ▪ He said he liked the show, but he was only being *polite*. [=he did not like the show, but he said that he did in order to show good manners] ▪ When she called the painting "unique" that was just a *polite* [=*nice*] way of saying she didn't like it. ▪ She received some *polite* applause despite the mistakes in her performance. ▪ They had been fighting, but they were able to make *polite* [=*civil*] conversation at dinner.
2 *always used before a noun* : socially correct or proper ▪ ***polite speech*** [=somewhat formal speech that is not offensive and can be used in all situations] ▪ Certain words should not be used in ***polite society/company***. [=with people who value good manners]
– **po•lite•ly** *adv* ▪ She asked them *politely* to leave. = She *politely* asked them to leave. ▪ He is not, ***to put it politely*** [=to say this in a way that shows good manners], the best guitar player in the world. – **po•lite•ness** *noun* [*noncount*] ▪ She

only did it ***out of politeness*** [=to be polite; because she wanted to show good manners]

pol·i·tic /ˈpɑːləˌtɪk/ *adj* [*more* ~; *most* ~] *formal* **: showing good judgment especially in dealing with other people** ▪ It would not be *politic* to ignore them. ▪ a *politic* [=*tactful*] answer/decision — see also BODY POLITIC

po·lit·i·cal /pəˈlɪtɪkəl/ *adj*

1 : of or relating to politics or government ▪ the American *political* system [=the way the American government is officially organized, managed, etc.] ▪ The senator has changed *political* parties. ▪ Health care has become a major *political* issue in recent years. ▪ a *political* leader ▪ *political* ambition ▪ a group of *political* activists ▪ economic and *political* power ▪ *political* reform ▪ We need a *political* solution rather than a military solution.

2 [*more* ~; *most* ~] **: interested in or active in politics** ▪ She is very *political*.

3 *always used before a noun* **: involving, concerned with, or accused of acts against a government** ▪ *political* prisoners [=people who are put in prison because of their political beliefs and activities] ▪ a *political* crime

4 : relating to the things people do to gain or keep power or an advantage within a group, organization, etc. ▪ His promotion was entirely *political*. [=he was promoted because a powerful person wanted him to be promoted and not because he was qualified] ▪ She claims that she was fired for *political* reasons.

political football see FOOTBALL

– po·lit·i·cal·ly /pəˈlɪtɪkli/ *adv* ▪ She's *politically* liberal/conservative. ▪ It is a *politically* sensitive issue. ▪ *Politically*, the country is divided. ▪ The students are very *politically* active. ▪ a *politically* motivated crime

political action committee *noun, pl* ~ **-tees** [*count*] *US* **: a group that is formed to give money to the political campaigns of people who are likely to make decisions that would benefit the group's interests** ▪ The governor received over $3 million in campaign contributions from *political action committees*. — called also *PAC*

politically correct *adj* [*more* ~; *most* ~] *sometimes disapproving* **: agreeing with the idea that people should be careful to not use language or behave in a way that could offend a particular group of people** ▪ *politically correct* language/terms ▪ He later realized that his response was not *politically correct*. — abbr. *PC*

– political correctness *noun* [*noncount*]

politically incorrect *adj* [*more* ~; *most* ~] **: not avoiding language or behavior that could offend a particular group of people** ▪ a *politically incorrect* comment ▪ *politically incorrect* humor

– political incorrectness *noun* [*noncount*]

political science *noun* [*noncount*] **: the study of governments and how they work** ▪ a degree in *political science*

– political scientist *noun, pl* ~ **-tists** [*count*] ▪ *Political scientists* offered their views on the President's policies.

pol·i·ti·cian /ˌpɑːləˈtɪʃən/ *noun, pl* **-cians** [*count*] **: someone who is active in government usually as an elected official**

po·lit·i·cize *also Brit* **po·lit·i·cise** /pəˈlɪtəˌsaɪz/ *verb* **-cizes; -cized; -ciz·ing** [+ *obj*]

1 *disapproving* **: to relate (an idea, issue, etc.) to politics in a way that makes people less likely to agree** ▪ They have *politicized* the budget process. — often used as *(be) politicized* ▪ Many people have expressed concerns that the investigation has *been politicized*. ▪ Health care has become a highly *politicized* issue in recent years.

2 : to cause (someone) to become involved or interested in government or politics — usually used as *(be) politicized* ▪ students *politicized* by the war

– po·lit·i·ci·za·tion *also Brit* **po·lit·i·ci·sa·tion** /pəˌlɪtəsəˈzeɪʃən, *Brit* pəˌlɪtəˌsaɪˈzeɪʃən/ *noun* [*noncount*] ▪ the *politicization* of religion

pol·i·tick·ing /ˈpɑːləˌtɪkɪŋ/ *noun* [*noncount*] *often disapproving* **: political activity that is done especially in order to win support or gain an advantage** ▪ She won the nomination after a lot of behind-the-scenes *politicking*.

po·lit·i·co /pəˈlɪtɪˌkoʊ/ *noun, pl* **-cos** [*count*] *somewhat informal + often disapproving* **:** POLITICIAN ▪ a *politico* who will do anything to win an election

pol·i·tics /ˈpɑːləˌtɪks/ *noun*

1 [*noncount*] **: activities that relate to influencing the actions and policies of a government or getting and keeping power in a government** ▪ He is an important figure in American *politics*. ▪ The students discussed the latest news in national/local *politics*. ▪ *Politics* has always interested her. = She's always been interested in *politics*. — often used with a plural verb ▪ *Politics* have always interested her. ▪ He talked about the ways in which global *politics* are changing. ▪ The mayor's *politics* [=the political decisions the mayor made] were often criticized during her time in office. — see also PARTY POLITICS, POWER POLITICS

2 [*noncount*] **: the work or job of people (such as elected officials) who are part of a government** ▪ *Politics* is a competitive profession. ▪ She plans on ***going into politics***. = She plans on ***entering politics***. [=she plans on getting a job that involves politics]

3 [*plural*] **: the opinions that someone has about what should be done by governments : a person's political thoughts and opinions** ▪ She has changed her *politics*. ▪ His *politics* are very liberal/conservative. [=he believes that governments should be liberal/conservative]

4 [*noncount*] *often disapproving* **: the activities, attitudes, or behaviors that are used to get or keep power or an advantage within a group, organization, etc.** ▪ I don't want to get involved in ***office politics***. ▪ She wrote a book about ***sexual politics*** [=the way men and women deal with and behave toward each other] in the academic world.

5 [*noncount*] *chiefly Brit* **:** POLITICAL SCIENCE ▪ a degree in *politics*

play politics *disapproving* **: to say or do things for political reasons instead of doing what is right or what is best for other people** ▪ She's been accused of *playing politics* with the investigation. ▪ Legislators need to stop *playing politics* with our future.

pol·i·ty /ˈpɑːləti/ *noun, pl* **-ties** *formal*

1 [*count*] **: something (such as a country or state) that has a government : a politically organized unit** ▪ the *polities* of medieval Italy

2 [*noncount*] **: a form of government** ▪ the American *polity*

pol·ka /ˈpoʊlkə, *Brit* ˈpɒlkə/ *noun, pl* **-kas** [*count*]

1 : a lively dance for couples ▪ We danced a *polka*.

2 : the music for a polka ▪ The band played a *polka*.

pol·ka dot /ˈpoʊkə-/ *noun, pl* ~ **dots** [*count*] **: one of a series of dots that make a pattern especially on fabric or clothing** — usually plural ▪ The dress has *polka dots* on it. — see color picture on page C12

– polka–dot *or* **pol·ka–dot·ted** /ˈpoʊkəˌdɑːtəd/ *adj* ▪ a *polka-dotted* skirt [=a skirt with a pattern of polka dots]

¹poll /ˈpoʊl/ *noun, pl* **polls**

1 [*count*] **: an activity in which several or many people are asked a question or a series of questions in order to get information about what most people think about something** ▪ The magazine conducted a *poll* to find out the favorite 100 movies of all time. ▪ A recent *poll* shows a decrease in the number of teenagers who smoke. — see also EXIT POLL, OPINION POLL, STRAW POLL

2 a [*count*] **: the record of votes that were made by people in an election** — usually plural ▪ The *polls* show that she's ahead with 55 percent of the votes. = She's ahead ***in the polls*** with 55 percent of the votes. **b** [*noncount*] *Brit* **: the number of votes made in an election** ▪ The candidate won with 55 percent of the *poll*. [=(*US*) *vote*]

3 ***the polls*** **: the places where people vote during an election** ▪ *The polls* are open until 8:00 tonight. ▪ Voters ***went to the polls*** today. [=people voted today] ▪ He was defeated ***at the polls***. [=he lost the election]

²poll *verb* **polls; polled; poll·ing** [+ *obj*]

1 : to ask (several or many people) a question or a series of questions in order to get information about what most people think about something ▪ The magazine *polled* its readers on their eating habits. [=the magazine took/conducted a poll of its readers to find out about their eating habits] ▪ About half of the people *polled* had tried smoking.

2 : to receive (a specified number or percentage of votes) in an election ▪ The conservative candidate *polled* more than 10,000 votes in the last election.

pol·len /ˈpɑːlən/ *noun* [*noncount*] **: the very fine usually yellow dust that is produced by a plant and that is carried to other plants of the same kind usually by wind or insects so that the plants can produce seeds**

pollen count *noun, pl* ~ **counts** [*count*] **: a number that indicates the amount of pollen in the air and that is used by people who get sick from breathing in pollen** ▪ The weather forecast said that the *pollen count* will be high tomorrow.

pol·li·nate /ˈpɑːləˌneɪt/ *verb* **-nates; -nat·ed; -nat·ing** [+ *obj*] **: to give (a plant) pollen from another plant of the same**

P

kind so that seeds will be produced ▪ The plants/flowers are *pollinated* by bees.
– **pol·li·na·tion** /ˌpɑːləˈneɪʃən/ *noun* [*noncount*] ▪ *Pollination* is required for plants to produce seeds. – **pol·li·na·tor** /ˈpɑːləˌneɪtɚ/ *noun, pl* **-tors** [*count*] ▪ Honeybees are a common *pollinator* of flowers.

polling *noun* [*noncount*]
1 : the act of asking a person a question as part of a survey or poll ▪ The *polling* was done by telephone.
2 *chiefly Brit* **:** the act of voting in an election ▪ *Polling* starts at 8 a.m. ▪ (*Brit*) It's ***polling day*** [=(*US*) *election day*] today.

polling booth *noun, pl* ~ **booths** [*count*] *Brit* **:** VOTING BOOTH

polling place *noun, pl* ~ **places** [*count*] *US* **:** a building where people go to vote in an election — called also (*Brit*) *polling station*

pol·li·wog *also* **pol·ly·wog** /ˈpɑːliˌwɑːg/ *noun, pl* **-wogs** [*count*] *US* **:** TADPOLE

poll·ster /ˈpoʊlstɚ/ *noun, pl* **-sters** [*count*] **:** someone who makes questions for a poll, asks questions in a poll, or collects and presents results from a poll

poll tax *noun, pl* ~ **tax·es** [*count*] **:** a tax that each adult has to pay in order to vote in an election ✧ Poll taxes are no longer legal in the U.S.

pol·lut·ant /pəˈluːtn̩t/ *noun, pl* **-ants** [*count*] **:** a substance that makes land, water, air, etc., dirty and not safe or suitable to use **:** something that causes pollution ▪ air/water *pollutants* ▪ environmental/industrial *pollutants* ▪ chemical/toxic *pollutants*

pol·lute /pəˈluːt/ *verb* **-lutes; -lut·ed; -lut·ing** [+ *obj*] **:** to make (land, water, air, etc.) dirty and not safe or suitable to use ▪ Waste from the factory had *polluted* [=*contaminated*] the river. ▪ Miles of beaches were *polluted* by the oil spill. ▪ Car exhaust *pollutes* the air. — often used figuratively ▪ Violence on television is *polluting* the minds of children.
– **polluted** *adj* [*more* ~; *most* ~] ▪ *polluted* beaches/air ▪ The river is *polluted*. – **pol·lut·er** *noun, pl* **-ers** [*count*] ▪ *Polluters* will be fined. ▪ The company is one of the worst *polluters* in the country.

pol·lu·tion /pəˈluːʃən/ *noun* [*noncount*]
1 : the action or process of making land, water, air, etc., dirty and not safe or suitable to use ▪ industrial practices that have caused *pollution* of the air and water
2 : substances that make land, water, air, etc., dirty and not safe or suitable to use ▪ The tests showed high levels of *pollution* in the water/air. ▪ The fish are dying of/from *pollution*. — see also LIGHT POLLUTION, NOISE POLLUTION

Pol·ly·an·na /ˌpɑːliˈænə/ *noun, pl* **-nas** [*count*] *disapproving* **:** someone who thinks good things will always happen and finds something good in everything ▪ I'm no *Pollyanna*, but I do think some good will come out of this.
– **Pol·ly·an·na·ish** /ˌpɑːliˈænəɪʃ/ *also* **Pol·ly·an·nish** /ˌpɑːliˈænɪʃ/ *adj* ▪ *Pollyannaish* illusions/beliefs

pollywog *variant spelling of* POLLIWOG

po·lo /ˈpoʊloʊ/ *noun* [*noncount*] **:** a game played by two teams of four players who ride horses while using long mallets to hit a wooden ball into a goal — see also WATER POLO

polo neck *noun, pl* ~ **necks** [*count*] *Brit* **:** TURTLENECK 1

polo shirt *noun, pl* ~ **shirts** [*count*] **:** a shirt with a collar and a few buttons at the neck that you put on by pulling over your head — see color picture on page C14

pol·ter·geist /ˈpoʊltɚˌgaɪst/ *noun, pl* **-geists** [*count*] **:** a ghost that makes strange noises and causes objects to move

poly- *combining form* **:** many ▪ *polygamous* ▪ *polyglot*

poly·es·ter /ˌpɑːliˈɛstɚ/ *noun* [*noncount*] **:** a material that is made from a chemical process and that is used for making many different products including fabrics ▪ The shirt is made of *polyester*. ▪ a *polyester* shirt ▪ The sheets are a cotton and *polyester* blend.

poly·eth·yl·ene /ˌpɑːliˈɛθəˌliːn/ *noun* [*noncount*] *US* **:** a light and strong plastic that is used mainly in sheets for packaging — called also (*Brit*) *polythene*

po·lyg·a·my /pəˈlɪgəmi/ *noun* [*noncount*] **:** the state or practice of being married to more than one person at the same time ▪ Some cultures practice *polygamy*. — compare MONOGAMY
– **po·lyg·a·mist** /pəˈlɪgəmɪst/ *noun, pl* **-mists** [*count*] ▪ He/She is a *polygamist*. – **po·lyg·a·mous** /pəˈlɪgəməs/ *adj* ▪ a *polygamous* marriage

poly·glot /ˈpɑːliˌglɑːt/ *adj, formal*
1 : knowing or using several languages **:** MULTILINGUAL ▪ *polyglot* travelers ▪ a *polyglot* population
2 : made up of people or things from different cultures, countries, etc. ▪ a *polyglot* community made up of many cultures
– **polyglot** *noun, pl* **-glots** [*count*] ▪ She was a *polyglot* who was fluent in four languages.

poly·gon /ˈpɑːliˌgɑːn/ *noun, pl* **-gons** [*count*] *mathematics* **:** a flat shape that has three or more straight lines and angles ▪ Pentagons, hexagons, and octagons are all kinds of *polygons*. — see picture at GEOMETRY

poly·graph /ˈpɑːliˌgræf, *Brit* ˈpɒliˌgrɑːf/ *noun, pl* **-graphs** [*count*]
1 : LIE DETECTOR ▪ They hooked him up to the *polygraph* and began the test.
2 *US* **:** a test that is done with a lie detector to see if someone is telling the truth ▪ She was asked to take a *polygraph*.

poly·math /ˈpɑːliˌmæθ/ *noun, pl* **-maths** [*count*] *formal* **:** someone who knows a lot about many different things

poly·mer /ˈpɑːləmɚ/ *noun, pl* **-mers** [*count*] *chemistry* **:** a chemical compound that is made of small molecules that are arranged in a simple repeating structure to form a larger molecule

poly·mor·phous /ˌpɑːliˈmoɚfəs/ *adj, formal + technical* **:** having or occurring in many different forms, styles, or stages of development ▪ a *polymorphous* rash ▪ *polymorphous* sexuality

pol·yp /ˈpɑːləp/ *noun, pl* **-yps** [*count*]
1 *medical* **:** a small lump that grows inside your body (such as inside your colon or on your vocal cords)
2 : a small sea animal (such as a coral) that has a body shaped like a tube

poly·syl·lab·ic /ˌpɑːlisəˈlæbɪk/ *adj, technical* **:** having more than three syllables ▪ *polysyllabic* words

poly·tech·nic /ˌpɑːliˈtɛknɪk/ *noun, pl* **-nics** [*count*] **:** a college or university that provides training in technical and practical sciences
– **polytechnic** *adj, always used before a noun* ▪ a *polytechnic* university/institute

poly·the·ism /ˈpɑːliˌθiːˌɪzəm/ *noun* [*noncount*] **:** the belief that there is more than one god
– **poly·the·ist** /ˈpɑːliˌθiːjɪst/ *noun, pl* **-ists** [*count*] – **poly·the·is·tic** /ˌpɑːliθiˈɪstɪk/ *adj* ▪ *polytheistic* religions

poly·thene /ˈpɑːləˌθiːn/ *noun* [*noncount*] *Brit* **:** POLYETHYLENE

poly·un·sat·u·rat·ed /ˌpɑːliˌʌnˈsætʃəˌreɪtəd/ *adj, technical* — used to describe a type of oil or fat that is found especially in nuts and fish and that is better for your health than saturated fats and trans fats ▪ *polyunsaturated* fats/oils — compare MONOUNSATURATED, UNSATURATED

poly·ure·thane /ˌpɑliˈjɚəˌθeɪn/ *noun* [*noncount*] **:** a type of plastic that is used to make various products and especially to make a clear liquid that is spread on a surface (such as a wooden floor) and that becomes hard when it dries ▪ The floor will need two coats of *polyurethane*.

polyvinyl chloride *noun* [*noncount*] *technical* **:** PVC

po·made /poʊˈmeɪd, *Brit* pəˈmɑːd/ *noun, pl* **-mades** [*count*] **:** a thick substance that is used to style hair

pome·gran·ate /ˈpɑːməˌgrænət/ *noun, pl* **-ates** [*count*] **:** a round, red fruit that has a thick skin and many large seeds

pom·mel /ˈpʌməl/ *noun, pl* **-mels** [*count*] **:** a high, round part on the front of a saddle

pommel horse *noun, pl* ~ **horses** [*count*] **:** a large piece of equipment used in gymnastics that is like a very thick bench with two handles on top of it — called also *horse*

pomp /ˈpɑːmp/ *noun* [*noncount*] **:** the impressive decorations, music, clothing etc., that are part of some formal events ▪ the *pomp* [=*splendor*] of a royal ceremony
pomp and circumstance **:** impressive formal activities or ceremonies ▪ The prime minister was greeted with *pomp and circumstance*. ▪ the *pomp and circumstance* of a presidential inauguration

pom·pa·dour /ˈpɑːmpəˌdoɚ/ *noun, pl* **-dours** [*count*] *chiefly US* **:** a hairstyle worn especially by men in which the hair is combed into a high mound at the front of the head — called also (*Brit*) *quiff*

pom–pom /ˈpɑːmˌpɑːm/ *noun, pl* **-poms** [*count*]
1 : a small, soft ball that is used as a decoration especially on clothing ▪ The hat had a *pom-pom* [=(*chiefly Brit*) *bobble*] on top.
2 : a large collection of plastic strings attached to a handle that is waved by cheerleaders

P

pomp·ous /ˈpɑːmpəs/ *adj* [*more* ~; *most* ~] *disapproving* : having or showing the attitude of people who speak and behave in a very formal and serious way because they believe that they are better, smarter, or more important than other people • a *pompous* [=*self-important*] politician • a *pompous* remark • She found it difficult to talk about her achievements without sounding *pompous*.
– **pom·pos·i·ty** /ˌpɑːmˈpɑːsəti/ *noun, pl* **-ties** [*noncount*] theatrical *pomposity* [*count*] the *pomposities* [=pompous remarks and actions] of elected officials – **pomp·ous·ly** *adv* • a suggestion she had *pompously* dismissed

[1]**ponce** /ˈpɑːns/ *noun, pl* **ponc·es** [*count*] *Brit, informal*
1 : PIMP
2 *offensive* : a homosexual man or a man who dresses and behaves in a way that seems feminine

[2]**ponce** /ˈpɑːns/ *verb* **ponces; ponced; ponc·ing**
ponce about/around [*phrasal verb*] *Brit, informal* : to spend time doing things that are not useful or serious : to waste time doing silly things • It's time to stop *poncing about* and get busy.

pon·cho /ˈpɑːnʧoʊ/ *noun, pl* **-chos** [*count*] : a piece of clothing that is used as a coat and that is made of a single piece of cloth or plastic with a hole in the middle for a person's head to go through

pond /ˈpɑːnd/ *noun, pl* **ponds**
1 [*count*] : an area of water that is surrounded by land and that is smaller than a lake
2 ***the pond*** *informal* : the Atlantic Ocean • They moved here from across *the pond*.
a big fish in a small pond see [1]FISH

pon·der /ˈpɑːndɚ/ *verb* **-ders; -dered; -der·ing** : to think about or consider (something) carefully [+ *obj*] He *pondered* the question before he answered. • The team *pondered* their chances of success. • We *pondered* whether we could afford the trip. [*no obj*] — + *on, over,* or *about* • She paused to *ponder on* the situation. • We *pondered over/about* what to do.

pon·der·ous /ˈpɑːndərəs/ *adj* [*more* ~; *most* ~]
1 : very boring or dull • students struggling to stay awake during a *ponderous* lecture
2 : slow or awkward because of weight and size • the elephant's *ponderous* movements
– **pon·der·ous·ly** *adv* • a *ponderously* technical lecture • He walked *ponderously* up the stairs. – **pon·der·ous·ness** *noun* [*noncount*]

[1]**pong** /ˈpɑːŋ/ *noun, pl* **pongs** [*count*] *Brit, informal* : an unpleasant smell • the *pong* of stale cigarette smoke

[2]**pong** *verb* **pongs; ponged; pong·ing** [*no obj*] *Brit, informal* : to have an unpleasant smell • foods that make your breath *pong* a bit

pon·tiff *or* **Pon·tiff** /ˈpɑːntəf/ *noun, pl* **-tiffs** [*count*] *formal* : POPE

pon·tif·i·cal /pɑnˈtɪfɪkəl/ *adj, always used before a noun, formal* : of, relating to, or coming from a pope • *pontifical* authority

[1]**pon·tif·i·cate** /pɑnˈtɪfəˌkeɪt/ *verb* **-cates; -cat·ed; -cat·ing** [*no obj*] *disapproving* : to speak or express your opinion about something in a way that shows that you think you are always right • We had to listen to her *pontificate* about/on the best way to raise children.

[2]**pon·tif·i·cate** /pɑnˈtɪfəkət/ *noun, pl* **-cates** [*count*]
1 : the position of a pope • He was elected to the *pontificate* last year.
2 : the period of time during which a particular person is pope • during the *pontificate* of Pope John Paul II

pon·toon /pɑnˈtuːn/ *noun, pl* **-toons** [*count*] : a large hollow container filled with air that is used to make a structure (such as a boat, airplane, or bridge) float on top of water • The boat had two *pontoons*. • They built a ***pontoon bridge*** [=a bridge that floats on the water and is held up by pontoons] • a ***pontoon plane*** [=an airplane that has pontoons on the bottom so that it can float on water]

[1]**po·ny** /ˈpoʊni/ *noun, pl* **po·nies** [*count*] : a small horse • He rode a *pony*. — see also ONE-TRICK PONY
dog and pony show see [1]DOG

[2]**pony** *verb* **po·nies; po·nied; po·ny·ing**
pony up [*phrasal verb*] *US, informal* **1** : to pay money for something • When the bill came, we all had to *pony up*. [=*pay up*] = We all had to *pony up* for the bill. **2** ***pony up (something)*** : to pay (money) for something • We *ponied up* $160 for the concert tickets.

po·ny·tail /ˈpoʊniˌteɪl/ *noun, pl* **-tails** [*count*] : a way of arranging hair by gathering it together at the back of the head and letting it hang down freely • She usually wears her hair pulled/tied back in a *ponytail*. — see picture at HAIR

Pon·zi scheme /ˈpɑːnzi-/ *noun, pl* ~ **schemes** [*count*] *US* : PYRAMID SCHEME

poo /ˈpuː/ *noun, informal*
1 [*noncount*] : solid waste passed out of the body : FECES • dog *poo* [=*poop*]
2 [*singular*] : the act of passing solid waste from the body — used especially by children in the phrases ***take a poo*** and ***do a poo***
– **poo** *verb* **poos; pooed; poo·ing** [*no obj*] • The dog *pooed* on the lawn.

-poo /ˌpuː/ *combining form, US, informal* + *disapproving* — used to suggest that something is small, unimportant, or childish in some way • They all have these cutesy-*poo* nicknames I find so annoying.

poo–bah *variant spelling of* POOH-BAH

pooch /ˈpuːʧ/ *noun, pl* **pooch·es** [*count*] *informal* : a dog • What a cute little *pooch*!

poo·dle /ˈpuːdl/ *noun, pl* **poodles** [*count*] : a type of dog that has thick, curly hair — see picture at DOG

[1]**poof** /ˈpuːf/ *interj* — used to say that something has happened suddenly or that someone or something has disappeared • One minute she was here, then *poof*, she was gone. • I took a pill and *poof*—my headache vanished.

[2]**poof** *noun, pl* **poofs** [*count*] *Brit, informal* + *offensive* : a homosexual man

poof·ter /ˈpuːftɚ/ *noun, pl* **-ters** [*count*] *Brit, informal* + *offensive* : a homosexual man

pooh /ˈpuː/ *interj, informal*
1 — used to show that you think an idea, suggestion, etc., is not very good • Oh, *pooh*, that's a terrible idea!
2 *Brit* — used to express disgust at an unpleasant smell • *Pooh*! What stinks?

pooh–bah *also* **poo–bah** /ˈpuːˌbɑː/ *noun, pl* **-bahs** [*count*] *often disapproving* : a person who has a lot of power or influence • an annual gathering of airline industry *pooh-bahs*

pooh–pooh /ˈpuːˌpuː/ *verb* **-poohs; -poohed; -pooh·ing** [+ *obj*] *informal* : to think or say that (something) is not very good or not true • They *pooh-poohed* my idea/suggestion. • He *pooh-poohed* the idea that the house was haunted. • The campers *pooh-poohed* our warnings about the storm.

[1]**pool** /ˈpuːl/ *noun, pl* **pools** [*count*]
1 : SWIMMING POOL • She dove into the *pool*. • an indoor *pool* • Is it an aboveground *pool* or an inground *pool*?
2 a : a small area of water • tide *pools* on the beach — see also WADING POOL **b** : a small amount of liquid or light that is on a surface — often + *of* • They found a *pool* [=*puddle*] *of* blood on the floor. • They stood in a *pool of* light. — sometimes used figuratively • Her eyes were *pools of* blue.
– compare [3]POOL

[2]**pool** *verb* **pools; pooled; pool·ing** [*no obj*] : to form a pool or puddle • Water *pooled* on the floor. — compare [4]POOL

[3]**pool** *noun, pl* **pools**
1 [*count*] : the money that is bet by people on an event (such as a sports game) • He won the weekly football *pool*. • The *pool* was split among three people.
2 [*noncount*] : a game played on a long table in which players use a long stick and a white ball to hit 15 colored balls into one of six pockets around the table • He enjoys playing/shooting *pool*. • a *pool* table • a *pool* cue — called also *pocket billiards*; compare BILLIARDS, SNOOKER
3 [*count*] : an amount of money that has been collected from many people for some purpose • They each put $20 into the *pool*. • an investment *pool*
4 [*count*] : a supply of things or people that are available for use • The team has a *pool* of talent waiting in the minor leagues. • a *pool* of jurors • We dipped into our *pool* of resources. — see also GENE POOL, MOTOR POOL
5 [*count*] : a group of people who do the same job or activity together • The President answered questions from journalists in the press *pool*. • the secretarial *pool* — see also CAR POOL
– compare [1]POOL

[4]**pool** *verb* **pools; pooled; pool·ing** [+ *obj*] : to combine (something) to form a supply which can be used by a group of people • We *pooled* our money together and rented a car. • We can do more when we *pool* our ideas and resources. — compare [2]POOL

pool·room /ˈpuːlˌruːm/ *noun, pl* **-rooms** [*count*] : a room that has a pool table or many pool tables : a room where people play pool

P

pool·side /ˈpuːlˌsaɪd/ *noun* [*noncount*] **:** the area next to or near the side of a swimming pool ▪ We had lunch at the *poolside*. — often used before another noun ▪ a *poolside* barbecue/bar
– **poolside** *adv* ▪ Sunbathers were relaxing *poolside*. ▪ We had lunch *poolside*.

[1]**poop** /ˈpuːp/ *verb* **poops; pooped; poop·ing** [*no obj*] *US, informal* **:** to pass solid waste from the body **:** DEFECATE ▪ The dog *pooped* on the lawn. — compare [3]POOP

[2]**poop** *noun, US, informal*
1 [*noncount*] **:** solid waste passed out of the body **:** FECES ▪ dog *poop*
2 [*singular*] **:** the act of passing solid waste from the body ▪ The dog did a *poop* on the lawn.

[3]**poop** *verb* **poops; pooped; pooping**
poop out [*phrasal verb*] *US, informal* **1 :** to stop working properly ▪ The old radio finally *pooped out*. **2 a :** to become very tired ▪ We worked all morning but we *pooped out* in the afternoon. **b *poop (someone) out* :** to make (someone) very tired ▪ That hike really *pooped* me *out*. ▪ I'm all *pooped out*.
– compare [1]POOP

poop deck *noun, pl* **~ decks** [*count*] **:** the flat surface on the raised structure at the rear of a ship

pooped *adj, not used before a noun, US, informal* **:** very tired ▪ We were *pooped* after a long day of work.

poop·er–scoop·er /ˈpuːpɚˌskuːpɚ/ *noun, pl* **-ers** [*count*] *informal* **:** a device that is used for picking up dog feces so that it can be thrown away

poor /ˈpuɚ/ *adj* **poor·er; -est** [*also more ~; most ~*]
1 : having little money or few possessions **:** not having enough money for the basic things that people need to live properly ▪ We were too *poor* to buy new clothes. ▪ The organization helps *poor* families/people. ▪ a *poor* country/neighborhood — opposite RICH
2 : having a very small amount of something ▪ a *poor* crop ▪ She has a *poor* vocabulary. — often + *in* ▪ Junk food is *poor in* vitamins and nutrients. — opposite RICH
3 : not good in quality or condition **:** BAD ▪ a *poor* effort ▪ It was a *poor* attempt at a joke. ▪ a *poor* performance ▪ He is in *poor* condition/health. ▪ She couldn't read the sign because her vision was too *poor*. ▪ The joke was in *poor* taste. [=the joke was offensive or not polite] ▪ He has a *poor* opinion of her. [=he does not think she is good; he does not like her]
4 : not skilled at something **:** not able to do something well ▪ He was such a *poor* plumber that he couldn't fix a simple leak. ▪ a *poor* golfer ▪ She is a *poor* judge of character. ▪ I am *poor* [=(more commonly) *bad*] at math.
5 *always used before a noun* — used to refer to someone or something in a way that shows sympathy ▪ The *poor* kitten hurt its paw. ▪ Leave the *poor* guy alone. ▪ You're all by yourself, you *poor* thing. ▪ *Poor* John has been sick for days.
a poor second/third (etc.) — used to say that someone finished a race or contest a long way behind the winner ▪ He came in *a poor second* in the race. [=he finished second but was far behind the winner] ▪ She was *a poor second* in the tournament.
make a poor fist of see FIST
poor man's **1** — used to refer to someone (such as a performer) who is like another person in some ways but not as talented or successful ▪ a young actor who is said to be the *poor man's* James Dean **2** — used to refer to something that is like something else but not as expensive ▪ Pewter is the *poor man's* silver.
***the poor* :** poor people ▪ He gave money to *the poor*.

poor·house /ˈpuɚˌhaʊs/ *noun, pl* **-hous·es** [*count*] *old-fashioned* **:** a place for poor people to live that is paid for by the taxes, donations, etc., of other people

[1]**poor·ly** /ˈpuɚli/ *adv* **:** in a poor or bad manner **:** in a way that is not good or satisfactory ▪ The essay was so *poorly* [=*badly*] written that it made no sense. ▪ a *poorly* run business

[2]**poorly** *adj, Brit, informal* **:** somewhat ill ▪ feeling *poorly*

[1]**pop** /ˈpɑːp/ *verb* **pops; popped; pop·ping**
1 a : to suddenly break open or come away from something often with a short, loud noise [*no obj*] The balloon *popped*. [=*burst*] ▪ We heard the sound of corks *popping* as the celebration began. ▪ One of the buttons *popped* off my sweater. [+ *obj*] Don't *pop* that balloon! ▪ She *popped* the cork on the champagne. [=she opened the bottle of champagne by removing the cork] **b** [*no obj*] **:** to make a short, loud noise ▪ Guns were *popping* in the distance.
2 : to cook (popcorn) [+ *obj*] We *popped* some popcorn in the microwave. [*no obj*] The popcorn is done *popping*.
3 [*no obj*] *informal* **a :** to come from, into, or out of a place suddenly or briefly ▪ I didn't mean to say that—it just *popped* out. ▪ Her shoulder *popped* out of its socket. ▪ He opened the box, and out *popped* a mouse. ▪ A funny thought just *popped* into my head. [=I just thought of something funny] ▪ The cathedral suddenly *popped* into view. [=I could suddenly see the cathedral] ▪ Her father *pops* in and out of her life. [=her father is sometimes involved in her life and sometimes not] **b** *always followed by an adverb or preposition* **:** to go to or from a place quickly, suddenly, or briefly ▪ If you are busy, I can *pop* back in later. ▪ She *popped* over for a cup of tea. = (*Brit*) She *popped* round for a cup of tea. ▪ My neighbor *popped* in for a visit. ▪ I need to *pop* into the drugstore for some film. ▪ She *popped* out for a minute. She should be back soon. ▪ I'll *pop* down to the post office during my break.
4 *always followed by an adverb or preposition* [+ *obj*] *informal* **:** to put (something) in, into, or onto a place suddenly or briefly ▪ She *popped* a CD in the player. ▪ He *popped* a quarter in the jukebox. ▪ I *popped* a grape into my mouth. ▪ He *popped* [=*stuck*] his head out the window.
5 ✧ When your ***ears pop***, you feel a sudden change of pressure in your ears as you are going up or down in an airplane, on a steep road, etc.
6 ✧ If your ***eyes pop***, they open very wide because you are surprised, afraid, excited, etc. ▪ When I saw the new car, my *eyes* practically *popped* out of my head.
7 [+ *obj*] *US, informal* **:** to hit (someone) ▪ I felt like *popping* him (one).
8 [*no obj*] *baseball* **:** to hit a pop fly ▪ He *popped* [=*popped up*] to the second baseman in the first inning. ▪ The batter ***popped out***. [=hit a pop fly that was caught for an out]
9 [+ *obj*] *US, informal* **:** to open and drink (a bottle or can of beer) ▪ They stopped at a bar to *pop* a few beers after work.
pop off [*phrasal verb*] *informal* **1 :** to die especially in a sudden or unexpected way ▪ The old man *popped off* before he could rewrite his will. **2** *US* **:** to talk loudly or angrily to someone ▪ The hockey player was ejected from the game for *popping off* to the referee.
pop on [*phrasal verb*] *Brit, informal* ***pop on (something)*** *or* ***pop (something) on* :** to put on (clothing) quickly ▪ *pop on* a hat
pop open **1 :** to open suddenly and quickly ▪ The suitcase/lid *popped open*. **2 :** to open (something) suddenly and quickly ▪ She *popped* the umbrella *open*. ▪ He *popped open* a cold beer.
pop pills *informal* **:** to take a lot of pills regularly ▪ I've been *popping pills* all week for this cold. ▪ He spends his time getting drunk and *popping pills*.
pop the question *informal* **:** to ask someone to marry you ▪ He *popped the question* on Christmas Day.
pop up [*phrasal verb*] *informal* **1 :** to appear in usually a sudden or unexpected way ▪ Coffee shops seem to be *popping up* everywhere. ▪ New evidence has been *popping up* every day in the trial. ▪ Problems kept *popping up*. **2** *baseball* **:** to hit a high fly ball that does not go very far **:** to hit a pop fly ▪ The batter *popped up* [=*popped*] to the second baseman. — see also POP-UP

[2]**pop** *noun, pl* **pops**
1 [*count*] **:** a short, loud sound ▪ We heard a loud *pop* when the lights went out.
2 *informal* **:** SODA POP [*noncount*] a bottle of *pop* [=*soda*] [*count*] Two *pops*, please.
3 [*count*] *baseball* **:** POP FLY
a pop *US, informal* **:** for each one **:** APIECE ▪ The tickets are selling at $50 *a pop*.
take a pop at *informal* **1 :** to try to hit (someone) ▪ Some drunk *took a pop at* me. **2** *chiefly Brit* **:** to criticize (someone) publicly ▪ He *took a pop at* his rival.
– compare [4]POP, [5]POP

[3]**pop** *adj, always used before a noun*
1 : of or relating to things that are popular and often talked about on television, in newspapers, etc. ▪ *pop* culture/psychology/fiction
2 : of or relating to popular music ▪ *pop* rock ▪ a *pop* artist/singer/star [=a person who sings popular music]

[4]**pop** *noun, pl* **pops**
1 [*noncount*] **:** music that is popular ▪ The radio station plays *pop*.
2 *Pops* [*noncount*] *US* **:** an orchestra that plays popular music — used in names ▪ the Boston/Cincinnati *Pops*
– compare [2]POP, [5]POP

P

[5]**pop** *noun, pl* **pops** *US, informal + old-fashioned*
1 [*count*] : a person's father — usually singular • Hey *Pop*, can I borrow one of your ties? • My *pop* likes watching football.
2 pops *often humorous* — used as a form of address for an old man • Need help with that package, *pops*? — see also MOM-AND-POP
– compare [2]POP, [4]POP

pop. *abbr* population

pop art *or* **Pop Art** *noun* [*noncount*] : art in which common objects (such as road signs, hamburgers, comic strips, or soup cans) are used or shown
– pop artist *or* **Pop artist** *noun, pl* **~ -ists** [*count*]

pop·corn /ˈpɑːpˌkoɚn/ *noun* [*noncount*] : corn in the form of hard yellow seeds that burst open and become soft and white when they are heated • We watched a movie and ate (a bag of) *popcorn*.

popcorn

pope *or* **Pope** /ˈpoʊp/ *noun, pl* **popes** *or* **Popes** [*count*] : the head of the Roman Catholic Church • The cardinals elected a new *pope*. • *Pope* Benedict XVI

pop–eyed /ˈpɑːpˌaɪd/ *adj*
1 : having eyes that stick out • *pop-eyed* bullfrogs
2 : having eyes that are open very wide because of surprise, fear, excitement, etc. • He stared *pop-eyed* as the huge wave came straight towards the boat.

pop fly *noun, pl* **~ flies** [*count*] *baseball* : a very high fly ball that does not go very far • He hit a high *pop fly* to the second baseman. — called also *pop, pop-up*

pop·gun /ˈpɑːpˌgʌn/ *noun, pl* **-guns** [*count*] : a toy gun that shoots corks and makes a loud noise

pop·lar /ˈpɑːplɚ/ *noun, pl* **-lars** [*count*] : a tall, thin tree that has rough bark, soft wood, and very small groups of flowers

pop·lin /ˈpɑːplən/ *noun* [*noncount*] : a strong cotton cloth

pop·over /ˈpɑːpˌoʊvɚ/ *noun, pl* **-overs** [*count*] *US* : a type of bread roll that is very light and that is made from eggs, milk, and flour

poppa *variant spelling of* PAPA

pop·per /ˈpɑːpɚ/ *noun, pl* **-pers** [*count*]
1 : a pan or electric machine for making popcorn • a popcorn *popper*
2 *Brit* : [2]SNAP 3

pop·pet /ˈpɑːpət/ *noun, pl* **-pets** [*count*] *Brit, informal* — used to talk in a loving way to or about a child • It's time for bed, *poppet*.

pop·py /ˈpɑːpi/ *noun, pl* **-pies** [*count*] : a type of plant that has bright red or orange flowers and that is the source of opium; *also* : its flower

pop·py·cock /ˈpɑːpiˌkɑːk/ *noun* [*noncount*] *informal + old-fashioned* : foolish words or ideas : NONSENSE • That's a lot of *poppycock*!

poppy seed *noun, pl* **~ seeds** [*count*] : the small, black seed of a poppy that is used in baked goods (such as breads and cakes) • Sprinkle *poppy seeds* on the bread before baking. • a *poppy seed* cake

pop quiz *noun, pl* **~ quiz·zes** [*count*] *US* : a short test that a teacher gives to students without warning

Pop·si·cle /ˈpɑːpsɪkəl/ *trademark* — used for flavored and colored water frozen on a stick

pop–top /ˈpɑːpˌtɑːp/ *noun, pl* **-tops** [*count*] *US* : the part of a can's top that can be removed by pulling a ring

pop·u·lace /ˈpɑːpjələs/ *noun* [*singular*] *formal* : the people who live in a country or area • The *populace* has suffered greatly. • a diverse/educated *populace* • the general *populace* [=the ordinary or common people]

pop·u·lar /ˈpɑːpjəlɚ/ *adj*
1 [*more ~; most ~*] **a** : liked or enjoyed by many people • They have names that were *popular* a century ago. • He is a *popular* guy in school. • a *popular* actor • Spicy foods have become increasingly *popular*. • This is our most *popular* [=*best-selling*] brand of sneaker. — often + *with* or *among* • The bar is *popular with* college students. • This TV show is especially *popular among* women. — opposite UNPOPULAR **b** : accepted, followed, used, or done by many people • That is a very *popular* misconception. • The word "groovy" was *popular* in the 1960s but it's outdated now. • Her theories are *popular* among social scientists. • ***Contrary to popular belief/opinion*** [=in spite of what many people believe], fame does have its drawbacks. — opposite UNPOPULAR
2 *always used before a noun* : of, relating to, or coming from most of the people in a country, society, or group • *popular* government • *popular* culture • the *popular* vote — see also *popular demand* at [1]DEMAND
3 *always used before a noun, somewhat formal* : designed or intended for the average person : capable of being understood by ordinary people • *popular* mechanics • a *popular* history of physics

pop·u·lar·i·ty /ˌpɑːpjəˈlerəti/ *noun* [*noncount*] : state of being liked, enjoyed, accepted, or done by a large number of people : the quality or state of being popular • Acupuncture has grown/gained (in) *popularity* [=has become more popular] in the West. • the increasing *popularity* of cell phones • The candidate is winning/losing *popularity* with/among voters. [=is becoming more/less popular with/among voters]

popularity contest *noun, pl* **~ -tests** [*count*] : a contest or situation in which the person who wins or is most successful is the one who is most popular rather than the one who is most skillful, qualified, etc. • The election was just a *popularity contest*. Voters didn't really care about the issues. — often used to say that someone or something is not popular • After laying off hundreds of workers, the company isn't going to win any *popularity contests* around here. [=the company is not well liked after laying off hundreds of workers]

pop·u·lar·ize *also Brit* **pop·u·lar·ise** /ˈpɑːpjələˌraɪz/ *verb* **-iz·es; -ized; -iz·ing** [+ *obj*]
1 : to cause (something) to be liked, enjoyed, accepted, or done by many people : to make (something) popular • a phrase that was *popularized* by its use in a hit TV show • Dream analysis was *popularized* by Sigmund Freud.
2 : to make (something that is difficult or complicated) simpler and easier to understand for the average person • The book presents a *popularized* version of American history.
– pop·u·lar·i·za·tion *also Brit* **pop·u·lar·i·sa·tion** /ˌpɑːpjələrəˈzeɪʃən, *Brit* ˌpɒpjəˌlaˌraɪˈzeɪʃən/ *noun* [*noncount*] • the *popularization* of yoga

pop·u·lar·ly /ˈpɑːpjələli/ *adv*
1 : by many people or most people • a *popularly* held belief • The polygraph machine is more *popularly* [=*commonly*] known as a "lie detector."
2 : by being chosen or voted for by most of the people • He was the country's first ***popularly elected*** leader. [=the country's first leader who was chosen in an election rather than in some other way]

pop·u·late /ˈpɑːpjəˌleɪt/ *verb* **-lates; -lat·ed; -lat·ing** [+ *obj*] : to live in (a country, city, area, etc.) : to make up the population of (a place) • Immigrants began to *populate* the area in the late 19th century. • Strange creatures *populate* the ocean depths. — often used as *(be) populated* • The country *is populated* by many ethnic groups. — often used figuratively • The area *is populated* by small farms. [=the area has many small farms] • His stories *are populated* with real-life characters.
– populated *adj* [*more ~; most ~*] • a densely/heavily *populated* area [=an area where many people live] • a sparsely/thinly *populated* area [=an area where few people live] • The most *populated* region of the country [=the region where most people live] is in the south.

pop·u·la·tion /ˌpɑːpjəˈleɪʃən/ *noun, pl* **-tions**
1 : the number of people who live in a place [*count*] The world's *population* has increased greatly. — often + *of* • The *population of* New York City is over eight million. [*noncount*] The city has experienced an increase in *population*. — often used before another noun • *population* growth/control • a ***population explosion/boom*** [=a sudden large increase in the number of people or animals in an area]
2 [*count*] : a group of people or animals of a particular kind that live in a place • There has been a sharp reduction in the bat *population* in this region. • the rural *population* of America • the educated/Jewish/adult *population*

pop·u·list /ˈpɑːpjəlɪst/ *adj* : of or relating to a political party that claims to represent ordinary people • *populist* leaders
– pop·u·lism /ˈpɑːpjəˌlɪzəm/ *noun* [*noncount*] • His *populism* appeals to a broad range of voters. **– populist** *noun, pl* **-ists** [*count*] • She is a *populist*.

pop·u·lous /ˈpɑːpjələs/ *adj* [*more ~; most ~*] *formal* : having a large population • a *populous* seaport • the most *populous* state in the U.S.

[1]**pop–up** /ˈpɑːpˌʌp/ *adj, always used before a noun*
1 : having a picture that stands up when a page is opened • a *pop-up* book • a *pop-up* card

2 *computers* **:** appearing on the screen over another window or document ▪ a *pop-up* menu ▪ *pop-up* ads

2pop–up *noun, pl* **-ups** *[count]*
1 *baseball* **:** POP FLY ▪ He hit a high *pop-up* that was caught by the shortstop. — see also *pop up* at 1POP
2 *computers* **:** a window that appears on the screen over other windows or documents and that often advertises something ▪ The Web site is full of *pop-ups.*

por·ce·lain /ˈpoɚsələn/ *noun [noncount]* **:** a hard, white substance that is very delicate and that is made by baking clay ▪ The bowl is made of/from *porcelain.* ▪ a *porcelain* bowl/doll

porch /ˈpoɚtʃ/ *noun, pl* **porch·es** *[count]*
1 *US* **:** a structure attached to the entrance of a building that has a roof and that may or may not have walls ▪ The house has a large front/back *porch.* ▪ an enclosed *porch* [=a porch that has walls] — see picture at HOUSE
2 *Brit* **:** an entrance to a building that has a separate roof

por·cine /ˈpoɚˌsaɪn/ *adj [more ~; most ~] formal* **:** of, relating to, or like a pig ▪ *porcine* pets ▪ his *porcine* face

por·cu·pine /ˈpoɚkjəˌpaɪn/ *noun, pl* **por·cu·pines** *also* **porcupine** *[count]* **:** a small animal that has very stiff, sharp parts (called quills) all over its body — see picture at RODENT

1pore /ˈpoɚ/ *verb* **pores; pored; por·ing**
pore over *[phrasal verb]* ***pore over (something)*** **:** to read or study (something) very carefully ▪ He *pored over* the map for hours.

2pore *noun, pl* **pores** *[count]*
1 : a very small opening on the surface of your skin that liquid comes out through when you sweat
2 : a small opening on the surface of a plant, a rock, etc.

pork /ˈpoɚk/ *noun [noncount]*
1 : the meat of a pig that is used for food ▪ roast *pork* ▪ *pork* chops
2 *US, informal + disapproving* **:** government money that is spent on projects done to help the political careers of elected officials ▪ We need to cut the *pork* out of the federal budget.

pork barrel *noun [noncount] US, informal + disapproving* **:** government projects that benefit people in a particular part of the country and that are done in order to help the political careers of elected officials — often used before another noun ▪ *pork barrel* projects/spending

pork·er /ˈpoɚkɚ/ *noun, pl* **-ers** *[count] informal*
1 : a very fat pig used for food
2 : a fat person

pork rind *noun, pl* **~ rinds** *[count, noncount] US* **:** a small piece of pig skin that is fried and eaten cold as a snack

1porky /ˈpoɚki/ *adj* **pork·i·er; -est** *[also more ~; most ~] informal* **:** 1FAT ▪ He's looking a little *porky* these days.

2porky *noun, pl* **pork·ies** *[count] Brit slang* **:** 4LIE ▪ He told a *porky.*

porn /ˈpoɚn/ *also* **por·no** /ˈpoɚnoʊ/ *noun [noncount] informal* **:** PORNOGRAPHY ▪ making/selling *porn* — often used before another noun ▪ a *porn* movie ▪ the *porn* industry

por·no·graph·ic /ˌpoɚnəˈgræfɪk/ *adj [more ~; most ~] often disapproving* **:** showing or describing naked people or sex in a very open and direct way in order to cause sexual excitement ▪ *pornographic* magazines/movies ▪ *pornographic* Web sites

por·nog·ra·phy /poɚˈnɑːgrəfi/ *noun [noncount] often disapproving* **:** movies, pictures, magazines, etc., that show or describe naked people or sex in a very open and direct way in order to cause sexual excitement ▪ If you ask me, his movies are just high-class *pornography.*
— por·nog·ra·pher /poɚˈnɑːgrəfɚ/ *noun, pl* **-phers** *[count]*

po·rous /ˈporəs/ *adj [more ~; most ~]*
1 : having small holes that allow air or liquid to pass through ▪ *porous* rock ▪ a *porous* membrane/surface
2 : easy to pass or get through ▪ The country has a *porous* border.
— po·ros·i·ty /pəˈrɑːsəti/ *noun [noncount] technical* ▪ the *porosity* of the membrane

por·poise /ˈpoɚpəs/ *noun, pl* **-pois·es** *[count]* **:** a small usually gray and white whale that has a rounded nose — see picture at DOLPHIN

por·ridge /ˈporɪdʒ/ *noun [noncount] Brit* **:** OATMEAL 2

1port /ˈpoɚt/ *noun, pl* **ports**
1 : a town or city where ships stop to load and unload cargo *[count]* Boston is a major U.S. *port.* *[noncount]* The ship is now in *port* but will be leaving *port* soon.
2 : a place where ships can find shelter from a storm *[count]* The ship reached the *port* safely. *[noncount]* The ship spent two days in *port.*
any port in a storm — used to say that you will use anyone or anything for comfort, help, etc., when you are in a bad situation ▪ "I know she's lonely, but I can't believe she's going out with that guy." "Well, you know what they say: *any port in a storm.*"
— compare 2PORT, 3PORT, 4PORT

2port *noun [noncount]* **:** the side of a ship or aircraft that is on the left when you are looking toward the front ▪ The ship turned to *port.* — compare STARBOARD — compare 1PORT, 3PORT, 4PORT
— port *adj* ▪ the *port* side ▪ the *port* engine

3port *noun, pl* **ports** *[count, noncount]* **:** a strong, sweet, usually dark red wine that is made in Portugal — compare 1PORT, 2PORT, 4PORT

4port *noun, pl* **ports** *[count]* **:** a place where you can connect a piece of equipment (such as a printer or mouse) to a computer — compare 1PORT, 2PORT, 3PORT

Port. *abbr* Portugal

portabella *variant spelling of* PORTOBELLO

por·ta·ble /ˈpoɚtəbəl/ *adj [more ~; most ~]* **:** easy to carry or move around ▪ a *portable* television/radio ▪ *Portable* devices such as MP3 players are becoming increasingly popular.
— portable *noun, pl* **-tables** *[count]* ▪ laptop computers and other *portables* **— por·ta·bil·i·ty** /ˌpoɚtəˈbɪləti/ *noun [noncount]* ▪ *Portability* is the main advantage of laptops.

por·tal /ˈpoɚtl/ *noun, pl* **-tals** *[count]*
1 *formal + literary* **:** a large door or gate to a building (such as a church)
2 *computers* **:** a Web site that helps you find other sites ▪ a Web *portal* for baseball fans

port·cul·lis /poɚtˈkʌləs/ *noun, pl* **-lis·es** *[count] formal + literary* **:** a heavy iron gate that can be raised or lowered at the entrance to a castle

por·tend /poɚˈtɛnd/ *verb* **-tends; -tend·ed; -tend·ing** *[+ obj] formal + literary* **:** to be a sign or warning that something usually bad or unpleasant is going to happen ▪ The distant thunder *portended* a storm. ▪ If you're superstitious, a black cat *portends* trouble.

por·tent /ˈpoɚˌtɛnt/ *noun, pl* **-tents** *[count] formal + literary* **:** a sign or warning that something usually bad or unpleasant is going to happen ▪ a *portent* of evil

por·ten·tous /poɚˈtɛntəs/ *adj [more ~; most ~]*
1 *formal + literary* **:** giving a sign or warning that something usually bad or unpleasant is going to happen ▪ a *portentous* dream/event
2 *formal + disapproving* **:** trying to seem important, serious, or impressive **:** POMPOUS ▪ a *portentous* manner/tone
— por·ten·tous·ly *adv*

por·ter /ˈpoɚtɚ/ *noun, pl* **-ters**
1 *[count]* **:** a person whose job is to carry bags or luggage at a hotel, airport, etc. ▪ The *porter* helped her with her luggage.
2 *[count] US* **:** a person whose job is to help passengers on a train
3 *[count] Brit* **:** a person whose job is to let people into a hotel, college, hospital, etc. ▪ the night *porter*
4 *[count] Brit* **:** a person whose job is to move patients from one part of a hospital to another
5 *[count, noncount]* **:** a heavy, dark brown beer ▪ a glass of *porter*

port·fo·lio /poɚtˈfouliˌoʊ/ *noun, pl* **-lios** *[count]*
1 : a flat case for carrying documents or drawings
2 : a set of drawings, paintings, or photographs that are presented together in a folder ✧ Artists present *portfolios* of their work to possible employers or to people who might buy or show their art.
3 *finance* **:** the investments that are owned by a person or organization ▪ an investment/retirement *portfolio* ▪ a *portfolio* manager
4 *Brit* **:** the responsibilities of a minister of state or member of a cabinet ▪ That's not part of his *portfolio.*

port·hole /ˈpoɚtˌhoul/ *noun, pl* **-holes** *[count]* **:** a small round window in the side of a ship or aircraft

por·ti·co /ˈpoɚtɪˌkou/ *noun, pl* **-coes** *or* **-cos** *[count] formal* **:** a row of columns supporting a roof at the entrance of a building

1por·tion /ˈpoɚʃən/ *noun, pl* **-tions** *[count]*
1 : a part of a larger amount, area, etc. ▪ A *portion* of the donations will be given to the orphanage. ▪ *Portions* of land

were used for farming. ▪ A considerable/significant *portion* of the city was flooded.

2 : a part of something that is shared with other people — usually singular ▪ A *portion* of the blame belongs to you. ▪ He took on a large *portion* of the work.

3 : the amount of food that is served to a person at one time ▪ The restaurant gives large/generous *portions*. ▪ I'll just have a small *portion* [=*serving*] of meat. ▪ She divided the pie into six equal *portions*.

[2]**portion** *verb* **-tions; -tioned; -tion·ing** [+ *obj*] **:** to divide (something) into parts and give those parts to people ▪ The work was *portioned* to each member of the staff. — usually + *out* ▪ They *portioned* the supplies *out* equally. ▪ The supplies were *portioned out* among the troops.

port·ly /ˈpoətli/ *adj* **port·li·er; -est** [*also more* ~; *most* ~] *somewhat formal* **:** having a round and somewhat fat body ▪ a *portly* gentleman

port·man·teau /poətˈmæntoʊ/ *noun, pl* **-teaus** *or* **-teaux** /poətˈmæntoʊz/ [*count*] *old-fashioned* **:** a large suitcase that opens into two parts

por·to·bel·lo /ˌpoətəˈbɛloʊ/ *also* **por·ta·bel·la** /ˌpoətəˈbɛlə/ *noun, pl* **-los** *also* **-las** [*count*] *chiefly US* **:** a large brown mushroom used in cooking

port of call *noun, pl* **ports of call** [*count*] **:** a place where a ship stops during a journey ▪ The island is a busy *port of call*. ▪ Our next *port of call* is Jamaica.

port of entry *noun, pl* **ports of entry** [*count*] **:** a place (such as a city or airport) where people or goods enter a country

por·trait /ˈpoətrət/ *noun, pl* **-traits**

1 [*count*] **:** a painting, drawing, or photograph of a person that usually only includes the person's head and shoulders ▪ black-and-white *portraits* ▪ a family *portrait* ▪ The queen posed for her *portrait*. — see also SELF-PORTRAIT

2 [*count*] **:** a detailed description of something or someone ▪ The book/film presents a *portrait* of life in a small town.

3 [*noncount*] **:** a way of printing a page so that the shorter sides are on the top and bottom and the longer sides are on the left and right — compare LANDSCAPE

por·trait·ist /ˈpoətrətɪst/ *noun, pl* **-ists** [*count*] **:** a person who paints or draws portraits

por·trai·ture /ˈpoətrəʧɚ/ *noun* [*noncount*]

1 : the art of making portraits ▪ a painter who is master at *portraiture*

2 : portraits of people painted or drawn by artists ▪ The museum is exhibiting *portraiture* from the late 19th century.

por·tray /poəˈtreɪ/ *verb* **-trays; -trayed; -tray·ing** [+ *obj*]

1 : to describe (someone or something) in a particular way ▪ The White House has *portrayed* the President as deeply conflicted over the matter. ▪ The lawyer *portrayed* his client as a victim of child abuse. ▪ He *portrayed* himself as a victim.

2 : to show (someone or something) in a painting, book, etc. ▪ The painting *portrays* the queen in a purple robe. ▪ The novel *portrays* [=*depicts*] life in a small southern town.

3 : to play (a character) in a film, play, or television show ▪ Laurence Olivier *portrayed* Hamlet beautifully.

por·tray·al /poəˈtrejəl/ *noun, pl* **-als** [*count*]

1 : the act of showing or describing someone or something especially in a painting, book, etc. — often + *of* ▪ We will examine Edgar Allan Poe's *portrayal of* women in his stories. ▪ The book is an accurate *portrayal of* his life. ▪ I don't accept his *portrayal of* himself as an innocent victim. [=I don't believe that he is an innocent victim, as he claims to be]

2 : the way in which an actor plays a character — often + *of* ▪ Laurence Olivier's *portrayal of* Hamlet was brilliant.

[1]**Por·tu·guese** /ˌpoəʧəˈgiːz/ *adj* **:** of or relating to Portugal, its people, or their language ▪ *Portuguese* customs/food

[2]**Portuguese** *noun*

1 [*noncount*] **:** the language spoken in Portugal and Brazil ▪ She is teaching her son *Portuguese*.

2 ***the Portuguese*** **:** the people of Portugal **:** Portuguese people ▪ the customs of *the Portuguese*

Portuguese man–of–war *noun, pl* **~ man–of–wars** *or* **~ men–of–war** [*count*] **:** a large sea animal that has a very soft body, many long, soft parts (called tentacles) that hang down from its body, and a poisonous sting

pos. *abbr* **1** position **2** positive

[1]**pose** /ˈpoʊz/ *verb* **pos·es; posed; pos·ing**

1 [+ *obj*] **:** to be or create (a possible threat, danger, problem, etc.) ▪ Smog *poses* a threat to our health. [=smog threatens our health] ▪ His careless behavior *poses* a hazard to others. [=his careless behavior is dangerous to others] ▪ Physical sports *pose* a risk of injury. ▪ The weather should not *pose* a problem for us. ▪ Decreasing the unemployment rate *poses* a serious challenge to/for the new governor.

2 [+ *obj*] **:** to ask or suggest (a question) ▪ My mother *posed* a question to me that I still can't answer to this day: "What do you want to do with your life?" ▪ The contradictions in his argument *pose* [=*raise*] questions about his credibility.

3 : to stand, sit, or lie down in a particular position as a model for a photograph, painting, etc. [*no obj*] — usually + *for* ▪ Everyone *posed for* the group photo. ▪ She *posed* nude *for* the magazine. [+ *obj*] The photographer *posed* her on the steps of the courthouse.

pose as [*phrasal verb*] ***pose as (someone or something)*** **:** to pretend to be (someone or something) in order to deceive people ▪ She *posed as* a student to get free admission to the museum. ▪ undercover cops *posing as* drug dealers

[2]**pose** *noun, pl* **poses** [*count*]

1 : the position in which someone stands, sits, lies down, etc., especially as a model for a photograph, painting, etc. ▪ The photographs show the models in both clothed and nude *poses*. ▪ Hold that *pose*. It will make a great photograph.

2 *disapproving* **:** a kind of behavior that is intended to impress other people and that is not sincere ▪ His disapproval of the war looks good to voters, but I bet it's just a *pose*.

[1]**pos·er** /ˈpoʊzɚ/ *noun, pl* **-ers** [*count*] *disapproving* **:** a person who dresses or behaves in a deceptive way that is meant to impress other people ▪ He's not really interested in rap music. He's just a *poser*. — called also **poseur** — compare [2]POSER

[2]**poser** *noun, pl* **-ers** [*count*] *informal* **:** a difficult question or problem ▪ Here's a *poser* for you—what is good art? — compare [1]POSER

po·seur /poʊˈzɚ/ *noun, pl* **-seurs** [*count*] *disapproving* **:** [1]POSER

posh /ˈpɑːʃ/ *adj* **posh·er; -est** [*also more* ~; *most* ~] *informal*

1 : very attractive, expensive, and popular ▪ They live in a *posh* neighborhood. ▪ I stayed at a *posh* [=*elegant, luxurious*] hotel.

2 *Brit* **:** typical of people who have high social status ▪ a *posh* accent ▪ The family is very *posh*.

— posh *adv, Brit* ▪ They laugh when I try to ***talk posh***.

pos·it /ˈpɑːzət/ *verb* **-its; -it·ed; -it·ing** [+ *obj*] *formal* **:** to suggest (something, such as an idea or theory) especially in order to start a discussion ▪ Some astronomers have *posited* [=*proposed, postulated*] that the universe is made up of mysterious dark matter.

[1]**po·si·tion** /pəˈzɪʃən/ *noun, pl* **-tions**

1 a [*count*] **:** the place where someone or something is in relation to other people or things ▪ From this *position*, you can see all of New York City's skyline. ▪ The chart shows the *positions* [=*locations*] of the constellations in the night sky. **b** [*noncount*] **:** the place where someone or something should be — used after *in, into,* or *out of* ▪ The actors were all *in position*. ▪ The nail fell *out of position* before I could hammer it. ▪ He maneuvered the car *into position*. ▪ The defensive players fell back *into position*. ▪ Police were *in position* to catch the fleeing suspect. ▪ The switch is *in* the on *position*, but nothing is happening.

2 a : the way someone stands, sits, or lies down [*count*] Actors, please assume/take your *positions*. The show is about to begin. ▪ The child fell asleep in a sitting *position*. ▪ I was in an uncomfortable *position* and had to move. [*noncount*] I was uncomfortable, so I shifted *position*. — see also FETAL POSITION **b** [*count*] **:** the way something is arranged or placed ▪ Return your seat to an upright *position* for landing.

3 [*count*] **:** the situation that someone or something is in — usually singular ▪ I've been in your *position* before, so I think I can help you. ▪ The company's financial *position* has worsened over the past year. ▪ The manager was placed in the awkward/difficult *position* of having to lay off dozens of workers. ▪ Put yourself in my *position* for a moment. What would you do? ▪ He is in a *position* of power/authority. ▪ I'm ***in no position to*** lend you any money. [=I cannot lend you any money]

4 [*count*] **:** an opinion or judgment on a particular subject ▪ The Supreme Court has taken the *position* that the First Amendment does not apply in these kinds of cases. ▪ Allow me to explain my *position*. — often + *on* ▪ I was forced to rethink my *positions on* certain issues. ▪ He criticized his opponent for not taking a *position on* gun control.

5 : the rank or role of someone or something in an organiza-

P

tion or society [*count*] He rose to a *position* of leadership and authority. ▪ They dedicated their lives to improving the *position* of women in a male-dominated society. [*noncount*] Wealth and *position* are not important to her.

6 [*count*] **:** JOB ▪ Does your company have any entry-level *positions* available? ▪ The *position* has been filled. [=someone has been hired for the job] ▪ Requirements for the *position* include a master's degree and at least five years of work experience. ▪ She was named to the *position* of senior vice president of marketing.

7 : the place of someone or something in a race, contest, competition, etc. [*count*] She finished the race in fourth *position*. [*noncount*] The cars ***jockeyed for position*** in the first lap of the race. [=each car tried to get into a better position in the first lap of the race] ▪ The candidates *jockeyed for position* in the debates. [=they tried to do better than others in the debates] — see also POLE POSITION

8 [*count*] *sports* **: the particular place and job of a player on a sports team** ▪ I think goalie is the hardest *position* to play in hockey.

9 [*count*] **: a place where an army has put soldiers, guns, etc.** — usually plural ▪ Artillery bombarded our *positions*.

[2]position *verb* **-tions; -tioned; -tion·ing** [+ *obj*] **: to put (something or someone) in a particular position** ▪ He *positioned* the chairs around the table. ▪ The company is *positioning* itself to take advantage of a new market. ▪ The shortstop was *positioned* well to make the play. ▪ She *positioned* herself by the door.

po·si·tion·al /pəˈzɪʃənəl/ *adj, always used before a noun* **: relating to the position of someone or something** ▪ *positional* changes ▪ a *positional* advantage

position paper *noun, pl* **~ -pers** [*count*] **: a written report from an organization or government that discusses a particular issue and suggests what should be done**

[1]pos·i·tive /ˈpɑːzətɪv/ *adj*

1 [*more ~; most ~*] **: good or useful** ▪ Did you have a *positive* [=*pleasant*] experience working with that company? ▪ The book had a *positive* influence on me. ▪ He has been a *positive* role model for his brother. ▪ Nothing *positive* came out of that experience. ▪ What are some of the *positive* things about your job? ▪ The low unemployment rate is a *positive* sign for the economy. ▪ The company took *positive* steps to create a safer workplace. — opposite NEGATIVE

2 [*more ~; most ~*] **: thinking about the good qualities of someone or something : thinking that a good result will happen : hopeful or optimistic** ▪ You've got to have a *positive* attitude/outlook to do well in life. ▪ You should try to be more *positive* about the whole situation. ▪ ***On the positive side***, you will be making more money. ▪ To end ***on a positive note***, we are seeing an increase in sales this month. — opposite NEGATIVE

3 *not used before a noun* **: completely certain or sure that something is correct or true** ▪ We were *positive* that we would win the game. ▪ "That is the street we need to take." "Are you sure?" "(I'm) *Positive*." ▪ I'm not (absolutely) *positive*, but I think they won the World Series in 1954.

4 [*more ~; most ~*] **: showing or expressing support, approval, or agreement** ▪ Most of the response from the public has been *positive* [=*favorable*] so far. ▪ The reviews were mostly *positive*. ▪ *positive* feedback ▪ The new Web site has received a *positive* response from its visitors. — opposite NEGATIVE

5 : unable to be doubted : certainly true ▪ There is no *positive* [=*definite, conclusive*] proof that life exists on other planets. ▪ The police have not yet made a *positive* identification of the victim. ▪ The fact that the DNA samples did not match is ***proof positive*** that he is not the father.

6 : showing the presence of a particular germ, condition, or substance ▪ He tested *positive* for steroids. [=the test showed that he had used steroids] ▪ The test results were *positive*. ▪ HIV *positive* patients — opposite NEGATIVE

7 a *mathematics* **: greater than zero** ▪ a *positive* integer — opposite NEGATIVE **b : more than the amount of money spent or invested** ▪ We got a *positive* return on our investment. [=we made a profit on our investment] — opposite NEGATIVE

8 *technical* **a : containing or producing electricity that is charged by a proton** ▪ a *positive* charge/current — opposite NEGATIVE **b : having more protons than electrons** ▪ a *positive* ion/particle — opposite NEGATIVE

9 *always used before a noun, informal* **: absolute or complete**

position

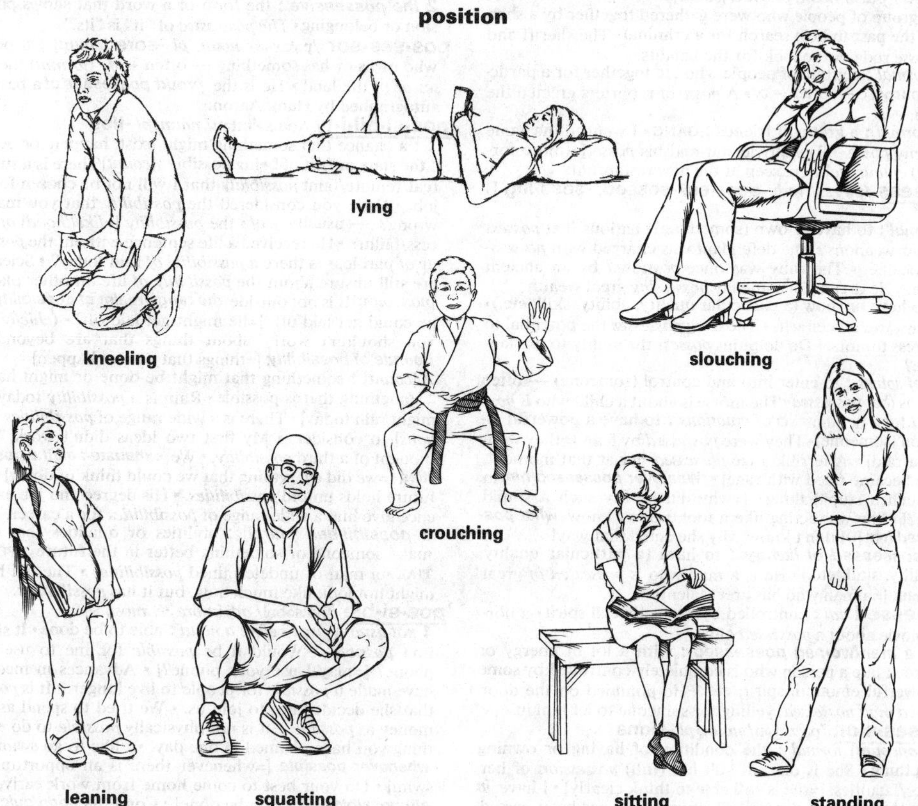

P

— used to make a statement more forceful • The way poor people are treated in this country is a *positive* disgrace.

[2]**positive** *noun, pl* **-tives** *[count]*
1 : something that is good or useful • The *positives* of living in the city include access to public transportation and many interesting restaurants. • The *positives* of the job outweigh the negatives. [=there are more good things about the job than bad things] — opposite NEGATIVE
2 : the result from a test that shows that a particular germ, condition, or substance is present • The test showed a *positive*. • The test produced too many ***false positives*** [=results that showed something was present when it really was not] to be reliable. — opposite NEGATIVE
3 : a photograph that shows light and dark areas or colors as they look in real life — compare NEGATIVE

positive discrimination *noun [noncount] Brit* : AFFIRMATIVE ACTION

pos•i•tive•ly /ˈpɑːzətɪvli/ *adv*
1 a — used to stress the truth of a statement • The new City Hall building is *positively* [=*downright*] ugly. • Driving a car without wearing a seatbelt is *positively* stupid. **b** — used to stress that you really mean what you are saying • "Are you going out with him?" "*Positively* [=*certainly*] not!" • This is *positively* [=*definitely*] the last time I'm going to bail you out!
2 *[more ~; most ~]* **:** in a positive way: such as **a :** in a way that shows that you are hopeful and thinking about the good qualities of a situation • If you start thinking *positively*, you might feel better. **b :** in a way that shows that you agree with or approve of someone or something • Only 35 percent of survey respondents view the state of the economy *positively*. • Customers responded *positively* to the new product. **c :** in a certain or definite way • No one was able to *positively* identify the corpse.
3 *technical* — used to say that something has a positive electric charge • *positively* charged ions

pos•i•tron /ˈpɑːzəˌtrɑːn/ *noun, pl* **-trons** *[count] physics* **:** a very small particle of matter that has a positive charge of electricity and that travels around the nucleus of an atom

poss. *abbr* possible

pos•se /ˈpɑːsi/ *noun, pl* **-ses** *[count]*
1 : a group of people who were gathered together by a sheriff in the past to help search for a criminal • The sheriff and his *posse* rode out to look for the bandits.
2 *informal* **:** a group of people who are together for a particular purpose — often + *of* • A *posse of* reporters greeted the coach.
3 *informal* **:** a group of friends **:** GANG • I went to the game with my *posse*. • The movie star and his *posse* [=(more formally) *entourage*] were seen at the new restaurant.

pos•sess /pəˈzɛs/ *verb* **-sess•es; -sessed; -sess•ing** *[+ obj]*
1 *formal* **:** to have or own (something) • nations that *possess* nuclear weapons • The defendant was charged with *possessing* cocaine. • The ruby was once *possessed* by an ancient queen. • He dreams of someday *possessing* great wealth.
2 : to have or show (a particular quality, ability, skill, etc.) • He *possesses* a keen wit. • The drug *possesses* the potential to suppress tumors. • Do dolphins *possess* the ability to use language?
3 a *of spirits* **:** to enter into and control (someone) — often used as *(be) possessed* • The movie is about a child who *is possessed* by a demon. **b** *of emotions* **:** to have a powerful effect on (someone) • They were *possessed* by fear. [=they were very afraid] • A terrible rage *possessed* her at that moment. [=she became filled with rage] • ***Whatever possessed him*** to say such a stupid thing? [=why did he say such a stupid thing?] • She was acting like a fool. I don't know ***what possessed her***. [=I don't know why she acted that way]
be possessed of *literary* **:** to have (a particular quality, ability, skill, etc.) • He is a man who is *possessed of* great talent. [=a man who has great talent]

possessed *adj* **:** controlled by a usually evil spirit • a horror movie about a *possessed* child
like a man/woman possessed **:** with a lot of energy or force **:** like a person who is completely controlled by some powerful emotion, spirit, etc. • He pounded on the door *like a man possessed*, yelling for someone to let him in.

pos•ses•sion /pəˈzɛʃən/ *noun, pl* **-sions**
1 *[noncount] formal* **:** the condition of having or owning something • She is old but still has (full) *possession* of her senses/faculties. [=she is still able to think clearly] • I have ***in my possession*** [=I possess] silverware that has been passed down in my family for generations. • The city can ***take possession of*** the abandoned buildings. • She ***came into possession of*** a rare silver coin.
2 *[count]* **:** something that is owned or possessed by someone • The family lost all of its *possessions* in the fire. • This ring was my mother's most precious *possession*. • personal *possessions* [=*belongings*]
3 *[noncount] law* **:** the crime of having something that is illegal (such as a drug or weapon) • The defendant was charged with heroin *possession*. • *possession* of stolen property
4 *[count]* **:** a country that is controlled or governed by another country • The U.S. has several *possessions* in the Pacific Ocean.
5 *sports* **a** *[noncount]* **:** control of the ball or puck in a game • He took too long to shoot and lost *possession* of the puck. • He did not have *possession* of the ball before he was knocked out of bounds. **b** *[count] American football* **:** a time when a team has control of the ball and is trying to score • They scored a touchdown on each of their first two *possessions*.
6 *[noncount]* **:** the state of being controlled by a usually evil spirit • demonic *possession*

[1]**pos•ses•sive** /pəˈzɛsɪv/ *adj*
1 *[more ~; most ~]* **:** not willing to share things with or lend things to other people — often + *about* • She is very *possessive about* her toys. — often + *of* • He is quite *possessive of* his DVD collection.
2 *[more ~; most ~]* **:** wanting all of someone's attention and love • If you marry him, he is only going to become even more jealous and *possessive* than he is now. • a *possessive* boyfriend — often + *of* • a mother who was very *possessive of* her son
3 *grammar* **:** relating to a word or a form of a word that shows that something or someone belongs to something or someone else • The *possessive* form of "dog" is "dog's." • "His" and "her" are ***possessive pronouns***.
— **pos•ses•sive•ly** *adv* • "It's mine!" he said *possessively*.
— **pos•ses•sive•ness** *noun [noncount]*

[2]**possessive** *noun, pl* **-sives** *grammar*
1 *[count]* **:** a possessive word or phrase • "Your" and "yours" are *possessives*.
2 ***the possessive*** **:** the form of a word that shows possession or belonging • *The possessive* of "it" is "its."

pos•ses•sor /pəˈzɛsɚ/ *noun, pl* **-sors** *[count]* **:** a person who owns or has something — often + *of* • (*formal*) the *possessor of* the land • He is the ***proud possessor of*** a baseball autographed by Hank Aaron.

pos•si•bil•i•ty /ˌpɑːsəˈbɪləti/ *noun, pl* **-ties**
1 : a chance that something might exist, happen, or be true **:** the state or fact of being possible *[count]* There is a strong/real/remote/faint *possibility* that I will not be chosen for the job. • Have you considered the *possibility* that you may be wrong? — usually + *of* • the *possibility* [=*likelihood*] *of* success/failure • He received a life sentence without the *possibility of* parole. • Is there a *possibility of* rain today? • Scientists are still unsure about the *possibility of* life on other planets. *[noncount]* It is not outside ***the range/realm of possibility*** that he could get laid off. [=he might get laid off] • (*chiefly Brit*) You shouldn't worry about things that are beyond ***the bounds of possibility***. [=things that cannot happen]
2 *[count]* **:** something that might be done or might happen **:** something that is possible • Rain is a *possibility* today. [=it might rain today] • There is a wide range of *possibilities* [=*options*] to consider. • My first two ideas didn't work, but I thought of a third *possibility*. • We ***exhausted all/the possibilities*** [=we did everything that we could think of doing] • The future holds untold *possibilities*. • His degree and job experience give him a wide range of *possibilities* for a career.
3 ***possibilities*** *[plural]* **:** abilities or qualities that could make someone or something better in the future **:** POTENTIAL • a man of undetermined *possibilities* • The old house might not look like much now, but it has *possibilities*.

[1]**pos•si•ble** /ˈpɑːsəbəl/ *adj [more ~; most ~]*
1 *not usually used before a noun* **:** able to be done • It simply isn't *possible*. • Would it be *possible* for me to use your phone? [=may I use your phone?] • Advances in medicine have made it *possible* for people to live longer. • It is *possible* that she decided not to join us. • We tried to spend as little money as *possible*. • It is not physically *possible* to do everything you have planned in one day. • I like to go swimming ***whenever possible*** [=whenever there is an opportunity to swim] • Do your best to come home from work early, ***if (at all) possible*** [=if it can be done] • Come ***as soon/quickly as***

(humanly) possible [=as soon as you can] — opposite IMPOSSIBLE
2 : able to happen or exist ▪ We need to plan against *possible* dangers. [=dangers that may occur] ▪ The weather report warned of *possible* thunderstorms tonight. ▪ Thunderstorms are *possible* but not probable tonight. ▪ The highest *possible* score is 100. ▪ How *possible* [=*likely*] is rain today? ▪ What *possible* good can it do to argue? ▪ He is in the worst *possible* situation. ▪ It is *possible* that life exists on other planets.
3 ***always used before a noun*** **: able or suited to be or to become something specified** ▪ I found a *possible* site for a camp. ▪ She suggested a *possible* solution to the problem.
4 : reasonable to believe : perhaps true ▪ It's *possible* that your computer has a virus. ▪ Robbery is one *possible* motive for the murder.

²possible *noun, pl* **-sibles**
1 [*count*] **: someone or something that might be suitable or acceptable for a particular job, purpose, etc.** ▪ We have two *possibles* for the job.
2 ***the possible*** **: something that can be done** ▪ Finishing the job today is not outside the realm of *the possible*. [=is not impossible]

pos·si·bly /ˈpɑːsəbli/ *adv*
1 — used to say something might happen, exist, or be true but is not certain ▪ The exam will probably take you the whole hour to complete, *possibly* [=*perhaps, maybe*] even longer. ▪ The doctor says I might *possibly* regain full use of my hand. ▪ The fire could *possibly* have been caused by faulty wiring. ▪ It's *possibly* the worst movie I've ever seen. ▪ "Is it going to rain?" "***Quite possibly.***"
2 — used to show shock or surprise at something ▪ That cannot *possibly* be true. [=it is not possible that it is true] ▪ How could anyone *possibly* have done such a thing?
3 — used to ask for something politely ▪ Could you *possibly* get me some bread and milk while you're out?
4 — used to say that someone will do or has done everything that can be done to achieve something ▪ I will come as soon as I *possibly* can. ▪ I did all I *possibly* could to get here on time, but I got caught in traffic.
5 — used in negative statements to emphasize that something cannot or could not happen or be done ▪ I can't *possibly* tell you that. It's a secret. ▪ You couldn't *possibly* understand what I'm going through. ▪ You could not have *possibly* finished your homework in such a short amount of time.

pos·sum /ˈpɑːsəm/ *noun, pl* **pos·sums** *also* **possum** [*count*] **: OPOSSUM**
play possum informal **1 : to pretend to be asleep or dead** ▪ The wounded soldier *played possum*, hoping the enemy would pass him by. **2 : to pretend to be helpless or less effective in order to deceive an opponent or save strength** ▪ The boxer *played possum* [=pretended to be weaker than he was] for the first few rounds, letting his opponent tire himself out.

¹post /ˈpoʊst/ *noun, pl* **posts** [*count*]
1 : a piece of wood or metal that is set in an upright position into or on the ground especially as a support or marker ▪ fence *posts* — see picture at HOUSE
2 : a pole that marks the starting or finishing point of a horse race — usually singular ▪ a horse's ***post position*** [=the position of a horse in the line of horses at the start of a race] ▪ (*Brit*) The horses galloped toward the ***finishing post***
3 : GOALPOST — usually singular ▪ The shot hit the *post*.
from pillar to post see PILLAR
– compare ³POST, ⁴POST

²post *verb* **posts; post·ed; post·ing**
1 [+ *obj*] **a : to put up (a sign, notice, etc.) so that it can be seen by many people** ▪ When we lost our cat, we *posted* (up) signs all over the neighborhood asking if people had seen him. ▪ The professor *posted* (up) the students' exam grades outside her office. **b : to make (something) officially known to many people** ▪ A snowstorm warning was *posted* [=*announced*] for the New England area. ▪ The company *posted* [=*reported*] increased profits for the third quarter.
2 : to add (a message) to an online message board [+ *obj*] I read through the previous messages, then *posted* a quick response. [*no obj*] She *posts* regularly to several newsgroups.
3 [+ *obj*] ***chiefly Brit*** **: to send (a letter or package) by mail** ▪ If you find anything I've left behind, just *post* [=*mail*] it to me.
keep (someone) posted **: to regularly give (someone) the most recent news about something** ▪ *Keep me posted* on how the project is coming along. ▪ We don't know her condition yet, but we'll *keep you posted.*
post bail see ¹BAIL
– compare ⁵POST

³post *noun, pl* **posts**
1 [*noncount*] ***chiefly Brit*** **a : POSTAL SERVICE** ▪ We don't have a telephone at the cottage, so contact us by *post*. [=*mail*] ▪ There are strict rules against sending dangerous materials through the *post*. **b : letters or packages sent by post : MAIL** ▪ He got a summer job delivering the *post*. ▪ Has the *post* come yet? ▪ After lunch, she sat and read the *post*. ▪ I put the payment in the *post* [=I mailed the payment] this morning. — see also PARCEL POST
2 [*count*] **: a message on an online message board** ▪ The Internet newsgroup is very active, with over 50 *posts* per day. — called also *posting*
by return of post see ²RETURN
– compare ¹POST, ⁴POST

⁴post *noun, pl* **posts**
1 [*count*] **a : the place where a soldier or guard is told to be** ▪ No matter what happens, do not abandon your *post*. [=do not leave your assigned area] ▪ a command *post* **b : the place where someone does a job** ▪ The bartender returned to her *post* behind the counter. **c : a place where soldiers are sent to live for a period of time : CAMP** ▪ My cousin's Army unit was recently sent to a *post* in Alaska. ▪ The large *post* houses over 25,000 people. — see also STAGING POST
2 [*count*] **: a usually important job or position in a large organization** ▪ Our old supervisor just retired, so they're looking for someone to fill his *post*. ▪ He resigned from his *post* as superintendent of public schools. ▪ She applied for a government/administrative *post*.
3 [*count*] **: TRADING POST**
4 ***the post basketball*** **a : the area on a basketball court that is near the basket** ▪ He was standing in *the post* all alone. **b : the position of a player who is in the post** ▪ She usually plays *the post*.
– compare ¹POST, ³POST

⁵post *verb* **posts; posted; post·ing** [+ *obj*]
1 ***always followed by an adverb or preposition*** **: to assign (someone, such as a guard) to stand or stay at a particular place** ▪ Paramedics were *posted* nearby. ▪ The general *posted* a guard outside the door to his tent.
2 ***chiefly Brit*** **: to send (someone) to a place to work for a long period of time as part of a job — usually + *to*** ▪ Her company is *posting* her *to* New York City. — usually used as *(be) posted* ▪ He *was posted to* Munich, Germany.
– compare ²POST

post- /ˌpoʊst/ *prefix* **: after or later than** ▪ the *post*war period [=the time after a war] ▪ *post*date ▪ the *post*industrial economy ▪ *post*-1990

post·age /ˈpoʊstɪʤ/ *noun* [*noncount*]
1 : the cost of sending a letter or package by mail ▪ How much is the *postage* for this package? ▪ Enclose two dollars for *postage* and handling.
2 : the stamps attached to a letter or package ▪ I hope I put enough *postage* on the package.

postage meter *noun, pl* **~ -ters** [*count*] **: a machine that stamps pieces of mail to show that postage has been paid**

postage–paid *adj*, ***always used before a noun*** **: costing nothing to mail because the postage has been paid already** ▪ a *postage-paid* envelope/postcard

postage stamp *noun, pl* **~ stamps** [*count*] **: ¹STAMP 1**

post·al /ˈpoʊstl/ *adj*, ***always used before a noun*** **: relating to or involved in the sending, handling, and delivery of mail** ▪ *postal* workers [=post office employees] ▪ *Postal* rates are going up. ▪ The city worked to quickly restore *postal* service.
go postal US, informal **: to suddenly behave in a very violent or angry way** ▪ She suddenly *went postal* and started yelling at the customers. ▪ If he calls me this late again, I'm going to *go postal* on him.

postal address *noun, pl* **~ -dresses** [*count*] **: MAILING ADDRESS**

postal order *noun, pl* **~ -ders** [*count*] ***Brit*** **: MONEY ORDER**

Postal Service *noun*
the Postal Service US **: the U.S. government department in charge of collecting and delivering mail** ▪ *the* United States *Postal Service*

post·bag /ˈpoʊstˌbæg/ *noun, pl* **-bags** ***Brit***
1 [*count*] **: MAILBAG**
2 [*singular*] **: the total number of letters received by a person, business, or organization at a particular time** ▪ We re-

ceived a huge *postbag* on the spelling mistakes in our newsletter.

post·box /ˈpoʊstˌbɑːks/ *noun, pl* **-boxes** [*count*] *Brit* : MAILBOX 1

post·card /ˈpoʊstˌkaɚd/ *noun, pl* **-cards** [*count*] : a card on which a message may be sent by mail without an envelope and that often has a picture on one side — see picture at MAIL; see also PICTURE POSTCARD

post·code /ˈpoʊstˌkoʊd/ *noun, pl* **-codes** [*count*] *Brit* : a group of numbers and letters that is used especially in the United Kingdom and Australia as part of an address to identify a mail delivery area — compare ZIP CODE

post·date /ˌpoʊstˈdeɪt/ *verb* **-dates; -dat·ed; -dat·ing** [+ *obj*]
1 : to give (something) a date that is later than the actual or current date ▪ *postdate* a check ▪ We sent the company a *postdated* check for next month's payment. — opposite ANTEDATE
2 : to exist, happen, or be made at a later time than (something) ▪ These buildings *postdate* World War II. [=they were built after World War II] — opposite ANTEDATE, PREDATE

post·doc·tor·al /ˌpoʊstˈdɑːktərəl/ *adj, always used before a noun* : relating to work that is done after a PhD has been completed ▪ a *postdoctoral* fellowship ▪ *postdoctoral* research

post·er /ˈpoʊstɚ/ *noun, pl* **-ers** [*count*]
1 a : a usually large printed notice often having a picture on it that is put in a public place to advertise something ▪ *Posters* for the concert have been going up all over town. ▪ campaign *posters* **b** : a usually large picture that is put on walls as a decoration ▪ His walls were covered with *posters* of his favorite bands.
2 : a person who writes messages on an online message board

poster boy *noun, pl* ~ **boys** [*count*] : a male poster child

poster child *noun, pl* ~ **children** [*count*] *US*
1 : a child who has a particular disease and is shown in posters to raise money to help fight that disease
2 : a person who represents or is identified with something (such as a cause or product) ▪ She was a stirring speaker and activist and soon became the *poster child* of the antiwar movement. ▪ (*humorous*) My brother is the *poster child* for laziness. [=he is very lazy]

poste res·tante /ˌpoʊstˌrɛˈstɑːnt/ *noun* [*noncount*] *chiefly Brit* : GENERAL DELIVERY

poster girl *noun, pl* ~ **girls** [*count*] : a female poster child

[1]**pos·te·ri·or** /poʊˈstirijɚ/ *adj, technical* : near or toward the back of something (such as the body) ▪ the *posterior* part of the brain — opposite ANTERIOR

[2]**pos·te·ri·or** /pɑˈstirijɚ/ *noun, pl* **-ors** [*count*] *humorous* : the part of the body above the legs that is used for sitting : BUTTOCKS ▪ The man squeezed his large *posterior* into the chair.

pos·ter·i·ty /pɑˈsterəti/ *noun* [*noncount*] *formal* : people in the future ▪ *Posterity* will remember her as a woman of courage and integrity. ▪ A record of the events was ***preserved for posterity***. ▪ The truth about what happened will be known/lost ***to posterity***.

post exchange *noun, pl* ~ **-changes** [*count*] *US* : a store at a military post — abbr. *PX*

post–free /ˈpoʊstˈfriː/ *adj, always used before a noun, chiefly Brit* : POSTPAID ▪ *post-free* delivery
— **post–free** *adv* ▪ They sent me a brochure *post-free*.

post·game /ˈpoʊstˈgeɪm/ *adj, always used before a noun, US* : happening immediately or very soon after the end of a sports game ▪ a *postgame* interview/celebration

[1]**post·grad·u·ate** /ˌpoʊstˈgræʤəwət/ *adj, always used before a noun* : of or relating to studies done after earning a bachelor's degree or other degree ▪ After college, she spent her first *postgraduate* year studying abroad. ▪ a *postgraduate* [=(*US*) *graduate*] student/course/program

[2]**postgraduate** *noun, pl* **-ates** [*count*] *chiefly Brit* : a student who continues to study for an advanced degree after earning a bachelor's degree or other first degree : a graduate student

post·haste /ˈpoʊstˈheɪst/ *adv, literary* : very quickly : with great speed — used after a verb ▪ They sent *posthaste* for the doctor. = They sent for the doctor *posthaste*.

post·hu·mous /ˈpɑːsʧəməs/ *adj, always used before a noun* : happening, done, or published after someone's death ▪ She received a *posthumous* award for her life of philanthropy. ▪ her *posthumous* fame/reputation ▪ a *posthumous* novel/anthology/memoir
— **post·hu·mous·ly** *adv* ▪ The Army *posthumously* awarded him a medal for bravery. ▪ Her last book was published *posthumously*. [=after her death]

pos·tie /ˈpoʊsti/ *noun, pl* **-ties** [*count*] *Brit, informal* : LETTER CARRIER

post·ing /ˈpoʊstɪŋ/ *noun, pl* **-ings** [*count*]
1 *US* : a public announcement of something ▪ the company's latest *posting* of profits ▪ a job *posting* [=an announcement telling people that a position is open]
2 *chiefly Brit* : the act of sending someone to a place to work for a long period of time as part of a job ▪ military *postings* ▪ a Foreign Service *posting* in Paris
3 : [3]POST 2

Post–it /ˈpoʊstˌɪt/ *trademark* — used for a small, colored slip of paper with a sticky edge

post·man /ˈpoʊstmən/ *noun, pl* **-men** /-mən/ [*count*] : a man who collects and delivers mail : MAILMAN

[1]**post·mark** /ˈpoʊstˌmaɚk/ *noun, pl* **-marks** [*count*] : a mark placed over the stamp on a piece of mail that shows when the mail was sent and where it was sent from and that makes it impossible to use the stamp again — see picture at MAIL

[2]**postmark** *verb* **-marks; -marked; -mark·ing** [+ *obj*] : to put a postmark on (something) ▪ The package was *postmarked* 13 February.

post·mas·ter /ˈpoʊstˌmæstɚ, *Brit* ˈpəʊstˌmɑːstə/ *noun, pl* **-ters** [*count*] : a person who is in charge of a post office

Postmaster General *noun, pl* **Postmasters General** [*count*] : the person who is in charge of the U.S. Postal Service

post·men·o·paus·al /ˌpoʊstˌmɛnəˈpɑːzəl/ *adj, medical*
1 : having gone through menopause ▪ *postmenopausal* women
2 : happening after menopause ▪ *postmenopausal* symptoms

post·mis·tress /ˈpoʊstˌmɪstrəs/ *noun, pl* **-tress·es** [*count*] *old-fashioned* : a woman who is in charge of a post office

post·mod·ern /ˌpoʊstˈmɑːdɚn/ *adj* : of or relating to postmodernism ▪ *postmodern* architecture/literature

post·mod·ern·ism /ˌpoʊstˈmɑːdɚˌnɪzəm/ *noun* [*noncount*] : a style of art, architecture, literature, etc., that developed after modernism and that differs from modernism in some important way (such as by combining traditional materials and forms with modern ones or by having an ironic tone or attitude)
— **post·mod·ern·ist** /ˌpoʊstˈmɑːdɚnɪst/ *adj* ▪ a *postmodernist* author ▪ *postmodernist* art — **postmodernist** *noun, pl* **-ists** [*count*] ▪ The author is a *postmodernist*.

[1]**post·mor·tem** /ˌpoʊstˈmoɚtəm/ *adj, always used before a noun, medical* : happening after death ▪ a *postmortem* examination

[2]**postmortem** *noun, pl* **-tems** [*count*]
1 *medical* : an examination of a dead body to find out the cause of death : AUTOPSY ▪ A *postmortem* showed that the man had been poisoned.
2 : a discussion or analysis of something (such as an event) after it has ended ▪ Party leaders are conducting a *postmortem* of the election to try to find out what went wrong.

post·na·tal /ˌpoʊstˈneɪtl/ *adj, always used before a noun, medical* : relating to the period of time following the birth of a child ▪ *postnatal* care/depression

post office *noun, pl* ~ **-fices**
1 [*count*] : a building where the mail for a local area is sent and received — abbr. *P.O.*
2 ***the Post Office*** : the government department in charge of collecting and delivering mail ▪ She works for *the Post Office*. [=(*US*) *the Postal Service*]

post office box *noun, pl* ~ **boxes** [*count*] : P.O. BOX

post–op /ˈpoʊstˈɑːp/ *adj, always used before a noun, medical* : POSTOPERATIVE ▪ a *post-op* procedure/patient

post·op·er·a·tive /ˌpoʊstˈɑːprətɪv/ *adj, always used before a noun, medical*
1 : happening after an operation ▪ *postoperative* care
2 : having had an operation recently ▪ a *postoperative* patient

post·paid /ˈpoʊstˈpeɪd/ *adj* : costing nothing to mail because the postage has been paid already ▪ The shoes are $40 *postpaid*. ▪ a *postpaid* card

post·par·tum /ˌpoʊstˈpaɚtəm/ *adj, always used before a noun, medical* : relating to or happening in the period of time following the birth of a child ▪ a *postpartum* examination/care

postpartum depression *noun* [*noncount*] *chiefly US, medical* : a feeling of deep sadness, anxiety, etc., that a woman feels after giving birth to a child

post·pone /ˌpoustˈpoun/ *verb* **-pones; -poned; -pon·ing** [+ *obj*] : to decide that something which had been planned for a particular time will be done at a later time instead ▪ We had to *postpone* our vacation. = We had to *postpone* going on our vacation. ▪ The baseball game was *postponed* until/to tomorrow because of rain.

– **post·pone·ment** /ˌpoustˈpounmənt/ *noun, pl* **-ments** [*count*] After many *postponements*, the wedding finally took place. [*noncount*] The rain caused *postponement* of the baseball game.

post·pran·di·al /poustˈprændijəl/ *adj, always used before a noun, formal + humorous* : happening after a meal ▪ *postprandial* nausea ▪ a *postprandial* coffee/nap

post·script /ˈpoustˌskrɪpt/ *noun, pl* **-scripts** [*count*]

1 : a note or series of notes added at the end of a letter, article, or book ▪ In a *postscript* to her letter, she promised to write again soon. — abbr. *PS*

2 : an additional fact or piece of information about a story that occurs after the main part ▪ An interesting *postscript* to the story is that the two people involved later got married.

post·sea·son /ˈpoustˌsiːzn̩/ *noun, pl* **-sons** [*count*] *US, sports* : a period of time immediately after the regular season when teams play against each other in a series of games to determine a champion ▪ The team has never played in the *postseason*. — often used before another noun ▪ *postseason* games

post–traumatic stress disorder *noun* [*noncount*] *medical* : a mental condition that can affect a person who has had a very shocking or difficult experience (such as fighting in a war) and that is usually characterized by depression, anxiety, etc. — abbr. *PTSD* — called also *post-traumatic stress syndrome*

[1]**pos·tu·late** /ˈpɑːstʃəˌleɪt/ *verb* **-lates; -lat·ed; -lat·ing** [+ *obj*] *formal* : to suggest (something, such as an idea or theory) especially in order to start a discussion ▪ The theory *postulates* [=*claims, posits*] that carbon dioxide emissions contribute to global warming. ▪ Scientists have *postulated* the existence of water on the planet.

[2]**pos·tu·late** /ˈpɑːstʃələt/ *noun, pl* **-lates** [*count*] *formal* : a statement that is accepted as being true and that is used as the basis of a theory, argument, etc. ▪ Einstein's theory of relativity was deduced from two *postulates*.

pos·ture /ˈpɑːstʃɚ/ *noun, pl* **-tures**

1 : the way in which your body is positioned when you are sitting or standing [*count*] Human beings have an upright *posture*. ▪ a rigid/stiff *posture* [*noncount*] He has good/bad/poor *posture*.

2 [*count*] *formal* : the attitude a person or group has toward a subject — usually singular ▪ The country has taken an aggressive *posture* on immigration. ▪ She took a neutral *posture* in the argument.

– **pos·tur·al** /ˈpɑːstʃərəl/ *adj, always used before a noun, formal* ▪ poor *postural* habits

pos·tur·ing /ˈpɑːstʃərɪŋ/ *noun* [*noncount*] *disapproving* : behavior that is intended to impress other people and that is not sincere ▪ Don't be fooled by his macho *posturing*. He's really a coward at heart.

post·war /ˈpoustˌwoɚ/ *adj, always used before a noun* : happening, existing, or made after a war ▪ the *postwar* generation ▪ *postwar* architecture; *especially* : happening, existing, or made after World War II ▪ *postwar* Europe — opposite PREWAR

post·wom·an /ˈpoustˌwʊmən/ *noun, pl* **-wom·en** /-ˌwɪmən/ [*count*] : a woman who collects or delivers mail : a female letter carrier

po·sy /ˈpouzi/ *noun, pl* **-sies** [*count*] *old-fashioned*

1 : a small bunch of flowers ▪ a *posy* of violets

2 : a single cut flower ▪ a pocket full of *posies*

[1]**pot** /ˈpɑːt/ *noun, pl* **pots**

1 [*count*] **a** : a deep, round container that is used for cooking ▪ a soup *pot* ▪ He scrubbed the *pots* and pans. — see picture at KITCHEN **b** : a container that is used for storing or holding something ▪ clay *pots* ▪ (*Brit*) a yogurt/paint *pot* ▪ He is growing tomato plants in *pots*. — see also CHAMBER POT, CHIMNEY POT, COFFEEPOT, FLOWERPOT, LOBSTER POT, MELTING POT, STOCKPOT, TEAPOT

2 [*count*] : the amount of something held by a pot — often + *of* ▪ She made a *pot of* tea.

3 [*count*] *informal* : a large amount of something — usually + *of* ▪ She earned a *pot of* money on that job. ▪ His comments have stirred up a *pot of* trouble. — often plural ▪ She earned *pots of* money.

4 ***the pot*** *chiefly US* **a** : the total amount of money that can be won in a card game and that is made up of all the bets put together : KITTY ▪ He took *the pot*. [=he won all the money that was bet] ▪ There is over $100 in *the pot*. **b** : the total amount of money that has been gathered from many people for some purpose : KITTY ▪ A donor added $1,000 to *the pot* in support of the theater company.

5 [*count*] *informal* : POTBELLY — usually singular ▪ I'm so out of shape—look at this *pot*!

6 [*count*] *informal* : TOILET — usually singular ▪ sat on the *pot*

7 [*count*] *Brit* : a shot that causes a ball to fall into a pocket in games like snooker and pool

a watched pot never boils see [1]BOIL

go to pot *informal* : to be ruined : to fail ▪ Their business is *going to pot*.

– compare [2]POT

[2]**pot** *noun* [*noncount*] *informal* : MARIJUANA ▪ an ounce of *pot* ▪ a *pot* smoker/plant — compare [1]POT

[3]**pot** *verb* **pots; pot·ted; pot·ting** [+ *obj*]

1 : to plant (something) in a pot ▪ She spent the afternoon *potting* tulip bulbs.

2 *Brit* : to shoot (a ball) into a pocket in games like snooker and pool ▪ He *potted* [=*pocketed, sank*] the winning shot.

3 *Brit* : to shoot and kill (an animal) ▪ She *potted* a bird.

po·ta·ble /ˈpoutəbəl/ *adj* [*more* ~; *most* ~] *technical* : safe to drink ▪ *potable* water

pot·ash /ˈpɑːtˌæʃ/ *noun* [*noncount*] : a form of potassium that is used especially to improve soil or to make soap

po·tas·si·um /pəˈtæsijəm/ *noun* [*noncount*] : a soft, silver-white metal that is used especially in farming and industry

po·ta·to /pəˈteɪtou/ *noun, pl* **-toes**

1 : a round root of a plant that has brown, yellow, or red skin and white or yellow flesh and that is eaten as a vegetable [*count*] baked/mashed/roasted/boiled *potatoes* [*noncount*] slices of *potato* ▪ mashed *potato* ▪ *potato* salad — see color picture on page C4; see also JACKET POTATO, SWEET POTATO

2 [*count*] : the plant that produces potatoes ▪ She's growing carrots and *potatoes* in her garden this year.

– see also COUCH POTATO, HOT POTATO, MEAT AND POTATOES, SMALL POTATOES

potato chip *noun, pl* ~ **chips** [*count*] *US* : a thin slice of potato that is fried or sometimes baked and usually salted ▪ I had a sandwich and a bag of *potato chips* for lunch. — called also (*Brit*) *crisp*, (*Brit*) *potato crisp*

potato pancake *noun, pl* ~ **-cakes** [*count*] *chiefly US* : a fried, flat cake consisting of potato mixed with egg and usually onion and spices

pot·bel·lied /ˈpɑːtˌbɛlid/ *adj* : having a large, round stomach that sticks out ▪ a *potbellied* man

potbellied pig *noun, pl* ~ **pigs** [*count*] : a small pig with a large belly and usually a black or white coat

potbellied stove *noun, pl* ~ **stoves** [*count*] *US* : a stove with a large, rounded body — called also *potbelly stove*

pot·bel·ly /ˈpɑːtˌbɛli/ *noun, pl* **-lies** [*count*]

1 : a large, round stomach that sticks out ▪ a man with a *potbelly*

2 : POTBELLIED STOVE

potbelly stove *noun, pl* ~ **stoves** [*count*] : POTBELLIED STOVE

pot·boil·er /ˈpɑːtˌbɔɪlɚ/ *noun, pl* **-ers** [*count*] : a book, movie, etc., that is made in usually a cheap way in order to make money rather than for artistic reasons

po·ten·cy /ˈpoutn̩si/ *noun, pl* **-cies**

1 [*noncount*] : the power to influence someone ▪ Her words had *potency*. — often + *of* ▪ I can't deny the *potency of* his argument.

2 : the strength or effectiveness of something [*count*] drugs of high *potencies* [*noncount*] vitamins of high *potency*

3 [*noncount*] : the ability of a man to have sex ▪ The drug can improve ***sexual potency***.

po·tent /ˈpoutn̩t/ *adj* [*more* ~; *most* ~]

1 a : very effective or strong ▪ *potent* medicine ▪ The tea was *potent*. **b** : having a very powerful effect or influence on someone ▪ He had *potent* arguments for going to war. ▪ Her story serves as a *potent* reminder of the dangers of drug use.

2 *of a man* : able to have sex — opposite IMPOTENT

– **po·tent·ly** *adv* ▪ a *potently* meaningful speech

P

po·ten·tate /ˈpoʊtn̩ˌteɪt/ *noun, pl* **-tates** [*count*] *literary* : a powerful ruler ▪ medieval *potentates*

[1]**po·ten·tial** /pəˈtɛnʃəl/ *adj, always used before a noun* : capable of becoming real : POSSIBLE ▪ Doctors are excited about the new drug's *potential* benefits. ▪ Critics say the factory poses a *potential* threat to the environment. ▪ the school's *potential* growth ▪ He is a *potential* candidate for president. ▪ The project has *potential* risks/advantages.

– po·ten·tial·ly *adv* ▪ a *potentially* deadly virus

[2]**potential** *noun, pl* **-tials**

1 [*count*] : a chance or possibility that something will happen or exist in the future — usually singular; usually + *for* ▪ Wet roads increase the *potential for* an accident. [=make an accident more likely to happen] ▪ If you study hard, there is a greater *potential for* success.

2 a : a quality that something has that can be developed to make it better [*count*] Scientists are exploring the *potentials* of the new drug. ▪ The stock's earning *potential* is high. [=the stock is likely to earn a lot of money] ▪ The new technology has the *potential* to transform the industry. [*noncount*] There is *potential* in the new technology, but it will be a long time before it can actually be used. ▪ The company has a lot of *potential* for future growth. **b** [*noncount*] : an ability that someone has that can be developed to help that person become successful ▪ The team's newest player shows great *potential*. [=*promise*] ▪ He has the *potential* to be one of the team's best players. ▪ She has leadership *potential*. [=she could become a successful leader] ▪ He shows enormous *potential* as an athlete. ▪ The school tries to help students ***reach/realize their full potential***. [=to become the best they can be]

3 [*count, noncount*] *technical* : the amount of work that is required to move a quantity of electricity from one point on a circuit to another ✧ This kind of work is usually measured in volts. ▪ The instrument is used to measure the changing electrical *potentials*.

potential energy *noun* [*noncount*] *physics* : the energy that something has because of its position or the way its parts are arranged ✧ Potential energy is energy that is not yet being used.

po·ten·ti·al·i·ty /pəˌtɛnʃiˈæləti/ *noun, pl* **-ties** *formal*

1 : a quality that can be developed to make someone or something better [*count*] They underestimated his *potentialities*. [*noncount*] The teacher sees *potentiality* [=*potential*] in every student.

2 [*count*] : a chance or possibility that something will happen or exist in the future — usually singular ▪ There is a/the *potentiality* for good in all people.

pot·head /ˈpɑːtˌhɛd/ *noun, pl* **-heads** [*count*] *US, informal* : a person who smokes a lot of marijuana

pot·hold·er /ˈpɑːtˌhoʊldɚ/ *noun, pl* ~ **-ers** [*count*] *US* : a small, thick cloth pad that people use to protect their hands when they are holding hot cooking pots, pans, etc. — see picture at KITCHEN

pot·hole /ˈpɑːtˌhoʊl/ *noun, pl* **-holes** [*count*] : a deep, round hole in a road or some other surface (such as the bottom of a river) — sometimes used figuratively ▪ The project hit a big *pothole* a few weeks ago.

– pot·holed /ˈpɑːtˌhoʊld/ *adj* ▪ the city's *potholed* streets

po·tion /ˈpoʊʃən/ *noun, pl* **-tions** [*count*] : a drink that is meant to have a special or magical effect on someone ▪ He drank the fatal *potion*. ▪ The hero in the play is given a magic/love *potion* so that he will fall in love with the princess. ▪ medical *potions* ▪ sleeping *potions*

pot·luck (*US*) *or Brit* **pot luck** /ˈpɑːtˈlʌk/ *noun, pl* **-lucks**

1 [*count*] *US* : a meal to which everyone who is invited brings food to share ▪ He organized a neighborhood *potluck* for next Saturday. — often used before another noun ▪ a *potluck* dinner/supper

2 [*noncount*] *chiefly Brit* : a meal for a guest that is prepared from whatever is available ▪ I wasn't expecting you for dinner, so you'll have to ***take pot luck***. — often used figuratively ▪ We don't have definite plans. We're just going to *take pot luck*. [=we're just going to take/accept whatever is available and hope that it is good]

pot·pie /ˈpɑːtˈpaɪ/ *noun, pl* **-pies** [*count*] *US* : a mixture of meat and vegetables that is covered with a layer of pastry and cooked in a deep dish ▪ a chicken/turkey *potpie*

pot plant *noun, pl* ~ **plants** [*count*]

1 *chiefly US, informal* : a marijuana plant

2 *Brit* : HOUSEPLANT

pot·pour·ri /ˌpoʊpʊˈriː/ *noun, pl* **-ris**

1 [*count, noncount*] : a mixture of dried flower petals, leaves, and spices that is used to make a room smell pleasant

2 [*singular*] : a collection of different things ▪ The festival was a musical *potpourri*—performances included folk, jazz, blues, and rap music. — often + *of* ▪ The book is a *potpourri* [=*assortment, medley*] *of* stories about family, religion, and food.

pot roast *noun, pl* ~ **roasts** [*count, noncount*] : a piece of beef that is cooked slowly in a pot

pot·shot /ˈpɑːtˌʃɑːt/ *noun, pl* **-shots** [*count*] : a gunshot that is fired in a careless way or at an easy target ▪ A sniper was on the roof ***taking potshots*** at passing cars. — often used figuratively to describe a careless or unfair criticism ▪ She uses her newspaper column to *take potshots* at anyone who disagrees with her. ▪ a verbal *potshot*

pot·tage /ˈpɑːtɪʤ/ *noun* [*noncount*] *old-fashioned* : a thick soup of vegetables and often meat

a mess of pottage : something that has little or no value ▪ They sold/traded their birthright for *a mess of pottage*.

pot·ted /ˈpɑːtəd/ *adj, always used before a noun*

1 : growing in a pot rather than in the ground ▪ *potted* palms/plants/herbs

2 : cooked and then preserved in a pot, jar, or can ▪ *potted* meats

3 *chiefly Brit, informal* : giving only the most important information about something : brief and simplified ▪ The book gives a *potted* history of the Industrial Revolution in the first chapter. ▪ a *potted* summary/version

[1]**pot·ter** /ˈpɑːtɚ/ *noun, pl* **-ters** [*count*] : a person who makes pots, bowls, plates, etc., out of clay : a person who makes pottery by hand

[2]**potter** *verb* **-ters; -tered; -ter·ing**

potter around/about [*phrasal verb*] *Brit* : to spend time in a relaxed way doing small jobs and other things that are not very important ▪ He spent his vacation ***pottering around*** [=(*US*) *puttering around*] the house/garden.

– pot·ter·er /ˈpɑːtərɚ/ *noun, pl* **-ers** [*count*]

potter's wheel *noun, pl* ~ **wheels** [*count*] : a machine with a flat disk on which a potter shapes wet clay into pots as it spins

pot·tery /ˈpɑːtəri/ *noun, pl* **-ter·ies**

1 [*noncount*] : objects (such as bowls, plates, etc.) that are made out of clay usually by hand and then baked at high temperatures so that they become hard ▪ He has collected *pottery* for years. ▪ a glazed *pottery* jar

2 [*noncount*] : the art or activity of making objects out of clay ▪ She was a painter for years before she discovered *pottery*. ▪ a *pottery* class ▪ *pottery* techniques

3 [*count*] : a place where potters make objects out of clay

potting shed *noun, pl* ~ **sheds** [*count*] : a small building in which plants are grown in pots until they are ready to be planted outside

potting soil *noun* [*noncount*] *US* : a mixture of dirt and other substances that people use when placing plants in pots

[1]**pot·ty** /ˈpɑːti/ *noun, pl* **-ties** *informal*

1 [*count*] : a pot that children use as a toilet until they are big enough to use a toilet

2 ***the potty*** : the toilet or bathroom — used by children or when talking to children ▪ Mommy, I need to use *the potty*.

go potty *US, informal* : to use the toilet — used by children or when talking to children. ▪ Be sure to *go potty* before we leave the house. ▪ I have to *go potty*.

[2]**potty** *adj* **pot·ti·er; -est** [*also more* ~; *most* ~] *Brit, informal*

1 : CRAZY ▪ I think he's ***gone a little potty***. ▪ All this noise is ***driving me potty***!

2 : very interested in or excited about someone or something ▪ She's just *potty* about this new dance class.

pot·ty–mouthed /ˈpɑːtiˌmaʊðd/ *adj* [*more* ~; *most* ~] *US, informal* : using indecent or offensive language : FOUL-MOUTHED ▪ *potty-mouthed* comedians

– potty mouth *noun, pl* ~ **mouths** [*count*] *US, informal* ▪ a comedian who has/is a *potty mouth* [=a comedian who uses a lot of offensive language]

potty training *noun* [*noncount*] : TOILET TRAINING

– potty–train *verb* **-trains; -trained; -training** [+ *obj*] ▪ She's trying to *potty-train* her daughter. **– potty–trained** *adj* ▪ The twins are *potty-trained* now.

pouch /ˈpaʊʧ/ *noun, pl* **pouch·es** [*count*]

1 a : a small bag ▪ He carried his money in a small leather *pouch* in his pocket. ▪ a tobacco *pouch* **b** : a bag often with a lock that is used to carry letters or important papers ▪ a mail *pouch*

2 a : a pocket of skin on the stomachs of some female animals (such as kangaroos and koalas) that is used to carry young **b :** a pocket of skin inside the mouths of some animals (such as squirrels and hamsters) that is used to carry food

– pouchy /ˈpaʊʧi/ *adj* **pouch·i·er; -est** • *pouchy* [=*baggy*] eyes

pouf *also* **pouffe** /ˈpu:f/ *noun, pl* **poufs** *also* **pouffes** [*count*] *Brit* **:** OTTOMAN

poul·tice /ˈpoʊltəs/ *noun, pl* **-tic·es** [*count*] **:** a soft, usually heated substance that is spread on cloth and then placed on the skin to heal a sore or reduce pain

poul·try /ˈpoʊltri/ *noun* [*noncount*]

1 : birds (such as chickens and ducks) that are raised on farms for their eggs or meat

2 : meat from a bird • This wine goes well with *poultry.*

pounce /ˈpaʊns/ *verb* **pounc·es; pounced; pounc·ing** [*no obj*]

1 : to suddenly jump toward and take hold of someone or something • The cat crouched low and waited for the moment to *pounce.* — usually + *on* • As the boys rounded the corner, a group of kids *pounced on* them. — often used figuratively • A salesperson *pounced on* me [=quickly approached me] as soon as I walked into the store. • When a few documents showed that the mayor had avoided paying his taxes, the press *pounced on* [=*attacked*] him. • She lost control of the ball, and the other team *pounced on* the opportunity to score. • He *pounced on* the job offer.

2 : to act or move quickly and suddenly • Movie studios are ready to *pounce* as soon as she announces that she's making movies again. • She *pounced* at the phone when it rang.

¹pound /ˈpaʊnd/ *noun, pl* **pounds** *also* **pound**

1 [*count*] **:** a unit of weight that is equal to 16 ounces or 0.4536 kilograms • The recipe calls for a *pound* of ground beef. • a 50-*pound* dog = a dog that weighs 50 *pounds* • Chicken is on sale this week for $3 per/a *pound.* • I gained some weight last winter and I'm trying to lose a few *pounds.* • ***Pound for pound,*** it's the most valuable crop being grown in the state. [=when comparing a pound of this crop with a pound of other crops, a pound of this crop is more valuable]

2 a [*count*] **:** a basic unit of money in the United Kingdom and some other countries • The bill came to 30 *pounds* 10 pence. • Rent for the flat is 600 *pounds* per/a month. • a five-*pound* note **b** [*count*] **:** a bill or coin that is worth one pound • "Do you have any cash on you?" "I've got a few *pounds* in my wallet." **c *the pound*** *technical* **:** the value of a pound when it is compared to another unit of money • The dollar dropped sharply against *the pound.* • the strength/weakness of *the pound*

in for a penny, in for a pound see PENNY

pile on the pounds see ²PILE

pound of flesh **:** an amount that is owed to someone who demands to be paid • When the creditors came to collect their *pound of flesh,* he had nothing to give them.

– compare ²POUND, ³POUND; see also POUND CAKE

²pound *noun, pl* **pounds** [*count*]

1 : a place where dogs and cats that are found on the streets without an owner are kept until their owners come and get them

2 : a place to which cars that have been parked illegally are towed and kept until their owners pay to get them back

– compare ¹POUND, ³POUND

³pound *noun, pl* **pounds** [*count*] *US* **:** the symbol # • To record a message, press *pound.* = To record a message, press the ***pound key.*** [=press the button/key labeled "#"] — called also (*US*) *pound sign,* (*Brit*) *hash,* (*Brit*) *hash sign* — compare ¹POUND, ²POUND

⁴pound *verb* **pounds; pound·ed; pound·ing**

1 : to hit (something or someone) with force again and again [+ *obj*] Heavy waves *pounded* the shore. • The metal is heated and then *pounded* into shape. • She *pounded* [=*drove*] the nails into the wood. • He got frustrated and started to *pound* the piano keys. • He *pounded* his fist on the table. • The boxers were really *pounding* each other. [*no obj*] Someone is *pounding* [=*banging*] at the door. • Waves *pounded* against the side of the boat. — often + *on* • He began to *pound on* a drum.

2 [+ *obj*] **:** to crush or break (something) into very small pieces by hitting it again and again • The wheat is *pounded* into flour. • *Pound* the herbs and garlic until they form a paste.

3 *always followed by an adverb or preposition* [*no obj*] **:** to walk or run with heavy and loud steps • He came *pounding* down the stairs. • The horses *pounded* up the track.

4 [*no obj*] **:** to work hard at something for a long time — usually + *away* • He *pounded away* all night at his computer, writing the report. • I don't feel like I'm making much progress, but I keep *pounding away.*

5 [*no obj*] **:** to beat loudly and quickly • He woke from the dream in a cold sweat with his heart *pounding* (in his ears). • I took an aspirin because my head was *pounding.* • a *pounding* [=*throbbing*] headache

6 [+ *obj*] **:** to bomb (an area) many times • Bombers *pounded* the city all night.

7 [+ *obj*] *US, informal* **:** to drink (something) quickly • They *pounded* (back) a few beers at the bar.

pound out [*phrasal verb*] ***pound out (something) or pound (something) out*** **1 :** to make or produce (something) quickly • Every week he *pounds out* [=*bangs out*] another column for the newspaper. **2 :** to play (a song, melody, etc.) loudly on a musical instrument (such as a piano) • The band's lead singer was *pounding out* [=*banging out*] a tune on the piano.

pound the streets/pavement **:** to walk or run on the street especially in search of something • She's out there every day *pounding the pavement,* looking for work. • Hard-core joggers will *pound the streets* in all kinds of weather.

pound·age /ˈpaʊndɪʤ/ *noun* [*noncount*]

1 *technical* **:** an amount charged for every pound that something weighs

2 *informal* **:** body weight • She's carrying some extra *poundage* after the holidays.

pound cake *noun, pl* **~ cakes** [*count, noncount*] *US* **:** a rich cake made with a large amount of butter and eggs

pound·er /ˈpaʊndɚ/ *noun, pl* **-ers** [*count*]

1 : a person or thing that has a specified weight in pounds — used in combination • The fish was a 22-*pounder.* [=the fish weighed 22 pounds] • He's the team's only 300-*pounder.* [=a person who weighs 300 pounds]

2 : a gun that fires a shell of a specified weight • a 64-*pounder*

pound–fool·ish /ˈpaʊndˈfu:lɪʃ/ *adj*

penny-wise and/but pound-foolish see PENNY-WISE

pounding *noun, pl* **-ings**

1 [*count*] **:** the act of hitting someone or something with force again and again — usually singular • We could hear the *pounding* of waves against the shore. • There was a *pounding* [=*banging*] on/at my door early the next morning. • The boxer ***took a pounding*** [=*took a beating*] in the ring. — often used figuratively • They gave us a *pounding* in the first half of the game. • The company's stocks *took a pounding.*

2 [*singular*] **:** the act of beating loudly and quickly • I could feel a *pounding* in my chest. = I could feel the *pounding* of my heart in my chest.

pound sign *noun, pl* **~ signs** [*count*]

1 : the symbol £ that represents the British pound

2 *US* **:** ³POUND

pound sterling *noun, pl* **pounds sterling** [*count*] **:** a basic unit of money in the United Kingdom **:** POUND

pour /ˈpoɚ/ *verb* **pours; poured; pour·ing**

1 [+ *obj*] **:** to cause (something) to flow in a steady stream from or into a container or place • He carefully *poured* the water into her glass. • *Pour* the sauce over the pasta. • She *poured* salt into the palm of her hand and then sprinkled it over the stew. • The smokestacks *poured* out thick clouds of black smoke. • The burst pipe *poured* out water. • The concrete foundation has been *poured.* — sometimes used figuratively • She ***poured scorn on*** the plan. [=she talked about the plan in a very critical and scornful way]

2 : to fill a cup or glass with a drink for someone [+ *obj*] Will you *pour* (out) the wine? [=will you fill everyone's glass with wine?] • *Pour* a drink for me, please. = *Pour* me a drink, please. • Can I *pour* you some lemonade? • He *poured* [=*served*] himself a (cup of) coffee. [*no obj*] Could you please *pour?*

3 *always followed by an adverb or preposition* [*no obj*] **:** to flow or move continuously in a steady stream • Light *poured* [=*streamed*] down from the hole in the roof. • Smoke *poured* out from the chimney. • Sweat was *pouring* from her brow. — often used figuratively • Music *pours* out of the dance clubs at night. • All of his pent-up emotion came *pouring* out. • She started crying, and then the whole story of what happened came *pouring* out. • Orders for the soap have started to *pour* in. • Thousands of people *poured* into the stadium for the game. • People *poured* out of the subway.

4 [*no obj*] **a :** to rain heavily • It *poured* all day. • It was *pouring* the whole time we were there. • (*Brit*) It is **pouring (down)**

P

with rain. **b** *of rain* **:** to come down heavily ▪ The rain ***poured down.*** ▪ We had to wait for hours in the ***pouring rain.***

pour cold water on see [1]WATER

pour into *[phrasal verb]* ***pour (something) into (something)*** **:** to spend (a large amount of money, time, energy, etc.) on something ▪ She has *poured* thousands (of dollars) *into* the business. ▪ He has been *pouring* all his time/resources *into* the project.

pour oil on troubled waters *chiefly Brit* **:** to try to make peace between people who are arguing

pour on *[phrasal verb]* **1** ***pour on (something)*** *or* ***pour (something) on*** **:** to produce a lot of (something) in order to achieve something ▪ The defense *poured on* the pressure in the second half of the game. ▪ He really *poured on* the charm to get her to have dinner with him. **2** ***pour it on*** *informal* **a :** to talk about something in an emotional way that is not sincere in order to get sympathy, attention, etc. ▪ When he saw that she felt sorry for him, he really *poured it on.* **b** *chiefly US* **:** to do something in a very energetic and effective way ▪ After they took the lead in the second half, they really started to *pour it on.* [=they started to score a lot of points very quickly]

pour out *[phrasal verb]* ***pour out (something)*** *or* ***pour (something) out*** **:** to freely express (an emotion) **:** to talk freely about (something personal) ▪ I listened while he *poured out* his anger and frustration. ▪ I'm sorry about *pouring out* my troubles like this. ▪ She *poured out* the whole story.

pour your heart/soul out *or* ***pour out your heart/soul*** **:** to speak very freely to someone about how your private and most deeply felt emotions ▪ He'll *pour his heart out* to anyone who will listen.

when it rains, it pours *or* ***it never rains but it pours*** see [2]RAIN

pout /ˈpaʊt/ *verb* **pouts; pout•ed; pout•ing**

1 : to push out your lips to show that you are angry or annoyed or to look sexually attractive *[+ obj]* She *pouted* her lips and stared at him angrily. *[no obj]* The boy didn't want to leave—he stomped his feet and *pouted.* ▪ The model *pouted* for the cameras. ▪ Her lips *pouted,* and she began to cry.

2 *[no obj] chiefly US* **:** to refuse to talk to people because you are angry or annoyed about something ▪ Whenever he doesn't get his own way, he *pouts.* [=*sulks*] ▪ Quit *pouting!*

– pout *noun, pl* **pouts** *[count]* ▪ She had a sultry *pout* on her lips. **– pouted** *adj* ▪ *pouted* lips **– pouty** /ˈpaʊti/ *adj* **pout•i•er; -est** ▪ *pouty* lips ▪ He had a *pouty* look on his face.

POV *abbr, chiefly US* point of view

pov•er•ty /ˈpɑːvəti/ *noun*

1 *[noncount]* **:** the state of being poor ▪ rural/urban *poverty* ▪ families living in *poverty* ▪ He came from *poverty.* ▪ He was born in/into *poverty.*

2 *[singular] formal* **:** a lack *of* something ▪ There is a *poverty of* information about the disease. ▪ a *poverty of* imagination

poverty line *noun*

the poverty line **:** the level of income that makes it possible for a person to pay for basic food, clothing, and shelter ▪ Many families in the city are living below/at *the poverty line.* — called also *poverty level*

pov•er•ty–strick•en /ˈpɑːvətiˌstrɪkən/ *adj* **:** very poor ▪ *poverty-stricken* neighborhoods/families

poverty trap *noun, pl* **~ traps** *[count]* **:** a situation in which a person who is poor is unable to escape from poverty; *especially, chiefly Brit* **:** a situation in which a poor person who gets a job will remain poor because the amount of money that person receives from the government will be reduced

pow /ˈpaʊ/ *interj*

1 — used to express the sound of an explosion, a gun firing, or a person hitting another person ▪ We were talking and then . . . *Pow!* Someone hit him from behind.

2 — used to show that something has happened suddenly ▪ I was relaxing with a cup of tea and then—*pow!* I suddenly remembered where I was supposed to be.

POW /ˌpiːˌoʊˈdʌbəlˌjuː/ *noun, pl* **POWs** *[count]* **:** PRISONER OF WAR ▪ missing *POWs* ▪ a *POW* camp

[1]**pow•der** /ˈpaʊdɚ/ *noun, pl* **-ders**

1 : a dry substance made up of very tiny pieces of something *[noncount]* garlic/chili/cocoa *powder* *[count]* The *powder* is made from the roots of the plant. ▪ Mix together the different *powders.* ▪ She crushed the peppercorns into a fine *powder.* — see also BAKING POWDER, CHILI POWDER, CURRY POWDER, FIVE-SPICE POWDER, SOAP POWDER

2 *[noncount]* **:** a very fine, dry substance that is put on your body or face especially to make it dry or less shiny ▪ The girls put on their lipstick and (face) *powder* before heading out to the dance. ▪ We're running low on ***baby powder*** and diapers. — see picture at GROOMING; see also TALCUM POWDER

3 *[noncount]* **:** snow that is very light and dry ▪ We woke this morning to several inches of fresh *powder* on the ground. — often used before another noun ▪ *powder* skiing/snow

4 *[noncount]* **:** GUNPOWDER — see also POWDER KEG

keep your powder dry *old-fashioned* **:** to be calm and ready for a possible problem in the future ▪ They don't know how the election will turn out, so for now they're just *keeping their powder dry.*

take a powder *US, informal + old-fashioned* **:** to leave suddenly and quickly ▪ The boys decided to *take a powder* as soon as they saw there was work to be done.

[2]**powder** *verb* **-ders; -dered; -der•ing** *[+ obj]* **:** to put powder on (your face or body) ▪ She *powdered* her face and put on lipstick.

powder your nose *somewhat old-fashioned* — used by women as a polite way of excusing themselves from a table, conversation, etc., to go to the bathroom ▪ Excuse me. I'm just going to go *powder my nose.* I'll be right back.

powder blue *noun [noncount]* **:** a pale blue color — see color picture on page C2

pow•dered *adj, always used before a noun*

1 : in the form of a powder: such as **a :** made into a dry powder by having all the water removed ▪ *powdered* milk/ink **b :** having been crushed or ground into a powder ▪ *powdered* shells/charcoal

2 : covered in powder ▪ *powdered* wigs/cheeks

powdered sugar *noun [noncount] US* **:** sugar that has been ground into a fine powder — called also *(US) confectioners' sugar, (Brit) icing sugar*

powder keg *noun, pl* **~ kegs** *[count]*

1 : a small container that is used to hold gunpowder

2 : a place or situation that is likely to become dangerous or violent soon ▪ Political instability has made the region a *powder keg.*

powder puff *noun, pl* **~ puffs** *[count]* **:** a small, round piece of soft material that is used to put powder on your face or body

powder room *noun, pl* **~ rooms** *[count]*

1 *US* **:** a small bathroom especially for guests that has a toilet and sink but not a bathtub or shower

2 : a public bathroom for women in a restaurant, hotel, etc.

pow•dery /ˈpaʊdəri/ *adj*

1 : like powder ▪ *powdery* ashes ▪ the beach's *powdery* white sand

2 : covered with powder ▪ We skied down the *powdery* slopes.

[1]**pow•er** /ˈpawɚ/ *noun, pl* **-ers**

1 *[noncount]* **:** the ability or right to control people or things ▪ She is from a very wealthy family with a lot of social *power.* ▪ a politician who is hungry for *power* = a *power*-hungry politician ▪ The company abused its *power,* forcing workers to work overtime without pay. ▪ The company was almost destroyed in a ***power struggle*** between its two founders. ▪ She had them ***in her power.*** [=she controlled them] ▪ I'm sorry, but I don't have it *in my power* to help you. [=I don't have the power to help you; I can't help you] — often + *over* ▪ He has no *power over* me.

2 *[noncount]* **:** political control of a country or area ▪ After the emperor died, *power* passed to his eldest son. ▪ the peaceful transfer of *power* to the newly elected president ▪ The president was removed from *power* in the recent uprising. ▪ The new government has ***taken power.*** ▪ The latest elections put a new (political) party ***in power.*** ▪ The rebels ***rose/came to power*** several years ago. — see also BLACK POWER, FLOWER POWER

3 *[count]* **a :** a person or organization that has a lot of control and influence over other people or organizations ▪ A small company with only a few products has grown to become a *power* in the industry. ▪ Our state is now the region's leading economic *power.* **b :** a country that has a lot of influence and military strength ▪ a foreign *power* ▪ the European *powers* — see also GREAT POWER, SUPERPOWER, WORLD POWER

4 *[noncount]* **a :** physical force or strength ▪ Getting the floor clean required lots of muscle *power.* — often + *of* ▪ I was impressed by the sheer *power of* her tennis serve. ▪ the *power of* hurricane winds **b :** military force ▪ They are threatening to use air/military *power* to resolve the conflict.

P

— see also BALANCE OF POWER, FIREPOWER, SEA POWER **c** : the energy or force that someone or something can produce for movement, work, etc. ▪ He could not walk ***under his own power.*** [=he could not walk without help] ▪ The machines are running ***at full power.*** [=are doing as much work as they can possibly do]

5 a : an ability to do something [*count*] It's an old story, but it still has the *power* to frighten children. ▪ You have the *power* to change your life. ▪ I'll do everything ***within/in my power*** to help. [=I'll do everything that I can to help] ▪ It's ***in your power*** [=you have the ability] to change the way things are done here. — often + *of* ▪ He's studying the healing *powers of* various plants. ▪ She lost the *power of* speech. [=she was no longer able to speak] ▪ Some things are beyond the *power of* human understanding. ▪ He used all of his *powers of* persuasion, but she still would not agree. [*noncount*] Each member of the club has equal voting *power.* ▪ The new computer is tiny but has more computing *power* than many desktop computers. ▪ His position gives him great bargaining *power.* — see also BUYING POWER, PURCHASING POWER, STAYING POWER **b** [*noncount*] : the ability to influence or affect people or things ▪ It was a speech of great *power.* ▪ A good lawyer is able to argue with *power* and conviction. — often + *of* ▪ the *power of* art/love/religion/television ▪ Great poetry reminds us of the *power of* language. — see also DRAWING POWER, PULLING POWER

6 : the right to do something : legal or official authority to do something [*count*] You have the *power* to decide whether or not you'll agree to do it. ▪ The President has the *power* to veto laws passed by Congress. [*noncount*] The board of directors has given her *power* to negotiate the contract. — see also POWER OF ATTORNEY

7 [*noncount*] **a** : energy that can be collected and used to operate machines ▪ electrical/nuclear/solar/wind/battery *power* ▪ The car's engine yields more *power* while using less fuel. — see also HORSEPOWER, MANPOWER **b** : the electricity that people use ▪ We lost *power* during the storm. ▪ Do you know how many watts of *power* your refrigerator uses per day?

8 [*count*] *mathematics* **a** : the number of times that a number is to be multiplied by itself ▪ 5 (raised) to the third *power* is 125. [=5 x 5 x 5 = 125] **b** : a number that results from multiplying a number by itself ▪ 8 is a *power* of 2 because 2 x 2 x 2 is equal to 8.

9 [*noncount*] *technical* : the ability of an optical device (such as a telescope) to make objects look bigger ▪ the *power* [=*magnification*] of a microscope/telescope ▪ a telescope of high *power*

do (someone) a power of good *Brit, informal + old-fashioned* : to help someone physically or mentally : to make someone feel better ▪ I think spending a day outside in the sunshine would *do you a power of good.* [=(*US*) *do you a world of good*]

more power to you (*US*) *or Brit* ***more power to your elbow*** *informal* — used to say that you approve of what someone is doing and hope it will be successful ▪ If he wants to write a book, *more power to him*!

the corridors/halls of power : places where people talk about issues and make important decisions especially about political matters ▪ *the corridors of power* in Washington, D.C.

the power behind the throne : the person who secretly controls a country, organization, etc., by controlling the actions and decisions of the official leader ▪ He's the company president, but his assistant is *the (real) power behind the throne.*

the powers that be : the people who decide what is allowed or acceptable in a group, organization, etc. ▪ The students wanted to have a big party, but *the powers that be* didn't approve. ▪ I applied for the job, but I guess *the powers that be* didn't think I was qualified.

> ***synonyms*** POWER, AUTHORITY, JURISDICTION, COMMAND, and DOMINION mean the right or ability to govern, rule, or strongly influence people or situations. POWER is a general word that suggests the ability to control or influence what is done, felt, etc. ▪ the *power* of the throne ▪ the *power* to appoint judges ▪ The movie has the *power* to shape public opinion. AUTHORITY suggests power that has been given to someone for a specific purpose and that has certain limits. ▪ She gave her nephew the *authority* to manage the estate on her behalf. JURISDICTION refers to official, legal power that has certain limits. ▪ This matter is outside the court's *jurisdiction.* COMMAND refers to the power that someone (such as a military officer) has to make decisions and to force people to behave in a desired way. ▪ He was given *command* of the regiment. DOMINION is a formal word that stresses the greatest or highest power or authority. ▪ The country no longer has *dominion* over the island.

²power *verb* **-ers; -ered; -er·ing**

1 [+ *obj*] : to supply (something) with power — usually used as *(be) powered* ▪ The entire village *is powered* by wind. — see also POWERED

2 *always followed by an adverb or preposition* : to move with great speed or force [*no obj*] The running back *powered* through the defensive line. — often used figuratively ▪ The band *powered* through a number of new songs before playing some of their classics. [+ *obj*] He *powered* the ball past the goalie. ▪ She ***powered her way*** to the finish line.

power up [*phrasal verb*] ***power up (something) or power (something) up*** : to make (a machine) ready for use by supplying it with electricity ▪ I *powered up* [=*started up, turned on*] the computer.

³power *adj, always used before a noun*

1 : of or relating to electrical power ▪ a *power* supply/source/failure/outage ▪ Someone from the *power* [=*electric*] company called. ▪ *Power* lines [=wires that carry electricity] run along the west side of the street.

2 : operated by using electricity rather than a person's strength ▪ a *power* drill/saw ▪ *power* tools ▪ The car comes equipped with *power* windows.

3 : having great strength or power ▪ a *power* running back ▪ a *power* pitcher

4 a : involving important people who meet to discuss business or political affairs ▪ a *power* breakfast/lunch **b** *of clothing* : having a formal or impressive quality that is meant to make you look powerful and important ▪ a *power* suit ▪ (*US*) He was wearing a red *power* tie.

power–assisted steering *noun* [*noncount*] : POWER STEERING

power base *noun, pl* **~ bases** [*count*] : the area or group of people that provides the main support for a particular political candidate ▪ Both candidates are doing whatever they can to raise money from their *power bases.* ▪ Most of her *power base* is in the city.

pow·er·boat /ˈpawɚˌbout/ *noun, pl* **-boats** [*count*] : MOTORBOAT; *especially* : SPEEDBOAT

power broker *noun, pl* **~ -kers** [*count*] : a person who has a lot of influence and control in a particular activity (such as politics)

power cut *noun, pl* **~ cuts** [*count*] *Brit* : OUTAGE

pow·ered /ˈpawɚd/ *adj* : operated by a specified kind of power ▪ electrically *powered* vehicles — usually used in combination ▪ nuclear-*powered* submarines ▪ a battery-*powered* motor — see also HIGH-POWERED

power forward *noun, pl* **~ -wards** [*count*] *basketball* : a forward whose size and strength are used mainly to control play near the basket

pow·er·ful /ˈpawɚfəl/ *adj* [*more ~; most ~*]

1 : having the ability to control or influence people or things ▪ rich and *powerful* people ▪ a *powerful* ally ▪ The country is becoming more and more *powerful.*

2 : having a strong effect on someone or something ▪ *powerful* drugs that attack cancer cells ▪ The cash bonus provides a *powerful* incentive to workers. ▪ *powerful* emotions/images ▪ The perfume has a *powerful* smell. ▪ It's a very *powerful* movie. ▪ He gave a *powerful* [=*moving*] speech. ▪ a *powerful* [=*convincing, compelling*] argument

3 : having or producing a lot of physical strength or force ▪ *powerful* magnets ▪ a *powerful* machine/motor/force ▪ The dog has a *powerful* body. ▪ She has a *powerful* voice. ▪ The weapons are very *powerful.* ▪ The aardvark uses its *powerful* claws to dig for food.

4 : capable of doing many things in a fast and efficient way ▪ His new computer is more *powerful* than the one I have.

the powerful : powerful people ▪ the weak and *the powerful*

– pow·er·ful·ly *adv* ▪ a *powerfully* built man [=a man with a body that looks very strong] ▪ a *powerfully* written speech/book

pow·er·house /ˈpawɚˌhaus/ *noun, pl* **-hous·es** [*count*]

1 : a group of people or an organization that has a lot of power ▪ The country is an economic *powerhouse.* ▪ Their company became a *powerhouse* in the video game industry.

P

2 : a person, team, etc., that has a lot of energy, strength, and skill • an intellectual *powerhouse* • She's a *powerhouse* on the tennis court. • This year's team is a *powerhouse* that's winning its games easily. • a *powerhouse* gymnast
3 *chiefly US* : someone or something that is full *of* a particular thing • Seaweed is a *powerhouse of* vitamins and minerals. • He is a *powerhouse of* ideas.

pow•er•less /ˈpawɚləs/ *adj* : having no power : unable to do something or to stop something • *powerless* victims • She felt *powerless* [=*helpless*] lying in the hospital bed. — often + *against* • He felt *powerless against* the rumors that people were spreading about him. — often followed by *to* + *verb* • Studies show that people are not *powerless to prevent* heart disease.
– **pow•er•less•ness** *noun* [*noncount*]

power of attorney *noun, pl* **powers of attorney** *law*
1 [*count, noncount*] : the right to act and make decisions for another person in business and legal matters • Mrs. Flagg gave her son (a) *power of attorney* over all her accounts when she entered the nursing home.
2 [*count*] : a document that gives someone the right of power of attorney

power pack *noun, pl* ~ **packs** [*count*] : a small case that contains the power supply for an electronic device

power plant *noun, pl* ~ **plants** [*count*] *US* : a building or group of buildings in which electricity for a large area is produced — called also *power station*

power play *noun, pl* ~ **plays** [*count*] *US*
1 *ice hockey* : a situation in which one team has more players on the ice than the other team for a period of time because of a penalty • They scored their first goal on a *power play*.
2 : an attempt by a person, group, or organization to use power in a forceful and direct way to get or do something • He made a *power play* to seize control of the company.

power point *noun, pl* ~ **points** [*count*] *Brit* : OUTLET 4

power politics *noun* [*noncount*] : politics based on the use of military or economic power to influence the actions and decisions of other governments

power steering *noun* [*noncount*] : a steering system in cars that uses power from the engine to make it easier to turn the steering wheel — called also *power-assisted steering*

power strip *noun, pl* ~ **strips** [*count*] *US* : an electrical device that has a series of outlets attached to a cord with a plug on one end — see picture at COMPUTER

power structure *noun, pl* ~ **-tures** [*count*] *US* : a group of people who have control of a government, organization, etc., or the way in which those people are organized • The parade won't happen without the approval of the city's *power structure*. • Women in the company are struggling for equality against the male *power structure*. • They are making changes to the *power structure* of the church/university.

power trip *noun, pl* ~ **trips** [*count*] : an activity or way of behaving that makes a person feel powerful : something that a person does for the pleasure of using power to control other people • She's been ***on a power trip*** since she was promoted to manager.

power walk *verb* ~ **walks**; ~ **walked**; ~ **walking** [*no obj*] : to walk quickly for exercise especially while carrying or wearing weights
– **power walking** *noun* [*noncount*]

pow•wow /ˈpaʊˌwaʊ/ *noun, pl* **-wows** [*count*]
1 : a social gathering of Native Americans that usually includes dancing
2 *informal* : a meeting for people to discuss something • We'll talk about vacation plans at the family *powwow*.

pox /ˈpɑːks/ *noun*
1 [*singular*] : a disease that causes a rash on the skin — see also CHICKEN POX
2 [*noncount*] *old-fashioned* **a** : SYPHILIS **b** : SMALLPOX
3 [*singular*] *old-fashioned* + *humorous* — used to say that you hope something bad will happen to someone or something • ***A pox on*** all who don't believe me!

poxy /ˈpɑːksi/ *adj, always used before a noun, Brit slang* : not important : having little value • a *poxy* job

pp *abbr* **1** *pp.* pages • The article is on *pp.* 22–27. **2** per person • The tickets are $55 *pp.* **3** *Brit* by proxy ✧ This abbreviation is used before a person's name on a document to show that the signature is not of that person but of a person who has signed the document with the other person's permission. **4** pianissimo

PPO /ˌpiːˌpiːˈoʊ/ *noun, pl* **PPOs** [*count*] *US* : an organization that provides health care to people at a lower cost if they use the doctors, hospitals, etc., that belong to the organization • I'm not sure if that doctor belongs to my *PPO*. ✧ *PPO* is an abbreviation of "preferred provider organization." — compare HMO

PPS *abbr* an additional postscript — used before a second note that is added to the end of a letter after the writer has signed it; compare PS

¹PR /ˈpiːˈɑɚ/ *noun* [*noncount*] : PUBLIC RELATIONS • a job in *PR* — often used before another noun • a *PR* agency/firm/representative

²PR *abbr* **1** proportional representation **2** Puerto Rico

prac•ti•ca•ble /ˈpræktɪkəbəl/ *adj* [*more* ~; *most* ~] : able to be done or used • There's no *practicable* [=*feasible*] way to do the experiment with the current technology. • The idea is interesting but not *practicable*, I'm afraid. • Someday it may be *practicable* [=*possible*] to efficiently use waste as fuel.
– **prac•ti•ca•bil•i•ty** /ˌpræktɪkəˈbɪləti/ *noun* [*noncount*] • To be honest, I doubt the *practicability* of the idea. – **prac•ti•ca•bly** /ˈpræktɪkəbli/ *adv*

¹prac•ti•cal /ˈpræktɪkəl/ *adj* [*more* ~; *most* ~]
1 : relating to what is real rather than to what is possible or imagined • We can speculate about the future, but on a more *practical* level, we have to admit that we simply don't know what will happen. • An engineer will address the design's *practical* problems. • She has a lot of *practical* experience in dealing with these kinds of problems. • The *practical* [=*actual*] effect of the change has been very slight. — opposite THEORETICAL
2 **a** : likely to succeed and reasonable to do or use • The books suggests some *practical* ways to save money. • *practical* solutions to complicated problems • He thinks wind can be a *practical* source of renewable energy. **b** : appropriate or suited for actual use • The machine is too big to be *practical* for most private homes. • The shoes are nice, but they're not very *practical*. **c** : relating to what can or should be done in an actual situation • The book is a *practical* guide to car care. • He gave me some *practical* advice/help on finding a job. • One of the *practical* advantages of living in the city is that you have access to public transportation. • I have enough *practical* knowledge of German to get by. **d** : logical and reasonable in a particular situation • We could try to continue, but it's more *practical* to start over. • We left early for *practical* reasons—there's less traffic then and it's cooler.
3 *of a person* **a** : tending to make good decisions and to deal with daily life in a sensible way • He is a very *practical* person with no interest in expensive cars or clothes. • Try to be more *practical* about money. **b** : good at making or repairing things • My husband is not very *practical* around the house.
for (all) practical purposes — used to say that one thing has the same effect or result as something else • His effort to hide the document was, *for practical purposes* [=*in effect*], an admission that he had made a mistake. • During the blizzard, the town was, *for all practical purposes* [=*virtually, practically*], shut down.

²practical *noun, pl* **-cals** [*count*] *chiefly Brit* : an examination in which students have to do or make something to show what they have learned • We have our zoology *practicals* next week.

prac•ti•cal•i•ty /ˌpræktɪˈkæləti/ *noun, pl* **-ties**
1 [*noncount*] : the quality of being likely to succeed and reasonable to do or use • Panelists will debate the *practicality* of wind as a source of renewable energy.
2 [*noncount*] : the quality of being appropriate or suited for actual use • The size of the machine makes me doubt its *practicality* [=*suitability*] for use in the home. • I know you like the dressy shoes better than the sneakers, but I think you should choose based on *practicality*, not style.
3 [*noncount*] : the quality of being sensible in making decisions and dealing with the problems of daily life • His optimism and *practicality* make him a skilled businessman.
4 ***practicalities*** [*plural*] : the facts about something : the real things that have to be done or dealt with in a particular situation — usually + *of* • New teachers often find the *practicalities* [=*realities*] *of* teaching very different from the theories they learned in college.

practical joke *noun, pl* ~ **jokes** [*count*] : a joke involving something that is done rather than said : a trick played on someone • One of the children filled the sugar bowl with salt as a *practical joke*.
– **practical joker** *noun, pl* ~ **-kers** [*count*]

prac·ti·cal·ly /ˈpræktɪkli/ *adv*
1 : almost or nearly • *Practically* [=*virtually*] everyone went to the game. • The room's ceiling was so low that we *practically* had to crawl. • I talk to him *practically* everyday. • The project is *practically* complete. • Football is *practically* a religion in some places.
2 [*more* ~; *most* ~] **:** in a way that is reasonable or logical **:** in a practical way • We need to discuss the issue *practically* [=*sensibly*] before we make any decisions. • *Practically* speaking, Alaska is too far to go for just a few days.

practical nurse *noun, pl* ~ **nurses** [*count*] *US* **:** a nurse who cares for sick people but does not have as much training or experience as a registered nurse — compare REGISTERED NURSE; see also LICENSED PRACTICAL NURSE

[1]**prac·tice** (*US*) *or Brit* **prac·tise** /ˈpræktəs/ *verb* **-tic·es; -ticed; -tic·ing**
1 : to do something again and again in order to become better at it [*no obj*] To be a good musician, you have to *practice* a lot. [+ *obj*] Have you been *practicing* your lines for the play? • She had to *practice* flying in various weather conditions before she could get her pilot's license.
2 [+ *obj*] **:** to do (something) regularly or constantly as an ordinary part of your life • He *practices* yoga daily. • The monks *practice* celibacy. • Grandmother taught us to *practice* good manners. • ***Practice what you preach***—don't smoke if you tell your children not to smoke.
3 [+ *obj*] **:** to live according to the customs and teachings of (a religion) • Their family *practices* Buddhism. • a *practicing* Catholic
4 : to have a professional medical or legal business [+ *obj*] My cousin plans to *practice* medicine/law/dentistry. [=plans to be a doctor/lawyer/dentist] [*no obj*] There are thousands of lawyers *practicing* in this city. • a *practicing* physician

[2]**practice** *noun, pl* **-tices**
1 a [*noncount*] **:** the activity of doing something again and again in order to become better at it • Being a good musician takes a lot of *practice*. • I'm sure you'll learn your lines for the play with enough *practice*. • They'll get better with *practice*. • If you want to be a good musician, you have to stay ***in practice***. [=you have to practice enough to improve and keep your skills] • I used to be pretty good at playing the piano, but I'm ***out of practice*** now. [=I haven't practiced so my skills are not as good as they were] • If you want to be a good writer, you should write every day. Remember, ***practice makes perfect***. [=you become better at something if you practice it often] **b :** a regular occasion at which you practice something [*noncount*] I'm late for trumpet/ballet/soccer *practice*. • The marching band has/holds *practice* every Wednesday afternoon. [*count*] The team's *practices* usually last two hours. — **often used before another noun** • The team was on the *practice* field at dawn. • a *practice* session
2 : something that is done often or regularly [*count*] She has made a *practice* of volunteering at a homeless shelter one weekend a month. • It is his *practice* [=*habit*] to read the newspaper each morning. • The company has been accused of unfair labor *practices*. [=of treating its workers unfairly] • The country's poor sanitation *practices* have led to widespread disease. • Burial *practices* vary around the world. [*noncount*] It is common *practice* among my friends to not use capital letters in e-mail. • It's ***good practice*** [=it is wise; it is a good idea] to always carry a few dollars in cash. • Letting the car get/run very low on fuel is ***bad practice***. [=is a bad/unwise thing to do]
3 [*noncount*] **:** the action of doing or using something • the theory and *practice* of teaching • the *practice* of law/medicine • Her advice is good, but it's hard to ***put into practice***. [=to use it in actual situations] • He worked on a farm during the summer to *put* his knowledge of agriculture *into practice*.
4 [*count*] **:** a professional medical or legal business • a pharmacist's *practice* • Her law *practice* is in the downtown area. — see also FAMILY PRACTICE, GROUP PRACTICE, PRIVATE PRACTICE
in practice — used to say what is actually done or what the actual effect or result of something is • The software is designed to block pornographic Web sites, but *in practice* [=*in reality*], it blocks many other sites as well. • *In* actual *practice*, people sometimes forget to take their medication.

practiced (*US*) *or Brit* **practised** *adj*
1 : good at doing something because you have done it many times • a *practiced* chef • Only a few of the dancers are *practiced* in traditional ballet. • The diamonds may look identical to you and me, but to a ***practiced eye*** [=someone who has a lot of knowledge and experience with diamonds], one is obviously a fake.
2 *always used before a noun* **:** learned by doing something again and again • He split the log with *practiced* skill.

prac·ti·cum /ˈpræktɪkəm/ *noun, pl* **-cums** [*count*] *US* **:** a course of study for teachers, doctors, nurses, etc., that involves actually working in the area of study and using the knowledge and skills that have been learned in a school

prac·ti·tion·er /prækˈtɪʃənə/ *noun, pl* **-ers** [*count*] *formal*
1 : a person who works in a professional medical or legal business • a health *practitioner* • legal *practitioners* — see also FAMILY PRACTITIONER, GENERAL PRACTITIONER, MEDICAL PRACTITIONER, NURSE PRACTITIONER
2 : a person who regularly does an activity that requires skill or practice • yoga *practitioners* — often + *of* • *practitioners of* the art of glassblowing

prag·mat·ic /prægˈmætɪk/ *adj* [*more* ~; *most* ~] *formal* **:** dealing with the problems that exist in a specific situation in a reasonable and logical way instead of depending on ideas and theories • a *pragmatic* [=*practical*] approach to health care • His *pragmatic* view of public education comes from years of working in city schools. • a *pragmatic* leader
— prag·mat·i·cal·ly /prægˈmætɪkli/ *adv* • She approaches problems *pragmatically*.

prag·mat·ics /prægˈmætɪks/ *noun* [*noncount*] *linguistics* **:** the study of what words mean in particular situations

prag·ma·tism /ˈprægməˌtɪzəm/ *noun* [*noncount*] *formal* **:** a reasonable and logical way of doing things or of thinking about problems that is based on dealing with specific situations instead of on ideas and theories • The right person for the job will balance vision with *pragmatism*.
— prag·ma·tist /ˈprægmətɪst/ *noun, pl* **-tists** [*count*]

prai·rie /ˈpreri/ *noun, pl* **-ries :** a large, mostly flat area of land in North America that has few trees and is covered in grasses [*count*] Millions of buffalo once roamed the *prairies*. [*noncount*] The train tracks extend over miles of *prairie*. — often used before another noun • *prairie* grasses/flowers

prairie dog *noun, pl* ~ **dogs** [*count*] **:** a small animal that lives on the prairies of the central and western U.S. — see picture at RODENT

[1]**praise** /ˈpreɪz/ *verb* **prais·es; praised; prais·ing** [+ *obj*]
1 : to say or write good things about (someone or something) **:** to express approval of (someone or something) • Critics *praised* her as both an actor and director. • He *praised* her cooking. • A good teacher *praises* students when they do well. • His poems *praise* nature. — **opposite** CRITICIZE
2 : to express thanks to or love and respect for (God) • We *praise* God for your safe arrival. • *Praise* Allah that you are safe! [=I thank Allah that you are safe] • People gather in churches to *praise* the Lord.
praise (someone or something) to the skies **:** to praise someone or something very much • Critics have *praised* the play *to the skies*.

[2]**praise** *noun, pl* **praises**
1 : spoken or written words about the good qualities of someone or something **:** an expression of approval for someone or something [*noncount*] He deserves *praise* for the way he's handled this crisis. • He won critical *praise* [=*acclaim*] for his performance. • "Good job" is ***high praise*** coming from her. She rarely compliments anyone's work. • I have ***nothing but praise*** for the hospital staff. • The poem is ***in praise of*** nature. [=the poem praises nature] [*plural*] The critics ***heaped praises on*** her performance. = The critics ***sang the praises of*** her performance. = The critics ***sang her praises***. [=the critics praised her performance in a very enthusiastic way]
2 : an expression of thanks to or love and respect for God [*plural*] People gathered in the church to sing *praises* to the Lord. [*noncount*] hymns/songs of *praise* • You made it here safely. ***Praise be to God***. [=thank God] • We were not, ***praise be*** [=*thankfully*], required to join hands and sing songs.
damn with faint praise see [2]DAMN

praise·wor·thy /ˈpreɪzˌwəði/ *adj* **:** deserving praise **:** worthy of praise • *praiseworthy* efforts to develop an AIDS vaccine

pra·line /ˈprɑːˌliːn/ *noun, pl* **-lines** [*count, noncount*] **:** a candy made of nuts and boiled sugar

pram /ˈpræm/ *noun, pl* **prams** [*count*] *Brit* **:** BABY CARRIAGE

prance /ˈpræns/ *verb* **pranc·es; pranced; pranc·ing** [*no obj*]
1 *always followed by an adverb or preposition* **:** to walk or

P

move in a lively and proud way ▪ The singer *pranced* around on stage. ▪ The little boy *pranced* across the room in his cowboy costume.

2 *of a horse* **:** to move by taking high steps **:** to lift each hoof up high when moving

prang /ˈpræŋ/ *verb* **prangs; pranged; prang·ing** [+ *obj*] *Brit, informal* **:** to damage (a vehicle) in an accident ▪ She *pranged* her car.

– prang *noun, pl* **prangs** [*count*] ▪ a minor *prang* [=*accident*] in a car park

prank /ˈpræŋk/ *noun, pl* **pranks** [*count*] **:** a trick that is done to someone usually as a joke ▪ a childish *prank* ▪ He enjoys playing *pranks* on his friends. ▪ (*US*) He's always ***pulling pranks***.

prank·ster /ˈpræŋkstɚ/ *noun, pl* **-sters** [*count*] **:** a person who plays pranks on other people

prat /ˈpræt/ *noun, pl* **prats** [*count*] *Brit, informal* **:** a stupid or foolish person ▪ He acts like a real *prat* sometimes.

prate /ˈpreɪt/ *verb* **prates; prat·ed; prat·ing** [*no obj*] **:** to talk for a very long about something that is not very important or interesting ▪ She kept *prating* (on) about what she did over the weekend.

prat·fall /ˈprætˌfɑːl/ *noun, pl* **-falls** [*count*]
1 : a sudden fall in which you end up sitting on the ground ▪ He slipped and took a *pratfall* into the mud.
2 : an embarrassing mistake or accident ▪ a politician who's known for his verbal *pratfalls* [=*blunders*]

prat·tle /ˈprætl/ *verb* **prattles; prattled; prattling** [*no obj*] **:** to talk for very long about something that is not important or interesting ▪ They *prattled* on into the night, discussing school, music, and friends.

– prattle *noun* [*noncount*] ▪ I was tired of listening to their *prattle*.

prawn /ˈprɑːn/ *noun, pl* **prawns** [*count*]
1 a *US* **:** a large shrimp **b** *Brit* **:** SHRIMP
2 : a small lobster with long, slender claws

pray /ˈpreɪ/ *verb* **prays; prayed; pray·ing**
1 a : to speak to God especially in order to give thanks or to ask for something [*no obj*] *praying* to God/Allah daily ▪ There's little else to do now but hope and *pray*. ▪ The minister said, "***Let us pray***." — often + *for* ▪ We *prayed* (to God) *for* their safe return. ▪ *pray for* forgiveness [+ *obj*] The family *prayed* (to God) that she wouldn't need surgery. ▪ He *prayed* that they would have the strength to go on. **b :** to hope or wish very much for something to happen [*no obj*] — usually + *for* ▪ She's *praying* [=*hoping*] *for* a chance to play in the game. [+ *obj*] He *prayed* that he would find a parking spot.
2 [+ *obj*] *old-fashioned* **:** to seriously ask (someone) to do something ▪ I *pray* [=*beg*] you, tell me where they went. ▪ I *pray* you be careful. [=please be careful] — used to introduce a question or request in a polite or deliberately old-fashioned way ▪ *Pray* be careful. ▪ *Pray* [=*please*] tell me what to do. ▪ Why should I trust them, ***pray tell***? [=tell me why I should trust them; I do not think that they should be trusted]

prayer /ˈpreɚ/ *noun, pl* **prayers**
1 [*count*] **a :** words spoken to God especially in order to give thanks or to ask for something ▪ Father said a *prayer*, and then we began to eat. ▪ She told the children to say their *prayers* before they went to sleep. ▪ We've been praying for her safe return, and now our ***prayers have been answered***. = We've been praying for her safe return, and now God has ***answered our prayers***. [=she has returned safely] — often + *for* ▪ a *prayer for* peace ▪ I'm very nervous about the surgery. Will you say a *prayer for* me? **b :** a fixed set of words that are spoken to God ▪ a *prayer* of thanksgiving ▪ We joined hands and recited the *prayer* together. ▪ a book of hymns and *prayers* — see also LORD'S PRAYER
2 [*noncount*] **:** the act of speaking to God **:** the act of praying ▪ The people were kneeling in *prayer*. ▪ a moment of silent *prayer*
3 [*count*] **:** a strong hope or wish ▪ It's our *prayer* that peace will come to the region soon. ▪ The house seemed like the ***answer to all my prayers***. [=the house had everything that I hoped for]
4 ***prayers*** [*plural*] **:** a meeting at which people pray together ▪ Refreshments will be served following morning *prayers*.
5 [*singular*] *informal* **:** a slight chance of doing or getting something — usually used in negative statements ▪ No one thought the team had a *prayer* (of winning). ▪ "Do you think he'll get the job." "No. He doesn't have a *prayer*."
on a wing and a prayer see [1]WING

prayer book *noun, pl* **~ books** [*count*] **:** a book that contains prayers and other writings used in church services

prayer·ful /ˈpreɚfəl/ *adj, formal*
1 [*more* ~; *most* ~] **:** tending to pray often **:** DEVOUT ▪ a *prayerful* man
2 : involving prayer ▪ They gave their *prayerful* support to the victims of the tragedy.
– prayer·ful·ly *adv*

prayer rug *noun, pl* **~ rugs** [*count*] **:** a small rug that Muslims kneel on when they pray — called also *prayer mat*

prayer shawl *noun, pl* **~ shawls** [*count*] **:** a shawl that is worn over the head or shoulders by Jewish men especially during morning prayers

prayer wheel *noun, pl* **~ wheels** [*count*] **:** a round container that is filled with prayers written on paper and that turns on a tall pole ✧ Prayer wheels are used by Tibetan Buddhists.

praying mantis *noun, pl* **~ mantises** [*count*] **:** a large insect that eats other insects by holding them in its raised front legs — called also *mantis*; see color picture on page C10

pre- /priː/ *prefix*
1 : earlier than **:** before ▪ *pre*historic ▪ *pre*season
2 : in advance ▪ *pre*pay

preach /ˈpriːtʃ/ *verb* **preach·es; preached; preach·ing**
1 : to make a speech about religion in a church or other public place **:** to deliver a sermon [*no obj*] Have you ever heard that minister *preach*? ▪ The minister *preached* to the congregation about/on the need for tolerance. [+ *obj*] His followers listened to him *preach* the gospel. ▪ The priest *preached* a regular sermon that Sunday.
2 : to write or speak about (something) in an approving way **:** to say that (something) is good or necessary [+ *obj*] Some people have begun to complain about the project delays, but the mayor continues to *preach* patience. [=to say that people should be patient] ▪ Although he once *preached* revolution [=said that there should be a revolution], he now claims to be a man of peace. ▪ Their mother has always *preached* the value/virtues of a good education. ▪ ***Practice what you preach*** — don't smoke if you tell your children not to smoke. [*no obj*] The mayor continues to *preach* about the need for patience.
3 [*no obj*] **:** to write or speak in an annoying way about the right way to behave ▪ It's important to give teenagers helpful advice without *preaching* (to/at them). ▪ I don't like being *preached* at/to about how I should live my life.
preach to the choir (*chiefly US*) ***or preach to the converted*** **:** to speak for or against something to people who already agree with your opinions ▪ The speeches he makes to his supporters won't win him any more votes. He's just *preaching to the choir*.

preach·er /ˈpriːtʃɚ/ *noun, pl* **-ers** [*count*] **:** a person who speaks publicly about religious subjects in a Christian church or other public place

preachy /ˈpriːtʃi/ *adj* **preach·i·er; -est** [*also more* ~; *most* ~] *informal + disapproving* **:** trying to teach something (such as proper or moral behavior) in a way that is annoying or unwanted ▪ We were put off by the speaker's *preachy* tone. ▪ a boring and *preachy* writer

pre·ad·o·les·cent /ˌpriːˌædəˈlɛsn̩t/ *adj* **:** of or relating to the period of life before a child begins to develop into an adult **:** of or relating to the period of life before adolescence ▪ *preadolescent* boys/girls ▪ my *preadolescent* interests
– pre·ad·o·les·cence /ˌpriːˌædəˈlɛsn̩s/ *noun* [*noncount*]
– preadolescent *noun, pl* **-scents** [*count*] ▪ Is this movie appropriate for *preadolescents*?

pre·am·ble /ˈpriːˌæmbəl/ *noun, pl* **-am·bles** *somewhat formal*
1 : a statement that is made at the beginning of something (such as a legal document) and usually gives the reasons for the parts that follow [*count*] The *preamble* to the U.S. Constitution begins by saying "We the People of the United States, in order to form a more perfect union, . . ." [*noncount*] He told us the news ***without preamble***. [=without saying anything else first]
2 [*count*] **:** something that comes before and leads to something else ▪ His early travels were just a *preamble* to his later adventures.

pre·ap·prove /ˌpriːjəˈpruːv/ *verb* **-proves; -proved; -prov·ing** [+ *obj*] **:** to say that you will say yes to (someone or something) when a final or official request is made **:** to approve (someone or something) in advance ▪ The bank has *preapproved* our loan. = The bank has *preapproved* us for a loan. = We've been/gotten *preapproved* for a loan.
– pre·ap·prov·al /ˌpriːjəˈpruːvəl/ *noun* [*noncount*] **– pre-**

approved *adj* ▪ Participants in the program can purchase certain *preapproved* medications at a discounted price.

pre·ar·range /ˌpriːjəˈreɪnʤ/ *verb* **-rang·es; -ranged; -rang·ing** [+ *obj*] : to plan or decide (something) before it happens : to arrange (something) in advance ▪ The details of the ceremony were carefully *prearranged.*

– **prearranged** *adj* ▪ They met at a *prearranged* time and place. ▪ a *prearranged* meeting – **pre·ar·range·ment** /ˌpriːjəˈreɪnʤmənt/ *noun, pl* **-ments** [*noncount*] They met by *prearrangement* at the restaurant. [*count*] There's no need to make *prearrangements.*

pre·cal·cu·lus /ˌpriːˈkælkjələs/ *noun* [*noncount*] *US* : an introductory course that prepares students for the study of calculus ▪ She is taking *precalculus* this semester.

– **precalculus** *adj, always used before a noun* ▪ a *precalculus* course ▪ *precalculus* students

pre·can·cer·ous /ˌpriːˈkænsərəs/ *adj, medical* : likely to become cancerous ▪ a *precancerous* growth/lesion

pre·car·i·ous /prɪˈkerijəs/ *adj* [*more* ~; *most* ~] : not safe, strong, or steady ▪ He earned a *precarious* livelihood/living by gambling. ▪ She was in a state of *precarious* [=*delicate*] health. ▪ The government is in a *precarious* position. [=a dangerous position that must be dealt with carefully] ▪ The strong wind almost knocked him off of his *precarious* perch on the edge of the cliff.

– **pre·car·i·ous·ly** *adv* ▪ The vase was placed *precariously* close to the edge of the table. – **pre·car·i·ous·ness** *noun* [*noncount*]

pre·cast /ˌpriːˈkæst, *Brit* ˌpriːˈkɑːst/ *adj, technical* : made into shapes that are ready to be used to build something ▪ The wall is built with *precast* concrete panels.

pre·cau·tion /prɪˈkɑːʃən/ *noun, pl* **-tions** [*count*] : something that is done to prevent possible harm or trouble from happening in the future ▪ Be sure to follow the usual safety *precautions* when cooking outdoors. ▪ When driving, she always wears her seatbelt as a *precaution.* ▪ Every home owner should ***take precautions*** against fire. ▪ She *took the precaution* of packing extra medicine for the trip.

– **pre·cau·tion·ary** /prɪˈkɑːʃəˌneri, *Brit* prɪˈkɔːʃənri/ *adj* ▪ The beaches were closed as a *precautionary* measure.

pre·cede /prɪˈsiːd/ *verb* **-cedes; -ced·ed; -ced·ing** [+ *obj*] *somewhat formal*

1 : to happen, go, or come before (something or someone) ▪ Riots *preceded* the civil war. ▪ She *preceded* him into the room. ▪ The country became more conservative in the years that *preceded* his election. ▪ The new mayor is very different from the person who *preceded* her in office. ▪ The meeting was *preceded* by a brief welcoming speech. — see also PRECEDING

2 : to do or say something before (something) ▪ The chairman *preceded* the meeting with a brief welcoming speech.

pre·ce·dence /ˈprɛsədəns/ *noun* [*noncount*] *somewhat formal* : the condition of being more important than something or someone else and therefore coming or being dealt with first ▪ The guests were introduced in order of *precedence.* [=the most important guests were introduced first] ▪ The safety of the children ***has/takes precedence over*** [=is more important than] everything else. ▪ Many small businesses complain that the government's policies ***give precedence to*** large corporations. [=treat large corporations as more important]

prec·e·dent /ˈprɛsədənt/ *noun, pl* **-dents** *somewhat formal*

1 : a similar action or event that happened at an earlier time [*count*] There are no *precedents* for these events. [=nothing like these events has ever happened before] [*noncount*] There isn't any *precedent* for these events. = These events are ***without precedent.***

2 : something done or said that can be used as an example or rule to be followed in the future [*count*] The judge's ruling was based on a *precedent* established by an earlier decision. ▪ He says that the government will set/establish a dangerous *precedent* if it refuses to allow the protesters to hold a rally. [*noncount*] The judge's ruling was based/founded on legal *precedent.*

3 [*noncount*] : the usual or traditional way of doing something ▪ The voters ***broke (with) precedent*** [=they did something that had not been done before] when they elected a woman to the position.

pre·ced·ing /prɪˈsiːdɪŋ/ *adj* : existing, happening, or coming before : PREVIOUS ▪ The *preceding* week he had been on vacation. ▪ the *preceding* year ▪ the *preceding* chapter

pre·cept /ˈpriːˌsɛpt/ *noun, pl* **-cepts** *formal* : a rule that says how people should behave [*count*] the basic/moral *precepts* of a religion [*noncount*] I was taught by *precept* and by example.

pre·cinct /ˈpriːˌsɪŋkt/ *noun, pl* **-cincts** [*count*]

1 *US* : any one of the sections that a town or city is divided into when people vote in an election ▪ an electoral *precinct*

2 *US* **a** : any one of the sections that a city is divided into for organizing the city's police forces ▪ a police *precinct* ▪ a *precinct* captain/station **b** : a police station of a precinct ▪ She was taken to the (police) *precinct* for questioning.

3 *Brit* : an area in a town or city where people may walk and vehicles are not allowed ▪ a pedestrian/shopping *precinct*

4 : the area that is near or around a place — usually plural; often + *of* ▪ within the *precincts of* the college — sometimes used figuratively ▪ the private *precincts of* the heart/mind

¹pre·cious /ˈprɛʃəs/ *adj* [*more* ~; *most* ~]

1 : rare and worth a lot of money ▪ diamonds and other *precious* stones ▪ *precious* jewels/jewelry ✧ A ***precious metal*** is an expensive metal (such as gold) that is used especially for jewelry. — see also SEMIPRECIOUS

2 : very valuable or important : too valuable or important to be wasted or used carelessly ▪ We can save *precious* time by taking this shortcut. ▪ They were able to be together for only a few *precious* hours/days. ▪ *precious* resources

3 : greatly loved, valued, or important ▪ *precious* memories ▪ the family's most *precious* moments ▪ a very *precious* [=*dear*] friend

4 *US, informal* : having a very pleasing and usually youthful appearance or quality : CUTE ▪ Aren't those children *precious*?

5 *formal + disapproving* : having a too careful, precise, or polite quality that seems false or annoying ▪ The sometimes *precious* writing makes the book difficult to read. ▪ *precious* manners

– **pre·cious·ly** *adv* ▪ a somewhat *preciously* written book ▪ We have *preciously* [=*precious*] little time left. – **pre·cious·ness** *noun* [*noncount*] ▪ The *preciousness* of the writing annoys me.

²precious *adv* : very or extremely ▪ She had ***precious little*** to say. ▪ There are ***precious few*** hours of sunlight left.

prec·i·pice /ˈprɛsəpəs/ *noun, pl* **-pic·es** [*count*]

1 : a very steep side of a mountain or cliff ▪ He stood on the edge of the *precipice.*

2 : a point where danger, trouble, or difficulty begins — usually singular ▪ He is ***on the precipice of*** a midlife crisis. ▪ The company is now ***on the edge of a precipice.*** [=the company is close to a very bad or dangerous situation]

¹pre·cip·i·tate /prɪˈsɪpəˌteɪt/ *verb* **-tates; -tat·ed; -tat·ing**

1 [+ *obj*] *formal* : to cause (something) to happen quickly or suddenly ▪ Her death *precipitated* a family crisis. ▪ The budget problem was *precipitated* by many unexpected costs.

2 *technical* **a** [*no obj*] : to become separated from a liquid especially by a chemical process ▪ minerals that *precipitate* from seawater **b** [+ *obj*] : to cause (something solid) to become separated from a liquid especially by a chemical process ▪ *precipitate* minerals from seawater

– **precipitating** *adj* ▪ *precipitating* events/factors [=events/factors that cause something to happen]

²pre·cip·i·tate /prɪˈsɪpətət/ *noun, pl* **-tates** [*count*] *technical* : a solid substance that is separated from a liquid especially by a chemical process

³pre·cip·i·tate /prɪˈsɪpətət/ *adj* [*more* ~; *most* ~] *formal* : happening very quickly or too quickly without enough thought or planning ▪ a *precipitate* [=*precipitous*] attack/decision

– **pre·cip·i·tate·ly** *adv* ▪ He says the police acted *precipitately* in making the arrest.

pre·cip·i·ta·tion /prɪˌsɪpəˈteɪʃən/ *noun, pl* **-tions**

1 [*noncount*] : water that falls to the ground as rain, snow, etc. ▪ The weather forecast calls for some sort of frozen *precipitation* tomorrow—either snow or sleet. ▪ a 50 percent chance of *precipitation*

2 [*count, noncount*] *technical* : the process of separating a solid substance from a liquid ▪ Minerals are separated from the seawater by *precipitation.*

pre·cip·i·tous /prɪˈsɪpətəs/ *adj* [*more* ~; *most* ~] *formal*

1 : very steep ▪ a *precipitous* slope

2 : happening in a very quick and sudden way ▪ There has been a *precipitous* decline/drop in home sales recently. ▪ People were shocked by his *precipitous* fall from political power.

P

3 : done too quickly and without enough thought or planning ▪ a *precipitous* [=*precipitate*] action
– **pre·cip·i·tous·ly** *adv* ▪ The slope dropped away *precipitously*. ▪ Home sales are declining/dropping *precipitously*.
– **pre·cip·i·tous·ness** *noun* [*noncount*]

pré·cis /preɪˈsiː/ *noun, pl* **pré·cis** /preɪˈsiːz/ [*count*] : a brief summary of the main points and ideas of a piece of writing or speech ▪ a *précis* of the book's plot
– **précis** *verb* **-cis·es** /preɪˈsiːz/; **-cised; -cis·ing** [+ *obj*] *Brit* ▪ She is skilled at *précising* complex theories.

pre·cise /prɪˈsaɪs/ *adj*
1 a [*more* ~; *most* ~] : very accurate and exact ▪ Be sure to take *precise* measurements before you cut the cloth. ▪ The dating of very old materials has become more *precise* with new instruments. ▪ a *precise* definition ▪ The word has a very *precise* meaning. ▪ Can you find a more *precise* term than "good" to describe the movie? ▪ Could you be a little more *precise* about what happened? **b** *always used before a noun* — used to refer to an exact and particular time, location, etc. ▪ She quietly closed the door to the baby's room, and at just that *precise* moment the phone began to ring.
2 [*more* ~; *most* ~] : very careful and exact about the details of something ▪ She is very *precise* in her work.
to be precise — used to indicate that a statement is accurate and specific ▪ one night in early summer—June 22, *to be precise*
– **pre·cise·ly** *adv* ▪ It is *precisely* [=*exactly*] two o'clock. ▪ He knows *precisely* how much money he has. ▪ "Do you mean that the system is outdated?" "*Precisely*." = "Yes, that's *precisely* what I mean." ▪ The king was popular *precisely* because he was so kind and generous. ▪ I have a doctor's appointment this afternoon, or, ***more precisely***, at two o'clock this afternoon. – **pre·cise·ness** *noun* [*noncount*] ▪ the *preciseness* of the measurements ▪ She does her work with *preciseness*. [=*precision*]

[1]**pre·ci·sion** /prɪˈsɪʒən/ *noun* [*noncount*] : the quality of being precise : exactness or accuracy ▪ I admire the *precision* of her work. — often used after *with* ▪ The work was done *with* surgical *precision*. [=was done in a very precise way] ▪ The cause of the fire cannot be determined ***with any (degree of) precision***.

[2]**precision** *adj, always used before a noun*
1 : designed for very accurate measurement or operation ▪ a *precision* instrument
2 : done in a very careful and exact way ▪ *precision* drilling ▪ The airplane made a *precision* approach for landing.

pre·clude /prɪˈkluːd/ *verb* **-cludes; -clud·ed; -clud·ing** [+ *obj*] *formal*
1 : to make (something) impossible : to prevent (something) from happening ▪ She suffered an injury that *precluded* the possibility of an athletic career. ▪ Bad weather *precluded* any further attempts to reach the summit.
2 : to prevent (someone) from doing something — + *from* ▪ The injury *precluded* her *from* having an athletic career.

pre·co·cious /prɪˈkoʊʃəs/ *adj* [*more* ~; *most* ~] *of a child* : having or showing the qualities or abilities of an adult at an unusually early age ▪ She was a *precocious* child who could read before she went to school. ▪ A *precocious* musician, he was giving concerts when he was seven.
– **pre·co·cious·ly** *adv* ▪ a *precociously* mature child – **pre·co·cious·ness** *noun* [*noncount*] ▪ the child's *precociousness* – **pre·coc·i·ty** /prɪˈkɑːsəti/ *noun* [*noncount*] ▪ the child's *precocity*

pre·con·ceived /ˌpriːkənˈsiːvd/ *adj, always used before a noun* : formed before having actual knowledge about something or before experiencing something — often + *about* or *of* ▪ I didn't have any *preconceived* ideas/notions *about/of* what the job would be like when I first started.

pre·con·cep·tion /ˌpriːkənˈsɛpʃən/ *noun, pl* **-tions** [*count*] : an idea or opinion that someone has before learning about or experiencing something directly ▪ I came to the lecture without any *preconceptions*. — often + *about* or *of* ▪ He's changing people's *preconceptions about/of* modern art.

pre·con·di·tion /ˌpriːkənˈdɪʃən/ *noun, pl* **-tions** [*count*] : something that must exist or happen before something else can exist or happen ▪ An education is an essential/important/necessary *precondition* [=*prerequisite*] for getting a good job. ▪ They insist on a guarantee as a *precondition* of/to the deal.

pre·cook /ˌpriːˈkʊk/ *verb* **-cooks; -cooked; -cook·ing** [+ *obj*] : to cook (food) partially or entirely at an earlier time ▪ He *precooked* the chicken before he grilled it. ▪ The pasta should be *precooked* and allowed to cool. ▪ *precooked* meals/meats

pre·cur·sor /prɪˈkɚsɚ/ *noun, pl* **-sors** [*count*] *somewhat formal* : something that comes before something else and that often leads to or influences its development — often + *of* or *to* ▪ Rhythm and blues was a *precursor of* rock music. ▪ Small tremors may be *precursors to* big earthquakes.

pre·date /ˌpriːˈdeɪt/ *verb* **-dates; -dat·ed; -dat·ing** [+ *obj*] : to exist or happen at an earlier time than (something or someone) ▪ modes of transportation that *predate* the car ▪ the native people who *predated* European settlers in America — opposite POSTDATE

pre·da·tion /prɪˈdeɪʃən/ *noun* [*noncount*] *technical* : the act of killing and eating other animals : the act of preying on other animals ▪ *predation* by lions

pred·a·tor /ˈprɛdətɚ/ *noun, pl* **-tors** [*count*]
1 : an animal that lives by killing and eating other animals : an animal that preys on other animals ▪ *predators* like bears and wolves ▪ The population of rabbits is controlled by natural *predators*.
2 : a person who looks for other people in order to use, control, or harm them in some way ▪ a sexual *predator* [=a person who commits sexual crimes against other people] ▪ a corporate *predator* acquiring business rivals

pred·a·to·ry /ˈprɛdəˌtori, *Brit* ˈprɛdətri/ *adj*
1 *technical* : living by killing and eating other animals ▪ *predatory* animals/birds/insects
2 [*more* ~; *most* ~] : wrongly harming or using others for pleasure or profit ▪ *predatory* business practices ▪ *predatory* acts of sexual violence ▪ *predatory* men/women

pre·de·cease /ˌpriːdɪˈsiːs/ *verb* **-ceas·es; -ceased; -ceas·ing** [+ *obj*] *formal* : to die before (someone) ▪ She was *predeceased* by her husband. [=her husband died before she did]

pre·de·ces·sor /ˈprɛdəˌsɛsɚ, *Brit* ˈpriːdəˌsɛsə/ *noun, pl* **-sors** [*count*]
1 : a person who had a job or position before someone else ▪ The company's new president has changed many of the policies that were introduced by his *predecessor*. [=by the previous president] — opposite SUCCESSOR
2 : something that comes before something else ▪ Today's computers are much faster than their *predecessors* were.

pre·des·ti·na·tion /ˌpriːˌdɛstəˈneɪʃən/ *noun* [*noncount*] : the belief that everything that will happen has already been decided by God or fate and cannot be changed

pre·des·tined /ˌpriːˈdɛstənd/ *adj* : certain to do or be something or certain to happen ▪ He felt he was *predestined* [=*destined*] to marry her when they first met. ▪ The course of her life seemed to be *predestined*. ▪ a *predestined* outcome

pre·de·ter·mine /ˌpriːdəˈtɚmən/ *verb* **-mines; -mined; -min·ing** [+ *obj*] : to decide (something) before it happens or in advance ▪ The sex of the child is *predetermined* when the egg is fertilized.
– **predetermined** *adj* ▪ They were to meet at a *predetermined* time and place. [=a time and place that they had agreed on earlier]

pre·de·ter·min·er /ˌpriːdəˈtɚmənɚ/ *noun, pl* **-ers** [*count*] *grammar* : a word (such as "both" or "all") that comes before a determiner in a phrase ▪ In the phrase "for all their trouble," the word "their" is a determiner and the word "all" is a *predeterminer*.

pre·dic·a·ment /prɪˈdɪkəmənt/ *noun, pl* **-ments** [*count*] : a difficult or unpleasant situation ▪ The governor has gotten himself into quite a *predicament*. ▪ I don't know how to get out of the *predicament* I'm in.

[1]**pred·i·cate** /ˈprɛdəˌkeɪt/ *verb* **-cates; -cat·ed; -cat·ing** [+ *obj*] *formal* : to base (something) *on* or *upon* something else — usually used as *(be) predicated* ▪ His theory *is predicated on* faulty assumptions.

[2]**pred·i·cate** /ˈprɛdəkət/ *noun, pl* **-cates** [*count*] *grammar* : the part of a sentence that expresses what is said about the subject ▪ In the sentence "The child threw the ball," the subject is "the child" and the *predicate* is "threw the ball."

[3]**pred·i·cate** /ˈprɛdəkət/ *adj, always used before a noun, grammar* : used after a linking verb to describe a noun that comes before the verb ▪ In "the sun is hot," "hot" is a *predicate* adjective. — compare ATTRIBUTIVE

pred·i·ca·tive /ˈprɛdəkətɪv, *Brit* prɪˈdɪkətɪv/ *adj, grammar* : [3]PREDICATE ▪ a *predicative* adjective
– **pred·i·ca·tive·ly** *adv*

pre·dict /prɪˈdɪkt/ *verb* **-dicts; -dict·ed; -dict·ing** [+ *obj*]

P

: to say that (something) will or might happen in the future • All the local forecasters are *predicting* rain for this afternoon. • She claims that she can *predict* future events. • It's hard to *predict* how the election will turn out. • Many people *predicted* that the store would fail, but it has done very well. • She won the election, as I *predicted* (she would). • Sales are *predicted* to be the same as last year.

pre·dict·able /prɪˈdɪktəbəl/ *adj* [*more* ~; *most* ~]
1 : capable of being known before happening or being done • The results of the study were completely *predictable*. [=the results were exactly what we guessed or expected they would be] • They did their work at a steady and *predictable* rate. • She writes novels with very *predictable* plots.
2 : behaving in a way that is expected • I knew he would say that. He's so *predictable*.
– **pre·dict·abil·i·ty** /prɪˌdɪktəˈbɪləti/ *noun* [*noncount*] • We were disappointed by the *predictability* of the movie. – **pre·dict·ably** /prɪˈdɪktəbli/ *adv* • They work quickly and *predictably*. • It was a *predictably* bad movie. [=it was not surprising that the movie was bad] • *Predictably* [=as you would expect], he denied knowing anything about the scandal.

pre·dic·tion /prɪˈdɪkʃən/ *noun, pl* **-tions**
1 [*count*] **:** a statement about what will happen or might happen in the future • Journalists have begun making *predictions* about the winner of the coming election. • Despite *predictions* that the store would fail, it has done very well.
2 [*noncount*] **:** the act of saying what will happen in the future **:** the act of predicting something • The figures and statistics are used for the *prediction* of future economic trends.

pre·dic·tive /prɪˈdɪktɪv/ *adj* [*more* ~; *most* ~] *formal* **:** making it possible to predict what will happen **:** useful in the prediction of something • The test does not have much *predictive* value. • High blood pressure is *predictive* of future heart problems.

pre·dic·tor /prɪˈdɪktɚ/ *noun, pl* **-tors** [*count*] *formal* **:** something that shows whether or not something is likely to happen **:** something that is useful in the prediction of something — often + *of* • High blood pressure can be a strong *predictor* [=*indicator*] *of* future heart problems.

pre·di·lec·tion /ˌprɛdəˈlɛkʃən, *Brit* ˌpriːdəˈlɛkʃən/ *noun, pl* **-tions** [*count*] *formal* **:** a natural liking for something **:** a tendency to do or to be attracted to something • She followed her own *predilections*. [=she did the things she liked/wanted to do] — often + *for* • They shared a *predilection for* adventure stories. • He has a *predilection for* trouble. [=he often gets into trouble]

pre·dis·pose /ˌpriːdɪˈspoʊz/ *verb* **-pos·es; -posed; -pos·ing** [+ *obj*] *formal* **:** to cause (someone) to be more likely to behave in a particular way or to be affected by a particular condition • Past experiences have *predisposed* her to distrust people. • Researchers have identified a gene that may *predispose* some people to (develop/developing) the disease. — often used as *(be) predisposed* • Researchers have determined that some patients *are* genetically *predisposed* to (develop/developing) the disease. • He believes that some people *are predisposed* to/toward criminal behavior.
– **pre·dis·po·si·tion** /ˌpriːˌdɪspəˈzɪʃən/ *noun, pl* **-tions** [*count*] — usually singular • He has a *predisposition* to be cynical. • patients with a *predisposition* toward cancer [*noncount*] She is at risk for breast cancer because of genetic *predisposition*.

pre·dom·i·nance /prɪˈdɑːmənəns/ *noun*
1 [*noncount*] **:** the state of being more powerful or important than other people or things • a group of young reformers who have gained/won *predominance* within the government • The tribe fought to maintain its *predominance*.
2 [*singular*] **:** a situation in which there is a greater number or amount of a particular type of person or thing than of other people or things — often + *of* • There is a *predominance of* older people in the neighborhood. [=most of the people in the neighborhood are older]

pre·dom·i·nant /prɪˈdɑːmənənt/ *adj* [*more* ~; *most* ~] **:** more important, powerful, successful, or noticeable than other people or things • Red is the *predominant* [=*main*] color in the painting. • Religion is the *predominant* theme of the play. • She is *predominant* among new writers. • Older people are *predominant* in that neighborhood. [=most of the people in that neighborhood are older]
– **pre·dom·i·nant·ly** *adv* • The speech was *predominantly* [=*mainly, primarily*] about tax cuts. • The people in that neighborhood are *predominantly* [=*mostly*] older.

[1]**pre·dom·i·nate** /prɪˈdɑːməˌneɪt/ *verb* **-nates; -nat·ed; -nat·ing** [*no obj*]
1 : to be more successful or powerful than other people or things — often + *over* • One ethnic group *predominates over* others in that country.
2 : to be greater in number or amount than other types of people or things • Cottages *predominate* along the beach. [=most of the buildings along the beach are cottages] • Older people *predominate* in that neighborhood. • Rain *predominates* [=there is a great deal of rain] in the tropical regions.

[2]**pre·dom·i·nate** /prɪˈdɑːmənət/ *adj* [*more* ~; *most* ~] **:** PREDOMINANT • the *predominate* color in the painting • the *predominate* reason for the change
– **pre·dom·i·nate·ly** /prɪˈdɑːmənətli/ *adv* • The people in that neighborhood are *predominately* [=*mostly, predominantly*] older.

pre·eclamp·sia /ˌpriːjɪˈklæmpsijə/ *noun* [*noncount*] *medical* **:** a serious condition that causes a pregnant women to develop very high blood pressure — called also *toxemia*

pree·mie /ˈpriːmi/ *noun, pl* **-mies** [*count*] *US, informal* **:** a baby that is born before it has fully developed **:** a premature baby

pre·em·i·nent /priˈɛmənənt/ *adj* [*more* ~; *most* ~] *formal* **:** more important, skillful, or successful than others **:** better than others • She's the *preeminent* chef in a city that has many good ones. • The poem is a *preeminent* example of his work.
– **pre·em·i·nence** /priˈɛmənəns/ *noun* [*noncount*] • the nation's *preeminence* in world affairs • military *preeminence*

pre·em·i·nent·ly /priˈɛmənəntli/ *adv, formal* **:** to a very great degree • He is *preeminently* qualified for the position.

pre·empt /priˈɛmpt/ *verb* **-empts; -empt·ed; -empt·ing** [+ *obj*]
1 *formal* **:** to prevent (something) from happening • The contract *preempts* lawsuits by the company's clients.
2 *formal* **:** to take the place of (something) • The state law was *preempted* by a federal law.
3 *US* **:** to be shown instead of (another television program) • The President's speech *preempted* regular programming.
– **pre·emp·tion** /priˈɛmpʃən/ *noun, pl* **-tions** [*noncount*] federal *preemption* of state jurisdiction • Some viewers complained about the *preemption* of regular programming. [*count*] *preemptions* of regular programming

pre·emp·tive /priˈɛmptɪv/ *adj* **:** done to stop an unwanted act by another group, country, etc., from happening • The country took *preemptive* action against the perceived enemy. • a *preemptive* attack/strike by the army
– **pre·emp·tive·ly** *adv*

preen /ˈpriːn/ *verb* **preens; preened; preen·ing**
1 *of a bird* **:** to use the beak to clean and arrange feathers [+ *obj*] The bird was *preening* its feathers. = The bird was *preening* itself. [*no obj*] The bird was *preening*.
2 : to make (yourself) neat and tidy [+ *obj*] She stood *preening* herself in front of the mirror. [*no obj*] She stood *preening* in front of the mirror.
3 *disapproving* **:** to act in a way that shows you are very proud about something or pleased with yourself [*no obj*] The award-winners were *preening* backstage. [+ *obj*] They are *preening* themselves on their success.

pre·ex·ist·ing /ˌpriːɪgˈzɪstɪŋ/ *adj* **:** existing at an earlier time **:** existing before something else • The insurance does not cover *preexisting* medical conditions. • They made changes to the *preexisting* law.

pre·ex·is·tent /ˌpriːɪgˈzɪstənt/ *adj* **:** PREEXISTING

[1]**pre·fab** /ˌpriːˈfæb/ *adj, informal* **:** PREFABRICATED • a *prefab* home

[2]**prefab** *noun, pl* **-fabs** [*count*] *informal* **:** a prefabricated building (such as a house) • The company sells hundreds of *prefabs* every year.

pre·fab·ri·cated /ˌpriːˈfæbrɪˌkeɪtəd/ *adj* **:** made of parts that are made at a factory and that can be put together later • *prefabricated* buildings/houses

[1]**pref·ace** /ˈprɛfəs/ *noun, pl* **-ac·es** [*count*] **:** an introduction to a book or speech • The book's *preface* was written by the author.

[2]**preface** *verb* **-aces; -aced; -ac·ing** [+ *obj*] **:** to introduce (a piece of writing, a speech, a remark, etc.) by writing or saying something • Each chapter in the book is *prefaced* by a suitable quotation. [=there is a suitable quotation at the beginning of each chapter] — often + *with* • She *prefaces* the book *with* a short account of what influenced her to write it. • He *prefaced* his remarks *with* a short biographical sketch.

P

pref·a·tory /ˈprɛfəˌtori, *Brit* ˈprɛfətri/ *adj, always used before a noun, formal* **:** included at the beginning of a book, speech, etc., as an introduction ▪ The speaker made some *prefatory* remarks. ▪ Each chapter in the book has a *prefatory* quotation.

pre·fect /ˈpriːˌfɛkt/ *noun, pl* **-fects** [*count*]
1 : a chief officer or government official who is responsible for a particular area in some countries (such as Japan and France)
2 *chiefly Brit* **:** an older student who is given the job of helping to watch and control younger students in a school

pre·fec·ture /ˈpriːˌfɛktʃɚ/ *noun, pl* **-tures** [*count*] **:** any one of the areas into which some countries (such as Japan and France) are divided for local government **:** the area that is governed by a prefect

pre·fer /prɪˈfɚ/ *verb* **-fers; -ferred; -fer·ring** [+ *obj*]
1 : to like (someone or something) better than someone or something else ▪ Some people like vanilla ice cream, but I *prefer* chocolate. ▪ I *prefer* shopping online. ▪ She tends to *prefer* small college campuses. ▪ I *prefer* this dictionary because of its helpful examples. ▪ I would *prefer* it if you smoked outside. = I would *prefer* you to smoke outside. ▪ Which one is the *preferred* alternative? ▪ What is the *preferred* pronunciation of her name? — often + *to* or *over* ▪ He *prefers* sports *to* reading. ▪ He *prefers* a good book *to* a movie. ▪ She *prefers* chocolate *over* vanilla. — often followed by *to* + *verb* ▪ I suggested that we play a game, but they *preferred to watch* TV. ▪ I would *prefer* not *to know* about it.
2 *law* **:** to make (a charge) against someone in a court of law ▪ They *preferred* [=*brought*] charges against him for manslaughter. [=they formally accused him of the crime of manslaughter]

pref·er·a·ble /ˈprɛfrəbəl/ *adj* [*more* ~; *most* ~] **:** better or more desirable ▪ the *preferable* choice — often + *to* ▪ As far as I'm concerned, physical therapy is greatly/infinitely *preferable to* surgery. ▪ The book is far/much *preferable to* the movie. [=is much better than the movie]

pref·er·a·bly /ˈprɛfrəbli/ *adv* — used to say what is most wanted or preferred ▪ I'd like to have the work done soon, *preferably* by the end of the week. ▪ Applicants should hold a college degree, *preferably* with experience in the lab.

pref·er·ence /ˈprɛfrəns/ *noun, pl* **-enc·es**
1 : a feeling of liking or wanting one person or thing more than another person or thing [*count*] Car buyers have recently shown a growing/strong *preference* for smaller vehicles. ▪ When it comes to music, everyone has their own *preferences*. [*noncount*] Some people like small cars and some people like big cars. It's a matter of personal *preference*. ▪ She listed her favorite restaurants in order of *preference*. ▪ He has tried not to show *preference* in giving out jobs.
2 [*noncount*] **:** an advantage that is given to some people or things and not to others ▪ The policy of the school is to ***give preference*** to minority candidates.
3 [*count*] **:** something that is liked or wanted more than another thing **:** something that is preferred ▪ We could drive to New York, but my (personal) *preference* is to go by train. [=I would prefer to go by train] ▪ "We could go to an Italian or Chinese restaurant tonight. What's your *preference*?" "Either one is fine. I don't have a *preference*."
4 : the sexual feelings that a person has **:** a person's identity as homosexual, bisexual, or heterosexual [*count*] people with different (sexual) *preferences* [=*orientations*] [*noncount*] The company claims it does not discriminate on the basis of sexual *preference*.
in preference to **:** instead of (something or someone) **:** rather than (something or someone) ▪ They chose her *in preference to* me.

pref·er·en·tial /ˌprɛfəˈrɛnʃəl/ *adj* [*more* ~; *most* ~] **:** giving an advantage to a particular person or group ▪ powerful people who demand/get/receive ***preferential treatment*** from politicians
– **pref·er·en·tial·ly** *adv* ▪ The manager's friends are treated *preferentially*.

pre·fer·ment /prɪˈfɚmənt/ *noun* [*noncount*] *formal* **:** the act of moving someone to a higher or more important position or rank in an organization ▪ He has hopes for *preferment*.

preferred provider *noun, pl* ~ **-ers** [*count*] *US* **:** a doctor, hospital, etc., that is part of a PPO

preferred provider organization *noun, pl* ~ **-tions** [*count*] *US* **:** PPO

pre·fig·ure /ˌpriːˈfɪgjɚ, *Brit* ˌpriːˈfɪgə/ *verb* **-ures; -ured; -ur·ing** [+ *obj*] *formal* **:** to show or suggest (something that will happen or exist at a future time) ▪ His style of painting *prefigured* the development of modern art.

[1]**pre·fix** /ˈpriːˌfɪks/ *noun, pl* **-fix·es** [*count*]
1 : a letter or group of letters that is added at the beginning of a word to change its meaning ▪ Add the *prefix* "re-" to form the words "retell" and "recall." — compare AFFIX, SUFFIX
2 *old-fashioned* **:** a title (such as "Mr." or "Dr.") that is used before a person's name

[2]**pre·fix** /ˌpriːˈfɪks/ *verb* **-fix·es; -fixed; -fix·ing** [+ *obj*] **:** to add a letter, number, or symbol at the beginning of a word or number ▪ *Prefix* "un" to "do" to form the word "undo." ▪ The cost of the item was *prefixed* by/with a dollar sign.

pre·game /ˈpriːˈgeɪm/ *adj, always used before a noun, US* **:** happening before the beginning of a sports game ▪ a *pregame* interview

preg·nan·cy /ˈprɛgnənsi/ *noun, pl* **-cies :** the condition of a woman or female animal that is going to have a baby or babies **:** the condition of a pregnant woman or female animal [*count*] women who have had multiple *pregnancies* [=women who have been pregnant many times] ▪ an unwanted/unplanned *pregnancy* [*noncount*] She's being careful about what she eats during (her) *pregnancy*. ▪ a ***pregnancy test*** [=a medical test to see if a woman is pregnant]

preg·nant /ˈprɛgnənt/ *adj*
1 *of a woman or female animal* **:** having a baby or babies developing inside the body ▪ *pregnant* women ▪ She got/became *pregnant* soon after her marriage. ▪ He got his girlfriend *pregnant*. [=he caused his girlfriend to become pregnant] — often + *with* ▪ His wife is *pregnant with* twins. [=she is going to give birth to twins] ▪ She is *pregnant with* her first child.
2 *formal* **:** filled with meaning or emotion because of what is going to happen or be said ▪ There was a *pregnant* pause/silence before the winner was announced. — often + *with* ▪ The moment was *pregnant with* excitement.

pre·heat /ˌpriːˈhiːt/ *verb* **-heats; -heat·ed; -heat·ing** [+ *obj*] **:** to heat (an oven) to a particular temperature before putting food to be cooked inside ▪ *Preheat* the oven to 375 degrees before you put the roast in.

pre·hen·sile /priːˈhɛnsəl, *Brit* priːˈhɛnsajəl/ *adj, technical* **:** capable of grabbing or holding something by wrapping around it ▪ The monkey has a *prehensile* tail. ▪ The elephant has a *prehensile* trunk.

pre·his·tor·ic /ˌpriːhɪˈstorɪk/ *also* **pre·his·tor·i·cal** /ˌpriːhɪˈstorɪkəl/ *adj*
1 : of, relating to, or existing in the time before people could write ▪ *prehistoric* animals/remains ▪ *prehistoric* times
2 [*more* ~; *most* ~] *informal* + *disapproving* **:** very old or outdated ▪ His attitudes about women are downright *prehistoric*.

pre·his·to·ry /ˌpriːˈhɪstəri/ *noun, pl* **-to·ries**
1 [*noncount*] **:** the period of time in the past before people could write **:** the time before history was written down ▪ We are learning about the *prehistory* of North America.
2 [*count*] **:** the time and events that came before and led to the development of something — usually singular ▪ the *prehistory* of the Internet

pre·judge /ˌpriːˈdʒʌdʒ/ *verb* **-judg·es; -judged; -judg·ing** [+ *obj*] **:** to form an opinion about (someone or something) before you have enough understanding or knowledge ▪ Officials complain that some reporters have *prejudged* the outcome of the investigation. ▪ She was wrong for *prejudging* him.

[1]**prej·u·dice** /ˈprɛdʒədəs/ *noun, pl* **-dic·es**
1 : an unfair feeling of dislike for a person or group because of race, sex, religion, etc. [*noncount*] The organization fights against racial *prejudice*. — often + *against* ▪ evidence of *prejudice against* women and minorities [*count*] religious, racial, and sexual *prejudices*
2 [*count*] **:** a feeling of like or dislike for someone or something especially when it is not reasonable or logical ▪ We tend to make these kinds of decisions according to our own *prejudices*. ▪ He has a *prejudice* against fast-food restaurants.

[2]**prejudice** *verb* **-dices; -diced; -dic·ing** [+ *obj*]
1 : to cause (someone) to have an unfair feeling of dislike for someone or something ▪ The incident *prejudiced* [=*biased*] consumers against the company.
2 *formal* **:** to have a harmful effect on (something, such as a legal case) ▪ The defense claims that the media coverage *prejudiced* the trial. [=damaged the trial so that the result of the trial is not valid]

prejudiced *adj* [*more* ~; *most* ~]
1 : having or showing an unfair feeling of dislike for a per-

P

son or group because of race, sex, religion, etc. ▪ a *prejudiced* person ▪ *prejudiced* comments ▪ Most Americans deny being *prejudiced* against people of other races.

2 : having a feeling or like or dislike for something or someone ▪ I was *prejudiced* against the movie because of its title.

prej·u·di·cial /ˌprɛʤəˈdɪʃəl/ *adj* [*more* ~; *most* ~]

1 : showing an unfair feeling of dislike for a person or group because of race, sex, religion, etc. : showing prejudice ▪ *prejudicial* feelings

2 *formal* : causing or likely to cause injury or harm to someone or something ▪ The judge ruled that the *prejudicial* effect of the evidence outweighed its value. — often + *to* ▪ The appeals court ruled that the testimony was unfairly *prejudicial to* the defendant.

pre–K /ˈpriːˈkeɪ/ *noun* [*noncount*] *US* : PREKINDERGARTEN ▪ Her daughter is in *pre-K* this year.

pre·kin·der·gar·ten /ˌpriːˈkɪndɚˌgɑɚtn̩/ *noun* [*count, noncount*] *US*

1 : a class or program that is for children who are usually three or four years old

2 : PRESCHOOL

prel·ate /ˈprɛlət/ *noun, pl* **-ates** [*count*] *formal* : a high-ranking Christian priest : a bishop, cardinal, etc.

[1]**pre·lim·i·nary** /prɪˈlɪməˌneri, *Brit* prɪˈlɪmənri/ *adj* : coming before the main part of something ▪ *Preliminary* findings/studies/tests show that the drug could help patients with skin cancer. ▪ The *preliminary* [=*early*] results of the experiment are encouraging. ▪ a *preliminary* hearing ▪ The team was eliminated in the *preliminary* round of the tournament. ▪ research that is *preliminary* to the study

[2]**preliminary** *noun, pl* **-nar·ies** [*count*]

1 : something that comes first in order to prepare for or introduce the main part of something else — often + *to* ▪ There will be a short briefing about topics to be discussed as a *preliminary to* the meeting. — usually plural ▪ There were the usual *preliminaries* before the ceremony.

2 : a game that is played before the main part of a competition to decide which players or teams will be allowed to continue playing — usually plural ▪ the World Cup *preliminaries*

pre·lude /ˈprɛlˌjuːd/ *noun, pl* **-ludes** [*count*]

1 : something that comes before and leads to something else — usually singular; often + *to* ▪ The dark clouds were a *prelude to* the storm. ▪ Drinks and appetizers were offered as a *prelude to* dinner.

2 : a short piece of music that introduces a longer piece

pre·mar·i·tal /ˌpriːˈmerətl̩/ *adj, always used before a noun* : happening before marriage ▪ *premarital* sex ▪ *premarital* counseling

pre·ma·ture /ˌpriːməˈtuɚ, ˌpriːməˈʧuɚ, *Brit* ˈprɛməʧə/ *adj*

1 : happening too soon or earlier than usual ▪ Her *premature* death at age 30 stunned her family and friends. ▪ Too much exposure to the sun can cause the *premature* aging of skin. ▪ His retirement seems *premature*. ▪ It is *premature* to say [=too soon to say] what the cause of the fire was. ▪ a *premature* birth

2 : born before the normal time ▪ *premature* babies ▪ The baby was three weeks *premature*. [=the baby was born three weeks before it was expected to be born]

– pre·ma·ture·ly *adv* ▪ She died *prematurely*. ▪ He was *prematurely* gray. = His hair went gray *prematurely*. ▪ The child was born *prematurely*.

pre·med /ˈpriːˈmɛd/ *noun* [*noncount*] *US* : a course of study at a college or university that prepares students to enter medical school ▪ She majored in *premed*.

– premed *adj, always used before a noun* ▪ *premed* students/classes

pre·med·i·tat·ed /ˌpriːˈmɛdəˌteɪtəd/ *adj* : done or made according to a plan : planned in advance ▪ *premeditated* murder ▪ The attack was *premeditated*.

pre·men·stru·al /ˌpriːˈmɛnstrəwəl/ *adj* : happening just before a woman's menstrual period : before menstruation ▪ *premenstrual* symptoms

premenstrual syndrome *noun* [*noncount*] : a condition experienced by some women before menstruation that may include tiredness, irritability, anxiety, depression, headache, and stomach pain — called also *(US) PMS, (Brit) PMT, (Brit) premenstrual tension*

[1]**pre·mier** /prɪˈmiɚ, *Brit* ˈprɛmiə/ *noun, pl* **-miers** [*count*] : PRIME MINISTER ▪ the Russian *premier*

> Do not confuse *premier* with *premiere*.

[2]**premier** *adj, always used before a noun* : most important or best ▪ the city's *premier* restaurant ▪ a concert by one of the world's *premier* [=*leading*] pianists

[1]**pre·miere** *also* **pre·mière** /prɪˈmiɚ, *Brit* ˈprɛmiˌɛə/ *noun, pl* **-mieres** *also* **-mières** [*count*] : the first time a film, play, television show, etc., is shown or performed ▪ The movie will have its *premiere* next week. ▪ We saw the Chicago *premiere* of the play. [=the first public performance of the play in Chicago] ▪ the ***world premiere*** [=the first public performance anywhere in the world] of a new symphony

> Do not confuse *premiere* with *premier*.

[2]**premiere** *also* **première** *verb* **-mieres** *also* **-mières**; **-miered** *also* **-mièred**; **-mier·ing** *also* **-mièr·ing**

1 [*no obj*] *of a movie, play, television show, etc.* : to be shown or performed for the first time ▪ The movie/play *premieres* next week.

2 [+ *obj*] : to show or perform (a movie, play, television show, etc.) for the first time — usually used as *(be) premiered* ▪ The movie *was premiered* at a film festival.

pre·mier·ship /prɪˈmiɚˌʃɪp, *Brit* ˈprɛmiəˌʃɪp/ *noun, pl* **-ships** [*count*] : the job of a prime minister or the period of time when a person is prime minister — usually singular ▪ a businessman who is seeking the *premiership* [=trying to be elected prime minister] ▪ Her *premiership* ends this year.

prem·ise /ˈprɛməs/ *noun, pl* **-is·es**

1 ***premises*** [*plural*] : a building and the area of land that it is on ▪ They were asked to leave the *premises*. ▪ The company leases part of the *premises* to smaller businesses. ▪ The *premises* were searched by the police.

2 *also Brit* **pre·miss** [*count*] *formal* : a statement or idea that is accepted as being true and that is used as the basis of an argument ▪ He disagreed with her *premise*. ▪ the basic *premises* of the argument ▪ a theory based on the simple *premise* that what goes up must come down

off the premises *also* ***off premises*** : away from or outside of a building or on the area of land that it is on ▪ Police escorted her *off the premises*. ▪ The printing of the books is done *off the premises*. [=at another place]

on the premises *also* ***on premises*** : inside a building or on the area of land that it is on ▪ The hotel has a restaurant *on the premises*. [=inside the hotel] ▪ No smoking is allowed *on the premises*.

pre·mised /ˈprɛməst/ *adj*

premised on/upon : based on (a particular idea or belief) ▪ The plan is *premised on* the belief that people are willing to pay more to use alternative fuel sources.

[1]**pre·mi·um** /ˈpriːmijəm/ *noun, pl* **-ums**

1 [*count*] : the price of insurance ▪ Health insurance *premiums* went up again this year. : the amount paid for insurance ▪ The monthly *premium* for your health insurance is deducted from your paycheck.

2 [*singular*] : a price that is higher than the regular price ▪ There is a *premium* [=higher price] for hotel rooms that have views of the beach. ▪ Many customers are willing to pay a *premium* for organic vegetables. ▪ Land in the county is selling ***at a premium***. [=for a high price] — see also AT A PREMIUM (below)

3 [*singular*] : a high or extra value ▪ Publishers ***put/place a premium*** on accuracy. [=publishers value accuracy very highly]

at a premium : difficult to get because there is little available ▪ We bought bunk beds because space in the apartment is *at a premium*. ▪ Overnight delivery is available when time is *at a premium*. [=when something needs to happen or be done very soon]

[2]**premium** *adj, always used before a noun*

1 : high or higher than normal ▪ Customers are willing to pay *premium* [=*high*] prices for products that are reliable. ▪ The hotel charges *premium* [=*higher*] rates during the summer.

2 : of high or higher than normal quality ▪ *premium* cigars/gasoline

pre·mo·ni·tion /ˌpriːməˈnɪʃən/ *noun, pl* **-tions** [*count*] : a feeling or belief that something is going to happen when there is no definite reason to believe it will ▪ *premonitions* of disaster ▪ She had a *premonition* that he would call.

pre·na·tal /ˌpriːˈneɪtl̩/ *adj, always used before a noun, medical* : relating to pregnant women and their unborn babies ▪ *prenatal* [=*(Brit) antenatal*] care/development/testing/diagnosis ▪ *prenatal* vitamins

– pre·na·tal·ly *adv* ▪ The baby was tested *prenatally* for hereditary diseases.

P

pre·nup /ˈpriːˌnʌp/ *noun, pl* **-nups** [*count*] : PRENUPTIAL AGREEMENT

pre·nup·tial agreement /ˌpriːˈnʌpʃəl-/ *noun, pl* ~ **-ments** [*count*] *law* : an official agreement that two people make before they marry in which they state how much of each other's property each will receive if they divorce or if one of them dies ▪ Did you sign a *prenuptial agreement*? [=*prenup*]

pre·oc·cu·pa·tion /ˌpriːˌɑːkjəˈpeɪʃən/ *noun, pl* **-tions** [*count*]
1 : a state in which you give all your attention to something — usually + *with* ▪ I don't understand her *preoccupation with* her appearance.
2 : something that you give all or most of your attention to ▪ We need to better understand the problems and *preoccupations* of our clients.

pre·oc·cu·pied /ˌpriːˈɑːkjəˌpaɪd/ *adj* [*more* ~; *most* ~] : thinking about something a lot or too much — often + *with* ▪ She is too *preoccupied with* family problems to focus on her work.

pre·oc·cu·py /ˌpriːˈɑːkjəˌpaɪ/ *verb* **-pies**; **-pied**; **-py·ing** [+ *obj*] : to be thought about or worried about by (someone) very often or constantly ▪ The question of life after death has *preoccupied* many philosophers. ▪ Her family problems continue to *preoccupy* her. [=she continues to spend a lot of time thinking/worrying about her family problems]

pre–op /ˈpriːˈɑːp/ *adj, medical* : PREOPERATIVE ▪ a *pre-op* evaluation/consultation

pre·op·er·a·tive /ˌpriːˈɑːprətɪv/ *adj, medical* : happening before an operation ▪ *preoperative* assessment/diagnosis/care

pre·or·dained /ˌpriːjoɚˈdeɪnd/ *adj, formal* : decided in advance and certain to happen ▪ a *preordained* conclusion ▪ Although such an outcome is likely, it is by no means *preordained*. [=it is not certain]

pre–owned /ˌpriːˈoʊnd/ *adj* : owned by someone else before : previously owned ▪ They sell quality *pre-owned* [=*used, secondhand*] cars. ▪ The car is *pre-owned*.

¹prep /ˈprɛp/ *verb* **preps**; **prepped**; **prep·ping** *US, informal* : PREPARE: such as **a** : to make yourself ready for something — usually + *for* [*no obj*] She spent all night *prepping for* the test. [+ *obj*] The runners are *prepping* themselves *for* the race. **b** [+ *obj*] : to make (someone or something) ready for something ▪ It took me about 20 minutes to *prep* the vegetables. — often + *for* ▪ Teachers spent the week *prepping* students *for* the test. ▪ The patient is being *prepped for* surgery.

²prep *noun* [*noncount*] *informal*
1 *US* : PREPARATION ▪ Painting a room involves a lot of *prep*. — usually used before another noun ▪ These recipes require minimal *prep* time. [=you need only a little time to make these recipes] ▪ college *prep* courses [=classes that students take to get ready for college]
2 *US* : PREP SCHOOL — usually used before another noun ▪ *prep* students [=students who attend a prep school] ▪ *prep* sports
3 *Brit* : HOMEWORK

³prep *abbr* preposition

pre·pack /ˌpriːˈpæk/ *verb* **-packs**; **-packed**; **-pack·ing** [+ *obj*] : PREPACKAGE — usually used as *(be) prepacked* ▪ The sandwiches *are prepacked*. ▪ *prepacked* meals

pre·pack·age /ˌpriːˈpækɪʤ/ *verb* **-ag·es**; **-aged**; **-ag·ing** [+ *obj*] : to put (a product) in a package before selling it — usually used as *(be) prepackaged* ▪ The meals *are prepackaged* and ready to eat. ▪ *prepackaged* software ▪ *prepackaged* salads — sometimes used figuratively ▪ a *prepackaged* speech [=a speech that is not original or special]

prepaid *past tense and past participle of* PREPAY

prep·a·ra·tion /ˌprɛpəˈreɪʃən/ *noun, pl* **-tions**
1 [*noncount*] : the activity or process of making something ready or of becoming ready for something ▪ The festival involves a lot of *preparation*. ▪ food/meal *preparation* ▪ To complete this recipe, plan on about 30 minutes of *preparation* and 40 minutes of baking. ▪ Plans for the next edition are already ***in preparation***. [=are already being prepared/made] — often + *for* ▪ Her *preparation for* the role included training in karate. ▪ The boxer exercised daily ***in preparation for*** the fight. [=to prepare for the fight]
2 ***preparations*** [*plural*] : things that are done to make something ready or to become ready for something ▪ The staff is ***making preparations*** to move to another building. [=the staff is doing things to become ready to move to another building] ▪ ***Preparations are under way*** [=things are being done to become ready] for the move to the new building. — often + *for* ▪ *Preparations for* the parade are almost completed. ▪ They are busy with *preparations for* their wedding.
3 [*count*] : a substance (such as a cream or lotion) that you use as medicine or to improve your appearance ▪ a vitamin E *preparation* ▪ skin care *preparations*

pre·pa·ra·to·ry /prɪˈperəˌtori, *Brit* prɪˈpærətri/ *adj, always used before a noun* : used or done to prepare for something ▪ The new employees have begun *preparatory* [=*introductory*] training. ▪ There is a lot of *preparatory* work involved in teaching.
preparatory to formal : as a way of becoming ready for (something) : in preparation for (something) ▪ *Preparatory to* the job interview, I researched the company.

preparatory school *noun, pl* ~ **schools** [*count*] : PREP SCHOOL

pre·pare /prɪˈpeɚ/ *verb* **-pares**; **-pared**; **-par·ing**
1 a [+ *obj*] : to make (someone or something) ready for some activity, purpose, use, etc. ▪ The teacher *prepared* the students for the test. ▪ Your room is being *prepared* now and should be ready soon. ▪ The nurses *prepared* the patient for surgery. ▪ Farmers are busy *preparing* the soil for planting. **b** : to make yourself ready for something that you will be doing, something that you expect to happen, etc. [*no obj*] They'll be arriving soon. We don't have much more time to *prepare*. — often + *for* ▪ We don't have much more time to *prepare for* their arrival. ▪ He *prepares for* games by studying tapes of the opposing team. ▪ At this time of year, most animals are *preparing for* winter. [+ *obj*] We don't have much more time to *prepare* ourselves *for* their arrival. ▪ She tried to *prepare* herself *for* bad news. ▪ The sailors are *preparing* themselves *for* a long voyage.
2 [+ *obj*] : to make or create (something) so that it is ready for use ▪ She *prepared* [=*made*] dinner. ▪ *Prepare* a salad. ▪ He *prepared* [=*wrote*] a report for his boss. ▪ The pharmacist *prepared* the prescription.

prepared *adj*
1 : made at an earlier time for later use : made ready in advance ▪ The president read a *prepared* statement. ▪ The store sells a selection of *prepared* foods.
2 : ready for something : in a suitable condition for some purpose or activity ▪ I got so nervous. I guess I just wasn't *prepared*. ▪ She was well-*prepared* and scored high on the test. — often + *for* ▪ Be *prepared* [=*ready*] *for* a long wait. ▪ The campers were not *prepared for* the rain.
3 *not used before a noun* : willing *to do* something ▪ How much are you *prepared to pay*? ▪ I wasn't *prepared to spend* that much money. ▪ I'm *prepared to listen*.

pre·pared·ness /prɪˈperədnəs/ *noun* [*noncount*] *formal* : the fact of being ready for something : the state of being prepared ▪ The police have been criticized for their lack of *preparedness*. [=for not being prepared] ▪ emergency *preparedness* [=being ready for an emergency] ▪ The military is in a state of *preparedness*.

pre·pay /ˌpriːˈpeɪ/ *verb* **-pays**; **-paid** /-ˈpeɪd/; **-pay·ing** [+ *obj*]
1 : to pay for (something) before you receive or use it ▪ Special orders must be *prepaid*.
2 : to pay (something) before you are required to pay it ▪ There is no penalty for *prepaying* the loan. [=for paying what you owe sooner than you have agreed to]
– prepaid *adj* ▪ a *prepaid* calling card ▪ a *prepaid* envelope [=an envelope for which the postage has already been paid]
– pre·pay·ment /ˌpriːˈpeɪmənt/ *noun, pl* **-ments** [*count*] loan *prepayments* [*noncount*] We have the option of *prepayment* without a penalty. — often used before another noun ▪ a *prepayment* penalty

pre·pon·der·ance /prɪˈpɑːndərəns/ *noun* [*singular*] *formal* : a greater amount or number of something ▪ A *preponderance* of the evidence [=most of the evidence] shows that the accused is guilty. ▪ The *preponderance* [=*majority*] of visitors to the museum are from outside the country.

pre·pon·der·ant /prɪˈpɑːndərənt/ *adj, formal* : greater in number, force, or importance ▪ A *preponderant* number of visitors [=most of the visitors] are from outside the country. ▪ the country's *preponderant* [=*dominant*] power
– pre·pon·der·ant·ly *adv* ▪ Visitors to the museum are *preponderantly* [=*predominantly*] foreign.

prep·o·si·tion /ˌprɛpəˈzɪʃən/ *noun, pl* **-tions** [*count*] *grammar* : a word or group of words that is used with a noun, pronoun, or noun phrase to show direction, location, or time, or to introduce an object ▪ The *preposition* "on" in "The keys are on the table" shows location. ▪ The *preposition* "in" in "The movie starts in one hour" shows time.

prep•o•si•tion•al phrase /ˌprɛpəˈzɪʃənl-/ *noun, pl* ~ **phrases** [*count*] *grammar* : a phrase that begins with a preposition and ends in a noun, pronoun, or noun phrase ▪ In "He is from Russia," "from Russia" is a *prepositional phrase*.

pre•pos•sess•ing /ˌpriːpəˈzɛsɪŋ/ *adj* [*more* ~; *most* ~] *somewhat formal* : having qualities that people like : appealing or attractive ▪ a *prepossessing* young musician ▪ She lives in one of the least *prepossessing* parts of the city.

pre•pos•ter•ous /prɪˈpɑːstərəs/ *adj* : very foolish or silly ▪ a *preposterous* excuse ▪ The whole idea is *preposterous*!
– **pre•pos•ter•ous•ly** *adv* ▪ The prices are *preposterously* [=*absurdly*] high. – **pre•pos•ter•ous•ness** *noun* [*noncount*] ▪ She laughed at the *preposterousness* [=*absurdity*] of my suggestion.

prep•py *or* **prep•pie** /ˈprɛpi/ *noun, pl* **-pies** [*count*] *US, informal + often disapproving* : someone who dresses or acts like a student at a prep school (such as by wearing neat, somewhat formal clothing or by using particular words and phrases) ▪ a rich *preppy*
– **preppy** *or* **preppie** *adj* ▪ *preppy* clothes

prep school *noun, pl* ~ **schools** [*count*]
1 *US* : a private school that prepares students for college
2 *Brit* : a private school for children between the ages of 7 and 13

pre•pu•bes•cent /ˌpriːpjuˈbɛsn̩t/ *adj, always used before a noun, formal* : relating to or being in the period of life just before puberty ▪ *prepubescent* growth ▪ *prepubescent* children

pre•quel /ˈpriːkwəl/ *noun, pl* **-quels** [*count*] : a movie, book, etc., that tells the part of a story that happened before the story in another movie, book, etc. ▪ His next film will be a *prequel* to last year's hit movie. — compare SEQUEL

pre•re•cord /ˌpriːrɪˈkoəd/ *verb* **-cords**; **-cord•ed**; **-cord•ing** [+ *obj*] : to record (something, such as a radio or television program) before showing it to the public, broadcasting it, etc. ▪ The television show *prerecords* most of its interviews. ▪ a *prerecorded* program/interview

pre•reg•is•ter /ˌpriːˈrɛʤəstɚ/ *verb* **-ters**; **-tered**; **-ter•ing** [*no obj*] *chiefly US* : to put your name on an official list in order to become a participant in something (such as a college course) before the usual time during which this list is made : to register before the official registration period ▪ Students can *preregister* online. — often + *for* ▪ I *preregistered for* the class.
– **pre•reg•is•tra•tion** /ˌpriːˌrɛʤəˈstreɪʃən/ *noun* [*noncount*] ▪ *Preregistration* begins tomorrow.

pre•req•ui•site /ˌpriːˈrɛkwəzət/ *noun, pl* **-sites** [*count*] : something that you officially must have or do before you can have or do something else : REQUIREMENT — often + *for* or *to* ▪ Citizenship is a *prerequisite for* voting. ▪ The introductory course is a *prerequisite for* the advanced-level courses. ▪ Having good credit is a *prerequisite to* applying for a loan.

pre•rog•a•tive /prɪˈrɑːgətɪv/ *noun, pl* **-tives** [*count*] *formal* : a right or privilege ▪ If you'd rather sell the tickets than use them, that's your *prerogative*. ▪ It's a writer's *prerogative* to decide the fate of her characters.; *especially* : a special right or privilege that some people have ▪ presidential *prerogatives* [=the rights or privileges a president has] — often + *of* ▪ Education was once only the *prerogative of* the wealthy.

pres. *abbr* **1** present **2** president

pre•sage /ˈprɛsɪʤ/ *verb* **-sag•es**; **-saged**; **-sag•ing** [+ *obj*] *formal* : to give or be a sign of (something that will happen or develop in the future) ▪ Many investors are worried that the current slowdown could *presage* another recession. ▪ events that *presaged* the civil rights movement

Pres•by•te•ri•an /ˌprɛzbəˈtirijən/ *adj* : of or relating to a Christian church in Scotland, the U.S., and other countries that is officially led by a group of ministers and elders (called a presbytery) ▪ a *Presbyterian* doctrine/church ▪ The minister is *Presbyterian*.
– **Presbyterian** *noun, pl* **-ans** [*count*] – **Pres•by•te•ri•an•ism** /ˌprɛzbəˈtirijəˌnɪzəm/ *noun* [*noncount*]

pres•by•tery /ˈprɛzbəˌteri, *Brit* ˈprɛzbətri/ *noun, pl* **-ter•ies** [*count*]
1 : a group of ministers and elders who are the leaders of the Presbyterian churches in a particular area
2 : the house where a Roman Catholic priest lives : RECTORY

[1]**pre•school** /ˈpriːˌskuːl/ *noun, pl* **-schools** [*count, noncount*] *chiefly US* : a school for very young children — called also *nursery school*

[2]**preschool** *adj, always used before a noun* : relating to the time in a child's life when the child is old enough to talk and walk but is not ready to go to school ▪ *preschool* age/education/children

pre•school•er /ˈpriˌskuːlɚ/ *noun, pl* **-ers** [*count*] *US*
1 : a child who is old enough to talk and walk but who is too young to go to school
2 : a child who goes to a preschool

pre•science /ˈprɛʃijəns, *Brit* ˈprɛsiəns/ *noun* [*noncount*] *formal* : the ability to know what will or might happen in the future : FORESIGHT ▪ He predicted their response with amazing *prescience*. ▪ Her *prescience* as an investor is impressive.

pre•scient /ˈprɛʃijənt, *Brit* ˈprɛsiənt/ *adj* [*more* ~; *most* ~] *formal* : having or showing an ability to know what will happen before it does ▪ She was remarkably *prescient* about the outcome of the elections. ▪ a *prescient* remark
– **pre•scient•ly** *adv*

pre•scribe /prɪˈskraɪb/ *verb* **-scribes**; **-scribed**; **-scrib•ing** [+ *obj*]
1 : to officially tell someone to use (a medicine, therapy, diet, etc.) as a remedy or treatment ▪ My doctor *prescribed* this medicine. = This medicine was *prescribed* by my doctor. ▪ This drug should not be *prescribed* to children. ▪ a drug commonly *prescribed* to treat rashes ▪ The doctor *prescribed* three months of physical therapy for my leg injury.
2 : to make (something) an official rule ▪ The law *prescribes* a prison sentence of at least five years for the crime. ▪ The regulations *prescribe* that all employees must pass a physical examination. ▪ We must follow the rules as *prescribed* by the government.
– **prescribed** *adj, always used before a noun* ▪ the *prescribed* dosage of a drug ▪ Members must obey the *prescribed* rules of conduct.

pre•scrip•tion /prɪˈskrɪpʃən/ *noun, pl* **-tions**
1 a : a written message from a doctor that officially tells someone to use a medicine, therapy, etc. [*count*] The drug is only sold with a *prescription*. — often + *for* ▪ The doctor wrote me a *prescription for* cough syrup. [*noncount*] (*US*) The drug is only available ***by prescription***. = (*Brit*) The drug is only available ***on prescription***. [=you can only get the drug if you have a prescription] **b** [*count*] : a medicine or drug that a doctor officially tells someone to use ▪ I have to pick up my *prescription*. — often used before another noun ▪ *prescription* drugs/medicine/costs
2 [*count*] : something that is suggested as a way to do something or to make something happen — + *for* ▪ a *prescription for* economic recovery ▪ a *prescription for* improving the educational system

pre•scrip•tive /prɪˈskrɪptɪv/ *adj*
1 [*more* ~; *most* ~] : giving exact rules, directions, or instructions about how you should do something ▪ Critics claim the new rules/regulations are too *prescriptive*.
2 *technical* : providing rules and opinions that tell people how language should be used ▪ *prescriptive* dictionaries — opposite DESCRIPTIVE

pre•sea•son /ˌpriːˈsiːzn̩/ *noun, pl* **-sons** [*count*] *sports* : a period of time before the regular season when players train and people or teams play against each other in unofficial games ▪ The team only won two games during the *preseason*. ▪ *preseason* training/games

pres•ence /ˈprɛzn̩s/ *noun, pl* **-enc•es**
1 [*count*] : the fact of being in a particular place : the state of being present — usually singular ▪ The test results showed the *presence* of bacteria in the water. [=showed that there were bacteria in the water] ▪ No one was aware of the stranger's *presence*. ▪ His very *presence* on the basketball court intimidated opponents. ▪ She talked about the growing *presence* of women in the construction industry. [=the increasing number of women working in the construction industry]
2 [*noncount*] : the area that is close to someone — used to describe being in the same place as someone ▪ Please don't smoke ***in my presence***. [=near me; when I am present] ▪ She asked them not to talk about the accident *in her presence*. ▪ Their daughter is shy ***in the presence of*** [=*around*] strangers. ▪ The contract was signed *in the presence of* two witnesses.
3 [*count*] : someone or something that is seen or noticed in a particular place, area, etc. — usually singular ▪ Her mother was a constant *presence* at the swim meets. [=her mother always went to the swim meets] ▪ There is a heavy military

P

presence in the city. [=there are a lot of soldiers, military vehicles, etc., in the city] • The company is an important *presence* on the Internet.

4 [*singular*] **: a way of moving, standing, speaking, etc.** • He'll be remembered as a caring teacher with a warm *presence*. [=a kind and gentle way of speaking, behaving, etc.] • an actor with a commanding *presence* on the stage = an actor with a commanding ***stage presence*** [=an actor with a powerful quality that attracts attention on the stage]

5 [*count*] *literary* **: something (such as a spirit) that you cannot see but that you feel or believe is present — usually singular** • She felt a ghostly *presence* in the room.

grace (a person, group, etc.) with your presence see ²GRACE

make your presence felt/heard/known **: to make people aware of you by gaining power or influence over them** • Women are *making their presence felt* in the industry. • The Internet service is *making its presence known* by doing a lot of advertising.

presence of mind *noun* [*noncount*] **: the ability to think clearly and act quickly especially in an emergency — usually followed by *to* + verb** • The child had the *presence of mind to call* for an ambulance. • He had the *presence of mind to write* down the license plate number of the car.

¹pres·ent /ˈprɛzn̩t/ *noun, pl* **-ents** [*count*] **: something that you give to someone especially as a way of showing affection or thanks : GIFT** • a birthday/Christmas/anniversary/wedding *present* • Here's a *present* for you from John. • I gave/got her a book as a *present*. • Did you wrap the *presents*? — compare ⁴PRESENT

²pre·sent /prɪˈzɛnt/ *verb* **-sents; -sent·ed; -sent·ing**

1 [+ *obj*] **: to give something to someone in a formal way or in a ceremony** • He *presented* the queen with a diamond necklace. • He was *presented* with a medal at the ceremony. • She *presented* a check for $5,000 to the charity.

2 a : to formally talk about (something you have written, studied, etc.) to a group of people [+ *obj*] The scientist *presented* his results/report to the committee. • She will be *presenting* a paper on methods for teaching ESL at the conference. [*no obj*] What time will you be *presenting*? **b** [+ *obj*] **: to make (something) available to be used or considered** • The defense will *present* [=*produce*] evidence refuting the charges. • An offer was *presented* for our consideration. • The opportunity ***presented itself*** [=became available], and she took advantage of it.

3 [+ *obj*] **: to make (something, such as a play or show) available to be seen by the public** • The Main Street Theater Company is *presenting* Shakespeare's *Othello* next month. • The museum is *presenting* an exhibition of paintings by Monet.

4 [+ *obj*] **: to show (something) to someone** • He *presented* his ID to the security guard. • You'll be required to *present* a passport when you cross the border.

5 [+ *obj*] **: to describe or show (someone or something) in a particular way** • No matter how the government tries to *present* what happened, it was a tragic mistake. • The article *presents* an accurate picture of the contemporary lives of Japanese women. • The candidate tried to *present* a more upbeat image of himself. • She *presents* herself as a very ambitious person.

6 [+ *obj*] **: to create (a problem, challenge, etc.) for someone or something** • Storing these delicate artifacts *presents* [=*poses*] a challenge for the college. • The conflicting information *presents* a dilemma (for us): which numbers are correct? • The shortages *presented* a serious problem to the government. = The shortages *presented* the government with a serious problem. • We have been *presented* with a difficult task.

7 [+ *obj*] **a : to introduce (someone or something) to an audience** • I am pleased to *present* our first comedian of the night. **b** *formal* **: to introduce (someone) to a person who is important, of high rank, etc.** • He was *presented* as ambassador to the king.

8 [+ *obj*] *formal* **: to bring (yourself) to a particular place** • She was ordered to *present* herself at court [=to go to court] the next day.

9 [+ *obj*] *formal* **: to express (something, such as an apology)** • Please allow me to *present* my apologies (to you). • Let me *present* my congratulations and best wishes (to you) on this happy occasion.

10 [+ *obj*] *Brit* **: to introduce the different parts of (a radio or television program)** • She *presents* [=(*US*) *hosts*] a popular game show.

– pre·sent·er *noun, pl* **-ers** [*count*] • the *presenter* of the award • The *presenter* spoke well. • (*Brit*) the *presenter* [=(*US*) *host*] of the game show

³pres·ent /ˈprɛzn̩t/ *adj*

1 a : not past or future : existing or happening now • the *present* [=*current*] situation • No further changes are planned ***at the present time***. [=*now*] • The game has existed in its ***present form*** for more than 300 years. **b — used to say what someone or something is now** • the company's *present* [=(more commonly) *current*] employees • the *present* leadership of the Senate [=the people who have positions of power in the Senate now] • The ceremony honors our soldiers, ***past and present***. [=people who were soldiers in the past and people who are soldiers now]

2 a : at the particular place or event that is being referred to — often + *at* • She was *present at* the meeting. **— often + *in*** • There was a large crowd *present in* the auditorium. **— sometimes used as an interjection** • "John Smith?" "*Present!*" [=*here*] **b : existing in something — usually + *in*** • There were high levels of lead *present in* the water. [=the water contained high levels of lead]

all present and accounted for (*US*) *or Brit* ***all present and correct*** **— used to say that all the people who are supposed to be at a place or event are there** • The students are ***all present and accounted for***.

present company excepted/excluded **— used to say that a critical comment you have made about a group of people does not include the person or people you are with** • Men are such jerks—*present company excepted/excluded*, of course.

present writer *somewhat formal* **— used to refer to yourself as the person who is writing something** • No one—*present writer* included—thought the plan would work. [=no one, including me, thought the plan would work] • She is promoting her latest movie, which ***the present writer*** has not yet seen. [=which I have not yet seen]

⁴pres·ent /ˈprɛzn̩t/ *noun*

1 [*noncount*] **: the period of time that exists now : the present time** • Past, *present*, and future are all linked together. **— usually used with *the*** • the past, *the present*, and the future • Let's leave things as they are for *the present*. We may change them in the future. • I have worked here from 2000 to *the present*. • Geologists believe that *the present* is the key to the past. • There's ***no time like the present*** for getting things done! [=it is best to get things done right away instead of waiting until later]

2 [*count*] **: the current condition or situation of someone or something — usually singular** • He was trying to escape his *present* by living in the past. • She moved the company out of a troubled past and into a profitable *present*.

3 ***the present*** *grammar* **: PRESENT TENSE** • The verb is in *the present*.

at present **: at or during this time : at the present time : NOW** • Things were bad then but they're better *at present*. • *At present* I am working as a substitute teacher.

– compare ¹PRESENT

pre·sent·able /prɪˈzɛntəbəl/ *adj* [*more* ~; *most* ~] **: in good enough condition to be seen by someone : not too dirty, messy, etc., to be seen** • I have to make myself *presentable* before our guests arrive. • a *presentable* appearance

pre·sen·ta·tion /ˌpriːzɛnˈteɪʃən/ *noun, pl* **-tions**

1 [*count*] **: an activity in which someone shows, describes, or explains something to a group of people** • The charts and graphs helped me understand the *presentation*. • She will take your questions after she has ***made her presentation***. • The senior accountant ***gave a presentation*** at the meeting.

2 [*noncount*] **: the way in which something is arranged, designed, etc. : the way in which something is presented** • The *presentation* of the food made it look very appetizing.

3 a : the act of giving something to someone in a formal way or in a ceremony [*noncount*] The choir sang during the *presentation of* the gifts. [*count*] The awards were given out last night, and the mayor was on hand to ***make the presentations***. [=to present the awards] **b** [*count*] **: a ceremony in which something (such as an award) is given to someone in a formal way** • an awards *presentation*

4 [*noncount*] **: the act of showing or presenting something to someone so that it can be seen or considered** • The state has a law that prohibits the *presentation* of new evidence 30 days after conviction.

5 [*count*] **: the performance of a play** • We are going to see an outdoor *presentation* of the play.

6 [*count*] *medical* **: the position of a baby inside its mother just before the baby is born** • abnormal birth *presentations*

– pre·sen·ta·tion·al /ˌprɛznˌteɪʃənl/ *adj* ▪ *presentational* skills

present day *noun*

the present day : the period of time that exists now : the present time ▪ The English of *the present day* is different from the English of the past.

– pres·ent–day /ˈprɛzn̩tˈdeɪ/ *adj, always used before a noun* ▪ *present-day* [=*contemporary, modern*] English

pre·sen·ti·ment /prɪˈzɛntəmənt/ *noun, pl* **-ments** [*count*] *formal* : a feeling or belief that something is going to happen ▪ a *presentiment* [=*premonition*] of death/danger

pres·ent·ly /ˈprɛzn̩tli/ *adv*

1 : during the time that is happening now : at the present time : NOW ▪ She is *presently* [=*currently*] at work on a new novel.

2 : after a short time : SOON ▪ He'll be here *presently*.

present participle *noun, pl* ~ **-ciples** [*count*] *grammar* : a verb form that ends in "-ing" and that is used with "be" to refer to action that is happening at the time of speaking or a time spoken of ▪ The verbs "dancing" in "He was dancing" and "crying" in "The baby is crying" are *present participles*. ✧ The present participle can also be used before a noun like an adjective. ▪ the crying baby ▪ the quickly rising tide

present perfect *noun*

the present perfect *grammar* : a verb tense that is used to refer to an action that began in the past and is completed at the time of speaking ✧ The *present perfect* in English is formed with "has" and "have" and the past participle of a verb, as in "He has left," and "They have found what they were looking for."

present tense *noun, pl* ~ **tenses** [*count*] : a verb tense that is used to refer to the present

pres·er·va·tion /ˌprɛzɚˈveɪʃən/ *noun* [*noncount*]

1 : the act of preserving something: such as **a** : the act of keeping something in its original state or in good condition — often + *of* ▪ *preservation of* the city's historical buildings ▪ the *preservation of* land for wildlife ▪ (*Brit*) a ***preservation order*** [=an official order by a court that makes it illegal to destroy or change a building, tree, view, etc.] **b** : the act of keeping something safe from harm or loss ▪ wildlife *preservation* — often + *of* ▪ the *preservation of* music programs in public schools ▪ the *preservation of* cultural traditions **c** : the act of using a particular treatment on a food so that it can be eaten in the future ▪ methods of food *preservation*, such as canning and freezing

2 : the degree to which something is kept safe from harm or ruin ▪ The ancient paintings were found in a perfect ***state of preservation***. [=they were perfectly preserved] ▪ The buildings are in a good *state of preservation*. — see also SELF-PRESERVATION

pres·er·va·tion·ist /ˌprɛzɚˈveɪʃənɪst/ *noun, pl* **-ists** [*count*] : someone who works to preserve something (such as a building or an area of land)

pre·ser·va·tive /prɪˈzɚvətɪv/ *noun, pl* **-tives** [*count, noncount*] : a substance that is used to preserve something: such as **a** : a chemical that is added to food to keep it fresh longer ▪ This food does not contain any artificial *preservatives*. **b** : a substance that is used on wood to prevent it from decaying ▪ The wood was treated with *preservative*.

[1]**pre·serve** /prɪˈzɚv/ *verb* **-serves; -served; -serv·ing** [+ *obj*]

1 : to keep (something) in its original state or in good condition ▪ The committee is in charge of *preserving* [=*maintaining*] the city's historical buildings. ▪ The fossil was well *preserved*.

2 : to keep (something) safe from harm or loss : PROTECT ▪ These laws are intended to help *preserve* our natural resources. ▪ They are fighting to *preserve* their rights as citizens. ▪ a subtance that helps *preserve* wood

3 : to prevent (food) from decaying ▪ The peaches are *preserved* in syrup. ▪ Salt can be used to *preserve* meat.

– pre·serv·er *noun, pl* **-ers** [*count*] ▪ The police should be *preservers* of law and order. — see also LIFE PRESERVER

[2]**preserve** *noun, pl* **-serves**

1 : a sweet food made of fruit cooked in sugar [*count*] — usually plural ▪ a jar of strawberry *preserves* [*noncount*] a jar of strawberry *preserve*

2 [*count*] : an area where plants, animals, minerals, etc., are protected ▪ nature/wildlife *preserves* [=*reserves*] ▪ Game *preserves* allow only carefully controlled hunting and fishing.

3 [*singular*] : an activity, job, interest, etc., that is available to or considered suitable for only a particular group of people ▪ The military was once an all-male *preserve*. — often + *of* ▪ Raising children used to be the (exclusive) *preserve of* women. [=used to be thought of as something done only by women]

pre·side /prɪˈzaɪd/ *verb* **-sides; -sid·ed; -sid·ing** [*no obj*] : to be in charge of something (such as a trial) ▪ Court is now in session, Justice Raul Fernandez *presiding*. — often + *at* ▪ She will *preside* as judge *at* the trial.

preside over [*phrasal verb*] ***preside over (something)*** 1 : to be in charge of something (such as a meeting or organization) ▪ The vice president *presided over* the meeting. ▪ The Chief Justice *presides over* the Supreme Court. ▪ He has *presided over* the company for 15 years. 2 : to be in charge of a country, company, etc., during (a particular time or activity) ▪ She *presided over* a period of relative peace and prosperity.

– presiding *adj* ▪ the *presiding* judge/officer

pres·i·den·cy /ˈprɛzədənsi/ *noun, pl* **-cies** [*count*] : the job of a president or the period of time when a person is president — usually singular ▪ candidates for the *presidency* [=people who are trying to be elected president] ▪ the third year of his *presidency*

pres·i·dent /ˈprɛzədənt/ *noun, pl* **-dents** [*count*]

1 : the head of the government in some countries ▪ The *President* will hold a news conference tomorrow. ▪ *President* Abraham Lincoln — often + *of* ▪ the *President of* the United States

2 : someone who has the highest position in an organization or business ▪ a bank/college *president* — often + *of* ▪ the *president of* the club — compare VICE PRESIDENT

– pres·i·den·tial /ˌprɛzəˈdɛnʃəl/ *adj, always used before a noun* ▪ a *presidential* candidate/election/government

president–elect *noun, pl* **-elects** [*count*] : a person who has been elected president but who has not officially become president yet

Presidents' Day *noun* [*noncount*] : the third Monday in February celebrated in most states of the U.S. as a holiday in honor of the birthdays of George Washington and Abraham Lincoln — compare WASHINGTON'S BIRTHDAY

[1]**press** /ˈprɛs/ *noun, pl* **press·es**

1 **a** [*noncount*] : newspapers, magazines, and radio and television news reports ▪ American/foreign/local *press* ▪ Reports in the *press* suggested there had been many casualties. ▪ ***freedom of the press*** [=the right of newspapers, magazines, etc., to report news without being controlled by the government] — often used before another noun ▪ The murder trial has drawn a lot of *press* coverage. ▪ *press* reports/clippings **b** ***the press*** : the people (such as reporters and photographers) who work for newspapers, magazines, etc. ▪ She refused to talk to *the press*. ▪ members of *the press* ▪ (*US*) *The press* was waiting outside the courtroom. = (*Brit*) *The press* was/were waiting outside the courtroom. — see also PRESS CONFERENCE **c** — used to talk about how often or how well or badly someone or something is described in newspapers, magazines, etc. [*noncount*] The trial has been getting a lot of *press*. [=there have been a lot of press reports about the trial] ▪ The new edition of the dictionary is getting good *press*. ▪ He has gotten a lot of bad *press* lately. [*singular*] (*Brit*) The new edition of the dictionary is getting a good *press*.

2 **a** [*count*] : PRINTING PRESS ▪ The pages rolled off the *presses*. ▪ Stop the *presses*! — see also *hot off the press* at [1]HOT **b** [*noncount*] : the act or the process of being printed ▪ The book is ***on press*** now and due out soon. ▪ The story is ***going to press***. [=the story is about to be printed] ▪ He did not return our call by/before ***press time***. [=the time when the story was printed] **c** [*count*] : a printing or publishing business ▪ a university *press* ▪ The book is published by Federal Street *Press*.

3 [*count*] : a machine that uses pressure to shape, flatten, or squeeze something ▪ a cookie/cider/garlic *press* ▪ a trouser *press*

4 [*count*] : the act of pushing or flattening something with your finger or hand or with a device (such as an iron) — usually singular ▪ The machine turns on with the *press* [=*push*] of a button. ▪ (*chiefly Brit*) Your shirt needs a *press*. [=your shirt needs pressing; your shirt needs to be ironed]

5 [*singular*] : a large group of people gathered together in one place : CROWD — often + *of* ▪ We were caught in the *press of* people outside the theater.

– see also FULL-COURT PRESS

[2]**press** *verb* **presses; pressed; press·ing**

1 **a** : to push (something) with strong or steady force [+ *obj*]

She *pressed* the pieces of clay together. ▪ The machine *presses* the metal/plastic into sheets. ▪ People were *pressed* against each other in the crowd. ▪ The little girl *pressed* her face against the window. ▪ Dad took me aside and *pressed* some money into my hand. [*no obj*] He lightly *pressed* (down) on her stomach to feel the baby move. **b :** to push (something, such as a button or lever on a machine) with your finger or hand [+ *obj*] Don't *press* that button. ▪ *Press* "Play" to start the movie. [*no obj*] *Press* here to release the buckle.

2 [+ *obj*] **:** to force or try to persuade (someone) to do something especially by repeatedly asking for it to be done ▪ She *pressed* him to go with her to the ballet. ▪ I *pressed* her for more details. ▪ He is *pressing* [=*pressuring*] us for a decision. = He is *pressing* us to make a decision. ▪ After the scandal, the CEO was *pressed* into resigning. ▪ When *pressed*, he tends to give in.

3 [+ *obj*] **:** to repeat (something) often in a way that is annoying to show that it is very important ▪ I don't want to *press* [=*push*] the issue, but it is important and needs to be addressed immediately. ▪ He kept ***pressing the point*** that something needs to be done immediately. ▪ They're trying to ***press home*** their message. [=trying to make their message clear and forceful] ▪ Laborers are ***pressing their case*** for higher wages.

4 [+ *obj*] **:** to flatten or smooth out (something) with your hand, an iron, etc. ▪ She *pressed* the ball of dough flat. ▪ He *pressed* [=*ironed*] his shirt and pants.

5 [+ *obj*] **:** to push down on a fruit or vegetable to make juice come out of it ▪ He *pressed* the apples to make cider. ▪ The machine *presses* the juice out of the grapes. ▪ freshly *pressed* [=(more commonly) *squeezed*] orange juice

6 a *always followed by an adverb or preposition* [*no obj*] **:** to continue moving forward in a forceful or steady way ▪ The explorers *pressed* deeper into the jungle. ▪ The troops *pressed* [=*pushed*] on/forward in spite of the snow. **b :** to continue to do something especially in a determined way [*no obj*] — usually + *on* or *ahead* ▪ Now that we have answered that question, let's *press on*. ▪ The city *pressed ahead* with plans to build a casino. [+ *obj*] She saw an opening and *pressed* (home) her attack/advantage.

7 *always followed by an adverb or preposition* [*no obj*] **:** to crowd closely around or against someone or something **:** to move in a large group toward or near someone or something ▪ Reporters *pressed* around/about the players as they left the field.

press charges **:** to take legal action against someone **:** to officially accuse someone of a crime ▪ He was caught shoplifting, but the store owner didn't *press charges*.

press for [*phrasal verb*] ***press for (something)*** **:** to make a demand for (something) ▪ Laborers are *pressing for* higher wages.

press on *also* ***press upon*** [*phrasal verb*] ***press (something) on/upon (someone)*** **:** to force (someone) to take or accept (something) ▪ I tried to *press* money *on* him for my half of the bill, but he refused to take it. ▪ She's always *pressing* her opinions *on* us. — see also ²PRESS 6b (above)

press (someone or something) into service **:** to use (someone or something) for a particular job or purpose when a special need occurs ▪ Retired doctors and nurses were *pressed into service* to help care for the wounded. ▪ The backup computer was *pressed into service* when the main computer failed.

press the flesh *informal* **:** to greet and shake hands with people especially while campaigning for a political office

press agency *noun, pl* **~ -cies** [*count*] **:** NEWS AGENCY

press agent *noun, pl* **~ agents** [*count*] **:** a person whose job is to give information about an important or famous person or organization to news reporters

press box *noun, pl* **~ boxes** [*count*] **:** a special area or section of seats where reporters sit at a sports event

press clipping *noun, pl* **~ -pings** [*count*] **:** CLIPPING 1

press conference *noun, pl* **~ -ences** [*count*] **:** a meeting in which someone gives information to news reporters and answers questions ▪ The President will hold/give a *press conference* later today. — called also *news conference*

press corps *noun, pl* **~ corps** [*count*] **:** a group of news reporters who are located in a particular place or who follow a particular person ▪ the White House *press corps*

pressed /ˈprɛst/ *adj, not used before a noun* **:** lacking something that is needed or desired — + *for* ▪ I am really *pressed for* time/money right now. ▪ He's *pressed for* space in his new apartment. — see also HARD-PRESSED

press gallery *noun, pl* **~ -ler·ies** [*count*] **:** an area especially in a court of law where news reporters sit

press gang *noun, pl* **~ gangs** [*count*] **:** a group of men who in the past would take men and force them to join the navy or army

– press–gang /ˈprɛsˌgæŋ/ *verb* **-gangs; -ganged; -gang·ing** [+ *obj*] — often + *into* ▪ He was *press-ganged into* the navy. [=he was forced by a press gang to join the navy] — often used figuratively in British English ▪ He was *press-ganged into* working throughout the holiday.

press·ing /ˈprɛsɪŋ/ *adj* [*more* ~; *most* ~] **:** very important and needing immediate attention **:** URGENT ▪ a *pressing* problem/concern ▪ a *pressing* need for reform

press kit *noun, pl* **~ kits** [*count*] **:** a collection of photographs, documents, etc., that is given to newspapers, magazines, television news programs, and radio stations **:** a package of information about someone or something that is given to the press

press·man /ˈprɛsmən/ *noun, pl* **-men** /-mən/ [*count*] *Brit* **:** NEWSPAPERMAN

press office *noun, pl* **~ -fices** [*count*] **:** the office of an organization (such as a political party or a government department) that gives information to newspapers, magazines, television news programs, and radio stations

press officer *noun, pl* **~ -cers** [*count*] **:** a person who works in a press office

press release *noun, pl* **~ -leases** [*count*] **:** an official statement that gives information to newspapers, magazines, television news programs, and radio stations

press·room /ˈprɛsˌruːm/ *noun, pl* **-rooms** [*count*]

1 : a room where someone talks to news reporters

2 : a room that contains printing presses

press secretary *noun, pl* **~ -tar·ies** [*count*] **:** a person whose job is to give information about an important or famous person or organization to news reporters ▪ the White House *press secretary*

press stud *noun, pl* **~ studs** [*count*] *Brit* **:** ²SNAP 3

press–up /ˈprɛsˌʌp/ *noun, pl* **-ups** [*count*] *Brit* **:** PUSH-UP

¹pres·sure /ˈprɛʃɚ/ *noun, pl* **-sures**

1 a : the weight or force that is produced when something presses or pushes against something else [*noncount*] Keep steady *pressure* on the cap as you turn it. [=press on the cap as you turn it] ▪ Apply *pressure* to the wound to stop the bleeding. ▪ the *pressure* of the compressed air inside the chamber ▪ high/low ***water pressure*** [=a force that makes a flow of water strong/weak] ▪ Check the car's ***tire pressure.*** [=the amount of air inside the tires] ▪ The contents of the bottle are ***under pressure.*** [=the contents are tightly pressed into the bottle] [*singular*] The animal's jaws can exert a *pressure* of more than 750 pounds per square inch. — see also BLOOD PRESSURE **b** [*noncount*] **:** the action of pressing or pushing against something ▪ The horse will respond to the slightest *pressure* of a rider's knee. ▪ The fruit yields to gentle *pressure* when it's ripe.

2 [*noncount*] **:** the weight of the air in the Earth's atmosphere ▪ the normal air *pressure* at sea level ▪ atmospheric *pressure* ▪ *Pressure* fell [=the air became lighter] as the storm approached. ▪ An area of ***high/low pressure*** [=heavy/light air] is moving over the west coast.

3 : the force that you feel when people are trying to persuade or force you to do something by using arguments, threats, etc. [*noncount*] He felt *pressure* from his father to become a doctor. = His father put *pressure* on him to become a doctor. [=his father was trying to persuade/force him to become a doctor] ▪ The mayor is ***under pressure*** to resign. [=people are trying to force the mayor to resign] [*count*] He gave in to the social *pressures* to act and dress like everybody else. ▪ She felt a constant *pressure* to earn more money. — see also PEER PRESSURE

4 : a feeling of stress or anxiety because you have too much to do or because people are depending on you for something [*count*] She was dealing with the *pressures* of everyday life. [*noncount*] Can he handle the *pressure* of the job? ▪ She's been experiencing a lot of *pressure* at work lately. ▪ They both work well ***under pressure.*** [=they work well when the job is stressful] ▪ Her job is ***high pressure.*** [=her job is very stressful] — see also HIGH-PRESSURE

²pressure *verb* **-sures; -sured; -sur·ing** [+ *obj*] *chiefly US* **:** to use pressure to force or try to force (someone) to do something — often followed by *into* + *-ing verb* ▪ The defense *pressured* the quarterback *into throwing* a bad pass. ▪ They *pressured* him *into resigning*. [=they forced him to resign] —

often followed by *to + verb* ▪ They're *pressuring* him *to make* a decision. ▪ They *pressured* him *to resign.* [=they tried to force him to resign by putting pressure on him] — often used as *(be) pressured* ▪ Doctors are *being pressured* by the insurance companies. ▪ She felt *pressured* to make a decision.

pressure cooker *noun, pl* ~ **-ers**
1 *[count]* : a special pot that is used to cook food quickly by using the pressure of steam
2 *[singular] informal* : a situation or place that causes you to feel a lot of stress or pressure ▪ The new boss has turned the office into a *pressure cooker.*
– pressure–cooker *adj, always used before a noun* ▪ the *pressure-cooker* [=*high-pressure*] atmosphere of law school

pressure group *noun, pl* ~ **groups** *[count]* : a group of people who share an interest, concern, or set of opinions and who try to influence politics or the policies of government, business, etc. ▪ a *pressure group* trying to reduce taxes

pressure point *noun, pl* ~ **points** *[count]*
1 : a place on your body that can be pressed to stop tension or pain
2 : a place on your body where a blood vessel is near the bone and can be pressed to stop bleeding
3 : a place, area, or situation that is a source or possible source of problems : a point where pressure is applied or felt ▪ economic *pressure points*

pres·sur·ize *also Brit* **pres·sur·ise** /ˈprɛʃəˌraɪz/ *verb* **-iz·es; -ized; -iz·ing** *[+ obj]*
1 *technical* **a** : to press (something) tightly into a space or container ▪ A pump is used to *pressurize* the fuel. **b** : to cause the air pressure inside (something, such as an airplane) to be the same as or close to the pressure of air on the Earth's surface ▪ The system that *pressurizes* the airplane's cabin failed to operate correctly.
2 *Brit* : ²PRESSURE ▪ Don't let them *pressurize* you to do anything you don't want to do.
– pres·sur·i·za·tion *also Brit* **pres·sur·i·sa·tion** /ˌprɛʃərəˈzeɪʃən, *Brit* ˌprɛʃəˌraɪˈzeɪʃən/ *noun [noncount] technical* ▪ airplane cabin *pressurization* **– pressurized** *also Brit* **pres·sur·ised** *adj* ▪ the airplane's *pressurized* cabin ▪ The fuel is stored in *pressurized* containers. [=containers that are designed to hold liquids, gases, etc., that are under high pressure]

pres·tige /prɛˈstiːʒ/ *noun [noncount]* : the respect and admiration that someone or something gets for being successful or important ▪ Her career as a diplomat has brought her enormous *prestige.* ▪ The job has low pay and low *prestige.* ▪ The family has wealth and social *prestige.*
– pres·ti·gious /prɛˈstɪʤəs/ *adj [more ~; most ~]* ▪ a *prestigious* college/university ▪ a *prestigious* award

pres·to /ˈprɛstoʊ/ *interj, US* : suddenly as if by magic ▪ A wave of the hand and, *presto* [=*(Brit) hey presto*], it's gone.

pre·sum·ably /prɪˈzuːməbli, *Brit* prɪˈzjuːməbli/ *adv* : very likely — used to say what you think is likely to happen or be true even though you are not sure ▪ *Presumably,* he'll come later. = He'll *presumably* come later. = He'll come later, *presumably.* [=it is reasonable to think that he will come later] ▪ There was hardly any furniture in the house, *presumably* [=*probably*] because they didn't have much money.

pre·sume /prɪˈzuːm, *Brit* prɪˈzjuːm/ *verb* **-sumes; -sumed; -sum·ing** *[+ obj]*
1 a : to think that (something) is true without knowing that it is true ▪ I *presume* [=*assume, expect*] (that) you'll fly to Chicago rather than drive. ▪ I *presume* (that) the car was very expensive. = The car was very expensive, I *presume.* ▪ "Is she still at work?" "I *presume* so, since she's not home." **b** : to accept legally or officially that something is true until it is proved not true ▪ A person is *presumed* (to be) innocent until proven guilty in a court of law. ▪ The court must *presume* innocence until there is proof of guilt. ▪ After the earthquake several people were missing and ***presumed dead.*** [=believed to be dead]
2 *formal* : to do (something) that you do not have the right or permission to do — followed by *to + verb* ▪ How can you *presume* [=*dare*] *to speak* for her? ▪ I'm not going to *presume to tell* you how to do your job.
3 : to expect that someone has (a certain level of knowledge, skill, etc.) ▪ The course *presumes* familiarity with basic computer programming. [=people who take the course should know basic computer programming]
presume on/upon *[phrasal verb]* ***presume on/upon (something) formal*** : to expect too much from (a relationship) in a way that shows that you do not understand your role in the relationship : to go beyond the proper limits of (a relationship) ▪ I don't want to *presume on/upon* our friendship by asking for too many favors.

pre·sump·tion /prɪˈzʌmpʃən/ *noun, pl* **-tions**
1 *[count]* : a belief that something is true even though it has not been proved — often *+ that* ▪ The *presumption* is *that* the thief had a key to the store. ▪ There was a widespread *presumption that* she would appoint him as her successor. ▪ the *presumption that* all students learn in the same way ▪ Thousands of people used this drug ***on the presumption that*** it was safe. [=they used it because they believed that it was safe]
2 *law* : an act of accepting that something is true until it is proved not true — often *+ of* *[noncount]* The trial was unfair from the beginning because there was no *presumption of* innocence. *[singular]* a defendant's right to a *presumption of* innocence
3 *[noncount] formal* : willingness to do something without the right or permission to do it ▪ You don't know anything about my situation, and yet you have the *presumption* [=*(more commonly) gall, nerve*] to tell me what to do!

pre·sump·tu·ous /prɪˈzʌmpʃəwəs/ *adj [more ~; most ~] formal* : too confident especially in a way that is rude ▪ It would be *presumptuous* (of me) to tell the manager how to do things. : done or made without permission, right, or good reason ▪ a *presumptuous* question
– pre·sump·tu·ous·ly *adv* **– pre·sump·tu·ous·ness** *noun [noncount]*

pre·sup·pose /ˌpriːsəˈpoʊz/ *verb* **-pos·es; -posed; -pos·ing** *[+ obj] formal*
1 : to be based on the idea that something is true or will happen ▪ The rule *presupposes* a need to restrict student access to the library. — often *+ that* ▪ The plan *presupposes that* the state has enough money to carry it out.
2 : to require or depend on (something) in order to be true or exist ▪ Prayer *presupposes* a belief in a higher being. [=in order to pray you must believe that a higher being exists]
– pre·sup·po·si·tion /ˌpriːˌsʌpəˈzɪʃən/ *noun, pl* **-tions** *[count]* We can't be afraid to examine/question our *presuppositions.* [=*assumptions*] ▪ The argument is based on the *presupposition* [=*presumption*] that there is life in outer space. *[noncount]* The argument is based on prejudice and *presupposition.*

pre·tax /ˌpriːˈtæks/ *adj* : before taxes have been taken away from a total ▪ *pretax* profits/income/earnings/dollars

pre·teen /ˈpriːˈtiːn/ *noun, pl* **-teens** *[count]* : a boy or girl who is 11 or 12 years old
– preteen *adj, always used before a noun* ▪ a *preteen* girl/boy ▪ *preteen* clothing

¹pre·tend /prɪˈtɛnd/ *verb* **-tends; -tend·ed; -tend·ing**
1 : to act as if something is true when it is not true *[+ obj]* She *pretended* (that) she didn't care what other people said about her. ▪ I'm going to *pretend* (that) we never had this conversation. ▪ He had a big stain on his shirt, but I *pretended* not to notice. ▪ The children *pretended* to be asleep. ▪ She *pretended* to be angry. = She *pretended* (that) she was angry. ▪ He *pretended* to be blind. = He *pretended* [=*(more commonly) feigned*] blindness. ▪ I don't *pretend* to have all the answers. [=I don't claim that I have all the answers] ▪ *(formal)* He was *pretending* an emotion he really couldn't feel. *[no obj]* I don't like having to *pretend.* = I don't like *pretending.* ▪ She looked like she was enjoying the party but she was just *pretending.* ▪ It was a mistake, and to ***pretend otherwise*** would be foolish.
2 : to imagine and act out (a particular role, situation, etc.) *[+ obj]* *Pretend* (that) I'm your boss. What would you say? ▪ The children were *pretending* to be animals. ▪ He *pretended* to make a phone call. *[no obj]* Let's just *pretend* for a moment. I'm your boss. What would you say to me?
pretend to *[phrasal verb]* ***pretend to (something) formal*** : to claim that you have (something, such as a quality or ability) ▪ She *pretends to* a deep religious devotion, but I don't believe her. — usually used in negative statements ▪ I don't *pretend to* any expertise in these matters.
– pretended *adj* ▪ I wasn't fooled by her *pretended* indifference.

²pretend *adj, informal* : not real : IMAGINARY ▪ The little girl has a *pretend* [=*make-believe*] friend. ▪ The children played on a *pretend* train.

pre·tend·er /prɪˈtɛndɚ/ *noun, pl* **-ers** *[count]* : someone who claims to have the right to a particular title or position (such as king or queen) when others do not agree — usually *+ to* ▪ a *pretender to* the throne

P

pre·tense (*US*) *or Brit* **pre·tence** /ˈpriːˌtɛns, *Brit* prɪˈtɛns/ *noun, pl* **-tens·es**

1 [*count*] **: a false reason or explanation that is used to hide the real purpose of something : PRETEXT** ▪ He called her ***under/on the pretense*** of asking about the homework assignment. [=asking about the homework assignment was not the real reason he called her] ▪ A reporter obtained documents from the company ***under false pretenses***. [=by saying something that was not true, by pretending something, etc.]

2 : an act or appearance that looks real but is false [*singular*] Their indifference is only a *pretense*. [=they are only pretending to be indifferent] ▪ We tried to keep up the *pretense* that everything was fine. ▪ She couldn't even ***make a pretense*** of liking him. [=she disliked him so much that she was unable to pretend that she liked him] [*noncount*] Their indifference is merely *pretense*. ▪ He ***abandoned/dropped all pretense at*** politeness. [=he stopped pretending or trying to be polite]

3 [*count*] *formal* **: a claim of having a particular quality, ability, condition, etc. — usually singular** ▪ I make no *pretense* of being a history expert. [=I do not claim/pretend to be a history expert]

pre·ten·sion /prɪˈtɛnʃən/ *noun, pl* **-sions** *formal*

1 [*noncount*] **: the unpleasant quality of people who think of themselves as more impressive, successful, or important than they really are** ▪ He spoke about his achievements without *pretension*. ▪ I admire his honesty and lack of *pretension*. ▪ The restaurant offers excellent food without *pretension*.

2 [*count*] **: a desire to do something or a claim to be something that is impressive or important — usually plural** ▪ The movie has no artistic *pretensions*. = The movie has no *pretensions* to/of being great art. [=the movie is not trying/claiming to be artistic] ▪ She has serious literary *pretensions*. [=*aspirations*]

pre·ten·tious /prɪˈtɛnʃəs/ *adj* [*more* ~; *most* ~] *disapproving* **: having or showing the unpleasant quality of people who want to be regarded as more impressive, successful, or important than they really are** ▪ He's a *pretentious* snob. ▪ a *pretentious* restaurant/movie ▪ The houses in the neighborhood are large and *pretentious*. ▪ He uses *pretentious* language.

— pre·ten·tious·ly *adv* ▪ a *pretentiously* decorated hotel **— pre·ten·tious·ness** *noun* [*noncount*]

pre·ter·nat·u·ral /ˌpriːtəˈnætʃərəl/ *adj, formal* **: very unusual in a way that does not seem natural** ▪ He is a young man with *preternatural* [=*exceptional*] good looks. ▪ She has a *preternatural* ability to charm people. ▪ There was a *preternatural* quiet in the house.

— pre·ter·nat·u·ral·ly *adv* ▪ The house was *preternaturally* [=*strangely*] quiet.

pre·text /ˈpriːˌtɛkst/ *noun, pl* **-texts** [*count*] **: a reason that you give to hide your real reason for doing something : PRETENSE** ▪ The leaders used a minor clash at the border as a *pretext* for war. [=as a reason/excuse for starting a war] ▪ She always managed to visit him ***on*** one ***pretext*** or another. [=she found various reasons to visit him] ▪ She went back to her friend's house ***on/under the pretext that*** she had forgotten her purse.

pre·trial /ˈpriːˈtrajəl/ *adj, always used before a noun, chiefly US, law* **: before a trial** ▪ *pretrial* publicity ▪ a *pretrial* hearing

pret·ti·fy /ˈprɪtəˌfaɪ/ *verb* **-fies; -fied; -fy·ing** [+ *obj*]

1 : to make (something) pretty ▪ The city is trying to *prettify* its downtown.

2 *disapproving* **: to make (something) seem better or more attractive than it really is** ▪ The movie *prettified* what was in reality a very bloody battle.

[1]pret·ty /ˈprɪti/ *adj* **pret·ti·er; -est** [*also more* ~; *most* ~]

1 a : attractive to look at usually in a simple or delicate way ▪ a *pretty* dress ▪ *pretty* flowers **— used especially of a girl or woman** ▪ She has a *pretty* face. ▪ I've never seen her looking so happy or so *pretty*. **b : pleasant to look at or listen to** ▪ a *pretty* sunset/room/voice/name/poem ▪ That song is *pretty*. = That's a *pretty* song. ***synonyms*** see BEAUTIFUL

2 *always used before a noun* **: large or impressive** ▪ He made a *pretty* profit selling his antique car. ▪ She received a *pretty* sum of money.

3 : pleasant to see or experience ▪ What a *pretty* [=*nice*] day. **— usually used in negative statements** ▪ The game was*n't pretty* but at least we won. ▪ It isn't going to be *pretty* when the mayor finds out his son has been arrested. ▪ The kitchen was ***not a pretty sight*** [=the kitchen was very messy] after we finished making breakfast.

4 *always used before a noun, old-fashioned* **: very unpleasant** ▪ What a *pretty* [=*terrible*] mess you've gotten us into! ▪ a *pretty* [=*miserable*] state of affairs

a pretty penny see PENNY

(as) pretty as a picture *old-fashioned* **: very attractive or pleasant to look at : very pretty** ▪ She is as *pretty as a picture*!

pretty face ✧ Someone who is ***not just a/another pretty face*** or ***more than (just) a pretty face*** is attractive but also has other good qualities, such as intelligence. ▪ If he wants to get people to vote for him, he's got to prove he's *more than just a pretty face*.

— pret·ti·ly /ˈprɪtəli/ *adv* ▪ She dresses/sings *prettily*. **— pret·ti·ness** /ˈprɪtinəs/ *noun* [*noncount*]

[2]pretty *adv*

1 : to some degree or extent but not very or extremely : FAIRLY ▪ The house was *pretty* [=*moderately, rather*] big. ▪ It's *pretty* cold outside. ▪ "Did you put the keys on the table?" "I'm *pretty* sure I did." ▪ The teams are *pretty* equally matched. ▪ The work is *pretty* hard. ▪ I have to leave *pretty* soon. ▪ The movie was *pretty* good but not great. ▪ (*US*) I'm ***pretty near/nearly*** done. [=I'm almost done]

2 : to a great degree or extent : VERY ▪ His injury was *pretty* bad. [=his injury was bad] ▪ We got *pretty* [=*quite*] close. ▪ They've accomplished some *pretty* amazing things. ▪ She was driving *pretty* fast.

pretty much/well *informal* **: not completely but mostly** ▪ His ideas were *pretty much* ignored at the meeting. ▪ It is *pretty much* the same color. ▪ The engine is *pretty well* shot. [=the engine is almost completely useless] ▪ "Are you finished yet?" "*Pretty much*." [=*just about*]

sit pretty see SIT

[3]pretty *verb* **-ties; -tied; -ty·ing** [+ *obj*] **: to make (something) pretty** ▪ She *prettied* the cake with icing, sprinkles, and nuts. **— usually + *up*** ▪ The curtains *pretty up* the room. ▪ Landscapers *prettied* the park *up* with flowers and bushes.

pretty boy *noun, pl* **~ boys** [*count*] *informal + disapproving* **: a man who is very attractive** ▪ Movie critics seem to finally agree that this *pretty boy* can act.

pret·zel /ˈprɛtsəl/ *noun, pl* **-zels** [*count*] **: a long, thin piece of bread that is usually salted and shaped like a knot or stick**

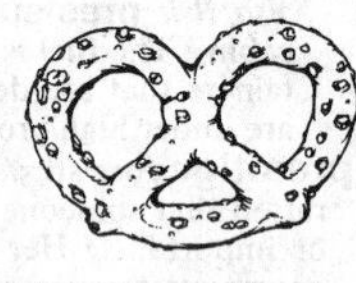

pretzel

pre·vail /prɪˈveɪl/ *verb* **-vails; -vailed; -vail·ing** [*no obj*] *formal*

1 : to defeat an opponent especially in a long or difficult contest ▪ Our soccer team *prevailed* [=*won*] despite the bad weather. **— often + *against* or *over*** ▪ He *prevailed against/over* last year's champion. ▪ She *prevailed* in a lawsuit *against* her doctor. [=she won a lawsuit against her doctor] **— often used figuratively** ▪ Justice will *prevail*. ▪ Truth will always *prevail* [=*triumph*] *over* lies.

2 : to be usual, common, or popular ▪ Mutual respect *prevails* among students and teachers here. ▪ The house was built in the style that *prevailed* in the 1980s.

3 : to be or continue to be in use ▪ The tribal custom still *prevails* [=*persists*] after hundreds of years. ▪ The law still *prevails* in some states.

prevail on/upon [*phrasal verb*] ***prevail on/upon (someone)*** **: to ask or persuade (someone) to do something** ▪ They *prevailed on/upon* me to play a few tunes on the piano.

prevailing *adj, always used before a noun* **: usual, common, or popular** ▪ the *prevailing* opinion/fashion ▪ She disagrees with *prevailing* [=*current*] ideas/notions about raising children. ▪ The ***prevailing wind*** in this region is from the east. [=the wind in this region usually comes from the east]

prev·a·lent /ˈprɛvələnt/ *adj* [*more* ~; *most* ~] **: accepted, done, or happening often or over a large area at a particular time : common or widespread** ▪ *prevalent* beliefs ▪ a custom that was once *prevalent* here ▪ Those teaching methods are still *prevalent* at some schools. ▪ a fashion that is *prevalent* among teenagers

— prev·a·lence /ˈprɛvələns/ *noun* [*noncount*] *formal* **— usually + *of*** ▪ the *prevalence of* the disease

pre·var·i·cate /prɪˈverəˌkeɪt/ *verb* **-cates; -cat·ed; -cat·ing** [*no obj*] *formal* **: to avoid telling the truth by not directly answering a question** ▪ Government officials *prevaricated* about the real costs of the project.

— pre·var·i·ca·tion /prɪˌverəˈkeɪʃən/ *noun, pl* **-tions** [*noncount*] Please answer clearly, without *prevarication*. [*count*] You've answered with nothing but half-truths and *prevarications*.

pre·vent /prɪˈvɛnt/ *verb* **-vents; -vent·ed; -vent·ing** [+ *obj*]
1 : to stop (something) from happening or existing ▪ Seatbelts in cars often *prevent* serious injuries. ▪ Can exercise and a healthy diet *prevent* heart disease? ▪ The accident could have been *prevented.*
2 : to make (someone or something) not do something **:** to stop (someone or something) *from* doing something ▪ He grabbed my arm to *prevent* me *from* falling. ▪ Bad weather *prevented* us *from* leaving. ▪ How are you going to *prevent* him *from* finding out about the party? — often used without *from* in British English ▪ Her injury will *prevent* her competing this year.
– **pre·vent·able** /prɪˈvɛntəbəl/ *adj* ▪ Many of these deaths were *preventable.* [=*avoidable*] ▪ a *preventable* disease
– **pre·vent·er** *noun, pl* **-ers** [*count*] ▪ She applied a rust *preventer* to the metal frame.

pre·ven·ta·tive /prɪˈvɛntətɪv/ *adj* **:** PREVENTIVE ▪ *preventative* measures
– **preventative** *noun, pl* **-tives** [*count*]

pre·ven·tion /prɪˈvɛnʃən/ *noun* [*noncount*] **:** the act or practice of stopping something bad from happening **:** the act of preventing something ▪ Exercise and diet play a role in the *prevention* of heart disease. ▪ crime/fire *prevention* ▪ (*US*) ***an ounce of prevention is worth a pound of cure*** = (*Brit*) ***prevention is better than cure*** [=it is better and easier to stop a problem, illness, etc., from happening than to stop or correct it after it has started]

pre·ven·tive /prɪˈvɛntɪv/ *adj* **:** used to stop something bad from happening ▪ Farmers are covering their crops as a *preventive* measure against frost. ▪ *preventive* medicine [=medicine that stops you from getting sick; medicine that keeps you healthy] ▪ We'll take whatever *preventive* action is necessary.
– **preventive** *noun, pl* **-tives** [*count*] ▪ The drug is used as a *preventive* against cancer.

[1]**pre·view** /ˈpriːˌvjuː/ *noun, pl* **-views** [*count*]
1 : a special show or performance that allows some people to see a movie, play, etc., before it is shown to the public ▪ We saw the movie at a special *preview.* — see also SNEAK PREVIEW
2 *US* **:** a selected group of scenes that are shown to advertise a movie or television show ▪ After seeing the *preview* [=*trailer*], I can't wait to see the movie. ▪ Before the movie starts they always show *previews* of coming attractions. ▪ There are *previews* of the next week's episode at the end of each show.
3 : a description of something that will happen or be available in the future ▪ They gave a *preview* of the upcoming football season. ▪ The magazine includes a *preview* of the newest fall fashions.
4 : an example of what something will look like ▪ You can see a *preview* of the page/photo before you print it.

[2]**preview** *verb* **-views; -viewed; -view·ing** [+ *obj*]
1 : to see, hear, or show something (such as a movie) before it is available to the public ▪ Critics have not yet *previewed* [=*seen, watched*] the new movie. ▪ The designers will *preview* their new lines at the fashion show.
2 : to give a general description of (something that will happen in the future) ▪ They *previewed* the upcoming football season.
3 : to see an example of what something will look like ▪ You can *preview* the page/photo before you print it.

pre·vi·ous /ˈpriːvijəs/ *adj*
1 : existing or happening before the present time ▪ She has a child from a *previous* marriage. ▪ She has made *previous* attempts to quit smoking. [=she has tried to quit smoking before] ▪ No *previous* [=*past*] experience is necessary. ▪ I can't go to the party because of a *previous* [=*prior*] engagement. [=because I agreed to be somewhere else before I knew about the party]
2 a : earlier in time or order ▪ In *previous* [=*past*] years, we always went to the beach for vacation. ▪ a *previous* album/book [=an album/book made before the current album/book] ▪ The two characters met in a *previous* chapter. ▪ the *previous* owners of the house **b :** immediately before in time or order ▪ It was Tuesday, and we'd met for lunch the *previous* day. [=the day immediately before; Monday]
previous to *somewhat formal* **:** before (a time, event, etc.) ▪ I lived in Boston for a while and *previous to* [=*prior to*] that, I lived in Miami.
– **pre·vi·ous·ly** *adv* ▪ *Previously,* the state paid for the program. ▪ The author's new book includes some *previously* published material.

pre·war /ˌpriːˈwoɚ/ *adj* **:** happening or existing before a war; *especially* **:** happening or existing before World War II ▪ the *prewar* years ▪ *prewar* Europe/buildings — opposite POSTWAR

prexy /ˈprɛksi/ *also* **prex** /ˈprɛks/ *noun, pl* **prex·ies** *also* **prex·es** [*count*] *US slang* **:** PRESIDENT

[1]**prey** /ˈpreɪ/ *noun* [*noncount*]
1 : an animal that is hunted or killed by another animal for food ▪ The lion stalked its *prey.* ▪ The bird circled above looking for *prey.* ▪ The seals are ***easy prey*** for sharks. — see also BIRD OF PREY
2 : someone who is easily harmed or affected in a bad way by someone or something **:** VICTIM ▪ Too often elderly people are ***easy prey*** for swindlers and other criminals.
be/fall prey to **1 :** to be killed by (an animal, disease, etc.) ▪ The deer *fell prey to* coyotes. ▪ Many people *fell prey to* disease. **2 :** to be harmed or affected in a bad way by (someone or something) ▪ After the accident, she *was prey to* all kinds of anxieties. ▪ Some of his friends *fell prey to* drugs. ▪ She *fell prey to* an online scam.

[2]**prey** *verb* **preys; preyed; prey·ing**
prey on/upon [*phrasal verb*] **1** ***prey on/upon (something)*** **:** to hunt and kill (something) for food ▪ The wolves *prey on* small animals. **2** ***prey on/upon (someone)*** **:** to hurt, cheat, or steal from (someone) ▪ criminals who *prey on* lonely elderly people ▪ Gangs are known to *prey on* tourists in the city. **3** ***prey on/upon someone's mind*** **:** to make someone worry **:** to be constantly on someone's mind ▪ Her growing debts *preyed on her mind.* [=she worried about her growing debts] ▪ The thought that he could have done better *preyed on his mind.* ▪ a question that *preys on the minds* of many of us

prez /ˈprɛz/ *noun, pl* **prez·es** [*count*] *US slang* **:** PRESIDENT

[1]**price** /ˈpraɪs/ *noun, pl* **pric·es**
1 : the amount of money that you pay for something or that something costs [*count*] oil/gas *prices* ▪ You paid a high/low/reasonable *price* for the car. ▪ We bought the house at a good *price.* ▪ Can you give me a *price* for the car? [=can you tell me how much the car costs?] ▪ If the *price* is right/reasonable, I'll buy it. = If it's the right *price,* I'll buy it. ▪ The *price* of milk rose/increased/fell/dropped. ▪ With the coupon you can buy two loaves of bread for the *price* of one. [=for the same amount of money it costs to buy one] ▪ I won't sell the house. ***Not at any price***. [=I won't sell the house no matter how much money someone offers me for it] [*noncount*] High-definition television sets should come down in *price* over the next few years. [=they should start to cost less over the next few years] ▪ What is the difference in *price* between the two cars? ▪ Children who are older than 12 years old have to pay ***full price***. [=the main or highest price] ▪ Air-conditioning is included in the car's ***base price***. [=the basic price you pay for something without adding anything extra] — often used before another noun ▪ *price* cuts/increases ▪ a *price* list for computer components — see also ASKING PRICE, CONSUMER PRICE INDEX, HALF PRICE, LIST PRICE, MARKET PRICE, PURCHASE PRICE, RESERVE PRICE, RETAIL PRICE INDEX, SELLING PRICE, STICKER PRICE
2 [*singular*] **:** the thing that is lost, damaged, or given up in order to get or do something ▪ A loss of privacy is often the *price* (you pay) for being famous. ▪ Giving up alcohol was ***a small price (to pay) for*** keeping his family together. ▪ Five years in prison is ***a high price (to pay) for*** one mistake. ▪ We won the war, but at ***what price***? [=did we lose or give up too much in order to win the war?] ▪ ***What price glory/fame***? [=is glory/fame worth what you have to lose or give up in order to get it?]
3 [*noncount*] **:** the amount of money needed to persuade someone to do something ▪ I know he said he wouldn't do it, but I think it's just a matter of finding his *price.*
a price on someone's head **:** an amount of money that will be given to anyone who kills or captures someone ▪ The group's leader has been in hiding since the government put *a price on his head.*
at any price **1 :** for any amount of money ▪ We think it's the best education you can get *at any price.* ▪ I wouldn't work for her again. Not *at any price.* **2 :** without caring about what might be lost or given up ▪ people who want peace *at any price*
at a price **1 :** by losing or giving up something or doing something unpleasant ▪ Success came *at a price.* **2 :** for a very large amount of money ▪ The chocolate is available by

P

mail order, but *at a price*. [=it is expensive to have the chocolate mailed to you]

beyond price literary **:** extremely valuable or important ▪ Her friendship is a treasure *beyond price*. [=a priceless treasure]

put a price on **1 :** to ask for a particular amount of money for (something you are selling) ▪ The owners have not yet *put a price on* the house. **2 :** to say how important or valuable something is — usually used in negative statements to say that something is extremely important and valuable ▪ You *can't put a price on* true love. ▪ The teachers there really care about the students, and I *don't* think you can *put a price on* (something like) that.

> ***synonyms*** PRICE, CHARGE, COST, and FEE mean the amount of money that is asked for or given as payment for something. PRICE refers to how much money is asked for goods. ▪ What is the *price* of the car? CHARGE refers to the amount that you pay for using something or for a service. ▪ There is no *charge* for parking here. ▪ What are these phone *charges* on the bill? COST is used to refer to what is paid for something by the buyer rather than what is asked for by the seller. ▪ The *cost* of the repairs seemed very high. COST may also be used to refer to prices in general. ▪ The *cost* of living is higher in big cities. FEE refers to an amount that is set by law, a business, etc., for doing something or for a particular service. ▪ There is a $50 *fee* for the license.

[2]**price** *verb* **prices; priced; pric·ing** [+ *obj*]

1 : to say or decide how much something costs : to give a price to (something) ▪ They *priced* the house too high. — usually used as *(be) priced* ▪ The house *is priced* too high. ▪ The computer *is priced* at $2,000. ▪ a reasonably *priced* car ▪ high-*priced* televisions [=expensive televisions]

2 : to put a price on (something) : to attach a price tag to (something) ▪ Workers quickly *priced the* new merchandise.

3 : to learn the price of (something that you are thinking about buying) ▪ I've been *pricing* TVs [=comparing the prices of different TVs] and I know which one we should buy.

price (someone) out of the market **:** to make the price of something too high for (someone) ▪ The high rents are *pricing* some people *out of the market*.

price yourself out of the market **:** to make the price of your services, products, etc., too high ▪ If your fee is too high, you may find that you've *priced yourself out of the market*. [=people may stop wanting to pay for your services because they cost too much]

– pricing *noun* [*noncount*] ▪ The store uses low *pricing* to attract customers. ▪ The company is changing its *pricing* policy/strategy.

price–fix·ing /ˈpraɪsˌfɪksɪŋ/ *noun* [*noncount*] **:** the usually illegal act or practice of agreeing with business competitors to set prices at a particular level instead of allowing prices to be determined by competition

price·less /ˈpraɪsləs/ *adj*

1 : extremely valuable or important : INVALUABLE ▪ The painting is *priceless*. ▪ a *priceless* piece of information ▪ Good health is *priceless*.

2 *informal* **:** very funny ▪ The look on his face was *priceless*.

price point *noun, pl* **~ points** [*count*] *business* **:** a product's regular price as set by the manufacturer

price tag *noun, pl* **~ tags** [*count*]

1 : a piece of paper or plastic that is attached to a product and that has the product's price written or printed on it ▪ The *price tag* is missing so I don't know how much this sweater costs.

2 : the amount of money that something costs ▪ The car has a $30,000 *price tag*. = The car has a *price tag* of $30,000. [=the price of the car is $30,000] ▪ The equipment carries a ***hefty price tag***. [=it is expensive] ▪ You can't ***put a price tag on*** the safety of our children. [=the safety of our children is worth any amount of money; it is extremely important]

price war *noun, pl* **~ wars** [*count*] **:** a situation in which companies or stores compete with each other by lowering their prices on goods or services in order to attract more customers ▪ The airlines are engaged in another *price war*.

pricey *also* **pricy** /ˈpraɪsi/ *adj* **pric·i·er; -est** [*also more ~; most ~*] *informal* **:** EXPENSIVE ▪ The car is a little *pricey*. ▪ a *pricey* restaurant/store

[1]**prick** /ˈprɪk/ *verb* **pricks; pricked; prick·ing**

1 [+ *obj*] **:** to make a very small hole in (something) with a sharp pointed object ▪ She *pricked* her finger with a pin. = The pin *pricked* her (finger). ▪ The nurse *pricked* my finger and squeezed out a drop of blood.

2 a [+ *obj*] **:** to cause a sharp, painful feeling on or in (part of your body) ▪ The sharp shells *pricked* the bottoms of our feet. **b** *literary* ✧ If ***tears prick your eyes***, you begin to feel tears in your eyes.

3 [+ *obj*] **:** to make (someone) feel guilt, shame, regret, etc. ▪ She was *pricked* by doubt/guilt/jealousy. ▪ The photographs of the flood victims ***pricked my conscience*** [=made me feel guilty] and I knew I had to do something to help. ▪ His ***conscience pricked him***. [=he felt guilty; he felt that he had done something wrong]

4 *of an animal* **:** to cause (the ears) to point upward [+ *obj*] The dog *pricked* (*up*) its ears at the sound. [*no obj*] The dog's ears *pricked up* at the sound. — used figuratively of people ▪ Her ***ears pricked (up)*** when they said her name. = She ***pricked up her ears*** [=she started to listen carefully] when they said her name.

[2]**prick** *noun, pl* **pricks** [*count*]

1 : an act of making a small hole in something with a sharp pointed object ▪ The nurse gave my finger a (little) *prick* (with a needle) and squeezed out a drop of blood.

2 a : a feeling of pain caused by being touched by something sharp or pointed ▪ She felt a *prick* as the thorn jabbed her foot. ▪ He felt the *prick* of the needle. **b :** a slight, sharp feeling *of* sadness, regret, etc. ▪ She felt a *prick of* jealousy. ▪ He felt a ***prick of conscience***. [=a feeling of guilt]

3 *informal + offensive* **:** PENIS

4 *informal + offensive* **:** a very bad or unpleasant man

[1]**prick·le** /ˈprɪkəl/ *noun, pl* **prick·les** [*count*]

1 : one of usually many stiff, sharp points that grow on some plants : THORN ▪ vines covered in *prickles*

2 : a slight, sharp feeling *of* an emotion ▪ She felt a *prickle of* fear as the stranger came closer to her. ▪ He felt the familiar *prickle of* excitement as the game began.

[2]**prickle** *verb* **prickles; prick·led; prick·ling :** to cause or experience an unpleasant feeling that is like the feeling of having many small, sharp points against your skin [+ *obj*] The burrs were *prickling* my arm. ▪ The wool sweater *prickled* my skin. [*no obj*] My skin *prickled* with fear. ▪ The hair *prickled* on the back of my neck. ▪ She felt a *prickling* sensation in her shoulder.

prick·ly /ˈprɪkli/ *adj* **prick·li·er; -est**

1 : having many sharp points ▪ a *prickly* cactus/bush ▪ The plant's leaves are *prickly*.

2 a : caused or seeming to be caused by something that has many small, sharp points ▪ a *prickly* feeling/sensation **b :** causing a prickly feeling on your skin ▪ a *prickly* wool sweater

3 : very difficult or complicated : requiring careful treatment ▪ a *prickly* [=*sensitive*] issue ▪ a *prickly* [=*thorny*] question

4 : easily annoyed or angered ▪ He's a *prickly* old man. ▪ a *prickly* [=*touchy*] personality

– prick·li·ness *noun* [*noncount*]

prickly heat *noun* [*noncount*] *medical* **:** a skin rash that people sometimes get during hot weather : HEAT RASH ▪ suffering from *prickly heat*

prickly pear *noun* [*count, noncount*] **:** a cactus that has yellow flowers and fruits shaped like pears; *also* **:** the fruit of this plant

pricy *variant spelling of* PRICEY

[1]**pride** /ˈpraɪd/ *noun, pl* **prides**

1 [*noncount*] **a :** a feeling that you respect yourself and deserve to be respected by other people : SELF-RESPECT ▪ Being able to work again gave him his *pride* back. ▪ Getting caught cheating stripped him of his *pride*. ▪ *Pride* would not allow her to give up. ▪ It's a matter of *pride* that he does the work all by himself. **b :** a feeling that you are more important or better than other people ▪ The novel is about a family consumed with *pride* and vanity. ▪ They needed help, but their *pride* wouldn't let them ask for it. ▪ I had to ***swallow my pride*** and admit I made a mistake.

2 a : a feeling of happiness that you get when you or someone you know does something good, difficult, etc. [*noncount*] The sight of her son holding the trophy filled her with *pride*. [=made her very proud] ▪ She spoke with *pride* [=she spoke proudly] about her son's achievements. ▪ She looked at her painting with *pride*. [=*satisfaction*] ▪ He ***takes pride in*** [=is proud of] his work. [*singular*] He showed a great/immense *pride* in his family. **b** [*singular*] **:** a person or thing that makes you feel proud ▪ These young people are the *pride* of their community.

3 [*count*] : a group of lions

pride and joy : someone or something that makes you very proud and happy • Our children are our *pride and joy.* • The car is his *pride and joy.*

pride of place : the highest position or best place • The Nobel Prize winner was given *pride of place* at the conference. • The statue has *pride of place* in the center of town. • A picture of their children took *pride of place* on the wall.

– **pride·ful** /ˈpraɪdfəl/ *adj* [*more* ~; *most* ~] *US* • a *prideful* [=*proud*] parent • He was too *prideful* to accept their help.

– **pride·ful·ly** *adv, US*

[2]**pride** *verb* **prides; prid·ed; prid·ing**

pride yourself on : to be proud because of having (an ability, quality, etc.) • I *pride myself on* my math skills. [=I am proud of my math skills] • The restaurant *prides itself on* having the best pizza in town.

priest /ˈpriːst/ *noun, pl* **priests** [*count*] : a person who has the authority to lead or perform ceremonies in some religions and especially in some Christian religions • He was ordained as a Roman Catholic *priest.* • a parish *priest*

priest·ess /ˈpriːstəs/ *noun, pl* **-ess·es** [*count*] : a woman who leads or performs religious ceremonies in some religions • a tribal *priestess*

priest·hood /ˈpriːstˌhʊd/ *noun, pl* **-hoods**

1 ***the priesthood*** : the job of being a priest • He is ***entering the priesthood.*** [=becoming a priest] • He decided to ***leave the priesthood.*** [=stop being a priest]

2 : a group of priests in a particular religion [*count*] an ancient civilization that was ruled by a *priesthood* [*noncount*] What is the influence of the *priesthood* in today's society?

priest·ly /ˈpriːstli/ *adj* **priest·li·er; -est** : of or relating to a priest or to priests as a group • the *priestly* class • *priestly* robes/vows • *priestly* power : like a priest • He is a kind, *priestly* man.

prig /ˈprɪg/ *noun, pl* **prigs** [*count*] *disapproving* : someone who annoys people by being very careful about proper behavior and by criticizing the behavior of other people • She is too much of a *prig* for my liking.

– **prig·gish** /ˈprɪgɪʃ/ *adj* [*more* ~; *most* ~] • She is too *priggish.* • *priggish* people – **prig·gish·ly** *adv* – **prig·gish·ness** *noun* [*noncount*]

prim /ˈprɪm/ *adj* **prim·mer; prim·mest** [*or more* ~; *most* ~]

1 *sometimes disapproving* **a** : very formal and proper • a *prim* manner • He has *prim* views on religion. **b** : easily shocked or upset by rude behavior, comments, etc. • a *prim* [=*prudish*] young lady • Her aunts were very ***prim and proper.***

2 : very neat in appearance • a *prim* little house

– **prim·ly** *adv* • She was *primly* dressed. • She spoke to him *primly.* – **prim·ness** *noun* [*noncount*]

pri·ma ballerina /ˈpriːmə-/ *noun, pl* ~ **-nas** [*count*] : the main female dancer in a ballet company

pri·ma·cy /ˈpraɪməsi/ *noun* [*noncount*] *formal* : the state of being most important or strongest • Civil law took *primacy* over religious law. • She has established *primacy* in her field of study. — often + *of* • He believes in the *primacy of* the family over the state.

pri·ma don·na /ˌprɪməˈdɑːnə, *Brit* ˌpriːməˈdɒnə/ *noun, pl* ~ **-nas** [*count*]

1 : the main female singer in an opera company : DIVA

2 *disapproving* : a person who thinks she or he is better than everyone else and who does not work well as part of a team or group • The actress is a temperamental *prima donna.* • We are looking for team players, not *prima donnas.*

primaeval *Brit spelling of* PRIMEVAL

pri·ma fa·cie /ˌpraɪməˈfeɪʃə, *Brit* ˌpraɪməˈfeɪʃi/ *adj, always used before a noun, law* : based on what is known or seen when something is first considered or dealt with • a *prima facie* case • There is strong *prima facie* evidence that she committed perjury. [=when we look at the situation now, there is strong evidence that she committed perjury, although it is possible that we will find out that she did not commit perjury when we learn more]

pri·mal /ˈpraɪməl/ *adj* [*more* ~; *most* ~] *formal* : very basic and powerful — used especially to describe feelings that are like the feelings of animals and that seem to come from a part of human nature that has existed since ancient times • *primal* urges/instincts

pri·mar·i·ly /praɪˈmerəli, *Brit* ˈpraɪmərəli/ *adv* — used to indicate the main purpose of something, reason for something, etc. • The game is designed *primarily* [=*mainly*] for younger children. • They seemed *primarily* [=*mostly*] interested in getting rich.

[1]**pri·ma·ry** /ˈpraɪˌmeri, *Brit* ˈpraɪməri/ *adj, always used before a noun*

1 **a** : most important : MAIN • our *primary* [=*principal*] objective/goal • The economy was the *primary* focus of the debate. • Your safety is our *primary* [=*foremost*] concern. **b** : most basic or essential • *primary* needs • The family is the *primary* social unit of human life. • The *primary* function of our schools is to educate our young people. — compare SECONDARY, TERTIARY

2 : happening or coming first • the *primary* [=*initial*] stage of a civilization • We just started our *primary* flight training. — compare SECONDARY, TERTIARY

3 : not coming from or dependent on something else • The book is based mainly on *primary* sources rather than secondary sources.

4 *chiefly Brit* : relating to the education of young children • *primary* [=(*US*) *elementary*] education/teachers

[2]**primary** *noun, pl* **-ries** [*count*] *US* : an election in which members of the same political party run against each other for the chance to be in a larger and more important election • a presidential *primary* — called also (*US*) *primary election*

primary care *noun* [*noncount*] : medical care from the doctor who sees a patient first and provides basic treatment or decides that the patient should see another doctor • He provides *primary care* to inner-city patients. • (*US*) a *primary care* physician/provider

primary color (*US*) *or Brit* **primary colour** *noun, pl* ~ **-ors** [*count*] : one of the three colors red, yellow, or blue which can be mixed together to make other colors — compare SECONDARY COLOR

primary school *noun, pl* ~ **schools** : a school for young children [*count*] a new *primary school* [=(*US*) *elementary school*, (*US*) *grade school*] [*noncount*] She goes to *primary school.* — compare SECONDARY SCHOOL

pri·mate /ˈpraɪˌmeɪt/ *noun, pl* **-mates** [*count*]

1 : any member of the group of animals that includes human beings, apes, and monkeys

2 *or* ***Primate formal*** : the highest ranking priest in a particular country or area in some Christian churches (such as the Church of England) • the *Primate* of England and Wales

[1]**prime** /ˈpraɪm/ *adj, always used before a noun*

1 : most important : PRIMARY • our *prime* responsibility • The wine industry is of *prime* importance to the California economy. • The police have not yet named the *prime* suspect in the murder investigation.

2 : of the highest quality or value : EXCELLENT • *prime* beef • The house is expensive because it's in a *prime* location. • *prime* farmland

3 — used to say that someone or something is a very good example of a particular kind of person or thing • The melting of ice caps is a ***prime example*** of the effects of global warming. • Orson Welles is a *prime example* of the movie director as artist. • a ***prime specimen*** of a racehorse

4 : most likely or very likely to be chosen for something, to experience something, etc. • The mayor has become a *prime* target for criticism. • Her father was unhealthy and looked like a *prime* candidate for a heart attack. [=he looked like someone who was likely to have a heart attack]

[2]**prime** *noun*

1 [*singular*] : the period in life when a person is best in health, strength, etc. : the most active or successful time of a person's life • young college graduates ***in the prime of life*** • She just retired, but she's still ***in her prime.*** [=still active and in good health] • He was a great pitcher once, but he's ***past his prime.*** [=is no longer as good as he was when he was younger]

2 [*noncount*] *technical* : PRIME RATE • The interest rate is two percent plus/over *prime.*

[3]**prime** *verb* **primes; primed; prim·ing** [+ *obj*]

1 : to make (someone) ready to do something : PREPARE • She was obviously *primed* for the questions at the press conference. • Both teams are *primed* for battle and ready to play.

2 : to make (something) ready for use • *prime* a bomb/gun • *prime* a pump • *prime* an engine

3 : to cover (a surface) with special paint in order to prepare it for the final layer of paint • We sanded and *primed* the woodwork before painting.

prime the pump : to do something that will help a thing to grow or develop • The government has to *prime the pump* to get the economy going. • That sort of language will only *prime the pump* for an ugly argument later.

P

prime interest rate *noun, pl* ~ **rates** [*count*] : PRIME RATE

prime meridian *noun*
the prime meridian : an imaginary line that runs from the North Pole to the South Pole through Greenwich, England

prime minister *or* **Prime Minister** *noun, pl* ~ **-ters** [*count*] : the head of the government in some countries ▪ the *Prime Minister* of England — abbr. *PM*

prime mover *noun, pl* ~ **-ers** [*count*] : a person or thing that starts something or that has a very powerful influence on something ▪ She was the *prime mover* behind the town's annual summer festival.

prime number *noun, pl* ~ **-bers** [*count*] *mathematics* : a number (such as 2, 3, or 5) that can only be exactly divided by itself and by 1

[1]**prim·er** /ˈprɪmɚ, *Brit* ˈpraɪmə/ *noun, pl* **-ers** [*count*]
1 *chiefly US* : something (such as a book) that provides basic information on a particular subject ▪ The article is an excellent *primer* on foreign policy.
2 : a small book that helps teach children how to read
– compare [2]PRIMER

[2]**prim·er** /ˈpraɪmɚ/ *noun, pl* **-ers** [*count, noncount*] : a kind of paint that is used to prepare a surface for a final layer of a different paint — compare [1]PRIMER

prime rate *noun, pl* ~ **rates** [*count*] : the lowest interest rate that banks will give to people who borrow money from them — called also *prime, prime interest rate*

prime time *noun* [*noncount*]
1 a : the time in the evening when the largest number of people are watching television ▪ The program is being shown during *prime time.* ▪ a *prime-time* program **b** : the television shows that are on during prime time ▪ He's the best actor in *prime time.*
2 *chiefly US, informal* : the highest or most difficult level of use ▪ This software isn't ready for *prime time.* [=it is not yet good enough to be used; it has problems that need to be corrected]

pri·me·val *also Brit* **pri·mae·val** /praɪˈmiːvəl/ *adj* [*more* ~; *most* ~]
1 : very old or ancient ▪ *primeval* forests ▪ the forest *primeval*
2 *formal* : basic and powerful : PRIMAL ▪ our *primeval* instincts

[1]**prim·i·tive** /ˈprɪmətɪv/ *adj* [*more* ~; *most* ~]
1 : of, belonging to, or seeming to come from an early time in the very ancient past ▪ the time when *primitive* man first learned to use fire ▪ *primitive* animals/plants [=animals/plants that lived in ancient times or that have not changed much since ancient times]
2 : not having a written language, advanced technology, etc. ▪ *primitive* societies/cultures
3 : very simple and basic : made or done in a way that is not modern and that does not show much skill ▪ *primitive* [=*crude*] tools ▪ The technology they used was *primitive* and outdated. ▪ The camp had only a *primitive* outdoor toilet.
4 : coming from the part of a person that is wild or like an animal : not based on reason ▪ *primitive* instincts/feelings/fears
– **prim·i·tive·ly** *adv* – **prim·i·tive·ness** *noun* [*noncount*]

[2]**primitive** *noun, pl* **-tives** [*count*] *formal*
1 : an artist who makes art in a simple style that is childlike; *also* : the art made by such an artist ▪ The museum is known for its collection of American *primitives.*
2 *old-fashioned* : someone who belongs to a primitive society ▪ a Stone Age *primitive*

pri·mo /ˈpriːmoʊ/ *adj, US slang* : of the best quality : EXCELLENT ▪ I found a *primo* parking space right out front.

pri·mor·di·al /prɪˈmoɚdijəl/ *adj, formal* : existing from the beginning of time : very ancient ▪ *primordial* gases in space ▪ *primordial* [=*primeval*] forests

primp /ˈprɪmp/ *verb* **primps; primped; primp·ing** : to try to make yourself more attractive by making small changes to your clothes, hair, etc., especially while looking at yourself in a mirror [*no obj*] The girls spent hours *primping* in front of the mirror. [+ *obj*] He *primped* his hair while waiting for his date.

prim·rose /ˈprɪmˌroʊz/ *noun, pl* **-ros·es** [*count*] : a small plant with flowers that are usually a pale yellow color
primrose path : an easy way of living or proceeding that will lead to problems later ▪ The mayor is leading us down a/the *primrose path* by refusing to maintain the roads and only repairing them after they fail.

prince /ˈprɪns/ *noun, pl* **princ·es** [*count*]
1 a : a male member of a royal family; *especially* : the son or grandson of a king or queen **b** : a male ruler or monarch in some countries ▪ the *Prince* of Monaco
2 : a man who is the best in his class, profession, etc. — usually singular ▪ He was the *prince* of poets. ▪ He is a *prince* among men. [=he is a very good man]

Prince Charming *noun* [*singular*] *often humorous* : a man who is handsome, brave, polite, etc., and would be a perfect husband or boyfriend ▪ She was still waiting to meet her *Prince Charming.* ▪ He's no *Prince Charming*, but he's okay.

prince·ly /ˈprɪnsli/ *adj*
1 : very large or impressive ▪ a *princely* gift ▪ Their summer house cost a ***princely sum***. [=their summer house was very expensive]
2 : of, relating to, or suitable for a prince ▪ a display of *princely* courtesy ▪ *princely* duties

prin·cess /ˈprɪnsəs, *Brit* ˌprɪnˈses/ *noun, pl* **-cess·es** [*count*]
1 : a female member of a royal family; *especially* : a daughter or granddaughter of a king or queen
2 : the wife of a prince ▪ *Princess* Diana
3 *informal + sometimes disapproving* : a usually attractive girl or woman who is treated with special attention and kindness ▪ a pop music *princess* ▪ She's just a stuck-up *princess.*

[1]**prin·ci·pal** /ˈprɪnsəpəl/ *adj, always used before a noun* : most important : CHIEF ▪ Vegetables are the *principal* ingredients in this soup. ▪ My *principal* [=*main*] reason for moving is to have a shorter drive to work. ▪ She is the *principal* cellist of the orchestra.
– **prin·ci·pal·ly** /ˈprɪnsəpəli/ *adv* ▪ He is *principally* [=*chiefly, mainly*] known as a composer.

[2]**principal** *noun, pl* **-pals** [*count*]
1 a *US* : the person in charge of a public school ▪ the new high school *principal* **b** *Brit* : the person in charge of a university or college
2 : an amount of money that is put in a bank or lent to someone and that can earn interest — usually singular ▪ Our monthly mortgage payment covers the interest on our loan as well as some of the *principal.*
3 a : the main performer in a group of performers ▪ The ballet featured the two *principals.* [=lead dancers] **b** : the most important person in a group ▪ One of the *principals* in the assassination plot has been arrested.

> Do not confuse *principal* with *principle.*

prin·ci·pal·i·ty /ˌprɪnsəˈpæləti/ *noun, pl* **-ties** [*count*] *formal* : a small area or country that is ruled by a prince

principal parts *noun* [*plural*] *grammar* : the main forms of a verb ▪ The *principal parts* of the verb "write" include the infinitive "write," the past tense "wrote," the past participle "written," and the present participle "writing."

prin·ci·ple /ˈprɪnsəpəl/ *noun, pl* **-ciples**
1 : a moral rule or belief that helps you know what is right and wrong and that influences your actions [*count*] He has good *principles.* ▪ It's ***against my principles*** to cheat. [=I believe that cheating is wrong] [*noncount*] As ***a matter of principle***, he would not accept the gift. [=he did not feel that it was right to accept the gift] ▪ She refused ***on principle*** [=because of her beliefs] to give toy guns to the children.
2 [*count*] : a basic truth or theory : an idea that forms the basis of something ▪ well-established economic *principles* ▪ His investment strategy is based on the *principle* that the stock market offers the best returns for long-term investors.
3 [*count*] : a law or fact of nature that explains how something works or why something happens ▪ the basic *principles* of hydraulics/magnetism
in principle **1** — used to say that something which has not yet happened or been done should be possible according to what is known ▪ *In principle*, making the changes should be a simple matter, but there may be problems we haven't thought of. **2** : in a general way and without giving attention to details ▪ They accepted the offer *in principle.*

> Do not confuse *principle* with *principal.*

prin·ci·pled /ˈprɪnsəpəld/ *adj* [*more* ~; *most* ~] : having, based on, or relating to strong beliefs about what is right and wrong ▪ a *principled* person [=a person who has strong moral principles; a person who tries to do what is morally right] ▪ She took a *principled* stand/position on funding public education.

[1]**print** /ˈprɪnt/ *verb* **prints; print·ed; print·ing**
1 : to cause (words, images, etc.) to appear on paper or cloth

by using a machine (called a printer) [+ *obj*] We *printed* 50 invitations before we ran out of ink. • Could you *print* (up) another copy of last quarter's report? • The new machine *prints* 30 pages per minute. • Your tickets are being *printed* now. • a slogan *printed* on a bumper sticker • We *printed* the new logo on the T-shirts. = We *printed* the T-shirts with the new logo. [*no obj*] Your tickets are *printing* now. • This printer allows you to *print* on both sides of a sheet of paper.

2 [+ *obj*] **: to use a machine (called a printing press) to produce (books, newspapers, magazines, etc.)** • They *printed* 10,000 copies of the book's new edition.

3 [+ *obj*] **: to include (something) in a book, newspaper, magazine, etc. : PUBLISH** • I'm surprised they *printed* that cartoon/story in the paper. • Her picture was *printed* in a magazine last month.

4 : to write (something) using separate letters that do not join together [+ *obj*] *Print* your name and address in the space provided. [*no obj*] Once you learn how to *print*, then you can move on to cursive writing.

5 [+ *obj*] **: to produce (a photograph) on paper** • Please *print* two copies of all the pictures on that roll. • Our vacation pictures are on my computer, but I haven't *printed* them yet.

a license to print money see [1]LICENSE

print out *also* ***print off*** [*phrasal verb*] ***print (something) out/off*** *or* ***print out/off (something)*** **: to produce a paper copy of (a document that is on a computer)** • Could you *print out* another copy for me? — see also PRINTOUT

– printed *adj, always used before a noun* • *printed* documents • Fewer people these days are getting their news from the ***printed page/word***. [=from newspapers, magazines, books, and other printed sources]

[2]**print** *noun, pl* **prints**

1 [*noncount*] **: the process of making a book, magazine, newspaper, etc.** • The editor's job is to prepare the manuscript ***for print***. [=for publication] • He was glad to get one of his poems ***into print***. [=into a published magazine, book, etc.] • Her first novel is still ***in print***. [=her first novel is still being printed for sale] • His biography has been ***out of print*** for years. [=his biography is no longer being printed] • When is the book scheduled to ***go to print***? [=when is the book supposed to be sent to the printer?]

2 [*noncount*] **: the letters, numbers, or symbols used in printing something : TYPE** • books with large *print* = large-*print* books [=books with large letters for people who have difficulty seeing] • What is the *print* size of your book? — see also FINE PRINT, SMALL PRINT

3 [*count*] **a : a photograph that is printed on paper** • black-and-white *prints* • She bought a *print* [=a photographic copy] of the painting for her room. **b : a picture made from pressing an inked surface on paper** • a woodblock *print* • an exhibit of 16th-century German *prints*

4 [*count*] **: a mark made on the surface of something: such as a : FINGERPRINT** • The detectives found his *prints* on the wine glass. • Police dusted the house for *prints*. **b : FOOTPRINT** • A muddy *print* on the sidewalk matched the tread on the suspect's boots.

5 [*count*] **: cloth that has a pattern printed on it** • The fabric store had a variety of plaids and *prints* available. • a floral *print* dress

[3]**print** *adj, always used before a noun* **: of, relating to, or writing for books, magazines, newspapers, etc.** • *print* journalists/journalism • *print* ads/media

print·able /ˈprɪntəbəl/ *adj*

1 : suitable to be printed or published • The paper's editor isn't looking for a great article, just something *printable*. • The coach yelled insults at his team, none of which are *printable*. [=the words he used were too offensive to be shown in print]

2 : able to be printed by using a computer's printer • There are *printable* maps on the Web site.

printed circuit *noun, pl* ~ **-cuits** [*count*] *technical* **: a circuit that uses thin strips of metal on a thin board to carry electricity**

print·er /ˈprɪntɚ/ *noun, pl* **-ers** [*count*]

1 : a machine that is used for printing documents, photographs, etc. • I need a new *printer* for my office. — see picture at OFFICE; see also INK-JET PRINTER, LASER PRINTER

2 : a person or company whose business is printing books, magazines, etc. • Benjamin Franklin was originally a *printer*. • The manuscript was sent to the *printer* yesterday.

print·ing /ˈprɪntɪŋ/ *noun, pl* **-ings**

1 [*noncount*] **: the process of producing books, magazines, etc. by using machinery** • color *printing* • a *printing* error

2 [*count*] **: the act or process of printing a set number of copies of a book at one time** • The book is already in its second *printing*, and a third printing is scheduled for later this year. • The book has had two *printings* of 100,000 copies each.

3 [*noncount*] **: handwriting that uses separate letters that do not join together** • Her *printing* is very neat.

printing press *noun, pl* ~ **press·es** [*count*] **: a machine that prints books, magazines, newspapers, etc., usually in large numbers**

print·out /ˈprɪntˌaʊt/ *noun, pl* **-outs** [*count*] **: a copy of a document produced by a printer** • She gave me a *printout* of the directions. • a computer *printout* — see also ***print out*** at [1]PRINT

[1]**pri·or** /ˈprajɚ/ *adj, always used before a noun*

1 : existing earlier in time : PREVIOUS • *prior* approval • in *prior* years • Do you have a *prior* history of back problems? • The job requires *prior* experience in advertising. • The defendant had a *prior* record of convictions. • I'm sorry, but we have a *prior* commitment and can't come tonight. • The contract was canceled ***without prior notice***. [=the contract was canceled right away]

2 *formal* **: more important than something else because it came first** • We have a *prior* claim to the estate.

prior to *somewhat formal* **: before (a time, event, etc.)** • *Prior to* dinner, photographs of the wedding party will be taken. • My parents were married just *prior to* the war.

[2]**prior** *noun, pl* **-ors** [*count*]

1 a : a monk who is the head of a religious house or order b : a priest whose rank is just below that of an abbot

2 *US, informal* **: a previous time of being arrested for or found guilty of a crime** • The suspect has two *priors* for robbery. [=the suspect had been arrested/convicted twice before for robbery]

pri·or·ess /ˈprajərəs/ *noun, pl* **-ess·es** [*count*] **: a nun who is head of a religious house or order**

pri·or·i·tize *also Brit* **pri·or·i·tise** /praɪˈorəˌtaɪz/ *verb* **-tiz·es; -tized; -tiz·ing**

1 : to organize (things) so that the most important thing is done or dealt with first [+ *obj*] It's always difficult to *prioritize* work, school, and family. [*no obj*] If you want to do your job efficiently, you have to learn to *prioritize*.

2 [+ *obj*] **: to make (something) the most important thing in a group** • The town council hopes to *prioritize* the bridge construction project at the next meeting.

pri·or·i·ty /praɪˈorəti/ *noun, pl* **-ties**

1 [*count*] **: something that is more important than other things and that needs to be done or dealt with first** • Reorganizing the sales force will be a top *priority* for the new president. • Getting the work done on time is a *priority* for me. • Exercising is not very high on her list of *priorities*. [=it's not among the things she thinks are important]

2 *priorities* [*plural*] *US* **: the things that someone cares about and thinks are important** • He has terrible *priorities*. [=he doesn't care about the things that are truly important] • You need to ***get your priorities straight*** and go back to school. [=you need to realize that going back to school is the most important thing for you to do] • She decided to go to the party instead of studying? ***Where are her priorities***?

3 [*noncount*] **: the condition of being more important than something or someone else and therefore coming or being dealt with first** • These problems are important and should be ***given priority*** (over others). [=they should be dealt with first] • I know you want to buy a new stereo, but right now, saving for college has to ***take priority***. • Health concerns should ***have priority*** over comfort. [=health concerns are more important than comfort]

pri·o·ry /ˈprajəri/ *noun, pl* **-ries** [*count*] **: a place where a group of monks or nuns live : a religious house that is under the direction of a prior or prioress**

prism /ˈprɪzəm/ *noun, pl* **prisms** [*count*] **: a transparent glass or plastic object that usually has three sides and that separates the light that passes through it into different colors — often used figuratively to describe a way of looking at or thinking about something that causes you to see or understand it in a different way** • The novel is a history of early 19th-century America told ***through the prism of*** one life.

pris·mat·ic /prɪzˈmætɪk/ *adj, technical* **: using, containing, or shaped like a prism** • a *prismatic* lens • *prismatic* crystals

pris·on /ˈprɪzn̩/ *noun, pl* **-ons**

1 : a building where people are kept as punishment for a crime or while they are waiting to go to court [*count*] a

P

state/federal *prison* • The state plans to build two more *prisons*. [*noncount*] He was ***in prison*** at the time. • If caught, they're all ***going to prison***. • She was ***sent/sentenced to prison*** for robbery. • He was ***released from prison***. • He's scheduled to get ***out of prison*** next month. — often used before another noun • a *prison* cell • a *prison* guard • an investigation into *prison* conditions • an overhaul of the *prison* system • *prison* reform • the *prison* population • an eight-year *prison* sentence/term • ***prison time*** [=the time someone spends in prison] ***synonyms*** see [1]JAIL

2 [*count*] : a place or situation from which you cannot escape • Her marriage became a *prison* to her.

prison camp *noun, pl* **~ camps** [*count*] : a camp where a large group of prisoners are kept especially during a war

pris·on·er /ˈprɪzn̩ɚ/ *noun, pl* **-ers** [*count*]

1 : a person who is kept in a prison • The *prisoners* [=*inmates*] have two hours of exercise per day. • a ***political prisoner*** [=a person put in prison because of his or her political beliefs]

2 : a person who has been captured and is being kept somewhere • He was captured by rebel forces and kept as their *prisoner* for several months before they set him free. • They ***took him prisoner***. = He was ***taken prisoner***. [=they captured him and made him their prisoner] • The families were ***held/kept prisoner*** for four days. — sometimes used figuratively • She's a *prisoner* of her fears. [=she is controlled by her fears]

take no prisoners : to deal with the people you are competing with or trying to defeat in a very harsh way without mercy • He *takes no prisoners* when it comes to running the business. — see also TAKE-NO-PRISONERS

prisoner of conscience *noun, pl* **prisoners of conscience** [*count*] : someone who is held in prison because of his or her political or religious beliefs

prisoner of war *noun, pl* **prisoners of war** [*count*] : a soldier who has been captured during a war by the enemy — called also *POW*

pris·sy /ˈprɪsi/ *adj* **pris·sier**; **-est** [*also more ~; most ~*] *informal + disapproving* : having or showing the annoying attitude of people who care too much about dressing and behaving properly and who are easily upset by other people's behavior, language, etc. • She was too *prissy* to wear jeans. • a *prissy* do-gooder

– pris·si·ly /ˈprɪsəli/ *adv* **– pris·si·ness** /ˈprɪsinəs/ *noun* [*noncount*]

pris·tine /ˈprɪˌstiːn/ *adj* [*more ~; most ~*]

1 : in perfect condition : completely clean, fresh, neat, etc. • My office is a mess but her office is always *pristine*. • He was wearing a *pristine* white shirt. • The car is 10 years old but it's still in ***pristine condition***. [=it still looks the way it did when it was new]

2 : not changed by people : left in its natural state • a *pristine* forest

P

pri·va·cy /ˈpraɪvəsi, *Brit* ˈprɪvəsi/ *noun* [*noncount*]

1 : the state of being alone : the state of being away from other people • She went upstairs for some *privacy*. • I don't care about what you do in the *privacy* of your own home. [=I don't care what you do when you are at home by yourself or with your family]

2 : the state of being away from public attention • Celebrities have a right to *privacy*. • She felt that the guard's request to search her was an ***invasion of (her) privacy***. [=she felt the search did not respect her privacy]

[1]**pri·vate** /ˈpraɪvət/ *adj* [*more ~; most ~*]

1 : for the use of a single person or group : belonging to one person or group : not public • a *private* beach/club/property • He returned to the country on his *private* [=*personal*] jet. • It was the first time many had seen works from the artist's *private* collection. • a room with a ***private bath*** [=a bathroom that is not shared between several rooms]

2 : not relating to a person's official position or job • At work he was always very serious, but in his *private* life, he was actually very funny and relaxed.

3 a : not known by the public or by other people : SECRET • *private* dealings/meetings • Please keep all my personal information *private*. • They shared a ***private joke***. [=a joke only understood by the few people who know what it refers to] **b** : not telling others about yourself : keeping your personal information secret • He's a very *private* person.

4 : away from other people : out of the sight and hearing of other people • Let's go somewhere *private*. • They were sitting in a *private* corner of the restaurant.

5 *always used before a noun* : not holding a public or elected office • *private* individuals • a ***private citizen***

6 a : not paid for or controlled by the government • tax policies to encourage *private* industry • a *private* hospital/college • The mayor hired a *private* contractor rather than using city workers to do the job. **b** : not having stocks traded on the open market • a *private* company

7 : involving or done with a single person rather than a group • She had years of *private* piano study/lessons. • *private* students [=students who are given private lessons]

– pri·vate·ly *adv* • a *privately* held/owned company • The two leaders met *privately* to discuss trade policy.

[2]**private** *noun, pl* **-vates**

1 [*count*] : a person of the lowest rank in the U.S. or British Army or the U.S. Marines

2 privates [*plural*] *informal* : PRIVATE PARTS

in private : out of the sight and hearing of other people : in a private place • We would like to speak to you *in private*. [=*privately*] • The group always met *in private*.

private enterprise *noun* [*noncount*] : FREE ENTERPRISE

pri·va·teer /ˌpraɪvəˈtiɚ/ *noun, pl* **-teers** [*count*] : a ship used in the past to attack and rob other ships; *also* : a sailor on a privateer

private investigator *noun, pl* **~ -tors** [*count*] : someone who works as a detective and who is not a member of a police force • She hired a *private investigator* to follow her husband. — called also *private detective, (informal) private eye*

private member *noun, pl* **~ -bers** [*count*] *Brit* : a member of the British House of Commons who is not a minister in the government

private member's bill *noun, pl* **~ bills** [*count*] *Brit* : a bill prepared or introduced in the British House of Commons by a private member

private parts *noun* [*plural*] *informal* : a person's external sexual organs — used as a polite way of referring to the sexual organs without having to say their names • He used a towel to cover his *private parts*. — called also *privates*

private patient *noun, pl* **~ -tients** [*count*] *Brit* : a person who gets and pays for medical treatment outside of the National Health Service

private practice *noun, pl* **~ -tices** : a professional business (such as that of a lawyer or doctor) that is not controlled or paid for by the government or a larger company (such as a hospital) [*noncount*] After years as attorney general, he returned to *private practice*. • He is now ***in private practice***. [*count*] She left the hospital clinic and now has a *private practice*.

private school *noun, pl* **~ schools** [*count*] : a school that does not get money from the government and that is run by a group of private individuals — compare PUBLIC SCHOOL

private sector *noun* [*singular*] : the part of an economy which is not controlled or owned by the government • The *private sector* is growing. • *private-sector* businesses/gains — compare PUBLIC SECTOR

pri·va·tion /praɪˈveɪʃən/ *noun, pl* **-tions** *formal* : a lack or loss of the basic things that people need to live properly [*noncount*] The country has suffered through long periods of economic *privation*. [*count*] the *privations* of poverty

pri·vat·ize *also Brit* **pri·vat·ise** /ˈpraɪvəˌtaɪz/ *verb* **-iz·es**; **-ized**; **-iz·ing** [*+ obj*] : to remove (something) from government control and place it in private control or ownership • The city decided to *privatize* the municipal power company. • a proposal to *privatize* the health-care system — opposite NATIONALIZE

– pri·vat·i·za·tion *also Brit* **pri·vat·i·sa·tion** /ˌpraɪvətəˈzeɪʃən, *Brit* ˌpraɪvəˌtaɪˈzeɪʃən/ *noun* [*noncount*] • the *privatization* of health care

priv·et /ˈprɪvət/ *noun* [*noncount*] : a bush with green leaves that is often used for hedges

[1]**priv·i·lege** /ˈprɪvlɪʤ/ *noun, pl* **-leg·es**

1 [*count*] : a right or benefit that is given to some people and not to others • The prisoner's exercise *privileges* were taken away. [=the prisoner was no longer allowed to exercise] • Good health care should be a right and not a *privilege*.

2 [*singular*] : a special opportunity to do something that makes you proud • Meeting the President was a *privilege*. [=*honor*] • We had the *privilege* of being invited to the party. • I had the *privilege* of knowing your grandfather.

3 [*noncount*] *somewhat formal* : the advantage that wealthy and powerful people have over other people in a society • He lived a life of wealth and *privilege*. • children of *privilege* [=privileged children; children from wealthy families with high social status]

4 [*noncount*] : the right to keep important information private ▪ attorney-client *privilege* [=the right an attorney has to keep information shared by a client secret] ▪ During the investigation, the President invoked ***executive privilege***.

5 [*noncount*] *Brit* : the right to say or do something without being punished for it ▪ parliamentary *privilege*

[2]**privilege** *verb* **-leges; -leged; -leg·ing** [+ *obj*] *formal* : to give an advantage that others do not have to (someone or something) ▪ The new tax laws unfairly *privilege* the rich.

privileged *adj*

1 [*more ~; most ~*] *sometimes disapproving* : having special rights or advantages that most people do not have ▪ He comes from a very *privileged* background. ▪ The town attracts people who are wealthy and *privileged*. ▪ The President's adviser has a *privileged* position of trust. ▪ She had *privileged* access to the files. ▪ Only ***the privileged few*** can become members of the club. ▪ I ***was privileged*** to be part of the winning team. [=I had the good fortune of being part of the winning team]

2 *law* : known only by the people who need to know ▪ *privileged* [=*confidential*] information

[1]**privy** /ˈprɪvi/ *adj*

privy to : allowed to know about (something secret) ▪ I wasn't *privy to* their plans. [=I didn't know about their plans]

[2]**privy** *noun, pl* **priv·ies** [*count*] *old-fashioned* : a small outdoor building that is used as a toilet

Privy Council *noun*

the Privy Council : the group of people chosen by the British king or queen to serve as advisers

privy purse *noun*

the privy purse : the amount of money given to the British king or queen for personal expenses

[1]**prize** /ˈpraɪz/ *noun, pl* **priz·es** [*count*]

1 : something that is won in a contest or given as an award ▪ $500 was the *prize* for first place. ▪ She won a *prize* for guessing correctly how many jelly beans there were in the jar. ▪ He won first/second/third *prize*. ▪ The ***grand prize*** [=the best prize] of the drawing went to his daughter. — see also BOOBY PRIZE, CONSOLATION PRIZE, DOOR PRIZE, NOBEL PRIZE, PULITZER PRIZE

2 : something that is very valuable or desirable and that is difficult to get ▪ This picture would be the *prize* of any museum's collection.

[2]**prize** *adj, always used before a noun*

1 **a** : given as an award or prize ▪ *prize* money **b** : winning a prize ▪ a *prize* [=(more commonly) *prizewinning*] essay ▪ the *prize* pig

2 : very good or impressive : deserving an award or prize ▪ Dad brought back his *prize* catch, a three-foot striped bass. ▪ a *prize* student

3 *Brit, informal* : real or complete ▪ I felt a *prize* fool for making such a stupid mistake.

[3]**prize** *verb* **prizes; prized; priz·ing** [+ *obj*] : to value (someone or something) very highly ▪ I know that you *prize* our friendship. ***synonyms*** see APPRECIATE — compare [4]PRIZE

[4]**prize** (*US*) *or Brit* **prise** /ˈpraɪz/ *verb* **priz·es; prized; priz·ing** [+ *obj*] *somewhat formal* : to open or move (something) with a tool ▪ I tried to *prize* [=(*US*) *pry*] the lid off the jar. ▪ She *prized* the door open with the crowbar. — often used figuratively ▪ He tried to *prize* the information out of me. [=he tried to force me to give him the information] — compare [3]PRIZE

prized *adj, always used before a noun* : very valuable or important ▪ These are some of my *prized* possessions. ▪ She was a highly *prized* employee.

prize·fight /ˈpraɪzˌfaɪt/ *noun, pl* **-fights** [*count*] : a fight between two professional boxers for money

– **prize·fight·er** /ˈpraɪzˌfaɪtɚ/ *noun, pl* **-ers** [*count*] – **prize·fight·ing** /ˈpraɪzˌfaɪtɪŋ/ *noun* [*noncount*] ▪ He wrote a history of American *prizefighting*.

prize–giving *noun, pl* **-ings** [*count*] *Brit* : a ceremony at which prizes are awarded

prize·win·ner /ˈpraɪzˌwɪnɚ/ *noun, pl* **-ners** [*count*] : someone or something that wins a prize

– **prize·win·ning** /ˈpraɪzˌwɪnɪŋ/ *adj, always used before a noun* ▪ a *prizewinning* director ▪ a *prizewinning* recipe

[1]**pro** /ˈproʊ/ *noun, pl* **pros** [*count*] : an argument for something : a reason to do something — usually plural ▪ Make a list of the *pros* and a list of the cons and then compare them. ▪ The *pros* outweigh the cons. [=there are more advantages than disadvantages] ▪ Congress weighed the ***pros and cons*** of the new tax plan. [=the arguments for and against the new tax plan]

2 : a person who supports or is in favor of something ▪ When the new law was proposed, we began hearing arguments from both the *pros* and the cons. [=from the people who supported it and the people who opposed it]

– compare [3]PRO

[2]**pro** *adv* : in favor of something ▪ Much was written ***pro and con*** about the law. [=both for and against the law]

[3]**pro** *noun, pl* **pros** [*count*]

1 : someone who is paid to participate in a sport or activity : PROFESSIONAL ▪ tennis/golf *pros* ▪ He just ***turned pro*** this year. [=he just became a professional this year]

2 : someone who has a lot of experience or skill in a particular job or activity ▪ He is a *pro* when it comes to household repairs. ▪ She handled that tricky situation like an ***old pro***.

the pros US, somewhat informal : the professional level of competition in a sport ▪ He is playing in *the pros* now.

– compare [1]PRO

[4]**pro** *adj, always used before a noun*

1 : paid to participate in a sport or activity : PROFESSIONAL ▪ a *pro* athlete/wrestler

2 : done by people who are paid to play or compete in a sport or activity : PROFESSIONAL ▪ *pro* football/basketball

pro- *prefix* : in favor of : supporting — often used with a hyphen ▪ *pro*-Democracy — opposite ANTI-

pro·ac·tive /proʊˈæktɪv/ *adj* [*more ~; most ~*] : controlling a situation by making things happen or by preparing for possible future problems ▪ A survey was given out to customers so that the company could take *proactive* steps to improve their service. ▪ The city is taking a *proactive* approach to fighting crime by hiring more police officers. — compare REACTIVE

– **pro·ac·tive·ly** *adv* ▪ Regular exercise is one way to fight heart disease *proactively*.

pro–am /ˈproʊˈæm/ *noun, pl* **-ams** [*count*] : an event or tournament in which both professionals and amateurs compete

– **pro–am** *adj, always before a noun* ▪ a *pro-am* tournament/race

prob·a·bil·i·ty /ˌprɑːbəˈbɪləti/ *noun, pl* **-ties**

1 : the chance that something will happen [*count*] The *probability* [=*likelihood*] of an earthquake is low/high. ▪ There is a low/high *probability* that you will be chosen. [*noncount*] There is some *probability* of rain tomorrow.

2 [*singular*] : something that has a chance of happening ▪ With the dark clouds moving in, rain seems more like a *probability* than a possibility.

3 : a measure of how often a particular event will happen if something (such as tossing a coin) is done repeatedly [*count*] The *probability* of a coin coming up heads is one out of every two tries. [*noncount*] the laws of *probability*

in all probability : almost certainly : very likely ▪ *In all probability*, he will go home tomorrow. ▪ We will contact you, *in all probability*, next week.

prob·a·ble /ˈprɑːbəbəl/ *adj* [*more ~; most ~*] : likely to happen or to be true but not certain ▪ a *probable* result/explanation ▪ His account of what happened is more *probable* than not. [=his account of what happened is probably true] ▪ It is *probable* that life exists outside of our planet.

probable cause *noun* [*noncount*] *chiefly US, law* : evidence that gives someone a reason to think that a crime has been or is being committed ▪ The lawyer argued that there was a lack of *probable cause* for a search warrant. ▪ The police had *probable cause* to arrest him.

prob·a·bly /ˈprɑːbəbli/ *adv* : very likely : almost certainly ▪ It will *probably* rain today. ▪ They will *probably* be here soon. ▪ You are *probably* right. ▪ It was *probably* the best concert I've ever been to. ▪ There were *probably* about 150 people at the wedding. ▪ "Are you going to the picnic?" "*Probably*." ▪ "Can you finish painting the room today?" "*Probably* not."

[1]**pro·bate** /ˈproʊˌbeɪt/ *noun* [*noncount*] *law*

1 : the process of proving in court that the will of a person who has died is valid ▪ Her will was offered for *probate* by the relatives.

2 : PROBATE COURT ▪ The case will now go to *probate*.

[2]**probate** *verb* **-bates; -bat·ed; -bat·ing** [+ *obj*] *US, law* : to prove that (a will) is valid before a probate court ▪ The court will *probate* the will. ▪ The will was *probated*.

probate court *noun, pl* **~ courts** [*count, noncount*] *US, law* : a court that proves wills are valid

pro·ba·tion /proʊˈbeɪʃən/ *noun*

P

1 : a situation or period of time in which a person who is starting a new job is tested and watched to see if that person is able to do the job properly [*noncount*] As a new employee, I will be ***on probation*** for three months. [*singular*] There is a three-month *probation* (period) for new employees.
2 [*noncount*] *law* **:** a situation or period of time in which a person who has committed a crime is allowed to stay out of prison if that person behaves well, does not commit another crime, etc. ▪ He hoped that the judge would grant him *probation.* ▪ He was sentenced to one year's *probation.* ▪ He was sent back to prison for violating his *probation.* ▪ She was arrested while ***on probation.***
3 [*noncount*] *US* **:** a situation or period of time in which a person who has made a serious mistake or done something bad is watched and must behave well in order not to be seriously punished ▪ Instead of firing her, they ***put/placed her on probation.*** ▪ The student was *placed on probation* for copying test answers.

probation officer *noun, pl* ~ **-cers** [*count*] *law* **:** a person who is in charge of watching, working with, and helping people who have been placed on probation

[1]**probe** /ˈproʊb/ *verb* **probes; probed; prob·ing**
1 : to ask a lot of questions in order to find secret or hidden information about someone or something [*no obj*] His questions made it clear he was *probing* for information. ▪ He didn't like the police *probing* into his past. ▪ Firefighters are still *probing* [=*looking*] for the cause of the fire. [+ *obj*] He didn't like the police *probing* him about his past.
2 [+ *obj*] **a :** to touch or reach into (something) by using your finger, a long tool, etc., in order to see or find something ▪ The doctor *probed* the wound with his finger. ▪ Searchers *probed* the mud with long poles. **b :** to look into or examine (something) carefully ▪ She *probed* the files for evidence that would help the investigation.
– probing *adj* ▪ The reporter asked a lot of *probing* questions. ▪ Her father gave her a *probing* look. ▪ a *probing* mind

[2]**probe** *noun, pl* **probes** [*count*]
1 : a careful examination or investigation of something ▪ The FBI *probe* did not produce any new evidence.
2 : a thin, long instrument that is used especially for examining parts of the body
3 : SPACE PROBE

pro·bi·ty /ˈproʊbəti/ *noun* [*noncount*] *formal* **:** the quality of a person who is completely honest ▪ a person of *probity*

[1]**prob·lem** /ˈprɑːbləm/ *noun, pl* **-lems**
1 [*count*] **:** something that is difficult to deal with **:** something that is a source of trouble, worry, etc. ▪ Racism and sexism are major social *problems.* ▪ The company is having financial *problems.* ▪ She has a drug *problem.* [=she is addicted to drugs] ▪ He has chronic health/medical *problems.* ▪ She has a weight *problem.* [=her weight is not healthy] ▪ The mechanic fixed the *problem* with the car. ▪ There are a few *problems* with your argument. ▪ We have to find a way to solve this *problem.* ▪ She is bothered by family/personal/marriage *problems.* ▪ We didn't have any *problems* getting here. ▪ I have my own *problems* to deal with. ▪ Mosquitoes are a *problem* in the summer. ▪ When he drinks too much, he causes *problems.* ▪ The *problem* with you is that you're too stubborn. ▪ We would love to have a dog. ***The only problem is (that)*** [=the reason that would be difficult is] we don't have the time to take care of it. ▪ The fact that you're late is ***not my problem.*** [=I am not responsible for helping you deal with the problem of being late]
2 [*singular*] **a :** difficulty in understanding something ▪ I'm having a *problem* following your argument. **b :** a feeling of not liking or wanting to do something ▪ "We'll have to leave a little early." "OK, I don't ***have a problem with*** that." [=that doesn't bother me] ▪ "He says he won't go." "***What's his problem?***" [=why is he being so unreasonable?]
3 [*count*] **:** a mathematical question to be solved ▪ a math *problem* ▪ Solve these *problems* for homework.
no problem *also* ***not a problem*** *informal* — used to say that you are happy to do something or that you are not bothered by something ▪ "Thanks for your help." "*No problem.*" ▪ "I'm sorry for interrupting you." "*No problem.*" ▪ "Can you get this done by lunchtime?" "*No problem.*" ▪ "I would like to pay with my credit card." "*Not a problem.*"

[2]**problem** *adj, always used before a noun* **:** difficult to deal with ▪ a ***problem child***

prob·lem·at·ic /ˌprɑːbləˈmætɪk/ *also* **prob·lem·at·i·cal** /ˌprɑːbləˈmætɪkəl/ *adj* [*more* ~; *most* ~] **:** difficult to understand, solve, or fix ▪ a *problematic* [=*puzzling*] situation ▪ Rules of grammar are more *problematic* for non-native speakers.

problem–solving *noun* [*noncount*] **:** the process or act of finding a solution to a problem ▪ Let's do some *problem-solving* and see if we can't figure out what to do. ▪ mathematical *problem-solving* ▪ *problem-solving* skills

pro bono /ˌproʊˈboʊnoʊ/ *adj, always used before a noun, law* **:** involving or doing legal work for free ▪ *pro bono* work ▪ a *pro bono* case/lawyer
– pro bono *adv* ▪ The lawyer defended him *pro bono.* [=for free]

pro·bos·cis /prəˈbɑːsəs/ *noun, pl* **-bos·cis·es** *also* **-bos·ci·des** /-ˈbɑːsəˌdiːz/ [*count*]
1 *biology* **:** the long, thin nose of some animals (such as an elephant)
2 *biology* **:** a long, thin tube that forms part of the mouth of some insects (such as a butterfly)
3 *humorous* **:** a person's nose especially when it is very long or big

pro·ce·dure /prəˈsiːʤɚ/ *noun, pl* **-dures**
1 : a series of actions that are done in a certain way or order **:** an established or accepted way of doing something [*count*] Installing a car battery is a simple *procedure.* ▪ What is the *procedure* for applying for a loan? ▪ New employees are taught the proper safety *procedures.* [*noncount*] We must follow proper court/legal/parliamentary *procedure.* ▪ An identity check is standard police *procedure.*
2 [*count*] **:** a medical treatment or operation ▪ the *procedure* for treating a burn ▪ surgical *procedures* ▪ The *procedure* will take two hours.
– pro·ce·dur·al /prəˈsiːʤərəl/ *adj, always used before a noun, formal* ▪ *procedural* steps ▪ Congress will vote on a *procedural* matter/bill.

pro·ceed /proʊˈsiːd/ *verb* **-ceeds; -ceed·ed; -ceed·ing**
1 [*no obj*] **a :** to continue to do something ▪ After the interruption, she *proceeded* with her presentation. ▪ "Before we *proceed* further, does anyone have any questions?" ▪ We will *proceed* according to plan. ▪ We may not be able to *proceed* as planned. ▪ How should we *proceed*? ▪ After inspecting the house, the couple decided to *proceed* [=*go ahead*] with the sale. ▪ When we've finished this part of the project, we can *proceed* [=*go on*] to the next step. **b :** to continue being done ▪ The problems have been fixed and the work can now *proceed.* ▪ The work is *proceeding* [=*going*] well.
2 [+ *obj*] **:** to do something after you have done something else — often used to describe behavior that is surprising, annoying, etc.; followed by *to + verb* ▪ He said he didn't have much time and then *proceeded to spend* the next half hour talking about his vacation.
3 *always followed by an adverb or preposition* [*no obj*] *formal* **:** to go or move in a particular direction ▪ All passengers must *proceed* to the baggage claim area. ▪ The crowd *proceeded* toward the exits. ▪ The troops *proceeded* north along the river.
proceed against [*phrasal verb*] ***proceed against (someone)*** *law* **:** to start a legal case against (someone) ▪ They threatened to *proceed against* him.
proceed from [*phrasal verb*] ***proceed from (something)*** *formal* **:** to come from (a source) ▪ Strange noises *proceeded from* the house.

pro·ceed·ing /proʊˈsiːdɪŋ/ *noun, pl* **-ings**
1 [*count*] *law* **:** the process of appearing before a court of law so a decision can be made about an argument or claim **:** a legal action ▪ a court *proceeding* — usually plural ▪ bankruptcy/divorce/criminal *proceedings* ▪ The bank is undertaking legal *proceedings* against him.
2 ***proceedings*** [*plural*] **a :** things that are said or done at a meeting, conference, ceremony, etc. ▪ The secretary kept a record of the *proceedings* at/of the meeting. ▪ She started the *proceedings* with a brief welcoming speech. **b** *formal* **:** an official record of the things said or done at a meeting, conference, etc. ▪ The *proceedings* of the conference will be published.

pro·ceeds /ˈproʊˌsiːdz/ *noun* [*plural*] **:** the total amount of money or profit that is made ▪ The *proceeds* of the concert will go to charity. ▪ Half the *proceeds* will be donated to the church. ▪ He took the *proceeds* from the sale of his business and invested in stocks.

[1]**pro·cess** /ˈprɑːˌsɛs, *Brit* ˈprəʊˌsɛs/ *noun, pl* **-cess·es** [*count*]
1 : a series of actions that produce something or that lead to a particular result ▪ costly manufacturing *processes* ▪ How

does the election *process* work? • Learning a foreign language can be a long/slow/difficult *process*. • We're remodeling our house. The whole *process* is expected to take a few months. • She figured out who he was by the ***process of elimination*** [=by considering and rejecting each possible choice until only one was left] — see also DUE PROCESS

2 : a series of changes that happen naturally • the *process* of growth • the aging *process* • Breathing and the circulation of blood are life *processes*.

3 *medical* **:** something that sticks out of something else • a bony *process* on the foot

in process **:** being worked on or done • The book is still *in process*.

in the process **1 :** while doing something • He scored the goal but was injured *in the process*. **2** ✧ If you are ***in the process of*** doing something, you are doing something that takes a certain amount of time to do. • I am *in the process of* buying a new car/house.

²process *verb* **-cesses; -cessed; -cess·ing** [+ *obj*]

1 a : to change (something) from one form into another by preparing, handling, or treating it in a special way • Food is often *processed* before it is packaged and sold. • He brought the film to be *processed*. [=*developed*] • The sewage plant *processes* waste. **b :** to deal with (something, such as an official document or request) by using a particular method or system • Her job includes *processing* insurance claims. • Your application will be *processed* in 5 to 10 business days.

2 : to take in and use (information) • Computers *process* data. • The brain *processes* the information that is taken in by our senses. • It took me a minute to *process* [=*understand*] what he was saying.

– processing *noun* [*noncount*] • food *processing* • the *processing* of insurance claims • information *processing* — see also DATA PROCESSING, WORD PROCESSING

pro·ces·sion /prəˈsɛʃən/ *noun, pl* **-sions**

1 : an organized group or line of people or vehicles that move together slowly as part of a ceremony [*count*] a funeral/wedding *procession* • There was a *procession* of children carrying candles. [*noncount*] The cars moved ***in procession*** to the cemetery.

2 [*count*] **:** a number of people or things that come or happen one after another **:** SERIES — + *of* • We have had a *procession of* visitors today. • The new employee had a *procession of* meetings to go to.

¹pro·ces·sion·al /prəˈsɛʃənl/ *adj, always used before a noun* **:** of, relating to, or used for a procession • *processional* music

²processional *noun, pl* **-als** [*count*]

1 : a piece of music that is played during a procession • a wedding *processional*

2 : PROCESSION 1 • He led a slow *processional* into the church.

pro·ces·sor /ˈprɑːˌsɛsɚ/ *noun, pl* **-sors** [*count*]

1 : a machine, company, etc., that treats, prepares, or handles something • a film *processor* • the largest seafood *processor* in the country • a film *processor* — see also FOOD PROCESSOR

2 : CPU — see also MICROPROCESSOR, WORD PROCESSOR

pro–choice /proʊˈʧoɪs/ *adj* **:** believing that pregnant women should have the right to choose to have an abortion • *pro-choice* supporters/groups • The governor has taken a *pro-choice* position. = The governor is *pro-choice*. — compare PRO-LIFE

pro·claim /proʊˈkleɪm/ *verb* **-claims; -claimed; -claim·ing** [+ *obj*]

1 : to say or state (something) in a public, official, or definite way **:** to declare or announce (something) • She *proclaimed* that she will run for governor. • The President *proclaimed* a national day of mourning. • He took command of the government and *proclaimed* himself emperor. • The magazine *proclaimed* him to be the best player in baseball. • He *proclaimed* his love for her in a poem. • She continues to *proclaim* her innocence. [=to say that she is innocent]

2 *formal* **:** to show (something) clearly • His behavior *proclaimed* his good upbringing.

proc·la·ma·tion /ˌprɑːkləˈmeɪʃən/ *noun, pl* **-tions** *somewhat formal*

1 : the act of saying something in a public, official, or definite way **:** the act of proclaiming something [*count*] No one believed her *proclamations* of innocence. [=her statements that she was innocent] [*noncount*] the *proclamation* of martial law

2 [*count*] **:** an official statement or announcement made by a person in power or by a government • The President issued a *proclamation* which freed the slaves.

pro·cliv·i·ty /proʊˈklɪvəti/ *noun, pl* **-ties** [*count*] *formal* **:** a strong natural liking for something that is usually bad **:** a tendency to do something that is usually bad — usually singular • Why do some people have a *proclivity* for violence? [=why are some people violent?] • She has a *proclivity* [=*tendency*] to assume the worst. • He shows no *proclivity* towards aggression. [=he is not aggressive]

pro·cras·ti·nate /prəˈkræstəˌneɪt/ *verb* **-nates; -nat·ed; -nat·ing** [*no obj*] **:** to be slow or late about doing something that should be done **:** to delay doing something until a later time because you do not want to do it, because you are lazy, etc. • He *procrastinated* and missed the submission deadline. • He told her to stop *procrastinating* and get to work.

– pro·cras·ti·na·tion /prəˌkræstəˈneɪʃən/ *noun* [*noncount*] • She is not prone to *procrastination*. **– pro·cras·ti·na·tor** /prəˈkræstəneɪtɚ/ *noun, pl* **-tors** [*count*] • Some people are *procrastinators* when it comes to paying their bills.

pro·cre·ate /ˈproʊkriˌeɪt/ *verb* **-ates; -at·ed; -at·ing** [*no obj*] *formal* **:** to produce children or offspring **:** REPRODUCE • Animals have a natural instinct to *procreate*.

– pro·cre·ation /ˌproʊkriˈeɪʃən/ *noun* [*noncount*]

proc·tor /ˈprɑːktɚ/ *verb* **-tors; -tored; -tor·ing** *US* **:** to watch students who are taking an examination [+ *obj*] Volunteers *proctored* [=(*Brit*) *invigilated*] the exam. [*no obj*] Teachers volunteered to *proctor*.

– proctor *noun, pl* **-tors** [*count*] • The *proctor* [=(*Brit*) *invigilator*] will collect the exams when time is up.

pro·cure /prəˈkjɚ/ *verb* **-cures; -cured; -cur·ing** [+ *obj*] *formal*

1 : to get (something) by some action or effort **:** OBTAIN • She managed to *procure* a ticket to the concert. • The CIA believes the group is *procuring* weapons. • They still need to *procure* a marriage license.

2 : to find or provide (a prostitute) for someone • He was charged with illegally *procuring* young women for wealthy clients.

– pro·cur·able /prəˈkjɚrəbəl/ *adj* • easily *procurable* goods **– pro·cure·ment** /prəˈkjɚmənt/ *noun* [*noncount*] • the *procurement* of materials and supplies • Birth certificates are needed for *procurement* of a marriage license. **– pro·cur·er** /prəˈkjɚrɚ/ *noun, pl* **-ers** [*count*] • The company is the largest *procurer* of building materials in the area.

¹prod /ˈprɑːd/ *verb* **prods; prod·ded; prod·ding**

1 : to push someone or something with your finger or a pointed object **:** POKE [+ *obj*] She *prodded* him in the ribs to get his attention. [*no obj*] — often + *at* • He *prodded at* the snake with a stick.

2 [+ *obj*] **:** to persuade or try to persuade (someone) to do something • His parents kept *prodding* [=*urging*] him to go back to school. • She was *prodded* into joining the team.

– prodding *noun* [*noncount*] • He didn't need any *prodding* to try again.

²prod *noun, pl* **prods** [*count*]

1 a : the act of pushing someone or something with your finger or a pointed object **:** POKE • She gave him a sharp *prod* in the back. **b :** something (such as a long stick) that is used to prod an animal • He picked up a stick and used it as a *prod* to get the donkey moving. — see also CATTLE PROD

2 : something said or done to encourage or remind someone to do something • He needed a few *prods* to remember his lines. • She called me and ***gave me a prod*** about finishing the report.

prod·i·gal /ˈprɑːdɪgəl/ *adj, always used before a noun, formal* **:** carelessly and foolishly spending money, time, etc. • a *prodigal* spender • a *prodigal* lifestyle

prodigal son/daughter **:** a son/daughter who leaves his or her parents to do things that they do not approve of but then feels sorry and returns home — often used figuratively • He left the company several years ago, but now the *prodigal son* has returned.

– prodigal *noun, pl* **-gals** [*count*] • The *prodigal* [=*prodigal son/daughter*] has returned.

pro·di·gious /prəˈdɪʤəs/ *adj, formal*

1 : amazing or wonderful **:** very impressive • a *prodigious* achievement/effort/talent

2 : very big • a *prodigious* amount

– pro·di·gious·ly *adv, formal* • He is *prodigiously* talented/wealthy.

prod·i·gy /ˈprɑːdəʤi/ *noun, pl* **-gies** [*count*] **:** a young per-

P

son who is unusually talented in some way ▪ child *prodigies* ▪ a chess/tennis/math *prodigy*

[1]**pro·duce** /prəˈduːs, *Brit* prəˈdjuːs/ *verb* **-duc·es; -duced; -duc·ing**

1 [+ *obj*] **a :** to make (something) especially by using machines ▪ The factory *produces* [=*manufactures*] steel. ▪ Thousands of cars are *produced* here each year. — see also MASS-PRODUCE **b :** to make or create (something) by a natural process ▪ The tree *produces* good fruit. ▪ Honey is *produced* by bees. ▪ twins *produced* from a single egg

2 [+ *obj*] **:** to cause (something) to exist or happen **:** to cause (a particular result or effect) ▪ The insect bite *produced* a rash. ▪ His suggestion *produced* the desired results.

3 [+ *obj*] **:** to be the source of (something or someone) **:** to be the place where (something or someone) comes from ▪ The region *produces* large amounts of cotton and tobacco. ▪ The college has *produced* some well-known scientists.

4 : to be in charge of making and usually providing the money for (a play, movie, television show, record, etc.) [+ *obj*] She is *producing* her first play/film. ▪ He has *produced* many albums. ▪ He *produced* and directed the movie. [*no obj*] On most of her movies, she both *produces* and directs.

5 [+ *obj*] **a :** to show (something) **:** to cause (something) to appear or be seen ▪ He *produced* his ID for the security guard. ▪ He suddenly *produced* a gun and told the cashier to hand over all the money. **b :** to provide (something that is wanted or needed) ▪ They could not *produce* evidence that proved he was at the scene of the crime. ▪ He'll be in trouble if he doesn't *produce* the money he owes them.

[2]**pro·duce** /ˈproʊˌduːs, *Brit* ˈprɒˌdjuːs/ *noun* [*noncount*] **:** fresh fruits and vegetables ▪ fresh/local/organic *produce*

pro·duc·er /prəˈduːsɚ, *Brit* prəˈdjuːsə/ *noun, pl* **-ers** [*count*]

1 : someone who is in charge of making and usually providing the money for a play, movie, record, etc. ▪ a record *producer* ▪ the *producer* of the play ▪ He is the director and *producer*.

2 : someone or something that grows or makes particular goods or products ▪ wine *producers* ▪ the nation's grain *producers* ▪ The country is the world's leading oil *producer*.

prod·uct /ˈprɑːˌdʌkt/ *noun, pl* **-ucts**

1 : something that is made or grown to be sold or used [*count*] dairy/software *products* ▪ my favorite skin-care *products* ▪ The company's newest *product* is selling well. [*noncount*] (*technical*) The company needs to find a way to sell more *product*. — often used before another noun ▪ *product* design/development — see also GROSS DOMESTIC PRODUCT, GROSS NATIONAL PRODUCT

2 [*count*] **:** something that is the result of a process ▪ The sap used to make maple syrup is a natural *product*. ▪ This book is the *product* of many years of hard work. ▪ The ***finished/end product*** was a beautiful vase. — see also BY-PRODUCT, WASTE PRODUCT

3 [*count*] **:** someone or something that is produced or influenced by a particular environment or experience — + *of* ▪ People are often *products of* their surroundings and upbringing. ▪ Her politeness is a *product of* good parenting. ▪ My grandfather was a *product of* his times. [=my grandfather was like other people who grew up with him]

4 [*count*] *mathematics* **:** the number that is the result of multiplying two or more numbers ▪ 15 is the *product* of 3 and 5.

pro·duc·tion /prəˈdʌkʃən/ *noun, pl* **-tions**

1 [*noncount*] **a :** the process of making or growing something for sale or use ▪ agricultural/food/steel *production* ▪ the *production* of grain/cars/nuclear weapons ▪ Next year's car models are already ***in production***. = Next year's car models have already ***gone into production***. [=next year's car models are already being made] ▪ The airplane is ***out of production***. = The airplane has ***gone out of production***. [=the airplane is no longer being made] — often used before another noun ▪ *production* costs/problems ▪ the *production* process/schedule — see also MASS PRODUCTION **b :** the process of making something naturally ▪ the body's *production* of red blood cells **c :** the process of making a play, movie, television show, record, etc. ▪ I took a course in film/video *production*. ▪ He has a job in television *production*. ▪ The sequel to the movie is ***in production***. [=is being made]

2 [*count*] **:** a show (such as a play or movie) that is presented to the public ▪ We saw a stage *production* of the novel. ▪ The director wants her in his next *production*.

3 [*count*] **:** the amount of something that is made or grown for sale or use ▪ the annual *production* of coal/steel/food ▪ a rise/fall in oil *production* ▪ *Production* levels are low/high.

4 [*singular*] *informal* **:** something that is very difficult or complicated ▪ It can be a major *production* to get the kids ready for school in the morning. ▪ Getting home turned out to be a real *production* because of all the delays at the airport. ▪ The picnic was quite a *production*. There were clowns, music, and fireworks.

production line *noun, pl* **~ lines** [*count*] **:** a line of machines, equipment, workers, etc., in a factory that builds a product by passing work from one station to the next until the product is finished ▪ He works on the *production line* at the local factory. — called also *assembly line, line*

pro·duc·tive /prəˈdʌktɪv/ *adj* [*more ~; most ~*]

1 : doing or achieving a lot **:** working hard and getting good results ▪ a *productive* meeting ▪ I had a very *productive* day. ▪ I am most *productive* in the morning. ▪ a highly *productive* [=*successful*] sales team ▪ Some staff members are more *productive* than others.

2 *always used before a noun* **:** producing or able to produce something especially in large amounts ▪ *productive* fishing waters ▪ *productive* farmland

3 *formal* **:** causing or resulting in something — + *of* ▪ Your efforts have been *productive of* many benefits. [=have produced many benefits]

– pro·duc·tive·ly *adv* ▪ The farmers learned to use their land more *productively*. ▪ The team worked *productively*.

pro·duc·tiv·i·ty /ˌproʊdəkˈtɪvəti/ *noun* [*noncount*] **:** the rate at which goods are produced or work is completed ▪ The country has low/high agricultural *productivity*. ▪ The company is looking for ways to improve worker *productivity*. ▪ There has been an increase in *productivity*.

prof /ˈprɑːf/ *noun, pl* **profs** [*count*] *informal* **:** PROFESSOR ▪ a Harvard *prof*

Prof. *abbr* professor ▪ *Prof.* Smith

[1]**pro·fane** /proʊˈfeɪn/ *adj* [*more ~; most ~*] *formal*

1 : having or showing disrespect for religious things ▪ *profane* language

2 : relating to ordinary life **:** not religious or spiritual **:** SECULAR ▪ sacred and *profane* customs

[2]**profane** *verb* **-fanes; -faned; -fan·ing** [+ *obj*] *formal + literary* **:** to treat (a holy place or object) with great disrespect ▪ Vandals *profaned* [=*desecrated*] the temple.

pro·fan·i·ty /proʊˈfænəti/ *noun, pl* **-ties**

1 [*noncount*] **:** offensive language ▪ The comic uses too much *profanity*. ▪ My mom will not tolerate *profanity*.

2 [*count*] **:** an offensive word ▪ I have never heard my father utter a single *profanity*. — usually plural ▪ The song is filled with *profanities*.

pro·fess /prəˈfɛs/ *verb* **-fess·es; -fessed; -fess·ing** [+ *obj*] *formal*

1 : to say or declare (something) openly ▪ He *professes* confidence in his friend. ▪ They *profess* loyalty to the king. ▪ He *professes* himself (to be) unsatisfied with their decision.

2 : to say that you are, do, or feel something when other people doubt what you say **:** CLAIM — followed by *to + verb* ▪ They *professed to be* our friends. ▪ She *professed to know* nothing about the missing money. ▪ She *professed to be* pleased with the outcome, but we knew the truth.

3 *old-fashioned* **:** to believe in (a particular religion) ▪ He *professes* Judaism/Catholicism/Islam.

pro·fessed /prəˈfɛst/ *adj, always before a noun, formal* **:** openly said or declared ▪ He is a *professed* enemy of the king. ▪ a *professed* Jew/Catholic/Muslim — often used to suggest that what someone says is not true or should be doubted ▪ His *professed* reason for resigning was to spend time with his family, but we heard rumors that he was caught stealing. — see also SELF-PROFESSED

pro·fes·sion /prəˈfɛʃən/ *noun, pl* **-sions**

1 [*count*] **:** a type of job that requires special education, training, or skill ▪ The doctor talked to students who are thinking about entering/joining the *profession*. ▪ the legal *profession* ▪ Most *professions* in the medical field require years of training. ▪ He is a carpenter ***by profession***. = His *profession* is carpentry. ▪ (*humorous*) She works in ***the (world's) oldest profession***. [=she is a prostitute]

2 [*singular*] **:** the people who work in a particular profession ▪ Their daughter recently became a member of the medical *profession*. ▪ The teaching *profession* opposes the new law. = (*Brit*) The teaching *profession* oppose the new law.

3 [*count*] *formal* **:** the act of declaring or saying something openly — often + *of* ▪ She made a *profession of* religious faith.

[1]**pro·fes·sion·al** /prəˈfɛʃənl̩/ *adj*

1 *always used before a noun* **a :** relating to a job that re-

quires special education, training, or skill ▪ Do you have any *professional* experience? ▪ *professional* people/photographers/electricians/soldiers ▪ a *professional* career **b :** done or given by a person who works in a particular profession ▪ *professional* services ▪ You need *professional* help. ▪ You should seek *professional* advice.
2 *always used before a noun* **a :** paid to participate in a sport or activity ▪ *professional* athletes/golfers ▪ a *professional* poker player ▪ a golfer who recently ***turned professional*** **b :** done by people who are paid to play or compete ▪ *professional* sports/football/poker
3 [*more* ~; *most* ~] **:** having or showing the skill, good judgment, and polite behavior that is expected from a person who is trained to do a job well ▪ He deals with the customers in a very *professional* way. = He is very *professional* in dealing with the customers. ▪ I was impressed by the calm and *professional* way she handled the crisis. ▪ The presentation was very *professional.*

[2]**professional** *noun, pl* **-als** [*count*]
1 : someone who does a job that requires special training, education, or skill **:** someone who is a member of a profession ▪ medical/legal *professionals* ▪ The bathtub was installed by a *professional.*
2 : someone who is paid to participate in a sport or activity ▪ The tournament is open to both amateurs and *professionals.* ▪ a golfer who recently became a *professional* ▪ a golf/tennis *professional* [=a skillful golf/tennis player whose job is to teach other people how to play] — compare AMATEUR
3 : someone who has a lot of experience or skill in a particular job or activity ▪ She handled the situation like a *professional.*

professional foul *noun, pl* ~ **fouls** [*count*] *Brit, soccer* **:** a foul that is made on purpose especially to prevent the other team from scoring a goal

pro·fes·sion·al·ism /prəˈfɛʃənəˌlɪzəm/ *noun* [*noncount*] **:** the skill, good judgment, and polite behavior that is expected from a person who is trained to do a job well ▪ A high level of *professionalism* is expected when working with clients. ▪ She is highly respected for her *professionalism.*

pro·fes·sion·al·ize (*US*) *also Brit* **pro·fes·sion·al·ise** /prəˈfɛʃənəˌlaɪz/ *verb* **-iz·es; -ized; -iz·ing** [+ *obj*] *formal* **:** to make (an activity) into a job that requires special education, training, or skill ▪ The country is *professionalizing* the military. — often used as *(be) professionalized* ▪ Childcare has *been professionalized.*
– pro·fes·sion·al·i·za·tion (*US*) *also Brit* **pro·fes·sion·al·i·sa·tion** /prəˌfɛʃənələˈzeɪʃən, *Brit* prəˌfɛʃənəˌlaɪˈzeɪʃən/ *noun* [*noncount*] ▪ the *professionalization* of sports

pro·fes·sion·al·ly /prəˈfɛʃənəli/ *adv*
1 : in a way that relates to someone's profession ▪ *Professionally,* she is very successful, but her personal life is unhappy.
2 : by someone who has the special education, training, or skill that is required to do a particular job ▪ The bathtub was *professionally* installed. [=was installed by a professional] ▪ a *professionally* trained staff
3 : as a paid job ▪ He plays soccer *professionally.*
4 : in a way that shows the skill, good judgment, and polite behavior that is expected from a person who is trained to do a job well ▪ The problem was dealt with very *professionally.*

pro·fes·sor /prəˈfɛsɚ/ *noun, pl* **-sors** [*count*] **:** a teacher especially of the highest rank at a college or university ▪ a chemistry/history *professor* = a *professor* of chemistry/history ▪ *Professor* Williams will be teaching the class.
– pro·fes·so·ri·al /ˌproufəˈsorijəl/ *adj* ▪ *professorial* duties/appointments ▪ He had a *professorial* look to him. = He looked *professorial.* [=he looked like a professor]

pro·fes·sor·ship /prəˈfɛsɚˌʃɪp/ *noun, pl* **-ships** [*count*] **:** the job or duties of a professor ▪ He accepted a *professorship* of poetry at the university.

prof·fer /ˈprɑːfɚ/ *verb* **-fers; -fered; -fer·ing** [+ *obj*] *formal* **:** to offer or give (something) to someone ▪ He *proffered* advice on how best to proceed. ▪ Many explanations were *proffered.* ▪ the *proffered* testimony/evidence

pro·fi·cient /prəˈfɪʃənt/ *adj* [*more* ~; *most* ~] **:** good at doing something **:** SKILLFUL ▪ a *proficient* reader ▪ He has become very *proficient* at computer programming. ▪ She is *proficient* in two foreign languages.
– pro·fi·cien·cy /prəˈfɪʃənsi/ *noun* [*noncount*] ▪ a test in reading *proficiency* = a reading *proficiency* test [=a test to see how well you can read] ▪ He shows a high level of *proficiency* in Spanish.

[1]**pro·file** /ˈprouˌfajəl/ *noun, pl* **-files**
1 a : the shape of a head or face that is seen or drawn from the side [*count*] His *profile* is very unusual. ▪ An image of the President's *profile* appears on the coin. [*noncount*] The drawing showed her head ***in profile.*** [=the drawing showed the shape of her head as it is seen from the side] **b** [*count*] **:** the shape of something that is seen against a background — usually singular ▪ The artist painted the *profile* of a boat against the setting sun.

profile

2 [*count*] **:** a brief written description that provides information about someone or something ▪ I read a *profile* of her in a magazine. ▪ patient *profiles* ▪ *profiles* of American colleges
high/low profile — used to describe the amount of attention that someone or something is given ▪ The actor's *high profile* helped promote the movie. ▪ The company has kept a *high profile* in the computer industry. ▪ I don't really like attention, so I try to keep/maintain a *low profile* around here. [=I try to avoid doing things that will cause people to notice me]

[2]**profile** *verb* **-files; -filed; -fil·ing** [+ *obj*] **:** to give a brief description that provides information about (someone or something) ▪ The mayor was *profiled* in the magazine last month.

profiling *noun* [*noncount*]
1 : the act or process of learning information about someone based on what is already known ▪ consumer *profiling*
2 : the act or practice of regarding particular people as more likely to commit crimes because of their appearance, race, etc. ▪ racial *profiling*

[1]**prof·it** /ˈprɑːfət/ *noun, pl* **-its**
1 : money that is made in a business, through investing, etc., after all the costs and expenses are paid **:** a financial gain [*count*] The company made/turned a *profit* this year. ▪ *Profits* are up/down from last year. ▪ There was a rise/fall/increase/decrease in *profits* this year. ▪ The *profits* from CD sales were donated to charity. ▪ We sold the house ***at a profit.*** [=we made a profit when we sold our house] [*noncount*] The organization is not run for *profit.* ▪ The film made $1,000,000 in *profit.* — opposite LOSS
2 [*noncount*] *formal* **:** the advantage or benefit that is gained from doing something ▪ The book can be read with *profit* by anyone who wants to understand how the system works.

[2]**profit** *verb* **-its; -it·ed; -it·ing**
1 a [*no obj*] **:** to get an advantage or benefit from something — often + *by* or *from* ▪ He *profited by* his experience/mistake. [=he learned something useful from his experience/mistake] ▪ Everyone can *profit from* reading this book. **b** [+ *obj*] **:** to be an advantage to (someone) **:** to help (someone) ▪ It would *profit* him to take some computer classes.
2 [*no obj*] **:** to earn or get money *by* or *from* something ▪ The company has *profited by* selling its products online. ▪ He *profited* greatly *from* his investments. ▪ The island *profits from* tourism.

prof·it·able /ˈprɑːfətəbəl/ *adj* [*more* ~; *most* ~]
1 : making money ▪ a *profitable* business ▪ The movie was very *profitable.*
2 : producing good or helpful results or effects ▪ a *profitable* [=*beneficial*] experience ▪ The agreement was *profitable* [=*advantageous*] for everyone.
– prof·it·abil·i·ty /ˌprɑːfətəˈbɪləti/ *noun* [*noncount*] ▪ trying to improve the company's *profitability* [=to make the company more profitable] **– prof·it·ably** /ˈprɑːfətəbli/ *adv* ▪ He invested his money *profitably.* ▪ Computers can be *profitably* used in schools.

prof·i·teer·ing /ˌprɑːfəˈtirɪŋ/ *noun* [*noncount*] *disapproving* **:** the act of making money by selling things at very high prices at a time when they are hard to get ▪ The company was accused of *profiteering* during the crisis.
– prof·i·teer /ˌprɑːfəˈtiɚ/ *noun, pl* **-teers** [*count*]

pro·fit·er·ole /prəˈfɪtəˌroul/ *noun, pl* **-oles** [*count*] *Brit* **:** CREAM PUFF 1

prof·it·less /ˈprɑːfətləs/ *adj* **:** not making a profit or producing a useful result ▪ a *profitless* company ▪ a *profitless* argument

profit margin *noun, pl* ~ **-gins** [*count*] **:** the difference between the cost of buying or making something and the price at which it is sold ▪ The company has one of the highest/lowest *profit margins* in the industry.

profit sharing *noun* [*noncount*] **:** a system in which employees receive a part of the company's profits

P

prof·li·gate /ˈprɑːflɪgət/ *adj* [*more* ~; *most* ~] *formal* **:** carelessly and foolishly wasting money, materials, etc. **:** very wasteful ▪ She was very *profligate* in her spending. ▪ *profligate* energy use
— **profligate** *noun, pl* **-gates** [*count*] — **prof·li·ga·cy** /ˈprɑːflɪgəsi/ *noun* [*noncount*]

pro for·ma /proʊˈfoɚmə/ *adj* **:** done or existing as something that is usual or required but that has little true meaning or importance ▪ The meeting was strictly *pro forma*, since the decision had already been made.

pro forma invoice *noun, pl* ~ **-voices** [*count*] *business* **:** a document that is provided before or with a shipment of goods and that describes the items shipped or the terms of the sale

pro·found /prəˈfaʊnd/ *adj* [*more* ~; *most* ~]
1 a : having or showing great knowledge or understanding ▪ a *profound* thinker ▪ His knowledge of history is *profound*. ▪ Her books offer *profound* insights into the true nature of courage. **b :** difficult to understand **:** requiring deep thought or wisdom ▪ the *profound* mysteries of outer space ▪ *profound* questions
2 a : very strongly felt ▪ *profound* sorrow ▪ a *profound* sense of loss **b :** very great ▪ Computer technology has made *profound* [=*major, significant*] changes in our lives. ▪ His paintings have had a *profound* effect/impact/influence on her own work.
3 *somewhat formal* **:** absolute or complete ▪ a *profound* silence/sleep/deafness
— **pro·found·ly** *adv* ▪ She was influenced *profoundly* by his art. ▪ The discovery is *profoundly* important. ▪ Their beliefs are *profoundly* different. ▪ *profoundly* deaf people

pro·fun·di·ty /prəˈfʌndəti/ *noun, pl* **-ties** *formal*
1 [*noncount*] **:** the quality being profound: such as **a :** the quality of showing great knowledge or understanding ▪ the *profundity* of his thoughts/insights ▪ Her books are a mixture of playfulness and *profundity*. **b :** the quality of being very strongly felt ▪ the depth and *profundity* of her feelings
2 [*count*] **:** a statement that shows great knowledge or understanding — usually plural ▪ philosophical *profundities*

pro·fuse /prəˈfjuːs/ *adj* [*more* ~; *most* ~] **:** given, produced, or existing in large amounts ▪ He offered *profuse* apologies for being late. ▪ They were *profuse* in their thanks. ▪ *profuse* bleeding/sweating
— **pro·fuse·ly** *adv* ▪ He apologized *profusely*. ▪ She was bleeding *profusely* when she was brought to the hospital.

pro·fu·sion /prəˈfjuːʒən/ *noun, formal* **:** a large amount of something [*singular*] — often + *of* ▪ a *profusion of* flowers/colors [*noncount*] The flowers grow ***in profusion***.

pro·gen·i·tor /proʊˈʤɛnətɚ/ *noun, pl* **-tors** [*count*]
1 *formal* **a :** someone who first thinks of or does something **:** a person who begins something ▪ the *progenitors* of modern art **b :** something that is a model for something else **:** something that begins the development of something else ▪ a mechanical *progenitor* [=*precursor*] *of* the modern computer
2 *biology* **:** a person or animal in the past that is related to a person or animal living now **:** ANCESTOR ▪ wild cats that were the *progenitors* of the house cat

P

prog·e·ny /ˈprɑːʤəni/ *noun, pl* **progeny** [*count*]
1 a : a person who comes from a particular parent or family **:** the child or descendant of someone ▪ Many Americans are the *progeny* of immigrants. **b :** the young of an animal or plant ▪ The small plants are the *progeny* of an oak tree.
2 : something that is the product of something else ▪ Their work is the *progeny* of many earlier studies.

pro·ges·ter·one /proʊˈʤɛstəˌroʊn/ *noun* [*noncount*] *medical* **:** a substance (called a hormone) that occurs naturally in women and female animals ✧ Progesterone prepares the body for having a baby.

prog·no·sis /prɑgˈnoʊsəs/ *noun, pl* **-no·ses** /-ˈnoʊˌsiːz/ [*count*]
1 : a doctor's opinion about how someone will recover from an illness or injury ▪ Right now, doctors say his *prognosis* is/isn't good. — compare DIAGNOSIS
2 : a judgment about what is going to happen in the future ▪ The president had a hopeful *prognosis* about the company's future.

prog·nos·tic /prɑgˈnɑːstɪk/ *adj, always used before a noun, formal* **:** relating to or used for making a judgment about what is going to happen in the future ▪ *prognostic* information/factors/signs ▪ a *prognostic* weather chart

prog·nos·ti·ca·tion /prɑgˌnɑːstəˈkeɪʃən/ *noun, pl* **-tions** [*count*] *formal* **:** a statement about what is going to happen in the future ▪ His *prognostications* [=*predictions*] are usually right.
— **prog·nos·ti·ca·tor** /prɑgˈnɑːstəˈkeɪtɚ/ *noun, pl* **-tors** [*count*] *formal* ▪ Political *prognosticators* believe she will lose the election.

[1]pro·gram (*US*) *or Brit* **pro·gramme** /ˈproʊˌgræm/ *noun, pl* **-grams** [*count*]
1 : a plan of things that are done in order to achieve a specific result ▪ government *programs* ▪ a *program* of regular dental checkups ▪ a workout *program*
2 : a set of instructions that tell a computer what to do ▪ a sorting *program* ▪ He writes computer *programs*. ✧ In this sense, the spelling *program* is used in both U.S. and British English.
3 : a thin book or a piece of paper that gives information about a concert, play, sports game, etc. ▪ a theater *program*
4 : something that is broadcast on television or radio ▪ a news *program* [=*show*] ▪ the morning *program*
5 *US* **:** a group of classes that lead to a degree **:** a course of study ▪ The university has a great graduate *program*. ▪ I enrolled in the teaching *program*.
get with the program *informal* **:** to start doing what others need or want you to do **:** to become involved and active in a useful and effective way ▪ His boss told him that he'd better *get with the program* if he wants to keep his job.

[2]program (*US*) *or Brit* **programme** *verb* **-grams; -grammed** *or* **-gramed; -gram·ming** *or* **-gram·ing**
1 a : to give (a computer) a set of instructions to perform a particular action **:** to create a program for (a computer) [+ *obj*] He *programmed* the computer to calculate his monthly expenses and earnings. — often used as *(be) programmed* ▪ The computer *is programmed* to create monthly sales reports. [*no obj*] She is learning how to *program* in school. ✧ In this sense, the spelling *program* is used in both U.S. and British English. **b** [+ *obj*] **:** to give (a machine) a set of instructions to perform a particular action ▪ Can you help me *program* my cell phone? ▪ *program* a VCR
2 [+ *obj*] **:** to make (a person or animal) behave or think in a particular way — often used as *(be) programmed* ▪ Some people *are programmed* to be violent. [=some people have a natural or acquired tendency to be violent] ▪ instinctive behaviors that are genetically *programmed* in animals
— **pro·gram·ma·ble** /ˈproʊˌgræməbəl/ *adj* ▪ a *programmable* calculator

pro·gram·ma·tic /ˌproʊgrəˈmætɪk/ *adj, formal* **:** of, relating to, resembling, or having a program ▪ *programmatic* changes/reforms

pro·gram·mer /ˈproʊˌgræmɚ/ *noun, pl* **-mers** [*count*] **:** a person who creates computer programs

pro·gram·ming /ˈproʊˌgræmɪŋ/ *noun* [*noncount*]
1 : the act or job of creating computer programs
2 : a schedule of television or radio broadcasts ▪ television/radio *programming* ▪ The news conference interrupted regular television *programming*.

[1]prog·ress /ˈprɑːgrəs, *Brit* ˈprəʊˌgrɛs/ *noun* [*noncount*]
1 : movement forward or toward a place ▪ the rapid *progress* of the ship ▪ He made slow *progress* down the steep cliff.
2 : the process of improving or developing something over a period of time ▪ the *progress* of science ▪ The project showed slow but steady *progress*. ▪ She offered a ***progress report*** [=a report about how much work has been done on something] ▪ We're not finished yet, but we're ***making progress***. [=we are moving forward in our work; our work is proceeding/progressing]
in progress **:** happening or being done ▪ Several projects are now *in progress*. ▪ The filming is already *in progress*.

[2]pro·gress /prəˈgrɛs/ *verb* **-gress·es; -gressed; -gress·ing** [*no obj*]
1 : to move forward in time ▪ It became colder as the day *progressed*. [=*went on*]
2 : to improve or develop over a period of time ▪ The project has been *progressing* slowly. ▪ The work is *progressing* and should be completed soon.
3 *always followed by an adverb or preposition, formal* **:** to move forward or toward a place ▪ The caravan *progressed* slowly across the desert.

pro·gres·sion /prəˈgrɛʃən/ *noun, pl* **-sions** [*count*]
1 : the process of developing over a period of time ▪ Doctors were surprised by the rapid *progression* of the disease. ▪ the natural *progression* of his musical talent
2 : a continuous and connected series of actions, events, etc. **:** SEQUENCE ▪ a *progression* of activities

[1]pro·gres·sive /prəˈgrɛsɪv/ *adj*
1 : moving forward ▪ the *progressive* movements of the hands of a clock
2 : happening or developing gradually over a period of time ▪ a *progressive* disease
3 [*more* ~; *most* ~] **:** using or interested in new or modern ideas especially in politics and education ▪ a *progressive* community/school ▪ a *progressive* candidate
4 *grammar* **:** of or relating to the progressive tense of a verb ▪ a *progressive* verb form
– pro·gres·sive·ly *adv* ▪ The situation grew *progressively* worse.

[2]progressive *noun, pl* **-sives**
1 [*count*] **:** a person who favors new or modern ideas especially in politics and education ▪ social *progressives*
2 ***the progressive*** *grammar* **:** PROGRESSIVE TENSE ▪ "*Believe*" is never used in *the progressive*.

progressive tense *noun, pl* **~ tenses** [*count*] *grammar* **:** a verb tense that is used to refer to an action or a state that is continuing to happen ✧ A progressive verb form in English consists of a form of the verb "be" followed by the main verb's present participle.

pro·hib·it /proʊˈhɪbət/ *verb* **-its; -it·ed; -it·ing** [+ *obj*]
1 a : to order (someone) not to use or do something — + *from* ▪ The town *prohibited* teenagers *from* being in the streets after 10 p.m. **b :** to say that (something) is not allowed ▪ The rules *prohibit* dating a coworker. ▪ The town *prohibits* [=*forbids*] parking on that street. — often used as *(be) prohibited* ▪ Flash photography *is prohibited* inside the museum. ▪ Alcohol *is prohibited* in the park.
2 : to make (something) impossible to do ▪ The prison's electric fence *prohibits* escape.

pro·hi·bi·tion /ˌprowəˈbɪʃən/ *noun, pl* **-tions**
1 [*noncount*] **:** the act of not allowing something to be used or done ▪ the city's *prohibition* of smoking in restaurants
2 [*count*] **:** a law or order that stops something from being used or done ▪ a *prohibition* against parking on the street
3 ***Prohibition*** [*noncount*] **:** the period of time from 1920 to 1933 in the U.S. when it was illegal to make or sell alcohol

pro·hi·bi·tion·ist /ˌprowəˈbɪʃənɪst/ *noun, pl* **-ists** [*count*] **:** someone who supported the laws that made the production and sale of alcohol illegal in the U.S. during Prohibition

pro·hib·i·tive /proʊˈhɪbətɪv/ *adj*
1 [*more* ~; *most* ~] **:** so high that people are prevented from using or buying something ▪ the *prohibitive* cost of rent ▪ The price was *prohibitive*. [=too high]
2 *US* **:** almost certain to perform, win, etc., in the expected way ▪ She is the *prohibitive* favorite to win the nomination. [=she is almost certain to win the nomination]
3 *formal* **:** stopping people from using or doing something ▪ a *prohibitive* ruling ▪ *prohibitive* legislation
– pro·hib·i·tive·ly *adv* ▪ The price was *prohibitively* high.

[1]proj·ect /ˈprɑːˌʤɛkt/ *noun, pl* **-ects** [*count*]
1 : a planned piece of work that has a specific purpose (such as to find information or to make something new) and that usually requires a lot of time ▪ an ambitious *project* ▪ a research/construction *project* ▪ The repair turned out to be quite a *project*. [=it took a lot of time and effort to do]
2 : a task or problem in school that requires careful work over a long period of time ▪ a science *project*
3 *US* **:** HOUSING PROJECT — usually plural ▪ They grew up in ***the projects***.

[2]pro·ject /prəˈʤɛkt/ *verb* **-jects; -ject·ed; -ject·ing**
1 [+ *obj*] **:** to plan, calculate, or estimate (something) for a time in the future ▪ He *projected* next year's costs as being slightly higher than this year's. ▪ It's difficult to *project* funding needs so far into the future. — often used as *(be) projected* ▪ The new building *is projected* to be finished in the fall. ▪ The actual cost was much higher than the *projected* cost. ▪ What is the *projected* [=*expected*] date of completion?
2 [+ *obj*] **:** to cause (light, a picture, a movie, etc.) to appear on a surface — often + *on* or *onto* ▪ The machine *projects* motion pictures *on/onto* a screen.
3 [+ *obj*] **:** to have or show (a particular quality, image, etc., that can be seen by other people) ▪ He *projects* strength. ▪ an athlete who *projects* a positive image to young people ▪ We need an actor who *projects* a tough-guy image. ▪ He tried to ***project himself*** as a strong leader. [=to act in a way that would make people see him as a strong leader]
4 *always followed by an adverb or preposition* [*no obj*] **:** to stick out beyond an edge or surface ▪ Two balconies *projected* [=*extended*] out over the seats below.
5 [+ *obj*] **:** to send or throw (something) forward, upward, or outward ▪ The fountain *projects* a slender column of water high into the air. ▪ You need to ***project your voice*** better if you want to be an actor. [=you need to speak louder and more clearly if you want to be an actor] — often used figuratively ▪ The success of his first movie suddenly *projected* [=*threw*] him into an unfamiliar world of wealth and fame.
project onto [*phrasal verb*] ***project (something) onto (someone)*** **:** to believe or imagine that (your ideas, feelings, etc.) are shared by (another person) ▪ She *projected* her fears *onto* him. [=she thought that he had the same fears she had]

pro·jec·tile /prəˈʤɛktajəl/ *noun, pl* **-tiles** [*count*] *formal*
1 : something (such as a bullet or rocket) that is shot from a weapon ▪ The cannon fires a ten-pound *projectile*.
2 : something (such as a rock) that is thrown as a weapon ▪ Someone threw a *projectile* at her car.

pro·jec·tion /prəˈʤɛkʃən/ *noun, pl* **-tions**
1 [*count*] **:** an estimate of what might happen in the future based on what is happening now ▪ He gave a *projection* of future expenses.
2 [*count*] **:** something that sticks out from a surface ▪ *projections* on the rock wall
3 [*noncount*] **:** the act or process of causing a picture, movie, etc., to appear on a surface ▪ movie *projection* ▪ *projection* equipment
4 [*count*] *technical* **:** a type of map or drawing which shows all the parts of something that is curved or solid (such as the earth) on a flat surface ▪ a *projection* map
5 [*noncount*] **:** the act of speaking, singing, or producing sounds in a way that can be heard over a great distance ▪ You need to work on voice/vocal *projection*. ▪ sound *projection*
6 [*noncount*] *psychology* **:** the act of imagining that someone else has the same ideas, feelings, etc., that you have ▪ An example of *projection* is when someone thinks that everyone hates them because they hate themselves.
7 [*count*] **:** something that is imagined or created from your ideas, thoughts, feelings, etc. — often + *of* ▪ The image that we have of strangers is often just a *projection of* our own fears and desires.

pro·jec·tion·ist /prəˈʤɛkʃənɪst/ *noun, pl* **-ists** [*count*] **:** a person who operates a machine (called a projector) that shows movies on a screen in a theater ▪ a movie *projectionist*

pro·jec·tor /prəˈʤɛktɚ/ *noun, pl* **-tors** [*count*] **:** a machine that projects a movie or picture onto a screen ▪ a movie/slide *projector* — see also OVERHEAD PROJECTOR

pro·lapse /proʊˈlæps/ *noun* [*noncount*] *medical* **:** a condition in which an organ in your body moves down below its normal position ▪ *prolapse* of the uterus

prole /ˈproʊl/ *noun, pl* **proles** [*count*] *Brit, old-fashioned* + *impolite* **:** a person who has low social status **:** a member of the working class **:** PROLETARIAN

pro·le·tar·i·an /ˌproʊləˈterijən/ *noun, pl* **-ans** [*count*] **:** a person who has low social status **:** a member of the working class
– proletarian *adj* ▪ He was proud of his *proletarian* origins. ▪ a *proletarian* novel [=a novel about working-class people]

pro·le·tar·i·at /ˌproʊləˈterijət/ *noun*
the proletariat **:** the lowest social or economic class of a community; *especially* **:** the working class ▪ a member of *the proletariat*

pro–life /proʊˈlaɪf/ *adj* **:** opposed to abortion ▪ the *pro-life* movement ▪ The governor has taken a *pro-life* position. = The governor is *pro-life*. — compare PRO-CHOICE
– pro–lifer *noun, pl* **-lifers** [*count*]

pro·lif·er·ate /prəˈlɪfəˌreɪt/ *verb* **-ates; -at·ed; -at·ing** [*no obj*] **:** to increase in number or amount quickly ▪ New problems have *proliferated* in recent months. [=many new problems have occurred in recent months]
– pro·lif·er·a·tion /prəˌlɪfəˈreɪʃən/ *noun* [*noncount*] cancer cell *proliferation* ▪ trying to halt (the) *proliferation* of nuclear weapons [*singular*] There has been a recent *proliferation* of medical advertising on TV.

pro·lif·ic /prəˈlɪfɪk/ *adj* [*more* ~; *most* ~] **:** producing a large amount of something ▪ a *prolific* author [=an author who writes many books] ▪ a *prolific* inventor ▪ She's a *prolific* scorer. [=she scores many points/goals] ▪ a very *prolific* orchard [=an orchard that produces a very large amount of fruit] ▪ The tree is a *prolific* bloomer. [=the tree produces many flowers]
– pro·lif·i·cal·ly /prəˈlɪfɪkli/ *adv*

pro·lix /proʊˈlɪks/ *adj* [*more* ~; *most* ~] *formal* + *disapprov-*

ing : using too many words : VERBOSE • The speech was unnecessarily *prolix*. • a somewhat *prolix* writer

pro·logue /ˈproʊˌlɑːg/ *noun, pl* **-logues** [*count*] : an introduction to a book, play, etc. • a brief, one-page *prologue* • the *prologue* to his autobiography — often used figuratively • events that were a *prologue* to war [=events that came before and led to war] — compare EPILOGUE

pro·long /prəˈlɑːŋ/ *verb* **-longs; -longed; -long·ing** [+ *obj*] : to make (something) last or continue for a longer time • Chemotherapy helped to *prolong* [=*extend*] her life. • Additives are used to *prolong* the shelf life of packaged food. • High interest rates were *prolonging* the recession.

– pro·lon·ga·tion /proʊˌlɑːŋˈgeɪʃən/ *noun, pl* **-tions** [*count, noncount*] • a *prolongation* of life/suffering

prolonged *adj, always used before a noun* [*more ~; most ~*] : lasting longer than usual or expected : continuing for a long time • a *prolonged* absence • a *prolonged* period of uncertainty • *prolonged* applause/discussions • a *prolonged* illness • a *prolonged* period of rain

prom /ˈprɑːm/ *noun, pl* **proms** [*count*]

1 *US* : a formal dance for high school students usually at the end of the school year • the junior/senior *prom* • the high school *prom* • Are you going to the *prom*? — often used before another noun • the *prom* queen • *prom* night

2 *Brit, informal* : PROMENADE CONCERT

[1]**prom·e·nade** /ˌprɑːməˈneɪd, ˌprɑːməˈnɑːd/ *noun, pl* **-nades** [*count*]

1 *Brit, somewhat old-fashioned* : a public place for walking especially along a beach

2 *old-fashioned* : a walk taken in a public place for pleasure • They went for a *promenade* around town.

[2]**promenade** *verb* **-ades; -ad·ed; -ad·ing** [*no obj*] *old-fashioned* : to walk in a public place for pleasure • They *promenaded* along the beach.

promenade concert *noun, pl* **~ -certs** [*count*] *Brit* : a musical concert during which many people who are listening stand instead of sit

prom·i·nence /ˈprɑːmənəns/ *noun* : the state of being important, well-known, or noticeable : the state of being prominent [*noncount*] She is a scholar of considerable *prominence*. [=*distinction*] • He quickly gained *prominence* [=became well-known] in medical circles. • The company rose to *prominence* in the 1990s. [*singular*] The publicity has given him a *prominence* he doesn't deserve.

prom·i·nent /ˈprɑːmənənt/ *adj* [*more ~; most ~*]

1 : important and well-known • socially/politically *prominent* families • The new policy is opposed by *prominent* [=*leading*] members of the faculty. • He quickly became *prominent* in the music industry.

2 a : easily noticed or seen • He placed the award in a *prominent* position on his desk. • the disease's *prominent* symptoms **b** : sticking out in a way that is easily seen or noticed • He has a *prominent* nose/chin. • *prominent* cheekbones • the most *prominent* peak in the mountain range

– prom·i·nent·ly *adv* • He figured *prominently* in the band's history. [=he had an important part in the band's history] • The award is *prominently* positioned where everyone can see it.

P

pro·mis·cu·ous /prəˈmɪskjəwəs/ *adj* [*more ~; most ~*] *disapproving*

1 : having or involving many sexual partners • a *promiscuous* man/woman • *promiscuous* behavior • *promiscuous* sex

2 *formal* : including or involving too many people or things : not limited in a careful or proper way • He was *promiscuous* with his apologies. [=he apologized often for many different reasons] • a *promiscuous* selection of poems

– pro·mis·cu·i·ty /ˌprɑːməˈskjuːwəti/ *noun* [*noncount*] • sexual *promiscuity* **– pro·mis·cu·ous·ly** *adv*

[1]**prom·ise** /ˈprɑːməs/ *noun, pl* **-is·es**

1 [*count*] : a statement telling someone that you will definitely do something or that something will definitely happen in the future • I'll be here early tomorrow, and that's a *promise*. [=I promise that I'll be here early tomorrow] • Do I have your *promise* that you'll support me? [=do you promise to support me?] • She gave me her *promise*. • I don't believe his *promise* of further tax cuts. = I don't believe his *promise* to cut taxes further. • He ***made a promise*** to help her. = He *made a promise* that he would help her. [=he promised to help her] • He ***kept/fulfilled his promise***. [=he did what he said he would do] • He ***broke his promise***. = He ***went back on his promise***. [=he didn't do what he said he would do] • She never *made a promise* that she didn't intend to keep.

2 [*noncount*] : an indication of future success or improvement • a young artist who ***shows (a lot of) promise*** [=who seems talented and likely to do good work in the future] • Her early novels were ***full of promise***. [=were very promising] • The new drug ***holds/has promise***. [=the new drug could be effective or successful]

3 : a reason to expect that something will happen in the future — + *of* [*noncount*] There is little *promise of* relief in the forecast. • They were attracted by the *promise of* success. [*singular*] a sunny morning that gives every *promise of* a fine day • There is a *promise of* better days ahead.

a lick and a promise see [2]LICK

[2]**promise** *verb* **-ises; -ised; -is·ing**

1 : to tell someone that you will definitely do something or that something will definitely happen in the future [+ *obj*] He *promised* to buy his son a new bicycle. = He *promised* his son a new bicycle. = He *promised* a new bicycle to his son. • *Promise* me that you won't tell anyone. • I can't *promise* you that I'll be able to go, but I'll do my best. • The governor *promised* that the prisoners would receive a fair trial. • She *promised* to announce the results tomorrow. • International organizations have *promised* aid. • I *promise* to be careful. [*no obj*] You always *promise*, but you never do what you say you will. • "I won't tell anyone." "*Promise*?" "Yes, I *promise*."

2 [+ *obj*] *somewhat formal* : to make (something) seem likely : to show signs of (something that is likely or expected to happen) • Those gray skies *promise* rain. ✧ Something that ***promises to be*** good, exciting, etc., is expected to be good, exciting, etc. • The race *promises to be* the most exciting of the season. • It *promises to be* a good game. [=it should be a good game]

I (can) promise you — used to emphasize a statement • He's only concerned about himself, *I promise* [=*assure*] *you*. • *I can promise you*, you won't be disappointed.

promise (someone) the stars/moon/earth/world : to promise (someone) that you will do or give something great or wonderful even though it is not possible • He *promised her the stars and the moon*, but he never even bought her flowers. • Politicians will *promise the earth* when they're trying to get elected.

Promised Land *noun*

the Promised Land **1** : the land that was given to Abraham and his descendants according to the promise God made in the Bible **2** *or* ***the promised land*** : a happy place or condition that someone wants to reach : a place where dreams or hopes can come true • They came to America searching for *the promised land*.

promising *adj* [*more ~; most ~*] : likely to succeed or to be good : full of promise • a *promising* student • a *promising* start/debut • The neighborhood didn't look very *promising*.

– prom·is·ing·ly *adv* • His career as a quarterback began *promisingly* (enough) but was cut short by injuries.

prom·is·so·ry note /ˈprɑːməˌsori-, *Brit* ˈprɒməsri-/ *noun, pl* **~ notes** [*count*] *business* : a written promise to pay an amount of money before a particular date

pro·mo /ˈproʊmoʊ/ *noun, pl* **-mos** [*count*] *informal* : something (such as an announcement, a brief film, or an appearance) that is used to advertise or promote something (such as a new book or movie) • radio/television *promos* — often used before another noun • a *promo* photo/shoot/appearance

prom·on·to·ry /ˈprɑːmənˌtori, *Brit* ˈprɒməntri/ *noun, pl* **-ries** [*count*] : a high area of land or rock that sticks out into the sea • a rocky/steep *promontory*

pro·mote /prəˈmoʊt/ *verb* **-motes; -mot·ed; -mot·ing** [+ *obj*]

1 a : to change the rank or position of (someone) to a higher or more important one • I was *promoted* today! • He was *promoted* to senior editor. • The army major was *promoted* to lieutenant colonel. — opposite DEMOTE **b** *Brit* : to move (a sports team) to a higher position in a league • The team have been *promoted* to the First Division. — opposite RELEGATE

2 : to help (something) happen, develop, or increase • The President's visit was intended to *promote* [=*further*] foreign trade. • Mediators were present to *promote* dialogue. • Good soil *promotes* plant growth. • The school distributed pamphlets *promoting* good dental hygiene.

3 : to make people aware of (something, such as a new product) through advertising : to make (something) more popular, well-known, etc. • The marketing department is busy *promoting* the new line of men's clothes for fall. • The island is being *promoted* as a destination for romantic getaways.

pro·mot·er /prəˈmoʊtɚ/ *noun, pl* **-ers** [*count*]
1 : a person or organization that organizes or provides money for a sports event, a musical performance, etc. ▪ a boxing *promoter* [=a person who organizes boxing matches] ▪ concert/club *promoters*
2 : a person or organization that helps something to happen, develop, or increase — often + *of* ▪ the *promoters of* the congressional bill ▪ The company is a major *promoter of* alternative fuels.

pro·mo·tion /prəˈmoʊʃən/ *noun, pl* **-tions :** the act of promoting someone or something: such as **a :** the act of moving someone to a higher or more important position or rank in an organization [*noncount*] There was little chance for/of *promotion* within the company. [*count*] She was given a well-deserved *promotion*. **b** [*noncount*] *Brit* **:** the act of moving a sports team to a higher position in a league **c :** something (such as advertising) that is done to make people aware of something and increase its sales or popularity [*noncount*] — often + *of* ▪ the *promotion of* a new brand of ice cream [*count*] The company is offering a special *promotion* to increase sales. **d** [*noncount*] **:** the activity of helping something to happen, develop, or increase ▪ the *promotion* of better relations between neighboring countries

pro·mo·tion·al /prəˈmoʊʃənl̩/ *adj* **:** done or used to make people aware of something (such as a new product or book) and increase its sales or popularity ▪ *promotional* displays/materials ▪ She went on a *promotional* tour for her novel.

[1]prompt /ˈprɑːmpt/ *verb* **prompts; prompt·ed; prompt·ing** [+ *obj*]
1 a : to cause (someone) to do something ▪ Curiosity *prompted* her to ask a few questions. **b :** to be the cause of (something) ▪ Pride *prompted* his angry response. ▪ The evidence *prompted* a criminal investigation.
2 a : to say (something that encourages a person to talk) ▪ "Did you hear me?" he *prompted* when his friend did not respond to his first question. **b :** to say the lines of a play to (an actor who has forgotten them) **:** to give a prompt to (an actor) ▪ The actor had to be *prompted* by someone who was standing offstage.
3 *computers* **:** to show a message that tells (a user) to do something ▪ The computer/program *prompted* me to type in a number.
– prompt·er *noun, pl* **-ers** [*count*]

[2]prompt *adj* **prompt·er; -est** [*also more* ~; *most* ~]
1 : done or given without delay ▪ The victims need *prompt* [=*immediate*] medical assistance. ▪ We always get *prompt* service at that restaurant. ▪ He was offered *prompt* access to the data he needed.
2 : arriving or doing something at the expected time or without delay ▪ They were very *prompt* about responding to my request. ▪ Please try to be *prompt* [=*punctual*] about keeping appointments.
– prompt·ness *noun* [*noncount*] ▪ I was surprised by the *promptness* of their response.

[3]prompt *noun, pl* **prompts** [*count*]
1 : the lines of a play that are said to an actor who has forgotten them ▪ The actor was given a *prompt* by someone offstage.
2 *computers* **:** a message that appears on a computer screen asking the user to do something or to provide information ▪ a computer *prompt*

[4]prompt *adv, Brit* **:** exactly at the time stated ▪ The meeting will begin at 9 a.m. *prompt*. [=(*US*) *sharp*]

prompt·ly /ˈprɑːmptli/ *adv*
1 : in a prompt manner **:** without delay ▪ He reacted *promptly* during the emergency. ▪ The student was *promptly* [=*immediately*] expelled.
2 : exactly at a particular or the correct time ▪ She arrived *promptly* at 7:00 p.m. as we had agreed.

pro·mul·gate /ˈprɑːməlˌgeɪt/ *verb* **-gates; -gat·ed; -gat·ing** [+ *obj*]
1 *formal* **:** to make (an idea, belief, etc.) known to many people ▪ Her ideas/theories have been widely *promulgated* on the Internet.
2 *technical* **:** to make (a new law) known officially and publicly ▪ The law was *promulgated* in April 1988.
– pro·mul·ga·tion /ˌprɑːməlˈgeɪʃən/ *noun* [*noncount*]

prone /ˈproʊn/ *adj*
1 [*more* ~; *most* ~] **:** likely to do, have, or suffer from something — usually + *to* ▪ They are *prone to* (making) errors/mistakes. = They are error-*prone*/mistake-*prone*. [=they make many errors/mistakes] ▪ Tests showed that the machine is *prone to* failure/fail. ▪ He is somewhat *prone to* depression. ▪ People in my family are *prone to* heart disease. ▪ He is *prone to* (having) accidents. = He is ***accident-prone***. [=he has many accidents] ▪ an athlete who is ***injury-prone*** [=who is often injured]
2 : lying with the front of your body facing downward ▪ He was lying on the floor in a *prone* position. = He was (lying) *prone* on the floor. — compare SUPINE
– prone·ness /ˈproʊnnəs/ *noun* [*noncount*] ▪ *proneness* to accidents/depression

prong /ˈprɑːŋ/ *noun, pl* **prongs** [*count*]
1 : one of the long points of a fork or similar object **:** TINE
2 : one of the small metal parts of an electrical plug that fit into the holes in an outlet

pronged /ˈprɑːngd/ *adj*
1 : having a specified number of prongs — used in combination ▪ a three-*pronged* fork/outlet/plug
2 : having a specified number of parts — used in combination ▪ The company has a two-*pronged* strategy for improving sales in the coming year.

prong·horn /ˈprɑːŋˌhoɚn/ *noun, pl* **-horn** *or* **-horns** [*count*] **:** a large animal of western North America that looks like an antelope — called also *pronghorn antelope*

pronghorn

pro·nom·i·nal /proʊˈnɑːmənl̩/ *adj, grammar* **:** relating to a pronoun or used like a pronoun ▪ the *pronominal* adjective "this" in "this dog"
– pro·nom·i·nal·ly *adv*

pro·noun /ˈproʊˌnaʊn/ *noun, pl* **-nouns** [*count*] *grammar* **:** a word (such as *I, he, she, you, it, we,* or *they*) that is used instead of a noun or noun phrase — see also PERSONAL PRONOUN

pro·nounce /prəˈnaʊns/ *verb* **-nounc·es; -nounced; -nounc·ing**
1 [+ *obj*] **a :** to make the sound of (a word or letter) with your voice ▪ She practices *pronouncing* foreign words. ▪ The "k" in "know" is not *pronounced*. [=the "k" in "know" is silent] **b :** to say or speak (a word) correctly ▪ I'm sorry. I can't *pronounce* your name.
2 [+ *obj*] *formal* **a :** to say or announce (something) in an official or formal way ▪ The priest *pronounced* a blessing on their home. ▪ The judge ***pronounced sentence***. [=stated the punishment for a criminal] **b :** to say or state that (someone or something) is something in usually an official or definite way ▪ After reviewing the replay of the race's finish, the horse was *pronounced* the winner. [=was declared to be the winner] ▪ I now *pronounce* you man and wife. [=I now declare that you are married] ▪ She *pronounced* the party a success. [=she said that the party was a success] ▪ The doctors *pronounced* him fit to go back to work. ▪ He was *pronounced* dead upon arrival at the hospital.
3 [*no obj*] *formal* **a :** to state an opinion on something — + *on* or *upon* ▪ As a grammarian, he freely *pronounces on* questions of proper English. ▪ The senator *pronounced upon* the major issues in the election. **b :** to give a judgment for or against someone or something ▪ Many senators are *pronouncing* in favor of the bill. ▪ The judge *pronounced* for/against the defendant.

pro·nounce·able /prəˈnaʊnsəbəl/ *adj* **:** capable of being pronounced or said ▪ His name is not easily *pronounceable*.

pro·nounced /prəˈnaʊnst/ *adj* [*more* ~; *most* ~] **:** very noticeable ▪ He walked with a *pronounced* limp. ▪ There has been a *pronounced* [=*decided, definite*] improvement in her condition. ▪ The symptoms of the disease have become steadily more *pronounced*.

pro·nounce·ment /prəˈnaʊnsmənt/ *noun, pl* **-ments** [*count*] *formal* **:** an official public statement ▪ He made some important *pronouncements* on government policy.

pron·to /ˈprɑːnˌtoʊ/ *adv, informal* **:** without delay **:** right away ▪ He told me to get there *pronto*. [=*quickly, immediately*]

pro·nun·ci·a·tion /prəˌnʌnsiˈeɪʃən/ *noun, pl* **-tions**
1 : the way in which a word or name is pronounced [*count*] What is the correct *pronunciation* of his name? [*noncount*] I haven't learned proper *pronunciation* of French words.
2 [*singular*] **:** a particular person's way of pronouncing a word or the words of a language ▪ He has flawless *pronuncia-*

tion. [=he pronounces words flawlessly]

[1]proof /ˈpruːf/ *noun, pl* **proofs**
1 [*noncount*] **: something which shows that something else is true or correct** ▪ The document was *proof* that her story was true. ▪ He claims that he was home when the murder was committed, but he has no *proof*. ▪ The photograph is ***proof positive*** [=definite proof] that the accident happened the way he described. ▪ I'm ***living proof*** that success is possible. [=my success shows that other people can succeed too] — **often + *of*** ▪ The evidence gave *proof of* her statement. [=the evidence proved her statement] ▪ Do you have any *proof of* identity? ▪ Keep the receipt as ***proof of purchase***. [=evidence showing/proving that you bought something]
2 [*count*] **a : an act or process of showing that something is true** ▪ The ***burden of proof*** [=the need to show that something is true] is on the prosecuting lawyer of the case. **b** *mathematics* **: a test which shows that a calculation is correct** ▪ The *proof* shows that the theorem is true. ▪ mathematical *proofs*
3 [*count*] *technical* **: a copy of something that is going to be printed which is examined and used to make corrections before the final printing is done — usually plural** ▪ He edited the *proofs* of the manuscript.
4 [*noncount*] **: a measurement of how much alcohol is in an alcoholic drink** ▪ The whiskey is 80 *proof*.
the proof is in the pudding see PUDDING

[2]proof *adj, formal* **: designed or made to prevent or protect *against* something harmful** ▪ The seal of the bottle is *proof against* tampering. [=the seal prevents tampering] — **usually used in combination** ▪ water*proof* ▪ bullet*proof*

[3]proof *verb* **proofs; proofed; proof·ing** [+ *obj*] **:** PROOFREAD ▪ She *proofed* the story carefully.

proof·read /ˈpruːfˌriːd/ *verb* **-reads; -read** /-ˌrɛd/; **-read·ing** [+ *obj*] **: to read and correct mistakes in (a written or printed piece of writing)** ▪ He *proofread* the essay carefully.
— **proof·read·er** *noun, pl* **-ers** [*count*] ▪ She's an excellent *proofreader*. — **proof·read·ing** *noun* [*noncount*]

[1]prop /ˈprɑːp/ *verb, always followed by an adverb or preposition* **props; propped; prop·ping** [+ *obj*] **: to support (something) by placing it against something else or by placing something under it** ▪ She *propped* the rake against a tree. ▪ We *propped* the shed's roof with poles. ▪ The window was *propped* open.
prop up [*phrasal verb*] **1 *prop up (something) or prop (something) up* : to stop (something) from falling or slipping by placing something under or against it** ▪ We *propped up* the beams with long boards. **2 *prop (someone) up or prop up (someone)* : to give help, encouragement, or support to (someone)** ▪ His faith *propped* him *up* in times of crisis.

[2]prop *noun, pl* **props** [*count*]
1 : something that is used to support something and keep it in position ▪ He used rocks as *props* to keep up the fence post.
2 : someone or something that gives help or support to someone or something else ▪ His wife was his emotional *prop* during his depression. ▪ He used his inheritance money as a *prop* to start his own business.
3 *rugby* **: a player who plays in a forward position on a rugby team — called also *prop forward***
— compare [3]PROP, [4]PROP

[3]prop *noun, pl* **props** [*count*] **: an object that is used by a performer or actor or that is used to create a desired effect in a scene on a stage, in a movie, etc.** ▪ The performers used different *props* in their comedy routine. ▪ The only stage *props* were a hanging lightbulb and a wooden chair. — compare [2]PROP, [4]PROP

[4]prop *noun, pl* **props** [*count*] *informal* **:** PROPELLER — compare [2]PROP, [3]PROP

pro·pa·gan·da /ˌprɑːpəˈgændə/ *noun* [*noncount*] *usually disapproving* **: ideas or statements that are often false or exaggerated and that are spread in order to help a cause, a political leader, a government, etc.** ▪ He was accused of spreading *propaganda*. ▪ a *propaganda* campaign ▪ The report was nothing but lies and *propaganda*.
— **pro·pa·gan·dist** /ˌprɑːpəˈgændɪst/ *noun, pl* **-dists** [*count*] — **pro·pa·gan·dis·tic** /ˌprɑːpəˌgænˈdɪstɪk/ *adj* ▪ *propagandistic* writing

pro·pa·gan·dize *also Brit* **pro·pa·gan·dise** /ˌprɑːpəˈgænˌdaɪz/ *verb* **-diz·es; -dized; -diz·ing** *formal* **: to spread propaganda** [+ *obj*] They were *propagandized* into believing what the government wanted them to believe. [*no obj*] He uses his movies to *propagandize* for the state.

prop·a·gate /ˈprɑːpəˌgeɪt/ *verb* **-gates; -gat·ed; -gat·ing**
1 [+ *obj*] *formal* **: to make (something, such as an idea or belief) known to many people** ▪ The group *propagates* [=*promotes*] its antigovernment doctrine on the Web.
2 *technical* **: to produce (a new plant)** [+ *obj*] We are discovering new ways to *propagate* plants without seeds. ▪ He *propagated* the apple tree by grafting. [*no obj*] The plants failed to *propagate*.
— **prop·a·ga·tion** /ˌprɑːpəˈgeɪʃən/ *noun* [*noncount*] ▪ the *propagation* of plants/ideas — **prop·a·ga·tor** /ˈprɑːpəˌgeɪtɚ/ *noun, pl* **-tors** [*count*] ▪ a *propagator* of new ideas ▪ plant *propagators*

pro·pane /ˈproʊˌpeɪn/ *noun* [*noncount*] **: a colorless gas that is used for cooking and heating**

pro·pel /prəˈpɛl/ *verb* **-pels; -pelled; -pel·ling** [+ *obj*] **: to push or drive (someone or something) forward or in a particular direction** ▪ He grabbed him and *propelled* him through the door. ▪ The train is *propelled* by steam. — **often used figuratively** ▪ She was *propelled* [=*motivated*] by greed when she stole the money. ▪ The album *propelled* the band to fame. — see also JET-PROPELLED

pro·pel·lant *also* **pro·pel·lent** /prəˈpɛlənt/ *noun, pl* **-lants** [*count, noncount*] *technical*
1 : a gas under pressure in a can that is used to spray out the contents when the pressure is released
2 : a fuel or an explosive substance that is used to make something (such as a rocket) go forward ▪ rocket *propellant*

pro·pel·ler /prəˈpɛlɚ/ *noun, pl* **-lers** [*count*] **: a device with two or more blades that turn quickly and cause a ship or aircraft to move**

propelling pencil *noun, pl* **~ -cils** [*count*] *Brit* **:** MECHANICAL PENCIL

pro·pen·si·ty /prəˈpɛnsəti/ *noun, pl* **-ties** [*count*] *formal* **: a strong natural tendency to do something** ▪ Why do some people have a *propensity* for/toward violence? [=why are some people violent?; why do some people have a tendency to be violent?] ▪ He had a *propensity* for crime. ▪ She has a *propensity* to assume the worst. [=she tends to assume the worst]

[1]prop·er /ˈprɑːpɚ/ *adj*
1 [*more ~; most ~*] **a : correct according to social or moral rules** ▪ That is not the *proper* [=*acceptable*] way to dress for school. ▪ It is not *proper* to speak that way. ▪ The children need to learn *proper* behavior. ▪ It would not be *proper* for you to borrow the ladder without asking first. **b : behaving in a way that is correct according to social or moral rules** ▪ She is a very prim and *proper* young lady.
2 *always used before a noun* **: exactly correct** ▪ Is this the *proper* spelling of your name? ▪ *proper* punctuation
3 *always used before a noun* **: right or suitable for some purpose or situation** ▪ He didn't have the *proper* [=*appropriate*] training for the job. ▪ You need to eat a *proper* meal instead of junk food. ▪ Each step must be done in the *proper* order/sequence. ▪ You need to get a *proper* [=*real, decent*] job. ▪ Please put your shoes in their *proper* place. [=please put your shoes where they belong]
4 *always used after a noun* **— used to emphasize that you are referring to the specific thing that is being named** ▪ Her family lived outside the city *proper*. [=lived in an area that was close to the city but was not actually in the city]
5 *always used before a noun, chiefly Brit* **: complete or absolute** ▪ I felt a *proper* fool after making that mistake. ▪ We are in a *proper* mess now.
proper to *formal* **: belonging to or suited to (something)** ▪ Are such violent emotions *proper to* poetry?

[2]proper *adv, chiefly Brit, informal* **: in a complete way** ▪ We sure have messed things up *proper*. [=*thoroughly, completely*] ▪ They beat us ***good and proper***.

prop·er·ly /ˈprɑːpəli/ *adv*
1 : in a way that is acceptable or suitable ▪ The children must learn how to behave *properly* [=*appropriately*] in church. ▪ He doesn't know how to *properly* tie a necktie. ▪ The can opener is not working *properly*. [=*right*]
2 : in a way that is accurate or correct ▪ The boxes were not *properly* labeled. ▪ Did I spell your name *properly*? ▪ *Properly* speaking, whales are not fish. ▪ The house *properly* belongs to his sister.

proper name *noun, pl* **~ names** [*count*] **:** PROPER NOUN

proper noun *noun, pl* **~ nouns** [*count*] **: a word or group of words (such as "Noah Webster," "Kentucky," or "U.S. Congress") that is the name of a particular person, place, or thing and that usually begins with a capital letter — called**

also *proper name*; compare COMMON NOUN

prop·er·tied /ˈprɑːpɚtid/ *adj, always used before a noun, formal* : owning a lot of property or land ▪ the wealthy, *propertied* classes

prop·er·ty /ˈprɑːpɚti/ *noun, pl* **-ties**

1 [*noncount*] **: something that is owned by a person, business, etc.** ▪ Those books are my *property*. [=I own those books] ▪ We are not responsible for the loss of ***personal property***. ▪ The library is ***public property***. [=the library is owned by the city, town, or state] ▪ He was trying to sell ***stolen property***. — see also INTELLECTUAL PROPERTY

2 : a piece of land often with buildings on it that is owned by a person, business, etc. [*noncount*] He was caught trespassing on private *property*. ▪ She owns all sorts of *property* around town. ▪ The students were caught smoking on school *property*. [*count*] He owns several valuable *properties* in the area. ▪ a developer of commercial/residential *properties* — often used before another noun ▪ *Property* values are going up. ▪ a *property* tax

3 [*count*] *somewhat formal* **: a special quality or characteristic of something** ▪ One of the *properties* of helium is its lightness. ▪ A unique *property* of garlic is its strong odor. ▪ The two plants have similar physical *properties*. ▪ The herb has medicinal *properties*. ▪ the chemical *properties* of water

hot property see [1]HOT

prop forward *noun, pl* **~ -wards** [*count*] *rugby* **:** [2]PROP 3

proph·e·cy /ˈprɑːfəsi/ *noun, pl* **-cies**

1 [*count*] **: a statement that something will happen in the future : PREDICTION** ▪ The *prophecies* of the author have all come true. ▪ His *prophecy* was fulfilled. [=the thing that he said would happen did happen]

2 [*noncount*] **: the power or ability to know what will happen in the future** ▪ She has the gift of *prophecy*.

proph·e·sy /ˈprɑːfəˌsaɪ/ *verb* **-sies; -sied; -sy·ing** [+ *obj*] **: to state that something will happen in the future : PREDICT** ▪ He *prophesied* the government's failure. = He *prophesied* that the government would fail. ▪ The book claims that modern events were *prophesied* in ancient times.

proph·et /ˈprɑːfət/ *noun, pl* **-ets**

1 [*count*] **: a member of some religions (such as Christianity, Judaism, and Islam) who delivers messages that are believed to have come from God** ▪ the Old Testament *prophets* ▪ the words of the *prophet* ▪ the *Prophet* Isaiah/Muhammad

2 *the Prophet* — used as another name for Muhammad, the founder of Islam

3 a *the Prophets* : the writers of the books of the Bible that describe what will happen in the future b *Prophets* : the part of the Bible that includes the books written by the Prophets.

4 [*count*] **: a person who states that something will happen in the future** ▪ a stock market *prophet* [=a person who predicts what will happen in the stock market] ▪ the local weather *prophet* ▪ a ***prophet of doom*** [=someone who says that bad things will happen]

5 [*count*] **: a person who teaches or spreads a new idea or belief** ▪ a *prophet* of socialism

proph·et·ess /ˈprɑːfətəs/ *noun, pl* **-ess·es** [*count*] **: a woman who is a prophet**

pro·phet·ic /prəˈfɛtɪk/ *adj*

1 : correctly stating what will happen in the future ▪ Her warning proved to be *prophetic*. [=the thing that she warned would/could happen did happen] ▪ a *prophetic* statement

2 : of or relating to a prophet or to prophecy ▪ the *prophetic* books of the Old Testament

— **pro·phet·i·cal·ly** /prəˈfɛtɪkli/ *adv* ▪ The coach *prophetically* promised a victory in the next game.

[1]**pro·phy·lac·tic** /ˌproʊfəˈlæktɪk, *Brit* ˌprɒfəˈlæktɪk/ *adj, medical* **: designed to prevent disease** ▪ a *prophylactic* drug/treatment/regimen ▪ the *prophylactic* use of antibiotics

[2]**prophylactic** *noun, pl* **-tics** [*count*]

1 *medical* **: something that is designed to prevent the spread of disease or infection**

2 *US* **: CONDOM**

pro·pi·ti·ate /proʊˈpɪʃiˌeɪt/ *verb* **-ates; -at·ed; -at·ing** [+ *obj*] *formal* **: to make (someone) pleased or less angry by giving or saying something desired : APPEASE** ▪ He made an offering to *propitiate* the angry gods.

— **pro·pi·ti·a·tion** /proʊˌpɪʃiˈeɪʃən/ *noun* [*noncount*] — **pro·pi·tia·to·ry** /proʊˈpɪʃijəˌtori, *Brit* prəʊˈpɪʃiətri/ *adj* ▪ a *propitiatory* offering to the gods

pro·pi·tious /prəˈpɪʃəs/ *adj* [*more ~; most ~*] *formal* **: likely to have or produce good results** ▪ conditions that are *propitious* for growth [=conditions that make growth likely] ▪ Now is a *propitious* time to start a business.

pro·po·nent /prəˈpoʊnənt/ *noun, pl* **-nents** [*count*] **: a person who argues for or supports something : ADVOCATE** ▪ a civil rights *proponent* — often + *of* ▪ He is a leading *proponent of* gun control. — opposite OPPONENT

pro·por·tion /prəˈpoɚʃən/ *noun, pl* **-tions**

1 [*count*] **: an amount that is a part of a whole** ▪ Some of the money goes to cover expenses, but a large *proportion* [=*portion, percentage*] is donated to charity. — usually + *of* ▪ These expenses account for only a small *proportion of* our budget. ▪ The *proportion of* people who own their own homes is slowly increasing. ▪ The solution was made from equal *proportions of* water and bleach. ▪ A high *proportion of* high school students enroll in college. ▪ A large *proportion of* the proceeds are donated to charity. ▪ A small *proportion of* people in the group was left-handed.

2 : the relationship that exists between the size, number, or amount of two things [*count*] — usually singular; often + *of* ▪ The *proportion* [=*ratio*] *of* boys to girls in our class is three to one. [=there are three boys for each girl in our class] [*noncount*] Your share of the profits will be ***in proportion to*** the amount of work that you do. [=if you do more work, you will get a larger share of the profits]

3 : the correct or appropriate relationship between the size, shape, and position of the different parts of something [*noncount*] His head is large ***in proportion to*** his body. [=the size of his head seems large when compared to the size of his body] ▪ The garage is not *in proportion to* the house. [=the garage is too small/big for the house] ▪ His ears were drawn ***out of proportion with*** his head. ▪ The size of the window seems *out of proportion with* the height of the wall. [*count*] — usually plural ▪ The cathedral has classic *proportions*.

4 *proportions* [*plural*] **: the size, shape, or extent of something** ▪ The carpet did not fit the *proportions* [=*dimensions*] of the room. ▪ It's a problem of huge/massive *proportions*. ▪ It was a disaster of biblical/epic *proportions*. [=it was a terrible disaster that affected many people]

5 [*noncount*] **a : the importance of something when it is compared to other things : the relative importance of things** ▪ He has no ***sense of proportion***. **b** ✧ **If you *keep things in proportion*, you understand which things are truly important and you do not become upset by small things that are not important.** ▪ Let's *keep things in proportion*. You should be able to wait one more day after you have waited two months already. **c** ✧ **If something *gets out of proportion* or is *blown out of proportion*, it becomes larger than it should be or it is treated as something worse or more important than it really is.** ▪ Their fears have *gotten* (totally/completely) *out of proportion*. ▪ The story was *blown out of proportion* in the newspapers. ▪ You are ***blowing things*** (all/way) ***out of proportion***.

pro·por·tion·al /prəˈpoɚʃənl̩/ *adj*

1 : having a size, number, or amount that is directly related to or appropriate for something ▪ If you increase the size of the picture, keep the length and width *proportional*. [=increase the length and width by the same percentage so that they are related to each other in the same way] — often + *to* ▪ Keep the length *proportional to* the width. ▪ Your share of the profits will be *proportional to* the amount of work you did. ▪ The taxi fare is *proportional to* the length of the ride. — see also DIRECTLY PROPORTIONAL, INVERSELY PROPORTIONAL

2 : having parts that are the correct or appropriate size in relation to each other ▪ The features of the face in the drawing are *proportional*. — often + *to* ▪ The head was not *proportional to* the body. [=the head was too large/small for the body] ▪ The sleeves were not *proportional to* the length of the blouse.

— **pro·por·tion·al·ly** /prəˈpoɚʃənl̩i/ *adv* ▪ The profits were divided *proportionally*. ▪ The ears were not drawn *proportionally* with the head.

proportional representation *noun* [*noncount*] **: a system in which the number of seats held by members of a political party in a legislature (such as a parliament) is determined by the number of votes its candidates receive in an election**

pro·por·tion·ate /prəˈpoɚʃənət/ *adj* **: PROPORTIONAL 1** ▪ Each investor will receive a *proportionate* share of the profits. — often + *to* ▪ The property tax is *proportionate to* the size of the house.

— **pro·por·tion·ate·ly** *adv* ▪ The profits were divided *proportionately*. ▪ If your sales increase, then your salary will be adjusted *proportionately*.

P

pro·por·tioned /prəˈpoɚʃənd/ *adj* **: having parts that relate in size to the other parts in a particular way** ▪ The sculpture was poorly *proportioned*. ▪ She has a well-*proportioned* figure.

pro·pos·al /prəˈpoʊzəl/ *noun, pl* **-als**
1 [*count*] **: something (such as a plan or suggestion) that is presented to a person or group of people to consider** ▪ Everyone thought the *proposal* made sense. ▪ They rejected/accepted/considered/approved my *proposal*. ▪ The committee is reviewing the *proposal* for the new restaurant. ▪ They put forth a *proposal* to sell the company. ▪ a business *proposal*
2 [*noncount*] **: the act of presenting a plan, suggestion, etc., to a person or group of people** ▪ These problems have led to the *proposal* of a new law.
3 [*count*] **: the act of asking someone to marry you** ▪ She accepted his *proposal* (of marriage). ▪ a marriage *proposal*

pro·pose /prəˈpoʊz/ *verb* **-pos·es; -posed; -pos·ing**
1 [+ *obj*] **: to suggest (something, such as a plan or theory) to a person or group of people to consider** ▪ The scientists *proposed* a new theory. ▪ The mayor *proposed* a plan for a new bridge. ▪ Several senators have *proposed* raising the tax. ▪ I *propose* that we revise the bylaws.
2 [+ *obj*] **: to plan or intend to do (something)** ▪ They *propose* to buy a new house. ▪ How do you *propose* solving this problem?
3 [+ *obj*] **: to suggest (someone) for a job, position, office, etc.** ▪ The chairman *proposed* the young executive as a candidate for promotion. ▪ She *proposed* [=(more commonly) *nominated*] her teacher for the award.
4 : to ask someone to marry you — often + *to* [*no obj*] He *proposed to* his girlfriend. [+ *obj*] He ***proposed marriage to*** his girlfriend.
propose a toast **: to publicly wish a person future health, happiness, and success and ask others to raise their glasses and join in a drink** ▪ I would like to *propose a toast* to the bride and groom.
— **proposed** *adj, always used before a noun* ▪ They rejected the *proposed* offer/plan. — **pro·pos·er** *noun, pl* **-ers** [*count*] ▪ He is the original *proposer* of the theory.

[1]**prop·o·si·tion** /ˌprɑːpəˈzɪʃən/ *noun, pl* **-tions** [*count*]
1 : something (such as a plan or offer) that is presented to a person or group of people to consider ▪ He made an attractive business *proposition*. ▪ The other company rejected their *proposition*.
2 : a statement to be proved, explained, or discussed ▪ Her theory rejects the basic *proposition* that humans evolved from apes. ▪ If we accept *proposition* "A" as true, then we must accept *proposition* "B" as false.
3 : something that someone intends to do or deal with ▪ Fixing the engine will not be an easy/simple *proposition*. [=*matter*] ▪ The election will be a tough *proposition* for the mayor. ▪ The farm will never be a paying *proposition*. [=the farm will never make money]
4 *US* **: a suggestion for a change in the law on which people must vote** ▪ The town voted in favor of a *proposition* calling for a ban on smoking in public spaces. ▪ He expects *Proposition* 12 to pass by a wide margin.

[2]**proposition** *verb* **-tions; -tioned; -tion·ing** [+ *obj*] **: to offer to have sex with (someone) in a direct and often offensive way** ▪ He was *propositioned* by a prostitute. ▪ He got drunk and *propositioned* a woman sitting next to him in the bar.

pro·pound /prəˈpaʊnd/ *verb* **-pounds; -pound·ed; -pound·ing** [+ *obj*] *formal* **: to suggest (an idea, theory, etc.) to a person or group of people to consider : PROPOSE** ▪ Her new book expands upon the theory *propounded* in her first book.
— **pro·pound·er** *noun, pl* **-ers** [*count*]

pro·pri·e·tary /prəˈprajəˌteri, *Brit* prəˈprajətri/ *adj, formal*
1 : of or like that of an owner ▪ The publisher has *proprietary* rights [=the rights of an owner] to the manuscript. ▪ The investors have a *proprietary* interest in the land.
2 : used, made, or sold only by the particular person or company that has the legal right to do so ▪ The computer comes with the manufacturer's *proprietary* software. ▪ a *proprietary* drug ▪ "Merriam-Webster" is a *proprietary* name.
3 : kept private by an owner ▪ The journalist tried to get access to *proprietary* information.

pro·pri·e·tor /prəˈprajətɚ/ *noun, pl* **-tors** [*count*] *formal* **: a person who owns a business or property** ▪ She is the *proprietor* of the store. ▪ a restaurant *proprietor*
— **pro·pri·e·tor·ship** /prəˈprajətɚˌʃɪp/ *noun, pl* **-ships** [*count*] The business is a sole *proprietorship* and not a partnership. [*noncount*] He was given *proprietorship* of the store.

pro·pri·e·tress /prəˈprajətrəs/ *noun, pl* **-tress·es** [*count*] *formal* **: a woman who is a proprietor**

pro·pri·e·ty /prəˈprajəti/ *noun, pl* **-ties** *formal*
1 [*noncount*] **: behavior that is accepted as socially or morally correct and proper** ▪ She acted with *propriety*. ▪ He went beyond the bounds of *propriety*. [=he acted improperly] ▪ She conducted herself with *propriety*.
2 [*noncount*] **: the state or quality of being correct and proper** ▪ They debated the *propriety* of the punishment that he was given.
3 ***proprieties*** [*plural*] **: rules of correct social behavior** ▪ When attending a wedding, there are certain *proprieties* that must be observed. ▪ the social *proprieties*

props /ˈprɑːps/ *noun* [*plural*] *US slang*
1 : something that is said to publicly thank and give special attention to someone for doing something : credit or recognition ▪ *Props* to everyone that made this movie a success. ▪ All of the performers deserve ***mad props***. [=very enthusiastic praise] — often + *for* ▪ He gave *props* to his brother *for* his help with the project.
2 : RESPECT ▪ The teacher earned our *props*.

pro·pul·sion /prəˈpʌlʃən/ *noun* [*noncount*] *technical* **: the force that moves something forward : the force that propels something** ▪ rocket/electric *propulsion* ▪ Sailboats use wind as their source/means of *propulsion*. ▪ a *propulsion* system — see also JET PROPULSION
— **pro·pul·sive** /prəˈpʌlsɪv/ *adj* ▪ *propulsive* forces

pro ra·ta /proʊˈreɪtə/ *adj, formal* **: calculated according to the specific amount that someone has done, used, etc.** ▪ Each investor will receive a *pro rata* share of the profits. [=a share based on how much money each person invested]
— **pro rata** *adv* ▪ The fee will be paid *pro rata* to the people who did the work.

pro·rate /proʊˈreɪt/ *verb* **-rates; -rat·ed; -rat·ing** [+ *obj*] *US* **: to calculate (something) according to the specific amount that someone has done, used, etc.** ▪ We will *prorate* your monthly rent for the remaining 10 days on your lease. [=you will pay 10 days' worth of a month's rent] ▪ The player's annual salary was *prorated* because he only played for the last three months of the season.
— **pro·ra·tion** /proʊˈreɪʃən/ *noun* [*noncount*]

pro·sa·ic /proʊˈzejɪk/ *adj* [*more* ~; *most* ~] *formal* **: dull or ordinary** ▪ He has a *prosaic* writing style. ▪ the *prosaic* life of a hardworking farmer ▪ She believes the noises are made by ghosts, but I think there's a more *prosaic* explanation.
— **pro·sa·i·cal·ly** /proʊˈzejəkli/ *adv*

pro·sce·ni·um /proʊˈsiːnijəm/ *noun, pl* **-ums** [*count*] **: the part of a stage that is in front of the curtain** ▪ The host walked onto the *proscenium*. ▪ a ***proscenium arch*** [=an arch that is over the front of a stage]

pro·sciut·to /proʊˈʃuːtoʊ/ *noun* [*noncount*] **: a type of spicy Italian ham**

pro·scribe /proʊˈskraɪb/ *verb* **-scribes; -scribed; -scrib·ing** [+ *obj*] *formal* **: to make (something) illegal : to not allow (something)** ▪ The principal *proscribed* [=*banned, prohibited*] the use of cell phones in school. ▪ acts that are *proscribed* by law ▪ *proscribed* conduct
— **pro·scrip·tion** /proʊˈskrɪpʃən/ *noun, pl* **-tions** [*count, noncount*]

prose /ˈproʊz/ *noun* [*noncount*] **: writing that is not poetry : ordinary writing** ▪ She writes in very clear *prose*. — often used before another noun ▪ She has a unique *prose* style. ▪ He is a talented *prose* writer. ▪ a *prose* narrative

pros·e·cute /ˈprɑːsɪˌkjuːt/ *verb* **-cutes; -cut·ed; -cut·ing**
1 *law* **: to hold a trial against a person who is accused of a crime to see if that person is guilty** [*no obj*] The store's owner agreed not to *prosecute* if the boy returned the stolen goods. [+ *obj*] Shoplifters will be *prosecuted*.
2 : to work as a lawyer to try to prove a case against someone accused of a crime [+ *obj*] The case is being *prosecuted* by the assistant district attorney. [*no obj*] the *prosecuting* lawyer/counsel
3 [+ *obj*] *formal* **: to continue to do (something) : to proceed with (something)** ▪ She criticized the government for the way it has *prosecuted* the war.
— **pros·e·cut·able** /ˌprɑːsəˈkjuːtəbəl/ *adj* ▪ a *prosecutable* offense

prosecuting attorney *noun, pl* ~ **-neys** [*count*] *US* **: DISTRICT ATTORNEY**

pros·e·cu·tion /ˌprɑːsɪˈkjuːʃən/ *noun, pl* **-tions**

1 : the act or process of holding a trial against a person who is accused of a crime to see if that person is guilty [*count*] There has been an increase in *prosecutions* for gun-related crimes. [*noncount*] The defendant is awaiting *prosecution*.

2 *the prosecution* : the side of a legal case which argues that a person who is accused of a crime is guilty : the lawyer or lawyers who prosecute someone in a court case • *The prosecution* called their first witness. • *The prosecution* rests, Your Honor. • The defense told the jury that *the prosecution* had not proved its case. — often used before another noun • *prosecution* attorneys/lawyers — compare DEFENSE

3 [*noncount*] *formal* : the act of doing or continuing to do something — usually + *of* • the *prosecution of* the war

pros·e·cu·tor /ˈprɑːsɪˌkjuːtɚ/ *noun, pl* **-tors** [*count*] : a lawyer who represents the side in a court case that accuses a person of a crime and who tries to prove that the person is guilty

pros·e·ly·tize *also Brit* **pros·e·ly·tise** /ˈprɑːsələˌtaɪz/ *verb* **-tiz·es; -tized; -tiz·ing** *formal + often disapproving* : to try to persuade people to join a religion, cause, or group [*no obj*] He uses his position to *proselytize* for the causes that he supports. [+ *obj*] *proselytize* a faith/religion

pro shop *noun, pl* **~ shops** [*count*] : a shop where equipment for a sport (such as golf or tennis) is sold usually by people who play or teach the sport professionally

pros·o·dy /ˈprɑːsədi/ *noun* [*noncount*] *technical* : the rhythm and pattern of sounds of poetry and language

[1]pros·pect /ˈprɑːˌspɛkt/ *noun, pl* **-pects**

1 : the possibility that something will happen in the future [*singular*] the frightening *prospect* of going to war • She is excited by the *prospect* of returning to school. • Bankruptcy is an unlikely *prospect* for the company. [*noncount*] There was no/little *prospect* that the two parties would reach an agreement anytime soon.

2 [*count*] : an opportunity for something to happen — usually plural • He has few *prospects* for employment. • She has a lot of business *prospects*. = She has a lot of *prospects* for doing business.

3 [*count*] : someone or something that is likely to succeed or to be chosen • a young baseball player who's considered a top *prospect* • We haven't decided which car to buy yet. We're still looking at a few *prospects*.

4 [*count*] *formal* : a wide view of an area from usually a high place — usually singular; usually + *of* • a wide *prospect of* the surrounding country

in prospect *formal* : possible or likely to exist or happen in the future • A great medical breakthrough is *in prospect*. [=expected in the future]

[2]pros·pect /ˈprɑːˌspɛkt, *Brit* prəˈspɛkt/ *verb* **-pects; -pect·ed; -pect·ing** [*no obj*] : to search an area for gold, minerals, oil, etc. — often + *for* • Men were *prospecting for* gold along the river. — sometimes used figuratively • The team actively *prospects for* talented players.

— **pros·pec·tor** /ˈprɑːˌspɛktɚ/ *noun, pl* **-tors** [*count*] • a gold/oil *prospector* — **prospecting** *noun* [*noncount*] • oil *prospecting*

pro·spec·tive /prəˈspɛktɪv/ *adj, always used before a noun*

1 : likely to be or become something specified in the future • a seminar for *prospective* home buyers [=people who are likely to buy a home fairly soon] • *prospective* parents/students/employers

2 *formal* : likely to happen • The new law has many *prospective* [=*expected*] benefits.

pro·spec·tus /prəˈspɛktəs/ *noun, pl* **-tus·es** [*count*]

1 : a printed statement that describes something (such as a new business or investment) and that is sent to people who may want to be involved in it or invest in it

2 *chiefly Brit* : a book or document that provides information about a school, business, etc. : BROCHURE

pros·per /ˈprɑːspɚ/ *verb* **-pers; -pered; -per·ing** [*no obj*]

1 : to become very successful usually by making a lot of money • She *prospered* as a real estate agent. • He hopes his business will *prosper*.

2 : to become very active, healthy, or strong • The city *prospered* [=*flourished, thrived*] as a center for trade. • No crop can *prosper* in this heat. • The economy is *prospering*.

pros·per·i·ty /prɑˈspɛrəti/ *noun* [*noncount*] : the state of being successful usually by making a lot of money • a period of *prosperity* for our nation • economic *prosperity*

pros·per·ous /ˈprɑːspərəs/ *adj* [*more ~; most ~*] : having success usually by making a lot of money • The company had a *prosperous* year. • He predicted a *prosperous* future. • *prosperous* [=*affluent*] merchants • a *prosperous* town

pros·tate /ˈprɑːˌsteɪt/ *noun, pl* **-tates** [*count*] : PROSTATE GLAND • enlargement of the *prostate* — often used before another noun • *prostate* cancer

prostate gland *noun, pl* **~ glands** [*count*] : an organ found in men and male animals that produces the liquid in which sperm is carried

pros·the·sis /prɑsˈθiːsəs/ *noun, pl* **-the·ses** /-ˌsiːz/ [*count*] *medical* : an artificial device that replaces a missing or injured part of the body • She was fitted with a *prosthesis* to replace her missing leg. • a dental/optical *prosthesis*

— **pros·thet·ic** /prɑsˈθɛtɪk/ *adj* • She wears a *prosthetic* leg.

[1]pros·ti·tute /ˈprɑːstəˌtuːt, *Brit* ˈprɒstəˌtjuːt/ *noun, pl* **-tutes** [*count*] : a person who has sex with someone in exchange for money

[2]prostitute *verb* **-tutes; -tut·ed; -tut·ing** [+ *obj*] : to use (something valuable, such as talent) in a way that is not appropriate or respectable and especially to earn money • a writer who *prostituted* his talents by writing commercials

prostitute yourself **1** : to work as a prostitute : to offer yourself for sex in exchange for money • She *prostituted herself* for drug money. **2** : to do something that is below your level of skill or ability in order to make money • a writer who *prostituted himself* by writing commercials

pros·ti·tu·tion /ˌprɑːstəˈtuːʃən, *Brit* ˌprɒstəˈtjuːʃən/ *noun*

1 [*noncount*] : the work of a prostitute : the act of having sex in exchange for money • She was arrested for *prostitution*.

2 [*singular*] : the use of a skill or ability in a way that is not appropriate or respectable • Writing commercials was a *prostitution* of his talents.

[1]pros·trate /ˈprɑːˌstreɪt/ *adj*

1 : lying with the front of your body turned toward the ground • The police found the body in a *prostrate* position. • a *prostrate* body • She was ***lying prostrate*** on the bed.

2 : so tired, upset, etc., that you are unable to do anything • They were *prostrate* from/with the heat. • He was *prostrate* with grief. [=he was completely overcome by grief]

[2]pros·trate /ˈprɑːˌstreɪt, *Brit* prəˈstreɪt/ *verb* **-trates; -trat·ed; -trat·ing** [+ *obj*] : to make (someone) weak or powerless — usually used as *(be) prostrated* • She *was prostrated* [=*overcome*] with/by grief.

prostrate yourself : to lie down with your face turned toward the ground • The worshippers *prostrated themselves* on the ground before the shrine.

— **pros·tra·tion** /prɑˈstreɪʃən/ *noun, pl* **-tions** [*count, noncount*] • The campers suffered from ***heat prostration***. [=physical exhaustion caused by heat]

pro·tag·o·nist /proʊˈtægənɪst/ *noun, pl* **-nists** [*count*]

1 : the main character in a novel, play, movie, etc.

2 : an important person who is involved in a competition, conflict, or cause • She was a leading *protagonist* in the civil rights movement.

pro·te·an /ˈproʊtijən/ *adj* [*more ~; most ~*] *literary + formal* : able to change into many different forms or able to do many different things • a *protean* organism • a *protean* actor

pro·tect /prəˈtɛkt/ *verb* **-tects; -tect·ed; -tect·ing**

1 : to keep (someone or something) from being harmed, lost, etc. [+ *obj*] He had no raincoat to *protect* himself from the rain. • She keeps her jewelry *protected* in a safe. • You have to *protect* your business against fraud. • New laws have been passed to *protect* your privacy. • The forest is *protected* by/under federal law. • The high taxes on imported goods are intended to *protect* domestic producers. [*no obj*] Sunscreen helps to ***protect against*** sunburn.

2 : to save (someone) from financial loss caused by fire, injury, damage, etc. — usually + *against* [+ *obj*] The insurance *protects* you *against* flooding. [*no obj*] The insurance does not *protect against* damage caused by earthquakes.

3 [+ *obj*] *sports* : to try to stop opponents from scoring at (your goal) • The goalie slipped and fell, but the defenseman was there to *protect* [=*defend*] the goal.

— **protected** *adj, always used before a noun* [*more ~; most ~*] • a *protected* area/species • *protected* industries/markets

pro·tec·tion /prəˈtɛkʃən/ *noun, pl* **-tions**

1 [*noncount*] : the state of being kept from harm, loss, etc. : the state of being protected • He fights for the *protection* of the environment. • Hard hats provide *protection* for the workers' heads. • The witness was placed ***under police protection***. — often + *against* • The ointment offers *protection against* infection. — often + *from* • The law ensures your *protection from* illegal searches.

2 : something that keeps a person or thing from being

P

harmed, lost, etc. : something that protects someone or something [*count*] legal *protections* — often + *against* ▪ *protections against* sexual harassment — often + *from* ▪ She used her briefcase as a *protection from* the rain. [*noncount*] — often + *against* ▪ She used her briefcase as *protection against* the rain. — often + *from* ▪ The rabbit's white fur serves as *protection from* predators during the winter.

3 [*noncount*] : a device (such as a condom) that is used during sex to prevent pregnancy or the spread of diseases ▪ Do you have *protection*?

4 [*noncount*] : insurance against financial loss caused by fire, injury, damage, etc. — often + *against* ▪ The policy offers complete *protection against* fire and theft.

5 [*noncount*] : a situation in which people (such as store owners) pay money to criminals so that the criminals will not hurt them or damage their property ▪ His store was burned down because he refused to pay for *protection*. — often used before another noun ▪ *protection* money ▪ a *protection* racket

pro·tec·tion·ism /prəˈtɛkʃəˌnɪzəm/ *noun* [*noncount*] : the practice of helping businesses and industries in your own country by making laws that limit and tax products imported from other countries

– **pro·tec·tion·ist** /prəˈtɛkʃənɪst/ *noun, pl* **-ists** [*count*] ▪ *Protectionists* are in favor of the new tariff. – **protectionist** *adj* ▪ *protectionist* policies

pro·tec·tive /prəˈtɛktɪv/ *adj*

1 *always used before a noun* : used to protect someone or something : giving or meant to give protection ▪ He put a *protective* cover over the car. ▪ *protective* clothing/gear ▪ The police are keeping her in **protective custody** [=in jail and away from others so that she will not be harmed]

2 [*more ~; most ~*] : having or showing a strong desire to protect someone or something from harm ▪ an overly *protective* mother — often + *of* ▪ She is very *protective of* her children.

– **pro·tec·tive·ly** *adv* ▪ She kept her hand *protectively* on her purse. – **pro·tec·tive·ness** *noun* [*noncount*]

pro·tec·tor /prəˈtɛktɚ/ *noun, pl* **-tors** [*count*] : a person or thing that protects someone or something ▪ She sees her older brother as her *protector*. ▪ a *protector* of free speech ▪ ear *protectors* — see also SURGE PROTECTOR

pro·tec·tor·ate /prəˈtɛktərət/ *noun, pl* **-ates** [*count*] : a small country that is controlled and protected by a larger one

pro·té·gé /ˈproʊtəˌʒeɪ/ *noun, pl* **-gés** [*count*] : a young person who is taught and helped by someone who has a lot of knowledge and experience ▪ He was a *protégé* of the great composer.

pro·té·gée /ˈproʊtəˌʒeɪ/ *noun, pl* **-gées** [*count*] : a woman who is a protégé

pro·tein /ˈproʊˌtiːn/ *noun, pl* **-teins** : a substance found in foods (such as meat, milk, eggs, and beans) that is an important part of the human diet [*noncount*] You need more *protein* in your diet. ▪ These foods are an excellent source of *protein*. [*count*] These foods have all of the essential *proteins*.

pro tem /ˌproʊˈtɛm/ *adv, formal* : for the present time but not permanently ▪ He is serving as the chairman *pro tem*. [=*temporarily*]

– **pro tem** *adj* ▪ the president *pro tem* [=the temporary president] of the U.S. Senate

pro tem·po·re /proʊˈtɛmpəri/ *adv, formal* : PRO TEM

– **pro tempore** *adj*

¹pro·test /prəˈtɛst/ *verb* **-tests; -test·ed; -test·ing**

1 a : to show or express strong disagreement with or disapproval of something [*no obj*] The victim's family *protested* at/against the judge's sentence. ▪ There is no use *protesting*. I will not change my mind. [+ *obj*] (*US*) ▪ The coach *protested* the referee's call. ▪ The decision was *protested* by dozens of people. **b** /ˈproʊˌtɛst/ : to show or express strong disapproval of something at a public event with other people [*no obj*] Students *protested* at the civil rights rally. ▪ They were *protesting* against the death penalty. [+ *obj*] (*US*) ▪ Peace activists *protested* the war.

2 [+ *obj*] : to say (something that other people do not agree with or believe) in a forceful way ▪ The defendant *protested* [=*declared*] his innocence in court. ▪ She *protested* that the law was unfair. ▪ "But I'm innocent!" he *protested*.

– **pro·test·er** *or* **pro·tes·tor** /prəˈtɛstɚ, ˈproʊˌtɛstɚ/ *noun, pl* **-ers** *or* **-tors** [*count*] ▪ student *protesters*

²pro·test /ˈproʊˌtɛst/ *noun, pl* **-tests**

1 : something said or done that shows disagreement with or disapproval of something [*count*] He heard *protests* from the crowd. ▪ She told him to go to bed despite his *protests* that he wasn't tired. [*noncount*] There were cries/howls of *protest* when the verdict was announced. ▪ The suspect surrendered his gun without *protest*. ▪ She was so upset by their decision that she resigned ***in protest*** ▪ He paid the fine ***under protest*** [=he paid the fine although he objected to it]

2 [*count*] : an event at which people gather together to show strong disapproval about something ▪ The students launched/held/staged a *protest* against the tuition increase. ▪ an antiwar *protest* ▪ a *protest* march/demonstration/rally

Prot·es·tant /ˈprɑːtəstənt/ *noun, pl* **-tants** [*count*] : a member of one of the Christian churches that separated from the Roman Catholic Church in the 16th century

– **Protestant** *adj* ▪ a *Protestant* minister – **Prot·es·tant·ism** /ˈprɑːtəstənˌtɪzəm/ *noun* [*noncount*]

pro·tes·ta·tion /ˌprɑːtəˈsteɪʃən/ *noun, pl* **-tions** [*count*] *formal* : a strong statement that something is true when other people do not believe it is true ▪ Despite his *protestations* to the contrary, he appears to be guilty. — often + *of* ▪ The police ignored his *protestations of* innocence.

pro·to·col /ˈproʊtəˌkɑːl/ *noun, pl* **-cols**

1 : a system of rules that explain the correct conduct and procedures to be followed in formal situations [*noncount*] The soldier's actions constitute a breach of military *protocol*. [*count*] They did not follow the proper diplomatic *protocols*. ▪ What is the proper *protocol* for declining a job offer?

2 [*count*] : a plan for a scientific experiment or for medical treatment ▪ an experimental *protocol* ▪ a simplified treatment *protocol*

3 [*count*] *formal* : a document that describes the details of a treaty or formal agreement between countries ▪ the Geneva *Protocol* of 1925

4 [*count*] *computers* : a set of rules used in programming computers so that they can communicate with each other ▪ an Internet *protocol*

pro·ton /ˈproʊˌtɑːn/ *noun, pl* **-tons** [*count*] *physics* : a very small particle of matter that is part of the nucleus of an atom and that has a positive electrical charge

pro·to·plasm /ˈproʊtəˌplæzəm/ *noun* [*noncount*] *biology* : the usually colorless substance that is the living part of animal and plant cells

pro·to·type /ˈproʊtəˌtaɪp/ *noun, pl* **-types** [*count*]

1 : an original or first model of something from which other forms are copied or developed ▪ They tested the *prototype* of the car. ▪ He is developing a *prototype* for his invention.

2 a : someone or something that has the typical qualities of a particular group, kind, etc. ▪ He is the *prototype* of a conservative businessman. **b** : a first or early example that is used as a model for what comes later ▪ The Sherlock Holmes stories are the *prototypes* of modern detective stories.

pro·to·typ·i·cal /ˌproʊtəˈtɪpɪkəl/ *adj* : having the typical qualities of a particular group or kind of person or thing : very typical ▪ a *prototypical* gangster ▪ *prototypical* horror movies

pro·to·zo·an /ˌproʊtəˈzowən/ *noun, pl* **-ans** [*count*] : a tiny organism whose body is a single cell ▪ Amoebas are *protozoans*.

pro·to·zo·on /ˌproʊtəˈzoʊˌɑːn/ *noun, pl* **-zoa** /-ˈzowə/ [*count*] : PROTOZOAN

pro·tract·ed /proʊˈtræktəd/ *adj* [*more ~; most ~*] : lasting a long time : continuing longer than necessary or expected ▪ They reached an agreement after *protracted* [=*lengthy*] negotiations. ▪ a *protracted* battle/conflict/war

pro·trac·tor /proʊˈtræktɚ/ *noun, pl* **-tors** [*count*] : a device that has the form of a half circle and that is used for drawing and measuring angles

pro·trude /proʊˈtruːd/ *verb* **-trudes; -trud·ed; -trud·ing** [*no obj*] : to stick out ▪ His lower jaw *protrudes* slightly. ▪ A handkerchief *protruded* from his shirt pocket.

– **protruding** *adj* ▪ He has a *protruding* jaw.

pro·tru·sion /proʊˈtruːʒən/ *noun, pl* **-sions**

1 [*count*] : a part that sticks out ▪ bony *protrusions* on the outside of the elbow ▪ a roof with many *protrusions*

2 [*count, noncount*] : the act of sticking out or the condition of something that sticks out ▪ The pain was caused by a/the *protrusion* of a disc in his lower back.

pro·tu·ber·ance /proʊˈtuːbərəns, *Brit* prəʊˈtjuːbərəns/ *noun, pl* **-anc·es** [*count*] : a usually rounded part that sticks out from a surface ▪ There was a small *protuberance* [=*bulge*] on the skull.

pro·tu·ber·ant /proʊˈtuːbərənt, *Brit* prəʊˈtjuːbərənt/ *adj* [*more ~; most ~*] **:** sticking out from a surface usually with a curved or rounded shape ▪ slightly *protuberant* [=*bulging*] eyes/lips

proud /ˈpraʊd/ *adj* **proud·er; -est** [*or more ~; most ~*]
1 a : very happy and pleased because of something you have done, something you own, someone you know or are related to, etc. **:** feeling pride ▪ They are the *proud* parents of a hero. ▪ I was *proud* that I never gave in. ▪ She's the *proud* owner of a new car. — often + *of* ▪ I am *proud of* what we have accomplished. ▪ She's very *proud of* her daughter. ▪ He has a record to be *proud of.* — sometimes followed by *to + verb* ▪ I'm *proud to know* him. **b :** causing someone to feel very happy and pleased **:** causing a feeling of pride ▪ It was one of the *proudest* moments of my life. [=when I felt most proud] ▪ Her *proudest* accomplishment was to finish school.
2 *disapproving* **:** having or showing the attitude of people who think that they are better or more important than others **:** having or showing too much pride ▪ He has a *proud* manner. ▪ a *proud* and opinionated person
3 : not wanting to lose the respect of other people **:** not willing to accept help from other people ▪ She's too *proud* to accept their charity.
4 : excellent or impressive ▪ They have a *proud* record of public service. ▪ a *proud* [=large and impressive] castle
5 *literary, of an animal* **:** having a lot of strength and spirit ▪ a *proud* horse/stallion
do (someone) proud* :** to give someone a reason to feel proud ▪ It *did me proud* [=made me feel proud] to watch her graduate from college. ▪ She *did her family proud* by standing up for her beliefs. ▪ His performance in the game *did us* (all) *proud.* ▪ She ***did herself proud. [=she did well; she did something that she can be proud of]
– proud·ly *adv* ▪ The new citizen was standing *proudly* and happily with his family. ▪ He spoke *proudly* of his son's achievements. ▪ She *proudly* showed off her awards. ▪ The building stands *proudly* on a hillside.

prove /ˈpruːv/ *verb* **proves; proved; proved** *or chiefly US* **prov·en** /ˈpruːvən/; **prov·ing**
1 [+ *obj*] **:** to show the existence, truth, or correctness of (something) by using evidence, logic, etc. ▪ The charges against him were never *proved* in court. ▪ The government failed to *prove* its case. ▪ We have evidence that will *prove* his guilt. = We have evidence that will *prove* that he is guilty. ▪ It could not be *proven* that the suspect stole the money. ▪ A person who is charged with a crime is considered innocent until *proved/proven* guilty. ▪ mathematicians trying to *prove* a theorem ▪ He climbed the mountain just to *prove* [=*show*] (that) he could. ▪ ***What are you trying to prove*** by behaving so recklessly? [=why are you behaving so recklessly?] ▪ I've accomplished everything I wanted to; ***I've got nothing left to prove.*** [=I do not have to do anything more to show that I am skillful, successful, etc.] ▪ He's willing to do almost anything to ***prove a point.*** [=to show that he is right about something] ▪ To ***prove her point,*** she got out the old research. — opposite DISPROVE
2 [+ *obj*] **:** to show that (someone or something) has a particular quality, ability, etc. ▪ We have evidence that will *prove* him (to be) guilty. [=that will prove that he is guilty] ▪ The tests *proved* the vaccine to be effective. ▪ Her second album was a hit that *proved* her critics wrong.
3 [*linking verb*] **:** to turn out to be — used to say that something or someone is eventually found to have a particular quality, ability, etc. ▪ The new drug may *prove* (to be) beneficial/effective. ▪ The vaccine has *proven* (to be) effective after years of tests. ▪ It may *prove* difficult/impossible to do this. ▪ The report of the war's end *proved* (to be) false. ▪ The book should *prove* helpful to many people. ▪ The new system could *prove* to be as bad as the old one was.
***prove yourself* :** to show that you are able to do something or to succeed ▪ She was eager to *prove herself* in her new job. ▪ She has *proven herself* (to be) capable of excellent work. [=she has shown that she is capable of excellent work]
– prov·able /ˈpruːvəbəl/ *adj* ▪ The case will not be easily *provable.*

prov·e·nance /ˈprɑːvənəns/ *noun, pl* **-nanc·es** *formal* **:** the origin or source of something [*count*] Has anyone traced the *provenances* of these paintings? ▪ The saying has its *provenance* in [=comes from] Greek myth. [*noncount*] The artifact is of unknown *provenance.*

prov·en·der /ˈprɑːvəndɚ/ *noun* [*noncount*] *old-fashioned* **:** FOOD ▪ a supply of *provender*

prov·erb /ˈprɑːˌvɚb/ *noun, pl* **-erbs** [*count*] **:** a brief popular saying (such as "Too many cooks spoil the broth") that gives advice about how people should live or that expresses a belief that is generally thought to be true

pro·ver·bi·al /prəˈvɚbijəl/ *adj*
1 : of, relating to, or resembling a proverb ▪ *proverbial* wisdom ▪ a *proverbial* expression/phrase
2 : commonly spoken of **:** widely known ▪ the *proverbial* beginner's luck ▪ His generosity is *proverbial.*
– pro·ver·bi·al·ly *adv*

pro·vide /prəˈvaɪd/ *verb* **-vides; -vid·ed; -vid·ing**
1 [+ *obj*] **a :** to make (something) available **:** to supply (something that is wanted or needed) ▪ The Web site *provides* information about local activities. ▪ The curtains on the windows *provide* privacy. ▪ The school *provided* new uniforms for the band. ▪ The goal is to *provide* health care to/for as many people as possible. ▪ The store *provides* excellent service (to its customers). ▪ Coffee and doughnuts will be *provided* at the meeting. **b :** to give something wanted or needed to (someone or something) **:** to supply (someone or something) *with* something ▪ The Web site *provides* users *with* information about local activities. ▪ The school *provided* the band *with* new uniforms. ▪ The store *provides* its customers *with* excellent service. ▪ Workers were *provided with* gloves for protection.
2 [+ *obj*] *formal* **:** to say that something will or should happen **:** to make it certain or possible that something will happen or be done ▪ The contract *provides* that certain deadlines will be met. ▪ The law *provides* that minors will be treated differently from adults.
3 [*no obj*] **:** to supply what is needed for someone to live ▪ All we can do is work hard and trust that the Lord will *provide.*
provide against [*phrasal verb*] ***provide against (something)*** **:** to do what is needed to prepare for (something bad that might happen) ▪ We should store extra supplies now to *provide against* a possible scarcity in the coming months.
provide for [*phrasal verb*] **1** ***provide for (something)*** **:** to cause (something) to be available or to happen in the future ▪ The contract *provides for* 10 paid holidays. ▪ The grant *provides for* more research. ▪ The law *provides for* the appointment of a new official. **2** ***provide for (something or someone)*** **:** to supply what is needed for (something or someone) ▪ It's hard to make enough money to *provide for* such a large family. ▪ They agreed to *provide for* the child's education.

provided *conj* **:** IF — used to say that one thing must happen or be true in order for another thing to happen ▪ You can make the change if you want, *provided* (that) the change makes sense. ▪ You can still get health care, *provided* (that) you pay the cost yourself.

Prov·i·dence /ˈprɑːvədəns/ *noun* [*noncount*] **:** God or fate thought of as the guide and protector of all human beings ▪ He put his faith in divine *Providence.*

prov·i·dent /ˈprɑːvədənt/ *adj* [*more ~; most ~*] *formal* **:** careful about planning for the future and saving money for the future ▪ *provident* people ▪ a more *provident* policy
– prov·i·dent·ly *adv*

prov·i·den·tial /ˌprɑːvəˈdɛnʃəl/ *adj* [*more ~; most ~*] *formal* **:** happening at a good time because of luck **:** LUCKY ▪ We had made a *providential* escape. ▪ It seemed *providential* that he should arrive at just that moment.
– prov·i·den·tial·ly *adv*

pro·vi·der /prəˈvaɪdɚ/ *noun, pl* **-ders** [*count*]
1 : a group or company that provides a specified service ▪ health-care *providers* ▪ an Internet *provider* = a *provider* of Internet service
2 : a person (such as a mother or father) who earns the money that is needed to support a family ▪ She works hard and is a good *provider.* ▪ He is the sole *provider* for his family.

providing *conj* **:** IF — used to say that one thing must happen or be true in order for another thing to happen ▪ We can have a picnic tomorrow, *providing* [=*as long as*] it doesn't rain. ▪ *Providing* we have the money, we'll travel to Europe.

prov·ince /ˈprɑːvəns/ *noun, pl* **-inces**
1 [*count*] **:** any one of the large parts that some countries are divided into ▪ the Canadian *provinces*
2 [*count*] **:** a subject or area of interest that a person knows about or is involved in — usually singular ▪ It's a legal question that is/falls outside my *province.* [=it does not relate to the area that I know about] ▪ That subject is the special *province* of this magazine. ▪ Study in that area had once been the exclusive/sole *province* of academics.

3 ***the provinces*** : the parts of a country that are away from large cities ▪ They left the city for life in *the provinces*.

[1]**pro•vin•cial** /prəˈvɪnʃəl/ *adj*

1 : of, relating to, or coming from a province ▪ a *provincial* official ▪ She speaks with a *provincial* accent.

2 [*more* ~; *most* ~] *disapproving* : not knowing or caring about people and events in other places : having narrow or limited concerns or interests ▪ an artist who has been criticized for being *provincial* and old-fashioned ▪ His *provincial* attitude was a source of irritation for her. ▪ She is too *provincial* to try foreign foods.

– pro•vin•cial•ism /prəˈvɪnʃəˌlɪzəm/ *noun, pl* **-isms** *disapproving* [*noncount*] He grew tired of the narrow *provincialism* of his hometown. [*count*] the prejudices and *provincialisms* of his hometown

[2]**provincial** *noun, pl* **-cials** [*count*] : a person who lives in or comes from a place that is far away from large cities — often used in a disapproving way to suggest that such a person has narrow or limited concerns or interests ▪ an artist who has been dismissed as a *provincial*

proving ground *noun, pl* ~ **grounds** [*count*]

1 : a place where things or people are tested or tried out for the first time — often + *for* ▪ The local racetrack became a *proving ground for* new jockeys.

2 : a place where scientific testing is done

[1]**pro•vi•sion** /prəˈvɪʒən/ *noun, pl* **-sions**

1 [*noncount*] : the act or process of supplying or providing something ▪ They saw to the *provision* of transportation for the trip. [=they made sure that transportation was provided]

2 : something that is done in advance to prepare for something else [*count*] *Provisions* should be made for regular inspections. ▪ He made *provisions* to donate part of his fortune to charity after he died. [*noncount*] You should ***make provision*** for emergencies.

3 ***provisions*** [*plural*] : a supply of food and other things that are needed ▪ I carried my *provisions* in one large backpack. ▪ We brought enough *provisions* to last the entire trip.

4 [*count*] : a condition that is included as part of an agreement or law ▪ You can enroll in the book club with the *provision* that you buy more books. [=you can enroll if you agree to buy more books] ▪ Under the *provisions* of the contract, the work must be completed in two months.

[2]**provision** *verb* **-sions; -sioned; -sion•ing** [+ *obj*] : to supply (someone or something) with provisions and especially with food ▪ They stopped to *provision* the ship.

pro•vi•sion•al /prəˈvɪʒənl̩/ *adj* [*more* ~; *most* ~] : existing or accepted for the present time but likely to be changed : TEMPORARY ▪ a *provisional* government ▪ *provisional* arrangements ▪ The government has given *provisional* approval for the use of the new drug.

– pro•vi•sion•al•ly *adv* ▪ The government has *provisionally* approved the use of the new drug.

provisional licence *noun, pl* ~ **-cences** [*count*] *Brit* : LEARNER'S PERMIT

pro•vi•so /prəˈvaɪzoʊ/ *noun, pl* **-sos** [*count*] : a condition that must be accepted in order for someone to agree to do something ▪ He accepted the job with one *proviso*: he would work alone.

prov•o•ca•tion /ˌprɑːvəˈkeɪʃən/ *noun, pl* **-tions** : an action or occurrence that causes someone to become angry or to begin to do something [*count*] He can turn violent at the least/slightest/smallest *provocation*. ▪ Her calmness in the face of repeated *provocations* impressed her friends. [*noncount*] With hardly any *provocation*, the crowd began to chant.

pro•voc•a•tive /prəˈvɑːkətɪv/ *adj* [*more* ~; *most* ~]

1 : causing discussion, thought, argument, etc. ▪ a thoughtful and *provocative* book/essay/idea ▪ *provocative* comments ▪ It was one of his more *provocative* suggestions. ▪ an intentionally *provocative* style

2 : causing sexual feelings or excitement : SEXY ▪ She was wearing a very *provocative* outfit.

– pro•voc•a•tive•ly *adv* ▪ a *provocatively* thoughtful work ▪ She was dressed *provocatively*.

pro•voke /prəˈvoʊk/ *verb* **-vokes; -voked; -vok•ing** [+ *obj*]

1 : to cause the occurrence of (a feeling or action) : to make (something) happen ▪ His remarks *provoked* both tears and laughter. ▪ His insults were intended to *provoke* [=*start*] a fight. ▪ The results of the election have *provoked* [=*generated*] a lot of discussion. ▪ ideas that are likely to *provoke* [=*stimulate*] change

2 : to cause (a person or animal) to become angry, violent, etc. ▪ He just says those things because he's trying to *provoke* you. ▪ The animal will not attack unless it is *provoked*. — sometimes + *into* ▪ He was *provoked into* a violent reaction by their taunts.

pro•vost /ˈproʊˌvoʊst, *Brit* ˈprɒvəst/ *noun, pl* **-vosts** [*count*]

1 *US* : an official of high rank at a university

2 *Brit* : the head of a college at a university

3 : the head of a Scottish town

prow /ˈpraʊ/ *noun, pl* **prows** [*count*] : the front of a ship

prow•ess /ˈprawəs/ *noun* [*noncount*] : great ability or skill ▪ He is known for his *prowess* on the football field. ▪ athletic/physical/technical *prowess* ▪ their naval and military *prowess*

[1]**prowl** /ˈprawəl/ *verb* **prowls; prowled; prowl•ing**

1 *of an animal* : to move quietly through an area while hunting [*no obj*] a tiger *prowling* in the jungle ▪ wolves *prowling* in packs [+ *obj*] He moved like a tiger *prowling* the jungle.

2 : to move through a place or area especially while searching for something often in a quiet or secret way [+ *obj*] The police were *prowling* the streets in their patrol cars. ▪ He liked to *prowl* the streets late at night. ▪ I *prowled* the store looking for sales. [*no obj*] I *prowled* through the store looking for sales.

[2]**prowl** *noun* [*singular*] : an act of moving through a place while searching for something : an act of prowling ▪ a *prowl* through the bookshop

on the prowl : searching for something often in a quiet or secret way ▪ My cat was *on the prowl*. [=my cat was prowling] ▪ reporters *on the prowl* for a good story

prowl•er /ˈprawlɚ/ *noun, pl* **-ers** [*count*]

1 : a person who moves through an area in a quiet way in order to commit a crime ▪ There were reports of a *prowler* in the neighborhood.

2 : an animal that moves through an area while hunting or searching for food ▪ Raccoons are night *prowlers*.

prox•i•mate /ˈprɑːksəmət/ *adj, always used before a noun, formal* : coming or happening immediately before or after something in a way that shows a very close and direct relationship ▪ the *proximate* cause of the fire ▪ the *proximate* result

prox•im•i•ty /prɑkˈsɪməti/ *noun* [*noncount*] : the state of being near ▪ People are attracted to the area by the *proximity* [=*nearness*] of several beaches. — often + *to* ▪ I like the *proximity* of the bus stop *to* my home. ▪ The bus stop is located ***in close proximity to*** [=*near to*] my home. ▪ family members who live *in close proximity* (*to* each other)

proxy /ˈprɑːksi/ *noun, pl* **prox•ies**

1 [*count*] : a person who is given the power or authority to do something (such as to vote) for someone else ▪ Since I wouldn't be available to vote, I nominated him to act as my *proxy*. — often + *for* ▪ He served as a *proxy for* his uncle.

2 [*noncount*] : power or authority that is given to allow a person to act for someone else — usually used in the phrase ***by proxy*** ▪ I voted *by proxy*. [=by giving another person the authority to vote for me]

– proxy *adj, always used before a noun* ▪ a *proxy* vote

prude /ˈpruːd/ *noun, pl* **prudes** [*count*] *disapproving* : a person who is easily shocked or offended by things that do not shock or offend other people ▪ He is too much of a *prude* to enjoy movies containing sex and violence.

– prud•ish /ˈpruːdɪʃ/ *adj* [*more* ~; *most* ~] ▪ She's very *prudish* about sex. **– prud•ish•ly** *adv* **– prud•ish•ness** *noun* [*noncount*]

pru•dence /ˈpruːdəns/ *noun* [*noncount*] : careful good judgment that allows someone to avoid danger or risks ▪ act with ordinary/reasonable *prudence* ▪ He always exercises *prudence* with his finances.

pru•dent /ˈpruːdn̩t/ *adj* [*more* ~; *most* ~] : having or showing careful good judgment ▪ He always listened to her *prudent* advice. ▪ You made a *prudent* choice/decision. ▪ She's a *prudent* investor. — opposite IMPRUDENT

– pru•dent•ly *adv* ▪ The money was *prudently* invested.

pru•den•tial /pruˈdɛnʃəl/ *adj* [*more* ~; *most* ~] *formal* + *old-fashioned* : having or showing careful good judgment : PRUDENT ▪ a *prudential* approach to managing money

– pru•den•tial•ly *adv*

prud•ery /ˈpruːdəri/ *noun* [*noncount*] *disapproving* : the behavior or thinking of people who are too easily shocked or offended : prudish behavior or attitudes ▪ sexual *prudery*

[1]**prune** /ˈpruːn/ *noun, pl* **prunes** [*count*] : a dried plum that is often cooked before it is eaten ▪ stewed *prunes* ▪ *prune* juice

[2]**prune** *verb* **prunes; pruned; prun•ing** [+ *obj*]

1 : to cut off some of the branches of (a tree or bush) so that it will grow better or look better ▪ She carefully *pruned* the hedge. ▪ Those trees need to be *pruned* every year. — often + *back* ▪ You should *prune back* the unwanted branches.
2 : to reduce (something) by removing parts that are not necessary or wanted ▪ The students were asked to *prune* their essays. ▪ The budget needs to be *pruned*.
– **pruning** *noun* [*noncount*] ▪ The bushes need *pruning*.

prun·er *noun, pl* **-ers**
1 [*count*] : a person who prunes something ▪ She's a skillful *pruner*.
2 ***pruners*** [*plural*] *US* : PRUNING SHEARS

pruning shears *noun* [*plural*] *US* : a garden tool that is used for cutting off the branches of trees and bushes ▪ a pair of *pruning shears* — called also (*US*) *pruners*, (*Brit*) *secateurs*; see picture at GARDENING

pru·ri·ent /ˈprɚrijənt/ *adj* [*more* ~; *most* ~] *formal* + *usually disapproving* : having or showing too much interest in sex ▪ He took a *prurient* interest in her personal life. ▪ a book that appealed to the *prurient* curiosity of its readers
– **pru·ri·ence** /ˈprɚrijəns/ *noun* [*noncount*] – **pru·ri·ent·ly** *adv*

prus·sic acid /ˈprʌsɪk-/ *noun* [*noncount*] : a very poisonous acid

[1]**pry** /ˈpraɪ/ *verb* **pries; pried; pry·ing** [*no obj*] : to try to find out about other people's private lives ▪ I was curious, but I didn't want to *pry*. — usually + *into* ▪ He claims that the government is improperly *prying into* his affairs. ▪ They were trying to *pry into* my past. — compare [2]PRY

[2]**pry** *verb, always followed by an adverb or preposition* **pries; pried; prying** [+ *obj*] *US* : to raise, move, or open (something) with a tool ▪ *pry* off a tight lid ▪ *pry* up a floorboard ▪ They *pried* open the door with a crowbar. — often used figuratively ▪ I couldn't *pry* the secret out of her. [=I couldn't get her to reveal the secret] — compare [1]PRY

prying *adj* [*more* ~; *most* ~] : trying to find out about other people's private lives ▪ She tried to escape the *prying* eyes of her neighbors. ▪ *prying* questions

PS *abbr* **1** postscript — used to introduce an added comment that comes after your name at the end of a letter **2** *US* public school

psalm /ˈsɑːm/ *noun, pl* **psalms** [*count*] : a song or poem used in worship and especially one from the Bible

psalm·ist /ˈsɑːmɪst/ *noun, pl* **-ists** [*count*] : a writer of psalms

psal·ter /ˈsɑːltɚ/ *noun, pl* **-ters** [*count*] : a book that contains a collection of psalms for worship

pseud /ˈsuːd/ *noun, pl* **pseuds** [*count*] *Brit, informal* + *disapproving* : a person who pretends to have a lot of knowledge : PSEUDO-INTELLECTUAL ▪ a pompous *pseud*

pseud- *or* **pseudo-** *combining form* : not real : fake ▪ *pseudo*nym ▪ *pseudo*-intellectual

pseu·do /ˈsuːdoʊ/ *adj, always used before a noun, chiefly US* : not real or genuine : FAKE ▪ a *pseudo* event

pseu·do–in·tel·lec·tu·al /ˌsuːdoʊˌɪntəˈlɛkʧəwəl/ *noun, pl* **-als** [*count*] *disapproving* : a person who wants to be thought of as having a lot of intelligence and knowledge but who is not really intelligent or knowledgeable ▪ She thinks her classmates are just a bunch of *pseudo-intellectuals*.
– **psuedo–intellectual** *adj*

pseu·do·nym /ˈsuːdəˌnɪm/ *noun, pl* **-nyms** [*count*] : a name that someone (such as a writer) uses instead of his or her real name ▪ Mark Twain is the *pseudonym* of the American writer Samuel L. Clemens. ▪ She preferred to write ***under a pseudonym***. [=using a false name instead of her real name] — compare [2]ALIAS
– **pseu·don·y·mous** /suˈdɑːnəməs/ *adj* ▪ a *pseudonymous* author

psi *abbr* pounds per square inch

pso·ri·a·sis /səˈrajəsəs/ *noun* [*noncount*] *medical* : a skin disease that causes areas of your skin to become red and rough and to fall off

psst /ˈpst/ *interj* — used to get someone's attention ▪ *Psst!* I'm over here.

[1]**psych** /ˈsaɪk/ *verb* **psychs; psyched; psych·ing** [+ *obj*] *informal* : to make (yourself or another person) mentally ready to perform or compete ▪ He was trying to *psych* himself before the race. — usually + *up* ▪ He was trying to *psych* himself *up* before the race. — see also PSYCHED
psych out [*phrasal verb*] ***psych (someone) out*** *or* ***psych out (someone)*** *informal* : to make (someone) feel nervous or unable to perform well : to say or do something to make (someone) feel uncomfortable or less confident ▪ She has a way of *psyching out* the competition. ▪ He was trying to *psych* me *out* by reminding me of the last time he beat me.

[2]**psych** *abbr* psychology

psy·che /ˈsaɪki/ *noun, pl* **psy·ches** [*count*] *formal* : the soul, mind, or personality of a person or group ▪ some hidden corner within your *psyche* ▪ the female/male/human *psyche* ▪ the nation's *psyche*

psyched /ˈsaɪkt/ *adj* [*more* ~; *most* ~] *informal* : very eager, ready, or excited about something ▪ Are you *psyched* for this party? ▪ I'm so *psyched* about my vacation!

psy·che·de·lia /ˌsaɪkəˈdiːljə/ *noun* [*noncount*] : the art, music, style of living, etc., that is associated with psychedelic drugs and especially with the time in the 1960s when many people were using psychedelic drugs ▪ the tie-dyed fashions of *psychedelia* ▪ music ranging from jazz to disco to '60s *psychedelia*

[1]**psy·che·del·ic** /ˌsaɪkəˈdɛlɪk/ *adj*
1 a — used to describe a drug (such as LSD) that affects your thinking and causes you to see things that are not real ▪ *psychedelic* drugs **b** : caused by the use of psychedelic drugs ▪ a *psychedelic* experience ▪ *psychedelic* visions
2 : suggesting the effects of psychedelic drugs by having bright colors, strange sounds, etc. ▪ hippies wearing *psychedelic* clothing ▪ *psychedelic* color schemes ▪ *psychedelic* dance music ▪ strange *psychedelic* images
– **psy·che·del·i·cal·ly** /ˌsaɪkəˈdɛlɪkli/ *adv*

[2]**psychedelic** *noun, pl* **-ics** [*count*] : a psychedelic drug (such as LSD)

psy·chi·a·trist /saɪˈkajətrɪst/ *noun, pl* **-trists** [*count*] : a doctor who treats mental or emotional disorders : a doctor of psychiatry

psy·chi·a·try /saɪˈkajətri/ *noun* [*noncount*] : a branch of medicine that deals with mental or emotional disorders
– **psy·chi·at·ric** /ˌsaɪkiˈætrɪk/ *adj* ▪ a *psychiatric* clinic/hospital ▪ *psychiatric* ailments

[1]**psy·chic** /ˈsaɪkɪk/ *adj*
1 a *also* **psy·chi·cal** /ˈsaɪkɪkəl/ — used to describe strange mental powers and abilities (such as the ability to predict the future, to know what other people are thinking, or to receive messages from dead people) that cannot be explained by natural laws ▪ people with *psychic* abilities/powers ▪ reports of *psychic* phenomena **b** *of a person* : having strange and unnatural mental abilites : having psychic powers ▪ She claims to be *psychic*. ▪ (*humorous*) "How did you know that would happen?" "I'm *psychic*."
2 *also* **psychical** : of or relating to the mind ▪ suffered *psychic* disturbances ▪ *psychic* disorders
– **psy·chi·cal·ly** /ˈsaɪkɪkli/ *adv*

[2]**psychic** *noun, pl* **-chics** [*count*] : a person who has strange mental powers and abilities (such as the ability to predict the future, to know what other people are thinking, or to receive messages from dead people) : a person who has psychic powers ▪ She claims to be a *psychic*.

psy·cho /ˈsaɪkoʊ/ *noun, pl* **-chos** [*count*] *informal* : a person who is mentally ill and often dangerous or violent : PSYCHOPATH ▪ He plays a drug-dealing *psycho* in the movie.
– **psycho** *adj* ▪ *psycho* creeps/killers ▪ She can turn *psycho* at any minute.

psy·cho·anal·y·sis /ˌsaɪkowəˈnæləsəs/ *noun* [*noncount*] : a method of explaining and treating mental and emotional problems by having the patient talk about dreams, feelings, memories, etc. ▪ The doctor recommended *psychoanalysis*.
– **psy·cho·an·a·lyt·ic** /ˌsaɪkoʊˌænəˈlɪtɪk/ *also* **psy·cho·an·a·lyt·i·cal** /ˌsaɪkoʊˌænəˈlɪtɪkəl/ *adj* ▪ *psychoanalytic* explanations of behavior ▪ She studied *psychoanalytic* theory. – **psy·cho·an·a·lyt·i·cal·ly** /ˌsaɪkoʊˌænəˈlɪtɪkli/ *adv*

psy·cho·an·a·lyst /ˌsaɪkoʊˈænəlɪst/ *noun, pl* **-lysts** [*count*] : a doctor who helps people with mental and emotional problems by talking to them about their dreams, memories, etc. : a doctor who practices psychoanalysis

psy·cho·an·a·lyze *also Brit* **psy·cho·an·a·lyse** /ˌsaɪkoʊˈænəˌlaɪz/ *verb* **-lyz·es; -lyzed; -lyz·ing** [+ *obj*] : to treat the mental and emotional problems of (a patient) by having the patient talk about dreams, feelings, memories, etc. : to treat (someone) by means of psychoanalysis

psy·cho·bab·ble /ˈsaɪkoʊˌbæbəl/ *noun* [*noncount*] *informal* + *disapproving* : language that is used by people who talk about mental and emotional problems and that is seen as silly or meaningless : psychological jargon ▪ a popular book filled with the usual *psychobabble*

psy·cho·log·i·cal /ˌsaɪkəˈlɑːʤɪkəl/ *also US* **psy·cho·log·ic** /ˌsaɪkəˈlɑːʤɪk/ *adj*
1 : of or relating to the mind **:** MENTAL • *psychological* anguish • *psychological* disorders • a *psychological* rather than a physical condition • emotional and *psychological* states
2 : of or relating to the study of the mind **:** of or relating to psychology • *psychological* analysis/research/tests • a *psychological* clinic
psychological warfare **:** things that are done to make someone (such as an enemy or opponent) become less confident or to feel hopeless, afraid, etc. • The army used radio broadcasts into enemy territory as a form of *psychological warfare*.
– psy·cho·log·i·cal·ly /ˌsaɪkəˈlɑːʤɪkli/ *adv* • a *psychologically* healthy person • The abuse left him *psychologically* scarred.

psy·chol·o·gist /saɪˈkɑːləʤɪst/ *noun, pl* **-gists** [*count*] **:** a scientist who specializes in the study and treatment of the mind and behavior **:** a specialist in psychology

psy·chol·o·gy /saɪˈkɑːləʤi/ *noun, pl* **-gies**
1 [*noncount*] **:** the science or study of the mind and behavior • She studied *psychology* in college.
2 : the way a person or group thinks [*noncount*] the *psychology* of an athlete • mob *psychology* • the *psychology* of crowd behavior [*count*] We need to understand the *psychologies* of the two people involved in the incident.
– see also REVERSE PSYCHOLOGY

psy·cho·path /ˈsaɪkəˌpæθ/ *noun, pl* **-paths** [*count*] **:** a person who is mentally ill, who does not care about other people, and who is usually dangerous or violent • a murderous *psychopath*
– psy·cho·path·ic /ˌsaɪkəˈpæθɪk/ *adj* • violent and *psychopathic* behavior • a *psychopathic* murderer

psy·cho·sis /saɪˈkousəs/ *noun, pl* **-cho·ses** /-ˈkouˌsiːz/ [*count, noncount*] **:** a very serious mental illness that makes you behave strangely or believe things that are not true • The patient suffers from some kind of *psychosis*.

psy·cho·so·ma·tic /ˌsaɪkousəˈmætɪk/ *adj* **:** caused by mental or emotional problems rather than by physical illness • The doctor told her that her stomach problems were *psychosomatic*. • *psychosomatic* disorders/illness/symptoms
– psy·cho·so·mat·i·cal·ly /ˌsaɪkousəˈmætɪkli/ *adv*

psy·cho·ther·a·py /ˌsaɪkouˈθerəpi/ *noun, pl* **-pies** [*count, noncount*] **:** treatment of mental or emotional illness by talking about problems rather than by using medicine or drugs • the benefits of *psychotherapy*
– psy·cho·ther·a·pist /ˌsaɪkouˈθerəpɪst/ *noun, pl* **-pists** [*count*] • a trained *psychotherapist*

[1]**psy·chot·ic** /saɪˈkɑːtɪk/ *adj* **:** having or relating to a very serious mental illness that makes you act strangely or believe things that are not true **:** relating to or suffering from psychosis • *psychotic* behavior/symptoms • *psychotic* patients • He was diagnosed as *psychotic*.
– psy·chot·i·cal·ly /saɪˈkɑːtɪkli/ *adv*

[2]**psychotic** *noun, pl* **-ics** [*count*] **:** a person who suffers from a very serious mental illness **:** a psychotic person • His father is a *psychotic*.

psy·cho·tro·pic /ˌsaɪkəˈtroupɪk/ *adj, technical* **:** having an effect on how the mind works • *psychotropic* drugs

pt *or* **Pt** *abbr* **1** part • Add 1 *pt* gin. • Shakespeare's Henry IV, *Pt* 1 **2** pint • 2 qts, 1 *pt* **3** ***pt.*** *or* ***Pt.*** point • Score 1 *pt.* per question for a maximum score of 20 *pts*. • Our address is 47 Sunfish *Pt*. **4** ***Pt.*** port • *Pt.* Royale

PT *abbr* **1** part-time • typist position, *PT* **2** *US* physical therapist; physical therapy • My *PT* told me not to overdo it. • a course of *PT* after the injury **3** *Brit* physical training

PTA *abbr* Parent-Teacher Association • He joined the *PTA*. • a *PTA* meeting

Pte *abbr, Brit* private • *Pte* Daniel Kyle

ptero·dac·tyl /ˌterəˈdæktl/ *noun, pl* **-tyls** [*count*] **:** a large flying animal that lived long ago when dinosaurs were alive

PTO *abbr* **1** *US* Parent-Teacher Organization • The *PTO* is raising money for a new playground. • a *PTO* meeting **2** *chiefly Brit* please turn over ✧ *PTO* is written on the bottom of a page to tell the reader to continue reading on the back of that page.

PTSD *abbr* post-traumatic stress disorder

Pty *abbr, Brit* proprietary ✧ *Pty* is used after the names of companies in Australia, New Zealand, and South Africa. • Laura Russ Yachts, *Pty* Ltd

pub /ˈpʌb/ *noun, pl* **pubs** [*count*] **:** a building or room especially in Britain or Ireland where alcoholic drinks and often food are served • We ate at a lot of good *pubs* on our trip to England last summer. • an Irish *pub*

pub. *abbr* published; publisher; publishing • a rare first ed., *pub*. 1841 • the Kavanagh *Pub*. Co.

pub crawl *noun, pl* **~ crawls** [*count*] *informal* **:** a visit to several or many pubs or bars in one night • She invited me to join them on a *pub crawl*.

pu·ber·ty /ˈpjuːbəti/ *noun* [*noncount*] **:** the period of life when a person's sexual organs mature and he or she becomes able to have children • He reached/entered *puberty* later than most of his classmates.

pu·bes·cent /pjuˈbɛsn̩t/ *adj* **:** beginning to physically develop into an adult **:** having reached puberty • *pubescent* boys/girls

pu·bic /ˈpjuːbɪk/ *adj, always used before a noun* **:** of, relating to, or near the sexual organs • *pubic* hair • the *pubic* bone

[1]**pub·lic** /ˈpʌblɪk/ *adj*
1 *always used before a noun* **:** of, relating to, or affecting all or most of the people of a country, state, etc. • *public* opinion • *Public* outrage over the scandal eventually forced him to resign. • The ads are intended to increase *public* awareness of the risks of smoking. • a study of ***public policy*** [=government policies that affect the whole population] • He is the director of ***public affairs***. [=his work involves events, activities, etc., that a company does for the public]
2 *always used before a noun* **a :** of, relating to, paid for by, or working for a government • She was elected to a *public* office. • *public* spending/funding • *public* education/housing • a *public* corporation • a *public* prosecutor/officer • He was in Congress for many years but he recently retired from *public* life. **b :** supported by money from the government and from private contributors rather than by commercials • *public* television/radio
3 a : able to be used by anyone **:** open or available to people in general rather than to just a few people • a *public* library/restroom/telephone/beach • *public* property • They decided on a nearby restaurant as a convenient *public* place to meet. • The government has allowed *public* access to the documents. • The city council is holding a *public* meeting. **b :** able to be seen or heard by many people • This will be her first *public* performance in five years. • a *public* apology • Her trial will be *public*.
4 : known to many people • As a celebrity, she is trying to keep her private life separate from her *public* life. • The scandal ruined his ***public image***. [=the scandal caused many people to change their opinion of him from good to bad] • a ***public figure*** [=a well-known person] • The results of the study have been ***made public***. [=have been announced, published, etc., so that they are generally known]
5 : offering shares or stock that can be traded on the open market • a *public* corporation/company — opposite PRIVATE; see also INITIAL PUBLIC OFFERING
go public **1 :** to make something known to many people **:** to make something generally known by announcing it, publishing it, etc. • He *went public* with his research. **2 :** to offer shares or stock that can be freely traded on the open market • The company plans to *go public*.
in the public eye see [1]EYE
public knowledge see KNOWLEDGE

[2]**public** *noun* [*singular*]
1 ***the public*** **:** the people of a country, state, etc. • *the* American *public* • The beach is open to *the public*. • (*US*) *The public* is angry with the President = (*Brit*) *The public* are angry with the President. • ***The general public*** is in favor of the law. • ***Members of the public*** called for the mayor's resignation.
2 : a group of people who have a shared interest, quality, etc. • He has once again won the approval of his *public* [=his supporters/fans] with his latest movie. • the reading *public* [=people who read a lot; people who enjoy reading]
in public **:** in a place where you can be seen by many people **:** in a public place • They were seen kissing *in public*. • The former actress is now rarely seen *in public*.

public access *noun* [*noncount*] *chiefly US* **:** a television channel on which any person can broadcast a program • The city council meeting will be broadcast on *public access*. — often used before another noun • *public access* television • a *public access* channel

public address system *noun, pl* **~ -tems** [*count*] **:** [2]PA 1

pub·li·can /ˈpʌblɪkən/ *noun, pl* **-cans** [*count*] *Brit, formal* **:** someone who owns or manages a pub

public assistance *noun [noncount] US* **: money that the government gives to people who are poor, old, or disabled** ▪ Our family had to ***go on public assistance*** [=receive money from the government] when my parents lost their jobs.

pub·li·ca·tion /ˌpʌbləˈkeɪʃən/ *noun, pl* **-tions**
1 *[noncount]* **: the act or process of producing a book, magazine, etc., and making it available to the public** ▪ The company specializes in the *publication* of dictionaries. ▪ the book's date of *publication* = the book's *publication* date [=the date when the book was published] ▪ My novel has been accepted ***for publication***. [=my book will be published and sold to the public]
2 *[count]* **: a book, magazine, etc., that has been printed and made available to the public** ▪ She has a very impressive list of *publications*. ▪ a scholarly/scientific *publication*
3 *[noncount]* **: the act of printing something (such as an article or photograph) in a magazine, newspaper, etc. — often + *of*** ▪ the *publication of* a photo ▪ The *publication of* their findings created an immediate controversy.

public convenience *noun, pl* **~ -niences** *[count] Brit, formal* **: a room in a public place with a sink and toilet : RESTROOM**

public defender *noun, pl* **~ -ers** *[count] US* **: a lawyer who is paid by the government to defend people who are accused of a crime and are unable to pay for a private lawyer**

public domain *noun*
the public domain **1 : the state of something that is not owned by a particular person or company and is available for anyone to use** ▪ The software has entered *the public domain*. ▪ The software is ***in the public domain***. **2** *US* **: land that is owned by the government** ▪ The forests are part of *the public domain*.
– public domain *adj* ▪ *public domain* software ▪ The software became *public domain*. ▪ The forests are *public domain*.

public health *noun [noncount]*
1 : the health of people in general ▪ a disease that poses a serious threat to *public health*
2 *US* **: the science of caring for the people of a community by giving them basic health care and health information, improving living conditions, etc.** ▪ She got her degree in *public health*. ▪ *Public health* officials warned of an influenza outbreak.

public house *noun, pl* **~ houses** *[count] Brit, formal* **: PUB**

pub·li·cist /ˈpʌbləsɪst/ *noun, pl* **-cists** *[count]* **: a person whose job is to give information about an important or famous person or organization to news reporters** ▪ The actor's *publicist* [=*press agent*] declined to comment.

pub·lic·i·ty /pəˈblɪsəti/ *noun [noncount]*
1 : something that attracts the attention of the public ▪ His public appearances are good *publicity* for the new movie. ▪ An arrest for drunk driving is bad *publicity* for any celebrity.
2 : attention that is given to someone or something by newspapers, magazines, television news programs, etc. ▪ The film has gotten some good/bad *publicity*. ▪ She has received a lot of *publicity* for her latest novel.
3 : the activity or business of getting people to give attention to someone or something ▪ The studio spent a lot of money on *publicity* for the movie. ▪ Her antics on the show were just a ***publicity stunt***. [=something done just to get publicity]

pub·li·cize *also Brit* **pub·li·cise** /ˈpʌbləˌsaɪz/ *verb* **-cizes; -cized; -ciz·ing** *[+ obj]* **: to cause (something) to be publicly known : to give information about (something) to the public** ▪ The company neglected to *publicize* the side effects of the new drug. ▪ He is busy *publicizing* [=*promoting*] his book. ▪ a highly *publicized* murder trial

public land *noun, pl* **~ lands** *US* **: land that is owned and taken care of by the government** *[count]* the management of *public lands* *[noncount]* The government will auction off 20 parcels of *public land*.

pub·lic·ly /ˈpʌblɪkli/ *adv*
1 a *[more ~; most ~]* **: in a way that is meant be heard or seen by many people** ▪ He *publicly* announced his resignation. = He announced his resignation *publicly*. ▪ She very *publicly* acknowledged/admitted her mistake. **b : in a way that can be used, seen, bought, etc., by anyone** ▪ The information is *publicly* available/accessible. ▪ a *publicly* traded stock [=a stock that the general public can buy or sell] ▪ a *publicly* owned company [=a company that is owned by the people who own its stock; a company that anyone can buy a share of]
2 : by a government ▪ *publicly* funded research ▪ *publicly* owned land
3 : by all or most of the people of a country, state, etc. ▪ The policies have been *publicly* approved.

public relations *noun*
1 *[noncount]* **: the activity or job of providing information about a particular person or organization to the public so that people will regard that person or organization in a favorable way** ▪ He is very experienced in *public relations*. ▪ a *public relations* firm **— called also *PR***
2 *[plural]* **: the relationship between an organization and the public** ▪ Sponsoring community events is always good for *public relations*. **— called also *PR***

public school *noun, pl* **~ schools** *[count, noncount]*
1 *US* **: a school that gets money from and is controlled by a local government** ▪ Both of their sons attend *public school*.
2 *Brit* **: a private school that prepares students for college or for public service**

public sector *noun [singular]* **: the part of an economy which is controlled or owned by the government** ▪ She has a job in the *public sector*. **— compare PRIVATE SECTOR**

public servant *noun, pl* **~ -vants** *[count]* **: a government official or employee**

public service *noun, pl* **~ -vices**
1 *[count, noncount]* **: the business of supplying something (such as electricity, gas, or transportation) to the members of a community** ▪ The cost of *public services* is on the rise.
2 : something that is done to help people rather than to make a profit *[count]* The station is running antismoking commercials as a *public service*. *[noncount]* The company is heavily involved in *public service*. ▪ The TV station showed a ***public service announcement*** [=an announcement made for the good of the public] on drunk driving.
3 *[noncount]* **: work that someone does as part of a government : the work done by public servants** ▪ He works in *public service*. ▪ She has devoted her life to *public service*.

public speaking *noun [noncount]* **: the act or skill of speaking to a usually large group of people** ▪ He has a fear of *public speaking*. ▪ She has a gift for *public speaking*. ▪ a book on *public speaking*
– public speaker *noun, pl* **~ -ers** *[count]* ▪ She's a gifted *public speaker*.

public–spirited *adj [more ~; most ~] somewhat formal* **: having or showing a desire to help other people** ▪ a *public-spirited* person/act

public transit *noun [noncount] US* **: MASS TRANSIT**

public utility *noun, pl* **~ -ties** *[count]* **: a company (such as an electric company) that provides a public service and must follow special rules made by the government**

public works *noun [plural]* **: buildings and structures (such as schools, highways, and docks) that are built and owned by a government**

pub·lish /ˈpʌblɪʃ/ *verb* **-lish·es; -lished; -lish·ing**
1 *[+ obj]* **: to prepare and produce (a book, magazine, etc.) for sale** ▪ It's a small company that only *publishes* about four books a year. ▪ The university press *publishes* academic titles. ▪ The newspaper is *published* daily.
2 : to have something you wrote included in a book, magazine, newspaper, etc. *[no obj]* There is a lot of pressure for professors to *publish* regularly. *[+ obj]* He has not *published* anything for a long time.
3 *[+ obj]* **: to include (an article, letter, photograph, etc.) in a magazine or newspaper** ▪ The magazine *published* two of my stories.
4 *[+ obj] formal* **: to make (something) known to many people : to make a public announcement of (something)** ▪ The committee plans on *publishing* their findings.
– pub·lish·able /ˈpʌblɪʃəbəl/ *adj [more ~; most ~]* ▪ My professor said that my essay is *publishable*. ▪ a *publishable* quote

pub·lish·er /ˈpʌblɪʃɚ/ *noun, pl* **-ers** *[count]* **: a person or company that produces books, magazines, etc.** ▪ He submitted the manuscript to *publishers* of children's books.

pub·lish·ing /ˈpʌblɪʃɪŋ/ *noun [noncount]* **: the business of producing books, magazines, etc., to sell to the public** ▪ He was hoping to get a job in *publishing* after college. ▪ Her sister works for a well-known *publishing* company/house.

puck /ˈpʌk/ *noun, pl* **pucks** *[count]* **: the small, hard, rubber object that is used in ice hockey** ▪ a hockey *puck*

puck·er /ˈpʌkɚ/ *verb* **-ers; -ered; -er·ing : to pull the sides of (something, such as skin or cloth) together so that folds or wrinkles are formed** *[+ obj]* He ***puckered his lips*** [=he

squeezed his lips together in the way people do when they are going to kiss someone] and kissed her on the cheek. [*no obj*] His skin *puckered* a little around the scar. ▪ She ***puckered up*** [=puckered her lips] and gave him a big smooch.
– puckered *adj* ▪ a *puckered* seam ▪ his *puckered* [=*wrinkled*] face/skin

puck·ish /ˈpʌkɪʃ/ *adj* [*more* ~; *most* ~] *literary* : having or showing a desire to cause trouble in a playful or harmless way : MISCHIEVOUS ▪ He had a *puckish* smile/look on his face.

pud /ˈpʊd/ *noun, pl* **puds** [*count, noncount*] *Brit, informal* : PUDDING ▪ What's for *pud*? ▪ a steak and kidney *pud*

pud·ding /ˈpʊdɪŋ/ *noun, pl* **-dings** [*count, noncount*]
1 *US* : a thick, sweet, soft, and creamy food that is usually eaten cold at the end of a meal ▪ chocolate/vanilla/butterscotch *pudding*
2 : a sweet, soft food that is made of rice, bread, etc. ▪ rice/bread *pudding* ▪ tapioca *pudding*
3 *Brit* : DESSERT ▪ What's for *pudding*?
4 *Brit* : a hot dish like a pie that has a mixture of meat or vegetables inside of it ▪ steak and kidney *pudding*
the proof is in the pudding *also* ***the proof of the pudding is in the eating*** — used to say that you can only know if something is good or bad by trying it
– see also BLACK PUDDING, CHRISTMAS PUDDING, PEASE PUDDING, PLUM PUDDING

pud·dle /ˈpʌdl̩/ *noun, pl* **pud·dles** [*count*] : a small amount of water, mud, etc., on the ground ▪ She accidentally stepped in a *puddle* and got her shoes wet. ▪ After the storm, the road was covered in deep *puddles*.

pu·den·dum /pjʊˈdɛndəm/ *noun, pl* **-den·da** /-ˈdɛndə/ [*count*] *technical* : the sexual organs on the outside of a person's body — used especially to refer to a woman's sexual organs; usually plural ▪ the female *pudenda*

pudgy /ˈpʌʤi/ *adj* **pudg·i·er; -est** [*also more* ~; *most* ~] *informal* : somewhat fat ▪ The baby wrapped its *pudgy* [=*plump*, (*Brit*) *podgy*] little hand around my finger. ▪ a *pudgy* little man

pueb·lo /ˈpwɛbloʊ/ *noun, pl* **-los**
1 [*count*] : a group of Native American homes that have flat roofs and that were used in the past in the southwestern U.S.
2 *Pueblo* [*count, noncount*] : a member of any of several groups of Native Americans from the southwestern U.S.

pu·er·ile /ˈpjɚrəl/ *adj* [*more* ~; *most* ~] *formal + disapproving* : silly or childish especially in a way that shows a lack of seriousness or good judgment ▪ a *puerile* comedy ▪ *puerile* behavior

¹puff /ˈpʌf/ *verb* **puffs; puffed; puff·ing**
1 : to breathe smoke from a cigarette, pipe, etc., in and out of the lungs [*no obj*] She sat on the porch *puffing* on a cigarette. ▪ The men spent the evening *puffing* (away) at cigars. [*+ obj*] He *puffed* [=*smoked*] a pipe.
2 a : to produce or send out small clouds of smoke or steam [*+ obj*] He *puffed* [=*blew*] smoke into my face. ▪ The chimney *puffed* white smoke into the sky. [*no obj*] Steam *puffed* (out) from the pot. **b** *always followed by an adverb or preposition* [*no obj*] : to move in a particular direction while producing clouds of steam or smoke ▪ We watched the train *puff* away on its journey west.
3 [*no obj*] *informal* **a** : to breathe loudly especially because of hard physical activity ▪ He was *puffing* and panting from running. **b** *always followed by an adverb or preposition* : to move or do something while breathing loudly ▪ The bikers *puffed* up the hill.
4 a [*no obj*] : to become larger and rounder than normal — usually *+ up* ▪ Her face *puffed up* [=*swelled*] from an allergic reaction to the almonds. ▪ The cake *puffed up* as it baked in the oven. **b** [*+ obj*] : to make (something) larger and rounder than normal ▪ He *puffed* his chest and swaggered into the room. — usually *+ up* ▪ The frog *puffed* itself *up*. ▪ He *puffed up* his chest and swaggered into the room.
huff and puff see ¹HUFF
puff out [*phrasal verb*] ***puff (something) out*** *or* ***puff out (something)*** : to make (something) larger and rounder by filling it with air ▪ She *puffed out* her cheeks, made a wish, and blew out the candles on her cake. ▪ A gust of wind *puffed out* the boat's sails.
puff (up) with pride ◊ When you *puff (up) with pride* or when you are *puffed (up) with pride*, you are very proud and stand or sit up straighter because of it. ▪ When his daughter's name was announced as the winner, he *puffed up with pride*.
– puffed *adj* ▪ The baby wore an adorable little dress with *puffed* sleeves. [=sleeves made so that they puff out]

²puff *noun, pl* **puffs**
1 [*count*] : an act of breathing something (such as smoke or medicine) into your lungs ▪ He let me have a *puff* off his pipe. ▪ She took two *puffs* on her inhaler before going for a run.
2 [*count*] : a movement of gas, smoke, or air that can be seen or felt ▪ She blew out the candles in a single *puff*. [=an outward breath of air] — usually *+ of* ▪ The magician disappeared in a *puff of* smoke. ▪ We saw *puffs of* smoke billowing from the chimney. ▪ A sudden *puff of* cold air hit the back of my neck.
3 [*count*] : a light, round pastry that contains a sweet filling ▪ *puffs* filled with cream cheese and apricot jam — see also CREAM PUFF
4 *Brit, informal + disapproving* : speech or writing that praises someone or something too much [*noncount*] The story was just a lot of public relations *puff*. [*count*] The story was just a PR *puff*. [=(*chiefly US*) *puff piece*]
5 [*noncount*] *Brit, informal* : BREATH 1 ▪ Halfway up the hill, I was already ***out of puff***.
– see also POWDER PUFF

puff·er /ˈpʌfɚ/ *noun, pl* **-ers** [*count*] : a type of poisonous fish that can inflate its body with air so that it forms a ball — called also *puffer fish*

puf·fin /ˈpʌfən/ *noun, pl* **-fins** [*count*] : a black-and-white seabird that lives in the north Atlantic and has a large, colorful bill

puff pastry *noun* [*noncount*] : dough that is made of thin layers that puff up during baking

puff piece *noun, pl* ~ **pieces** [*count*] *chiefly US, informal + disapproving* : a story, news report, etc., that praises someone or something too much ▪ The story was just another *puff piece* to help the mayor get reelected.

puffy /ˈpʌfi/ *adj* **puff·i·er; -est** [*also more* ~; *most* ~]
1 : larger than normal : SWOLLEN ▪ When I first wake up in the morning, my eyes are *puffy*.
2 : soft and light ▪ *puffy* clouds ▪ *puffy*, white hair
– puff·i·ness /ˈpʌfinəs/ *noun* [*noncount*]

pug /ˈpʌg/ *noun, pl* **pugs** [*count*] : a small dog that has short fur, a tightly curled tail, and a wide wrinkled face — see picture at DOG

pu·gi·list /ˈpju:ʤəlɪst/ *noun, pl* **-lists** [*count*] *old-fashioned + somewhat formal* : a professional boxer ▪ a talented *pugilist*
– pu·gi·lism /ˈpju:ʤəˌlɪzəm/ *noun* [*noncount*] ▪ He made a career out of *pugilism*. **– pu·gi·lis·tic** /ˌpju:ʤəˈlɪstɪk/ *adj* ▪ a *pugilistic* career

pug·na·cious /ˌpʌgˈneɪʃəs/ *adj* [*more* ~; *most* ~] *formal* : showing a readiness or desire to fight or argue ▪ There's one *pugnacious* member on the committee who won't agree to anything.
– pug·na·cious·ly *adv* **– pug·nac·i·ty** /ˌpʌgˈnæsəti/ *noun* [*noncount*] ▪ a player who's known for his *pugnacity*

¹puke /ˈpju:k/ *verb* **pukes; puked; puk·ing** *informal* : to empty what is in your stomach through your mouth : VOMIT [*no obj*] I think I'm going to *puke*. [=*throw up*] ▪ Her snobby attitude ***makes me (want to) puke***. [=makes me sick; makes me very angry, annoyed, etc.] [*+ obj*] — usually *+ up* ▪ He *puked up* [=*threw up*] his breakfast.

²puke *noun* [*noncount*] *informal* : the food, liquid, etc., that comes out of your body through your mouth when you vomit : VOMIT ▪ a puddle of dog *puke*

puk·ka /ˈpʌkə/ *adj, Brit, informal* : very good ▪ They assured us that everything's *pukka*. [=*OK*] ▪ a *pukka* meal

Pu·lit·zer Prize /ˈpʊlətsɚ-/ *noun, pl* ~ **Prizes** [*count*] : one of a number of prizes that are awarded in the U.S. each year for excellent work in writing, reporting, or music composition — called also *Pulitzer*

¹pull /ˈpʊl/ *verb* **pulls; pulled; pull·ing**
1 : to hold onto and move (someone or something) in a particular direction and especially toward yourself [*+ obj*] He *pulled* the door open and ran out. ▪ The cat will scratch you if you keep *pulling* its tail. ▪ Make a knot in the rope and *pull* it tight. ▪ *Pull* the baby's chair closer to the table. ▪ She *pulled* the blanket over her head. [*no obj*] We tried pushing and *pulling* but couldn't get the couch to move. ▪ Grab the end of the rope and *pull* as hard as you can.
2 [*+ obj*] : to remove (something) by gripping it and using force ▪ We spent the morning in the garden *pulling* weeds. ▪ I accidentally *pulled* one of the buttons off my shirt. ▪ The dentist said I have to have two teeth *pulled*. [=*extracted*] ▪ He

pulled the cork (out) and poured the wine. ▪ He *pulled* the plug out of the socket.
3 [+ *obj*] **a :** to cause (something you are holding or something that is attached to you) to move with you as you go in a particular direction ▪ Horses *pull* carriages around the park. ▪ She was *pulling* a wagon behind her. **b :** to cause (something) to move or be directed toward something ▪ The colors *pull* [=*draw*] the eye toward the center of the painting.
4 *always followed by an adverb or preposition* **a** [*no obj*] *of a car, train, etc.* **:** to move from or to a particular place ▪ The car *pulled* out of the driveway. ▪ The train *pulled* into the station [=arrived at the station] right on time. ▪ I made it to the bus stop just when the bus was *pulling* away/out. [=was leaving] **b :** to move a vehicle from or to a particular place [*no obj*] Look both ways before *pulling* out (into traffic). ▪ It's a tight squeeze, so be careful *pulling* in. ▪ He *pulled* into the parking space. ▪ We'll have to *pull* off the highway. ▪ She *pulled* away from the curb and into traffic. [+ *obj*] He slowly *pulled* the car into traffic. ▪ *Pull* the car into the garage.
5 *always followed by an adverb or preposition* [*no obj*] *of a car, wheel, etc.* **:** to move to the left or right instead of straight ahead when traveling forward ▪ I need to get the alignment of the car fixed because when I drive it *pulls* [=*drifts*] to the right/left. ▪ The wheel *pulls* left.
6 *always followed by an adverb or preposition* **:** to move (your body or a part of your body) in a particular direction or to a particular position [+ *obj*] She wore her hair *pulled* back in a ponytail. ▪ At my age, it can be hard to *pull* yourself up from the couch. ▪ I tried to grab his hand but he *pulled* it away. [*no obj*] When I leaned over to kiss her, she *pulled* away.
7 [+ *obj*] **:** to move (a trigger, lever, etc.) in order to operate a device or machine ▪ He *pulled* the trigger, but the gun didn't fire. ▪ She dropped in a quarter and *pulled* the slot machine's lever.
8 : to move a boat through water using oars **:** ROW [*no obj*] The crew *pulled* toward shore. [+ *obj*] The crew *pulled* the boat toward shore.
9 [+ *obj*] **a :** to remove (someone or something) from a place or situation ▪ The pitcher was *pulled* (from the game) [=was taken out of the game] in the third inning. **b :** to take (something) away ▪ The police *pulled* his driver's license for drunk driving. = He had his license *pulled* for drunk driving. ▪ The project was well-funded until a few companies *pulled* [=*withdrew*] their sponsorship.
10 [+ *obj*] **:** to take (a weapon) out of a pocket or other hidden place ▪ He went into the store and *pulled* a gun on the cashier. [=took out a gun and pointed it at the cashier] ▪ Somone *pulled* a knife on him and threatened to stab him.
11 [+ *obj*] **:** to do (something) ▪ They *pulled* [=*carried out*] a robbery. ▪ I *pulled* [=*worked*] two double shifts at the restaurant this week. ▪ She loved to *pull* [=*play*] tricks/jokes on her brother. ▪ Don't you ever *pull* a crazy stunt like that again! ▪ To finish my paper for class, I had to ***pull an all-nighter***. [=stay awake all night working]
12 [+ *obj*] **:** to hurt (a muscle, tendon, or ligament) by stretching it too much ▪ She *pulled* [=*strained*] a muscle in her back when she tried to reach the top shelf.
13 [+ *obj*] *sports* **:** to hit (a ball) toward the left from a right-handed swing or toward the right from a left-handed swing ▪ (*baseball*) He *pulled* the ball down the left-field line. ▪ (*golf*) She *pulled* her drive into the rough. — compare PUSH
14 [+ *obj*] *informal* **:** to behave like (a particular person) ▪ Whenever anyone forgot where they had parked the car, we'd say they *"pulled* a Dave." [=they did something that Dave often does]
15 *Brit, informal* **:** to attract (someone) sexually [+ *obj*] He had a brief affair with a girl he *pulled* in a bar. [*no obj*] She's wearing a short skirt hoping it will help her *pull* tonight.

> In addition to the phrases shown below, *pull* occurs in many idioms that are shown at appropriate entries throughout the dictionary. For example, *pull a face* can be found at [1]FACE, *pull someone's leg* can be found at [1]LEG, and *pull the wool over someone's eyes* can be found at WOOL.

pull a fast one *informal* **:** to deceive or trick someone ▪ Be careful. Someone might try to *pull a fast one* on you.
pull ahead [*phrasal verb*] **:** to take the lead in a race, competition, contest, etc. ▪ The two runners were side by side until one *pulled ahead*. ▪ She *pulled ahead* in the race. ▪ He has *pulled ahead* of the other candidates in the election polls.
pull apart [*phrasal verb*] **1 a :** to be separated into parts or pieces by pulling ▪ The rolls *pull apart* easily. **b *pull (something) apart or pull apart (something)* :** to separate or break (something) into parts or pieces ▪ She *pulled* the rolls *apart* with her hands. — sometimes used figuratively ▪ His gambling problem is *pulling* the family *apart*. [=is destroying the family] **2 *pull (people or animals) apart or pull apart (people or animals)* :** to separate (people or animals) in order to stop a fight ▪ Customers stepped in and *pulled* the two men *apart*. [=separated the two men who were fighting]
pull aside [*phrasal verb*] ***pull (someone) aside* :** to take (someone) to one side away from other people for a private conversation ▪ The reporter *pulled* me *aside* and asked if I knew who was in charge.
pull at [*phrasal verb*] ***pull at (something)*** **1 :** to hold onto and pull (something) repeatedly ▪ When she gets nervous, she *pulls at* [=*pulls on*] her ear. **2 :** to breathe in the smoke from (a cigarette, pipe, etc.) ▪ He rocked back and forth, *pulling at* [=*pulling on*] his pipe.
pull away [*phrasal verb*] **:** to begin to move farther ahead in a race, competition, contest, etc. ▪ They *pulled away* in the second half and won the game easily. — often + *from* ▪ In the final lap, he *pulled away from* the other cars and won.
pull back [*phrasal verb*] **1 :** to decide not to do something that you had intended to do or started to do ▪ The buyers of the house *pulled back* [=*pulled out*] at the last minute. **2 *pull back or pull back (someone or something) or pull (someone or something) back* :** to move back from a place or position or to cause (someone or something) to move back from a place or position ▪ The soldiers were outnumbered and were forced to *pull back*. [=*retreat, withdraw*] ▪ The general *pulled* his army *back*. **3 *pull (something) back or pull back (something)*** *Brit, sports* **:** to score (a goal, point, etc.) so that you are not as far behind in a game as you were before ▪ They were behind 2–0 but they *pulled back* a goal [=they scored a goal to make the score 2–1] early in the second half.
pull down [*phrasal verb*] **1 *pull down (something) or pull (something) down* a :** to move (something) down ▪ I *pulled down* the shade. ▪ He always wears his baseball cap *pulled down* over his eyes. **b :** to destroy (a building) completely ▪ The wreckers *pulled down* [=*demolished*] the building. **c :** to make (something) smaller in amount or number **:** to reduce or lower (something) ▪ The rumors that the company was filing for bankruptcy *pulled* stock prices *down*. **2 *pull down (someone) or pull (someone) down*** *US, informal* **:** to cause (someone) to become sad or depressed ▪ The loss really *pulled* the team *down*. [=brought the team down] **3 *pull down (something)*** *informal* **a :** to earn (a particular and usually large amount of money) ▪ He *pulls down* [=*makes, pulls in*] more than a million dollars a year. **b :** to get (something) ▪ The show has *pulled down* high ratings.
pull for [*phrasal verb*] ***pull for (someone or something)*** *US, informal* **:** to say or show that you hope (someone or something) will succeed, get well, etc. ▪ I hope you're feeling better soon. We're all *pulling for* you (to get well). ▪ I'm *pulling* [=*rooting*] *for* the home team.
pull in [*phrasal verb*] **1 :** to arrive at a place and come to a stop ▪ "When are our guests coming?" "I think they just *pulled in*." ▪ The train *pulled in* on time. **2 *pull in (someone or something) or pull (someone or something) in* :** to attract (someone or something) ▪ We hope the display will *pull* customers *in* from the street. ▪ She's trying to *pull in* more votes. **3 *pull in (something) also pull (something) in*** *informal* **:** to earn (a particular and usually large amount of money) ▪ After just a couple of years at the firm, she was *pulling in* [=*pulling down, making*] more than $100,000. **4 *pull (someone) in* :** to bring (someone) to a police station **:** to arrest (someone) ▪ The police *pulled* him *in* for questioning.
pull off [*phrasal verb*] ***pull off (something) or pull (something) off*** **1 :** to remove (something) from something else **:** to take off (something) ▪ He *pulled off* the covers of the bed. ▪ She *pulled* her boots *off*. **2** *informal* **:** to do (something difficult) successfully ▪ We were doubtful the plan would work, but he managed to *pull* it *off*. ▪ The team *pulled off* a win/upset.
pull on [*phrasal verb*] **1 *pull on (something)* :** to hold onto and pull (something) repeatedly ▪ When she gets nervous, she *pulls on* [=*pulls at*] her ear. **2 :** to breathe in the smoke from (a cigarette, pipe, etc.) ▪ He rocked back and forth, *pulling on* [=*pulling at*] his pipe. **3 *pull on (something) or pull (something) on* :** to dress yourself in (clothing) ▪ She

P

quickly *pulled on* [=*put on*] her clothes/sweater.

pull out [*phrasal verb*] **1 : to decide not to do something that you had intended to do or started to do** ▪ The buyers of the house *pulled out* at the last minute. **2 *pull out or pull out (someone or something) or pull (someone or something) out* : to leave a place or position or to cause (someone or something) to leave a place or position** ▪ The invading army was outnumbered and was forced to *pull out*. [=*withdraw*] ▪ Military leaders have decided to *pull* the troops *out* of the war zone. ▪ Organizations are *pulling out* of the country [=are leaving the country] due to threats of civil war. — see also PULLOUT

pull over [*phrasal verb*] **1 *pull over or pull over (something) or pull (something) over* : to move a vehicle to the side of the road and stop** ▪ Let's *pull over* and look at the map. ▪ He *pulled* the car *over* to look at the map. **2 *pull over (someone or something) or pull (someone or something) over* : to force (a driver or vehicle) to move to the side of the road and stop** ▪ He was *pulled over* (by the police) for speeding.

pull through [*phrasal verb*] **1 : to survive a serious illness, injury, operation, etc.** ▪ We sat in the hospital waiting room praying that he would *pull through*. [=*live*] **2 a *pull through or pull through (something)* : to get through a difficult situation** ▪ I'm sure that the company will *pull through*, just as it has in difficult times in the past. ▪ It was a bad time for my family, but we managed to *pull through* it. **b *pull (someone or something) through* : to help (someone or something) to continue to live or succeed in a dangerous or difficult situation** ▪ His determination *pulled* him *through*. ▪ Outside financial help is needed to *pull* the company *through* its troubles.

pull together [*phrasal verb*] **1 : to work together as a group in order to get something done** ▪ It was amazing to see so many people *pull together* to help the poor. **2 a *pull together (someone or something) or pull (someone or something) together* : to bring (people or things) together and organize them in order to make or do something** ▪ She managed to *pull* a team of researchers *together*. ▪ He started his research by *pulling together* all the available data. **b *pull together (something) or pull (something) together* : to make (something) by bringing together different things** ▪ The chef *pulled together* a menu of American and Italian cuisine. ▪ The boss asked her to *pull* a brief sales report *together*. **3 *pull (yourself) together* : to become calm again : to control your emotions and behavior after you have been very upset, emotional, etc.** ▪ I know you're upset, but you need to *pull yourself together*. [=*calm down*]

pull up [*phrasal verb*] **1 *pull up (something) or pull (something) up* a : to move (something) up** ▪ I *pulled up* the shade. **b : to move (something) forward or into a position where it can be seen, used, etc.** ▪ *Pull up* a chair and make yourself comfortable. ▪ Give me a moment to *pull up* your file on the computer. **2 *pull up or pull (something) up or pull up (something)* : to stop a vehicle at a particular place** ▪ We *pulled up* in front of the house. ▪ He *pulled up* next to me at the stoplight. ▪ He *pulled* the car *up* in front of the house. **3 *pull up* : to stop suddenly before completing something** ▪ A muscle spasm caused him to *pull up* halfway through the race. ▪ She started to answer and then ***pulled up short*** **4 *pull (someone) up Brit, informal* : to criticize (someone) severely for doing something** ▪ Her boss *pulled* her *up* for/on being late.

P

²pull *noun, pl* **pulls**

1 [*count*] **: the act of moving or trying to move something by holding it and bringing it toward you : the act of pulling something** ▪ She gave the door a few hard *pulls* and it opened. ▪ Give the rope a *pull*. ▪ I felt a couple *pulls* [=*tugs*] on the fishing line.

2 [*noncount*] **: special influence and power over other people** ▪ He has a lot of *pull* in local political circles.

3 [*count*] **: an ability or power to attract someone or to make someone want to go somewhere, do something, etc. — usually singular** ▪ She has great box-office *pull*. [=she attracts a lot of people to her movies] ▪ She resisted the *pull* to abandon her principles to make more money. ▪ the irresistible *pull* of Hollywood for/on young actors and actresses

4 [*singular*] **: a natural force that causes one thing (such as a planet) to be pulled toward another** ▪ The planet has a strong gravitational *pull*. ▪ the *pull* of gravity

5 [*count*] **: an injury that is caused by stretching a muscle, tendon, or ligament too much** ▪ He is recovering from a muscle/groin *pull*.

6 [*count*] **a : the act of breathing in smoke from a cigarette, cigar, pipe, etc.** ▪ He just looked at me and ***took a pull on/off/at*** his cigarette before answering. **b : the act of taking a long drink of something** ▪ He ***took a long pull on*** his beer.

7 [*count*] **: something (such as a handle or cord) that opens or operates something when it is pulled** ▪ a drawer/bell *pull*

8 [*count*] *chiefly Brit* **: a difficult climb up a steep hill — usually singular** ▪ a long *pull* uphill

pull·back /ˈpʊlˌbæk/ *noun, pl* **-backs** [*count*]
1 : an act of removing military troops from a position or an area ▪ the *pullback* [=*withdrawal*] of forces from the border
2 *formal* **: an act of doing less or becoming less involved in something** ▪ a *pullback* in consumer spending

pull–down menu *noun, pl* **~ menus** [*count*] *computers* **:** DROP-DOWN MENU

pul·let /ˈpʊlət/ *noun, pl* **-lets** [*count*] **: a young chicken and especially one that is less than a year old**

pul·ley /ˈpʊli/ *noun, pl* **-leys** [*count*] **: a wheel or set of wheels that is used with a rope, chain, etc., to lift or lower heavy objects**

pulley

pulling power *noun* [*noncount*] *chiefly Brit* **:** DRAWING POWER ▪ a performer with a lot of *pulling power*

Pull·man /ˈpʊlmən/ *noun, pl* **-mans** [*count*] **: a comfortable railroad car that carries people and is used especially for overnight travel**

pull·out /ˈpʊlˌaʊt/ *noun, pl* **-outs** [*count*]
1 : an act of removing military troops from a position or an area ▪ A *pullout* of troops from the region has begun.
2 : a section of a newspaper, magazine, etc., that is meant to be removed and looked at separately ▪ That article is in the special *pullout* (section). ▪ a ten-page *pullout* — see also *pull out* at ¹PULL

pull·over /ˈpʊlˌoʊvɚ/ *noun, pl* **-overs** [*count*] **: a piece of clothing (such as a sweater) that is put on by pulling it over your head** ▪ She was wearing a light *pullover*. ▪ a *pullover* jacket/sweater — see color picture on page C15

pull tab *noun, pl* **~ tabs** [*count*] *US* **: a small metal ring on the top of a can or other container that you pull to open the container — called also (*Brit*) *ring pull***

pull–up /ˈpʊlˌʌp/ *noun, pl* **-ups** [*count*] **: an exercise in which you hold onto a bar above your head and then pull your body up until your chin is above the bar** ▪ doing *pull-ups* ▪ a *pull-up* bar — called also (*US*) *chin-up*

pul·mo·nary /ˈpʊlməˌneri, *Brit* ˈpʊlmənri/ *adj, always used before a noun, medical* **: relating to the lungs** ▪ the *pulmonary* arteries/veins

¹pulp /ˈpʌlp/ *noun, pl* **pulps**
1 a [*noncount*] **: the inner, juicy part of a fruit or vegetable** ▪ The fruit has sweet, juicy *pulp* and hard, black seeds. ▪ the *pulp* of an orange **b** [*noncount*] **: the substance that is left after the liquid has been squeezed from a fruit or vegetable** ▪ I like to strain the *pulp* out of my orange juice. **c : a soft, wet substance that is made by crushing something** [*noncount*] The grain was mashed into *pulp*. [*singular*] mashed to a *pulp*
2 [*noncount*] **: a soft material that is made mostly from wood and is used in making paper** ▪ The boxes will be turned back into *pulp* and be made into newspapers. ▪ a *pulp* mill ▪ This paper is made from inexpensive ***wood pulp***.
3 [*count*] *US* **: a magazine, book, etc., that is cheaply made and that deals with sex, drugs, violence, etc., in a shocking way** ▪ He made a little extra money by writing stories for a science fiction *pulp*. — often used before another noun ▪ a *pulp* magazine ▪ ***pulp fiction***
4 [*count, noncount*] *technical* **: the soft tissue that is inside a tooth**

to a pulp **— used to say that someone or something is very badly beaten, mashed, smashed, etc.** ▪ He threatened to ***beat them to a (bloody) pulp***.

– pulpy /ˈpʌlpi/ *adj* **pulp·i·er; -est** [*also more ~; most ~*] ▪ *pulpy* orange juice ▪ *pulpy* magazines

²pulp *verb* **pulps; pulped; pulp·ing** [+ *obj*] **: to crush (something) until it is soft and wet : to make (something) into pulp** ▪ They will *pulp* the unsold copies of the book. [=turn them into pulp for making paper] ▪ the wood *pulping* process

pul·pit /ˈpʊlˌpɪt/ *noun, pl* **-pits** [*count*] **:** a raised platform where a priest or minister stands when leading a worship service — usually singular • The pastor ascended the *pulpit.* — often used figuratively • The war crimes were denounced ***from the pulpit***. [=by priests and church leaders] • People have different opinions about women ***in the pulpit***. [=as priests or church leaders; in the priesthood] — see also BULLY PULPIT

pulpit

pul·sar /ˈpʌlˌsɑɚ/ *noun, pl* **-sars** [*count*] *technical* **:** a type of star that gives off a rapidly repeating series of radio waves

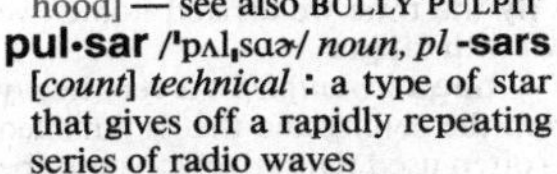

pul·sate /ˈpʌlˌseɪt, *Brit* ˌpʌlˈseɪt/ *verb* **-sates; -sat·ed; -sat·ing** [*no obj*]

1 : to make strong and regular beats, sounds, flashes, etc. • The lights *pulsated* with the music. • People danced to the *pulsating* sounds of hip-hop.

2 : to be filled with activity or a feeling • Virtually every scene of the movie *pulsates* with suspense.

– **pul·sa·tion** /ˌpʌlˈseɪʃən/ *noun, pl* **-tions** [*count, noncount*] • artery *pulsations*

¹pulse /ˈpʌls/ *noun, pl* **puls·es** [*count*]

1 : the regular movement of blood through your body that is caused by the beating of your heart and that can be felt by touching certain parts of your body — usually singular • This machine measures *pulse* rate and blood pressure. • a strong/weak *pulse* • My *pulse* quickened when I heard the exciting news. = The exciting news set my *pulse* racing. [=the exciting news made my heart beat faster] • She has a resting *pulse* of 60. [=when she is resting, her heart beats 60 times per minute] • The nurse ***checked/took/felt my pulse***. [=measured how fast my heart was beating]

2 : a strong, regular beat or pattern of sounds in music — usually singular • the strong *pulse* of the music

3 : a brief increase in an amount of electricity, light, or sound • light *pulses* = *pulses* of light • *pulse* waves

4 : the ideas, feelings, or opinions that are shared by a particular group of people — usually singular • Her book is a good analysis of the political *pulse* of the nation.

finger on the pulse see ¹FINGER

²pulse *verb* **pulses; pulsed; puls·ing** [*no obj*]

1 a : to move with strong, regular beats • When he gets angry, the veins in his forehead *pulse*. [=*throb*] • He could feel the blood *pulsing* through his veins. — often used figuratively • A rush of excitement *pulsed* through her body. [=she felt a sudden rush of excitement] **b :** to produce a strong, regular beat • Dance music *pulsed* from the speakers.

2 : to be filled with activity or a feeling • The city *pulses* with life.

pul·ver·ize *also Brit* **pul·ver·ise** /ˈpʌlvəˌraɪz/ *verb* **-iz·es; -ized; -iz·ing** [+ *obj*]

1 *technical* **:** to crush, beat, or grind (something) into powder or dust • The mower *pulverizes* grass clippings. • Bits of *pulverized* rock filled the air.

2 *informal* **:** to destroy or defeat (someone or something) completely • They *pulverized* the opposition.

pu·ma /ˈpuːmə, *Brit* ˈpjuːmə/ *noun, pl* **pu·mas** *also* **puma** [*count*] **:** COUGAR

pum·ice /ˈpʌməs/ *noun* [*noncount*] **:** a gray stone that comes from volcanoes, is full of small holes, has a very light weight, and is used especially for smoothing and polishing things or for softening the skin — called also *pumice stone*

pum·mel /ˈpʌməl/ *verb* **-mels;** *US* **-meled** *or Brit* **-melled;** *US* **-mel·ing** *or Brit* **-mel·ling** [+ *obj*] **:** to repeatedly hit or punch (someone or something) very hard • He *pummeled* [=*beat*] the intruder. • She *pummeled* the steering wheel (with her fists). — often used figuratively • They *pummeled* the opposition. • Her last movie was *pummeled* by the critics.

¹pump /ˈpʌmp/ *noun, pl* **pumps** [*count*]

1 : a device that forces liquid, air, or gas into or out of something • an air *pump* • a water *pump* • a foot/hand *pump* [=a pump that you operate by using your foot/hand] • a bicycle *pump* [=a small pump used for putting air in bicycle tires] • (*US*) a ***gas pump*** = (*Brit*) a ***petrol pump*** — see picture at BICYCLE

2 : the act of pumping something • Three more *pumps* and the tire should be full enough.

at the pump *also* ***at the pumps*** *US, informal* **:** at the places where customers buy gasoline for their cars • Prices are higher *at the pump*. [=gas prices are higher] • Expect long lines *at the pumps* this weekend. [=expect long lines at gas stations this weekend]

prime the pump see ³PRIME

– compare ³PUMP

²pump *verb* **pumps; pumped; pump·ing**

1 a : to move something (such as water, air, or gas) to or from a particular place with a pump [+ *obj*] He *pumped* the water up from the bottom of the boat. — often used figuratively • The President hoped the tax cuts would help *pump* money back into the economy. • She *pumped* all of her resources into starting her own business. [*no obj*] The machine suddenly stopped *pumping*. **b** [+ *obj*] **:** to remove water, air, etc., from (something) with a pump • We *pumped* the boat dry. • We had to *pump* the basement out. **c** [+ *obj*] **:** to remove the contents of (someone's stomach) by using a tube and a small pump • Doctors had to *pump* (out) her stomach after she swallowed poison.

2 *of the heart* **:** to move (blood) through your body by beating [+ *obj*] Your heart *pumps* blood all over your body. [*no obj*] My heart started *pumping* [=*beating*] fast.

3 *always followed by an adverb or preposition* [*no obj*] *of a liquid* **:** to flow in a series of movements caused by the action of a pump, by the beating of your heart, etc. • I could feel the blood *pumping* through my veins. • Blood *pumped* out of the cut.

4 : to move (something) up and down or in and out quickly and repeatedly [+ *obj*] He *pumped* his arms up and down as he ran. • She *pumped* the handle of the well. • *pump* the brake pedal [*no obj*] His leg nervously *pumped* up and down under the table.

5 [+ *obj*] *informal* **:** to question (someone) again and again to try to find out information — often + *for* • The detective *pumped* them *for* information on the murder.

pump iron *informal* **:** to lift weights in order to make your muscles stronger • I'm going to the gym to *pump* some *iron*.

pump out [*phrasal verb*] ***pump out (something)*** *or* ***pump (something) out*** *informal* **:** to produce (something) quickly and frequently • The author *pumps out* a book every year.

pump (someone or something) full of (something) **:** to fill (someone or something) with (something) by using a pump • They *pumped* the balloon *full of* helium. — often used figuratively • He pulled out a gun and threatened to *pump* them *full of* bullets/lead. [=threatened to shoot them] • She was *pumped full of* antibiotics/caffeine.

pump up [*phrasal verb*] **1** ***pump (something) up*** *or* ***pump up (something)*** **:** to fill (something, such as a tire) with air by using a pump **:** INFLATE • I'll be ready to go for a bike ride after I *pump up* my tires. **2** ***pump (something) up*** *or* ***pump up (something)*** *informal* **:** to increase the amount, size, or value of (something) • The company is trying hard to *pump up* sales. • All of the praise *pumped up* her ego. **3** ***pump (someone) up*** *or* ***pump up (someone)*** **:** to fill (someone) with excitement or enthusiasm • The coach made a speech to try and *pump up* his players. • The team was (all) *pumped up* for the game.

³pump *noun, pl* **pumps** [*count*]

1 *US* **:** a woman's dress shoe with a high heel — usually plural • She wore black leather *pumps* with her suit. — called also (*Brit*) *court shoe*

2 *Brit* **:** a light, soft shoe that is worn for dancing or exercise • ballet *pumps*

– compare ¹PUMP

pumped /ˈpʌmpt/ *adj, US, informal* **:** excited and enthusiastic about something • I'm *pumped* [=*pumped up*] for tonight's concert.

pum·per·nick·el /ˈpʌmpɚˌnɪkəl/ *noun* [*noncount*] **:** a heavy and dark type of bread made from rye

pump·kin /ˈpʌmpkən/ *noun, pl* **-kins** [*count, noncount*] **:** a large, round, orange vegetable used as food and sometimes as a decoration — often used before another noun • *pumpkin* pie • *pumpkin* soup — see color picture on page C4

¹pun /ˈpʌn/ *noun, pl* **puns** [*count*] **:** a humorous way of using a word or phrase so that more than one meaning is suggested • She made a *pun*. • The delicatessen is sandwiched, if you'll ***pardon/excuse/forgive the pun***, between two stores. • She's a skillful pilot whose career has—***no pun intended***—really taken off. — often + *on* • The name "Dew Drop Inn" is a *pun on* "do drop in."

P

²pun *verb* **puns; punned; pun·ning :** to make a pun [*no obj*] a *punning* headline — often + *on* ▪ *Punning on* her daughter's first name, she said, "Mary Christmas!" [+ *obj*] "Firefighting sparks my interest," he *punned*.

¹punch /ˈpʌntʃ/ *verb* **punch·es; punched; punch·ing** [+ *obj*]
1 : to hit (someone or something) hard with your fist ▪ Stop *punching* your sister! ▪ He *punched* my face/nose/mouth/arm. ▪ He *punched* me in the face/nose/mouth/eye/belly. ▪ She *punched* him on the chin/jaw/arm.
2 *chiefly US* **:** to press or push (something) with a short, quick movement ▪ He quickly *punched* the buttons on his telephone.
3 : to make (a hole, dent, etc.) by pressing or cutting *in, into*, or *through* something ▪ She *punched* an opening *through* the dough with her finger. ▪ The tool *punches* holes *in* paper.
4 : to make a hole in (something, such as a ticket) by using a special tool ▪ The conductor *punched* my railway pass.
***punch holes in* :** to weaken or destroy (an idea, plan, belief, etc.) by proving that parts of it are wrong ▪ Lawyers tried to *punch holes in* her argument.
punch in [*phrasal verb*] *US* **1 :** to place a card in a time clock at the beginning of a workday so that the time is recorded on the card ▪ The crew *punched in* [=(*chiefly Brit*) *clocked in*] at 8:00. **2** ***punch (something) in or punch in (something)* :** to enter (information, such as words or numbers) into a computer or other machine by pressing buttons or keys ▪ She *punched in* her secret code.
punch out [*phrasal verb*] *US* **1 :** to place a card in a time clock at the end of a workday so that the time is recorded on the card ▪ It's time to *punch out*. **2** ***punch (someone) out or punch out (someone)*** *informal* **:** to hit (someone) repeatedly in order to cause pain or injury : to beat (someone) up ▪ He threatened to *punch* me *out* if I talked to his girlfriend again.
punch someone's lights out *informal* **:** to hit someone's face hard with your fist ▪ It's a good thing he's not here, or I'd *punch his lights out*.
punch up [*phrasal verb*] ***punch (something) up or punch up (something)*** *US, informal* **:** to make (something) more lively, exciting, attractive, etc. ▪ New owners *punched up* the newspaper with color photographs. ▪ The steak was *punched up* with a pepper sauce.
– punch·er *noun, pl* **-ers** [*count*] ▪ a card *puncher* ▪ He was the greatest *puncher* in the history of boxing.

²punch *noun, pl* **punches**
1 [*count*] **:** a quick hit with your fist ▪ throw/land a *punch* ▪ kicks and *punches* ▪ He gave me a *punch* in the nose. [=he punched me in the nose] — see also RABBIT PUNCH, SUCKER PUNCH
2 [*noncount*] **:** energy or forcefulness ▪ The team was well trained but lacked *punch*. ▪ The last sentence in your essay needs more *punch*.
(as) pleased as punch see PLEASED
***beat (someone) to the punch* :** to do or achieve something before someone else is able to ▪ We were working on a new product but our competition *beat us to the punch*. [=our competition started selling a similar product before we did]
pack a punch see ²PACK
pull punches* :** to express criticism in a mild or kind way — usually used in negative statements ▪ When he has something bad to say about a movie, he doesn't *pull* his/any *punches*. [=he does not try to make his criticisms seem less harsh than they are] ▪ The report ***pulls no punches in blaming the government for this crisis.
roll with the punches see ¹ROLL
– compare ³PUNCH, ⁴PUNCH

³punch *noun, pl* **punches :** a drink made usually by mixing different fruit juices and often flavored with wine or liquor [*count*] a fruit *punch* [*noncount*] They plan to serve *punch* at the party. ▪ a bowl/glass of *punch* — see also PUNCH BOWL — compare ²PUNCH, ⁴PUNCH

⁴punch *noun, pl* **punches** [*count*]
1 : a tool or machine for cutting holes in paper, cardboard, leather, etc. ▪ a paper *punch*
2 : a hole made by a cutting tool or machine ▪ He got an extra *punch* on his discount card.
– compare ²PUNCH, ³PUNCH

Punch–and–Judy show /ˌpʌntʃənˈʤu:di-/ *noun, pl* ~ **shows** [*count*] **:** a comic puppet show in which a puppet named Punch fights with his wife Judy

punch bag *noun, pl* ~ **bags** [*count*] *Brit* **:** PUNCHING BAG

punch bowl *noun, pl* ~ **bowls** [*count*] **:** a large bowl from which punch is served at a party

punch card *noun, pl* ~ **cards** [*count*] **:** a card with holes that have been punched in different positions to represent information ▪ old-fashioned computer *punch cards* — called also *punched card*

punch–drunk /ˈpʌntʃˌdrʌŋk/ *adj* [*more* ~; *most* ~]
1 *of a boxer* **:** confused and unable to speak or move normally because of being punched many times in the head ▪ *punch-drunk* fighters
2 *informal* **:** unable to think or act normally because you are very tired, excited, etc. ▪ By the time we arrived home, we were *punch-drunk* [=*dazed*] with fatigue.

punching bag *noun, pl* ~ **bags** [*count*] *US* **:** a very heavy bag that usually hangs from the ceiling and that is punched for exercise or training — often used figuratively to describe someone who is often criticized, hit, or defeated by another person ▪ I'm tired of being your *punching bag*. — called also (*Brit*) *punch bag*

punch line *noun, pl* ~ **lines** [*count*] **:** the words at the end of a joke or story that make it funny, surprising, etc. ▪ She didn't understand the *punch line*.

punch–up /ˈpʌntʃˌʌp/ *noun, pl* **-ups** [*count*] *Brit, informal* **:** a fight in which people punch each other

punchy /ˈpʌntʃi/ *adj* **punch·i·er; -est** *informal*
1 : very exciting or lively ▪ *punchy* colors ▪ a *punchy* tune ▪ *punchy* dialogue ▪ shrimp in a *punchy* sauce
2 *US* **:** PUNCH-DRUNK ▪ a *punchy* ex-fighter ▪ She was *punchy* with fatigue.

punc·til·i·ous /ˌpʌŋkˈtɪlijəs/ *adj* [*more* ~; *most* ~] *formal* **:** very careful about behaving properly and doing things in a correct and accurate way ▪ She's very *punctilious* about grammar. ▪ a *punctilious* [=*meticulous*] caretaker
– punc·til·i·ous·ly *adv* ▪ They do their jobs *punctiliously*. **– punc·til·i·ous·ness** *noun* [*noncount*]

punc·tu·al /ˈpʌŋktʃəwəl/ *adj* [*more* ~; *most* ~] **:** arriving or doing something at the expected or planned time ▪ The trains were *punctual*. ▪ a *punctual* employee
– punc·tu·al·i·ty /ˌpʌŋktʃəˈwæləti/ *noun* [*noncount*] ▪ Workers received bonuses for *punctuality*. **– punc·tu·al·ly** *adv* ▪ She arrived *punctually* at 7:00.

punc·tu·ate /ˈpʌŋktʃəˌweɪt/ *verb* **-ates; -at·ed; -at·ing** [+ *obj*]
1 : to use punctuation marks in (a piece of writing) ▪ Do you know how to *punctuate* a sentence correctly? ▪ an improperly *punctuated* sentence
2 : to interrupt or occur in (something) repeatedly — usually used as *(be) punctuated* ▪ Her speech *was punctuated* by frequent applause.

punc·tu·a·tion /ˌpʌŋktʃəˈweɪʃən/ *noun* [*noncount*] **:** the marks (such as periods and commas) in a piece of writing that make its meaning clear and that separate it into sentences, clauses, etc. ▪ grammar, *punctuation*, and spelling

punctuation mark *noun, pl* ~ **marks** [*count*] **:** any one of the marks (such as a period, comma, or question mark) used to divide a piece of writing into sentences, clauses, etc.

¹punc·ture /ˈpʌŋktʃə/ *noun, pl* **-tures** [*count*]
1 : a hole or wound made by a sharp point ▪ a slight *puncture* of the skin
2 : a small hole in a tire that causes it to lose air ▪ I got/had a *puncture* [=(*US*) *flat, flat tire*] on the way to the airport.

²puncture *verb* **-tures; -tured; -tur·ing**
1 : to make a hole in (something) with a sharp point [+ *obj*] A nail *punctured* the tire. = The tire was *punctured* by a nail. [*no obj*] Worn tires *puncture* easily.
2 [+ *obj*] **:** to weaken, damage, or destroy (something, such as an argument or a person's feelings, pride, etc.) suddenly or in a way that causes surprise or embarrassment ▪ *puncture* an argument ▪ Their criticism *punctured* [=*hurt, wounded*] his self-esteem.
3 [+ *obj*] *of a sound* **:** to interrupt (silence) in a sudden and unexpected way ▪ The silence was *punctured* [=*broken, shattered*] by her cry.
– punctured *adj* ▪ a *punctured* [=*perforated*] eardrum ▪ *punctured* tires

pun·dit /ˈpʌndət/ *noun, pl* **-dits** [*count*] **:** a person who knows a lot about a particular subject and who expresses ideas and opinions about that subject publicly (such as by speaking on television and radio shows) ▪ political *pundits* ▪ a television *pundit*

pun·gent /ˈpʌnʤənt/ *adj* [*more* ~; *most* ~]

1 : having a strong, sharp taste or smell ▪ a *pungent* herb ▪ a *pungent* aroma/odor ▪ a *pungent* sauce
2 : having a strong effect on the mind because of being clever and direct ▪ a play with *pungent* dialogue ▪ a *pungent* satire of/on current politics
– pun·gen·cy /ˈpʌnʤənsi/ *noun* [*noncount*] ▪ The delightful *pungency* of Thai, Indian, and Mexican food comes from chili peppers and spices. **– pun·gent·ly** *adv* ▪ a *pungently* sweet aroma

pun·ish /ˈpʌnɪʃ/ *verb* **-ish·es; -ished; -ish·ing** [+ *obj*]
1 a : to make (someone) suffer for a crime or for bad behavior ▪ I think that murderers should be *punished* by/with life imprisonment. ▪ She was *punished* for lying. ▪ His parents *punished* him by taking away his allowance. **b :** to make someone suffer for (a crime or bad behavior) ▪ How should I *punish* my child's misbehavior? ▪ State law *punishes* fraud with fines. ▪ The law states that treason shall be *punished* by death. [=that the punishment for treason is death]
2 : to treat (someone or something) severely or roughly ▪ I don't understand why women continue to *punish* [=*damage*] their feet by wearing high-heeled shoes.

pun·ish·able /ˈpʌnɪʃəbəl/ *adj* **:** able to be punished **:** calling for or deserving punishment ▪ Jaywalking is a *punishable* offense in this city. ▪ a crime *punishable* by death [=a crime that has death as a possible punishment]

punishing *adj* [*more* ~; *most* ~] **:** very harsh, difficult, or extreme ▪ Few people can handle Antarctica's *punishing* cold. ▪ She had a *punishing* schedule of six classes last semester.

pun·ish·ment /ˈpʌnɪʃmənt/ *noun, pl* **-ments**
1 : the act of punishing someone or a way of punishing someone [*count*] I took away my daughter's car keys as a *punishment* for her bad behavior. ▪ The *punishments* that the government has inflicted/imposed on the protesters are severe and unjust. ▪ The *punishment* for murder is life imprisonment. [*noncount*] I took away my daughter's car keys as (a form of) *punishment* for her bad behavior. ▪ ***cruel and unusual punishment*** [=punishment that is very painful or harsh or that is too severe for a particular crime] — see also CAPITAL PUNISHMENT, CORPORAL PUNISHMENT
2 [*noncount*] **:** the state of being punished ▪ Some religions teach that wicked people will suffer eternal *punishment* in hell after they die.
3 [*noncount*] **:** rough physical treatment ▪ These hiking boots are tough enough to take any amount of *punishment*. [=the boots will not be ruined even if they are used very roughly] ▪ He keeps playing football despite all his injuries. I guess he's a ***glutton/sucker for punishment***. [=he is attracted to pain, suffering, difficulty, etc.]

pu·ni·tive /ˈpju:nətɪv/ *adj*
1 : intended to punish someone or something ▪ The federal government will take *punitive* action against the company that polluted the river. ▪ *punitive* measures ▪ The plaintiff will receive $50,000 in compensatory damages and $300,000 in ***punitive damages***. [=money that someone is ordered to pay as a punishment for causing harm]
2 [*more* ~; *most* ~] **:** extremely or unfairly severe or high ▪ Lobbyists complain that the bill would impose ***punitive taxes*** on the industry.
– pu·ni·tive·ly *adv*

punk /ˈpʌŋk/ *noun, pl* **punks**
1 [*count*] *US, informal + disapproving* **:** a rude and violent young man ▪ Why can't the police do more to get the *punks* off our streets?
2 [*noncount*] **a :** a kind of loud and intense rock music that was most popular from the late 1970s to the early 1980s — often used before another noun ▪ a *punk* musician ▪ a *punk* band — called also *punk rock* **b** [*count*] **:** a person who plays punk rock or who is a fan of punk rock — called also *punk rocker*

pun·net /ˈpʌnət/ *noun, pl* **-nets** [*count*] *Brit* **:** a small box that is used to hold soft fruits (such as strawberries and blueberries)

[1]punt /ˈpʌnt/ *verb* **punts; punt·ed; punt·ing**
1 *sports* **:** to drop a ball and kick it before it touches the ground in sports like American football and rugby [+ *obj*] The kicker *punted* the ball 40 yards. [*no obj*] They *punted* from midfield.
2 *US, informal* **:** to avoid dealing with a problem or answering a question [*no obj*] The legislature has *punted* on important issues like health-care funding and tax reform. [+ *obj*] The judges are *punting* the decision to Congress. [=the judges are not making the decision themselves and are saying that Congress should decide]
– compare [4]PUNT

[2]punt *noun, pl* **punts** [*count*] *sports* **:** a kick made by dropping a ball and kicking it before it touches the ground **:** the act of punting a ball in sports like American football and rugby ▪ a 40-yard *punt* — compare [3]PUNT, [5]PUNT, [6]PUNT

[3]punt *noun, pl* **punts** [*count*] **:** a long, thin boat with a flat bottom and square ends that is moved by pushing a long pole against the bottom of a river, canal, etc. — compare [2]PUNT, [5]PUNT, [6]PUNT

[4]punt *verb* **punts; punt·ed; punt·ing** [*no obj*] *chiefly Brit* **:** to go on a river, canal, etc. in a long, thin boat (called a punt) ▪ Do you want to ***go punting*** tomorrow? — compare [1]PUNT

[5]punt /ˈpʊnt/ *noun, pl* **punts** [*count*] **:** the basic unit of money used in the Republic of Ireland before the euro — compare [2]PUNT, [3]PUNT, [6]PUNT

[6]punt /ˈpʌnt/ *noun, pl* **punts** [*count*] *Brit, informal* **:** [1]BET 1 ▪ Maybe I'll take a *punt* on that horse. [=maybe I'll make/place a bet on that horse] — compare [2]PUNT, [3]PUNT, [5]PUNT

punt·er /ˈpʌntɚ/ *noun, pl* **-ters** [*count*]
1 *American football* **:** a player whose job is to punt the ball ▪ He was one of the greatest *punters* in NFL history.
2 *Brit, informal* **:** someone who makes a bet **:** BETTOR
3 *Brit, informal* **:** CUSTOMER ▪ Effective marketing means getting the *punters* to buy what you want them to buy. ▪ The sale attracted more than 1,000 *punters*.
4 *chiefly Brit* **:** a person who goes on a river, canal, etc., in a long, thin boat (called a punt)

pu·ny /ˈpju:ni/ *adj* **pu·ni·er; -est** *somewhat informal*
1 : small and weak ▪ a *puny* little guy ▪ I wouldn't mess with him—he makes bodybuilders look *puny* in comparison.
2 : not very large, impressive, or effective ▪ *puny* weapons ▪ a *puny* little car ▪ We laughed at their *puny* attempt to trick us.

pup /ˈpʌp/ *noun, pl* **pups** [*count*] **:** a young dog **:** PUPPY ▪ a cute little *pup*; *also* **:** one of the young of various animals other than dogs ▪ seal *pups*
buy/sell a pup *Brit, informal + old-fashioned* ◊ To *buy a pup* means to pay too much money for something or to buy something that is worthless. To *sell (someone) a pup* means to trick someone into paying too much for something or into buying something that is worthless.

pu·pa /ˈpju:pə/ *noun, pl* **pu·pae** /ˈpju:ˌpi:/ [*count*] *biology* **:** an insect that is in the stage of development between larva and adult
– pu·pal /ˈpju:pəl/ *adj, always used before a noun* ▪ the *pupal* stage of an insect's life

pu·pate /ˈpju:ˌpeɪt/ *verb* **-pates; -pat·ed; -pat·ing** [*no obj*] *biology* **:** to become a pupa ▪ Unlike most butterflies, this species *pupates* underground.

[1]pu·pil /ˈpju:pəl/ *noun, pl* **-pils** [*count*]
1 : a child or young person who is being taught **:** STUDENT ▪ There are 22 *pupils* in the kindergarten class.
2 : someone who is taught especially artistic or musical skills by a usually famous person **:** DISCIPLE ▪ a painting by a *pupil* of Rubens ▪ Both Rimsky-Korsakov and his *pupil* Stravinsky are renowned composers of classical music. ▪ Aristotle was Plato's most brilliant *pupil*.
– compare [2]PUPIL

[2]pupil *noun, pl* **-pils** [*count*] **:** the small, black, round area at the center of the eye — see picture at EYE — compare [1]PUPIL

pup·pet /ˈpʌpət/ *noun, pl* **-pets** [*count*]
1 : a doll that is moved by putting your hand inside it or by pulling strings or wires that are attached to it
2 : a person or an organization that is controlled by another person or organization ▪ a dictator who was perceived as being an American *puppet* ▪ a ***puppet regime*** [=a government controlled by the government of another country]

puppet

pup·pe·teer /ˌpʌpəˈtiɚ/ *noun, pl* **-teers** [*count*] **:** a person who uses puppets in performances to entertain people

pup·pet·ry /ˈpʌpətri/ *noun* [*noncount*] **:** the skill or activity of using puppets in performances

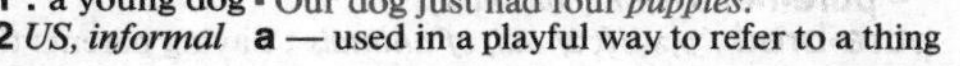

pup·py /ˈpʌpi/ *noun, pl* **-pies** [*count*]
1 : a young dog ▪ Our dog just had four *puppies*.
2 *US, informal* **a** — used in a playful way to refer to a thing

▪ Why isn't the grill on? Fire that *puppy* up! [=turn on the grill] ▪ This is a big program. You'll need a lot of RAM to run this *puppy* on your computer. **b** — used in a playful way to refer to a person ▪ If they thought the new mayor would be easy to bribe, they picked the wrong *puppy*. [=the wrong guy] ▪ That guy is ***one sick puppy***. [=that guy is crazy, cruel, or disgusting] ▪ I was ***one tired puppy*** [=I was very tired] after a long day of hiking.

puppy fat *noun* [*noncount*] *Brit* : BABY FAT

puppy love *noun* [*noncount*] : romantic love that is felt by a child or teenager and that is not considered by adults to be real love

pup tent *noun, pl* **~ tents** [*count*] *US* : a small tent for usually two people

[1]**pur·chase** /ˈpɚtʃəs/ *verb* **-chas·es; -chased; -chas·ing** [+ *obj*] *formal* : to buy (property, goods, etc.) : to get (something) by paying money for it ▪ *purchase* a house ▪ He *purchased* a new suit for a hundred dollars. ▪ Souvenirs can be *purchased* at the gift shop. = You can *purchase* souvenirs at the gift shop.

— **pur·chas·er** *noun, pl* **-ers** [*count*] — **purchasing** *adj, always used before a noun* ▪ *purchasing* agents ▪ the company's ***purchasing department*** [=the people in a company who buy the company's supplies]

[2]**purchase** *noun, pl* **-chases**

1 : an act of buying something [*count*] credit card *purchases* ▪ cash *purchases* [*noncount*] The CD player is guaranteed for one year from the date of *purchase*. ▪ Getting a rebate requires ***proof of purchase***. [=something, such as a receipt, that proves that you bought something]

2 [*count*] : something that is bought ▪ The car was an expensive *purchase*. ▪ He displayed his recent *purchases* with pride.

3 : a firm hold or grip that makes movement possible [*singular*] The ice made it impossible for the car's wheels to ***gain/get a purchase*** on the road. [*noncount*] The surface was so slick that the wheels couldn't *gain purchase*. — sometimes used figuratively ▪ I couldn't *get a purchase* on the problem. [=I couldn't get a good understanding of the problem]

purchase order *noun, pl* **~ -ders** [*count*] : a formal document that is used by an employee to request that something be purchased by a company

purchase price *noun, pl* **~ prices** [*count*] : the amount of money someone pays for something (such as a house)

purchasing power *noun* [*noncount*]

1 : the amount of money that a person or group has available to spend ▪ Inflation decreases consumer *purchasing power*. — called also *buying power*

2 : the value of money thought of as how much it can buy ▪ a decline in the *purchasing power* of the dollar

pur·dah /ˈpɚdə/ *noun* [*noncount*] : a custom among Muslims and some Hindus in which women stay separate from men or keep their faces and bodies covered when they are near men ▪ Most of the women ***keep purdah***. [=live according to the rules of purdah]

pure /ˈpjɚ/ *adj* **pur·er; -est** [*also more ~; most ~*]

1 : not mixed with anything else ▪ *pure* gold/silver ▪ *pure* silk/cotton/wool/cashmere ▪ *pure* orange juice ▪ *pure* honey ▪ *pure* maple syrup ▪ *pure* olive oil ▪ *pure* white ▪ I was acting on *pure* intuition/instinct. [=only because of intuition/instinct and not for any other reason]

2 : clean and not harmful in any way ▪ The company bottles only the *purest* water. ▪ *pure* mountain air

3 : having a smooth and clear sound that is not mixed with any other sounds ▪ the *pure* notes of the flute

4 *always used before a noun* : COMPLETE, TOTAL — used for emphasis ▪ *pure* [=*utter*] nonsense/folly/fantasy ▪ *pure* joy/delight ▪ *pure* evil ▪ It was *pure* coincidence/chance/luck that we met. ▪ The story was *pure* fiction.

5 : morally good : free from sexual or evil thoughts ▪ a *pure* and upright man ▪ a *pure* heart ▪ *pure* intentions ▪ Don't expect me to believe you're ***(as) pure as the driven snow***. [=morally perfect]

6 *always used before a noun* : relating to theory and knowledge rather than to the practical uses of something ▪ the *pure* sciences ▪ *pure* mathematics

7 : PUREBRED ▪ a *pure* Arabian horse ▪ a *pure* breed of cattle

pure and simple : with nothing other than what has been mentioned — used after a noun or phrase to add emphasis ▪ It was fraud, *pure and simple*. ▪ The relationship is over, *pure and simple*. [=the relationship is completely over]

— **pure·ness** *noun* [*noncount*]

pure·bred /ˈpjɚˌbrɛd/ *adj, of animals* : having parents that are of the same breed ▪ *purebred* cattle ▪ a *purebred* horse

— **purebred** *noun, pl* **-breds** [*count*] ▪ The dog is not a *purebred*.

[1]**pu·ree** *or* **pu·rée** /pjʊˈreɪ, *Brit* ˈpjʊəreɪ/ *noun, pl* **-rees** : a thick liquid made by crushing usually cooked food (such as fruits or vegetables) [*noncount*] a spoonful of apple *puree* [*count*] a *puree* of sweet potatoes and carrots ▪ vegetable/fruit *purees*

[2]**puree** *or* **purée** *verb* **-rees; -reed; -ree·ing** [+ *obj*] : to crush (food) until it is a thick liquid : to make a puree of (food) ▪ She used a blender to *puree* the soup.

— **pureed** *or* **puréed** *adj* ▪ *pureed* carrots/vegetables ▪ a sauce made with *pureed* berries/beans

pure·ly /ˈpjɚli/ *adv* : completely or only ▪ They met *purely* by accident/coincidence. ▪ a selection based *purely* on merit ▪ He reads *purely* [=*simply, merely*] for enjoyment. [=he reads only because he enjoys reading] ▪ The organization's mission, ***purely and simply***, is to provide food to people who need it. ▪ It was *purely and simply* a matter of greed.

pur·ga·tive /ˈpɚgətɪv/ *noun, pl* **-tives** [*count*] *medical* : a medicine or food that causes the bowels to empty

pur·ga·to·ry /ˈpɚgəˌtori, *Brit* ˈpɜːgətri/ *noun, pl* **-ries**

1 ***Purgatory*** [*singular*] : a state after death according to Roman Catholic belief in which the souls of people who die are made pure through suffering before going to heaven

2 : a place or state of suffering [*noncount*] the *purgatory* of drug abuse [*count*] The marathons were jokingly referred to as one-day *purgatories*.

[1]**purge** /ˈpɚʤ/ *verb* **purg·es; purged; purg·ing** [+ *obj*]

1 : to remove people from an area, country, organization, etc., often in a violent and sudden way ▪ *purge* a country of an ethnic group = *purge* an ethnic group from a country ▪ High-ranking officials were *purged* from the company following the merger.

2 : to cause something to leave the body ▪ medicines that *purge* the body of toxins = medicines that *purge* toxins from the body

binge and purge see [2]BINGE

purge yourself : to free yourself of something (such as a bad feeling or memory) ▪ He *purged himself* of his old fears. [=he got rid of his old fears; he overcame his old fears]

[2]**purge** *noun, pl* **purges** [*count*] : the often violent and sudden removal of people from an area, country, organization, etc. ▪ Stalin's *purges* ▪ brutal postwar *purges* ▪ a corporate *purge*

pu·ri·fi·er /ˈpjɚrəˌfajɚ/ *noun, pl* **-ers** [*count*] : a device that is used for removing dirty or harmful substances ▪ We installed a water/air *purifier* in our home.

pu·ri·fy /ˈpjɚrəˌfaɪ/ *verb* **-fies; -fied; -fy·ing** [+ *obj*] : to make (something or someone) pure: such as **a** : to remove dirty or harmful substances from (something) ▪ We *purified* the water by boiling it. ▪ You can *purify* the air with a filtration system. ▪ a bottle of *purified* water **b** : to free (someone) from guilt or evil thoughts ▪ *purify* the mind/soul ▪ She believed she could *purify* herself through constant prayer.

— **pu·ri·fi·ca·tion** /ˌpjɚrəfəˈkeɪʃən/ *noun* [*noncount*] ▪ air/water *purification* ▪ the *purification* of souls

pur·ist /ˈpjɚrɪst/ *noun, pl* **-ists** [*count*] : a person who has very strong ideas about what is correct or acceptable and who usually opposes changes to traditional methods and practices ▪ jazz/music *purists* ▪ a *purist* who only drinks European wines ▪ a grammatical *purist*

— **pur·ism** /ˈpjɚˌɪzəm/ *noun* [*noncount*]

pu·ri·tan /ˈpjɚrətən/ *noun, pl* **-tans** [*count*]

1 ***Puritan*** : a member of a Protestant group in England and New England in the 16th and 17th centuries that opposed many customs of the Church of England

2 : a person who follows strict moral rules and who believes that pleasure is wrong ▪ moral *puritans* ▪ She's a *puritan* about sex.

— **Puritan** *adj* ▪ *Puritan* values/traditions/attitudes ▪ a *Puritan* influence ▪ the *Puritan* work ethic

pu·ri·tan·i·cal /ˌpjɚrəˈtænɪkəl/ *adj* [*more ~; most ~*] *disapproving* : very strict especially concerning morals and religion ▪ *puritanical* rules ▪ *puritanical* attitudes about sex

pu·ri·tan·ism /ˈpjɚrətənˌɪzəm/ *noun* [*noncount*]

1 ***Puritanism*** : the beliefs and practices of Puritans

2 *often disapproving* : the beliefs and practices of people who follow very strict moral and religious rules about the proper way to behave and live ▪ moral *puritanism*

pu·ri·ty /ˈpjɚrəti/ *noun* [*noncount*] : the quality or state of being pure: such as **a** : lack of dirty or harmful substances ▪

P

water *purity* **b :** lack of guilt or evil thoughts ▪ moral/religious/sexual *purity*

purl /ˈpɚl/ *noun* [*noncount*] **:** a stitch used in knitting — usually used before another noun ▪ a *purl* stitch

– purl *verb* **purls; purled; purl·ing** [+ *obj*] ▪ *Purl* two stitches. [*no obj*] *Purl* across the row.

pur·lieu /ˈpɚlˌjuː/ *noun, pl* **-lieus** [*count*] *formal* **:** the area surrounding a place — usually plural ▪ the *purlieus* of the old fortress

pur·loin /pɚˈlɔɪn/ *verb* **-loins; -loined; -loin·ing** [+ *obj*] *formal + humorous* **:** to take (something that belongs to someone else) **:** STEAL ▪ He managed to *purloin* [=*filch*] a bottle of whiskey when no one was looking.

– purloined *adj* ▪ *purloined* [=*stolen*] love letters

[1]**pur·ple** /ˈpɚpəl/ *noun, pl* **pur·ples** [*count, noncount*] **:** a color that is between red and blue — see color picture on page C1

[2]**purple** *adj* **pur·pler; pur·plest**

1 : of the color purple ▪ *purple* grapes/tulips

2 *disapproving* **:** using many fancy words ▪ The book contains a few *purple* passages. ▪ Her writing was full of ***purple prose***.

Purple Heart *noun, pl* **~ Hearts** [*count*] **:** a U.S. military award that is given to a soldier who is wounded or killed in battle

purple patch *noun* [*singular*] *Brit, informal* **:** a period of good luck or success ▪ The team enjoyed a *purple patch* in the first half.

pur·plish /ˈpɚpəlɪʃ/ *adj* [*more ~; most ~*] **:** somewhat purple ▪ a *purplish* blue

[1]**pur·port** /ˈpɚˌpoɚt/ *noun* [*noncount*] *formal* **:** the main or general meaning of something (such as a speech or a person's actions) ▪ the *purport* of the book/visit ▪ The letter was not read aloud, but all present were informed of its *purport*.

[2]**pur·port** /pɚˈpoɚt/ *verb* **-ports; -port·ed; -port·ing** [+ *obj*] **:** to claim to be or do a particular thing when this claim may not be true — followed by *to + verb* ▪ The report *purports to be* objective. [=it claims to be objective, but it may not be] ▪ The program *purports to meet* the needs of gifted students. ▪ The survey does not *purport to be* conclusive.

pur·port·ed /pɚˈpoɚtəd/ *adj, always used before a noun* **:** said to be true or real but not definitely true or real ▪ the *purported* [=*alleged*] crime ▪ the *purported* value of the estate

– pur·port·ed·ly *adv* ▪ diaries *purportedly* [=*supposedly*] written by a famous author

pur·pose /ˈpɚpəs/ *noun, pl* **-pos·es**

1 [*count*] **:** the reason why something is done or used **:** the aim or intention of something ▪ The *purpose* of the new resort is to attract more tourists. ▪ There's little/no *purpose* in restarting the process. [=there is little/no reason to start the process again] ▪ These ancient mounds were probably used for ceremonial *purposes*. [=were probably used in ceremonies] ▪ Please keep a record of your receipts for tax/business *purposes*. [=for situations involving taxes/business] ▪ Everything on the boat ***serves a purpose***. [=everything has a particular use or function] ▪ The loans are small but they ***serve a good purpose***. ▪ We were happy to know that the money was being used ***for a good purpose***. [=for something useful, important, etc.] ▪ She used her skills ***to (no) good purpose***. [=she used her skills in a way that was (not) good or helpful] ▪ Changes had suddenly been made ***for no apparent purpose***. [=for no clear reason] ▪ ***For the purpose(s) of*** this discussion, let's assume that sales will increase next year.

2 [*noncount*] **:** the feeling of being determined to do or achieve something ▪ She wrote with *purpose*. [=she knew exactly what she wanted to write] ▪ Sometimes his life seemed to lack *purpose* or meaning. ▪ He was a man of *purpose*. [=he was very clear about what he wanted to do and how to do it] ▪ We started work again with a renewed ***sense of purpose***. ▪ He showed great ***strength of purpose***. [=he showed that he was very determined to achieve his goals]

3 [*count*] **:** the aim or goal of a person **:** what a person is trying to do, become, etc. ▪ She knew from a young age that her sole *purpose* (in life) was to be a writer. [=she knew that all she wanted (in life) was to be a writer] ▪ We shared a ***common purpose***. [=we had the same goals] ▪ He was searching for ***a higher purpose***. [=a more meaningful reason to live, work, etc.]

for (all) practical purposes see [1]PRACTICAL

on purpose **:** in a way that is planned or intended **:** in a deliberate way ▪ Someone set the fire *on purpose*. [=*purposely, intentionally*] ▪ I knew she hadn't done it *on purpose*.

to/for all intents and purposes see [1]INTENT

to the purpose *old-fashioned* **:** appropriate to the situation ▪ He didn't say much *to the purpose*. [=he didn't say much that was useful or helpful]

pur·pose–built /ˌpɚpəsˈbɪlt/ *adj, Brit* **:** designed and built for a particular use ▪ The art is housed in a *purpose-built* structure that provides a controlled environment.

pur·pose·ful /ˈpɚpəsfəl/ *adj* [*more ~; most ~*] **:** having a clear aim or purpose ▪ *purposeful* activity ▪ a *purposeful* glance/grin

– pur·pose·ful·ly *adv* ▪ She strode *purposefully* to the door and knocked loudly. **– pur·pose·ful·ness** *noun* [*noncount*]

pur·pose·less /ˈpɚpəsləs/ *adj* **:** having or seeming to have no purpose or reason ▪ I have to go to another *purposeless* [=(more commonly) *pointless, useless*] meeting tonight. ▪ *purposeless* suffering

pur·pose·ly /ˈpɚpəsli/ *adv* **:** in a way that is planned or intended **:** in a deliberate way ▪ She *purposely* [=*intentionally*] raised her voice to attract attention.

[1]**purr** /ˈpɚ/ *noun, pl* **purrs** [*count*]

1 : the low, soft sound that a cat makes when it is happy

2 : a sound that is like the purr of a cat ▪ the soft *purr* of a car engine

[2]**purr** *verb* **purrs; purred; purr·ing**

1 [*no obj*] **:** to make a purr or a sound like a purr ▪ The cat was *purring* contentedly in my lap. ▪ The cars were *purring* along the highway. ▪ The engine *purred* smoothly.

2 [+ *obj*] **:** to say (something) in a soft, low voice especially when you are pleased or trying to persuade someone to do something ▪ "You look tense. Let me buy you a drink," he *purred*.

[1]**purse** /ˈpɚs/ *noun, pl* **purs·es**

1 [*count*] **a** *US* **:** a usually leather or cloth bag used by women for carrying money and personal things **:** HANDBAG **b** *chiefly Brit* **:** CHANGE PURSE

2 [*singular*] **:** an amount of money that a person, organization, or government has available to use ▪ Many believe the work should be financed by the ***public purse***. [=should be paid for by the government]

3 [*count*] **:** an amount of money that is offered as a prize in a competition (such as a horse race, a golf tournament, or a boxing match) ▪ a golf tournament with a million dollar *purse*

purse strings ✧ A person, organization, or government that ***holds/controls the purse strings*** makes the decisions about how money is spent. ▪ The museum's board of directors *holds/controls the purse strings*. When a person, organization, or government ***tightens the purse strings***, less money is available for spending. ▪ School administrators are already *tightening (the) purse strings*. When a person, organization, or government ***loosens the purse strings***, more money is available for spending. ▪ Companies are expected to *loosen the purse strings* as the economy improves.

[2]**purse** *verb* **purses; pursed; purs·ing** [+ *obj*] **:** to form (your lips) into a tight circle or line ▪ She *pursed* her lips in concentration. ▪ His lips were tightly *pursed*.

purs·er /ˈpɚsɚ/ *noun, pl* **-ers** [*count*] **:** an officer on a ship whose job is to handle matters relating to money for the passengers and crew and to make sure passengers are comfortable and have what they need

pur·su·ance /pɚˈsuːwəns, *Brit* pəˈsjuːəns/ *noun*

in pursuance of *formal* **:** in order to do (something) or to do what is required by (something) ▪ The changes will be made *in pursuance of* the contract.

pur·su·ant to /pɚˈsuːwənt-, *Brit* pəˈsjuːənt-/ *prep, formal* **:** in a way that agrees with or follows (something) **:** in accordance with (something) ▪ *Pursuant to* the terms of the sale, the owner shall be solely responsible for damages.

pur·sue /pɚˈsuː, *Brit* pəˈsjuː/ *verb* **-sues; -sued; -su·ing** [+ *obj*]

1 : to follow and try to catch or capture (someone or something) for usually a long distance or time ▪ Hounds *pursued* the fox for miles. ▪ The criminal is being *pursued* by police.

2 : to try to get or do (something) over a period of time ▪ He chose to *pursue* a college degree. ▪ She wants to *pursue* a legal career.

3 : to be involved in (an activity) ▪ *pursue* a hobby

4 : to move along (a course) ▪ The ship *pursued* [=*followed*] a northerly course.

5 : to make an effort to find out more about (something) ▪ I'll be meeting with my lawyer to *pursue* this matter further. ▪

My associate is interested in *pursuing* the case.
– **pur·su·er** *noun, pl* **-ers** [*count*] ▪ He changed direction to confuse his *pursuers*.

pur·suit /pɚˈsu:t, *Brit* pəˈsju:t/ *noun, pl* **-suits**
1 [*noncount*] **: the act of pursuing someone or something: such as a : the act of following or chasing someone or something** ▪ The hounds were running in the woods ***in pursuit of*** a fox. ▪ The escaped prisoner ran through the park with the police ***in full pursuit*** [=ran through the park while being chased/pursued by the police] ▪ A car raced past us with the police ***in hot/close pursuit*** [=following very closely behind] **b : an attempt to find, achieve, or get something** — *+ of* ▪ the *pursuit of* excellence/knowledge ▪ the *pursuit of* happiness ▪ the *pursuit of* a college degree ▪ He would do anything ***in pursuit of*** wealth and fame. [=he would do anything to achieve wealth and fame]
2 [*count*] **: an activity that is done for pleasure** ▪ She enjoys reading, knitting, and other quiet *pursuits*.

pu·ru·lent /ˈpjɚrələnt/ *adj, medical* **: containing or producing pus** ▪ a *purulent* wound/discharge
– **pu·ru·lence** /ˈpjɚrələns/ *noun* [*noncount*]

pur·vey /pɚˈveɪ/ *verb* **-veys; -veyed; -vey·ing** [*+ obj*] *formal* **: to make (something, such a product) available : to supply or provide (something) for use** ▪ a shop *purveying* handmade merchandise ▪ *purvey* information

pur·vey·or /pɚˈvejɚ/ *noun, pl* **-ors** [*count*] *formal* **: a person or business that sells or provides something** ▪ a *purveyor* of kitchen supplies ▪ a software *purveyor*

pur·view /ˈpɚˌvju:/ *noun* [*noncount*] *formal* **: an area within which someone or something has authority, influence, or knowledge** ▪ The case is within the court's *purview*. ▪ That question is outside/beyond my *purview*. ▪ The moral dilemmas of the early settlers are beyond the *purview* of this book.

pus /ˈpʌs/ *noun* [*noncount*] *medical* **: a thick, yellowish substance that is produced when a part of the body or a wound becomes infected** ▪ *Pus* oozed from the cat's injured ear.

[1]**push** /ˈpʊʃ/ *verb* **push·es; pushed; push·ing**
1 : to use force to move (someone or something) forward or away from you [*+ obj*] Please stop *pushing* me. ▪ Do you want to *push* the shopping cart? ▪ *Push* [=*press*] the button to turn on the computer. ▪ He slowly *pushed* the door open. ▪ She *pushed* back her chair and stood up. ▪ She *pushed* him aside and marched into the boss's office. ▪ He *pushed* her out of the way. ▪ He *pushed* me into the table. ▪ He was *pushed* off the sidewalk into the street. ▪ She *pushed* her wet hair back/away from her face. ▪ The bulldozer *pushed* the rubble over the edge of the pit. — **often used figuratively** ▪ Larger companies are *pushing* [=*forcing*] smaller ones into bankruptcy. ▪ Poverty *pushed* them to the breaking point. ▪ He ***pushed aside*** [=*put aside*] his fear of rejection and asked her out on a date. ▪ She ***pushed*** her doubts ***to the back of her mind*** = She ***pushed*** her doubts ***out of her mind*** [=she tried not to think about her doubts] [*no obj*] No matter how hard I *pushed*, I couldn't move the boulder. ▪ He *pushed* and pulled to loosen the post from the ground. ▪ She *pushed* against the door, but it wouldn't open.
2 : to go forward while using your hands, arms etc., to forcefully move people or things that are blocking you [*no obj*] Quit (your) ***pushing and shoving*** Can't you see there are a lot of people ahead of you in line? — **often +** ***through*** ▪ The paramedics *pushed through* the crowd. [*+ obj*] They ***pushed their way*** to the front row.
3 [*+ obj*] **a : to force or try to force or persuade (someone) to do something** ▪ He *pushed* his son to play football. ▪ He *pushed* them to accept his plan. ▪ She *pushed* him into trying out for the team. **b : to force (someone) to work hard at something in order to achieve success** ▪ The coach tends to *push* his players too hard. ▪ Her teachers *pushed* her to succeed. ▪ She was tired but she ***pushed herself*** to keep working. **c : to do or say things that cause trouble for (someone)** ▪ He kept *pushing* his parents until they had no choice but to punish him. ▪ If you *push* him too far, you'll regret it.
4 [*no obj*] **a** ***always followed by an adverb or preposition*** **: to continue moving forward in a forceful or steady way** ▪ The explorers *pushed* (along) deep into the jungle. — **usually +** ***ahead, forward,*** **or** ***on*** ▪ The army *pushed* [=*pressed*] *on* in spite of the snow. ▪ They were tired, but they kept *pushing ahead*. **b : to continue to do something especially in a determined way** ▪ If we want to succeed, we have to keep *pushing*. — **usually +** ***ahead, forward,*** **or** ***on*** ▪ The city *pushed* [=*pressed*] *ahead/forward* with its plans to build a casino. ▪ They *pushed on* with their plans.
5 ***always followed by an adverb or preposition*** [*+ obj*] **: to force (someone or something) to move away from a place** ▪ The troops *pushed* the enemy from the city. ▪ Settlers *pushed* the native people off their land.
6 [*+ obj*] **: to cause (something) to be accepted, completed, etc., by making a special effort** ▪ The senators are trying to *push* the bill through Congress. ▪ All of the editorial staff helped to *push* the project to completion.
7 [*no obj*] **: to make a strong, continuous effort to get or do something — often +** ***for*** ▪ The workers are *pushing* hard *for* higher wages. — **often followed by** ***to + verb*** ▪ Town residents are *pushing to prevent* the shopping mall from being built.
8 [*+ obj*] **a : to make a strong effort to sell (something)** ▪ We're *pushing* last year's models to make room for this year's. **b : to try to make (something) more popular, well-known, etc., by talking about it** ▪ He went on the talk show to *push* [=*promote*] his new film. **c : to repeat (something) in order to show that it is important** ▪ They kept *pushing* [=*pressing*] the issue. ▪ We need to get them to do something, but we don't want to ***push the point*** too much.
9 [*+ obj*] *informal* **: to sell (illegal drugs)** ▪ He was arrested for *pushing* drugs.
10 [*+ obj*] **a : to go up to and often beyond (a limit)** ▪ His humor *pushes* the limits of bad taste. ▪ She is always *pushing* her body's limits with new physical challenges. **b** *informal* **: to get close to (an age or number) — always used as** ***(be) pushing*** ▪ She must *be pushing* 80. [=she must be almost 80 years old] ▪ The game was played in front of a crowd *pushing* 50,000. [=a crowd of almost 50,000 people]
11 ***always followed by an adverb or preposition*** [*+ obj*] **: to cause or force (something) to change in a specified way** ▪ The cost of oil has *pushed* gas prices higher/up. [=has raised gas prices] ▪ Stock prices have been *pushed* down. [=have been lowered] ▪ Gas prices have been *pushed* [=*raised*] to record levels.
12 [*+ obj*] *sports* **: to hit (a ball) toward the right from a right-handed swing or toward the left from a left-handed swing** ▪ (*golf*) She *pushed* her drive into the rough. — **compare** PULL

be pushing up daisies see DAISY

push around *also Brit* ***push about*** [*phrasal verb*] ***push (someone) around/about*** **: to try to force (someone) to do what you want by making threats, using force, etc.** ▪ Don't let the bigger boys *push* you *around*—stand up for yourself!

push back [*phrasal verb*] ***push back (something) or push (something) back*** **: to change (a planned event) to start at a later date or time** ▪ The date of the meeting has been *pushed back* from Tuesday to Thursday. ▪ The start time of the game has been *pushed back* from 1 p.m. to 3 p.m.

push in [*phrasal verb*] *Brit* **: to move in front of other people who are waiting in a line** ▪ He *pushed in* at the head of the queue. [=(*US*) he cut in at the head of the line]

push it/things *informal* **: to continue to do or to try to do something when you should stop** ▪ If your mom already said "no" two times, don't *push it*. [=don't keep asking her] You'll just make her mad. ▪ You've won a lot of money, but don't *push it* [=don't push your luck] or you could lose it all. ▪ She *pushed things* too far and lost all her winnings.

push off [*phrasal verb*] **1 : to move from a place or position by pushing against a surface with something** ▪ She *pushed off* (from shore) with her oar and started paddling. ▪ His ankle injury prevented him from *pushing off* with his left foot when he was skating. **2** *Brit, informal* **: to go away : LEAVE — used in speech as a rude or angry way of telling someone to go away** ▪ *Push off* [=*get lost*], mate.

push on [*phrasal verb*] ***push (something) on (someone)*** **: to force (someone) to accept (something)** ▪ He's always trying to *push* his political beliefs *on* other people. — **see also** [1]PUSH 4 (above)

push over [*phrasal verb*] **1** ***push over (someone or something) or push (someone or something) over*** **: to make (someone or something) fall to the ground by pushing** ▪ He *pushed* the smaller child *over*. ▪ She *pushed over* the statue. **2** *US, informal* **: to move so that there is room for someone else to sit or stand next to you** ▪ *Push over* [=*shove over*] so that I can sit down, too.

push paper(s) see [1]PAPER
push the envelope see ENVELOPE
push your luck see [1]LUCK

[2]**push** *noun, pl* **pushes** [*count*]
1 : an act of pushing something or someone — usually singular ▪ He gave me a *push*. [=he pushed me] ▪ Give the door a *push* to open it. ▪ The computer starts with the ***push of a but-***

ton. • At the *push of a button*, you can change a color photo into a black-and-white one.

2 : a large, organized military attack — usually singular • They're making a final *push* against enemy forces. • The army has launched a *push* toward the capital. — often used figuratively • The company is making a *push* into foreign markets. [=the company is entering foreign markets]

3 : a strong, continuous effort to get or achieve something — usually singular • Despite a multimillion dollar marketing *push*, the movie flopped. — often + *for* • Workers are making a determined *push for* higher wages. — often followed by *to* + *verb* • a *push to improve* public schools

at a push *Brit, informal* : with some difficulty : by making a special effort • We can fit five people in the car, six *at a push*.

get the push *Brit, informal* : to lose your job : to be fired from your job • The employees with less experience *got the push*. [=were fired; *got the ax*]

give (someone) the push *Brit, informal* : to dismiss (someone) from a job : to fire (someone) • His boss *gave him the push*. [=*gave him the ax*]

push comes to shove *informal* — used to describe what happens when a situation becomes very serious or difficult and action needs to be taken • He backed down ***when push came to shove***. • He'll surrender ***if push comes to shove***.

push–bike /ˈpʊʃˌbaɪk/ *noun, pl* **-bikes** [*count*] *Brit, old-fashioned* : BICYCLE

push button *noun, pl* ~ **-tons** [*count*] : a small button or knob that is pushed to operate a machine
– **push–button** *adj, always used before a noun* • a *push-button* phone

push·cart /ˈpʊʃˌkaɚt/ *noun, pl* **-carts** [*count*] *US* : a cart that is pushed by a person — used especially to describe a cart that is used for selling something outdoors • selling fruits and vegetables from a *pushcart*

push button

push·chair /ˈpʊʃˌʧeɚ/ *noun, pl* **-chairs** [*count*] *Brit* : STROLLER 1

pushed *adj, not used before a noun, Brit, informal*

1 — used to say that it is difficult to do something • You'd be (hard) *pushed* [=*hard-pressed*] to find a better place to spend your holiday.

2 : lacking something that is needed or desired : PRESSED — usually + *for* • I am really *pushed for* time/money right now.

3 : busy or active • We've been a bit *pushed* lately.

push·er /ˈpʊʃɚ/ *noun, pl* **-ers** [*count*] : someone who sells illegal drugs • junkies and *pushers* • a drug *pusher* — see also PAPER PUSHER, PEN PUSHER

push·over /ˈpʊʃˌoʊvɚ/ *noun, pl* **-overs** [*count*] *informal*

1 : an opponent that is easy to defeat • They thought the first team they played would be a *pushover*.

2 : something that is easy to do • The exam was a *pushover*.

3 : someone who is easy to persuade or influence • Dad's a *pushover*. He'll let me do anything I want.

4 : someone who is unable to resist the attraction or appeal of something : SUCKER — usually + *for* • I'm a *pushover for* guys with big muscles. • He's a *pushover for* kung fu movies.

push·pin /ˈpʊʃˌpɪn/ *noun, pl* **-pins** [*count*] *US* : a short pin that has a large head and that is used to attach things (such as papers or photographs) to a wall or bulletin board — see picture at OFFICE; compare THUMBTACK

push–up /ˈpʊʃˌʌp/ *noun, pl* **-ups** [*count*] *chiefly US* : an exercise in which you lay on your stomach and raise and lower your body by straightening and bending your arms — called also (*Brit*) *press-up*

pushy /ˈpʊʃi/ *adj* **push·i·er; -est** [*also more* ~; *most* ~] *disapproving* : using forceful methods to make others do what you want them to do : aggressive and rude • a *pushy* salesperson
– **push·i·ness** /ˈpʊʃinəs/ *noun* [*noncount*]

pu·sil·lan·i·mous /ˌpjuːsəˈlænəməs/ *adj* [*more* ~; *most* ~] *formal* : weak and afraid of danger : COWARDLY • a *pusillanimous* leader

[1]**puss** /ˈpʊs/ *noun, pl* **puss·es** [*count*] *informal* : FACE • I felt like smacking him right in the *puss*. [=like punching him right in the face] — see also SOURPUSS — compare [2]PUSS

[2]**puss** *noun* [*singular*] *Brit, informal* : a cat or kitten • Come here, *puss*. [=(*US*) *kitty*] — compare [1]PUSS

[1]**pussy** /ˈpʊsi/ *noun, pl* **puss·ies** [*count*] *informal* : a cat or kitten : PUSSYCAT — used especially by children or when talking to children — compare [2]PUSSY, [3]PUSSY

[2]**pus·sy** /ˈpʊsi/ *noun, pl* **pus·sies** [*count*] *informal* + *offensive* : a woman's sex organs; *also* : sexual intercourse with a woman ✧ These uses of *pussy* are very offensive and should be avoided. — compare [1]PUSSY, [3]PUSSY

[3]**pus·sy** /ˈpʊsi/ *noun, pl* **pus·sies** [*count*] *chiefly US, informal* + *impolite* : a weak and cowardly man : SISSY • He got into a fight when someone called him a *pussy*. — compare [1]PUSSY, [2]PUSSY

pussy·cat /ˈpʊsiˌkæt/ *noun, pl* **-cats** [*count*] *informal*

1 : a cat or kitten — used especially by children or when talking to children • Look at the cute little *pussycat*!

2 : a person who has a kind and gentle nature • He looks tough, but he's really a *pussycat*.

pussy·foot /ˈpʊsiˌfʊt/ *verb* **-foots; -foot·ed; -foot·ing** [*no obj*] *informal* + *disapproving* : to avoid making a definite decision or stating a definite opinion because of fear, doubt, etc. • He should stop *pussyfooting* and tell us what he wants to do. — often + *around* • He's been *pussyfooting around* for months because he's afraid of offending anyone.

pussy willow *noun, pl* ~ **-lows** [*count*] : a small tree with large, soft flowers; *also* : the flower of this tree

pus·tule /ˈpʌsˌʧuːl/ *noun, pl* **-tules** [*count*] *medical* : a small bump on the skin that contains or produces pus

[1]**put** /ˈpʊt/ *verb* **puts; put; put·ting** [+ *obj*]

1 *always followed by an adverb or preposition* **a :** to cause (someone or something) to be in a particular place or position • She *put* [=*placed, set*] the plant near the window. • *Put* the car in the garage. • I *put* the keys on the table. • He *put* his arms around her and held her tight. **b :** to cause (something) to go into or through something in a forceful way • He fell and accidentally *put* his hand through a window. **c :** to cause (someone) to be in a particular place or send (someone) to a particular place • The illness *put* her in the hospital for three days. • They *put* her in prison for forgery. • Her parents decided to *put* her in a special school for deaf children. • If she drove 55 mph for 20 minutes, that would *put* her about halfway there by now. **d :** to show that (someone or something) is in a particular place • The evidence/report *puts* the defendant at the scene of the crime. [=it shows that the defendant was at the scene of the crime]

2 : to write (something) with a pen or pencil in or on something • Don't forget to *put* your signature on the check. • He *put* his phone number on a napkin. • *Put* a circle around the correct answer. • I wrote that the answer was option B. What did you *put*? • She had always dreamed of writing a novel, but she never actually ***put pen to paper***. [=started writing]

3 *always followed by an adverb or preposition* **:** to cause (someone or something) to be in a particular state or condition • Not exercising *puts* you at greater risk of developing heart disease. • *Put* the TV on channel 5, please. • Who *put* you in charge/command/control? • I told her some jokes to *put* her in/into a good mood. • His careless spending *put* him in/into debt. • Their actions have *put* them in serious danger. • Her reassuring words ***put us at ease***. [=made us feel calm and relaxed] • ***Put*** that idea ***out of your mind***. [=stop thinking about that idea] • They said they shot the injured horse to ***put it out of its misery***. [=so that it would not continue to suffer] • They have ***put*** their competitors ***out of business***. • The new technology could ***put him out of a job***. = It could ***put him out of work***. [=it could make him lose his job] • He's ***putting*** the children ***to bed***. [=helping them get into their beds]

4 *always followed by an adverb or preposition* **a :** to cause (someone or something) to do work or perform a task — often + *to* • She *put* the kids *to* work cleaning the basement. **b :** to use (something) • They are ready to *put* the plan in action/motion. • *putting* an idea into action/effect/practice • The new weapon was immediately ***put to use*** by the military. • I don't need this camera, but maybe you can ***put it to good use***.

5 *always followed by an adverb or preposition* **:** to cause (something) to have an effect on someone or something — usually + *on* • He *puts* [=*places*] great emphasis *on* the need for new leadership. [=he strongly emphasizes the need for new leadership] • She has been *putting* pressure *on* us to finish the project early. • Another child would *put* a heavy strain *on* their finances. [=would strain their finances very much] • A special tax/duty/surcharge was *put on* luxury items. • They want to *put* a limit *on* government spending.

6 : to say or express (something) • As she *put* it, "You can't please everyone." • How should I *put* this? I don't think you're cut out for this job. • Well *put*! • Let me *put* it another

P

way. ▪ I think you're incompetent, ***to put it bluntly***. ▪ It was a difficult experience, ***to put it mildly***. [=it was a very difficult experience] ▪ She finds it hard to ***put her feelings into words***. [=to say what her feelings are]
7 *always followed by an adverb or preposition* **a :** to ask (a question) or make (a suggestion) to someone ▪ Let me *put* this question to you [=let me ask you this question]: what do we do now? ▪ I *put* my plan/proposal before the board of directors for consideration. **b :** to ask a group of people to formally vote on (something) ▪ They plan on *putting* the motion/resolution to a/the vote this afternoon.
8 : to add music to (words) ▪ She writes the lyrics and he *puts* [=*sets*] them to music.
9 *sports* **:** to throw (a shot put)
I wouldn't put it past (someone) see ²PAST
put about [*phrasal verb*] **1** ***put (something) about or put about (something)*** *Brit* **:** to tell many people about (something) ▪ They *put about* the news that he was resigning. = They *put* it *about* that he was resigning. **2 a** *of a boat or ship* **:** to change direction ▪ The ship *put about* and sailed back out to sea. **b** ***put (something) about*** **:** to cause (a boat or ship) to change direction ▪ a boat that can be *put about* quickly
put across [*phrasal verb*] **1** ***put (something) across or put across (something)*** **:** to cause (something) to be clearly understood **:** to get (something) across ▪ She has had trouble *putting* her message *across* to voters. **2** ***put (yourself) across as (something)*** **:** to cause (yourself) to appear to be (a particular type of person) ▪ He tries to *put himself across as* [=to make other people believe that he is] a nice guy.
put a foot wrong see ¹FOOT
put aside [*phrasal verb*] ***put (something) aside or put aside (something)*** **1 :** to save or keep (something, such as money) to be used at a later time ▪ She's been *putting aside* some money for a vacation. ▪ Can you *put* a few minutes *aside* for a short meeting? **2 :** to stop worrying or thinking about (something) ▪ We need to *put* these problems *aside* for now and get the work done. ▪ It's time to *put aside* our differences and start working together.
put at [*phrasal verb*] ***put (something) at (something)*** **:** to guess or estimate (something) to be (something) ▪ The coroner *put* his time of death *at* 7:00. [=the coroner estimated that the time of his death was 7:00] ▪ Recent estimates *put* the number of unreported cases *at* 2,000 each year.
put away [*phrasal verb*] **1** ***put (something) away or put away (something)*** **a :** to return (something) to the place where it belongs ▪ He washed, dried, and *put away* the dishes after dinner. ▪ She *put* the pictures *away* for safekeeping. ▪ *Put* your notes *away*. It's time for the test. **b :** to save or keep (something, such as money) to be used at a later time ▪ Her parents started *putting away* money for her education the year she was born. **c** *informal* **:** to eat (a large amount of food) ▪ I used to *put away* huge meals before I went on a diet. ▪ That guy can really ***put it away***! **2** ***put (someone) away or put away (someone)*** *informal* **:** to cause (someone) to be kept in a prison or mental hospital ▪ He's a vicious criminal. I hope they *put* him *away* for the rest of his life.
put back [*phrasal verb*] ***put (something) back or put back (something)*** **1 :** to return (something) to the place where it belongs ▪ Remember to *put* the vacuum cleaner *back* in the closet after you've used it. ▪ The books had been *put back* neatly on the shelf. **2** *Brit* **:** to change (a planned event) to start at a later date or time ▪ They *put back* [=*pushed back, postponed*] the game until next week. ▪ The meeting has been *put back* from 1 p.m. to 3 p.m.
put before [*phrasal verb*] ***put (something) before (someone or something)*** **:** to ask (a person or group) to make a decision about (something) ▪ The problem of downtown parking was *put before* the mayor/council. ▪ We should *put* this question *before* the voters.
put behind [*phrasal verb*] ***put (something) behind you*** **:** to stop worrying about or being upset by (something that happened in the past) ▪ It was a disappointing loss, but we need to *put it behind us* and focus on winning the next game. ▪ *Put* the past *behind you*.
put by [*phrasal verb*] ***put (something) by or put by (something)*** *chiefly Brit* **:** to save (money) for a later time ▪ She has *put* some money *by* [=*put aside*] for emergencies.
put down [*phrasal verb*] **1** ***put (someone or something) down also put down (someone or something)*** **a :** to place (someone or something that you have been holding or carrying) on a table, on the floor, etc. ▪ She carefully *put* the vase *down* on the table. ▪ The police ordered him to *put down* the gun. ▪ I don't need you to carry me. *Put* me *down*! **b :** to add (someone or something) to a list ▪ Don't forget to *put down* milk and bread on the shopping list. **c** *informal* **:** to say critical or insulting things about (someone or something) ▪ He frequently *puts down* her work. ▪ Her parents are always *putting* her *down*. ▪ He ***puts himself down*** a lot, but he's really quite an attractive man. — see also PUT-DOWN **2** ***put (something) down or put down (something)*** **a :** to write (something) **:** to record (something) in writing ▪ She says that the reporter *put* her quote *down* incorrectly. ▪ Every night, he *puts* his thoughts *down* in a journal. ▪ I need to *put down* my thoughts on paper before I forget them. ▪ What answer did you *put down* on the test? **b :** to give (an amount of money) as a first payment when you are buying something that costs a lot of money ▪ We *put* 10 percent *down* on the house. = We *put down* a 10 percent deposit on the house. ▪ *Put* no money *down* and pay no interest on the car until next year. **c :** to put (something) in place on the floor or ground ▪ *Putting down* [=*installing*] a new hardwood floor would greatly increase the value of your home. ▪ We *put down* a layer of mulch in the rose garden. **d :** to stop (a violent or dangerous activity) by using force ▪ Federal troops were brought in to help *put down* the riot. ▪ *put down* a rebellion/revolt/uprising **e :** to kill (an animal) in a way that causes it little pain usually because it is injured or sick ▪ They had to have their dog *put down* [=*put to sleep*] by the vet. **f** *Brit* **:** to end a telephone connection ▪ She said goodbye and ***put down the phone***. [=*hung up the phone*] ▪ She ***put the phone down on him***. [=she hung up the phone while he was still talking to her] **g** *Brit* **:** to formally suggest (something) as an idea to be discussed and voted on by a group of people **:** to propose or introduce (something) ▪ *putting down* an amendment in Parliament **3** ***put down or put (something) down or put down (something)*** *chiefly Brit* **:** to land or to cause (an airplane) to land ▪ Our plane *put down* [=*landed*] in New York around 2 p.m. ▪ The pilot was forced to *put* [=*set*] the plane *down* in a field. **4** ***put (someone) down or put down (someone)*** **:** to place (a baby or child) in a bed to sleep ▪ He *put* the baby *down* (in her crib) for a nap. **5** ***put (someone) down as (something)*** **:** to think of (someone) as (a specified kind of person or thing) ▪ Most people *put* him *down as* [=believe that he is] a fanatic. **6** ***put (someone) down for (something)*** **:** to write the name of (someone) on a list of people who will do or give (something) ▪ Can I *put you down for* a donation? [=can I write that you will give a donation?] ▪ Sure, *put me down for* $20. **7** ***put (something) down to (something)*** **:** to say or think that (something) happened because of (something) ▪ Let's *put* the mistake *down to* your inexperience and forget about it. ▪ The mistake was *put down to* [=*attributed to*] his inexperience.
put forth [*phrasal verb*] ***put forth (something) or put (something) forth*** *somewhat formal* **1 :** to suggest (an idea, plan, etc.) for people to think about or consider ▪ The same argument has been *put forth* by many people in the opposition. ▪ I would like to *put forth* some alternatives. ▪ *putting forth* a plan/proposal/theory **2 :** to use (something, such as energy) for a particular purpose ▪ She *put forth* all her energy to win the race. ▪ They *put forth* a good effort. **3** *of a plant* **:** to produce or send out (something) by growing ▪ The trees are starting to *put forth* new leaves.
put forward [*phrasal verb*] ***put (something) forward or put forward (something)*** *somewhat formal* **:** to suggest (something) for consideration **:** PROPOSE ▪ He *put forward* [=*put forth*] a theory about how the accident may have occurred.
put in [*phrasal verb*] **1** ***put (something) in or put in (something)*** **a :** to make (something) ready to be used in a certain place **:** INSTALL ▪ We *put in* new cabinets just last year. ▪ In order to fix the car they have to *put in* a new engine. **b :** to add (a comment) to a conversation or argument ▪ She *put* a quick comment *in* about her busy schedule. ▪ I'd like to *put in* a few words on his behalf. [=to say something that supports him] ▪ Would you mind ***putting in a good word for*** me? [=would you say something good about me?] ▪ You will each have a chance to ***put in your two cents***. [=to express your opinion] **c :** to make an official statement, offer, or request ▪ She *put in* a plea of not guilty. [=she pleaded not guilty] ▪ I need to *put in* [=*make, submit*] a report about this. ▪ You have two weeks to *put in* [=*submit*] a claim with the insurance company. ▪ They are *putting in* [=*making*] a $300,000 offer for the house. ▪ I'd like to *put in* [=*place*] an order for a dozen roses. ▪ Contractors have begun *putting in* bids for the job. **d :** to perform (a particu-

P

lar action) • They *put in* an amazing performance last night. • The prime minister **put in a call to** [=*called*] the White House. • I won't be able to stay at the party long, but I'll at least try to **put in an appearance**. [=to go to the party for a short time] **e** : to work or do something for (an amount of time) • She *put in* 10 hours at the office yesterday. • She *put in* a long day at work. • He has *put in* his time (in jail), and now he is a free man. **2 put in (something) or put (something) in (something)** : to use (a certain amount of energy or effort) when doing something • If we *put in* a little more effort, we could finish by this afternoon. • He *puts* a lot of energy *in* his performances. **3 put (something) in (something) a** : to invest (money) into (something) • She *put* her money *in* stocks and bonds. **b** — used to say what causes you to have faith, confidence, etc. • He *puts* his faith *in* reason/science. • *putting* her trust *in* God **4 put in for (something)** : to ask for (something) in an official way : to formally request (something) • He *put in for* a leave of absence. • *putting in for* a promotion **5** *of a boat or ship* : to enter a harbor or port • The ship *put in* at Sydney.

put into [*phrasal verb*] **put (something) into (something) 1** : to use (a certain amount of energy or effort) when doing (something) • He *puts* a lot of energy *into* his performances. • She **put her heart into** (writing) the letter. [=she expressed her feelings in a very open and honest way] **2** : to invest (time, money, etc.) in (something) • They *put* their entire life savings *into* the company. • We *put* a lot of money *into* (fixing up) that house.

put it there *or* **put her there** *informal + old-fashioned* — used to invite someone to shake hands with you • *Put her there*, pal!

put off [*phrasal verb*] **1 put (something) off or put off (something)** : to decide that (something) will happen at a later time : POSTPONE • The meeting has been *put off* until next week. = We *put off* (holding) the meeting until next week. • I've been meaning to call him, but I keep *putting* it *off*. • I've been *putting off* calling him. **2 put (someone) off or put off (someone) a** : to cause (someone) to wait • I need to come up with an excuse to *put off* the bill collector. • She finally called him after *putting* him *off* all week. **b** : to cause (someone) to dislike someone or something • Don't let the restaurant's dingy appearance *put* you *off*—their food is great. • I was *put off* by his rudeness. • (*chiefly Brit*) His rudeness **put me off him** [=made me dislike him] at once. — see also OFF-PUTTING **c** *Brit* : to allow (someone) to get off a bus or other vehicle • Could you *put* [=*let*] me *off* (the bus) at the next stop, please?

put on [*phrasal verb*] **1 put (something) on or put on (something) a** : to dress yourself in (clothing) • She *put on* her new dress. • *Put on* a hat and gloves. • I'll *put* some clothes *on* and be right there. **b** : to apply (something) to your face or body • *putting on* lipstick/mascara/lotion • She *puts on* far too much makeup. • We tried to **put on a happy/brave face** [=we tried to appear happy/brave] despite our concern. **c** : to add to or increase the amount of (something) • The fire was getting low and we needed to *put on* more wood. • She *put on* [=*gained*] 40 pounds during her pregnancy. • He's *put on* some weight recently. **d** : to cause (a machine, a light, etc.) to begin to work • Would you mind if I *put* [=*turned*] the TV *on*? • Somebody *put on* the lights. **e** : to cause (something) to begin to be heard, seen, produced, etc. • *put on* a record/CD/album • *putting on* some music • We *put on* the air-conditioning/heat in the car. **f** : to start cooking or making (something) • Let me know when to *put on* the rice. • He *put on* a pot of coffee for his guests. **g** : to produce (something that entertains people, such as a play, a party, etc.) • They're *putting on* a concert. • He always *puts on* a great show/performance. • The town *puts on* a fireworks display every Independence Day. • We are *putting on* a barbecue for everyone in the neighborhood. **2 put (something) on (someone or something) a** : to say that (someone or something) is responsible for or guilty of (something) • Responsibility for the accident was *put on* the other driver. • He *puts* much of the blame for his problems *on* the government. **b** : to bet (an amount of money) on (someone or something) • We *put* $2 *on* the favorite to win. • *putting* money *on* horse races **3 put (someone or something) on (something)** : to add (someone or something) to (a list or group of related things) • She asked to have her name *put on* the list of candidates. • They *put* her *on* the list. • We *put* several new dishes *on* the menu. • "Bartender, I'll have another beer." "Okay, I'll *put* it *on* your bill." **4 put (someone) on or put on (someone)** *chiefly US, informal* : to say things that are not true to (someone) in a joking way : to trick or fool (someone) for amusement • He said he knew the President, but I think he was just *putting me on*. [=(*Brit*) *having me on*] — see also ²PUT-ON **5** — used to say that you would like to speak to someone on the phone • Hi Dad. Could you *put* Mom *on*? [=could you give Mom the phone so that I can speak to her?] • *Put* Dave *on* the phone, please. **6 put (someone) on (something)** : to tell (someone) to use or do (something) • Her doctor *put* her *on* medication. [=her doctor prescribed medication for her] • He decided to *put* himself *on* a diet. [=to go on a diet] **7 put (someone) on to (something)** : to give (someone) information about (something) : to tell (someone) about (something that he or she did not know about before) • A friend of mine *put* me *on to* this book in high school.

put out [*phrasal verb*] **1 put (something) out or put out (something) a** : to cause (something) to stop burning : EXTINGUISH • She *put* the fire *out* by pouring water on it. • She *put out* her cigarette in an ashtray. **b** : to stop (something) from working • Who *put out* [=*turned off*] the lights? **c** : to take (something) outside and leave it there • I *put* the dog *out* in the backyard before leaving the house. • *putting* horses *out* to graze • (*US*) Don't forget to *put out* the trash/garbage. = (*Brit*) Don't forget to *put out* the rubbish. **d** : to extend (something) outward • I *put out* my hand and he shook it eagerly. • She *put out* her arm for them to stop. **e** : to place (something) where people may use it • He always *put out* a bowl of candy for the grandchildren. • We should *put out* a few extra chairs in case more people arrive. **f** : to produce (something) • This small radiator *puts out* a surprising amount of heat. • They will have to *put out* considerable effort to meet the deadline. • It was early spring, and the trees were just starting to *put out* their leaves. **g** : to make (something) available to be bought, used, etc. • She plans to *put out* a new album in March. • They need to be *putting out* cars that get better gas mileage. • The information was given in a pamphlet *put out* by the university's health department. • Researchers recently *put out* a report/study on the issue. • The police have *put out* [=*issued*] a warrant for his arrest. • Someone **put the word out** [=started telling people] that the police were looking for her. **2 put (someone) out or put out (someone) a** : to annoy or bother (someone) • All the attention didn't seem to *put* her *out* at all. • I'm a little *put out* that no one called to tell me they would be late. **b** : to cause (someone) to do extra work : to cause trouble for (someone) • I hope my visit didn't *put* you *out*. [=didn't inconvenience you] • Please don't *put* yourself *out* just for us. **c** : to make (someone) unconscious • The anesthesia *put* him *out* for a little over three hours. **d** *sports* : to cause (someone) to be out in baseball or cricket • The runner was *put out* at second base. — see also PUTOUT **3** *chiefly US, informal + impolite* : to have sex with someone • Did she *put out* last night? **4** *of a boat or ship* : to leave a harbor or port • The ship *put out* to sea.

put over [*phrasal verb*] **1 put (something) over or put over (something)** : to cause (something) to be clearly understood : to put (something) across • He *puts over* very complicated concepts in a way that his students can understand. **2 put (yourself) over as (something)** : to cause (yourself) to appear to be (a particular type of person) • She *puts herself over as* [=makes other people believe that she is] a modern, independent woman. **3 put (something) over on (someone)** : to lie about (something) to (someone) : to trick or deceive someone • Don't try to *put* anything *over on* her. She'll see right through you.

put paid to see ²PAID

put (someone) in mind of see ¹MIND

put through [*phrasal verb*] **1 put (something) through or put through (something)** : to cause (something) to be accepted or done successfully • They *put through* a number of reforms. • tax cuts that were *put through* by former administrations • I asked Human Resources to help me *put through* [=to help me get] a transfer to a different department. **2 put (someone) through (something)** : to pay for (someone) to attend (school) • She has a full-time job and is *putting* herself *through* college. **3 put (someone or something) through (something)** : to cause (someone or something) to experience (something) • His doctor *put* him *through* a series of tests. • She *put* her parents *through* a lot when she was a teenager. • You've been *put through* quite an ordeal. • I've been *put through* hell! • We *put* that truck

P

through a lot when we owned it. ▪ The new software still needs to be ***put through its paces*** [=it still needs to be tested] before it can be made available to the public. **4 *put (someone or something) through*** *or* ***put through (someone or something)*** **a** : to cause a phone call from (someone) to be sent to another person's phone ▪ Please hold while I *put* you *through* (to the manager). **b** : to cause (a phone call) to be sent to another person's phone ▪ Please hold while I *put* your call *through* (to the manager).

put to death see DEATH

put together [*phrasal verb*] **1 *put (something) together*** *or* ***put together (something)*** **a** : to create (something) by joining or gathering parts together ▪ You'll need a screwdriver to *put* the toy *together.* ▪ They *put* their first band *together* when they were in high school. ▪ Help me *put together* a list of what we need at the store. ▪ She *put* a proposal *together* to give to the committee for consideration. ▪ Her outfit was very well *put together.* [=the parts looked good together] **b** — used to say that someone or something is greater than the total of all the other people or things mentioned ▪ You're smarter than all of those other guys *put together.* **2 *put (something) together with (something)*** : to add or combine (something) with (something) ▪ I never would have thought of *putting* this wine together *with* fish. ▪ The lack of rain *put together with* [=along with, combined with] the heat ruined many of the region's crops.

put up [*phrasal verb*] **1 *put (something) up*** *or* ***put up (something)*** **a** : to place (something) in a higher position ▪ They *put up* the flag in the morning and take it down at night. ▪ Sit down. *Put* your feet *up* and relax. ▪ If you have a question, please *put up* [=*raise*] your hand. ▪ Stop! *Put* your hands *up* (over your head)! ▪ When she goes to work, she usually *puts* her hair *up* (in a ponytail). **b** : to cause (something) to be on a wall, to hang from a ceiling, etc. ▪ She went around town *putting up* posters for the concert. ▪ I just *put up* new curtains. **c** : to set or place (something) so that it stands up ▪ *putting up* a tent ▪ They *put up* a display of new products. ▪ They *put up* a "for sale" sign in front of their house. **d** : to build (something) ▪ They're *putting up* a new office building on Main Street. ▪ *putting up* a fence **e** : to make (something) available for people to buy or have ▪ The lamps were *put up* at auction. — often + *for* ▪ They *put* all of their possessions *up for* sale. ▪ They *put* the puppies *up for* adoption. **f** : to provide (money, property, etc.) in order to pay for something ▪ They decided not to *put up* the money for her bail. ▪ They *put up* the company's assets as collateral on the loan. **g** : to offer (something) as a prize ▪ The police have *put up* a $1,000 reward for information leading to his capture. **h** *chiefly Brit* : to increase (something) : RAISE ▪ They are likely to *put up* interest rates again this year. **i** *US* : to return (something) to the place where it belongs ▪ It's time to *put up* [=*put away*] your toys and get ready for bed. ▪ He washed, dried, and *put up* the dishes after dinner. **j** *chiefly US* : to preserve (fruits, vegetables, etc.) to be used later : CAN ▪ Their grandmother spent the afternoon *putting up* peaches. **2 *put up (something)*** **a** : to do (something) as a way of resisting or struggling against someone or something ▪ We're not leaving without *putting up* a fight. [=without fighting] ▪ As expected, the kids *put up* a fuss when we said it was time for bed. ▪ They are likely to *put up* stiff resistance to any new proposals. **b** : to offer (something) as an argument, a suggestion, etc. ▪ She *put up* a good/solid argument in his defense. ▪ *putting up* a proposal **c** : to score (points) ▪ They *put up* 20 points in the first half. ▪ She needs to *put up* big numbers [=to score a lot of points] in today's game. **3 a *put (someone) up*** : to give food and shelter to (someone) : to allow or pay for (someone) to stay in someone's home, a hotel, etc., for the night ▪ Could you *put* me *up* for the night? ▪ His employers *put* him *up* at a hotel. ▪ We *put* our guests *up* in the spare bedroom. **b** *chiefly Brit* : to stay in someone's home, a hotel, etc., for the night ▪ He *put up* with a friend while he was in town. ▪ *putting up* at a hotel **4 *put (someone) up*** *or* ***put up (someone)*** : to choose or suggest (someone) to be a candidate or competitor ▪ The party *put* her *up* (as its candidate) for governor. ▪ They *put up* their best man to compete against the champion. **5 *put (someone) up to (something)*** : to convince (someone) to do (something stupid or foolish) ▪ His friends *put* him *up to* (playing) the prank. ▪ Who *put* you *up* to this? **6 *put up with (something or someone)*** : to allow (someone or something unpleasant or annoying) to exist or happen : TOLERATE ▪ At this school, we will not *put up with* bad behavior. ▪ I can't *put up with* much more of this. **7 *put up or shut up*** *informal* — used to tell someone in a somewhat rude way to start doing something or to stop talking about it ▪ You've complained long enough. It's time to *put up or shut up.*

²**put** *noun, pl* **puts** [*count*] *sports* : the act of throwing a shot put

³**put** *adj*

stay put : to stay where you are : to not move or go anywhere ▪ *Stay put* until I get back.

– see also HARD PUT

pu·ta·tive /ˈpjuːtətɪv/ *adj, always used before a noun, formal* : generally believed to be something ▪ a *putative* expert ▪ the child's *putative* father [=the man who is believed to be the child's father]

– **pu·ta·tive·ly** *adv*

put–down /ˈpʊtˌdaʊn/ *noun, pl* **-downs** [*count*] : a statement that criticizes or insults someone ▪ humiliating *put-downs* — see also *put down* at ¹PUT

¹**put–on** /ˈpʊtˈɑːn/ *adj, always used before a noun* : not real or genuine : FAKE ▪ a *put-on* British accent — see also *put on* at ¹PUT

²**put–on** /ˈpʊtˌɑːn/ *noun, pl* **-ons** [*count*] *chiefly US* : the act of saying things that are not true in a joking way ▪ He said he knew the President, but I'm sure that was just a *put-on.* [=I'm sure he was just putting me on] — see also *put on* at ¹PUT

put·out /ˈpʊtˌaʊt/ *noun, pl* **-outs** [*count*] *baseball* : an action that causes a batter or runner on the opposite team to be out ▪ The shortstop fielded the grounder and threw to first base for the *putout.* — see also *put out* at ¹PUT

pu·tre·fac·tion /ˌpjuːtrəˈfækʃən/ *noun* [*noncount*] : the process or result of decaying ▪ the smell/stench of *putrefaction*

pu·tre·fy /ˈpjuːtrəˌfaɪ/ *verb* **-fies; -fied; -fy·ing** [*no obj*] *formal* : to be slowly destroyed by natural processes : to rot and become putrid ▪ *putrefying* meat/flesh ***synonyms*** see ¹DECAY

pu·trid /ˈpjuːtrəd/ *adj*

1 : decayed with usually a very bad or disgusting smell ▪ *putrid* [=*rotten*] meat ▪ a *putrid* odor/smell/stench [=a bad smell that something has when it is decaying]

2 *informal* : very ugly, bad, or unpleasant ▪ a *putrid* shade of green ▪ a *putrid* performance

putt /ˈpʌt/ *verb* **putts; putt·ed; putt·ing** [*no obj*] : to hit a golf ball with a special club (called a putter) so that it rolls along the ground toward the hole

– **putt** *noun, pl* **putts** [*count*] ▪ Her *putt* was a few feet short of the hole. ▪ She made/sank/holed the *putt.* [=she putted the ball and it went in the hole] ▪ She missed the *putt.* [=she putted the ball and it did not go in the hole] – **putting** *noun* [*noncount*] ▪ Her *putting* has improved considerably.

¹**putt·er** /ˈpʌtɚ/ *noun, pl* **-ers** [*count*]

1 : a golf club that is used to putt the ball

2 : a person who putts golf balls ▪ a golfer who's a good/bad *putter* [=a golfer who putts well/badly]

²**put·ter** /ˈpʌtɚ/ *verb* **-ters; -tered; -ter·ing** [*no obj*] *Brit* : to make small popping sounds while moving slowly ▪ the motorboat *puttered* across the lake

putter around [*phrasal verb*] *US* : to spend time in a relaxed way doing small jobs and other things that are not very important ▪ I didn't do much last weekend. I just *puttered around.* [=(*Brit*) *pottered around/about*] ▪ He spent his vacation *puttering around* the house/garden.

– **put·ter·er** *noun, pl* **-ers** [*count*]

¹**put·ting** *present participle of* ¹PUT

²**putt·ing** *present participle of* PUTT

putt·ing green /ˈpʌtɪŋ-/ *noun, pl* ~ **greens** [*count*] *golf* : an area covered with very short grass around the hole into which the ball must be played : GREEN; *also* : a similar area that has many holes and that is used for practice

put·ty /ˈpʌti/ *noun* [*noncount*] : a soft, sticky substance that becomes hard when it dries and that is used for holding glass in window frames or for filling small holes in wood

putty in your hands ✧ If someone is *putty in your hands,* you are able to control that person very easily. ▪ He does whatever she wants. He's *putty in her hands.*

– **putty** *verb* **put·ties; put·tied; put·ty·ing** [+ *obj*] ▪ She *puttied* the window to stop drafts.

put–up job *noun, pl* ~ **jobs** [*count*] *informal + disapproving* : something that is secretly arranged or decided at an earlier time in order to trick or deceive someone ▪ That talent contest was a *put-up job*: you never had a chance to win!

P

put–up•on /ˈpʊtəˌpɑːn/ *adj* [*more* ~; *most* ~] **:** feeling that someone is taking advantage of you or treating you unfairly ▪ I was beginning to feel rather *put-upon* by the end of their visit. ▪ a *put-upon* secretary

putz /ˈpʌts/ *noun, pl* **putz•es** [*count*] *US, informal* **:** a stupid or foolish person who is not well liked ▪ I can't believe what a *putz* that guy is.

[1]**puz•zle** /ˈpʌzəl/ *noun, pl* **puz•zles** [*count*]
1 a : a question or problem that requires thought, skill, or cleverness to be answered or solved ▪ a book of puns, riddles, and *puzzles* — see also CROSSWORD PUZZLE **b :** JIGSAW PUZZLE — often used figuratively ▪ The restaurant is trying to attract more customers, and the new menu is an important ***piece of the puzzle.*** [=an important part of what is being done] ▪ Researchers are close to finding a solution, but they haven't found the final *pieces of the puzzle.*
2 : something or someone that is difficult to understand — usually singular ▪ The cause of the explosion was a *puzzle.* [=no one knew what caused the explosion] ▪ His strange behavior is a *puzzle* to his friends. [=his friends don't understand the reason for his strange behavior]

[2]**puzzle** *verb* **puzzles; puz•zled; puz•zling** [+ *obj*] **:** to confuse (someone) **:** to be difficult for (someone) to understand ▪ The question *puzzled* me. [=I did not know the answer to the question] ▪ The cause of the accident has *puzzled* investigators. ▪ I was *puzzled* by his behavior. [=I did not understand the reason for his behavior]
puzzle out [*phrasal verb*] ***puzzle (something) out or puzzle out (something)*** **:** to understand or find (something, such as the answer to a difficult problem) by careful thinking ▪ She *puzzled out* the meaning of the strange phrase.
puzzle over [*phrasal verb*] ***puzzle over (something)*** **:** to think or worry for a long time about (something) ▪ He's been *puzzling over* whether to buy a new car. ▪ We *puzzled over* the best arrangement for the furniture.

puzzled *adj* [*more* ~; *most* ~] **:** feeling or showing confusion because something is difficult to understand ▪ Investigators are *puzzled* about the cause of the accident. ▪ He had a very *puzzled* [=*confused*] look on his face.

puz•zle•ment /ˈpʌzəlmənt/ *noun, formal*
1 [*noncount*] **:** a feeling of being confused because something is difficult to understand ▪ The cause of the accident has been a source of *puzzlement.* ▪ The explanation only increased their *puzzlement.*
2 [*singular*] *chiefly US* **:** something that is difficult to understand ▪ The cause of the accident is a *puzzlement.* [=*puzzle*]

puz•zler /ˈpʌzələ/ *noun, pl* **puz•zlers** [*count*] *informal* **:** something that is confusing or difficult to understand — usually singular ▪ The question is a real *puzzler.*

puz•zling /ˈpʌzəlɪŋ/ *adj* [*more* ~; *most* ~] **:** causing or likely to cause confusion **:** difficult to solve or understand ▪ *puzzling* questions ▪ a *puzzling* metaphor/statement/event ▪ The directions are somewhat *puzzling.*

PVC /ˌpiːˌviːˈsiː/ *noun* [*noncount*] **:** a type of plastic used for pipes that carry water and for many other products ✧ *PVC* is an abbreviation of "polyvinyl chloride."

Pvt. *abbr, US* private ▪ *Pvt.* David Logan

PX *abbr, US* post exchange

[1]**pyg•my** *also* **pig•my** /ˈpɪgmi/ *noun, pl* **-mies** [*count*]
1 ***Pygmy*** **:** a member of a group of very small people who live in Africa
2 *disapproving* **:** a person who is regarded as very weak, stupid, etc. ▪ an intellectual *pygmy*

[2]**pygmy** *also* **pigmy** *adj, always used before a noun, biology* — used to describe a type of plant or animal that is smaller than the usual size ▪ a *pygmy* elephant

pyjamas *Brit spelling of* PAJAMAS

py•lon /ˈpaɪˌlɑːn/ *noun, pl* **-lons** [*count*]
1 a : a tall tower or similar structure ▪ The bridge is supported by concrete *pylons.* **b :** a tall, metal structure that is part of a series of structures supporting a long stretch of electrical wire ▪ a row of electricity *pylons*
2 *US* **:** TRAFFIC CONE
3 *American football* **:** one of the upright markers that are positioned at the corners of the end zone

pyr•a•mid /ˈpirəˌmɪd/ *noun, pl* **-mids** [*count*]
1 a : a very large structure built especially in ancient Egypt that has a square base and four triangular sides which form a point at the top ▪ the ancient *pyramids* of Egypt **b :** a shape, object, or pile that is wide near the bottom and narrows gradually as it reaches the top ▪ a *pyramid* of apples/oranges — see picture at GEOMETRY
2 : something that resembles a pyramid in the way its parts are arranged or organized ▪ the social *pyramid* ▪ (*US*) the ***food pyramid*** [=a drawing or chart that is shaped like a pyramid and that shows the type of food you should eat for a healthy diet]
– py•ra•mi•dal /pəˈræmədl/ *adj* ▪ a *pyramidal* structure

pyramid scheme *noun, pl* ~ **schemes** [*count*] **:** a dishonest and usually illegal business in which many people are persuaded to invest their money and the money of later investors is used to pay the people who invested first — called also (*US*) *Ponzi scheme*

pyre /ˈpajə/ *noun, pl* **pyres** [*count*] **:** a pile of wood for burning a dead body ▪ a funeral *pyre*

Py•rex /ˈpaɪˌrɛks/ *trademark* — used for a type of special glass that can get very hot without breaking

py•rite /ˈpaɪˌraɪt/ *noun* [*noncount*] **:** a common mineral that is shiny and pale yellow in color

py•ro•ma•nia /ˌpaɪroʊˈmeɪnijə/ *noun* [*noncount*] **:** a mental illness that makes people have a strong desire to set fires
– py•ro•ma•ni•ac /ˌpaɪroʊˈmeɪniˌæk/ *noun, pl* **-acs** [*count*] ▪ The fire was set by a *pyromaniac.*

py•ro•tech•nics /ˌpaɪrəˈtɛknɪks/ *noun* [*plural*]
1 : a bright display of fireworks
2 : a very impressive show or display that requires great skill ▪ The visual *pyrotechnics* of the film are stunning. ▪ verbal/musical *pyrotechnics*

Pyr•rhic victory /ˈpirɪk-/ *noun, pl* ~ **-ries** [*count*] **:** a victory that is not worth winning because so much is lost to achieve it ▪ The company won the lawsuit, but it was a *Pyrrhic victory* because of all the bad publicity they received during the trial.

py•thon /ˈpaɪˌθɑːn/ *noun, pl* **-thons** [*count*] **:** a very large snake that kills the animals it eats by wrapping itself around them

Q

q *or* **Q** /ˈkjuː/ *noun, pl* **q's** *or* **qs** *or* **Q's** *or* **Qs :** the 17th letter of the English alphabet [*count*] The word "quart" begins with a *q.* [*noncount*] The word "quart" begins with *q.*
mind your p's and q's see [1]P

QA *abbr* quality assurance

Q and A *or* **Q & A** *noun, pl* **Q and A's** *or* **Q & A's** [*count*] **:** a period of time or an occasion when someone answers questions that are asked by a reporter, by the people in an audience, etc. ▪ There will be a brief *Q and A* following the speech. — often used before another noun ▪ a *Q and A* session

QB *abbr* quarterback

QC *abbr* **1** quality control **2** *Brit* Queen's Counsel

QED /ˌkjuːˌiːˈdiː/ *abbr* — used to say that something (such as a particular fact or a logical statement) proves what you were trying to prove ✧ *QED* is an abbreviation of the Latin phrase "quod erat demonstrandum," /ˌkwɑːdˈeəˌɑːtˌdɛmənˈstrændəm/ which means "which was to be demonstrated."

qt. *abbr* quart

q.t. /ˌkjuːˈtiː/
on the q.t. or on the Q.T. informal **:** in a secret or quiet way ▪ All the arrangements were made *on the q.t.* ▪ She told me about it *on the q.t.* ▪ This information is private, so ***keep it on the q.t.*** [=don't tell anyone about it]

Q–tips /ˈkjuːˌtɪps/ *trademark* — used for short sticks that have pieces of soft cotton at both ends

qtr. *abbr* quarter

qty. *abbr* quantity

qua /ˈkwɑː/ *prep, formal* **:** in the character or role of (someone or something) **:** AS — used to indicate that someone or something is being referred to or thought about in a particular way ▪ The artist *qua* artist is less interesting to me than the artist as a human being. — see also SINE QUA NON

[1]**quack** /ˈkwæk/ *verb* **quacks; quacked; quack·ing** [*no obj*] *of a duck* **:** to make a loud sound ▪ We could hear the ducks *quacking*.

[2]**quack** *noun, pl* **quacks** [*count*] **:** the loud sound that is made by a duck — compare [3]QUACK

[3]**quack** *noun, pl* **quacks** [*count*] *informal*

1 *disapproving* **:** an unskillful doctor or a person who falsely claims to have medical skills ▪ That *quack* almost killed me by prescribing the wrong medication. ▪ Her doctor turned out to be a real *quack*.

2 *Brit* — used in usually a negative or humorous way to refer to a doctor ▪ a visit to the *quack*

– compare [2]QUACK

– **quack** *adj, always used before a noun* ▪ *quack* medicines ▪ a *quack* doctor

quack·ery /ˈkwækəri/ *noun* [*noncount*] *disapproving* **:** the methods and treatments used by unskillful doctors or by people who pretend to be doctors ▪ His cure was nothing but *quackery*.

quad /ˈkwɑːd/ *noun, pl* **quads** [*count*] *informal*

1 : QUADRANGLE 2 ▪ Meet me at the *quad* after class.

2 : QUADRICEPS ▪ She suffered a *quad* injury. — usually plural ▪ I overworked my *quads* at the gym.

3 : QUADRUPLET ▪ She gave birth to *quads*.

quad·ran·gle /ˈkwɑːˌdræŋgəl/ *noun, pl* **-ran·gles** [*count*]

1 *geometry* **:** a flat shape that has four sides and four angles **:** QUADRILATERAL

2 : an open square or rectangular area at a college, school, etc., that is surrounded by buildings on all four sides

quad·rant /ˈkwɑːdrənt/ *noun, pl* **-rants** [*count*] **:** one part of something that is evenly divided into four parts ▪ Draw two intersecting lines that divide the page into four *quadrants*. ▪ The town is located in the northwest *quadrant* of the state.; *especially, geometry* **:** one part of a circle that is evenly divided into four parts

qua·drat·ic equation /kwɑˈdrætɪk-/ *noun, pl* **~ -tions** [*count*] *mathematics* **:** an equation in which the highest unknown variable is multiplied by itself only once ▪ $x^2 + 4x + 4 = 0$ is a *quadratic equation*.

quad·ri·ceps /ˈkwɑːdrəˌsɛps/ *noun, pl* **quadriceps** [*count*] **:** a large muscle at the front of your upper leg ▪ He felt a pain in his right *quadriceps*. ▪ My *quadriceps* are sore.

quad·ri·lat·er·al /ˌkwɑːdrəˈlætərəl/ *noun, pl* **-als** [*count*] *geometry* **:** a flat shape that has four sides and four angles

– **quadrilateral** *adj* ▪ The sheet of metal was cut into even *quadrilateral* shapes.

qua·drille /kwɑˈdrɪl/ *noun, pl* **-drilles** [*count*] **:** a dance for four couples who each form one side of a square ✧ This dance was popular in the 18th and 19th centuries.

qua·dril·lion /kwɑˈdrɪljən/ *noun, pl* **quadrillion** *or* **qua·dril·lions** [*count*] **:** the number 1,000,000,000,000,000 **:** one thousand trillion

quad·ri·ple·gia /ˌkwɑːdrəˈpliːʤijə/ *noun* [*noncount*] *medical* **:** a condition in which you are permanently unable to move or feel your arms and legs and most of your body because of injury or illness

quad·ri·ple·gic /ˌkwɑːdrəˈpliːʤɪk/ *noun, pl* **-gics** [*count*] *medical* **:** a person who is permanently unable to move or feel both arms and both legs because of injury or illness — compare PARAPLEGIC

– **quadriplegic** *adj, always used before a noun* ▪ *quadriplegic* patients

quad·ru·ped /ˈkwɑːdrəˌpɛd/ *noun, pl* **-peds** [*count*] *technical* **:** an animal that has four feet ▪ Horses and cows are *quadrupeds*. — compare BIPED

[1]**qua·dru·ple** /kwɑˈdruːpəl/ *verb* **-dru·ples; -dru·pled; -dru·pling**

1 [*no obj*] **:** to become four times bigger in value or number ▪ The value of the stock has *quadrupled* in the past year. ▪ The town's population has *quadrupled* in the past 50 years.

2 [*+ obj*] **:** to cause (something) to become four times bigger ▪ He *quadrupled* his winnings. ▪ The company has *quadrupled* the number of its employees.

[2]**quadruple** *adj*

1 : four times bigger in size or amount ▪ She ordered a *quadruple* espresso.

2 *always used before a noun* **:** having four parts or including four people or things ▪ a *quadruple* murder [=a murder of four people]

qua·dru·plet /kwɑˈdruːplət/ *noun, pl* **-plets** [*count*] **:** one of four babies that are born at the same time to the same mother — usually plural ▪ She had (a set of) *quadruplets*. [=she gave birth to four babies] — compare QUINTUPLET, SEXTUPLET, TRIPLET, TWIN

quaff /ˈkwɑːf/ *verb* **quaffs; quaffed; quaff·ing** [*+ obj*] *old-fashioned + literary* **:** to drink a large amount of (something) quickly ▪ We stopped at a bar and *quaffed* a few beers.

quag·mire /ˈkwægˌmajɚ/ *noun, pl* **-mires** [*count*]

1 : an area of soft, wet ground — usually singular ▪ After a lot of rain, the dirt road becomes a *quagmire*.

2 : a situation that is hard to deal with or get out of **:** a situation that is full of problems — usually singular ▪ The trial became a legal *quagmire*. ▪ She's caught in a *quagmire* of debt.

qua·hog /ˈkoʊˌhɑːg/ *noun, pl* **-hogs** [*count*] *US* **:** a type of large clam that is eaten as food

[1]**quail** /ˈkweɪl/ *noun, pl* **quail** *or* **quails**

1 [*count*] **:** a kind of small wild bird that is often hunted

2 [*noncount*] **:** the meat of quail eaten as food ▪ We had *quail* for dinner.

[2]**quail** *verb* **quails; quailed; quail·ing** [*no obj*] *literary* **:** to feel afraid and often to show your fear in a way that can be clearly seen ▪ Other politicians *quailed* before him. ▪ He *quailed* at the thought of seeing her again.

quail

quaint /ˈkweɪnt/ *adj* **quaint·er; -est** [*or more* ~; *most* ~] **:** having an old-fashioned or unusual quality or appearance that is usually attractive or appealing ▪ The fishing village was very *quaint*. ▪ The writer talks about the *quaint* customs of the natives. ▪ They have some *quaint* [=*outdated*] notions about how women should behave.

– **quaint·ly** *adv* ▪ The town is *quaintly* old-fashioned.

[1]**quake** /ˈkweɪk/ *verb* **quakes; quaked; quak·ing** [*no obj*]

1 : to shake because of fear, anger, etc. **:** TREMBLE ▪ He *quaked* with fear. ▪ She was *quaking* with rage.

2 : to shake violently ▪ The explosion made the whole house *quake*.

[2]**quake** *noun, pl* **quakes** [*count*] *informal* **:** EARTHQUAKE

Quak·er /ˈkweɪkɚ/ *noun, pl* **-ers** [*count*] **:** a member of a Christian religious group whose members dress simply, are against violence, and have meetings without any special ceremony or priests — called also *Friend*

– **Quaker** *adj* ▪ a *Quaker* school/family

qual·i·fi·ca·tion /ˌkwɑːləfəˈkeɪʃən/ *noun, pl* **-tions**

1 [*count*] **a :** a special skill or type of experience or knowledge that makes someone suitable to do a particular job or activity — usually plural ▪ He has the best *qualifications* for the job. ▪ She has the proper *qualifications* to teach. ▪ academic/educational/technical *qualifications* **b :** something that is necessary in order for you to do, have, or be a part of something — usually plural ▪ What are the *qualifications* for owning a gun? ▪ He met all the health *qualifications* for joining the army.

2 *formal* **:** something that is added to a statement to limit or change its effect or meaning [*noncount*] I agree with the statement without *qualification*. [=I agree completely] [*count*] They will agree to the deal only with the *qualification* [=*stipulation*] that they get 40 percent of the profits.

3 [*count*] *Brit* **:** an official record or document (such as a degree, certificate, or diploma) which shows that you have completed a course of study or training and are qualified to do something ▪ She is finishing up her *qualification* in marketing. ▪ He is studying for his teaching *qualification*. ▪ Students working towards their *qualifications*. ▪ Her ***paper qualifications*** [=her qualifications on paper; her qualifications as shown by documents] make her a good candidate, but do you think she has the right personality for the job?

4 [*noncount*] **:** the act of qualifying for something or the fact of having qualified for something ▪ Your credit card will be sent to you by mail upon *qualification*. [=when you have qualified to receive it] ▪ The team earned *qualification* for the tournament. [=the team qualified to play in the tournament]

qual·i·fied /ˈkwɑːləˌfaɪd/ *adj*

Q

1 [*more* ~; *most* ~] : having the necessary skill, experience, or knowledge to do a particular job or activity : having the qualifications to do something ▪ She is highly *qualified* for the job. ▪ He is *qualified* [=*eligible*] to run for president. ▪ She is *qualified* [=*licensed*] to practice law in this state. ▪ fully *qualified* teachers/nurses ▪ I'm not *qualified* to give you advice about what you should do.

2 *formal* : not complete : limited in some way : PARTIAL ▪ She gave a *qualified* yes to the question. ▪ The plan was given *qualified* approval.

qual·i·fi·er /ˈkwɑːləˌfajɚ/ *noun, pl* **-ers** [*count*]

1 : a person or team that has defeated others to enter a competition ▪ She's one of the *qualifiers* for the tournament.

2 : a game or contest that a person or team must win in order to enter a particular competition ▪ She'll be playing in the tournament this year after winning the *qualifier*.

3 *grammar* : a word (such as an adjective or adverb) or phrase that describes another word or group of words : MODIFIER

qual·i·fy /ˈkwɑːləˌfaɪ/ *verb* **-fies; -fied; -fy·ing**

1 a [+ *obj*] : to give (someone) the necessary skill or knowledge to do a particular job or activity ▪ His experience *qualifies* him for the job. ▪ The training will *qualify* you to sell insurance. **b** [*no obj*] : to have the necessary skill or knowledge to do a particular job or activity : to have the qualifications to do something ▪ They both *qualify* for the job.

2 [*no obj*] : to pass an exam or complete a course of study that is required in order to do something ▪ Lawyers may only work in the state in which they *qualified*. [=passed the exam] — often + *as* ▪ He has just *qualified as* a doctor/pilot.

3 a [*no obj*] : to have the right to do, have, or be a part of something ▪ Did she *qualify* to receive financial aid? ▪ Financial assistance is available for those who *qualify*. — often + *for* ▪ Town residents *qualify for* a discount on the tickets. ▪ To *qualify for* the contest, you must be at least 18 years old. **b** [+ *obj*] : to give (someone) the right to do, have, or be a part of something ▪ The win *qualifies* her to compete in the final race. ▪ The certification *qualifies* you to teach only in this state. — often + *for* ▪ The insurance plan *qualifies* you *for* an eye exam every two years. ▪ Further education will *qualify* you *for* a pay raise.

4 [*no obj*] : to have the skills that are required or do the things that are required to become a member of a team or to be allowed in a competition ▪ Only those racers who *qualify* will continue to the next round. ▪ She tried to get into the tournament, but she failed to *qualify*. — often + *for* ▪ She *qualified for* the Olympic team.

5 a [*no obj*] : to have all the necessary qualities to be thought of or described in a particular way — + *as* ▪ Does this shirt *qualify as* business attire? ▪ Living in a camper for a weekend does not *qualify as* outdoor camping. ▪ A 10–3 victory *qualifies as* a blowout. ▪ The book is too short to *qualify as* a novel. **b** [+ *obj*] : to give (someone or something) the right to be thought of or described in a particular way — + *as* ▪ His brief time in the army doesn't *qualify* him *as* a military expert.

6 [+ *obj*] *formal* : to make (a statement) more specific or limited in meaning or effect ▪ I would like to *qualify* [=*modify*] what I said earlier to avoid any misinterpretation.

7 [+ *obj*] *grammar* : to limit or describe the meaning of (a word or group of words) : MODIFY ▪ Adjectives *qualify* nouns.

qual·i·ta·tive /ˈkwɑːləˌteɪtɪv/ *adj* : of or relating to how good something is : of or relating to the quality of something ▪ a *qualitative* analysis of the product [=an analysis concerned with the quality of the product] ▪ The research showed a *qualitative* difference between the two teaching methods. [=showed that one teaching method is better than the other] — compare QUANTITATIVE

– **qual·i·ta·tive·ly** *adv*

[1]**qual·i·ty** /ˈkwɑːləti/ *noun, pl* **-ties**

1 [*noncount*] : how good or bad something is ▪ Pollution affects air/water *quality*. ▪ The restaurant serves food of high *quality*. [=the food at the restaurant is very good] ▪ The dress material is of poor *quality*. [=the dress material is not good] — often + *of* ▪ The *quality of* the service we received was very good. ▪ The *quality of* their products has gone down. ▪ His attention to detail shows in the *quality of* his work. ▪ She has raised/improved her ***quality of life*** [=she has become more successful] with her new career. ▪ The drug is used to improve the *quality of life* for patients who have chronic illnesses. [=to make their lives more pleasant and enjoyable]

2 [*count*] : a characteristic or feature that someone or something has : something that can be noticed as a part of a person or thing ▪ Honesty is a desirable *quality*. ▪ Stubbornness is one of his bad *qualities*. ▪ She has strong leadership *qualities*. ▪ The house has many fine *qualities*. ▪ His music has a primitive *quality*. — often + *of* ▪ Hardness is a *quality of* steel. ▪ He considered the good and bad *qualities of* the car before buying it.

3 [*noncount*] : a high level of value or excellence ▪ wine of *quality* [=very good wine] ▪ They offer *quality* at a reasonable price.

[2]**quality** *adj, always used before a noun*

1 : very good or excellent ▪ The restaurant offers *quality* service. ▪ The store sells *quality* furniture at reasonable prices. ▪ It can be difficult to find *quality* childcare. ▪ He had a *quality* education.

2 *Brit* : intended for people who are educated and who care about serious matters ▪ a *quality* newspaper/paper ▪ the *quality* press

quality assurance *noun* [*noncount*] : the activity of checking goods or services to make sure that they are good — abbr. *QA*

quality control *noun* [*noncount*] : the activity of checking goods as they are produced to make sure that the final products are good — abbr. *QC*

quality time *noun* [*noncount*] : time that you spend giving all of your attention to someone who is close to you (such as your child) ▪ Spending some *quality time* after work with your children is very important. ▪ Dad and I spent some *quality time* together.

qualm /ˈkwɑːm/ *noun, pl* **qualms** [*count*] : a feeling of doubt or uncertainty about whether you are doing the right thing ▪ He accepted their offer without a *qualm*. — usually plural; often + *about* ▪ She had/felt some *qualms about* moving to the big city. ▪ He had no *qualms about* accepting their offer.

quan·da·ry /ˈkwɑːndri/ *noun, pl* **-ries** [*count*] *formal* : a situation in which you are confused about what to do ▪ The unexpected results of the test have created a *quandary* for researchers. ▪ He was ***in a quandary*** [=*unsure, confused*] about which candidate to choose.

quan·go /ˈkwæŋˌgoʊ/ *noun, pl* **-gos** [*count*] *Brit* : an organization that deals with public matters and is supported by the government but that works independently and has its own legal powers ✧ *Quango* was formed as an abbreviation of "quasi-nongovernmental organization."

quanta *plural of* [1]QUANTUM

quan·ti·fi·er /ˈkwɑːntəˌfajɚ/ *noun, pl* **-ers** [*count*] *grammar* : a word or number (such as "many," "few," "some," "two," or "2") that is used with a noun to show the amount of something ▪ "Five" in "the five men" is a *quantifier*.

quan·ti·fy /ˈkwɑːntəˌfaɪ/ *verb* **-fies; -fied; -fy·ing** [+ *obj*] *formal* : to find or calculate the quantity or amount of (something) ▪ It is difficult to *quantify* intelligence. ▪ Doctors have *quantified* the risks of smoking cigarettes. ▪ It is impossible to *quantify* the number of Web sites on the Internet.

– **quan·ti·fi·able** /ˌkwɑːntəˈfajəbəl/ *adj* ▪ The health risks are not *quantifiable*. ▪ *quantifiable* benefits

quan·ti·ta·tive /ˈkwɑːntəˌteɪtɪv/ *adj* : of or relating to how much there is of something : of or relating to the quantity or amount of something ▪ a *quantitative* analysis/measurement ▪ Scientists are gathering *quantitative* information about human intelligence. — compare QUALITATIVE

– **quan·ti·ta·tive·ly** *adv*

quan·ti·ty /ˈkwɑːntəti/ *noun, pl* **-ties**

1 : an amount or number of something [*count*] The wine is made in small/large *quantities*. — often + *of* ▪ I ate a large *quantity of* food. [=I ate a lot of food] ▪ Farmers grow large *quantities of* wheat and corn. ▪ Add a half a cup of oil, and the same *quantity of* vinegar. [*noncount*] The boss is worried about *quantity* as well as quality. ▪ Production saw an increase ***in quantity***. [=there was an increase in the amount produced] — abbr. *qty*.

2 : a large amount or number of something [*count*] — + *of* ▪ Police found *quantities of* drugs and guns in the house. ▪ There is a *quantity of* information [=a lot of information] available on this topic. [*noncount*] Blood cells are produced ***in quantity***. [=in large amounts] ▪ The family buys food *in quantity*.

known quantity : someone or something whose abilities or characteristics are well known ▪ When she was cast in the role of the princess, she was already a *known quantity* from her work in several films.

Q

unknown quantity : someone or something whose abilities or characteristics are not yet known • If you've never been published before, you're an *unknown quantity*, so you're going to have difficulty selling your first novel.

quantity surveyor *noun, pl* ~ **-ors** [*count*] *Brit* : someone whose job is to estimate the amount and cost of materials needed for building something and how long it will take to build

[1]**quan·tum** /ˈkwɑːntəm/ *noun, pl* **quan·ta** /ˈkwɑːntə/ [*count*] *physics* : the smallest amount of many forms of energy (such as light)

[2]**quantum** *adj, always used before a noun, physics* : of, relating to, or using the principles of quantum theory • *quantum* physics

quantum leap *noun, pl* ~ **leaps** [*count*] : a sudden large change, development, or improvement • Prices have taken a *quantum leap* upward. • The new drug is a *quantum leap* in the fight against cancer. — called also *quantum jump*

quantum mechanics *noun* [*noncount*] *physics* : a branch of physics that deals with the structure and behavior of very small pieces of matter

quantum theory *noun* [*noncount*] *physics* : a theory in physics that is based on the idea that energy (such as light) is made of small separate units of energy

[1]**quar·an·tine** /ˈkworənˌtiːn/ *noun* [*noncount*]

1 : the period of time during which a person or animal that has a disease or that might have a disease is kept away from others to prevent the disease from spreading • a six-month *quarantine*

2 : the situation of being kept away from others to prevent a disease from spreading • The infected people were put into *quarantine*. • The cows will be kept/held ***in quarantine*** for another week. • The dog was put/placed ***under quarantine***

[2]**quarantine** *verb* **-tines; -tined; -tin·ing** [+ *obj*] : to keep (a person or animal) away from others to prevent a disease from spreading : to put or keep (a person or animal) in quarantine • The hospital *quarantined* the infected patients. • The dog was immediately *quarantined*.

quark /ˈkwoɚk/ *noun, pl* **quarks** [*count*] *physics* : any one of several types of very small particles that make up matter

[1]**quar·rel** /ˈkworəl/ *noun, pl* **-rels** [*count*]

1 : an angry argument or disagreement • a lover's *quarrel* = a *quarrel* between lovers • They had a *quarrel* about/over money. • a *quarrel* between husband and wife • She had a *quarrel* with her mother.

2 : a reason to disagree with or argue about something — + *with* • I have a few *quarrels with* your plan. • I have ***no quarrel with*** [=I do not object to] your plan. • It would be foolish to ***pick a quarrel*** [=start a quarrel] ***with*** him.

[2]**quarrel** *verb* **-rels**; *US* **-reled** *or Brit* **-relled**; *US* **-rel·ing** *or Brit* **-rel·ling** [*no obj*] : to argue about or disagree with something • The children *quarrel* all the time. • She and her husband are always *quarreling* about/over money. • I don't want to *quarrel* with you. • I won't *quarrel* [=*disagree*] with your version of what happened.

quar·rel·some /ˈkworəlsəm/ *adj* [*more* ~; *most* ~] : ready or likely to argue or disagree • She is very *quarrelsome*. • a *quarrelsome* person

[1]**quar·ry** /ˈkwori/ *noun* [*singular*] : an animal or person that is being hunted or chased • The dogs chased their *quarry*. • The detective followed his *quarry* into a nightclub. — compare [2]QUARRY

[2]**quarry** *noun, pl* **quar·ries** [*count*] : a place where large amounts of stone are dug out of the ground • a limestone *quarry* — compare [1]QUARRY

[3]**quarry** *verb* **-ries; -ried; -ry·ing**

1 : to dig or take (stone or other materials) from a quarry [+ *obj*] — often used as *(be) quarried* • Limestone *is quarried* in this area. • The stone used for these buildings *was quarried* from a nearby site. [*no obj*] an area where workers are *quarrying* for limestone

2 [+ *obj*] : to make a quarry in (a place) — usually used as *(be) quarried* • This area has *been quarried* for limestone.

– quarrying /ˈkworijɪŋ/ *noun* [*noncount*]

quart /ˈkwoɚt/ *noun, pl* **quarts** [*count*]

1 *US* : a unit of liquid measurement equal to two U.S. pints or 0.946 liters — abbr. *qt.*

2 *Brit* : a unit of liquid measurement equal to two British pints or 1.14 liters — abbr. *qt.*

[1]**quar·ter** /ˈkwoɚtɚ/ *noun, pl* **-ters**

1 [*count*] : one of four equal parts of something • Cut the pie into *quarters*. • A *quarter* [=*fourth*] of the class voted "no."

2 [*count*] : a unit of something (such as weight or length) that equals one fourth of some larger unit • an inch and a *quarter* • a *quarter* of a cup of sugar • It happened three *quarters* of a century ago. [=75 years ago]

3 [*count*] : one of four divisions of an hour : a period of 15 minutes • He was three *quarters* of an hour early. • It is now ***(a) quarter to*** four. = (*US*) It is now ***(a) quarter of*** four. [=it is 15 minutes before four o'clock] • The alarm went off at ***(a) quarter past*** six. = (*US*) The alarm went off at ***(a) quarter after*** six. [=15 minutes after six o'clock]

4 [*count*] : one of four divisions of a year : a period of three months • The company's profits rose in the second *quarter*. • (*Brit*) ***quarter day*** [=the first day of a financial quarter when payments are due]

5 [*count*] : one of four divisions of a school term usually lasting about 12 weeks • She received her grades for the first *quarter*. — compare SEMESTER, TERM, TRIMESTER

6 [*count*] : one of the four equal parts of the playing time of a game (such as basketball or American football) • There are two minutes left in the third *quarter*. • The final *quarter* of the game was very exciting.

7 [*count*] : a coin of the United States and Canada that is worth 25 cents • Do you have a *quarter* for the parking meter?; *also* : the sum of 25 cents • The candy costs a *quarter*.

8 [*count*] : a person or group of people or an area in which people live • Concern has been expressed in many *quarters*. [=many people have expressed concern] • The move was met with dismay in this *quarter*. • My brother and I have not spoken in years so I expect no help from that *quarter*. [=I expect no help from my brother] • Complaints came ***from all quarters*** [=from many people or places]

9 [*count*] : a part or area of a city • She lives in the historic *quarter*. [=*district*]

10 ***quarters*** [*plural*] : the place where someone lives • Our living *quarters* were very comfortable. • soldiers'/servants' *quarters*

11 [*count*] : one of the two times during a month when a quarter of the moon's surface can be seen • The moon was in its/the first *quarter*. • a *quarter* moon

at/in close quarters : close together usually in a very small space • The sailors were living *in close quarters*. • We could observe the behavior of all the animals *at close quarters*. [=from a short distance]

no quarter *literary* : no pity or mercy — used to say that an enemy, opponent, etc., is treated in a very harsh way • The soldiers showed/gave *no quarter* to the enemy. • They received *no quarter* or sympathy.

[2]**quarter** *verb* **-ters; -tered; -ter·ing** [+ *obj*]

1 : to divide or separate (something) into four parts • The hunters *quartered* the deer. • She *quartered* the potatoes.

2 : to provide (someone) with a place to stay for a usually short period of time : to provide living quarters for (someone) • We were *quartered* in log cabins at the camp.

[3]**quarter** *adj, always used before a noun* : equal or about nearly equal in size, value, amount, etc., to one fourth of something • a *quarter* century ago • a *quarter* acre of land • They live less than a *quarter* mile from us.

[1]**quar·ter·back** /ˈkwoɚtɚˌbæk/ *noun, pl* **-backs** [*count*] *American football* : a player who leads a team's attempts to score usually by passing the ball to other players — abbr. *QB*; see also MONDAY-MORNING QUARTERBACK

[2]**quarterback** *verb* **-backs; -backed; -back·ing** [+ *obj*] *US*

1 *American football* : to play the position of quarterback for (a team) • He *quarterbacked* his high school team.

2 : to lead or organize (something) by making important decisions • She *quarterbacked* the company's latest ad campaign.

quarterback sneak *noun, pl* ~ **sneaks** [*count*] *American football* : a play in which the quarterback runs forward immediately after receiving the ball instead of handing it or throwing it to another player • He ran a *quarterback sneak* up the middle for a touchdown.

quar·ter·deck /ˈkwoɚtɚˌdɛk/ *noun, pl* **-decks** [*count*] : the upper level of a ship's deck that is located toward the rear of the ship and that is used mainly by officers

quar·ter·final (*US*) *or Brit* **quar·ter–final** /ˌkwoɚtɚˈfaɪnl/ *noun, pl* **-nals** [*count*] : one of four matches, games, or contests to decide the four people or teams that will continue playing in a competition (such as a tennis tournament) • He lost in the *quarterfinal*. — often plural ▪ She won in the *quarterfinals* but lost in the semifinals. — often used before another noun ▪ a *quarterfinal* match

quarter horse *noun, pl* ~ **horses** [*count*] : a small, strong horse that can run very fast for short distances

quarter hour *noun, pl* ~ **hours** [*count*] : 15 minutes ▪ Trains depart every *quarter hour*. : a period of time that lasts for 15 minutes ▪ I waited a *quarter hour* in line.

[1]**quar·ter·ly** /ˈkwoɚtɚli/ *adj* : happening, done, or produced four times a year ▪ The company holds *quarterly* meetings. ▪ a *quarterly* report
– **quarterly** *adv* ▪ The payments are made *quarterly*. [=four times a year] ▪ The interest on the account is compounded *quarterly*.

[2]**quarterly** *noun, pl* **-lies** [*count*] : a magazine that is published four times a year ▪ a literary *quarterly*

quar·ter·mas·ter /ˈkwoɚtɚˌmæstɚ, *Brit* ˈkwɔːtəˌmɑːstə/ *noun, pl* **-ters** [*count*]
1 : an army officer who provides clothing and supplies for soldiers
2 : a navy officer who is in charge of the steering of a ship and the use of signals on a ship

quarter note *noun, pl* ~ **notes** [*count*] *US* : a musical note equal in time to ¼ of a whole note — called also (*Brit*) *crotchet*

quar·tet /kwoɚˈtɛt/ *noun, pl* **-tets** [*count*]
1 : a group of four singers or musicians who perform together ▪ He is a member of a jazz *quartet*.
2 : a song or piece of music performed by four singers or musicians ▪ a string *quartet* by Beethoven
3 : a group or set of four people or things ▪ The author wrote a *quartet* of novels about the same character.

quartz /ˈkwoɚts/ *noun* [*noncount*] : a mineral that is often found in the form of a hard crystal and that is used especially to make clocks and watches

qua·sar /ˈkweɪˌzɑɚ/ *noun, pl* **-sars** [*count*] *astronomy* : a very bright object in space that is similar to a star and that is very far away from the Earth and gives off powerful radio waves

quash /ˈkwɑːʃ/ *verb* **quash·es; quashed; quash·ing** [+ *obj*]
1 : to stop (something) from continuing by doing or saying something ▪ The riot was *quashed* by police. ▪ The couple *quashed* rumors that they were engaged.
2 *law* : to decide that (a ruling, decision, etc.) is wrong and no longer valid ▪ The judge *quashed* [=*overturned*] the verdict of the lower court and ordered a new trial.

qua·si- /ˈkweɪˌzaɪ, ˈkwɑːzi/ *combining form* : in some way or sense but not in a true, direct, or complete way ▪ His appearance on TV earned him *quasi*-celebrity [=*near*-celebrity] status. ▪ a *quasi*-historical novel ▪ a *quasi*-official organization [=an organization that is like an official organization but that is not actually official]

qua·train /ˈkwɑːˌtreɪn/ *noun, pl* **-trains** [*count*] : a poem or verse that has four lines

[1]**qua·ver** /ˈkweɪvɚ/ *verb* **-vers; -vered; -ver·ing** [*no obj*] *of your voice* : to produce sound in an unsteady way especially because you are afraid or nervous : TREMBLE ▪ Her voice *quavered* during the speech. ▪ He spoke in *quavering* tones.
– **qua·very** /ˈkweɪvəri/ *adj* ▪ a *quavery* voice

[2]**quaver** *noun, pl* **-vers** [*count*]
1 : an unsteady sound in someone's voice that is caused by fear or other strong emotions ▪ There was a *quaver* in his voice.
2 *Brit* : EIGHTH NOTE

quay /ˈkiː/ *noun, pl* **quays** [*count*] : a structure built on the land next to a river, lake, or ocean that is used as a place for boats to stop for loading and unloading freight and passengers

quay·side /ˈkiːˌsaɪd/ *noun, pl* **-sides** [*count*] : the area of land next to a quay ▪ a *quayside* café

quea·sy /ˈkwiːzi/ *adj* **quea·si·er; -est** [*also more* ~; *most* ~]
1 : having a sick feeling in the stomach : suffering from nausea ▪ The boat ride made me a little *queasy*. ▪ She complained of a *queasy* stomach. ▪ a *queasy* sensation
2 : having an unpleasantly nervous or doubtful feeling ▪ He feels *queasy* about taking the test. ▪ She had the *queasy* feeling that she was being watched.
– **quea·si·ness** *noun* [*noncount*]

queen /ˈkwiːn/ *noun, pl* **queens** [*count*]
1 a : a woman who rules a country and who usually inherits her position and rules for life ▪ She was crowned *queen* of England. ▪ the reign of *Queen* Elizabeth **b** : the wife of a king ▪ the king and his *queen*
2 a : a girl or woman who is highly respected and very successful or popular ▪ She's a fashion *queen*. ▪ the *queen* of the blues **b** : a girl or woman who is awarded the highest honor for an event or contest ▪ She was voted *queen* of the prom. ▪ the homecoming *queen* **c** : something that is thought of as female and that is considered better than all others ▪ This ship is the *queen* of all the ocean liners.
3 : the most powerful piece in the game of chess that can move any number of free squares in any direction — see picture at CHESS
4 : a playing card that has a picture of a queen ▪ the *queen* of hearts/spades/clubs/diamonds — see picture at PLAYING CARD
5 : a female insect (such as a bee or ant) that lays eggs ▪ a *queen* bee
6 *informal* + *offensive* : a homosexual man who usually acts like a woman — see also DRAG QUEEN

queen·ly /ˈkwiːnli/ *adj* : resembling a queen or suitable for a queen ▪ She maintained a *queenly* posture. ▪ *queenly* dignity

Queen Mother *noun*
the Queen Mother : the widow of a king who is the mother of the current king or queen

Queen's Counsel *noun, pl* ~ **-sels** [*count*] : a barrister who is chosen to represent the British royal family in a court of law — used when Britain is ruled by a queen; abbr. *QC*

Queen's evidence *noun*
turn Queen's evidence *Brit, law* ◊ If you are charged with a crime and you *turn Queen's evidence* (or *turn King's evidence*), you agree to give information (such as the names of other criminals) to the court in order to reduce your own punishment. ▪ One of the gang members *turned Queen's evidence* [=(*US*) *turned state's evidence*] and testified against the other members.

queen–size /ˈkwiːnˌsaɪz/ *or* **queen–sized** /ˈkwiːnˌsaɪzd/ *adj, US, of a bed* : having a size of about 60 inches by 80 inches (about 1.5 by 1.9 meters) — compare FULL-SIZE, KING-SIZE, TWIN-SIZE

[1]**queer** /ˈkwiɚ/ *adj* **queer·er; -est**
1 *old-fashioned* : odd or unusual ▪ The sky was a *queer* shade of red. ▪ a *queer* odor ▪ I had a *queer* feeling that something bad was about to happen. ▪ He's a bit *queer* in the head. [=he's mentally strange or unwell; he's slightly crazy] — see also *queer fish* at [1]FISH
2 *informal* + *usually offensive* : HOMOSEXUAL ◊ *Queer* in this sense is offensive in most of its uses, but it is also now sometimes used in a neutral or positive way especially by some homosexual and bisexual people. ▪ *queer* culture ▪ She is interested in taking a class in ***queer studies***.
– **queer·ly** *adv* ▪ a *queerly* shaped cloud ▪ He looked at her *queerly*. – **queer·ness** *noun* [*noncount*]

[2]**queer** *noun, pl* **queers** [*count*] *informal* + *usually offensive* : a homosexual person

[3]**queer** *verb* **queers; queered; queer·ing** [+ *obj*] *informal* : to spoil or ruin (something) ▪ The sudden storm *queered* our plans. ▪ (*US*) Something ***queered the deal***. ▪ (*Brit*) The unexpected delay ***queered his pitch***. [=ruined his plans]

quell /ˈkwɛl/ *verb* **quells; quelled; quell·ing** [+ *obj*]
1 : to end or stop (something) usually by using force ▪ Police *quelled* [=*quashed*] the riot.
2 : to calm or reduce (something, such as fear or worry) ▪ The president's remarks *quelled* [=*eased*] employees' fears.

quench /ˈkwɛntʃ/ *verb* **quench·es; quenched; quench·ing** [+ *obj*] *formal* : to stop (a fire) from burning : to put out (a fire) ▪ Firefighters *quenched* [=*extinguished*] the flames.
quench your thirst : to cause you to stop feeling thirsty ▪ a drink that will *quench your thirst* ▪ He *quenched his thirst* by drinking a bottle of water.

quer·u·lous /ˈkwerələs/ *adj* [*more* ~; *most* ~] *formal* : complaining in an annoyed way ▪ The child said in a *querulous* [=*whining*] voice that he didn't like carrots. ▪ *querulous* customers
– **quer·u·lous·ly** *adv* – **quer·u·lous·ness** *noun* [*noncount*]

[1]**que·ry** /ˈkwiri/ *noun, pl* **que·ries** [*count*] : a question or a request for information about something ▪ I have a *query* about my order. ▪ an Internet *query* ▪ The librarian responded to my *query*.

[2]**query** *verb* **queries; que·ried; que·ry·ing** [+ *obj*]

1 *chiefly US* **: to ask (someone) a question** ▪ The reporter *queried* [=*questioned*] several citizens about the tax hike. ▪ They conducted a survey in which several hundred people were *queried* about their dietary habits.

2 : to ask questions or express doubt about (something) ▪ She *queried* [=*questioned*] the teacher's decision.

3 : to ask (a question) ▪ "What's that?" he *queried*.

que•sa•dil•la /ˌkeɪsəˈdiːjə/ *noun, pl* **quesadillas** [*count*] **: a Mexican food which consists of a flat piece of bread (called a tortilla) that is folded around a filling of meat, cheese, or other ingredients and usually fried**

[1]**quest** /ˈkwɛst/ *noun, pl* **quests** [*count*] *formal + literary*

1 : a journey made in search of something ▪ They went on a *quest* for gold.

2 : a long and difficult effort to find or do something ▪ a *quest* for answers ▪ The team's *quest* to win a championship finally came to an end. ▪ He refuses to give up his *quest* to discover the truth.

in quest of **: searching for (something)** ▪ She is *in quest of* the perfect wine.

[2]**quest** *verb* **quests; quest•ed; quest•ing** [*no obj*] *formal + literary* **: to go on a journey to find something** ▪ They were *questing* for gold.

[1]**ques•tion** /ˈkwɛstʃən/ *noun, pl* **-tions**

1 [*count*] **: a sentence, phrase, or word that asks for information or is used to test someone's knowledge** ▪ Can I ask you a personal *question*? ▪ Please answer my *question*. ▪ I don't understand the *question*. ▪ Are there any more *questions*? ▪ I have a couple of legal *questions* (for you). ▪ In answer to your *question*, our next meeting will be on Friday. ▪ The essay *questions* on the test were easy/hard. ▪ There are 10 multiple-choice *questions* on the exam. ▪ The exam included several *questions* on/about current events. ▪ The *question* arose as to who would be responsible for caring for our grandmother. ▪ I expected him to ask where I worked, but the *question* never came up. ▪ I am sure to get a raise. The *question* is [=what I want to know is], how much it will be? ▪ The key *question* in solving the mystery is, how did the murderer enter the house? ▪ One *question* still remains: Do we have the funding for this project? ▪ (*formal*) She posed the *question* of [=she asked] whether we could get funding for the project. ▪ Stop avoiding the *question* and answer me! ▪ She hoped to avoid awkward/embarrassing *questions* about her personal life during the interview. ▪ Whether voters will support him remains an ***open question***. [=no one knows yet whether voters will support him] ▪ There are still many ***unanswered questions*** about his past. ▪ It was a ***rhetorical question***. I didn't expect an answer. ▪ "How can we reduce expenses without cutting important programs?" "(That's a) ***good question***." [=I don't know] ▪ The ***big question*** [=the thing everyone would like to know] is, will he be number one in the football draft? ▪ There will be a ***question and answer session*** [=a period of time when people can have their questions answered] following the speech. ▪ (*formal*) The lawyer would like to ***put another question to*** the defendant. [=ask the defendant another question] — see also LEADING QUESTION

2 [*count*] **: a matter or problem that is being discussed : a subject or topic** ▪ Her paper raises several *questions* [=*issues*] that need to be discussed/addressed. ▪ It is still an ***open question*** whether or not you may go. — **often + *of*** ▪ The class discussed the *question of* stem cell research. ▪ The *question of* buying or leasing a car is really up to the buyer to decide on.

3 [*noncount*] **a : doubt or uncertainty about something** ▪ There was little *question* of her being able to do the work. ▪ There is considerable *question* about the actual value of the property. — **often used in negative statements** ▪ There is no *question* but that there will be some protest about his decision. ▪ There was no *question* of/about his loyalty. ▪ There is no *question* that he was one of the greatest players of the game. ▪ There's ***no question about it***—that girl has talent! ▪ ***Without question***, it was his best performance by far. [=it was definitely his best performance ever] ▪ She trusted him *without question*. **b : a state of doubt or uncertainty** ▪ The results of the study have ***come into question***. = The results of the study have been ***called into question***. [=people are expressing doubts about the results] ▪ The fact that he plagiarized ***throws/brings/calls into question*** the authenticity of his earlier writings.

4 [*noncount*] **: the possibility or chance *of* something happening or *of* someone doing something — used in negative statements** ▪ ***There was no question of*** escape. [=escape was not possible] ▪ *There was no question of* him forgetting about what happened.

a question of **— used to say that one thing results from or requires another** ▪ "I can't go!" "If it's just *a question of* money [=if money is the only problem], I can let you borrow some." ▪ It's only *a question of* time [=a matter of time] before/until we catch him. ▪ Is success all just *a question of* being in the right place at the right time?

beg the question see BEG

beyond question **1 : completely certain or definite** ▪ His genius is *beyond question*. **2 : in a way that is completely certain : without any doubt** ▪ The new evidence establishes his innocence *beyond* (all) *question*.

in question **1 — used to indicate the specific thing that is being discussed or referred to** ▪ The painting *in question* is by Rembrandt. ▪ What is *in question* is not the candidate's private life but her policies. ▪ Where were you on the Sunday *in question*? **2 : in a state of doubt or uncertainty** ▪ His suitability for the job is *in question*. ▪ The results of the study are *in question*.

open to question **: not known for sure : UNCERTAIN** ▪ Her intentions are *open to question*. ▪ The author's exact meaning is *open to question*.

out of the question **: not possible or allowed** ▪ Asking my father for money was completely *out of the question*. ▪ Wearing a stained blouse to dinner was *out of the question*.

pop the question see [1]POP

[2]**question** *verb* **-tions; -tioned; -tion•ing** [+ *obj*]

1 : to ask (someone) questions about something ▪ The reporter *questioned* her at length on her life as the First Lady. ▪ The witness was *questioned* by the defense. ▪ Police *questioned* [=*interrogated*] the suspect carefully. — **often + *about*** ▪ She was *questioned about* her husband's mysterious disappearance.

2 : to have or express doubt about (something) ▪ I could tell that she was *questioning* my decision. ▪ He began to *question* his ability to do the job. ▪ I trusted him and I never *questioned* what he told me. ▪ The lawyer *questioned* the truth of the witness's statement. ▪ He began to *question* whether the things she had said were really true.

– ques•tion•er *noun, pl* **-ers** [*count*] ▪ The mayor's first *questioner* at the town meeting asked about the new parking regulations.

ques•tion•able /ˈkwɛstʃənəbəl/ *adj*

1 : not likely to be true or correct : giving reason to doubt or question something ▪ The truth of the statements was highly *questionable*. ▪ a *questionable* conclusion ▪ It is *questionable* whether this is the right decision. [=I question/doubt whether this is the right decision]

2 : likely to be bad : not worthy of trust ▪ The water available in the village is of *questionable* quality. ▪ a man of *questionable* character ▪ They acquired the money through *questionable* means.

3 : not certain : unknown or undecided ▪ The company is facing a *questionable* future.

– ques•tion•ably /ˈkwɛstʃənəbli/ *adv* ▪ *questionably* obtained money

[1]**questioning** *adj* **: showing a feeling of doubt or a desire to ask a question in order to get information** ▪ She gave him a *questioning* look.

– ques•tion•ing•ly *adv* ▪ She looked at him *questioningly*.

[2]**questioning** *noun* [*noncount*] **: the activity or process of asking questions** ▪ The police took him in for *questioning*. ▪ the *questioning* of authority

question mark *noun, pl* **~ marks** [*count*]

1 : the punctuation mark ? that is used after a direct question or to indicate that something (such as a birth date) is uncertain

2 a *chiefly US* **: someone or something that causes feelings of doubt or uncertainty** ▪ The future of the company remains a *question mark*. [=no one knows what will happen in the company's future] ▪ His leg is still sore and he remains a *question mark* for next week's game. [=it is not certain that he will be able to play in next week's game] ▪ The team's pitching is a big *question mark* this season. **b** ◊ If there is ***a question mark over something***, there is doubt about it. ▪ Her injured elbow puts *a* big *question mark over* her chances in the tournament.

question master *noun, pl* **~ -ters** [*count*] *Brit* **: QUIZMASTER**

ques•tion•naire /ˌkwɛstʃəˈneɚ/ *noun, pl* **-naires** [*count*] **: a written set of questions that are given to people in order to collect facts or opinions about something** ▪ (*US*) Would you please fill out this *questionnaire*? = (*Brit*) Would you please fill in this *questionnaire*?

[1]**queue** /ˈkjuː/ *noun, pl* **queues** [*count*]

1 *chiefly Brit* : a line of people who are waiting for something • The people formed a *queue* [=(*US*) *line*] at the ticket window. • We were forced to stand/wait in a *queue*. • a bus/taxi *queue*

2 *computers* : a series of instructions that are stored in a computer so that they can be processed later • Three jobs remain in the printer *queue*.

jump the queue *Brit* : to go ahead of the other people in a queue : to go to the front of a queue instead of waiting • He tried to *jump the queue* but they wouldn't let him. — see also QUEUE-JUMPING

[2]**queue** *verb* **queues; queued; queu·ing** *or* **queue·ing** [*no obj*] *chiefly Brit* : to form or wait in a line • Hundreds of people *queued* [=(*US*) *lined up*] for a chance to meet him. • The crowd was *queuing* at the snack bar. — often + *up* • The crowd was *queuing up* at the snack bar.

queue–jumping *noun* [*noncount*] *Brit* : the act of going ahead of other people in a queue instead of waiting your turn • Police say that the fight broke out over *queue-jumping*. [=(*US*) *cutting in line*] — see also *jump the queue* at [1]QUEUE

[1]**quib·ble** /ˈkwɪbəl/ *verb* **quib·bles; quib·bled; quib·bling** [*no obj*] : to argue or complain about small, unimportant things — usually + *about* or *over* • People ignored the main point of the speech and *quibbled about* its length. • Why are you *quibbling over* such a small amount of money?

[2]**quibble** *noun, pl* **quibbles** [*count*] : a small complaint or criticism usually about something unimportant • Our only *quibble* about the trip was that it rained a lot. • a minor *quibble*

quiche /ˈkiːʃ/ *noun, pl* **quich·es** [*count, noncount*] : a pie made with eggs, milk, cheese, and vegetables or meat

[1]**quick** /ˈkwɪk/ *adj* **quick·er; -est**

1 : done or happening in a short amount of time • a *quick* look/glance • They had a *quick* drink at the bar. • She took a *quick* shower. • She gave him a *quick* kiss. • You're back already? That was *quick*! • We made a *quick* decision, but it turned out to be a good one. • He got a *quick* reply to his inquiry. • The car made a *quick* [=*sudden*] left turn.

2 : fast in thinking, learning, or understanding • a *quick* mind/learner • *quick* students • His *quick* thinking/wits allowed him to escape trouble. • (*US*) She is a ***quick study*** who learned her job easily. • Her friends admired her ***quick wit***.

3 a : fast in moving or reacting • He walked with *quick* steps. • She has *quick*, agile hands. • Please be *quick*. We can't wait much longer. • He has a ***quick temper***. [=he gets angry very quickly and easily] **b** : tending to do something very quickly or too quickly — followed by *to* + *verb* • He is always *quick to criticize* other people, but he gets angry if anyone criticizes him. • She was *quick to excuse* her son's behavior.

4 : able to be done, obtained, or achieved easily and in a short amount of time • a *quick* and easy recipe • He made a *quick* profit/buck selling the car. • There is no ***quick fix*** for these problems. [=there is no fast and easy solution for these problems]

be quick on the draw see [2]DRAW

quick off the mark see [1]MARK

the quick and the dead *literary* : living people and dead people

– quick·ness *noun* [*noncount*] • The track coach was impressed with her *quickness*. • He is known for his *quickness* of wit. • The child amazes me with his *quickness* to learn.

[2]**quick** *adv* **quicker; -est** *informal* : in a fast or quick manner : QUICKLY • a scheme to get rich *quick* • "Come *quick*!" she shouted. • I got used to living with a roommate pretty *quick*. • I can't run any *quicker*. • The new student learned (the) *quickest*. • *Quick*! [=come/move quickly] The train is leaving. • They came ***quick as a flash***. [=very quickly] — often used in combination • *quick*-growing birches • a *quick*-thinking rescuer

[3]**quick** *noun*

cut (someone) to the quick : to make (someone) very upset • Her harsh words *cut him to the quick*. [=he was deeply hurt by her harsh words]

the quick : the very sensitive area of flesh under a fingernail or toenail • He had bitten his nails to *the quick*.

quick·en /ˈkwɪkən/ *verb* **-ens; -ened; -en·ing**

1 a [+ *obj*] : to make (something) faster • She *quickened* [=*hastened*] her steps. • We *quickened* the pace. [=we started to walk faster] • Stimulants can *quicken* the heart rate. **b** [*no obj*] : to become faster • His pulse *quickened* at the thought of seeing her again. • a *quickening* tempo

2 *formal + literary* **a** [+ *obj*] : to make (something, such as a feeling) stronger or more active • The approach of the deadline *quickened* our sense of urgency. **b** [*no obj*] : to become stronger or more active • The drama *quickened* when police arrived at the scene.

quick–fire *adj, always used before a noun, chiefly Brit* : done or coming very quickly one after another : RAPID-FIRE • *quick-fire* responses/questions/jokes

quick·ie /ˈkwɪki/ *noun, pl* **-ies** [*count*] *informal*

1 : something that is done very quickly • "Do you have any other questions?" "Just a *quickie*." • I would like to have a meeting. It'll be a *quickie*. — often used before another noun • a *quickie* divorce/marriage

2 : an act of sexual intercourse that is done in a very short amount of time

quick·lime /ˈkwɪkˌlaɪm/ *noun* [*noncount*] : [2]LIME

quick·ly /ˈkwɪkli/ *adv* [*more ~; most ~*] : in a fast or quick manner • They *quickly* moved away when they saw the oncoming car. • The investigators must act *quickly*. • Please get here as *quickly* as possible. • We ate too/very *quickly*. • They *quickly* settled the dispute.

quick·sand /ˈkwɪkˌsænd/ *noun, pl* **-sands**

1 [*noncount*] : deep, wet sand into which heavy objects sink easily

2 : a situation that is dangerous and difficult to escape from [*noncount*] the *quicksand* of depression [*plural*] freed from the *quicksands* of war

[1]**quick·sil·ver** /ˈkwɪkˌsɪlvɚ/ *noun* [*noncount*] *old-fashioned + literary* : MERCURY 1a

[2]**quicksilver** *adj, always used before a noun, literary* : changing quickly and often • his *quicksilver* [=*mercurial*] temperament

quick–tem·pered /ˈkwɪkˈtɛmpɚd/ *adj* [*more ~; most ~*] : becoming angry quickly and easily : having a quick temper • a *quick-tempered* coach

quick–wit·ted /ˈkwɪkˈwɪtəd/ *adj* [*more ~; most ~*] : having or showing the ability to think and understand things quickly • a *quick-witted* opponent/defendant • *quick-witted* humor • a *quick-witted* reply — opposite SLOW-WITTED

quid /ˈkwɪd/ *noun, pl* **quid** *also* **quids** [*count*] *Brit, informal* : one pound in money • We lost a few *quid* on the horses. • The ticket costs five *quid*.

quids in *Brit, informal* ✧ If you are *quids in*, you have made a good profit. • I was *quids in* by the time I left the horse races.

quid pro quo /ˌkwɪdˌproʊˈkwoʊ/ *noun, pl* **quid pro quos** [*count*] : something that is given to you or done for you in return for something you have given to or done for someone else • If he helps us, he'll expect a *quid pro quo*. [=he'll expect us to do something for him]

qui·es·cent /kwaɪˈɛsn̩t/ *adj*

1 *formal* : not active : QUIET • a *quiescent* state

2 *medical* : not now developing or causing symptoms • *quiescent* disease • a *quiescent* virus

– qui·es·cence /kwaɪˈɛsn̩s/ *noun* [*noncount*] • long periods of *quiescence*

[1]**qui·et** /ˈkwajət/ *adj* **qui·et·er; -est** [*also more ~; most ~*]

1 : making very little noise • a *quiet* engine • the *quiet* hum of the refrigerator • He spoke in a very *quiet* voice. • She was ***as quiet as a mouse***. [=very quiet]

2 a : not talking • Surprisingly, the class was *quiet*. • "Be *quiet*!" she scolded. • Can't you be *quiet* for one minute? [=can't you stop talking?] • She suddenly turned/became/went *quiet*. [=she suddenly stopped talking] **b** : tending not to talk very much • He's a very *quiet* person. • She has a *quiet* disposition/temperament.

3 : not having much activity or movement • a *quiet* [=*calm*] sea • During the morning, business was *quiet*. • Some days at the store are *quieter* than others. • a *quiet* town/village/neighborhood • a *quiet* stretch of road • He led a *quiet* life.

4 : not disturbed by noise or people • We enjoyed a *quiet* [=*peaceful*] dinner for two. • I was looking forward to a *quiet* cup of tea. • I decided to do a little *quiet* reading.

5 : not shown or done in an obvious way • She worked with *quiet* determination. • There is a *quiet* confidence about him. • He was filled with *quiet* desperation/rage. • A *quiet* revolution was underway.

keep quiet **1** : to not say anything or make any noise • Please *keep quiet* during the movie. • He thought about telling the police what he knew, but he decided to *keep quiet*.

Q

[=he decided not to say anything] **2** ***keep quiet about (something) or keep (something) quiet*** : to not say anything about (something) ▪ She *kept quiet about* her plans to change jobs. ▪ She *kept* her plans *quiet*. **3** ***keep (someone) quiet*** **a** : to prevent (someone) from speaking or to prevent (someone or something) from making noise ▪ She gave the dog a bone to *keep him quiet*. **b** : to prevent (someone) from revealing information about something ▪ They paid money to the witness to *keep him quiet*. ▪ What'll it take to *keep you quiet*?

– qui·et·ly *adv* [*more ~; most ~*] ▪ He spoke/moved *quietly*. ▪ She was *quietly* reading in her room. ▪ He is *quietly* confident that he will win. ▪ She *quietly* retired from the sport. **– qui·et·ness** *noun* [*noncount*] ▪ the *quietness* of the forest/neighborhood ▪ His *quietness* bothered her.

[2]**quiet** *verb* **-ets; -et·ed; -et·ing** [+ *obj*] *chiefly US* : to make (someone or something) quieter, calmer, or less intense ▪ The announcer was trying to *quiet* [=(*Brit*) *quieten*] the crowd. ▪ She tried to *quiet* [=*calm, soothe*] the crying baby. ▪ Her comments have done nothing to *quiet* [=*lessen*] the controversy. ▪ Unfortunately, his efforts did little to *quiet* [=*dispel*] our doubts. — often + *down* ▪ The announcer was trying to *quiet down* [=(*Brit*) *quieten down*] the crowd.

quiet down [*phrasal verb*] *chiefly US* : to become quiet or quieter : to become calmer or less noisy ▪ The children started to *quiet down* [=(*Brit*) *quieten down*] after dinner. ▪ He told the crowd to *quiet down*. ▪ Things are *quieting down* in town. [=the town is becoming less busy]

[3]**quiet** *noun* [*noncount*] : the quality or state of being quiet or calm ▪ the *quiet* of a wooded trail ▪ Can I have some *quiet* here? I'm trying to study. ▪ I need a little ***peace and quiet***.

on the quiet : in a secret or quiet way : without people knowing ▪ The deal was made *on the quiet*.

qui·et·en /ˈkwajətən/ *verb* **-ens; -ened; -en·ing** [+ *obj*] *Brit* : [2]QUIET ▪ trying to *quieten* (down) the crowd

quieten down [*phrasal verb*] *Brit* : to become quiet or quieter ▪ The children *quietened down* after dinner.

qui·etude /ˈkwajəˌtuːd, *Brit* ˈkwajəˌtjuːd/ *noun* [*noncount*] *literary* : the state of being quiet or calm : QUIETNESS ▪ the *quietude* [=*calm*] of the forest

quiff /ˈkwɪf/ *noun, pl* **quiffs** [*count*] *Brit* : hair at the front of a person's head that is brushed upward; *also* : POMPADOUR

quill /ˈkwɪl/ *noun, pl* **quills** [*count*]
1 a : the hollow central part of a feather **b** : a large, stiff feather from the wing or tail of a bird
2 : a pen that is made from a feather — called also *quill pen*
3 : one of the hollow, sharp parts on the back of a porcupine

quilt /ˈkwɪlt/ *noun, pl* **quilts** [*count*] : a bed cover with stitched designs that is made of two layers of cloth filled with wool, cotton, or soft feathers

quilt·ed /ˈkwɪltəd/ *adj* : having two layers of stitched cloth filled with wool, cotton, or soft feathers ▪ a *quilted* jacket/coat

quilt·er /ˈkwɪltɚ/ *noun, pl* **-ers** [*count*] : a person who makes quilts

quilt·ing /ˈkwɪltɪŋ/ *noun* [*noncount*]
1 : the activity or process of making a quilt ▪ Her hobbies include knitting and *quilting*.
2 : the material or stitching that is used in making quilts ▪ diamond *quilting*

quin /ˈkwɪn/ *noun, pl* **quins** [*count*] *Brit, informal* : QUINTUPLET

quince /ˈkwɪns/ *noun, pl* **quinc·es**
1 [*count, noncount*] : the yellow fruit of an Asian tree that is used for making jam, jelly, etc.
2 [*count*] : the tree that produces quince ▪ a flowering *quince*

qui·nine /ˈkwaɪˌnaɪn, *Brit* ˈkwɪˌniːn/ *noun* [*noncount*] : a drug that is made from the bark of a tree and used especially to treat malaria

quint /ˈkwɪnt/ *noun, pl* **quints** [*count*] *US, informal* : QUINTUPLET

quin·tes·sence /kwɪnˈtɛsn̩s/ *noun*
the quintessence *formal* **1** : the most important part of something ▪ *The quintessence* of music is the melody. **2** : the perfect example of something ▪ He was *the quintessence* of calm. [=he was perfectly calm]

– quint·es·sen·tial /ˌkwɪntəˈsɛnʃəl/ *adj* ▪ He was the *quintessential* cowboy. [=he was the perfect example of a cowboy] ▪ She's the *quintessential* New Yorker. **– quint·es·sen·tial·ly** *adv* ▪ The humor in the movie is *quintessentially* British.

quin·tet /kwɪnˈtɛt/ *noun, pl* **-tets** [*count*]
1 : a group of five singers or musicians who perform together ▪ a famous brass/jazz *quintet*
2 : a piece of music for five singers or musicians ▪ a piano/string *quintet*

[1]**quin·tu·ple** /kwɪnˈtʌpəl, *Brit* ˈkwɪntjʊpl/ *verb* **-tu·ples; -tu·pled; -tu·pling**
1 [*no obj*] : to become five times bigger in value or number ▪ The town's population has *quintupled* in the past 50 years.
2 [+ *obj*] : to cause (something) to become five times bigger ▪ We *quintupled* our earnings. ▪ The company has *quintupled* the number of its employees.

[2]**quintuple** *adj*
1 : five times bigger in size or amount ▪ Share prices are *quintuple* what they were a few days ago.
2 *always used before a noun* : having five parts or including five people or things ▪ a *quintuple* homicide/murder [=a murder of five people]

quin·tu·plet /kwɪnˈtʌplət, *Brit* ˈkwɪntjʊplət/ *noun, pl* **-plets** [*count*] : one of five babies that are born at the same time to the same mother — usually plural ▪ She had (a set of) *quintuplets*. [=she gave birth to five babies] — compare QUADRUPLET, SEXTUPLET, TRIPLET, TWIN

[1]**quip** /ˈkwɪp/ *noun, pl* **quips** [*count*] : a clever remark ▪ witty/amusing *quips* ▪ They ***traded quips*** over a beer.

[2]**quip** *verb* **quips; quipped; quip·ping** [+ *obj*] : to make (a clever remark)

quirk /ˈkwɚk/ *noun, pl* **quirks** [*count*]
1 : an unusual habit or way of behaving ▪ Everyone has their little *quirks*.
2 : something strange that happens by chance ▪ Their meeting was a (strange) ***quirk of fate/nature***.

quirky /ˈkwɚki/ *adj* **-i·er; -est** [*also more ~; most ~*] : unusual especially in an interesting or appealing way ▪ *quirky* ideas/behavior ▪ He has a *quirky* sense of humor. ▪ a *quirky* new sitcom

quis·ling /ˈkwɪzlɪŋ/ *noun, pl* **-lings** [*count*] *old-fashioned* : a person who helps an enemy that has taken control of his or her country : TRAITOR — often used before another noun ▪ a *quisling* regime/government

quit /ˈkwɪt/ *verb* **quits; quit** *also* **quit·ted; quit·ting**
1 *informal* : to leave (a job, school, career, etc.) [+ *obj*] He *quit* his job. ▪ She *quit* college after one semester. ▪ She decided to *quit* show business. ▪ He *quit* teaching after five years. [*no obj*] Many workers are *quitting* because of poor pay. ▪ She hates her job and she's thinking about *quitting*. ▪ I *quit*!
2 *chiefly US, informal* : to stop doing (an action or activity) [+ *obj*] She *quit* smoking/drinking years ago. ▪ I wish you would *quit* bothering her. ▪ He angrily told her to ***quit it*** [=to stop doing what she was doing] [*no obj*] We're going to *quit* for the day. It's too hot to keep working.
3 [*no obj*] *informal* : to stop working ▪ The engine suddenly *quit*. ▪ The car *quit* [=*broke down*] a few miles down the road.
4 *formal* : to leave (the place where you live) [+ *obj*] They *quit* the city for a quiet life in the country. ▪ The landlord gave the tenants ***notice to quit*** the premises. [=the landlord formally told them that they had to leave] [*no obj*] The landlord gave the tenants *notice to quit*.

quite /ˈkwaɪt/ *adv*
1 a : to a very noticeable degree or extent : VERY ✧ *Quite* is a more forceful word than *fairly* but it is a less forceful word than *extremely*. It is used more often in British English than in U.S. English, but it is not an unusual or rare word in U.S. English. ▪ She did *quite* well. ▪ He is *quite* ill/rich/busy. ▪ The room is *quite* large/small. ▪ They were *quite* surprised. ▪ Blue jays are *quite* common in this area. ▪ We go out to dinner *quite* frequently. ▪ The entertainment was *quite* good. ▪ We live *quite* near the school. ▪ *Quite* frankly, we felt it was not our responsibility. ▪ *Quite* simply, we do not have the resources. ▪ She sings *quite* wonderfully. **b** — used to make a statement more forceful ▪ I *quite* liked/enjoyed the music. ▪ "We're sorry for the trouble." "That's ***quite all right***." ▪ The work has value in itself, ***quite apart from*** the good effects it produces. ▪ I haven't seen her for ***quite some time***. [=a long period of time] ▪ I decided I had heard ***quite enough***. ▪ It was ***quite something*** [=a major event] for a small-town boy to be interviewed for the national news. — often used with *a, an,* or *the* before a noun ▪ She is *quite a* beauty. [=she's very beautiful] ▪ The news was *quite a* shock. [=the news was very shocking] ▪ My promotion was *quite a* surprise. ▪ We had *quite a* lot of food at the dinner party. ▪ It was *quite an* eventful week. ▪ We were in line for *quite a* while. ▪ She has made *quite a* career for herself. [=she has had a very successful ca-

reer] ▪ The award is *quite an* honor. [=is a very impressive honor]
2 : completely or entirely ▪ "Are you *quite* finished?" "Not *quite*." ▪ We *quite* agree. ▪ I am *quite* capable of doing it myself, thank you. ▪ They assured me that I was *quite* mistaken. ▪ Something wasn't *quite* right. ▪ We hadn't *quite* made up our minds. ▪ She's *quite* right, you know. ▪ I *quite* forgot your birthday.
3 : exactly or precisely ▪ No one realized *quite* what was happening. ▪ *Quite* why he left is unclear. ▪ That is not *quite* what I said.
4 *Brit* — used to express agreement ▪ "We need to let children be children." "*Quite*." ▪ "There is little violence in his films." "***Quite so.***" ▪ "They have no one but themselves to blame." "***Quite right.***"
quite a bit see [1]BIT
quite a few see [1]FEW
quite the contrary see [1]CONTRARY

quits /ˈkwɪts/ *adj, chiefly Brit, informal* **:** having nothing owed by either side ▪ Here's the money I owed you. Now, we're *quits*. [=*even*]
call it quits *informal* **:** to quit or end something (such as a job, relationship, or activity) ▪ She decided to *call it quits* after many years in office. ▪ After eight years of marriage, she and her husband are *calling it quits*. ▪ I'm ready to *call it quits*.
double or quits see [3]DOUBLE

quit·ter /ˈkwɪtɚ/ *noun, pl* **-ters** [*count*] *informal + disapproving* **:** a person who easily gives up or stops doing something **:** a person who quits ▪ Don't be a *quitter*. I know you can do it.

[1]**quiv·er** /ˈkwɪvɚ/ *verb* **-ers; -ered; -er·ing** [*no obj*] **:** to shake because of fear, cold, nervousness, etc. **:** TREMBLE ▪ Her lips *quivered* when she heard the bad news. — often + *with* ▪ He was *quivering with* excitement/rage.

[2]**quiver** *noun, pl* **-vers** [*count*]
1 : a shaking sound, movement, or feeling that is caused by fear or other strong emotions — usually singular ▪ I could hear a *quiver* [=*quaver*] in her voice. — often + *of* ▪ He felt a *quiver of* excitement/anticipation.
2 : a case used for carrying arrows

quix·ot·ic /kwɪkˈsɑːtɪk/ *adj* [*more ~; most ~*] *formal* **:** hopeful or romantic in a way that is not practical ▪ a *quixotic* solution/pursuit ▪ They had *quixotic* dreams/visions about the future.

[1]**quiz** /ˈkwɪz/ *noun, pl* **quiz·zes** [*count*]
1 *US* **:** a short spoken or written test that is often taken without preparation ▪ The teacher gave us a *quiz* on the material we studied yesterday. — see also POP QUIZ
2 : a set of questions about a particular subject that people try to answer as a game or competition ▪ a trivia/health *quiz*

[2]**quiz** *verb* **quizzes; quizzed; quiz·zing** [+ *obj*]
1 : to ask (someone) questions about something — usually + *on* or *about* ▪ They *quizzed* him *on* his knowledge of old jazz tunes. ▪ He is being *quizzed* by investigators *about* his possible involvement in the crime.
2 *US* **:** to give (someone) a quiz — usually + *on* ▪ The teacher *quizzed* us *on* the material we studied yesterday.

quiz·mas·ter /ˈkwɪzˌmæstɚ, *Brit* ˈkwɪzˌmɑːstə/ *noun, pl* **-ters** [*count*] **:** a person who asks the questions for people to answer on a quiz show — called also (*Brit*) *question master*

quiz show *noun, pl* **~ shows** [*count*] **:** a radio or television program during which people compete with each other by trying to answer questions ▪ a popular TV *quiz show* ▪ a *quiz show* contestant/host

quiz·zi·cal /ˈkwɪzɪkəl/ *adj* [*more ~; most ~*] **:** showing that you do not understand something or that you find something strange or amusing ▪ He gave me a *quizzical* look. ▪ There was a *quizzical* expression on his face. ▪ She raised a *quizzical* eyebrow when she saw what he was wearing.
— quiz·zi·cal·ly /ˈkwɪzɪkli/ *adv* ▪ He looked at me *quizzically*.

quoit /ˈkwoɪt/ *noun, pl* **quoits**
1 ***quoits*** [*noncount*] **:** a game in which players try to throw rings over a small post that is standing upright in the ground
2 [*count*] **:** a ring that is used in quoits

Quon·set /ˈkwɑːnsət/ *trademark* — used for a type of metal shelter that has a curved roof

quo·rum /ˈkworəm/ *noun* [*singular*] **:** the smallest number of people who must be present at a meeting in order for decisions to be made ▪ We need five people to make a *quorum*.

quo·ta /ˈkwoʊtə/ *noun, pl* **-tas** [*count*]
1 : an official limit on the number or amount of people or things that are allowed ▪ import/export *quotas* ▪ The agency imposes strict fishing/hunting *quotas*. ▪ The company has imposed *quotas* on hiring. ▪ He lost his driver's license because he exceeded the *quota* of traffic violations.
2 : a specific amount or number that is expected to be achieved ▪ The department set new sales *quotas* in January. ▪ They filled/met their *quota* for new members. [=they got the number of new members that they were trying to get]

quot·able /ˈkwoʊtəbəl/ *adj* [*more ~; most ~*] **:** deserving to be quoted **:** interesting or clever enough to be quoted ▪ a *quotable* phrase/author

quo·ta·tion /kwoʊˈteɪʃən/ *noun, pl* **-tions**
1 [*count*] **:** something that a person says or writes that is repeated or used by someone else in another piece of writing or a speech ▪ literary/illustrative *quotations* [=*quotes*] ▪ He gathered *quotations* from the trial transcript to prove his point. ▪ a well-known *quotation* attributed to Abraham Lincoln ▪ a book of humorous *quotations*
2 [*noncount*] **:** the act of using quotations in a piece of writing or a speech ▪ She relied heavily on *quotation* in her essays, which made them less original.
3 [*count*] **:** a written statement of how much money a particular job will cost to do ▪ The builder gave us several price *quotations* [=*quotes*] for the new housing complex.
4 [*count*] *finance* **:** a statement of the current value of stocks, bonds, or goods ▪ foreign stock *quotations* [=*quotes*]

quotation mark *noun, pl* **~ marks** [*count*] **:** one of a pair of punctuation marks " " or ' ' that are used to show the beginning and the end of a quotation, to show that something is a title, to show that a word or phrase is being used in a special way, etc. — usually plural ▪ There were *quotation marks* around the phrase. = The phrase was ***in quotation marks***. ▪ Titles of newspaper articles should be placed/put *in quotation marks*. — called also (*Brit*) *inverted comma*

[1]**quote** /ˈkwoʊt/ *verb* **quotes; quot·ed; quot·ing**
1 a [+ *obj*] **:** to repeat (something written or said by another person) exactly — often + *from* ▪ She *quoted* a passage *from* the book in her article. **b** [+ *obj*] **:** to write or say the exact words of (someone) ▪ He began his speech by *quoting* Shakespeare. ▪ Can I ***quote you on that***? [=can I tell other people that you said that?] ▪ He was ***quoted as saying*** that there would be further delays. [=it was reported that he said that there would be further delays] ▪ The reporter *quoted* the police chief *as saying* that an investigation would be launched soon. **c :** to write or say a line or short section from (a piece of writing or a speech) [+ *obj*] He *quotes* the Bible frequently. [*no obj*] — + *from* ▪ He *quotes from* the Bible frequently. **d** — used in speech to show that you are exactly repeating someone else's words. ▪ When I asked him if he'd be seeing her again, he said, *quote*, "Not if I can help it." ▪ He said, and I *quote*, "Not if I can help it." — often followed by *unquote* ▪ She said it was *quote*, "time for a change," *unquote*. ▪ He said he's been living under, ***quote, unquote***, "intense pressure."
2 [+ *obj*] **:** to mention (something) as an example to support an idea or statement ▪ She said this kind of occurrence is common, and she *quoted* [=*cited*] several instances of almost identical behavior.
3 [+ *obj*] **a :** to tell someone the price at which something can be bought or done — often + *for* ▪ The sales associate *quoted* (us) an unreasonably high price *for* the car. **b** *finance* **:** to state the current price of (something, such as a stock) — usually used as *(be) quoted* ▪ Shares for the stock are *being quoted* at $68. ▪ a list of companies that *are quoted* on the stock exchange [=companies whose stocks are sold on the stock exchange]

[2]**quote** *noun, pl* **quotes** [*count*]
1 : QUOTATION ▪ Each chapter of the book began with an inspirational *quote*. ▪ She included *quotes* from the poem in her essay. ▪ The article included *quotes* from the mayor and several councilors. ▪ The price *quotes* exceeded our expectations. ▪ I checked the stock *quotes* online.
2 : QUOTATION MARK ▪ The phrase was ***in quotes***. [=there were quotation marks around it] ▪ Titles of newspaper articles should be placed/put *in quotes*.

quoth /ˈkwoʊθ/ *verb, old-fashioned + literary* — used to mean "said" in phrases like *quoth I, quoth he*, etc. ▪ "What a fool," *quoth* he. [="what a fool," he said] ▪ ". . . *Quoth* the raven, 'Nevermore.'" —Edgar Allan Poe, "The Raven" (1845)

quo·tid·i·an /kwoʊˈtɪdijən/ *adj, formal + literary*
1 : ordinary or very common ▪ a *quotidian* existence/life

Q

2 : done each day ▪ *quotidian* [=*everyday*] routines

quo·tient /ˈkwoʊʃənt/ *noun, pl* **-tients** [*count*]
1 *mathematics* : the number that results when one number is divided by another
2 : the degree to which a specific quality or characteristic exists ▪ an actress whose likability *quotient* is high [=an actress who is very likable] — see also INTELLIGENCE QUOTIENT

R

1r *or* **R** /ˈɑɚ/ *noun, pl* **r's** *or* **rs** *or* **R's** *or* **Rs** : the 18th letter of the English alphabet [*count*] There are two *r's* in "tomorrow." [*noncount*] "River" begins and ends with *r*. — see also THREE R'S
roll your r's see 1ROLL

2r *abbr* **1** radius **2** *or R* right ▪ L or *R*

1R — used as a special mark to indicate that people over the age of 17 or 18 may see a particular movie but that younger people may only see the movie in a movie theater with a parent or guardian ▪ The movie is rated *R*. — compare G, NC-17, PG, PG-13, X; see also R-RATED

2R *abbr* **1** registered trademark **2** Republican ▪ Sen. Jane Smith *R*-PA **3** *R.* river ▪ *R.* Trent

rab·bi /ˈræˌbaɪ/ *noun, pl* **-bis** [*count*] : a person who is trained to make decisions about what is lawful in Judaism, to perform Jewish ceremonies, or to lead a Jewish congregation ▪ He is a *rabbi*. ▪ *Rabbi* Jane Smith

rab·bin·ic /rəˈbɪnɪk/ *or* **rab·bin·i·cal** /rəˈbɪnɪkəl/ *adj, always used before a noun* : of or relating to rabbis, their writings, or their teachings ▪ *rabbinic* commentaries/texts ▪ *rabbinical* traditions

1rab·bit /ˈræbət/ *noun, pl* **rab·bits** *or* **rabbit**
1 [*count*] : a small animal that usually lives in holes in the ground and has long ears, soft fur, and back legs that are longer than its front legs ▪ We keep *rabbits* as pets. ▪ a *rabbit* hutch ▪ a *rabbit* hole
2 [*noncount*] : the fur or meat of a rabbit ▪ a stew made with *rabbit* ▪ a *rabbit* stew ▪ a *rabbit* coat

rabbit

2rabbit *verb* **-bits; -bit·ed; -bit·ing**
rabbit on [*phrasal verb*] *Brit, informal* : to talk for too long about something that is not important or interesting — often + *about* ▪ He *rabbited on about* all his problems.

rabbit punch *noun, pl* ~ **punches** [*count*] : a quick punch to the back of the neck or the kidneys that is illegal in boxing

rabbit warren *noun, pl* ~ **-rens** [*count*]
1 : a series of underground tunnels where rabbits live
2 : a building or place with many connected rooms, passages, etc., where you can get lost very easily ▪ The Pentagon is a *rabbit warren* of corridors.

rab·ble /ˈræbəl/ *noun, disapproving*
1 [*singular*] : a large group of loud people who could become violent : MOB ▪ an angry/unruly *rabble*
2 ***the rabble*** : ordinary or common people who do not have a lot of money, power, or social status — often used in a humorous or exaggerated way to suggest the attitudes of wealthy and powerful people ▪ celebrities who live in beautiful homes far away from *the rabble*

rab·ble–rous·er /ˈræbəlˌraʊzɚ/ *noun, pl* **-ers** [*count*] *disapproving* : a person who makes a group of people angry, excited, or violent (such as by giving speeches) especially in order to achieve a political or social goal
– rab·ble–rous·ing /ˈræbəlˌraʊzɪŋ/ *adj* ▪ a *rabble-rousing* speech/politician **– rabble–rousing** *noun* [*noncount*]

ra·bid /ˈræbəd/ *adj*
1 : affected with rabies ▪ *rabid* dogs
2 [*more* ~; *most* ~] : having or expressing a very extreme opinion about or interest in something ▪ a politician with *rabid* supporters ▪ Her husband is a *rabid* baseball fan.
– ra·bid·ly *adv* ▪ Photographers *rabidly* pursued her wherever she went.

ra·bies /ˈreɪbiz/ *noun* [*noncount*] : a very serious and often fatal disease that affects animals (such as dogs) and that can be passed on to people if an infected animal bites them

rac·coon /ræˈkuːn/ *noun, pl* **raccoon** *or* **rac·coons**
1 [*count*] : a small North American animal with grayish-brown fur that has black fur around its eyes and black rings around its tail
2 [*noncount*] : the fur of a raccoon ▪ a *raccoon* coat

raccoon

1race /ˈreɪs/ *noun, pl* **rac·es**
1 a [*count*] : a competition between people, animals, vehicles, etc., to see which one is fastest ▪ a bicycle/boat/car/yacht *race* — see also DRAG RACE, FOOTRACE, HORSE RACE, RAT RACE, SACK RACE **b** ***the races*** : an event at which there is a series of horse races ▪ Let's go to *the races* this weekend.
2 [*count*] : a contest or competition in which different people or teams try to win something or to do something first ▪ the *race* for governor ▪ a baseball pennant *race* ▪ the *race* to find a cure for the disease
3 [*singular*] : a situation in which someone has to do something very quickly because there is not much time ▪ It was a ***race against time*** to disarm the bomb. ▪ It was a ***race against the clock*** to finish the job on time.
— compare 3RACE

2race *verb* **races; raced; rac·ing**
1 a [*no obj*] : to compete in a race ▪ Eight horses will *race* for the cup. ▪ That horse will never *race* again. **b** [+ *obj*] : to compete in a race against (someone) ▪ She's going to *race* the champion. ▪ They *raced* each other home. ▪ I'll *race* you to see who gets there first.
2 [+ *obj*] : to drive or ride (something) in a race ▪ She *races* cars/horses for a living.
3 [*no obj*] : to go, move, or function at a very fast speed ▪ The people *raced* [=(more commonly) *ran*] for safety. ▪ The flood *raced* through the valley. ▪ His heart was *racing*. [=was beating very fast] ▪ Her mind was *racing*. [=she had many thoughts going quickly through her mind] ▪ The truck's engine was *racing*. ▪ The dog *raced* ahead of me.
4 [+ *obj*] : to cause (the engine of a vehicle) to go very fast ▪ The drivers *raced* [=*revved*] their engines while waiting at the starting line.
5 [*no obj*] : to try to do something very quickly because there is not much time ▪ She is ***racing against the clock*** to be sure the assignment is handed in on time. ▪ Researchers are ***racing (against time)*** to find a cure.

3race *noun, pl* **races**
1 : one of the groups that people can be divided into based on certain physical qualities (such as skin color) [*count*] It is their hope that the *races* can live in harmony. [*noncount*] The company does not discriminate on grounds of *race*, age, sex, or religion. — often used before another noun ▪ Politicians are trying to improve *race* relations. ▪ *race* discrimination — see also HUMAN RACE
2 [*count*] : a group of people who share the same history, language, culture, etc. ▪ the English *race* ▪ She is the descen-

R

dant of a noble *race*. ▪ a mythical *race* of giants
3 [*count*] **: a group of related or similar animals or plants** ▪ a distinct *race* of birds
— compare [1]RACE

race–bait·ing /ˈreɪsˌbeɪtɪŋ/ *noun* [*noncount*] *US, disapproving* **: the unfair use of statements about race to try to influence the actions or attitudes of a particular group of people** ▪ a politician who is being accused of *race-baiting*

race car *noun, pl* **~ cars** [*count*] *US* **: a very fast car that is used in professional auto racing** — called also *racing car*; see picture at CAR

race course (*US*) *or Brit* **race·course** /ˈreɪsˌkoəs/ *noun, pl* **~ cours·es** [*count*] **: a course or track that is used for racing;** *especially, chiefly Brit* **: a grass track that is used for horse racing**

race·go·er /ˈreɪsˌgowɚ/ *noun, pl* **-ers** [*count*] *chiefly Brit* **: a person who goes to a race**

race·horse /ˈreɪsˌhoəs/ *noun, pl* **-hors·es** [*count*] **: a horse that is bred and trained for racing**

rac·er /ˈreɪsɚ/ *noun, pl* **-ers** [*count*]
1 : a person or animal that races ▪ He is a stock car *racer*. ▪ His horse will be a great *racer*.
2 : a car, boat, etc., that is used in racing

race riot *noun, pl* **~ -ots** [*count*] **: a violent fight between people of different races : a riot that is caused by racial anger, hatred, etc.**

race·track /ˈreɪsˌtræk/ *noun, pl* **-tracks** [*count*] **: a track or course that is used for racing** ▪ a bicycle *racetrack*; *especially, US* **: a track that is used for horse racing**

race·way /ˈreɪsˌweɪ/ *noun, pl* **-ways** [*count*] *chiefly US* **: a course or track that is used for racing : RACETRACK**

ra·cial /ˈreɪʃəl/ *adj*
1 : relating to or based on race ▪ *racial* stereotypes/prejudices ▪ What is your *racial* identity? ▪ a *racial* minority
2 *always used before a noun* **: existing or happening between people of different races** ▪ striving for *racial* equality/harmony ▪ There was *racial* tension on campus. ▪ *racial* segregation
– ra·cial·ly *adv* ▪ a *racially* mixed population

ra·cial·ism /ˈreɪʃəˌlɪzəm/ *noun* [*noncount*] *chiefly Brit, old-fashioned* **: RACISM**
– ra·cial·ist /ˈreɪʃəlɪst/ *noun, pl* **-ists** [*count*] **– racialist** *adj* [*more ~; most ~*] ▪ *racialist* [=*racist*] thinking

racing *noun* [*noncount*] **: the sport or profession of racing horses, cars, etc.** ▪ auto/yacht *racing* — often used before another noun ▪ his *racing* career ▪ *racing* fans

racing car *noun, pl* **~ cars** [*count*] **: RACE CAR**

rac·ism /ˈreɪˌsɪzəm/ *noun* [*noncount*] *disapproving*
1 : poor treatment of or violence against people because of their race ▪ Have you experienced *racism*? ▪ a protest against *racism*
2 : the belief that some races of people are better than others ▪ the *racism* that was the basis of apartheid
– rac·ist /ˈreɪsɪst/ *noun, pl* **-ists** [*count*] ▪ *racists* and bigots **– racist** *adj* [*more ~; most ~*] ▪ He was accused of making a *racist* remark. ▪ *racist* attitudes/practices

[1]**rack** /ˈræk/ *noun, pl* **racks**
1 [*count*] **: a frame or stand that has shelves, hooks, slots, etc., in which or on which you place things** ▪ a bike/hat/luggage/magazine/wine *rack* ▪ The store has *racks* of dresses. ▪ Place the pie on the middle *rack* in the oven. ▪ During the store's sales, the clothes were ***flying off the rack***. [=people were buying the clothes very quickly] — see also DISH RACK, ROOF RACK
2 ***the rack*** **: a machine used in the past to hurt people by stretching their bodies** ▪ The prisoners were tortured on *the rack*. — sometimes used figuratively ▪ The interviewer put me on *the rack* and asked some really tough questions.
3 [*count*] *technical* **: a bar with teeth that fit into a gear or a wheel in a machine** ▪ a car with ***rack and pinion*** steering
4 [*count*] **: a pair of antlers** ▪ a deer with a huge *rack*
5 [*count*] *US, informal* **:** [1]BED 1 ▪ soldiers heading back to the *rack* after a long day
6 [*count*] *US* **a : a triangular frame that is used to group the balls together in a billiard game b : a group of billiard balls that have been set up with a rack** ▪ a tight/loose *rack*
off the rack *US* **: in a store where clothes are sold in different sizes that are not made to fit a particular person** ▪ He bought that suit *off the rack*. [=(*Brit*) *off the peg*] — see also OFF-THE-RACK
on the rack *Brit, informal* **: in a very bad or difficult situation** ▪ They had their opponents *on the rack* in the first half.
– compare [3]RACK, [4]RACK

[2]**rack** *verb* **racks; racked; rack·ing** [*+ obj*]
1 : to cause (someone or something) to suffer pain or damage — usually used as *(be) racked* ▪ He *was racked* with/by jealousy [=he was very jealous] when he saw his ex-wife with another man. ▪ a body *racked* by disease ▪ The team has *been racked* by dissension. [=the team has experienced a lot of dissension] ▪ The country *was racked* by civil war.
2 *US* **: to put (balls) in a rack for a game of billiards** ▪ *Rack* the balls (up) and we'll play some pool.
rack up [*phrasal verb*] ***rack up (something)*** *informal* **: to achieve or get (something) as time passes : ACCUMULATE** ▪ I wanted to *rack up* as many points as possible. ▪ The company has *racked up* huge losses/sales.
rack your brain/brains **: to think very hard in order to try to remember something, solve a problem, etc.** ▪ I've been *racking my brain*, but I can't remember his name.

[3]**rack** *noun, pl* **racks** [*count, noncount*] **: a cut of meat from a lamb or pig that includes some of the ribs** ▪ We had (a) ***rack of lamb*** for dinner. — compare [1]RACK, [4]RACK

[4]**rack** *noun* [*noncount*] **: the state of being destroyed or ruined** ▪ The old house has ***gone to rack and ruin***. [=has become ruined] — compare [1]RACK, [3]RACK

[1]**rack·et** *or* **rac·quet** /ˈrækət/ *noun, pl* **rackets** *or* **racquets** [*count*] **: a piece of sports equipment that is used to hit a ball or other object in games like tennis, badminton, squash, etc.** ▪ a tennis *racket* — compare [2]RACKET

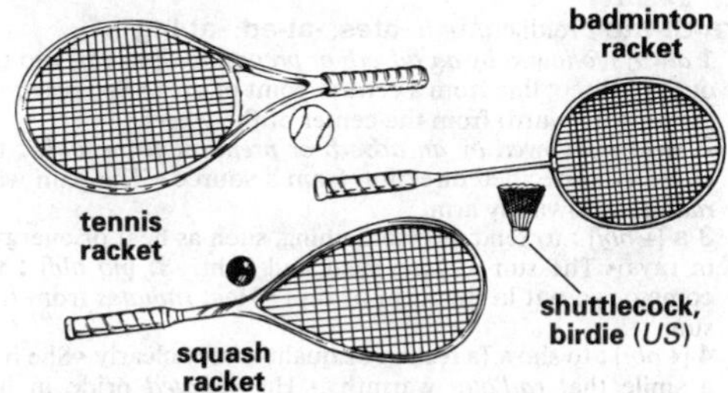

[2]**racket** *noun, pl* **-ets**
1 [*singular*] **: a loud, unpleasant noise** ▪ The kids have been making a terrible *racket*. ▪ What's all the *racket*?
2 [*count*] **: a business that makes money through illegal activities** ▪ He was a member of a criminal *racket*. ▪ He ran protection *rackets* for the mob.
3 [*singular*] *US, informal* **a : an easy way to make money** ▪ Is that all you do for a living? What a *racket*. **b : a job or business** ▪ Acting has got to be a tough *racket* to succeed in.
– compare [1]RACKET

rack·e·teer /ˌrækəˈtiɚ/ *noun, pl* **-teers** [*count*] **: a person who makes money through illegal activities**

rack·e·teer·ing /ˌrækəˈtirɪŋ/ *noun* [*noncount*] **: the act or crime of making money through illegal activities** ▪ He was arrested and charged with *racketeering*.

ra·con·teur /ˌræˌkɑːnˈtɚ/ *noun, pl* **-teurs** [*count*] *formal* **: someone who is good at telling stories**

rac·quet·ball /ˈrækətˌbɑːl/ *noun, pl* **-balls**
1 [*noncount*] **: a game played on a court with four walls by two or four players who use rackets to hit a soft ball against the walls** ▪ They were playing (a game of) *racquetball*.
2 [*count*] **: the ball that is used in racquetball**

racy /ˈreɪsi/ *adj* **rac·i·er; -est** [*also more ~; most ~*] **: exciting, lively, or amusing often in a way that is slightly shocking** ▪ a *racy* [=*risqué*] novel/movie ▪ *racy* humor
– rac·i·ly /ˈreɪsəli/ *adv* ▪ a *racily* explicit movie **– rac·i·ness** /ˈreɪsinəs/ *noun* [*noncount*]

rad /ˈræd/ *adj* **rad·der; rad·dest** [*also more ~; most ~*] *US slang* **: very appealing or good** ▪ The party was totally *rad*. [=*awesome, cool*]

ra·dar /ˈreɪˌdɑɚ/ *noun, pl* **-dars : a device that sends out radio waves for finding out the position and speed of a moving object (such as an airplane)** [*count*] a powerful *radar* [*noncount*] The approaching planes were detected by *radar*. — often used figuratively in informal U.S. English ▪ A career in politics wasn't even ***on my radar (screen)*** at that point. [=I wasn't thinking at all about a career in politics] ▪ an actor who has ***fallen off the radar*** [=who has stopped being noticed or talked about] ▪ He tried to stay ***under the radar*** [=*unnoticed*] as he went about his business.

radar gun *noun, pl* **~ guns** [*count*] **: a small device that**

uses radar to measure the speed of a moving object (such as a car or a ball)

[1]**ra·di·al** /ˈreɪdijəl/ *adj* : arranged or having parts arranged in straight lines coming out from the center of a circle ▪ the *radial* form of a starfish
– **ra·di·al·ly** *adv* ▪ The streets extend *radially* from the city's center.

[2]**radial** *noun, pl* **-als** [*count*] : a type of strong tire in which cords underneath the rubber run across the tire's surface — called also *radial tire*

ra·di·ance /ˈreɪdijəns/ *noun*
1 : a quality of brightness and happiness that can be seen on a person's face [*singular*] She had a youthful *radiance* about her. [*noncount*] Her face glowed with *radiance*.
2 [*singular, noncount*] : a warm, soft light that shines from something ▪ the *radiance* of the rising sun

ra·di·ant /ˈreɪdijənt/ *adj*
1 [*more ~; most ~*] : having or showing an attractive quality of happiness, love, health, etc. ▪ a *radiant* smile ▪ She had a *radiant* inner glow. ▪ She looked *radiant* at her wedding.
2 [*more ~; most ~*] : bright and shining ▪ the *radiant* sun ▪ *radiant* blue skies
3 *always used before a noun, technical* : sent out from something in rays or waves that you cannot see ▪ *radiant* heat ▪ *radiant* energy
– **ra·di·ant·ly** *adv* ▪ She smiled *radiantly* as she accepted the award.

ra·di·ate /ˈreɪdiˌeɪt/ *verb* **-ates; -at·ed; -at·ing**
1 *always followed by an adverb or preposition* [*no obj*] : to go out in a direct line from a central point or area ▪ Spokes *radiate* (out/outward) from the center of the wheel.
2 *always followed by an adverb or preposition* [*no obj*] : to move in a specified direction from a source ▪ The pain was *radiating* down my arm.
3 a [*+ obj*] : to send out (something, such as heat or energy) in rays ▪ The sun *radiates* heat and light. **b** [*no obj*] : to come or go out in the form of rays ▪ Heat *radiates* from the sun.
4 [*+ obj*] : to show (a feeling or quality) very clearly ▪ She has a smile that *radiates* warmth. ▪ He *radiated* pride in his achievements.

ra·di·a·tion /ˌreɪdiˈeɪʃən/ *noun* [*noncount*]
1 : a type of dangerous and powerful energy that is produced by radioactive substances and nuclear reactions ▪ She was exposed to high levels of *radiation*.
2 *medical* : the use of controlled amounts of radiation for the treatment of diseases (such as cancer) ▪ He goes in for *radiation* next week. — called also *radiation therapy, radiotherapy*
3 a : energy that comes from a source in the form of waves or rays you cannot see ▪ ultraviolet *radiation* **b** *technical* : the process of giving off energy in the form of waves or rays you cannot see ▪ the sun's *radiation* of heat

radiation sickness *noun* [*noncount*] *medical* : an illness that results from exposure to too much radiation

ra·di·a·tor /ˈreɪdiˌeɪtɚ/ *noun, pl* **-tors** [*count*]
1 : a large, metal device that is next to the wall in a room and that becomes hot and provides heat for the room when hot water passes through it
2 : a device that is used to keep the engine of a vehicle from getting too hot — see picture at CAR

[1]**rad·i·cal** /ˈrædɪkəl/ *adj* [*more ~; most ~*]
1 a : very new and different from what is traditional or ordinary ▪ The computer has introduced *radical* innovations. ▪ *radical* ideas about education **b** : very basic and important ▪ There are some *radical* differences between the two proposals. ▪ The new president has made some *radical* changes to the company. ▪ *radical* reforms
2 : having extreme political or social views that are not shared by most people ▪ *radical* liberals/conservatives ▪ a *radical* wing of extremists
3 *US slang, somewhat old-fashioned* : very appealing or good ▪ The party was totally *radical*! [=*cool*]
– **rad·i·cal·ly** /ˈrædɪkli/ *adv* ▪ She has proposed a *radically* different approach to the problem. ▪ The hurricane *radically* changed the landscape. ▪ *radically* new technology
– **rad·i·cal·ness** *noun* [*noncount*]

[2]**radical** *noun, pl* **-cals** [*count*] : a person who favors extreme changes in government : a person who has radical political opinions ▪ He was a *radical* when he was young, but now he's much more moderate.

rad·i·cal·ism /ˈrædɪkəˌlɪzəm/ *noun* [*noncount*] : the opinions and behavior of people who favor extreme changes especially in government : radical political ideas and behavior ▪ political *radicalism*

rad·i·cal·ize *also Brit* **rad·i·cal·ise** /ˈrædɪkəˌlaɪz/ *verb* **-iz·es; -ized; -iz·ing** [*+ obj*] : to cause (someone or something) to become more radical especially in politics ▪ The war has *radicalized* an entire generation of young people.

ra·dic·chio /ræˈdɪkijoʊ/ *noun, pl* **-chios** [*count, noncount*] : a plant which has reddish or green leaves that have a bitter taste and that are eaten in salads

radii *plural of* RADIUS

[1]**ra·dio** /ˈreɪdiˌoʊ/ *noun, pl* **-di·os**
1 [*noncount*] : the system or process that is used for sending and receiving signals through the air without using wires ▪ The news was sent/received by/over *radio*. — often used before another noun ▪ *radio* communications/signals
2 [*noncount*] : programs that are broadcast by radio ▪ I listen to the *radio* all the time. ▪ I heard the news/song ***on the radio***. — often used before another noun ▪ *radio* programs/shows/stations — see also TALK RADIO
3 [*count*] **a** : a device that is used to receive the signals that are broadcast by radio ▪ There's a problem with the car's *radio*. ▪ a portable/transistor *radio* ▪ The *radio* was playing very loudly. ▪ Turn up/down/on/off the *radio*. **b** : a device that is used to send and receive messages by radio ▪ two-way *radios* ▪ The pilot's *radio* wasn't working.
4 [*noncount*] : the business that makes and broadcasts radio programs ▪ He became the most popular talk show host in *radio*. ▪ She is a powerful force in *radio*.

[2]**radio** *verb* **-dios; -di·oed; -dio·ing** : to send a message to someone by radio [*no obj*] The police *radioed* for backup. ▪ The stranded sailors were *radioing* for help. ▪ The pilot *radioed* in to the control tower. [*+ obj*] The police *radioed* a report back to the station. ▪ They *radioed* the Coast Guard for help.

ra·dio·ac·tive /ˌreɪdijoʊˈæktɪv/ *adj* [*more ~; most ~*] : having or producing a powerful and dangerous form of energy (called radiation) ▪ Uranium and plutonium are *radioactive*. ▪ *radioactive* material/waste
– **ra·dio·ac·tive·ly** *adv* – **ra·dio·ac·tiv·i·ty** /ˌreɪdijowækˈtɪvəti/ *noun* [*noncount*] ▪ the *radioactivity* of certain elements

ra·dio·car·bon dating /ˌreɪdijoʊˈkɑɚbən-/ *noun* [*noncount*] *technical* : CARBON DATING

radio–controlled *adj* : controlled by radio signals sent from somewhere else ▪ a *radio-controlled* toy car

ra·di·og·ra·phy /ˌreɪdiˈɑːgrəfi/ *noun* [*noncount*] *medical* : the process of taking a photograph of the inside of a person's body by using X-rays
– **ra·di·og·ra·pher** /ˌreɪdiˈɑːgrəfɚ/ *noun, pl* **-phers** [*count*] *medical*

ra·di·ol·o·gist /ˌreɪdiˈɑːləʤɪst/ *noun, pl* **-gists** [*count*] *medical* : a doctor who is trained in radiology

ra·di·ol·o·gy /ˌreɪdiˈɑːləʤi/ *noun* [*noncount*] *medical* : a branch of medicine that uses some forms of radiation (such as X-rays) to diagnose and treat diseases

radio telescope *noun, pl* **~ -scopes** [*count*] *technical* : a piece of equipment that receives radio waves from space and that is used for finding stars and other objects

ra·dio·ther·a·py /ˌreɪdioʊˈθerəpi/ *noun* [*noncount*] *medical* : RADIATION 2
– **ra·dio·ther·a·pist** /ˌreɪdioʊˈθerəpɪst/ *noun, pl* **-pists** [*count*]

radio wave *noun, pl* **~ waves** [*count*] : an electromagnetic wave that is used for sending signals through the air without using wires

rad·ish /ˈrædɪʃ/ *noun, pl* **-ish·es** [*count*] : a small, round vegetable that is red or white, is eaten raw in salads, and has a sharp spicy taste; *also* : the plant that produces this vegetable — see color picture on page C4; see also HORSERADISH

ra·di·um /ˈreɪdijəm/ *noun* [*noncount*] : a radioactive element that is used medically in cancer treatments

ra·di·us /ˈreɪdijəs/ *noun, pl* **ra·dii** /ˈreɪdiˌaɪ/ [*count*]
1 *technical* : a straight line from the center of a circle or sphere to any point on the outer edge ▪ Measure the *radius* of the circle.; *also* : the length of this line ▪ a *radius* of 10 inches — see picture at GEOMETRY; compare DIAMETER
2 : an area that goes outward in all directions from a particular place ▪ The new museum is expected to draw people from a wide *radius*. ▪ More than 100,000 students live *within* a 10-mile *radius* of the university. [=within 10 miles of the

university] • There are three restaurants *within* a one-block *radius* of our apartment.
3 *medical* : the bone in the lower part of your arm on the same side as your thumb — see picture at HUMAN

ra·don /ˈreɪˌdɑːn/ *noun* [*noncount*] : a radioactive element which is a gas that is used medically in cancer treatments

RAF *abbr* Royal Air Force

raf·fia /ˈræfijə/ *noun* [*noncount*] : material that looks like string, is made from palm leaves, and is used to make baskets, hats, etc.

raff·ish /ˈræfɪʃ/ *adj* [*more* ~; *most* ~] : not completely acceptable or respectable but interesting and attractive • *raffish* charm • *raffish* behavior • He's a *raffish* character.
– raff·ish·ly *adv* **– raff·ish·ness** *noun* [*noncount*]

[1]**raf·fle** /ˈræfəl/ *noun, pl* **raf·fles** [*count*] : a contest that a group or organization uses to earn money and that involves people buying numbered tickets in exchange for a chance to win a prize • We're having a *raffle* to raise money for new playground equipment. • We are selling ***raffle tickets***.

[2]**raffle** *verb* **raf·fles; raf·fled; raf·fling** [+ *obj*] : to give (something) as a prize in a raffle — usually + *off* • Our church will *raffle off* turkeys this Thanksgiving.

[1]**raft** /ˈræft, *Brit* ˈrɑːft/ *noun, pl* **rafts** [*count*]
1 : a flat structure that is used for floating or sailing on water
2 : a plastic or rubber boat that you have to fill with air in order to use — see also LIFE RAFT
– compare [2]RAFT

[2]**raft** *noun, pl* **rafts** [*count*] : a large amount or number or people or things • a *raft* of political supporters — compare [1]RAFT

[1]**raf·ter** /ˈræftɚ, *Brit* ˈrɑːftə/ *noun, pl* **-ters** [*count*] : one of the large, long pieces of wood that support a roof — usually plural • a room with beautiful exposed *rafters* — compare [2]RAFTER

[2]**rafter** *noun, pl* **-ters** [*count*] : a person who makes or travels in a raft • whitewater *rafters* — compare [1]RAFTER

raft·ing /ˈræftɪŋ, *Brit* ˈrɑːftɪŋ/ *noun* [*noncount*] : the activity of traveling down a river on a raft • whitewater *rafting* — often used before another noun • a *rafting* trip • *rafting* equipment

[1]**rag** /ˈræg/ *noun, pl* **rags**
1 [*count*] : a piece of cloth that is old and no longer in good condition : a scrap of cloth • She used a *rag* to mop up the spill. • I tore the old towel into *rags*. — see also DO-RAG
2 *rags* [*plural*] **a** *informal* : CLOTHES • expensive French *rags* — see also GLAD RAGS **b** : clothing that is in poor condition • He threw away a bunch of old *rags*. • a homeless person wearing *rags* = a homeless person (dressed) ***in rags***
3 [*count*] *informal* : a newspaper of poor quality • He's a writer for our local *rag*.
4 [*count*] : a piece of ragtime music • a piano *rag*
a red rag to a bull see [1]RED
chew the rag see [1]CHEW
from rags to riches : from being poor to being wealthy : from a state of having very little money to a state of having a lot of money • She went *from rags to riches* overnight.

[2]**rag** *verb* **rags; ragged; rag·ging** *informal* : to laugh at and make jokes about (someone) [+ *obj*] The other kids *ragged* [=*teased, razzed*] him for having a crush on the teacher. [*no obj*] (*US*) — + *on* • The other kids were always *ragging on* me because I wasn't good at sports.

rag·a·muf·fin /ˈrægəˌmʌfən/ *noun, pl* **-fins** [*count*] *somewhat old-fashioned* : a child who is dressed in rags and is usually dirty and poor

rag·bag /ˈrægˌbæg/ *noun, pl* **-bags** [*count*] *chiefly Brit* : a collection of very different things • a *ragbag* of ideas

rag doll *noun, pl* ~ **dolls** [*count*] : a soft doll made of cloth

[1]**rage** /ˈreɪʤ/ *noun, pl* **rag·es**
1 **a** [*noncount*] : a strong feeling of anger that is difficult to control • Her note to him was full of *rage*. • He was shaking with *rage*. • a fit of *rage* — see also ROAD RAGE ***synonyms*** see [1]ANGER **b** [*count*] : a sudden expression of violent anger • She was seized by a murderous *rage*. • His *rages* rarely last more than a few minutes. • He ***flew into a rage*** [=he suddenly became extremely angry]
2 [*singular*] **a** : something that is suddenly very popular • Karaoke is ***(all) the rage*** these days. [=karaoke is very popular] **b** : a strong desire by many people to have or do something — + *for* • I don't understand the current *rage for* flavored coffee. [=I don't understand why flavored coffee is so popular]

[2]**rage** *verb* **rages; raged; rag·ing** [*no obj*]
1 : to talk in an extremely angry way • She *raged* about the injustice of their decision. • Protesters and activists have *raged* against the company [=have angrily criticized the company] for years. : to shout loudly and angrily • The manager *raged* at the umpire.
2 : to happen or continue in a destructive, violent, or intense way • A storm was *raging* outside, but we were warm and comfortable indoors. • The fire *raged* for hours. — often + *on* • The debate *rages on* in Congress.

rag·ged /ˈrægəd/ *adj* [*more* ~; *most* ~]
1 : having an edge or surface that is not straight or even • a *ragged* outline • *ragged* [=(more commonly) *jagged*] cliffs
2 **a** : in bad condition especially because of being torn • a *ragged* dress • a boy in *ragged* jeans • the notebook's *ragged* [=*tattered*] pages **b** : wearing clothes that are torn and in poor condition • a *ragged* orphan
3 : tired from effort or stress • You look a little *ragged*—did you have a rough week?
4 : not as good as possible : having good parts and bad parts • a *ragged* performance
5 : harsh and not regular : not smooth or even • The patient's breathing is *ragged*. • a *ragged* cough/breath
on the ragged edge *US, informal* : very close to failure • We are running *on the ragged edge* financially. • Our budget is *on the ragged edge* as it is.
run (someone) ragged *informal* : to make (someone) very tired • All this travel is *running* me *ragged*! • He was *run ragged* [=*worn out*] with/by all the travel.
– rag·ged·ly *adv* • coughing *raggedly* • dressed *raggedly*
– rag·ged·ness *noun* [*noncount*]

rag·gedy /ˈrægədi/ *adj* **rag·ged·i·er; -est** [*or more* ~; *most* ~] *informal* : not in good condition : RAGGED • a *raggedy* old doll • *raggedy* clothes • a *raggedy* group of soldiers

raging *adj, always used before a noun*
1 : very wild and violent • a *raging* storm • The fire quickly turned into a *raging* inferno.
2 : very great, strong, or impressive • *raging* ambition • The book was a *raging* success.
3 : causing a lot of pain or distress • a *raging* headache • her *raging* anguish

rag·lan /ˈræglən/ *adj, always used before a noun* : attached at a line that goes from your neck to the area under your arm • a sweater with *raglan* sleeves; *also* : having sleeves like this • a *raglan* sweater/shirt

ra·gout /ræˈguː/ *noun, pl* **-gouts** [*count, noncount*] : a stew of meat, vegetables, and spices

rag·tag /ˈrægˌtæg/ *adj, always used before a noun, informal* : made up of different people or things and not organized or put together well • a *ragtag* group of musicians

rag·time /ˈrægˌtaɪm/ *noun* [*noncount*] : a type of lively music that is often played on the piano and that was very popular in the U.S. in the early part of the 20th century

rag·top /ˈrægˌtɑːp/ *noun, pl* **-tops** [*count*] *chiefly US, informal + somewhat old-fashioned* : a car with a roof that can be folded down : CONVERTIBLE

rag trade *noun*
the rag trade *chiefly Brit, informal* : the business of designing, making, and selling clothes : the fashion industry

rag·weed /ˈrægˌwiːd/ *noun* [*noncount*] : any one of a group of North American plants that release a lot of pollen into the air and that can cause allergic reactions in some people

rah–rah /ˈrɑːˌrɑː/ *adj, always used before a noun, chiefly US, informal* : showing a lot of enthusiasm usually in a way that is annoying • We were getting sick of his *rah-rah* attitude about the school. • *rah-rah* cheerleaders

[1]**raid** /ˈreɪd/ *noun, pl* **raids** [*count*]
1 : a surprise attack on an enemy by soldiers or other military forces • They launched/mounted a *raid* against the enemy. • The building was destroyed in a ***bombing raid*** [=a surprise attack in which bombs are used] — see also AIR RAID
2 : an occurrence in which police suddenly enter a place in a forceful way to find criminals, illegal drugs, etc. • Weapons were also seized during the drug *raid*. • They caught five smugglers in the *raid*.
3 *chiefly Brit* : an act of going into a place (such as a bank) in order to steal something : HEIST • a bank *raid*

[2]**raid** *verb* **raids; raid·ed; raid·ing** [+ *obj*]
1 : to attack (a place or group) in a sudden and unexpected way • The village was *raided* often by neighboring tribes.
2 **a** : to enter (a place) suddenly in a forceful way in order to look for someone or something • Police *raided* the house and

found drugs. • Federal agents *raided* the warehouse, seizing stolen property and arresting five smugglers. **b : to enter (a place) in order to steal or take something** • Two armed men *raided* [=(more commonly) *robbed*] the bank on Tuesday. • The boys *raided* the fridge [=took food from the refrigerator] when they got home from soccer practice. • She *raided* her sister's closet to find something to wear to the party.

– raiding *adj* • The village needs protection from *raiding* tribes. • a ***raiding party*** [=a group of people who attack a place or group]

raid·er /ˈreɪdɚ/ *noun, pl* **-ers** [*count*]
1 : a person who suddenly and unexpectedly attacks a place or group • The village needs protection from enemy *raiders*.
2 : a person who enters a place in order to steal or take something • *Raiders* had emptied the tomb of treasure.
3 : a person who tries to take control of a business by buying a lot of its stock • He made his fortune as a ***corporate raider***.

[1]**rail** /ˈreɪl/ *noun, pl* **rails**
1 [*count*] **a : a bar that goes from one post or support to another and that is used to form a barrier** • She leaned over the *rail* of the ship. • We sat on the fence *rail* and watched the cows. — see picture at HOUSE; see also GUARDRAIL, HANDRAIL **b : a bar used to hang something from** • He hung the curtains on the *rail*.
2 a [*count*] **: one of the bars of steel that form a train's track — usually plural** • The train went off the *rails*. = (*chiefly Brit*) The train jumped the *rails*. — see also THIRD RAIL **b** [*noncount*] **:** [1]RAILROAD • transportation by *rail* • ***commuter rail*** [=part of a railroad made especially for people who work in a city but live outside it] — **often used before another noun** • *rail* travel • ***passenger rail*** service [=trains that take passengers rather than cargo] between the two cities — see also MONORAIL
go off the rails informal **: to lose control and start to behave in a way that is not normal or acceptable** • He was a promising student but he *went off the rails* after he started taking drugs. • The government has *gone* (completely) *off the rails*.

[2]**rail** *verb* **rails; railed; rail·ing** [*+ obj*] **: to use rails to create a barrier around or at the edge of (something) — usually + *off*** • They've *railed off* [=(more commonly) *fenced off*] the garden. — compare [3]RAIL
– railed *adj* • a *railed* balcony/platform

[3]**rail** *verb* **rail; railed; railing** [*no obj*] *formal* **: to complain angrily about something** • old men *railing* at/against the government • The workers *railed* about the unfair treatment they'd received. — compare [2]RAIL

rail·card /ˈreɪlˌkɑɚd/ *noun, pl* **-cards** [*count*] *Brit* **: a card that you can use to buy railroad tickets at a price that is lower than the usual price** • a student *railcard*

rail·ing /ˈreɪlɪŋ/ *noun, pl* **-ings** [*count*] **: a barrier that is made of rails supported by posts** • He leaned on the deck's *railing* and watched the sun set. — see picture at HOUSE

rail·lery /ˈreɪləri/ *noun* [*noncount*] *formal* **: friendly joking about or with somebody** • affectionate *raillery*

rail·man /ˈreɪlmən/ *noun, pl* **-men** [*count*] *Brit* **:** RAILWAYMAN

[1]**rail·road** /ˈreɪlˌroʊd/ *noun, pl* **-roads** [*count*] *US*
1 : a system of tracks on which trains travel • a transcontinental *railroad* [=(*chiefly Brit*) *railway*] — **often used before another noun** • a *railroad* station • *railroad* cars/workers/travel
2 : a company that owns and operates trains • an employee of the *railroad* [=(*chiefly Brit*) *railway*]

[2]**railroad** *verb* **-roads; -road·ed; -road·ing** [*+ obj*]
1 : to force (something) to be officially approved or accepted without much discussion or thought • a controversial law that is being ***railroaded through*** Congress • a bill that was ***railroaded into*** law
2 *US* **: to convict (someone) of a crime unfairly** • They claim she was *railroaded*.
3 : to force (someone) into doing something quickly or without enough information — usually + *into* • He *railroaded* her *into* signing the contract. • She's trying to *railroad* us *into* buying the house.
– rail·road·er *noun, pl* **-ers** [*count*] *US* • He worked as a *railroader* [=a person who works for a railroad company] all his life. **– rail·road·ing** *noun* [*noncount*] • the history of *railroading* [=of trains, railroads, the people who work on them, etc.]

railroad crossing *noun, pl* **~ -ings** [*count*] *US* **: a place where a road crosses railroad tracks — called also (*Brit*) *level crossing***

rail·way /ˈreɪlˌweɪ/ *noun, pl* **-ways** [*count*] *chiefly Brit* **:** [1]RAILROAD

rail·way·man /ˈreɪlˌweɪmən/ *noun, pl* **-men** [*count*] *Brit* **: a man who works for a railroad company**

rai·ment /ˈreɪmənt/ *noun* [*noncount*] *literary* **:** CLOTHING • gorgeous/glamorous *raiment*

[1]**rain** /ˈreɪn/ *noun, pl* **rains**
1 : water that falls in drops from clouds in the sky [*noncount*] The weatherman forecasts *rain* for this afternoon. • We could hear the sound of (the) *rain* on the roof. • Everyone went inside when the *rain* began to fall. • He was standing outside in the ***pouring rain***. [=rain falling in large drops and with a lot of force] • Take an umbrella with you. It ***looks like rain***. [=the sky looks the way it does when there is going to be rain] [*count*] spring/summer *rains* • What the garden needs is a good, soaking *rain*. • A ***light/heavy rain*** began to fall. • There has been some flooding due to the recent *heavy rains*. — see also ACID RAIN
2 [*noncount*] **: weather in which there is a lot of rain : rainy weather** • We've had a week of *rain*.
3 ***rains*** [*plural*] **: large amounts of rain that fall at a particular time of year** • The *rains* came and flooded the valley.
4 [*singular*] **: a large amount *of* something falling from above** • a *rain of* ash/ashes
(as) right as rain see [1]RIGHT
rain or shine *or* ***come rain, come shine*** *or* ***come rain or come shine*** **— used to say that something will happen even it rains** • The party will be on Tuesday, *rain or shine*. **— sometimes used figuratively** • I'll always love you, *come rain or come shine*. [=I will love you no matter what happens]
– rain·less *adj* • a *rainless* week

[2]**rain** *verb* **rains; rained; rain·ing**
1 [*no obj*] **— used with *it* to say that rain is falling** • Take an umbrella with you. *It's raining*. [=rain is falling from the sky] • The weatherman said *it* will *rain* later this afternoon. • *It rained* all day. • *It's raining* (pretty) hard/heavily. [=there is a lot of rain falling] • *It's raining* lightly. [=there is a small amount or rain falling]
2 ***always followed by an adverb or preposition*** [*no obj*] **: to fall from above in large amounts** • Ashes *rained* (down) from the volcano. • Sparks from the fireworks *rained* on the field.
3 [*+ obj*] **: to cause (something) to fall in large amounts** • The volcano *rained* ashes on the city. • The boxers ***rained blows/punches*** on each other. [=the boxers hit each other many times]
be rained out (*US*) *or Brit* ***be rained off*** **: to be canceled because of rain** • Today's game *was rained out* and will be played tomorrow instead.
rain cats and dogs *informal* **: to rain very hard**
rain on someone's parade *US, informal* **: to spoil someone's pleasure** • I don't mean to *rain on your parade*, but I have some bad news.
when it rains, it pours (*US*) *or chiefly Brit* ***it never rains but it pours*** *informal* **— used to say that when something bad happens other bad things usually happen at the same time** • The team not only lost the game but three of its best players were injured. *When it rains, it pours*.

[1]**rain·bow** /ˈreɪnˌboʊ/ *noun, pl* **-bows** [*count*] **: a curved line of different colors that sometimes appears in the sky when the sun shines through rain**

[2]**rainbow** *adj, always used before a noun* **: of, relating to, or including people of different races, cultures, etc.** • a *rainbow* coalition

rain check *noun, pl* **~ checks** [*count*] *US*
1 : a ticket given to people so that they can go to another event (such as a baseball game) if the one they were watching or planning to go to is canceled or stopped because of rain
2 : a promise to allow someone to buy or do something in the future because it is not possible to buy or do it now • The store offered *rain checks* when the sale items had all sold. • She asked if she could ***have/take a rain check*** on the invitation for dinner. [=she said she wasn't able to come to dinner and asked if she could be invited again at a future time] • "Would you like to go to lunch with me?" "I'm afraid I can't today. Can I *take a rain check*?" [=can I go to lunch with you another day?]

rain·coat /ˈreɪnˌkoʊt/ *noun, pl* **-coats** [*count*] **: a coat that you wear when it rains in order to stay dry — see color picture on page C15**

rain date *noun, pl* **~ dates** [*count*] *US* **: a date for some-**

R

thing to happen if it cannot happen on its original date because of rain • The bike trip is scheduled for May 18th, with a *rain date* of May 25th.

rain·drop /ˈreɪnˌdrɑːp/ *noun, pl* **-drops** [*count*] : a single drop of rain

rain·fall /ˈreɪnˌfɑːl/ *noun, pl* **-falls** : the amount of rain that falls on a particular area [*count*] This area has an average annual *rainfall* of 12 inches. • areas with heavy *rainfalls* [*noncount*] an increase in annual *rainfall*

rain forest *noun, pl* ~ **-ests** [*count, noncount*] : a tropical forest that receives a lot of rain and that has very tall trees • the Amazon *rain forest* — called also *tropical rain forest*

rain·proof /ˈreɪnˌpruːf/ *adj* : able to keep rain out : not allowing rain to come through • a *rainproof* jacket • The tent is *rainproof*.

rain·storm /ˈreɪnˌstoɚm/ *noun, pl* **-storms** [*count*] : a storm that produces rain

rain·wa·ter /ˈreɪnˌwɑːtɚ/ *noun* [*noncount*] : water that falls as rain • a bucket filled with *rainwater*

rain·wear /ˈreɪnˌweɚ/ *noun* [*noncount*] : clothing that you wear when it rains in order to stay dry

rainy /ˈreɪni/ *adj* **rain·i·er; -est** [*also more ~; most ~*] : having a lot of rain • It's been *rainy* all day today. [=rain has been falling all day] • *rainy* weather

for a rainy day informal : for a time in the future when something will be needed • He set a little money aside *for a rainy day*. [=he saved a little money so that he would have it if he needed it in the future] • I have some money that I'm saving *for a rainy day*.

[1]**raise** /ˈreɪz/ *verb* **rais·es; raised; rais·ing** [+ *obj*]

1 a : to lift or move (something or someone) to a higher position • *Raise* your hand if you know the answer. • *Raise* your arms above your head. • He *raised* his head and looked around. • She *raised* her eyes from her book and stared at him. • He *raised* the cup to his lips and drank. • I *raised* the lid and peeked inside. • Let's *raise* the windows and get some fresh air in here. • We *raised* the flag to the top of the pole. **b** : to lift or move (something or someone) to a standing or more upright position • They *raised* [=*erected, put up*] a flagpole in the quadrangle. • I carefully *raised* her to a sitting position. • She *raised* herself onto her knees. — often + *up* • He slowly *raised* himself *up* off the floor. • The men *raised up* the barn's walls with pulleys. — opposite LOWER

2 a : to increase the amount or level of (something) • Our landlord is *raising* the rent. • The store is *raising* its prices. • The governor wants to *raise* the minimum wage. • He matched the bet and then *raised* it. • The college is *raising* its standards for admission. • Exercise *raises* your body temperature. • The ad campaign is intended to *raise* awareness of the importance of a healthy diet. • Exposure to secondhand smoke *raises* the risk of lung cancer. • The captain tried to *raise* the spirits of his crew. [=the captain tried to cheer them up] **b** : to increase the quality of (something) • She needs to *raise* her game in the play-offs. [=she needs to play better in the play-offs]

3 : to collect (money) from people for a particular cause • The organization is *raising* money to help the hurricane victims. — usually + *for* • The students are *raising* money *for* their school.

4 : to form (something, such as an army) by gathering a group of people together • The rebels were able to ***raise an army*** quickly.

5 a : to mention (something) for people to think or talk about • The issue of money was never *raised*. • I'm sorry that I have to *raise* this subject, but we can't ignore it any longer. **b** : to cause people to think about or be aware of (something) • The book *raises* many questions about our biological origins. • The discovery ***raises the possibility*** of a cure for the disease. [=the discovery makes it possible that a cure for the disease will be found]

6 : to cause (something) to happen or exist : to produce (something) • The news *raised* hopes for peace. • The news *raised* fears of war. • Her comment *raised* a few smiles/laughs. • He was so tired he could barely *raise* a smile. [=he could barely smile] • The laws were passed without *raising* much opposition. • A passerby saw the intruders and *raised* [=*sounded*] the alarm. • The audience *raised* a cheer [=the audience cheered] at the end of the speech. • Some people are ***raising a ruckus/fuss/stink*** [=are complaining or objecting very angrily] about the proposed tax.

7 *chiefly US* : to take care of and teach (a child) : to bring up or rear (a child) • We have *raised* two wonderful girls. • They have *raised* their children to be well-mannered. • She was *raised* by her grandparents. • He was *raised* (as) a Baptist. = He was *raised* Baptist. • My dad was *raised* on a farm. • Some kids are *raised* on (a diet of) junk food. • I was ***born and raised*** here. • This is a wonderful place to ***raise a family***.

8 : to keep and take care of (animals or crops) • He *raises* [=*breeds*] chickens on his farm. • They're *raising* [=*growing*] corn this year.

9 : to cause (a dead person) to live again : RESURRECT • He claimed that he could *raise* people from the dead. = He claimed that he could ***raise the dead***. • That noise is loud enough to *raise the dead*.

10 *formal* : to stop or remove (something that is preventing or blocking an activity) often for only a short period of time • They *raised* the siege/embargo/blockade. • The city has temporarily *raised* [=*lifted*] its ban on smoking in bars.

11 : to build (a monument, statue, etc.) : ERECT • The city *raised* a monument in his honor.

12 *mathematics* : to multiply (a number) by itself a specified number of times • *Raise* two to the fourth power. • Two *raised* to the fourth power is 16.

13 : to get (someone) to speak with you on a radio : to contact (someone) by radio • We tried to *raise* him on the radio, but we couldn't get through.

14 : to bet more than (a previous player in a card game) • I'll match that bet and *raise* you five. [=I'll increase your bet by 5]

raise a glass see [1]GLASS

raise an/your eyebrow, raise eyebrows see EYEBROW

raise Cain US, old-fashioned **1** : to behave wildly and make a lot of noise • They were always getting drunk and *raising Cain*. **2** : to complain in a loud or angry way • The townsfolk *raised Cain* [=*raised hell*] about the tax increase.

raise hell see HELL

raise its ugly head see [1]HEAD

raise the bar see [1]BAR

raise the roof see [1]ROOF

raise your voice : to speak loudly especially because you are angry • Don't you *raise your voice* at me! • The baby is sleeping, so try not to *raise your voice*. • Many people *raised their voices* [=*spoke out*] in protest. = Many ***voices were raised*** in protest.

[2]**raise** *noun, pl* **raises** [*count*] *US* : an increase in the amount of your pay • I asked my boss for a *raise*. [=(*Brit*) *rise*] • a *raise* in salary = a ***pay raise***

raised *adj* : higher than the surrounding area or surface • a *raised* platform • a *raised* flower bed • a plaque with *raised* lettering

raised ranch *noun, pl* ~ **ranches** [*count*] *US* : a house that has two floors with its front entry located between the floors

rai·sin /ˈreɪzn̩/ *noun, pl* **-sins** [*count*] : a dried grape used for food — see also GOLDEN RAISIN

rai·son d'être /ˌreɪˌzoʊnˈdɛtrə/ *noun, pl* **rai·sons d'être** /ˌreɪˌzoʊnzˈdɛtrə/ [*count*] *formal* : the thing that is most important to someone or something : the reason for which a person or organization exists • Art is his *raison d'être*.

ra·ja *or* **ra·jah** /ˈrɑːʤə/ *noun, pl* **-jas** *or* **-jahs** [*count*] : a king or prince in India

[1]**rake** /ˈreɪk/ *noun, pl* **rakes** [*count*] : a tool that has a series of metal, wooden, or plastic pieces at the end of a long handle and that is used to gather leaves, break apart soil, make ground smooth, etc. • a leaf *rake* — compare [3]RAKE, [4]RAKE

[2]**rake** *verb* **rakes; raked; rak·ing**

1 : to use a rake to gather leaves, break apart soil, make ground smooth, etc. [+ *obj*] *rake* (up) leaves • I *raked* the gravel smooth. • *Rake* (out) the soil until it's level. • *rake* the lawn [=use a rake to remove leaves, sticks, etc., from the lawn] [*no obj*] We *raked* all afternoon.

2 *always followed by an adverb or preposition* [+ *obj*] : to move (your fingers or something similar) through or along something • He *raked* his fingers through his hair. • The cat *raked* its claws along/down the post.

3 [+ *obj*] : to shoot many bullets along (something) • Two men *raked* the car with gunfire.

4 [*no obj*] *Brit, informal* : to search through something by using your hand • He *raked* [=*rifled*] through the drawers, trying to find the letter. • She *raked* around in her handbag.

rake in [*phrasal verb*] ***informal*** **1** ***rake (something) in*** or ***rake in (something)*** : to earn or receive (a large amount of money) • The movie *raked in* over $300 million. **2** ***rake it in***

: to earn a lot of money • The owners of that restaurant must be really *raking it in*.

rake over [*phrasal verb*] ***rake over (something)*** *chiefly Brit, informal* : to continue to think or talk about (something that happened in the past) • Don't spend so much time *raking over* the past.

rake (someone) over the coals see COAL

rake up [*phrasal verb*] ***rake (something) up*** *or* ***rake up (something)*** *informal* : to talk about (something unpleasant that happened in the past) • There's no need to *rake* those old controversies *up* again. • She didn't like to *rake up* [=*dredge up*] bad memories.

[3]**rake** *noun* [*singular*] : an upward or downward slant : SLOPE • the slight/steep *rake* of the stage • the forward *rake* of the barge — compare [1]RAKE, [4]RAKE

[4]**rake** *noun, pl* **rakes** [*count*] *old-fashioned* : a man who leads an immoral life and is mainly interested in pleasure • a selfish *rake* — compare [1]RAKE, [3]RAKE

rake–off /ˈreɪkˌɑːf/ *noun, pl* **-offs** [*count*] *chiefly Brit, informal* : a share of a profit that is usually earned illegally • The bookmaker took a 20 percent *rake-off*.

rak•ish /ˈreɪkɪʃ/ *adj* [*more ~; most ~*]

1 *somewhat old-fashioned* : having an unusual quality that is attractive and stylish • a *rakish* smile • He wore his hat at a ***rakish angle***. [=tipped to one side in a way that is attractive]

2 *old-fashioned, of a man* : immoral and devoted to pleasure • a *rakish* [=*dissolute*] aristocrat

— **rak•ish•ly** *adv* • He smiled *rakishly*.

[1]**ral•ly** /ˈræli/ *noun, pl* **-lies** [*count*]

1 : a public meeting to support or oppose someone or something • a political *rally* • Supporters held a *rally* for the candidate. • Protesters staged an antiwar *rally*. • a ***youth rally*** [=a public meeting for teenagers and young adults] — see also PEP RALLY

2 *finance* : an increase in price or value after a decrease in price or value • Stock prices are up after the dollar's *rally* yesterday.

3 *sports* : an occurrence in which a team or player that has been behind or playing badly begins to play well • The team's late-game *rally* [=*comeback*] helped them win the game.

4 *sports* : a continuous series of hits back and forth between players in tennis or a similar game • She ended the *rally* with a hard overhand shot to the far corner.

5 : a car race that is usually held on public roads • a road *rally* • a professional *rally* driver

[2]**rally** *verb* **-lies; -lied; -ly•ing**

1 a [*no obj*] : to meet publicly to support or oppose something : to come together for a rally • His supporters will *rally* tomorrow morning outside the capitol. **b** [+ *obj*] : to cause (people) to join together to publicly support or oppose something • The group is trying to *rally* voters for the election. • The shootings *rallied* protesters who say the city neglects poorer neighborhoods.

2 [*no obj*] : to publicly support or oppose something or someone as a group • Many people in the community have *rallied* to the mayor's side. [=have publicly shown support for the mayor] • Parents ***rallied for/behind*** [=publicly showed support for] the new dress code guidelines. • Students ***rallied against*** [=publicly showed opposition to] the new dress code guidelines.; *also* : to join together as a group to do something • Concerned people around the country have *rallied* (together) to help raise money for the victims.

3 [+ *obj*] : to cause (a group of people) to have new energy and enthusiasm in a difficult time or situation • The coach *rallied* his players for the second half of the game. • As the deadline approached, it was clear that we needed to ***rally the troops***. [=to urge everyone to work harder]

4 [*no obj*] : to improve suddenly after a period of weakness, failure, etc. • We were trailing for most of the game, but we *rallied* in the fourth quarter and ended up winning. • Stocks *rallied* [=increased in price or value] at the close of trading today. • The patient briefly *rallied* [=got healthier] but then became much worse and died a few days later.

rally around *or chiefly Brit* ***rally round*** [*phrasal verb*] ***rally around/round (someone or something)*** : to join together to support (someone or something) in a difficult time or situation • We *rallied around* our neighbors when their house burned down. • When the town library lost its funding, the community *rallied around* it.

rallying cry *noun, pl* **~ cries** [*count*] : a word or phrase that is used to make people join together to support an idea, cause, etc. • the *rallying cry* of a political movement • "We believe!" became the *rallying cry* of the fans.

rallying point *noun, pl* **~ points** [*count*] : someone or something that makes people join together to support a person, cause, etc. • His promise to improve education has become a *rallying point* for his supporters.

[1]**ram** /ˈræm/ *noun, pl* **rams** [*count*]

1 : an adult male sheep — compare EWE, [1]LAMB

2 a : a piece of machinery that is used to hit or lift something else • a hydraulic *ram* **b** : BATTERING RAM

[2]**ram** *verb* **rams; rammed; ram•ming**

1 a : to forcefully hit something [+ *obj*] His car/boat *rammed* mine. • They deliberately *rammed* my car from behind. [*no obj*] They *rammed* [=*crashed*] into my car from behind. • The car slid and *rammed* against the wall. **b** [+ *obj*] : to cause (something) to forcefully hit something • He deliberately *rammed* his car into mine. • She *rammed* her fist against the wall in anger.

2 *always followed by an adverb or preposition* [+ *obj*] : to push (something) into a position or place with force • She *rammed* the cork into the barrel. • He opened the chute and *rammed* the clothes down. — sometimes used figuratively • The law was *rammed* [=*pushed*] through Congress.

ram (something) down someone's throat see THROAT

ram (something) home : to make (something) very clear and obvious in a forceful way • He tried to *ram home* the importance of meeting the deadline. • She hoped that the pictures and examples would *ram* her point *home*.

RAM /ˈræm/ *noun* [*noncount*] *computers* : the part of a computer in which information is stored temporarily when a program is being used • My computer is slow because it needs more *RAM*. — called also *random-access memory*; compare ROM

Ram•a•dan /ˈrɑːməˌdɑːn, *Brit* ˈræməˌdæn/ *noun, pl* **-dans** [*count, noncount*] : the ninth month of the Islamic year when Muslims do not eat or drink anything between sunrise and sunset

[1]**ram•ble** /ˈræmbəl/ *verb* **ram•bles; ram•bled; ram•bling** [*no obj*]

1 *always followed by an adverb or preposition* : to walk or go from one place to another place without a specific goal, purpose, or direction • He often *rambled* [=*roamed*] around/about the countryside in an old truck. • She *rambled* [=*wandered*] along the riverbank. — sometimes used figuratively • The trail *rambles* [=*meanders*] *through* the woods for miles.

2 : to go from one subject to another without any clear purpose or direction • She *rambled* for several minutes before introducing the main speaker. • He's funny, but he tends to *ramble*. — often + *on* • The novel's first chapter *rambles on* for about 100 pages.

[2]**ramble** *noun, pl* **rambles** [*count*]

1 *chiefly Brit* : a long walk for pleasure • We went for a *ramble* along the beach. • He encountered many interesting people in his *rambles* in the country.

2 : a long speech or piece of writing that goes from one subject to another without any clear purpose or direction • The first chapter is a 100-page *ramble*. • We had to listen to another one of his long *rambles* about politics and religion.

ram•bler /ˈræmblɚ/ *noun, pl* **-blers** [*count*]

1 *chiefly Brit* : a person who goes on long walks for pleasure

2 : a plant that grows up and over fences, walls, etc. • These roses are *ramblers*, so they will eventually cover the fence.

[1]**ram•bling** /ˈræmbəlɪŋ/ *adj* [*more ~; most ~*]

1 *of a building* : big and having many rooms that are arranged in an irregular shape • a *rambling* old farmhouse

2 : not having a specific goal, purpose, or direction • a *rambling* car ride • a *rambling* lecture

3 *of a plant* : growing up and over fences, walls, etc., in an irregular way • *rambling* roses

[2]**rambling** *noun, pl* **-blings**

1 [*noncount*] *chiefly Brit* : the activity of walking for pleasure : HIKING • She enjoys *rambling*, swimming, and biking. • Would you like to ***go rambling***?

2 **ramblings** [*plural*] : spoken or written words that go from one subject to another without any clear purpose or direction • We ignored her drunken *ramblings*.

ram•bunc•tious /ræmˈbʌŋkʃəs/ *adj* [*more ~; most ~*] *US* : uncontrolled in a way that is playful or full of energy • a class full of *rambunctious* [=*boisterous*, (*Brit*) *rumbustious*] children • a *rambunctious* crowd/audience

ram•e•kin /ˈræməkən/ *noun, pl* **-kins** [*count*] : a small, usually round bowl that has steep sides and that is used for cooking and serving food for one person

ra·men /ˈrɑːmən/ *noun* [*noncount*] : very thin, long noodles used in Asian cooking • a bowl of *ramen*

ram·i·fi·ca·tion /ˌræməfəˈkeɪʃən/ *noun, pl* **-tions** [*count*] *formal* : something that is the result of an action, decision, etc. — usually plural • They discussed the possible *ramifications* [=*consequences*] of the new treaty. • The government's actions in this case could have major political *ramifications*.

[1]**ramp** /ˈræmp/ *noun, pl* **ramps** [*count*]
1 *US* : a usually sloping road that connects a road to a highway • an exit/entrance *ramp* — called also (*Brit*) *slip road*; see also OFF-RAMP, ON-RAMP
2 : a piece of equipment with a slope that is used to join two surfaces that are at different levels or heights • The loading dock has a *ramp*. • a ***wheelchair ramp*** [=a ramp for someone in a wheelchair to use instead of stairs to enter into a building]

[2]**ramp** *verb* **ramps; ramped; ramp·ing**
ramp up [*phrasal verb*] ***ramp up or ramp up (something) or ramp (something) up*** : to increase or to cause (something) to increase in speed, size, etc. • Work started slowly, but now we're *ramping up* to full speed. • The company has been *ramping up* production. • The work is going too slowly. We need to ***ramp it up*** a bit.

[1]**ram·page** /ˈræmˌpeɪʤ/ *noun, pl* **-pag·es** [*count*] : an occurrence of wild and usually destructive behavior • a murderous *rampage* • (*chiefly US*) Rioters were/went ***on a rampage***, looting shops and setting fires. = (*chiefly Brit*) Rioters were/went ***on the rampage***.

[2]**rampage** *verb* **-pages; -paged; -pag·ing** [*no obj*] : to act or move in a wild and usually destructive way • Rioters *rampaged* through the streets of the city. • *rampaging* soccer fans

ram·pant /ˈræmpənt/ *adj* [*more* ~; *most* ~]
1 *usually disapproving* — used to describe something that is very common or that is spreading very quickly and in a way that is difficult to control • There is evidence of *rampant* corruption in the local government. • *rampant* crime/disease • Rumors of her engagement were *rampant*. = Rumors of her engagement ***ran rampant***. [=there were many rumors that she was engaged to be married]
2 : growing quickly and in a way that is difficult to control • a weed that's *rampant* in this area
— **ram·pant·ly** *adv*

ram·part /ˈræmˌpɑɚt/ *noun, pl* **-parts** [*count*] : a tall, thick stone or dirt wall that is built around a castle, town, etc., to protect it from attacks — usually plural • The city's *ramparts* crumbled long ago.

ram–raiding *noun* [*noncount*] *Brit* : the crime of driving a car or truck into a store window in order to steal the things that are in the store

ram·rod /ˈræmˌrɑːd/ *noun, pl* **-rods** [*count*] : a metal bar that is used to push explosive material down into the barrel of some old-fashioned guns
straight as a ramrod or ramrod straight : in a very straight and stiff way — used especially to describe the way someone stands or sits • The guard stood *straight as a ramrod*. • He sat in the saddle, *ramrod straight*.

ram·shack·le /ˈræmˌʃækəl/ *adj* [*more* ~; *most* ~]
1 : in a very bad condition and needing to be repaired • a *ramshackle* [=*dilapidated*] old house • a *ramshackle* [=*rundown*] neighborhood
2 : not carefully made or put together • The movie's *ramshackle* plot is confusing and not believable.

ran *past tense of* [1]RUN

[1]**ranch** /ˈrænʧ, *Brit* ˈrɑːnʧ/ *noun, pl* **ranch·es** [*count*]
1 : a large farm especially in the U.S. where animals (such as cattle, horses, and sheep) are raised — see also DUDE RANCH
2 *chiefly US* : a farm for a special crop or kind of animal • an almond *ranch* • a cattle/mink *ranch*
3 *US* : RANCH HOUSE 2 — see also RAISED RANCH

[2]**ranch** *verb* **ranches; ranched; ranch·ing**
1 : to live or work on a ranch [*no obj*] My grandfather started *ranching* here 150 years ago. [+ *obj*] The family has *ranched* 10,000 acres here for the past 150 years.
2 [+ *obj*] *chiefly US* : to raise (an animal) on a ranch • The family has been *ranching* cattle here for 150 years.

ranch dressing *noun, pl* ~ **-ings** [*count, noncount*] *US* : a creamy salad dressing

ranch·er /ˈrænʧɚ, *Brit* ˈrɑːnʧə/ *noun, pl* **-ers** [*count*] : a person who lives or works on a ranch • a cattle *rancher*

ranch house *noun, pl* ~ **houses** [*count*]
1 : the main house on a ranch
2 *US* : a house that has a single story and a roof that is not very steep

ranching *noun* [*noncount*] : the activity of raising animals on a ranch • cattle *ranching* • The land is highly suitable for *ranching*.

ran·cid /ˈrænsəd/ *adj* [*more* ~; *most* ~]
1 *of food* : having a strong and unpleasant smell or taste from no longer being fresh • *rancid* butter • Some foods become/go/turn *rancid* quickly.
2 *chiefly US* : full of anger and bitterness • The argument turned *rancid*.

ran·cor (*US*) *or Brit* **ran·cour** /ˈræŋkɚ/ *noun* [*noncount*] *formal* : an angry feeling of hatred or dislike for someone who has treated you unfairly • She answered her accusers calmly and without *rancor*. • In the end, the debate created a degree of *rancor* among the committee members.
— **ran·cor·ous** (*US*) *or Brit* **ran·cour·ous** /ˈræŋkərəs/ *adj* [*more* ~; *most* ~] • a *rancorous* debate

rand /ˈrænd/ *noun, pl* **rand** [*count*] : the basic unit of money in the Republic of South Africa

R & B *abbr* rhythm and blues • an *R & B* band = a band that plays *R & B*

R & D *abbr* research and development • She works for a computer firm doing *R & D*. • She works in the *R & D* department.

ran·dom /ˈrændəm/ *adj* [*more* ~; *most* ~] : chosen, done, etc., without a particular plan or pattern • a *random* sequence of letters • A *random* sample/sampling/selection of doctors from around the country were selected for the study. • We tasted the wines in *random* order and then rated each. • a *random* collection of buttons • *random* drug testing • She collects *random* photographs that she finds in antique shops. • Pick a *random* word on the page. • The computer program generates a list of *random* numbers.
at random : in a way that does not follow a particular plan or pattern • Our names were chosen/selected/picked *at random* from the list. • People drifted in and out of the gallery *at random* all evening.
— **ran·dom·ly** *adv* • The ropes had been cut *randomly* to different lengths. • We were each asked to *randomly* pick a word on the page. — **ran·dom·ness** *noun* [*noncount*]

random–access memory *noun* [*noncount*] : RAM

ran·dom·ize *also Brit* **ran·dom·ise** /ˈrændəˌmaɪz/ *verb* **-iz·es; -ized; -iz·ing** [+ *obj*] *technical* : to arrange or choose (something) in a random way or order : to make (something) random • The numbers have been *randomized*. • a *randomized* selection/sequence • A *randomized* study of patients treated with the drug showed it to be effective.

R & R *abbr* rest and recreation; rest and recuperation; rest and relaxation • We rented a cottage in the country to get a little *R & R*.

randy /ˈrændi/ *adj* **rand·i·er; -est** [*also more* ~; *most* ~] *chiefly Brit, informal* : sexually excited • a *randy* [=*horny*] bachelor • She was feeling a little *randy*.

rang *past tense of* [3]RING

[1]**range** /ˈreɪnʤ/ *noun, pl* **rang·es**
1 [*count*] : a group or collection of different things or people that are usually similar in some way — usually singular; usually + *of* • We'll be covering a *range of* topics in this class. • The rugs are available in a *range of* colors. • The new computer system should solve a whole *range of* problems.
2 [*count*] : a series of numbers that includes the highest and lowest possible amounts — usually singular • What's the salary *range* for the job? [=what are the highest and lowest salaries that people are paid for the job?] • The car is out of our price *range*. [=it is too expensive] • Bicycles come in every price *range*. • The game is designed for children in the 7 to 13 age *range*. • His blood pressure is in the normal *range*. • Tickets cost in the $200 *range*. [=tickets cost approximately $200]
3 [*count*] : the total amount of ability, knowledge, experience, etc., that a person has — usually singular • an actor with an impressive *range* [=an impressive ability to act many roles] • The technical vocabulary is a little outside my *range* (of expertise).
4 [*count*] : all of the notes that a particular person can sing or that a particular musical instrument can make — usually singular • The song is out of my vocal *range*. • The singer's *range* has gotten broader over the years.
5 a : a specified distance [*noncount*] The photograph was taken at close/short *range*. [=taken from a close distance] • You can see the whole playing field at long *range*. [=from far away] [*count*] Both photographs were shot at close *ranges*.

b : the distance over which someone or something can see, hear, or reach someone or something else [*noncount*] We were within the siren's *range*. = We were within *range* of the siren. [=we could hear the siren] • I can't get the radio station west of the mountains because I'm out of *range* there. • She told the children not to wander out of *range* of her voice/vision. • The troops were within *range* of the enemy's artillery. [*count*] a missile with a 400-mile *range* = a missile with a *range* of 400 miles • The antenna gives the radio a *range* of about 20 miles. **c** [*count*] : the distance that an airplane or other vehicle can travel before it needs more fuel • The airplane has a 1,200-mile *range*. = The airplane has a *range* of 1,200 miles.

6 [*count*] : a series of mountains or hills in a line • the northern and southern mountain *ranges* — sometimes used in the names of mountain ranges • the Cascade *Range*

7 *US* : open land that farm animals (such as cows and sheep) use for grazing and roaming : RANGELAND [*noncount*] the areas of open *range* in Wyoming [*count*] The book identifies plants that grow on the western *ranges*.

8 [*noncount*] : the ability to move around • He wears loose clothing to give his arms and legs free *range* of motion.

9 [*count*] : the area in which an animal or plant naturally lives • The grizzly bear's *range* is largely limited to the northwestern parts of North America.

10 [*count*] **a** : a place where people can practice shooting guns • a firing/shooting/rifle *range* **b** : a place where weapons are tested • a missile *range* **c** : a place where people can practice hitting golf balls : DRIVING RANGE

11 [*count*] *US* : a large piece of kitchen equipment that consists of an oven and a stove • a gas/electric *range* [=(*Brit*) *cooker*] — see picture at KITCHEN

12 [*count*] *chiefly Brit* : a group of related products that are sold by one company • The company has a wide product *range*. • a full *range* [=*line*] of electrical supplies

²range *verb* **ranges; ranged; rang·ing**

1 [*no obj*] : to include everything between specified limits • The selection of food *ranged* from mild to very spicy. • The game is designed for children whose ages *range* between 7 and 13. = The game is designed for children *ranging* in age from 7 to 13. • The rugs *range* in size/price/color. [=there is a variety of rugs in different sizes/prices/colors] • Items on the menu *range* from American fare like hamburgers and hot dogs to Italian pasta dishes.

2 [*no obj*] : to live or grow in a particular area • Grizzly bears *range* over a much smaller area than they once did. • The plant once *ranged* across the island.

3 [*no obj*] : to move around an area • The tribe *ranged* [=*roamed*] far and wide in search of good land. • The farmers let the horses *range* [=*rove*] freely. — often used figuratively • The essay *ranges* widely over a variety of topics.

4 [+ *obj*] *formal* : to arrange (people or things) in a particular place or area • The children *ranged* themselves around the teacher's chair to listen to the story. — usually used as *(be) ranged* • Chairs *were ranged* along the edge of the garden. • Soldiers *were ranged* along the palace walls.

5 [+ *obj*] *formal* : to join with other people who support or oppose someone or something • They have ***ranged themselves*** in opposition to the proposed new law. — often used as *(be) ranged* • Several groups *are ranged* against the proposed new law. [=several groups have joined together to fight/oppose the proposed new law]

range·land /ˈreɪnʤˌlænd/ *noun, pl* **-lands** [*count, noncount*] *US* : open land that farm animals (such as cows and sheep) use for grazing and roaming

rang·er /ˈreɪnʤɚ/ *noun, pl* **-ers** [*count*]

1 a : a person in charge of managing and protecting part of a public forest • She's now a *ranger* at a national forest in Montana. — called also *forest ranger* **b** : a person in charge of managing and protecting part of a national park • We were fortunate enough to get a tour from a *ranger* when we visited Yellowstone National Park. — called also *park ranger*

2 : a soldier in the U.S. Army who has special training especially in fighting at close range

3 ***Ranger*** *Brit* : a girl between the ages of 14 and 19 who is a member of the Girl Guides organization — called also *Ranger Guide*

rangy /ˈreɪnʤi/ *adj* **rang·i·er; -est** [*also more* ~; *most* ~]

1 *of a person* : tall and thin • a *rangy* teenager

2 *of an animal* : having a long body and long legs • *rangy* cattle

3 *of a plant* : tall and having few leaves • a *rangy* shrub • the plant's *rangy* stems

¹rank /ˈræŋk/ *noun, pl* **ranks**

1 a : a position in a society, organization, group, etc. [*noncount*] people of high *rank* and profession • She's not concerned about *rank* or wealth. • Unlike in chess, all the game pieces in checkers are of equal *rank*. [=*value*] [*count*] officers with the *rank* of captain • He rose to the *rank* of partner in the law firm. • He longed to join the upper social *ranks*. • military *ranks* such as private, corporal, and sergeant • He moved up/rose through the *ranks* to become vice president of the company. • a photographer in the ***front rank*** [=an excellent photographer] • a writer of the ***first rank*** [=an excellent writer] **b** [*noncount*] : a high position in a society, organization, group, etc. — usually used after *of* • Expensive cars are sometimes seen as a badge *of rank*. • The guest lecturer is a novelist *of rank* [=of high regard; of esteem] who has won many prestigious awards.

2 ranks [*plural*] **a** : the people or things that belong to a particular organization or group • A company spokesperson announced that the company will be decreasing its *ranks* by 200. [=laying off 200 employees] • The organization's *ranks* have doubled in the past two years. • The restaurant has made it to the city's ***front ranks***. [=the restaurant is one of the best in the city] — often + *of* • More older adults are choosing to join the *ranks of* college students. • the growing/swelling *ranks of* vegetarians **b** : the people in the army, navy, air force, etc., who are not officers • The flu swept through the *ranks*, infecting almost every soldier. • Several men were selected from the *ranks*.

3 [*count*] : a row of people or things • The troops stood in *ranks*. • Twelve soldiers stood in the front *rank*. — compare ⁵FILE

4 [*count*] *Brit* : TAXI STAND

break ranks *also* ***break rank*** **1** : to step out of a line • The soldier was disciplined for *breaking ranks*. **2** : to no longer agree with or support a person or group — often + *with* • The senator decided to *break ranks with* others in his party and support the proposal. • One scientist has *broken ranks with* her colleagues and questioned the research.

close ranks : to join together to support or protect someone or something that is in trouble • The police officers *closed ranks* when their captain was being investigated for misconduct. • The family *closed ranks* to protect one of their own.

pull rank : to use your high position in a society, organization, group, etc., to order someone to do something or to get special treatment or privileges • He's their boss, but he doesn't like to *pull rank* (on them) if he can avoid it.

²rank *verb, not used in progressive tenses* **ranks; ranked; rank·ing**

1 a [+ *obj*] : to place (someone or something) in a particular position among a group of people or things that are being judged according to quality, ability, size, etc. • A magazine recently *ranked* the school as one of the best in the country. — often used as *(be) ranked* • The museum *is ranked* among the best in the U.S. • The young gymnast *is ranked* fifth in the world. — see also OUTRANK **b** [*no obj*] : to have a particular position in a group of people or things that are being judged according to quality, ability, size, etc. • The city currently *ranks* as the world's largest. • Our professor *ranks* with/among the best in her field. [=is one of the best in her field] • This kind of mistake *ranks* right up there with [=is as bad as] forgetting your mother's birthday. • Students who *rank* in the top third of their class have a better chance of being accepted to the college of their choice.

2 [+ *obj*] : to arrange (people or things) in a line or row — usually used as *(be) ranked* • The books *were* neatly *ranked* in rows.

³rank *adj*

1 [*more* ~; *most* ~] : having a strong, unpleasant smell • the *rank* [=*foul*] smell of the alley • a *rank* odor

2 a [*more* ~; *most* ~] : very bad and obvious • His *rank* [=*flagrant*] dishonesty makes it impossible to trust him. • *rank* [=*glaring*] hypocrisy **b** *always used before a noun* : complete or total • You can't expect a *rank* beginner like her to know all the rules of the game.

3 *of plants* : growing too quickly and over too much land • *rank* weeds

rank and file *noun*

the rank and file **1** : the people in the army, navy, air force, etc., who are not officers **2** : the members of a group or organization who are not leaders • *The rank and file* is/are unhappy with the chairman's decision. • *the rank and file* of the union

– **rank–and–file** *adj, always used before a noun* ▪ *rank-and-file* members

[1]**rank·ing** /ˈræŋkɪŋ/ *adj, always used before a noun, chiefly US* **:** having a high position or the highest position in a group or organization ▪ a *ranking* news analyst ▪ Who is the *ranking* officer here? ▪ the country's *ranking* law school — see also HIGH-RANKING, LOW-RANKING, TOP-RANKING

[2]**ranking** *noun, pl* **-ings**
1 *rank·ings [plural]* **:** a list of people or things that are ordered according to their quality, ability, size, etc. ▪ She is currently fifth in the world gymnastics *rankings.* [=she is ranked as the fifth best gymnast in the world] ▪ He is number two in the class *rankings.*
2 *[count]* **:** the position of a person or thing in the rankings ▪ The new coach led the team to a No. 1 *ranking.*

ran·kle /ˈræŋkəl/ *verb* **ran·kles; ran·kled; ran·kling :** to cause (someone) to feel angry or irritated especially for a long time *[+ obj]* The joke about her family *rankled* her. *[no obj]* The fact that he never repaid the money still *rankles* (with her) years later.

ran·sack /ˈrænˌsæk/ *verb* **-sacks; -sacked; -sack·ing** *[+ obj]* **:** to search (a place) for something in a way that causes disorder or damage ▪ Robbers *ransacked* the apartment looking for money. ▪ The room had been *ransacked.*

[1]**ran·som** /ˈrænsəm/ *noun, pl* **-soms :** money that is paid in order to free someone who has been captured or kidnapped *[count]* The kidnappers demanded a *ransom* of one million dollars. *[noncount]* The family is willing to pay *ransom* for his release. ▪ The *ransom* note explained the terms under which she would be released. ▪ *ransom* money/payment ▪ (*chiefly US*) A group of men is holding the ship's crew ***for ransom.*** = (*Brit*) A group of men is holding the ship's crew ***to ransom.*** — sometimes used figuratively ▪ (*Brit*) The boy used his bad temper to hold his mother *to ransom,* forcing her to buy him sweets. — see also KING'S RANSOM

[2]**ransom** *verb* **-soms; -somed; -som·ing** *[+ obj]* **:** to pay money in order to free (a person who has been captured or kidnapped) ▪ He was held captive for a week before he was *ransomed* and returned to his family.

rant /ˈrænt/ *verb* **rants; rant·ed; rant·ing :** to talk loudly and in a way that shows anger **:** to complain in a way that is unreasonable *[no obj]* "You can ***rant and rave*** all you want," she said, "but it's not going to change things." — often + *about* ▪ He always *rants about* the evils of the film industry. — often + *on* ▪ She *ranted on* for hours *about* the smoking ban. *[+ obj]* He *ranted* that they were out to get him.
– **rant** *noun, pl* **rants** *[count]* ▪ We had to listen to his *rant* about the evils of the film industry.

rant·ings /ˈræntɪŋz/ *noun [plural]* **:** loud and angry comments that continue for a long time ▪ the *rantings* of a crazy person

[1]**rap** /ˈræp/ *noun, pl* **raps**
1 *[count]* **:** a quick hit or knock ▪ I was startled by a sharp *rap* on/against/at the window/door. ▪ He gave me a *rap* on the knee.
2 *[count] US, informal* **:** a statement by police or the government saying that someone has committed a crime — usually singular ▪ She faces a murder *rap* [=*charge*] for the death of her boyfriend. — see also BEAT THE RAP (below)
3 *the rap informal* **:** the blame or punishment for something ▪ He ***took the rap*** for his brother in order to protect him.
4 *[count] US, informal* **:** a complaint ***against*** someone or something **:** something that someone or something is criticized for — usually singular ▪ The main *rap against* him is that he isn't totally honest about what he knows.
a rap on/over/across the knuckles *informal* **:** criticism or punishment that is given in a gentle way for something that you did wrong ▪ I received *a rap on the knuckles* for missing the meeting.
beat the rap *US, informal* **:** to avoid being sent to jail for a crime ▪ He was arrested for assault, but he *beat the rap.*
bum rap *informal* **1** *US* **:** an unfair claim that someone has committed a crime or done something wrong ▪ The defendant was sent to jail on a *bum rap.* **2** *chiefly US* **:** a criticism or bad opinion that is not deserved or fair ▪ The teenagers say they've all ***gotten a bum rap*** because one person damaged some property. ▪ She thinks motorboats *get a bum rap* from environmentalists. ▪ He was ***given a bum rap*** by reviewers.
– compare [3]RAP

[2]**rap** *verb* **raps; rapped; rap·ping**
1 : to quickly hit or knock (something) several or many times *[+ obj]* The teacher *rapped* the desk with her knuckles. ▪ The boy teased the dog by *rapping* a stick on the fence. *[no obj]* Someone was *rapping* on the door.
2 *[+ obj] chiefly Brit* **:** to say (something) quickly and forcefully — usually + *out* ▪ The officer *rapped out* [=*barked out*] a command.
3 *[+ obj]* **:** to criticize (someone or something) publicly ▪ The report *raps* the organization for failing to develop a plan.
rap someone on/over/across the knuckles or rap someone's knuckles **:** to criticize or punish someone in a gentle way for doing something wrong ▪ The boss *rapped me over/on the knuckles* for missing the meeting.
– compare [4]RAP

[3]**rap** *noun, pl* **raps**
1 *[noncount]* **:** a type of music that has words that are spoken with the rhythm instead of being sung ▪ He listens mostly to *rap.* — often used before another noun ▪ a *rap* album/artist/group/song ▪ *rap* music
2 *[count]* **:** a rap song ▪ He performed a *rap.*
– compare [1]RAP

[4]**rap** *verb* **raps; rapped; rapping** *[no obj]*
1 : to perform rap music or a rap song ▪ The band has been *rapping* at local clubs. ▪ He *raps* in the band.
2 *informal* **:** to talk in a free and informal way ▪ I enjoyed *rapping* with him about sports.
– compare [2]RAP

ra·pa·cious /rəˈpeɪʃəs/ *adj [more ~; most ~] formal* **:** always wanting more money, possessions, etc. **:** wanting more than is needed or deserved ▪ a *rapacious* thief ▪ a *rapacious* [=*greedy*] businessman
– **ra·pa·cious·ly** *adv* – **ra·pa·cious·ness** *noun [noncount]* – **ra·pac·i·ty** /rəˈpæsəti/ *noun [noncount]*

[1]**rape** /ˈreɪp/ *verb* **rapes; raped; rap·ing** *[+ obj]* **:** to force (someone) to have sex with you by using violence or the threat of violence ▪ He is accused of *raping* the girl. ▪ She was *raped* by a fellow student.

[2]**rape** *noun, pl* **rapes**
1 : the crime of forcing someone to have sex with you by using violence or the threat of violence *[noncount]* He has been charged with (committing) *rape.* *[count]* There has been a decrease in the number of reported *rapes.* ▪ a *rape* trial [=the trial of someone who has been accused of rape] ▪ *rape* victims — see also DATE RAPE, GANG RAPE, STATUTORY RAPE
2 *[noncount] literary* **:** the act of ruining or destroying something — usually + *of* ▪ the *rape of* the land ▪ the *rape of* privacy
– compare [3]RAPE

[3]**rape** *noun [noncount]* **:** a plant that is grown as food for farm animals and as a source of oil ▪ *rape* oil — called also (*chiefly Brit*) *oilseed rape, rapeseed* — compare [2]RAPE

rape·seed /ˈreɪpˌsiːd/ *noun, pl* **-seeds**
1 *[noncount]* **:** [3]RAPE
2 *[count]* **:** the seed of the rape plant

rap·id /ˈræpəd/ *adj [more ~; most ~]*
1 : happening in a short amount of time **:** happening quickly ▪ a *rapid* [=*quick*] change in temperature ▪ There's been *rapid* growth in the number of new businesses in the town. ▪ Scientists are concerned about the *rapid* disappearance of the island's coral reefs.
2 : having a fast rate ▪ a *rapid* heartbeat ▪ *rapid* breathing
3 : moving quickly ▪ She carefully guided the boat through the *rapid* water.
– **ra·pid·i·ty** /rəˈpɪdəti/ *noun [noncount]* ▪ Doctors were amazed by the *rapidity* [=*speed*] of his recovery. – **rap·id·ly** *adv* ▪ the *rapidly* [=*quickly*] changing temperature ▪ He was breathing *rapidly.* ▪ Her heart beat *rapidly.*

rapid eye movement sleep *noun [noncount]* **:** REM SLEEP

rap·id–fire /ˌræpədˈfajɚ/ *adj, always used before a noun*
1 : coming quickly one after another ▪ The comedian's *rapid-fire* jokes kept the audience laughing. ▪ *rapid-fire* changes
2 *of a weapon* **:** able to quickly shoot bullets one after another ▪ a *rapid-fire* rifle

rap·ids /ˈræpədz/ *noun [plural]* **:** a part of a river where the water flows very fast usually over rocks
shoot the rapids see [1]SHOOT

rapid transit *noun [noncount] chiefly US* **:** the system that is used in cities for quickly bringing people to and from places on trains, buses, etc. ▪ We'll use *rapid transit* to get from the airport to the hotel.

R

[1]ra·pi·er /ˈreɪpijɚ/ *noun, pl* **-ers** [*count*] : a straight sword that has a narrow blade with sharp edges

[2]rapier *adj, always used before a noun* : extremely sharp • his *rapier* wit

rap·ist /ˈreɪpɪst/ *noun, pl* **-ists** [*count*] : a person who rapes someone : a person who commits rape • a convicted *rapist*

rap·pel /rəˈpɛl/ *verb* **-pels; -pelled; -pel·ling** [*no obj*] *US* : to move down a steep cliff, rock, etc., by pushing your feet against its surface and sliding down a rope • They *rappelled* [=(*chiefly Brit*) *abseiled*] down the rock's face.

rap·per /ˈræpɚ/ *noun, pl* **-pers** [*count*] : a person who performs rap music or speaks the words of a rap song

rap·port /ræˈpoɚ/ *noun, formal* : a friendly relationship [*singular*] He quickly developed a good *rapport* with the other teachers. [*noncount*] She works hard to build *rapport* with her patients. • There is a lack of *rapport* between the members of the group.

rap·por·teur /ˌræˌpoɚˈtɚ/ *noun, pl* **-teurs** [*count*] : a person whose job is to do research and present official reports on a particular subject • He was selected to be the UN's *rapporteur* on nuclear energy.

rap·proche·ment /ˌræˌproʊʃˈmɑːnt, *Brit* ræˈprɒʃmɒŋ/ *noun, formal* : the development of friendlier relations between countries or groups of people who have been enemies [*singular*] Officials hope that these talks will lead to a *rapprochement* with the rebels. [*noncount*] The possibility of *rapprochement* between the two countries seems unlikely.

rap session *noun, pl* **~ -sions** [*count*] *US, informal* : a meeting at which a group of people talk informally about a particular subject • a *rap session* for teenagers about/on drunk driving

rap sheet *noun, pl* **~ sheets** [*count*] *US, informal* : a list kept by the police of all the times a person has been arrested • He has a long *rap sheet*. [=he has been arrested many times] — called also (*Brit*) *charge sheet*

rapt /ˈræpt/ *adj, literary + formal* : showing complete interest in something • The students listened with *rapt* attention. • *rapt* audiences • The children sat *rapt* as the puppets danced.
— **rapt·ly** *adv* • The students listened *raptly*.

rap·tor /ˈræptɚ/ *noun, pl* **-tors** [*count*] *technical*
1 : a bird (such as an eagle or hawk) that kills and eats other animals for food : BIRD OF PREY
2 : a small or medium-sized dinosaur that ate other animals

rap·ture /ˈræptʃɚ/ *noun, pl* **-tures** *literary + formal* : a state or feeling of great happiness, pleasure, or love [*noncount*] We listened with *rapture* as the orchestra played. • a smile of *rapture* • He listened to the wind in the trees, his eyes closed ***in rapture***. [*count*] — usually plural • This dessert will send people who like chocolate ***into raptures***. [=this dessert will be loved by people who like chocolate] • Critics ***went into raptures*** over her performance.

rap·tur·ous /ˈræptʃərəs/ *adj* : showing extreme pleasure, love, or enthusiasm for someone or something • The novel has received *rapturous* [=*ecstatic*] reviews. • *rapturous* applause • a *rapturous* description of the landscape
— **rap·tur·ous·ly** *adv*

[1]rare /ˈreɚ/ *adj* **rar·er; -est** [*also more ~; most ~*]
1 : not common or usual : not often done, seen, or happening • She has the *rare* [=*uncommon*] ability to make people feel comfortable even in difficult situations. • These colors are *rare* [=*infrequent*] among birds of North America. • a *rare* disease • It is still *rare* [=*unusual*] for a woman to hold an executive position in some industries. • He had the *rare* opportunity of meeting the President. • Only in *rare* instances is surgery necessary to treat the condition. • He eats meat only on *rare* occasions.
2 : having only a few of its kind in existence • a collection of *rare* books • a list of *rare* and endangered species • a *rare* [=*scarce*] gem
3 *technical, of air* : not having much oxygen : RAREFIED • It's difficult to breathe in the *rare* air at these heights.
— compare [2]RARE
— **rare·ness** *noun* [*noncount*] • The gem's *rareness* [=*rarity, scarcity*] makes it very expensive.

[2]rare *adj, of meat* : cooked for only a short time so that the inside is still red • *rare* roast beef • I like my steak *rare*. — compare MEDIUM, WELL-DONE — compare [1]RARE
— **rare** *adv* • "How would you like your steak cooked/done?" "*Rare*, please."

rare bird *noun, pl* **~ birds** [*count*] : an unusual or uncommon person or thing • The little diner is a *rare bird* in a city full of expensive restaurants.

rare·bit /ˈreɚbət/ *noun, pl* **-bits** [*count, noncount*] : WELSH RAREBIT

rar·e·fied /ˈrerəˌfaɪd/ *adj* [*more ~; most ~*]
1 *often disapproving* : understood by only a small group of people : only for people who know about a particular thing • She has never been comfortable in the *rarefied* [=*esoteric*] world of art dealers.
2 *technical, of air* : not having much oxygen because of being high up in the atmosphere • It's difficult to breathe in the *rarefied* air near the mountain's peak.

rare·ly /ˈreɚli/ *adv* [*more ~; most ~*] : not very often • She *rarely* talks about her past. • These machines only need to be fixed very *rarely*. = These machines *rarely* need to be fixed. • The temperature *rarely* [=*seldom*] drops below freezing here. • *Rarely* do we see this kind of weather in our area. • ***Only rarely*** is surgery necessary to treat this condition.
rarely ever see EVER
rarely if ever see EVER

rar·ing /ˈrerən/ *adj, informal* : ready and excited to start *to do* something : very eager • The kids are *raring* to get to work on the tree house. • She's been ***raring to go*** since dawn.

rar·i·ty /ˈrerəti/ *noun, pl* **-ties**
1 [*count*] : a person or thing that is not common or usual : a person or thing that is not seen or does not happen often • In most sports, athletes over the age of 50 are *rarities*. • Snow is a *rarity* in this part of the world.
2 [*count*] : something that is valuable because there are few of its kind • He is selling most of his collection, keeping only the real *rarities*.
3 [*noncount*] : the quality of being rare • The *rarity* of the disease makes it difficult to diagnose.

ras·cal /ˈræskəl, *Brit* ˈrɑːskəl/ *noun, pl* **-cals** [*count*]
1 *informal + humorous* : a person and especially a young person who causes trouble or does things that annoy people • Which one of you *rascals* woke me up?
2 *old-fashioned* : a cruel or dishonest man • a lying *rascal*
— **ras·cal·ly** *adj, old-fashioned* • *rascally* kids • a *rascally* man

[1]rash /ˈræʃ/ *noun, pl* **rash·es**
1 : a group of red spots on the skin that is caused by an illness or a reaction to something [*count*] The baby has a skin *rash*. • The doctor said she developed the *rash* because of the medicine. • an itchy *rash* • I ***break out in a rash*** if I eat shellfish. [*noncount*] Symptoms of the disease include *rash* and fever. — see also DIAPER RASH, HEAT RASH
2 [*singular*] : a series *of* usually unpleasant things or events that happen in a short period of time • There has been a *rash of* robberies in the city this summer. • a *rash of* fires

[2]rash *adj*
1 : done or made quickly and without thought about what will happen as a result • He later regretted having made such a *rash* [=*hasty*] promise. • Their *rash* actions resulted in a serious accident that could have killed someone. • a *rash* statement • Please don't do anything *rash*. [=*foolish*]
2 *not used before a noun* : doing something quickly and without thinking carefully about what will happen as a result • Don't be *rash* about this decision. Take your time. • It was *rash* of you to make that promise.
— **rash·ly** *adv* • He had promised *rashly* to take care of the farm for her. — **rash·ness** *noun* [*noncount*]

rash·er /ˈræʃɚ/ *noun, pl* **-ers** [*count*] *chiefly Brit* : a thin piece of bacon or ham • We were served eggs, a few *rashers* (of bacon), and coffee.

[1]rasp /ˈræsp, *Brit* ˈrɑːsp/ *verb* **rasps; rasped; rasp·ing**
1 [*+ obj*] : to speak in a way that sounds rough or harsh • "Let go of my arm," she *rasped*.
2 [*no obj*] : to make a rough, harsh sound • The metal boxes *rasped* as they were dragged across the floor.
3 [*+ obj*] : to rub (something) with a rough object or substance • I used a rock to *rasp* (away) the rough parts of the stick.
— **rasping** *adj* • a *rasping* [=*rough, harsh*] voice

[2]rasp *noun, pl* **rasps**
1 [*count*] : a metal tool that has sharp points and that is used to make rough surfaces smooth
2 [*singular*] : a rough, harsh sound — often *+ of* • He heard the *rasp of* metal boxes being dragged across the floor.

rasp·ber·ry /ˈræzˌberi, *Brit* ˈrɑːzbri/ *noun, pl* **-ries** [*count*]
1 : a soft, red berry that is sweet and juicy • ice cream with *raspberries* • *raspberry* jam — see color picture on page C5
2 *informal* : a rude sound made by pushing your tongue outside your lips and blowing air out of your mouth • One of the

children made/blew a *raspberry* at him. — called also (*US*) *Bronx cheer*

raspy /ˈræspi, *Brit* ˈrɑːspi/ *adj* **rasp·i·er**; **-est** [*also more* ~; *most* ~] : having a rough, harsh sound ▪ Her voice was *raspy* from yelling so much.

Ras·ta /ˈrɑːstə, *Brit* ˈræstə/ *noun, pl* **-tas** [*count*] *informal* : RASTAFARIAN

Ras·ta·far·i·an /ˌrɑːstəˈfɑrijən, *Brit* ˌræstəˈferiən/ *noun, pl* **-ans** [*count*] : a member of a religious movement among black Jamaicans which teaches that black people will eventually return to Africa and which worships Haile Selassie, the former Emperor of Ethiopia ✧ Rastafarians usually wear dreadlocks and do not eat meat.

– **Ras·ta·far·i·an·ism** /ˌrɑːstəˈfɑrijəˌnɪzəm, *Brit* ˌræstəˈferiəˌnɪzəm/ *noun* [*noncount*]

[1]**rat** /ˈræt/ *noun, pl* **rats** [*count*]

1 : a small animal that has a pointed nose and a long, thin tail ▪ a dirty old building infested by *rats* and mice ▪ a ***lab/laboratory rat*** [=a rat that is used by scientists for experiments] ▪ He came in from the rain looking like a ***drowned rat***. [=looking very wet and miserable] — see picture at RODENT

2 *informal* **a** : a person who is not loyal or who cannot be trusted ▪ I can't believe that *rat* turned us in to the police! **b** : a person who is bad or cruel ▪ No one understands why she's with a *rat* like him.

3 *US, informal* : a person who spends a lot of time in a specified place ▪ a mall *rat* ▪ Every night he goes to work out with the other gym *rats*.

smell a rat *informal* : to think or suspect that something is wrong about a situation ▪ She *smelled a rat* when her husband came home with lipstick on his collar.

– see also PACK RAT, RUGRAT

[2]**rat** *verb* **rats**; **rat·ted**; **rat·ting** *informal* : to tell someone in authority (such as the police) about something wrong that someone has done : to betray someone [*no obj*] The teacher knows what we did, which means that somebody *ratted*. — often + *on* ▪ I am trying to find out who *ratted on* me. [+ *obj*] (*US*) — + *out* ▪ Someone *ratted* him *out* to the police. ▪ They accused him of *ratting out* his own brother.

rat–arsed /ˈræt-ˌɑɚst/ *adj, not used before a noun, Brit slang* : very drunk

rat–a–tat /ˈrætəˌtæt/ *or* **rat–a–tat–tat** /ˌrætəˌtætˈtæt/ *noun* [*singular*] : a quick series of knocking, tapping, or cracking sounds ▪ the *rat-a-tat* of gunfire

ra·ta·tou·ille /ˌræˌtæˈtwiː/ *noun* [*noncount*] : a thick stew that is made of vegetables (such as eggplant, tomatoes, and squash) and sometimes meat

[1]**ratch·et** /ˈrætʃət/ *noun, pl* **-ets** [*count*] : a device made up of a wheel or bar with many teeth along its edge in between which a piece fits so that the wheel or bar can move only in one direction

[2]**ratchet** *verb* **-ets**; **-et·ed**; **-et·ing** [+ *obj*] : to increase or decrease (something) especially by a series of small steps or amounts — usually + *up* or *down* ▪ Banks are *ratcheting up* interest rates. ▪ A little salt will *ratchet up* the flavor. ▪ The company *ratcheted down* costs by using cheaper materials.

[1]**rate** /ˈreɪt/ *noun, pl* **rates** [*count*]

1 : the speed at which something happens over a particular period of time ▪ The cold weather meant a slower growing *rate* for many crops. ▪ At the *rate* we're moving, it will be morning before we arrive. ▪ People work at different *rates*. ▪ Gun violence is increasing at an alarming *rate*. ▪ Snow was falling at a *rate* of three inches per hour. ▪ There has been a fall in the *rate* of inflation.

2 : the number of times something happens or is done during a particular period of time ▪ There is a high success *rate* for this surgery. [=this surgery is often/usually successful] ▪ Economists are concerned about the city's rising unemployment *rate*. [=the increasing number of people who are unemployed] ▪ Crime *rates* have declined in recent years. ▪ The nurse will check your ***heart/pulse rate***. [=the number of times your heart beats in a minute] — see also BIRTHRATE, DEATH RATE

3 : an amount that is paid : a price or amount to be paid that is set according to a scale or standard ▪ The hotel's *rates* start at $65/night. [=the least expensive rooms at the hotel cost $65 for one night's stay and other rooms cost more than $65] ▪ What's the interest *rate* on the loan? ▪ tax *rates* ▪ Regular admission to the theater is $12, the student *rate* is $8, and the *rate* for senior citizens is $6. — see also EXCHANGE RATE, PRIME RATE

at any rate — used to indicate that something is true or certain regardless of what else has happened or been said ▪ This restaurant has the best food—or *at any rate*, the best pasta dishes—in the city. ▪ *At any rate* [=*in any case*], cooking with fresh ingredients makes everything taste better. ▪ It is possible that she was nervous. *At any rate*, her singing was still good.

at a rate of knots *Brit, informal* : very fast or quickly ▪ We were bowling along the motorway *at a rate of knots*.

at this/that rate : if things continue to happen in the same way they have been happening ▪ *At this rate*, the town's farmland will be gone within 20 years.

going rate : the average or usual price that is charged for something ▪ What's the *going rate* for a new computer? ▪ You can hire a babysitter for a *going rate* of $10/hour.

[2]**rate** *verb* **rates**; **rat·ed**; **rat·ing**

1 a [+ *obj*] : to make a judgment about the quality, ability, or value of (someone or something) ▪ On a scale of 1 to 5, I'd *rate* the book at/a 4. ▪ Judges *rated* each song according to a number of criteria. — often used as *(be) rated* ▪ The school *is rated* above average. ▪ the highest *rated* [=*ranking*] radio show — see also OVERRATE, UNDERRATE **b** [*no obj*] : to be judged as having a particular level of quality, ability, or value ▪ The car *rates* as one of the best on the market. [=the car is one of the best on the market] ▪ The movie *rates* among the worst ever. ▪ The shoes *rate* high as far as comfort goes, but they're not very stylish.

2 [+ *obj*] : to consider something or someone to be (something) ▪ The boat is just large enough to be *rated* a ship. ▪ Based on recent polls, the policy should be *rated* a failure.

3 [+ *obj*] : to officially state that a movie, video game, etc., is appropriate for a specific audience — usually used as *(be) rated* ▪ The movie *is rated* G for general audiences.

4 [+ *obj*] : to state the normal power or limit of (a machine, engine, etc.) — usually used as *(be) rated* ▪ The submarine *is rated* to withstand tons of pressure. — usually + *at* ▪ The engine *is rated at* 500 horsepower. ▪ an outlet *rated at* 15 amps

5 [+ *obj*] : to deserve (something) because of being important, good, etc. ▪ The new museum *rates* a visit. [=the new museum is worth visiting] ▪ I don't understand why the ceremony didn't even *rate* [=*merit*] a mention in the newspaper. [=I don't understand why the ceremony wasn't mentioned in the newspaper]

6 [*no obj*] *US, informal* : to be liked by someone and get special treatment or privileges — usually + *with* ▪ He really *rates with* the boss. [=the boss really likes him]

7 [+ *obj*] *Brit, informal* : to think of (someone or something) as being good or of a high quality : LIKE ▪ I don't *rate* their chances (of winning). ▪ They didn't *rate* him as a player.

rate of exchange *noun, pl* **rates of exchange** [*count*] : EXCHANGE RATE

rath·er /ˈræðɚ, *Brit* ˈrɑːðə/ *adv*

1 : to some degree or extent ▪ Yesterday was a *rather* [=*fairly*] hot day. ▪ That sounded *rather* [=quite a bit] like thunder. ▪ a *rather* [=*quite*] common flower ▪ It's getting *rather* [=*pretty*] late. We'd better get to bed. ▪ The movie is a comedy, but *rather* a dull one. ▪ a *rather* [=*somewhat*] serious condition ▪ I think the children watch *rather* too much television. ▪ It *rather* annoyed me that he was late picking me up. — often used to make a statement less forceful ▪ He has been spending *rather* a lot of money lately. ▪ She *rather* likes chocolate. ▪ To tell you the truth, I *rather* think you are wrong. ▪ You're driving *rather* fast, don't you think?

2 a — used to introduce a statement that indicates what is true after you have said what is not true ▪ I don't like chocolate—*rather*, I love chocolate. ▪ What matters is not how often you call, ***but rather*** what you say. ▪ It wasn't red *but rather* a shade of bright orange. **b** — used to introduce a statement that corrects what you have just said ▪ We can take the car, ***or rather***, the van. ▪ My father, *or rather*, my stepfather, will be visiting soon.

3 *Brit, old-fashioned* — used to express agreement ▪ "Wasn't the show fantastic?" "*Rather*!"

rather than **1** : in place of (something or someone) : instead of (something or someone) ▪ He writes at a table *rather than* a desk. ▪ Why do one thing *rather than* another? ▪ *Rather than* using dried herbs, he picked fresh ones from the garden. : and not ▪ She reacted by laughing *rather than* by getting upset. ▪ He was happy *rather than* sad. **2** — used to say what is not chosen or done because something else is chosen or done instead ▪ *Rather than* continue the argument, she walked away. ▪ I chose to sing *rather than* play an instrument.

would rather — used to indicate what you want or prefer to

R

do, have, etc. • She *would rather* drive than take the train. • I *would rather* you didn't tell them. [=I would prefer it if you didn't tell them] • We'*d rather* go somewhere warm. [=we'd prefer to go somewhere warm] • "If you'*d rather*, we can go outside." "No, thanks—I'*d rather* not." • Which beach *would* you *rather* [=would you like to] go to?

rat•i•fy /ˈrætəˌfaɪ/ *verb* **-fies; -fied; -fy•ing** [+ *obj*] **:** to make (a treaty, agreement, etc.) official by signing it or voting for it • A number of countries have refused to *ratify* the treaty.

– **rat•i•fi•ca•tion** /ˌrætəfəˈkeɪʃən/ *noun* [*noncount*] • *ratification* of the treaty

rating *noun, pl* **-ings**

1 [*count*] **:** a measurement of how good, difficult, efficient, etc., something or someone is • The President's approval *rating* is lower than it was a month ago. [=fewer people approve of the President this month] • The school has an above-average academic *rating*. • The article compares the fuel-economy *ratings* of various cars. — see also CREDIT RATING

2 ***the ratings*** **:** numbers that show how many people watch or listen to a particular television or radio program • "How is the show doing in *the ratings*?" "It's down in *the ratings* [=few people are watching it]. I think it'll be canceled."

3 [*count*] **:** a symbol that is officially given to a movie, video game, etc., to tell people what audience it is appropriate for • Both movies received G *ratings*. [=both movies are rated G; both movies are appropriate for people of all ages]

4 [*count*] **:** a statement about the normal power or limit of a machine, engine, etc. • a 15 amp *rating* • The car has a horsepower *rating* of 500.

5 [*count*] *Brit* **:** someone in the navy who is not an officer

ra•tio /ˈreɪʃiˌoʊ/ *noun, pl* **-tios** [*count*] **:** the relationship that exists between the size, number, or amount of two things and that is often represented by two numbers • The college has a 12:1 *ratio* between students and teachers. = The college's student-to-teacher *ratio* is 12 to 1. [=for every 12 students, there is one teacher] • What is the length-to-width *ratio*? — often + *of* • The *ratio of* students to teachers is 12 to 1. • Women outnumbered men by a *ratio of* three to two. [=for every three women, there were two men] • The office has a high *ratio of* males to females. [=there are many more males that work at the office than females] — see also ASPECT RATIO

[1]ra•tion /ˈræʃən/ *noun, pl* **-tions**

1 a [*count*] **:** a particular amount of food that is given to one person or animal for one day • The soldiers were given their *rations* for the day. • The horse was fed its *ration* of oats. • The prisoners were kept ***on short rations***. [=were given very little to eat each day] **b** ***rations*** [*plural*] **:** food or supplies • The campers were getting low on *rations*. [=had used most of their food]

2 [*count*] **:** a particular amount of something (such as gasoline or food) that the government allows you to have when there is not enough of it • a gas *ration* • weekly sugar and butter *rations*

[2]ration *verb* **-tions; -tioned; -tion•ing** [+ *obj*] **:** to control the amount of (something, such as gasoline or food) that people are allowed to have especially when there is not enough of it • During the war, the government *rationed* gasoline. — often used as *(be) rationed* • Gasoline *was rationed* during the war.

– **rationing** *noun* [*noncount*] • The drought has forced the government to institute water *rationing*.

ra•tio•nal /ˈræʃənl/ *adj*

1 : based on facts or reason and not on emotions or feelings • a *rational* decision/choice • I'm sure there is a *rational* [=*sensible, reasonable*] explanation for his decision.

2 : having the ability to reason or think about things clearly • No *rational* [=*sane*] person would behave like that. • Humans are *rational* beings. [=are able to use reason when thinking about something] — opposite IRRATIONAL

– **ra•tio•nal•i•ty** /ˌræʃəˈnæləti/ *noun* [*noncount*] *formal* • The *rationality* of that statement is questionable. – **ra•tio•nal•ly** *adv* • Think about the problem *rationally*. • She stayed calm and acted *rationally*. [=*sensibly*]

ra•tio•nale /ˌræʃəˈnæl/ *noun, pl* **-nales** [*count*] *somewhat formal* **:** the reason or explanation for something — usually singular • That was a strange decision. What was their *rationale*? — often + *for, behind,* or *of* • What was her *rationale for* leaving school? • He explained the *rationale behind* his early retirement. • I don't understand the *rationale of* his decision.

ra•tio•nal•ism /ˈræʃənəˌlɪzəm/ *noun* [*noncount*] *philosophy* **:** the belief that reason and experience and not emotions or religious beliefs should be the basis for your actions, opinions, etc.

– **ra•tio•nal•ist** /ˈræʃənəlɪst/ *noun, pl* **-ists** [*count*] – **rationalist** *or* **ra•tio•nal•is•tic** /ˌræʃənəˈlɪstɪk/ *adj, always used before a noun* • a *rationalist* philosophy/thinker

ra•tio•nal•ize *also Brit* **ra•tio•nal•ise** /ˈræʃənəˌlaɪz/ *verb* **-iz•es; -ized; -iz•ing**

1 : to think about or describe something (such as bad behavior) in a way that explains it and makes it seem proper, more attractive, etc. [+ *obj*] She tried to *rationalize* her grandson's strange behavior by blaming it on the boy's father. • He couldn't *rationalize* buying such an expensive car. [*no obj*] She knows she shouldn't have done it—she's just trying to *rationalize*.

2 [+ *obj*] *chiefly Brit* **:** to find ways to make (something, such as an industry, a company, etc.) waste less time, effort, and money • Management is thinking of ways to *rationalize* our system of production.

– **ra•tio•nal•i•za•tion** *also Brit* **ra•tio•nal•i•sa•tion** /ˌræʃənələˈzeɪʃən, *Brit* ˌræʃənəˌlaɪˈzeɪʃən/ *noun, pl* **-tions** [*count, noncount*] • Listening to his *rationalizations* [=*excuses*] makes me angry.

rat race *noun*

the rat race **:** the unpleasant life of people who have jobs that require them to work very hard in order to compete with others for money, power, status, etc. • She is quitting *the rat race* to spend time with her family. • He wants to get out of *the rat race*.

rat run *noun, pl* **~ runs** [*count*] *Brit, informal* **:** a small street that connects larger roads and that drivers use to get more quickly to the place they are going

rats /ˈræts/ *interj, informal* — used to express disappointment or annoyance • *Rats*! I lost again. • *Rats*! I left my pocketbook in the car.

rat•tan /ræˈtæn/ *noun* [*noncount*] **:** a plant with very long, strong stems that are woven together to make baskets, furniture, etc. • baskets made of *rattan* — often used before another noun • a *rattan* [=*wicker*] chair

[1]rat•tle /ˈrætl/ *verb* **rat•tles; rat•tled; rat•tling**

1 a [*no obj*] **:** to hit against something repeatedly and make a quick series of short, loud sounds • The window *rattled* as the truck drove by. • The coins *rattled* in the box. **b** [+ *obj*] **:** to cause (something) to move or shake and make a series of noises **:** to cause (something) to rattle • She *rattled* the jar with the coins in it. = She *rattled* the coins in the jar.

2 *always followed by an adverb or preposition* [*no obj*] **:** to make quick, short, loud sounds while moving • The old truck *rattled* down the street. • The train *rattled* by.

3 [+ *obj*] **:** to upset or disturb (someone) • The question *rattled* [=*unnerved*] the speaker. — often used as *(be) rattled* • I *was rattled* by his questions. • He's an experienced performer who *is* not easily *rattled*.

rattle around [*phrasal verb*] ***rattle around or rattle around (something) informal*** **:** to live or spend time in a place that is very big • Her husband died last year, and now she's just *rattling around* in that huge house by herself. • *rattle around* the house • We *rattled around* Europe last summer. — sometimes used figuratively • An old song has been *rattling around* in my head all day.

rattle off [*phrasal verb*] ***rattle (something) off or rattle off (something) informal*** **:** to say (something) quickly or easily from memory • The teacher *rattled off* the answers. • She *rattled off* the names of all 50 states.

rattle on [*phrasal verb*] *informal* **:** to talk for a long time about things that are not interesting or important — often + *about* • Grandpa would *rattle on* [=*go on*] *about* his childhood for hours. • She ***rattled on and on about*** the party. [=she talked for a long time about the party]

rattle someone's cage see CAGE

rattle through [*phrasal verb*] ***rattle through (something) Brit*** **:** to do (something) quickly • We *rattled through* the meeting.

— see also SABER-RATTLING

[2]rattle *noun, pl* **rattles** [*count*]

1 : a series of short, loud sounds — usually singular • We heard a *rattle* from inside the box. • the *rattle* of machine guns

2 : a baby's toy that makes a series of short sounds when it is shaken

3 : the group of hard, loose pieces (called scales) that cover the end of a rattlesnake's tail

R

rat·tler /ˈrætlɚ/ *noun, pl* **rat·tlers** [*count*] *informal* : RATTLESNAKE

rat·tle·snake /ˈrætlˌsneɪk/ *noun, pl* **-snakes** [*count*] : a poisonous American snake with a group of hard, loose pieces (called scales) at the end of its tail that it shakes to make a noise

rat·tle·trap /ˈrætlˌtræp/ *noun, pl* **-traps** [*count*] *US, informal* : something (such as a car) that is old, noisy, and not in good condition • Are you still driving that old *rattletrap*? — often used before another noun • a *rattletrap* car/bus

rattling /ˈrætlɪŋ/ *adv, Brit, informal + old-fashioned* : very or extremely • a *rattling* good story

rat·ty /ˈræti/ *adj* **rat·ti·er**; **-est** *informal*
1 *US* : in very bad condition • a *ratty* [=*shabby*] old sweater • *ratty* [=*unkempt*] hair • Those shoes are getting pretty *ratty*.
2 *Brit* : easily angered or annoyed • She gets *ratty* [=(*chiefly US*) *cranky*] if she doesn't get enough sleep.

rau·cous /ˈrɑːkəs/ *adj* [*more* ~; *most* ~]
1 : loud and unpleasant to listen to • *raucous* shouts/laughter
2 : behaving in a very rough and noisy way • a *raucous* crowd
– **rau·cous·ly** *adv* – **rau·cous·ness** *noun* [*noncount*]

raunch /ˈrɑːntʃ/ *noun* [*noncount*] *informal + sometimes disapproving* : something that deals with or relates to sex in usually a shocking or offensive way • a movie full of *raunch*

raun·chy /ˈrɑːntʃi/ *adj* **raun·chi·er**; **-est** [*also more* ~; *most* ~] *informal*
1 : dealing with or suggesting sex in a way that is somewhat shocking • a *raunchy* [=*dirty*] magazine/movie/joke
2 *US, disapproving* : very dirty, smelly, etc. • *raunchy* old sneakers • a *raunchy* smell
– **raun·chi·ness** /ˈrɑːntʃinəs/ *noun* [*noncount*]

rav·age /ˈrævɪʤ/ *verb* **rav·ag·es**; **rav·aged**; **rav·ag·ing** [+ *obj*] *formal* : to damage or harm (something) very badly • The enemy *ravaged* [=*plundered*] the village. — often used as *(be) ravaged* • The village *was ravaged* [=*devastated*] by the plague. • The forest *was ravaged* by fire. • the *ravaged* people/city/land

rav·ages /ˈrævɪʤəz/ *noun* [*plural*] *literary* : destruction or damage — usually + *of* • the *ravages of* war/disease — sometimes used figuratively • Her face showed ***the ravages of time***. [=her face looked old, wrinkled, etc.]

¹rave /ˈreɪv/ *verb* **raves**; **raved**; **rav·ing**
1 : to talk or write about someone or something in an excited or enthusiastic way [*no obj*] — usually + *about* or *over* • Critics *raved about* the new play. • Customers *rave over* the restaurant's pizza. [+ *obj*] "It's his best performance yet," *raved* one movie critic.
2 [*no obj*] : to talk loudly in an angry or wild way • The guy on the corner was *raving* like a madman. • The coach ***ranted and raved*** at the referee.

²rave *noun, pl* **raves** [*count*]
1 : a statement of enthusiastic praise or approval • Her review of the movie was a *rave*. — often plural in U.S. English • The movie got *raves* from the critics. [=the critics praised the movie very enthusiastically] — often used in the phrase ***rave review*** • The movie got *rave reviews* from the critics. [=was highly praised by the critics] • My kids give my cooking *rave reviews*.
2 : a large party that lasts all night in which people dance to electronic dance music

rav·el /ˈrævəl/ *verb* **-els**; *US* **-eled** *or chiefly Brit* **-elled**; *US* **-el·ing** *or chiefly Brit* **-el·ling** [*no obj*] *formal + literary* : to become divided into separate threads : UNRAVEL • The fabric will *ravel*.
– **raveled** (*US*) *or chiefly Brit* **ravelled** *adj* • a *ravelled* edge • a *raveled* sleeve

¹ra·ven /ˈreɪvən/ *noun, pl* **-vens** [*count*] : a bird that has shiny black feathers and looks like a crow but is larger

²raven *adj, always used before a noun, literary* : shiny and black • *raven* hair

rav·en·ing /ˈrævənɪŋ/ *adj, always used before a noun, literary* : hungry and eager to kill • *ravening* wolves — often used figuratively • the *ravening* paparazzi

rav·en·ous /ˈrævənəs/ *adj* [*more* ~; *most* ~] : very hungry • By the time dinner was ready, we were *ravenous*. • a *ravenous* wolf • After hiking all day, I had a ***ravenous appetite***. [=I was extremely hungry] — sometimes used figuratively • She was *ravenous* for public attention.
– **rav·en·ous·ly** *adv* • I felt *ravenously* hungry. • The birds were feeding *ravenously* after their long flight.

rav·er /ˈreɪvɚ/ *noun, pl* **-ers** [*count*]
1 : someone who goes to a rave
2 *Brit* : someone who goes to many parties

ra·vine /rəˈviːn/ *noun, pl* **-vines** [*count*] : a small, deep, narrow valley

¹raving *adj, always used before a noun, informal*
1 : talking or acting in a crazy way • a *raving* lunatic
2 : very great — used to make a description more forceful • She's cute, but she's no *raving* beauty. • a *raving* success

²raving *adv, informal* : completely or fully • That guy is ***(stark) raving mad***. [=that guy is completely insane]

rav·ings /ˈreɪvɪŋz/ *noun* [*plural*] : statements that have no meaning or that sound crazy • Don't listen to her *ravings*. • the *ravings* of a madman

rav·i·o·li /ˌræviˈoʊli/ *noun, pl* **ravioli** *also* **rav·i·o·lis** [*count, noncount*] : pasta that is shaped like a square and is filled with meat, cheese, or vegetables • a plate of *ravioli* • These *ravioli* are delicious. — see picture at PASTA

rav·ish /ˈrævɪʃ/ *verb* **-ish·es**; **-ished**; **-ish·ing** [+ *obj*] *literary*
1 : to fill (someone) with pleasure, joy, or happiness — usually used as *(be) ravished* • She *was ravished* by the country's beauty. • He *was ravished* by her charm.
2 : to force (a woman) to have sex with you by using violence or the threat of violence : RAPE

rav·ish·ing /ˈrævɪʃɪŋ/ *adj* : very beautiful • She looked *ravishing*. [=*stunning*] • She is a *ravishing* beauty. • a *ravishing* view of the ocean
– **rav·ish·ing·ly** *adv* • She is *ravishingly* beautiful.

¹raw /ˈrɑː/ *adj* **raw·er**; **raw·est**
1 : not cooked • *raw* meat/vegetables • You can eat carrots *raw*. = You can eat *raw* carrots.
2 a : in a natural state : not treated or prepared • *raw* silk/steel • *raw* sewage • Fold the *raw* [=*unfinished*] edge of the fabric under. — see also RAW MATERIAL **b** : not yet organized or changed in any way • He entered the *raw* data into a spreadsheet.
3 : very sore : damaged and painful from harsh conditions, rubbing, etc. • hands *raw* from windburn • The shoes rubbed my heels *raw*. • His throat was *raw* from the cold air. — sometimes used figuratively • The article touched/struck/hit a ***raw nerve***. [=the article hurt or upset the people who read it]
4 : powerful and not controlled • I was impressed by the *raw* energy of his performance. • The town was destroyed by the *raw* power of the tornado. • *raw* emotion/anger
5 : having no experience or training • *raw* [=*green*] recruits/soldiers • The team has a lot of *raw* talent. [=the team has a lot of talented but inexperienced players]
6 : wet and cold • a *raw* winter day
7 *US* : rude or offensive • *raw* language
– **raw·ness** *noun* [*noncount*]

²raw *noun*
in the raw **1** : in a natural or unfinished state • The sculpture is still *in the raw*. • a firsthand look at poverty *in the raw* **2** : not wearing clothes : NAKED • He sleeps *in the raw*. [=*in the nude*]

raw bar *noun, pl* ~ **bars** [*count*] *US* : an area in a restaurant where uncooked shellfish is served

raw·boned /ˈrɑːˌboʊnd/ *adj* [*more* ~; *most* ~] *US* : thin with bones that show under the skin • He was tall and *rawboned*.

raw deal *noun, pl* ~ **deals** [*count*] : an unfair way of treating someone — usually singular • We're getting a *raw deal* [=are being treated unfairly] with the new tax laws.

raw·hide /ˈrɑːˌhaɪd/ *noun* [*noncount*] : the skin of a cow before it has been prepared or made into leather

raw material *noun, pl* ~ **-als** [*count, noncount*] : the basic material that can be used to make or create something • Wheat and rye are the *raw materials* for a flour mill. • His experiences during the war were the *raw material* for the story.

¹ray /ˈreɪ/ *noun, pl* **rays** [*count*]
1 a : one of the lines of light that you can see coming from an object • A *ray* of sunlight shone on her face. • We were blinded by the sun's *rays*. • *Rays* of light reflected off the mirror. ✧ In informal English, if you ***catch some rays***, ***catch a few rays***, ***soak up a few rays***, etc., you sit or lie in the sun. • I'm going to the beach to *catch some rays*. [=to sunbathe] **b** *technical* : a thin beam of energy (such as heat or light) that moves in the form of waves • harmful ultraviolet *rays* — see also CATHODE-RAY TUBE, DEATH RAY, GAMMA RAY, X-RAY
2 : a very small amount *of* something • I saw a tiny *ray of* rec-

R

ognition in his eyes. • We're finally starting to see a ***ray of hope*** [=a reason to start being hopeful] • The announcement is/brings a *ray of hope* to all of us who have been fighting this disease.

ray of sunshine : someone or something that makes a person happier or a place more cheerful • Their baby girl was their own little *ray of sunshine*. • He was a *ray of sunshine* to his patients.

– compare ²RAY

²ray *noun, pl* **rays** [*count*] : a fish with a flat body and a long, narrow tail — see color picture on page C8; see also STINGRAY — compare ¹RAY

ray·on /ˈreɪˌɑːn/ *noun* [*noncount*] : a smooth fiber that is used in making clothing • The shirt is made of *rayon*. • a *rayon* shirt

raze /ˈreɪz/ *verb* **raz·es; razed; raz·ing** [+ *obj*] : to destroy (something, such as a building) completely : DEMOLISH — often used as *(be) razed* • The old factory *was razed* to make room for a parking lot.

ra·zor /ˈreɪzɚ/ *noun, pl* **-zors** [*count*] : a tool or device with a sharp edge that is used to shave or cut hair from the face, body, or head • an electric *razor* • a disposable/safety *razor* — see picture at GROOMING

razor's edge *or* ***razor edge*** — used in various phrases to refer to a dangerous position or a position in which two different things are carefully balanced • He's a thrill-seeker who likes living ***on the razor's edge***. • The country's future is ***balanced on a razor's edge***. • He ***walks a/the razor edge*** [=*walks a/the fine line*] between humor and bad taste in his comedy.

razor blade *noun, pl* **~ blades** [*count*] : a small, thin, sharp piece of metal that is used in a razor — see picture at GROOMING

razor–sharp *adj* [*more ~; most ~*]

1 : very sharp • Sharks have *razor-sharp* teeth.

2 : showing a lot of intelligence or the ability to think quickly • She was *razor-sharp* in the debate. • He has a *razor-sharp* wit/mind.

razor–thin *adj, always used before a noun, chiefly US* : very small or thin • *razor-thin* models • He won by a *razor-thin* margin. • It was a *razor-thin* victory. [=a victory that was won by a very small margin or amount]

razor wire *noun* [*noncount*] : strong wire that has many sharp metal pieces on it and is put around an area to keep people out or in

razz /ˈræz/ *verb* **razz·es; razzed; razz·ing** [+ *obj*] *US, informal* : to make playful or unkind comments about (someone) : TEASE • We *razzed* the other team's pitcher. • Quit *razzing* me!

raz·zle–daz·zle /ˌræzəlˈdæzəl/ *noun* [*noncount*]

1 : noisy and exciting activity meant to attract attention • The kids enjoyed the *razzle-dazzle* of the circus.

2 *American football* : an action, movement, etc., that is done to confuse an opponent • The team used a little *razzle-dazzle* to score the winning touchdown.

– razzle–dazzle *adj, always used before a noun* • a *razzle-dazzle* dance routine • some *razzle-dazzle* piano work

razz·ma·tazz /ˌræzməˈtæz/ *also chiefly Brit* **razz·a·ma·tazz** /ˌræzəməˈtæz/ *noun* [*noncount*] : noisy and exciting activity meant to attract attention • show-business *razzmatazz*

RBI /ˌɑɚbiˈaɪ/ *noun, pl* **RBIs** *or* **RBI** [*count*] *baseball* : a run that is scored as a result of a specific batter's hit, walk, etc. ✧ *RBI* is an abbreviation of "run batted in." • A runner scored from third base on his long fly out, so he'll get (credited with) an *RBI* on that play. • He leads the league in *RBIs*.

RC *abbr* Roman Catholic

Rd *or* **Rd.** *abbr* road • 14 Wisteria *Rd*.

RD *abbr, US* rural delivery ✧ The U.S. Postal Service chooses official routes for the delivery of mail in rural areas, where houses are fairly far apart. • John Smith lives on *RD* 2. [=on the rural mail-delivery route numbered 2 in his town] • John Smith, *RD* 2, Box 237

-rd — used in writing after the number 3 for the word *third* • my 3*rd* [=*third*] try • I placed 43*rd* in the class.

RDA *abbr, US* recommended daily allowance; recommended dietary allowance • 50 percent of the U.S. *RDA* of iron

¹re /ˈreɪ/ *noun* [*noncount*] *music* : the second note of a musical scale • do, *re*, mi, fa, sol, la, ti

²re /ˈreɪ, ˈriː/ *prep, formal* : on the subject of : regarding or concerning — used in business and legal writing and e-mail before a word or phrase that states the subject you will be discussing • *re* your letter of last month • *Re*: Changes in procedure

RE *abbr, Brit* religious education • He teaches *RE* at the local school.

re- /ri/ *prefix*

1 : again • *re*fill [=fill again] • *re*do [=do over; do again]

2 : back to an original place, condition, etc. • *re*call [=call something back]

¹reach /ˈriːʧ/ *verb* **reach·es; reached; reach·ing**

1 a : to be able to touch, pick up, or grab (something) by moving or stretching [+ *obj*] She couldn't *reach* the apple. She was too short. • He couldn't *reach* the apple, even with a stick. • Can you *reach* me that pencil? = Can you *reach* that pencil for me? [=can you pick up that pencil and give it to me?] [*no obj*] It's no good. I can't *reach*. [=I can't touch what I'm trying to touch] **b** : to move or stretch (your hand, arm, etc.) when you are trying to touch or grab something [+ *obj*] — + *out, into, up*, etc. • I *reached* my hand *out* (to her). = I *reached out* my hand (to her). • She *reached* her hand *into* her purse to get her wallet. [*no obj*] She can't *reach* that far. — usually + *out, into, up*, etc. • I *reached up* to pull the cord. • She *reached into* her purse. • He was *reaching out* to grab the railing when he fell.

2 [+ *obj*] : to arrive at (a place that you have been traveling to) • We *reached* California after driving for two days. • The rescue team *reached* the stranded hikers this morning. [=the rescue team arrived this morning at the place where the hikers were stranded] — often used figuratively • He *reached* [=*got to*] the play-offs but was eliminated in the first round.

3 — used to say that something is big or long enough to touch a certain place or point [+ *obj*] Their land *reaches* the river. • The phone cord doesn't *reach* the table. = The phone cord isn't long enough to *reach* the table. • When she is sitting, her feet don't *reach* the ground. [=her feet don't touch the ground because her legs are short] [*no obj*] Skirts must *reach* (down) below the knees. • Their land *reaches* to the river. • The phone cord doesn't *reach*.

4 [+ *obj*] **a** : to grow, develop, or increase to (a particular amount, size, etc.) • You are an adult when you *reach* [=*become*] 18. • The lottery is expected to *reach* $50 million. • The temperature could *reach* 100°F this afternoon. • These plants can *reach* (up to) 6 feet tall. • The winds could *reach* 60 mph. **b** : to come to (a particular situation or condition) • The situation has *reached* [=*gotten to, arrived at*] a critical point. • We've *reached* a crisis in the negotiations. **c** : to succeed in achieving (something) after making an effort over a period of time • The school has *reached* their goal of raising $10,000. • They are still trying to ***reach an agreement***. • Have you ***reached a decision***? • Has the jury ***reached a verdict***?

5 *not used in the progressive tenses* [+ *obj*] **a** : to be seen or heard by (someone) • Your letter *reached* me yesterday. [=I received your letter yesterday] • The news just *reached* us. [=we just heard the news] • The news won't *reach* his parents until tomorrow. • She left a message for her boss, but it didn't *reach* him. **b** : to call or write to (someone) : to communicate with (someone) • I tried to *reach* [=*contact*] you by phone. • You can *reach* me by e-mail.

6 [+ *obj*] : to get the attention or interest of (someone) • The company is using TV commercials to *reach* a bigger audience. • Her music *reaches* young people.

7 [+ *obj*] *informal* : to make (someone) understand or accept something • I don't think I'm *reaching* my son.

reach for [*phrasal verb*] **1** ***reach for (someone or something)*** : to move your hand in order to get or touch (someone or something) • She *reached for* the salt and pepper. • He *reached* into his pocket *for* a dime. • She *reached* inside the bag *for* a pen. • The frog jumped as she *reached for* it. **2** ***reach for (something)*** : to try hard to achieve or succeed at (something) • Success won't come to you, you have to *reach for* it. — see also *reach for the moon* at ¹MOON, *reach for the stars* at ¹STAR

reach out [*phrasal verb*] **1** : to make an effort to do something for other people • The church is *reaching out* to help the poor. **2** ***reach out to (someone)*** **a** : to offer help or support to (someone) • The students are *reaching out to* the homeless. • a community *reaching out to* refugees **b** : to try to get the attention and interest of (someone) • He's *reaching out to* young voters.

– reach·able /ˈriːʧəbəl/ *adj* • The island is only *reachable* by boat. • a *reachable* goal • She is always *reachable* by cell phone. • Some children are just not *reachable*. [=some children refuse to accept what their parents, teachers, etc., tell them]

R

[2]reach *noun, pl* **reaches**

1 : the distance that you can stretch your arm to touch, pick up, or grab something [*singular*] The toy was ***within/in her reach***. [=she was able to touch/reach the toy] • Keep chemicals ***out of the reach of*** [=*away from*] children. • The ball was just ***out of her reach***. [=she was not quite able to touch or grab the ball] • The ball was ***beyond her reach***. [=the ball was too far away for her to grab] • The boxer has a ***long reach***. [=can reach a long way; has long arms] [*noncount*] He kept a dictionary ***within reach***. [=*nearby*] • The child tried to grab anything ***in reach***. [=anything that was close enough to touch] • The ball was just ***out of reach***.

2 : the ability or power of someone or something to do, achieve, or control something [*singular*] Victory was ***within their reach***. [=they were close to victory] • Buying a new car is ***beyond our reach*** right now. [=we do not have enough money to buy a new car right now] • His illness was ***beyond the reach of*** medicine. [=medicine could not cure his illness] [*noncount*] Victory was ***within reach***. • Their goal is ***out of reach***.

3 ***reaches*** [*plural*] **a :** the parts of an area that are a long way from the center • The country's farthest *reaches* had not been explored. — often + *of* • the outer *reaches of* the universe • the further *reaches of* the valley • the northern *reaches of* the country — sometimes used figuratively • Scientists are still discovering the far *reaches of* the human mind. **b :** levels *of* an organization • the upper/higher/lower *reaches of* the business **c :** a straight part of a stream or river • the upper/lower *reaches* of the river

within (easy) reach of **:** close to (something) • Our house is *within easy reach of* the highway.

re·act /riˈækt/ *verb* **-acts; -act·ed; -act·ing** [*no obj*]

1 : to behave or change in a particular way when something happens, is said, etc. • When I told her what happened, she *reacted* with anger. • I didn't expect him to *react* that way. • The firefighters *reacted* quickly when they heard the alarm. — often + *to* • She *reacted to* the news by getting angry. • Most people *reacted* positively *to* the smoking ban. — see also OVERREACT

2 *of a chemical substance* **:** to change after coming into contact with another substance — often + *with* • The chemicals *react with* each other to form a gas. — often + *together* • Ozone is formed in the atmosphere when sunlight and hydrocarbons *react together*.

3 *medical* **:** to be affected by a drug, food, etc., in usually a bad way • He *reacted* badly to the drug.

react against [*phrasal verb*] ***react against (someone or something)*** **:** to do things that are opposed to (something or someone that you disagree with) • He belonged to a group of artists who *reacted against* convention by doing things in a completely new way.

re·ac·tant /riˈæktənt/ *noun, pl* **-tants** [*count*] *chemistry* **:** a substance that changes when it is combined with another substance in a chemical reaction

re·ac·tion /riˈækʃən/ *noun, pl* **-tions**

1 : the way someone acts or feels in response to something that happens, is said, etc. [*count*] Their *reaction* to the news was positive. • When I told him what happened, his immediate *reaction* was one of shock. • The announcement produced an angry/stunned *reaction* from most of the people at the meeting. • My first *reaction* when I met him was not to trust him. • There has been a ***mixed reaction*** [=people have reacted in different ways] to the new policy. [*noncount*] There hasn't yet been much *reaction* to the announcement. • The newspaper received many angry letters ***in reaction to*** [=in response to] the editorial.

2 : an action or attitude that shows disagreement with or disapproval of someone or something [*count*] — usually singular; often + *against* • The modernist movement in literature was a *reaction against* traditional literary conventions. [*noncount*] There has been strong *reaction against* the government's policies.

3 ***reactions*** [*plural*] **:** the ability to act and move quickly in order to avoid sudden danger • A good driver has quick *reactions*. • The speed of his *reactions* saved his life.

4 *medical* **:** an occurrence in which your body is affected by a drug, food, etc., in usually a bad way [*count*] I had/suffered a (bad) *reaction* to the medicine. • Something she ate caused/triggered an allergic *reaction*. [*noncount*] There is a risk of adverse *reaction* to the medicine.

5 a *chemistry* **:** a chemical change that occurs when two or more substances combine to form a new substance [*count*] The *reaction* of hydrogen with oxygen makes water. • chemical *reactions* [*noncount*] a substance produced by chemical *reaction* **b** [*count, noncount*] *physics* **:** a process in which the nucleus of an atom is changed by being split apart or joined with the nucleus of another atom — called also *nuclear reaction*; see also CHAIN REACTION

6 [*count, noncount*] *physics* **:** a physical force that opposes the action of an equal and opposite force • For every action, there is an equal and opposite *reaction*.

7 [*noncount*] *formal* **:** a strong tendency or desire to oppose new political or social ideas • They have had to fight against the forces of *reaction*.

re·ac·tion·ary /riˈækʃəˌneri, *Brit* riˈækʃənri/ *noun, pl* **-aries** [*count*] *disapproving* **:** a person who is strongly opposed to new political or social ideas

– reactionary *adj* [*more* ~; *most* ~] • *reactionary* views/opinions/ideas • a *reactionary* politician

re·ac·ti·vate /riˈæktəˌveɪt/ *verb* **-vates; -vat·ed; -vat·ing** [+ *obj*] **:** to cause (something) to start working or happening again **:** to activate (something) again • *reactivate* the alarm • Once his debt was paid, his account was *reactivated*.

re·ac·tive /riˈæktɪv/ *adj*

1 [*more* ~; *most* ~] **:** done in response to a problem or situation **:** reacting to problems when they occur instead of doing something to prevent them • a *reactive* strategy • The government's response to the problem was *reactive* rather than proactive. — compare PROACTIVE

2 *chemistry* **:** tending to change into something else when mixed with another substance • a *reactive* chemical/substance

re·ac·tor /riˈæktɚ/ *noun, pl* **-tors** [*count*] *physics* **:** a large device that produces nuclear energy — called also *nuclear reactor*

[1]read /ˈriːd/ *verb* **reads; read** /ˈrɛd/; **read·ing** /ˈriːdɪŋ/

1 a : to look at and understand the meaning of letters, words, symbols, etc. [*no obj*] She learned to *read* at a very early age. [+ *obj*] Can you *read* decimals/music/Braille? • I can't *read* your handwriting. • He claimed that he could ***read my palm***. [=look at the lines on the palm of my hand and tell me what was going to happen to me in the future] **b :** to read the words of (a book, magazine, etc.) [+ *obj*] He likes *reading* the newspaper. • She *reads* a lot of mystery novels. • We will be *reading* (works by) Milton in the class. • She starts work every day by *reading* her e-mail. • Didn't you *read* the instructions? [*no obj*] He likes to *read*. • She doesn't *read* much. • Please *read* from Chapter 5 through Chapter 10. **c :** to speak aloud the words of (something written) [+ *obj*] He *read* the poem aloud. • The teacher *read* a story to us. = The teacher *read* us a story. • He wrote down the address I gave him and *read* it back to me. [*no obj*] Her mother *read* to her every night at bedtime. — see also READ OUT (below)

2 : to learn information about something from a book, newspaper, etc. [*no obj*] — often + *about* • I *read about* the fire in the newspaper. — sometimes + *of* • I have *read of* such things happening elsewhere. [+ *obj*] — + *that* • I *read* somewhere *that* he's making a new movie. • I *read that* they got married.

3 [+ *obj*] **a :** to learn information about (someone) by looking at how that person behaves • I can't *read* her—I'm not sure if she likes me or not. • You're an easy person to *read*. **b :** to learn information about (something) by looking at particular characteristics • A good canoeist can *read* the rapids. • (*golf*) She missed the putt because she didn't *read* the green correctly. • (*American football*) The quarterback *read* the defense correctly.

4 [+ *obj*] **:** to understand (something) in a particular way • The way I *read* it, we're supposed to show up at 3 p.m. • The situation is hard to *read*. [=*interpret*] — often + *as* • I *read* his actions *as* a cry for help.

5 [+ *obj*] **a :** to show (words) for someone to read • The sign *reads* [=*says*] "No Trespassing." **b :** to show (a temperature, weight, number, etc.) • The thermometer *reads* 90 degrees. • The clock *read* 4:30.

6 [*no obj*] **:** to be written in a particular way • The definition *reads* awkwardly. [=the definition is awkwardly written] • This essay will *read* better if you reorganize it. • The speech *reads* well. [=the speech is written well] • The first chapters *read* like a lecture.

7 [+ *obj*] **:** to get information from (something) • Someone *reads* the water meter once a month. • A scanner *reads* the bar codes on packages. • The computer can't *read* that disk.

8 [+ *obj*] **:** to hear and understand (someone) over a radio • Can you *read* me now? • I *read* you loud and clear.

R

9 [+ *obj*] **: to replace (a word or number) with another word or number — used to indicate how something written or said should be changed or corrected** • In the second problem, *read* 5 instead of 3. [=the number should be 5, not 3]

10 *Brit* **: to study (a subject) especially at a university** [+ *obj*] He *read* history at Oxford. [*no obj*] — often + *for* • She is *reading for* a business degree.

read between the lines **: to look for or find a hidden meaning that is not directly stated or obvious in something that someone writes or says** • Her letter seemed pretty cheerful, but if you *read between the lines*, you can tell that she's not really happy.

read into [*phrasal verb*] ***read into (something)*** **: to think of (something, such as a comment or situation) as having a meaning or importance that does not seem likely or reasonable** • You're *reading* too much *into* her remarks. [=her remarks do not have the meaning or importance that you think they have]

read lips **: to understand what people are saying by watching the movement of their lips : LIP-READ** • deaf people who know how to *read lips* • I couldn't hear what he was saying, but I was able to *read* his *lips*. ✧ People who tell you to ***read their lips*** mean that you should pay close attention to what they are saying. • "Can't I please go?" "*Read my lips*: you're not going, and that's final!"

read out [*phrasal verb*] ***read (something) out*** *or* ***read out (something)*** **: to read (something) aloud especially to other people** • I *read out* the names on the list.

read over [*phrasal verb*] ***read over (something)*** *or* ***read (something) over*** **: to read (something) from beginning to end especially to look for mistakes or check details** • He *read over* [=*read through*] the directions/contract carefully.

read (someone) like a book **: to easily understand the true thoughts and feelings of (someone) by looking at how that person acts or behaves** • My mom always knows when I'm lying. She can *read me like a book*.

read someone's thoughts *or* ***read someone's mind*** **: to know or guess what someone is thinking** • She looked deep into his eyes, trying to *read his thoughts*. • "I think we should go out to a movie tonight." "You *read my mind*. I was thinking the same thing."

read (someone) the riot act see [1]RIOT

read through [*phrasal verb*] ***read through (something)*** *or* ***read (something) through*** **: to read (something) from beginning to end especially to look for mistakes or check details** • Remember to *read through* [=*read over*] the essay before you hand it in. • He *read* the instructions *through* twice before he tried to assemble the bicycle.

read up on [*phrasal verb*] ***read up on (something)*** **: to read a lot about (something) in order to learn about it** • I *read up on* the history of the war.

take (something) as read *Brit* **: to accept or assume that something is true and does not need to be proved** • You can *take it as read* [=you can be sure] that there's nothing really new in their proposal.

[2]**read** /ˈriːd/ *noun, pl* **reads** [*count*] *informal*

1 : something (such as a book) that is read — usually singular • The book is an easy *read*. [=the book is easy to read; reading the book is easy] • The book is a good/quick/enjoyable *read*.

2 : an act of reading something (such as a book, article, etc.) • He reviewed the book after several *reads*. **— usually singular** • Give this article a *read* [=read this article] and tell me what you think of it.

3 *chiefly Brit* **: a period of time spent reading** • She was lying in bed having a peaceful *read*.

[3]**read** /ˈrɛd/ *adj* **: having knowledge that has been gained from reading books, articles, etc. — used after an adverb** • He is well-*read*. • He is better *read* than most people. • She is widely *read* in [=she has read a lot of] American literature.

read·able /ˈriːdəbəl/ *adj* [*more* ~; *most* ~]

1 : easy and enjoyable to read • a highly *readable* book • The travel guide is very *readable*.

2 : clear and easy to read • She has such beautiful, *readable* [=*legible*] handwriting. **— opposite** UNREADABLE; **see also** MACHINE-READABLE

– read·abil·i·ty /ˌriːdəˈbɪləti/ *noun* [*noncount*] • I enjoy the clarity and *readability* of his writing style.

read·er /ˈriːdɚ/ *noun, pl* **-ers** [*count*]

1 : a person who reads a book, magazine, newspaper, etc. • The book's ending leaves *readers* to draw their own conclusions. • She's a fast/slow/avid/voracious *reader*. • He's not much of a *reader*. [=he doesn't enjoy reading books, magazines, etc.] • a magazine with three million *readers* **— often +** ***of*** • a *reader of* science fiction • regular *readers of* the newspaper **— see also** MIND READER, NEWSREADER

2 : a machine that is used for reading text or information that is stored on film, tape, etc. • a microfilm *reader* • a card *reader*

3 : a book that is used to learn how to read or to practice reading in your own language or in a foreign language • a first-grade *reader*

4 *or* ***Reader*** *Brit* **: a teacher at a university who ranks just below a professor**

read·er·ship /ˈriːdɚˌʃɪp/ *noun, pl* **-ships** [*count*]

1 : the number or group of people who read a particular newspaper or magazine — usually singular • The magazine's *readership* decreased when the editors changed the format. • an enthusiastic/devoted *readership* • The newspaper has a *readership* of around 5,000.

2 *or* ***Readership*** *Brit* **: the position of a reader at a university** • She holds/has a *readership* in chemistry.

read·i·ly /ˈrɛdəli/ *adv* [*more* ~; *most* ~]

1 : quickly and easily • *readily* understandable/available • simple instructions that anyone can *readily* understand

2 : in a way that shows you are willing to do something : without hesitation or complaint • She *readily* [=*willingly*] admits that she is to blame. • He *readily* agreed to help us.

read·i·ness /ˈrɛdinəs/ *noun* [*noncount*]

1 : the state of being ready or prepared for something • The soldier lay ***in readiness***. **— often +** ***for*** • They're unsure of their daughter's *readiness for* kindergarten.

2 : the state of being willing to do something — usually followed by ***to + verb*** • He showed a *readiness* [=*willingness*] *to help* us.

read·ing /ˈriːdɪŋ/ *noun, pl* **-ings**

1 a [*count*] **: the act of reading something** • She gave the manuscript a careful *reading*. [=she read the manuscript carefully] • The family attended the *reading* of her will. • The speech ended with a *reading* from his latest novel. • After several *readings*, I finally understood the meaning of the poem. **b** [*noncount*] **: the activity of reading a book, magazine, etc.** • He needs help in *reading*. • They both love *reading*. • The teacher gave us a list of books for further *reading* on the subject. • The book makes for interesting/good *reading*. [=the book is interesting/good] • He has done a lot of *reading* on this subject. **— often used before another noun** • *reading* glasses • a *reading* light

2 a : a book, article, etc., that is being read or that is intended to be read [*count*] The *reading* for today is about human cloning. **— often plural** • The teacher assigned several *readings* to the class. • What are the *readings* for the next class? [*noncount*] *Moby-Dick* is required *reading* for any scholar of 19th-century American literature. • Shakespeare is not exactly ***light reading***. [=the works of Shakespeare are not easy to read] **— often used before another noun** • Did you bring any *reading* material/matter for the trip? • Students were given a summer *reading* list. • What is your child's *reading* level? [=how difficult are the books, articles, etc., that your child reads?] **b** [*count*] **: a part of the Bible that is read aloud as part of a religious service** • The pastor selected a *reading* for tonight's service.

3 [*count*] **: a particular opinion or understanding of something** • We need to get a better *reading* on [=a better idea of] what they intend to do. **— often +** ***of*** • I disagree with his *reading* [=*interpretation*] *of* what happened. • Her *reading of* the text is that the main character is depressed. • The judge made his ruling according to a strict *reading of* the law.

4 [*count*] **: an event at which something is read aloud to an audience** • a poetry/book *reading*

5 [*count*] **: the temperature, weight, number, etc., that is shown on a measuring instrument** • The thermometer *reading* was 20 degrees. • Meter *readings* are taken once a month. • The scale gave an inaccurate *reading*.

6 [*count*] **: an occurrence in which a proposed bill is discussed in a legislature before it becomes law**

re·ad·just /ˌriːjəˈʤʌst/ *verb* **-justs; -just·ed; -just·ing**

1 [*no obj*] **: to change in order to work or do better in a new situation : to get used to a new situation or change** • It takes time to *readjust* after a loved one dies. **— often +** ***to*** • The children need time to *readjust to* the new school.

2 [+ *obj*] **: to change or move the position of (something) slightly** • She was constantly *readjusting* her glasses. • He *readjusted* the picture on the wall.

– re·ad·just·ment /ˌriːjəˈʤʌstmənt/ *noun, pl* **-ments**

R

[*count*] She was constantly making *readjustments* to her glasses. [*noncount*] After the divorce, he had a tough period of *readjustment*.

re·ad·mit /ˌriːjədˈmɪt/ *verb* **-mits; -mit·ted; -mit·ting** [+ *obj*]

1 : to allow (someone) to again join a club, group, etc., or enter a place • They refused to *readmit* her to/into the club. • Only people who have ticket stubs will be *readmitted* (to the theater).

2 : to take (someone) into a hospital as a patient again • He was *readmitted* soon after being discharged.

read–only *adj, computers* **:** capable of being viewed but not of being changed or deleted • a *read-only* file/document

read–only memory *noun* [*noncount*] *computers* **:** ROM

read·out /ˈriːdˌaʊt/ *noun, pl* **-outs** [*count*] *computers* **:** a small screen that shows information • The calculator has a digital *readout*.; *also* **:** the information shown on such a screen • He checked the *readout* on the screen.

[1]ready /ˈrɛdi/ *adj* **read·i·er; -est** [*also more* ~; *most* ~]

1 *not used before a noun* **:** prepared to do something • I'll be *ready* in 10 minutes. • "Can we leave now?" "I'm ***ready when you are***" • We didn't have much time to ***get ready*** [=to prepare] before they arrived. • (*somewhat formal*) We need more time to ***make ready*** — often followed by *to + verb* • We are *ready to make* changes. • The kids are *ready to go/leave*. • Are you *ready to learn/listen*? • The boss is *ready to speak* to you now. • She got/made herself *ready to go*. • Doctors are ***ready and waiting*** *to give* help when it's needed. — often + *for* • She's busy getting the children *ready for* school. • Are you *ready for* your test? • We need time to get/make *ready for* the long trip. • The soldiers are ***ready for anything*** that the enemy might do.

2 *not used before a noun* **:** properly prepared or finished and available for use • Dinner is *ready*. • The college's new dormitory will be *ready* (by) next year. • Your prescription will be *ready* in about 20 minutes. • The car won't be *ready* until tomorrow. • We got everything *ready* for the party before the guests arrived.

3 *not used before a noun* **:** almost about *to do* something • He looked like he was *ready to cry*. [=like he was about to start crying] • I was *ready to walk* out of the room [=I felt like walking out of the room] when he said that.

4 *not used before a noun* **a :** willing and eager to do something • She's always *ready* with advice. = She's always *ready* to give advice. [=she likes to give advice] • He is always *ready* to help his friends. • He was angry and *ready* for a fight. **b :** needing or wanting something as soon as possible — usually + *for* • I'm tired and *ready for* bed. [=I want to go to bed] • The house looks like it's *ready for* a paint job. [=looks like it needs to be painted]

5 *always used before a noun* **:** quick and clever • a *ready* answer/wit

6 *always used before a noun* **:** available for immediate use • *ready* money/cash • (*Brit*) a *ready* meal • She has *ready* access to the files. [=she can get and use the files very quickly and easily]

(get) ready, (get) set, go *also Brit* ***ready, steady, go*** — used as a command to start a race

ready to roll see [1]ROLL

[2]ready *verb* **read·ies; read·ied; ready·ing** [+ *obj*] *formal* **:** to prepare (someone or something) • They *readied* the room for guests. • She *readied* herself to speak. • We have to *ready* ourselves for a tough fight ahead.

[3]ready *noun, pl* **readies**

at the ready **:** available for immediate use • The tourists kept their cameras *at the ready*.

the ready *or* ***the readies*** *Brit, informal* **:** money that can be used immediately • I'm a bit short of *the ready* just now.

ready–made /ˌrɛdiˈmeɪd/ *adj*

1 : prepared in advance for immediate use • *ready-made* clothing/meals

2 *always used before a noun* **:** already created or provided • The snowstorm gave us a *ready-made* excuse not to go to the party. • a *ready-made* solution

ready–to–wear *adj* **:** made in a standard size and not made for a particular person • a *ready-to-wear* suit

re·af·firm /ˌriːjəˈfəm/ *verb* **-firms; -firmed; -firm·ing** [+ *obj*] **:** to formally state (something) again in order to emphasize that it is true • The President *reaffirmed* his commitment to cutting taxes. • She *reaffirmed* her stance on the issue.

– re·af·fir·ma·tion /riˌæfəˈmeɪʃən/ *noun, pl* **-tions** [*count, noncount*]

re·agent /riˈeɪʤənt/ *noun, pl* **-agents** [*count*] *chemistry* **:** a substance that is used to test for the presence of another substance by causing a chemical reaction with it

[1]re·al /ˈriːjəl/ *adj*

1 : actually existing or happening **:** not imaginary • The movie is based on *real* events. • The detective Sherlock Holmes is not a *real* person. • He has no *real* power; he is just a figurehead. • The battle scenes in the movie seemed very *real* to me. • The team has a *real* chance at winning. • There is a very *real* possibility that we will be moving to Maine. • In ***real life*** relationships are not perfect. • The actor looks taller on TV than he does in *real life*. • I finally got to talk to a ***real live*** person [=an actual person] instead of a machine. • He's always daydreaming and seems to be out of touch with ***the real world*** • Their son finally went out into *the real world* [=the world where people have to work, deal with daily problems, etc.] and got a job.

2 : not fake, false, or artificial • *real* [=*genuine*] leather • a *real* diamond • Your *real* friends [=the people who are truly your friends] would be here to help you. • What is his *real* name? • Tell me the *real* reason you need the money.

3 : important and deserving to be regarded or treated in a serious way • This is a very *real* problem/danger/concern. • They have avoided talking about the *real* issues. • There is no *real* reason to worry.

4 *always used before a noun* — used for emphasis • There's a *real* surprise at the end of the movie. • Receiving this award is a *real* thrill. • He's being a *real* jerk.

5 : strong and sincere • I have no *real* interest in sports. [=I'm not very interested in sports] • He made a *real* effort to improve his grades. • There was a look of *real* [=*genuine*] astonishment on her face. • She showed *real* delight/happiness when I told her the good news.

6 *always used before a noun, finance* **:** measured by what money can actually buy at a particular time • a *real* increase in wages as compared to inflation • Charitable donations declined in *real* dollars last year.

for real *informal* **1 :** true and genuine • The information is *for real*. **2** *US* **a :** honest and serious • He convinced us that he was *for real* and really wanted to help. • Is that guy *for real*? **b :** genuinely good, skillful, etc. • The team has proven that it's *for real* this year. [=has proven that it's good and has a real chance of winning] **3 :** seriously or truly • He's in trouble *for real*. [=he's really in trouble] • They were just pretending to argue before, but now they're doing it *for real*.

get real *informal* **:** to start to think in a serious or reasonable way **:** to stop having foolish ideas, hopes, etc. • We have to *get real* about this problem. • You think you can get into Harvard with those grades? *Get real*.

keep it real *informal* **:** to talk and behave in an honest and serious way that shows who you really are • He says he's just trying to *keep it real*.

the real deal see [3]DEAL

the real McCoy see MCCOY

the real thing see THING

– re·al·ness *noun* [*noncount*] • The jeweler verified the *realness* [=*genuineness*] of the diamond. • The audience was impressed by the *realness* [=*realism*] of the movie.

[2]real *adv, chiefly US, informal* **:** very or really • We had a *real* good time. • The water is *real* warm. • He is *real* fast. • We went to bed *real* late. • a *real* old car

real estate *noun* [*noncount*] *chiefly US*

1 : property consisting of buildings and land • He sells *real estate*. — often used before another noun • a *real estate* broker/business/investment • *real estate* prices/values

2 : the business of selling land and buildings • She works in *real estate*.

real estate agent *noun, pl* **~ agents** [*count*] *chiefly US* **:** a person in the business of selling land and buildings — called also (*Brit*) *estate agent*

re·align /ˌriːjəˈlaɪn/ *verb* **-aligns; -aligned; -align·ing** [+ *obj*]

1 : to change the position or direction of (something) slightly usually in relation to something else • She *realigned* the mirror. • We had to *realign* the text to fit it on the page. • The car's wheels were *realigned*.

2 : to organize (something) in a different way • The company has *realigned* [=*reorganized*] several departments.

realign yourself **:** to begin to have different opinions, beliefs, practices, etc. **:** to become a member or supporter of

R

a different group • She has *realigned herself* with the conservatives.

– **re·align·ment** /ˌriːjəˈlaɪnmənt/ *noun, pl* **-ments** [*count*] His car is due for a *realignment*. [*noncount*] the benefits of corporate *realignment*

re·al·ism /ˈriːjəˌlɪzəm/ *noun* [*noncount*]

1 : the quality of a person who understands what is real and possible in a particular situation and is able to deal with problems in an effective and practical way • He has a sense of *realism* about what can be done to improve the economy.

2 : the quality of being very much like real life **:** the quality of seeming to be real • The *realism* of her dream was alarming.

3 : a style of art or literature that shows or describes people and things as they are in real life • the stark *realism* of the play/painting

re·al·ist /ˈriːjəlɪst/ *noun, pl* **-ists** [*count*]

1 : a person who understands what is real and possible in a particular situation **:** a person who accepts and deals with things as they really are • I'd like to think that these problems can be solved easily, but I'm a *realist*. I know that a lot of hard work will be needed.

2 : an artist or writer who shows or describes people and things as they are in real life

– **realist** *adj, always used before a noun* • a *realist* [=*realistic*] approach to the problem • a *realist* painting

re·al·is·tic /ˌriːjəˈlɪstɪk/ *adj* [*more ~; most ~*]

1 : able to see things as they really are and to deal with them in a practical way • He tried to be *realistic* about the situation. • We have to be *realistic* and accept the fact that these problems cannot be solved easily. — opposite UNREALISTIC

2 : based on what is real rather than on what is wanted or hoped for **:** sensible and appropriate • The plan is not very *realistic*. • a *realistic* approach/goal • It's not *realistic* to expect people to spend that much money on wedding gifts. — opposite UNREALISTIC

3 : showing people and things as they are in real life • a *realistic* painting/novel/description • The battle scene in the movie was very *realistic*. [=it seemed very much like a real battle] — opposite UNREALISTIC

– **re·al·is·ti·cal·ly** /ˌriːjəˈlɪstɪkli/ *adv* • We need to deal with these problems *realistically*. • We can't *realistically* expect the war to end soon. = *Realistically*, we can't expect the war to end soon. • The movie portrayed the battle very *realistically*.

[1]**re·al·i·ty** /riˈæləti/ *noun, pl* **-ties**

1 [*noncount*] **:** the true situation that exists **:** the real situation • He refused to face/accept *reality*. [=the truth] • the difference between fiction/fantasy and *reality* • She's out of touch with *reality*. [=she does not know what is really true] • The *reality* is that we can't afford to buy a house. • He used television as an escape from *reality*.

2 [*count*] **:** something that actually exists or happens **:** a real event, occurrence, situation, etc. • The movie shows the harsh/grim/stark *realities* of war. [=the things that really happen in a war] • Her dream of competing in the Olympics became a *reality*. [=she competed in the Olympics, as she had dreamed of doing] • They made the plan a *reality*. — see also VIRTUAL REALITY

***in reality* :** in truth — used to stress that something is true or real especially when it is different from what was believed or expected • They talked as if they had accomplished a lot, but *in reality* they did very little. • *In reality*, she was 15 years younger than she looked.

[2]**reality** *adj, always used before a noun* — used to describe television shows in which people who are not actors are shown living with, dealing with, and often competing against each other in real-life situations • *reality* television/TV/shows

reality check *noun, pl* **~ checks** [*count*] *informal* **:** something which shows you that the real situation is different from what you believed or hoped — usually singular • Her friends gave her a *reality check* about her boyfriend. [=told her the truth about her boyfriend] • He was starting to think he was infallible, so the criticism from his boss served as a *reality check*.

re·al·iz·able *also Brit* **re·al·is·able** /ˌriːjəˈlaɪzəbəl/ *adj*

1 : possible to achieve • a *realizable* goal/plan

2 *finance* **:** in a form that can be easily sold for money • *realizable* assets

re·al·i·za·tion *also Brit* **re·al·i·sa·tion** /ˌriːjələˈzeɪʃən, *Brit* ˌrɪəˌlaɪˈzeɪʃən/ *noun, pl* **-tions**

1 [*singular*] **:** the state of understanding or becoming aware of something • There is a growing *realization* that changes need to be made to the coaching staff. • She had a/the sudden *realization* [=she suddenly realized] that things had changed between them. • He ***came to the realization*** [=he realized] that he was adding up the wrong numbers.

2 [*count*] *formal* **:** the act of achieving something that was planned or hoped for — usually singular; usually + *of* • He was thrilled by the *realization of* his lifelong dream.

3 [*noncount*] *finance* **:** the act of selling property in order to get money • the *realization* of assets

re·al·ize *also Brit* **re·al·ise** /ˈriːjəˌlaɪz/ *verb* **-iz·es; -ized; -iz·ing** [+ *obj*]

1 : to understand or become aware of (something) • They did not *realize* the risk/danger that was involved. • He finally *realized* the scope of the problem. • I *realize* (that) this is an unusual situation. • She *realizes* how much things have changed. • Do you *realize* how difficult that stunt is? • You just have to *realize* that you can't always get what you want. • She slowly *realized* what he was trying to say.

2 : to cause (something) to become real — usually used as *(be) realized* • Our worst fears have *been realized*. [=the things that we most feared have actually happened]

3 *formal* **:** to achieve (something, such as a goal, dream, etc.) • He *realized* a lifelong dream/goal by winning an Olympic medal. • He finally *realized* his ambition to start his own business. • She hasn't yet *realized* her potential as a golfer. [=she hasn't become as good as she can be]

4 *formal* **:** to earn or get (money) by sale or effort • We can *realize* a profit by selling the stock. • The furniture of the estate *realized* $10,000 at the auction.

real–life *adj, always used before a noun* **:** happening in the real world rather than in a story **:** happening in the real life of someone • *real-life* problems/events • a *real-life* drama

re·al·lo·cate /ˌriˈæləˌkeɪt/ *verb* **-cates; -cat·ed; -cat·ing** [+ *obj*] **:** to move or direct (something) so that it can be used for a different purpose • After the class trip was canceled, the money was *reallocated* to cover the cost of the dance. • We need to *reallocate* our resources.

– **re·al·lo·ca·tion** /ˌriˌæləˈkeɪʃən/ *noun, pl* **-tions** [*count, noncount*]

re·al·ly /ˈriːjəli/ *adv*

1 — used to refer to what is true or real • She didn't *really* mean it. • Is that *really* a word? • It turned out that the bone wasn't *really* broken. • He might *really* be the one she's going to marry. • They *really* are twins. • What *really* happened? • There are *really* only two choices. • Who *really* cares? • I'm not hurt—*really*. [=I am being honest when I say I'm not hurt] • Did you *really* [=*honestly*] think I wouldn't notice?

2 : without question or doubt — used to make a statement more definite or forceful • You should *really* see a doctor about your back pains. • I *really* believe she's not coming back. • You *really* should try some of this cake. • She *really* is a nice person. • We *really* need the extra money. • He *really* likes her. [=he likes her very much]

3 : to a great degree **:** VERY • The dog runs *really* fast. • The water is *really* hot/cold. • She's a *really* nice person. • It's a *really* [=*truly*] beautiful day. • a *really* frightening/funny story • I had a *really* good time at the party.

4 — used to reduce the force of a negative statement • I don't *really* agree with you. • It *really* doesn't matter.

5 — used in speech to show surprise, doubt, or interest • "They're getting divorced." "*Really*?" [=I am surprised to hear that and would like to hear more] • "I think she likes me." "Oh, *really*?" [=I am doubtful that she really likes you]

6 *US* — used in speech to express agreement with what someone has just said • "He shouldn't be allowed to do that." "Yeah, *really*. Who does he think he is?"

7 — used in speech to show that you are annoyed • *Really*, you could have mentioned it sooner. • *Really*, you're being ridiculous.

not really — used to say "no" in a way that is not very forceful or definite • "Was the movie good?" "*Not really*." [=the movie wasn't very good] • "Do you want to go to a movie?" "No, *not really*." [=no, I am not very interested in going]

realm /ˈrɛlm/ *noun, pl* **realms** [*count*]

1 : an area of activity, interest, or knowledge • new discoveries in the *realm* of medicine • in political and legal *realms* • the *realm* of art/science/education • A victory by the team seems ***within the realm of possibility***. [=a victory seems possible] • It's not ***beyond the realm of possibility*** [=it's not impossible] that he will return.

2 : a country that is ruled by a king or queen ▪ a peaceful *realm*

re·al·po·li·tik /reɪˈɑːlˌpoulɪˌtiːk/ *noun* [*noncount*] **:** a system of politics based on a country's situation and its needs rather than on ideas about what is morally right and wrong

real–time *adj, always used before a noun* **:** happening or shown at the speed at which a computer receives and processes information ▪ *real-time* data/chatting/video

— **real time** *noun* [*noncount*] ▪ We chatted online in *real time.*

Re·al·tor /ˈriːjəltɚ/ *service mark* — used for a real estate agent who is a member of a national licensing association

re·al·ty /ˈriːjəlti/ *noun* [*noncount*] *US* **:** REAL ESTATE

[1]**ream** /ˈriːm/ *noun, pl* **reams**

1 [*count*] **:** an amount of paper that equals 480, 500, or 516 sheets

2 ***reams*** [*plural*] *informal* **:** a large amount of writing — usually + *of* ▪ She took *reams of* notes. [=she took a very large amount of notes]

[2]**ream** *verb* **reams; reamed; ream·ing** [+ *obj*] *US, informal* **:** to criticize (someone) in an angry way ▪ He ***got reamed*** in the press for his comments. — often + *out* ▪ She *reamed* him *out* for leaving the lights on.

re·an·i·mate /ˌriːˈænəˌmeɪt/ *verb* **-mates; -mat·ed; -mat·ing** [+ *obj*] **:** to give new life or energy to (something) ▪ The touchdown *reanimated* the crowd. ▪ She knows how to *reanimate* a dull conversation.

reap /ˈriːp/ *verb* **reaps; reaped; reap·ing**

1 [+ *obj*] **:** to get (something, such as a reward) as a result of something that you have done ▪ She is now *reaping* the benefits/rewards of her hard work. ▪ He *reaped* large profits from his investments.

2 : to cut and collect (a plant, crop, etc.) from a field [+ *obj*] The workers were out *reaping* the crops. [*no obj*] The workers were out *reaping* in the fields.

reap what you sow **:** to experience the same kind of things that you have caused other people to experience ▪ If you're rude to everyone, you'll *reap what you sow.* [=people will be rude to you]

reap·er /ˈriːpɚ/ *noun, pl* **-ers** [*count*] **:** a person or machine that cuts and collects crops — see also GRIM REAPER

re·ap·pear /ˌriːjəˈpiɚ/ *verb* **-pears; -peared; -pear·ing** [*no obj*] **:** to appear again after not being seen, felt, etc., for a period of time ▪ We watched the fireflies in the field vanish and then *reappear.* ▪ Call the doctor if the symptoms *reappear.* [=come back]

— **re·ap·pear·ance** /ˌriːjəˈpirəns/ *noun, pl* **-anc·es** [*count*] — usually singular ▪ The bird was believed to be extinct until its recent *reappearance.* [*noncount*] The vaccine prevents *reappearance* of the disease.

re·ap·ply /ˌriːjəˈplaɪ/ *verb* **-plies; -plied; -ply·ing**

1 [+ *obj*] **:** to put or spread (something) again on a surface, a part of the body, etc. ▪ She *reapplied* her makeup. ▪ The finish needs to be *reapplied.*

2 [*no obj*] **:** to ask formally for something (such as a job, admission to a school, a loan, etc.) again usually in writing ▪ She plans to *reapply* to the school. ▪ He *reapplied* for the job.

3 [+ *obj*] **:** to cause (force, pressure, etc.) to have an effect or to be felt again ▪ The defense *reapplied* the pressure in the second half.

re·ap·praise /ˌriːjəˈpreɪz/ *verb* **-prais·es; -praised; -prais·ing** [+ *obj*] *formal*

1 : to make a new judgment about the value of (something) ▪ Our house is being *reappraised* for tax purposes.

2 : to think about (something) again in order to decide whether you should change your opinion about it **:** REASSESS ▪ The bad economic news is forcing many people to *reappraise* their investment strategies.

— **re·ap·prais·al** /ˌriːjəˈpreɪzəl/ *noun, pl* **-als** [*count*] tax *reappraisals* [*noncount*] The situation has changed and requires some careful *reappraisal.*

[1]**rear** /ˈriɚ/ *noun, pl* **rears**

1 [*noncount*] **:** the part of something that is opposite to or away from the front part **:** the back part of something ▪ There are two bedrooms at the *rear.* — often + *of* ▪ The store is in the *rear of* the building. ▪ We sat toward the *rear of* the train/boat.

2 [*count*] *informal* **:** the part of your body that you sit on **:** BUTTOCKS — usually singular ▪ He slipped and fell on his *rear.* [=*rear end*]

bring up the rear **:** to be in the last position in a group, line, etc. ▪ At this point in the voting, Jones is leading with Smith in second place and Johnson *bringing up the rear.* ▪ They entered the room first and I *brought up the rear.*

[2]**rear** *adj, always used before a noun* **:** at or near the back of something ▪ The car's *rear* bumper was damaged. ▪ We used the *rear* [=*back*] entrance of the hotel. ▪ the horse's *rear* [=*hind*] legs ▪ the car's *rear* lights/window

[3]**rear** *verb* **rears; reared; rear·ing**

1 [+ *obj*] **:** to take care of (a young person or animal) ▪ His family *rears* [=*raises*] cattle. ▪ They *reared* [=*brought up*, (*chiefly US*) *raised*] their children to be polite and well-mannered. ▪ books on child-*rearing* — often + *on* ▪ The kitten was *reared on* special food. ▪ He was *reared on* comic books. [=he read a lot of comic books when he was young]

2 [*no obj*] *of an animal* **:** to rise up on the back legs with the front legs in the air ▪ The horse *reared* (up) in fright.

3 [*no obj*] **:** to rise high in the air ▪ The cliff wall *reared* (up) above us.

rear its ugly head see [1]HEAD

rear admiral *noun, pl* **~ -als** [*count*] **:** an officer of high rank in the navy

rear end *noun, pl* **~ ends** [*count*]

1 : the part of the body you sit on **:** BUTTOCKS ▪ She stood up and brushed off her *rear end.*

2 : the back part of something (such as a vehicle) ▪ The car's *rear end* was badly damaged in the accident.

rear–end /ˈriɚˈɛnd/ *verb* **-ends; -end·ed; -end·ing** [+ *obj*] *chiefly US, informal* **:** to drive into the back of (a vehicle) ▪ Someone *rear-ended* my car at a stoplight. = My car was *rear-ended* at a stoplight. ▪ I got *rear-ended.*

rear guard *noun, pl* **~ guards** [*count*] **:** a group of soldiers who are placed at the back of an army and who protect the army from being attacked from behind

rear·guard /ˈriɚˌgɑɚd/ *adj, always used before a noun* **:** fought or conducted by a group of soldiers at the rear of an army especially during a retreat ▪ a *rearguard* battle/defense ▪ The army fought a courageous *rearguard* action. — often used figuratively to describe an effort or fight to change or stop something that is very close to happening or being done ▪ The town has been fighting a *rearguard* action to prevent the multiplex from being built.

re·arm /riˈɑɚm/ *verb* **-arms; -armed; -arm·ing**

1 [*no obj*] **:** to obtain new weapons ▪ The treaty forbids the country to *rearm.*

2 [+ *obj*] **:** to supply (someone or something) with new weapons ▪ Another country was *rearming* their enemies.

— **re·ar·ma·ment** /riˈɑɚməmənt/ *noun* [*noncount*] ▪ naval *rearmament* ▪ They announced plans for *rearmament.*

rear·most /ˈriɚˌmoust/ *adj, always used before a noun* **:** at the very rear of something **:** farthest back from the front ▪ the *rearmost* part of the building ▪ the *rearmost* seats

re·ar·range /ˌriːjəˈreɪnʤ/ *verb* **-rang·es; -ranged; -rang·ing** [+ *obj*]

1 a : to change the position or order of (things) ▪ He *rearranged* the furniture. ▪ She *rearranged* the letters of her name to spell different words. **b :** to change the position or order of the things in (something) ▪ Because of the cancellation, he had to *rearrange* his schedule. ▪ *rearrange* the living room

2 : to change the time or location of (something) ▪ He asked his secretary to *rearrange* [=*reschedule*] the appointment.

— **re·ar·range·ment** /ˌriːjəˈreɪnʤmənt/ *noun, pl* **-ments** [*count, noncount*] ▪ Her schedule required *rearrangement.*

rear·view mirror /ˈriɚˌvjuː-/ *noun, pl* **~ -rors** [*count*] **:** a mirror in a vehicle that allows the driver to see what is behind the vehicle — see picture at CAR

[1]**rear·ward** /ˈriɚwɚd/ *adj, somewhat formal*

1 : located at, near, or toward the back of something ▪ the *rearward* section of the store

2 : directed toward the rear of something **:** BACKWARD ▪ a *rearward* glance ▪ *rearward* motion

[2]**rear·ward** (*chiefly US*) /ˈriɚwɚd/ *or chiefly Brit* **rear·wards** /ˈriɚwɚdz/ *adv, somewhat formal* **:** at, near, or toward the rear ▪ He glanced *rearward.* [=*backward*]

rear–wheel drive *noun* [*noncount*] **:** a system that applies engine power to the rear wheels of a vehicle ▪ a car with *rear-wheel drive*

[1]**rea·son** /ˈriːzn̩/ *noun, pl* **-sons**

1 [*count*] **:** a statement or fact that explains why something is the way it is, why someone does, thinks, or says something, or why someone behaves a certain way ▪ I gave a *reason* for my absence. ▪ Is there a *reason* for your strange behavior? ▪ There is a *reason* why they don't want to come. ▪ I can't give you the report for the simple *reason* that it isn't yet finished.

• She explained her *reasons* for deciding to change jobs. • He wanted to know the *reason* for their decision. • "Why don't you want to go to the party?" "No (particular) *reason*. I just feel like staying home tonight." • Give me one good *reason* why I should believe you. • For obvious *reasons*, we can't do that yet. • For *reasons* of space, some of the charts and graphs have been omitted from the article. • She resigned for personal *reasons*. • He is always late, ***for some/whatever reason***. [=he is always late, and no one knows why] • He tends to get upset ***for no reason***. • She did things ***for no good reason***. [=there was no acceptable explanation for her actions]

2 [*noncount*] **: a fact, condition, or situation that makes it proper or appropriate to do something, feel something, etc.** • There is no *reason* [=*cause*] to panic. • There's no *reason* for you to feel that way. • I had sufficient/adequate/enough *reason* [=*justification*] to leave. • He saw no *reason* to pursue the issue any further. • They want to try something different, and that's *reason* enough for the change. • He was found not guilty ***by reason of*** insanity. [=not guilty because he was insane when he committed the crime] • We have ***(every) reason*** to believe he is lying. • The company fired him ***with/without reason***. [=there was/wasn't a good reason for the company to fire him] • She decided, *with reason*, to find somewhere else to live. • Poor work conditions are ***all the more reason*** to find another job.

3 [*noncount*] **: the power of the mind to think and understand in a logical way** • Human beings possess the power of *reason*. • (*old-fashioned*) He ***lost his reason***. [=he became insane]

4 [*noncount*] **: ideas and opinions that are fair, sensible, and appropriate** • I can't get him to ***listen to (the voice of) reason***. = I can't get him to ***see reason***. • He is not ***open to reason***. [=he is not listening to logical or sensible thinking]

rhyme or reason see [1]RHYME

stand to reason **: to be sensible or understandable** • If her friends don't want to go, ***it stands to reason*** [=it makes sense] that she won't want to go either.

within reason **: within reasonable or sensible limits** • You can do anything you want, *within reason*. • The price is *within reason*.

[2]**reason** *verb* **-sons; -soned; -son·ing**

1 [*no obj*] **: to think in a logical way** • He lost the ability to *reason*.

2 [+ *obj*] **: to form (a conclusion or judgment) by thinking logically** • He *reasoned* that both statements couldn't be true. • She *reasoned* that something must be wrong.

reason out [*phrasal verb*] ***reason (something) out*** or ***reason out (something)*** **: to find an explanation or solution to (something, such as a problem, question, mystery, etc.) by thinking about the possibilities** • He *reasoned out* [=*worked out*] the problem by himself.

reason with [*phrasal verb*] ***reason with (someone)*** **: to talk with (someone) in a sensible way in order to try to change that person's thoughts or behavior** • They tried to *reason with* him, but he wouldn't listen.

rea·son·able /ˈriːznəbəl/ *adj*

1 [*more ~; most ~*] **: fair and sensible** • We have *reasonable* cause not to believe him. • She offered a *reasonable* compromise. • Your idea sounds *reasonable*. • It's not *reasonable* to expect perfect weather. • Please be more *reasonable*. There is no way I'll be able to finish all this work in so little time. • A *reasonable* man would not expect such a thing. • Our boss has *reasonable* expectations of his employees. • The request/offer seems *reasonable*. • We finished within a *reasonable* [=*acceptable*] amount of time. — opposite UNREASONABLE

2 : fairly or moderately good • The team has a *reasonable* chance of winning. • He makes a *reasonable* amount of money. — see also *reasonable facsimile* at FACSIMILE

3 [*more ~; most ~*] **: not too expensive** • The store's prices are *reasonable*. • The hotel offers excellent accommodations at *reasonable* rates. — opposite UNREASONABLE

– rea·son·able·ness /ˈriːznəbəlnəs/ *noun* [*noncount*] • We appreciated the *reasonableness* of his decision.

rea·son·ably /ˈriːznəbli/ *adv*

1 : to a fair or moderate degree : FAIRLY • The estimate was *reasonably* accurate. • They're doing a *reasonably* good job. • He is doing *reasonably* well in school. • The food is *reasonably* affordable/inexpensive/cheap. • She is *reasonably* intelligent. • I'm *reasonably* sure that the work will be done soon.

2 [*more ~; most ~*] **: in a logical and sensible way** • "Why don't we take turns?" she suggested *reasonably*. • We might *reasonably* assume he'll be available. • The judge *reasonably* believes that some form of punishment is necessary. • We need to discuss this problem *reasonably*.

3 [*more ~; most ~*] **: in a fair or appropriate way** • a *reasonably* priced car [=a car that is not too expensive] • She can *reasonably* be expected to show up on time.

reasoned *adj, always used before a noun* **: based on sensible and logical thinking** • a *reasoned* argument/conclusion • a *reasoned* appeal • a place for *reasoned* debate

rea·son·ing /ˈriːznɪŋ/ *noun* [*noncount*]

1 : the process of thinking about something in a logical way in order to form a conclusion or judgment • Could you explain your *reasoning*? • They told everyone the *reasoning* behind the decision. • a conclusion based on fallacious/flawed/false/sound *reasoning* • scientific/logical/legal *reasoning* • a method/mode/pattern of *reasoning* • She chose to follow a particular ***line of reasoning***. [=she chose to use a specific set of reasons in order to reach a conclusion]

2 : the ability of the mind to think and understand things in a logical way • Humans possess the power of *reasoning*.

re·as·sem·ble /ˌriːjəˈsɛmbəl/ *verb* **-sem·bles; -sem·bled; -sem·bling**

1 [+ *obj*] **: to put the parts of (something) back together : to assemble (something) again** • She *reassembled* the puzzle.

2 [*no obj*] **: to meet as a group again after a period of time : to assemble again** • The committee will *reassemble* [=*reconvene*] next month.

re·as·sert /ˌriːjəˈsɚt/ *verb* **-serts; -sert·ed; -sert·ing** [+ *obj*]

1 : to make other people accept or respect (something that has been in doubt) • He tried to *reassert* his authority/leadership/power/control.

2 : to state or declare (something) more strongly or clearly : to state again that (something) is true • She *reasserted* her innocence. = She *reasserted* that she was innocent.

reassert itself **: to start to have an effect again after a period of not having an effect** • Traditional values have *reasserted themselves*. • An earlier pattern may *reassert itself*.

– re·as·ser·tion /ˌriːjəˈsɚʃən/ *noun, pl* **-tions** [*count, noncount*]

re·as·sess /ˌriːjəˈsɛs/ *verb* **-sess·es; -sessed; -sess·ing** [+ *obj*] **: to think about (something) again in order to decide whether to change your opinion or judgment of it : to assess (something) again** • The doctor *reassessed* the injury. • She convinced him to *reassess* the issue.

– re·as·sess·ment /ˌriːjəˈsɛsmənt/ *noun, pl* **-ments** [*count, noncount*]

re·as·sur·ance /ˌriːjəˈʃərəns/ *noun, pl* **-anc·es : something that is said or done to make someone feel less afraid, upset, or doubtful** [*count*] Experts offered their *reassurances* that the accident wouldn't happen again. [*noncount*] He received *reassurance* from his family. • Children need a lot of *reassurance*.

re·as·sure /ˌriːjəˈʃɚ/ *verb* **-sures; -sured; -sur·ing** [+ *obj*] **: to make (someone) feel less afraid, upset, or doubtful** • Experts *reassured* the public that the accident wouldn't happen again. • I tried to *reassure* myself that the children were safe. • The news didn't *reassure* him.

reassuring *adj* [*more ~; most ~*] **: making someone feel less afraid, upset, or doubtful** • The news was somewhat/slightly *reassuring*. • a *reassuring* change • She gave me a *reassuring* smile. • It was deeply *reassuring* to hear his voice.

– re·as·sur·ing·ly *adv* • She smiled *reassuringly*.

re·bate /ˈriːˌbeɪt/ *noun, pl* **-bates** [*count*]

1 : an amount of money that is paid back to you because you have paid too much • a tax *rebate* [=*refund*]

2 : an amount of money that a business or company pays back to you because you have bought a particular product or service • a mail-in/store *rebate* • There is a $50 *rebate* offered with the printer.

[1]**reb·el** /ˈrɛbəl/ *noun, pl* **-els** [*count*]

1 : a person who opposes or fights against a government • The government captured six armed *rebels*. — often used before another noun • a *rebel* army/leader • *rebel* forces/groups • the *rebel* movement

2 : a person who opposes a person or group in authority • He was a *rebel* against the school administration. **: a person who does not obey rules or accept normal standards of behavior, dress, etc.** • He is a typical teenage *rebel*. • a fashion *rebel*

[2]**re·bel** /rɪˈbɛl/ *verb* **-bels; -belled; -bel·ling** [*no obj*]

1 : to oppose or fight against a government • When the government imposed more taxes, the people *rebelled*. • The protesters are *rebelling* against the new tax law.

2 : to oppose a person or group in authority • Children often

R

rebel against their parents. **: to refuse to obey rules or accept normal standards of behavior, dress, etc.** • He *rebeled* against the social conventions of his time.

re·bel·lion /rɪˈbɛljən/ *noun, pl* **-lions**

1 : an effort by many people to change the government or leader of a country by the use of protest or violence [*count*] The king's army suppressed/quelled/crushed the *rebellion*. • The unfair tax laws sparked a *rebellion*. • A *rebellion* broke out. [*noncount*] The peasants rose in *rebellion*.

2 : open opposition toward a person or group in authority [*count*] She's the head of a *rebellion* against the leaders of the party. [*noncount*] Recent election losses have led to open *rebellion* among some party members, who are calling for a complete change of leadership.

3 [*noncount*] **: refusal to obey rules or accept normal standards of behavior, dress, etc.** • signs of teenage *rebellion*

re·bel·lious /rɪˈbɛljəs/ *adj*

1 : fighting against a government • a *rebellious* army • *rebellious* peasants

2 [*more ~; most ~*] **: refusing to obey rules or authority or to accept normal standards of behavior, dress, etc. : having or showing a tendency to rebel** • a *rebellious* child • a *rebellious* look • He's always had a ***rebellious streak***. [=he has always been inclined to disobey]

– re·bel·lious·ly *adv* • She glared back *rebelliously*. • He responded *rebelliously*. **– re·bel·lious·ness** *noun* [*noncount*]

re·birth /riˈbɚθ/ *noun, pl* **-births** [*count*]

1 : a period in which something becomes popular again after a long period of time when it was not popular — often + *of* • the *rebirth of* pop music • The war generated a *rebirth* [=*revival, renaissance*] *of* patriotic feeling.

2 : a period of new life, growth, or activity • the natural cycle of birth, death, and *rebirth* in plants • the *rebirth* [=*revival, renaissance*] of the old shopping district • a spiritual *rebirth*

re·boot /riˈbuːt/ *verb* **-boots; -boot·ed; -boot·ing** *computers* **: to turn off a computer and then immediately turn it on** [+ *obj*] She tried to *reboot* her computer after it froze. [*no obj*] After you install the software, you will have to *reboot*.

re·born /riˈboɚn/ *adj* **: having new or stronger religious beliefs** • a *reborn* Christian

be reborn **: to be born again : to become alive again after death** • The phoenix is a mythical bird that *is reborn* from its own ashes. **— often used figuratively to describe something that becomes active or popular again** • After years of renovations and improvements, the city has *been reborn* as a tourist destination.

¹re·bound /ˈriːˌbaʊnd/ *noun, pl* **-bounds** [*count*]

1 : the act of bouncing back after hitting something • The fielder caught the ball ***on the rebound*** off the wall. [=caught the ball when it rebounded off the wall]

2 : a ball, puck, etc., that bounces back after hitting something • He caught/grabbed the *rebound*.

3 *basketball* **: the act of catching the ball after a shot has missed going in the basket** • He led the league in *rebounds* last year.

4 : an increase or improvement after a decrease or decline • There has been a recent *rebound* in stock prices.

on the rebound **1 : sad and confused because a romantic relationship has recently ended** • She refused to date him while he was still *on the rebound*. **2** *chiefly US* **: getting better** • His health is *on the rebound*.

²rebound *verb* **-bounds; -bound·ed; -bound·ing**

1 [*no obj*] **: to bounce back *off* something after hitting it** • The baseball *rebounded off* the wall.

2 [*no obj*] **: to increase or improve after a recent decrease or decline** • Share prices are *rebounding*. • She *rebounded* quickly from the loss. • He is *rebounding* [=*recovering*] from the injury well.

3 *basketball* **: to catch the ball after a shot has missed going in the basket** [*no obj*] She is good at both shooting and *rebounding*. [+ *obj*] He *rebounded* the ball and quickly passed it to a teammate.

re·buff /rɪˈbʌf/ *verb* **-buffs; -buffed; -buff·ing** [+ *obj*] *formal* **: to refuse (something, such as an offer or suggestion) in a rude way** • Our suggestion was immediately *rebuffed*. • The company *rebuffed* the bid. • She *rebuffed* him when he asked her for a date.

– rebuff *noun, pl* **-buffs** [*count*] • Our suggestion was met with a sharp *rebuff*.

re·build /riˈbɪld/ *verb* **-builds; -built** /riˈbɪlt/; **-build·ing**

1 : to build (something) again after it has been damaged or destroyed [+ *obj*] He *rebuilt* his house after it was destroyed by a fire. [*no obj*] They tried to *rebuild* after the earthquake.

2 : to make important improvements or changes in (something) [+ *obj*] They are *rebuilding* [=*renovating, remodeling*] an old house. • He is trying to *rebuild* [=*restore*] his reputation. • The new owner plans to *rebuild* the franchise. [*no obj*] The team is *rebuilding* after losing most of its top players.

re·buke /rɪˈbjuːk/ *verb* **-bukes; -buked; -buk·ing** [+ *obj*] *formal* **: to speak in an angry and critical way to (someone) — often + *for*** • She was *rebuked* [=*reprimanded*] *for* being late. • The boss *rebuked* us *for* talking too much.

– rebuke *noun, pl* **-bukes** [*count*] • He was stunned by the harsh *rebuke* from his father.

re·bus /ˈriːbəs/ *noun, pl* **-bus·es** [*count*] **: a riddle or puzzle made up of letters, pictures, or symbols whose names sound like the parts or syllables of a word or phrase**

re·but /rɪˈbʌt/ *verb* **-buts; -but·ted; -but·ting** [+ *obj*] *formal* **: to prove (something) is false by using arguments or evidence** • Her lawyer attempted to *rebut* the witness's testimony.

– re·but·tal /rɪˈbʌtl/ *noun, pl* **-tals** *formal* [*count*] Her report is a *rebuttal* of some common misconceptions. • In an angry *rebuttal*, the researchers claimed they were being unfairly scrutinized. [*noncount*] He said ***in rebuttal*** that he hadn't cheated.

re·cal·ci·trant /rɪˈkælsətrənt/ *adj* [*more ~; most ~*] *formal* **: stubbornly refusing to obey rules or orders** • a *recalcitrant* prisoner

– re·cal·ci·trance /rɪˈkælsətrəns/ *noun* [*noncount*]

¹re·call /rɪˈkɑːl/ *verb* **-calls; -called; -call·ing**

1 *not used in progressive tenses, somewhat formal* **: to remember (something) from the past** [+ *obj*] She wanted to send him a letter but couldn't *recall* his address. • I don't *recall* what time they said they would be here. • It is important to *recall* that not very long ago cell phones did not exist. • From what I *recall*, I think the library is two blocks down on the left. • "The first time we met," he *recalled*, "we got into a big argument." [*no obj*] As you may *recall*, we had agreed that decisions would require prior approval. • "What's his address?" "I don't *recall*."

2 [+ *obj*] **a : to ask or order (someone) to return** • The government *recalled* the soldiers to active duty. = The soldiers were *recalled* to active duty. • The ambassador was *recalled* from abroad. **b : to ask people to return (a product with a defect or problem)** • The factory is *recalling* all the cars because of a problem with the brakes. • Officials *recalled* two tons of contaminated meat today.

3 *not used in progressive tenses* [+ *obj*] **: to cause (something) to be thought of : to bring (an image, idea, etc.) into your mind** • The old stone town hall *recalls* [=*resembles*] a stone house from medieval Europe. • Seeing her again *recalled* memories of the happy times we spent together.

²re·call /ˈriːˌkɑːl/ *noun, pl* **-calls**

1 [*singular*] **: an official order for someone or something to return** • They issued a *recall* of workers after the layoff.

2 [*count*] **: a request by a company for people to return a product that has a defect or problem** • The factory has issued a *recall* of all cars with the defective brakes. • a beef *recall*

3 [*noncount*] **: the ability to remember what has been learned or experienced in the past** • She did mental exercises meant to improve her *recall*. • He has ***total recall***. [=the ability to remember all the details of things exactly as they happened]

4 [*singular*] *US* **: a way in which a public official may be removed from office by a special vote of the people** • Many people are calling for a *recall* of the mayor. • a *recall* election

beyond recall **: impossible to bring back : not able to be brought back or remembered** • Her youth was (gone) *beyond recall*. [=her youth was gone and could not be brought back] • events that are now *beyond recall*

re·cant /rɪˈkænt/ *verb* **-cants; -cant·ed; -cant·ing** *formal* **: to publicly say that you no longer have an opinion or belief that you once had** [*no obj*] Church officials asked the minister/priest to *recant*. [+ *obj*] Witnesses threatened to *recant* their testimony when the court released their names to the paper.

– re·can·ta·tion /ˌriːˌkænˈteɪʃən/ *noun, pl* **-tions** [*count, noncount*]

re·cap /ˈriːˌkæp/ *verb* **-caps; -capped; -cap·ping : to give a brief summary of what has been done or said before** [+ *obj*] At the end of the program, the announcer *recapped* the

R

day's news. • Before we continue, let's *recap* what we have done so far. [*no obj*] Before we continue, let's *recap*.
– **recap** *noun, pl* **-caps** [*count*] • The article provides a short *recap* of recent political developments. • Before we continue, here's a *recap* of what we have done so far.

re·ca·pit·u·late /ˌriːkəˈpɪtʃəˌleɪt/ *verb* **-lates; -lat·ed; -lat·ing** *formal* **:** to give a brief summary of something **:** RECAP [+ *obj*] To *recapitulate* what was said earlier, we need to develop new ways to gain customers. [*no obj*] We understood your point, there's no need to *recapitulate*.
– **re·ca·pit·u·la·tion** /ˌriːkəˌpɪtʃəˈleɪʃən/ *noun, pl* **-tions** [*count*] She provided a *recapitulation* [=*summary*] of events leading up to this point. [*noncount*] His speech was so complex that *recapitulation* is impossible.

re·cap·ture /riˈkæptʃɚ/ *verb* **-tures; -tured; -tur·ing** [+ *obj*]
1 : to catch (someone or something that has escaped) • The guards *recaptured* the escaped prisoner.
2 : to gain control of (a place or position) again after losing it • The soldiers *recaptured* the hill they had lost the day before. • In the final lap of the race, he *recaptured* the lead.
3 : to experience or bring back (a feeling, quality, or situation) again • They are trying to *recapture* those happy times they had together. • The documentary *recaptures* the social tensions of the 1960s.
– **recapture** *noun* [*noncount*] • The escaped prisoners have so far avoided *recapture*.

re·cast /riˈkæst, *Brit* riˈkɑːst/ *verb* **-casts; -cast; -cast·ing** [+ *obj*]
1 a : to change the actors in (a play, movie, or television show) • The director decided to *recast* the movie with unknowns. **b :** to give a new role to (an actor) • When she quit the movie, I was *recast* in the leading role. • The director *recast* some of the actors in the play.
2 : to present (something) in a different way • You should *recast* the last sentence in your essay to make it clearer. • He *recast* his political image to fit the times.

rec·ce /ˈrɛki/ *noun, pl* **-ces** [*count, noncount*] *Brit, informal* **:** RECONNAISSANCE

rec'd *abbr* received • your letter *rec'd* March 3

re·cede /rɪˈsiːd/ *verb* **-cedes; -ced·ed; -ced·ing** [*no obj*]
1 : to move away gradually • The floodwaters slowly *receded*. • I felt sad as I watched the ship *recede* from view.
2 : to become smaller or weaker • We listened as the sound of the sirens *receded* [=*faded*] into the distance. • The pain from my headache slowly began to *recede*.
3 ✧ If your hair is *receding*, you are gradually losing the hair that is at the front of your head. • His hair started *receding* when he was in his thirties. • He has a ***receding hairline***.
4 ✧ A ***receding chin/forehead*** is a chin/forehead that slants backward.

re·ceipt /rɪˈsiːt/ *noun, pl* **-ceipts**
1 [*count*] **:** a piece of paper on which the things that you buy or the services that you pay for are listed with the total amount paid and the prices for each • Keep your *receipt* in case you need to return anything.
2 [*noncount*] *formal* **:** the act of receiving something • The form should be completed and returned within 30 days of *receipt*. • Open immediately ***upon/on receipt of*** the package. • I am ***in receipt of*** your instructions. [=I have received your instructions]
3 ***receipts*** [*plural*] **:** money that a business, bank, or government receives • Our company deposits cash *receipts* every day.

re·ceiv·able /rɪˈsiːvəbəl/ *adj, always used after a noun, business* **:** not yet paid • ***accounts receivable*** [=the amounts of money that people and (other) businesses owe you]

re·ceiv·ables /rɪˈsiːvəbəlz/ *noun* [*plural*] *business* **:** the amounts of money that other people and businesses owe you • Our *receivables* are down this quarter.

re·ceive /rɪˈsiːv/ *verb* **-ceives; -ceived; -ceiv·ing**
1 [+ *obj*] **:** to get or be given (something) • You will be charged a late fee if the electric company does not *receive* your payment on time. • I *received* a letter/call from her yesterday. • You will *receive* a discount if you spend over $100. • This spring he'll *receive* [=be awarded] his PhD in physics.
2 [+ *obj*] **:** to react to (something) in a specified way • She *received* the news of his death with remarkable calmness. — often used as *(be) received* • Her new book *was* well/poorly *received* by the critics. [=the critics liked/disliked her new book] • The results of the study *were received* with considerable skepticism.
3 [+ *obj*] *formal* **:** to welcome (someone) in usually a formal way • The ambassador *received* [=*greeted*] his guests as they arrived at the party.
4 [+ *obj*] **:** to accept (someone) as a member of an organization, church, etc. — + *into* • She was *received into* the church/university.
5 [+ *obj*] **a :** to suffer (an injury) • He *received* [=*got*] a broken nose when he slipped and fell on the ice. **b :** to be given (a punishment) • She *received* a heavy sentence from the judge.
6 [+ *obj*] **:** to experience or take (a medical treatment) • He *receives* an injection once a week to treat his allergies. • Only one of the patients *receiving* the new treatment is experiencing bad side effects. • He *received* a kidney transplant.
7 [+ *obj*] **a :** to get (signals that are sent to a television, radio, etc.) • We were unable to *receive* the broadcast. • A satellite *receives* the signals and then sends them back to earth. **b :** to be able to hear (someone who is talking to you on a radio) • I'm *receiving* you loud and clear.
8 *American football* **:** to be the player or team to which the ball is kicked when play begins [*no obj*] They won the coin toss and chose to *receive*. [+ *obj*] They chose to *receive* the kickoff.
9 [+ *obj*] *law* **:** to buy or take (goods that have been stolen) illegally • He was found guilty of *receiving* stolen goods.
on/at the receiving end ✧ If you are *on/at the receiving end* of something bad or unpleasant, you are the person it is directed at. • It's not often that I find myself *on the receiving end* of such insults.

received *adj, always used before a noun, formal* **:** widely accepted • What was radical thinking in times past has become ***received wisdom*** today.

Received Pronunciation *noun* [*noncount*] **:** the British pronunciation of words that is based on the speech of educated people and is sometimes considered to be the standard pronunciation — abbr. *RP*

re·ceiv·er /rɪˈsiːvɚ/ *noun, pl* **-ers** [*count*]
1 : the part of a telephone that you pick up and hold near your face when you are making or receiving a phone call • She angrily slammed down the phone's *receiver*.
2 : radio or television equipment that changes signals into sound and pictures • a satellite *receiver*
3 *American football* **:** a player who catches passes thrown by the quarterback — see also WIDE RECEIVER
4 *law* **:** a person who is chosen to take control of a bankrupt business or its property • She was listed as the *receiver* in the bankruptcy proceedings.
5 *law* **:** a person who buys or takes goods knowing that they have been stolen • a *receiver* of stolen property

re·ceiv·er·ship /rɪˈsiːvɚˌʃɪp/ *noun* [*noncount*] *law* **:** the state of a business that has been placed under the control of a receiver because it is bankrupt • Years of financial difficulty eventually placed the company into *receivership*.

receiving line *noun, pl* **~ lines** [*count*] *US* **:** a group of family members and friends who stand in line at a wedding, funeral, or other formal occasion to welcome or greet guests and receive their good wishes, their sympathy, etc.

re·cent /ˈriːsn̩t/ *adj* [*more ~; most ~*] **:** happening or beginning not long ago • *Recent* events have brought attention to the problem. • I usually watch that show every week, but I missed the most *recent* episode. • Medical science has made amazing progress in *recent* decades/years. • She's a *recent* college graduate. [=she graduated from college a short time ago] • The change was *recent*. • That was the biggest earthquake ***in recent history/memory***.

re·cent·ly /ˈriːsn̩tli/ *adv* [*more ~; most ~*] **:** during the period of time that has just passed **:** not long ago • She *recently* graduated from college. • I was going to paint the room white, but more *recently* I've been considering a light blue. • I saw him *recently* for the first time in many years. • Only *recently* did they decide to move. • Until *recently* I had no idea where I would end up finding a job.

re·cep·ta·cle /rɪˈsɛptɪkəl/ *noun, pl* **-ta·cles** [*count*]
1 *formal* **:** a container that is used to hold something • She used the box as a *receptacle* for her jewelry. • a trash *receptacle* — sometimes used figuratively • He became a *receptacle* for his father's love and kindness.
2 *US* **:** a device into which an electric cord can be plugged in order to provide electricity for a lamp, television, etc. • an electrical *receptacle* [=*outlet*]

re·cep·tion /rɪˈsɛpʃən/ *noun, pl* **-tions**
1 [*count*] **:** the kind of welcome that someone or something

is given — usually singular • The performers did not get the warm *reception* they had hoped for. • His suggestion was given a cool *reception*. [=people were not enthusiastic about his suggestion]

2 [*count*] **:** a social gathering to celebrate something or to welcome someone • The school held a *reception* for the new students and their families. • a wedding *reception*

3 [*noncount*] **:** the act or process of receiving, welcoming, or accepting something or someone • He decided to run for a seat on the school committee only a year after his *reception* into the community. • Her job is to deal with the *reception* of donations.

4 [*noncount*] — used to describe how well or badly a radio, television, etc., is able to receive signals • Our TV gets poor *reception* because of all the trees around the house. • My cell phone *reception* is terrible.

5 [*noncount*] **:** a desk or area in a hotel, office building, etc., where visitors first go after entering • Check in at *reception* when you arrive. = Check in at the ***reception desk*** when you arrive. • I waited in the ***reception area***. [=*lobby*]

6 [*count*] *American football* **:** the act of catching a forward pass • He had three *receptions* [=he caught three passes] in today's game.

reception class *noun, pl* **~ classes** [*count*] *Brit* **:** a class for young children who are just starting to go to school

re·cep·tion·ist /rɪˈsɛpʃənɪst/ *noun, pl* **-ists** [*count*] **:** a person whose job is to deal with the people who call or enter an office, hotel, etc.

reception room *noun, pl* **~ rooms** [*count*] *Brit* **:** a room in a house (such as a living room) that is used for sitting and not for cooking, sleeping, etc. • For sale: house with 2 bedrooms, 1 bathroom, and 2 *reception rooms*.

re·cep·tive /rɪˈsɛptɪv/ *adj* [*more ~; most ~*] **:** willing to listen to or accept ideas, suggestions, etc. • I was happy to be speaking before such a *receptive* audience. — often + *to* • He was *receptive to* the idea of going back to school.

— re·cep·tive·ness *noun* [*noncount*] • He was pleased by the *receptiveness* of the audience. **— re·cep·tiv·i·ty** /ˌriːˌsɛpˈtɪvəti/ *noun* [*noncount*] • the audience's *receptivity* to his theories

re·cep·tor /rɪˈsɛptɚ/ *noun, pl* **-tors** [*count*] *biology* **:** a nerve ending that senses changes in light, temperature, pressure, etc., and causes the body to react in a particular way

¹re·cess /ˈriːˌsɛs/ *noun, pl* **-cess·es**

1 [*noncount*] *US* **:** a short period of time during the school day when children can play • The students play outside after lunch and at/during *recess*. • Do you have morning *recess*? — called also (*Brit*) *playtime*

2 : a usually brief period of time during which regular activity in a court of law or in a government stops [*count*] The judge called for a *recess* [=*break*] for lunch. • The Senate debates will continue after the August *recess*. [*noncount*] The Senate wanted to vote on the bill before *recess*.

3 [*count*] **:** a dark, hidden place or part — usually plural; often + *of* • the dark *recesses of* the forest • He buried the memory in the deepest *recesses of* his mind.

4 [*count*] **:** a part of a wall that is set back from the rest of the wall

²recess *verb* **-cesses; -cessed; -cess·ing** *US* **:** to stop regular activity in a court of law or in a government for a usually short period of time [*no obj*] The trial *recessed* for the holidays. [+ *obj*] The judge decided to *recess* the trial for the holidays.

recessed *adj* **:** set back into a wall or ceiling • The shelf is *recessed* into the wall. • The room has *recessed* lights/lighting. • *recessed* shelves

re·ces·sion /rɪˈsɛʃən/ *noun, pl* **-sions**

1 : a period of time in which there is a decrease in economic activity and many people do not have jobs [*count*] Many people lost their jobs during the recent *recession*. • an economic *recession* [*noncount*] The economy is in deep *recession*. • The President helped pull the country out of *recession*.

2 [*noncount*] *formal* **:** the act of moving back or away slowly **:** the act of receding • the *recession* of the floodwaters

re·ces·sion·ary /rɪˈsɛʃəˌneri, *Brit* rɪˈsɛʃənri/ *adj* **:** of or relating to an economic recession • in these *recessionary* times

re·ces·sive /rɪˈsɛsɪv/ *adj, biology* **:** causing or relating to a characteristic or condition that a child will have only if both of the child's parents have it • *recessive* genes • Red hair is a *recessive* trait. = Red hair is *recessive*. — opposite DOMINANT

re·charge /riˈʧɑɚʤ/ *verb* **-charg·es; -charged; -charg·ing**

1 : to refill (a battery) with electricity [+ *obj*] When the computer beeps, you need to *recharge* the battery. [*no obj*] It takes about an hour for the battery to *recharge*.

2 [*no obj*] **:** to regain your energy and strength • Take a break to give yourself time to *recharge*.

recharge your batteries *informal* **:** to rest and relax in order to regain your energy and strength • We took a nap after work to *recharge our batteries* before going out dancing.

— re·charge·able *adj* • *rechargeable* batteries

re·charg·er /riˈʧɑɚʤɚ/ *noun, pl* **-ers** [*count*] **:** a machine that recharges batteries • The digital camera has a built-in *recharger*.

re·cher·ché /rəˌʃeəˈʃeɪ, *Brit* rəˈʃɛəˌʃeɪ/ *adj* [*more ~; most ~*] *formal* **:** unusual and not understood by most people • *recherché* references

re·cid·i·vist /rɪˈsɪdəvɪst/ *noun, pl* **-vists** [*count*] *formal* **:** a person who continues to commit crimes even after being caught and punished

— re·cid·i·vism /rɪˈsɪdəˌvɪzəm/ *noun* [*noncount*] • We hope the new program will lower *recidivism* rates.

rec·i·pe /ˈrɛsəpi/ *noun, pl* **-pes** [*count*]

1 : a set of instructions for making food • The *recipe* calls for fresh thyme. • I didn't read the *recipe* carefully. • This is one of my grandmother's *recipes*. • a ***recipe book*** [=*cookbook*] — often + *for* • a *recipe for* beef stew

2 : a way of doing something that will produce a particular result — + *for* • He says he has an infallible *recipe for* success. • "She's planning to do the plumbing herself." "That's a ***recipe for disaster***." [=that will result in disaster]

re·cip·i·ent /rɪˈsɪpijənt/ *noun, pl* **-ents** [*count*] *formal* **:** a person who receives something • welfare *recipients* — often + *of* • She is the *recipient of* many honors. [=she has received many honors]

re·cip·ro·cal /rɪˈsɪprəkəl/ *adj* — used to describe a relationship in which two people or groups agree to do something similar for each other, to allow each other to have the same rights, etc. • a *reciprocal* trade agreement between two countries • a *reciprocal* exchange of information • The plan will only work if both sides fulfill their *reciprocal* [=*mutual*] obligations.

— re·cip·ro·cal·ly /rɪˈsɪprəkli/ *adv*

re·cip·ro·cate /rɪˈsɪprəˌkeɪt/ *verb* **-cates; -cat·ed; -cat·ing**

1 a : to do (something) for or to someone who has done something similar for or to you [*no obj*] She was harshly criticized, but she did not defend herself or *reciprocate* in any way. [=she did not criticize the people who criticized her] [+ *obj*] They appreciated her kindness but were not ready to *reciprocate* the gesture. **b** [+ *obj*] **:** to have (a feeling) for someone who has the same feeling for you • It broke his heart to learn that his love was not *reciprocated*. [=that the person he loved did not love him]

2 [*no obj*] *technical* **:** to move back and forth again and again • a *reciprocating* saw

— re·cip·ro·ca·tion /rɪˌsɪprəˈkeɪʃən/ *noun* [*noncount*]

rec·i·proc·i·ty /ˌrɛsəˈprɑːsəti/ *noun* [*noncount*] *formal* **:** a situation or relationship in which two people or groups agree to do something similar for each other, to allow each other to have the same rights, etc. **:** a reciprocal arrangement or relationship • The proposal calls for *reciprocity* in trade relations.

re·cit·al /rɪˈsaɪtl/ *noun, pl* **-als** [*count*]

1 : a dance or musical performance • piano *recitals* • a dance *recital*

2 : the act of reading something out loud or saying something from memory usually for an audience • a poetry *recital* — often + *of* • He gave a *recital of* his own poems before a large group of students.

3 : a long description or list that includes many things — often + *of* • Her speech was actually just a long *recital of* names, places, and dates.

rec·i·ta·tion /ˌrɛsəˈteɪʃən/ *noun, pl* **-tions :** the act of reciting something: such as **a :** the act of saying or repeating something out loud for an audience [*noncount*] the *recitation* of poetry/prayers [*count*] a poetry *recitation* **b** [*count*] **:** the act of describing or listing many things in a series — often + *of* • a *recitation of* our successes and failures • dry *recitations of* statistics

rec·i·ta·tive /ˌrɛsətəˈtiːv/ *noun, pl* **-tives** *music* **:** a passage in vocal music (such as an opera) in which the words are sung in a way that resembles speech [*count*] the second *recitative* of Act II [*noncount*] The opera made use of *recitative*.

R

re·cite /rɪˈsaɪt/ *verb* **-cites; -cit·ed; -cit·ing**
1 : to read (something) out loud or say (something) from memory usually for an audience [+ *obj*] He *recited* the poem/passage with great feeling. [*no obj*] He began to *recite* from the Koran.
2 [+ *obj*] **:** to say or describe (a series or list of things) • He can easily *recite* all the facts about any player on the team.

reck·less /ˈrɛkləs/ *adj* [*more* ~; *most* ~] **:** not showing proper concern about the possible bad results of your actions • He is a wild and *reckless* young man. • She has gotten two tickets for ***reckless driving*** [=driving a car in a dangerous manner] • He showed a ***reckless disregard for*** the safety of others. • He spends money ***with reckless abandon***.
– reck·less·ly *adv* • They *recklessly* threw themselves into battle. **– reck·less·ness** *noun* [*noncount*] • financial *recklessness*

reck·on /ˈrɛkən/ *verb* **-ons; -oned; -on·ing** [+ *obj*]
1 *informal* **:** to think or suppose (something) **:** to believe that (something) is true or possible • I *reckon* that we'll have to leave early. • Do you *reckon* you'll be able to go to the grocery store after work? • We'll have to leave early, I *reckon*. • "Do you think it will rain?" "(I) *Reckon* so." [=I think it will]
2 : to calculate or guess (an amount, number, value, etc.) **:** to have or form a general idea about (something) • They *reckoned* that they would reach their destination by noon. • I *reckon* [=*estimate*] the height of the building to be 70 feet. • Losses were *reckoned* to be over a million dollars.
3 : to think of (someone or something) as being something specified — usually used as *(be) reckoned* • She *was reckoned* [=*considered*] to be among the group's leaders. = She *was reckoned* as one of the group's leaders.
reckon on [*phrasal verb*] ***reckon on (something)*** **:** to expect (something) to happen **:** to plan on (something) • The train was an hour late, which was something we hadn't *reckoned on*. • She *reckoned on* winning the election. [=she expected to win the election]
reckon up [*phrasal verb*] ***reckon up (something) or reckon (something) up*** *chiefly Brit* **:** to calculate the total number or amount of (something) • He *reckoned up* the bill.
reckon with [*phrasal verb*] **1** ***reckon with (something)*** **:** to consider or think about (something) when you are making plans • They hadn't *reckoned with* all the paperwork that went along with buying a new house. **2** ***reckon with (someone or something)*** **:** to deal with (someone or something that can cause problems or trouble) • Anyone who tries to change the system will have to *reckon with* me. = Anyone who tries to change the system will have me to *reckon with*. [=I will oppose/fight anyone who tries to change the system] ✧ If you are a ***person/force to be reckoned with*** or a ***person/force to reckon with***, you are someone who is strong and cannot be ignored. • When he won his first three matches, the other players realized that he was *a force/man to be reckoned with*.
reckon without [*phrasal verb*] ***reckon without (something or someone)*** *chiefly Brit* **:** to fail to consider (something or someone) when making plans • They thought they could defeat him, but they *reckoned without* his determination.

reckoning *noun*
1 [*noncount*] **:** the act of calculating the amount of something • I was more than $10 off in my *reckoning*. • ***By my reckoning*** [=by my calculations], he should be in his 80s by now.
2 a [*noncount*] **:** the time when your actions are judged as good or bad and you are rewarded or punished • When the ***day of reckoning*** comes, we will have to face some unpleasant truths. **b** [*count*] **:** the act of judging something — usually singular • In the ***final reckoning*** her earliest books are the best.
3 [*noncount*] *Brit* **:** the group of people or things that are considered likely to win or be successful • Our football team hardly comes ***into the reckoning*** • Because of his injury, he is ***out of the reckoning*** • The team is still ***in the reckoning***

re·claim /rɪˈkleɪm/ *verb* **-claims; -claimed; -claim·ing** [+ *obj*]
1 : to get back (something that was lost or taken away) • Sons and daughters are proudly *reclaiming* the traditions that their parents had forgotten. • She *reclaimed* the title of world champion this year. • You might be able to *reclaim* some of the money you contributed.
2 : to make (land) available for use by changing its condition • Environmental groups have been *reclaiming* contaminated sites. • Acres of land were *reclaimed* by conservationists. • *reclaimed* swampland
3 : to get (a usable material) from materials that have been used before • The factory *reclaims* fibers from textile wastes. • These bottles were made from *reclaimed* [=(more commonly) *recycled*] plastic.
– rec·la·ma·tion /ˌrɛkləˈmeɪʃən/ *noun* [*noncount*] • land *reclamation*

re·cline /rɪˈklaɪn/ *verb* **-clines; -clined; -clin·ing**
1 [*no obj*] *formal* **:** to sit back or lie down in a relaxed manner • She was *reclining* on the sofa, watching TV.
2 : to lean backward [*no obj*] Does that chair *recline*? • The theater has *reclining* seats. [+ *obj*] He *reclined* his seat so that he could nap more comfortably.

re·clin·er /rɪˈklaɪnɚ/ *noun, pl* **-ers** [*count*] **:** a comfortable chair which has a back that can lean back at an angle — see picture at LIVING ROOM

re·cluse /ˈrɛˌklu:s, *Brit* rɪˈklu:s/ *noun, pl* **-cluses** [*count*] **:** a person who lives alone and avoids other people • My neighbor is a *recluse*—I only see him about once a year.
– re·clu·sive /rɪˈklu:sɪv/ *adj* [*more* ~; *most* ~] • my *reclusive* neighbor • a *reclusive* lifestyle

rec·og·ni·tion /ˌrɛkɪgˈnɪʃən/ *noun*
1 a : the act of accepting that something is true or important or that it exists [*noncount*] The procedure is gaining *recognition* as the latest advance in organ transplant surgery. • The Olympic Committee gave official/formal *recognition* to the sport. [*singular*] His smile was a *recognition* that things were not so bad. **b** [*noncount*] **:** the act of accepting someone or something as having legal or official authority — often + *of* • the *recognition of* the territory as a state • They demand legal *recognition of* their rights.
2 [*noncount*] **:** the act of knowing who or what someone or something is because of previous knowledge or experience • She somehow escaped *recognition*. [=she was not recognized; no one knew who she was when they saw her] • The renovations changed the house ***beyond (all) recognition*** [=changed the house so much that it looked completely different and could not be recognized as the same house]
3 [*noncount*] **:** special attention or notice especially by the public for someone's work or actions • Her paintings received *recognition* from her fellow artists. • All she wanted was some *recognition* for her work. • He finally received the *recognition* that he deserved. • They were awarded medals ***in recognition of*** their bravery.
4 [*noncount*] *computers* **:** the ability of a computer to understand and process human speech or writing • speech/voice/handwriting *recognition*

re·cog·ni·zance /rɪˈkɑ:gnəzəns/ *noun* [*noncount*] *US, law* **:** a legal promise made by someone before a court of law that must be kept to avoid being punished • He was released ***on his own recognizance*** [=he promised to do what the court wanted him to do and the court let him go]

rec·og·nize *also Brit* **rec·og·nise** /ˈrɛkɪgˌnaɪz/ *verb* **-nizes; -nized; -niz·ing** [+ *obj*]
1 *not used in progressive tenses* **:** to know and remember (someone or something) because of previous knowledge or experience • I didn't *recognize* you at first with your new haircut. • I can always *recognize* him from far away by/from the way he walks. • They *recognized* the odor at once.
2 : to accept or be aware that (something) is true or exists • It's important to *recognize* [=be aware of] your own faults. • They started talking and quickly *recognized* [=*realized*] how much they had in common.
3 : to accept and approve of (something) as having legal or official authority • The U.S. government has now *recognized* the newly formed country. • They refused to *recognize* the treaty.
4 : to think of (someone or something) as being something specified • The institute is an internationally *recognized* authority on eye surgery. • Walt Whitman is *recognized* as one of America's great poets.
5 : to publicly give special attention or notice to (someone or something) • They *recognized* her years of service with a special award. • We want to find an appropriate way to *recognize* his achievements.
– rec·og·niz·able *also Brit* **rec·og·nis·able** /ˈrɛkɪgˌnaɪzəbəl/ *adj* [*more* ~; *most* ~] • She has one of the most *recognizable* faces in the movie industry. • The bird is easily *recognizable* because of its bright red feathers.
– rec·og·niz·ably *also Brit* **rec·og·nis·ably** /ˈrɛkɪgˌnaɪzəbli/ *adv* • *recognizably* different versions

¹re·coil /rɪˈkojəl/ *verb* **-coils; -coiled; -coil·ing** [*no obj*]

1 : to quickly move away from something that is shocking, frightening, or disgusting **:** to react to something with shock or fear • We *recoiled* in horror at the sight of his wounded arm. • He *recoiled* from her touch. — often used figuratively • We *recoiled* at the prospect of having to spend that much money to fix the car.

2 *of a gun* **:** to move back suddenly when fired • The rifle *recoiled* and bruised my shoulder.

²re·coil /ˈriːˌkojəl/ *noun* [*singular*] **:** the sudden backward movement of a gun that happens when the gun is fired • The gun has a sharp *recoil*.

rec·ol·lect /ˌrɛkəˈlɛkt/ *verb* **-lects; -lect·ed; -lect·ing** [+ *obj*] **:** to remember (something) • I've been trying to *recollect* what happened. • I don't *recollect* telling him anything, but maybe I did. • She couldn't *recollect* who had mentioned his name in the first place. • From what I *recollect*, they said four of them were coming.

rec·ol·lec·tion /ˌrɛkəˈlɛkʃən/ *noun, pl* **-tions**

1 [*noncount*] **:** the act of remembering something or the ability to remember something • Her *recollection* of the accident is very different from mine. • ***To the best of my recollection*** [=from what I can remember], I only met them once.

2 [*count*] **:** something from the past that is remembered **:** MEMORY • She has only a vague *recollection* of her seventh birthday party. • His novel is largely based on his own *recollections* of his childhood in the inner city. • He says he ***has no recollection*** of what happened. [=he doesn't remember what happened]

re·com·mence /ˌriːkəˈmɛns/ *verb* **-menc·es; -menced; -menc·ing** *formal* **:** to begin (something) again after stopping [+ *obj*] The countries agreed to *recommence* the peace talks. [*no obj*] Production will *recommence* in early fall.

rec·om·mend /ˌrɛkəˈmɛnd/ *verb* **-mends; -mend·ed; -mend·ing** [+ *obj*]

1 : to say that (someone or something) is good and deserves to be chosen • A friend *recommended* this restaurant. • I can't decide between the lasagna and the salmon. Which do you *recommend*? • They *recommended* her for a promotion after only two years. • The film is *recommended* to anyone who liked her earlier movies.

2 : to suggest that someone do (something) • It is strongly *recommended* that you change the oil in your car every 5,000 miles. • Take only the *recommended* dose of cough syrup. • I *recommend* [=*suggest*] getting to the theater an hour early to be sure you get tickets. = I *recommend* that you get to the theater an hour early. • You may decide to pursue the matter in court, but I wouldn't *recommend* it.

3 : to make (something or someone) seem attractive or good • As a vacation destination, the area ***has much to recommend it*** [=there are many things that make it a good vacation destination] • He ***has little/nothing to recommend him*** as a political candidate. [=he has little/nothing that suggests he would be an attractive or successful candidate]

rec·om·men·da·tion /ˌrɛkəmənˈdeɪʃən/ *noun, pl* **-tions**

1 [*noncount*] **:** the act of saying that someone or something is good and deserves to be chosen • My boss wrote me a glowing ***letter of recommendation*** • We picked this restaurant ***on his recommendation*** [=because he recommended it] • Employees are frequently hired ***on the recommendation of*** a friend in the company.

2 [*count*] **:** a suggestion about what should be done • The report made very specific *recommendations* for policy reform. • He rejected his doctor's *recommendation* [=*advice*] that he work less and exercise more. • The committee's *recommendation* to hire a new director has been well received.

3 [*count*] *chiefly US* **:** a formal letter that explains why a person is appropriate or qualified for a particular job, school, etc. • The application requires two written *recommendations*. [=*references*]

¹rec·om·pense /ˈrɛkəmˌpɛns/ *noun, formal* **:** something that is given to or done to thank or reward someone or to pay someone for loss or suffering [*singular*] He is asking for a just/fair *recompense* for the work he's done. [*noncount*] She is seeking *recompense* [=*compensation*] for medical fees. • He received $10,000 ***in recompense*** for his injuries.

²recompense *verb* **-pens·es; -pensed; -pens·ing** [+ *obj*] *formal* **:** to give something (such as money) to (someone) as a reward or as a payment for loss or suffering • The company has agreed to *recompense* [=(more commonly) *compensate*] her for the injuries she sustained on the job.

re·con /ˈriːˌkɑːn/ *noun, pl* **-cons** [*count, noncount*] *US, informal* **:** RECONNAISSANCE

rec·on·cile /ˈrɛkənˌsajəl/ *verb* **-ciles; -ciled; -cil·ing** *formal*

1 [+ *obj*] **:** to find a way of making (two different ideas, facts, etc.) exist or be true at the same time • I'm afraid her story cannot be *reconciled* with the proven facts. [=her story must be false because it does not agree with the proven facts] • You'll need to *reconcile* [=*settle*] your differences with her. • It can be difficult to *reconcile* your ideals with reality.

2 : to cause people or groups to become friendly again after an argument or disagreement [+ *obj*] His attempt to *reconcile* his friends (with each other) was unsuccessful. — often used as *(be) reconciled* • After many years, they *are* finally *reconciled* (with each other). [=they are friendly again] [*no obj*] We will never *reconcile*. • After many years, they finally *reconciled* (with each other).

reconcile to [*phrasal verb*] ***reconcile (someone) to (something)*** **:** to cause (someone) to accept (something unpleasant) • He eventually became *reconciled to* his position in life. • I *reconciled* myself *to* the loss.

– rec·on·cil·able /ˌrɛkənˈsaɪləbəl/ *adj* • Your theory is easily *reconcilable* with our results.

rec·on·cil·i·a·tion /ˌrɛkənˌsɪliˈeɪʃən/ *noun, pl* **-tions** *formal*

1 : the act of causing two people or groups to become friendly again after an argument or disagreement [*noncount*] Signing the trade agreement was praised as an act of *reconciliation* between the two countries. [*count*] He contacted us in hopes of a *reconciliation*.

2 : the process of finding a way to make two different ideas, facts, etc., exist or be true at the same time [*noncount*] The differences in their philosophies are beyond *reconciliation*. [=cannot be reconciled] [*count*] a *reconciliation* of opposing views

re·con·dite /ˈrɛkənˌdaɪt/ *adj, formal* **:** not understood or known by many people • a *recondite* subject/fact

re·con·di·tion /ˌriːkənˈdɪʃən/ *verb* **-tions; -tioned; -tion·ing** [+ *obj*] **:** to return (something) to good condition by repairing it, cleaning it, or replacing parts • He *reconditioned* the old car. • a *reconditioned* engine

re·con·fig·ure /ˌriːkənˈfɪgjɚ, *Brit* ˌriːkənˈfɪgə/ *verb* **-ure; -ures; -ur·ing** [+ *obj*] **:** to change the way (something) is arranged or prepared for a particular purpose • We *reconfigured* the floor space to make it easier to work in. • The network has been *reconfigured*.

re·con·nais·sance /riˈkɑːnəzəns/ *noun, pl* **-sanc·es :** military activity in which soldiers, airplanes, etc., are sent to find out information about an enemy [*noncount*] There are two helicopters available for *reconnaissance*. • *reconnaissance* missions/aircraft [*count*] They did/conducted a *reconnaissance* of the enemy's position.

re·con·noi·ter (*US*) *or Brit* **re·con·noi·tre** /ˌriːkəˈnoɪtɚ/ *verb* **-ters; -tered; -ter·ing :** to go to (a place or area) in order to find out information about a military enemy **:** to do a reconnaissance of (a place) [+ *obj*] An expedition *reconnoitered* the coast to find out the exact location of enemy forces. [*no obj*] They were sent ahead to *reconnoiter*.

re·con·sid·er /ˌriːkənˈsɪdɚ/ *verb* **-ers; -ered; -er·ing :** to think carefully about (someone or something) again especially in order to change a choice or decision you have already made [+ *obj*] She refused to *reconsider* her decision not to loan us the money. • Local opposition has forced the company to *reconsider* building a new warehouse here. [*no obj*] We hope you will *reconsider*.

– re·con·sid·er·a·tion /ˌriːkənˌsɪdəˈreɪʃən/ *noun, pl* **-tions** [*count, noncount*] • The plan was sent back to the board for *reconsideration*.

re·con·sti·tute /riˈkɑːnstəˌtuːt, *Brit* riˈkɒnstəˌtjuːt/ *verb* **-tutes; -tut·ed; -tut·ing** [+ *obj*]

1 *formal* **:** to form (an organization or group) again in a different way • They have plans to *reconstitute* the bankrupt company. • a newly *reconstituted* committee

2 *technical* **:** to return (something, such as dried food) to a former state by adding water • *reconstituted* potatoes

– re·con·sti·tu·tion /riˌkɑːnstəˈtuːʃən, *Brit* riˌkɒnstəˈtjuːʃən/ *noun* [*noncount*]

re·con·struct /ˌriːkənˈstrʌkt/ *verb* **-structs; -struct·ed; -struct·ing** [+ *obj*]

1 : to build (something damaged or destroyed) again • After the earthquake, many houses needed to be *reconstructed*. • Archaeologists were able to *reconstruct* most of the ancient village from their findings.

R

2 : to find out and describe or show the way an event or series of events happened • They are attempting to *reconstruct* the events that led to the bridge's collapse. • Police *reconstructed* the crime.

re·con·struc·tion /ˌriːkənˈstrʌkʃən/ *noun, pl* **-tions**
1 [*noncount*] **:** the act or process of building something that was damaged or destroyed again • the *reconstruction* of the dam
2 [*noncount*] **:** the process of putting something (such as a country) back into a good condition • the *reconstruction* of postwar Europe • *reconstruction* of the health-care system
3 : a process in which an event or series of events is carefully examined in order to find out or show exactly what happened [*noncount*] They were able to determine the cause of the accident by careful *reconstruction* of the events leading up to it. [*count*] The police staged a *reconstruction* of the crime/accident.
4 *or* ***Reconstruction*** [*noncount*] *US* **:** the period from 1867 to 1877 when the southern states joined the northern states again after the American Civil War

re·con·struc·tive /ˌriːkənˈstrʌktɪv/ *adj, medical* **:** done on a body part to return it to a former shape or to change the way that it looks • a *reconstructive* operation • His face was badly damaged and will require ***reconstructive surgery***.

re·con·vene /ˌriːkənˈviːn/ *verb* **-venes; -vened; -ven·ing**
1 [*no obj*] **:** to meet again after a break • Congress/Parliament will *reconvene* after the holiday.
2 [+ *obj*] **:** to cause (a group of people) to meet again after a break • The association *reconvened* the conference every three years.

[1]**rec·ord** /ˈrɛkəd/ *noun, pl* **-ords** [*count*]
1 : an official written document that gives proof of something or tells about past events • There is no *record* of their first meeting. • Please submit your school *records* [=an official list of your classes, grades, etc.] with your application. • dental/medical/financial/court *records* • Unfortunately, there is no *record* of the transaction. • keep/maintain (good) *records*
2 a — used to talk about the things that someone or something has done in the past • The candidate has a strong environmental *record*. [=has a history of voting for laws, supporting projects, etc., that help the environment] • a voting *record* • She has a good driving *record*. [=she has not had any car accidents, traffic tickets, etc.] • The company has a perfect safety *record*. [=the company has had no accidents, injuries, etc.] • The team had a ***losing/winning record*** last season. [=the team lost/won most of the games it played last season] — see also TRACK RECORD **b :** CRIMINAL RECORD • The defendant does not have a *record*. [=has not been arrested in the past for a crime]
3 : a performance or achievement that is the best of its kind • a new *record* for the high jump • He ***broke the record*** for the high jump. [=he jumped higher than anyone else had ever jumped] • She ***set a record*** for the most sales in the history of the company. [=she made more sales for the company than anyone else ever had] • He ***holds the world/Olympic record*** for the shot put. [=he has thrown the shot put farther than anyone else in the world/Olympics] • She *holds the* (team/school's) *record* for the most strikeouts in a game.
4 a : a flat, round disc on which sound or music is recorded • He has a collection of old *records*. • play a *record* — sometimes used figuratively • He sounds like a ***broken record***. [=he keeps saying the same thing over and over again] **b :** a musical recording on a record, CD, etc. • Have you heard the band's latest *record*? • a ***hit record*** [=a record or CD that is very popular and sells many copies] — often used before another noun • an independent *record* label/company [=a company that produces musical recordings] • She just signed her first *record* [=(more commonly) *recording*] contract.
a matter of record see [1]MATTER
for the record **1** — used to indicate that a statement will be written down in an official record • The judge asked her to state her name *for the record*. **2** — used to indicate that you are making a statement which is important and should be remembered • I'll do what you want, but (just) *for the record*, I don't think this is a good idea.
off the record — used to describe a statement that is not official and should not be repeated or made public by being used in a newspaper, magazine, etc. • Government officials did speak to reporters, but only *off the record*. [=the reporters were not allowed to publish the things the officials said] • Her remarks were strictly *off the record*. • *Off the record*, I don't think he has any real chance of winning.
of record *formal* **1 :** having an official status • his attorney *of record* • the company's shareholders *of record* **2 :** regarded as an accurate and trusted source of information • a newspaper *of record*
on record **1** — used to indicate that someone is making or has made an official or public statement • She is *on record* as supporting the program. [=she has publicly stated that she supports the program] • The judge's opinion is *on record*. • The governor ***went on record*** as being opposed to higher taxes. **2 :** included or described in official records • This has been one of the worst years *on record* [=one of the worst years ever recorded] for winter storms.
on the record — used to describe a statement that is official and can be repeated or made public by being used in a newspaper, magazine, etc. • The reporter made it clear that the interview was *on the record*.
set/put the record straight **:** to provide the facts about something that people have a false understanding or idea about • Let me *set the record straight* about what really happened last week.

[2]**re·cord** /rɪˈkoəd/ *verb* **-cords; -cord·ed; -cord·ing**
1 [+ *obj*] **:** to write (something) down so that it can be used or seen again in the future **:** to produce a record of (something) • Be sure to *record* all your business expenditures. • He *recorded* the incident in his journal. = The incident was *recorded* in his journal. = His journal *recorded* the incident. • The first *recorded* [=*known*] case of the disease occurred two years ago. • There are similar events all throughout ***recorded history***.
2 [+ *obj*] **:** to show a measurement of (something) **:** to indicate (something) • The thermometer *recorded* 40 degrees below zero. • A seismograph is a device that measures and *records* the intensity of earthquakes.
3 : to store (something, such as sounds, music, images, etc.) on tape or on a disk so that it can be heard or seen later **:** to produce a recording of (something) [+ *obj*] Please *record* the television program for me. • He *recorded* the birthday party with his new video camera. • He just *recorded* his latest album. • The show is *recorded* in front of a live audience. [*no obj*] The band spent all night *recording*. — see also PRERECORD

[3]**rec·ord** /ˈrɛkəd/ *adj, always used before a noun* **:** best or most remarkable among other similar things • We've had *record* temperatures. [=temperatures that are higher/lower than temperatures have ever been at this time of year] • He finished in *record* time. [=in the least amount of time ever] • A *record* number [=the highest number ever] of voters turned out for the election. • Gas prices are at a *record* high. [=higher than they have ever been]

record book *noun, pl* **~ books** [*count*] **:** a book that has records of the best or most remarkable performances or achievements in a particular sport or activity — usually used figuratively • His long jump earned him a place in the *record book*. [=his long jump set a record] • That game was one for the *record books*. [=many records were set during that game]

record–breaking *adj, always used before a noun* **:** better, greater, higher, etc., than any other in the past **:** beyond any previous record • a *record-breaking* high jump • The outdoor concert drew a *record-breaking* crowd to the park. [=the largest crowd to ever be at the park]
– record breaker *noun, pl* **~ -ers** [*count*]

recorded delivery *noun* [*noncount*] *Brit* **:** CERTIFIED MAIL • I sent the package by *recorded delivery*.

re·cord·er /rɪˈkoədə/ *noun, pl* **-ers** [*count*]
1 : a device that records sounds or images or both so that they can be heard or seen again — see also COCKPIT VOICE RECORDER, FLIGHT RECORDER, TAPE RECORDER
2 : a musical instrument that is shaped like a tube with holes and that is played by blowing into the top of the tube — see picture at WOODWIND
3 : a judge in some courts of law
4 : a person whose job is to record official information • She works as the clerk and *recorder* at the county courthouse.

record holder *noun, pl* **~ -ers** [*count*] **:** the person or thing that has achieved something no other person or thing has achieved **:** a person or thing that holds a record • He is the marathon world *record holder*. [=he has run a marathon in less time than any other person in the world] • They're developing an airplane that is expected to be faster than the current *record holder*.

re·cord·ing /rɪˈkoədɪŋ/ *noun, pl* **-ings**
1 [*count*] **:** music, sounds, or images that have been stored on

a record, CD, computer, etc., so that they can be heard or seen again • a digital *recording* • early *recordings* of jazz
2 [*noncount*] **: the act or process of storing sounds or images on tape or a disk — usually used before another noun** • a *recording* studio/session • a ***recording artist*** [=a person who performs music for recordings]

record player *noun, pl* **~ -ers** [*count*] **: a device used for playing musical records**

[1]re·count /rɪˈkaʊnt/ *verb* **-counts; -count·ed; -count·ing** [+ *obj*] *formal* **: to tell someone about (something that happened) : to describe or give an account of (an event)** • John later *recounted* how he got lost on the way home. • He *recounted* the conversation that he had with his boss. — compare [2]RECOUNT

[2]re·count /riˈkaʊnt/ *verb* **-counts; -count·ed; -count·ing** [+ *obj*] **: to count (something) again** • They carefully *recounted* the votes. • We *recounted* the money to make sure it was all there. — compare [1]RECOUNT

[3]re·count /ˈriːˌkaʊnt/ *noun, pl* **-counts** [*count*] **: a second count of the votes in a very close election** • The election was very close and the loser demanded a *recount*.

re·coup /rɪˈkuːp/ *verb* **-coups; -couped; -coup·ing** [+ *obj*] **: to get back (money that has been spent, invested, lost, etc.) : RECOVER** • It will be hard for us to *recoup* the loss. • Movie studios can turn to video sales to *recoup* the costs of a movie that does poorly at the box office. • She *recouped* only a portion of her investment.

re·course /ˈriːˌkoɚs, *Brit* rɪˈkɔːs/ *noun* [*noncount*] **: an opportunity or choice to use or do something in order to deal with a problem or situation** • His only *recourse* [=the only thing he can do] is to file a complaint with the management. • She has no legal *recourse* against the magazine. [=there is no legal action she can take against the magazine] • He had no *recourse* to legal help. [=he was not able to get legal help] • The dispute was settled ***without recourse to*** law.

re·cov·er /rɪˈkʌvɚ/ *verb* **-ers; -ered; -er·ing**
1 [*no obj*] **a : to become healthy after an illness or injury : to return to normal health** • She had a heart attack but is *recovering* well. — often + *from* • He's at home *recovering from* the flu. • I feel fully *recovered from* my surgery. **b : to return to a normal state after a period of difficulty** • Share prices will be down until the economy *recovers*. — often + *from* • The team never *recovered from* the devastating loss. • The city will *recover from* this recession eventually.
2 [+ *obj*] **a : to get (something, such as an ability or feeling) again** • He'll try again when he *recovers* [=*regains*] his confidence. • She *recovered* consciousness in the hospital. • I slipped, but somehow *recovered* my balance. • He suffered a stroke and hasn't yet *recovered* the use of his left arm. **b : to get back (something stolen or lost)** • The police *recovered* his stolen wallet. • The program helps users *recover* computer files that have been deleted. • a *recovered* computer file — often + *from* • Very little was *recovered from* the wrecked ship. **c : to get back (money that has been spent, invested, etc.)** • The author gets no royalties until the publisher *recovers* [=*recoups*] the expenses of publication. • He may sue the company to ***recover damages*** for injuries caused by the device. [=to get money from the company to make up for being injured by the device]
– re·cov·er·able /rɪˈkʌvərəbəl/ *adj*

re–cov·er /riˈkʌvɚ/ *verb* **-ers; -ered; -er·ing** [+ *obj*] **: to cover (something) again : to put a new cover on (something)** • She *re-covered* the old chair with a new fabric.

re·cov·er·ing /rɪˈkʌvərɪŋ/ *adj, always used before a noun* **: in a state in which you have stopped or are trying to stop a behavior (such as drinking alcohol or using drugs) that you have been doing for a long time and that is harmful to you** • a *recovering* alcoholic • *recovering* drug addicts • (*humorous*) He describes himself as "a *recovering* politician."

re·cov·ery /rɪˈkʌvəri/ *noun, pl* **-er·ies**
1 [*count*] **: the act or process of becoming healthy after an illness or injury : the act or process of recovering — usually singular** • The patient made a miraculous *recovery*. • Therapy played a vital role in his *recovery*. • The card said, "Best wishes for a ***speedy recovery***." [=a quick return to health] • She is expected to ***make a complete/full recovery***. [=to recover fully; to have no lasting health problems] • She's ***on the road to recovery***. [=in the process of becoming healthy again]
2 : the act or process of returning to a normal state after a period of difficulty [*count*] **— usually singular** • the forest's natural *recovery* after a fire • The army helped with the *recovery* efforts after the storm. • We should see a gradual economic *recovery* in the next few months. [*noncount*] This policy may slow the pace of economic *recovery*.
3 [*noncount*] **: the return of something that has been lost, stolen, etc.** • We hope for the *recovery* of the stolen paintings. • Their mission was the *recovery* of the space capsule. • programmers trained in ***data recovery*** [=getting back computer files that are or seem to be lost]
4 [*noncount*] **: the act or process of stopping the use of drugs, alcohol, etc., and returning to a healthy way of living** • Admitting that you are addicted to a drug is an important step toward *recovery*. • She's battled alcoholism most of her life, but she's ***in recovery*** now.
5 [*noncount*] **: the act of getting something (such as oil, gas, gold, etc.) out of a substance that is deep in the ground** • a technique used in oil and gas *recovery*

recovery room *noun, pl* **~ rooms** [*count*] **: a room in a hospital where patients are taken for special care after an operation**

re–cre·ate /ˌriːkriˈeɪt/ *verb* **-ates; -at·ed; -at·ing** [+ *obj*] **: to make (something from the past) exist or seem to exist again : to create (something) again** • The movie set *re-creates* a London street of 1895. • The scene of the crime was *re-created* based upon police photographs.
– re–cre·a·tion /ˌriːkriˈeɪʃən/ *noun, pl* **-tions** [*count*] a perfect *re-creation* of a colonial village [*noncount*] The investigation involved careful *re-creation* of the crime scene.

rec·re·a·tion /ˌrɛkriˈeɪʃən/ *noun, pl* **-tions : something people do to relax or have fun : activities done for enjoyment** [*noncount*] The fields next to the school are used for *recreation*. • a *recreation* center/area/facility [*count*] Hiking and gardening are our favorite *recreations*. [=*pastimes*]

rec·re·a·tion·al /ˌrɛkriˈeɪʃənl̩/ *adj*
1 : done for enjoyment • *recreational* activities
2 *of a drug* **: used for pleasure instead of for medical purposes** • Marijuana is a *recreational* drug. • *recreational* drug users

recreational vehicle *noun, pl* **~ -cles** [*count*] *US* **: a large vehicle that often has a bathroom, kitchen, and beds for use during travel and camping;** *especially* **: MOTOR HOME — called also** *RV*; **compare CAMPER**

recreation ground *noun, pl* **~ grounds** [*count*] *Brit* **: an area of public land that is used for sports and outdoor games**

recreation room *noun, pl* **~ rooms** [*count*]
1 : a public room in a school, hospital, etc., that is used for games and social activities
2 *US* **: a room in a house that is used for playing games, watching television, etc. — called also (*informal*) *rec room***

re·crim·i·na·tion /rɪˌkrɪməˈneɪʃən/ *noun, pl* **-tions : an angry statement in which you accuse or criticize a person who has accused or criticized you** [*count*] The discussion turned into a heated debate with *recriminations* flying back and forth. [*noncount*] The meeting ended with bitterness and *recrimination*. • words of *recrimination*

rec room /ˈrɛk-/ *noun, pl* **~ rooms** [*count*] *US, informal* **: RECREATION ROOM**

[1]re·cruit /rɪˈkruːt/ *verb* **-cruits; -cruit·ed; -cruit·ing**
1 a : to find suitable people and get them to join a company, an organization, the armed forces, etc. [+ *obj*] He was *recruited* by the army after high school. • Public schools are *recruiting* new teachers. • College football coaches spend a lot of time *recruiting* high school athletes. [*no obj*] College football coaches spend a lot of time *recruiting*. • Some parents don't think the military should be *recruiting* from high schools. **b** [+ *obj*] **: to form or build (a group, team, army, etc.) by getting people to join** • We *recruited* a crew of volunteers to help us. • *recruit* a regiment • *recruit* an army
2 [+ *obj*] **: to persuade (someone) to join you in some activity or to help you** • I *recruited* my brother to drive us to the concert. • She *recruited* four friends to distribute food to the homeless with her.
– re·cruit·er *noun, pl* **-ers** [*count*] • an army *recruiter* **– re·cruit·ment** /rɪˈkruːtmənt/ *noun* [*noncount*] • *recruitment* of college graduates

[2]recruit *noun, pl* **-cruits** [*count*]
1 : a person who has recently joined the armed forces • army *recruits*
2 : a person who has recently joined a company, organization, etc. • the newest *recruit* on the team • She's one of the department's new *recruits*.

rec·tal /ˈrɛktl/ *adj, medical* **: relating to, affecting, or located near the rectum** • *rectal* cancer

rect·an·gle /ˈrɛkˌtæŋgəl/ *noun, pl* **-an·gles** [*count*] *geometry* **: a four-sided shape that is made up of two pairs of paral-**

R

lel lines and that has four right angles; *especially* : a shape in which one pair of lines is longer than the other pair• squares and *rectangles* — see picture at GEOMETRY

– **rect·an·gu·lar** /rɛkˈtæŋgjələ/ *adj*• a *rectangular* shape

rec·ti·fy /ˈrɛktəˌfaɪ/ *verb* **-fies; -fied; -fy·ing** [+ *obj*] *formal* : to correct (something that is wrong)• The hotel management promised to *rectify* the problem/situation.

– **rec·ti·fi·ca·tion** /ˌrɛktəfəˈkeɪʃən/ *noun* [*noncount*]

rec·ti·lin·e·ar /ˌrɛktəˈlɪnijə/ *adj, technical* : made with straight lines • *rectilinear* forms/designs/shapes : having many straight lines• the *rectilinear* skyline/architecture of a modern city

rec·ti·tude /ˈrɛktəˌtu:d, *Brit* ˈrɛktəˌtju:d/ *noun* [*noncount*] *formal* : the quality of being honest and morally correct• No one questioned his moral *rectitude*. [=*integrity*]

rec·tor /ˈrɛktə/ *noun, pl* **-tors** [*count*]

1 : a priest or minister who is in charge of a church or parish
2 *chiefly Brit* : a person who is in charge of a university or school

rec·to·ry /ˈrɛktəri/ *noun, pl* **-ries** [*count*] : the house where the rector of a Christian church lives

rec·tum /ˈrɛktəm/ *noun, pl* **-tums** [*count*] *medical* : the end of the tube in your body that helps digest food : the last part of the large intestine — see picture at HUMAN

re·cum·bent /rɪˈkʌmbənt/ *adj, formal* : lying down • The Egyptian sphinx has the body of a *recumbent* lion. • a *recumbent* position

re·cu·per·ate /rɪˈku:pəˌreɪt, *Brit* rɪˈkju:pəˌreɪt/ *verb* **-ates; -at·ed; -at·ing**

1 [*no obj*] : to return to normal health or strength after being sick, injured, etc. : RECOVER• She took a day off to *recuperate*. — often + *from*• Dad is *recuperating from* knee surgery.
2 [+ *obj*] *Brit* : to get back (money that has been spent, invested, lost, etc.)• The company is expected to *recuperate* [=*recoup, recover*] its losses in the next two months.

– **re·cu·per·a·tion** /rɪˌku:pəˈreɪʃən, *Brit* rɪˌkju:pəˈreɪʃən/ *noun* [*noncount*]

re·cu·per·a·tive /rɪˈku:pəˌreɪtɪv, *Brit* rɪˈkju:pərətɪv/ *adj, formal* : helping you to return to normal health or strength : helping you to recuperate• the *recuperative* [=*healing*] powers of the body [=the body's ability to heal]

re·cur /rɪˈkə/ *verb* **-curs; -curred; -cur·ring** [*no obj*] : to happen or appear again : to occur again• There is only a slight chance that the disease will *recur*. • The same problem keeps *recurring*.

– **recurring** *adj*• She suffers from *recurring* headaches. • a *recurring* injury/nightmare

re·cur·rence /rɪˈkərəns/ *noun, pl* **-renc·es** : a new occurrence of something that happened or appeared before [*count*]We hope to prevent a *recurrence* of the disease. [*noncount*]high/low rates of *recurrence*

re·cur·rent /rɪˈkərənt/ *adj* : happening or appearing again and again• a *recurrent* fever/infection • The loss of innocence is a *recurrent* theme in his stories.

– **re·cur·rent·ly** *adv*

re·cy·cle /riˈsaɪkəl/ *verb* **-cy·cles; -cy·cled; -cy·cling**

1 a [+ *obj*] : to make something new from (something that has been used before) • The company *recycles* plastic. • They're studying various ways to *recycle* garbage into fuel. • The oil is *recycled*. • The doormat is made from *recycled* tires.
b : to send (used newspapers, bottles, cans, etc.) to a place where they are made into something new [+ *obj*]Town residents are required to *recycle* cans and bottles. [*no obj*]We make efforts to *recycle*.
2 [+ *obj*] : to use (something) again• The author *recycles* a familiar story in her latest novel.

– **re·cy·cla·ble** /riˈsaɪkləbəl/ *adj* • *recyclable* bottles
– **recyclable** *noun, pl* **-cla·bles** [*count*] • Put all *recyclables* [=recyclable materials] in the green bin.
– **recycling** *noun* [*noncount*]• The *recycling* of plastics is encouraged. • (*US*) Put the *recycling* [=the materials that can be recycled] out by the curb in the morning. — often used before another noun • a *recycling* plant [=a factory that recycles materials] • the city's *recycling* program

[1]red /ˈrɛd/ *adj* **red·der; red·dest** [*also more* ~; *most* ~]

1 : having the color of blood• a shiny *red* fire truck • bright *red* shoes • dark *red* apples
2 : reddish brown or reddish orange in color• She has *red* hair. [=she is a redhead] • a *red* fox
3 *of a person's face* : pink because of embarrassment, anger, etc.• His face turns *red* when he gets angry. • When she realized her mistake, she turned ***beet red*** [=she blushed] • (*Brit*) His face ***went red*** with embarrassment.
4 *of eyes* : having many red lines from lack of sleep, drunkenness, etc. : BLOODSHOT• Her eyes were *red* from crying.
5 *somewhat old-fashioned, informal + disapproving* : supporting Communism : COMMUNIST

a red rag to a bull *Brit, informal* : something that makes a person very angry• Just mentioning his poor marks to him was waving *a red rag to a bull*.

not one red cent see CENT

paint the town red see [2]PAINT

– **red·ness** /ˈrɛdnəs/ *noun* [*noncount*]• There was swelling and *redness* around the site of the bee sting.

[2]red *noun, pl* **reds**

1 : the color of blood [*noncount*]The artist uses *red* to symbolize passion. • a lady dressed in *red* [*count*] the *reds* and oranges of autumn leaves — see color picture on page C1
2 [*count, noncount*] : RED WINE
3 *Red* [*count*] *somewhat old-fashioned, informal + disapproving* : a Communist or someone who supports Communists

in the red : spending and owing more money than is being earned • Apparently the company had been *in the red* [=had been losing money] for some time before it went out of business. — compare *in the black* at [2]BLACK

see red *informal* : to become very angry• The construction delays on the highway have many commuters *seeing red*.

red alert *noun, pl* ~ **alerts** : a warning that there is great danger [*count*] — usually singular• The commander issued a *red alert*. • A *red alert* was sounded on the island as the storm approached. [*noncount*]The troops have been put ***on red alert***

red blood cell *noun, pl* ~ **cells** [*count*] : a red-colored blood cell that carries oxygen from the lungs to other parts of the body — called also *red blood corpuscle, red cell, red corpuscle*; compare WHITE BLOOD CELL

red–blood·ed /ˈrɛdˈblʌdəd/ *adj* [*more* ~; *most* ~] *informal* : full of energy, strength, and strong emotion• Every *red-blooded* teenager wants a car. • your average *red-blooded* sports fan • I did what any *red-blooded* woman would do: I demanded an apology.

red·brick /ˈrɛdˌbrɪk/ *adj, always used before a noun*

1 : made of red bricks• a historic *redbrick* mansion
2 *Brit* — used to describe British universities that were created in the late 19th or early 20th century and that have buildings made of red bricks• He attended a *redbrick* university. — compare OXBRIDGE

red card *noun, pl* ~ **cards** [*count*] *soccer* : a red card that a referee holds in the air to indicate that a player who has broken the rules of the game will not be allowed to continue playing — compare YELLOW CARD

red carpet *noun*

roll out the red carpet : to formally greet or welcome an important guest who has just arrived• The governor *rolled out the red carpet* for his dinner guests.

– **red–carpet** *adj, always used before a noun*• a *red-carpet* welcome • We got the ***red-carpet treatment*** [=we were treated like very important people] when we arrived.

red cell *noun, pl* ~ **cells** [*count*] : RED BLOOD CELL

red·coat /ˈrɛdˌkoʊt/ *noun, pl* **-coats** [*count*] : a British soldier of the 18th and early 19th centuries and especially during the American Revolution

red corpuscle *noun, pl* ~ **-puscles** [*count*] : RED BLOOD CELL

Red Crescent *noun*

the Red Crescent : an organization in Islamic countries that helps people who are suffering because of a war or natural disaster

Red Cross *noun*

the Red Cross : an international organization that helps people who are suffering because of a war or natural disaster

red deer *noun, pl* ~ **deer** [*count*] : a large kind of deer with big antlers that lives in Europe, Asia, and Africa — compare ELK 1

red·den /ˈrɛdn̩/ *verb* **-dens; -dened; -den·ing** : to make something red or to become red [+ *obj*]First-degree burns *redden* the skin. [*no obj*]Her face *reddened* when her name was announced.

red·dish /ˈrɛdɪʃ/ *adj* [*more* ~; *most* ~] : somewhat red• the *reddish* clay • She has *reddish*-brown hair.

re·dec·o·rate /riˈdɛkəˌreɪt/ *verb* **-rates; -rat·ed; -rat·ing** : to change the appearance of the inside of a house, building, or room by painting the walls, changing the furniture, etc.

[+ *obj*] They *redecorated* [=*redid*] three rooms in their house. [*no obj*] She helped us *redecorate*.

– re·dec·o·ra·tion /riˌdɛkəˈreɪʃən/ *noun* [*noncount*]

re·deem /rɪˈdi:m/ *verb* **-deems; -deemed; -deem·ing** [+ *obj*]

1 : to make (something that is bad, unpleasant, etc.) better or more acceptable ▪ The exciting ending partially *redeems* what is otherwise a very dull movie. ▪ The restaurant's excellent service is not enough to *redeem* [=*compensate for*] the mediocre food. ▪ He wants to ***redeem his reputation***.

2 : to exchange (something, such as a coupon or lottery ticket) for money, an award, etc. ▪ You can *redeem* this coupon at any store. ▪ You have 90 days to *redeem* your winning lottery ticket. ▪ This voucher can be *redeemed* for a free meal at several local restaurants.

3 : to buy back (something, such as a stock or bond) ▪ The government will pay you interest when it *redeems* the bonds you bought. ▪ The company *redeemed* some of its stock.

4 : to pay back (money that is owed) ▪ *redeem* a debt

5 *formal* **:** to do what is required by (a pledge or a promise) **:** FULFILL ▪ The President *redeemed* his campaign promise. [=he did what he promised to do]

6 *Christianity* **:** to save (people) from sin and evil ▪ They believe that Jesus Christ was sent here to *redeem* us from sin.

redeem yourself **:** to succeed or do something good after you have failed or done something bad ▪ They can *redeem themselves* for yesterday's loss by winning today's game.

re·deem·able /rɪˈdi:məbəl/ *adj*

1 : able to be exchanged for money or goods ▪ The gift certificate is *redeemable* at any store location. ▪ (*Brit*) The voucher is ***redeemable against*** any purchase.

2 *US* **:** able to make something that is bad or unpleasant more acceptable, enjoyable, etc. ▪ That movie had no *redeemable* [=*redeeming*] qualities whatsoever. [=nothing about the movie was good, enjoyable, etc.]

re·deem·ing /rɪˈdi:mɪŋ/ *adj* **:** making a bad or unpleasant thing or person better or more acceptable ▪ He had few *redeeming* qualities. [=he had few good qualities to offset his bad qualities] ▪ The job's only *redeeming* feature is the employee discount.

re·deem·er /rɪˈdi:mɚ/ *noun, pl* **-ers**

1 [*count*] **:** a person who brings goodness, honor, etc., to something again **:** a person who redeems something ▪ He was considered the *redeemer* of the family's reputation/virtue.

2 ***the Redeemer*** **:** JESUS CHRIST

re·demp·tion /rɪˈdɛmpʃən/ *noun, pl* **-tions :** the act, process, or result of redeeming something or someone: such as **a** [*noncount*] **:** the act of making something better or more acceptable ▪ the *redemption* of his reputation ▪ The situation is ***beyond/past redemption***. [=it is too bad to be corrected or improved] **b :** the act of exchanging something for money, an award, etc. [*count*] stock *redemptions* [*noncount*] the *redemption* of coupons **c** [*noncount*] *Christianity* **:** the act of saving people from sin and evil ▪ the *redemption* of sinners **:** the fact of being saved from sin or evil ▪ a sinner's search for *redemption* ▪ bad people who are ***beyond/past redemption*** [=who cannot be saved]

– re·demp·tive /rɪˈdɛmptɪv/ *adj* ▪ the *redemptive* power of art/love/sports

re·de·ploy /ˌri:dɪˈploɪ/ *verb* **-ploys; -ployed; -ploy·ing**

1 : to move (soldiers or equipment) to a new area [+ *obj*] The soldiers were *redeployed* to the country's capital. [*no obj*] Most units will *redeploy* to their home bases.

2 [+ *obj*] *formal* **:** to move (something, such as money) from one area or activity to another ▪ They *redeployed* their assets into mutual funds.

– re·de·ploy·ment /ˌri:dɪˈploɪmənt/ *noun, pl* **-ments** [*count, noncount*]

re·de·sign /ˌri:dɪˈzaɪn/ *verb* **-signs; -signed; -sign·ing** [+ *obj*] **:** to change the design of (something) ▪ The book's cover has been *redesigned* for the new edition. ▪ We're *redesigning* our kitchen. ▪ a newly *redesigned* Web site

– redesign *noun, pl* **-signs** [*count, noncount*] ▪ The *redesign* of the Web site has been a great success.

re·de·vel·op /ˌri:dɪˈvɛləp/ *verb* **-ops; -oped; -op·ing**

1 : to change the appearance of an area especially by repairing and adding new buildings, stores, roads, etc. [+ *obj*] The city has plans to *redevelop* the neighborhood. — often used as (*be*) *redeveloped* ▪ A portion of the property is *being redeveloped* into condos. [*no obj*] The city has plans to *redevelop*.

2 [*no obj*] **:** to happen or develop again ▪ We need to make sure that these problems don't *redevelop*.

– re·de·vel·op·ment /ˌri:dɪˈvɛləpmənt/ *noun, pl* **-ments** [*count, noncount*] ▪ urban *redevelopment*

red–eye /ˈrɛdˌaɪ/ *noun, pl* **-eyes**

1 [*count*] *US, informal* **:** a flight in a passenger airplane that happens late at night or that continues through the night ▪ He caught/took the *red-eye* to Los Angeles. ▪ a *red-eye* flight

2 [*noncount*] **:** the appearance of a person's eyes as red in a photograph that was taken with a flash ▪ The digital photo editing program can be used to remove *red-eye*.

red–faced *adj* [*more* ~; *most* ~] **:** having or showing a red face especially because you are embarrassed, angry, or ashamed ▪ I was *red-faced* [=very embarrassed] when I realized the stupid mistake I'd made. ▪ He was *red-faced* with rage/shame.

red flag *noun, pl* ~ **flags** [*count*] **:** a warning sign **:** a sign that there is a problem that should be noticed or dealt with ▪ Gaps in your employment history are *red flags* to employers.

red giant *noun, pl* ~ **giants** [*count*] *astronomy* **:** a very large star that has a reddish color

red–hand·ed /ˈrɛdˈhændəd/ *adv* **:** while doing something wrong or illegal ▪ The robbers were ***caught red-handed*** by the police. [=the robbers were caught while they were stealing]

red·head /ˈrɛdˌhɛd/ *noun, pl* **-heads** [*count*] **:** a person who has red hair ▪ Her brothers are both *redheads*.

– red·head·ed /ˈrɛdˌhɛdəd/ *adj* ▪ a *redheaded* actress

red herring *noun, pl* ~ **-rings** [*count*] **:** something unimportant that is used to stop people from noticing or thinking about something important ▪ The argument is a *red herring*. It actually has nothing to do with the issue. ▪ The plot of the mystery was full of *red herrings*.

red–hot /ˈrɛdˈhɑ:t/ *adj*

1 a : glowing red because of being very hot ▪ *red-hot* coals **b :** extremely hot ▪ a *red-hot* iron ▪ a bowl of *red-hot* chili

2 *informal* **a :** very active or successful ▪ The local economy has been *red-hot*. ▪ The team is *red-hot* again this year. **b :** extremely popular ▪ a *red-hot* vacation destination **c :** new and exciting ▪ *red-hot* news

re·dial /ˈri:ˌdajəl/ *verb* **-dials;** *US* **-dialed** *or Brit* **-dialled;** *US* **-dial·ing** *or Brit* **-dial·ling :** to select a series of numbers on a telephone again **:** to dial again [+ *obj*] Did you *redial* the number? [*no obj*] The number was busy, so she *redialed*.

– redial *noun* [*noncount*] ▪ The phone has a *redial* function. ▪ You can dial the same number again by pressing the *redial* button.

redid *past tense of* REDO

red ink *noun* [*noncount*] *chiefly US* — used to describe a situation in which a business, organization, etc., is spending more money than it is earning and has a lot of debt ▪ The company was ***drowning/awash in red ink***. [=deeply in debt]

re·di·rect /ˌri:dəˈrɛkt/ *verb* **-rects; -rect·ed; -rect·ing** [+ *obj*]

1 : to change the path or direction of (something) ▪ They dug trenches near the river to *redirect* the flow of the water. ▪ Traffic will be *redirected* to avoid downtown. ▪ Visitors to the old Web site address are *redirected* automatically to the new one. ▪ I tried to *redirect* their attention to the other painting.

2 : to use (something) for a different purpose ▪ *redirect* tax dollars ▪ It's time to *redirect* your energy to your homework.

3 *Brit* **:** to send (a letter or package) to a new mailing address **:** FORWARD

– re·di·rec·tion /ˌri:dəˈrɛkʃən/ *noun* [*noncount*]

re·dis·cov·er /ˌri:dɪˈskʌvɚ/ *verb* **-ers; -ered; -er·ing** [+ *obj*] **:** to find (something lost or forgotten) again **:** to discover (something) again ▪ She *rediscovered* her love of ballet when she was in her 50s.

re·dis·trib·ute /ˌri:dɪˈstrɪˌbju:t/ *verb* **-utes; -ut·ed; -ut·ing** [+ *obj*] **:** to divide (something) among a group in a different way ▪ Unused federal funds will be *redistributed* to other states. ▪ The government *redistributed* the land to the settlers.

– re·dis·tri·bu·tion /riˌdɪstrəˈbju:ʃən/ *noun* [*noncount*] ▪ the *redistribution* of wealth

re·dis·trict /riˈdɪstrɪkt/ *verb* **-tricts; -trict·ed; -trict·ing** [+ *obj*] *US* **:** to divide (a town, state, etc.) into new political or school districts ▪ The town was *redistricted* last year.

red–letter day *noun, pl* ~ **days** [*count*] *informal* **:** a very happy and important day ▪ Yesterday was a *red-letter day* for the graduating class.

red–light *adj, always used before a noun* **:** having many prostitutes ▪ the city's *red-light* district/area

R

red meat *noun* [*noncount*] **:** meat that is red when it is raw — used especially to refer to beef; compare WHITE MEAT

red·neck /ˈrɛdˌnɛk/ *noun, pl* **-necks** [*count*] *US, informal + usually disapproving* **:** a white person who lives in a small town or in the country especially in the southern U.S., who typically has a working-class job, and who is seen by others as being uneducated and having opinions and attitudes that are offensive
– **redneck** *also* **red·necked** /ˈrɛdˌnɛkt/ *adj* • a *redneck* sheriff • a *redneck* town

re·do /riˈduː/ *verb* **-does** /riˈdʌz/; **-did** /riˈdɪd/; **-done** /riˈdʌn/; **-do·ing** /riˈduːwɪŋ/ [+ *obj*]
1 : to do (something) again especially in order to do it better • Let's hope we don't have to *redo* our paperwork.
2 : to change (something, such as a room or part of a room) so that it looks new or different • I want to *redo* the kitchen and put in new cabinets and new appliances.
– **re·do** /ˈriːˌduː/ *noun, pl* **-dos** [*count*] *informal* • There are no *redos* in the Olympics. [=there are no opportunities to do something again if you do not like how you did it the first time]

red·o·lent /ˈrɛdələnt/ *adj* [*more* ~; *most* ~] *literary + formal*
1 : having a strong smell **:** full of a fragrance or odor • a *redolent* bouquet — often + *of* • a room *redolent of* spices — often + *with* • The sauce was *redolent with* the smell of basil.
2 : causing thoughts or memories *of* something • a room *redolent* [=*reminiscent*] *of* the 1940s

re·dou·ble /riˈdʌbəl/ *verb* **-dou·bles; -dou·bled; -dou·bling :** to greatly increase the size or amount of (something) [+ *obj*] They *redoubled* their efforts to finish the work on time. [*no obj*] Their efforts to finish the work *redoubled* as the deadline drew near.

re·doubt /rɪˈdaʊt/ *noun, pl* **-doubts** [*count*]
1 : a small building or area that gives protection to soldiers under attack
2 : a safe or protected place • The refugees gathered in a hilly *redoubt* several miles outside the city.

re·doubt·able /rɪˈdaʊtəbəl/ *adj, literary + formal* **:** causing or deserving great fear or respect **:** very powerful, impressive, etc. • a *redoubtable* [=*formidable*] warrior • There is a new biography of the *redoubtable* Winston Churchill.

re·dound /rɪˈdaʊnd/ *verb* **-dounds; -dound·ed; -dound·ing** [*no obj*] *formal* **:** to have a particular result — used especially to describe how something affects someone or something or affects the opinion that people have about someone or something; + *to* • It ***redounds to his credit*** that he worked so hard to prevent this crisis. [=he deserves credit for working so hard] • a policy that may ***redound to the advantage of*** our competitors [=that may help our competitors]

red panda *noun, pl* ~ **panda** *also* ~ **pandas** [*count*] **:** a small Asian animal that has reddish-brown fur and a long tail

red pepper *noun, pl* ~ **-pers**
1 [*count*] **:** a type of hollow vegetable (called a pepper) that is red and that can be eaten raw or cooked
2 [*count*] **:** a hot pepper that is red and that is added to food to make it spicy; *also* [*noncount*] **:** CAYENNE PEPPER

re·draft /riˈdræft, *Brit* riˈdrɑːft/ *verb* **-drafts; -draft·ed; -draft·ing** [+ *obj*] **:** to make a new version of (a document, plan, etc.) • A meeting was called to *redraft* the state budget proposal.

re·draw /riˈdrɑː/ *verb* **-draws; -drew; -drawn; -draw·ing** [+ *obj*] **:** to draw (something) again usually in a different way • The company is *redrawing* its logo. — often used figuratively • The country's borders were *redrawn* after the war. [=the borders were changed]

[1]**re·dress** /rɪˈdrɛs/ *verb* **-dress·es; -dressed; -dress·ing** [+ *obj*] *formal* **:** to correct (something that is unfair or wrong) • We hope that all these grievances/problems will be *redressed* [=*remedied*] immediately. • It is time to *redress* the injustices of the past. • They've been treated unfairly, and it's time to ***redress the balance***. [=make the situation fair]

[2]**redress** *noun* [*noncount*] *formal* **:** something (such as money) that is given to someone to make up for damage, trouble, etc. • Their lawyer has said that they intend to seek *redress* [=*compensation*] through the courts.

red·shirt /ˈrɛdˌʃɚt/ *noun, pl* **-shirts** [*count*] *US, sports* **:** a college athlete who practices with a team but does not play any official games ✧ Since college athletes are only officially allowed to play for four years, being a redshirt for a year makes it possible for an athlete to attend the school for five years and play for four of those years. • a *redshirt* freshman
– **redshirt** *verb* **-shirts; -shirt·ed; -shirt·ing** [+ *obj*] He was *redshirted* his freshman year. [*no obj*] He *redshirted* (during) his freshman year.

red·skin /ˈrɛdˌskɪn/ *noun, pl* **-skins** [*count*] *informal + offensive* **:** NATIVE AMERICAN ✧ The word *redskin* is very offensive and should be avoided.

red–tailed hawk /ˈrɛdˌteɪld-/ *noun, pl* ~ **hawks** [*count*] **:** a type of American hawk that has a reddish tail — called also *redtail*

red tape *noun* [*noncount*] *disapproving* **:** a series of actions or complicated tasks that seem unnecessary but that a government or organization requires you to do in order to get or do something • bureaucratic *red tape* • You would not believe the *red tape* involved in getting the required permits.

re·duce /rɪˈduːs, *Brit* rɪˈdjuːs/ *verb* **-duc·es; -duced; -duc·ing**
1 [+ *obj*] **:** to make (something) smaller in size, amount, number, etc. **:** DECREASE • The medicine *reduces* the risk of infection. • We are trying to *reduce* our debt. • Stricter speed limit enforcement has *reduced* the number of car accidents. • Her prison sentence was *reduced* from 15 years to 10. • a drastically *reduced* price
2 [+ *obj*] **a :** to cause (someone) to be in a specified state or condition — + *to* • The movie's ending ***reduced them to tears***. [=made them cry] • The crowd was ***reduced to silence***. [=became suddenly silent] **b :** to cause (something) to be in a specified form by breaking it, burning it, etc. — + *to* • *reduce* stone *to* powder • mountains that will someday be *reduced to* sand • Their house was ***reduced to ashes*** [=was completely burned/destroyed] by the fire. • The city was ***reduced to rubble/ruins*** by the bombing. **c :** to force (someone) to do something that causes shame, embarrassment, etc. — followed by *to* + *-ing verb* • The museum has been *reduced to begging* for funding.
3 [+ *obj*] **:** to describe (something) in a way that includes only some of the facts and details — + *to* • You're *reducing* religion *to* a list of do's and don'ts. • Her argument can be *reduced to* a few essential points.
4 : to boil (a liquid) so that there is less of it [+ *obj*] Simmer the broth until it is *reduced* to 2 cups. [=until there are only two cups of it] [*no obj*] Simmer the broth until it *reduces* to 2 cups.
5 [+ *obj*] **:** to change (someone's rank) to a lower or less important one • As part of her sentence, the sergeant's rank was *reduced* to private.
6 [*no obj*] *US, informal* **:** to gradually decrease your weight by eating less • He's on a (weight) *reducing* diet.
7 [+ *obj*] *mathematics* **:** to change (a fraction) so that it is written with the lowest possible numbers • You can *reduce* $\frac{2}{4}$ to $\frac{1}{2}$.
reduced circumstances *formal* **:** a situation in which you have less money than you used to have • He found himself living in *reduced circumstances* after he lost his job. • We will have to adjust to our *reduced circumstances*.
– **re·duc·er** *noun, pl* **-ers** [*count*] • a fever *reducer* • noise/weight *reducers* – **re·duc·ible** /rɪˈduːsəbəl, *Brit* rɪˈdjuːsəbəl/ *adj* • The theories are not *reducible* to easy interpretation. • The fraction is *reducible*.

re·duc·tion /rɪˈdʌkʃən/ *noun, pl* **-tions**
1 : the act of making something smaller in size, amount, number, etc. **:** the act of reducing something [*count*] a drastic/marked/sharp/significant *reduction* in size • troop *reductions* = *reductions* in the number of troops • cost/price/rate *reductions* [*noncount*] Many voters want to see some *reduction* of the deficit.
2 [*count*] **:** an amount by which something is reduced • There is a 20 percent *reduction* on selected items during this sale.

re·duc·tive /rɪˈdʌktɪv/ *adj, formal + often disapproving* **:** dealing with or describing something complicated in a simple or too simple way • a *reductive* interpretation of the theory • *reductive* methods of analysis

re·dun·dan·cy /rɪˈdʌndənsi/ *noun, pl* **-cies**
1 a [*noncount*] **:** the act of using a word, phrase, etc., that repeats something else and is therefore unnecessary • Avoid *redundancy* in your writing. **b** [*count*] **:** a word, phrase, etc., that repeats something else and is therefore unnecessary **:** a redundant word, phrase, etc. • Try to avoid using *redundancies* in your writing.
2 *technical* **:** a part in a machine, system, etc., that has the same function as another part and that exists so that the entire machine, system, etc., will not fail if the main part fails [*count*] The design incorporates several *redundancies*. [*noncount*] a system with a high level of *redundancy*

R

3 *Brit* **a** : the act of ending the employment of a worker or group of workers [*count*] compulsory/voluntary *redundancies* [=*layoffs*] [*noncount*] The restructuring is expected to result in the *redundancy* of several hundred workers. **b** [*noncount*] : the fact of being dismissed from a job because you are no longer needed • The workers are now facing *redundancy*.

re·dun·dant /rɪˈdʌndənt/ *adj*
1 : repeating something else and therefore unnecessary • He edited the paper and removed any *redundant* information or statements. • Avoid *redundant* expressions in your writing. • Some people say that since all adages are old, the phrase "old adage" is *redundant*.
2 *technical* — used to describe part of a machine, system, etc., that has the same function as another part and that exists so that the entire machine, system, etc., will not fail if the main part fails • The design incorporates several *redundant* features.
3 *Brit* : dismissed from a job because you are no longer needed • More than 200 of the company's employees have already been ***made redundant***. [=*laid off*]
– re·dun·dant·ly *adv* • In the phrase "old adage," "old" is sometimes thought of as being used *redundantly*.

red wine *noun, pl* ~ **wines** [*count, noncount*] : wine that has a red color

red·wood /ˈrɛdˌwʊd/ *noun, pl* **-woods**
1 [*count*] : a very tall evergreen tree
2 [*noncount*] : the wood of a redwood

red zone *noun*
the red zone *American football* : the area of the field that is inside an opponent's 20-yard line • The team has had trouble scoring when it gets into *the red zone*.

reed /ˈriːd/ *noun, pl* **reeds** [*count*]
1 : a tall, thin grass that grows in wet areas • the *reeds* along the edge of a pond
2 a : a thin strip of wood, metal, or plastic inside some musical instruments (such as clarinets and oboes) that makes a sound when you blow over it **b** : a musical instrument that has a reed • the orchestra's *reeds* • the *reed* section of the orchestra

re·ed·u·cate /riˈɛʤəˌkeɪt/ *verb* **-cates; -cat·ed; -cat·ing** [+ *obj*]
1 : to teach (someone) to do or understand something in a new way • The program *reeducates* people about how to eat in a more healthful way. • (*disapproving*) camps that were used to "*reeducate*" political prisoners [=to force political prisoners to accept the official ideas and beliefs of the government]
2 : to train (someone) for a different job • We need to *reeducate* the workers who lost their jobs when the factory closed.
– re·ed·u·ca·tion /riˌɛʤəˈkeɪʃən/ *noun* [*noncount*] • a need for *reeducation* about how to eat in a more healthful way • ***reeducation camps*** for political prisoners

reedy /ˈriːdi/ *adj* **reed·i·er; -est** [*also more* ~; *most* ~]
1 : full of or covered with reeds • a *reedy* marsh
2 : having a weak, high-pitched sound • *reedy* music/voices
3 *US* : long and thin • *reedy* legs/arms

reef /ˈriːf/ *noun, pl* **reefs** [*count*] : a long line of rocks or coral or a high area of sand near the surface of the water in the ocean — see also BARRIER REEF, CORAL REEF

ree·fer /ˈriːfɚ/ *noun, pl* **-fers** *informal* + *old-fashioned*
1 [*noncount*] : MARIJUANA • smoking *reefer*
2 [*count*] : a marijuana cigarette • smoking a *reefer*

reef knot *noun, pl* ~ **knots** [*count*] *chiefly Brit* : SQUARE KNOT

reek /ˈriːk/ *verb* **reeks; reeked; reek·ing** [*no obj*]
1 : to have a very strong and unpleasant smell • The garbage *reeks*. [=*stinks*] — often + *of* • The room *reeked of* smoke.
2 *usually disapproving* — used to say that it is very obvious that someone or something has a lot of a specified thing; usually + *of* • a neighborhood that *reeks of* poverty [=a neighborhood in which everyone is clearly very poor] • She *reeks of* money. [=she dresses, acts, etc., in a way that shows that she has a lot of money]

¹reel /ˈriːl/ *noun, pl* **reels** [*count*]
1 a : a device shaped like a cylinder that a string, cord, etc., is wrapped around • a garden hose *reel* • (*Brit*) a cotton *reel* [=(*US*) a spool of thread] **b** : a device that is attached to the handle of a fishing pole and used to wrap and release the line • He bought a new rod and (fishing) *reel*. — see picture at FISHING **c** : an object that is used to hold and release film or tape • a *reel* of film
2 : a part of a movie that is on a reel of film • There's an exciting chase scene in the movie's second *reel*.
— compare ⁴REEL

²reel *verb* **reels; reeled; reel·ing**
reel in [*phrasal verb*] ***reel (something) in or reel in (something)*** : to pull in (a fish that is caught on a hook on the end of a fishing line) by turning the reel of a fishing rod
reel off [*phrasal verb*] ***reel (something) off or reel off (something)*** : to say (something) easily and quickly • She *reeled off* the right answers without hesitation.
— compare ³REEL

³reel *verb* **reels; reeled; reeling** [*no obj*]
1 : to be very shocked, confused, and upset • Still *reeling* from the death of her husband, she was now dealing with having to find a new job. • I couldn't believe what I was hearing. My head *reeled*.
2 : to move or fall back suddenly • He suddenly *reeled* back against the wall. • The surprise attack sent the enemy *reeling*.
3 : to move or walk in a way that is very unsteady • He was *reeling* drunkenly down the street. • They *reeled* around the room, laughing hysterically. • When she opened her eyes, the room was *reeling*. [=the room looked like it was moving in an unsteady way]
– compare ²REEL

⁴reel *noun, pl* **reels** [*count*] : a lively dance originally from Scotland and Ireland; *also* : the music for this dance — see also VIRGINIA REEL — compare ¹REEL

re·elect /ˌriːjəˈlɛkt/ *verb* **-elects; -elect·ed; -elect·ing** [+ *obj*] : to elect (someone) again • The town *reelected* her (to be) mayor. • He was *reelected* to the school committee.
– re·elec·tion /ˌriːjəˈlɛkʃən/ *noun, pl* **-tions** [*count, noncount*] • The senator decided to run for *reelection*.

re·emerge /ˌriːjɪˈmɚʤ/ *verb* **-emerg·es; -emerged; -emerg·ing** [*no obj*]
1 : to come out of something you have entered • The rescuers didn't *reemerge* from the cave until hours later.
2 : to be seen or known again • an old style that has *reemerged* [=has become popular again] • The former actor has *reemerged* as a candidate for mayor.

re·en·act /ˌriːjəˈnækt/ *verb* **-acts; -act·ed; -act·ing** [+ *obj*] : to repeat the actions of (an event) • The group *reenacted* a famous American Civil War battle.
– re·en·act·ment /ˌriːjəˈnæktmənt/ *noun, pl* **-ments** [*count, noncount*]

re·en·ter /riˈɛntɚ/ *verb* **-ters; -tered; -ter·ing** : to enter again: such as **a** : to go into (a place you have left) again [+ *obj*] They've *reentered* the country. • The space shuttle has safely *reentered* the Earth's atmosphere. [*no obj*] If you leave the theater, you won't be allowed to *reenter* without showing a ticket stub. **b** [+ *obj*] : to go back into (a game that you were participating in earlier) • The quarterback *reentered* the game in the second half. **c** [+ *obj*] : to type in (words, data, etc.) again on a computer • The original file was corrupted, so they had to *reenter* the data.
– re·en·try /riˈɛntri/ *noun, pl* **-tries** [*noncount*] *Reentry* to the theater will be permitted with a ticket stub. • The space shuttle needs to be controlled precisely during *reentry*. [*count*] shuttle *reentries*

re·es·tab·lish /ˌriːjɪˈstæblɪʃ/ *verb* **-lish·es; -lished; -lish·ing** [+ *obj*] : to establish (someone or something) again: such as **a** : to cause (someone or something) to be widely known and accepted again • The city is trying to *reestablish* itself as a tourist destination. **b** : to make (something) exist again • The school was *reestablished* last year in a new town. • She is working hard to *reestablish* her political influence. • The crew has *reestablished* communication with the ship.
– re·es·tab·lish·ment /ˌriːjɪˈstæblɪʃmənt/ *noun* [*noncount*]

re·eval·u·ate /ˌriːjɪˈvæljəˌweɪt/ *verb* **-ates; -at·ed; -at·ing** [+ *obj*] : to judge the value or condition of (someone or something) again • We will *reevaluate* your progress after six months.

re·ex·am·ine /ˌriːɪgˈzæmən/ *verb* **-ines; -ined; -in·ing** [+ *obj*] : to examine (someone or something) again usually in a new or different way • The book *reexamines* traditional family roles.

ref /ˈrɛf/ *noun, pl* **refs** [*count*] *informal* : a referee in a game or sport

ref. *abbr* reference

re·fec·to·ry /rɪˈfɛktəri/ *noun, pl* **-ries** [*count*] : a large room where meals are served at a place (such as a seminary or monastery) where many people live

re·fer /rɪˈfɚ/ *verb* **-fers; -ferred; -fer·ring** [+ *obj*] : to send

R

(someone or something) to a particular person or place for treatment, help, advice, etc. • How can doctors *refer* patients for treatment without examining them first? • Most of the patients we see here were *referred* by other doctors. — usually + *to* • My doctor *referred* me *to* a specialist. • The Senate bill has been *referred to* the Finance Committee. • The company is *referring* people *to* its Web site for more information.

refer to [*phrasal verb*] **1** ***refer to (something)*** : to look at or in (something) for information • She often *refers to* her notes when giving a speech. • Please *refer to* our Web site for more information. **2** ***refer to (something)*** : to have a direct connection or relationship to (something) • The word "finch" *refers to* a kind of bird. • The numbers shown in the text *refer to* footnotes at the bottom of the page. **3 a** ***refer to (someone or something)*** : to talk about or write about (someone or something) especially briefly : to mention (someone or something) in speech or in writing • No one *referred to* the incident. **b** ***refer to (something or someone) as (something)*** : to call (something or someone) by (a specified name or title) • The victim was *referred to* only *as* "John Doe." • At one time, people *referred to* the city *as* the Paris of the East.

[1]ref·er·ee /ˌrɛfəˈriː/ *noun, pl* **-ees** [*count*]

1 : a person who makes sure that players act according to the rules of a game or sport • a football/soccer *referee*

2 *Brit* : [1]REFERENCE 3a

[2]referee *verb* **-ees**; **-eed**; **-ee·ing** *sports* : to act as a referee in (a game or sport) [+ *obj*] She *refereed* the basketball game. [*no obj*] He has *refereed* for several years now.

[1]ref·er·ence /ˈrɛfrəns/ *noun, pl* **-enc·es**

1 : the act of mentioning something in speech or in writing : the act of referring *to* something or someone [*count*] *references to* an earlier event • Bob's nickname was "Elvis," a *reference to* the way he styled his hair. [=people called Bob "Elvis" because he styled his hair in the same way Elvis Presley did] [*noncount*] She ***made reference to*** our agreement. [=she mentioned our agreement] • The numbers were calculated ***by reference to*** the most recent census. — see also FRAME OF REFERENCE, POINT OF REFERENCE

2 [*noncount*] : the act of looking at or in something for information • The report was filed for future *reference*. [=so that people could look at it later] • *Reference* to a map will make the position clear. — see also CROSS-REFERENCE

3 a [*count*] : a person who can be asked for information about another person's character, abilities, etc. • She listed her former teacher as a *reference* when she applied for the job. — called also (*Brit*) *referee* **b** : a statement about someone's character, abilities, etc. [*count*] Her former teacher gave her a *reference* when she applied for the job. [*noncount*] Her teacher gave her a ***letter of reference***.

4 [*count*] : something (such as a book, dictionary, encyclopedia, etc.) that people can look at or in to find information about something • a small dictionary that is a handy *reference* • How many *references* do you use in your essay?

in reference to *or* ***with reference to*** *formal* : about or concerning (something or someone) : in relation to • I have something further to add *with reference to* [=*with respect to*, *in regard to*] what was said earlier. • I am writing *in reference to* your recent letter. • The course covers ancient history *with* special *reference to* the Roman Empire. [=the course is about ancient history and especially about the Roman Empire]

terms of reference see [1]TERM

[2]reference *verb* **-ences**; **-enced**; **-enc·ing** [+ *obj*] : to mention (something or someone) in speech or in writing : to refer to (something or someone) • The book *references* many other authors who have written on this topic.

[3]reference *adj, always used before a noun*

1 : used to find information about something • a *reference* book • a list of *reference* materials/sources

2 : used to tell people where information can be found • a *reference* mark/number

reference library *noun, pl* ~ **-braries** [*count*]

1 : a collection of books often about a particular subject • a *reference library* of science

2 : a library that lets you use books while you are there but does not allow you to take the books home — compare LENDING LIBRARY

reference point *noun, pl* ~ **points** [*count*] : POINT OF REFERENCE

ref·er·en·dum /ˌrɛfəˈrɛndəm/ *noun, pl* **-da** /-də/ *or* **-dums** : an event in which the people of a county, state, etc., vote for or against a law that deals with a specific issue : a public vote on a particular issue [*count*] They are having/holding a *referendum* to decide the issue. = They are having/holding a *referendum* on the issue. [*noncount*] The issue was decided by *referendum*.

re·fer·ral /rɪˈfərəl/ *noun, pl* **-rals** [*count*] : the act of sending someone to another person or place for treatment, help, advice, etc. • She got a *referral* (to a specialist) from her doctor. = Her doctor gave her a *referral*.

[1]re·fill /riˈfɪl/ *verb* **-fills**; **-filled**; **-fill·ing**

1 [+ *obj*] : to fill (something) again • He *refilled* his glass from the nearby pitcher. • I need to *refill* my prescription. [=to get more of a prescribed medicine]

2 [*no obj*] : to be filled again • The reservoir will *refill* once it begins raining.

— **re·fill·able** /riˈfɪləbəl/ *adj* • a *refillable* propane tank • The prescription is *refillable*.

[2]re·fill /ˈriːˌfɪl/ *noun, pl* **-fills** [*count*] : a new supply of something • The restaurant advertised free *refills* (of soda). • prescription *refills*

re·fi·nance /ˌriːfəˈnæns, riˈfaɪˌnæns/ *verb* **-nanc·es**; **-nanced**; **-nanc·ing** [+ *obj*] : to get a new loan to pay (an older debt) : to finance (something) again • *refinance* a mortgage • They're *refinancing* their home.

re·fine /rɪˈfaɪn/ *verb* **-fines**; **-fined**; **-fin·ing** [+ *obj*]

1 : to remove the unwanted substances in (something) • *refine* oil/sugar

2 : to improve (something) by making small changes • The inventor of the machine spent years *refining* the design. • The class is meant to help you *refine* your writing style.

— **re·fin·er** *noun, pl* **-ers** [*count*] • oil/sugar *refiners* [=companies that refine oil/sugar] — **refining** *noun* [*noncount*] • oil production and *refining*

refined *adj*

1 : free of unwanted substances : PURE • *refined* flour/metals/oil/sugar

2 [*more* ~; *most* ~] : improved to be more precise or exact • She has become more *refined* in her painting technique. • *refined* testing methods

3 [*more* ~; *most* ~] : having or showing the good education, polite manners, etc., that are expected in people who belong to a high social class • *refined* and civilized people • He has very *refined* manners. • *refined* and elegant works of art

re·fine·ment /rɪˈfaɪnmənt/ *noun, pl* **-ments**

1 [*noncount*] : the act or process of removing unwanted substances from something : the act or process of making something pure • oil *refinement*

2 [*noncount*] : the act or process of improving something — often + *of* • the *refinement of* testing methods

3 [*count*] : an improved version of something — often + *of* • The game is a *refinement of* last year's version.

4 [*count*] : a small change that improves something • Several engine *refinements* have resulted in increased efficiency.

5 [*noncount*] : the quality of a person who has the good education, polite manners, etc., that are expected in people who belong to a high social class • a person of great *refinement*

re·fin·ery /rɪˈfaɪnəri/ *noun, pl* **-er·ies** [*count*] : a place where the unwanted substances in something (such as oil or sugar) are removed : a place where something is refined • oil/sugar *refineries*

re·fin·ish /riˈfɪnɪʃ/ *verb* **-ish·es**; **-ished**; **-ish·ing** [+ *obj*] *US* : to remove the coating on the surface of (furniture, a floor, etc.) and put on a new coating : to put a new finish on (something) • She made her living repairing and *refinishing* wood floors. • *refinished* antique furniture

re·fit /riˈfɪt/ *verb* **-fits**; **-fit·ted**; **-fit·ting** [+ *obj*] : to make (something, such as a boat) ready for use again especially by adding new parts • *refit* a ship for service • They're *refitting* the building with hardwood floors.

— **re·fit** /ˈriːˌfɪt/ *noun, pl* **-fits** [*count*] • The ship was in port for a *refit*. — **refitting** *noun, pl* **-tings** [*count, noncount*]

re·flect /rɪˈflɛkt/ *verb* **-flects**; **-flect·ed**; **-flect·ing**

1 a [*no obj*] *of light, sound, etc.* : to move in one direction, hit a surface, and then quickly move in a different and usually opposite direction — usually + *off* • The light *reflected off* the mirror. • The sound of our voices *reflected off* the walls of the tunnel. **b** [+ *obj*] ✧ When a surface *reflects* light, sound, or heat, it causes the light, sound, or heat that hits it to move or bounce away in a different direction. • A polished surface *reflects* light. • The tiles are used to *reflect* heat. • The moon shines with *reflected* light. [=the moon shines because it is reflecting the light that shines on it from the sun]

2 [+ *obj*] **: to show the image of (something) on a surface** • The old church is *reflected* in the glass exterior of the skyscraper. • The clouds were *reflected* [=*mirrored*] in the surface of the lake.

3 [+ *obj*] **: to show (something) : to make (something) known** • Her book clearly *reflects* her beliefs. • Where you learned a language is *reflected* in your accent.

4 [*no obj*] **a : to cause people to think of someone or something in a specified way — + *on* or *upon*** • The book leaves out things that might *reflect* badly/poorly *on* him. [=things that might make him look bad] • Your achievement *reflects* well *on* your school. = Your achievement ***reflects credit on*** your school. [=your achievement shows that your school taught you well] **b : to cause people to disapprove of someone or something — + *on* or *upon*** • His bad behavior *reflects on* all of us.

5 a [*no obj*] **: to think carefully about something** • You should take some time to *reflect* before you make a decision. — often + *on* or *upon* • I've been *reflecting on* my experiences here. **b** [+ *obj*] **: to think or say (something) after careful thought** • She was disappointed with their decision, but she *reflected* that it could have been worse. • "It could have been worse," she *reflected*.

reflected glory *noun* [*noncount*] **: respect or admiration that you get because of something that someone else has done** • He enjoyed basking in the *reflected glory* of his famous brother's success.

re·flec·tion *or chiefly Brit* **re·flex·ion** /rɪˈflɛkʃən/ *noun, pl* **-tions**

1 [*count*] **: an image that is seen in a mirror or on a shiny surface** • She was looking at her *reflection* in the mirror. • He saw the *reflections* of the clouds on the lake.

2 [*count*] **: something that shows the effect, existence, or character of something else — often + *of*** • The high crime rate is a *reflection of* the violence of our society. • artistic styles that are *reflections of* different cultures • The movie is an accurate *reflection of* what life is like in small towns.

3 [*singular*] **: something that causes people to disapprove of a person or thing — + *on* or *upon*** • His bad behavior is a *reflection on* all of us. [=it makes people think badly of all of us] • You're not to blame for these problems. They're ***no reflection on*** you. [=they do not show anything about your character]

4 [*noncount*] **: careful thought about something** • She had no time for *reflection*. • spending time in quiet *reflection* • ***On/Upon reflection*** [=after thinking about it], I decided to accept their offer.

5 [*count*] **: an opinion that you form or a remark that you make after carefully thinking about something — usually plural** • The book features the writer's *reflections* on America and its people. • personal *reflections*

re·flec·tive /rɪˈflɛktɪv/ *adj*

1 a [*more ~; most ~*] **: causing light, sound, or heat to move away : reflecting light, sound, or heat** • The material is highly *reflective*. [=it easily reflects light] • *reflective* surfaces **b : relating to or caused by light that reflects off a surface** • the *reflective* glare of the shiny metal

2 [*more ~; most ~*] **: thinking carefully about something : THOUGHTFUL** • She was in a very *reflective* mood.

3 — used to say that one thing shows what something else is like; + *of* • The school is *reflective of* society: the same problems that exist in society exist at the school.

– re·flec·tive·ly *adv* • He spoke softly and *reflectively* about his experiences.

re·flec·tor /rɪˈflɛktɚ/ *noun, pl* **-tors** [*count*] **: an object that is used to reflect light** • safety devices such as bicycle *reflectors* • *Reflectors* are placed along the lanes of the highway.

re·flex /ˈriːˌflɛks/ *noun, pl* **-flex·es**

1 [*count*] **: an action or movement of the body that happens automatically as a reaction to something** • the cough/gag *reflex* • *reflexes* such as swallowing and blinking • a *reflex* action/response

2 [*count*] **: something that you do without thinking as a reaction to something** • Disagreeing with my suggestions has become almost a *reflex* for him.

3 *reflexes* [*plural*] **: the natural ability to react quickly** • an athlete with great/quick *reflexes* • My *reflexes* are slower now that I'm older.

re·flex·ive /rɪˈflɛksɪv/ *adj*

1 *grammar* : showing that the action in a sentence or clause happens to the person or thing that does the action • In "I hurt myself," the verb "hurt" is *reflexive*. • In the sentence "We forced ourselves to finish the assignment," the word "ourselves" is a *reflexive* pronoun.

2 : happening or done without thinking as a reaction to something • For many people, the *reflexive* response to this kind of demand is to say no. • music that triggers *reflexive* toe tapping

– re·flex·ive·ly *adv* • Many people respond *reflexively* to this kind of demand by saying no.

re·flex·ol·o·gy /ˌriːˌflɛkˈsɑːləʤi/ *noun* [*noncount*] **: a method of relieving pain or curing illness by pressing on particular parts of a person's hands or feet**

– re·flex·ol·o·gist /ˌriːˌflɛkˈsɑːləʤɪst/ *noun, pl* **-gists** [*count*]

re·flux /ˈriːˌflʌks/ *noun* [*noncount*] *medical* **: a backward flow of the contents of the stomach into the esophagus that causes heartburn** • acid *reflux*

re·fo·cus /riˈfoʊkəs/ *verb* **-cus·es; -cused; -cus·ing : to focus again: such as a : to adjust (something, such as a camera or a lens) again to make an image clear** [+ *obj*] She *refocused* the camera. [*no obj*] The camera *refocuses* automatically. **b : to cause (something, such as attention) to be directed at something different** [+ *obj*] She *refocused* her energies toward a career in music. • He needs to *refocus* his attention on his schoolwork. [*no obj*] Sports are not a priority now. You need to *refocus* and improve your grades.

re·for·es·ta·tion /riˌforəˈsteɪʃən/ *noun* [*noncount*] **: the act of planting tree seeds or young trees in an area where there used to be a forest — compare DEFORESTATION**

– re·for·est /riˈforəst/ *verb* **-ests; -est·ed; -est·ing** [+ *obj*] • They are *reforesting* the burned areas of land.

[1]re·form /rɪˈfoɚm/ *verb* **-forms; -formed; -form·ing**

1 [+ *obj*] **: to improve (someone or something) by removing or correcting faults, problems, etc.** • The program is designed to *reform* prisoners. • They want to *reform* campaign spending. • The laws need to be *reformed*.

2 [*no obj*] **: to improve your own behavior or habits** • The program is designed to help former gang members who are trying to *reform*.

– re·form·able /rɪˈfoɚməbəl/ *adj* • Some prisoners are not *reformable*. **– reformed** *adj, always used before a noun* • *reformed* tax laws • a *reformed* criminal

[2]reform *noun, pl* **-forms**

1 [*noncount*] **: the improvement of something by removing or correcting faults, problems, etc.** • A group of senators are calling for *reform* of the nation's health-care system. • economic/educational/political/tax *reform* • a *reform* movement

2 [*count*] **: an action, plan, rule, etc., that is meant to improve something** • He has proposed a list of political *reforms*.

Re·form /rɪˈfoɚm/ *adj* **: accepting and following only some of the traditional beliefs and customs of Judaism** • *Reform* Judaism • a *Reform* congregation

re–form /riˈfoɚm/ *verb* **-forms; -formed; -form·ing : to form (something) again** [+ *obj*] They decided to *re-form* the band. [=to bring the members of the band together again] [*no obj*] The ice *re-formed* on the lake. [=ice formed on the lake again]

ref·or·ma·tion /ˌrɛfɚˈmeɪʃən/ *noun, pl* **-tions**

1 *formal* : the act or process of improving something or someone by removing or correcting faults, problems, etc. [*noncount*] the *reformation* of our justice system • education *reformation* [=(more commonly) *reform*] [*count*] — usually singular • a radical *reformation* of society

2 *the Reformation* : the 16th-century religious movement that led to the establishment of the Protestant churches

re·for·ma·to·ry /rɪˈfoɚməˌtori, *Brit* rɪˈfɔːmətri/ *noun, pl* **-ries** [*count*] *US, old-fashioned* **: REFORM SCHOOL**

re·form·er /rɪˈfoɚmɚ/ *noun, pl* **-ers** [*count*] **: a person who works to change and improve a society, government, etc.** • an economic/educational/social *reformer*

re·form·ist /rɪˈfoɚmɪst/ *adj*

1 : wanting to change and improve a society, government, etc. • a *reformist* group/movement

2 : of or relating to the work of a reformer • *reformist* efforts/views

reform school *noun, pl* **~ schools** [*count*] *US, old-fashioned* **: a place where young people who have committed crimes are sent to live and be taught to behave in ways that are socially acceptable**

re·fract /rɪˈfrækt/ *verb* **-fracts; -fract·ed; -fract·ing** [+ *obj*] *technical, of an object or substance* **: to make (light) change direction when it goes through at an angle** • Prisms *refract* light. • Light is *refracted* when it hits water.

– re·frac·tion /rɪˈfrækʃən/ *noun, pl* **-tions** [*count, noncount*] ▪ the *refraction* of light through water **– re·frac·tive** /rɪˈfræktɪv/ *adj* ▪ the *refractive* properties of the glass

re·frac·to·ry /rɪˈfræktəri/ *adj* [*more ~; most ~*]
1 *medical* **: difficult to treat or cure** ▪ a *refractory* disease
2 *formal* **: difficult to control or deal with** ▪ a *refractory* [=*disobedient*] child

¹re·frain /rɪˈfreɪn/ *verb* **-frains; -frained; -frain·ing** [*no obj*] *formal* **: to stop yourself from doing something that you want to do** ▪ I was going to make a joke but I *refrained*. — usually + *from* ▪ Please *refrain from* smoking. ▪ She *refrained from* saying what she truly felt.

²refrain *noun, pl* **-frains** [*count*]
1 : a phrase or verse that is repeated regularly in a poem or song : CHORUS
2 : a comment or statement that is often repeated ▪ A common/familiar *refrain* among teachers these days is that the schools need more funding.

re·fresh /rɪˈfrɛʃ/ *verb* **-fresh·es; -freshed; -fresh·ing** [+ *obj*]
1 : to make (someone) have more energy and feel less tired or less hot ▪ A cold shower should *refresh* you. [=make you feel better] ▪ Sleep *refreshes* the body.
2 : to give someone more of (a drink) : to fill (someone's glass, cup, etc.) again ▪ Can I *refresh* your drink? [=would you like me to fill your glass again?]
3 *computers* **: to put (something, such as a page on the Internet) into a computer's memory again in order to show any new information : to cause an updated version of (something, such as an Internet page) to appear on a computer screen** ▪ Try *refreshing* [=*reloading*] the home page.
refresh someone's memory **: to remind someone about something : to help someone to remember something** ▪ I'm not sure of the address. Can you *refresh my memory*? [=can you remind me?]
– refreshed *adj* [*more ~; most ~*] ▪ I felt very *refreshed* after taking a nap.

re·fresh·er /rɪˈfrɛʃɚ/ *noun, pl* **-ers** [*count*] *chiefly US* **: something that helps you to remember something you have forgotten : a reminder about something** — usually singular; usually + *on* ▪ Before we play, I need a *refresher on* the rules. [=I need someone to remind me about the rules] ▪ Some people need a *refresher on* how to be polite.

refresher course *noun, pl* **~ courses** [*count*] **: a training class which helps people review information or learn new skills needed for their jobs** ▪ The staff is required to take *refresher courses* every three years.

re·fresh·ing /rɪˈfrɛʃɪŋ/ *adj* [*more ~; most ~*]
1 : pleasantly new, different, or interesting ▪ Working on the new project was a *refreshing* change. ▪ It is *refreshing* to hear some good news about him.
2 : making you feel more rested, energetic, cool, etc. ▪ a *refreshing* glass of cold water ▪ My swim was very *refreshing*.
– re·fresh·ing·ly *adv* ▪ *refreshingly* different/honest ▪ The water was *refreshingly* cool.

re·fresh·ment /rɪˈfrɛʃmənt/ *noun, pl* **-ments**
1 ***refreshments*** [*plural*] **: drinks and small amounts of food** ▪ Light *refreshments* will be served/provided at the meeting. ▪ They provided plenty of ***liquid refreshments***. [=drinks, especially alcoholic drinks]
2 [*noncount*] **: food and drink** ▪ The workers were in need of *refreshment*. ▪ (*humorous*) Would you like some ***liquid refreshment***? [=an alcoholic drink]
3 [*noncount*] **: the process of becoming rested and regaining strength or energy** ▪ We went camping for relaxation and *refreshment*.

re·fried beans /ˈriːˌfraɪd-/ *noun* [*plural*] **: a Mexican food that consists of beans that are cooked with seasonings, fried, then mashed and fried again**

re·frig·er·ate /rɪˈfrɪʤəˌreɪt/ *verb* **-ates; -at·ed; -at·ing** [+ *obj*] **: to put or keep (something, such as food) in a refrigerator in order to make it cold or keep it fresh** ▪ *Refrigerate* the mixture for an hour before serving. ▪ The potato salad needs to be (kept) *refrigerated*.
– refrigerated *adj* ▪ Ice cream is delivered in a *refrigerated* truck. [=a truck that has a refrigerator for keeping things cold] **– re·frig·er·a·tion** /rɪˌfrɪʤəˈreɪʃən/ *noun* [*noncount*] ▪ The salad does not need *refrigeration*.

re·frig·er·a·tor /rɪˈfrɪʤəˌreɪtɚ/ *noun, pl* **-tors** [*count*] **: a device or room that is used to keep things (such as food and drinks) cold** — called also *fridge*; see picture at KITCHEN

re·fu·el /riˈfjuːl/ *verb* **-els;** *US* **-eled** *or Brit* **-elled;** *US* **-el·ing** *or Brit* **-el·ling : to add fuel to (an airplane, a truck, etc.)** [+ *obj*] The crew *refueled* the airplane. — often used as *(be) refueled* ▪ The airplane needs to *be refueled*. [*no obj*] The airplane landed to *refuel*.

ref·uge /ˈrɛˌfjuːʤ/ *noun, pl* **-ug·es**
1 [*noncount*] **: shelter or protection from danger or trouble** ▪ They were seeking *refuge*. = They were seeking a ***place of refuge***. [=a safe place] — often + *in* or *from* ▪ We ***took refuge in*** [=we took shelter in, we went into] a nearby barn during the storm. = We ***found refuge from*** the storm in a nearby barn. ▪ They ***sought refuge in*** another country. [=went to another country for protection] — often used figuratively ▪ After the death of her husband, she *took/sought/found refuge in* her music.
2 [*count*] **: a place that provides shelter or protection** ▪ wildlife *refuges* [=areas where wild animals are protected] — often + *for* ▪ The area is a *refuge for* wildlife. ▪ The shelter is a *refuge for* abused women.

ref·u·gee /ˌrɛfjʊˈʤiː/ *noun, pl* **-gees** [*count*] **: someone who has been forced to leave a country because of war or for religious or political reasons** ▪ Thousands of *refugees* have fled the area. ▪ *refugee* camps

¹re·fund /rɪˈfʌnd/ *verb* **-funds; -fund·ed; -fund·ing** [+ *obj*] **: to give back money that someone paid for something (such as a product that was returned or a service that was not acceptable)** ▪ If you are not completely satisfied, we will *refund* the purchase price. ▪ We will *refund* (you) your money. ▪ They refused to *refund* the ticket. [=to give back the money that I had paid for the ticket]
– re·fund·able /rɪˈfʌndəbəl/ *adj* ▪ The fee is not *refundable*. ▪ a *refundable* security deposit

²re·fund /ˈriːˌfʌnd/ *noun, pl* **-funds** [*count*] **: an amount of money that is given back to someone who has returned a product, paid too much, etc.** ▪ No *refunds* or exchanges are allowed. ▪ She demanded a *refund*. ▪ The store gave me a ***full refund***. [=gave me back all the money I paid] ▪ We received a ***tax refund*** this year. [=this year we paid too much income tax so we got some money back]

re·fur·bish /rɪˈfɚbɪʃ/ *verb* **-bish·es; -bished; -bish·ing** [+ *obj*] **: to repair and make improvements to (something, such as a building)** ▪ They are *refurbishing* [=*renovating*] the old house. ▪ They sell *refurbished* computers. [=old computers that have been repaired so that they are in good condition]
– re·fur·bish·ment /rɪˈfɚbɪʃmənt/ *noun, pl* **-ments** [*count, noncount*] ▪ The hotel is closed for *refurbishment*. [=*renovation*]

re·fus·al /rɪˈfjuːzəl/ *noun, pl* **-als** [*count*] **: an act of saying or showing that you will not do, give, or accept something : an act of refusing** ▪ My request for more money was met with a flat/firm *refusal*. — often + *of* ▪ Her *refusal of* the job surprised us. — often followed by *to* + *verb* ▪ She worried about his stubborn/steadfast *refusal to eat*.
(the right of) first refusal **: the right to accept or refuse something before it is offered to anyone else** ▪ If we decide to sell the house, we'll give our tenants *first refusal*. [=we will offer to sell the house to our tenants before offering to sell to other people]

¹re·fuse /rɪˈfjuːz/ *verb* **-fus·es; -fused; -fus·ing**
1 : to say that you will not accept (something, such as a gift or offer) [+ *obj*] He *refused* the job. [=he did not accept the job] ▪ I ***could hardly refuse*** [=could not refuse] the money. ▪ The offer was ***too good to refuse***. [=the offer was so good that I had to accept it] [*no obj*] When they offered me the money, I couldn't *refuse*.
2 : to say or show that you are not willing to do something that someone wants you to do [*no obj*] They asked her to help but she *refused*. [+ *obj*] — usually followed by *to* + *verb* ▪ He *refused to answer* the question. ▪ She flatly/stubbornly/steadfastly *refused to help*. ▪ They *refuse to accept* the truth.
3 [+ *obj*] **: to not allow someone to have (something)** ▪ They were *refused* [=*denied*] admittance to the game. ▪ They *refused* him a visa. [=they did not give him a visa]

²ref·use /ˈrɛˌfjuːs/ *noun* [*noncount*] *formal* **: something (such as paper or food waste) that has been thrown away : trash or garbage** ▪ a pile of *refuse* [=*rubbish*]

re·fute /rɪˈfjuːt/ *verb* **-futes; -fut·ed; -fut·ing** [+ *obj*] *formal*
1 : to prove that (something) is not true ▪ The lawyer *refuted* the testimony of the witness. ▪ *refute* an argument/claim
2 : to say that (something) is not true ▪ He *refuted* [=*denied*] the rumor about him. ▪ He *refutes* the notion that he's planning to retire soon. ▪ She *refuted* the allegations against her.

– **ref·u·ta·tion** /ˌrɛfjʊˈteɪʃən/ *noun, pl* **-tions** [*count, noncount*] *formal* ▪ a *refutation* of the theory

[1]**reg** /ˈrɛg/ *noun, pl* **regs** [*count*] *US, informal* : REGULATION ▪ a list of proposed *regs*

[2]**reg** *abbr* **1** register; registered; registration **2** regular

re·gain /riˈgeɪn/ *verb* **-gains; -gained; -gain·ing** [+ *obj*]

1 : to get (something) again : to get back (something that you lost) ▪ I *regained* [=*recovered*] my health/strength. ▪ She fell into a coma and never *regained* consciousness. ▪ He slipped but quickly *regained* his footing. ▪ The actor has recently *regained* some of his former popularity. ▪ The pilot struggled to *regain* control of the plane. ▪ The home team attempted/tried to *regain* possession of the ball.

2 *literary* : to get back to (something) : to reach (a place) again ▪ They finally *regained* the shore.

re·gal /ˈriːgəl/ *adj* [*more ~; most ~*] : of, relating to, or suitable for a king or queen ▪ He has a *regal* bearing. [=he is very dignified, authoritative, etc.] ▪ a ceremony of *regal* [=*royal*] splendor

– **re·gal·ly** /ˈriːgəli/ *adv* ▪ She waved *regally* to the crowd.

re·gale /rɪˈgeɪl/ *verb* **-gales; -galed; -gal·ing**

regale with [*phrasal verb*] ***regale (someone) with (something)*** *somewhat formal* : to entertain or amuse (someone) by telling stories, describing experiences, etc. ▪ He *regaled* his party guests *with* stories of his adventures abroad.

re·ga·lia /rɪˈgeɪljə/ *noun* [*noncount*]

1 : special clothes and decorations (such as a crown or scepter) for official ceremonies ▪ Her royal/ceremonial *regalia* was quite impressive. ▪ The queen was in ***full regalia***.

2 : special clothing of a particular kind ▪ The war *regalia* of the tribe is on display at the museum. ▪ He was dressed in cowboy *regalia*.

[1]**re·gard** /rɪˈgaəd/ *noun, pl* **-gards**

1 [*noncount*] : care or concern for someone or something — often + *for* or *to* ▪ He has no *regard for* my feelings. [=he doesn't care at all about my feelings] ▪ She seems to have little *regard for* her health. ▪ Would you please show some *regard for* others? ▪ The company acted ***without regard for*** the safety of its workers. ▪ She was hired ***without regard to*** race, age, or gender. [=race, age, and gender did not influence the decision to hire her] ▪ The President acted ***with due regard to*** [=with the proper care for] the welfare of the nation.

2 : a feeling of respect and admiration for someone or something [*singular*] — often + *for* ▪ I have a great *regard for* his ability. ▪ The students ***have a high regard for*** their teacher. [=the students respect and admire their teacher very much] [*noncount*] She has won the *regard* [=*esteem, respect*] of the other scientists in her field. ▪ I have no/little *regard* for his opinions. ▪ His work is ***held in high regard***. [=his work is greatly respected]

3 ***regards*** [*plural*] : friendly greetings ▪ Give/Send them my (warm/kind) *regards*. [=greet them for me; tell them I am thinking of them]— sometimes used to end a letter ▪ I look forward to seeing you soon. *Regards*, John.

in that/this regard *formal* — used to refer to something just mentioned ▪ He is studying law and *in that regard* he is doing very well. [=he is doing well studying law] ▪ We will take care of supplying the food, so you have nothing to worry about *in that regard*.

in/with regard to *formal* : relating to (something) ▪ This letter is *in regard to* your unpaid balance. [=this letter concerns your unpaid balance] ▪ I have a question *with regard to* [=*concerning, regarding*] your last statement.

[2]**regard** *verb* **-gards; -gard·ed; -gard·ing** [+ *obj*]

1 : to think of (someone or something) in a particular way ▪ He is highly *regarded* by his coworkers. [=his coworkers have a very high opinion of him]— often + *as* ▪ She *regards* him *as* a friend. [=she considers him a friend] ▪ He *regards* himself *as* an expert. ▪ The book is widely *regarded as* his best. [=many people think the book is the best that he has ever written]

2 *formal* : to look at (someone or something) ▪ The police officer *regarded* the group of teenagers with suspicion.

as regards *formal* : relating to (something) : in or with regard to (something) ▪ *As regards* [=*regarding*] your first question, we cannot assist you.

regarding *prep, somewhat formal* : relating to (something) : ABOUT ▪ The teacher talked to the students *regarding* their homework. ▪ I have a question *regarding* your earlier comments.

re·gard·less /rɪˈgaədləs/ *adv* : in spite of difficulty, trouble, etc. : without being stopped by difficulty, trouble, etc. ▪ It may rain, but I will go *regardless*. [=I will go even if it rains; I will not be stopped from going] ▪ It was raining, but we went for a walk *regardless*. [=*anyway*]

regardless of : without being stopped or affected by (something) ▪ He runs every day *regardless of* the weather. [=he runs every day no matter what the weather is like] ▪ *Regardless of* [=*despite*] our request, he would not alter his plans.

re·gat·ta /rɪˈgɑːtə, *Brit* rɪˈgætə/ *noun, pl* **-tas** [*count*] : a race or a series of races between boats (such as sailboats)

re·gen·cy /ˈriːʤənsi/ *noun, pl* **-cies** [*count*] : a government or period of time in which a person (called a regent) rules in place of a king or queen ▪ The people supported the *regency*. ▪ Peace was restored during the *regency*.

Re·gen·cy /ˈriːʤənsi/ *adj, always used before a noun* : of, relating to, or like the styles in Britain during the period 1811–20 ▪ an example of *Regency* furniture/architecture/style

re·gen·er·ate /rɪˈʤɛnəˌreɪt/ *verb* **-ates; -at·ed; -at·ing**

1 *biology* : to grow again after being lost, damaged, etc. [*no obj*] The lizard's tail can *regenerate*. ▪ The tissue cells *regenerated*. [+ *obj*] The lizard is able to *regenerate* its tail. ▪ The tissue cells can ***regenerate themselves***.

2 [+ *obj*] *formal* : to give new life to (something) ▪ The land is *regenerated* [=*renewed*] by the rotation of the crops. ▪ The plan is meant to *regenerate* [=*revive*] the economy.

– **re·gen·er·a·tion** /rɪˌʤɛnəˈreɪʃən/ *noun* [*noncount*] – **re·gen·er·a·tive** /rɪˈʤɛnəˌreɪtɪv, *Brit* rɪˈʤɛnərətɪv/ *adj* ▪ the *regenerative* process

re·gent /ˈriːʤənt/ *noun, pl* **-gents** [*count*] : a person who rules a kingdom when the king or queen is not able to rule because he or she is sick, too young, etc.

Regent *adj, always used after a noun* : ruling because the king or queen is unable to rule : acting as a regent ▪ the Prince *Regent*

reg·gae /ˈrɛgeɪ/ *noun* [*noncount*] : popular music that is originally from Jamaica and that combines native styles with elements of rock and soul music

reg·i·cide /ˈrɛʤəˌsaɪd/ *noun, pl* **-cides**

1 [*noncount*] : the crime of killing a king or queen

2 [*count*] : someone who kills a king or queen

re·gime /reɪˈʒiːm/ *noun, pl* **-gimes** [*count*]

1 : a form of government ▪ a socialist/Communist/military *regime* : a particular government ▪ The new *regime* is sure to fall.

2 : a system of management ▪ Under the new *regime*, all workers must file a weekly report.

3 : REGIMEN ▪ He was put on a strict exercise *regime*.

reg·i·men /ˈrɛʤəmən/ *noun, pl* **-mens** [*count*] : a plan or set of rules about food, exercise, etc., to make someone become or stay healthy ▪ a daily training/exercise *regimen* ▪ a strict treatment/drug *regimen*— often + *of* ▪ a *regimen of* daily exercise

[1]**reg·i·ment** /ˈrɛʤəmənt/ *noun, pl* **-ments** [*count*] : a military unit that is usually made of several large groups of soldiers (called battalions) ▪ infantry/cavalry *regiments*

– **reg·i·men·tal** /ˌrɛʤəˈmɛntl/ *adj, always used before a noun* ▪ the *regimental* commander/headquarters

[2]**reg·i·ment** /ˈrɛʤəˌmɛnt/ *verb* **-ments; -ment·ed; -ment·ing** [+ *obj*]

1 : to organize and control (something) strictly ▪ They carefully *regiment* their son's diet/schedule/life.

2 : to control the behavior of (people) strictly ▪ She criticized the way the school *regiments* its students by having strict rules.

– **reg·i·men·ta·tion** /ˌrɛʤəmənˈteɪʃən/ *noun* [*noncount*] ▪ She did not like the school's *regimentation*. – **regimented** *adj* [*more ~; most ~*] ▪ The school was highly *regimented*. ▪ a *regimented* schedule/routine/lifestyle ▪ He's following a *regimented* diet.

re·gion /ˈriːʤən/ *noun, pl* **-gions**

1 [*count*] : a part of a country, of the world, etc., that is different or separate from other parts in some way ▪ The bird returns to this *region* every year. ▪ The plant grows in tropical *regions*. [=*areas*] ▪ He's the company sales manager for the entire Southwest *region*.— often + *of* ▪ the agricultural/coastal/mountainous *regions of* the country ▪ the Amazon *region of* South America ▪ the desert *regions of* the world ▪ the winemaking *regions of* France ▪ the unknown *regions of* outer space

2 [*count*] : a place on your body : an area that is near a specified part of your body ▪ She has a pain in the lower back *re-*

gion. — often + *of* ▪ He felt a pain in the *region* [=*vicinity*] *of* his heart.

3 ***the regions*** *Brit* **: the parts of a country that are not close to the capital city** ▪ attempts to go outside of London and stimulate cultural life in *the regions*

(somewhere) in the region of **: close to (an amount)** ▪ He makes *somewhere in the region of* [=*about, approximately*] $100,000 a year.

– re·gion·al /ˈriːʤənl/ *adj* ▪ He spoke with a *regional* accent. [=an accent that occurs in a particular region] ▪ a *regional* newspaper/school **– re·gion·al·ly** *adv* ▪ The newspaper is sold *regionally*. ▪ a *regionally* based newspaper

re·gion·al·ism /ˈriːʤənəˌlɪzəm/ *noun, pl* **-isms**

1 [*noncount*] **: interest in or loyalty to a particular region** ▪ The residents have a strong sense of *regionalism*.

2 [*count*] **: a word that is used in a particular region** ▪ The word "pop" for "soda" is a Midwest *regionalism*.

[1]**reg·is·ter** /ˈrɛʤəstɚ/ *noun, pl* **-ters** [*count*]

1 : an official list, book, or system for keeping records of something — often + *of* ▪ The church keeps a *register of* births, marriages, and deaths. ▪ a national *register of* historic places ▪ a *register* [=(*US*) *registry*] *of* voters ▪ (*Brit*) After the students were seated, the teacher ***called/took the register*** [=read a list of the students' names out loud and noted which students were there and which were not]

2 *formal* **: a part of the range of musical notes that a person's voice or an instrument can reach** ▪ a singer's upper/middle/lower *register*

3 : CASH REGISTER ▪ She works at the *register* in a grocery store.

4 *US* **: a cover on an opening (such as a heating vent) that has parts which can be opened or closed to control the flow of air**

[2]**register** *verb* **-ters; -tered; -ter·ing**

1 a [+ *obj*] **: to record information about (something) in a book or system of public records** ▪ He *registered* the birth of his child. ▪ She *registered* her new car. ▪ The car was *registered* under my name. ▪ The company *registered* its trademark. ▪ Only 32 cases of the disease have been *registered*. **b : to put your name on an official list** [*no obj*] Did you *register* to vote? — often + *at* or *for* ▪ We *registered at* the hotel. ▪ Patients must *register at* the front desk. ▪ The students *registered for* classes. [=the students enrolled in classes] ▪ All men between the ages of 18 and 25 must *register for* the draft. [+ *obj*] She is busy *registering* the students/voters/guests. — see also PREREGISTER ◊ If you ***register as something*** or if you ***are registered as something***, you enter or have entered your name on an official list which indicates what group you belong to. ▪ He *registered as* a Republican. = He *is registered* (to vote) *as* a Republican. ▪ She *registered as* unemployed/disabled.

2 [+ *obj*] **: to show or record (an amount, value, etc.)** ▪ Roast the meat for two hours or until the meat thermometer *registers* 140 degrees. ▪ an earthquake that *registered* 6.3 on the Richter scale

3 [+ *obj*] **: to get or reach (something) :** ACHIEVE ▪ The team finally *registered* a victory after losing three games in a row. ▪ The company *registered* over one billion dollars in sales.

4 a [*no obj*] **: to be recognized or remembered** ▪ It took a moment for what she was saying to *register*. [=it took a moment before I understood what she was saying] — often used in negative statements ▪ The name didn't *register* with me. [=I didn't recognize the name] **b** [+ *obj*] **: to notice or realize (something)** — often used in negative statements ▪ She didn't *register* my presence until I spoke to her.

5 *formal* **: to show (a feeling or emotion)** [+ *obj*] Her face *registered* anger/fear/surprise. ▪ Fear was *registered* on her face. [*no obj*] Fear *registered* on her face.

6 [+ *obj*] **: to send (a letter, package, etc.) by registered mail to protect it from damage or loss** ▪ Please *register* this letter.

7 [+ *obj*] *formal* **: to make (something) known officially and publicly** ▪ I want to *register* a protest over their decision.

registered *adj*

1 a : having the owner's name entered in an official list or register ▪ a *registered* trademark/security **b : having your name entered in an official list or register** ▪ Are you a *registered* voter?

2 : sent by registered mail ▪ a *registered* letter

registered mail *noun* [*noncount*] **: mail that is recorded in the post office where it is mailed and then recorded again in each post office it reaches and that is treated with special care** — called also (*Brit*) *registered post*; compare CERTIFIED MAIL

registered nurse *noun, pl* **~ nurses** [*count*] **: a nurse who has more training and experience than a licensed practical nurse and who has passed a special exam** — called also *RN* — compare LICENSED PRACTICAL NURSE, PRACTICAL NURSE

register office *noun, pl* **~ -fices** [*count*] *Brit* **:** REGISTRY OFFICE

reg·is·trar /ˈrɛʤəˌstrɑɚ/ *noun, pl* **-trars** [*count*]

1 : someone who is in charge of keeping records especially of births, marriages, and deaths

2 : an officer of a college or university who is in charge of registering students and keeping academic records

3 *Brit* **: a doctor who is training at a hospital to become a specialist in a particular field of medicine :** RESIDENT

reg·is·tra·tion /ˌrɛʤəˈstreɪʃən/ *noun, pl* **-tions**

1 a : the act or process of entering information about something in a book or system of public records [*noncount*] — often + *of* ▪ the *registration of* motor vehicles ▪ the *registration of* trademarks [*count*] trademark *registrations* **b : the act or process of entering names on an official list** [*noncount*] Student *registration* (for courses) ends today. ▪ Voter *registration* begins today. ▪ A $75 *registration* fee is due. [*count*] *Registrations* for the test/course are lower this year than they were last year. [=fewer people have registered for the test/course this year]

2 [*count*] *US* **: a document showing that something (such as a vehicle) has been officially registered** ▪ The police officer asked to see my driver's license and *registration*.

registration number *noun, pl* **~ -bers** [*count*] *Brit* **:** LICENSE NUMBER

reg·is·try /ˈrɛʤəstri/ *noun, pl* **-tries** [*count*]

1 : a place where official records are kept ▪ the Massachusetts *Registry* of Motor Vehicles

2 *US* **: a book or system for keeping an official list or record of items** ▪ a voter *registry* [=*register*] ▪ a ***gift registry*** [=a list kept by a store of the things that someone wants as gifts]

registry office *noun, pl* **~ -fices** [*count*] *Brit* **: a place where marriages are performed and where records of births, marriages, and deaths are kept**

re·gress /ˈriːˌgrɛs/ *verb* **-gress·es; -gressed; -gress·ing** [*no obj*] *technical* **: to return to an earlier and usually worse or less developed condition or state** ▪ The patient is *regressing* to a childlike state.

– re·gres·sion /rɪˈgrɛʃən/ *noun, pl* **-sions** [*count, noncount*]

[1]**re·gret** /rɪˈgrɛt/ *verb* **-grets; -gret·ted; -gret·ting** [+ *obj*]

1 : to feel sad or sorry about (something that you did or did not do) : to have regrets about (something) ▪ Don't say anything you might *regret* later. ▪ I deeply *regret* what I said. ▪ She does not *regret* leaving him. ▪ He *regrets* not traveling more when he was younger. ▪ He says he doesn't *regret* anything that he's done in his life. ▪ If you don't travel now, you might ***live to regret it*** [=you might feel sorry or disappointed about it in the future]

2 *not used in progressive tenses* — **used formally and in writing to express sad feelings about something that is disappointing or unpleasant** ▪ We *regret* to inform you [=we are sorry to tell you] that we have offered the job to someone else. ▪ We *regret* any inconvenience these delays may cause. ▪ Dr. Smith *regrets* that she will be unable to attend. [=Dr. Smith cannot attend] ▪ It is to be *regretted* [=it is regrettable/unfortunate] that the program has lost its funding.

[2]**regret** *noun, pl* **-grets**

1 : a feeling of sadness or disappointment about something that you did or did not do [*count*] She has no *regrets* about leaving him. ▪ My greatest *regret* is not going to college. [*noncount*] She expressed (her) *regret* for calling me a liar. ▪ ***To my regret*** I never visited Europe. ▪ It is ***with deep regret*** that he is announcing his resignation. ▪ ***Much to the regret of*** my parents, I decided not to go to college. = ***Much to*** my parents' ***regret*** I decided not to go to college. [=my parents were disappointed that I did not go to college]

2 ***regrets*** [*plural*] **: a statement saying politely that you will not be able to go to a meeting, party, etc.** ▪ My coworker ***gives/sends her regrets*** for not being able to attend the meeting.

re·gret·ful /rɪˈgrɛtfəl/ *adj* [*more ~; most ~*] **: feeling or showing regret : sad or disappointed** ▪ He is *regretful* about not coming with us.

re·gret·ful·ly /rɪˈgrɛtfəli/ *adv* [*more ~; most ~*]

R

1 : with regret **:** with sadness or disappointment ▪ "I must leave now," he said *regretfully.* ▪ I must *regretfully* decline your invitation.

2 — used to say that something is regretted ▪ *Regretfully* [=*regrettably, unfortunately*], we can't go. [=we are disappointed that we can't go]

re·gret·ta·ble /rɪˈgrɛtəbəl/ *adj* [*more* ~; *most* ~] **:** causing sadness or disappointment **:** UNFORTUNATE ▪ His decision to quit is *regrettable.* ▪ It was a *regrettable* mistake.

re·gret·ta·bly /rɪˈgrɛtəbli/ *adv* [*more* ~; *most* ~]

1 — used to say that something is disappointing or regrettable ▪ *Regrettably* [=*unfortunately*], I cannot go. ▪ *Regrettably,* the movie theater was shut down.

2 : to an extent that causes disappointment or regret ▪ There has been a *regrettably* [=*disappointingly*] large decline in wages. ▪ The progress of the work was *regrettably* slow.

re·group /riˈgruːp/ *verb* **-groups; -grouped; -group·ing**

1 : to form into a group again [*no obj*] Members of the search party will *regroup* in the morning. [+ *obj*] The general *regrouped* his forces after the retreat.

2 [*no obj*] **:** to stop for a short time and prepare yourself before you continue doing something that is difficult **:** to stop and think, reorganize, etc., before continuing ▪ Let's *regroup* and try this again. ▪ Wait a minute. I need to *regroup.* ▪ The coach called a time-out to give his players time to *regroup.*

[1]**reg·u·lar** /ˈrɛgjələ/ *adj*

1 a : happening over and over again at the same time or in the same way **:** occurring every day, week, month, etc. ▪ He works *regular* hours. [=he works at the same time every work day] ▪ He has never held a *regular* [=*steady*] job. ▪ Most days she follows a *regular* routine/schedule. ▪ The music has a *regular* [=*steady*] beat. **b :** happening at times that are equally separated ▪ The town holds *regular* meetings. ▪ five *regular* payments of $100 ▪ His breathing/heartbeat is *regular.* [=*normal*] ▪ The sales team meets ***on a regular basis*** [=*regularly*] ▪ The buses run from 4 a.m. to midnight ***at regular intervals.*** [=there is the same amount of time between buses] — opposite IRREGULAR

2 *always used before a noun* **a :** happening or done very often ▪ Seeing wildlife is a *regular* [=*common*] occurrence where she lives. ▪ We made *regular* use of the pool. ▪ Getting *regular* exercise is important. ▪ Exercise has become a *regular* part of my lifestyle. ▪ The theater was ***in regular use*** [=was used continuously] for over 20 years. **b :** doing the same thing or going to the same place very often ▪ He is a *regular* contributor to the magazine. ▪ She is a *regular* [=*frequent*] guest on the TV show. ▪ He is one of the store's ***regular customers*** [=customers who shop at the store frequently]

3 : spaced an equal distance apart ▪ The seedlings were planted in *regular* rows. ▪ The wallpaper has a *regular* pattern of stripes. ▪ The boards are placed ***at regular intervals.*** [=the space between each board is the same]

4 *always used before a noun* **a :** normal or usual ▪ Our *regular* business/office hours are from 9 a.m. to 5 p.m. ▪ The *regular* price is $45, but it is on sale for $30. ▪ I saw a different doctor because my *regular* doctor was on vacation. ▪ He is substituting today for the *regular* quarterback. ▪ The class will meet at the *regular* time tomorrow. ▪ The *regular* [=*scheduled*] television programming was interrupted by a special report. ▪ The *regular* season for football begins soon. ▪ Parties are a *regular* feature of college life. ▪ He sat down in his *regular* spot. **b** *chiefly US* **:** not special or unusual ▪ Do you use *regular* or premium gas in your car? ▪ Would you like a *regular* [=normal size] soda or a large? ▪ He's a *regular* [=*average, ordinary*] guy. ▪ It's nothing special, just a *regular* [=*basic*] stereo. = It's just a ***regular old*** stereo. ▪ He drinks ***regular coffee.*** [=coffee that has caffeine]

5 [*more* ~; *most* ~] **a :** having a shape that is smooth or even ▪ a *regular* surface/outline **b :** having parts that are arranged in an even or balanced way ▪ He has very *regular* features.

6 *grammar* **:** following the normal patterns by which word forms (such as the past tenses of verbs) are usually created ▪ "Talk" is a *regular* verb because its past tense is "talked." ▪ nouns with *regular* plural forms

7 *always used before a noun, informal* — used for emphasis ▪ She's become a *regular* [=*real*] expert on fitness.

8 : able to have normal bowel movements **:** not constipated ▪ Eating plenty of fiber helps me keep/stay *regular.*

9 [*more* ~; *most* ~] **:** having or being menstrual cycles that usually last the same number of days each time ▪ She is very *regular.* = Her cycle is very *regular.*

10 *always used before a noun* **:** belonging to a country's official army ▪ the *regular* army/troops/soldiers

[2]**regular** *noun, pl* **-lars**

1 [*count*] **:** someone who goes somewhere very often ▪ They are *regulars* at the bar/restaurant.

2 [*count*] **:** someone who often or usually performs, plays, etc. ▪ He is a *regular* on the television show. ▪ the *regulars* on a baseball team

3 *US* **:** something that is average or usual in quality or size [*noncount*] Do you drink decaf or *regular*? [=regular coffee] ▪ "What kind of gas do you put in your car?" "I use *regular.*" [*count*] We'll have one large soda and two *regulars.*

4 [*count*] **:** a soldier who belongs to a country's permanent army — usually plural ▪ The *regulars* were called to battle. — compare IRREGULAR

reg·u·lar·i·ty /ˌrɛgjəˈlerəti/ *noun, pl* **-ties**

1 [*noncount*] **:** the quality of being regular: such as **a :** the quality of something that happens very often or with the same amount of time between each occurrence — often + *of* ▪ the *regularity of* the seasons — often used after *with* ▪ She appears *with regularity* [=appears regularly] on the show. ▪ Fights break out *with* some *regularity.* ▪ Robberies have been occurring *with* increasing/alarming *regularity.* **b :** the quality of something that has parts which are arranged in an even or balanced way ▪ the *regularity* of his features

2 [*count*] **:** something that happens very often or with the same amount of time between each occurrence ▪ Scientists analyzed *regularities* [=*patterns*] in the sun's emissions.

reg·u·lar·ize *also Brit* **reg·u·lar·ise** /ˈrɛgjələˌraɪz/ *verb* **-izes; -ized; -iz·ing** [+ *obj*] **:** to make (something, such as a situation) regular, legal, or officially accepted ▪ Under the program, illegal immigrants would be able to apply to *regularize* their status.

reg·u·lar·ly /ˈrɛgjələli/ *adv* [*more* ~; *most* ~]

1 a : at the same time every day, week, month, etc. **:** on a regular basis ▪ The sales team meets *regularly.* ▪ We go to church *regularly.* ▪ a *regularly* scheduled program **b :** very often ▪ They play golf *regularly.* ▪ She goes out to dinner quite *regularly.*

2 : with the same amount of space between each thing ▪ a series of *regularly* [=*evenly*] spaced lines

reg·u·late /ˈrɛgjəˌleɪt/ *verb* **-lates; -lat·ed; -lat·ing** [+ *obj*]

1 : to set or adjust the amount, degree, or rate of (something) **:** CONTROL ▪ The dam *regulates* the flow of water into the river. ▪ The thermostat *regulates* the room's temperature. = The room's temperature is *regulated* by the thermostat.

2 a : to bring (something) under the control of authority ▪ We need better laws to *regulate* the content of the Internet. ▪ Laws have been made to *regulate* working conditions. **b :** to make rules or laws that control (something) ▪ The government *regulates* how much lead may be found in our water supply. ▪ The department *regulates* foreign trade.

[1]**reg·u·la·tion** /ˌrɛgjəˈleɪʃən/ *noun, pl* **-tions**

1 [*count*] **:** an official rule or law that says how something should be done ▪ safety *regulations* [=*codes*] ▪ Builders must comply with the *regulations.* ▪ federal/state/government *regulations* ▪ *regulations* on the disposal of waste ▪ Each agency has its own set of ***rules and regulations.*** ***synonyms*** see LAW

2 [*noncount*] **:** the act of regulating something — + *of* ▪ the *regulation of* gun sales by the government ▪ the body's *regulation of* blood pressure

[2]**regulation** *adj* **:** in agreement with the official rules ▪ a *regulation* [=*official*] baseball ▪ Students must wear *regulation* uniforms. ▪ The length of the field is not *regulation.* = The field is not *regulation* size.

reg·u·la·tor /ˈrɛgjəˌleɪtə/ *noun, pl* **-tors** [*count*]

1 : a device for controlling the level or amount of something (such as speed or temperature) ▪ a pressure *regulator*

2 : an official who works for the part of the government that controls a public activity (such as banking or insurance) by making and enforcing rules ▪ federal/state *regulators*

reg·u·la·to·ry /ˈrɛgjələˌtori, *Brit* ˌrɛgjəˈleɪtri/ *adj, always used before a noun, formal* **:** making or concerned with making official rules about what is acceptable in a particular business, activity, etc. ▪ a *regulatory* agency/authority ▪ They are seeking *regulatory* approval for the merger.

re·gur·gi·tate /riˈgədʒəˌteɪt/ *verb* **-tates; -tat·ed; -tat·ing**

1 : to bring food that has been swallowed back to and out of the mouth [*no obj*] The bird *regurgitates* to feed its young. [+ *obj*] The bird *regurgitates* food to feed its young. ▪ *regurgitated* food

2 [+ *obj*] *disapproving* **:** to repeat (something, such as a fact, idea, etc.) without understanding it ▪ She memorized the historical dates only to *regurgitate* them on the exam. • The speaker was just *regurgitating* facts and figures.

– **re·gur·gi·ta·tion** /rɪˌgɚdʒəˈteɪʃən/ *noun* [*noncount*]

[1]**re·hab** /ˈriːˌhæb/ *noun* [*noncount*] *informal*

1 : a program for helping people who have problems with drugs, alcohol, etc. — often used after *in* or *into* • He is *in rehab*. • She checked herself *into rehab*. — compare DETOX

2 : the process of helping someone (such as an injured patient or a drug user) to become healthy again **:** the process of rehabilitating someone • He has had two months of *rehab*. = He has been/gone through two months of *rehab*. • The *rehab* for his leg injury is going well. • a *rehab* center/program

[2]**rehab** *verb* **-habs; -habbed; -hab·bing** *US, informal* **:** REHABILITATE [+ *obj*] It could take him several months to *rehab* his knee. • trying to *rehab* drug addicts • They're planning to *rehab* that old building. [*no obj*] He's still *rehabbing* from the injury.

re·ha·bil·i·tate /ˌriːjəˈbɪləˌteɪt/ *verb* **-tates; -tat·ed; -tat·ing**

1 : to bring (someone or something) back to a normal, healthy condition after an illness, injury, drug problem, etc. [+ *obj*] The clinic *rehabilitates* drug addicts. • He's still *rehabilitating* the knee he injured last summer. • They try to *rehabilitate* horses that have suffered injuries. [*no obj*] She's still *rehabilitating* [=*recovering*] from her ankle injury.

2 [+ *obj*] **:** to teach (a criminal in prison) to live a normal and productive life • The program is intended to *rehabilitate* criminals.

3 [+ *obj*] **:** to bring (someone or something) back to a good condition **:** RESTORE • The country has *rehabilitated* its image since the war. • The city plans to *rehabilitate* its slum areas.

– **re·ha·bil·i·ta·tion** /ˌriːjəˌbɪləˈteɪʃən/ *noun* [*noncount*] • His *rehabilitation* was successful. • the *rehabilitation* of drug abusers/criminals • a *rehabilitation* [=*rehab*] center/program

re·hash /riˈhæʃ/ *verb* **-hash·es; -hashed; -hash·ing** [+ *obj*] *disapproving*

1 : to present (something) again in a slightly different form • You're just *rehashing* the same argument all over again.

2 : to talk about or discuss (something) again • *rehashing* old memories

– **re·hash** /ˈriːˌhæʃ/ *noun, pl* **-hash·es** [*count*] • The newest book is just a *rehash* of her earlier work.

re·hears·al /rɪˈhɚsəl/ *noun, pl* **-als :** an event at which a person or group practices an activity (such as singing, dancing, or acting) in order to prepare for a public performance [*noncount*] She was 15 minutes late to *rehearsal*. • The production of *King Lear* has been ***in rehearsal*** for nearly a month. [=the actors have been practicing their parts in the play together for nearly a month] [*count*] There are only three more *rehearsals* before the concert. — often used figuratively • This tournament is a *rehearsal* for the Olympics. — see also DRESS REHEARSAL, WEDDING REHEARSAL

rehearsal dinner *noun, pl* **~ -ners** [*count*] *US* **:** a formal meal after a wedding rehearsal for the people participating in a wedding ceremony

re·hearse /rɪˈhɚs/ *verb* **-hears·es; -hearsed; -hears·ing**

1 a : to prepare for a public performance of a play, a piece of music, etc., by practicing the performance [+ *obj*] The orchestra is *rehearsing* a piece by Schumann. • *rehearse* a play/scene/dance [*no obj*] The band stayed up late *rehearsing* for the big show. **b** [+ *obj*] **:** to direct (a group of people) as they prepare for a public performance • We were allowed to watch the director *rehearse* the dancers.

2 [+ *obj*] **:** to say or do (something) several times in order to practice • lawyers *rehearsing* their closing arguments • He *rehearsed* his dance moves in front of the mirror.

– **rehearsed** *adj* • well-*rehearsed* dancers [=dancers who have been rehearsed well; dancers who have been directed well during rehearsal] • a *rehearsed* statement • Her story sounded *rehearsed*. [=it seemed like a story she had practiced telling; it did not sound natural or true]

re·heat /riˈhiːt/ *verb* **-heats; -heat·ed; -heat·ing** [+ *obj*] **:** to make (cooked food that has become cool) hot again • I'm just going to *reheat* some leftovers for dinner.

re·hire /riˈhajɚ/ *verb* **-hires; -hired; -hir·ing** [+ *obj*] **:** to hire (someone) back into the same company or job • His contract expired, but the company decided to *rehire* him for another project.

re·house /riˈhaʊz/ *verb* **-hous·es; -housed; -hous·ing** [+ *obj*] *Brit* **:** to give (a person or animal) a different and usually better place to live • The organization is working to *rehouse* families who were displaced in the fire.

[1]**reign** /ˈreɪn/ *noun, pl* **reigns** [*count*]

1 : the period of time during which a king, queen, emperor, etc., is ruler of a country • She was a popular ruler throughout her *reign*. • the *reign* of Queen Elizabeth

2 : the period of time during which someone is in charge of a group or organization • his *reign* as department chairperson • her *reign* as team president

3 : the period of time during which someone or something is the best or the most important, powerful, etc. • his *reign* as heavyweight boxing champion • the *reign* of digital technology

[2]**reign** *verb* **reigns; reigned; reign·ing** [*no obj*]

1 : to rule as a king, queen, emperor, etc. • The king *reigned* in a time of peace and prosperity. — often + *over* • She *reigned over* her kingdom for many decades.

2 : to be the best or the most powerful or important person or thing • The lion *reigns* as king of the jungle. • As a director, he still ***reigns supreme***. [=he is still the best]

3 — used to say that a quality exists to such a degree in a place or situation that it affects everything about that place or situation • Silence *reigns* in the old library's dusty aisles. • Chaos *reigned* in the city [=chaos was everywhere in the city] after the military coup.

– **reigning** *adj* • the *reigning* king/queen • She remains the *reigning* diva of pop music. • the *reigning* champion

re·ig·nite /ˌriːɪgˈnaɪt/ *verb* **-nites; nit·ed; nit·ing**

1 : to begin to burn again or to cause (something) to begin to burn again [*no obj*] Be careful that the embers don't *reignite*. [+ *obj*] Heat will *reignite* the smoldering rags.

2 [+ *obj*] **a :** to give new life or energy to (someone or something) • The incident *reignited* racial tensions. **b :** to cause (something) to suddenly occur again • The study has *reignited* debate on the issue.

reign of terror *noun, pl* **reigns of terror** [*count*] **:** a period during which a person or group commits violent acts against many people and causes a lot of fear • The dictator seized power and began a *reign of terror*. • The sheriff put an end to the killer's *reign of terror*. — often used figuratively • a temperamental CEO's *reign of terror*

re·im·burse /ˌriːjəmˈbɚs/ *verb* **-burs·es; -bursed; -burs·ing** [+ *obj*] **:** to pay someone an amount of money equal to an amount that person has spent — often + *for* • We will *reimburse* you *for* your travel expenses. = We will *reimburse* your travel expenses. • I should be *reimbursed for* the fees.

– **re·im·burs·able** /ˌriːjəmˈbɚsəbəl/ *adj* • *reimbursable* expenses – **re·im·burse·ment** /ˌriːjəmˈbɚsmənt/ *noun, pl* **-ments** [*count, noncount*] • I received a partial *reimbursement* for my travel expenses.

[1]**rein** /ˈreɪn/ *noun, pl* **reins** [*count*]

1 : a strap that is fastened to a device (called a bridle) placed on the head of an animal (such as a horse) and that is used to guide and control the animal — usually plural • The rider pulled on the *reins* to stop his horse. — see picture at HORSE

2 a : the ability to limit or control something • We need to ***keep a rein on*** our spending. [=we need to limit/control our spending] • He has people working for him, but he ***has/keeps a tight rein on*** every part of the process. **b :** the power to guide or control someone or something — usually plural • They ***held the reins*** of government/power. [=they controlled the government] • She ***handed the reins*** of the company to her successor. = She ***handed over the reins*** of the company to her successor. • The President-elect will officially ***take the reins*** [=take control] in January.

***free/full rein* :** the opportunity to act freely • The studio gave the director *free rein* [=complete control] over the movie. • Give *full rein* to your imagination.

[2]**rein** *verb* **reins; reined; rein·ing**

rein in [*phrasal verb*] ***rein (someone or something) in*** or ***rein in (someone or something)*** **1 :** to limit or control (someone or something) • Congress must *rein in* spending. • You had better *rein* that kid *in* before she gets hurt. **2 :** to make (an animal) stop by using reins • The rider *reined in* his horse.

re·in·car·nate /ˌriːjənˈkɑɚˌneɪt/ *verb* **-nates; -nat·ed; -nat·ing**

***be reincarnated* :** to be born again with a different body after death • Some religions teach that we *are reincarnated* [=*reborn*] many times on the way to enlightenment. — sometimes used figuratively • The old mill is *being reincarnated* as a condominium complex.

– **reincarnated** *adj* • They believe that the boy is their *reincarnated* leader.

re•in•car•na•tion /ˌriːjənˌkɑɚˈneɪʃən/ *noun, pl* **-tions**
1 [*noncount*] : the idea or belief that people are born again with a different body after death • Many people believe in *reincarnation*.
2 [*count*] : someone who has been born again with a different body after death — often + *of* • They believe that the boy is the *reincarnation of* their leader. — sometimes used figuratively • The café is a *reincarnation of* an eatery of the same name that existed across town years ago.

rein•deer /ˈreɪnˌdiɚ/ *noun, pl* **reindeer** [*count*] : a large type of deer that lives in northern parts of the world : CARIBOU • a large herd of *reindeer*

re•in•force /ˌriːjənˈfoɚs/ *verb* **-forc•es; -forced; -forc•ing** [+ *obj*]
1 : to strengthen (a group of people) with new supplies or more people • The captain sent out another squad to *reinforce* the troops. • Our camp is *reinforced* with supplies flown in by helicopter.
2 : to strengthen (something, such as clothing or a building) by adding more material for support • She *reinforced* the elbows of the jacket. [=she sewed more material onto the elbows of the jacket] • The soldiers *reinforced* [=*strengthened*] the barricades with sandbags. • The levees will need to be *reinforced*.
3 : to encourage or give support to (an idea, behavior, feeling, etc.) • The bad weather forecast only *reinforces* our decision to leave early tomorrow. • Some critics say that the movie *reinforces* negative stereotypes about the military. • We do our best to *reinforce* good conduct in the classroom.

reinforced concrete *noun* [*noncount*] : concrete that has metal bars inside of it to make it stronger

re•in•force•ment /ˌriːjənˈfoɚsmənt/ *noun, pl* **-ments**
1 ***reinforcements*** [*plural*] : people and supplies that are sent to help or support an army, military force, etc. • "We're outnumbered! Call for *reinforcements*!" • We need to prevent enemy *reinforcements* from reaching the front line.
2 a [*noncount*] : the act of strengthening or encouraging something • The bridge is in need of *reinforcement*. • the *reinforcement* of stereotypes **b** [*count*] : a thing that strengthens or encourages something • The teacher introduced the new vocabulary words and then used a game as a *reinforcement*. [=as something that would help the students understand/remember the words]
3 : a response to someone's behavior that is intended to make that person more likely to behave that way again [*count*] positive/negative *reinforcements* [*noncount*] You should encourage good behavior with positive *reinforcement*.

re•in•state /ˌriːjənˈsteɪt/ *verb* **-states; -stat•ed; -stat•ing** [+ *obj*]
1 : to put (someone) back in a job or position that had been taken away • After his name was cleared, he was *reinstated* as committee chairperson. • The company promised to *reinstate* [=*rehire*] the employees that had been laid off.
2 : to begin using or dealing with (a law, policy, system, etc.) again • The school board voted to *reinstate* the school's uniform policy. • the year the death penalty was *reinstated* • The court case was dismissed by the judge but *reinstated* [=*reopened*] on appeal.
– **re•in•state•ment** /ˌriːjənˈsteɪtmənt/ *noun* [*noncount*] • the *reinstatement* of the death penalty

re•in•sure /ˌriːjənˈʃɚ/ *verb* **-sures; -sured; -sur•ing** [+ *obj*] : to insure (something) again so that the insurance is shared by more than one company
– **re•in•sur•ance** /ˌriːjənˈʃɚrəns/ *noun* [*noncount*] – **re•in•sur•er** /ˌriːjənˈʃɚrɚ/ *noun, pl* **-ers** [*count*]

re•in•ter•pret /ˌriːjənˈtɚprət/ *verb* **-prets; -pret•ed; -pret•ing** [+ *obj*] : to understand and explain or show (something) in a new or different way • New information may force us to *reinterpret* the evidence. • The director wants to *reinterpret* the old play for a modern audience.
– **re•in•ter•pre•ta•tion** /ˌriːjənˌtɚprəˈteɪʃən/ *noun, pl* **-tions** [*count*] modern *reinterpretations* of Shakespeare's plays [*noncount*] These works of art are always ***open to reinterpretation***. [=can always be explained or understood in a different way]

re•in•tro•duce /ˌriːjɪntrəˈduːs, *Brit* ˌriːjɪntrəˈdjuːs/ *verb* **-duc•es; -duced; -duc•ing** [+ *obj*]
1 : to begin using (something) again • The school has decided to *reintroduce* some of its old policies.
2 : to return (an animal or plant) to the area where it used to live • Several species of endangered fish are being *reintroduced* into the river.
– **re•in•tro•duc•tion** /ˌriːˌɪntrəˈdʌkʃən/ *noun, pl* **-tions** [*count, noncount*]

re•in•vent /ˌriːjənˈvɛnt/ *verb* **-vents; -vent•ed; -vent•ing** [+ *obj*]
1 : to make major changes or improvements to (something) • The candidate promised to *reinvent* Social Security.
2 : to present (something) in a different or new way • chefs who *reinvent* regional favorites using exotic ingredients
reinvent the wheel *informal* : to waste time trying to do something that has already been done successfully by someone else • When designing new software, there's no need to *reinvent the wheel*.
reinvent yourself : to become a different kind of person, performer, etc. • She's a classical singer who's trying to *reinvent herself* as a pop artist.
– **re•in•ven•tion** /ˌriːjənˈvɛnʃən/ *noun, pl* **-tions** [*count, noncount*] • the *reinvention* of the education system

re•in•vest /ˌriːjənˈvɛst/ *verb* **-vests; -vest•ed; -vest•ing**
1 a : to use (the profits of an investment) to buy more investments [+ *obj*] Many investors *reinvest* their dividends. [*no obj*] Before you *reinvest*, consider your options carefully. **b** [+ *obj*] : to use (money that a business has earned) to improve the business • The company *reinvests* a portion of its profits in new products.
2 [*no obj*] *US* : to spend money, time, energy, etc., to make improvements to something valuable — often + *in* • We need to *reinvest in* our neighborhoods.
– **re•in•vest•ment** /ˌriːjənˈvɛstmənt/ *noun, pl* **-ments** [*count, noncount*] • the *reinvestment* of earnings/dividends • neighborhood/community *reinvestment*

re•is•sue /riˈɪˌʃuː/ *verb* **-is•sues; -is•sued; -is•su•ing** [+ *obj*] : to publish or produce (something, such as a book or recording) again : to issue (something) again • The publisher has decided to *reissue* the author's out-of-print books. • My favorite album is being *reissued* on CD. [=my favorite album is being produced again as a CD]
– **reissue** *noun, pl* **-is•sues** [*count*] • That's not the original album—it's a *reissue*.

re•it•er•ate /riˈɪtəˌreɪt/ *verb* **-ates; -at•ed; -at•ing** [+ *obj*] *somewhat formal* : to repeat something you have already said in order to emphasize it • *reiterate* a claim/view/point • She avoided answering our questions directly, instead *reiterating* that the answers could be found in her book. • Allow me to *reiterate*: if I am elected, I will not raise taxes.
– **re•it•er•a•tion** /riˌɪtəˈreɪʃən/ *noun, pl* **-tions** [*count*] The report was nothing more than a *reiteration* of statements by officials. [*noncount*] the *reiteration* of certain themes in the author's books

[1]**re•ject** /rɪˈʤɛkt/ *verb* **-jects; -ject•ed; -ject•ing** [+ *obj*]
1 : to refuse to believe, accept, or consider (something) • My teacher *rejected* my excuse for being late. • The committee *rejected* my proposal/idea/suggestion/motion. • I agree with several points of her argument, while *rejecting* [=disagreeing with] her conclusions. • She *rejected* the package/letter [=she did not accept the delivery of the package, letter, etc.] and returned it unopened.
2 : to decide not to publish (something) or make (something) available to the public because it is not good enough • My article/book/paper was *rejected*. • The produce inspector *rejected* several crates of berries that had begun to grow mold.
3 a : to refuse to allow (someone) to join a club, to attend a school, etc. • The college *rejects* hundreds of applicants each year. **b** : to decide not to offer (someone) a job or position • We *rejected* 5 of the 10 job applicants right away.
4 : to refuse to love, care for, or give attention to (someone) • The mother cat *rejected* the smallest kitten and refused to feed it. • *Rejected* by society, these street kids have to fend for themselves. • He still loves her even though she's *rejected* him before. • He wanted to ask her on a date, but he was afraid of being *rejected*.
5 *medical, of a person's body* : to produce substances that try to harm or destroy (a transplanted organ, a skin graft, etc.) • The patient's immune system *rejected* the transplanted heart. = The patient *rejected* the transplanted heart.
– **re•jec•tion** /rɪˈʤɛkʃən/ *noun, pl* **-tions** [*count*] The committee was unanimous in its *rejection* of my proposal. • After many *rejections*, her novel was finally accepted for publication. [*noncount*] In any transplant operation, there is a risk of organ *rejection*. • a ***rejection letter*** [=a letter say-

R

ing that you or something you have written, made, etc., has been rejected]

²re·ject /ˈriːˌʤɛkt/ *noun, pl* **-jects** [*count*]

1 : something that is not good enough for some purpose **:** something that cannot be used or accepted ▪ Stack the promising applications here, and put the *rejects* over there. ▪ One way to save on clothing costs is to buy (factory) *rejects*. [=clothes that are sold for a lower price because they have flaws]

2 : a person who is not accepted or liked by other people ▪ the *rejects* of society = society's *rejects* ▪ (*informal*) Ignore him, he's a (total/complete) *reject*.

re·jig /rɪˈʤɪg/ *verb* **-jigs; -jigged; -jig·ging** [+ *obj*] *Brit, informal* **:** REJIGGER

re·jig·ger /rɪˈʤɪgɚ/ *verb* **-jig·gers; -jig·gered; -jig·ger·ing** [+ *obj*] *US, informal* **:** to change or adjust (something) **:** REARRANGE ▪ We'll have to *rejigger* [=(*Brit*) *rejig*] the family finances to pay for the new car. ▪ The TV network is *rejiggering* its schedule.

re·joice /rɪˈʤoɪs/ *verb* **-joic·es; -joiced; -joic·ing** [*no obj*] **:** to feel or show that you are very happy about something ▪ We all *rejoiced* over/about/in/at our friend's good luck. ▪ The fans *rejoiced* when their team finally won the World Series. = The fans *rejoiced* in their team's World Series victory.

rejoice in the name/title of *Brit, humorous* **:** to have a name/title that makes people laugh or smile ▪ a woman who *rejoices in the name of* Eugenia Whelpbottom

– rejoicing *noun* [*noncount*] ▪ There was much *rejoicing* when the soldiers returned home.

re·join *verb* **-joins; -joined; -join·ing**

1 /ˌriːˈʤoɪn/ **:** to become a member of (a group or organization) again [+ *obj*] I'll be *rejoining* my family for the last part of our vacation. ▪ Now that the kids are in school, I'm ready to *rejoin* the workforce. [*no obj*] The original drummer left the band in 2000 but *rejoined* two years later.

2 /rɪˈʤoɪn/ **:** to come together with (something) again [+ *obj*] This trail eventually *rejoins* the main trail. [*no obj*] The river divides here, but the two streams *rejoin* downstream.

3 /ˌriːˈʤoɪn/ [+ *obj*] *formal* **:** to reply to (something said or written) especially in a rude or angry way ▪ "You're a fine one to talk," she *rejoined*. [=*replied, retorted*]

re·join·der /rɪˈʤoɪndɚ/ *noun, pl* **-ders** [*count*] *formal* **:** a usually rude or angry reply to something written or said ▪ The article was a stinging *rejoinder* to her critics. ▪ a witty *rejoinder*

re·ju·ve·nate /rɪˈʤuːvəˌneɪt/ *verb* **-nates; -nat·ed; -nat·ing** [+ *obj*]

1 : to make (someone) feel or look young, healthy, or energetic again ▪ The spa treatment *rejuvenated* me.

2 : to give new strength or energy to (something) ▪ Each candidate claims to have a plan to *rejuvenate* the sagging economy. ▪ Her efforts to *rejuvenate* her career have so far been unsuccessful.

– rejuvenated *adj* [*more* ~; *most* ~] ▪ I felt *rejuvenated* [=*refreshed*] after a nap and a shower. ▪ a *rejuvenated* economy **– rejuvenating** *adj* [*more* ~; *most* ~] ▪ *rejuvenating* face cream ▪ The swim was very *rejuvenating*. **– re·ju·ve·na·tion** /rɪˌʤuːvəˈneɪʃən/ *noun* [*noncount*] physical/economic *rejuvenation* [*singular*] The city has experienced a *rejuvenation*.

re·kin·dle /riˈkɪndl/ *verb* **-kin·dles; -kin·dled; -kin·dling** [+ *obj*] **:** to cause (something, such as a feeling) to be strong or active again ▪ The movie has *rekindled* public interest in the trial. ▪ The court's controversial decision is sure to *rekindle* debate about this issue. ▪ *rekindle* an old romance

– rekindling *noun* [*singular*] ▪ a *rekindling* of interest/debate

¹re·lapse /ˈriːˌlæps/ *noun, pl* **-laps·es**

1 : the return of an illness after a period of improvement [*count*] Everyone thought she was well until a sudden *relapse* sent her back to the hospital. [*noncount*] Patients who stop taking the medication have a higher risk of *relapse*. [=they are more likely to get sick again]

2 : a return to bad behavior that you had stopped doing [*count*] a drug addict who has had a *relapse* [*noncount*] a drug addict who has a history of *relapse* ▪ The program has a low rate of *relapse*. [=most people who use the program do not return to the bad behavior they had stopped doing]

²re·lapse /rɪˈlæps/ *verb* **-laps·es; -lapsed; -laps·ing** [*no obj*]

1 a : to become ill again after a period of improvement in health ▪ If you don't continue your treatment, you could *relapse*. **b** *of an illness* **:** to return or become worse after leaving or improving for a period of time ▪ Malaria can *relapse* years after the original infection.

2 : to return to a bad condition, form of behavior, etc. ▪ The country soon *relapsed* into chaos. ▪ She stayed out of trouble for a long time, but then she *relapsed* into her old ways. ▪ Many former smokers *relapse* [=begin smoking again] in times of stress.

re·lat·able /rɪˈleɪtəbəl/ *adj* [*more* ~; *most* ~] *US* **:** possible to understand because of being like something you have known, experienced, etc. ▪ The show has likable characters in *relatable* situations. [=in situations that people can relate to]

re·late /rɪˈleɪt/ *verb* **-lates; -lat·ed; -lat·ing**

1 [+ *obj*] **:** to show or make a connection between (two or more things) ▪ *relate* cause and effect — often + *to* ▪ Few of the people who became sick *related* their symptoms *to* the food they'd eaten the day before.

2 [*no obj*] **:** to understand and like or have sympathy for someone or something ▪ You must be feeling awful. I went through something similar myself last year, so I can *relate*. — usually + *to* ▪ I can *relate to* your feelings. ▪ I've never been able to *relate to* him very well. ▪ The audience needs to be able to *relate to* the characters in the story. ▪ He writes songs that people can really *relate to*.

3 [+ *obj*] *formal* **:** to tell (something, such as a story) ▪ The book *relates* [=*recounts*] a tale of jealousy and heartache. ▪ We listened eagerly as she *related* the whole exciting story.

4 [*no obj*] — used to describe how people talk to, behave toward, and deal with each other; usually + *to* or *with* ▪ The way a child *relates to* [=*interacts with*] her teacher can affect her education. ▪ They are very formal in the way they *relate* [=*interact*] *with* each other.

relate to [*phrasal verb*] ***relate to (someone or something)*** **:** to be connected with (someone or something) **:** to be about (someone or something) ▪ The readings *relate to* the class discussions. ▪ Their grudge *relates* back *to* a misunderstanding that took place years ago. ▪ other information *relating to* his performance — often used as *(be) related to* ▪ The survey suggests that financial success *is* closely/strongly/directly *related to* a person's level of education. — see also RELATE 1, 2, 4 (above)

related *adj*

1 : connected in some way ▪ ancient history and other *related* subjects/areas/fields ▪ drug-*related* crimes [=crimes that are connected to illegal drugs]

2 *not used before a noun* **:** in the same family ▪ I just found out that my best friend and I are *related* through distant cousins. ▪ We all call her "auntie," but we're not actually *related*. [=we're not in the same family] ▪ My stepmother and I are not ***related by blood***. [=my stepmother and I do not share biological ancestors; our biological families are different] ▪ My sister-in-law and I are ***related by marriage***. [=my sister-in-law is married to someone in my family]

3 : belonging to the same group because of shared characteristics, qualities, etc. ▪ Horses and donkeys are *related*. ▪ closely/distantly *related* species ▪ The words "play" and "playful" are *related*.

re·la·tion /rɪˈleɪʃən/ *noun, pl* **-tions**

1 ***relations*** [*plural*] **a :** the way in which two or more people, groups, countries, etc., talk to, behave toward, and deal with each other ▪ The incident led to tense international *relations*. — see also INDUSTRIAL RELATIONS **b** *formal* **:** SEXUAL INTERCOURSE ▪ ***sexual relations*** outside of marriage

2 : the way in which two or more people or things are connected [*count*] the *relations* [=(more commonly) *relationships*] between weather events and erosion [*noncount*] This movie ***bears no relation to*** the book by the same title. [=it is not connected to the book at all; the movie and the book do not tell the same story, have the same characters, etc.]

3 : a person who is a member of your family [*count*] We threw a big party for all our friends and *relations*. [=*relatives*] ▪ Is he a *relation* of yours? [=are you related to him?] [*noncount*] I'm Jill Jones, and this is Mike Jones—***no relation***. [=we have the same last name but we are not related; we are not members of the same family]

in relation to *formal* **1 —** used to talk about what something is like by comparing it to something else or by seeing how it is related to something else ▪ The monkey's eyes are large *in relation to* its head. ▪ understanding literature *in relation to* history **2 :** about (something or someone) ▪ I have several comments to make *in relation to* [=*in/with reference to, regarding*] the subject at hand.

re·la·tion·ship /rɪˈleɪʃənˌʃɪp/ *noun, pl* **-ships**

1 [*count*] **:** the way in which two or more people, groups, countries, etc., talk to, behave toward, and deal with each other • The *relationship* between the two countries has improved. • She has a close *relationship* with her sister. • We have a good ***working relationship***. [=we work well together] • I have a ***love-hate relationship*** with my ex. [=I have strong feelings of both love and hatred for my ex]

2 [*count*] **:** a romantic or sexual friendship between two people • She has had many bad *relationships*. • I am not in a *relationship* right now.

3 : the way in which two or more people or things are connected [*count*] the *relationship* between mental and physical health • the doctor-patient *relationship* [*noncount*] "What is your *relationship* to the witness?" "He is my father/friend/boss." • Her earlier paintings ***bear little relationship*** to her later work. [=her earlier paintings are very different from her later work; her earlier paintings are not obviously connected to her later work]

[1]**rel·a·tive** /ˈrɛlətɪv/ *noun, pl* **-tives** [*count*]

1 : a member of your family • At the family reunion, I saw *relatives* I haven't seen in years. • He inherited a small piece of land from a distant *relative*.

2 : something that belongs to the same group as something else because of shared characteristics, qualities, etc. • The donkey is a *relative* of the horse.

[2]**relative** *adj*

1 a : compared to someone or something else or to each other • the *relative* value of two houses • What are the *relative* advantages of the different methods? [=what are the advantages of each method compared to the others?] • the *relative* positions of the islands • We discussed the ***relative merits*** of each school. • The car might seem expensive, but ***it's all relative***. [=the car is expensive compared to some cars but not to other cars] **b :** seeming to be something when compared with others • I'm a *relative* newcomer to the area. [=I am not really new to the area but I am more of a newcomer than many people] • We did it with *relative* [=*comparative*] ease.

2 *grammar* **:** referring to a noun, a part of a sentence, or a sentence that was used earlier • "Who," "whom," "whose," "which," and "that" are all ***relative pronouns***. • The phrase "that won" in "the book that won" is a ***relative clause***.

relative to *formal* **1 —** used to describe what someone or something is like when compared with or measured against someone or something else • Dolphins have large brains *relative to* their body size. • The value of the house is low *relative to* similar houses in the area. **2 :** concerning or about (something) **:** referring to (something) • We will discuss matters *relative to* peace and security.

rel·a·tive·ly /ˈrɛlətɪvli/ *adv* **:** when compared to others • The car's price is *relatively* high/low. [=the car's price is fairly/somewhat high/low when compared to the price of other cars] • We've had a *relatively* [=*comparatively*] warm/cool/dry spring. • There were *relatively* few people [=a fairly small number of people] at the meeting last night. • The house is *relatively* [=*fairly*] new.

relatively speaking **1 :** when compared to others that are similar • The procedure was quick, *relatively speaking*. • This is a pretty good college, *relatively speaking*. • *Relatively speaking*, the movie wasn't bad. **2 —** used to say that something is true or correct as a general statement even if it is not entirely true or correct • The trip was, *relatively speaking*, a disaster.

rel·a·tiv·ism /ˈrɛlətɪˌvɪzəm/ *noun* [*noncount*] **:** the belief that different things are true, right, etc., for different people or at different times • moral/cultural *relativism*

– rel·a·tiv·ist /ˈrɛlətɪvɪst/ *noun, pl* **-ists** [*count*] • cultural *relativists* **– relativist** *also* **rel·a·tiv·is·tic** /ˌrɛlətɪˈvɪstɪk/ *adj* • a *relativist* view

rel·a·tiv·i·ty /ˌrɛləˈtɪvəti/ *noun* [*noncount*] *physics* **:** a theory developed by Albert Einstein which says that the way that anything except light moves through time and space depends on the position and movement of someone who is watching

re·launch /riˈlɑːntʃ/ *verb* **-launch·es; -launched; -launch·ing** [+ *obj*] **:** to launch (something) again: such as **a :** to send or shoot (something, such as a rocket) into the air or water or into outer space again • *relaunch* the space shuttle **b :** to offer or sell a new version of (something, such as a product) • The company is preparing to *relaunch* its software. • The editor *relaunched* the magazine with a new title and a better format.

– re·launch /ˈriːˌlɑːntʃ/ *noun, pl* **-launch·es** [*count*] • The company has announced the *relaunch* of its software.

re·lax /rɪˈlæks/ *verb* **-lax·es; -laxed; -lax·ing**

1 : to become or to cause (something) to become less tense, tight, or stiff [*no obj*] Her grip on my hand *relaxed* [=*loosened*] only after the roller coaster had come to a complete stop. • The muscles in my neck and shoulders should *relax* after a nice hot shower. [+ *obj*] When the roller coaster stopped, she *relaxed* [=*loosened*] her grip on my hand. • A hot shower *relaxed* the tight muscles in my neck and shoulders. **— sometimes used figuratively** • Winter has finally *relaxed* its grip on the country.

2 [*no obj*] **:** to stop feeling nervous or worried • I can't *relax* with all this noise! • Just *relax*, there's nothing to worry about. • Try to *relax* and enjoy the ride.

3 [*no obj*] **:** to spend time resting or doing something enjoyable especially after you have been doing work • After work I like to come home and *relax* [=*unwind*] for a while in front of the television. • She likes to *relax* with a glass of wine [=to have a glass of wine] before bed.

4 : to become or to cause (something, such as a rule or law) to become less severe or strict [+ *obj*] The commission has voted to *relax* industry regulations/restrictions/standards. [*no obj*] Fashion rules have *relaxed* a lot in recent years.

5 [+ *obj*] *formal* **:** to allow (something, such as your attention or concentration) to become weaker • We mustn't *relax* our vigilance for a moment!

6 [+ *obj*] *chiefly US* **:** to use a chemical treatment on (hair) in order to make it straight or straighter

re·lax·ant /rɪˈlæksənt/ *noun, pl* **-ants** [*count*] **:** a substance (such as a drug) that relaxes you, your muscles, etc. • a ***muscle relaxant***

re·lax·a·tion /ˌriːˌlækˈseɪʃən/ *noun, pl* **-tions**

1 [*noncount*] **a :** a way to rest and enjoy yourself • I like to play the guitar for *relaxation*. **b :** time that you spend resting and enjoying yourself • What I need is some rest and *relaxation*.

2 : something that you do to stop feeling nervous, worried, etc. [*noncount*] *relaxation* techniques/exercises [*count*] (*Brit*) Her favourite *relaxation* is listening to music.

3 [*noncount*] **:** the act of making something (such as a muscle) less tense, tight, or stiff • the *relaxation* of muscles = muscle *relaxation* **— sometimes used figuratively** • the *relaxation* of winter's grip on the country

4 : the act of becoming or causing something to become less severe or strict [*noncount*] Workers demanded the *relaxation* of the company's strict dress code. [*count*] a *relaxation* of rules • *relaxations* of safety regulations

re·laxed /rɪˈlækst/ *adj* [*more* ~; *most* ~]

1 : calm and free from stress, worry, or anxiety **:** not worried or tense • Nothing makes me feel more *relaxed* than a nice hot bath. • I used to get really nervous performing, but I'm pretty *relaxed* about it now. • He's a very *relaxed* guy.

2 : informal and comfortable **:** CASUAL • The restaurant had a *relaxed* atmosphere. • The seminar was very *relaxed*—we met at the professor's house instead of the lecture hall. • We have a *relaxed* dress code at the office.

3 : not strict or carefully controlled • a *relaxed* set of rules • He has a *relaxed* attitude towards his studies. [=he is not very serious about his studies]

4 *chiefly US, of hair* **:** made straight or straighter with a chemical treatment • *relaxed* hair

5 *of clothing* **:** not tight • *relaxed* [=loose-fitting] jeans

re·lax·er /rɪˈlæksɚ/ *noun, pl* **-ers** [*count, noncount*] *chiefly US* **:** a chemical treatment that is used to make curly hair straight or straighter

re·lax·ing /rɪˈlæksɪŋ/ *adj* [*more* ~; *most* ~] **:** helping you to rest and to feel less tense, worried, nervous, etc. • quiet, *relaxing* music • We spent three *relaxing* days at the beach.

[1]**re·lay** /ˈriːˌleɪ/ *noun, pl* **-lays** [*count*]

1 : a race between teams in which each team member runs, swims, etc., a different part of the race • I'm running (in) the *relay* at tomorrow's track meet. • the 4x100 *relay* [=a relay with four parts that are 100 meters each] • Our *relay* team is training for next weekend's race.

2 : the act of passing something from one person or device to another • a satellite *relay* of a television signal • (*baseball*) The shortstop's *relay* (throw) from center field was too late to catch the runner at home.; *also* **:** a system for doing this • We set up a *relay* to carry buckets of water to the campsite. • a satellite *relay* system

3 : a group of people, horses, etc., that takes the place of others so that something (such as a job or an activity) is done

R

continuously • They worked ***in relays*** to clear the rubble.

4 *technical* **: a device that is used to cause a switch to open or close automatically when there is a change in the current that is flowing through a circuit** • an electromagnetic *relay*

²re·lay /rɪˈleɪ/ *verb* **-lays; -layed; -lay·ing** [+ *obj*] **: to pass (something, such a message or information) from one person or device to another** • Messengers on horseback *relayed* battle plans to the front lines. • Please *relay* the news to the rest of the team. — often used as *(be) relayed* • This report is *being relayed* to us by our crew at the scene of the accident. • Data *relayed* from the aircraft will be recorded on the ground.

¹re·lease /rɪˈliːs/ *verb* **-leas·es; -leased; -leas·ing** [+ *obj*]

1 a : to allow (a person or animal) to leave a jail, cage, prison, etc. : to set (someone or something) free • The hostages have been *released*. • The judge *released* the prisoner. • The lion was *released* from its cage. • There is a lot of controversy over whether or not wolves should be *released* into the park. **b : to stop holding (someone or something)** • The hot-air balloon pilot signaled the ground crew to *release* [=*let go of*] the ropes. • I *released* my son's hand, and he ran out onto the playground. **c : to allow (a substance) to enter the air, water, soil, etc.** • Plastic *releases* [=*emits*] dangerous chemicals when it burns. • The factory faced serious fines for *releasing* dangerous chemicals into the river. • Heat is *released* into the atmosphere by cars. • During exercise, the body *releases* chemicals in the brain that make you feel better. **d : to cause (an emotion, a feeling, etc.) to go away by expressing it or dealing with it in some way** • She started to cry, *releasing* all of her repressed emotion. • Exercise is a good way to *release* stress/tension.

2 : to free (someone) from a duty, responsibility, etc. • The contract was declared null, and we were *released* from our agreement/obligation. • I *released* him from his promise. [=I said that he did not have to do what he had promised to do]

3 : to give up control or possession of (something) • The local police *released* the evidence to the FBI.

4 : to make (something) available to the public • The band hopes to *release* their new album by next summer. • The police will not *release* the names of the teenagers involved in the robbery. • They *released* a statement this afternoon.

5 : to allow (part of a machine, device, etc.) to go back to its normal position • The camera's shutter will stay open until the button is *released*. • *release* [=*disengage*] the parking brake

²release *noun, pl* **-leases**

1 : the act of releasing someone or something: such as a : the act of allowing a person or animal to leave a jail, cage, prison, etc. [*noncount*] the *release* of the hostages • The prisoner is eligible for early *release*. • There was a controversy over the *release* of wolves into the park. [*count*] The prisoner was given an early *release*. **b : the act of allowing a substance to enter the air, water, soil, etc.** [*noncount*] the *release* of heat into the atmosphere • Exercise triggers the *release* of chemicals in the brain that make you feel better. [*count*] an accidental *release* of pollutants into the river **c : the act of freeing someone from a duty, responsibility, etc.** [*noncount*] They've filed a request for *release* from the contract. [*count*] They're requesting a *release* from their contractual obligations. **d** [*noncount*] **: the act of making something available to the public** • The *release* of the book is scheduled for next month. • The government has tried to bar the *release* of the documents. • The film's ***general release*** is Friday. [=the film will begin to be shown in theaters on Friday] • (*Brit*) The film is ***on general release***. [=the film is being shown in theaters]

2 a [*singular*] **: a way of dealing with and getting rid of unpleasant emotions, feelings, etc.** • Dancing is a great *release* (from stress). • activities that offer a *release* from stress **b** *formal* **: an end to pain, distress, etc.** [*noncount*] We mourned her death, but were glad it brought her *release* from pain. • a feeling of *release* [*singular*] Her death brought her a *release* from pain.

3 [*count*] **: something (such as a new product or an official statement) that is made available to the public** • new product *releases* • the band's latest *release* • the year's top CD *releases* • The company has issued a *release* about the new software. — see also PRESS RELEASE

4 [*count*] **: an official document which states that a company, person, etc., is not responsible if you are hurt while doing something** • The company requires visitors to the mine to sign a *release* before they go below ground. • a *release* form

5 [*count*] **: a device that allows a part of a machine to move freely** • the shutter *release* on a camera

6 [*count*] *US, sports* **: the action or manner of throwing a ball** — usually singular • The quarterback has a quick *release*.

rel·e·gate /ˈrɛləˌgeɪt/ *verb* **-gates; -gat·ed; -gat·ing** [+ *obj*]

1 *formal* **: to put (someone or something) in a lower or less important position, rank, etc. — usually used as *(be) relegated*; usually + *to*** • an important historical figure who *is* usually *relegated to* footnote status • The team's best player has *been relegated to* a backup role because of injuries. • old books *relegated to* the attic

2 *formal* **: to give (something, such as a job or responsibility) *to* another person or group** • The bill has been *relegated to* committee for discussion.

3 *Brit* **: to move (a sports team) to a lower position in a league — usually used as *(be) relegated*; usually + *to*** • The team have *been relegated to* the Second Division. — opposite PROMOTE

— **rel·e·ga·tion** /ˌrɛləˈgeɪʃən/ *noun* [*noncount*] • her *relegation* to a backup role

re·lent /rɪˈlɛnt/ *verb* **-lents; -lent·ed; -lent·ing** [*no obj*] *somewhat formal*

1 : to agree to do or accept something that you have been resisting or opposing • Our application was initially refused, but the city *relented* in the end and the permit was issued. • They had refused to pay and *relented* only after being threatened with a lawsuit.

2 : to become less severe, harsh, strong, determined, etc. • He will not *relent* [=*give up*] in his effort to clear his name. • The winds would not *relent*.

re·lent·less /rɪˈlɛntləs/ *adj* [*more* ~; *most* ~]

1 : continuing without becoming weaker, less severe, etc. • Her *relentless* optimism held the team together. • *relentless* winds

2 : remaining strict or determined • The hunter was *relentless* in pursuit of his prey. • a *relentless* opponent of deregulation

— **re·lent·less·ly** *adv* • She is *relentlessly* optimistic. • a hunter *relentlessly* pursuing his prey [=pursuing without stopping]

rel·e·vant /ˈrɛləvənt/ *adj* [*more* ~; *most* ~] **: relating to a subject in an appropriate way** • a *relevant* [=*pertinent*] question • The ideas and observations expressed in the book are still *relevant* today. — often + *to* • Her comments were not *relevant* [=(more formally) *germane*] *to* the discussion. • Do you have any experience that is *relevant to* this job? — opposite IRRELEVANT

— **rel·e·vance** /ˈrɛləvəns/ *or* **rel·e·van·cy** /ˈrɛləvənsi/ *noun* [*noncount*] • The question lacks *relevance*. — **rel·e·vant·ly** *adv* • It's a funny story, and more *relevantly*, it's true.

re·li·able /rɪˈlajəbəl/ *adj* [*more* ~; *most* ~]

1 : able to be trusted to do or provide what is needed : able to be relied on • a *reliable* car • a *reliable* source of safe drinking water [=a way to get safe drinking water every time you need it] • He's not very *reliable*. You can't always count on him to do what he says he'll do.

2 : able to be believed : likely to be true or correct • a *reliable* witness • It's a rumor, but I heard it from a *reliable* source. [=someone who is likely to have accurate information] • We can't write a report without *reliable* data. • We need more *reliable* information before we can take action.

— **re·li·abil·i·ty** /rɪˌlajəˈbɪləti/ *noun* [*noncount*] • These cars are known for their *reliability*. — **re·li·ably** /rɪˈlajəbli/ *adv* • How can I get my computer to work *reliably*? • Few analysts can *reliably* estimate corporate profits.

re·li·ance /rɪˈlajəns/ *noun* [*singular*] **: the state of needing someone or something for help, support, etc. — usually + *on* or *upon*** • The region's *reliance on* tourism has only grown in recent years. • Some farmers are taking steps to reduce their *reliance on* pesticides.

re·li·ant /rɪˈlajənt/ *adj* [*more* ~; *most* ~] **: needing someone or something for help, support, etc. : DEPENDENT — usually + *on* or *upon*** • Most college students remain *reliant on* their parents' support. • Students have become too *reliant on/upon* calculators and don't truly understand basic mathematical principles. — see also SELF-RELIANT

rel·ic /ˈrɛlɪk/ *noun, pl* **-ics** [*count*]

1 : something that is from a past time, place, culture, etc. — often + *of* or *from* • *relics of* ancient China • *relics from* the war • This law is a *relic of* a bygone era. • Typewriters are a ***relic of the past***. [=typewriters are no longer used or considered modern]

2 : an object (such as a piece of clothing or the bone of a

R

saint) that is considered holy ▪ holy/sacred *relics*

re·lief /rɪˈliːf/ *noun, pl* **-liefs**

1 : a pleasant and relaxed feeling that someone has when something unpleasant stops or does not happen [*noncount*] I felt such a sense of *relief* after I finished my thesis. ▪ He expressed *relief* that the crisis was finally over. ▪ Much to everyone's *relief*, the airplane took off without any problems. ▪ She ***breathed a sigh of relief***. [=she no longer felt tension, worry, fear, etc.] [*singular*] What a *relief* it is to be back home.

2 [*noncount*] **:** the removal or reducing of something that is painful or unpleasant ▪ I want *relief* from my headaches. [=I want my headaches to stop] ▪ pain *relief* ▪ Exercise is an excellent source of stress *relief*. ▪ Both candidates promised tax *relief* for middle-class families.

3 [*noncount*] **a :** things (such as food, money, or medicine) that are given to help people who are victims of a war, earthquake, flood, etc. ▪ disaster/famine *relief* ▪ Countries from around the world have been sending *relief* to the flood victims. ▪ *Relief* workers [=people whose job it is to provide aid] delivered medical supplies. ▪ We donated to the *relief* effort for the hurricane victims. **b** *chiefly US, old-fashioned* **:** money that is given by the government to poor people **:** WELFARE ▪ My father lost his job and we had to go on *relief*.

4 [*noncount*] **:** a person or group that replaces another person or group that needs rest or has finished a period of work ▪ 30,000 troops will be sent abroad as *relief* for the deployed soldiers. — often used before another noun ▪ The *relief* driver took over after the midway point of the race. ▪ a *relief* crew

5 : something that is enjoyable and that replaces for a short time something that is boring, unpleasant, or difficult [*singular*] Just one day of sunshine would be a welcome *relief* from the rainy weather we've been having lately. [*noncount*] His character provides a little ***comic relief*** in what is otherwise a very serious and dramatic movie.

6 a [*noncount*] **:** a way of decorating wood, stone, metal, etc., with designs that stick out above the surface ▪ Each gold coin depicts the queen's head in *relief* on the front. **b** [*count*] **:** a work of art with designs that stick out above the surface ▪ ancient marble *reliefs* — see also BAS-RELIEF

7 [*noncount*] **:** a situation in which something is more noticeable when it is compared to something else ▪ The trees stood in stark *relief* against the sky. ▪ Her political activism throws the apathy of others into sharp *relief*. [=makes the apathy of others very noticeable]

relief map *noun, pl* **~ maps** [*count*] **:** a map that uses different colors or textures to show the height or depth of mountains, hills, valleys, etc.

relief pitcher *noun, pl* **~ -ers** [*count*] *baseball* **:** a pitcher who comes into a game when another pitcher is removed from the game — called also *reliever*

relief road *noun, pl* **~ roads** [*count*] *Brit* **:** a road that can be used to avoid a busy area, another road with heavy traffic, etc.

re·lieve /rɪˈliːv/ *verb* **-lieves; -lieved; -liev·ing** [+ *obj*]

1 : to reduce or remove (something, such as pain or an unpleasant feeling) ▪ I took a pill to *relieve* my headache. ▪ I wish I could *relieve* your suffering. ▪ What's the best way to *relieve* stress? ▪ She tried to *relieve* the tension by making a joke.

2 : to make (a problem) less serious ▪ an effort to *relieve* traffic congestion ▪ *relieve* poverty ▪ We need to find ways to *relieve* overcrowding in our schools.

3 : to take the place of (someone who has been working, fighting, etc.) ▪ I've come to *relieve* the guard on duty. ▪ The soldiers were *relieved* by 30,000 fresh troops. ▪ (*baseball*) He *relieved* the starting pitcher in the sixth inning.

4 : to make (something) less boring, dull, etc., by including a part that is different ▪ His latest book is a long, serious novel *relieved* only by the occasional joke.

relieve of [*phrasal verb*] ***relieve (someone) of (something)*** **1** *formal* **:** to take (something that is difficult or unpleasant) from (someone) ▪ She signed a contract that *relieved* him *of* all responsibility regarding the business. ▪ The law *relieves* you *of* any liability. [=under the law, you will not be liable] **2** *informal + humorous* **:** to steal (something) from (someone) ▪ Someone *relieved* him *of* his wallet. [=someone stole his wallet] **3 :** to remove (someone who has done something wrong) from (a post, duty, job, etc.) ▪ The general was *relieved of* his command.

relieve yourself **:** to pass waste from your body ▪ He stopped the car and went out into the woods to *relieve himself*. [=*urinate*] ▪ The puppy *relieved himself* on the carpet.

relieved *adj* [*more ~; most ~*] **:** feeling relaxed and happy because something difficult or unpleasant has been stopped, avoided, or made easier **:** feeling relief ▪ I was *relieved* to hear that you're feeling better. ▪ He was greeted at the door by his much *relieved* mother.

re·liev·er /rɪˈliːvɚ/ *noun, pl* **-ers** [*count*]

1 : something that relieves pain, stress, etc. ▪ pain *relievers* like aspirin and ibuprofen ▪ Exercise is a good stress *reliever*.

2 *baseball* **:** RELIEF PITCHER

re·li·gion /rɪˈlɪʤən/ *noun, pl* **-gions**

1 [*noncount*] **:** the belief in a god or in a group of gods ▪ Many people turn to *religion* for comfort in a time of crisis.

2 : an organized system of beliefs, ceremonies, and rules used to worship a god or a group of gods [*count*] There are many *religions*, such as Buddhism, Christianity, Hinduism, Islam, and Judaism. ▪ Shinto is a *religion* that is unique to Japan. ▪ I think that children should be taught about different *religions*. [=*faiths*] ▪ It is against my *religion* [=my beliefs do not allow me] to drink alcohol. [*noncount*] They advocated for ***freedom of religion***. [=the right to choose what religion to follow and to worship without interference] ▪ She no longer participates in ***organized religion***. [=a belief system that has large numbers of followers and a set of rules that must be followed]

3 *informal* **:** an interest, a belief, or an activity that is very important to a person or group [*count*] Hockey is a *religion* in Canada. ▪ Politics are a *religion* to him. [*noncount*] Where I live, high school football is *religion*. ▪ Food is *religion* in this house.

find/get religion *informal + sometimes disapproving* **1 :** to become religious **:** to decide to follow a particular religion ▪ Lots of people *get religion* in prison. ▪ My dad *found religion* after surviving a car accident. **2 :** to stop doing something that others think is wrong and begin to do something others think is good or correct ▪ Automakers have *found religion*, finally bringing more hybrid vehicles to market. ▪ The mayor *got religion* on public transit and is now pushing plans to build a new subway.

re·li·gi·os·i·ty /rɪˌlɪʤiˈɑːsəti/ *noun* [*noncount*] *sometimes disapproving* **:** the state of being religious ▪ a man of deep *religiosity* [=a very/deeply religious man]

re·li·gious /rɪˈlɪʤəs/ *adj* [*more ~; most ~*]

1 : of or relating to religion ▪ My *religious* beliefs forbid the drinking of alcohol. ▪ *religious* groups/organizations/schools ▪ *Religious* leaders called for an end to the violence.

2 : believing in a god or a group of gods and following the rules of a religion ▪ She is very *religious*. ▪ My grandfather was a deeply *religious* [=*spiritual*] man. ▪ His wife is very active in the church, but he's not *religious* himself.

3 *informal* **a :** very careful to do something whenever it can or should be done — usually + *about* ▪ She's *religious about* using her seatbelt [=she always uses her seatbelt] when she drives. **b :** very interested in or involved with something — usually + *about* ▪ The people here are *religious about* college football.

re·li·gious·ly /rɪˈlɪʤəsli/ *adv* [*more ~; most ~*]

1 : concerned or connected with religion ▪ He is *religiously* observant. ▪ Voters in this part of the country tend to be *religiously* and socially liberal.

2 : very regularly or carefully ▪ She swims and lifts weights *religiously*. ▪ I read the classified ads *religiously*. ▪ This recipe must be followed *religiously*.

re·lin·quish /rɪˈlɪŋkwɪʃ/ *verb* **-quish·es; -quished; -quish·ing** [+ *obj*] *formal* **:** to give up (something) **:** to give (something, such as power, control, or possession) to another person or group ▪ I will not *relinquish* my rights. ▪ She was forced to *relinquish* control of the project. ▪ The court ordered him to *relinquish* custody of his child.

— re·lin·quish·ment /rɪˈlɪŋkwɪʃmənt/ *noun* [*noncount*]

rel·i·quary /ˈrɛləˌkweri/ *noun, pl* **-quar·ies** [*count*] **:** a container that is used to hold holy objects (called relics)

[1]**rel·ish** /ˈrɛlɪʃ/ *noun, pl* **-ish·es**

1 [*count, noncount*] **:** a seasoned sauce that is used to add flavor to other foods and that is made of chopped fruit or vegetables ▪ mango *relish*; *especially* **:** such a sauce made from pickles ▪ I like to eat hot dogs with mustard and *relish*.

2 a [*noncount*] **:** enjoyment of or delight in something ▪ She plays the role with great *relish*. ▪ He took particular *relish* in pointing out my error. **b** [*singular*] **:** a feeling of liking something ▪ He showed little *relish* for the job. [=he did not like the job]

²relish *verb* **-ishes; -ished; -ish·ing** [+ *obj*] **:** to enjoy or take pleasure in (something) ▪ I *relish* traveling to new places. ▪ I don't *relish* the idea/prospect/thought of working late tonight. ▪ He *relishes* the chance/opportunity to compete again.

re·live /riˈlɪv/ *verb* **-lives; -lived; -liv·ing** [+ *obj*] **:** to experience (something) again in your imagination **:** to remember (something) so clearly that the same emotions you felt in the past are felt again ▪ an athlete trying to *relive* his glory days ▪ He would sometimes *relive* the battle in his dreams.

re·load /riˈloʊd/ *verb* **-loads; -load·ed; -load·ing**

1 : to put bullets, film, etc., into something (such as a gun or camera) again [+ *obj*] They *reloaded* their rifles. ▪ I need to *reload* the camera. [*no obj*] The soldiers *reloaded*.

2 : to put data into a computer's memory again [+ *obj*] If the images don't display, *reload* the page. [*no obj*] Exit the program and *reload*.

re·lo·cate /riˈloʊˌkeɪt/ *verb* **-cates; -cat·ed; -cat·ing :** to move to a new place [*no obj*] He *relocated* to Los Angeles for his new job. ▪ How can we convince more businesses to *relocate* to/in this city? [+ *obj*] The company decided to *relocate* its headquarters.

– re·lo·ca·tion /ˌri:loʊˈkeɪʃən/ *noun, pl* **-tions** [*count, noncount*] ▪ corporate *relocations*

re·luc·tant /rɪˈlʌktənt/ *adj* [*more ~; most ~*] **:** feeling or showing doubt about doing something **:** not willing or eager to do something ▪ We were *reluctant* to get involved. ▪ He might agree but seems *reluctant* to admit it. ▪ a *reluctant* participant

– re·luc·tance /rɪˈlʌktəns/ *noun* [*singular*] They have shown a *reluctance* to take risks. [*noncount*] He agreed to help us with much/great *reluctance*. **– re·luc·tant·ly** *adv* ▪ She *reluctantly* agreed to pay the fine.

re·ly /rɪˈlaɪ/ *verb* **-lies; -lied; -ly·ing**

rely on/upon [*phrasal verb*] **1** ***rely on/upon (someone or something)*** **a :** to need (someone or something) for support, help, etc. **:** to depend on (someone or something) ▪ My mother *relied on* me for financial support. ▪ They *rely on* a well for all their water. ▪ She *relies on* her sister to drive her to school. ▪ He no longer *relies upon* his parents for money. **b :** to trust or believe (someone or something) ▪ She's someone you can *rely on*. ▪ You can *rely on* him to do it right. ▪ I *relied* heavily *upon* your advice. ▪ You could always *rely on* [=*count on*] him to disagree. [=you could always be sure that he would disagree] **2** ***rely on/upon (something)*** **:** to expect (something) with confidence **:** to be certain that (something) will happen or exist ▪ The economy may improve next year, but it's not something you can *rely on*.

REM /ˈrɛm, ˌɑɚˌi:ˈɛm/ *noun* [*noncount*] **:** REM SLEEP

re·main /rɪˈmeɪn/ *verb* **-mains; -mained; -main·ing**

1 [*no obj*] **:** to be left when the other parts are gone or have been used ▪ Little *remained* after the fire. ▪ Only two minutes still *remain* in the game. ▪ The memory of that day will *remain* [=*stay*] with me for the rest of my life.

2 *not used in progressive tenses* [*no obj*] **:** to be something that still needs to be done, dealt with, etc. ▪ The question/mystery *remains*: who fired the shot? — often followed by *to* + *verb* ▪ Much work *remains to be* done. [=there is much work still to be done] ▪ It ***remains to be seen*** [=it is uncertain] whether or not she was lying.

3 *always followed by an adverb or preposition* [*no obj*] *somewhat formal* **:** to stay in the same place or with the same person or group **:** to stay after others have gone ▪ She *remained* in Boston after she finished college. ▪ The soldiers were ordered to *remain* at their posts. ▪ I *remained* behind after the class had ended. ▪ He *remained* with the team.

4 *not used in progressive tenses* [*linking verb*] **:** to continue in a specified state, condition, or position ▪ She *remained* [=*kept, stayed*] calm. ▪ Please *remain* standing/seated. **:** to continue to be something specified ▪ It *remains* true that the best wines are not always the most expensive. ▪ The weather *remained* cold. ▪ The victim's identity *remains* a mystery. ▪ They have *remained* friends. [=they are still friends]

the fact remains see FACT

– remaining *adj* ▪ Add the *remaining* ingredients to the sauce. ▪ a few *remaining* guests

¹re·main·der /rɪˈmeɪndɚ/ *noun, pl* **-ders**

1 ***the remainder*** **:** the part that is left when the other people or things are gone, used, etc. ▪ Most of the university's students live on campus and *the remainder* [=*the rest*] rent apartments in town. — often + *of* ▪ The players will be suspended for *the remainder of* the season. ▪ The *remainder of* the money will be donated to charity.

2 [*count*] *mathematics* **a :** the number that is left when one number is subtracted from another number ▪ 2 subtracted from 5 gives a *remainder* of 3. **b :** the number that is left over when one number does not divide evenly into another number ▪ 5 goes into 29 five times with a *remainder* of 4.

3 [*count*] **:** a book that is sold at a reduced price by the publisher **:** a book that is remaindered

²remainder *verb* **-ders; -dered; -der·ing** [+ *obj*] **:** to sell (a book) at a reduced price because not many copies are being sold and no more copies will be produced ▪ The book did not sell well and ended up being *remaindered*.

re·mains /rɪˈmeɪnz/ *noun* [*plural*]

1 : the dead body of a person or animal ▪ Her *remains* will be returned to her family for burial. ▪ fossil *remains* of prehistoric animals ▪ human *remains*

2 : the parts of something that are left when the other parts are gone or used ▪ These photos show the *remains* of a star that exploded thousands of years ago. ▪ the *remains* of a medieval castle

mortal remains *formal* **:** the dead body of a person

¹re·make /riˈmeɪk/ *verb* **-makes; -made** /-ˈmeɪd/; **-mak·ing** [+ *obj*]

1 : to make a new or different version of (something, such as a movie, song, etc.) ▪ They will be *remaking* the film with American actors.

2 : to make (something) into something else ▪ The city is trying to *remake* [=*transform*] itself into a regional center for arts and tourism.

²re·make /ˈri:ˌmeɪk/ *noun, pl* **-makes** [*count*] **:** a new or different version of a movie, song, etc. ▪ The director's next project will be a *remake* of King Kong.

re·mand /rɪˈmænd, *Brit* rɪˈmɑ:nd/ *verb* **-mands; -mand·ed; -mand·ing** [+ *obj*] *law*

1 *US* **:** to send (a case) back to another court of law to be tried or dealt with again ▪ The judge *remanded* the case for further consideration.

2 *always followed by a preposition* **:** to order (someone) to go somewhere — usually used as *(be) remanded* ▪ He *was remanded* into custody [=he was sent to prison to wait for his trial] until the end of the month. ▪ She *was remanded* to drug rehab as part of her sentencing. ▪ (*Brit*) She *was* ***remanded on bail*** [=she was allowed to post bail and wait for her trial at home instead of in prison]

– remand *noun, pl* **-mands** [*count, noncount*] ▪ (*US*) The appellate court will hear the case on *remand*. [=the case has been remanded and will be heard by the appellate court] ▪ (*Brit*) He's in prison on *remand* awaiting trial. [=he has been remanded to prison and is awaiting trial]

remand centre *noun, pl* **~ -tres** [*count*] *Brit, law* **:** a jail for people who are waiting for trial or sentencing

¹re·mark /rɪˈmɑɚk/ *noun, pl* **-marks**

1 [*count*] **:** something that someone says or writes to express an opinion or idea **:** COMMENT ▪ I was offended by his *remark*. ▪ I've heard many disparaging *remarks* about him. ▪ an author known for making witty/clever *remarks*

2 [*noncount*] *formal* **:** the act of noticing or making a comment about something ▪ The incident passed without *remark*.

3 ***remarks*** [*plural*] **:** a short speech or a part of a speech ▪ opening/closing *remarks*

> ***synonyms*** REMARK, OBSERVATION, and COMMENT mean something that is said or written and that gives an opinion. REMARK often suggests a quick thought or an informal judgment. ▪ He made a casual *remark* about the food. OBSERVATION often suggests an opinion expressed after looking closely at and thinking about something. ▪ She published her *observations* on whales after 10 years of study. COMMENT often suggests a remark that is meant to explain or criticize. ▪ I asked her to give me her *comments* on the book when she finished it.

²remark *verb* **-marks; -marked; -mark·ing :** to make a statement about someone or something **:** to make a remark [+ *obj*] "It's so hot today," she *remarked*. ▪ He *remarked* [=*commented*] that the movie was disappointing. [*no obj*] — + *on* or *upon* ▪ The mayor *remarked on/upon* how quickly the construction of the new civic center was progressing.

re·mark·able /rɪˈmɑɚkəbəl/ *adj* [*more ~; most ~*] **:** unusual or surprising **:** likely to be noticed ▪ Competing in the

Olympics is a *remarkable* achievement. ▪ a *remarkable* new theory ▪ The girl has a *remarkable* talent.

– re•mark•ably /rɪˈmɑɚkəbli/ *adv* ▪ *Remarkably* (enough), no one was hurt. ▪ They were *remarkably* successful.

re•mar•ry /riˈmeri/ *verb* **-ries; -ried; -ry•ing : to marry again** [*no obj*] I'm not sure if I'll ever *remarry*. ▪ She never *remarried* after her husband died. [+ *obj*] Is he going to *remarry* his ex-wife?

– re•mar•riage /riˈmerɪʤ/ *noun, pl* **-riag•es** [*count, noncount*]

re•mas•ter /riˈmæstɚ, *Brit* riˈmɑːstə/ *verb* **-ters; -tered; -ter•ing** [+ *obj*] *technical* **: to make a new copy of (a recording or film) with the sound or image improved** ▪ The movie was ***digitally remastered*** [=improved using digital technology] for release on DVD.

re•match /ˈriːˌmæʧ/ *noun, pl* **-match•es** [*count*] **: a match or game that is played by the same people or teams after an earlier match or game — usually singular** ▪ After he lost the first game he demanded a *rematch*.

re•me•di•a•ble /rɪˈmiːdijəbəl/ *adj, formal* **: capable of being solved or cured** ▪ This problem is easily *remediable*.

re•me•di•al /rɪˈmiːdijəl/ *adj*

1 a : done to correct or improve something : done to make something better ▪ Officials have pledged *remedial* action/measures to repair damaged bridges. **b : done to cure or treat someone** ▪ *remedial* therapy

2 : involving students who need special help to improve in a particular subject ▪ Thirty percent of the new students need *remedial* classes/courses in math. ▪ *remedial* education ▪ He's taking a course in *remedial* reading. ▪ (*US*) a *remedial* student [=a student who is taking a remedial class]

[1]rem•e•dy /ˈrɛmədi/ *noun, pl* **-dies**

1 [*count*] **: a medicine or treatment that relieves pain or cures a usually minor illness** ▪ a *remedy* for fever ▪ The store now sells ***herbal remedies***. [=medicines made from plants] ▪ a shelf of ***cold remedies*** [=medicines to take when you have a cold] ▪ Do you know of a good ***home remedy*** [=a medicine made at home] for heartburn? ▪ ***folk remedies*** [=traditional medicines that are not prescribed by a doctor]

2 : a way of solving or correcting a problem [*count*] Building more roads isn't always the best *remedy* for traffic congestion. ▪ You may have no ***legal remedy*** [=way of finding a solution using the law] in this dispute. [*noncount*] The problem was beyond *remedy*. ▪ She was left without *remedy* since the court did not recognize her claim.

[2]remedy *verb* **-dies; -died; -dy•ing** [+ *obj*] **: to solve, correct, or improve (something)** ▪ Something must be done to *remedy* the problem/situation. ▪ The conflict can be *remedied* by scheduling the meeting for next week.

re•mem•ber /rɪˈmɛmbɚ/ *verb* **-bers; -bered; -ber•ing**

1 : to have or keep an image or idea in your mind of (something or someone from the past) : to think of (something or someone from the past) again [+ *obj*] I *remember* my first day of school like it was yesterday. ▪ Do you *remember* me? I used to work with you many years ago. ▪ *Remember* when we went hiking last summer? ▪ I *remember* telling him not to do it, but he did it anyway. ▪ I *remember* what that felt like. ▪ It was a day ***to remember***. [=it was a special/memorable day] [*no obj*] ***As far as I can remember***, I've never been late to a meeting. ▪ My family has lived in New York ***for as long as I can remember***. [=for a very long time]

2 : to cause (something) to come back into your mind [+ *obj*] I couldn't *remember* how to spell her name. ▪ I can't *remember* where I put that book. ▪ I *remembered* that I had left my wallet at home. ▪ Sorry, I don't *remember* your name. [=I have forgotten your name] [*no obj*] What was it that I was going to ask him? I can't *remember*.

3 : to keep (information) in your mind : to not forget (something) [+ *obj*] *Remember* the dates for the test. ▪ Thank you for *remembering* my birthday. ▪ I *remembered* to feed the cat. ▪ *Remember*, the trains stop running at 12:30 a.m. ▪ Please *remember* to take out the trash tomorrow. ▪ (*formal*) ***It should be remembered*** [=it is important to keep in mind] that he made many important contributions to the campaign. [*no obj*] I don't need to write it down, I'll *remember*. — see also ***remember your manners*** at MANNER

4 [+ *obj*] **: to think about (someone who has died) in a respectful way** ▪ On this day, let us *remember* our nation's veterans. ▪ We should *remember* the victims of the tragedy. ▪ She is *remembered* for her contributions to physics.

5 [+ *obj*] **: to give money or a gift to (someone)** ▪ Her brother was *remembered* in her will. [=she wrote in her will that her brother should receive some of her things after her death] ▪ They *remembered* him on his birthday.

remember me to *old-fashioned* **— used to ask someone to give your greetings to another person** ▪ *Remember me to* your aunt when you see her today.

re•mem•brance /rɪˈmɛmbrəns/ *noun, pl* **-branc•es** *literary*

1 [*noncount*] **: the act of remembering a person, thing, or event** ▪ a time for *remembrance* — often + *of* ▪ The *remembrance of* his loss seemed to darken his mood.

2 [*noncount*] **: something that is done or made to honor the memory of a person, thing, or event — often + *of*** ▪ The dinner was held ***in remembrance of*** my mother.

3 [*count*] **: a memory of a person, thing, or event — often + *of*** ▪ I have many fond *remembrances of* my youth.

Remembrance Sunday *noun, pl* **~ -days** [*count, noncount*] *Brit* **: a holiday that is observed on the Sunday closest to November 11 to honor the people who were killed in the two World Wars — called also *Remembrance Day***

re•mind /rɪˈmaɪnd/ *verb* **-minds; -mind•ed; -mind•ing** [+ *obj*] **: to make (someone) think about something again : to cause (someone) to remember something** ▪ She'll forget to call the doctor if you don't *remind* her. ▪ *Remind* me to buy some groceries after work. ▪ I constantly have to be *reminded* how to pronounce her name. ▪ I had to *remind* him that we were supposed to leave early. ▪ The audience was *reminded* to turn their cell phones off in the theater. ▪ (*humorous*) "We have a test tomorrow." "***Don't remind me.***" [=I don't want to hear about it because it's something unpleasant that I'm trying not to think about] ▪ The mail just arrived. ***That reminds me***, did you mail that letter I gave you yesterday?

remind of [*phrasal verb*] **1 *remind (someone) of (something)*** **: to cause (someone) to remember (something)** ▪ I *reminded* him *of* his promise to help me. [=I reminded him that he had promised to help me] ▪ This song *reminds* me *of* our wedding day. **2 *remind (someone) of (someone or something)*** **: to cause (someone) to think of (a similar person or thing)** ▪ He *reminds* me *of* my uncle. [=he is like my uncle; he looks/acts like my uncle] ▪ This painting *reminds* me *of* a picture I saw at the Metropolitan Museum.

re•mind•er /rɪˈmaɪndɚ/ *noun, pl* **-ers** [*count*] **: something that causes you to remember or to think about something** ▪ The accident was a sobering *reminder* of the dangers of climbing. ▪ a constant *reminder* of his past ▪ She sent him an e-mail *reminder* about the meeting. ▪ I wrote myself a *reminder* to take out the trash.

rem•i•nisce /ˌrɛməˈnɪs/ *verb* **-nisc•es; -nisced; -nisc•ing** [*no obj*] **: to talk, think, or write about things that happened in the past** ▪ He *reminisced* with old buddies at his high school reunion. ▪ She *reminisced* about her time in Europe.

rem•i•nis•cence /ˌrɛməˈnɪsn̩s/ *noun, pl* **-cenc•es** *formal*

1 [*count*] **: a story that someone tells about something that happened in the past — usually plural; often + *of*** ▪ I listened to my grandmother's *reminiscences of* her childhood.

2 [*noncount*] **: the act of remembering or telling about past experiences** ▪ a time for *reminiscence*

rem•i•nis•cent /ˌrɛməˈnɪsn̩t/ *adj*

1 : reminding you of someone or something else : similar to something else — often + *of* ▪ His singing is *reminiscent of* the crooners of the '40s and '50s. ▪ It had a taste *reminiscent of* spinach.

2 *always used before a noun, literary + formal* **: thinking about the past : having many thoughts of the past** ▪ I'm in a *reminiscent* mood.

re•miss /rɪˈmɪs/ *adj* [*more* ~; *most* ~] *formal* **: not showing enough care and attention** ▪ It would be *remiss* (of me) if I forgot to mention them in my lecture. ▪ I was *remiss* in paying my bills. [=I neglected to pay my bills]

re•mis•sion /rɪˈmɪʃən/ *noun, pl* **-sions**

1 : a period of time during a serious illness when the patient's health improves [*noncount*] Her cancer has ***gone into remission***. = Her cancer is ***in remission***. [=the symptoms of her cancer have become much less severe] ▪ The patient is *in remission*. [*count*] a temporary *remission* of symptoms

2 *formal* **: the act of reducing or canceling the amount of money that you owe** [*noncount*] The university offers tuition *remission* to teaching assistants. [=teaching assistants do not have to pay tuition] [*count*] tax *remissions* ▪ fee *remissions*

3 [*noncount*] *Brit* **: the reduction of a prison sentence** ▪ He was given *remission* for good behavior.

[1]re•mit /rɪˈmɪt/ *verb* **-mits; -mit•ted; -mit•ting** [+ *obj*] *formal*

R

1 : to send (money) as a payment ▪ Please *remit* $1,000 upon receipt of this letter. ▪ Payment can be *remitted* by check.
2 : to cancel or free someone from (a punishment, debt, etc.) ▪ The governor *remitted* the remainder of her life sentence.
remit to [*phrasal verb*] ***remit (something) to (someone or something)*** : to send (something, such as a dispute or a court case) to an authority that can make a decision about it — often used as *(be) remitted to* ▪ The matter *was remitted to* a new committee for discussion. ▪ The case *was remitted to* the state court.

²remit *noun, pl* **-mits** [*count*] *Brit, formal* : an area of responsibility and authority — usually singular ▪ The problem was outside/beyond our *remit.* ▪ She will have a wide *remit* to reform the company.

re·mit·tance /rɪˈmɪtn̩s/ *noun, pl* **-tanc·es** *formal*
1 [*count*] : an amount of money that is sent as a payment for something ▪ Please return the form with your *remittance.* [=*payment*]
2 [*noncount*] : the act of sending money as a payment for something ▪ *Remittance* can be made by check or credit card.

re·mix /ˈriːˌmɪks/ *noun, pl* **-mix·es** [*count*] : a new or different version of a recorded song that is made by changing or adding to the original recording of the song ▪ dance *remixes* of rock songs
– re·mix /riˈmɪks/ *verb* **-mix·es; -mixed; -mix·ing** [+ *obj*] ▪ He *remixed* the song for the new album. **– re·mix·er** *noun, pl* **-ers** [*count*] ▪ He is the band's *remixer.*

rem·nant /ˈrɛmnənt/ *noun, pl* **-nants** [*count*]
1 : the part of something that is left when the other parts are gone — usually plural; often + *of* ▪ These villages are the last surviving *remnants of* a great civilization. ▪ A new police force was formed from the *remnants of* the army.
2 : a small piece of cloth that is left after the rest of the cloth has been sold ▪ *Remnants* go on sale next week.

re·mod·el /riˈmɑːdl/ *verb* **-els;** *US* **-eled** *or Brit* **-elled;** *US* **-el·ing** *or Brit* **-el·ling** [+ *obj*] : to change the structure, shape, or appearance of (something) ▪ We *remodeled* the kitchen last year.
– remodeled (*US*) *or Brit* **remodelled** *adj* ▪ newly *remodeled* [=*renovated*] bathrooms **– remodeling** (*US*) *or Brit* **remodelling** *noun* [*noncount*] ▪ The office will be closed during *remodeling.*

re·mold (*US*) *or Brit* **re·mould** /riˈmoʊld/ *verb* **-molds; -mold·ed; -mold·ing** [+ *obj*] *formal* : to change (something, such as an idea, a system, or a habit) ▪ She resisted the efforts to *remold* her image. ▪ The company needs to ***remold itself*** [=transform itself] into a smaller and more competitive business.

re·mon·strance /rɪˈmɑːnstrəns/ *noun, pl* **-stranc·es** *formal* : a protest or complaint about something [*count*] an angry *remonstrance* [*noncount*] Many residents wrote letters of *remonstrance* to city officials.

re·mon·strate /ˈrɛmənˌstreɪt, rɪˈmɑːnˌstreɪt/ *verb* **-strates; -strat·ed; -strat·ing** [*no obj*] *formal* : to disagree and argue or complain about something ▪ He got angry when I politely *remonstrated* with him about littering.
– re·mon·stra·tion /ˌrɛmənˈstreɪʃən, rəˌmɑːnˈstreɪʃən/ *noun, pl* **-tions** [*count*] an official *remonstration* [=*protest, complaint*] [*noncount*] letters of *remonstration*

re·morse /rɪˈmoɚs/ *noun* [*noncount*] : a feeling of being sorry for doing something bad or wrong in the past : a feeling of guilt ▪ I could forgive him for what he did if he showed some *remorse.* — often + *for* ▪ She was filled with *remorse for* not visiting her father more often. [=she was very sorry that she did not visit her father more often] ▪ I felt a bit of *remorse* [=*regret*] *for* being so impatient.
– re·morse·ful /rɪˈmoɚsfəl/ *adj* ▪ She seemed truly *remorseful* for what she had done. **– re·morse·ful·ly** /rɪˈmoɚsfəli/ *adv* ▪ She *remorsefully* pleaded guilty.

re·morse·less /rɪˈmoɚsləs/ *adj*
1 : very cruel and showing no pity or sympathy for other people : MERCILESS ▪ a *remorseless* murderer
2 : continuing in a way that does not end or that seems impossible to stop ▪ his *remorseless* pursuit of justice
– re·morse·less·ly *adv* ▪ She attacked her opponent's position *remorselessly.*

re·mort·gage /riˈmoɚgɪʤ/ *verb* **-gag·es; -gaged; -gag·ing** : to get a second mortgage on a house or to change the mortgage that you have [+ *obj*] We had to *remortgage* our house. [*no obj*] I'd like to *remortgage* at a lower rate.

¹re·mote /rɪˈmoʊt/ *adj* **re·mot·er; -est** [*or more* ~; *most* ~]
1 a : far away : DISTANT ▪ She enjoys reading about *remote* lands. ▪ *remote* galaxies **b** : far away from other people, houses, cities, etc. ▪ a *remote* island/village ▪ The mission is to transport medical supplies to *remote* areas/places/regions of the globe.
2 *always used before a noun* : far away in time : happening a long time ago or far into the future ▪ a tradition that dates back to *remote* antiquity ▪ an invention that may be available in the *remote* future
3 : very small : SLIGHT ▪ There is a *remote* possibility that I'll be free Friday night. ▪ a ***remote chance*** [=a very small possibility]
4 *always used before a noun* : not closely related ▪ *remote* ancestors
5 : very different *from* something ▪ Their traditions are *remote from* our own.
6 : not friendly or involved with other people : distant or cold in manner ▪ She became very *remote* in her old age.
7 *always used before a noun* **a** *computers* : connected to a computer system from another place ▪ a *remote* computer/machine/terminal ▪ *Remote* users cannot access these files. ▪ The computer is capable of ***remote access.*** [=it is possible to become connected to this computer from another place] **b** : capable of being controlled from a distance ▪ a *remote* camera ▪ *remote* sensors
– re·mote·ness *noun* [*noncount*] ▪ The *remoteness* of his location made it hard for rescuers to reach him. ▪ his *remoteness* as a father

²remote *noun, pl* **-motes** [*count*] *informal* : REMOTE CONTROL

remote control *noun, pl* ~ **-trols**
1 [*count*] : a small device that is used to operate electronic equipment (such as a television) from a distance by using electronic signals ▪ Where did you put the *remote control*? — called also (*informal*) *remote,* (*chiefly US, informal*) *clicker,* (*Brit, informal*) *zapper*
2 [*noncount*] : a process or system that makes it possible to control something from a distance by using electronic signals ▪ The bomb was detonated by *remote control.* ▪ a DVD player with *remote control* ▪ a *remote control* camera
– remote–controlled *adj* ▪ a *remote-controlled* toy car

re·mote·ly /rɪˈmoʊtli/ *adv*
1 : to a very small degree ▪ It's *remotely* [=*barely*] possible that they could have met, but I don't think it's very likely. — usually used in negative statements ▪ I've never seen anything *remotely* like it. [=never seen anything that was like it at all] ▪ I wasn't even *remotely* involved in that decision. ▪ Nothing he said was even *remotely* true. [=nothing he said was at all true]
2 *technical* : from a distance ▪ I can log in *remotely* to my computer. [=I can log in to my computer by using another computer that is connected to it] ▪ a *remotely* operated submarine ▪ They can *remotely* monitor the building. ▪ The door can be unlocked *remotely.*

remote sensing *noun* [*noncount*] *technical* : the use of satellites to collect information about and take photographs of the Earth

remould *Brit spelling of* REMOLD

re·mount /riˈmaʊnt/ *verb* **-mounts; -mount·ed; -mount·ing**
1 [+ *obj*] : to attach (something) to a support again ▪ a diamond *remounted* in a new setting ▪ I had to *remount* the tires on my car. ▪ I had trouble *remounting* the door.
2 : to get on a horse, bicycle, motorcycle, etc., again after getting off or falling off [*no obj*] She fell off her horse but quickly *remounted.* [+ *obj*] She *remounted* her horse and finished her ride.

re·mov·able /rɪˈmuːvəbəl/ *adj* : able to be removed : made to be detached or taken out ▪ The hard drive is *removable.* ▪ I'm looking for a digital camera with a *removable* lens.

re·mov·al /rɪˈmuːvəl/ *noun, pl* **-als**
1 [*noncount*] : the act of moving or taking something away from a place ▪ We arranged for the *removal* of the old car. ▪ The city is having problems with trash/waste/snow *removal.* ▪ Surgical *removal* of the tumor might be necessary.
2 [*noncount*] : the act of making something go away so that it no longer exists ▪ stain *removal* ▪ the *removal* of doubt
3 [*noncount*] : the act of forcing someone to leave a job ▪ *removal* from office ▪ The scandal resulted in the director's *removal.* [=*dismissal*]
4 [*count*] *Brit* : the act of moving furniture and other things from one house to another ▪ Local *removals* [=(*US*) *moves*] can be done cheaply. — often used before another noun ▪ a

removal [=(*US*) *moving*] company • *removal* expenses

removal van *noun, pl* ~ **vans** [*count*] *Brit* : MOVING VAN

¹re•move /rɪˈmu:v/ *verb* **-moves; -moved; -mov•ing** [+ *obj*]

1 : to move or take (something) away from a place • *Remove* the trash from the front yard. • My tonsils were *removed* when I was five years old. • Trees help to *remove* carbon dioxide from the atmosphere.

2 : to cause (something) to no longer exist • These new findings should *remove* any doubt about his innocence. • What's a good way to *remove* stains from a silk dress? • The new law would *remove* obstacles to obtaining a work permit.

3 : to force (someone) to leave a job : to dismiss (someone) from a job • He was *removed* from office.

4 *somewhat formal* **:** to take off (something, such as a piece of your clothing) • Please *remove* your shoes. • He *removed* his sunglasses.

²remove *noun, pl* **-moves** *formal* : a distance separating one person or thing from another — used with *at* [*count*] — usually singular • His anger remains, even *at* a *remove* of 20 years. [=even after 20 years have passed] • He keeps the children *at* a safe *remove* from the dangers of the city. [*noncount*] She thrives when she's *at* some *remove* from mainstream society.

removed *adj, not used before a noun*

1 : away from something : DISTANT • We're looking for an apartment somewhat *removed* from the noise of downtown.

2 : of a younger or older generation • The child of your first cousin is your first cousin once *removed.*

far removed from : very different from (something) • a pampered life *far removed from* the poverty of his youth • Hockey and soccer are not that *far removed from* each other.

re•mov•er /rɪˈmu:vɚ/ *noun, pl* **-ers** [*count*]

1 : something (such as a chemical) that removes something unwanted from something else • paint/stain *remover* • nail polish *remover*

2 *Brit* **:** a person or company that is hired to take furniture and possessions from one place to another — usually plural • Don't let the *removers* [=(*US*) *movers*] pack your dishes.

REM sleep *noun* [*noncount*] : a stage of sleep during which you dream and your eyes make quick movements — called also *rapid eye movement sleep, REM*

re•mu•ner•ate /rɪˈmju:nəˌreɪt/ *verb* **-ates; -at•ed; -at•ing** [+ *obj*] *formal* : to pay someone for work that has been done • They were *remunerated* for their services. = Their services were *remunerated.*

re•mu•ner•a•tion /rɪˌmju:nəˈreɪʃən/ *noun, pl* **-tions** *formal* : an amount of money paid to someone for the work that person has done [*noncount*] an increase in *remuneration* • a *remuneration* package [*count*] She was given generous *remunerations* for her work.

re•mu•ner•a•tive /rɪˈmju:nərətɪv/ *adj* [*more* ~; *most* ~] *formal* : paying a lot of money : PROFITABLE • Our investors are seeking more *remunerative* opportunities.

re•nais•sance /ˈrɛnəˌsɑ:ns, *Brit* rɪˈneɪsn̩s/ *noun*

1 ***the Renaissance*** **:** the period of European history between the 14th and 17th centuries when there was a new interest in science and in ancient art and literature especially in Italy • a book on *the Renaissance* — often used as *Renaissance* before another noun • a *Renaissance* scholar/painter • *Renaissance* art

2 [*singular*] **a :** a situation or period of time when there is a new interest in something that has not been popular in a long time • The magazine began when the country was undergoing a culinary *renaissance.* [=*rebirth*] • The city has experienced a *renaissance* [=*renewal, revival*] of interest in historic preservation. **b :** a period of new growth or activity • the city's economic *renaissance* [=*revival, rebirth*]

Renaissance man *noun, pl* ~ **men** [*count*] : a man who is interested in and knows a lot about many things

Renaissance woman *noun, pl* ~ **-men** [*count*] : a woman who is interested in and knows a lot about many things

re•nal /ˈri:nl/ *adj, always used before a noun, medical* : relating to or involving the kidneys • *renal* disease/failure

re•name /riˈneɪm/ *verb* **-names; -named; -nam•ing** [+ *obj*] : to give a new name to (someone or something) • Ceylon was *renamed* Sri Lanka in 1972. • The bridge is being *renamed* in honor of the city's former mayor.

re•na•scent /rɪˈnæsn̩t/ *adj, formal* : existing, happening, or popular again • *renascent* inflation/nationalism

rend /ˈrɛnd/ *verb* **rends; rent** /ˈrɛnt/ *also US* **rend•ed; rend•ing** [+ *obj*] *literary* : to tear (something) into pieces with force or violence • They *rent* the cloth to shreds. • mourners *rending* their clothes/garments in grief — sometimes used figuratively • a family *rent* [=*torn apart*] by divorce

ren•der /ˈrɛndɚ/ *verb* **-ders; -dered; -der•ing** [+ *obj*]

1 *formal* **:** to cause (someone or something) to be in a specified condition • Depression can *render* a person helpless. • Both passengers were *rendered* unconscious in the accident. • The sight of her *rendered* him speechless. • The virus *rendered* the computer useless.

2 *formal* **:** to give (something) to someone • *render* an apology • He witnessed a car accident and stopped to *render* aid/assistance. • a fee/payment ***for services rendered*** [=for something that a person, company, etc., has done for you]

3 *law* **:** to officially report or declare (a legal judgment, such as a verdict) • The jury *rendered* a verdict of not guilty.

4 *formal* **:** to present or perform (something) • The novel *renders* a portrait of life in ancient Rome. • poems *rendered* in the original German • perfectly *rendered* songs

5 *formal* **:** TRANSLATE • *render* Latin into English • The word was incorrectly *rendered* as "light."

6 : to melt (fat) especially as a way of removing it from meat • It's important to *render* the fat from the duck.

7 : to change (something) *into* a different substance by some process • trees *rendered into* wood pulp • animal fat *rendered into* tallow

ren•der•ing /ˈrɛndərɪŋ/ *noun, pl* **-ings** [*count*] *formal*

1 : a performance of a song, play, etc. • She gave an emotional *rendering* [=*rendition*] of the national anthem.

2 : a description, explanation, or translation • The book is a faithful *rendering* of life in a rural community. • a new *rendering* of the text in English

¹ren•dez•vous /ˈrɑ:ndɪˌvu:/ *noun, pl* **ren•dez•vous** /ˈrɑ:ndɪˌvu:z/ [*count*]

1 : a meeting with someone that is arranged for a particular time and place and that is often secret • a romantic *rendezvous* • He was late for their *rendezvous.*

2 a : a place where people agree to meet at a particular time • The restaurant will be our *rendezvous.* **b :** a place where many people go to spend time • This park/café is a popular/favorite *rendezvous* [=*hangout, haunt*] for local teens.

²ren•dez•vous /ˈrɑ:ndɪˌvu:/ *verb* **-vouses** /-ˌvu:z/; **-voused** /-ˌvu:d/; **-vous•ing** /-ˌvu:wɪŋ/ [*no obj*] : to meet at a particular time and place • The cousins *rendezvoused* in New York before they flew to London.

ren•di•tion /rɛnˈdɪʃən/ *noun, pl* **-tions** [*count*]

1 : a performance of something • a moving *rendition* of an old gospel song

2 : TRANSLATION • a new *rendition* of the text in English

ren•e•gade /ˈrɛnɪˌgeɪd/ *noun, pl* **-gades** [*count*]

1 : a person who leaves one group, religion, etc., and joins another that opposes it • *renegades* from the Republican/Democratic Party — usually used before another noun • a *renegade* Republican/Democrat

2 : someone or something that causes trouble and cannot be controlled • stories about pirates and *renegades* on the high seas — often used before another noun • drugs that attack *renegade* cells in cancer patients

re•nege /rɪˈnɛg, *Brit* rɪˈni:g/ *verb* **-neges; -neged; -neg•ing** [*no obj*] : to refuse to do something that you promised or agreed to do • They had promised to pay her tuition but later *reneged.* — usually + *on* • They *reneged on* their promise to pay her tuition.

re•ne•go•ti•ate /ˌri:nɪˈgoʊʃiˌeɪt/ *verb* **-ates; -at•ed; -at•ing :** to discuss again the details of a formal agreement especially in order to change them : to negotiate (something) again [+ *obj*] *renegotiate* a contract/lease/agreement [*no obj*] The deal is done. I won't *renegotiate.*

– re•ne•go•ti•a•tion /ˌri:nɪˈgoʊʃiˌeɪʃən/ *noun, pl* **-tions** [*count, noncount*]

re•new /rɪˈnu:, *Brit* rɪˈnju:/ *verb* **-news; -newed; -new•ing** [+ *obj*]

1 : to make (something) new, fresh, or strong again • When you sleep, your body has a chance to *renew* itself. • This discussion has *renewed* my hope of finding a solution to the problem. • At the start of each school year, we *renew* our commitment to helping students succeed.

2 : to make (a promise, vow, etc.) again • She *renewed* her promise to come see me. • They celebrated their 25th wedding anniversary by *renewing* their wedding vows.

3 : to begin (something) again especially with more force or enthusiasm • They have *renewed* their efforts to find a peace-

R

ful solution. ▪ The incident has *renewed* hostilities between the groups. ▪ We hope to *renew* [=(more commonly) *resume*] negotiations soon. ▪ They recently ***renewed their acquaintance/friendship*** after more than 10 years apart. ▪ If you haven't listened to this music since the 1960s, it's time to *renew your acquaintance* with these songs.
4 : **to put in a fresh supply of (something) :** REPLACE ▪ You should *renew* the water in the fish tank once a week.
5 : **to cause (something) to continue to be effective or valid for an additional period of time** ▪ The landlord agreed to *renew* our lease for another year. ▪ You can *renew* your driver's license online. ▪ He forgot to *renew* his passport and now it's expired. ▪ You should *renew* your magazine subscription before it runs out. ▪ She *renewed* the library book. [=she had the library extend the period of time that she can borrow the book]
– **renewed** *adj* ▪ She wrote with *renewed* [=*fresh*] enthusiasm after meeting with her editor. ▪ We felt *renewed* [=*restored, revived*] after a good night's sleep. ▪ There was more violence in spite of *renewed* efforts to make peace. ▪ We have a *renewed* sense of pride in our town. ▪ High fuel prices have led to *renewed* interest in electric cars.

re·new·able /rɪˈnuːwəbəl, *Brit* rɪˈnjuːwəbəl/ *adj*
1 : **able to be extended for another time period : able to be renewed** ▪ a *renewable* life insurance policy ▪ a *renewable* lease
2 : **restored or replaced by natural processes : able to be replaced by nature** ▪ Forests are *renewable* natural resources, but they must be treated with care. ▪ Wind and water are *renewable* fuel sources. — opposite NONRENEWABLE

re·new·al /rɪˈnuːwəl, *Brit* rɪˈnjuːwəl/ *noun, pl* **-als**
1 : **the act of extending the period of time when something is effective or valid : the act of renewing something** [*count*] The lease calls for yearly *renewals*. ▪ License *renewals* can be done online. ▪ You can get a 10 percent savings on subscription *renewals*. [*noncount*] His contract is ***up for renewal*** at the end of the season. [=it will be time to consider renewing his contract at the end of the season]
2 : **the state of being made new, fresh, or strong again : the state of being renewed** [*singular*] High fuel prices have led to a *renewal* of interest in electric cars. [*noncount*] She uses flowers in her art as symbols of rebirth and *renewal*. — see also URBAN RENEWAL

re·nom·i·nate /riˈnɑːməˌneɪt/ *verb* **-nates; -nat·ed; -nat·ing** [+ *obj*] **: to nominate (someone) again** ▪ The President is likely to be *renominated* for a second term. ▪ The President has *renominated* a judge that Congress previously rejected.
– **re·nom·i·na·tion** /riˌnɑːməˈneɪʃən/ *noun, pl* **-tions** [*count, noncount*]

re·nounce /rɪˈnaʊns/ *verb* **-nounc·es; -nounced; -nounc·ing** [+ *obj*]
1 : **to say especially in a formal or official way that you will no longer have or accept (something) : to formally give up (something)** ▪ The king *renounced* [=*abdicated*] the throne. ▪ She *renounced* her inheritance. ▪ We will not deal with them until they *renounce* (the use of) violence/terrorism.
2 : **to say in a formal or definite way that you refuse to follow, obey, or support (someone or something) any longer** ▪ Many of his former supporters have *renounced* him. ▪ He *renounced* his old way of life. ▪ psychiatrists who *renounce* [=*reject*] the teachings of Freud

ren·o·vate /ˈrɛnəˌveɪt/ *verb* **-vates; -vat·ed; -vat·ing** [+ *obj*] **: to make changes and repairs to (an old house, building, room, etc.) so that it is back in good condition** ▪ *renovate* an old farmhouse ▪ a newly *renovated* theater ▪ It's an old factory that has been *renovated* as office space. ▪ We *renovated* the kitchen three years ago.
– **ren·o·va·tion** /ˌrɛnəˈveɪʃən/ *noun, pl* ~ **tions** [*count*] a costly *renovation* — often plural ▪ The restaurant is closed for *renovations*. [*noncount*] The park will be closed during *renovation*. – **ren·o·va·tor** /ˈrɛnəˌveɪtɚ/ *noun, pl* **-tors** [*count*] ▪ good advice for home *renovators*

re·nown /rɪˈnaʊn/ *noun* [*noncount*] *somewhat formal* **: great fame and respect** ▪ He achieved/gained/won great *renown* for his discoveries. ▪ Her photographs have earned her international *renown*. ▪ writers ***of renown*** [=renowned writers]

re·nowned /rɪˈnaʊnd/ *adj* [*more* ~; *most* ~] **: known and admired by many people for some special quality or achievement** ▪ a restaurant *renowned* for its wine list ▪ a *renowned* scientist

¹rent /ˈrɛnt/ *noun, pl* **rents : money that you pay in return for being able to use property and especially to live in an apartment, house, etc., that belongs to someone else** [*noncount*] How much do you pay in *rent*? ▪ *Rent* is due on the first of the month. [*count*] Our landlord raised the *rent*. ▪ *Rents* near the college have risen.
for rent chiefly US **: available for use in return for payment : available to be rented** ▪ houses *for rent* [=*to let*] ▪ bicycles/costumes/rooms *for rent*
– compare ⁴RENT

²rent *verb* **rents; rent·ed; rent·ing**
1 : **to pay money in return for being able to use (something that belongs to someone else)** [+ *obj*] We *rented* our friends' cottage for the month of August. ▪ (*US*) We *rented* tables and chairs for the wedding. ▪ (*US*) We *rented* [=(*Brit*) *hired*] a car at the airport. ▪ (*US*) Do you want to *rent* a movie/DVD/video tonight? [*no obj*] When they first moved to town, they *rented*. [=they lived in a house, apartment, etc., that was rented] ▪ Do you own or *rent*?
2 [+ *obj*] **: to allow someone to use (something) in return for payment** ▪ They *rented* [=*let*] their cottage to friends. ▪ We *rented* them the upstairs apartment in our house. ▪ We *rent* (out) a room in our house to a college student.
3 [*no obj*] **: to be available for use in return for payment : to be for rent** ▪ The cottage *rents* for $400 a week.
– **rent·able** /ˈrɛntəbəl/ *adj* ▪ *rentable* storage space ▪ The house is *rentable* in the winter. – **rent·er** *noun, pl* **-ers** [*count*] ▪ *Renters* don't get the tax breaks that home owners get. ▪ The company is the largest car *renter* in the area.

³rent *past tense and past participle of* REND

⁴rent *noun, pl* **rents** [*count*] *formal + literary* **: a hole made by tearing something** ▪ a *rent* in the fabric — compare ¹RENT

rent·al /ˈrɛntl̩/ *noun, pl* **-als**
1 : **the amount of money paid or collected as rent** [*count*] — usually singular ▪ The average *rental* is $400 per month. [*noncount*] thousands of dollars paid in *rental* ▪ *rental* fees/income ▪ (*Brit*) ***line rental*** [=money that you pay to use a telephone line]
2 : **the act of renting something** [*count*] There are restrictions against *rentals* to people with pets. [*noncount*] The movie is available for *rental*. ▪ a *rental* agreement
3 [*count*] *chiefly US* **: something that can be rented** ▪ Boat *rentals* are available on the island. ▪ a two-bedroom *rental* ▪ I had a *rental* while my car was being repaired. ▪ a *rental* car

rent control *noun* [*noncount*] *chiefly US* **: a system in which the government determines how much rent can be charged for an apartment, house, etc.**
– **rent–controlled** *adj* ▪ *rent-controlled* housing ▪ a *rent-controlled* apartment

re·nun·ci·a·tion /rɪˌnʌnsiˈeɪʃən/ *noun, pl* **-tions : the act of renouncing something or someone** [*count*] the king's *renunciation* of the throne [*noncount*] *renunciation* of violence ▪ Their vows include *renunciation* of all wealth.

re·open /riˈoʊpən/ *verb* **-opens; -opened; -open·ing**
1 : **to open again after being closed** [*no obj*] The restaurant will *reopen* in April. ▪ I'm sorry, but the store is closed. We *reopen* at nine on Monday. ▪ The cut on his knee *reopened* when he tried to run. [+ *obj*] The company announced plans to *reopen* its Detroit factory. ▪ a procedure to *reopen* a clogged artery — sometimes used figuratively ▪ Telling that story will only ***reopen old wounds***. [=cause people to think of things from the past that make them sad, angry, etc.]
2 a : **to start (something) again after a period without activity** [+ *obj*] They *reopened* [=*resumed*] the negotiations. ▪ The district attorney *reopened* the murder case because new evidence was found. [*no obj*] The negotiations have *reopened*. **b** [+ *obj*] *US* **: to discuss and make changes to (something that had been considered finished) again** ▪ He wants the team to *reopen* his contract.
– **reopening** *noun* [*singular*] The mayor was present for the library's official *reopening*. ▪ a *reopening* of negotiations [*noncount*] The factory is set for *reopening*.

re·or·der /riˈoɚdɚ/ *verb* **-ders; -dered; -der·ing**
1 : **to order (something) again** [+ *obj*] I had to *reorder* the shirt because they sent the wrong size. ▪ The book sold out the first day, and the store *reordered* 500 copies. [*no obj*] Call us when you're ready to *reorder*.
2 [+ *obj*] **: to arrange (something) in a different order** ▪ You need to *reorder* your priorities. ▪ The coach *reordered* the batting lineup. ▪ After her husband's death, she *reordered* her life.

re·or·ga·nize *also Brit* **re·or·ga·nise** /riˈoɚgəˌnaɪz/ *verb* **-niz·es; -nized; -niz·ing : to organize (something) again or in a different way** [+ *obj*] The staff is still *reorganizing* the

files according to the new system. • The company was *reorganized* after it went bankrupt. [*no obj*] The company is *reorganizing* as a corporation. • The club had to *reorganize* when most of its members moved away.
– **re·or·ga·ni·za·tion** *also Brit* **re·or·ga·ni·sa·tion** /riˌoɚgənəˈzeɪʃən, *Brit* riˌɔ:gəˌnaɪˈzeɪʃən/ *noun* [*noncount*]

¹rep /ˈrɛp/ *noun, pl* **reps** [*count*] *informal* : REPRESENTATIVE • sales *reps* — compare ²REP, ³REP

²rep *noun, pl* **reps** [*count*] *informal* : a motion or exercise that is repeated — usually plural • When he does push-ups, he does 3 sets of 12 *reps*. [=*repetitions*] — compare ¹REP, ³REP

³rep *noun, pl* **reps** [*count*] *US slang* : REPUTATION • He's worried about protecting his *rep*. — compare ¹REP, ²REP

Rep. *abbr* **1** Republican **2** representative • a letter to *Rep.* Richard Jones

re·pack·age /riˈpækɪʤ/ *verb* **-ag·es; -aged; -ag·ing** [+ *obj*]
1 : to put (something) into a new package • Large pieces of meat are cut and *repackaged* at the butcher's shop.
2 : to present (something) to the public in a new or more attractive way • *repackage* newspaper comic strips as books • TV studios *repackage* real-life dramas as entertainment.

¹re·pair /rɪˈpeɚ/ *verb* **-pairs; -paired; -pair·ing** [+ *obj*]
1 : to put (something that is broken or damaged) back into good condition : FIX • He *repairs* clocks. • This old lawn mower isn't worth *repairing*. • She *repaired* an old chest that was coming apart. • He underwent surgery to *repair* a torn ligament in his knee. • There was no hope of *repairing* the damage—she had to buy a new car.
2 : to correct or improve (something, such as a relationship or reputation) • The school is trying to *repair* its damaged reputation. • Can their marriage be *repaired*?
– compare ³REPAIR
– **re·pair·able** /rɪˈperəbəl/ *adj* • The computer is not *repairable*. – **re·pair·er** /rɪˈperɚ/ *noun, pl* **-ers** [*count*] • a *repairer* of clocks

²repair *noun, pl* **-pairs**
1 : the act or process of repairing something [*noncount*] The roof is in need of *repair*. [=the roof needs to be repaired; the roof is damaged, in poor condition, etc.] • a shoe/car *repair* shop • The car was damaged ***beyond repair***. [=the car was so damaged that it could not be repaired] [*count*] The *repairs* were expensive. • We had to ***make repairs*** to the roof. • He *made* a few *repairs* to the stairs.
2 [*noncount*] : a specified physical condition • His job is to keep the buildings in good *repair*. [=in good condition] • The roof is in poor *repair*. • The fence is in excellent *repair*.

³repair *verb* **-pairs; -paired; -pairing**
repair to [*phrasal verb*] ***repair to (a place)*** *old-fashioned + formal* : to go to (a place) • After dinner, the guests *repaired to* the drawing room for coffee. • (*humorous*) Shall we *repair to* the coffee shop?
– compare ¹REPAIR

re·pair·man /rɪˈpeɚˌmæn/ *noun, pl* **-men** /-mən/ [*count*] : a person (especially a man) whose job is to repair things • a TV *repairman*

rep·a·ra·ble /ˈrɛpərəbəl/ *adj, formal* : capable of being repaired • The roof is *reparable*. [=(more commonly) *repairable*] • The situation is serious but *reparable*. — opposite IRREPARABLE

rep·a·ra·tion /ˌrɛpəˈreɪʃən/ *noun, pl* **-tions**
1 ***reparations*** [*plural*] : money that a country or group that loses a war pays because of the damage, injury, deaths, etc., it has caused • The country paid millions in *reparations*.
2 *formal* : something that is done or given as a way of correcting a mistake that you have made or a bad situation that you have caused [*noncount*] They've offered no apologies and seem to have no thoughts of *reparation*. [*plural*] She says she's sorry and wants to ***make reparations***.

rep·ar·tee /ˌrɛpəˈti:, *Brit* ˌrɛpɑ:ˈti:/ *noun* [*noncount*] : conversation in which clever statements and replies are made quickly • The two comedians engaged in witty *repartee*.

re·past /rɪˈpæst, *Brit* rɪˈpɑ:st/ *noun, pl* **-pasts** [*count*] *literary* : MEAL • our traditional Thanksgiving *repast* • She offered us a light *repast* before we set out on our trip.

re·pa·tri·ate /riˈpeɪtriˌeɪt, *Brit* riˈpætriˌeɪt/ *verb* **-ates; -at·ed; -at·ing** [+ *obj*]
1 : to return (someone) to his or her own country • Countries are required to *repatriate* prisoners of war when conflict has ended. • *repatriated* refugees
2 *business* : to send (money) back to your own country • *repatriate* capital/profits
– **re·pa·tri·a·tion** /riˌpeɪtriˈeɪʃən, *Brit* riˌpætriˈeɪʃən/ *noun, pl* **-tions** [*count*] forced *repatriations* of political refugees [*noncount*] displaced persons seeking *repatriation*

re·pay /rɪˈpeɪ/ *verb* **-pays; -paid** /-ˈpeɪd/; **-pay·ing** [+ *obj*]
1 a : to pay back (money that you have borrowed) • *repay* a loan/debt • You can *repay* the mortgage over 30 years. **b** : to make a payment to (a person or organization that has loaned you money) • She would rather have to *repay* the bank than borrow from her parents and have to *repay* them.
2 a : to do or give something in return for (something) • How can I ever *repay* your kindness? • He *repaid* her kindness with cruelty. [=he was cruel to her after she had been kind to him] : to provide something in return for (work, effort, etc.) • Our efforts will be *repaid* [=our effort will have been worthwhile] if even one person who has never voted before votes on election day. **b** : to do something for (someone) in return for what that person has done for you • How can I ever *repay* you for your kindness?

re·pay·able /rɪˈpejəbəl/ *adj, not used before a noun* — used to describe how a loan can be or should be repaid • The loan is *repayable* in monthly installments. • These loans are *repayable* over 10 years.

re·pay·ment /rɪˈpeɪmənt/ *noun, pl* **-ments**
1 [*noncount*] : the act or process of paying back money that you have borrowed • *Repayment* on education loans begins when you are no longer a student. • The company will use the money for debt *repayment*. • a *repayment* plan/program
2 [*count*] *chiefly Brit* : an amount of money that is paid regularly in order to pay back a loan • monthly *repayments* [=*payments*]

re·peal /rɪˈpi:l/ *verb* **-peals; -pealed; -peal·ing** [+ *obj*] : to officially make (a law) no longer valid • The state legislature eventually *repealed* [=*rescinded*] the tax (law).
– **repeal** *noun, pl* **-peals** [*count, noncount*] • Most voters oppose the *repeal* of the law.

¹re·peat /rɪˈpi:t/ *verb* **-peats; -peat·ed; -peat·ing**
1 [+ *obj*] **a** : to say (something) again • Will you *repeat* the question? • He kept *repeating* the same thing over and over. • He often has to ask people to *repeat themselves* because he's a little deaf. • The group's message is one that ***bears repeating***. [=is important enough to state more than once] — sometimes used in speech to emphasize a word or phrase • "There are five—(I) *repeat*—five ways to do this." **b** : to say (something) after someone else has said it • *Repeat* after me: "I promise to do my best . . ." • You are simply *repeating*, in slightly different words, what has been said already.
2 [+ *obj*] : to say (something that you have memorized) : RECITE • My five-year-old can *repeat* her favorite stories word for word.
3 [+ *obj*] : to tell (something that you have heard) to someone else • Please don't *repeat* what I've told you (to anyone).
4 a : to make, do, or achieve (something) again [+ *obj*] The doctors had to *repeat* the operation. • We need to avoid *repeating* the mistakes of the past. • I'm not so sure the team can *repeat* the success they had last season. • I had trouble in school when I was young and had to *repeat* (the) third grade. [=I had to stay in the third grade for another year] • She's been absent so much that she is going to have to *repeat* her sophomore year. • They won the championship last year. Will ***history repeat itself*** this year? [=will the same thing happen again?; will they win the championship again this year?] [*no obj*] (*US*) • They're trying to *repeat* as champions this year. [=to win the championship again after winning it last year] **b** [+ *obj*] : to present (something) again • The workshop will be *repeated* in the fall. • The radio station broadcasts the show live on Saturday mornings, and then *repeats* it on Wednesday nights.
5 [*no obj*] : to begin again • The cycle *repeats* every 24 hours. • The pattern on the wallpaper *repeats* every foot or so.
repeat yourself : to say again what you have already said • I've already told you what to do, and I'm not going to *repeat myself*.

²re·peat /rɪˈpi:t, ˈri:ˌpi:t/ *noun, pl* **-peats** [*count*]
1 a : an occurrence in which something happens or is done again — usually + *of* • We're hoping to avoid a *repeat of* last year's budget problems. **b** : something that happens or is done again — usually used before another noun • a *repeat* win • The company gets a lot of *repeat* business. [=business from customers who have bought something from the company before] **c** : someone who does something again • Most of the customers are *repeats*. — usually used before another noun • *repeat* customers • There are tougher penalties for *re-*

R

peat offenders [=people who have committed a crime more than once]
2 : a radio or television show that is broadcast again • No, I don't want to watch that. It's a *repeat*.
3 *music* **:** a section of music that is repeated; *also* **:** the symbol in written music that shows that a section should be repeated

re·peat·able /rɪˈpi:təbəl/ *adj*
1 : appropriate to say again to someone else • He said things that aren't *repeatable* in front of the children. [=things that are too impolite, offensive, etc., to say again in front of the children]
2 : possible to do or make again • *repeatable* test results

re·peat·ed /rɪˈpi:təd/ *adj, always used before a noun* **:** said, done, or happening again and again • The landlord ignored her *repeated* requests to have the stove repaired. • He never succeeded in spite of *repeated* attempts. • *repeated* failures
– re·peat·ed·ly *adv* • I've told her *repeatedly* [=many times] to shut the gate when she goes out.

re·peat·er /rɪˈpi:tɚ/ *noun, pl* **-ers** [*count*] **:** a gun that fires several times without needing to be reloaded

re·pel /rɪˈpɛl/ *verb* **-pels; -pelled; -pel·ling** [*+ obj*]
1 : to keep (something) out or away • a fabric that *repels* water • The candle *repels* insects.
2 : to force (an enemy, attacker, etc.) to stop an attack and turn away • Their superior forces *repelled* the invasion.
3 *physics* **:** to force (something) to move away or apart • one electron *repelling* another • Two positive electrical charges *repel* each other. • Magnets can both *repel* and attract one another. — opposite ATTRACT 5
4 : to cause (someone) to feel disgust • Everyone was *repelled* [=*repulsed*] by the sight.

[1]re·pel·lent *also* **re·pel·lant** /rɪˈpɛlənt/ *adj*
1 : keeping something out or away • The candle has a *repellent* effect on insects. — often used in combination • a water-*repellent* fabric [=a fabric that repels water]
2 [*more ~; most ~*] *formal* **:** causing someone to feel disgust **:** REPULSIVE • a *repellent* sight • ideas that are *repellent* to me [=ideas that disgust me]
– re·pel·len·cy /rɪˈpɛlənsi/ *noun* [*noncount*] • a fabric known for its water *repellency*

[2]repellent *also* **repellant** *noun, pl* **-lents** *also* **-lants :** a substance that is used to keep something out or away [*noncount*] a can of insect *repellent* [*count*] a mosquito *repellent* • Coat the exterior with a water *repellent*.

re·pent /rɪˈpɛnt/ *verb* **-pents; -pent·ed; -pent·ing** *formal* **:** to feel or show that you are sorry for something bad or wrong that you did and that you want to do what is right [*no obj*] The preacher told us that we would be forgiven for our sins if we *repented*. • criminals who have *repented* for their crimes — sometimes + *of* • We must *repent of* our sins/wrongdoings. [*+ obj*] The preacher told us that we would be forgiven if we *repented* our sins.
– re·pen·tance /rɪˈpɛntn̩s/ *noun* [*noncount*] • His behavior is a sign of true *repentance*. • a holy day of fasting, prayer, and *repentance* **– re·pen·tant** /rɪˈpɛntn̩t/ *adj* [*more ~; most ~*] • He seemed genuinely *repentant*. • *repentant* sinners

re·per·cus·sion /ˌri:pɚˈkʌʃən/ *noun, pl* **-sions** [*count*] **:** something usually bad or unpleasant that happens as a result of an action, statement, etc., and that usually affects people for a long time — usually plural • We didn't expect the decision to have such serious/enormous/tremendous *repercussions*. [=*consequences*] • We did not consider the possible *repercussions* of our actions.

rep·er·toire /ˈrɛpɚˌtwɑɚ/ *noun, pl* **-toires** [*count*]
1 : all the plays, songs, dances, etc., that a performer or group of performers knows and can perform • The band's *repertoire* includes both classic and modern jazz.
2 : all the things that a person is able to do • He has a limited *repertoire* when it comes to cooking. — often + *of* • She has quite a *repertoire of* funny stories.

rep·er·to·ry /ˈrɛpɚˌtori, *Brit* ˈrɛpətri/ *noun, pl* **-ries**
1 : an organized group of actors that performs many kinds of plays with each play being performed for only a short time [*noncount*] She acted in *repertory* for many years. • *repertory* theater [*count*] Several *repertories* perform here.
2 [*count*] **:** REPERTOIRE 1 • a ballet company's *repertory*

rep·e·ti·tion /ˌrɛpəˈtɪʃən/ *noun, pl* **-tions**
1 [*noncount*] **:** the act of saying or doing something again **:** the act of repeating something • Sometimes *repetition* is necessary to drive a point home. • Find a synonym for "nice" in order to avoid *repetition*. [=using the same word again] • Children's songs involve lots of *repetition*. • I quit my job at the factory because I hated the mindless *repetition*.
2 [*count*] **:** something that is done or said again • the poem's rhythmic *repetitions* • Let's determine what caused the error in order to avoid a *repetition* (of it). • When he does push-ups, he does 3 sets of 12 *repetitions*. [=(*informal*) *reps*]

rep·e·ti·tious /ˌrɛpəˈtɪʃəs/ *adj* [*more ~; most ~*] **:** having parts, actions, etc., that are repeated many times in a way that is boring or unpleasant **:** having too much repetition • He was bored by the *repetitious* work. • *repetitious* lyrics • Her writing can be *repetitious*.
– rep·e·ti·tious·ly *adv* **– rep·e·ti·tious·ness** *noun* [*noncount*]

re·pet·i·tive /rɪˈpɛtətɪv/ *adj*
1 : happening again and again **:** repeated many times • an injury caused by *repetitive* wrist movements • a *repetitive* pattern • *repetitive* stress/strain
2 : having parts, actions, etc., that are repeated many times in a way that is boring or unpleasant **:** REPETITIOUS • She left the job because the work was too *repetitive*. • At the risk of being/sounding *repetitive*, I must remind you again to be careful.
– re·pet·i·tive·ly *adv* • an injury caused by *repetitively* flexing the wrist **– re·pet·i·tive·ness** *noun* [*noncount*]

re·phrase /riˈfreɪz/ *verb* **-phras·es; -phrased; -phras·ing** [*+ obj*] **:** to say or write (something) again using different words in order to make the meaning clearer • Let me *rephrase* the question.

re·place /rɪˈpleɪs/ *verb* **-plac·es; -placed; -plac·ing** [*+ obj*]
1 a : to be used instead of (something) • Will computers ever completely *replace* books? • Paper bags have been largely *replaced* by plastic bags. **b :** to do the job or duty of (someone) • She was hired to *replace* the previous manager.
2 : to put someone or something new in the place or position of (someone or something) • I *replaced* the old rug with a new one. • They recently *replaced* the old phone system. • The team's manager was *replaced* last season. • The patient needed a transfusion to *replace* lost blood. • They've appointed a new minister to *replace* the one who just retired. • I guess it's finally time to *replace* the stove.
3 : to put (something) where it was before • He carefully *replaced* the vase on the shelf.
– re·place·able /rɪˈpleɪsəbəl/ *adj* • Don't worry about the broken vase—it's easily *replaceable*. — opposite IRREPLACEABLE

re·place·ment /rɪˈpleɪsmənt/ *noun, pl* **-ments**
1 [*noncount*] **:** the act of replacing something • She underwent a hip *replacement*. [=a doctor replaced her hip with an artificial hip] • Is your old dictionary in need of *replacement*? [=do you need a new dictionary?] • Your car's *replacement* cost is less than the cost to repair it. [=it costs less to buy a new car than it does to fix your car]
2 [*count*] **:** a person or thing that replaces someone or something else • I'm training my *replacement*. • We need a *replacement* for our old vacuum cleaner. • Where can we get *replacement* parts for the tractor?

[1]re·play /ˈri:ˌpleɪ/ *noun, pl* **-plays** [*count*]
1 : a game that is played again because there was no winner in a previous game • They scheduled the *replay* for Saturday.
2 : a recording of something (such as an action in a sports event) that is being shown again • You could see the fumble on the *replay*. — see also ACTION REPLAY, INSTANT REPLAY
3 : an occurrence in which something happens or is done again **:** REPEAT — often + *of* • We don't want a *replay of* that unfortunate incident.

[2]re·play /riˈpleɪ/ *verb* **-plays; -played; -play·ing** [*+ obj*]
1 : to play (a game) again because there was no winner in a previous game • The tied game will be *replayed* on Saturday.
2 : to play (recorded images, sounds, etc.) • The game's highlights were *replayed* on the evening news. • The footage has been ***played and replayed*** on television. — often used figuratively • That night I *replayed* the conversation in my mind. [=I thought carefully about what had been said during the conversation]

re·plen·ish /rɪˈplɛnɪʃ/ *verb* **-ish·es; -ished; -ish·ing** [*+ obj*] *somewhat formal* **:** to fill or build up (something) again • An efficient staff of workers *replenished* the trays of appetizers almost as quickly as guests emptied them. • He *replenished* his supply of wood in preparation for the winter. • Drink this—you need to *replenish* your fluids after your

R

hike. • plants that *replenish* soil nutrients

– re·plen·ish·ment /rɪˈplɛnɪʃmənt/ *noun* [*noncount*] • The clinic's drug supply is in serious need of *replenishment*. • the *replenishment* of soil nutrients

re·plete /rɪˈpliːt/ *adj, not used before a noun, formal*

1 : having much or plenty of something **:** filled *with* something • The book is *replete with* photographs. • The country's history is *replete with* stories of people who became successful by working hard.

2 : having had plenty to eat **:** pleasantly full • feeling *replete*

rep·li·ca /ˈrɛplɪkə/ *noun, pl* **-cas** [*count*] **:** an exact or very close copy of something • We toured a *replica* of the ship. • It's an authentic/exact/faithful/perfect *replica* of an ancient Greek urn.

rep·li·cate /ˈrɛpləˌkeɪt/ *verb* **-cates; -cat·ed; -cat·ing** *formal* **:** to repeat or copy (something) exactly [+ *obj*] Scientists have failed to *replicate* [=*duplicate*] the results of his experiment. • They are working on computer-generated speech that *replicates* the human voice. • DNA *replicates* itself in the cell nucleus. [*no obj*] DNA *replicates* in the cell nucleus.

– rep·li·ca·tion /ˌrɛpləˈkeɪʃən/ *noun, pl* **-tions** [*count, noncount*]

¹re·ply /rɪˈplaɪ/ *verb* **-plies; -plied; -ply·ing :** to say, write, or do something as an answer or response [*no obj*] I wrote to him, but he never *replied*. [=wrote back] • He never *replied* [=*responded*] to my letter/e-mail/invitation. • I called out to them, but no one *replied*. • He didn't *reply* to her greeting. • The company has *replied* to the recent protests by posting an ad in the local newspaper. • She *replied* to the accusation with a stack of documents proving her innocence. [+ *obj*] "Do you feel better?" "A little," he *replied*. [=*answered*] • He *replied* politely that he felt a little better.

²reply *noun, pl* **-plies :** something said, written, or done as an answer or response [*count*] A timely *reply* will be appreciated. • His *reply* was rude. • The invitations have been sent, but we haven't received any *replies* yet. [*noncount*] I asked her what was wrong. ***In reply***, she handed me a letter. • He wrote a brief note ***in reply to*** her letter.

reply–paid *adj, always used before a noun, Brit* **:** POSTAGE-PAID • a *reply-paid* envelope

re·po /ˈriːˌpoʊ/ *adj, always used before a noun, US, informal* **:** of or relating to the business of taking property from people who have stopped making the payments that they agreed to make to pay for it • a *repo* company • Their car was taken/repossessed by the ***repo man***. [=a man whose job is to take things from people who are not paying for them]

¹re·port /rɪˈpoɚt/ *noun, pl* **-ports** [*count*]

1 : a story in a newspaper or on radio or television that is about something that happened or that gives information about something • a news/weather/financial *report* • a special *report* on/about health • a *report* from our correspondent in China

2 a : a written or spoken description of a situation, event, etc. • She wrote/made a *report* of the meeting. • He gave a detailed/full *report* on/about the project. • a medical *report* • a book *report* • She filled out a police *report* at the scene of the accident. • Can you give us a quick ***progress report***? [=an explanation of how something is developing] **b :** an official document that gives information about a particular subject • the government's *report* on crime in 2006 • The company issued/published/released its annual (business) *report*.

3 : a written or spoken statement about something that may or may not be true • Unconfirmed *reports* state that over 100 people were hurt. • Police have received *reports* of gang activity in the neighborhood. • ***By/from all reports***, you are a very hard worker. [=everyone says that you are a very hard worker]

4 *formal* **:** a loud noise made by a gun or an explosion • the sharp *report* of a rifle

5 *Brit* **:** REPORT CARD

²report *verb* **-ports; -port·ed; -port·ing**

1 : to give information about (something) in a newspaper or on television or radio [+ *obj*] The murder was *reported* in the national news. • Several TV stations are *reporting* that the police are close to making an arrest. • Their job is to *report* the news accurately and fairly. • It was *reported* (on the news) that two people died in the fire. = Two people were *reported* to have died in the fire. [*no obj*] — often + *on* • He *reports on* political news for a local TV station.

2 : to tell people about (something) **:** to make a report about (something) [+ *obj*] He was asked to *report* the details of the meeting. • Tomorrow the committee will *report* its findings on air pollution. [*no obj*] — often + *on* • She *reported on* the project to her manager.

3 [+ *obj*] **a :** to describe (a feeling, condition, etc.) • He *reported* feeling depressed. = He *reported* that he felt depressed. [=he said that he felt depressed] • The doctor *reported* some improvement in her condition. **b** ✧ Something that ***is reported*** is said by people and may or may not be true. • Her manner *was reported* as arrogant. = Her manner *was reported* to be arrogant. [=people said that she was arrogant] • It *is reported* that the herb helps reduce anxiety.

4 [+ *obj*] **:** to tell the police, fire department, etc., about (something, such as a crime or accident). • He called 911 and *reported* a fire. • She *reported* the burglary to the police. • They *reported* their son missing. [=they told the police that their son was missing]

5 [+ *obj*] **:** to tell someone with authority about (someone who has broken a rule, done something wrong, etc.) • They threatened to *report* him to the police. — often + *for* • The teacher *reported* him to the principal *for* misbehaving in class.

6 [*no obj*] **:** to go somewhere and tell someone that you have arrived — usually + *for* or *to* • The new recruits are expected to *report for* duty next week. • Please *report to* the office immediately when you arrive. • He was asked to *report for* work at 7:00 a.m.

report back [*phrasal verb*] **1 :** to return to a place in order to report information you have found, do more work, etc. • *Report back* to my office in two hours. = *Report back* (to me) in two hours. • Patients must *report back* to the center for a second treatment. **2 *report back or report back (something) or report (something) back* :** to give (information that you have found) to someone • The policeman *reported back* that he found nothing wrong. • A committee will study the matter and *report back* their findings. — often + *to* • Each researcher *reports* his results *back to* the project director.

***report sick* :** to tell your boss, employer, etc. that you are sick and cannot work • He *reported sick* on Friday (to his supervisor).

report to [*phrasal verb*] ***report to (someone)*** ✧ The person you *report to* at your job is the person who is directly in charge of what you do, who reviews your work, etc. • She *reports to* the president of the company.

– reported *adj, always used before a noun* • the *reported* findings/facts • a *reported* crime • The company has suffered losses of a *reported* two million dollars.

re·port·able /rɪˈpoɚtəbəl/ *adj, US* **:** required by law to be publicly reported to the government • a *reportable* disease • *reportable* income

re·port·age /rɪˈpoɚtɪʤ/ *noun* [*noncount*] *formal* **:** REPORTING • war *reportage* • *reportage* of the news

report card *noun, pl* ~ **cards** [*count*] *US* **:** a written statement of a student's grades that is given to the student's parents — called also (*Brit*) *report*

re·port·ed·ly /rɪˈpoɚtədli/ *adv* **:** according to what has been said — used to indicate what has been said or reported • The medication's side effects are *reportedly* few and mild. • They *reportedly* stole one million dollars.

re·port·er /rɪˈpoɚtɚ/ *noun, pl* **-ers** [*count*] **:** a person who writes news stories for a newspaper, magazine, etc., or who tells people the news on radio or television • a news/television *reporter* • She's a *reporter* for one of the major networks. — see also CUB REPORTER

reporting *noun* [*noncount*] **:** the act or activity of telling people the news in a newspaper or on television or radio • firsthand *reporting* • She is very skilled at *reporting*.

¹re·pose /rɪˈpoʊz/ *noun* [*noncount*] *formal + literary* **:** a state of resting or not being active • His face ***in repose*** [=*at rest*] is serious and thoughtful.

²repose *verb* **-pos·es; -posed; -pos·ing** *formal + literary*

1 *always followed by an adverb or preposition* **:** to rest or lay (something) somewhere [+ *obj*] She *reposed* her head on a cushion. [*no obj*] I found her *reposing* [=*relaxing*] on the couch.

2 : to place (trust, hope, confidence, etc.) *in* someone or something • They *reposed* confidence *in* their leader. [=they had confidence in their leader]

re·pos·i·to·ry /rɪˈpɑːzəˌtori, *Brit* rɪˈpɒzətri/ *noun, pl* **-ries** [*count*] *formal*

1 : a place where a large amount of something is stored • a *repository* for nuclear waste • huge *repositories* of data

2 : a person who possesses a lot of information, wisdom, etc.

▪ He is the *repository of* many secrets. ▪ She is the *repository of* her family's history.

re·pos·sess /ˌriːpəˈzɛs/ *verb* **-sess·es; -sessed; -sess·ing** [+ *obj*] **: to take (something) back from a buyer because payments are not being made** ▪ The bank *repossessed* her truck.

– repossessed *adj* ▪ a *repossessed* house/car ▪ *repossessed* property **– re·pos·ses·sion** /ˌriːpəˈzɛʃən/ *noun, pl* **-sions** [*count, noncount*] ▪ The judge allowed *repossession* of the house.

rep·re·hen·si·ble /ˌrɛprɪˈhɛnsəbəl/ *adj* [*more ~; most ~*] *formal* **: very bad : deserving very strong criticism** ▪ *reprehensible* [=*contemptible*] acts

– rep·re·hen·si·bly /ˌrɛprɪˈhɛnsəbli/ *adv* ▪ They behaved *reprehensibly*.

rep·re·sent /ˌrɛprɪˈzɛnt/ *verb* **-sents; -sent·ed; -sent·ing**

1 [+ *obj*] **a : to act or speak officially for (someone or something)** ▪ He *represented* his company at the meeting. ▪ She hired an agent to *represent* her in the contract negotiations. **b : to have a government position in which you speak or act for (a particular group, state, etc.)** ▪ Senator Smith *represents* the state of Connecticut. **c : to speak or act for (someone or something) in a court of law** ▪ He *represented* himself at the trial. [=he spoke for himself at the trial and did not have a lawyer] ▪ The company is *represented* by a local law firm.

2 [+ *obj*] **a : to be part of a sports event or other competition for (a particular country, city, school, etc.)** ▪ She *represented* the United States in figure skating at the Olympics. **b** ***be represented* — used to say that people from a particular place or group are present at an event, meeting, etc.** ▪ The town *was* well *represented* at the meeting. [=there were many people from the town at the meeting]

3 ***not used in progressive tenses*** [***linking verb***] **: to form or be something** ▪ The money he makes from his investments *represents* [=*constitutes*] over half his income. ▪ The court's decision *represents* a victory for small businesses. ▪ The new prices *represent* a substantial increase over last year's prices.

4 [+ *obj*] **: to be an example of (someone or something)** ▪ He *represents* everything I dislike about politics/politicians. ▪ They have a collection of animals *representing* more than 50 species.

5 [+ *obj*] **: to be a sign or symbol of (someone or something)** ▪ The flag *represents* our country. ▪ Letters *represent* sounds. ▪ High and low temperatures are *represented* by colored lines on the graph. ▪ She is beginning to question the company and everything it *represents*. [=*stands for*]

6 [+ *obj*] **: to show (someone or something) in a picture, painting, photograph, etc.** ▪ This painting *represents* [=*portrays, depicts*] Queen Elizabeth.

7 [+ *obj*] **: to describe (someone or something) in a particular way** ▪ The politician was angry with the newspaper for *representing* [=*portraying*] his party negatively. **— often used to suggest that a description is false** ▪ He *represented* himself as poor, but I saw him driving an expensive new car.

rep·re·sen·ta·tion /ˌrɛprɪˌzɛnˈteɪʃən/ *noun, pl* **-tions**

1 [*noncount*] **: a person or group that speaks or acts for or in support of another person or group** ▪ He had no legal *representation* [=he did not have a lawyer] during the trial. ▪ Each state has equal *representation* in the Senate. **— see also** PROPORTIONAL REPRESENTATION

2 [*count*] **: something (such as a picture or symbol) that stands for something else** ▪ The letters of the alphabet are *representations* of sounds.

3 [*count*] **: a painting, sculpture, etc., that is created to look like a particular thing or person** ▪ carved *representations* of flowers

4 [*noncount*] **: the act of presenting or describing a person or thing in a particular way** ▪ the film's heroic *representation* of America ▪ We discussed the *representation* of women in Jane Austen's novels.

5 [*count*] *formal* **a : a statement made to influence the opinions or actions of others** ▪ Her *representation* of the situation was very confusing. ▪ He was accused of making false *representations*. **b** *chiefly Brit* **: a formal and official complaint about something** ▪ Our ambassador has ***made representations*** to their government.

rep·re·sen·ta·tion·al /ˌrɛprɪˌzɛnˈteɪʃənl/ *adj* **: showing people and things as they appear in real life : REALISTIC** ▪ *representational* art ▪ a *representational* painter

¹rep·re·sen·ta·tive /ˌrɛprɪˈzɛntətɪv/ *adj* [*more ~; most ~*]

1 : typical of a particular group of people or of a particular thing ▪ a *representative* example ▪ The paintings are *representative* of English art in the early 19th century.

2 : including examples of the different types of people or things in a group ▪ The students chosen for the survey are a fairly *representative* sample/sampling of college students from across the U.S.

3 : having people who are chosen in elections to act or speak for or in support of the people who voted for them ▪ *representative* government ▪ *representative* democracy

– rep·re·sen·ta·tive·ness *noun* [*noncount*]

²representative *noun, pl* **-tives** [*count*]

1 a : someone who acts or speaks for or in support of another person or group ▪ a sales *representative* [=a salesperson] ▪ the actor's personal *representative* [=*agent*] **b : a member of the House of Representatives of the U.S. Congress or of a state government** ▪ Do you know who your *representatives* are? ▪ state *representatives* ▪ The bill was introduced by *Representative* Smith.

2 : a person or thing that is typical of a group ▪ a *representative* of her age group

re·press /rɪˈprɛs/ *verb* **-press·es; -pressed; -press·ing** [+ *obj*]

1 : to not allow yourself to do or express (something) ▪ She *repressed* a laugh. [=she stopped herself from laughing] ▪ He *repressed* his anger.

2 : to not allow yourself to remember (something, such as an unpleasant event) ▪ *repress* a painful memory

3 : to control (someone or something) by force ▪ The dictator brutally *repressed* [=*subdued, suppressed*] political disagreement. ▪ Religious groups were severely *repressed*.

re·pressed /rɪˈprɛst/ *adj* [*more ~; most ~*]

1 : stopped from being expressed or remembered ▪ *repressed* sexuality/anger ▪ a *repressed* memory

2 : having feelings or desires that are not allowed to be expressed ▪ a *repressed* child ▪ a sexually *repressed* man

3 : kept under control by force ▪ a *repressed* minority

re·pres·sion /rɪˈprɛʃən/ *noun* [*noncount*]

1 a : the act of using force to control someone or something ▪ the state's *repression* of its citizens **b : the state of being controlled by force** ▪ They survived 60 years of political *repression*.

2 : the act of not allowing a memory, feeling, or desire to be expressed ▪ sexual *repression*

re·pres·sive /rɪˈprɛsɪv/ *adj* [*more ~; most ~*]

1 : controlling people by force ▪ a *repressive* government

2 : not allowing certain feelings or desires to be expressed ▪ a sexually *repressive* culture

– re·pres·sive·ly *adv* **– re·pres·sive·ness** *noun* [*noncount*]

¹re·prieve /rɪˈpriːv/ *noun, pl* **-prieves** [*count*]

1 : an official order that delays the punishment of a prisoner who is sentenced to death ▪ He won/got a (temporary) *reprieve* from his death sentence.

2 a : a delay that keeps something bad from happening ▪ They wanted to close the library, but we managed to get/secure a *reprieve* for it. **b : a period of relief from pain, trouble, etc.** ▪ This warm spell has given us a *reprieve* from the winter cold.

²reprieve *verb* **-prieves; -prieved; -priev·ing** [+ *obj*]

1 : to delay the punishment of (someone, such as a prisoner who is sentenced to death) ▪ He was sentenced to death but then *reprieved*.

2 : to prevent (something) from being closed, destroyed, etc., for a period of time ▪ The library has been *reprieved* and will remain open for at least another year.

rep·ri·mand /ˈrɛprəˌmænd, *Brit* ˈrɛprəˌmɑːnd/ *verb* **-mands; -mand·ed; -mand·ing** [+ *obj*] **: to speak in an angry and critical way to (someone who has done something wrong, disobeyed an order, etc.)** ▪ The soldiers were severely *reprimanded*. **— often + *for*** ▪ She was *reprimanded for* being late. ▪ The boss *reprimanded* us *for* talking too much.

– reprimand *noun, pl* **-mands** [*count*] a severe/mild *reprimand* [*noncount*] a letter of *reprimand*

¹re·print /riˈprɪnt/ *verb* **-prints; -print·ed; -print·ing** [+ *obj*] **: to print (something, such as a book, article, etc.) again** ▪ She gave permission to *reprint* her article.

²re·print /ˈriːˌprɪnt/ *noun, pl* **-prints** [*count*]

1 : the act of printing more copies of a book ▪ The novel is already on its fifth *reprint*. ▪ The publisher does *reprints* of books written in the early 1900s.

2 : a book, story, etc., that is printed again ▪ This is a *reprint*

R

of an article that was originally published in the *New York Times*.

re·pri·sal /rɪˈpraɪzəl/ *noun, pl* **-sals :** something that is done to hurt or punish someone who has hurt you or done something bad to you [*count*] Enemy officers suffered harsh *reprisals*. ▪ The allies threatened economic *reprisals* against the invading country. [*noncount*] The prisoners kept silent for fear of *reprisal*. [=*punishment*] ▪ The hostages were taken ***in reprisal*** for the bombing.

[1]**re·prise** /rɪˈpri:z/ *noun, pl* **-pris·es** [*count*] **:** something (such as a piece of music) that is repeated ▪ They ended their performance with a *reprise* of the opening number. ▪ The team is hoping to avoid a *reprise* of last year's defeat.

[2]**reprise** *verb* **-prises; -prised; -pris·ing** [+ *obj*] **:** to repeat (something, such as a performance of a piece of music) ▪ *reprise* a song/play/film ▪ He will *reprise* his role in the play.

[1]**re·proach** /rɪˈproʊʧ/ *noun, pl* **-proach·es** *formal*

1 : a expression of disapproval or disappointment [*noncount*] She looked at him with *reproach*. ▪ His actions were ***above/beyond reproach***. [=his actions could not be criticized] [*count*] Accusations and *reproaches* from both parties made it difficult to pursue discussions.

2 [*noncount*] **:** loss of reputation **:** DISGRACE ▪ His conduct has brought shame and *reproach* to his family.

3 [*count*] **:** something that causes shame or disgrace — usually singular ▪ This situation is a scandal and a *reproach* to the entire country.

– re·proach·ful /rɪˈproʊʧfəl/ *adj* [*more ~; most ~*] ▪ a *reproachful* look **– re·proach·ful·ly** /rɪˈproʊʧfəli/ *adv* ▪ She shook her head *reproachfully*.

[2]**reproach** *verb* **-proaches; -proached; -proach·ing** [+ *obj*] *formal* **:** to speak in an angry and critical way to (someone) **:** to express disapproval or disappointment to (someone) — often + *for* ▪ She *reproached* her daughter *for* her selfishness.

reproach yourself **:** to feel shame or regret because of something you have done ▪ He *reproached himself for* not telling the truth.

rep·ro·bate /ˈrɛprəˌbeɪt/ *noun, pl* **-bates** [*count*] *formal* **:** a person who behaves in a morally wrong way ▪ drunken *reprobates*

– reprobate *adj* [*more ~; most ~*] ▪ a *reprobate* lifestyle

re·pro·duce /ˌri:prəˈdu:s, *Brit* ˌri:prəˈdju:s/ *verb* **-duc·es; -duced; -duc·ing**

1 [+ *obj*] **a :** to make a copy of (something) ▪ *reproduce* a photograph ▪ The concert will be *reproduced* on compact disc. **b :** to produce something that is the same as or very similar to (something else) ▪ Sound effects can *reproduce* the sound of thunder.

2 [+ *obj*] **:** to cause (something) to happen again in the same way ▪ They haven't been able to *reproduce* the results of the first experiment.

3 : to produce babies, young animals, new plants, etc. [*no obj*] Flies *reproduce* rapidly. [+ *obj*] Salmon return to the stream to *reproduce* offspring. ▪ The virus is able to ***reproduce itself*** very rapidly.

– re·pro·duc·ible /ˌri:prəˈdu:səbəl, *Brit* ˌri:prəˈdju:səbəl/ *adj* ▪ The results of the experiment were not *reproducible*.

re·pro·duc·tion /ˌri:prəˈdʌkʃən/ *noun, pl* **-tions**

1 [*noncount*] **:** the process that produces babies, young animals, or new plants ▪ sexual/asexual *reproduction*

2 [*noncount*] **:** the act of copying something (such as a document, book, or sound) ▪ the mass *reproduction* of fine art ▪ methods of sound *reproduction*

3 [*count*] **:** something that is made to look exactly like an original **:** COPY ▪ photographic/digital *reproductions* ▪ a *reproduction* of the painting

re·pro·duc·tive /ˌri:prəˈdʌktɪv/ *adj, always used before a noun* **:** relating to or involved in the production of babies, young animals, or new plants ▪ the *reproductive* tract/organs/system/cycle ▪ *reproductive* health/success ▪ (*US*) He is a leading supporter of ***reproductive rights***. [=a woman's right to choose whether or not she will have a baby]

re·proof /rɪˈpru:f/ *noun, pl* **-proofs** *formal*

1 [*noncount*] **:** criticism or blame ▪ The fear of *reproof* prevented them from complaining.

2 [*count*] **:** a statement that criticizes or blames someone ▪ She responded to their *reproofs* [=*rebukes*] by walking off angrily.

re·prove /rɪˈpru:v/ *verb* **-proves; -proved; -prov·ing** [+ *obj*] *formal* **:** to criticize or correct (someone) usually in a gentle way ▪ The teacher *reproved* the student for being late.

– reproving *adj* [*more ~; most ~*] ▪ a long *reproving* speech ▪ He gave me a *reproving* look. **– re·prov·ing·ly** *adv* ▪ She looked at me *reprovingly*.

rep·tile /ˈrɛpˌtajəl/ *noun, pl* **-tiles** [*count*]

1 : an animal (such as a snake, lizard, turtle, or alligator) that has cold blood, that lays eggs, and that has a body covered with scales or hard parts

2 *informal* **:** a person who cannot be trusted or who is not likable ▪ He called the governor's top aide a *reptile*.

– rep·til·ian /rɛpˈtɪlijən/ *adj* ▪ a *reptilian* brain/jawbone/claw ▪ The bird was *reptilian* in appearance. ▪ a *reptilian* smile

re·pub·lic /rɪˈpʌblɪk/ *noun, pl* **-lics** [*count*] **:** a country that is governed by elected representatives and by an elected leader (such as a president) rather than by a king or queen ▪ an independent *republic* ▪ an eastern European *republic* — see also BANANA REPUBLIC

[1]**re·pub·li·can** /rɪˈpʌblɪkən/ *noun, pl* **-cans** [*count*]

1 ***Republican*** **:** a member of the Republican party of the U.S. ▪ Our state representative is a *Republican*. ▪ The state's voters are mostly *Republicans*. — compare DEMOCRAT 2

2 : a person who believes in or supports a republican form of government

3 ***Republican*** **:** a person from Northern Ireland who believes that Northern Ireland should be part of the Republic of Ireland rather than the United Kingdom — opposite LOYALIST

[2]**republican** *adj* [*more ~; most ~*]

1 ***Republican US*** **:** of or relating to one of the two major political parties in the U.S. ▪ *Republican* candidates/proposals/voters ▪ the leader of the ***Republican Party*** — compare DEMOCRATIC 2

2 : relating to or based on a form of government in which representatives are elected and there is no king or queen ▪ *republican* reforms ▪ a *republican* government

– re·pub·li·can·ism *or* **Republicanism** /rɪˈpʌblɪkəˌnɪzəm/ *noun* [*noncount*] ▪ moderate/conservative *Republicanism* ▪ Roman *republicanism*

re·pu·di·ate /rɪˈpju:diˌeɪt/ *verb* **-ates; -at·ed; -at·ing** [+ *obj*] *formal*

1 : to refuse to accept or support (something) **:** to reject (something or someone) ▪ a generation that has *repudiated* the values of the past ▪ He has publicly *repudiated* the government's policies.

2 : to say or show that (something) is not true ▪ He published an article that *repudiates* the study's claims. ▪ She says she has evidence which *repudiates* the allegations.

– re·pu·di·a·tion /rɪˌpju:diˈeɪʃən/ *noun, pl* **-tions** [*count, noncount*] ▪ His statements are a *repudiation* of the government's policies.

re·pug·nance /rɪˈpʌgnəns/ *noun* [*noncount*] *formal* **:** a strong feeling of dislike or disgust ▪ They expressed their *repugnance* at the idea. ▪ They felt nothing but *repugnance* for the group's violent history.

re·pug·nant /rɪˈpʌgnənt/ *adj* [*more ~; most ~*] *formal* **:** causing a strong feeling of dislike or disgust **:** REPULSIVE ▪ a morally *repugnant* act — often + *to* ▪ The idea was completely *repugnant to* us.

re·pulse /rɪˈpʌls/ *verb* **-puls·es; -pulsed; -puls·ing** [+ *obj*] *formal*

1 : to force (someone) to stop attacking you **:** REPEL ▪ The troops *repulsed* the attack. ▪ The invaders were *repulsed*. [=*driven back*]

2 : to cause dislike or disgust in (someone) ▪ I was *repulsed* by the movie's violence. ▪ The moldy bread *repulsed* him.

3 : to reject (someone or something) in a rude or unfriendly way ▪ He *repulsed* all attempts to help him.

re·pul·sion /rɪˈpʌlʃən/ *noun, pl* **-sions**

1 : a feeling of strong dislike or disgust [*noncount*] I read about what happened with a feeling of shock and *repulsion*. [*singular*] She felt a *repulsion* for politics.

2 *physics* **:** a force that pushes something away from something else [*noncount*] magnetic *repulsion* [*count*] a *repulsion* between the particles — opposite ATTRACTION

3 [*noncount*] **:** the act of pushing someone or something away **:** the act of repulsing something or someone ▪ their successful *repulsion* of the attack/attackers

re·pul·sive /rɪˈpʌlsɪv/ *adj* [*more ~; most ~*]

1 : causing strong dislike or disgust ▪ *repulsive* and evil acts ▪ a *repulsive* [=*repellent*] man ▪ The rotten meat was *repulsive*. [=*nauseating, revolting*]

2 *physics* **:** of or relating to the force that pushes something

away from something else • Magnets have a *repulsive* effect on each other.
– **re·pul·sive·ly** *adv* • a *repulsively* hideous man – **re·pul·sive·ness** *noun* [*noncount*] • physical *repulsiveness*

re·pur·pose /riˈpɚpəs/ *verb* **-pos·es; -posed; -pos·ing** [+ *obj*] : to change (something) so that it can be used for a different purpose • finding ways to *repurpose* old computer equipment

rep·u·ta·ble /ˈrɛpjətəbəl/ *adj* [*more* ~; *most* ~] : respected and trusted by most people : having a good reputation • a *reputable* source/brand/company • *reputable* businessmen/scientists/writers — opposite DISREPUTABLE

rep·u·ta·tion /ˌrɛpjəˈteɪʃən/ *noun, pl* **-tions** : the common opinion that people have about someone or something : the way in which people think of someone or something [*count*] This car dealership has a good/bad *reputation*. [=people think that the car dealership is good/bad] • He has earned/established/acquired a *reputation* as a first-class playwright. • a teacher with a *reputation* for patience • Poor customer service has ruined/damaged/destroyed the company's *reputation*. • The cruise ship ***lived up to its reputation***. [=the cruise ship was as good, enjoyable, etc., as we were told it would be] [*noncount*] I know that the restaurant, by *reputation*, is excellent. [=the restaurant has an excellent reputation]

re·pute /rɪˈpjuːt/ *noun* [*noncount*] *formal*
1 : REPUTATION • They are held in high/good/bad/low *repute*. [=they have a good/bad reputation]
2 : good reputation • a scientist of *repute* [=*distinction*]
ill repute : bad reputation • She was a ***woman of ill repute***. [=*prostitute, whore*] • a ***house of ill repute*** [=*brothel, whorehouse*]

re·put·ed /rɪˈpjuːtəd/ *adj* : said to be true, to exist, to have a specified identity, etc. • He is *reputed* to be a millionaire. [=people say that he is a millionaire] • a *reputed* gang member • She was hired for her *reputed* talents as a manager.
– **re·put·ed·ly** *adv* • Their pizza is *reputedly* the best in town. [=people say that their pizza is the best in town]

[1]**re·quest** /rɪˈkwɛst/ *noun, pl* **-quests**
1 : an act of politely or formally asking for something [*count*] They made a *request* to begin work immediately. • She filed/sent/submitted a formal *request* for more information. • He denied/refused/rejected her *request*. • He fulfilled/granted her *request*. • The radio program ***takes requests***. [=people can ask for certain songs to be played] • ***At your request***, I am enclosing a full refund of your payment. • Troops were sent ***at the request of*** our allies. [*noncount*] Catalogs are available ***by/on/upon request***. [=you can get a catalog by requesting one]
2 [*count*] : something (such as a song) that a person asks for • The radio station plays *requests*. [=songs that people ask the radio station to play] • This next song is a *request* from one of our listeners.

[2]**request** *verb* **-quests; -quest·ed; quest·ing** [+ *obj*]
1 : to ask for (something) in a polite or formal way • He *requested* a table near the window. [=he asked to be seated at a table near the window] • The governor will *request* that the legislature raise taxes.
2 : to ask (someone) to do something in a polite or formal way • Gentlemen are *requested* to wear a jacket and tie. • I am sending your medical records ***as requested***. [=as I have been asked to do]

re·qui·em *or* **Requiem** /ˈrɛkwijəm/ *noun, pl* **-ems** [*count*]
1 : a Christian religious ceremony for a dead person — called also *Requiem Mass*
2 : a piece of music for a requiem

re·quire /rɪˈkwajɚ/ *verb* **-quires; -quired; -quir·ing** [+ *obj*] *formal*
1 : to need (something) • We *require* your assistance. • He is very sick and *requires* constant care. [=he has to be given constant care] — used to say that something is necessary • The game *requires* great skill and coordination. [=you must have great skill and coordination to play the game] • It *requires* great strength to lift 500 pounds. = Lifting 500 pounds *requires* great strength. • Experience is *required* for this job. [=you must have experience for this job] • English is a *required* course. [=a course that must be taken in order to graduate] • The newspaper is ***required reading*** [=reading that must be done] in my politics course.
2 : to make it necessary for someone to do something • The law *requires* everyone to pay the tax. = The law *requires* that everyone pay the tax. • What will be *required* of me if I accept the job? = What will I be *required* to do if I accept the job? • The truck driver carries a special license, as the law *requires* (him to do). = The truck driver carries a special license, ***as required by*** law.

re·quire·ment /rɪˈkwajɚmənt/ *noun, pl* **-ments** [*count*]
1 : something that is needed or that must be done • nutritional *requirements* • a legal/statutory *requirement* • (*Brit*) Her services were ***surplus to requirements***. [=more than what was needed]
2 : something that is necessary for something else to happen or be done • He has met the basic/minimum *requirements* for graduation. • She has fulfilled/satisfied the general *requirements* of the course.

[1]**req·ui·site** /ˈrɛkwəzət/ *adj, formal* : needed for a particular purpose • She has the *requisite* [=*necessary, required*] skills/experience for the job.

[2]**requisite** *noun, pl* **-sites** [*count*] *formal* : something that is needed for a particular purpose • Five years of previous experience is a *requisite* for this job.

req·ui·si·tion /ˌrɛkwəˈzɪʃən/ *verb* **-tions; -tioned; -tion·ing** [+ *obj*] *formal* : to ask for or demand and take (something) for your use • The officer *requisitioned* supplies for his troops. • The car was *requisitioned* by the police.
– **requisition** *noun, pl* **-tions** [*count*] • The office manager made a *requisition* [=an official request] for supplies.

re·quite /rɪˈkwaɪt/ *verb* **-quites; -quit·ed; -quit·ing** [+ *obj*] *formal* : to give or do something in return for (something that another person has given or done) • His love for her was not *requited*. [=she did not return his love; she did not love him] — compare UNREQUITED

re·read /riˈriːd/ *verb* **-reads; -read; -read·ing** [+ *obj*] : to read (something) again • We carefully *reread* the contract.

re·route /riˈruːt/ *verb* **-routes; -rout·ed; -rout·ing** [+ *obj*] : to change the normal route of (something) • The airplanes were *rerouted* due to bad weather.

[1]**re·run** /ˈriːˌrʌn/ *noun, pl* **-runs** [*count*]
1 : a television program or movie that is shown again • She spent her vacation watching summer *reruns*.
2 : an occurrence in which something happens or is done again • Voters do not want a *rerun* [=*repeat*] of the last election.

[2]**re·run** /riˈrʌn/ *verb* **-runs; -ran** /-ˈræn/; **-run; -run·ning** [+ *obj*]
1 : to show (a television program or movie) again • Last week's show is being *rerun* tomorrow night.
2 : to do or run (something) again • They *reran* the race, but the result was the same. • He *reran* the software on my computer. • They *reran* [=*repeated*] the lab tests.

re·sale /ˈriːˌseɪl/ *noun, pl* **-sales** : the act of selling something that you have bought [*count*] They earned thousands of dollars on *resales* of the baseball tickets. [*noncount*] He buys baseball collectibles and then holds them for *resale*. • The *resale* price/value of the car is $8,000.

re·sched·ule /riˈskɛˌʤuːl, *Brit* riˈʃɛˌdjuːl/ *verb* **-ules; -uled; -ul·ing** [+ *obj*]
1 : to schedule (something) for a different time or date • She called to *reschedule* her appointment. • The meeting was *rescheduled* for Tuesday.
2 : to arrange (a loan or debt) to be paid back at a later date than was originally planned • He *rescheduled* his college loans.

re·scind /rɪˈsɪnd/ *verb* **-scinds; -scind·ed; -scind·ing** [+ *obj*] *formal* : to end (a law, contract, agreement, etc.) officially : to say officially that (something) is no longer valid • The navy *rescinded* its ban on women sailors. • The company later *rescinded* its offer/decision.

[1]**res·cue** /ˈrɛskju/ *verb* **-cues; -cued; -cu·ing** [+ *obj*] : to save (someone or something) from danger or harm • The survivors were *rescued* by the Coast Guard. — often + *from* • A fireman *rescued* three children *from* the burning building. — sometimes used figuratively • She *rescued* an old chair *from* the trash.
– **res·cu·er** *noun, pl* **-ers** [*count*] • *Rescuers* struggled to free the young man from the car wreck.

[2]**rescue** *noun, pl* **-cues** [*count*] : an act of saving someone or something from danger, harm, or trouble • The lifeguard performed a heroic *rescue*. • The policeman ***came/went to the rescue of*** the lost boy. [=the policeman rescued the lost boy] • When her brother lost his job, she ***came to his rescue*** by paying his rent. — often used before another noun • a *rescue* team/squad • a *rescue* operation/mission

[1]**re·search** /ˈriːˌsɚʧ/ *noun, pl* **-search·es**
1 : careful study that is done to find and report new knowl-

edge about something [*noncount*] cancer/AIDS/drug *research* • medical/scientific/scholarly *research* • She conducts *research* into/on the causes of Alzheimer's disease. • Recent *research* shows/indicates that the disease is caused in part by bad nutrition. • The study is an important piece of *research*. — often used before another noun • *research* data/findings • a *research* group/organization/scientist • a *research* assistant • a *research* program/project • a *research* lab/laboratory/library/center • a *research* paper/report [*plural*] (*formal* + *old-fashioned*) We read about Sigmund Freud's *researches* into the human psyche.

2 [*noncount*] **: the activity of getting information about a subject** • He did a lot of *research* before buying his car. — see also MARKET RESEARCH

– re·search·er *noun, pl* **-ers** [*count*] • Medical *researchers* say that the drug is useless.

²re·search /rɪˈsɚtʃ/ *verb* **-search·es; -searched; -search·ing** [+ *obj*]

1 : to study (something) carefully • She is *researching* [=*investigating*] the relationship between stress and heart disease. • He spent the summer *researching* his dissertation.

2 : to collect information about or for (something) • Before going out to eat, she *researched* area restaurants. • The reporter made hundreds of telephone calls while *researching* the story.

research and development *noun* [*noncount*] **:** studies and tests that are done in order to design new or improved products • The company spends millions of dollars each year on *research and development*. — abbr. *R & D*

research park *noun, pl* ~ **parks** [*count*] *US* **:** an area where companies have offices and laboratories and do work involving science and technology — called also *technology park*, (*chiefly Brit*) *science park*

re·sell /riˈsɛl/ *verb* **-sells; -sold; -sell·ing** [+ *obj*] **:** to sell (something that you bought) • He repaired the motorcycle and *resold* it for a profit.

re·sem·blance /rɪˈzɛmbləns/ *noun, pl* **-blanc·es**

1 : the state of looking or being like someone or something else [*singular*] He bears/has a close/striking/strong/uncanny *resemblance* to his father. [=he looks a lot like his father] • When she showed me her niece's picture, I immediately saw a/the ***family resemblance***. [=a similarity in the way they look because they are related] [*noncount*] He doesn't look exactly like his father, but there is some *resemblance*. • There is no *resemblance* between her and her sister.

2 [*count*] **:** something that makes one person or thing like another **:** SIMILARITY • I noticed some *resemblances* between them. [=I noticed some ways in which they resemble each other]

re·sem·ble /rɪˈzɛmbəl/ *verb, not used in progressive tenses* **-sem·bles; -sem·bled; -sem·bling** [+ *obj*] **:** to look or be like (someone or something) • He strongly *resembles* his father in appearance and in temperament. • Terrier dogs closely *resemble* each other. • We couldn't find anything *resembling* [=*like*] a good restaurant. [=we couldn't find a good restaurant]

re·sent /rɪˈzɛnt/ *verb* **-sents; -sent·ed; -sent·ing** [+ *obj*] **:** to be angry or upset about (someone or something that you think is unfair) • I *resent* that remark. • She *resented* being told what to do. • He *resented* his boss for making him work late.

re·sent·ful /rɪˈzɛntfəl/ *adj* [*more* ~; *most* ~] **:** having or showing a feeling of anger or displeasure about someone or something unfair • She is *resentful* about being demoted. • He's *resentful* of his boss. = He feels *resentful* toward his boss. • a *resentful* child • She gave me a *resentful* glare. • a *resentful* letter to the editor

– re·sent·ful·ly *adv* **– re·sent·ful·ness** *noun* [*noncount*]

re·sent·ment /rɪˈzɛntmənt/ *noun* [*noncount*] **:** a feeling of anger or displeasure about someone or something unfair • She bore/felt/harbored bitter feelings of *resentment* toward her ex-husband. • He's filled with *resentment* at/against his boss. • He expressed his *resentment* of the new policies.

res·er·va·tion /ˌrɛzɚˈveɪʃən/ *noun, pl* **-tions**

1 [*count*] **:** an arrangement to have something (such as a room, table, or seat) held for your use at a later time • We made dinner *reservations* at the restaurant for 6 o'clock. • I have a hotel *reservation*.

2 : a feeling of doubt or uncertainty about something [*count*] My only *reservation* about buying the car was its high price. — often plural • She had *reservations* about changing jobs. [*noncount*] He supported her decision ***without reservation***. [=he completely supported her decision]

3 [*count*] **:** an area of land in the U.S. that is kept separate as a place for Native Americans to live • a Navajo *reservation*

4 [*count*] *US* **:** an area of land on which hunting animals is not allowed • a wildlife *reservation* [=*reserve*]

¹re·serve /rɪˈzɚv/ *verb* **-serves; -served; -serv·ing** [+ *obj*]

1 : to make arrangements so that you will be able to use or have (something, such as a room, table, or seat) at a later time • We *reserved* a hotel room. • This table is *reserved* for someone else. • The seats are *reserved* under my name.

2 : to keep (something) for a special or future use • We will *reserve* this wine for a special occasion. • She usually *reserved* her best dishes for very important dinners. • She spoke in a tone of voice that she usually *reserved* for her students. [=that she usually only used for her students]

3 : to choose to do (something) at a later time **:** DEFER • I will ***reserve judgment*** [=will not make a judgment/decision] until I know the full story.

4 : to have or keep (something, such as a right) for possible use at a future time • We *reserve* the right to make further changes to the agreement if necessary.

²reserve *noun, pl* **-serves**

1 [*count*] **:** a supply of something that is stored so that it can be used at a later time • oil *reserves* • a cash *reserve* • He had to call upon his inner *reserves* of strength to keep going.

2 [*count*] **:** a military force that is additional to the regular forces and that is available if it is needed • the army *reserve* — often plural • He is a member of the *reserves*.

3 [*count*] **:** an area of land where animals and plants are given special protection • a forest/wildlife *reserve* — see also NATURE RESERVE

4 [*count*] **:** an area of land where Native Americans live **:** RESERVATION • a Navajo *reserve*

5 [*noncount*] **:** the quality of a person who does not express feelings, opinions, etc., in an easy and open way • His natural *reserve* is sometimes mistaken for unfriendliness.

6 [*count*] **:** a player on a team who takes the place of a regular player who is injured or cannot play • the *reserves* on a football team

in reserve **:** kept for future or special use • She has a lot of money (kept) *in reserve* in case problems arise.

without reserve **:** in a free and complete way • They trusted him *without reserve*. [=trusted him completely]

re·served /rɪˈzɚvd/ *adj*

1 [*more* ~; *most* ~] **:** not openly expressing feelings or opinions • She is a very *reserved* young woman.

2 : kept for use only by a particular person or group • a *reserved* parking space • The front row is *reserved* for faculty.

reserve price *noun, pl* ~ **prices** [*count*] **:** the lowest price that a seller will accept for the thing that is being sold at an auction

re·serv·ist /rɪˈzɚvɪst/ *noun, pl* **-ists** [*count*] **:** a member of a military reserve • an army *reservist*

res·er·voir /ˈrɛzəˌvwɑɚ/ *noun, pl* **-voirs** [*count*]

1 : a usually artificial lake that is used to store a large supply of water for use in people's homes, in businesses, etc.

2 : a place (such as a part of a machine) where a liquid is stored • The pen has a large ink *reservoir*. • the engine's oil *reservoir*

3 : an extra supply of something • Colleges and universities provide *reservoirs* of talent for job recruiters. • She found the *reservoirs* of energy she needed to finish the job.

re·set /riˈsɛt/ *verb* **-sets; -set; -set·ting** [+ *obj*] **:** to set (something) again: such as **a :** to move (something) back to an original place or position • The machine *reset* the bowling pins. **b :** to put (a broken bone) back in the correct position for healing • His broken leg had to be *reset*. **c :** to put (a gem) into a new piece of jewelry • *reset* a diamond **d :** to change (something) so that it shows a different time or can be used again • He *reset* his watch. • *reset* the timer to 10 minutes • The fire alarm was *reset*. • *reset* a trap

re·set·tle /riˈsɛtl/ *verb* **-set·tles; -set·tled; -set·tling**

1 : to begin to live in a new area after leaving an old one **:** to settle again [*no obj*] They left town and *resettled* out west. [+ *obj*] He *resettled* his family in the valley.

2 [+ *obj*] **:** to begin to use (an area) again as a place to live — usually used as *(be) resettled* • The area *was resettled* in the 1800s.

– re·set·tle·ment /riˈsɛtlmənt/ *noun* [*noncount*]

re·shape /riˈʃeɪp/ *verb* **-shapes; -shaped; -shap·ing** [+ *obj*] **:** to give a new form or shape to (something) • The body of the car was *reshaped* to allow for more cargo space. •

R

These changes will *reshape* the future. ▪ He *reshaped* the plot of his story.

re·shuf·fle /riˈʃʌfəl/ *verb* **-shuf·fles; -shuf·fled; -shuf·fling** [+ *obj*]
1 : to shuffle (cards) again ▪ The dealer *reshuffled* the cards.
2 : to change the way the parts of (something) are arranged or organized ▪ The President *reshuffled* his Cabinet. [=changed the jobs/positions of the people in his Cabinet] ▪ We had to *reshuffle* [=*rearrange*] our schedule.
– reshuffle *noun, pl* **-shuffles** [*count*] ▪ There has been a major *reshuffle* in the department.

re·side /riˈzaɪd/ *verb* **-sides; -sid·ed; -sid·ing** [*no obj*] *formal*
1 : to live in a particular place ▪ He *resides* in St. Louis. ▪ He still *resides* at his parents' house.
2 : to exist or be present ▪ The power of veto *resides* with the President. [=the President has the power of veto] ▪ Meaning *resides* within the text of the poem. ▪ The importance of this decision *resides* in the fact that it relates to people across the country.

res·i·dence /ˈrɛzədəns/ *noun, pl* **-denc·es** *formal*
1 [*noncount*] **:** the state of living in a particular place ▪ He recently ended his *residence* at the apartment complex. ▪ Birds have ***taken up residence*** [=established a home] in the barn. ▪ (*US*) a ***residence hall*** = (*Brit*) a ***hall of residence*** [=a place where students live at a college or university]
2 [*count*] **:** the place where someone lives ▪ a two-story *residence* ▪ Police surrounded the *residence*. — often used to refer especially to a large and impressive house where an important or wealthy person lives ▪ He spent three months at his summer *residence*. ▪ the prime minister's *residence*
3 [*noncount*] **:** legal permission to live in a country ▪ They were granted/denied *residence* in this country.
in residence **1 :** living in a particular place at a particular time ▪ The Queen was not *in residence* at the palace when the fire broke out. **2 :** having an official position as a writer, artist, etc., who has been chosen to live and work at a college or other institution for a period of time ▪ She is the artist *in residence* at the museum this summer.

res·i·den·cy /ˈrɛzədənsi/ *noun, pl* **-cies** *formal*
1 a [*noncount*] **:** the state or fact of living in a place ▪ proof of *residency* [=*residence*] ▪ You must meet the town's *residency* requirement in order to vote. **b** [*singular*] **:** a period of time when someone lives in a place ▪ a four-year *residency* in the country
2 [*count*] **:** legal permission to live in a place ▪ He was granted/denied *residency*. [=*residence*]
3 [*count, noncount*] *chiefly US* **:** a period when a doctor receives advanced training at a hospital in order to become a specialist in a particular field of medicine ▪ She recently completed her *residency* in pediatrics. ▪ a *residency* program
4 [*count, noncount*] **:** a period of time when a writer, artist, etc., lives and works at a college or other institution

[1]**resident** /ˈrɛzədənt/ *noun, pl* **-dents** [*count*]
1 : someone who lives in a particular place ▪ She is a *resident* of New York. [=she lives in New York] ▪ apartment *residents*
2 *US* **:** a doctor who is training at a hospital to become a specialist in a particular field of medicine ▪ a first-year *resident*

R

[2]**res·i·dent** *adj*
1 : living in a particular place usually for a long period of time ▪ the city's *resident* voters ▪ Several tribes are *resident* in this part of the country.
2 *always used before a noun* **:** working regularly at a particular place ▪ the magazine's *resident* critic — often used humorously to refer to the person in a group who has a particular skill, area of knowledge, etc. ▪ He is our *resident* trivia expert.

res·i·den·tial /ˌrɛzəˈdɛnʃəl/ *adj*
1 : containing mostly homes instead of stores, businesses, etc. ▪ a *residential* area/street/neighborhood
2 : used as a place to live ▪ *residential* property
3 : of or relating to the places where people live ▪ The company offers insurance for commercial and *residential* customers. ▪ *residential* insurance policies
4 a : providing students a place to live ▪ *residential* colleges **b :** requiring students to live at a school while taking classes ▪ *residential* study ▪ a *residential* course
5 a : provided to patients who are staying at a place for medical care ▪ *residential* drug treatment **b :** requiring patients to stay while they are receiving medical care ▪ a *residential* treatment center

re·sid·u·al /rɪˈzɪʤəwəl/ *adj, formal* **:** remaining after a process has been completed or something has been removed ▪ She's still dealing with the *residual* effects of the accident.

re·sid·u·als /rɪˈzɪʤəwəlz/ *noun* [*plural*] **:** additional payments that are made to a person (such as a writer or actor) who worked on a commercial or television program every time the commercial or program is shown again ▪ She earns a lot in *residuals*.

res·i·due /ˈrɛzəˌdu:, *Brit* ˈrɛzəˌdju:/ *noun, pl* **-dues**
1 : a usually small amount of something that remains after a process has been completed or a thing has been removed [*count*] The grill was covered in a greasy *residue* from the hamburgers. ▪ The divorce left a *residue* of pain in the family. [*noncount*] There was some kind of sticky *residue* on the floor.
2 [*count*] *formal* **:** the amount of something valuable (such as an estate) that is left after all debts have been paid ▪ She left the *residue* of her estate to her daughter.

re·sign /rɪˈzaɪn/ *verb* **-signs; -signed; -sign·ing :** to give up (a job or position) in a formal or official way [+ *obj*] The senator was forced to *resign* his position. [*no obj*] The newspaper's editor *resigned* after the scandal. ▪ He *resigned* from his job as principal of the school.
resign yourself **:** to make yourself accept something that is bad or that cannot be changed — usually + *to* ▪ We *resigned ourselves to* the fact that we were going to lose the game. ▪ You don't have to *resign yourself to* doing a job that you don't enjoy. — see also ***resigned to*** at RESIGNED

res·ig·na·tion /ˌrɛzɪgˈneɪʃən/ *noun, pl* **-tions**
1 : an act of giving up a job or position in a formal or official way [*count*] The chairman accepted their *resignations*. [*noncount*] a letter of *resignation*
2 [*count*] **:** a letter which states that a person has given up a job or position ▪ The manager received *resignations* from three members of the staff.
3 [*noncount*] **:** the feeling that something unpleasant is going to happen and cannot be changed ▪ We accepted the news with *resignation*. ▪ a sigh of *resignation*

resigned *adj, always used before a noun* **:** feeling or showing acceptance that something unpleasant will happen or will not change ▪ She gave a *resigned* sigh. ▪ "OK, you can go," he said, in a *resigned* voice.
resigned to ✧ If you are *resigned to* something, you accept a bad situation that cannot be changed. ▪ She was *resigned to* a long visit with his mother. ▪ I'm *resigned to* having to work this weekend. ▪ He was ***resigned to the fact*** that an expensive vacation would have to wait.
– re·sign·ed·ly /rɪˈzaɪnədli/ *adv* ▪ She shook her head and sighed *resignedly* when he told her the news.

re·sil·ience /rɪˈzɪljəns/ *noun* [*noncount*]
1 : the ability to become strong, healthy, or successful again after something bad happens ▪ The rescue workers showed remarkable *resilience* in dealing with the difficult conditions.
2 : the ability of something to return to its original shape after it has been pulled, stretched, pressed, bent, etc. ▪ the *resilience* of rubber ▪ Cold temperatures caused the material to lose *resilience*.

re·sil·ien·cy /rɪˈzɪljənsi/ *noun* [*noncount*] **:** RESILIENCE

re·sil·ient /rɪˈzɪljənt/ *adj* [*more* ~; *most* ~]
1 : able to become strong, healthy, or successful again after something bad happens ▪ *resilient* young people ▪ *resilient* competitors ▪ The local economy is remarkably *resilient*.
2 : able to return to an original shape after being pulled, stretched, pressed, bent, etc. ▪ a *resilient* material
– re·sil·ient·ly *adv*

res·in /ˈrɛzn̩/ *noun, pl* **-ins** [*count, noncount*]
1 : a yellow or brown sticky substance that comes from some trees and that is used to make various products
2 : an artificial substance that is similar to natural resins and that is used to make plastics — compare ROSIN
– res·in·ous /ˈrɛzn̩əs/ *adj* [*more* ~; *most* ~] ▪ a *resinous* substance

re·sist /rɪˈzɪst/ *verb* **-sists; -sist·ed; -sist·ing**
1 [+ *obj*] **:** to fight against (something) **:** to try to stop or prevent (something) ▪ He was charged with *resisting* arrest. ▪ Many people *resisted* [=*opposed*] the efforts of lawmakers to raise taxes.
2 [+ *obj*] **:** to remain strong against the force or effect of (something) **:** to not be affected or harmed by (something) ▪ These windows can *resist* very high winds. ▪ The drug will help your body *resist* infection.
3 : to prevent yourself from doing something that you want to do [+ *obj*] She couldn't *resist* telling us what she'd heard. ▪

He was able to *resist* the urge to tell her his secret. • It was hard *resisting* the temptation to open the box. • The offer was hard to *resist*. [*no obj*] I know I shouldn't have any more cake, but I can't *resist*.

– re·sist·er /rɪˈzɪstɚ/ *noun, pl* **-ers** [*count*] • military draft *resisters*

re·sis·tance /rɪˈzɪstəns/ *noun*

1 : refusal to accept something new or different [*noncount*] — often + *from* • She sensed *resistance from* some of the staff regarding the changes in policy. — often + *to* • There was a lot of *resistance to* the plan when it was first suggested. [*singular*] They have shown a stubborn *resistance to* change.

2 [*noncount*] **:** effort made to stop or to fight against someone or something • He offered no *resistance* when he was arrested. [=he did not try to prevent himself from being arrested] • The troops met heavy/stiff *resistance* as they approached the city. — see also PASSIVE RESISTANCE

3 : the ability to prevent something from having an effect [*noncount*] The paint shows good weather *resistance*. — often + *to* • the body's *resistance to* disease [*singular*] Over time the patient/infection could develop a *resistance to* the drug.

4 [*noncount*] **:** a force that slows down a moving object (such as an airplane) by going against the direction in which the object is moving • reducing wind *resistance*

5 *or* ***Resistance*** [*singular*] **:** a secret organization that fights against enemy forces who have gained control of a region, country, etc. • a member of the French *Resistance* • *resistance* forces

6 [*noncount*] *technical* **:** the ability of a substance to prevent electricity from passing through it • electrical *resistance*

take/follow the path/line of least resistance **:** to choose the easiest way to do something instead of trying to choose the best way • She tends to *follow the path of least resistance* instead of going after what she really wants.

re·sis·tant /rɪˈzɪstənt/ *adj* [*more ~; most ~*]

1 : opposed to something **:** wanting to prevent something from happening — usually + *to* • People are often *resistant to* change.

2 : not affected or harmed by something • These plants are *resistant to* cold temperatures. • He became *resistant to* the medication. — often used in combination • a water-*resistant* watch

re·sis·tor /rɪˈzɪstɚ/ *noun, pl* **-tors** [*count*] *technical* **:** a device that is used to control the flow of electricity in an electric circuit

re·sit /riˈsɪt/ *verb* **re·sits; re·sat** /riˈsæt/; **re·sit·ting** [+ *obj*] *Brit* **:** to take (an examination) again • He has to *resit* [=*retake*] the exam he failed.

– re·sit /ˈriːˌsɪt/ *noun, pl* **-sits** [*count*] • He passed the *resit*.

res·o·lute /ˈrɛzəˌluːt/ *adj* [*more ~; most ~*] **:** very determined **:** having or showing a lot of determination • She is a *resolute* competitor. • He has remained *resolute* in his opposition to the bill. • a leader with a stern and *resolute* manner

– res·o·lute·ly *adv* • The senator is *resolutely* opposed to the bill.

res·o·lu·tion /ˌrɛzəˈluːʃən/ *noun, pl* **-tions**

1 a [*noncount*] **:** the act of finding an answer or solution to a conflict, problem, etc. **:** the act of resolving something • a court for the *resolution* of civil disputes • conflict *resolution* **b** [*count*] **:** an answer or solution to something • We found a *resolution* to the dispute.

2 : the ability of a device to show an image clearly and with a lot of detail [*count*] computer screens with high *resolutions* [*noncount*] The monitor has excellent *resolution*. • a high-*resolution* copier/monitor/camera

3 [*count*] **:** a promise to yourself that you will make a serious effort to do something that you should do • He made a *resolution* to lose weight. [=he resolved to lose weight] • Her ***New Year's resolution*** [=her promise to do something differently in the new year] is to exercise regularly.

4 [*noncount*] **:** the quality of being very determined to do something **:** DETERMINATION • They admired his courage and *resolution*. [=*resolve*]

5 [*count*] **:** a formal statement that expresses the feelings, wishes, or decision of a group • The assembly passed a *resolution* calling for the university president to step down.

6 [*noncount*] **:** the point in a story at which the main conflict is solved or ended • the *resolution* of the plot

¹re·solve /rɪˈzɑːlv/ *verb* **-solves; -solved; -solv·ing**

1 [+ *obj*] **:** to find an answer or solution to (something) **:** to settle or solve (something) • The brothers finally *resolved* their conflict. • The issue of the book's authorship was never *resolved*. • His speech did nothing to *resolve* doubts about the company's future. • They haven't been able to *resolve* their differences.

2 [+ *obj*] **:** to make a definite and serious decision to do something • She *resolved* to quit smoking. • He *resolved* that he would start dating again.

3 [+ *obj*] **:** to make a formal decision about something usually by a vote • The committee *resolved* to override the veto.

4 *formal* **:** to change *into* separate parts or a different form by usually a gradual process [+ *obj*] The mixture was *resolved into* two parts. [*no obj*] The image eventually *resolved into* the shape of a person's body.

– re·solv·able /rɪˈzɑːlvəbəl/ *adj* [*more ~; most ~*] • a *resolvable* conflict

²resolve *noun* [*noncount*] **:** a strong determination to do something • His comments were intended to weaken her *resolve* but they only served to strengthen it.

resolved /rɪˈzɑːlvd/ *adj* **:** feeling strong determination to do something • I was *resolved* [=*determined*] to find out the truth.

res·o·nance /ˈrɛzənəns/ *noun* [*noncount*]

1 *formal* **:** the quality of a sound that stays loud, clear, and deep for a long time • the *resonance* of the singer's voice

2 *formal* **:** a quality that makes something personally meaningful or important to someone • His story didn't have much *resonance* with the audience.

3 *technical* **:** a sound or vibration produced in one object that is caused by the sound or vibration produced in another

res·o·nant /ˈrɛzənənt/ *adj* [*more ~; most ~*]

1 : producing a loud, clear, deep sound • a *resonant* church bell • the *resonant* tones of the piano • He has a deep, *resonant* voice.

2 : strongly affecting someone especially with a particular quality • *resonant* images of heroism • His words were *resonant* with meaning.

– res·o·nant·ly *adv*

res·o·nate /ˈrɛzəˌneɪt/ *verb* **-nates; -nat·ed; -nat·ing** [*no obj*]

1 : to continue to produce a loud, clear, deep sound for a long time • The siren *resonated* throughout the city.

2 : to have particular meaning or importance for someone **:** to affect or appeal to someone in a personal or emotional way — usually + *with* • Her speech *resonated with* voters. [=voters liked and were impressed by her speech]

res·o·na·tor /ˈrɛzəˌneɪtɚ/ *noun, pl* **-tors** [*count*] **:** a device used to make something (such as a musical instrument) louder

¹re·sort /rɪˈzoɚt/ *noun, pl* **-sorts**

1 [*count*] **:** a place where people go for vacations • a ski/beach/golf *resort* • a *resort* hotel

2 [*count*] **:** something that you choose for help • "We may have to ask them for more time." "That should be our ***last resort***." [=that should be something we do only if nothing else works] • Our ***first resort*** was to go to the police. • The company will only declare bankruptcy ***as a last/final resort***. = (*Brit*) The company will only declare bankruptcy ***in the last resort***. • a ***weapon of last resort*** [=a weapon that is only used if its use cannot be avoided]

3 [*noncount*] **:** the act of doing or using something especially because no other choices are possible — usually + *to* • The police hope to end the standoff ***without resort to*** force. [=without using force]

²resort *verb* **-sorts; -sort·ed; -sort·ing**

resort to [*phrasal verb*] ***resort to (something)*** **:** to do or use (something) especially because no other choices are possible • We want to resolve this crisis without *resorting to* violence. • He had to *resort to* asking his parents for money.

re·sound /rɪˈzaʊnd/ *verb* **-sounds; -sound·ed; -sound·ing** [*no obj*]

1 : to become filled with sound — usually + *with* • The hall *resounded with* cheers.

2 : to make a loud, deep sound • The organ *resounded* throughout the church.

3 : to make a strong impression or have a great effect on people • His speech *resounded* throughout the world.

re·sound·ing /rɪˈzaʊndɪŋ/ *adj* [*more ~; most ~*]

1 : producing a loud, deep sound that lasts for a long time • a *resounding* crash

2 : leaving no doubt **:** very definite • The play was a *resounding* [=*great, huge*] success. • a *resounding* victory • The class answered with a *resounding* no.

– re·sound·ing·ly *adv*

R

re·source /ˈriːˌsoɚs, *Brit* rɪˈzɔːs/ *noun, pl* **-sourc·es**
1 [*count*] **: something that a country has and can use to increase its wealth** ▪ Oil is essentially their only *resource.* — **usually plural** ▪ The country has vast mineral *resources.* ▪ coal, oil, and other ***natural resources***
2 [*plural*] **: a supply of something (such as money) that someone has and can use when it is needed** ▪ Their financial *resources* are severely limited. [=they do not have much money] ▪ If we ***pool our resources*** [=if we combine our money] we can buy the car. — **see also** HUMAN RESOURCES
3 [*count*] **: a place or thing that provides something useful** ▪ The library/Internet is a useful *resource* [=*source*] for information. ▪ The computer laboratory is an essential *resource* for students.
4 a [*count*] **: an ability or quality that allows you to do the things that are necessary — usually plural** ▪ Does he have the intellectual *resources* to do the job? ▪ During his illness she discovered vast ***inner resources*** that gave her the strength she needed. **b** [*noncount*] *formal* **: an ability to deal with and find solutions for problems** ▪ She is a worker of tremendous *resource.* [=*resourcefulness*]

re·source·ful /rɪˈsoɚsfəl, *Brit* rɪˈzɔːsfəl/ *adj* [*more* ~; *most* ~] **: able to deal well with new or difficult situations and to find solutions to problems** ▪ a *resourceful* leader
— **re·source·ful·ly** *adv* ▪ She handled the problem very *resourcefully.* — **re·source·ful·ness** *noun* [*noncount*]

[1]re·spect /rɪˈspɛkt/ *noun, pl* **-spects**
1 : a feeling of admiring someone or something that is good, valuable, important, etc. [*noncount*] He has earned/gained/won their *respect.* ▪ The soldier saluted as a sign of *respect.* ▪ Despite our differences, I have enormous *respect* for him. ▪ She has a lot of *respect* for his opinion. [=she values his opinion very highly] [*singular*] I have a great *respect* for his accomplishments.
2 : a feeling or understanding that someone or something is important, serious, etc., and should be treated in an appropriate way [*noncount*] She showed no *respect* [=*consideration*] for my feelings. ▪ I expect to be treated with *respect.* ▪ He has no *respect* for the rules. [=he does not obey/follow the rules; he disregards the rules] [*count*] He has a healthy *respect* for the dangers of the work he does. [=he is aware of the dangers and does the work in a careful way]
3 [*count*] **: a particular way of thinking about or looking at something** ▪ The show was perfect in all *respects.* [=in every way] ▪ Your theory makes sense in one *respect.* ▪ In many *respects* [=in many ways], her life has been a hard one.
4 *respects* [*plural*] **: a polite greeting or expression of kind feelings** ▪ Please ***give/send my respects*** to your parents. [=please tell your parents I said hello] ▪ I ***paid my respects*** [=offered my condolences] to the family at the funeral. ▪ We went to his funeral to ***pay our last/final respects***
with (all) (due) respect **— used as a polite or formal way of saying that you disagree with someone** ▪ I have to say, *with all respect,* that I don't think your solution will work. ▪ *With all due respect,* I must disagree with your conclusions.
with respect to *also* ***in respect to*** *or chiefly Brit* ***in respect of*** *formal* **: about or concerning (something or someone) : in relation to (something or someone)** ▪ There is a question *with respect to* your earlier comments. ▪ There have been problems *with respect to* transferring the data from the old computer to the new one.

[2]respect *verb* **-spects; -spect·ed; -spect·ing** [+ *obj*]
1 : to feel admiration for (someone or something) : to regard (someone or something) as being worthy of admiration because of good qualities ▪ The students *respect* the principal for his honesty. ▪ I *respect* what she has accomplished.
2 : to act in a way which shows that you are aware of (someone's rights, wishes, etc.) ▪ He *respected* my wish for quiet. [=he was quiet because he knew that was what I wanted] ▪ Please *respect* my privacy. ▪ You must learn to *respect* other people's property.
3 a : to treat or deal with (something that is good or valuable) in a proper way ▪ We need to *respect* the environment. **b : do what is required by (a law, rule, etc.)** ▪ She always *respects* [=*observes*] the speed limit.
as respects *formal* **: about or concerning (something) : with respect to (something)** ▪ She is very liberal *as respects* human rights.
— **re·spect·er** /rɪˈspɛktɚ/ *noun, pl* **-ers** [*count*] ▪ He wants to be seen as a *respecter* of the environment. ▪ (*formal*) The law is ***no respecter of persons*** [=the law applies to all people in the same way]

re·spect·able /rɪˈspɛktəbəl/ *adj* [*more* ~; *most* ~]
1 : considered to be good, correct, or acceptable : decent or correct in character, behavior, or appearance ▪ *respectable* people ▪ She comes from a very *respectable* family. ▪ wearing *respectable* clothes
2 : fairly good ▪ She makes a *respectable* [=*decent*] salary. ▪ Her grades were *respectable* [=*satisfactory*] but not great.
— **re·spect·abil·i·ty** /rɪˌspɛktəˈbɪləti/ *noun* [*noncount*] ▪ He has an air of *respectability* about him. — **re·spect·ably** /rɪˈspɛktəbli/ *adv* ▪ He was *respectably* dressed.

respected *adj* [*more* ~; *most* ~] **: admired by many people** ▪ She is a highly *respected* professor. ▪ He is one of the most *respected* people in the film industry.

re·spect·ful /rɪˈspɛktfəl/ *adj* [*more* ~; *most* ~] **: showing or having respect** ▪ a *respectful* manner **— often + *of*** ▪ Children should be *respectful of* their elders.
— **re·spect·ful·ly** /rɪˈspɛktfəli/ *adv* ▪ He *respectfully* removed his hat when he entered the building. — **re·spect·ful·ness** *noun* [*noncount*]

re·spect·ing /rɪˈspɛktɪŋ/ *prep, formal* **: about or relating to (something) : with respect to (something)** ▪ We have heard no information *respecting* [=*concerning, regarding*] the path of the storm.

re·spec·tive /rɪˈspɛktɪv/ *adj* **: belonging or relating to each one of the people or things that have been mentioned** ▪ The brother and sister returned to their *respective* [=*own*] bedrooms. ▪ They are all very successful in their *respective* [=*individual*] fields.
— **re·spec·tive·ly** /rɪˈspɛktɪvli/ *adv* ▪ The boy and girl are 12 and 13 years old *respectively.* [=the boy is 12 and the girl is 13]

res·pi·ra·tion /ˌrɛspəˈreɪʃən/ *noun* [*noncount*] *medical* **: the act or process of breathing** ▪ The doctor checked his heartbeat and *respiration.* — **see also** ARTIFICIAL RESPIRATION

res·pi·ra·tor /ˈrɛspəˌreɪtɚ/ *noun, pl* **-tors** [*count*]
1 : a device that you wear over your mouth and nose so that you can breathe when there is a lot of dust, smoke, etc., in the air
2 *medical* **: a device that helps people to breathe when they are not able to breathe naturally** ▪ The doctors put her on a *respirator.*

re·spi·ra·to·ry /ˈrɛspərəˌtori, *Brit* rɪˈspɪrətri/ *adj, medical* **: of or relating to breathing or the organs of the body that are used in breathing** ▪ *respiratory* diseases/illnesses/infections ▪ the *respiratory* system [=the lungs or other organs used in respiration]

re·spire /rɪˈspajɚ/ *verb* **-spires; -spired; -spir·ing** [*no obj*] *technical* **:** BREATHE **1** ▪ Fish use their gills to *respire.*

re·spite /ˈrɛspət, *Brit* ˈrɛˌspaɪt/ *noun, pl* **-spites : a short period of time when you are able to stop doing something that is difficult or unpleasant or when something difficult or unpleasant stops or is delayed** [*count*] **— usually singular** ▪ The weekend provided a nice *respite* from the pressures of her job. ▪ a temporary *respite* [*noncount*] The bad weather has continued without *respite.*

re·splen·dent /rɪˈsplɛndənt/ *adj* [*more* ~; *most* ~] *literary* **: very bright and attractive** ▪ The fields were *resplendent* with flowers. ▪ She looked *resplendent* in her green evening gown. ▪ a bird with *resplendent* yellow feathers
— **re·splen·dent·ly** *adv*

re·spond /rɪˈspɑːnd/ *verb* **-sponds; -spond·ed; -spond·ing**
1 : to say or write something as an answer to a question or request : REPLY [*no obj*] She hasn't yet *responded* to my letter. ▪ My mother *responded* to my request with a firm no. ▪ The teacher asked a question, but the student didn't *respond.* [+ *obj*] "Are you ready?" he asked. "No," she *responded.* ▪ When I asked him what he was doing, he *responded* that it was none of my business.
2 [*no obj*] **: to do something as a reaction to something that has happened or been done** ▪ Police quickly *responded* to the call for help. ▪ She *responded* to their decision by threatening to quit. **: to have a particular reaction to something** ▪ He doesn't *respond* [=*react*] well to criticism. ▪ Most readers *responded* favorably to the book. [=most readers liked the book]
3 [*no obj*] **: to have a good or desired reaction to something** ▪ The patient is *responding* to the treatment. [=the patient is getting better because of the treatment]

re·spon·dent /rɪˈspɑːndənt/ *noun, pl* **-dents** [*count*] **: a person who gives a response or answer to a question that is asked especially as part of a survey** ▪ A majority of *respondents* said they disagreed with the mayor's plan.

R

re•sponse /rɪˈspɑ:ns/ *noun, pl* **-spons•es**
1 : something that is said or written as a reply to something [*count*] He got a *response* to his letter. [*noncount*] I am writing ***in response to*** your letter of July 17. • She asked him but he ***gave/made no response***. [=he did not answer]
2 : something that is done as a reaction to something else [*count*] When I told him my plan, I wasn't expecting such an enthusiastic *response*. • Her *response* to their decision was to threaten to quit her job. • The patient suffered an adverse *response* to the medication. [=the patient became worse after taking the medication] [*noncount*] When you knocked on the door, was there any *response*?

re•spon•si•bil•i•ty /rɪˌspɑ:nsəˈbɪləti/ *noun, pl* **-ties**
1 [*noncount*] **:** the state of being the person who caused something to happen • He accepted full *responsibility* for the accident. [=he admitted that the accident was his fault] • The boys denied any *responsibility* for the damage to the fence. • A terrorist group has claimed *responsibility* for the bombing.
2 a : a duty or task that you are required or expected to do [*count*] The janitor has many *responsibilities*. • Mowing the lawn is your *responsibility*. • She has to deal with a lot of family and work *responsibilities*. • It is your *responsibility* to give the company two weeks notice if you decide to leave. • A teacher's most important *responsibility* is to help her students. = A teacher's first *responsibility* is to/toward her students. [*noncount*] In her new position, she will have much more *responsibility*. **b** [*count*] **:** something that you should do because it is morally right, legally required, etc. • We have a *responsibility* to protect the environment. • The government's *responsibility* is to serve the public.
3 [*noncount*] **:** the state of having the job or duty of dealing with and taking care of something or someone • The principal has *responsibility* for 450 students and a staff of 35.
4 [*noncount*] **:** the quality of a person who can be trusted to do what is expected, required, etc. • She is completely lacking in *responsibility*. • The boy developed a ***sense of responsibility*** with his first job.
on your own responsibility ◇ To do something *on your own responsibility* is to do it without being told to and to accept the blame if it has a bad result. • He changed the schedule *on his own responsibility*.

re•spon•si•ble /rɪˈspɑ:nsəbəl/ *adj*
1 — used to describe the person or thing that causes something to happen • Those *responsible* will be punished/rewarded. **—** usually + *for* • The technicians found the glitch that was *responsible for* [=that caused] the computer crash. • Police caught the youths *responsible for* the vandalism. • Who was *responsible for* the accident? • She's *responsible for* most of the improvements here in recent months. • He ***holds me responsible for*** [=blames me for] the project's failure.
2 : having the job or duty of dealing with or taking care of something or someone **—** + *for* • She is *responsible for* the company's publicity. • Each child is *responsible for* his or her own belongings. • The committee is *responsible for* organizing the dance. • You are *responsible for* mowing the lawn. • Who was *responsible for* choosing this location? • Parents are *responsible for* their own children.
3 [*more ~; most ~*] **:** able to be trusted to do what is right or to do the things that are expected or required • She is a very *responsible* worker. • Is he *responsible* enough to have a car? **—** opposite IRRESPONSIBLE
4 [*more ~; most ~*] **:** involving important duties, decisions, etc., that you are trusted to do • She got a higher salary and a more *responsible* position at the company.
5 : working under the direction and authority of a particular person **—** + *to* • I am *responsible to* her, and she is directly *responsible to* the company president.
– re•spon•si•bly /rɪˈspɑ:nsəbli/ *adv* [*more ~; most ~*] • Our leaders must act *responsibly*.

re•spon•sive /rɪˈspɑ:nsɪv/ *adj* [*more ~; most ~*]
1 : reacting in a desired or positive way • The patient was not *responsive* to the treatment. • They weren't very *responsive* to my suggestion. [=they did not respond very favorably to my suggestion]
2 : quick to react or respond • The store is very *responsive* to the needs of its customers. • a car with *responsive* steering [=steering that works quickly when you move the steering wheel]
– re•spon•sive•ly *adv* **– re•spon•sive•ness** *noun* [*noncount*]

¹rest /ˈrɛst/ *noun*
the rest **:** the part that is left when other people or things are gone, used, etc. • You bring these bags in, and I'll bring *the rest*. [=*the remainder*] • Thanks for your help. I can handle *the rest*. • Linda, Joan, Donna, and *the rest* **—** often + *of* • He would regret that decision for *the rest of* his life. • She went shopping and spent *the rest of* her money on dinner. • We finished *the rest of* the cake. • He worked in the morning and relaxed (for) *the rest of* the day.
– compare ²REST

²rest *noun, pl* **rests**
1 : a period of time in which you relax, sleep, or do nothing after you have been active or doing work [*noncount*] a day of *rest* • I was ordered to get some *rest*. • None of us had/got much *rest* last night. [*count*] **—** usually singular • I need a *rest*. [=*break*] • The coach canceled practice to give his team a *rest*. • a 10-minute *rest* period **—** see also BED REST
2 [*noncount*] **:** a state in which there is no motion • an object in a state of *rest*
3 [*count*] **:** an object that is designed to support or hold something • a knife/spoon *rest* • the violin's chin *rest* **—** see also ARMREST, FOOTREST, HEADREST
4 [*count*] **a :** a period of silence between musical notes **b :** a symbol in music that shows a period of silence between notes
at rest **1 :** not moving • The object is *at rest*. [=*motionless*] **2 :** no longer living **:** DEAD • After years of suffering, she is finally *at rest*. **3 :** in a relaxed and comfortable state • You can ***set/put your mind at rest*** [=you can relax and stop worrying]
come to rest **:** to stop moving • The ball *came to rest* against the curb. • Her eyes *came to rest* on a mysterious man. [=she stopped looking around and looked at the mysterious man]
give it a rest *informal* **—** used to tell someone to stop talking about something • Oh, *give it a rest*! I don't want to hear it.
give (something) a rest *informal* **:** to stop doing or using (something) • Hey, *give the TV remote a rest* and go outside to play!
lay (someone) to rest **:** to bury (someone who has died) **—** usually used as *(be) laid to rest* • She *was laid to rest* in the church's graveyard.
lay/put to rest (something) *or* ***lay/put (something) to rest*** **:** to make someone stop thinking about or believing (something) by showing it is not true • I want to *lay/put to rest* any lingering doubts about my decision.
– compare ¹REST

³rest *verb* **rests; rest•ed; rest•ing**
1 [*no obj*] **:** to stop doing work or an activity • We will not *rest* until we discover the truth. **:** to spend time relaxing, sleeping, or doing nothing after you have been active or doing work • The workers were *resting* in the shade. • They expect to *rest* [=*relax*] while on vacation. • He is *resting* comfortably after his ordeal. • She went to her room to *rest* for a while.
2 [+ *obj*] **a :** to give rest to (someone) • The coach canceled practice to *rest* his team. • May God *rest* her soul. [=I pray that God will give her soul peace now that she has died] **b :** to stop using (something) so that it can become strong again • He *rested* his horse before continuing the journey. • You should *rest* your eyes after all that reading. • The pitcher needs to *rest* his arm.
3 *always followed by an adverb or preposition* **a** [*no obj*] **:** to sit or lie on something • The spoon was *resting* in the cup. • The house *rests* on a concrete foundation. **—** often used figuratively • The real authority *rests* with the committee. • The blame *rests* (solely) on/with me. [=I am to blame; I am responsible for what happened] **b** [+ *obj*] **:** to place (something) on or against something else • He *rested* his hand on her shoulder. • She *rested* her bike against a tree. • He *rested* his chin in his hands. • Don't *rest* your elbows on the table.
4 [*no obj*] **:** to lie in a grave after death • My grandfather *rests* [=is buried] next to my grandmother. • May she ***rest in peace***. [=may she have peace in her death]
5 : to stop presenting evidence in a legal case [*no obj*] The defense *rests*, Your Honor. [+ *obj*] The defense *rested* its case. **—** see also *I rest my case* at ¹CASE
let (something) rest **:** to stop mentioning or talking about (something) • You just won't *let* this *rest*, will you? • They told them their decision, but he won't *let* the matter *rest*.
rest easy **:** to stop worrying about something **:** to not worry about something • I can *rest easy* knowing that he will be in charge.
rest on/upon [*phrasal verb*] **1** ***rest on/upon (someone or something)*** **a :** to depend or rely on (someone or something) • All our hopes *rested on* one man. **b :** to stop mov-

R

ing and look at (someone or something) • His eyes/gaze *rested on* the letter. **2 *rest on/upon (something)*** : to be based on (something) • His theory *rested upon* two important pieces of evidence.

rest on your laurels see LAUREL

rest with [*phrasal verb*] ***rest with (someone or something)*** : to be the responsibility of (someone or something) • The final decision *rests with* you.

rest area *noun, pl* ~ **-eas** [*count*] *US* : an area next to a highway where people can stop to rest, use the bathroom, get food, etc. — called also (*US*) *rest stop*

re·start /riˈstɑɚt/ *verb* **-starts; -start·ed; -start·ing**

1 : to make (something) start again after it has stopped [+ *obj*] *Restart* your computer. • *restart* the video game • They plan to *restart* negotiations next week. [*no obj*] After you *restart* [=restart your computer], go to the main menu.

2 [*no obj*] : to start again after stopping • The tournament will *restart* tomorrow. • The tractor won't *restart*.

– restart *noun, pl* **-starts** [*count*] • a computer *restart*

re·state /riˈsteɪt/ *verb* **-states; -stat·ed; -stat·ing** [+ *obj*] : to say (something) again or in a different way especially to make the meaning clearer • She needs to *restate* her arguments.

– re·state·ment /riˈsteɪtmənt/ *noun, pl* **-ments** [*count, noncount*] • a *restatement* of familiar ideas

res·tau·rant /ˈrɛstəˌrɑːnt/ *noun, pl* **-rants** [*count*] : a place where you can buy and eat a meal • a Mexican/Italian/Chinese *restaurant* [=a restaurant that serves Mexican/Italian/Chinese food]

restaurant car *noun, pl* ~ **cars** [*count*] *chiefly Brit* : DINING CAR

res·tau·ra·teur /ˌrɛstərəˈtɚ/ *also* **res·tau·ran·teur** /ˌrɛstəˌrɑːnˈtɚ/ *noun, pl* **-teurs** [*count*] : a person who owns or manages a restaurant

rest·ed /ˈrɛstəd/ *adj* [*more* ~; *most* ~] : having had enough rest or sleep • They were (well) *rested* after a long vacation. • She appears *rested* and sharp. • I want to be *rested* for the exam.

rest·ful /ˈrɛstfəl/ *adj* [*more* ~; *most* ~] : peaceful and quiet in a way that makes you relax • It's *restful* by the stream. • a *restful* weekend

– rest·ful·ly *adv*

rest home *noun, pl* ~ **homes** [*count*] : a place where people who are old or who are unable to take care of themselves can live and be taken care of : NURSING HOME

rest·ing /ˈrɛstɪŋ/ *adj, always used before a noun, technical* : taken or measured when you are relaxed and not moving much • your *resting* heart rate • the *resting* metabolic rate

resting place *noun, pl* ~ **places** [*count*]

1 : a place where you can stop and rest • We found a good *resting place* by the side of the trail.

2 : a place where someone is buried • This is her ***final/last resting place***.

3 : a place where something has been put • The monument was moved to a new *resting place*.

res·ti·tu·tion /ˌrɛstəˈtuːʃən, *Brit* ˌrɛstəˈtjuːʃən/ *noun* [*noncount*] *formal*

1 : the act of returning something that was lost or stolen to its owner • the *restitution* of her stolen property

2 : payment that is made to someone for damage, trouble, etc. • He was ordered to make *restitution* to the victim.

res·tive /ˈrɛstɪv/ *adj* [*more* ~; *most* ~] *formal* : feeling bored or impatient while waiting for something to happen or change • a *restive* audience • The audience grew/became *restive*.

– res·tive·ly *adv* **– res·tive·ness** *noun* [*noncount*]

rest·less /ˈrɛstləs/ *adj* [*more* ~; *most* ~]

1 : feeling nervous or bored and tending to move around a lot : not relaxed or calm • *restless* children who can't sit still • The audience was becoming *restless*.

2 : unhappy about a situation and wanting change • He started to feel *restless* and discontent in his job.

3 : having little or no rest or sleep • a *restless* night

– rest·less·ly *adv* • They searched *restlessly* for something new to do. • He tossed *restlessly* in bed. **– rest·less·ness** *noun* [*noncount*] • the *restlessness* of the crowd

re·stock /riˈstɑːk/ *verb* **-stocks; -stocked; -stock·ing** [+ *obj*] : to provide a new supply of something to replace what has been used, sold, taken, etc. • We *restocked* the merchandise after the store closed. • The shelves need to be *restocked*. • The pond is *restocked* with trout every spring.

res·to·ra·tion /ˌrɛstəˈreɪʃən/ *noun, pl* **-tions**

1 : the act or process of returning something to its original condition by repairing it, cleaning it, etc. [*noncount*] The building is undergoing *restoration*. [*count*] — often + *of* • They have undertaken a careful *restoration of* the building.

2 *somewhat formal* : the act of bringing back something that existed before — usually + *of* [*noncount*] the *restoration of* peace after war • the *restoration of* law and order by the police [*count*] The town called for a *restoration of* the law.

3 [*count, noncount*] *somewhat formal* : the act of returning something that was stolen or taken — often + *of* • (a) *restoration of* stolen property

4 *the Restoration* : the period in 17th-century English history when Charles II was king after a long period of no king or queen on the throne • The play was written during *the Restoration*. — often used as *Restoration* before another noun • a *Restoration* play

¹re·stor·ative /rɪˈstorətɪv/ *adj, formal* : having the ability to make a person feel strong or healthy again • the *restorative* powers of rest • a *restorative* herb

²restorative *noun, pl* **-atives** [*count*] *formal* : something that makes a person feel strong or healthy again • Sleep is a powerful *restorative*.

re·store /rɪˈstoɚ/ *verb* **-stores; -stored; -stor·ing** [+ *obj*]

1 : to give back (someone or something that was lost or taken) : to return (someone or something) — often + *to* • The police *restored* the stolen purse *to* its owner. • The police *restored* the lost child *to* her parents.

2 : to put or bring (something) back into existence or use • Surgery will *restore* his hearing. [=surgery will let him hear again] • The police *restored* law and order. • The team's victory has *restored* a sense of pride to the community. [=the team's victory has made the community feel proud again] • The government needs to *restore* confidence in the economy.

3 : to return (something) to an earlier or original condition by repairing it, cleaning it, etc. • The crew is trying to *restore* the old house (to its original condition). • He *restores* old paintings. • an antique car that is being carefully *restored* • newly/recently *restored* churches

4 a : to bring (someone) back to an earlier and better condition — usually + *to* • Her care *restored* the child *to* health. **b** : to put (someone) back in a position — usually + *to* • His allies *restored* the king *to* the throne.

– re·stor·able /rɪˈstorəbəl/ *adj* • The car is in *restorable* condition. **– re·stor·er** *noun, pl* **-ers** [*count*] • an art *restorer* • a *restorer* of antique furniture

re·strain /rɪˈstreɪn/ *verb* **-strains; -strained; -strain·ing** [+ *obj*]

1 : to prevent (a person or animal) from doing something • He could not *restrain* the dog from attacking. • I wanted to have another serving, but I somehow *restrained* myself. = I somehow *restrained* myself from having another serving. • He could *restrain* himself no longer.

2 : to prevent (a person or animal) from moving by using physical force • Hospital orderlies needed to *restrain* the patient. • He was *restrained* and placed in a holding cell.

3 : to keep (something) under control • He could barely *restrain* his anger. • The manufacturer took measures to *restrain* costs.

re·strained /rɪˈstreɪnd/ *adj* [*more* ~; *most* ~]

1 : showing careful self-control • She was admired for her *restrained* behavior. • a *restrained* smile

2 : not too colorful or fancy • a *restrained* style of architecture • The room was decorated with *restrained* colors.

restraining order *noun, pl* ~ **-ders** [*count*] *US, law* : a legal order saying that someone is not allowed to go near a particular person • The judge issued a *restraining order*. — often + *against* • She took out a *restraining order against* her former husband.

re·straint /rɪˈstreɪnt/ *noun, pl* **-straints**

1 [*count*] *somewhat formal* : a way of limiting, controlling, or stopping something — usually plural; often + *on* • The government has placed/put/imposed *restraints on* imports.

2 [*count*] *formal* : a device that limits a person's movement • Make sure the child safety *restraint* is in place. • The prisoner was placed ***in restraints***.

3 [*noncount*] : control over your emotions or behavior • His angry response showed a lack of *restraint*. • The government has acted with *restraint* in dealing with this crisis. • You should exercise *restraint*.

4 [*noncount*] *formal* : physical force that prevents someone from moving • (*US*) She was charged with ***unlawful restraint***. • He was placed ***under restraint***. [=he was restrained]

R

re•strict /rɪˈstrɪkt/ *verb* **-stricts; -strict•ed; -strict•ing** [+ *obj*]
1 : to limit the amount or range of (something) ▪ Her eye problem *restricts* her reading. ▪ She was told to *restrict* the amount of salt she uses. ▪ They want to *restrict* access to the beach. [=they want to limit who can use the beach] ▪ The new law *restricts* smoking in public places. ▪ They have accused the government of trying to *restrict* free speech. — often used as *(be) restricted* ▪ Visits *are restricted* to 30 minutes. [=visits cannot be longer than 30 minutes] ▪ The damage from the fire *was restricted* to the rear of the building. [=the rear of the building was the only part damaged by the fire]
2 : to prevent (someone) from doing something ▪ They say the government is trying to *restrict* them from speaking out.
3 : to allow (someone) to only have or do a particular thing — usually + *to* ▪ The doctor *restricted* her *to* a low-fat diet. [=she was only allowed to eat a low-fat diet] ▪ He *restricts* himself *to* one cup of coffee a day. [=he allows himself to have only one cup of coffee a day]

re•strict•ed /rɪˈstrɪktəd/ *adj*
1 : having a set limit ▪ Only a *restricted* [=*limited*] number of students will be allowed in the class.
2 [*more ~; most ~*] **:** having definite rules about what or who is allowed and not allowed ▪ He is on a severely/very *restricted* diet. ▪ The beach has *restricted* access. [=only certain people can go on the beach]
3 : allowing use or entry by only certain people ▪ a *restricted* country club ▪ You have entered a *restricted* area.
4 : kept secret from all but a few people **:** CLASSIFIED ▪ a *restricted* document ▪ That information is *restricted*.

re•stric•tion /rɪˈstrɪkʃən/ *noun, pl* **-tions**
1 [*count*] **:** a law or rule that limits or controls something ▪ Building in that area came with some *restrictions*. ▪ travel *restrictions* ▪ They placed/imposed *restrictions* on smoking indoors. ▪ They will lift/remove export *restrictions*.
2 [*noncount*] **:** the act of limiting or controlling something ▪ illegal *restriction* of free speech

re•stric•tive /rɪˈstrɪktɪv/ *adj*
1 [*more ~; most ~*] **:** limiting or controlling someone or something ▪ *restrictive* laws/regulations ▪ a very *restrictive* diet
2 *grammar, of a word or group of words* **:** giving information about a person or thing that is needed to understand which person or thing is meant ▪ In the sentence "The book that you ordered is out of print," "that you ordered" is a ***restrictive clause***. — compare NONRESTRICTIVE

rest•room /ˈrɛstˌruːm/ *noun, pl* **-rooms** [*count*] *US* **:** a room in a public place with a sink and toilet **:** BATHROOM 2 ▪ a public *restroom*

re•struc•ture /riˈstrʌktʃɚ/ *verb* **-tures; -tured; -tur•ing** [+ *obj*] **:** to change the basic organization or structure of (something) ▪ You should *restructure* this sentence to make its meaning clearer. ▪ The college is *restructuring* its Humanities Department.
– restructuring *noun, pl* **-ings** [*count, noncount*] ▪ A *restructuring* of the health-care system is needed.

rest stop *noun, pl* **~ stops** [*count*] *US* **:** REST AREA

[1]re•sult /rɪˈzʌlt/ *noun, pl* **-sults**
1 : something that is caused by something else that happened or was done before [*count*] The book is the *result* of years of hard work and dedication. ▪ The ***end/final result*** of his work was a classic American novel. ▪ ***As a result of*** [=because of] the accident, he was out of work for three months. ▪ He sprained his wrist and, ***as a result*** [=because of this], he will not be playing in the tournament. ▪ Bad weather caused several delays ***with the result that*** the work was not completed on time. [=the work was not completed on time because bad weather caused delays] [*noncount*] The investigation continued without *result*.
2 [*count*] **a :** the final score or a description of who won and lost in a game, election, etc. ▪ What was the *result* of last night's game? [=who won last night's game?] — often plural ▪ Election *results* will be posted later. ▪ The play-off roster depends on the *results* of tonight's game. **b** *Brit, informal* **:** a win especially in a soccer match — usually singular ▪ After several drawn matches, we finally ***got a result***. [=we finally won]
3 [*count*] *Brit* **:** the grade received on a test or examination — usually plural ▪ Have you gotten your exam *results* yet?
4 [*count*] **:** information that you get from a scientific or medical test ▪ My blood test *result* was fine.
5 ***results*** [*plural*] **:** something you want that is achieved successfully ▪ We are waiting for the experiment to produce *results*. ▪ This method ***gets results***. [=this method is effective and successful]

[2]result *verb* **-sults; -sult•ed; -sult•ing** [*no obj*] **:** to happen because of something else that happened or was done before **:** to be caused by something else ▪ If you take this drug, side effects may *result*. — usually + *from* ▪ The fire *resulted from* an explosion.
result in [*phrasal verb*] ***result in (something)*** **:** to cause (something) to happen ▪ The disease *resulted in* his death. **:** to produce (something) as a result ▪ The trial *resulted in* an acquittal.
– resulting *adj, always used before a noun* ▪ the accident and his *resulting* death

re•sul•tant /rɪˈzʌltn̩t/ *adj, always used before a noun, formal* **:** coming from or caused by something else ▪ She deserves credit for the increase in sales and the *resultant* increase in profit.

re•sume /rɪˈzuːm, *Brit* rɪˈzjuːm/ *verb* **-sumes; -sumed; -sum•ing** *formal*
1 : to begin again after stopping [*no obj*] The game *resumed* after the rain stopped. ▪ Negotiations have *resumed*. [+ *obj*] After the rain stopped, the teams *resumed* play. ▪ She sat down and *resumed* her work.
2 [+ *obj*] **:** to take (a seat, place, position, etc.) again **:** to go back to (something) ▪ He shook his visitor's hand and *resumed* his seat. ▪ I *resumed* my place at the podium. ▪ She will be *resuming* her position at the company.

ré•su•mé *or* **re•su•me** *also* **re•su•mé** /ˈrɛzəˌmeɪ, *Brit* ˈrezjʊˌmeɪ/ *noun, pl* **-més** *or* **-mes** [*count*]
1 *US* **a :** a short document describing your education, work history, etc., that you give an employer when you are applying for a job ▪ If you would like to be considered for the job, please submit your *résumé*. — called also (*chiefly Brit*) *curriculum vitae* **b :** a list of achievements ▪ His musical *résumé* includes performances at Carnegie Hall, a stint with the New York Philharmonic, and two Grammys.
2 *formal* **:** a short description of things that have happened **:** SUMMARY ▪ a brief *résumé* of the news

re•sump•tion /rɪˈzʌmpʃən/ *noun, formal* **:** an act of starting something again after it has stopped **:** an act of resuming something — usually + *of* [*singular*] The rain has stopped, but we're still waiting for the *resumption of* the game. [*noncount*] *Resumption of* peace talks is expected soon.

re•sur•face /riˈsɚfəs/ *verb* **-fac•es; -faced; -fac•ing**
1 [*no obj*] **:** to rise to the surface again after being underwater or underground ▪ The submarine *resurfaced*.
2 [*no obj*] **:** to suddenly be found or appear again ▪ A few of the writer's journals have *resurfaced*. ▪ His resentment toward her *resurfaced*.
3 [+ *obj*] **:** to put a new surface on (something) **:** to refinish or repair the surface of (something) ▪ He *resurfaced* the table. ▪ The road needs to be *resurfaced*.

re•sur•gence /rɪˈsɚʤəns/ *noun* **:** a growth or increase that occurs after a period without growth or increase [*singular*] a *resurgence* of interest/popularity [*noncount*] There has been some *resurgence* in economic activity recently.

re•sur•gent /rɪˈsɚʤənt/ *adj, formal* **:** becoming popular, active, or successful again after a period of being less popular, active, or successful ▪ a *resurgent* stock market ▪ a *resurgent* politician

res•ur•rect /ˌrɛzəˈrɛkt/ *verb* **-rects; -rect•ed; -rect•ing** [+ *obj*]
1 : to bring (a dead person) back to life ▪ The story is about a scientist who claimed that he could *resurrect* the dead.
2 : to cause (something that had ended or been forgotten or lost) to exist again, to be used again, etc. ▪ He is trying to *resurrect* his acting career. ▪ an old government program that is being *resurrected* ▪ Her reputation has been *resurrected*. [=*restored*]

res•ur•rec•tion /ˌrɛzəˈrɛkʃən/ *noun*
1 *in Christianity* **a *the Resurrection*** **:** the event told about in the Bible in which Jesus Christ returned to life after his death **b *the resurrection*** *or* ***the Resurrection*** **:** the event told about in the Bible in which dead people will be brought back to life before the day of final judgment
2 [*singular*] **:** the act of causing something that had ended or been forgotten or lost to exist again, to be used again, etc. ▪ He was enjoying the *resurrection* of his career. ▪ a *resurrection* of an old theory

re•sus•ci•tate /rɪˈsʌsəˌteɪt/ *verb* **-tates; -tat•ed; -tat•ing** [+ *obj*] **:** to bring (someone who is unconscious, not breathing, or close to death) back to a conscious or active state

R

again • The patient stopped breathing but doctors were able to *resuscitate* him. — often used figuratively • He is trying to *resuscitate* his political career.

– **re·sus·ci·ta·tion** /rɪˌsʌsəˈteɪʃən/ *noun, pl* **-tions** [*count, noncount*] • The patient stopped breathing and required emergency *resuscitation.* — see also CARDIOPULMONARY RESUSCITATION, MOUTH-TO-MOUTH RESUSCITATION

ret. *or* **Ret.** *abbr* retired • General Smith, U.S. Army (*Ret.*)

¹retail /ˈriːˌteɪl/ *noun* [*noncount*] : the business of selling things directly to customers for their own use • She has a job in *retail.* — compare WHOLESALE

²retail *adj* : relating to the business of selling things directly to customers for their own use • a *retail* establishment/shop/store • the manufacturer's suggested *retail* price [=the price of something when it is sold to the final customer] • Is that price *retail* or wholesale?

³retail *adv* : in a store that sells things directly to customers for their own use : from a retailer • You usually have to pay more if you buy something *retail* than if you buy it wholesale. • The product sells *retail* for about $100.

⁴re·tail *verb* **-tails; -tailed; -tail·ing**

1 [+ *obj*] : to sell (something) to customers for their own use • We *retail* clothing at the best possible prices.

2 [*no obj*] : to be sold to the final customer for a specified price • jewelry that *retails* from $100 — often + *at* • The item *retails at* $59.

3 [+ *obj*] *formal* : to tell (something) to one person after another : to tell (something) again • *retailing* [=*retelling*] gossip

re·tail·er /ˈriːˌteɪlɚ/ *noun, pl* **-ers** [*count*] : a person or business that sells things directly to customers for their own use • The company is a leading *retailer* of women's clothing.

re·tail·ing /ˈriːˌteɪlɪŋ/ *noun* [*noncount*] : the business of selling things directly to customers for their own use • She works in *retailing.*

retail park *noun, pl* ~ **parks** [*count*] *Brit* : a large shopping area that contains many different kinds of stores

retail price index *noun*

the retail price index *Brit* : CONSUMER PRICE INDEX

re·tain /rɪˈteɪn/ *verb* **-tains; -tained; -tain·ing** [+ *obj*] *formal*

1 : to continue to have or use (something) : KEEP • A landlord may *retain* part of your deposit if you break the lease. • They insisted on *retaining* old customs. • You will *retain* your rights as a citizen. • The TV show has *retained* its popularity for many years.

2 : to keep (someone) in a position, job, etc. • The company's goal is to attract and *retain* good employees. • The team failed to *retain* him, and he became a free agent.

3 : to pay for the work of (a person or business) • They have decided to *retain* a firm to conduct a survey. • You may need to *retain* an attorney.

4 : to keep (something) in your memory especially for a long period of time • I studied French in college, but I haven't *retained* much of what I learned. • She has a remarkable ability to *retain* odd facts.

5 : to continue to hold (something, such as heat or moisture) as time passes • Topping the soil with mulch will help it to *retain* moisture.

re·tain·er /rɪˈteɪnɚ/ *noun, pl* **-ers**

1 : an amount of money that you pay to someone (such as a lawyer) to make sure that you will have that person's services when you need them [*count*] They paid a *retainer* to the lawyer. • They have her on a *retainer.* [*noncount*] They have/keep the lawyer ***on retainer.***

2 [*count*] *US* : a device that you put in your mouth to keep your teeth in the correct position especially after you have had braces

3 [*count*] *old-fashioned* : a servant in a wealthy home • a faithful old *retainer*

retaining wall *noun, pl* ~ **walls** [*count*] : a wall that is built to keep the land behind it from sliding

¹re·take /riˈteɪk/ *verb* **-takes; -took** /-ˈtʊk/; **-tak·en** /-ˈteɪkən/; **-tak·ing** [+ *obj*] : to take (something) again • They helped their party *retake* the Senate. • He *retook* the lead close to the finish line. • We will have to *retake* the photograph. • Students can *retake* the test.

²re·take /ˈriːˌteɪk/ *noun, pl* **-takes** [*count*]

1 : the act of filming, photographing, or recording something again • The director called for a *retake.*

2 *Brit* : an examination that a student takes again after failing or doing poorly the first time

re·tal·i·ate /rɪˈtæliˌeɪt/ *verb* **-ates; -at·ed; -at·ing** [*no obj*] : to do something bad to someone who has hurt you or treated you badly : to get revenge against someone • After the company announced plans to reduce benefits, the union threatened to *retaliate* by calling for a strike.

– **re·tal·i·a·tion** /rɪˌtæliˈeɪʃən/ *noun, pl* **-tions** [*noncount*] They lived under the threat of *retaliation.* • The union has threatened a strike ***in retaliation for*** the company's plans to reduce benefits. [*count*] a quick *retaliation* – **re·tal·ia·to·ry** /rɪˈtæljəˌtori/ *adj* • *retaliatory* attacks

¹re·tard /rɪˈtɑɚd/ *verb* **-tards; -tard·ed; -tard·ing** [+ *obj*] *formal* : to slow down the development or progress of (something) • The chemical will *retard* the spread of fire. • The problems have *retarded* the progress of the program.

²re·tard /ˈriːˌtɑɚd/ *noun, pl* **-tards** [*count*] *informal + offensive* : a person who has slow mental development; *also* : a stupid or foolish person

re·tar·dant /rɪˈtɑɚdn̩t/ *adj, always used before a noun, technical* : able to slow down the progress or development of something — usually used in combination • flame-*retardant* fabrics [=fabrics that do not catch fire easily]

– **retardant** *noun, pl* **-dants** [*count*] • a fire *retardant*

re·tar·da·tion /ˌriːˌtɑɚˈdeɪʃən/ *noun* [*noncount*]

1 *old-fashioned + sometimes offensive* : an unusual slowness of mental development • The child suffered severe mental *retardation.*

2 *formal* : an act of slowing down the development or progress of something • The chemical induced a *retardation* of cell growth.

re·tard·ed /rɪˈtɑɚdəd/ *adj, old-fashioned + often offensive* : slow or limited in mental development • mentally *retarded*

retch /ˈrɛtʃ/ *verb* **retch·es; retched; retch·ing** [*no obj*] : to vomit or feel as if you are about to vomit • I nearly *retched.* • The smell made him *retch.* [=gag]

re·tell /riˈtɛl/ *verb* **-tells; -told** /-ˈtoʊld/; **-tell·ing** [+ *obj*] : to tell (a story) again especially in a different way • The movie *retells* the story of Romeo and Juliet.

– **retelling** *noun, pl* **-ings** [*count*] • The story is a *retelling* of a Greek legend.

re·ten·tion /rɪˈtɛnʃən/ *noun* [*noncount*] *formal*

1 a : the act of keeping someone or something • the recruitment and *retention* of good employees • the *retention* of profits from all sales **b** : the act of keeping extra liquid, heat, etc., inside the body • pills to offset water *retention* • the *retention* of fluid

2 : the ability to keep something • The fabric has good color *retention.* [=the fabric's colors do not fade]

3 : the ability to remember things easily or for a long time • the *retention* of things learned in school • They say the herb promotes memory *retention.*

re·ten·tive /rɪˈtɛntɪv/ *adj* [*more* ~; *most* ~] *formal* : having the ability to remember things easily or for a long time • a *retentive* mind/memory — see also ANAL-RETENTIVE

– **re·ten·tive·ness** *noun* [*noncount*]

re·think /riˈθɪŋk/ *verb* **-thinks; -thought** /-ˈθɑːt/; **-think·ing** : to think carefully about (someone or something) again especially in order to change a choice or decision : RECONSIDER [+ *obj*] You had better *rethink* your decision. • The government is *rethinking* its policy. [*no obj*] He took a moment to *rethink.*

– **re·think** /ˈriːˌθɪŋk/ *noun* [*singular*] • The situation calls for a *rethink* of the government's policy. – **rethinking** *noun* [*noncount*] • The problem demands some careful/serious *rethinking.*

ret·i·cent /ˈrɛtəsənt/ *adj* [*more* ~; *most* ~] : not willing to tell people about things • a quiet, *reticent* [=*reserved*] person — often + *about* • He is *reticent about* discussing his past.

– **ret·i·cence** /ˈrɛtəsəns/ *noun* [*noncount*]

ret·i·na /ˈrɛtənə/ *noun, pl* **-nas** [*count*] : the sensitive tissue at the back of the eye that receives images and sends signals to the brain about what is seen

– **ret·i·nal** /ˈrɛtənəl/ *adj, technical* • the *retinal* image • a *retinal* detachment

ret·i·nue /ˈrɛtəˌnuː, *Brit* ˈrɛtəˌnjuː/ *noun, pl* **-nues** [*count*] : a group of helpers, supporters, or followers • the king and his *retinue* • a pop star traveling with his *retinue* • a *retinue* of servants

re·tire /rɪˈtajɚ/ *verb* **-tires; -tired; -tir·ing**

1 a [*no obj*] : to stop a job or career because you have reached the age when you are not allowed to work anymore or do not need or want to work anymore • I want to be healthy when I *retire.* • She plans to *retire* (from her job) in two years. • We plan to *retire* in/to Florida. = We plan to *re-*

R

tire and move to Florida. • The boxer *retired* undefeated. **b** [+ *obj*] : to cause (someone, such as a military officer) to end a job or career — usually used as *(be) retired* • The general *was retired* with honors.
2 [*no obj*] : to stop playing in a game, competition, etc., especially because of injury • She had to *retire* during the first set because of a muscle strain.
3 [+ *obj*] : to take (something) out of use, service, or production • The Navy is *retiring* the old battleship. • The manufacturer plans to *retire* that car model in a few years. • The team is *retiring* his jersey number in honor of his great career.
4 [*no obj*] *formal* : to move *to* a different place • He *retired to* the library to study. • Shall we *retire to* the parlor?
5 [*no obj*] *literary* : to go to bed • She *retired* for the night.
6 [*no obj*] *formal* : to move away from action or danger : RETREAT • The army was forced to *retire* from the battlefield.
7 [+ *obj*] *baseball* : to cause (a batter) to be out • The pitcher *retired* seven batters in a row. • She was *retired* on a fly ball to center field. • He struck out Jones to ***retire the side***. [=to end the inning by getting the final out]

retired *adj* : not working anymore : having ended your working or professional career • elderly *retired* people • She's a *retired* teacher.

re·tir·ee /rɪˌtaɪˈriː/ *noun, pl* **-ees** [*count*] *US* : someone who has permanently stopped working in a job or profession : a person who has retired • a group of elderly *retirees*

[1]**re·tire·ment** /rɪˈtajəmənt/ *noun, pl* **-ments**
1 a [*count*] : the act of ending your working or professional career : the act of retiring • She decided to take an early *retirement*. • Many fans were surprised by the champion's *retirement*. • The staff is smaller because of several *retirements*. **b** [*noncount*] : the state of being retired • I'm looking forward to *retirement*. • He is ready for *retirement*. • He ***came out of retirement*** to play baseball again.
2 : the period after you have permanently stopped your job or profession [*noncount*] She has remained very active during *retirement*. [*singular*] The staff all wished her a long and happy *retirement*.
3 [*noncount*] *US* : the age at which a person usually retires • She reaches *retirement* [=(more commonly) *retirement age*] next May.
4 [*noncount*] *US* : money that you receive from a savings plan or pension once you retire from a job or profession • We can't live on his *retirement* alone.

[2]**retirement** *adj, always used before a noun* : of, relating to, or designed for people who are retired • a *retirement* community [=a place for people who are retired] • *retirement* benefits/age

retirement home *noun, pl* **~ homes** [*count*] : a place where retired people can live and sometimes be taken care of

retirement plan *noun, pl* **~ plans** [*count*] *US* : a system for saving money for use during your retirement • My employer offers a good *retirement plan*.

retiring *adj*
1 [*more ~; most ~*] : quiet and shy • a shy, *retiring* young woman
2 — used to describe a person who will be retiring from a job or profession soon • A banquet was held to honor the *retiring* senator.

re·tool /riˈtuːl/ *verb* **-tools; -tooled; -tool·ing**
1 [+ *obj*] : to change or replace the tools or machines in (a factory, workshop, etc.) • The factory has been *retooled*.
2 *US* : to make changes to (something) in order to improve it [+ *obj*] The company is *retooling* its sales strategies. [*no obj*] The company is *retooling* for the future.

[1]**re·tort** /rɪˈtoɚt/ *verb* **-torts; -tort·ed; -tort·ing** [+ *obj*] : to reply to something in a quick and often angry way • "That's not true!" she *retorted*. • She *retorted* angrily that it wasn't true.

[2]**retort** *noun, pl* **-torts** [*count*] : a quick and often angry reply • He hurled a *retort* at his accuser. • She made a clever *retort*.

re·touch /riˈtʌʧ/ *verb* **-touch·es; -touched; -touch·ing** [+ *obj*] : to make small changes to (something, such as a photograph) in order to improve the way it looks • The photo had been *retouched* to remove the wrinkles around his eyes. • a *retouched* photograph
– retouching *noun* [*noncount*] • They did a lot of *retouching* to her picture.

re·trace /riˈtreɪs/ *verb* **-trac·es; -traced; -trac·ing** [+ *obj*]
1 : to go back along the same course, path, etc., that you or someone else has taken earlier • *retrace* a path/route • The crew will attempt to *retrace* the last voyage of Captain Cook. • He carefully ***retraced his steps/footsteps*** back to the road.
2 : to find out about and describe (someone's past movements or actions) • Her biographer carefully *retraced* her childhood. • The police are attempting to *retrace* his movements on the night of the robbery.

re·tract /rɪˈtrækt/ *verb* **-tracts; -tract·ed; -tract·ing**
1 : to pull (something) back into something larger that usually covers it [+ *obj*] A cat can *retract* its claws. • The pilot *retracted* the plane's landing gear. [*no obj*] The plane's landing gear failed to *retract*.
2 [+ *obj*] : to say that something you said or wrote is not true or correct • The newspaper *retracted* [=*withdrew*] the story. • She was forced to *retract* [=*take back*] her statement.
3 [+ *obj*] *formal* : to take back (something, such as an offer or promise) • Their college grants were *retracted*. • They *retracted* the job offer.
– re·tract·able /rɪˈtræktəbəl/ *adj* • the plane's *retractable* landing gear • The stadium's roof is *retractable*.

re·trac·tion /rɪˈtrækʃən/ *noun, pl* **-tions** *formal*
1 [*count*] : a statement saying that something you said or wrote at an earlier time is not true or correct • His charges were false, and he was forced to make/issue a *retraction*.
2 [*noncount*] : the act of moving something back into a larger part that usually covers it : the act of retracting something • the *retraction* of the plane's landing gear

re·train /riˈtreɪn/ *verb* **-trains; -trained; -train·ing**
1 [+ *obj*] : to teach (someone) new skills : to train (someone) again • The organization *retrains* people who have lost their jobs.
2 [*no obj*] : to learn new skills especially for a different job • He is *retraining* for another job. • He *retrained* as a mechanic.

re·tread /ˈriːˌtrɛd/ *noun, pl* **-treads** [*count*]
1 : an old tire whose surface has been given a new layer of rubber
2 *US, informal + disapproving* : something that uses ideas, stories, etc., that have been used before • The show is just another TV sitcom *retread*.

[1]**re·treat** /rɪˈtriːt/ *noun, pl* **-treats**
1 : movement by soldiers away from an enemy because the enemy is winning or has won a battle [*noncount*] The forces are now ***in (full) retreat***. [*count*] The army passed through the town on/during its *retreat* (from the battlefield). • He ***sounded/signaled the retreat***. [=made the signal telling soldiers to begin a retreat]
2 [*count, noncount*] : movement away from a place or situation especially because it is dangerous, unpleasant, etc. • Some of her friends were surprised by her *retreat* from public life following her defeat in the election. • He ***made/beat a hasty retreat*** [=he left quickly] when he realized he had entered the wrong office.
3 [*count*] : the act of changing your opinion or position on something because it is unpopular — usually singular • The mayor was forced to make a *retreat* from his earlier position.
4 : the act or process of moving away [*count*] — usually singular • Scientists continue to measure the slow *retreat* of the glacier. • the *retreat* of the floodwaters [*noncount*] Studies show the glaciers are ***in retreat***. — sometimes used figuratively • Her political influence has been *in retreat* since the scandal.
5 a [*count*] : a place that is quiet and private • She went to her mountain *retreat* for a quiet weekend. • an idyllic/island/isolated *retreat* **b** : a trip to a place where you can quietly pray, think, study, etc. [*count*] We went on a corporate/spiritual *retreat*. • The church offers *retreats* several times a year. [*noncount*] She went ***on retreat*** for several weeks last year.

[2]**retreat** *verb* **-treats; -treat·ed; -treat·ing** [*no obj*]
1 : to move back to get away from danger, attack, etc. • When the enemy attacked, our troops were forced to *retreat*. • They *retreated* behind trees for safety.
2 : to move or go away from a place or situation especially because it is dangerous, unpleasant, etc. • He quickly *retreated* from the room. • After her defeat, she *retreated* from politics.
3 : to change your opinion or statement about something because it is unpopular — usually + *from* • The mayor was forced to *retreat from* his original position.
4 : to move backward • As the temperatures warm, the glaciers begin to *retreat*. • The floodwaters are *retreating*.
5 : to go to a place that is quiet and private • They *retreated* into the next room to talk privately.

re·trench /rɪˈtrɛnʧ/ *verb* **-trench·es; -trenched;**

R

-**trench•ing** [*no obj*] *formal* : to change the way things are done in order to spend less money • When the economy slowed, the company was forced to *retrench*.
– **re•trench•ment** /rɪˈtrɛntʃmənt/ *noun, pl* **-ments** [*count, noncount*] • The company is going through a (period of) *retrenchment*.

re•tri•al /riˈtrajəl/ *noun, pl* **-als** : a second trial in a court of law in order to make a new judgment on a case that has been judged before [*noncount*] His case is coming up for *retrial*. [*count*] a series of *retrials*

ret•ri•bu•tion /ˌrɛtrəˈbjuːʃən/ *noun* [*noncount*] *formal* : punishment for doing something wrong • The killer acted without fear of *retribution*. • ***divine retribution*** [=punishment by God] — often + *for* • They are seeking *retribution for* the killings.
– **re•trib•u•tive** /rɪˈtrɪbjətɪv/ *adj* • *retributive* justice

re•triev•al /rɪˈtriːvəl/ *noun* [*noncount*] : the act or process of getting and bringing back something : the act or process of retrieving something • the *retrieval* of stolen goods • property *retrieval* • The system allows quick storage and *retrieval* of data.
beyond retrieval **1** : not able to be brought back • The satellite is *beyond retrieval*. • The old data is now *beyond retrieval*. **2** : not able to be corrected, cured, etc. • The patient may be *beyond retrieval*. [=the patient may die; the patient may not be able to be saved] • The situation is *beyond retrieval*.

re•trieve /rɪˈtriːv/ *verb* **-trieves; -trieved; -triev•ing**
1 [+ *obj*] **a** : to get and bring (something) back from a place • Many archaeological relics were *retrieved* from the site. • Police *retrieved* his stolen car. **b** : to find and get (information) from a computer or disk • You can quickly *retrieve* data/information. • The files were *retrieved* from the computer. • He was able to *retrieve* the document.
2 : to find and bring birds or animals that have been shot back to a hunter [*no obj*] The dog is learning how to *retrieve*. [+ *obj*] The dog has been trained to *retrieve* birds.
3 [+ *obj*] *formal* : to keep (something) from failing or becoming worse • They were able to *retrieve* [=*save*] the situation. • Can their relationship be *retrieved*? [=*salvaged*]
– **re•triev•able** /rɪˈtriːvəbəl/ *adj* • The data should be *retrievable*.

re•triev•er /rɪˈtriːvɚ/ *noun, pl* **-ers** [*count*] : a dog that is used for retrieving birds or animals that have been shot by a hunter — see also GOLDEN RETRIEVER, LABRADOR RETRIEVER

ret•ro /ˈrɛtroʊ/ *adj* [*more* ~; *most* ~] : looking like or relating to styles or fashions from the past • the *retro* look in fashion • *retro* music
– **retro** *noun* [*noncount*] • *Retro* is in.

retro- *prefix* : backward : back • *retro*grade

ret•ro•ac•tive /ˌrɛtroʊˈæktɪv/ *adj, formal* : effective from a particular date in the past • They all received a *retroactive* pay raise. • The new tax will be *retroactive* to January 1.
– **ret•ro•ac•tive•ly** *adv* • The new law will be applied *retroactively*.

ret•ro•fit /ˌrɛtroʊˈfɪt/ *verb* **-fits; -fit•ted; -fit•ting** [+ *obj*] : to provide (something) with new parts that were not available when it was originally built • The factory has been *retrofitted* to meet the new safety regulations. • We can *retrofit* your car with the new fuel system.

R

ret•ro•grade /ˈrɛtrəˌgreɪd/ *adj* [*more* ~; *most* ~]
1 *formal* : returning to an earlier and usually worse state or condition • a *retrograde* policy that would leave more people poorer than they are now
2 *technical* : moving backward • *retrograde* motion

ret•ro•gres•sive /ˌrɛtrəˈgrɛsɪv/ *adj* [*more* ~; *most* ~] *formal* : causing a return to an earlier and usually worse state • *retrogressive* [=(more commonly) *regressive*] government policies

ret•ro•spect /ˈrɛtrəˌspɛkt/ *noun*
in retrospect : when thinking about the past or something that happened in the past • *In retrospect*, I made the right decision. • What is interesting *in retrospect* is how wrong our assumptions were.

ret•ro•spec•tion /ˌrɛtrəˈspɛkʃən/ *noun* [*noncount*] *formal* : the act of thinking about the past or something that happened in the past • This is a time of *retrospection* for many people.

[1]**ret•ro•spec•tive** /ˌrɛtrəˈspɛktɪv/ *adj*
1 : of or relating to the past or something that happened in the past • They issued a *retrospective* report. • a *retrospective* analysis of what went wrong • The museum is having a *retrospective* exhibit of the artist's early works.
2 : effective from a particular date in the past • *retrospective* [=(more commonly) *retroactive*] laws
– **ret•ro•spec•tive•ly** *adv* • Their actions could only be understood *retrospectively*. • The new law will be applied *retrospectively*.

[2]**retrospective** *noun, pl* **-tives** [*count*] : an exhibition of work that an artist has done in the past • The museum is featuring a *retrospective* of Picasso's early works.

re•try /riˈtraɪ/ *verb* **-tries; -tried; -try•ing** [+ *obj*]
1 : to try (something) again • He *retried* (entering) the password.
2 : to judge (a court case) for a second time • The judge will *retry* the case. • The case will be *retried*.

[1]**re•turn** /rɪˈtɚn/ *verb* **-turns; -turned; -turn•ing**
1 [*no obj*] : to come or go to a place again : to come back or go back again • We waited for you to *return*. • She is *returning* home tomorrow. • I'm leaving but will *return* at 2 p.m. • She left home ***never to return***. [=she never went home again] — often + *from* or *to* • No one was home when I *returned from* work. • He *returned from* his trip last night. • I *returned to* Paris 10 years later. • The bird *returns to* this area each spring. • He ***returned to find*** the house empty. [=he returned and found that the house was empty] — see also RETURN TO (below)
2 [+ *obj*] **a** : to bring, give, send, or take (something) to the place that it came from or the place where it should go • I have to *return* a book to the library. • I'm *returning* your ladder. Thanks for letting me borrow it. • *Return* [=*bring*] this application to me when you have filled it out. • Please fill out the application and *return* [=*send*] it to the address below. • She *returned* the gun to its holster. [=she put the gun in its holster] **b** : to bring or send (something that you bought) to the place that it came from because it does not work or fit properly, because it is damaged, etc. • The dishes were broken when they were delivered, so I had to *return* them. • I had to *return* the shirt and get a bigger size. **c** : to bring (empty bottles or cans) to a place that collects them so that they can be used again • I'm going to *return* these bottles and cans (for recycling).
3 [*no obj*] : to happen or exist again • The pain *returned* [=*recurred, came back*] about two hours after I took the pill. • His jealousy *returned* when he saw his ex-wife with her new husband. • Hope has *returned* to the city. [=the city's people are hopeful again]
4 [+ *obj*] : to respond to (something) in the same way • He smiled at her, and she *returned* the smile. [=she smiled at him] • When I told her that she looked beautiful, she *returned* [=*repaid*] the compliment by saying that I looked very handsome. • He never *returned* my phone calls. [=he did not call me back] • Thanks for helping me. I'll be sure to ***return the favor***. [=I will help you when you need help] • When the suspect started shooting, the police were forced to ***return fire***. [=to shoot back at the suspect]
5 [+ *obj*] *formal* : to make an official report of (a decision or order) • The jury *returned* a verdict of guilty.
6 [+ *obj*] *tennis* : to hit back (a ball that was hit to you) • He *returned* her serve. • Her serve is difficult to *return*.
7 [+ *obj*] *American football* : to run with the ball after getting it because of a kick, fumble, etc. • He *returned* the ball/kick 50 yards.
8 [+ *obj*] *Brit* : to elect (someone) to office — usually used as *(be) returned* • He *was returned* to Parliament. — often + *as* • She *was returned as* prime minister.
9 [+ *obj*] *finance* : to produce or earn (something, such as a profit or loss) • The investment *returned* a huge profit. • bonds that *return* [=*yield*] five percent annually
return to [*phrasal verb*] ***return to (something)*** **1** : to go to (a place where you work, study, etc.) again after being away for a time • When do you *return to* school? • She hopes to *return to* the office next week. — see also [1]RETURN 1 (above) **2** : to start doing or using (something) again especially after a long time • She hopes to *return to* work [=to start working again] next week. • She hopes to *return to* working at home next week. • He *returned to* the old ways of farming. **3** : to start an activity again that relates to (something) • He *returned to* his book [=he started reading his book again] after feeding the cat. • Let's *return to* your first question. [=let's discuss the first question you asked earlier] • He *returned to* football not as a player but as a coach. **4** : to change back to (an earlier or original condition or state) • She soon *returned* [=*reverted*] *to* her old hab-

its. • His breathing ***returned to normal.*** [=his breathing became normal again]

[2]**return** *noun, pl* **-turns**

1 [*singular*] **:** the act of coming or going back to the place you started from or to a place where you were before • We are looking forward to your *return.* • We're looking forward to our *return* to Europe. • What is the date of her *return* from Mexico? [=when is she coming back from Mexico?] • ***Upon/on his return*** [=(less formally) when he returned; when he came back], he found a note taped to the door. • The bad weather delayed his ***return home.*** [=his return to his home] • I stopped by your house ***on my return home.*** [=on my way home] • She became sick ***on her return from*** America. [=she became sick at the time she returned from America]

2 [*singular*] **:** the act of going back to an activity, job, situation, etc. **:** the act of starting to do something again after stopping • The team looked forward to his *return* to coaching. • a *return* to the old ways of farming • He managed the team last year, so his ***return as*** a player [=his return to the team as a player and not as a manager] was a surprise.

3 [*singular*] **a :** the fact that something (such as a condition, feeling, or situation) happens again — + *of* • the *return of* peace to the region • Scientists noticed a *return* [=*recurrence*] *of* the disease in the monkeys. • She noticed a *return of* his old habits. • the *return of* spring **b :** the fact that someone or something changes *to* a condition or state that existed before • the department's *return to* normal • The people celebrated their leader's *return to* power.

4 [*singular*] **:** the act of taking someone or something back to the proper place — + *of* • The police arranged for the *return of* the stolen goods. [=for the goods to be taken to the place they were stolen from] • The mother demanded a ***safe return*** *of* her child. [=demanded that her child would be brought back to her and not be hurt]

5 a [*count*] **:** something that is brought or sent back to a store or business because it does not work or fit properly, is damaged, is not needed, etc. • The store does not accept *returns* more than 30 days after purchase. **b *returns*** [*plural*] *chiefly US* **:** empty cans or bottles that are brought back to a store so that they can be used again

6 *finance* **:** the profit from an investment or business [*count*] Investors are promised a *return.* • The company had poor *returns* last year. — often + *on* • He received a large *return on* his investment. [=he made a lot of money on his investment] [*noncount*] The stock has had a high rate of *return.* — sometimes used figuratively • Her son's success in college was an excellent *return* on her investment. • She expected some *return* from the company for all her years of loyal service.

7 *returns* [*plural*] **:** a report of the results of voting • election *returns*

8 [*count*] **:** a report that you send to the government about the money that you have earned and the taxes that you have paid in one year • He has copies of his *returns* for the last 15 years. • We filed our ***(income) tax return.*** [=we sent our tax return to the government] • He filed his 2007 *tax return* in February of 2008.

9 [*count*] *sports* **:** the act of returning a ball • (*tennis*) She hit a powerful *return.* [=she hit back the ball that was served to her very hard] • (*American football*) a 50-yard kickoff/punt/fumble *return* [=a 50-yard run with the ball after getting it on a kickoff/punt/fumble]

10 [*count*] *Brit* **:** a ticket for a trip that takes you to a place and back to the place you started from **:** a round-trip ticket • One *return* is often less expensive than buying two one-way tickets. • a ***day return*** [=a reduced-price ticket for traveling to a place and back on the same day]

by return *or* ***by return of post*** *Brit* **:** immediately by mail • I replied *by return of post.* • I wrote you *by return.*

happy returns *old-fashioned* — used for wishing someone a happy birthday and to express the hope that he or she will live to celebrate many more birthdays in the future • They wished me (many) *happy returns.*

in return **:** in payment or exchange • He helps out and expects nothing *in return.* • He will not help unless he gets something *in return.* • The prisoner told the police who had ordered the killing. *In return,* his sentence was reduced by two years. — often + *for* • I will lend you the money *in return for* a favor. • He worked *in return for* a free meal.

– see also POINT OF NO RETURN

[3]**return** *adj, always used before a noun*

1 : used in or taken for returning to a place • a *return* flight/trip • the *return* road • a ***return envelope*** [=an envelope that has an address on it and that you can use to mail something back to the person who sent it to you]

2 : happening or done for the second time • a *return* visit

3 *chiefly Brit* **:** used or paying for a trip that takes you to a place and back to the place you started from • a *return* [=(*US*) *round-trip*] ticket/fare

re·turn·able /rɪˈtɚnəbəl/ *adj*

1 : allowed to be exchanged for a small amount of money at a place that collects empty bottles and cans so that they can be used again • *returnable* bottles/cans

2 : allowed to be returned • Sale items are not *returnable.*

return address *noun, pl* **~ -dress·es** [*count*] **:** an address on an envelope or package that shows where the envelope or package should be returned to if it cannot be delivered — see picture at MAIL

re·turn·ee /rɪˌtɚˈniː/ *noun, pl* **-ees** [*count*] **:** someone who returns to a place or activity; *especially* **:** someone who returns to a country after being in another country in prison, in military service, etc.

re·turn·er /rɪˈtɚnɚ/ *noun, pl* **-ers** [*count*]

1 *Brit* **:** someone who goes back to work after not working for a long period of time

2 *American football* **:** a player who returns a punt or kickoff • a punt *returner*

return game *noun, pl* **~ games** [*count*] **:** a second game played between the same players or teams — called also (*chiefly Brit*) *return match*

returning officer *noun, pl* **~ -cers** [*count*] *Brit* **:** an official who organizes an election and announces the result

return mail *noun* [*noncount*] *US* **:** mail that answers or responds to something • We received a lot of *return mail* after the announcement. • Fill out the enclosed form and send it back ***by return mail.*** [=(*Brit*) *by return of post*] [=immediately; as soon as possible]

Reu·ben /ˈruːbən/ *noun, pl* **-bens** [*count*] *US* **:** a grilled sandwich that is made from a kind of sliced beef (called corned beef), cheese, and prepared sour cabbage (called sauerkraut)

re·uni·fy /riˈjuːnəˌfaɪ/ *verb* **-fies; -fied; -fy·ing :** to make (something, such as a divided country) whole again **:** to unify (something) again [+ *obj*] Our goal is to *reunify* [=*reunite*] this family by returning the children to their parents. — often used as *(be) reunified* • East and West Germany *were reunified* in 1990. [*no obj*] Germany *reunified* in 1990.

– re·uni·fi·ca·tion /riˌjuːnəfəˈkeɪʃən/ *noun* [*noncount*] • the *reunification* of Germany **– reunified** *adj, always used before a noun* • a *reunified* Germany

re·union /riˈjuːnjən/ *noun, pl* **-unions** [*count*]

1 : an act of getting people together again after they have been apart **:** an act of reuniting • an emotional *reunion* between mother and son • He dreamed of a *reunion* with his son.

2 : an organized gathering of people who have not been together for a long time • We attended a ***family reunion.*** [=a usually large gathering for family members] • (*US*) a ***high school reunion*** [=a *reunion* of people who studied at a high school at the same time] • (*US*) Are you going to our 20th ***class reunion?*** [=a *reunion* of the people who graduated with us 20 years ago]

re·unite /ˌriːjʊˈnaɪt/ *verb* **-unites; -unit·ed; -unit·ing**

1 [+ *obj*] **:** to bring (people or things) together again especially after they have been apart for a long time • The police *reunited* the woman and her son. • We need a candidate who can *reunite* the party. — often + *with* • The police *reunited* her *with* her son. — often used as *(be) reunited* • She *was reunited with* her son.

2 [*no obj*] **:** to be together again after being apart for a long time • The band *reunited* for a special concert.

re–up /riˈʌp/ *verb* **-ups; -upped; -up·ping** *US, informal*

1 [*no obj*] **:** to officially agree to stay in the military, on a team, with a company, etc., for an additional period of time • When war broke out last year, many soldiers *re-upped.* • The team's top scorer has *re-upped* for another three years.

2 [+ *obj*] **:** to officially agree or persuade someone to officially agree that an existing arrangement will continue for an additional period of time • Now I have to decide if I should *re-up* [=*renew*] my lease/contract. • The team wants to *re-up* their star player for another two years.

re·use /riˈjuːz/ *verb* **-us·es; -used; -us·ing** [+ *obj*] **:** to use (something) again • I can *reuse* that container.

– re·use /riˈjuːs/ *noun* [*noncount*] • the *reuse* of packing materials as insulation • The motor oil has been processed for *reuse.* **– re·us·able** /riˈjuːzəbəl/ *adj* • *reusable* containers

[1]**rev** /ˈrɛv/ *verb* **revs; revved; rev•ving** [+ *obj*] : to cause (an engine) to run more quickly : to increase the revolutions per minute of (a motor in a vehicle) • She sat in the car and *revved* the engine [=she pressed the car's accelerator when the engine was on but the car was not in gear] while she waited for us. — often + *up* • He *revved up* the motorcycle by making adjustments to its engine.

rev up [*phrasal verb*] *informal* **1** : to become more active • The campaign is *revving up*. **2** ***rev (someone or something) up*** *or* ***rev up (someone or something)*** : to make (someone or something) more active or effective • Big business spending is *revving up* the economy. • The company is getting *revved up* for the launch of its new product line. — see also REVVED UP

[2]**rev** *noun, pl* **revs** [*count*] *informal* : a complete turn of an engine part : REVOLUTION — usually plural • a motor with a speed of 5,000 ***revs per minute***

Rev. (*US*) *or Brit* **Rev** *or Brit* **Revd** *abbr* reverend • *Rev*. Antonio Weiss • the *Revd* Peter Smith

re•val•ue /riˈvælju/ *verb* **-ues; -ued; -u•ing**

1 *finance* : to change the value of a country's money so that it is worth less or more when it is traded for another country's money [+ *obj*] Three of the nations are expected to *revalue* their currencies soon. [*no obj*] Most analysts predict that the country will *revalue* before the end of the year.

2 [+ *obj*] : to make a new judgment about the value of (something, such as a house or an investment) • Under state law, the town is required to *revalue* [=*reassess*] residential properties every five years.

– re•val•u•a•tion /riˌvæljəˈweɪʃən/ *noun, pl* **-tions** [*count, noncount*]

re•vamp /riˈvæmp/ *verb* **-vamps; -vamped; -vamp•ing** [+ *obj*] : to make (something) better or like new again • The company has *revamped* the design of its best-selling car. • They are *revamping* [=*renovating*] the old house.

– revamp *or* **revamping** *noun, pl* **-vamps** *or* **-vampings** [*count*] — usually singular • They gave the car's design a *revamp*. • a complete *revamping* [=*reorganization*] of our department

re•veal /rɪˈviːl/ *verb* **-veals; -vealed; -veal•ing** [+ *obj*]

1 a : to make (something) known • She would not *reveal* the secret. • The test *revealed* the true cause of death. • It was *revealed* that they stole over $1 million. • They *revealed* the plans for the new building. — opposite CONCEAL **b** : to show or prove that (someone) is a particular type of person — often + *to be* • The book *reveals* him *to be* an expert at chess. • She *revealed* herself *to be* a talented pianist. — often + *as* • She *revealed* the reporter *as* a liar.

2 : to show (something) plainly or clearly : to make (something that was hidden) able to be seen • The expression on his face *revealed* how he felt. • The curtain was lifted to *reveal* the grand prize. • Pulling up the carpeting *revealed* the home's beautiful hardwood floors. — opposite CONCEAL

re•veal•ing /rɪˈviːlɪŋ/ *adj* [*more ~; most ~*]

1 : giving information about something that was not known before • The book is a *revealing* account of being part of a gang. • Her comments about her childhood were *revealing*.

2 : showing parts of the body that are usually hidden from view • She wore a very *revealing* shirt. • That skirt is much too *revealing*.

– re•veal•ing•ly *adv* • The actor talked *revealingly* about his life.

rev•eil•le /ˈrɛvəli, *Brit* rɪˈvæli/ *noun* [*noncount*] *military* : a signal given on a musical instrument (such as a bugle or drum) in the early morning to call soldiers or sailors to duty • He awoke at *reveille*.

[1]**rev•el** /ˈrɛvəl/ *verb* **rev•els;** *US* **rev•eled** *or Brit* **rev•elled;** *US* **rev•el•ing** *or Brit* **rev•el•ling**

revel in [*phrasal verb*] ***revel in (something)*** : to enjoy (something) very much • She *reveled in* her success. • He *reveled in* other people's misfortune.

[2]**revel** *noun, pl* **-els** [*count*] *literary + old-fashioned* : a noisy and wild celebration — usually plural • holiday *revels*

rev•e•la•tion /ˌrɛvəˈleɪʃən/ *noun, pl* **-tions**

1 [*count*] : a usually secret or surprising fact that is made known • The book includes many shocking/startling *revelations* about the mayor's personal life. • damaging personal *revelations* • The *revelation* that she was a drug user was not a surprise to me.

2 [*count*] : an act of making something known : an act of revealing something in usually a surprising way • *Revelations* by the newspaper caused a scandal. — often + *of* • His outburst was a *revelation of* his true character. • The *revelation of* her gambling problem followed her bankruptcy.

3 [*singular*] : something that surprises you • Her talent ***came as a revelation***. [=was completely unexpected] — often + *to* • The movie was a *revelation to* me. I didn't know he was such a good actor.

4 : a sign or message from God [*count*] a divine *revelation* [*noncount*] a prophecy made known by *revelation*

re•ve•la•to•ry /ˈrɛvələˌtori, *Brit* ˌrɛvəˈleɪtri/ *adj, formal* : making something known : revealing something in usually a surprising way • a *revelatory* experience/biography

rev•el•er (*US*) *or Brit* **rev•el•ler** /ˈrɛvələ/ *noun, pl* **-ers** [*count*] : a person who is celebrating with other people in usually a wild and noisy way : a person who is taking part in revelry • The streets were crowded with *revelers* on New Years Eve.

rev•el•ry /ˈrɛvəlri/ *noun, pl* **-ries** : a wild and noisy celebration [*count*] a drunken *revelry* [*noncount*] a night of *revelry*

[1]**re•venge** /rɪˈvɛnʤ/ *noun* [*noncount*]

1 : the act of doing something to hurt someone because that person did something that hurt you • an act of *revenge* • She swore that she would have her *revenge*. • She wants *revenge* against her enemies. • He got his *revenge*. • *revenge* attacks/killings • He swore to ***take (his) revenge on*** his enemies. [=to harm his enemies] • He is ***seeking revenge for*** his father's murder. [=he wants to harm the person who killed his father] • The bombing was ***in revenge for*** the assassination of their leader.

2 : the act of defeating an opponent who has defeated you in the past • The team is seeking *revenge for* the loss earlier in the season.

– re•venge•ful /rɪˈvɛnʤfəl/ *adj* [*more ~; most ~*]

[2]**revenge** *verb* **-veng•es; -venged; -veng•ing**

revenge yourself on *formal* : to do something to hurt (someone who has hurt you) : to take revenge on (someone) • She vowed to *revenge herself on* her father's killer.

rev•e•nue /ˈrɛvəˌnuː, *Brit* ˈrɛvəˌnjuː/ *noun, pl* **-nues** *finance*

1 : money that is made by or paid to a business or an organization [*noncount*] The factory lost *revenue* because of the strike by the workers. • The company receives millions of dollars in advertising *revenue*. [=money paid by advertisers] • The firm is looking for another source of *revenue*. [*plural*] advertising and sales *revenues*

2 : money that is collected for public use by a government through taxes [*noncount*] Government officials have reported a decrease in *revenue*. [*plural*] state and federal ***tax revenues*** — see also INLAND REVENUE, INTERNAL REVENUE SERVICE

re•ver•ber•ate /rɪˈvəbəˌreɪt/ *verb* **-ates; -at•ed; -at•ing** [*no obj*] *somewhat formal*

1 : to continue in a series of quickly repeated sounds that bounce off a surface (such as a wall) • Her voice *reverberated* [=*echoed*] throughout the stadium. — often used figuratively • The effects of that event still *reverberate* today.

2 : to become filled with a sound • The room *reverberated* [=*echoed, rang*] with laughter.

re•ver•ber•a•tion /rɪˌvəbəˈreɪʃən/ *noun, pl* **-tions**

1 *somewhat formal* : a sound that echoes [*count*] the *reverberations* of her voice [*noncount*] Although the room was very big, her voice could be heard with little *reverberation*.

2 [*count*] : an effect or result that is not wanted — usually plural • The *reverberations* [=*repercussions*] of his actions will be felt for years to come. • economic/political *reverberations*

re•vere /rɪˈviə/ *verb* **-veres; -vered; -ver•ing** [+ *obj*] *formal* : to have great respect for (someone or something) : to show devotion and honor to (someone or something) • The family *reveres* old traditions. — often + *as* • The town *reveres* him *as* a hero. — often used as *(be) revered* • He *is revered as* a hero. • Her poems *are revered* by other poets.

rev•er•ence /ˈrɛvərəns/ *noun, formal* : honor or respect that is felt for or shown to (someone or something) [*noncount*] Her poems are treated with *reverence* by other poets. — often + *for* • a feeling of *reverence for* tradition [*singular*] Their religion has/shows a deep *reverence for* nature.

rev•er•end /ˈrɛvərənd/ *noun, pl* **-ends** [*count*] : a priest or minister in the Christian church

Reverend *adj, always used before a noun* — used as a title for a priest or minister in the Christian church • We welcome *Reverend John Smith* as our guest. — often used after *the* • *the Reverend* Mr. Smith • *the Reverend* John Smith — abbr. *Rev*. or (*Brit*) *Revd*

Reverend Mother *noun, pl* **~ -ers** [*count*] : a woman who is the head of a convent : MOTHER SUPERIOR • I will ask the *Reverend Mother* what to do. — often used as a form of address • Good morning, *Reverend Mother*.

rev•er•ent /ˈrɛvərənt/ *adj* [*more* ~; *most* ~] *formal* : showing a lot of respect : very respectful • a *reverent* crowd of worshippers • a *reverent* tone of voice — opposite IRREVERENT

– **rev•er•ent•ly** *adv* • They all spoke of her *reverently*.

rev•er•en•tial /ˌrɛvəˈrɛnʃəl/ *adj* [*more* ~; *most* ~] *formal* : showing or having a lot of respect : REVERENT • a *reverential* attitude

– **rev•er•en•tial•ly** *adv*

rev•er•ie /ˈrɛvəri/ *noun, pl* **-er•ies** *formal + literary* : a state in which you are thinking about pleasant things [*count*] I drifted into a *reverie*. [=*daydream*] [*noncount*] He was lost in *reverie*. [=he was daydreaming]

re•ver•sal /rɪˈvəsəl/ *noun, pl* **-sals** : a change to an opposite state, condition, decision, etc. [*count*] In a sudden *reversal*, the mayor has decided not to run for reelection. • the *reversal* of a decision/position/policy • a surprising/sudden *reversal* in the value of the stock • We had a ***role reversal***; I became the leader and he became the follower. • In a ***reversal of roles***, he is now taking care of his mother. [*noncount*] *Reversal* of the decision is unlikely. ✧ *Reversal* often means a change to a worse state or condition. • He suffered a financial *reversal*. • The company had a complete ***reversal of fortune*** and went bankrupt.

[1]**re•verse** /rɪˈvəs/ *verb* **-vers•es; -versed; -vers•ing**

1 [+ *obj*] : to change (something) to an opposite state or condition • Our roles as caregiver and patient have been *reversed*. [=*switched*] • The runners *reversed* their direction on the track. • The Supreme Court *reversed* [=*overturned*] the decision. • The college is trying to *reverse* the decline in applicants. [=the college is trying to get more people to apply] • ***Had our situations been reversed*** [=if I had been in the situation that you were in], I would have done things differently.

2 [+ *obj*] : to cause (something, such as a process) to stop or return to an earlier state • We cannot *reverse* [=*undo*] the damage that is already done. • The medicine may *reverse* the course of this disease. [=the medicine may stop this disease from getting worse] • There is no way to *reverse* the aging process. • The operation cannot be *reversed*. [=*undone*] • Can anything ***reverse the trend*** toward higher prices?

3 [+ *obj*] **a** : to change the order or position of (two things or a series) • *Reverse* the "i" and "e" in "recieve" to spell "receive" correctly. • My mother and I *reversed* our roles. Now I'm taking care of her. • We're going to *reverse* our usual order and start with Z. **b** : to switch the positions of the top and bottom or the front and back of (something) • You need to *reverse* the paper [=to turn the paper around] in the printer so that the letterhead is up. • *Reverse* that painting [=turn that painting over] so that I can see the back.

4 *chiefly Brit* : to drive (a vehicle) backward [+ *obj*] *Reverse* [=(*US*) *back, back up*] the car into/out of the parking space. [*no obj*] *Reverse* [=(*US*) *back, back up*] into/out of the parking space. • The car *reversed*. [=(*US*) *backed up*]

reverse the charges or reverse the charge *Brit* : to arrange to have the cost of a phone call paid by the person who is called • He telephoned and *reversed the charges*. [=(*US*) he called collect]

reverse yourself *US, formal* : to change your decision or opinion about something • The mayor has *reversed himself* on the issue of raising taxes.

[2]**reverse** *noun, pl* **-verses**

1 ***the reverse*** : something that is opposite to something else • The river flows south to north, rather than *the reverse*. [=north to south] • Women may play in the men's league, but not *the reverse*. [=but men cannot play in the women's league] • I thought she would like the movie, but actually ***the reverse was true***. [=she didn't like the movie] • You don't owe me any money. If anything, *the reverse is true*. [=I owe you money] • "Did you think it would be difficult?" "***Quite the reverse***. [=*quite the contrary*] I thought it would be easy." — often + *of* • The ending of the book was *the reverse of* what I expected.

2 ***the reverse*** : the back side of a coin, document, etc. • The building appears on *the reverse* of the coin. • Please sign your name on *the reverse*.

3 [*noncount*] : REVERSE GEAR • I put the car ***in/into reverse*** and backed out of the garage. — sometimes used figuratively • The economy seems to be stuck *in reverse*. [=the economy is continuing to get worse]

4 [*count*] *formal* : a change that makes something worse • The loss of their support was a serious *reverse* for the project. — usually plural • The company has had some financial *reverses*. [=*setbacks*]

5 [*count*] *American football* : a play in which one player gives the ball to another player who is moving in the opposite direction

in reverse **1 a** : in an order in which the last part is first and the first part is last : BACKWARD • In her latest film, the story is told *in reverse*. We see the main character as an adult in the beginning and as a child at the end. • The winners were called *in reverse* from last place to first place. **b** : in a way that is opposite to what is normal or to what happened earlier • Ten years ago, American tourists flocked to Europe. But now that the dollar is weak, we have the same situation *in reverse*. Europeans are coming to the U.S. in record numbers. **2** : toward an opposite or worse state or condition • The talks between the labor union and workers seem to be moving *in reverse*.

into reverse : into an opposite state or condition • The decrease in profit has been put *into reverse*. • The economy has gone *into reverse*. [=*has gotten worse*]

[3]**reverse** *adj, always used before a noun*

1 : opposite to what is usual or stated • Can you say the alphabet in *reverse* order? • The wheel will not turn in the *reverse* [=*other*] direction. • The drug is used to lower blood pressure but may have the *reverse* effect in some patients.

2 : opposite to the front • Please sign your name on the *reverse* [=*back*] side.

reverse–charge *adj, Brit* : [2]COLLECT • a *reverse-charge* phone call

reverse discrimination *noun* [*noncount*] : the practice of making it more difficult for a certain type of person (such as a white man) to get a job, to go to a school, etc., because other people who were treated unfairly in the past are now being given an advantage • He claimed that *reverse discrimination* was to blame for his unemployment.

reverse engineer *verb* ~ **-neers;** ~ **-neered;** ~ **-neer•ing** [+ *obj*] *technical* : to study the parts of (something) to see how it was made and how it works so that you can make something that is like it • They *reverse engineered* the software.

– **reverse engineering** *noun* [*noncount*]

reverse gear *noun, pl* ~ **gears** : a part (called a gear) that makes a motor move a vehicle in a backward direction [*noncount*] Put the car ***in/into reverse gear***. — sometimes used figuratively • The economy seems to be stuck *in reverse gear*. [=the economy seems to be getting worse] [*count*] — usually singular • The tractor does not have a *reverse gear*.

reverse mortgage *noun, pl* ~ **-gages** [*count*] *chiefly US, finance* : a legal agreement in which a bank pays you an amount of money equal to the part of your home's value that you actually own, and you agree that when you sell your home or when you move or die, that amount of money plus interest will be paid to the bank

reverse psychology *noun* [*noncount*] : a method of getting someone to do what you want by pretending not to want it or by pretending to want something else

re•vers•ible /rɪˈvəsəbəl/ *adj*

1 a : able to be changed back to an earlier or original state • a *reversible* chemical reaction **b** : able to be stopped and not causing permanent damage or changes • Some diseases are *reversible*. • Fortunately, the damage is *reversible*. — opposite IRREVERSIBLE

2 a : having two sides that can be used • *reversible* fabrics • The rug is *reversible*. **b** : able to be worn with either side facing outward • This coat is *reversible*.

– **re•vers•ibil•i•ty** /rɪˌvəsəˈbɪləti/ *noun* [*noncount*]

re•ver•sion /rɪˈvəʒən, *Brit* rɪˈvə:ʃən/ *noun, pl* **-sions**

1 *technical + formal* : an act or process of returning to an earlier condition or state — usually + *to* [*count*] — usually singular • a *reversion to* a primitive state • a *reversion to* old customs/habits [*noncount*] His photos document the land's *reversion to* swamp.

2 [*count, noncount*] *law* : the returning of property to a former owner or to a person who received the right to it when the former owner died • the *reversion* of the estate

re•vert /rɪˈvət/ *verb* **-verts; -vert•ed; -vert•ing**

revert to [*phrasal verb*] ***revert to (something)*** **1** : to go back or return to (an earlier state, condition, situation, etc.) • She has *reverted* (back) *to* her old habits. • My blood pressure has ***reverted to normal***. [=has returned to normal; has become normal again] • After playing badly in the last two games, he seems to have ***reverted to form***. [=he is now playing as well as he usually does] • (*chiefly Brit*) After this one atypical comedy, will he ***revert to type*** [=will he do what he usually does] in his next film? **2** ***revert to (someone or something)*** *law, of property* : to be given to (a former owner or a former owner's heir) • The estate *reverted to* a distant cousin.

[1]**re·view** /rɪˈvjuː/ *noun, pl* **-views**

1 : an act of carefully looking at or examining the quality or condition of something or someone : examination or inspection [*count*] Changes to the building had to be made after the *review* by the safety inspectors. — often + *of* • a *review of* the case • a *review of* their research/evidence • a *review of* the policy/rules/regulations • I was disappointed with my ***salary/pay review***. [=a review of an employee's work and performance by an employer to decide by how much his or her pay or salary should be increased] [*noncount*] After hours of *review*, the committee made its decision. • a *review* board/committee • The medical records were sent to the doctor ***for review***. • The grant application is ***up for review***. [=the application for the grant will be looked at] • The book/policy/ruling is ***under review***. [=is being reviewed] • (*formal*) ***On review of*** [=after reviewing] the evidence, the jury finds the defendant guilty. • ***Upon further review*** of your situation [=after spending more time looking at and thinking about your situation], we have decided to grant your request. • The decision is ***subject to review*** by a higher authority. [=the decision might be studied and then changed by someone who has more power] — see also PEER REVIEW

2 a : a report that gives someone's opinion about the quality of a book, performance, product, etc. [*count*] I read the book/film *reviews* in the newspaper. • *Reviews* of the play were good. [=the people who wrote the reviews liked the play] • Critics gave the new album mixed *reviews*. [=some critics liked the album, while other critics did not] • a favorable *review* • The movie received ***rave reviews***. [=reviews that say it is excellent] [*noncount*] Copies of the book were sent to critics ***for review***. = ***Review copies*** of the book were sent to critics. [=copies of the book were sent to critics so that they could read it and then write reviews about it] • The educational software was sent to teachers *for review*. **b** [*count*] : a magazine filled mostly with reviews and articles that describe the writer's thoughts or opinions about a subject — often used in titles • He wrote an article for *The Annual Review of Biology*. • *The Western New England Law Review*

3 [*count*] : a class, a book, an article, etc., that studies or describes something (such as events from a particular time) : SURVEY — usually + *of* • a *review of* 19th-century American art • a *review of* the year's major events • The seminar is a *review of* the writer's career.

4 *US* : the act of studying information that was studied before [*count*] The teacher allowed one more *review* of our notes before the test. [*noncount*] I haven't done enough *review* [=(*Brit*) *revision*] for the exam.

5 [*count*] *military* : a formal inspection by officers of high rank or by an important person • a *review* of the cadets

Do not confuse *review* with *revue*.

[2]**review** *verb* **-views; -viewed; -view·ing**

1 a [+ *obj*] : to look at or examine (something) carefully especially before making a decision or judgment • Scientists are *reviewing* the results of the study. • I need time to *review* the situation. • The ruling will be *reviewed* by the Supreme Court. • The committee *reviewed* the applications/regulations. • The television show will *review* last year's major events. **b** *US* : to study or look at (something) again [+ *obj*] She *reviewed* her notes for the speech. • Please *review* [=*go over, check*] your answers before handing in your test. • I need to *review* [=(*Brit*) *revise*] chemistry. [*no obj*] Students were given time to *review* [=(*Brit*) *revise*] for the test. **c** [+ *obj*] : to describe or show (a series of things or events from the past) • The television show will *review* last year's major events. • The biography *reviewed* her accomplishments.

2 [+ *obj*] : to report on or judge the quality of a book, show, product, etc. • Critics have not yet *reviewed* the movie/play. • The book/album/car was *reviewed* in this magazine.

3 [+ *obj*] *military* : to make an official inspection of (someone or something) • The President *reviewed* the troops.

– **re·view·er** /rɪˈvjuːwɚ/ *noun, pl* **-ers** [*count*] • the newspaper's movie/book *reviewer*

re·vile /rɪˈvajəl/ *verb* **-viles; -viled; -vil·ing** [+ *obj*] *formal* : to speak about (someone or something) in a very critical or insulting way • Many people *reviled* him for his callous behavior. — usually used as *(be) reviled* • The committee's decision *was reviled* by reporters. • The policy ***was reviled as*** racist. [=people said that the policy was racist]

re·vise /rɪˈvaɪz/ *verb* **-vis·es; -vised; -vis·ing**

1 [+ *obj*] : to make changes especially to correct or improve (something) • Please *revise* this essay. • We have to *revise* our plans because of the delays. • I would like to *revise* my estimate. • You need to buy the *revised* [=corrected and updated] edition of the textbook.

2 *Brit* : to study (something) again [+ *obj*] She *revised* [=(*US*) *reviewed*] chemistry. [*no obj*] I need to *revise* [=(*US*) *review*] for the exam.

re·vi·sion /rɪˈvɪʒən/ *noun, pl* **-sions**

1 : a change or a set of changes that corrects or improves something [*count*] This edition is filled with *revisions*. • A *revision* of the theory will be necessary. • They made *revisions* to the book. [*noncount*] The essay needs *revision*. • The teacher gave me some suggestions for *revision*.

2 [*count*] : a new version of something : something (such as a piece of writing or a song) that has been corrected or changed • This is the original version, not the *revision*. • Here is my *revision* of the paragraph.

3 [*noncount*] *Brit* : study of information that was studied before • Have you done enough *revision* [=(*US*) *review*] for the exam?

re·vi·sion·ism /rɪˈvɪʒəˌnɪzəm/ *noun* [*noncount*] *formal* + *often disapproving* : support of ideas and beliefs that differ from and try to change accepted ideas and beliefs especially in a way that is seen as wrong or dishonest • She rejects the author's historical *revisionism*. [=the author's new interpretation of history]

– **re·vi·sion·ist** /rɪˈvɪʒənɪst/ *noun, pl* **-ists** [*count*] – **revisionist** *adj* • a *revisionist* argument/view

re·vis·it /riˈvɪzət/ *verb* **-its; -it·ed; -it·ing** [+ *obj*]

1 : to go to (a place) again especially after a long period of time • He *revisited* his old house. • The police *revisited* the crime scene.

2 : to think about or look at (something) again • The police *revisited* the case of the unsolved murder. • The book/idea is worth *revisiting*. • The judge said that he will *revisit* [=*reconsider*] his decision.

re·vi·tal·ize *also Brit* **re·vi·tal·ise** /riˈvaɪtəˌlaɪz/ *verb* **-izes; -ized; -iz·ing** [+ *obj*] : to make (someone or something) active, healthy, or energetic again • The mayor hopes to *revitalize* the city. • This shampoo *revitalized* my hair. [=made my hair look healthy] • The drink *revitalized* me. [=made me feel full of energy]

– **re·vi·tal·i·za·tion** *also Brit* **re·vi·tal·i·sa·tion** /riˌvaɪtələˈzeɪʃən, *Brit* riˌvaɪtəˌlaɪˈzeɪʃən/ *noun* [*noncount*] economic *revitalization* • *revitalization* efforts/plans [*singular*] a *revitalization* of the city

re·viv·al /rɪˈvaɪvəl/ *noun, pl* **-als**

1 [*count*] : a period in which something becomes popular again after a long period of time • a jazz *revival* • a *revival* of biographical writing • a *revival* in Gothic architecture • Fashions from the 1970s are ***enjoying a revival***.

2 : the growth of something or an increase in the activity of something after a long period of no growth or activity [*count*] — usually singular • After four slow years, our business is seeing a *revival*. • the recent ***revival of interest*** in mythology [*noncount*] The city is showing signs of *revival*.

3 [*count*] : the showing of a play, a movie, etc., to the public usually many years after it was last shown : a new production of an old show • There are three musical *revivals* on Broadway this season. • The opera company is staging a *revival* of Verdi's *Don Carlos*.

4 [*count*] *US, religion* : REVIVAL MEETING

re·viv·al·ist /rɪˈvaɪvəlɪst/ *noun, pl* **-ists** [*count*]

1 *religion* : someone who organizes and leads a revival meeting

2 *formal* : someone who uses or practices something that was popular in the past • a musical *revivalist*

– **re·viv·al·ism** /rɪˈvaɪvəˌlɪzəm/ *noun* [*noncount*] • religious *revivalism* – **revivalist** *adj, always used before a noun* • a *revivalist* preacher/movement

revival meeting *noun, pl* **~ -ings** [*count*] : a meeting or series of meetings led by a preacher to make people interested in a Christian religion — called also (*US*) *revival*

re·vive /rɪˈvaɪv/ *verb* **-vives; -vived; -viv·ing**

1 a [+ *obj*] : to make (someone or something) strong, healthy, or active again • The doctors were trying to *revive*

R

the patient. [=to make the unconscious patient conscious again] • Visiting my old house has *revived* [=*brought back*] childhood memories. • The water *revived* [=*refreshed*] the flowers. • The success of the movie has *revived* her career. • The government is trying to *revive* the economy. • Our spirits were *revived* by his enthusiasm. **b** [*no obj*] **:** to become strong, healthy, or active again • The store's business is beginning to *revive*.
2 [+ *obj*] **:** to bring (something) back into use or popularity • The family is trying to *revive* an old custom.
3 [+ *obj*] **:** to arrange to have (an old play, opera, etc.) performed in front of an audience • He has decided to *revive* Molière's *Tartuffe*.

re•viv•i•fy /rɪˈvɪvəˌfaɪ/ *verb* **-fies; -fied; -fy•ing** [+ *obj*] *formal* **:** to make (someone or something) strong, healthy, or active again **:** REVIVE • looking for ways to *revivify* the city's economy

re•voke /rɪˈvoʊk/ *verb* **-vokes; -voked; -vok•ing** [+ *obj*] *formal* **:** to officially cancel the power or effect of (something, such as a law, license, agreement, etc.) **:** to make (something) not valid • The judge *revoked* her driver's license. • Their work permits were *revoked*. • He threatened to *revoke* [=*retract, cancel*] his offer. • Their privileges were *revoked* after they misbehaved.
– re•vo•ca•tion /ˌrɛvəˈkeɪʃən/ *noun, pl* **-tions** [*count, noncount*] • Not paying the fine may mean *revocation* of your driver's license.

[1]re•volt /rɪˈvoʊlt/ *verb* **-volts; -volt•ed; -volt•ing**
1 [*no obj*] **:** to fight in a violent way against the rule of a leader or government • The group threatened to *revolt*. — often + *against* • The peasants *revolted against* the king. • They *revolted against* the government.
2 [*no obj*] **:** to act in a way that shows that you do not accept the control or influence of someone or something — often + *against* • Teenagers tend to *revolt* [=*rebel*] *against* their parents. • He *revolted against* [=*disobeyed*] religious traditions.
3 [+ *obj*] **:** to cause (someone) to feel disgust or shock • All the violence *revolted* me. — often used as ***(be) revolted*** • He *was revolted* by the smell.

[2]revolt *noun, pl* **-volts**
1 : violent action against a ruler or government **:** REBELLION [*count*] the *revolt* of/by the slaves • The peasants' *revolt* was crushed by the king. • They ***staged a revolt***, but it was quickly put down. [=they started a revolt, but it was quickly defeated] — often + *against* • a *revolt against* the government [*noncount*] The leader of the group called for *revolt*. • The people rose (up) ***in revolt*** (***against*** the king). [=the people fought against the king]
2 : something which shows that you will not accept something or will not agree to be controlled or influenced by someone or something [*count*] a *revolt* by consumers over high prices = a consumer *revolt* over high prices — often + *against* • His book is a *revolt against* conservative thinking. [*noncount*] Consumers are ***in revolt against*** high prices.

re•volt•ing /rɪˈvoʊltɪŋ/ *adj* [*more ~; most ~*] **:** extremely unpleasant or offensive • a *revolting* [=*disgusting*] smell • The bloody scenes in the movie were positively *revolting*.
– re•volt•ing•ly *adv* • The movie was *revoltingly* violent.

rev•o•lu•tion /ˌrɛvəˈluːʃən/ *noun, pl* **-tions**
1 a : the usually violent attempt by many people to end the rule of one government and start a new one [*count*] the American/French *Revolution* • The group started a *revolution*. [*noncount*] The king knew that there was a threat of *revolution*. — see also COUNTERREVOLUTION **b** [*count*] **:** a sudden, extreme, or complete change in the way people live, work, etc. • This new theory could cause a *revolution* in elementary education. • the computer *revolution* [=the changes created by the widespread use of computers] • The growth of the middle class forced a social *revolution*. [=a major change in society] • the sexual *revolution* [=a major change in people's attitudes about sex] — see also INDUSTRIAL REVOLUTION
2 *technical* **a :** the action of moving around something in a path that is similar to a circle **:** ROTATION [*count*] the *revolution* of the Earth around the Sun [*noncount*] The period of *revolution* of the Earth around the Sun is equal to one year. **b** [*count*] **:** a complete turn that is made by something around its center point or line • The Earth makes one *revolution* on its axis in about 24 hours. • This motor operates at a speed of 5,000 ***revolutions per minute***.

[1]rev•o•lu•tion•ary /ˌrɛvəˈluːʃəˌneri, *Brit* ˌrɛvəˈluːʃənri/ *adj*
1 *always used before a noun* **:** relating to, involving, or supporting a political revolution • a *revolutionary* war/movement • a *revolutionary* leader/party
2 [*more ~; most ~*] **:** causing or relating to a great or complete change • *revolutionary* [=*radical*] ideas • The invention was *revolutionary*. • a *revolutionary* new product

[2]revolutionary *noun, pl* **-aries** [*count*] **:** someone who leads, joins, or wants a revolution

rev•o•lu•tion•ize *also Brit* **rev•o•lu•tion•ise** /ˌrɛvəˈluːʃəˌnaɪz/ *verb* **-iz•es; -ized; -iz•ing** [+ *obj*] **:** to change (something) very much or completely **:** to cause a revolution in (something) • The invention of the airplane *revolutionized* travel. • This new drug may *revolutionize* cancer treatment. • This discovery has *revolutionized* our understanding of how the human brain works.

re•volve /rɪˈvɑːlv/ *verb* **-volves; -volved; -volv•ing :** to turn around a center point or line **:** ROTATE [*no obj*] As the gear *revolves*, it turns the other gears. • The Earth *revolves* on its axis. [+ *obj*] The software allows you to *revolve* images.
revolve around [*phrasal verb*] **1 *revolve around (something)*** **:** to move around (something) in a path that is similar to a circle • The planets *revolve around* the sun. **2 *revolve around (someone or something)*** **:** to have (someone or something) as a main subject or interest • The discussion *revolved around* the question of how much money should be given to each department. • Her world *revolves around* her work/son. [=her work/son is extremely important to her] • His life *revolves around* playing basketball. [=he plays basketball a lot] • He thinks ***the world revolves around*** him. [=he thinks that he is the most important person in the world] • The world ***does not revolve around*** you. [=you are not the most important person in the world]

re•volv•er /rɪˈvɑːlvɚ/ *noun, pl* **-ers** [*count*] **:** a small gun with a container for bullets that turns after the gun is fired and puts another bullet into position to be fired next

revolving *adj, always used before a noun* **:** able to be turned around a center point • The band played on a *revolving* stage.

revolving door *noun, pl* **~ doors**
1 [*count*] **:** a type of door that turns in its frame when it is used and allows people to go both in and out of a large building at the same time
2 [*singular*] **a** — used to describe a situation in which the people who have a particular job or position are constantly or frequently changing • The team has gone through a *revolving door* of coaches. [=has had many different coaches] • The manager's position has become a *revolving door*. **b** — used to describe a situation in which someone leaves and returns to a place or position many times • criminals who have entered a *revolving door* of arrest, prison, release, and then arrest again
– revolving–door *adj, always used before a noun* • *revolving-door* management • a *revolving-door* roster of players

re•vue /rɪˈvjuː/ *noun, pl* **-vues** [*count*] **:** a show in a theater that includes funny songs, dances, short plays, etc., usually about recent events

> Do not confuse *revue* with *review*.

re•vul•sion /rɪˈvʌlʃən/ *noun, somewhat formal* **:** a very strong feeling of dislike or disgust [*noncount*] She was struck with *revulsion* at the sight of the dead animal. • I felt *revulsion* at the thought of [=I was revolted by] his cruelty. [*singular*] a growing *revulsion* to war

revved up *adj* [*more ~; most ~*] *informal* **:** very excited • a rousing song that got the crowd all *revved up* • He came home all *revved up* because he had won the tournament. • She is *revved up* for [=ready for and excited about] her trip. — see also *rev up* at [1]REV

[1]re•ward /rɪˈwoɚd/ *noun, pl* **-wards :** money or another kind of payment that is given or received for something that has been done or that is offered for something that might be done [*count*] The contest offered a cash *reward* to the first person who could breed a blue rose. • Hard work brings its own *rewards*. • She is ***reaping the rewards*** of success. [=is getting all the good things that come with success] — often + *for* • You deserve a *reward for* being so helpful. • A (cash) *reward* is being offered *for* the return of the lost dog. • The police are offering a *reward for* information leading to the capture of the fugitive. • You can go to bed late tonight ***as a reward for*** doing so well on that test. • Winning the game was a ***just reward*** [=an appropriate result] *for* the team's effort. • That lying crook got his ***just rewards***. [=*just deserts*] [*noncount*] Members will receive a discount ***in reward for*** getting friends

R

or family to join. • Her success is ***just reward for*** her hard work. [=she deserves her success because of her hard work]

[2]**reward** *verb* **-wards; -ward·ed; -ward·ing** [+ *obj*] **:** to give money or another kind of payment to (someone or something) for something good that has been done • She *rewarded* herself by buying a new pair of shoes. — often + *for* or *with* • She *rewarded* her children *with* ice cream *for* being so patient. — often used as *(be) rewarded* • She *was rewarded with* a cash bonus. • He *was rewarded for* his effort. = His effort *was rewarded.*

re·ward·ing /rɪˈwoɚdɪŋ/ *adj* [*more* ~; *most* ~]
1 : giving you a good feeling that you have done something valuable, important, etc. • It was a *rewarding* [=*valuable*] experience. • Nursing is a very *rewarding* [=*satisfying*] career.
2 : giving you money or profit • The investment has been very *rewarding.* [=*profitable*] • Her work is financially *rewarding.*

[1]**re·wind** /riˈwaɪnd/ *verb* **-winds; -wound** /-ˈwaʊnd/; **-wind·ing** [+ *obj*] **:** to make (a recording) go backwards • *Rewind* the tape so that we can hear that song again. — opposite [2]FAST-FORWARD

[2]**re·wind** /ˈriːˌwaɪnd/ *noun* [*noncount*] **:** a function that causes a recording (such as an audiotape or a videotape) to go backwards • Hit the *rewind* button. — opposite [1]FAST-FORWARD

re·wire /riˈwajɚ/ *verb* **-wires; -wired; -wir·ing** [+ *obj*] **:** to put new electrical wires in (a building, machine, etc.) • He *rewired* the entire house.

re·word /riˈwɚd/ *verb* **-words; -word·ed; -word·ing** [+ *obj*] **:** to state (something) again using different and often simpler words • You should *reword* this sentence. • Let me *reword* [=*rephrase*] the question. • They *reworded* the rule.

re·work /riˈwɚk/ *verb* **-works; -worked; -work·ing** [+ *obj*] **:** to make changes to (something, such as a piece of writing or music) in order to improve it • The teacher told me to *rework* [=*revise*] my essay. • The design has been completely *reworked.*

re·write /riˈraɪt/ *verb* **-writes; -wrote** /-ˈrout/; **-writ·ten** /-ˈrɪtn̩/; **-writ·ing** [+ *obj*] **:** to write (something) again especially in a different way in order to improve it or to include new information • The teacher asked him to *rewrite* the essay. • I had to *rewrite* the computer program/code. — sometimes used figuratively • You can't ***rewrite history.*** [=you can't change the past]
– re·write /ˈriːˌraɪt/ *noun, pl* **-writes** [*count*] • I usually do several *rewrites* of my essays.

RH *abbr* right hand

rhap·so·dize *also Brit* **rhap·so·dise** /ˈræpsəˌdaɪz/ *verb* **-diz·es; -dized; -diz·ing** [*no obj*] *formal* **:** to praise or describe something or someone with a lot of enthusiasm and emotion — usually + *about* or *over* • He *rhapsodized about* his favorite musician. • She *rhapsodizes over* the food at that restaurant.

rhap·so·dy /ˈræpsədi/ *noun, pl* **-dies** [*count*]
1 : a piece of music that is meant to express a lot of emotion and does not have a regular form
2 : a written or spoken expression of great enthusiasm, praise, etc. • The mayor launched/went into a long *rhapsody* about his plans for the city. • *rhapsodies* of praise
– rhap·sod·ic /ræpˈsɑːdɪk/ *adj* [*more* ~; *most* ~] • They waxed *rhapsodic* [=they became very enthusiastic] about the beauty of the area. • *rhapsodic* music

Rhe·sus factor /ˈriːsəs-/ *noun* [*noncount*] *medical* **:** RH FACTOR

rhe·sus monkey /ˈriːsəs-/ *noun, pl* ~ **-keys** [*count*] **:** a small monkey that is often used in medical research

rhet·o·ric /ˈrɛtərɪk/ *noun* [*noncount*] *formal*
1 *often disapproving* **:** language that is intended to influence people and that may not be honest or reasonable • absolutist/activist/racist *rhetoric* • angry *rhetoric* • a speech free of (empty) *rhetoric* • the *rhetoric* of politics
2 : the art or skill of speaking or writing formally and effectively especially as a way to persuade or influence people • a college course in *rhetoric* • classical *rhetoric*
– rhet·o·ri·cian /ˌrɛtəˈrɪʃən/ *noun, pl* **-cians** [*count*] *formal* • an expert *rhetorician* [=a person who is able to use language in a very effective way]

rhe·tor·i·cal /rɪˈtorɪkəl/ *adj*
1 : of, relating to, or concerned with the art of speaking or writing formally and effectively especially as a way to persuade or influence people • a *rhetorical* device/style
2 *of a question* **:** asked in order to make a statement rather than to get an answer • "Should we be leaving soon?" "Is that a ***rhetorical question***?" [=is that a question you're asking as a way to say that we should be leaving soon?] • My question was *rhetorical.* I wasn't really expecting an answer.
– rhe·tor·i·cal·ly /rɪˈtorɪkli/ *adv* • "Why does it have to rain?" she asked *rhetorically.*

rheumatic fever *noun* [*noncount*] *medical* **:** a serious disease especially of young people that causes fever, swelling and pain in the joints, and sometimes damage to the heart

rheu·ma·tism /ˈruːməˌtɪzəm/ *noun* [*noncount*] *medical* **:** a disease that causes stiffness and pain in the muscles and swelling and pain in the joints
– rheu·mat·ic /rʊˈmætɪk/ *adj* • a *rheumatic* disease • *rheumatic* pain

rheu·ma·toid arthritis /ˈruːməˌtoɪd-/ *noun* [*noncount*] *medical* **:** a serious disease that continues to become worse over a long period of time and that causes the joints to become very painful, stiff, and swollen

Rh factor /ˌɑɚˈeɪtʃ-/ *noun* [*noncount*] *medical* **:** a substance that is present in the red blood cells of most people ✧ If you do not have Rh factor in your blood, you can become ill by receiving blood from someone who has Rh factor. — called also *Rhesus factor*; see also RH-NEGATIVE, RH-POSITIVE

rhine·stone /ˈraɪnˌstoun/ *noun, pl* **-stones** [*count*] **:** a small stone that is made to look like a diamond and that is used in jewelry or for decoration

rhi·no /ˈraɪnou/ *noun, pl* **rhi·nos** *also* **rhino** [*count*] *somewhat informal* **:** RHINOCEROS

rhi·noc·er·os /raɪˈnɑːsərəs/ *noun, pl* **rhi·noc·er·os·es** *also* **rhinoceros** [*count*] **:** a large, heavy animal of Africa and Asia that has thick skin and either one or two large horns on its nose

rhinoceros

rhi·zome /ˈraɪˌzoum/ *noun, pl* **-zomes** [*count*] *botany* **:** a thick plant stem that grows underground and has shoots and roots growing from it

Rh–neg·a·tive /ˌɑɚˌeɪtʃˈnɛgətɪv/ *adj, medical* **:** not having Rh factor in the blood • The baby is *Rh-negative.* • *Rh-negative* blood

rho·do·den·dron /ˌroudəˈdɛndrən/ *noun, pl* **-drons** [*count*] **:** an evergreen bush that has large, bright flowers and that is often grown in gardens

rhom·boid /ˈrɑːmˌboɪd/ *noun, pl* **-boids** [*count*] *geometry* **:** a shape with four sides where only the opposite sides and angles are equal

rhom·bus /ˈrɑːmbəs/ *noun, pl* **-bus·es** [*count*] *geometry* **:** a shape with four sides that are equal in length and with four angles that are not always right angles

Rh–pos·i·tive /ˌɑɚˌeɪtʃˈpɑːzətɪv/ *adj, medical* **:** having Rh factor in the blood • The baby is *Rh-positive.* • *Rh-positive* blood

rhu·barb /ˈruːˌbɑɚb/ *noun, pl* **-barbs**
1 [*noncount*] **:** a plant with large green leaves and with thick pink or red stems that are cooked and used in pies, jams, etc. • *rhubarb* pie
2 [*count*] *US, informal + old-fashioned* **:** an angry argument • The coach got into a *rhubarb* with the umpire.

rhumba *variant spelling of* RUMBA

[1]**rhyme** /ˈraɪm/ *noun, pl* **rhymes**
1 [*count*] **:** one of two or more words or phrases that end in the same sounds • She used "moon" as a *rhyme* for "June." • He couldn't think of a *rhyme* for "orange."
2 [*count*] **:** a poem or song whose lines end in rhymes • children's *rhymes* • a catchy *rhyme* — see also NURSERY RHYME
3 [*noncount*] **:** the use of rhymes in a poem or song • They're learning about meter and *rhyme.* • He delivered the speech in *rhyme.* [=he used words that rhyme in the speech] • poems that use *rhyme*
rhyme or reason **:** a good reason or explanation for something — used in negative statements • There seems to be ***no rhyme or reason*** to/for some of the things he does. • She does things ***without rhyme or reason.***

[2]**rhyme** *verb* **rhymes; rhymed; rhym·ing**
1 [*no obj*] **:** to have or end with the same sounds • Please find the two lines that *rhyme.* • words that don't *rhyme* — often + *with* • "Bug" *rhymes with* "rug."
2 [*no obj*] **:** to have lines that end with the same sounds • po-

R

ems that *rhyme* • *rhyming* verse/couplets
3 [+ *obj*] : to use (a rhyme) in a poem, song, etc. • She *rhymed* "moon" with "June."

rhythm /ˈrɪðəm/ *noun, pl* **rhythms**
1 : a regular, repeated pattern of sounds or movements [*count*] The music has a fast/slow/steady *rhythm*. [=*beat*] • African/Caribbean *rhythms* — often + *of* • the *rhythm of* the poetry • the *rhythm of* his breathing • the *rhythm of* the tides [*noncount*] the composer's use of jazz *rhythm* • He can't play/dance ***in rhythm***. = He has no ***sense of rhythm***. [=he cannot play/dance at the correct speed to stay with the rhythm of the music]
2 [*count*] : a regular, repeated pattern of events, changes, activities, etc. • She enjoyed the *rhythms* of country life. • Travel can disrupt your body's daily/biological/circadian *rhythm*.

rhythm and blues *noun* [*noncount*] : a type of popular music performed by African-Americans that was developed originally by combining elements of blues and jazz — abbr. *R & B*

rhyth·mic /ˈrɪðmɪk/ *or* **rhyth·mi·cal** /ˈrɪðmɪkəl/ *adj* : having a regular repeated pattern of sounds or movements • We could hear a *rhythmic* drumming/chant outside.
– **rhyth·mi·cal·ly** /ˈrɪðmɪkli/ *adv* • She *rhythmically* tapped her feet.

rhythm method *noun* [*singular*] *medical* : a method of birth control in which a couple does not have sexual intercourse during the time when pregnancy is most likely to happen

rhythm section *noun, pl* ~ **-tions** [*count*] : the part of a band that plays the rhythm in a piece of music and that typically includes drums and bass

RI *abbr* Rhode Island

[1]**rib** /ˈrɪb/ *noun, pl* **ribs** [*count*]
1 : any one of the curved bones of the chest that connect to the spine — see picture at HUMAN
2 : a piece of meat from an animal that includes a rib and that is used as food — see also SPARERIB
3 : a long curved piece of metal, wood, etc., that forms the frame of a boat, roof, etc. • the *ribs* of an umbrella

[2]**rib** *verb* **ribs; ribbed; rib·bing** [+ *obj*] *informal* : to make jokes about (someone) in a friendly way : to kid or tease (someone) — often + *about* or *over* • They *ribbed* him *about/over* his silly outfit.

rib·ald /ˈrɪbəld/ *adj* [*more* ~; *most* ~] *formal* : referring to sex in a rude but amusing way • *ribald* jokes/comments/songs
– **rib·ald·ry** /ˈrɪbəldri/ *noun, pl* **-dries** [*count*] comedians exchanging *ribaldries* [=ribald remarks/jokes] [*noncount*] a scandal that has been the subject of much *ribaldry*

ribbed *adj* : having raised lines • *ribbed* fabric • a *ribbed* sweater

ribbing *noun* [*noncount*]
1 : friendly jokes about someone • a little good-natured *ribbing* between friends — usually used with *take* • He *took* some *ribbing* for the silly hat he was wearing. • I've *taken* a lot of *ribbing* about my accent.
2 : raised lines on a surface • the *ribbing* on a sweater

rib·bon /ˈrɪbən/ *noun, pl* **-bons**
1 : a narrow piece of cloth (such as silk) that is used to tie things or for decoration [*count*] She wore pink *ribbons* in her hair. • She tied a *ribbon* around the present. [*noncount*] a length/piece of *ribbon* • The present was tied with *ribbon*.
2 [*count*] : a short piece of cloth that is given as a military award • The soldier proudly wore his *ribbons* and medals.
3 [*count*] *chiefly US* : a piece of colored cloth that is given as an award in a competition • Her pie won a *ribbon* at the county fair. — see also BLUE RIBBON
4 [*count*] : something that is long and narrow like a strip of cloth • a *ribbon* of road
5 [*count*] : a long and narrow piece of cloth with ink that is used for producing printed characters in a typewriter or printer
6 ***ribbons*** [*plural*] : narrow pieces of something that has been cut or torn apart • Her pants were ***torn/cut to ribbons***. [=*to pieces*]

rib cage *noun, pl* ~ **cages** [*count*] *medical* : the curved wall of ribs that surrounds and protects the chest

rib eye *noun, pl* ~ **eyes** [*count, noncount*] : a large, tender cut of beef from the outer side of the rib — called also *rib eye steak*

ri·bo·fla·vin /ˌraɪbəˈfleɪvən/ *noun* [*noncount*] *technical* : a natural substance (called a vitamin) that is found in certain foods (such as milk, eggs, and leafy vegetables) and that helps your body to be healthy — called also *vitamin* B_2

ri·bo·nu·cle·ic acid /ˌraɪbounuˈkliːjɪk-, *Brit* ˌraɪbəunjuˈkliːjɪk-/ *noun* [*noncount*] *technical* : RNA

rice /ˈraɪs/ *noun* [*noncount*]
1 : small white or brown grains that come from a southeast Asian plant and that are used for food • a bowl/grain of *rice* • steamed/fried *rice* • brown/white *rice*
2 : the plant that produces rice • *Rice* is the main crop of the country. • a field of *rice* = a *rice* field/paddy

rice paper *noun* [*noncount*]
1 : a type of thin paper that is made from an Asian plant
2 : a food that looks like paper and that is used for wrapping other foods

rice pudding *noun* [*noncount*] : a sweet food made of rice cooked with milk and sugar

rich /ˈrɪʧ/ *adj* **rich·er; -est** [*also more* ~; *most* ~]
1 : having a lot of money and possessions : WEALTHY • a *rich* person • Her investments have made her *rich*. • a *rich* country/area/neighborhood • She is very *rich*. • (*informal + often disapproving*) She is ***filthy rich***. = She is ***stinking rich***. [=she is extremely rich; she has so much money that her wealth is disgusting or offensive] • He wrote a book on how to ***get rich quick***. [=how to make a large amount of money quickly] — opposite POOR
2 : very expensive and beautiful, impressive, etc. • *rich* [=*luxurious*] robes • *rich* decorations
3 a : having or supplying a large amount of something that is wanted or needed • The dictionary is a *rich* source of information. • a *rich* gold mine • *rich* [=*fertile*] soils • protein-*rich* foods [=foods that contain a lot of protein] — often + *in* or *with* • a land *rich in* resources • foods that are *rich in* protein • He had a life *rich with* blessings. **b** : containing a large amount of fat, oil, etc. : having a lot of flavor and making your stomach feel full • *rich* [=*heavy*] foods • a *rich* and spicy soup • The food was a little too *rich* for me. **c** : very interesting and full of many different things • Their country has a *rich* cultural heritage. • This area has a *rich* history. • She has a *rich* vocabulary.
4 : having a pleasingly strong quality • a *rich* [=dark and vivid] red • a singer with a full, *rich* voice • *rich* perfumes
5 *informal* — used to say that a person's comment or criticism is surprising or amusing because the same comment or criticism could be made about that person • His remarks about the importance of saving money are pretty *rich* coming from a man who just bought another new car. • "She says we're working too slowly." "Oh, ***that's rich***. She's the one who keeps delaying things with all her meetings."
strike it rich see [1]STRIKE
the rich : people who are rich • *the rich* and famous/powerful
– **rich·ness** /ˈrɪʧnəs/ *noun* [*noncount*] • the *richness of* the soil • the *richness of* the food • the *richness of* the painter's colors

rich·es /ˈrɪʧəz/ *noun* [*plural*]
1 : large amounts of money and possessions • He acquired *riches* [=*wealth*] and fame.
2 : good things that are available to use or choose • We live in a culture that offers many *riches*. • With so many fine restaurants in the city, diners are faced with an ***embarrassment of riches***. [=there are so many fine restaurants that it is difficult to choose one]
from rags to riches see [1]RAG

rich·ly /ˈrɪʧli/ *adv* [*more* ~; *most* ~]
1 : in a beautiful and expensive way • The room was *richly* decorated/ornamented. • *richly* dressed
2 : in a pleasingly strong way • *richly* fragrant/colored/flavored • a *richly* rewarding [=very satisfying] experience
3 : in a generous way • They were *richly* rewarded for their efforts.
4 : completely or fully • The reward/punishment he received was ***richly deserved***.
5 : having a large amount of something • The book is *richly* illustrated. [=the book has many illustrations] • a *richly* detailed description

Rich·ter scale /ˈrɪktɚ-/ *noun*
the Richter scale *technical* : a system of measurement used for showing the strength of an earthquake • The earthquake was a 4.5 on *the Richter scale*. = The earthquake measured 4.5 on *the Richter scale*.

rick /ˈrɪk/ *verb* **ricks; ricked; rick·ing** [+ *obj*] *Brit* : to injure

R

(a body part) by twisting it • I *ricked* [=*sprained, wrenched*] my back/neck.

rick·ets /ˈrɪkəts/ *noun* [*noncount*] *medical* **:** a disease in children that is caused by a lack of vitamin D and that causes bones to become soft and to bend

rick·ety /ˈrɪkəti/ *adj* [*more* ~; *most* ~] **:** not strong or stable and likely to break • *rickety* stairs • a *rickety* little/old table

rick·shaw /ˈrɪkˌʃɑː/ *noun, pl* **-shaws** [*count*] **:** a small, light vehicle with two wheels that is pulled by one person on foot or on a bicycle and that is used in some Asian countries

[1]ric·o·chet /ˈrɪkəˌʃeɪ/ *verb* **-chets; -cheted** /-ˌʃeɪd/; **-chet·ing** /-ˌʃejɪŋ/ [*no obj*] **:** to bounce off a surface and continue moving in a different direction • The bullet *ricocheted* off the wall.

[2]ricochet *noun, pl* **-chets**
1 [*count*] **:** something (such as a bullet or stone) that ricochets off a surface • He was hit by a *ricochet*.
2 [*noncount*] **:** the action of ricocheting off a surface • the *richochet* of the bullet off the wall

ri·cot·ta /rɪˈkɑːtə/ *noun* [*noncount*] **:** a soft, white Italian cheese — called also *ricotta cheese*

rid /ˈrɪd/ *verb* **rids; rid** *also* **rid·ded; rid·ding**
be rid of **:** to no longer have or be affected or bothered by (someone or something that is unwanted or annoying) • I thought I'd never *be rid of* that cold. [=I thought that cold would never go away] • He thought he'd never *be rid of* her. • It's just as well that he left you. You're ***well rid of*** him. [=you're better off without him]
get rid of **:** to do something so that you no longer have or are affected or bothered by (something or someone that is unwanted) • It's time to *get rid of* [=*throw away*] our old computer and buy a new one. • I *got rid of* some old furniture by selling/giving it to my nephew. • I've tried everything to *get rid of* this cold, but it just won't go away. • He kept talking and talking. She finally *got rid of* him [=she finally got him to leave] by saying she had to make dinner.
rid of [*phrasal verb*] ***rid (someone or something) of (someone or something)*** **:** to cause (someone or something) to no longer have or be affected by (someone or something unwanted) • The police are trying to *rid* the town *of* drug dealers. • *rid* the garden *of* pests • She went to the beach to relax and ***rid herself of*** all her worries.
want rid of *chiefly Brit* **:** to want to no longer have or be affected or bothered by (something or someone unwanted) **:** to want to be rid of (something or someone) • I could tell that he *wanted rid of* me.

rid·dance /ˈrɪdn̩s/ *noun*
good riddance — used to say that you are glad that someone is leaving or that something has gone • "Did you hear? Jack is leaving for a new job." "Well, *good riddance* (to him)! We'll be better off without him!" • Winter is finally over, and I say *good riddance*!

[1]rid·den /ˈrɪdn̩/ *adj* **:** filled with or containing something unpleasant or unwanted • He was *ridden* with guilt. [=he felt very guilty] — usually used in combination • a flea-*ridden* dog • a slum-*ridden* city • He was/felt guilt-*ridden* for the way he had neglected his son.

[2]ridden *past participle of* [1]RIDE

[1]rid·dle /ˈrɪdl̩/ *noun, pl* **rid·dles** [*count*]
1 : a difficult question that is asked as a game and that has a surprising or funny answer • The first person to solve the *riddle* wins a candy bar. — sometimes used figuratively • Stop speaking in *riddles*. [=stop speaking in a confusing way]
2 : someone or something that is difficult to understand or solve • the *riddle* of the origins of the universe • My brother has always been a *riddle* to me.

[2]riddle *verb* **riddles; rid·dled; rid·dling** [+ *obj*]
1 : to make many holes in (something or someone) *with* something • The robbers *riddled* the car *with* bullets.
2 : to fill (something) with something that is bad or unpleasant — usually used as *(be) riddled with* • The book *is riddled with* mistakes. [=the book has many mistakes] • Their theory *is riddled with* contradictions.

[1]ride /ˈraɪd/ *verb* **rides; rode** /ˈroʊd/; **rid·den** /ˈrɪdn̩/; **rid·ing**
1 : to sit on and control the movements of (a horse, motorcycle, bicycle, etc.) [+ *obj*] She learned how to *ride* a horse when she was young. • Most children learn to *ride* a bicycle at an early age. • He *rides* his motorcycle to work every day. [*no obj*] I never *rode* on a horse before. • She got on her bicycle and *rode* away.
2 a : to travel to a place as a passenger on or in (something that is moving, such as a bus, a train, or an elevator) [+ *obj*] (*chiefly US*) • He decided to walk to the movies instead of *riding* the bus. • She *rides* the subway home from school. • They *rode* the elevator/escalator to the second floor. [*no obj*] We *rode* through the park in a horse-drawn carriage. • The dog *rode* in the back of the truck. • He has never *ridden* aboard a cruise ship. **b :** to go on a mechanical ride at an amusement park or similar place [*no obj*] We *rode* on the Ferris wheel. [+ *obj*] We *rode* the roller coaster five times.
3 [+ *obj*] *chiefly US* **:** to travel over or on (a road, railway, trail, etc.) in a car, on a train, on a bicycle, etc. • He spends hours *riding* the back roads in his truck. • *riding* the rails • We *rode* the bike trails for hours.
4 [*no obj*] *of a vehicle* **:** to move over the surface of a road in a specified way • The car *rides* smoothly/well.
5 [+ *obj*] **:** to be supported or carried on (a wave) **:** to move on (a wave) • We watched the surfers *riding* the waves.
6 [+ *obj*] *US, informal* **:** to criticize or make jokes about (someone) constantly or frequently in usually a harsh or annoying way • The fans have been *riding* him pretty hard.
be riding for a fall *informal* **:** to be doing something that is likely to lead to failure or disaster • They're feeling pretty confident now, but if you ask me, they'*re riding for a fall*.
be riding high *informal* **1 :** to be very happy and excited • She'*s riding high* [=*flying high*] after her recent win. **2 :** to be very successful • The company's stock *was riding high* after the merger.
let (something) ride *informal* **:** to allow (something) to go unnoticed **:** to ignore (something) • He made a rude remark, but I *let* it *ride*. • You have to *let* his comment *ride*.
ride herd on *US, informal* **:** to keep (someone or something) under close watch or control • We had to *ride herd on* them to make sure they completed the work on time.
ride on [*phrasal verb*] ***ride on (something or someone)*** **1 :** to depend on (something or someone) • The future of the company *rides on* the success of this deal. • Our hopes are *riding on* you. **2** ✧ If you have money *riding on* something or someone, you have bet money on that thing or person. • I have a lot of money *riding on* this game. • There is a lot of money *riding on* the outcome of the race.
ride out [*phrasal verb*] ***ride (something) out*** *or* ***ride out (something)*** **:** to succeed in surviving or getting through (something dangerous or harmful that cannot be stopped or avoided) • The ship/crew *rode out* the storm. • We managed to *ride out* the stock market downturn.
ride shotgun *informal* **:** to ride in the front passenger seat of a vehicle • You can drive, but only if I can *ride shotgun*.
ride up [*phrasal verb*] *of clothing* **:** to move up your body as you move • These jeans keep *riding up* on me. • Her skirt *rode up* when she sat down.

[2]ride *noun, pl* **rides** [*count*]
1 a : a usually short journey in or on a vehicle • a two-hour car *ride* • We went for a *ride* in the country. • He took me for a *ride* on his motorcycle. = He gave me a *ride* on his motorcycle. • I had my first *ride* in a limousine. • Can I take your bike for a *ride*? = Can I go for a *ride* on your bike? [=can I ride your bike?] • Can you give me a *ride* [=*lift*] back to town? • I need a *ride* to work. • She caught/hitched a *ride* with her coworker. — see also HAYRIDE, JOYRIDE **b :** a usually short journey on a horse or other animal • We went on a horseback *ride*. • The kids had a *ride* on a horse. • They offered pony *rides* at the fair.
2 — used to describe what the experience of riding in a car or other vehicle is like; usually singular • The car has/offers a smooth/comfortable *ride*. • The road wasn't paved, so we had a pretty bumpy *ride*. — often used figuratively • Investors are preparing for a bumpy/rough *ride* [=a difficult time] in the stock market.
3 a : a large machine at an amusement park, fair, etc., that people ride on for enjoyment • The Ferris wheel is my favorite *ride*. **b :** the act of riding on such a machine • We went for a *ride* on the roller coaster. — see also FREE RIDE
along for the ride *informal* **:** doing something with other people without being seriously involved in it or having a serious interest in it • He wasn't really interested in buying anything when we went to the store; he was just *along for the ride*. • He wasn't really interested, but he ***came/went along for the ride***.
take (someone) for a ride *informal* **:** to trick or fool (someone) especially in order to get money • I figured out that he was *taking* me *for a ride*.

rid·er /ˈraɪdɚ/ *noun, pl* **-ers** [*count*]
1 : a person who rides something • a horseback *rider* • Watch

out for bike *riders* while driving. ▪ *riders* on the bus — see also DISPATCH RIDER
2 a : an official document that is attached to another document and that adds to or changes information in the original document ▪ She added a *rider* to her life insurance policy that increased her coverage. **b :** an additional part added to a legislative bill ▪ Congress added a *rider* to the health insurance bill.

ridge /ˈrɪʤ/ *noun, pl* **ridg·es** [*count*]
1 : a long area of land that is on top of a mountain or hill ▪ We hiked along the *ridge*.
2 : a raised part or area on the surface of something ▪ the *ridges* on the sole of a boot
3 : the place where two sloping surfaces meet ▪ the *ridge* of a roof
4 *weather* **:** a long area of high atmospheric pressure ▪ A *ridge* of high pressure is coming up from the south. — compare TROUGH 4

ridged /ˈrɪʤd/ *adj* **:** having ridges ▪ *ridged* potato chips

¹rid·i·cule /ˈrɪdəˌkjuːl/ *noun* [*noncount*] **:** the act of making fun of someone or something in a cruel or harsh way **:** harsh comments made by people who are laughing at someone or something ▪ She didn't show anyone her artwork for fear of *ridicule*. ▪ He was a ***subject/object of ridicule*** to his coworkers. [=he was ridiculed by his coworkers] ▪ They ***held him up to (public) ridicule*** [=they made fun of him publicly]

²ridicule *verb* **-cules; -culed; -cul·ing** [+ *obj*] **:** to laugh at and make jokes about (someone or something) in a cruel or harsh way **:** to make fun of (someone or something) ▪ The other kids *ridiculed* him for the way he dressed. ▪ They *ridiculed* all of her suggestions.

ri·dic·u·lous /rəˈdɪkjələs/ *adj* [*more* ~; *most* ~] **:** extremely silly or unreasonable ▪ She looks *ridiculous* in that outfit. ▪ Don't be *ridiculous*! ▪ It was a *ridiculous* suggestion. ▪ That's an absolutely *ridiculous* price for that sweater. ▪ He makes a *ridiculous* amount [=an extremely large amount] of money.
– **ri·dic·u·lous·ly** *adv* ▪ The movie was *ridiculously* long.
– **ri·dic·u·lous·ness** *noun* [*noncount*]

¹rid·ing /ˈraɪdɪŋ/ *noun* [*noncount*] **:** the sport or activity of riding a horse, bicycle, motorcycle, etc. ▪ (*US*) horseback *riding* = (*Brit*) horse *riding* ▪ We'll ***go riding*** after the rain stops.

²riding *adj, always used before a noun*
1 : related to or used for riding and especially for riding a horse ▪ *riding* lessons/gear/boots ▪ a *riding* helmet
2 *US* **:** controlled by a person who sits on it ▪ a *riding* lawnmower [=a lawnmower that you ride on]

rife /ˈraɪf/ *adj, not used before a noun* **:** very common and often bad or unpleasant ▪ She visited a country where malaria was *rife*. [=*widespread*] ▪ Speculation about who would be fired ***ran rife*** for weeks.
rife with **:** having a large amount of (something bad or unpleasant) **:** full of (something bad or unpleasant) ▪ The school was *rife with* rumors. ▪ a history *rife with* scandal

¹riff /ˈrɪf/ *noun, pl* **riffs** [*count*]
1 *music* **:** a short and usually repeated pattern of notes in a song ▪ a guitar *riff* ▪ He stole that *riff* from another song.
2 *US, informal* **:** a short set of comments on a particular subject — often + *on* ▪ a comedian's *riff on* modern love

²riff *verb* **riffs; riffed; riff·ing** [*no obj*]
1 *music* **:** to play a riff ▪ The guitarist *riffed* over the bass line.
2 *US, informal* **:** to talk about a particular subject in usually a quick and lively way **:** to deliver a riff on or about a particular subject ▪ He *riffed* on/about how great the economy was doing.

rif·fle /ˈrɪfəl/ *verb* **rif·fles; rif·fled; rif·fling** *chiefly Brit* **:** to look through something quickly and not very closely [*no obj*] He ***riffled through*** [=*rifled through*] her purse while she was out of the room. ▪ I *riffled through* [=flipped through] the magazine. [+ *obj*] He *riffled* the pages of the magazine.

riff·raff /ˈrɪfˌræf/ *noun* [*noncount*] *disapproving* **:** people who are not respectable **:** people who have very low social status ▪ Try not to associate with that *riffraff*. — often used in a humorous or exaggerated way to suggest the attitudes of wealthy and powerful people ▪ The doorman kept the *riffraff* out of the hotel.

¹ri·fle /ˈraɪfəl/ *noun, pl* **ri·fles** [*count*] **:** a gun that has a long barrel and that is held against your shoulder when you shoot it — see picture at GUN; see also AIR RIFLE, ASSAULT RIFLE

²rifle *verb* **rifles; ri·fled; ri·fling :** to search through something quickly and carelessly often in order to take or steal something [+ *obj*] He *rifled* the papers on his desk. ▪ Someone *rifled* his wallet and took his money. [*no obj*] He ***rifled through*** the papers on his desk. — compare ³RIFLE

³rifle *verb* **rifles; rifled; rifling** [+ *obj*] **:** to throw or hit (a ball) with a lot of speed and force ▪ The shortstop *rifled* a throw to second base for the out. ▪ The forward *rifled* the ball toward the goal. — compare ²RIFLE

ri·fle·man /ˈraɪfəlmən/ *noun, pl* **-men** /-mən/ [*count*]
1 : a soldier who carries a rifle
2 : a person who is skilled at shooting a rifle

rift /ˈrɪft/ *noun, pl* **rifts** [*count*]
1 : a situation in which two people, groups, etc., no longer have a friendly relationship ▪ The fight will only widen the *rift* with his brother. — often + *between* ▪ Nothing could heal the *rift between* them.
2 a : a deep crack or opening in the ground, a rock, etc. ▪ the *rift* in the rock ▪ We could see some stars through the *rifts* in the clouds. **b** *geology* **:** a break in the Earth's crust ▪ Scientists are studying the Mid-Atlantic *Rift*.

rift valley *noun, pl* ~ **-leys** [*count*] *geology* **:** a long, steep valley formed when two parallel rifts form in the Earth's crust and the land between them sinks

¹rig /ˈrɪg/ *verb* **rigs; rigged; rig·ging** [+ *obj*] **:** to control or affect (something, such as a game or election) in a dishonest way in order to get a desired result ▪ They are suspected of *rigging* [=*fixing*] the election. — compare ³RIG
– **rigged** *adj* ▪ The boxing match was *rigged*. ▪ a *rigged* election

²rig *noun, pl* **rigs** [*count*]
1 : equipment or machinery that is used for a particular purpose ▪ an oil-drilling *rig* = an oil *rig* ▪ a radio *rig*
2 *US* **:** a large truck that is attached to a trailer ▪ He drives a big *rig*.
3 : the way the sails and masts are arranged on a ship or boat ▪ the *rig* of a schooner

³rig *verb* **rigs; rigged; rigging** [+ *obj*]
1 a : to build or set up (something) usually quickly and for temporary use ▪ We *rigged* (up) a lean-to. ▪ Aid workers *rigged* (up) a shelter for the hurricane victims. — see also JERRY-RIGGED, JURY-RIG **b :** to place (something) in the proper position for use ▪ The stage crew *rigged* (up) the lights.
2 : to provide (a boat or ship) with ropes, sails, etc. ▪ They *rigged* (up) the ship and prepared to set sail.
3 a : to provide (someone or something) with particular clothing or equipment — usually + *out* ▪ They *rigged* the volunteer firefighters *out* in nonflammable suits. **b :** to put something secretly in (a place) — usually + *with* ▪ They *rigged* the enemy base *with* explosives.
– compare ¹RIG
– **rigged** *adj* ▪ a fully-*rigged* ship

rigamarole *variant spelling of* RIGMAROLE

rig·a·to·ni /ˌrɪgəˈtoʊni/ *noun* [*noncount*] **:** a type of pasta that is shaped like short, wide tubes

rig·ging /ˈrɪgɪŋ/ *noun* [*noncount*]
1 : the ropes and chains that are used on a ship to help support the masts and sails ▪ They checked the *rigging* before they set sail.
2 : equipment that is used for supporting and using lights, curtains, etc., in a theater

¹right /ˈraɪt/ *adj*
1 *usually not used before a noun* **:** morally or socially correct or acceptable ▪ Stealing is not *right*. ▪ You can't treat me like this! It's not *right*! ▪ You were *right* to tell the teacher about the girl who you saw cheating. ▪ Telling the teacher was the ***right thing*** to do. ▪ (*chiefly Brit*) "After I was treated so rudely, I complained to the management." "And ***quite right*** too!" [=complaining was the right thing to do] ▪ Since they helped him, it's ***only right*** that he should help them too. [=since they helped him, he should help them too] — opposite WRONG
2 a : agreeing with the facts or truth **:** accurate or correct ▪ the *right* answer ▪ "Is that clock *right*? Is it noon already?" "Yes. That's *right*." ▪ There's something not quite *right* about his story. ▪ Their theory was proved *right*. ▪ ***Let me get this right***—you want me to lend you $1,000?! — opposite WRONG **b** *not used before a noun* **:** speaking, acting, or judging in a way that agrees with the facts or truth ▪ You're *right*; the answer is six. ▪ I bet you like baseball. Am I *right*? ▪ Am I *right* in thinking that he should have never loaned her the money? ▪ We thought it was a bad idea, and time proved us *right*. — often + *about* ▪ He was *right about* her not having a job. ▪ "Relationships aren't easy." "You're definitely *right about* that." ▪ Let me ***put/set you right about*** one thing: I did

R

not start this argument! — often followed by *to* + *verb* • You're *right to take* things slowly with your new boyfriend. — opposite WRONG **c** — used in speech to ask if a statement is correct or to say that a statement is correct • "You took the dog out for a walk, *right*?" "Yes, I did." • "We met her at the party." "(That's) *Right*. Now I remember." • "I'll pay for the damages." "(You're) ***Damn right*** you will!" [=(more politely) you certainly will] • (*Brit*) "I'll pay for the damages." "***Too right*** you will." • (*Brit*) "Things are going from bad to worse." "*Too right*, mate!" **d** — used in speech to say you understand and accept what someone has said • "It's getting late." "Oh, *right*. I'll be ready in a minute." • "I'd like a coffee, please." "*Right*." = "***Right you are***." **e** — used for emphasis at the beginning of a statement • *Right*. [=*all right, OK*] Let's get this over with. **f** — used in speech to express disbelief • "I'm actually quite famous." "*Right*. And I'm the Pope." "No, it's true." "***Yeah, right***. I don't believe you."

3 : suitable or appropriate for a particular purpose, situation, or person • She is the *right* person for the job. • They're not *right* for each other. • You made the *right* decision. • Let me show you the *right* way to do it. • He kept practicing his technique until he got it *right*. • Hold the bat like this—that's *right*! • This apartment is just the *right* size. • That picture would be just *right* [=*perfect*] for my living room. • I need to find the *right* moment to ask him for the money. • I don't have the *right* tools to do the job. • I'll buy the car if the price is *right*. • He knows all the *right* people to succeed in this business. • Becoming a star is often a matter of being in ***the right place at the right time***. • He always knows the ***right thing*** to say. — opposite WRONG; see also MR. RIGHT

4 a : in a normal or healthy state or condition • I don't feel quite *right*. [=I feel somewhat ill] • The fish you bought doesn't smell *right*. [=it doesn't smell the way it should] • (*informal*) That boy is not ***right in the head***. • She is not in her ***right mind***. [=she is mentally ill] **b** *not used before a noun* **:** in a proper state or condition • Things are not *right* between them. [=they do not have a good/happy relationship] • He apologized and tried to ***put/set things right*** (with her).

5 *always used before a noun* **a :** located on the side of your body that is away from your heart • He felt a pain in his *right* side. • her *right* hand/leg **b :** done with your right hand • He hit him with a *right* hook to the jaw. **c :** located nearer to the right side of your body than to the left • on the *right* side of the street • a chair's *right* arm • taking a *right* turn — opposite LEFT

6 *US* — used to refer to the side of something that is meant to be on top, in front, or on the outside • The CD fell and landed ***right side up/down***. • He turned his socks ***right side out***. — opposite WRONG

7 *always used before a noun, Brit, informal* **:** complete or total — used for emphasis • I felt a *right* fool after making that mistake! • We were in a *right* mess!

(as) right as rain *informal* **:** in excellent health or condition • After a few days of rest, you'll be *right as rain* again.

get off on the right foot see [1]FOOT

give your right arm see [1]GIVE

push the right buttons see [1]BUTTON

– see also ALL RIGHT

– **right·ness** *noun* [*noncount*] • She questioned the *rightness* of his actions/decision.

R

[2]**right** *adv*

1 : in the exact location, position, or moment that is mentioned • The keys are *right* where I said they would be. • "Where are my keys?" "They're *right* here/there." • The bank is *right* next to the pharmacy. • The parking lot is *right* in front/back of the building. • He left his bags *right* in the middle of the floor. • She was waiting *right* outside the door. • The ball hit me *right* in the face. • We arrived *right* at noon. • I'm *right* behind you. • You are ***right on time***. • When the boss yelled at him, he quit ***right then and there***. • If you need me, I am ***right here*** for you. [=I am available to support/help you]

2 : in a direct course or manner • We went *right* [=*straight, directly*] home after the game. • He walked *right* past me without saying hello. • Come *right* this way, please. • She came *right* out and said it. [=she said it without hesitating]

3 : in a way that agrees with the facts or truth **:** CORRECTLY • You guessed *right*. • You heard *right*. I got the job. — opposite WRONG

4 : in a suitable, proper, or desired way • He eats *right* and exercises daily. • You're not doing it *right*. [=*correctly*] • Nothing is ***going right*** for me today. — opposite WRONG

5 : all the way • We stayed up to watch the game *right* to the very end. • The car went *right* [=*completely*] off the road. • The baby slept *right* through the night.

6 : without delay **:** very soon or immediately • She got pregnant *right* after they got married. • I'll be *right* with you. • He stepped out for a moment, but he'll be *right* back.

7 a : toward the right • Turn *right*. • She looked *right* and then left. • Please move *right*. • She ran *right* and caught the ball. **b :** towards the political right • a political party that has shifted *right* • His political views are slightly ***right of center***. [=are slightly conservative] **c** *US* **:** using the right hand • He bats/throws *right*. [=*right-handed*] — opposite LEFT

8 : in a complete manner • He felt *right* [=*completely*] at home at his new job. • She knew *right* [=(more commonly) *very*] well what was happening.

play your cards right see [1]CARD

right and left *or Brit* ***right, left, and centre*** **:** in a very quick and uncontrolled way • She has been spending money *right and left*. **:** in all directions • He was calling out names *right and left*. • The police were stopping cars *right and left*.

right away *also* ***right off*** **:** without delay or hesitation **:** IMMEDIATELY • Please send out this letter *right away*. • I could tell *right off* that he was lying.

right now **1 :** in the next moment **:** IMMEDIATELY • Please clean up this mess *right now*. **2 :** at the present time • He is out of the office *right now*.

serve someone right see [1]SERVE

[3]**right** *noun, pl* **rights**

1 : behavior that is morally good or correct [*noncount*] He's old enough to know the difference between *right* and wrong. = He's old enough to know ***right from wrong***. • You ***did right*** [=you did the right thing] to tell the teacher. • (*old-fashioned*) He always tried to ***do right by*** his employees. [=to treat his employees fairly] [*count*] We discussed the ***rights and wrongs*** of genetic cloning. — opposite WRONG

2 [*count*] **:** something that a person is or should be morally or legally allowed to have, get, or do • women fighting for equal *rights* • The government has denied the people their *rights*. [=has not allowed the people to do the things that they should be allowed to do] • Knowing the truth is her *right*. — often followed by *to* + *verb* • She has a *right to know* the truth. • They demanded the *right to vote*. • You have no *right to order* me around! • What gives you the *right to read* my diary? • He has every *right to be* angry. • You are ***within your rights*** *to demand* a refund. [=you have the right to demand a refund] — often + *of* • The government must protect the *rights of* its citizens. • the constitutional *right of* privacy — see also BILL OF RIGHTS, BIRTHRIGHT, BRAGGING RIGHTS, CIVIL RIGHTS, DIVINE RIGHT, HUMAN RIGHT, WOMEN'S RIGHTS

3 ***rights*** [*plural*] **:** the legal authority to reproduce, publish, broadcast, or sell something • broadcast *rights* • movie *rights* — often + *to* • The poet's family owns the publishing *rights to* all his books. — see also COPYRIGHT

4 a [*noncount*] **:** a location closer to the right side of your body than to the left **:** the right side • Swing the bat from *right* to left. — often used with *on* • As you come down the street, my house will be *on* your/the *right*. — often used with *to* • Move it *to* the *right*. • The picture is ***to the right of*** the window. **b** [*count*] **:** a turn or movement toward the right • Take a *right* at the next intersection. = (*US*) Make/hang a *right* at the next intersection. • two *rights* and then a left

5 [*count*] **:** a punch made with the right hand • He hit him with a left to the stomach followed by a *right* to the jaw.

6 a ***the Right*** **:** political groups who favor traditional attitudes and practices and conservative policies • His nomination is opposed by *the* country's *Right*. • The new law is disliked by *the Right*. • Members of *the Right* have voiced their opinions on this matter. **b** ***the right*** **:** the position of people who support the beliefs and policies of the political Right • The party has shifted to *the right*. [=has become more conservative] — compare LEFT; see also *the far right* at [2]FAR

by right **:** according to what is legally or morally correct • The money is mine *by right*. [=I have the right to have the money]

by rights *also* ***by all rights*** **:** according to what is proper and reasonable • *By rights*, you should have been the one to receive the promotion.

dead to rights *US* **1** *or Brit* ***bang to rights*** **:** with proof that you are guilty • The police had him *dead to rights*. • She was caught *dead to rights* on a bribery charge. **2** *sports* **:** with no chance of winning or succeeding • The other team had us *dead to rights* by the end of the first half.

in its own right **:** because of its own special qualities and not because of a connection with something else • Though it's based on a best-selling novel, the movie is great *in its own right*.

in the right : in the position or situation of being right • You are *in the right* to demand a refund/apology. • The judge agreed that he was *in the right*.

in your own right : because of your own efforts, talent, etc., and not because of your connection with someone else • Her husband is a well-known novelist, but she is a successful writer *in her own right*.

might makes right see ²MIGHT

of right *formal* : according to what is legally or morally correct • The estate belongs *of right* to him. • (*law*) The federal court may intervene ***as of right*** [=the federal court has a right to intervene]

put/set (something) to rights : to put (something) back into the normal or proper condition • He helped his mother *put* things *to rights* [=put things in order] after his father died.

two wrongs don't make a right see ³WRONG

⁴right *verb* **rights; right•ed; right•ing** [+ *obj*]

1 : to make (something) right : to correct (something wrong or unjust) • It was time to *right* an old wrong. • No one can *right* all the wrongs in the world.

2 : to return (something) to a proper state or condition • The government needs to do something to *right* the economy.

3 : to put (something or someone) back in an upright position • They *righted* the capsized boat. • He quickly *righted* himself after he fell off the chair.

right angle *noun, pl* **~ angles** [*count*] : an angle formed by two lines that are perpendicular to each other : an angle that measures 90° • A square has four *right angles*. • Hold the nail ***at a right angle to*** the board. • The two boards are joined ***at right angles to*** each other.

right–angled triangle *noun, pl* **~ -angles** [*count*] *Brit* : RIGHT TRIANGLE

right–click *verb* **-clicks; -clicked; -clicking** [*no obj*] *computers* : to press the button on the right side of a mouse or similar device in order to make something happen on a computer • *Right-click* on the icon and select "Open" from the menu. — compare ¹CLICK 2

righ•teous /ˈraɪtʃəs/ *adj, formal*

1 : morally good : following religious or moral laws • a *righteous* person • leading a *righteous* life

2 *always used before a noun* : caused by something that you believe is not morally right or fair • *righteous* anger/indignation — see also SELF-RIGHTEOUS

– righ•teous•ly *adv* **– righ•teous•ness** *noun* [*noncount*]

right field *noun* [*noncount*] : the part of a baseball outfield that is to the right when you are looking out from home plate • a fly ball to (deep/shallow) *right field*; *also* : the position of the player defending right field • He plays *right field*.

– right fielder *noun, pl* **~ -ers** [*count*]

right•ful /ˈraɪtfəl/ *adj, always used before a noun, formal*

1 : according to the law • The property should be returned to its *rightful* owner.

2 : proper or appropriate • He will be given his ***rightful place*** in the history books.

– right•ful•ly *adv* • The property is *rightfully* mine. • She was *rightfully* praised for all the work she did.

right–hand /ˈraɪtˌhænd/ *adj, always used before a noun*

1 : located closer to your right hand : located on the right side • Our building will be on the *right-hand* side. • Please write your name on the bottom *right-hand* corner of the page. • Take a *right-hand* turn. — compare LEFT-HAND

2 : made for the right hand • *right-hand* [=(more commonly) *right-handed*] tools — compare LEFT-HAND

right–hand•ed /ˈraɪtˈhændəd/ *adj*

1 : using the right hand more easily than the left hand • a *right-handed* person/pitcher • Most people in my family are *right-handed*, but I'm left-handed.

2 a : made for the right hand • a *right-handed* glove **b** : using or done with the right hand • a *right-handed* pitch/punch

3 : swinging from the right side of the body to the left side in sports like baseball and golf • a *right-handed* batter/hitter

– right–handed *adv* • She bats *right-handed*. **– right–hand•ed•ness** *noun* [*noncount*]

right–hand•er /ˈraɪtˈhændɚ/ *noun, pl* **-ers** [*count*] : a right-handed person; *especially* : a right-handed pitcher in baseball • The team has more *right-handers* than left-handers.

right–hand man *noun* [*singular*] : a very important assistant who helps someone do a job • He/She is the CEO's *right-hand man*.

Right Honourable *adj, Brit* — used as a title for a member of Parliament

right•ist *or* **Right•ist** /ˈraɪtɪst/ *noun, pl* **-ists** [*count*] : a person who belongs to or supports the political Right — compare LEFTIST

– rightist *or* **Rightist** *adj* [*more ~; most ~*] • a *rightist* government • *rightist* intellectuals

right•ly /ˈraɪtli/ *adv*

1 : in a way that is correct : CORRECTLY • If I remember *rightly*, today is his birthday. • She *rightly* anticipated a decline in the value of the stock. • He points out, ***quite rightly***, that there are flaws in the theory. • Many people, ***rightly or wrongly***, believe the economy will soon improve.

2 : for a good reason : in a way that is proper or appropriate • She *rightly* admires his paintings. • People are *rightly* upset about the city's rising crime rate. • ***Quite rightly***, the police commissioner is being blamed for the city's rising crime rate. • She is proud of her children, ***and rightly so***.

3 *informal* : with certainty : for sure — usually used in negative statements • I ***don't rightly know*** where she went. [=I don't know where she went; I'm not sure where she went] • I ***can't rightly say*** what happened.

right–mind•ed /ˈraɪtˈmaɪndəd/ *adj* [*more ~; most ~*] : having beliefs, opinions, etc., that most people think are morally or socially right • *right-minded* citizens

righto /ˌraɪtˈoʊ/ *interj, Brit, informal + old-fashioned* — used to say that you agree with, understand, or accept something that you have been told • "We need to leave soon." "*Righto*. I'll get ready."

right–of–way /ˌraɪtəvˈweɪ/ *noun, pl* **rights–of–way** *also* **right–of–ways**

1 [*noncount*] : the right to move onto or across a road before other people or vehicles • The other car has the *right-of-way*. • Pedestrians have the *right-of-way* here.

2 [*count*] **a** : a legal right to go across another person's land **b** : a path on a person's land which other people have a legal right to use **c** : a long, narrow area of land that is used for a road, railway, etc. • a railroad *right-of-way*

right on *adj*

1 *US* **a** : exactly correct • Her assessment of the situation was *right on*. **b** *informal + somewhat old-fashioned* — used to say that you agree completely with what someone has said • "Make love, not war!" "*Right on*, man!"

2 *usually* **right-on** [*more ~; most ~*] *chiefly Brit, informal + sometimes disapproving* : having or supporting liberal or left-wing beliefs and opinions about how people should be treated • one of the *right-on* people

Right Reverend *adj* — used as a title for a high-ranking member of the clergy

right•size /ˈraɪtˌsaɪz/ *verb* **-siz•es; -sized; -siz•ing** : to make a company smaller and more efficient by reducing the number of workers : DOWNSIZE [*no obj*] The company plans to *rightsize*. [+ *obj*] The company has *rightsized* [=*downsized*] its staff.

right–to–life /ˈraɪttəˈlaɪf/ *adj, always used before a noun* : opposed to abortion • *right-to-life* groups/activists

– right–to–lif•er /ˈraɪttəˈlaɪfɚ/ *noun, pl* **-ers** [*count*]

right triangle *noun, pl* **~ -angles** [*count*] *US* : a triangle that has a right angle — called also (*Brit*) *right-angled triangle*

right•ward (*chiefly US*) /ˈraɪtwəd/ *or chiefly Brit* **right•wards** /ˈraɪtwədz/ *adv* : toward the right • Turn the boat *rightward*. • She stepped *rightward* into the light. • He has moved *rightward* in his political beliefs. — opposite LEFTWARD

– rightward *adj* • a *rightward* turn

right wing *noun* [*singular*] : the part of a political group that consists of people who support conservative or traditional ideas and policies : the part of a political group that belongs to or supports the Right • His nomination is supported by the party's left wing but opposed by the *right wing*.

right–wing /ˈraɪtˈwɪŋ/ *adj* : of, relating to, or belonging to the political Right : having or supporting ideas and policies that are associated with conservative groups • *right-wing* politics/politicians

– right–wing•er /ˈraɪtˈwɪŋɚ/ *noun, pl* **-ers** [*count*] • a policy opposed by *right-wingers*

righty /ˈraɪti/ *noun, pl* **right•ies** [*count*] *chiefly US, informal* : RIGHT-HANDER • Our starting pitcher is a *righty*. — compare LEFTY

rig•id /ˈrɪdʒəd/ *adj* [*more ~; most ~*]

1 : not able to be bent easily : STIFF • a *rigid* steel beam • The patient's legs were *rigid*.

R

2 : not easily changed ▪ a *rigid* procedure ▪ The periodical has *rigid* [=*strict, inflexible*] guidelines for submissions. ▪ a *rigid* [=*strict, unwavering*] adherence to the rules

3 : not willing to change opinions or behavior ▪ He is a *rigid* disciplinarian.

– ri·gid·i·ty /rəˈʤɪdəti/ *noun* [*noncount*] ▪ the *rigidity* of the plant's stem ▪ the *rigidity* of the guidelines **– rig·id·ly** *adv* ▪ The law was *rigidly* enforced. ▪ The soldiers stood *rigidly* at attention.

rig·ma·role *or US* **rig·a·ma·role** /ˈrɪgəməˌroʊl, ˈrɪgməˌroʊl, *Brit* ˈrɪgməˌrəʊl/ *noun* **:** a long, complicated, and annoying process, description, etc. [*singular*] We had to go through the *rigmarole* of installing, registering, and activating the software before we found out it wouldn't work. [*noncount*] He just told us what to do without all the usual *rigamarole*.

rig·or (*US*) *or Brit* **rig·our** /ˈrɪgɚ/ *noun, pl* **-ors**

1 ***rigors*** [*plural*] **:** the difficult and unpleasant conditions or experiences that are associated with something ▪ They underwent the *rigors* of military training. ▪ the *rigors* of life in the wilderness

2 [*noncount*] **:** the quality or state of being very exact, careful, or strict ▪ They conducted the experiments with scientific *rigor*. ▪ a scholar known for her intellectual *rigor*

rig·or mor·tis /ˌrɪgɚˈmoɚtəs/ *noun* [*noncount*] **:** a temporary stiffness of the body that happens soon after death

rig·or·ous /ˈrɪgərəs/ *adj* [*more* ~; *most* ~]

1 : very strict and demanding ▪ *rigorous* enforcement of the rules ▪ *rigorous* training ▪ a *rigorous* course of study

2 : done carefully and with a lot of attention to detail ▪ We subjected the data to a *rigorous* analysis. ▪ a *rigorous* investigation

3 : difficult to endure because of extreme conditions ▪ a harsh, *rigorous* climate

– rig·or·ous·ly *adv* ▪ The rules must be *rigorously* followed. ▪ The data was *rigorously* analyzed. **– rig·or·ous·ness** *noun* [*noncount*]

rile /ˈrajəl/ *verb* **riles; riled; ril·ing** [+ *obj*]

1 : to make (someone) angry **:** to irritate or annoy (someone) ▪ Her comments *riled* the professor. — usually + *up* ▪ It doesn't take much to get him *riled up*. [=*angry*]

2 *US, informal* **:** to make (someone) very excited — usually + *up* ▪ His antics got the kids all *riled up*.

¹rim /ˈrɪm/ *noun, pl* **rims** [*count*]

1 : the outer edge of a usually round object ▪ There were chips on the *rim* of the plate. ▪ eyeglasses with wire *rims* ▪ The basketball bounced off the *rim* (of the hoop). ▪ the *rim* of the volcano

2 : the part of a wheel that the tire is put on ▪ He bought stainless steel *rims* for his new car. — see picture at BICYCLE

– rim·less /ˈrɪmləs/ *adj* ▪ *rimless* glasses

²rim *verb* **rims; rimmed; rim·ming** [+ *obj*] **:** to form or put a rim around (something) ▪ Sharp rocks *rimmed* [=*bordered*] the pond. ▪ She *rimmed* her eyes with eyeliner. ▪ a porcelain bowl *rimmed* with gold

rime /ˈraɪm/ *noun* [*noncount*] **:** FROST ▪ a heavy coating of *rime* ▪ *rime* ice

rimmed /ˈrɪmd/ *adj* **:** having a particular type of rim — used in combination ▪ horn-*rimmed* glasses ▪ dark-*rimmed* glasses ▪ a gold-*rimmed* plate

rind /ˈraɪnd/ *noun, pl* **rinds**

1 : the tough, outer skin of some fruits that is usually removed before the fruit is eaten [*count*] an orange *rind* ▪ the *rind* of a watermelon [*noncount*] grated lemon *rind* — see color picture on page C5

2 [*count, noncount*] **:** a tough, outer surface of some foods (such as certain cheeses) ▪ the *rind* of a cheese ▪ bacon *rind* — see also PORK RIND

¹ring /ˈrɪŋ/ *noun, pl* **rings** [*count*]

1 a : a piece of jewelry that is worn usually on a finger ▪ He gave her an engagement/diamond *ring*. — see color picture on page C11 **b :** a piece of jewelry that is shaped like a circle and worn in a special hole made in the skin ▪ a navel/nose *ring* — see also EARRING

2 a : something that is shaped like a circle ▪ He blew smoke *rings*. ▪ the *rings* of the planet Saturn ▪ Put the napkins in/through the napkin *rings*. ▪ I can't find my ***key ring***. [=a metal circle to which keys are attached] — see also ONION RING, TEETHING RING **b :** something that forms a circle around something else ▪ They built a *ring* of houses around an open area. ▪ The moon was surrounded by a *ring* of clouds. **c :** a circular or curved mark or shape ▪ a white *ring* around the dog's eye ▪ a *ring* of dirt in the bathtub ▪ I hadn't slept all night and had dark *rings* [=(more commonly) *circles*] under my eyes.

3 : an area that is used for shows and contests and is usually surrounded by ropes or a fence ▪ a circus/rodeo *ring* ▪ a boxing/wrestling *ring* — see also BULLRING

4 : a group of people who are involved in some illegal or dishonest activity ▪ Police broke up a *ring* of car thieves. ▪ a smuggling *ring*

5 *Brit* **:** the part on the top of a stove where the heat or flame is produced **:** BURNER

rings around — used in phrases like ***run rings around*** to say that one person or thing is much better than others ▪ There's an architect in our firm who *runs rings around* [=does much better work than] the rest of us. ▪ These are talented kids who can *dance rings around* [=dance much better than] most of their peers.

throw/toss your hat in/into the ring see HAT

– compare ⁴RING

²ring *verb* **rings; ringed; ring·ing** [+ *obj*]

1 : to form a circle around (something or someone) **:** to surround (something or someone) ▪ Police *ringed* the building. ▪ Little cottages *ring* the lake.

2 *Brit* **:** to draw a circle around (something) ▪ He *ringed* [=*circled*] the words that were misspelled.

– compare ³RING

– ringed /ˈrɪŋd/ *adj* ▪ a bird with a *ringed* bill ▪ Saturn, the *ringed* planet

³ring *verb* **rings; rang** /ˈræŋ/; **rung** /ˈrʌŋ/; **ringing**

1 a [+ *obj*] **:** to cause (an object or device, such as a bell) to make a sound ▪ She *rang* the little bell. ▪ *Ring* the doorbell. ▪ When she discovered the fire she immediately *rang* [=(more commonly) *sounded*] the alarm. **b** [*no obj*] *of an object or device* **:** to make a sound especially as a signal of something ▪ The church bells were *ringing*. ▪ The alarm/doorbell is *ringing*. ▪ Excuse me, my cell phone is *ringing*. [=my cell phone is making the sound which signals that someone is calling] **c** [*no obj*] **:** to call someone or something by ringing a bell ▪ You *rang*, madam? [=you rang a bell to call for me; how can I help you?] — usually + *for* ▪ She *rang for* the servants. ▪ He *rang for* a nurse.

2 [*no obj*] **a :** to fill a place or area with sound ▪ Cheers *rang* through the hall as the winner was announced. ▪ Gunshots *rang* in the air. — sometimes used figuratively ▪ His words were still ***ringing in my ears/head***. [=I was still thinking about or remembering what he had said] ▪ She entered cautiously, the teacher's warning *ringing in her ears*. **b :** to be filled *with* the sound of something ▪ The hall *rang with* their cheers. — sometimes used figuratively ▪ The whole town *rang with* news of the victory. [=many people in the town were talking about the victory] **c** ***of the ears*** **:** to be filled with a sound that other people cannot hear ▪ His ears were *ringing* after the concert.

3 [*no obj*] **:** to seem to have a specified quality or character ▪ Her explanation didn't ***ring true***. = Her explanation ***rang false***. [=her explanation didn't seem true; it seemed false] ▪ His apology ***rang hollow***. [=his apology did not sound sincere]

4 *chiefly Brit* **:** to make a telephone call to someone or something **:** CALL [+ *obj*] I'll *ring* you (up) tomorrow. ▪ He called me yesterday, and I *rang* him back today. [*no obj*] I *rang* this morning. ▪ He's not here right now. Can you *ring* back later?

have/get your bell rung see BELL

ring a bell *informal* **:** to be familiar ▪ Yes, that name *rings a bell*. ▪ The term didn't *ring a bell* with me.

ring in [*phrasal verb*] **1** ***ring in (something)*** *also* ***ring (something) in*** **:** to celebrate the beginning of (something, such as a new year) ▪ How did you *ring in* the new millennium? ▪ We're going to New York to ***ring in the New Year***. **2** *chiefly Brit* **a :** to make a telephone call to a place (such as the place where you work) ▪ She ***rang in sick*** [=(*US*) *called in sick*] yesterday. [=she telephoned the place where she works to say that she was sick and would not be coming to work] **b :** to make a telephone call to a radio or television program ▪ Thousands of people *rang in* [=(*US*) *called in*] to make a donation. **3** ***ring in at (an amount)*** **:** to cost (a certain amount of money) ▪ These hats *ring in at* 200 dollars.

ring off [*phrasal verb*] *Brit* **:** to end a telephone call **:** to hang up ▪ He said he didn't have time to talk and quickly *rang off*.

ring off the hook *US, of a telephone* **:** to ring constantly or frequently ▪ The phone was *ringing off the hook* all morning. [=many people called during the morning]

R

ring out [*phrasal verb*] **:** to be heard loudly and clearly ▪ A shot *rang out.* [=a loud shot was heard] ▪ Cheers *rang out* as the winner was announced.

ring the changes *Brit* **:** to make changes in order to do something differently, make it more interesting, etc. ▪ The team's manager *rang the changes* at halftime so that more players would have a chance to play.

ring up [*phrasal verb*] ***ring (something) up*** *or* ***ring up (something)*** **1 :** to use a special machine (called a cash register) to calculate the cost of (something, such as goods or services) ▪ The cashier *rang up* our purchases. **2 :** to achieve (something) ▪ The company *rang up* huge profits last quarter. ▪ She *rang up* another tournament win.

– compare [2]RING

[4]**ring** *noun, pl* **rings**

1 [*count*] **a :** the sound that a bell makes ▪ the *ring* of the doorbell **b :** the act of making a bell ring ▪ He gave the doorbell a *ring.* [=he rang the doorbell]

2 [*count*] **a :** the sound that a telephone makes when someone is calling ▪ The telephone's *ring* is loud. — compare RINGTONE **b :** one of the sounds in the series of sounds that a telephone makes when someone is calling ▪ She waited until the third *ring* to answer the phone.

3 [*singular*] **:** a specified quality ▪ Her story had a *ring* of truth about it. [=her story seemed true] ▪ His name had a familiar *ring* to it. [=his name was familiar]

give (someone) a ring *chiefly Brit* **:** to make a telephone call to (someone) ▪ I'll *give you a ring* [=*give you a call*] tomorrow.

– compare [1]RING

ring binder *noun, pl* **~ -ers** [*count*] **:** a cover for sheets of paper that are fastened into rings that pass through holes on the edge of the paper

ring·er /ˈrɪŋɚ/ *noun, pl* **-ers** [*count*]

1 : someone who rings a bell ▪ a bell *ringer*

2 : the part of a telephone that rings to signal that someone is calling ▪ Turn off the *ringer* on the telephone.

3 *informal* **:** a person or animal that enters a contest illegally by using a false name, pretending not to have much skill, etc. ▪ One of the players on the winning team was a *ringer.*

4 *informal* **:** someone who looks very much like another person ▪ He's a *ringer* for the President. ▪ She's a ***dead ringer*** for my cousin Julie. [=she looks exactly like my cousin Julie]

ring–fence *verb* **-fenc·es; -fenced; -fenc·ing** [+ *obj*] *Brit* **:** to put (an amount of money) aside for a specific purpose **:** EARMARK ▪ The money was *ring-fenced* for education programs.

ring finger *noun, pl* **~ -gers** [*count*] **:** the third finger especially of your left hand when you count the index finger as the first finger — see picture at HAND

ring·ing /ˈrɪŋɪŋ/ *adj, always used before a noun*

1 a : very loud and clear ▪ a *ringing* voice **b :** like the sound a bell or alarm makes ▪ Do you hear that *ringing* sound?

2 : made forcefully or with confidence ▪ a *ringing* endorsement/condemnation

ring·lead·er /ˈrɪŋˌliːdɚ/ *noun, pl* **-ers** [*count*] **:** the leader of a group that causes trouble or is involved in an illegal activity ▪ the *ringleader* of a gang of criminals

ring·let /ˈrɪŋlət/ *noun, pl* **-lets** [*count*] **:** a long curl of hair — usually plural ▪ She wore her hair in *ringlets.*

ring·mas·ter /ˈrɪŋˌmæstɚ, *Brit* ˈrɪŋˌmɑːstə/ *noun, pl* **-ers** [*count*] **:** a person whose job is to introduce the performers in a circus and to talk to the audience between performances

ring pull *noun, pl* **~ pulls** [*count*] *Brit* **:** PULL TAB

ring road *noun, pl* **~ roads** [*count*] *Brit* **:** a road that goes around a city or town

ring·side /ˈrɪŋˌsaɪd/ *noun* [*noncount*] **:** the area that is closest to the space used for circus acts, boxing matches, etc. **:** the seats that are closest to the ring ▪ We were seated at *ringside.*

– ringside *adj, always used before a noun* ▪ We had *ringside* seats. **– ringside** *adv* ▪ We sat *ringside.*

ring·tone /ˈrɪŋˌtoʊn/ *noun, pl* **-tones** [*count*] **:** the sound that a cell phone makes when someone is calling

ring toss *noun, pl* **~ tosses** [*count, noncount*] *US* **:** a game in which players try to throw a ring so that it will fall over an upright stick

ring·worm /ˈrɪŋˌwɚm/ *noun* [*noncount*] **:** a disease that causes ring-shaped marks to appear on the skin

rink /ˈrɪŋk/ *noun, pl* **rinks** [*count*] **:** an often enclosed area that has a special surface of ice, smooth pavement, etc., and that is used for skating ▪ an ice-skating/roller-skating *rink* ▪ a hockey *rink* ▪ The hockey team is practicing at the *rink.*

rinky–dink /ˈrɪŋkiˌdɪŋk/ *adj, US, informal + disapproving* **:** not very large or important **:** involving only a few people or only a small area ▪ a *rinky-dink* operation/business ▪ a *rinky-dink* [=*small-time*] drug dealer

[1]**rinse** /ˈrɪns/ *verb* **rins·es; rinsed; rins·ing** [+ *obj*]

1 a : to wash (something) with clean water and without soap ▪ I *rinsed* my face in the sink. ▪ *Rinse* out your mouth. ▪ *Rinse* (off) the apple before you eat it. ▪ *rinse* (out) a cup ▪ He washed the dishes and then *rinsed* them thoroughly. **b :** to wash (something) with a liquid other than clean water ▪ The tools were *rinsed* in alcohol.

2 *always followed by an adverb or preposition* **:** to remove (something) from an object by washing the object with clean water ▪ She *rinsed* the dirt off the lettuce. ▪ He *rinsed* the soap out of the cup.

[2]**rinse** *noun, pl* **rinses**

1 [*count*] **:** an act of washing something with a liquid and especially with clean water ▪ Give the apple a *rinse* [=rinse the apple] before you eat it.

2 : liquid that is used for rinsing something [*count*] a mouth *rinse* [*noncount*] She dunked the dish in the *rinse* water. ▪ Use sanitizing *rinse* on the scissors.

3 [*count, noncount*] **:** a dye that you put on your hair to change its color for a short time ▪ a bottle of hair *rinse*

[1]**ri·ot** /ˈrajət/ *noun, pl* **ri·ots**

1 [*count*] **:** a situation in which a large group of people behave in a violent and uncontrolled way ▪ The news about the election caused/started/sparked a *riot* in the city. ▪ a prison *riot* ▪ A lot of property was damaged in the recent *riots.* ▪ *riot* gear/police

2 [*singular*] **:** a place that is filled with something ▪ The field was a *riot* of wildflowers. [=the field was filled with many kinds of wildflowers] ▪ The woods are a ***riot of color*** in the autumn.

3 [*singular*] *informal* **:** someone or something that is very funny ▪ She's a *riot.* ▪ The movie was an absolute *riot.*

read (someone) the riot act **:** to speak in an angry and critical way to (someone who has done something wrong) **:** to tell (someone) that bad behavior will be severely punished if it continues ▪ His boss *read him the riot act* for making careless mistakes.

run riot **:** to behave in a violent and uncontrolled way ▪ People were *running riot* in the streets. — often used figuratively ▪ Crazy thoughts were *running riot* through my head. ▪ The weeds have *run riot* over our poor garden. [=the weeds in our garden have grown quickly and have taken over the garden]

[2]**riot** *verb* **riots; ri·ot·ed; ri·ot·ing** [*no obj*] *of a group of people* **:** to behave in a violent and uncontrolled way ▪ Students *rioted* after their team lost the football game.

– ri·ot·er *noun, pl* **-ers** [*count*] ▪ *Rioters* looted the store. **– rioting** *noun* [*noncount*] ▪ Police stopped the *rioting.*

ri·ot·ous /ˈrajətəs/ *adj* [*more ~; most ~*] *formal*

1 *of a group of people* **:** behaving in a violent and uncontrolled way ▪ a *riotous* assembly/crowd

2 : very exciting, fun, or full of energy ▪ a *riotous* party/celebration ▪ *riotous* humor

3 : existing or occurring in large amounts **:** ABUNDANT ▪ a *riotous* profusion of flowers

– ri·ot·ous·ly *adv* ▪ The fans celebrated *riotously.* ▪ He gave a *riotously* funny performance.

[1]**rip** /ˈrɪp/ *verb* **rips; ripped; rip·ping**

1 a [+ *obj*] **:** to tear, split, or open (something) quickly or violently ▪ She *ripped* the fabric in half. ▪ He *ripped* open the package. ▪ The dog ***ripped*** the pillow ***to shreds/pieces.*** ▪ The dog ***ripped a hole*** [=made a hole] in the pillow. ▪ The force of the explosion *ripped a hole* in the wall. **b** [*no obj*] **:** to become torn or split ▪ Her coat *ripped* when it caught on the doorknob. ▪ The seam has *ripped.*

2 *always followed by an adverb or preposition* [+ *obj*] **:** to remove (something) quickly or violently ▪ I *ripped* the poster off the wall. ▪ The sink had been *ripped* from the wall. ▪ He *ripped* the page out of the magazine. ▪ She *ripped* off her mask. ▪ He *ripped* the letter from my hands.

3 [*no obj*] **:** to go or move very quickly *through* or *into* something ▪ The fire *ripped through* the forest. ▪ an epidemic that *ripped through* the region ▪ The bullet *ripped into* her leg.

4 [+ *obj*] **:** to criticize (someone or something) in a very harsh or angry way ▪ (*US*) The coach *ripped* [=*ripped into*] his team for their sloppy play. ▪ His latest movie was ***ripped to shreds/pieces*** by the critics.

R

let rip *informal* **1 :** to do something in a way that is full of anger or energy • For the concert finale, the band *let rip* with a fantastic version of the song that made them famous. • I don't think anyone expected the senator to *let rip* at the press conference like that. [=to speak in such an angry way] **2** ***let (something) rip*** **:** to make (a car, boat, machine, etc.) go very fast — usually used in phrases like ***let it rip*** and ***let her/'er rip*** • Once we got the boat out into the open water, we *let it rip*.

rip apart [*phrasal verb*] **1** ***rip (something) apart*** *or* ***rip apart (something)*** **:** to completely destroy (something) by tearing it into pieces • The child *ripped* the toy *apart*. • Strong winds had *ripped apart* many of the little beach bungalows. — often used figuratively • a tragedy/scandal that almost *ripped* the family *apart* **2** ***rip (someone or something) apart*** *or* ***rip apart (someone or something)*** **:** to criticize (someone or something) in a very harsh or angry way especially by describing weaknesses, flaws, etc. • Critics *ripped* the author's latest novel *apart*. • an article that *rips apart* the mayor's plan

rip into [*phrasal verb*] ***rip into (someone or something)*** **:** to criticize (someone or something) in a very harsh or angry way • The coach *ripped into* [=*tore into*] the team after the game. • She *ripped into* the band's last performance.

rip off [*phrasal verb*] *informal* **1** ***rip (someone) off*** *or* ***rip off (someone)*** **:** to steal from or cheat (someone) • Hundreds of people were *ripped off* in a scam involving two people who claimed to be collecting money for disaster victims. • The store had been *ripping* customers *off* for years. • I wasn't trying to *rip* you *off*. I thought $50 was a fair price. **2** ***rip (something) off*** *or* ***rip off (something)*** **a :** to steal (something) • The organization's treasurer *ripped off* almost $6,000 before being caught. • Somebody *ripped off* [=*stole*] all our equipment. = All our equipment got *ripped off*. [=*stolen*] **b** *disapproving* **:** to copy or imitate (something) improperly **:** to make something that is too much like (something made by someone else) • The film has done well, but its makers have been accused of *ripping off* another movie made 30 years ago. — see also RIP-OFF

rip up [*phrasal verb*] ***rip (something) up*** *or* ***rip up (something)*** **:** to completely destroy (something) by tearing it into pieces • He *ripped up* the letter.

²rip *noun, pl* **rips** [*count*] **:** a long tear in something • She has a *rip* in her coat.

R.I.P. *or chiefly Brit* **RIP** /ˌɑɚˌaɪˈpiː/ *abbr* rest in peace ✧ *R.I.P.* is often written on a gravestone as a wish that the person buried there will have peace in death.

rip cord *noun, pl* **~ cords** [*count*] **:** a cord or wire that is pulled to open a parachute

ripe /ˈraɪp/ *adj* **rip·er; rip·est** [*also more ~; most ~*]
1 *of fruits and vegetables* **:** fully grown and developed and ready to be eaten • a *ripe* tomato • The apples are nearly *ripe*. — sometimes used figuratively • the violin's full, *ripe* sound • a story ***ripe with*** details [=a story that includes many details] — opposite UNRIPE
2 *not used before a noun* **:** ready or suitable for something — usually + *for* • The army was *ripe for* action. • a system that is ***ripe for abuse*** [=a system that is in such bad condition that it could easily be used wrongly] • The ***time was ripe for*** proposing his plan. • We'll make these changes when the *time is ripe*.
3 *of food and especially cheese* **:** brought to full flavor or the best state by being stored for a period of time • a *ripe* cheese
4 : having a strong and unpleasant smell • Those old sneakers smell pretty *ripe*.
ripe old age **:** a very old age • She took up painting at the *ripe old age* of 85. • They both lived to a *ripe old age*. — sometimes used humorously • She decided at the *ripe old age* of 23 that she'd learned all there was to know about human nature.
– ripe·ness *noun* [*noncount*] • Check the *ripeness* of the fruit before you buy it. • the cheese's *ripeness*

rip·en /ˈraɪpən/ *verb* **-ens; -ened; -en·ing**
1 [*no obj*] **:** to become ripe and ready to eat • The tomatoes finished *ripening* on the windowsill.
2 [+ *obj*] **:** to make (something) ripe • You can *ripen* the fruit by placing it in a paper bag and storing it at room temperature for a few days.

rip–off /ˈrɪpˌɑːf/ *noun, pl* **-offs** [*count*] *informal + disapproving*
1 : something that is too expensive **:** something that is not worth its price • The food was decent but the drinks were a *rip-off*. • The bike turned out to be a real *rip-off*.
2 : something that is too much like something made by someone else • The song is an obvious *rip-off*. • His new movie's just a *rip-off* of another movie made 30 years ago. — see also *rip off* at ¹RIP

ri·poste /rɪˈpoʊst/ *noun, pl* **-postes** [*count*] *formal* **:** a quick and clever reply • a witty *riposte* [=*retort*]

ripped *adj*
1 : having rips **:** torn, split, or opened • She was wearing *ripped* jeans.
2 *US, informal* **:** having a strong and muscular body or shape with little fat • *ripped* [=*chiseled*] abs • a *ripped* body • He is *ripped*.

¹rip·ple /ˈrɪpəl/ *verb* **rip·ples; rip·pled; rip·pling**
1 : to move in small waves [*no obj*] Water *rippled* under the dock. • We could see the lion's muscles *ripple*. [+ *obj*] A cool breeze *rippled* the water.
2 *always followed by an adverb or preposition* [*no obj*] **:** to pass or spread through or over (someone or something) • Fear/excitement *rippled* through the room. [=people in the room suddenly felt fear/excitement] • Economists predict that these costs will *ripple* through the economy. [=will affect the entire economy]

²ripple *noun, pl* **ripples** [*count*]
1 a : a small wave on the surface of a liquid • The pebble made *ripples* in the pond when I threw it in. **b :** a shape or pattern having small waves • *ripples* of sand
2 : a sound that gradually becomes louder and then quieter — usually + *of* • *ripples of* laughter
3 : something that passes or spreads through or over someone or something — usually singular; often + *of* • A *ripple of* fear/excitement spread through the room. [=people in the room suddenly felt fear/excitement]

ripple effect *noun, pl* **~ -fects** [*count*] **:** a situation in which one event causes a series of other events to happen • These kinds of crimes create a *ripple effect* throughout the city. [=they cause more crimes, problems, etc.] • These costs will have a huge/major *ripple effect* on the economy. [=the costs will cause important changes in the economy]

rip–roar·ing /ˈrɪpˈrorɪŋ/ *adj, informal* **:** very loud, lively, and exciting • a *rip-roaring* party
– rip–roaring *adv* • He was *rip-roaring* drunk. [=he was very drunk in a lively and noisy way]

rip·tide /ˈrɪpˌtaɪd/ *noun, pl* **-tides** [*count*] **:** a strong usually narrow current of water that flows away from a shore

¹rise /ˈraɪz/ *verb* **ris·es; rose** /ˈroʊz/; **ris·en** /ˈrɪzn̩/; **ris·ing** /ˈraɪzɪŋ/ [*no obj*]
1 a : to move upward • Smoke was *rising* into the air. • Bubbles *rose* to the surface of water. • The airplane *rose* [=(more formally) *ascended*] into the sky. — often + *up* • Smoke was *rising up* into the air. • The airplane *rose up* from the runway. — sometimes used figuratively • His ***spirits rose*** [=he began to feel happier] when he heard the good news. **b :** to become higher • The tide *rose* and fell. • The river is *rising*. **c :** to slope or extend upward • The land *rises* as you move away from the coast. • The road *rose* gently/steeply. • a tower *rising* above the little town • steeply/sharply *rising* mountain peaks — often + *up* • The mountains *rose up* before us.
2 : to advance to a higher level or position **:** to become more popular, successful, etc. • a politician who *rose* to fame/power/prominence very quickly • Empires *rise* [=become powerful, important, etc.] and fall. • The book has *risen* to the top of best-seller lists. • She ***rose through the ranks*** of the company to become president. [=she began her career with the company with little power or authority and gradually gained more power and authority until she had become president] • She ***has risen in my estimation***. [=I think more highly of her; I respect/admire her more]
3 a : to increase in amount, number, level, etc. **:** to become more • Sales have *risen* [=*increased*] in recent months. • People are angry about *rising* gasoline prices. • The population has been *rising* [=*growing*] dramatically/sharply/markedly. • Stocks *rose* (by) several points in early trading today. • The market is continuing to *rise*. **b :** to become stronger **:** to increase in strength • The wind *rose* in the afternoon. • My anger *rose* as I thought about what she had said. **c :** to become louder **:** to increase in volume • The music *rose* and fell. • Her voice *rose* to an angry shout.
4 a : to stand up • He *rose* slowly (to his feet). • She quickly *rose* from the chair and began to walk away. **b :** to get up from sleeping in a bed • He *rose* refreshed after a good night's sleep. • ***Rise and shine!*** [=wake up and get out of bed]
5 *of the sun or moon* **:** to appear above the horizon • The sun

R

rises [=*comes up*] in the morning and sets at night. ▪ We watched as the moon *rose* in the eastern sky. — opposite [1]SET 11

6 *of bread, cake, etc.* **:** to become bigger because of being filled with air bubbles made through a chemical process ▪ Yeast will make the dough *rise*.

7 : to begin to fight in order to remove a ruler or government ▪ The people *rose* in rebellion/revolt. — often + *up* ▪ He told the people that they should *rise up* and overthrow the corrupt government.

8 : to live again after dying **:** to come back to life ▪ a belief that the dead will ***rise again*** [=will live again] ▪ Christians believe that Jesus Christ ***rose from the dead***.

rise above [*phrasal verb*] ***rise above (something)*** **1 :** to not allow yourself to be hurt or controlled by (something bad or harmful) ▪ We need to *rise above* our anger/frustration and find a way to get along with each other. ▪ She *rose above* the prejudice of her time to become a great civil rights leader. ▪ It's time to *rise above* petty bickering/politics. **2 :** to be or become better than (something) ▪ The quality of the food never *rises above* average.

rise to the occasion/challenge **:** to make the special effort that is required to successfully deal with a difficult situation ▪ No one was sure if he could handle the pressure of making a speech, but he *rose to the occasion* and did an excellent job. ▪ When the company needed to increase its sales, its employees *rose to the challenge*.

your gorge rises see [1]GORGE

[2]rise *noun, pl* **rises**

1 [*count*] **:** an increase in amount, number, level, etc. — usually singular ▪ There has been a sharp/dramatic *rise* in property values. ▪ The town's population has grown by 200—a *rise* of more than 20 percent. ▪ a steady *rise* [=*increase*] in the number of available jobs ▪ a *rise* in prices/taxes = (*chiefly Brit*) a price/tax *rise* — opposite DECREASE

2 [*singular*] **:** an upward movement ▪ We watched the *rise* and fall of the waves.

3 [*singular*] **:** the act of advancing to a higher level or position **:** the process by which something or someone becomes established, popular, successful, etc. ▪ The book describes the empire's *rise* and fall. ▪ the meteoric/sudden *rise* of the Internet ▪ a politician's *rise* to fame/power/prominence ▪ the *rise* of nationalism/feminism

4 [*count*] **a :** an upward slope ▪ There was a gentle/steep *rise* in the road as we approached the town. **b :** an area of ground that is higher than the ground around it **:** a small hill ▪ We could see the valley below us as we came over the *rise*.

5 [*count*] *Brit* **:** an increase in the amount of money paid to a worker **:** RAISE ▪ I asked my boss for a *rise*. ▪ a pay *rise*

get a rise out of *informal* **:** to cause (someone) to react in an angry way **:** to make (someone) angry or upset ▪ Ignore her. She's just trying to *get a rise out of* you.

give rise to **:** to cause or produce (something) ▪ His strange behavior *gave rise to* rumors about his health. ▪ The recent increase in prices has *given rise to* concerns about inflation.

on the rise **1 :** increasing in amount, number, level, etc. ▪ Prices were falling last year, but now they are *on the rise* again. ▪ The water level in the lake is *on the rise*. **2 :** becoming more successful, popular, etc. ▪ an actress whose career is *on the rise*

ris·er /ˈraɪzɚ/ *noun, pl* **-ers**

1 [*count*] **:** a person who gets out of bed after sleeping — used in the phrases ***early riser*** and ***late riser*** ▪ I'm an *early/late riser*. [=I get out of bed early/late in the morning]

2 [*count*] *technical* **:** the upright board between two stairs

3 ***risers*** [*plural*] *US* **:** a set of tall and wide steps for standing or sitting on ▪ The school choir stood on the *risers* for the concert.

ris·i·ble /ˈrɪzəbəl/ *adj* [*more* ~; *most* ~] *formal + disapproving* **:** deserving to be laughed at **:** very silly or unreasonable ▪ a *risible* [=(more commonly) *ridiculous*] title ▪ The suggestion was downright *risible*.

rising *noun, pl* **-ings** [*count*] *chiefly Brit* **:** a violent attempt by a group of people in a country to remove a leader or government **:** UPRISING ▪ He was the leader of an armed *rising* against the elected government.

rising star *noun, pl* ~ **stars** [*count*] **:** a person who is quickly becoming popular, successful, etc. ▪ a politician who is a *rising star* in the Republican/Democratic Party

[1]risk /ˈrɪsk/ *noun, pl* **risks**

1 : the possibility that something bad or unpleasant (such as an injury or a loss) will happen [*noncount*] I prefer not to expose my money to too much *risk*. ▪ The degree of *risk* is minimal. ▪ All investments have/involve an ***element of risk***. [*count*] The trip didn't seem like much of a *risk*. ▪ I'm aware of the *risks* associated with this treatment. ▪ There is a *risk* of liver damage with this medication. ▪ Wearing a seatbelt greatly reduces the *risk* of injury or death in a car accident. ▪ We feel that this product presents a significant *risk* to public health. ▪ To me, skydiving is not ***worth the risk***.

2 [*count*] **:** someone or something that may cause something bad or unpleasant to happen ▪ Smoking is a *risk* to your lungs. ▪ Kids think it's fun, but they don't realize the *risks* involved. ▪ Excess body fat is a serious/significant health *risk*. ▪ The government claims she is a *risk* to national security. — see also SECURITY RISK

3 [*count*] **:** a person or thing that someone judges to be a good or bad choice for insurance, a loan, etc. ▪ Drivers who are considered poor *risks* have to pay more for car insurance. ▪ The bank will determine if a potential borrower is a good/bad ***credit risk***. [=someone who is likely/unlikely to pay back money the bank loans]

at risk **:** in a dangerous situation **:** in a situation in which something bad or harmful could happen ▪ They believe that the policy puts the country *at risk*. ▪ people who are *at risk* of developing heart disease [=who might develop heart disease] ▪ The program is designed for students who are *at risk* for/of failure. [=who are in danger of failing] ▪ Many residents remain *at risk* from floodwaters. ▪ He placed his life *at risk* to save them. [=he risked his life to save them] ▪ The firefighter went back into the burning building to save the dog—*at* considerable *risk* to his own life.

at the risk of (doing something) **:** despite the possibility of (doing something that could be considered improper, wrong, etc.) ▪ *At the risk of* being/sounding rude, I have to ask you how old you are. [=I have to ask how old you are even though you may consider me rude for asking] ▪ *At the risk of* sounding repetitive, I want to say again that our basic problem is a lack of effective leadership.

at your own risk **:** with full understanding that what you are doing is dangerous and that you are responsible for your own safety ▪ There's no lifeguard here, so if you swim you'll be doing it *at your own risk*.

calculated risk see CALCULATED

run a risk **:** to do something that may result in loss, failure, etc. ▪ He is not afraid of *running risks*. [=(more commonly) *taking risks*]

run the risk of **:** to do something that may result in (something bad or unpleasant happening) ▪ You *run the risk of* being misunderstood if you don't explain your purpose carefully. ▪ That strategy *runs the risk of* undermining their authority. ▪ It's a dangerous policy that *runs the risk of* failure/failing.

take a risk **:** to do something that may result in loss, failure, etc. ▪ Every time you invest money, you're *taking a risk*.

[2]risk *verb* **risks; risked; risk·ing** [+ *obj*]

1 : to put (something) in a situation in which it could be lost, damaged, etc. ▪ She *risked* her life to save her children. ▪ He *risked* all his money on starting his own business. — see also *risk life and limb* at [1]LIFE, *risk your neck* at [1]NECK

2 : to do something that could result in (something bad or unpleasant) ▪ He *risked* breaking his neck. ▪ She's *risking* being considered too sentimental. ▪ The country *risked* a war. ▪ brave people who *risked* being killed to help others ▪ I'm not willing to *risk* getting lost. I'm going to buy a map. ▪ The company is *risking* the loss of millions of dollars.

3 : to do (something that may have harmful or bad results) ▪ It's not wise to *risk* traveling so soon after surgery. ▪ We should stop for more gas. We probably have enough, but I don't want to ***risk it***. [=I don't want to possibly not have enough gas]

risk factor *noun, pl* ~ **-tors** [*count*] **:** something that increases risk; *especially* **:** something that makes a person more likely to get a particular disease or condition ▪ Age is one of the *risk factors* for this disease.

risk–taking *noun* [*noncount*] **:** the act or fact of doing something that involves danger or risk in order to achieve a goal ▪ Starting a business always involves some *risk-taking*.

– risk–taker *noun, pl* **-ers** [*count*] ▪ I'm not much of a *risk-taker*. [=I don't like to take risks]

risky /ˈrɪski/ *adj* **risk·i·er; -est** [*also more* ~; *most* ~] **:** involving the possibility of something bad or unpleasant happening **:** involving risk ▪ The proposal seems *risky*. ▪ It's not as *risky* [=*dangerous*] as people think. ▪ a less/slightly *risky* investment ▪ Her plan is too *risky*. ▪ Love is a ***risky business***.

[=love involves the possibility of being hurt] • It's a ***risky move*** [=an action that may result in something bad or unpleasant happening] for the company.

– risk·i·ness *noun* [*noncount*] • I don't like the *riskiness* of the plan.

ri·sot·to /rɪˈsɑːtoʊ/ *noun, pl* **-tos** [*count, noncount*] : an Italian dish made with rice and often vegetables or meat

ris·qué /rɪˈskeɪ/ *adj* [*more ~; most ~*] : referring to sex in a rude and slightly shocking way • a *risqué* joke/topic • a song with *risqué* lyrics

ris·sole /ˈrɪˌsoʊl/ *noun, pl* **-soles** [*count*] *Brit* : a small mass or ball of chopped and fried meat

Rit·a·lin /ˈrɪtələn/ *trademark* — used for a drug that is given to people who suffer from attention deficit disorder

rite /ˈraɪt/ *noun, pl* **rites** [*count*] : an act that is part of a usually religious ceremony • Incense is often burned in their religious *rites*. • funeral/purification *rites* • Police suspect that the crime was a gang ***initiation rite***. [=an act that someone must do in order to officially join a gang] — see also LAST RITES

rite of passage *noun, pl* **rites of passage** [*count*] : an act that is a symbol of an important change in someone's life • Her ears were pierced as a *rite of passage*. • For many, going to college is a *rite of passage*.

¹rit·u·al /ˈrɪtʃəwəl/ *noun, pl* **-als**

1 : a formal ceremony or series of acts that is always performed in the same way [*count*] a religious *ritual* • an ancient fertility *ritual* • The priest will perform the *ritual*. [*noncount*] He was buried simply, without ceremony or *ritual*.

2 : an act or series of acts done in a particular situation and in the same way each time [*count*] the daily *ritual* of preparing breakfast • the bird's mating *ritual* [*noncount*] His day-to-day life is based on *ritual*.

²ritual *adj, always used before a noun*

1 : done as part of a ceremony or ritual • a *ritual* dance • perform a *ritual* purification

2 : always done in a particular situation and in the same way each time • *ritual* acts • a *ritual* greeting/gesture

– rit·u·al·ly *adv*

rit·u·al·is·tic /ˌrɪtʃəwəˈlɪstɪk/ *adj* [*more ~; most ~*] *formal* : relating to or done as part of a rite or ritual • *ritualistic* acts • the *ritualistic* use of incense

– rit·u·al·is·ti·cal·ly /ˌrɪtʃəwəˈlɪstɪkli/ *adv*

ritzy /ˈrɪtsi/ *adj* **ritz·i·er; -est** [*also more ~; most ~*] *informal* : very fashionable and expensive often in a showy way • a *ritzy* resort/club/wedding

¹ri·val /ˈraɪvəl/ *noun, pl* **-vals** [*count*]

1 : a person or thing that tries to defeat or be more successful than another • The teams have been longtime *rivals*. • The men are romantic *rivals* for her affection. • her *rival* [=*competitor, opponent*] in the election • the company's ***chief/main rival*** — often used before another noun • a *rival* team/gang/candidate/company/school • He told a *rival* version of the story. [=a version that disagrees with another version]

2 : something or someone that is as good or almost as good as another person or thing • The company's paper is the *rival* of any in the world. [=it is as good as any paper in the world] • The company's latest cell phone has no *rival/rivals*. [=the company's newest cell phone is much better than all others available]

²rival *verb* **rivals**; *US* **ri·valed** *or Brit* **ri·valled**; *US* **ri·val·ing** *or Brit* **ri·val·ling** [*+ obj*] : to be as good or almost as good as (someone or something) • The company manufactures paper that *rivals* the world's best. • The new museum will *rival* the largest in the world.

ri·val·ry /ˈraɪvəlri/ *noun, pl* **-ries** : a state or situation in which people or groups are competing with each other [*count*] There is a bitter/friendly *rivalry* between the two groups. [*noncount*] a strong sense of *rivalry* • In our family there was plenty of ***sibling rivalry***. [=competition or jealousy between sisters and brothers]

rive /ˈraɪv/ *verb* **rives**; **rived**; **riv·en** /ˈrɪvən/; **riv·ing** [*+ obj*] *formal* : to divide or split (something) especially in a forceful or violent way — usually used as *(be) riven* • The country *was riven* by civil war. • a family *riven* with jealousy

riv·er /ˈrɪvɚ/ *noun, pl* **-ers** [*count*]

1 : a large natural flow of water that crosses an area of land and goes into an ocean, a lake, etc. • the Mississippi *River* • The raft is too small to use on this part of the *river*. • They have a house on the *river*. [=on land next to the river] • Large boats came ***up/down the river***. [=in the opposite/same direction that the river is flowing] • the ***mouth of the river*** = the ***river's mouth*** = the ***river mouth*** [=the place where the river enters the ocean] — see color picture on page C7; compare STREAM

2 : a large flow of something • *Rivers* of mud flowed down the hillside. — often *+ of* • The jet stream is a *river of* air. • I cried a *river of* tears. [=I cried a lot]

sell (someone) down the river see ¹SELL

up the river *US, old-fashioned + informal* : to prison • They sent him *up the river* for 10 years.

riv·er·bank /ˈrɪvɚˌbæŋk/ *noun, pl* **-banks** [*count*] : the ground at the edge of a river • They set up their camp next to the *riverbank*. [=next to the edge of the river]

riv·er·bed /ˈrɪvɚˌbɛd/ *noun, pl* **-beds** [*count*] : the ground at the bottom of a river

riv·er·boat /ˈrɪvɚˌboʊt/ *noun, pl* **-boats** [*count*] : a boat that is used on a river

riv·er·front /ˈrɪvɚˌfrʌnt/ *noun, pl* **-fronts** [*count*] *chiefly US* : the land that is next to a river • We went for a walk down at the *riverfront*. — often used before another noun • *riverfront* property

riv·er·side /ˈrɪvɚˌsaɪd/ *noun, pl* **-sides** [*count*] : the land that is next to a river • We walked along the *riverside*. — often used before another noun • a *riverside* community/camp

¹riv·et /ˈrɪvət/ *noun, pl* **-ets** [*count*] : a special kind of metal bolt or pin that is used to hold pieces of metal together

²rivet *verb* **-ets**; **-et·ed**; **-et·ing** [*+ obj*]

1 : to attract and hold all of someone's attention — usually used as *(be) riveted* • I *was riveted* by her story. [=her story was so interesting that I was giving all of my attention to it] • All eyes *were riveted* on her as she walked past. [=everyone watched her as she walked past] • the kind of performance that keeps an audience *riveted*

2 : to make (someone) unable to move because of fear, shock, etc. — usually used as *(be) riveted* • He *was* ***riveted to the spot*** with fright/amazement. • She stood ***riveted in place***, staring straight ahead.

3 : to fasten (something) with rivets • The iron plates are *riveted* rather than welded.

– riv·et·er *noun, pl* **-ers** [*count*] • He worked as a *riveter* in an airplane factory.

riv·et·ing /ˈrɪvətɪŋ/ *adj* [*more ~; most ~*] : very exciting or interesting • The movie/book/narrative was *riveting*. • a *riveting* story

Ri·vi·era /ˌrɪviˈerə/ *noun*

the Riviera : an area by the sea that has warm weather and is a popular place for people to go for vacations • *the* French/Italian *Riviera*

riv·u·let /ˈrɪvjələt/ *noun, pl* **-lets** [*count*] : a small stream of water or liquid • *rivulets* of water/sweat

rm. *abbr* room

¹RN /ˌɑɚˈɛn/ *noun, pl* **RNs** [*count*] : REGISTERED NURSE

²RN *abbr, Brit* Royal Navy

RNA /ˌɑɚˌɛnˈeɪ/ *noun* [*noncount*] *technical* : a substance in the cells of plants and animals that helps make proteins — called also *ribonucleic acid*; compare DNA

¹roach /ˈroʊtʃ/ *noun, pl* **roach·es** [*count*]

1 *US* : COCKROACH

2 *informal* : the part of a marijuana cigarette that is left after it has been smoked

– compare ²ROACH

²roach *noun, pl* **roach** *also* **roaches** [*count*] : a small European fish that lives in rivers and lakes — compare ¹ROACH

road /ˈroʊd/ *noun, pl* **roads**

1 : a hard flat surface for vehicles, people, and animals to travel on [*count*] a paved/gravel/dirt *road* • We'll cross the *road* up ahead at the crosswalk. • He drove off the *road*. • We parked by the side of the *road*. • There are lots of cars on the *road* this morning. • The *roads* around here are pretty bad. [=the roads are in bad condition] • This is a busy *road*. [=many cars, trucks, etc., use this road] • These country/mountain *roads* are beautiful. • icy *roads* • The post office is ***up/down this road*** a bit. [=a short distance further on this road] • There's likely to be a lot of traffic on the ***main/major roads*** [=the roads most commonly used], so you may want to take ***back/side roads***. [=roads that are less commonly used and that do not go through the main part of a city, town, etc.] • the county's ***public/private roads*** — often used in names • The library is on River *Road*. [*noncount*] a desolate stretch of *road* • Miles of *road* lay ahead. • The cabin is accessible ***by road***. • traveling on ***the open road*** [=on roads that are away from cities and towns] — see also MIDDLE-OF-THE-

ROAD, OFF-ROAD, SERVICE ROAD
2 [count] : a process or a course of action that leads to a certain result ▪ the *road* to riches/success/victory ▪ They're heading down a dangerous *road*. [=they're following a course of action that could lead to a bad result] ▪ She had a stroke recently but is on ***the road to recovery***. [=in the process of becoming healthy again] ▪ I've been/gone ***down this road*** before. [=I've had this kind of experience before; I've done this kind of thing before] — see also HIGH ROAD
down the road : in or into the future ▪ We don't know what the situation will be like a month/year *down the road*. ▪ They hope to expand the business ***somewhere down the road***. [=at some time in the future]
for the road — used to refer to an alcoholic drink that you have quickly before leaving a place ▪ I'll just have ***one (more) for the road***. [=I'll have one more drink before I leave]
get the/this show on the road see ²SHOW
hit the road *informal* : to begin a journey ▪ We got up early and *hit the road* around 7:00. : to go away : LEAVE ▪ Well, I guess it's time to *hit the road*. ▪ She angrily told him to *hit the road*. [=get lost]
on the road **1** : traveling especially in a car, truck, bus, etc. ▪ We've been *on the road* since Tuesday. ▪ Musicians often spend many months *on the road*. **2** *of a vehicle* **a** : being used ▪ You don't see too many of those cars *on the road* anymore. **b** : in good enough condition to be legally driven ▪ It will cost $1,500 to get the car back *on the road*.
the end of the road see ¹END

road·block /ˈroʊdˌblɑːk/ *noun, pl* **-blocks** [count]
1 : a place where police or military officers stop drivers especially in order to examine vehicles
2 *US* : something that stops progress ▪ That's the one *roadblock* to the plan. ▪ *roadblocks* on the path to success

road hog *noun, pl* ~ **hogs** [count] *informal + disapproving* : someone who drives a vehicle in a way that blocks other drivers

road·house /ˈroʊdˌhaʊs/ *noun, pl* **-houses** [count] *US, old-fashioned* : a restaurant or bar that is on a main road outside a city or town

road·ie /ˈroʊdi/ *noun, pl* **-ies** [count] *informal* : a person whose job is to help move and set up the equipment of traveling musicians

road·kill /ˈroʊdˌkɪl/ *noun* [noncount] : animals that have been killed by being hit by cars and other vehicles ▪ There is a lot of *roadkill* along the highway.

road map *noun, pl* ~ **maps** [count]
1 : a map that shows the roads in a particular area ▪ Did you bring a *road map*?
2 *chiefly US* : a plan for achieving a goal ▪ a *road map* to/for peace

road rage *noun* [noncount] : anger and aggressive behavior by a driver who is upset by how another person is driving

road·run·ner /ˈroʊdˌrʌnɚ/ *noun, pl* **-ners** [count] : a North American bird that lives in the desert and runs very fast

road show *noun, pl* ~ **shows** [count] : a group of people who travel to different places to entertain people or to advertise something

road·side /ˈroʊdˌsaɪd/ *noun* [noncount] : the land that is along a road : the area beside a road ▪ a hamburger stand on/by/at the *roadside* — often used before another noun ▪ a *roadside* restaurant ▪ *roadside* vegetation

road sign *noun, pl* ~ **signs** [count] : a sign near a road that has information for drivers

road·ster /ˈroʊdstɚ/ *noun, pl* **-sters** [count] : a car that has two seats and a fabric top that folds back

road test *noun, pl* ~ **tests** [count]
1 : a test to see how well a vehicle works when it is driven on roads ▪ The car performed well on the *road test*.
2 *US* : a test to see how well someone is able to drive a car or other vehicle ▪ I have to take a *road test* [=driving test] before I can get my license.
– **road test** *verb* ~ **tests**; ~ **tested**; ~ **testing** [+ obj] ▪ The car has not yet been *road tested*.

road trip *noun, pl* ~ **trips** [count] *US*
1 : a long trip in a car, truck, etc. ▪ a cross-country *road trip*
2 : a trip that is taken by a sports team in order to play one or more games ▪ The team won three of five games on its *road trip*.

road warrior *noun, pl* ~ **-riors** [count] *chiefly US, informal* : a person who travels a lot especially as part of his or her job ▪ a lightweight laptop computer that's perfect for *road warriors*

road·way /ˈroʊdˌweɪ/ *noun, pl* **-ways** [count] : the part of a road that is used by vehicles ▪ Police cleared the *roadway* for the parade.

road·work /ˈroʊdˌwɚk/ *noun* [noncount] *US* : work that is done to build or repair roads ▪ The *roadwork* caused a backup in traffic. — called also (*Brit*) *roadworks*

road·wor·thy /ˈroʊdˌwɚði/ *adj* : safe and suitable for using on a road ▪ a *roadworthy* vehicle — compare AIRWORTHY, SEAWORTHY
– **road·wor·thi·ness** *noun* [noncount] ▪ The trucks were all tested for *roadworthiness*.

roam /ˈroʊm/ *verb* **roams**; **roamed**; **roam·ing** : to go to different places without having a particular purpose or plan [no obj] The cattle *roamed* in search of water. ▪ Goats *roam* free on the mountain. ▪ He *roamed* about in search of work. ▪ The chickens are able to *roam* around freely in the farmyard. ▪ We *roamed* around town for a while before dinner. ▪ She liked to *roam* through the woods. [+ obj] Sheep *roamed* the hills. ▪ Tourists *roamed* the streets. ▪ She spent the day *roaming* [=surfing] the Internet. ▪ His ***eyes roamed*** [=he looked carefully around] the room in search of the cat.

roaming *noun* [noncount] : the use of a cell phone in an area that is outside the usual area and that requires the use of a different network ▪ There are high fees for *roaming*. — often used before another noun ▪ *roaming* charges/fees

roan /ˈroʊn/ *noun, pl* **roans** [count] : a horse that has white hairs mixed in with hairs of a darker color
– **roan** *adj, always used before a noun* ▪ a roan horse/mare/colt

¹**roar** /ˈroɚ/ *verb* **roars**; **roared**; **roar·ing**
1 [no obj] **a** : to make the loud sound of a wild animal (such as a lion) ▪ We heard a lion *roar* in the distance. **b** : to make a long, loud sound ▪ The guns/siren *roared*. ▪ The fans were *roaring* [=yelling and cheering loudly] after their team scored. ▪ The campfire was *roaring*. [=the campfire was burning brightly and loudly] ▪ The engine suddenly ***roared (back) to life***. [=it made the loud sound of an engine and began running well] — sometimes used figuratively ▪ His career suddenly *roared back to life*.
2 [no obj] : to laugh loudly ▪ The joke got the crowd *roaring*. ▪ The audience *roared* with laughter. [=the audience laughed loudly for a long time]
3 : to shout (something) very loudly [+ obj] "Watch out," he *roared*. ▪ The crowd *roared* its approval. — often + *out* ▪ The general *roared out* his orders. [no obj] She *roared* at him for being late.
4 *always followed by an adverb or preposition* [no obj] : to move noisily and quickly ▪ The truck *roared* away/off. ▪ The car *roared* down the street. ▪ The wind *roared* through the open barn. — sometimes used figuratively ▪ The team came *roaring* back in the second half to win the game.

²**roar** *noun, pl* **roars** [count]
1 : the loud sound of a wild animal (such as a lion)
2 : a loud, low sound that continues for a long time ▪ the *roar* of the airplane engines ▪ the *roar* of the river/crowd ▪ *roars* of laughter/approval

¹**roaring** /ˈrorɪŋ/ *adj, always used before a noun* : very loud, active, or strong ▪ the *roaring* river ▪ a *roaring* fire ▪ The store does a ***roaring business/trade***. [=the store is very busy and successful] ▪ The show was a ***roaring success***. [=a very great success] ▪ life during the ***roaring twenties*** [=the 1920s, when many people lived in a very wild and lively way]

²**roaring** *adv, informal* : extremely or very ▪ We had a *roaring* good time. ▪ He was ***roaring drunk***. [=very drunk]

¹**roast** /ˈroʊst/ *verb* **roasts**; **roast·ed**; **roast·ing**
1 a : to cook (food such as chicken, potatoes, or beef) with dry heat in an oven or over a fire [+ obj] He *roasted* the chicken. [no obj] The chicken is *roasting* in the oven. — compare BAKE, GRILL **b** : to dry (something, such as a bean or nut) with heat [+ obj] We *roasted* the peanuts over the fire. [no obj] The peanuts *roasted* over the fire.
2 [no obj] *informal* : to be very hot ▪ We were *roasting* in the hot sun. ▪ You must be *roasting* [=baking, sweltering] in that sweater.
3 [+ obj] *informal* : to criticize (someone or something) severely ▪ The movie is being *roasted* by the critics.
4 [+ obj] *US, informal* : to criticize (someone who is being honored at a special event) in a friendly or joking way : to tell jokes or funny stories about (someone) ▪ Friends and family *roasted* him at his 40th birthday party.

R

– **roasted** *adj* • *roasted* potatoes/garlic/tomatoes • *roasted* coffee beans • *roasted* peanuts – **roasting** *adj* • the smell of *roasting* meat • a ***roasting pan*** [=a pan used for roasting]

²roast *noun, pl* **roasts**
1 : a piece of meat that is roasted [*count*] She made a *roast* for dinner. [*noncount*] We're having pork *roast* for dinner. — see also POT ROAST
2 [*count*] *US* **:** an outdoor party at which food is cooked over an open fire • a pig *roast*
3 [*count*] *US* **:** an event at which someone is honored and people tell jokes or funny stories about that person in a friendly way • a celebrity *roast*

³roast *adj, always used before a noun* **:** cooked by roasting • *roast* [=*roasted*] chicken/pork/potatoes

roast·er /ˈroʊstɚ/ *noun, pl* **-ers** [*count*]
1 : a device used for roasting meat
2 *chiefly US* **:** a young chicken that is suitable for roasting — compare BROILER, FRYER

roasting *noun* [*singular*] *Brit* **:** the act of severely criticizing someone • My father ***gave me a roasting*** [=yelled at me] for coming home late. • He ***got a roasting*** from his boss. [=his boss criticized him severely]

rob /ˈrɑːb/ *verb* **robs; robbed; rob·bing** [+ *obj*]
1 : to take money or property from (a person or a place) illegally and sometimes by using force, violence, or threats • Someone tried to *rob* me. • They *robbed* the bank. • The cashier was *robbed* at gunpoint. — often + *of* • They *robbed* her *of* her life savings. • He was *robbed of* all his money. — sometimes used figuratively • You paid $300 to fix that old car? You ***got robbed***. [=you were overcharged; you spent too much]
2 : to keep (someone) from getting something expected or wanted • He made a great shot, but the goalie *robbed* him. [=the goalie blocked his shot and prevented him from scoring a goal] — often + *of* • The other team *robbed* them *of* a victory by getting a last-minute goal. • The center fielder made a great catch to *rob* him *of* a home run. • Her illness *robbed* her *of* a normal childhood. [=she wasn't able to have a normal childhood because of her illness]
rob Peter to pay Paul **:** to take money that was meant for one person or thing and use it to pay someone else or to pay for something else • She was trying to keep her creditors at bay by *robbing Peter to pay Paul*. [=using one credit card to make the payments on another credit card]
rob (someone) blind **:** to steal a lot of things or money from someone • If you're not careful, they'll *rob you blind*.
rob the cradle see ¹CRADLE

rob·ber /ˈrɑːbɚ/ *noun, pl* **-bers** [*count*] **:** a criminal who steals money or property **:** a thief who robs people • The store was held up by a gang of *robbers*. • a bank *robber*

robber baron *noun, pl* **~ -ons** [*count*] *old-fashioned* **:** a wealthy person who tries to get land, businesses, or more money in a way that is dishonest or wrong

rob·bery /ˈrɑːbəri/ *noun, pl* **-ber·ies :** the crime of stealing money or property **:** the crime of robbing a person or place [*count*] a series of armed *robberies* • They foiled a bank *robbery*. [*noncount*] He is charged with attempted *robbery*. • She was arrested for *robbery*. — see also HIGHWAY ROBBERY

robe /ˈroʊb/ *noun, pl* **robes** [*count*]
1 : a long, loose piece of clothing that is worn on top of other clothes to show that someone has a high rank or an important job • The priest wore a purple *robe*. — often plural • a judge's *robes* • The king was dressed in red *robes*.
2 *chiefly US* **:** a loose piece of clothing that wraps around your body and that you wear before or after bathing, swimming, etc., or while resting at home — called also *dressing gown*; see also BATHROBE

robed /ˈroʊbd/ *adj* **:** covered with a robe **:** dressed in robes • The priests were *robed* in black. • *robed* monks

rob·in /ˈrɑːbən/ *noun, pl* **-ins** [*count*]
1 : a North American bird with a grayish back and reddish breast — see color picture on page C9
2 : a small European bird with a brownish back and orange face and breast

ro·bot /ˈroʊˌbɑːt/ *noun, pl* **-bots** [*count*]
1 : a real or imaginary machine that is controlled by a computer and is often made to look like a human or animal • a talking toy *robot* • science fiction *robots* • a *robot* dog — sometimes used figuratively to describe a person who seems to do things automatically or who seems to have no feelings or emotions • He answered the questions like a *robot*.
2 : a machine that can do the work of a person and that works automatically or is controlled by a computer • The cars are assembled by *robots*. • *robot* technology
– **ro·bot·ic** /roʊˈbɑːtɪk/ *adj* • A *robotic* arm is used to mix the chemicals. • *robotic* movements – **ro·bot·i·cal·ly** /roʊˈbɑːtɪkli/ *adv* • The cars are assembled *robotically*. • He answered their questions *robotically*.

ro·bot·ics /roʊˈbɑːtɪks/ *noun* [*noncount*] **:** technology that is used to design, build, and operate robots

ro·bust /roʊˈbʌst/ *adj* [*more ~; most ~*]
1 : strong and healthy • *robust* young men and women • He is in *robust* health.
2 a : strongly formed or built • *robust* furniture **b :** successful or impressive and not likely to fail or weaken • a *robust* company • a *robust* economy • She offered a *robust* [=*forceful*] argument against the plan. **c :** impressively large • a *robust* [=*hearty*] dinner • *robust* profits
3 : having a rich, strong flavor • a *robust* [=*full-bodied*] wine • The sauce has a *robust* flavor.
– **ro·bust·ly** *adv* • *robustly* healthy young men and women • The food was *robustly* seasoned. – **ro·bust·ness** /roʊˈbʌstnəs/ *noun, pl* **-nesses** [*count, noncount*]

¹rock /ˈrɑːk/ *verb* **rocks; rocked; rock·ing**
1 : to move (someone or something) back and forth or from side to side [+ *obj*] She gently *rocked* the baby to sleep. • Waves *rocked* the boat. [*no obj*] He *rocked* back and forth while he stood waiting. • The boat *rocked* back and forth on the waves.
2 [+ *obj*] **:** to cause (something) to shake violently • An earthquake *rocked* the town. • The building was *rocked* by an explosion. — sometimes used figuratively • The discovery *rocked* [=*shook*] the very foundations of their theory.
3 [+ *obj*] *informal* **a :** to cause (someone or something) to be upset or shocked • The news of the murders *rocked* the town. **b :** to affect or influence (someone or something) very powerfully • Their invention *rocked* the computer industry. **c :** to entertain (someone) in a very powerful and effective way • The band *rocked* the crowd. • His performance ***rocked the house***. [=the audience loved his performance] • The new video game will ***rock your world***. [=you will really like the new video game]
4 [*no obj*] *informal* **:** to sing, dance to, or play rock music • We were *rocking* all night long.
5 [*no obj*] *slang* **:** to be very enjoyable, pleasing, or effective • Her new car really *rocks*. [=her new car is really great]
rock out [*phrasal verb*] *informal* **:** to play music in a loud or energetic way • The band *rocks out* on their new album.
rock the boat see ¹BOAT
– **rocking** *noun, pl* **-ings** [*count, noncount*] • a slow *rocking*

²rock *noun, pl* **rocks**
1 a [*noncount*] **:** the hard, solid material that the surface of the Earth is made of • They drilled through several layers of solid *rock*. • Moss can grow on bare *rock*. • The miners made a tunnel through the *rock*. • volcanic *rock* — often used before another noun • The mountain had many amazing *rock* formations. — see also BEDROCK, SHEETROCK **b** [*count*] **:** a piece of rock • a flat *rock* • (*US*) We threw *rocks* [=*stones*] into the water. • a pile of *rocks* **c** [*count*] **:** a large piece of rock that sticks up from the surface of the Earth • She climbed the *rock*. • The ship crashed into the *rocks*.
2 — used in phrases to say that something is very hard, steady, etc. • This bread is (as) ***hard as a rock***. = The bread is ***rock-hard***. [=the bread is very hard] • Her hand was ***steady as a rock***. [=her hand was very steady] • His muscles are ***solid as a rock***. [=very strong/solid] • The frozen chicken is ***rock-solid***. • The beat of the drum was ***rock-steady***.
3 [*singular*] *informal* **a :** a strong person who can be relied on • We could always count on him—he was our *rock*. **b :** someone whose ideas, values, ways of doing things, etc., do not change • Once she makes up her mind, she's (like) a *rock*. [=nobody can change her mind once she decides something]
4 [*count*] *informal* **:** a diamond or other jewel • Look at the size of that *rock* on her finger.
5 [*noncount*] *Brit* **:** hard candy that is made in a stick • a stick of *rock* — compare ROCK CANDY
6 [*count*] *informal* **:** a small hard piece of a drug • a *rock* of crack cocaine
between a rock and a hard place *informal* **:** in a very difficult or bad position or situation with no good way of getting out of it • He is caught/stuck *between a rock and a hard place*.
get your rocks off *informal* **1** *of a man* **:** to have an orgasm **2 :** to feel great pleasure or satisfaction • He *gets his rocks off* bossing everyone around.

R

live under a rock : to be unaware of things that most people know about • How could you have not heard about it? Do you *live under a rock*?

on the rocks **1** : having a lot of problems and likely to fail • Their marriage is *on the rocks.* [=*in trouble*] **2** *of an alcoholic drink* : with ice cubes • He ordered a whiskey/Scotch *on the rocks.*

– compare [3]ROCK

[3]**rock** *noun* [*noncount*] : a kind of popular music with a strong beat that is played on instruments that are made louder electronically • My favorite types of music are jazz and *rock.* — often used before another noun • *rock* music • a *rock* concert/band/star — see also HARD ROCK, SOFT ROCK — compare [2]ROCK

rock·a·bil·ly /ˈrɑːkəˌbɪli/ *noun* [*noncount*] : a kind of popular music that combines rock and country music

rock and roll *or* **rock 'n' roll** /ˌrɑːkənˈroʊl/ *noun* [*noncount*] : rock music

– **rock and roll·er** *or* **rock 'n' roll·er** /ˌrɑːkənˈroʊlɚ/ *noun, pl* **~ -ers** [*count*]

rock bottom *noun* [*noncount*] : the lowest possible level or point • Prices have ***hit/reached rock bottom*** [=have reached the lowest point they can reach] • After years of heavy drug use, she has finally *reached rock bottom.* • Their marriage has *hit rock bottom.*

rock–bottom *adj, always used before a noun, of a price* : very low • The furniture is being sold at *rock-bottom* prices.

rock candy *noun* [*noncount*] *US* : hard candy that is made on a string

rock climbing *noun* [*noncount*] : the sport or activity of climbing the steep sides of a mountain or cliff • a book about *rock climbing* • We are going *rock climbing.*

– **rock climb** *verb* **~ climbs; ~ climbed; ~ climbing** [*no obj*] • He *rock climbs* and skydives. – **rock climber** *noun, pl* **~ -ers** [*count*] • She's a skillful *rock climber.*

rock·er /ˈrɑːkɚ/ *noun, pl* **-ers** [*count*]

1 : a curved piece of wood or metal on which an object (such as a cradle or chair) moves back and forth or from side to side

2 *chiefly US* : ROCKING CHAIR

3 a : someone who plays or performs rock music **b** : someone who enjoys listening to rock music

off your rocker *informal* : CRAZY • You must be *off your rocker* if you think I'm going to do that!

rock·ery /ˈrɑːkəri/ *noun, pl* **-er·ies** [*count*] *chiefly Brit* : ROCK GARDEN

[1]**rock·et** /ˈrɑːkət/ *noun, pl* **-ets**

1 [*count*] : a type of very powerful engine that is powered by gases that are released from burning fuel • a car powered by a *rocket* = a *rocket*-powered car — often used before another noun • a *rocket* engine

2 [*count*] : a spacecraft or missile that is powered by a rocket engine • a moon *rocket* • antiaircraft *rockets* • a *rocket* launcher

3 [*count*] : a firework that goes high in the air before exploding — called also *skyrocket*

4 [*noncount*] *Brit* : ARUGULA

[2]**rocket** *verb* **-ets; -et·ed; -et·ing**

1 [*no obj*] : to increase quickly and suddenly • Prices *rocketed.* [=*skyrocketed*] • Sales *rocketed* from 1,000 units last week to 5,000 units this week. — often + *up* • Interest rates have been *rocketing up.*

2 *always followed by an adverb or preposition* : to move or rise quickly [*no obj*] The train *rocketed* through the tunnel. • The spacecraft *rocketed* into outer space. • He *rocketed* to stardom. • Her novel *rocketed* to the top of the best-seller list. • Their album *rocketed* up the charts. [+ *obj*] His role in the movie *rocketed* him to fame.

rocket science *noun* [*noncount*]

1 : the science of designing or building rockets

2 : something that is very difficult to learn or understand • The job is challenging, but it's not exactly *rocket science.*

– **rocket scientist** *noun, pl* **~ -tists** [*count*] • You don't have to be a *rocket scientist* [=you don't have to be unusually smart] to understand the instructions.

rocket ship *noun, pl* **~ ships** [*count*] : a spaceship that is powered by rockets

rock garden *noun, pl* **~ -dens** [*count*] : a garden in which plants grow between rocks — called also (*chiefly Brit*) *rockery*

rocking chair *noun, pl* **~ chairs** [*count*] : a chair that moves back and forth on rockers that are attached to its legs — see picture at LIVING ROOM

rocking horse *noun, pl* **~ horses** [*count*] : a toy horse that is attached to rockers and that moves back and forth while a child sits on it

rock 'n' roll *variant spelling of* ROCK AND ROLL

rock salt *noun* [*noncount*] : salt that is in the form of large pieces or crystals • I put some *rock salt* on the sidewalk to melt the ice.

rock·slide /ˈrɑːkˌslaɪd/ *noun, pl* **-slides** [*count*] : a large mass of rocks that suddenly and quickly moves down the side of a mountain or hill • a dangerous *rockslide*

rocky /ˈrɑːki/ *adj* **rock·i·er; -est** [*also more ~; most ~*]

1 : full of rocks : having many rocks • The soil is very *rocky.* • a *rocky* coastline

2 : full of problems or difficulties • a *rocky* journey/marriage • The team had a *rocky* start this season. • He knew he had a long ***rocky road*** ahead of him if he wanted to become a doctor. [=he knew that becoming a doctor would be very difficult]

ro·co·co /rəˈkoʊkoʊ/ *adj* : of or relating to a style of artistic expression that involves fancy curved forms and much decoration and was popular in the 18th century • The chairs are carved in a *rococo* style. • *rococo* art

rod /ˈrɑːd/ *noun, pl* **rods** [*count*]

1 : a straight, thin stick or bar • a curtain *rod* — see also LIGHTNING ROD, RAMROD

2 : a pole with a line and usually a reel that is used in fishing • a fishing *rod*

3 *old-fashioned* : a stick used to hit or whip someone as a form of punishment • He grew up in a time when people still believed in the old saying: spare the *rod* and spoil the child. [=believed that children should be physically punished for bad behavior in order to be raised correctly]

rule with a rod of iron see [2]RULE

– see also HOT ROD

rode *past tense of* [1]RIDE

ro·dent /ˈroʊdn̩t/ *noun, pl* **-dents** [*count*] : a small animal (such as a mouse, rat, squirrel, or beaver) that has sharp front teeth — see picture on next page

ro·deo /ˈroʊdiˌoʊ, roʊˈdeɪoʊ/ *noun, pl* **-de·os** [*count*] : an event in which people compete at riding horses and bulls, catching animals with ropes, etc.

roe /ˈroʊ/ *noun, pl* **roes** [*count, noncount*] : the eggs of a fish or sea animal • salmon *roe*

rog·er /ˈrɑːʤɚ/ *interj* — used to say that a message has been received and understood when you are talking to someone on a radio

[1]**rogue** /ˈroʊg/ *noun, pl* **rogues** [*count*]

1 *old-fashioned* : a man who is dishonest or immoral • a lying *rogue* [=*scoundrel*]

2 : a man who causes trouble in a playful way • He's a lovable old *rogue.*

[2]**rogue** *adj, always used before a noun* — used to describe something or someone that is different from others in usually a dangerous or harmful way • A *rogue* wave flipped the boat over. • *rogue* police officers [=dishonest police officers who commit crimes] • *rogue* states/regimes [=dangerous states/regimes that do not obey international laws] • a ***rogue elephant*** [=a dangerous elephant that lives apart from other elephants]

rogues' gallery *noun* [*singular*]

1 : a collection of pictures of criminals

2 : a collection or list of bad or dangerous people or things • a *rogues' gallery* of dictators • a *rogues' gallery* of deadly viruses

rogu·ish /ˈroʊgɪʃ/ *adj* [*more ~; most ~*] : showing in a playful way that you have done something wrong • a *roguish* wink/smile

– **rogu·ish·ly** *adv*

roil /ˈrojəl/ *verb* **roils; roiled; roil·ing** *chiefly US*

1 [+ *obj*] : to upset (someone or something) very much : to cause (someone or something) to become very agitated or disturbed • Financial markets have been *roiled* by the banking crisis.

2 [*no obj*] : to move in a violent and confused way • *roiling* river rapids — often used figuratively • A lot of different emotions were *roiling* (around) inside her. [=she was experiencing many emotions in a way that was disturbing or confusing]

role /ˈroʊl/ *noun, pl* **roles** [*count*]

1 : the character played by an actor • He plays the *role* of the

R

rodent

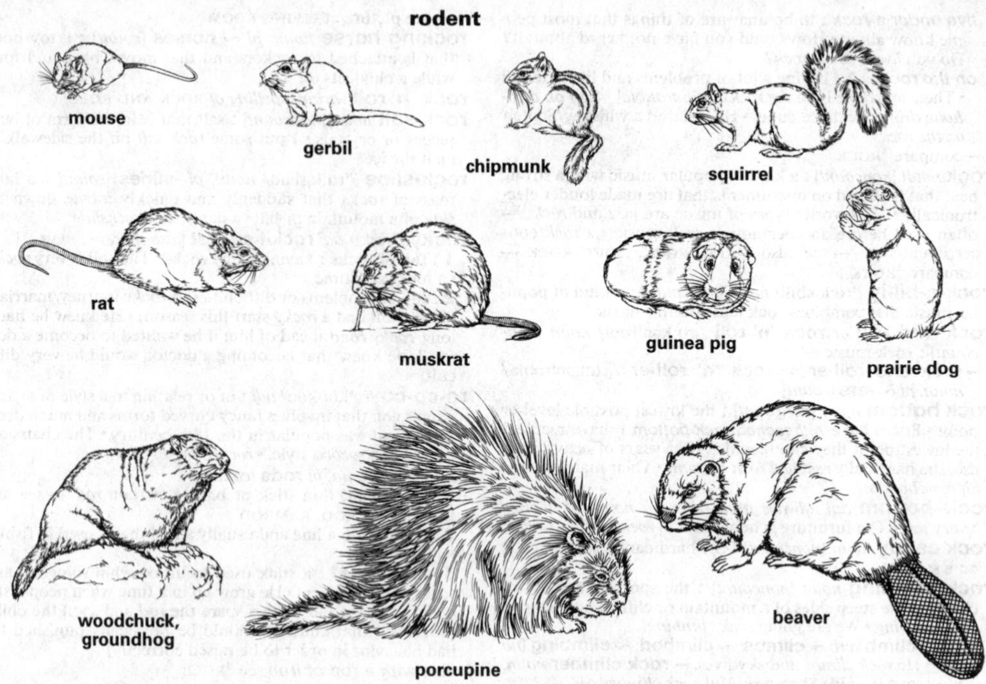

villain. • She was given the starring/lead/leading *role*. • I had a minor/major *role* in the play.

2 a : **a part that someone or something has in a particular activity or situation** — usually + *in* • Everyone had a *role* [=*hand*] *in* winning the game. [=everyone helped to win the game] • The government is taking an active *role in* improving public schools. [=the government is actively involved in improving public schools] • He had a key *role in* designing the bridge. • She talked about the *roles* of exercise and a healthy diet *in* preventing heart disease. • Newspapers play a major *role in* determining how people think about politics. • Religion plays an important *role in* his life. [=religion is very important to him] **b :** **the part that someone has in a family, society, or other group** • After her husband left her, she had to take on the dual *role* of mother and father for her children. • She likes to play the *role* of matchmaker with her friends. • She challenged the traditional *roles* assigned to women. • We'll switch/reverse *roles* this time, and you can wash the dishes while I dry them. • It was a case of ***role reversal***: the father stayed home with the children while the mother worked.

role model *noun, pl* **~ -els** [*count*] **:** **someone who another person admires and tries to be like** • Parents need to be good *role models* (for their children). • Athletes should remember that they are *role models*.

role–play /ˈroʊlˌpleɪ/ *noun, pl* **-plays :** **an activity in which people do and say things while pretending to be someone else or while pretending to be in a particular situation** [*noncount*] The teacher used *role-play* to show how people should act at an interview. [*count*] The students did *role-plays* to practice for their interviews.

– role–play *verb* **-plays; -played; -play·ing** [*no obj*] • children learning to *role-play* **– role–playing** *noun* [*noncount*] • We do a lot of *role-playing* in this class.

[1]**roll** /ˈroʊl/ *verb* **rolls; rolled; roll·ing**

1 a : **to move across the ground or another surface by turning over and over** [*no obj*] The children *rolled* down the hill. • The ball *rolled* slowly to a stop. [+ *obj*] She *rolled* the dice. • He *rolled* the ball to me. = He *rolled* me the ball. **b :** **to turn over one or more times** [*no obj*] He *rolled* (over) onto his back. • The pigs *roll* (around) in the mud to keep cool. • The car *rolled* (over) into the ditch. [+ *obj*] *Roll* the chicken wings in the batter. • The paramedics *rolled* him onto the gurney. • (*US*) He *rolled* his car in the accident.

2 : **to move smoothly on wheels** [*no obj*] The car *rolled* slowly to a stop. • A police car *rolled* up next to us. [+ *obj*] The children *rolled* the toy car to each other. • The patient was *rolled* into the emergency room.

3 [*no obj*] **:** **to move in a smooth, continuous way** • We left the movie theater as the final credits *rolled*. [=were moving across the screen] • The fog soon *rolled* away. • The clouds *rolled* past.

4 [+ *obj*] **a :** **to form (something) into the shape of a ball or tube** • She *rolled* the dough into a ball. • He *rolled* up the newspaper and swatted the fly. **b :** **to put (something) inside a tube** • He *rolled* the coins. **c :** **to wrap up (something or someone) in a way that forms the shape of a tube** • He *rolls* his own cigarettes. — often + *up* • She *rolled up* the meat in a tortilla. • He lay there snugly *rolled up* in blankets.

5 : **to form your body into a ball** — usually + *up* [*no obj*] He lay down on the bed and *rolled* [=*curled*] *up* (into a ball). [+ *obj*] He ***rolled himself up*** (into a ball).

6 [+ *obj*] **a :** **to make (something) smooth, even, or flat with a special tool (called a roller or rolling pin)** • She *rolled* (out) the dough. • He *rolled* the clay flat. • *rolled* steel/oats **b :** **to spread (something) *on* a surface with a special tool (called a roller)** • She *rolled* the paint *on* (the wall).

7 *always followed by an adverb or preposition* [*no obj*] **:** **to move forward along the normal course of time** • The days *rolled* [=*passed*] quickly by. • It got hotter as the day *rolled* on/along.

8 [*no obj*] **:** **to move or lean from side to side** • The ship heaved and *rolled* in the storm. • He walked with a *rolling* gait.

9 [*no obj*] **a :** **to make a deep, continuous sound** • Thunder *rolled* in the distance. • *rolling* thunder **b :** **to make a continuous, quick, beating sound** • The drums *rolled*.

10 : **to operate (something, such as a movie camera)** [+ *obj*] *Roll* the cameras when I say "action." [*no obj*] The camera was not *rolling* [=*filming*] at the time.

11 [*no obj*] **:** **to have a series of successes** • The team *rolled* through the play-offs.

12 : **to cause (your eyes) to look up toward the sky in an expression which shows that you think someone or something is foolish or annoying** [+ *obj*] He ***rolled his eyes*** at her suggestion. [*no obj*] Her eyes *rolled* when he told her his idea.

get rolling *informal* **1 :** **to leave** • We ought to *get rolling* if we don't want to be late. **2 :** **to start doing something** • You should *get rolling* on that assignment. • The project finally *got rolling*. [=got started]

get/set/start the ball rolling see [1]BALL

heads roll see [1]HEAD

keep the ball rolling see [1]BALL

let's roll *chiefly US, informal* — used to tell another person or a group of people to start leaving a place or to start doing something • *"Let's roll,"* the sergeant shouted to his men.

ready to roll *informal* **1 :** ready to leave • I am all packed and *ready to roll.* **2 :** ready to start doing something • After we got the loan approved, we were *ready to roll.*

roll around *also Brit* ***roll about*** [*phrasal verb*] *informal* **:** to arrive or happen again • By the time Friday *rolls around,* I'm ready for the weekend. • We'll be better prepared the next time the elections *roll around.*

roll back [*phrasal verb*] ***roll back (something) or roll (something) back*** *chiefly US* **1 :** to reduce (something, such as a price) • The store is *rolling back* its prices for this weekend only. **2 :** to change (something) back to the way it was at an earlier time **:** to reverse or undo (something) • The manufacturers are lobbying to *roll back* [=*rescind*] environmental regulations. • His proposal would ***roll back the clock*** on civil rights.

roll down [*phrasal verb*] ***roll down (something) or roll (something) down*** **1 :** to move (something) down especially by turning a handle • She *rolled down* the car window. **2 :** to unfold the edge of (something, such as a shirt sleeve or pants leg) to make it longer • He *rolled down* his sleeves.

rolled into one **:** combined together into one thing or person • It's a shopping center, amusement park, and nightclub (all) *rolled into one.*

roll in [*phrasal verb*] *informal* **1** ***be rolling in (something)*** **:** to have a large amount of (something) • They *were rolling in* money/cash. = They ***were rolling in (the) dough***. = They ***were rolling in it***. **2 :** to appear or arrive in large numbers or amounts • The money has been *rolling in.* • Donations *rolled in* to help the hurricane victims. **3 :** to arrive at a place especially later than usual or expected • Delegates *rolled in* from all parts of the country. • He finally *rolled in* at 3:30 in the morning.

rolling in the aisles see AISLE

roll off the tongue see [1]TONGUE

roll on *Brit, informal* — used to say that you want a time or event to come quickly • *Roll on* Friday. I can't wait for the weekend!

roll out [*phrasal verb*] ***roll out (something) or roll (something) out*** **1 :** to offer or sell (something) for the first time • The company is expected to *roll out* [=*launch*] several new products next year. — see also ROLLOUT **2 :** to make (something that has been rolled into the shape of a tube) long and flat again • He *rolled out* [=*unrolled*] the sleeping bags.

roll out of bed *informal* **:** to rise after sleeping in a bed and especially after sleeping later than usual • She *rolled out of bed* just before noon.

roll out the red carpet see RED CARPET

roll over [*phrasal verb*] **1** *informal* **:** to allow yourself to be easily defeated or controlled **:** to make no effort to fight or compete • I'm not going to just *roll over* and let them do what they want. **2** ***roll over (something) or roll (something) over*** **a :** to delay the payment of (something, such as a debt) • He wanted to *roll over* the repayment of the loan until later. **b :** to place (invested money) in a new investment of the same kind • She *rolled over* her investments from one fund to another. — see also ROLLOVER

roll the dice see [1]DICE

roll up [*phrasal verb*] **1** ***roll up (something) or roll (something) up*** **a :** to move (something) up especially by turning a handle • She *rolled up* the car window. **b :** to fold up the ends of (something, such as a shirt sleeve or pants leg) to make it shorter • She *rolled up* her jeans and stepped into the water. **2** *informal* **:** to arrive at a place in a vehicle • Celebrities *rolled up* in their limousines. **3** *Brit* — used to invite people to gather around to see a show or to buy things • *Roll up, roll up* [=(*chiefly US*) *step right up*]— you won't find cheaper watches anywhere else! — see also [1]ROLL 4c, 5 (above)

roll up your sleeves *informal* **:** to prepare to work hard • It's time to *roll up our sleeves* and get the job done. • Congress needs to *roll up its sleeves* and pass the bill now.

roll with the punches *informal* **:** to not allow yourself to become upset by things that happen • *Roll with the punches* and don't let life get you down!

roll your r's **:** to pronounce the sound /r/ with a trill • He *rolls his r's* when he speaks Spanish.

[2]roll /ˈroʊl/ *noun, pl* **rolls** [*count*]

1 : a long piece of cloth, paper, film, tape, etc., that is rolled to form the shape of a tube or ring • There are two photos left on this *roll.* • *rolls* of film/tape • a *roll* of toilet paper

2 : a paper tube that holds candies, coins, etc., inside • a *roll* of mints/quarters

3 a : a small loaf of bread for one person to eat • a dinner *roll* • tuna salad (served) on a *roll* • a hamburger *roll* [=*bun*] **b :** a sandwich made with a bread roll • a ham/cheese *roll* • (*US*) a clam/lobster *roll* **c :** a usually round sweet cake • cinnamon/sweet *rolls* — compare STICKY BUN; see also JELLY ROLL, SWISS ROLL

4 : a food that is rolled up for cooking or serving • cabbage/sausage/sushi *rolls* • *rolls* of sliced ham/turkey — see also EGG ROLL

5 : a thick fold of fat, skin, etc. • A *roll* of fat stuck out from under his shirt. • *rolls* of flesh/skin

6 : an official list of names • the voter *rolls* = (*US*) the election *rolls* [=a list of the people who can vote in an election] • welfare *rolls* [=a list of people on welfare] • The teacher called out the names on the *roll.* = The teacher ***called/took the roll***. — see also HONOR ROLL, PAYROLL

– compare [3]ROLL; see also BANKROLL

[3]roll *noun, pl* **rolls** [*count*]

1 : a sound that is produced by a series of quick hits on a drum • a *roll* of the drum — see also DRUM ROLL

2 : a deep, continuous sound • We heard the *roll* of thunder/cannons in the distance.

3 : an act of rolling something • With a *roll of* the dice, he won $100. • She showed her annoyance with a *roll of* her eyes. [=showed her annoyance by rolling her eyes]

4 *chiefly US* **:** a movement in which your body makes a complete turn forward or backward on the ground • a forward/backward *roll* [=*somersault*]

5 : the act of moving or leaning from side to side • We felt the *roll* of the ship.

6 : a movement of an airplane in which the airplane is turned upside down and then right side up again

a roll in the hay *informal + old-fashioned* **:** an act of having sex with someone

a roll of the dice see [1]DICE

on a roll *informal* **:** experiencing a series of successes • The team has been *on a roll* [=has been playing well and winning many games] since midseason. • He's a funny guy, and last night he was really *on a roll.* [=he was saying many funny things]

– compare [2]ROLL; see also ROCK AND ROLL

roll•back /ˈroʊlˌbæk/ *noun, pl* **-backs** [*count*] *chiefly US* **:** the act of rolling back something: such as **a :** a reduction or decrease in something • *rollbacks* in mortgage rates • a government-ordered *rollback* of gasoline prices • a *rollback* in environmental regulations **b :** the act of reversing or undoing something • a *rollback* of previous wage concessions

roll bar *noun, pl* ~ **bars** [*count*] **:** a metal bar in the roof of a car or other vehicle that is designed to protect riders if the vehicle rolls over

roll call *noun, pl* ~ **calls**

1 : the act of saying each of the names on a list to find out who is present [*count*] — usually singular • The sergeant began a/the *roll call.* [*noncount*] Two students missed *roll call.*

2 [*count*] **:** a list of people or things — usually singular • The policy is supported by an impressive *roll call* of scientists.

roll•er /ˈroʊlɚ/ *noun, pl* **-ers** [*count*]

1 a : a part that rolls and is used to move, press, shape, spread, or smooth something • the *rollers* of a conveyor belt • They moved the monument on *rollers.* • He flattened the clay with a *roller.* • a paint *roller* — see also STEAMROLLER **b :** a cylinder or rod on which something (such as a window shade or a map) is rolled up

2 : a small plastic or metal tube around which hair is wrapped to make it curl • Her hair was in *rollers.* [=*curlers*]

3 : a long, powerful ocean wave

4 : a ball that rolls slowly along the ground • (*baseball*) He hit a slow *roller* to the shortstop.

– see also HIGH ROLLER

Roll•er•blade /ˈroʊlɚˌbleɪd/ *trademark* — used for a skate that has wheels set in a straight line on the bottom

roll•er coast•er /ˈroʊlɚˌkoʊstɚ/ *noun, pl* ~ **-ers** [*count*]

1 : a ride at an amusement park which is like a small, open train with tracks that are high off the ground and that have sharp curves and steep hills • We went for a ride on the *roller coaster.* • a *roller-coaster* ride

2 : a situation or experience that involves sudden and extreme changes • The divorce was an emotional *roller coaster*

R

roller coaster

for both of them. • He's had a *roller-coaster* career. [=a career with many ups and downs]

Roller Derby *service mark* — used for a sports event in which two teams skate on roller skates around an oval track

roller rink *noun, pl* **~ rinks** [*count*] *chiefly US* : an enclosed area with a smooth floor that is used for roller-skating

roller skate *noun, pl* **~ skates** [*count*] : a shoe that has wheels on the bottom and that you wear on your foot in order to skate on a flat surface — usually plural • a pair of *roller skates* — see picture at SKATE

roller–skate *verb* **-skates; -skat·ed; -skat·ing** [*no obj*] : to skate on a flat surface with roller skates • I had never *roller-skated* until last week.
– **roller skater** *noun, pl* **~ -ers** [*count*] – **roller–skating** *noun* [*noncount*] • She loves *roller-skating.* • Let's ***go roller-skating.***

[1]rol·lick·ing /ˈrɑːlɪkɪŋ/ *adj, always used before a noun, informal* : enjoyable in a lively or noisy way • We had a *rollicking* good time. • a *rollicking* tale/tune

[2]rollicking *noun, pl* **-ings** [*count*] *Brit, informal* : the act of angrily criticizing someone who has done something wrong • Their boss ***gave them a rollicking.*** [=*scolding, tongue-lashing*] = They ***got a rollicking*** from their boss.

rolling /ˈroulɪŋ/ *adj, always used before a noun* : having gentle slopes or hills • *rolling* hills/prairies

rolling pin *noun, pl* **~ pins** [*count*] : a long cylinder that is used for making dough flat and smooth — see picture at KITCHEN

rolling stock *noun* [*noncount*] : the wheeled vehicles that are owned and used by a railroad

roll of honour *noun, pl* **rolls of honour** [*count*] *Brit* : HONOR ROLL

roll–on /ˈroulˌɑːn/ *adj, always used before a noun* : rubbed or spread on the body with a bottle that has a rolling ball set into its top • a *roll-on* deodorant/antiperspirant
– **roll–on** *noun, pl* **-ons** [*count*] • deodorants sold as *roll-ons*, sprays, or sticks

roll·out /ˈroulˌaʊt/ *noun, pl* **-outs** [*count, noncount*] : an occasion when a new product or service is first offered for sale or use • the national *rollout* of a new wireless service — see also *roll out* at [1]ROLL

roll·over /ˈroulˌouvɚ/ *noun, pl* **-overs** [*count, noncount*]
1 a : the act of delaying the payment of a debt **b** : the act of placing invested money in a new investment of the same kind — see also *roll over* at [1]ROLL
2 *chiefly US* : an accident in which a car, truck, etc., turns over • He was injured in a *rollover* (accident) on the highway.
3 *chiefly Brit* : prize money in a lottery that is not won and so is added to the prize money of the next lottery

roll·up /ˈroulˌʌp/ *noun, pl* **-ups** [*count*] : something that is rolled into the shape of a tube: such as **a** *US* : a food that is rolled up for cooking or serving **b** *usually* ***roll-up*** *Brit* : a cigarette that you roll yourself
– **roll–up** *adj* • *roll-up* blinds

[1]ro·ly–po·ly /ˌrouliˈpouli/ *adj, informal* : short and fat • a *roly-poly* man

[2]roly–poly *noun, pl* **-lies** [*count, noncount*] *Brit* : a sweet dough that is spread with jam, rolled up, and baked or steamed — called also *roly-poly pudding*

ROM /ˈrɑːm/ *noun* [*noncount*] : the part of a computer in which information that cannot be changed is stored — called also *read-only memory*; compare RAM; see also CD-ROM

ro·maine /rouˈmeɪn/ *noun* [*noncount*] *US* : a type of lettuce that has long, crisp leaves — called also (*US*) *romaine lettuce*, (*Brit*) *cos lettuce*; see color picture on page C4

[1]Ro·man /ˈroumən/ *noun, pl* **-mans**
1 [*count*] **a** : a person born, raised, or living in Rome **b** : a citizen of the ancient Roman Empire
2 ***roman*** [*noncount*] : letters, numbers, etc., that stand upright instead of slanting : roman type • The type should be set in *roman.* — see picture at FONT

[2]Roman *adj*
1 a : of or relating to Rome or the people of Rome • the *Roman* population • the *Roman* skyline **b** : of or relating to the ancient Roman Empire • a *Roman* emperor • *Roman* law
2 ***roman*** : having letters, numbers, etc., that stand upright instead of slanting • These words are roman. • *roman* type

Roman alphabet *noun*
the Roman alphabet : the alphabet that was used for writing Latin and that is now used for writing English and many other European languages

Roman candle *noun, pl* **~ -dles** [*count*] : a firework that is a long tube that shoots out balls or stars of fire one at a time

Roman Catholic *adj* : belonging or relating to the Christian church that is led by the pope • a *Roman Catholic* priest
– **Roman Catholic** *noun, pl* **~ -lics** [*count*] • Most of the people in this part of the country are *Roman Catholics.*
– **Roman Catholicism** *noun* [*noncount*]

[1]ro·mance /rouˈmæns/ *noun, pl* **-manc·es**
1 : an exciting and usually short relationship between lovers [*count*] They had a brief *romance* when they were younger. • a summer *romance* • They've ended their *romance.* [*noncount*] Their friendship blossomed into *romance.* • a tale of love and *romance*
2 [*noncount*] : the feeling of being in love • After only three years together, the *romance* in their relationship was gone.
3 [*count*] **a** : an exciting story often set in the past • a medieval *romance* **b** : a love story • She likes reading paperback *romances.* • an old-fashioned Hollywood *romance* — often used before another noun • a *romance* novel
4 [*noncount*] **a** : the quality of something that makes it exciting and attractive • the *romance* of the old West • The novel evoked the *romance* of Paris in the 20s. **b** : the excitement or emotional attraction that people feel for something • a book about America's *romance* with the open road

[2]romance *verb* **-mances; -manced; -manc·ing**
1 [+ *obj*] : to have or try to have a romantic relationship with (someone) • He was always *romancing* younger women. • She was *romanced* by several wealthy young men.
2 [+ *obj*] *US* : to give special attention to (someone) in order to get something that you want from that person • The museum's director spends a lot of time *romancing* potential donors. • a college athlete who's being *romanced* by several pro teams
3 [*no obj*] : to talk about something in a way that makes it seem better than it really is • They were *romancing* about the past.

Ro·mance language /rouˈmæns-/ *noun, pl* **~ -guages** [*count*] : a language (such as French, Italian, or Spanish) that developed from Latin

Ro·man·esque /ˌroumәˈnɛsk/ *adj* : of or relating to a style of architecture that was used in Europe during the 11th and 12th centuries and that included round arches, thick and heavy walls, and small windows • a *Romanesque* cathedral

Roman nose *noun, pl* **~ noses** [*count*] : a large nose that curves outward at the top

Roman numeral *noun, pl* **~ -als** [*count*] : one of the letters that were used by the ancient Romans to represent numbers and that are still used today • In *Roman numerals* "X" is equal to the number 10. — compare ARABIC NUMERAL

[1]ro·man·tic /rouˈmæntɪk/ *adj* [*more* ~; *most* ~]
1 a : of, relating to, or involving love between two people • She had *romantic* feelings for him. • He had a *romantic* relationship with a coworker. • Her latest movie is a *romantic* comedy. [=a comedy about two people who fall in love with each other] • His brother was having *romantic* troubles at the time. • She won't discuss her *romantic* life with the press. **b** : making someone think of love : suitable for romance • a *romantic* sunset/dinner/song **c** : thinking about love and doing and saying things to show that you love someone • Why can't you be more *romantic*?
2 : not realistic or practical : not based on what is real • He has some *romantic* notions about life on a farm. • She had a lot of big *romantic* dreams of becoming an actress.

3 *Romantic* : of or relating to Romanticism : stressing or appealing to the emotions or imagination • the *Romantic* poets/movement • Beethoven was the first great *Romantic* composer.
– ro•man•ti•cal•ly /roʊˈmæntɪkli/ *adv* • They were *romantically* involved. [=they had a romantic/sexual relationship with each other]

²romantic *noun, pl* **-tics** [*count*]
1 : a person who thinks a lot about love and does and says things that show strong feelings of love for someone • She married a real *romantic* who brings her roses every day.
2 : someone who is not realistic or practical : someone who thinks that things are better or more exciting than they really are • Law school is no place for idealists and *romantics.* • She's a hopeless/incurable *romantic.*
3 *Romantic* : a writer, musician, or artist whose work stresses emotion and imagination : a writer, musician, or artist of Romanticism • Beethoven was the first great *Romantic* among composers.

ro•man•ti•cism /roʊˈmæntəˌsɪzəm/ *noun* [*noncount*]
1 *Romanticism* : a style of art, literature, etc., during the late 18th and early 19th centuries that emphasized the imagination and emotions
2 : the quality or state of being impractical or unrealistic : romantic feelings or ideas • Try not to discourage the *romanticism* of college students.

ro•man•ti•cize *also Brit* **ro•man•ti•cise** /roʊˈmæntəˌsaɪz/ *verb* **-ciz•es; -cized; -ciz•ing :** to think about or describe something as being better or more attractive or interesting than it really is : to show, describe, or think about something in a romantic way [+ *obj*] The movie *romanticizes* [=*idealizes*] the old South. • He has *romanticized* notions of army life. • a *romanticized* view of politics [*no obj*] We were *romanticizing* about the past.

Rom•a•ny /ˈrɑːməni, ˈroʊməni/ *noun, pl* **-nies**
1 [*count*] **:** GYPSY
2 [*noncount*] **:** the language of the Gypsies
– Romany *adj*

Ro•meo /ˈroʊmijoʊ/ *noun, pl* **-me•os** [*count*] **:** a man who has many lovers or who shows strong feelings of love by doing romantic things • He was quite a *Romeo* when he was younger.

¹romp /ˈrɑːmp/ *noun, pl* **romps** [*count*] *informal*
1 : an enjoyable time of rough and noisy play • The dogs love a good *romp* through the woods.
2 : an easy victory • The game turned into a *romp* in the second half.
3 : an enjoyable and lively movie, book, play, etc. • His latest film is a wildly amusing *romp.*
4 *often humorous* **:** an act of sexual intercourse • a movie about a businessman having a *romp* with his secretary

²romp *verb* **romps; romped; romp•ing** [*no obj*]
1 : to play in a rough and noisy way • The kids were *romping* in the yard.
2 : to easily win a race, contest, etc. — often + *to* • The home team *romped to* a 21–6 win/victory. • (*chiefly Brit*) He is now the favorite to ***romp home*** (*to* victory) in the upcoming election.
3 *informal* **:** to move, go, or proceed in a quick, easy, or playful way — usually + *through* • Hundreds of fans *romped through* the streets. • She *romped through* the early rounds of the tournament. • The team *romped through* the season undefeated.

romp•er /ˈrɑːmpɚ/ *noun, pl* **-ers** [*count*] *chiefly US* **:** a piece of clothing that consists of a shirt with attached pants and that is worn especially by children — usually plural • a little girl wearing *rompers* — called also (*chiefly Brit*) *romper suit*

ron•do /ˈrɑːndoʊ/ *noun, pl* **-dos** [*count*] **:** a type of music for instruments in which the main tune at the beginning is repeated after each of the other tunes that are used

¹roof /ˈruːf/ *noun, pl* **roofs** [*count*]
1 : the cover or top of a building, vehicle, etc. • a shingle/slate/tile *roof* • The *roof* is leaking. • the *roof* of a car • The *roof* of the old barn collapsed. • We don't have much money, but at least we ***have a roof over our heads.*** [=at least we have somewhere to live] • You'll do what I say as long as you're living ***under my roof.*** [=as long as you are living in my house] • They all live ***under the same roof.*** [=in the same house] • We hope to have sales and service ***under one roof*** [=at the same location] in the near future. — see also MOONROOF, SUNROOF
2 : the top of the inside of a tunnel, cave, etc.
3 : the top of the inside of your mouth • He bit into a hot slice of pizza and burned the *roof* of his mouth.
go through the roof *informal* **1 :** to become very angry or upset • When they realized he'd lied to them, his parents *went through the roof.* **2 :** to rise to a very high level • Sales of their new CD have *gone through the roof.*
hit the roof see ¹HIT
raise the roof *informal* **:** to make a lot of noise by playing music, celebrating, shouting, etc. • The crowd *raised the roof* when the winning goal was scored. • His mother *raised the roof* when he came home late.
through the roof *chiefly US, informal* **:** at an extremely high level • Ticket prices are *through the roof.*
– roof•less /ˈruːfləs/ *adj* • a *roofless* stadium

²roof *verb* **roofs; roofed; roof•ing** [+ *obj*] **:** to cover (something, such as a building) with a roof — often + *over* or *in* • We *roofed over/in* the patio. — often used as *(be) roofed* • Our house *is roofed* with asphalt shingles.
– roofed /ˈruːft/ *adj* • a *roofed* front porch • thatch-*roofed* houses

roof•er /ˈruːfɚ/ *noun, pl* **-ers** [*count*] **:** a person who builds or repairs roofs

roof•ing /ˈruːfɪŋ/ *noun* [*noncount*]
1 : material that is used for building or repairing a roof • asphalt shingles used for *roofing*
2 : the work of building or repairing roofs • He did some *roofing* in the summer. • a *roofing* contractor

roof•line /ˈruːfˌlaɪn/ *noun, pl* **-lines** [*count*] **:** the outline or outer edge of a roof

roof rack *noun, pl* **~ racks** [*count*] **:** a frame that is attached to the roof of a vehicle and that is used for holding luggage, bicycles, skis, etc.

roof•top /ˈruːfˌtɑːp/ *noun, pl* **-tops** [*count*] **:** the upper surface of a roof • They have a garden on the *rooftop* of the apartment building. • He wanted to ***shout from the rooftops*** when he got the job. — often used before another noun • a *rooftop* television antenna • a *rooftop* garden

rook /ˈrʊk/ *noun, pl* **rooks** [*count*]
1 : a large, black European bird that is related to the crow
2 : a piece in the game of chess that looks like a castle tower : CASTLE — see picture at CHESS

rook•ie /ˈrʊki/ *noun, pl* **-ies** [*count*] *chiefly US*
1 : a first-year player in a professional sport • There are three *rookies* in the starting lineup. — often used before another noun • a *rookie* quarterback • This is his *rookie* season. [=his first season playing]
2 : a person who has just started a job or activity and has little experience : BEGINNER • an experienced policeman whose partner is a *rookie* — often used before another noun • a *rookie* cop

¹room /ˈruːm/ *noun, pl* **rooms**
1 [*count*] **a :** a part of the inside of a building that is divided from other areas by walls and a door and that has its own floor and ceiling • Cigarette smoke filled the *room.* • I could hear the TV from the next *room.* • The salesman went into the ***back room*** [=a room in the back of a building] to get another pair of shoes for me to try. **b :** a room in a house, hotel, etc., where someone sleeps • a double *room* [=a room in a hotel where two people can sleep] • Go to your *room!* • He rents *rooms* to college students. — see also BEDROOM, GUEST ROOM
2 [*noncount*] **:** space that is used for something • We're running out of *room* in the office. • The sofa takes up too much *room.* • In the backyard there is enough *room* to run and play. • Is there enough *room* to turn the car around? • There's only *room* for five people in the car. • Don't eat too much. You should leave some *room* for dessert. • There's no more *room* on the computer disk to save the file. • Can we ***make/find room*** in the garage for the bicycles? — see also ELBOW ROOM, HEADROOM, LEGROOM, STANDING ROOM
3 [*singular*] **:** the people in a room • The whole *room* cheered/applauded.
4 [*noncount*] **:** the possibility for something to happen or exist — often + *for* • There is *room for* improvement in your essay. [=your essay is not as good as it could be] • There is no *room for* doubt about his guilt. [=his guilt is certain]
5 *rooms* [*plural*] *Brit, old-fashioned* **:** APARTMENT • I visited his *rooms* in London.

²room *verb* **rooms; roomed; room•ing** [*no obj*] *US* **:** to live in a room, apartment, or house with another person — + *together* or *with* • We *roomed together* in college. [=we were

R

roommates in college] • He *roomed with* his brother for several years.

room and board *noun [noncount] chiefly US* : a place to stay with meals provided and included in the price • We paid $50 (for) *room and board*. [=(*chiefly Brit*) *bed and board*]

room·er /ˈruːmɚ/ *noun, pl* **-ers** [*count*] *US* : a person who pays rent to live in a house with its owner

room·ful /ˈruːmfəl/ *noun, pl* **room·fuls** /ˈruːmfəlz/ *also* **rooms·ful** /ˈruːmzfəl/ [*count*] : the amount of people or things that are in a room — usually + *of* • a *roomful of* strangers • A *roomful of* wiring and circuits can now be reduced to a tiny computer chip.

room·ie /ˈruːmi/ *noun, pl* **-ies** [*count*] *US, informal* : ROOMMATE • She was my *roomie* in college.

rooming house *noun, pl* ~ **houses** [*count*] *US* : a house where rooms with furniture are rented to people to live in • After losing his job, he moved to a cheap *rooming house*.

room·mate /ˈruːmˌmeɪt/ *noun, pl* **-mates** [*count*] : a person who shares a room, apartment, or house with someone else • She was my college *roommate*. = We were *roommates* in college.

room service *noun [noncount]* : the service that is provided to hotel guests so that they can have food, drinks, etc., brought to their rooms • *Room service* is available. • He ordered a meal from *room service*. • She called *room service*.

room temperature *noun [noncount]* : a comfortable temperature that is not too hot or too cold • Store the wine at *room temperature*.

roomy /ˈruːmi/ *adj* **room·i·er; -est** [*also more* ~; *most* ~] : having plenty of space or room • The car was *roomy* [=*spacious*] inside.

– **room·i·ness** *noun [noncount]* • the *roominess* of the car

¹roost /ˈruːst/ *noun, pl* **roosts** [*count*] : a place where birds rest or sleep

rule the roost *informal* : to have the most control or authority in a group • In my small elementary school, bullies *ruled the roost*.

²roost *verb* **roosts; roost·ed; roost·ing** [*no obj*] *of a bird* : to rest or sleep somewhere • Pigeons *roost* on the building's ledge.

come home to roost ♦ If something from your past *comes home to roost* or ***your/the chickens come home to roost***, you experience problems that you deserve because they are caused by your past actions or are like the problems you have caused for other people. • Her bad decisions are *coming home to roost*. • He's been cheating people for years but now *the chickens are* (finally) *coming home to roost*. [=he is getting what he deserves]

roost·er /ˈruːstɚ/ *noun, pl* **-ers** [*count*] *chiefly US* : an adult male chicken • We heard the crow of a *rooster*. — called also *cock*; compare HEN

¹root /ˈruːt/ *noun, pl* **roots**

1 [*count*] : the part of a plant that grows underground, gets water from the ground, and holds the plant in place • Elm trees have shallow *roots*. • Pull weeds up by the *roots* so that they don't grow back. — see color picture on page C6

2 [*count*] : the part of a tooth, hair, fingernail, etc., that is attached to the body • You can tell that she dyes her hair blonde because her dark *roots* are showing.

3 [*count*] **a** : the cause or source of something — usually singular • He believes that money is the *root* of all evil. [=money causes people to do bad things] • We need to get to the *root* of the problem. = We need to get to the ***root cause*** of the problem. • Simple greed was ***at the root of*** the robbery. [=was the reason for the robbery] **b** : the origin of something — usually plural • Rock-and-roll music has its *roots* in blues music. [=rock-and-roll music originated/developed from blues music]

4 ***roots*** [*plural*] **a** : the family history of a person or a group of people • They have traced their *roots* [=*ancestry*] back several generations. **b** : a special connection to something — + *in* • She's a dedicated teacher with *roots in* the community. • His family has *roots in* the New York theater scene. • a novelist with *roots* deep *in* Southern life — see also GRASS ROOTS

5 [*count*] *mathematics* : a number that is multiplied by itself a certain number of times to produce another number • 2 is the 4th *root* of 16. [=2 x 2 x 2 x 2 = 16] — see also CUBE ROOT, SQUARE ROOT

6 [*count*] : a word from which other words are formed • "Butler" and "bottle" come from the same Latin *root*. • "Hold" is the *root* of "holder."

put down roots : to become a member of a community and begin to feel that it is your home : to settle and live in one place • The family *put down roots* in New England. [=they made New England their home]

root and branch *chiefly Brit* **1** : complete or thorough • a *root and branch* overhaul of local schools **2** : completely or thoroughly • The laws were reformed *root and branch*.

take root **1** *of a plant* : to grow and develop roots • There isn't enough time for the grass to *take root* before winter. **2** : to begin to develop • The classroom should be a place where creativity can *take root* and flourish. • It was years before democratic ideals *took root* in that part of the world.

²root *verb* **roots; root·ed; root·ing**

1 *of a plant* **a** [*no obj*] : to grow and develop roots • The plants had difficulty *rooting* in the poor soil. **b** [+ *obj*] : to make (a plant) grow and develop roots • She *rooted* the seedlings in pots before planting them in the garden. • The lichen *rooted* itself to the rock. • The lichen was *rooted* to the rock.

2 [+ *obj*] : to make (someone) unable to move • Fear *rooted* me to my chair. — usually used as *(be) rooted* • I *was rooted* to my chair by/with fear.

root in [*phrasal verb*] ***root (something) in (something)*** : to form, make, or develop (something) by using (something) as a basis • He *roots* his art *in* reality. [=bases his art on the real world] — usually used as *(be) rooted in* • His art *is rooted in* reality. • Her opinions *are* deeply *rooted in* her faith. • a dance *rooted in* African tradition

– compare ³ROOT, ⁴ROOT

³root *verb* **roots; rooted; rooting** [*no obj*]

1 *always followed by an adverb or preposition* : to search for something by moving around or by turning things over • We *rooted* through the desk drawers for the phone bill. • She *rooted* around in her purse to find her keys. • I think I'll *root* around for some leftovers in the fridge.

2 *of animals* : to look for food under the ground by digging with the nose : GRUB • a *rooting* pig

root out [*phrasal verb*] ***root (something or someone) out*** *or* ***root out (something or someone)*** **1** : to find and remove (something or someone) • The mayor was determined to *root out* corruption in city government. **2** : to find (something or someone) after searching for a long time • He finally *rooted out* the cause of the problem.

– compare ²ROOT, ⁴ROOT

⁴root *verb* **roots; rooted; rooting**

root for [*phrasal verb*] ***root for (someone or something)*** : to express or show support for (a person, a team, etc.) • They always *root for* the home team. • We're *rooting for* the underdog. : to hope for the success of (someone or something) • Remember that we're all *rooting for* you. [=we all want to see you succeed]

root on [*phrasal verb*] ***root (someone or something) on*** *US* : to help (someone or something) to win or succeed by expressing or showing strong support • The team is playing for the championship tomorrow, and thousands of fans will be there to *root* them *on*. • Her friends and family were there to *root* her *on* to victory.

– compare ²ROOT, ³ROOT

– **root·er** /ˈruːtɚ/ *noun, pl* **-ers** [*count*]

root beer *noun, pl* ~ **beers** [*count, noncount*] : a sweet, brown drink that is flavored with roots and herbs and that contains bubbles • a bottle of *root beer*

root canal *noun, pl* ~ **-nals** [*count*] : a dental procedure to save a tooth by removing the diseased or injured tissue in its root • I need to have a *root canal*.

root cellar *noun, pl* ~ **-lars** [*count*] *chiefly US* : a room or large hole in the ground where vegetables (such as potatoes and carrots) are kept

root·less /ˈruːtləs/ *adj* : having no home or connection to a place • He was leading a *rootless* existence. • a *rootless* drifter

– **root·less·ness** *noun [noncount]*

root vegetable *noun, pl* ~ **-tables** [*count*] : a vegetable (such as a carrot or potato) that grows under the ground

¹rope /ˈroʊp/ *noun, pl* **ropes**

1 : a strong, thick string that is made by twisting many thin strings or fibers together [*count*] Tie the end of the *rope* to the post. • She made a knot in the *rope*. [*noncount*] a six-foot length of *rope* • We used *rope* to tie down the furniture in the trailer. • The hostages were tied up with *rope*. — see also JUMP ROPE, SKIPPING ROPE, TIGHTROPE, TOWROPE

2 [*count*] : a string on which a number of similar things are held together • a *rope* of pearls

3 *the ropes* : the special way things are done at a particular place or in a particular activity • The veteran cop showed the rookie *the ropes*. • It will take a few weeks for new employees to ***learn the ropes*** • someone who ***knows the ropes***
4 *the ropes* : a fence made of rope that encloses a boxing or wrestling ring • The boxer was pushed back against *the ropes*.
jump/skip rope *US* : to jump over a rope that is being swung near the ground for exercise or as a game • He *jumps rope* to warm up before the game. • The kids are outside *jumping rope*.
money for old rope see MONEY
on the ropes *informal* : in a very bad position or situation : very close to failure or defeat • The company is *on the ropes* and in danger of closing.
the end of your rope see [1]END

[2]**rope** *verb* **ropes; roped; rop·ing** [+ *obj*]
1 *always followed by an adverb or preposition* : to bind, fasten, or tie (something or someone) with a rope • The dog was *roped* to the fence. • The boats were *roped* together at the dock. • Mountain climbers often *rope* themselves together for safety.
2 *chiefly US* : to catch (an animal) by throwing a circle of rope around it : LASSO • He tried to *rope* the calf.
3 *informal* : to use clever or tricky methods to get (someone) to do something — + *in* or *into* • I didn't want to go to the party, but my friends somehow *roped* me *in*. • My friends *roped* me *into* going to the party. • I always seem to get *roped into* driving.
rope off [*phrasal verb*] ***rope off (something)*** or ***rope (something) off*** : to separate (an area) from another area with rope • The police *roped off* the street for the summer festival. • Part of the exhibit had been *roped off*.

rope ladder *noun, pl* ~ **-ders** [*count*] : a ladder that has short pieces (called rungs) which are held between two long ropes

ropy *also* **rop·ey** /ˈroupi/ *adj* **rop·i·er; -est** [*also more* ~; *most* ~]
1 : similar to rope : like rope in appearance • *ropy* noodles/vines
2 *Brit, informal* **a** : in bad condition • a *ropy* [=*worn*] suit : of bad quality • *ropy* [=*shoddy*] plumbing **b** : ill or unwell • The passengers looked a bit *ropy* after the bumpy flight.

ro–ro /ˈrouˌrou/ *noun, pl* **ro–ros** [*count*] *Brit* : a ship that is designed and equipped to allow vehicles (such as cars or tanks) to be driven on and off ✧ *Ro-ro* is an abbreviation of "roll on, roll off."

Ror·schach test /ˈroɚˌʃɑːk-/ *noun, pl* ~ **tests** [*count*] *technical* : a personality and intelligence test in which someone looks at ink blots of different shapes and then describes what the shapes look like

ro·sa·ry /ˈrouzəri/ *noun, pl* **-ries**
1 [*count*] : a string of beads that are used by Roman Catholics for counting prayers
2 *the Rosary* : a set of Roman Catholic prayers that are repeated in a specific order • recite/say *the Rosary*

[1]**rose** *past tense of* [1]RISE

[2]**rose** /ˈrouz/ *noun, pl* **ros·es**
1 [*count*] : a flower with a sweet smell that is usually white, yellow, red, or pink and that grows on a bush which has thorns on the stems • a bouquet of *roses* • He sent a dozen red *roses* to his girlfriend on Valentine's Day. — see color picture on page C6; see also BED OF ROSES
2 [*noncount*] : a slightly purplish-pink color — see color picture on page C3
come out/up smelling like a rose or ***come out/up smelling like/of roses*** *informal* : to have success or good fortune in a situation in which you were likely to fail, be harmed, etc. • The scandal forced several board members to resign, but the chairman *came out smelling like a rose*. [=the chairman's reputation was not damaged at all]
coming up roses *informal* : turning out to be good • Now that he finally has a job, everything's *coming up roses* for him. [=many good things are happening in his life]
(stop and) smell the roses *informal* : to stop being busy and enjoy the pleasant things in life • You shouldn't work so hard. You need to take some time to *stop and smell the roses*.
wake up and smell the roses see [1]WAKE

ro·sé /rouˈzeɪ, *Brit* ˈrəuzeɪ/ *noun, pl* **-sés** [*count, noncount*] : wine that has a pink color

ro·se·ate /ˈrouzijət/ *adj, literary* : having a pink color • a bird with *roseate* feathers

rose·bud /ˈrouzˌbʌd/ *noun, pl* **-buds** [*count*] : the flower of a rose that has not opened : the bud of a rose

rose·bush /ˈrouzˌbuʃ/ *noun, pl* **-bush·es** [*count*] : a bush that produces roses

rose–col·ored (*US*) *or Brit* **rose–col·oured** /ˈrouzˌkʌlɚd/ *adj*
1 : having a pink color • a *rose-colored* wine
2 : tending to think of things as being better than they really are • They always take a *rose-colored* view of the problem. ✧ If you see or view something through ***rose-colored glasses/spectacles***, you think of it as being better than it really is. • He looks at the world through *rose-colored glasses*. [=he looks at the world in an overly optimistic way]

rose hip *noun, pl* ~ **hips** [*count*] : a small fruit that grows on some rosebushes

rose·mary /ˈrouzˌmeri/ *noun* [*noncount*] : an herb that has a sweet smell and that is used in cooking and perfumes • The recipe calls for a tablespoon of *rosemary*. — see color picture on page C6

rose–tint·ed /ˈrouzˌtɪntəd/ *adj* : ROSE-COLORED

ro·sette /rouˈzet/ *noun, pl* **-settes** [*count*]
1 : a badge or ornament that is made of ribbon and folded in the shape of a rose
2 : a design shaped like a rose that is used as a decoration • a *rosette* of chocolate frosting • *Rosettes* are carved in the base of the statue.

rose water *noun* [*noncount*] : liquid made from roses that has a pleasant smell and is used as a perfume or flavoring

rose window *noun, pl* ~ **-dows** [*count*] : a circular window in a church that is made from stained glass with a decorative pattern

rose·wood /ˈrouzˌwud/ *noun* [*noncount*] : the hard, dark, red wood of some tropical trees that is used especially for making furniture and musical instruments

Rosh Ha·sha·nah /ˌrɑːʃhəˈʃɑːnə/ *noun* [*noncount*] : the Jewish New Year observed as a religious holiday in September or October

ros·in /ˈrɑːzn̩/ *noun* [*noncount*] : a hard and slightly sticky substance that has various uses (such as to make the bows of violins and similar instruments move more easily across the strings) — compare RESIN

[1]**ros·ter** /ˈrɑːstɚ/ *noun, pl* **-ters** [*count*]
1 a : a list of the people or things that belong to a particular group, team, etc. • His name has been added to the team *roster*. • a membership *roster* **b** *US* : a group of people or things whose names are included on a roster • The team has a *roster* of 40 players.
2 : a list that shows the order in which a job or duty is to be done by the members of a group • a duty *roster*

[2]**roster** *verb* **-ters; -tered; -ter·ing** [+ *obj*] *Brit* : to include (someone) on a roster of people who will be doing work • He was *rostered* for extra duty.

ros·trum /ˈrɑːstrəm/ *noun, pl* **ros·trums** *or* **ros·tra** /ˈrɑːstrə/ [*count*] *formal* : a small raised platform on a stage

rosy /ˈrouzi/ *adj* **ros·i·er; -est** [*also more* ~; *most* ~]
1 : having a pink color • *rosy* cheeks/peaches
2 : having or producing hope for success or happiness in the future • A young man with a *rosy* [=*promising*] future. • She has a *rosy* [=*optimistic*] outlook on life. • He ***painted a rosy picture*** of the company's future. [=he made the company's future sound very good]

[1]**rot** /ˈrɑːt/ *verb* **rots; rot·ted; rot·ting** : to slowly decay or cause (something) to decay [*no obj*] The wood had *rotted* away. • The apples were left to *rot*. • the smell of *rotting* garbage — often used figuratively • He was ***left to rot*** in jail. [=he was left in jail for a very long time] • I hope he ***rots in hell*** [+ *obj*] Eating too much candy can *rot* your teeth. — sometimes used figuratively • Too much TV will *rot* your brain. ***synonyms*** see [1]DECAY

[2]**rot** *noun* [*noncount*]
1 : the process of rotting or the condition that results when something rots • They found a lot of *rot* in the house's roof. — often used figuratively • moral *rot* • (*chiefly Brit*) ***The rot set in*** [=things started getting really bad] when the factory closed down. • (*Brit*) The team ***stopped the rot*** [=stopped things from getting worse] with a 5–0 win last night. — see also DRY ROT
2 *informal + somewhat old-fashioned* : foolish words or ideas : NONSENSE • That's a lot of *rot*! • all that *rot*

ro·ta /ˈroutə/ *noun, pl* **-tas** [*count*] *Brit* : a list that shows who must do a certain job • a *rota* of housekeeping duties

R

Ro·tar·i·an /roʊˈterijən/ *noun, pl* **-ans** [*count*] : a member of a Rotary Club

[1]**ro·ta·ry** /ˈroʊtəri/ *adj, always used before a noun*

1 : turning around a central point like a wheel ▪ a *rotary* blade ▪ the *rotary* action of the wheel

2 : having a part that turns around a central point like a wheel ▪ an old-fashioned *rotary* phone [=a phone with a dial that turns around a central point]

[2]**rotary** *noun, pl* **-ries** [*count*] *US* : TRAFFIC CIRCLE

Rotary Club *noun, pl* **~ Clubs** [*count*] : an international organization of businesspeople who raise money to help the sick or poor in their local area

ro·tate /ˈroʊˌteɪt, *Brit* rəʊˈteɪt/ *verb* **-tates; -tat·ed; -tat·ing**

1 : to move or turn in a circle [*no obj*] As the gear *rotates*, it turns the other gears. ▪ The Earth *rotates* on its axis. ▪ The planets *rotate* around the sun. ▪ a *rotating* propeller [+ *obj*] The software allows you to *rotate* images. ▪ *Rotate* the sheet of paper 90 degrees.

2 : to regularly change the person who does a particular job so that all the members of a group do it at different times [+ *obj*] The staff *rotates* the weekend shift. [*no obj*] We *rotate*—she does the dishes one week; I do them the next. ▪ The work is done by volunteers ***on a rotating basis***. [=the volunteers take turns doing the work]

3 : to regularly change the place or position of things or people so that each takes the place of another [+ *obj*] You should *rotate* your car's tires once a year. ▪ (*US*) The soldier was *rotated* home after six months. [=the soldier was sent home after six months and another soldier took his place] [*no obj*] The seasons *rotate*.

4 [+ *obj*] **:** to regularly change (crops grown on one piece of land) to make sure the soil stays healthy ▪ They *rotate* alfalfa and/with corn. [=grow alfalfa one year and corn the next]

– ro·tat·able /ˈroʊˌteɪtəbəl, *Brit* rəʊˈteɪtəbəl/ *adj* ▪ a *rotatable* platform

ro·ta·tion /roʊˈteɪʃən/ *noun, pl* **-tions**

1 a [*noncount*] **:** the act or process of moving or turning around a central point ▪ the *rotation* of the Earth around its axis ▪ the *rotation* of the Moon around the Earth **b** [*count*] **:** a complete turn around a central point ▪ The Earth makes one *rotation* every day.

2 a [*noncount*] **:** the act of regularly changing something by replacing it with something else ▪ crop *rotation* ▪ Alfalfa and corn are planted ***in rotation***. **b :** the act of regularly changing the place or position of things or people so that each takes the place of another [*noncount*] the *rotation* of the job of club president [*count*] The car needs a tire *rotation*.

3 [*count*] *US* **:** the group of people who take turns doing something ▪ Where are we in the *rotation*? [=when is it our turn?] ▪ (*baseball*) The team has a good (starting) *rotation*. [=group of pitchers who start games]

– ro·ta·tion·al /roʊˈteɪʃənl/ *adj, always used before a noun, technical* ▪ the *rotational* axis ▪ *rotational* motion

ro·ta·tor cuff /ˈroʊˌteɪtɚ-/ *noun, pl* **~ cuffs** [*count*] *chiefly US, medical* **:** a group of muscles and tendons that are around your shoulder and that allow it to move in all directions

ROTC /ˌɑɚˌoʊˌtiːˈsiː, ˈrɑːtsi/ *noun* [*noncount*] *US* **:** a military program that provides training and financial assistance for college students who become officers in the military at the end of the program ▪ He joined (the) *ROTC*. ▪ *ROTC* training begins tomorrow. ✧ *ROTC* is an abbreviation of "Reserve Officers' Training Corps."

rote /ˈroʊt/ *noun* [*noncount*] **:** the process of learning something by repeating it many times without thinking about it or fully understanding it ▪ The children learned the words to the poem ***by rote***.

– rote *adj, always used before a noun* ▪ *rote* learning/memorization

ro·tis·ser·ie /roʊˈtɪsəri/ *noun, pl* **-ies** [*count*] **:** a piece of equipment that turns meat over a source of heat so that it cooks on all sides ▪ a chicken cooked on a *rotisserie* = a *rotisserie* chicken

ro·tor /ˈroʊtɚ/ *noun, pl* **-tors** [*count*] *technical* **:** a part of a machine that turns around a central point ▪ the *rotor* (blade) of a helicopter ▪ brake *rotors*

[1]**rot·ten** /ˈrɑːtn/ *adj* [*more ~; most ~*]

1 : having rotted or decayed and no longer able to be used, eaten, etc. ▪ *rotten* wood ▪ *rotten* teeth ▪ *rotten* eggs ▪ The bananas ***went rotten***. — sometimes used figuratively ▪ The whole political system is *rotten*. [=*corrupt*]

2 *informal* **a :** very bad or unpleasant ▪ What *rotten* [=*lousy*] luck! ▪ They did a *rotten* job. ▪ We played a *rotten* game. [=we did not play well] ▪ What *rotten* weather we're having. **b** *not used before a noun* **:** not well or healthy ▪ I feel *rotten* today. **c** *not used before a noun* **:** not happy or pleased ▪ I feel *rotten* [=I feel guilty; I am upset] about what I said. **d :** not morally good **:** not honest, kind, etc. ▪ He was a *rotten* husband. [=he was not a very good husband] ▪ She's ***rotten to the core***. [=she's a very bad person; she's a very dishonest person] — see also *rotten apple* at APPLE

3 *always used before a noun, informal* — used for emphasis when you are angry ▪ You can keep your *rotten* money!

– rot·ten·ness /ˈrɑːtnnəs/ *noun* [*noncount*]

[2]**rotten** *adv, informal*

1 : very badly or poorly ▪ He treats her *rotten*.

2 : very much ▪ (*Brit*) He fancies you (something) *rotten*. [=he likes you very much] ▪ Those kids were ***spoiled rotten*** by their mother.

rot·ter /ˈrɑːtɚ/ *noun, pl* **-ters** [*count*] *Brit, informal + old-fashioned* **:** a very bad person ▪ a selfish *rotter*

Rott·wei·ler /ˈrɑːtˌwailɚ/ *noun, pl* **-lers** [*count*] **:** a type of large dog that is often used as a guard dog — see picture at DOG

ro·tund /roʊˈtʌnd/ *adj* [*more ~; most ~*] *literary + humorous* **:** fat and round ▪ a *rotund* face ▪ a short, *rotund* man

– ro·tun·di·ty /roʊˈtʌndəti/ *noun* [*noncount*]

ro·tun·da /roʊˈtʌndə/ *noun, pl* **-das** [*count*] **:** a large, round room and especially one covered by a dome ▪ We stood inside the *rotunda* of the U.S. Capitol Building.

rouble *chiefly Brit spelling of* RUBLE

rouge /ˈruːʒ/ *noun* [*noncount*] *old-fashioned* **:** a red powder or cream that is used to make your cheeks pinker ▪ She was wearing too much *rouge*.

– rouged /ˈruːʒd/ *adj* ▪ *rouged* ladies ▪ heavily *rouged* cheeks

[1]**rough** /ˈrʌf/ *adj* **rough·er; -est** [*also more ~; most ~*]

1 : having a surface that is not even ▪ *rough* tree bark ▪ a cat's *rough* tongue ▪ He trimmed the *rough* edge of the paper. ▪ We traveled over *rough* dirt roads. ▪ They hiked through *rough* terrain/country. — opposite SMOOTH

2 : having or causing sudden, violent movements ▪ a *rough* [=*bumpy*] ride on an old wooden roller coaster ▪ We were a bit shaken from the plane's *rough* landing. — opposite SMOOTH

3 *somewhat informal* **:** difficult or unpleasant to deal with ▪ She's had a *rough* [=*tough*] life/year/time. ▪ He went through a *rough* patch/period after his divorce. ▪ They've hit a few *rough* spots in their marriage. ▪ Despite a *rough* start, the team won more games this season than last. ▪ I had a *rough* night last night. [=I did not sleep well] ▪ It was ***rough going*** [=things were difficult] for a while. ▪ Our ancestors ***had it rough*** [=had a difficult existence] compared to us. ▪ He's ***having a rough time (of it)***. = He's ***going through a rough time***. [=he is having a difficult time; his life has been difficult recently]

4 : not calm **:** having large waves, strong winds, storms, etc. ▪ The sea is *rough* today. ▪ *rough* waters off the coast ▪ We ran into some *rough* [=*stormy*] weather.

5 : not gentle or careful **:** causing or likely to cause harm or injury ▪ These dishes are not made to withstand *rough* handling. ▪ The prisoners complained about *rough* treatment by the guards. ▪ She says the kids are too *rough* [=*rowdy*] when they play. ▪ He doesn't like *rough* sports like hockey. ▪ All right kids—no ***rough stuff***. [=no behaving or playing in a rough way] ▪ Don't ***be so rough on them*** [=don't punish or criticize them so harshly] for making a mistake.

6 : having a lot of crime or danger ▪ I live in a pretty *rough* neighborhood/area.

7 : made or done in a way that is simple or that needs further changes, improvements, etc. ▪ He made a *rough* sketch of the house. ▪ They built a *rough* [=*crude*] shelter out of branches. ▪ He submitted a ***rough draft*** of the article. ▪ The project still has a few ***rough edges***. [=the project still has a few things that need to be changed or finished] ▪ The design is still a bit ***rough around the edges***.

8 *always used before a noun* **:** not precise or exact **:** not including all the details ▪ If I were to make a *rough* guess, I might say there were 100,000 people at the parade. ▪ a *rough* translation of a Chinese proverb ▪ This sketch will give you a *rough* idea of what the house looks like.

9 : having a harsh sound ▪ She has a *rough* voice.

10 *Brit, informal* **:** not well ▪ I'm feeling too *rough* to go out tonight.

R

– **rough·ness** *noun [noncount]* ▪ the *roughness* of the waves ▪ surfaces with varying degrees of *roughness* and smoothness

²rough *adv*
1 : in a rough way ▪ The engine is running a little *rough*. ▪ Life has been treating her pretty *rough*. ▪ He ***plays rough*** with the dog.
2 *Brit* : outside and without shelter ▪ people ***living/sleeping rough*** on the streets

³rough *noun, pl* **roughs**
1 ***the rough golf*** : an area on a golf course covered with tall grass that makes it difficult to hit the ball ▪ He hit his drive into *the rough*.
2 *[count]* : something (such as a drawing) that is done quickly and is not detailed or finished ▪ He showed me a few *roughs* of the new building.
3 *[count] informal + old-fashioned* : a person who is loud and violent ▪ a gang of *roughs* [=*rowdies, hoodlums*]
in rough Brit : in an unfinished form ▪ The plans were done *in rough* for preapproval.
in the rough chiefly US : in an unfinished or rough state ▪ Some of the turquoise is polished and some is *in the rough*. [=not polished] ▪ He admired the beauty of nature *in the rough*. — see also DIAMOND IN THE ROUGH
take the rough with the smooth chiefly Brit : to accept and deal with the bad or unpleasant things that happen in addition to the good or pleasant things ▪ In this business, you have to learn to *take the rough with the smooth*.

⁴rough *verb* **roughs; roughed; rough·ing** *[+ obj] American football + ice hockey* : to hit (a player) very hard in a way that is not allowed by the rules ▪ He was called for *roughing* the kicker/passer.
rough in *[phrasal verb]* ***rough (something) in or rough in (something)*** : to make a rough or unfinished version of (something, such as a design) as the first step in creating the finished version ▪ *Rough in* the lettering on your poster. ▪ He *roughed in* the frame of the new door.
rough it informal : to live usually for a short time without the normal things that make life comfortable ▪ She was *roughing it* in the wilderness.
rough out *[phrasal verb]* ***rough (something) out or rough out (something)*** : to make (something, such as a drawing or a list) quickly and without including all the details ▪ We'll *rough out* a general plan.
rough up *[phrasal verb]* ***rough (someone) up or rough up (someone) informal*** : to hit and hurt (someone) ▪ The prisoner claimed that he was *roughed up* by the guards.

rough·age /ˈrʌfɪʤ/ *noun [noncount]* : plant material that cannot be digested but that helps you to digest other food : FIBER

rough–and–ready /ˌrʌfənˈrɛdi/ *adj [more ~; most ~]*
1 : not complete but good enough to be used ▪ a *rough-and-ready* solution/method
2 : not having polite manners or fancy skills but ready and able to do what needs to be done ▪ *rough-and-ready* soldiers

rough–and–tum·ble /ˌrʌfənˈtʌmbəl/ *adj, always used before a noun [more ~; most ~]*
1 : disorderly, loud, and rough ▪ a *rough-and-tumble* group of soccer fans ▪ a *rough-and-tumble* game
2 : very competitive and aggressive ▪ the *rough-and-tumble* world of politics ▪ a *rough-and-tumble* competitor
– **rough–and–tumble** *noun [noncount]* ▪ the *rough-and-tumble* of our neighborhood soccer games ▪ She joined the *rough-and-tumble* of politics.

rough diamond *noun, pl* ~ **-monds** *[count] Brit* : DIAMOND IN THE ROUGH 1

rough–edged /ˈrʌfˈɛʤd/ *adj* : having a rough quality : not smooth or refined ▪ *rough-edged* blues music ▪ *rough-edged* writing

rough·en /ˈrʌfən/ *verb* **-ens; -ened; -en·ing** : to become rough or cause (something) to become rough *[+ obj] Roughen* the surface with a file before you apply the glue. ▪ Her hands were *roughened* by years of hard work. *[no obj]* Age caused his skin to *roughen*.

rough–hewn /ˈrʌfˈhjuːn/ *adj*
1 : having a rough and uneven surface ▪ *rough-hewn* ceiling beams
2 : not polite or educated ▪ a *rough-hewn* peasant

rough·house /ˈrʌfˌhaus/ *verb* **-hous·es; -housed; -hous·ing** *[no obj] US, informal* : to play in a rough and noisy way ▪ The kids were *roughhousing* in the living room.

rough·ly /ˈrʌfli/ *adv*
1 : not exactly but close in number, quality, meaning, etc. ▪ *Roughly* translated, it means "hurry up!" ▪ The new product is modeled *roughly* on an earlier design. ▪ *Roughly* [=*approximately*] 20 percent of our land is farmland.
2 *[more ~; most ~]* **a** : in a way that is not gentle or careful ▪ He threw the package *roughly* in the truck. ▪ The guard told us *roughly* that we had to stand back. ▪ He pushed her *roughly*. **b** : in a very simple or basic way ▪ a *roughly* [=*crudely*] built shelter ▪ *roughly* sketched drawings **c** : in a way that produces a rough surface ▪ *roughly* cut timber

rough·neck /ˈrʌfˌnɛk/ *noun, pl* **-necks** *[count] chiefly US, informal*
1 : someone who behaves in a rough, rude, or aggressive way ▪ a town overrun by *roughnecks*
2 : someone who works on an oil rig or at an oil well

rough paper *noun [noncount] Brit* : SCRAP PAPER

rough·shod /ˈrʌfˌʃɑːd/ *adv* : without thinking or caring about the opinions, rights, or feelings of others ▪ They accused the government of ***riding roughshod*** over international law. [=of completely ignoring international law] ▪ *(US)* He achieved success by ruthlessly ***running roughshod*** over anyone who got in his way.

rou·lette /ruˈlɛt/ *noun [noncount]* : a game in which a small ball is dropped onto a numbered wheel that is spinning and players bet on which numbered section the ball will rest in — see also RUSSIAN ROULETTE

¹round /ˈraund/ *adj* **round·er; -est** *[also more ~; most ~]*
1 : shaped like a circle or ball ▪ The Earth is *round*. ▪ little *round* meatballs ▪ a *round* table ▪ The baby has a *round* face. ▪ the owl's big, *round* eyes
2 : shaped like a cylinder ▪ a *round* peg
3 : having curves rather than angles ▪ He has *round* shoulders. ▪ a shirt with a *round* collar ▪ The corners are *round*. ▪ the plant's round *leaves*
4 : slightly fat : PLUMP ▪ a large, *round* man ▪ his big, *round* belly
5 *always used before a noun* **a** ◇ A *round* number is a whole number that often ends in 0 or 5 and that is used instead of a more exact number. ▪ The total actually came to $33.02, but the cashier made it a *round* $33. ▪ ***In round numbers/figures***, the cost of the project adds up to two million dollars. ▪ "How much do you want for it?" "How about 50 dollars? That's a ***nice round number***." **b** : exact or complete ▪ a *round* dozen/million
– **round·ness** /ˈraundnəs/ *noun [noncount]* ▪ the perfect *roundness* of the stone

²round *adv*
1 *chiefly Brit* : AROUND
2 : from beginning to end ▪ The bush stays green ***all year round***. [=stays green throughout the entire year] — see also YEAR-ROUND

³round *noun, pl* **rounds**
1 *[count]* **a** : one of a series of similar events — often *+ of* ▪ A new *round of* negotations is scheduled to begin next week. ▪ Her second *round of* chemotherapy recently ended. **b** : a series of similar actions, events, or things — usually *+ of* ▪ She prepared herself for a *round of* appearances on television and radio shows. ▪ an endless *round of* business meetings **c** : a regular series of activities — usually *+ of* ▪ my usual *round of* chores
2 ***rounds*** *[plural]* : a series of regular or similar visits or stops ▪ The doctor is on her *rounds* at the hospital. ▪ *(US)* The doctor is ***making/doing her rounds*** at the hospital. [=the doctor is visiting the different patients she sees every day at the hospital] ▪ *(US)* She *made the rounds of* the stores [=she went to many different stores] looking for bargains.
3 : a route that is regularly covered as part of a job *[plural] (chiefly US)* The mailman was on his *rounds*. *[count] (Brit)* The postman was on his *round*.
4 *[count]* **a** : a stage of a sports competition in which each player or team plays against an opponent and the winner is allowed to continue to the next stage ▪ The team made it to the final *round* of the play-offs. ▪ He made it to the next *round*. **b** : one of the three-minute periods into which a boxing match is divided ▪ The match lasted five *rounds*. **c** : a complete set of holes played in golf : 18 holes of golf ▪ a *round* of golf
5 *[count]* : a number of drinks that are served at the same time to each person in a group ▪ I'll buy the next *round* (of drinks).
6 *[singular]* : a usually short period of applause, cheering, etc. ▪ The winner got a huge *round* of applause.

R

7 [*count*] **a :** a shot fired from a weapon ▪ Several *rounds* were fired. **b :** a bullet for one shot ▪ There was only one *round* left in the gun.

8 [*count*] *music* **:** a song in which three or more singers sing the same melody and words but start at different times

9 [*count*] **:** a round shape ▪ Cut the carrots into *rounds*. [=round slices] ▪ a *round* [=*wheel*] of cheese

10 [*count*] *Brit* **a :** a whole slice of bread or toast **b :** a sandwich that is made with two whole slices of bread — usually + *of* ▪ a *round of* ham sandwich [=a ham sandwich]

in the round **1 :** in a position that allows something to be seen from all sides ▪ a sculpture *in the round* **2 :** with a center stage surrounded by an audience ▪ The play was presented *in the round*. ▪ a theater *in the round*

make the rounds (*US*) *or chiefly Brit* ***do/go the rounds*** ✧ When a rumor, a piece of news, etc. *makes/does/goes the rounds*, it is passed from one person to another person and becomes widely known. ▪ Rumors about his resigning as CEO were *making the rounds*. [=were spreading] — see also [3]ROUND 2 (above)

[4]**round** *verb* **rounds; round·ed; round·ing** [+ *obj*]

1 : to go or pass around (something) ▪ When we *rounded* the bend (in the road), we saw two deer in a field. ▪ He slipped when he was *rounding* first base.

2 : to finish or complete (something) in a good or suitable way — + *off* or *out* ▪ They *rounded off* the meal with coffee and dessert. ▪ Winning the tournament was the perfect way to *round out* her career. ▪ Two Nobel Prize winners *round out* the distinguished staff.

3 : to cause (something) to have a round shape — often + *off* ▪ He *rounded off* the corners of the table.

4 *mathematics* **:** to increase or decrease (a number) to the nearest whole or round number ▪ He *rounded* 10.6 (up) to 11 and 10.3 (down) to 10. — often + *off* ▪ You can *round off* the amounts to the nearest dollar.

round on [*phrasal verb*] ***round on (someone)*** *Brit* **:** to suddenly turn toward and attack (someone) — usually used figuratively to describe suddenly beginning to speak to someone in an angry or critical way ▪ She *rounded on* him and called him a liar.

round up [*phrasal verb*] ***round up (someone or something) or round (someone or something) up*** **:** to find and gather together (people, animals, or things) ▪ They *rounded up* the cattle. ▪ The police *rounded up* all the suspects. ▪ She *rounded up* people to play basketball. — see also ROUNDUP

[5]**round** *prep, chiefly Brit*

1 : AROUND

2 : all during **:** THROUGHOUT ▪ The bush stays green ***(all) round the year*** [=(more commonly) *year-round*]

[1]**round·about** /ˈraʊndəˌbaʊt/ *adj* [*more* ~; *most* ~]

1 : not direct ▪ He took a *roundabout* route to town.

2 : not simple, clear, or plain **:** long and confusing ▪ a *roundabout* explanation ▪ In a *roundabout* way, he told me that my help was not wanted.

[2]**roundabout** *noun, pl* **-abouts** [*count*] *Brit*

1 : TRAFFIC CIRCLE

2 : MERRY-GO-ROUND

round·ed /ˈraʊndəd/ *adj*

1 : having a round or curving shape ▪ a countertop with *rounded* corners ▪ Her shoulders are *rounded*. ▪ *rounded* leaves

2 : fully developed ▪ a wine with a *rounded* character ▪ The novel gives a *rounded* picture of life as an illegal immigrant in the U.S. — see also WELL-ROUNDED

roun·del /ˈraʊndl/ *noun, pl* **-dels** [*count*] *chiefly Brit* **:** a round figure or object

round·er /ˈraʊndɚ/ *noun, pl* **-ers**

1 [*count*] **:** a boxing match lasting a specified number of rounds ▪ a 10-*rounder* [=a boxing match that lasts 10 rounds]

2 ***rounders*** [*plural*] *Brit* **:** a game that is played with a ball and bat and that is like baseball

round·ly /ˈraʊndli/ *adv*

1 a : thoroughly or completely ▪ He was *roundly* defeated. **b :** by nearly everyone **:** WIDELY ▪ Her leadership is *roundly* praised. ▪ He was *roundly* disliked/ignored.

2 : using plain or strong language ▪ She *roundly* criticized the plan. ▪ He told them *roundly* [=*bluntly*] that they would get no help.

round–rob·in /ˈraʊndˌrɑːbən/ *noun, pl* **-ins** [*count*] *sports* **:** a competition in which every player or team plays once against every other player or team

round–shoul·dered /ˈraʊndˌʃoʊldɚd/ *adj* **:** having shoulders that slope downward or forward

round·ta·ble /ˈraʊndˌteɪbəl/ *noun, pl* **-tables** [*count*] **:** a meeting at which people discuss something and everyone has an equal chance to express an opinion — often used before another noun ▪ a *roundtable* discussion/conference

round–the–clock *adj, always used before a noun* **:** AROUND-THE-CLOCK

round trip *noun, pl* ~ **trips** [*count*] **:** a trip to a place and back usually over the same route ▪ It's a 50-mile *round trip* to my parents' house.

— **round trip** *adv, US* ▪ The drive is 50 miles *round trip*.

— **round–trip** /ˈraʊndˌtrɪp/ *adj, always used before a noun, US* ▪ a ***round-trip ticket*** [=(*Brit*) *return*]

round·up /ˈraʊndˌʌp/ *noun, pl* **-ups** [*count*]

1 a : the act or process of gathering together animals (such as cattle) by circling around them in vehicles or on horses **b :** the act or process of finding and gathering together people or things of the same kind ▪ The police ordered a *roundup* of all the suspects. — see also *round up* at [4]ROUND

2 : a brief statement of the most important information **:** SUMMARY ▪ Here's a *roundup* of today's news.

round·worm /ˈraʊndˌwɚm/ *noun, pl* **-worms** [*count*] **:** a small worm with a long, round body that lives inside the bodies of people and animals

rouse /ˈraʊz/ *verb* **rous·es; roused; rous·ing** [+ *obj*] *somewhat formal*

1 : to wake (someone) from sleep ▪ He was *roused* (from sleep) by a loud crash. ▪ I've been unable to *rouse* her. — sometimes used figuratively ▪ He stood staring into space until he was *roused* by a tap on his shoulder. ▪ The music *roused* their spirits.

2 : to cause (someone who is tired or not interested) to become active ▪ What will it take to *rouse* voters (from their indifference)? ▪ I was so tired I could barely ***rouse myself*** to prepare dinner.

3 a : to cause (an emotional response) in someone ▪ His comments *roused* [=*aroused*] the anger of many military leaders. **b :** to make (a person or animal) angry ▪ These animals are dangerous when *roused*. ▪ She was ***roused to anger*** by their indifference.

4 : to cause (something) to happen ▪ The report *roused* [=(more commonly) *aroused*] speculation.

rousing *adj, always used before a noun*

1 : done or said with great enthusiasm or excitement ▪ She was met with a *rousing* reception. ▪ a *rousing* speech

2 : causing great emotion, excitement, or enthusiasm ▪ They played a *rousing* [=*stirring*] rendition of the national anthem. ▪ a *rousing* finale/victory

3 : unusually good ▪ The play was a *rousing* [=*remarkable*] success.

roust /ˈraʊst/ *verb* **rousts; roust·ed; roust·ing** [+ *obj*] *US* **:** to force (someone or something) to move from a place ▪ The soldiers were *rousted* from their beds before sunrise.

roust·about /ˈraʊstəˌbaʊt/ *noun, pl* **-abouts** [*count*] *chiefly US* **:** a worker in an oil field, at a circus, etc., whose job requires strength but little skill

[1]**rout** /ˈraʊt/ *noun, pl* **routs**

1 [*count*] **:** a game or contest in which the winner easily defeats the loser by a large amount ▪ The game turned into a *rout* in the second half. ▪ After they scored their fourth goal, ***the rout was on*** [=the game became a rout]

2 : a confused and disorderly retreat from a place [*count*] — usually singular ▪ the attack and the *rout* that followed [*noncount*] They put the enemy ***to rout*** [=they forced the enemy to run away]

[2]**rout** *verb* **routs; rout·ed; rout·ing** [+ *obj*]

1 : to defeat (someone) easily and completely in a game or contest ▪ The reigning champion *routed* the contender. ▪ The Nationalist party was *routed* in the polls.

2 : to force (someone or something) to move from a place ▪ The army *routed* the enemy from their stronghold. — often + *out* ▪ People were *routed out* of their homes by the soldiers.

[1]**route** /ˈruːt, ˈraʊt/ *noun, pl* **routes** [*count*]

1 a : a way to get from one place to another place ▪ We didn't know what *route* to take/follow. ▪ an escape *route* in case of fire ▪ a parade *route* ▪ We took ***the scenic route*** [=a way that is not the fastest way but that has beautiful scenery] **b :** a way that someone or something regularly travels along ▪ a major bird migratory *route* ▪ a bus/truck *route* ▪ a mail *route* ▪ (*US*) She has a ***paper route*** [=(*Brit*) *paper round*; a job of delivering newspapers to the same places every day]

2 : a way of achieving or doing something ▪ the *route* [=*road*]

to success • You could take a different *route* and still arrive at the same conclusion. • I decided to ***go/take the traditional route*** [=do the traditional thing] and have a big wedding.

3 *US* : a usually minor highway • Take *Route* 2 into town. • We live on a rural *route*.

²route *verb* **routes; rout·ed; rout·ing** [+ *obj*] : to send (someone or something) along a particular route • Traffic was *routed* around the accident. • When the doctor is out, his calls are *routed* to his answering service.

rout·er *noun, pl* **-ers** [*count*]

1 /ˈrautɚ/ : a machine used for cutting a groove into the surface of wood or metal

2 /ˈruːtɚ, ˈrautɚ/ *technical* : a device that sends data from one place to another within a computer network or between computer networks

¹rou·tine /ruˈtiːn/ *noun, pl* **-tines**

1 : a regular way of doing things in a particular order [*count*] Grandma gets upset if we change her *routine*. • A brisk walk is part of her morning *routine*. • The job will be easier once you settle into a *routine*. • You must go through the whole *routine* [=all the steps] of disarming the alarm. • an exercise *routine* [=a set of exercises always done in the same order] [*noncount*] We keep a copy of all correspondence as ***a matter of routine***. [=as a standard procedure]

2 [*noncount*] : a boring state or situation in which things are always done the same way • The meeting was a welcome break from *routine*. [=the meeting was different from what we normally do] • the boring *routine* of paperwork

3 [*count*] **a** : a series of things (such as movements or jokes) that are repeated as part of a performance • a comedy/dance/gymnastics *routine* **b** *informal* : something that is said or done the same way very often — usually singular • Every time I ask him to do something, I get the old "I'm too busy" *routine*. [=he says "I'm too busy"]

4 [*count*] : a set of instructions that will perform a particular job on a computer • the installation *routine*

²routine *adj*

1 [*more* ~; *most* ~] : done very often • The surgery has become a very *routine* operation and poses little danger. • He criticized her *routine* absence from important meetings.

2 : done or happening as a normal part of a job, situation, or process • a *routine* luggage search • a *routine* annual physical • *routine* [=*ordinary*] business practices

3 [*more* ~; *most* ~] **a** : easily done according to a set way or method • The more you do it, the more *routine* it becomes. • They hire high-school students for *routine* work such as filing. **b** *disapproving* : boring because of always being done in the same way • Data entry becomes *routine* very quickly.

– rou·tine·ly *adv* • They *routinely* turn down at least half the applicants.

rove /ˈrouv/ *verb* **roves; roved; rov·ing** *literary* : to go to different places without having a particular purpose or plan [*no obj*] We *roved* [=*roamed, wandered*] around town/Europe. [+ *obj*] They *roved* [=*roamed, wandered*] the streets of the village. • His ***eyes roved*** the room [=he looked around the room] in search of her.

rov·er /ˈrouvɚ/ *noun, pl* **-ers** [*count*]

1 *literary* : a person who wanders to different places • an aimless *rover*

2 : a vehicle used for exploring the surface of a moon, planet, etc. • the Mars *rover*

roving *adj, always used before a noun* : going to many different places • a *roving* reporter • *roving* bands of Gypsies

roving eye ✧ If you have a *roving eye*, you tend to look at and have sexual thoughts about other people even though you already have a wife, husband, etc. • His wife wasn't willing to tolerate his *roving eye*. [=*wandering eye*]

¹row /ˈrou/ *noun, pl* **rows** [*count*]

1 : a straight line of people or things that are next to each other • *rows* of corn • The desks are arranged in six *rows*. • The table of figures should include totals at the end of each *row* and column. • The bookstore has ***row upon row*** [=many rows] of self-help books.

2 : a line of seats in a theater, stadium, etc. • I see three empty seats in the second/front/back *row*. • We have front-*row* seats for the concert.

3 ***Row*** : a street or road — used in names • I live on Vassar *Row*. • a house on Church *Row*

a tough/hard row to hoe : something that is difficult to do or deal with • I am considering becoming a doctor, but I know that it's *a tough row to hoe*.

in a row : following one after another • There are three blue houses *in a row*. • She had her birthday party at the bowling alley three years *in a row*. [=three consecutive years]

– compare ³ROW, ⁴ROW; see also DEATH ROW, SKID ROW

²row *verb* **rows; rowed; row·ing**

1 : to move a boat through water using oars [*no obj*] Let's *row* (over) to the island after lunch. • We'll take turns *rowing*. [+ *obj*] They *rowed* the boat all the way across the lake.

2 [+ *obj*] : to carry (someone or something) in a boat that you row • I *rowed* the kids out to the island.

– compare ⁵ROW

³row *noun* [*singular*] : an act of rowing a boat • I went for a *row* on the lake. — compare ¹ROW, ⁴ROW

⁴row /ˈrau/ *noun, pl* **rows** *chiefly Brit, informal*

1 [*count*] : a noisy argument • She got into a terrible *row* [=*quarrel*] with her boyfriend.

2 [*count*] : a lot of loud arguing or complaining usually involving many people • The proposal to build a new nuclear energy plant caused a huge *row*. [=*uproar*]

3 [*singular*] : a loud, unpleasant noise • The children got hold of the drums and made an awful *row*. [=*racket*]

– compare ¹ROW, ³ROW

⁵row *verb* **rows; rowed; row·ing** [*no obj*] *Brit* : to have a noisy argument with someone • They were *rowing* again. • He's always *rowing with* his wife about/over trivial things. — compare ²ROW

row·an /ˈrawən, ˈrowən/ *noun, pl* **-ans** [*count, noncount*] *Brit* : MOUNTAIN ASH

row·boat /ˈrouˌbout/ *noun, pl* **-boats** [*count*] *US* : a small boat that is moved through water using oars — called also (*Brit*) *rowing boat*; see picture at BOAT

¹row·dy /ˈraudi/ *adj* **row·di·er; -est** [*also more* ~; *most* ~] : rough or noisy • a *rowdy* crowd • *rowdy* children • a *rowdy* game of basketball

– row·di·ness /ˈraudinəs/ *noun* [*noncount*]

²rowdy *noun, pl* **-dies** [*count*] : a person who causes trouble in a noisy way — usually plural • a gang of young *rowdies*

– row·dy·ism /ˈraudiˌɪzəm/ *noun* [*noncount*] • *rowdyism* among sports fans

row·er /ˈrowɚ/ *noun, pl* **-ers** [*count*] : a person who rows a boat : OARSMAN, OARSWOMAN • Olympic *rowers*

row house /ˈrou-/ *noun, pl* ~ **houses** [*count*] *US* : a house in a row of houses that shares a wall with the houses next to it — called also (*Brit*) *terraced house*

row·ing /ˈrowɪŋ/ *noun* [*noncount*]

1 : the sport of racing in long, narrow boats that are moved by using oars • She was on the *rowing* team.

2 : the activity of moving a boat by using oars • *Rowing* is good exercise.

rowing boat *noun, pl* ~ **boats** [*count*] *Brit* : ROWBOAT

rowing machine *noun, pl* ~ **-chines** [*count*] : an exercise machine that you use by moving your body as if you are rowing a boat — see picture at GYM

row·lock /ˈrɑːlək/ *noun, pl* **-locks** [*count*] *chiefly Brit* : OARLOCK

¹roy·al /ˈrojəl/ *adj, always used before a noun*

1 : of or relating to a king or queen • the *royal* family/household/palace • He comes from *royal* blood. [=he is in some way related to a king or queen]

2 ***Royal*** — used in names of organizations that are supported by or that serve a king or queen • the *Royal* Army • the *Royal* College of Art • the *Royal* National Theatre

3 : suitable for a king or queen : elaborate or impressive • They received a *royal* welcome as they stepped off the plane. • The hotel gave us ***the royal treatment***. [=they treated us like very important people]

4 *chiefly US, informal* — used to make a statement more forceful • My little brother is a *royal* pain in the neck.

the royal "we" : the word "we" used by a king or queen instead of "I" • When Queen Victoria said, "We are not amused," she was using *the royal "we."*

²royal *noun, pl* **-als** [*count*] *informal* : a member of a royal family • magazine stories about the private lives of *royals*

royal blue *noun* [*noncount*] : a bright purplish blue — see color picture on page C2

– royal blue *adj* • a *royal blue* shirt

Royal Commission *noun, pl* ~ **-sions** [*count*] : a group of people chosen by the British government to examine a particular topic or issue and recommend changes in the law • a *Royal Commission* on the death penalty

royal flush *noun, pl* ~ **flushes** [*count*] : a set of cards that a player has in a card game (such as poker) that are all of the same suit (such as diamonds) and are the most valuable cards (the ace, king, queen, jack, and ten) in that suit

Royal Highness *noun, pl* ~ **-nesses** [*count*] — used as a title for a member of a royal family; used with *his, her, their,* or *your* • *their Royal Highnesses*, the Prince and Princess of Wales • *Her/His Royal Highness* will receive you now. • Thank you, *your Royal Highness*.

roy·al·ist /ˈrojəlɪst/ *noun, pl* **-ists** [*count*] : a person who believes that a country should have a king or queen or who supports a particular king or queen

– **royalist** *adj*

roy·al·ly /ˈrojəli/ *adv*

1 : by a king or queen • a *royally* appointed prime minister

2 : in a way suitable for a king or queen • We were treated *royally*. [=we were treated like very important people]

3 *US, informal* — used to add emphasis to statements that usually express anger, frustration, etc. • (*impolite*) He's *royally* pissed. [=he's extremely angry] • I screwed up *royally*. [=very badly]

roy·al·ty /ˈrojəlti/ *noun, pl* **-ties**

1 [*noncount*] : members of a royal family • It was an honor and a privilege to dine with *royalty*. • On our wedding day, we were treated ***like royalty***.

2 [*count*] **a** : an amount of money that is paid to the original creator of a product, book, or piece of music based on how many copies have been sold — usually plural • After he died, his family continued to collect *royalties* on/from his books. • The book has earned $40,000 ***in royalties***. • ***royalty checks/payments*** for artists **b** : an amount of money that is paid by a mining or oil company to the owner of the land the company is using — usually plural • The company pays *royalties* to the government for drilling rights.

RP *abbr* **1** *Brit* Received Pronunciation **2** *baseball* relief pitcher

rpm *abbr* revolutions per minute ✧ *Rpm* is used after a number to indicate how many times something turns one complete circle during one minute. • The engine produces 187 horsepower at 6,000 *rpm*. • a 78-*rpm* record

RR *abbr* **1** railroad • Turn left at the *RR* crossing. **2** *or* **R.R.** *US* rural route ✧ The abbreviation *RR* is used in mailing addresses to places that are located in the country to show which delivery route the mailbox is located on. • *RR* 5, Box 653

R–rated *adj, US, of a movie* : having a rating of R : not suitable to be seen by children because of violence, offensive language, or sexual activity • an *R-rated* movie — often used figuratively • an *R-rated* joke

RSI *abbr* repetitive strain injury; repetitive stress injury

[1]**RSVP** *abbr* please reply — used on invitations to ask the invited guests to indicate whether they will be able to attend ✧ *RSVP* comes from the French phrase "répondez s'il vous plaît."

[2]**RSVP** /ˌɑɚˌɛsˌviːˈpiː/ *verb* **RSVP's** *or* **RSVPs**; **RSVP'd** *or* **RSVPed**; **RSVP'·ing** *or* **RSVP·ing** [*no obj*] *chiefly US* : to respond to an invitation • They asked us to *RSVP* by this Friday. • Have you *RSVP'd*?

Rt *or* **Rt.** *abbr, US* route • Take *Rt* 70 west.

Rte. *or* **Rte** *abbr, US* route • Take *Rte.* 70 west.

Rt Hon *abbr, Brit* Right Honourable

[1]**rub** /ˈrʌb/ *verb* **rubs**; **rubbed**; **rub·bing**

1 : to move something (such as your hand or an object) back and forth along the surface of (something) while pressing [+ *obj*] Could you *rub* my shoulders? • He blinked and *rubbed* his eyes. • The cat *rubbed* itself against my leg. [*no obj*] The cat *rubbed* against my leg. • Don't *rub* too hard or you'll tear the paper.

2 : to move (two things) back and forth against each other [+ *obj*] He *rubbed* his hands with glee. — often + *together* • I *rubbed* my hands *together* to warm them up. • The sound you hear is the crickets *rubbing* their legs *together*. • We learned how to *rub* two sticks *together* to start a fire. [*no obj*] There was a squeak when the boards *rubbed* together.

3 : to move back and forth many times against something in a way that causes pain or damage [*no obj*] The back of my shoe is *rubbing* against my heel and giving me a blister. • There are marks where the chair has *rubbed* against the wall. [+ *obj*] There are marks where the chair has been *rubbing* the wall. • I *rubbed* my knees raw scrambling over the rocks.

4 [+ *obj*] : to spread (something) over and into a surface by pressing firmly with your hands • We *rubbed* the steaks with spices before we grilled them. = We *rubbed* spices onto the steaks before we grilled them. • I *rubbed* the ointment onto my sore muscles.

rub along [*phrasal verb*] *Brit, informal* : to work, play, etc., together with little or no difficulty • We *rub along* [=*get along*] well enough, but we're not really close friends.

rub down [*phrasal verb*] ***rub (someone or something) down*** *or* ***rub down (someone or something)*** : to rub (a person or animal's body) with your hands in order to clean, dry, or massage it • The trainer *rubbed down* the players after the game to keep them from getting sore. — see also RUBDOWN

rub elbows with (*US*) *or* ***rub shoulders with*** *informal* : to meet and talk with (someone) in a friendly way • The award dinner gave me the opportunity to *rub elbows with* some of today's greatest American poets.

rub in [*phrasal verb*] ***rub (something) in*** *or* ***rub in (something)*** *informal* : to keep reminding someone of (something that person would like to forget) • She keeps *rubbing in* the fact that she makes more money than I do. • I know I made a mistake, but you don't have to ***rub it in***.

rub off [*phrasal verb*] **1** : to come off of a surface and often stick to another surface when the surfaces touch each other • Be careful that the ink doesn't *rub off* on your fingers. • The paint on the desk is beginning to *rub off*. — often used figuratively • Her positive attitude *rubbed off* on other people. [=other people began to have a positive attitude from being around her] • I wish some of your good luck would *rub off* on me. [=I wish that I would start having good luck too] **2** ***rub (something) off*** *or* ***rub off (something)*** : to remove (something) from a surface by rubbing • I *rubbed* the dirt *off* (of) the penny.

rub out [*phrasal verb*] **1** ***rub (something) out*** *or* ***rub out (something)*** *chiefly Brit* : to remove (something) by rubbing especially with an eraser • She *rubbed out* [=(*chiefly US*) *erased*] the wrong answer from her paper and filled in the correct one. **2** ***rub (someone) out*** *or* ***rub out (someone)*** *US, informal* : to murder (someone) • They say that the Mafia *rubbed* him *out*.

rub salt in/into someone's wounds *or* ***rub salt in/into the wound*** *informal* : to make a difficult situation even worse for someone • It's bad enough that he beat me, but the way he keeps talking about it is just *rubbing salt in the wound*.

rub someone's nose in *informal* : to repeatedly remind someone of (a mistake, failure, etc.) • He beat us all in the race and then *rubbed our noses in it*.

rub (someone) the wrong way (*US*) *or Brit* ***rub (someone) up the wrong way*** *informal* : to cause (someone) to be angry or annoyed : IRRITATE • She meant to be helpful but her suggestion really *rubbed me the wrong way*.

[2]**rub** *noun, pl* **rubs**

1 [*count*] : an act of rubbing a surface with your hands or an object — usually singular • After the car was washed, they gave the windshield a quick *rub* with a dry cloth. • Let me give you a ***back rub***. [=let me rub/massage your back]

2 ***the rub*** *formal* : something that causes a difficulty or problem • Therein/There lies *the rub*. [=that's the problem] • She's an amazing cook, but she rarely has time to make meals. There's *the rub*.

3 [*count*] *US* : a combination of spices that is rubbed into the surface of meat before the meat is cooked • He used his favorite *rub* on the steaks. • a dry *rub* for chicken

[1]**rub·ber** /ˈrʌbɚ/ *noun, pl* **-bers**

1 [*noncount*] : a strong substance that stretches and that is made out of chemicals or from the juice of a tropical tree • tires made of *rubber* — often used before another noun • He was wearing *rubber* gloves and safety goggles. • shoes with *rubber* soles • a red *rubber* ball • a *rubber* raft — see also FOAM RUBBER

2 [*count*] *Brit* : ERASER

3 ***rubbers*** [*plural*] *US, informal + old-fashioned* : shoes or boots that are made of rubber and that fit over your regular shoes to keep them dry — compare GALOSHES

4 [*count*] *US, informal* : CONDOM

5 [*count*] *baseball* : a flat piece of hard, white rubber on which the pitcher stands while pitching

burn rubber *informal* : to drive very fast • They were *burning rubber* up and down the road.

– compare [2]RUBBER

[2]**rubber** *noun, pl* **-bers** [*count*]

1 : a contest that consists of a series of games and that is won by the player or team that wins the most games (such as two games out of three) • Let's play a *rubber* of bridge.

2 *US, sports* : a game that decides who will be the winner of a

R

series of games — usually used before another noun • The teams will play today in the ***rubber game*** of the series. – compare ¹RUBBER

rubber band *noun, pl* ~ **bands** [*count*] : a thin, flexible loop that is made of rubber and used to hold things together — called also (*US*) *elastic,* (*Brit*) *elastic band*; see picture at OFFICE

rubber boot *noun, pl* ~ **boots** [*count*] *US* : a tall boot that is made out of rubber and that keeps your feet and lower legs dry — called also (*Brit*) *Wellington*

rubber bullet *noun, pl* ~ **-lets** [*count*] : a bullet that is made out of rubber so that it hurts but does not kill people and that is used by the police and military to control a crowd

rubber cement *noun* [*noncount*] : a thick, stretchy glue that contains rubber

rub·ber·ized *also Brit* **rub·ber·ised** /ˈrʌbəˌraɪzd/ *adj, always used before a noun* : coated or soaked with rubber • *rubberized* clothing

rub·ber·neck /ˈrʌbəˌnɛk/ *verb* **-necks; -necked; -neck·ing** [*no obj*] *chiefly US, informal* : to look around or stare with great curiosity; *especially* : to slow down while you are driving in order to stare at something (such as an accident) • She was *rubbernecking* and almost got in an accident herself.
– **rub·ber·neck·er** /ˈrʌbəˌnɛkə/ *noun, pl* **-ers** [*count*] • a traffic jam caused by *rubberneckers*

rubber plant *noun, pl* ~ **plants** [*count*] : a plant with large, shiny, dark green leaves that is often grown indoors

rubber stamp *noun, pl* ~ **stamps** [*count*]
1 : a small tool that consists of a handle attached to a piece of carved rubber and that is dipped in ink and then pressed on paper to print a date, name, symbol, etc.
2 *disapproving* : a person or organization that automatically approves everything that someone does or decides • The legislature has been nothing more than a *rubber stamp* for the President.

rubber stamp

rubber–stamp *verb* **-stamps; -stamped; -stamp·ing** [+ *obj*] *usually disapproving* : to approve or allow (something) without seriously thinking about it • They expected the proposal to be *rubber-stamped* by the legislature.

rub·bery /ˈrʌbəri/ *adj* [*more* ~; *most* ~]
1 : similar to rubber • The hard-boiled eggs were tough and *rubbery*. • a *rubbery* material
2 *of legs or knees* : bending like rubber : weak, shaky, and unstable • Her legs were/felt *rubbery* when she stepped off the roller coaster.

rubbing *noun, pl* **-bings** [*count*] : an image of a surface that is made by placing paper over it and rubbing the paper with a pencil, crayon, etc. • He made a *rubbing* of the old tombstone.

rubbing alcohol *noun* [*noncount*] *US* : a liquid that contains alcohol and water and that is used to clean wounds or skin — called also (*Brit*) *surgical spirit*

¹rub·bish /ˈrʌbɪʃ/ *noun* [*noncount*]
1 : things that are no longer useful or wanted and that have been thrown out : TRASH • Please, pick the *rubbish* up off the ground. • (*Brit*) We saw a rat run through the ***rubbish tip/dump.*** [=(*US*) garbage dump; an area of land where people can dump their rubbish] • (*chiefly Brit*) Put the potato peels in the ***rubbish bin.*** [=(*US*) *garbage can,* (*chiefly US*) *trash can*]
2 *chiefly Brit, informal* : words or ideas that are foolish or untrue • I think what he says is absolute *rubbish*! • That's (a load of) *rubbish*! I didn't cheat on the test. • "I'm sorry, but I had to do it." "*Rubbish!*"
3 *informal* : something that is worthless, unimportant, or of poor quality • The food at that restaurant is complete *rubbish*. • I can't believe you waste your time reading that *rubbish*. [=*garbage*]

²rubbish *verb* **-bish·es; -bished; -bish·ing** [+ *obj*] *Brit, informal* : to severely criticize (someone or something) • The critics *rubbished* [=(*US*) *trashed*] her new book.

rub·bishy /ˈrʌbəʃi/ *adj* [*more* ~; *most* ~] *Brit, informal* : of very low quality • a *rubbishy* film/book

rub·ble /ˈrʌbəl/ *noun* [*noncount*] : broken pieces of stone, brick, etc., from walls or buildings that have fallen • Rescue workers managed to pull two injured people out of the *rubble*. • The earthquake reduced the whole town to *rubble*.

rub·down /ˈrʌbˌdaʊn/ *noun, pl* **-downs** [*count*] *chiefly US* : an act of rubbing someone's body to relax the muscles • The trainer gave him a *rubdown* after the game. — see also *rub down* at ¹RUB

rube /ˈruːb/ *noun, pl* **rubes** [*count*] *US, informal* : an uneducated person who is usually from the country • They treated us as if we were a bunch of *rubes*.

Rube Gold·berg /ˈruːbˈgoʊldˌbəg/ *adj, always used before a noun, US* : doing something simple in a very complicated way that is not necessary • a *Rube Goldberg* [=(*Brit*) *Heath Robinson*] contraption/device/machine ✧ Rube Goldberg was an American cartoonist who was known especially for drawing humorously complicated machines that performed very simple tasks.

ru·bel·la /ruˈbɛlə/ *noun* [*noncount*] *medical* : GERMAN MEASLES

Ru·bi·con /ˈruːbɪˌkɑːn/ *noun*
the Rubicon : a limit or point that you reach when the results of your actions cannot be changed • Once you've ***crossed the Rubicon*** there's no going back. ✧ This word comes from the name of a stream that separated Gaul from Italy. In 49 B.C., Julius Caesar started a war by illegally marching his army across the Rubicon and into Italy.

ru·bi·cund /ˈruːbəkənd/ *adj, literary* : having red or pink skin : RUDDY • the *rubicund* face/features of his father

ru·ble (*chiefly US*) *or chiefly Brit* **rou·ble** /ˈruːbəl/ *noun, pl* **ru·bles**
1 [*count*] : the basic unit of money of Russia • It costs 40 *rubles*. • a hundred-*ruble* bill
2 [*count*] : a coin representing one ruble • She gave the driver a *ruble*. • a handful of *rubles*
3 ***the ruble*** *technical* : the value of the ruble compared with the value of the money of other countries • *The ruble* fell against the U.S. dollar.

ru·bric /ˈruːbrɪk/ *noun, pl* **-brics** [*count*] *formal*
1 : a name or heading under which something is classified • They classify very different problems under a general *rubric*. [=*category*]
2 : an explanation or a set of instructions at the beginning of a book, a test, etc.

ru·by /ˈruːbi/ *noun, pl* **-bies**
1 [*count*] : a deep red stone that is used in jewelry • diamonds and *rubies* — see color picture on page C11
2 [*count, noncount*] : a dark red color — see color picture on page C3
– **ruby** *adj* • her *ruby* lips • *ruby* red

ruched /ˈruːʃt/ *adj, of fabric or clothing* : gathered into folds • a *ruched* skirt

ruck /ˈrʌk/ *noun, pl* **rucks**
1 [*count*] *rugby* : a group of players who are trying to get the ball while it is on the ground
2 ***the ruck*** *Brit* : ordinary or normal people or events • Her outstanding poetry eventually allowed her to emerge from *the ruck*. [=the crowd]
3 [*singular*] *Brit, informal* : a fight especially among a group of people • He got drunk and started a *ruck* with the police.

ruck·sack /ˈrʌkˌsæk/ *noun, pl* **-sacks** [*count*] *chiefly Brit* : BACKPACK

ruck·us /ˈrʌkəs/ *noun* [*singular*] *chiefly US, informal* : a noisy argument, fight, etc. • They caused quite a *ruckus* [=(*Brit*) *rumpus*] with their yelling. • He ***raised a ruckus*** [=got upset and complained very loudly] over the cost of the repairs.

ruc·tions /ˈrʌkʃənz/ *noun* [*plural*] *chiefly Brit* : angry arguments or complaints • There were *ructions* over how the opera should be staged.

rud·der /ˈrʌdə/ *noun, pl* **-ders** [*count*] : a flat, movable piece usually of wood or metal that is attached to a ship, boat, airplane, etc., and is used in steering — see picture at BOAT

rud·der·less /ˈrʌdələs/ *adj* : without a leader, plan, or goal • When the Speaker of the House resigned, the party was left *rudderless*. • a *rudderless* young man

¹rud·dy /ˈrʌdi/ *adj*
1 : having a healthy reddish color • She has a *ruddy* face/complexion. • *ruddy* cheeks
2 *literary* : RED • the *ruddy* surface of Mars
3 *always used before a noun, Brit, informal* — used to make an angry or critical statement more forceful • The *ruddy* squirrels keep eating my birdseed! • He's a *ruddy* fool!
– **rud·di·ness** /ˈrʌdinəs/ *noun* [*noncount*]

²ruddy *adv, Brit, informal* : VERY, EXTREMELY — used to

R

make an angry or critical statement more forceful • It's *ruddy* awful!

ruddy well *Brit, informal* — used before a verb to stress anger, annoyance, or disapproval • I can *ruddy well* do as I like.

rude /ˈruːd/ *adj* **rud·er**; **rud·est** [*also more ~; most ~*]

1 : not having or showing concern or respect for the rights and feelings of other people **:** not polite • He made *rude* remarks/gestures. • I was shocked by her *rude* behavior. • I can't believe that he was so *rude* to me. • It is *rude* (of/for you) to always keep us waiting for you.

2 : relating to sex or other body functions in a way that offends others • *rude* jokes • I heard someone make ***a rude noise***.

3 *always used before a noun* **:** happening suddenly in usually an unpleasant or shocking way • If you think this job is going to be easy, you're in for a ***rude shock***. [=you will be unpleasantly shocked when you find out that this job is not easy at all] • He's about to have a ***rude awakening***. [=he's about to find out something that will shock him unpleasantly]

4 *literary* **:** made or done in a simple or rough way **:** CRUDE • a *rude* stone farmhouse

in rude health *Brit, old-fashioned* **:** strong and healthy • We hope to find you *in rude health* when we arrive.

– rude·ly *adv* • He *rudely* interrupted me. • I was *rudely* [=suddenly and unpleasantly] awakened from my nap. **– rude·ness** *noun* [*noncount*] • I was shocked by his *rudeness*.

ru·di·men·ta·ry /ˌruːdəˈmɛntəri/ *adj* [*more ~; most ~*] *formal*

1 : basic or simple • This class requires a *rudimentary* knowledge of human anatomy. • He speaks *rudimentary* English.

2 : not very developed or advanced • *rudimentary* technology • When baseball was in its *rudimentary* stages, different teams played by different rules. • Some insects have only *rudimentary* wings.

ru·di·ments /ˈruːdəmənts/ *noun* [*plural*] *formal* **:** basic facts or skills • the *rudiments* of grammar/government

rue /ˈruː/ *verb* **rues**; **rued**; **ru·ing** [+ *obj*] *formal* **:** to feel sorrow or regret for (something) • He must be *ruing* his decision now. • I ***rue the day*** (that) I signed that contract.

rue·ful /ˈruːfəl/ *adj* **:** showing or feeling regret for something done • He gave me a *rueful* smile and apologized.

– rue·ful·ly *adv* • "I still have a scar from the accident," he said *ruefully*.

ruff /ˈrʌf/ *noun, pl* **ruffs** [*count*]

1 : a large, round collar of folded fabric that was worn by men and women in the 16th and 17th centuries

2 : a mass of fur or feathers growing around or on the neck of an animal or bird

ruf·fi·an /ˈrʌfijən/ *noun, pl* **-ans** [*count*] *old-fashioned* **:** a strong and violent person (especially a man) who threatens and hurts other people • a gang of *ruffians*

¹ruf·fle /ˈrʌfəl/ *verb* **ruf·fles**; **ruf·fled**; **ruf·fling** [+ *obj*]

1 : to move or lift (something) so that it is no longer smooth • Her hair was *ruffled* by the wind. • The bird *ruffled* (up) its feathers.

2 : to make (someone) irritated, annoyed, worried, etc. • He *ruffled* some people with his constant complaining. — usually used as *(be) ruffled* • That boy is a lot of trouble. It's a good thing his parents *aren't* easily *ruffled*. [=don't become upset easily] • The actress *was* obviously *ruffled* by the reporter's question.

ruffle feathers *informal* **:** to upset or offend someone • His critical remarks ***ruffled some feathers***. = His critical remarks ***ruffled a few feathers***. • His critical remarks ***ruffled the feathers of*** the board members. • Her research has been ***ruffling feathers*** [=upsetting people] for years. • I agreed to do what they wanted because I didn't want to ***ruffle any feathers***.

²ruffle *noun, pl* **ruffles** [*count*] **:** a piece of cloth that is gathered together along one edge and used to decorate something • The dress has a *ruffle* around the collar.

– ruffled /ˈrʌfəld/ *adj* • a *ruffled* collar

rug /ˈrʌg/ *noun, pl* **rugs** [*count*]

1 : a piece of thick, heavy material that is used to cover usually a section of a floor • I accidentally spilled wine on the *rug*. — see picture at LIVING ROOM; see also PRAYER RUG, THROW RUG

2 *chiefly US, informal* **:** a small wig that is usually worn by a man to cover a bald spot **:** TOUPEE • You could tell that he was wearing a *rug*.

3 *Brit* **:** a blanket that you put over your lap and legs to keep them warm

cut a rug see ¹CUT

pull the rug (out) from under *informal* **:** to very suddenly take something needed or expected from (someone or something) • We were ready to start work on the project when the mayor *pulled the rug out from under* us and cut the funding.

sweep (something) under the rug see ¹SWEEP

rug·by *also* **Rugby** /ˈrʌgbi/ *noun* [*noncount*] **:** a game played by two teams in which each team tries to carry or kick a ball over the other team's goal line — called also (*chiefly Brit*) *rugby football*; see picture at BALL

Rugby League *noun* [*noncount*] **:** a type of rugby played with 13 people on each team

Rugby Union *noun* [*noncount*] **:** a type of rugby played with 15 people on each team

rug·ged /ˈrʌgəd/ *adj*

1 : having a rough, uneven surface • the *rugged* surface of the moon • She did a painting of the region's *rugged* coastline.

2 *of a man's face* **:** having rough but attractive features • People are attracted to his ***rugged good looks***.

3 : strong and determined • *rugged* pioneers • I admire her *rugged* individualism.

4 : made to be strong and tough • The chair is made of *rugged* plastic. • The fabric is lightweight but *rugged*.

5 : involving great difficulties or challenges **:** testing your physical, mental, or moral strength • a long and *rugged* winter • a *rugged* climb to the top of the mountain • the *rugged* life of a sailor

– rug·ged·ly *adv* • a *ruggedly* handsome man **– rug·ged·ness** *noun* [*noncount*] • the *ruggedness* of the terrain

rug·ger /ˈrʌgɚ/ *noun, pl* **-gers**

1 [*count*] *US, informal* **:** a person who plays rugby • college *ruggers*

2 [*noncount*] *Brit, informal* **:** RUGBY UNION • He plays *rugger*.

rug·rat /ˈrʌgˌræt/ *noun, pl* **-rats** [*count*] *US slang* **:** a young child • a mother and her little *rugrats*

¹ru·in /ˈruːwən/ *verb* **-ins**; **-ined**; **-in·ing** [+ *obj*]

1 : to damage (something) so badly that it is no longer useful, valuable, enjoyable, etc. **:** to spoil or destroy (something) • Moths *ruined* the sweater. • Years of computer use *ruined* his eyesight. [=made his eyesight very poor] • The bad weather *ruined* the party. • I *ruined* the sauce by adding too much garlic. • His low test scores *ruined* his chances of getting into a good school. • Poor customer service *ruined* the company's reputation. • You *ruined* my life! [=you made my life very difficult or unpleasant]

2 : to cause (someone) to lose money, social status, etc. • He was *ruined* by debt. • The scandal *ruined* the mayor.

²ruin *noun, pl* **-ins**

1 [*noncount*] **:** a state of complete destruction **:** a state of being ruined • The incident led to the *ruin* of their relationship. • The abandoned town had gone to *ruin*. • Don't let the house your grandfather built fall into *ruin*.

2 [*count*] **:** the remaining pieces of something that was destroyed • The castle is now a *ruin*. — usually plural • the *ruins* of the ancient city • We saw the (ancient) Mayan/Roman *ruins*. — sometimes used figuratively • He searched through the *ruins* of his childhood for the cause of his unhappiness.

3 [*noncount*] **:** the state of having lost money, social status, etc. • The drought brought economic/financial *ruin* to local farmers. • Her drug addiction brought her to the brink of *ruin*.

4 [*singular*] **:** something that badly damages someone physically, morally, economically, or socially • Her drug addiction was her *ruin*. • Street violence is the *ruin* of too many young people today.

in ruins **:** destroyed with some pieces or parts remaining • The building was/lay *in ruins*. — sometimes used figuratively • After her death, the family was *in ruins*.

ru·in·a·tion /ˌruːwəˈneɪʃən/ *noun* [*noncount*] *formal* **:** the act or process of destroying something • Water pollution is causing the *ruination* of the fishing industry.

ruined *adj, always used before a noun* **:** destroyed or badly damaged so that only parts remain • *ruined* buildings • a *ruined* Greek temple

ru·in·ous /ˈruːwənəs/ *adj, formal*

1 : causing or likely to cause damage or destruction • Smoking is *ruinous* [=(more commonly) *dangerous, hazardous*] to

your health. • *ruinous* effects/consequences
2 : costing far too much money • *ruinous* price increases
3 *chiefly Brit, formal* : falling apart : badly damaged • a *ruinous* building • The house has fallen into a *ruinous* state.
– ru·in·ous·ly *adv* • Funding the project would be *ruinously* expensive.

[1]rule /ˈruːl/ *noun, pl* **rules**
1 [*count*] **a** : a statement that tells you what is or is not allowed in a particular game, situation, etc. • I understand the basic *rules* of chess. • As long as you're living under our roof, you'll follow/obey our *rules*. • The college has strict *rules* for qualifying for financial assistance. • The new *rule* allows/permits employees to dress casually on Fridays. • Under the new *rules*, casual dress is now allowed. • the company's ***rules and regulations*** • It's important to learn the ***rules of the road*** before taking your driving test. • It's ***against the rules*** to eat during class. • He violated the ***unwritten/unspoken rule*** that you must thank your host before you leave a party. • We cannot ***bend/stretch the rules*** [=change or ignore the rules] just for you. • If you ***break the rules***, you'll be asked to leave. — see also GAG RULE, GROUND RULE ***synonyms*** see LAW
b : a statement that tells you what is allowed or what will happen within a particular system (such as a language or science) • the *rules* of grammar • the *rules* of geometry
2 [*count*] : a piece of advice about the best way to do something • Your speech will go well as long as you follow one simple *rule*: be confident. • The first *rule* of driving is to pay attention. • A good *rule* to follow when traveling is to do as the locals do.
3 [*singular*] : the way something usually is done or happens • ***As a rule***, I don't drive in the snow. [=I don't usually drive in the snow] • ***As a general rule***, electronic gadgets become smaller as they develop. • Friendly customer service seems to be ***the exception rather than the rule*** nowadays. [=friendly customer service seems to be rare these days] • They ***make it a rule*** to treat everyone fairly. [=they always treat everyone fairly]
4 [*noncount*] : the control and power that a particular person, group, or government has over a country or area • Today we celebrate the anniversary of the country's independence from colonial *rule*. • Under her *rule*, the country prospered. — see also HOME RULE, MAJORITY RULE
5 [*count*] *old-fashioned* : a stick used for measuring things : RULER — see also SLIDE RULE
by the rules : in the way that is most common, expected, and acceptable • After years of boredom, he grew tired of living *by the rules*. • She has always ***played by the rules*** throughout her career.
rule of law : a situation in which the laws of a country are obeyed by everyone • The courts uphold the *rule of law*.
rule of thumb **1** : a method of doing something that is based on experience and common sense rather than exact calculation • A good *rule of thumb* for keeping your closet organized is to get rid of any clothes you haven't worn in the past year. **2** : a principle that is believed and followed and that is based on the way something usually happens or is done • As a *rule of thumb*, stocks that involve greater risk also have the potential of earning you more money.

[2]rule *verb* **rules; ruled; rul·ing**
1 : to have control and power over a country, area, group, etc. [*no obj*] The queen *ruled* for 25 years. • A dynasty *ruled* over this region during the 11th century. — sometimes used figuratively • After the overthrow of the government, chaos *ruled*. [=there was a lot of chaos] [+ *obj*] Who will be the next leader to *rule* the country? — sometimes used figuratively • That summer, his band *ruled* the airwaves.
2 [+ *obj*] : to have great influence over (someone) • Football *ruled* their lives. • All of his actions were *ruled* by his religion.
3 : to make a legal decision about something [*no obj*] The court ***ruled in favor of*** the defendant. • The jury ***ruled against*** the tobacco companies. • How will the court ***rule on*** the motion? [+ *obj*] The Supreme Court *ruled* the law unconstitutional. • The board *ruled* that her behavior was cheating.
4 *not used in progressive tenses* [*no obj*] *slang* : to be very good or popular — used to express strong admiration for someone or something • That movie *rules*! [=that movie is great] • Your new sneakers *rule*.
divide and rule see [1]DIVIDE
rule out [*phrasal verb*] **1** ***rule (someone or something) out or rule out (someone or something)*** : to no longer consider (someone or something) as a possibility after careful thought or study • The police *ruled* them *out* as suspects when it was proved that they were out of town when the crime was committed. • There are some diseases your doctor will want to *rule out* before making a diagnosis. **2** ***rule (something) out or rule out (something)*** : to make (something) impossible : to prevent (something) from happening • The bad weather *ruled out* a picnic. **3** ***rule (someone) out*** : to remove (someone) from a competition, contest, etc. • He applied for the job, but his lack of experience quickly *ruled* him *out*. • (*chiefly Brit*) She has been *ruled out* of today's game with a broken thumb.
rule the roost see [1]ROOST
rule with an iron fist/hand (*chiefly US*) *or Brit* ***rule with a rod of iron*** : to rule a country, area, group, etc., in a very strict and often cruel way • The dictator *ruled* (the island) *with an iron fist*.

rule book *noun, pl* **~ books** [*count*] : a book that contains the official set of rules that must be followed in a game, job, etc. — usually singular • If you're not sure what to do, look in the *rule book*. — often used figuratively • The *rule book* says [=the rules say] that once the puck fully crosses the line it is a goal.

ruled *adj* : printed with lines on which to write • a *ruled* notebook • wide-*ruled* notebook paper

rul·er /ˈruːlɚ/ *noun, pl* **-ers** [*count*]
1 : a person (such as a king or queen) who rules a country, area, group, etc. • a summit attended by a number of *rulers* from around the world
2 : a straight piece of plastic, wood, or metal that has marks on it to show units of length and that is used to measure things • This *ruler* shows inches and centimeters. — see picture at CARPENTRY

[1]ruling *noun, pl* **-ings** [*count*] : an official decision made by a judge, referee, etc. • The decision overturns the Supreme Court's earlier *ruling*. • She disputed the referee's *ruling*.

[2]ruling *adj, always used before a noun* : having control and power over a country, area, group, etc. • members of the *ruling* class • the *ruling* family/party

[1]rum /ˈrʌm/ *noun, pl* **rums** [*count, noncount*] : an alcoholic drink that is made from sugar • a bottle/glass of *rum* • *rum* punch

[2]rum *adj, Brit, old-fashioned + informal* : strange or odd • They're a pretty *rum* lot.

rum·ba *also* **rhum·ba** /ˈrʌmbə/ *noun, pl* **-bas**
1 [*count*] : a type of dance originally from Cuba in which dancers move their hips a lot • They danced a/the *rumba*.
2 : the music for a rumba [*count*] The band played a *rumba*. [*noncount*] The band plays *rumba*.

[1]rum·ble /ˈrʌmbəl/ *verb* **rum·bles; rum·bled; rum·bling**
1 [*no obj*] : to make a low, heavy, continuous sound or series of sounds • Thunder *rumbled* in the distance. • I got hungry and my stomach started *rumbling*. [=*growling*] • *rumbling* machines
2 *always followed by an adverb or preposition* [*no obj*] : to move along with a low, heavy, continuous sound • The train *rumbles* through town twice a day. • We watched as the trucks *rumbled* past/by.
3 [*no obj*] *US, informal + old-fashioned* : to fight especially in the street • The gangs *rumbled* in the alley.
4 [+ *obj*] *Brit, informal* : to reveal or discover the true character of (someone) • He knows I've *rumbled* him.
rumble on [*phrasal verb*] : to continue for a long period of time • The debate *rumbled on* through newspaper articles.

[2]rumble *noun, pl* **rumbles** [*count*]
1 : a low, heavy sound or series of sounds • I was awakened by the *rumble* of a train passing by.
2 *US, informal + old-fashioned* : a fight in the street especially between gangs

rumble seat *noun, pl* **~ seats** [*count*] *US, old-fashioned* : a seat in the back of a car that folds down and is not covered by the top ✧ Rumble seats were most common in cars made during the 1920s and 1930s.

rumble strip *noun, pl* **~ strips** [*count*] : a set of grooves along the edge of a highway or across a road that cause noise and shaking when they are driven over and that are used to warn drivers that they need to slow down or are too close to the edge of the road

rum·bling /ˈrʌmbəlɪŋ/ *noun, pl* **-blings**
1 [*count*] : a low, heavy, continuous sound or series of sounds • *rumblings* of thunder — usually singular • The *rumbling* of the thunder frightened the cat. • the *rumbling* of distant traffic
2 ***rumblings*** [*plural*] : written or spoken comments showing that people are unhappy about something • There were *rum-*

R

blings about rising prices. • the *rumblings* of revolution

rum·bus·tious /ˌrʌmˈbʌstʃəs/ *adj [more ~; most ~] Brit* : RAMBUNCTIOUS

ru·mi·nant /ˈruːmənənt/ *noun, pl* **-nants** *[count] technical* : an animal (such as a cow or sheep) that has more than one stomach and that swallows food and then brings it back up again to continue chewing it

– **ruminant** *adj* • *ruminant* animals

ru·mi·nate /ˈruːməˌneɪt/ *verb* **-nates; -nat·ed; -nat·ing** *[no obj]*

1 *formal* : to think carefully and deeply about something • The question got us *ruminating* on the real value of wealth. • He *ruminated* over/about the implications of their decision.

2 *technical, of an animal* : to bring up and chew again what has already been chewed and swallowed • a *ruminating* cow

– **ru·mi·na·tion** /ˌruːməˈneɪʃən/ *noun, pl* **-tions** *[count]* *ruminations* on the meaning of life *[noncount]* Cows break down their food by *rumination*.

ru·mi·na·tive /ˈruːməˌneɪtɪv/ *adj [more ~; most ~] formal* : showing careful thought about something : very thoughtful • The poem is dark and *ruminative*. • She was in a *ruminative* mood.

[1]rum·mage /ˈrʌmɪʤ/ *verb, always followed by an adverb or preposition* **-mag·es; -maged; -mag·ing** *[no obj]* : to search for something especially by moving and looking through the contents of a place • He *rummaged* through the attic for his baseball card collection. • He *rummaged* in his pocket for the receipt. • I heard you *rummaging* around/about in the refrigerator.

[2]rummage *noun [singular] chiefly Brit* : the act of looking for something among a group of things • ***Have a rummage*** through the box [=look through the box] and see if you can find the toy you're looking for.

rummage sale *noun, pl* **~ sales** *[count] US* : a sale of used items (such as old clothes or toys) especially to raise money for a church, school, charity, etc. — called also *(Brit) jumble sale*

rum·my /ˈrʌmi/ *noun [noncount]* : a card game in which each player tries to collect groups of three or more cards — see also GIN RUMMY

ru·mor *(US) or Brit* **ru·mour** /ˈruːmɚ/ *noun, pl* **-mors** : information or a story that is passed from person to person but has not been proven to be true *[count]* There are *rumors* that they are making a new film. • She accused him of starting/spreading *rumors* about her. • Ever since his sudden resignation, *rumors* have been flying. • I heard a *rumor* that they broke up. • "Did you hear that they broke up?" "That's just/only a *rumor*." • The *rumor* turned out to be false/unfounded. *[noncount]* You can't fire him solely based on *rumor*. • ***Rumor has it*** that they broke up.

the rumor mill : a group of people who start and spread rumors • That news should keep *the rumor mill* churning/running/going for a while!

ru·mored *(US) or Brit* **ru·moured** /ˈruːmɚd/ *adj* — used to describe what is being said in rumors • The estate sold for a *rumored* $12 million. [=people say that it sold for $12 million, but that may not be true] • It ***was rumored that*** the factory was going to move overseas, but that turned out to be false. • The new boss ***is rumored to be*** a bit of a tyrant.

ru·mor·mon·ger *(US) or Brit* **ru·mour·mon·ger** /ˈruːmɚˌmɑːŋgɚ, ˈruːmɚˌmʌŋgɚ/ *noun, pl* **-gers** *[count] disapproving* : a person who enjoys spreading rumors

rump /ˈrʌmp/ *noun, pl* **rumps**

1 a *[count]* : the back part of an animal's body where the thighs join the hips • a horse's/cow's *rump* **b** *[count, noncount]* : a piece of meat that comes from the rump of a cow — called also *rump steak*

2 *[count] humorous* : the part of the body you sit on : BOTTOM • I slipped and fell on my *rump*.

3 *[singular] chiefly Brit* : the part of a group that remains after most of the members of that group have left or been forced to leave

rum·ple /ˈrʌmpəl/ *verb* **rum·ples; rum·pled; rum·pling** *[+ obj]* : to make (something) messy or wrinkled • He *rumpled* her hair affectionately.

– **rumpled** *adj* • She put on a *rumpled* shirt she had worn the day before. • a *rumpled* bed

rum·pus /ˈrʌmpəs/ *noun [singular] chiefly Brit, informal* : a noisy argument, fight, etc. : RUCKUS • They caused a *rumpus* [=*commotion*] with their fighting.

rumpus room *noun, pl* **~ rooms** *[count] US, somewhat old-fashioned* : a room usually in the basement of a house that a family uses for games, parties, etc.

[1]run /ˈrʌn/ *verb* **runs; ran** /ˈræn/; **run; run·ning**

1 *[no obj]* **a** : to move with your legs at a speed that is faster than walking • How fast can you *run*? • He *runs* faster than anyone else on the team. • She *ran* up the stairs to get her jacket. • We *ran* for the train—but missed it. • I heard her scream and *ran* to help. • She *ran* to me for help. • The dog *ran* away from me. • The dog *ran* toward me. • When I called the dog, he ***came running***. • Don't expect me to *come running* every time you want something. I'm not your servant. • The chickens were ***running loose*** in the yard. • The horses ***ran wild***. • He ***ran at*** me with a knife. [=he ran toward me with a knife in his hand] — often used figuratively • He *ran* back to his ex-girlfriend after I dumped him. • You can't keep *running* away from your problems. • Don't *come running* to me when you get in trouble. • Don't let your imagination *run wild*. I'm sure nothing bad has happened. **b** : to leave a place quickly by running • When the alarm sounded, the robbers *ran*. • He dropped the gun and *ran*. • Quick! *Run* and get a doctor! • The ambushed soldiers *ran* for cover. • They had the enemy *running* scared. — often + *away* • When she saw all the people in the audience, she had a sudden urge to *run away*. • They *ran away* screaming. — often + *off* • When they saw the police, they quickly *ran off*.

2 a : to run as part of a sport, for exercise, or in a race *[no obj]* He *ran* on the track team in college. • She's *running* in the marathon this year. • The horse will not be *running* in this race. *[+ obj]* I *run* six miles every day. • She *ran* a great race. [=she ran very well in the race] • He *ran* track in college. • She's *running* the marathon this year. • The marathon will be *run* tomorrow. [=people will be running the marathon tomorrow] **b** *American football* : to carry and run with (the ball) *[+ obj]* He *ran* the football for a 20-yard gain. • He *ran* the kick back to the 40-yard line. *[no obj]* He *ran* for 15 yards. **c** *baseball* : to run from base to base *[no obj]* He *runs* well and might attempt a steal. *[+ obj]* He ***runs the bases*** well.

3 *[+ obj]* : to cause (an animal) to run • He *ran* the horse through the fields.

4 *[no obj] chiefly US* : to be a candidate in an election for a particular office — often + *for* • She is *running* [=*(Brit) standing*] *for* mayor. — often + *against* • He is *running against* her in the upcoming election.

5 *[+ obj]* **a** : to direct the business or activities of (something) • She *runs* [=*manages*] the restaurant/hotel/store. • He *runs* the after-school program. • The President is doing a good job *running* the country. • The company is badly/privately *run*. • state/family-*run* companies • I'm old enough to ***run my own life***. [=make my own decisions] **b** : to do (a test or check) on someone or something • The doctors need to *run* some more tests. — often + *on* • The doctors *ran* some tests *on* the blood samples. • The police *ran* a security check *on* him.

6 a *[+ obj]* : to use and control (something) • I'm not licensed to *run* [=*operate*] a forklift. **b** *[+ obj]* : to put (something) into operation • You should *run* the engine for a few minutes before you start driving. • He *ran* the program (on the computer). **c** *[no obj]* : to function or operate • Never leave your car unattended while the engine is *running*. • He didn't know the camera was still *running*. • He had his new computer ***up and running*** in no time. — often + *on* • This software *runs on* most computers. • The car *runs on* [=*uses*] diesel.

7 a *usually followed by an adverb or preposition [no obj]* : to go on a particular route or at particular times • The bus/ferry *runs* every hour. • The train *runs* between New York and Washington. • Trains no longer *run* on this track. • The buses are ***running late***. [=the buses are late] **b** *[+ obj]* : to have (a bus, train, ferry, etc.) traveling on a route • They *run* extra trains on Saturdays.

8 a *[no obj]* : to make a quick trip *to* a place for something • She *ran* (up/down) *to* the store for bread and milk. • He *ran* over *to* the neighbors for some sugar. **b** *[+ obj]* : to drive (someone) a short distance *to* a place or event • I have to *run* the kids *to* soccer practice. **c** *always followed by an adverb or preposition [+ obj]* : to bring (something) quickly to someone who is at a particular place • Wait here. I'm just going to *run* this in/inside to her. • He *ran* an umbrella out to her before she drove off. **d** *[+ obj]* : to do (something that involves making a quick trip) : to do (an errand) • I have a few errands to *run* after I leave work today.

9 *always followed by an adverb or preposition* **a** *[+ obj]* : to cause (a driver or vehicle) to move in a particular direction • That car tried to *run* me off the road! • She *ran* her car off the road. • He *ran* the car into a tree. **b** [*no obj*] *of a driver or vehicle* **:** to move in a particular direction • His car *ran* off the road. = He *ran* off the road. — see also RUN INTO (below), RUN OVER (below)

10 *always followed by an adverb or preposition* **a** [+ *obj*] **:** to cause (something) to pass through, over, along, or into something else • She *ran* her fingers through my hair. • He *ran* a brush over the dog's fur. • I quickly *ran* my eyes over/down the list of names. **b** [*no obj*] **:** to travel or spread in a fast or uncontrolled way • Whispers *ran* through the crowd. • A chill *ran* up/down my spine.

11 *always followed by an adverb or preposition* [*no obj*] **a :** to go or extend in a particular direction • The boundary line *runs* east. • The road *runs* through the mountain. • The highway *runs* from Boston to New York. — sometimes used figuratively • My tastes in novels *run to/toward* science fiction and thrillers. [=I tend to like science fiction and thrillers] • Such behavior *runs* counter to [=such behavior does not agree with] the values of our society. • He does nothing that would *run* against [=go against] his moral principles. **b —** used to describe the position of a road, path, etc. • The highway *runs* close to the shore. • The route *runs* the length of the eastern coast. • A path *runs* along the ridge. • The pipes *run* beneath the floor. • There was a scratch *running* down the side of the car.

12 [+ *obj*] **:** to cause (something, such as a wire or cable) to go or extend from one point to another • He *ran* the wires up from the basement.

13 [+ *obj*] **:** to bring (something) from one country into another country illegally and secretly • He was arrested for *running* [=*smuggling*] drugs into the country.

14 a [*no obj*] **:** to flow • He left the water *running*.**:** to flow in a particular direction • The river *runs* down to the valley. • The river *runs* into the gulf. • The tide was *running* out. • Sand *ran* out of the bag. • Steam *runs* through the pipes. • Blood was *running* down his leg. **b** [+ *obj*] **:** to cause (something) to flow or to produce a flow of water • She *ran* the tap/faucet. • *Run* the water until it gets hot. **c** [+ *obj*] **:** to prepare (a bath) by running a faucet • She *ran* a hot bath for her husband. = She *ran* her husband a hot bath.

15 [*no obj*] **a :** to produce a flow of liquid • Chopping the onions made my eyes *run*. [=*water*] • I knew I was getting sick when my nose started to *run*. • a *running* sore **b :** to spread or flow into another area • Your eyeliner is *running*. • Mascara *ran* from her eyes. • The paint *ran* in some spots. • The writing was blurred where the ink *ran*. **c :** to have a color that spreads onto other pieces of clothing when clothes are washed together • Her red shirt *ran* and made my blue jeans look purple. • colors that *run*

16 *always followed by an adverb or preposition* [*no obj*] **:** to continue or remain effective for a particular period of time • His contract *runs* until next season. • She received six months on each charge, and the sentences are to *run* concurrently. • The course *runs* over a six-week period of time. • The televised game *ran* 30 minutes over the scheduled time. • The play has *run* for six months. • Things *ran* smoothly at the office while the boss was away.

17 [*no obj*] **:** to be or to begin to be something specified • The well has ***run dry***. • Her creativity has *run dry*. • We are ***running low on*** fuel. [=our supply of fuel is getting low] • Supplies were ***running low/short***. • We ***ran short of*** money. [=we did not have enough money] • I have to hurry. I'm ***running late***. [=I'm late; I'm behind schedule] • The project is ***running behind schedule***.

18 [*no obj*] **:** to include everything between specified limits **:** RANGE • The prices for tickets *run* from $10 to $50.

19 [+ *obj*] **:** to allow charges on (a bill) to add up before paying • He ***ran a tab*** at the bar.

20 a [+ *obj*] **:** to have (an amount of money) as a price • The rooms *run* [=*cost*] $100 a night. **b** [*no obj*] **:** to have or reach a particular length, size, or amount • The book *runs* (to) nearly 500 pages. • Their annual budget *runs* to about 5 million dollars. • Their yearly income *runs* into/to six figures. [=their yearly income is more than $100,000] • Gas is ***running at*** over $4 per gallon. [=gas prices are over $4 per gallon]

21 a [+ *obj*] **:** to print or broadcast (something) • Every newspaper in the city *ran* the story. • The ad was *run* in yesterday's newspaper. • The news station *ran* a feature on how to eat healthier. **b** [*no obj*] **:** to appear in print or on television • Many of his stories *ran* in national magazines. • The show has *run* for five seasons.

22 [+ *obj*] **:** to produce (a copy of a document, newspaper, etc.) using a printer or copying machine • 10,000 copies were *run* for the first edition. — see also RUN OFF (below)

23 a [+ *obj*] **:** to have (particular words) in writing or print • "We Will Not Lose" *ran* the headline. [=the headline was/said "We Will Not Lose"] **b** [*no obj*] **:** to be expressed in words • The definition *runs* as follows . . .

24 [+ *obj*] **:** to drive past or through (a stop sign or red traffic light) illegally without stopping • He *ran* a red light. = He *ran* the light. • She *ran* the stop sign.

25 [*no obj*] *US, of stockings* **:** to start to have a long hole that continues to get longer • The nylons are guaranteed not to *run*. [=(*Brit*) *ladder*]

26 [+ *obj*] *chiefly Brit* **:** to own and maintain (a vehicle) • I can't afford to *run* a car on my salary.

> In addition to the phrases shown below, *run* occurs in many idioms that are shown at appropriate entries throughout the dictionary. For example, *cut and run* can be found at [1]CUT and *run a tight ship* can be found at [1]SHIP.

run across [*phrasal verb*] ***run across (someone or something)*** **:** to meet (someone) or find (something) by chance • I *ran across* [=*ran into*] an old roommate of mine today. • I *ran across* some old photos from when I was a kid.

run a fever/temperature ✧ If you are ***running a fever/temperature***, you have a body temperature that is higher than normal.

run after [*phrasal verb*] **1** ***run after (someone or something)*** **:** to run toward (someone or something) in an attempt to catch that person or thing • The dog *ran after* [=*chased*] the squirrel. **2** ***run after (someone)*** *informal + disapproving* **:** to try to start a romantic relationship with (someone) • He's always *running after* younger women.

run along [*phrasal verb*] *informal + somewhat old-fashioned* **:** to go away **:** LEAVE • He told the boy to *run along* home. • *Run along* now, kid. This doesn't concern you.

run around *or chiefly Brit* ***run about*** *or* ***run round*** [*phrasal verb*]

1 : to run in an area while playing • The children were *running around* outside. **2** *informal* **:** to go from place to place in a busy or hurried way • I spent the whole day *running around* doing errands. **3** ***run around/about/round with (someone)*** *informal + disapproving* **:** to spend a lot of time with (someone) • He *runs around with* younger women.

run away [*phrasal verb*] **1 :** to leave your home suddenly without permission and go somewhere else to live • He *ran away* (from home) at a young age. • They *ran away* [=*ran off*] together because their families objected to their marriage. — see also RUNAWAY **2 :** to avoid a person or situation that makes you feel uncomfortable • You shouldn't keep *running away*. You should face your mom and tell her how you feel. **3 a** ***run away with (someone)*** *disapproving* **:** to leave a person or place in order to live with and have a sexual relationship with (someone) • He left his wife and *ran away with* [=*ran off with*] his secretary. • She *ran away with* a man old enough to be her father. **b** ***run away with (something)*** **:** to leave a place with (something that does not belong to you) • The butler *ran away with* [=*stole, ran off with*] the family silver. **4** ***run away with (something)*** *informal* **a :** to be the best or most popular performer in (a performance) • She *ran away with* [=*stole*] the show. **b :** to win (something) very easily • She *ran away with* the election. • He *ran away with* first place. **5** ***run away with (someone)*** **:** to make (someone) do something that is not sensible or reasonable • Don't let your imagination *run away with* you. [=don't let yourself imagine all kinds of things that aren't true] — see also [1]RUN 1b (above)

run by/past [*phrasal verb*] ***run (something) by/past (someone)*** **:** to tell (something) to (someone) so that it can be considered, approved, etc. • You'd better *run* this *past* the boss. [=you'd better tell the boss about this and find out if he/she thinks it is a good idea] • He *ran* some ideas *by* her. • (*informal*) Can you *run* that *by* me again? [=can you repeat what you just said?]

run down [*phrasal verb*] **1** ***run (someone or something) down*** *or* ***run down (someone or something)*** **:** to hit and knock down (a person or animal) with a vehicle • He says she deliberately tried to *run* him *down*. **2 a** ***run (someone or something) down*** *or* ***run down (someone or something)*** **:** to chase after and catch (a person or animal) • The cops *ran* the robber *down* in an alley. **b :** to find (someone or something) after searching • He wasn't in his office, but I finally *ran* him *down* in the faculty lounge. **3** ***run down*** *or* ***run down (something)*** *or* ***run (something) down*** **a :** to use

R

up or cause (something) to use up all of its power • The clock *ran down.* [=the clock slowed down and stopped working because it did not have any more power] • The watch's battery *ran down.* • Turn off the radio so you don't *run down* the batteries. **b** *Brit* **:** to become or cause (something, such as a business or activity) to become gradually smaller • The company has been *running down* for decades. • The company has been *running down* its factories/ inventory. **4** ***run (someone or something) down or run down (someone or something) informal*** **:** to criticize (someone or something) in usually an unfair way • Don't keep *running* yourself *down* like that: you have a lot to offer! **5** ***run down (something)*** **:** to say or repeat (a list of people or things) from the beginning to the end • Let me just *run down* all the things we need to do. • He *ran down* the list of names. — see also RUNDOWN

run for it informal **:** to run to avoid being caught • It's the cops! *Run for it!*

run high **:** to be or become very strong or intense • Passions often *run high* in these debates. [=people often get very angry in these debates] • Emotions are *running high* between the two teams.

run in [*phrasal verb*] **1** ***run (someone) in or run in (someone) informal + somewhat old-fashioned*** **:** to arrest (someone) • The police *ran* him *in* for being drunk and disorderly. **2** ***run (something) in or run in (something) Brit*** **:** to drive (a new vehicle) carefully for a period of time until it is ready for regular use • You shouldn't drive a new car too fast while you're *running* it *in.* [=breaking it in]

run into [*phrasal verb*] **1** ***run into (someone or something)*** **:** to move into (someone or something) in a sudden or forceful way • He went off the road and *ran into* a tree. = His car went off the road and *ran into* a tree. • Some guy on a bike almost *ran into* me! • She wasn't paying attention and *ran* right *into* the table. **2** ***run into (someone)*** **:** to meet (someone) by chance • I *ran into* [=*ran across*] an old classmate the other day. **3** ***run into (something)*** **:** to experience (something that is unpleasant or difficult) **:** ENCOUNTER • We *ran into* some bad weather on our way home. • We *ran into* some problems setting up the computer.

run its course ✧ When something *runs its course,* it begins, continues for a time, and then ends. • The disease usually *runs its course* in a few days.

run off [*phrasal verb*] **1 a :** to leave or abandon a person or place • Her husband *ran off* and left her with two small children to care for. — see also [1]RUN 1b (above) **b** ***run off with (someone or something) informal*** **:** to leave a place with (someone or something) **:** to run away with (someone or something) • Her husband *ran off* with his secretary. • She *ran off with* all the money. **2** ***run off (something) or run (something) off*** **:** to repeat or produce (something) quickly • Would you please *run off* five copies of this letter? — see also [1]RUN 22 (above) **3** ***run (someone or something) off or run off (someone or something) US*** **:** to force (a person or animal) off your land • He *ran* us *off* his property.

run on [*phrasal verb*] **1 :** to talk about something for a long time • He *ran on* (and on) about politics until everybody was bored. **2 :** to keep going without being stopped or interrupted for a long period of time • The meeting *ran on* for hours.

run out [*phrasal verb*] **1 a :** to come to an end • Time *ran out* [=*expired*] before we could tie the game. • My contract will *run out* soon. **b :** to become used up • The gasoline *ran out* before we got to Denver. • Our money finally *ran out.* [=our money was all used; we had no more money] **2** ***run (someone) out or run (someone) out of (something) old-fashioned*** **:** to force (someone) to leave a place • An angry mob *ran* him *out of* town. **3** ***run out (something) or run (something) out baseball, of a batter*** **:** to run hard to first base after hitting (a batted ball) • His manager got angry because he failed to *run out* a grounder. **4** ***run out or run out of (something)*** **:** to use up the available supply of (something) • We're low on gas. We'd better stop before we *run out.* • He *ran out of* space and had to put his address on the other side of the paper. • You have to work faster. We're *running out* of time. **5** ***run out on (someone) informal*** **:** to leave (someone you should stay with) **:** to abandon or desert (someone) • She *ran out on* her husband and children to be with a man old enough to be her father.

run over [*phrasal verb*] **1 :** to go beyond a limit • The meeting *ran over.* [=the meeting was longer than it was expected or planned to be] **2 a :** to flow over the top or edge of something **:** OVERFLOW • The water was *running over* onto the floor. **b** *of a container* **:** to have a liquid flow over its edge **:** OVERFLOW • His cup *ran over.* **3** ***run over (someone or something) or run (someone or something) over*** **a :** to knock down and drive over or go over (someone or something) • The dog was *run over* by a car. • The running back *ran over* two defenders. **b :** to read, repeat, or practice (something) quickly • Let's *run* the lines *over* together one more time. • Can you *run over* the instructions again?

run past see RUN BY (above)

run through [*phrasal verb*] **1** ***run through (something)*** **a :** to spend or use up (something) quickly **:** SQUANDER • He *ran through* his winnings in a short time. **b** ***run through (something)*** **:** to read, repeat, or practice (something) quickly • Let's *run through* our lines one more time. • He quickly *ran through* the dance routine. — see also RUNTHROUGH **c :** to occur repeatedly in (something) or throughout (something) • The song has been *running through* my head all morning. • Thoughts and memories of home kept *running through* his mind. • A note of despair *runs through* the narrative. **2** ***run (something) through (something)*** **:** to enter (information) into (a computer) for processing • She *ran* his name *through* the police computer to see if he had any previous arrests. • He *ran* the data *through.* **3** ***run (someone) through literary*** **:** to push a sword through (someone) • He *ran* him *through* with his sword.

run up [*phrasal verb*] **1** ***run up (something) or run (something) up*** **a :** to raise (a flag) to the top of a flagpole • To celebrate our victory, we *ran up* our flag. **b :** to achieve (a large score or lead) • Our team *ran up* a big lead in the first quarter. • (*US*) She angrily accused the other coach of deliberately ***running up the score*** [=continuing to try to score more points even though they are not needed to win a game] **c :** to increase the amount of (something) • These extras will *run* the bill *up* another $100. **d :** to get (a large bill, debt, etc.) by buying many things without making payments — often + *up* • She *ran up* a large phone bill. • He *ran up* a lot of debt on his credit cards. **2** ***run up against (something)*** **:** to experience (something difficult) **:** ENCOUNTER • She has *run up against* a lot of opposition. • He has *run up against* a bug in his computer program.

run with [*phrasal verb*] ***run with (something) informal*** **:** to use (something) in a very energetic, enthusiastic, and effective way • He took the idea and *ran with* it.

run your mouth informal **:** to talk too much and in a foolish way • He's always *running his mouth* about what a great athlete he is.

walk before you (can) run see [1]WALK

[2]run *noun, pl* **runs**

1 [*count*] **:** an act of running • He goes for a six-mile *run* every evening. • She took the dogs out for a *run.* • When they realized they might miss the train, they ***broke into a run*** [=started running] • The robbers heard the police sirens and ***made a run for it*** [=ran away to avoid being captured] • The dog was coming toward us ***at a run*** [=the dog was running toward us] — see also HIT-AND-RUN

2 [*count*] **a :** a continuous series of similar things — often + *of* • We had a long *run of* cloudy days. • a *run of* good/bad luck • a long *run of* wins/losses **b :** a continuous series of performances or showings • The play had a *run* of six months on Broadway. = The play had a six-month *run* on Broadway.

3 [*count*] **:** the amount of a product that is produced at one time — often + *of* • The book had a print *run of* 10,000 copies. [=10,000 copies of the book were printed at the one time]

4 [*count*] *US* **:** an attempt to win or do something • The team is ***making a run*** at the championship. [=the team is playing well and has a chance to win the championship] • She ***made an unsuccessful run*** for a seat in the Senate. [=she tried to be elected to a seat in the Senate, but she lost the election] • (*informal*) "I can't solve this math problem." "Let me ***take a run at it***" [=let me try it]

5 [*singular*] **:** the usual or normal kind of person or thing • She's not like the ***average/normal/general/usual run of*** students. [=she's not like most students] • The place is different from the *usual run of* restaurants.

6 [*count*] **a :** a score made in baseball when a player reaches home plate after going around the bases • The home team took the lead with three *runs* in the bottom of the fifth (inning). • a three-*run* lead — see also HOME RUN **b :** a score made in cricket

7 [*count*] *American football* **:** a play in which a player tries to

R

move the ball forward by running with it • He scored on a 25-yard *run*.
8 a [*count*] : a regular journey that is made by a bus, train, etc. • The bus makes four *runs* daily. • a delivery *run* • (*Brit*) the ***school run*** [=a regular trip in which parents take their children to or from school each day] • The planes were sent out on a ***bomb/bombing run***. **b** [*singular*] : a short trip in a vehicle • I have to make a quick *run* to the store.
9 [*count*] : a track that slopes down and that is used for skiing, sledding, etc. • a ski *run* [=*slope*] • a bobsled *run*
10 [*count*] : a path that is used regularly by animals • a deer *run* — see also RAT RUN
11 [*count*] : an enclosed area for animals where they feed and exercise • a chicken *run*
12 [*count*] *US* : a long hole in a stocking • She had a *run* in her stocking/nylons. — called also (*Brit*) *ladder*
13 [*count*] *music* : a series of notes that are sung or played quickly up or down a scale
14 [*count*] : a situation in which many people want to have, get, or do something at the same time — usually singular; usually + *on* • There's been a big *run on* tickets for the game. [=a lot of people have been trying to get tickets for the game] • There was a ***run on the bank***. [=a lot of people were taking their money out of the bank because they were afraid that the bank would fail]
15 [*count*] : the general way in which something is moving or changing • Investors are anxiously watching the *run of* the stock market. [=are watching to see if the stock market is going up or down]
16 ***the runs*** *informal* : DIARRHEA • a bad case of *the runs*
17 [*count*] *technical* : an occurrence in which a large number of fish (such as salmon) swim up a river to return to the place where they were hatched and produce young • a salmon *run*
a run for your money ✧ Someone who ***gives you a (good) run for your money*** in a game or contest makes it difficult for you to win by trying hard and playing or performing well. • Though they lost, they *gave* last year's champions a *run for their money*.
on the run **1 a** : running away from someone in order to avoid being captured • an escaped convict *on the run* • He is *on the run* from the cops. **b** : running away because you are about to be defeated • The army had the enemy *on the run*. **2** : while going somewhere or while doing something else • We ate lunch *on the run*. **3** *informal* : continuously busy • He's always *on the run*.
the run of : the freedom to go anywhere or do anything you want in (a place) • With his parents gone, he had *the run of* the house.
– see also DRY RUN, DUMMY RUN, LONG RUN, SHORT RUN, TRIAL RUN

run·about /ˈrʌnəˌbaʊt/ *noun, pl* **-abouts** [*count*]
1 *chiefly US* : a small motorboat
2 *chiefly Brit* : a small car

run·around /ˈrʌnəˌraʊnd/ *noun*
the runaround *informal* ✧ If someone ***gives you the runaround*** or you ***get the runaround***, you are not given the information or help that you need because someone will not answer your questions or deal with your problem directly. • I'm tired of *getting the runaround* from your customer representatives. • They keep *giving me the runaround*.

[1]run·away /ˈrʌnəˌweɪ/ *noun, pl* **-aways** [*count*] : someone (such as a child) who leaves home without permission : someone who runs away from home • teenage *runaways* — see also *run away* at [1]RUN

[2]runaway *adj, always used before a noun*
1 — used to describe a person who has left home without permission or who has escaped from someplace • *runaway* teenagers • a *runaway* slave
2 : operating, running, increasing, etc., in a fast and dangerous way that cannot be controlled • a *runaway* horse/train • a *runaway* oil well • *runaway* inflation
3 : extremely successful • a *runaway* best seller • The play was a *runaway* success.
4 a : won very easily by a large amount • a *runaway* victory **b** : having won very easily by a large amount • She was the *runaway* winner of the race.

run batted in *noun, pl* **runs batted in** [*count*] *baseball* : RBI

run–down /ˈrʌnˈdaʊn/ *adj* [*more* ~; *most* ~]
1 : in very bad condition because of age or lack of care • They lived in a *run-down* farmhouse in rural Maine.
2 *not used before a noun* : in poor health or physical condition : worn-out or exhausted • You look *run-down*.

run·down /ˈrʌnˌdaʊn/ *noun, pl* **-downs** [*count*]
1 : a quick report about the main parts of something • They gave us a *rundown* on/of the main points of the news.
2 *Brit* : a gradual reduction in the size of a business, activity, etc. • a *rundown* of/in our public services — see also *run down* at [1]RUN
3 *baseball* : a play in which a runner is chased by two or more opposing players who throw the ball to each other in an attempt to tag the runner out • He was caught in a *rundown*.

rune /ˈruːn/ *noun, pl* **runes** [*count*] : any of the characters in the alphabets that were used in ancient times by people of Northern Europe
– **ru·nic** /ˈruːnɪk/ *adj* • a *runic* inscription

[1]rung *past participle of* [3]RING

[2]rung /ˈrʌŋ/ *noun, pl* **rungs** [*count*]
1 : a piece of wood or metal that is placed between the legs of a chair for support
2 : one of the pieces of wood or metal that is used as a step on a ladder
3 : a position or level within a group, organization, etc., that is higher or lower than others • He was on the bottom *rung* on the corporate ladder. • the top *rung* of society • the lowest/highest *rung* of the pay scale

run–in /ˈrʌnˌɪn/ *noun, pl* **-ins** [*count*] *informal* : an angry argument — usually + *with* • He had a *run-in with* the cops.

run·nel /ˈrʌnl/ *noun, pl* **-nels** [*count*] *formal* + *literary* : a small stream

run·ner /ˈrʌnɚ/ *noun, pl* **-ners** [*count*]
1 a : a person who runs as part of a sport, for exercise, or in a race • a long-distance/cross-country/marathon *runner* • She's a fast *runner*. **b** : an animal (such as a horse) that runs in a race
2 a : a person who delivers messages, reports, materials, or products either within a business or organization or to outside locations : MESSENGER **b** : a person who brings drugs, guns, etc., to a place illegally and secretly • a drug *runner*
3 *baseball* : a player who is on base or is trying to reach a base : BASE RUNNER • The *runner* slid into third base.
4 : a long, thin piece or part on which something (such as a sled, skate, or drawer) slides
5 : a stem of a plant that grows along the ground and that forms new plants • a plant that spreads by sending out *runners*
6 a : a long, narrow carpet for a hall or staircase **b** : a narrow cloth cover for a table or other piece of furniture
do a runner *Brit, informal* : to leave a place quickly by running especially to avoid paying a bill or to escape punishment

run·ner–up /ˈrʌnɚˌʌp/ *noun, pl* **run·ners–up** /ˈrʌnɚzˌʌp/ [*count*] : a person or team that does not win first place in a competition but that does well enough to get a prize • the first and second *runners-up* in the beauty pageant; *especially* : a person or team that finishes in second place • The winner will receive $1,000 and the *runner-up* will receive $100.

[1]run·ning /ˈrʌnɪŋ/ *noun* [*noncount*]
1 : the activity or sport of running • He took up *running* for exercise. • long-distance *running* • They ***go running*** every evening.
2 : the activity of managing or operating something — usually + *of* • She's in charge of the day-to-day *running of* the entire operation. • the smooth *running of* the events
3 : the activity of bringing drugs, guns, etc., to a place illegally and secretly • drug *running*
in the running **1** : competing in a contest • The enthusiasm of his supporters made him decide to stay *in the running* for mayor. **2** : having a chance to win a contest • She is still *in the running* for the prize.
out of the running **1** : not competing in a contest • He declared himself officially *out of the running* for mayor. **2** : having no chance to win a contest • She is now *out of the running* for the prize.

[2]running *adj, always used before a noun*
1 : operating or flowing • Never add fuel to a *running* engine. • a *running* faucet — see also RUNNING WATER
2 : going on steadily or repeatedly for a long period of time • The farmer had a *running* battle with pests and disease. • a ***running joke/gag*** [=a joke/gag that is repeated many times in slightly different ways]

R

3 : made during the course of a process or activity • The major television stations provided *running* commentaries on the election results. • She kept a *running* total of their expenses on the trip.
4 : done while running or immediately after running • a *running* catch/jump
5 *American football* — used to describe play in which the ball is moved forward by running rather than by passing • a *running* play • The team has a strong *running* game. [=the team is good at moving the ball by running with it]
6 : designed for use by runners • a *running* track • *running* shoes

³running *adv, always used after a noun* : following or happening one after the other • It has rained (for) three days *running*. [=for three days in a row; for three consecutive days] • He has won the competition three times *running*.

running back *noun, pl* **~ backs** [*count*] *American football* : a player who carries the football on running plays

running board *noun, pl* **~ boards** [*count*] : a long, narrow board that is attached to the side of a vehicle to make it easier for people to get in and out

running mate *noun, pl* **~ mates** [*count*] *chiefly US* : the person who runs with someone in an election (such as an election to choose a new president) and who is given the less important position (such as vice president) if they are elected • When John F. Kennedy ran for president, his *running mate* was Lyndon Johnson.

running start *noun* [*singular*] *chiefly US* — used to say that a person or animal is running at the start of a race, jump, etc. • How fast can you cover 100 meters if you have a *running start*? [=if you are already running when you pass the starting point of that 100 meters?] • The sprinters were given a *running start*. [=were allowed to be running at the start of the race] — often used figuratively • The new mayor is off to a *running start*. [=*flying start*] [=the new mayor has been successful very quickly] • The company was given a *running start* [=*head start, advantage*] by its experience with similar projects in the past.

running time *noun, pl* **~ times** [*count, noncount*] : the amount of time that a movie, performance, recording, etc., lasts from beginning to end

running water *noun* [*noncount*] : water that comes into a building through pipes • a cabin with hot and cold *running water*

run•ny /ˈrʌni/ *adj* **run•ni•er; -est**
1 *of a food* : soft and with a lot of liquid • The scrambled eggs are *runny*. • The pudding is *runnier* than I like it.
2 : having a thin flow of liquid flowing out • a little boy with a *runny* nose • My eyes felt itchy and *runny*.

run•off /ˈrʌnˌɑːf/ *noun, pl* **-offs**
1 [*count*] : an additional race, contest, or election that is held because an earlier one has not resulted in a winner
2 [*noncount*] : water from rain or snow that flows over the surface of the ground into streams

run–of–the–mill /ˌrʌnəvðəˈmɪl/ *adj, often disapproving* : average or ordinary • a *run-of-the-mill* performance

runt /ˈrʌnt/ *noun, pl* **runts** [*count*]
1 : the smallest animal in a group that is born to one mother at the same time • the *runt* of the litter
2 *informal + disapproving* : a very small or weak person • a skinny little *runt*
– **runty** /ˈrʌnti/ *adj* **-i•er; -i•est** • a *runty* kid

run–through /ˈrʌnˌθruː/ *noun, pl* **-throughs** [*count*] : an activity in which you quickly do or read all the different parts of something especially in order to practice or prepare for something (such as a performance) • She gave her lines/notes a quick *run-through*. • They did a *run-through* [=*rehearsal*] of the play. — see also *run through* at ¹RUN

run–up /ˈrʌnˌʌp/ *noun, pl* **-ups** [*count*]
1 : a usually sudden increase in price • a *run-up* in stock prices
2 : the period immediately before an action or event • during the *run-up* to the war/election

run•way /ˈrʌnˌweɪ/ *noun, pl* **-ways** [*count*]
1 : a long strip of ground where airplanes take off and land
2 *US* : a raised structure along which models walk in a fashion show : CATWALK

ru•pee /ruˈpiː/ *noun, pl* **-pees** [*count*] : the basic unit of money in some Asian countries including India and Pakistan

ru•pi•ah /ruˈpiːjə/ *noun, pl* **rupiah** *or* **ru•pi•ahs** [*count*] : the basic unit of money in Indonesia

¹rup•ture /ˈrʌptʃə/ *noun, pl* **-tures**
1 [*count, noncount*] : a crack or break in something (such as a pipe) • A *rupture* in the pipeline resulted in major water damage.
2 *medical* **a** : a break or tear in a part of the body [*count*] a *rupture* of an artery [*noncount*] an infection that could cause *rupture* of the eardrum **b** [*count*] : HERNIA
3 [*count*] : a break in good relations between people or countries • The conflict caused a *rupture* in relations between the former allies. • They're trying to heal the *rupture* in their relationship.

²rupture *verb* **-tures; -tured; -tur•ing**
1 **a** : to break or burst [*no obj*] The pipe *ruptured* because of high water pressure. [*+ obj*] High water pressure *ruptured* the pipe. **b** [*+ obj*] *medical* : to cause a break or tear in (a part of the body) • The impact *ruptured* his liver. • a *ruptured* eardrum • I almost ***ruptured myself*** [=I almost gave myself a hernia] trying to lift that heavy box.
2 [*+ obj*] : to damage or destroy (a relationship, situation, etc.) • The scandal *ruptured* relations between the two countries. • The crime *ruptured* the peace of a small town.

ru•ral /ˈrərəl/ *adj* [*more ~; most ~*] : of or relating to the country and the people who live there instead of the city • She lives in a *rural* area. • a *rural* community/setting • *rural* voters — opposite URBAN

ruse /ˈruːs, *Brit* ˈruːz/ *noun, pl* **rus•es** [*count*] : a trick or act that is used to fool someone • His act was just a clever *ruse* to get me to go out with him.

¹rush /ˈrʌʃ/ *verb* **rush•es; rushed; rush•ing**
1 [*no obj*] : to move or do something very quickly or in a way that shows you are in a hurry • Firefighters *rushed* to the accident scene. • The children *rushed* down the stairs. • She *rushed* past me. • I *rushed* home from work to get ready for the party. • She *rushed* through dinner. • I'm getting everything ready tonight so I won't have to *rush* (around) in the morning. • She *rushed* to close the window when she heard the rain. • We were *rushing* to catch the bus.
2 **a** [*+ obj*] : to cause or force (someone) to do something too quickly • He got nervous because they *rushed* him. • Please stop *rushing* me! — often + *into* • They *rushed* her *into* making a bad decision. **b** [*no obj*] : to do something too quickly and often with little thought, attention, or care • He *rushed* through his work and made a lot of careless mistakes. — often + *into* • She *rushed into* (making) a bad decision. • After the divorce, he *rushed into* another marriage.
3 *always followed by an adverb or preposition* [*no obj*] : to flow or move very quickly in a particular direction • Water *rushed* through the pipes. • The *rushing* water broke through the barrier. — often used figuratively • When he saw her photo, memories came *rushing* back.
4 *always followed by an adverb or preposition* [*+ obj*] : to bring or send (someone or something) very quickly to a particular place • He *rushed* his wife to the hospital. • Supplies for the victims were *rushed* in. — sometimes used figuratively • Lawmakers *rushed* the bill through Congress.
5 [*+ obj*] : to do (something) quickly in a short period of time • He asked the clerk to *rush* his order.
6 [*+ obj*] : to run toward (someone or something) very quickly • Several hostages *rushed* the gunman and knocked him to the ground. • The crowd *rushed* the stage at the concert.
7 [*+ obj*] *US* **a** : to go through the process of becoming a member of (a fraternity or sorority) • She is *rushing* a sorority. **b** : to try to get (a student) to join a fraternity or sorority • He is being *rushed* by a fraternity.
8 *American football* : to move a football down the field by running with it instead of throwing it [*no obj*] He *rushed* [=*ran*] for 100 yards in last week's game. = He had 100 yards *rushing* in last week's game. • The team has a strong *rushing* defense/attack. [*+ obj*] He *rushed* [=*ran*] the ball for 100 yards in last week's game.

rush out [*phrasal verb*] ***rush (something) out or rush out (something)*** : to produce (something) very quickly • We had to *rush* the manuscript *out* so that it could be copied. • Reporters *rushed out* the story for the morning edition of the newspaper.

²rush *noun, pl* **rushes**
1 [*singular*] **a** : a quick, strong, or fast movement • He made a sudden *rush* toward the door. **b** : a quick and forceful movement of air, water, etc. • We felt a *rush* of cold/hot air from the vent. • When the levees broke, the *rush* of water flooded the area.
2 [*singular*] : a situation in which someone is doing some-

R

thing very quickly or hurrying ▪ In his *rush* to get out the door, he forgot his hat. [=he forgot his hat because he was rushing/hurrying to get out the door] ▪ We are in no *rush* [=*hurry*] to finish.

3 [*count*] : a situation in which a large number of people move to or toward one place at the same time usually to do a specific thing or to search for something ▪ Shop early to avoid the Christmas/holiday *rush*. [=the time when everyone else is doing their shopping] — see also GOLD RUSH

4 [*count*] : a sudden demand for something by many people ▪ There is always a *rush* for fans and air conditioners during the first heat wave.

5 [*count*] *US* : the process of finding new people to join a fraternity or sorority ▪ a fraternity *rush*

6 ***rushes*** [*plural*] : the first prints of scenes of a film or movie that have not been edited ▪ The director and the actors watched the *rushes* from the previous day's filming.

7 [*count*] : a strong feeling or emotion caused by a drug or by something exciting ▪ The roller-coaster ride gave me a *rush*. [=*thrill*] ▪ an adrenaline *rush* [=*high*] ▪ I felt a *rush* of relief after hearing the news.

– compare ³RUSH

³rush *noun, pl* **rushes** [*count*] : a tall plant similar to grass that grows in wet areas and that is used to make baskets and other things when dried — compare ²RUSH

rush·er /ˈrʌʃɚ/ *noun, pl* **-ers** [*count*] : someone or something that rushes; *especially, American football* : a player who carries the ball during running plays ▪ He was the team's leading *rusher* last year.

rush hour *noun, pl* **~ hours** [*count, noncount*] : a time during the day early in the morning or late in the afternoon when many people are traveling on roads to get to work or to get home from work ▪ We got caught in the morning *rush hour*. ▪ *rush hour* traffic

rusk /ˈrʌsk/ *noun, pl* **rusks** [*count*] *chiefly Brit* : a dry, hard cookie that is eaten especially by young children

rus·set /ˈrʌsət/ *noun* [*noncount*] : a reddish-brown color — see color picture on page C3

Rus·sian /ˈrʌʃən/ *noun, pl* **-sians**

1 [*count*] **a** : a person born, raised, or living in Russia **b** : a person whose family is from Russia

2 [*noncount*] : the language of the Russian people

– **Russian** *adj* ▪ *Russian* food/literature

Russian dressing *noun* [*noncount*] *US* : a type of salad dressing that typically contains chili sauce, chopped pickles, or pimientos

Russian roulette *noun* [*noncount*] : a dangerous game in which people fire a gun with a single bullet at their heads without knowing if the bullet will be shot or not — often used figuratively ▪ He was ***playing Russian roulette*** with his life. [=he was doing something that was very foolish and dangerous and that could destroy or end his life]

¹rust /ˈrʌst/ *noun* [*noncount*]

1 : a reddish substance that forms on iron or some other metal usually when it comes in contact with moisture or air ▪ an old pump covered in *rust* ▪ *rust* spots/patches

2 : a disease that causes plants to develop reddish-brown spots

3 : a reddish-brown color

²rust *verb* **rusts; rust·ed; rust·ing**

1 [*no obj*] : to form rust : to become rusty ▪ Your bicycle will *rust* if you leave it out in the rain. ▪ *rusting* nails ▪ The paint prevents *rusting*.

2 [+ *obj*] : to cause rust to form on (something) ▪ The moist air *rusted* the latch on the door. ▪ The old iron fence was *rusted*.

Rust·belt /ˈrʌstˌbɛlt/ *noun*

the Rustbelt : the northeastern and midwestern states of the U.S. in which many factories (such as steel mills) have closed because of changes in the economy ▪ Many people have moved from *the Rustbelt* to the Sunbelt.

¹rus·tic /ˈrʌstɪk/ *adj* [*more* ~; *most* ~]

1 : of, relating to, or suitable for the country or people who live in the country ▪ The inn has a *rustic* atmosphere. ▪ a *rustic* village

2 : made of rough wood ▪ simple, *rustic* furniture

– **rus·tic·i·ty** /ˌrʌˈstɪsəti/ *noun* [*noncount*] ▪ the *rusticity* of the inn

²rustic *noun, pl* **-tics** [*count*] : a person who lives in the country

¹rus·tle /ˈrʌsəl/ *verb* **rus·tles; rus·tled; rus·tling**

1 a [*no obj*] : to make a soft, light sound because parts of something are touching or rubbing against each other ▪ The trees *rustled* in the wind. ▪ Her skirt *rustled* as she walked. **b** [+ *obj*] : to cause (something) to make a soft, light sound ▪ He *rustled* the papers on his desk.

2 [+ *obj*] : to steal (animals) from a farm or ranch ▪ *rustle* sheep/cattle

rustle up [*phrasal verb*] ***rustle (something) up or rustle up (something)*** *informal* **1** : to prepare (food, a meal, etc.) quickly ▪ He *rustled up* a full meal in no time. **2** : to find or get (something) ▪ I'll see if I can *rustle up* some information about that for you.

– **rus·tler** /ˈrʌsələ/ *noun, pl* **rus·tlers** [*count*] ▪ a cattle *rustler* – **rustling** *noun* [*singular*] He heard a *rustling* in the bushes. [*noncount*] They were accused of cattle *rustling*.

²rustle *noun* [*singular*] : a quick series of soft, light sounds caused when things (such as leaves or pieces of paper) rub against each other ▪ He heard a *rustle* of leaves behind him.

rust·proof /ˈrʌstˌpruːf/ *adj* : protected against rusting ▪ a *rustproof* pipe

rusty /ˈrʌsti/ *adj* **rust·i·er; -est** [*also more* ~; *most* ~]

1 : covered with rust ▪ a *rusty* old car ▪ *rusty* nails

2 : not as good as usual or as in the past because you have not done or practiced something for a long time ▪ My tennis skills are a little *rusty*. ▪ The singers were a bit *rusty* after the long break.

3 : of the color of rust : reddish brown ▪ *rusty* hair

– **rust·i·ness** /ˈrʌstinəs/ *noun* [*noncount*]

¹rut /ˈrʌt/ *noun, pl* **ruts**

1 [*count*] : a long, narrow mark made by the wheels of a vehicle passing over an area ▪ The truck left deep *ruts* in the muddy ground.

2 [*singular*] : a situation or way of behaving that does not change ▪ She was ***stuck in a rut*** at her old job, so she quit work and went back to school. ▪ It is easy to ***get into a rut*** if you're not careful.

– compare ²RUT

– **rut·ted** /ˈrʌtəd/ *adj* ▪ a *rutted* dirt road – **rut·ty** /ˈrʌti/ *adj* ▪ a *rutty* track/road

²rut *noun* [*noncount*] : the time when male animals (such as deer) become sexually active ▪ Bucks will defend their territory during the *rut*. ▪ a stag ***in rut*** — compare ¹RUT

– **rut·ting** /ˈrʌtɪŋ/ *adj* ▪ a *rutting* elk/buck ▪ the *rutting* season

ru·ta·ba·ga /ˌruːtəˈbeɪgə/ *noun, pl* **-gas** [*count, noncount*] *US* : a large, yellowish root vegetable that is a type of turnip — called also (*Brit*) *swede*

ruth·less /ˈruːθləs/ *adj* [*more* ~; *most* ~] : having no pity : cruel or merciless ▪ a *ruthless* killer ▪ The journalist was *ruthless* in his criticism.

– **ruth·less·ly** *adv* ▪ The slaves were *ruthlessly* abused by their owners. – **ruth·less·ness** *noun* [*noncount*]

RV /ˌɑɚˈviː/ *noun, pl* **RVs** [*count*] : RECREATIONAL VEHICLE

Rx /ˌɑɚˈɛks/ *noun, pl* **Rx's** [*count*] *US* : a doctor's prescription ▪ an *Rx* for heartburn — often used figuratively ▪ an *Rx* for boredom [=a way to stop being bored] ✧ *Rx* comes from the Latin word "recipe," which means "take." It traditionally appears in places where medicines are sold and is often used on signs, in newspaper headlines, etc.

-ry *noun suffix* : -ERY ▪ wizard*ry* ▪ citizen*ry*

rye /ˈraɪ/ *noun*

1 [*noncount*] : a type of grass that is grown as a grain and used to make flour or whiskey

2 [*count, noncount*] *US* : bread that is made from rye flour ▪ a ham sandwich on *rye* — called also *rye bread*

3 [*count, noncount*] : whiskey that is made from rye ▪ a bottle of *rye* — called also *rye whiskey*

R

S

[1]s *or* **S** /ˈɛs/ *noun, pl* **s's** *or* **S's** : the 19th letter of the English alphabet *[count]* a word that starts with an *s* *[noncount]* a word that starts with *s*

[2]s *or* **S** *abbr* **1** small — usually used for a clothing size ▪ The shirt comes in *S*, M, L, or XL. **2** ***S*** south, southern

[1]-s *noun plural suffix*
1 — used to form the plural of most nouns ▪ head*s* ▪ book*s* ▪ boy*s* ▪ belief*s* ▪ mother*s*-in-law ▪ the Taylor*s*
2 — used with or without a preceding apostrophe to form the plural of abbreviations, numbers, letters, and symbols that are used as nouns ▪ MC*s* ▪ PhD*'s* ▪ the 1940*'s* ▪ men in their 50*s* — compare [1]-ES

[2]-s *verb suffix* — used to form the third person singular present tense of most verbs ▪ fall*s* ▪ take*s* ▪ play*s* — compare [2]-ES

's /s *after* p, t, k, f, *or* θ; əz *after* s, z, ʃ, ʒ, ʧ, *or* ʤ; z *elsewhere*/ *verb* — used as a contraction of *is, was, has,* and *does* ▪ She*'s* here. [=she is here] ▪ When*'s* [=when was] the last time you ate? ▪ He*'s* [=he has] seen them already. ▪ What*'s* he want? [=what does he want?]

-'s /s *after* p, t, k, f, *or* θ; əz *after* s, z, ʃ, ʒ, ʧ, *or* ʤ; z *elsewhere*/ *noun suffix or pronoun suffix* — used to form the possessive of singular nouns, of plural nouns not ending in *s*, of some pronouns, and of word groups that function as nouns or pronouns ▪ The boy*'s* books were missing. ▪ I called the doctor*'s* (office). ▪ children*'s* clothes ▪ anyone*'s* dog ▪ the man on the corner*'s* hat ▪ someone else*'s* car ✧ The possessive of a plural noun that ends in *s* is formed by adding an apostrophe alone instead of *'s*. ▪ The boys*'* books were missing. The possessive of singular nouns and names that end in *s* can usually be formed by adding *'s*. If adding *'s* would make the word difficult to say, an apostrophe alone may be used instead. ▪ James*'s* mother ▪ Moses*'* mother

Sa. *abbr* Saturday

Sab·bath /ˈsæbəθ/ *noun*
the Sabbath : a weekly day of rest and worship that is observed on Sunday by most Christians and on Saturday (from Friday evening to Saturday evening) by Jews and some Christians ▪ Our family ***keeps/observes the Sabbath***. [=obeys the rules about what should be done on the Sabbath] ▪ We are careful not to ***break the Sabbath***.
– **Sabbath** *adj, always used before a noun* ▪ *Sabbath* day/dinner/observances

sab·bat·i·cal /səˈbætɪkəl/ *noun, pl* **-cals** : a period of time during which someone does not work at his or her regular job and is able to rest, travel, do research, etc. *[count]* Several professors will be taking *sabbaticals* this year. ▪ She recently returned to work after a two-year *sabbatical* from her acting career. ▪ a paid *sabbatical* *[noncount]* Several professors will be ***on sabbatical*** this year.
– **sabbatical** *adj, always used before a noun* ▪ I chose to take *sabbatical* leave next year. ▪ a *sabbatical* year

sa·ber *(US) or Brit* **sa·bre** /ˈseɪbɚ/ *noun, pl* **-bers** *[count]*
1 : a long, heavy sword with a curved blade
2 : a lightweight sword that is used in fencing

saber–rattling *(US) or Brit* **sabre–rattling** *noun [noncount]* : actions and statements that are meant to frighten or threaten an enemy by suggesting the possible use of force

saber–toothed tiger *(US) or Brit* **sabre–toothed tiger** *noun, pl* **~ -gers** *[count]* : a type of large cat that lived in very ancient times and had long, curved teeth — called also *saber-toothed cat*

sa·ble /ˈseɪbəl/ *noun, pl* **sa·bles** *or* **sable**
1 *[count]* : a small animal that lives in northern Asia and has soft, brown fur
2 *[noncount]* : the fur of the sable ▪ a brush/coat made of *sable*
– **sable** *adj* ▪ a *sable* brush/coat

[1]sab·o·tage /ˈsæbəˌtɑːʒ/ *noun [noncount]* : the act of destroying or damaging something deliberately so that it does not work correctly ▪ Angry workers were responsible for the *sabotage* of the machines. ▪ terrorists engaging in (deliberate) acts of *sabotage* ▪ Officials have not yet ruled out *sabotage* as a possible cause of the crash. ▪ industrial *sabotage*

[2]sabotage *verb* **-tag·es; -taged; -tag·ing** *[+ obj]*
1 : to destroy or damage (something) deliberately so that it does not work correctly ▪ They *sabotaged* the enemy's oil fields. ▪ The airplane crashed because it was *sabotaged*.
2 : to cause the failure of (something) deliberately ▪ The lawyer is trying to *sabotage* the case by creating confusion. ▪ The deal was *sabotaged* by an angry employee. — sometimes used figuratively ▪ Bad weather *sabotaged* [=*ruined*] our plans.

sab·o·teur /ˌsæbəˈtɚ/ *noun, pl* **-teurs** *[count]* : a person who destroys or damages something deliberately : a person who performs sabotage ▪ The car's tires were slashed by *saboteurs*.

sac /ˈsæk/ *noun, pl* **sacs** *[count]* : a part inside the body of an animal or plant that is shaped like a bag and that usually contains liquid or air ▪ a food storage *sac* ▪ an air/egg *sac*

sac·cha·rin /ˈsækərən/ *noun [noncount]* : a very sweet, white substance that does not have any calories and that is used instead of sugar to sweeten food ▪ soft drinks flavored with *saccharin*

sac·cha·rine /ˈsækərən, *Brit* ˈsækəˌriːn/ *adj [more ~; most ~] formal* : too sweet or sentimental : sweet or sentimental in a way that does not seem sincere or genuine ▪ a *saccharine* smile ▪ a *saccharine* love story

sa·chet /sæˈʃeɪ, *Brit* ˈsæʃeɪ/ *noun, pl* **-chets** *[count]*
1 : a small bag that has a powder or a mixture of dried flowers and spices inside it and that is used to give a pleasant smell to clothes, sheets, etc.
2 *Brit* : a small, thin package : PACKET ▪ a *sachet* of shampoo/sugar

[1]sack /ˈsæk/ *noun, pl* **sacks**
1 *[count]* : a bag that is made of strong paper, cloth, or plastic ▪ a *sack* containing flour = a *sack* of flour ▪ *sacks* of cement ▪ a grocery *sack* — see also GUNNYSACK, RUCKSACK
2 *[count]* : the amount that is contained in a sack ▪ We peeled an entire *sack* [=*sackful*] of potatoes.
3 ***the sack*** *chiefly US, informal* : a person's bed ▪ He's still in *the sack*. Do you want me to wake him? ▪ It's time to ***hit the sack***. [=go to bed] ▪ She has a reputation for being ***good/great in the sack***. [=for being a good sexual partner] ▪ He's ready to ***jump/climb in the sack*** [=have sex] with any woman who'll have him.
4 ***the sack*** *informal* : a sudden dismissal from a job ▪ She ***got the sack*** [=she was fired] for always being late. ▪ The company ***gave him the sack*** [=fired him] for improper conduct.
5 *[count] American football* : the act of tackling the quarterback behind the line of scrimmage ▪ He was credited with three *sacks* in yesterday's game.
– compare [4]SACK; see also SAD SACK

[2]sack *verb* **sacks; sacked; sack·ing** *[+ obj]*
1 *informal* : to dismiss (someone) from a job ▪ They *sacked* [=*fired*] her for always being late.
2 *American football* : to tackle (the quarterback) behind the line of scrimmage ▪ The quarterback was *sacked* twice during the game.
3 *US, informal* : to put (something) in a sack ▪ Let me *sack* [=*bag*] those groceries for you.
sack out *[phrasal verb] US, informal* : to lie down for sleep ▪ I went upstairs to *sack out*. ▪ He *sacked out* on the living room couch. ✧ A person who ***is sacked out*** is sleeping. ▪ He *was sacked out* on the living room couch.
– compare [3]SACK

[3]sack *verb* **sacks; sacked; sack·ing** *[+ obj]* : to destroy and take things from (a place, such as a city or town) especially during a war ▪ The invading army *sacked* [=*plundered, pillaged*] the city. — compare [2]SACK

[4]sack *noun [singular]* : the act of destroying and taking things from a place (such as a city or town) especially during a war : the act of sacking a place — usually + *of* ▪ the *sack of* Rome — compare [1]SACK

sack·cloth /ˈsækˌklɑːθ/ *noun [noncount]* : rough cloth that is used for making sacks
sackcloth and ashes ✧ To ***don/wear sackcloth and ashes*** means to publicly express or show sorrow or regret for having done something wrong. ▪ He should be forced to *wear sackcloth and ashes* and apologize for his lies.

sack·ful /ˈsækˌfʊl/ *noun, pl* **-fuls** *[count]* : the amount that is contained in a sack • a *sackful* [=*sack*] of mail/potatoes

sack race *noun, pl* ~ **races** [*count*] : a race in which people stand inside large sacks and move forward by jumping • a children's *sack race*

sac·ra·ment /ˈsækrəmənt/ *noun, pl* **-ments**
1 [*count*] : an important Christian ceremony (such as baptism or marriage)
2 ***the Sacrament*** : the bread and wine that are eaten and drunk during the Christian ceremony of Communion • They stood in line to receive *the Sacrament*.
– **sac·ra·men·tal** /ˌsækrəˈmɛntl/ *adj* • *sacramental* wine

sa·cred /ˈseɪkrəd/ *adj* [*more* ~; *most* ~]
1 : worthy of religious worship : very holy • a *sacred* shrine • The burial site is *sacred* ground. • the *sacred* image of the Virgin Mary — often + *to* • The shrine is *sacred to* millions of worshippers.
2 : relating to religion • *sacred* scriptures/songs/texts
3 : highly valued and important : deserving great respect • the *sacred* pursuit of liberty • We have a *sacred* duty to find out the truth. • Freedom is a *sacred* right. • They'll make jokes about anything. ***Nothing is sacred*** to those guys. • I can't believe they would do that. ***Is nothing sacred***?
– **sa·cred·ly** *adv* • *sacredly* held beliefs – **sa·cred·ness** *noun* [*noncount*]

sacred cow *noun, pl* ~ **cows** [*count*] *disapproving* : someone or something that has been accepted or respected for a long time and that people are afraid or unwilling to criticize or question • The old government program has become a *sacred cow*.

[1]**sac·ri·fice** /ˈsækrəˌfaɪs/ *noun, pl* **-fic·es**
1 : the act of giving up something that you want to keep especially in order to get or do something else or to help someone [*count*] The war required everyone to make *sacrifices*. • No *sacrifice* is too great when it comes to her children. • He made many personal *sacrifices* to provide help to the city's homeless people. • He ***made the final/supreme/ultimate sacrifice*** [=he died] for his country. [*noncount*] The war required much *sacrifice* from everyone. • He provided help to the city's homeless people ***at great personal sacrifice*** (to himself).
2 a : an act of killing a person or animal in a religious ceremony as an offering to please a god [*count*] a place where priests performed human/animal *sacrifices* in ancient rituals [*noncount*] a place where people were offered (up) ***in sacrifice*** to the gods **b** [*count*] : a person or animal that is killed in a sacrifice • The villagers hoped the gods would accept their *sacrifice*. • The goat was offered as a *sacrifice*.
3 [*count*] *baseball* : SACRIFICE BUNT • The runner went to second base on a *sacrifice*.

[2]**sacrifice** *verb* **-fices; -ficed; -fic·ing**
1 : to give up (something that you want to keep) especially in order to get or do something else or to help someone [+ *obj*] She's had to *sacrifice* a lot for her family. • He *sacrificed* his personal life in order to get ahead in his career. • I want to follow a diet that is healthful without *sacrificing* taste. • She was able to ask for their help without *sacrificing* her dignity. • They ***sacrificed their lives*** [=they died] for their country. [*no obj*] She was willing to suffer, *sacrifice*, and work for success.
2 [+ *obj*] : to kill (a person or animal) in a religious ceremony as an offering to please a god • a place where people/animals were *sacrificed* in ancient rituals
3 *baseball* **a** [*no obj*] : to make a sacrifice bunt • He *sacrificed* in his first at bat. **b** [+ *obj*] : to cause (a base runner) to go to the next base by making a sacrifice bunt — usually used as *(be) sacrificed* • The runner *was sacrificed* to second base.

sacrifice bunt *noun, pl* ~ **bunts** [*count*] *baseball* : a bunt that allows a runner to go to the next base while the batter is put out — called also *sacrifice, sacrifice hit*

sacrifice fly *noun, pl* ~ **flies** [*count*] *baseball* : a fly ball that is caught by a fielder but allows a base runner to score after it is caught

sac·ri·fi·cial /ˌsækrəˈfɪʃəl/ *adj* : of, relating to, or involving sacrifice • *sacrificial* rites/rituals/offerings • a *sacrificial* altar • their *sacrificial* acts of self-denial
– **sac·ri·fi·cial·ly** *adv* • a *sacrificially* slaughtered animal

sac·ri·lege /ˈsækrəlɪʤ/ *noun* : an act of treating a holy place or object in a way that does not show proper respect [*singular*] They accused him of committing a *sacrilege*. [*noncount*] They accused him of *sacrilege*. • an act of *sacrilege* against the church — often used figuratively • It would be (a) *sacrilege* to cut down such beautiful trees.
– **sac·ri·le·gious** /ˌsækrəˈlɪʤəs/ *adj* • a *sacrilegious* act

sac·ro·sanct /ˈsækroʊˌsæŋkt/ *adj* [*more* ~; *most* ~] *formal* : too important and respected to be changed, criticized, etc. • the government's most *sacrosanct* institutions • The tradition is regarded as *sacrosanct*.

sad /ˈsæd/ *adj* **sad·der; -dest** [*also more* ~; *most* ~]
1 : not happy : feeling or showing grief or unhappiness • He's feeling *sad* because his pet died. • People were *sad* that he was leaving. • The experience left her *sadder* but wiser. • big *sad* eyes
2 : causing a feeling of grief or unhappiness • Have you heard the *sad* news about his wife's illness? • It'll be a *sad* day when you leave us. • a *sad* love song • a *sad* poem • a movie with a *sad* ending • He lived a *sad* life.
3 : causing feelings of disappointment or pity • The *sad* fact/truth of the matter is that they are right. • I live a pretty *sad* [=*pathetic*] life. I never go out on the weekend. • The government is in *sad* [=*bad*] shape. • The new version is a *sad* imitation of the original movie. • He's a *sad* excuse for a father. [=he's not a good father] • a *sad*-looking birthday cake • We needed more money but, ***sad to say***, there wasn't any. • ***Sad but true***, we couldn't afford to go away for even a weekend at the beach. — see also SAD SACK
– **sad·ness** *noun* [*noncount*] His leaving caused much *sadness*. [*singular*] I felt a deep *sadness* upon hearing the news.

sad·den /ˈsædn̩/ *verb* **-dens; -dened; -den·ing**
1 [+ *obj*] : to cause (someone) to be sad • It *saddens* me that we could not agree. • We were *saddened* to see how ill she looks. • She was *saddened* over/by the death of her friend.
2 [*no obj*] : to become sad : to show sadness • Her face/eyes *saddened* when she heard the news.
– **saddening** *adj* [*more* ~; *most* ~] • Her death is a *saddening* loss.

[1]**sad·dle** /ˈsædl̩/ *noun, pl* **sad·dles** [*count*]
1 : a leather-covered seat that is put on the back of a horse — see picture at HORSE
2 : a seat on a bicycle or motorcycle — see picture at BICYCLE
a burr in/under the saddle see BURR
in the saddle **1** : riding on a horse • a cowboy *in the saddle*
2 : in control : in a position to decide what happens • After a few setbacks, he's ***back in the saddle*** again.

[2]**saddle** *verb* **saddles; sad·dled; sad·dling** [+ *obj*] : to put a saddle on (a horse) • He *saddled* his horse and mounted it. — often + *up* • He *saddled up* his horse.
saddle up [*phrasal verb*] : to get on a horse • He *saddled up* and rode away.
saddle with [*phrasal verb*] ***saddle (someone or something) with (something)*** : to cause (someone or something) to have (a problem, burden, responsibility, etc.) • His actions have *saddled* the company *with* too much debt. • My boss *saddled* me *with* the task of organizing the conference. — often used as *(be) saddled with* • The company *is saddled with* an enormous amount of debt. • She *is saddled* [=*burdened*] *with* a reputation for not being dependable.

sad·dle·bag /ˈsædl̩ˌbæg/ *noun, pl* **-bags** [*count*] : one of a pair of bags that are laid across the back of a horse behind the saddle or that hang over the rear wheel of a bicycle or motorcycle

saddle horse *noun, pl* ~ **horses** [*count*] *US* : a horse that is used for riding

sad·dler /ˈsædlɚ/ *noun, pl* **-dlers** [*count*] : a person who makes, repairs, or sells saddles and other equipment for horses

sad·dlery /ˈsædləri/ *noun, pl* **-dler·ies**
1 [*noncount*] : the work of making, repairing, or selling saddles and other equipment for horses
2 [*noncount*] : saddles and other equipment for horses
3 [*count*] : a place where saddles and other equipment for horses is sold or stored

saddle shoe *noun, pl* ~ **shoes** [*count*] *US* : a shoe that has one color on the toe and heel and a different color on the middle part

saddle sore *noun, pl* ~ **sores** [*count*]
1 : a sore on the back of a horse caused by a saddle that is not fitted correctly
2 : a sore area on a horse rider's body that is caused by rubbing against the saddle

sa·dism /ˈseɪˌdɪzəm/ *noun* [*noncount*] : enjoyment that someone gets from being violent or cruel or from causing

pain; *especially* : sexual enjoyment from hurting or punishing someone ▪ sexual *sadism* — compare MASOCHISM
– **sa·dist** /ˈseɪdɪst/ *noun, pl* **-dists** [*count*] ▪ sexual *sadists* – **sa·dis·tic** /səˈdɪstɪk/ *adj* [*more ~; most ~*] ▪ *sadistic* behavior ▪ a *sadistic* criminal – **sa·dis·ti·cal·ly** /səˈdɪstɪkli/ *adv*

sad·ly /ˈsædli/ *adv* [*more ~; most ~*]
1 : in a way that shows sadness or unhappiness ▪ She shook her head *sadly*.
2 : in a way that causes feeling of sadness, disappointment, regret, etc. ▪ A cohesive plot was *sadly* lacking from the novel. ▪ Her work had been *sadly* neglected. — sometimes used for emphasis ▪ If you think she'll forgive you, you are ***sadly mistaken***
3 : UNFORTUNATELY — used to say that something is disappointing, sad, etc. ▪ I tried to help but, *sadly*, nothing could be done. ▪ *Sadly*, her negative attitude began to spread to other people.

sa·do·mas·och·ism /ˌseɪdoʊˈmæsəˌkɪzəm/ *noun* [*noncount*] : sexual behavior that involves getting pleasure from causing or feeling pain
– **sa·do·mas·och·ist** /ˌseɪdoʊˈmæsəkɪst/ *noun, pl* **-ists** [*count*] – **sa·do·mas·och·is·tic** /ˌseɪdoʊˌmæsəˈkɪstɪk/ *adj* ▪ *sadomasochistic* sexual practices

sad sack *noun, pl* **~ sacks** [*count*] *US, informal + old-fashioned* : a person who is not successful or able to do things well : an inept person who causes feelings of pity or disgust in other people ▪ The team is just a bunch of *sad sacks*. [=*losers*]
– **sad–sack** *adj, always used before a noun* ▪ a *sad-sack* team ▪ a *sad-sack* performance

SAE *abbr* **1** self-addressed envelope **2** stamped addressed envelope

sa·fa·ri /səˈfɑri/ *noun, pl* **-ris** : a journey to see or hunt animals especially in Africa [*count*] He went on a *safari* in Africa last year. [*noncount*] a group of hunters ***on safari***

safari jacket *noun, pl* **~ -ets** [*count*] : a type of lightweight jacket that usually has a belt and four large pockets

safari park *noun, pl* **~ parks** [*count*] *chiefly Brit* : a park in which wild animals move around freely and are watched by people from their vehicles

¹safe /ˈseɪf/ *adj* **saf·er; -est** [*also more ~; most ~*]
1 *not used before a noun* **a** : not able or likely to be hurt or harmed in any way : not in danger ▪ I don't feel *safe* in this neighborhood. ▪ The kids were *safe* in the cabin. ▪ We need to make sure that the children are ***safe and sound*** **b** : not able or likely to be lost, taken away, or given away ▪ "Is the money *safe*?" "Yes, it's in the bank." ▪ Be sure to keep your wallet *safe*. [=keep it in a place where it can't be stolen] ▪ The election is next week, and the polls show that her lead is *safe*. [=her lead is large; she will not lose her lead] ▪ Don't worry. Your secret is *safe* with me. [=I will not tell anyone else your secret]
2 a : not involving or likely to involve danger, harm, or loss ▪ a world made *safe* from war ▪ Is it *safe* to walk here? ▪ He wished us a *safe* trip. ▪ We are all hoping for their ***safe return*** [=hoping that they will return without being harmed] **b** : providing protection from danger, harm, or loss ▪ I found a *safe* place to take shelter from the storm. ▪ They live in a perfectly/relatively *safe* neighborhood. ▪ a *safe* harbor ▪ We watched the fireworks from a *safe* distance. ▪ You should keep your money in a *safe* [=*secure*] place. ▪ Bigger cars tend to be *safer* than smaller ones. ▪ the *safest* way to travel ▪ The shelter provides a ***safe haven*** for the homeless.
3 : not causing harm : not dangerous ▪ *safe* medicine ▪ a *safe* vaccine ▪ *safe* drinking water ▪ The book describes which mushrooms are *safe* to eat and which are not.
4 a : not likely to cause a bad result : not risky ▪ a *safe* investment/bet **b** : not likely to take risks : cautious or careful ▪ She's a very *safe* driver. ▪ It's probably not necessary to check the figures again, but ***(it's) better (to be) safe than sorry*** [=it is better to be careful now so that problems do not occur later on] ▪ ***To be on the safe side***, I checked the figures again. = ***To be safe***, I checked the figures again. ▪ I decided to ***play it safe*** [=to be careful and avoid risk or danger] and leave early so that I would be sure to arrive on time.
5 : not likely to cause disagreement or argument ▪ That's a *safe* assumption. ▪ It's *safe* to assume that she isn't married. ▪ Politics is not a *safe* subject around him. He's always angry about something. ▪ I think ***it's safe to say*** that he won't be causing any further problems. ▪ She is a ***safe bet*** to win the tournament. [=she will probably win the tournament]
6 *baseball* : successful at getting to a base without being put out ▪ The runner was *safe* on a close play at first base.
in safe hands see ¹HAND
– **safe·ly** *adv* ▪ We arrived home *safely*. [=without experiencing any problems, accidents, etc.] ▪ Be sure to drive *safely*. ▪ I can *safely* say that he won't be causing any further problems.

²safe *adv, chiefly US, informal* : in a safe way ▪ Be sure to drive *safe*. [=*safely*]

³safe *noun, pl* **safes** [*count*] : a strong metal box with a lock that is used to store money or valuable things

safe–con·duct /ˈseɪfˈkɑːndəkt/ *noun, pl* **-ducts** : protection from the government, police, etc., that is given to a person who is passing through an area that might be dangerous [*noncount*] They were given *safe-conduct* through the city. [*count*] The rebels' leader was granted a *safe-conduct* to talk with the president.

safe·crack·er /ˈseɪfˌkrækɚ/ *noun, pl* **-ers** [*count*] *chiefly US* : a person who steals things by opening safes ▪ The bank was robbed by a professional *safecracker*.

safe–deposit box *noun, pl* **~ boxes** [*count*] : a strong metal box in a bank that has a lock and that is used to store money or other valuable things — called also *safety-deposit box*

¹safe·guard /ˈseɪfˌgɑɚd/ *noun, pl* **-guards** [*count*] *formal* : something that provides protection against possible loss, damage, etc. ▪ The new law has *safeguards* to protect the rights of citizens. ▪ There are many *safeguards* built into the system to prevent fraud. ▪ Practicing good nutrition can be an important *safeguard* [=*defense*] against cancer.

²safeguard *verb* **-guards; -guard·ed; -guard·ing** *formal* : to make (someone or something) safe or secure : PROTECT [+ *obj*] laws that *safeguard* the rights of citizens ▪ You need to *safeguard* your computer against viruses. [*no obj*] There are steps you can take to *safeguard* against identity theft.

safe house *noun, pl* **~ houses** [*count*] : a place where a person hides from the police, stays to be protected by the police, or is involved in secret activities

safe·keep·ing /ˈseɪfˈkiːpɪŋ/ *noun* [*noncount*]
1 : the act of keeping something safe ▪ I gave her my jewelry ***for safekeeping*** while I was away. [=I gave her my jewelry so that she could keep it safe while I was away]
2 : the state of being kept safe ▪ His will is in *safekeeping* with his lawyer.

safe seat *noun, pl* **~ seats** [*count*] *Brit* : a seat in Parliament that is very unlikely to be lost to the opposition in an election

safe sex *noun* [*noncount*] : sexual activity in which people protect themselves from diseases (such as AIDS) by using condoms or by other methods ▪ a book advising young people to practice *safe sex*

safe·ty /ˈseɪfti/ *noun, pl* **-ties**
1 [*noncount*] : freedom from harm or danger : the state of being safe ▪ The changes were made in the interest of public *safety*. ▪ He made some suggestions about how to improve airline *safety*. ▪ bike/traffic *safety* ▪ I'm worried about the *safety* of the people who were left behind. ▪ He sought *safety* in a church. [=he went into a church to be safe] ▪ She fears for her own *safety*. [=she is afraid because she thinks she is in danger] ▪ We were reluctant to leave the relative *safety* of our hotel. ▪ She was only a mile from the *safety* of her home when the accident occurred. ▪ The climbers were roped together for *safety*. = The climbers were roped together ***for safety's sake*** ▪ There is ***safety in numbers***. [=you are safer in a group of people than you are when you are alone] ▪ "***Safety first***" [=the most important thing is to be safe]—that's what I always say. — often used before another noun ▪ *safety* experts/hazards/precautions ▪ a *safety* violation ▪ a *safety* harness/catch ▪ *safety* devices/features ▪ *safety* glasses/goggles
2 [*noncount*] : the state of not being dangerous or harmful ▪ The car has been redesigned for improved/added/increased *safety*. ▪ The toys are inspected for *safety*.
3 [*noncount*] : a place that is free from harm or danger : a safe place ▪ They were led/pulled/dragged ***to safety*** by the rescuers. ▪ The injured hiker was finally able to ***reach safety***.
4 [*count*] *US* : a device that prevents a gun from being fired accidentally — called also *safety catch*
5 [*count*] *American football* **a** : a defensive player whose position is far back from the line of scrimmage **b** : a score of two points for the defensive team when an offensive player who has the ball is tackled behind his own team's goal line

safety belt *noun, pl* **~ belts** [*count*]

1 : a belt that is used to prevent someone from falling or getting injured by holding that person in place
2 : SEAT BELT

safety–deposit box *noun, pl* ~ **boxes** [*count*] : SAFE-DEPOSIT BOX

safety glass *noun* [*noncount*] : a type of strong glass that breaks into tiny pieces that are not sharp when it is hit hard

safety net *noun, pl* ~ **nets** [*count*]
1 : a net that is placed below acrobats to catch them if they fall
2 : something that helps someone who is in a difficult situation ▪ a financial *safety net* ▪ The program provides a *safety net* for people who have lost their jobs.

safety pin *noun, pl* ~ **pins** [*count*] : a metal pin that is used for attaching things and that has a point at one end and a cover at the other into which the pointed end fits

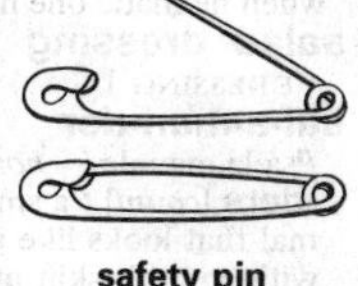
safety pin

safety razor *noun, pl* ~ **-zors** [*count*] : a razor with a cover for part of the blade to prevent deep cuts in the skin

safety valve *noun, pl* ~ **valves** [*count*]
1 : a part in a machine that opens automatically to release steam, water, gas, etc., when pressure becomes too great
2 : something that allows someone to release mental stress and tension in a harmless way ▪ His hobbies act as a *safety valve*, relieving some of the pressure he feels from his job.

saf·fron /ˈsæˌfrɑːn, *Brit* ˈsæfrən/ *noun* [*noncount*]
1 : an orange powder that is made from a type of flower (called a crocus) and that is used to color and flavor food
2 : an orange to orange-yellow color — see color picture on page C3

sag /ˈsæg/ *verb* **sags**; **sagged**; **sag·ging** [*no obj*]
1 : to bend or hang down in the middle especially because of weight or weakness ▪ The roof is *sagging* in the middle. ▪ Her cheeks *sagged* [=*drooped*] with age. ▪ The shelf *sagged* [=*bowed*] under the weight of so many books. ▪ a *sagging* mattress
2 : to become weaker or fewer ▪ The economy began to *sag*. ▪ As all our efforts failed, our spirits *sagged*. ▪ the company's *sagging* sales
– sag *noun, pl* **sags** [*count*] ▪ a *sag* in sales

sa·ga /ˈsɑːgə/ *noun, pl* **-gas** [*count*]
1 : a long and complicated story with many details ▪ the *saga* of a shipwrecked crew ▪ Her first novel was a family *saga* set in Iowa.
2 : a long and complicated series of events ▪ Getting our car back turned into quite a *saga*.
3 : a long story about past heroes from Norway and Iceland

sa·ga·cious /səˈgeɪʃəs/ *adj* [*more* ~; *most* ~] *formal* : having or showing an ability to understand difficult ideas and situations and to make good decisions : WISE ▪ a *sagacious* old man ▪ *sagacious* advice/counsel
– sa·ga·cious·ly *adv* **– sa·gac·i·ty** /səˈgæsəti/ *noun* [*noncount*] ▪ The old man was respected for his *sagacity*. [=*wisdom*]

[1]**sage** /ˈseɪʤ/ *noun, pl* **sag·es** [*count*] *formal* : a person who is very wise — compare [3]SAGE

[2]**sage** *adj, always used before a noun* **sag·er**; **sag·est** [*also more* ~; *most* ~] *formal* : very wise ▪ *sage* advice
– sage·ly *adv* ▪ He *sagely* suggested that she wait a few days.

[3]**sage** *noun* [*noncount*]
1 : an herb that has grayish-green leaves which are used in cooking
2 : a light grayish-green color — see color picture on page C6
— compare [1]SAGE

sage·brush /ˈseɪʤˌbrʌʃ/ *noun* [*noncount*] : a small plant that has leaves with a strong smell and that grows in dry areas of the western U.S.

sag·gy /ˈsægi/ *adj* **sag·gi·er**; **-est** [*also more* ~; *most* ~] *informal* : bending or hanging down too much : not firm ▪ a *saggy* mattress

Sag·it·tar·i·us /ˌsæʤəˈteriəs/ *noun, pl* **-us·es**
1 [*noncount*] : the ninth sign of the zodiac : the sign that comes between Scorpio and Capricorn and that has a centaur shooting a bow and arrow as its symbol
2 [*count*] : a person born under the sign Sagittarius : a person born between November 22 and December 21 ▪ Are you a *Sagittarius* or a Capricorn?

sa·go /ˈseɪgoʊ/ *noun, pl* **-gos** [*count*] : a substance that is made from a type of palm tree and used especially in cooking

[1]**said** *past tense and past participle of* [1]SAY

[2]**said** /ˈsɛd/ *adj, always used before a noun, formal + law* : mentioned or referred to before ▪ The following is a description of how *said* property [=the property mentioned before] is divided. ▪ by order of the judge of *said* court

[1]**sail** /ˈseɪl/ *verb* **sails**; **sailed**; **sail·ing**
1 **a** : to travel on water in a ship or boat [*no obj*] *sail* across/on/over the sea/ocean ▪ We'll *sail* along/up/down the coast. ▪ He *sailed* around the world on a luxury liner. [+ *obj*] She *sailed* the Atlantic coastline. **b** : to control a ship or boat (especially one that has sails) while traveling on water [+ *obj*] She's *sailing* a boat in tomorrow's race. ▪ The ship was *sailed* by a crew of 8. [*no obj*] I've been *sailing* since I was a child. ▪ learning to *sail* **c** *of a ship or boat* : to travel on water [+ *obj*] a ship that has *sailed* the seven seas [*no obj*] We sat on the shore watching boats *sail* by.
2 [*no obj*] : to begin a journey on water in a ship or boat ▪ We *sail* at 9 a.m. tomorrow. ▪ They *sail* for/to San Francisco next week. ▪ The ship will be ready to *sail* in a week.
3 *always followed by an adverb or preposition* [*no obj*] : to move or proceed in an easy, quick, and smooth way ▪ He *sailed* into the room. [=he walked quickly into the room in a very confident and easy way] ▪ The ball *sailed* [=*flew*] over the shortstop's head. ▪ The bill ***sailed through*** the legislature. [=the bill passed through the legislature very easily; the bill quickly became a law] ▪ She *sailed through* the exam/course. [=she easily passed the exam/course]
sail close to the wind *Brit* : to do something that is dangerous or that may be illegal or dishonest ▪ The company was *sailing close to the wind*, but it's not clear if they were breaking the law or not.

[2]**sail** *noun, pl* **sails**
1 [*count*] : a large piece of strong cloth that is connected to a ship or boat and that is used to catch the wind that moves the ship or boat through the water ▪ Wind filled the *sails* and our journey had begun. ▪ raising and lowering the ship's *sails* — see picture at BOAT
2 [*singular*] : a trip in a ship or boat ▪ a *sail* to San Francisco
in full sail *also* ***at full sail*** *of a ship or boat* : moving through the water by using all of its sails ▪ a yacht *in full sail*
set sail : to begin a journey on water in a ship or boat ▪ They *set sail* for/from San Francisco tomorrow.
take the wind out of someone's sails see [1]WIND
under sail *of a ship or boat* : moving through the water by using sails ▪ a ship *under sail*

sail·board /ˈseɪlˌboɚd/ *noun, pl* **-boards** [*count*] : a flat board that has a sail and that you stand on to ride over the surface of water : a board that is used for windsurfing — see picture at BOAT
– sail·board·er /ˈseɪlˌboɚdɚ/ *noun, pl* **-ers** [*count*] ▪ We watched the *sailboarders* [=*windsurfers*] from the shore.
– sail·board·ing /ˈseɪlˌboɚdɪŋ/ *noun* [*noncount*] ▪ He likes *sailboarding*. [=*windsurfing*]

sail·boat /ˈseɪlˌboʊt/ *noun, pl* **-boats** [*count*] *US* : a boat that has a sail — called also (*Brit*) *sailing boat*; see picture at BOAT

sail·ing /ˈseɪlɪŋ/ *noun* [*noncount*] : the sport or activity of traveling on water in a sailboat ▪ She likes *sailing*. ▪ They're ***going sailing*** next week.
clear sailing (*US*) *or chiefly US* ***smooth sailing*** *or chiefly Brit* ***plain sailing*** : easy progress : progress that is not blocked by anything ▪ Now that the permit has been approved, we expect to have *clear sailing* from here on. [=we expect that we will not have any problems from here on] ▪ Her time at college wasn't all *smooth sailing*. [=she had some problems/difficulties during her time at college]

sailing ship *noun, pl* ~ **ships** [*count*] : a ship that has sails

sail·or /ˈseɪlɚ/ *noun, pl* **-ors** [*count*]
1 : a person who works on a boat or ship as part of the crew ▪ He worked as a *sailor* on a cargo ship.
2 : someone who controls a boat or ship that has sails ▪ She's a skillful *sailor*.

sailor suit *noun, pl* ~ **suits** [*count*] : a suit especially for a child that looks like an old-fashioned sailor's uniform

saint /ˈseɪnt/ *noun, pl* **saints** [*count*]
1 : a person who is officially recognized by the Christian church as being very holy because of the way he or she lived ▪ He was declared a *saint* in the fifth century. — used as a ti-

S

tle before a saint's name• *Saint* Anne — abbr. *St.*; see also PATRON SAINT

2 : a person who is very good, kind, or patient• The salesperson was a *saint* for putting up with them. • a teacher with ***the patience of a saint***[=a very patient teacher]

– saint·hood /ˈseɪntˌhʊd/ *noun* [*noncount*]• The Pope elevated four people to *sainthood.* [=he made four people saints] • She recently entered the *sainthood.* [=she recently became a saint]

Saint Ber·nard /ˈseɪntbɚˈnɑɚd/ *noun, pl* **~ -nards** [*count*] **:** a very large, strong dog that was used in the past to find and help lost travelers

saint·ed /ˈseɪntəd/ *adj*

1 *old-fashioned* **:** unusually good, kind, or patient• my *sainted* old grandmother

2 : admired by many people• They believed whatever they were told by their *sainted* leader.

saint·ly /ˈseɪntli/ *adj* **saint·li·er; -est** [*also more ~; most ~*] **:** like a saint **:** very good and kind• a *saintly* old man • a *saintly* smile [=a smile that is like the smile of a saint]

– saint·li·ness *noun* [*noncount*]

Saint Pat·rick's Day /ˌseɪntˈpætrɪks-/ *noun* [*noncount*] **:** March 17 celebrated in honor of Saint Patrick

saint's day *noun* [*singular*] **:** a day of the year on which a particular saint is remembered

Saint Valentine's Day *noun* [*noncount*] **:** VALENTINE'S DAY

[1]sake /ˈseɪk/ *noun, pl* **sakes** [*count*]

1 : the benefit of someone or something — used in phrases with *for* to say that something is done to help a particular person or thing• Please do it *for her sake.* [=do it for her; do it to help her] • They sacrificed their lives *for all our sakes.* [=to help all of us] • We must do it *for the sake of* our country. — used in phrases with *for* to say that something is done for a particular purpose or to achieve a particular goal or result• *For simplicity's sake* [=to make this discussion simpler], we'll consider these two options as basically the same. • Let's assume, *for argument's sake*, that it was a mistake. = Let's assume, *for the sake of* argument, that it was a mistake. [=let's say for now that it was a mistake so that we can see how that will affect our discussion] • *For the sake of* clarity [=in order to be clear], I've listed each item separately. • They'll do anything *for the sake of* (making a) profit. • scholars who pursue knowledge *for its own sake* [=because they want to learn] • I don't paint for money. My motto is "***Art for art's sake***" [=I believe in making art for no other reason than that art is important]

2 *informal* — used in phrases with *for* to express anger, annoyance, surprise, etc.• ***For heaven's/Pete's sake***, could you hurry up? • Stop asking me questions, ***for God's sake***! • ***For pity's/God's/Christ's sake***, what's taking so long? • "You won!" "Oh, ***for goodness'/heaven's/Pete's sake***, I can't believe it!" ✧ The use of *God* and *Christ* in these phrases is offensive to some people.

for old times' sake ✧ If you do something *for old times' sake*, you do it because you did it in the past and you want to experience it again.• He and his old friends from college went back to the bar *for old times' sake*.

for the sake of it **:** for no particular reason• We drove around town just *for the sake of it*.

– compare [2]SAKE

[2]sa·ke *or* **sa·ki** /ˈsɑːki/ *noun, pl* **-kes** *or* **-kis** [*count, noncount*] **:** a Japanese alcoholic drink that is made from rice — compare [1]SAKE

sal·able *or* **sale·able** /ˈseɪləbəl/ *adj* [*more ~; most ~*] **:** capable of being sold **:** good enough to be sold• We'll have to repaint the house for it to be *salable*. • a *salable* commodity/product

– sal·abil·i·ty /ˌseɪləˈbɪləti/ *noun* [*noncount*]

sa·la·cious /səˈleɪʃəs/ *adj* [*more ~; most ~*] *formal + disapproving* **:** relating to sex in a way that is excessive or offensive • a song with *salacious* lyrics • *salacious* pictures/messages

– sa·la·cious·ly *adv* **– sa·la·cious·ness** *noun*

sal·ad /ˈsæləd/ *noun, pl* **-ads**

1 : a mixture of raw green vegetables (such as different types of lettuce) usually combined with other raw vegetables [*count*]For dinner we had roast chicken and a *salad*. • a *salad* of fresh/local greens • a spinach *salad* • I tossed the *salad* with some oil and vinegar and set it on the table. [*noncount*] a bowl of *salad* • Would you like soup or *salad* with your sandwich? • ***salad greens*** [=vegetables that are grown for their leaves and commonly used in salads]

2 [*count, noncount*] **:** a mixture of small pieces of raw or cooked food (such as pasta, meat, fruit, eggs, or vegetables) combined usually with a dressing and served cold• a delicious pasta/potato/fruit *salad* • chicken/tuna *salad*

salad bar *noun, pl* **~ bars** [*count*] **:** a place in a restaurant where there is a selection of ingredients that customers can use to make their own salads

salad cream *noun* [*noncount*] *Brit* **:** a thick liquid that is eaten on salads, sandwiches, etc.

salad days *noun* [*plural*] *somewhat old-fashioned*

1 : the period of life when someone is young and does not have much experience• during her *salad days* as a young reporter in New York city

2 : an early period of success• in his *salad days* as an actor, when he made one hit movie after another

salad dressing *noun, pl* **~ -ings** [*count, noncount*] **:** DRESSING 1

sal·a·man·der /ˈsæləˌmændɚ/ *noun, pl* **-ders** [*count*] **:** a small animal that looks like a lizard with smooth skin and that lives both on land and in water

salamander

sa·la·mi /səˈlɑːmi/ *noun, pl* **-mis** [*count, noncount*] **:** a large, spicy, and dry sausage that is usually eaten cold

sal·a·ried /ˈsælərid/ *adj*

1 *of a person* **:** receiving a salary• *salaried* employees

2 *of a job* **:** giving payment in the form of a salary• a *salaried* position

sal·a·ry /ˈsæləri/ *noun, pl* **-ries :** an amount of money that an employee is paid each year ✧ A salary is divided into equal amounts that are paid to a person usually once every two weeks or once every month. [*count*] She was offered a *salary* of $50,000 a year. [*noncount*] Employees receive an annual increase in *salary*. — compare [1]WAGE

sale /ˈseɪl/ *noun, pl* **sales**

1 a [*count*] **:** the act of selling something **:** the exchange of goods, services, or property for money• They profited from the *sale* of the house. • the company's online/Internet *sales* • Salespeople are paid a commission whenever they ***make a sale*** [=sell something] **b** ***sales*** [*plural*] **:** the total amount of money that a business receives from selling goods or services• *Sales* are up by $6,000 this month. • the company's annual *sales* • The company made over one million dollars ***in sales*** this quarter. • an increase/decrease *in sales* • disappointing ***sales figures***[=numbers that show how much money was made from sales]

2 [*count*] **:** an event or occasion during which a business sells goods or services at prices that are lower than usual• The store is having/holding a spring *sale*. • Everything in the store will be 15 percent off during the *sale*. • There is a *sale* on flights between New York and Paris. • (*Brit*) I bought these shoes ***in the sales*** [=at a time when many stores have a sale] — see also CLEARANCE SALE

3 ***sales*** [*plural*] **:** the business or activity of selling goods or services• He has a job in *sales*. • The department is in charge of *sales* and marketing. — often used before another noun• the *sales* department/manager • a new *sales* campaign

4 [*count*] **:** a public event at which things are sold• They're having/holding a *sale* of fine antiques next week. — see also GARAGE SALE, RUMMAGE SALE, TAG SALE, YARD SALE

for sale **:** available to be bought• That painting is not *for sale*. • The restaurant is (up) *for sale*. • houses *for sale*

on sale **1 :** available to be bought• These shoes are *on sale* at most department stores. • Tickets ***go on sale***[=become available to be bought] next week. **2** *chiefly US* **:** selling at a price that is lower than usual• I bought a shirt *on sale* for $5. • All computers will ***go on sale***[=will be sold for a reduced price] later this month.

on sale or return *Brit, business* **:** with the agreement that products which are not sold will be taken back without having to be paid for• The bookstore operates *on sale or return*. [=books in the store can be returned to the book supplier if the store does not sell them]

saleable *variant spelling of* SALABLE

sale·room /ˈseɪlˌruːm/ *noun, pl* **-rooms** [*count*] *Brit* **:** SALESROOM 2

sales·clerk /ˈseɪlzˌklɚk, *Brit* ˈseɪlzˌklɑːk/ *noun, pl* **-clerks** [*count*] *US* **:** a person whose job is to sell things in a store

sales·girl /ˈseɪlzˌgɚl/ *noun, pl* **-girls** [*count*] *old-fashioned +*

sometimes offensive : a woman (especially a young woman) whose job is to sell things • a *salesgirl* in a department store

sales•man /ˈseɪlzmən/ *noun, pl* **-men** /-mən/ [*count*] : a person (especially a man) whose job is to sell things • a car *salesman* • He was the company's best *salesman* last year.

sales•man•ship /ˈseɪlzmənˌʃɪp/ *noun* [*noncount*] : the skill of persuading people to buy things or to accept or agree to something • good/poor *salesmanship* • political *salesmanship*

sales•per•son /ˈseɪlzˌpɚsn̩/ *noun, pl* **sales•peo•ple** /ˈseɪlzˌpi:pəl/ *also* **sales•per•sons** [*count*] : a person whose job is to sell things • The company is hiring new *salespeople*.

sales pitch *noun, pl* **~ pitches** [*count*] : a speech that you give in order to persuade someone to buy something • He's good at getting customers to listen to his *sales pitch*. — sometimes used figuratively • It's not clear if voters liked the governor's *sales pitch* enough to reelect her.

sales•room /ˈseɪlzˌru:m/ *noun, pl* **-rooms** [*count*] *US*
1 : a place where things that are for sale are displayed • a car *salesroom* [=(more commonly) *showroom*]
2 : a room in which things are sold at an auction — called also (*Brit*) *saleroom*

sales slip *noun, pl* **~ slips** [*count*] *US* : a piece of paper on which a list of the things that you have bought is printed with the price for each item : RECEIPT

sales tax *noun, pl* **~ taxes** [*count, noncount*] : a tax that is added to the price of goods and services

sales•wom•an /ˈseɪlzˌwʊmən/ *noun, pl* **-wom•en** /-ˌwɪmən/ [*count*] : a woman whose job is to sell things • a retail *saleswoman*

sa•lient /ˈseɪljənt/ *adj* [*more ~; most ~*] *formal* : very important or noticeable • the *salient* facts • a *salient* characteristic/feature
– salience *noun* [*noncount*]

¹sa•line /ˈseɪˌli:n, *Brit* ˈseɪˌlaɪn/ *adj, technical* : containing salt • a *saline* solution • a *saline* lake
– sa•lin•i•ty /seɪˈlɪnəti/ *noun* [*noncount*] • testing the *salinity* of the water

²saline *noun* [*noncount*] *technical* : a mixture of salt and water

sa•li•va /səˈlaɪvə/ *noun* [*noncount*] : the liquid produced in your mouth that keeps your mouth moist and makes it easier to swallow food
– sal•i•vary /ˈsæləˌveri/ *adj, technical* • a *salivary* enzyme

salivary gland *noun, pl* **~ glands** [*count*] *medical* : a small organ that produces saliva in your mouth

sal•i•vate /ˈsæləˌveɪt/ *verb* **-vates; -vat•ed; -vat•ing** [*no obj*]
1 : to have a lot of saliva produced in your mouth because you see or smell food that you want to eat • The smell alone was enough to make me *salivate*.
2 : to have great interest in or desire for something • She was *salivating* at the prospect of traveling to Europe. • He *salivated* [=(informally) *drooled*] over his neighbor's new car.
– sal•i•va•tion /ˌsæləˈveɪʃən/ *noun* [*noncount*]

sal•low /ˈsæloʊ/ *adj* : slightly yellow in a way that does not look healthy • a *sallow* complexion/face • The child looked *sallow*.
– sal•low•ness *noun* [*noncount*]

¹sal•ly /ˈsæli/ *noun, pl* **-lies** [*count*] *formal*
1 : a clever and funny remark • a witty *sally* [=*quip*]
2 : a sudden attack in which a group of soldiers rush forward against an enemy

²sally *verb* **-lies; -lied; -ly•ing**
sally forth *also* ***sally out*** [*phrasal verb*] *literary* : to leave a place • After having breakfast and packing our bags, we *sallied forth* on the next leg of our trip.

salm•on /ˈsæmən/ *noun, pl* **salmon**
1 [*count, noncount*] : a large fish that is born in streams but that lives most of its life in the ocean and that is commonly used for food — see color picture on page C8
2 [*noncount*] : SALMON PINK — see color picture on page C3

sal•mo•nel•la /ˌsælməˈnɛlə/ *noun* [*noncount*] : a kind of bacteria that is sometimes in food and that makes people sick

salmon pink *noun* [*noncount*] : an orange-pink color — see color picture on page C3

sa•lon /səˈlɑ:n, *Brit* ˈsæˌlɒn/ *noun, pl* **-lons** [*count*]
1 : a business that gives customers beauty treatments (such as haircuts) • a hair/tanning/nail *salon* — see also BEAUTY SALON
2 *old-fashioned* : a large room in a fashionable house that is used for entertaining guests
3 : a regular meeting of writers, artists, etc., at someone's home ♦ Salons were common in the 18th and 19th centuries. • a literary *salon*

sa•loon /səˈlu:n/ *noun, pl* **-loons** [*count*]
1 : a place where alcoholic drinks are served; *especially* : such a place in the western U.S. during the 19th century
2 : a large, comfortable room on a ship where passengers can talk, relax, etc.
3 *Brit* : SEDAN — called also (*Brit*) *saloon car*
4 *Brit* : a comfortable room in a pub

sal•sa /ˈsɑ:lsə/ *noun, pl* **-sas**
1 : a spicy sauce made with tomatoes, onions, and hot peppers that is commonly served with Mexican food [*noncount*] a jar of *salsa* • chips and *salsa* [*count*] a delicious *salsa*
2 [*count, noncount*] **a** : a type of popular Latin-American music • The band was playing *salsa*. • a *salsa* band **b** : dancing that is done to salsa music • We're taking classes in *salsa*.

¹salt /ˈsɑ:lt/ *noun, pl* **salts**
1 [*noncount*] : a natural white substance that is used especially to flavor or preserve food • The soup needs a little more *salt*. • Season the meat with *salt* and pepper. • Add a ***pinch of salt*** [=a small amount of salt] — see also SEA SALT, TABLE SALT
2 [*count*] *technical* : a chemical compound formed when part of an acid is replaced by a metal or something like a metal • mineral/potassium *salts*
rub salt in/into someone's wounds see ¹RUB
take (something) with a grain/pinch of salt *informal* : to not completely believe (something) : to be doubtful about the truth or accuracy of (something) • He seems confident, but you should *take* what he says *with a grain of salt*.
the salt of the earth : a very good and honest person or group of people • These folks are *the salt of the earth*.
worth your salt : worthy of ordinary respect — used to say what should be expected from someone who does a job properly, from something that is as good as it should be, etc. • A detective writer *worth his salt* [=a good detective writer] keeps his readers from solving the mystery. • Any doctor *worth her salt* [=any good/capable doctor] would have advised you to get a second opinion before having major surgery.
– see also EPSOM SALT, SMELLING SALTS

²salt *verb* **salts; salt•ed; salt•ing** [+ *obj*]
1 : to flavor or preserve (food) with salt • He *salted* his potatoes. • The meat was preserved by being *salted* and smoked.
2 : to put salt on (a surface) especially in order to melt ice • The city *salted* the roads after the snowstorm.
salt away [*phrasal verb*] ***salt (something) away*** *or* ***salt away (something)*** *informal* **1** : to put (money) in a safe place especially secretly or dishonestly • He *salted* millions *away* in a foreign bank account. **2** *US* : to make your victory in (a game, contest, etc.) certain • They *salted away* the game by scoring 21 points in the last quarter.
salt with [*phrasal verb*] ***salt (something) with (something)*** : to put something in many places in (a story, speech, etc.) • She *salted* her speech *with* many religious references. • The book is *salted with* witty anecdotes. [=the book has many witty anecdotes throughout it]

³salt *adj, always used before a noun*
1 : containing salt • *salt* water
2 : preserved or seasoned with salt • *salt* [=*salted*] pork

salt–and–pepper *adj* : having many small spots of black and white • He has a *salt-and-pepper* beard. • His hair had turned *salt-and-pepper*.

salt•box /ˈsɑ:ltˌbɑ:ks/ *noun, pl* **-box•es** [*count*] *US* : a house that has two or more levels in the front, one level in the back, and a steep roof that slopes down from the front to the back

salt cel•lar /ˈsɑ:ltˌsɛlɚ/ *noun, pl* **~ -lars** [*count*] *Brit* : SALT SHAKER

salted *adj*
1 : having salt added • Cook the pasta in boiling *salted* water. • *salted* butter/peanuts — opposite UNSALTED
2 : preserved with salt • *salted* fish/meat/pork

sal•tine /sɑlˈti:n/ *noun, pl* **-tines** [*count*] *US* : a thin, salty cracker

salt•pe•ter (*US*) *or Brit* **salt•pe•tre** /ˈsɑ:ltˈpi:tə/ *noun* [*noncount*] : a white powder that exists naturally in some soils and that is used especially as a fertilizer, in medicine, and to make gunpowder

S

salt shak·er /ˈsɑːltˌʃeɪkɚ/ *noun, pl* ~ **-ers** [*count*] *US* : a small container that has holes in its top and that is used for sprinkling small amounts of salt onto food — called also (*Brit*) *salt cellar*; see picture at PLACE SETTING

salt·wa·ter /ˈsɑːltˌwɑːtɚ/ *adj, always used before a noun* : of, relating to, or living in salt water ▪ *saltwater* fish ▪ a *saltwater* pond — compare FRESHWATER

salty /ˈsɑːlti/ *adj* **salt·i·er; -est** [*also more* ~; *most* ~]

1 : containing salt or too much salt ▪ *salty* foods ▪ a *salty* lake ▪ I think the soup tastes *salty*.

2 *US, old-fashioned* : somewhat rude or shocking ▪ *salty* language/talk

– salt·i·ness /ˈsɑːltinəs/ *noun* [*noncount*] ▪ the *saltiness* of tears

sa·lu·bri·ous /səˈluːbrijəs/ *adj* [*more* ~; *most* ~] *formal* : making good health possible or likely ▪ *salubrious* weather ▪ a *salubrious* climate/area

sal·u·tary /ˈsæljəˌteri, *Brit* ˈsæljətri/ *adj* [*more* ~; *most* ~] *formal* : having a good or helpful result especially after something unpleasant has happened ▪ The accident should be a *salutary* lesson to be more careful. ▪ a *salutary* effect

sal·u·ta·tion /ˌsæljəˈteɪʃən/ *noun, pl* **-tions**

1 [*count*] : a word or phrase (such as "Gentlemen," "Dear Sir," "Dear Madam," or "To whom it may concern") that is used to begin a letter

2 *formal* : the act of greeting someone [*count*] A handshake and saying "hello" are common *salutations*. [*noncount*] Shaking hands is a form of *salutation*.

sa·lu·ta·to·ri·an /səˌluːtəˈtorijən/ *noun, pl* **-ans** [*count*] *US* : the student who has the second best grades in a graduating class — compare VALEDICTORIAN

[1]**sa·lute** /səˈluːt/ *verb* **-lutes; -lut·ed; -lut·ing**

1 : to give a sign of respect to (a military officer, flag, etc.) by moving your right hand to your forehead : to give a salute to (someone or something) [+ *obj*] He *saluted* the officer. ▪ *Salute* the flag. [*no obj*] The officer *saluted*.

2 [+ *obj*] : to show respect for (someone or something) : to publicly praise (someone or something) ▪ We *salute* our country's soldiers. ▪ The players *saluted* the fans. ▪ The president *saluted* her bravery.

[2]**salute** *noun, pl* **-lutes**

1 : the act of moving your right hand to your forehead as a sign of respect to a military officer, flag, etc. [*count*] The officers gave the general a *salute*. [*noncount*] They raised their hands ***in salute***.

2 : an act or ceremony that shows respect for someone [*count*] a 21-gun *salute* [=a military ceremony where 21 guns are fired in the air to honor someone] ▪ The concert was a *salute* to country music legends. [*noncount*] Twenty-one guns were fired ***in salute***. ▪ We raise our glasses ***in salute*** to the newlyweds.

[1]**sal·vage** /ˈsælvɪʤ/ *noun* [*noncount*]

1 : the act of saving something (such as a building, a ship, or cargo) that is in danger of being completely destroyed ▪ The ship was beyond *salvage*. ▪ *salvage* attempts/efforts/operations

2 : something (such as cargo) that is saved from a wreck, fire, etc. ▪ the *salvage* from the wrecked ship ▪ (*US*) I got the part from an auto *salvage* place. [=from a junkyard; from a place where broken cars are taken so that their parts can be removed and sold]

[2]**salvage** *verb* **-vag·es; -vaged; -vag·ing** [+ *obj*]

1 : to remove (something) from a place so that it will not be damaged, destroyed, or lost ▪ Divers *salvaged* some of the sunken ship's cargo. ▪ Few of their possessions were *salvaged* from the fire.

2 : to save (something valuable or important) : to prevent the loss of (something) ▪ He is trying to *salvage* his marriage/reputation.

– sal·vage·able /ˈsælvɪʤəbəl/ *adj* ▪ The marriage was not *salvageable*.

sal·va·tion /sælˈveɪʃən/ *noun* [*noncount*]

1 *in Christianity* : the act of saving someone from sin or evil : the state of being saved from sin or evil ▪ Pray for *salvation*.

2 : something that saves someone or something from danger or a difficult situation ▪ The new medication has been her *salvation*. [=has saved her] ▪ Tourism has been the *salvation* of the island.

Salvation Army *noun*

the Salvation Army : an international Christian group that helps poor people

[1]**salve** /ˈsæv, *Brit* ˈsælv/ *noun, pl* **salves** [*count, noncount*] : a creamy substance that you put on a wound to heal it or to make it less painful ▪ a *salve* for rashes/sunburns

[2]**salve** *verb* **salves; salved; salv·ing** [+ *obj*] : to make (something) less painful ▪ The lotion *salved* the pain. ▪ He bought her flowers to *salve* his guilty conscience.

sal·ver /ˈsælvɚ/ *noun, pl* **-vers** [*count*] *chiefly Brit* : a tray that is used for serving food or drinks on formal occasions

sal·vo /ˈsælvoʊ/ *noun, pl* **sal·vos** *or* **sal·voes** [*count*]

1 : the act of firing several guns or bombs at the same time ▪ We were driven back by a *salvo* of cannon fire.

2 : a sudden occurrence of applause, laughter, etc., from many people ▪ a *salvo* [=*burst*] of cheers

3 : a strong or sudden attack ▪ The newspaper article was intended as a *salvo* against the mayor's policies. ▪ He fired the ***opening salvo*** of the debate.

Sa·mar·i·tan /səˈmerətən/ *noun, pl* **-tans** [*count*] : GOOD SAMARITAN ▪ A *Samaritan* called a tow truck for us.

sam·ba /ˈsæmbə/ *noun* [*singular*] : a lively Brazilian dance ▪ They danced the *samba*.; *also* : the music for this dance ▪ The band played a *samba*.

[1]**same** /ˈseɪm/ *adj, always used before a noun*

1 : not different — used when referring to a particular person or thing that is connected to more than one person, time, place, etc. ▪ He has lived in the *same* city all his life. [=he has only lived in one city] ▪ She and her cousin go to the *same* school. [=she goes to a particular school, and her cousin also goes to that school] ▪ We graduated the *same* year. ▪ She saw the *same* man at several different times and places yesterday. ▪ I'd met him earlier that ***exact same*** day. = (*US*) I'd met him earlier that ***same exact*** day. ▪ "Puma" and "cougar" are different names for the ***very same*** animal. ▪ The restaurant's owner and chef are ***one and the same*** person. [=the owner is also the chef]

2 a : exactly like someone or something else ▪ The words "their" and "there" are pronounced in exactly the *same* way but spelled differently. ▪ They were wearing the ***exact same*** shirt. = (*US*) They were wearing the ***same exact*** shirt. ▪ He should help us—and ***the same thing goes for*** you! [=and you should help us too] **b** : not changed : exactly like an earlier version, event, etc. ▪ She gave the *same* answer as before. ▪ He eats the *same* breakfast every day. ▪ The *same* thing happened to me yesterday. ▪ She is not the *same* person (that) she used to be—she's changed.

3 — used to describe a quality or characteristic that is shared by more than one person or thing ▪ two people of the *same* sex [=two people who are both male or both female] ▪ The buildings are the *same* age/style. ▪ She has the *same* dark hair and eyes as her father.

at the same time see [1]TIME

same difference see DIFFERENCE

the same old *informal + usually disapproving* — used to refer to something that has not changed ▪ I was hoping for something different, but all I got was more of *the same old* thing. ▪ They brought up *the same old* argument/story yet again!

the same thing — used to say that two things are alike or have the same meaning ▪ Lying and cheating amount to much *the same thing*.

two sides of the same coin see [1]COIN

[2]**same** *pronoun*

1 ***the same*** **a** : someone or something that is exactly like another person or thing being discussed or referred to ▪ He ordered the salmon, and I had *the same*. [=I also had the salmon] ▪ "I'll have a coffee with cream and two sugars." "Make mine *the same*." ▪ Your idea is *the same* as his. ▪ (*chiefly Brit*) "Would you like another drink?" "Yes. (*The*) ***Same again***, please." [=please bring me another drink that is like the one you have already brought me] ▪ All of your classmates have begun their projects, and I suggest you ***do the same***. ▪ The band's last album was a bunch of bubble-gum pop, and their new release is just ***more of the same***. ▪ He should help us—and ***the same goes for*** you! [=and you should help us too] **b** ✧ Two or more things that are *the same* are exactly like each other or very similar to each other. ▪ The lunch specials are always *the same*. ▪ No two fingerprints are ever *the same*. ▪ The two cars are basically *the same*.

2 ***the same*** : someone or something that has not changed : something that is exactly like it was at an earlier time ▪ After the accident, he was never quite *the same* again. ▪ Things would never be *the same* without you! ▪ Things are very much *the same* as before.

S

all the same** or **just the same : despite what has just been said : NEVERTHELESS ▪ Of course it won't be easy. But you should try *all the same.* ▪ I'm afraid I can't accept your offer. But thank you *just the same.*

all the same to — used to say that someone does not care about what is chosen or done in a particular situation ▪ We can do it either today or tomorrow—it's *all the same to* me. [=I am willing to do it either today or tomorrow] ▪ I'd like to go fishing tomorrow morning, if it's *all the same to* you. [=if you don't object to that]

one and the same : one person or thing and not two ▪ The restaurant's owner and chef are *one and the same.* [=the owner is also the chef]

same here *informal* — used to say that you think, feel, or want the same thing as someone else ▪ "I'm tired." "*Same here.*" [=me too; I'm tired too] ▪ "I'll have a coffee." "*Same here,* please."

the same to you — used to return a greeting or insult ▪ "Merry Christmas!" "(And) *the same to you!*" [=Merry Christmas to you too] ▪ "Go to hell!" "*The same to you!*"

[3]**same** *adv* : in a way that is alike or very similar — usually used after *the* ▪ The two brands of soda taste *the same* [=*alike*] to me. ▪ The words "their" and "there" are pronounced *the same* but spelled differently. ▪ I feel exactly ***the same as*** I did yesterday. ▪ I don't like to dress *the same as* everyone else. ▪ The business is run much *the same as* it was 50 years ago. ▪ He ate a sandwich and apple for lunch, ***same as usual.*** [=as he usually does]

same·ness /ˈseɪmnəs/ *noun* [*singular*] : the quality or state of being alike or of not changing ▪ the *sameness* of the two methods ▪ There is a *sameness* to his stories that makes them too predictable. ▪ the *sameness* [=*monotony*] of daily life

same–sex *adj, always used before a noun* : involving members of the same sex ▪ *same-sex* twins [=twins that are both boys or both girls] ▪ *same-sex* couples/relationships ▪ *same-sex* marriages/unions

samey /ˈseɪmi/ *adj, Brit, informal* : similar and boring ▪ He has written five *samey* novels.

[1]**sam·ple** /ˈsæmpəl, *Brit* ˈsɑːmpəl/ *noun, pl* **sam·ples** [*count*]

1 : a small amount of something that gives you information about the thing it was taken from ▪ a blood/water/soil *sample* ▪ We would like to see a *sample* of your work.

2 : a small amount of something that is given to people to try ▪ I tasted a *sample* of the new cereal. ▪ ***Free samples*** were handed out at the store.

3 : a group of people or things that are taken from a larger group and studied, tested, or questioned to get information ▪ The *sample* included 96 women over the age of 40. ▪ a *sample* group ▪ A ***random sample*** of people filled out the survey. ▪ We looked at a ***representative sample*** of public schools.

4 : a small part of a recording (such as a song) that is used in another performer's recording

[2]**sample** *verb* **samples; sam·pled; sam·pling** [+ *obj*]

1 : to taste a small amount of (something) ▪ We *sampled* the wine/food.

2 : to try or experience (something) ▪ She *sampled* everything the resort had to offer, from golfing to yoga.

3 *technical* : to test, study, or question (a group of people or things taken from a larger group) to get information ▪ A low percentage of the women *sampled* said that they smoked during pregnancy. ▪ Five of the 20 schools *sampled* did not meet the standards.

4 : to use a small part of (a recording, such as a song) in another recording ▪ The rap group *sampled* the song.

[3]**sample** *adj, always used before a noun* : used as an example of something ▪ The teacher handed out a *sample* essay/exam. ▪ Here are some *sample* questions for the test.

sam·pler /ˈsæmplɚ, *Brit* ˈsɑːmplə/ *noun, pl* **-plers** [*count*]

1 : a piece of cloth with letters and words sewn in different kinds of stitches and made as an example of a person's sewing skill

2 : a collection that includes different examples of a particular type of thing ▪ a chocolate *sampler* ▪ The collection serves as a *sampler* of American poetry.

sam·pling /ˈsæmplɪŋ, *Brit* ˈsɑːmplɪŋ/ *noun, pl* **-plings**

1 [*count*] : a small group of people or things taken from a larger group and used to represent the larger group ▪ The reporter asked a *sampling* of people about their eating habits. ▪ a *sampling* of the menu's entrées

2 [*count*] : a small amount of something that is offered to someone to try ▪ We were given a *sampling* of the food.

3 [*noncount*] : the act of using a small part of a recording (such as a song) as part of another recording ▪ The band does a lot of *sampling.*

sam·u·rai /ˈsæməˌraɪ/ *noun, pl* **samurai** [*count*] : a member of a Japanese military class in the past ▪ a powerful *samurai* ▪ a *samurai* sword/warrior

san·a·to·ri·um /ˌsænəˈtorijəm/ *noun, pl* **-to·ri·ums** *or* **-to·ria** /-ˈtorijə/ [*count*] *old-fashioned* : a place for the care and treatment of people who are recovering from illness or who have a disease that will last a long time — called also (*US*) *sanitarium,* (*US*) *sanitorium*

sanc·ti·fy /ˈsæŋktəˌfaɪ/ *verb* **-fies; -fied; -fy·ing** [+ *obj*] *formal*

1 : to make (something) holy ▪ The priest *sanctified* their marriage.

2 : to give official acceptance or approval to (something) ▪ The constitution *sanctified* the rights of the people.

– sanc·ti·fi·ca·tion /ˌsæŋktəfəˈkeɪʃən/ *noun* [*noncount*] ▪ the *sanctification* of their marriage

sanc·ti·mo·nious /ˌsæŋktəˈmounijəs/ *adj* [*more* ~; *most* ~] *formal* + *disapproving* : pretending to be morally better than other people ▪ *sanctimonious* politicians ▪ a *sanctimonious* speech/lecture

– sanc·ti·mo·nious·ly *adv* ▪ She *sanctimoniously* criticized our plans.

[1]**sanc·tion** /ˈsæŋkʃən/ *noun, pl* **-tions** *formal*

1 [*count*] : an action that is taken or an order that is given to force a country to obey international laws by limiting or stopping trade with that country, by not allowing economic aid for that country, etc. — usually plural ▪ The United Nations has decided to impose trade/economic *sanctions* on the country. — often + *against* ▪ *Sanctions against* the country have been lifted.

2 [*noncount*] : official permission or approval ▪ The country acted without the *sanction* of the other nations. ▪ Their policy has/lacks legal *sanction.*

[2]**sanction** *verb* **-tions; -tioned; -tion·ing** [+ *obj*] *formal* : to officially accept or allow (something) ▪ The government has *sanctioned* the use of force. ▪ His actions were not *sanctioned* by his superiors.

sanc·ti·ty /ˈsæŋktəti/ *noun* [*noncount*] : the quality or state of being holy, very important, or valuable — often + *of* ▪ the *sanctity* [=*sacredness*] *of* marriage/life/tradition

sanc·tu·ary /ˈsæŋktʃəˌweri, *Brit* ˈsæŋktʃuəri/ *noun, pl* **-aries**

1 [*count*] : a place where someone or something is protected or given shelter ▪ wildlife/bird *sanctuaries* ▪ The house was a *sanctuary* for runaway teens. — often used figuratively ▪ Her garden was a *sanctuary* from the stress of daily life. [=she felt relaxed and free from stress when she was in her garden]

2 [*noncount*] : the protection that is provided by a safe place ▪ The refugees ***found/sought sanctuary*** when they crossed the border.

3 [*count*] **a** *US* : the room inside a church, synagogue, etc., where religious services are held **b** : the most sacred or holy part of a religious building ▪ The *sanctuary* contains the altar of sacrifice.

sanc·tum /ˈsæŋktəm/ *noun, pl* **-tums** [*count*] *somewhat formal*

1 : a place where you are not bothered by other people ▪ Her office was her *sanctum.* — see also INNER SANCTUM

2 : a holy or sacred place ▪ the *sanctum* of a church

[1]**sand** /ˈsænd/ *noun, pl* **sands**

1 [*noncount*] : the very tiny, loose pieces of rock that cover beaches, deserts, etc. ▪ The beaches are covered with pinkish *sand.* ▪ a grain of *sand* ▪ I have *sand* in my shoe. — see also QUICKSAND

2 a [*noncount*] : an area of sand ▪ The children are playing in the *sand.* ▪ She walked across the hot *sand.* **b sands** [*plural*] *literary* : the beach or desert ▪ Tourists walked the *sands.* ▪ They journeyed across the (desert) *sands.*

head in the sand see [1]HEAD

shifting sands — used to refer to changes that happen as time passes ▪ the *shifting sands* of war

the sands of time — used to refer to the passage of time ▪ Many civilizations have been buried by *the sands of time.* [=many civilizations have been forgotten because of the passage of time]

[2]**sand** *verb* **sands; sand·ed; sand·ing**

1 : to make the surface of something smooth by rubbing it with sandpaper [+ *obj*] You should *sand* the shelf before painting it. — often + *down* ▪ *Sand down* the table. [*no obj*] Be sure to *sand* before you paint the shelf.

2 [+ *obj*] *US* : to spread sand over (an icy street, sidewalk, etc.) : to cover (something) with sand ▪ The streets are slippery because they haven't been *sanded* yet.

san·dal /ˈsændl/ *noun, pl* **-dals** [*count*] : a shoe with a bottom part that is held in place with straps around the foot and sometimes the ankle ▪ a pair of *sandals* ▪ I'm missing a *sandal.* — see picture at SHOE

san·dal·wood /ˈsændl̩ˌwʊd/ *noun* [*noncount*] : a yellowish wood with a pleasant smell that is often used to make carved objects and whose oil is used in making perfumes and soaps; *also* : the tree that this wood comes from

¹sand·bag /ˈsændˌbæg/ *noun, pl* **-bags** [*count*] : a bag filled with sand and used as a weight or to build temporary walls, dams, etc.

²sandbag *verb* **-bags; -bagged; -bag·ging**
1 [+ *obj*] : to put sandbags around, on, or in (something) ▪ They *sandbagged* (the area around) the house to protect it from the flood.
2 [+ *obj*] *chiefly US, informal* : to hit (someone) with a sandbag — usually used figuratively to describe treating or criticizing someone unfairly ▪ He would have won the election but he got *sandbagged* by the media.
3 *US, informal* : to hide your true abilities or purpose in order to deceive people, gain an advantage, etc. [*no obj*] He claimed he was playing badly because of an injury, but I think he was *sandbagging.* [+ *obj*] I think he was *sandbagging* us.
– **sand·bag·ger** *noun, pl* **-ers** [*count*] *chiefly US*

sand·bank /ˈsændˌbæŋk/ *noun, pl* **-banks** [*count*] : a raised area of sand in a river, ocean, etc. ▪ The ship ran aground on a *sandbank.*

sand·bar /ˈsændˌbɑɚ/ *noun, pl* **-bars** [*count*] : a raised area of sand with a top that is near or just above the surface of the water in an ocean, lake, or river ▪ We walked out onto the *sandbar* at low tide.

sand·blast /ˈsændˌblæst, *Brit* ˈsændˌblɑːst/ *verb* **-blasts; -blast·ed; blast·ing** [+ *obj*] : to clean, polish, or decorate the surface of (something) by spraying sand on it with a powerful machine ▪ *sandblast* a building ▪ The metal was *sandblasted* to remove old paint. = The old paint was *sandblasted* off the metal.
– **sand·blast·er** *noun, pl* **-ters** [*count*]

sand·box /ˈsændˌbɑːks/ *noun, pl* **-box·es** [*count*] *US* : a low box filled with sand that children can play in — called also (*Brit*) *sandpit*; see picture at PLAYGROUND

sand castle *noun, pl* ~ **castles** [*count*] : a small model of a castle or other building that is made with wet sand on a beach

sand dollar *noun, pl* ~ **-lars** [*count*] *US* : the round, flat shell of a small sea animal; *also* : the small sea animal itself

sand dune *noun, pl* ~ **dunes** [*count*] : DUNE

sand·er /ˈsændɚ/ *noun, pl* **-ers** [*count*]
1 : an electric tool that is used to make a surface smooth — see picture at CARPENTRY
2 *US* : a machine that is used for spreading sand on icy roads

S&H *abbr, US* shipping and handling

S&L *noun, pl* **S&Ls** [*count*] *US* : SAVINGS AND LOAN ASSOCIATION — usually used before another noun ▪ *S&L* executives

sand·lot /ˈsændˌlɑːt/ *noun, pl* **-lots** [*count*] *US* : an empty area of land in a city where children play games or sports
– **sandlot** *adj, always used before a noun* ▪ *sandlot* games/baseball

S and M *or* **S&M** *noun* [*noncount*] : SADOMASOCHISM

sand·man /ˈsændˌmæn/ *noun*
the sandman — used to refer to sleep as an imaginary man who makes people sleepy by sprinkling sand in their eyes ▪ The kids are fighting off *the sandman.* [=the kids are trying not to fall asleep]

¹sand·pa·per /ˈsændˌpeɪpɚ/ *noun* [*noncount*] : stiff paper that has a rough surface on one side and that is rubbed against something (such as a piece of wood) to make it smooth

²sandpaper *verb* **-pers; -pered; -per·ing** [+ *obj*] : to make (something) smooth by rubbing it with sandpaper ▪ You should *sandpaper* [=(more commonly) *sand*] the shelf before you paint it.

sand·pip·er /ˈsændˌpaɪpɚ/ *noun, pl* **-ers** [*count*] : a type of bird that has long legs and a long bill and that lives near the sea

sand·pit /ˈsændˌpɪt/ *noun, pl* **-pits** [*count*] *Brit* : SANDBOX

S

sand·stone /ˈsændˌstoʊn/ *noun, pl* **-stones** [*count, noncount*] : a type of soft stone that is made from grains of sand stuck together

sand·storm /ˈsændˌstoɚm/ *noun, pl* **-storms** [*count*] : an occurrence in which very strong winds blow sand around very forcefully in the desert ▪ They were caught in a *sandstorm.*

sandpiper

sand trap *noun, pl* ~ **traps** [*count*] *US, golf* : an area on a golf course that is filled with sand : BUNKER

¹sand·wich /ˈsændˌwɪtʃ, *Brit* ˈsænˌwɪdʒ/ *noun, pl* **-wich·es** [*count*]
1 : two pieces of bread with something (such as meat, peanut butter, etc.) between them ▪ I had a ham *sandwich* for lunch. ▪ a peanut butter and jelly *sandwich* — see also CLUB SANDWICH, OPEN-FACED SANDWICH
2 : two or more cookies, crackers, or slices of cake with something between them ▪ (*chiefly US*) an ice-cream *sandwich* [=two cookies with ice cream between them]

sandwich

²sandwich *verb* **-wiches; -wiched; -wich·ing** [+ *obj*] *somewhat informal* : to put (someone or something) in the space between two other things or people — usually used as *(be) sandwiched between* ▪ The little boy *was sandwiched between* his brother and sister in the back seat of the van. ▪ a thin sheet of aluminum *sandwiched between* two pieces of plastic ▪ She lives in an old neighborhood *sandwiched between* the river and the railroad tracks.

sandwich board *noun, pl* ~ **boards** [*count*] : two signs that are worn on the front and back of a person's body and that are used especially for advertising something

sandwich course *noun, pl* ~ **courses** [*count*] *Brit* : a course of study in a college or university during which the students spend some time working in a business or industry

sandy /ˈsændi/ *adj* **sand·i·er; -est** [*also more* ~; *most* ~]
1 : full of or covered with sand ▪ The soil in my garden is very *sandy.* ▪ a *sandy* beach
2 : having a yellowish-gray or yellowish-brown color ▪ *sandy* hair
– **sand·i·ness** *noun* [*noncount*] ▪ the *sandiness* of the soil

sane /ˈseɪn/ *adj* **san·er; san·est** [*also more* ~; *most* ~]
1 : having a healthy mind : able to think normally ▪ He is perfectly *sane.* [=he is not mentally ill] ▪ No *sane* person could do something so horrible. ▪ Trips to the beach keep me *sane.* [=keep me feeling happy and able to deal with life without becoming too upset, nervous, etc.] ▪ It's hard to stay/remain *sane* [=to stay relaxed, calm, etc.] when I'm so busy. — opposite INSANE
2 : based on reason or good judgment : rational or sensible ▪ Leaving was the only *sane* option she had. ▪ a *sane* policy/decision
– **sane·ly** *adv* ▪ He spoke *sanely.*

sang *past tense of* SING

sang·froid /ˌsɑːŋˈfrwɑː/ *noun* [*noncount*] *literary* : the ability to stay calm in difficult or dangerous situations ▪ He displayed remarkable *sangfroid* when everyone else was panicking during the crisis.

san·gria /sæŋˈgriːjə/ *noun* [*noncount*] : an alcoholic drink made of red wine, fruit juice, and often soda water

san·guine /ˈsæŋgwən/ *adj* [*more* ~; *most* ~] *formal* : confident and hopeful ▪ She has a *sanguine* disposition/temperament. ▪ He is *sanguine* about the company's future.

san·i·tar·i·um /ˌsænəˈterijəm/ *noun, pl* **-i·ums** *or* **-ia** /-ijə/ [*count*] *US, old-fashioned* : SANATORIUM

san·i·tary /ˈsænəˌteri, *Brit* ˈsænətri/ *adj*
1 *always used before a noun* : of or relating to good health or protection from dirt, infection, disease, etc. ▪ *sanitary* laws ▪ poor *sanitary* conditions [=conditions that are likely to give people diseases or infection] ▪ The park had clean ***sanitary facilities.*** [=*bathrooms*]
2 [*more* ~; *most* ~] : free from dirt, infection, disease, etc. ▪ The public bathrooms were not very *sanitary.* [=*clean*] ▪ *san-*

itary packaging — opposite INSANITARY, UNSANITARY

sanitary napkin *noun, pl* ~ **-kins** [*count*] *US* : a thick piece of soft material that is used to absorb blood during menstruation — called also *sanitary pad, (Brit) sanitary towel*; compare TAMPON

san·i·ta·tion /ˌsænəˈteɪʃən/ *noun* [*noncount*] : the process of keeping places free from dirt, infection, disease, etc., by removing waste, trash and garbage, by cleaning streets, etc. ▪ Diseases can spread from poor *sanitation*. — often used before another noun ▪ *sanitation* workers/trucks

san·i·tize *also Brit* **san·i·tise** /ˈsænəˌtaɪz/ *verb* **-tiz·es; -tized; -tiz·ing** [+ *obj*]

1 : to make (something) free from dirt, infection, disease, etc., by cleaning it : to make (something) sanitary ▪ The housekeeping staff *sanitized* the bathroom.

2 *often disapproving* : to make (something) more pleasant and acceptable by taking things that are unpleasant or offensive out of it ▪ They're trying to *sanitize* the news.

– **sanitized** *also Brit* **sanitised** *adj* ▪ He gave them a *sanitized* account of his life that did not include his time in prison. – **sanitizing** *also Brit* **sanitising** *adj* ▪ *sanitizing* equipment

san·i·to·ri·um /ˌsænəˈtorijəm/ *noun, pl* **-to·ri·ums** *or* **-to·ria** /-ˈtorijə/ [*count*] *US, old-fashioned* : SANATORIUM

san·i·ty /ˈsænəti/ *noun* [*noncount*]

1 : the condition of having a healthy mind : the condition of being sane ▪ People have begun to doubt his *sanity*. ▪ She is the mother of six children but somehow keeps her *sanity*. ▪ I need a vacation to regain/recover my *sanity*. [=to begin to feel normal and relaxed again] — opposite INSANITY

2 : the condition of being based on reason or good judgment ▪ The *sanity* of the decision was never in question.

sank *past tense of* [1]SINK

sans /ˈsænz/ *prep* : WITHOUT ▪ She went to the party *sans* her husband.

San·skrit /ˈsænˌskrɪt/ *noun* [*noncount*] : a language that was spoken many years ago in India and is still used in the practice of Hinduism ▪ chanting in *Sanskrit*

– **Sanskrit** *adj, always before a noun* ▪ a *Sanskrit* word/verse/scholar

sans ser·if /sænˈserəf/ *noun* [*noncount*] *technical* : one of a group of typefaces that do not have short lines across the top and bottom of the long parts of the letters — see picture at FONT; compare SERIF

San·ta Claus /ˈsæntəˌklɑːz/ *noun* [*singular*] : an imaginary fat man with a white beard and a red suit who gives toys to children at Christmas — called also *Santa, (Brit) Father Christmas*

[1]**sap** /ˈsæp/ *noun, pl* **saps**

1 [*noncount*] : a watery juice inside a plant that carries the plant's food ▪ *Sap* is taken from maple trees to make syrup.

2 [*count*] *chiefly US, informal* : a person who is easily tricked or cheated ▪ The poor *sap* believed everything she told him.

[2]**sap** *verb* **saps; sapped; sap·ping** [+ *obj*]

1 : to use up the supply of (something, such as a person's courage, energy, strength, etc.) ▪ Moving the couch up the stairs *sapped* her strength. ▪ Months of rejections after job interviews *sapped* his confidence.

2 : to cause (someone) to lose courage, energy, strength, etc. — usually + *of* ▪ The illness *sapped* him *of* his strength. ▪ Her last three losses have *sapped* her *of* her confidence.

sap·ling /ˈsæplɪŋ/ *noun, pl* **-lings** [*count*] : a young tree

sap·per /ˈsæpɚ/ *noun, pl* **-pers** [*count*] *Brit* : a member of a military unit that builds structures to defend and protect a position

sap·phic /ˈsæfɪk/ *adj, always used before a noun, formal + literary* : of or relating to sexual relations between women : LESBIAN ▪ a *sapphic* relationship ▪ *sapphic* lovers

sap·phire /ˈsæˌfajɚ/ *noun, pl* **-phires**

1 [*count, noncount*] : a clear, usually deep blue jewel — see color picture on page C11

2 [*noncount*] : a deep blue color

sap·py /ˈsæpi/ *adj* **sap·pi·er; -est** [*also more* ~; *most* ~]

1 *US, informal* **a** : sad or romantic in a foolish or exaggerated way ▪ The movie was pretty *sappy*. [=*sentimental*] ▪ a *sappy* [=(*Brit*) *soppy*] love story **b** : foolish or silly : not thinking clearly or showing good judgment ▪ She gets all *sappy* when she is around babies. ▪ a *sappy* idea

2 : full of sap ▪ *sappy* wood

Sa·ran Wrap /səˈræn-/ *trademark, US* — used for a thin sheet of clear plastic that is used to wrap food

sar·casm /ˈsɑɚˌkæzəm/ *noun* [*noncount*] : the use of words that mean the opposite of what you really want to say especially in order to insult someone, to show irritation, or to be funny ▪ biting/dry *sarcasm* ▪ a voice full of *sarcasm* — compare IRONY

sar·cas·tic /sɑɚˈkæstɪk/ *adj* [*more* ~; *most* ~] : using or showing sarcasm ▪ a *sarcastic* person/remark/reply

– **sar·cas·ti·cal·ly** /sɑɚˈkæstɪkli/ *adv*

sar·coph·a·gus /sɑɚˈkɑːfəgəs/ *noun, pl* **-gi** /-ˌgaɪ/ *also* **-gus·es** [*count*] : a stone coffin from ancient times ▪ Egyptian/Roman *sarcophagi*

sar·dine /sɑɚˈdiːn/ *noun, pl* **-dines** [*count*] : a very small fish that is used for food and is usually packed in a can

like sardines : without enough room to move around ▪ A large crowd of reporters was ***crammed/packed like sardines*** into a small room.

sar·don·ic /sɑɚˈdɑːnɪk/ *adj* [*more* ~; *most* ~] *formal* : showing that you disapprove of or do not like someone or something : showing disrespect or scorn for someone or something ▪ The movie is a *sardonic* look at modern life. ▪ *sardonic* humor/comments ▪ a *sardonic* expression/smile

– **sar·don·i·cal·ly** /sɑɚˈdɑːnɪkli/ *adv* ▪ She smiled *sardonically* when she heard what had happened.

sarge /ˈsɑɚʤ/ *noun* [*singular*] *informal* : SERGEANT — usually used as a form of address ▪ What should I do, *Sarge*?

sa·ri /ˈsɑri/ *noun, pl* **-ris** [*count*] : a long piece of cloth that is wrapped around the body and head or shoulder and worn by women in southern Asia — see color picture on page C16

sarky /ˈsɑɚki/ *adj* **sark·i·er; -est** [*also more* ~; *most* ~] *Brit, informal* : SARCASTIC ▪ *sarky* comments/remarks

sar·nie /ˈsɑɚni/ *noun, pl* **-nies** [*count*] *Brit, informal* : SANDWICH ▪ a bacon/jam *sarnie*

sa·rong /səˈrɑːŋ/ *noun, pl* **-rongs** [*count*] : a long strip of cloth that is wrapped loosely around the body and worn by men and women of Malaysia and many Pacific islands — see color picture on page C16

SARS /ˈsɑɚz/ *noun* [*noncount*] : a serious disease that is caused by a virus and that affects your ability to breathe ✧ *SARS* is an abbreviation of "severe acute respiratory syndrome."

sar·sa·pa·ril·la /ˌsæspəˈrɪlə, *Brit* ˌsɑːspəˈrɪlə/ *noun, pl* **-las** [*count, noncount*] *old-fashioned* : a sweetened drink that is flavored with a substance made from the root of a plant

sar·to·ri·al /sɑɚˈtorijəl/ *adj, always used before a noun, formal* : of or relating to clothes ▪ They accused him of having poor *sartorial* taste. ▪ The wedding party arrived in *sartorial* splendor.

– **sar·to·ri·al·ly** *adv* ▪ my *sartorially* conservative friend [=my friend who wears conservative clothes]

SAS /ˌɛsˌeɪˈɛs/ *noun*

the SAS : a part of the British military that consists of soldiers who are specially trained for difficult and secret duties — called also *the Special Air Service*; compare SPECIAL FORCES

SASE *abbr, US* self-addressed stamped envelope

[1]**sash** /ˈsæʃ/ *noun, pl* **sash·es** [*count*] : a long piece of cloth that you wear around your waist or over one shoulder — compare [2]SASH

[2]**sash** *noun, pl* **sashes** [*count*] : the frame that holds glass in a window and that allows the window to open or close by sliding up and down — see picture at WINDOW — compare [1]SASH

sa·shay /sæˈʃeɪ/ *verb, always followed by an adverb or preposition* **-shays; -shayed; -shay·ing** [*no obj*] : to walk in a slow and confident way that makes people notice you ▪ The model *sashayed* down the runway. ▪ She *sashayed* into the room.

sa·shi·mi /ˈsɑːʃəmi, sɑˈʃiːmi/ *noun* [*noncount*] : a Japanese food made of thinly sliced raw fish

sash window *noun, pl* ~ **-dows** [*count*] *Brit* : DOUBLE-HUNG WINDOW — compare CASEMENT

Sas·quatch /ˈsæˌskwæʧ/ *noun* [*singular*] : a large, hairy creature that walks on two feet like a man and that some people claim to have seen in the northwestern U.S. and western Canada — called also *bigfoot*; compare ABOMINABLE SNOWMAN

sass /ˈsæs/ *verb* **sass·es; sassed; sass·ing** [+ *obj*] *chiefly US, informal* : to talk to (someone) in a rude way that does not show proper respect ▪ He got drunk and *sassed* a cop.

– **sass** *noun* [*noncount*] ▪ Don't give me any *sass*. [=*back talk, (Brit) backchat*]

sas·sa·fras /ˈsæsəˌfræs/ *noun, pl* **sassafras**
1 [*count, noncount*] : a tall tree of eastern North America
2 [*noncount*] : the dried bark from the root of the sassafras that is used in medicine and as a flavoring

Sas·se·nach /ˈsæsəˌnæk/ *noun, pl* **-nachs** [*count*] *Scotland, disapproving + humorous* : an English person

sassy /ˈsæsi/ *adj* **sass·i·er; -est** [*also more* ~; *most* ~] *chiefly US, informal*
1 : having or showing a rude lack of respect ▪ *sassy* children ▪ a *sassy* answer
2 : very stylish ▪ her *sassy* new hairdo ▪ She bought some *sassy* high heels.
3 : confident and energetic ▪ the heroine's *sassy* charm

¹sat *past tense and past participle of* SIT

²sat *abbr* satellite

Sat. *abbr* Saturday

SAT *abbr* Scholastic Assessment Test

Sa·tan /ˈseɪtn̩/ *noun* [*noncount*] : DEVIL 1a ▪ He went to the Halloween party dressed up as *Satan*. [=*the Devil*]

sa·tan·ic /seɪˈtænɪk/ *adj*
1 : of, relating to, or worshipping the Devil ▪ a *satanic* cult/rite
2 : very cruel or evil ▪ a *satanic* serial killer

sa·tan·ism /ˈseɪtəˌnɪzəm/ *noun* [*noncount*] : worship of the Devil
– **sa·tan·ist** /ˈseɪtənɪst/ *noun, pl* **-ists** [*count*]

satch·el /ˈsætʃəl/ *noun, pl* **-els** [*count*] : a small bag that is carried over your shoulder and that is used for carrying clothes, books, etc.

sate /ˈseɪt/ *verb* **sates; sat·ed; sat·ing** [+ *obj*] *formal*
1 : to fill (someone) with food so that no more is wanted — usually used as *(be) sated* ▪ He ate until he *was* completely *sated*. [=*full*] ▪ feel *sated*
2 : to end (something, such as hunger or curiosity) by providing everything that is required or wanted : SATISFY ▪ The meal was more than enough to *sate* his hunger/appetite. ▪ The information *sated* their curiosity.

sa·teen /sæˈtiːn/ *noun* [*noncount*] : smooth cloth that is like satin

sat·el·lite /ˈsætəˌlaɪt/ *noun, pl* **-lites**
1 a [*count*] : an object (such as a moon) that moves around a much larger planet **b** : a machine that is sent into space and that moves around the earth, moon, sun, or a planet ✧ Satellites are used for radio, television, and other types of communication and for studying the objects they move around. [*count*] *Satellites* help meteorologists predict the weather. [*noncount*] Images of the planet are sent by *satellite*. — often used before another noun ▪ *satellite* broadcasting/channels/images/radio/TV
2 [*count*] : a country, organization, etc., that is controlled by a larger and more powerful country, organization, etc.

satellite dish *noun, pl* ~ **dishes** [*count*] : a device that is shaped like a large dish and that receives television signals from a satellite high above the earth

satellite dish

sa·ti·ate /ˈseɪʃiˌeɪt/ *verb* **-ates; -at·ed; -at·ing** [+ *obj*] *formal* : to satisfy (a need, desire, etc.) fully ▪ Her curiosity was never *satiated*. [=*sated*]
– **sa·ti·a·tion** /ˌseɪʃiˈeɪʃən/ *noun* [*noncount*]

sa·ti·ety /səˈtajəti/ *noun* [*noncount*] *technical* : a feeling or condition of being full after eating food ▪ eating beyond the point of *satiety*

¹sat·in /ˈsætn̩/ *noun* [*noncount*] : cloth that has a smooth, shiny surface ▪ a dress made of *satin*

²satin *adj*
1 : made of or covered with satin ▪ *satin* sheets/shoes
2 : having a smooth and shiny surface : SATINY ▪ *satin* paint

sat·iny /ˈsætn̩i/ *adj* : smooth and shiny like satin ▪ There's a *satiny* feel to the material. ▪ a smooth *satiny* finish/texture

sat·ire /ˈsæˌtajə/ *noun, pl* **-ires**
1 [*noncount*] : a way of using humor to show that someone or something is foolish, weak, bad, etc. : humor that shows the weaknesses or bad qualities of a person, government, society, etc. ▪ His movies are known for their use of *satire*.
2 [*count*] : a book, movie, etc., that uses satire ▪ The movie is a political/social *satire*.
– **sa·tir·ic** /səˈtirɪk/ *or* **sa·tir·i·cal** /səˈtɪrɪkəl/ *adj* ▪ The play is a *satiric/satirical* comedy. ▪ her dry *satiric/satirical* wit ▪ a *satiric/satirical* novel – **sa·tir·i·cal·ly** /səˈtɪrɪkli/ *adv* ▪ a political subject that is usually treated *satirically*

sat·i·rist /ˈsætərɪst/ *noun, pl* **-rists** [*count*] : a person who uses satire in books, movies, etc. ▪ social *satirists* of the American Dream ▪ the great British *satirist*, Jonathan Swift

sat·i·rize *also Brit* **sat·i·rise** /ˈsætəˌraɪz/ *verb* **-riz·es; -rized; -riz·ing** [+ *obj*] : to show that (someone or something) is foolish, weak, bad, etc., by using satire ▪ The book *satirizes* contemporary life.

sat·is·fac·tion /ˌsætəsˈfækʃən/ *noun, pl* **-tions**
1 : a happy or pleased feeling because of something that you did or something that happened to you [*noncount*] He gets/derives great *satisfaction* from volunteering. ▪ the *satisfaction* of a job well done ▪ There is some *satisfaction* in knowing I was right. [*singular*] She finds a certain *satisfaction* in helping others. — opposite DISSATISFACTION
2 [*noncount*] : the act of providing what is needed or desired : the act of satisfying a need or desire ▪ sexual *satisfaction* ▪ the *satisfaction* of his deep craving for love
3 [*noncount*] *formal* : a result that deals with a problem or complaint in an acceptable way ▪ I complained to the manager about the poor service but did not get any *satisfaction*.
4 [*count*] *US* : something that makes you happy, pleased, or satisfied ▪ Helping others is one of the greatest *satisfactions* of my life.
to someone's satisfaction : so that someone is happy, pleased, or satisfied ▪ The work was not done *to my satisfaction*. [=I was not satisfied with the work] ▪ The charge must be proved *to the satisfaction* of the court. [=the court must be convinced that the charge is true]

sat·is·fac·to·ry /ˌsætəsˈfæktəri/ *adj* [*more* ~; *most* ~] : good enough for a particular purpose : ACCEPTABLE ▪ The job requires a *satisfactory* level of performance. ▪ Results are less *satisfactory* than had been anticipated. ▪ He gave a *satisfactory* account/explanation of how the accident had happened. ▪ The movie was brought to a *satisfactory* close/conclusion/end. ▪ His work has been *satisfactory*, but not outstanding. — opposite UNSATISFACTORY
– **sat·is·fac·to·ri·ly** /ˌsætəsˈfæktərəli/ *adv* ▪ My questions had been answered *satisfactorily*. ▪ They performed *satisfactorily* on the exam.

satisfied *adj* [*more* ~; *most* ~]
1 : having a happy or pleased feeling because of something that you did or something that happened to you ▪ a *satisfied* customer ▪ There was a *satisfied* look/smile on her face. ▪ She sat back from the table, *satisfied*. — often + *with* ▪ He's *satisfied with* things as they are. ▪ They were *satisfied with* the compromise. — opposite DISSATISFIED
2 *not used before a noun* : completely certain or sure about something : CONVINCED ▪ He was *satisfied* that she was not lying to him. ▪ You're quite *satisfied* that he's right?

sat·is·fy /ˈsætəsˌfaɪ/ *verb* **-fies; -fied; -fy·ing** [+ *obj*]
1 : to cause (someone) to be happy or pleased ▪ His job *satisfies* him. ▪ Nothing *satisfies* her so much as doing a good job. ▪ The movie's ending failed to *satisfy* audiences. — opposite DISSATISFY
2 : to provide, do, or have what is required by (someone or something) ▪ He ate a little food, but not enough to *satisfy* his hunger. [=not enough to stop him from being hungry] ▪ His curiosity was *satisfied* by their explanation. ▪ He has *satisfied* all of his graduation requirements. [=he has done all the things required for graduation] ▪ She *satisfied* [=*fulfilled*] all conditions for approval of the loan.
3 *formal* : to cause (someone) to believe that something is true : CONVINCE ▪ They have *satisfied* themselves that the story is only a rumor.

satisfying *adj* [*more* ~; *most* ~] : making you feel satisfied : giving you what you want or need ▪ You can have a very *satisfying* lunch at that restaurant. ▪ a totally *satisfying* movie/novel ▪ It is one of the most *satisfying* jobs I've ever had.
– **sat·is·fy·ing·ly** *adv* ▪ The movie has a *satisfyingly* happy ending.

sat·u·rate /ˈsætʃəˌreɪt/ *verb* **-rates; -rat·ed; -rat·ing** [+ *obj*]
1 : to make (something) very wet ▪ *Saturate* the sponge with water. ▪ That last rain really *saturated* [=*soaked*] the ground.
2 : to fill (something) completely with something ▪ Images of the war *saturated* the news. ▪ Their new products are *saturating* the market.

sat·u·rat·ed /ˈsætʃəˌreɪtəd/ *adj* [*more* ~; *most* ~]
1 : completely wet ▪ a *saturated* sponge/towel ▪ His shirt was *saturated* with sweat.

2 : completely filled with something ▪ the area's already *saturated* freeways — often + *with* ▪ Newspapers were *saturated with* stories about the election. ▪ The room was *saturated with* the smell of her perfume.
3 *technical* — used to describe a type of oil or fat that is found in foods such as meat and butter and that is bad for your health ▪ *Saturated* fats are not easily processed by the body. — compare UNSATURATED

sat·u·ra·tion /ˌsætʃəˈreɪʃən/ *noun* [*noncount*]
1 : the act or result of making something very wet ▪ Heavy rains resulted in the *saturation* of the soil.
2 : the act or result of supplying so much of something that no more is wanted ▪ the *saturation* of advertising on television ▪ a product that has reached market *saturation* [=a product that has saturated the market] — often used before a noun ▪ *saturation* coverage of a news story ▪ The number of game shows on TV may have reached the ***saturation point***. [=the point at which there are so many that no more can be added successfully]
3 : the act of using military force over a whole area — usually used before another noun ▪ ***saturation bombing*** [=bombing in which a very large number of bombs are dropped to cover an entire area instead of being aimed at a specific target]

Sat·ur·day /ˈsætəˌdeɪ/ *noun, pl* **-days :** the day of the week between Friday and Sunday [*count*] They left last *Saturday*. ▪ He will arrive next/this *Saturday*. ▪ His birthday falls on a *Saturday* this year. ▪ (*Brit*) He will arrive on the *Saturday* and leave on the Wednesday. ▪ The club meets on *Saturdays*. = The club meets every *Saturday*. [*noncount*] I will arrive on *Saturday*. = (*chiefly US*) I will arrive *Saturday*. — abbr. *Sat.*
– Sat·ur·days /ˈsætəˌdeɪz/ *adv* ▪ He visits his parents *Saturdays*. [=he visits his parents every *Saturday*]

Sat·urn /ˈsætən/ *noun* [*singular*] **:** the planet that is sixth in order from the sun and that is surrounded by large rings

sat·ur·nine /ˈsætəˌnaɪn/ *adj* [*more ~; most ~*] *literary* **:** very serious and unhappy ▪ his *saturnine* [=*sullen*] looks ▪ He is *saturnine* in temperament.

sa·tyr *or* **Sa·tyr** /ˈseɪtə, *Brit* ˈsætə/ *noun, pl* **-tyrs** [*count*] **:** one of the forest gods in Greek mythology who have faces and bodies like men and ears, legs, and tails like goats

sauce /ˈsɑːs/ *noun, pl* **sauc·es**
1 : a thick liquid that is eaten with or on food to add flavor to it [*count*] a delicious spaghetti/meat *sauce* ▪ She tried several *sauces* before she found one she liked. ▪ chicken in/with a cream *sauce* ▪ Cover the strawberries with the chocolate *sauce*. [*noncount*] This pizza needs more *sauce*. — see also SOY SAUCE, TARTAR SAUCE, WHITE SAUCE
2 [*count*] **:** boiled or canned fruit ▪ cranberry *sauce* — see also APPLESAUCE
3 [*singular*] *chiefly Brit, informal + old-fashioned* **:** rude or impolite language or actions ▪ I've had enough of your *sauce*!
4 ***the sauce*** *US slang* **:** alcoholic drinks **:** LIQUOR ▪ He's been ***off the sauce*** [=he has not drunk any alcohol] for a month now. ▪ He's back ***on the sauce***. [=he's drinking alcohol again]
what's sauce for the goose is sauce for the gander see [1]GOOSE

sauce·boat /ˈsɑːsˌboʊt/ *noun, pl* **-boats** [*count*] **:** a long and narrow container that has a handle and a special curved end for pouring and that is used for serving a sauce or gravy with a meal

sauce·pan /ˈsɑːsˌpæn, *Brit* ˈsɔːspən/ *noun, pl* **-pans** [*count*] **:** a deep, round cooking pan with a handle — see picture at KITCHEN

sau·cer /ˈsɑːsə/ *noun, pl* **-cers** [*count*] **:** a small, round dish that you put a cup on — see picture at PLACE SETTING; see also FLYING SAUCER

saucy /ˈsɑːsi/ *adj* **sauc·i·er; -est** [*also more ~; most ~*]
1 *somewhat old-fashioned* **:** rude usually in a lively and playful way ▪ a *saucy* actress ▪ *saucy* language
2 : served with a sauce ▪ *saucy* foods ▪ a *saucy* dish
– sauc·i·ly /ˈsɑːsəli/ *adv* ▪ He spoke *saucily*. **– sauc·i·ness** /ˈsɑːsinəs/ *noun* [*noncount*]

sau·er·kraut /ˈsawəˌkraʊt/ *noun* [*noncount*] **:** a German food made of a vegetable (called a cabbage) that is cut into small pieces and soaked in a salty and sour liquid

sau·na /ˈsɑːnə/ *noun, pl* **-nas** [*count*]
1 : a special heated room in which people sit or lie down in order to get hot and sweat ▪ The health club has a pool and a *sauna*.
2 : a health treatment in which people sit or lie down in a sauna ▪ He talked about the benefits of taking/having a *sauna* regularly.

saun·ter /ˈsɑːntə/ *verb, always followed by an adverb or preposition* **-ters; -tered; -ter·ing** [*no obj*] **:** to walk along in a slow and relaxed manner **:** STROLL ▪ They *sauntered* slowly down the street. ▪ Some girls *sauntered* by. ▪ He *sauntered* into the store.
– saunter *noun* [*singular*] ▪ We took a *saunter* around the town.

sau·sage /ˈsɑːsɪdʒ/ *noun, pl* **-sag·es :** spicy ground meat (such as pork) that is usually stuffed into a narrow tube of skin or made into a small flat cake [*noncount*] Would you like any/some *sausage*? [*count*] breakfast *sausages* ▪ They bought *sausages* for the picnic.
not a sausage *Brit, informal + old-fashioned* **:** NOTHING ▪ What did they find? *Not a sausage*.

sausage dog *noun, pl* **~ dogs** [*count*] *Brit, informal* **:** DACHSHUND

[1]sau·té /sɑˈteɪ, *Brit* ˈsəʊˌteɪ/ *verb* **-tés** *also* **-tes; -téed** *also* **-teed; -té·ing** *also* **-te·ing** [*+ obj*] **:** to fry (food) in a small amount of fat ▪ *Sauté* the onion and garlic. ▪ peppers *sautéed* in olive oil ▪ meat *sautéed* with herbs

[2]sauté *noun, pl* **-tés** [*count*] **:** a food that is fried in a small amount of fat ▪ a shrimp *sauté* = (*US*) a *sauté* of shrimp
– sauté *adj, always used before a noun* ▪ *sauté* [=*sautéed*] potatoes

[1]sav·age /ˈsævɪdʒ/ *adj* [*more ~; most ~*]
1 *of an animal* **:** not under human control **:** WILD ▪ *savage* [=*wild*] beasts
2 : very cruel or violent ▪ a *savage* criminal ▪ He was the victim of a *savage* attack/beating. ▪ a *savage* battle ▪ The coast was lashed by *savage* storms.
3 : very critical or harsh ▪ *savage* criticism ▪ He wrote *savage* satires about people he didn't like.
4 *old-fashioned + offensive* **:** having a way of life that is simple and not highly advanced **:** uncivilized or primitive ▪ a *savage* country/tribe
– sav·age·ly *adv* ▪ She was *savagely* attacked by the dog. ▪ He was *savagely* beaten. **– sav·age·ness** *noun* [*noncount*] ▪ the *savageness* [=(more commonly) *savagery*] of the battle/crime

[2]savage *noun, pl* **-ag·es** [*count*]
1 *old-fashioned + offensive* **:** a person who has a way of life that is simple and not highly advanced ▪ a wild *savage*
2 : a person who is very violent or cruel ▪ What kind of *savage* could have committed such a terrible crime?

[3]savage *verb* **-ages; -aged; -ag·ing** [*+ obj*] **:** to attack or treat (someone or something) in a very cruel, violent, or harsh way ▪ He looked like he'd been *savaged* by a wild animal. ▪ A hurricane *savaged* the city. ▪ The newspapers *savaged* his reputation.

sav·age·ry /ˈsævɪdʒəri/ *noun, pl* **-ries**
1 [*noncount*] **:** a cruel or violent quality **:** a savage quality ▪ The *savagery* of the attack was horrifying. ▪ an act of pure *savagery*
2 [*count*] **:** a cruel or violent act or action ▪ the *savageries* committed by the soldiers ▪ the *savageries* of war

sa·van·na *also* **sa·van·nah** /səˈvænə/ *noun, pl* **-nas** *also* **-nahs** [*count*] **:** a large flat area of land with grass and very few trees especially in Africa and South America

sa·vant /sæˈvɑːnt, *Brit* ˈsævənt/ *noun, pl* **-vants** [*count*] *formal*
1 : a person who knows a lot about a particular subject ▪ a computer *savant*
2 : a person who does not have normal intelligence but who has very unusual mental abilities that other people do not have

S

[1]save /ˈseɪv/ *verb* **saves; saved; sav·ing**
1 [*+ obj*] **a :** to keep (someone or something) safe **:** to stop (someone or something) from dying or being hurt, damaged, or lost ▪ He risked his life to *save* his friend (from drowning). ▪ The organization is dedicated to *saving* [=*protecting*] endangered animals. ▪ We need to *save* the rain forests (from destruction). ▪ He grabbed her arm to *save* her from falling. [=to stop/prevent her from falling so that she would not be hurt] ▪ The doctors managed to *save* the soldier's wounded leg. [=to keep the leg from having to be cut off] **b :** to stop (something) from ending or failing **:** to make (something that is in danger of failing) successful ▪ He is trying to *save* his marriage by going to counseling for his drug addiction. ▪ The new CEO *saved* the company (from bankruptcy). ▪ She *saved* a tense situation by staying calm.

2 : to keep (something) from being lost or wasted [+ *obj*] This new plan will help us *save* time. = The new plan will *save* us some time. ▪ Thinner computer monitors *save* space. [*no obj*] — + *on* ▪ A more efficient furnace will *save on* energy.
3 a : to keep money instead of spending it : to put money away especially in a bank so that you will have it in the future [*no obj*] She would rather *save* than spend. ▪ He has been *saving* (up) for a new car. [+ *obj*] *Save* a little money for later. ▪ She *saves* part of her pay every week. ▪ I *saved* $20,000 for a down payment on the house. **b** : to spend less money [*no obj*] Buy now and *save*! — often + *on* ▪ *Save on* everything in the store! ▪ He *saved on* [=spent less money for] his car insurance by switching to a different insurance company. [+ *obj*] She *saved* $15 at the grocery store by using coupons. — often + *on* ▪ We're trying to *save* money *on* our electric bill.
4 [+ *obj*] **a** : to keep (something) available for use in the future ▪ Be sure to *save* some cookies for your sister. ▪ You need to *save* (up) your energy for tomorrow. ▪ He *saves* his best jacket for special occasions. [=he only wears his best jacket on special occasions] ▪ The runners *saved* their energy for the last lap. = The runners ***saved themselves*** for the last lap. **b** : to keep (something) for someone to use or have ▪ She *saved* a seat for her friend. ▪ Please *save* the next dance for me. = Please *save* me the next dance. [=please don't plan to dance the next dance with anyone but me]
5 [+ *obj*] : to make (something) unnecessary ▪ Check that you have everything before you leave. It will *save* your having to go back again. ▪ The shortcut *saves* an hour's driving.
6 [+ *obj*] : to keep (someone) from doing something ▪ Thanks for sending out that package. It *saved* me a trip to the post office. ▪ I'll make the appointment for you to ***save you the trouble/bother.*** [=so that you don't have to do it yourself] — often + *from* ▪ You should cut up the vegetables to *save* you *from* doing it later when the guests are here.
7 [+ *obj*] : to collect or keep (something) ▪ She *saved* all his letters.
8 : to store (data) in a computer or on a storage device (such as a CD) so that it can be used later [+ *obj*] You should *save* your work on/to a disk. ▪ *save* a file [*no obj*] Don't forget to *save* before you close the file.
9 [+ *obj*] *sports* **a** : to stop (an opponent's shot) from scoring a goal ▪ He *saved* the penalty kick/shot. **b** : to keep (a game) from being lost to an opponent ▪ The relief pitcher *saved* the game.
10 *in Christianity* : to protect or free (someone) from sin or evil [+ *obj*] He believes that Jesus Christ will *save* him. [*no obj*] Jesus *saves*.
a penny saved (is a penny earned) see PENNY
save face see [1]FACE
save someone's bacon/hide/neck/skin *informal* : to save someone : to help someone get out of a dangerous or difficult situation ▪ You really *saved my bacon* by helping out yesterday. ▪ He doesn't care what happens to us. All he's worried about is *saving his own skin/neck.* [=saving himself]
save someone's life **1** *or* ***save a life*** : to stop (someone) from dying or being killed : to rescue (someone) who is in terrible danger ▪ She thanked the firefighters who *saved her life.* [=rescued her] ▪ a surgical procedure that has *saved the lives* of thousands of people ▪ The use of seat belts can *save lives.* ▪ If you donate blood, you might *save a life.* **2** *informal* : to help (someone) in an important way — often used to thank someone who helped you ▪ Thanks for covering for me. You really *saved my life.*
save the day : to make a bad situation end successfully ▪ Just when things looked hopeless, my brother came along and *saved the day.*
save your breath see BREATH
to save your life *informal* ✧ If you ***cannot do something to save your life,*** you are completely unable to do it. ▪ She *can't sing to save her life.* [=she is a very bad singer]

[2]**save** *noun, pl* **saves** [*count*]
1 : a play that stops an opponent from scoring a goal ▪ The goalie made a spectacular *save.*
2 *baseball, of a relief pitcher* : the act of keeping a team's lead when replacing another pitcher at the end of a game ▪ He leads the league in *saves.*

[3]**save** *prep, formal* : other than : but or except ▪ We had no hope *save* one.
save for : not including (someone or something) : except for (someone or something) ▪ The park was deserted *save for* a few joggers.

[4]**save** *conj, formal* : EXCEPT ▪ Little is known about his early years *save* that he left home when he was very young.

sav·er /ˈseɪvɚ/ *noun, pl* **-ers** [*count*]
1 : someone who saves money for future use ▪ He is a compulsive *saver* who always watches his spending.
2 : something that prevents unnecessary waste or loss — used in combination ▪ This recipe is a real time-*saver.* [=this recipe saves a lot of time] ▪ The new product is an energy-*saver.*
— see also LIFESAVER

[1]**saving** *noun, pl* **-ings**
1 [*count*] : an amount of something that is not spent or used ▪ The new system will provide a *saving* in labor. ▪ a *saving* on fuel — often plural ▪ a *savings* of 50 percent ▪ The investment offers tax *savings.* ▪ The *savings* at the end of the first year will be considerable.
2 ***savings*** [*plural*] : the amount of money that you have saved especially in a bank over a period of time ▪ How much money do you have in *savings*? ▪ She has her *savings* in stocks. ▪ They were able to retire on their *savings.* ▪ His parents lost their ***life savings*** [=all the money they had] when the stock market crashed.

[2]**saving** *adj*
1 : preventing the unnecessary waste or loss of something — used in combination ▪ energy-*saving* technology ▪ space-*saving* furniture
2 : preventing the unnecessary spending of money — used in combination ▪ money-*saving* tips ▪ cost-*saving* strategies

saving grace *noun, pl* ~ **graces** [*count*] : a good quality that makes a bad or unpleasant person or thing better or more acceptable ▪ It's expensive, but the machine's *saving grace* is its ease of operation. ▪ One of her *saving graces* is a good sense of humor.

savings account *noun, pl* ~ **-counts** [*count*] : a bank account in which people keep money that they want to save ▪ She opened a *savings account.*

savings and loan association *noun, pl* ~ **-tions** [*count*] *US* : a business that is like a bank and that holds and invests the money saved by its members and makes loans to home buyers — called also *savings and loan, S&L*

savings bank *noun, pl* ~ **banks** [*count*] : a business where people keep money that they are saving in order to earn interest on it and where they can borrow money to buy homes, cars, etc.

savings bond *noun, pl* ~ **bonds** [*count*] *finance* : a bond sold by the U.S. government that comes in values of $50 to $10,000

sav·ior (*US*) *or Brit* **sav·iour** /ˈseɪvjɚ/ *noun, pl* **-iors**
1 [*count*] : someone who saves something or someone from danger, harm, failure, etc. ▪ We all felt that she was our *savior.* ▪ Many people expected him to be the *savior* of his (political) party.
2 ***Savior*** (*US*) *or Brit* ***Saviour*** — used by Christians to refer to Jesus Christ ▪ saying a prayer to the/our *Savior*

sa·voir faire /ˌsævˌwɑɚˈfeɚ/ *noun* [*noncount*] *formal* : the ability to behave in a correct and confident way in different situations ▪ I admire her sophistication and *savoir faire.* ▪ He handled the problem with his usual *savoir faire.*

[1]**sa·vor** (*US*) *or Brit* **sa·vour** /ˈseɪvɚ/ *noun, pl* **-vors** *formal*
1 [*count*] : a good taste or smell — usually singular ▪ She enjoys the *savor* of a baking pie. ▪ There was a *savor* to the dish that I couldn't identify. ▪ a *savor* of mint ▪ an earthy *savor*
2 [*noncount*] *literary* : the quality that makes something interesting or enjoyable ▪ Without her love, life has lost its *savor* for me.

[2]**savor** (*US*) *or Brit* **savour** /ˈseɪvɚ/ *verb* **-vors; -vored; -vor·ing** *formal*
1 [+ *obj*] : to enjoy the taste or smell of (something) for as long as possible ▪ He *savored* the aroma of the baking pies. ▪ They *savored* every last morsel of food.
2 [+ *obj*] : to enjoy (something) for a long time ▪ She was just *savoring* the moment. ▪ The team is still *savoring* its victory. ▪ He *savored* the memories of his vacation.
savor of [*phrasal verb*] ***savor of (something)*** *formal* : to seem to suggest or involve (something unpleasant) ▪ That suggestion *savors of* [=*smacks of*] hypocrisy.

[1]**sa·vory** (*US*) *or Brit* **sa·voury** /ˈseɪvəri/ *adj* [*more* ~; *most* ~] *formal*
1 : having a pleasant taste or smell ▪ a *savory* aroma
2 : having a spicy or salty quality without being sweet ▪ They prepared an assortment of both sweet and *savory* foods.
3 : morally good — usually used in negative statements ▪ His

reputation was anything but *savory.* [=his reputation was unsavory] ▪ her less *savory* friend

[2]**savory** (*US*) *or Brit* **savoury** *noun, pl* **-vor·ies** [*count*] *formal* : a small serving of food that is spicy or salty but not sweet : a savory food ▪ They prepared assorted sweets and *savories.*

[1]**sav·vy** /ˈsævi/ *noun* [*noncount*] : practical understanding or knowledge of something ▪ He is admired for his business *savvy.* [=*shrewdness*]

[2]**savvy** *adj* **sav·vi·er; -est** [*also more ~; most ~*] *US* : having practical understanding or knowledge of something ▪ She's a very *savvy* investor. ▪ He is *savvy* about computers.

[1]**saw** *past tense of* [1]SEE

[2]**saw** /ˈsɑː/ *noun, pl* **saws** [*count*] : a tool that has a blade with sharp teeth and that is used to cut through wood, metal, and other hard material ▪ a power *saw* — see picture at CARPENTRY; see also CHAIN SAW, CIRCULAR SAW, HACKSAW, HANDSAW, JIGSAW — compare [4]SAW

[3]**saw** *verb* **saws; sawed** /ˈsɑːd/; **sawed** *or Brit* **sawn** /ˈsɑːn/; **saw·ing** /ˈsɑːɪŋ/ : to cut or shape (wood, metal, etc.) with a saw [+ *obj*] He *sawed* the boards in half. [*no obj*] This blade is too dull for *sawing.*

saw at [*phrasal verb*] ***saw at (something)*** : to try to cut (something) by moving a saw, knife, etc., backwards and forwards ▪ She was *sawing* (away) *at* the turkey with a dull knife. — sometimes used figuratively ▪ The violinist *sawed* (away) *at* the strings.

saw down [*phrasal verb*] ***saw down (something) or saw (something) down*** : to cut (something) with a saw and bring it to the ground : to cut (something) down ▪ The trees were *sawed down.*

saw off [*phrasal verb*] ***saw off (something) or saw (something) off*** : to remove (something) by cutting it with a saw ▪ She *sawed off* the branch.

saw up [*phrasal verb*] ***saw up (something) or saw (something) up*** : to cut (something) into pieces with a saw ▪ He *sawed up* the boards into foot-long pieces.

[4]**saw** *noun, pl* **saws** [*count*] : a common saying : PROVERB ▪ His grandfather recited the old *saw* about an apple a day keeping the doctor away. — compare [2]SAW

saw·dust /ˈsɑːˌdʌst/ *noun* [*noncount*] : tiny particles of wood that are formed from sawing or sanding wood

sawed–off shotgun *noun, pl* **~ -guns** [*count*] *US* : a shotgun that has a shorter barrel than a regular shotgun — called also (*Brit*) *sawn-off shotgun*

saw·horse /ˈsɑːˌhoɚs/ *noun, pl* **-hors·es** [*count*] : a frame on which wood is placed when it is being cut with a saw

saw·mill /ˈsɑːˌmɪl/ *noun, pl* **-mills** [*count*] : a mill or factory where logs are sawed to make boards

sax /ˈsæks/ *noun, pl* **sax·es** [*count*] *informal* : SAXOPHONE ▪ a tenor *sax*

Sax·on /ˈsæksən/ *noun, pl* **-ons** [*count*] : a member of the Germanic people who entered and conquered England in the fifth century A.D. — see also ANGLO-SAXON

– **Saxon** *adj* ▪ *Saxon* kings

sax·o·phone /ˈsæksəˌfoʊn/ *noun, pl* **-phones** [*count*] : a musical instrument that has a curved metal tube and that is played by blowing into a mouthpiece and pressing keys with your fingers — see picture at WOODWIND

sax·o·phon·ist /ˈsæksəˌfoʊnɪst, *Brit* sækˈsɒfənɪst/ *noun, pl* **-ists** [*count*] : someone who plays the saxophone

[1]**say** /ˈseɪ/ *verb* **says** /ˈsɛz/; **said** /ˈsɛd/; **say·ing** /ˈsejɪŋ/

1 : to use your voice to express (something) with words [+ *obj*] "Is anybody there?" he *said.* ▪ "Good morning," *said* the woman behind the counter. ▪ I *said* three words before he interrupted me again. ▪ I just stopped by to *say* hello. ▪ He left without *saying* goodbye. ▪ I wanted to *say* thank you for all you've done for me. ▪ She *said* something about going to the store after work. ▪ He *said* something in French. ▪ Anything you *say* to the police can be used as evidence against you. ▪ Don't believe a word he *says.* ▪ Please be quiet. I have something to *say.* ▪ Listen closely, because I'm not going to *say* this again/twice. ▪ What did you *say*? ▪ Who shall I *say* is calling, Sir? ▪ Did she *say* how to get there? ▪ I *said* to myself, "I can do it." ▪ He *said* (that) he was a doctor. ▪ I can honestly *say* (that) I had never seen that man before today. ▪ I already *said* (that) I was sorry. ▪ You know what they *say,* "If you can't beat 'em, join 'em." ▪ As people/they *say,* "You can't teach an old dog new tricks." ▪ Her eyes are hazel, ***which is to say*** [=which means that] they are greenish brown. ▪ "A word of advice: don't mention the war." "***Say no more*** [=I understand you; you do not need to explain it further]—I'll stay off the subject!" [*no obj*] "What happened next?" "I'd rather not *say.*"

2 [+ *obj*] : to express (an opinion) ▪ She thinks I should break up with him. What do you *say*? [=what's your opinion?] ▪ What would/do you *say* to seeing a movie tonight? [=would you like to see a movie tonight?] ▪ "After all, he was the last person to see her alive." "Are you *saying* that (you think) he killed her?" ▪ I *say* you're wrong. [=my opinion is that you're wrong] ▪ I wouldn't *say* (that) he's a great guitarist [=I don't think he's a great guitarist]; he's just OK. ▪ They *say* (that) you should drink eight glasses of water a day. = It's *said* that you should drink eight glasses of water a day. [=the opinion of people who know about this subject is that you should drink eight glasses of water a day] ▪ New England is *said* to be [=many people think New England is] very beautiful in the Fall. ▪ "Is the island nice?" "***So they/people say.***" ▪ ***I must say*** it was quite a surprise to hear from him. = ***I have to say*** it was quite a surprise to hear from him. ▪ I'm not *saying* we shouldn't buy the car. ***All I'm saying*** is that we should think about it some more. ▪ I didn't really enjoy the movie, but ***that's not to say*** it was bad. ▪ ***Say what you like*** (about it), I thought it was a good movie. ▪ Seeing your reaction, ***I would say*** that you're jealous that he has a new girlfriend. ▪ The dress seems too fancy for the party, ***wouldn't you say***? [=don't you agree?; do you think the same thing?] ▪ ***I'll say this for him***—he's very generous with his money. ▪ "She's a great singer!" "***If you say so.***"

3 : to express (a fact) with certainty [+ *obj*] No one can *say* for sure whether it will happen. ▪ It is ***hard to say*** what caused the injury. ▪ ***There's no saying*** [=it is impossible to know] how many people died in the earthquake. [*no obj*] "When will you be done?" "***I couldn't/can't say.***" [=I don't know] ✧ This sense is often used in indirect questions beginning with *who* to express disagreement or to say that something cannot be known for sure. ▪ Who *says* I can't do it? I can do anything if I put my mind to it. ▪ Who's to *say* they wouldn't have won if their team was healthy? ▪ Who can *say* what will happen? [=no one knows what will happen]

4 : to give (an order) : to tell someone to do (something) [+ *obj*] I *said* leave me alone! ▪ "Why do we have to go?" "Because your father and I *said* so." ▪ Mom *said* to wait here. ▪ She's the boss. ***What she says goes***! [=you have to do what she tells you to do] ▪ "Let's try installing the program one more time." "***Whatever you say***—you're the expert." ▪ "Don't you ever bring that subject up again, do you hear me?!" "Okay, okay. *Whatever you say.*" [*no obj*] Don't start until I *say* (so/to).

5 [+ *obj*] : to pronounce (a word) ▪ How do you *say* your name?

6 [+ *obj*] : to repeat or recite (something) ▪ We always *say* our prayers before going to bed. ▪ Can you *say* the poem from memory? ▪ A new priest *said* Mass this morning.

7 [+ *obj*] : to use written words to give (information) ▪ What does the card *say*? ▪ Does the article *say* how the fire happened? ▪ The letter *says* that I've been accepted to the college. ▪ It *says* here that there will be a special guest at the concert. ▪ The instructions *say* to add two eggs.

8 [+ *obj*] : to show or indicate (something) by using numbers, pictures, etc. ▪ The clock *says* five minutes after ten. ▪ The calendar *says* that Christmas falls on a Monday.

9 [+ *obj*] : to express (a meaning, emotion, etc.) without using words ▪ She likes art that really *says* something. ▪ The kind of car you drive *says* a lot about the kind of person you are. ▪ The look on her face *said* "I'm sorry." ▪ His face ***said it all.*** = His face ***said everything.*** [=his face showed how he felt]

10 a — used to suggest an example or possibility ▪ Let's pick a math problem. *Say* problem number 3. ▪ *Say* you do get accepted to the college. Will you go? ▪ We could leave on any day—*say* on Monday. ▪ ***Let's say*** you're right, for argument's sake. ▪ Suppose you won, ***shall we say,*** one million dollars. What would you do with it? **b** — used to suggest a possible or approximate amount, value, etc. ▪ The property is worth, *say,* four million dollars. = The property is worth four million dollars, *say.* [=the property is worth about four million dollars]

can't say fairer than that *Brit, informal* — used to say that you cannot make a better offer than the one you have made ▪ What do you think? I *can't say fairer than that,* now, can I?

enough said see [3]ENOUGH

fair to say see [1]FAIR

go without saying : to be obvious and true ▪ It *goes without saying* that I'll do whatever I can to help you.

S

hasten to say see HASTEN
have anything/something (etc.) to say about **1** : to have an opinion to express about (something) • I asked what she thought about the movie, but she didn't *have anything to say about* it. **2** : to have the ability to influence (something) • "I'm going to the party." "Not if I *have anything/something to say about it*." [=not if I can stop you]
have something/nothing/much (etc.) to say for yourself : to be able or unable to say something that explains what you are doing, have done, etc. • I asked him about school, but he didn't *have much to say for himself*. • Your teacher says you were caught cheating. What do you *have to say for yourself*?
having said that or ***that said*** : despite what I just said • Their work has been fairly good. *Having said that*, I still think there's a lot of room for improvement. • Much of the book was very dull. *That said*, I have to admit that the ending was extremely clever.
I dare say see [1]DARE
if I may say so also ***if I might say so*** — used to express criticism or disagreement in a polite way • The whole affair—*if I may say so*—was a waste of time.
if I say so myself — used when you are saying something that praises your own work, skill, etc. • I did a fine job painting the room, *if I say so myself*. • I'm a pretty good golfer, *if I say so myself*.
I hear what you're saying see HEAR
I'll say *informal* — used to indicate that you completely agree with something just said • "Isn't it hot today!" "*I'll say* (it is). It's unbearable!"
I say *Brit, old-fashioned* **1** — used to express surprise, shock, etc. • *I say*! Isn't that your friend over there? • *I say*! That's a wonderful idea. **2** — used to attract the attention of someone • *I say* (there). Can you help me?
needless to say see NEEDLESS
never say die see [1]DIE
never say never see NEVER
not to say — used to introduce a more forceful or critical way of describing someone or something • His manner was discourteous, *not to say* offensive. • He was impolite, *not to say* downright rude!
say cheese see CHEESE
say no : to say that you will not accept or agree to something • We requested more time, but she *said no*. [=she refused to allow us to have more time] — often + *to* • She *said no to* our request. • I never *say no to* dessert.
say something/little/a lot (etc.) for : to show that (someone or something) does or does not deserve to be praised, admired, etc. • It *says a lot for* her that she stayed in the game even though she was injured. • The students' low test scores don't *say much for* the education they're receiving. [=the low test scores show/suggest that the students are not getting a good education]
say the word see [1]WORD
say what *US, informal* — used to express surprise at what someone has just said • "I'm moving out." "*Say what*?"
say yes : to say that you accept or agree to something — often + *to* • They *said yes to* our plan.
say your piece see [1]PIECE
suffice (it) to say see SUFFICE
that is to say see [1]THAT
that said see HAVING SAID THAT (above)
that's not saying much — used to indicate that a fact, achievement, etc., is not unusual or impressive • He is a better golfer than me, but *that's not saying much* (because I'm not a good golfer).
there is something/a lot/much (etc.) to be said for — used to indicate that something has advantages which deserve to be considered when you are thinking about what to do • *There is something to be said for* small weddings. • It is not necessary, but *there is something to be said for* traveling abroad to learn a language.
to say nothing of — used when referring to another thing that relates to what you have just said • We need more time, *to say nothing of* [=not to mention] money. [=we also need more money] • The restaurant makes its own delicious bread, *to say nothing of* a great spaghetti sauce.
to say the least see [2]LEAST
when all is said and done see [3]ALL
you can say that again *informal* — used to indicate that you completely agree with something just said • "She's in a bad mood." "*You can say that again*." [=she certainly is]
you don't say — used to express surprise • "She ran off with another man." "*You don't say*!" — often used ironically to show that you are not at all surprised by something • "They lost again." "*You don't say*. What's that, eight in a row?"
you might say — used to suggest a possible way of describing or thinking about something • The experience was, *you might say*, a glimpse into the future.
you said it *informal* — used to indicate that you completely agree with something just said • "That was a pretty selfish thing for him to do." "*You said it*." • "Let's grab something to eat." "*You said it*. I'm starving."

[2]**say** *noun*
1 [*singular*] : an opportunity to express your opinion • Everybody ***had a say*** at the meeting. • We won't make a decision until all members have *had their say*.
2 : the power to decide or help decide something [*singular*] The judge will have the ***final say*** on/over the divorce settlement. — usually + *in* • The students want a greater *say in* decisions that affect their education. [*noncount*] He had no/some/little *say in* the matter.

[3]**say** *interj, chiefly US, informal*
1 — used to express surprise, shock, etc. • *Say*, isn't that your friend over there? • *Say*, that's a wonderful idea.
2 — used to attract the attention of someone • *Say* there. Can you help me? • *Say*, do you want to see a movie tonight?

say·ing /ˈsejɪŋ/ *noun, pl* **-ings** [*count*] : an old and well-known phrase that expresses an idea that most people believe is true • "Two minds are better than one," as the (old) *saying* goes.

say–so /ˈseɪˌsoʊ/ *noun* [*noncount*] *informal*
1 : a statement that is not supported by any proof • He said he did the work himself, but we have only his *say-so* that that's what actually happened.
2 : permission that is given by a person who has authority • She left the hospital on the *say-so* of her doctor. • Nothing was done without his *say-so*.
3 : the power to decide something • She has the ultimate *say-so* on/over what will be taught.

S–bend /ˈɛsˌbɛnd/ *noun, pl* **-bends** [*count*] *Brit* : a bend in a road or pipe in the shape of the letter S

SC *abbr* **1** South Carolina **2** supreme court

scab /ˈskæb/ *noun, pl* **scabs** [*count*]
1 : a hard covering of dried blood that forms over a wound to cover and protect it as it heals
2 *informal + disapproving* : a worker who does not join a strike or who takes the place of another worker who is on strike

scab·bard /ˈskæbəd/ *noun, pl* **-bards** [*count*] : a protective case for a sword that covers the blade

sca·bies /ˈskeɪbiz/ *noun* [*plural*] : a disease that is caused by small insects and that causes itching and red spots on the skin

sca·brous /ˈskæbrəs/ *adj* [*more ~; most ~*]
1 *technical* : having a rough surface • *scabrous* skin/leaves
2 *formal* : referring to sex in a rude or shocking way • a movie with *scabrous* humor

scads /ˈskædz/ *noun* [*plural*] *informal* : a large amount of something — usually + *of* • We have *scads* [=*lots*] *of* time left. • *scads of* money

scaf·fold /ˈskæfəld/ *noun, pl* **-folds** [*count*]
1 : a temporary or movable platform or structure on which a person stands or sits while working high above the floor or ground
2 : a platform or structure on which criminals are killed by being hanged or beheaded • The condemned man was led to the *scaffold*.

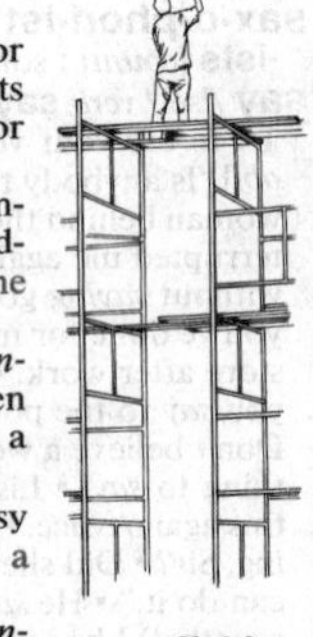
scaffold

scaf·fold·ing /ˈskæfəldɪŋ/ *noun* [*noncount*] : the metal poles and wooden boards that are used to build or support a scaffold (sense 1)

scal·able /ˈskeɪləbəl/ *adj, technical* : easy to make larger, more powerful, etc. • a *scalable* computer network
— scal·abil·i·ty /ˌskeɪləˈbɪləti/ *noun* [*noncount*]

scal·a·wag (*US*) or *chiefly Brit* **scal·ly·wag** /ˈskælɪˌwæg/ *noun, pl* **-wags** [*count*] *informal + somewhat old-fashioned* : a usually young person who causes trouble : RASCAL • an amusing little *scalawag*

[1]**scald** /ˈskɑːld/ *verb* **scalds; scald·ed; scald·ing** [+ *obj*]

1 : to burn (someone or something) with hot liquid or steam • The steam *scalded* his skin. — sometimes used figuratively • Tears *scalded* her face.
2 a : to put (something) in hot liquid or steam for a brief time • *Scald* the tomatoes in boiling water so that you can peel them more easily. b : to heat (a liquid) until it is very hot but not boiling • *scald* milk

[2]**scald** *noun, pl* **scalds** [*count*] : a burn left on the skin that is caused by hot liquid or steam

scald·ing /ˈskɑːldɪŋ/ *adj* [*more* ~; *most* ~]
1 : very hot • The men worked in the *scalding* sun. • *scalding* hot water • a *scalding* bowl of soup
2 : very critical : very harsh or severe • a *scalding* [=*scathing*] review of the book

[1]**scale** /ˈskeɪl/ *noun, pl* **scales** : a device that is used for weighing people or things [*count*] (*US*) a bathroom *scale* [*plural*] (*Brit*) He stepped onto the bathroom *scales*. — see picture at BATHROOM
tip the scales see [1]TIP
– compare [2]SCALE, [4]SCALE

[2]**scale** *noun, pl* **scales** [*count*] : one of many small thin plates that cover the bodies of some animals (such as fish or snakes) — compare [1]SCALE, [4]SCALE

[3]**scale** *verb* **scales; scaled; scal·ing** [+ *obj*] : to remove the scales from (a fish) • You should *scale*, bone, and clean the fish before you cook it. — compare [5]SCALE

[4]**scale** *noun, pl* **scales**
1 [*count*] : a series of musical notes that go up or down in pitch • the C-minor *scale* • a major *scale*
2 [*count*] : a line on a map or chart that shows a specific unit of measure (such as an inch) used to represent a larger unit (such as a mile) : the relationship between the distances on a map and the actual distances • The map uses a *scale* of one centimeter for every 10 kilometers.
3 [*count*] : a range of numbers that is used to show the size, strength, or quality of something — usually singular • ***On a scale of*** 1 to 10, I give the movie a 9. [=the movie was extremely good] • *On a scale of* 1 to 5—1 being mild pain and 5 being extreme pain—tell me how much pain you are in. — see also RICHTER SCALE
4 [*count*] : a range of levels of something from lowest to highest • He is at the top of the pay *scale* for his position. • Primates are high up on the evolutionary *scale*. — see also SLIDING SCALE
5 [*noncount*] — used to describe a model, drawing, etc., in which all of the parts of something relate to each other in the same way that they do in the larger form • The model of the new city hall is ***to scale***. [=the model shows exactly how the parts will relate to each other when it is built] • The diagram was not drawn *to scale*. • a ***scale model*** of a car
6 [*singular*] : the size or level of something especially in comparison to something else • The company does things on a larger *scale* than most others. • The mayor surveyed the full *scale* [=*extent*] of the damage. • The war could impact the economy ***on a global scale***. [=could impact the economy of the entire world] • They exposed fraud ***on a grand scale***. — see also FULL-SCALE, LARGE-SCALE, SMALL-SCALE
7 [*noncount*] *technical* : a hard substance that is formed in pipes or containers holding water
8 [*noncount*] *Brit* : a hard substance that forms on teeth : TARTAR • buildup of plaque and *scale* on the teeth
– compare [1]SCALE, [2]SCALE

[5]**scale** *verb* **scales; scaled; scaling** [+ *obj*] : to climb to the top of (something) • Hikers *scaled* the mountain. — sometimes used figuratively • She ***scaled the heights of*** the publishing industry. [=she rose to a very high position in the publishing industry]
scale back/down [*phrasal verb*] ***scale back/down (something) or scale (something) back/down*** : to decrease the size, amount, or extent of (something) • The committee *scaled down* the budget. • The company has *scaled back* production. • We *scaled back* our original plans.
scale up [*phrasal verb*] ***scale up (something) or scale (something) up*** : to increase the size, amount, or extent of (something) • The company hopes to *scale up* production soon.
– compare [3]SCALE

scal·lion /ˈskæljən/ *noun, pl* **-lions** [*count*] *US* : GREEN ONION

scal·lop /ˈskɑːləp, ˈskæləp/ *noun, pl* **-lops** [*count*]
1 : a type of shellfish that has a flat, round shell with two parts and that is often eaten as food — see color picture on page C8
2 : one of a series of similar curves that form a decorative edge on something

scal·loped /ˈskɑːləpt, ˈskæləpt/ *adj*
1 : baked in a sauce usually with bread crumbs on top • *scalloped* potatoes
2 : having a series of similar, decorative curves along the edge • a *scalloped* lace collar • Her skirt had a *scalloped* hem.

scallywag *chiefly Brit spelling of* SCALAWAG

[1]**scalp** /ˈskælp/ *noun, pl* **scalps** [*count*]
1 : the skin on the top of your head where hair grows
2 : hair and skin that is cut or torn from the head of an enemy as a sign of victory — often used figuratively • His boss ***wants his scalp***. [=wants to fire him] • Parents of some students are ***(going) after the principal's scalp***.

[2]**scalp** *verb* **scalps; scalped; scalp·ing** [+ *obj*]
1 : to remove the hair and skin from the head of (an enemy) as a sign of victory • Some members of the tribe were *scalped* by the attacking warriors.
2 *US* : to buy tickets for an event and resell them at a much higher price • People were *scalping* [=(*Brit*) *touting*] tickets outside the stadium.
– **scalp·er** *noun, pl* **-ers** [*count*] *US* • ticket *scalpers* [=(*Brit*) *ticket touts*]

scal·pel /ˈskælpəl/ *noun, pl* **-pels** [*count*] : a small knife with a thin, sharp blade that is used in surgery

scaly /ˈskeɪli/ *adj* **scal·i·er; -i·est** [*also more* ~; *most* ~] : covered with scales or flakes • a *scaly* crocodile • His skin was dry and *scaly*.

[1]**scam** /ˈskæm/ *noun, pl* **scams** [*count*] : a dishonest way to make money by deceiving people • She was the victim of an insurance *scam*. • a sophisticated credit card *scam* • a *scam* artist

[2]**scam** /ˈskæm/ *verb* **scams; scammed; scam·ming** [+ *obj*]
1 : to deceive and take money from (someone) • The company *scammed* hundreds of people out of their life savings. • I could tell they were *scamming* you and charging too much.
2 : to get (something, such as money) by deceiving someone • They *scammed* a lot of money from unwary customers.
– **scam·mer** *noun, pl* **-mers** [*count*]

scamp /ˈskæmp/ *noun, pl* **scamps** [*count*] *old-fashioned* : a child who causes trouble usually in a playful way : RASCAL • a mischievous little *scamp*

scam·per /ˈskæmpɚ/ *verb, always followed by an adverb or preposition* **-pers; -pered; -per·ing** [*no obj*] : to run or move quickly and often playfully • The kids were *scampering* around the yard. • A mouse *scampered* across the floor.

scam·pi /ˈskæmpi/ *noun* [*noncount*]
1 *US* : a dish of large shrimp prepared with a garlic-flavored sauce • shrimp *scampi*
2 *Brit* : large shrimp that are often breaded and fried • *scampi* and chips

scam·ster /ˈskæmstɚ/ *noun, pl* **-sters** [*count*] *informal* : a person who deceives people to get their money : a person who scams people • con artists, swindlers, and *scamsters*

[1]**scan** /ˈskæn/ *verb* **scans; scanned; scan·ning**
1 [+ *obj*] : to look at (something) carefully usually in order to find someone or something • He *scanned* the field with binoculars. • He *scanned* the audience looking for his parents. • She *scanned* his face for any clue to what he was thinking. • The program is *scanning* [=*searching*] the computer's files.
2 : to look over or read (something) quickly [+ *obj*] She quickly *scanned* the pages of the newspaper. [*no obj*] She ***scanned through*** the list to find her name.
3 [+ *obj*] : to look at the inside of (something) by using a special machine • Their bags were *scanned* at the airport. • This machine *scans* a patient's brain.
4 : to use a special machine to read or copy (something, such as a photograph or a page of text) into a computer [+ *obj*] She *scanned* her photos into her computer. • *scan* in the number • The cashier *scanned* the bar code on the box. [*no obj*] The bar code won't *scan*. [=the machine is unable to read the bar code]
5 [*no obj*] *technical, of a poem* : to have a correct or regular rhythm • These lines do not *scan*.

[2]**scan** *noun, pl* **scans** [*count*]
1 : the act or process of scanning something: such as a : the act of looking at something carefully or quickly — usually singular • a careful *scan* of the area • The investigator did a full *scan* of the computer's files. • She gave the list a quick *scan*. b : the act or process of using a special machine to

S

see the inside of something (such as a part of the body) • The patient underwent a brain *scan*.
2 : a picture of the inside of something that is made by a special machine • The doctor examined the bone *scans*. — see also CAT SCAN

scan·dal /ˈskændl/ *noun, pl* **-dals**
1 : an occurrence in which people are shocked and upset because of behavior that is morally or legally wrong [*count*] There was a major *scandal* involving the mayor's ties with the Mob. • Government officials were caught in an embezzlement *scandal*. • Her behavior caused a *scandal* at school. • a drug/sex *scandal* [*noncount*] His actions brought *scandal* on the team. [=his actions disgraced the team] • There was never a hint/trace of *scandal* during her time in office.
2 [*noncount*] : talk about the shocking or immoral things that people have done or are believed to have done • The gossip magazine is filled with rumors and *scandal*.
3 [*singular*] : something that is shocking, upsetting, or unacceptable • The high price of gas these days is a *scandal*. • It's a *scandal* that this city doesn't have a movie theater.

scan·dal·ize *also Brit* **scan·dal·ise** /ˈskændəˌlaɪz/ *verb* **-iz·es; -ized; -iz·ing** [+ *obj*] : to shock or offend (someone) by doing something immoral or illegal • She was *scandalized* by her son's behavior.

scan·dal·ous /ˈskændələs/ *adj* [*more* ~; *most* ~]
1 : shocking or offensive • *scandalous* behavior • Sex was a *scandalous* subject back then. • The magazine published *scandalous* pictures of the movie star. • The high price of gas these days is *scandalous*.
2 : involving immoral or shocking things that a person has done or is believed to have done • *scandalous* allegations • She was spreading *scandalous* rumors about him.
— **scan·dal·ous·ly** *adv* • *scandalously* high prices

Scan·di·na·vian /ˌskændəˈneɪvijən/ *noun, pl* **-vians** [*count*] : a person born, raised, or living in the countries of Scandinavia (Sweden, Norway, and Denmark)
— **Scandinavian** *adj* • *Scandinavian* furniture

scan·ner /ˈskænɚ/ *noun, pl* **-ners** [*count*] : a device that scans things: such as **a** : a device that reads or copies information or images into a computer • a price *scanner* at a supermarket • a photo *scanner* **b** : a device that is used to see inside something • a luggage *scanner* **c** : a radio receiver that searches for a signal • a police *scanner* [=a device that is used for listening to the police as they talk to each other over the radio]

scant /ˈskænt/ *adj* : very small in size or amount • Food was in *scant* supply. • She paid *scant* attention to the facts. • Police found *scant* evidence of fraud.

scanty /ˈskænti/ *adj* **-i·er; -est** [*also more* ~; *most* ~] : very small in size or amount • The cheerleaders wore *scanty* outfits. • *scanty* data ***synonyms*** see MEAGER
— **scant·i·ly** /ˈskæntəli/ *adv* • *scantily* dressed/clad dancers [=dancers wearing very little clothing]

scape·goat /ˈskeɪpˌgoʊt/ *noun, pl* **-goats** [*count*] : a person who is unfairly blamed for something that others have done • The CEO was ***made the scapegoat*** for the company's failures.
— **scapegoat** *verb* **-goats; -goat·ed; -goat·ing** [+ *obj*] • He was *scapegoated* for the company's failures. • He's a victim of *scapegoating*.

scap·u·la /ˈskæpjələ/ *noun, pl* **-lae** /-ˌliː/ *or* **-las** [*count*] *medical* : SHOULDER BLADE

S

[1]**scar** /ˈskɑɚ/ *noun, pl* **scars** [*count*]
1 : a mark that is left on your skin after a wound heals • The operation left a *scar* on his stomach. • the soldier's battle *scars* • *scar* tissue
2 : a mark on something showing where it has been damaged • The table had several *scars* on its top.
3 : a feeling of great emotional pain or sadness that is caused by a bad experience and that lasts for a long time • The divorce left her with deep emotional *scars*.

[2]**scar** *verb* **scars; scarred; scar·ring** [+ *obj*]
1 : to mark (something) with a scar • His arm was badly *scarred* after the accident.
2 : to cause (someone) to feel great emotional pain or sadness because of a bad experience • The tragedy left her emotionally *scarred*. • Divorce can *scar* a child for life. = Divorce can leave a child ***scarred for life***.
3 : to make marks on (something) that show damage or wear • Your shoes are *scarring* the floor. • The fence was *scarred* by rust.

scar·ab /ˈskerəb/ *noun, pl* **-abs** [*count*] : a large beetle with a black shell ✧ In ancient Egypt the scarab was a symbol of good luck and eternal life.

[1]**scarce** /ˈskeɚs/ *adj* **scarc·er; scarc·est** [*also more* ~; *most* ~] : very small in amount or number : not plentiful • Food was getting *scarce* during the drought. • *scarce* resources
make yourself scarce informal : to leave so that you will not be seen in a certain place • You'd better *make yourself scarce* before my parents get home.
— **scarce·ness** *noun* [*noncount*] • The *scarceness* [=*scarcity*] of the metal made it valuable.

[2]**scarce** *adv, literary* : almost not at all : scarcely or hardly • I could *scarce* believe what I was hearing.

scarce·ly /ˈskeɚsli/ *adv*
1 : almost not at all : HARDLY • He could *scarcely* control his joy. • *Scarcely* a day goes by when they don't see or talk to each other.
2 : by only a small amount of time, space, etc. : BARELY • I had *scarcely* [=only just] closed the door when the doorbell rang again. • The truck *scarcely* [=*just*] made it underneath the low bridge. • He had *scarcely* enough money.
3 : certainly not • This is *scarcely* a time to laugh. • I could *scarcely* tell them they were wrong.
scarcely ever see EVER

scar·ci·ty /ˈskeɚsəti/ *noun, pl* **-ties** : a very small supply : the state of being scarce [*count*] — usually singular • There was a *scarcity* of food. [=there was very little food; there was not enough food] • wartime *scarcities* [*noncount*] *Scarcity* of food forced the herds to move.

[1]**scare** /ˈskeɚ/ *verb* **scares; scared; scar·ing**
1 [+ *obj*] : to cause (someone) to become afraid : FRIGHTEN • You *scared* me. I didn't see you there. • Stop that, you're *scaring* the children. • The loud noise *scared* them. = They were *scared* by the loud noise. • You nearly ***scared me to death***. [=you scared me very much]
2 [*no obj*] : to become afraid • I don't ***scare easily***.
scare away/off [*phrasal verb*] ***scare (someone or something) away/off*** *or* ***scare away/off (someone or something)*** : to cause (someone or something) to go away and stay away because of fear or because of possible trouble, difficulty, etc. • The dog *scared* the prowler *away*. • The noise *scared off* the birds. • Tourists have been *scared off* by the recent violence in the city. [=tourists have not visited the city because of the recent violence there] • She finally found a man who's not *scared away* by the fact that she is a single mom raising two children.
scare into [*phrasal verb*] ***scare (someone) into (something)*** : to cause (someone) to do (something) because of fear • The police *scared* him *into* confessing his crime. • They tried to *scare* us *into* buying more insurance.
scare up [*phrasal verb*] ***scare (someone or something) up*** *or* ***scare up (someone or something) US, informal*** : to find or get (someone or something) with some difficulty • We managed to *scare up* [=*scrape up*] the money. • Let's try to *scare up* some people to play football.

[2]**scare** *noun, pl* **scares** [*count*]
1 : a sudden feeling of fear • You gave me (quite) a *scare*. [=you scared me] • She had a pregnancy *scare*. [=she was afraid she was pregnant]
2 : a situation in which a lot of people become afraid because of some threat, danger, etc. • There have been *scares* about the water supply being contaminated. • a ***bomb scare*** [=a situation in which people are afraid because someone says that a bomb is going to explode]
— **scare** *adj, always used before a noun* • a ***scare story*** about a possible epidemic • They used ***scare tactics*** to teach their children not to smoke cigarettes.

scare·crow /ˈskeɚˌkroʊ/ *noun, pl* **-crows** [*count*] : an object that looks like a person and that is placed in a field to scare birds away from crops

scared *adj* [*more* ~; *most* ~] : afraid of something : nervous or frightened • The rabbit looked *scared*. • I am really *scared* about speaking in front of the class. • He was *scared* that his mother wouldn't let him go to the movies with his friends. • She's *scared* to walk alone at night. • The children ***got scared*** [=became frightened] and ran away. — often + *of* • He was *scared of* asking her out. • She's *scared of* snakes. • I want to look in the file, but I'm *scared of* what I'll find. • She was ***scared to death of*** flying. = She was ***scared stiff of*** flying. [=she was very scared of flying]

scaredy–cat /ˈskeɚdiˌkæt/ *noun, pl* **-cats** [*count*] *informal* : someone who is very afraid of something — used mainly by children or when speaking to children • Don't be a *scaredy-cat*. The frog won't hurt you.

scare·mon·ger·ing /ˈskeəˌmɑːŋgərɪŋ, ˈskeəˌmʌŋgərɪŋ/ *noun* [*noncount*] *formal + disapproving* : the act or practice of saying things to make people afraid ▪ They used *scaremongering* about the economy to influence voters.

– **scare·mon·ger** /ˈskeəˌmɑːŋgə, ˈskeəˌmʌŋgə/ *noun, pl* **-gers** [*count*] ▪ *scaremongers* warning the public of global catastrophe

[1]**scarf** /ˈskɑəf/ *noun, pl* **scarves** /ˈskɑəvz/ *or* **scarfs** [*count*] : a long piece of cloth that is worn on your shoulders, around your neck, or over your head — see color picture on page C15

[2]**scarf** *verb* **scarfs; scarfed; scarf·ing** [+ *obj*] *US, informal* : to eat (something) quickly ▪ I *scarfed* [=(*chiefly Brit*) *scoffed*] a big breakfast. — often + *down* ▪ He *scarfed down* his lunch and went right back outside.

scarf up [*phrasal verb*] ***scarf (something) up*** *or* ***scarf up (something)*** *US, informal* : to take (something) in a quick and eager way ▪ People *scarfed up* [=*snapped up*] the free gifts.

scar·let /ˈskɑələt/ *noun, pl* **-lets** [*count, noncount*] : a bright red color — see color picture on page C3

– **scarlet** *adj* ▪ a bird with *scarlet* feathers

scarlet fever *noun* [*noncount*] : a very serious disease that causes a fever, sore throat, and a red rash

scary /ˈskeri/ *adj* **scar·i·er; -est** [*also more* ~; *most* ~] : causing fear ▪ a *scary* [=*frightening*] movie ▪ The stranger is *scary* looking. = He looks *scary*. = He's *scary* looking.

– **scar·i·ly** /ˈskerəli/ *adv* ▪ a *scarily* accurate prediction ▪ *Scarily*, the story is true. – **scar·i·ness** *noun* [*noncount*]

[1]**scat** /ˈskæt/ *interj* — used to scare away an animal

[2]**scat** *noun* [*noncount*] : jazz singing with sounds or words that mean nothing

scath·ing /ˈskeɪðɪŋ/ *adj* [*more* ~; *most* ~] *somewhat formal* : very harsh or severe ▪ a *scathing* review of the book ▪ a *scathing* look/comment

– **scath·ing·ly** *adv*

scat·o·log·i·cal /ˌskætəˈlɑːʤɪkəl/ *adj* [*more* ~; *most* ~] *formal* : relating to things that are disgusting or offensive ▪ *scatological* humor

[1]**scat·ter** /ˈskætə/ *verb* **-ters; -tered; -ter·ing**

1 a [+ *obj*] : to cause (things or people) to separate and go in different directions ▪ The wind *scattered* the pile of leaves. **b** [*no obj*] : to separate and go in different directions ▪ The crowd *scattered* [=*dispersed*] when the police arrived. ▪ The marbles *scattered* across the floor.

2 [+ *obj*] : to place or leave (things) in different places ▪ He *scattered* [=*spread*] the grass seed over the soil. ▪ She *scattered* the books on the table. ▪ He *scatters* his toys all around the house.

[2]**scatter** *noun* [*singular*] : a small number or group of things placed or found apart from each other — usually + *of* ▪ There was a *scatter of* empty cans and bottles on the lawn. ▪ a *scatter of* houses along the river

scat·ter·brain /ˈskætəˌbreɪn/ *noun, pl* **-brains** [*count*] *informal* : a person who is unable to concentrate or think clearly ▪ Where did I put my keys? I'm such a *scatterbrain* today.

– **scat·ter·brained** /ˈskætəˌbreɪnd/ *adj* [*more* ~; *most* ~] ▪ *scatterbrained* people ▪ *scatterbrained* ideas

scatter cushion *noun, pl* ~ **-ions** [*count*] *Brit* : THROW PILLOW

scattered *adj* : placed or found far apart ▪ The toys were *scattered* all over the house. ▪ Clothes were *scattered* about the room. ▪ The weather forecast calls for *scattered* [=*occasional*] showers all day. ▪ Houses are *scattered* along the river. ▪ My family is *scattered* throughout the country.

scat·ter·ing /ˈskætərɪŋ/ *noun, pl* **-ings** [*count*] : a small number or group of things or people that are seen or found at different places or times — usually + *of* ▪ The museum had a *scattering of* visitors last week. ▪ There were *scatterings of* geese in the park.

scatter rug *noun, pl* ~ **rugs** [*count*] : THROW RUG

scat·ty /ˈskæti/ *adj* **scat·ti·er; -est** [*also more* ~; *most* ~] *Brit, informal* : not having or showing the ability to think clearly ▪ My *scatty* [=*scatterbrained*] mother is always losing her keys.

scav·enge /ˈskævənʤ/ *verb* **-eng·es; -enged; -eng·ing**

1 *of an animal* : to search for food to eat [*no obj*] Rats *scavenged* in the trash. — often + *for* ▪ The bears *scavenged for* food in the woods. [+ *obj*] The bears *scavenged* the woods *for* food.

2 : to search through waste, junk, etc., for something that can be saved or used [*no obj*] — often + *for* ▪ They *scavenged for* antiques at the flea market. [+ *obj*] He *scavenged* the town dump *for* automobile parts.

– **scav·en·ger** /ˈskævənʤə/ *noun, pl* **-gers** [*count*]

scavenger hunt *noun, pl* ~ **hunts** [*count*] : a game in which players try to find specified items within a particular period of time

sce·nar·io /səˈnerijoʊ, *Brit* səˈnɑːriəʊ/ *noun, pl* **-ios** [*count*]

1 : a description of what could possibly happen ▪ A possible *scenario* would be that we move to the city. ▪ The most likely *scenario* is that he goes back to school in the fall. ▪ The ***best-case scenario*** would be for us to finish the work by tomorrow. ▪ In the ***worst-case scenario***, we would have to start the project all over again.

2 *formal* : a written description of a play, movie, opera, etc.

scene /ˈsiːn/ *noun, pl* **scenes**

1 [*count*] **a** : a division of an act in a play during which the action takes place in a single place without a break in time ▪ The play's opening *scene* takes place in the courtyard. ▪ Act I, *Scene* 3 **b** : a part of a play, movie, story, etc., in which a particular action or activity occurs ▪ a famous love/fight/chase *scene* ▪ The actor was nervous about his big *scene*.

2 [*count*] : a view or sight that looks like a picture ▪ a winter *scene* ▪ *scenes* [=*images*] of poverty

3 [*count*] : the place of an event or action ▪ This is the *scene* [=*location*] where the movie was filmed. ▪ a crime *scene* ▪ Police are now ***at/on the scene***. — often + *of* ▪ the *scene of* the crime/attack/accident ▪ The *scene* [=*setting*] *of* the story is New York City in the 1920s.

4 [*count*] : an occurrence in which someone becomes angry and loud in a noticeable way in a public place — usually singular ▪ There was quite an ugly/angry *scene* at the restaurant. ▪ The little boy ***made a scene*** because his mother wouldn't buy him candy.

5 [*noncount*] **a** : a particular area of activity that involves many people ▪ The music *scene* is changing in the city. ▪ The nightclub *scene* isn't for me. = (*informal*) Nightclubs are ***not my scene***. [=I do not like to go to nightclubs] ▪ He is new to the political *scene*. [=*arena*] ▪ After years of making movies, she suddenly vanished from the *scene*. **b** : someone's usual area of activity or surroundings : the place where someone lives, works, etc. — used in the phrase ***change of scene*** ▪ I'm sick of the cold weather. I need a *change of scene*. [=I need to go somewhere else]

6 [*count*] : something that happens : an event or occurrence ▪ The book describes *scenes* [=*episodes*] from his childhood. — often + *of* ▪ *scenes of* violence ▪ a *scene of* celebration

behind the scenes : in or into a private or secret place where things are done without being seen or known by the public ▪ The workers *behind the scenes* have made the event a success. ▪ They made the deal *behind the scenes*. ▪ We were taken *behind the scenes* to see the making of the movie. — see also BEHIND-THE-SCENES

enter the scene see ENTER

on the scene — used to say that someone or something is or has become an important part of a situation, activity, etc. ▪ She was lonely for a while, but now there's a new boyfriend *on the scene*. [=she has a new boyfriend] ▪ a popular singer who first ***burst on the scene*** last year ▪ Our lives have changed a lot since computers have ***come/appeared on the scene***. — see also SCENE 3 (above)

set the scene **1** : to give someone information that is needed to understand something ▪ Before I tell the story, let me *set the scene* (for you). **2** : to create the conditions in which something can happen ▪ His comments *set the scene* for an argument.

scen·ery /ˈsiːnəri/ *noun* [*noncount*]

1 : the walls, furniture, trees, etc., that are used on a stage during a play or other performance to show where the action is taking place ▪ She designed the *scenery* for the play. ▪ The *scenery* showed a forest/bedroom.

2 : a view of natural features (such as mountains, hills, valleys, etc.) that is pleasing to look at ▪ beautiful mountain *scenery* ▪ We went for a drive to enjoy the *scenery*.

3 : the things that can be seen where a person lives, works, etc. — used in the phrase ***change of scenery*** ▪ He was looking for a new job because he felt he needed a *change of scenery*. [=he needed to be in a different place] ▪ We decided to go to a new restaurant for a *change of scenery*.

S

sce·nic /ˈsiːnɪk/ *adj* [*more* ~; *most* ~] **:** having, providing, or relating to a pleasing or beautiful view of natural scenery (such as mountains, hills, valleys, etc.) ▪ the *scenic* beauty of the countryside ▪ Our hotel had a *scenic* view of the lake. ▪ a *scenic* route/drive ▪ The country around here is very *scenic.*

[1]**scent** /ˈsɛnt/ *noun, pl* **scents**

1 [*count*] **a :** a pleasant smell that is produced by something ▪ The flower has a wonderful *scent.* ▪ the *scent* of flowers/perfume **b :** a smell that is left by an animal or person and that can be sensed and followed by some animals (such as dogs) ▪ The dogs followed the fox's *scent.* ▪ The prisoner escaped because the dogs lost his *scent.* — often used figuratively ▪ The reporter was ***on the scent of*** a big story. [=was following/investigating a big story] ▪ Scientists are *on the scent of* a cure. [=are looking for and are close to finding a cure] ▪ He was being investigated by federal officials but he somehow managed to ***put them off the/his scent***

2 [*singular*] **a :** a slight indication of something that is going to happen or that might happen ▪ There was a *scent* [=*hint*] of trouble in the air. [=trouble was developing] **b :** a quality that suggests or shows the existence of something ▪ Her story has a/the *scent* of truth. [=her story seems to be true]

3 [*count, noncount*] **:** a liquid that is put on your body to give it a pleasant odor **:** PERFUME ▪ a bottle of *scent*

[2]**scent** *verb* **scents; scent·ed; scent·ing** [+ *obj*]

1 : to become aware of (something) by smell ▪ The dog *scented* a rabbit. — often used figuratively ▪ We *scented* [=*sensed, detected*] trouble and left. ▪ The reporter *scented* a big story.

2 : to give (something) a pleasing smell ▪ Roses *scented* [=*perfumed*] the air. ▪ She *scented* her handkerchief. ▪ She *scented* the air with perfume. — often used as *(be) scented* ▪ The room *was scented* by the flowers. ▪ The air *was scented* with/by her perfume.

scent·ed /ˈsɛntəd/ *adj* **:** having a pleasing smell ▪ sweetly *scented* flowers/oils ▪ The soap is *scented.* ▪ a pine-*scented* candle

scep·ter (*US*) *or Brit* **scep·tre** /ˈsɛptɚ/ *noun, pl* **-ters** [*count*] **:** a long decorated stick that is carried by a king or queen

sceptic, sceptical, scepticism *chiefly Brit spellings of* SKEPTIC, SKEPTICAL, SKEPTICISM

scha·den·freu·de /ˈʃɑːdn̩ˌfrɔɪdə/ *noun* [*noncount*] *formal* **:** a feeling of enjoyment that comes from seeing or hearing about the troubles of other people

[1]**sched·ule** /ˈskɛˌʤuːl, *Brit* ˈʃɛˌdjuːl/ *noun, pl* **-ules**

1 : a plan of things that will be done and the times when they will be done [*count*] I have a hectic/busy/full *schedule* this week. ▪ Students are planning their class/course *schedules* for next year. ▪ I have a flexible *schedule* [=I can change the times when I need to do things], so I can meet you at any time. ▪ Sorting the mail is part of her daily *schedule.* ▪ We have a ***tight schedule*** to get this project done. [=we have a small amount of time to finish the project] [*noncount*] The bus arrived ***on schedule*** [=*on time*; arrived at the time it was expected] ▪ So far, everything is *on schedule.* [=everything is happening at the time that was planned] ▪ The builders were ***ahead of schedule*** [=the builders were completing work earlier than planned] ▪ If we get too far ***behind/off schedule*** [=if we do things later than planned] we will not be able to catch up later. ▪ The project is ***going according to schedule*** [=things are happening as planned]

2 [*count*] **a :** a written or printed list of things and the times when they will be done ▪ I lost my class/course *schedule.* **b** *US* **:** a list of the times when buses, trains, airplanes, etc., leave or arrive ▪ a bus/train/airplane/flight *schedule* [=(*Brit*) *timetable*] **c :** a list of the television or radio programs that are on a particular channel and the times that they begin ▪ a programming *schedule* **d :** a list of prices or rates ▪ the doctor's fee *schedule* ▪ a tax *schedule*

[2]**schedule** *verb* **-ules; -uled; -ul·ing** [+ *obj*] **:** to plan (something) at a certain time ▪ We *scheduled* a meeting for next week. ▪ I need to *schedule* a doctor's appointment. — often used as *(be) scheduled* ▪ The release of the movie/album *is scheduled* for next month. ▪ The bus arrived earlier than (it was) *scheduled.* ▪ I *am scheduled* to arrive at noon. ▪ The test *is scheduled* to begin in one hour. ▪ The train will be leaving ***as scheduled*** [=*on time*; will be leaving at the planned time]

– scheduled *adj* ▪ a list of the *scheduled* events ▪ The plane's *scheduled* arrival/departure is midnight.

sche·mat·ic /skɪˈmætɪk/ *adj, technical* **:** showing the main parts of something usually in the form of a simple drawing or diagram ▪ a *schematic* diagram/representation of their business model

[1]**scheme** /ˈskiːm/ *noun, pl* **schemes** [*count*]

1 : a clever and often dishonest plan to do or get something ▪ a *scheme* [=*plot*] to seize control of the government ▪ a *scheme* to cheat people out of their money — see also PYRAMID SCHEME

2 *chiefly Brit* **:** an official plan or program of action ▪ The company has a new *scheme* for insurance coverage. ▪ a *scheme* to improve the economy ▪ a training/pension/marketing *scheme*

3 : the way that something is arranged or organized ▪ the color/decorative *scheme* of a room ▪ a poem's rhyme *scheme*

the scheme of things **:** the general way that things are organized and relate to each other ▪ Everyone has their role to play in *the (overall) scheme of things.* ▪ Our problems aren't really that important in *the grand scheme of things.* [=aren't really that important when you think about the larger situation]

[2]**scheme** *verb* **schemes; schemed; schem·ing** [*no obj*] **:** to make plans to do or get something in a secret and often dishonest way ▪ He felt that the other men were *scheming* against him. ▪ He was betrayed by a *scheming* friend. — often followed by *to + verb* ▪ She *schemed* [=*plotted*] *to take* control of the company from her brother.

– schem·er *noun, pl* **-ers** [*count*]

scher·zo /ˈskeɚtsoʊ/ *noun, pl* **-zos** [*count*] *formal* **:** a lively, humorous piece of music that is played quickly

schism /ˈsɪzəm, ˈskɪzəm/ *noun, pl* **schisms** *formal* **:** a division among the members of a group that occurs because they disagree on something [*count*] a *schism* between leading members of the party ▪ The controversy created a *schism* [=*rift*] in the group. [*noncount*] The church was divided by *schism.*

– schis·mat·ic /ˌsɪzˈmætɪk, ˌskɪzˈmætɪk/ *adj* ▪ *schismatic* groups

schist /ˈʃɪst/ *noun* [*noncount*] *technical* **:** a type of rock that can be broken into thin, flat pieces

schiz·oid /ˈskɪtˌsɔɪd/ *adj*

1 *technical* **:** relating to or having schizophrenia ▪ *schizoid* symptoms/patients

2 : changing frequently between opposite states ▪ With his *schizoid* nature, you never know whether he will disagree or agree with you. ▪ The biography shows how *schizoid* [=*changeable, varied*] his career has been.

schizo·phre·nia /ˌskɪtsəˈfriːnijə/ *noun* [*noncount*] *technical* **:** a very serious mental illness in which someone cannot think or behave normally and often experiences delusions

[1]**schizo·phren·ic** /ˌskɪtsəˈfrɛnɪk/ *adj*

1 *technical* **:** relating to or having schizophrenia ▪ *schizophrenic* symptoms/patients ▪ She has been diagnosed as *schizophrenic.*

2 : changing frequently between opposite states ▪ He criticized the government's *schizophrenic* foreign policy.

[2]**schizophrenic** *noun, pl* **-ics** [*count*] **:** a person who has schizophrenia

schlep *or* **schlepp** /ˈʃlɛp/ *verb* **schleps** *or* **schlepps; schlepped; schlep·ping** [+ *obj*] *US, informal* **:** to carry or pull (something) with difficulty **:** to drag or haul (something) ▪ We *schlepped* our luggage through the airport.

schlock /ˈʃlɑːk/ *noun* [*noncount*] *US, informal + usually disapproving* **:** things that are of low quality or value ▪ a film director who's known as a master of *schlock*

– schlock *adj* ▪ *schlock* horror movies **– schlocky** /ˈʃlɑːki/ *adj* **schlock·i·er; -est** [*also more* ~; *most* ~] ▪ a movie with *schlocky* special effects

schmaltz *also* **schmalz** /ˈʃmɑːlts/ *noun* [*noncount*] *informal + disapproving* **:** music, art, etc., that is very sad or romantic in usually a foolish or exaggerated way ▪ The movie has too much *schmaltz* for me. ▪ orchestral *schmaltz*

– schmaltzy /ˈʃmɑːltsi/ *adj* **schmaltz·i·er; -est** [*also more* ~; *most* ~] ▪ a *schmaltzy* love story ▪ The music is very *schmaltzy.*

schmo *or* **schmoe** /ˈʃmoʊ/ *noun, pl* **schmoes** [*count*] *US slang* **:** an ordinary person who is not interesting or unusual in any way ▪ They treated us like a bunch of *schmoes.* ▪ I'm just an ordinary *schmo* trying to make a living.

schmooze *or* **shmooze** /ˈʃmuːz/ *verb* **schmooz·es** *or* **shmooz·es; schmoozed** *or* **shmoozed; schmooz·ing** *or* **shmooz·ing** *informal* **:** to talk with someone in a friendly way often in order to get some advantage for yourself [*no obj*] People will have time to *schmooze* during the cocktail

hour. — often + *with* • She *schmoozed with* the reporters/boss. [+ *obj*] He *schmoozed* his teachers.
– schmooz·er /ˈʃmuːzɚ/ *noun, pl* **-ers** [*count*]

schmuck /ˈʃmʌk/ *noun, pl* **schmucks** [*count*] *US slang* : a stupid or foolish person : JERK • I can't believe what a *schmuck* that guy is.

schnapps /ˈʃnæps/ *noun, pl* **schnapps** [*count, noncount*] : a type of strong liquor

schol·ar /ˈskɑːlɚ/ *noun, pl* **-ars** [*count*]
1 : a person who has studied a subject for a long time and knows a lot about it : an intelligent and well-educated person who knows a particular subject very well • a biblical/classical/literary/Shakespearean *scholar* • She's a renowned *scholar* of African-American history.
2 : someone who has been given a scholarship • a Rhodes *scholar*

schol·ar·ly /ˈskɑːlɚli/ *adj*
1 : concerned with or relating to formal study or research • His writings have been recently given *scholarly* attention. • She has a *scholarly* interest in music. • a *scholarly* study of words and their origins • *scholarly* journals/work/writings
2 [*more* ~; *most* ~] : having the characteristics of a scholar • a very serious and *scholarly* young man [=a young man who studies serious subjects and who is learning or has learned a lot about those subjects]

schol·ar·ship /ˈskɑːlɚˌʃɪp/ *noun, pl* **-ships**
1 [*count*] : an amount of money that is given by a school, an organization, etc., to a student to help pay for the student's education • She got/received/won a *scholarship* to Yale University. • The organization is offering five $5,000 *scholarships*. • He is going to college on a football *scholarship*. [=a scholarship offered for his ability to play football] • She is attending college on a ***full scholarship***. [=a scholarship that pays fully for a student's tuition]
2 [*noncount*] : serious formal study or research of a subject • The essay is a work of serious *scholarship*. • standards of academic *scholarship* • The book is about his life and *scholarship*. • biblical/literary *scholarship*

Scholarship level *noun, pl* ~ **levels** [*count*] *Brit* : S LEVEL

scho·las·tic /skəˈlæstɪk/ *adj, always used before a noun* : of or relating to education • *scholastic* achievement/aptitude

[1]**school** /ˈskuːl/ *noun, pl* **schools**
1 a : a place where children go to learn [*count*] He is going to a different *school* this year. • The town is building a new *school*. [*noncount*] Where do you go to *school*? • He learned to play the flute at/in *school*. • Their daughter will start attending *school* next year. • He left/quit *school* [=he stopped going to school] when he was 16. — often used before another noun • the *school* building/newspaper • *school* lunches/functions/plays/friends • The town has an excellent *school* system. [=the schools in the town are excellent] **b** *US* : a college or university [*count*] He is transferring to a different *school* next semester. [*noncount*] He goes to *school* in New York. • He is attending law/business/medical *school*. • She is away at *school*. **c** [*count*] : a division within a university or college for study and research in a particular area of knowledge — usually singular • She is a student at the law/business/medical *school*. — often + *of* • the *school of* art/engineering **d** [*count*] : a place where people go to learn a particular skill • acting/driving/language *schools*
2 [*noncount*] **a :** the activity or process of learning or teaching in a school • *School* is hard for her. • Their daughter will start *school* next year. • (*US*) Where do you teach *school*? • (*US*) My parents won't let me get a job while I'm ***in school***. = (*Brit*) My parents won't let me get a job while I'm ***at school***. [=while I am a student in a school] • Stay *in school* and get your diploma. • He never did well *in school*. **b :** the period of time during which students are in school • I missed *school* yesterday. • He was late for *school*. [=he was not at the school on time] • Let's meet after *school*. • *School* starts at 8:00 a.m. — often used before another noun • the *school* day/year
3 [*count*] : the students or students and teachers of a school • The whole *school* was at the assembly. • Five *schools* donated money to the homeless shelter.
4 [*count*] : a group of people who share the same opinions, beliefs, or methods • artists from the Impressionist/Romantic *school* — often + *of* • the German *school of* philosophers/philosophy • a new *school of* painters/painting • The two authors come from different *schools of* writing. • There are two main ***schools of thought*** [=ways of thinking] on that topic. – compare [3]SCHOOL

[2]**school** *verb* **schools; schooled; school·ing** [+ *obj*] *somewhat old-fashioned* : to teach or train (someone or something) to do something • They *schooled* their children at home. — often + *in* • She *schooled* herself *in* patience. — often used as *(be) schooled* • He *is schooled in* five different languages. • The horse *is* well *schooled*. [=*trained*]

[3]**school** *noun, pl* **schools** [*count*] : a large group of fish or other ocean animals that are swimming together • Fish swim in *schools*. — often + *of* • a *school of* fish/dolphins — compare [1]SCHOOL

school age *noun* [*noncount*] : the age when a child is allowed to go to a school • children of *school age*
– school–age *adj, always used before a noun* • *school-age* children

school·bag /ˈskuːlˌbæg/ *noun, pl* **-bags** [*count*] : a bag for carrying schoolbooks and school supplies

school board *noun, pl* ~ **boards** [*count*] *US* : a group of people who are in charge of local schools — called also (*US*) *school committee*

school·book /ˈskuːlˌbʊk/ *noun, pl* **-books** [*count*] : a book that is used in schools : TEXTBOOK

school·boy /ˈskuːlˌbɔɪ/ *noun, pl* **-boys** [*count*] : a boy who goes to a school
– schoolboy *adj, always used before a noun* • *schoolboy* [=*childish, childlike*] pranks/humor

school bus *noun, pl* ~ **buses** [*count*] : a bus for carrying children to and from a school

school·child /ˈskuːlˌʧajəld/ *noun, pl* **-children** [*count*] : a child who goes to a school

school district *noun, pl* ~ **-tricts** [*count*] *US* : an area or region containing the schools that a school board is in charge of

school·girl /ˈskuːlˌgɚl/ *noun, pl* **-girls** [*count*] : a girl who goes to a school

school·house /ˈskuːlˌhaʊs/ *noun, pl* **-houses** [*count*] : a building that is used as a school

schooling *noun* [*noncount*] : teaching that is done in a school : EDUCATION • public *schooling* • He has had little *schooling*.

school·kid /ˈskuːlˌkɪd/ *noun, pl* **-kids** [*count*] *informal* : a child or teenager who goes to a school

school–leav·er /ˈskuːlˌliːvɚ/ *noun, pl* **-ers** [*count*] *Brit* : someone who has left school usually after completing a course of study instead of continuing on to a college or university • *School-leavers* are having trouble finding jobs.

school·marm /ˈskuːlˌmɑɚm/ *also* **school·ma'am** /ˈskuːlˌmæm/ *noun, pl* **-marms** *or* **-ma'ams** [*count*] *US, old-fashioned* : a woman who teaches in a school in a small town or in the country • a New England *schoolmarm*

school·mas·ter /ˈskuːlˌmæstɚ, *Brit* ˈskuːlˌmɑːstə/ *noun, pl* **-ters** [*count*] *old-fashioned* : a man who teaches in a school

school·mate /ˈskuːlˌmeɪt/ *noun, pl* **-mates** [*count*] : someone who goes to or went to the same school as you • my old *schoolmates*

school·mis·tress /ˈskuːlˌmɪstrəs/ *noun, pl* **-tress** [*count*] *old-fashioned* : a woman who teaches in a school

school·room /ˈskuːlˌruːm/ *noun, pl* **-rooms** [*count*] : a room where classes meet in a school : CLASSROOM

school·teach·er /ˈskuːlˌtiːʧɚ/ *noun, pl* **-ers** [*count*] : someone who teaches in a school

school·work /ˈskuːlˌwɚk/ *noun* [*noncount*] : work that is done in classes in a school or given to students to be done at home — compare HOMEWORK

school·yard /ˈskuːlˌjɑɚd/ *noun, pl* **-yards** [*count*] : the area next to or surrounding a school where children play

schoo·ner /ˈskuːnɚ/ *noun, pl* **-ners** [*count*]
1 : a ship that has usually two masts with the larger mast located toward the center and the shorter mast toward the front
2 : a large, tall glass • (*US*) a *schooner* of beer/ale • (*Brit*) a *schooner* of sherry

schtick *variant spelling of* SHTICK

schwa /ˈʃwɑː/ *noun, pl* **schwas** [*count*] *technical*
1 : a vowel that has the sound of the first and last vowels of the English word *America*
2 : the symbol ə that is used for the schwa sound

sci·at·ic /saɪˈætɪk/ *adj, medical* : relating to or near the hip • *sciatic* pains

sci·at·i·ca /saɪˈætɪkə/ *noun* [*noncount*] *medical* : pain in the lower back, hip, and especially the back of the thigh that is caused by pressure on the sciatic nerve

S

sciatic nerve *noun, pl* ~ **nerves** [*count*] *medical* : a nerve that goes from the lower back down the back of the leg

sci•ence /ˈsajəns/ *noun, pl* **-enc•es**
1 [*noncount*] : knowledge about or study of the natural world based on facts learned through experiments and observation ▪ modern *science* ▪ the laws of *science* ▪ The program encourages students to pursue a career in *science*. ▪ a list of terms commonly used in *science* ▪ a new branch/field of *science* ▪ advances in ***science and technology*** — often used before another noun ▪ *science* teachers/students/classes ▪ Each student is required to complete two *science* projects.
2 [*count*] : a particular area of scientific study (such as biology, physics, or chemistry) : a particular branch of science ▪ Students are required to take two *sciences*. ▪ students majoring in a *science* — see also COMPUTER SCIENCE, LIFE SCIENCE, NATURAL SCIENCE, PHYSICAL SCIENCE, ROCKET SCIENCE
3 [*count*] : a subject that is formally studied in a college, university, etc. ▪ the *science* of linguistics — see also POLITICAL SCIENCE, SOCIAL SCIENCE
4 [*singular*] : an activity that is done by using methods that are known to produce particular results ▪ Proper pitching is a *science*. ▪ Cooking is both a *science* and an art. ▪ He travels so much that he has packing his clothes ***down to a science***. [=he can pack his clothes very quickly and efficiently because he does it so often]

science fair *noun, pl* ~ **fairs** [*count*] : an event at which science projects created by students are shown and often judged for prizes ▪ She won first place at the *science fair*.

science fiction *noun* [*noncount*] : stories about how people and societies are affected by imaginary scientific developments in the future ▪ Time travel exists only in the realm of *science fiction*. ▪ a *science-fiction* movie/writer

science park *noun, pl* ~ **parks** [*count*] *chiefly Brit* : RESEARCH PARK

sci•en•tif•ic /ˌsajənˈtɪfɪk/ *adj*
1 : of or relating to science ▪ *scientific* techniques/knowledge/research ▪ the *scientific* community
2 [*more* ~; *most* ~] : done in an organized way that agrees with the methods and principles of science ▪ *scientific* thinking/reasoning ▪ a *scientific* approach — opposite UNSCIENTIFIC
– sci•en•tif•i•cal•ly /ˌsajənˈtɪfɪkli/ *adv*

scientific method *noun*
the scientific method *technical* : the process that is used by scientists for testing ideas and theories by using experiments and careful observation

sci•en•tist /ˈsajəntɪst/ *noun, pl* **-tists** [*count*] : a person who is trained in a science and whose job involves doing scientific research or solving scientific problems ▪ a soil/marine/computer *scientist*

sci–fi /ˈsaɪˈfaɪ/ *noun* [*noncount*] *informal* : SCIENCE FICTION ▪ She enjoys watching *sci-fi*.
– sci–fi *adj* ▪ a *sci-fi* novel/story/movie

scim•i•tar /ˈsɪmɪtɚ/ *noun, pl* **-tars** [*count*] : a sword with a curved blade that was used in the past especially in the Middle East and western Asia

scin•til•la /sɪnˈtɪlə/ *noun* [*singular*] : a very small amount *of* something — usually used in negative statements ▪ There's not even a *scintilla of* evidence to support his story.

scin•til•lat•ing /ˈsɪntəˌleɪtɪŋ/ *adj* [*more* ~; *most* ~] : very clever, amusing, and interesting ▪ a *scintillating* lecture/discussion

sci•on /ˈsajən/ *noun, pl* **-ons** [*count*]
1 *formal* : a person who was born into a rich, famous, or important family ▪ He's a *scion* of a powerful family.
2 *botany* : a piece of a plant that is attached to part of another plant

scis•sors /ˈsɪzɚz/ *noun* [*plural*] : a tool used for cutting paper, cloth, etc., that has two blades joined together in the middle so that the sharp edges slide against each other ▪ He handed her the *scissors*. = He handed her a pair of *scissors*.

scissors

scle•ro•sis /skləˈroʊsəs/ *noun* [*noncount*] *medical* : a disease in which soft parts inside the body (such as arteries or muscles) become hard — see also MULTIPLE SCLEROSIS
– scle•rot•ic /skləˈrɑːtɪk/ *adj* ▪ *sclerotic* patients/tissue

¹scoff /ˈskɑːf/ *verb* **scoffs; scoffed; scoff•ing** : to laugh at and talk about someone or something in a way that shows disapproval and a lack of respect [*no obj*] He *scoffed* when she told him that she planned to become an actress. ▪ He *scoffed* at the idea/notion/suggestion of her becoming an actress. [+ *obj*] "You! An actress?!" he *scoffed*. "You have no more talent than I do!" — compare ²SCOFF

²scoff *verb* **scoffs; scoffed; scoffing** [+ *obj*] *chiefly Brit, informal* : to eat (something) quickly ▪ She *scoffed* [=(*US*) *scarfed*] her breakfast. — compare ¹SCOFF

¹scold /ˈskoʊld/ *verb* **scolds; scold•ed; scold•ing** [+ *obj*] : to speak in an angry or critical way to (someone who has done something wrong) ▪ He *scolded* [=*reprimanded*] the children for making a mess. ▪ The article *scolds* [=(more formally) *berates, upbraids*] the United Nations for not doing enough about the situation. ▪ "You should never have done that," she *scolded*.
– scolding *noun, pl* **-ings** [*count*] — usually singular ▪ The children ***got a scolding*** for making a mess. [*noncount*] *Scolding* was not necessary.

²scold *noun, pl* **scolds** [*count*] : a person who often criticizes other people in an angry way : someone who scolds other people too often ▪ He can be a bit of a *scold* sometimes.

sconce /ˈskɑːns/ *noun, pl* **sconc•es** [*count*] : an object that is attached to a wall and that holds a candle or an electric light — see picture at LIGHTING

scone /ˈskoʊn, ˈskɑːn/ *noun, pl* **scones** [*count*] : a small, often sweet bread that sometimes has pieces of dried fruit in it — see picture at BAKING

¹scoop /ˈskuːp/ *noun, pl* **scoops**
1 [*count*] **a** : a kitchen tool like a spoon that has a usually thick handle and a deep bowl for taking something from a container ▪ an ice-cream *scoop* ▪ a flour *scoop* **b** : something that is shaped like a bowl or bucket and used to pick up and move things ▪ a backhoe with a large *scoop* ▪ the *scoop* of a shovel [=the part of a shovel that is like a bowl] **c** : the amount of something that is held in a scoop ▪ a *scoop* [=*scoopful*] of ice cream
2 [*count*] : a news story that is reported before other news reporters know about it ▪ The story turned out to be the political *scoop* of the year.
3 ***the scoop*** *US, informal* : information about something that is currently important or happening or that is interesting to many people ▪ Did you talk to him? What's *the scoop*? [=what did he say?; what is happening?] ▪ She always knows *the scoop*. ▪ Here's *the scoop* on how to clean leather. ▪ I was with them when it happened, so I've got ***the inside scoop***. [=information known only by a particular group of people]
4 [*count*] : the act of picking up something with a quick, continuous motion : the act of scooping something ▪ With one *scoop*, he gathered up all the clothes on the floor.
– scoop•ful /ˈskuːpˌfʊl/ *noun, pl* **-fuls** [*count*] ▪ a *scoopful* [=*scoop*] of ice cream ▪ *scoopfuls* of dirt

²scoop *verb* **scoops; scooped; scoop•ing** [+ *obj*]
1 a : to pick up and move (something) with a scoop, a spoon, etc. ▪ She has a job *scooping* ice cream. ▪ He *scooped* flour into the bowl. ▪ A backhoe was *scooping* dirt from the hole. ▪ The children *scooped* handfuls of marbles from the pile. — often + *out* ▪ Cut the melon in half and *scoop* the seeds *out*. ▪ He *scooped out* the leaves from the pool with the net. **b** : to pick up (something or someone) in one quick, continuous motion ▪ He *scooped* the dice off the table and rolled again. — often + *up* ▪ She quickly *scooped up* her child. ▪ The shortstop *scooped* the ball *up* and threw it to first base.
2 : to make (a hole, hollow, etc.) by using a scoop, spoon, etc. ▪ *Scoop* a hole in the dough for the filling. — often + *out* ▪ The mother turtle *scoops* [=*digs*] *out* a hollow in the sand and lays her eggs in it. ▪ a lake that was *scooped out* by glaciers long ago
3 : to report a news story before (any other newspaper, news program, etc.) ▪ The city's biggest newspaper got *scooped* by a weekly paper that released the story a full day before.
4 *Brit, informal* : to win (something, such as a large prize or reward) ▪ He managed to *scoop* first place.
scoop up [*phrasal verb*] ***scoop up (something) or scoop (something) up*** *informal* : to take or buy (something) in a quick and eager way ▪ Customers *scooped up* [=*scarfed up*] the free samples. — see also ²SCOOP 1b (above)
– scoop•er *noun, pl* **-ers** [*count*] ▪ an ice-cream *scooper*

scoop neck *noun, pl* ~ **necks** [*count*] : a round, low neckline on a woman's shirt or dress — called also *scoop neckline*

scoot /ˈskuːt/ *verb* **scoots; scoot·ed; scoot·ing** *informal*
1 [*no obj*] **:** to go or leave suddenly and quickly ▪ I'm late, so I have to *scoot*. [=*run*] ▪ She talked to us for a few minutes before *scooting* off to some appointment.
2 *always followed by an adverb or preposition, chiefly US* **:** to move (yourself, your chair, etc.) a short distance in a particular direction [+ *obj*] She *scooted* her chair back a few inches. [*no obj*] He *scooted* closer to the table. — often + *over* ▪ She *scooted over* so he could sit down. ▪ Can you *scoot over* a little?

scoot·er /ˈskuːtɚ/ *noun, pl* **-ers**
[*count*]
1 : a child's vehicle that is made of a narrow board with two small wheels attached underneath and an upright handle attached on top and that is moved by pushing with one foot while holding onto the handle
2 : MOTOR SCOOTER

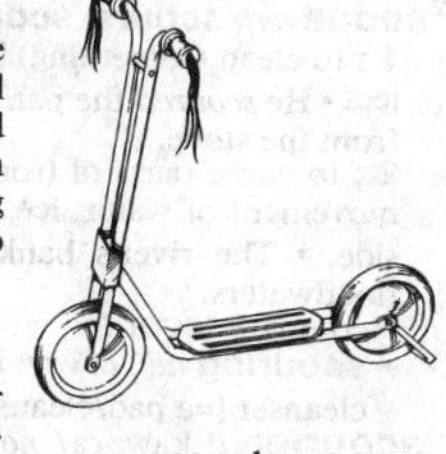
scooter

¹scope /ˈskoʊp/ *noun*
1 : the area that is included in or dealt with by something [*noncount*] The essay is sweeping/comprehensive in *scope*. [=the essay includes information, ideas, etc., about many topics] ▪ The law is of limited *scope*. [=the law applies only to a few situations, people, etc.] ▪ I was impressed by the size and *scope* of the book. ▪ That problem is somewhat beyond the *scope* of this discussion. ▪ We want to widen the *scope* of the study. [*singular*] This study has a wider/broader *scope* than previous studies on the subject have had.
2 [*noncount*] **:** space or opportunity for action, thought, etc. ▪ A bigger budget will allow more *scope* [=*room*] for innovation. ▪ The work has been good, but there's still some *scope* for improvement.
— compare ²SCOPE

²scope *noun, pl* **scopes** [*count*] *chiefly US* **:** an instrument (such as a telescope or microscope) that is used to look at things ▪ We looked through the *scope* at the moon. ▪ the *scope* of a rifle — compare ¹SCOPE

³scope *verb* **scopes; scoped; scop·ing**
scope out [*phrasal verb*] ***scope (someone or something) out*** *or* ***scope out (someone or something)*** *US, informal* **:** to look at (someone or something) especially in order to get information ▪ They *scoped out* [=*checked out*] the area before setting up the tent. ▪ Players were *scoping out* the competition. ▪ He wants to *scope out* [=*consider, examine*] all of the possibilities before deciding what to do.

¹scorch /ˈskoɚtʃ/ *verb* **scorch·es; scorched; scorch·ing**
1 a [+ *obj*] **:** to burn the surface of (something) ▪ Roast the peanuts while being careful not to *scorch* them. ▪ The hot pan *scorched* the table. **b** [*no obj*] **:** to be burned on the surface ▪ The fabric/material *scorches* at high temperatures.
2 [+ *obj*] **:** to damage (something) by making it extremely dry ▪ The hot sun *scorched* the grass. ▪ The land was *scorched* by drought.
3 *always followed by an adverb or preposition* [*no obj*] *Brit, informal* **:** to travel very fast ▪ The car went *scorching* down the street.
— **scorched** *adj* ▪ Dinner is a bit *scorched*. [=*burned*] ▪ *scorched* grass

²scorch *noun, pl* **scorches** [*count*] **:** a damaged area or mark that is caused by burning ▪ There was a *scorch* (mark) on the tabletop.

scorched–earth /ˈskoɚtʃtˈɚθ/ *adj* — used to describe a military policy in which all the houses, crops, factories, etc., in an area are destroyed so that an enemy cannot use them ▪ The retreating army adopted a ***scorched-earth policy***.

scorch·er /ˈskoɚtʃɚ/ *noun, pl* **-ers** [*count*] *informal* **:** a very hot day ▪ Tomorrow is going to be a real *scorcher*.

scorching *adj* **:** very hot ▪ several days of *scorching* heat ▪ a *scorching* summer afternoon
— **scorching** *adv* ▪ The day was ***scorching hot***. [=extremely hot]

¹score /ˈskoɚ/ *noun, pl* **scores**
1 [*count*] **a :** the number of points, goals, runs, etc., that each player or team has in a game or contest ▪ The *score* was tied at 1–1 [=each team had scored one run] after the second inning. ▪ The *score* (of the game) at halftime was 21–14. ▪ What's the *score*? ▪ The ***final score*** was 4–3. [=the score was 4–3 at the end of the game] **b** *chiefly US* **:** the number of points that someone gets for correct answers on a test, exam, etc. ▪ students with low/high test *scores* ▪ Only one person had/got a ***perfect score*** on the test. [=only one person answered all the questions correctly]
2 [*count*] **a :** a document showing all the notes of a piece of music ▪ a musical/orchestral *score* **b :** the music that is written for a movie or play ▪ The film's *score* is by a famous composer.
3 [*count*] **:** a mark or cut that is made in a surface with a sharp object
4 *pl* **score** [*count*] *formal + literary* **a :** the number 20 ▪ She has written more than a *score* of books. [=more than 20 books] **b :** a group of 20 people or things ▪ three *score* years [=60 years] ▪ A *score* of people were in attendance. — see also FOURSCORE, THREESCORE
5 ***scores*** [*plural*] *formal* **:** a large number or amount of people or things — usually + *of* ▪ We have received *scores of* suggestions.
by the score **:** in large numbers or amounts ▪ Factories are closing *by the score*. [=a lot of factories are closing] ▪ He's had girlfriends *by the score*. [=he has had lots of girlfriends]
even the score **1 :** to get enough points, goals, runs, etc., to have the same score as your opponent **:** to tie the score in a game ▪ They *evened the score* at 5–5. ▪ We *evened the score* in the second quarter. **2 :** to harm or punish someone who has harmed you ▪ She felt they had mistreated her, and she was determined to *even the score*.
keep score **:** to officially record the number of points, goals, runs, etc., that each player or team gets in a game or contest ▪ We'll just play for fun. We won't even *keep score*. ▪ Who's *keeping score*? — sometimes used figuratively ▪ If you're *keeping score* at home, this is the third time that he has run for mayor and lost.
know the score *informal* **:** to have a good understanding of a situation ▪ Now that she *knows the score*, she won't make the same mistake again.
on that/this score **:** with regard to the thing that is being discussed ▪ The work will be done on time. You have nothing to worry about *on that score*.
settle a/the score **:** to harm or punish someone who has harmed you ▪ The movie is about a woman who seeks out an old enemy to *settle a score*. ▪ He says he has a few (old) *scores to settle*. ▪ She wants to *settle the score* with her ex-husband.

²score *verb* **scores; scored; scor·ing**
1 a : to get points, goals, runs, etc., in a game or contest [*no obj*] She *scored* twice in the game. [+ *obj*] He *scored* a run/goal/touchdown. **b** [+ *obj*] **:** to be worth (a particular number of points) in a game or contest ▪ Each correct answer *scores* two points. ▪ In American football, a touchdown *scores* six points.
2 : to officially record the number of points, goals, runs, etc., that each player or team gets in a game or contest [*no obj*] Who's going to *score*? [=*keep score*] [+ *obj*] Who's going to *score* the game?
3 : to give (someone or something) a grade or a particular number of points based on the number of correct answers on a test, the quality of a performance, etc. [+ *obj*] Judges will *score* the performances based on their artistic and technical features. [*no obj*] Which judges are *scoring* tonight?
4 [+ *obj*] **:** to write the music for (a movie, play, etc.) ▪ The movie was *scored* by a famous composer.
5 [+ *obj*] **:** to mark or cut the surface of (something) with a sharp object ▪ He used a sharp blade to *score* the glass.
6 [+ *obj*] **:** to achieve or earn (something) ▪ He *scored* a big success/hit in his first movie.
7 [*no obj*] **:** to have success ▪ He has *scored* again with his latest thriller.
8 a *slang* **:** to buy or get (illegal drugs) [+ *obj*] He couldn't *score* any drugs. [*no obj*] Druggies come downtown looking to *score*. **b** [+ *obj*] *US, informal* **:** to get (something) ▪ I managed to *score* a couple of tickets to the game.
9 [*no obj*] *slang* **:** to have sex with someone and especially with someone you do not know well ▪ Did you *score* (with her) last night?
score off [*phrasal verb*] ***score off (someone)*** *Brit, informal* **:** to say or do something in order to get an advantage over (someone) ▪ They're always trying to *score off* each other.

score·board /ˈskoɚˌboɚd/ *noun, pl* **-boards** [*count*] **:** a large board on which the score of a game or contest is shown

score·card /ˈskoɚˌkɑɚd/ *noun, pl* **-cards** [*count*]
1 : a card on which the score of a game or contest is record-

S

ed • a golfer's *scorecard* • I always like to keep a *scorecard* when I watch a baseball game.
2 *US* : a report that gives information about the status, condition, or success of someone or something • The candidate rates highly on the magazine's legislative *scorecard*.

score·keep·er /ˈskoɚˌkiːpɚ/ *noun, pl* **-ers** [*count*] *chiefly US* : a person who records the official score in a game or contest

score·less /ˈskoɚləs/ *adj*
1 — used to describe a game in which no points, goals, runs, etc., have been scored • The game was *scoreless* after three innings. • a *scoreless* game
2 — used to describe a player or team that has not scored • He has been held *scoreless* in the past three games.

score·line /ˈskoɚˌlaɪn/ *noun, pl* **-lines** [*count*] *Brit* : the score and especially the final score of a game or contest

scor·er /ˈskorɚ/ *noun, pl* **-ers** [*count*]
1 : a person who scores points, goals, runs, etc., in a game or contest • He's the team's leading/high/top *scorer*.
2 : SCOREKEEPER

score·sheet /ˈskoɚˌʃiːt/ *noun, pl* **-sheets** [*count*] : a piece of paper on which the score of a game or contest is recorded • an official *scoresheet*

[1]**scorn** /ˈskoɚn/ *noun* [*noncount*]
1 : a feeling that someone or something is not worthy of any respect or approval • I have nothing but *scorn* [=*contempt*] for people who are cruel to animals. • They treated his suggestion with *scorn*. • an expression full of *scorn*
2 : harsh criticism that shows a lack of respect or approval for someone or something • Her political rivals have ***poured/heaped scorn on*** her ideas for improving the tax system.

[2]**scorn** *verb* **scorns; scorned; scorn·ing** [+ *obj*]
1 : to show that you think (someone or something) is not worthy of respect or approval : to feel or express scorn for (someone or something) • He *scorns* anyone who earns less money than he does. • Her actions were *scorned* by many people. • They were *scorned* as fanatics.
2 *formal* : to refuse or reject (someone or something that you do not think is worthy of respect or approval) • She *scorned* his invitation. — sometimes followed by *to + verb* • He *scorned to reply* to their accusations.

scorn·ful /ˈskoɚnfəl/ *adj* [*more* ~; *most* ~] : feeling or showing scorn • a *scornful* look/expression/laugh • He's *scornful* of anyone who disagrees with his political beliefs.
– **scorn·ful·ly** *adv* • She stared at him *scornfully*.

Scor·pio /ˈskoɚpiˌoʊ/ *noun, pl* **-pios**
1 [*noncount*] : the eighth sign of the zodiac that comes between Libra and Sagittarius and that has a scorpion as its symbol — see picture at ZODIAC
2 [*count*] : a person born under the sign of Scorpio : a person born between October 24 and November 21 • I'm a Virgo, and my sister is a *Scorpio*.

scor·pi·on /ˈskoɚpijən/ *noun, pl* **-ons** [*count*] : a small animal related to spiders that has two front claws and a curved tail with a poisonous stinger at the end — see color picture on page C10

Scot /ˈskɑːt/ *noun, pl* **Scots** [*count*] : a person born, raised, or living in Scotland

scotch /ˈskɑːtʃ/ *verb* **scotch·es; scotched; scotch·ing** [+ *obj*] : to stop (something) from continuing by doing or saying something • The administration did everything possible to *scotch* [=*squelch*] the rumors.

S

[1]**Scotch** *or* **scotch** /ˈskɑːtʃ/ *noun, pl* **Scotch·es** *or* **scotch·es** : a kind of whiskey that is made in Scotland [*noncount*] a bottle of *Scotch* [*count*] I'll have another *Scotch* [=a glass of Scotch], please.

[2]**Scotch** *adj, old-fashioned* : of or relating to Scotland or its people : SCOTTISH

[3]**Scotch** *trademark* — used for a type of adhesive tape

scot–free /ˈskɑːtˈfriː/ *adj, informal* : without the punishment that is deserved • It's not fair. I was punished and they ***got off scot-free***. [=they were not punished at all]

Scot·land Yard /ˌskɑːtləndˈjɑɚd/ *noun* [*noncount*] : the detective department of the London police • The case is being investigated by *Scotland Yard*.

[1]**Scots** /ˈskɑːts/ *adj* : of or relating to Scotland or its people : SCOTTISH • a *Scots* accent • *Scots* law

[2]**Scots** *noun* [*noncount*] : the English language of Scotland

Scots·man /ˈskɑːtsmən/ *noun, pl* **-men** /-mən/ [*count*] : a man born, raised, or living in Scotland

Scots·wom·an /ˈskɑːtsˌwʊmən/ *noun, pl* **-wom·en** /-ˌwɪmən/ [*count*] : a woman born, raised, or living in Scotland

Scot·tish /ˈskɑːtɪʃ/ *adj* : of or relating to Scotland or its people • He spoke with a *Scottish* accent. • the *Scottish* countryside • Robert Burns was a great *Scottish* poet.

scoun·drel /ˈskaʊndrəl/ *noun, pl* **-drels** [*count*] *old-fashioned* : a person (especially a man) who is cruel or dishonest • He's a rotten *scoundrel*.

[1]**scour** /ˈskawɚ/ *verb* **scours; scoured; scour·ing** [+ *obj*] : to search (something) carefully and thoroughly • We *scoured* the woods for the missing child. • I *scoured* the book for information. — compare [2]SCOUR

[2]**scour** *verb* **scours; scoured; scouring** [+ *obj*]
1 : to clean (something) by rubbing it hard with a rough object • He *scoured* the pan with steel wool. • She *scoured* spots from the stove.
2 : to cause parts of (something) to be carried away by the movement of water, ice, etc. • Spring rains *scoured* the hillside. • The river's banks had been *scoured* [=*eroded*] by floodwaters.
– compare [1]SCOUR
– **scouring** *adj, always used before a noun* • a *scouring* pad/cleanser [=a pad/cleanser that is used to scour something]

scour·er /ˈskawɚrɚ/ *noun, pl* **-ers** [*count*] *Brit* : a small, rough object that is used to clean dishes, pans, etc.

[1]**scourge** /ˈskɚʤ/ *noun, pl* **scourg·es** [*count*]
1 *formal + literary* : someone or something that causes a great amount of trouble or suffering • a city ravaged by the *scourge* of unemployment/poverty • The disease continues to be a *scourge* in the developing world. • Spelling is the *scourge* of learners of English. [=spelling is very difficult for people who are learning English]
2 : a whip that was used to punish people in the past

[2]**scourge** *verb* **scourges; scourged; scourg·ing** [+ *obj*] *formal + literary*
1 : to cause a lot of trouble or suffering for (someone or something) • a neighborhood *scourged* by crime
2 : to hit (someone) with a whip as punishment • The prisoner was *scourged* with a whip.

[1]**scout** /ˈskaʊt/ *noun, pl* **scouts** [*count*]
1 *or* ***Scout*** **a** : BOY SCOUT **b** : GIRL SCOUT
2 : a soldier, airplane, etc., that is sent to get information about the size, location, equipment, etc., of an enemy
3 : a person whose job is to search for talented performers, athletes, etc. • a baseball *scout* — see also TALENT SCOUT
good scout *US, informal + somewhat old-fashioned* : a person who is friendly, kind, helpful, etc. • He's a *good scout*. [=*good egg*]

[2]**scout** *verb* **scouts; scout·ed; scout·ing**
1 a *always followed by an adverb or preposition* [*no obj*] : to search an area or place for something or someone • Two small ships were sent to *scout* for information about the enemy. • My brother set up the tent while I *scouted* (around) for firewood. • We *scouted* around the store to see if anyone was available to help us. **b** [+ *obj*] : to explore (an area) in order to find information about it • Several soldiers were sent ahead to *scout* the area. • She *scouted* out the town to see if she'd like to live there.
2 : to watch or look at (someone or something) in order to decide if that person or thing is suited for a particular job or purpose [+ *obj*] He's a talented pitcher who is being *scouted* by several major-league teams. • She *scouts* young musicians for one of the country's top orchestras. • The site is being *scouted* as a possible location for the factory. [*no obj*] She *scouts* for one of the country's top orchestras.

scout·ing *or* **Scouting** /ˈskaʊtɪŋ/ *noun* [*noncount*] : the activities of Boy Scout and Girl Scout groups

scout·mas·ter /ˈskaʊtˌmæstɚ, *Brit* ˈskaʊtˌmɑːstə/ *noun, pl* **-ters** [*count*] : the leader of a group of Boy Scouts

[1]**scowl** /ˈskawəl/ *verb* **scowls; scowled; scowl·ing** [*no obj*] : to look at someone or something in a way that shows anger or disapproval • The teacher *scowled* [=*glowered*] at me when I walked in late. • She *scowled* [=*frowned*] in response to his question.

[2]**scowl** *noun, pl* **scowls** [*count*] : an expression on someone's face that shows anger or disapproval • The teacher gave me a *scowl* when I walked in late. • She responded to his question with a *scowl*.

scrab·ble /ˈskræbəl/ *verb, always followed by an adverb or preposition* **scrab·bles; scrab·bled; scrab·bling** [*no obj*] : to move the hands or feet in an awkward and hurried way in order to find or do something • She *scrabbled* around in her handbag for a pen. • He *scrabbled* at the slippery rock. — see also HARDSCRABBLE

scrag·gly /ˈskrægəli/ *adj* **scrag·gli·er; -est** [*also more ~; most ~*] *chiefly US, informal* : growing in a way that is not neat and even : having a ragged appearance • a *scraggly* beard • *scraggly* hair/bushes

scrag·gy /ˈskrægi/ *adj* **scrag·gi·er; -est** [*also more ~; most ~*] *informal*

1 *Brit* : very thin in a way that does not look healthy : SCRAWNY • a *scraggy* mongrel • her *scraggy* neck

2 : having a ragged appearance : SCRAGGLY • a *scraggy* beard

scram /ˈskræm/ *verb, not used in progressive tenses* **scrams; scrammed; scram·ming** [*no obj*] *informal + old-fashioned* : to leave immediately • The vandals *scrammed* before the police could arrive. — often used as a command to tell a person or animal to leave • *Scram!* You're not wanted here!

¹scram·ble /ˈskræmbəl/ *verb* **scram·bles; scram·bled; scram·bling**

1 [*no obj*] **a** *always followed by an adverb or preposition* : to move or climb over something quickly especially while also using your hands • We *scrambled* over the boulders and kept climbing up the mountain. • He *scrambled* up the ramp. **b** : to move or act quickly to do, find, or get something often before someone else does • reporters *scrambling* to finish stories by deadline • Both players *scrambled* for the ball. • News of the factory closing found workers *scrambling* to find jobs. • It started to rain, and we all *scrambled* for cover.

2 [+ *obj*] : to prepare (eggs) by mixing the white and yellow parts together and then stirring the mixture in a hot pan • I'll *scramble* some eggs for breakfast.

3 [+ *obj*] : to put (parts of something) in the wrong order — often used as *(be) scrambled* • The letters of the words *are scrambled*. [=*mixed up*]

4 [+ *obj*] : to change (a radio or electronic signal) so that whoever receives it will not be able to understand it • We will have to *scramble* our radio communications. • The cable company *scrambles* the channels that you do not pay for.

5 [*no obj*] *American football, of a quarterback* : to run with the ball while being chased by defensive players • The quarterback *scrambled* for a 5-yard gain.

– **scrambled** *adj* • *scrambled* eggs and toast • a *scrambled* signal

²scramble *noun, pl* **scrambles** : an act of scrambling: such as **a** [*singular*] : the act of moving or climbing over something quickly especially while also using your hands • a quick *scramble* over boulders **b** [*singular*] : the act of moving or acting quickly to do, find, or get something • the *scramble* for power in the country • a *scramble* for the ball • There was a ***mad scramble*** to fill vacant positions at the school. **c** [*count*] *American football* : a play in which the quarterback runs with the ball while being chased by defensive players — usually singular • He gained 10 yards on a *scramble*.

scram·bler /ˈskræmbələ/ *noun, pl* **-blers** [*count*] : a person or thing that scrambles: such as **a** : a device that is used to change a radio or electronic signal so that whoever receives it will not be able to understand it • Spies used a *scrambler* to encode their messages. **b** *American football* : a quarterback who scrambles well • Our quarterback is a great *scrambler*.

¹scrap /ˈskræp/ *noun, pl* **scraps**

1 [*singular*] : a very small amount — usually used in negative statements • After the scandal, he had no *scrap* of dignity left. [=he had no dignity left at all] • There is not a *scrap* [=*shred*] of evidence that she committed the crime.

2 ***scraps*** [*plural*] : pieces of food that are not eaten and could be thrown away • The dogs begged for *scraps* from the table. • *scraps* of dough

3 [*count*] : a small piece of something that is left after you have used the main part • a *scrap* (piece) of paper • She made a quilt from fabric *scraps*. • All that is left of the blanket is a *scrap* or two. • *scrap* fabric — see also SCRAP PAPER

4 [*noncount*] : things from an unwanted or broken object (such as a car) that are useful only in making or fixing something else • *scrap* metal • He sold the car for *scrap*. [=he sold it to someone who wanted the parts of the car] — compare ³SCRAP

²scrap *verb* **scraps; scrapped; scrap·ping** [+ *obj*] : to get rid of (something) because it is damaged, no longer useful, etc. • He *scrapped* his car after the accident. • The company had to *scrap* plans for the new building. • Should we *scrap* the idea?

³scrap *noun, pl* **scraps** [*count*] *informal* : a physical fight • I got into quite a few *scraps* when I was a kid. — compare ¹SCRAP

scrap·book /ˈskræpˌbʊk/ *noun, pl* **-books** [*count*] : a book with blank pages to which you attach photographs, letters, newspaper stories, etc., that help you remember a person or time • My mother keeps a *scrapbook* of all the articles I've ever written.

¹scrape /ˈskreɪp/ *verb* **scrapes; scraped; scrap·ing**

1 [+ *obj*] : to damage (the surface of something) or hurt (a part of your body) by rubbing something rough or sharp against it or by making it rub against something rough or sharp • Someone had *scraped* the car with a key. • I *scraped* one of the chairs while bringing it up the stairs. • I *scraped* my knee when I fell.

2 *always followed by an adverb or preposition* : to rub or cause (something) to rub against a hard surface and make a harsh and usually unpleasant sound [*no obj*] fingernails *scraping* against a blackboard • the sound of chairs *scraping* on the floor as people stood to leave • The boat *scraped* against the edge of the dock. [+ *obj*] She *scraped* her fingernails across the blackboard. • The deer *scraped* its antlers against the tree.

3 a [+ *obj*] : to remove (something) from a surface by rubbing an object or tool against it • *Scrape* the seeds into a bowl. • *Scrape* the paint from the wood. — often + *off* • The tool was used to *scrape* hair *off* buffalo skins. • *Scrape* the scales *off* the fish. • He *scraped off* the dirt from his shoes. **b** : to clean (something) by rubbing an object or tool against it • Please *scrape* your plate into the trash.

4 [+ *obj*] : to barely succeed in collecting or gathering (something needed or wanted) by making an effort — + *together* or *up* • He managed to *scrape up* enough money for lunch. • We *scraped* enough players *together* to play basketball.

bow and scrape see ¹BOW

scrape by also scrape along [*phrasal verb*]

1 : to live with barely enough money : to be able to buy only the things you need most • Money was tight, but we somehow managed to *scrape by*. [=*survive*] • She's *scraping along* on just a few hundred dollars a month. **2** *or* ***scrape through*** : to succeed at doing something but just barely • He didn't study for the exam and just barely *scraped by*. [=he passed the exam but came very close to failing]

²scrape *noun, pl* **scrapes** [*count*]

1 : a mark or injury that is caused by something rubbing against something else • There's a *scrape* on the fender that wasn't there yesterday. • I got a *scrape* on my knee when I fell. • We survived the accident with a few minor bumps and *scrapes*.

2 *informal* : a bad, dangerous, or unpleasant situation • legal/financial *scrapes* • She got into a few *scrapes* with the police/law when she was younger.

3 : a harsh and usually unpleasant sound that is made when something rubs against a hard surface • the *scrape* of fingernails on a blackboard

scrap·er /ˈskreɪpə/ *noun, pl* **-ers** [*count*] : a tool that is used to scrape something off a surface • a paint *scraper*

scrap heap *noun, pl* **~ heaps** [*count*] : a place where broken or useless things are taken and left • Her car was sent off to the *scrap heap* [=*dump*] after the accident. — often used figuratively • He may be past his prime, but he's not ready for the *scrap heap* yet. • a minor event consigned to the *scrap heap* of history

scra·pie /ˈskreɪpi/ *noun* [*noncount*] : a usually fatal brain disease that affects sheep

scrap·ing /ˈskreɪpɪŋ/ *noun, pl* **-ings** [*count*] : an object or substance that has been removed from a surface by rubbing an object or tool against it : something that is scraped off of a surface — usually plural • The carpenter brushed the *scrapings* aside as she worked. • DNA tests on fingernail *scrapings* from the victim's hands [=on material scraped from the underside of the victim's fingernails] were inconclusive.

scrap paper *noun* [*noncount*] : paper that is partly used or is of poor quality but that you can use for unimportant things • Please take out a piece of *scrap paper* and practice the math problems on the board. — called also (*Brit*) *rough paper*, (*US*) *scratch paper*

scrap·per /ˈskræpə/ *noun, pl* **-pers** [*count*] *chiefly US, informal* : a person who fights or struggles against something or to do something • He's quite a *scrapper*.

scrap·ple /ˈskræpəl/ *noun* [*noncount*] *US* : a dish of meat mixed with spices, broth, and boiled cornmeal that is placed in a mold and served sliced and fried

scrap·py /ˈskræpi/ *adj* **scrap·pi·er**; **-est** [*also more* ~; *most* ~] *informal*

1 *US* : ready or eager to fight ▪ He's a *scrappy* guy you don't want to mess with.

2 *US* : willing to work hard in order to succeed : determined and tough ▪ a *scrappy* football player ▪ a *scrappy* journalist

3 *chiefly Brit* : not organized or done well ▪ a *scrappy* essay that should be rewritten

scrap·yard /ˈskræpˌjɑɚd/ *noun, pl* **-yards** [*count*] *chiefly Brit* : JUNKYARD

[1]**scratch** /ˈskrætʃ/ *verb* **scratch·es**; **scratched**; **scratch·ing**

1 a : to rub your skin with something sharp (such as your fingernails) especially in order to stop an itch [+ *obj*] Will you *scratch* my back for me? ▪ *Scratching* the itch only makes it worse. ▪ The dog *scratched* its ear. — sometimes used figuratively ▪ Maybe it's time to ***scratch the/that itch*** to travel I've had since I was a kid. [=maybe it's time to satisfy the urge I've had to travel] [*no obj*] You shouldn't *scratch*. It'll just make your itch worse. — see also SCRATCH SOMEONE'S BACK (below) **b** : to make a shallow and narrow cut in (your skin) with something sharp (such as fingernails, claws, etc.) [+ *obj*] The cat *scratched* me. ▪ Thorns *scratched* our legs as we climbed through the briars. [*no obj*] Careful, the cat will *scratch*. **c** [*no obj*] : to rub a surface or object with something sharp or rough in a way that produces a harsh sound ▪ The dog was *scratching* at the door.

2 [+ *obj*] **a** : to make a line or mark in the surface of (something) by rubbing or cutting it with something rough or sharp ▪ Be careful not to *scratch* the table. ▪ Someone *scratched* the paint on my car. **b** : to make (something, such as a line or letters) in the surface of something by using a stick, a sharp tool, etc. ▪ The little boy *scratched* lines in the dirt with a stick. ▪ They *scratched* their initials in the old bridge. **c** : to write (something) in a quick and untidy way ▪ She *scratched* a note to herself on a napkin.

3 [+ *obj*] *informal* **a** : to decide not to do or continue with (something) ▪ We had to *scratch* our picnic plans because of the weather. ▪ We should go to the movies tonight. No, *scratch* [=*forget*] that. Let's rent a DVD instead. **b** : to remove (someone) from the list of players who will be playing in a game ▪ She was *scratched* from the starting lineup.

scratch a living *or US* ***scratch out a living*** : to earn barely enough money to live ▪ He *scratched out a living* as a farmer.

scratch off [*phrasal verb*] ***scratch (something) off*** *or* ***scratch off (something)*** **1** : to remove (something) from an object or surface by rubbing with a sharp edge or tool ▪ *Scratch off* the gray box on the ticket to see if you've won! ▪ She *scratched* the gum *off* her shoe with a stick. **2** : to draw a line through (something that is written down) ▪ He *scratched* his name *off* the list.

scratch out [*phrasal verb*] ***scratch (something) out*** *or* ***scratch out (something)*** : to draw a line through (something that is written down) ▪ I *scratched out* the mistake.

scratch someone's back *informal* : to do something that helps someone else but that is often wrong or difficult to do ▪ ***You scratch my back, and I'll scratch yours.*** [=if you do something to help me, I'll do something to help you]

scratch the surface : to deal with or learn about only a small part of something ▪ If you think she only did it for the money, you haven't even *scratched the surface*. [=there are many other factors, reasons, etc., involved] ▪ There's so much to learn about this subject. I feel like I've only *scratched the surface*.

scratch your head *informal* : to be confused about something : to think about something you do not understand ▪ His odd behavior left us all *scratching our heads*. [=we could not understand his odd behavior]

– **scratch·er** *noun, pl* **-ers** [*count*] ▪ a long-handled back *scratcher* [=a device you can use to scratch your back]

[2]**scratch** *noun, pl* **scratches**

1 [*count*] **a** : a line or mark in the surface of something that is caused by something rough or sharp rubbing against it ▪ There's a *scratch* in the paint on the new car! ▪ The table is an antique but it doesn't have any dents or *scratches*. **b** : a shallow and narrow cut in the skin that is caused by something sharp ▪ I got a *scratch* on my leg when I climbed the fence. ▪ He escaped the fire ***without a scratch***. [=without getting hurt; without any injuries]

2 [*count*] : the sound made when something sharp rubs against a surface or object ▪ The only sound in the room during the test was the *scratch* of pencils on paper.

3 [*noncount*] *US slang* : MONEY ▪ We don't have the *scratch* to buy a new car.

from scratch **1** : with ingredients you have prepared yourself rather than with a prepared mixture of ingredients bought from a store ▪ bread/cookies made *from scratch* ▪ I used a frozen pie crust rather than making one *from scratch*. **2** : from a point at which nothing has been done yet ▪ We will have to start the project *from scratch*. ▪ He built the company *from scratch*.

up to scratch *chiefly Brit, informal* : good enough : as good as expected or wanted — usually used in negative statements ▪ Her performance wasn't *up to scratch*. [=(*US*) *up to snuff*]

[3]**scratch** *adj, always used before a noun*

1 *of a golfer* : having no handicap ▪ a *scratch* golfer [=an excellent golfer whose score is usually close to par]

2 *chiefly Brit* : put together quickly and without enough planning or thought ▪ a *scratch* team

scratching post *noun, pl* ~ **posts** [*count*] : an upright piece of wood that is covered with carpet and kept in a house for a pet cat to scratch

scratch pad *noun, pl* ~ **pads** [*count*] *US* : a small book of blank paper that is used for writing notes, brief messages, etc.

scratch paper *noun* [*noncount*] *US* : SCRAP PAPER

scratch ticket *noun, pl* ~ **tickets** [*count*] *chiefly US* : a small card that has covered areas that you remove by rubbing with the edge of a coin, fingernail, etc., to see if you have won a prize (such as money) — called also (*chiefly Brit*) *scratch card*

scratchy /ˈskrætʃi/ *adj* **scratch·i·er**; **-est**

1 : having a rough sound : having a sound like the sound made when something sharp or rough rubs against a surface or object ▪ listening to *scratchy* old records ▪ He has a *scratchy* [=*gravelly*] voice.

2 *informal* : rough and irritating to the skin : likely to make you itch ▪ The costume is made from *scratchy* material.

3 : swollen and sore ▪ He is sick with a *scratchy* throat.

4 : written in a careless way that is difficult to read ▪ I could barely read her *scratchy* notes.

[1]**scrawl** /ˈskrɑːl/ *verb, always followed by an adverb or preposition* **scrawls**; **scrawled**; **scrawl·ing** [+ *obj*] : to write or draw (something) very quickly or carelessly ▪ She *scrawled* her signature on the receipt.

[2]**scrawl** *noun, pl* **scrawls** [*count*] : something that has been written or drawn very quickly or carelessly ▪ Her signature was just a *scrawl*.

scraw·ny /ˈskrɑːni/ *adj* **scraw·ni·er**; **-est** [*also more* ~; *most* ~] : very thin in a way that is not attractive or healthy ▪ a *scrawny* [=*skinny*] kid ▪ The only plants in their yard were a couple of *scrawny* bushes.

[1]**scream** /ˈskriːm/ *verb* **screams**; **screamed**; **scream·ing**

1 a [*no obj*] : to suddenly cry out in a loud and high voice because of pain, surprise, etc. ▪ She *screamed* when the door suddenly slammed shut. ▪ This is so irritating I could *scream*. ▪ The crowd *screamed* with excitement. ▪ He was dragged, ***kicking and screaming***, from the room. **b** : to say (something) in a loud and high voice because you are angry, afraid, etc. [*no obj*] He *screamed* at/for her to stop. [+ *obj*] "Help!" he *screamed*. — often + *out* ▪ The general *screamed out* orders. **c** [*no obj*] : to make a very loud, high sound ▪ Sirens were *screaming* in the distance.

2 *always followed by an adverb or preposition* [*no obj*] : to move very quickly through a place while making a lot of noise ▪ Police cars *screamed* down the street.

3 [*no obj*] : to speak, write, or express something in a way that shows intense or uncontrolled emotion ▪ Newspaper headlines *screamed* about the spike in crime.

4 [+ *obj*] : to bring (an idea, word, etc.) into your mind very clearly ▪ The amount she paid in taxes was so low that it practically *screamed* "fraud." [=it very strongly suggested that she had committed fraud] ▪ That big white dress *screams* "Marry me."

scream bloody murder (*US*) *or Brit* ***scream blue murder*** *informal* : to scream, yell, or complain in a very loud or angry way ▪ His political opponents *screamed bloody murder* when he was appointed to office.

scream for [*phrasal verb*] ***scream for (something)*** *informal* **1** : to demand or need (something) ▪ People are *screaming*

S

for news about the virus. • These policies just ***scream (out) for*** reform. [=these policies very badly need to be reformed] **2 :** to be very suitable or appropriate for (something) • Hot summer days like this just *scream for* ice cream and visits to the pool.

[2]**scream** *noun, pl* **screams**
1 [*count*] **:** a loud and high cry or sound • She let out a piercing *scream.* — often + *of* • *screams of* terror • the *screams of* the fire trucks as they raced by
2 [*singular*] *informal + old-fashioned* **:** a person or thing that is very funny • She's an absolute *scream.*

scream·er /ˈskri:mɚ/ *noun, pl* **-ers** [*count*] *informal*
1 : something that moves or works very quickly • The batter hit a *screamer* right at the shortstop. • She kicked a *screamer* into the net. • My last computer was pretty fast, but this one's a real *screamer.*
2 : a person who tends to scream **:** a person who screams more often or more easily than most people • Don't startle her—she's a *screamer.*

scream·ing /ˈskri:mɪŋ/ *adj, always used before a noun*
1 : very noticeable and difficult to ignore • The room's walls were painted in a *screaming* yellow. • *screaming* headlines • a *screaming* need for reform • (*US*) I have a *screaming* headache.
2 *US* **:** very fast or powerful • The batter hit a *screaming* line drive right at the shortstop.

scream·ing·ly /ˈskri:mɪŋli/ *adv, informal* **:** very or extremely • a *screamingly* funny film

scree /ˈskri:/ *noun, pl* **screes** [*count, noncount*] **:** an area of loose stones on the side of a mountain

[1]**screech** /ˈskri:ʧ/ *noun, pl* **screech·es** [*count*]
1 : a loud and very high cry that usually expresses extreme pain, anger, or fear • With a loud *screech,* she smashed the plate against the wall.
2 : a loud and very high sound • the *screech* of brakes

[2]**screech** *verb* **screeches**; **screeched**; **screech·ing**
1 : to cry out or shout in a loud and very high voice because of extreme pain, anger, fear, etc. [*no obj*] I *screeched* when I saw the mouse. • He kept *screeching* at the children to pay attention. [+ *obj*] "You can't do this to me!" she *screeched.*
2 [*no obj*] **:** to make a loud and very high sound • The car ***screeched to a halt/stop.*** [=made a loud and very high sound as it stopped] — often used figuratively • Her promising career *screeched to a halt* [=suddenly stopped/ended] when she was caught stealing.
— **screeching** *adj* • The car came to a ***screeching halt*** • The project came to a *screeching halt.*

screech owl *noun, pl* ~ **owls** [*count*] **:** a kind of small American owl that has bunches of feathers that look like ears on the sides of its head

screed /ˈskri:d/ *noun, pl* **screeds** [*count*] *disapproving* **:** a long and often angry piece of writing that usually accuses someone of something or complains about something • In her *screed* against the recording industry, she blamed her producer for ruining her career.

[1]**screen** /ˈskri:n/ *noun, pl* **screens**
1 [*count*] **a :** the usually flat part of a television or computer monitor that shows the images or text **:** the part of a television or computer that you look at when you are using it • Don't sit too close to the *screen* or you'll get a headache. • A pop-up ad appeared on the *screen.* • a television/TV *screen* • a computer/display *screen* — see picture at COMPUTER **b :** a large, flat, white surface on which images or movies are shown • When I go to the movies, I like to sit close to the *screen.*
2 [*noncount*] **:** the art or profession of acting in movies • a star of stage and *screen* [=a famous actor who acts in plays and movies] • The two actors perform well together ***on screen*** [=in movies or on TV] — often used before another noun • a *screen* actor • She has tremendous ***screen presence*** [=a powerful quality that attracts attention in movies] — see also BIG SCREEN, SILVER SCREEN
3 [*count*] *chiefly US* **:** a sheet that is made of very small wire or plastic strings which are woven together and that is set in a frame in a window, door, etc., to let air in but keep insects out • a window *screen* • a *screen* door [=a door that has a screen built into it]
4 [*count*] **:** something that is used to hide, protect, cover, or block a person or thing: such as **a :** a group of trees or plants that separates one area from another • We planted a *screen* of shrubs so the neighbors couldn't see into our yard. **b :** a large, thin piece of wood, paper, or cloth that is set in a frame and used to separate one room or part of a room from another • You can change your clothes behind the *screen.* **c :** something that hides the real nature of an activity, feeling, etc. • His activities were just a *screen* for his real plans. **d** *sports* **:** a planned action in some sports (such as basketball or ice hockey) in which a player or a player's view is legally blocked by an opponent • The goalie couldn't see the puck because of the *screen.* — see also SMOKE SCREEN, SUNSCREEN, WINDSCREEN
5 [*count*] *American football* **:** SCREEN PASS • The quarterback threw a *screen* to the halfback.
— see also SILK SCREEN

[2]**screen** *verb* **screens**; **screened**; **screen·ing** [+ *obj*]
1 : to examine (people or things) in order to decide if they are suitable for a particular purpose • A committee will *screen* candidates for the job, but the final hiring decision will be made by Ms. Brown. • someone who *screens* luggage at the airport [=someone who examines the luggage of airplane passengers in order to make sure that nothing dangerous is brought onto an airplane] • We *screen* the kids' music so that we can approve what they listen to. • He usually ***screens his (telephone/phone) calls*** [=he usually lets his answering machine answer his phone so that he can hear who is calling before he decides to talk to whoever it is]
2 a : to do a test on (someone) to find out if that person has or is likely to develop a disease — usually + *for* • All blood donors are *screened for* AIDS. • She was *screened for* breast cancer. **b :** to do a test on (a person's blood, urine, etc.) to find out if the person has been using an illegal substance — usually + *for* • All athletes will be *screened for* performance-enhancing drugs prior to the events.
3 : to show (a movie, television show, etc.) to the public on a screen • We'll be *screening* his latest film in two weeks.
4 : to hide, protect, cover, or block (someone or something) with a screen • I was *screened* by the cars so no one saw me. • The altar was *screened.* • We planted a row of shrubs to *screen* our backyard from the neighbors. • The goalie was *screened* on that play. [=players blocked the goalie from seeing the puck] • a ***screened porch*** [=a porch that has walls made of screens] — often used figuratively • We try to *screen* our children from the violence on TV.

screen out [*phrasal verb*] **1** ***screen (someone or something) out*** or ***screen out (someone or something)*** **:** to remove (someone or something that is not suitable for a particular purpose) from a group that is being examined • Not all students will be allowed to participate. Students receiving a D or lower will be *screened out.* **2** ***screen (something) out*** or ***screen out (something)*** **:** to prevent (something harmful) from passing through • The lotion is supposed to *screen out* [=*block*] the sun's harmful rays.

screen·er /ˈskri:nɚ/ *noun, pl* **-ers** [*count*] **:** a person or thing that screens something or someone; *especially* **:** a person whose job is to examine airplane passengers and their luggage in order to make sure that nothing dangerous is brought onto an airplane • Airline *screeners* found a suspicious package in his luggage which turned out to be a bomb.

screen·ing /ˈskri:nɪŋ/ *noun, pl* **-ings :** the act of screening people or things: such as **a** [*count*] **:** an event in which a movie is shown to an audience • We were late for the (movie) *screening.* **b :** the act of doing a test on a person or a person's blood, urine, etc., to look for evidence of a disease, illegal drug, etc. [*noncount*] methods of *screening* for cancer [*count*] Players must pass three random drug *screenings.* **c :** the act of examining people or things in order to decide if they are suitable for a particular purpose [*noncount*] Federal agents handle passenger and luggage *screening* at the airport. [*count*] The company will be conducting applicant *screenings* Wednesday.

screen pass *noun, pl* ~ **passes** [*count*] *American football* **:** a pass to a receiver who is behind the line of scrimmage and is protected by a line of blockers

screen·play /ˈskri:nˌpleɪ/ *noun, pl* **-plays** [*count*] **:** the written form of a movie that also includes instructions on how it is to be acted and filmed **:** the script for a movie • an award for best *screenplay*

screen saver *noun, pl* ~ **-ers** [*count*] **:** a computer program that shows a moving image or set of images on a computer screen when the computer is on but is not being used

screen test *noun, pl* ~ **tests** [*count*] **:** a recording of a short performance by an actor that is made with a movie or video camera and that is used to decide if that person should be given a part in a movie

screen·writ·er /ˈskriːn,raɪtɚ/ *noun, pl* **-ers** [*count*] **:** a person who writes screenplays

[1]**screw** /ˈskruː/ *noun, pl* **screws** [*count*]
1 : a narrow, pointed metal cylinder that has a wide flat or rounded top and a ridge (called a thread) that goes around it in a spiral ✧ A screw is used to hold things together or to attach things. It is inserted into wood, metal, etc., by being turned. • Tighten the *screws.* — see picture at CARPENTRY; compare [1]NAIL 1
2 : an object that has a thread like a screw which is used to attach or connect it to something — usually used before another noun • The bottle has a ***screw cap/top***. [=a cap/top that is attached and removed by turning it]
3 *informal + offensive* **a :** an act of sexual intercourse **b :** a sexual partner
4 *slang* **:** a prison guard
have a screw loose *or* ***have a loose screw*** *informal* **:** to be crazy • He acts like he *has a screw loose.* • You've got to *have a loose screw* to think that's a good idea. = You've got to ***have a few loose screws*** to think that's a good idea.
put the screws on/to (someone or something) *informal* **:** to use force or the threat of force to make (someone or something) do what you want • The government is finally *putting the screws to* an industry that's been evading environmental laws for years.
tighten the screws *informal* **:** to put more pressure on someone or something to do something • We need to *tighten the screws* on people who've been evading the tax.

[2]**screw** *verb* **screws; screwed; screw·ing**
1 *always followed by an adverb or preposition* [+ *obj*] **:** to attach (something) with a screw • I *screwed* the boards together. • The cupboards are *screwed* to the wall.
2 *always followed by an adverb or preposition* **a** [+ *obj*] **:** to turn (something) so that it attaches or connects to something • *Screw* the cap on tight. • *Screw* the light bulb into the fixture. **b** [*no obj*] **:** to fit onto or into something by being turned • The lid *screws* onto the jar. • The light bulb *screws* right in.
3 *informal + offensive* **a** [*no obj*] **:** to have sex **b** [+ *obj*] **:** to have sex with (someone)
4 [+ *obj*] *informal* **a :** to take something from (someone) by lying or breaking a rule • I'd given them all of my savings before I realized I was being *screwed.* [=*cheated*] — often + *out of* • The company *screwed* them *out of* thousands of dollars of investment money. **b :** to prevent (someone) from having or getting something that is deserved or expected • He will *screw* you if you give him the chance. — often + *out of* or (*US*) *over* • She was *screwed out of* the job. [=she should have gotten the job but she didn't get it] • The company changed its return policy and (totally) *screwed* me *over.*
5 [+ *obj*] *informal + impolite* — used to express anger, disgust, etc. • She doesn't like it? Well, *screw* her. • ***Screw it*** [=*forget it*], I'm not waiting around forever.
6 [+ *obj*] **:** to press or squeeze (something) so that it is no longer flat or smooth — often + *up* • He *screwed* [=*crumpled*] *up* the letter into a ball and threw it into the trash.
have/get your head screwed on right/straight see [1]HEAD
screw around [*phrasal verb*] *chiefly US, informal* **1 :** to do things that are not useful or serious **:** to waste time • Quit *screwing around* [=*messing around, fooling around*] and get back to work. **2 :** to have sex with someone who is not your husband, wife, or regular partner • She found out he's been *screwing around.* [=*fooling around*] — often + *with* • She was *screwing around with* her boss. **3 :** to use or do something in a way that is not very serious • I spent the afternoon *screwing around* [=*messing around*] on the piano. — often + *with* • *screwing around with* paints **4** ***screw around with (something)*** **:** to handle or play with (something) in a careless or foolish way • It's really dangerous to *screw around with* your cell phone while you're driving.
screw up [*phrasal verb*] *informal* **1 a :** to make a mistake **:** to do something incorrectly • Sorry about that, I *screwed up.* • You really *screwed up* this time. **b** ***screw (something) up or screw up (something)*** **:** to make a mistake in (something) • The waiter *screwed up* our order. • This performance is important, so don't *screw* it *up.* **2** ***screw (something) up or screw up (something)*** **:** to damage or ruin (something) • Drugs *screwed up* her life. **:** to damage or change (something) so that it does not work properly • I don't know what I did, but I somehow *screwed up* the computer. **3** ***screw (someone) up or screw up (someone)*** **:** to make (someone) very upset and unhappy for a long time • The divorce really *screwed* him *up.* **4** ***screw (something) up or screw up (something)*** **:** to tighten the muscles of (your face or eyes) • He *screwed* his face *up* into a frown. • She *screwed up* her eyes [=she squinted] and tried to read the sign. **5** ***screw up the/your courage*** **:** to make yourself brave enough to do something difficult • I finally *screwed up the courage* to tell them that I was quitting. — see also [2]SCREW 6

[1]**screw·ball** /ˈskruː,bɑːl/ *noun, pl* **-balls** [*count*]
1 *baseball* **:** a pitch that is thrown with spin so that the ball curves in a direction that is opposite to the direction of a curveball
2 *chiefly US, informal* **:** a crazy person **:** a person who is not able to think in a clear or sensible way • She really did that? What a *screwball.*

[2]**screwball** *adj, always used before a noun, US, informal* **:** funny in a very silly and strange way • a *screwball* comedy

screw·driv·er /ˈskruː,draɪvɚ/ *noun, pl* **-ers** [*count*] **:** a tool that is used for turning screws — see picture at CARPENTRY

screwed–up *adj* [*more ~; most ~*] *informal* **:** not right or normal **:** not acting or functioning the way a person or thing should • He's a pretty *screwed-up* kid. • Our computer network is all *screwed-up.*

screw–top *adj, always used before a noun* **:** having a top or lid that that it can be attached and removed by being turned • a *screw-top* jar [=a jar with a top that screws on]

screw·up /ˈskruː,ʌp/ *noun, pl* **-ups** [*count*] *informal + disapproving*
1 : a mistake or error • That was a major *screwup.*
2 : a person who often makes mistakes especially about important things **:** someone who often screws up • She's a *screwup* who can't hold down a job.

screwy /ˈskruːwi/ *adj* **screw·i·er; -est** [*also more ~; most ~*] *informal*
1 : different from what you expect because of being strange or unusual • I knew something was *screwy.* • a *screwy* idea
2 : not sensible or reasonable • *screwy* people • a *screwy* foreign policy

[1]**scrib·ble** /ˈskrɪbəl/ *verb* **scrib·bles; scrib·bled; scrib·bling**
1 : to write (something) quickly and in a way that makes it difficult to read [+ *obj*] She *scribbled* a note to him and then dashed off to her meeting. • He *scribbled* down his phone number. [*no obj*] Students *scribbled* furiously as the professor lectured. • She was *scribbling* away in a notebook.
2 [*no obj*] **:** to draw lines, shapes, etc., that have no particular meaning in a quick and careless way • The toddler *scribbled* all over the paper.
– scribbling *noun, pl* **scribblings** [*count*] • I couldn't read the doctor's illegible *scribblings.*

[2]**scribble** *noun, pl* **scribbles**
1 [*noncount*] **:** writing that is difficult to read because it has been done quickly or carelessly • She could barely make out the doctor's *scribble.*
2 ***scribbles*** [*plural*] **:** lines, shapes, etc., that have no particular meaning and are drawn in a quick and careless way • The chalkboard was adorned with the children's *scribbles.*

scrib·bler *noun, pl* **-blers** [*count*] *humorous + disapproving* **:** a writer or author • My wife's a banker, but I'm just a *scribbler* who writes for the newspaper.

[1]**scribe** /ˈskraɪb/ *noun, pl* **scribes** [*count*]
1 : a person in the past whose job was to copy manuscripts and books • Medieval *scribes* were often monks.
2 *chiefly US, informal* **:** a journalist or writer • She was interviewed for the newspaper by a local *scribe.*

[2]**scribe** *verb* **scribes; scribed; scrib·ing** [+ *obj*] **:** to make (a shape, design, mark, etc.) in something by cutting or scratching with a sharp pointed tool • *Scribe* a line along the board where you will be trimming it.

[1]**scrim·mage** /ˈskrɪmɪʤ/ *noun, pl* **-mag·es**
1 [*noncount*] *American football* **:** the point in a game at which the center passes or throws the ball to the quarterback • The first play from *scrimmage* netted them a touchdown. — see also LINE OF SCRIMMAGE
2 [*count*] *US* **:** an informal game that is played for practice **:** a game that is not official • a preseason *scrimmage*

[2]**scrimmage** *verb* **-mages; -maged; -mag·ing** [*no obj*] *US* **:** to play in a scrimmage • We *scrimmage* every Saturday. • Last weekend we *scrimmaged* against Bell High.

scrimp /ˈskrɪmp/ *verb* **scrimps; scrimped; scrimp·ing** [*no obj*] **:** to spend as little money as you can **:** to be careful about spending money • They ***scrimped and saved*** for their big vacation.

S

[1]scrip /ˈskrɪp/ *noun, pl* **scrips** [*count*] *technical*
1 : a document which says that the person who has the document has the right to something (such as stock or land)
2 : special money that a government makes during an emergency and that can only be used for a short period of time – compare [2]SCRIP

[2]scrip *noun, pl* **scrips** [*count*] *US, informal* **:** PRESCRIPTION 1a • I need to get my *scrip* filled. — compare [1]SCRIP

[1]script /ˈskrɪpt/ *noun, pl* **scripts**
1 [*count*] **a :** the written form of a play, movie, television show, etc. • The actors haven't had time to study the *script*. • She sent her *script* to several television production studios. • an early version of the *script* **b :** a plan for what is going to be done or said in a particular situation • When questioned, officials followed the *script* and declined comment.
2 a [*noncount*] **:** a type of handwriting in which all the letters in a word are connected to each other • She wrote in *script* [=*cursive*] instead of printing. **b :** a particular style of writing or printing **:** a way that a particular set of letters, numbers, etc., is written or printed [*noncount*] words written in cuneiform *script* [*count*] roman and italic *scripts* **c :** the letters of a language arranged in their usual order **:** ALPHABET [*noncount*] languages that use the Cyrillic *script* [*count*] The message was written in a foreign *script*.

[2]script *verb* **scripts; script·ed; script·ing** [+ *obj*]
1 : to write the script for (a play, movie, television show, etc.) • I *scripted* three episodes of the show. — often used as *(be) scripted* • The actors' dialogue *was* carefully *scripted*.
2 : to plan how (something) will happen, be done, etc. • The discussion couldn't have gone better if we had *scripted* it. • The trip didn't go as *scripted*.

scripted *adj* **:** written at an earlier time • a *scripted* speech/joke; *also* **:** planned in a careful way at an earlier time • a *scripted* campaign • Her public appearances are all *scripted* events.

scrip·ture /ˈskrɪptʃɚ/ *noun, pl* **-tures**
1 ***Scripture or the Scriptures*** **:** the books of either the Old Testament or the New Testament or of both **:** the Bible • someone who frequently quotes *Scripture* • Each day they read (from) *the Scriptures*. • *the* Hebrew *Scriptures*
2 ***scriptures*** [*plural*] **:** the sacred writings of a religion • sacred/holy *scriptures*
– scrip·tur·al /ˈskrɪptʃərəl/ *adj* • a *scriptural* passage

script·writ·er /ˈskrɪptˌraɪtɚ/ *noun, pl* **-ers** [*count*] **:** a person who writes the written form of a play, movie, television show, etc. **:** a person who writes a script • Hollywood *scriptwriters*

scrod /ˈskrɑːd/ *noun, pl* **scrod** [*count, noncount*] *US* **:** a young fish (such as a cod or a haddock) that is eaten as food

[1]scroll /ˈskroʊl/ *noun, pl* **scrolls** [*count*]
1 : a long piece of paper that rolls around one or two cylinders and that usually has something written or drawn on it • the Dead Sea *Scrolls* • He read from the *scroll*.
2 : a decoration that looks like the curled ends of a scroll • a scarf with lovely green *scrolls* on it

scroll

[2]scroll *verb* **scrolls; scrolled; scroll·ing** *computers* **:** to move text or images of a Web page, document, etc., up, down, or to the side on a computer screen so that you can see all of it [*no obj*] *scroll* through an e-mail • She *scrolled* (down) to the bottom of the screen. [+ *obj*] You have to *scroll* the screen to see the bottom of the Web page.

scroll bar *noun, pl* **~ bars** [*count*] *computers* **:** a narrow bar along the bottom or side of a window that you click on with a mouse to see parts of the window that are hidden

scroll saw *noun, pl* **~ saws** [*count*] *US* **:** a machine that has a narrow blade for cutting curves and decorative patterns in wood, metal, plastic, etc.

Scrooge *or* **scrooge** /ˈskruːdʒ/ *noun, pl* **Scroog·es** *or* **scrooges** [*count*] *informal* **:** a selfish and unfriendly person who is not willing to spend or give away money — usually singular • His boss is a real *Scrooge* who never gives people raises. ✧ ***Scrooge*** is from the name of Ebenezer Scrooge, the main character in the story *A Christmas Carol* by Charles Dickens.

scro·tum /ˈskroʊtəm/ *noun, pl* **scro·tums** *or* **scro·ta** /ˈskroʊtə/ [*count*] **:** the sack of skin that contains the testicles of men and male animals

scrounge /ˈskraʊndʒ/ *verb* **scroung·es; scrounged; scroung·ing**
1 : to persuade someone to give you (something) for free [+ *obj*] I managed to *scrounge* enough money for a bus ticket. — often + *off* or *from* • I *scrounged* a few bucks *off* my friend for lunch. • She *scrounged* some money *from* her folks. [*no obj*] He's always *scrounging off* his friends instead of paying for things himself.
2 *US* **:** to get or find something by looking in different places, asking different people, etc. [*no obj*] We *scrounged* around for firewood. [+ *obj*] We managed to *scrounge* some firewood. — often + *up* • I tried to *scrounge up* some tickets to the show, but I didn't have any luck.
– scroung·er *noun, pl* **-ers** [*count*]

[1]scrub /ˈskrʌb/ *noun* [*noncount*]
1 : small bushes and trees • A chipmunk hid in the *scrub*.
2 : land that is covered with small bushes and trees • In the desert *scrub*, temperatures can reach well over 100 degrees. – compare [2]SCRUB

[2]scrub *noun, pl* **scrubs**
1 [*count*] **a :** the act of rubbing something hard with a rough object or substance and often with soap in order to clean it **:** the act of scrubbing something — usually singular • He gave the pan a good *scrub*. [=he scrubbed the pan] **b :** a powerful cleanser that is used to clean the skin • a face *scrub*
2 ***scrubs*** [*plural*] *US* **:** special loose clothing that is worn by people who work in hospitals • hospital/surgical *scrubs*
– compare [1]SCRUB

[3]scrub *verb* **scrubs; scrubbed; scrub·bing**
1 : to rub (something) hard with a rough object or substance and often with soap in order to clean it [+ *obj*] She *scrubbed* the potatoes. [*no obj*] We *scrubbed* and *scrubbed* until the floor was clean.
2 [+ *obj*] *informal* **:** to decide that (something, such as a game, performance, etc.) will not happen **:** to cancel (something) • They *scrubbed* the game because of the bad weather.
scrub off [*phrasal verb*] ***scrub off (something) or scrub (something) off*** **:** to remove (something) from a surface by scrubbing • I *scrubbed off* the heavy stage makeup. • *scrubbing* dirt and grime *off* the walls
scrub out [*phrasal verb*] ***scrub out (something) or scrub (something) out*** **1 :** to remove (something) from an object by scrubbing • a stain in the carpet that was impossible to *scrub out* **2 :** to scrub the inside of (something) • She *scrubbed out* the flower pots and filled them with fresh soil.
scrub up [*phrasal verb*] **:** to wash your hands and arms thoroughly • The doctor *scrubbed up* for surgery.

scrub·ber /ˈskrʌbɚ/ *noun, pl* **-bers** [*count*]
1 : a tool or machine that is used for scrubbing something • a vegetable *scrubber* [=a brush that is used for scrubbing vegetables] • a floor *scrubber*
2 : a person whose job is to scrub something • She got a job as a pot *scrubber*.
3 *technical* **:** a machine that removes a dangerous substance from air, water, etc. • The *scrubbers* will reduce the power plant's sulfur emissions.

scrub brush (*US*) *or Brit* **scrubbing brush** *noun, pl* **~ brushes** [*count*] **:** a small brush with stiff bristles that is used for scrubbing things

scrub·by /ˈskrʌbi/ *adj* **scrub·bi·er; -est** [*also more ~; most ~*]
1 : covered with small bushes and trees • *scrubby* land
2 : small and not growing well • *scrubby* trees/bushes

scrub·land /ˈskrʌbˌlænd/ *noun, pl* **-lands :** land that is covered with small bushes and trees [*noncount*] a large area of *scrubland* [*count*] the *scrublands* of the American West

scruff /ˈskrʌf/ *noun* [*singular*] **:** the skin on the back of the neck • She held the kitten ***by the scruff of its neck***.

scruffy /ˈskrʌfi/ *adj* **scruff·i·er; -est** [*also more ~; most ~*] *informal* **:** not neat, clean, or orderly • a *scruffy* beard • *scruffy* college students • The neighborhood is full of dilapidated houses with *scruffy* backyards.

scrum /ˈskrʌm/ *noun, pl* **scrums** [*count*]
1 *rugby* **a :** a way of starting play again in which players from each team come together and try to get control of the ball by pushing against each other and using their feet when the ball is thrown in between them **b :** the group of players who are involved in a scrum
2 : a large group of people who are close together in one place • He pushed through the *scrum* [=*crowd, throng*] of holiday shoppers. • The actress was caught in a media *scrum*. [=a crowd of reporters, photographers, etc.]

scrump·tious /ˈskrʌmpʃəs/ *adj* [*more ~; most ~*] *informal*

S

: very pleasant to taste : DELICIOUS ▪ a *scrumptious* cake

scrunch /ˈskrʌntʃ/ *verb* **scrunch·es; scrunched; scrunch·ing**

1 *always followed by an adverb or preposition* [*no obj*] : to make your body lower or shorter by bending your legs, making your back bend forward, lowering your head, etc. ▪ I *scrunched* down in the chair. ▪ I spent the night *scrunched* (up) in the back of the car.

2 [+ *obj*] : to tighten the muscles of (your face or nose) — usually + *up* ▪ She *scrunched up* her face/nose.

3 [+ *obj*] **a** : to put (several or many people or things) in a space that is too small — usually used as *(be) scrunched* ▪ The restaurant's tables *are* all *scrunched* together. **b** : to press or squeeze (something) so that it is no longer flat or smooth ▪ I *scrunched* the fabric in my hand. — often + *up* ▪ He *scrunched* [=*crumpled*] *up* the paper and threw it away.

4 *always followed by an adverb or preposition* [*no obj*] : to make the loud sound of something being crushed ▪ The snow was *scrunching* [=(more commonly) *crunching*] under our feet.

scrunch·ie *or* **scrunchy** /ˈskrʌntʃi/ *noun, pl* **scrunch·ies** [*count*] *US* : a piece of elastic in the shape of a circle that is covered with fabric and used to hold hair back in a ponytail, bun, etc. — see picture at GROOMING

¹scru·ple /ˈskruːpəl/ *noun, pl* **scruples** : a feeling that prevents you from doing something that you think is wrong [*count*] — usually plural ▪ They seem to have no *scruples* [=*qualms*] about distorting the truth. ▪ moral/religious *scruples* ▪ a woman without *scruples* [*noncount*] She acted without *scruple*.

²scruple *verb* **scruples; scru·pled; scru·pling** [+ *obj*] *formal* : to be unwilling *to do* something because you think it is improper, morally wrong, etc. — usually used in negative statements ▪ He did not *scruple to lie* about it. [=he was willing to lie about it; lying about it did not bother him]

scru·pu·lous /ˈskruːpjələs/ *adj* [*more* ~; *most* ~]

1 : very careful about doing something correctly ▪ She was always *scrupulous* about her work. ▪ The work requires *scrupulous* attention to detail. ▪ They were *scrupulous* [=*meticulous*] in their testing.

2 : careful about doing what is honest and morally right ▪ Less *scrupulous* companies find ways to evade the law.

— **scru·pu·lous·ly** *adv* ▪ a *scrupulously* clean house

scru·ti·nize *or Brit* **scru·ti·nise** /ˈskruːtəˌnaɪz/ *verb* **-niz·es; -nized; -niz·ing** [+ *obj*] : to examine (something) carefully especially in a critical way ▪ I closely *scrutinized* my opponent's every move. ▪ Her performance was carefully *scrutinized* by her employer.

scru·ti·ny /ˈskruːtəni/ *noun, formal* : the act of carefully examining something especially in a critical way : the act of scrutinizing something [*noncount*] the close/careful *scrutiny* of data ▪ judicial/public/scientific *scrutiny* ▪ I'd never faced that kind of *scrutiny* before. ▪ Because of their past crimes, everything they do now will be subject to *scrutiny*. ▪ Their behavior is ***under scrutiny*** again. = Their behavior has ***come under scrutiny*** again. [=people are examining their behavior in a critical way again] [*singular*] Her opinion is based on a careful *scrutiny* of the text.

scu·ba /ˈskuːbə/ *adj, always used before a noun* : used in scuba diving ▪ *scuba* gear ▪ a *scuba* tank

scuba diving *noun* [*noncount*] : a sport or activity in which you swim underwater using an air tank and a special breathing machine that you strap on your body ▪ Her hobbies include sailing and *scuba diving*. ▪ We ***went scuba diving*** for the first time this summer.

— **scuba dive** *verb* ~ **dives;** ~ **dived;** ~ **div·ing** [*no obj*] ▪ He plans to *scuba dive* while on vacation. — **scuba diver** *noun, pl* ~ **-ers** [*count*] ▪ He's an expert *scuba diver*.

scud /ˈskʌd/ *verb, always followed by an adverb or preposition* **scuds; scud·ded; scud·ding** [*no obj*] *literary* : to move or go quickly ▪ Clouds *scudded* across the sky.

¹scuff /ˈskʌf/ *verb* **scuffs; scuffed; scuff·ing**

1 [+ *obj*] : to make a mark or scratch in the surface of (something) by scraping it ▪ I *scuffed* (up) my new shoes the very first time I wore them.

2 *always followed by an adverb or preposition* [*no obj*] : to walk without lifting your feet : to drag your feet while you walk ▪ She *scuffed* down the hall towards her room.

— **scuffed** *adj* ▪ *scuffed* shoes/boots ▪ an old, *scuffed* leather jacket

²scuff *noun, pl* **scuffs**

1 [*count*] : a mark that is made by scuffing something ▪ I tried to rub the *scuff* (mark) out of my shoe.

2 ***scuffs*** [*plural*] *US* : slippers that are open at the heel ▪ She slid into her *scuffs* and headed into the kitchen.

scuf·fle /ˈskʌfəl/ *verb* **scuf·fles; scuf·fled; scuf·fling** [*no obj*]

1 : to fight briefly and usually not very seriously ▪ Children *scuffled* on the playground. ▪ Protesters and police *scuffled*.

2 *always followed by an adverb or preposition* : to move quickly and with short steps : SCURRY ▪ Small creatures *scuffled* in the underbrush.

— **scuffle** *noun, pl* **scuf·fles** [*count*] ▪ They got in/into a *scuffle*. ▪ A *scuffle* broke out between the players.

¹scull /ˈskʌl/ *noun, pl* **sculls**

1 [*count*] : a long and very narrow boat that is usually rowed by one or two people ▪ a double *scull* [=a scull for two people]

2 ***sculls*** [*plural*] : a race using sculls ▪ He took first place in the single *sculls*.

²scull *verb* **sculls; sculled; scull·ing** [*no obj*] : to row a scull or other small boat ▪ She *sculled* along the river.

— **scull·er** *noun, pl* **-ers** [*count*] ▪ He's one of the top *scullers* in the state. — **scull·ing** *noun* [*noncount*] ▪ She joined the *sculling* team. ▪ He ***went sculling*** early that morning.

scul·lery /ˈskʌləri/ *noun, pl* **-ler·ies** [*count*] *old-fashioned* : a room that is near the kitchen in a large and usually old house and that is used for washing dishes, doing messy kitchen tasks, etc.

sculpt /ˈskʌlpt/ *verb* **sculpts; sculpt·ed; sculpt·ing**

1 : to make (something) by carving or molding clay, stone, etc. : to make (a sculpture) [+ *obj*] She carefully *sculpted* the wood. — often used as *(be) sculpted* ▪ The figures *were sculpted* from wood. ▪ The statue *was sculpted* in ice. — often used figuratively ▪ She carefully *sculpted* the narrative of the story. [*no obj*] The children painted and *sculpted* all morning.

2 [+ *obj*] *chiefly US* : to make (a part of your body) more muscular by doing exercises ▪ *Sculpt* your back with push-ups.

sculpt·ed /ˈskʌlptəd/ *adj*

1 a : carved or molded into a particular shape from wood, stone, clay, etc. ▪ a *sculpted* facade **b** : made into a particular shape by someone or something ▪ her *sculpted* bangs ▪ a wind-*sculpted* rock formation

2 a : having a clear shape ▪ *sculpted* cheekbones **b** *chiefly US* : very muscular and attractive ▪ a lean, *sculpted* athlete/body

sculp·tor /ˈskʌlptɚ/ *noun, pl* **-tors** [*count*] : a person who makes sculptures

sculp·tress /ˈskʌlptrəs/ *noun, pl* **-tress·es** [*count*] *somewhat old-fashioned* : a woman who makes sculptures

sculp·ture /ˈskʌlptʃɚ/ *noun, pl* **-tures**

1 : a piece of art that is made by carving or molding clay, stone, metal, etc. [*count*] a *sculpture* of an elephant ▪ an abstract *sculpture* [*noncount*] an exhibit of African *sculpture* — compare STATUE

2 [*noncount*] : the process or art of carving or molding clay, stone, metal, etc., into a sculpture ▪ She's studying *sculpture*.

— **sculp·tur·al** /ˈskʌlptʃərəl/ *adj* ▪ the *sculptural* arts ▪ a *sculptural* piece

sculp·tured /ˈskʌlptʃɚd/ *adj* : carved or molded into a particular shape from wood, stone, clay, etc. ▪ a *sculptured* [=(more commonly) *sculpted*] facade

scum /ˈskʌm/ *noun, pl* **scums**

1 [*noncount*] : a layer of something unpleasant or unwanted

that forms on top of a liquid ▪ Boil the chicken and use a spoon to remove any *scum* that floats to the surface. ▪ ***pond scum*** [=a layer of algae on top of a pond]
2 *informal* : a dishonest, unkind, or unpleasant person [*noncount*] Ignore him; he's *scum*. ▪ They are the ***scum of the earth***. [=the worst people on the earth] [*count*] He's a complete *scum*.
– **scum·my** /ˈskʌmi/ *adj* **scum·mi·er; -est** [*also more ~; most ~*] ▪ *scummy* water ▪ a *scummy* person

scum·bag /ˈskʌmˌbæg/ *noun, pl* **-bags** [*count*] *slang* : a dishonest, unkind, or unpleasant person ▪ She's a total *scumbag*.

[1]**scup·per** /ˈskʌpɚ/ *verb* **-pers; -pered; -per·ing** [+ *obj*] *Brit* : to cause (something) to stop or fail ▪ The boss *scuppered* [=(*US*) *scuttled*] the plan. ▪ The latest information could *scupper* the peace talks.

[2]**scupper** *noun, pl* **-pers** [*count*] *technical* : a hole in the side of a boat that allows water to drain from the deck

scur·ri·lous /ˈskɚrələs/ *adj* [*more ~; most ~*] *formal* : said or done unfairly to make people have a bad opinion of someone ▪ *scurrilous* attacks on the senator ▪ *scurrilous* rumors
– **scur·ri·lous·ly** *adv*

scur·ry /ˈskɚri/ *verb, always followed by an adverb or preposition* **-ries; -ried; -ry·ing** [*no obj*] : to move quickly and with short steps ▪ She *scurried* off to finish the job. ▪ Mice *scurried* around the house.

scur·vy /ˈskɚvi/ *noun* [*noncount*] : a disease that is caused by not eating enough fruits or vegetables that contain vitamin C

[1]**scut·tle** /ˈskʌtl/ *verb* **scut·tles; scut·tled; scut·tling** [+ *obj*]
1 *US* : to cause (something) to end or fail ▪ He tried to *scuttle* [=(*Brit*) *scupper*] the conference/sale.
2 : to sink (a ship) by putting holes in the bottom or sides
– compare [2]SCUTTLE

[2]**scuttle** *verb, always followed by an adverb or preposition* **scuttles; scuttled; scuttling** [*no obj*] : to move quickly and with short steps ▪ Crabs *scuttled* along the ocean floor. ▪ He *scuttled* away to find his hat. — compare [1]SCUTTLE

[3]**scuttle** *noun, pl* **scuttles** [*count*] : a metal pail for carrying coal

scut·tle·butt /ˈskʌtlˌbʌt/ *noun* [*noncount*] *US, informal* : talk or stories about someone that may not be true ▪ There's some *scuttlebutt* [=there's a rumor] that he might be planning to leave his wife.

scuz·zy /ˈskʌzi/ *adj* **scuz·zi·er; -est** [*also more ~; most ~*] *US slang* : dirty, dishonest, or unpleasant ▪ He is a *scuzzy* guy. ▪ a *scuzzy* bathroom

[1]**scythe** /ˈsaɪð/ *noun, pl* **scythes** [*count*] : a farming tool with a curved blade and long handle that is used for cutting grass, grain, etc.

[2]**scythe** *verb* **scythes; scythed; scyth·ing** : to cut (something, such as grass or grain) with a scythe [+ *obj*] *scything* the wheat — often used figuratively ▪ Her hands *scythed* [=*cut through*] the air. [*no obj*] — usually used figuratively ▪ Her hands *scythed* through the air.

scythe

SD *abbr* South Dakota

SE *abbr* southeast; southeastern

sea /ˈsiː/ *noun, pl* **seas**
1 a : the salt water that covers much of the Earth's surface [*noncount*] We traveled ***by sea***. [=on a ship] — often used with *the* ▪ The ship sank to the bottom of *the sea*. [=*the ocean*] ▪ creatures of *the sea* ▪ He was sailing ***the open sea***. [=sailing far away from land] — often used before another noun ▪ a *sea* voyage ▪ a *sea* animal/creature ▪ the *sea* floor [*plural*] (*literary*) ▪ the uncharted *seas* — see also HIGH SEAS **b** *or* **Sea** [*count*] : a large body of water that is part of the sea or that has land around part or all of it ▪ the Mediterranean *Sea* ▪ the *seas* of the Southern Hemisphere — see color picture on page C7; see also SEVEN SEAS
2 [*count*] : an area of the sea — used to describe the movement of the water in the sea ▪ a calm/rough *sea* — often plural ▪ We sailed in heavy *seas*. [=in very large waves]
3 [*count*] : a large amount or number *of* people or things spread over a large area — usually singular ▪ a *sea of* screaming fans ▪ a golden *sea of* wheat — sometimes used figuratively ▪ a *sea of* sadness
4 *or* **Sea** [*count*] *technical* : one of the large, flat areas on the moon or on Mars ▪ lunar *seas* ▪ the *Sea* of Tranquility
at sea **1** : sailing or traveling on the sea ▪ The navy spent as much time in port as they did *at sea*. ▪ The crew was ***lost at sea***. [=the crew disappeared while traveling on the sea] **2** : confused and not confident ▪ She felt completely *at sea* when she started her new job.
between the devil and the deep blue sea see DEVIL
fish in the sea see [1]FISH
go to sea *somewhat old-fashioned* : to become a sailor ▪ He *went to sea* at a young age.
out to sea : toward or into a part of the ocean that is far away from land ▪ The boat headed *out to sea*. ▪ He fell overboard and was ***swept out to sea***.
put (out) to sea : to leave a port, harbor, etc., and begin traveling on the sea ▪ The ship *put to sea*. ▪ We will dock tonight and *put out to sea* tomorrow.

sea air *noun* [*noncount*] : the air near the sea ▪ He breathed in the *sea air*.

sea anemone *noun, pl* **~ -nes** [*count*] : a small, brightly colored sea animal that looks like a flower and sticks to rocks, coral, etc.

sea·bed /ˈsiːˌbɛd/ *noun*
the seabed : the ground that is at the bottom of the sea

sea·bird /ˈsiːˌbɚd/ *noun, pl* **-birds** [*count*] : a bird that lives on or near the sea and finds food in it ▪ gulls and other *seabirds*

sea·board /ˈsiːˌboɚd/ *noun, pl* **-boards** [*count*] : the part of a country that is along or near the sea ▪ He lives on the eastern *seaboard*. ▪ a *seaboard* city

sea·borne /ˈsiːˌboɚn/ *adj, always used before a noun*
1 : carried in a ship sailing across the sea ▪ *seaborne* cargo
2 : involving or using ships that sail across the sea ▪ *seaborne* trade

sea breeze *noun, pl* **~ breezes** [*count*] : a light wind that blows from the sea toward land

sea captain *noun, pl* **~ -tains** [*count*] : the captain of a ship that travels on the sea

sea change *noun, pl* **~ changes** [*count*] : a big and sudden change — usually singular ▪ There's been a *sea change* in public opinion. ▪ Her attitude has undergone a *sea change* [=her attitude has changed completely] in recent months.

sea·coast /ˈsiːˌkoʊst/ *noun, pl* **-coasts** : the land along the edge of a sea [*count*] a beautiful *seacoast* ▪ the eastern *seacoast* [*noncount*] a stretch of *seacoast* [=*coast, shore, shoreline*] ▪ a *seacoast* [=*coastal*] town

sea dog *noun, pl* **~ dogs** [*count*] *old-fashioned + literary* : an experienced sailor

sea·far·er /ˈsiːˌferɚ/ *noun, pl* **-ers** [*count*] *old-fashioned* : someone who works or travels on a boat or ship on the sea : SAILOR

sea·far·ing /ˈsiːˌferɪŋ/ *noun* [*noncount*] : the activity of traveling on the sea especially while working on a boat or a ship ▪ He began a life of *seafaring*.
– **seafaring** *adj, always used before a noun* ▪ He always tells stories from his *seafaring* days. ▪ a *seafaring* people ▪ a *seafaring* adventure

sea·floor /ˈsiːˌfloɚ/ *noun, pl* **-floors** [*count*] : the ground that is at the bottom of the sea — usually singular ▪ a sunken ship lying on the *seafloor*

sea·food /ˈsiːˌfuːd/ *noun* [*noncount*] : fish and shellfish that live in the ocean and are used for food ▪ I'm allergic to *seafood*. ▪ a *seafood* dish/restaurant

sea·front /ˈsiːˌfrʌnt/ *noun, pl* **-fronts** [*count*] : the part of a town, area, etc., that is near the sea — usually singular ▪ hotels on/along the *seafront* — often used before another noun ▪ *seafront* [=(*US*) *oceanfront*] property

sea·go·ing /ˈsiːˌgowɪŋ/ *adj, always used before a noun* : made or used for traveling on the sea ▪ a *seagoing* [=*oceangoing*] ship/craft/vessel

sea green *noun* [*noncount*] : a bluish-green color like the sea — see color picture on page C2
– **sea–green** *adj* ▪ She has *sea-green* eyes.

sea·gull /ˈsiːˌgʌl/ *noun, pl* **-gulls** [*count*] : a large, common, usually gray and white bird that lives near the ocean : GULL — see color picture on page C9

sea horse *noun, pl* **~ horses** [*count*] : a small fish that has a head that looks like a horse's head and that swims with its head above its body and tail

[1]**seal** /ˈsiːl/ *verb* **seals; sealed; seal·ing**
1 a [+ *obj*] : to close (something) tightly so that air, liquid, etc., cannot get in or out ▪ He *sealed* the jar. — often + *up* ▪ He *sealed up* the cracks in the wall. **b** [+ *obj*] : to close (an envelope, bag, etc.) by sticking or pressing two of its parts to-

S

gether ▪ Would you *seal* this envelope? **c** [*no obj*] : to become closed tightly ▪ Make sure the bag *seals* properly.
2 [+ *obj*] : to cover the surface of (something) with a substance that will protect it ▪ We used a sealant/sealer to *seal* the wood to make it waterproof.
3 [+ *obj*] : to make (something) definite and final ▪ His home run *sealed* the victory. [=his home run made it certain that his team would win] ▪ (*informal*) They finally ***sealed the deal.*** [=they finally reached an agreement and made a deal] ▪ Their decision ***sealed her fate.*** = Once they made their decision, ***her fate was sealed.*** [=their decision made it certain that something bad or unwanted would happen to her]
4 [+ *obj*] : to prevent someone from going into or through (an area or place) ▪ Troops have *sealed* the border between the two countries. ▪ The room/chamber has been *sealed* and no one can enter.
my lips are sealed see LIP
seal in [*phrasal verb*] ***seal (something) in*** or ***seal in (something)*** : to prevent (something that is in something else) from getting out or escaping ▪ He seared the steak to *seal in* the juices.
seal off [*phrasal verb*] ***seal off (something)*** or ***seal (something) off*** : to prevent people from entering or leaving (an area or place) ▪ Police *sealed off* the crime scene.
– **sealed** *adj* ▪ a *sealed* jar

²seal *noun, pl* **seals** [*count*]
1 a : an official mark that is stamped on paper or on a small piece of wax to show that something (such as a document) is genuine and has been officially approved ▪ The paperwork must have a notary's *seal.* **b** : a small piece of stamped wax or a small sticker that is put on a letter or envelope to keep it closed or to show that it has not been opened
2 : a device with a raised design that can be pressed into something (such as paper or wax) to make a seal
3 a : a piece of material (such as rubber) that is used on the lid of a container to keep air, water, etc., out of the container or to show the container has not been opened ▪ a rubber *seal* on the jar ▪ The plastic *seal* on the bottle was broken. **b** : the state of being closed tightly so that no air, water, etc., can pass through ▪ The caulk gives the window an airtight *seal.*
seal of approval : an action or statement that shows approval or official acceptance ▪ The bill has the President's *seal of approval.* ▪ Fans have given the band's new song their *seal of approval.* [=fans like the band's new song]
set the seal on *Brit, formal* : to make (something) final or definite ▪ The goal *set the seal on* their victory. [=the goal sealed/assured their victory]
under seal *law, formal* : having an official seal that prevents the public from seeing or reading it ▪ a document/contract *under seal*
– compare ³SEAL

³seal /ˈsiːl/ *noun, pl* **seals**
1 [*count*] : a large animal that lives in the sea near coasts, has flippers, and eats fish
2 [*noncount*] : the skin of a seal usually used for fur ▪ a jacket made of *seal*
– compare ²SEAL

seal

SEAL /ˈsiːl/ *noun, pl* **SEALs** [*count*] *US* : a soldier in the U.S. Navy who has special training and belongs to a small group that performs dangerous missions ▪ a Navy *SEAL*

sea lane /ˈsiːˌleɪn/ *noun, pl* ~ **lanes** [*count*] : a route that ships regularly take across the sea

seal·ant /ˈsiːlənt/ *noun, pl* **-ants** [*count*] : a substance that is put on a surface in order to protect it from air, water, etc. — called also *sealer*

sea legs *noun* [*plural*] : the ability to walk steadily and not feel sick while traveling on a boat or ship ▪ When I first started sailing, it took me a while to get my *sea legs.*

¹seal·er /ˈsiːlɚ/ *noun, pl* **-ers** [*count*] : SEALANT — compare ²SEALER

²sealer *noun, pl* **-ers** [*count*]
1 : a person who hunts seals
2 : a ship that is used in hunting seals
– compare ¹SEALER

sea level *noun* [*noncount*] : the average height of the sea's surface ✧ Sea level is a standard level that is used when measuring the height or depth of a place on land ▪ The city is a mile above *sea level.* ▪ The valley sits well below *sea level.*

seal·ing /ˈsiːlɪŋ/ *noun* [*noncount*] : the activity of hunting seals

sealing wax *noun* [*noncount*] : a type of wax used especially in the past for making seals on letters and documents

sea lion *noun, pl* ~ **lions** [*count*] : a large seal that lives near coasts in the Pacific Ocean

seam /ˈsiːm/ *noun, pl* **seams** [*count*]
1 a : a line where two pieces of cloth or other material are sewn together ▪ the *seams* of a dress **b** : a line where two pieces of wood, metal, dough, etc., are joined together ▪ the *seams* of a boat
2 *technical* : a layer of coal, rock, etc., that is between two other layers of rock underground ▪ coal *seams* ▪ a rich *seam* of iron ore — sometimes used figuratively to describe a good source of something valuable ▪ The book is a rich *seam of* information about the history of baseball.
be bursting at the seams see ¹BURST
come/fall apart at the seams *informal* : to break into parts or pieces — usually used figuratively to describe someone or something that is in very bad condition ▪ The plan/company is *falling apart at the seams.* ▪ She looks like she's going to *come apart at the seams.*

sea·man /ˈsiːmən/ *noun, pl* **-men** [*count*]
1 : an experienced sailor
2 : a sailor in the U.S. or British Navy or the U.S. Coast Guard who is not an officer

sea·man·ship /ˈsiːmənˌʃɪp/ *noun* [*noncount*] : skill in sailing or operating a ship ▪ The captain shows great *seamanship.*

seamed /ˈsiːmd/ *adj*
1 : having a visible line where two pieces of material are joined together ▪ *seamed* stockings
2 : having deep lines or wrinkles ▪ her *seamed* face

seam·less /ˈsiːmləs/ *adj*
1 : having no seams ▪ a *seamless* rug/boat
2 : moving from one thing to another easily and without any interruptions or problems ▪ The transitions from scene to scene were *seamless.* ▪ a *seamless* transfer of power
3 : perfect and having no flaws or errors ▪ a *seamless* [=*flawless*] performance
– **seam·less·ly** *adv* ▪ The speaker moved from one subject to the next *seamlessly.*

seam·stress /ˈsiːmstrəs/ *noun, pl* **-stress·es** [*count*] : a woman who sews clothes, curtains, etc., as a job

seamy /ˈsiːmi/ *adj* **seam·i·er; -est** [*also more* ~; *most* ~] : of or relating to unpleasant and usually illegal things (such as crime, drugs, etc.) ▪ the *seamy* [=*seedy*] side of the city ▪ She was involved in a *seamy* corruption scandal.

sé·ance /ˈseɪˌɑːns/ *also* **se·ance** *noun, pl* **-anc·es** [*count*] : a meeting where people try to communicate with the spirits of dead people ▪ They're having/holding a *séance.*

sea·plane /ˈsiːˌpleɪn/ *noun, pl* **-planes** [*count*] : an airplane that can take off from and land on water

sea·port /ˈsiːˌpoɚt/ *noun, pl* **-ports** [*count*] : a town or city with a harbor where ships stop to load and unload cargo : PORT ▪ Boston is a major *seaport* in the northeastern U.S.

sea power *noun, pl* ~ **-ers**
1 [*count*] : a country that has a large and powerful navy ▪ Britain was the world's greatest *sea power* at one time.
2 [*noncount*] : the strength and size of a country's navy ▪ a massive increase in *sea power*

sear /ˈsiɚ/ *verb* **sears; seared; sear·ing** [+ *obj*]
1 : to burn and damage the surface of (something) with strong and sudden heat ▪ The tree was *seared* by lightning. ▪ The flames *seared* my skin. — often used figuratively ▪ That image was *seared* [=*burned*] into my memory. [=I cannot forget that image] — see also SEARING
2 *US* : to cook the surface of (something, such as a piece of meat) quickly with intense heat ▪ The steak was *seared* over a hot grill.

¹search /ˈsɚʧ/ *noun, pl* **search·es**
1 : an attempt to find someone or something : the act or process of looking for someone or something [*count*] a thorough/exhaustive/quick *search* ▪ We will begin/launch/con-

duct a *search* for a new manager this week. • A ***search and rescue team*** [=a group of people trained to find and help lost people] was sent out for the hikers. — often + *for* • The *search for* the crew was called off. • Police are continuing their *search for* the killer. [*noncount*] Scientists are ***in search of*** the answer. [=scientists are searching for the answer] — see also STRIP SEARCH

2 [*count*] : an attempt to find information in a database, network, Web site, etc., by using a computer program • I performed a *search* for the file. • I did a Web *search* for restaurants in that area.

²search *verb* **searches; searched; search·ing**

1 a [*no obj*] : to carefully look for someone or something : to try to find someone or something • They haven't found him yet, so they have to keep *searching*. • They *searched* among/through the wreckage (for survivors). • We *searched* [=*looked*] everywhere but we couldn't find the keys. — often + *for* • They're still *searching for* the lost child. — often used figuratively • Scientists are *searching for* a cure. [=are doing research to try to find a cure] • He *searched for* the words to comfort her. [=he tried to think of words that he could say to comfort her] • She *searched for* an answer to his question. **b** [+ *obj*] : to carefully look for someone or something in (something) • Police *searched* the vehicle. — often + *for* • He *searched* his room *for* his wallet. **c** [+ *obj*] : to carefully look through the clothing of (someone) for something that may be hidden • The police *searched* her for concealed weapons. • He was *searched* by the guard before he was allowed to enter the courtroom.

2 : to use a computer to find information in (a database, network, Web site, etc.) [+ *obj*] The software allows you to *search* thousands of sites at the same time. — often + *for* • She *searched* the Web *for* information about the car. [*no obj*] She *searched for* information on the Web.

3 [+ *obj*] : to look carefully at (something) in order to get information about it • He *searched* her face, hoping to see some glimmer of emotion.

search me *informal* — used in speech to say that you do not know the answer to a question • "Why did they do that?" "*Search me*." [=I don't know]

search out [*phrasal verb*] ***search (someone or something) out*** or ***search out (someone or something)*** : to find (someone or something) by carefully looking • She *searched out* the relevant information.

— search·er *noun, pl* **-ers** [*count*] • *Searchers* couldn't find the lost hikers.

search engine *noun, pl* ~ **-gines** [*count*] : a computer program that is used to look for information on the Internet

searching *adj, always used before a noun* : carefully made, done, asked, etc., in order to find out more information about someone or something • a *searching* question • a *searching* gaze/look

— search·ing·ly *adv* • She looked *searchingly* at us.

search·light /ˈsɚʧˌlaɪt/ *noun, pl* **-lights** [*count*] : a very bright light that can be aimed in different directions and that is used to find people or things in the dark

search party *noun, pl* ~ **parties** [*count*] : an organized group of people who are looking for someone or something that is missing • If the hikers don't return by tomorrow, a *search party* will be sent out.

search warrant *noun, pl* ~ **-rants** [*count*] : a legal document that gives the police permission to search a place for evidence

sear·ing /ˈsirɪŋ/ *adj* [*more* ~; *most* ~]

1 : very hot • the *searing* heat of the fire

2 : extremely intense, severe, etc. • She felt a *searing* pain in her foot. • (*chiefly US*) It was a *searing* experience.

3 *of writing or speech* : very strong and critical • a *searing* review • She made/launched a *searing* attack on her political enemies.

— sear·ing·ly *adv* • *searingly* hot food

sea salt *noun* [*noncount*] : a type of salt that is made from seawater and is used in cooking

sea·scape /ˈsiːˌskeɪp/ *noun, pl* **-scapes** [*count*] : a picture or painting of the sea • an artist known for her *seascapes*

sea·shell /ˈsiːˌʃɛl/ *noun, pl* **-shells** [*count*] : the hard, empty shell of a small sea creature (such as a clam) • She collects *seashells*.

sea·shore /ˈsiːˌʃoɚ/ *noun*

the seashore : the land along the edge of the sea that is usually covered with sand or rocks • They built a house near *the seashore*.

— seashore *adj, always used before a noun* • the *seashore* ecosystem

sea·sick /ˈsiːˌsɪk/ *adj* [*more* ~; *most* ~] : feeling sick because of the movement of a boat or ship that you are traveling on • The storm/waves made her *seasick*.

— sea·sick·ness *noun* [*noncount*] • The medicine prevents *seasickness*.

¹sea·side /ˈsiːˌsaɪd/ *adj, always used before a noun* : located in the area near the sea • a *seaside* hotel • a quaint *seaside* town/community

²seaside *noun*

the seaside *chiefly Brit* : the areas or towns along or near the sea • a trip to *the seaside*

¹sea·son /ˈsiːzn̩/ *noun, pl* **-sons**

1 [*count*] : one of the four periods (spring, summer, autumn, and winter) into which the year is commonly divided • Spring is my favorite *season* (of the year). • I enjoy watching the *seasons* change every year.

2 : a particular period of time during the year: such as **a** [*count*] : a period of time when a particular sport is being played • the baseball/football *season* • The team had a good *season* last year. [=the team played well last year] — see also OFF-SEASON, POSTSEASON, PRESEASON **b** : a period of time when a particular event, process, activity, etc., occurs [*count*] These plants have a short growing *season*. • the ***breeding/mating season*** [=the period of time when animals, birds, etc., are mating] • the ***Christmas season*** • (*US*) the ***holiday season*** [=the time from late November through January when several holidays (such as Christmas, Hanukkah, and New Year's Eve) happen] [*noncount*] The article talks about ways to stay healthy during ***flu season***. [=the time of year, and especially the winter, when many people get influenza and other mild illnesses] • June marks the beginning of ***tourist season***. [=the time when many people go to visit places as tourists] • During ***peak season*** [=the time when tourists visit the most], the island is very crowded. **c** [*count, noncount*] : a period of time when people are legally allowed to hunt, fish, etc. • Deer *season* starts next week. • lobster *season* • hunting/fishing *season* — see also OPEN SEASON **d** [*count, noncount*] : the time of the year during which something grows and can be harvested • blueberry *season* **e** : a time of the year during which a particular type of weather usually happens [*count*] the hot/dry/rainy *season* [*noncount*] Monsoon *season* is coming soon. **f** [*singular*] : a time of the year when a new fashion, color, hair style, etc., is popular • This *season's* fashions are very feminine. • Pink is in style this *season*. **g** [*noncount*] : a period of time when a series of new television shows, plays, etc., are being shown or performed • I can't wait until the new (television) *season* starts. • The theater company will be putting on plays by Shakespeare this *season*. • one of the shows in the network's *season* lineup

in season/out of season **1** ✧ When fruits and vegetables are *in season*, it is the time of year when they are being harvested and are easily available. When they are *out of season*, they are not being harvested in a place near you and are more difficult or expensive to get. • Strawberries are *in season*. • They import asparagus when it is *out of season* here. **2** ✧ When animals, fish, etc., are *in season*, it is the time of year when they can be legally hunted, caught, etc. When they are *out of season*, they cannot be legally hunted, caught, etc. • Deer may only be hunted *in season*. • That fish is not *in season*. = That fish is *out of season*.

Season's Greetings — used in writing as a greeting in the time of year when Christmas and several other holidays happen near each other

²season *verb* **-sons; -soned; -son·ing**

1 : to add salt, pepper, spices, etc., to (something) to give it more flavor [+ *obj*] He *seasoned* the stew. [*no obj*] ***Season to taste***. [=add as much seasoning as you like so it tastes good to you]

2 [+ *obj*] : to make (wood) ready for use by slowly drying it • You must *season* the firewood.

sea·son·able /ˈsiːzn̩əbəl/ *adj, of weather* : normal for a certain time of year • We've been having *seasonable* weather. • These temperatures are *seasonable*. — opposite UNSEASONABLE

— sea·son·ably /ˈsiːzn̩əbli/ *adv* • The weather has been *seasonably* cool.

sea·son·al /ˈsiːzn̩əl/ *adj*

1 : happening or needed during a particular time of the year • The rise in gas prices is *seasonal*. • The store hires *seasonal* workers during the holidays.

S

2 : normal for a certain time of year • *seasonal* decorations • I have *seasonal* allergies.
— **sea·son·al·i·ty** /ˌsiːzəˈnæləti/ *noun [noncount] technical* • We tracked the *seasonality* of rainfall levels. — **sea·son·al·ly** *adv* • The restaurant changes its menu *seasonally*.

seasonal affective disorder *noun [noncount] medical* : an illness that makes people feel sad and tired during the winter because there is less light during the day

seasoned *adj*
1 *of food* : having a lot of spices, herbs, salt, pepper, etc., added • a highly *seasoned* stew
2 *always used before a noun* : having a lot of experience doing something • a *seasoned* actor/writer/traveler
3 *of wood* : dry and ready for use • *seasoned* lumber

sea·son·ing /ˈsiːzṇɪŋ/ *noun, pl* **-ings** : a substance (such as salt, pepper, a spice, or an herb) that is used to add flavor to food [*count*] My favorite *seasonings* are black pepper and oregano. [*noncount*] Add some *seasoning* to the marinade. • The soup needs more *seasoning*.

season ticket *noun, pl* ~ **-ets** [*count*] : a ticket for a certain place, activity, or series of events (such as sports contests) that you can use many times during a particular period of time • I have/hold *season tickets* for our team's games. • I get a *season ticket* for the commuter train from my employer. • *season ticket* holders

[1]**seat** /ˈsiːt/ *noun, pl* **-seats**
1 [*count*] : something (such as a chair) that you sit on : a place for sitting • There were *seats* for six people at the table. • an uncomfortable bicycle *seat* • a car with leather *seats* • He used the box as a *seat*. • He couldn't find his *seat* in the concert hall. • The city recently built a new 1,000-*seat* theater. • She booked/reserved a *seat* on the next flight to Rome. • Please ***have/take a seat*** [=please sit down] • The teacher asked us to ***take our seats***. [=sit down in our usual or assigned places] — see picture at BICYCLE; see also BACKSEAT, CATBIRD SEAT
2 a [*count*] : the part of a chair or other piece of furniture that a person sits on • The stool's *seat* is broken. • The chairs have woven *seats*. **b** [*singular*] : the part of a piece of clothing (such as a skirt or pair of pants) that you sit on — + *of* • You have a tear in the *seat of* your pants. **c** [*count*] *somewhat old-fashioned* : the part of the body on which you sit • I fell off the horse and had a sore *seat* [=*bottom*] for weeks.
3 [*count*] : an official position within an organization and the right to be present when that organization meets • The Democrats gained two more *seats* in the last election. • She won a Senate *seat*. • a *seat* on the federal court • a *seat* on the board • (*chiefly Brit*) He ***took his seat***[=began his official duties as a member] in Parliament.
4 [*singular*] **a** : a place or area where a particular activity, function, etc., occurs — + *of* • The university has been a *seat of* learning since the Middle Ages. • the part of the brain that is the *seat of* reasoning **b** : a place (such as a city) where the people who run a government, religion, etc., are based — + *of* • the *seat of* government/power • The Vatican is the *seat of* the Roman Catholic Church. — see also COUNTY SEAT
by the seat of your pants : by using your own judgment and feelings to deal with each new problem or task without planning, preparation, or help from others • He was running the company *by the seat of his pants*. • We were ***flying by the seat of our pants*** when we started our business. — see also SEAT-OF-THE-PANTS
get/put bums on seats see [5]BUM
in the driver's seat see DRIVER
on the edge of your seat see [1]EDGE

[2]**seat** *verb* **seats; seat·ed; seat·ing** [+ *obj*]
1 : to give (a person) a place to sit • I could *seat* you here if you wish. — often used as *(be) seated* • Please *be seated*. [=please sit down] • She *was seated* in the front row.
2 : to have enough seats for (a certain number of people) • The restaurant *seats* 120 (people). • The plans call for a stadium *seating* 30,000 people.

seat belt *noun, pl* ~ **belts** [*count*] : a strap on a vehicle's seat that holds a person in the seat if there is an accident • Fasten your *seat belt*. — see picture at CAR

seat·er /ˈsiːtə/ *noun, pl* **-ers** [*count*] : something (such as a vehicle) that has a specified number of seats — used in combination • Our couch is a three-*seater*. — see also TWO-SEATER

seat·ing /ˈsiːtɪŋ/ *noun, pl* **-ings**
1 [*noncount*] : seats or places to sit • There won't be enough *seating* for everyone. • The auditorium has *seating* for 400. • There is additional *seating* on the deck. • The auditorium has a *seating* capacity of 400. • Here is the ***seating arrangement/plan*** [=a plan that shows where people should sit] for our wedding reception.
2 [*count*] : a scheduled time when people are allowed into a performance, a meal, etc. • There are two *seatings* for tea. • We bought tickets for the 5:30 *seating* of the show.

seat·mate /ˈsiːtˌmeɪt/ *noun, pl* **-mates** [*count*] *US* : a person who sits next to you in a bus, airplane, etc. • My *seatmate* on the flight to Rome was very friendly.

seat–of–the–pants *adj, always used before a noun, chiefly US* : done or made by using your own judgment and feelings without planning, preparation, or help from others • It was a *seat-of-the-pants* decision.

sea turtle *noun, pl* ~ **turtles** [*count*] : a type of large turtle that lives in the sea

sea urchin *noun, pl* ~ **-chins** [*count*] : a small sea animal that lives on the ocean floor and is covered in sharp spines

sea·wall /ˈsiːˌwɑːl/ *noun, pl* **-walls** [*count*] : a wall built to keep sea waves from coming up onto land

sea·ward /ˈsiːwəd/ *also* **sea·wards** /ˈsiːwədz/ *adv* : toward the sea • We drifted *seaward*. • She gazed *seaward*.
— **seaward** *adj, always used before a noun* • the *seaward* slope of the mountain

sea·wa·ter /ˈsiːˌwɑːtə/ *noun [noncount]* : water in or from the sea

sea·weed /ˈsiːˌwiːd/ *noun, pl* **-weeds** [*count, noncount*] : a type of plant that grows in the sea

sea·wor·thy /ˈsiːˌwəði/ *adj [more ~; most ~]* : fit or safe to travel on the sea • a *seaworthy* ship — compare AIRWORTHY, ROADWORTHY
— **sea·wor·thi·ness** /ˈsiːˌwəðinəs/ *noun [noncount]* • He doubted the ship's *seaworthiness*.

se·ba·ceous /sɪˈbeɪʃəs/ *adj, always used before a noun, biology* : producing an oily substance in the body • *sebaceous* glands

[1]**sec** *abbr* **1** second, seconds • 2 min, 45 *sec* **2** section • *Sec* 2, Row K, Seat 45 **3 Sec.** secretary • *Sec.* of Internal Affairs

[2]**sec** /ˈsɛk/ *noun [singular] informal* : a very brief time : SECOND • Wait just a *sec*.

SEC *abbr, US* Securities and Exchange Commission ✧ The Securities and Exchange Commission is a part of the U.S. federal government that enforces laws about securities like stocks.

sec·a·teurs /ˌsɛkəˈtəz/ *noun [plural] Brit* : PRUNING SHEARS

se·cede /sɪˈsiːd/ *verb* **-cedes; -ced·ed; -ced·ing** [*no obj*] : to separate from a nation or state and become independent • South Carolina *seceded* from the Union in 1860.

se·ces·sion /sɪˈsɛʃən/ *noun, pl* **-sions** [*count*] : the act of separating from a nation or state and becoming independent • the *secession* of the Southern states

se·ces·sion·ist /sɪˈsɛʃənɪst/ *noun, pl* **-ists** [*count*] : a person who thinks that a nation, state, etc., should separate from another and become independent

se·clude /sɪˈkluːd/ *verb* **-cludes; -clud·ed; -clud·ing** [+ *obj*] : to keep (someone) away from other people • He *secluded* himself in his room to study for the exam.

secluded *adj [more ~; most ~]*
1 : hidden from view : private and not used or seen by many people • a *secluded* beach • We looked for a *secluded* spot in the park to have our picnic.
2 : placed apart from other people • She led a *secluded* [=*solitary*] life on the family farm.

se·clu·sion /sɪˈkluːʒən/ *noun [noncount]*
1 : the act of placing or keeping someone away from other people : the act of secluding someone • the *seclusion* of women that occurs in some countries
2 : the state of being away from other people : a secluded state or condition • I enjoyed the *seclusion* of the island. • After his wife died he lived ***in seclusion***. [=he lived by himself and kept away from other people]

[1]**sec·ond** /ˈsɛkənd/ *adj, always used before a noun*
1 a : occupying the number two position in a series • We sat in the *second* row. • the *second* house on the left • the author's *second* novel • B is the *second* letter in the alphabet. • That's the *second* time I've seen him today. • The office is on the ***second floor***. [=(*US*) the floor just above the lowest floor; (*Brit*) the floor that is two floors above the lowest floor] **b** : next to the first in importance or rank • Chocolate is my first choice; vanilla is my *second* choice. • I won *second* prize.

c : another of the same kind ▪ They needed a *second* car. [=they needed two cars] ▪ The chair needs a *second* coat of paint. ▪ The word has a *second* meaning. [=the word has two meanings] ▪ She took a *second* helping [=she took another serving] of carrots. ▪ English as a ***second language*** [=a language that you learn in addition to the language you first learned when you were a young child] ▪ I could have fired him, but I gave him a ***second chance*** [=I gave him another chance] ▪ I recommend you get a ***second opinion*** [=advice from another doctor to make sure the first advice is right] ▪ He passed her by without (giving her) a ***second glance*** [=he didn't notice her] ▪ She liked the house enough to give it a ***second look*** [=she looked at the house again]

2 — used to refer to the forward gear or speed of a vehicle that is next to the lowest forward gear ▪ You should put the car in *second* gear when you go up the hill. — sometimes used figuratively ▪ The movie never really gets out of *second* gear. ▪ The program is shifting into *second* gear now that all the proposals have been approved.

3 : having or playing the part in a group of instruments that is one level lower than the first ▪ She plays *second* violin in the city orchestra. — see also *play second fiddle* at [1]FIDDLE

every second — used to indicate how often a repeated activity happens or is done ▪ We elect a mayor *every second* year. [=in alternate years; every other year]

second only to : only less important than (something or someone) ▪ Rice is *second only to* corn as the state's major crop.

second to none see [1]NONE

[2]**second** *adv*

1 : in a position that only comes after one other in time, order, or importance ▪ The university ranks *second* in the nation. ▪ This is the *second* most common error made by job applicants. ▪ Milan is Italy's *second* largest city. ▪ I placed/finished *second* in the race. = (*US*) I came in *second* in the race. = (*Brit*) I came *second* in the race. ▪ The misspelled word is in the ***second to last*** paragraph. [=in the paragraph that comes just before the last one] — see also SECOND BEST

2 — used to introduce a statement that is the second in a series of statements ▪ It's pointless to plan a trip—first, we can't afford one, and *second*, we don't have time to take one.

[3]**second** *noun, pl* **-onds**

1 [*singular*] : something that is second : the second thing in a series ▪ His birthday is on the *second* of June. [=on June 2] ▪ The win was his *second* of the year. — see also *a close second* at [2]CLOSE

2 seconds [*plural*] : another serving of food taken after you are finished with the first serving ▪ Who wants *seconds*?

3 [*singular*] : a statement made to support or approve a motion in a meeting ▪ There's been a motion to vote on the proposal. Do I hear a *second*?

4 [*count*] : a product that is cheaper than normal because it is damaged or imperfect — usually plural ▪ These curtains are *seconds*. ▪ The store sells factory *seconds*.

5 [*noncount*] : the forward gear or speed in a vehicle that is one speed higher than first gear ▪ Put the car/bicycle in *second* when you go up the hill.

6 [*count*] *Brit* : an undergraduate degree of the second highest level from a British university ▪ He took/received a *second* in history.

7 [*noncount*] *baseball* : SECOND BASE ▪ He stole *second*. ▪ There's a runner on *second*.

8 [*count*] : a person whose job is to help someone who is fighting in a boxing match or duel

– compare [4]SECOND

[4]**second** *noun, pl* **-onds** [*count*]

1 a : a unit of time that is equal to ¹⁄₆₀ of a minute ▪ There was a delay of several *seconds*. ▪ a 30-*second* TV commercial ▪ phone lines transmitting data at 1,200 bits per *second* ▪ The sound came on for a *second* or two and then went off again. **b** *informal* : a very brief period of time ▪ For a *second* (there) I thought you were kidding. ▪ This will (just/only) take a *second*. ▪ I'll be back in a *second*. [=I'll be back very soon] ▪ I can't come ***right this second*** [=at this very moment] ▪ "Did you enjoy her visit?" "I enjoyed ***every second***" [=I enjoyed the entire visit] ▪ I expect her back ***any second now*** [=very soon] ▪ It could happen ***at any second*** [=at any time] — see also SPLIT SECOND

2 *technical* : one of 60 equal parts into which a minute can be divided for measuring angles ▪ 40 degrees, 27 minutes, and 45 *seconds*

just a second see [2]JUST

just this second see [2]JUST

– compare [3]SECOND

[5]**second** *verb* **sec·onds; sec·ond·ed; sec·ond·ing** [+ *obj*]

1 a : to approve (something, such as a motion) during a meeting so that discussion or voting can begin ▪ I would like to *second* the motion to adjourn. **b** *informal* : to agree with (a suggestion or statement) ▪ "Let's call it a day." "I'll *second* that."

2 /sɪˈkɑːnd/ *Brit* : to move (someone) from a regular job to a different place, department, etc., for a short period of time — usually used as *(be) seconded* ▪ She *was seconded* to the Birmingham office for six months.

– **sec·ond·er** *noun, pl* **-ers** [*count*] ▪ Nomination forms must be signed by a nominator and a *seconder*.

[1]**sec·ond·ary** /ˈsɛkənˌderi, *Brit* ˈsɛkəndri/ *adj*

1 : not as important or valuable as something else ▪ Winning is *secondary*—we play for the fun of the sport. ▪ There are some *secondary* issues/considerations which must be taken into account as well. ▪ *secondary* goals ▪ I want a car that's reliable; the color is of *secondary* importance. ▪ The *secondary* roads are indicated on the map with a green line. — often + *to* ▪ In some children's books, the text is *secondary to* the illustrations. — compare PRIMARY, TERTIARY

2 : of or relating to education of students who have completed primary school ▪ This job requires at least a *secondary* [=high school] education. ▪ a *secondary* English textbook — see also SECONDARY SCHOOL

3 : caused by or coming from something else ▪ a *secondary* infection ▪ Better gas mileage is a *secondary* benefit of reduced speed limits. ▪ The biography uses mostly *secondary* sources. [=information that did not come from original/primary sources but came from research done by others]

– **sec·ond·ari·ly** /ˌsɛkənˈderəli/ *adv* ▪ The building planners are only *secondarily* concerned with accessibility.

[2]**secondary** *noun, pl* **-aries** [*count*] *American football* : the players on the defense who are positioned away from the line of scrimmage and who mainly try to stop forward passes by the offense ▪ The team has a strong *secondary*.

secondary color *noun, pl* ~ **-ors** [*count*] : a color (such as green, orange, or purple) that is formed by mixing two primary colors

secondary school *noun, pl* ~ **schools** [*count*]

1 *US* : HIGH SCHOOL 1 ▪ a job that requires at least a *secondary school* education

2 *Brit* : a school for children between the ages of 11 and 16 or 18 — compare PRIMARY SCHOOL

second banana *noun, pl* ~ **-nanas** [*count*] *US, informal* : a someone who is not as important or powerful as another person ▪ an actor who always plays (the) *second banana* to some big star — compare TOP BANANA

second base *noun* [*singular*] *baseball* : the base that must be touched second by a base runner ▪ He slid into *second base*.; *also* : the position of the player who defends the area near second base ▪ He used to play *second base* for the Red Sox. — compare FIRST BASE, HOME PLATE, THIRD BASE

second baseman *noun, pl* ~ **-men** [*count*] *baseball* : the player who defends the area near second base : the fielder who plays second base

second best *noun* [*noncount*] : something that is good but not the best ▪ He won't settle for *second best*.

come off second best *chiefly Brit* : to finish in second place : to fail to win ▪ Our team *came off second best*.

– **sec·ond–best** /ˌsɛkəndˈbest/ *adj, always used before a noun* ▪ We were seated at the *second-best* table. ▪ He was considered the team's *second-best* pitcher.

second childhood *noun* [*noncount*] : a time when an old person whose mind is failing begins to behave like a child again ▪ an old man going through his *second childhood*

second class *noun*

1 [*noncount*] **a** : a level of service on a train, ship, etc., that is just below first class ▪ The airline offers special services for travelers in first and *second class*. **b** : a class of mail in the U.S. that includes newspapers, magazines, etc. **c** : a class of mail in the UK that costs less and takes longer to arrive than first class

2 [*singular*] *Brit* : an undergraduate degree of the second highest level given by a British university ▪ She got an upper *second class* in English at Oxford.

second–class *adj*

1 : of or relating to second class ▪ a *second-class* seat ▪ *second-class* postage

S

2 a : not given the same rights or treatment as the rest of the people in a society • They complained that they were being treated like ***second-class citizens***. [=being treated as if they were less important and deserving of respect than other people] **b** : not of the best quality • They received *second-class* treatment. • a *second-class* mind/intellect
– second–class *adv* • She always travels *second-class*.

Second Coming *noun*
the Second Coming : the time when Christians believe that Jesus Christ will return to judge humanity at the end of the world

second cousin *noun, pl* **~ -sins** [*count*] : a child of your parent's cousin • Susan is my *second cousin*. — compare FIRST COUSIN

second–degree *adj, always used before a noun*
1 *US, of a crime* : of a level of seriousness that is less than first-degree : deserving punishment but not the most severe punishment • *second-degree* assault/murder
2 : causing a moderate level of injury • He received/suffered *second-degree* burns. • a *second-degree* concussion — compare FIRST-DEGREE, THIRD-DEGREE
– second degree *noun* [*singular*] *US* • He was charged with assault in the *second degree*.

sec•ond–guess /ˌsɛkəndˈgɛs/ *verb* **-guess•es; -guessed; -guess•ing** [+ *obj*]
1 *US* : to criticize or question the actions or decisions of someone • Don't *second-guess* the umpire. = Don't *second-guess* the umpire's decision.
2 : to try to guess or predict what (someone or something) will do • He gave up trying to *second-guess* the stock market.
– sec•ond–guess•er *noun, pl* **-ers** [*count*] *chiefly US* • He received criticism from *second-guessers* in the media.

sec•ond•hand /ˈsɛkəndˈhænd/ *adj*
1 a : having had a previous owner : USED • He buys *secondhand* CDs. • a dealer in *secondhand* furniture **b** : buying or selling things that have already been owned or used • He's always haunting the *secondhand* shops for bargains. • a *secondhand* bookstore
2 : not original : taken from someone who was not directly involved • *secondhand* information/reports — compare FIRSTHAND
– secondhand *adv* • She buys all her clothes *secondhand*. • I heard about the news *secondhand*.

second hand *noun, pl* **~ hands** [*count*] : the hand that marks the seconds on a watch or clock — compare HOUR HAND, MINUTE HAND

secondhand smoke *noun* [*noncount*] : smoke from a cigarette, cigar, pipe, etc., that can be inhaled by people who are near the person who is smoking

second–in–command *noun, pl* **seconds–in–command** [*count*] : someone who is ranked second in a group or organization • He served as *second-in-command* to the sheriff. • the police chief's *second-in-command*

second lieutenant *noun, pl* **~ -ants** [*count*] : an officer in the U.S. Army, Air Force, or Marine Corps who ranks below a first lieutenant

sec•ond•ly /ˈsɛkəndli/ *adv* — used to introduce a statement that is the second statement in a series • I'm moving because, for one thing, my apartment is too small, and, *secondly*, I found one closer to my job.— compare FIRSTLY, THIRDLY

se•cond•ment /sɪˈkɑːndmənt/ *noun* [*noncount*] *Brit* : a period of time when you are away from your regular job while you do another job • She returned to London after her *secondment* in/to Birmingham.

S

second nature *noun* [*noncount*] : something you can do easily or without much thought because you have done it many times before • After a while, using the gearshift becomes *second nature*.

second person *noun* [*noncount*]
1 *grammar* : a set of words or forms (such as pronouns or verb forms) that refer to the person that the speaker or writer is addressing — often used before another noun • "You" is the *second person* singular and plural pronoun in English.
2 : a writing style that uses second person pronouns and verbs • The author begins the story in the *second person* with the sentence "You open the door and step into the room." — compare FIRST PERSON, THIRD PERSON

sec•ond–rate /ˌsɛkəndˈreɪt/ *adj* : not very good : of ordinary or inferior quality • a *second-rate* education • The meal was only *second-rate*.

sec•ond–string /ˌsɛkəndˈstrɪŋ/ *adj, always used before a noun, chiefly US, sports* : not used as one of the regular players on a team • a *second-string* quarterback — compare FIRST-STRING
– second stringer *noun, pl* **~ -ers** [*count*] *chiefly US*

second thought *noun, pl* **~ thoughts** [*count*] : a feeling of guilt, doubt, worry, etc., that you have after you have decided to do something or after something has happened • After she agreed to lend him the money, she had *second thoughts*. • She was having *second thoughts* about getting married. • They throw away perfectly good food ***without (so much as) a second thought***. [=without worrying about it] • Don't ***give a second thought to*** [=don't worry about] that broken vase. • He hardly ***gave it a second thought***.
on second thought (*US*) *or Brit* ***on second thoughts*** : after thinking about something again • *On second thought*, I think I'll go after all.

second wind *noun* [*singular*] : a feeling of new energy that allows you to continue to do something after you had begun to feel tired • The sight of the finish line gave the runners a *second wind*. • He suddenly got his *second wind* and was able to complete the project on time.

se•cre•cy /ˈsiːkrəsi/ *noun* [*noncount*]
1 : the act of keeping information secret • She ***swore him to secrecy***. [=made him promise to keep a secret]
2 : the quality or state of being hidden or secret • The project was cloaked/shrouded in *secrecy*. [=the true nature of the project was kept secret]

[1]**se•cret** /ˈsiːkrət/ *adj*
1 : kept hidden from others : known to only a few people • the robbers' *secret* hideout • a *secret* compartment/passage/cave • a *secret* formula/ingredient • Her *secret* wish is to become a senator. • The message was written in *secret* code. • I don't know the *secret* password. • He was sent on a *secret* mission. • They engaged in *secret* negotiations with the enemy. • She tried to keep her marriage *secret*. • She has a ***secret admirer***. [=someone admires her but she does not know who it is] • She has a ***secret lover***. [=a lover that no one else knows about]— see also SECRET AGENT, SECRET POLICE, SECRET SERVICE, TOP SECRET
2 [*more ~; most ~*] : keeping information hidden from others : SECRETIVE • They've been very *secret* about their plans.
– se•cret•ly *adv* • She wrote to him *secretly*. • He was *secretly* delighted by their decision. • They got married *secretly*.

[2]**secret** *noun, pl* **-crets** [*count*]
1 : a fact or piece of information that is kept hidden from other people • Don't tell him about the party—it's a *secret*. • I'm going to tell you a *secret*, but you have to promise not to tell anyone else. • They're getting married. The *secret* is out. [=everyone now knows that they're getting married] • He knows how to ***keep a secret***. [=if you tell him a secret he won't tell it to anyone else] • This wine may be Italy's ***best-kept secret***. [=something very good that not many people know about] • ***It's no secret*** [=many people know] that he has connections to the Mafia. • I'll ***let you in on a (little) secret***. [=I'll tell you a secret] • The report disclosed the company's ***dirty little secret***. [=something bad that the company does not want people to know] • Don't worry. ***Your secret is safe with me***. [=I won't tell anyone your secret]— see also TRADE SECRET
2 : a special or unusual way of doing something to achieve a good result • You always look great. What's your *secret*? • She shared her beauty *secrets* with the group. • The *secret* to/of a good sauce is the base. • What is the ***secret to your success***? [=why are you so successful?]
3 : something that cannot be explained • the *secrets* of the universe • one of nature's greatest *secrets*
in secret : in a private place or manner • They met *in secret*. [=*secretly*]
make no secret of : to show or express (something) openly : to not try to hide (something) • She *made no secret of* her dislike for him.

secret agent *noun, pl* **~ agents** [*count*] : a person who tries to get secret information about another country, government, etc. • He was accused of being a *secret agent* for a foreign government.

sec•re•tar•i•at /ˌsɛkrəˈterijət/ *noun, pl* **-ats** [*count*] : a department in a governmental organization that is headed by a secretary or a secretary-general • the United Nations *secretariat*

sec•re•tary /ˈsɛkrəˌteri, *Brit* ˈsɛkrətri/ *noun, pl* **-tar•ies** [*count*]
1 : a person whose job is to handle records, letters, etc., for another person in an office • You can set up an appointment

with my *secretary*. ▪ He works as a legal *secretary*. ▪ She is our ***executive/administrative secretary*** [=a secretary with some management duties] — see also PRESS SECRETARY

2 : a person in a club or other organization who is in charge of keeping letters and records ▪ He was the club's *secretary*.

3 a *US* : an official who is selected by the President and is in charge of a particular department of the government ▪ the *Secretary* of Commerce ▪ the Treasury *Secretary* **b** *Brit* : a government official who helps a minister, an ambassador, etc. ▪ He is a junior *secretary* at the embassy. **c** *Brit* : SECRETARY OF STATE 2 — see also FOREIGN SECRETARY

– sec·re·tar·i·al /ˌsɛkrəˈterijəl/ *adj* ▪ *secretarial* duties

Secretary–General *noun, pl* **Secretaries–General** [*count*] : an official who is in charge of an organization ▪ the *Secretary-General* of the United Nations

Secretary of State *noun, pl* **Secretaries of State** [*count*]

1 : the head of the U.S. government department that is in charge of how the country relates to and deals with foreign countries ▪ The President appointed the *Secretary of State*.

2 : the head of one of several important departments of the British government ▪ the *Secretary of State* for Home Affairs

¹se·crete /sɪˈkriːt/ *verb* **-cretes; -cret·ed; -cret·ing** [+ *obj*] *biology* : to produce and give off (a liquid) ▪ glands that *secrete* saliva — compare ²SECRETE

²secrete *verb* **-cretes; -creted; -creting** [+ *obj*] *somewhat formal* : to put (something) in a hidden place ▪ He *secreted* [=*hid*] the money under the mattress. — compare ¹SECRETE

se·cre·tion /sɪˈkriːʃən/ *noun, pl* **-tions** *biology*

1 [*noncount*] : the production of a liquid by part of a plant or animal ▪ the *secretion* of stomach acids ▪ insulin *secretion*

2 [*count*] : a substance produced and given off by a plant or animal part ▪ gastric *secretions* ▪ root *secretions* that repel insects

se·cre·tive /ˈsiːkrətɪv/ *adj* [*more* ~; *most* ~] : not letting people see or know what you are doing or thinking : tending to act in secret ▪ a highly *secretive* organization ▪ He's very *secretive* about his work.

– se·cre·tive·ness *noun* [*noncount*]

secret police *noun*

the secret police : a police organization that is run by a government and that operates in a secret way to control the actions of people who oppose the government

secret service *noun*

1 ***the Secret Service*** : a U.S. government department in charge of protecting elected leaders of the U.S. and visiting leaders

2 [*singular*] : a government department that protects a country's secrets and obtains secret information about other countries ▪ the British *secret service*

sect /ˈsɛkt/ *noun, pl* **sects** [*count*]

1 : a religious group that is a smaller part of a larger group and whose members all share similar beliefs ▪ Buddhist *sects* ▪ a *sect* of Judaism

2 : a religious or political group that is connected to a larger group but that has beliefs that differ greatly from those of the main group ▪ a fundamentalist Christian *sect* ▪ radical Muslim *sects*

sec·tar·i·an /sɛkˈterijən/ *adj* : relating to religious or political sects and the differences between them ▪ *sectarian* movements ▪ The country was split along *sectarian* lines. ▪ *sectarian* violence

– sec·tar·i·an·ism /sɛkˈterijəˌnɪzəm/ *noun* [*noncount*] ▪ The country was split by *sectarianism*.

¹sec·tion /ˈsɛkʃən/ *noun, pl* **-tions**

1 [*count*] **a** : one of the parts that form something ▪ the upper *section* of the bridge ▪ This *section* of the road is closed. **b** : a particular area that is part of a larger place ▪ the frozen food *section* in the supermarket ▪ the library's reference *section* ▪ the Crown Heights *section* of Brooklyn ▪ Do you want to sit in the nonsmoking *section*? **c** : a part of a newspaper, play, book, etc. ▪ Can I see the sports *section* (of the newspaper)? ▪ The dictionary includes a *section* on signs and symbols. ▪ *Section* 1123 of the bankruptcy code **d** : a part of a group of people ▪ ads that target one *section* of the population ▪ He had his own ***cheering section*** in the stands. [=his own group of people who were cheering for him]

2 [*count*] : one of several parts made so that something can be put together easily ▪ The siding comes in five-foot *sections*.

3 [*count*] : a part of a band or orchestra that has instruments of a particular kind ▪ the brass *section* ▪ the rhythm *section*

4 [*count*] *US* : one of the parts of an orange, grapefruit, or similar fruit that can be easily separated from each other ▪ a *section* of grapefruit — see color picture on page C5

5 [*count*] *medical* : a layer cut from a part of the body ▪ He examined tissue *sections* of the brain under a microscope. — see also CESAREAN SECTION

6 a [*noncount*] : a diagram showing how something would look if it was cut from the top to the bottom : CROSS SECTION ▪ a drawing of a ship ***in section*** **b** [*count*] *mathematics* : a shape that is made when a line cuts through a solid figure ▪ a conical *section*

7 [*count*] *US* : a piece of land that is one mile wide and one mile long

²section *verb* **-tions; -tioned; -tion·ing** [+ *obj*]

1 : to divide (something) into parts ▪ Peel and *section* the orange. ▪ *Section* the chicken and marinate the parts.

2 *Brit* : to officially send (a mentally ill person) to a psychiatric hospital ▪ She was *sectioned* by the judge.

section off [*phrasal verb*] ***section (something) off or section off (something)*** : to separate (an area) from a larger area ▪ Part of the field was *sectioned off* for parking.

¹sec·tion·al /ˈsɛkʃənl/ *adj*

1 : showing how something would look if it were cut from the top to the bottom ▪ a *sectional* drawing/view of a ship

2 : concerned only with one part of a group or community ▪ *sectional* [=(more commonly) *local*] interests ▪ *sectional* conflict

3 : made up of sections that can be put together or taken apart easily ▪ *sectional* shelving

²sectional *noun, pl* **-als** [*count*] *US* : a type of long seat (called a sofa) that has three or more separate sections ▪ a leather *sectional* — called also *sectional sofa*

sec·tion·al·ism /ˈsɛkʃənəˌlɪzəm/ *noun* [*noncount*] *chiefly US* : a tendency to be more concerned with the interests of your particular group or region than with the problems and interests of the larger group, country, etc. ▪ a nation divided by *sectionalism*

sec·tor /ˈsɛktɚ/ *noun, pl* **-tors** [*count*]

1 : an area of an economy : a part of an economy that includes certain kinds of jobs ▪ the industrial/agricultural/service *sector* — see also PRIVATE SECTOR, PUBLIC SECTOR

2 : an area for which someone (such as a military commander) is responsible ▪ He was assigned to the northern *sector*.

3 *computers* : one of the parts that a computer disk is divided into ▪ Data is stored on the disk in 512-byte *sectors*.

4 *geometry* : an area in a circle that lies between two straight lines drawn from the center of the circle to the edge of the circle ▪ a 90-degree *sector*

sec·u·lar /ˈsɛkjəlɚ/ *adj*

1 a [*more* ~; *most* ~] : not spiritual : of or relating to the physical world and not the spiritual world ▪ *secular* concerns **b** : not religious ▪ *secular* music ▪ a *secular* society ▪ Both *secular* and religious institutions can apply for the funds. **c** : of, relating to, or controlled by the government rather than by the church : CIVIL ▪ *secular* courts

2 — used to describe a member of the clergy who lives in ordinary society and not in a monastery ▪ a *secular* priest

secular humanism *noun* [*noncount*] *chiefly US* : HUMANISM; *especially* : humanism viewed as a system of values and beliefs that are opposed to the values and beliefs of traditional religions

– secular humanist *noun, pl* **~ -ists** [*count*]

sec·u·lar·ism /ˈsɛkjələˌrɪzəm/ *noun* [*noncount*] : the belief that religion should not play a role in government, education, or other public parts of society

– sec·u·lar·ist /ˈsɛkjələrɪst/ *noun, pl* **-ists** [*count*]

– secularist *or* **sec·u·lar·is·tic** /ˌsɛkjələˈrɪstɪk/ *adj* [*more* ~; *most* ~] ▪ the more *secularist* wing of the party ▪ a *secularistic* view

sec·u·lar·ize *also Brit* **sec·u·lar·ise** /ˈsɛkjələˌraɪz/ *verb* **-iz·es; -ized; -iz·ing** [+ *obj*]

1 : to take religion out of (something) : to make (something) secular ▪ attempts to *secularize* the government ▪ a *secularized* society

2 : to transfer the ownership or control of (something) from a religious organization to the state ▪ The government *secularized* the hospital.

– sec·u·lar·i·za·tion *also Brit* **sec·u·lar·i·sa·tion** /ˌsɛkjələrəˈzeɪʃən, *Brit* ˌsɛkjəˌlaɪˈzeɪʃən/ *noun* [*noncount*]

¹se·cure /sɪˈkjɚ/ *adj* **se·cur·er; -est** [*or more* ~; *most* ~]

1 a : protected from danger or harm ▪ We need to make our network more *secure* against attacks by hackers. ▪ The children were safe and *secure* in their beds. ▪ A safe is provided

S

to keep your valuables *secure* from potential thieves. **b :** providing protection from danger or harm • You should store your valuables in a *secure* place. • How *secure* is your front door? **c :** guarded so that no one can enter or leave without approval • You are now entering a *secure* area. • (*chiefly Brit*) a ***secure unit*** for young offenders

2 : feeling safe and free from worries or doubt : CONFIDENT • I'm feeling *secure* about my place in the company. • I was ***secure in the belief/knowledge*** that I had done all I could. [=I felt confident because I believed/knew that I had done all I could] • They are ***financially secure***. [=they have enough money to live on; they do not have to worry about money] — opposite INSECURE

3 a : firmly attached • Is that shelf *secure*? • Make sure the door is *secure*. [=shut tightly] **b :** in a firm position that prevents unwanted movement • a *secure* grip • *secure* footing **c :** not in danger of being lost or taken away • The company has established a *secure* foothold in the market. • He believes his job is *secure*. • a *secure* investment • They didn't begin to celebrate until they knew their victory was *secure*.

4 : known only to certain people • You can access your bank account online using a *secure* [=*secret*] password.

[2]**secure** *verb* **-cures; -cured; -cur·ing** [+ *obj*] *somewhat formal*

1 a : to make (something) safe by guarding or protecting it • Police *secured* the building. • We must *secure* the country's borders. **b :** to put (something) in a place or position so that it will not move • *Secure* your belongings under the seat. • *secure* a child safety seat • The metal rod is *secured* (in place) with a pin. • The seat is *secured* to the base by three screws.

2 : to make (something) certain • She scored a goal to *secure* the team's victory. • She *secured* the zoo's future with a handsome bequest.

3 : to guarantee that (an amount owed) will be paid usually by offering your property if you cannot pay • He *secured* a loan using his house as collateral.

4 : to get (something) by using effort : OBTAIN • We *secured* permission to visit the school. • I *secured* a place in the final round. • He *secured* a position with the insurance company. • He *secured* her release.

se·cure·ly /sɪˈkjɚli/ *adv* [*more ~; most ~*]

1 : not loosely : so as not to move or be removed : FIRMLY • He made sure the balloon was *securely* fastened to his little girl's wrist. • Tie the boat *securely* to the dock. • Place your items *securely* in the overhead bins.

2 a : so as not to be found • The jewels were *securely* [=*safely*] hidden. **b :** in a manner that prevents secret information from being seen by others • insuring that everyone can vote *securely* • You can shop and bank *securely* on the Internet.

se·cu·ri·ty /sɪˈkjɚrəti/ *noun, pl* **-ties**

1 [*noncount*] **a :** the state of being protected or safe from harm • We must insure our national *security*. — often used before another noun • an electronic *security* system • random *security* checks • *security* measures **b :** things done to make people or places safe • The college failed to provide adequate *security* on campus after dark. • increased *security* at airports • There was a lapse in *security* and the inmates escaped. **c :** the area in a place (such as an airport) where people are checked to make sure they are not carrying weapons or other illegal materials • We have to go through *security* at the airport. **d :** the part of a company or other organization that provides protection for workers, equipment, etc. • We called *security* when we found the door open.

2 [*noncount*] **:** the state of being closely watched or guarded • The meeting was held under tight *security*. • The prisoner was being kept under maximum *security*.

3 [*noncount*] **:** the state of being free from anxiety or worry **:** the state of being or feeling secure • financial *security* • She is concerned about job *security*. [=about the possibility of losing her job] • I like the *security* of knowing there will be someone there to help me when I need help. • Growing up in a close family gave her a sense of *security*.

4 [*count*] **a :** something given as proof of a promise to make a payment later • *security* for a loan **b :** a document showing that someone owns or has invested in a company, organization, etc. • government *securities*

— see also SOCIAL SECURITY

security blanket *noun, pl* **~ -kets** [*count*] **:** a blanket that is carried by a child because it makes the child feel safe — often used figuratively • The job was her *security blanket*. [=the job was the thing that made her feel safe and secure]

security deposit *noun, pl* **~ -its** [*count*] **:** an amount of money that you pay when you begin to rent property (such as an apartment) and that can be used to pay for any damage that you cause to the property

security guard *noun, pl* **~ guards** [*count*] **:** a person whose job is to guard a place (such as a store or museum) and make sure the people and things in it are not harmed

security risk *noun, pl* **~ risks** [*count*]

1 : someone who could damage an organization by giving information to an enemy or competitor • We can't let him see this information—he's a *security risk*.

2 : someone or something that is a risk to safety • Any package left unattended will be deemed a *security risk*.

se·dan /sɪˈdæn/ *noun, pl* **-dans** [*count*] *US* **:** a car that has four doors and that has room for four or more people — called also (*Brit*) *saloon*, (*Brit*) *saloon car*; see picture at CAR; compare COUPE

sedan chair *noun, pl* **~ chairs** [*count*] **:** a covered chair that is carried on poles by two people and that was used in the past for carrying a passenger through the streets of a city

[1]**se·date** /sɪˈdeɪt/ *adj* [*more ~; most ~*]

1 : slow and relaxed • We walked the beach at a *sedate* pace.

2 : quiet and peaceful : CALM • a *sedate* neighborhood/town • the *sedate* countryside • He remained *sedate* under pressure. • a *sedate* horse

[2]**sedate** *verb* **-dates; -dat·ed; -dat·ing** [+ *obj*] **:** to give (a person or animal) drugs that cause relaxation or sleep • The doctor *sedated* the patient heavily. — often used as (*be*) *sedated* • The patient had to *be sedated*. • The animal *was* heavily *sedated* during the procedure.

se·da·tion /sɪˈdeɪʃən/ *noun* [*noncount*]

1 : a relaxed, calm, or sleepy condition that results from taking a drug (called a sedative) • Patients are kept ***under (heavy) sedation*** during the surgery.

2 : the act of giving a person or animal a drug that causes calmness or relaxation • For some patients, *sedation* may be necessary.

sed·a·tive /ˈsɛdətɪv/ *noun, pl* **-tives** [*count*] **:** a drug that calms or relaxes someone • The patient was given a powerful *sedative*. — often used before another noun • *sedative* drugs/medicine • the *sedative* effects of the drug

sed·en·tary /ˈsɛdn̩ˌteri, *Brit* ˈsɛdn̩tri/ *adj* [*more ~; most ~*]

1 : doing or involving a lot of sitting : not doing or involving much physical activity • Editing the dictionary is a *sedentary* job. • The work is very *sedentary*. • Their health problems were caused by their *sedentary* lifestyles/lives. • He became *sedentary* later on in his life.

2 : staying or living in one place instead of moving to different places • *sedentary* birds • *sedentary* tribes/people

se·der *or* **Se·der** /ˈseɪdɚ/ *noun, pl* **-ders** [*count*] **:** a Jewish religious service and dinner that is held on the first or first and second evenings of the Passover

sedge /ˈsɛʤ/ *noun, pl* **sedg·es** [*count, noncount*] **:** a plant like grass that grows in wet ground or near water

sed·i·ment /ˈsɛdəmənt/ *noun, pl* **-ments** [*count, noncount*]

1 : material that sinks to the bottom of a liquid • There was a layer of *sediment* in the bottom of the tank.

2 : material (such as stones and sand) that is carried into water by water, wind, etc.

sed·i·men·ta·ry /ˌsɛdəˈmɛntəri/ *adj, technical* **:** made from material that sinks to the bottom of a liquid : made from sediment • *sedimentary* layers/deposits • Sandstone is a *sedimentary* rock. [=a type of rock formed when sediments that were deposited in ancient times were pressed together and became hard]

sed·i·men·ta·tion /ˌsɛdəmənˈteɪʃən/ *noun* [*noncount*] *technical* **:** the natural process in which material (such as stones and sand) is carried to the bottom of a body of water and forms a solid layer • rock formed by *sedimentation*

se·di·tion /sɪˈdɪʃən/ *noun* [*noncount*] *formal* **:** the crime of saying, writing, or doing something that encourages people to disobey their government • The leaders of the group have been arrested and charged with *sedition*.

— **se·di·tious** /sɪˈdɪʃəs/ *adj* [*more ~; most ~*] • He was arrested for making *seditious* statements.

se·duce /sɪˈduːs, *Brit* sɪˈdjuːs/ *verb* **-duc·es; -duced; -duc·ing** [+ *obj*]

1 : to persuade (someone) to have sex with you • He tried to *seduce* her. • She was *seduced* by an older man.

2 : to persuade (someone) to do something • The other team *seduced* him with a better offer. — often + *into* • He *seduced* people *into* following him by telling them lies. — often used

S

as *(be) seduced* ▪ The people *were seduced into* thinking/believing that he was a prophet. ▪ She *was seduced (into* acting) by thoughts of fame and fortune. ▪ He *was seduced into* a life of crime.

– **se·duc·er** /sɪˈduːsɚ, *Brit* sɪˈdjuːsə/ *noun, pl* **-ers** [*count*] ▪ the *seducer* of a young woman

se·duc·tion /sɪˈdʌkʃən/ *noun, pl* **-tions**

1 : the act of persuading someone to have sex with you [*count*] The book describes his *seductions* of young women. [*noncount*] a story of *seduction*

2 [*count*] **:** something that interests and attracts people — usually plural ▪ Tourists cannot resist the *seductions* of the island. ▪ the *seductions* of fame and fortune

se·duc·tive /sɪˈdʌktɪv/ *adj* [*more* ~; *most* ~]

1 : sexually attractive ▪ a *seductive* woman/smile/voice/dress ▪ He looks *seductive*.

2 : making someone do or want something **:** very attractive ▪ The idea of moving to New York City is highly/very *seductive*. [=*tempting*] ▪ The wine has a *seductive* [=*alluring*] aroma. ▪ the *seductive* power of advertising

– **se·duc·tive·ly** *adv* ▪ She walks/talks *seductively*. ▪ She was dressed *seductively*. ▪ The desserts sound *seductively* sweet. – **se·duc·tive·ness** *noun* [*noncount*]

se·duc·tress /sɪˈdʌktrəs/ *noun, pl* **-tress·es** [*count*] **:** an attractive woman who seduces someone

[1]**see** /ˈsiː/ *verb* **sees; saw** /ˈsɑː/; **seen** /ˈsiːn/; **see·ing** /ˈsiːjɪŋ/

1 a : to notice or become aware of (someone or something) by using your eyes [+ *obj*] It was so dark that I couldn't *see* anything. ▪ I can't *see* a thing without my glasses. ▪ Would you turn on the light? I can hardly *see* a thing. ▪ Let me *see* what you're holding in your hand. ▪ I *saw* your sister at the party, but I didn't talk to her. ▪ I *saw* her take the money. ▪ Nobody *saw* the accident happen. ▪ He was last *seen* leaving his house yesterday morning. ▪ This is the prettiest garden I've ever *seen*! = I've never *seen* such a pretty garden (before)! ▪ You have to *see* it to believe it. ▪ "He says he's coming." "I'll believe it when I *see* it." ▪ It's nice to *see* you (looking) so happy! ▪ I can *see* how happy you are. ▪ I could *see* (that) she was tired. ▪ I *see* (that) you bought a new car. = You bought a new car, I *see*. ▪ This club is the place to be *seen* (at) these days. [=this club is the place where people go to be noticed by important or fashionable people] ▪ "Have you met the new guy yet?" "No, but I've ***seen him around***." [=I have noticed him in some of the places I often go to] ▪ A mall's a mall. ***If you've seen one, you've seen them all***. [=all shopping malls look the same] [*no obj*] It was so dark that I couldn't *see*. ▪ He can no longer *see* to read without his glasses. ▪ I couldn't *see* through/out the foggy window. ▪ I can't *see* over the person in front of me. ▪ On a clear day, you can *see* for miles from the top of the mountain. ▪ "He broke his leg." "***So I see***." [=I can see that his leg is broken] ▪ If you don't believe me, go and ***see for yourself***. **b** [*no obj*] **:** to have the ability to see **:** to have the power of sight ▪ She doesn't/can't *see* very well. ▪ She cannot *see*. [=she is blind]

2 : to be or become aware of (something) [+ *obj*] He *saw* the opportunity and took it. ▪ He only *sees* [=*notices*] my faults. ▪ I *saw* a big difference in her behavior. ▪ It was easy to *see* that she was lying. ▪ Can't you *see* that he needs help? ▪ Anyone can *see* that they're in love. ▪ I can *see* there has been a mistake. ▪ I *see* that the school has raised its tuition again. ▪ He claims that he can *see* the future. [=that he knows what will happen in the future] ▪ I *see* by/from the newspaper that they've won the election. ▪ Looking at the sales figures, we can *see* a steady rise in profits. ▪ Investors never *saw* this turn in the stock market coming. ▪ The book's ending is so predictable that you can ***see it coming a mile away/off***. [*no obj*] He claims that he can *see* into the future. ▪ ***As you can see***, the sales figures show a steady rise in profits.

3 : to learn or find out (something) especially by looking or waiting [+ *obj*] Please *see* who's at the door. ▪ It will be interesting to *see* if the team can pull off a win. ▪ I'm not sure if I'm going to the party. I have to *see* how I feel tomorrow. ▪ You should try on the dress to *see* if it fits. ▪ Can you check to *see* if the car needs oil? ▪ She brought the car to a mechanic to *see* what was wrong with it. ▪ I'll *see* what I can do to help. ▪ We'll have to *see* how it goes. ▪ We *saw*, in the previous lecture, how Newton came up with his theory. ▪ He called to *see* if we would be home tonight. ▪ I have to ***wait and see*** whether or not I got the job. ▪ It ***remains to be seen*** [=it is uncertain] whether or not she was lying. [*no obj*] "Can you fix the car?" "I will have to *see*." ▪ "Can I go to the party?" "***We'll see***." [=*maybe, perhaps*] ▪ Things will get better, ***you'll see***.

4 [+ *obj*] **a** *not used in progressive tenses* **:** to read (something written or printed) ▪ Have you *seen* today's newspaper? ▪ I *saw* in the newspaper that the team lost. ▪ I need to *see* your license. ▪ He posted his journal online ***for all (the world) to see***. **b** — used to tell someone where to look for information ▪ For further information, *see* Appendix A. ▪ *See* the explanatory notes at the beginning of the book. ▪ *See* [=*look*] below for details.

5 [+ *obj*] **a :** to watch (a television program, movie, etc.) ▪ Did you *see* the baseball game (on TV) last night? ▪ I *saw* that movie, too. **b :** to go to and watch (a performance, play, event, etc.) ▪ We *saw* the parade. ▪ We are *seeing* a play tonight.

6 [*no obj*] — used in speech to direct someone's attention to something or someone ▪ *See*, I told you it would rain. ▪ *See*, the bus is coming.

7 [+ *obj*] **a :** to think of (someone or something) in a certain way ▪ Looking back, I *see* things differently now. ▪ I *see* myself to be an understanding person. ▪ I *see* you now for what you really are: a liar and cheat. ▪ Try to *see* things from my point of view. ▪ In order to understand them, you have to ***see the world through their eyes***. — often + *as* ▪ She *saw* herself *as* an independent woman. [=she thought of herself as independent] ▪ He is *seen as* one of the best players in baseball. ▪ I *see* the job *as* a great opportunity. **b** — used to say what your opinion is about something ▪ "Can we do it?" "I ***don't see why not***." [=yes, I believe that we can do it] ▪ ***As I see it***, you have only two choices. ▪ ***The way he sees it***, we should be done by Friday. [=he thinks we should be done by Friday]

8 [+ *obj*] **a :** to imagine (someone) as being or doing something specified ▪ Can you really *see* yourself any happier than you are now? ▪ I can't *see* her becoming a doctor. ▪ I can't *see* him objecting to our plan, can you? — often + *as* ▪ She *sees* herself *as* a doctor in the future. ▪ I can still *see* her *as* she was years ago. ▪ Somehow, I just couldn't *see* him *as* a banker. **b :** to form a mental picture of (something) ▪ He *saw* a great future for himself in baseball. ▪ I can *see* it now in my mind: you and her married with two kids.

9 : to understand (something) [+ *obj*] I *see* what you mean. ▪ I can *see* why/how you would feel that way. ▪ I don't *see* the point of your story. ▪ What's so funny? I don't *see* the joke. ▪ I don't *see* why we have to do that. ▪ I don't *see* how/that/why it matters. ▪ I can't get him to ***see reason/sense***. [*no obj*] "You should hold the club like this." "Oh, ***I see***."

10 [+ *obj*] **a :** to meet with (someone) ▪ I can *see* you later this afternoon. ▪ I'll be *seeing* my lawyer on Friday. ▪ Do you *see* your dentist regularly? ▪ The doctor is *seeing* a patient at the moment. ▪ He has been *seeing* a psychotherapist. — often + *about* ▪ You should *see* a doctor *about* your rash. ▪ What would you like to *see* me *about*? **b :** to visit (someone) ▪ I *saw* him at the hospital. ▪ I am *seeing* an old friend tomorrow. **c :** to allow yourself to be visited by (someone) ▪ He's not *seeing* anyone today. **d :** to be with and talk to (someone) ▪ I can't tell you how glad/pleased I am to *see* you again! ▪ We'll *see* you again real soon. ▪ They *see* each other less [=they spend less time together] now that he has a new job. **e** — used in phrases like ***see more/less of*** and ***see a lot of*** to describe how much time people spend with each other ▪ I'd like to *see more of* you. [=I'd like to spend more time with you] ▪ They've been *seeing a lot of* each other lately. [=they've been spending a lot of time together lately]

11 [+ *obj*] **:** to spend time with (someone) as part of a romantic relationship — usually used as *be seeing* ▪ They've *been seeing* each other for over a year. ▪ *Are* you *seeing* [=*dating*] anyone right now?

12 [+ *obj*] **:** to make sure (something) is done **:** to check that (something) is done ▪ *See* (that) the work gets finished on time. [=make sure that the work is finished on time] ▪ *See* that the door is locked before you leave the building.

13 [+ *obj*] **:** to experience (something) ▪ He *saw* a lot of action during the war. ▪ I never thought I would live to *see* the day when gas would cost so much. ▪ Nothing bothers him—he's *seen* it all before. ▪ Oil prices have *seen* a large increase.

14 [+ *obj*] **:** to be the place or time in which (something) happens ▪ The city has *seen* a lot of growth in recent years. [=the city has grown a lot in recent years] ▪ This year has *seen* a drop in profits. [=profits have dropped this year] ▪ The last decade *saw* many technological advances.

15 *always followed by an adverb or preposition* [+ *obj*] **:** to go somewhere with (someone) ▪ I'll *see* [=*accompany*] you home. ▪ They *saw* [=*escorted*] him out (of the club). ▪ My secretary will *see* you to the door. ▪ I can ***see myself out***, thank you. [=I can leave without having anyone show me where to

S

go] • He kissed her goodbye and *saw* her onto the plane. [=he watched her get onto the plane] — see also SEE OFF (below)
16 [+ *obj*] : to help or support (someone or something) for a particular period of time • We had enough supplies to *see* us (out) to the end of winter. [=the supplies were enough to last until the end of winter] — usually + *through* • The support of his friends *saw* him *through* his depression. [=helped him to get through his depression] • The legislators vowed to *see* the bill *through* Congress to make sure that it became a law. • They have enough money to *see* them *through*.
17 [+ *obj*] : to make a bet that is equal to (another player's bet) in poker • I'll *see* your 10 and raise you 10. • I'll *see* you and raise 10.

has seen better days see ¹BETTER
I'll be seeing you *informal* — used to say goodbye
let me see, let's see see ¹LET
long time no see see ¹LONG
not see the forest/wood for the trees see TREE
see about [*phrasal verb*] ***see about (something)*** **1** : to do what is required for (something) : to deal with (something) • She is *seeing about* getting tickets to the concert. • I should *see about* [=*attend to*] dinner soon. **2** ***we'll (soon) see about that*** — used in speech to say that you are not going to allow someone to do something or to behave in a particular way • "He says that he's not going." "Well, *we'll (soon) see about that*."
see after [*phrasal verb*] ***see after (someone or something)*** : to take care of (someone or something) • *See after* [=*look after*] the baggage, while I see if our flight is on time. • Can you *see after* the baby for me?
see and be seen : to see and be noticed by important or fashionable people • We go to the club to *see and be seen*.
see around/round [*phrasal verb*] ***see around/round (something)*** *Brit* : to move about while looking at (something) : to tour (something) • If you'd like to *see around* [=*look around*] the factory, someone can accompany you.
see double see ⁴DOUBLE
see eye to eye : to have the same opinion : AGREE — usually used in negative statements • They don't *see eye to eye* on this issue.
see fit see ¹FIT
see here — used to introduce a statement when you want someone to notice what you are saying • *See here* [=*look here*], you need to start behaving more responsibly.
see if I care see ²CARE
see in [*phrasal verb*] ***see (something) in (someone or something)*** : to notice or perceive (something good or attractive) in (someone or something) • She *saw* great musical talent *in* her son. • I think their plan is crazy, but he apparently *sees* something *in* it. • I can't understand what she *sees in* him. = I don't know what she *sees in* him. [=I don't know why she likes/admires him]
seeing is believing see BELIEVE
see off [*phrasal verb*] ***see (someone) off*** or ***see off (someone)*** **1** : to go to an airport, train station, etc., with (someone who is leaving) in order to say goodbye • She *saw* him *off* at the train station. **2** *Brit* **a** : to chase or force (someone) away from a place • The police finally *saw* them *off*. **b** : to defeat or stop (an enemy, opponent, etc.) • They *saw off* the opposition.
see out [*phrasal verb*] ***see (something) out*** : to continue to work at (something) until it is completed • He *saw* the project *out* to its very end.
see over [*phrasal verb*] ***see over (something)*** *Brit* : to walk around and examine (a place) carefully • They went to *see* the house *over*. [=look the house over]
see red see ²RED
see stars see ¹STAR
see the back of see ¹BACK
see the light, see the light of day see ¹LIGHT
see things : to see things that do not really exist : HALLUCINATE • There's no one there—you must be *seeing things*.
see through [*phrasal verb*] **1** ***see through (someone or something)*** : to realize the true nature of (someone or something) • She *saw through* his lies. [=she knew he was lying] • I can't lie to her—she'd ***see right through*** me. **2** ***see (something) through*** : to continue to work at (something) until it is completed • He *saw* the project *through* to the end. — see also ¹SEE 16 (above)
see to [*phrasal verb*] **1** ***see to (something)*** : to do or provide what is needed for (something) • His uncle *saw to* his education. [=his uncle made the necessary payments, arrangements, etc., for his education] • The hotel staff *saw to* [=*attended to*] my every need. : to deal with (something) • I have to *see to* [=*attend to*] dinner. • I'll *see to* your order at once. • You really ought to have that rash *seen to* by a doctor. **2** ***see to it*** : to make sure that something is done • Can you *see to it* that everyone gets a copy of this memo?
see you or ***see you around*** or ***see you later*** *informal* — used to say goodbye • "I guess I'll be going now." "OK. (I'll) *See you later*."
see your way (clear) to see ¹WAY
what/who should you see but see SHOULD

²see *noun, pl* **sees** *formal*
1 [*count*] : the area in which a bishop has authority : DIOCESE
2 [*noncount*] : the authority or power of a bishop
3 [*count*] : the office of a bishop

¹seed /ˈsiːd/ *noun, pl* **seeds**
1 : a small object produced by a plant from which a new plant can grow [*count*] a packet of sunflower *seeds* • He planted/sowed the *seeds* three inches apart. • (*US*) apple/orange *seeds* [=(*Brit*) *pips*] [*noncount*] She raked the grass *seed* into the soil. • She grows her plants ***from seed*** [=by planting seeds rather than by some other method] — see color picture on page C5
2 [*count*] : the beginning of something which continues to develop or grow • Her comment ***planted/sowed a seed of*** doubt in his mind. [=caused him to begin to have doubts] • The government's policies *planted/sowed the seeds of* war/destruction. [=created a situation that led to war/destruction]
3 [*count*] : a player or team that is ranked as one of the best in a competition (such as a tennis tournament) in order to be sure that the best players or teams do not play against each other in the early part of the competition • The top *seed* won the tournament. • Our team is the number one *seed*. • She is ranked as the third *seed*.
4 [*noncount*] **a** *literary* : all the children, grandchildren, etc., of a particular man • the *seed* of Abraham **b** *old-fashioned + humorous* : a man's semen • a man spreading his *seed* [=fathering many children]
go to seed or ***run to seed*** **1** : to produce seeds • The flowers will *go to seed* and spread. • The plant *runs to seed* rapidly in hot weather. **2** : to become less attractive, effective, etc., because of age or lack of care • He let himself *go to seed* after he lost his job.

²seed *verb* **seeds; seed·ed; seed·ing**
1 [+ *obj*] : to plant (an area of ground) with seeds • We *seeded* the field with corn. • a newly *seeded* lawn
2 [*no obj*] *of a plant* : to produce seeds • These plants will *seed* late in the fall.
3 [+ *obj*] : to remove (seeds) from a fruit or vegetable • After you wash and *seed* the peppers you can chop them.
4 [+ *obj*] : to give (a player or team) a particular rank which shows how likely that person or team is to win a competition (such as a tennis tournament) — usually used as *(be) seeded* • The team/player *was seeded* first/last in the tournament. • the top-*seeded* player
seed itself *of a plant* : to produce new plants from its own seeds • This plant spreads quickly because it *seeds itself*.

³seed *adj, always used before a noun* : used for producing a new crop of plants • *seed* corn/potatoes

seed·bed /ˈsiːdˌbɛd/ *noun, pl* **-beds** [*count*] : an area of soil prepared for planting seeds — sometimes used figuratively • a *seedbed* for innovation [=a place/situation in which innovation can occur]

seed·less /ˈsiːdləs/ *adj* : having no seeds inside • *seedless* grapes • a *seedless* orange

seed·ling /ˈsiːdlɪŋ/ *noun, pl* **-lings** [*count*] : a young plant that is grown from seed

seed money *noun* [*noncount*] : money that is used for starting a new business, program, project, etc. • He provided *seed money* for the campaign. — called also *seed capital*

seedy /ˈsiːdi/ *adj* **seed·i·er; -est** [*also more* ~; *most* ~]
1 : dirty or in bad condition • a *seedy* motel • He was wearing a *seedy* suit.
2 : not respectable or decent • a *seedy* bar • a *seedy* area of the city
3 : having bad morals : DISHONEST • a *seedy* lawyer
4 : having a lot of seeds • *seedy* fruit

see·ing /ˈsiːjɪŋ/ *conj* — used to explain the reason for a statement • *Seeing* how often she gets into trouble [=since she gets into trouble so often], I don't think we should help her this time. — often + *that* or *as* • There's not much we can do, *seeing that* [=*since*] they've already made their decision. • *See-*

S

ing as you've met my family, don't you think I should meet yours? • ***Seeing as how*** [=*since*] I'm not busy right now, I can help you.

Seeing Eye *trademark, US* — used for a dog that is trained to guide a blind person

seek /ˈsiːk/ *verb* **seeks; sought** /ˈsɑːt/; **seek·ing** [+ *obj*] *somewhat formal*

1 : to search for (someone or something) : to try to find (someone or something) • He is *seeking* employment. [=he is looking for a job] • The office is *seeking* a salesperson. • The prince is *seeking* a wife. • Snakes *seek* the sun to warm their bodies. • thrill-*seeking* travelers [=travelers who want to have very exciting/thrilling experiences]

2 : to ask for (help, advice, etc.) • You should visit your doctor and *seek* his advice. • You should *seek* medical help immediately if you experience any chest pain or shortness of breath. • The church is *seeking* donations/volunteers.

3 a : to try to get or achieve (something) • He *sought* revenge for his son's murder. • During the war, she *sought* asylum in Spain. • They *sought* refuge in Canada. • The company is *seeking* new ways to improve service. • The mayor is *seeking* reelection. • She *seeks* perfection in her work. • attention-*seeking* behavior • Immigrants come to America to ***seek their fortune***. [=to try to become rich] • They are ***seeking compensation/damages*** [=they are trying to get money] for their loss. **b :** to make an attempt *to do* something • Doctors have been *seeking* [=*trying*] *to find* a cure. • The builders *sought to make* the bridge stronger.

seek out [*phrasal verb*] ***seek (someone or something) out*** or ***seek out (someone or something)* :** to search for and find (someone or something) • His parents *sought out* the best doctors in the field. • White blood cells *seek out* and destroy infections.

– see also HEAT-SEEKING

– **seek·er** *noun, pl* **-ers** [*count*] • *seekers* of perfection • job/thrill/pleasure/autograph *seekers*

seem /ˈsiːm/ *verb* **seems; seemed; seem·ing** [*linking verb*]

1 : to appear to be something or to do something : to have a quality, appearance, etc., that shows or suggests a particular characteristic, feeling, etc. • She *seemed* happy. • He didn't *seem* interested. • Their request *seems* reasonable/strange. • What they're doing doesn't *seem* right to me. • The letter *seems* important. • Her story *seems* true. — often followed by *to + verb* • Her story *seems to be* true. • She *seems to know* our secret. [=I have the feeling/impression that she knows our secret] • He didn't *seem to remember* that part of the story. — often used in the phrases ***seem like, seem as if***, and ***seem as though*** • He *seems like* a nice man. = He *seems* (to be) a nice man. • We waited for what *seemed like* hours. • Buying a new car *seemed like* a good idea at the time. • It *seemed as if/though* the work would never end.

2 — used with *it* to make a statement about what appears to be true based on what is known • *It seems* (that) they forgot about the meeting. • The concert will not take place, *it seems*. • "Are we on schedule?" "***So it seems.***" [=yes, I think that we are on schedule] • They are very rude, or *so it seems* (to me).

3 — used to make a statement less definite or more polite; followed by *to + verb* • I *seem to remember* that you said you'd help me. — often used in negative statements • I can't *seem to solve* the problem. [=I have tried to solve the problem, but I can't] • I couldn't *seem to hit* the ball straight. • What *seems to be* the problem? [=what is the problem?]

seem·ing /ˈsiːmɪŋ/ *adj, always used before a noun, somewhat formal* : appearing to be true but not being true or certain : APPARENT • Parents discussed the teacher's *seeming* lack of interest in the students. • I was fooled by the *seeming* simplicity of the instructions.

– **seem·ing·ly** *adv* • *seemingly* contradictory statements [=statements that seem to be contradictory] • a *seemingly* impossible stunt • a *seemingly* simple job

seem·ly /ˈsiːmli/ *adj* **seem·li·er; -est** [*or more* ~; *most* ~] *formal + old-fashioned* : proper or appropriate for the situation • *seemly* behavior • a *seemly* reply — opposite UNSEEMLY

seen *past participle of* [1]SEE

seep /ˈsiːp/ *verb, always followed by an adverb or preposition* **seeps; seeped; seep·ing** [*no obj*] : to flow or pass slowly through small openings in something • Blood was *seeping* through the bandage. • The chemicals *seeped* into the ground. • Water was *seeping* in (through the cracks). — sometimes used figuratively • The secret *seeped* out.

seep·age /ˈsiːpɪʤ/ *noun, pl* **-ag·es** *formal* : an occurrence in which a liquid or gas flows or passes slowly through small openings [*count*] gas/oil *seepages* • the *seepage* of water [*noncount*] Check for *seepage* in the basement.

seer /ˈsiɚ/ *noun, pl* **seers** [*count*] : someone who predicts things that will happen in the future • prophets and *seers* • political *seers* [=people who make predictions about politics]

seer·suck·er /ˈsiɚˌsʌkɚ/ *noun* [*noncount*] : a light type of cloth that has an uneven surface and a pattern of lines — often used before another noun • a *seersucker* dress/jacket/suit

[1]**see·saw** /ˈsiːˌsɑː/ *noun, pl* **-saws**

1 [*count*] : a long, flat board that is balanced in the middle so that when one end goes up the other end goes down ✧ Children play on a seesaw by sitting on each of its ends and moving each other up and down by pushing off the ground with their feet. • Let's play/ride on the *seesaw*. — called also (*US*) *teeter-totter*; see picture at PLAYGROUND

2 [*singular*] : a situation in which something keeps changing from one state to another and back again • Their relationship was an emotional *seesaw*. — often used before another noun • a *seesaw* battle for power • a *seesaw* economy

[2]**seesaw** *verb* **-saws; -sawed; -saw·ing** [*no obj*] : to keep changing from one state or condition to another and then back again • The lead *seesawed* between the two runners right up to the finish line. • Stock prices have continued to *seesaw*. [=to go up and down]

seethe /ˈsiːð/ *verb* **seethes; seethed; seeth·ing** [*no obj*]

1 : to feel or show strong emotion (such as anger) even though you try to control it • He *seethed* at his brother's success. — often + *with* • He *seethed with* anger/jealousy. • The letter *seethes with* resentment. • a *seething* letter

2 : to be in a state of constant activity • We found ourselves in the middle of a *seething* crowd. — often used as *(be) seething with* • The island *is seething with* tourists. [=there are very many tourists moving around on the island] • The field *was seething with* crickets. • His brain *was seething with* ideas.

see–through /ˈsiːˌθruː/ *adj* : thin enough to be seen through • a *see-through* blouse/container • The plastic is *see-through*. [=*transparent*]

[1]**seg·ment** /ˈsɛgmənt/ *noun, pl* **-ments** [*count*]

1 : one of the parts into which something can be divided : SECTION • The railroad track is divided into *segments*. — often + *of* • in the final *segment of* the book • The *segment of* the population over 70 years of age is growing larger. • The company controls a large *segment of* the market. • the *segments of* an orange

2 *geometry* **a :** a part of a circle formed by drawing a straight line between two points on the circle **b :** a part of a straight line between two points

[2]**seg·ment** /ˈsɛgˌmɛnt, *Brit* sɛgˈmɛnt/ *verb* **-ments; -ment·ed; -ment·ing** [+ *obj*] : to divide (something) into parts • Market researchers have *segmented* the population into different age groups.

– **segmented** *adj* • a worm that has a *segmented* body = a *segmented* worm [=a worm whose body is made of different segments or sections]

seg·men·ta·tion /ˌsɛgmənˈteɪʃən/ *noun* [*noncount*] : the process of dividing something into parts or segments • the *segmentation* of the population

seg·re·gate /ˈsɛgrɪˌgeɪt/ *verb* **-gates; -gat·ed; -gat·ing** [+ *obj*]

1 : to separate groups of people because of their particular race, religion, etc. • The civil rights movement fought against practices that *segregated* blacks and whites. — often + *from* • He grew up at a time when blacks were *segregated from* whites. • During religious services, women are *segregated from* men. — opposite INTEGRATE

2 : to not allow people of different races to be together in (a place, such as a school) • Many states at that time continued to *segregate* public schools. • racially *segregated* schools • a *segregated* neighborhood — opposite INTEGRATE

seg·re·ga·tion /ˌsɛgrɪˈgeɪʃən/ *noun* [*noncount*] : the practice or policy of keeping people of different races, religions, etc., separate from each other • racial/religious *segregation* • They fought to end the *segregation* of public schools. • the *segregation* of men and women

seg·re·ga·tion·ist /ˌsɛgrɪˈgeɪʃənɪst/ *noun, pl* **-ists** [*count*] : a person who supports racial segregation • *segregationists* versus integrationists • a *segregationist* politician/state/attitude/view

se·gue /ˈsɛˌgweɪ/ *verb* **se·gues; se·gued; se·gue·ing** [*no obj*] : to move without stopping from one activity, topic, song, etc., to another ▪ She quickly *segued* to the next topic. ▪ The band smoothly *segued* from one song to the next. ▪ In the movie, a shot of the outside of the house *segued* neatly to/into a shot of the family inside the house.

– **segue** *noun, pl* **segues** [*count*] ▪ a nice *segue* to the next song ▪ She used the question as a *segue* to her next topic.

seis·mic /ˈsaɪzmɪk/ *adj, always used before a noun*

1 *technical* **:** of, relating to, or caused by an earthquake ▪ *seismic* activity/data/waves/zones

2 [*more ~; most ~*] **:** very great or important ▪ *Seismic* social changes have occurred. ▪ The discovery caused a ***seismic shift*** [=a great change] in public attitudes.

– **seis·mi·cal·ly** /ˈsaɪzmɪkli/ *adv* ▪ a *seismically* active region [=a region where many earthquakes occur]

seis·mo·graph /ˈsaɪzməˌgræf, *Brit* ˈsaɪzməˌgrɑːf/ *noun, pl* **-graphs** [*count*] **:** a device that measures and records the movement of the earth during an earthquake

seis·mol·o·gy /saɪzˈmɑːləʤi/ *noun* [*noncount*] **:** the scientific study of earthquakes

– **seis·mo·log·i·cal** /ˌsaɪzməˈlɑːʤɪkəl/ *adj* ▪ *seismological* research – **seis·mol·o·gist** /saɪzˈmɑːləʤɪst/ *noun, pl* **-gists** [*count*]

seize /ˈsiːz/ *verb* **seiz·es; seized; seiz·ing** [+ *obj*]

1 a : to use legal or official power to take (something) ▪ Police *seized* [=*confiscated*] the weapons and drugs. ▪ The bank *seized* their property. **b :** to get or take (something) in a forceful, sudden, or violent way ▪ The army has *seized* control of the city. ▪ A rebel group attempted to *seize* power. ▪ He suddenly *seized* the lead in the final lap of the race. **c :** to attack and take control of (a place) by force or violence ▪ The soldiers *seized* [=*captured*] the fort.

2 a : to forcefully take and hold (someone or something) with your hand or arms **:** GRAB ▪ He *seized* her by the arm. ▪ He tried to *seize* the gun from him. ▪ She ***seized hold of*** my hand. [=she seized my hand] **b :** to take (someone) as a prisoner ▪ The police *seized* [=*arrested*] the robbers. ▪ *Seize* that man! ▪ She was *seized* by kidnappers and carried off to a hidden location.

3 : to take or use (something, such as a chance or opportunity) in a quick and eager way ▪ He ***seized the chance/initiative/opportunity*** to present his ideas to his boss. ▪ My father taught me to ***seize the day***. [=to do the things I want to do when I have the chance instead of waiting for a later time] ▪ ***Seizing the moment***, she introduced herself to the famous film director.

4 a : to begin to affect (someone) suddenly ▪ Panic *seized* him. = He was *seized* by panic. **b :** to have a powerful effect on (someone) ▪ His movies *seized* the public's imagination. [=the public became very interested in and enthusiastic about his movies] ▪ She was suddenly *seized* with the idea [=she suddenly had the idea] of owning her own restaurant.

seize on/upon [*phrasal verb*] ***seize on/upon (something)*** **:** to take or use (something, such as a chance or opportunity) in a quick and eager way ▪ His critics have *seized on* the scandal to call for his resignation. ▪ She ***seized on the opportunity*** to tell her side of the story.

seize up [*phrasal verb*] **:** to stop working because the moving parts can no longer move ▪ The engine/brakes suddenly *seized up*. — sometimes used figuratively ▪ Her brain *seized up* when she tried to answer the question.

sei·zure /ˈsiːʒɚ/ *noun, pl* **-zures**

1 [*noncount*] **:** the act of taking control of something especially by force or violence ▪ the *seizure* of power by the rebels

2 *law* **:** the act of taking something by legal authority [*noncount*] property that is protected from *seizure* ▪ the *seizure* of evidence by the police [*count*] Not all searches and *seizures* by the police require a warrant.

3 [*count*] *medical* **:** an abnormal state in which you become unconscious and your body moves in an uncontrolled and violent way ▪ an epileptic *seizure* [=*fit*] ▪ The patient has been experiencing *seizures*. [=*convulsions*]

sel·dom /ˈsɛldəm/ *adv* **:** not often **:** almost never ▪ We *seldom* [=*rarely*] eat pork. ▪ We *seldom* go to the movies. ▪ This type of turtle *seldom* grows over four inches in length. ▪ We seldom agree. = (*somewhat formal*) *Seldom* do we agree. ▪ I have seldom had to wait so long. = (*somewhat formal*) *Seldom* have I had to wait so long.

seldom ever see EVER

seldom if ever see EVER

[1]se·lect /səˈlɛkt/ *verb* **-lects; -lect·ed; -lect·ing**

1 : to choose (someone or something) from a group [+ *obj*] Please *select* one item from the list. ▪ The school will only *select* 12 applicants for enrollment. — often used as *(be) selected* ▪ People *were selected* at random to take the survey. ▪ The restaurant *was* recently *selected* as one of the best in the area. ▪ She *was selected* to work on the project. ▪ The book is a collection of *selected* essays and letters. [*no obj*] Knowing the importance of making the right choice, he *selected* carefully.

2 [+ *obj*] *computers* **:** to choose (a particular action, section of text, etc.) especially by using a mouse ▪ Use the mouse to *select* [=*highlight*] the text you want to copy. ▪ Copy the *selected* text. ▪ *Select* "Insert" from the "Edit" menu.

[2]select *adj* [*more ~; most ~*]

1 : chosen from a group to include the best people or things ▪ Only a few *select* employees attended the meeting. ▪ A *select* committee was formed to plan the project. ▪ The group was small and *select*. ▪ A *select* number of people are invited. ▪ Only a ***select few*** will be accepted into the program.

2 *always used before a noun* **:** of the highest quality ▪ a *select* hotel ▪ The statue was made from a *select* [=*choice*] piece of marble. ▪ He only drinks *select* wines.

se·lec·tion /səˈlɛkʃən/ *noun, pl* **-tions**

1 [*noncount*] **:** the act of choosing something or someone from a group ▪ The *selection* of the best poem was difficult. ▪ His *selection* as athlete of the year surprised many people. [=people were surprised when he was selected/chosen as athlete of the year] ▪ It was not easy to ***make my selection***. [=it was not easy to choose] — sometimes used before another noun ▪ the *selection* process/committee/criteria — see also NATURAL SELECTION

2 [*count*] **a :** someone or something that is chosen from a group ▪ Who is your *selection* [=*choice*] for president? ▪ She sang *selections* from her new album. [=she sang songs that she selected from her new album] **b :** a collection of things chosen from a group of similar things — usually singular; usually + *of* ▪ The pub has a wide *selection of* beers. [=has many different beers]

se·lec·tive /səˈlɛktɪv/ *adj* [*more ~; most ~*]

1 : careful to choose only the best people or things ▪ He is very *selective* [=*picky, choosy*] about which tomatoes to use for the sauce. ▪ The club is *selective* in choosing members. ▪ The college has a highly *selective* admissions process.

2 : involving the selection of people or things from a group ▪ *selective* breeding ▪ She has a ***selective memory***. [=she remembers only what she wants to remember]

– **se·lec·tive·ly** *adv* ▪ The advertisement *selectively* targets men between the ages of 18 and 24. ▪ The dog is *selectively* bred for its calm temperament. – **se·lec·tiv·i·ty** /səˌlɛkˈtɪvəti/ *noun* [*noncount*]

se·lec·tor /səˈlɛktɚ/ *noun, pl* **-tors** [*count*]

1 : a device used for choosing a function, setting, etc., on a piece of equipment ▪ a channel *selector* ▪ a gear *selector* ▪ the input/output *selector* — often used before another noun ▪ Flip the *selector* switch from 25 volts to 70 volts.

2 *Brit* **:** someone who chooses the best or most suitable people for a sports team ▪ a *selectors* committee

se·le·ni·um /səˈliːnijəm/ *noun* [*noncount*] *technical* **:** a chemical element that is used in electronic devices to make them sensitive to light

self /ˈsɛlf/ *noun, pl* **selves** /ˈsɛlvz/

1 [*count*] **:** the person that someone normally or truly is — used to describe the way someone acts or feels ▪ He's just not his usual/normal *self* today. ▪ She was her ***old self*** again after some sleep. [=she returned to behaving/feeling as she normally did after some sleep] ▪ He was a mere ***ghost/shadow of his former self*** after the illness. [=he was much weaker after his illness] ▪ She showed her ***true/real self***. [=she stopped pretending and showed what type of person she really was]

2 [*count*] **:** a particular part of your personality or character that is shown in a particular situation ▪ She showed her better *self* at the party. ▪ Her public *self* is very different from her private *self*. ▪ He started taking yoga and meditation classes to get in touch with his ***inner self***. [=the emotional and spiritual part of himself]

3 [*noncount*] **:** the personality or character that makes a person different from other people **:** the combination of emotions, thoughts, feelings, etc., that make a person different from others ▪ We each develop a unique sense of *self*. [=a unique idea about who we are] ▪ Philosophers have written about the conception/idea of the *self*.

4 [*noncount*] *formal* **:** your own personal interest or advantage ▪ She helped without any thought of *self*. [=without any thought of trying to make things better for herself]

5 [*count*] — used to refer to a person ▪ a photo of her younger *self* • He puts his whole *self* into each and every game. [=he tries very hard to play his best in each game] • (*informal*) "Go get me another beer." "You can get it your (own) damn *self*!" • (*informal*) I could barely drag my sorry *self* out of bed.

self- /ˌsɛlf/ *combining form*
1 a : yourself or itself • *self*-pitying **b :** of yourself or itself • *self*-destructive • *self*-sacrifice
2 : by, to, with, for, or toward yourself or itself • *self*-made • *self*-evident • *self*-propelled • *self*-addressed • *self*-respect

self–ab•sorbed /ˌsɛlfəbˈsoəbd/ *adj* [*more ~; most ~*] *disapproving* **:** only caring about and interested in yourself • *self-absorbed* people • He's so (completely/totally) *self-absorbed* that he didn't even notice I was crying!
– self–ab•sorp•tion /ˌsɛlfəbˈsoəpʃən/ *noun* [*noncount*]

self–abuse /ˌsɛlfəˈbjuːs/ *noun* [*noncount*]
1 : things that you do that harm your own body or health • drug addiction and other forms of *self-abuse*
2 *old-fashioned + disapproving* **:** MASTURBATION

self–ac•tu•al•i•za•tion *also Brit* **self–ac•tu•al•i•sa•tion** /ˌsɛlfˌækʧəwələˈzeɪʃən, *Brit* ˌsɛlfˌækʧuəˌlaɪˈzeɪʃən/ *noun* [*noncount*] *formal* **:** the process of fully developing and using your abilities

self–ad•dressed /ˌsɛlfəˈdrɛst/ *adj* **:** having the sender's address on it so that it can be sent back to that person • a *self-addressed* envelope

self–ad•he•sive /ˌsɛlfədˈhiːsɪv/ *adj* **:** able to stick to something without first being made wet • *self-adhesive* labels/stamps

self–ap•point•ed /ˌsɛlfəˈpoɪntəd/ *adj, disapproving* **:** thinking of yourself as having a particular position, job, responsibility, etc., without considering the opinions or wishes of other people • a *self-appointed* guardian of public morals

self–as•sem•bly /ˌsɛlfəˈsɛmbli/ *adj, always used before a noun, Brit* — used to describe a product that is bought in parts that you have be put together • *self-assembly* furniture
– self–assembly *noun* [*noncount*] • The box says "*self-assembly* [=*assembly*] required."

self–as•ser•tive /ˌsɛlfəˈsɚtɪv/ *adj* [*more ~; most ~*] **:** very confident and willing to express opinions • a bold and *self-assertive* young lawyer
– self–as•ser•tive•ness *noun* [*noncount*]

self–as•ser•tion /ˌsɛlfəˈsɚʃən/ *noun* [*noncount*] **:** the act of expressing or defending your rights, claims, or opinions in a confident or forceful way

self–as•sess•ment /ˌsɛlfəˈsɛsmənt/ *noun, pl* **-ments** [*count, noncount*] **:** the act or process of judging your own achievements or progress

self–as•sur•ance /ˌsɛlfəˈʃərəns/ *noun* [*noncount*] **:** confidence in yourself and your abilities • I was impressed by his *self-assurance*.

self–as•sured /ˌsɛlfəˈʃəd/ *adj* [*more ~; most ~*] **:** having or showing confidence in yourself and your abilities • She was calm and *self-assured*. • He has a *self-assured* manner.

self–aware•ness /ˌsɛlfəˈweənəs/ *noun* [*noncount*] **:** knowledge and awareness of your own personality or character • Her *self-awareness* was unusual in such a young child.
– self–aware /ˌsɛlfəˈweə/ *adj* [*more ~; most ~*] • a remarkably *self-aware* child

self–ca•ter•ing /ˌsɛlfˈkeɪtərɪŋ/ *adj, Brit* **:** provided with equipment that allows you to cook your own food while you are on holiday • a *self-catering* cottage/apartment • *self-catering* holidays
– self–catering *noun* [*noncount*] *Brit* • Prices start at £199 for a week's *self-catering*.

self–cen•tered (*US*) *or Brit* **self–cen•tred** /ˌsɛlfˈsɛntəd/ *adj* [*more ~; most ~*] *disapproving* **:** too interested in yourself and not caring about the needs or feelings of other people **:** SELFISH • I think he's a *self-centered* and opinionated jerk.
– self–cen•tered•ness (*US*) *or Brit* **self–cen•tred•ness** *noun* [*noncount*]

self–con•cept /ˈsɛlfˈkɑːnˌsɛpt/ *noun, pl* **-cepts** [*count*] *formal* **:** the idea that you have about the kind of person you are • Children need to develop a positive *self-concept*.

self–con•fessed /ˌsɛlfkənˈfɛst/ *adj, always used before a noun* **:** freely and openly admitting that you are a particular type of person • a *self-confessed* forger • a *self-confessed* television addict

self–con•fi•dent /ˌsɛlfˈkɑːnfədənt/ *adj* [*more ~; most ~*] **:** having or showing confidence in yourself and your abilities • a quietly *self-confident* man • She has a *self-confident* look about her.
– self–con•fi•dence /ˌsɛlfˈkɑːnfədəns/ *noun* [*noncount*] • He lacks the *self-confidence* to speak his mind. **– self–con•fi•dent•ly** *adv*

self–con•grat•u•la•tion /ˌsɛlfkənˌgræʧəˈleɪʃən, ˌsɛlfkənˌgræʤəˈleɪʃən/ *noun* [*noncount*] *usually disapproving* **:** a way of behaving or speaking which shows that you are very happy about something that you have done • The president's speech was full of *self-congratulation* about making the company profitable again.
– self–con•grat•u•la•to•ry /ˌsɛlfkənˈgræʧələˌtori, ˌsɛlfkənˈgræʤələˌtori, *Brit* ˌsɛlfkənˌgræʧəˈleɪtri/ *adj* [*more ~; most ~*] • a *self-congratulatory* attitude/tone

self–con•scious /ˌsɛlfˈkɑːnʃəs/ *adj* [*more ~; most ~*]
1 : uncomfortably nervous about or embarrassed by what other people think about you • She's *self-conscious* whenever she has to give a speech. — often + *about* • He's very *self-conscious about* his appearance.
2 *usually disapproving* **:** done in a way that shows an awareness of the effect that is produced **:** done in a deliberate way • the *self-conscious* irony in the play • a *self-conscious* attempt to win people's sympathy
– self–con•scious•ly *adv* • He *self-consciously* smoothed his hair. **– self–con•scious•ness** *noun* [*noncount*]

self–con•tained /ˌsɛlfkənˈteɪnd/ *adj*
1 : not requiring help or support from anyone or anything else **:** complete by itself • a *self-contained* community [=a community that provides all the supplies, services, etc., that people need for everyday life] • This machine is a *self-contained* unit/system.
2 [*more ~; most ~*] **:** tending to keep thoughts and feelings private and to deal with things without help from other people • He is a very *self-contained* young man.
3 *Brit* **:** having a kitchen and bathroom • a *self-contained* flat

self–con•tra•dic•to•ry /ˌsɛlfˌkɑːntrəˈdɪktəri/ *adj* **:** having two or more parts that disagree with each other • Your argument is *self-contradictory*. • a *self-contradictory* statement

self–con•trol /ˌsɛlfkənˈtroul/ *noun* [*noncount*] **:** control over your feelings or actions • a lack of *self-control* • You have to show/learn a little *self-control*. • He lost his *self-control* and lashed out at the other player. • When it comes to chocolate, I ***lose all self-control***. [=I cannot stop myself from eating too much chocolate]
– self–con•trolled /ˌsɛlfkənˈtrould/ *adj* [*more ~; most ~*]

self–crit•i•cism /ˌsɛlfˈkrɪtəˌsɪzəm/ *noun, pl* **-cisms :** criticism of your own faults and weaknesses [*noncount*] His autobiography is full of *self-criticism*. [*count*] There are many *self-criticisms* in his autobiography.
– self–crit•i•cal /ˌsɛlfˈkrɪtɪkəl/ *adj* • a *self-critical* evaluation

self–de•cep•tion /ˌsɛlfdɪˈsɛpʃən/ *noun, pl* **-tions** [*count, noncount*] **:** the act of making yourself believe something that is not true • He was unaware of his own *self-deceptions*.

self–de•feat•ing /ˌsɛlfdɪˈfiːtɪŋ/ *adj*
1 : meant to solve a problem but actually causing the same or another problem **:** causing more problems than it solves • Violence is a *self-defeating* solution. • a *self-defeating* strategy/policy
2 : preventing you from doing or achieving something • Don't just assume you'll fail! That's a *self-defeating* attitude.

self–de•fense (*US*) *or Brit* **self–de•fence** /ˌsɛlfdɪˈfɛns/ *noun* [*noncount*]
1 : the act of defending yourself, your property, etc. • He argued that shooting the burglar was *self-defense*. • She hit back ***in self-defense***.
2 : skills that make you capable of protecting yourself during an attack • Women are advised to take at least one class in *self-defense*. • a *self-defense* instructor

self–de•ni•al /ˌsɛlfdɪˈnajəl/ *noun* [*noncount*] **:** the act of not allowing yourself to have or do something you want • Dieting is an exercise in *self-denial*. • The monks lead a life of *self-denial*. = The monks practice *self-denial*.

self–dep•re•cat•ing /ˌsɛlfˈdɛprɪˌkeɪtɪŋ/ *adj* [*more ~; most ~*] *formal* **:** meant to make yourself or the things you do seem unimportant • He spoke in a *self-deprecating* tone. • *self-deprecating* humor
– self–dep•re•ca•tion /ˌsɛlfˌdɛprɪˈkeɪʃən/ *noun* [*noncount*] • his humble *self-deprecation*

self–de•struct /ˌsɛlfdɪˈstrʌkt/ *verb* **-structs; -struct•ed; -struct•ing** [*no obj*] **:** to destroy itself • The missile automatically *self-destructs* if it goes off course. — often used figuratively • The team had a large lead most of the game but *self-*

S

destructed in the ninth inning and lost. • a rock star who *self-destructed* on drugs
– **self–destruct** *adj, always used before a noun* • a *self-destruct* button/mechanism/system

self–de·struc·tion /ˌsɛlfdɪˈstrʌkʃən/ *noun, pl* **-tions** [*count*] : the act of hurting or killing yourself • an act of *self-destruction* • His drinking started him ***on the path/road to self-destruction***.
– **self–de·struc·tive** /ˌsɛlfdɪˈstrʌktɪv/ *adj* [*more ~; most ~*] • *self-destructive* behavior

self–de·ter·mi·na·tion /ˌsɛlfdɪˌtəməˈneɪʃən/ *noun* [*noncount*]
1 : the right of the people of a particular place to choose the form of government they will have
2 : the freedom to make your own choices

self–dis·ci·pline /ˌsɛlfˈdɪsəplən/ *noun* [*noncount*] : the ability to make yourself do things that should be done • It's hard to exercise every day. You have to have a lot of *self-discipline*. • a lack of *self-discipline*
– **self–dis·ci·plined** /ˌsɛlfˈdɪsəplənd/ *adj* [*more ~; most ~*] • *self-disciplined* students

self–dis·cov·ery /ˌsɛlfdɪˈskʌvəri/ *noun* [*noncount*] : the act or process of gaining knowledge or understanding of your abilities, character, and feelings • She was on a voyage of *self-discovery*.

self–doubt /ˈsɛlfˈdaʊt/ *noun, pl* **-doubts** : a feeling of doubt about your own abilities or actions [*noncount*] a moment of *self-doubt* [*count*] Right before the start of the race, all his *self-doubts* returned.

self–drive /ˈsɛlfˈdraɪv/ *adj, always used before a noun, Brit*
1 *of a car* : rented from a company • a *self-drive* [=(*chiefly US*) *rental*] car
2 : done by driving yourself • a *self-drive* holiday/tour

self–ed·u·cat·ed /ˌsɛlfˈɛʤəˌkeɪtəd/ *adj* : educated by your own efforts (such as by reading books) rather than in a school • a *self-educated* businessman

self–ef·fac·ing /ˌsɛlfɪˈfeɪsɪŋ/ *adj* [*more ~; most ~*] *formal* : not trying to get attention or praise for yourself or your abilities : MODEST • He has a *self-effacing* manner. • She is quiet and *self-effacing*.
– **self–ef·face·ment** /ˌsɛlfɪˈfeɪsmənt/ *noun* [*noncount*]

self–em·ployed /ˌsɛlfɪmˈplɔɪd/ *adj* : earning income from your own business or profession rather than by working for someone else • a *self-employed* businessman
– **self–em·ploy·ment** /ˌsɛlfɪmˈplɔɪmənt/ *noun* [*noncount*]

self–es·teem /ˌsɛlfəˈstiːm/ *noun* [*noncount*] : a feeling of having respect for yourself and your abilities • low/high *self-esteem* • programs to raise/build *self-esteem* among children

self–ev·i·dent /ˌsɛlfˈɛvədənt/ *adj* [*more ~; most ~*] *formal* : clearly true and requiring no proof or explanation • The meaning is *self-evident*. • *self-evident* truths
– **self–ev·i·dent·ly** *adv*

self–ex·am /ˌsɛlfɪgˈzæm/ *noun, pl* **-ams** [*count*] : SELF-EXAMINATION

self–ex·am·i·na·tion /ˌsɛlfɪgˌzæməˈneɪʃən/ *noun, pl* **-tions**
1 [*noncount*] : careful examination of your own behavior and beliefs to see whether they are good or bad • the process of *self-examination*
2 [*count*] *medical* : the act or practice of checking your body for symptoms of illness • Doctors recommend a breast *self-examination* once a month.

self–ex·plan·a·to·ry /ˌsɛlfɪkˈsplænəˌtori, *Brit* ˌsɛlfɪkˈsplænətri/ *adj* : easy to understand without explanation • a *self-explanatory* phrase • The chapter titles of the book are *self-explanatory*.

self–ex·pres·sion /ˌsɛlfɪkˈsprɛʃən/ *noun* [*noncount*] : the expression of your thoughts or feelings especially through artistic activities (such as painting, writing, dancing, etc.) • a form/means/medium/mode of *self-expression* • The strict rules leave little room for *self-expression*.

self–flag·el·la·tion /ˌsɛlfˌflæʤəˈleɪʃən/ *noun* [*noncount*] : the act of hitting yourself with a whip as a way to punish yourself or as part of a religious ritual — often used figuratively • journalists engaging in *self-flagellation* [=journalists cricitizing themselves very harshly]

self–ful·fill·ing /ˌsɛlffʊlˈfɪlɪŋ/ *adj*
1 : becoming real or true because it was predicted or expected • The prediction of a rise in the stock market became a ***self-fulfilling prophecy*** when investors heard the report and began buying stock.
2 [*more ~; most ~*] : providing happiness and satisfaction : FULFILLING • She finds running her own business very *self-fulfilling*.

self–ful·fill·ment (*US*) *or Brit* **self–ful·fil·ment** /ˌsɛlffʊlˈfɪlmənt/ *noun* [*noncount*] : the feeling of being happy and satisfied because you are doing something that fully uses your abilities and talents • She found *self-fulfillment* [=*fulfillment*] by starting her own business.

self–gov·ern·ing /ˌsɛlfˈgʌvənɪŋ/ *adj* : controlled or ruled by its own members : having self-government • a *self-governing* territory/body

self–gov·ern·ment /ˌsɛlfˈgʌvənmənt/ *noun* [*noncount*] : government or control of a country, group, etc., by its own members rather than by the members of a different country, group, etc. • the island's right to *self-government*

self–help /ˈsɛlfˈhɛlp/ *noun* [*noncount*] : the action or process of doing things to improve yourself or to solve your problems without the help of others • books on *self-help*
– **self–help** *adj, always used before a noun* • *self-help* books/manuals

self·hood /ˈsɛlfˌhʊd/ *noun* [*noncount*] : the quality that makes a person or thing different from others : INDIVIDUALITY

self–iden·ti·fi·ca·tion /ˌsɛlfaɪˌdɛntəfəˈkeɪʃən/ *noun* [*noncount*]
1 : the feeling that you share and understand the problems or experiences of someone else • the young teacher's *self-identification* [=*identification*] with his students
2 : the act of identifying yourself as a particular kind of person • the teenager's *self-identification* as a rebel

self–iden·ti·ty /ˌsɛlfaɪˈdɛntəti/ *noun* [*noncount*] : the quality that makes a person or thing different from others : INDIVIDUALITY

self–im·age /ˈsɛlfˈɪmɪʤ/ *noun* [*noncount*] : the way you think about yourself and your abilities or appearance • She has a positive/negative/strong/poor *self-image*.

self–im·por·tant /ˌsɛlfɪmˈpoətn̩t/ *adj* [*more ~; most ~*] *disapproving* : having too high an opinion of your own importance • a *self-important* businessman
– **self–im·por·tance** /ˌsɛlfɪmˈpoətns/ *noun* [*noncount*]

self–im·posed /ˌsɛlfɪmˈpoʊzd/ *adj* : required by you of yourself : not given to you by someone else • a *self-imposed* task/deadline/limit • *self-imposed* exile/isolation/punishment

self–in·dul·gent /ˌsɛlfɪnˈdʌlʤənt/ *adj* [*more ~; most ~*] *disapproving* : allowing yourself to have or do whatever you want in a way that is excessive or wasteful • a *self-indulgent* lifestyle • a *self-indulgent* millionaire
– **self–in·dul·gence** /ˌsɛlfɪnˈdʌlʤəns/ *noun, pl* **-gen·ces** [*noncount*] a moment of *self-indulgence* [*count*] a small *self-indulgence*

self–in·flict·ed /ˌsɛlfɪnˈflɪktəd/ *adj* : caused by your own actions • a *self-inflicted* wound • His problems are mainly *self-inflicted*.

self–in·ter·est /ˌsɛlfˈɪntrəst/ *noun* [*noncount*]
1 *disapproving* : concern only for getting what you want or need and not about what happens to other people • They acted out of *self-interest* and fear.
2 : your own interest or advantage • Our *self-interest* demands that we help them. [=it benefits us to help them]
– **self–in·ter·est·ed** /ˌsɛlfˈɪntrəstəd/ *adj* • *self-interested* behavior

self·ish /ˈsɛlfɪʃ/ *adj* [*more ~; most ~*] *disapproving* : having or showing concern only for yourself and not for the needs or feelings of other people • *selfish* behavior/motives • a *selfish* man • She's interested only in her own *selfish* concerns. • I wish he'd spend less time with his friends and more time with me. Am I being *selfish*?
– **self·ish·ly** *adv* • He *selfishly* kept the money for himself. • She acted *selfishly*. – **self·ish·ness** *noun* [*noncount*] • the *selfishness* of their behavior

self·less /ˈsɛlfləs/ *adj* [*more ~; most ~*] : having or showing great concern for other people and little or no concern for yourself • a *selfless* act • *selfless* dedication/devotion/love
– **self·less·ly** *adv* • He *selflessly* volunteered to help.
– **self·less·ness** *noun* [*noncount*]

self–made /ˈsɛlfˈmeɪd/ *adj* : made rich and successful by your own efforts • a *self-made* man

self–mu·ti·la·tion /ˌsɛlfˌmjuːtəˈleɪʃən/ *noun* [*noncount*] *medical* : the act of wounding yourself on purpose especially because you are mentally ill

self–per·cep·tion /ˌsɛlfpəˈsɛpʃən/ *noun, pl* **-tions** [*count*, *noncount*] : the idea that you have about the kind of person you are ▪ People's *self-perceptions* are often very different from the way other people perceive them.

self–pity /ˈsɛlfˈpɪti/ *noun* [*noncount*] *disapproving* : a feeling of pity for yourself because you believe you have suffered more than is fair or reasonable ▪ He was wallowing in *self-pity*. ▪ She spoke without a trace/hint of *self-pity*.
– self–pity·ing /ˈsɛlfˈpɪtijɪŋ/ *adj* ▪ a *self-pitying* complainer

self–por·trait /ˌsɛlfˈpoətrət/ *noun, pl* **-traits** [*count*] : a painting or drawing of yourself that is done by yourself

self–pos·sessed /ˌsɛlfpəˈzɛst/ *adj* [*more ~; most ~*] : having or showing control of your feelings or actions especially in a difficult situation ▪ She is a remarkably calm and *self-possessed* young woman.
– self–pos·ses·sion /ˌsɛlfpəˈzɛʃən/ *noun* [*noncount*]

self–pres·er·va·tion /ˌsɛlfˌprɛzəˈveɪʃən/ *noun* [*noncount*] : protection of yourself from harm or death ▪ We all have an instinct for *self-preservation*.

self–pro·claimed /ˌsɛlfprouˈkleɪmd/ *adj, always used before a noun, usually disapproving* : giving yourself a particular name, title, etc., usually without any reason or proof that would cause other people to agree with you ▪ the *self-proclaimed* king of pop ▪ a *self-proclaimed* expert

self–pro·fessed /ˌsɛlfprəˈfɛst/ *adj, always used before a noun, usually disapproving*
1 : SELF-PROCLAIMED ▪ *self-professed* experts
2 : SELF-CONFESSED ▪ a *self-professed* sports junkie

self–pro·pelled /ˌsɛlfprəˈpɛld/ *adj* : able to move itself by means of a motor ▪ a *self-propelled* lawn mower [=a lawn mower that you do not have to push]

self–rais·ing flour /ˈsɛlfˈreɪzɪŋ-/ *noun* [*noncount*] *Brit* : SELF-RISING FLOUR

self–re·al·i·za·tion /ˌsɛlfˌriːjələˈzeɪʃən, *Brit* ˌsɛlfˌrɪəˌlaɪˈzeɪʃən/ *noun* [*noncount*] : the act of achieving the full development of your abilities and talents ▪ Work is often a means of *self-realization*.

self–re·flec·tion /ˌsɛlfrɪˈflɛkʃən/ *noun* [*noncount*] : careful thought about your own behavior and beliefs : SELF-EXAMINATION ▪ a moment of *self-reflection*

self–re·li·ant /ˌsɛlfrɪˈlajənt/ *adj* [*more ~; most ~*] : confident in your own abilities and able to do things for yourself : not needing help from other people ▪ She worked very hard to be *self-reliant*. ▪ a *self-reliant* adult
– self–re·li·ance /ˌsɛlfrɪˈlajəns/ *noun* [*noncount*]

self–re·spect /ˌsɛlfrɪˈspɛkt/ *noun* [*noncount*] : proper respect for yourself as a human being ▪ a sense of dignity and *self-respect* ▪ I lost my job, but not my *self-respect*.

self–re·spect·ing /ˌsɛlfrɪˈspɛktɪŋ/ *adj, always used before a noun* : having proper respect for yourself as a human being ▪ No *self-respecting* person would do something like that.

self–re·straint /ˌsɛlfrɪˈstreɪnt/ *noun* [*noncount*] : control over your own actions or feelings that keeps you from doing things you want to do but should not do ▪ I know you like to shop, but you need to exercise/show some *self-restraint*.

self–righ·teous /ˌsɛlfˈraɪʧəs/ *adj* [*more ~; most ~*] *disapproving* : having or showing a strong belief that your own actions, opinions, etc., are right and other people's are wrong ▪ a *self-righteous* person/tone ▪ *self-righteous* indignation ▪ It's OK to criticize, but don't be/get *self-righteous* about it.
– self–righ·teous·ly *adv* **– self–righ·teous·ness** *noun* [*noncount*]

self–ris·ing flour /ˈsɛlfˈraɪzɪŋ-/ *noun* [*noncount*] *US* : a mixture of flour, salt, and baking powder — called also (*Brit*) *self-raising flour*

self–rule /ˈsɛlfˈruːl/ *noun* [*noncount*] : SELF-GOVERNMENT

self–rul·ing /ˈsɛlfˈruːlɪŋ/ *adj* : SELF-GOVERNING

self–sac·ri·fice /ˈsɛlfˈsækrəˌfaɪs/ *noun* [*noncount*] : the act of giving up something that you want to have or keep in order to help someone else ▪ We should honor the courage and *self-sacrifice* of the brave soldiers who died for our country.
– self–sa·cri·fic·ing /ˈsɛlfˈsækrəˌfaɪsɪŋ/ *adj* ▪ *self-sacrificing* parents who put their children first

self·same /ˈsɛlfˌseɪm/ *adj, always used before a noun, literary* : exactly the same ▪ These *selfsame* [=very same] people who complain about the problem also refuse to help correct it.

self–sat·is·fac·tion /ˌsɛlfˌsætəsˈfækʃən/ *noun* [*noncount*] *usually disapproving* : a feeling of being very pleased or satisfied with yourself and what you have done ▪ his smug *self-satisfaction*

self–sat·is·fied /ˌsɛlfˈsætəsˌfaɪd/ *adj* [*more ~; most ~*] *usually disapproving* : feeling or showing self-satisfaction ▪ a *self-satisfied* young woman ▪ a *self-satisfied* smirk

self–seek·ing /ˌsɛlfˈsiːkɪŋ/ *adj* [*more ~; most ~*] *disapproving* : concerned only about getting what you want or need and not caring about what happens to other people ▪ a *self-seeking* opportunist ▪ *self-seeking* behavior/motives
– self–seek·er /ˌsɛlfˈsiːkɚ/ *noun, pl* **-ers** [*count*] ▪ He's a *self-seeker* who'll do anything to get ahead.

self–ser·vice /ˌsɛlfˈsɚvəs/ *adj* : allowing or requiring customers to serve themselves without help from workers ▪ a *self-service* café ▪ a *self-service* gas station
– self–service *noun* [*noncount*] ▪ The gas station only has *self-service*.

self–serv·ing /ˌsɛlfˈsɚvɪŋ/ *adj* [*more ~; most ~*] *disapproving* : having or showing concern only about your own needs and interests ▪ *self-serving* motives ▪ a *self-serving* politician

self–start·er /ˌsɛlfˈstɑɚtɚ/ *noun, pl* **-ers** [*count*] : a person who is able to work without needing a lot of instruction or help ▪ The job requires a highly motivated *self-starter*.

self–styled /ˌsɛlfˈstajəld/ *adj, always used before a noun* : called a particular thing by yourself : SELF-PROCLAIMED ▪ *self-styled* experts

self–suf·fi·cient /ˌsɛlfsəˈfɪʃənt/ *adj* [*more ~; most ~*] : able to live or function without help or support from others ▪ *self-sufficient* villages/farms ▪ His new job allowed him to become more *self-sufficient*.
– self–suf·fi·cien·cy /ˌsɛlfsəˈfɪʃənsi/ *noun* [*noncount*] ▪ economic *self-sufficiency*

self–sup·port·ing /ˌsɛlfsəˈpoətɪŋ/ *adj* : earning enough money to live without getting help from other people ▪ She hopes to find a better job so she'll finally be *self-supporting*.

self–taught /ˈsɛlfˈtɑːt/ *adj*
1 : educated by your own efforts (such as by reading books) rather than by a teacher ▪ a *self-taught* musician
2 : learned by your own efforts rather than at school ▪ *self-taught* knowledge

self–willed /ˈsɛlfˈwɪld/ *adj* [*more ~; most ~*] *disapproving* : determined to do what you want even though other people may not want you to do it ▪ a stubborn and *self-willed* child

self–worth /ˈsɛlfˈwɚθ/ *noun* [*noncount*] : a feeling that you are a good person who deserves to be treated with respect : SELF-ESTEEM ▪ a healthy sense of *self-worth*

[1]sell /ˈsɛl/ *verb* **sells; sold** /ˈsould/; **sell·ing**
1 : to exchange (something) for money [+ *obj*] He *sold* his car. ▪ He buys and remodels houses and then *sells* them at a profit. ▪ She *sold* him a watch for $20. = She *sold* a watch to him for $20. [*no obj*] Stock prices are increasing, so now is a good time to *sell*. — opposite BUY
2 [+ *obj*] : to make (something) available to be bought ▪ Only a few stores *sell* that type of equipment. ▪ She *sells* insurance. [=she has the job of selling insurance to people] ▪ He is *selling* his car for $1,000. [=he is offering his car for sale at a price of $1,000]
3 [*no obj*] : to be able to be bought for a particular price — + *for* or *at* ▪ Those cookies *sell for* a dollar apiece. ▪ All items in the store are *selling at* half price.
4 a [*no obj*] : to be bought by someone or by many people ▪ That house still hasn't *sold*. [=no one has bought that house] ▪ The houses in that neighborhood aren't *selling*. [=people aren't buying the houses that are for sale in that neighborhood] ▪ They hope the new version will *sell* better than the old one. [=they hope that more people will buy the new version] ▪ The dictionary is *selling* well. [=many people are buying copies of the dictionary] ▪ The newest model just didn't *sell*. [=very few people bought it] **b** [+ *obj*] — used to say how many copies of something have been sold ▪ Their first album *sold* more than a a million copies. [=more than a million copies of the album were bought]
5 : to cause people to want to buy (something) : to cause the sale of (something) [+ *obj*] His name on the cover *sells* the book. [*no obj*] Good advertising *sells*.
6 [+ *obj*] : to persuade someone to accept or approve of (something or someone) ▪ He had a difficult time *selling* his theory to other scientists. ▪ You will really have to *sell* yourself at the interview to get that job.

sell a pup see PUP

sell off [*phrasal verb*] ***sell (something) off*** *or* ***sell off (something)*** : to sell (something) especially for a low price in order to get rid of it quickly or to get money that you need ▪ He *sold off* his car so he could move overseas. ▪ The family plans to *sell* some of the property *off*. — see also SELL-OFF

sell on [*phrasal verb*] ***sell (someone) on (something)*** : to per-

S

suade (someone) to be interested in and excited about (something) ▪ He tried to *sell* them *on* the value of the project he was proposing. — often used as *(be) sold on* ▪ She *wasn't sold on* the idea. [=she wasn't convinced that it was a good idea]

sell out *[phrasal verb]* **1 a :** to be bought until no more are available : to be entirely sold ▪ Tickets to the concert *sold out* quickly. ▪ The book has *sold out* in stores across the country. **b :** to sell the entire amount of something ▪ Many stores *sold out* quickly when the book was first published. ▪ The concert *sold out* quickly. [=all the tickets to the concert were quickly bought] **c *be sold out* :** to have sold the entire amount of something ▪ "Are there any more tickets?" "No, I'm sorry, We're (all) *sold out.*" [=we've sold all the tickets] — often + *of* ▪ The store *was sold out of* milk again. [=there was no milk at the store because it had all been sold] **d *sell (something) out or sell out (something)*** : to sell all of (something) ▪ The tickets were (all) *sold out* quickly. [=all of the tickets were sold quickly] **2 :** to sell all that you own of a business, company, etc. ▪ In the end, the other owners forced her to *sell out.* **3** *disapproving* **:** to do something that does not agree with your beliefs, values, etc., especially in order to make money ▪ Many of the band's fans accused them of *selling out* when they started appearing in television commercials. ▪ The union sees the deal as *selling out* to management. [=the union sees the deal as going against their principles and favoring management] **4 *sell (someone) out or sell out (someone)*** *informal* **:** to do something that harms or causes trouble for (someone who trusted you) in order to get something for yourself : to betray (someone) ▪ She *sold out* her accomplices [=she told police who her accomplices were] in exchange for a lower sentence. — see also SELLOUT, SOLD-OUT

sell (someone) down the river *informal* **:** to do something that harms (someone who trusted you) especially in order to get something for yourself : to betray (someone) ▪ I can't believe my best friend would *sell* me *down the river.*

***sell (someone or something) short* :** to put too low a value on the ability, importance, or quality of (someone or something) ▪ Don't *sell* yourself *short.* You have some great skills and experience. ▪ I think you're *selling* the book *short*; it's a lot more interesting than that.

sell up *[phrasal verb] Brit* **:** to sell your possessions, business, etc., especially so that you can move away ▪ They were forced to *sell up* and go out of business.

***sell your body* :** to accept money in exchange for sex

***sell your soul (to the devil)* :** to gain wealth, success, power, etc., by doing something bad or dishonest ▪ He has *sold his soul (to the devil)* for fame and prosperity.

[2]**sell** *noun, pl* **sells** *[count] chiefly US* **:** something that is sold — used to say that it is easy or difficult to get people to buy or accept something; usually singular ▪ Her new novel was an easy *sell.* [=her new novel sold well; many people wanted to buy it] ▪ We need to raise taxes, but that's a tough *sell.* [=it's hard to persuade people to accept a tax increase] — see also HARD SELL, SOFT SELL

sell–by date *noun, pl* **~ dates** *[count]* **:** a date that is printed on food packages which shows the last day on which the food can be sold — sometimes used figuratively ▪ He wants to get married before he's past his *sell-by date.* [=before he's too old]

sell·er /ˈsɛlɚ/ *noun, pl* **-ers** *[count]*

1 : a person or business that sells something ▪ a ticket *seller* ▪ The *seller* said that the car was in excellent condition. ▪ We're the number one *seller* of appliances in the country. — opposite BUYER; see also BOOKSELLER

2 : a product that sells in a particular way or amount ▪ Her new CD is a hot *seller.* [=a lot of people are buying her new CD] ▪ That book is our top/biggest *seller.* — see also BEST SELLER

seller's market *noun [singular]* **:** a situation in which few things of the same kind are for sale, prices are high, and sellers have an advantage over buyers — opposite BUYER'S MARKET

selling point *noun, pl* **~ points** *[count]* **:** a quality or feature that makes people want to buy something ▪ The car's new sound system is a *selling point.* ▪ The house's big/main/major *selling point* is its location.

selling price *noun [singular]* **:** the price for which something actually sells ▪ They asked $200,000 for the house, but the eventual *selling price* was $175,000. — compare ASKING PRICE

sell–off /ˈsɛlˌɑːf/ *noun [noncount]*

1 *US* **:** the sale of a large number of stocks or shares that causes their price to drop ▪ The decline in technology stocks prompted a *sell-off* that made matters even worse. — see also *sell off* at [1]SELL

2 *Brit* **:** the sale of an industry that is owned by the government to private buyers

Sellotape /ˈsɛləˌteɪp/ *trademark, Brit* — used for a type of adhesive tape

sell·out /ˈsɛlˌaʊt/ *noun, pl* **-outs** *[count]*

1 : a game, concert, etc., for which all seats are sold ▪ The concert/game/performance was a *sellout.*

2 a : an occurrence in which you do something that does not agree with your beliefs, values, etc., especially in order to make money ▪ The union sees the deal as a *sellout.* **b :** someone who does something that does not agree with that person's beliefs or values especially in order to make money ▪ Angry fans called him a *sellout* when he started appearing in television commercials. — see also *sell out* at [1]SELL

selt·zer /ˈsɛltsɚ/ *noun [noncount]* **:** water that has bubbles added to it

selves *plural of* SELF

se·man·tic /sɪˈmæntɪk/ *adj, linguistics*

1 : of or relating to the meanings of words and phrases ▪ the process of *semantic* development/change

2 : of or relating to semantics ▪ *semantic* theory ▪ a *semantic* analysis/interpretation

– se·man·ti·cal·ly /sɪˈmæntɪkli/ *adv* ▪ The words are *semantically* related.

se·man·tics /sɪˈmæntɪks/ *noun [noncount] linguistics*

1 : the study of the meanings of words and phrases in language

2 : the meanings of words and phrases in a particular context ▪ The whole controversy is a matter of *semantics.* [=the controversy was caused by people understanding the same words in different ways]

– se·man·ti·cist /sɪˈmæntəsɪst/ *noun, pl* **-cists** *[count]*

sema·phore /ˈsɛməˌfoɚ/ *noun [noncount]* **:** a system used for sending signals by using two flags that are held in your hands

sem·blance /ˈsɛmbləns/ *noun [singular]* **:** the state of being somewhat like something but not truly or fully the same thing — usually + *of* ▪ They found it hard to maintain any *semblance of* control. [=to maintain any appearance of having control; to maintain any control at all] ▪ Her life finally returned to some *semblance of* order/normality. [=her life finally became a little more ordered/normal]

se·men /ˈsiːmən/ *noun [noncount]* **:** the sticky, whitish liquid containing sperm that is produced by a male's sex organs

se·mes·ter /səˈmɛstɚ/ *noun, pl* **-ters** *[count] US* **:** one of two usually 18-week periods that make up an academic year at a school or college — compare QUARTER, TERM, TRIMESTER

semi *noun, pl* **sem·is** *[count] informal*

1 /ˈsɛˌmaɪ/ **:** SEMIFINAL — usually plural ▪ The team made it to the *semis.*

2 /ˈsɛˌmaɪ/ *US* **:** a short, heavy truck that has a long trailer attached to the back and that is used to move goods : SEMITRAILER

3 /ˈsɛmi/ *Brit* **:** a house that is attached to another house : a semidetached house

semi- *prefix*

1 : half ▪ a *semi*circle ▪ *semi*circular

2 : happening twice during a particular period of time ▪ *semi*annual ▪ *semi*monthly

3 : partly : not completely ▪ *semi*tropical

4 : partial : not complete ▪ *semi*consciousness

semi·an·nu·al /ˌsɛmiˈænjəwəl/ *adj, chiefly US* **:** happening or produced every six months or twice in each year ▪ my *semiannual* visit to my cousin ▪ a *semiannual* journal/report

– semi·an·nu·al·ly *adv*

semi·au·to·mat·ic /ˌsɛmiˌɑːtəˈmætɪk/ *adj, of a gun* **:** able to fire bullets one after the other quickly but not automatically ▪ a *semiautomatic* rifle/weapon/pistol

– semiautomatic *noun, pl* **-ics** *[count]* ▪ The police found a *semiautomatic* in his car.

semi·breve /ˈsɛmiˌbriːv/ *noun, pl* **-breves** *[count] Brit* **:** WHOLE NOTE

semi·cir·cle /ˈsɛmiˌsɚkəl/ *noun, pl* **-cir·cles** *[count]*

1 : half of a circle
2 : an arrangement of people or things that forms a semicircle • The children sat in a *semicircle.* • The houses are built in a *semicircle.*
– **semi·cir·cu·lar** /ˌsɛmiˈsɚkjəlɚ/ *adj* • a *semicircular* driveway

semi·co·lon /ˈsɛmiˌkoulən/ *noun, pl* **-lons** [*count*] : the punctuation mark ; that is used to separate major parts in a sentence and to separate items in a series if the items contain commas

semi·con·duc·tor /ˌsɛmikənˈdʌktɚ/ *noun, pl* **-tors** [*count*] : a material or object that allows some electricity or heat to move through it and that is used especially in electronic devices • Silicon is a *semiconductor.*
– **semi·con·duct·ing** /ˌsɛmikənˈdʌktɪŋ/ *adj, always used before a noun* • *semiconducting* materials/properties

semi·con·scious /ˌsɛmiˈkɑːnʃəs/ *adj* : partially conscious : only somewhat awake and able to understand what is happening around you • The victim was *semiconscious* and could barely talk.

semi·de·tached /ˌsɛmidɪˈtætʃt/ *adj, Brit* : attached to another house by a shared wall on one side • a *semidetached* house/villa
– **semidetached** *noun* [*singular*] • He lives in a *semidetached.*

semi·fi·nal /ˈsɛmiˌfaɪnl/ *noun, pl* **-nals** [*count*] : either one of two matches, games, or contests to decide which people or teams will be in the final part of a competition (such as a series of races or a tennis tournament) • She played against a lesser-known rival in the (women's) *semifinal.* — often plural • She won in the quarterfinals but lost in the *semifinals.* — often used before another noun • the *semifinal* round • *semifinal* teams
– **semi·fi·nal·ist** /ˌsɛmiˈfaɪnlɪst/ *noun, pl* **-ists** [*count*] • She was a *semifinalist* in the tennis tournament.

semi·for·mal /ˌsɛmiˈfoɚməl/ *adj, US* : somewhat formal : not informal but not highly formal • She wore a *semiformal* gown to the wedding. • a *semiformal* dinner party • a *semiformal* meeting/proposal

semi·month·ly /ˌsɛmiˈmʌnθli/ *adj* : happening or produced two times in each month • a *semimonthly* meeting/newsletter

sem·i·nal /ˈsɛmənl/ *adj*
1 *formal* : having a strong influence on ideas, works, events, etc., that come later : very important and influential • a *seminal* book/work/writer
2 *always used before a noun, medical* : of or containing semen • *seminal* fluid • the *seminal* duct

sem·i·nar /ˈsɛməˌnɑɚ/ *noun, pl* **-nars** [*count*]
1 : a meeting in which you receive information on and training in a particular subject • a writing *seminar* • a *seminar* on career planning • educational/investment *seminars*
2 : a class offered to a small group of students at a college or university • a graduate/philosophy *seminar* • a *seminar* room

sem·i·nar·i·an /ˌsɛməˈnerijən/ *noun, pl* **-ans** [*count*] : someone who is studying at a seminary

sem·i·nary /ˈsɛməˌneri, *Brit* ˈsɛmənəri/ *noun, pl* **-nar·ies** [*count*] : a school for training religious leaders (such as priests, ministers, and rabbis)

se·mi·o·tics /ˌsiːmiˈɑːtɪks, sɛmiˈɑːtɪks/ *noun* [*noncount*] *technical* : the study of signs and symbols and how they are used
– **se·mi·o·tic** /ˌsiːmiˈɑːtɪk, sɛmiˈɑːtɪk/ *adj* • a *semiotic* analysis/theory

semi·pre·cious /ˌsɛmiˈprɛʃəs/ *adj, of a jewel* : fairly valuable : having somewhat less value than a precious stone • *semiprecious* stones such as aquamarines and garnets

semi·pri·vate /ˌsɛmiˈpraɪvət/ *adj*
1 : available to a small number of people : providing some but not complete privacy • a *semiprivate* terrace/pool
2 : shared by two patients • a *semiprivate* room in a hospital

semi·pro /ˈsɛmiˌprou/ *adj, always used before a noun* : SEMIPROFESSIONAL
– **semipro** *noun, pl* **-pros** [*count*]

semi·pro·fes·sion·al /ˌsɛmiprəˈfɛʃənəl/ *adj, always used before a noun*
1 : paid to participate in a sport or activity but not doing it as a full-time job • a *semiprofessional* pitcher/musician
2 : involving semiprofessional athletes • *semiprofessional* soccer/football
– **semiprofessional** *noun, pl* **-als** [*count*]

semi·qua·ver /ˈsɛmiˌkweɪvɚ/ *noun, pl* **-vers** [*count*] *Brit* : SIXTEENTH NOTE

semi·retired /ˌsɛmirɪˈtajɚd/ *adj, US* : working only part-time at a career, job, etc., especially because you have reached the age at which you no longer need or want to work full-time • a *semiretired* executive/nurse

semi·skilled /ˌsɛmiˈskɪld/ *adj* : having or requiring some training : having or requiring less training than skilled labor and more than unskilled labor • *semiskilled* labor/jobs • *semiskilled* and unskilled assembly workers

semi–skimmed milk /ˌsɛmiˈskɪmd-/ *noun* [*noncount*] *Brit* : milk from which some of the cream has been removed — compare SKIM MILK

semi·sweet /ˌsɛmiˈswiːt/ *adj, US* : slightly sweet • *semisweet* chocolate

Sem·ite /ˈsɛˌmaɪt, *Brit* ˈsiːˌmaɪt/ *noun, pl* **-ites** [*count*] : a member of a group of people originally of southwestern Asia that includes Jews and Arabs

Se·mit·ic /səˈmɪtɪk/ *adj*
1 : of or relating to the language family that includes Hebrew and Arabic
2 : of or relating to the Semites

semi·tone /ˈsɛmiˌtoun/ *noun, pl* **-tones** [*count*] *music* : a difference in sound that is equal to $\frac{1}{12}$ of an octave — called also (*US*) *half step*

semi·trail·er /ˈsɛˌmaɪˌtreɪlɚ/ *noun, pl* **-ers** [*count*] *US*
1 : a long trailer that has wheels at the rear and is attached at its forward end to a large truck
2 : a large truck with a long trailer attached to the back of it — see picture at TRUCK

semi·trop·i·cal /ˌsɛmiˈtrɑːpɪkəl/ *adj* : SUBTROPICAL

semi·week·ly /ˌsɛmiˈwiːkli/ *adj* : happening twice a week • *semiweekly* classes

sem·o·li·na /ˌsɛməˈliːnə/ *noun* [*noncount*]
1 : a type of wheat flour that is often used to make pasta
2 *Brit* : a sweet dessert made from semolina and milk

sen. *abbr* **1** senate; senator **2** senior

sen·ate /ˈsɛnət/ *noun, pl* **-ates**
1 ***the Senate*** : the smaller group of the two groups of people who meet to discuss and make the laws of a country, state, etc. • *the* New York State *Senate*; *especially* : the smaller group of the two groups that form the U.S. Congress • *The Senate* approved the bill. • *The Senate* voted to repeal the tax cut. — often used before another noun • The *Senate* bill was approved. • the *Senate* race • the *Senate* majority leader • a *Senate* aide — compare HOUSE OF REPRESENTATIVES
2 [*count*] : a group of people who govern some colleges and universities
3 ***the Senate*** : the group of officials who led the ancient Roman government

sen·a·tor /ˈsɛnətɚ/ *noun, pl* **-tors** [*count*] : a member of a senate or the Senate • Democratic/Republican *senators* • a former *senator* • *Senator* Inouye

sen·a·to·ri·al /ˌsɛnəˈtorijəl/ *adj* : of or relating to a senator or a senate • *senatorial* offices/candidates

send /ˈsɛnd/ *verb* **sends; sent** /ˈsɛnt/; **send·ing** [+ *obj*]
1 : to cause (a letter, an e-mail, a package, etc.) to go or to be carried from one place or person to another • I *sent* [=*mailed*] the letter/package/check to her. • (*US*) I *sent* it to her by mail. = (*Brit*) I *sent* it to her by post. • Please fill out the form and *send* it back (to us). • He *sent* me an e-mail. = He *sent* an e-mail to me. • Supplies were *sent* (out) to the troops. • Satellites receive signals in space and *send* them back to Earth.
2 : to give (a message) to someone • Please *send* my compliments to the chef. [=tell the chef that I enjoyed the food] • Tell her that I *send* my love. [=tell her that I think of her in a loving way] • When you write to him, please *send* him my very best wishes. • ***Send word*** to the others [=tell the others] that we'll be late.
3 : to tell or cause (someone or something) to go to a place • He became ill and was *sent* home from school. • She *sent* the kids to bed immediately after supper. • He was *sent* to prison for armed robbery. • He *sent* me (to the store) for bread and milk. • The company *sent* me to the conference. • "There is a Ms. Jones here to see you." "*Send* her in." • He was *sent* on a secret mission. • Helicopters were *sent* (out) to search for the lost hikers. • They *sent* a limo to pick her up at the airport. • He asked us to *send* a taxi for him.
4 : to make the arrangements and payments that allow (someone) to attend a school, camp, etc. • They are able to *send* both their children to private school. • They *sent* their daughter to soccer camp during the summer. • They are

sending their son (away/off) to military school.
5 : to tell (someone or something) to go *to* a particular person or place for treatment, help, information, etc. • She *sent* him *to* the information desk. • The teacher *sent* [=*referred*] the students *to* the dictionary for the meaning of the word. • My doctor *sent* me *to* a specialist. • The Senate *sent* the bill *to* a committee.
6 *always followed by an adverb or preposition* : to cause (someone or something) to move in a particular direction or manner • News of the strike *sent* stock prices down. • The surprise attack *sent* the enemy running. • The punch *sent* him to the floor. • He *sent* the ball into right field. • Her performance **sent a chill/shiver up/down my spine** [=made me feel very excited and emotional]
7 : to put (someone) into a particular state or condition • Her lectures often *send* students to sleep. — usually + *into* • Their decision *sent* him *into* a rage.

send away for [*phrasal verb*] **send away for (something)** or **send away to (someone) for (something)** : to ask to receive (something) by sending a letter, coupon, etc., to someone by mail • I *sent away for* [=*sent off for*] a free sample. • You will have to *send away to* the manufacturer *for* a refund.

send down [*phrasal verb*] **send down (someone)** or **send (someone) down** *Brit, informal* : to send (someone) to prison • He was *sent down* for six years for the robbery.

send for [*phrasal verb*] **1 send for (someone)** : to ask (someone) to come to a place • Someone should *send for* a doctor. **2 send for (something)** : to ask someone to bring or send (something) to you • *Send for* our free product catalog. • The general has already *sent for* reinforcements. • She *sent for* help.

send forth [*phrasal verb*] **send forth (something)** *formal* **1** : to cause (something) to be heard • She *sent forth* [=*emitted*, (less formally) *let out*] a loud cry. **2** : to cause (light, heat, etc.) to move outward from a source • The tropical flowers *sent forth* [=*emitted*, (less formally) *gave off*] a wonderful fragrance. **3** : to produce (something) in the process of growing or developing • The plant began to *send forth* [=*send out*] its shoots.

send in [*phrasal verb*] **1 send in (someone)** or **send (someone) in a** : to tell (someone) to go to a place to deal with a difficult situation • Police were *sent in* to restore order. **b** : to tell (a player) to enter a game • He was *sent in* to replace the starting goaltender. **2 send in (something)** or **send (something) in** : to mail or e-mail (something) to a place • Please *send in* your poems by October 1.

send off [*phrasal verb*] **1 send off (something)** or **send (something) off** : to send (something) by mail or another service • I *sent off* the package yesterday. **2 send off (someone)** or **send (someone) off** *chiefly Brit* : to order (a player who has broken a rule) to leave the field for the remainder of the game • He was *sent off* [=*ejected*] for striking another player. **3 send off for (something)** : to ask to receive (something) by sending a letter, coupon, etc., to someone by mail • I *sent off for* [=*sent away for*] a sample.

send on [*phrasal verb*] **send on (something)** or **send (something) on** : to cause (something) to go or to be carried from one place to another • I had my mail/post *sent on* [=*forwarded, sent*] to my new address. • He had his baggage *sent on* ahead. [=sent to the place he is going to]

send out [*phrasal verb*] **1 send out (something)** or **send (something) out a** : to mail (something) to many different people or places • Have you *sent out* the invitations yet? **b** : to cause (a signal) to go out • The pilot *sent out* a distress signal. **c** : to cause (light, heat, etc.) to move outward from a source • The coals *sent out* [=*gave off*] a reddish glow. **d** : to produce (something) in the process of growing or developing • The plant began to *send out* its shoots. **2 send out for (something)** : to ask a restaurant to deliver (food) to you • We *sent out for* pizza.

send (someone or something) packing *informal* : to force (someone or something) to leave a place or situation • We were *sent packing* after the first day of tryouts. • A loss in tomorrow's game will *send* them *packing*. [=will eliminate them from the competition]

send up [*phrasal verb*] **1 send up (something)** or **send (something) up a** : to cause (something) to be heard • He *sent up* a loud cry. [=he cried out loudly] **b** : to cause (something) to move upward • The campfire *sent up* sparks. • If you need help, *send up* a flare so that we can locate you. **c** : to produce (something) in the process of growing or developing • plants *sending up* new shoots **d** : to suggest or propose (something) to a more powerful person or group so that a decision can be made • The bill has been *sent up* to the Senate for a vote. • They are *sending up* a new name/applicant for consideration. **2 send up (someone or something)** or **send (someone or something) up** *chiefly Brit, informal* : to imitate (someone or something) in an amusing way • The show *sends up* [=*parodies*] soap operas. — see also SEND-UP

send•er /ˈsɛndɚ/ *noun, pl* **-ers** [*count*] : a person who sends a letter, package, message, etc. • He wrote "return to *sender*" on the package.

send–off /ˈsɛndˌɑːf/ *noun, pl* **-offs** [*count*] : an occasion when people gather together to say goodbye to someone who is leaving — usually singular • A crowd of friends gave them a fine *send-off*.

send–up /ˈsɛndˌʌp/ *noun, pl* **-ups** [*count*] *informal* : a movie, song, etc., that imitates the style of someone or something else in an amusing way — often + *of* • a *send-up* [=*parody*] *of* horror films — see also *send up* at SEND

se•nes•cence /sɪˈnɛsn̩s/ *noun* [*noncount*] *technical + formal* : the state of being old or the process of becoming old • premature *senescence*
– se•nes•cent /sɪˈnɛsn̩t/ *adj* • *senescent* cells

se•nile /ˈsiːˌnajəl/ *adj* [*more ~; most ~*] : showing a loss of mental ability (such as memory) in old age • a *senile* man in his eighties • Her mother is becoming/getting/going *senile*.
– se•nil•i•ty /sɪˈnɪləti/ *noun* [*noncount*] • Paranoia is a possible sign of *senility*.

senile dementia *noun* [*noncount*] *medical* : a condition that affects the mind of aging people and causes them to be confused, to forget things, etc.

¹se•nior /ˈsiːnjɚ/ *adj*
1 *not used before a noun, US* **a** : older in age — usually + *to* • She is five years *senior to* me. = She is *senior to* me by five years. [=she is five years older than I am] **b** — used chiefly in its abbreviated form *Sr.* to identify a father who has the same name as his son. • John Smith, Jr. and John Smith, *Sr.* — compare JUNIOR
2 : higher in standing or rank than another person in the same position • a *senior* officer/manager/executive • the *senior* vice president of marketing • She is a *senior* aide to the president. • a *senior* editor for the magazine • He recently became a *senior* partner in the accounting/consulting firm. — often + *to* • He is *senior to* me. — compare JUNIOR
3 *always used before a noun* **a** : of, relating to, or designed for older people • a *senior* center • *senior* housing **b** : designed for or done by adults or people over a certain age • the men's *senior* baseball league • *senior* golf

²senior *noun, pl* **-niors** [*count*]
1 : a person who is older than another person • She is five years my *senior*. = She is my *senior* by five years. [=she is five years older than I am] — compare JUNIOR
2 : a person who is of a higher rank than another person • As his *senior*, she commanded quite a bit of respect. • She was his *senior* in rank.
3 *US* : a student in the final year of high school or college • high school juniors and *seniors* — often used before another noun • the *senior* class/yearbook/prom • She skipped her *senior* year and went straight to college. • the *senior* captain of a team — compare FRESHMAN, JUNIOR, SOPHOMORE
4 *chiefly US* : SENIOR CITIZEN

senior citizen *noun, pl* **~ -zens** [*count*] *chiefly US* : an old person • programs/activities for *senior citizens* : a person who is at least a certain age (such as 55) • *Senior citizens* qualify for a discount at the movie theater.

senior high school *noun, pl* **~ schools** [*count*] *US* : a school that includes the 10th, 11th, and 12th grades and often also the 9th grade : HIGH SCHOOL — compare JUNIOR HIGH SCHOOL

se•nior•i•ty /sinˈjorəti/ *noun* [*noncount*]
1 : the amount of time you have worked at a job or for a company compared to other employees • Promotions are based on merit and *seniority*. • a teacher with less/more *seniority* • He has worked here longer than I have, so he **has seniority over** me.
2 : the state of having a higher rank than another person • a position of *seniority*

sen•sa•tion /sɛnˈseɪʃən/ *noun, pl* **-tions**
1 [*count*] : a particular feeling or effect that your body experiences • I experienced a stinging/prickling/tingling *sensation* in my arm. • She felt a burning *sensation* in her throat. • visual/bodily *sensations* • a *sensation* of hunger • She craved new experiences and *sensations*.

2 [*count*] : a particular feeling or experience that may not have a real cause ▪ I had a *sensation* of falling. [=I felt as if I were falling] ▪ She had the strange *sensation* that someone was watching her. ▪ I couldn't quite shake the *sensation* that I'd been fooled.

3 [*noncount*] : the ability to feel things through your physical senses ▪ Her injury left her with no *sensation* in her legs.

4 [*count*] **a** : a lot of excitement and interest — usually singular ▪ The news created (quite) a *sensation*. ▪ News of the corporate merger caused a *sensation* on the stock market. **b** : someone or something that causes a lot of excitement and interest — usually singular ▪ The rave reviews turned the book into a nationwide *sensation* overnight. ▪ a music/pop *sensation*

sen·sa·tion·al /sɛnˈseɪʃənl/ *adj* [*more* ~; *most* ~]

1 : causing very great excitement or interest with shocking details ▪ a particularly *sensational* trial/crime ▪ *sensational* headlines ▪ *sensational* news stories

2 : very excellent or great ▪ a *sensational* performance/idea ▪ a *sensational* (new) talent

3 *informal* : very attractive ▪ She looked *sensational* in her new dress.

— **sen·sa·tion·al·ly** *adv* ▪ The books sold *sensationally* well.

sen·sa·tion·al·ism /sɛnˈseɪʃənəˌlɪzəm/ *noun* [*noncount*] *disapproving* : the use of shocking details to cause a lot of excitement or interest ▪ The network was accused of *sensationalism* in its reporting.

— **sen·sa·tion·al·ist** /sɛnˈseɪʃənəlɪst/ *also chiefly US* **sen·sa·tion·al·is·tic** /sɛnˌseɪʃənəˈlɪstɪk/ *adj* [*more* ~; *most* ~] ▪ *sensationalist* tabloids/reporting ▪ *sensationalistic* newspaper stories

sen·sa·tion·al·ize *also Brit* **sen·sa·tion·al·ise** /sɛnˈseɪʃənəˌlaɪz/ *verb* **-iz·es**; **-ized**; **-iz·ing** [+ *obj*] *disapproving* : to describe or show something in a way that makes it seem more shocking than it really is ▪ Journalists should report the news accurately without trying to *sensationalize* it.

— **sensationalized** *adj* ▪ a *sensationalized* story of a kidnapping

[1]**sense** /ˈsɛns/ *noun, pl* **sens·es**

1 **a** [*count*] : one of the five natural powers (touch, taste, smell, sight, and hearing) through which you receive information about the world around you ▪ All of my *senses* were on the alert for danger. — often + *of* ▪ The dog lost his *sense of* smell. ▪ an acute/poor *sense of* hearing — see also SIXTH SENSE **b** [*singular*] : a physical feeling : something that your body experiences — usually + *of* ▪ a *sense of* fatigue/hunger ▪ Ear problems can sometimes affect a person's ***sense of balance***.

2 **a** [*singular*] : a particular feeling : an emotion that you are aware of ▪ We had a *sense* that something wasn't quite right. — usually + *of* ▪ Once the speech was over, he was filled with a tremendous *sense of* relief. ▪ a *sense of* loss/urgency/pride ▪ a *sense of* well-being ▪ Their *sense of* accomplishment was obvious. ▪ We felt a growing *sense of* danger. ▪ The gun gave him a ***false sense of security***. [=made him feel safer than he really was] ▪ She has a strong ***sense of self***. [=she has strong ideas about who she is] **b** [*count*] : a personal quality : a specific quality that is part of your personality — usually singular; + *of* ▪ He had a great *sense of* adventure. [=he liked adventure very much] ▪ a *sense of* order/duty ▪ She lacked any *sense of* responsibility about financial matters. ▪ He had no *sense of* purpose [=he did not know what he wanted to do with his life] after his divorce. ▪ She has a great ***sense of humor***. [=she says funny things and can see the funny side of things] ▪ He has no *sense of humor*. [=he does not find things amusing] ▪ His excellent ***sense of direction*** [=ability to find his way around easily in a new place] was useful during our travels. ▪ The chairman's speech gave us a clear *sense of direction*. [=helped us to know what we should try to accomplish]

3 ***senses*** [*plural*] : the ability to think clearly or in a reasonable way ▪ His *senses* were clear despite his illness. ▪ They hoped recent events would ***bring them to their senses***. [=make them act sensibly] ▪ I was scared ***out of my senses***. [=I was so scared that I couldn't think clearly] ▪ (*chiefly Brit*) Are you ***out of your senses***? [=*out of your mind*]

4 [*noncount*] : a proper or reasonable way of thinking about something : an awareness of what is appropriate ▪ He had the *sense* to leave when the crowd got rowdy. [=he acted in a sensible way and left when the crowd got rowdy] ▪ She had the ***good sense*** to stop before she said too much. ▪ I wish she would ***see sense*** [=act in a sensible way] and go to college. — see also COMMON SENSE, HORSE SENSE

5 [*noncount*] : a reason for doing something : a reason why something was done ▪ There's no *sense* [=*point*] in waiting. ▪ I fail to see the *sense* of/in that decision. [=I fail to see why that decision was made]

6 [*count*] : the meaning of something (such as a word or phrase) ▪ Many words have more than one *sense*. ▪ in the biblical/religious/legal *sense* of the word ▪ an abstract/broad *sense* ▪ The American *sense* of this word differs from the British *sense*. ▪ He learned the speech by heart but missed the *sense* entirely. [=he memorized the speech but he did not understand it] — often + *of* ▪ The oldest *sense of* the word dates from 1890. ▪ The intended *sense of* the passage was lost in translation. ▪ The book is a classic ***in every sense of the word***. [=in every possible way]

come to your senses : to begin to think in a sensible or correct way after being foolish or wrong ▪ He finally *came to his senses* and gave up his plans to quit his job and become an artist. ▪ When will you *come to your senses*? Don't you realize that she's been lying to you?

in a/one sense : in one way : from one point of view ▪ *In one sense* [=*in a way*], he was correct.

in no sense : in no way : definitely not ▪ This book is *in no sense* intended for beginners. = *In no sense* is this book intended for beginners. [=this book is too hard or advanced for beginners]

in some senses : in some ways ▪ *In some senses*, it was a wasted effort.

knock some sense into someone's head *or* ***knock some sense into someone*** *informal* : to cause someone to stop thinking or behaving foolishly ▪ I tried to *knock some sense into the boy's head*, but he just wouldn't see reason.

make (any) sense of : to understand (something) ▪ We couldn't *make (any) sense of* the instructions. ▪ Were you able to *make any sense of* what he said?

make sense 1 : to have a clear meaning : to be easy to understand ▪ We read the recommendations and thought they *made* (perfect) *sense*. ▪ The instructions don't *make any sense* (at all). = The instructions ***make no sense*** (at all). = The instructions ***make little sense***. ▪ You're ***not making much sense*** (to me). [=I can't understand what you're saying] 2 : to be reasonable ▪ It *makes sense* to leave early to avoid traffic. ▪ It ***makes little/no sense*** to continue. [=there is little/no point in continuing] ▪ Why would he do such an awful thing? It *makes no sense* (to me).

take leave of your senses see [2]LEAVE

talk (some) sense into/to *informal* : to cause (someone) to stop thinking or behaving foolishly ▪ I couldn't *talk sense to* him. ▪ He *talked (some) sense into* her and she promised she would get rid of that dangerous car.

[2]**sense** *verb* **senses**; **sensed**; **sens·ing** [+ *obj*]

1 *not used in progressive tenses* : to understand or be aware of (something) without being told about it or having evidence that it is true ▪ We *sensed* danger. ▪ She immediately *sensed* my dislike. — often + *that, what, when*, etc. ▪ He *sensed what* was going on and decided to intervene. ▪ I *sensed that* I may have offended you. ▪ My mother told me later that even though she was miles away, she could *sense* [=*tell*] *that* something wasn't right at home. ▪ People can *sense* [=*perceive*] *when* someone isn't being honest.

2 *of a machine* : to detect the presence or occurrence of (something) ▪ A motion detector can *sense* movement. ▪ a device that *senses* (the presence of) fine particles in the air — often + *that, when, whether*, etc. ▪ The system can *sense if* there is a readable CD in the drive.

sense·less /ˈsɛnsləs/ *adj*

1 : done or happening for no reason ▪ a *senseless* crime/tragedy ▪ *senseless* deaths ▪ *senseless* acts of violence

2 — used after *beat, knock*, etc., to say that someone is hurt badly and becomes unconscious ▪ I was *knocked senseless* by the fall. [=I fell and hit my head and lost consciousness] ▪ They beat him *senseless*. = He was beaten *senseless*. [=he was beaten until he was unconscious]

3 : stupid or foolish ▪ a *senseless* practical joke ▪ Don't be such a *senseless* idiot!

— **sense·less·ly** *adv* — **sense·less·ness** *noun* [*noncount*]

sense organ *noun, pl* ~ **-gans** [*count*] : a part of your body (such as your eyes, ears, nose, or tongue) that you use to see, hear, smell, taste, or feel things

sen·si·bil·i·ty /ˌsɛnsəˈbɪləti/ *noun, pl* **-ties** *formal*

1 [*count*] : the kinds of feelings that you have when you hear, see, read, or think about something ▪ The speaker gave no thought to the *sensibilities* of his audience. [=the speaker did not worry about how his audience would feel about what he said] ▪ We don't want to offend the viewers' *sensibilities*.

[=we don't want to upset the people who watch this]
2 [*count*] **:** the kinds of feelings that a certain type of person tends to have • This movie appeals to people with a feminist *sensibility*. [=this movie appeals to feminists] • The cartoon seems out of line with modern *sensibilities*. [=the cartoon seems strange or offensive to modern people]
3 : the ability to feel and understand emotions [*count*] The writer is remembered most for his *sensibility*. [*noncount*] She's a woman of poetic/artistic *sensibility*.

sen·si·ble /ˈsɛnsəbəl/ *adj* [*more* ~; *most* ~]
1 : having or showing good sense or judgment **:** REASONABLE • *sensible* people • a *sensible* choice/solution/diet • *sensible* prices • a *sensible* answer/question • My teacher gave me some *sensible* advice. • She was *sensible* enough to stop driving when she got too tired.
2 : designed to be comfortable, useful, etc., rather than stylish • *sensible* shoes/clothes • She wore a *sensible* coat.
– sen·si·bly /ˈsɛnsəbli/ *adv* • My doctor advised me to eat *sensibly*. • He was *sensibly* dressed.

sen·si·tive /ˈsɛnsətɪv/ *adj* [*more* ~; *most* ~]
1 a : easily upset by the things that people think or say about you • a moody, *sensitive* teenager • He acts like a tough guy, but he's really very *sensitive* to criticism. — often + *about* • She's painfully/overly *sensitive about* her looks. [=she cares very/too much about what people say or think about her looks] • a ***sensitive soul*** [=a person who is easily hurt emotionally] — opposite INSENSITIVE **b :** likely to cause people to become upset • *sensitive* [=*touchy*] topics/issues • a politically *sensitive* decision
2 a : aware of and understanding the feelings of other people • I found him to be a *sensitive* and caring person. — often + *to* • She was *sensitive to* the fears of her patients. — opposite INSENSITIVE **b :** having an understanding of something **:** aware of something — + *to* • We are *sensitive to* the need to act quickly in this situation.
3 : easily affected by something in a way that is not pleasant or good **:** reacting to something in, on, or around you in a bad way • *sensitive* skin — often + *to* • She is *sensitive to* pollen (in the air). • My teeth are *sensitive to* cold foods. • I am *sensitive to* wheat. [=I become ill when I eat wheat] • Now that I'm older, I'm more *sensitive to* (the) cold. [=I feel colder in cold surroundings now than I did in the past]
4 : able to express thoughts and feelings through writing, music, dance, etc. • a *sensitive* poet/artist • an exquisitely *sensitive* dance performance
5 *technical* **a :** able to sense very small changes in something • a highly *sensitive* device/instrument • *sensitive* scales **b :** changing in response to something • light-*sensitive* film = film that is *sensitive* to light
6 : needing to be handled in a careful or secret way in order to protect someone or something • highly *sensitive* information [=information that could be harmful if many people knew it; information that should be kept secret] • *sensitive* financial data
– sen·si·tive·ly *adv* • The problem was handled *sensitively*.

sen·si·tiv·i·ty /ˌsɛnsəˈtɪvəti/ *noun, pl* **-ties**
1 a : the tendency to become upset about things that are done to you, are said about you, or relate to you [*noncount*] I was surprised by her extreme *sensitivity* about even the smallest suggestions that we made. — often + *to* • his *sensitivity to* criticism [*count*] Their *sensitivities* were inflamed by his remarks. [=they became very upset by his remarks] **b** [*noncount*] **:** the tendency to cause people to be upset • the racial *sensitivity* of this issue [=the tendency of people of certain races to become upset about this issue] • This is a matter of great political *sensitivity*.
2 a : an awareness and understanding of the feelings of other people [*noncount*] He handled the situation with great *sensitivity*. • Her decision shows a lack of *sensitivity*. • I would have appreciated a little more *sensitivity* from you. [*singular*] — often + *to* • She has shown a great *sensitivity to* the needs of her students. **b :** an awareness of the details or qualities of something — often + *to* • He displays a remarkable *sensitivity to* the subtle nuances of language.
3 : the quality of being easily affected by something in a bad or unpleasant way [*noncount*] skin *sensitivity* [=the skin's tendency to react in a bad way to substances that touch it] • drug *sensitivity* = *sensitivity* to drugs/medications [*count*] He has chemical *sensitivities*. [=his body reacts badly to certain chemicals] • He has food *sensitivities*. [=he can't eat certain kinds of food] — often + *to* • a *sensitivity to* light/pollen
4 [*singular*] **:** the ability to express your thoughts and feelings through writing, music, etc. • Her singing is characterized by a rich emotional *sensitivity*.
5 [*noncount*] **:** the quality of needing to be handled in a careful or secret way • the *sensitivity* of this document/data
6 [*noncount*] *technical* **:** the ability of a device to sense very small changes in something • The new refinements have improved the *sensitivity* of the motion detector.

sen·si·tize *also Brit* **sen·si·tise** /ˈsɛnsəˌtaɪz/ *verb* **-tiz·es; -tized; -tiz·ing** [+ *obj*] **:** to make (someone or something) sensitive or more sensitive: such as **a :** to make (someone) more aware of something — usually + *to* • The program is intended to *sensitize* students *to* the dangers of drug use. **b** *medical* **:** to cause (someone) to become sensitive to a substance and to react to it in a bad way — usually + *to*; usually used as *(be) sensitized* • If you have become *sensitized to* an allergen, even an extremely small amount of the allergen in your environment can trigger an attack.
– sen·si·ti·za·tion *also Brit* **sen·si·ti·sa·tion** /ˌsɛnsətəˈzeɪʃən, *Brit* ˌsɛnsəˌtaɪˈzeɪʃən/ *noun* [*noncount*]

sen·sor /ˈsɛnˌsoɚ, ˈsɛnsɚ/ *noun, pl* **-sors** [*count*] **:** a device that detects or senses heat, light, sound, motion, etc., and then reacts to it in a particular way • a motion/optical *sensor* • ***Image sensors*** are used in digital cameras. • ***Infrared sensors*** can track an object's movement.

sen·so·ry /ˈsɛnsəri/ *adj* **:** of or relating to your physical senses • A study was conducted on *sensory* stimulation and its effects on the brain. • *sensory* perceptions • *sensory* deprivation

sen·su·al /ˈsɛnʃəwəl/ *adj* [*more* ~; *most* ~] **:** relating to, devoted to, or producing physical or sexual pleasure • *sensual* desires/pursuits/excesses • a very *sensual* man/woman • Certain fragrances apparently heighten *sensual* experiences. • a *sensual* mouth • *sensual* delights
– sen·su·al·i·ty /ˌsɛnʃəˈwæləti/ *noun* [*noncount*] • The actress exuded *sensuality* on screen. **– sen·su·al·ly** /ˈsɛnʃəwəli/ *adv* [*more* ~; *most* ~] • a *sensually* pleasing experience

sen·su·ous /ˈsɛnʃəwəs/ *adj* [*more* ~; *most* ~] **:** affecting the senses in a pleasing way **:** pleasant, attractive, or appealing in a way that produces or suggests feelings of physical or sexual pleasure • a *sensuous* voice/mouth • her *sensuous* lips • The *sensuous* sounds of soul music created a warm atmosphere. • A gentle, *sensuous* breeze caressed our faces.
– sen·su·ous·ly *adv* [*more* ~; *most* ~] • a *sensuously* smooth finish **– sen·su·ous·ness** *noun* [*noncount*]

sent *past tense and past participle of* SEND

[1]sen·tence /ˈsɛntn̩s/ *noun, pl* **-tenc·es**
1 [*count*] **:** a group of words that expresses a statement, question, command, or wish ✧ Sentences usually contain a subject and verb. In written English, the first word of a sentence is capitalized and the sentence ends with a period, question mark, or exclamation point. • write/construct/analyze a *sentence* • complete/incomplete *sentences*
2 *law* **:** the punishment given by a court of law [*count*] a harsh/lenient *sentence* • a prison/jail *sentence* • He is serving a 10-year *sentence* for armed robbery. [*noncount*] The judge ***passed/pronounced sentence on*** him. [=announced what his punishment would be] — see also DEATH SENTENCE, LIFE SENTENCE, SUSPENDED SENTENCE

[2]sentence *verb* **-tences; -tenced; -tenc·ing** [+ *obj*] *law* **:** to officially state the punishment given to (someone) by a court of law • The defendant was *sentenced* and fined. — usually + *to* • The judge *sentenced* him *to* prison.
– sentencing /ˈsɛntn̩sɪŋ/ *noun* [*noncount*] • He will return to the court on Wednesday for *sentencing*. — often used before another noun • *sentencing* laws/guidelines

sentence adverb *noun, pl* ~ **-verbs** [*count*] *grammar* **:** an adverb that limits or describes the meaning of an entire statement rather than just a single word or phrase • "Similarly" and "hopefully" often function as *sentence adverbs*.

sentence fragment *noun, pl* ~ **-ments** [*count*] *grammar* **:** a group of words that is written out as a sentence but that lacks a subject or verb

sen·ten·tious /sɛnˈtɛnʃəs/ *adj* [*more* ~; *most* ~] *formal* + *disapproving* **:** having or expessing strong opinions about what people should and should not do • a smug and *sententious* writer • a *sententious* speech
– sen·ten·tious·ly *adv* • He spoke *sententiously*.

sen·tient /ˈsɛnʃijənt/ *adj, technical* + *formal* **:** able to feel, see, hear, smell, or taste • *sentient* beings

sen·ti·ment /ˈsɛntəmənt/ *noun, pl* **-ments**
1 : an attitude or opinion [*count*] His criticism of the court's

S

decision expresses a *sentiment* that is shared by many people. ▪ an expression of antiwar *sentiments* ▪ a noble *sentiment* ▪ "The lecture was interesting, but it was much too long." "***My sentiments exactly!***" [=I agree with you completely] [*noncount*] A good politician understands public *sentiment*. [=understands the opinions held by many or most people]
2 [*noncount*] : feelings of love, sympathy, kindness, etc. ▪ She likes warmth and *sentiment* in a movie. ▪ You have to be tough to succeed in the business world. There's no room for *sentiment*.

sen·ti·men·tal /ˌsɛntəˈmɛntl/ *adj* [*more* ~; *most* ~]
1 : based on, showing, or resulting from feelings or emotions rather than reason or thought ▪ He has a *sentimental* attachment to his old high school. ▪ She saved her wedding gown for *sentimental* reasons. ▪ He has *sentimental* ideas about the past. ✧ A ***sentimental journey*** is a visit to a place that was once very familiar and that brings back memories of the past. ▪ They took a *sentimental journey* to England, the country where they had met. ✧ Something that has ***sentimental value*** is important to someone because of its connection with a happy time of life, a special person, etc. ▪ I keep this picture because it has *sentimental value* for me.
2 a : appealing to the emotions especially in an excessive way ▪ a *sentimental* melodrama **b** : having or expressing strong feelings of love, sadness, etc., in a way that may seem foolish or excessive ▪ a *sentimental* person ▪ I tend to get very *sentimental* when I think about my childhood.
– **sen·ti·men·tal·ly** *adv*

sen·ti·men·tal·ism /ˌsɛntəˈmɛntəˌlɪzəm/ *noun* [*noncount*] : a tendency to have or express feelings of love, sadness, etc., especially in a way that seems foolish or excessive : a sentimental quality ▪ the *sentimentalism* of 19th-century art
– **sen·ti·men·tal·ist** /ˌsɛntəˈmɛntəlɪst/ *noun, pl* **-ists** [*count*]

sen·ti·men·tal·i·ty /ˌsɛntəˌmɛnˈtæləti/ *noun* [*noncount*] : the quality of being sentimental especially in an excessive way ▪ the *sentimentality* of Romantic poetry

sen·ti·men·tal·ize *also Brit* **sen·ti·men·tal·ise** /ˌsɛntəˈmɛntəˌlaɪz/ *verb* **-iz·es**; **-ized**; **-iz·ing** : to describe or show (something) in an emotional way that makes it seem more attractive or interesting than it really is : to describe or show (something) in a sentimental way [+ *obj*] The movie *sentimentalizes* the past. ▪ *sentimentalized* stories of childhood [*no obj*] He does not *sentimentalize* in his biography.

sen·ti·nel /ˈsɛntənəl/ *noun, pl* **-nels** [*count*] : SENTRY ▪ armed *sentinels* — sometimes used figuratively ▪ The trees ***stand sentinel*** [=stand in a row like soldiers] on the cliffs.

sen·try /ˈsɛntri/ *noun, pl* **-tries** [*count*] : a soldier who guards a door, gate, etc. ▪ The general placed/posted an armed *sentry* at the bridge. ▪ The company hired a policeman to ***stand sentry*** [=be a guard] by the door.

Sep. *abbr* September

sep·a·ra·ble /ˈsɛpərəbəl/ *adj* : capable of being separated ▪ The top and bottom sections are easily *separable* (from each other). ▪ His religious and political beliefs are not always *separable* from each other. — opposite INSEPARABLE
– **sep·a·ra·bil·i·ty** /ˌsɛpərəˈbɪləti/ *noun* [*noncount*]

[1]**sep·a·rate** /ˈsɛpərət/ *adj*
1 : not joined, connected, or combined : placed or kept apart ▪ two *separate* building ▪ There are *separate* restrooms for men and women. ▪ The boys/girls have *separate* rooms. ▪ They slept in *separate* beds. ▪ We use the same Internet service provider but have *separate* accounts. ▪ The company broke up into three *separate* [=*independent*] entities. ▪ Each state has a *separate* set of laws [=has its own set of laws] concerning marriage. ▪ He tries to keep his private life and public life *separate* (from each other). = He tries to keep his private life *separate* from his public life.
2 : different from something else ▪ I met him on four *separate* [=*different*] occasions. : not related ▪ That's an entirely *separate* issue.
go your separate ways **1** : to end a relationship with someone ▪ After 20 years of marriage, they decided to *go their separate ways*. **2** : to go in different directions after being together ▪ After dinner we *went our separate ways*.
under separate cover see [2]COVER
– **sep·a·rate·ness** *noun* [*noncount*]

[2]**sep·a·rate** /ˈsɛpəˌreɪt/ *verb* **-rates**; **-rat·ed**; **-rat·ing**
1 [+ *obj*] : to cause (two or more people or things) to stop being together, joined, or connected : to make (people or things) separate ▪ He *separated* the fighters (from each other). ▪ They described the process used to *separate* cream from milk. ▪ (*US*) He fell and *separated* [=*dislocated*] his shoulder. [=caused the bone in his shoulder to move out of its proper position]
2 [+ *obj*] : to be between (two things or people) ▪ A river *separates* the two towns. = The two towns are *separated* by a river. [=there is a river between the two towns] ▪ A great distance *separated* the sisters from each other.
3 [*no obj*] : to stop being together, joined, or connected : to become separate ▪ They walked together to the corner, but then they *separated* and went their separate ways. ▪ The main group *separated* into several smaller groups. ▪ Oil and water *separate* when combined together. ▪ The oil *separated* from the water. ▪ The salt crystals *separated* out of the liquid.
4 [*no obj*] : to stop living with a husband, wife, or partner ▪ They *separated* six months after their wedding. ▪ She *separated* from her boyfriend last week.
5 [+ *obj*] : to see or describe the differences between (two things) ▪ We need to *separate* [=*distinguish*] fact and/from fiction.
6 [+ *obj*] : to be the quality that makes (people or things) different : DIFFERENTIATE ▪ Their personalities and political beliefs *separate* them. ▪ Our ability to reason is what *separates* us from animals.
7 [+ *obj*] — used to describe how much difference there is in the scores or positions of people or teams in a race, game, etc. ▪ One goal *separated* the teams at the beginning of the third period. ▪ Polls show that the candidates are *separated* by only a narrow margin as the election approaches.
separate off [*phrasal verb*] ***separate (someone or something) off*** or ***separate off (someone or something)*** : to cause (someone or something) to be separate from other people or things ▪ He *separated* himself *off* from the crowd in the subway.
separate out [*phrasal verb*] ***separate out (someone or something)*** or ***separate (someone or something) out*** : to remove (someone or something) from a group ▪ Before you put out the trash, you have to *separate out* the bottles and cans. ▪ Most schools *separate out* children with learning problems.
separate the men from the boys : to show which people are really strong, brave, etc., and which are not ▪ The competition has been easy to this point, but now it gets tough and we'll really begin to *separate the men from the boys*.
separate the sheep from the goats or ***separate the wheat from the chaff*** *chiefly Brit* : to judge which people or things in a group are bad and which ones are good ▪ The magazine describes many different products and then *separates the sheep from the goats*.

separated *adj*
1 : not living with a husband, wife, or partner ▪ My sister is *separated* from her husband. = My sister and her husband are *separated*.
2 *US, medical* : not attached because of an injury : DISLOCATED ▪ He suffered a *separated* shoulder.
3 : located far apart from each other ▪ The birds live on two widely *separated* islands.

sep·a·rate·ly /ˈsɛpərətli/ *adv* : not together with someone or something else ▪ The two vegetables should be cooked *separately*. ▪ The software is sold *separately* from the hardware. ▪ The professor met with each student *separately*.

sep·a·rates /ˈsɛpərəts/ *noun* [*plural*] : pieces of women's clothing that can be worn with other pieces in different combinations to form different outfits

sep·a·ra·tion /ˌsɛpəˈreɪʃən/ *noun, pl* **-tions**
1 : the act of separating people or things or the state of being separated [*count*] After a *separation* of 30 years, she visited her family in Cuba. [*noncount*] Moving away meant *separation* from his family. ▪ The U.S. Constitution calls for the ***separation of church and state***. [=calls for government and religion to be kept separate from each other]
2 [*count*] : a situation in which a husband and wife live apart from each other — usually singular ▪ She wanted a *separation* from her husband.

separation anxiety *noun* [*noncount*] : a feeling of strong fear and anxiety that is experienced by a young child when the child is separated from a parent

sep·a·rat·ist /ˈsɛpərətɪst/ *noun, pl* **-ists** [*count*] : a member of a group of people who want to form a new country, religion, etc., that is separate from the one they are in now
– **sep·a·rat·ism** /ˈsɛpərəˌtɪzəm/ *noun* [*noncount*] ▪ religious *separatism* – **separatist** *adj* ▪ a *separatist* movement/group/leader

sep·a·ra·tor /ˈsɛpəˌreɪtɚ/ *noun, pl* **-tors** [*count*] : someone

S

or something that separates two or more things from each other

se·pia /ˈsiːpijə/ *noun* [*noncount*] : a reddish-brown color
– **sepia** *adj* • *sepia* photographs/prints

sep·sis /ˈsɛpsəs/ *noun* [*noncount*] *medical* : illness caused by an infection in a part of the body • She was treated for *sepsis* of the urinary tract.

Sept. *abbr* September

Sep·tem·ber /sɛpˈtɛmbɚ/ *noun, pl* **-bers** : the ninth month of the year [*noncount*] early/mid-/late *September* • early/late in *September* • School begins on *September* the fifth. = (*US*) School begins on *September* fifth. = School begins on the fifth of *September*. [*count*] The weather has been very mild during the past two *Septembers*.

sep·tet /sɛpˈtɛt/ *noun, pl* **-tets** [*count*]
1 : a group of seven singers or musicians who perform together
2 : a piece of music that is meant to be performed by seven people

sep·tic /ˈsɛptɪk/ *adj, chiefly Brit, medical* : infected with bacteria • a *septic* leg • The cut ***went septic***. [=the cut became infected]

sep·ti·ce·mia (*US*) *or Brit* **sep·ti·cae·mia** /ˌsɛptəˈsiːmijə/ *noun* [*noncount*] *medical* : a dangerous infection of the blood : BLOOD POISONING

septic tank *noun, pl* **~ tanks** [*count*] : a tank under the ground that holds human waste from toilets

sep·tu·a·ge·nar·i·an /sɛpˌtuːwəʤəˈnerijən, *Brit* ˌsɛpˌtjuːəʤəˈnɛəriən/ *noun, pl* **-ans** [*count*] : a person who is between 70 and 79 years old

se·pul·chral /səˈpʌlkrəl/ *adj*
1 [*more ~; most ~*] *literary* : very sad and serious : very dismal or gloomy • *sepulchral* silence/darkness
2 *always used before a noun* : of or relating to a sepulchre • *sepulchral* walls • a *sepulchral* inscription

sep·ul·chre *or US* **sep·ul·cher** /ˈsɛpəlkɚ/ *noun, pl* **-chres** *or US* **-chers** [*count*] *old-fashioned* : a place of burial : TOMB

se·quel /ˈsiːkwəl/ *noun, pl* **-quels** [*count*]
1 : a book, movie, etc., that continues a story begun in another book, movie, etc. • The new film is a *sequel* to the very successful comedy that came out five years ago. • He is busy writing the book's *sequel*. — compare PREQUEL
2 : something that happens after and usually as a result of a previous event • There is an interesting *sequel* to my date with her that I'll share with you later.

se·quence /ˈsiːkwəns/ *noun, pl* **-quenc·es**
1 : the order in which things happen or should happen [*count*] a *sequence* of events [*noncount*] He listened to the telephone messages ***in sequence***. • After she dropped the photographs, they were ***out of sequence***. [=not in order, out of order]
2 [*count*] : a group of things that come one after the other : SERIES • a *sequence* of numbers/thoughts/poems/photographs
3 [*count*] : a part of a movie, television show, etc., that deals with one subject, action, or idea • a chase *sequence* in a spy movie • I enjoyed the movie's opening *sequence*.

se·quen·tial /sɪˈkwɛnʃəl/ *adj, formal*
1 : of, relating to, or arranged in a particular order or sequence • *sequential* filing systems • Put the cards in *sequential* order.
2 : happening in a series or sequence • *sequential* actions/events
– **se·quen·tial·ly** *adv* • I arranged the photos *sequentially*.

se·ques·ter /sɪˈkwɛstɚ/ *verb* **-ters; -tered; -ter·ing** [+ *obj*]
1 *formal* : to keep (a person or group) apart from other people • The jury was *sequestered* until a verdict was reached. • He was *sequestered* in his room.
2 *law* : to take (property) until a debt has been paid • Their property was *sequestered*.

sequestered *adj, literary* : located in a quiet and private place : SECLUDED • a *sequestered* house/village

se·ques·trate /ˈsiːkwəˌstreɪt/ *verb* **-trates; trat·ed; -trat·ing** [+ *obj*] *chiefly Brit, law* : SEQUESTER 2

se·ques·tra·tion /ˌsiːkwəˈstreɪʃən/ *noun* [*noncount*]
1 *US* : the act of keeping a person or group apart from other people or the state of being kept apart from other people • the *sequestration* of a jury • During their *sequestration*, jurors were not allowed to speak to reporters.
2 *chiefly Brit, law* : the act of taking someone's property until a debt has been paid • the *sequestration* of property

se·quin /ˈsiːkwən/ *noun, pl* **-quins** [*count*] : a small piece of shiny metal or plastic that is sewn onto clothes as a decoration
– **se·quined** *or* **se·quinned** /ˈsiːkwənd/ *adj* • a *sequined* dress/gown

se·quoia /sɪˈkwojə/ *noun, pl* **-quoi·as** [*count*] : a very tall evergreen tree that grows in California

sera *plural of* SERUM

ser·aph /ˈsɛrəf/ *noun, pl* **ser·a·phim** /ˈsɛrəˌfɪm/ *or* **seraphs** [*count*] : a type of angel that is described in the Bible : an angel of the highest rank

se·raph·ic /səˈræfɪk/ *adj, literary* : very beautiful or pure like that of an angel • a *seraphic* smile • her *seraphic* face

[1]**ser·e·nade** /ˌserəˈneɪd/ *noun, pl* **-nades** [*count*] : a love song that is sung or played outdoors at night for a woman

[2]**serenade** *verb* **-nades; -nad·ed; -nad·ing** [+ *obj*] : to sing or play a serenade for (someone) • He *serenaded* her from the garden below her window. — sometimes used figuratively • The crickets *seranaded* us all night long.

ser·en·dip·i·ty /ˌserənˈdɪpəti/ *noun* [*noncount*] *literary* : luck that takes the form of finding valuable or pleasant things that are not looked for • They found each other by pure *serendipity*.
– **ser·en·dip·i·tous** /ˌserənˈdɪpətəs/ *adj* • a *serendipitous* discovery

se·rene /səˈriːn/ *adj* [*more ~; most ~*] : calm and peaceful • a *serene* face • *serene* music/skies
– **se·rene·ly** *adv* • She smiled *serenely*. • The sunset was *serenely* beautiful. – **se·ren·i·ty** /səˈrɛnəti/ *noun* [*noncount*] • a feeling of peace and *serenity*

serf /ˈsɚf/ *noun, pl* **serfs** [*count*] : a person in the past who belonged to a low social class and who lived and worked on land owned by another person • medieval *serfs*

serf·dom /ˈsɚfdəm/ *noun* [*noncount*] : the state of being a serf

serge /ˈsɚʤ/ *noun* [*noncount*] : a strong cloth that is used to make clothes • a coat made of *serge* • a blue *serge* suit

ser·geant /ˈsɑɚʤənt/ *noun, pl* **-geants** [*count*]
1 : an officer of low rank in the army or marines — see also STAFF SERGEANT
2 : an officer in a police force with a rank below captain or lieutenant — abbr. *Sgt.*

sergeant major *noun, pl* **sergeants major** *or* **sergeant majors** [*count*] : an officer of low rank in the U.S. Army or Marines Corps

[1]**se·ri·al** /ˈsirijəl/ *adj, always used before a noun*
1 : arranged or happening in a series • The pictures are numbered and arranged in *serial* order. • Scientists made *serial* observations over a period of two weeks.
2 a *of a crime* : committed many times usually in the same way • *serial* murders/rapes **b** *of a criminal* : committing a series of crimes • a *serial* killer/rapist
3 : broadcast or published in separate parts over a period of time • a *serial* story/novel/publication
4 *computers* : designed for a computer system in which very small pieces of information are sent one at a time over a single wire • a *serial* cable/connection/port/printer — compare [1]PARALLEL 3
– **se·ri·al·ly** *adv* • *serially* numbered items • *serially* connected printers • The story was published *serially*.

[2]**serial** *noun, pl* **-als** [*count*] : a story that is broadcast on television or radio or that is published in a magazine in separate parts over a period of time • a daytime television *serial*

se·ri·al·ize *also Brit* **se·ri·al·ise** /ˈsirijəˌlaɪz/ *verb* **-iz·es; -ized; -iz·ing** [+ *obj*] : to broadcast or publish (something, such as a story) in separate parts over a period of time • Her story was *serialized* in the magazine.
– **se·ri·al·i·za·tion** *also Brit* **se·ri·al·i·sa·tion** /ˌsirijələˈzeɪʃən, *Brit* ˌsɪəriəˌlaɪˈzeɪʃən/ *noun, pl* **-tions** [*count, noncount*]

serial number *noun, pl* **~ -bers** [*count*] : a number that is put on a product and that is used to identify it • the *serial number* of a computer

se·ries /ˈsiriz/ *noun, pl* **series** [*count*]
1 : a number of things or events that are arranged or happen one after the other — usually singular • the summer concert *series* at the park — often + *of* • a *series of* experiments/explosions • We've had a *series of* problems with our computer network. • an unusual *series of* events
2 a : a set of regularly presented television shows involving

the same group of characters or the same subject • a popular television *series* • a five-part *series* on/about the history of baseball **b** : a set of books, articles, etc., that involve the same group of characters or the same subject • a comic book *series* • a *series* of articles on global warming

3 *sports* : a set of games that are played between two teams one after the other on different days • The Yankees played a three-game *series* against the Red Sox last week. • The ***play-off series*** between the two teams begins next week. — see also WORLD SERIES

in series : one after the other in a particular order • She placed the items *in series*.

ser•if /ˈserəf/ *noun, pl* **-ifs** [*count*] *technical* : one of the short lines near the top and bottom of the long parts of some printed letters — see picture at FONT; see also SANS SERIF

se•ri•ous /ˈsirijəs/ *adj* [*more* ~; *most* ~]

1 : having an important or dangerous possible result • a *serious* injury/illness/condition • "You sound terrible." "It's just a bad cold. Nothing *serious*." • *serious* risks • For my brother, not going to college was a *serious* mistake. • Crime is a *serious* problem in this neighborhood.

2 : involving or deserving a lot of thought, attention, or work • a *serious* study • The team is a *serious* contender for the championship. • If you want to quit smoking, you have to make a *serious* effort. • They had a *serious* conversation about their relationship. • a *serious* novel about modern life • The story raises *serious* questions about our system of justice. • Dog shows are a *serious* business.

3 : giving a lot of attention or energy to something • *serious* musicians • She is a *serious* cyclist who rides 200 miles each week. • *Serious* journalists do not pry into the personal lives of famous people. • When it comes to fishing, he's very *serious*. = He's very *serious* about fishing. • My sister is *serious* about her grades.

4 : not joking or funny • a *serious* story/opera • Don't laugh. I'm *serious*! • Can you be *serious* just this once? This is important. • He is *serious* about moving down South. [=he truly wants/intends to move down South] • "He says he won't do it." "***Are you serious***?" • "I'm joining the army." "***You can't be serious***." [=you have to be joking; I can't believe that you're really joining the army]

5 *always used before a noun, informal* : large or impressive in quality or amount • After business school, he started making some *serious* money. [=he started making a large amount of money] • These are *serious* shoes! • They did some *serious* drinking at the bar. [=they drank a lot]

6 : having or involving strong romantic feelings • Their romance is quite *serious*. They're even talking about marriage. • We've dated a few times, but it's nothing *serious*. • They are a *serious* couple. • He's never really had a *serious* relationship with a woman. — often + *about* • She and her boyfriend are *serious about* each other.

7 : thoughtful or quiet in appearance or manner • He looks like a *serious* person. • You look *serious*. What's the matter?

se•ri•ous•ly /ˈsirijəsli/ *adv* [*more* ~; *most* ~]

1 : in a serious way • No one was *seriously* injured in the accident. • I thought *seriously* about death while I was in the hospital. • You should *seriously* consider buying a new car. • You don't mean that *seriously*, do you? • If you like arguing so much, you should be a lawyer! *Seriously*, you would be good at it. [=I was joking when I said you should be a lawyer, but I actually think you would be good at it] • It was so hot that we nearly melted. But *seriously*, it was hotter than I've ever experienced. • (*informal*) "I'll pay for dinner." "*Seriously*?" [=are you being serious when you say that you'll pay for dinner?]

2 : to a large or great degree or extent • I think you are *seriously* mistaken. • During her first year in the United States, she was *seriously* [=*very, extremely*] unhappy. • She's a *seriously* beautiful woman. [=a very beautiful woman]

take (someone or something) seriously : to treat (someone or something) as being very important and deserving attention or respect • He *takes* his religious faith *seriously*. • She's well qualified for the job, so she hopes the company will *take* her *seriously*. • His parents threatened to punish him, but he didn't *take* them *seriously*. [=he didn't believe that they would actually punish him] • Police are *taking* the matter very *seriously*. • Don't *take* him *seriously*—he loves to say crazy things. • Most politicians ***take themselves too seriously***. [=think of themselves as being more important than they really are]

se•ri•ous•ness /ˈsirijəsnəs/ *noun* [*noncount*] : the quality or state of being serious • We were shocked by the *seriousness* of her illness. • The child's *seriousness* was surprising. • You have to consider the *seriousness* of the charges against you. • She spoke with great *seriousness*.

in all seriousness : in a serious way — used to stress that a statement, question, etc., is not a joke • "I was the queen of England in a previous life," she said *in all seriousness*. • *In all seriousness*, if he does propose, what will you say?

ser•mon /ˈsɚmən/ *noun, pl* **-mons** [*count*]

1 : a speech about a moral or religious subject that is usually given by a religious leader • He preached/delivered/gave a *sermon* on the importance of kindness.

2 *informal + usually disapproving* : a serious talk about how someone should behave • Dad gave me a *sermon* yesterday about doing my homework.

ser•mon•ize *also Brit* **ser•mon•ise** /ˈsɚməˌnaɪz/ *verb* **-iz•es; -ized; -iz•ing** [*no obj*] : to give a sermon to someone; *especially, disapproving* : to give someone unwanted advice about good moral behavior • She's a teacher who can talk to her students about serious subjects without *sermonizing*.

ser•pent /ˈsɚpənt/ *noun, pl* **-pents** [*count*] *literary* : a usually large snake

ser•pen•tine /ˈsɚpənˌtiːn, *Brit* ˈsɜːpənˌtaɪn/ *adj* [*more* ~; *most* ~] : having many bends and turns • a *serpentine* [=*twisting*] path through the woods

ser•rat•ed /ˈseəˌeɪtəd, səˈreɪtəd/ *adj* : having a row of small points or teeth along the side like a saw • a knife with a *serrated* blade/edge

ser•ried /ˈserid/ *adj, always used before a noun, literary* : crowded or pressed together • Flowers came up every spring in their *serried* ranks.

se•rum /ˈsirəm/ *noun, pl* **se•rums** *or* **se•ra** /ˈsirə/

1 [*noncount*] *medical* : the part of blood that is like water and that contains substances (called antibodies) that fight disease • blood *serum*

2 *medical* : serum from an animal's blood that can be added to a person's blood to prevent or cure disease [*noncount*] The patient was administered *serum*. [*count*] mouse *sera*

3 [*noncount*] *biology* : the watery part of a fluid found in a plant

ser•vant /ˈsɚvənt/ *noun, pl* **-vants** [*count*]

1 : a person who is hired to do household or personal duties such as cleaning and cooking • domestic/household *servants* — see also CIVIL SERVANT, PUBLIC SERVANT

2 : a person who is devoted to or guided by something — often + *of* • a *servant of* the truth • She is a *servant of* her religion.

[1]serve /ˈsɚv/ *verb* **serves; served; serv•ing**

1 a [+ *obj*] : to give (food or drink) to someone at a meal, in a restaurant, etc. • Soup was *served* as the first course. • The waiter *served* our meals quickly. • The restaurant *serves* excellent Italian food. • Dinner is *served*. [=dinner is on the table and ready to be eaten] — see also SERVE UP (below) **b** : to give food or drink to (someone) [+ *obj*] The waiter who *served* us was very nice. • Feel free to *serve* yourself at the salad bar. [*no obj*] You carve the turkey, and I'll *serve*.

2 [+ *obj*] : to be enough food for (a particular number of people) • We need to make enough soup to *serve* [=*feed*] eight people. • The roast should *serve* six.

3 [+ *obj*] : to provide service to (a customer) : to help (a customer) make purchases • I'm afraid all of our salespeople are *serving* other customers right now. • What can we do to *serve* our customers better?

4 [*no obj*] **a** : to be used or seen in a particular way — + *as* • The trees can *serve as* shelter from the rain. • The organization *serves as* a model of social responsibility. • The accident *serves as* [=*is*] a reminder of the dangers of drunk driving. • Let that *serve as* [=*be*] a lesson to you. **b** : to have a particular result or effect — often + *as* • Babysitting his nieces *served as* a test of his patience. — often followed by *to + verb* • She tried hard but her efforts only *served to bring* more attention to her lack of experience.

5 a [+ *obj*] : to be useful or helpful to (someone) • Her quick wit has *served* her well on many occasions. **b** : to provide what is needed by or for (someone or something) [+ *obj*] The library *serves* the community. = The library ***serves the needs*** of the community. [=provides things that the community needs] • He argued that government too often ***serves the interests*** of big business. [=does things to help big business instead of ordinary people] • Arguing with him ***serves no purpose***. [=is not useful or helpful in any way] • ***If (my) memory serves me (right/correctly)*** [=if I remember correctly], she is from Los Angeles. [*no obj*] ***If memory serves***, she is from Los Angeles. • Many people do not believe that ***justice has been served*** in his case. [=that he has been given proper punishment or fair treatment by the legal system] — see also SELF-SERVING **c** [+ *obj*] **: to provide (an area or group of people) with a particular service** • This neighborhood is not *served* with/by garbage collection. • Two elementary schools *serve* the town.

6 : to hold a particular office, position, etc. : to perform a duty or job [*no obj*] They *served* on the jury. • She *served* on the city council for years. • He *served* as the club's adviser. • He *served* for five years in the army. = He *served* in the army for five years. • She was elected to *serve* for a second term. [+ *obj*] We honor those who *serve* our country. • She *served* a two-year apprenticeship.

7 [+ *obj*] **: to be in prison for or during (a period of time)** • He's *serving* two years for robbery. • She is *serving* a life/10-year sentence. • He has ***served time*** [=spent time in prison] for drug possession.

8 [+ *obj*] *law* **: to send or give (someone) official legal papers** • He *served* her with divorce papers. • The police officer *served* a summons/writ on him.

9 [+ *obj*] **: to give respect and service to (someone or something)** • She dedicated her whole life to *serving* God.

10 *sports* **: to throw a ball into the air and hit it over a net to start play in tennis, volleyball, etc.** [*no obj*] It's your turn to *serve*. [+ *obj*] They flipped a coin to decide who would *serve* the ball first.

first come, first served see ²FIRST

serve out [*phrasal verb*] ***serve (something) out*** *or* ***serve out (something)*** **: to complete (a term in office, a prison sentence, etc.)** • He vowed that he would *serve out* his five-year term as chairperson. • She *served out* her sentence in a prison in New York.

serve (someone) right **— used to say that someone who has behaved badly deserves a particular punishment, problem, etc.** • "I hear his wife is divorcing him." "***It serves him right*** after the way he's treated her." • "He won't even talk to me." "(*It*) *Serves you right* for lying to him."

serve two masters **: to give equal support to two different causes, groups, etc.** • You cannot *serve two masters*.

serve up [*phrasal verb*] ***serve up (something)*** *or* ***serve (something) up*** **: to give (food) to someone at a meal, in a restaurant, etc.** • That little restaurant *serves up* some of the best Indian food in the city. — sometimes used figuratively • The movie *serves up* a ton of laughs. [=the movie is very funny]

²**serve** *noun, pl* **serves** [*count*] *sports* **: the act or action of throwing a ball into the air and hitting it over a net to start play in tennis, volleyball, etc.** • She started the game with a powerful *serve*. • It's your *serve*. [=it's your turn to serve the ball]

serv·er /ˈsɚvɚ/ *noun, pl* **-ers** [*count*]

1 *US* **: a person who brings your food and drinks at a restaurant : a waiter or waitress** • She asked our *server* for another glass of wine.

2 : the main computer in a network which provides files and services that are used by the other computers • the file/mail/Web *server*

3 : the player who begins play in tennis, volleyball, etc., by serving the ball

4 : something (such as a tray or spoon) that is used to serve food

S

serv·ery /ˈsɚvəri/ *noun, pl* **-er·ies** [*count*] *Brit* **: a counter in a restaurant where customers pick up their food and bring it back to their tables**

¹**ser·vice** /ˈsɚvəs/ *noun, pl* **-vic·es**

1 [*count*] **: an organization, company, or system that provides something to the public** • the National Park *Service* • the National Weather *Service* [=a government agency that provides information about the weather] • Students go to health *services* for medical attention. • He runs a landscaping *service*. • Their housing is provided through government *services*. — see also ANSWERING SERVICE, CIVIL SERVICE, DATING SERVICE, FOREIGN SERVICE, INTERNAL REVENUE SERVICE, POSTAL SERVICE, PUBLIC SERVICE, SECRET SERVICE, SOCIAL SERVICES, WIRE SERVICE

2 : work done by an organization or person that does not involve producing goods [*count*] Take advantage of their free delivery *service*. • bus/Internet/telephone *service* — often plural • He offered his *services* as a babysitter [=he offered to be a babysitter] during the party. • The lawyers offer their *services* for free to those who cannot afford to pay. • We received a bill for *services* rendered. [=for work that had been done] • the consumption of ***goods and services*** [*noncount*] We guarantee excellent *service*. • They have jobs in the ***service industries*** [=jobs that involve providing services to customers and not producing a product]

3 [*noncount*] **a : work done for a business or organization : EMPLOYMENT** • She retired from the company after 34 years of *service*. • Pay is determined by length of *service*. **b : work done for your country, government, etc.** • a family tradition of public *service* • Reporters began investigating his record of ***military service*** [=time spent serving in the army, navy, air force, etc.] — see also COMMUNITY SERVICE **c** *old-fashioned* **: employment as a servant** • He entered the queen's *service*. • In those days it wasn't unusual for a person to ***go into service*** [=become a servant] as a child. • He was ***in service*** all his life.

4 [*noncount*] **: the act of helping or serving customers at a restaurant, hotel, store, etc.** • The food was good but the *service* was terribly slow. • The company is known for its excellent customer *service*. — see also FULL-SERVICE, LIP SERVICE, ROOM SERVICE

5 [*noncount*] **: use of a machine or vehicle** • Our car has given us great *service* over the years. [=has served us very well over the years] **: the state of being available for use** • The copier is currently ***out of service*** [=*out of order*] • The new planes will be ***put into service*** [=will begin being used] next year.

6 : work that is done to repair something (such as a vehicle) or to keep it in good condition [*noncount*] He brought his car in for *service*. • The store provides television sales and *service*. [*count*] (*Brit*) He brought his car in for a *service*.

7 : a regularly scheduled trip on a bus, airplane, boat, etc. [*count*] The 10:30 bus *service* to Boston is canceled today. [*noncount*] There is ferry *service* to the island four times a day. [=the ferry goes to the island four times a day]

8 [*count*] **: a religious ceremony** • a funeral/memorial/burial *service* • She goes to the synagogue for *services* on Friday nights.

9 *US* ***the service*** *or Brit* ***the services*** **: a country's military forces : a country's army, navy, air force, etc.** • He entered/joined *the service* when he was 19. • She was in *the service* for 20 years.

10 [*count*] **: a set of dishes, cups, etc., that match each other** • a tea *service* • I have a china/dinner *service* for 12 people.

11 [*count*] *sports* **: the act of serving the ball in tennis, volleyball, etc. : SERVE** • a first/second *service*

12 [*noncount*] *law* **: the act of giving legal papers to someone** • the *service* of a subpoena

13 ***services*** *Brit* **: a place along a highway for drivers to get food, gasoline, etc. — used both as a singular noun and as a plural noun** • We stopped at a *services*.

at someone's service **: ready or available for someone's use** • I am happy to be *at your service* if you have any questions. • They made sure there was a car *at her service* when she got there.

be of service **: to be helpful or useful to someone** • I am glad to *be of service*. • May I *be of service* to you?

do (someone) a service **: to do something that helps (someone)** • The journalists *did* the public *a service* by exposing the corruption. • You are *doing us no service* by criticizing everything.

²**service** *verb* **-vices; -viced; -vic·ing** [+ *obj*]

1 : to do the work that is needed to keep (a machine or vehicle) in good condition • I need to get my car *serviced*. • The shop *services* sewing machines and old typewriters.

2 *technical* **: to pay interest on (a loan or debt)** • The company was unable to *service* the loan.

3 : to provide (someone) with something that is needed or wanted • The bookstore primarily *services* people looking for out-of-print books.

ser·vice·able /ˈsɚvəsəbəl/ *adj* **: ready to use or able to be used** • I bought an old but still *serviceable* bicycle.

service area *noun, pl* **~ areas** [*count*] *chiefly Brit* **: REST AREA**

service charge *noun, pl* **~ charges** [*count*]

1 : an amount of money that is charged for a particular service in addition to a basic fee • Tickets are $25 each plus a $3 *service charge* per ticket. — called also (*US*) *service fee*

2 *Brit* **: an amount of money that is paid to the owner of an apartment building for services (such as garbage collection)**

3 *Brit* **: a charge added to a bill in a restaurant to pay for the work of the waitress or waiter**

service club *noun, pl* ~ **clubs** [*count*] *US* : a national organization that is made up of groups of local people who work to improve their communities

ser·vice·man /ˈsɚvəsˌmæn/ *noun, pl* **-men** /-ˌmɛn/ [*count*] : a man who is a member of the military

service mark *noun, pl* ~ **marks** [*count*] : a name, word, symbol, etc., that an organization uses to identify its services — compare TRADEMARK

service road *noun, pl* ~ **roads** [*count*] : a road that is near and parallel to a major road and that allows people to go to local stores, houses, etc.

service station *noun, pl* ~ **-tions** [*count*] : GAS STATION

ser·vice·wom·an /ˈsɚvəsˌwʊmən/ *noun, pl* **-wom·en** /-ˌwɪmən/ [*count*] : a woman who is a member of the military

servicing *noun* [*noncount*] : work done to repair a machine or vehicle or to keep it in good condition • The photocopier needs *servicing*.

ser·vi·ette /ˌsɚviˈɛt/ *noun, pl* **-ettes** [*count*] *Brit* : NAPKIN

ser·vile /ˈsɚvəl, *Brit* ˈsəːˌvaɪl/ *adj* [*more* ~; *most* ~] *formal* + *disapproving* : very obedient and trying too hard to please someone • In the presence of an authority, he immediately adopted a *servile* [=*submissive*] attitude. • a *servile* assistant
– **ser·vil·i·ty** /sɚˈvɪləti/ *noun* [*noncount*]

[1]**serving** *noun, pl* **-ings** [*count*] : an amount of food or drink that is enough for one person • This recipe makes four *servings* [=*helpings*] of rice and beans. • This is my third *serving* of mashed potatoes. • According to the package, one ***serving size*** is 6 ounces.

[2]**serving** *adj, always used before a noun* : used to serve or give out food • a *serving* bowl • *serving* utensils

ser·vi·tude /ˈsɚvəˌtuːd, *Brit* ˈsəːvəˌtjuːd/ *noun* [*noncount*] *formal* : the condition of being a slave or of having to obey another person • indentured/involuntary *servitude*

ses·a·me /ˈsɛsəmi/ *noun* [*noncount*] : a plant that is grown in warm regions and that produces small flat seeds that are used in cooking and as a source of oil — often used before another noun • *sesame* seeds • *sesame* oil — see also OPEN SESAME

ses·sion /ˈsɛʃən/ *noun, pl* **-sions**

1 [*count*] : a period of time that is used to do a particular activity • a practice *session* • Her health insurance will cover 12 one-hour *sessions* of therapy per year. • a recording/photo *session* • After the speech there will be a ***question and answer session***. [=a period of time when people can have their questions answered] — see also BULL SESSION, JAM SESSION, RAP SESSION

2 : a formal meeting or series of meetings of a group of people (such as a court of law or legislature) [*count*] the U.N. Special *Session* on Disarmament [*noncount*] The board met in ***closed session*** [=with no one else present] for four hours to discuss the issue. • Congress is ***in session*** [=is meeting] right now.

3 *US* : a period of time during the year in which a school, college, or university has classes [*count*] I'm going to take classes during the summer *session*. [*noncount*] School will be back ***in session*** at the beginning of September. [=school will start again at the beginning of September]

[1]**set** /ˈsɛt/ *verb* **sets; set; set·ting**

1 *always followed by an adverb or preposition* [+ *obj*] **a** : to put (something) in a place or position • *Set* your books (down) on the table. • We need to *set* some extra chairs around the table. • He *set* the ladder against the wall and walked away. • I remember *setting* my bag right here. **b** : to put (something) into the surface of something • They *set* the bricks along the walkway. — often used as *(be) set* • The posts *are set* firmly in the ground. • The tiles *are set* into the wall. **c** : to attach (something, such as a jewel) to a piece of jewelry or other decoration • The jeweler can *set* the stone several different ways. — often used as *(be) set* • Her wedding ring *is set* [=*inlaid*] with seven diamonds. • a diamond *set* in a simple gold band

2 *always followed by an adverb or preposition* [+ *obj*] : to cause the action of (a film, story, etc.) to happen in a certain place or during a certain time — often used as *(be) set* • The play *is set* in Verona, Italy. [=the action of the play takes place in Verona] • The novel *is set* in 1943. • a novel *set* during World War II • The story ***is set against*** (the backdrop of) the Second World War. [=the story takes place during the Second World War]

3 [+ *obj*] **a** : to make (something) ready to be used : to put (something) in a position to be used • He turned off the car and *set* the parking brake. • Rangers will *set* a trap to catch the bear. **b** : to put plates, forks, spoons, knives, etc., on a table before serving a meal • Would you please *set* [=(*Brit*) *lay*] the table? • We *set* an extra place at the table for our guest. • The table was *set* for two. [=it had two place settings]

4 [+ *obj*] : to cause (a clock) to show a particular time • We *set* the clocks ahead one hour for daylight saving time. : to cause the controls of (a clock or other device) to be in a particular position • The alarm was *set* for 7:00 a.m. = The alarm was *set* to go off at 7:00 a.m. • I *set* the timer for/to twenty minutes. • *Set* the oven to 350 degrees. • In the winter, she *sets* the thermostat at/to 68 degrees.

5 [+ *obj*] : to decide on or choose (something) • I *set* a goal (for myself) to lose 15 pounds by the end of the year. • The company must meet certain conditions *set* by the government in order to stay in business. • She will be *setting* the agenda for this afternoon's meeting. • *setting* boundaries/limits/rules • NASA has not yet *set* [=*named*] the date for the shuttle launch. • He has ***set his sights on*** becoming [=he has decided to try to become] the next president. • We don't have enough time to do everything. We have to ***set priorities***. [=to decide which things are most important to do]

6 [+ *obj*] **a** : to give (a particular price or value) to something • An antiques appraiser *set* the value of the chair at $500. • If you *set* your prices too high, no one will buy your products. • Her bail was *set* at $10,000. = The judge *set* (her) bail at $10,000. [=the judge decided that she will have to pay $10,000 or stay in jail until her trial] **b** : to give (a high value or importance) to something • They *set* a high value on their privacy. [=they value their privacy very highly] • Our family ***sets great store by/on*** tradition. [=our family believes that tradition is very important]

7 [+ *obj*] **a** : to cause (something) to be accepted as an example, rule, etc. : to establish (a standard, trend, etc.) for others to follow or try to copy • They are improving the safety of their vehicles and *setting* a higher standard for other companies (to follow). • His style of directing has *set* a new trend in moviemaking. [=other directors are copying his way of making movies] • His behavior ***sets a good/bad example*** for the rest of the children. • The ruling is likely to ***set a precedent*** for how future cases are decided. [=future cases will be decided based on this case] • Her lighthearted question ***set the tone*** for the rest of the interview. [=it gave the rest of the interview a light and easy feeling] **b** : to establish (a record) as the performance or achievement that is the best of its kind • She *set* a record for the most sales in the company's history. [=she made more sales for the company than anyone else ever had] • He *set* the world record for/in the 100-meter dash.

8 [+ *obj*] : to cause (someone or something) to be in a specified condition • The slaves were *set* free. • He made a raft and *set* it afloat in the river. • They ***set*** the house ***on fire***. = They ***set fire to*** the house. = (more formally) They *set* the house afire/aflame/ablaze. [=they caused the house to begin burning] • I wish I knew how to ***set your mind at ease***. [=to help you stop worrying] • She ***set him right/straight*** about what happened. [=she told him that he was wrong and explained what really happened] • We should ***set our own house in order*** [=correct the way we do things] before we criticize them.

9 : to cause (someone or something) to start doing something [+ *obj*] We have no idea what *set* [=*got*] her crying. — often + *to* • Her question *set* me *to* wondering if I had made the right decision. • They are ready to ***set*** the plan ***in motion***. [=they are ready to cause the plan to start happening] • The plan has been *set in motion*. • Sources say that the governor has ***set the wheels in motion*** for a run for the presidency. [=the governor has started to run for president] [*no obj*] He immediately ***set to work*** [=started working] on the project.

10 [+ *obj*] *Brit* : to give (someone) a particular job : to require someone to do (a task) • My boss *set* me to organizing the files. • She *set* [=*assigned*] her students the task of writing a three-page report. • *setting* homework for the children

11 [*no obj*] *of the sun or moon* : to move down in the sky and go below the horizon • We sat on the beach and watched the sun *set*. — opposite [1]RISE 5

12 [+ *obj*] : to put and hold (your jaw, mouth, etc.) firmly into a certain position • She crossed her arms, *set* her jaw, and refused to answer any questions. • He *set* his lips firmly.

13 a [*no obj*] *of a liquid* : to become thick or hard • The gelatin needs a few hours to *set*. • My nail polish is still *setting*. • a quick-*setting* cement **b** : to become permanent [*no obj*] If you don't wash your shirt right away, the stain will *set*. [=you will not be able to remove the stain] [+ *obj*] Hot water will *set* the stain.

14 : to put (a broken bone) into its normal position so it can heal [+ *obj*] Doctors *set* her broken leg last week. [*no obj*] The bones will take several weeks to *set*. [=grow together]

15 [+ *obj*] **:** to give a particular style to (someone's hair) by wetting it, putting it in curlers or clips, and drying it • She gets her hair *set* and styled twice a week.

16 [+ *obj*] **:** to type or print (a word, sentence, etc.) in a particular form or style • a word *set* in italics

17 [+ *obj*] **:** to add music to (words) **:** to create (music) to accompany words — usually + *to* • She wrote the lyrics, and he *set* them *to* music.

set about [*phrasal verb*] ***set about (something)*** **:** to begin to do (something) • They *set about* (the task of) creating a new Web site. — sometimes followed by *to + verb* • They *set about to create* a new Web site.

set against [*phrasal verb*] **1** ***set (something) against (something)*** **a :** to compare (something) to (something else) • Let's *set* the advantages *against* the disadvantages. — often used as *(be) set against* • The challenges of fixing the problem now must *be set against* the dangers of waiting until later to act. • The fines were small when *set against* the company's huge annual profits. — see also [1]SET 2 (above) **b** *Brit* **:** to list (something) as an expense in order to reduce (income for which you must pay tax) • You can *set* your mortgage payments *against* your rental income. **2** ***set (yourself) against (someone or something)*** **:** to decide that you do not support (something or someone) **:** to be or become opposed to (something or someone) • She *set herself against* the prevailing beliefs of the time. • He has *set himself against* (joining) them. **3** ***set (someone) against (someone)*** **:** to cause (someone) to disagree with or oppose (someone) • The incident *set* brother *against* sister.

set apart [*phrasal verb*] **1** ***set (someone or something) apart*** **:** to be a quality that makes (someone or something) better than or different from other people or things — usually + *from* • What *sets* her *apart* (*from* the other teachers) is her great passion for her work. • His great height *set* him *apart from* the other men in his family. **2** ***set (something) apart*** **:** to keep or save (something) for a particular purpose — often used as *(be) set apart*; usually + *for* • A few acres of the city *were set apart for* a park.

set aside [*phrasal verb*] ***set (something) aside or set aside (something)*** **1 :** to move (something) to the side because you are not working on it, dealing with it, etc. • Mix the dry ingredients in a small bowl and *set* the mixture *aside*. **:** to wait until later to use or deal with (something) • I've *set* your memo *aside* for now but I'll read it this afternoon. • The committee *set aside* discussion of the proposal until their next meeting. **2 :** to keep or save (something) for a particular purpose • The hotel *set aside* [=*set apart*] 20 rooms for the guests of the bride and groom. • We need to *set* some money *aside* for our vacation. **3 :** to stop thinking about, talking about, or being affected by (something) • They decided to *set aside* their differences and work together. • *Setting aside* the fact that the meal was extremely expensive, dinner was very enjoyable. **4** *law* **:** to change or reverse (a legal decision, conviction, etc.) • The verdict was *set aside* [=*overturned*] by the court.

set back [*phrasal verb*] **1** ***set (something or someone) back or set back (something or someone)*** **:** to make the progress of (something or someone) slower or more difficult **:** to cause (something or someone) to go back to an earlier or worse condition • A recent lack of funding has *set back* research on the disease. • If the law is reversed, it will *set* us *back* 20 years. [=it will undo 20 years of progress] • *setting back* progress **2** ***set (someone) back*** *informal* **:** [2]COST • A new suit will *set* you *back* at least $200.

set down [*phrasal verb*] **1** ***set down (something)*** **:** to create or establish (a rule, requirement, etc.) • All participants must follow the guidelines *set down* [=*established*] by the organization. • Once she *sets down* the rules, there's no changing her mind. **2** ***set (something) down or set down (something)*** **a :** to record (something) by writing it down • She took out her notebook and started *setting down* her thoughts. • When an idea for a song comes to me, I *set* it *down* on paper. • *setting* an agreement *down* in writing **b :** to land (an airplane) on the ground or water • We had to *set* the plane *down* in a field. **3** ***set (someone) down*** **:** to allow (someone) to get off a bus, airplane, etc. • I asked the taxi driver to *set* me *down* [=*drop me off*, (*US*) *let me off*] in front of the library.

set eyes on see [1]EYE

set foot in/on see [1]FOOT

set forth [*phrasal verb*] **1** *literary* **:** to begin a journey • We will *set forth* [=*set out*] at dawn. **2** ***set forth (something) or set (something) forth*** *formal* **:** to explain or describe (something) in an organized way • The author *sets forth* [=*states*] the book's premise in its first two pages.

set forward [*phrasal verb*] ***set (something) forward or set forward (something)*** **:** to explain or describe (something) so that it can be considered • She has *set forward* [=*presented*] an ambitious plan to fix the nation's health-care system.

set in [*phrasal verb*] **:** to begin to be present, seen, etc. — used of something unpleasant or unwanted that often lasts for a long time • The kids should go outside and play before the rain *sets in* again. • An infection *set in* after the surgery. • Reality was starting to *set in*. [=become obvious] We were not going to win.

set in stone see [1]STONE

set loose see *let loose* at [2]LOOSE

set off [*phrasal verb*] **1 :** to begin traveling in a particular direction • We *set off* for home. • They *set off* in a different direction. • In the first chapter, the hero *sets off* on a long voyage across the ocean. **2** ***set off (something) also set (something) off*** **:** to cause (something) to start or happen • *set off* an explosion • Her comments *set off* [=*touched off*] a chain of events that led to two people losing their jobs. • The incident *set off* a debate about how public land should be used. **3** ***set off (something) or set (something) off*** **a :** to cause (something) to begin making noise • The thick smoke *set off* the school's fire alarms. • Your watch will probably *set* the metal detectors *off*. **b :** to cause (fireworks, a bomb, etc.) to explode • They were accused of *setting off* the bomb that destroyed the building. • It was *set off* by remote control. **c :** to make (something) easy to see or notice • The blue in your sweater *sets off* [=*accents*] your eyes. • Bright yellow police tape *set off* the area where the crime occurred. • a quote *set off* by quotation marks **4** ***set (someone) off*** **:** to cause (someone) to suddenly start yelling, crying, laughing, etc. • I wonder what *set* her *off*.

set on [*phrasal verb*] ***set (someone or something) on (someone)*** **:** to make (a person or animal) suddenly attack (someone) • Police dogs were *set on* the protesters. • She *set* her friends *on* him.

set out [*phrasal verb*] **1 a :** to begin traveling in a particular direction • We got out of the car and *set out* for the nearest gas station. • They *set out* toward the east. **b :** to start doing something **:** to begin an activity or effort with a particular plan or purpose • She *set out* with the goal of going to the Olympics. — often followed by *to + verb* • She accomplishes whatever she *sets out* [=*intends*] *to do*. • I never *set out to hurt* you. [=I was not trying to hurt you] • He *set out to become* a lawyer but ended up teaching history instead. **2** ***set (something) out or set out (something)*** **a :** to explain or describe (something) • In the article, the group *sets out* the role of parents in a child's education. • He *set out* the basic argument between the two groups. **b :** to move and organize (a group of things) so that they can be seen or used • We'll need to *set* a few extra chairs *out* for our guests. • They *set out* maps and travel brochures for the tourists to take.

set pen to paper see [1]PEN

set sail see [2]SAIL

set the pace see [1]PACE

set the record straight see [1]RECORD

set the scene see SCENE

set the stage see [1]STAGE

set to [*phrasal verb*] *Brit, literary* **:** to begin doing something in an active and serious way • We *set to* and soon finished the work.

set up [*phrasal verb*] **1 :** to prepare for something by putting things where they need to be • We have one hour left to *set up* for the party. • We had better start *setting up*. **2** ***set up (something) or set (something) up*** **a :** to create or establish (something) for a particular purpose • A panel needs to be *set up* to investigate the issue. • She hopes that in a few years she can *set up* a private practice of her own. • A foundation was *set up* for people with the disease. • The church *set up* a school for the city's homeless children. • The hikers **set up camp** [=they prepared an area where they could sleep outside] just before sunset. **b :** to arrange and plan (an event or activity) • I'll ask my secretary to *set up* a meeting with our clients. • Let's *set up* a time to get together. • He was the one who *set up* the bank robbery. **c :** to put (something) in an upright position • They *set up* flags along the street for the parade. • Help me *set* the tent *up*. **d :** to make (a machine, system, etc.) ready to be used • They *set up* the movie camera next to the door. • This computer wasn't *set up* to run so many programs at one time. **3** ***set (someone) up*** *or* ***set up (someone)*** **a :** to cause (someone) to be in a bad situation or to appear guilty • Those aren't his drugs. Someone must have *set* him *up*! [=framed him; made it look like the drugs were his] • He claimed he was *set up* by the police. **b** *Brit* **:** to help (someone) feel healthy and full of energy • She says that daily exercise has *set* her *up* to face the challenges of getting old. **c :** to give (someone) a job, a place to live, etc. • She *set* me *up* in a great apartment in the city. • He *set* his son *up* with a job at his company. **d :** to do something that makes it likely or possible for (someone) to do, get, or experience something • The team's excellent defense *set* them *up* to score the winning touchdown. — usually + *for* • I think you're just *setting* yourself *up for* a big disappointment. [=you're expecting something that won't happen and you will be disappointed when it doesn't] **e :** to cause (someone) to meet someone in order to start a romantic relationship • "How did you first meet your husband?" "My best friend *set* us *up*." — often + *with* • She wants to *set* him *up with* her sister. **4** ***set (yourself) up as (something)*** **a :** to try to make people believe that you are (something) • She has *set herself up as* the best alternative to the current administration. • He *sets himself up as* a defender of the people, but he's really only interested in getting more power. **b** *also* ***set up as (something)*** *or* ***set up in (something)*** **:** to start your own business • She *set (herself) up as* a wedding planner. [=she began working as a wedding planner] • He ***set up in business*** after finishing college. — see also SETUP

set up house see [1]HOUSE

set upon [*phrasal verb*] ***set (someone or something) upon (someone)*** **:** to attack (someone or something) — often used as *(be) set upon* • The protesters *were set upon* by police dogs.

set up shop see [1]SHOP

set your heart on see HEART

set your mind to see [1]MIND

set your teeth on edge see TOOTH

[2]**set** *noun, pl* **sets**

1 [*count*] **a :** a group of similar things that belong together — often + *of* • an extra *set of* keys • There were two *sets of* footprints leading to the door. • Her parents bought her a complete *set of* Shakespeare. [=all of the poems and plays written by Shakespeare] • a *set of* instructions • a complex *set of* emotions/ideas **b :** a group of things that are used together • I need to buy a new *set* of golf clubs. • a *set* of dishes • a chess *set* • an electric train *set* • a dining (room) *set* [=a group of furniture for a dining room] — see also TEA SET

2 [*count*] **:** a piece of electronic equipment • a radio/stereo *set* • a television *set* = (*US*) a TV *set* • The kids are allowed to watch two hours of television. After that, I turn off the *set*. — see also HEADSET

3 [*count*] **a :** a place where a movie or television program is filmed or a play is performed • We met on the *set* of *Hamlet*. • The actors got along well both on and off the *set*. [=while they were performing and while they were not] • Quiet on the *set*! **b :** the rooms, painted backgrounds, furniture, etc., that are used for a scene in a movie, television program, or play • elaborate stage *sets* • a *set* designer — called also (*US*) *setting*

4 [*count*] **:** one of the parts into which a tennis or volleyball match is divided **:** a group of tennis or volleyball games • He won a five-*set* match by three *sets* to two. — see also SET POINT

5 [*count*] **:** a group of songs or pieces that a musician or band performs at a concert • Her band opened the show with a 30-minute *set*.

6 [*singular*] *somewhat old-fashioned* **:** a group of people who have similar interests or characteristics • His music has become especially popular with the college *set*. [=with college students] • the younger *set* • the town's wealthy ***horsey set*** [=people who are interested in riding horses] — see also JET SET

7 [*count*] *Brit* **:** a group of students who perform at the same level in a particular subject • She's in the ***top set*** for science.

8 [*count*] *mathematics* **:** a group of numbers, points, etc. • the *set* of positive integers • a finite *set* of points

9 [*count*] **:** the number of times that you perform a group of repeated movements when you exercise • He did 3 *sets* of 12 push-ups.

10 [*singular*] **:** the way you move or hold your body, shoulders, etc. • The *set* of her shoulders suggested confidence and strength. • the firm *set* of his jaw — see also MIND-SET

11 [*count*] **:** a small bulb that you use to grow a new plant • onion *sets*

[3]**set** *adj*

1 : having a particular position or location • Her college is *set* in the countryside. • Their house is *set* back from the road. • a man with deep-*set* eyes — see also CLOSE-SET

2 : particular and not changing — used to describe something that has been decided by someone with authority • All the cars on our lot have a *set* [=*fixed*] price. • All contestants must write a 200-word essay on a *set* subject. • Schools must be in session a *set* number of days each year. • The office is open at *set* hours during the week. • (*Brit*) The book is now a ***set book/text*** [=a book that students must read] in schools. • (*chiefly Brit*) The restaurant has a very good ***set menu*** [=a menu with items that cannot be changed]

3 [*more ~; most ~*] **:** not likely to change • She has very *set* ideas about how children should behave. • We're both getting older and more ***set in our ways*** [=more unwilling to change the way we do or think about things]

4 *of a person's face or expression* **:** in a firm position that does not move or change • He stared at me with angry eyes and a *set* jaw. • a *set* smile • a crowd of *set* faces

5 *not used before a noun, informal* **:** ready or prepared for something • Is everyone *set* to go? • We're ***all set*** • She's *all set* for an early-morning start. • If we win the lottery, we'll be ***set for life*** [=we will have everything we need for the rest of our lives]

6 *not used before a noun* **:** scheduled or supposed to happen at a certain time — often + *for* • Your package is *set* [=*slated*] *for* delivery on the 11th. • Her trial is *set for* October. • The album is *set for* an early March release. — often followed by *to* + *verb* • The album is *set to be* released in early March. • The game is *set to begin* at 6:00.

be set against **:** to feel strongly that you do not want (something) or will not do (something) • Everyone was *set against* going. • He was ***dead set against*** the deal. [=he was very strongly opposed to the deal]

be set on **:** to feel strongly that you want (something) or will do (something) • She has *been set on* becoming a doctor since she was a child. • I'm not completely *set on* red for this room.

(get) ready, (get) set, go see [1]READY

have your heart set on see HEART

have your mind set on see [1]MIND

set in stone see [1]STONE

set–aside /ˈsɛtəˌsaɪd/ *noun, pl* **-asides**

1 [*count*] **:** something that is saved and used for a particular purpose; *especially, US* **:** a program that requires jobs, money, etc., to be saved for people who have not been given as much as others in the past • minority *set-asides*

2 *Brit* **a** [*noncount*] **:** a plan in the European Union in which farmers are paid not to grow a certain crop on a piece of land so that the price for that crop will not decrease too much **b** [*count*] **:** a piece of land on which the crop is not grown

set·back /ˈsɛtˌbæk/ *noun, pl* **-backs** [*count*] **:** a problem that makes progress more difficult or success less likely • Despite some early *setbacks*, they eventually became a successful company. • a serious/minor/temporary *setback*

set piece *noun, pl* **~ pieces** [*count*]

1 : a scene in a movie or play, an image in a painting, a piece of music, etc., that has a familiar style or pattern and that creates a particular and usually dramatic effect • a movie with some lovely *set pieces*

2 *chiefly Brit* **:** a carefully planned and performed group of movements in sports • She scored with a *set piece*.

set point *noun, pl* **~ points** *tennis* **:** a situation in which one player or team can win the set by winning the next point [*count*] He won with an ace on his second *set point*. [*noncount*] He won with an ace on/at *set point*.; *also* [*count*] **:** the point that must be won to win a set

set square *noun, pl* **~ squares** [*count*] *Brit* **:** TRIANGLE 5

sett /ˈsɛt/ *noun, pl* **setts** [*count*] *Brit* **:** a hole in the ground in which a badger lives

set·tee /sɛˈtiː/ *noun, pl* **-tees** [*count*]

1 : a long seat that has a back and arms and that two or more people can sit on

2 *Brit* **:** SOFA

set·ter /ˈsɛtɚ/ *noun, pl* **-ters** [*count*]

1 : a person or thing that determines or establishes some-

S

thing ▪ As a teenager, she was a style *setter* for her younger sister. [=her younger sister copied her style] ▪ world record *setters* [=people who set world records] — often used in combination ▪ I like to use the joke as a ***tone-setter*** for my speeches. [=use the joke to set the tone for my speeches] — see also PACESETTER, TRENDSETTER

2 : a large dog that has long ears and long, smooth hair ▪ English/Irish *setters*

set·ting /ˈsɛtɪŋ/ *noun, pl* **-tings** [*count*]

1 : the place and conditions in which something happens or exists ▪ This would be a beautiful/perfect/ideal *setting* for a picnic. ▪ You will have the opportunity to view the animals in their natural *setting*. [=*environment*] ▪ He tends to be shy in social *settings*. ▪ dining in a casual/formal *setting* ▪ urban versus rural *settings*

2 a : the time, place, and conditions in which the action of a book, movie, etc., takes place ▪ The movie changes the play's *setting* from the late 18th century to the year 2000. ▪ She uses modern-day Los Angeles as the *setting* for her book. **b** *US* **:** the rooms, painted backgrounds, furniture, etc., that are used for a scene in a movie or play **:** SET ▪ stage *settings*

3 : a particular way of positioning the controls of a machine, system, etc., in order to produce a desired result ▪ Save money by turning the temperature *settings* up in the summer and down in the winter. ▪ She just learned how to change the *settings* on her camera.

4 : the metal that attaches a stone or jewel to a piece of jewelry ▪ The ring has a single diamond in a gold *setting*.

5 : PLACE SETTING

6 : the music that is written to go with a piece of writing ▪ the musician's *settings* of poems by W. B. Yeats

[1]**set·tle** /ˈsɛtl̩/ *verb* **set·tles; set·tled; set·tling**

1 : to end (something, such as an argument) by reaching an agreement [+ *obj*] They were determined to *settle* the dispute/argument before going home for the day. ▪ *settle* a case/lawsuit ▪ The two sides have ***settled their differences***. [*no obj*] He agreed to *settle* out of court. [=to reach an agreement about a legal case without going to court]

2 [+ *obj*] **:** to make a final decision about (something) **:** DECIDE ▪ We need to *settle* this question once and for all. ▪ ***That settles it***. I can't take the day off from work, so I'm not going. — often used as *(be) settled* ▪ *It's settled* then: you pay for dinner and I'll pay for the movie.

3 : to move to a place and make it your home [*no obj*] His grandparents were immigrants from Germany who *settled* in Pennsylvania. ▪ He always thought he'd leave the city and *settle* in the country. [+ *obj*] the people who *settled* the West — often used as *(be) settled* ▪ The region *was settled* by German immigrants. ▪ The area *was settled* in the 18th century.

4 a *always followed by an adverb or preposition* **:** to put or place (someone) in a comfortable position [+ *obj*] He *settled* the baby into its crib. ▪ She ***settled herself*** behind the wheel and pulled the car out of the driveway. [*no obj*] He *settled* back into his chair. **b** [*no obj*] **:** to begin to feel comfortable in a new place, job, position, etc. — + *in* or *into* ▪ I'm glad to finally be *settling in* at my new job. ▪ The children are *settling into* their new school just fine.

5 a [+ *obj*] **:** to make (someone or something) quiet or calm ▪ Rocking *settled* the baby. ▪ She had a drink to *settle* her nerves. **b** [*no obj*] **:** to become quiet or calm ▪ I'm still waiting for my nerves to *settle*. [=*settle down*]

6 [+ *obj*] **:** to relieve pain and discomfort in (the stomach) ▪ Ginger and peppermint tea are good for *settling* the/your stomach.

7 [*no obj*] **a :** to move slowly downward **:** to sink gradually ▪ The foundation of the house has *settled* a little. ▪ an area where the ground has *settled* **b :** to go or fall down to a surface ▪ Dust *settled* on the shelves. ▪ The cocoa *settled* to the bottom of the mug. ▪ Some of the contents (of the package) may have *settled* during shipping. ▪ Fog *settles* [=*collects*] in the valley. — see also *the dust settles* at [1]DUST **c :** to stop flying, moving, etc., and rest on something — often + *on* ▪ The birds *settled on* a branch. ▪ His eyes *settled on* the woman in the red dress. [=his eyes stopped moving and he looked at the woman in the red dress] — often used figuratively ▪ A hush *settled on* the crowd. = A hush *settled* over the room. [=everyone in the crowd/room became quiet] ▪ Boredom *settled on* the faces of the students. [=the students began to look bored]

8 : to pay money that is owed [*no obj*] — often + *with* or *up* ▪ Before moving he *settled with* the utility company. ▪ We can *settle up* later. [+ *obj*] We *settled* the bill. ▪ When do you intend to ***settle your account***? [=pay what you owe]

9 [+ *obj*] **a :** to arrange who will be given control or ownership of (a property, business, etc.) ▪ She had to *settle* her aunt's estate after her death. **b :** to put (something) in order so that nothing else needs to be done ▪ He *settled* his affairs before entering the army.

settle a/the score see [1]SCORE

settle down [*phrasal verb*] **1 a :** to become quiet, calm, or orderly ▪ *Settle down*, children. ▪ When things *settle down* here, I'll come for a visit. **b *settle (someone or something) down or settle down (someone or something)*** **:** to make (someone or something) quiet, calm, or orderly ▪ He managed to *settle* the dog *down* long enough to give her the medicine. **2 :** to begin to live a quiet and steady life by getting a regular job, getting married, etc. ▪ They swore they would never *settle down* and get married. **3 :** to put yourself into a comfortable position ▪ She *settled down* on the bed. ▪ He *settled down* for the night. **4 :** to become quiet and begin giving your attention to something ▪ They quickly *settled down* to their work.

settle for [*phrasal verb*] ***settle for (something)*** **:** to be happy or satisfied with (something) **:** to accept (something) ▪ Neither team would *settle for* a tie score. ▪ He asked his parents if he could borrow $20 but *settled for* $10. [=he accepted $10 because that was all they would give him] ▪ I'm determined to win the championship and I won't *settle for* less.

settle on/upon [*phrasal verb*] **1 *settle on/upon (something or someone)*** **:** to choose (something or someone) after thinking about other possible choices ▪ We weren't sure what color we'd paint the kitchen, but we finally *settled on* a soft yellow. ▪ Hours later, they *settled on* a plan. **2 *settle (something) on (someone) chiefly Brit*** **:** to arrange to give (money or property) to (someone) ▪ She *settled* her whole fortune *on* her grandchildren.

[2]**settle** *noun, pl* **settles** [*count*] **:** a long wooden bench with arms, a high solid back, and often with space under the seat which can be used to store things

settled *adj* [*more* ~; *most* ~]

1 : not likely to move or change ▪ *settled* peoples ▪ She had to adjust to the *settled* habits of her new coworkers. ▪ He hated moving so often and longed for a more *settled* life.

2 : comfortable or happy with your home, job, etc. ▪ You'll feel more *settled* once you make some new friends.

3 : having people living in it ▪ *settled* areas of the country ▪ a densely/sparsely *settled* neighborhood [=a neighborhood where many/few people live]

set·tle·ment /ˈsɛtl̩mənt/ *noun, pl* **-ments**

1 a [*count*] **:** a formal agreement or decision that ends an argument or dispute ▪ I got the house in the divorce *settlement*. ▪ The parties have not been able to reach/negotiate a *settlement* in the case. ▪ an ***out-of-court settlement*** [=an agreement made to avoid a court case]; *also* **:** an amount of money that someone receives as part of such an agreement ▪ a cash *settlement* ▪ a *settlement* of two million dollars = a two-million-dollar *settlement* **b** [*singular*] **:** the act or process of settling an argument or disagreement ▪ We were hoping for a quick *settlement* of the dispute between the neighbors.

2 [*noncount*] **:** the act of paying back money that is owed — often + *of* ▪ the *settlement of* our debts ▪ He paid $20,000 in *settlement of* a loan.

3 a [*count*] **:** a place where people have come to live and where few or no people lived before ▪ English *settlements* in North America ▪ This was the island's first colonial *settlement*. **b** [*noncount*] **:** the act or process of moving to a new area or place to live there **:** the act or process of settling an area or place — often + *of* ▪ The rifle played a big role in the early *settlement of* North America. **c** [*count*] **:** a small village ▪ They came upon the ruins of an ancient *settlement*.

settlement house *noun, pl* ~ **houses** [*count*] *US* **:** a place or organization that provides various community services to people in a crowded part of a city

set·tler /ˈsɛtl̩ɚ/ *noun, pl* **-tlers** [*count*] **:** a person who goes to live in a new place where usually there are few or no people ▪ The town was established by British *settlers* [=*colonists*] in 1769.

set–to /ˈsɛtˌtuː/ *noun, pl* **-tos** [*count*] *chiefly Brit* **:** a usually short fight or argument ▪ He left after a *set-to* with his girlfriend. — see also *set to* at [1]SET

set–top box *noun, pl* ~ **boxes** [*count*] **:** a device that is connected to a television so that the television can receive digital signals

set·up /ˈsɛtˌʌp/ *noun, pl* **-ups**

1 : the process of making something (such as a machine or

computer program) ready to be used [*count*] an online account *setup* [*noncount*] The tent is designed for quick and easy *setup*. [=is designed to be set up quickly and easily] • *Setup* of the new software is a breeze. — often used before another noun • How much *setup* time is needed? • Run the *setup* program on your computer.
2 [*count*] : the way that something is done or organized • It took me a while to learn the *setup* of the office's filing system. • We had a great *setup*. On my days off, my wife would work from home while I took care of the kids. • The software makes it easy to create custom *setups*.
3 [*count*] *informal* : a situation in which someone is deliberately put in a bad position or made to look guilty — usually singular • Those aren't my drugs. This is a *setup*! Someone is trying to frame me!
4 [*count*] : the beginning of a story, joke, etc., that explains and leads to what follows — usually singular • This sounds like the *setup* to one of your jokes. • the *setup* for a television crime drama — see also *set up* at [1]SET

sev·en /ˈsɛvən/ *noun, pl* **-ens**
1 [*count*] : the number 7
2 [*count*] : the seventh in a set or series • the *seven* of hearts
3 [*noncount*] : seven o'clock • "What time is it?" "It's *seven*." • I leave each day at *seven*.
at sixes and sevens see SIX
– seven *adj* • waiting for *seven* hours **– seven** *pronoun* • *Seven* (of them) passed the test.

sev·en·fold /ˈsɛvənˌfoʊld/ *adj* : seven times as great or as many • There has been a *sevenfold* increase in membership in the past year.
– sevenfold *adv* • Membership has increased *sevenfold*.

seven seas *noun* [*plural*] : all the waters or oceans of the world • He sailed the *seven seas*.

sev·en·teen /ˌsɛvənˈtiːn/ *noun, pl* **-teens** [*count*] : the number 17
– seventeen *adj* • They lived together for *seventeen* years. **– seventeen** *pronoun* • We interviewed *seventeen* (of them). **– sev·en·teenth** /ˌsɛvənˈtiːnθ/ *noun, pl* **-teenths** [*count*] • I'll see you on the *seventeenth* of April. • The bill is due on the *seventeenth* (of the month). • one *seventeenth* of the total **– seventeenth** *adj* • The paintings were made in the *seventeenth* century. • He finished in *seventeenth* place. **– seventeenth** *adv* • She finished *seventeenth* in the race.

[1]**sev·enth** /ˈsɛvənθ/ *noun, pl* **-enths**
1 [*singular*] : number seven in a series • I'll be flying in on the *seventh*. [=the seventh day of the month] • (*baseball*) He got a base hit in the *seventh*. [=the seventh inning]
2 [*count*] : one of seven equal parts of something • Only about a *seventh* of the town voted for her.

[2]**seventh** *adj* : occupying the number seven position in a series • on the *seventh* day • the book's *seventh* edition • her *seventh* goal of the season • I finished in *seventh* place in the competition.
– seventh *adv* • She finished *seventh* in the race. • the nation's *seventh* largest city

seventh heaven *noun* [*singular*] *informal* : a state of extreme happiness and joy • When I told her she was going to be a grandmother, she was ***in seventh heaven***. [=she was very happy]

sev·en·ty /ˈsɛvənti/ *noun, pl* **-ties**
1 [*count*] : the number 70
2 ***seventies*** [*plural*] **a** : the numbers ranging from 70 to 79 • a salary in the low *seventies* [=between $70,000 and $74,000] **b** : a set of years ending in digits ranging from 70 to 79 • She grew up in the *seventies*. [=1970–1979] • She is in her *seventies*.
– sev·en·ti·eth /ˈsɛvəntijəθ/ *noun, pl* **-eths** [*count*] • one *seventieth* of the total **– seventieth** *adj* • his *seventieth* birthday **– seventy** *adj* • *seventy* books **– seventy** *pronoun* • *Seventy* (of them) came to the performance. • *seventy* of her classmates

sev·er /ˈsɛvɚ/ *verb* **-ers; -ered; -er·ing** [*+ obj*]
1 : to cut off (something) : to remove or separate (something) by cutting • He *severed* the lowest tree limbs. • His finger was *severed* in the accident. • a *severed* head/hand
2 : to end (a relationship, connection, etc.) completely • When she went off to college, she *severed* [=*cut off*] (all) ties with her high school friends. • Activists are asking the government to *sever* all diplomatic relations with the country.

[1]**sev·er·al** /ˈsɛvərəl/ *adj, always used before a noun*
1 : more than two but not very many • It took *several* days/weeks for the package to arrive. • He arrived *several* hours ago. • *several* million people • We added *several* more names to the list. • The meat can be cooked *several* ways. • There are *several* similar stores at the mall.
2 *formal* : different and separate • a federal union of the *several* states • After college, we each ***went our several ways***. [=(more commonly) *went our separate ways*; stopped being together]
– sev·er·al·ly /ˈsɛvərəli/ *adv, formal + law* • Both spouses are ***jointly and severally*** liable for the tax. [=are liable both together and separately]

[2]**several** *pronoun* : more than two but not very many • *Several* of the guests left early. • I haven't read all of her books, but I've read *several*.

sev·er·ance /ˈsɛvərəns/ *noun* [*singular*] *formal*
1 : the act of ending someone's employment • a *severance* of employment — usually used before another noun • ***severance pay*** [=money given to someone who has been fired or laid off from a job] • She received a good ***severance package*** [=money and other benefits given when employment is ended] when she was laid off.
2 : the act of ending a relationship, connection, etc. — usually *+ of* • a *severance of* diplomatic relations

se·vere /səˈviɚ/ *adj* **se·ver·er; -est** [*or more ~; most ~*]
1 a : very bad, serious, or unpleasant • *severe* weather conditions • The storm caused *severe* damage to the roof. • a *severe* economic depression • The patient is in *severe* pain. • children with *severe* learning disabilities • In the most *severe* cases, the disease can lead to blindness. **b** : causing a lot of physical pain or suffering • He suffered a *severe* head injury. • a *severe* cold/infection • *severe* burns/wounds
2 : very harsh • He faces *severe* penalties for his actions. • The punishment was *severe*. • *severe* criticism • a *severe* critic
3 : requiring great effort • The war was a *severe* test of his leadership. • a *severe* challenge
4 : very formal, strict, and serious • a *severe* young woman • He's very generous despite his somewhat *severe* manner.
5 : not having much decoration : very plain • a very *severe* style of architecture • *severe* clothing • a *severe* hairstyle
– se·vere·ly *adv* • *severely* injured/punished • The accident has *severely* limited her mobility. **– se·ver·i·ty** /səˈverəti/ *noun* [*noncount*] • At first, they didn't understand the *severity* of the problem/situation. • We were shocked at the *severity* of the penalty. • Treatment varies according to the *severity* of the symptoms.

sew /ˈsoʊ/ *verb* **sews; sewed; sewn** /ˈsoʊn/ *or* **sewed; sew·ing** : to make or repair something (such as a piece of clothing) by using a needle and thread [*+ obj*] She *sews* her own dresses by hand. • He *sewed* a patch onto his sleeve. • I *sewed* the button back on the shirt. • The surgeon *sewed* the wound shut. [*no obj*] She designs her own dresses and *sews* in her free time.
sew up [*phrasal verb*] ***sew (something) up or sew up (something)*** **1** : to close or repair (something) by using a needle and thread • He *sewed up* the tear in his shirt. • The surgeon *sewed up* the wound. **2** *informal* **a** : to do the final things that are needed to complete (something) in a successful way • They're *sewing up* the details of the agreement. — often used as *(be) sewn/sewed up* • The deal *was sewn up* by lunchtime. **b** : to make (something, such as a victory) certain • He scored a touchdown that *sewed up* the win/game. — often used as *(be) sewn/sewed up* • They felt they *had* the win/game *sewn up*. [=they felt that they were certainly going to win] • It looks like he has the nomination all *sewn up*.

sew·age /ˈsuːwɪʤ/ *noun* [*noncount*] : waste material (such as human urine and feces) that is carried away from homes and other buildings in a system of pipes • raw *sewage*

sewage treatment plant *noun, pl* **~ plants** [*count*] *chiefly US* : a place where sewage is cleaned so that it is not harmful or dangerous to the environment — called also (*US*) *sewage plant*, (*Brit*) *sewage farm*, (*Brit*) *sewage treatment works*, (*Brit*) *sewage works*

[1]**sew·er** /ˈsuːwɚ, *Brit* ˈsjuːə/ *noun, pl* **-ers** [*count*] : a pipe that is usually underground and that is used to carry off water and sewage • a *sewer* pipe • The water ran into the *sewer*. — compare [2]SEWER

[2]**sew·er** /ˈsowɚ/ *noun, pl* **-ers** [*count*] : someone who sews things • Both of the children were good *sewers* and cooks. — compare [1]SEWER

sew·er·age /ˈsuːwərɪʤ, *Brit* ˈsjuːərɪʤ/ *noun* [*noncount*]
1 : a system or process used for carrying away water and sewage • municipal *sewerage*

S

2 : SEWAGE ▪ raw *sewerage*

sewing *noun [noncount]*

1 : the act or process of using a needle and thread to make or repair something (such as a piece of clothing) ▪ She enjoys *sewing.*

2 : things that are used for sewing or that are being sewn ▪ She left her *sewing* in the living room.

sewing machine *noun, pl* **~ machines** *[count]* **:** a machine that is used for sewing things

sewn *past participle of* SEW

sex /ˈsɛks/ *noun, pl* **sexes**

1 *[noncount]* **:** the state of being male or female **:** GENDER ▪ The form asks for your name, age, and *sex.* ▪ The couple didn't know what the *sex* of their baby would be. ▪ How do you tell the *sex* of a hamster? ▪ discrimination on the basis of *sex* ▪ the female/male *sex* ▪ a ***sex change***(operation) [=an operation in which a man's body is changed to be like a woman's body or a woman's body is changed to be like a man's]

2 *[count]* **:** men or male animals as a group or women or female animals as a group ▪ This movie will appeal to both *sexes.* [=will appeal to both men and women] ▪ a battle of the *sexes* [=a battle between men and women] ▪ Some feel men are the more aggressive *sex.* ▪ a single-*sex* dormitory [=a dormitory where only women or men stay] — see also OPPOSITE SEX

3 *[noncount]* **:** physical activity in which people touch each other's bodies, kiss each other, etc. **:** physical activity that is related to and often includes sexual intercourse ▪ All he ever thinks about is *sex.* ▪ Her mom talked to her about *sex.* ▪ She doesn't like all the *sex* and violence in movies. ▪ premarital *sex* ▪ He ***had sex*** with his girlfriend. — often used before another noun ▪ He has a low ***sex drive*** [=he does not have a strong desire to have sex] ▪ a ***sex shop*** [=a store that sells items relating to sex] ▪ She has an active ***sex life*** [=she has sex often] — see also PHONE SEX, SAFE SEX

sex act *noun, pl* **~ acts** *[count]* **:** an action performed with another person for sexual pleasure ▪ paid to perform a *sex act* ▪ a pair of actors simulating ***the sex act*** [=*sexual intercourse*]

sex·a·ge·nar·i·an /ˌsɛksədʒəˈnerijən/ *noun, pl* **-ans** *[count]* **:** a person who is between 60 and 69 years old

sex appeal *noun [noncount]* **:** the quality of being sexually attractive ▪ an actor with a lot of *sex appeal*

sexed /ˈsɛkst/ *adj [more ~; most ~]* — used to describe how much sexual interest or desire a person has ▪ a highly *sexed* man/woman [=a man/woman who has a strong desire for sex]

sex education *noun [noncount]* **:** education in schools about sex — called also *(informal) sex ed*

sex gland *noun, pl* **~ glands** *[count]* **:** GONAD

sex·ism /ˈsɛkˌsɪzəm/ *noun [noncount]* **:** unfair treatment of people because of their sex; *especially* **:** unfair treatment of women ▪ Have you experienced *sexism*? ▪ the problem of *sexism* in language

— sex·ist /ˈsɛksɪst/ *adj [more ~; most ~]* ▪ He was accused of being *sexist.* ▪ Many people thought the ad was *sexist.* ▪ a *sexist* remark **— sexist** *noun, pl* **-ists** *[count]* ▪ He was accused of being a *sexist.*

sex·less /ˈsɛksləs/ *adj*

1 : not having sexual activity **:** not including sex ▪ a *sexless* marriage

2 : not looking like either a male or female ▪ *sexless* dolls

— sex·less·ness *noun [noncount]*

sex object *noun, pl* **~ -jects** *[count]* **:** someone who is thought of only as being sexually attractive or desirable ▪ movies that portray/treat women as *sex objects*

sex offender *noun, pl* **~ -ers** *[count]* **:** a person who is guilty of a crime involving sex (such as rape)

sex symbol *noun, pl* **~ -bols** *[count]* **:** a usually famous person who is very sexually attractive ▪ a Hollywood *sex symbol*

sex·tant /ˈsɛkstənt/ *noun, pl* **-tants** *[count]* **:** an instrument used to determine the position of a ship or airplane by measuring the positions of the stars and sun

sex·tet /sɛkˈstɛt/ *noun, pl* **-tets** *[count]*

1 : a piece of music written for six performers

2 : a group of six people or things; *especially* **:** a group of six singers or musicians who perform together

sex·ton /ˈsɛkstən/ *noun, pl* **-tons** *[count]* **:** a person who takes care of church buildings and property and often rings the church's bell during services

sex·tu·plet /sɛkˈstʌplət, *Brit* ˈsɛkstjʊplət/ *noun, pl* **-plets** *[count]* **:** one of six babies born at the same time to the same mother ▪ She gave birth to *sextuplets.* — compare QUADRUPLET, QUINTUPLET, TRIPLET, TWIN

sex·u·al /ˈsɛkʃəwəl/ *adj*

1 : of, relating to, or involving sex ▪ *sexual* activity/reproduction ▪ *sexual* abuse/desire/attraction ▪ a person's *sexual* organs ▪ He denied that he had a *sexual* relationship with her. ▪ *sexual* partners [=people who have sex with each other]

2 : of or relating to males and females ▪ *sexual* differences/characteristics ▪ *sexual* roles

— sex·u·al·ly /ˈsɛkʃəwəli/ *adv* ▪ Some teenagers are *sexually* active. [=some teenagers have sex] ▪ The movie has some *sexually* explicit scenes. [=the movie has scenes that show sex]

sexual intercourse *noun [noncount]* **:** sexual activity between two people; *especially* **:** sexual activity in which a man puts his penis into the vagina of a woman ▪ a doctor who is accused of having *sexual intercourse* with one of his patients — called also *intercourse*

sex·u·al·i·ty /ˌsɛkʃəˈwæləti/ *noun [noncount]* **:** the sexual habits and desires of a person ▪ She is comfortable with her *sexuality.* ▪ a study of male *sexuality*

sexually transmitted disease *noun, pl* **~ -eases** *[count] medical* **:** STD

sexual orientation *noun [count]* **:** a person's sexual preference or identity as bisexual, heterosexual, or homosexual

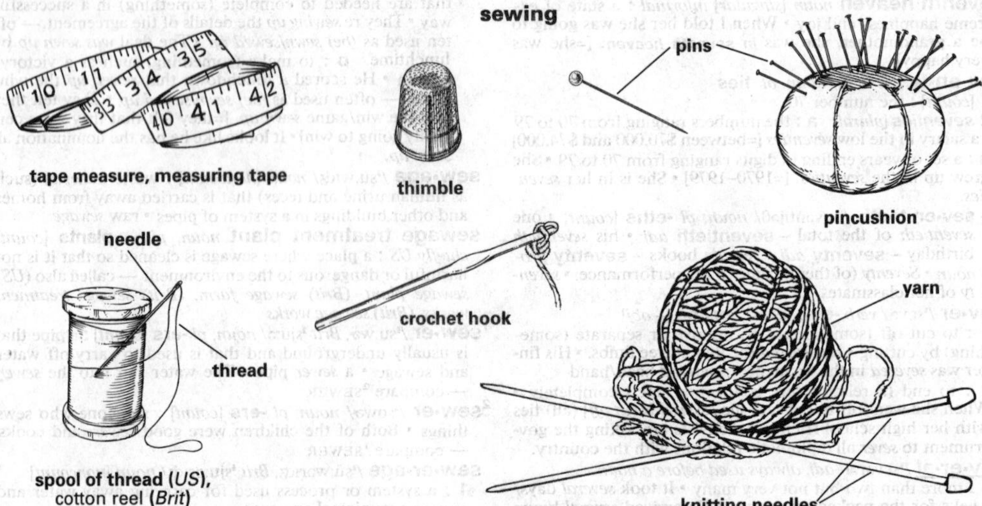

S

: the state of being bisexual, heterosexual, or homosexual • His *sexual orientation* has never been a problem for him at work. • people of different *sexual orientations* — called also *orientation*

sexy /ˈsɛksi/ *adj* **sex·i·er; -est** [*also more ~; most ~*]
1 : sexually appealing, attractive, or exciting • She wore a *sexy* skirt. • a *sexy* young actor • Her legs are long and *sexy*. • a *sexy* photograph
2 : having interesting or appealing qualities • a *sexy* story • *sexy* music
– sex·i·ly /ˈsɛksəli/ *adv* • *sexily* dressed dancers **– sex·i·ness** /ˈsɛksinəs/ *noun* [*noncount*]

SF *abbr* science fiction

Sgt. *abbr* sergeant

sh *or* **shh** *or* **shhh** /ʃ *often prolonged*/ *interj* — used to tell someone to be quiet • *Shh!* The baby is sleeping.

shab·by /ˈʃæbi/ *adj* **shab·bi·er; -est** [*also more ~; most ~*]
1 : in poor condition especially because of age or use • The furniture was old and *shabby*. • He wore a *shabby* coat. • Her first apartment was pretty *shabby*.
2 : dressed in clothes that are old and worn • *shabby* workmen
3 *informal* **:** not fair, generous, or reasonable • They complained about the *shabby* treatment they received at the hotel. • Backing out of the deal was a *shabby* thing to do.
not (too) shabby *informal* **:** fairly good or quite good • He came in second in the race. That's *not too shabby* for an inexperienced runner. [=that's not bad at all for an inexperienced runner]
– shab·bi·ly /ˈʃæbəli/ *adv* • The man was *shabbily* dressed.
– shab·bi·ness /ˈʃæbinəs/ *noun* [*noncount*]

[1]shack /ˈʃæk/ *noun, pl* **shacks** [*count*] **:** a small house or building that is not put together well • an old *shack* in the woods

[2]shack *verb* **shacks; shacked; shacking**
shack up [*phrasal verb*] *informal* **:** to live with someone without being married • She *shacked up* with her boyfriend. • young couples *shacking up*

[1]shack·le /ˈʃækəl/ *noun, pl* **shack·les**
1 [*count*] **:** one of two rings or bands that are placed around a person's wrists or ankles and that are connected by a chain — usually plural • The prisoner was placed in *shackles*.
2 *shackles* [*plural*] **:** something that prevents people from acting freely — *+ of* • The country was freed from the *shackles of* tyranny.

[2]shackle *verb* **shackles; shack·led; shack·ling** [*+ obj*] **:** to put shackles on (someone or something) • The guard *shackled* the prisoner. — often used as *(be) shackled* • Their legs *were shackled* together. — often used figuratively • The people *were shackled* by poverty.

[1]shade /ˈʃeɪd/ *noun, pl* **shades**
1 [*noncount*] **:** an area of slight darkness that is produced when something blocks the light of the sun • The buildings cast *shade* on the plaza. • The tree provided plenty of *shade*. • These plants grow well in *shade*. • It was a hot sunny day, but luckily their seats for the game were ***in the shade***. • We sat ***in the shade of*** a willow tree.
2 [*count*] **a :** something that is used to block strong light • He used his hand as a *shade* as he looked out into the bright sunlight. • an eye *shade* **b :** LAMPSHADE • a lamp with a broken *shade* **c** *US* **:** WINDOW SHADE • She pulled down the *shades*.
3 *shades* [*plural*] *informal* **:** SUNGLASSES • She was wearing a cool pair of *shades*.
4 [*noncount*] **:** a darkened area in a drawing, painting, etc. • a painting with contrasting areas of light and *shade*
5 [*count*] **:** a particular type of a color that is lighter, darker, etc., than other types — usually *+ of* • different *shades of* brown • lipstick in several *shades of* red • a bright *shade of* blue
6 [*count*] **:** a particular form of something that is usually slightly different from other forms • The word has many *shades* of meaning.
7 [*count*] **:** a very small amount • He saw *shades* [=*traces*] of himself in his son. • He is just ***a shade*** [=*a bit, a little*] taller than his brother. • The shirt is *a shade* too large for me.
draw the shades on see [1]DRAW
have it made in the shade *US, informal* **:** to have a very easy life or to be in a very good situation • She had to work hard for many years to achieve success, but now she *has it made in the shade*.
put (someone or something) in the shade *chiefly Brit, informal* **:** to be much better than (someone or something) • Their performance really *put ours in the shade*.
shades of — used to say what or who you are reminded of when you look at or think about someone or something • a former actor who's now a politician—*shades of* Ronald Reagan
– shade·less *adj* • Their yard is bare and *shadeless*.

[2]shade *verb* **shades; shad·ed; shad·ing** [*+ obj*]
1 : to shelter (something) from strong light and especially from sunlight • He *shaded* his eyes (with his hand). [=he placed his hand near his eyes to block the sun] • Several large trees *shade* the house.
2 : to make an area in a drawing, on a graph, etc., darker than other areas • She *shaded* the drawing to give it depth. • The *shaded* part of the graph represents the amount of sales. — sometimes *+ in* • *Shade in* the circle that indicates the correct answer.
3 *US* **:** to change (something, such as the truth) slightly in order to deceive people • The article *shaded* the truth by revealing only one side of the story. • *shading* the facts
shade into [*phrasal verb*] ***shade into (something)*** **:** to slowly or gradually change into (something) or become the same as (something) • as day *shades into* night

shading *noun, pl* **-ings**
1 [*noncount*] **:** the use of dark areas in a drawing, on a graph, etc.
2 *shadings* [*plural*] **:** small differences • *shadings of* blue • subtle *shadings* of meaning

[1]shad·ow /ˈʃædoʊ/ *noun, pl* **-ows**
1 [*count*] **:** a dark shape that appears on a surface when someone or something moves between the surface and a source of light • The tree cast/threw a long *shadow* across the lawn. • You can see your own *shadow* on a sunny day. — often used figuratively • a town located in the *shadow* of the Rocky Mountains [=a town located very close to the Rocky Mountains] • The bad news cast a *shadow* on the party. [=made the party much less enjoyable] • His death left a *shadow* over her heart. • For years they lived under the *shadow* of a dictator. [=they were ruled by a dictator] • He couldn't escape his father's *shadow*. [=he couldn't escape the influence of his powerful/successful father] • She grew up ***in the shadow of*** her very popular sister. [=people did not notice her because of all the attention that was given to her sister]
2 : an area of darkness created when a source of light is blocked [*noncount*] Part of the valley was in *shadow*. [*plural*] He saw something moving in the *shadows*.
3 [*singular*] **:** a very small amount of something • I sensed a *shadow* of disappointment in his expression. • There is not ***a shadow of (a) doubt*** [=there is no doubt] that he is lying.
4 [*count*] **:** someone who follows another person or who is always seen with another person • He is the President's adviser and *shadow*.
5 [*count*] **:** a dark area of skin under a person's eyes — usually plural • She woke up with dark *shadows* [=*circles*] under her eyes.
6 [*count*] **:** someone or something that is now much weaker, less impressive, etc., than in the past — *+ of* • The city today is just/only a *shadow of* what it once was. • He was once a great player, but now he's just ***a shadow of his former self***.
— see also EYE SHADOW, FIVE-O'CLOCK SHADOW

[2]shadow *verb* **-ows; -owed; -ow·ing** [*+ obj*]
1 : to cover (something) with a shadow — usually used as *(be) shadowed* • The yard *was shadowed* [=*shaded*] by trees.
2 a : to follow and watch (someone) especially in a secret way **:** TRAIL • Police *shadowed* the suspect for several days. **b :** to follow and watch (someone who is doing a job) in order to learn how to do the job yourself • She spent the night *shadowing* other waiters at the restaurant.

[3]shadow *or* **Shadow** *adj, always used before a noun* — used to describe the members of the main opposition party in British politics who would be given important positions in the government if their party won a national election • the *shadow* cabinet/Chancellor • *Shadow* Ministers

shad·ow·box /ˈʃædoʊˌbɑːks/ *verb* **-box·es; -boxed; -box·ing** [*no obj*] **:** to box with an imaginary opponent as a form of training • He was *shadowboxing* to stay in shape.
– shadowboxing *noun* [*noncount*]

shad·owy /ˈʃædowi/ *adj* [*more ~; most ~*]
1 : full of shade or shadows • a *shadowy* lane
2 : dark and mysterious • She was pursued by a *shadowy* figure.

S

3 : not clearly seen or understood ▪ He had only a *shadowy* idea of what they wanted him to do.

shady /ˈʃeɪdi/ *adj* **shad·i·er; -est** [*also more* ~; *most* ~]
1 a : giving or providing shade ▪ a *shady* tree **b :** sheltered from the sun's light : having shade ▪ Their backyard is nice and *shady*. ▪ a *shady* area
2 *informal* : seeming to be dishonest ▪ a *shady* business deal ▪ I don't trust him. He seems like a pretty *shady* character.

¹shaft /ˈʃæft, *Brit* ˈʃɑːft/ *noun, pl* **shafts**
1 [*count*] : the long, narrow part of a weapon, tool, instrument, etc. ▪ the *shaft* of a spear ▪ the *shaft* of a golf club
2 [*count*] : a bar in a machine which holds or turns other parts that move or spin ▪ a propeller *shaft* — see also DRIVESHAFT
3 [*count*] : one of two poles between which a horse is tied to pull a vehicle (such as a carriage)
4 [*count*] **a :** an opening or passage straight down through the floors of a building ▪ an air/elevator *shaft* **b :** an opening or passage in a mine ▪ a mine *shaft*
5 [*count*] *formal + literary* : a narrow beam of light ▪ They stood in a *shaft* of sunlight.
6 ***the shaft*** *US, informal* : harsh or unfair treatment ▪ Her boss really ***gave her the shaft*** [=treated her unfairly] when he promoted someone less experienced instead of her. ▪ He got promoted and she ***got the shaft***

²shaft *verb* **shafts; shaft·ed; shaft·ing** [+ *obj*] *chiefly US, informal* : to treat (someone) unfairly or harshly ▪ You really ***got shafted*** in that deal.

¹shag /ˈʃæg/ *noun, pl* **shags**
1 [*noncount*] : long pieces of material (such as wool) that are twisted together to make a rug or carpet — often used before another noun ▪ a *shag* rug ▪ *shag* carpeting
2 [*noncount*] : a type of strong tobacco that is cut into very small pieces
3 [*count*] *chiefly Brit* : a black bird that lives near the sea : CORMORANT
– compare ⁴SHAG

²shag *verb* **shags; shagged; shag·ging** [+ *obj*] *US* : to catch or retrieve (a ball that someone has hit) ▪ (*baseball*) They *shagged* fly balls in the outfield during batting practice. — compare ³SHAG

³shag *verb* **shags; shagged; shag·ging** *Brit, informal + impolite* : to have sexual intercourse with (someone) [+ *obj*] He *shagged* her last night. [*no obj*] They *shagged* all night. — compare ²SHAG

⁴shag *noun, pl* **shags** [*count*] *chiefly Brit, informal + impolite* : an act of sexual intercourse ▪ a quick *shag* — compare ¹SHAG

shag·gy /ˈʃægi/ *adj* **shag·gi·er; -est** [*also more* ~; *most* ~]
1 : long and tangled ▪ *shaggy* hair ▪ the dog's *shaggy* coat
2 : covered with hair or fur that is long and tangled ▪ a *shaggy* dog

shaggy–dog story /ˌʃægiˌdɑːg-/ *noun, pl* ~ **-ries** [*count*] *old-fashioned* : a long story or joke with an ending that is disappointing or that makes no sense

shah /ˈʃɑː/ *noun, pl* **shahs** [*count*] : a king of Iran in past times

¹shake /ˈʃeɪk/ *verb* **shakes; shook** /ˈʃʊk/; **shak·en** /ˈʃeɪkən/; **shak·ing**
1 a : to move sometimes violently back and forth or up and down with short, quick movements [*no obj*] The ground *shook* during the earthquake. ▪ The house *shook* as the train rumbled by. [+ *obj*] The earthquake *shook* the ground. ▪ *Shake* the salad dressing well before using it. ▪ He ***shook his fist*** (in the air) and yelled at the driver who cut them off. **b** [*no obj*] : to move or have parts of your body move in short, quick movements and in a way that you are not able to control ▪ His hand *shook* [=*trembled*] as he reached for the phone. ▪ He was *shaking* [=*shivering*] with cold. ▪ She was *shaking* with laughter [=laughing very hard] as he told us the story. ▪ I could see that he was *shaking* with anger/rage. [=he was so angry that he was shaking] ▪ I was so nervous that I was ***shaking like a leaf***. ▪ She was ***shaking in her boots/shoes*** [=she was very nervous] as she waited for the doctor.
2 [+ *obj*] : to free yourself from (someone or something) : to get away from or get rid of (someone or something) ▪ The fugitive couldn't *shake* the police. ▪ It's hard to *shake* the feeling that I'm forgetting something. — sometimes + *off* ▪ He is trying to *shake off* a cold.
3 [+ *obj*] : to cause (a belief, feeling, etc.) to become weaker ▪ The news did nothing to *shake* my belief that things will be okay. ▪ Her confidence was badly *shaken* by the accident. [=she became much less confident because of the accident] ▪ Nothing could *shake* his faith in God.
4 [+ *obj*] : to cause (someone) to feel fear, anxiety, shock, etc. ▪ The whole town was *shaken* by the news. — see also SHAKE UP 1 (below)
5 [+ *obj*] : to force (something) out of something by shaking ▪ He *shook* (out) the sand from his sandals.
6 : to grasp (someone's hand) with your hand and move it up and down when you are meeting or saying goodbye to each other or as a sign of friendship or agreement [+ *obj*] I *shook* his hand. = I ***shook hands*** with him. = (*somewhat old-fashioned*) I *shook* him by the hand. [*no obj*] They ***shook on*** the deal. = They ***shook on it***. [=they shook hands to show that they agreed]
7 [*no obj*] *of your voice* : to produce sound in an unsteady way because you are nervous, angry, sad, etc. ▪ His voice *shook* as he started his speech. ▪ Her voice *shook* with rage.
more than you can shake a stick at *chiefly US, informal* : more than you can count ▪ She has *more* cats *than you can shake a stick at*. [=she has a lot of cats]
shake a leg *informal* : to move or go quickly ▪ It's time to *shake a leg*—we're running late. — often used as a command ▪ "*Shake a leg*! We're going to be late."
shake down [*phrasal verb*] *US, informal* **1** ***shake (someone) down or shake down (someone)*** : to get money from (someone) by using deception or threats ▪ mobsters *shaking down* store owners for protection **2** ***shake (someone or something) down or shake down (someone or something)*** : to search (someone or something) thoroughly ▪ The police *shook* the car *down* looking for illegal drugs.
shake out [*phrasal verb*] **1** *informal* : to happen or end in a particular way ▪ We are just going to wait to see how things *shake out*. [=*turn out*] **2** ***shake (something) out or shake out (something)*** : to shake (something) back and forth or up and down in order to remove dirt, wrinkles, etc., from it ▪ She *shook out* the clothes as she took them from the dryer. ▪ He *shook* the rug *out*.
shake up [*phrasal verb*] **1** ***shake (someone) up or shake up (someone)*** : to upset (someone) : to shock or frighten (someone) ▪ The accident *shook up* both drivers. ▪ She was *shaken up* when she heard what happened. ▪ The layoffs *shook up* the whole department. — see also ¹SHAKE 4 (above) **2** ***shake (something) up or shake up (something)*** : to make many changes in (something, such as a company or organization) ▪ The coach *shook* things *up* by hiring new assistants. ▪ The new CEO *shook up* the company by asking some senior managers to leave. — see also SHAKE-UP
shake your head : to turn your head from side to side as a way of answering "no" or of showing disagreement or refusal ▪ When I asked her if she wanted help, she just *shook her head*.

²shake *noun, pl* **shakes**
1 [*count*] : a short, quick movement back and forth or up and down ▪ He responded to the question with a *shake* of his head. ▪ Give the dice a *shake*.
2 ***the shakes*** *informal* : a condition in which parts of your body move in a way that you are not able to control ▪ The whole experience gave me *the shakes*. [=made me shake with fear/nervousness] ▪ He drank too much coffee and got a bad case of *the shakes*.
3 [*count*] : MILKSHAKE ▪ a chocolate *shake*
a fair shake *informal* : a fair deal : fair treatment ▪ The judge ***gave him a fair shake***. [=the judge treated him fairly] ▪ She expected to ***get a fair shake*** from her boss.
in two shakes *informal* : very quickly or soon ▪ I'll be ready to go *in two shakes*.
no great shakes *informal* : not very good or skillful at something ▪ He's *no great shakes* as a poker player. = He's *no great shakes* at playing poker.

shake·down /ˈʃeɪkˌdaʊn/ *noun, pl* **-downs** [*count*] *informal*
1 *US* : the act of taking something (such as money) from someone by using threats or deception ▪ He was the victim of a *shakedown* by a street gang.
2 *US* : a thorough search of something ▪ The guards conducted a *shakedown* of the prisoners' cells to look for weapons.
3 : a thorough test of a new ship, airplane, etc., in order to make sure there are no problems or defects ▪ They're putting the system through a *shakedown*. — often used before another noun ▪ a *shakedown* cruise/flight

shak·er /ˈʃeɪkɚ/ *noun, pl* **-ers** [*count*]

S

1 : a container that is shaken to mix something or to make something come out ▪ a cocktail *shaker* ▪ a *shaker* of salt ▪ a dice *shaker* — see also PEPPER SHAKER, SALT SHAKER
2 Shaker : a member of a U.S. religious group that is known for living simply in close communities ▪ a member of ***the Shakers***
movers and shakers see MOVER
– Shaker *adj, always used before a noun* ▪ a *Shaker* village/community ▪ *Shaker* furniture [=furniture made in the simple style used by Shakers]

Shake·spear·ean /ʃeɪkˈspirijən/ *adj* **:** of or relating to William Shakespeare or his writings ▪ *Shakespearean* drama ▪ a *Shakespearean* actor

shake–up /ˈʃeɪkˌʌp/ *noun, pl* **-ups** [*count*] **:** an important change or series of changes in the way a company or other organization is organized or run ▪ There has been a major *shake-up* in the company. ▪ a management *shake-up* — see also *shake up* at [1]SHAKE

shaky /ˈʃeɪki/ *adj* **shak·i·er; -est** [*also more ~; most ~*]
1 : not strong or steady in movement, sound, etc. **:** tending to shake because of weakness, strong emotion, etc. ▪ I was so nervous that my hands were *shaky*. [=*shaking, trembling*] ▪ She took a few *shaky* steps before she collapsed. ▪ His voice was *shaky*.
2 : weak and likely to break down, collapse, or fail ▪ a *shaky* ladder ▪ The company's future is looking pretty *shaky*. [=the company's future does not look good] ▪ a *shaky* economy ▪ Her commitment to the cause seems *shaky*. ▪ His argument/theory rests ***on shaky ground***. [=his argument/theory is not supported by strong evidence] ▪ Their marriage is *on shaky ground*.
3 : not impressive or effective ▪ the pitcher's *shaky* performance ▪ The team has performed better lately after getting off to a *shaky* start. ▪ My memory of that day is a little *shaky*. [=I don't remember exactly what happened on that day]
– shak·i·ly /ˈʃeɪkəli/ *adv* ▪ He stood *shakily* on the ladder. ▪ The pitcher started the game *shakily*. **– shak·i·ness** /ˈʃeɪkinəs/ *noun* [*noncount*] ▪ the *shakiness* of her voice

shale /ˈʃeɪl/ *noun* [*noncount*] **:** a soft kind of rock that splits easily into flat pieces

shall /ˈʃæl, ʃəl/ *verb, past tense* **should** /ˈʃʊd, ʃəd/ *present tense for both singular and plural* **shall**; *negative* **shall not or shan't** /ˈʃænt, *Brit* ˈʃɑ:nt/ [*modal verb*] *formal*
1 — used to say that something is expected to happen in the future ▪ We *shall* [=*will*] arrive tomorrow evening. ▪ I *shall not* mention it again. = I *shan't* mention it again. ▪ Perhaps it will happen. We *shall* see.
2 — used to ask for someone's opinion ▪ "*Shall* [=*should*] I call a taxi?" "Please do." ▪ When *shall* we leave? [=when do you think we should leave?] ▪ *Shall* we dance? [=would you like to dance?] ▪ Let's dance, *shall* we?
3 — used to give a command or to say that you will or will not allow something to happen ▪ You *shall* leave at once! ▪ They *shall* not pass.
4 — used in laws or rules to say that something is required ▪ It *shall* be unlawful to carry firearms. ▪ The jury alone *shall* decide the verdict. ▪ There *shall* be no talking during the test. — see also SHALT

shal·lot /ʃəˈlɑ:t, ˈʃælət/ *noun, pl* **-lots** [*count, noncount*] **:** a small type of onion that is used in cooking — see color picture on page C4

shal·low /ˈʃæloʊ/ *adj* **shal·low·er; -est** [*also more ~; most ~*]
1 a : having a small distance to the bottom from the surface or highest point ▪ a *shallow* dish/pond/grave ▪ The *shallow* end of the pool is only three feet deep. — opposite DEEP **b :** not going far inward from the outside or the front edge of something ▪ a *shallow* closet — opposite DEEP
2 *disapproving* **:** not caring about or involving serious or important things ▪ Her boyfriends were all *shallow* creeps. ▪ She is only interested in *shallow* [=*superficial*] things like clothes and money.
3 : taking in a small amount of air ▪ She could only take *shallow* breaths. ▪ His breathing became very *shallow*. — opposite DEEP
4 *sports* **:** located near the inside edges of an area ▪ (*baseball*) He hit a fly ball to *shallow* right field. — opposite DEEP
– shal·low·ly *adv* ▪ He was breathing *shallowly*. **– shal·low·ness** *noun* [*noncount*] ▪ They measured the *shallowness* of the water. ▪ She could no longer tolerate his *shallowness*.

shal·lows /ˈʃæloʊz/ *noun* [*plural*] **:** a shallow area in a river, lake, etc. ▪ The fish lay their eggs in the *shallows* of the river.

shalt /ˈʃælt, ʃəlt/ *second person singular present tense of* SHALL, *old-fashioned* — used after *thou* ▪ *Thou shalt* not kill.

[1]**sham** /ˈʃæm/ *noun, pl* **shams**
1 [*count*] **a :** something that is not what it appears to be and that is meant to trick or deceive people ▪ He claims that the trial was a *sham*. ▪ Their marriage was a *sham*. **b :** someone who deceives people by pretending to be a particular kind of person, to have a particular skill, etc. ▪ Many people believed he could help them, but I knew he was a *sham*.
2 [*noncount*] **:** words or actions that are not sincere or honest ▪ She exposed their *sham* and hypocrisy.

[2]**sham** *adj, always used before a noun* **:** not real **:** FALSE, FAKE ▪ *sham* marriages ▪ *sham* pearls ▪ a *sham* doctor

[3]**sham** *verb* **shams; shammed; sham·ming :** to act in a way that is meant to trick or deceive people [*no obj*] She wasn't really hurt; she was only *shamming*. [+ *obj*] He was *shamming* illness to avoid work.

sha·man /ˈʃɑ:mən, ˈʃeɪmən/ *noun, pl* **-mans** [*count*] **:** someone who is believed in some cultures to be able to use magic to cure people who are sick, to control future events, etc.

sham·ble /ˈʃæmbəl/ *verb* **sham·bles; sham·bled; sham·bling** [*no obj*] **:** to walk in an awkward, unsteady way without lifting your feet very high off the ground ▪ He *shambled* into the room.

sham·bles /ˈʃæmbəlz/ *noun* **:** a place or state in which there is great confusion, disorder, or destruction [*singular*] The city was a *shambles* after the hurricane. ▪ This room is a *shambles*. [=*mess*] ▪ His life was a *shambles* after the divorce. [*noncount*] The room was ***in shambles***.

sham·bol·ic /ʃæmˈbɑ:lɪk/ *adj* [*more ~; most ~*] *chiefly Brit* **:** very messy or disorganized ▪ a *shambolic* system of public transportation

[1]**shame** /ˈʃeɪm/ *noun*
1 [*noncount*] **:** a feeling of guilt, regret, or sadness that you have because you know you have done something wrong ▪ He felt *shame* for his lies. ▪ The defendant ***hung his head in shame***. [=looked down because he was ashamed] ▪ ***Shame on you*** [=you should feel shame] for being so rude.
2 [*noncount*] **:** ability to feel guilt, regret, or embarrassment ▪ How could you be so rude? ***Have you no shame***?
3 [*noncount*] **:** dishonor or disgrace ▪ Her crimes brought *shame* upon her family. ▪ There is no *shame* in admitting your mistakes. [=you should not feel ashamed/embarrassed about admitting your mistakes] ▪ He had to endure the *shame* of being fired.
4 [*singular*] **:** something that is regretted **:** PITY ▪ It would be a *shame* to give up now. We're so close to the end. ▪ It's a *shame* that you'll miss the show. ▪ What a *shame* that they lost the game. ▪ I heard you lost your job. That's (such) a *shame*.
a crying shame see CRYING
put (someone or something) to shame **:** to be much better than (someone or something) ▪ Her art project *put mine to shame*. [=her art project was much better than mine]

[2]**shame** *verb* **shames; shamed; sham·ing** [+ *obj*]
1 : to cause (someone) to feel ashamed ▪ Her crimes *shamed* [=*disgraced*] her family. ▪ He was *shamed* by his behavior at the party.
2 : to force (someone) to act in a specified way by causing feelings of shame or guilt + *into* ▪ The suspects were *shamed into* confessing. ▪ My sister *shamed* me *into* giving the money back.

shame·faced /ˈʃeɪmˌfeɪst/ *adj* [*more ~; most ~*] **:** feeling or showing shame ▪ He stood there, looking *shamefaced*. ▪ a *shamefaced* apology/grin
– shame·faced·ly /ˈʃeɪmˌfeɪsədli/ *adv* ▪ He *shamefacedly* apologized for breaking the window.

shame·ful /ˈʃeɪmfəl/ *adj* [*more ~; most ~*] **:** very bad **:** bad enough to make someone ashamed ▪ There is no excuse for such *shameful* behavior. ▪ a *shameful* scandal ▪ What a *shameful* sight.
– shame·ful·ly /ˈʃeɪmfəli/ *adv* ▪ He has behaved *shamefully*. [=very badly; disgracefully] ▪ She looked away *shamefully*. [=she looked away because she was ashamed] ▪ He *shamefully* turned himself in to the police. **– shame·ful·ness** *noun* [*noncount*]

shame·less /ˈʃeɪmləs/ *adj* [*more ~; most ~*] **:** having or showing no shame ▪ The actor made a *shameless* plug for his movie. ▪ a *shameless* display of poor sportsmanship
– shame·less·ly *adv* ▪ He *shamelessly* gave himself a raise. **– shame·less·ness** *noun* [*noncount*]

S

¹sham·poo /ʃæmˈpuː/ *noun, pl* **-poos**
1 [*count, noncount*] **a** : a special liquid that is used for cleaning your hair • a bottle of *shampoo* **b** : a special liquid used for cleaning rugs, carpets, etc.
2 [*count*] : an act of cleaning hair, a carpet, etc., with shampoo — usually singular • She gets a *shampoo* every morning.

²shampoo *verb* **-poos; -pooed; -poo·ing** [+ *obj*] : to clean (something, such as hair, a carpet, etc.) with shampoo • She *shampoos* her hair every morning. • We need to *shampoo* the rug.

sham·rock /ˈʃæmˌrɑːk/ *noun, pl* **-rocks** [*count*] : a small plant with three leaves on each stem that is the national symbol of Ireland

shandy /ˈʃændi/ *noun, pl* **-dies** [*count, noncount*] *Brit* : a drink made of beer mixed with lemonade

shang·hai /ʃæŋˈhaɪ/ *verb* **-hais; -haied; -hai·ing** [+ *obj*] *somewhat old-fashioned*
1 : to bring (someone) onto a ship by force • a *shanghaied* sailor
2 *informal* : to make (someone) do something by using force or tricks — usually + *into* • I somehow got *shanghaied into* babysitting for my sister's kids.

shank /ˈʃæŋk/ *noun, pl* **shanks** [*count*]
1 : the straight, narrow part of a tool that connects the part that does the work with the part that you hold • the *shank* of a drill bit
2 : a piece of meat cut from the upper part of the leg • a lamb/beef *shank*
3 : the part of the leg between the knee and the ankle — usually plural • an old man with skinny *shanks*

shan't /ˈʃænt, *Brit* ˈʃɑːnt/ *chiefly Brit* : shall not

¹shan·ty /ˈʃænti/ *noun, pl* **-ties** [*count*] : a small, simple building that is roughly made from sheets of wood, plastic, etc., and that is used as a house by poor people — compare ²SHANTY

²shanty *noun, pl* **-ties** [*count*] : a song that sailors sang in the past while they worked — compare ¹SHANTY

shan·ty·town /ˈʃæntiˌtaʊn/ *noun, pl* **-towns** [*count*] : a town or a part of a town where the people are poor and live in shanties

¹shape /ˈʃeɪp/ *noun, pl* **shapes**
1 : the form or outline of an object [*count*] circles, squares, triangles, and other geometric *shapes* • The cake has a rectangular/circular *shape*. • The pieces came in many different sizes and *shapes*. • a cookie ***in the shape of*** a heart [=a cookie shaped like a heart] • The cloud ***took the shape of*** a dog. [=the cloud looked like a dog] [*noncount*] The pieces were sorted by size and *shape*. • The cloud kept changing *shape*. • The cake was rectangular/circular ***in shape***. • The bike's rim was bent ***out of shape***. [=it was bent so that it was not its usual round shape]
2 [*noncount*] **a** : the condition of something or someone — usually used with *in* • The car was *in* good/bad/poor *shape*. • He's *in* better/worse *shape* now. • All the players are in top/exellent *shape*. • She has had quite a few glasses of wine and is *in* no *shape* to drive. [=she shouldn't drive because she has drunk too much wine] • Their marriage is *in* bad/good *shape*. **b** : a physically strong and healthy condition • I need to start exercising and get back ***in shape***. • I'm ***out of shape*** because I haven't been exercising. • The players were in poor condition, but the coach quickly ***whipped/licked/knocked/got them into shape***. • She ***stays/keeps in shape*** by exercising daily and eating well. — often used figuratively • It will cost billions of dollars to get the company back *in shape*. [=back into good condition]
3 [*noncount*] : the way something is done : the form of something • Computer technology has changed the *shape* of communication. • They offered help ***in the shape of*** [=in the form of] a loan. [=the help they offered was a loan] • That behavior is not acceptable ***in any way, shape, or form***. [=it is not at all acceptable] • Another newspaper has stopped publication. Is this the ***shape of things to come*** in the newspaper business? [=is this what the future of the newspaper business is going to be like?]
4 [*noncount*] : a definite form or arrangement of something • The plan is finally ***taking shape***. • His discussions with fellow professors and his students ***gave shape to*** his book.
5 [*count*] : a person or thing that cannot be seen clearly • I saw a vague *shape* [=*figure*] in the dark. • dark *shapes* moving in the shadows
bent out of shape see ¹BENT

²shape *verb* **shapes; shaped; shap·ing** [+ *obj*]
1 : to give a particular form or shape to (something) : to work with (a material) in order to make something from it • The artist *shaped* the stone with a hammer and chisel. — often + *into* • *Shape* the dough *into* loaves.
2 : to influence the development of (something) : to help (something) become what it is • Schools *shape* the minds of future leaders. • Ads help *shape* public opinion.
3 : to make (something, such as a plan) by a process of careful thought • They have *shaped* [=*devised*] a careful strategy for winning the election.
shape up [*phrasal verb*] *informal* **1** : to happen or develop in a particular way • Our plans are *shaping up* nicely. • This is *shaping up* to be an exciting year. [=it looks like this will be an exciting year] **2 a** : to start behaving in a better or more acceptable way • You'd better *shape up* and start studying. • If he doesn't *shape up*, he's going to be fired. ✧ In informal U.S. English, if you are told to ***shape up or ship out***, you will have to leave your job, position, etc., if you do not improve your behavior. **b** ***shape up (someone or something) or shape (someone or something) up*** : to cause (someone or something) to start behaving in a better or more acceptable way • She has really *shaped up* the sales department. **3** : to make your body stronger and healthier by exercising • He has been *shaping up* at the gym.
– shap·er *noun, pl* **-ers** [*count*]

shaped /ˈʃeɪpt/ *adj*
1 : having a particular shape or form • a cookie *shaped* like a heart — often used in combination • an egg-*shaped* toy • a shirt with a V-*shaped* collar
2 : shaped or formed in a particular way • a carefully *shaped* ice sculpture

shape·less /ˈʃeɪpləs/ *adj*
1 **a** : not having a particular or definite shape • a *shapeless* blob **b** : not having the usual or normal shape • an old, *shapeless* baseball cap
2 : not organized or arranged in a way that is clear and understandable • a *shapeless* essay/argument
– shape·less·ly *adv* **– shape·less·ness** *noun* [*noncount*]

shape·ly /ˈʃeɪpli/ *adj* **shape·li·er; -est** [*also more* ~; *most* ~] : having an attractive shape or form • She has a *shapely* figure.
– shape·li·ness *noun* [*noncount*]

shard /ˈʃɑɚd/ *also* **sherd** /ˈʃɚd/ *noun, pl* **shards** *also* **sherds** [*count*] : a sharp piece of something (such as glass or pottery) — often + *of* • *shards of* glass

¹share /ˈʃeɚ/ *verb* **shares; shared; shar·ing**
1 [+ *obj*] : to have or use (something) with others • We *share* a house/car (together). — often + *with* • I *share* an office *with* two other people.
2 [+ *obj*] *of two or more people* : to divide (something) into parts and each take or use a part • They *shared* the last cookie. • We *shared* the money equally.
3 : to let someone else have or use a part of (something that belongs to you) [+ *obj*] The children need to learn to *share* their toys. — often + *with* • He doesn't *share* his toys with other kids. • *Share* the cookies *with* your sister. [*no obj*] The children need to learn to *share* (*with* each other).
4 : to have (something that someone or something else also has) : to have (something) in common [+ *obj*] We *share* an interest in baseball. [=we are both interested in baseball] • The two countries *share* a border. • I know you're worried about the schedule, but I don't *share* your concerns. [=I don't have the same concerns that you have; I am not worried about the schedule] — often + *with* • I *share* these concerns *with* others in the group. [*no obj*] — + *in* • I don't *share* *in* your concerns about the schedule.
5 : to tell someone about (your feelings, opinions, thoughts, etc.) [+ *obj*] Please *share* any ideas that you may have. — often + *with* • Would you like to *share* your feelings *with* the group? • Thanks for *sharing* that (*with* me). [*no obj*] Thanks for *sharing*.
6 : to have equal responsibility for or involvement in (something) [+ *obj*] I *share* the blame for what happened. [*no obj*] — + *in* • We all *share in* the responsibility for this tragedy. • The whole family *shares in* the household chores.
share out [*phrasal verb*] ***share out (something) or share (something) out*** *chiefly Brit* : to divide (something) into parts and give the parts to different people • In her will, she *shared out* her property to her nephews and nieces. — see also SHARE-OUT
– shar·er *noun, pl* **-ers** [*count*]

²share *noun, pl* **shares**

1 [*singular*] : a part of something that has been divided into parts and given to different people • I deserve a *share* in the winnings. — often + *of* • I sold my *share* [=*portion*] *of* the business. • I got my *share of* the profits. — see also LION'S SHARE, TIME-SHARE
2 [*count*] : any of the equal parts into which the ownership of a property or business is divided • 100 *shares* of stock — see also MARKET SHARE
3 [*singular*] : the amount of something that someone owes or deserves or is responsible for — often + *of* • Everybody should have to pay their *share* [=*portion*] *of* the dinner bill. • Everyone must accept their *share of* the blame. • I've done my (fair) *share of* the work.
a share of the pie see PIE

share·crop·per /ˈʃeɚˌkrɑːpɚ/ *noun, pl* **-pers** [*count*] : a farmer especially in the southern U.S. who raises crops for the owner of a piece of land and is paid a portion of the money from the sale of the crops

share·hold·er /ˈʃeɚˌhoʊldɚ/ *noun, pl* **-ers** [*count*] : someone who owns shares in a company or business : STOCKHOLDER

share·hold·ing /ˈʃeɚˌhoʊldɪŋ/ *noun* [*noncount*] : the amount of shares that someone owns in a company or business • He has a substantial *shareholding* [=he owns a large number of shares] in the company.

share option *noun, pl* ~ **-tions** [*count*] *Brit* : STOCK OPTION

share–out *noun, pl* **-outs** [*count*] *Brit* : an act of dividing something into parts and giving them to two or more people — usually singular • There was an equal *share-out* of the money. — see also *share out* at ¹SHARE

share·ware /ˈʃeɚˌweɚ/ *noun* [*noncount*] : computer software that you can try for free for a certain period of time before choosing whether or not to buy it — compare FREEWARE

sha·ria /ʃəˈriːjə/ *noun* [*noncount*] : the religious laws based on the Koran that Muslims follow

shark /ˈʃɑɚk/ *noun, pl* **sharks** [*count*]
1 : a large and often dangerous sea fish with very sharp teeth — see color picture on page C8
2 *informal* : a person who gets money from people by deceiving or cheating them; *especially* : a person who wins money in a game by playing well and by being dishonest • a pool *shark* • a card *shark* — see also LOAN SHARK
– shark·like /ˈʃɑɚkˌlaɪk/ *adj* • a *sharklike* smile/appetite

¹**sharp** /ˈʃɑɚp/ *adj* **sharp·er; -est** [*also more ~; most ~*]
1 : having a thin edge that is able to cut things or a fine point that is able to make a hole in things • a *sharp* knife/pencil • *sharp* teeth/claws — opposite BLUNT, DULL; see also RAZOR-SHARP
2 **a** : sudden and quick • a *sharp* drop/rise/decrease/increase in temperature • a *sharp* break from tradition [=a sudden change from the traditional way of doing things] **b** : involving a sudden change in direction • He took a *sharp* left turn. • a *sharp* curve in the road
3 **a** : clear and easy to see • a *sharp* image/picture/photograph [=an image/picture/photograph in which the small details can be clearly seen] **b** : very noticeable • a *sharp* difference/distinction • Her cheerful mood ***stands in sharp contrast*** to her dreary surroundings.
4 : having or showing a quick ability to notice and understand things • a *sharp* student • *sharp* questions • You have *sharp* eyes.
5 : very sudden and severe • a *sharp* pain • a *sharp* disappointment
6 : critical or harsh • a *sharp* reply/attack/criticism/rebuke • He was very *sharp* with her. [=he spoke to her in a very harsh way] • She has ***a sharp tongue*** [=she tends to say very critical things to people]
7 : loud, short, and sudden • a *sharp* noise
8 *of cheese* : having a strong odor and flavor • *sharp* cheddar cheese
9 : very strong and cold • a *sharp*, biting wind
10 *disapproving* : clever in a bad or dishonest way • *sharp* business practices
11 : ending in a point or edge • a *sharp* nose • *sharp* mountain peaks
12 *informal* : stylish or fashionable • He's a *sharp* dresser. • a *sharp* outfit • You're looking very *sharp* today.
13 *music* **a** : higher than the true pitch • Her singing was slightly *sharp*. **b** : higher than a specified note by a semitone • F *sharp* — compare ¹FLAT 10, ¹NATURAL 8
keep a sharp eye on : to watch (someone or something) carefully • *Keep a sharp eye on* the kids to make sure they don't hurt themselves.
– sharp·ness *noun* [*noncount*]

²**sharp** *adv*
1 : EXACTLY — used to refer to an exact time • It's four o'clock *sharp*.
2 : above the correct musical pitch • He sang slightly *sharp*. — compare ³FLAT 4
3 : SUDDENLY • turn *sharp* [=*sharply*] left/right
look sharp *informal* : to act quickly : HURRY • You'd better *look sharp* if you want to be ready on time.

³**sharp** *noun, pl* **sharps** [*count*] : a musical note that is one semitone higher than a specified note • C *sharp*; *also* : a written symbol ♯ that is placed before a note to show that it should be played a semitone higher — compare ²FLAT 3, ²NATURAL 2

sharp·en /ˈʃɑɚpən/ *verb* **-ens; -ened; -en·ing**
1 [+ *obj*] : to make (something) sharp or sharper • *sharpen* a knife/pencil
2 **a** [+ *obj*] : to make (something) clearer or more distinct • Can you *sharpen* the image? • The lecture *sharpened* my understanding of the topic. **b** [*no obj*] : to become clearer or more distinct • The outlines of the mountains *sharpened* as we got closer.
3 [+ *obj*] : to improve (something) • I took a course to *sharpen* (up) my computer skills.
4 [*no obj*] : to become more severe • The pain suddenly *sharpened*.
sharpen up [*phrasal verb*] : to become better, smarter, more skillful, etc. • You'd better *sharpen up* if you want to keep your job.

sharp·en·er /ˈʃɑɚpənɚ/ *noun, pl* **-ers** [*count*] : a tool or machine that makes something sharp • a pencil/knife *sharpener*

sharp–eyed /ˈʃɑɚpˈaɪd/ *adj*
1 : having very good eyesight • a *sharp-eyed* bird
2 : having a strong ability to notice things • A *sharp-eyed* [=*perceptive*] reader will notice the book's repeating themes.

sharp·ish /ˈʃɑɚpɪʃ/ *adv, Brit, informal* : QUICKLY • getting the work done *sharpish*

sharp·ly /ˈʃɑɚpli/ *adv* [*more ~; most ~*]
1 : in a harsh, critical, or angry way • He spoke *sharply* to the children and made them cry. • He criticized her *sharply*.
2 : suddenly and by a large amount • The temperature dropped/fell/rose *sharply*. • Prices are expected to increase/decline *sharply*. • The car turned/veered *sharply* to the left. • a *sharply* angled curve in the road
3 : clearly or distinctly • a *sharply* defined image • Her cheerful mood contrasts *sharply* with her dreary surroundings.
4 : loudly and suddenly • She cried out *sharply*.
5 : with a very sharp edge or point • The knife is *sharply* pointed.

sharp·shoot·er /ˈʃɑɚpˌʃuːtɚ/ *noun, pl* **-ers** [*count*] : someone who is skilled at shooting a target with a gun
– sharp·shoot·ing /ˈʃɑɚpˌʃuːtɪŋ/ *noun* [*noncount*]

sharp–tongued /ˈʃɑɚpˈtʌŋd/ *adj* [*more ~; most ~*] : tending to say very critical things to people : having a sharp tongue • a comedy about a mild man and his *sharp-tongued* wife

sharp–wit·ted /ˈʃɑɚpˈwɪtəd/ *adj* [*more ~; most ~*] : having or showing an ability to think and react very quickly • a *sharp-witted* young woman • a *sharp-witted* reply

shat *past tense and past participle of* SHIT

shat·ter /ˈʃætɚ/ *verb* **-ters; -tered; -ter·ing**
1 : to break suddenly into many small pieces [*no obj*] The window *shattered* (into a thousand pieces) when it was hit by a rock. [+ *obj*] The rock *shattered* the window. • She *shattered* her leg [=she broke her leg very badly] in a fall.
2 [+ *obj*] : to damage (something) very badly • His dreams were *shattered* by their rejection. • The end of his marriage *shattered* him emotionally.

shattered *adj*
1 : very shocked and upset • The end of his marriage left him emotionally *shattered*.
2 *Brit, informal* : very tired • I was *shattered* when I got home from work.

shattering *adj* : very shocking and upsetting • The end of his marriage was an emotionally *shattering* experience.

shat·ter·proof /ˈʃætɚˌpruːf/ *adj* : made so that it does not break easily and will not form sharp, dangerous pieces if it does break • *shatterproof* glass

[1]shave /ˈʃeɪv/ *verb* **shaves; shaved; shaved** *or* **shav·en** /ˈʃeɪvən/; **shav·ing**
1 a : to cut the hair, wool, etc., off (someone or something) very close to the skin [*+ obj*] He *shaves* himself [=cuts off the hair that grows on his face] every morning before breakfast. ▪ He *shaved* his head. ▪ She cut herself while *shaving* her legs. ▪ The sheep were all *shaved*. ▪ *shaved/shaven* heads/legs [*no obj*] He *shaves* every morning before breakfast. ▪ I cut myself *shaving* this morning. **b** [*+ obj*] **:** to cut off (hair, wool, a beard, etc.) very close to the skin ▪ He *shaved* his beard. ▪ She *shaves* her dog's fur in the summer. — often *+ off* ▪ He *shaved off* his beard.
2 [*+ obj*] **:** to remove a thin layer of (something) from something ▪ He *shaved* some butter from the container. — usually *+ off* ▪ *Shave* the bark *off* the tree.
3 [*+ obj*] **:** to reduce something by taking away (a small amount) — usually *+ off* ▪ Can you *shave* a little *off* the price? [=can you reduce the price by a small amount?] ▪ She was able to *shave* a few seconds *off* the record. [=to beat the record by a few seconds]

[2]shave *noun, pl* **shaves** [*count*] **:** an act of shaving — usually singular ▪ He gave himself a *shave*. [=he shaved himself] — see also CLOSE SHAVE

shaven *adj* **:** having had the hair, wool, etc., removed : having been shaved ▪ a *shaven* head — see also CLEAN-SHAVEN

shav·er /ˈʃeɪvɚ/ *noun, pl* **-ers** [*count*]
1 : a tool or device that is used to shave hair from your face, body, or head ▪ an electric *shaver* [=*razor*] — see picture at GROOMING
2 : a person who shaves ▪ a careful *shaver*
3 *old-fashioned* **:** a young boy ▪ when he was just a *shaver*

shaving *noun, pl* **-ings** [*count*] **:** a very thin piece removed from something with a sharp tool — usually plural ▪ wood *shavings*

shaving cream *noun* [*noncount*] **:** a special cream or foam that is spread over your face or another part of your body before shaving — called also *shaving foam*

Sha·vu·ot /ʃəˈvuːˌoʊt/ *noun* [*noncount*] **:** a Jewish holiday celebrated 50 days after the first day of Passover

shawl /ˈʃɑːl/ *noun, pl* **shawls** [*count*] **:** a piece of cloth that is used especially by women as a covering for the head or shoulders

[1]she /ˈʃiː/ *pronoun*
1 : that female — used to indicate a female person or animal that is the subject of a verb ▪ *She* is my mother. ▪ Ask your sister where *she* is going. ▪ *She* has been planning this trip since January. ▪ (*on the telephone*) "Hello, I'd like to speak with Jane." "This is *she*." [=I (the person who answered the phone) am Jane] — compare HE
2 *somewhat old-fashioned* — used to refer to something (such as a ship) that is thought of as having female qualities ▪ *She* was a fine ship.

[2]she *noun* [*singular*] **:** a girl, woman, or female animal ▪ "Somebody called when you were out, but I can't remember who." "Was it a he or a *she*?" — sometimes used in combination ▪ a little black *she*-cat [=a little, black female cat]

s/he /ˈʃiːˈhiː, ˈʃiːjɚˈhiː, ˈʃiːˌslæʃˈhiː/ *pronoun* **:** she or he — used in writing as a pronoun when the subject of the sentence can be either female or male ▪ Once a student has chosen a project, *s/he* should write a brief description of it.

sheaf /ˈʃiːf/ *noun, pl* **sheaves** /ˈʃiːvz/ [*count*]
1 : a bunch of stalks and ears of grain that are tied together after being cut ▪ *sheaves* of wheat
2 : a group of things fastened together ▪ a *sheaf* of arrows/papers

shear /ˈʃiɚ/ *verb* **shears; sheared; sheared** *or* **shorn** /ˈʃoɚn/; **shear·ing** [*+ obj*]
1 a : to cut the hair, wool, etc., off (an animal) ▪ The farmers *sheared* the sheep. **b :** to cut off (an animal's hair, wool, etc.) ▪ The farmers *sheared* the wool from the sheep. — often *+ off* ▪ The farmers *sheared off* the wool from the sheep.
2 : to cut off a person's hair — usually used as *(be) shorn* ▪ His long locks *were shorn*. ▪ the monk's *shorn* head
3 *literary* **:** to take something away from (someone) — usually used as *(be) shorn* ▪ a tyrant who has *been shorn* of power [=a tyrant whose power has been taken away]
shear off [*phrasal verb*] **1 :** to become separated suddenly because of great force ▪ The excess weight caused the bolt to *shear off*. **2 *shear (something) off or shear off (something)* :** to remove (something) with great force ▪ The impact of the crash *sheared off* the airplane's wing.
– shear·er *noun, pl* **-ers** [*count*]

shears /ˈʃiɚz/ *noun* [*plural*] **:** a large, heavy pair of scissors — see also PINKING SHEARS

sheath /ˈʃiːθ/ *noun, pl* **sheaths** /ˈʃiːðz/ [*count*]
1 : a cover for the blade of a knife, sword, etc. ▪ the *sheath* of a sword
2 : a protective covering ▪ a piece of wire covered with a plastic *sheath* ▪ a nerve *sheath*
3 *Brit* **:** CONDOM
4 : a close-fitting dress that does not usually have a belt

sheathe /ˈʃiːð/ *verb* **sheathes; sheathed; sheath·ing** [*+ obj*]
1 *literary* **:** to put (something, such as a sword) into a sheath ▪ He *sheathed* his sword.
2 : to cover (something) with something that protects it — usually used as *(be) sheathed* ▪ The ship's bottom *is sheathed* with/in copper.

sheath·ing /ˈʃiːðɪŋ/ *noun* [*noncount*] **:** a protective outer covering ▪ copper *sheathing*

she·bang /ʃɪˈbæŋ/ *noun*
***the whole shebang informal* :** the whole thing : everything that is included in something ▪ You can buy *the whole shebang* for just $50.

[1]shed /ˈʃɛd/ *verb* **sheds; shed; shed·ding**
1 [*+ obj*] **:** to get rid of (something) ▪ I've been trying to *shed* some extra pounds. ▪ The company has had to *shed* many jobs. ▪ She hasn't been able to *shed* her image as a troublemaker. [=to make people stop thinking of her as a troublemaker]
2 : to lose (leaves, skin, fur, etc.) naturally [*+ obj*] Snakes *shed* their skin. ▪ The dog is *shedding* its fur. ▪ The trees are *shedding* their leaves. [*no obj*] The cat is *shedding*.
3 [*+ obj*] **a :** to take off (something you are wearing) ▪ He quickly *shed* his hat and coat. **b** *Brit* **:** to lose or drop (a load, cargo, etc.) ▪ The lorry *shed* its load.
4 [*+ obj*] **:** to cause (water) to flow off instead of soaking into something ▪ Raincoats *shed* water.
shed blood see BLOOD
shed light on see [1]LIGHT
shed tears see [3]TEAR

[2]shed *noun, pl* **sheds** [*count*]
1 : a small, simple building that is used especially for storing things — see also COWSHED, POTTING SHED, TOOLSHED, WOODSHED
2 *Brit* **:** a large industrial building ▪ a railway *shed*

she'd /ˈʃiːd, ʃɪd/ — used as a contraction of *she had* or *she would* ▪ *She'd* [=*she had*] already eaten by the time we arrived. ▪ *She'd* [=*she would*] prefer to wait until next week.

sheen /ˈʃiːn/ *noun* [*singular*] **:** a soft, smooth, shiny quality ▪ Her hair has a *sheen* to it. ▪ the *sheen* of satin

sheep /ˈʃiːp/ *noun, pl* **sheep** [*count*]
1 : an animal with a thick woolly coat that is often raised for meat or for its wool and skin ▪ a flock of *sheep*
2 : a person who does what other people say to do ▪ They followed every new fad like (a flock of) *sheep*.
a wolf in sheep's clothing see [1]WOLF
separate the sheep from the goats see [2]SEPARATE
— see also BLACK SHEEP

sheep

sheep·dog /ˈʃiːpˌdɑːg/ *noun, pl* **-dogs** [*count*] **:** a dog that is trained to control sheep

sheep·herd·er /ˈʃiːpˌhɚdɚ/ *noun, pl* **-ers** [*count*] **:** a person who controls a flock of sheep : a person who herds sheep

sheep·ish /ˈʃiːpɪʃ/ *adj* [*more ~; most ~*] **:** showing or feeling embarrassment especially because you have done something foolish or wrong ▪ a *sheepish* look/grin/smile ▪ He felt a little *sheepish*.
– sheep·ish·ly *adv* ▪ He *sheepishly* admitted his mistake. ▪ She grinned at us *sheepishly*.

sheep·skin /ˈʃiːpˌskɪn/ *noun, pl* **-skins**
1 [*count, noncount*] **a :** the skin of a sheep usually with the wool still on it **b :** a type of leather made from the skin of a sheep ▪ a bag/coat made of *sheepskin*
2 [*count*] *US, informal + humorous* **:** a diploma from a college or university ▪ jobs that don't require a *sheepskin*

[1]sheer /ˈʃiɚ/ *adj*
1 *always used before a noun* — used to emphasize the large

amount, size, or degree of something • The *sheer* amount of work was staggering. • The *sheer* number of questions overwhelmed her. • The *sheer* force of the wind knocked me to the ground.
2 *always used before a noun* : complete and total • *sheer* [=*utter*] nonsense • *sheer* [=*pure*] luck/coincidence/joy
3 : very steep : almost straight up and down • a *sheer* drop to the sea • *sheer* cliffs/walls
4 : very thin • *sheer* stockings/curtains

²sheer *adv* : straight up or down • mountains rising *sheer* from the plains

³sheer *verb, always followed by an adverb or preposition* **sheers; sheered; sheer·ing** [*no obj*] : to turn suddenly • The boat *sheered* [=*swerved*] *away* from the rocks.

¹sheet /ˈʃiːt/ *noun, pl* **sheets** [*count*]
1 a : a large piece of cloth that is used to cover something • We used *sheets* to protect the furniture when we painted. **b** : a large piece of thin cloth used on a bed • The *sheets* are changed daily at the hotel. • He slid between the *sheets* and went to sleep. — called also *bedsheet*; see picture at BED
2 : a usually rectangular piece of paper — see also BALANCE SHEET, RAP SHEET, SPREADSHEET, TIME SHEET, WORKSHEET, *clean sheet* at ¹CLEAN
3 : a thin, flat, rectangular or square piece of something • a *sheet* of iron/glass — see also BAKING SHEET, COOKIE SHEET
4 : a wide, flat surface or area of something • A *sheet* of ice covered the driveway. — see also ICE SHEET
5 : a large moving area of something (such as fire or water) • a *sheet* of flame • *sheets* of rain
– compare ²SHEET

²sheet *noun, pl* **sheets** [*count*] *technical* : a rope or chain attached to the lower corner of a sail and used to change the position of the sail
three sheets to the wind *old-fashioned + humorous* : very drunk • When he staggered out of the bar, he was *three sheets to the wind.*
– compare ¹SHEET

sheet·ing /ˈʃiːtɪŋ/ *noun* [*noncount*]
1 : material (such as plastic) in the form of thin layers used to cover or protect something • We covered the wall with clear plastic *sheeting.*
2 : cloth that is used to make sheets for a bed

sheet lightning *noun* [*noncount*] : lightning that appears as a wide flash of light over a large area of sky

sheet metal *noun* [*noncount*] : thin, flat pieces of metal

sheet music *noun* [*noncount*] : music printed on sheets of paper that are not bound together

Sheet·rock /ˈʃiːtˌrɑːk/ *trademark* — used for drywall

sheikh *or* **sheik** /ˈʃiːk/ *noun, pl* **sheikhs** *or* **sheiks** [*count*]
1 : an Arab chief, ruler, or prince
2 : a leader of a Muslim organization or group

sheikh·dom *or* **sheik·dom** /ˈʃiːkdəm/ *noun, pl* **-doms** [*count*] : an area ruled by a sheikh

shei·la /ˈʃiːlə/ *noun, pl* **-las** [*count*] *Australia + New Zealand, informal* : a girl or young woman

shek·el /ˈʃɛkəl/ *noun, pl* **-els** [*count*] : the basic unit of money in Israel

shelf /ˈʃɛlf/ *noun, pl* **shelves** /ˈʃɛlvz/ [*count*]
1 : a flat board which is attached to a wall, frame, etc., and on which objects can be placed • Put the vase on the *shelf.* • the top/bottom *shelf* of the kitchen cabinet • Will you get that book down off the *shelf*? • We don't have much *shelf* space. — see also BOOKSHELF
2 *geology* : a flat area of rock, sand, etc., especially underwater • a coastal *shelf* — see also CONTINENTAL SHELF
off the shelf : directly from a store without having to be specially made or ordered • The dress was a perfect fit right *off the shelf.* • equipment purchased *off the shelf*
on the shelf : in an inactive state : not active or being used • They put their plan to remodel the house *on the shelf* for the time being. • The quarterback remains *on the shelf* [=is still not playing] with a severe injury.

shelf life *noun, pl* **~ lives** [*count*]
1 : the length of time that food may be stored and still be good to eat — usually singular • Rice has a long *shelf life.*
2 : the length of time during which something or someone lasts or remains popular — usually singular • a movie with a short *shelf life*

¹shell /ˈʃɛl/ *noun, pl* **shells**
1 a : the hard outer covering of an animal, insect, etc., that protects it [*count*] a turtle's *shell* • the *shell* of a crab • We collected *shells* at the beach. [*noncount*] jewelry made of *shell* — see also SEASHELL, TORTOISESHELL **b** : the hard outer covering of an egg : EGGSHELL [*count*] broken *shells* [*noncount*] a piece of *shell* **c** : the hard outer covering of a nut, fruit, or seed [*count*] a coconut *shell* [*noncount*] pieces of walnut *shell*
2 [*count*] *US* : something (such as pasta) that is shaped like a shell • We're going to have stuffed *shells* for dinner.
3 [*count*] : the hard outer structure of a building, car, airplane, etc. — usually singular • the *shell* of an unfinished house • the *shell* of an airplane • The building was just a bombed-out *shell.*
4 [*count*] *chiefly US* : a hard or crisp piece of bread, dough, etc., that is used to hold a filling • a pastry/pie *shell* • taco/tortilla *shells*
5 [*count*] **a** : a metal case that is filled with an explosive and that is shot from a cannon • mortar *shells* **b** *chiefly US* : a metal tube that you put into a gun and that holds an explosive and a bullet : CARTRIDGE • The police found several spent *shells* at the scene of the shooting.
6 a — used in phrases that describe becoming less shy and more willing to talk to other people • Making new friends helped her ***come out of her shell***. = Making new friends ***brought her out of her shell***. **b** — used in phrases that describe becoming quieter, less active, etc. • He lost confidence in himself and ***retreated/withdrew into his shell***.

²shell *verb* **shells; shelled; shell·ing** [+ *obj*]
1 : to remove the shell or outer covering of (something) • *shell* peanuts/peas
2 : to shoot shells at (someone or something) using large guns • They *shelled* the enemy troops. • The town was *shelled* during the battle.
3 *US, informal* : to score heavily against (a pitcher) in baseball — usually used as *(be) shelled* • He *was shelled* in the second inning.
shell out [*phrasal verb*] ***shell out*** *or* ***shell out (money)*** *informal* : to pay a large amount of money for something — usually + *for* • I'm going to have to *shell out for* these shoes. • He *shelled out* $400 *for* the tickets.

she'll /ˈʃiːl, ʃɪl/ — used as a contraction of *she will* • *She'll* be home soon.

¹shel·lac /ʃəˈlæk/ *noun, pl* **-lacs** [*count, noncount*] : a clear liquid that dries into a hard coating and that is put on a surface to protect it

²shellac *verb* **-lacks; -lacked; -lack·ing** [+ *obj*]
1 : to coat (something) with shellac • *shellac* the table
2 *US, informal* : to defeat (a person or team) easily and completely — usually used as *(be) shellacked* • They *were shellacked* 14–2 in yesterday's game.

shellacking *noun, pl* **-ings** [*count*] *US, informal* : a very bad defeat • They took a *shellacking* in yesterday's game.

shelled /ˈʃɛld/ *adj*
1 : having a shell especially of a specified kind • pink-*shelled* • hard-*shelled*
2 : having the shell removed • *shelled* nuts/oysters

shell·fire /ˈʃɛlˌfajə/ *noun* [*noncount*] : the firing of shells from large guns • The soldiers traded *shellfire.* [=the soldiers fired shells at each other] • The town came under *shellfire.*

shell·fish /ˈʃɛlˌfɪʃ/ *noun, pl* **shellfish** : an animal (such as a crab or an oyster) that has a hard outer shell and that lives in water [*count*] lobsters, crabs, and other *shellfish* [*noncount*] a serving of *shellfish* — see color picture on page C8

shell game *noun, pl* **~ games** [*count*] *US* : a dishonest betting game in which someone hides a ball under one of three cups or shells, moves the cups or shells around quickly, and asks an observer to guess which one the ball is under — often used figuratively to describe dishonest actions that are done to trick people • The company was playing an elaborate *shell game.*

shelling *noun* [*noncount*] : the firing of shells from large guns • The town sustained weeks of heavy *shelling.*

shell shock *noun* [*noncount*] *old-fashioned* : BATTLE FATIGUE

shell–shocked *adj*
1 *old-fashioned* : affected with battle fatigue • a *shell-shocked* veteran
2 [*more ~; most ~*] : very confused, upset, or exhausted because of something that has happened : very shocked • She was *shell-shocked* when she heard the news.

shell suit *noun, pl* **~ suits** [*count*] *Brit* : a pair of usually brightly colored light, nylon pants and a matching jacket

¹shel·ter /ˈʃɛltə/ *noun, pl* **-ters**

S

1 a [*count*] : a structure that covers or protects people or things ▪ a bomb/fallout *shelter* ▪ We made a *shelter* from branches. **b** [*count*] : a place that provides food and protection for people or animals that need assistance ▪ a *shelter* for battered women ▪ an animal *shelter* ▪ homeless *shelters* **c** [*noncount*] : a place to live ▪ The organization provides food and *shelter* for homeless people.

2 [*noncount*] : the state of being covered and protected from danger, bad weather, etc. ▪ The crowd ran for *shelter* when the rain started. ▪ They sought *shelter* from the storm. ▪ They ***found/took shelter*** in a cave during the storm. [=they went into a cave to get out of the storm]

— see also TAX SHELTER

²shelter *verb* **-ters; -tered; -ter·ing**

1 [+ *obj*] : to protect (someone) from danger, bad weather, etc. : to provide shelter for (someone) ▪ A cave *sheltered* the climbers during the storm. ▪ They were accused of *sheltering* a criminal. [=giving a criminal a place to hide] — often + *from* ▪ They *sheltered* themselves *from* the sudden rain. — often used figuratively ▪ Most parents want to *shelter* their children *from* pain and sadness. [=to prevent their children from experiencing pain and sadness] ▪ Investors are trying to *shelter* themselves *from* rising interest rates.

2 [*no obj*] : to be in a place that provides protection from danger, bad weather, etc. : to take shelter ▪ They *sheltered* in a cave while they waited for the storm to pass.

sheltered *adj*

1 : providing protection from bad weather ▪ *sheltered* bays/harbors ▪ The flowers were planted in a *sheltered* location.

2 [*more* ~; *most* ~] *sometimes disapproving* : protected from dangerous or unpleasant experiences in the world ▪ She has lived a very *sheltered* life.

3 *always used before a noun, Brit* : providing care for people (such as old or disabled people) who need help with daily activities ▪ They are moving to *sheltered* accommodation/housing. ▪ *sheltered* employment

shel·tie *or* **shel·ty** /ˈʃɛlti/ *noun, pl* **-ties** [*count*] : SHETLAND SHEEPDOG

shelve /ˈʃɛlv/ *verb* **shelves; shelved; shelv·ing** [+ *obj*]

1 : to put (something) on a shelf ▪ He *shelved* the books/products. ▪ The books were *shelved* according to category.

2 : to stop doing or thinking about (something) for a period of time ▪ The idea/plan/project was *shelved*.

3 *US* : to make (someone) unable to play or perform — usually used as *(be) shelved* ▪ He *was shelved* by injury last year. [=he was unable to play because he was injured]

shelves *plural of* SHELF

shelving *noun* [*noncount*] : shelves or the materials that are used to make shelves ▪ a laundry room with *shelving* ▪ We need more *shelving* to finish the bookcase.

she·nan·i·gans /ʃəˈnænɪgənz/ *noun* [*plural*] *informal* : activity or behavior that is not honest or proper ▪ They were engaging in some political/financial *shenanigans*.

¹shep·herd /ˈʃɛpəd/ *noun, pl* **-herds** [*count*] : a person whose job is to take care of sheep — sometimes used figuratively ▪ He was a good *shepherd* to new students. — see also GERMAN SHEPHERD

²shepherd *verb* **-herds; -herd·ed; -herd·ing** [+ *obj*] : to guide (someone or something) ▪ She carefully *shepherded* the children across the street. ▪ They *shepherded* the bill through Congress.

shep·herd·ess /ˈʃɛpədəs/ *noun, pl* **-ess·es** [*count*] *old-fashioned* : a woman whose job is to take care of sheep

shepherd's pie *noun, pl* ~ **pies** [*count, noncount*] : a dish of meat and sometimes vegetables covered with a crust of mashed potatoes

sher·bet /ˈʃəbət/ *also US* **sher·bert** /ˈʃəbət/ *noun, pl* **-bets** *also* **-berts**

1 [*count, noncount*] *US* : a frozen sweet dessert made from fruit or fruit juices ▪ a lemon *sherbet*

2 [*noncount*] *Brit* : a sweet powder used to make a bubbly drink or eaten by itself

sherd *variant spelling of* SHARD

sher·iff /ˈʃerəf/ *noun, pl* **-iffs** [*count*]

1 : an elected official who is in charge of enforcing the law in a county or town of the U.S.

2 *Brit* : the highest official in a county or shire in England or Wales who represents the king or queen and who attends ceremonies and has legal duties — called also *High Sheriff*

3 : the most important judge in a county or district in Scotland

Sher·pa *or* **sher·pa** /ˈʃəpə/ *noun, pl* **-pas** [*count*] : a member of a people who live in the Himalayas and who are often hired to help guide mountain climbers and carry their equipment

sher·ry /ˈʃeri/ *noun, pl* **-ries** [*count, noncount*] : a type of strong wine with a nutty flavor that is made especially in Spain

she's /ˈʃiːz, ʃɪz/ — used as a contraction of *she is* or *she has* ▪ *She's* [=*she is*] quite right! ▪ *She's* [=*she has*] been teaching for several years.

Shet·land pony /ˈʃɛtlənd-/ *noun, pl* ~ **pon·ies** [*count*] : a type of small, strong horse

Shetland sheepdog *noun, pl* ~ **-dogs** [*count*] : a type of small dog that has a long, thick coat — called also *sheltie*

Shia *or* **Shi·'a** /ˈʃiːˌɑː/ *noun, pl* **Shia** *or* **Shi'a** *also* **Shi·as** *also* **Shi·'as**

1 [*noncount*] : one of the two main branches of Islam — often used before a noun ▪ the *Shia* faith/tradition — compare SUNNI

2 [*count*] : a Muslim who is a member of the Shia branch of Islam : SHIITE

Shi·at·su /ʃiˈɑːtsu/ *noun* [*noncount*] : a Japanese method of relieving pain or curing illness by pressing on particular points on a person's body with the fingertips or thumbs

shib·bo·leth /ˈʃɪbələθ/ *noun, pl* **-leths** [*count*]

1 : an old idea, opinion, or saying that is commonly believed and repeated but that may be seen as old-fashioned or untrue ▪ She repeated the old *shibboleth* that time heals all wounds.

2 : a word or way of speaking or behaving which shows that a person belongs to a particular group

shied *past tense and past participle of* SHY

¹shield /ˈʃiːld/ *noun, pl* **shields** [*count*]

1 : a large piece of metal, wood, etc., carried by someone (such as a soldier or police officer) for protection

2 : something that defends or protects someone or something ▪ the heat *shield* on a space shuttle ▪ The thief tried to use a hostage as a ***human shield*** [=the thief hid behind the hostage so the police would not shoot] ▪ Exercise and good nutrition are a ***shield against*** disease. [=exercise and good nutrition protect you from disease] — see also WINDSHIELD

3 *US* : a police officer's badge

4 : a picture shaped like a soldier's shield that has a coat of arms on it

5 *Brit* : an award for winning a competition or game

²shield *verb* **shields; shield·ed; shield·ing** [+ *obj*]

1 : to cover and protect (someone or something) ▪ She *shielded* her eyes. — often + *from* ▪ She lifted her hand to *shield* her eyes *from* the glare. ▪ He was *shielded from* the rain. — often used figuratively ▪ I think she's *shielded* her child *from* the real world for too long. ▪ His friends tried to *shield* him *from* the press.

2 : to prevent (someone or something) from being seen — usually + *from* ▪ A line of trees *shields* the house *from* view.

¹shift /ˈʃɪft/ *verb* **shifts; shift·ed; shift·ing**

1 : to move or to cause (something or someone) to move to a different place, position, etc. [+ *obj*] I *shifted* the bag to my other shoulder. ▪ She *shifted* her position slightly so she could see the stage better. ▪ I *shifted* [=*turned*] my gaze toward the horizon. ▪ They *shifted* him to a different department. [*no obj*] The wind *shifted*. ▪ He nervously *shifted* from foot to foot. ▪ She *shifted* in her seat. ▪ The population is *shifting* [=*moving*] away from the city.

2 : to change or to cause (something) to change to a different opinion, belief, etc. [*no obj*] Public opinion has *shifted* dramatically in recent months. [+ *obj*] Their efforts to *shift* public opinion have failed. ▪ She refused to ***shift her ground*** [=she refused to change her opinion]

3 : to go or to cause (something) to go from one person or thing to another [+ *obj*] I wanted to *shift* the discussion back to the main point. ▪ They tried to *shift* the blame onto/to us. ▪ Their attempts at *shifting* attention away from the controversy seemed to be working. ▪ The mayor plans to *shift* some resources to the development project. [*no obj*] The focus of the debate quickly *shifted* to more controversial topics. ▪ *shifting* alliances/demands/patterns

4 *US* : to change the gear you are using in a vehicle [*no obj*] She *shifted* into first gear. ▪ I hear a loud noise when the car *shifts*. [+ *obj*] She *shifted* the car into low gear. — see also DOWNSHIFT, UPSHIFT, *shift gears* at ¹GEAR

5 [+ *obj*] *Brit, informal* : to get rid of (something) ▪ I can't seem to *shift* this cold. ▪ This detergent will *shift* even the most stubborn stains.

S

shift for yourself : to do things without help from others • She left them to *shift for themselves.* [=*fend for themselves*]
shifting sands see [1]SAND
shift the goalposts see GOALPOST
shift yourself *Brit, informal* : to move quickly : HURRY • We need to *shift ourselves* [=*get moving*] if we're going to make it home before dark.

[2]**shift** *noun, pl* **shifts** [*count*]
1 a : a change in position or direction • There will be a *shift* of responsibility when she takes the new position.— often + *in* • a *shift in* the wind • unpredictable *shifts in* weather • The *shift in* leadership will take place at the end of the year. **b** *always followed by an adverb or preposition* : a change in how something is done or how people think about something • a *shift* away from tradition • a gradual *shift* toward more liberal policies • a *shift* in voter opinion
2 a : a group of people who work together during a scheduled period of time • The day/night *shift* worked overtime. • The restaurant needed only one *shift* for lunch. **b** : the scheduled period of time during which a person works • He works the day/night *shift.* • waiters working long *shifts*— see also GRAVEYARD SHIFT, SWING SHIFT
3 : SHIFT KEY
4 : a woman's loose, straight dress

shift·er /ˈʃɪftɚ/ *noun, pl* **-ers** [*count*] *US* : GEARSHIFT

shift key *noun, pl* **~ keys** [*count*] : a key on a computer keyboard or a typewriter that you press to type capital letters — called also *shift*

shift·less /ˈʃɪftləs/ *adj, disapproving* : lacking ambition and energy • a lazy, *shiftless* person
– shift·less·ness *noun* [*noncount*]

shifty /ˈʃɪfti/ *adj* **shift·i·er; -est** [*also more ~; most ~*] *informal*
1 : having an appearance or way of behaving that seems dishonest • a *shifty* salesman • *shifty* eyes
2 *US* : difficult to catch : able to move and change directions quickly • a *shifty* runner
– shift·i·ly /ˈʃɪftəli/ *adv* • He eyed them *shiftily.* **– shift·i·ness** /ˈʃɪftinəs/ *noun* [*noncount*]

shii·ta·ke /ʃiˈtɑːki/ *noun, pl* **-kes** [*count*] *chiefly US* : a type of Asian mushroom used in cooking

Shi·ite *or* **Shi·'ite** /ˈʃiːˌaɪt/ *noun, pl* **-ites** *or* **-'ites** [*count*] : a Muslim who is a member of the Shia branch of Islam — compare SUNNI
– Shiite *or* **Shi'ite** *adj, always used before a noun* • a *Shiite* Muslim • the *Shiite* community

shill /ˈʃɪl/ *verb* **shills; shilled; shill·ing** [*no obj*] *US, informal + disapproving* : to talk about or describe someone or something in a favorable way because you are being paid to do it — often + *for* • celebrities *shilling for* politicians
– shill *noun, pl* **shills** [*count*] • He's just a political *shill.*

shil·ling /ˈʃɪlɪŋ/ *noun, pl* **-lings** [*count*]
1 : a British coin used before 1971 that was equal to 1/20 of a British pound
2 : the basic unit of money in Kenya, Somalia, Tanzania, and Uganda

shilly–shally /ˈʃɪliˌʃæli/ *verb* **-shal·lies; -shal·lied; -shal·ly·ing** [*no obj*] *informal + disapproving* : to hesitate and take a long time to do or decide something • They continue to *shilly-shally* about what to do.
– shilly–shallying *noun* [*singular*] • Congress should stop all the *shilly-shallying* and just vote.

shim·mer /ˈʃɪmɚ/ *verb* **-mers; -mered; -mer·ing** [*no obj*] : to shine with a light that seems to move slightly • The road *shimmered* in the heat. • The landscape *shimmers* [=*glimmers*] with light. • *shimmering* colors/light
– shimmer *noun* [*singular*] • the *shimmer* of the jewels
– shim·mery /ˈʃɪməri/ *adj* • a *shimmery* glow/luster

shim·my /ˈʃɪmi/ *verb* **-mies; -mied; -my·ing**
1 : to move or shake your body from side to side [*no obj*] They were *shimmying* on the dance floor. • I *shimmied* into my jacket. [+ *obj*] She *shimmied* her hips.
2 [*no obj*] *US* : to vibrate or move very quickly from side to side • One of the car's wheels was *shimmying.*
– shimmy *noun, pl* **-mies** [*count*] • She gave her hips a *shimmy.*

[1]**shin** /ˈʃɪn/ *noun, pl* **shins** [*count*] : the front part of the leg below the knee • She kicked him in the *shin.* • a *shin* pad/guard— see picture at HUMAN

[2]**shin** *verb* **shins; shinned; shin·ning** [*no obj*] *Brit* : SHINNY — + *up* or *down* • The sailor *shinned up* the mast. • He *shinned down* the drainpipe.

shin·bone /ˈʃɪnˌboʊn/ *noun, pl* **-bones** [*count*] : the large bone at the front of the leg between the knee and the ankle : TIBIA

shin·dig /ˈʃɪnˌdɪg/ *noun, pl* **-digs** [*count*] *informal* : a big party • an informal *shindig*

[1]**shine** /ˈʃaɪn/ *verb* **shines; shone** /ˈʃoʊn, *Brit* ˈʃɒn/ *or chiefly US* **shined; shin·ing**
1 [*no obj*] : to give off light • The moon/stars *shined* brightly. • The sun was *shining* through the clouds. • lamps *shining* from the windows
2 [*no obj*] : to have a smooth surface that reflects light • He polished the silver until it *shone.* [=*gleamed*]
3 *not used in progressive tenses* [*no obj*] : to be very good or successful at an activity • She found a sport where she can really *shine.*
4 [*no obj*] : to have a bright, glowing appearance • Her face was *shining* with joy/excitement. • His eyes were *shining.*
5 [+ *obj*] : to point (something that produces light) in a particular direction • Please *shine* the flashlight over here.
6 *past tense and past participle* **shined** [+ *obj*] : to make (something) bright and shiny by polishing • I *shined* my shoes. • He had his shoes *shined.*
make hay while the sun shines see HAY
rise and shine *informal* — used to tell someone to wake up and get out of bed • C'mon, kids! *Rise and shine!*
shine through [*phrasal verb*] : to be seen, expressed, or shown clearly • Once she relaxed, her talent really began to *shine through.*

[2]**shine** *noun* [*singular*]
1 : the brightness that results when light is reflected from a surface • the *shine* of polished silver • He had a nice *shine* on his shoes.— see also SUNSHINE
2 : the act of polishing a pair of shoes • Would you like a *shine?*— see also SHOESHINE
rain or shine see [1]RAIN
take a shine to *informal* : to begin to like (someone or something) • She really *took a shine to* [=*took a liking to*] her new neighbor.

shin·er /ˈʃaɪnɚ/ *noun, pl* **-ers** [*count*] *US, informal* : BLACK EYE • He got a *shiner* during a fight at school.

[1]**shin·gle** /ˈʃɪŋgəl/ *noun, pl* **shin·gles** [*count*] : a small, thin piece of building material that is used to cover the roof or sides of a building
hang out your shingle *US, informal* : to start your own business especially as a doctor or lawyer • She graduated from law school and *hung out her shingle.*
— compare [3]SHINGLE

shingles

[2]**shingle** *verb* **shin·gles; shin·gled; shin·gling** [+ *obj*] : to cover (something) with shingles • *shingle* a house/roof • a house *shingled* with cedar

[3]**shingle** *noun* [*noncount*] : small stones that form a beach • She walked along the *shingle.* • a *shingle* beach— compare [1]SHINGLE
– shin·gly /ˈʃɪŋgəli/ *adj* • a strip of *shingly* beach

shin·gles /ˈʃɪŋgəlz/ *noun* [*noncount*] *medical* : a disease that causes pain and red marks on your skin along the path of a nerve

shining *adj*
1 : producing or reflecting a bright, steady light • a *shining* star
2 : excellent or perfect • Her latest movie is a *shining* example of what a film can be. • a *shining* success

shin·ny /ˈʃɪni/ *verb* **-nies; -nied; -ny·ing** [*no obj*] *US* : to climb up or down something (such as a pole) by grasping it with your arms and legs — + *up* or *down* • He *shinnied up* [=(*Brit*) *shinned up*] the tree to get a better look. • She *shinnied down* the drainpipe.

Shin·to /ˈʃɪnˌtoʊ/ *noun* [*noncount*] : the traditional religion of Japan — called also *Shin·to·ism* /ˈʃɪnˌtoʊˌɪzəm/

shiny /ˈʃaɪni/ *adj* **shin·i·er; -est** [*also more ~; most ~*] : having a smooth, shining, bright appearance • *shiny* black shoes • a *shiny* new car
– shin·i·ness *noun* [*noncount*]

[1]**ship** /ˈʃɪp/ *noun, pl* **ships**
1 : a large boat used for traveling long distances over the sea [*count*] a sailing/cruise/merchant *ship* • the captain of the

S

ship [*noncount*]He will travel by *ship*. — see also FLAGSHIP, STEAMSHIP, TALL SHIP, TROOPSHIP, WARSHIP
2 [*count*] : a large airplane or spacecraft — see also AIRSHIP, ROCKET SHIP, SPACESHIP
abandon ship see [1]ABANDON
jump ship **1** : to leave a ship without the captain's permission ▪ He planned to *jump ship* at the next port. **2** : to suddenly or unexpectedly leave a group, team, etc. ▪ She *jumped ship* when the competition offered her a better job.
run a tight ship : to manage or handle a group of people in a strict and effective way ▪ The boss *runs a tight ship*.
ship comes in ✧ When ***your ship comes in***, you become very successful or wealthy. ▪ She's still waiting for *her ship to come in*.

[2]ship *verb* **ships; shipped; ship·ping**
1 a : to send (something) to a customer [+ *obj*]The goods were *shipped* from a foreign port. ▪ We *shipped* the items to you last week. = We *shipped* you the items last week. [*no obj*]Your order is expected to *ship* soon. **b** : to send (a new product) to stores so that it can be bought by customers [+ *obj*]The company will *ship* its new software next month. [*no obj*]The software will *ship* next month.
2 *always followed by an adverb or preposition* [+ *obj*] : to send (someone) to a place that is usually far away ▪ The soldiers were *shipped* overseas for duty. ▪ Her parents are *shipping* her (off) to boarding school.
3 [+ *obj*] *of a ship or boat* : to take in (water) over the side ▪ When the waves increased, the boat began *shipping* water.
ship out [*phrasal verb*] : to leave one place and go to another for military duties ▪ The troops will be *shipping out* next month. — see also *shape up or ship out* at [2]SHAPE

-ship /ˌʃɪp/ *noun suffix*
1 : the state or condition of being something ▪ friend*ship* ▪ apprentice*ship*
2 : the position, status, or duties of something ▪ professor*ship*
3 : skill or ability as someone or something ▪ horseman*ship* ▪ penman*ship*

ship·board /ˈʃɪpˌboɚd/ *adj, always used before a noun* : happening or existing on a ship ▪ *shipboard* entertainment/meals ▪ a *shipboard* romance
on shipboard : on a ship ▪ They celebrated their honeymoon *on shipboard*.

ship·build·er /ˈʃɪpˌbɪldɚ/ *noun, pl* **-ers** [*count*] : a person or company that designs and builds ships
– ship·build·ing /ˈʃɪpˌbɪldɪŋ/ *noun* [*noncount*] ▪ a *shipbuilding* company

ship·load /ˈʃɪpˈloʊd/ *noun, pl* **-loads** [*count*] : an amount or number that will fill a ship ▪ a *shipload* of corn ▪ *Shiploads* of settlers came to the New World.

ship·mate /ˈʃɪpˌmeɪt/ *noun, pl* **-mates** [*count*] : a sailor who works or sails on the same ship as another sailor

ship·ment /ˈʃɪpmənt/ *noun, pl* **-ments**
1 [*count*] : a load of goods that are being sent to a customer, store, etc. ▪ We sent out another *shipment* of books. ▪ arms/grain/oil *shipments* ▪ My order was delivered in two *shipments*.
2 [*noncount*] : the act of sending something to a customer, store, etc. ▪ This box is ready for *shipment*.

ship·per /ˈʃɪpɚ/ *noun, pl* **-pers** [*count*] : a person or company that ships goods or products ▪ fruit/oil/wine *shippers*

ship·ping /ˈʃɪpɪŋ/ *noun* [*noncount*]
1 : the act or business of sending goods to people, stores, etc. ▪ The fruit was ready for *shipping*. ▪ a ***shipping clerk*** [=a person whose job involves shipping things] ▪ What do you charge for ***shipping and handling***? [=for packaging and sending something to a customer]
2 *formal* : a group of ships ▪ They protected our *shipping* from submarines during wartime. ▪ international *shipping* lanes [=paths through the sea that commercial ships can take]

ship·shape /ˌʃɪpˈʃeɪp/ *adj, not used before a noun* : clean, neat, and tidy : organized and in good condition ▪ I like to keep my car *shipshape*. ▪ Everything had to be *shipshape* before we could sell the house.

ship·wreck /ˈʃɪpˌrɛk/ *noun, pl* **-wrecks**
1 : the destruction or sinking of a ship at sea [*count*]Only a few sailors survived the *shipwreck*. [*noncount*]The crew narrowly avoided *shipwreck*.
2 [*count*] : a ruined or destroyed ship ▪ Divers searched the sunken *shipwreck*. — sometimes used figuratively ▪ His marriage was a *shipwreck*.
– shipwreck *verb* **-wrecks; -wrecked; -wreck·ing** [+ *obj*] — usually used as *(be) shipwrecked* ▪ The boat *was shipwrecked* on the reef. ▪ *shipwrecked* sailors ▪ a *shipwrecked* boat

ship·yard /ˈʃɪpˌjɑɚd/ *noun, pl* **-yards** [*count*] : a place where ships are built or repaired

shire /ˈʃajɚ/ *noun, pl* **shires** [*count*]
1 *Brit* : a county in England — used in the names of British counties ▪ Northampton*shire*
2 *or* **Shire** : a type of tall, strong horse used for pulling heavy loads — called also *shire horse*

shirk /ˈʃɚk/ *verb* **shirks; shirked; shirk·ing** : to avoid doing something that you are supposed to do [+ *obj*]He's too conscientious to *shirk* his duty/responsibility. [*no obj*]He never *shirked* from doing his duty. ▪ They did their duty without *shirking* or complaining.
– shirk·er *noun, pl* **-ers** [*count*] ▪ She's no *shirker*.

shirt /ˈʃɚt/ *noun, pl* **shirts** [*count*] : a piece of clothing for the upper body that has sleeves and usually a collar and buttons down the front — see also NIGHTSHIRT, POLO SHIRT, STUFFED SHIRT, SWEATSHIRT, T-SHIRT, UNDERSHIRT
keep your shirt on *informal* — used to tell someone to calm down or be more patient ▪ "Aren't you ready yet?" "*Keep your shirt on*! I'll be ready in a minute."
lose your shirt *chiefly US, informal* : to lose a lot of money because of a bad bet or investment ▪ He *lost his shirt* betting on football games. ▪ Many investors *lost their shirts* when the market crashed.
put your shirt on *chiefly Brit, informal* : to bet a lot of money on (someone or something) ▪ I *put my shirt on* a horse in the second race.
the shirt off your back *informal* ✧ People who would ***give you the shirt off their back*** would do anything to help you. ▪ She'd *give me the shirt off her back* if I ever needed help.

[1]shirt·sleeve /ˈʃɚtˌsliːv/ *noun, pl* **-sleeves** [*count*] : the sleeve of a shirt
in (your) shirtsleeves : wearing a shirt but no coat or jacket ▪ a man *in his shirtsleeves* ▪ It was hot and most of the crowd was *in shirtsleeves*.

ship

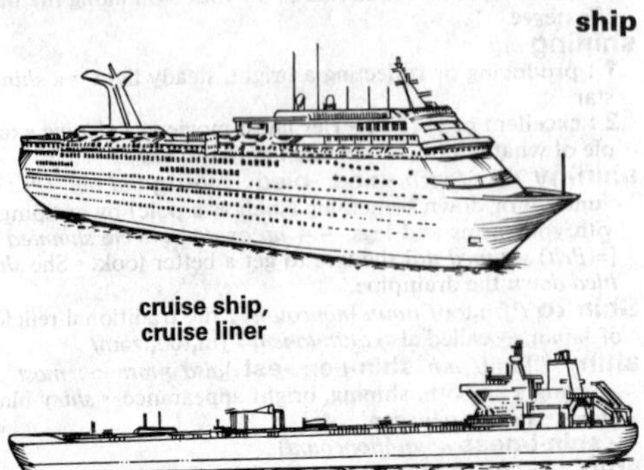

cruise ship, cruise liner

tanker

container ship

freighter, cargo ship

S

²shirtsleeve *also* **shirt·sleeves** /ˈʃɚtˌsliːvz/ *adj, always used before a noun, US*
1 : not wearing a coat or jacket ▪ a *shirtsleeve* crowd
2 : warm enough so that you do not need a coat or jacket ▪ *shirtsleeves* weather
3 : informal and direct ▪ *shirtsleeve* diplomacy

shirt·tail /ˈʃɚtˌteɪl/ *noun, pl* **-tails** [*count*] **:** the part of a shirt that hangs below the waist especially in the back — usually plural ▪ His *shirttails* were untucked.

shirty /ˈʃɚti/ *adj* **shirt·i·er; -est** *Brit, informal* **:** angry or irritated ▪ *shirty* letters of complaint ▪ He was/got *shirty* with the people who arrived late.

shish ke·bab /ˈʃɪʃkəˌbɑːb, *Brit* ˈʃɪʃkəˌbæb/ *noun, pl* ~ **-babs** [*count*] **:** KEBAB

¹shit /ˈʃɪt/ *noun, pl* **shits** *informal*
1 *offensive* **a** [*noncount*] **:** solid waste that is passed out of the body **b** [*singular*] **:** the act of passing solid waste from the body — used in the phrases ***take a shit*** and (*Brit*) ***have a shit*** **c** ***the shits* :** DIARRHEA
2 [*noncount*] *offensive* **:** foolish or untrue words or ideas **:** NONSENSE ▪ Don't give me that *shit!* ▪ Why are you telling me this *shit?* ▪ Just ***cut the shit*** [=stop saying meaningless things] and get to the point. ▪ He's ***full of shit*** [=he is lying]
3 [*noncount*] *offensive* **:** something that is worthless, unimportant, etc. ▪ That movie was total *shit.* ▪ We need to get rid of all that *shit* [=*junk*] in the basement. ▪ There's always some *shit* going on.
4 [*noncount*] *offensive* **:** bad or unfair behavior or treatment ▪ Do what I say, and don't ***give me any shit.*** ▪ He's a tough teacher who won't ***take shit*** from anyone.
5 [*count*] *offensive* **:** a very bad or annoying person ▪ He's been acting like a total *shit.*
6 *offensive* **a** ***the shit*** — used for emphasis after words like *beat, scare, surprise,* etc. ▪ I'm going to *beat/kick the* (living) *shit* out of you! ▪ She *surprised the shit* out of me. **b** — used as an interjection ▪ *Shit!* I dropped my coffee! ▪ Oh, *shit.* Here she comes.
get/pull your shit together *US, offensive* **:** to begin to live in a good and sensible way **:** to stop being confused, foolish, etc. ▪ I really need to *get my shit together* and start looking for a job. ▪ He can never seem to *pull his shit together* enough to keep a job.
give a shit *offensive* **:** to care at all about someone or something — usually used in negative statements ▪ I *don't give a shit* what happens.
in deep shit *also Brit* ***in the shit*** *offensive* **:** in a lot of trouble ▪ If his parents find out, he'll be *in deep shit.*
like shit *offensive* **:** very bad ▪ The food tasted *like shit.* **:** very badly ▪ She treats him *like shit.* ✧ If you ***feel like shit***, you feel very sick, unhappy, etc. ▪ I got drunk at the party, and the next morning I *felt like shit.* [=I felt sick] ▪ When I saw how badly I had hurt his feelings, I *felt like shit.*
no shit *offensive* — used to show that you are surprised or impressed by what has been said ▪ "They got married." "*No shit!*" — often used in an ironic way when someone makes an obvious statement ▪ "It's cold out there." "*No shit.*" [=*no kidding*]
shit happens *offensive* — used to say that bad things happen as part of life and cannot be prevented
the shit hits the fan *offensive* — used to describe what happens when people find out about something that makes them very angry ▪ I told him I was dropping out of school and *the shit hit the fan.*

²shit *verb* **shits; shit** *or* **shat** /ˈʃæt/; **shit·ting** *informal*
1 [*no obj*] *offensive* **:** to pass solid waste from the body **:** DEFECATE
2 [+ *obj*] *US, offensive* **:** to try to deceive or trick (someone) ▪ Are you *shitting* me?!
shit yourself *or US* ***shit your pants*** *offensive* **:** to become so afraid, surprised, worried, etc., that you defecate ▪ He jumped out from behind a tree and I nearly *shit my pants.*

shit–faced *adj, US, informal + offensive* **:** very drunk ▪ He went out last night and got *shit-faced.*

shit·head /ˈʃɪtˌhɛd/ *noun, pl* **-heads** [*count*] *informal + offensive* **:** a very annoying, stupid, or unpleasant person ▪ He's acting like a complete *shithead.*

shit·less /ˈʃɪtləs/ *adv, informal + offensive* **:** very much **:** to a very high degree — used for emphasis ▪ I was bored/scared *shitless.*

shit·load /ˈʃɪtˌloʊd/ *noun, pl* **-loads** [*count*] *informal + offensive* **:** a very large amount of something ▪ You're in a *shitload* of trouble. ▪ They have *shitloads* of money.

shit·ty /ˈʃɪti/ *adj* **shit·ti·er; -est** [*also more* ~; *most* ~] *informal + offensive*
1 : very bad or unpleasant ▪ What *shitty* weather!
2 : cruel or unkind ▪ He's been pretty *shitty* to her lately.

¹shiv·er /ˈʃɪvɚ/ *verb* **-ers; -ered; -er·ing** [*no obj*] **:** to shake slightly because you are cold, afraid, etc. ▪ It was so cold that I was *shivering.* ▪ She was *shivering* [=*trembling*] with fear/excitement.

²shiver *noun, pl* **-ers** [*count*] **:** a small shaking movement caused by cold or strong emotion ▪ She felt a *shiver* of delight/pleasure when she opened the gift. ▪ Her performance was so brilliant that it ***sent shivers up (and down) my spine.*** [=it thrilled or excited me] ▪ The look in his eyes ***gave me the shivers.*** [=made me very afraid]

shiv·ery /ˈʃɪvəri/ *adj*
1 : shaking because of cold, fear, illness, etc. ▪ He woke up feeling sweaty and *shivery.*
2 *always used before a noun, US, informal* **:** causing shivers ▪ *shivery* [=*cold*] weather ▪ a *shivery* [=*scary*] horror story

shmooze *variant spelling of* SCHMOOZE

¹shoal /ˈʃoʊl/ *noun, pl* **shoals** [*count*]
1 : an area where the water in a sea, lake, or river is not deep ▪ fish lurking in the *shoals*
2 : a small, raised area of sand just below the surface of the water ▪ The boat ran aground on the *shoal.*
— compare ²SHOAL

²shoal *noun, pl* **shoals** [*count*] **:** a large group or number — often + *of* ▪ a *shoal* [=(more commonly) *school*] *of* fish ▪ (*chiefly Brit*) a *shoal of* letters from angry readers — compare ¹SHOAL

¹shock /ˈʃɑːk/ *noun, pl* **shocks**
1 a [*count*] **:** a sudden usually unpleasant or upsetting feeling caused by something unexpected — usually singular ▪ If you haven't been there for a while, prepare yourself for a *shock:* the place has changed a lot. ▪ a terrible/nasty *shock* ▪ You're ***in for a big/rude shock*** if you think this job will be easy. — often + *of* ▪ the *shock of* discovering that someone you love has betrayed you ▪ He got the ***shock of his life*** [=he was very unpleasantly surprised] when he saw his own name on the list. — see also CULTURE SHOCK, STICKER SHOCK **b** [*count*] **:** something unexpected that causes a sudden usually unpleasant or upsetting feeling — usually singular ▪ Seeing his parents at the rock concert was a *shock.* ▪ Her death ***came as a shock*** to the family. ▪ It *came as* quite *a shock.* ▪ It is ***something of a shock*** to learn/discover that she is guilty. **c** [*noncount*] **:** a state in which you are experiencing a sudden usually unpleasant or upsetting feeling because of something unexpected ▪ She stood there ***in shock*** as he told her what had happened. ▪ They were ***in a state of shock*** after hearing the news. = They were *in shock* over the news. **d** [*count*] **:** a sudden bad change in something ▪ Unfortunately, it's the poor who are most vulnerable to this kind of economic *shock.* ▪ oil/energy price *shocks*
2 [*noncount*] *medical* **:** a serious condition in which the body is not able to get enough blood to all the parts of the body ✧ Shock is caused by a severe injury, a large loss of blood, etc. ▪ She was treated/hospitalized for *shock* after the accident. ▪ He was ***in (a state of) shock.*** = He was ***suffering from shock.*** — see also SHELL SHOCK, TOXIC SHOCK SYNDROME
3 [*count*] **:** the effect of a strong charge of electricity passing through the body of a person or animal — usually singular ▪ When the wires touched, I got a *shock.* ▪ an electric *shock* ▪ I walked across the carpet and then got a *shock* when I touched the metal doorknob.
4 [*count*] **:** SHOCK ABSORBER — usually plural ▪ The car needs new *shocks.*
5 : a violent shake [*count*] an earthquake *shock* ▪ The building is made to withstand large *shocks.* — often + *of* ▪ the *shock of* the explosion [*noncount*] The car's bumper absorbs *shock* on impact.
a shock to the/your system **:** something that has a sudden and usually unpleasant effect on you ▪ The cold weather was *a shock to my system* after being in the tropics. ▪ For freshmen, college life can be *a* real *shock to the system.*
— compare ⁴SHOCK

²shock *verb* **shocks; shocked; shock·ing**
1 [+ *obj*] **:** to surprise and usually upset (someone) ▪ The attack *shocked* the world. ▪ His anger *shocked* us. — often used as *(be) shocked* ▪ They *were shocked* to discover/learn that their son was taking drugs. — often + *at* or *by* ▪ I *am shocked at/by* how easy it was to do. ▪ Everyone *was* deeply *shocked at/by* her behavior. ▪ We *were shocked by* the news of her

S

death. — often + *into* ▪ We *were shocked into* silence by what we saw. [=we were so surprised and upset by what we saw that we could not say anything] ▪ The news was so upsetting that people *were* finally *shocked into* (taking) action.

2 : to cause (someone) to feel horror or disgust [+ *obj*] He enjoys *shocking* his readers. ▪ I was *shocked* by their bad language. [*no obj*] The art exhibit is meant to *shock*.

– **shocked** *adj* ▪ She had a *shocked* look on her face. ▪ He stood in *shocked* silence after hearing the news.

³shock *adj, always used before a noun* — used to describe something that surprises and usually upsets people ▪ Bikinis have lost their *shock* effect. [=bikinis no longer shock people] ▪ It was a *shock* [=very surprising] defeat/victory for the team. ▪ He dresses as a woman for ***shock value***. [=in order to shock people] ▪ I don't think there's anything wrong with using ***shock tactics*** [=actions, images, stories, etc., that surprise and upset people] to discourage people from driving while drunk. ▪ ***shock radio/TV*** [=radio/television programs that are meant to shock and usually offend people]

shock horror *Brit, informal* — used to say that you are surprised by something unpleasant or upsetting when you really are not ▪ Teenagers are—*shock horror*—having sex.

⁴shock *noun, pl* **shocks** [*count*] : a thick and full mass of hair — usually singular ▪ a *shock of* hair — compare ¹SHOCK

shock absorber *noun, pl* ~ **-ers** [*count*] : a device that is connected to the wheel of a vehicle in order to reduce the effects of traveling on a rough surface ▪ The car needs new *shock absorbers*.

shock·er /ˈʃɑːkɚ/ *noun, pl* **-ers** [*count*] *informal* : something that shocks people ▪ The ending of the movie is a real *shocker*. ▪ Their divorce was a *shocker*.

shock·ing /ˈʃɑːkɪŋ/ *adj* [*more* ~; *most* ~]

1 : very surprising and upsetting or causing a sudden feeling of horror or disgust ▪ a *shocking* crime ▪ The fact that he was married to another woman was a *shocking* discovery. = It was *shocking* to discover that he was married to another woman. ▪ *shocking* news ▪ The number of young teenagers who smoke is *shocking*.

2 *chiefly Brit, informal* : very bad ▪ a *shocking* waste of money/time ▪ The building is in a *shocking* state.

– **shock·ing·ly** *adv* ▪ The movie was *shockingly* violent.

shocking pink *noun* [*noncount*] : a very bright pink color

– **shocking–pink** *adj* ▪ a *shocking-pink* dress

shock jock *noun, pl* ~ **jocks** [*count*] *chiefly US* : a person who talks on the radio and says things that are offensive to many people : a radio disc jockey who says shocking things

shock·proof /ˈʃɑːkˌpruːf/ *adj* : not damaged if dropped, hit, etc. : resistant to shock ▪ The watch is supposed to be waterproof and *shockproof*.

shock therapy *noun* [*noncount*] : a treatment for mental illness in which the patient is given electric shocks — called also *ECT, electroconvulsive therapy, shock treatment*

shock troops *noun* [*plural*]

1 : troops who are specially trained for sudden attacks against an enemy ▪ *Shock troops* were sent in for a surprise attack.

2 : a group of people who are very active in fighting for a cause ▪ the *shock troops* of the civil rights movement

shock wave *noun, pl* ~ **waves** [*count*]

1 : a movement of extremely high air pressure that is caused by an explosion, an earthquake, etc.

2 : a usually negative response or reaction that many people have to a particular thing ▪ The decision created a *shock wave* of criticism. — usually plural ▪ The court's ruling sent *shock waves* throughout the nation.

shod /ˈʃɑːd/ *adj, literary* : wearing shoes — often + *in* ▪ His feet were *shod in* slippers. = He was *shod in* slippers. [=he was wearing slippers]

shod·dy /ˈʃɑːdi/ *adj* **shod·di·er; -est** : poorly done or made ▪ *shoddy* work/workmanship/furniture/goods ▪ They gave a *shoddy* performance. ▪ *shoddy* journalism

– **shod·di·ly** /ˈʃɑːdəli/ *adv* ▪ a *shoddily* built barn ▪ a *shoddily* managed business – **shod·di·ness** /ˈʃɑːdinəs/ *noun* [*noncount*]

¹shoe /ˈʃuː/ *noun, pl* **shoes**

1 [*count*] : an outer covering for your foot that usually has a stiff bottom part called a sole with a thicker part called a heel attached to it and an upper part that covers part or all of the top of your foot ▪ She bought a pair of *shoes*. ▪ He took off his *shoes* and socks. ▪ high-heeled *shoes* ▪ dress *shoes* [=shoes for formal events or times] ▪ athletic/running *shoes* ▪ *shoe* polish ▪ a *shoe* store/shop

2 *shoes* [*plural*] : another person's situation or position ▪ I wouldn't want to be ***in his shoes*** right now. ▪ Anyone *in her shoes* would have done the same thing. ▪ Try to ***put yourself in their shoes*** [=try to imagine yourself in their situation] and think of how you would want to be treated. ▪ I don't think anyone will be able to ***fill her shoes*** [=do what she does as well as she does it] after she retires. ▪ He ***stepped into the shoes*** [=took the role] of president with ease.

3 [*count*] : a flat U-shaped piece of iron that is nailed to the bottom of a horse's hoof : HORSESHOE

4 [*count*] : the part of a brake that presses on the wheel of a vehicle — usually plural ▪ The brake *shoes* are worn out.

if the shoe fits or ***if the shoe fits, wear it*** *US* — used to say that something said or suggested about a person is true and that the person should accept it as true ▪ "Are you calling me a cheater?" "Well, *if the shoe fits, wear it*." [=(*Brit*) *if the cap fits, wear it*]

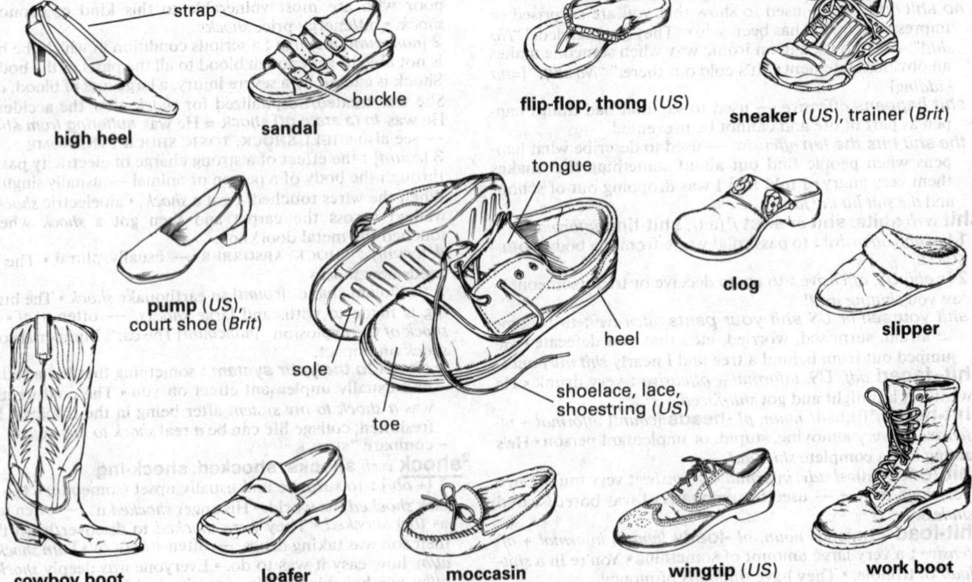

S

the shoe is on the other foot see [1]FOOT

[2]**shoe** *verb* **shoes; shod** /ˈʃɑːd/ *also chiefly US* **shoed** /ˈʃuːd/; **shoe·ing** /ˈʃuːwɪŋ/ [+ *obj*] **:** to put a horseshoe on (a horse) ▪ The blacksmith *shod* the horse. ▪ The horse was taken to be *shod*.

shoe·box /ˈʃuːˌbɑːks/ *noun, pl* **-box·es** [*count*]
1 : a box that shoes are sold in
2 : a very small home, apartment, room, etc. ▪ Their apartment was just a *shoebox*.

[1]**shoe·horn** /ˈʃuːˌhoɚn/ *noun, pl* **-horns** [*count*] **:** a curved device that you use to slide the heel of your foot into a shoe

[2]**shoehorn** *verb* **-horns; -horned; -horn·ing** [+ *obj*] **:** to force (something or someone) into a small space, a short period of time, etc. ▪ A parking garage has been *shoehorned* between the buildings. ▪ She's trying to *shoehorn* a year's worth of classes into a single semester. ▪ I don't know how they managed to *shoehorn* everyone into that little room.

shoe·lace /ˈʃuːˌleɪs/ *noun, pl* **-lac·es** [*count*] **:** a long, thin material like a string that is used for fastening a shoe ▪ Tie your *shoelaces*. ▪ Your *shoelace* is undone/untied. — called also *lace, (US) shoestring*; see picture at SHOE

shoe·mak·er /ˈʃuːˌmeɪkɚ/ *noun, pl* **-ers** [*count*] **:** someone who makes or repairs shoes
– shoe·mak·ing /ˈʃuːˌmeɪkɪŋ/ *noun* [*noncount*]

shoe·shine /ˈʃuːˌʃaɪn/ *noun, pl* **-shines** [*count*] **:** the act of polishing someone's shoes in exchange for money — usually singular ▪ Mister, would you like a *shoeshine*? — often used before another noun ▪ a *shoeshine* boy/man [=a boy/man who earns money by polishing/shining shoes] ▪ a *shoeshine* stand

shoe·string /ˈʃuːˌstrɪŋ/ *noun, pl* **-strings**
1 [*count*] *US* **:** SHOELACE
2 [*singular*] *informal* **:** a small amount of money — usually used in the phrase ***on a shoestring*** ▪ She started/began the business *on a shoestring*. [=using very little money] ▪ The newspaper operates/runs *on a shoestring*. ▪ The movie was made *on a shoestring*. — often used before another noun ▪ The business is operating on a *shoestring* budget. ▪ The store is a *shoestring* operation right now.

shoestring catch *noun, pl* **~ catches** [*count*] *baseball* **:** a catch made when the ball is just above the ground ▪ The left fielder made a *shoestring catch*.

shoestring potatoes *noun* [*plural*] *US* **:** potatoes cut into very thin long pieces and fried in deep fat **:** very thin french fries

shoe tree *noun, pl* **~ trees** [*count*] **:** a device shaped like a foot that is placed inside a shoe when it is not being worn to keep it the right shape

sho·gun /ˈʃoʊgən/ *noun, pl* **-guns** [*count*] **:** any one of the military leaders who ruled Japan until the revolution of 1867–68

shone *past tense and past participle of* [1]SHINE

[1]**shoo** /ˈʃuː/ *interj* — used when repeatedly moving your hand away from you in a short motion with your fingers down to tell an animal or person to leave ▪ *Shoo*! Get out of here!

[2]**shoo** *verb* **shoos; shooed; shoo·ing** [+ *obj*] **:** to tell (an animal or person) to leave ▪ We tried to help her, but she *shooed* us away. ▪ He *shooed* the cat out of the house.

shoo–in /ˈʃuːˌɪn/ *noun, pl* **-ins** [*count*] *chiefly US, informal* **:** someone or something that will win easily or is certain to win ▪ The horse is a *shoo-in* to win the race. — often + *for* ▪ a *shoo-in for* the tournament/job/award

shook *past tense of* [1]SHAKE

[1]**shoot** /ˈʃuːt/ *verb* **shoots; shot** /ˈʃɑːt/; **shoot·ing**
1 a : to cause a bullet, arrow, etc., to move forward with great force from a weapon [*no obj*] Does this gun *shoot* accurately? ▪ Don't *shoot*. I surrender. ▪ He *shot* at the deer. ▪ The enemy was *shooting* at the rescue helicopter. ▪ The sniper was ***shooting to kill***. [=shooting with the purpose of killing someone] [+ *obj*] She *shot* the arrow into the air. ▪ I tried *shooting* a gun for the first time. ▪ He *shot* a spitball into the girl's hair. ▪ a stunt in which she was *shot* from a cannon **b** [+ *obj*] **:** to wound or kill (a person or animal) with a bullet, arrow, etc., that is shot from a weapon ▪ He *shot* two deer this hunting season. ▪ The police *shot* the suspect in the leg. ▪ She accidentally *shot* herself in the foot. ▪ Two people were ***shot dead*** [=killed with bullets] during the robbery. ▪ The guards were ordered to ***shoot on sight*** anyone who tried to escape. [=to immediately shoot anyone they saw trying to escape] **c** [+ *obj*] **:** to remove or destroy (something) with a bullet, rocket, etc., that is shot from a weapon — often + *off* ▪ He *shot* the lock *off* the door. — often + *out* ▪ She *shot out* the lights.
2 *always followed by an adverb or preposition* **a :** to go, move, or pass quickly and suddenly in a particular direction or to a particular place [*no obj*] They *shot* past us on skis. ▪ A cat *shot* [=*darted*] across the street. ▪ Sparks from the fire were *shooting* all over. ▪ A sharp pain *shot* through her chest. ▪ The album *shot* straight to number one on the charts. [+ *obj*] The frog *shot* out its tongue at a fly. ▪ The album *shot* the band straight to the top of the charts. **b :** to flow forcefully or to cause (something) to flow forcefully in a particular direction or to a particular place [*no obj*] Blood was *shooting* [=*spurting*] from her neck. [+ *obj*] The snake *shot* venom into his eyes.
3 a *sports* **:** to kick, hit, or throw (a basketball, hockey puck, etc.) toward or into a goal [+ *obj*] She *shot* the ball from midfield. ▪ He *shot* the eight ball into the side pocket. [*no obj*] He *shoots*; he scores! ▪ You can't really play hockey if you don't have a goal to *shoot* at. **b** [+ *obj*] *basketball* **:** to score (a goal) by shooting ▪ He *shot* 10 field goals during the game. ▪ She is outside ***shooting baskets***. [=practicing basketball] **c** [+ *obj*] *golf* **:** to achieve (a particular score) ▪ She *shot* an 81. ▪ He *shot* a hole in one. **d** [+ *obj*] **:** to play (a sport or game) ▪ They are in the back *shooting* craps/dice. ✧ This sense is usually used with sports or games that involve shooting a ball. ▪ They *shot* a round of golf. ▪ Let's *shoot* some pool. ▪ (*US, informal*) Let's *shoot* some hoops. [=let's play basketball]
4 : to film or photograph (something) [+ *obj*] The movie was *shot* in Australia. ▪ The scene was *shot* in slow motion. ▪ Where did you *shoot* [=*take*] this photo? [*no obj*] The director says we'll begin *shooting* [=*filming*] next week.
5 [+ *obj*] **:** to direct (a look, comment, etc.) at (someone) quickly and suddenly ▪ She *shot* her sister a disapproving glance/look. — usually + *at* ▪ She *shot* a disapproving glance/look *at* her sister. ▪ He *shot* some angry words *at* me when the others left the room.
6 [*no obj*] *US, informal* — used to tell someone to begin to speak ▪ You wanted to tell me something? OK, *shoot*. ▪ "Can I ask you a few questions?" "*Shoot*."
7 [+ *obj*] *informal* **:** to inject (an illegal drug) into a vein ▪ She began *shooting* heroin when she was 20.

have shot your bolt see [1]BOLT

shoot daggers at see DAGGER

shoot down [*phrasal verb*] **1** ***shoot down (something)*** *or* ***shoot (something) down*** **a :** to cause (something) to fall to the ground by hitting it with a bullet, rocket, etc., that is shot from a weapon ▪ The helicopter was *shot down*. **b :** to end or defeat (something) ▪ The bill was *shot down* in the Senate. ▪ Her hopes were *shot down*. **c :** to reject (something) completely ▪ My idea was immediately *shot down*. = My idea was ***shot down in flames***. **2** ***shoot down (someone)*** *or* ***shoot (someone) down*** **a :** to kill (someone) with a bullet shot from a gun ▪ He was *shot down* in cold blood. ▪ Someone *shot* him *down*. **b** *informal* **:** to refuse to accept the offer made by (someone) ▪ I asked her on a date, but she *shot* me *down*. [=she said no to me]

shoot for [*phrasal verb*] ***shoot for (something)*** *chiefly US, informal* **:** to have (something) as a goal ▪ "When would you like to have this completed by?" "Let's *shoot for* [=*aim for*] Friday."

shoot for the moon see [1]MOON

shoot from the hip **:** to act or speak quickly without thinking about the possible results ▪ I admit I'm *shooting from the hip* here, but I think it's a decent idea.

shoot it out **:** to shoot guns at someone during a fight until one side is killed or defeated ▪ The two gangs *shot it out* in the street. — often + *with* ▪ The escaped convict *shot it out with* the police. — see also SHOOT-OUT

shoot off [*phrasal verb*] *Brit, informal* **:** to leave a place quickly and suddenly ▪ I have to *shoot off* to my next appointment.

shoot the breeze *also* ***shoot the bull*** *US, informal* **:** to talk informally about unimportant things ▪ I enjoy *shooting the breeze* with my neighbors.

shoot the messenger see MESSENGER

shoot the rapids **:** to move quickly in a river where the water flows very fast usually over rocks ▪ whitewater rafters *shooting the rapids*

shoot the shit *US, informal + offensive* **:** to talk informally about unimportant things **:** to shoot the breeze

shoot up [*phrasal verb*] **1 :** to grow or increase quickly and suddenly • He *shot up* to six feet tall over the summer. • Sales have *shot up* this month. **2 shoot up or shoot up (something)** *informal* : to inject an illegal drug into a vein • They *shot up* before the party. • *shooting up* heroin **3 shoot up (something) or shoot (something) up** : to shoot many bullets at or inside (something) • He walked in and just started *shooting up* the place. • He *shot* the place *up*.

shoot your mouth off *also* **shoot off at the mouth** *informal* : to talk foolishly, carelessly, or too much about something • She tends to *shoot her mouth off*. • Try not to *shoot your mouth off* about this to anyone.

shoot yourself in the foot *informal* : to do or say something that causes trouble for yourself • By complaining about this you're only bringing attention to your mistakes. You're *shooting yourself in the foot*.

[2]**shoot** *noun, pl* **shoots** [*count*]

1 a : the part of a new plant that is just beginning to grow above the ground **b** : a new branch and its leaves on an established plant • Small green *shoots* grew from the base of the tree.

2 a : an occasion when a movie, television show, etc., is being filmed • She is currently on a ***movie shoot*** in London. **b** : PHOTO SHOOT

3 *chiefly Brit* **a** : an occasion when people hunt and kill wild animals • They went on a duck *shoot*. [=*hunt*] **b** : a piece of usually privately owned land that is used for hunting • a 5,000-acre *shoot*

[3]**shoot** *interj, US* — used to show that you are annoyed or surprised • "We've missed the train!" "Oh, *shoot*!"

shoot·around /ˈʃu:təˌraʊnd/ *noun, pl* **-arounds** [*count*] *US* : a usually informal basketball practice

shoot–'em–up /ˈʃu:təmˌʌp/ *noun, pl* **-ups** [*count*] *informal* : a movie, television show, or video game that has a lot of killing with guns, bombs, etc.

shoot·er /ˈʃu:tɚ/ *noun, pl* **-ers** [*count*]

1 a : a person who shoots a weapon • The police are looking for the *shooter*. — see also SHARPSHOOTER **b** : a person who throws, kicks, or hits a ball or puck

2 : a small amount (called a shot) of liquor (such as whiskey or tequila) often mixed with another liquid • a whiskey *shooter*

— see also SIX-SHOOTER, TROUBLESHOOTER

[1]**shooting** *adj, always used before a noun*

1 a : relating to the act of shooting a gun • a *shooting* range **b** : relating to an occurrence in which a person is shot with a gun • The *shooting* victims [=the people who were shot] remain hospitalized. • a *shooting* death [=a death caused by being shot]

2 : relating to the action of photographing or filming someone or something • the movie's *shooting* schedule

3 : moving through part of your body in sudden painful bursts • I've been having *shooting* pains in my leg.

[2]**shooting** *noun, pl* **-ings**

1 [*count*] : an occurrence in which a person is shot with a gun • There was a *shooting* last night.

2 [*noncount*] : the activity or sport of killing wild animals with a gun • They are ***going shooting*** [=(more commonly) *going hunting*] this weekend.

3 [*noncount*] : the action of photographing or filming someone or something • *Shooting* of the movie begins next week.

shooting gallery *noun, pl* ~ **-ler·ies** [*count*] : a place where people shoot guns at objects for practice or to win prizes

S

shooting guard *noun, pl* ~ **guards** [*count*] *basketball* : a player who is one of the two guards on a team and whose main role is to score points

shooting match *noun*

the whole shooting match *informal* : the entire thing : EVERYTHING • They said that they would pay for the food, music, decorations—*the whole shooting match*.

shooting star *noun, pl* ~ **stars** [*count*] : a streak of light in the night sky that looks like a star falling but that is actually a piece of rock or metal (called a meteor) falling from outer space into the Earth's atmosphere

shoot–out /ˈʃu:tˌaʊt/ *noun, pl* **-outs** [*count*]

1 : a fight in which people shoot guns at each other until one side is killed or defeated

2 *soccer or hockey* : a competition that is used to decide the winner at the end of a tie game by giving each team a particular number of chances to shoot the ball or puck into the goal

3 : a competition between two people or groups that remains very close until the end • The two studios are in a *shoot-out* for the movie rights to the novel.

[1]**shop** /ˈʃɑ:p/ *noun, pl* **shops**

1 [*count*] **a** : a building or room where goods and services are sold — see also BARBERSHOP, BOOKSHOP, COFFEE SHOP, PAWNSHOP, PRO SHOP, SPECIALTY SHOP, THRIFT SHOP

> ***usage*** In U.S. English, *store* is more common than *shop*. When *shop* is used, it is usually for particular types of small businesses that sell one kind of product or service. *Store* is used for both small and large businesses, especially ones that sell many kinds of goods and services. In British English *store* is only used for large businesses that sell many kinds of goods and services and for a few types of smaller business that sell equipment. • (*US + Brit*) a gift/sandwich/doughnut/flower *shop* • (*US + Brit*) an antique *shop* [=(*US*) *store*] • (*US + Brit*) a pet/card *shop* [=(*US*, more commonly) *store*] • (*Brit*) a computer *shop* [=(*US + Brit*) *store*] • (*Brit*) a hardware *shop* [=(*US + Brit*) *store*] • (*Brit*) The *shops* [=(*US*) *stores*] are always crowded around the holiday season. • (*Brit*) I'm going to ***the shops*** this afternoon. [=(*US*) I'm going shopping this afternoon; I'm going to stores to look at and buy things]

b : the place where a specified kind of worker works : a worker's place of business • (*US*) the butcher *shop* = (*Brit*) the butcher's *shop* • (*Brit*) a ***chemist's shop*** [=(*US*) *drugstore*]

2 [*count*] : a place for making or repairing goods, machinery, vehicles, etc. • a repair *shop* • I took the car to the *shop* to get new brakes. — see also BODY SHOP, MACHINE SHOP, SWEATSHOP, WORKSHOP

3 [*noncount*] *US* : a class in school in which students are taught to work with tools and machinery • I am taking *shop* this semester. • I made a table in *shop*.; *also* [*count*] : a room in which a shop class is taught • The wood/metal *shop* is down the hall.

4 [*noncount*] *informal* : talk that is related to or about your work or special interests : SHOPTALK • They are always ***talking shop***.

5 [*singular*] *Brit, informal* : the activity of shopping for food or other things that are needed regularly • I did my weekly *shop*. [=(*US*) (*grocery/food*) *shopping*]

a bull in a china shop see [1]BULL

all over the shop *Brit* : all over the place : EVERYWHERE

close up shop see [1]CLOSE

mind the shop see [2]MIND

set up shop : to start a business or activity in a particular place • The restaurant *set up shop* three blocks from here. • He moved to France, where he *set up shop* as a writer. • I *set up shop* in the living room and made phone calls all afternoon.

[2]**shop** *verb* **shops; shopped; shop·ping**

1 : to visit places where goods are sold in order to look at and buy things [*no obj*] Where do you like to *shop*? • I like to *shop* at locally owned stores. • They *shopped* all day. = They spent the day *shopping*. • She is *shopping* for a new car. • He is out *shopping*. • Many people now *shop* online. [*+ obj*] (*US*) They ***shopped the store(s)*** in search of gift ideas. [=looked throughout the store(s) for a gift to buy] — see also COMPARISON SHOP, WINDOW-SHOP

2 [*+ obj*] *US* : to try to get a company to publish or produce (something) • She's *shopping* her idea for a film. — often + *around* • He *shopped* his manuscript *around*, but no publishers were interested.

3 [*+ obj*] *Brit, informal* : to give information about the secret or criminal activity of (someone) to an authority (such as the police) • His own mother *shopped* him to the police.

shop around [*phrasal verb*] : to visit several different places where a thing is sold in order to find the most suitable item or service for the lowest price • She is *shopping around* for a new car. • *Shop around* first before you buy a car. • She is *shopping around* for a bank with low fees. — see also [2]SHOP 2 (above)

– shop·per /ˈʃɑ:pɚ/ *noun, pl* **-pers** [*count*] • The stores were crowded with *shoppers*. • Christmas *shoppers* [=people who are shopping for Christmas gifts]

shop·a·hol·ic /ˌʃɑ:pəˈhɑ:lɪk/ *noun, pl* **-ics** [*count*] *informal* : a person who likes to shop very much

shop–bought *adj, Brit* : STORE-BOUGHT

shop floor *noun* [*singular*] *Brit* : the area where products are made in a factory • proper safety procedures for the *shop floor* • managerial control of the *shop floor* [=of the workers in a factory]

shop front *noun, pl* ~ **fronts** [*count*] : STOREFRONT

shop·keep·er /ˈʃɑːpˌkiːpɚ/ *noun, pl* **-ers** [*count*] : someone who owns or manages a shop or store : STOREKEEPER

shop·lift /ˈʃɑːpˌlɪft/ *verb* **-lifts; -lift·ed; -lift·ing** : to steal things from a shop or store [*no obj*] The manager saw the kids *shoplift* and called the police. ▪ He was caught *shoplifting*. [+ *obj*] The kids *shoplifted* candy from the store.
– **shop·lift·er** /ˈʃɑːpˌlɪftɚ/ *noun, pl* **-ers** [*count*] ▪ Police watched for *shoplifters*. – **shoplifting** *noun* [*noncount*] ▪ She was arrested for *shoplifting*.

shoppe /ˈʃɑːp/ *noun, pl* **shoppes** [*count*] *old-fashioned* : [1]SHOP 1a — used in the names of small businesses that sell one type of product or service ▪ Amy's Toy *Shoppe* ▪ a new mall called "The *Shoppes* at Woodford Hills"

shopping *noun* [*noncount*]
1 : the activity of visiting places where goods are sold in order to look at and buy things (such as food, clothing, etc.) ▪ We ***do*** (our) grocery ***shopping*** once a week. = We ***go*** grocery ***shopping*** once a week. [=we shop for groceries once a week] ▪ I can *do* your *shopping* for you. ▪ When are you going to *do* the *shopping*? ▪ I'm *going shopping*. [=(*Brit*) *going to the shops*] ▪ We *went shopping* for a gift at the mall. — often used before another noun ▪ a *shopping* area/basket/cart ▪ We're going on a *shopping* trip in New York City. ▪ a ***shopping bag*** [=(*Brit*) *carrier bag*; a bag that a store gives you to carry any items you have bought there] ▪ We went on a ***shopping spree***. [=we bought a lot of things in a short period of time]
2 *Brit* : the things that are bought at a shop or store ▪ Put the *shopping* in the car.

shopping cart *noun, pl* ~ **carts** [*count*] : [1]CART 2

shopping center (*US*) *or Brit* **shopping centre** *noun, pl* ~ **-ters** [*count*] : a group of shops or stores in one area — called also *shopping plaza*

shopping list *noun, pl* ~ **lists** [*count*]
1 : a list of things to be bought at a shop or store
2 : a long list of related things ▪ a *shopping list* [=*laundry list*] of things to be fixed around the house

shopping mall *noun, pl* ~ **malls** [*count*] *chiefly US* : a large building or group of buildings containing many different stores : MALL

shop–soiled /ˈʃɑːpˌsojəld/ *adj, Brit* : SHOPWORN

shop steward *noun, pl* ~ **-ards** [*count*] : a member of a labor union in a factory or company who is elected by the other members to meet with the managers

shop·talk /ˈʃɑːpˌtɑːk/ *noun* [*noncount*] *chiefly US* : talk that is related to your work or special interests ▪ There was a lot of *shoptalk* at the office party.

shop·worn /ˈʃɑːpˌwoɚn/ *adj, US*
1 : faded or damaged from being in a shop or store for too long ▪ *shopworn* [=(*Brit*) *shop-soiled*] books/goods
2 : not interesting because of being used too often ▪ *shopworn* [=(*Brit*) *shop-soiled*] stories/sayings/clichés

[1]**shore** /ˈʃoɚ/ *noun, pl* **shores**
1 : the land along the edge of an area of water (such as an ocean, lake, etc.) [*count*] a rocky/sandy *shore* [=*coast*] ▪ Houses were built on the *shores* of the lake. ▪ The boat ***hugged the shore***. [=stayed close to the shore] [*noncount*] We swam to *shore*. ▪ The boat was about a mile from *shore*. ▪ The boat headed for *shore*.
2 ***shores*** [*plural*] *literary* : a country that touches a sea or ocean : a country that has a coast ▪ My family came to these *shores* [=came to this country] 100 years ago. ▪ The plant was brought to our *shores* from Europe. ▪ We arrived on American/British *shores*.

[2]**shore** *verb* **shores; shored; shor·ing**
shore up [*phrasal verb*] ***shore (something) up*** *or* ***shore up (something)*** **1** : to support (something) or keep (something) from falling by placing something under or against it ▪ They *shored up* [=*propped up*] the roof/wall. **2** : to support or help (something) ▪ The tax cuts are supposed to *shore up* the economy. ▪ The new player should *shore up* the team's defense.

shore leave *noun* [*noncount*] : official permission for a sailor to leave a ship and go onto land for a period of time

shore·line /ˈʃoɚˌlaɪn/ *noun, pl* **-lines** : the land along the edge of an area of water (such as an ocean, lake, etc.) : a coast or shore [*count*] rocky *shorelines* ▪ The road runs along the *shoreline*. [*noncount*] 1,000 miles of *shoreline*

shorn *past participle of* SHEAR

[1]**short** /ˈʃoɚt/ *adj* **short·er; -est**
1 a : extending a small distance from one end to the other end : having little length : not long ▪ Her hair is *short*. = She has *short* hair. ▪ It's just a *short* distance from here. = It's just a *short* distance away. ▪ the *shortest* rope ▪ One of my legs is slightly *shorter* than the other. ▪ The coat is *short* on him. = The coat is too *short* for him. [=the coat should be longer in order to fit him correctly] **b** : not great in distance ▪ a *short* walk/drive/trip ▪ This way is *shorter*. **c** : having little height : not tall ▪ He is *short* for his age. ▪ a *short* girl
2 a : lasting or continuing for a small amount of time : BRIEF ▪ a *short* delay/vacation/speech ▪ the *shortest* day of the year ▪ Life's too *short* to worry about the past. ▪ The movie/meeting was very *short*. ▪ You have done a lot in a *short* space/period of time. ▪ a *short* burst of speed ▪ I've only lived here for a *short* time/while. ▪ It's just a *short* walk from here. [=you can walk there from here in a few minutes] ▪ She has a very ***short memory***. [=she forgets about events, conversations, etc., soon after they happen] **b** *always used before a noun* : seeming to pass quickly ▪ She has made great progress in a few *short* years. ▪ He visited for two *short* weeks.
3 : having few pages, items, etc. ▪ a *short* book/poem ▪ I have a list of things I need to do before we go, but it's pretty *short*. ▪ *short* sentences
4 *of clothing* : covering only part of the arms or legs ▪ boys in *short* pants ▪ a shirt with *short* sleeves [=sleeves that end at or above the elbows] ▪ a *short* skirt [=a skirt that ends above the knees and especially several inches above the knees]
5 a : existing in less than the usual or needed amount ▪ We should hurry. Time is *short*. [=we don't have much time] ▪ Money has been *short* lately. [=I haven't had enough money lately] ▪ Gasoline is ***in short supply***. [=little gasoline is available] ▪ (*US*) We can be ready ***on short notice***. = (*Brit*) We can be ready ***at short notice***. [=very quickly] ▪ (*US*) Thank you for meeting with me ***on such short notice***. = (*Brit*) Thank you for meeting with me ***at such short notice***. [=even though you did not know that I wanted to meet with you until a short time ago] **b** *not used before a noun* : having less than what is needed : not having enough of something ▪ I can't pay the bill. I'm a little *short* (of money). [=I don't have enough money] ▪ The team was *short* (by) two players. = The team was two players *short*. — often + *on* ▪ *short on* time/food/money ▪ She's a little *short on* patience today. [=she is feeling somewhat impatient] ▪ He's not *short on* self-confidence. [=he has plenty of self-confidence] ▪ He was long on criticism but *short on* useful advice. [=he was very critical but did not give any useful advice] **c** : less than — used in the phrase ***nothing short of*** to give emphasis to a statement or description ▪ His recovery is *nothing short of* a miracle. = His recovery is *nothing short of* miraculous. [=his recovery is a miracle; his recovery is miraculous] **d** : not reaching far enough ▪ The throw to first base was *short*. ▪ a *short* throw
6 : made smaller by having part removed ▪ a *short* tax form — often + *for* ▪ "Doc" is *short for* "doctor." ▪ "Ben" is *short for* "Benjamin." ▪ "www" is *short for* "World Wide Web."
7 *not used before a noun* : talking to someone in a very brief and unfriendly way : rudely brief ▪ I'm sorry I was *short* [=*abrupt, curt*] with you.
8 *linguistics, of a vowel* — used to identify certain vowel sounds in English ▪ long and *short* vowels ▪ the *short* "a" in "bad" ▪ the *short* "e" in "bet" ▪ the *short* "i" in "sit" ▪ the *short* "o" in "hot" ▪ the *short* "u" in "but" — compare [1]LONG 6
a short fuse see [2]FUSE
draw the short straw see [1]DRAW
fall short see [1]FALL
in short order : quickly and without delay ▪ *In short order* the group set up camp. ▪ The papers were organized *in short order*.
make short work of see [2]WORK
short and sweet : pleasantly brief : not lasting a long time or requiring a lot of time ▪ That's the way we like the meetings—*short and sweet*. ▪ I've got a few announcements, but I'll keep it *short and sweet*. [=I will talk for only a few minutes]
short of breath ✧ If you are *short of breath*, it is difficult for you to breathe. ▪ He is overweight and gets *short of breath* [=*out of breath*] just walking to his car. ▪ She was *short of breath* and unable to talk after her run.
the short end of the stick see [1]STICK
– **short·ness** /ˈʃoɚtnəs/ *noun* [*noncount*] ▪ I was surprised by the *shortness* of the meeting. ▪ One symptom is ***shortness of breath***.

[2]**short** *adv* **short·er; -est**
1 : to or at a point that is not as far as expected or desired : to a point not reaching what is needed for something ▪ The

S

ball fell *short.* ▪ He threw the ball *short.* ▪ He began to run/answer and then ***pulled up short*** [=stopped suddenly and did not finish] ▪ We made as many cookies as we could, but we ***came up short*** [=we had fewer than we needed to have] and there weren't enough for everyone. ▪ Time is ***running short*** [=there is little time left to do, accomplish, etc., something] — often + *of* ▪ He finished in 30 seconds—just one second *short of* the world record. [=he finished in 30 seconds and the world record is 29 seconds] ▪ She quit school a month *short of* [=*before*] graduation. ▪ We ***came up short of*** [=we did not achieve] our goal. ▪ Sales for the month ***came short of*** our estimates. [=we sold less than we had predicted we would sell] ▪ The attack was ***just short of*** a full invasion. ▪ She's *just short of* six feet tall. [=she is almost six feet tall] ▪ The performance was *just short of* perfection. = The performance was (only a) ***little short of*** perfect. ▪ The running back was ***stopped short of*** the goal line. [=was stopped just before the goal line] ▪ He ***stopped well short of*** the line. [=long before reaching the line] ▪ The boss said that she was unhappy with some employees, but she ***stopped short of*** naming which ones. [=but she did not say which employees she was unhappy with] ▪ We have plenty of shirts left, but we're ***running short of*** [=*running out of*] smaller sizes. [=the available supply of smaller sizes is almost used up]

2 : in a sudden manner ▪ The hunter stopped *short* [=*suddenly*] when he saw the deer. ▪ I was wandering through the exhibit when I was ***brought up short*** by a striking photograph. [=when a striking photograph made me suddenly stop]

3 : for or during a short time ▪ Her career was *short*-lasting.

4 : in a way that makes something short ▪ Keep the grass mowed *short.* ▪ Her dark hair was cut/cropped *short.* [=she had short hair]

caught short see [1]CATCH

cut short **:** to end (something) earlier than expected ▪ We had to *cut* our vacation *short.* ▪ The speech was *cut short.* [=the speech was interrupted and not finished]

fall short see [1]FALL

sell (someone or something) short see [1]SELL

short of **:** except for (something) **:** other than (something) ▪ *Short of* replacing the motor, I have tried everything to fix the car. ▪ *Short of* a catastrophe [=unless something terrible happens], I think we'll succeed.

taken/caught short *Brit, informal* **:** suddenly needing to use a toilet when there is no toilet available

[3]short *noun, pl* **shorts**

1 ***shorts*** [*plural*] **a :** pants that end at or above the knees ▪ a pair of *shorts* ▪ Your *shorts* are dirty. ▪ short *shorts* [=shorts that cover very little of the legs] — see color picture on page C14; see also BERMUDA SHORTS **b :** BOXER SHORTS

2 [*count*] **:** a short movie ▪ The *short* before the main movie was very funny.

3 [*count*] **:** SHORT CIRCUIT

4 [*noncount*] *baseball, informal* **:** SHORTSTOP ▪ Who's playing *short*?

5 [*count*] *Brit* **:** a small amount of liquor that you drink quickly **:** SHOT ▪ a *short* of vodka

for short **:** in a shorter form **:** as an abbreviation ▪ My name is Benjamin, or Ben *for short.*

in short **:** in a few words — used to indicate that you are saying something in as few words as possible ▪ The trip was, *in short,* a disaster. ▪ *In short* [=*in summary*], the company is doing extremely well.

the long and (the) short of it see [3]LONG

[4]short *verb* **shorts; short·ed; short·ing**

1 [+ *obj*] **:** to cause (something) to have a short circuit **:** SHORT-CIRCUIT ▪ The lightning *shorted* the TV. — often + *out* in U.S. English ▪ Water *shorted out* the flashlight.

2 [*no obj*] **:** to stop working because of a short circuit **:** SHORT-CIRCUIT ▪ The hair dryer must have *shorted.* — often + *out* in U.S. English ▪ The toaster oven *shorted out.*

short·age /ˈʃoɚtɪʤ/ *noun, pl* **-ag·es :** a state in which there is not enough of something that is needed [*count*] a gasoline/water *shortage* — often + *of* ▪ a *shortage of* cash/gasoline/teachers/water ▪ ***There is no shortage of*** restaurants [=there are many restaurants] in the city. [*noncount*] (*chiefly Brit*) ▪ periods of food *shortage*

short·bread /ˈʃoɚtˌbrɛd/ *noun* [*noncount*] **:** a thick cookie made of flour, sugar, and a lot of butter or other shortening

short·cake /ˈʃoɚtˌkeɪk/ *noun* [*noncount*]

1 *chiefly US* **:** a dessert made with a rich cake that is served with sweetened fruit on top ▪ strawberry *shortcake*

2 *chiefly Brit* **:** SHORTBREAD

short·change /ˈʃoɚtˈʧeɪnʤ/ *verb* **-chang·es; -changed; -chang·ing** [+ *obj*]

1 : to give (someone) less than the correct amount of change ▪ The cashier *shortchanged* me. I gave her 10 dollars to pay for an $8.95 book, and she only gave me a dollar back.

2 : to give (someone) less than what is expected or deserved ▪ The band *shortchanged* its fans by playing for only 30 minutes. — often used as *(be) shortchanged* ▪ He *was shortchanged* [=*was cheated*] out of a promotion (by the company). ▪ Many people felt they were *being shortchanged* by the policy. = Many people ***felt shortchanged*** by the policy.

short circuit *noun, pl* **~ circuits** [*count*] **:** the failure of electricity to flow properly in a circuit because the wires or connections in the circuit are damaged or not connected properly ▪ The fire was caused by a *short circuit.*

short–circuit *verb* **-circuits; -circuited; -circuiting**

1 a [+ *obj*] **:** to cause (something) to have a short circuit ▪ The lightning *short-circuited* the TV. **b** [*no obj*] **:** to stop working because of a short circuit ▪ The lamp must have *short-circuited.*

2 [+ *obj*] **:** to avoid doing (something) ▪ The owners *short-circuited* [=*bypassed, circumvented*] the required inspection.

3 [+ *obj*] **:** to stop (efforts, plans, etc.) from succeeding ▪ The lawyers *short-circuited* [=*frustrated, impeded*] any attempt to sue the company.

short·com·ing /ˈʃoɚtˌkʌmɪŋ/ *noun, pl* **-ings** [*count*]

1 : a weakness in someone's character **:** a personal fault or failing ▪ Her lack of attention to detail is her biggest *shortcoming.* — usually plural ▪ He has many more strengths than *shortcomings.*

2 : a bad feature **:** a flaw or defect in something ▪ The main/major *shortcoming* of this camera is that it uses up batteries quickly.

short·cut /ˈʃoɚtˌkʌt/ *noun, pl* **-cuts** [*count*]

1 : a shorter, quicker, or easier way to get to a place ▪ Wait, I know a *shortcut.* Turn left here. ▪ We ***took*** a ***shortcut*** home. ▪ Let's *take* the *shortcut* through the woods.

2 : a quicker or easier way to do something ▪ I used a *shortcut* to calculate the total weight. ▪ There are no *shortcuts* to/for learning another language. ▪ Mistakes were made because too many ***shortcuts*** were ***taken.***

short·en /ˈʃoɚtn̩/ *verb* **-ens; -ened; -en·ing**

1 [*no obj*] **:** to become shorter ▪ The days have begun to *shorten.* [=last for a smaller amount of time]

2 [+ *obj*] **:** to make (something) shorter ▪ *shorten* a pair of pants ▪ He had to *shorten* the speech. ▪ Not changing the oil regularly will *shorten* the life of the engine. [=will cause the engine to fail sooner] ▪ "Franklin D. Roosevelt" is often *shortened* to "FDR."

– shortened *adj* ▪ "I've" is the *shortened* form of "I have." ▪ I heard a *shortened* version of the song on the radio.

short·en·ing /ˈʃoɚtnɪŋ/ *noun* [*noncount*] **:** a fat (such as butter) that is used in cooking or baking

short·fall /ˈʃoɚtˌfɑːl/ *noun, pl* **-falls** [*count*] *formal* **:** a failure to get what is expected or needed ▪ a *shortfall* in milk production ▪ profit *shortfalls* ▪ We had a budget *shortfall.* [=our costs were higher than the available amount of money]; *also* **:** the amount of such a failure ▪ a $2 million *shortfall* = a *shortfall* of $2 million [=$2 million less than is needed]

short·hair /ˈʃoɚtˌheɚ/ *noun, pl* **-hairs** [*count*] **:** a cat that has short, thick fur — compare LONGHAIR

short–haired *adj* **:** having short fur or hair ▪ *short-haired* cats ▪ a *short-haired* student — opposite LONG-HAIRED

short·hand /ˈʃoɚtˌhænd/ *noun* [*noncount*]

1 : a method of writing quickly by using symbols or abbreviations for sounds, words, or phrases **:** STENOGRAPHY ▪ The notes were written ***in shorthand.*** [=using special symbols] ▪ The secretary ***takes shorthand.*** [=writes in shorthand] — compare LONGHAND

2 : a short or quick way of showing or saying something — usually + *for* ▪ "ASAP" is *shorthand for* "as soon as possible."

– shorthand *adj, always used before a noun* ▪ *shorthand* symbols ▪ a ***shorthand reporter*** [=someone whose job is to record in shorthand exactly what is said in a court of law or in a meeting] ▪ (*Brit*) a ***shorthand typist*** [=(*chiefly US*) *stenographer*; someone whose job is to record in shorthand what is said and then type it] ▪ "The Far East" is a *shorthand* term for all the countries of eastern Asia and the Malay Archipelago.

short·hand·ed /ˌʃoɚtˈhændəd/ *adj*

1 [*more* ~; *most* ~] **:** having fewer than the usual number of people available ▪ The crew was *shorthanded.* [=someone who is usually in the crew wasn't there] • a *shorthanded* staff • We're very *shorthanded* this week. [=many people who are usually here are not here this week]

2 *always used before a noun, ice hockey* : made when a team member is off the ice for a penalty • a *shorthanded* goal

short–haul /ˈʃoɚtˌhɑːl/ *adj, always used before a noun* : traveling or involving a short distance • *short-haul* flights

shortie *variant spelling of* SHORTY

short list *noun, pl* ~ **lists** [*count*] : a list of a small number of people or things that have been selected from a larger group and are being considered to receive an award, to get a job, etc. — usually singular • She is on the *short list* for the Nobel Prize. • The book is on the *short list* for the National Book Award.

– **short–list** *verb* **-lists; -list·ed; -list·ing** [+ *obj*] — usually used as *(be) short-listed* • He's *been short-listed* for the position. [=he has been put on a short list for the position] • The novel *was short-listed* to win the award.

short–lived /ˈʃoɚtˈlɪvd/ *adj* **short·er–lived; short·est–lived** [*or more* ~; *most* ~] : living or lasting for a short time • *short-lived* insects • Her happiness was *short-lived.* — compare LONG-LIVED

short·ly /ˈʃoɚtli/ *adv*

1 : in or within a short time : SOON • They should arrive *shortly.* • I'll be ready *shortly.* • He left *shortly* after/before you did. • ***Shortly after*** [=soon after] she hung up, the phone rang again.

2 : in a very brief and unfriendly way • "I can't help you right now," he said *shortly.*

short–or·der /ˈʃoɚtˌoɚdɚ/ *adj, always used before a noun* : making or serving food that can be cooked quickly when a customer orders it • a *short-order* cook

short–range /ˈʃoɚtˈreɪnʤ/ *adj, always used before a noun* **short·er–range; short·est–range**

1 : able to travel or be used over short distances • *short-range* missiles/weapons • a *short-range* radio

2 : involving a short period of time • *short-range* [=*short-term*] goals • a *short-range* weather forecast

short run *noun*

the short run : a short period of time at the beginning of something • One plan had advantages ***over the short run***. — usually used in the phrase ***in the short run*** • It won't make any difference *in the short run.* [=when a small amount of time has passed] • These changes may improve profits *in the short run* [=*in the short term, in the near future*], but they are going to cost us money in the long run. — compare LONG RUN

– **short–run** *adj, always used before a noun* • *short-run* benefits [=benefits that will exist or continue for a short period of time]

short–sheet *verb* **-sheets; -sheet·ed; -sheet·ing** [+ *obj*] *US*

1 : to arrange the top sheet on a bed in a way that leaves no space for the feet of a person getting into the bed ✧ Short-sheeting a bed is a playful trick. • Somebody *short-sheeted* my bed at summer camp.

2 : to give (someone) less than what is expected or deserved • Our school district was *short-sheeted* [=(more commonly) *shortchanged*] by the state government.

short shrift *noun* [*noncount*] : little or no attention or thought • He ***gives short shrift*** to the author's later works. • The lower classes have ***gotten/received short shrift*** from the city government. [=the city government has not paid attention to the problems of the people in the lower classes]

short·sight·ed /ˈʃoɚtˌsaɪtəd/ *adj* [*more* ~; *most* ~]

1 a : not considering what will or might happen in the future • *shortsighted* politicians who only care about how they do in the next election **b** : made or done without thinking about what will happen in the future • The plan was dangerously *shortsighted.* • *shortsighted* policies/investments — opposite (*US*) FARSIGHTED, (*Brit*) LONG-SIGHTED

2 *Brit* : NEARSIGHTED

– **short·sight·ed·ness** *noun* [*noncount*] • We're victims of our own *shortsightedness.*

short–staffed *adj* [*more* ~; *most* ~] : having fewer than the usual number of people available • The team/department is *short-staffed.* [=*shorthanded*] • a *short-staffed* hospital

short–stay *adj, always used before a noun, Brit*

1 : providing a specified service for short periods of time • a *short-stay* car park

2 : staying at a place (such as a hospital or nursing home) for a short period of time • *short-stay* patients/residents

short·stop /ˈʃoɚtˌstɑːp/ *noun, pl* **-stops** [*count*] *baseball* : the player who defends the area between second and third base • an all-star *shortstop*

short story *noun, pl* ~ **-ries** [*count*] : a short written story usually dealing with few characters : a short work of fiction

short temper *noun, pl* ~ **-pers** [*count*] : a tendency to become angry easily • She has a *short temper.*

short–tem·pered /ˌʃoɚtˈtɛmpɚd/ *adj* [*more* ~; *most* ~] : easily made angry • *short-tempered* children • She is *short-tempered.*

short term *noun*

the short term : a short period of time at the beginning of something • It will meet our needs, at least for *the short term.* • His plan has advantages ***over the short term***. — usually used in the phrase ***in the short term*** • It won't make any difference *in the short term.* [=when a small amount of time has passed] • These changes may improve profits *in the short term* [=*in the near future, in the short run*], but they are going to cost us money in the long term. — compare LONG TERM

short–term /ˈʃoɚtˌtɚm/ *adj* : lasting for, relating to, or involving a short period of time • the *short-term* effects of the plan • The company is using a *short-term* plan/strategy to increase profits. • Her memory of events that happened long ago is still okay, but her *short-term* memory is failing. [=it is difficult for her to remember things that happened recently] • a *short-term* contract/investment • *short-term* [=*short-range*] goals — opposite LONG-TERM

short time *noun* [*noncount*] *Brit* : a work schedule in which an employee works fewer hours than usual • The company hasn't laid anyone off, but a number of employees have been put on *short time.*

short·wave /ˈʃoɚtˌweɪv/ *noun, pl* **-waves** [*count*]

1 : a radio wave with a wavelength between 10 and 100 meters

2 : a radio or receiver that uses shortwaves

– **shortwave** *adj, always used before a noun* • *shortwave* frequencies • a *shortwave* radio/receiver

shorty *or* **short·ie** /ˈʃoɚti/ *noun, pl* **short·ies** [*count*] *informal* : someone who is not tall : a short person • when I was just a *shorty* — often used as a form of address • How are you today, *shorty*? ✧ *Shorty* is often used humorously but can be insulting.

¹shot /ˈʃɑːt/ *noun, pl* **shots**

1 [*count*] : an act of shooting a gun • Two *shots* were heard. = Two *shots* rang out. • She fired a warning *shot* into the air. [=she fired/shot a gun into the air as a warning] • He ***took a shot*** at the deer. [=he tried to shoot the deer; he fired a gun at the deer] — see also GUNSHOT, POTSHOT

2 [*noncount*] **a** : BUCKSHOT **b** : the objects (called ammunition) that are shot from cannons and other old-fashioned weapons • musket/cannon *shot* — see also SLINGSHOT

3 [*count*] : a person who shoots a gun • She is a very good *shot.* [=she is skilled in shooting a gun] • You're not a bad *shot.* [=you are able to shoot a gun fairly well] — see also BIG SHOT

4 [*count*] : a critical or hurtful remark • They ***took shots*** at each other throughout the debate. • As her ***parting shot*** [=her final critical comment], she said that the other candidate simply did not understand the needs of the city's citizens. — see also CHEAP SHOT, POTSHOT

5 [*count*] : the act of hitting someone or something with your hand or an object • The boxer got in a few good *shots* on his opponent. • She ***took a shot*** at me [=tried to hit me] with a snowball but missed.

6 [*count*] **a** : an act of kicking, hitting, or throwing a ball or puck toward or into a goal • She scored on a perfect *shot* from the right wing. • Wow! That was a good/great *shot!* • He ***made the shot***. [=got the ball or puck in the goal] • He ***took a shot*** [=threw the ball toward the goal] but missed. **b** : a ball or puck that is kicked, hit, or thrown toward or into a goal • The *shot* went between the goalie's legs. • Her *shot* landed on the putting green. — see also CHIP SHOT, FOUL SHOT, JUMP SHOT, SLAP SHOT

7 [*count*] **a** : an attempt to do something successfully — usually singular • You should ***give it a shot***. [=you should try to do it] • I'll *give* you one more *shot.* [=I'll let you try one more time] • They lost, but at least they *gave it* their best *shot.* [=*try, effort*] — often + *at* • ***Take*** another ***shot at*** the math problem. • I never changed a tire before, but I'll ***have a shot at*** it. • I *took/had a shot at* (guessing) the answer and guessed right. **b** : a chance that something will happen or be

S

achieved — usually singular • The horse has a 12 to 1 *shot* of winning. • It's a 10 to 1 *shot* that he'll be on time. — often + *at* • The team has a good *shot at* winning. • She has a *shot at* (winning) the title. — see also LONG SHOT
8 [*count*] *informal* : [1]PHOTOGRAPH — often + *of* • I got some good *shots* [=*pictures*] *of* the kids. • Be sure to take/get a couple *shots of* the car. — see also MUG SHOT, SNAPSHOT
9 [*count*] : a part of a movie or a television show that is filmed by one camera without stopping • the movie's opening *shot* • a close-up *shot* of a beehive
10 [*count*] *chiefly US* : an act of putting something (such as medicine or vaccine) into the body with a needle : INJECTION • a flu *shot* — often + *of* • a *shot of* morphine/Novocain
11 [*count*] **a** : a small amount of a drink and especially a strong alcoholic drink • tequila *shots* • a *shot* glass — often + *of* • a *shot of* whisky/espresso — called also (*Brit*) *short* **b** : a small amount of something — often + *of* • The pilot took a *shot of* oxygen. • My speech could use a *shot of* humor.
12 [*count*] : a heavy metal ball that people throw as far as they can in the athletic event called the shot put
a shot *US, informal* : for each one : APIECE • They cost $5 *a shot.*
a shot across the/someone's bow(s) : a warning to not do something or to stop doing something • The fine is a *shot across the bow* to an industry that thinks it can ignore the law.
a shot in the arm : something that makes someone or something stronger or more active, confident, etc. • The award has given the school a much needed *shot in the arm.*
a shot in the dark **1** : a guess that is based on very little or no information or evidence • Estimating the cost of a project like this is often a *shot in the dark.* **2** : an attempt that is not likely to succeed • I know it's a *shot in the dark,* but I still think we can convince them to join us.
call the shots *informal* : to be in charge or control of something • Who's the one who *calls the shots* around here?
like a shot : immediately and very quickly • He started the car and took off *like a shot.*

[2]shot *past tense and past participle of* [1]SHOOT

[3]shot *adj, not used before a noun*
1 *informal* : in a very bad condition • The tires on the car are *shot.* • It's such a stressful job—my nerves are ***shot (to pieces)***
2 a *of a fabric* : having threads of a different color woven in — often + *with* • The dress is blue *shot with* silver. • blue fabric ***shot through with*** silver thread **b** : having a particular color, quality, feature, etc., throughout — usually + *with* • His stories are *shot with* comedy. • black hair ***shot through with*** gray
shot of *Brit, informal* : no longer having someone or something that you do not want • I'm ready to get/be *shot of* [=*rid of*] this job. • The band wants to be *shot of* its manager.

shot clock *noun, pl* **~ clocks** [*count*] *basketball* : a clock that shows how much time a player has left to shoot the ball

shot·gun /ˈʃɑːtˌgʌn/ *noun, pl* **-guns** [*count*]
1 : a gun with a long barrel that shoots a large number of small metal balls (called buckshot) — see picture at GUN; see also SAWED-OFF SHOTGUN
2 *American football* : an offensive formation in which the quarterback is a few yards behind the line of scrimmage at the start of a play
ride shotgun see [1]RIDE

shotgun wedding *noun, pl* **~ -dings** [*count*] : a wedding that happens because the bride is pregnant — called also *shotgun marriage*

shot put *noun*
the shot put : an athletic event in which people compete by trying to throw a heavy metal ball (called a shot) as far as possible
– shot–put·ter /ˈʃɑːtˌpʊtɚ/ *noun, pl* **-ters** [*count*]

shot put

should /ˈʃʊd, ʃəd/ *verb, past tense of* SHALL [*modal verb*]
1 a — used to say or suggest that something is the proper, reasonable, or best thing to do • You *should* [=*ought to*] get some rest. • They *should* be punished. • We *should* leave a few minutes early to make sure we get there on time. • Maybe you *should* consider finding a new job. • I *should* emphasize that these numbers are only estimates. • My friends say that I *should* quit the team. • What time *should* we meet? [=what is the best time for us to meet?; what time do you want to meet?] • Patients *should* inform the receptionist upon their arrival. **b** — used with *have* to say that something was the proper, reasonable, or best thing to do but was not done • You *should have* been more careful. • She *shouldn't have* spoken to him so rudely. • What *should* I *have* done? • *Should* I not *have* gone? [=was it wrong for me to go?] • I *should have* known that he would be late. [=I didn't know that he would be late, but it would have been reasonable for me to expect it because he is often late] **c** — used with *have* to say that you wish someone had seen, heard, or experienced something • You *should have* seen her face [=I wish that you had seen her face] when she opened the present. • It was so funny. You *should have* been there.
2 — used to ask for someone's opinion • *Should* [=(more formally) *shall*] I turn the music down? • What *should* we have for lunch?
3 — used to say that something is expected or correct • Everyone *should* [=*ought to*] have a copy of the handout. • There *should* be four place settings at the table, not six. • "He feels very sorry about what happened." "Well, he *should*!" • You *should* be ashamed of yourself, behaving so rudely to our guests! • They *should* be here by now. = They *should* have arrived by now. [=I expected them to be here by now]
4 a — used when saying that you feel a specified way about someone's words or behavior • I'm surprised that he *should* intentionally be so rude to you. • It's strange (that) you *should* say that. • Funny you *should* mention it. [=I think it's odd/strange that you mentioned it] I've been thinking the same thing. **b** — used to emphasize what you believe, think, hope, etc. • I *should* imagine it won't take more than two hours to drive there. [=I am fairly certain that it won't take more than two hours] • I *should* think not. [=I really don't think so] • I *should* hope that she would apologize. [=I expect her to apologize] • "She apologized for her rude behavior." "Well, I ***should hope so***"
5 — used with *have* in negative statements as a polite way of thanking someone for doing something • You really *should* not *have* gone to all that trouble on my account—but I'm glad you did! • Flowers for me? You *shouldn't have.*
6 *somewhat formal* — used to talk about the result or effect of something that may happen or be true • *Should* [=*if*] you change your mind, please let us know. • I will feel very guilty *should* anything go wrong. [=if anything goes wrong] — usually used with *if* • I will feel very guilty *if* anything *should* [=*were to*] go wrong. • *If* he *should* call [=if he calls], tell him I'm not home. • *If* you *should* see them [=if you see them], say hello for me.
7 *Brit* — used to say that you would do or feel something if something specified happened; only used after *I* or *we* • If my husband treated me like that, I *should* [=*would*] divorce him. • I *should* be surprised if many people go to the fair on such a rainy day. • I *should* not be surprised if no one goes. • I *shouldn't* [=*wouldn't*] be surprised at all.
8 *Brit* — used when giving someone advice; only used after *I* or *we* • I *should* [=*would*] see a doctor if I were you.
9 *Brit* — used to say that you want to do or want to have something; only used after *I* or *we* • "They really need some help." "Well, I *should* be glad to help them." • I ***should like*** to call my lawyer. • "Would you care for a drink?" "I *should like* one very much."
how/why should I/we know — used to say that you do not know the answer to a question and are surprised that you were asked it • "Where did they go?" "*How should I know*?"
what/who should you see but — used to say that you are surprised to see something or someone • I looked up and *what should I see but* a hummingbird hovering over my head. • They were walking along when *who should they see but* Kim!

[1]shoul·der /ˈʃoʊldɚ/ *noun, pl* **-ders**
1 [*count*] : the part of your body where your arm is connected • He rested the baby's head on his *shoulder.* • He grabbed my *shoulder* and turned me around. • She carried a backpack on one *shoulder.* • He has broad *shoulders.* — often used figuratively • The responsibility for the failure falls squarely ***on her shoulders*** [=she is completely responsible for the failure] — see picture at HUMAN; see also COLD SHOULDER

2 a [*count*] **:** the part of an animal's body where a front leg is connected ▪ The horse is five feet high at the *shoulder*. **b :** a cut of meat from the shoulder of an animal [*count*] a *shoulder* of lamb [*noncount*] We had pork *shoulder* for dinner.
3 [*count*] **:** the part of a piece of clothing that covers your shoulders — usually plural ▪ The jacket is tight in the *shoulders*. ▪ The blouse has padded *shoulders*.
4 [*count*] **:** a part of something that is near the top and that resembles a person's shoulder in shape — often + *of* ▪ the *shoulder of* the hill/bottle
5 [*singular*] *US* **:** the outside edge of a road that is not used for travel ▪ They pulled over to the *shoulder* to fix the flat tire. — called also (*Brit*) *hard shoulder*
a good head on your shoulders see [1]HEAD
a shoulder to cry on **1 :** a person who gives you sympathy and support ▪ She's always been a sympathetic *shoulder to cry on*. **2 :** sympathy and support ▪ He offered me *a shoulder to cry on* when my husband left me.
have a chip on your shoulder see [1]CHIP
head and shoulders above see [1]HEAD
look over your shoulder **:** to worry or think about the possibility that something bad might happen, that someone will try to harm you, etc. ▪ You can never feel confident in this business. You always have to be *looking over your shoulder*.
rub shoulders with see [1]RUB
shoulder to shoulder **1 :** physically close together ▪ Everyone was standing/squeezed *shoulder to shoulder* on the crowded bus. **2 :** united together to achieve a shared goal ▪ I stand *shoulder to shoulder* with the other legislators in this effort.

[2]shoulder *verb* **-ders; -dered; -der·ing**
1 [+ *obj*] **:** to deal with or accept (something) as your responsibility or duty ▪ He *shouldered* the blame for the project's failure. ▪ The company will *shoulder* the costs of the repairs. ▪ She *shouldered* the full burden of raising three children.
2 a [+ *obj*] **:** to push (something) with your shoulder ▪ He *shouldered* the door open. **b** *always followed by an adverb or preposition* **:** to move forward by pushing through something with the shoulders [*no obj*] She *shouldered* through the crowd. [+ *obj*] She *shouldered* her way through the crowd.
3 [+ *obj*] **:** to place or carry (something) on your shoulder ▪ The soldiers *shouldered* their rifles and marched away.

shoulder bag *noun, pl* **~ bags** [*count*] **:** a bag that is designed to be carried on one shoulder by a strap

shoulder blade *noun, pl* **~ blades** [*count*] **:** one of the two flat, triangular bones of the shoulder that are located in the upper back — called also *scapula*; see picture at HUMAN

-shoul·dered /ˌʃouldəd/ *adj* **:** having shoulders of a specified kind — used in combination ▪ round-*shouldered* ▪ broad-*shouldered*

shoulder–high *adj* **:** reaching as high as your shoulder ▪ a *shoulder-high* wall

shoulder–length *adj, of a person's hair* **:** reaching your shoulders ▪ She has *shoulder-length* hair.

shoulder strap *noun, pl* **~ straps** [*count*] **:** a strap that is used to carry or hold something on your shoulder or to hold up a piece of clothing

shouldn't /ˈʃʊdnt/ — used as a contraction of *should not* ▪ You *shouldn't* do that.

should've /ˈʃʊdəv/ — used as a contraction of *should have* ▪ I *should've* known that she would come. ▪ He *should've* been ready to go.

[1]shout /ˈʃaʊt/ *verb* **shouts; shout·ed; shout·ing**
1 : to say (something) very loudly [+ *obj*] Protesters *shouted* [=*screamed, yelled*] insults as city officials passed by. ▪ Someone was *shouting* "Fire!" — often + *out* ▪ The general *shouted out* orders to his men. [*no obj*] There's no need to *shout* at me.
2 [*no obj*] **:** to make a sudden, loud cry ▪ They *shouted* [=*screamed*] with delight. — often + *out* ▪ He *shouted out* in pain when the doctor moved his broken ankle.
shout down [*phrasal verb*] ***shout (someone) down*** **:** to shout so that (someone who is speaking) cannot be heard ▪ The crowd *shouted* him *down* when he tried to give his speech. [=the crowd stopped him from giving his speech by shouting]
shout your head off see [1]HEAD
shout yourself hoarse **:** to make your voice hoarse by shouting ▪ He *shouted himself hoarse* at the game.

[2]shout *noun, pl* **shouts**
1 [*count*] **:** a sudden, loud cry — often + *of* ▪ She gave a *shout of* surprise.
2 [*singular*] *Brit, informal* **:** a person's turn to buy drinks ▪ It's your *shout*.
be in with a shout *Brit, informal* **:** to have a good chance of winning or achieving something ▪ We aren't too far behind, so we're still *in with a shout*.
give (someone) a shout *informal* **:** to tell (someone) about something when it happens or is ready to be done ▪ I'll *give you a shout* when it's time to leave.

shouting distance *noun* [*noncount*] *informal* **:** a short distance ▪ We live ***within shouting distance*** of my parents.

shouting match *noun, pl* **~ matches** [*count*] **:** a loud, angry argument in which people shout at each other ▪ He got into a *shouting match* with his neighbor.

shout–out /ˈʃaʊtˌaʊt/ *noun, pl* **-outs** [*count*] *US, informal* **:** an expression of greeting or praise that is given to someone in the presence of many people — usually singular ▪ I would like to ***give a shout-out*** to all the men and women in our armed forces. ▪ During his awards speech, the director *gave a shout-out* to his production crew.

[1]shove /ˈʃʌv/ *verb* **shoves; shoved; shov·ing**
1 [+ *obj*] **:** to push (something) with force ▪ He *shoved* the door until it finally opened.
2 : to push (someone or something) along or away in a rough or careless way [+ *obj*] A large man *shoved* me out of the way. ▪ She *shoved* her plate aside. ▪ He *shoved* me into the pool. [*no obj*] A group of security guards *shoved* through the crowd. ▪ The children were ***pushing and shoving*** to see the clowns.
shove it *US, informal + impolite* — used to say that you will not accept or do something ▪ They can take their suggestion and *shove it*.
shove off [*phrasal verb*] *informal* **:** to leave a place ▪ It's getting late, so I guess I should *shove off*. ▪ She angrily told him to *shove off*.
shove over *or chiefly Brit* ***shove up*** [*phrasal verb*] *informal* **:** to move over to make room for someone else ▪ *Shove over* [=*push over*] so that I can sit down, too.
shove (something) down someone's throat see THROAT

[2]shove *noun, pl* **shoves** [*count*] **:** a strong, forceful push ▪ He gave the door a *shove*, and it opened.
push comes to shove see [2]PUSH

[1]shov·el /ˈʃʌvəl/ *noun, pl* **-els** [*count*]
1 : a tool with a long handle that is used for lifting and throwing dirt, sand, snow, etc.
2 : the part of a machine (such as a backhoe) that picks up and moves dirt, sand, snow, etc. — see also STEAM SHOVEL

[2]shovel *verb* **-els;** *US* **-eled** *or Brit* **-elled;** *US* **-el·ing** *or Brit* **-el·ling**
1 [+ *obj*] **:** to lift and throw (dirt, sand, snow, etc.) with a shovel ▪ He is outside *shoveling* snow.
2 *US* **a :** to remove snow from (a sidewalk, driveway, etc.) with a shovel [+ *obj*] I have to *shovel* the driveway. [*no obj*] I had to *shovel* for an hour to clear the driveway. **b** [+ *obj*] **:** to create (a path) by removing snow with a shovel ▪ The snow was so deep we had to *shovel* a path to our front door.
3 [+ *obj*] *informal* **:** to put large amounts of (something, such as food) into something in a quick way ▪ Stop *shoveling* food into your mouth.

shov·el·ful /ˈʃʌvəlˌfʊl/ *noun, pl* **shov·el·fuls** /ˈʃʌvəlˌfʊlz/ *also* **shov·els·ful** /ˈʃʌvəlzˌfʊl/ [*count*] **:** the amount that a shovel will hold ▪ a *shovelful* of snow

shovel pass *noun, pl* **~ passes** [*count*] *American football* **:** a short pass made by throwing the ball underhand or with a sidearm motion

[1]show /ˈʃoʊ/ *verb* **shows; showed** /ˈʃoʊd/; **shown** /ˈʃoʊn/ *or* **showed; show·ing**
1 [+ *obj*] **:** to cause or allow (something) to be seen ▪ He *showed* her a picture. = He *showed* a picture to her. ▪ You have to *show* your tickets/passports at the gate. ▪ You're the only person that I've *shown* this letter to. ▪ Give them a chance to *show* (you) what they can do.
2 [+ *obj*] **:** to give information that proves (something) ▪ The study/research *shows* (that there is) a link between cigarettes and lung cancer. ▪ The medication has been *shown* [=*proven*] to reduce high blood pressure. ▪ They *showed* the theory to be faulty. ▪ He seemed perfectly healthy before he had his heart attack. That just ***goes to show*** [=*shows, proves*] that appearances can be deceptive.
3 [+ *obj*] **:** to teach (someone) how to do or use something especially by letting that person see you do or use it ▪ You will

have to *show* me how to play the game. • He *showed* them a card trick. • Definitions tell you the meanings of words; examples *show* you how the words are used.
4 [+ *obj*] : to tell (someone) what or where something is by touching or pointing to it • *Show* me which video game you want to play. • She *showed* me where Laos was on the globe. • *Show* me where it hurts. • The guide *showed* us the church. [=pointed to the different parts of the church and told us about them]
5 *always followed by an adverb or preposition* [+ *obj*] : to lead (someone) to a place • He *showed* us to our seats. • Please ***show him in/out.*** [=lead him to the entrance/exit] • She ***showed them the way*** to the door.
6 [+ *obj*] — used to describe what can be seen or noticed when you look at or examine something • Her grades have *shown* some improvement. [=her grades have improved] • The city's education system is ***showing signs of*** improvement. [=the city's education system seems to be improving]
7 [+ *obj*] : to have an image or picture of (someone or something) • The postcard *shows* a sunset on the beach. • The photograph *shows* her as a young woman.
8 : to give (information) in the form of numbers, pictures, etc. [+ *obj*] The thermostat *showed* 68 degrees. • The pie chart *shows* that 20 percent of the money is spent on supplies. [*no obj*] 3:15 *showed* on the clock.
9 a [*no obj*] : to be able to be seen or noticed • The sun *showed* through the clouds. • The scar hardly *shows.* • Pull down your skirt. Your slip is *showing.* [=I can see your slip] • He's been working out a lot, and it *shows.* — sometimes + *up* • The mountains *showed up* clearly against the sky. **b** [+ *obj*] : to cause or allow (something) to be easily seen or noticed • A light-colored carpet will *show* dirt.
10 a [+ *obj*] : to cause or allow (a feeling, quality, or condition) to be seen or known • The expression on his face *showed* how disappointed he was. • She is not afraid of *showing* her true feelings. • *Show* your support by wearing one of these yellow ribbons. • When you say you dislike computers, you're really *showing* your age. **b** [*no obj*] *of a feeling, quality, or condition* : to be able to be seen • His disappointment *showed* in his face.
11 [+ *obj*] : to give (mercy, respect, etc.) to someone • The judge *showed* no mercy. • Students must *show* respect for their teachers. = Students must *show* their teachers respect. • Please *show* some compassion.
12 [+ *obj*] : to cause (someone) to see your true ability, power, etc. • They think I'm too old to run the race, but ***I'll show them***! [=I'll run the race and prove that I'm not too old to do it] • He thinks he can tell me what to do, but I'll ***show him who's boss.***
13 : to make (a movie, television show, piece of art, etc.) available for the public to see [+ *obj*] Some news programs have decided not to *show* [=*air*] the video. • She is *showing* her paintings at an art gallery. [*no obj*] The movie is now *showing* [=*playing*] in local theaters. • She has *shown* at the art gallery several times.
14 [*no obj*] *chiefly US, informal* : to arrive or appear at a place • Many passengers failed to *show.* — usually + *up* • Everyone *showed up* on time. • He didn't *show up* for work today. — see also NO-SHOW
15 : to enter (an animal) in a competition in which it is judged against other animals of the same kind [+ *obj*] He breeds and *shows* poodles. [*no obj*] Two of our dogs will be *showing* in the national competition.
16 — used in phrases like ***have something/nothing to show for*** to say what someone has achieved or produced by doing something • We worked all day but *had nothing to show for* it. [=we worked all day but did not achieve/accomplish anything] • He invested millions of dollars into the company, but he *has little to show for* it. • She *has* two Olympic gold medals *to show for* her years of training and practice. [=she won two Olympic gold medals as a result of her years of training and practice]
show around *also Brit* ***show round*** [*phrasal verb*] ***show (someone) around/round*** : to act as a guide for someone who is visiting a place : to lead (someone) around a place and point to and talk about the interesting or important things you see • She *showed* us *around* (the city).
show off [*phrasal verb*] *informal* **1** *disapproving* : to try to impress someone with your abilities or possessions • The boys were *showing off* in front of the girls. • Stop trying to *show off.* **2** ***show off (someone or something) or show (someone or something) off*** : to cause (someone or something that you are proud of) to be seen or noticed by a lot of people • She *showed* her baby *off* at the office. • He drove around town, *showing off* his new car. **3** ***show off (something) or show (something) off*** : to make (something) very noticeable • She wears tight clothes that *show off* her figure. — see also SHOW-OFF
show (someone) the door, show (someone) to the door see DOOR
show the flag see [1]FLAG
show up [*phrasal verb*] ***show up (someone) or show (someone) up*** *informal* : to embarrass (someone) : to do something that makes (someone) look foolish, weak, etc. • He was deliberately trying to *show up* the boss. — see also [1]SHOW 9a, 14 (above)
show willing *Brit* : to show that you are willing and eager to do what is needed • I got in to work extra early to *show willing* and impress my boss.
show your face : to appear in public and allow people to see you • I don't know how he can stand to *show his face* around here after what happened.
show your hand *also* ***show your cards*** **1** : to put down your playing cards on a table so that their values can be seen **2** : to tell other people what you are planning to do, want to do, or are able to do • The company wants to avoid *showing its hand* about its decision until next month.
show yourself **1** : to move out from a hidden place so that you can be seen • The guard ordered him to *show himself.* **2** : to show that you are a particular kind of person, that you have a particular skill, etc. — followed by *to + verb* • They *showed themselves to be* cowards. [=they behaved in a cowardly way] • She has *shown herself to be* capable of running the company. [=has shown that she is capable of running the company]
show your stuff see [1]STUFF
show your true colors see [1]COLOR

[2]**show** *noun, pl* **shows**
1 [*count*] **a** : a performance in a theater that usually includes singing and dancing • We saw a *show* last night. = We went to a *show* last night. • a Broadway/musical *show* • She was the ***star of the show.*** **b** : a public performance that is intended to entertain people • a one-woman comedy *show* • a puppet *show* • The band always ***puts on a good show.*** — sometimes used figuratively • The team *put on a poor show* [=played poorly] in the second half. — see also FLOOR SHOW, HORROR SHOW, ICE SHOW, PEEP SHOW, PUNCH-AND-JUDY SHOW, ROAD SHOW, SIDESHOW
2 [*count*] : a television or radio program • my favorite (TV) *show* — see also GAME SHOW, QUIZ SHOW, TALK SHOW
3 [*count*] : an event at which things of the same kind are put on display for people to look at or buy • an agricultural *show* • fashion/auto/boat *shows* • a *show* of his early paintings — see also TRADE SHOW
4 [*singular*] **a** : an action, performance, etc., which clearly shows an ability, feeling, quality, etc. — usually + *of* • a *show of* the country's great military strength • a remarkable *show of* generosity • All of the students signed the petition in a *show of* unity/solidarity with their classmate. **b** : an event at which something is done or shown to impress or entertain people — usually + *of* • a spectacular *show of* fireworks
5 *disapproving* : an act of pretending to feel a particular way : an act of behaving a certain way in order to make others like or approve of you [*count*] — usually singular; usually + *of* • He made a great *show of* friendship. • She put on a big *show of* sympathy, but she really didn't care about his troubles. [*noncount*] Her friendliness is ***all show.*** [=she does not truly have friendly feelings toward others]
6 [*singular*] : an event, business, etc., and all of the activities that are involved in its success • The new president tried to ***run the whole show*** [=be in charge of everything] himself. • A new manager is *running the show.*
7 [*count*] : a competition at which animals of the same kind are judged against one another • a dog *show* • They have two ***show dogs.*** [=dogs that compete in dog shows] — see also HORSE SHOW
a show of hands : an occurrence in which people put a hand in the air to indicate that they want something, agree with something, etc. • Let me see *a show of hands*: how many people want a piece of cake?
dog and pony show see [1]DOG
for show **1** : intended to be seen but not used or bought • We're not supposed to eat the fruit on the table. It's just *for show.* [=it's just being used as decoration] **2** : done in order to make others like or approve of you • He says he en-

joys classical music, but it's only *for show*. [=he pretends to like classical music]

get the/this show on the road *informal* : to begin an activity or journey • Everyone ready? OK, let's *get this show on the road*!

on show : put somewhere for people to see • Her paintings are *on show* [=*on display*] at the art gallery. • The artifacts will be ***put on show*** in the museum. • His work ***goes on show*** tomorrow.

the show must go on *informal* — used to say that a performance, event, etc., must continue even though there are problems

show–and–tell /ˈʃowənˈtɛl/ *noun* [*noncount*] : a school activity in which children show an item to the class and talk about it • She brought in a seashell for *show-and-tell*.

show•biz /ˈʃoʊˌbɪz/ *noun* [*noncount*] *informal* : SHOW BUSINESS • Sometimes the critics love you and sometimes they hate you. That's *showbiz*.

¹show•boat /ˈʃoʊˌboʊt/ *noun, pl* **-boats** [*count*]
1 : a large boat that has a theater and a group of performers and that gives plays at towns and cities along a river
2 *chiefly US, informal + usually disapproving* : a person (such as an athlete) who behaves or performs in a way that is meant to attract the attention of a lot of people • The fans like him, but the other players think he's a *showboat*.

²showboat *verb* **-boats; -boat•ed; -boat•ing** [*no obj*] *chiefly US, informal + usually disapproving* : to behave or perform in a way that is meant to attract the attention of a lot of people • She was *showboating* for the cameras when she tripped and fell.

show business *noun* [*noncount*] : the entertainment industry involved in making movies, television shows, plays, etc. • She has been in *show business* for over 30 years. • actors trying to break into *show business* • *show business* executives

¹show•case /ˈʃoʊˌkeɪs/ *noun, pl* **-cas•es** [*count*]
1 : a box that has a glass top or sides and that is used for displaying objects in a store, museum, etc.
2 : an event, occasion, etc., that shows the abilities or good qualities of someone or something in an attractive or favorable way • The convention was a *showcase* of the company's new products. — usually *+ for* • The program is a *showcase for* up-and-coming musicians. • The movie is a *showcase for* her talents.

²showcase *verb* **-cases; -cased; -cas•ing** [*+ obj*] : to show (something or someone) in an attractive or favorable way • The program *showcases* up-and-coming musicians.

show•down /ˈʃoʊˌdaʊn/ *noun, pl* **-downs** [*count*]
1 : a meeting, argument, fight, etc., that will finally settle a disagreement between people or groups — often *+ with* • Supporters of the bill are in a *showdown with* the opposition.
2 : an important game or competition — often *+ with* • The team is getting ready for tonight's *showdown with* last year's champions.

¹show•er /ˈʃawɚ/ *noun, pl* **-ers** [*count*]
1 a : a device that produces a spray of water for you to stand under and wash your body **b** : a room or an enclosed area in a room that contains a shower • My hotel room had a *shower* but no bathtub. • a *shower* curtain/stall • I couldn't answer the phone because I was ***in the shower***. • The team ***hit the showers*** after practice. [=the team went to the locker room and used the *showers* there after practice] — see picture at BATHROOM **c** : the act of washing your body with a shower • She ***took a shower*** after her run. = (*Brit*) She ***had a shower*** after her run. • a ***shower cap*** [=a cap that you wear while you are taking a shower]
2 a : a brief fall of rain or snow over a small area • Light/Heavy *showers* are expected later today. — see also THUNDERSHOWER **b** : a large number of small things that fall or happen at the same time — often *+ of* • a *shower of* sparks/tears • He gave the baby a *shower of* kisses. [=he showered the baby with kisses]
3 *US* : a party where gifts are given to a woman who is going to be married or have a baby • a bridal/baby *shower*

²shower *verb* **-ers; -ered; -er•ing**
1 [*no obj*] : to wash yourself by using a shower • Please *shower* before using the pool.
2 : to fall on someone or something in the way that rain falls from the sky [*no obj*] Sparks from the machine *showered* onto the floor of the garage. • Rice *showered* down on the newlyweds as they left the church. [*+ obj*] A passing car *showered* her with muddy water. = A passing car *showered* muddy water on her.
3 [*+ obj*] : to provide (someone) with something in large amounts • He *showered* her with gifts/kisses. = He *showered* gifts/kisses on her. [=he gave her many gifts/kisses]

show•er•head /ˈʃawɚˌhɛd/ *noun, pl* **-heads** [*count*] : the device that controls the spray of water in a shower — see picture at BATHROOM

show•ery /ˈʃawəri/ *adj* [*more* ~; *most* ~] : having a lot of rain showers • Weve been having *showery* weather lately. • It may be *showery* [=*rainy*] tomorrow.

show•girl /ˈʃoʊˌgɚl/ *noun, pl* **-girls** [*count*] : a woman who sings or dances in a musical show

showing *noun, pl* **-ings** [*count*]
1 : the act of making a movie, television show, piece of art, etc., available for the public to see • The movie's last *showing* tonight is at 10:30.
2 : a performance or appearance of a particular kind — usually singular • He had a poor *showing* [=he performed poorly] in the tournament. • Both candidates are expected to make a good/strong *showing* [=to get many votes] in next week's election.

show jumping *noun* [*noncount*] : the sport of riding a horse over a set of fences as quickly and skillfully as possible

show•man /ˈʃoʊmən/ *noun, pl* **-men** /-mən/ [*count*] : a person who is good at entertaining people

show•man•ship /ˈʃoʊmənˌʃɪp/ *noun* [*noncount*] : the ability to attract attention and entertain people • political *showmanship*

shown *past participle of* ¹SHOW

show–off /ˈʃoʊˌɑːf/ *noun, pl* **-offs** [*count*] *informal + disapproving* : a person who tries to impress other people with his or her abilities or possessions — see also *show off* at ¹SHOW

show•piece /ˈʃoʊˌpiːs/ *noun, pl* **-piec•es** [*count*]
1 : something that is the best or most attractive thing being shown • The museum's *showpiece* is a painting by Picasso.
2 : something that is seen as an excellent or outstanding example of something • The house is an architectural *showpiece*.

show•place /ˈʃoʊˌpleɪs/ *noun, pl* **-plac•es** [*count*] : a beautiful or important place that people enjoy seeing • They have transformed their home into a *showplace*.

show•room /ˈʃoʊˌruːm/ *noun, pl* **-rooms** [*count*] : a large room where things that are for sale are displayed • a car *showroom* • The stereo was a *showroom* model.

show•stop•per /ˈʃoʊˌstɑːpɚ/ *noun, pl* **-pers** [*count*] : an act, song, or performer that receives so much applause that the performance is interrupted
– **show•stop•ping** /ˈʃoʊˌstɑːpɪŋ/ *adj, usually used before a noun* • a *showstopping* performance

show•time /ˈʃoʊˌtaɪm/ *noun* [*noncount*] : the time when a play, movie, etc., begins • We have five minutes until *showtime*. • *Showtime* is in five minutes. — often used figuratively in U.S. English • We've been making plans for months. Now it's *showtime*.

show trial *noun, pl* ~ **trials** [*count*] : a trial in a court of law in which the verdict has been decided in advance • They were forced to confess their guilt in public *show trials*.

show window *noun, pl* ~ **-dows** [*count*] : a large window in the front of a store that is used for displaying goods that are for sale

showy /ˈʃowi/ *adj* **show•i•er; -est** [*also more* ~; *most* ~] : having an appearance that attracts attention • *showy* blossoms • Perhaps you should wear something a little less *showy*. • (*disapproving*) *showy* [=*gaudy*] jewelry

shrank *past tense of* ¹SHRINK

shrap•nel /ˈʃræpnəl/ *noun* [*noncount*] : small metal pieces that scatter outwards from an exploding bomb, shell, or mine • He has a piece of *shrapnel* in his leg. • *Shrapnel* from the explosion wounded many people.

¹shred /ˈʃrɛd/ *noun, pl* **shreds**
1 [*count*] : a long, thin piece cut or torn off of something • The cats tore/ripped the curtain ***to shreds***. [=into many long, thin pieces] • The wallpaper is ***in shreds***. — often *+ of* • *shreds of* paper/cloth
2 ***shreds*** [*plural*] : a completely ruined condition • An air attack tore the village ***to shreds***. [=completely destroyed the village] • His reputation was ***in shreds*** after the arrest. • Critics ***picked/pulled/tore/ripped the movie to shreds***. [=criticized the movie very severely]
3 [*singular*] : a very small amount *of* something • He struggled to retain a *shred of* his dignity. — usually used in negative statements • There's not a *shred of* evidence showing that

S

he committed the crime. • She made the accusation without a *shred of* proof.

[2]**shred** *verb* **shreds; shred·ded; shred·ding** [+ *obj*] : to cut or tear (something) into long, thin pieces • He *shredded* the paper/cloth. • *Shred* the cabbage and add it to the salad. • He *shredded* the documents. [=he put the documents into a shredder to cut them into pieces]

shredded wheat *noun* [*noncount*] : a breakfast cereal that is made from cooked wheat that is shredded and formed into biscuits

shred·der /ˈʃrɛdɚ/ *noun, pl* **-ders** [*count*] : a machine used for cutting something (such as paper) into long, thin pieces • a document *shredder* — see picture at OFFICE

shrew /ˈʃruː/ *noun, pl* **shrews** [*count*]
1 : a small animal that looks like a mouse with a long, pointed nose
2 *old-fashioned* : an unpleasant, bad-tempered woman

shrewd /ˈʃruːd/ *adj* **shrewd·er; -est** [*also more* ~; *most* ~] : having or showing an ability to understand things and to make good judgments : mentally sharp or clever • a *shrewd* observer/businessman • She's *shrewd* about her investments. • a *shrewd* observation
— **shrewd·ly** *adv* — **shrewd·ness** *noun* [*noncount*]

shrew·ish /ˈʃruːwɪʃ/ *adj, old-fashioned, of a woman* : unpleasant and bad-tempered • a *shrewish* old hag

[1]**shriek** /ˈʃriːk/ *verb* **shrieks; shrieked; shriek·ing**
1 [*no obj*] : to make a loud, high-pitched cry • The birds were *shrieking* in the trees. • The baby *shrieked* [=*screamed*] with delight. • She *shrieked* when she saw a mouse.
2 [+ *obj*] : to say (something) in a loud, high-pitched voice • "Mommy!" she *shrieked*.

[2]**shriek** *noun, pl* **shrieks** [*count*] : a loud, high-pitched cry or sound • The baby gave a *shriek* [=*scream*] of delight. • the *shriek* of the train's brakes

shrift /ˈʃrɪft/ see SHORT SHRIFT

[1]**shrill** /ˈʃrɪl/ *adj* **shrill·er; -est** [*also more* ~; *most* ~]
1 : having a very loud, high-pitched sound • a *shrill* whistle/scream
2 : loud and difficult to ignore but often unreasonable • *shrill* protests/accusations
— **shrill·ness** *noun* [*noncount*] — **shril·ly** *adv* • He whistled *shrilly*.

[2]**shrill** *verb* **shrills; shrilled; shrill·ing**
1 [*no obj*] : to make a very loud, high-pitched sound • The bell *shrilled*.
2 [+ *obj*] : to say (something) in a very loud, high-pitched voice • "What!?" she *shrilled*.

shrimp /ˈʃrɪmp/ *noun, pl* **shrimp** *or* **shrimps** [*count*]
1 : a small shellfish that has a long body and legs and that is eaten as food — see color picture on page C8; compare PRAWN
2 *informal* : a very small or unimportant person • He's a little *shrimp* of a boy.

shrimp·ing *noun* [*noncount*] : the activity or business of catching shrimp

shrine /ˈʃraɪn/ *noun, pl* **shrines** [*count*]
1 : a place connected with a holy person or event where people go to worship • a Buddhist *shrine* • the *shrine* of Saint Mary • They erected a *shrine* to the saint.
2 : a place that people visit because it is connected with someone or something that is important to them • tourists visiting the *shrines* of American independence • The writer's house has become a *shrine* to/for his fans.

S

[1]**shrink** /ˈʃrɪŋk/ *verb* **shrinks; shrank** /ˈʃræŋk/ *or* **shrunk** /ˈʃrʌŋk/; **shrunk** *or* **shrunk·en** /ˈʃrʌŋkən/; **shrink·ing**
1 a [*no obj*] : to become smaller in amount, size, or value • The sweater *shrank* when it was washed. • Meat *shrinks* as it cooks. • The town's population *shrank* during the war. **b** [+ *obj*] : to make (something) smaller in amount, size, or value • Hot water *shrank* the sweater. • The treatment should *shrink* the tumor.
2 *always followed by an adverb or preposition* [*no obj*] : to quickly move away from something shocking, frightening, or disgusting • He *shrank* in horror when he saw the dead cat.
shrink from [*phrasal verb*] ***shrink from (something)*** : to try to avoid (something difficult or unpleasant) : to be unwilling to do (something) • He doesn't *shrink from* telling the truth, no matter how painful it may be. • She won't *shrink from* the task.

[2]**shrink** *noun, pl* **shrinks** [*count*] *informal* : a psychiatrist or psychologist • He is seeing a *shrink*.

shrink·age /ˈʃrɪŋkɪʤ/ *noun* [*noncount*]
1 : the amount by which something becomes smaller or less • The *shrinkage* in contributions is significant. • a *shrinkage* of 10 percent
2 : the act or process of becoming smaller in amount, size, or value • the *shrinkage* of the polar ice caps

shrinking violet *noun, pl* ~ **-lets** [*count*] *informal* : a person who is very shy • He's no *shrinking violet* when it comes to competition.

shrink–wrap /ˈʃrɪŋkˌræp/ *noun* [*noncount*] : tough, clear, thin plastic that is placed around a product (such as a book or a package of food) and shrunk in order to wrap it tightly
— **shrink–wrapped** /ˈʃrɪŋkˌræpt/ *adj* • a *shrink-wrapped* book

shriv·el /ˈʃrɪvəl/ *verb* **-els;** *US* **-eled** *or Brit* **-elled;** *US* **-el·ing** *or Brit* **-el·ling**
1 [*no obj*] : to become dry and wrinkled from heat, cold, or old age • plants *shriveling* in the heat — often + *up* • The leaves *shriveled up* in the hot sun.
2 [+ *obj*] : to cause (something) to become dry and wrinkled — often + *up* • The heat *shriveled up* the plant's leaves.
— **shriveled** *adj* • She was small and *shriveled* with age. • a *shriveled* grape

[1]**shroud** /ˈʃraʊd/ *noun, pl* **shrouds** [*count*]
1 : a cloth that is used to wrap a dead body
2 *literary* : something that covers or hides something — usually + *of* • covered in a *shroud of* secrecy/fog

[2]**shroud** *verb* **shrouds; shroud·ed; shroud·ing** [+ *obj*] *literary* : to cover or hide (something) • Fog *shrouded* the land. • The mountains were ***shrouded in*** fog. • Their work is *shrouded in* secrecy.

Shrove Tuesday /ˈʃroʊv-/ *noun* [*noncount*] : the day before the first day of the Christian holy period of Lent : the Tuesday before Ash Wednesday — called also (*US*) *Fat Tuesday*, (*Brit*) *Pancake Day*; compare MARDI GRAS

shrub /ˈʃrʌb/ *noun, pl* **shrubs** [*count*] : a plant that has stems of wood and is smaller than a tree : BUSH — see color picture on page C6

shrub·bery /ˈʃrʌbəri/ *noun, pl* **-ber·ies**
1 [*noncount*] : a group of shrubs planted together • a patch of tangled *shrubbery*
2 [*count*] : an area planted with shrubs • a large *shrubbery*

shrug /ˈʃrʌg/ *verb* **shrugs; shrugged; shrug·ging** : to raise and lower your shoulders usually to show that you do not know or care about something [*no obj*] I asked if he wanted to go out to dinner, and he just *shrugged*. [+ *obj*] He just ***shrugged his shoulders***.
shrug off [*phrasal verb*] ***shrug off (something)*** *or* ***shrug (something) off*** **1** : to think of or treat (something) as not important : to pay no attention to (something) • She *shrugged off* their concerns. • I warned him about the storm but he just *shrugged* it *off*. **2** : to take off (a piece of clothing) by moving your shoulders back and forth • She *shrugged off* her coat.
— **shrug** *noun, pl* **shrugs** [*count*] • The suggestion was met with nothing but *shrugs*. • She answered me with a *shrug* of the/her shoulders.

shrunk *past tense and past participle of* [1]SHRINK

shrunk·en /ˈʃrʌŋkən/ *adj* : made smaller or shorter • a *shrunken* old man [=a man who has gotten smaller/shorter in old age]

shtick *also* **schtick** /ˈʃtɪk/ *noun, pl* **shticks** *also* **schticks** [*count*] *US, informal*
1 : a usual way of performing, behaving, speaking, etc. • That joke is part of his *shtick*.
2 : something that a person likes to do or does well • Sports are just not my *shtick*.

[1]**shuck** /ˈʃʌk/ *noun, pl* **shucks** [*count*] *US*
1 : the outer covering of a nut or a plant (such as corn)
2 : the shell of an oyster or clam

[2]**shuck** *verb* **shucks; shucked; shuck·ing** [+ *obj*] *US* : to remove the outer covering of (a plant, such as corn) or the shell of (an oyster or clam) • *shuck* the corn/oysters
shuck off [*phrasal verb*] ***shuck off (something)*** *informal* : to remove and throw aside (something) • He *shucked off* his coat.

shucks /ˈʃʌks/ *interj, US, old-fashioned* — used to show that you are disappointed or embarrassed • Oh, *shucks*, I completely forgot.

shud·der /ˈʃʌdɚ/ *verb* **-ders; -dered; -der·ing** [*no obj*]
1 *of a person* : to shake because of fear, cold, etc. — often + *with* • He *shuddered* [=*quivered, trembled*] *with* fear when he

heard the scream. — often used figuratively ▪ I *shudder* at the thought of what might happen. = ***I shudder to think*** (of) what might happen. [=I am very worried/fearful about what might happen]

2 *of a thing* **:** to shake violently ▪ The old car *shuddered* to a halt. ▪ The house *shuddered* as a plane flew overhead.

– shudder *noun, pl* **-ders** [*count*] ▪ I felt a *shudder* [=*tremble*] in the floor as the truck drove by. ▪ a *shudder* of fear

¹shuf·fle /ˈʃʌfəl/ *verb* **shuf·fles; shuf·fled; shuf·fling**

1 : to slide your feet along the ground or back and forth without lifting them completely [*no obj*] He *shuffled* across the floor. [*+ obj*] She stood there, *shuffling* her feet, waiting for the bus to arrive.

2 a [*+ obj*] **:** to move things or people into a different order or into different positions ▪ She *shuffled* the papers on her desk. ▪ The manager *shuffled* the batting order. **b :** to mix (playing cards) before playing a game so that no one knows what order they are in [*+ obj*] He *shuffled* the cards/deck. [*no obj*] Whose turn is it to *shuffle* and deal?

²shuffle *noun, pl* **shuffles**

1 [*singular*] **:** the act of moving by sliding your feet without lifting them off the ground ▪ We heard the *shuffle* of feet outside the door.

2 [*count*] **:** the act of mixing the order of playing cards **:** the act of shuffling cards ▪ He gave the cards a good *shuffle* and then dealt. ▪ Whose *shuffle* is it? [=whose turn is it to shuffle?]

lost in the shuffle *US* **:** not noticed or given attention because there are many other people or things to consider or deal with ▪ With six older kids, the baby sometimes is/gets *lost in the shuffle*.

shuf·fle·board /ˈʃʌfəlˌboɚd/ *noun* [*noncount*] **:** a game in which players use a long stick with a curved piece at one end to slide discs into scoring areas that are marked on the ground

shun /ˈʃʌn/ *verb* **shuns; shunned; shun·ning** [*+ obj*] **:** to avoid (someone or something) ▪ He *shuns* parties and social events. ▪ After his divorce he found himself being *shunned* by many of his former friends.

shunt /ˈʃʌnt/ *verb* **shunts; shunt·ed; shunt·ing** [*+ obj*]

1 : to move (someone or something) to a different and usually less important or noticeable place or position ▪ The company *shunted* him (off) to the mail room. — often used figuratively ▪ Her suggestions were *shunted aside*. [=*ignored*]

2 : to move (a train or railway car) from one track to another

¹shush /ˈʃʌʃ, ˈʃʊʃ/ *verb* **shush·es; shushed; shush·ing** [*+ obj*] **:** to tell (someone) to be quiet ▪ The librarian *shushed* the noisy children.

²shush *interj* — used to tell someone to be quiet ▪ *Shush*! I can't hear the movie.

¹shut /ˈʃʌt/ *verb* **shuts; shut; shut·ting**

1 a [*+ obj*] **:** to close (something) ▪ Please *shut* the door/window/lid/drawer. ▪ He *shut* his eyes and went to sleep. ▪ She *shut* the book loudly. ▪ I accidentally *shut* the door on her fingers. **b** [*no obj*] **:** to become closed ▪ flowers that *shut* at night ▪ The door *shut* slowly behind me.

2 : to stop the services or activities of (a business, school, etc.) for a period of time or forever **:** CLOSE [*+ obj*] The owner is *shutting* the pub for the weekend. ▪ They plan to *shut* the factory by the end of the year. [*no obj*] (*Brit*) The restaurant *shuts* [=*closes*] at 11.

shut away [*phrasal verb*] ***shut (someone or something) away*** **:** to put (someone or something) in a place that is separate from others ▪ She was *shut away* in prison for three years. ▪ He *shut* himself *away* (in his room) to study.

shut down [*phrasal verb*] **1** ***shut down or shut down (something) or shut (something) down*** **a :** to close or to cause (a business, factory, etc.) to close for a period of time or forever ▪ They were forced to *shut down* the store. ▪ The factory *shut down*. ▪ The vendors started *shutting down* for the night. **b :** to stop operating or to cause (a machine) to stop operating ▪ The computer suddenly *shut down*. [=*turned off*] ▪ She *shut down* her computer and went home. — see also SHUTDOWN **2** ***shut down (someone or something) or shut (someone or something) down informal*** **:** to cause (an opponent) to be unsuccessful, unable to score, etc. ▪ The defense *shut down* the opposition.

shut in [*phrasal verb*] **1** ***shut (someone or something) in (something)*** **:** to put (someone or something) in a room and close or lock the door ▪ Someone *shut* the cat *in* the closet. ▪ He *shut* himself *in* his room to study. **2** ***shut (something) in (something)*** **:** to have (something, such as your hand or finger) in between the parts of (something, such as a door or window) when it closes ▪ He accidentally *shut* his hand *in* the car door.

shut off [*phrasal verb*] **1** ***shut off or shut off (something) or shut (something) off*** **:** to stop operating or to cause (a machine, light, etc.) to stop operating ▪ The camera *shuts off* [=*turns off*] automatically when not in use. ▪ She *shut off* the car. ▪ Who *shut off* the lights? ▪ *Shut* the television *off* and go to bed. **2** ***shut off (something) or shut (something) off*** **:** to stop the flow or supply of (something) ▪ Make sure to *shut off* the water/gas/electricity before beginning any work. **3** ***shut (yourself) off*** **:** to keep (yourself) in a place that is away from other people — usually *+ from* ▪ He *shut* himself *off from* his family. **4** ***shut (someone or something) off from (something)*** **:** to separate (someone or something) from (something) — usually used as *(be) shut off from* ▪ Here on the island, people *are shut off from* (contact with) the outside world.

shut out [*phrasal verb*] **1** ***shut out (someone or something) or shut (someone or something) out*** **:** to stop (someone or something) from entering a place ▪ She locked the door and *shut* him *out* of the room. ▪ He closed the curtain to *shut out* the sunlight. ▪ Try *shutting out* the draft by putting a blanket at the bottom of the door. — often used figuratively ▪ He tried to *shut out* the memory of that day. = He tried to *shut* the memory *out* of his mind. **2** ***shut out (someone) or shut (someone) out*** **:** to not allow (someone) to be involved in your life, to know your personal thoughts and feelings, etc. ▪ I can't help you if you keep *shutting* me *out*. — often *+ of* ▪ She *shut* him *out of* her life completely. **3** ***shut out (someone) or shut (someone) out chiefly US*** **:** to keep (a player or team) from scoring in a game or contest ▪ The team was *shut out* [=the team did not score any points] in the first half. — see also SHUTOUT

shut up [*phrasal verb*] **1** *informal* **a :** to stop talking, laughing, etc. ▪ He won't *shut up* about how he won the game. ▪ Can someone get that dog to *shut up*? — often used as a rude way to tell someone to stop talking ▪ *Shut up* for a second and listen to what I have to say. **b** ***shut (someone) up informal*** **:** to cause (someone) to stop talking, laughing, etc. ▪ Nothing *shuts* her *up*. **2** ***shut up (something) or shut (something) up*** **:** to close and lock all the doors of (a house, store, etc.) ▪ They *shut up* the house and left town. ✧ In British English, to ***shut up shop*** is to go out of business forever or stop performing all services or activities for a period of time. ▪ Rather than *shutting up shop* [=*closing up shop*] entirely, the company laid off half of its workers. ▪ The store has already *shut up shop* for the day. **3** ***shut (someone or something) up*** **:** to put (someone or something) in a place that is away from other people ▪ He *shut* himself *up* in his room all day to study.

shut your mouth or shut your face informal — used to tell someone in a rude way to stop talking ▪ She angrily told him to *shut his mouth*. ✧ This phrase is also used with other informal words for ***mouth***, such as ***yap, trap*** and ***gob***.

²shut *adj*

1 : not open **:** CLOSED ▪ She listened to the music with her eyes *shut*. ▪ The door slammed *shut*. ▪ Check to make sure that all the windows are *shut*. — see also OPEN-AND-SHUT

2 *Brit* **:** not operating or open to the public ▪ The store is *shut* [=*closed*] for remodeling.

keep your mouth shut see ¹MOUTH

with your eyes shut see ¹EYE

shut·down /ˈʃʌtˌdaʊn/ *noun, pl* **-downs** [*count*] **:** the act of stopping the operation or activity of a business, machine, etc., for a period of time or forever ▪ the *shutdown* of the factory ▪ a maintenance *shutdown* — see also *shut down* at ¹SHUT

shut–eye /ˈʃʌtˌaɪ/ *noun* [*noncount*] *informal* **:** SLEEP ▪ You'd better get some *shut-eye*.

shut–in /ˈʃʌtˌɪn/ *noun, pl* **-ins** [*count*] *US* **:** a sick or disabled person who rarely or never leaves home ▪ a service that delivers food to elderly *shut-ins*

shut·out /ˈʃʌtˌaʊt/ *noun, pl* **-outs** [*count*] *US* **:** a game or contest in which one side does not score ▪ They beat us in a 9–0 *shutout*. ▪ He pitched a *shutout*. — see also *shut out* at ¹SHUT

¹shut·ter /ˈʃʌtɚ/ *noun, pl* **-ters** [*count*]

1 : one of a pair of outside covers for a window that open and close like a door — usually plural ▪ She opened the *shutters*. — see picture at HOUSE

S

2 : the part of a camera that opens to allow light in when a picture is taken

²shutter *verb* **-ters; -tered; -ter·ing** [+ *obj*] *US*
1 : to cover (a window) with shutters • They locked the doors and *shuttered* the windows.
2 : to close (a business, store, etc.) for a period of time or forever • They declared bankruptcy and *shuttered* the store.

shut·ter·bug /ˈʃʌtɚˌbʌg/ *noun, pl* **-bugs** [*count*] *US, informal* : a person who enjoys taking photographs

shuttered *adj*
1 : having shutters or having closed shutters • *shuttered* windows • He kept the house *shuttered*.
2 *chiefly US* : closed for business for a period of time or forever • old, *shuttered* factories

¹shut·tle /ˈʃʌtl/ *noun, pl* **shut·tles** [*count*]
1 : a vehicle that travels back and forth between places • A *shuttle* takes people from the parking lot to the airport. — often used before another noun • a *shuttle* bus/train/service
2 : SPACE SHUTTLE
3 : a pointed tool that is used to weave cloth by pulling a thread from side to side across other threads

²shuttle *verb* **shuttles; shut·tled; shut·tling**
1 *always followed by an adverb or preposition* [*no obj*] : to travel back and forth between places • We *shuttled* between the city and the country all summer.
2 [+ *obj*] : to bring (people) back and forth between places • A bus *shuttled* people from the parking lot to the dock.

shut·tle·cock /ˈʃʌtlˌkɑːk/ *noun, pl* **-cocks** [*count*] : a light object shaped like a cone that is hit over the net in the game of badminton — called also (*US*) *birdie*; see picture at RACKET

shuttle diplomacy *noun* [*noncount*] : activity in which a person travels back and forth between two countries and talks to their leaders in order to bring about agreement, prevent war, etc.

¹shy /ˈʃaɪ/ *adj* **shi·er** *or* **shy·er** /ˈʃajɚ/; **shi·est** *or* **shy·est** /ˈʃajəst/ [*also more ~; most ~*]
1 a : feeling nervous and uncomfortable about meeting and talking to people • a *shy*, quiet girl • I was painfully *shy* as a teenager. • She was too *shy* to ask for help. **b** : showing that you are nervous and uncomfortable about meeting and talking to people • her *shy* manner • He gave her a *shy* smile.
2 : tending to avoid something because of nervousness, fear, dislike, etc. • publicity *shy* • camera *shy* — often + *of* • He was never *shy of* controversy.
3 : hesitant about taking what you want or need • Help yourself if you want more. Don't be *shy*.
4 *of an animal* : easily frightened : TIMID • animals that are nocturnal and *shy*
5 *chiefly US* : having less than a full or expected amount or number : SHORT • We were *shy* about 10 dollars. — usually + *of* • He was two weeks *shy of* his 19th birthday when he joined the army. • The ball stopped just a few inches *shy of* the hole. • He's three credits *shy of* his bachelor's degree.
fight shy of *Brit* : to try to avoid something • She has always *fought shy of* publicity.
once bitten, twice shy see ¹BITE
— **shy·ly** *adv* • He answered/smiled *shyly*. — **shy·ness** *noun* [*noncount*]

²shy *verb* **shies; shied; shy·ing** [*no obj*] : to move away from something because of fear • The horse *shied* when the gun went off.
shy from (*US*) *or* ***shy away from*** [*phrasal verb*] ***shy from (something)*** (*US*) *or* ***shy away from (something)*** : to try to avoid (something) because of nervousness, fear, dislike, etc. • They never *shied from* publicity. • She *shies away from* making any predictions. • He *shied away from* discussing his divorce.

shy·ster /ˈʃaɪstɚ/ *noun, pl* **-sters** [*count*] *chiefly US, informal* : a dishonest person; *especially* : a dishonest lawyer or politician — often used before another noun • a *shyster* lawyer

Si·a·mese cat /ˈsajəˌmiːz-/ *noun, pl* **~ cats** [*count*] : a type of cat that has blue eyes and short light-colored hair on the body with darker-colored ears, paws, tail, and face

Si·a·mese twin /ˈsajəˌmiːz-/ *noun, pl* **~ twins** [*count*] : CONJOINED TWIN

¹sib·i·lant /ˈsɪbələnt/ *adj, formal* : making or having a sound like the letters *s* or *sh* • *sibilant* consonants/whispers • the *sibilant* hiss of a snake

²sibilant *noun, pl* **-lants** [*count*] *technical* : a sibilant sound (such as \s\ or \z\)

sib·ling /ˈsɪblɪŋ/ *noun, pl* **-lings** [*count*] *formal* : a brother or sister • Do you have any *siblings*? [=brothers or sisters] • younger/older *siblings* • *sibling* relationships • There was barely any ***sibling rivalry*** [=competition between brothers and sisters] in our family.

¹sic /ˈsɪk/ *verb* **sics; sicced** /ˈsɪkt/; **sic·cing** [+ *obj*] *US, informal* : to attack (someone or something) — usually used as a command to a dog • *Sic* 'em, boy.
sic (something) on (someone or something) : to order (an animal, such as a dog) to attack (someone or something) • He *sicced* his dog *on* me. — often used figuratively • The company *sicced* their lawyers *on* me.

²sic — used in writing after an error (such as a spelling error) in a quotation to show that the error was made by the speaker or writer who is being quoted and not by you • His letter said the people were "very freindly [*sic*] to me."

¹sick /ˈsɪk/ *adj* **sick·er; -est** [*also more ~; most ~*]
1 : affected with a disease or illness : ILL • He is at home *sick* in bed. • She is *sick* with the flu. • I'm too *sick* to go to work. • a *sick* dog • The medicine just made me *sicker*. • The *sickest* patients are in intensive care. • My poor rosebush looks *sick*. • (*US*) I hardly ever ***get sick***. • (*US*) She has been ***out sick*** all week. = (*Brit*) She has been ***off sick*** all week. [=she has not been at work all week because she is sick] • (*formal*) Dozens of workers ***fell sick*** [=became ill] from exposure to the fumes. • (*old-fashioned*) He ***took sick*** [=became ill] and died. • (*informal*) He was (as) ***sick as a dog***. [=he was very sick] — sometimes used figuratively • a *sick* economy — see also AIRSICK, CARSICK, SEASICK
2 *always used before a noun* : of or relating to people who are ill • She has been on the *sick* list all week. • the hospital's *sick* ward
3 a *not used before a noun, informal* : very annoyed or bored by something because you have had too much of it — + *of* • He was *sick of* her lies. • I'm getting *sick of* this cold weather. • I'm *sick of* pizza—I had it three times this week already. • What are you most *sick of*? • I'm ***sick and tired of*** hearing you two argue. = I'm ***sick to death of*** hearing you two argue. **b** : very disgusted or angry • The way they treat people ***makes me sick***.
4 : not mentally normal or healthy • I know it sounds *sick*, but I like reading about murders. • He has a *sick* [=*perverted*] mind. • *sick* [=*morbid, disturbing*] thoughts
5 : relating to very unpleasant or offensive things • *sick* jokes/humor
6 a : very unpleasant • I had a *sick* feeling that we were hopelessly lost. **b** : powerfully affected by a strong and unpleasant emotion — usually + *with* • She was *sick with* shame/fear/longing/guilt. • We have been ***sick with worry*** about her. = We've been ***worried sick*** [=very worried] about her. — see also HOMESICK, LOVESICK
be sick : to vomit • I *was sick* [=*vomited, threw up*] several times. • The last time I ate oysters, I *was* violently *sick*. [=I vomited a lot] • Stop the car—I'm ***going to be sick***. [=I'm going to throw up]
call/phone in sick ◊ If you *call/phone in sick*, you make a phone call to your place of work to say you will not be working that day because you are sick. • Two of the waiters *called in sick*, so we're very short-staffed.
feel sick **1** *US* : to feel ill • I was *feeling sick*, so I went home early. **2** : to feel like you will vomit • After eating a whole plate of cookies, I *felt sick*. **3** *US* : to feel very upset • I *feel sick* about what happened.
report sick see ²REPORT
sick at heart see HEART
sick to your stomach **1** *US* : caused to vomit • I was *sick to my stomach* [=I vomited] last night. : feeling like you are going to vomit • When I had the flu, just the thought of eating made me *sick to my stomach*. [=*nauseous*] **2** : feeling very disgusted or angry • The way they treat people ***makes me sick to my stomach***.
the sick : people who are sick : sick people • She spent her life caring for *the sick* and dying.

²sick *noun* [*noncount*] *Brit, informal* : VOMIT

³sick *verb* **sicks; sicked; sick·ing**
sick up [*phrasal verb*] ***sick up (something)*** *or* ***sick (something) up*** *Brit, informal* : to vomit (something) • He *sicked up* [=*threw up*] his dinner.

sick bay *noun, pl* **~ bays** [*count*] : a place on a ship that is used to care for sick or injured people

sick·bed /ˈsɪkˌbɛd/ *noun, pl* **-beds** [*count*] : the bed on which a sick person lies • The general gave the orders from his *sickbed.*

sick day *noun, pl* ~ **days** [*count*] : a paid day in which an employee does not work because he or she is sick

sick·en /ˈsɪkən/ *verb* **-ens; -ened; -en·ing**

1 *somewhat formal* : to become sick or to cause (someone) to become sick [*no obj*] Many people *sickened* and died on the long voyage. [+ *obj*] The bacteria in the drinking water *sickened* the whole village.

2 [+ *obj*] : to cause (someone) to feel disgusted or angry • We were *sickened* by the reports of violence.

be sickening for *Brit, informal* : to be starting to have or suffer from (an illness) • I've been sneezing all day. I must *be sickening for* something.

sicken of [*phrasal verb*] ***sicken of (something)*** *US* : to lose interest in (something) because you have had too much of it • He soon *sickened of* [=got sick of] busy city life and moved out to the country.

sick·en·ing /ˈsɪkənɪŋ/ *adj* [*more* ~; *most* ~]

1 : causing you to feel sick • a *sickening* [=*nauseating*] odor/stench • We had reached a *sickening* [=*dizzying*] height.

2 : causing a strong feeling of disgust • a *sickening* display of selfishness • *sickening* cruelty

3 *of a sound* : causing great concern especially because someone or something may have been badly harmed • We heard the squeal of brakes and a *sickening* thud/crash.

– sick·en·ing·ly *adv* • The cake was *sickeningly* sweet. • a *sickeningly* familiar pattern of behavior

sick·ie /ˈsɪki/ *noun, pl* **-ies** [*count*] *informal*

1 *US* : SICKO • He's a real *sickie.*

2 *Brit* : a day when someone who is not really sick claims to be sick and does not go to work • He ***took/pulled/threw a sickie*** to go to the football game.

sick·le /ˈsɪkəl/ *noun, pl* **-les** [*count*] : a tool with a curved metal blade attached to a short handle that is used for cutting grass, grain, etc.

sick leave *noun* [*noncount*]

1 : the number of days per year for which an employer agrees to pay workers who are unable to work because they are sick • employee benefits such as vacation time and *sick leave* • We are allotted three weeks annual *sick leave.* — called also *sick time*

2 : an absence from work because of sickness • He's been on *sick leave* since last Thursday.

sickle–cell anemia (*US*) *or Brit* **sickle–cell anaemia** *noun* [*noncount*] *medical* : a serious disease that affects the red blood cells and occurs mostly in people of African, Mediterranean, or southwest Asian ancestry

sick·ly /ˈsɪkli/ *adj* **sick·li·er; -est** [*also more* ~; *most* ~]

1 a : often affected by a disease or illness : not healthy and strong • a *sickly* child • a *sickly* plant **b** : caused by or relating to sickness • a *sickly* complexion/appetite

2 a : causing a person to feel sick • A *sickly* [=*nauseating*] odor filled the room. **b** : causing feelings of dislike or disgust • The walls were painted a *sickly* yellow.

3 : weak and pale • The lamp gave off a *sickly* glow.

– sickly *adv* • The dessert has a *sickly* sweet taste.

sick·ness /ˈsɪknəs/ *noun, pl* **-ness·es**

1 [*noncount*] : unhealthy condition of body or mind : the state of being sick • She missed work due to *sickness.* [=*illness*]

2 [*count*] : a specific type of disease or illness • He died from an unknown *sickness.* — see also RADIATION SICKNESS, SLEEPING SICKNESS

3 [*noncount*] : the feeling you have in your stomach when you think you are going to vomit • The patient complained of *sickness* [=*nausea*] and stomach pains. — see also MORNING SICKNESS, MOTION SICKNESS, TRAVEL SICKNESS

sickness benefit *noun* [*noncount*] *Brit* : money that is paid by the government to someone who is too sick to work

sicko /ˈsɪkoʊ/ *noun, pl* **sick·os** [*count*] *informal* : a person who does disturbing things that a person who is mentally normal would not do • She was afraid to walk alone for fear some *sicko* might be lurking in the shadows.

sick pay *noun* [*noncount*] : money that is paid by an employer to a person who misses work because of sickness

sick·room /ˈsɪkˌruːm/ *noun, pl* **-rooms** [*count*] : a room in which a sick person stays • We brought father home from the hospital and converted a spare room into a *sickroom.*

sick time *noun* [*noncount*] : SICK LEAVE

[1]side /ˈsaɪd/ *noun, pl* **sides**

1 [*count*] : a place, space, or direction that is away from or beyond the center of something • The army was attacked from all *sides.* • the right-hand *side* of the street • the opposite *side* of the room • Move over. This is my *side* of the bed. — often used with *on* or *to* • You have some dirt *on* the *side* of your face. • The car was hit *on* the driver's *side.* • They live *on* the other *side* of town. • The cabins are *on* the east *side* of the lake. • Guards stood *on* either *side* of the gate. • The army was surrounded *on* every *side.* • He sat *on* the *side* [=*edge*] of the bed. • The statue is leaning *to* the *side.* • The dog tilted its head *to* one *side.* • Pull over *to* the *side* of the road.

2 [*count*] **a** : an outer surface or part of something • The box says, "THIS *SIDE* UP." — often + *of* • the dark *side of* the moon • You should season both *sides of* the steak before you grill it. **b** : one of the surfaces of an object that is not the front, back, top, or bottom — often + *of* • Nutritional information can be found on the *side of* the box. • Red cloth decorated the front and *sides of* the platform. • The *side of* the car was badly dented. **c** : one of the two surfaces of a thin object • Flip the record over and play the other *side.* — often + *of* • She wrote on both *sides of* the paper. • Look on the back *side of* the note.

3 [*count*] : a line that forms part of a geometric shape • A square has four *sides.* : a surface that forms part of a geometric object • A cube has six *sides.*

4 [*count*] : one of the slopes of a hill or mountain — often + *of* • the steep *side of* the hill • They built a house on the *side of* a mountain. — see also HILLSIDE, MOUNTAINSIDE

5 [*count*] **a** : the right or left part of your body • She likes to sleep on her right *side.* : the right or left part of your body from your shoulder to your hip • I have a pain in my left *side.* • We laughed so much that our *sides* hurt. **b** : the place directly to the right or left of someone — usually singular • I stood ***at/by her side*** as she spoke to reporters. • I was standing ***on her left side.*** • She set/put the book ***to the/one side*** and looked out the window. — often used figuratively • His wife ***stood at/by his side*** [=remained loyal to him] throughout the scandal. • Promise me that you will not ***leave my side.*** [=abandon me] — see also BLIND SIDE

6 [*count*] : one of two or more opinions, positions, etc., that disagree with each other • He listened to both *sides* of the argument. • My *side* [=*version*] of the story is different from his. • She has since changed *sides* on that issue. • You are both my friends, so I don't want to ***choose/pick/take sides.*** [=support one person and not the other] • Are you ***on my side*** or his? [=do you support me or him?] • ***Whose side are you on,*** anyway? • People ***on both sides*** of the dispute [=people who support one position and people who support the other position] agree that changes are necessary. — see also ON YOUR SIDE (below)

7 [*count*] : one of the two or more people or groups that are involved in an argument, war, etc. • All *sides* agreed on the treaty. • Each *side* accuses the other of delaying progress.

8 [*count*] **a** : a sports team • There are 11 players on each *side.* • Our *side* won the game. • (*Brit*) a football *side* • We need to ***choose/pick sides*** [=to decide which players will be on each team] before we start playing. **b** *baseball* : the players on a team who bat in an inning — usually singular • The pitcher struck out the *side* [=struck out three batters] in the first inning.

9 a [*count*] : a particular part or feature of something that is opposite to or different from another part or feature • There are good/positive and bad/negative *sides* to owning your own business. — often + *of* • He's learning about the sales *side of* the business. • She ***kept her side of the bargain/deal.*** [=she did what she agreed to do] — see also DOWNSIDE, FLIP SIDE, UPSIDE **b** — used in phrases like ***on the large side, on the heavy side,*** etc., to describe someone or something as somewhat heavy, large, etc. • She has always been a little *on the heavy side.* [=has always been somewhat heavy] • These pants are *on the tight side.* [=are a little tight] • The sauce is a bit *on the spicy side.* [=is a bit spicy] • Your boyfriend is *on the young side* for you, isn't he?

10 [*count*] **a** : a part of someone's personality that is opposite or different from another part • I have never seen this *side* of you before. • He is in touch with his feminine *side.* **b** — used in phrases like ***be/get on someone's good/bad side*** and ***be/get on the right/wrong side of someone*** to talk about doing things that cause someone to like you or dislike you • Trust me. You don't want to *get on his bad side.* [=you don't want to make him annoyed or angry] • She tries to *keep/stay on her boss's good side* by finishing all of her work on time. • If you *get on the wrong side of* him [=if you make him annoyed or angry] he can be very mean.

11 [*count*] : the ancestors or relatives of your mother or your father ▪ She gets her red hair from her mother's *side*. ▪ Both *sides* of his family are Irish. ▪ my grandfather on my father's *side* [=my father's father]
12 [*count*] *US* : a small amount of food that is ordered in addition to the main meal — often + *of* ▪ I ordered a *side of* fries with my hamburger.
13 [*count*] : one of the two halves of an animal that is eaten as food — usually + *of* ▪ a *side of* bacon/pork/beef
14 [*count*] *chiefly Brit* : a page of writing on one side of a piece of paper ▪ I wrote two *sides* in response to the question.
15 [*count*] *Brit, informal* + *old-fashioned* : a television channel — usually singular ▪ What's on the other *side*?
a thorn in the/your side see THORN
err on the side of see ERR
(from) side to side : moving to the left and then to the right ▪ She shook her head *from side to side* in disagreement. ▪ waving the flags *from side to side* ▪ He moved *side to side* on the tennis court.
let the side down *Brit* : to disappoint your family, friends, etc., by failing to do what is needed or expected ▪ I feel like I really *let the side down*. [=let everyone down]
on side *Brit* : included among the group of people who support a particular goal, project, etc. ▪ We need to keep everyone *on side*. [=on board]
on the bright side see BRIGHT
on the credit side see [1]CREDIT
on the debit side see [1]DEBIT
on the right/wrong side of 30, 40, 50 (etc.) *informal* : younger/older than 30, 40, 50 (etc.) ▪ She's still *on the right side of 40*. [=younger than 40]
on the side **1 a** : in addition to the main item in a meal ▪ We were served salmon with rice and grilled vegetables *on the side*. **b** : served next to something rather than on top of it ▪ For my salad, I'd like Italian dressing *on the side*. **2** : in addition to your main job ▪ She sells insurance *on the side*. **3** : as part of a secret romantic relationship that is outside of your marriage or main romantic relationship ▪ a married man with a girlfriend *on the side* ▪ She had a fiancé but was seeing another man *on the side*.
on the wrong/right side of the law — used to say that someone is or is not living the life of a criminal ▪ He has been *on the wrong side of* the law since he stole a car at the age of 17. ▪ Now that she's out of prison she's trying to stay *on the right side of the law*. [=trying not to get into trouble with the police]
on your side : as an advantage ▪ He is not a very tall basketball player, but he does have quickness *on his side*. : helping you to succeed ▪ Luck seems to be *on your side* tonight. ▪ Time is *on our side*. [=we have a lot of time to do what we need to do] — see also [1]SIDE 6 (above)
side by side **1** : next to each other and facing in the same direction ▪ We walked *side by side* down the hallway. ▪ They stood *side by side* at the altar. **2** : together or very close to each other ▪ The tribes have lived peacefully *side by side* for many years. ▪ People worked *side by side* to rescue the trapped coal miners.
split your sides (laughing) see [1]SPLIT
the other side of the coin see [1]COIN
the wrong side of the tracks see [1]TRACK
this side of **1 a** : very nearly (something) ▪ Their actions were just *this side of* illegal. [=were almost but not quite illegal] **b** : that is not (something) : other than (something) ▪ the worst punishment *this side of* death **2** *Brit* : BEFORE ▪ She's not likely to be back *this side of* Monday week.
to the/one side **1** : to a place that is on one side : ASIDE ▪ Please move/step *to the side*. I need to get past you. ▪ He put his luggage *to one side*. ▪ She took the boy *to the side* [=away from other people] and told him to behave. **2** : in a state in which something is not dealt with, done, or used until a later time : ASIDE ▪ Let's put/leave that question *to the side* for a moment. ▪ He set his household chores *to the side* to finish writing his essay. ▪ They managed to put some money *to the side* every month. — see also [1]SIDE 1 (above)
two sides of the same coin see [1]COIN
– compare [4]SIDE

[2]**side** *adj, always used before a noun*
1 : of or located on the side of something ▪ a front and *side* view of the car ▪ The jacket has *side* pockets. ▪ Please use the *side* door/entrance.
2 : happening or done in addition to the main or most important thing ▪ A *side* benefit of the drug is that it helps patients relax. ▪ She took on a *side* project/job during the summer. ▪ a *side* remark/issue
3 : in addition to the main meal ▪ a *side* salad ▪ I had a burger with a ***side order*** of fries. ▪ I'll have rice as a ***side dish***.

[3]**side** *verb* **sides; sid·ed; sid·ing** [+ *obj*] *US* : to cover the outside walls of (a building) with long pieces of material (called siding) ▪ They just *sided* their house.
side against [*phrasal verb*] ***side against (someone)*** : to not agree with (someone) : to not support the opinions or actions of (someone) ▪ They both *sided against* [=*opposed*] me. ▪ His father *sided* with his mother *against* him.
side with [*phrasal verb*] ***side with (someone)*** : to agree with or support the opinions or actions of (someone) ▪ She *sided with* her friend in the argument. ▪ They betrayed their country and *sided with* the enemy.

[4]**side** *noun* [*noncount*] *Brit, informal* : an unpleasantly proud attitude or way of behaving ▪ He was a war hero and yet there was ***no side to*** him. [=he was not arrogant or pretentious] — compare [1]SIDE

[1]**side·arm** /ˈsaɪdˌɑɚm/ *noun, pl* **-arms** [*count*] : a weapon (such as a sword or handgun) that is worn on your hip or in your belt

[2]**sidearm** *adj, chiefly US* : done with your arm moving out to the side ▪ The pitcher has a *sidearm* delivery. ▪ a *sidearm* pass
– sidearm *adv* ▪ He throws *sidearm*.

side·board /ˈsaɪdˌboɚd/ *noun, pl* **-boards**
1 [*count*] : a piece of furniture that has drawers and shelves for holding dishes, silverware, table linen, etc.
2 ***sideboards*** [*plural*] *Brit* : SIDEBURNS

side·burns /ˈsaɪdˌbɚnz/ *noun* [*plural*] : hair that grows on the side of a man's face in front of his ears — see picture at BEARD

side–by–side *adj, always used before a noun* : positioned next to each other ▪ *side-by-side* beds : involving things that are positioned next to each other ▪ a *side-by-side* comparison of the two paintings

side·car /ˈsaɪdˌkɑɚ/ *noun, pl* **-cars** [*count*] : a small vehicle that is attached to the side of a motorcycle for a passenger to ride in

sided *adj* : having sides usually of a specified number or kind — used in combination ▪ a two-*sided* letter ▪ glass-*sided* buildings — see also DOUBLE-SIDED, ONE-SIDED

side effect *noun, pl* **~ -fects** [*count*]
1 : an often harmful and unwanted effect of a drug or chemical that occurs along with the desired effect ▪ Nausea and diarrhea are the *side effects* of the drug. ▪ the harmful *side effects* of using chemicals to kill insects
2 : a result of an action that is not expected or intended ▪ The merger created positive *side effects* for both companies.

side·kick /ˈsaɪdˌkɪk/ *noun, pl* **-kicks** [*count*] *informal* : a person who helps and spends a lot of time with someone who is usually more important, powerful, etc. ▪ the mayor and his *sidekick*

side·light /ˈsaɪdˌlaɪt/ *noun, pl* **-lights** [*count*]
1 : a piece of information that is in addition to the main information ▪ The book includes some amusing *sidelights* about his childhood
2 *Brit* : PARKING LIGHT

[1]**side·line** /ˈsaɪdˌlaɪn/ *noun, pl* **-lines** [*count*]
1 a : a line that marks the outside edge of a sports field or court **b** : the space outside the area where a game is played on a field or court — usually plural ▪ We stood ***on the sidelines*** to watch the game. ▪ He was forced to watch the game ***from the sidelines***. — often used figuratively ▪ His injury has kept him *on the sidelines* [=has kept him from playing] this season. ▪ He stayed *on the sidelines* and let his daughter run the family business her way.
2 : a job that is done in addition to your main job ▪ She makes and sells jewelry ***as a sideline***.

[2]**sideline** *verb* **-lines; -lined; -lin·ing** [+ *obj*] : to prevent (a player) from playing in a game especially because of injury, illness, etc. — usually used as ***(be) sidelined*** ▪ He *was sidelined* with a knee injury. — often used figuratively ▪ a lawyer *sidelined* by illness ▪ Her career had *been sidelined* for several years by motherhood.

side·long /ˈsaɪdˌlɑːŋ/ *adj, always used before a noun* : made to the left or right or out of the corner of your eye ▪ a *sidelong* look/glance
– sidelong *adv* ▪ She glanced *sidelong* at her brother.

side road *noun, pl* **~ roads** [*count*] : a smaller road that is connected to a main road ▪ We like driving on *side roads* when we travel.

side·sad·dle /ˈsaɪdˌsædl/ *noun, pl* **-sad·dles** [*count*] : a

saddle that is made for a rider to sit with both legs on one side of the horse
– **sidesaddle** *adv* • She rode/sat *sidesaddle*. [=she rode/sat with both legs on one side of the horse]

side·show /ˈsaɪd,ʃoʊ/ *noun, pl* **-shows** [*count*]
1 : a smaller show that is performed in addition to a main show • a circus *sideshow*
2 : an activity or event that is less important than the main activity or event • Their disagreement is just a political *sideshow* when compared to the real issues at hand.

side·split·ting /ˈsaɪd,splɪtɪŋ/ *adj, informal* **:** very funny • a *sidesplitting* comedy/performance

side·step /ˈsaɪd,stɛp/ *verb* **-steps; -stepped; -step·ping**
1 : to avoid walking into or being hit by (someone or something) by stepping to the right or left [+ *obj*] She *sidestepped* the puddle. [*no obj*] He *sidestepped* to avoid (being hit by) his opponent.
2 [+ *obj*] **:** to avoid answering or dealing with (something) directly • She *sidestepped* the reporter's question. • They're *sidestepping* the real issue.

side street *noun, pl* ~ **streets** [*count*] **:** a smaller street that connects to and often ends at a main road • We live on a quiet *side street*.

[1]**side·swipe** /ˈsaɪd,swaɪp/ *verb* **-swipes; -swiped; -swip·ing** [+ *obj*] *US* **:** to hit the side of a vehicle with the side of another vehicle • The taxi *sideswiped* a parked car.

[2]**sideswipe** *noun, pl* **-swipes** [*count*] **:** a critical remark about someone or something that is made while talking about someone or something else • She ***took a sideswipe at*** the senator's voting record.

side table *noun, pl* ~ **tables** [*count*] **:** a table that is designed to be placed against a wall

side·track /ˈsaɪd,træk/ *verb* **-tracks; -tracked; -track·ing** [+ *obj*]
1 : to cause (someone) to talk about or do something different and less important — usually used as *(be/get) sidetracked* • Now, what was I saying? I *got sidetracked* by that phone call.
2 *US* **a :** to change the direction or use of (something) — usually used as *(be) sidetracked* • The grant money *was sidetracked* [=*diverted*] to fund unrelated research projects. **b :** to prevent (something) from being dealt with — usually used as *(be) sidetracked* • The real issue *has been sidetracked*.

side–view mirror *noun, pl* ~ **-rors** [*count*] *US* **:** a mirror on the outside of a vehicle that allows the driver to see what is behind and to the right or left of the vehicle • the right/left *side-view mirror* — called also *(Brit) wing mirror*

side·walk /ˈsaɪd,wɑːk/ *noun, pl* **-walks** [*count*] *US* **:** a usually concrete path along the side of a street for people to walk on • Bicycles are not allowed on the *sidewalk*. • *sidewalk* cafés • a ***sidewalk sale*** [=an event in which a store displays its goods outside on a sidewalk] — called also *(Brit) pavement*; see picture at STREET

side·ways /ˈsaɪd,weɪz/ *adv*
1 : with one side facing forward • We had to turn *sideways* to let them through the crowded hallway. • crabs walking *sideways* along the beach
2 : to or toward the right or left side • Helicopters can fly up, down, forward, backward, and *sideways*. • She fell *sideways* and landed on her shoulder. • I looked *sideways* at him to see if he was smiling.
– **sideways** *adj* • a *sideways* movement/glance

sid·ing /ˈsaɪdɪŋ/ *noun, pl* **-ings**
1 [*noncount*] *US* **:** long pieces of material that are used to cover the outside walls of a building • vinyl *siding* — called also *(chiefly Brit) cladding*
2 [*count*] **:** a short railroad track that is connected with the main track

si·dle /ˈsaɪdl̩/ *verb, always followed by an adverb or preposition* **si·dles; si·dled; si·dling** [*no obj*]
1 : to move close to someone in a quiet or secret way • He *sidled* up to me and slipped me a note. • She *sidled* over and whispered, "Do you see that guy?"
2 : to go or move with one side forward • The crab *sidled* away. • She *sidled* through the narrow opening.

SIDS *abbr* sudden infant death syndrome

siege /ˈsiːʤ/ *noun, pl* **sieg·es**
1 : a situation in which soldiers or police officers surround a city, building, etc., in order to try to take control of it [*count*] the *siege* of Paris • The castle was built to withstand a *siege*. [*noncount*] The city is in a ***state of siege***.
2 [*count*] **:** a serious and lasting attack *of* something — usually singular • He's recovering from a *siege of* depression. • a long *siege of* bitterly cold temperatures
lay siege to (something or someone) **1 :** to surround (a city, building, etc.) with soldiers or police officers in order to try to take control of it • The army *laid siege to* the city. **2 :** to attack (something or someone) constantly or repeatedly — usually used figuratively • Angry taxpayers *laid siege to* city hall with letters and phone calls.
under siege **1 :** surrounded with soldiers or police officers in a siege • The city was *under siege* and food was getting scarce. **2 :** very seriously attacked or criticized by many people • The newspaper has been *under siege* lately by its readers for printing a false story.

siege mentality *noun* [*singular*] **:** a strong feeling that you are in constant danger or are surrounded by enemies • Living in a high-crime area can create a *siege mentality*.

si·en·na /siˈɛnə/ *noun* [*noncount*]
1 : a brownish-yellow color
2 : a reddish-brown color

si·er·ra /siˈerə/ *noun, pl* **-ras** [*count*]
1 : a range of mountains with sharply pointed peaks • The *Sierra* Nevada is a mountain range in California.
2 : a mountain in a sierra — usually plural • The *sierras* rose up sharply before us.

si·es·ta /siˈɛstə/ *noun, pl* **-tas**
1 : a regular period of sleep or rest in the afternoon in some hot countries [*count*] Most of the shops were closed after lunch for a two-hour *siesta*. [*noncount*] The shops are closed during *siesta*. • It's *siesta* time.
2 [*count*] **:** a brief sleep **:** NAP • He's taking a little *siesta* out there on the patio.

[1]**sieve** /ˈsɪv/ *noun, pl* **sieves** [*count*] **:** a kitchen tool that has many small holes and that is used to separate smaller particles from larger ones or solids from liquids
have a memory/mind like a sieve *informal* **:** to have a very bad memory **:** to be unable to remember things • I'm sorry. I *have a memory like a sieve*. What was your name again?

[2]**sieve** *verb* **sieves; sieved; siev·ing** [+ *obj*] **:** to put (something) through a sieve • She *sieved* [=*sifted*] the flour into a mixing bowl.

sift /ˈsɪft/ *verb* **sifts; sift·ed; sift·ing**
1 [+ *obj*] **a :** to put (flour, sugar, etc.) through a sifter or sieve • *Sift* the flour into a mixing bowl. • *sifted* flour **b :** to separate or remove (something) by using a sifter or sieve • *Sift* the lumps from the sugar. — often + *out* • *Sift out* the rocks from the sand. — often used figuratively • The lawyer *sifted out* the relevant facts of the case.
2 : to go through (something) very carefully in order to find something useful or valuable [+ *obj*] The police *sifted* the evidence in hopes of finding a clue. [*no obj*] The police *sifted* for clues. • The lawyer ***sifted through*** the hundreds of pages of testimony. • Firefighters *sifted through* the debris.

sift·er /ˈsɪftɚ/ *noun, pl* **-ers** [*count*]
1 *chiefly US* **:** [1]SIEVE; *especially* **:** a special kitchen tool used for sifting flour, sugar, etc.
2 *Brit* **:** SHAKER 1

sigh /ˈsaɪ/ *verb* **sighs; sighed; sigh·ing**
1 [*no obj*] **:** to take in and let out a long, loud breath in a way that shows you are bored, disappointed, relieved, etc. • He *sighed* with/in relief when he saw that he passed the test.
2 [*no obj*] *literary* **:** to make a sound like sighing • The wind *sighed* through the trees.
3 [+ *obj*] **:** to say (something) with a sigh • "I may never see my old home again," she *sighed*.
– **sigh** *noun, pl* **sighs** [*count*] • She gave a long, weary *sigh*. • He sank into the chair with a *sigh*. — often + *of* • a *sigh of* disappointment • I can ***breathe a sigh of relief*** [=stop worrying] now that she's safe.

[1]**sight** /ˈsaɪt/ *noun, pl* **sights**
1 [*noncount*] **:** the sense through which a person or animal becomes aware of light, color, etc., by using the eyes **:** the ability to see • Your *sight* [=*vision, eyesight*] weakens as you get older. • She regained *sight* in her left eye. • He ***lost his sight*** [=he became blind] at a young age.
2 [*noncount*] **:** the act of seeing someone or something • I know him ***by sight*** [=I have seen him], but I don't know his name. • She hated him ***on sight***. [=she hated him the first time she saw him] • The officers were ordered to ***shoot on sight***. — often + *of* • The (mere) *sight of* her ex-boyfriend filled her with rage. • We ***lost sight of*** the plane. [=we could no longer see the plane] • He faints ***at the sight of*** [=when he sees] blood. • He ***can't stand/bear the sight of*** blood. • She

caught sight of an eagle gliding through the air. — often used figuratively • We must not *lose sight of* our goal. [=we must keep thinking about our goal]

3 [*noncount*] : a position in which someone or something can be seen • The ship came ***into sight***. [=*into view*] • When I looked out the door, there was no one ***in sight***. [=no one could be seen] • Keep ***out of sight*** until I tell you it's OK to come out. • The child wandered *out of sight*. • ***Get out of my sight***! [=go away from me; I don't want to see you] • Don't let the puppy *out of your sight*. • The rabbit ***disappeared from sight*** into the tall grass. • The controls are ***hidden from sight*** behind a panel. • She left her purse out ***in plain sight***. = Her purse was ***in plain sight of*** anyone passing by. • We finally ***came in/within sight of*** the mountains. [=we finally came to a place where we could see the mountains] • A large pole was directly in my ***line of sight***. [=a large pole was blocking my view] — sometimes used figuratively • The end of the project is finally *in/within sight*. [=the end of the project is finally near] ✧ The phrase ***out of sight, out of mind*** means that you stop thinking about something or someone if you do not see that thing or person for a period of time.

4 [*count*] **a** : someone or something that is seen • The old dog was a pathetic/sorry *sight*. • Deer are a common/familiar *sight* in this area. • I've seen what he looks like when he gets out of bed in the morning, and believe me, it's ***not a pretty sight***. • The birth of the calf was ***a sight to see/behold***. [=was an amazing or wonderful thing to see] • We enjoyed the ***sights and sounds*** of the casino. **b** : a famous or interesting place in an area — usually plural • Our tour guide showed us the *sights*. • We saw all the *sights* of/in the city.

5 [*singular*] *informal* : someone or something that is strange, funny, messy, etc. • I'd invite you in, but the living room is a *sight*. • He was all dressed up as a pirate. It was quite a *sight* (to see)! • (*chiefly Brit*) You should get some sleep. You ***look a sight***.

6 ***sights*** [*plural*] : a goal or expectation • The company has raised/lowered its *sights* for annual sales by five percent. • She has ***set her sights on*** becoming a doctor. [=she wants to become a doctor]

7 [*count*] : a device that is used to aim a gun • He adjusted the *sight* of the rifle. — usually plural • The deer was ***in her sights***. = She could see the deer *in her sights*. — sometimes used figuratively • He always had a law career *in his sights*. [=his goal was always to have a law career]

8 [*singular*] *informal* : a large amount or extent : a lot • The car is a *sight* less expensive and has better gas mileage. • The book is ***a far sight*** [=a great deal] better than the movie. • You'll have to work ***a damn/darn sight*** quicker than that if you want to get done on time.

a sight for sore eyes : a person or thing that you are very glad to see • After being away from home for so long, my friends and family were *a sight for sore eyes*.

at first sight see [1]FIRST

drop out of sight see [2]DROP

heave in/into sight see [1]HEAVE

no end in sight see [1]END

out of sight *US, informal + old-fashioned* : very good • The show was really *out of sight*.

sight gag see [2]GAG

sight unseen : without seeing or examining something • They bought the house *sight unseen*. [=they bought the house without first looking at it]

[2]**sight** *verb* **sights; sight·ed; sight·ing** [+ *obj*] : to see (something or someone that is being looked for or that is rarely seen or difficult to see) • They *sighted* a ship in the distance. • Several bears have been *sighted* in the area.

sight·ed /ˈsaɪtəd/ *adj* : able to see : not blind • blind and *sighted* people • partially *sighted* people [=people who are not blind but have only a limited ability to see] — see also CLEAR-SIGHTED, FARSIGHTED, LONG-SIGHTED, NEAR-SIGHTED, SHORTSIGHTED

sighting *noun, pl* **-ings** [*count*] : an act of seeing something or someone that is rarely seen or difficult to see — often + *of* • There have been several *sightings of* whales swimming off the island.

sight·less /ˈsaɪtləs/ *adj, literary* : not able to see : BLIND • *sightless* eyes

sight–read /ˈsaɪtˌriːd/ *verb* **-reads; -read** /-ˌrɛd/; **-read·ing** /-ˌriːdɪŋ/ : to perform (written music) while reading it for the first time without practicing it [+ *obj*] The orchestra hired her because she could *sight-read* even the most difficult scores. [*no obj*] She *sight-reads* well.

– sight reader *noun, pl* ~ **-ers** [*count*] **– sight–reading** *noun* [*noncount*]

sight·see·ing /ˈsaɪtˌsiːjɪŋ/ *noun* [*noncount*] : the activity of visiting the famous or interesting places of an area • We spent the afternoon *sightseeing*. • We did a lot of *sightseeing* on our vacation.

– sight·seer /ˈsaɪtˌsijə/ *noun, pl* **-seers** [*count*] • The church attracts a lot of *sightseers*.

sig·ma /ˈsɪgmə/ *noun, pl* **-mas** [*count*] : the 18th letter of the Greek alphabet — Σ or σ or ς

[1]**sign** /ˈsaɪn/ *noun, pl* **signs** [*count*]

1 : a piece of paper, wood, etc., with words or pictures on it that gives information about something • The *sign* in the store window says "OPEN." • After you get off the highway, follow the *signs* for Route 25. • road/street/traffic *signs* • He ran the stop *sign*. • There was a "For Sale" *sign* on the car.

2 : something (such as an action or event) which shows that something else exists, is true, or will happen • All the *signs* point to him as the guilty party. • She ignored me, which was a sure *sign* that she was mad at me. • "The company called me in for a second interview." "That's a ***good sign***." • It was a ***bad sign*** that he couldn't walk on the injured leg. • There are plenty of ***warning signs*** that the company is in danger of bankruptcy. — often + *of* • Chest pain could be a *sign of* a heart attack. • We remained alert for any *signs of* danger. • the telltale *signs of* the disease • the first *signs of* spring • The bartender called the police ***at the first sign of*** trouble. [=as soon as there was trouble] • The runner ***showed signs of*** fatigue. [=appeared to be tired] • His writing is *showing signs of* improvement. [=appears to be improving] • He ***showed no sign of*** remorse. • The planet *showed no signs of* life. [=there was no evidence of living things on the planet] — see also VITAL SIGNS

3 : a motion, action, or movement that you use to express a thought, command, or wish • They bowed before the king as a *sign* of respect. • The teacher made a *sign* for the students to be quiet. • a picture of the president giving the thumbs-up *sign* — see also SIGN OF THE CROSS

4 : any one of the hand movements that are used in sign language — often + *for* • Do you know the *sign for* "thank you"? • the *sign for* the letter B

5 : a symbol that is used to represent something especially in mathematics • The symbol ÷ is the *sign* for division. — see also CALL SIGN, DIVISION SIGN, DOLLAR SIGN, MINUS SIGN, MULTIPLICATION SIGN, PLUS SIGN

6 : STAR SIGN • What's your *sign*?

a sign of the times : something that shows the kinds of things that are happening, popular, important, etc., in a culture at a particular period in history • Having metal detectors in schools is *a sign of the times*.

[2]**sign** *verb* **signs; signed; sign·ing**

1 a : to write (your name) on something [+ *obj*] *Sign* your name on the bottom line. • She met with fans and *signed* autographs. [*no obj*] Please *sign* at the bottom of the application. • Make sure you get all the details before you ***sign on the dotted line***. [=officially agree to buy or do something by signing a document] **b** [+ *obj*] : to write your name on (something) especially to show that you accept, agree with, or will be responsible for something • You forgot to *sign* the document/letter/check. • He was forced to *sign* the confession. • The contract was *signed* by both parties. • The author will be *signing* copies of his books today. • a *signed* confession • The contract should be ***signed, sealed, and delivered*** by tomorrow. • The President ***signed*** the bill ***into law***. [=made the bill a law by signing an official document]

2 a [+ *obj*] : to hire (someone) to do something especially by having that person sign a contract • The team *signed* the pitcher to a three-year contract. • He is *signed* to a three-year contract. • The studio *signed* her to do another movie. = The studio *signed* her for another movie. — see also SIGN ON (below), SIGN UP (below) **b** [*no obj*] : to agree to work for or to produce something for an organization, business, etc., especially by signing a contract • She *signed* to direct two movies for the studio. — usually + *with* • She *signed with* the studio to direct two movies. • He *signed with* the team for one season. • The band *signed with* an independent label. — see also SIGN ON (below), SIGN UP (below)

3 : to communicate by using sign language [*no obj*] The child is learning how to *sign*. [+ *obj*] She *signed* "please."

sign away [*phrasal verb*] ***sign (something) away*** or ***sign away (something)*** : to give (something, such as rights or property) to someone by signing a document • He *signed away* his share of the property.

S

sign for [*phrasal verb*] ***sign for (something)*** : to sign a document to show that you have received (a package, letter, etc.) • I *signed for* the package when it was delivered.

sign in [*phrasal verb*] **1 a :** to sign your name on a list, in a book, etc., to show that you have arrived • All visitors must *sign in* upon arrival. **b *sign (someone) in*** *or* ***sign in (someone)*** : to write the name of (someone) on a list, in a book, etc., to show that they have arrived • The receptionist *signed* the guests *in*. **2 *sign (something) in*** *or* ***sign in (something)*** : to sign your name on a list, in a book, etc., to show that you have returned (something that you borrowed) • He *signed* the video equipment (back) *in*.

sign off [*phrasal verb*] **1 :** to end a letter or broadcast by signing or saying your name • She *signed off* with "Yours Truly, Maria." • "This is DJ Fresh *signing off*. Peace." • The radio station *signs off* [=stops broadcasting] at midnight. **2** *US* ***sign off*** *or Brit* ***sign (something) off*** *or Brit* ***sign off (something)*** : to approve something officially by signing your name • (*US*) She refused to *sign off* until the wording was changed. • (*Brit*) He inspected the memo before *signing* it *off*. — usually + *on* in U.S. English • He ***signed off on*** the memo [=he approved the memo by signing it] and gave it back to his secretary for distribution.

sign on [*phrasal verb*] **1 a :** to agree to do something (such as a job) especially by signing a contract • She *signed on* to the new project. • He *signed on* [=*signed up*] as a member of the crew. **b *sign (someone) on*** *or* ***sign on (someone)*** : to hire (someone) to do something especially by having that person sign a contract • The studio has *signed* her *on* [=*signed* her *up*] to do another movie. • She's *signed on* for another movie. — see also ²SIGN 2 (above) **2 :** to start a broadcast by saying your name • "This is DJ Fresh *signing on*." • The radio station *signs on* [=begins broadcasting] at 5:00 a.m. **3** *Brit* **:** to report officially that you are unemployed in order to receive money from the government • She lost her job and had to *sign on*.

sign out [*phrasal verb*] **1 a :** to sign your name on a list, in a book, etc., to show that you have left a place • Did the visitors *sign out*? **b *sign (someone) out*** *or* ***sign out (someone)*** : to write the name of (someone) on a list, in a book, etc., to show that they have left a place • The receptionist *signed* the guests *out*. **2 *sign (something) out*** *or* ***sign out (something)*** : to sign your name on a list, in a book, etc., to show that you have borrowed (something) • He *signed* the video equipment *out*. • The library book is *signed out*.

sign over [*phrasal verb*] ***sign (something) over*** *or* ***sign over (something)*** : to give (something that you own, such as rights or property) to someone by signing a document • He *signed over* the property to his brother.

sign up [*phrasal verb*] **1 a :** to sign your name on a document or list in order to get, do, or take something • She *signed up* for health insurance. • He *signed up* for tennis lessons. • Students can now *sign up* for classes. **b :** to indicate that you will definitely do a job, join a team, etc., especially by signing a contract • He *signed up* [=*signed on*] as an Army reservist. • She *signed up* with another team. **2 *sign (someone) up*** *or* ***sign up (someone)*** **a :** to add the name of (someone) to an official list in order for that person to get, do, or take something • The church has *signed up* more than enough volunteers for the festival. **b :** to hire (someone) to do something especially by having that person sign a contract • The team *signed up* [=*signed on*] several new players. • The record label *signed* the band *up*. — see also ²SIGN 2 (above)

sign·age /ˈsaɪnɪʤ/ *noun* [*noncount*] **:** signs or a system of signs used to show information about something (such as a business or a road) • Recent airport improvements include more lighting and better *signage*.

¹**sig·nal** /ˈsɪgnl/ *noun, pl* **-nals** [*count*]

1 : an event or act which shows that something exists or that gives information about something **:** SIGN • The change in his behavior is clearly a *signal* [=*indication*] that there is a problem. • He likes her but he is sending the wrong *signals* with his constant teasing. — often + *of* • Inflammation is a *signal of* infection.

2 : something (such as a sound, a movement of part of the body, or an object) that gives information about something or that tells someone to do something • Don't start until I give the *signal*. [=*sign*] • The teacher gave us the *signal* to finish what we were working on and hand in our tests. • The pilot sent out a ***distress signal*** [=a message that the airplane was in danger] before the plane crashed. • They communicated with each other by using ***hand signals***. [=movements of a person's hands that mean something]

3 : a piece of equipment with colored lights that is used on railways and roads to tell people when to go, to slow down, or to stop • Faulty wiring in the train station caused a *signal* to malfunction. • The ***traffic signal*** [=*traffic light*] was not working.

4 *technical* **a :** a message, sound, or image that is carried by waves of light or sound • The video/TV *signal* is scrambled. • Satellite dishes receive television *signals*. • a *digital* signal • The transmitter beams radio *signals* into space. **b :** a wave of light or sound that carries a message, sound, or image • We'll need better equipment to generate a 50 Hz *signal*.

busy signal see ¹BUSY

mixed signals see MIXED

²**signal** *verb* **-nals**; *US* **-naled** *or Brit* **-nalled**; *US* **-nal·ing** *or Brit* **-nal·ling**

1 [+ *obj*] **:** to be a sign of (something) **:** to show the existence of (something) • Robins *signal* the arrival of spring. • The election results surely *signal* the start/beginning of a new era. • He *signaled* [=*showed, communicated*] his irritation by sighing and rolling his eyes dramatically. • Redness, swelling, and painful itching *signal* [=*indicate*] an infection. • A lock on the suitcase might *signal* that there's something of value inside.

2 : to make a sound or motion that tells someone something [*no obj*] Did he *signal* before he made the left turn? • They *signaled* at me to come over to their table. • We *signaled* for help. [+ *obj*] He *signaled* us that it was time to begin the meeting. • The umpire *signaled* a strike.

³**signal** *adj, always used before a noun, formal* **:** very important or great **:** SIGNIFICANT • Is he worthy of such a *signal* honor? • The bill's passage was a *signal* [=*notable*] victory for environmentalists.

— **sig·nal·ly** /ˈsɪgnəli/ *adv* • The mayor has *signally* failed to do what he promised to do.

sig·nal·er (*US*) *or Brit* **sig·nal·ler** /ˈsɪgnələ/ *noun, pl* **-ers** [*count*] **:** SIGNALMAN 2

sig·nal·man /ˈsɪgnlmən/ *noun, pl* **-men** /-mən/ [*count*]

1 *chiefly Brit* **:** a person who has the job of operating signals on a railway

2 : a person in the military who is trained to send and receive signals

sig·na·to·ry /ˈsɪgnəˌtori, *Brit* ˈsɪgnətri/ *noun, pl* **-ries** [*count*] *formal* **:** a person, country, or organization that has signed an official document • *signatories* to the treaty/petition • a *signatory* of the Declaration of Independence

¹**sig·na·ture** /ˈsɪgnəʧə/ *noun, pl* **-tures**

1 [*count*] **:** a person's name written in that person's handwriting • There is a place for your *signature* at the bottom of the form. • If we can collect 200,000 *signatures* on our petition, then our candidate will be included on the ballot. • We presented the document to the president for her *signature*.

2 [*noncount*] *formal* **:** the act of signing something • The contract requires *signature* by both parties. [=must be signed by both parties] • The bill passed and went to the governor ***for signature*** a week ago.

3 [*count*] **:** something (such as a quality or feature) that is closely associated with someone or something — usually singular • Her latest movie includes the humor and fast pace that have become her *signature*.

²**signature** *adj, always used before a noun* **:** closely associated with someone or something **:** making a person or thing easy to recognize • the chef's *signature* dish • "Respect" is her *signature* song/tune. • The director's new movie is a return to his *signature* style.

sign·board /ˈsaɪnˌboəd/ *noun, pl* **-boards** [*count*] **:** a board with writing or a picture on it that gives information about something (such as a business)

sign·ee /ˌsaɪˈniː/ *noun, pl* **-ees** [*count*] *US, formal* **:** a person, organization, etc., that has signed an official document (such as a treaty or contract) • *signees* [=*signatories*] to the treaty/petition

sign·er /ˈsaɪnə/ *noun, pl* **-ers** [*count*]

1 : a person, country, or organization that has signed an official document • He was one of the *signers* of the Declaration of Independence.

2 : a person who uses sign language

sig·net ring /ˈsɪgnət-/ *noun, pl* **~ rings** [*count*] **:** a ring that is decorated with a special design and worn on the finger — see color picture on page C11

sig·nif·i·cance /sɪgˈnɪfɪkəns/ *noun*

1 : the quality of being important **:** the quality of having notable worth or influence [*noncount*] The discovery has great

S

significance to researchers. • His age is of little *significance*. • This building should be preserved because of its historical *significance*. • Does the ceremony have any religious *significance*? [*singular*] Her work has a *significance* that will last beyond her lifetime. — opposite INSIGNIFICANCE

2 : the meaning of something [*noncount*] I failed to understand/grasp/appreciate the *significance* of her remarks. • Does the date March 16 have some special *significance* to/for you? [*singular*] People in ancient times assigned a particular *significance* to the number seven.

sig·nif·i·cant /sɪgˈnɪfɪkənt/ *adj* [*more* ~; *most* ~]

1 : large enough to be noticed or have an effect • A *significant* number of customers complained about the service. • He won a *significant* amount of money. • There is a *significant* difference in prices between the two stores. • The study found a statistically *significant* decrease in symptoms in patients who had taken the drug. • His influence on me was *significant*. = He had a *significant* influence on me.

2 : very important • a *significant* event in the history of our nation • Fish is a *significant* part of their diet. • It is *significant* that she never mentioned him. — opposite INSIGNIFICANT

3 : having a special or hidden meaning • He gave us a *significant* wink/look. • a *significant* [=*suggestive*] glance

sig·nif·i·cant·ly /sɪgˈnɪfɪkəntli/ *adv*

1 : in a way that is large or important enough to be noticed or have an effect • People who smoke have a *significantly* greater risk of developing lung cancer than people who don't. • Another store sold the game for a *significantly* lower price. • If you take my advice, your chances of winning will increase/improve *significantly*.

2 [*more* ~; *most* ~] — used to say that something is important or meaningful • *Significantly*, William broke with family tradition and decided not to name his newborn son "William." • It was the first time I had ever traveled outside of the country, but, more *significantly*, it was the first time I had ever been outside of my parents' supervision.

3 : in a way that has a special or hidden meaning • He looked/glanced *significantly* in her direction when he said that some of us are not doing our jobs.

significant other *noun, pl* ~ **-ers** [*count*] : someone that you have a romantic relationship with : your husband, wife, boyfriend, or girlfriend • Before you make such an important decision, you should talk it over with your *significant other*. — abbr. *SO*

sig·ni·fy /ˈsɪgnəˌfaɪ/ *verb* **-fies; -fied; -fy·ing**

1 [+ *obj*] : to be a sign of (something) : to mean (something) • Black clothing *signifies* mourning. • A check mark next to your name *signifies* that you have met all the requirements. • The recent decline of the stock market does not necessarily *signify* the start of a recession.

2 [+ *obj*] : to show (your feelings, intentions, opinions, etc.) by doing something • He nodded to *signify* his approval. = He nodded to *signify* that he approved. • He gave her a diamond ring to *signify* his love.

3 [*no obj*] *formal + somewhat old-fashioned* : to have importance : MATTER • Whether he agrees or not does not *signify*.

sign·ing /ˈsaɪnɪŋ/ *noun, pl* **-ings**

1 [*noncount*] : the act of writing your name on something (such as a contract or document) to show that you agree to something — often + *of* • the *signing of* the Declaration of Independence • Two people witnessed the *signing of* the will.

2 [*noncount*] : the use of sign language • The child uses *signing* to communicate.

3 a [*noncount*] : the act of having someone sign a contract with a sports team, record company, etc. • The team has announced the *signing* of several new players. **b** [*count*] : someone who has signed a contract with a sports team, record company, etc. • a list of the team's recent *signings*

sign language *noun, pl* ~ **-guages** [*count, noncount*] : a system of hand movements used for communication especially by people who are deaf

sign of the cross

the sign of the cross : a movement of the hand that forms a cross shape and that is done as an expression of the Christian faith • She knelt and made *the sign of the cross*.

¹sign·post /ˈsaɪnˌpoʊst/ *noun, pl* **-posts** [*count*] : a sign beside a road showing the direction and distance to a place • The *signpost* says it is 10 miles to the city. — sometimes used figuratively • There are no *signposts* pointing to a solution.

²signpost *verb* **-posts; -post·ed; -post·ing** [+ *obj*] *chiefly Brit* : to provide (something) with signposts or guides • The road from here to London is well/clearly *signposted*. — sometimes used figuratively • His success has *signposted* the way for others.

Sikh /ˈsiːk/ *noun, pl* **Sikhs** [*count*] : a follower of Sikhism
— **Sikh** *adj*

Sikh·ism /ˈsiːˌkɪzəm/ *noun* [*noncount*] : a religion founded in India around 1500 that is based on the belief that there is one God

si·lage /ˈsaɪlɪʤ/ *noun* [*noncount*] : food for farm animals that is stored inside a silo

¹si·lence /ˈsaɪləns/ *noun, pl* **-lenc·es**

1 [*noncount*] : a lack of sound or noise : QUIET • I find it hard to sleep unless there is complete *silence*. • The *silence* was broken by the sound of footsteps in the hallway.

2 : a situation, state, or period of time in which people do not talk [*noncount*] We sat there in dead/total/complete *silence*. • My sister's revelation was met with stunned *silence*. • *Silence* fell/descended upon the room. [=the room became quiet] • The professor asked for *silence*. [*count*] There was an awkward *silence* after he confessed his love for her. • A long *silence* followed her reply.

3 : a situation or state in which someone does not talk about or answer questions about something [*noncount*] We must break 50 years of *silence* on issues like the government's involvement in assassination and espionage. • I will not be intimidated into *silence*. • You don't have to ***suffer in silence***. [=suffer or be unhappy without saying anything] [*singular*] She finally ended her *silence* and spoke to the media about what happened. — see also CONSPIRACY OF SILENCE

deafening silence see DEAFENING

silence is golden — used to say that it is often better to remain silent than to speak

²silence *verb* **-lences; -lenced; -lenc·ing** [+ *obj*]

1 : to cause (someone or something) to stop speaking or making noise : to cause (someone or something) to become silent • My sister's revelation *silenced* everyone around the table. • Police *silenced* the crowd. • Disconnecting the battery will *silence* the alarm.

2 a : to stop (someone) from expressing opinions that are opposed to your own or from telling people about bad things that you have done • The mayor tried to *silence* his critics. • I will not be *silenced*! **b** : to stop (something) from being expressed or revealed : SUPPRESS • It's obvious that the purpose of this law is to *silence* dissent.

si·lenc·er /ˈsaɪlənsɚ/ *noun, pl* **-ers** [*count*]

1 *US* : a device that is attached to a handgun to reduce the noise that the gun makes when it is fired

2 *Brit* : MUFFLER 1

si·lent /ˈsaɪlənt/ *adj*

1 : not speaking or making noise : QUIET • She was *silent* for a few minutes as she thought about how to answer him. • Please be *silent*. • The crowd ***fell silent*** as the horrible news was read aloud.

2 *always used before a noun* [*more* ~; *most* ~] : tending not to talk much • My father was a very *silent* man. • He was ***the strong, silent type***.

3 : not having or making any sound or noise • He said he would call me, but the phone was *silent* all day. • The radio went *silent*. [=*dead*] • A long, *silent* pause followed her reply.

4 *always used before a noun* : done, felt, or expressed without speaking • She offered a *silent* prayer of thanks for her family's safety. • They nodded their heads in *silent* agreement. • He turned his back on the president in *silent* protest.

5 : giving no information about something or refusing to discuss something • History books are *silent* about this shameful incident in our nation's past. • The president remained *silent* on the issue of funding. • You have the ***right to remain silent***. [=the legal right not to say anything when you are arrested]

6 *grammar* : written in the spelling of a word but not pronounced • There is a *silent* "e" in "cane." • The "b" in "debt" is *silent*.

7 *always used before a noun, of movies* **a** : not having spoken dialogue • *silent* movies/films **b** : of or relating to movies that have no spoken dialogue • filmmakers of the *silent* era

— **si·lent·ly** *adv* • She sat *silently* beside me. • The tiger moved *silently* through the jungle.

silent auction *noun, pl* ~ **-tions** [*count*] : an auction in which people write down their bids for the things being sold

silent majority *noun*

the silent majority : the largest part of a country's population that consists of people who are not actively involved in politics and do not express their political opinions publicly

silent partner *noun, pl* ~ **-ners** [*count*] *chiefly US* : a partner who invests money in a business but is not involved in running the business — called also (*Brit*) *sleeping partner*

silent treatment *noun*

the silent treatment : the act of ignoring someone because you are angry at him or her • I told him that I thought he was crazy and got *the silent treatment* for the rest of the day. [=he refused to talk to me for the rest of the day] • Whenever she gets mad at me, she ***gives me the silent treatment*** [=she does not speak to me]

[1]**sil·hou·ette** /ˌsɪləˈwɛt/ *noun, pl* **-ettes**

silhouette

1 a : a dark shape in front of a light background [*count*] the *silhouettes* of buildings against the sky [*noncount*] The buildings appeared ***in silhouette*** against the sky. **b** : a picture of something showing it as a dark shape on a light background; *especially* : such a picture showing a person's face from the side [*count*] My piano teacher has a framed *silhouette* of Mozart on her wall. [*noncount*] a portrait of my mother done ***in silhouette***

2 [*count*] : the shape or outline of something • He admired the sports car's sleek *silhouette.*

[2]**silhouette** *verb* **-ettes; -ett·ed; -ett·ing** [+ *obj*] : to make (someone or something) appear as a dark shape in front of a light background — often used as (*be*) *silhouetted* • The house *was silhouetted* against the sky.

sil·i·ca /ˈsɪlɪkə/ *noun* [*noncount*] : a chemical that contains silicon, that is found in sand and quartz, and that is used to make glass

sil·i·cate /ˈsɪləˌkeɪt/ *noun, pl* **-cates** [*count, noncount*] : a chemical that contains silicon and that is used in building materials (such as bricks, cement, and glass) • aluminum *silicate*

sil·i·con /ˈsɪlɪkən, ˈsɪləˌkɑːn/ *noun* [*noncount*] : a chemical element that is found in the Earth's crust and is used especially in computers and electronics

sil·i·cone /ˈsɪləˌkoʊn/ *noun* [*noncount*] : a chemical that does not let water or heat pass through and that is used to make rubber, grease, and in plastic surgery • a prosthesis made of *silicone* — often used before another noun • *silicone* breast implants

silk /ˈsɪlk/ *noun, pl* **silks**

1 : a smooth, soft, and shiny cloth that is made from thread produced by silkworms; *also* : the thread that is used to make silk [*count*] *silks* from China • a variety of *silks* and satins • embroidery *silks* [*noncount*] a dress (made) of blue *silk* • pure *silk* • The robe has butterflies embroidered in *silk* on the sleeves. • Her hair is ***as smooth as silk*** [=very smooth] — often used before another noun • a *silk* blouse/scarf

2 [*noncount*] : the thread that is produced by a spider • the *silk* of a spider's web • spider *silk*

3 [*noncount*] : the thin strings in an ear of corn • corn *silk*

4 ***silks*** [*plural*] : the cap and shirt worn by a jockey • the stable's red and green racing *silks*

5 *Brit* : a lawyer who has reached the highest rank : a Queen's Counsel or King's Counsel [*count*] She maintains a busy practice as a leading *silk* in employment law. [*noncount*] He ***took silk*** [=reached the highest barrister's rank] in 2001.

silk·en /ˈsɪlkən/ *adj*

1 : made of silk or a cloth that is like silk • *silken* [=*silk*] robes • a *silken* cord • *silken* cushions

2 : smooth, soft, and shiny like silk • her *silken* [=(more commonly) *silky*] black hair • the baby's *silken* skin

3 *of food* : smooth, soft, and rich • *silken* pudding/pâté

4 *of a sound* : smooth and pleasant to hear • his *silken* voice • the *silken* tones of his violin

silk screen *noun, pl* ~ **screens**

1 [*noncount*] : a method of printing in which ink or paint is forced through a stretched piece of silk cloth • artists who work ***in silk screen*** — often used before another noun • *silk screen* printing/designs

2 [*count*] : a print that is made by silk screen • He decorated the office with paintings and *silkscreens.*

— **silk–screen** *verb* **-screens; -screened; -screen·ing** [+ *obj*] • The logo was *silk-screened* onto T-shirts.

silk·worm /ˈsɪlkˌwɚm/ *noun, pl* **-worms** [*count*] : a caterpillar that produces silk which is used to make thread or cloth

silky /ˈsɪlki/ *adj* **silk·i·er; -est** [*also more* ~; *most* ~]

1 : made of silk or of material that is soft, smooth, and shiny like silk • *silky* lingerie/pantyhose • a *silky* nightgown

2 : smooth, soft, and shiny like silk • her *silky* brown hair • The cat has a *silky* coat. • The material has a *silky* feel.

3 *of food* : smooth, soft, and rich • *silky* chocolate mousse

4 *of a sound* : smooth and pleasant to hear • a *silky* voice

5 : having a smooth motion • This car gives a *silky* ride. • a golfer with a *silky* swing

— **silk·i·ly** /ˈsɪlkəli/ *adv* • a *silkily* smooth fabric — **silk·i·ness** /ˈsɪlkinəs/ *noun* [*noncount*] — **silky** *adv* • This lotion will make your skin feel smooth and *silky.* • The dog's fur is *silky* soft. • He has such a ***silky smooth*** voice.

sill /ˈsɪl/ *noun, pl* **sills** [*count*]

1 a : the shelf at the bottom of a window frame : WINDOWSILL — see picture at WINDOW **b** : a piece of wood, metal, or stone at the bottom of a door frame

2 : the part of the frame of a car that is directly under its doors

[1]**sil·ly** /ˈsɪli/ *adj* **sil·li·er; -est** [*also more* ~; *most* ~]

1 : having or showing a lack of thought, understanding, or good judgment : foolish or stupid • I hope I didn't make any *silly* mistakes. • The idea does seem a bit *silly.* • That's the *silliest* thing I've ever heard. • You drove in this weather? What a *silly* thing to do! • *Silly* me. I locked myself out of the car again. • Ask a *silly* question, and you get a *silly* answer. • He looks *silly* [=*ridiculous*] wearing that huge floppy hat. • "I can't ask you to do that." "***Don't be silly.*** It is my pleasure."

2 : not practical or sensible • What a *silly* little purse. It looks too small to hold everything that I'd need to carry.

3 a : not serious, meaningful, or important • I'm tired of watching *silly* movies. • The book was a *silly* waste of time. **b** : playful and funny • I like a man who can be *silly* without being immature. • He made a *silly* face. • He has a *silly* sense of humor.

4 *not used before a noun* : in a condition in which you are unable to think clearly • The ball hit him in the head and knocked him *silly.* • He was beaten *silly* by thugs. • They drank themselves *silly.* [=they got extremely drunk]

— **sil·li·ness** /ˈsɪlinəs/ *noun* [*noncount*] • the *silliness* of the whole idea

[2]**silly** *adv, informal* : to an extreme degree • I'm scared *silly* [=I'm very scared] of speaking to such a large group. • She was bored *silly* throughout much of the class.

[3]**silly** *noun* [*noncount*] *informal* — used to address someone who is being silly • No, *silly*, I don't need that one; I need the other one.

si·lo /ˈsaɪloʊ/ *noun, pl* **-los** [*count*]

silo

1 : a tower that is used to store food (such as grain or grass) for farm animals

2 : an underground structure that is used for storing and firing a missile

[1]**silt** /ˈsɪlt/ *noun* [*noncount*] : sand, soil, mud, etc., that is carried by flowing water and that sinks to the bottom of a river, pond, etc.

— **silty** /ˈsɪlti/ *adj* **silt·i·er; -est** • *silty* water

[2]**silt** *verb* **silts; silt·ed; silt·ing**

1 [*no obj*] : to become blocked, filled, or covered with silt • The marsh *silted* over. — often + *up* • The river delta has *silted up* over the centuries.

2 [+ *obj*] : to block, fill, or cover (something) with silt • The entrance to the creek had *silted* shut. • heavily *silted* areas — often + *up* • Sand had *silted up* the stream bed.

[1]**sil·ver** /ˈsɪlvɚ/ *noun, pl* **-vers**

1 [*noncount*] : a soft grayish-white metal that is very valuable and is used to make jewelry, coins, knives, forks, etc. • a bracelet made of *silver* • an artist who works in *silver* and gold • a wooden statue inlaid with *silver* • pure/sterling *silver*

2 [*noncount*] : objects (such as knives, forks, teapots, candlesticks, etc.) that are made of or covered with silver • We need to polish the *silver.*

3 [*noncount*] : coins that are made of silver • a bag of *silver*

4 [*count, noncount*] : a shiny light gray color

5 [*count*] : SILVER MEDAL • She won two *silvers* in the last Olympics.

[2]**silver** *adj*

1 a : made of silver • *silver* jewelry/coins • a *silver* teapot • a *silver* belt buckle **b** : containing silver • *silver* ore • a *silver*

S

mine **c** : of or relating to silver • *Silver* prices have risen.
2 [*more ~; most ~*] : having the whitish-gray color of silver • *silver* hair • a *silver* car • a dress trimmed with *silver* ribbon
3 *always used before a noun* : of or relating to the 25th anniversary of an important event (such as a marriage) • They will celebrate their ***silver (wedding) anniversary*** this year. = (*Brit*) They will celebrate their ***silver wedding*** this year. • a ***silver jubilee*** — compare DIAMOND, GOLDEN
born with a silver spoon in your mouth see BORN

[3]**silver** *verb* **-vers; -vered; -ver·ing** [+ *obj*]
1 *technical* : to cover (something, such as a mirror) with a thin layer of silver or something that looks like silver
2 *literary* : to make (something) shine like silver • The surface of the lake was *silvered* by the moonlight.
– silvered *adj* • a container lined with *silvered* glass

silver bullet *noun, pl* **~ -lets** [*count*] *US* : something that very quickly and easily solves a serious problem — usually singular • There is no *silver bullet* that will solve all our economic problems.

silver dollar *noun, pl* **~ -lars** [*count*] *US* : a large silver coin worth one dollar that was used in the past ✧ *Silver dollar* is now often used to describe the size of something. • He had a bald spot the size of a *silver dollar* on his head.

sil·ver·fish /ˈsɪlvɚˌfɪʃ/ *noun, pl* **silverfish** [*count*] : a small silver-colored insect that does not have wings and that lives inside houses

silver foil *noun* [*noncount*] *Brit* : a very thin sheet of metal (such as aluminum) : FOIL

silver lining *noun, pl* **~ -ings** [*count*] : something good that can be found in a bad situation • If there's a *silver lining* to losing my job, it's that I'll now be able to go to school full-time and finish my degree earlier.
every cloud has a silver lining — used to say that every bad situation holds the possibility of something good • When my closest friend moved away, my mother reminded me that "*every cloud has a silver lining.*"

silver medal *noun, pl* **~ -dals** [*count*] : a medal made of silver that is given as a prize to someone who wins second place in a contest • She won a *silver medal* in the Olympics. — compare BRONZE MEDAL, GOLD MEDAL

silver paper *noun* [*noncount*] *Brit*
1 : paper that is shiny on one side like silver and that is used for wrapping food (such as chocolate)
2 : SILVER FOIL

silver–plated *adj* : covered with a thin layer of silver • a *silver-plated* tray

silver screen *noun*
the silver screen *old-fashioned* **1** : a screen in a movie theater • one of the greatest films ever to hit *the silver screen* [=one of the greatest films ever shown in movie theaters] **2** : movies in general • stars of *the silver screen* [=movie stars]

sil·ver·smith /ˈsɪlvɚˌsmɪθ/ *noun, pl* **-smiths** [*count*] : a person who makes things out of silver

Silver Star *noun, pl* **~ Stars** [*count*] : a U.S. military award that is given to a soldier who is extremely brave in battle — called also *Silver Star Medal*

sil·ver–tongued /ˈsɪlvɚˌtʌŋd/ *adj* : able to speak in a way that makes other people do or believe what you want them to do or believe • a *silver-tongued* politician

sil·ver·ware /ˈsɪlvɚˌweɚ/ *noun* [*noncount*]
1 : objects (such as forks, knives, spoons, dishes, teapots, etc.) for serving food and drink that are made of or covered with silver
2 *US* : forks, knives, and spoons that are made of stainless steel, plastic, etc. — called also *flatware*
3 *Brit, informal* : something (such as a large cup or trophy) that is given as a prize in a sports contest • The team has gone two seasons without winning any *silverware*.

sil·very /ˈsɪlvəri/ *adj* [*more ~; most ~*] *literary*
1 : shiny and white or light gray in color like silver • a pond full of *silvery* fish • a dress of *silvery* gray/white silk • *Silvery* light reflected off the water.
2 *of sound* : high, clear, soft, and pleasant • The violinist played with a bright, *silvery* tone. • a singer with a beautiful *silvery* voice

[1]**sim·i·an** /ˈsɪmijən/ *adj*
1 *technical* : of or relating to monkeys or apes • a study of *simian* viruses
2 *literay* : like a monkey or ape • his *simian* facial features

[2]**simian** *noun, pl* **-ans** [*count*] *technical* : a monkey or ape

sim·i·lar /ˈsɪmələ/ *adj* [*more ~; most ~*] : almost the same as someone or something else • Our cats are *similar* in size/color/appearance. • You two look very/quite *similar* to each other. • They had *similar* experiences growing up, even though they came from vastly different backgrounds. • We got remarkably/strikingly *similar* results. • I was going to say something *similar*. • I would have reacted in a *similar* way if it had happened to me. — opposite DISSIMILAR

sim·i·lar·i·ty /ˌsɪməˈlerəti/ *noun, pl* **-ties** : a quality that makes one person or thing like another [*count*] I doubt that these words are related beyond a *similarity* in sound. • The books share a *similarity* of ideas. • I see a lot of *similarities* in them. — often + *between* • Have you noticed a *similarity between* these movies? • We discussed the *similarities between* the author's books. [*noncount*] Looking at these fossils, I see some *similarity* to modern-day birds. • I see very little *similarity between* your situation and his. • Both women have two children and like sports but ***there the similarity ends***. [=they are not alike in other ways]

sim·i·lar·ly /ˈsɪmələli/ *adv*
1 [*more ~; most ~*] : in a similar way : in almost the same way • My friend and I were *similarly* affected by the new tax law. • The houses are decorated *similarly*.
2 — used to say that two situations, actions, statements, etc., are alike • People still painted after photography became popular. *Similarly* [=*likewise*], there will still be people who prefer to shoot on film even after digital cameras become the norm.

sim·i·le /ˈsɪməli/ *noun, pl* **-les** *grammar* : a phrase that uses the words *like* or *as* to describe someone or something by comparing it with someone or something else that is similar [*count*] "She's as fierce as a tiger" is a *simile*, but "She's a tiger when she's angry" is a metaphor. [*noncount*] What do you think of the author's use of *simile*? — compare METAPHOR

[1]**sim·mer** /ˈsɪmɚ/ *verb* **-mers; -mered; -mer·ing**
1 : to cook (something) so that it is almost boiling for a certain period of time [+ *obj*] *Simmer* the stew for 40 minutes or until the sauce has thickened. • The chicken was *simmered* in a cream sauce. [*no obj*] Let the stew *simmer* (for) 40 minutes.
2 [*no obj*] **a** : to be filled with a strong feeling that is difficult to control or hide — usually + *with* • He was *simmering with* anger/resentment. **b** : to be felt strongly by someone without being directly shown or expressed • Anger *simmered* inside him.
3 [*no obj*] : to continue for a long time without producing a definite result • The dispute *simmered* for years before any progress was made. • It's a debate that has *simmered* for 30 years and is likely to continue. • *simmering* conflicts/controversies • Long-*simmering* tensions between the two groups eventually sparked violence.
4 [*no obj*] : to develop slowly • The idea for my novel *simmered* in my mind for quite some time.
simmer down [*phrasal verb*] : to become calm after being very angry or excited • After he *simmered down*, we were able to work out a solution to the problem. • "*Simmer down*! I was just joking. Don't take it so personally."

[2]**simmer** *noun* [*singular*] : a state of simmering : a way of cooking that is close to boiling • Bring the mixture to a *simmer*.

sim·per /ˈsɪmpɚ/ *verb* **-pers; -pered; -per·ing**
1 [*no obj*] : to smile in a way that is not sincere or natural • He *simpered* and smirked while he talked to the boss.
2 [+ *obj*] : to say (something) in a way that is not sincere or natural • She *simpered* that she had gone to all this trouble for a reason.
– simper *noun* [*singular*] • an annoying *simper* **– simper·ing** *adj* • a *simpering* reporter

sim·ple /ˈsɪmpəl/ *adj* **sim·pler; -plest** [*or more ~; most ~*]
1 : not hard to understand or do • a *simple* task • The solution to the problem was relatively *simple*. • The answer is really quite *simple*. • a *simple* [=*straightforward*] explanation • a *simple* recipe • There are three *simple* steps/rules to follow. • The camera is *simple* to use. • The directions seem *simple* enough. [=seem fairly simple] • Just press the button. It is ***as simple as that***. = Just press the button. It is ***that simple***. • Don't go into too much detail in the report. Just ***keep it simple*** and to the point.
2 : having few parts : not complex or fancy • The engine has a *simple* [=*basic*] design. • a *simple* machine • The melody is very *simple*. • She wore a *simple* [=*plain, unadorned*] black dress. • We don't want to spend a lot of money on the party,

so we're ***keeping it simple.*** [=we're not having an extravagant party]
3 *always used before a noun* : not special or unusual : ORDINARY • *simple* folks • I'm a *simple* farmer just trying to make a living. • He enjoys the ***simple pleasure*** of spending time with his wife and kids after work. • Relaxing on the beach and watching the sunset is one of ***life's simple pleasures.***
4 *always used before a noun* : complete and total — used for emphasis • I watch what I eat, but the *simple* truth is that I can't resist chocolate. • The *simple* fact is that he did not study for the exam. • I don't want to go ***for the simple reason that*** [=*because*] I'm very tired.
5 *grammar, of a sentence* : having only one main clause and no additional clauses • "Last summer was unusually hot" is a *simple* sentence.
6 *old-fashioned* : not very intelligent • a mentally *simple* man • She looked at me as if I were *simple*.
pure and simple see PURE
the simple life ✧ If you live *the simple life*, you do not own many things or use many modern machines and you usually live in the countryside. • He lives in a small cabin and enjoys *the simple life*.

simple fracture *noun, pl* **~ -tures** [*count*] *medical* : a break in a bone in which no parts stick out through the skin — compare COMPOUND FRACTURE

simple interest *noun* [*noncount*] *finance* : interest paid only on the original amount of money and not on the interest it has already earned — compare COMPOUND INTEREST

sim·ple·mind·ed /ˌsɪmpəlˈmaɪndəd/ *adj* [*more* ~; *most* ~]
1 : not very intelligent • a superstitious and very *simpleminded* man • He took a *simpleminded* approach to the problem.
2 : having or showing a lack of good sense or judgment • a *simpleminded* [=*stupid, silly*] mistake

sim·ple·ton /ˈsɪmpəltən/ *noun, pl* **-tons** [*count*] *old-fashioned* : someone who is not very intelligent or who does not have or show good sense or judgment • The instructions were so complicated I felt like a complete *simpleton*.

sim·plic·i·ty /sɪmˈplɪsəti/ *noun, pl* **-ties**
1 [*noncount*] : the quality of being easy to understand or use • People like the *simplicity* of the instructions/camera. • ***For simplicity's sake*** [=to make it simpler and easier], we have rounded off the numbers to the nearest whole number. = We have rounded off the numbers ***for the sake of simplicity.***
2 a [*noncount*] : the state or quality of being plain or not fancy or complicated • the *simplicity* of the music/writing/design **b** [*count*] : something that is simple or ordinary but enjoyable — usually plural • He loved the *simplicities* of country life.
3 [*noncount*] : something that is easy to do • Making the dish is ***simplicity itself.*** [=very easy]

sim·pli·fy /ˈsɪmpləˌfaɪ/ *verb* **-fies; -fied; -fy·ing** [+ *obj*] : to make (something) easier to do or understand • Microwave ovens have *simplified* cooking. • The new software should *simplify* the process. • The forms have been *simplified*.
– simplified *adj* [*more* ~; *most* ~] • Can you explain the problem in more *simplified* terms? • a *simplified* version of the instructions **– sim·pli·fi·ca·tion** /ˌsɪmpləfəˈkeɪʃən/ *noun, pl* **-tions** [*count, noncount*] • Voters are pushing for *simplification* of the tax code.

sim·plis·tic /sɪmˈplɪstɪk/ *adj* [*more* ~; *most* ~] *disapproving* : too simple : not complete or thorough enough : not treating or considering all possibilities or parts • a *simplistic* approach to a complicated problem • His interpretation of the theory was too *simplistic*. • *simplistic* thinking
– sim·plis·ti·cal·ly /sɪmˈplɪstɪkli/ *adv* • He described the problem too *simplistically*.

sim·ply /ˈsɪmpli/ *adv*
1 a : nothing more than : only, merely, or just • *Simply* add water to the mix and stir. • *Simply* click on the computer icon and follow the directions. • If he continues to bother you, *simply* ignore him. • You can order new checks *simply* by calling or going online. • It is *simply* a matter of time before something goes wrong. **b** : without any question — used to stress the simple truth of a description or statement • That is *simply* [=*just*] not true. • The opera was *simply* marvelous. • She *simply* can't sing. • I *simply* could not decide which one I wanted. • She *simply* does not understand the work that is involved. • There is *simply* not enough time to visit everyone. • We want to buy the car, but we *simply* can't afford it. • He is, ***quite simply***, one of the best players ever to play the game. • *Quite simply*, the countryside is beautiful.
2 a : in way that is clear and understandable • The instructions are *simply* written. **b** : in a way that is plain or not fancy or complicated • She dresses *simply*. • *simply* drawn figures • He lived *simply* on the farm. **c** : in a way that is direct and uses few words • The diner is called *simply* "Joe's." • "Sorry, I can't help you," he said *simply*. • The problem, ***put simply***, is money. • ***Simply put***, the movie was horrible. • ***Simply speaking***, he's not capable of doing the job.

sim·u·late /ˈsɪmjəˌleɪt/ *verb* **-lates; -lat·ed; -lat·ing** [+ *obj*] : to look, feel, or behave like (something) • The wall surface is made to *simulate* stone. = The wall surface *simulates* stone. • The model will be used to *simulate* the effects of an earthquake. • The material *simulates* [=*imitates*] the look and feel of real fur.

simulated *adj* : made to look, feel, or behave like something : not real • *simulated* leather • They are trained in *simulated* combat. • Dummies are used in *simulated* car crashes.

sim·u·la·tion /ˌsɪmjəˈleɪʃən/ *noun, pl* **-tions** : something that is made to look, feel, or behave like something else especially so that it can be studied or used to train people [*count*] — often + *of* • a computer *simulation of* spaceflight • *simulations of* body movements • a *simulation of* the planet's surface [*noncount*] They use computer *simulation* to predict weather conditions.

sim·u·la·tor /ˈsɪmjəˌleɪtɚ/ *noun, pl* **-tors** [*count*] : a machine that is used to show what something looks or feels like and is usually used to study something or to train people • a flight *simulator* used by pilots • an earthquake *simulator*

si·mul·cast /ˈsaɪməlˌkæst, *Brit* ˈsɪməlˌkɑːst/ *verb* **-casts; -cast; -cast·ing** [+ *obj*] : to broadcast (a program) by radio and television at the same time • The network will *simulcast* the game on its radio and television stations. — often used as *(be) simulcast* • The President's speech will *be simulcast* this afternoon.
– simulcast *noun, pl* **-casts** [*count*] • a TV/radio *simulcast* of the concert

si·mul·ta·neous /ˌsaɪməlˈteɪnijəs, *Brit* ˌsɪməlˈteɪniəs/ *adj* : happening at the same time • The two gunshots were *simultaneous*. • *simultaneous* events — often + *with* • The release of the new album will be *simultaneous with* the release of the DVD.
– si·mul·ta·neous·ly *adv* • The speech will be broadcast *simultaneously* on radio and TV.

¹sin /ˈsɪn/ *noun, pl* **sins**
1 : an action that is considered to be wrong according to religious or moral law [*count*] He committed the *sin* of stealing. • Murder is a *sin*. • I confessed my *sins*. [*noncount*] We are not free from *sin*. • a world of *sin* — see also CARDINAL SIN, DEADLY SIN, MORTAL SIN, ORIGINAL SIN, VENIAL SIN
2 [*count*] : an action that is considered to be bad — usually singular • It's a *sin* to waste food. — see also BESETTING SIN
(as) guilty/miserable/ugly as sin *informal* : very guilty/miserable/ugly • Even though he was acquitted, most people think he is *guilty as sin*. • That house is *as ugly as sin*.
for your sins *chiefly Brit, humorous* — used to say that you are doing something unpleasant, difficult, etc., as a form of punishment • *For my sins*, I was made chairman of the board.
live in sin see ¹LIVE

²sin *verb* **sins; sinned; sin·ning** [*no obj*] : to do something that is considered wrong according to religious or moral law : to commit a sin • Forgive me, for I have *sinned*.

¹since /ˈsɪns/ *prep* : in the time after (a specified time or event in the past) : from (a point in the past) until the present time • I haven't seen him *since* yesterday. • I haven't eaten *since* breakfast. • *Since* the party, she has not spoken to him at all. • The company has been in its present location *since* the beginning of the century. • We've been waiting for you *since* 10 o'clock. • We have been friends *since* [=*ever since*] college. • The company started as a small local business 10 years ago and has grown a lot ***since then***. [=within that time] • The house was built in 1919. ***Since that time*** [=from 1919 to the present], it has changed owners several times.
since the year one see YEAR
since when? — used to show that you are surprised and often angry, annoyed, or doubtful about what someone has said or done • "I'm a vegetarian." "*Since when*?" • "You told me to do it." "*Since when* did you start listening to me?" • *Since when* is it okay to cheat?

²since *conj*
1 : in the period after the time when • We've played better *since* you joined the team. • He has had two jobs *since* he graduated.

S

2 : from the time in the past when ▪ I have wanted to be a pilot *since* [=*ever since*] I was a child. ▪ He hasn't ridden a bike *since* he was a boy. ▪ (*US*) It has been over 10 years *since* I last visited Europe. = (*Brit*) It is over 10 years *since* I last visited Europe. ▪ They haven't won a championship *since* Truman was President.

3 — used to introduce a statement that explains the reason for another statement ▪ *Since* you've finished all your chores, you may go out and play. ▪ Should we invite someone else *since* he can't go?

[3]**since** *adv*

1 : from a past time until now ▪ He moved to New York one year ago and has lived there *since*. [=(more commonly) *ever since*]

2 : after a time in the past ▪ She graduated four years ago and has *since* married. ▪ He left home two years ago and has *since* become a soldier.

3 : before the present time ▪ I received your letter some time *since*. [=(more commonly) *ago*] — see also *long since* at [2]LONG

sin·cere /sɪnˈsiɚ/ *adj* **sin·cer·er; -est** [*or more* ~; *most* ~]

1 : having or showing true feelings that are expessesd in an honest way ▪ He sounded *sincere* in his promises. ▪ She seemed *sincere* in her commitment to finish school.

2 : genuine or real : not false, fake, or pretended ▪ She has a *sincere* interest in painting. ▪ He showed a *sincere* concern for her health. ▪ Her apology was *sincere*. ▪ He made a *sincere* attempt/effort to quit smoking. ▪ Please accept our *sincere* thanks. — opposite INSINCERE

– sin·cer·i·ty /sɪnˈserəti/ *noun* [*noncount*] ▪ Some people are questioning the *sincerity* of her promises. ▪ Her apology was spoken with *sincerity*. ▪ ***In all sincerity*** [=*in all honesty*], we could not have done this project without your help.

sin·cere·ly /sɪnˈsiɚli/ *adv*

1 : genuinely or truly : in a sincere or truthful way ▪ He *sincerely* apologized for breaking the vase. ▪ Do you *sincerely* [=*really*] believe that the country is better off now? ▪ I *sincerely* hope that you do a better job next time. ▪ I am *sincerely* sorry for your loss. ▪ He tried *sincerely* to make up for his mistake.

2 ✧ ***Sincerely, yours sincerely,*** and (*chiefly US*) ***sincerely yours*** are often used at the end of a formal letter before the sender's signature.

sine /ˈsaɪn/ *noun, pl* **sines** [*count*] *geometry* **:** the ratio between the long side (called the hypotenuse) and side that is opposite to an acute angle in a right triangle

si·ne·cure /ˈsaɪnɪˌkjɚ/ *noun, pl* **-cures** [*count*] *formal* **:** a job or position in which someone is paid to do little or no work

si·ne qua non /ˌsɪnɪˌkwɑːˈnɑːn/ *noun, pl* **~ nons** [*count*] *formal* **:** something that is absolutely needed ▪ Patience is a *sine qua non* for this job.

sin·ew /ˈsɪnˌjuː/ *noun, pl* **-ews** [*count, noncount*] **:** strong tissue that connects muscles to bones ▪ cutting through bone and *sinew* — often used figuratively ▪ the *sinews* of power

sin·ewy /ˈsɪnjəwi/ *adj* [*more* ~; *most* ~]

1 : having strong and lean muscles ▪ *sinewy* arms ▪ The lion has a *sinewy* body. — sometimes used figuratively ▪ *sinewy* writing

2 : tough and difficult to cut or chew ▪ a *sinewy* piece of meat

sin·ful /ˈsɪnfəl/ *adj* [*more* ~; *most* ~]

1 : wrong according to religious or moral law ▪ a *sinful* act [=an act that is a sin] ▪ It is *sinful* to steal.

2 : very bad or wicked ▪ *sinful* people

3 *informal* **:** extremely enjoyable in a way that makes you feel guilty ▪ a *sinful* chocolate cake

– sin·ful·ly *adv* ▪ They acted *sinfully*. ▪ The cake is *sinfully* delicious. ▪ *sinfully* rich chocolate **– sin·ful·ness** *noun* [*noncount*]

sing /ˈsɪŋ/ *verb* **sings; sang** /ˈsæŋ/ *or* **sung** /ˈsʌŋ/; **sung; sing·ing**

1 : to use your voice to make musical sounds in the form of a song or tune [*no obj*] She *sings* in the choir. ▪ The children danced and *sang*. ▪ She *sings* beautifully. ▪ He *sang* softly to the baby. ▪ She's a great actress, and she can dance and *sing*, too. [+ *obj*] We all stood and *sang* the national anthem. ▪ He *sang* a tune to us. = He *sang* us a tune. ▪ I can't *sing* the high notes. ▪ She *sang* the baby to sleep. [=she sang to the baby until it fell asleep]

2 [*no obj*] **:** to make pleasant sounds that sound like music ▪ Do you hear the birds *singing*?

3 [*no obj*] **:** to make a high-pitched whistling sound ▪ The kettle *sang* on the stove. ▪ The bullet *sang* past his helmet.

sing a different tune see [1]TUNE

sing along [*phrasal verb*] **:** to sing a song together with someone who is already singing or with a recording of the song ▪ If you know the words, *sing along* (with us). ▪ He loves to *sing along* with the radio. — see also SING-ALONG

sing of [*phrasal verb*] ***sing of (someone or something)*** *literary + old-fashioned* **:** to speak or write about (someone or something) especially with enthusiasm ▪ The poet *sang of* knights and medieval times.

sing out [*phrasal verb*] ***sing out*** *or* ***sing out (something)*** *or* ***sing (something) out*** **1 :** to say or shout something loudly ▪ If you need any help, just *sing out*. ▪ The children *sang out* [=*cried out*] "good morning" to the teacher. ▪ The crowd *sang out* insults. **2 :** to sing something loudly ▪ The singer stopped and the crowd *sang out* the rest of the chorus.

sing someone's/something's praises *or* ***sing the praises of someone/something*** **:** to say good things about someone or something ▪ His patients all *sing his praises*. ▪ They were *singing the praises* of their new equipment.

– singing *noun* [*noncount*] ▪ What beautiful *singing*. ▪ folk *singing* ▪ There was *singing* and dancing all night long.

– singing *adj* ▪ She has a wonderful *singing* voice. ▪ His *singing* career is ruined.

sing. *abbr* singular

sing–along /ˈsɪŋəˌlɑːŋ/ *noun, pl* **-alongs** [*count*] **:** an informal occasion or event at which people sing songs together ▪ a Christmas *sing-along* — called also (*Brit*) *singsong*; see also *sing along* at SING

singe /ˈsɪnʤ/ *verb* **sing·es; singed; singe·ing** [+ *obj*] **:** to burn (something) slightly ▪ The flame *singed* his hair. = His hair was *singed* by the flame. ▪ The wood was *singed* by the candle.

sing·er /ˈsɪŋɚ/ *noun, pl* **-ers** [*count*] **:** someone who sings ▪ My sister is a pretty good *singer*.; *especially* **:** a performer who sings ▪ He is the lead *singer* in the band. ▪ a country/opera/pop/rock *singer* — see also FOLKSINGER, TORCH SINGER

singer–songwriter *noun, pl* **-ers** [*count*] **:** a performer who writes songs and sings them

[1]**sin·gle** /ˈsɪŋgəl/ *adj*

1 *always used before a noun* **:** not having or including another : only one ▪ They lost by a *single* point. [=they lost by one point] ▪ A *single* shoe was found. ▪ It costs $10 for a *single* glass of wine! ▪ a *single* serving of carrots ▪ He earns $2,000 in a *single* week. ▪ There is a *single* [=*uniform*] standard for men and women. — sometimes used to emphasize the largeness or importance of something ▪ The fingerprint turned out to be the *single* most important piece of evidence. ▪ Tobacco is the *single* greatest/largest/biggest industry in the state. ▪ Drunk driving is the greatest/largest/biggest *single* killer of high school students. — sometimes used in negative statements to emphasize that there is a complete lack of something ▪ Not a *single* cookie was left. ▪ Not a *single* sound was heard. ▪ I could not hear a *single* word of what he said. ▪ We didn't get a *single* reply.

2 : not married or not having a serious romantic relationship with someone ▪ a club for *single* [=*unattached, unmarried*] people ▪ Are you *single*? ▪ a *single* parent/mother/father [=a mother or father who takes care of a child alone]

3 — used for emphasis after words like *any, each, every*, etc. ▪ He has more home runs than any other *single* player. [=than any other player] ▪ These laws apply to each *single* citizen. ▪ I drink milk every *single* day. ▪ She can't watch him every *single* minute.

4 *always used before a noun* **:** made for one person to use ▪ I stayed in a *single* room. ▪ I slept in a **single bed**. [=(*US*) *twin bed*]

5 *Brit* **:** ONE-WAY ▪ a *single* ticket ▪ How much is the *single* fare?

[2]**single** *noun, pl* **sin·gles**

1 [*count*] **:** an unmarried person and especially one who is young and socially active — usually plural ▪ The party is for *singles*. — often used before another noun ▪ a *singles* bar/club

2 [*count*] **a** *baseball* **:** a hit that allows the batter to reach first base ▪ He hit a *single* to right field. — compare DOUBLE, HOME RUN, TRIPLE **b** *cricket* **:** a hit that scores one run

3 ***singles*** [*plural*] **:** a game of tennis or a similar sport that is played between two players ▪ Do you want to play *singles* or doubles? ▪ a *singles* match

4 [*count*] : a music recording having one main song and sometimes one or more other songs • I bought the *single*.; *also* : one song from a recording that includes many songs • Have you heard the latest *single* from the album? • The song was released as a *single* before the album came out. — compare ALBUM
5 [*count*] : a room in a hotel, inn, etc., for one person • The hotel has only *singles* available. — compare DOUBLE
6 [*count*] *US* : a one-dollar bill • Do you have five *singles* for this five?
7 [*count*] *Brit* : a one-way ticket • A *single* to Bath, please.

[3]**single** *verb* **singles; sin·gled; sin·gling** [*no obj*] : to hit a single in baseball • He *singled* to right field.
single out [*phrasal verb*] ***single out (someone or something) or single (someone or something) out*** : to treat or to speak about (someone or something in a group) in a way that is different from the way you treat or speak about others • The teacher *singled* him *out* as the only student to get a perfect score on the test. • The coach *singled out* the players who played poorly. • The reviewer *singled* her performance *out* for praise/criticism. — often used as *(be) singled out* • She *was singled out* for special treatment.

single bond *noun, pl* **~ bonds** [*count*] *technical* : a chemical bond in which two atoms in a molecule share one pair of electrons — compare DOUBLE BOND, TRIPLE BOND

sin·gle–breast·ed /ˈsɪŋgəlˈbrɛstəd/ *adj, of a coat, jacket, or suit* : having one row of buttons • He wore a *single-breasted* blazer. — compare DOUBLE-BREASTED

sin·gle–deck·er /ˈsɪŋgəlˈdɛkɚ/ *noun, pl* **-ers** [*count*] *Brit* : a bus that has only one level — often used before another noun • a *single-decker* bus — compare DOUBLE-DECKER, TRIPLE-DECKER

single digits *noun* [*plural*] *chiefly US* : a number or percentage that is 9 or less • They won the game by *single digits*. [=by 9 points or fewer than 9 points] • The state's unemployment rate is in the *single digits*. — called also *single figures*
– sin·gle–dig·it /ˈsɪŋgəlˈdɪʤɪt/ *adj, always used before a noun* • the state's *single-digit* unemployment rate • a *single-digit* increase

single file *noun* [*noncount*] : a line of people, animals, or things arranged one behind another — used after *in* • They stood/walked *in single file*.
– single file *adv* • The students walked *single file* out of the classroom. • Boys and girls, please line up *single file*.

sin·gle–hand·ed /ˌsɪŋgəlˈhændəd/ *adj, always used before a noun*
1 : done by one person • *single-handed* sailing
2 : working alone • a *single-handed* sailor
– single–handed *adv* • He sailed the boat home *single-handed*. **– sin·gle–hand·ed·ly** *adv* • She raised the children *single-handedly*. [=she raised the children by herself] • He is credited with almost *single-handedly* saving the company from bankruptcy.

single malt *noun, pl* **~ malts** [*count, noncount*] : a kind of whiskey that comes from one place and that is not blended with other kinds of whiskey — often used before another noun • *single-malt* Scotch

single market *noun* [*singular*] *economics* : a group of countries that have an agreement which allows goods to be moved, bought, or sold between them very easily • the European Union's *single market*

sin·gle–mind·ed /ˌsɪŋgəlˈmaɪndəd/ *adj* [*more ~; most ~*] : having only one purpose, goal, or interest : focused on one thing • He worked with *single-minded* dedication/determination/devotion to help the poor. • She is very *single-minded* and determined to succeed.
– sin·gle–mind·ed·ly *adv* • He is *single-mindedly* devoted to his job. **– sin·gle–mind·ed·ness** *noun* [*noncount*]

sin·glet /ˈsɪŋglət/ *noun, pl* **-glets** [*count*] *chiefly Brit* : a shirt that has no sleeves or collar and that is worn for playing sports

sin·gly /ˈsɪŋgli/ *adv, formal* : without another • The birds can be seen *singly* or in groups. • The books in the set cannot be sold *singly*. [=(more commonly) *individually*]

sing·song /ˈsɪŋˌsɑːŋ/ *noun, pl* **-songs**
1 [*singular*] : a way of speaking in which the sound of your voice rises and falls in a pattern • They spoke in a *singsong*. — often used before another noun • a *singsong* voice
2 [*count*] *Brit* : SING-ALONG

[1]**sin·gu·lar** /ˈsɪŋgjəlɚ/ *adj*
1 *grammar* : showing or indicating no more than one thing • In the phrase "his car is red," the word "car" is a *singular* noun. • "Walks" in "she walks everyday" is a *singular* verb. — abbr. *sing.*; compare PLURAL
2 a *formal* : better or greater than what is usual or normal • the *singular* [=*exceptional*] beauty of the landscape • Her father noticed her *singular* [=*unique*] talent for music. • the *singular* [=*remarkable*] importance of the discovery • She showed a *singular* [=*noticeable, obvious*] lack of interest. **b** *literary* : strange or odd • He had a *singular* appearance. • *singular* customs
– sin·gu·lar·ly *adv* • a *singularly* important discovery • Passion was *singularly* [=*noticeably*] lacking in his music.

[2]**singular** *noun*
the singular : a form of a word that is used to refer to one person or thing • "Wolf" is the *singular* and "wolves" is the plural. • "Mouse" is the *singular* of "mice." • The verb should be ***in the singular***. • Rewrite the sentence *in the singular*. [=using singular forms of words]

sin·gu·lar·i·ty /ˌsɪŋgjəˈlerəti/ *noun* [*noncount*] *formal* : the quality of being strange or odd • People could not understand the *singularity* of his imagination.

Sin·ha·la /sɪnˈhɑːlə/ *noun* [*noncount*] : SINHALESE 2

Sin·ha·lese /ˌsɪnhəˈliːz/ *noun, pl* **Sinhalese**
1 [*count*] : a member of a group of people who live in Sri Lanka
2 [*noncount*] : the language of the Sinhalese people • He speaks *Sinhalese*.
– Sinhalese *adj*

sin·is·ter /ˈsɪnəstɚ/ *adj* [*more ~; most ~*] : having an evil appearance : looking likely to cause something bad, harmful, or dangerous to happen • There was something *sinister* about him. • He looked *sinister*. • *sinister* black clouds
– sin·is·ter·ly *adv*

[1]**sink** /ˈsɪŋk/ *verb* **sinks; sank** /ˈsæŋk/ *or* **sunk** /ˈsʌŋk/; **sunk; sink·ing**
1 a [*no obj*] : to go down below the surface of water, mud, etc. • The passengers were rescued from the boat before it *sank*. • a *sinking* ship • The rock *sank* to the bottom of the pool. • My foot *sank* into the deep mud. • She *sank* up to her knees in the snow. **b** [+ *obj*] : to cause (a ship or boat) to go down below the surface of water • The torpedo *sank* the ship.
2 [*no obj*] : to move down to a lower position • The sun *sank* behind the hills. • He *sank* to his knees and prayed. [=he knelt down and prayed] • She *sank* back into the cozy chair.
3 [*no obj*] : to become lower in amount, value, etc. : to decline or decrease • The temperature *sinks* quickly after the sun sets. • The lake's water level is slowly *sinking*. • His strength is slowly *sinking*. • The company's stock *sank* after it announced that profits were less than expected. • The currency's value is *sinking*.
4 [+ *obj*] : to use force to cause (something) to go into the ground or another surface — often + *into* • He *sank* [=*drove*] the fence posts *into* the ground. • He *sank* the ax *into* the tree. • The nail was *sunk* all the way *into* the wall. • The cat *sank* its claws *into* my arm.
5 [*no obj*] **a** : to do something that is morally wrong • How could you *sink* [=*stoop*] to cheating? • I never thought he could *sink* so low. [=do something so wrong] **b** : to begin to feel sad, depressed, etc. • She *sank* into a deep depression. • Her ***heart sank*** [=she became very sad] at the thought of moving so far away. • With a ***sinking heart*** [=with great sadness], she signed the papers to sell the house. • She got that ***sinking feeling*** [=a feeling of dread or discouragement] as she viewed the storm damage. **c** : to go or change to a worse or less active state — often + *into* • The patient *sank* *into* a coma. • He's ***sinking fast*** and won't live much longer.
6 [*no obj*] *of a person's voice* : to become quieter • Her voice *sank* to a whisper. [=she began to whisper]
7 a [*no obj*] : to become less successful : to move toward failure • The company is *sinking* under the weight of heavy debt. [=the company is failing because it has too much debt] **b** [+ *obj*] : to cause (someone or something) to fail • Bad weather *sank* their plans for a picnic. • If we don't get that money soon, we'll ***be sunk***.
8 [+ *obj*] : to make (a well, shaft, mine, etc.) by digging down into the earth • The workers are *sinking* a well.
9 [+ *obj*] : to spend (a lot of money, work, time, etc.) on something — + *in* or *into* • He *sank* [=*invested*] five million dollars *in* the new company. • He keeps *sinking* money *into* that old car. • She has *sunk* a lot of work *into* the project.
10 [+ *obj*] : to throw, hit, or roll (a ball) into a hole or basket • He *sank* [=*dropped, holed*] the putt. • In pool, you need to

sink [=*pocket*] the eight ball to win. • She *sank* the jump shot.
11 [+ *obj*] *chiefly Brit, informal* **:** to drink (something) completely • They *sank* [=*downed*] one more pint before leaving.
sink in [*phrasal verb*] **:** to become completely known, felt, or understood • I had to tell him what to do over and over before it finally *sank in.* • The fact that she's left me still hasn't really *sunk in.*
sink like a stone **:** to sink very suddenly and quickly • The ship hit an iceberg and *sank like a stone.* — often used figuratively • His last movie *sank like a stone.*
sink or swim ✧ A situation in which you either *sink or swim* is one in which you must succeed by your own efforts or fail completely. • They left me to *sink or swim* on my own. • In this job, it's *sink or swim.*
sink without a trace (*US*) *or Brit* ***sink without trace*** **:** to sink beneath the water to a place that cannot be seen or found • The boat *sank without a trace.* — often used figuratively • Her first album was a big success, but after that she *sank without a trace.*
sink your teeth into see TOOTH

[2]**sink** *noun, pl* **sinks** [*count*] **:** a wide bowl that has a faucet for water and a drain at the bottom and is usually positioned in a counter or on a pedestal • a kitchen *sink* • (*chiefly US*) a bathroom *sink* [=(*chiefly Brit*) *washbasin*] — see pictures at BATHROOM, KITCHEN

sink·er /ˈsɪŋkɚ/ *noun, pl* **-ers** [*count*]
1 : a weight used for holding a fishing line or net underwater
2 *baseball* **:** a fast pitch that drops lower as it reaches home plate — called also *sinker ball*
hook, line and sinker see [1]HOOK

sink·hole /ˈsɪŋkˌhoʊl/ *noun, pl* **-holes** [*count*] **:** a low area or hole in the ground that is formed especially when soil and rocks are removed by flowing water — sometimes used figuratively • The new highway is a financial *sinkhole.* [=something that constantly uses up money, resources, etc.]

sin·ner /ˈsɪnɚ/ *noun, pl* **-ners** [*count*] **:** someone who has done something wrong according to religious or moral law **:** someone who has sinned

Si·no- /ˈsaɪnoʊ/ *combining form* **:** Chinese and • *Sino-*Japanese relations [=relations between China and Japan]

sin·u·ous /ˈsɪnjəwəs/ *adj* [*more* ~; *most* ~] *formal + literary*
1 : having many twists and turns • a *sinuous* [=*winding*] road • *sinuous* vines
2 : moving and bending in a smooth and attractive way • a *sinuous* dancer • She moved with *sinuous* grace.
– sin·u·ous·ly *adv*

si·nus /ˈsaɪnəs/ *noun, pl* **-nus·es** [*count*] **:** any of several spaces in the skull that connect with the nostrils — usually plural • My *sinuses* are blocked. [=they are filled with mucus that will not drain properly] — often used before another noun • a *sinus* infection/problem

si·nus·itis /ˌsaɪnjəˈsaɪtəs/ *noun* [*noncount*] *medical* **:** painful swelling of the tissues inside the sinuses

Sioux /ˈsuː/ *noun, pl* **Sioux** /ˈsuː/ [*count*] **:** a member of a Native American people originally from the north central U.S.

sip /ˈsɪp/ *verb* **sips; sipped; sip·ping :** to drink (a liquid) slowly by taking only small amounts into your mouth [+ *obj*] She *sipped* her coffee while she watched the sun rise. [*no obj*] He *sipped* on the bottle of water. — sometimes + *at* • He *sipped at* his wine.
– sip *noun, pl* **sips** [*count*] • Have/take a *sip* of water.

[1]**si·phon** *also* **sy·phon** /ˈsaɪfən/ *noun, pl* **-phons** [*count*] **:** a bent tube used to move a liquid from one container into another container by means of air pressure

[2]**siphon** *also* **syphon** *verb* **-phons; -phoned; -phon·ing** [+ *obj*]
1 : to move (a liquid) from one container to another by using a siphon • The water needs to be *siphoned* from the pool. — often + *off* • He *siphoned off* gas from the car's tank.
2 : to take and use (something, such as money) for your own purpose • She illegally *siphoned* money out of other people's bank accounts. • Funds were *siphoned* from the schools to build a new stadium. • The large chain stores are *siphoning* profits from the small local stores.

sir /ˈsɚ/ *noun, pl* **sirs**
1 [*noncount*] **a** — used without a name as a form of polite address to a man you do not know • May I help you, *sir*? • *Sir,* your order is ready. — compare MA'AM, MADAM, MISS **b** — used without a name as a form of polite address to a man of rank or authority (such as a military or police officer, teacher, or master) • "At ease, lieutenant." "Yes *sir,* captain." • *Sir,* I don't think I was speeding. • *Sir,* can you help me with this math problem? • Dinner is ready, *sir.*
2 ***Sir*** [*count*] — used without a name as a form of address at the beginning of a formal letter • Dear *Sir* or Madam • Dear *Sir/Sirs*
3 ***Sir*** [*noncount*] — used as a title before the name of a knight or baronet • *Sir* Lancelot • *Sir* Charles • *Sir* Elton John • *Sir* Walter Scott
4 [*noncount*] *US, informal* — used in the phrases ***no sir*** and ***yes sir*** for emphasis, to show surprise, etc. • I will not have that man in my home, *no sir.* [=*no sirree*] • That was a wonderful dinner. *Yes sir.* [=*yes sirree*] • "She couldn't have said that to her mom." "*Yes sir,* she sure did." • "The teacher caught them kissing." "*No sir!* She did?"

[1]**sire** /ˈsajɚ/ *noun, pl* **sires**
1 [*noncount*] — used formerly to address a man of rank or authority (such as a king or lord) • Your horses are ready, *sire.* [=*my lord*]
2 [*count*] *technical* **:** a male parent of some animals (such as dogs and horses) • the foal's *sire* — compare [3]DAM

[2]**sire** *verb* **sires; sired; sir·ing** [+ *obj*]
1 *of an animal* **:** to become the father of (an animal) • The horse *sired* several champion racers.
2 *old-fashioned* **:** to become the father of (a child) • He *sired* [=*fathered*] six children.

si·ren /ˈsaɪrən/ *noun, pl* **-rens** [*count*]
1 : a piece of equipment that produces a loud, high-pitched warning sound • an ambulance *siren* • the wailing of air-raid *sirens* • We heard police *sirens.* [=sirens on police cars]
2 : a woman who is very attractive but also dangerous **:** TEMPTRESS • a Hollywood *siren*
3 ***Siren*** **:** one of a group of female creatures in Greek mythology whose singing attracted sailors and caused them to sail into dangerous water or toward rocks

siren song *noun, pl* **~ songs** [*count*] **:** something that is very appealing and makes you want to go somewhere or do something but that may have bad results — often + *of* • They could not resist the *siren song of* fame and money. — called also *siren call*

sir·loin /ˈsɚˌlɔɪn/ *noun, pl* **-loins** [*count, noncount*] **:** a piece of beef from the lower back area of a cow — often used before another noun • a *sirloin* steak • *sirloin* tips

sir·ree *also* **sir·ee** /səˈriː/ *noun* [*noncount*] *US, informal* — used in the phrases ***no sirree*** and ***yes sirree*** for emphasis, to show surprise, etc. • I won't let them do it. *No sirree.* [=*no sir*] • "Did you like the movie?" "*Yes sirree,* I sure did."

sis /ˈsɪs/ *noun* [*noncount*] *informal* **:** SISTER — used as a name for your sister especially when you are talking to her • *Sis,* can you help me with this?

si·sal /ˈsaɪsəl/ *noun* [*noncount*] **:** a strong white fiber made from a tropical plant — often used before another noun • *sisal* fibers/rope/twine • a *sisal* rug

sis·sy *also Brit* **cis·sy** /ˈsɪsi/ *noun, pl* **sis·sies** [*count*] *informal + disapproving*
1 : a boy who is weak or who likes things that girls usually like • The other kids laughed at him and called him a *sissy* because he didn't like sports.
2 : a person who is weak and fearful • Don't be such a *sissy.* [=*wimp*] It's just a frog.
– sissy *adj* • He thinks golf is a *sissy* sport.

[1]**sis·ter** /ˈsɪstɚ/ *noun, pl* **-ters**
1 [*count*] **:** a girl or woman who has one or both of the same parents as you • my little/younger *sister* • his big/older *sister* • She's my twin *sister.* • He has two *sisters.* — compare HALF SISTER, SISTER-IN-LAW, STEPSISTER
2 *informal* — used when talking to a woman • *Sister,* you have got to relax. • *Sister,* you don't need him in your life.
3 *or* ***Sister*** [*count*] **:** a member of a religious community of women **:** NUN • The *sisters* live in the convent. — often used as a title • the *Sisters* of St. Joseph • *Sister* Christine — abbr. *Sr.*
4 [*count*] **:** a woman who is from the same group or country as you • her college sorority *sisters* • We must support our brothers and *sisters* fighting overseas. • She speaks for her Asian *sisters.*
5 [*count*] *US, informal* **:** a black woman — used especially by African-Americans
6 *or* ***Sister*** [*count*] *chiefly Brit* **:** a nurse in a hospital ward or clinic
– see also WEAK SISTER

[2]**sister** *adj, always used before a noun* **:** belonging to the same kind or group **:** having similar qualities or characteristics •

The two cruise liners are *sister* ships. • *sister* companies/schools

sister city *noun, pl* ~ **cit·ies** [*count*] *US* : one of two cities or towns in different areas that have a special relationship and are usually similar in some way • A choir from our *sister city* in France is performing here next week. — called also (*Brit*) *twin town*

sis·ter·hood /ˈsɪstɚˌhʊd/ *noun, pl* **-hoods**
1 [*noncount*] : the close relationship among women based on shared experiences, concerns, etc. • The bonds of *sisterhood* have helped unite women to fight for social equality.
2 [*count*] : a community or society of women — usually singular • She is a member of the *sisterhood; especially* : a community of nuns — usually singular • Sister Katherine joined the *sisterhood* 10 years ago.

sis·ter–in–law /ˈsɪstɚrənˌlɑː/ *noun, pl* **sis·ters–in–law** /ˈsɪstɚzənˌlɑ/ [*count*]
1 : the sister of your husband or wife
2 : the wife of your brother

sis·ter·ly /ˈsɪstɚli/ *adj* [*more* ~; *most* ~] : showing or suggesting the closeness of a sister • She gave her brother a *sisterly* kiss on the cheek. • She received *sisterly* support from other women. • a *sisterly* friendship

sit /ˈsɪt/ *verb* **sits**; **sat** /ˈsæt/; **sit·ting**
1 a [*no obj*] : to be in a position in which your bottom is resting on a chair, the ground, etc., especially with your back upright • He was *sitting* in a chair next to the window. • She *sat* across from me during dinner. • The children *sat* cross-legged on the floor playing a game. • Are you going to *sit* there and watch TV all day? • Don't just *sit* there—do/say something! • You can't expect young children to ***sit still*** [=sit without moving around] for that long. **b** [*no obj*] : to begin to sit : to put yourself in a sitting position • He went over and *sat* [=*sat down*] in a chair next to the window. • She walked around the table and *sat* across from me. **c** *always followed by an adverb or preposition* [+ *obj*] : to cause (someone) to be seated : to put (someone) in a sitting position • She *sat* the toddler in the chair.
2 [*no obj*] **a** *of an animal* : to rest with the tail end of the body on the floor and the front legs straight • The cat likes to *sit* by the window. • He taught the dog to *sit* (on command). • *Sit*! Good dog! **b** *of a bird* : to rest on the top or the edge of something • The bird *sat* on the ledge.
3 *always followed by an adverb or preposition* [*no obj*] : to be or stay in a particular place, position, or condition • The limousine is *sitting* outside. • A vase *sat* on the table. • The sled *sits* unused in the garage during the summer.
4 [*no obj*] : to be a member of an official group that has meetings • She *sits* on the board of directors.
5 [*no obj*] : to meet in order to carry on official business : to hold a session • The court is now *sitting*. • Parliament will *sit* for four months.
6 [*no obj*] **a** : to take care of a child while the child's parents are away : BABYSIT • She *sits* for the neighbors' kids. = She *sits* for the neighbors. **b** : to take care of something while the owner is away — usually used in combination • Can you dog-*sit* [=take care of my dog] for me this weekend? — see also HOUSE-SIT
7 [+ *obj*] *US* : to have enough seats for (a certain number of people) • The car *sits* [=*seats*] five (people).
8 [*no obj*] : to pose *for* a portrait, photograph, etc. • She agreed to *sit for* the painting/painter.
9 *Brit* : to take (an examination) [+ *obj*] Students will *sit* the exam next week. [*no obj*] The course prepares students to *sit* for the exam.

sit around *also chiefly Brit* ***sit about*** [*phrasal verb*] : to spend time doing nothing useful • He *sits around* and does nothing while I do all the work. • She just *sits around* watching television all day.

sit back [*phrasal verb*] **1** : to get into a comfortable and relaxed position in a chair, seat, etc. • *Sit back* and enjoy the ride. **2** : to make no effort to do something • He *sat back* and watched us do all the work. • How can you just *sit back* and let him insult you like that?

sit by [*phrasal verb*] : to make no effort to stop something bad or unpleasant from happening • We cannot just *sit by* and watch him ruin his life. • I won't *sit* idly *by* while he ruins his life!

sit down [*phrasal verb*] **1** : to begin to sit : to put yourself into a sitting position • She called just as we were *sitting down* to eat. • Come on in and *sit down*. [=have a seat] • Please *sit down* and be quiet. — sometimes used figuratively • We need to ***sit down and*** figure this problem out. [=we need to give our attention to figuring this problem out] **2** ***be sitting down*** : to be in a sitting position • She made sure everyone *was sitting down* before she began. • I have some shocking news. *Are* you *sitting down*? **3** ***sit (someone) down*** : to cause (someone) to be seated : to put or get (someone) in a sitting position • He *sat* the child *down*. • You need to *sit* him *down* and have a talk with him. • She *sat* herself *down* on the couch.

sit in [*phrasal verb*] **1** : to take the place of someone who is not present • The President could not attend the meeting, so the Vice President is *sitting in*. = The Vice President is ***sitting in for*** the President. **2** ***sit in on (something)*** : to attend (something, such as a class or meeting) without officially participating • She's been asked to *sit in on* the meetings. • I would like to *sit in on* one of your classes.

sit on [*phrasal verb*] ***sit on (something) informal*** : to delay dealing with or talking about (something) • Let's *sit on* the problem for a while and see if anything changes. • They have been *sitting on* my insurance claim for months! • Let's just *sit on* this news for the time being.

sit on your hands : to make no effort to deal with or respond to something • She accused the administration of *sitting on its hands* while industries violated the law.

sit on your laurels see LAUREL

sit out [*phrasal verb*] ***sit out (something) or sit (something) out*** **1** : to stay in a place and wait for (something) to end • Though the movie was very boring, he *sat* it *out* to see how it ended. **2** : to not take part in (something) • She *sat out* several dances/practices. • You can start the game without me. I'm going to *sit* this one *out*.

sit pretty informal : to be in a very good or favorable situation • Our team *sits pretty* at the top of the rankings. — usually used as ***be sitting pretty*** • He bought stock in the company early on, and now he *is sitting pretty*.

sit through [*phrasal verb*] ***sit through (something)*** : to go to (something) and stay until the end • We had to *sit through* another boring meeting. • I can't believe the kids *sat through* the whole movie.

sit tight **1** : to not move or change your position : to stay where you are • *Sit tight*, I'll go get help. **2** : to not change your situation : to stay in the same situation • This isn't a good time to sell a house. Let's just *sit tight* and see if the market improves.

sit up [*phrasal verb*] **1** : to stay awake until late at night • They *sat up* talking until almost dawn. **2** : to sit with your back very straight • Quit slouching and *sit up* (straight). **3** ***sit up or sit (someone) up*** : to move or help (someone) to move into a sitting position • He *sat up* in bed. • She *sat* the child *up*.

sit up and take notice : to suddenly pay attention to (someone or something) • The news made them *sit up and take notice*.

sit well/comfortably (etc.) ◇ If something ***does not sit well/comfortably (etc.) with you***, you do not like it. • The decision *didn't sit well with* him. • That attitude *doesn't sit comfortably with* me.

si·tar /sɪˈtɑɚ/ *noun, pl* **-tars** [*count*] : a musical instrument from India that is like a guitar and that has a long neck and a round body

sit·com /ˈsɪtˌkɑːm/ *noun, pl* **-coms** [*count, noncount*] : a show that is on television regularly and that is about a group of characters who are involved in different funny situations — called also *situation comedy*

[1]sit–down /ˈsɪtˈdaʊn/ *adj, always used before a noun*
1 : done or used while sitting down • a *sit-down* job/interview • a *sit-down* lawn mower
2 a : served to people who are sitting down at a table • Will the reception be a *sit-down* dinner or a buffet? **b** : serving sit-down meals • a *sit-down* restaurant

[2]sit–down /ˈsɪtˌdaʊn/ *noun, pl* **-downs**
1 [*count*] : a strike or protest in which a group of people sit down to block a road, entrance, etc., and refuse to leave until they are given what they demand • The students staged a *sit-down*. — often used before another noun • a *sit-down* strike/protest
2 [*count*] *chiefly US* : a meeting held to talk about a problem or disagreement • The group arranged a *sit-down* with city officials.
3 [*singular*] *Brit* : a short rest while sitting down • I need a *sit-down* and a cup of tea.

[1]site /ˈsaɪt/ *noun, pl* **sites** [*count*]

1 : the place where something (such as a building) is, was, or will be located ▪ Hard hats must be worn on the construction *site*. ▪ They visited the *site* of their future house. ▪ The company has chosen a new *site* for its office building.
2 : a place where something important has happened ▪ the *site* of the battle ▪ Federal investigators combed through the crash *site*.
3 : a place that is used for a particular activity ▪ an archaeological *site* ▪ a nuclear test *site*
4 : WEB SITE

²**site** *verb, always followed by an adverb or preposition* **sites**; **sit·ed**; **sit·ing** [+ *obj*] *formal* : to place or build (something) in a particular location — usually used as *(be) sited* ▪ The office building will *be sited* on this lot.

sit–in /ˈsɪtˌɪn/ *noun, pl* **-ins** [*count*] : a strike or protest in which people sit or stay in a place and refuse to leave until they are given what they demand ▪ The activists staged a *sit-in* at the State House to protest the treatment of prisoners.

sit·ter /ˈsɪtɚ/ *noun, pl* **-ters** [*count*]
1 *chiefly US* : a person who takes care of a child while the child's parents are away : BABYSITTER ▪ They hired a *sitter* so they could go out.
2 : a person who poses for a portrait or photograph

¹**sit·ting** /ˈsɪtɪŋ/ *noun, pl* **-tings** [*count*]
1 : a period of time during which someone sits and does a particular activity ▪ I got through the book in one *sitting*.
2 : a period of time when a person poses for a portrait or photograph ▪ He finished the portrait in one *sitting*.
3 : a time when a meal is served to a number of people at the same time ▪ We'll eat at the second *sitting*. ▪ We have reservations for the 5:30 *sitting*.
4 : a formal meeting of a court of law, a legislature, etc. ▪ a *sitting* of the legislature

²**sitting** *adj, always used before a noun*
1 : currently holding an office ▪ a *sitting* President ▪ a *sitting* member of Parliament
2 : used in or for sitting ▪ a *sitting* position
3 : easily hit ▪ a *sitting* target

sitting duck *noun, pl* ~ **ducks** [*count*] : a person or thing that is easy to hit, attack, trick, etc. ▪ The tourists were *sitting ducks* for local thieves.

sitting room *noun, pl* ~ **rooms** [*count*] : LIVING ROOM

sitting tenant *noun, pl* ~ **-ants** [*count*] *Brit* : a person who is living in a rented house or apartment and has the legal right to stay there

sit·u·ate /ˈsɪʧəˌweɪt/ *verb* **-ates**; **-at·ed**; **-at·ing** [+ *obj*] *formal* : to place (someone or something) in a particular location ▪ They decided to *situate* the new office building near the airport. ▪ We *situated* ourselves in the seats nearest the exit. — often used figuratively ▪ You need to *situate* the events in the proper historical context.

situated *adj, formal*
1 : located in a particular place ▪ The building is *situated* in the bad part of town. ▪ *Situated* above the valley, the house offers beautiful views. ▪ beautifully/ideally/well *situated*
2 : in a particular living situation ▪ My parents are not rich, but they're comfortably *situated*.

sit·u·a·tion /ˌsɪʧəˈweɪʃən/ *noun, pl* **-tions** [*count*]
1 : all of the facts, conditions, and events that affect someone or something at a particular time and in a particular place ▪ He's in a bad/difficult/dangerous *situation*. ▪ You may find yourself in a *situation* where you lose control of the vehicle. ▪ How is your financial *situation*? ▪ I'm worried about the current political/economic *situation*. ▪ I've been in your *situation* [=*position*] before, so I think I can help you. ▪ My parents are retired and in a good *situation*.
2 : an important or sudden problem ▪ I have a *situation* that I have to deal with at the moment.
3 *somewhat formal + old-fashioned* : a place or location ▪ The house is in a wonderful *situation* overlooking the valley.
4 *old-fashioned* : JOB 1 ▪ She found a *situation* as a governess.

situation comedy *noun, pl* ~ **-dies** [*count*] : SITCOM

sit–up /ˈsɪtˌʌp/ *noun, pl* **-ups** [*count*] : an exercise in which you lie on your back and use your stomach muscles to raise the top part of your body to a sitting position ▪ She does 50 *sit-ups* every morning. — compare ²CRUNCH 4

six /ˈsɪks/ *noun, pl* **sixes**
1 [*count*] : the number 6
2 [*count*] : the sixth in a set or series ▪ the *six* of hearts
3 [*noncount*] : six o'clock ▪ "What time is it?" "It's *six*." ▪ I leave each day at *six*.
at sixes and sevens *chiefly Brit, informal* : disorganized and confused ▪ The change left everyone *at sixes and sevens*. ▪ Everything will be *at sixes and sevens* until our computer system is fixed.
hit/knock (someone) for six *Brit, informal* : to have an unpleasant and shocking effect on (someone) ▪ The news of the accident really *hit me for six*.
six of one, half (a) dozen of the other (*US*) *or chiefly Brit* ***six of one and half a dozen of the other*** *informal* — used to say that you do not see any real difference between two possible choices ▪ "Which do you prefer?" "I don't care; it's *six of one, half a dozen of the other*."
– six *adj* ▪ *six* possibilities/hours **– six** *pronoun* ▪ *Six* (of them) will be coming tonight.

six–figure *adj, always used before a noun* : in the hundreds of thousands : totaling 100,000 or more but less than one million ▪ a *six-figure* income/salary

six·fold /ˈsɪksˌfoʊld/ *adj* : six times as great or as many ▪ a *sixfold* increase
– six·fold /ˈsɪksˈfoʊld/ *adv* ▪ Membership has increased *sixfold*.

six–gun /ˈsɪksˌgʌn/ *noun, pl* **-guns** [*count*] : SIX-SHOOTER

six–pack /ˈsɪksˌpæk/ *noun, pl* **-packs** [*count*]
1 : a group of six cans or bottles sold together ▪ We bought/drank a *six-pack*. ▪ a *six-pack* of soda/beer
2 *informal* : a group of strong and well-shaped muscles that can be seen on a person's stomach ▪ Check out his *six-pack*. ▪ He has *six-pack* abs.

six·pence /ˈsɪkspəns/ *noun, pl* **sixpence** *or* **six·penc·es** [*count*] : a coin formerly used in Britain that was worth six pennies

six–shoot·er /ˈsɪksˌʃuːtɚ/ *noun, pl* **-ers** [*count*] : a type of gun (called a revolver) that can hold six bullets — used especially to describe guns used in the old American West ▪ a cowboy's *six-shooter* — called also *six-gun*

six·teen /ˌsɪkˈstiːn/ *noun, pl* **-teens** [*count*] : the number 16
– sixteen *adj* ▪ *sixteen* years **– sixteen** *pronoun* ▪ *Sixteen* (of them) will be coming tonight. **– six·teenth** /ˌsɪkˈstiːnθ/ *noun, pl* **-teenths** [*count*] ▪ I'll see you on the *sixteenth* of April. ▪ The bill is due on the *sixteenth* (of the month). ▪ one *sixteenth* of the total **– sixteenth** *adj* ▪ The paintings were made in the *sixteenth* century. ▪ He finished in *sixteenth* place. **– sixteenth** *adv* ▪ She finished *sixteenth* in the race. ▪ the nation's *sixteenth* largest city

sixteenth note *noun, pl* ~ **notes** [*count*] *US* : a musical note equal in time to 1/16 of a whole note — called also (*Brit*) *semiquaver*

¹**sixth** /ˈsɪksθ/ *noun, pl* **sixths**
1 [*singular*] : the number six in a series ▪ I'll be flying in on the *sixth*. [=the sixth day of the month] ▪ He got a base hit in the *sixth*. [=the sixth inning]
2 [*count*] : one of six equal parts of something ▪ Only about a *sixth* of the town voted for her.

²**sixth** *adj* : occupying the number six position in a series ▪ on the *sixth* day ▪ the book's *sixth* edition ▪ I finished in *sixth* place in the competition.
– sixth *adv* ▪ She finished *sixth* in the race. ▪ the nation's *sixth* largest city

sixth form *noun* [*singular*] *Brit* : the two final years of secondary school in Britain for students aged 16 to 18
– sixth–former *noun, pl* **-mers** [*count*] *Brit*

sixth form college *noun, pl* ~ **-leges** [*count*] *Brit* : a school in Britain providing education for students aged 16 to 18

sixth sense *noun* [*singular*] : a special ability to know something that cannot be learned by using the five senses (such as sight or hearing) ▪ She claimed to have a *sixth sense* for knowing when someone was about to call her.

six·ty /ˈsɪksti/ *noun, pl* **six·ties**
1 [*count*] : the number 60
2 ***sixties*** [*plural*] **a** : the numbers ranging from 60 to 69 **b** : a set of years ending in digits ranging from 60 to 69 ▪ She likes music from the *sixties*. [=from 1960 to 1969] ▪ He retired when he was in his *sixties*.
– six·ti·eth /ˈsɪkstijəθ/ *noun, pl* **-eths** [*count*] ▪ one *sixtieth* of the total **– sixtieth** *adj* ▪ his *sixtieth* birthday **– sixty** *adj* ▪ *sixty* books **– sixty** *pronoun* ▪ *Sixty* (of them) arrived this morning.

siz·able *or* **size·able** /ˈsaɪzəbəl/ *adj* : fairly large ▪ a *sizable* contribution/donation ▪ a *sizable* portion/percentage/proportion of the population ▪ He won by a *sizable* margin.
– siz·ably /ˈsaɪzəbli/ *adv, chiefly US* ▪ Costs have increased *sizably*.

S

[1]size /ˈsaɪz/ *noun, pl* **siz·es**
1 a : the total amount of physical space that a person or thing occupies : how large or small someone or something is [*count*] The *size* of the box is 12 inches long, 6 inches wide, and 5 inches tall. ▪ The bug was about the *size* of a dime. ▪ The twins are the same *size*. [=*height*] ▪ The tomatoes haven't quite reached their full *size*. ▪ The house is a good *size*. ▪ pieces of wood in all shapes and *sizes* ▪ televisions in large and small *sizes* [*noncount*] The cars are similar ***in size***. **b** : the total number of people or things in a group [*count*] I was impressed by the *size* of the audience. ▪ The *size* of the population keeps increasing. [*noncount*] There is a big difference ***in size*** between 50 people and a hundred! **c** [*noncount*] : the very large size of something ▪ It's hard to imagine the canyon's *size* until you see it in person. ▪ You should have seen ***the size of*** the shark they caught!
2 [*noncount*] : a specific size ▪ The lumber can be cut ***to size***. [=cut to the specific size you need]
3 : one of a series of standard measurements in which clothing, shoes, etc., are made [*count*] What is your shoe *size*? ▪ The dress is a *size* 12. ▪ Do you have this dress in a larger *size*? ▪ She's a *size* six. [=the clothes that fit her are size six] [*noncount*] Try this shoe on ***for size***. [=try this shoe on to see if it is the correct size]
down to size ✧ If people ***cut/bring (etc.) you down to size***, they make you realize that you are not as powerful and important as you thought you were. ▪ He thinks he's so smart! I wish someone would *cut him down to size*.
that's about the size of it *informal* — used to say that what has been stated about a situation is correct ▪ "So there's no chance of getting finished on time?" "*That's about the size of it*, I'm afraid."
– compare [4]SIZE

[2]size *verb* **sizes**; **sized**; **siz·ing** [+ *obj*]
1 : to make (something) a particular size ▪ The jeweler *sized* the ring (up/down) to fit her finger.
2 : to arrange or classify (things) in different groups according to size — usually used as *(be) sized* ▪ Men's pants *are sized* in inches.
size up [*phrasal verb*] ***size (something or someone) up*** or ***size up (something or someone)*** *informal* : to consider (something or someone) in order to form an opinion or conclusion ▪ The news media has been *sizing* the candidates *up*. ▪ She quickly *sized up* the situation.
– compare [5]SIZE

[3]size *adj* : having a specified size — used in combination ▪ medium-*size* cars ▪ a decent-*size* house

[4]size *noun* [*noncount*] : SIZING — compare [1]SIZE

[5]size *verb* **sizes**; **sized**; **siz·ing** [+ *obj*] : to cover (something, such as paper) with a sticky substance (called sizing) in order to make it stiff or smooth or to attach something else to it — compare [2]SIZE

sized /ˈsaɪzd/ *adj* : having a specified size — used in combination ▪ a small-*sized* dog ▪ a modest-*sized* apartment

sizing *noun* [*noncount*] : a sticky substance that is used to make a material (such as paper) stiff or smooth or to attach something (such as wallpaper) to a surface — called also *size*

siz·zle /ˈsɪzəl/ *verb* **siz·zles**; **siz·zled**; **siz·zling** [*no obj*]
1 : to make a hissing sound like the sound water makes when it hits hot metal ▪ bacon *sizzling* in the pan
2 *chiefly US, informal* : to be very exciting, romantic, etc. ▪ Their romance *sizzled* throughout the whole summer. ▪ The book *sizzles* with excitement.
– **sizzle** *noun* [*singular*] ▪ I heard the *sizzle* of frying bacon.

siz·zler /ˈsɪzlɚ/ *noun, pl* **-zlers** [*count*] *US, informal*
1 : a very hot day ▪ It looks like tomorrow's going to be another *sizzler*.
2 : something that is very exciting, thrilling, sexy, etc. ▪ a *sizzler* of a movie

sizzling *adj, chiefly US, informal*
1 : very hot ▪ a *sizzling* summer
2 : very exciting, romantic, etc. ▪ a *sizzling* love affair

ska /ˈskɑː/ *noun* [*noncount*] : a type of fast popular music that combines elements of traditional Caribbean rhythms and jazz

skank /ˈskæŋk/ *noun, pl* **skanks** [*count*] *chiefly US, informal + impolite* : a person and especially a woman who is very sexually active or dresses in an overly sexual way ▪ She was dressed like a *skank*.
– **skanky** /ˈskæŋki/ *adj* **skank·i·er**; **-est**

[1]skate /ˈskeɪt/ *noun, pl* **skates** [*count*] : a kind of shoe with blades or wheels on the bottom that allow you to glide or roll on a surface: such as **a** : ICE SKATE **b** : ROLLER SKATE **c** : IN-LINE SKATE
get/put your skates on *Brit, informal* — used to tell someone to hurry
– compare [3]SKATE

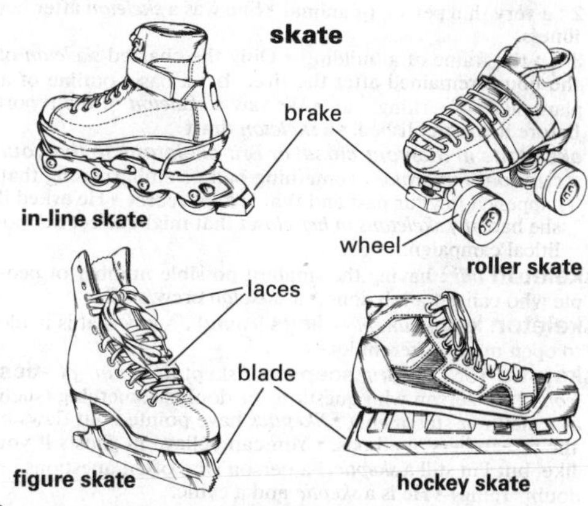

[2]skate *verb* **skates**; **skat·ed**; **skat·ing**
1 : to move or glide over a surface on skates [*no obj*] hockey players *skating* into position ▪ Couples *skated* around the rink. [+ *obj*] She *skated* an excellent program in the competition.
2 [*no obj*] : to ride or perform tricks on a skateboard ▪ We *skate* at the park.
3 [*no obj*] : to move or glide quickly along a surface ▪ The bugs *skated* along the surface of the water.
skate over/around [*phrasal verb*] ***skate over/around (something)*** : to avoid talking about (something) especially because it is difficult to talk about or embarrassing ▪ He *skated over* the issue/question.
– **skat·er** /ˈskeɪtɚ/ *noun, pl* **-ers** [*count*] ▪ She's a very good *skater*. ▪ Olympic ice *skaters*

[3]skate *noun, pl* **skates** [*count, noncount*] : a type of fish that has a flat, wide body and a long narrow tail — compare [1]SKATE

[1]skate·board /ˈskeɪtˌboɚd/ *noun, pl* **-boards** [*count*] : a short board that is on wheels and that a person stands on to move along a surface or to perform tricks

[2]skateboard *verb* **-boards**; **-board·ed**; **-board·ing** [*no obj*] : to ride or perform tricks on a skateboard ▪ He *skateboards* to school every day.
– **skate·board·er** /ˈskeɪtˌboɚdɚ/ *noun, pl* **-board·ers** [*count*]
– **skateboarding** *noun* [*noncount*] ▪ *Skateboarding* is not allowed in the parking lot.

skateboard

skate park *noun, pl* ~ **parks** [*count*] *chiefly US* : a place with special structures and surfaces on which people can roller-skate or skateboard

skating *noun* [*noncount*] : the activity or sport of gliding on skates or a skateboard ▪ No *skating* is allowed in the parking lot. ▪ We used to ***go skating*** on the pond every winter.

skating rink *noun, pl* ~ **rinks** [*count*] : an area or place that is used for skating

ske·dad·dle /skɪˈdædl/ *verb* **-dad·dles**; **-dad·dled**; **-dad·dling** [*no obj*] *informal + humorous* : to leave a place very quickly ▪ I've got to *skedaddle* or I'll be late.

skeet shooting /ˈskiːt-/ *noun* [*noncount*] *US* : the sport of shooting at targets (called clay pigeons) that are thrown in the air

skein /ˈskeɪn/ *noun, pl* **skeins** [*count*] : a long piece of yarn or thread that is loosely wound — compare HANK

skel·e·tal /ˈskɛlətl/ *adj*
1 *technical* : of or relating to a skeleton ▪ *skeletal* muscles ▪ the *skeletal* system ▪ The archaeologist found *skeletal* remains.
2 : very thin ▪ She was *skeletal* after her illness.

[1]skel·e·ton /ˈskɛlətən/ *noun, pl* **-tons** [*count*]

S

1 a : the structure of bones that supports the body of a person or animal ▪ They found the fossil *skeleton* of a mastodon. **b** : a set or model of all the bones in the body of a person ▪ He hung a plastic *skeleton* on the door for Halloween.— see picture at HUMAN
2 : a very thin person or animal ▪ She was a *skeleton* after her illness.
3 a : the frame of a building ▪ Only the charred *skeleton* of the house remained after the fire. **b** : a basic outline of a plan, piece of writing, etc. ▪ We saw a *skeleton* of the report before it was published. ▪ a *skeleton* draft
skeletons in the/your closet *or Brit* ***skeletons in the/your cupboard*** *informal* : something bad or embarrassing that happened in your past and that is kept secret ▪ He asked if she had any *skeletons in her closet* that might affect her political campaign.

²**skeleton** *adj* : having the smallest possible number of people who can get a job done ▪ a *skeleton* crew/staff

skeleton key *noun, pl* ~ **keys** [*count*] : a key that is made to open many different locks

skep·tic (*US*) *or Brit* **scep·tic** /ˈskɛptɪk/ *noun, pl* **-tics** [*count*] : a person who questions or doubts something (such as a claim or statement) ▪ *Skeptics* have pointed out flaws in the researchers' methods. ▪ You can believe in ghosts if you like, but I'm still a *skeptic*.: a person who often questions or doubts things ▪ He is a *skeptic* and a cynic.

skep·ti·cal (*US*) *or Brit* **scep·ti·cal** /ˈskɛptɪkəl/ *adj* [*more* ~; *most* ~] : having or expressing doubt about something (such as a claim or statement) ▪ She's highly *skeptical* of/about the researchers' claims. ▪ I'm *skeptical* that he can win. [=I doubt he can win] ▪ He says he can win, but I remain *skeptical*. ▪ When I said I'd finished my homework early, Mom looked *skeptical*.
– skep·ti·cal·ly (*US*) *or Brit* **scep·ti·cal·ly** /ˈskɛptɪkli/ *adv* ▪ People regarded the claims *skeptically*. ▪ She looked at me *skeptically*.

skep·ti·cism (*US*) *or Brit* **scep·ti·cism** /ˈskɛptəˌsɪzəm/ *noun* : an attitude of doubting the truth of something (such as a claim or statement) [*noncount*] She regarded the researcher's claims with *skepticism*. [*singular*] It's good to maintain a healthy *skepticism* about fad diets.

¹**sketch** /ˈskɛtʃ/ *noun, pl* **sketch·es** [*count*]
1 : a quick, rough drawing that shows the main features of an object or scene ▪ He made/drew a *sketch* of his house.
2 : a short description of something ▪ He wrote up a *sketch* of the plot. ▪ There is a biographical *sketch* of the author on the book's back cover. ▪ She gave us a ***thumbnail sketch*** [=short description] of the movie's plot.
3 : a short, funny performance ▪ a comedy *sketch*

²**sketch** *verb* **sketches; sketched; sketch·ing**
1 : to make a quick, rough drawing of (something) [+ *obj*] He *sketched* the trees outside his window. [*no obj*] He likes to sit outside and *sketch*.— often + *out* ▪ He *sketched out* the house's floor plans.
2 [+ *obj*] : to describe (something) briefly ▪ She *sketched* the plan for us.— often + *out* ▪ She *sketched out* the company's financial situation.
sketch in [*phrasal verb*] ***sketch in (something) or sketch (something) in*** : to add (something, such as details) to a drawing, description, etc. ▪ She looked over her picture and then *sketched in* a few more clouds. ▪ The author decided to *sketch in* some minor characters.

sketch·book /ˈskɛtʃˌbʊk/ *noun, pl* **-books** [*count*] : a book filled with paper that is used for drawing

sketch·pad /ˈskɛtʃˌpæd/ *noun, pl* **-pads** [*count*] : SKETCHBOOK

sketchy /ˈskɛtʃi/ *adj* **sketch·i·er; -est** [*also more* ~; *most* ~]
1 : not complete or clear ▪ The details about the accident are still a little *sketchy*. ▪ *sketchy* information/reports ▪ I have only a *sketchy* idea of how it works.
2 : done quickly without many details ▪ a *sketchy* drawing
3 *US, informal* : likely to be bad or dangerous ▪ a *sketchy* neighborhood
– sketch·i·ly /ˈskɛtʃəli/ *adv* ▪ a *sketchily* drawn figure
– sketch·i·ness /ˈskɛtʃinəs/ *noun* [*noncount*]

skew /ˈskjuː/ *verb* **skews; skewed; skew·ing** [+ *obj*]
1 : to change (something) so that it is not true or accurate ▪ They were accused of *skewing* the facts to fit their theory. ▪ A few unusual cases may have *skewed* the data. [=may have made the data show something that is not normal or typical]
2 : to make (something) favor a particular group of people in a way that is unfair ▪ He accused them of *skewing* the rules in their favor. — usually used as *(be) skewed*; usually + *toward* ▪ The tax cuts *are skewed toward* the wealthy.

skewed *adj* [*more* ~; *most* ~]
1 : not true or accurate ▪ *skewed* facts ▪ The ratio seems *skewed*.
2 : not straight ▪ The line is *skewed*.

¹**skew·er** /ˈskjuːwɚ/ *noun, pl* **-ers** [*count*] : a long pointed piece of metal or wood that is pushed through pieces of food to keep them together or hold them in place for cooking

²**skewer** *verb* **-ers; -ered; -ering** [+ *obj*]
1 : to push a skewer through (food) ▪ *skewer* a marshmallow
2 *chiefly US, informal* : to criticize (someone or something) very harshly ▪ Critics *skewered* the movie.

skew–whiff /ˌskjuːˈwɪf/ *adj* [*more* ~; *most* ~] *Brit, informal* : not straight : CROOKED ▪ a slightly *skew-whiff* door— often used figuratively ▪ Their plans went a little *skew-whiff*.

¹**ski** /ˈskiː/ *noun, pl* **skis** [*count*]
1 : one of a pair of long narrow pieces of wood, metal, or plastic that curve upward slightly in front, are attached to shoes, and are used for gliding over snow
2 : WATER SKI

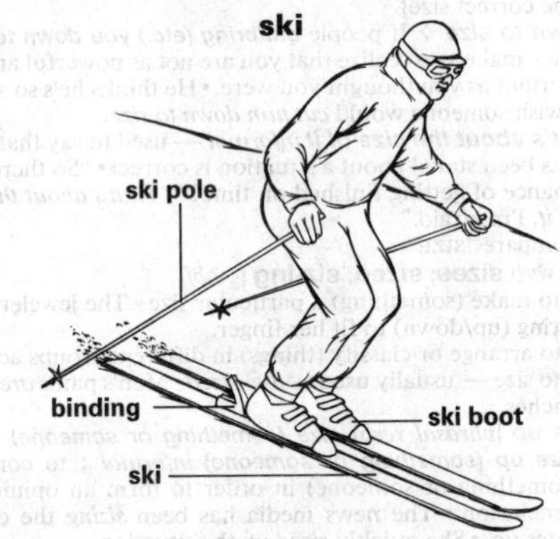

²**ski** *verb* **skies; skied; ski·ing** : to move or glide on skis over snow or water [*no obj*] He loves to *ski*. [+ *obj*] I have *skied* that mountain before.— see also WATER-SKI
– ski·er *noun, pl* **-ers** [*count*] ▪ My brother is a very good *skier*. ▪ *Skiers* love fresh snow.

³**ski** *adj, always used before a noun* : of, relating to, or used in skiing ▪ *ski* equipment/goggles ▪ a *ski* slope ▪ She is on her school's *ski* team. ▪ a *ski* instructor ▪ *ski* resorts/lodges

ski boot *noun, pl* ~ **boots** [*count*] : a boot or shoe made to be fastened to skis — see picture at SKI

¹**skid** /ˈskɪd/ *verb* **skids; skid·ded; skid·ding** [*no obj*] : to slide along a road or other surface in an uncontrolled way ▪ The truck *skidded* on/across the icy road. ▪ The car *skidded* off the road and into the gully. ▪ He slammed on the brakes, and the car *skidded* to a halt. ▪ I *skidded* on the ice and fell.

²**skid** *noun, pl* **skids** [*count*]
1 : a sudden, uncontrolled sliding movement ▪ The car hit a patch of ice and ***went into a skid***. ▪ The police measured the ***skid marks*** [=marks made by a skidding vehicle] on the road.
2 : one of a pair of long narrow parts on which a helicopter or airplane rests — usually plural ▪ the *skids* of a helicopter
3 *US, sports* : a series of losses that happen one after the other : a losing streak ▪ This victory ends a five-game *skid*.
4 : PALLET 1 ▪ They loaded the packages onto a *skid*.
hit the skids *informal* : to begin to fail or get worse very suddenly and quickly ▪ After he was injured his career *hit the skids*. ▪ The stock market has *hit the skids*.
on the skids *informal* : failing or getting worse : in a bad state or situation that is likely to result in failure ▪ The company is *on the skids*. ▪ Her marriage was *on the skids*.
put the skids under *Brit, informal* : to make (something or someone) likely or certain to fail ▪ He scored the goal that *put the skids under* our hopes for victory.

skid row *noun* [*noncount*] *chiefly US, informal* : a poor part of a town or city where people who are homeless or who drink too much often go
on skid row *chiefly US, informal* : having no money, job,

home, etc., and not able to take care of yourself • You'll end up on *skid row* if you don't stop drinking so much.

skiff /ˈskɪf/ *noun, pl* **skiffs** [*count*] : a small, light boat that is usually for only one person

skiing *noun* [*noncount*] : the activity or sport of gliding on skis • cross-country/downhill *skiing* • *Skiing* is my favorite winter activity. • We are planning to ***go skiing*** tomorrow.

ski jump *noun, pl* **~ jumps** [*count*] : a large, steep platform that slopes downward but curves upward slightly at the end so that skiers can glide down it and jump off the end
– **ski jumper** *noun, pl* **~ -ers** [*count*] – **ski jumping** *noun* [*noncount*] • He won a gold medal in Olympic *ski jumping*.

skilful *Brit spelling of* SKILLFUL

ski lift *noun, pl* **~ lifts** [*count*] : a series of seats or handles that are attached to a moving cable and that are used to carry skiers up a mountain

skill /ˈskɪl/ *noun, pl* **skills** : the ability to do something that comes from training, experience, or practice [*noncount*] Poker is a game of luck and *skill*. • I was impressed by her *skill* at writing. = I was impressed by her *skill* as a writer. • The work is difficult and requires a lot of *skill*. [*count*] Cooking is a useful *skill*. • He has excellent social *skills*. • reading and writing *skills* — see also PEOPLE SKILLS

skilled /ˈskɪld/ *adj*
1 [*more ~; most ~*] : having the training, knowledge, and experience that is needed to do something : having a lot of skill • *skilled* workers • a very *skilled* and talented writer • He is *skilled* at cooking.
2 *always used before a noun* : requiring training • Carpentry is a *skilled* trade. — opposite UNSKILLED

skil·let /ˈskɪlət/ *noun, pl* **-lets** [*count*] *chiefly US* : FRYING PAN

skill·ful (*US*) *or Brit* **skil·ful** /ˈskɪlfəl/ *adj*
1 [*more ~; most ~*] : having the training, knowledge, and experience that is needed to do something well : having a lot of skill • a *skillful* artist • He is *skillful* at diplomacy. • an artist *skillful* in the use of color
2 : showing or requiring skill • the *skillful* manner in which the doctor and nurses treated the patient • These issues require *skillful* handling.
– **skill·ful·ly** (*US*) *or Brit* **skil·ful·ly** *adv* • The furniture was *skillfully* made. • The manager handled the problem *skillfully*. – **skill·ful·ness** (*US*) *or Brit* **skil·ful·ness** *noun* [*noncount*] • the *skillfulness* of a craftsman

skim /ˈskɪm/ *verb* **skims; skimmed; skim·ming**
1 [+ *obj*] : to remove a layer of something from the surface of a liquid • I *skimmed* the fat from the broth. = I *skimmed* the broth to remove the fat. • He *skimmed* the leaves from the pool. • The cream is *skimmed* from the milk. • The milk is *skimmed* before it is bottled. — see also SKIM MILK
2 : to look over or read (something) quickly especially to find the main ideas [+ *obj*] She only *skimmed* the reading assignment. [*no obj*] She only ***skimmed through/over*** the reading assignment.
3 [+ *obj*] *Brit* : to throw (a flat stone) along the surface of water so that it bounces • He is really good at *skimming* [=(*US*) *skipping*] stones.
4 : to move quickly or lightly along, above, or near the surface of something [*no obj*] The ducks *skimmed* across/over the water before landing. [+ *obj*] The ducks *skimmed* the surface of the pond before landing.
skim off [*phrasal verb*] ***skim off (something) or skim (something) off*** : to take (something valuable) for yourself out of something else • He *skimmed off* some of the profits.

ski mask *noun, pl* **~ masks** [*count*] : a knitted fabric mask that covers your head, has openings for your eyes, mouth, and sometimes your nose, and is worn especially by skiers for protection from the cold

skim·mer /ˈskɪmɚ/ *noun, pl* **-mers** [*count*] : a spoon with holes in it that is used by cooks for skimming things

skim milk *noun* [*noncount*] *chiefly US* : milk from which all the cream and fat has been removed — called also (*chiefly Brit*) *skimmed milk*

skimp /ˈskɪmp/ *verb* **skimps; skimped; skimp·ing** [*no obj*] : to spend less time, money, etc., on something than is needed • Parents shouldn't *skimp* when it comes to their child's safety. — often + *on* • Don't *skimp on* sleep. • The book doesn't *skimp on* details. [=the book provides plenty of details] • The roof is already leaking because the builder *skimped on* materials. [=the builder bought cheap materials]

skimpy /ˈskɪmpi/ *adj* **skimp·i·er; -est** [*also more ~; most ~*] : very small in size or amount • a *skimpy* portion • *skimpy* evidence • a *skimpy* dress [=a dress which does not cover very much of the body]
– **skimp·i·ly** /ˈskɪmpəli/ *adv* • *skimpily* [=*scantily*] clad/dressed – **skimp·i·ness** /ˈskɪmpinəs/ *noun* [*noncount*] • I dislike the *skimpiness* of that restaurant's portions.

¹skin /ˈskɪn/ *noun, pl* **skins**
1 : the natural outer layer of tissue that covers the body of a person or animal [*noncount*] I have dry *skin*. • She has pale/dark/fair *skin*. • the rough *skin* of a shark • *skin* creams/lotions • *skin* cancer • Choose makeup that matches your *skin* tone. • The horrible things I saw ***made my skin crawl/creep*** [=made me feel disgusted, afraid, etc.] [*count*] These snakes shed their *skins* once a year.
2 : the skin of an animal that has been removed from the body often with its hair or feathers still attached and that is used to make things (such as clothes) [*count*] Native Americans had many uses for animal *skins*. [*noncount*] His boots are made of alligator *skin*.
3 : the outer covering of a fruit, vegetable, etc. [*count*] apple/sausage *skins* [*noncount*] Potato *skin* is very nutritious.
(a) thick/thin skin ✧ If you have *(a) thin skin*, you are easily upset or offended by the things other people say or do. • He has such *a thin skin* that he can't even take a little good-natured teasing. If you have *(a) thick skin*, you are not easily upset or offended by the things other people say and do. • She has pretty *thick skin* when it comes to criticism. • If you want to perform publicly, you'll need to ***grow a thicker skin*** [=become less sensitive to criticism]
by the skin of your teeth informal : only by a small difference in time, space, or amount : just barely • He escaped *by the skin of his teeth*. [=he just barely escaped] • She only passed the test *by the skin of her teeth*. [=she almost did not pass the test]
get under your skin informal **1** : to irritate or upset you • She really *gets under my skin*. **2** : to affect you emotionally even though you do not want or expect to be affected • I used to hate the city, but after a while it kind of *got under my skin*. [=I grew to like it] • The actress accepted the role because the character really *got under her skin*.
jump out of your skin informal ✧ If you almost/nearly (etc.) *jump out of your skin*, you are suddenly surprised or frightened very much by something. • I didn't hear her come in, so I nearly *jumped out of my skin* when she spoke to me.
no skin off my nose informal — used to say that you do not care or do not have a strong opinion about something • Go if you like—it's *no skin off my nose*.
save someone's skin see ¹SAVE
skin and bones or skin and bone informal : very thin in a way that is unattractive and unhealthy • After the illness, he was *skin and bones*. • The starving dog was ***nothing but skin and bones***.
– **skin·less** /ˈskɪnləs/ *adj* • *skinless* chicken breast

²skin *verb* **skins; skinned; skin·ning** [+ *obj*]
1 : to remove the skin of (an animal, fruit, or vegetable) • The hunter *skinned* the rabbit and prepared it for cooking. • *Skin* [=(more commonly) *peel*] the tomatoes/peppers.
2 : to scrape or rub off some of the skin from (a body part) • I *skinned* my knee when I fell.
keep your eyes skinned see ¹EYE
skin (someone) alive informal : to punish (someone) severely • Mom is going to *skin* me *alive* when she finds out about the broken window.

skin–deep /ˈskɪnˈdiːp/ *adj* : not very deep at all : relating to, affecting, or involving only the surface • Beauty is only *skin-deep*. • These reforms are more than *skin-deep*.

skin–dive *verb* **-dives; -dived; -div·ing** [*no obj*] : to swim underwater with special equipment (such as a face mask, snorkel, and flippers) but without a diving suit or air tank • We plan to *skin-dive* while on vacation.
– **skin diver** *noun, pl* **~ -ers** [*count*] – **skin diving** *noun* [*noncount*] • We ***went skin diving*** while on vacation.

skin·flint /ˈskɪnˌflɪnt/ *noun, pl* **-flints** [*count*] *informal + disapproving* : a person who hates to spend money • She is a penny-pinching *skinflint*.

skin·head /ˈskɪnˌhɛd/ *noun, pl* **-heads** [*count*] : a person with a shaved head; *especially* : a young white person who belongs to a gang whose members shave their heads and have racist beliefs

skinned /ˈskɪnd/ *adj* : having skin of a specified kind — used in combination • pale-*skinned* • dark-*skinned* • smooth-*skinned*

[1]skin·ny /ˈskɪni/ *adj* **skin·ni·er; -est** [*also more ~; most ~*] *informal* : very thin or too thin ▪ a *skinny* actress ▪ *skinny* arms/legs ***synonyms*** see [2]LEAN

[2]skinny *noun*
the skinny *US, informal* : the true information about someone or something that is not known by most people ▪ ***What's the skinny on*** their supposed breakup? ▪ Give me ***the inside/straight/real skinny.***

skin·ny–dip /ˈskɪniˌdɪp/ *verb* **-dips; -dipped; -dip·ping** [*no obj*] *informal* : to swim without wearing any clothes ▪ We used to *skinny-dip* in the lake.
– skinny–dip *noun, pl* **-dips** [*count*] ▪ They went for a *skinny-dip* in the lake. **– skin·ny–dip·per** /ˈskɪniˌdɪpɚ/ *noun, pl* **-pers** [*count*] **– skinny–dipping** *noun* [*noncount*] ▪ Let's ***go skinny-dipping.***

skint /ˈskɪnt/ *adj, Brit, informal* : having no money : BROKE ▪ I'm completely *skint.*

skin·tight /ˈskɪnˈtaɪt/ *adj* : very closely fitted to the body : very tight ▪ a *skintight* dress

[1]skip /ˈskɪp/ *verb* **skips; skipped; skip·ping**
1 [*+ obj*] : to not do (something that is usual or expected) ▪ He *skipped* the meeting. [=he didn't go to the meeting] ▪ I *skipped* breakfast, and now I'm really hungry. ▪ (*chiefly US*) They got in trouble for ***skipping school/class.*** — see also *skip bail* at [1]BAIL
2 : to not discuss, read, do, or deal with (something) and go instead to the next thing : to pass over or leave out (something) [*+ obj*] I *skipped* the boring parts of the book. ▪ If you are having trouble with one of the questions on the test, *skip* it and come back to it later. ▪ She will *skip* a grade and go right from the fourth to the sixth grade next September. — often *+ over* ▪ You can *skip over* the introduction if you want. [*no obj*] I don't like this song. Let's *skip* to the next one.
3 *always followed by an adverb or preposition* [*no obj*] **a** : to change quickly from one subject, place, etc., to another ▪ It's hard to understand him when he *skips* from topic to topic like that. ▪ The movie *skips* around in time. **b** ✧ If a CD, DVD, record, etc., *skips*, it fails to play part of a song or movie properly because it is damaged. ▪ The record keeps *skipping.*
4 [*no obj*] : to move forward in a light or playful way by taking short, quick steps and jumps ▪ The kids *skipped* happily down the street.
5 [*+ obj*] *informal* : to leave (a place) in a sudden and unexpected way especially to avoid trouble, punishment, etc. ▪ Police are afraid he might try to *skip* the country. ▪ They ***skipped town*** while awaiting trial.
6 *US* : to throw (a flat stone) along the surface of water so that it bounces [*+ obj*] She's really good at *skipping* [=(*Brit*) *skimming*] stones. [*no obj*] I got the rock to *skip* six times!
7 [*no obj*] *Brit* : to jump over a rope that is being swung near the ground for exercise or as a game ▪ The children are outside *skipping.* [=(*US*) *skipping rope, jumping rope*]
heart skips a beat see HEART
skip it *chiefly US, informal* — used to say that you do not want to do something, talk about something, etc. ▪ I meant to . . . oh, *skip it.* It's not important anyway.
skip out (*US*) *or Brit* ***skip off*** [*phrasal verb*] *informal* : to leave a place quickly in a secret and improper way ▪ They *skipped out* before the check arrived. ▪ She *skipped out* with all the money. — often *+ on* in U.S. English ▪ They *skipped out on* the bill/check. ▪ She *skipped out on* me and took all the money.
skip rope see [1]ROPE

S

[2]skip *noun, pl* **skips** [*count*]
1 : a short, quick step and jump forward ▪ a quick *skip*
2 *Brit* : a large metal container for putting trash in
a hop, skip, and (a) jump see [2]HOP

ski pole *noun, pl* **~ poles** [*count*] : one of two long sticks that are used to control your movements and balance while you are skiing — see picture at SKI

[1]skip·per /ˈskɪpɚ/ *noun, pl* **-pers** [*count*] *informal*
1 : the captain of a ship or boat
2 *informal* : someone who leads a group; *especially* : the manager of a baseball team

[2]skipper *verb* **-pers; -pered; -per·ing** [*+ obj*] *informal*
1 : to be the captain of (a ship or boat) ▪ The boat was *skippered* by a skilled veteran sailor.
2 : to be the person who leads or manages (a team) ▪ He *skippered* the team to their latest World Series win.

skipping rope *noun, pl* **~ ropes** [*count*] *Brit* : JUMP ROPE

[1]skir·mish /ˈskɚmɪʃ/ *noun, pl* **-mish·es** [*count*]
1 : a brief and usually unplanned fight during a war ▪ *Skirmishes* broke out between rebel groups. ▪ Violent *skirmishes* with the enemy continue despite talks of peace.
2 : a minor or brief argument or disagreement ▪ a political *skirmish*

[2]skirmish *verb* **-mishes; -mished; -mish·ing** [*no obj*] : to be involved in a skirmish ▪ Rebel groups are *skirmishing* with military forces. ▪ The presidential candidates *skirmished* over their economic plans.

[1]skirt /ˈskɚt/ *noun, pl* **skirts** [*count*]
1 a : a piece of clothing worn by women and girls that hangs from the waist down ▪ She was wearing a short/long *skirt.* — see color picture on page C14; see also MINISKIRT **b** : the part of a dress, coat, etc., that hangs from the waist down ▪ The *skirt* of her coat got caught in the car door. — sometimes plural ▪ He gathered up the *skirts* of his robe as he climbed the stairs. ▪ a dress with full *skirts*
2 : an outer covering that hangs down to protect something ▪ They put a protective *skirt* around the base of the machine.

[2]skirt *verb* **skirts; skirt·ed; skirt·ing**
1 : to avoid (something) especially because it is difficult or will cause problems [*+ obj*] The mayor *skirted* the issue by saying that a committee was looking into the problem. ▪ They tried to *skirt* the new regulations. [*no obj*] He tried to ***skirt around*** the question.
2 : to lie or go along the edge of (something) [*+ obj*] Pine trees *skirt* the northern edge of the pond. [*no obj*] The road ***skirts around*** the lake. ▪ We *skirted around* the edge of the city.

skirting board *noun, pl* **~ boards** [*count, noncount*] *Brit* : BASEBOARD — called also (*Brit*) *skirting*

skit /ˈskɪt/ *noun, pl* **skits** [*count*] : a short, funny story or performance ▪ One of the funniest *skits* in the show was about cheerleading.

skit·ter /ˈskɪtɚ/ *verb, always followed by an adverb or preposition* **-ters; -tered; -ter·ing** [*no obj*] : to move quickly and lightly along a surface ▪ Dry leaves *skittered* over the sidewalk. ▪ Mice *skittered* across the floor.

skit·tish /ˈskɪtɪʃ/ *adj* [*more ~; most ~*]
1 *of an animal* : easily frightened or excited ▪ a *skittish* horse
2 : nervous or fearful about doing something ▪ We've been *skittish* about taking on such a large mortgage. ▪ *skittish* consumers/investors
3 *chiefly US* : tending to change often : not dependable or stable ▪ a *skittish* stock market
– skit·tish·ly *adv* **– skit·tish·ness** *noun* [*noncount*]

skit·tle /ˈskɪtl̩/ *noun, pl* **skit·tles**
1 ***skittles*** [*noncount*] : a British game played by rolling a wooden ball toward a set of objects in order to knock over as many objects as possible
2 [*count*] : one of the objects that a player tries to knock over in a game of skittles

skive /ˈskaɪv/ *verb* **skives; skived; skiv·ing** *Brit, informal* : to avoid school or work by staying away or by leaving without permission — often *+ off* [*no obj*] He works for his mother and feels he can *skive off* whenever he feels like it. [*+ obj*] She *skived off* school twice last month.
– skiv·er /ˈskaɪvɚ/ *noun, pl* **-ers** [*count*]

Skiv·vies /ˈskɪviz/ *trademark, US* — used for men's underwear

skiv·vy /ˈskɪvi/ *noun, pl* **-vies** [*count*] *Brit, informal* : a female servant who does work that is dirty and unpleasant ▪ I'm tired of being treated like a *skivvy.*

skul·dug·gery *or* **skull·dug·gery** /ˌskʌlˈdʌgəri/ *noun* [*noncount*] *old-fashioned* : secret or dishonest behavior or activity ▪ tales of espionage and *skulduggery*

skulk /ˈskʌlk/ *verb, always followed by an adverb or preposition* **skulks; skulked; skulk·ing** [*no obj*] : to move or hide in a secret way especially because you are planning to do something bad ▪ A man was *skulking* around outside. ▪ She *skulked* into her sister's room.

skull /ˈskʌl/ *noun, pl* **skulls** [*count*] : the structure of bones that form the head and face of a person or animal ▪ He had a fractured *skull.* ▪ (*informal*) You need to ***get it into/through your thick skull*** [=you need to realize/understand] that you can't just sit there and expect everyone else to do your work for you! ▪ (*informal*) He can't seem to *get it through his skull* that I don't like him. — see picture at HUMAN

skull and cross·bones /ˌskʌlənˈkrɑːsˌbounz/ *noun* [*singular*] : a picture of a human skull above two crossed bones that was used on the flags of pirate ships in the past and is now used as a warning label on containers of poisonous or dangerous substances

skull·cap /ˈskʌlˌkæp/ *noun, pl* **-caps** [*count*]
1 : a small, round cap that fits on top of the head and that is worn especially by Jewish men and Catholic clergymen
2 : a tight-fitting cap that is made of material that stretches

skunk /ˈskʌŋk/ *noun, pl* **skunks** [*count*]
1 : a small black-and-white North American animal that produces a very strong and unpleasant smell when it is frightened or in danger
2 *US, informal* **:** a very bad or unpleasant person ▪ Her brother's a low-down, dirty *skunk.*

skunk

skunk cabbage *noun* [*noncount*] **:** a North American plant that grows in wet, shady areas and that produces a strong odor

sky /ˈskaɪ/ *noun, pl* **skies :** the space over the Earth where the sun, moon, stars, and clouds appear [*count*] a starry *sky* ▪ the night/desert *sky* ▪ There wasn't a cloud in the *sky.* ▪ Dark clouds moved quickly across the *sky.* ▪ Hailstones suddenly fell out of the *sky.* ▪ The sun/moon was high in the *sky.* ▪ The forecast is for sunny/blue/gray/overcast *skies* tomorrow. ▪ partly cloudy *skies* [*noncount*] a patch of blue *sky*
praise (someone or something) to the skies see [1]PRAISE
take to the sky/skies *chiefly US* **:** to begin flying ▪ The new airliner will *take to the skies* next year.
the sky's the limit see [1]LIMIT
— see also PIE IN THE SKY

sky blue *noun* [*noncount*] **:** a pale to light blue color — see color picture on page C2

sky·box /ˈskaɪˌbɑːks/ *noun, pl* **-box·es** [*count*] *US* **:** an area with a roof and private seats near the top of a sports stadium

sky·cap /ˈskaɪˌkæp/ *noun, pl* **-caps** [*count*] *US* **:** a person whose job is to carry people's luggage at an airport

sky·div·ing /ˈskaɪˌdaɪvɪŋ/ *noun* [*noncount*] **:** the sport of jumping from an airplane and falling through the sky before opening a parachute
— **sky·dive** /ˈskaɪˌdaɪv/ *verb* **-dives; -dived; -div·ing** [*no obj*] ▪ Have you ever *skydived?* — **sky·div·er** *noun, pl* **-ers** [*count*]

[1]**sky–high** /ˈskaɪˈhaɪ/ *adj* **:** extremely high ▪ *sky-high* prices ▪ Her blood pressure is *sky-high.*

[2]**sky–high** *adv* **:** to a very high degree, level, or amount ▪ Stock prices rose *sky-high.* ▪ Rubble was piled *sky-high.*

sky·lark /ˈskaɪˌlɑɚk/ *noun, pl* **-larks** [*count*] **:** a small bird of Europe, Asia, and northern Africa that sings while it flies

sky·light /ˈskaɪˌlaɪt/ *noun, pl* **-lights** [*count*] **:** a window in the roof of a house or on a ship's deck

sky·line /ˈskaɪˌlaɪn/ *noun, pl* **-lines** [*count*] **:** the outline of buildings, mountains, etc., against the background of the sky ▪ the New York City *skyline*

[1]**sky·rock·et** /ˈskaɪˌrɑːkət/ *verb* **-ets; -et·ed; -et·ing** [*no obj*] **:** to increase quickly to a very high level or amount ▪ Costs/Sales have *skyrocketed.* ▪ *skyrocketing* prices ▪ His popularity *skyrocketed* after his latest movie.

[2]**skyrocket** *noun, pl* **-ets** [*count*] **:** [1]ROCKET 3

sky·scrap·er /ˈskaɪˌskreɪpɚ/ *noun, pl* **-ers** [*count*] **:** a very tall building in a city

sky·ward /ˈskaɪwɚd/ *also chiefly Brit* **sky·wards** /ˈskaɪwɚdz/ *adv* **:** toward the sky **:** up into the sky ▪ Everyone looked *skyward* as the jets passed by. ▪ The bird soared *skyward.*

slab /ˈslæb/ *noun, pl* **slabs** [*count*]
1 : a thick, flat piece of a hard material (such as stone or wood) ▪ concrete *slabs* ▪ *slabs* of rock
2 : a thick, flat piece of food (such as bread or meat) ▪ a *slab* of bacon ▪ a thick *slab* of homemade bread

[1]**slack** /ˈslæk/ *adj*
1 : not stretched or held in a tight position **:** LOOSE ▪ *slack* rope ▪ His broken arm hung *slack* at his side. ▪ The rope suddenly ***went slack.*** ▪ Her jaw *went slack* [=fell open] in amazement.
2 : not busy **:** lacking the expected or desired activity ▪ The fall is our *slack* [=*slow*] season. ▪ a *slack* market
3 a : doing something poorly because you are not putting enough care or effort into it ▪ I've been a little *slack* [=*careless*] about taking my medication lately. **b :** done poorly and carelessly ▪ He accused the government of *slack* supervision of nuclear technology.
— **slack·ly** *adv* ▪ Streamers hung *slackly* from the walls.
— **slack·ness** *noun* [*noncount*] ▪ the *slackness* of the rope ▪ His *slackness* at work has been noticed.

[2]**slack** *noun, pl* **slacks**
1 [*noncount*] **:** the part of a rope, chain, etc., that hangs loosely ▪ Take in/up the *slack* of the rope. — sometimes used figuratively to describe a part of something that is available but not used ▪ We left some *slack* in the budget so that we can hire more people if we have to.
2 slacks [*plural*] *chiefly US* **:** pants or trousers ▪ He was wearing a white shirt and (a pair of) cotton *slacks.* ▪ She wore ***dress slacks*** and a nice blouse.
give/cut (someone) some slack *informal* **:** to treat (someone) in a less harsh or critical way ▪ Would you *give/cut me some slack?* I'm doing the best I can.
pick/take up the slack **:** to provide or do something that is missing or not getting done ▪ When he didn't get the pay raise he was expecting, he had to take another job to *pick up the slack.* [=to make up for the money he was not making] ▪ The manager has to *take up the slack* when employees don't do their jobs correctly.

[3]**slack** *verb* **slacks; slacked; slack·ing** [*no obj*] **:** to give little or no effort or attention to work ▪ They need to stop *slacking* and get down to work.
slack off [*phrasal verb*] **1 :** to do something with less effort or energy than you did it with before ▪ I was exercising regularly last summer, but I've been *slacking off* recently. **2 :** to become less active, forceful, etc. ▪ Their business has been *slacking off* in recent months.

slack·en /ˈslækən/ *verb* **-ens; -ened; -en·ing**
1 a [*no obj*] **:** to become slower or less active **:** to slow down ▪ Sales show no sign of *slackening.* ▪ The wind *slackened* (off) and the sky cleared. **b** [+ *obj*] **:** to make (something) slower or less active ▪ She *slackened* her speed/pace [=she slowed down] after she slipped on the ice.
2 : to become less tight or to make (something) less tight **:** LOOSEN [*no obj*] As he began to relax, his grip on the steering wheel *slackened.* [+ *obj*] He *slackened* his grip. ▪ The captain ordered us to *slacken* the sails.

slack·er /ˈslækɚ/ *noun, pl* **-ers** [*count*] *informal* **:** a person who avoids work and responsibilities ▪ The people I work with are a bunch of *slackers.*

[1]**slag** /ˈslæg/ *noun* [*noncount*] **:** the material that is left when rocks that contain metal are heated to get the metal out ▪ a ***slag heap*** [=a large pile of slag] — compare [2]SLAG

[2]**slag** *noun, pl* **slags** [*count*] *Brit slang, offensive* **:** a woman who has many sexual partners — compare [1]SLAG

[3]**slag** *verb* **slags; slagged; slag·ging**
slag off [*phrasal verb*] ***slag (someone) off*** *or* ***slag off (someone)*** *Brit slang* **:** to criticize (someone) harshly ▪ She often *slags off* other musicians to try to make herself look good.

slain *past participle of* SLAY

slake /ˈsleɪk/ *verb* **slakes; slaked; slak·ing** [+ *obj*] *literary* **:** to provide, do, or have what is required by (something) **:** SATISFY ▪ trying to *slake* his curiosity/lust
slake your thirst **:** to cause you to stop feeling thirsty **:** to quench your thirst ▪ They *slaked their thirst* with cold water.

sla·lom /ˈslɑːləm/ *noun, pl* **-loms** [*count, noncount*] **:** a race especially on skis over a winding course that is marked by flags — often used before another noun ▪ a *slalom* course/race ▪ *slalom* skiers/racers/skis

S

[1]**slam** /ˈslæm/ *verb* **slams; slammed; slam·ming**
1 : to close (something) in a forceful way that makes a loud noise [+ *obj*] He *slammed* the door in my face. ▪ She *slammed* the drawer shut. [*no obj*] He stepped inside and let the door *slam* behind him. ▪ The window *slammed* shut.
2 [+ *obj*] **:** to set or throw (something) in a forceful way that makes a loud noise ▪ In her anger, she *slammed* the ball against the fence. — usually + *down* ▪ He *slammed* the books *down* on the table and ran outside. ▪ She *slammed down* the phone.
3 *always followed by an adverb or preposition* [*no obj*] **:** to hit something with a lot of force ▪ The car slid on the ice and *slammed* into a tree. ▪ Her arm *slammed* against the table.
4 [+ *obj*] *informal* **:** to criticize (someone or something) harshly ▪ Her decision is getting *slammed* in the press. — often + *for* ▪ Many people have *slammed* the company *for* not paying its workers decent wages.
slam on the brakes **:** to press down hard on the brakes of a

car to make it stop suddenly • He *slammed on the brakes* to avoid hitting the dog.

²slam *noun, pl* **slams** [*count*]
1 a : an act of closing something in a forceful way that makes a loud noise — usually singular • He closed the book with a *slam*. **b :** a loud noise that is made when something is closed in a forceful way — usually singular • I heard the *slam* of a car door in the driveway.
2 *chiefly US* **:** a competition in which people read their poetry out loud so that it can be judged by other people • a poetry *slam* • *slam* poets
— see also GRAND SLAM

slam dunk *noun, pl* ~ **dunks** [*count*]
1 *basketball* **:** ²DUNK
2 *US, informal* **:** something that is sure to happen or be successful • The vote proved to be a *slam dunk* for our side with a 24 to 5 win. • There's no doubt that he's guilty. The case is a *slam dunk*.

slam–dunk *verb* **-dunks; -dunked; -dunk·ing** *basketball* **:** to jump high in the air and push (the ball) down through the basket **:** DUNK [+ *obj*] He *slam-dunked* the ball. [*no obj*] At his height, it's not so hard to *slam-dunk*.

slam·mer /ˈslæmɚ/ *noun*
the slammer informal **:** a prison or jail • He got 10 years ***in the slammer.***

¹slan·der /ˈslændɚ/ *noun, pl* **-ders**
1 [*noncount*] **:** the act of making a false spoken statement that causes people to have a bad opinion of someone • She is being sued for *slander*. • He was a target of *slander*. — compare LIBEL
2 [*count*] **:** a false spoken statement that is made to cause people to have a bad opinion of someone • We've heard countless unsupported *slanders* about her.
— **slan·der·ous** /ˈslændərəs/ *adj* • *slanderous* claims/attacks/allegations

²slander *verb* **-ders; -dered; -der·ing** [+ *obj*] **:** to make a false spoken statement that causes people to have a bad opinion of someone • She was accused of *slandering* her former boss.

slang /ˈslæŋ/ *noun* [*noncount*] **:** words that are not considered part of the standard vocabulary of a language and that are used very informally in speech especially by a particular group of people • American *slang* • local/military/street *slang*
— **slang** *adj* • a *slang* word/expression/term • The word "phat" is *slang*. — **slangy** /ˈslæŋi/ *adj* • *slangy* expressions

slang·ing match /ˈslæŋɪŋ-/ *noun, pl* ~ **matches** [*count*] *Brit, informal* **:** an angry argument in which people insult each other **:** SHOUTING MATCH

¹slant /ˈslænt/ *verb* **slants; slant·ed; slant·ing**
1 : to not be level or straight up and down [*no obj*] The floor *slants* [=*slopes*] down slightly. • a *slanting* table • His handwriting *slants* [=*leans*] to the left. • The sunlight *slanted* down through the leaves and branches of the trees. [+ *obj*] She *slanted* her hat a little to the right.
2 [+ *obj*] **:** to present (something, such as a news story) in a way that favors a particular group, opinion, etc. • They deliberately *slanted* the story to make themselves look good. — often used as *(be) slanted* • The media coverage of the strike *was slanted* against the union.
— **slanted** *adj* [*more* ~; *most* ~] • Her attic bedroom has *slanted* ceilings. • a *slanted* roof/floor • The news program claimed to be objective but was very *slanted*. [=*biased*]

²slant *noun, pl* **slants**
1 [*singular*] **:** a direction, line, or surface that is not level or straight up and down • The computer keyboard is positioned ***at a slant*** so that typing is more comfortable for the wrists. • He sliced the carrots ***on a/the slant***
2 [*count*] **:** a way of thinking about, describing, or discussing something — usually singular • The book offers a new *slant* on the history of the country. • The latest evidence puts an entirely different *slant* on the case. • His writings have a liberal/religious *slant*.

¹slap /ˈslæp/ *verb* **slaps; slapped; slap·ping**
1 a [+ *obj*] **:** to hit (someone or something) with the front or back of your open hand • She *slapped* him across/in the face. • She *slapped* his face. • He *slapped* me on the back and said "Good job!" • He called the dog by *slapping* his hand against his thigh. **b :** to hit something with a sound like the sound made when your hand slaps something [*no obj*] Waves were *slapping* against the side of the boat. [+ *obj*] Gentle waves *slapped* the side of the raft.
2 [+ *obj*] **:** to put (something) on a surface quickly or forcefully — + *down* or *on* • He *slapped* the book *down* on the desk. • She *slapped down* her cards and shouted "I win!" • He *slapped* a fresh coat of paint *on* (the wall). • I grabbed a slice of bread and *slapped on* some peanut butter.
3 [+ *obj*] *sports* **:** to hit (something) with a forceful swing of your arms, hands, etc. • (*ice hockey*) He *slapped* the puck into the net. • (*baseball*) She *slapped* a single to right field.
slap around [*phrasal verb*] ***slap (someone) around also slap around (someone) informal*** **:** to hit or slap (someone) many times • The children screamed when they saw him *slapping* her *around*. [=beating her up]
slap on [*phrasal verb*] ***slap (something) on or slap on (something) informal*** **:** to add (something, such as an extra charge) to an amount • The hotel *slapped* an extra $100 *on* his bill to cover the damage. • The judge *slapped on* an additional fine. — see also ¹SLAP 2 (above)
slap together [*phrasal verb*] ***slap together (something) or slap (something) together informal*** **:** to create (something) by putting parts together in a quick or careless way • I *slapped* a sandwich *together* as I was running out the door. • The company *slapped together* a Web site and then waited for the customers to come pouring in.
slap with [*phrasal verb*] ***slap (someone) with (something) US, informal*** **:** to punish (someone) with (a fine, lawsuit, etc.) • They were *slapped with* a lawsuit. • The judge *slapped* the company *with* a fine for polluting the river.

²slap *noun, pl* **slaps** [*count*]
1 : a hit with the front or back of your open hand • I was so angry that I felt like giving him a *slap*.
2 : a loud sound made when something hits a flat surface • I could hear the *slap* of the waves against the side of the boat.
a slap in the face **:** a surprising act that offends or insults someone • Her decision to leave the company to work for our competitors was *a slap in the face*.
a slap on the back **:** the act of slapping someone's back usually to express praise or approval • He gave me *a slap on the back* and said "Good job!"
a slap on the wrist **:** a mild punishment that is given to someone who should be punished more severely • Even though he was proven guilty, he got away with *a slap on the wrist*. • The fine was just *a slap on the wrist*.

³slap *adv, informal* **:** exactly or directly • I walked *slap* into the post. • Her apartment is *slap* in the middle of the city. = Her apartment is ***slap bang*** in the middle of the city.

slap·dash /ˈslæpˌdæʃ/ *adj* [*more* ~; *most* ~] **:** quick and careless • *slapdash* repairs • The writing is *slapdash*.

slap·hap·py /ˈslæpˌhæpi/ *adj* [*more* ~; *most* ~] *informal*
1 : PUNCH-DRUNK • a *slaphappy* boxer • We were all a bit *slaphappy* after staying up all night to finish the report.
2 : happy and careless • She has a *slaphappy* attitude about her work.

slap shot *noun, pl* ~ **shots** [*count*] *ice hockey* **:** a shot that is made by swinging your stick with a lot of force

slap·stick /ˈslæpˌstɪk/ *noun* [*noncount*] **:** comedy that involves physical action (such as falling down or hitting people) — often used before another noun • *slapstick* comedy

slap–up /ˈslæpˌʌp/ *adj, always used before a noun, Brit, informal, of a meal* **:** excellent and very large • a *slap-up* dinner

¹slash /ˈslæʃ/ *verb* **slash·es; slashed; slash·ing** [+ *obj*]
1 a : to make a long cut in (something) with a knife or other sharp weapon • Someone *slashed* his car's tires. • He threatened to *slash* the man's throat. **b :** to make (a path) by cutting plants • She *slashed* a path through the underbrush. • They ***slashed their way through*** the jungle.
2 : to reduce (something) by a large amount • The company has *slashed* prices to increase sales. • Funding for the program was *slashed*.
slash at [*phrasal verb*] ***slash at (someone or something)*** **:** to attack (someone or something) violently with a knife or other sharp weapon • He *slashed at* me with a knife.

²slash *noun, pl* **slashes**
1 [*count*] **:** a thin and usually long cut made with a knife or other sharp object • There was a horrible *slash* on his arm.
2 [*count*] **:** a quick movement with a sharp knife or weapon to cut someone or something • He cut my cheek with a quick *slash* of the knife.
3 [*count*] **:** a patch or line of bright light or color • *slashes* of sunlight on a wall • a dark painting with a *slash* of red
4 [*count*] **:** the mark / that is used to mean "or" (as in *and/or*), "and or" (as in *bottles/cans*), or "per" (as in *kilometers/hour*) or as a division sign in fractions (as in ¾) — called also *slash mark*, (*Brit*) *oblique*

S

5 [*singular*] *Brit slang* : an act of urinating ▪ He got out of the car to ***have/take a slash.***

slash–and–burn *adj*

1 : done by cutting down and burning trees and plants in order to clear an area of land and grow crops on it for usually a brief time ▪ *slash-and-burn* agriculture

2 : using extremely harsh methods : RUTHLESS ▪ *slash-and-burn* tactics/politics

slash·er /ˈslæʃɚ/ *noun, pl* **-ers** [*count*] : someone who kills people with a knife or other sharp weapon ▪ a *slasher* movie/film [=a movie in which many people are violently murdered by a slasher]

slat /ˈslæt/ *noun, pl* **slats** [*count*] : a thin, narrow strip of wood, plastic, or metal ▪ the *slats* of a venetian blind ▪ The fence has two broken *slats.*

– slat·ted /ˈslætəd/ *adj* ▪ *slatted* blinds

[1]**slate** /ˈsleɪt/ *noun, pl* **slates**

1 [*noncount*] : a type of hard rock that splits easily into thin layers ▪ Some school blackboards are made of *slate.*

2 [*count*] : a small sheet of slate in a wooden frame that was used in schools in the past for writing on with chalk — see also BLANK SLATE

3 [*count*] : a piece of slate that is used with others to cover a roof or wall ▪ roofing *slates* ▪ The house has a *slate* roof.

4 [*count*] *US* : a list of people who are trying to win an election ▪ The party has fielded an impressive *slate* of candidates this year.

clean slate see [1]CLEAN

wipe the slate clean see [1]WIPE

[2]**slate** *verb* **slates; slat·ed; slat·ing** [+ *obj*] *chiefly US* : to arrange or plan for something to happen, someone to be chosen, etc. — usually used as *(be) slated* ▪ The new art museum *is slated* [=*is scheduled*] to open next spring. ▪ She *is slated* to become the company's next president. — often + *for* ▪ Her latest album *is slated for* release in July. — compare [3]SLATE

[3]**slate** *verb* **slates; slated; slating** [+ *obj*] *Brit, informal* : to criticize (someone or something) very harshly ▪ The film/book was *slated* by most critics. — compare [2]SLATE

slate blue *noun* [*noncount*] : a grayish-blue color — see color picture on page C2

– slate blue *adj*

slate gray (*US*) *or Brit* **slate grey** *noun* [*noncount*] : a bluish-gray color — see color picture on page C2

– slate gray (*US*) *or Brit* **slate grey** *adj*

slath·er /ˈslæðɚ/ *verb* **-ers; -ered; -er·ing** [+ *obj*] : to cover something with a thick layer of a liquid, cream, etc. ▪ We ate lobster *slathered* with/in butter ▪ She *slathered* her skin with sunscreen. = She *slathered* sunscreen on her skin.

slat·tern /ˈslætən/ *noun, pl* **-terns** [*count*] *old-fashioned* : an untidy, dirty woman

– slat·tern·ly /ˈslætənli/ *adj* ▪ a *slatternly* housewife

[1]**slaugh·ter** /ˈslɑːtɚ/ *verb* **-ters; -tered; -ter·ing** [+ *obj*]

1 : to kill (an animal) for food ▪ *slaughter* cattle

2 : to kill (many people) in a very violent way ▪ Hundreds of people were *slaughtered* [=*massacred*] by the invaders.

3 *informal* : to defeat (someone or something) easily or completely ▪ Our team got *slaughtered* yesterday. ▪ They *slaughtered* us.

[2]**slaugh·ter** *noun* [*noncount*]

1 : the act of killing animals for their meat ▪ Thousands of cows are sent to (the) *slaughter* every day.

2 : the violent killing of a large number of people ▪ the *slaughter* of innocent people — see also MANSLAUGHTER

like a lamb to the slaughter see [1]LAMB

slaugh·ter·house /ˈslɑːtɚˌhaʊs/ *noun, pl* **-hous·es** [*count*] : a building where animals are killed for their meat — called also (*chiefly Brit*) *abattoir*

Slav /ˈslɑːv/ *noun, pl* **Slavs** [*count*] : a person from eastern Europe who speaks a Slavic language

[1]**slave** /ˈsleɪv/ *noun, pl* **slaves** [*count*]

1 : someone who is legally owned by another person and is forced to work for that person without pay ▪ freed/escaped/former *slaves* ▪ He treats her like a *slave.* ▪ Do it yourself! I'm not your *slave!*

2 *disapproving* : a person who is strongly influenced and controlled by something — + *to* or *of* ▪ She's a *slave to* fashion. ▪ a *slave of* desire

[2]**slave** *verb, always followed by an adverb or preposition* **slaves; slaved; slav·ing** [*no obj*] : to work very hard ▪ I *slaved* all morning to get the work done on time. ▪ I spent all day ***slaving over a hot stove.*** [=I spent all day cooking] ▪ She's been ***slaving away at*** her homework.

slave driver *noun, pl* ~ **-ers** [*count*]

1 : someone who is in charge of slaves and makes them work

2 *disapproving* : someone who makes people work very hard ▪ The new boss is a real *slave driver.*

slave·hold·er /ˈsleɪvˌhoʊldɚ/ *noun, pl* **-ers** [*count*] *US* : a person who owns slaves

– slave·hold·ing /ˈsleɪvˌhoʊldɪŋ/ *adj* ▪ *slaveholding* towns

slave labor (*US*) *or Brit* **slave labour** *noun* [*noncount*]

1 : work that is done by slaves or by people who are treated like slaves ▪ prisoners being forced to do *slave labor* ▪ a *slave labor* camp

2 : slaves doing work ▪ The pyramids were built by *slave labor.*

[1]**sla·ver** /ˈslævɚ/ *verb* **-vers; -vered; -ver·ing** [*no obj*] : to allow liquid to drip out of the mouth : DROOL ▪ The dog *slavered* [=(more commonly) *slobbered*] over his food.

[2]**slav·er** /ˈsleɪvɚ/ *noun, pl* **-ers** [*count*]

1 : a person who was involved in buying and selling slaves in the past

2 : a ship that was used to carry slaves from one place to another in the past

slav·ery /ˈsleɪvəri/ *noun* [*noncount*]

1 : the state of being a slave ▪ She was ***sold into slavery.***

2 : the practice of owning slaves ▪ the abolition of *slavery*

slave state *noun, pl* ~ **states** [*count*] : a state of the U.S. in which slavery was legal until the American Civil War

slave trade *noun* [*noncount*] : the activity or business of buying and selling slaves — used especially to refer to the business of buying and selling people as slaves before the American Civil War

[1]**Slav·ic** /ˈslɑːvɪk/ *noun* [*noncount*] : a group of related languages that includes Russian, Bulgarian, Czech, Polish, etc.

[2]**Slavic** *adj* : of or relating to the Slavs or their languages ▪ *Slavic* people/languages/lands/folklore

slav·ish /ˈsleɪvɪʃ/ *adj, disapproving* : copying or following someone or something completely without any attempt to be original or independent ▪ a politician and his *slavish* followers ▪ *slavish* obedience/imitation ▪ He has been criticized for his *slavish* devotion/adherence to the rules.

– slav·ish·ly *adv* ▪ He *slavishly* copies everything his older brother does. **– slav·ish·ness** *noun* [*noncount*]

Sla·von·ic /sləˈvɑːnɪk/ *noun* [*noncount*] : SLAVIC

– Slavonic *adj*

slaw /ˈslɑː/ *noun* [*noncount*] *US, informal* : COLESLAW

slay /ˈsleɪ/ *verb* **slays; slew** /ˈsluː/ *also* **slayed; slain** /ˈsleɪn/; **slay·ing** [+ *obj*]

1 a *literary* : to kill (someone or something) especially in a battle or war ▪ The knight *slew* the dragon. b *US* : to kill (someone) — used especially in newspaper stories and headlines; usually used as *(be) slain* ▪ The victims *were slain* in their homes. ▪ The headline read "Three *Slain* in Bank Robbery."

2 *chiefly US, informal + old-fashioned* : to delight or amuse (someone) very much ▪ That guy *slays* me. [=that guy kills me; I think he's very funny]

– slay·er *noun, pl* **-ers** [*count*] **– slaying** *noun, pl* **-ings** [*count*] *chiefly US* ▪ Police have arrested a man in connection with three *slayings* that happened last month.

sleaze /ˈsliːz/ *noun, pl* **sleaz·es**

1 [*noncount*] *somewhat informal* : behavior that is dishonest or immoral ▪ political *sleaze* and corruption ▪ The newspaper editorial addresses the ***sleaze factor*** [=*dishonesty*] in political campaigns.

2 [*count*] *US, informal* : a dishonest or immoral person ▪ He's a real *sleaze.*

sleaze·bag /ˈsliːzˌbæg/ *noun, pl* **-bags** [*count*] *informal* : a dishonest or immoral person ▪ She was involved with some *sleazebag.* ▪ a *sleazebag* lawyer

sleaze·ball /ˈsliːzˌbɑːl/ *noun, pl* **-balls** [*count*] *informal* : a dishonest or immoral person ▪ He is a lying *sleazeball.*

slea·zy /ˈsliːzi/ *adj* **slea·zi·er; -est** *informal*

1 : dishonest or immoral ▪ a *sleazy* lawyer/trick

2 : dirty and in bad condition from being neglected ▪ a *sleazy* neighborhood

3 : not decent or socially respectable ▪ *sleazy* nightclubs/tabloids ▪ a dancer in a *sleazy* outfit

– slea·zi·ness /ˈsliːzinəs/ *noun* [*noncount*]

[1]**sled** /ˈslɛd/ *noun, pl* **sleds** [*count*] *chiefly US* : a small vehicle that has a flat bottom or long, narrow strips of metal or wood on the bottom and that is used for moving over snow

S

or ice — called also *(Brit) sledge*; compare SLEIGH, TOBOGGAN; see also DOGSLED

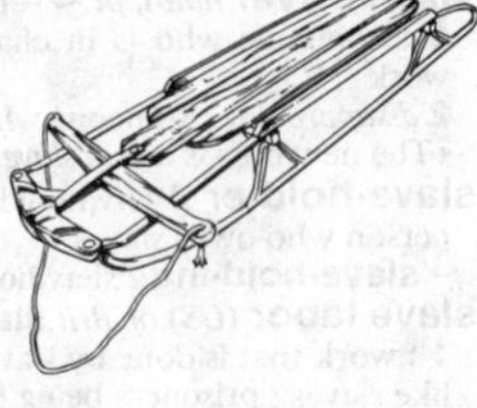
sled

²sled *verb* **sleds; sled·ded; sled·ding** *[no obj] chiefly US* : to ride on a sled especially down a hill • We went *sledding* [=*(Brit) sledging*] on the hill.
– **sled·der** *noun, pl* **-ders** *[count]*

sled dog *noun, pl* **~ dogs** *[count] chiefly US* : a dog that is trained to pull a sled — called also *(Brit) sledge dog*

¹sledge /ˈslɛʤ/ *noun, pl* **sledg·es** *[count] Brit* : ¹SLED

²sledge *verb* **sledges; sledged; sledg·ing** *[no obj] Brit* : ²SLED

sledge·ham·mer /ˈslɛʤˌhæmɚ/ *noun, pl* **-mers** *[count]* : a large, heavy hammer with a long handle — often used figuratively • The news hit me like a *sledgehammer*. [=I was shocked by the news]

sleek /ˈsliːk/ *adj* **sleek·er; -est** *[also more ~; most ~]*
1 : straight and smooth in design or shape • the *sleek* lines of a sports car • a *sleek*, modern building
2 : smooth and shiny • *sleek*, dark hair
3 : stylish and attractive • a *sleek* young executive
– **sleek·ly** *adv* • a *sleekly* modern building – **sleek·ness** *noun [noncount]*

¹sleep /ˈsliːp/ *verb* **sleeps; slept** /ˈslɛpt/; **sleep·ing**
1 *[no obj]* : to rest your mind and body by closing your eyes and becoming unconscious • I couldn't *sleep* last night. I was awake all night long. • I usually try to *sleep* for at least eight hours every night. • Did you *sleep* soundly/well last night? • I *slept* badly/poorly. • We were *sleeping* peacefully when a sudden loud noise woke us up. • I can never *sleep* on airplanes. • He ***has trouble sleeping***. [=finds it difficult to fall asleep] — sometimes used figuratively • New York is the city that never *sleeps*. [=a city that is full of activity all night]
2 *[+ obj]* : to have enough space for (a specified number of people) to sleep in it • The tent *sleeps* five adults.

let sleeping dogs lie see ¹DOG

sleep around *[phrasal verb] informal + disapproving* : to have sex with many different people • I heard he *sleeps around*.

sleep away *[phrasal verb]* ***sleep away (something)*** *or* ***sleep (something) away*** *chiefly US* : to spend (a period of time) sleeping • Don't *sleep* your day *away*.

sleep a wink *informal* : to sleep for even a very brief time — used in negative statements • I *didn't/couldn't sleep a wink* [=didn't/couldn't sleep at all] last night.

sleep in *[phrasal verb] informal* : to sleep past the time when you usually get up • On Sundays, we always *sleep in*.

sleep like a baby/log *informal* : to sleep very well • After a long day of skiing, I *slept like a baby/log* last night.

sleep off *[phrasal verb]* ***sleep (something) off*** *or* ***sleep off (something)*** *informal* : to sleep until the effects of alcohol, medication, etc., are no longer felt • She was *sleeping off* the anesthesia. • He had too much to drink, and I'm letting him ***sleep it off***.

sleep on it *informal* : to think more about something overnight and make a decision about it later • You've heard my offer. Why don't you *sleep on it* and let me know what you decide.

sleep over *[phrasal verb]* : to stay overnight at another person's house • My mother said that you could *sleep over* on Saturday. — see also SLEEPOVER

sleep through *[phrasal verb]* ***sleep through (something)*** : to sleep without being awakened by (something, such as a loud noise) • She *slept* (right) *through* the thunderstorm.

sleep tight : to sleep deeply and well • Good night. *Sleep tight*.

sleep together *[phrasal verb] informal* : to have sex with each other • She found out that her husband and his secretary were *sleeping together*.

sleep with *[phrasal verb]* ***sleep with (someone)*** *informal* : to have sex with (someone) • She found out that her husband was *sleeping with* his secretary.

²sleep *noun*
1 *[noncount]* : the natural state of rest during which your eyes are closed and you become unconscious • I just need to get some *sleep*. • How much *sleep* did you get last night? • He was diagnosed with a ***sleep disorder***. [=a medical problem that prevents him from sleeping normally] • Her roommate talks/walks ***in her sleep***. • The baby cried himself ***to sleep***. [=cried until he fell asleep] • She sang the baby *to sleep*. [=she sang to the baby until it fell asleep] — see also REM SLEEP
2 *[singular]* : a period of sleep especially of a particular kind • The noise woke her from a deep/light *sleep*. • Sometimes all you need to feel better is ***a good night's sleep***. [=a full night of sleep] • *(Brit)* I think I'll go to my bedroom and ***have a sleep***.
3 *[noncount] informal* : the dry substance that sometimes forms in the corners of your eyes while you are sleeping • He woke up and rubbed the *sleep* out of his eyes.

get to sleep : to succeed in beginning to sleep : to fall asleep • It took me almost an hour to *get to sleep* last night. • I woke up in the middle of the night, but I eventually ***got back to sleep***. [=started sleeping again]

go to sleep **1** : to begin sleeping • She lay down on the couch and *went* (right) *to sleep*. • Tell the kids it's time to *go to sleep*. [=*go to bed*] • After the party, I just wanted to *go to sleep*. **2** ✧ If a part of your body (such as a foot or leg) *goes to sleep*, it is not able to feel anything for a brief time, usually because you have kept it in an awkward position for too long. • I have to move because my foot is *going to sleep*.

in your sleep ✧ If you can do something *in your sleep*, you can do it very easily because you have done it many times before. • She could bake those cookies *in her sleep*. • I can drive that route *in my sleep*.

lose sleep over : to worry about (something) so much that you cannot sleep — usually used in negative statements • I'm disappointed about their decision, but I'm *not losing any sleep over* it. • I *wouldn't lose sleep over* it if I were you.

put to sleep **1** ***put (an animal) to sleep*** : to give (a sick or injured animal) drugs that will make it die without pain • We had to *put* my cat *to sleep* last week. **2** ***put (someone) to sleep*** **a** *informal* : to use a drug to make (someone) unconscious before a medical operation : to give (someone) anesthesia before a medical operation • The doctor *put* the patient *to sleep*. **b** : to get (someone) ready to sleep for the night • Did you *put* the kids *to sleep*? [=did you put the kids to bed?] **c** : to make someone fall asleep from boredom • That movie practically *put* me *to sleep*. • Her lectures used to *put* him *to sleep*.

sleep·away /ˈsliːpəˌweɪ/ *adj, always used before a noun, US* : providing beds and rooms so people can stay overnight for a number of nights • We sent the kids off to ***sleepaway camp*** for the week.

sleep·er /ˈsliːpɚ/ *noun, pl* **-ers** *[count]*
1 a : a person who sleeps in a particular way • a light *sleeper* [=someone who does not sleep well and wakes up easily] • a heavy *sleeper* [=someone who sleeps well and does not wake up easily] • a sound *sleeper* **b** : someone who is asleep • *Sleepers* were awakened by the sound of a loud crash.
2 a : a place or piece of furniture that can be used for sleeping — usually used before another noun • the *sleeper* cab of a truck • Our guests will use the ***sleeper sofa***. [=a sofa that folds out to form a bed] **b** : SLEEPING CAR
3 *chiefly US, informal* : someone or something that suddenly becomes successful in a way that was not expected • He may turn out to be the *sleeper* in this year's election. • The movie was the summer's *sleeper*. • The movie became the ***sleeper hit*** of the summer.
4 : a spy who lives and works for a long time like an ordinary person among the people he or she is spying on — often used before another noun • a *sleeper* agent • The police discovered a ***sleeper cell*** [=a small organized group of spies] that had been operating in the city for years.
5 *US* : a piece of clothing that covers the entire body including usually the feet and that is worn by a baby or small child
6 *Brit* : one of the heavy beams to which the rails of a railway are attached : TIE

sleeping bag *noun, pl* **~ bags** *[count]* : a warm, long bag that is used for sleeping outdoors or in a tent — see picture at CAMPING

sleeping car *noun, pl* **~ cars** *[count]* : a railroad car with beds for people to sleep in — called also *sleeper*

sleeping partner *noun, pl* **~ -ners** *[count] Brit* : SILENT PARTNER

sleeping pill *noun, pl* **~ pills** *[count]* : a pill that contains a drug which helps a person sleep

sleeping sickness *noun [noncount]* : a tropical disease that causes fever, sleepiness, and usually death

S

sleep·less /ˈsli:pləs/ *adj*
1 *always used before a noun* : without sleep • a *sleepless* night
2 *not used before a noun* : not able to sleep • He lay *sleepless* in bed.
– **sleep·less·ly** *adv* • He lay *sleeplessly*. – **sleep·less·ness** *noun* [*noncount*] • He suffers from *sleepnessness*. [=*insomnia*]

sleep·over /ˈsli:pˌoʊvɚ/ *noun, pl* **-overs** [*count*] : a party where one or more people (especially children) stay overnight at one person's house • Our daughter is having a *sleepover* for her friends tomorrow. — see also *sleep over* at [1]SLEEP

sleep·walk /ˈsli:pˌwɑ:k/ *verb* **-walks; -walked; -walk·ing** [*no obj*] : to walk around while you are asleep
– **sleep·walk·er** /ˈsli:pˌwɑ:kɚ/ *noun, pl* **-ers** [*count*]
– **sleepwalking** *noun* [*noncount*]

sleepy /ˈsli:pi/ *adj* **sleep·i·er; -est** [*also more* ~; *most* ~]
1 : tired and ready to fall asleep • She felt *sleepy* and went to bed.
2 : quiet and not active or busy • a *sleepy* little town
– **sleep·i·ly** /ˈsli:pəli/ *adv* • "Yes," she murmured *sleepily*.
– **sleep·i·ness** /ˈsli:pinəs/ *noun* [*noncount*]

sleepy·head /ˈsli:piˌhɛd/ *noun, pl* **-heads** [*count*] *chiefly US, informal* : a sleepy person — used especially to address someone (such as a child) • Are you ready for bed, *sleepyhead?*

[1]**sleet** /ˈsli:t/ *noun* [*noncount*] : frozen or partly frozen rain • The snow turned to *sleet* and made driving very dangerous.

[2]**sleet** *verb* **sleets; sleet·ed; sleet·ing** [*no obj*] — used with *it* to say that sleet is falling • *It's sleeting* outside. [=sleet is falling from the sky]

sleeve /ˈsli:v/ *noun, pl* **sleeves** [*count*]
1 : the part of a shirt, jacket, etc., that covers all or part of your arm • a shirt with long/short *sleeves* — see color picture on page C15; see also SHIRTSLEEVE
2 a : a part that fits over or around something to protect it or to hold its parts together • The joint is covered with a metal *sleeve*. • a plastic document *sleeve* **b** : JACKET 2b • a record/CD *sleeve*
an ace up your sleeve see [1]ACE
have/keep (something) up your sleeve *informal* : to have/keep a secret method, trick, etc., that you can use when it is needed • The coach always ***keeps a few tricks up his sleeve***. • They still ***have some surprises up their sleeves***.
laugh up your sleeve see [1]LAUGH
on your sleeve *informal* : in a way that can be clearly seen • Many politicians wear religion *on their sleeves*. [=show their religious beliefs in a very open way] • He ***wears his emotions/heart on his sleeve***. [=his emotions are easy to see]
roll up your sleeves see [1]ROLL
– **sleeved** /ˈsli:vd/ *adj* • a long-*sleeved* shirt – **sleeve·less** /ˈsli:vləs/ *adj* • a *sleeveless* dress

sleeve notes *noun* [*plural*] *Brit* : LINER NOTES

sleigh /ˈsleɪ/ *noun, pl* **sleighs** [*count*] : a large, open vehicle that is usually pulled by a horse over snow or ice

sleight of hand /ˈslaɪt-/ *noun* [*noncount*]
1 : quick or deceptive hand movements that are used especially to perform magic tricks • He performs *sleight of hand* with cards and books of matches.
2 : the act of tricking or deceiving someone in a clever way • Investigative journalists exposed the company's financial *sleight of hand*.

slen·der /ˈslɛndɚ/ *adj* **slen·der·er; -est** [*also more* ~; *most* ~]
1 a : thin especially in an attractive or graceful way • She has a *slender* figure. • Deer have *slender* legs. **b** : very narrow : not wide • a flower with a *slender* stem • an animal with a long, *slender* snout
2 : small or limited in amount or size • The President has a *slender* [=*narrow, slim*] lead in the polls. = The President leads by a *slender* margin in the polls. • (*formal*) young people of *slender* means [=young people who do not have much money]
– **slen·der·ness** *noun* [*noncount*]

slept *past tense and past participle of* [1]SLEEP

sleuth /ˈslu:θ/ *noun, pl* **sleuths** [*count*] *old-fashioned* : someone who looks for information to solve crimes : DETECTIVE • a clever *sleuth*
– **sleuth·ing** /ˈslu:θɪŋ/ *noun* [*noncount*] • He did some *sleuthing* to see if he could turn up any clues.

S level *noun, pl* **S levels** [*count*] *Brit* : the highest of three tests in a particular subject that students in England, Wales, and Northern Ireland take usually at the age of 18 • She got an A in her *S levels* in math, physics, and chemistry. — called also *Scholarship level*; compare A LEVEL, O LEVEL

[1]**slew** *past tense of* SLAY

[2]**slew** /ˈslu:/ *noun* [*singular*] *informal* : a large number *of* people or things • A whole *slew of* people [=a lot of people] were waiting. • He has written a *slew of* books.

[3]**slew** *verb, always followed by an adverb or preposition* **slews; slewed; slew·ing** : to turn or slide in another direction very quickly [*no obj*] His car *slewed* [=*skidded, veered*] sideways off the road. [+ *obj*] He *slewed* the telescope three degrees south.

[1]**slice** /ˈslaɪs/ *noun, pl* **slic·es** [*count*]
1 a : a thin piece of food that is cut from something larger • a *slice* of bread • thin *slices* of roast beef **b** : a piece that is cut from a pie, cake, etc. • They sell pizza by the *slice*. [=they sell individual pieces cut from a pizza] • a *slice* of pie **c** : a piece that is cut from a piece of fruit • *slices* of melon/cantaloupe
2 *informal* **a** : a part of something • A good *slice* [=*portion*] of the population saw the game on TV. **b** : an example of something • The Fourth of July parade was a real *slice of* Americana.
3 *sports* : a shot in golf and other games that curves to the side instead of going straight • He hit a *slice* into the right rough.
a slice of life : something (such as a story or movie) that shows what ordinary life is like • The story is/shows/presents a ***slice of life*** in a small Midwestern town. — see also SLICE-OF-LIFE
a slice of the action see ACTION
a slice of the cake see [1]CAKE
a slice of the pie see PIE

[2]**slice** *verb* **slices; sliced; slic·ing**
1 a : to cut something with a sharp object (such as a knife) [+ *obj*] She *sliced* the lemon in half. • He *sliced* the board in two. [=he cut the board into two pieces] • He *sliced* open his finger while cleaning the fish. [*no obj*] The knife *sliced* through the cake easily. — sometimes used figuratively • His jokes *sliced* [=*cut*] through the tension in a room. **b** [+ *obj*] : to cut (something) into pieces or slices • She *sliced* the bread/tomato/pie. — often + *up* • He *sliced up* a banana.
2 [+ *obj*] : to make (something) smaller by removing part of it • The university *sliced* [=*cut*] the research budget in half.
3 *sports* : to hit or kick (a ball or shot) in a way that causes it to curve : to hit a slice [+ *obj*] (*golf*) She *sliced* her drive into the rough. [*no obj*] (*golf*) The ball *sliced* into the rough.
4 : to move quickly and easily through something (such as air or water) [*no obj*] — usually + *through* • The ship's hull *sliced through* the waves. [+ *obj*] The conductor *sliced* the air with his arms.
any way you slice it or ***no matter how you slice it*** *US, informal* — used to say that the truth of a statement is not changed or affected by the way you describe or think about a situation • Losing is disappointing *no matter how you slice it*. [=losing is always disappointing] • *Any way you slice it*, online commerce is here to stay.
slice and dice *chiefly US* : to divide something into many small parts especially so you can use the result for your own purposes • You can *slice and dice* the data any way you want.
slice off [*phrasal verb*] ***slice off (something)*** or ***slice (something) off*** : to remove (something) by cutting : to cut off (something) with a sharp object (such as a knife) • *Slice off* the excess fat after you cook the steak. — often used figuratively • The salesperson *sliced* 10 percent *off* of the cost of the car.
the best/greatest thing since sliced bread *informal* — used to describe something or someone that you think is very good, useful, etc. • He thinks wireless Internet access is *the greatest thing since sliced bread*.
– **sliced** *adj* • thinly *sliced* beef • *sliced* bread – **slic·er** *noun, pl* **-ers** [*count*] • a bread *slicer*

slice–of–life *adj, always used before a noun* : showing what ordinary life is like • a *slice-of-life* drama

[1]**slick** /ˈslɪk/ *adj* **slick·er; -est** [*also more* ~; *most* ~]
1 : very smooth and slippery • Be careful as you drive home—the roads are *slick*.
2 : clever in usually a dishonest or deceptive way • a *slick* salesman • big corporations and their *slick* lawyers

S

3 a : skillful and clever ▪ The new kid had some *slick* moves on the basketball court. **b :** very good : of the highest quality ▪ The students did a *slick* job of promoting the concert. ▪ The video game has *slick* graphics. ▪ a *slick* Broadway-style production

– **slick·ly** *adv* ▪ very *slickly* done – **slick·ness** *noun* [*noncount*]

[2]**slick** *verb* **slicks; slicked; slick·ing** [+ *obj*] **:** to make (something) smooth and slippery ▪ The rain *slicked* the roads. ▪ rain-*slicked* roads

slick back/down [*phrasal verb*] ***slick back/down (hair) or slick (hair) back/down*** **:** to pull (hair) back and make it look smooth or shiny by using water or some wet substance (such as hair gel) ▪ He climbed out of the pool and *slicked back* his hair. ▪ He had long sideburns and dark *slicked-back* hair.

[3]**slick** *noun, pl* **slicks** [*count*]

1 : a thin layer of liquid that makes a surface very slippery; *especially* **:** OIL SLICK

2 : a smooth tire that is used in car racing ▪ racing *slicks*

slick·er /ˈslɪkɚ/ *noun, pl* **-ers** [*count*] *US* **:** a long, loose raincoat — see also CITY SLICKER

[1]**slide** /ˈslaɪd/ *verb* **slides; slid** /ˈslɪd/; **slid·ing**

1 a : to move smoothly along a surface [*no obj*] The door *slides* open easily. ▪ The firefighters *slid* down the pole to their trucks. [+ *obj*] He *slid* the bottle across the table. ▪ *Slide* your finger along the seam. ▪ She *slid* the paper under the door. **b** [*no obj*] **:** to move over ice or snow smoothly and often in a way that cannot be controlled ▪ He *slid* across the ice. ▪ Cars were slipping and *sliding* all over the roads during the snowstorm.

2 [*no obj*] **:** to slip and fall ▪ Her purse *slid* out of her hands. ▪ The strap of her dress kept *sliding* down/off.

3 *always followed by an adverb or preposition* **a :** to move or pass smoothly and easily into or out of something [*no obj*] She *slid* into the booth beside us. ▪ He *slid* into [=began doing] his impersonation of the president. [+ *obj*] He *slid* the key into his pocket. ▪ He always finds a way to *slide* in a reference to his new book. **b :** to move so you or your movements are not noticed [*no obj*] They *slid* [=*slipped*] out of the room when nobody was looking. [+ *obj*] He quietly *slid* the money into my hand.

4 [*no obj*] **:** to become gradually worse over time ▪ His parents are concerned that their son's grades have started to *slide*. [=*worsen*] ▪ Sales figures have been *sliding* [=*declining*] for the last three quarters. ▪ The restaurant's new management is really letting the quality of the food *slide*.

5 [*no obj*] *baseball* **:** to dive toward a base to avoid being tagged out ▪ He *slid* into second base.

let (something) slide *informal* **:** to do nothing about (something, such as another person's mistake or bad behavior) **:** to ignore (something) ▪ You were late this morning. I'll *let it slide* this time, but don't let it happen again. ▪ It may be best to ***let things slide*** this time.

[2]**slide** *noun, pl* **slides** [*count*]

1 : a movement to a lower or worse state or condition **:** DECLINE — usually singular ▪ The recent *slide* in the stock market has made investors nervous. ▪ The book describes her *slide into* depression. ▪ the *slide* in television ratings ▪ (*chiefly Brit*) Her career has been ***on the slide*** [=*on the decline*] for a couple of years.

2 : an act of moving along or over a surface by sliding — usually singular ▪ The car hit a patch of ice and went into a *slide*. [=began sliding] — see also LANDSLIDE, MUDSLIDE, ROCKSLIDE

3 : a structure with a slippery surface that children slide down ▪ a playground *slide* — see picture at PLAYGROUND; see also WATERSLIDE

4 *baseball* **:** the act of diving towards a base to avoid being tagged out ▪ a *slide* into home plate

5 : a small piece of film with an image on it that can be shown on a wall or screen by using a special machine (called a projector) ▪ They showed us *slides* from their vacation in Europe. ▪ a *slide* presentation/show/projector

6 : a small, thin, and usually rectangular piece of glass that holds an object to be looked at under a microscope ▪ She sent the *slides* to the lab.

7 : a part of a musical instrument or a machine that is moved backward or forward ▪ He oiled the *slide* of his trombone. ▪ The *slide* mechanism on the machine was broken.

8 *Brit* **:** BARRETTE

slid·er /ˈslaɪdɚ/ *noun, pl* **-ers** [*count*]

1 *baseball* **:** a fast pitch that curves slightly in the air

2 : something that slides

slide rule *noun, pl* **~ rules** [*count*] **:** an old-fashioned instrument that is like a ruler with a middle piece that slides back and forth and that is used to do calculations

sliding door *noun, pl* **~ doors** [*count*] **:** a door that opens and closes by sliding sideways instead of by swinging on hinges

sliding scale *noun, pl* **~ scales** [*count*] **:** a system in which the amount that people are required to pay in fees, taxes, etc., changes according to different situations or conditions — usually singular ▪ Patients at the clinic pay on a *sliding scale* based on their income.

[1]**slight** /ˈslaɪt/ *adj* **slight·er; -est**

1 : very small in degree or amount ▪ *slight* adjustments/errors ▪ a *slight* odor/cold/fever ▪ There is a *slight* chance of rain. ▪ Her head is tilted at a *slight* angle in the picture. ▪ The medication didn't have the *slightest* effect. [=did not have any effect] ▪ If you have even the *slightest* doubt, then don't do it. ▪ There is not the *slightest* danger [=there is no danger] of that happening.

2 : thin and not very strong or muscular ▪ a *slight* woman

not in the slightest **:** not at all : not in the least ▪ "Does it bother you?" "*Not in the slightest*."

[2]**slight** *verb* **slights; slight·ed; slight·ing** [+ *obj*] **:** to offend or insult (someone) : to treat (someone) with disrespect ▪ I'm sure he didn't mean to *slight* you. ▪ He was *slighted* by his colleagues.

– **slight** *noun, pl* **slights** [*count*] ▪ a deliberate *slight* ▪ The remark was not intended to be a *slight* on his character. – **slighting** *adj* ▪ He made *slighting* references to her book. ▪ a *slighting* remark

slight·ly /ˈslaɪtli/ *adv* **:** in a very small amount or degree : a little ▪ I got only a *slightly* better grade when I retook the test. ▪ I'm *slightly* confused. ▪ The sauce has a *slightly* bitter taste. ▪ The price has increased *slightly*. ▪ Keep your knees *slightly* bent. ▪ He seemed to move ***ever so slightly*** closer. [=he moved closer only by a very small amount]

slightly built **:** thin and not very strong or muscular ▪ a *slightly built* girl

[1]**slim** /ˈslɪm/ *adj* **slim·mer; -est** [*also more ~; most ~*]

1 : thin in an attractive way ▪ She looked *slim* and fit for her age. ▪ He has a *slim* build. ▪ I was a lot *slimmer* in those days.

2 : small in amount, size, or degree ▪ a *slim* majority ▪ They have only a *slim* chance of winning. ▪ "What are their chances of winning?" "***Slim to none***." [=they have almost no chance of winning]

– **slim·ly** *adv* [*more ~; most ~*] ▪ He was tall and *slimly* built. – **slim·ness** *noun* [*noncount*]

[2]**slim** *verb* **slims; slimmed; slim·ming**

1 [+ *obj*] **:** to make (something) thinner ▪ She started exercising to *slim* her thighs.

2 [*no obj*] *Brit* **:** [2]DIET ▪ I'll skip dessert; I'm *slimming*.

slim down [*phrasal verb*] **1 :** to lose weight : to become thinner ▪ She's been trying to *slim down*. ▪ He looks like he's really *slimmed down* since last year. **2 *slim down (something) or slim (something) down*** **:** to make (something) smaller **:** REDUCE ▪ We have to *slim down* the company's advertising budget.

slime /ˈslaɪm/ *noun, pl* **slimes**

1 [*noncount*] **:** a thick, slippery liquid ▪ Green *slime* covers the surface of the pond.

2 *US, informal* **:** a very bad, unpleasant, or dishonest person [*noncount*] That guy's *slime*. ▪ She thinks men are *slime*. [*count*] — usually singular ▪ That guy's a real *slime*.

slime·ball /ˈslaɪm,bɑːl/ *noun, pl* **-balls** [*count*] *informal* **:** a very bad, unpleasant, or dishonest person ▪ He's a real *slimeball* for leaving her.

slim·line /ˈslɪm,laɪn/ *adj, always used before a noun, chiefly Brit* **:** smaller or thinner in size than usual ▪ a *slimline* CD case

slim·mer /ˈslɪmɚ/ *noun, pl* **-ers** [*count*] *Brit* **:** a person who is trying to lose weight **:** DIETER

[1]**slimming** *adj*

1 [*more ~; most ~*] **:** making you look thinner ▪ That dress is *slimming* on you. ▪ Black suits are *slimming*.

2 *always used before a noun* **:** intended to help people lose weight ▪ a controversial *slimming* [=(more commonly) *diet*] drug ▪ *slimming* exercises

[2]**slimming** *noun* [*noncount*] *chiefly Brit* **:** the act of losing weight ▪ I know I'm in need of a little *slimming*.

slimy /ˈslaɪmi/ *adj* **slim·i·er; -est** [*also more ~; most ~*]

1 a : covered with slime ▪ a *slimy* rock/worm **b :** resembling slime ▪ *slimy* mud ▪ a *slimy* gel
2 *informal* **:** very dishonest, bad, or immoral ▪ a *slimy* businessman/politician ▪ *slimy* business practices
3 *informal* **:** causing disgust **:** OFFENSIVE ▪ Get your *slimy* fingers off my jacket.
– slim·i·ness *noun [noncount]*

[1]sling /ˈslɪŋ/ *verb* **slings; slung** /ˈslʌŋ/; **sling·ing** *[+ obj]*
1 : to throw (something) with a forceful sweeping motion ▪ She *slung* the bag over her shoulder. ▪ The protesters started *slinging* [=*flinging*] stones at the police. — often used figuratively ▪ They *slung* [=*hurled*] insults at each other. ▪ He was *slung* [=*thrown*] into jail for the night. — see also MUDSLINGING
2 : to hang (something) loosely ▪ He *slung* a hammock between two trees. — often used as *(be) slung* ▪ His guitar *was slung* around his neck. ▪ a low-*slung* belt
sling your hook *Brit, informal* **:** to go away **:** LEAVE ▪ She angrily told him to *sling his hook.*

[2]sling *noun, pl* **slings** *[count]*
1 : something that is used to lift, carry, or support something: such as **a :** a piece of cloth that hangs around your neck and is used to support an injured arm or hand ▪ He has to keep his arm ***in a sling*** **b :** a long strap attached to something ▪ a leather rifle *sling* **c :** a large piece of cloth that is worn usually around your neck and that forms a bag which is used to hold a baby close to you **d :** a large net, rope, chain, etc., that is used to lift heavy things ▪ We attached the *sling* to the crane.

sling

2 : a strap usually with a pocket in the middle that is used to throw something (such as a stone)
slings and arrows **:** the problems and criticisms that are experienced in someone's life ▪ Politicians must be willing to endure/suffer the *slings and arrows* of public life.

sling·back /ˈslɪŋˌbæk/ *noun, pl* **-backs** *[count]* **:** a woman's shoe that is open at the back and has a thin strap that goes around the heel

sling·shot /ˈslɪŋˌʃɑːt/ *noun, pl* **-shots** *[count] US* **:** a Y-shaped stick with an elastic band attached to it that is used for shooting small stones — called also *(Brit) catapult*

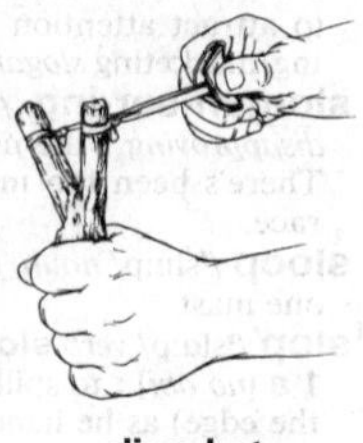
slingshot

slink /ˈslɪŋk/ *verb, always followed by an adverb or preposition* **slinks; slunk** /ˈslʌŋk/ *also US* **slinked; slink·ing** *[no obj]* **:** to move in a way that does not attract attention especially because you are embarrassed, afraid, or doing something wrong ▪ I thought I saw someone *slinking* [=*sneaking*] around outside. ▪ He *slinked* away in shame.

slinky /ˈslɪŋki/ *adj* **slink·i·er; -est**
1 : fitting closely to the body in a sexy way ▪ a *slinky* black dress ▪ The dancers wore *slinky* costumes.
2 : slow in a sexually attractive way ▪ the song's *slinky* rhythm ▪ *slinky* dance movements

[1]slip /ˈslɪp/ *verb* **slips; slipped; slip·ping**
1 *[no obj]* **:** to slide out of the proper position ▪ The ring was too big and *slipped* off my finger. ▪ The engine's belt continued to *slip.* ▪ The hammer *slipped* out of my hands. ▪ The knife *slipped* and she cut herself. ▪ My foot *slipped* on the stair and I fell.
2 *[no obj]* **:** to lose your balance especially on a slippery surface ▪ She *slipped* and fell. — often + *on* ▪ He *slipped on* the stairs. ▪ Be careful not to *slip on* the ice.
3 *always followed by an adverb or preposition* **:** to move easily across or over something *[no obj]* The drawer should just *slip* [=*slide*] into place. ▪ The bib *slips* over the baby's head. *[+ obj]* Help me *slip* the cover over the piano.
4 *always followed by an adverb or preposition [no obj]* **:** to move into or out of a place without being noticed ▪ Someone was able to *slip* through security. ▪ We'll *slip* out the back door. — see also SLIP AWAY (below)
5 *always followed by an adverb or preposition [no obj]* **:** to put on or take off a piece of clothing quickly or easily ▪ He stood up and *slipped* on his jacket. ▪ He *slipped* off his shoes. ▪ Let me just *slip* into my bathrobe. ▪ You should *slip* out of those wet clothes.
6 *[+ obj]* **a** *always followed by an adverb or preposition* **:** to put or place (something) somewhere in a quiet or secret way ▪ He *slipped* the key into his pocket. ▪ Someone *slipped* a drug into his drink. ▪ He managed to ***slip in*** [=*include*] a few jokes during his speech. **b :** to give (something) to someone in a quiet or secret way ▪ He *slipped* the envelope to his secretary. = He *slipped* his secretary the envelope.
7 *always followed by an adverb or preposition [no obj]* **:** to happen or pass without being noticed by someone or something ▪ Time keeps *slipping* away. ▪ Her birthday *slipped* by without us knowing. ▪ Despite all our efforts, some errors do *slip* past us. ▪ We didn't want to let the opportunity ***slip through our fingers*** [=we did not want to let the opportunity pass without taking advantage of it]
8 *[no obj]* **a :** to go from one state or condition to another ▪ She was *slipping* out of consciousness. — often + *into* ▪ The patient *slipped into* a coma. ▪ The word has *slipped into* disuse. ▪ The actor *slipped into* character. [=the actor began to behave, speak, etc., like the character he was playing] **b :** to move into a lower or worse state or condition ▪ The stock market has *slipped* to its lowest level in a month. ▪ I can't believe he beat me. I must be *slipping.* ▪ Test scores *slipped* [=*declined*] this year.
9 *[+ obj]* **a :** to escape (someone) **:** to get away from (someone) ▪ The thief *slipped* his pursuers. **b :** to get free from (something) ▪ The dog *slipped* its collar.
10 *[+ obj] medical* **:** to have (a part of your body) move out of its normal position especially in a joint ▪ I *slipped* a disc.
let (something) slip *or* ***let slip (something)*** **:** to say (something that you did not want to say) by mistake ▪ He *let slip* that he's looking for a better job. ▪ Don't *let* it *slip* that we hadn't planned on inviting her.
slip away *[phrasal verb]* **1 :** to pass out of existence ▪ The afternoon quietly *slipped away.* ▪ They saw their four-run lead *slip away.* ▪ Their grandmother *slipped away* [=*died*] in her sleep last night. **2 :** to leave a place without being noticed ▪ They *slipped away* from the party right after dinner.
slip out *[phrasal verb]* **:** to be said by mistake ▪ I didn't intend to tell them. It just *slipped out.*
slip through/between the cracks see [2]CRACK
slip through the net see [1]NET
slip up *[phrasal verb] informal* **:** to make a mistake ▪ Make sure you don't *slip up* again.
slip your mind/memory *informal* **:** to be forgotten ▪ Her birthday completely *slipped my mind.* [=I completely forgot about her birthday]

[2]slip *noun, pl* **slips** *[count]*
1 a : a small piece of paper ▪ He wrote the number on a ***slip of paper.*** **b :** a piece of paper that has a specified use or purpose ▪ a deposit *slip* ▪ a betting *slip* ▪ a rejection *slip* — see also PINK SLIP, SALES SLIP
2 : a mistake ▪ a careless *slip* ▪ Their performance was very good except for a few minor *slips.* — see also A SLIP OF THE TONGUE (below), FREUDIAN SLIP
3 : a movement to a lower or worse state or condition **:** DECLINE — usually singular ▪ a ratings *slip* = a *slip* in the ratings
4 : the act of losing your balance and falling especially on a slippery surface — usually singular ▪ The bruise is from a *slip* on the ice.
5 : a piece of woman's underwear that is like a thin dress or skirt and that is worn under a dress or skirt ▪ Her *slip* was showing. ▪ You will need a ***half slip*** [=a slip that only covers you from the waist down] for that dress. — see color picture on page C13
6 : a place for a ship or boat in the water between two piers ▪ She guided her boat into one of the *slips.*
a slip of the tongue **:** something that is said by mistake ▪ *a* careless *slip of the tongue*
give (someone) the slip *informal* **:** to escape (someone) **:** to get away from (someone) ▪ The intruder ran from the police and *gave them the slip.*
– compare [3]SLIP, [4]SLIP

[3]slip *noun [singular] old-fashioned* **:** a young, thin person or animal — + *of* ▪ He was a mere *slip of* a boy. [=he was just a small boy] ▪ She was a wee *slip of* a thing. — compare [2]SLIP, [4]SLIP

[4]slip *noun [noncount] technical* **:** thin, wet clay that is used in pottery — compare [2]SLIP, [3]SLIP

slip·case /ˈslɪpˌkeɪs/ *noun, pl* **-cas·es** *[count]* **:** a hard protective box for books or magazines that is open at one end

S

slip·cov·er /ˈslɪpˌkʌvɚ/ *noun, pl* **-ers** [*count*] *US* **:** a loose, removable cloth cover for a piece of furniture ▪ We put a *slipcover* on the sofa.

slip·knot /ˈslɪpˌnɑːt/ *noun, pl* **-knots** [*count*] **:** a knot that can slide along the rope around which it is made and that is tightened by pulling on one end

slip–on /ˈslɪpˌɑːn/ *noun, pl* **-ons** [*count*] **:** a shoe that does not have ties, buckles, etc., and that you can put on or take off very easily ▪ a pair of *slip-ons* ▪ *slip-on* sandals

slip·page /ˈslɪpɪʤ/ *noun, pl* **-pag·es** *formal*
1 : a movement downward **:** an act of moving into a lower or worse condition or state [*count*] price *slippages* ▪ a *slippage* [=*decrease*] in sales [*noncount*] There has been some *slippage* in the stock's price/value. [=the price/value of the stock has gone down]
2 : the act of sliding or slipping [*noncount*] The boot's sole prevents *slippage*. [*count*] an accidental *slippage*

slipped disc *also chiefly US* **slipped disk** *noun, pl* **~ discs** *also chiefly US* **~ disks** [*count*] *medical* **:** an injury to the spine in which one of the connecting parts between the bones slips out of its proper position and causes back pain

slip·per /ˈslɪpɚ/ *noun, pl* **-pers** [*count*] **:** a light, soft shoe that is easily put on and taken off and that is worn indoors — called also (*Brit*) *carpet slipper*; see picture at SHOE

slip·pery /ˈslɪpəri/ *adj* **slip·per·i·er; -est** [*also more* ~; *most* ~]
1 : difficult to stand on, move on, or hold because of being smooth, wet, icy, etc. ▪ The trails were muddy and *slippery*. ▪ The floor looks *slippery*. ▪ Fish are *slippery* to hold. ▪ The sign cautions: "***Slippery when wet.***"
2 : not easy to understand or identify in an exact way ▪ a *slippery* definition ▪ *slippery* concepts/notions
3 *informal* **:** not able to be trusted **:** TRICKY ▪ *slippery* politicians
– slip·per·i·ness *noun* [*noncount*]

slippery slope *noun* [*singular*] **:** a process or series of events that is hard to stop or control once it has begun and that usually leads to worse or more difficult things ▪ His behavior will lead him down a *slippery slope* to ruin.

slip road *noun, pl* **~ roads** [*count*] *Brit* **:** a short road that is used to get on or off a major road or highway **:** an on-ramp or off-ramp

slip·shod /ˈslɪpˈʃɑːd/ *adj* **:** very careless or poorly done or made ▪ *slipshod* construction ▪ He did a *slipshod* job. ▪ Her scholarship is *slipshod* at best.

slip·stream /ˈslɪpˌstriːm/ *noun, pl* **-streams** [*count*] *technical* **:** an area of low air pressure that is immediately behind a vehicle that is moving very fast and that other vehicles can ride in to go faster with less effort ▪ The motorcycle was riding the truck's *slipstream*.

slip·up /ˈslɪpˌʌp/ *noun, pl* **-ups** [*count*] **:** a careless mistake ▪ We were late because of a *slipup* in the schedule.

[1]**slit** /ˈslɪt/ *verb* **slits; slit; slit·ting** [+ *obj*] **:** to make a long, narrow cut or opening in (something) with a sharp object ▪ I *slit* the bag open at the top. ▪ The bag of seeds had been *slit* open. ▪ Someone tried to *slit* his throat. [=someone tried to kill him by cutting his throat] ▪ She tried to ***slit her wrists***. [=to kill herself by cutting her wrists]

[2]**slit** *noun, pl* **slits** [*count*] **:** a long, narrow cut or opening in something ▪ You could see through the *slit* in the fence. ▪ The skirt has a *slit* on one side. ▪ a dress with a *slit* skirt

S

slith·er /ˈslɪðɚ/ *verb* **-ers; -ered; -er·ing**
1 [*no obj*] **:** to move by sliding your entire body back and forth ▪ The snake *slithered* through the garden. ▪ To get under the porch, I lay on my stomach and *slithered* like a snake.
2 *always followed by an adverb or preposition* **:** to move smoothly, quietly, or secretly like a snake [*no obj*] She *slithered* quietly into the room. [+ *obj*] He *slithered* his hand around her waist.

slith·ery /ˈslɪðəri/ *adj* **slith·er·i·er; -est** [*also more* ~; *most* ~]
1 : having an unpleasantly slippery surface, feeling, or quality ▪ *slithery* reptiles
2 : having a flowing and smooth look or way of moving ▪ She wore a sexy, *slithery* dress.

[1]**sliv·er** /ˈslɪvɚ/ *noun, pl* **-ers** [*count*] **:** a small, thin piece that has been cut, torn, or broken from something larger — often + *of* ▪ My son has a *sliver* [=*splinter*] *of* wood in his finger. ▪ Just a *sliver* [=a very thin slice] *of* cake for me, please. — often used figuratively ▪ A *sliver of* light peeked through the curtains. ▪ a *sliver of* hope

[2]**sliver** *verb* **-ers; -ered; -er·ing** [+ *obj*] *somewhat formal* **:** to cut or break (something) into small, thin pieces ▪ The vase (*was*) *slivered* into thousands of shards when she dropped it.
– slivered *adj* ▪ *slivered* almonds

slob /ˈslɑːb/ *noun, pl* **slobs** [*count*] *informal*
1 *disapproving* **:** a person who is lazy and dirty or messy ▪ He's a disgusting *slob*.
2 : an ordinary person ▪ Some ***poor slob*** got robbed.

slob·ber /ˈslɑːbɚ/ *verb* **-bers; -bered; -ber·ing** [*no obj*] **:** to let saliva or liquid flow from your mouth **:** DROOL ▪ Her baby just *slobbered* on the blanket. ▪ The puppy *slobbered* all over me.
slobber over [*phrasal verb*] ***slobber over (someone or something)*** *informal* **:** to show that you like (someone or something) in an excessive and uncontrolled way ▪ His friends were *slobbering* (all) *over* his new sports car.
– slobber *noun* [*noncount*] ▪ I have dog *slobber* [=*saliva*] all over me.

slob·bery /ˈslɑːbəri/ *adj* **:** full of drool or saliva ▪ a big, *slobbery* (wet) kiss ▪ a *slobbery* dog **:** covered in drool or saliva ▪ The toy was all *slobbery* because the dog had been chewing on it.

[1]**slog** /ˈslɑːg/ *verb, always followed by a preposition or adverb* **slogs; slogged; slog·ging** *informal*
1 : to keep doing something even though it is difficult or boring **:** to work at something in a steady, determined way **:** PLOD [*no obj*] He *slogged* away at the paperwork all day. ▪ She *slogged* through her work. [+ *obj*] She *slogged* her way through her work.
2 : to walk slowly usually with heavy steps **:** PLOD [*no obj*] We've been *slogging* along for hours. ▪ He *slogged* through the deep snow. [+ *obj*] They *slogged* their way through the snow.
slog it out *Brit, informal* **:** to fight or compete until one side wins **:** to slug it out
– slog·ger *noun, pl* **-gers** [*count*]

[2]**slog** *noun* [*singular*] *informal*
1 : a long period of hard work or effort ▪ It will be a long, hard *slog* before everything is back to normal.
2 : a long, difficult walk ▪ It was a long *slog* up the mountain.

slo·gan /ˈsloʊgən/ *noun, pl* **-gans** [*count*] **:** a word or phrase that is easy to remember and is used by a group or business to attract attention ▪ political/campaign *slogans* ▪ advertising/marketing *slogans*

slo·gan·eer·ing /ˌsloʊgəˈnirɪŋ/ *noun* [*noncount*] *usually disapproving* **:** the use of slogans in advertising or politics ▪ There's been too much *sloganeering* in this year's mayoral race.

sloop /ˈsluːp/ *noun, pl* **sloops** [*count*] **:** a small sailboat with one mast

[1]**slop** /ˈslɑːp/ *verb* **slops; slopped; slop·ping**
1 a [*no obj*] **:** to spill from a container ▪ Water *slopped* (over the edge) as he handed her the glass. **b** *always followed by an adverb or preposition* [+ *obj*] **:** to splash or spill (a liquid) ▪ She *slopped* coffee on her sweater. ▪ Huge waves *slopped* water into the boat.
2 [+ *obj*] *US* **:** to feed slop to (an animal) ▪ *slop* the pigs
slop around/about [*phrasal verb*] *Brit, informal* **:** to move or act in a lazy or relaxed way **:** to spend time resting or relaxing ▪ He *slopped around* the house all day.

[2]**slop** *noun, pl* **slops**
1 : food that is fed to pigs and other animals [*noncount*] The pigs are fed *slop*. [*plural*] The pigs ate the *slops*.
2 [*noncount*] *informal* **:** soft, wet food that is very unappealing ▪ I won't eat that *slop*!
3 [*noncount*] *chiefly US, informal* **:** something that is worthless, foolish, etc. ▪ The movie is just a lot of sentimental *slop*. [=*garbage*]

[1]**slope** /ˈsloʊp/ *noun, pl* **slopes** [*count*]
1 a : ground that slants downward or upward **:** ground that slopes ▪ They climbed the steep *slope*. ▪ a slight/gentle *slope* **b :** an area of land on a mountain that is used for skiing ▪ a ski *slope* — often plural ▪ Let's ***hit the slopes***. [=let's go skiing] ▪ I love being ***on the slopes***. [=I love skiing]
2 : an upward or downward slant ▪ What is the angle of the *slope*? ▪ You can adjust the *slope* of the ramp. ▪ a *slope* of 30 degrees
— see also SLIPPERY SLOPE

[2]**slope** *verb* **slopes; sloped; slop·ing** [*no obj*]
1 : to not be level **:** to have a downward or upward slant ▪ The ground *sloped* downward. ▪ *sloping* mountainsides

2 : to not be straight : to lean or slant to the left or right • His handwriting *slopes* to the left.

slope off [*phrasal verb*] *Brit, informal* : to leave a place quietly or secretly • He *sloped off* to bed.

slop·py /ˈslɑːpi/ *adj* **slop·pi·er; -est**

1 : not careful or neat : showing a lack of care, attention, or effort • a *sloppy* effort/essay • *sloppy* handwriting • Your work has been very *sloppy* lately.

2 *informal* : romantic in a foolish or exaggerated way • a *sloppy* love song

3 : containing or involving a lot of liquid or too much liquid • *sloppy* food • a *sloppy* mixture/kiss

– slop·pi·ly /ˈslɑːpəli/ *adv* **– slop·pi·ness** *noun* [*noncount*]

sloppy joe /ˈslɑːpiˈʤoʊ/ *noun, pl* **~ joes** [*count*] *US* : ground beef that is cooked in a thick, spicy sauce and usually served on a bun

slosh /ˈslɑːʃ/ *verb, always followed by an adverb or preposition* **slosh·es; sloshed; slosh·ing**

1 [*no obj*] : to walk through water, mud, etc., in a forceful and noisy way • The children *sloshed* through the big puddle.

2 a [*no obj*] *of a liquid* : to move in a noisy or messy way • Water *sloshed* in the bottom of the boat as it rocked. • Juice *sloshed* over the rim of her glass. **b** [+ *obj*] : to cause (a liquid) to move in a noisy or messy way • The child *sloshed* the water in the tub.

sloshed /ˈslɑːʃt/ *adj* [*more ~; most ~*] *slang* : very drunk • They were/got totally *sloshed* last night.

[1]**slot** /ˈslɑːt/ *noun, pl* **slots** [*count*]

1 : a long, thin opening • a box with a *slot* in the top • He put three quarters into the machine's (coin) *slot*.

2 a : a period of time that is available or used for a particular occurrence, event, etc. • The doctor has an open *slot* at 2 p.m. • The network moved my favorite TV show to a different ***time slot***. **b** : a place or position in an organization, group, etc. • They offered him a regular *slot* on the newspaper's editorial page. • We need someone to fill an open *slot* in the marketing department.

3 *US* : SLOT MACHINE — usually plural • He likes to play the *slots*.

[2]**slot** *verb* **slots; slot·ted; slot·ting**

1 [+ *obj*] : to put (something) into a space which is made for it • He *slotted* the piece of wood into the groove.

2 [*no obj*] : to fit easily into something • Her ideas *slot* neatly into the theory.

slot in [*phrasal verb*] ***slot (someone or something) in*** *informal* : to find a place for (someone or something) in a schedule, plan, etc. • I can *slot* you *in* at 2 p.m.

sloth /ˈslɑːθ/ *noun, pl* **sloths**

1 [*noncount*] *formal* : the quality or state of being lazy : LAZINESS • the sins/vices of gluttony and *sloth*

2 [*count*] : a type of animal that lives in trees in South and Central America and that moves very slowly

sloth

sloth·ful /ˈslɑːθfəl/ *adj* [*more ~; most ~*] *formal* : LAZY • a *slothful* person • *slothful* behavior/habits

slot machine *noun, pl* **~ -chines** [*count*]

1 : a machine used for gambling that starts when you put coins into it and pull a handle or press a button — called also (*informal*) *one-armed bandit*, (*Brit*) *fruit machine*

2 *Brit* : VENDING MACHINE

slotted *adj* : having a slot or slots • a ***slotted spoon*** [=a spoon that has narrow holes in it so that liquid can pass through]

[1]**slouch** /ˈslaʊʧ/ *verb* **slouch·es; slouched; slouch·ing** [*no obj*] : to walk, sit, or stand lazily with your head and shoulders bent forward • Sit up straight. Please don't *slouch*. • She *slouched* into the room. • The boy was *slouching* over his school books.

[2]**slouch** *noun, pl* **slouches**

1 [*singular*] : a way of walking, sitting, or standing with the head and shoulders bent forward • She walks with a *slouch*.

2 [*count*] *informal* : a lazy or worthless person • (*chiefly US*) They're just a bunch of lazy *slouches*. — usually used in the phrase ***no slouch*** to say that someone is very good at a particular job, activity, etc. • She's *no slouch* when it comes to cooking. [=she's a very good cook] • He's *no slouch* as a director.

[1]**slough** /ˈslʌf/ *verb* **sloughs; sloughed; slough·ing** [+ *obj*] *formal*

1 : to lose a dead layer of (skin) • Snakes *slough* (off) their skin annually.

2 : to get rid of (something unwanted) — usually + *off* • We have to *slough off* our fears and face the challenge that confronts us.

[2]**slough** /ˈsluː, *Brit* ˈslaʊ/ *noun, pl* **sloughs**

1 [*singular*] : a sad or hopeless condition — usually + *of* • a *slough of* depression/frustration/sadness

2 [*count*] : an area of soft, wet ground or deep mud • a *slough* of mud

slov·en·ly /ˈslʌvənli/ *adj* [*more ~; most ~*]

1 : messy or untidy • *slovenly* clothes • a *slovenly* man • He dressed in a *slovenly* manner. • *slovenly* habits

2 : done in a careless way : SLOPPY • *slovenly* thinking/grammar

– slov·en·li·ness *noun* [*noncount*]

[1]**slow** /ˈsloʊ/ *adj* **slow·er; -est** [*also more ~; most ~*]

1 a : not moving quickly : not able to move quickly • a *slow*, old dog • a *slow* runner/pace/speed **b** : not happening quickly : taking more time than is expected or wanted • a *slow* growth/increase/process • Bureaucracy is always *slow*. **c** : not operating quickly • a *slow* computer **d** : not doing something quickly • The buyers were *slow* to act, and the house was sold to someone else. : not able to do something quickly • a *slow* reader/learner **e** : not allowing someone or something to move quickly • a *slow* racetrack/route

2 : not easily able to learn and understand things • He was a quiet boy who seldom spoke, and some people thought he was a little *slow*.

3 : not very busy or interesting • a *slow* market • Business is *slow* during the summer. • The first few chapters are *slow*, but after that it gets better.

4 *of a clock or watch* : showing a time that is earlier than the correct time • The clock is (five minutes) *slow*.

5 *photography* : not allowing photographs to be taken very quickly or when there is very little light • *slow* film

a slow start ✧ Someone or something that has *a slow start* is not successful at first but does well eventually. • Despite *a slow start* at the box office, the movie's popularity has increased steadily. • The team ***got off to a slow start*** this season but is playing well now.

do a slow burn see [2]BURN

slow off the mark see [1]MARK

– slow·ish /ˈsloʊɪʃ/ *adj* **– slow·ness** *noun* [*noncount*]

[2]**slow** *adv* **slower; -est** [*also more ~; most ~*] : in a slow way or at a low speed • go/move/walk/drive *slow* • My computer is working *slow*. — opposite FAST

[3]**slow** *verb* **slows; slowed; slow·ing**

1 a [*no obj*] : to begin to move at a lower speed • The car *slowed* and gradually came to a stop. — often + *down* or *up* • The car *slowed down* a little as it approached the intersection. • I *slowed up* and let the others catch up with me. **b** [+ *obj*] : to make (something, such as a car) move at a lower speed • The extra weight *slowed* the truck. — often + *down* or *up* • *Slow* the car *down* so that I can read the sign. • The extra weight *slowed up* the truck.

2 a [*no obj*] : to become slower • a *slowing* economy — often + *down* or *up* • Business *slowed down/up* after the holidays. **b** [+ *obj*] : to make (something) slower — often + *down* or *up* • They tried to *slow down/up* the process somewhat.

slow down [*phrasal verb*] : to stop being very active, talking very fast, etc. • You've been working too hard. You need to *slow down* and take it easy for a while. • *Slow down*! You're talking so fast I can hardly understand you.

– slowing *noun* [*singular*] There has been a *slowing* of job growth in recent months. [*noncount*] There has been some *slowing* of the economy.

slow·coach /ˈsloʊˌkoʊʧ/ *noun, pl* **-coach·es** [*count*] *Brit, informal* : SLOWPOKE

slow·down /ˈsloʊˌdaʊn/ *noun, pl* **-downs** [*count*] : a decrease in the speed at which something is moving or happening • an economic *slowdown* • The business had a *slowdown* after the holidays.

slow lane *noun, pl* **~ lanes**

1 [*count*] : a section of a highway for cars that are traveling at slower speeds • He's a nervous driver and always stays in the *slow lane*.

2 [*singular*] : a situation in which someone or something is not advancing as quickly as others or is not as successful as others • His career is still stuck in the *slow lane*.

S

slow·ly /ˈsloʊli/ *adv* [*more* ~; *most* ~] **:** in a slow way or at a low speed ▪ go/walk/drive *slowly* ▪ working/talking/moving *slowly* ▪ Things are *slowly* getting better.
 slowly but surely **:** by making slow but definite progress — used to stress that something is happening or being done even though it is not happening or being done quickly ▪ We're getting the work done, *slowly but surely*.

slow motion *noun* [*noncount*] **:** a way of showing action that has been filmed or photographed at a speed that is slower than the actual speed ▪ The scene was shot ***in slow motion.*** ▪ They showed the goal *in slow motion*.
 – slow–mo·tion /ˈsloʊˈmoʊʃən/ *adj* ▪ a *slow-motion* replay ▪ *slow-motion* photography

slow·poke /ˈsloʊˌpoʊk/ *noun, pl* **-pokes** [*count*] *US, informal* **:** a person who moves, acts, or works very slowly ▪ We're going to be late if that *slowpoke* doesn't hurry up. — called also (*Brit*) *slowcoach*

slow–wit·ted /ˈsloʊˈwɪtəd/ *adj* [*more* ~; *most* ~] **:** slow to learn or understand things ▪ a *slow-witted* child — opposite QUICK-WITTED

sludge /ˈslʌʤ/ *noun* [*noncount*]
 1 : thick, soft, wet mud
 2 : a soft, thick material that is produced in various industrial processes (such as in the treatment of sewage)
 3 : a thick material that can form in the oil in an engine and cause engine problems
 – sludgy /ˈslʌʤi/ *adj* **sludg·i·er; -est** ▪ *sludgy* ground

[1]**slug** /ˈslʌg/ *noun, pl* **slugs** [*count*]
 1 : a small, soft creature that is like a snail without a shell ▪ a garden *slug*
 2 *US, informal* **:** a lazy person ▪ He's such a *slug*.
 – compare [2]SLUG, [3]SLUG

slug

[2]**slug** *noun, pl* **slugs** [*count*]
 1 *US* **:** a small piece of metal that is fired from a gun **:** BULLET ▪ a .45 *slug*
 2 *US, informal* **:** a disc shaped like a coin that is used illegally instead of a coin in a machine
 3 *informal* **:** a small amount of liquor taken in one swallow — usually + *of* ▪ a *slug of* whiskey
 – compare [1]SLUG, [3]SLUG

[3]**slug** *noun, pl* **slugs** [*count*] *US* **:** a hard punch with the fist ▪ a *slug* to the jaw — compare [1]SLUG, [2]SLUG

[4]**slug** *verb* **slugs; slugged; slug·ging** [*no obj*] *informal* **:** to hit (someone or something) hard with your fist, a bat, etc. ▪ He said something nasty, and she *slugged* him. ▪ (*baseball*) He *slugged* two home runs in yesterday's game.
 slug it out *informal* **:** to fight or compete over something until one side wins ▪ The companies are *slugging it out* in court.

slug·ger /ˈslʌgɚ/ *noun, pl* **-gers** [*count*] **:** someone who hits someone or something hard: such as **a :** a boxer who punches hard **b** *baseball* **:** a batter who hits many home runs

slug·gish /ˈslʌgɪʃ/ *adj* [*more* ~; *most* ~] **:** moving slowly or lazily ▪ a *sluggish* lizard/stream ▪ The game picked up after a *sluggish* start.
 – slug·gish·ly *adv* ▪ The water flowed *sluggishly*. **– slug·gish·ness** *noun* [*noncount*]

[1]**sluice** /ˈsluːs/ *noun, pl* **sluic·es** [*count*]
 1 : an artificial passage for water to flow through with a gate for controlling the flow
 2 : a device (such as a floodgate) used for controlling the flow of water

[2]**sluice** *verb* **sluices; sluiced; sluic·ing**
 1 [+ *obj*] **:** to wash or spray (something or someone) with a stream of water ▪ He *sluiced* (down) the floor.
 2 *always followed by an adverb or preposition* [*no obj*] **:** to flow or pour down heavily ▪ Rain came *sluicing* down.

[1]**slum** /ˈslʌm/ *noun, pl* **slums**
 1 [*count*] **:** an area of a city where poor people live and the buildings are in bad condition ▪ a city *slum* ▪ He grew up in the *slums* of New York.
 2 [*singular*] *Brit, informal* **:** a very untidy place ▪ His house is a *slum*.

[2]**slum** *verb* **slums; slummed; slum·ming** [*no obj*] *informal* **:** to spend time in places or conditions that are much worse than your usual places or conditions ▪ She's never been one to *slum* around (in cheap hotels). ▪ He had no problem ***slumming (it)*** in cheap hotels. ▪ He sometimes likes to ***go slumming*** in bars around the city.

[1]**slum·ber** /ˈslʌmbɚ/ *verb* **-bers; -bered; -ber·ing** [*no obj*] *literary* **:** SLEEP ▪ The children quietly *slumbered*.

[2]**slumber** *noun, pl* **-bers** *literary* **:** SLEEP [*count*] a dreamless *slumber* [*noncount*] She fell into deep *slumber*.

slumber party *noun, pl* ~ **-ties** [*count*] *US* **:** a party where one or more people (usually girls) stay overnight at one person's house **:** SLEEPOVER ▪ My 12-year-old daughter is having a *slumber party* tonight.

slum·lord /ˈslʌmˌloəd/ *noun, pl* **-lords** [*count*] *chiefly US, disapproving* **:** a person who owns a building with apartments that are in bad condition and rents them to poor people

[1]**slump** /ˈslʌmp/ *verb* **slumps; slumped; slump·ing** [*no obj*]
 1 *always followed by an adverb or preposition* **a :** to sit or fall down suddenly and heavily ▪ She fainted and *slumped* to the floor. ▪ Exhausted, he *slumped* down into the chair. **b :** to move down or forward suddenly ▪ His shoulders *slumped* forward in disappointment.
 2 : to decrease suddenly and by a large amount ▪ Real estate prices *slumped* during the recession.
 – slumped *adj* ▪ The driver of the car was found *slumped* over the steering wheel unconscious. ▪ He was/sat *slumped* in front of the TV all afternoon.

[2]**slump** *noun, pl* **slumps** [*count*]
 1 : a sudden decrease in prices, value, amount, etc. ▪ a market *slump* — often + *in* ▪ a *slump in* real estate prices
 2 : a period of time when an economy is doing poorly ▪ The economy's been in a *slump* since last year.
 3 *US, sports* **:** a period of time when a team or player is doing poorly ▪ They've been in a *slump* ever since they traded their best player. ▪ He's in a batting *slump*.

slung *past tense and past participle of* [1]SLING

slunk *past tense and past participle of* SLINK

[1]**slur** /ˈslɚ/ *verb* **slurs; slurred; slur·ring**
 1 a [+ *obj*] **:** to say (something) in an unclear way especially because you are drunk or tired ▪ She was *slurring* her words. ▪ His speech was *slurred*. **b** [*no obj*] *of speech* **:** to become unclear especially because you are drunk or tired ▪ His speech/words *slurred* as he got drunker
 2 [+ *obj*] **:** to say critical and unfair things about (someone or someone's character) ▪ They tried to *slur* him by lying about his war record. ▪ They tried to *slur* his character/reputation.
 3 [+ *obj*] *music* **:** to sing or play musical notes so that each one runs smoothly into the next one

[2]**slur** *noun, pl* **slurs** [*count*]
 1 : an insulting remark about someone or someone's character ▪ a racial/ethnic *slur* [=an insult based on someone's race/ethnicity]
 2 *music* **:** a symbol in music that is used to show that notes are to be sung or played smoothly with no break in between them

slurp /ˈslɚp/ *verb* **slurps; slurped; slurp·ing** [+ *obj*] *informal* **:** to eat or drink (something) noisily or with a sucking sound ▪ He always *slurps* his soup/tea.
 – slurp *noun, pl* **slurps** [*count*] — usually singular ▪ a quick *slurp* of coffee

slur·ry /ˈslɚri/ *noun, pl* **-ries** [*count, noncount*] **:** a thick mixture of water and another substance (such as mud or lime)

slush /ˈslʌʃ/ *noun* [*noncount*]
 1 : partly melted snow ▪ a sidewalk covered with *slush*
 2 *informal* **:** something that is thought to be silly because it is too romantic or emotional ▪ The movie is just a lot of romantic/sentimental *slush*.
 – slushy /ˈslʌʃi/ *adj* **slush·i·er; -est** ▪ *slushy* snow

slush fund *noun, pl* ~ **funds** [*count*] **:** an amount of money that is kept secretly for illegal or dishonest purposes ▪ a political *slush fund* ▪ a secret *slush fund* for paying bribes

slut /ˈslʌt/ *noun, pl* **sluts** [*count*] *informal* + *offensive* **:** a woman who has many sexual partners
 – slut·ty /ˈslʌti/ *adj* **slut·ti·er; -est** ▪ a *slutty* woman ▪ *slutty* clothes

sly /ˈslaɪ/ *adj* **sli·er** *or* **sly·er; sli·est** *or* **sly·est** [*also more* ~; *most* ~]
 1 : clever in a dishonest way ▪ a *sly* con man ▪ a *sly* scheme
 2 : showing that you know a secret ▪ a *sly* wink/glance/smile
 on the sly *informal* **:** in a secret way ▪ They've been meeting each other *on the sly*. [=secretly]
 – sly·ly *adv* ▪ He winked *slyly*. **– sly·ness** *noun* [*noncount*]

sm. *abbr* small

S–M *or* **S/M** /ˌɛsəndˈɛm/ *abbr* sadomasochism

S

[1]smack /ˈsmæk/ *verb* **smacks; smacked; smack·ing** [+ *obj*]
1 : to slap or hit (someone or something) hard ▪ He *smacked* the child on the bottom. ▪ I was so angry I felt like *smacking* someone.
2 *always followed by an adverb or preposition* **:** to set or hit (something) on or against something else so that it makes a loud noise ▪ She *smacked* the plate down on the table. ▪ He accidentally *smacked* his head against the shelf.
3 *US, informal* **:** to kiss (someone) loudly ▪ His aunt likes to *smack* him on the cheek every time she comes over.
smack of [*phrasal verb*] ***smack of (something)*** **:** to seem to contain or involve (something unpleasant) ▪ That suggestion *smacks of* hypocrisy.
smack your lips **:** to close and open your lips noisily especially before or after eating or drinking ▪ She *smacked her lips* (together) and announced that dinner was delicious.

[2]smack *noun, pl* **smacks** [*count*]
1 : a hard slap or hit ▪ He gave the child a *smack* on the bottom.
2 : a loud noise that is made when something hits something else in a forceful way ▪ The dictionary fell to the floor with a *smack.*
3 *informal* **:** a loud kiss ▪ She gave him a *smack* on the cheek. — compare [3]SMACK, [5]SMACK, [6]SMACK

[3]smack *noun* [*noncount*] **:** a small, noticeable amount *of* a particular thing ▪ a *smack* [=*hint, trace*] *of* vanilla flavor ▪ There's a *smack of* condescension in the book's tone. — compare [2]SMACK, [5]SMACK, [6]SMACK

[4]smack *adv, informal* **:** exactly or directly ▪ She dropped the book *smack* in the middle of the table. ▪ The ball hit me *smack* in the face.

[5]smack *noun* [*noncount*] *slang* **:** HEROIN — compare [2]SMACK, [3]SMACK, [6]SMACK

[6]smack *noun, pl* **smacks** [*count*] *Brit* **:** a small fishing boat — compare [2]SMACK, [3]SMACK, [5]SMACK

smack–dab /ˈsmækˈdæb/ *adv, US, informal* **:** exactly or directly ▪ They planted a tree *smack-dab* in the center of the lawn.

smack·er /ˈsmækɚ/ *noun, pl* **-ers** [*count*] *informal*
1 : a U.S. dollar or British pound — usually plural ▪ I won 1,000 *smackers* gambling.
2 : a loud kiss ▪ She gave him a *smacker* right on the lips.

[1]small /ˈsmɑːl/ *adj* **small·er; -est** [*also more ~; most ~*]
1 : little in size ▪ They live in a *small* house. ▪ a *small* glass of soda ▪ She moved to a *smaller* town. ▪ The toy is *small* enough to fit in my pocket. ▪ He has *small* hands. ▪ This room is a little *smaller* than that one.
2 : few in number or little in amount ▪ a *small* crowd/group/company/party/school ▪ a *small* supply/number ▪ The movie was a *small* success. ▪ There is a *small* [=*slight*] chance that they can still win. — see also *small hours* at HOUR
3 : not very important **:** MINOR ▪ a *small* matter ▪ There are still a few *small* details we have to deal with. ▪ It's only a *small* mistake. ▪ The change had only a *small* impact on the community.
4 : very young ▪ I loved the playground when I was *small.* ▪ a *small* boy ▪ They have two *small* children.
5 : involving or including few people, things, etc. ▪ She works for a *small* company. ▪ *small* businesses/dealers/investors ▪ a *small* advertising campaign ▪ a *small* fund-raiser
6 : LOWERCASE ▪ The first letter is a capital, but the rest are *small.*
7 : very soft and quiet ▪ a *small* voice
8 : foolish or ashamed ▪ He's just trying to make you feel *small.* ▪ He felt very *small* to be caught cheating.
a big fish in a small pond see [1]FISH
in no small measure **:** to a great degree **:** largely or mostly ▪ A child's happiness is due *in no small measure* [=*in no small part*] to its parents.
(it's a) small world see [1]WORLD
not (in) the smallest bit see [1]BIT
– small·ish /ˈsmɑːlɪʃ/ *adj* **– small·ness** /ˈsmɑːlnəs/ *noun* [*noncount*]

[2]small *noun, pl* **smalls** [*count*] **:** something that is sold in a small size **:** something that is smaller than other things of the same kind ▪ These shirts are all *smalls.* ▪ "What size ice-cream cones do you want?" "We'll take three larges and a *small.*"
the small of the/your back **:** the lower part of your back that is smaller and narrower than the rest ▪ I felt a sharp pain in *the small of my back.*

small ad *noun, pl* **~ ads** [*count*] *Brit* **:** [2]CLASSIFIED

small arms *noun* [*plural*] **:** weapons (such as handguns and rifles) that are fired while being held in one hand or both hands

small beer *noun* [*noncount*] *Brit, informal* **:** SMALL POTATOES

small change *noun* [*noncount*]
1 : coins that are not worth a lot of money ▪ a pocket full of *small change*
2 *informal* **a :** an amount of money that is not large or important ▪ The fine is a lot of money to some people, but to him it's *small change.* **b :** something or someone that is not important ▪ My problems are *small change* compared to yours. ▪ He wasn't a major criminal. He was strictly *small change.*

small–claims court *noun, pl* **~ courts** [*count*] *law* **:** a court where legal disputes over small amounts of money are settled

small fry *noun, pl* **~ fries** *informal*
1 *US* **a** [*count*] **:** a child — usually singular ▪ I remember going to the beach when I was just a *small fry.* **b** [*noncount*] **:** CHILDREN ▪ fun activities for the *small fry*
2 [*noncount*] **:** people or things that are not important ▪ Big businesses are not concerned with the *small fry.*

small·hold·ing /ˈsmɑːlˌhoʊldɪŋ/ *noun, pl* **-ings** [*count*] *chiefly Brit* **:** a small farm
– small·hold·er /ˈsmɑːlˌhoʊldɚ/ *noun, pl* **-ers** [*count*]

small intestine *noun, pl* **~ -tines** [*count*] **:** the long, narrow upper part of the intestine in which food is digested after it leaves the stomach — see picture at HUMAN; compare LARGE INTESTINE

small–mind·ed /ˈsmɑːlˈmaɪndəd/ *adj* [*more ~; most ~*] *disapproving*
1 : not interested in new or different ideas **:** not willing to accept the opinions of other people ▪ *small-minded* people
2 : typical of a small-minded person ▪ a *small-minded* attitude
– small–mind·ed·ness *noun* [*noncount*]

small potatoes *noun* [*noncount*] *US, informal* **:** someone or something that is not important or impressive ▪ Last week's storm was *small potatoes* compared to the blizzard we had two years ago. ▪ These changes are *small potatoes.* [=(*Brit, informal*) small beer]

small·pox /ˈsmɑːlˌpɑːks/ *noun* [*noncount*] **:** a serious disease that causes fever and a rash and often death ✧ *Smallpox* is now very rare.

small print *noun* [*noncount*] *chiefly Brit* **:** FINE PRINT

small–scale /ˈsmɑːlˈskeɪl/ *adj*
1 : involving few people or things ▪ a *small-scale* production ▪ *small-scale* manufacturing
2 : covering or involving a small area ▪ a *small-scale* network ▪ a *small-scale* map

small screen *noun*
the small screen **:** TELEVISION ▪ a movie made for *the small screen*

small talk *noun* [*noncount*] **:** informal, friendly conversation about unimportant subjects ▪ They made *small talk* while waiting for the meeting to start.

small–time /ˈsmɑːlˈtaɪm/ *adj* **:** not very important or successful **:** PETTY ▪ *small-time* racketeering ▪ a *small-time* thief

small–town /ˈsmɑːlˌtaʊn/ *adj* **:** of or relating to a small town ▪ *small-town* values/life/charm **:** coming from or living in a small town ▪ a *small-town* girl — compare BIG-CITY

smarmy /ˈsmaɚmi/ *adj* **smarm·i·er; -est** *informal + disapproving* **:** behaving in a way that seems polite, kind, or pleasing but is not genuine or believable ▪ a *smarmy* salesman/politician ▪ *smarmy* politeness

[1]smart /ˈsmaɚt/ *adj* **smart·er; -est**
1 *chiefly US* **a :** very good at learning or thinking about things **:** INTELLIGENT ▪ He's a *smart* [=*bright, clever*] guy. ▪ Poodles are said to be *smart* dogs. — see also STREET-SMART **b :** showing intelligence or good judgment **:** WISE ▪ That was a *smart* investment. ▪ Taking that job was a ***smart move.*** [=a good decision]
2 *informal + disapproving* **:** behaving or talking in a rude or impolite way **:** showing a lack of respect for someone ▪ Don't ***get smart*** with me. [=don't be rude to me] ▪ He gave her a *smart* answer.
3 : very popular **:** stylish and fashionable — somewhat old-fashioned in U.S. English ▪ one of the *smartest* restaurants in town ▪ He hangs out with ***the smart set.*** [=the popular and usually rich people]

S

4 : very neat and clean — somewhat old-fashioned in U.S. English ▪ What a *smart* [=*beautiful, charming*] little kitchen you have! ▪ He looks *smart* [=(*US*) *sharp*] in his new suit.
5 : very quick and energetic ▪ I gave him a *smart* slap on the head. ▪ We continued along at a very *smart* pace.
6 : controlled by computers and able to do things that seem intelligent ▪ *smart* bombs/weapons
smart money — used to say who or what is expected to win, be successful, etc. ▪ ***The smart money is on*** Jones to win the election. [=people think that Jones will win the election]
– smart·ly *adv* ▪ She slapped him *smartly.* ▪ He was *smartly* dressed. **– smart·ness** *noun* [*noncount*]

²smart *verb* **smarts; smart·ed; smart·ing** [*no obj*]
1 : to feel a sudden sharp pain ▪ "Ouch! That *smarts*!" ▪ Her eyes were *smarting* from the smoke.
2 : to be upset about something — usually used as *(be) smarting* ▪ He's still *smarting* at/from/over losing the match last month.
smart off [*phrasal verb*] *US, informal* : to say rude and irritating things to someone ▪ Ignore her, she is just *smarting off* again.

³smart *adv* **smart·er; -est** : in a smart way : SMARTLY ▪ He plays *smart* and the fans appreciate that. ▪ I dress *smarter* than she does. ▪ ***Play it smart*** during the contract negotiations and you'll get more vacation time.

smart–al·eck /ˈsmɑɚtˌælɪk/ *noun, pl* **-ecks** [*count*] *informal + disapproving* : a person who says things that are clever or funny but that are also disrespectful or rude ▪ He's a nice kid but sometimes he can be a real *smart-aleck.* ▪ Don't be such a *smart-aleck.*
– smart–aleck *or* **smart–al·ecky** /ˈsmɑɚtˌælɪki/ *adj* [*more ~; most ~*] ▪ *smart-aleck* remarks ▪ a *smart-alecky* comment

smart–arse /ˈsmɑɚtˌɑɚs/ *noun, pl* **-ars·es** [*count*] *Brit, informal + impolite* : SMART-ALECK
– smart–arse *or* **smart–arsed** /ˈsmɑɚtˌɑɚst/ *adj* [*more ~; most ~*] ▪ *smart-arse* remarks

smart–ass /ˈsmɑɚtˌæs/ *noun, pl* **-ass·es** [*count*] *US, informal + impolite* : SMART-ALECK ▪ Quit being a *smart-ass* and behave yourself.
– smart–ass *or* **smart–assed** /ˈsmɑɚtˌæst/ *adj* [*more ~; most ~*] ▪ a *smart-assed* remark ▪ a *smart-ass* attitude

smart card *noun, pl* **~ cards** [*count*] : a plastic card (such as a credit card) that has a small computer chip for storing information

smart·en /ˈsmɑɚtn̩/ *verb* **-ens; -ened; -en·ing**
smarten up [*phrasal verb*] **1** *US* **a** : to become more intelligent or aware : to become smarter ▪ He told me to *smarten up* and pay attention to the teacher. ▪ He'd better *smarten up* [=*wise up*] or he'll get fired. **b** ***smarten (someone or something) up*** *or* ***smarten up (someone or something)*** : to make (someone or something) smarter or more aware ▪ Someone needs to *smarten* him *up* before he gets in trouble. **2** ***smarten (someone or something) up*** *or* ***smarten up (someone or something)*** : to make (someone or something) neat and attractive ▪ They *smartened* [=*spruced*] themselves *up* for the party. ▪ They *smartened up* the room for the party.

smart–mouth /ˈsmɑɚtˌmaʊθ/ *or* **smart–mouthed** /ˈsmɑɚtˌmaʊθt/ *adj, US, informal + disapproving* : saying rude or disrespectful things ▪ *smart-mouth* comments ▪ a bunch of *smart-mouthed* kids
– smart–mouth *noun, pl* **-mouths** [*count*] ▪ He's a real *smart-mouth.*

smarts /ˈsmɑɚts/ *noun* [*plural*] *US, informal* : INTELLIGENCE ▪ He's got the *smarts* [=*brains, know-how*] to do the job. — see also STREET SMARTS

smarty *or* **smart·ie** /ˈsmɑɚti/ *noun, pl* **smart·ies** [*count*] *US, informal*
1 : SMART-ALECK ▪ Don't be such a *smarty.*
2 : a smart person ▪ She's a real *smarty* and does her job very well.

smarty–pants /ˈsmɑɚtiˌpænts/ *noun* [*noncount*] *informal + disapproving* : a person who talks and behaves like someone who knows everything ▪ Go ahead, *smarty-pants,* tell us about your grade point average. ▪ Don't be such a *smarty-pants.* [=*know-it-all*]

¹smash /ˈsmæʃ/ *verb* **smash·es; smashed; smash·ing**
1 : to break (something) into many pieces : to shatter or destroy (something) [+ *obj*] He *smashed* the vase with a hammer. ▪ The ball *smashed* the window. [*no obj*] The vase fell and *smashed* to pieces. ▪ The window *smashed* [=*shattered*] when the baseball hit it.
2 a : to hit (something) violently and very hard [+ *obj*] She *smashed* [=*crushed*] her finger in the door. [*no obj*] He *smashed* into the wall. ▪ The car *smashed* [=*crashed*] into the rail. **b** [+ *obj*] : to hit (a ball) downward and very hard in tennis and other games ▪ She *smashed* the ball deep into the opposite corner.
3 [+ *obj*] : to destroy or beat (someone or something) easily or completely ▪ We *smashed* our opponents. ▪ He *smashed* the world record. [=he broke the world record by a large amount]
4 [+ *obj*] : to crash (a vehicle) ▪ He *smashed* his car. — often + *up* in U.S. English ▪ She *smashed up* her new car.
smash down [*phrasal verb*] ***smash (something) down*** *or* ***smash down (something)*** : to hit (something) hard so that it breaks and falls down ▪ Police *smashed down* the door.
smash in [*phrasal verb*] ***smash (something) in*** *or* ***smash in (something)*** : to hit (something) hard so that you break it or make a hole in it ▪ I *smashed in* the window. ▪ I was so mad I felt like *smashing* his face *in.*
smash up [*phrasal verb*] ***smash (something) up*** *or* ***smash up (something)*** : to break and destroy (something) in a deliberate way ▪ Vandals broke in and *smashed* the place *up.* — see also ¹SMASH 4 (above), SMASHUP
– smash·er *noun, pl* **-ers** [*count*]

²smash *noun, pl* **smashes** [*count*]
1 : someone or something that is very successful or popular ▪ The new movie is a *smash.* ▪ She was a *smash* at the party. ▪ His new song promises to be a ***smash hit.***
2 : the sound made when something hits a surface very violently ▪ The vase fell to the ground with a loud *smash.*
3 : a hard downward hit in tennis or other games ▪ She hit an overhand *smash* that won the match.
4 *Brit* : CRASH, SMASHUP ▪ a car *smash*

smash–and–grab *adj, always used before a noun, chiefly Brit* — used to describe a robbery that is done by breaking a window of a car, store, etc., and stealing whatever you can take quickly ▪ a *smash-and-grab* robbery/thief

smashed /ˈsmæʃt/ *adj*
1 : broken to pieces ▪ a *smashed* window
2 *not used before a noun* [*more ~; most ~*] *slang* : very drunk ▪ He had a few too many beers and was *smashed.*

smash·ing /ˈsmæʃɪŋ/ *adj* [*more ~; most ~*] *old-fashioned* : very good or impressive ▪ (*chiefly Brit*) You look *smashing* in that dress. = That dress looks *smashing* on you. ▪ The play was a *smashing* success. [=a very great success]

smash·up /ˈsmæʃˌʌp/ *noun, pl* **-ups** [*count*] *informal* : an accident that badly damages or destroys a vehicle : CRASH ▪ a four-car *smashup*

smat·ter·ing /ˈsmætərɪŋ/ *noun* [*singular*] : a small amount *of* something ▪ She only knows a *smattering of* German. ▪ a *smattering of* applause

¹smear /ˈsmiɚ/ *noun, pl* **smears** [*count*]
1 : a dirty mark, spot, streak, etc., made by touching or rubbing something ▪ There was a *smear* [=*smudge*] on the mirror.
2 *medical* : a very small sample of something (such as skin or blood) that someone examines with a microscope ▪ The blood *smear* revealed malaria. — see also PAP SMEAR
3 : an untrue story about a person that is meant to hurt that person's reputation ▪ a deliberate *smear* — often used before another noun ▪ a *smear* campaign ▪ His opponent did a *smear* job on him.

²smear *verb* **smears; smeared; smear·ing**
1 [+ *obj*] : to make (something) dirty by rubbing it with something else ▪ The children *smeared* the window with fingerprints.
2 [+ *obj*] : to spread (something) over a surface ▪ She *smeared* jam on her toast. ▪ Butter was *smeared* all over the counter. ▪ The axle was *smeared* [=*covered*] with grease. ▪ children with paint-*smeared* faces
3 a [*no obj*] : to spread or drip in an untidy way ▪ Her mascara *smeared* when she cried. ▪ The ink *smeared* [=*smudged*] when she folded the letter. **b** [+ *obj*] : to cause (something) to spread or drip in an untidy way ▪ Water *smeared* [=*smudged*] the ink so I could barely read the letter.
4 [+ *obj*] : to make untrue statements about someone in order to hurt that person's reputation ▪ political opponents *smearing* each other ▪ They deliberately tried to *smear* him by telling lies about his war record. ▪ They tried to *smear* his reputation.

S

smear test *noun, pl* **~ tests** [*count*] *Brit, medical* : PAP SMEAR

[1]**smell** /ˈsmɛl/ *noun, pl* **smells**
1 [*count*] **a** : the quality of a thing that you can sense with your nose : ODOR • the distinctive *smell* of onions • the *smell* [=*scent*] of her perfume **b** : an unpleasant odor • What is that *smell*?
2 [*noncount*] : the ability to notice or recognize odors : the ability to smell things • Dogs have a keen sense of *smell*.
3 [*singular*] : an act of smelling something • One *smell* [=*whiff*] of this perfume and you will fall in love with it.

[2]**smell** *verb* **smells; smelled** *or Brit* **smelt** /ˈsmɛlt/; **smell·ing**
1 a [+ *obj*] : to use your nose to sense smells • She leaned over and *smelled* the flowers. • She *smelled* [=*sniffed*] the milk to see if it was sour. **b** : to be able to use your nose to sense smells [*no obj*] I have a cold right now so I can't *smell*. [+ *obj*] I can't *smell* anything because I'm so stuffed up. **c** *not used in progressive tenses* [+ *obj*] : to notice something because of its smell • I could *smell* dinner cooking. • I think I *smell* gas.
2 a [*linking verb*] : to have a particular smell • This car *smells* like mold. • That soup *smells* good. — sometimes + *of* • He *smelled of* alcohol. **b** *not used in progressive tenses* [*no obj*] : to have a bad smell • Whew, what *smells*? • These sneakers *smell*. [=*stink*]
3 a [+ *obj*] : to sense or detect (something) : to think that (something) is going to happen • Can't you *smell* the profits? • As the end of the game got closer, our team began to *smell* victory. [=began to sense/feel that victory was very near] • I ***smell trouble***. [=I think there's going to be trouble] **b** [*no obj*] : to appear or seem to have a certain quality • Something doesn't *smell* [=*seem*] right about this deal.
come out/up smelling like a rose see [2]ROSE
smell a rat see [1]RAT
smell out [*phrasal verb*] ***smell (something) out*** *or* ***smell out (something)*** : to find (something) by smelling it • Police have trained the dogs to *smell out* [=*sniff out*] drugs.
(stop and) smell the roses see [2]ROSE

smelling salts *noun* [*plural*] : a chemical that has a strong smell and that is used to wake people up after they faint

smelly /ˈsmɛli/ *adj* **smell·i·er; -est** : having a bad smell • I don't like *smelly* cheese. • *smelly* sneakers • *smelly* [=*stinky*] feet

[1]**smelt** /ˈsmɛlt/ *noun, pl* **smelts** *or* **smelt** [*count*] : a type of small fish that can be eaten

[2]**smelt** *verb* **smelts; smelt·ed; smelt·ing** [+ *obj*] : to melt rock that contains metal in order to get the metal out • the process used for *smelting* iron ore

[3]**smelt** *Brit past tense and past participle of* [2]SMELL

smelt·er /ˈsmɛltɚ/ *noun, pl* **-ers** [*count*] : a machine used for smelting metal

smid·gen *also* **smid·geon** *also chiefly Brit* **smid·gin** /ˈsmɪʤən/ *or US* **smidge** /ˈsmɪʤ/ *noun* [*singular*] *informal* : a small amount • I'll just have a *smidgen* of ice cream. • a *smidgen* of dignity • Could you move just a *smidge* [=*bit*] to the left?

[1]**smile** /ˈsmajəl/ *noun, pl* **smiles** [*count*] : an expression on your face that makes the corners of your mouth turn up and that shows happiness, amusement, pleasure, affection, etc. • He greeted me with a big *smile*. • I like your *smile*. • She gave me a *smile*. [=she smiled at me] • a polite *smile* • a *smile* of pleasure/satisfaction
all smiles : happy and smiling • She was *all smiles* as she opened her birthday presents.
wipe that/the smile off someone's face see [1]WIPE

[2]**smile** *verb* **smiles; smiled; smil·ing**
1 [*no obj*] : to make a smile : to make the corners of your mouth turn up in an expression that shows happiness, amusement, pleasure, affection, etc. • The photographer asked us to *smile* for the camera. • She *smiled* when she saw him. • She hasn't had much to *smile* about lately. [=she hasn't had much reason to feel happy lately] • He ***smiled to himself*** [=he smiled or felt happy] as he looked at the photos. — often + *at* • She *smiled at* me. • I had to *smile at* his silly comments.
2 [+ *obj*] **a** : to show or express (something, such as approval, encouragement, etc.) by a smile • Both parents *smiled* their approval. • I *smiled* my encouragement. **b** : to say (something) with a smile • "Nice job," she *smiled*.
smile on/upon [*phrasal verb*] ***smile on/upon (someone or something)*** : to make (someone or something) have good luck or success • Fortune *smiled upon* us. [=we were lucky] • Lady Luck *smiled on* me and I won the jackpot.

[1]**smil·ey** /ˈsmaili/ *adj* [*more ~; most ~*] : happy and cheerful : smiling a lot • She's a very *smiley* kid.

[2]**smiley** *noun, pl* **smil·ies** [*count*] : SMILEY FACE

smiley face *noun, pl* **~ faces** [*count*] : a symbol used in typing, writing, or drawing that represents a person smiling • He ended his e-mail with a *smiley face*. • The teacher drew a *smiley face* on the student's homework. • a *smiley-face* button

smil·ing·ly /ˈsmailɪŋli/ *adv* [*more ~; most ~*] : with a smile : while smiling • "May I help you?" he asked *smilingly*. • The waiter *smilingly* described the specials.

smirk /ˈsmɚk/ *verb* **smirks; smirked; smirk·ing** [*no obj*] : to smile in an unpleasant way because you are pleased with yourself, glad about someone else's trouble, etc. • She tried not to *smirk* when they announced the winner. — often + *at* • She *smirked at* the thought of how this would hurt him.
– smirk *noun, pl* **smirks** [*count*] • He had a big *smirk* on his face when he told me the news.

smite /ˈsmaɪt/ *verb* **smites; smote** /ˈsmoʊt/; **smit·ten** /ˈsmɪtn̩/ *or* **smote; smit·ing** [+ *obj*] *literary + old-fashioned*
1 : to hurt, kill, or punish (someone or something) • He vowed that he would *smite* his enemy. • Misfortune *smote* him and all his family.
2 : to hit (someone or something) very hard • He *smote* the ball mightily.

smith /ˈsmɪθ/ *noun, pl* **smiths** [*count*] : a person who makes things (such as tools or horseshoes) with iron : BLACKSMITH • Ancient *smiths* developed the techniques needed to make metal tools. — see also GOLDSMITH, GUNSMITH, SILVERSMITH

smith·er·eens /ˌsmɪðəˈri:nz/ *noun* [*plural*] *informal* : small broken pieces : tiny bits • The car was ***blown to smithereens***. [=was completely destroyed by an explosion] • The vase was ***smashed to smithereens***. • An explosion here could *blow* us all *to smithereens*.

smithy /ˈsmɪθi/ *noun, pl* **smith·ies** [*count*]
1 : the place where a blacksmith works • They tore down the old *smithy* behind the general store.
2 : SMITH • In earlier times, the town *smithy* [=*blacksmith*] would repair pots and wagon wheels.

smit·ten /ˈsmɪtn̩/ *adj* [*more ~; most ~*]
1 : in love with someone or something • From the moment he saw her, he was *smitten*. — usually + *by* or *with* • He was *smitten with* her from the moment he laid eyes on her. • I was *smitten by* his good looks. • consumers *smitten with* the latest gadgets
2 : suddenly affected by something (such as a strong emotion or a serious illness) — usually + *by* or *with* • He was *smitten by* disaster. • She was *smitten with* terror.
– see also SMITE

smock /ˈsmɑ:k/ *noun, pl* **smocks** [*count*]
1 : a light and loose long shirt usually worn over your regular clothing to protect it from getting dirty • an artist's *smock* • The children's *smocks* were covered with paint. — called also (*Brit*) *overall*
2 : a long shirt usually worn by women

smock·ing /ˈsmɑ:kɪŋ/ *noun* [*noncount*] : a type of decoration for clothing that is made of many small folds that are sewn into place

smog /ˈsmɑ:g/ *noun* [*noncount*] : fog mixed with smoke : a cloud of dirty air from cars, factories, etc., that is usually found in cities

smog·gy /ˈsmɑ:gi/ *adj* **smog·gi·er; -est** [*also more ~; most ~*] : having a lot of smog • *smoggy* cities

[1]**smoke** /ˈsmoʊk/ *noun, pl* **smokes**
1 [*noncount*] : the cloud of black, gray, or white gases and dust that is produced by burning something • *Smoke* from the campfire stung my eyes. • cigarette *smoke* • We could see black *smoke* from the house fire. • I smell *smoke*. • *smoke* inhalation — see also SECONDHAND SMOKE
2 a [*count*] *informal* : a cigarette, cigar, etc. : something that people smoke • Hey, (have you) got a *smoke*? • Can I bum a few *smokes* off you? **b** [*singular*] : the act of smoking a cigarette, cigar, etc. • He went outside ***for a smoke***. = He went outside ***to have a smoke***. [=to smoke a cigarette, cigar, etc.]
blow smoke *chiefly US, informal* : to lie about something : to say things that are not true in order to fool or impress people • Don't listen to him. He's just *blowing smoke*.
go up in smoke **1** : to burn up completely • All their possessions *went up in smoke*. [=burned in a fire] **2** *informal*

S

: to end or disappear completely • When she hurt her back, all her dreams of being a dancer *went up in smoke.*

where there's smoke, there's fire (*chiefly US*) *or* ***there's no smoke without fire*** — used to say that if people are saying that someone has done something wrong there is usually a good reason for what they are saying • "Do you believe those rumors about the mayor?" "Well, you know what they say, *where there's smoke, there's fire.*"

[2]**smoke** *verb* **smokes; smoked; smok•ing**

1 : to suck the smoke from a cigarette, cigar, pipe, etc., into your mouth and lungs and then exhale it [+ *obj*] I caught her *smoking* a cigarette. • He was thrown out of school for *smoking* marijuana. [*no obj*] She *smokes* and drinks, but I don't. • Do you mind if I *smoke* in here? — see also CHAIN-SMOKE, SMOKING

2 [+ *obj*] **:** to produce smoke • That old car *smokes* when you start it up. • the *smoking* remains of a fire • Olive oil has a high ***smoking point***. [=it does not begin to produce smoke until it is heated to a high temperature]

3 [+ *obj*] **:** to use smoke to flavor and preserve (food, such as meat, cheese, or fish) • We *smoke* our hams over hickory. — see also SMOKED

4 [+ *obj*] *US, informal* **a :** to beat (someone or something) completely **:** DEFEAT • They *smoked* the competition. • We got *smoked*. **b :** to hit (a ball) very hard and fast • (*baseball*) He *smoked* a line drive into left field. • (*tennis*) She *smoked* a forehand down the line.

put/stick that in your pipe and smoke it see [1]PIPE

smoke like a chimney *chiefly US, informal* **:** to smoke a lot of cigarettes, cigars, etc. • She still *smokes like a chimney* despite warnings from her doctor.

smoke out [*phrasal verb*] ***smoke (someone or something) out*** *or* ***smoke out (someone or something)*** **:** to force (someone or something) to leave a place by filling the place with smoke • The hunters tried to *smoke* the foxes *out* of the den. — often used figuratively • She's determined to *smoke out* [=*find out*] the truth about what really happened.

smoke alarm *noun, pl* ~ **alarms** [*count*] **:** a device that makes a loud and harsh noise when smoke fills a room — called also *smoke detector*

smoke and mirrors *noun* [*plural*] *chiefly US* **:** something that seems good but is not real or effective and that is done especially to take attention away from something else that is embarrassing or unpleasant • The new proposal brings no real changes—it's all just *smoke and mirrors*.

smoke bomb *noun, pl* ~ **bombs** [*count*] **:** a bomb that produces a lot of smoke when it explodes • Police threw *smoke bombs* at the rioters.

smoked *adj* [*more* ~; *most* ~]

1 : treated with smoke to add flavor and prevent spoiling • *smoked* ham/mozzarella/salmon

2 : covered by a gray film **:** tinted gray • *smoked* glass/windows

smoke detector *noun, pl* ~ **-tors** [*count*] **:** SMOKE ALARM

smoke–filled room *noun, pl* ~ **rooms** [*count*] **:** a room or place where secret decisions are made by a small group of powerful people • political deals made in *smoke-filled rooms*

smoke–free *adj* [*more* ~; *most* ~] — used to describe a place where people are not allowed to smoke • We guarantee a *smoke-free* working environment.

smoke grenade *noun, pl* ~ **-nades** [*count*] *chiefly US* **:** SMOKE BOMB

smoke•house /ˈsmoʊkˌhaʊs/ *noun, pl* **-hous•es** [*count*] **:** a building where meat or fish is given flavor and kept from spoiling by the use of smoke • Hams hung from the rafters of the *smokehouse*.

smoke•less /ˈsmoʊkləs/ *adj* **:** not producing or containing smoke • *smokeless* powder • a *smokeless* cigarette

smokeless tobacco *noun* [*noncount*] **:** tobacco that is placed in the mouth between the cheek and the gum instead of being smoked

smok•er /ˈsmoʊkɚ/ *noun, pl* **-ers** [*count*]

1 : a person who smokes cigarettes, cigars, etc. • She's a heavy *smoker*.

2 : a piece of equipment used for smoking foods

smoke screen *noun, pl* ~ **screens** [*count*]

1 : something that you do or say to hide something or to take attention away from something • His campaign promises were just a *smoke screen*. • The truth was hidden behind a *smoke screen* of lies.

2 : a cloud of thick smoke that is used to hide ships, soldiers, etc.

[1]**smoke•stack** /ˈsmoʊkˌstæk/ *noun, pl* **-stacks** [*count*] **:** a tall chimney on a factory, ship, etc., for carrying smoke away — called also (*Brit*) *chimney stack*

[2]**smokestack** *adj, always used before a noun, chiefly US* **:** of or relating to companies that manufacture products in large factories • She invested in *smokestack* stocks. • Car manufacturing and other *smokestack industries* need to adapt to the global economy.

smoking /ˈsmoʊkɪŋ/ *noun* [*noncount*] **:** the activity of smoking a cigarette, cigar, pipe, etc. • There is no *smoking* allowed in this restaurant. • When did you start *smoking*? • Would you like to be seated in the ***smoking section***? [=an area where smoking is allowed] • You need to ***quit/stop smoking***. — see also NONSMOKING, PASSIVE SMOKING

smoking gun *noun, pl* ~ **guns** [*singular*] **:** a piece of evidence that clearly proves who did something or shows how something happened • This document is the *smoking gun* that proves that he was lying.

smoking jacket *noun, pl* ~ **-ets** [*count*] **:** a loose jacket or robe worn especially in the past by men at home

smoky *also* **smok•ey** /ˈsmoʊki/ *adj* **smok•i•er; -est**

1 : filled with smoke • a *smoky* bar • *smoky* rooms

2 : having a flavor, taste, or appearance of smoke • a *smoky*, full-bodied wine • *smoky* eyes • Her dress was a *smoky* blue.

3 : very attractive or sexy • Her *smoky* voice drew me in. • She gave him a *smoky* look.

– smok•i•ness /ˈsmoʊkinəs/ *noun* [*noncount*]

smol•der (*US*) *or Brit* **smoul•der** /ˈsmoʊldɚ/ *verb* **-ders; -dered; -der•ing** [*no obj*]

1 : to burn slowly without flames but usually with smoke • The remains of the campfire *smoldered*. • *smoldering* ruins • a *smoldering* fire

2 *literary* **a :** to feel a strong emotion but keep it hidden • He *smoldered* with lust. • Her eyes *smoldered* with anger. **b :** to be felt strongly by someone without being directly shown or expressed • Anger *smoldered* in my heart. • Their discontent *smoldered* [=*simmered*] for years.

3 : to be attractive in a sexy way • He gave her a *smoldering* look. [=he looked at her in a very sexy way]

smooch /ˈsmuːʧ/ *verb* **smooch•es; smooched; smooch•ing** *informal* **:** to kiss [*no obj*] They *smooched* while sitting on the porch swing. [+ *obj*] She *smooched* him while they were on the porch swing.

– smooch *noun, pl* **smooches** [*count*] • Give me a big *smooch* [=*kiss*] on the cheek before you go.

[1]**smooth** /ˈsmuːð/ *adj* **smooth•er; -est**

1 a : having a flat, even surface **:** not rough **:** not having any bumps, ridges, or uneven parts • *smooth* skin • They groomed the ski trail so it was *smooth*. • The river rocks had been worn *smooth* by the water. • The surface is ***(as) smooth as silk***. [=very smooth] **b** *of a liquid mixture* **:** not having any lumps **:** mixed together so there are no lumps • Whisk the flour into the gravy until it is *smooth*. • The milkshake was *smooth* and creamy.

2 : happening or done without any problems • With the aid of observers, the election process was a *smooth* one. • Our trip was *smooth* and uneventful.

3 a : even and regular without sudden movements • the *smooth* movements of a swimmer • She has a nice, *smooth* golf swing. **b :** not having or causing sudden, violent movements • His new car has a *smooth* ride. • Our flight was very *smooth*. — opposite ROUGH

4 *informal* **:** relaxed, confident, and pleasant in a way that may be intended to deceive people • I don't trust him—he's just too *smooth*. • He has a *smooth* manner. • He's a real ***smooth talker***. [=he says flattering things] • She's a ***smooth operator***. [=a person who is smooth] — see also SMOOTHIE

5 a : not sharp, bitter, or unpleasant in taste or smell • The wine was full and *smooth*. • a *smooth* cup of coffee **b :** pleasant to hear or listen to • He has a rich, *smooth* voice.

smooth sailing see SAILING

take the rough with the smooth see [3]ROUGH

– smooth•ness *noun* [*noncount*]

[2]**smooth** *verb* **smoothes; smoothed; smooth•ing** [+ *obj*]

1 : to make (something) smooth • He *smoothed* his tie and headed out the door. • The coin's date had been *smoothed* away over time. — often + *back* or *down* • She *smoothed back* her hair. • *Smooth* the surface *down* with sandpaper. — see also SMOOTH OUT (below)

2 : to remove problems or difficulties from a situation •

They **smoothed the way** for a quick end to the dispute. [=they made it easier to achieve a quick end to the dispute] • She has helped **smooth a path** [=has helped make it easier] for more women to run for office.

3 *always followed by an adverb or preposition* **:** to spread (something) over a surface (such as your skin) **:** to apply (something) by rubbing it on a surface • *Smooth* the cream on after your shower. • *Smooth* the wax over the wood before polishing. • She *smoothed* on some moisturizer before she put on her makeup. • He *smoothed* ointment over the cut.

smooth away [*phrasal verb*] ***smooth (something) away*** *or* ***smooth away (something)*** **:** to make (problems, difficulties, etc.) less serious **:** to remove (problems, difficulties, etc.) • We'll help *smooth away* any legal trouble.

smooth out [*phrasal verb*] ***smooth (something) out*** *or* ***smooth out (something)*** **1 :** to make (something) smooth or flat • Help me *smooth out* the tablecloth. • The ground was rocky, so we *smoothed out* the path with cedar chips. **2 :** to make (something) easier by removing or dealing with problems • We will *smooth out* the election process by next year. • She tried to ***smooth things out*** [=end an argument or disagreement] with her daughter-in-law, but the damage was done.

smooth over [*phrasal verb*] ***smooth (something) over*** *or* ***smooth over (something)*** **:** to make (a disagreement, problem, difficulty, etc.) seem less serious than it really is • Don't worry about missing the application deadline—we'll *smooth* that *over* with the office. • She *smoothed over* the objections to his candidacy.

smooth·ie *or* **smoothy** /ˈsmu:ði/ *noun, pl* **-ies** [*count*]
1 : a person who has a relaxed, polite, and confident way of speaking and behaving but who may not seem honest or sincere • He's a real *smoothie* around women.
2 : a thick, cold drink that is made of fruit mixed with milk, yogurt, or juice • fruit *smoothies*

smooth·ly /ˈsmu:ðli/ *adv* [*more* ~; *most* ~] **:** in a smooth way: such as **a :** without any problems or difficulties • The whole trip went very *smoothly*. • As long as things go *smoothly*, she'll be fine. **b :** without delays or sudden starts or stops • The accident has been cleaned up and traffic is flowing *smoothly* once again. • The software enables you to move *smoothly* from one screen to the next. **c :** with confidence and ease **:** in a relaxed and confident way • She made the jump shot *smoothly* and easily. • "Don't worry," she said *smoothly*, "Just leave it all to me."

smooth–talking *adj* [*more* ~; *most* ~] **:** talking in a friendly and pleasant way that is not completely honest or sincere • a *smooth-talking* salesman • *smooth-talking* politicians

s'more /ˈsmoɚ/ *noun, pl* **s'mores** [*count*] *US* **:** a sweet food that is made by putting a melted marshmallow and a piece of chocolate between two crackers

smor·gas·bord /ˈsmoɚgəsˌboɚd/ *noun* [*singular*]
1 : a meal with many different foods that are placed on a large table so that people can serve themselves **:** BUFFET
2 : a large mixture of many different things • We were presented with a *smorgasbord* [=*variety*] of options.

smote *past tense and past participle of* SMITE

smoth·er /ˈsmʌðɚ/ *verb* **-ers; -ered; -er·ing** [+ *obj*]
1 : to kill (someone) by covering the face so that breathing is not possible • He tried to *smother* her with a pillow.
2 : to cover (something) in order to keep it from growing or spreading • She *smothered* the fire with a blanket. — often used figuratively • She *smothered* her son with love/affection. [=she gave her son a lot of love and affection in a way that prevented him from feeling free to live his own life]
3 : to try to keep (something) from happening **:** to try to stop doing (something) • I tried to *smother* [=*stifle, suppress*] a yawn.
4 : to cover (something or someone) thickly or completely • She *smothers* her pancakes in/with syrup. [=she puts a lot of syrup on her pancakes] • The potatoes were *smothered* in gravy. • She *smothered* him with/in kisses. [=she kissed him many times]

smoulder *Brit spelling of* SMOLDER

[1]**smudge** /ˈsmʌʤ/ *noun, pl* **smudg·es** [*count*] **:** a dirty mark, spot, streak, etc. • His hand left a grimy *smudge* on the wall.
– smudgy /ˈsmʌʤi/ *adj* **smudg·i·er; -est**

[2]**smudge** *verb* **smudges; smudged; smudg·ing**
1 [+ *obj*] **:** to make a dirty mark, spot, streak, etc., on (something) • Don't *smudge* the picture with your dirty hands! • His face was *smudged* with grease.
2 a [*no obj*] **:** to become blurry and unclear by being touched or rubbed • Charcoal drawings *smudge* easily. **b** [+ *obj*] **:** to make (something) blurry or unclear by touching or rubbing it • Be careful not to *smudge* [=*smear*] the ink.

smug /ˈsmʌg/ *adj* **smug·ger; smug·gest** *disapproving* **:** having or showing the annoying quality of people who feel very pleased or satisfied with their abilities, achievements, etc. • It's OK to celebrate your success, but try not to be too *smug* about it. • You can wipe that *smug* look off your face. • a *smug* smile/expression
– smug·ly *adv* [*more* ~; *most* ~] • She smiled *smugly*.
– smug·ness *noun* [*noncount*]

smug·gle /ˈsmʌgəl/ *verb* **smug·gles; smug·gled; smug·gling** [+ *obj*]
1 : to move (someone or something) from one country into another illegally and secretly • He was arrested for *smuggling* drugs into the country. • They *smuggled* immigrants across the border. • The paintings had been *smuggled* out of the country before the war. • *smuggled* goods
2 *informal* **:** to take or bring (something) secretly • We *smuggled* his favorite sandwich past the nurse.
– smug·gler /ˈsmʌglɚ/ *noun, pl* **-glers** [*count*] • drug *smugglers*

smut /ˈsmʌt/ *noun* [*noncount*] *informal + disapproving* **:** language, pictures, or stories that deal with sex in a way that is offensive • *Smut* is not allowed in this house. • obscenity laws that aimed to stamp out *smut*

smut·ty /ˈsmʌti/ *adj* **smut·ti·er; -est** *informal + disapproving* **:** relating to sex in a way that is offensive • *smutty* jokes/humor • a *smutty* magazine

[1]**snack** /ˈsnæk/ *noun, pl* **snacks** [*count*] **:** a small amount of food eaten between meals • He had a *snack* of chips and dip. • between-meal *snacks* • I didn't have time for lunch so I just grabbed a quick/light *snack*. • peanuts, potato chips, and other ***snack foods***

[2]**snack** *verb* **snacks; snacked; snack·ing** [*no obj*] *informal* **:** to eat a small amount of food between meals **:** to eat a snack • She tries not to *snack* between meals. • I'll just *snack* on an apple if I'm hungry.

snack bar *noun, pl* ~ **bars** [*count*] **:** a public place where small meals and snacks are served usually at a counter • There's a *snack bar* at the pool where we can get nachos.

sna·fu /snæˈfu:/ *noun, pl* **-fus** [*count*] *chiefly US, somewhat informal* **:** a problem that makes a situation difficult or confusing • a major scheduling *snafu*

[1]**snag** /ˈsnæg/ *noun, pl* **snags** [*count*]
1 : an unexpected problem or difficulty • We ***hit a snag*** with our travel plans. = We ***ran into a snag*** with our travel plans. [=we had a problem with our travel plans]
2 : a sharp or broken part of something that sticks out from a smooth surface • I caught my sleeve on a *snag* and tore it.
3 : a thread that sticks out from a piece of cloth • My sweater has a *snag* where I caught it on a nail.
4 : a dead tree or tree stump that is still standing up • After the fire, there were a few *snags* still smoldering.

[2]**snag** *verb* **snags; snagged; snag·ging** [+ *obj*]
1 : to catch and tear (something) on something sharp • I *snagged* my favorite sweater on a nail.
2 *US, informal* **:** to catch, capture, or get (something or someone) by quick action or good luck • The shortstop *snagged* the grounder. • The police *snagged* the suspect as he was trying to run away. • I managed to *snag* the information I needed from/off the Internet. • Can I *snag* a ride from/with you?

S

snail /ˈsneɪl/ *noun, pl* **snails** [*count*] **:** a small animal that lives in a shell that it carries on its back, that moves very slowly, and that can live in water or on land
at a snail's pace **:** very slowly • The work is progressing *at a snail's pace*.

snail

snail mail *noun* [*noncount*] *informal + humorous* **:** ordinary mail that is delivered by a postal system **:** mail that is not e-mail • She still uses *snail mail* for paying bills. • I can be contacted by e-mail and *snail mail*.

[1]**snake** /ˈsneɪk/ *noun, pl* **snakes** [*count*]
1 : an animal that has a long, thin body and no arms or legs •

a poisonous *snake* — see also GARTER SNAKE, RATTLESNAKE

snake

2 *chiefly US, informal* : a bad person who tells lies and betrays other people • He's a dirty *snake*! • I thought she was my friend, but she turned out to be ***a snake in the grass***.

3 : a long thin tool that is used to clear out blocked pipes — called also *plumber's snake*

– snake·like /ˈsneɪkˌlaɪk/ *adj* [*more* ~; *most* ~]

²snake *verb* **snakes; snaked; snak·ing** : to move like a snake : to follow a twisting path with many turns [*no obj*] The road *snakes* through the mountains. • Cables *snaked* across the floor. [*+ obj*] Technicians *snaked* cables through the set. • He *snaked* his way through the crowd.

snake·bit /ˈsneɪkˌbɪt/ *also* **snake·bitten** /ˈsneɪkˌbɪtn̩/ *adj* [*more* ~; *most* ~] *US slang* : having bad luck : very unlucky • The team was *snakebit* this year, winning only 1 game out of 10. • He's so *snakebit* that nothing he does comes out right.

snake·bite /ˈsneɪkˌbaɪt/ *noun, pl* **-bites** [*count, noncount*] : the wound you get when a snake bites you

snake charmer *noun, pl* **~ -ers** [*count*] : someone who appears to make snakes move by playing music to them

snake oil *noun* [*noncount*] *chiefly US, informal + disapproving* : something that is sold as medicine but that is not really useful or helpful in any way • *snake oil* remedies — often used figuratively • He thinks politicians are just a bunch of *snake oil* salesmen. [=dishonest people]

snake·skin /ˈsneɪkˌskɪn/ *noun* [*noncount*] : leather made from the skin of a snake • boots made of *snakeskin* = *snakeskin* boots

snaky /ˈsneɪki/ *adj* [*more* ~; *most* ~]

1 : moving like a snake • the dancer's *snaky* movements

2 *chiefly US* : long, thin, or twisting like a snake • a *snaky* river • His hair was long and *snaky*.

– snak·i·ly /ˈsneɪkəli/ *adv*

¹snap /ˈsnæp/ *verb* **snaps; snapped; snap·ping**

1 : to break quickly with a short, sharp sound [*no obj*] The branch *snapped* and fell to the ground. • The cable suddenly *snapped*. • The earpiece of his glasses *snapped* off. [*+ obj*] She *snapped* the twig in two. • The boy *snapped* the wing off his toy airplane.

2 *always followed by an adverb or preposition* : to move into a specified position with a short, sharp sound [*no obj*] The trap *snapped* shut. • The bent tree *snapped* back into an upright position. • The pieces *snap* [=*click*] easily into place. [*+ obj*] I *snapped* the lid shut. • She *snapped* the pieces together.

3 *always followed by an adverb or preposition* [*+ obj*] : to close (something) with a fastener and especially with a snap • She *snapped* her handbag shut. • He *snapped* (up) his jacket.

4 [*+ obj*] : to turn (something) *on* or *off* with a switch • *snap on/off* the lights

5 : to make a short, sharp sound or to cause (something) to make a short, sharp sound [*no obj*] A fire *snapped* [=*crackled*] in the wood stove. [*+ obj*] The driver *snapped* [=*cracked*] the whip to get the horses moving. • a bored student *snapping* her chewing gum

6 : to use your thumb and fingers to make a short, sharp sound [*+ obj*] People ***snapped their fingers*** to the beat. • He *snapped his fingers* to get the waiter's attention. [*no obj*] People in the audience *snapped* to the beat.

7 [*+ obj*] *informal* : to take (a photograph) • tourists *snapping* pictures • The images were *snapped* by a satellite camera. : to photograph (someone or something) • A photographer *snapped* the famous couple leaving a London club last week.

8 : to speak using short, angry sentences or phrases [*no obj*] — usually + *at* • They argued and *snapped at* each other all the time. [*+ obj*] She *snapped* that I was lucky to have a job at all. • "Leave me alone!" he *snapped*.

9 [*no obj*] : to suddenly no longer be able to control your emotions because of a difficult situation, circumstance, etc. • She *snapped* under the pressure of the job. • He just *snapped* and started swearing at everybody.

10 : to move with a quick, short movement or to cause (something) to move with a quick, short movement [*no obj*] Flags *snapped* in the wind. [*+ obj*] When you're throwing, *snap* your wrist as you release the ball.

11 [*+ obj*] *US, informal* : to cause the end of (a series of wins, losses, successes, etc.) • They *snapped* [=*broke*] a 10-game losing streak. [=they won a game after losing 10 games] • His hitting streak was *snapped* at 18 games.

12 [*+ obj*] *American football* : to pass (the ball) back to a teammate and especially to the quarterback by passing it between your legs at the start of a play • The center *snapped* [=*hiked*] the ball.

13 [*no obj*] : to try to bite someone or something suddenly and quickly — usually + *at* • The dog *snapped at* a fly.

snap out of [*phrasal verb*] ***snap out of (something)*** *or* ***snap (someone) out of (something)*** *informal* : to stop being in or to cause (someone) to stop being in (an unhappy condition or mood, a daydream, etc.) • I don't know how to get her to *snap out of* her depression. [=to stop being depressed] • The sound of a door slamming *snapped me out of* my daydream. • Come on, ***snap out of it***! You can't let your breakup get you so depressed.

snap to attention ✧ A soldier who *snaps to attention* moves quickly to a position of standing silently with the body stiff and straight, the feet together, and both arms at the sides. The phrase is also used figuratively. • The children *snapped to attention* [=suddenly stopped moving around, talking, etc.] when the teacher clapped his hands.

snap to it *informal* : to start working harder or more quickly • You'll have to *snap to it* if you want to finish on time.

snap up [*phrasal verb*] ***snap (something or someone) up*** *or* ***snap up (something or someone)*** : to buy or take (something or someone) quickly or eagerly • Shoppers came to the store to *snap up* bargains after the holidays. • When they see your work history, they'll *snap* you *up*! [=hire you immediately]

²snap *noun, pl* **snaps**

1 [*count*] : a sudden, short, sharp sound caused by something breaking or moving into a new position — usually singular • We could hear the *snap* of twigs beneath our feet. • the *snap* of the alligator's jaws

2 [*count*] : the act of snapping your fingers or the sound made when you snap your fingers • I've trained the dog to come to me with a *snap* of my fingers.

3 [*count*] *US* : a device that fastens something by closing or locking with a short, sharp sound • The *snap* of the bracelet broke.; *especially* : a set of two metal or plastic pieces that fit tightly together when you press them • pockets with *snaps* — called also (*Brit*) *popper*, (*Brit*) *press stud*

snap

4 [*count*] : a thin, hard cookie — see also GINGERSNAP

5 [*singular*] *US, informal* : something that is very easy to do : CINCH • The software is a *snap* to install. = Installing the software is a *snap*. • The recipes are a *snap* (to prepare).

6 [*singular*] *US, informal* : a small amount of time • I'll be ready in a *snap*. [=*jiffy*]

7 [*count*] : a sudden brief period of a specified kind of weather • We had a ***cold snap*** [=a brief period of very cold weather] last week.

8 [*count*] : a quick, short movement • She pulled the rope taut with a *snap* [=*flick*] of her wrist.

9 [*count*] *chiefly Brit* : SNAPSHOT • family *snaps* [=informal photographs of family members that are taken quickly]

10 [*count*] *American football* : the act of snapping the ball back to a teammate and especially to the quarterback at the start of a play • the first *snap* of the game • The quarterback fumbled the *snap*. [=fumbled the ball when it was snapped to him]

11 [*noncount*] *Brit* : a card game in which players put down cards in a pile and try to be the first to say "snap" when two cards that are the same have been played

³snap *adj, always used before a noun* : done or made suddenly or without careful thought • a *snap* judgment/decision • (*chiefly Brit*) a *snap* election

⁴snap *interj, Brit* — used to express surprise when two things are alike • *Snap*! I ate spaghetti last night, too.

snap bean *noun, pl* **~ beans** [*count*] : any of several types of beans whose long green seed cases are eaten as a vegetable when they are young and tender

snap·drag·on /ˈsnæpˌdrægən/ *noun, pl* **-ons** [*count*] : a tall plant that has many usually pink, white, red, or yellow flowers

snap pea *noun, pl* **~ peas** [*count*] : SUGAR SNAP PEA

S

snap·per /ˈsnæpɚ/ *noun, pl* **-pers**
1 [*count, noncount*] **:** a type of fish that lives in the ocean and that is eaten as food • red *snapper*
2 [*count*] *chiefly Brit, informal* **:** PHOTOGRAPHER
3 [*count*] **:** SNAPPING TURTLE
4 [*count*] *American football* **:** the player who passes the ball to another player at the start of a play

snapping turtle *noun, pl* **~ turtles** [*count*] **:** a large American turtle that has strong jaws and that is sometimes used for food — called also *snapper*

snap·pish /ˈsnæpɪʃ/ *adj* [*more ~; most ~*] *chiefly US* **:** feeling or showing irritation • a *snappish* mood/remark • The shoppers were *snappish* and rude.
– **snap·pish·ly** *adv* • "I've been waiting for you," he said *snappishly*.

snap·py /ˈsnæpi/ *adj* **snap·pi·er; -est** [*also more ~; most ~*] *informal*
1 a : exciting or lively • *snappy* colors • a *snappy* tune **b :** moving or able to move quickly • a *snappy* pace • a car with a *snappy* engine
2 : fashionable or stylish • a *snappy* [=*sharp*] dresser • a *snappy* [=*snazzy*] bow tie
3 : clever and funny • a *snappy* [=*witty*] joke/remark • The show is well-acted, and the dialogue is *snappy*.
4 : feeling or showing irritation **:** SNAPPISH • He got pretty *snappy* about it. • She was awfully *snappy* with me.
make it snappy *or Brit* ***look snappy*** *informal* **:** to act, move, or go quickly **:** HURRY UP • Clean your room, and *make it snappy*! [=do it quickly]
– **snap·pi·ly** /ˈsnæpəli/ *adv* • *snappily* written essays • *snappily* dressed

snap·shot /ˈsnæp͵ʃɑːt/ *noun, pl* **-shots** [*count*]
1 : an informal photograph that is taken quickly • family *snapshots* — often + *of* • *snapshots of* the baby
2 : a quick view or a small amount of information that tells you a little about what someone or something is like — often + *of* • Television news presents only *snapshots of* the war. • We get a *snapshot of* 18th-century Japan in his letters.

¹snare /ˈsneɚ/ *noun, pl* **snares** [*count*]
1 : a device that has a loop (called a noose) which gets smaller when the end of it is pulled and that is used to catch animals **:** a kind of trap • a rabbit *snare*
2 : a position or situation from which it is difficult to escape • people caught in the *snare* of drug addiction
3 : SNARE DRUM

²snare *verb* **snares; snared; snar·ing** [+ *obj*]
1 a : to catch (an animal) in a snare • They caught fish and *snared* seabirds. — often used figuratively • Police *snared* the thief outside the bank. **b :** to cause (something) to become caught in something (such as a net or trap) • Unfortunately, the nets also *snare* turtles. — usually used as *(be/get) snared* • Thousands of turtles *get snared* [=*ensnared*] in the nets each year. — sometimes used figuratively • another politician *snared* [=*caught, entangled*] in another scandal
2 : to win or get (something) by skillful action or good luck • I was lucky enough to *snare* [=(more commonly) *snag*] a job with a good salary and benefits. • They *snared* first place in the contest. • trying to *snare* business from competitors
3 *US, sports* **:** to catch (a thrown or hit ball) usually by jumping • The shortstop *snared* a high throw from the outfield.

snare drum *noun, pl* **~ drums** [*count*] **:** a drum of a medium size that is played with special sticks (called drumsticks) — called also *snare*; see picture at PERCUSSION

¹snarl /ˈsnɑɚəl/ *noun, pl* **snarls** [*count*]
1 : a twisted knot of hairs, thread, etc. **:** TANGLE • a brush that smoothes out *snarls* • *snarls* of string/rope
2 : a situation in which you can no longer move or make progress • a traffic *snarl* • The project has been plagued by legal/bureaucratic *snarls*.
– compare ⁴SNARL

²snarl *verb* **snarls; snarled; snarl·ing :** to become twisted together **:** to form a snarl or snarls [*no obj*] Her hair *snarls* very easily. — sometimes used figuratively • Traffic *snarled* at the intersection after the accident. [+ *obj*] The rope had become *snarled* around the post. — sometimes used figuratively • The accident *snarled* traffic.
snarl up [*phrasal verb*] ***snarl (something) up*** *or* ***snarl up (something)*** *chiefly Brit* **:** to stop (something or someone) from moving or making progress • Traffic was *snarled up* because of the parade. — see also SNARL-UP
– compare ³SNARL

³snarl *verb* **snarls; snarled; snarling**
1 [*no obj*] **:** to growl and show the teeth — usually + *at* • The dog *snarled at* the postman.
2 : to say something in an angry or annoyed way [+ *obj*] "Get back to work," she *snarled*. — often + *at* • He *snarled* insults *at* other drivers. [*no obj*] The stranger *snarled at* her.
– compare ²SNARL

⁴snarl *noun, pl* **snarls** [*count*] **:** an act of growling and showing the teeth — usually singular • The dog gave a *snarl* when I reached for its bone. — compare ¹SNARL

snarl–up *noun, pl* **-ups** [*count*] *chiefly Brit* **:** a situation in which you can no longer move or make progress • a traffic *snarl-up* [=*snarl*]

¹snatch /ˈsnætʃ/ *verb* **snatch·es; snatched; snatch·ing** [+ *obj*]
1 : to take (something) quickly or eagerly • She *snatched* [=*grabbed*] the ball out of the air and ran down the court. • An eagle swooped down and *snatched* one of the hens. — often + *up* • She *snatched up* the last copy of the book. — often used figuratively • trying to *snatch* a few moments of rest • The company *snatched* him *up* [=hired him] as soon as he graduated from college.
2 : to take (something or someone) suddenly from a person or place often by using force • A man *snatched* [=*stole*] the old woman's purse. • Kidnappers *snatched* [=*abducted*] the girl from her bedroom. • She *snatched* the toy from his hands. — sometimes + *away* • She *snatched* her brother's toy *away*. — sometimes used figuratively • He *snatched* 30 rebounds in one game. • His life was *snatched away* (from him) by a tragic accident. [=he died in a tragic accident]
snatch at [*phrasal verb*] ***snatch at (something)*** **:** to grab or try to grab (something) quickly or eagerly • chaotic city streets where thieves *snatch at* tourists' wallets — often used figuratively • She was an ambitious person who *snatched at* every opportunity.

²snatch *noun, pl* **snatches** [*count*] **:** a small part of something — usually + *of* • I only caught a (short) *snatch of* the music/conversation/dialogue.
in snatches **:** for short periods of time • sleeping *in snatches* **:** in small amounts • The plot of the novel came to me *in snatches*.

snatch·er /ˈsnætʃɚ/ *noun, pl* **-ers** [*count*] **:** a person who takes something from someone else and runs away • a purse/briefcase *snatcher* [=*thief*] • a child/baby *snatcher* [=a person who kidnaps a child/baby]

snaz·zy /ˈsnæzi/ *adj* **snaz·zi·er; -est** [*also more ~; most ~*] *informal* **:** attractive and stylish • a *snazzy* new computer/car/stereo • a *snazzy* dresser/hotel/party/tie

¹sneak /ˈsniːk/ *verb* **sneaks; sneaked** *or chiefly US* **snuck** /ˈsnʌk/; **sneak·ing**
1 *always followed by an adverb or preposition* [*no obj*] **:** to move quietly and secretly in order to avoid being noticed • They tried to *sneak* into the movie without paying. • As a teenager she would *sneak* out (of her house/apartment) at night to visit her boyfriend. • He *sneaked* [=*crept*] past the guard.
2 [+ *obj*] **:** to take or bring (something) secretly and often quickly • She *sneaked* some cigars through customs. • He *snuck* a few cookies out of the jar while his mother wasn't looking. • They caught him trying to *sneak* food into the theater. • I *sneaked* a note to my friend in class. = I *sneaked* my friend a note in class. • I'm going to *sneak* a smoke. [=I'm going to smoke a cigarette while nobody is watching] • I was caught *sneaking* a look [=secretly looking] at my Christmas presents. • Can I ***sneak a peek*** at your quiz answers?
3 [*no obj*] *Brit, old-fashioned* **:** to tell someone (such as a parent or teacher) about something wrong that someone else has done • I got in trouble after she *sneaked* [=*squealed*, (*chiefly US*) *tattled*] on me.
sneak up on [*phrasal verb*] ***sneak up on (someone)*** **1 :** to approach (someone) quietly and secretly in order to avoid being noticed • My father likes to *sneak up on* my mother and tickle her. • Don't *sneak up on* me like that! **2 :** to approach, happen, or develop without being noticed • My birthday really *snuck up on* me this year. • This kind of problem can *sneak up on* you if you're not attentive.

²sneak *noun, pl* **sneaks** [*count*]
1 *US, informal* **:** a person who acts in a secret and usually dishonest way • What a rotten *sneak*! I should have known not to trust her.
2 *Brit, old-fashioned* **:** TATTLETALE
3 *American football* **:** QUARTERBACK SNEAK • He ran a *sneak* up the middle for a touchdown.

[3]**sneak** *adj, always used before a noun* : done while others are not paying attention • a *sneak* [=*surprise*] attack • She took a ***sneak peek*** [=a secret look] at the birthday presents hidden in the closet.

sneak·er /ˈsniːkɚ/ *noun, pl* **-ers** [*count*] *US* : a shoe with a rubber sole that is designed for people to wear while running, playing sports, etc. — called also (*Brit*) *trainer,* (*chiefly Brit*) *training shoe*; see picture at SHOE

sneaking *adj, always used before a noun*
1 : behaving in a secret and dishonest manner • a *sneaking* [=*sneaky*] eavesdropper
2 : not openly expressed — usually + *for* • He had a *sneaking* admiration *for* his opponent. • a *sneaking* fondness *for* bad movies
3 ✧ If you have a ***sneaking feeling/suspicion***, you think that something might be true or might happen even though you have no definite reason to think so. • I have a *sneaking feeling/suspicion* that we're going to have a test today. • I have a *sneaking suspicion* that he's lying.

sneak preview *noun, pl* ~ **-views** [*count*] : a special showing of something (such as a movie, play, or product) before it becomes available to the general public • A few prominent writers were invited to a *sneak preview* of the new film/play. • a *sneak preview* of this fall's fashions

sneaky /ˈsniːki/ *adj* **sneak·i·er; -est** [*also more* ~; *most* ~]
1 : behaving in a secret and usually dishonest manner • a *sneaky*, untrustworthy person
2 : done in a secret and dishonest manner • They make it look like you're getting a lot more than you really are. It's a *sneaky* trick. • It's a *sneaky* way of getting people to buy something they don't need.
– sneak·i·ly /ˈsniːkəli/ *adv* • a *sneakily* subversive movie
– sneak·i·ness /ˈsniːkinəs/ *noun* [*noncount*]

[1]**sneer** /ˈsniɚ/ *verb* **sneers; sneered; sneer·ing**
1 [*no obj*] **:** to smile or laugh at someone or something with an expression on your face that shows dislike and a lack of respect — usually + *at* • She *sneered at* me in disgust.
2 : to express dislike and a lack of respect for someone or something in a very open way [*no obj*] — usually + *at* • an academic who *sneers at* anyone who doesn't have a PhD • Critics *sneered at* his first novel. [+ *obj*] "You obviously don't know what you're talking about," she *sneered*.
– sneering *adj, always used before a noun* • the *sneering* villain of the comic book • *sneering* contempt **– sneer·ing·ly** *adv* • Critics *sneeringly* referred to the novel as "juvenile."

[2]**sneer** *noun, pl* **sneers** [*count*] : an expression on a person's face that is like a smile but that shows dislike and a lack of respect for someone or something • She looked at me with a *sneer* of disgust. • "They're paranoid," he said with a *sneer*.; *also* : a statement, criticism, etc., that shows dislike and a lack of respect • The novel elicited *sneers* from the critics.

sneeze /ˈsniːz/ *verb* **sneez·es; sneezed; sneez·ing** [*no obj*] : to suddenly force air out through your nose and mouth with a usually loud noise because your body is reacting to dust, a sickness, etc. • She was constantly *sneezing* and coughing.
sneeze at [*phrasal verb*] ***sneeze at (something)*** *not used in progressive tenses, informal* : to regard (something) as not important, worth noticing, etc. — always used in negative statements • The award is ***nothing to sneeze at***. = The award ***is not to be sneezed at***. [=the award is important]
– sneeze *noun, pl* **sneezes** [*count*] • Germs can be spread through a *sneeze* or a handshake.

snick·er /ˈsnɪkɚ/ *verb* **-ers; -ered; -er·ing** [*no obj*] *chiefly US* : to make a short, quiet laugh in a way that shows disrespect — usually + *at* • They *snickered* [=(*chiefly Brit*) *sniggered*] *at* my strange hat.
– snicker *noun, pl* **-ers** [*count*] • His crazy story drew/got *snickers* from the police. • She heard *snickers* behind her back.

snide /ˈsnaɪd/ *adj* [*more* ~; *most* ~] : unkind or insulting in an indirect way • *snide* remarks/comments/references • a *snide* tone
– snide·ly *adv* • "Are you having a problem?" she asked *snidely*.

[1]**sniff** /ˈsnɪf/ *verb* **sniffs; sniffed; sniff·ing**
1 a [*no obj*] : to take air into your nose in short breaths that are loud enough to be heard • She *sniffed* and wiped her nose with a tissue. **b :** to smell (something or someone) by putting your nose close to it and taking air in through your nose in short breaths [+ *obj*] She put perfume on her wrist and *sniffed* it. • The dog *sniffed* the carpet. [*no obj*] He held the flower up to his nose and *sniffed*. — often + *at* • The cat *sniffed at* the food and walked away. **c** [+ *obj*] : to take (something, such as fumes or a drug) into your body by inhaling it through your nose in order to get intoxicated • *sniffing* glue/ether • *sniffing* [=(more commonly) *snorting*] cocaine
2 a [+ *obj*] : to discover or find (something) by smelling — usually + *out* • dogs that are trained to *sniff out* drugs — often used figuratively • Several companies, *sniffing* [=*sensing*] profit potential, are investing in the area. • My mother is an expert at *sniffing out* trouble. • the ability to *sniff out* bargains • By asking around, we were able to *sniff out* the truth. **b** [*no obj*] : to search *for* something by smelling • A dog *sniffed* (around) *for* drugs in the car. — often used figuratively • The detective *sniffed for* clues. • She has been *sniffing* (around/about) *for* a new job.
3 [+ *obj*] : to say (something) in a way that shows dislike, disapproval, etc. • "I guess you don't need my help," she *sniffed*.
sniff around/round [*phrasal verb*] ***sniff around/round (someone)*** *Brit, informal* : to try to get (someone) as a romantic partner, employee, etc. • His engagement hasn't stopped him from *sniffing around* other girls. • Rival companies have been *sniffing around* her for years.
sniff at [*phrasal verb*] ***sniff at (something)*** : to show dislike or disapproval of (something) especially because you think it is not important or worthy of respect • Some people *sniff at* the idea of using fake flowers. • It's not a big profit, but it's ***not to be sniffed at***. = It's not a big profit, but it's ***nothing to sniff at***.

[2]**sniff** *noun, pl* **sniffs**
1 [*count*] : an act or the sound of drawing air into the nose especially in order to smell something or because you are sick or have been crying • He took a big *sniff* [=*whiff*] of the soup. • She said that she felt fine, but her *sniffs* and coughs told a different story.
2 [*singular*] : an expression of dislike or disapproval • "I refuse to answer that question," she said with a *sniff*.
3 [*singular*] : a small amount or sign *of* something • He wanted to avoid the slightest *sniff of* a scandal. • They ran away at the first *sniff* [=*hint*] *of* trouble. • There was still a *sniff of* hope left for the team.
4 [*singular*] : an opportunity to come close to achieving or experiencing something — usually + *of* • The team did not even get a *sniff of* the play-offs last year. [=did not even come close to reaching the play-offs]

sniff·er /ˈsnɪfɚ/ *noun, pl* **-ers** [*count*]
1 : someone who sniffs a drug or other substance in order to become intoxicated • a cocaine/glue/paint *sniffer*
2 : a dog that is trained to find people, illegal drugs, explosives, etc., by recognizing and following scents • *Sniffers* were brought in to search bags at the airport. — called also *sniffer dog*

[1]**snif·fle** /ˈsnɪfəl/ *verb* **snif·fles; snif·fled; snif·fling**
1 [*no obj*] : to repeatedly take air into your nose in short breaths that are loud enough to be heard because you are sick or have been crying • The children have been *sniffling* for a week now.
2 [+ *obj*] : to say (something) while crying or sniffling • "In your family's eyes," she *sniffled*, "I'm not good enough."

[2]**sniffle** *noun, pl* **sniffles** [*count*]
1 : an act or the sound of sniffling • He couldn't stop his *sniffles*.
2 ***the sniffles*** *informal* : a slight or mild cold that causes you to sniffle a lot • I have (a case of) *the sniffles*.

sniffy /ˈsnɪfi/ *adj* **sniff·i·er; -est** [*also more* ~; *most* ~] *chiefly Brit, informal + disapproving* : having or showing the attitude of people who believe that they are better or more important than other people • a *sniffy* [=*snooty*] man in an expensive suit • She wrote a *sniffy* letter rejecting his offer.

snif·ter /ˈsnɪftɚ/ *noun, pl* **-ters** [*count*] : a glass with a narrow rim, a wide bowl, and a short stem that is used especially for drinking brandy

snig·ger /ˈsnɪgɚ/ *verb* **-gers; -gered; -ger·ing** [*no obj*] *chiefly Brit* : SNICKER — usually + *at* • The class *sniggered at* her mistake.
– snigger *noun, pl* **-gers** [*count*] • His awkwardness drew *sniggers* from the other boys.

[1]**snip** /ˈsnɪp/ *noun, pl* **snips**
1 [*count*] : a small piece that is cut from something : a small piece that is snipped • a *snip* of yarn
2 [*count*] : an act or the sound of snipping something — usu-

ally singular • She removed the dead flowers with a *snip* of her scissors.
3 [*singular*] *Brit, informal* : something bought or sold for a good price • Tickets are a *snip* [=*bargain*] at only three euros each.
– see also SNIPS

[2]**snip** *verb* **snips; snipped; snip·ping** : to cut (something) with scissors : to remove (something) by cutting with scissors [+ *obj*] He *snipped* some fresh herbs from plants on the windowsill. • *snipping* pictures out of magazines • *Snip* the uneven ends off. = *Snip* off the uneven ends. [*no obj*] She *snipped* at the hanging strings.

[1]**snipe** /ˈsnaɪp/ *verb* **snipes; sniped; snip·ing**
1 [*no obj*] : to shoot *at* someone from a hidden place • Enemy fighters *sniped at* them from vacant buildings.
2 : to criticize someone or something in a harsh or unfair way [*no obj*] — usually + *at* • The candidates have been *sniping at* each other in speeches. [+ *obj*] One of the senators *sniped*, "What does he think this is, a monarchy?"
– sniping *noun* [*noncount*] • Soldiers took cover when the *sniping* started. • There has been a lot of *sniping* between the candidates.

[2]**snipe** *noun, pl* **snipes** *or* **snipe** [*count*] : a bird with a long thin beak that lives in wet areas

snip·er /ˈsnaɪpɚ/ *noun, pl* **-ers** [*count*] : a person who shoots at another person from a hidden place • The soldiers were attacked by a *sniper*. — often used before another noun • a *sniper* attack

snip·pet /ˈsnɪpət/ *noun, pl* **-pets** [*count*]
1 : a small piece of information or news — usually + *of* • *snippets of* gossip/information
2 : a small part of something (such as a piece of music, a conversation, etc.) • *snippets* from the author's newest novel — often + *of* • I heard only a *snippet of* their conversation.

snip·py /ˈsnɪpi/ *adj* **snip·pi·er; -est** [*also more ~; most ~*] *US, informal* : feeling or showing irritation • I'm sorry. I didn't mean to get *snippy* with you. • *snippy* comments

snips /ˈsnɪps/ *noun* [*plural*] : heavy scissors that are used especially for cutting metal • tin *snips*

snit /ˈsnɪt/ *noun*
have a snit *US, informal* : to become annoyed and angry usually about something minor • She's going to *have a snit* when she sees this mess.
in a snit *US, informal* : in a very annoyed and angry state usually because of something minor • He left *in a snit* when they told him he'd have to wait another hour. • She got *in a snit* when she found out he was late.

[1]**snitch** /ˈsnɪʧ/ *verb* **snitch·es; snitched; snitch·ing** *informal*
1 [*no obj*] *disapproving* : to tell someone in authority (such as the police or a teacher) about something wrong that someone has done • Someone must have *snitched* to the police. — usually + *on* • She *snitched* [=*tattled, squealed*] *on* her brother when he skipped school.
2 [+ *obj*] : to take or steal (something that is not very valuable) • He *snitched* a dime from the kid next door.

[2]**snitch** *noun, pl* **snitches** [*count*] *informal + disapproving* : a person who tells someone in authority (such as the police or a teacher) about something wrong that someone has done : someone who snitches — usually singular • Who's the *snitch* who ratted on me?

sniv·el /ˈsnɪvəl/ *verb* **-els;** *US* **-eled** *or Brit* **-elled;** *US* **-el·ing** *or Brit* **-el·ling** : to complain or cry in an annoying way [*no obj*] millionaires *sniveling* about their financial problems [+ *obj*] "Woe is me," she *sniveled*.
– sniveling *adj* • He's a *sniveling*, lying coward.

snob /ˈsnɑːb/ *noun, pl* **snobs** [*count*] *disapproving* : someone who tends to criticize, reject, or ignore people who come from a lower social class, have less education, etc. • Most of the people in the club are *snobs* who look down on people who attended public schools. • Don't be such a *snob*. • food/wine/art *snobs* [=people who think they are better than other people because they know about fine food/art/wine] • an intellectual *snob*
– snob·bism /ˈsnɑːˌbɪzəm/ *noun* [*noncount*] • She accused me of *snobbism*. [=she accused me of being a snob]

snob appeal *noun* [*noncount*] *disapproving* : a quality that makes something attractive to people who are snobs • Expensive cars have *snob appeal*. • old foreign films with *snob appeal* — called also (*Brit*) *snob value*

snob·bery /ˈsnɑːbəri/ *noun* [*noncount*] *disapproving* : the behavior or attitude of people who think they are better than other people : the behavior or attitude of snobs • the *snobbery* of some wine connoisseurs • (*chiefly US*) By a kind of ***reverse snobbery***, he hated people from educated families and bragged about his working-class relatives. • (*Brit*) ***inverted snobbery***

snob·bish /ˈsnɑːbɪʃ/ *adj* [*more ~; most ~*] *disapproving* : having or showing the attitude of people who think they are better than other people : of or relating to people who are snobs • a *snobbish* rich kid • a *snobbish* attitude
– snob·bish·ly *adv* • She *snobbishly* refused to watch mainstream movies. **– snob·bish·ness** *noun* [*noncount*]

snob·by /ˈsnɑːbi/ *adj* **snob·bi·er; -est** [*also more ~; most ~*] *informal + disapproving* : SNOBBISH • a *snobby* brat • *snobby* prep schools

sno–cone *variant spelling of* SNOW CONE

snog /ˈsnɑːg/ *verb* **snogs; snogged; snog·ging** *Brit, informal* : to kiss for a long time [*no obj*] They were *snogging* on the couch. [+ *obj*] They were *snogging* each other on the couch.
– snog *noun* [*singular*] • They were sharing a *snog*.

snook /ˈsnʊk, *Brit* ˈsnuːk/ see *cock a snook at* at [2]COCK

[1]**snook·er** /ˈsnʊkɚ, *Brit* ˈsnuːkə/ *noun* [*noncount*] : a version of the game of pool that is played chiefly in Britain with a cue ball, 15 red balls, and 6 balls of other colors on a table that has 6 pockets — often used before another noun • a *snooker* player/table — compare BILLIARDS, POOL

[2]**snooker** *verb* **-kers; -kered; -ker·ing** [+ *obj*] *informal*
1 *US* : to trick or deceive (someone) • She *snookered* [=*hoodwinked*] her parents into buying her a new car. — often used as *(be) snookered* • I have a feeling we've *been snookered*.
2 *Brit* : to prevent (someone) from doing or achieving something • He was ahead early in the match, but he ***snookered himself***. [=he caused his own defeat by performing badly] — often used as *(be) snookered* • They wanted to build a museum but *were snookered* [=*thwarted*] by city regulations.

[1]**snoop** /ˈsnuːp/ *verb* **snoops; snooped; snoop·ing** [*no obj*] *informal* : to look for private information about someone or something • She locks up her diary to keep her brother from *snooping*. • I caught her *snooping* (around) in my desk drawers. • Government agencies have been *snooping* on them for years. • She doesn't want reporters *snooping* into her personal life.
– snoop·er *noun, pl* **-ers** [*count*] **– snooping** *noun* [*noncount*] • electronic/government *snooping* **– snooping** *adj* • a *snooping* device/cop • *snooping* software/technology

[2]**snoop** *noun, pl* **snoops** *informal*
1 [*count*] : someone who looks for private information about someone or something : someone who snoops • No, I didn't read your e-mail. I'm no *snoop*.
2 [*singular*] : a secret look around a place • We had a *snoop* around their apartment.
– snoopy /ˈsnuːpi/ *adj* **snoop·i·er; -est** • a *snoopy* reporter

snoot /ˈsnuːt/ *noun, pl* **snoots** [*count*]
1 a : SNOUT 1 **b** *informal + humorous* : the nose of a person • She has a great big *snoot*.
2 *US, informal* : a snooty person : SNOB • That little *snoot* thinks he deserves only the best!

snooty /ˈsnuːti/ *adj* **snoot·i·er; est** [*also more ~; most ~*] *informal + disapproving* : having or showing the insulting attitude of people who think that they are better, smarter, or more important than other people • a *snooty* [=*snobbish*] rich girl • a *snooty* accent/attitude • a *snooty* restaurant
– snoot·i·ness /ˈsnuːtinəs/ *noun* [*noncount*]

[1]**snooze** /ˈsnuːz/ *verb* **snooz·es; snoozed; snooz·ing** [*no obj*] *informal* : to sleep lightly especially for a short period of time : DOZE • She lay down on the sofa and *snoozed* [=*napped*] for a while.

[2]**snooze** *noun* [*singular*] *informal*
1 : a short period of light sleep : NAP • take/catch a *snooze*
2 *US* : something that is dull or boring — usually singular • The novel was a real *snooze*. [=*bore*]
3 : SNOOZE BUTTON • Most mornings I hit (the) *snooze* at least twice.

snooze button *noun, pl* **~ -buttons** [*count*] *chiefly US* : a button on an alarm clock that stops the alarm from making noise for a short time so that the sleeper can rest for a few more minutes • He woke up and hit the *snooze button*. — called also (*chiefly US*) *snooze alarm*

snooz·er /ˈsnuːzɚ/ *noun, pl* **-ers** [*count*] *US, informal* : something that is dull and boring — usually singular • a *snoozer* of a film

S

[1]**snore** /ˈsnoɚ/ *verb* **snores; snored; snor·ing** [*no obj*] **:** to breathe noisily while sleeping ▪ My husband *snores*.
– **snor·er** *noun, pl* **-ers** [*count*] ▪ a loud *snorer* – **snoring** *noun* [*noncount*]

[2]**snore** *noun, pl* **snores** [*count*]
1 : an act of snoring or the sound made when someone is snoring ▪ a loud/soft *snore*
2 *US, informal* **:** something that is dull and boring — usually singular ▪ The movie was a real *snore*. [=*snooze, bore*]

[1]**snor·kel** /ˈsnoɚkəl/ *noun, pl* **-kels** [*count*] **:** a special tube that makes it possible to breathe while you are swimming with your head underwater — see picture at SCUBA DIVING

[2]**snorkel** *verb* **-kels;** *US* **-keled** *or Brit* **-kelled;** *US* **-kel·ing** *or Brit* **-kel·ling** [*no obj*] **:** to swim underwater while using a snorkel ▪ We *snorkeled* in the Caribbean on our vacation last year.
– **snor·kel·er** (*US*) *or Brit* **snor·kel·ler** *noun, pl* **-ers** [*count*] – **snorkeling** (*US*) *or Brit* **snorkelling** /ˈsnoɚkəlɪŋ/ *noun* [*noncount*] ▪ She **went snorkeling** with her sister.

[1]**snort** /ˈsnoɚt/ *verb* **snorts; snort·ed; snort·ing**
1 [*no obj*] **:** to force air noisily through your nose ▪ The old dog *snorted* like a pig when it smelled food. ▪ He *snorted* with disgust.
2 a [*no obj*] **:** to express dislike, disapproval, anger, or surprise by snorting ▪ She *snorted* at his suggestion that he could fix the sink himself. **b** [+ *obj*] **:** to say (something) with a snort or while snorting ▪ "Yeah, you're a writer, and I'm the King of Spain!" he *snorted*.
3 [+ *obj*] **:** to take (a drug) into your body by inhaling it through your nose ▪ They were *snorting* cocaine.

[2]**snort** *noun, pl* **snorts** [*count*]
1 : an act or the sound of noisily forcing air through the nose **:** an act or the sound of snorting ▪ the *snorts* of a pig/horse/bull ▪ a *snort* of laughter/derision/disapproval
2 : an amount of a drug taken into the body by inhaling it through the nose ▪ a *snort* of cocaine

snot /ˈsnɑːt/ *noun, pl* **snots** *informal + impolite*
1 [*noncount*] **:** mucus from the nose ▪ *Snot* was dripping from his nose.
2 [*count*] *disapproving* **:** a rude and annoying person ▪ an obnoxious little *snot*

snot·ty /ˈsnɑːti/ *adj* **-ti·er; -ti·est** [*also more* ~; *most* ~] *informal*
1 : rude and annoying — used especially to describe people who think they are better than other people ▪ a *snotty* reply/manner/person ▪ She was very *snotty* to me.
2 : covered or filled with mucus from the nose **:** dirty with mucus ▪ a *snotty* nose
– **snot·ti·ly** /ˈsnɑːtəli/ *adv* ▪ She took a bite and said *snottily*, "So you think you can cook?" – **snot·ti·ness** /ˈsnɑːtinəs/ *noun* [*noncount*]

snout /ˈsnaʊt/ *noun, pl* **snouts** [*count*]
1 : the long nose of some animals (such as pigs) ▪ The dog raised his *snout* and sniffed. — sometimes used figuratively ▪ The boat's *snout* bounced on the waves.
2 *informal + humorous* **:** the nose of a person ▪ a punch in the *snout*
have/get your snout in the trough see TROUGH

[1]**snow** /ˈsnoʊ/ *noun, pl* **snows**
1 : soft, white pieces of frozen water that fall to the ground from the sky in cold weather [*noncount*] *Snow* fell softly on the town. ▪ The mountains were blanketed/covered with *snow*. ▪ She took a walk in the *snow*. ▪ We got 12 inches of *snow*. [=we had a snowstorm that left 12 inches of snow on the ground] ▪ We haven't had much *snow* this year. ▪ The weatherman is forecasting ***heavy/light snow***. [=the weatherman is saying that a large/small amount of snow will fall] ▪ She went out to ***shovel the snow***. [*count*] Soon the warm spring sun will melt the winter *snows*. ▪ the *snows* of the Rocky Mountains ▪ A ***light/heavy snow*** was falling.
2 [*noncount*] **:** white dots that appear on the screen of a television when it is receiving a weak signal

[2]**snow** *verb* **snows; snowed; snow·ing**
1 [*no obj*] — used with *it* to say that snow is falling ▪ Look—*it's snowing*! [=snow is falling from the sky] ▪ *It snowed* all day. ▪ The weatherman says that *it* will *snow* tomorrow. ▪ *It* was *snowing* heavily, making it difficult to drive.
2 [+ *obj*] *US, informal* **:** to impress, deceive, or persuade (someone) — usually used as *(be) snowed* ▪ She *was* not *snowed* by the special treatment she received. ▪ I *was* completely *snowed* by the presentation. [=I was very impressed by it]
snowed in *also Brit* ***snowed up*** **1 :** unable to leave a place because a lot of snow is falling or has fallen ▪ We got *snowed in* at my sister's house. ▪ They were *snowed in* for a week. **2 :** blocked with snow ▪ The road was *snowed in*.
snowed under **:** having to deal with too much of something **:** overwhelmed by something ▪ He was *snowed under* with e-mail. [=he had a lot of e-mails to respond to]

[1]**snow·ball** /ˈsnoʊˌbɑːl/ *noun, pl* **-balls** [*count*] **:** a ball of snow that someone makes usually for throwing ▪ This snow is perfect for making *snowballs*. ▪ During recess, the children had a ***snowball fight***. [=a playful fight in which people throw snowballs at each other]
a snowball's chance in hell *informal* **:** any chance at all — used to say that something is extremely unlikely or impossible ▪ Let's be honest—there isn't *a snowball's chance in hell* that we'll win this game. [=there's no chance that we'll win] ▪ Unfortunately, he ***doesn't have a snowball's chance in hell*** of getting the job. [=there is no chance that he will get the job; he will not get the job]

[2]**snowball** *verb* **-balls; -balled; -ball·ing** [*no obj*] **:** to increase, grow, etc., at a faster and faster rate ▪ Problems *snowball* when early trouble signs are ignored. ▪ What started as a small annual concert has *snowballed* into a full-fledged music festival. ▪ consumers dealing with *snowballing* debt

snowball effect *noun* [*singular*] **:** a situation in which one action or event causes many other similar actions or events ▪ The city hopes that these improvements will have a *snowball effect* and spur private investment in the community.

snow·bank /ˈsnoʊˌbæŋk/ *noun, pl* **-banks** [*count*] **:** a pile of snow especially along the side of a road ▪ The car slid into a *snowbank*.

snow·bird /ˈsnoʊˌbɚd/ *noun, pl* **-birds** [*count*] *US* **:** someone who spends the winter months in a warm place ▪ Like many of the state's *snowbirds*, they live in Florida from November through March.

snow·blow·er /ˈsnoʊˌblowɚ/ *noun, pl* **-ers** [*count*] **:** a machine that picks up snow from a driveway, sidewalk, etc., and throws it aside

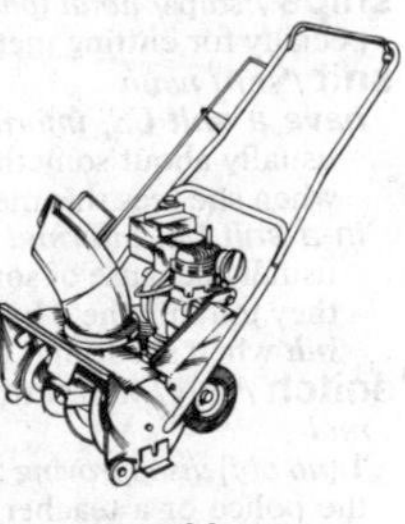
snowblower

[1]**snow·board** /ˈsnoʊˌboɚd/ *noun, pl* **-boards** [*count*] **:** a board like a wide ski that is used for sliding down hills of snow while standing

[2]**snowboard** *verb* **-boards; -board·ed; -board·ing** [*no obj*] **:** to slide down a hill of snow on a snowboard especially as a sport ▪ Do you *snowboard*?
– **snow·board·er** *noun, pl* **-ers** [*count*] ▪ She is an expert *snowboarder*. – **snowboarding** *noun* [*noncount*] ▪ *Snowboarding* is my favorite sport. ▪ He **went snowboarding** yesterday.

snow·bound /ˈsnoʊˈbaʊnd/ *adj*
1 : unable to leave a place because a lot of snow is falling or has fallen ▪ We were *snowbound* for a week.
2 : blocked with snow ▪ *snowbound* roads/airports

snow·capped /ˈsnoʊˌkæpt/ *adj* **:** having the top covered with snow ▪ *snowcapped* mountains

snow cone *or* **sno–cone** /ˈsnoʊˌkoʊn/ *noun, pl* ~ **cones** *or* **-cones** [*count*] *US* **:** a cone-shaped paper cup that contains very small pieces of ice flavored with a sweet syrup

snow day *noun, pl* ~ **days** [*count*] *US* **:** a day when schools and businesses are closed because a lot of snow is falling

snow·drift /ˈsnoʊˌdrɪft/ *noun, pl* **-drifts** [*count*] **:** a hill of snow that is formed by wind ▪ The car was almost buried in a *snowdrift*.

snow·drop /ˈsnoʊˌdrɑːp/ *noun, pl* **-drops** [*count*] **:** a small white flower that blooms in early spring

snow·fall /ˈsnoʊˌfɑːl/ *noun, pl* **-falls :** an amount of snow that falls in a single storm or in a particular period of time [*count*] The yearly *snowfall* here is over 30 feet! ▪ after a ***heavy snowfall*** [=after a large amount of snow has fallen] [*noncount*] 30 feet of annual *snowfall* ▪ The area is expecting ***heavy snowfall*** this weekend.

snow·field /ˈsnoʊˌfiːld/ *noun, pl* **-fields** [*count*] **:** a large flat area of fallen snow

snow·flake /ˈsnoʊˌfleɪk/ *noun, pl* **-flakes** [*count*] **:** a small,

soft piece of frozen water that falls from the sky as snow : a flake of snow
snow job *noun, pl* ~ **jobs** [*count*] *US, informal* : a strong effort to make someone believe something by saying things that are not true or sincere • They'd been promised a big return on their investments, but all they got was a *snow job.*
snow line *noun, pl* ~ **lines** [*count*] : an imaginary line on a mountain that marks the height above which snow does not completely melt • climbing above the *snow line*
snow·man /ˈsnoʊˌmæn/ *noun, pl* **-men** /-ˌmɛn/ [*count*] : a figure made of snow that is shaped to look like a person • The kids built a *snowman* in the front yard.
snow·melt /ˈsnoʊˌmɛlt/ *noun* [*noncount*] : water from melting snow that flows over the surface of the ground into streams and rivers
snow·mo·bile /ˈsnoʊmoʊˌbiːl/ *noun, pl* **-biles** [*count*] : a vehicle used for traveling on snow or ice
snow·mo·bil·ing /ˈsnoʊmoʊˌbiːlɪŋ/ *noun* [*noncount*] : the activity or sport of driving a snowmobile • The park has trails for *snowmobiling.* • Let's **go snowmobiling.**

snowmobile

– snow·mo·bil·er /ˈsnoʊmoʊˌbiːlɚ/ *noun, pl* **-ers** [*count*] • In winter the park is full of *snowmobilers.*
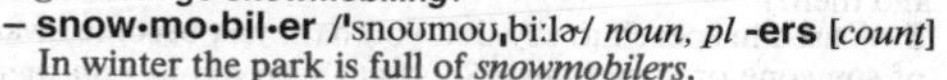
snow pea *noun, pl* ~ **peas** [*count*] *US* : a type of pea whose flat outer part and seeds may be eaten — called also (*Brit*) *mangetout*; see color picture on page C4
[1]**snow·plow** (*US*) *or Brit* **snow·plough** /ˈsnoʊˌplaʊ/ *noun, pl* **-plows** [*count*]
1 : a flat or curved piece of metal that is attached to the front of a vehicle and used for clearing snow from a road, driveway, etc.; *also* : a vehicle (such as a truck) that has a snowplow attached — see picture at PLOW
2 : a position in skiing in which the front ends of the skis are moved together in order to stop, slow down, or turn — often used before another noun • a *snowplow* turn/stop
[2]**snowplow** (*US*) *or Brit* **snowplough** *verb* **-plows; -plowed; -plow·ing** [*no obj*] : to move the front ends of your skis together in order to stop, slow down, or turn • He *snowplowed* to a stop.
[1]**snow·shoe** /ˈsnoʊˌʃuː/ *noun, pl* **-shoes** [*count*] : a light, wide frame that is attached to your shoe to make it easier to walk on soft snow without sinking
[2]**snowshoe** *verb* **-shoes; -shoed; -shoe·ing** [*no obj*] : to walk with snowshoes • We *snowshoed* through the woods.
– snowshoeing *noun* [*noncount*] • *Snowshoeing* is one of her favorite winter activities. • We **went snowshoeing** in the mountains.
– snow·sho·er /ˈsnoʊˌʃuːwɚ/ *noun, pl* **-ers** [*count*]

snowshoe

snow·storm /ˈsnoʊˌstoɚm/ *noun, pl* **-storms** [*count*] : a storm with a large amount of falling snow
snow·suit /ˈsnoʊˌsuːt/ *noun, pl* **-suits** [*count*] : a piece of clothing or a jacket and matching pants that is worn by children over their regular clothes when they go outdoors in the winter
snow thrower *noun, pl* ~ **-ers** [*count*] *US* : SNOWBLOWER
snow tire *noun, pl* ~ **tires** [*count*] *US* : a special tire that is used to give a vehicle better control when you are driving on snow and ice
snow–white /ˈsnoʊˈwaɪt/ *adj* : white as snow : completely white • *snow-white* hair
snowy /ˈsnowi/ *adj* **snow·i·er; -est** [*also more* ~; *most* ~]
1 a : having a lot of snow • a *snowy* day • This is the *snowiest* winter in years. **b** : covered in snow • *snowy* mountaintops/streets/fields
2 : white like snow • *snowy* hair • *snowy* white flower petals
Snr *abbr, Brit* senior • Dave Smith *Snr*
snub /ˈsnʌb/ *verb* **snubs; snubbed; snub·bing** [+ *obj*]
1 : to ignore (someone) in a deliberate and insulting way • She *snubbed* me in the hallway.
2 : to not accept or attend (something) as a way to show disapproval • He *snubbed* their job offer. • They deliberately *snubbed* the meeting.
– snub *noun, pl* **snubs** [*count*] • His refusal to accept the award/invitation was a deliberate *snub.* • Her name was left off the guest list by mistake, but she took it as a *snub.*
snub–nosed /ˈsnʌbˌnoʊzd/ *adj*
1 : having a short, wide nose • a *snub-nosed* child
2 *of a gun* : having a very short barrel • a *snub-nosed* revolver/handgun
snuck (*US*) *past tense and past participle of* [1]SNEAK
[1]**snuff** /ˈsnʌf/ *verb* **snuffs; snuffed; snuff·ing** [+ *obj*]
1 : to cause (something, such as a candle or cigarette) to stop burning by pressing it with your fingers, covering it, etc. • She *snuffed* the candles after everyone had left the table. — often + *out* • She *snuffed out* her cigarette.
2 *informal* **a** : to cause the end of (something) • The home run ended the game and *snuffed* their chances to win a championship. • Their hopes were *snuffed.* — often + *out* • Their chances of winning were *snuffed out.* • Her life was *snuffed out* by cancer. **b** : to kill (someone) • a gangster who was/got *snuffed* by a rival — often + *out* • They threatened to *snuff* him *out.*
snuff it *Brit, informal* : to die • He *snuffed it* at a young age.
[2]**snuff** *noun* [*noncount*] : a type of tobacco that is chewed, placed against the gums, or inhaled into the nose • He took a pinch of *snuff.*
up to snuff *US, informal* : good enough : as good as expected or wanted • I'm trying to get my math skills *up to snuff.* • The performances by the actors were not *up to snuff.*
snuf·fle /ˈsnʌfəl/ *verb* **snuf·fles; snuf·fled; snuf·fling** [*no obj*] : to breathe loudly because you have a cold or have been crying • The child was *snuffling* in his room.
[1]**snug** /ˈsnʌg/ *adj* **snug·ger; snug·gest** [*also more* ~; *most* ~]
1 : fitting closely and often too tightly • a *snug* coat • The shoes were too *snug.* • These jeans are *snug* around the hips.
2 : providing or enjoying warmth, shelter, and comfort : COZY • a *snug* little apartment/room • We were *snug* in the cabin. • She felt *snug* under the warm blanket. • The children were *snug* in their beds.
– snug·ly *adv* • The coat fits *snugly.* • The children slept *snugly* in bed.
[2]**snug** *noun, pl* **snugs** [*count*] *Brit* : a small private room in a pub
snug·gle /ˈsnʌgəl/ *verb, always followed by an adverb or preposition* **snug·gles; snug·gled; snug·gling**
1 [*no obj*] : to lie or sit close together in a comfortable position • The puppy *snuggled* up against the sleeping boy. • The boy *snuggled* close to his mother. • We *snuggled* (together) under a blanket.
2 [+ *obj*] : to place (something) close to or against someone or something : NESTLE • The dog *snuggled* its nose between the pillows. • The baby *snuggled* his head against my chest.
[1]**so** /ˈsoʊ/ *adv*
1 a : to a degree that is suggested or stated • She had never felt *so* happy. [=had never felt as happy as she did then] • You shouldn't eat *so* fast. [=you should eat more slowly] • I don't think they can score twice in *so* short a time. • It was hot last summer—but less *so* than this summer. [=but not as hot as it was this summer] • The play was impressive—***(all) the more so*** [=it was even more impressive] because the students had written it themselves. • There has always been an interest in genetic cloning, but ***never more so*** than in recent years. — often + *that* • She was *so* tired *that* she almost fell asleep at the dinner table. • The library is *so* large (*that*) you could get lost in it. — often used with *as* when making a comparison, when giving an example of some quality, or when describing someone or something • She had never been *so* [=*as*] nervous *as* when she performed for the queen. • His latest novel is not *so* suspenseful *as* his others. • How can you be *so* cruel *as* to criticize her weight? • Would you be *so* kind *as* to help me with my bags? [=would you please help me with my bags?] • Sailing is ***not so much*** a science ***as*** an art. [=sailing is more of an art than a science] — see also SO MUCH AS (below) **b** : to a great degree : very or extremely • He looked *so* handsome in his suit. • We are all *so* excited about the trip. • I'm *so* happy that you decided to join us for dinner. • He loves her *so.* [=very much] • ***Not so long ago*** [=a short time ago], she was the nation's best gymnast. • I feel ***so much*** better after taking that nap. • Thank you *so much* for your help. • The game is *so much* fun. [=is very enjoyable] • He dislikes her *so*

S

much that he won't even talk to her. ▪ The test was not ***so very*** hard after all. ✧ When this sense of *so* is used before an adjective alone, it is considered informal. ▪ The apple pie tasted *so* good. [=tasted very good] ▪ This computer is *so* out-of-date. **c** *informal* **: without any doubt — used to make a statement more forceful** ▪ I *so* don't believe you. ▪ I *so* wanted them to win. ▪ That was *so* not the right thing to say! ▪ That shirt is *so* you. [=it looks like something you would wear; it is very typical of your style] ▪ Her hairstyle is *so* 1980s. [=it's out of date and looks like the hairstyles that were popular in the 1980s] ▪ It's *so* not fair. [=it's very unfair]

2 : to a definite but not specified amount ▪ "He is about *so* tall," she said, raising her hand about six feet in the air. ▪ I can only move *so* fast. ▪ I have never seen ***so many*** geese on one pond before. ▪ I can only do *so many* things at a time. ▪ I can do only ***so much*** in a day. ▪ There is still *so much* to be done before the guests arrive. ▪ There is only *so much* negative criticism a person can take. [=a person can only take a certain amount of negative criticism] ▪ The house burned ***like so much*** paper. [=like something made of paper] ▪ The explanation sounded *like so much* [=like a lot of] nonsense.

3 : in the same way ▪ She was always a hard worker and *so* was her father. [=and her father was too] ▪ "I'm going to the concert." "*So* am I." [=I am also going] ▪ "I wish I had a coffee right now." "***So do I***" [=I do too] ▪ (*US, informal*) "I really like her music." "***So don't I***" [=so do I; I do too]

4 : in the way that is stated or suggested ▪ The bell rang, we took our seats, and *so* began another new school year. — often + *that* ▪ The football arena was *so* designed *that* every seat had a good view of the field. ▪ ***It (just) so happens that*** I know her son. [=I happen to know her son]

5 *informal* **: most certainly** ▪ "I never said that" "You did *so*." [=*too, indeed*] ▪ "You're not really leaving." "I am *so*."

and so forth *or* ***and so on*** **: and other things often of the same or similar kind** ▪ Magazines, newspapers, journals, *and so forth* are on the second floor of the library. ▪ She wanted to know about my family, my childhood, my hopes and fears, (and so on) *and so forth*. ▪ I bought milk, eggs, bread, *and so on*.

even so see ²EVEN

ever so see EVER

every so often see EVERY

how so see ¹HOW

never so much as see NEVER

so far see ¹FAR

so help me (God) see ¹HELP

so long see ²LONG

so much **: an amount, price, etc., that is not stated or known** ▪ You are charged *so much* a mile when renting a vehicle. ▪ You can only believe *so much* of what he says. [=you can only believe some of what he says]

so much as **— used after a negative word (such as *not* or a contraction of *not*) to stress the smallness of an amount or effort** ▪ We didn't hear *so much as* a word from her the whole time. [=we didn't hear a word from her] ▪ Not only did they not help, they didn't *so much as* [=*even*] offer to help! ▪ They ended their date without *so much as* a hug. — see also ¹SO 1a (above)

so much for *informal* **1 — used to say that everything that can be said about or done with something or someone has been said or done** ▪ *So much for* the history of the case. Now we'll look at its implications. ▪ Well, *so much for* that idea. [=that idea was not successful] We'll have to try something else. **2 — used to say that something has ended** ▪ Well, it's raining. *So much for* our perfect weather.

so much so (that) **: to the extent that** ▪ The twins look alike—*so much so that* even their parents sometimes confuse them. [=the twins look so alike that even their parents sometimes confuse them]

so much the better see ³BETTER

so to speak see SPEAK

²so *pronoun* **— used to refer to something that has just been stated or suggested** ▪ "Has she left?" "I believe *so*." [=I believe she has left] ▪ If you have not yet returned the form, please do *so* immediately. [=please return it immediately] ▪ "Is it true?" "I think/hope *so*." ▪ They're going to help us move, or *so* they said. ▪ If you wanted to leave early, you should have said *so*. ▪ "They're getting married." "Really? Who said *so*?" ▪ "I heard you're moving to New York." "Who told you *so*?" [=who told you that?] ▪ I didn't like the dress and told her *so*. [=told her I didn't like it] ▪ "Is he coming to the meeting?" "*So* he says." [=he says he's coming] ▪ "You were late this morning." "*So* I was—what's it to you?" ▪ I might be late. ***If so*** [=if I am late], please start the meeting without me. ▪ Fold the paper ***like so*** [=like this] ▪ If they insist on going, ***so be it*** [=if they insist on going, they will go, and there is nothing I can do to stop them] ▪ "Today is the first day of winter." "Why, ***so it is***"

if I may say so see ¹SAY

or so **— used to say that a number, amount, etc., is not exact** ▪ We plan to stay a week *or so*. [=we plan to stay about a week] ▪ Tickets cost $20 *or so*.

³so *conj*

1 : for that reason : and therefore ▪ We were bored with the movie, *so* we left. ▪ I don't want to go, *so* I won't. ▪ There are no more chairs available, *so* you'll have to stand.

2 — used to say the reason for something ▪ Please be quiet *so* I can study. ▪ She pulled him to the side ***so that*** no one else could hear their conversation. ▪ Let's get there early *so that* we can get good seats.

3 — used in speech to introduce a statement or question ▪ *So* here we are. ▪ *So*, we meet at last! ▪ *So*, as I was saying, the car is used but in good condition. ▪ *So*, how did the test go?

4 — used in speech to say in a somewhat rude or annoyed way that something is unimportant ▪ *So* I mispronounced the word. You still understood what I meant. ▪ "I'm taller than you!" "*So*?" ▪ She has a glass of wine now and then—***so what***? = *So what* if she has a glass of wine now and then? [=why should anyone object if she has a glass of wine now and then?]

5 — used in speech to say that you have just become aware of someone or something ▪ *So*, that's who did it! ▪ *So* there you are. I've been looking for you. ▪ "Goodbye, then." "*So* you're not coming with me after all!"

so as see ²AS

so far as see ¹FAR

so long as see ²LONG

⁴so *adj, not used before a noun* **: agreeing with actual facts : TRUE** ▪ You are saying things that are just not *so*. ▪ I heard you met the president—is that *so*? ▪ She thinks I'm angry at her, but that just isn't *so*. [=I'm not angry at her]

just so see ²JUST

⁵so /ˈsoʊ/ *noun [noncount] music* **: SOL**

So. *or* **so.** *abbr* south or southern

SO *abbr* **1** strikeout **2** significant other

¹soak /ˈsoʊk/ *verb* **soaks; soaked; soak·ing**

1 a : to put (something) in a liquid for a period of time [+ *obj*] *Soak* the beans overnight (in water). ▪ He *soaked* his feet (in a tub of warm water). ▪ You should *soak* those dirty clothes before you wash them. ▪ The cucumbers are *soaked* [=*marinated*] in vinegar. [*no obj*] The beans *soaked* in water overnight. **b** [*no obj*] **: to take a long bath** ▪ He relaxed and *soaked* in the tub. **c** [+ *obj*] **: to make (someone or something) very wet with water or another liquid** ▪ After planting the seeds, *soak* the soil. ▪ She *soaked* the dog with the hose. ▪ His shirt was *soaked* with sweat. ▪ I was/got *soaked* by the rain. ▪ My shirt and pants were ***soaked through*** [=made completely wet] by the rain. ▪ I was ***soaked to the skin*** [=made completely wet] within minutes.

2 [*no obj*] *of a liquid* **: to enter or pass *through* or *into* something** ▪ The oil *soaked into* the wood. ▪ Sweat *soaked through* his shirt. ▪ Rain *soaked through* her jacket. ▪ Blood *soaked through* the bandage.

3 [+ *obj*] *informal* **: to make (someone) pay a lot of money for something** ▪ People are getting *soaked* by city taxes. ▪ They're *soaking* their customers by charging high fees for routine services.

soak in [*phrasal verb*] *of a liquid* **: to enter something by a gradual process** ▪ Pour water around the base of the plant and allow it to *soak in*. — **often used figuratively** ▪ He sat quietly, letting her words *soak in*. ▪ Close your eyes and let the music *soak in*.

soak up [*phrasal verb*] ***soak up (something)*** *or* ***soak (something) up*** **1 : to take in (liquid) : ABSORB** ▪ The rag *soaked up* most of the water. ▪ This kind of paper *soaks up* ink easily. **2 : to enjoy feeling or experiencing (something pleasant) in usually a slow or relaxed way** ▪ We went to the beach and *soaked up* the sun/sunshine all afternoon. ▪ I sat at my table for an hour *soaking up* [=*savoring*] the atmosphere of the café. ▪ The performers stood on the stage, *soaking up* the applause. **3 : to learn and remember (something) quickly** ▪ He eagerly *soaked up* [=*took in*] every word she said. ▪ She has an ability to *soak up* new information very quickly. **4 : to use a large amount of (money, supplies, etc.) • This project is *soaking up* resources that could be used elsewhere.

[2]**soak** *noun [singular]*

1 : an act of letting something stay in a liquid for a long time in order to soften or clean it • This shirt needs a good *soak* [=needs to be soaked] to get out the stains.

2 *informal* **:** a long bath • I had a long, hot *soak* in the tub.

soaked *adj* **:** made completely wet by water or another liquid • a *soaked* towel • My socks are *soaked*. — often used in combination • a blood-*soaked* bandage • an oil-*soaked* rag • a rain-*soaked* field — sometimes used figuratively • a sun-*soaked* beach

soaking *noun [singular]*

1 : an act of leaving something in a liquid for a long time **:** SOAK • These dishes need a good *soaking*.

2 : an act of making someone or something very wet • People at the game got a *soaking* [=got soaked] from an unexpected rain shower.

– soaking *adj* • a *soaking* rain • I was *soaking* [=completely wet] after walking home in the rain. • I was ***soaking wet***.

so–and–so /ˈsowənˌsou/ *noun, pl* **so–and–sos** *or* **so–and–so's** /ˈsowənˌsouz/ *informal*

1 *[noncount]* — used when the name of a person is unknown or not important • She's always gossiping and telling people that *so-and-so* [=some person] is getting married or divorced or something. • Let's say Mr. *So-and-so*, who is related to you, asks to borrow $1,000. Would you give it to him?

2 *[count]* **:** a rude or annoying person • He's an arrogant *so-and-so*. • I can't believe that stupid *so-and-so* got the job.

[1]**soap** /ˈsoup/ *noun, pl* **soaps**

1 : a substance that is used for washing something *[noncount]* Make sure you use *soap* and water to wash your hands. • a bar of *soap* • dish/laundry *soap* [=*detergent*] • *soap* bubbles/scum • a *soap* dish/dispenser *[count]* The store sells many different brands of liquid/hand/antibacterial *soaps*. — see picture at GROOMING

2 *[count] informal* **:** SOAP OPERA • Her first acting job was on a *soap*. • a *soap* star

[2]**soap** *verb* **soaps; soaped; soap·ing** *[+ obj]* **:** to rub soap over or into (someone or something) • I *soap* my hair/body first when I take a shower. • He *soaped* and rinsed the car. — often + *up* • He *soaped up* the car.

soap·box /ˈsoupˌbɑːks/ *noun, pl* **-boxes** *[count]* **:** a box or small platform that someone stands on to give a speech to people in an outdoor, public place • a *soapbox* speech — often used figuratively to describe making speeches or expressing strong opinions • His fame as an actor provides him with a *soapbox* to encourage young people to vote. • He jumped ***on the soapbox*** and spoke out against the war. • She needs to get ***off her soapbox*** and stop telling people what to do.

soap opera *noun, pl* **~ -eras** *[count]* **:** a television or radio program that has continuing stories about the daily lives and problems of a group of people • She loves to watch daytime *soap operas*. — sometimes used figuratively • My life is a *soap opera*. [=my life has a lot of dramatic events and problems like the ones that occur in soap operas] — called also (*informal*) *soap*

soap powder *noun, pl* **~ -ders** *[count, noncount] chiefly Brit* **:** a powder that is made from soap and other substances and used for washing clothes

soap·stone /ˈsoupˌstoun/ *noun [noncount]* **:** a type of soft stone that feels like soap — often used before another noun • a *soapstone* sculpture

soap·suds /ˈsoupˌsʌdz/ *noun [plural]* **:** the bubbles that form when water is mixed with soap **:** SUDS

soapy /ˈsoupi/ *adj* **soap·i·er; -est** *[also more ~; most ~]*

1 : containing soap • *soapy* water

2 : like soap • The stone has a *soapy* feel.

soar /ˈsoɚ/ *verb* **soars; soared; soar·ing** *[no obj]*

1 : to increase very quickly in amount or price • The temperature *soared* to 100 degrees. • Stock prices are beginning to *soar*. • The oil shortage sent prices *soaring*. • The nation's divorce rate has *soared*. • Interest rates have *soared* (up) to new heights.

2 a : to fly or sail often at a great height by floating on air currents • The eagle *soared* above us. • A hang glider *soared* in the air. **b :** to rise quickly upward to a great height • The rocket *soared* into the sky. • The ball *soared* out of the stadium. — often used figuratively • The song is *soaring* in popularity. = The popularity of the song is *soaring*. • Her ***spirits soared*** [=she became very happy and excited] when she heard the news.

3 : to reach or rise to a great height • The mountain *soars* over 20,000 feet above sea level.

– soaring *adj, always used before a noun* • a *soaring* divorce rate • a *soaring* eagle • She is enjoying her *soaring* popularity. • *soaring* skyscrapers

sob /ˈsɑːb/ *verb* **sobs; sobbed; sob·bing**

1 *[no obj]* **:** to cry noisily while taking in short, sudden breaths • He began to *sob* uncontrollably. • She could not stop *sobbing*.

2 *[+ obj]* **:** to say (something) while sobbing • "I hate you," she *sobbed*. • She *sobbed* (out) her goodbye.

– sob *noun, pl* **sobs** *[count]* • "I don't know what I'll do," she said with a *sob*.

SOB /ˌɛsˌouˈbiː/ *noun, pl* **SOBs** *[count] chiefly US, informal* **:** SON OF A BITCH • I hate that miserable *SOB*.

[1]**so·ber** /ˈsoubɚ/ *adj* **so·ber·er; -est** *[or more ~; most ~]*

1 : not drunk • I'm driving, so I have to stay *sober* tonight. • She has been *sober* for three years. [=she stopped drinking alcohol three years ago] • I haven't been drinking at all. I'm ***(as) sober as a judge***. [=I'm completely sober] • He claims that he was ***stone cold sober*** [=completely sober] when the accident happened.

2 : having or showing a very serious attitude or quality • He is a *sober*, hardworking farmer. • The story is a *sober* look at drug abuse. • Illness is a *sober* reminder of our mortality. • The article is a *sober* reflection on the state of our nation.

3 : plain in color • a *sober* gray suit

– so·ber·ly *adv* • He talked *soberly* about his life. • She was *soberly* dressed.

[2]**sober** *verb* **-bers; -bered; -ber·ing** *[+ obj]* **:** to make (someone) serious or thoughtful • He returned home from the war, saddened and *sobered* by his experiences.

sober up *[phrasal verb]* ***sober up or sober (someone) up*** **:** to become sober or less drunk or to make (a drunk person) sober or less drunk • You need to *sober up* before you go. • I tried to *sober* her *up*. • I have to *sober* myself *up*.

so·ber·ing /ˈsoubərɪŋ/ *adj [more ~; most ~]* **:** making you feel serious and thoughtful • His death is a *sobering* reminder of the dangers of mountaineering. • a *sobering* fact/thought

so·bri·ety /səˈbrajəti/ *noun [noncount]*

1 : the state of not being drunk • The police tested him for *sobriety*. [=tested him to see if he was sober] • They did a *sobriety* test on him. • He has had 10 years of *sobriety*. [=he stopped drinking alchohol 10 years ago]

2 *formal* **:** the quality of being serious • the *sobriety* of the situation

so·bri·quet *also* **sou·bri·quet** /ˈsoubrɪˌkeɪ/ *noun, pl* **-quets** *[count] formal* **:** a name or phrase that describes the character of someone or something **:** NICKNAME • Baseball player Ty Cobb was also known by the *sobriquet* "The Georgia Peach."

sob story *noun, pl* **~ -ries** *[count] informal* **:** a sad story about yourself that you tell in order to make people feel sorry for you • She told a *sob story* about how she had to starve herself to pay for the rent. • I don't want to hear any of your *sob stories*.

soc. *abbr* **1** society **2** sociology

so–called /ˈsouˈkɑːld/ *adj, always used before a noun*

1 — used to indicate the name that is commonly or usually used for something • an epidemic of the *so-called* mad cow disease • *so-called* Generation Xers

2 — used to indicate a name or description that you think is not really right or suitable • I was lied to by a *so-called* friend. [=by someone who claims to be my friend but who is not really my friend] • The restaurant's *so-called* specials can be ordered any day of the week.

soc·cer /ˈsɑːkɚ/ *noun [noncount]* **:** a game played between two teams of 11 players in which a round ball is moved toward a goal usually by kicking • Both of their children play *soccer*. — often used before another noun • a *soccer* ball/player/team/coach/field/game — called also (*Brit*) *football*; see picture at BALL; see also TABLE SOCCER

soccer mom *noun, pl* **~ moms** *[count] US, informal* **:** a mother usually from the middle class who brings her children to soccer games and similar activities — often used to refer in a general way to such women as a group of people having similar interests, values, etc. • politicians trying to win the vote of *soccer moms*

so·cia·ble /ˈsouʃəbəl/ *adj [more ~; most ~]*

1 : liking to be with and talk to other people • They are *sociable* people who enjoy having parties. • Their daughter is very *sociable*. [=*friendly*]

S

2 : involving or allowing friendly and pleasant social relations ▪ They had a very *sociable* evening.
– **so·cia·bil·i·ty** /ˌsoʊʃəˈbɪləti/ *noun* [*noncount*]

[1]**so·cial** /ˈsoʊʃəl/ *adj*
1 a : relating to or involving activities in which people spend time talking to each other or doing enjoyable things with each other ▪ She has poor/good *social* skills. ▪ The vacation resort held a lot of *social* events. ▪ She has a busy/hectic ***social life*** [=she spends a lot of time doing things with her friends, going to parties, etc.] ▪ I joined the club to improve my *social life*. ▪ He's a ***social drinker*** [=he only drinks alcohol at parties and other social occasions] ▪ ***social drinking*** **b** [*more* ~; *most* ~] : liking to be with and talk to people : happy to be with people ▪ He's not feeling very *social* [=*sociable*] this evening. ▪ Her sister is much more *social* than she is. — opposite ANTISOCIAL
2 : of or relating to people or society in general ▪ *social* institutions like marriage and family ▪ Health care is a major *social* issue. ▪ Child abuse has become a serious *social* problem. ▪ Martin Luther King, Jr., fought for *social* change/reform.
3 : tending to form relationships and live together in groups : not solitary ▪ Most humans are *social* beings. ▪ Bees are *social* insects. ▪ Elephants are *social* animals.
4 *always used before a noun* : of, relating to, or based on rank in a particular society ▪ The established *social* order was challenged by the peasants' rebellion. ▪ Men and women are considered *social* equals in our culture. ▪ *Social* classes are based on wealth and property. ▪ The family's *social* status is middle class.
– **so·cial·ly** /ˈsoʊʃəli/ *adv* ▪ She's *socially* active in the community. ▪ I only know her *socially*. ▪ He only drinks *socially*. [=he only drinks alcohol at parties and other social events] ▪ *socially* unacceptable behavior ▪ *socially* disadvantaged families

[2]**social** *noun, pl* **-cials**
1 [*count*] : an informal social event for members of a group ▪ The club/church has *socials* every month.
2 ***the social*** *Brit, somewhat informal* : SOCIAL SECURITY ▪ He's living on *the social* now.

social climber *noun, pl* ~ **-ers** [*count*] *disapproving* : someone who tries to gain a higher social position or status (such as by becoming friendly with wealthy people)

social democracy *noun, pl* ~ **-cies** *formal*
1 [*noncount*] : a political movement that uses principles of democracy to change a capitalist country to a socialist one
2 [*count*] : a country that uses both capitalist and socialist practices
– **social democrat** *noun, pl* ~ **-crats** [*count*] – **social democratic** *adj*

social engineering *noun* [*noncount*] *formal* : the practice of making laws or using other methods to influence public opinion and solve social problems or improve social conditions
– **social engineer** *noun, pl* ~ **-neers** [*count*]

social housing *noun* [*noncount*] *Brit* : houses or apartments that are made available to be rented at a low cost by poor people

so·cial·ism /ˈsoʊʃəˌlɪzəm/ *noun* [*noncount*] : a way of organizing a society in which major industries are owned and controlled by the government rather than by individual people and companies — compare CAPITALISM, COMMUNISM

so·cial·ist /ˈsoʊʃəlɪst/ *noun, pl* **-ists** [*count*]
1 : a person who believes in socialism
2 ***Socialist*** : a member of a political party that supports socialism
– **socialist** *or* **Socialist** *adj* ▪ a *socialist* country/government ▪ *socialist* ideas ▪ the *Socialist* party – **so·cial·is·tic** /ˌsoʊʃəˈlɪstɪk/ *adj* ▪ *socialistic* countries/ideas

so·cial·ite /ˈsoʊʃəˌlaɪt/ *noun, pl* **-ites** [*count*] : someone who is well-known in fashionable society and is often seen at parties and other social events for wealthy people ▪ New York City *socialites*

so·cial·ize *also Brit* **so·cial·ise** /ˈsoʊʃəˌlaɪz/ *verb* **-iz·es**; **-ized**; **-iz·ing**
1 [*no obj*] : to talk to and do things with other people in a friendly way ▪ She danced and *socialized* at the party. — often + *with* ▪ He doesn't *socialize with* the other players on the team. ▪ She enjoys *socializing with* her coworkers.
2 [+ *obj*] *formal* : to teach (someone) to behave in a way that is acceptable in society — usually used as *(be) socialized* ▪ Children *are socialized* at an early age.
– **so·cial·i·za·tion** *also Brit* **so·cial·i·sa·tion** /ˌsoʊʃələˈzeɪʃən, *Brit* ˌsəʊʃəˌlaɪˈzeɪʃən/ *noun* [*noncount*] ▪ the *socialization* of children

socialized medicine *noun* [*noncount*] *chiefly US* : medical and hospital services that are provided by a government and paid for by taxes

social science *noun, pl* ~ **-ences**
1 [*noncount*] : the study of human society
2 [*count*] : a particular area of study that relates to human behavior and society ▪ Economics is a *social science*.
– **social scientist** *noun, pl* ~ **-tists** [*count*]

social security *noun* [*noncount*]
1 : a program in which the government provides money to people who are unable to work because they are old, disabled, or unemployed
2 *or* ***Social Security*** : a program in the U.S. that requires workers to make regular payments to a government fund which is used to make payments to people who are unable to work because they are old, disabled, or retired ▪ *Social Security* benefits/tax — abbr. *SS*
3 *or* ***Social Security*** : money that is paid out through a social security program ▪ She is living on *social security*. ▪ He began collecting/receiving *Social Security* checks.

Social Security number *noun, pl* ~ **-bers** [*count*] : a number that is given to each citizen of the U.S. by the government and that is used for the Social Security program and for official forms and records — abbr. *SSN*

social services *noun* [*plural*] : a program supported by a government or private organization that helps people who have financial or family problems ▪ the Department of *Social Services* ▪ Contact *social services* for help.
– **social service** *adj, always used before a noun* ▪ a *social service* agency/worker

social studies *noun* [*plural*] : a course of study that deals with human relationships and the way society works

social work *noun* [*noncount*] : the work done by someone who works for a government or private organization that helps people who have financial or family problems ▪ She is doing *social work*. ▪ He has a job in *social work*.
– **social worker** *noun, pl* ~ **-ers** [*count*]

so·ci·e·tal /səˈsajətl/ *adj, always used before a noun, formal* : of or relating to society : SOCIAL ▪ *societal* changes/needs/problems/values

so·ci·ety /səˈsajəti/ *noun, pl* **-et·ies**
1 [*noncount*] : people in general thought of as living together in organized communities with shared laws, traditions, and values ▪ Poverty hurts *society* as a whole.
2 : the people of a particular country, area, time, etc., thought of especially as an organized community [*count*] ancient/modern *societies* ▪ Christian/consumer *societies* ▪ We need to do more to help the poorer members of our *society*. [*noncount*] the values of Western/American *society* ▪ wealthy/poor members of *society* ▪ These problems affect only a small segment of *society*. [=only a small number of people] ▪ That kind of behavior isn't allowed in ***polite society***. [=among people of the middle and upper classes who speak and behave in a polite way]
3 [*noncount*] : people who are fashionable and wealthy ▪ She was introduced to *society* at a formal reception. ▪ The club's members are drawn from the ranks of ***high society***. — often used before another noun ▪ *society* ladies/fashions/parties ▪ the newspaper's *society* page
4 [*count*] : a group of people who work together or regularly meet because of common interests, beliefs, or activities ▪ a literary/musical *society* ▪ historical *societies* ▪ The American Cancer *Society* ▪ The *Society* of Newspaper Editors
5 [*noncount*] *formal* : the state of being with other people ▪ He avoided the *society* [=*company*] of other writers.

socio- *combining form*
1 : society ▪ *socio*logy
2 : social and ▪ *socio*economic

so·cio·eco·nom·ic /ˌsousijouˌɛkəˈnɑːmɪk/ *adj, formal* : of, relating to, or involving a combination of social and economic factors ▪ Their *socioeconomic* backgrounds are very different.
– **so·cio·eco·nom·i·cal·ly** /ˌsousijouˌɛkəˈnɑːmɪkli/ *adv*

so·ci·ol·o·gy /ˌsousiˈɑːləʤi/ *noun* [*noncount*] : the study of society, social institutions, and social relationships — abbr. *soc.*
– **so·cio·log·i·cal** /ˌsousijəˈlɑːʤɪkəl/ *adj* ▪ The problem is *sociological*. ▪ a *sociological* study – **so·cio·log·i·cal·ly** /ˌsousijəˈlɑːʤɪkli/ *adv* ▪ The experiment is *sociologically*

important. – **so•ci•ol•o•gist** /ˌsousiˈɑːlədʒɪst/ *noun, pl* **-gists** [*count*]

so•cio•path /ˈsousijəˌpæθ/ *noun, pl* **-paths** [*count*] : someone who behaves in a dangerous or violent way towards other people and does not feel guilty about such behavior
– **so•cio•path•ic** /ˌsousijəˈpæθɪk/ *adj* ▪ a *sociopathic* personality ▪ *sociopathic* behavior ▪ He is *sociopathic.*

[1]**sock** /ˈsɑːk/ *noun, pl* **socks** [*count*] : a piece of clothing that is worn on your foot and that covers your ankle and sometimes the lower part of your leg ▪ a white cotton *sock* — usually plural ▪ a pair of *socks* ▪ wool/ankle/athletic *socks* — see color picture on page C13; see also BOBBY SOCKS, TUBE SOCK
knock/blow your socks off informal : to affect or impress you in a very strong and favorable way ▪ This song will *knock your socks off.* [=you will enjoy this song very much]
put a sock in it informal — used to tell someone to stop talking ▪ I wish someone would tell him to *put a sock in it.*
— compare [2]SOCK

[2]**sock** *noun, pl* **socks** [*count*] *informal* : a hard hit with the fist : PUNCH — usually singular ▪ She gave him a *sock* in the jaw/stomach. — compare [1]SOCK

[3]**sock** *verb* **socks; socked; sock•ing** [+ *obj*] *informal* : to hit (someone or something) hard ▪ He *socked* [=*punched*] him in the eye/nose/jaw. ▪ (*baseball*) He *socked* a home run over the left-field wall. — often used figuratively ▪ The city was *socked* by a blizzard. ▪ He *socked* us with a huge lawsuit.
sock away [*phrasal verb*] ***sock away (something) or sock (something) away*** *US, informal* : to save (something, such as money) by putting it in a safe place ▪ My father had been *socking away* money since I was a young boy.
socked in *US* : affected by bad weather conditions that prevent people from leaving ▪ The whole metro region is *socked in* with snow. ▪ The airport was *socked in* by fog.
sock it to *informal* : to do or say something to (someone) in a strong and forceful way ▪ He really *socked it to* her. ▪ Legislators are getting ready to *sock it to* homeowners with high property tax increases.

sock•et /ˈsɑːkət/ *noun, pl* **-ets** [*count*]
1 a : a device in a wall into which an electric cord can be plugged : OUTLET ▪ She plugged the lamp into the *socket.* **b** : an opening on a piece of electrical equipment into which a plug, lightbulb, etc., fits ▪ He screwed the lightbulb into the *socket.*
2 : a hollow part in a bone that holds an eye, a tooth, or another bone ▪ an inflamed tooth *socket* ▪ the hip *socket* ▪ His shoulder popped out of its *socket.*

socket wrench *noun, pl* ~ **wrenches** [*count*] *US* : a tool that has a part which fits over the end of a bolt or nut and is used to turn it

So•crat•ic /səˈkrætɪk/ *adj, formal* : of or relating to the ancient Greek philosopher Socrates, his followers, or his method of asking questions to discover the truth ▪ *Socratic* questioning/thinking ▪ the ***Socratic method***

[1]**sod** /ˈsɑːd/ *noun, pl* **sods** *chiefly US*
1 [*noncount*] : the upper layer of soil that is made up of grass and plant roots ▪ The grounds crew repaired the *sod* [=*turf*] after the football game.
2 [*count, noncount*] : a piece of sod ▪ They were laying *sod* in the yard.
– compare [2]SOD

[2]**sod** *noun, pl* **sods** *Brit, informal*
1 [*count*] **a** *offensive* : a person who is unpleasant, offensive, or annoying ▪ He's a nasty old *sod.* **b** *impolite* : a man who you think is lucky, unlucky, etc. ▪ That poor old *sod* has been waiting there for hours.
2 [*singular*] *impolite* : something that is annoying or difficult ▪ The problem was a real *sod* to fix.
give a sod also care a sod *Brit, informal + impolite* : to care at all about someone or something — used in negative statements ▪ I don't *give/care a sod* about what people say.
odds and sods *Brit, informal* : ODDS AND ENDS ▪ The store sells art supplies and other *odds and sods.*
sod all *Brit, informal + impolite* : nothing at all ▪ You've done (sweet) *sod all* to help me! ▪ They were wearing *sod all.*
– compare [1]SOD

[3]**sod** *verb* **sods; sod•ded; sod•ding** [+ *obj*] *Brit, informal + impolite* — used to show that you are angry or annoyed at a person, thing, or situation ▪ *Sod* [=*damn*] you! I'm not going to do it. ▪ *Sod* this machine. ▪ ***Sod it (all).*** I can't be bothered with this.
sod off *Brit, informal + impolite* — used to tell someone to leave or go away ▪ *Sod off* or I'll call the police.

so•da /ˈsoudə/ *noun, pl* **-das**
1 a [*noncount*] : SODA WATER ▪ Scotch and *soda* **b** [*count, noncount*] *chiefly US* : SODA POP ▪ orange/grape *soda* ▪ I ordered fries and a *soda.* — often used before another noun ▪ a *soda* machine ▪ *soda* cans/bottles
2 [*count*] *US* : a drink made of soda water, flavoring, and often ice cream ▪ a chocolate *soda* ▪ an ice-cream *soda*
3 [*noncount*] : a white powdery substance that contains salt and is used in cooking and medicine — see also BAKING SODA, WASHING SODA

soda cracker *noun, pl* ~ **-ers** [*count*] *US* : a thin, usually salted cracker that is often served with soup

soda fountain *noun, pl* ~ **-tains** [*count*] *chiefly US, somewhat old-fashioned* : a counter usually in a store at which cold drinks, types of ice cream, etc., are prepared and served

soda jerk *noun, pl* ~ **jerks** [*count*] *US, old-fashioned* : a person who prepares and serves drinks and ice cream at a soda fountain

soda pop *noun, pl* ~ **pops** [*count, noncount*] *US* : a drink consisting of soda water, flavoring, and a sweet syrup — called also *pop,* (*chiefly US*) *soda*

soda water *noun, pl* ~ **-ters** [*count, noncount*] : water that has bubbles in it and that is often used to make other drinks — called also (*US*) *club soda, soda*

sod•den /ˈsɑːdn/ *adj* : very heavy and wet ▪ *sodden* sandbags/fields

sod•ding /ˈsɑːdɪŋ/ *adj, always used before a noun, Brit, informal + impolite*
1 — used to show that you are angry, annoyed, or surprised ▪ The *sodding* [=*damn*] thing broke again!
2 — used to emphasize a statement ▪ That *sodding* (great) lorry almost crashed into me.

so•di•um /ˈsoudijəm/ *noun* [*noncount*] : a soft silver-white element that is found in salt, baking soda, and other compounds

sodium bicarbonate *noun* [*noncount*] : BAKING SODA — called also *bicarbonate of soda*

sodium chloride *noun* [*noncount*] *technical* : the chemical compound that forms salt

sod•o•mite /ˈsɑːdəˌmaɪt/ *noun, pl* **-mites** [*count*] *old-fashioned* : a person who has anal sex with another person : someone who practices sodomy

sod•o•my /ˈsɑːdəmi/ *noun* [*noncount*] : anal sex with someone
– **sod•o•mize** *also Brit* **sod•o•mise** /ˈsɑːdəˌmaɪz/ *verb* **-miz•es; -mized; -miz•ing** [+ *obj*] *chiefly US*

Sod's Law *noun* [*noncount*] *Brit* : MURPHY'S LAW

so•fa /ˈsoufə/ *noun, pl* **-fas** [*count*] : a long and comfortable piece of furniture on which a person can sit or lie down — see picture at LIVING ROOM

sofa bed *noun, pl* ~ **beds** [*count*] : a sofa that can be folded out to form a bed — see picture at BED

[1]**soft** /ˈsɑːft/ *adj* **soft•er; -est**
1 : easy to press, bend, cut, etc. : not hard or firm ▪ a *soft* mattress ▪ *soft* cheese/dough ▪ The ground was *soft* after the heavy rain. ▪ Iron and lead are *soft* metals. — opposite HARD
2 : smooth and pleasant to touch ▪ *soft* skin ▪ a *soft* silk ▪ The rabbit's fur is *soft.*
3 a : having a very light color : not strong or bright in color or tone ▪ *soft* colors ▪ The room was painted in *soft* pink. ▪ *soft* blues **b** *of light* : not bright or harsh ▪ *soft* lighting [=lighting that is not too bright] ▪ the *soft* glow of the moon
4 a : gentle in manner : not harsh ▪ He has a *soft* touch. ▪ She gave him a *soft* kiss on the cheek. ▪ We decided to take a *softer* approach in disciplining the children. **b :** not strong or very forceful ▪ a *soft* [=*mild, gentle*] breeze ▪ A *soft* [=*light*] rain fell. **c :** having a low, gentle sound ▪ a *soft* voice
5 : having a curved or rounded outline ▪ *soft* rolling hills ▪ a sweater with *soft* shoulder lines
6 *disapproving* : not strict, harsh, or critical enough ▪ The students thought their teacher was *soft.* ▪ You're too *soft* with your children. — often + *on* ▪ Some people accuse the mayor of being *soft on* crime.
7 : involving little work or effort : EASY ▪ He has a pretty *soft* job. ▪ a *soft* life ▪ (*chiefly Brit*) Police insisted that community service work was not a ***soft option.***
8 a : not physically strong : not muscular ▪ He had grown *soft* from years of inactivity. **b :** not brave or tough ▪ He used to love adventure, but he has ***gone/gotten soft*** in his old age.

S

9 : feeling sympathy for other people : sympathetic and kind • He has a *soft* heart. — opposite HARD

10 : relating to matters that are not serious or important • *soft* news stories — opposite HARD

11 *of an illegal drug* : not as strong or harmful to the health as other drugs • Marijuana is a *soft* drug. — opposite HARD

12 *of water* : not containing many minerals and able to make bubbles with soap • *soft* water — opposite HARD

13 : sounding like the "c" in "ace" or the "g" in "gem" • The "c" in "cell" is *soft*, but the "c" in "cabbage" is hard. • the *soft* "g" in "general" — opposite HARD

soft in the head *informal* : stupid or crazy • He's a nice old man but he's a bit *soft in the head*. • Have you ***gone soft in the head***? [=are you crazy?]

soft on *informal + old-fashioned* : attracted to (someone) • I think he's a little *soft on* her. — see also [1]SOFT 6 (above)

– soft·ly *adv* • She spoke *softly* but firmly. • She chuckled/laughed *softly*. • a *softly* lit room • The ball landed *softly* in the grass. **– soft·ness** /ˈsɑːftnəs/ *noun* [*singular*] • the *softness* of silk • Her voice has a gentle *softness*.

[2]**soft** *adv* **soft·er; -est** *chiefly US*

1 : in a soft or gentle way • She kissed him *soft* [=(more commonly) *softly*] on the lips. • Can you please talk *softer*? [=more softly]

2 : in a way that is not strong or forceful • He hit the ball *soft*. [=(more commonly) *softly*] • a *soft*-hit ball

soft·ball /ˈsɑːftˌbɑːl/ *noun, pl* **-balls**

1 [*noncount*] : a sport that is similar to baseball but that is played on a smaller field and with a ball that is pitched underhand and that is larger and softer than a baseball • Do you want to play *softball*? • *softball* teams

2 [*count*] : the ball that is used in softball — see picture at BALL

3 [*count*] *US* : a question that is very easy to answer • All the questions in the interview were *softballs*. • The reporter threw him a *softball*. [=asked him an easy question] • *softball* questions.

soft–boiled /ˈsɑːftˈbojəld/ *adj, of an egg* : boiled until the white is solid but the yolk is liquid • *soft-boiled* eggs — compare HARD-BOILED

soft·bound /ˈsɑːftˌbaʊnd/ *adj, US, of a book* : having a flexible cover • *softbound* books — compare HARDBOUND

soft–core /ˈsɑːftˈkoɚ/ *adj* : showing or describing sex acts but not in an extremely open and shocking way — usually used before a noun • *soft-core* pornography — compare HARD-CORE

soft·cov·er /ˈsɑːftˌkʌvɚ/ *noun, pl* **-ers** *US* : a book that has a flexible cover [*count*] *Softcovers* sell quickly. [*noncount*] The novel is now available ***in softcover***. — often used before another noun • *softcover* books — compare HARDCOVER, PAPERBACK

soft drink *noun, pl* **~ drinks** [*count*] : a cold drink that is usually sweet, does not contain alcohol, and is often sold in bottles or cans

soft·en /ˈsɑːfən/ *verb* **-ens; -ened; -en·ing**

1 : to become less hard or firm or to make (something) less hard or firm [*no obj*] The butter will *soften* if left on the counter overnight. • The wax *softened* (up) quickly. [+ *obj*] The recipe called for one stick of butter, *softened*. • Heat *softens* (up) wax quickly.

2 [+ *obj*] : to make (something) less dry or rough • The oil is used to *soften* and preserve the leather. • The lotion *softens* dry skin.

3 a [+ *obj*] : to make (something) less severe, harsh, extreme, etc. • The company has *softened* its stance on dating in the workplace. • His arrogance is *softened* by a good sense of humor. [=his sense of humor makes his arrogance less annoying] • Passing clouds *softened* the glare of the sun. [=passing clouds made the sun less bright] **b** [*no obj*] : to become less harsh, severe, extreme, etc. • Her face/voice/expression *softened* when he entered the room. • His criticism of the president has *softened* in the past year. **c** [+ *obj*] : to make (something) less painful, forceful, or harmful • The grass *softened* my fall. — often used figuratively • Management tried to *soften* the impact of the layoffs by offering early retirement packages. = They tried to ***soften the blow*** by offering early retirement packages.

4 [+ *obj*] : to make (something) seem rounder or less sharp • Her new haircut *softened* her features.

soften up [*phrasal verb*] ***soften (someone) up*** *or* ***soften up (someone)*** **1 :** to treat (someone) very well or kindly in order to make that person more likely to help you, give you something, etc. • He tried to *soften* her *up* by buying her flowers. **2 :** to weaken (an enemy) through military attacks • They used artillery to *soften up* the enemy's defenses before launching a full-scale attack.

soft·en·er /ˈsɑːfənɚ/ *noun, pl* **-ers** [*count*] : a substance that makes something smoother or softer • a new skin *softener* — see also FABRIC SOFTENER

soft focus *noun* [*noncount*] : a way of producing a photograph so that the edges of the image are not completely clear or sharp

– soft–focus *adj* • used a *soft-focus* lens • *soft-focus* photography

soft fruit *noun, pl* **~ fruits** [*count, noncount*] *chiefly Brit* : small fruits (such as berries) that do not have pits or stones

soft furnishings *noun* [*plural*] *Brit* : things (such as curtains or rugs) that are made of cloth and used to decorate a room, house, etc.

soft·heart·ed /ˈsɑːftˌhɑɚtəd/ *adj* [*more ~; most ~*] : having feelings of kindness and sympathy for other people • He looks tough, but he's really very *softhearted*. • She's too *softhearted* to fire anyone. — compare HARD-HEARTED

– soft·heart·ed·ness *noun* [*noncount*]

soft·ie *or* **softy** /ˈsɑːfti/ *noun, pl* **soft·ies** [*count*] *informal* : a kind person : a softhearted person • He may look tough, but he is really a *softie* at heart.

soft landing *noun, pl* **~ -ings** [*count*] : a landing in which an airplane, a spacecraft, etc., touches the ground in a controlled and gradual way that does not damage it • The lunar module made a *soft landing* on the moon. — often used figuratively to describe an ending or solution that is not difficult or harmful • Market analysts are predicting a *soft landing* for the economy after the economic boom.

softly–softly *adj, Brit, informal* : careful and patient in dealing with someone or something • a *softly-softly* approach/strategy

softly–spoken *adj* [*more ~; most ~*] *chiefly Brit* : SOFT-SPOKEN

soft money *noun* [*noncount*] *chiefly US* : money that is given to a political party rather than to a particular candidate

soft–ped·al /ˈsɑːftˈpɛdl/ *verb* **-als;** *US* **-aled** *or Brit* **-alled;** *US* **-al·ing** *or Brit* **-al·ling** [+ *obj*] *chiefly US, informal* : to treat or describe (something) as less important than it really is • I'm not trying to *soft-pedal* the issue/problem.

soft rock *noun* [*noncount*] : rock music with a gentler sound and slower beat than hard rock — compare HARD ROCK

soft sell *noun* [*singular*] : a way of selling something that uses persuasion rather than aggressive pressure — often used before another noun • using *soft-sell* tactics • a *soft-sell* approach to marketing — compare HARD SELL

soft–shell /ˈsɑːftˈʃɛl/ *or* **soft–shelled** /ˈsɑːftˈʃɛld/ *adj, US* : having a shell that is soft or easily broken • *soft-shell* crabs

soft–soap /ˈsɑːftˈsoʊp/ *verb* **-soaps; -soaped; -soap·ing** [+ *obj*] *Brit, informal* : to try to persuade (someone) to do something by using praise, kind words, etc. — often + *into* • Don't be *soft-soaped into* going out with him.

– soft soap *noun* [*noncount*] *Brit, informal*

soft–spo·ken /ˈsɑːftˈspoʊkən/ *adj* [*more ~; most ~*] : having a gentle, quiet voice or manner • a *soft-spoken* teacher

soft spot *noun, pl* **~ spots** [*count*]

1 : a strong liking *for* someone or something — usually singular • He has a *soft spot for* children. [=he likes children very much] • She has a *soft spot for* chocolate ice cream.

2 : a weak point that can be attacked • They found a *soft spot* in the enemy's defenses.

soft target *noun, pl* **~ -gets** [*count*] : a target that can be attacked easily because it does not have military defenses • hospitals, schools, and other *soft targets* — often used figuratively • elderly people who are a *soft target* for criminals

soft–top *noun, pl* **-tops** [*count*] *informal* : a car with a roof made of thick fabric that can be lowered or removed : CONVERTIBLE — compare HARDTOP

soft touch *noun, pl* **~ touches** [*count*] *US, informal* : a person who is easily deceived or taken advantage of • His friends all know that he's a *soft touch*.

soft toy *noun, pl* **~ toys** [*count*] *Brit* : STUFFED ANIMAL

soft·ware /ˈsɑːftˌweɚ/ *noun* [*noncount*] : the programs that run on a computer and perform certain functions • word-processing *software* • antivirus *software* • I installed/loaded the *software*. — often used before another noun • the *soft-*

S

ware industry • *software* programs/development — compare HARDWARE

soft·wood /ˈsɑːftˌwʊd/ *noun, pl* **-woods**

1 [*count, noncount*] : the wood of a tree (such as a pine tree) that is soft and easy to cut — often used before another noun • *softwood* lumber

2 [*count*] : a tree that produces softwood • pines, firs, and other *softwoods* — compare HARDWOOD

softy *variant spelling of* SOFTIE

sog·gy /ˈsɑːgi/ *adj* **sog·gi·er; -est**

1 : heavy with water or moisture : completely wet and usually soft • The cereal got all *soggy.* • *soggy* bread

2 *informal* : RAINY • *soggy* weather

– sog·gi·ness /ˈsɑːginəs/ *noun* [*noncount*]

soh /ˈsoʊ/ *noun* [*noncount*] *chiefly Brit, music* : SOL

¹soil /ˈsojəl/ *noun, pl* **soils**

1 : the top layer of earth in which plants grow [*noncount*] This kind of plant grows well in moist *soil.* • The *soil* in this area is very fertile/sandy. • Cleaning up contaminated *soil* [=soil that has harmful chemicals in it] can be very costly. [*count*] Certain plants cannot live in poorly drained *soils.* — see also POTTING SOIL

2 [*noncount*] *formal + literary* : the land of a particular country • They have returned to their ***native soil*** [=the place they are originally from] • I had never set foot ***on Japanese/Italian soil*** before. [=I had never been to Japan/Italy before]

3 [*noncount*] : a place where something begins or develops • Poor neighborhoods can be ***fertile soil*** for crime. [=there is often a lot of crime in poor neighborhoods]

4 ***the soil*** *literary* : farming as a way of making a living • Her ancestors had felt a closeness to *the soil.*

²soil *verb* **soils; soiled; soil·ing** *formal*

1 [+ *obj*] : to make (something) dirty • I *soiled* my blouse/shirt at the cocktail party. • The ink *soiled* his hands. • Her clothes were *soiled* and very wet. • *soiled* linens/underwear/diapers — sometimes used figuratively • He refused to ***soil his hands*** [=do anything dishonest or wrong] for her.

2 [*no obj*] : to become dirty • This fabric *soils* easily.

soi·ree *or* **soi·rée** /swɑˈreɪ/ *noun, pl* **-rees** *or* **-rées** [*count*] : a formal party that is usually at night • a fashionable *soiree* at a fancy hotel

so·journ /ˈsoʊˌʤən/ *noun, pl* **-journs** [*count*] *formal* : a period of time when you stay in a place as a traveler or guest • Our family enjoyed a two-week *sojourn* in the mountains.

– sojourn *verb, always followed by an adverb or preposition* **-journs; -journed; -journ·ing** [*no obj*] *formal* • We *sojourned* for two weeks at a resort.

sol /ˈsoʊl/ *noun* [*noncount*] *music* : the fifth note of a musical scale • do, re, mi, fa, *sol,* la, ti — called also *so,* (*chiefly Brit*) *soh*

so·lace /ˈsɑːləs/ *noun, formal* : someone or something that gives a feeling of comfort to a person who is sad, depressed, etc. : a source of comfort [*singular*] Her presence was a great *solace* for/to me. [*noncount*] — often + *in* • We took/found *solace in* the knowledge that she hadn't been alone at the end. • I urged him not to seek *solace in* alcohol. [=I urged him not to drink to feel better]

so·lar /ˈsoʊlɚ/ *adj, always used before a noun*

1 : of or relating to the sun • a *solar* eclipse/phenomenon

2 : produced by or using the sun's light or heat • *solar* energy/power • a *solar* heating system

solar cell *noun, pl* **~ cells** [*count*] : a device that uses light or heat from the sun to produce electricity

so·lar·i·um /soʊˈlerijəm/ *noun, pl* **-ums** [*count*]

1 : a room with walls and a ceiling that are made of glass to allow in sunlight

2 *Brit* : a room where you can lie in the sun or get a tan

solar panel *noun, pl* **~ -els** [*count*] : a large, flat piece of equipment that uses the sun's light or heat to create electricity • All of the house's electricity is produced by *solar panels* on the roof.

so·lar plex·us /ˈsoʊlɚˈplɛksəs/ *noun*

the solar plexus : the area on the front of your body just below the ribs • He punched him in *the solar plexus.*

solar system *noun, pl* **~ -tems**

1 ***the solar system*** : our sun and the planets that move around it

2 [*count*] : a star other than our sun and the planets that move around it

sold *past tense and past participle of* ¹SELL

¹sol·der /ˈsɑːdɚ, *Brit* ˈsɒldə/ *noun* [*noncount*] : a mixture of metals (such as lead and tin) that is melted and used to join metal parts together

²solder *verb* **-ders; -dered; -der·ing** [+ *obj*] : to join (something made of metal) to something else with solder • Wires are *soldered* onto the circuit board.

soldering iron *noun, pl* **~ irons** [*count*] : a tool that is electrically heated and used for joining parts with solder

soldering iron

¹sol·dier /ˈsoʊlʤɚ/ *noun, pl* **-diers** [*count*] : a person who is in the military : a member of an army • Many *soldiers* were wounded in combat. • an American *soldier* • British/German *soldiers* — see also FOOT SOLDIER

²soldier *verb* **-diers; -diered; -dier·ing**

soldier on [*phrasal verb*] : to continue to do something or to try to achieve something even though it is difficult • We *soldiered on* to the end. • The researchers encountered many problems but they *soldiered on.*

sol·dier·ing /ˈsoʊlʤərɪŋ/ *noun* [*noncount*] : the life or job of a soldier

sol·dier·ly /ˈsoʊlʤəli/ *adj* [*more ~; most ~*] : suited to or typical of a good soldier • *soldierly* virtues • a *soldierly* manner

soldier of fortune *noun, pl* **soldiers of fortune** [*count*] : someone who will fight as a soldier for any country or person in return for payment

sol·diery /ˈsoʊlʤəri/ *noun* [*singular*] *old-fashioned* : a group of soldiers

sold–out /ˈsoʊldˈaʊt/ *adj* : having all the tickets sold completely • a *sold-out* show/performance/concert : of or relating to an event where all the tickets have been sold • A *sold-out* crowd attended the show. — see also *sell out* at ¹SELL

¹sole /ˈsoʊl/ *adj, always used before a noun*

1 : only or single • He became the *sole* heir to the property. • the *sole* owner • The *sole* aim/objective/purpose of the program is to help the poor. • She was the *sole* survivor of the tragedy. • Icy roads were the *sole* cause of the accident.

2 : belonging only to the person or group specified • She has the *sole* authority to hire new staff members. [=only she can hire new staff members] • He has *sole* jurisdiction of the area.

²sole *noun, pl* **soles** [*count*]

1 : the bottom part of the foot

2 : the part of a shoe, boot, etc., that touches the ground • shoes with slippery *soles* • heavy boots with thick rubber *soles* — see picture at SHOE

– compare ⁴SOLE

³sole *verb* **soles; soled; sol·ing** [+ *obj*] : to put a new sole on (a shoe, boot, etc.) • My shoes need to be *soled.*

⁴sole *noun, pl* **soles** [*count, noncount*] : a type of ocean fish that is eaten as food • fillet of *sole* — compare ²SOLE

so·le·cism /ˈsɑːləˌsɪzəm/ *noun, pl* **-cisms** [*count*] *formal*

1 : a mistake in speech or writing • a verbal *solecism*

2 : an impolite or improper way of behaving • a stylistic *solecism*

soled /ˈsoʊld/ *adj, of a shoe* : having a particular type of sole — used in combination • leather-*soled* shoes • thick-*soled* hiking boots

sole·ly /ˈsoʊlli/ *adv*

1 : without anything or anyone else involved • His rank was based *solely* on merit. • You will be held *solely* responsible for any damage. • The decision is *solely* [=*entirely*] yours.

2 : only or just • She did not write *solely* for money.

sol·emn /ˈsɑːləm/ *adj*

1 : very serious or formal in manner, behavior, or expression • a *solemn* occasion/moment • He spoke in a *solemn* and thoughtful manner. • a *solemn* religious ceremony/procession • He wore a very *solemn* expression on his face. • He recited the poem in a *solemn* voice.

2 : sad and serious • A *solemn* crowd gathered around the grave.

3 : done or made sincerely • a *solemn* declaration/oath • We made a *solemn* promise/vow to love each other forever.

– sol·emn·ly *adv* • We listened *solemnly* as the president spoke. • Do you *solemnly* swear to tell the truth?

so·lem·ni·ty /səˈlɛmnəti/ *noun, pl* **-ties** *formal*

1 [*noncount*] : the quality of being formal or serious • the *so-*

lemnity of the occasion • Her voice conveyed the *solemnity* of the passage. • The visiting statesman was welcomed with appropriate *solemnity*.

2 ***solemnities*** [*plural*] : formal ceremonies • Elaborate *solemnities* marked the 100th anniversary of the event.

sol•em•nize (*US*) *also Brit* **sol•em•nise** /ˈsɑːləmˌnaɪz/ *verb* **-niz•es; -nized; -niz•ing** [+ *obj*] *formal* : to mark or celebrate (something) officially or formally especially with a religious ceremony • The priest *solemnized* their marriage.

so•lic•it /səˈlɪsət/ *verb* **-its; it•ed; -it•ing** *formal*

1 a : to ask for (something, such as money or help) from people, companies, etc. [+ *obj*] The center is *soliciting* donations to help victims of the earthquake. • The company is *soliciting* bids from various firms. • The organization is *soliciting* new memberships/subscriptions. • The newspaper's editors want to *solicit* opinions/comments from readers. [*no obj*] The organization is *soliciting* for donations. **b** [+ *obj*] : to ask (a person or group) for money, help, etc. • Special interest groups are *soliciting* Congress for funds.

2 [+ *obj*] : to offer to have sex with (someone) in return for money • The prostitutes were arrested for *soliciting* customers.

– so•lic•i•ta•tion /səˌlɪsəˈteɪʃən/ *noun, pl* **-tions** *formal* [*count*] E-mail *solicitations* for comments didn't generate much response. [*noncount*] the *solicitation* of funds • *Solicitation* is not allowed in the store or its parking lot. **– soliciting** *noun* [*noncount*] • No *soliciting* is allowed on store property. • He was arrested for *soliciting*.

so•lic•i•tor /səˈlɪsətɚ/ *noun, pl* **-tors** [*count*]

1 *US* : a person whose job involves talking to many people and trying to persuade them to buy things, donate money, etc. • *Solicitors* will be arrested for trespassing.

2 : a lawyer in Britain who assists people in legal matters and who can represent people in lower courts of law — compare BARRISTER

3 *US* : a chief law officer of a city, town, or government department

solicitor general *noun, pl* **solicitors general** [*count*] : a law officer who assists an attorney general and is just below the attorney general in rank

so•lic•i•tous /səˈlɪsətəs/ *adj* [*more* ~; *most* ~] *formal* : showing concern or care for someone's health, happiness, etc. • I appreciated his *solicitous* inquiry about my health. • He had always been *solicitous* for the welfare of his family.

– so•lic•i•tous•ly *adv*

so•lic•i•tude /səˈlɪsəˌtuːd, *Brit* səˈlɪsəˌtjuːd/ *noun* [*noncount*] *formal* : concern that someone feels about someone's health, happiness, etc. • He expressed *solicitude* for my health.

¹sol•id /ˈsɑːləd/ *adj*

1 : firm or hard : not having the form of a gas or liquid • Concrete is a *solid* material. • particles of *solid* matter • When ice melts, it passes from a *solid* to a liquid form. • I was on a liquid diet when I was sick because I couldn't digest *solid* food. • His muscles are very *solid*. [=*hard*] • I was glad to get off the plane and back on *solid* ground. • The pond was ***frozen solid***.

2 : having no space inside : not hollow • a *solid* rubber ball • a *solid* object

3 a *always used before a noun* : made entirely from the specified material • The ring is *solid* gold/silver. • *solid* oak/cherry/mahogany furniture • a chunk of *solid* marble/granite **b** : consisting only of the color specified or only of one color • I prefer *solid* colors like blue or green instead of plaids and stripes. — see color picture on page C12

4 : having no breaks, spaces, or pauses • The road was divided by a *solid* yellow line. • We talked for three *solid* hours. [=we talked for three hours without stopping] — often used figuratively • The rain fell in *solid* sheets. [=the rain fell very heavily] • The stores are always ***packed solid*** [=very crowded] during the holidays. • The hotels in the city were ***booked solid*** for the conference.

5 [*more* ~; *most* ~] **a** : good and able to be trusted to do or provide what is needed • He plays *solid* defense. • The team's defense is very *solid*. • She gave a *solid* performance. • She's a good, *solid* player. **b** : having a strong basis : good and dependable • His friend gave him some good, *solid* advice. • The company has built/established a *solid* reputation. • She had *solid* reasons for her decision. • Students need a *solid* foundation in language skills. • The prosecution has no *solid* evidence. • He had a *solid* alibi. • Financially, the company is ***(as) solid as a rock***. [=the company is in very good condition]

6 [*more* ~; *most* ~] : strong and well-made • *solid* furniture • This chair is very *solid*.

7 *US* : agreeing with or supporting something (such as a political party) in a completely loyal and dependable way • She is a *solid* Democrat/Republican.

8 *geometry* : having length, width, and height : THREE-DIMENSIONAL • a *solid* geometric figure

– sol•id•ly *adv* • *solidly* constructed furniture • a *solidly* built athlete • She put her feet *solidly* [=*securely*] on the ground. • Her reputation was *solidly* established. • a *solidly* Republican area/suburb [=an area/suburb where most people vote for Republicans] • Environmentalists were *solidly* [=*completely*] opposed to drilling in the area. • The quarterback played *solidly* during the second half. **– sol•id•ness** *noun* [*noncount*]

²solid *noun, pl* **-ids**

1 [*count*] : a solid substance : a substance that is not a gas or a liquid

2 [*count*] *geometry* : an object that has length, width, and height : a three-dimensional object — see picture at GEOMETRY

3 ***solids*** [*plural*] : foods that are not liquid • She couldn't eat *solids* after the surgery.

sol•i•dar•i•ty /ˌsɑːləˈderəti/ *noun* [*noncount*] : a feeling of unity between people who have the same interests, goals, etc. • national *solidarity* • The vote was a ***show of solidarity***.

so•lid•i•fy /səˈlɪdəˌfaɪ/ *verb* **-fies; -fied; -fy•ing**

1 : to make (something) solid or hard or to become solid or hard [+ *obj*] Work is under way to *solidify* the concrete that supports the building. • *solidified* lava [*no obj*] Hot wax *solidifies* as it cools.

2 : to make (a plan, project, etc.) stronger and more certain or to become stronger and more certain [+ *obj*] Recent findings helped to *solidify* our position. • The international community is working to *solidify* its alliances. [*no obj*] Their plans have *solidified*.

– so•lid•i•fi•ca•tion /səˌlɪdəfəˈkeɪʃən/ *noun* [*noncount*]

so•lid•i•ty /səˈlɪdəti/ *noun* [*noncount*] : the quality or state of being solid • the *solidity* of stone/granite/concrete • The *solidity* of his convictions impressed us.

so•lil•o•quy /səˈlɪləkwi/ *noun, pl* **-quies** [*count, noncount*] : a long, usually serious speech that a character in a play makes to an audience and that reveals the character's thoughts

so•lip•sism /ˈsoʊləpˌsɪzəm/ *noun* [*noncount*] *technical* : a theory in philosophy that your own existence is the only thing that is real or that can be known

– so•lip•sis•tic /ˌsoʊləpˈsɪstɪk/ *adj* • a *solipsistic* view

sol•i•taire /ˈsɑːləˌteɚ/ *noun, pl* **-taires**

1 [*noncount*] *chiefly US* : a card game that is played by one person — called also (*Brit*) *patience*

2 [*count*] : a single jewel that is set alone in a piece of jewelry • a diamond *solitaire* bracelet

¹sol•i•tary /ˈsɑːləˌteri, *Brit* ˈsɒlətri/ *adj*

1 a : without anyone or anything else : not involving or including anyone or anything else • a *solitary* traveler • We saw one *solitary* [=*single*] figure coming over the horizon. — sometimes used in negative statements to emphasize a complete lack of something • I could not hear a *solitary* [=*single*] word of what he said. **b** : done by a person who is alone • He took a *solitary* walk/stroll on the beach. • a *solitary* job

2 : separate from other people or things • A *solitary* house stood on top of the cliff.

3 [*more* ~; *most* ~] : tending to live or spend time alone • Most cats are *solitary* creatures. • He's a very *solitary* man.

– sol•i•tar•i•ly /ˌsɑːləˈterəli, *Brit* ˈsɒlətrəli/ *adv* **– sol•i•tar•i•ness** /ˈsɑːləˌterinəs, *Brit* ˈsɒlətrinəs/ *noun* [*noncount*]

²solitary *noun* [*noncount*] : SOLITARY CONFINEMENT • The prisoner was kept in *solitary*.

solitary confinement *noun* [*noncount*] : the state of being kept alone in a prison cell away from other prisoners • He spent three months in *solitary confinement*.

sol•i•tude /ˈsɑːləˌtuːd, *Brit* ˈsɒləˌtjuːd/ *noun* [*noncount*] : a state or situation in which you are alone usually because you want to be • She wished to work on her novel in *solitude*. • He enjoyed the peace and *solitude* of the woods.

¹so•lo /ˈsoʊloʊ/ *noun, pl* **-los** [*count*]

1 : a piece of music that is performed by one singer or musician • a piano/guitar *solo* • an operatic *solo*

2 : something that is done without another person • She is learning to fly and she flew her first *solo* yesterday.

[2]**solo** *adj, always used before a noun*
1 a : done without another person • a student pilot's first *solo* flight **b :** involving or done by a single performer instead of a group • a *solo* performance • She left the band last year and started a *solo* career. • He just issued his first *solo* album. • a *solo* artist/performer [=a singer or musician who is not part of a group]
2 *baseball* **:** hit with no runners on base • a ***solo home run*** [=a home run that scores one run]
– solo *adv* • She is traveling *solo*. [=by herself] • The singer went *solo* after being with the band for 10 years.

[3]**solo** *verb* **-los; -loed; -lo·ing** [*no obj*]
1 : to perform a piece of music without another singer or musician • The guitarist *solos* on practically every song.
2 : to fly an airplane without an instructor • She *soloed* for the first time yesterday.

so·lo·ist /ˈsoʊlowɪst/ *noun, pl* **-ists** [*count*] **:** a person who performs a musical solo • a piano *soloist*

sol·stice /ˈsɑːlstəs/ *noun, pl* **-stic·es** [*count*] **:** one of the two times during the year when the sun is farthest north or south of the equator ✧ The ***summer solstice*** occurs around June 22 and the ***winter solstice*** occurs around December 22. — compare EQUINOX

sol·u·ble /ˈsɑːljəbəl/ *adj* [*more ~; most ~*]
1 : capable of being dissolved in a liquid • Sugar is *soluble* in water. • *soluble* fiber — sometimes used in combination • water-*soluble* vitamins/compounds — opposite INSOLUBLE
2 *formal* **:** capable of being solved or explained • a *soluble* [=(more commonly) *solvable*] problem
– sol·u·bil·i·ty /ˌsɑːljəˈbɪləti/ *noun* [*noncount*]

so·lu·tion /səˈluːʃən/ *noun, pl* **-tions**
1 a [*count*] **:** something that is used or done to deal with and end a problem **:** something that solves a problem • Medication may not be the best *solution* for the patient's condition. • The *solution* is simple/obvious: you need to spend less money. — often + *to* • There is no simple *solution to* the country's drug problem. • She suggested a number of creative *solutions to* the housing crisis. **b** [*noncount*] **:** the act of solving something • a problem that has so far resisted *solution* [=a problem that no one has been able to solve]
2 [*count*] **a :** a correct answer to a problem, puzzle, etc. — often + *to* • The *solutions to* the math problems are in the back of the book. • I can't figure out the *solution to* this puzzle. **b :** an explanation for something that is difficult to understand (such as a mystery) — often + *to* • The police haven't yet found a *solution to* this crime/mystery.
3 a : a liquid in which something has been dissolved [*count*] She made a *solution* of baking soda and water. • a 40 percent saline *solution* [*noncount*] He rinsed the contact lens with saline *solution*. **b** [*noncount*] **:** the act or process of dissolving a solid, liquid, or gas in a liquid • the *solution* of sucrose in water

solve /ˈsɑːlv/ *verb* **solves; solved; solv·ing** [+ *obj*]
1 : to find a way to deal with and end (a problem) • They are working to *solve* the traffic problem. • If they'll lend us the money we need, all our problems will be *solved*.
2 a : to find the correct answer to (something, such as a riddle) • She *solved* the riddle/puzzle. • He couldn't *solve* the math problem. **b :** to find the correct explanation for (something, such as a mystery) • The mystery/crime has been *solved*. • The FBI has been trying to *solve* the case for years.
– solv·able /ˈsɑːlvəbəl/ *adj* • an easily *solvable* mystery
– solv·er *noun, pl* **-ers** [*count*] • She's a good problem *solver*.

sol·ven·cy /ˈsɑːlvənsi/ *noun* [*noncount*] **:** the state of being able to pay debts • They reviewed financial records to measure the borrower's *solvency*.

[1]**sol·vent** /ˈsɑːlvənt/ *adj* [*more ~; most ~*] **:** able to pay debts • He couldn't stay/remain *solvent* after losing his business.

[2]**solvent** *noun, pl* **-vents** [*count, noncount*] *technical* **:** a liquid substance that is used to dissolve another substance • turpentine and other *solvents*

som·ber (*US*) *or Brit* **som·bre** /ˈsɑːmbɚ/ *adj* [*more ~; most ~*] *formal*
1 : very sad and serious • Her death put us in a *somber* mood. • The movie is a *somber* portrait of life on the streets.
2 : having a dull or dark color • He wore a *somber* suit.
– som·ber·ly *adv* • He shook his head *somberly* at the sad news. **– som·ber·ness** *noun* [*noncount*]

som·bre·ro /səmˈbreroʊ/ *noun, pl* **-ros** [*count*] **:** a type of hat with a very wide brim that is often worn in Mexico and the southwestern U.S. — see picture at HAT

[1]**some** /ˈsʌm, səm/ *adj, always used before a noun*
1 — used to refer to a person or thing that is not known, named, or specified • *Some* guy called while you were out. • She works for *some* company (or other/another) out west. • For *some* reason, the lights went out. • I tried to offer him *some* type/sort/kind of payment for the favor. • Could you call back *some* other time? I'm busy right now. • *Some* birds cannot fly. • I like *some* kinds of nuts but not all of them. • *Some* people believe it and others don't.
2 a : of an unspecified amount or number • Can I have *some* water? • I bought *some* apples. • She had *some* interest in the job. • I have *some* money left, but not much. • I hope I've been of *some* help. **b :** of a fairly large amount or number • Their decision was met with *some* surprise. [=people were fairly surprised by their decision] • It will be *some* time [=a considerable amount of time] before she comes back. • We met *some* years ago. • He spoke at *some* length about his problems.
3 *informal* **a —** used to express approval • That was *some* game! [=that was a very good/enjoyable game] **b —** used to express disapproval, disappointment, etc. • You have *some* nerve [=a lot of nerve] to say that! • You don't know how to get there? *Some* navigator you are! [=you're not a good navigator] • *Some* friend he is—he left me stranded at the train depot.

[2]**some** /ˈsʌm/ *pronoun* **:** an unspecified amount or number of people or things • *Some* of the apples are bruised. • *Some* of the people at the party had too much to drink. • This bakery makes *some* of the best bread in town. • Most birds can fly but *some* cannot. • *Some* [=some people] say that patience is a virtue. • I'm making coffee; do you want *some*?
and then some informal **:** and more in addition to that • I ran a mile *and then some*. • He got what he deserved *and then some*. [=he got more than he deserved]

[3]**some** /ˈsʌm, ˌsʌm/ *adv*
1 — used to indicate that a number is approximate • *Some* 80 people [=about 80 people] showed up for the lecture. — sometimes used in combination • The drug is illegal in 20-*some* states.
2 : to an unspecified amount or degree • Would you like ***some more*** potatoes? • I need to work on it *some more*. — often used informally in U.S. English without *more* • He needs to grow up *some* before he can live on his own. • The cut bled *some*. [=a little] • He helped me *some*.

[1]**-some** /səm/ *adj suffix*
1 : having a specified quality • burden*some*
2 : causing a specified feeling or condition • fear*some* • awe*some* • quarrel*some*

[2]**-some** *noun suffix* **:** a group of (so many) people or things • four*some* [=a group of four people]

[1]**some·body** /ˈsʌmˌbʌdi/ *pronoun* **:** a person who is not known, named, or specified **:** SOMEONE • *Somebody* left you a message. • The singer waved to *somebody* in the crowd. • We need *somebody* who can work nights and weekends. • Is that *somebody* you know? • *Somebody* has to do it. • After I turned down the job, she offered it to ***somebody else***.

[2]**somebody** *noun, pl* **-bod·ies** [*count*] **:** an important person — usually singular • The teacher convinced her that she could grow up to be *somebody*.

some·day /ˈsʌmˌdeɪ/ *adv* **:** at some time in the future • *Someday* we'll buy a house. • She hopes to publish her novel *someday*. • Let's have lunch *someday* next week.

some·how /ˈsʌmˌhaʊ/ *adv* **:** in a way that is not known or certain • *Somehow* (or other/another) we got lost. • She *somehow* managed to find her earring in the sand. • It will all work out *somehow*.

some·one /ˈsʌmˌwʌn/ *pronoun* **:** some person **:** SOMEBODY • *Someone* left you a message. • Is that *someone* you know? • We need *someone* who can work nights and weekends. • *Someone* took the last piece of cake. • I'll do it because *someone* has to. • She offered the job to ***someone else***. — compare ANYONE

some·place /ˈsʌmˌpleɪs/ *adv, US* **:** SOMEWHERE • Should we eat here or go *someplace* else? • I put my keys *someplace* but I can't remember where. — compare ANYPLACE

[1]**som·er·sault** /ˈsʌmɚˌsɑːlt/ *noun, pl* **-saults** [*count*] **:** a forward or backward movement of your body on the ground or in the air that is made by bringing your feet over your head • The gymnast turned/performed/did a *somersault*. • a forward/backward *somersault* — sometimes used figuratively •

S

His heart did a *somersault* when he heard the news.

[2]**somersault** *verb* **-saults; -sault·ed; -sault·ing** [*no obj*] **:** to make a complete turn forward or backward on the ground or in the air **:** to do a somersault • The diver *somersaulted* in midair. • He flew off his bike and *somersaulted* over the bushes.

[1]**some·thing** /ˈsʌmˌθɪŋ/ *pronoun*

1 : a thing that is not known, named, or specified • *Something* came in the mail for you. • I thought I heard *something* outside. • He said *something* that really bothered me. • I started to say *something* but she interrupted me. • I have *something* to tell you. • There's *something* wrong with my car. • *Something* is going on at the school, but I don't know what. • "The job doesn't pay very well and the hours are long." "I think you should look for *something* better." • I don't know what she studies, but it has *something* to do with computers. [=it relates to computers] • Would you like *something* [=*anything*] to drink? • Is there *something* [=*anything*] wrong? • Is there *something* [=*anything*] good on TV tonight? • I just got my tax refund. It's not much, but it's *something*. [=it's better than nothing] • "They won't give us an extra week to finish, but they'll give us a couple of days." "Well, that's *something* anyway." • Do you want pizza for dinner or ***something else***? [=or a different thing for dinner] • I got you ***a little something*** [=a small thing] for your birthday.

2 : a person or thing that is important or worth noticing • She thinks she's really *something* ever since her promotion. • That waterfall is really *something*, isn't it? • He decided to go back to college and ***make something of himself*** [=become successful]

3 : an amount that is more than a specified number — used in combination • His friends are all twenty*something* singles. [=his friends are single people between the ages of 20 and 29] • The bill came to fifty-*something* dollars.

4 — used to make a statement or description less forceful or definite • He is ***something of*** an expert [=he is an expert to some degree] with car repair. • We have *something of* a problem here. • The movie was *something of* [=*somewhat of*] a disappointment. [=was somewhat disappointing]

or something informal — used to suggest another name, choice, etc., that is not specified • Are you crazy *or something*? • You can probably clean that stain with club soda *or something*. [=or something like that] • The man wearing the badge must be a guard *or something*. • Can I get you a glass of wine *or something*?

something else informal **:** a person or thing that is special or impressive • That magician really is *something else*. • The Grand Canyon is *something else*, isn't it?

start something see [1]START

[2]**something** *adv*

1 : in a very small amount or degree **:** somewhat or slightly • The total repairs cost *something* over $300. • He does look ***something like*** his father. [=he resembles his father somewhat] • The movie was *something like* what I expected.

2 *informal* — used before an adjective that is being used like an adverb to add emphasis • He was snoring *something* awful/terrible [=was snoring very loudly] last night.

something fierce see FIERCE

[1]**some·time** /ˈsʌmˌtaɪm/ *adv*

1 : at an unspecified time in the future • We should get together *sometime*. • It's likely to happen *sometime* soon. • She will return from her trip *sometime* in December.

2 : at an unspecified or unknown time in the past • A burglar broke in *sometime* during the night. • The book was written *sometime* around the turn of the century.

[2]**sometime** *adj, always used before a noun*

1 *formal* — used to say what someone or something was in the past • the *sometime* [=*former*] prime minister

2 *US* — used to say what someone sometimes does or is • He is a talented pianist and *sometime* teacher of music. [=he sometimes teaches music]

some·times /ˈsʌmˌtaɪmz/ *adv* **:** at certain times **:** OCCASIONALLY • His jokes are funny, but *sometimes* he goes too far. • *Sometimes* I take the bus to work. • We all make mistakes *sometimes*. • She works nine hours a day, *sometimes* more than that. • The word is *sometimes* used figuratively.

some·way /ˈsʌmˌweɪ/ *adv* **:** SOMEHOW • We'll do it *someway*.

[1]**some·what** /ˈsʌmˌwʌt/ *adv* **:** in a small amount or degree **:** to some degree • He felt *somewhat* awkward in his suit. • The instructions were *somewhat* [=*slightly, a little*] confusing. • Our work has progressed *somewhat*. • The course is *somewhat* more difficult than I was told it would be.

[2]**somewhat** *pronoun* — used to make a statement or description less forceful or definite • We have ***somewhat of*** a problem. [=we have a slight/minor problem] • To say he has improved is *somewhat of* [=*something of*] an understatement.

[1]**some·where** /ˈsʌmˌweɚ/ *adv*

1 : in, at, or to a place not known, named, or specified • The boy ran off *somewhere*. • She lives *somewhere* in the city. • I've seen you *somewhere* before. • His house must be around here *somewhere*. • Do you want to go ***somewhere else***?

2 : close to a specified number, time, or amount — usually + *around* or *between* • We met up *somewhere around* nine o'clock. • There must be *somewhere around* 100 people here. • The event attracted *somewhere between* 300 and 500 people. • The car costs *somewhere around* $25,000 to $30,000.

get somewhere informal **:** to make progress • After hours of questioning, the police began to *get somewhere* with the suspect. • The work has been very slow, but I feel like we're finally *getting somewhere*.

[2]**somewhere** *noun* [*noncount*] **:** a place not known, named, or specified • We looked for *somewhere* to park the car. • I know *somewhere* nice where we can eat.

som·me·lier /ˌsʌməlˈjeɪ/ *noun, pl* **-liers** /ˌsʌməlˈjeɪz/ [*count*] **:** a waiter in a restaurant who is in charge of serving wine

som·no·lent /ˈsɑːmnələnt/ *adj* [*more* ~; *most* ~] *formal*

1 : tired and ready to fall alseep **:** SLEEPY • *somnolent* travelers — sometimes used figuratively • a *somnolent* little village

2 : causing a person to fall asleep **:** very boring • a *somnolent* lecture

— **som·no·lence** /ˈsɑːmnələns/ *noun* [*noncount*]

son /ˈsʌn/ *noun, pl* **sons**

1 [*count*] **:** a male child • She gave birth to a *son*. • They have two *sons* and a daughter. • He is the *son* of a lawyer and a doctor. • an adopted *son* — sometimes used figuratively • our town's own native *son* [=a boy/man who is from our town] — sometimes used by an older person to address a younger man or a boy • Slow down, *son*, I can't understand what you're saying. — see also FAVORITE SON, GODSON, GRANDSON, STEPSON

2 ***the Son*** **:** the second person of the Trinity in the Christian religion **:** Jesus Christ • the Father, *the Son* and the Holy Spirit

like father, like son see [1]FATHER

prodigal son see PRODIGAL

so·nar /ˈsoʊˌnɑɚ/ *noun* [*noncount*] **:** a device used for finding things that are underwater by using sound waves • They detected the submarine by using *sonar*. • a *sonar* signal

so·na·ta /səˈnɑːtə/ *noun, pl* **-tas** [*count*] *music* **:** a piece of music written for one or two instruments that has usually three or four large sections that are different from each other in rhythm and mood • a piano/cello *sonata*

song /ˈsɑːŋ/ *noun, pl* **songs**

1 [*count*] **:** a short piece of music with words that are sung • He sang a love *song*. • The *song* was playing on the radio. — see also FOLK SONG, SIREN SONG, SWAN SONG, THEME SONG, TORCH SONG

2 [*noncount*] **:** the act of singing • She suddenly burst/broke into *song*. [=began singing] • The event was celebrated in *song* by a folk group.

3 [*count, noncount*] **:** a series of musical sounds that are produced by a bird or an animal (such as a whale) • I could hear the *song* of a sparrow.

for a song chiefly US, informal **:** for a very small amount of money • This old car can be bought/had *for a song*.

song and dance *noun* [*singular*]

1 : a performance that combines singing and dancing

2 *US, informal + disapproving* **:** a long story, explanation, or excuse that may not be true or directly related to what is being discussed — often + *about* • When I asked him why the work wasn't finished, he gave me a long *song and dance about* some problem he's been having with his computer.

make a song and dance about (something) Brit, informal **1 :** to cause a lot of excitement about (something) • The film is nothing to *make a song and dance about*. **2 :** to complain about (something) in a way that is excessive or unnecessary • He was *making a* big *song and dance about* the new regulations.

song·bird /ˈsɑːŋˌbɚd/ *noun, pl* **-birds** [*count*]

1 : a bird that produces a series of musical sounds **:** a bird that sings especially in an appealing way

S

2 *chiefly US, somewhat old-fashioned* : a female singer ▪ a talented *songbird*

song·book /ˈsɑːŋˌbʊk/ *noun, pl* **-books** [*count*] : a book that contains the music and words to songs

song·fest /ˈsɑːŋˈfɛst/ *noun, pl* **-fests** [*count*] *US* : an informal gathering where people sing songs together

song·ster /ˈsɑːŋstɚ/ *noun, pl* **-sters** [*count*] : a person who sings usually very well ▪ a Broadway *songster*

song·stress /ˈsɑːŋstrəs/ *noun, pl* **-stress·es** [*count*] : a woman who sings usually very well ▪ a jazz *songstress*

song·writ·er /ˈsɑːŋˌraɪtɚ/ *noun, pl* **-ers** [*count*] : a person who writes the words or music to songs ▪ an award-winning singer and *songwriter* — see also SINGER-SONGWRITER

song·writ·ing /ˈsɑːŋˌraɪtɪŋ/ *noun* [*noncount*] : the act or process of writing the words or music to songs — often used before another noun ▪ a famous *songwriting* duo

son·ic /ˈsɑːnɪk/ *adj, always used before a noun* : of or relating to sound, sound waves, or the speed of sound ▪ *sonic* waves ▪ The concert was a *sonic* extravaganza. [=a very exciting and entertaining musical event]

sonic boom *noun, pl* ~ **booms** [*count*] : a very loud and explosive noise that is produced by an aircraft when it travels faster than the speed of sound

son–in–law /ˈsʌnənˌlɑː/ *noun, pl* **sons–in–law** /ˈsʌnzənˌlɑː/ [*count*] : the husband of your daughter

son·net /ˈsɑːnət/ *noun, pl* **-nets** [*count*] : a poem made up of 14 lines that rhyme in a fixed pattern

son·ny /ˈsʌni/ *noun, old-fashioned* — used by an older person to address a younger man or a boy ▪ Watch your mouth, *sonny*.

son of a bitch *noun, pl* **sons of bitches** *chiefly US, informal + impolite*

1 [*count*] : a person (especially a man) who you strongly dislike or hate ▪ That *son of a bitch* insulted my family. ▪ He's a mean *son of a bitch*.

2 — used to express surprise, disappointment, anger, etc. ▪ *Son of a bitch*! You won! ▪ We've run out of gas? *Son of a bitch*!

3 [*singular*] : something that is very difficult or unpleasant ▪ The test turned out to be a real *son of a bitch*.

son of a gun *noun, pl* **sons of guns** *US, informal*

1 [*count*] : a person (especially a man) or thing that you are annoyed with ▪ That *son of a gun* never called me back. ▪ I had to bring the car to the shop. The *son of a gun* broke down again.

2 *old-fashioned* — used by a man to address a male friend ▪ How are you, you old *son of a gun*?

3 — used to express mild surprise, disappointment, etc. ▪ *Son of a gun*, I lost a button. ▪ Well, *son of a gun*, you made it!

sono·gram /ˈsɑːnəˌgræm/ *noun, pl* **-grams** [*count*] *US, technical* : a picture that is taken of the inside of something (such as a person's body) by using a special machine : ULTRASOUND ▪ The *sonogram* showed that the fetus was developing normally.

so·no·rous /ˈsɑːnərəs/ *adj* [*more* ~; *most* ~] *formal* : having a sound that is deep, loud, and pleasant ▪ He has a deep, *sonorous* voice.

– so·nor·i·ty /səˈnorəti/ *noun, pl* **-ties** [*count, noncount*] ▪ the *sonority* of the singer's voice **– so·no·rous·ly** *adv* ▪ He sang *sonorously*.

soon /ˈsuːn/ *adv* **soon·er; -est**

1 a : at a time that is not long from now ▪ We will *soon* be making changes. ▪ I'll see you *soon*. ▪ The *soonest* I can get there is tomorrow. ▪ When is the *soonest* possible date of delivery? ▪ We'll find out the answer ***soon enough***. [=we'll find out the answer soon] ▪ We need to fix this problem ***sooner rather than later***. [=we need to fix this problem soon] **b** : in a short time after something happens ▪ The audience *soon* realized that it wasn't a stunt. ▪ She found a job ***soon after*** graduation. ▪ Please give me a call ***as soon as*** you get there. [=give me a call immediately when you get there] ▪ I had ***no sooner*** walked through the door when the phone rang. = *No sooner* did I walk through the door than the phone rang. [=the phone rang immediately after I walked through the door] ▪ I told them we needed more copies. ***No sooner said than done***. [=they immediately gave us more copies]

2 : in a quick way : QUICKLY ▪ How *soon* can you finish the job? ▪ The *sooner* you finish your homework, the *sooner* you can go outside and play. ▪ I will let you know ***as soon as possible***. ▪ I'll get there ***as soon as*** I can. ▪ The *sooner* [=more quickly] we get the pipe fixed, the better. = We need to get the pipe fixed, ***the sooner the better***.

sooner or later : at an unspecified time in the future : EVENTUALLY ▪ *Sooner or later*, we'll have to tell her the truth. ▪ The bus should be here *sooner or later*.

too soon : before the time that is proper, preferred, or specified ▪ I spoke *too soon*. ▪ It's *too soon* to tell what will happen. ▪ The show was over all *too soon*. ▪ The plumber arrived, and ***not a moment too soon***. [=the plumber arrived just in time; if the plumber had arrived later, it would have been too late]

would sooner or would just as soon — used to indicate what you want or prefer to do, have, etc. ▪ He *would sooner* [=*would rather*] lose everything than admit that he was wrong. ▪ We asked him to come with us, but he said he'*d just as soon* stay home.

soot /ˈsʊt/ *noun* [*noncount*] : a black powder that is formed when something (such as wood or coal) is burned

– sooty /ˈsuːti/ *adj* **soot·i·er; -est** ▪ the worker's *sooty* hands

soothe /ˈsuːð/ *verb* **soothes; soothed; sooth·ing** [+ *obj*]

1 : to cause (someone) to be calmer, less angry, etc. ▪ She played music to *soothe* [=*comfort*] the baby. ▪ The waiter tried to *soothe* the angry customer.

2 a : to cause (a part of the body) to feel better ▪ This cream *soothes* aching muscles. ▪ Her nerves were *soothed* by a warm bath. **b** : to cause (pain) to go away or become less severe ▪ Nothing can *soothe* their pain. — sometimes + *away* ▪ The massage *soothed away* my back pain.

soothing *adj* [*more* ~; *most* ~] : producing feelings of comfort or relief ▪ a *soothing* bath/cream/massage ▪ *soothing* words ▪ The music had a *soothing* effect on the baby.

– sooth·ing·ly *adv* ▪ She sang *soothingly* to the baby.

sooth·say·er /ˈsuːθˌsejɚ/ *noun, pl* **-ers** [*count*] *old-fashioned* : someone who makes predictions about what is going to happen in the future

¹sop /ˈsɑːp/ *noun, pl* **sops** [*count*] *disapproving* : something that is done or given to someone in order to prevent trouble, gain support, etc. — usually singular ▪ Critics say that the proposed tax cut is just a *sop* to wealthy taxpayers. — see also MILKSOP

²sop *verb* **sops; sopped; sop·ping**

sop up [*phrasal verb*] ***sop up (a liquid) or sop (a liquid) up*** : to remove (a liquid) from a surface by using soft paper, bread, etc. ▪ He *sopped up* the gravy with pieces of bread. ▪ The water was *sopped up* [=*mopped up*] with a mop.

soph. *abbr* sophomore

so·phis·ti·cate /səˈfɪstɪkət/ *noun, pl* **-cates** [*count*] *formal* : a person who has a lot of knowledge about the world and about culture, art, literature, etc. : a sophisticated person ▪ urban *sophisticates*

so·phis·ti·cat·ed /səˈfɪstəˌkeɪtəd/ *adj* [*more* ~; *most* ~]

1 a : having or showing a lot of experience and knowledge about the world and about culture, art, literature, etc. ▪ She was a *sophisticated* and well-traveled woman. ▪ She has *sophisticated* tastes. **b** : attractive to fashionable or sophisticated people ▪ a swank and *sophisticated* restaurant

2 : highly developed and complex ▪ a *sophisticated* computer network ▪ *sophisticated* technologies ▪ Her knitting technique is more *sophisticated* than mine.

– so·phis·ti·cat·ed·ly *adv* **– so·phis·ti·ca·tion** /səˌfɪstəˈkeɪʃən/ *noun* [*noncount*] ▪ She is admired for her *sophistication* and sense of style. ▪ the growing *sophistication* of new technologies

soph·ist·ry /ˈsɑːfəstri/ *noun, pl* **-ries** *formal*

1 [*noncount*] : the use of reasoning or arguments that sound correct but are actually false

2 [*count*] : a reason or argument that sounds correct but is actually false

soph·o·more /ˈsɑːfˌmoɚ/ *noun, pl* **-mores** [*count*] *US* : a student in the second year of high school or college ▪ She's a *sophomore* in high school. — often used before another noun ▪ Their son is in his *sophomore* year in college. ▪ The team's quarterback improved during his *sophomore* season. — compare FRESHMAN, JUNIOR, SENIOR

soph·o·mor·ic /ˌsɑːfˈmorɪk/ *adj* [*more* ~; *most* ~] *US, disapproving* : having or showing a lack of emotional maturity : foolish and immature ▪ a *sophomoric* joke ▪ His behavior at the party was *sophomoric*.

sop·o·rif·ic /ˌsɑːpəˈrɪfɪk/ *adj* [*more* ~; *most* ~] *formal* : causing a person to become tired and ready to fall asleep ▪ the *soporific* heat of summer ▪ a *soporific* drug

– soporific *noun, pl* **-ics** [*count*] ▪ a substance used as a *soporific*

S

sop·ping /ˈsɑːpɪŋ/ *adj, informal* : completely or thoroughly wet • His clothes were *sopping* from the rain. • a ***sopping wet*** sponge

sop·py /ˈsɑːpi/ *adj* **sop·pi·er; -est** [*also more* ~; *most* ~]
1 *US* : soaked through with water : very wet • *soppy* towels
2 *Brit, informal* **a** : sad or romantic in a foolish or exaggerated way • The radio played nothing but *soppy* [=(*US*) *sappy*] love songs. **b** : foolish or silly • She gets all *soppy* [=(*US*) *sappy*] when she's around babies.

[1]so·pra·no /səˈprænoʊ, səˈprɑːnoʊ/ *adj, always used before a noun*
1 : relating to the highest female singing voice or the highest voice part in a singing group • the *soprano* tones
2 : having a high sound range • a *soprano* saxophone

[2]soprano *noun, pl* **-nos** [*count*]
1 : the highest voice part in a singing group
2 : the highest female singing voice or a person with this voice • She sings in a high *soprano*. • an opera *soprano*
— compare ALTO, BASS, TENOR

sor·bet /soɚˈbeɪ/ *noun, pl* **-bets** [*count*] : a frozen sweet dessert that is made usually from fruit or fruit juices • a raspberry *sorbet* — called also (*Brit*) *water ice*

sor·cer·er /ˈsoɚsərɚ/ *noun, pl* **-ers** [*count*] : a person who practices sorcery : a wizard or warlock

sor·cer·ess /ˈsoɚsərəs/ *noun, pl* **-ess·es** [*count*] : a woman who practices sorcery : WITCH

sor·cery /ˈsoɚsəri/ *noun* [*noncount*] : the use of magical powers that are obtained through evil spirits : WITCHCRAFT

sor·did /ˈsoɚdəd/ *adj* [*more* ~; *most* ~] *formal*
1 : very bad or dishonest • He shared the *sordid* details of his past. • *sordid* business deals • a *sordid* scandal/affair
2 : very dirty : FILTHY • *sordid* living conditions

[1]sore /ˈsoɚ/ *adj* **sor·er; -est** [*also more* ~; *most* ~]
1 : feeling or affected by pain : PAINFUL • *sore* muscles • Her back felt *sore*. • After I fell I was *sore* [=*achy*] all over. • a dog limping on a *sore* leg • The patient has a ***sore throat***.
2 *always used before a noun* : causing emotional pain or distress • That's a *sore* subject to bring up. • The discussion touched on a *sore* spot.
3 *chiefly US, informal* : angry or upset • My neighbor is *sore* at me. • Are you still *sore* about what happened last night? • He's a ***sore loser***. [=he becomes very upset or angry when he loses]
a sight for sore eyes see [1]SIGHT
(like) a bear with a sore head see [1]BEAR
stick/stand out like a sore thumb *informal* : to be very noticeable in usually a bad way • I wasn't wearing the right clothes for the party, and I *stuck out like a sore thumb*.
— **sore·ness** *noun* [*noncount*] • muscle *soreness* • There will be some *soreness* after you get the injection.

[2]sore *noun, pl* **sores** [*count*] : a sore or painful spot on the body • He has a *sore* on his lip. — see also BEDSORE, CANKER SORE, COLD SORE, EYESORE

sore·head /ˈsoɚˌhɛd/ *noun, pl* **-heads** [*count*] *US, informal* + *disapproving* : a person who easily becomes angry or upset • Just because you lost, don't be a *sorehead*!
— **sore·head·ed** /ˈsoɚˈhɛdəd/ *adj* • a *soreheaded* loser

sore·ly /ˈsoɚli/ *adv* : very much : BADLY • You will be *sorely* missed. • She provided some *sorely* needed help. • The house is *sorely* in need of paint. • He is *sorely* lacking in social skills.

sor·ghum /ˈsoɚgəm/ *noun* [*noncount*] : a kind of tropical grass that is grown for food; *also* : the grain that grows on this grass

so·ror·i·ty /səˈrorəti/ *noun, pl* **-ties** [*count*] : an organization of female students at a U.S. college • She wanted to pledge/join a *sorority*. — compare FRATERNITY

[1]sor·rel /ˈsorəl/ *noun, pl* **-rels** [*count*] : a reddish-brown horse • a *sorrel* mare — compare [2]SORREL

[2]sorrel *noun* [*noncount*] : a plant that has sour juice and that is used in cooking — compare [1]SORREL

[1]sor·row /ˈsɑroʊ/ *noun, pl* **-rows**
1 [*noncount*] : a feeling of sadness or grief caused especially by the loss of someone or something • I felt *sorrow* at/over the death of my friend. • an expression of *sorrow* • (*chiefly Brit*) He spoke ***more in sorrow than in anger***. [=because of sadness or disappointment rather than anger]
2 [*count*] : a cause of grief or sadness • a life filled with joys and *sorrows* • She had a secret *sorrow*. • He went to the bar to ***drown his sorrows***. [=to forget about the things that were making him sad by getting drunk]

[2]sorrow *verb* **-rows; -rowed; -row·ing** [*no obj*] *formal* + *literary* : to feel or express sorrow • a *sorrowing* mother, grieving over the death of her son

sor·row·ful /ˈsɑrəfəl/ *adj* [*more* ~; *most* ~] *formal* + *literary* : feeling or showing sadness : full of sorrow • a *sorrowful* young man • a *sorrowful* goodbye • *sorrowful* eyes • Her expression was *sorrowful*.
— **sor·row·ful·ly** *adv*

sor·ry /ˈsɑri/ *adj* **sor·ri·er; -est** [*more* ~; *most* ~]
1 : feeling sorrow or regret • I'm *sorry* if I offended you. • She was *sorry* to hear about their divorce. • I'm *sorry* for your loss. • I'm *sorry* for saying that. • I'm *sorry* that I wasted your time. • He ***felt sorry for*** her. [=he felt sympathy for her because she was in a bad situation] • Stop ***feeling sorry for yourself***. [=feeling pity for yourself] • It's probably not necessary to check the figures again, but ***(it's) better (to be) safe than sorry***. [=it is better to be careful now so that problems do not occur later on]
2 a — used to express polite regret • *Sorry*, but I disagree. • *Sorry* [=*excuse me*], I didn't mean to interrupt you. **b** — used to introduce disappointing or bad news in a polite way • I'm *sorry*, but I couldn't find any information for you. • *Sorry*, but it's too late to change our plans. **c** — used as an apology for a minor fault or offense (such as bumping into someone) • *Sorry*. I didn't see you standing there. • I forgot to pick up the dry cleaning. ***Sorry about that***. [=I'm sorry; I apologize] **d** — used as a polite way of asking someone to repeat something spoken • *Sorry*? [=*Pardon*?] I couldn't hear what you said. **e** — used to introduce a correction to what you have said or written • (*humorous*) Any football nut—*sorry*, fan—will know what I mean.
3 *always used before a noun* **a** : very bad or poor • What a *sorry* state of affairs we're in now. • That's the *sorriest* excuse I've heard. **b** : causing feelings of disappointment or pity • The *sorry* [=*sad*] truth is that he was right all along. • I dragged my *sorry* [=*pitiful*] self out of bed.

[1]sort /ˈsoɚt/ *noun, pl* **sorts**
1 [*count*] : a group of people or things that have some shared quality : a particular kind or type of person or thing • animals of various *sorts* • What *sort* of car do you drive? • Is this some *sort* of a joke? [=is this a joke?]
2 [*singular*] : a person of a particular type • He's not a bad *sort*. • She's not the *sort* to complain.
3 [*count*] *technical* : the act of separating things and putting them in a particular order : the act of sorting things • The program did a numeric *sort* of the data.
all sorts of : a large number or variety of (things or people) : MANY • The movie appeals to *all sorts of* people. • They've been having *all sorts of* problems. [=they've been having a lot of problems]
of sorts or ***of a sort*** : in some ways but not entirely or exactly • It was a vacation *of sorts*. [=it was like a vacation in some ways, although it wasn't really a vacation] • He's a poet *of sorts*. [=he writes some poetry but he is not really a poet]
of the sort : like the person or thing mentioned • "You said you didn't like him." "I said nothing *of the sort*." [=I didn't say that at all] • I would like to go to a movie or a concert, or something *of the sort*. [=something like that]
out of sorts **1** : somewhat angry or unhappy • My boss is (feeling) *out of sorts* today. **2** : somewhat ill • I don't know what's wrong with me, but I'm feeling a little *out of sorts*.
sort of *informal* : to some small degree : slightly or somewhat • I feel *sort of* foolish. • I think he *sort of* likes me. • You look *sort of* like my cousin. • "Did you enjoy the movie?" "*Sort of*." • The walls were (painted) *sort of* blue. = The walls were (painted in) *sort of* a blue color.

[2]sort *verb* **sorts; sort·ed; sort·ing** [+ *obj*]
1 : to separate and put (people or things) in a particular order • She started to *sort* the mail. • They *sorted* the winners from the losers. • The program can *sort* data alphabetically or numerically. — often + *out* • He *sorted out* the socks by color. • I finally *sorted out* the mess in the attic.
2 *Brit, informal* : to deal with (something or someone) in a successful way • We need to get this problem *sorted*. [=*sorted out*]
sort out [*phrasal verb*] **1 *sort (something) out*** or ***sort out (something)*** **a** : to understand or find (something, such as a reason or a solution) by thinking • I'm trying to *sort out* [=*find out, figure out*] a way to do it. **b** : to find an answer or solution for (something) • He's still trying to *sort out* his problems. • We need to get these problems *sorted out* as soon as possible. **c** ✧ If something ***sorts itself out***, it stops being a problem without anyone having to do anything. •

They decided to wait until things *sorted themselves out*. **2** ***sort (someone) out or sort out (someone)*** **a** : to solve the problems of (someone) • They're still trying to *sort* their son *out*. [=trying to sort out their son's problems] • I just need a little more time to ***sort myself out***. **b** *Brit, informal* : to deal with (someone who is causing problems) in a forceful way • I told my brother they were bullying me, and he promised to *sort* them *out* (for me). — see also [2]SORT 1 (above)

sort through [*phrasal verb*] ***sort through (something)*** : to look at things and put them in a particular order especially while you are searching for something • He *sorted through* the papers.

– sort·er *noun, pl* **-ers** [*count*]

sorta /ˈsoɚtə/ — used in writing to represent the sound of the phrase *sort of* when it is spoken quickly • It's *sorta* cold out. ✧ The pronunciation represented by *sorta* is common in informal speech. The written form should be avoided except when trying to represent or record such speech.

sor·tie /ˈsoɚti/ *noun, pl* **-ties** [*count*]
1 : a sudden attack in which a group of soldiers rush forward against an enemy
2 : a mission or attack by a single plane

sort–out *noun* [*singular*] *Brit* : an activity in which you make a room, closet, etc., neat and organized • Let's have a *sort-out* of the attic.

SOS /ˌɛsˌoʊˈɛs/ *noun* [*singular*] : a signal used by ships and airplanes to call for help — often used figuratively • The team sent out an *SOS* for a replacement player. • The club has issued an *SOS* for volunteers. — compare MAYDAY

so–so /ˈsoʊˈsoʊ/ *adj, informal* : neither very good nor very bad : fair or average • The reviews were only *so-so*. • a *so-so* movie/performance • The food was good, but the service was just *so-so*.

sot /ˈsɑːt/ *noun, pl* **sots** [*count*] *old-fashioned* : a person who is often drunk : DRUNKARD • a pathetic old *sot*

sot·to vo·ce /ˌsɑːtoʊˈvoʊʧi/ *adv*
1 *formal* : in a very quiet voice • He gave his opinion *sotto voce*.
2 *music* : very softly • play the last part *sotto voce*
– sotto voce *adj* • *sotto voce* comments

sou /ˈsuː/ *noun* [*singular*] *chiefly Brit, informal* : a small amount of money • I'm not giving you anything. Not a *sou*.

soubriquet *variant spelling of* SOBRIQUET

souf·flé /suˈfleɪ/ *noun, pl* **-flés** : a food that is made with eggs, flour, and other ingredients (such as cheese, vegetables, fruit, or chocolate) and that is baked until its top rises and it becomes very light and fluffy [*count*] cheese *soufflés* [*noncount*] a serving of chocolate *soufflé*

sought *past tense and past participle of* SEEK

sought–after *adj* [*more* ~; *most* ~] : wanted by many people and hard to get or find • *sought-after* antiques • the most *sought-after* artists

souk /ˈsuːk/ *noun, pl* **souks** [*count*] : a marketplace in North Africa or the Middle East

soul /ˈsoʊl/ *noun, pl* **souls**
1 [*count*] **a** : the spiritual part of a person that is believed to give life to the body and in many religions is believed to live forever • salvation of the human *soul* [=*spirit*] • the *souls* of the dead **b** : a person's deeply felt moral and emotional nature • He could not escape the guilt that he felt in the inner recesses of his *soul*.
2 [*noncount*] : the ability of a person to feel kindness and sympathy for others, to appreciate beauty and art, etc. • She has no *soul*.
3 [*count*] : a human being : PERSON • a brave/gentle/kind *soul* • Some poor *soul* was asking for handouts on the street. • There wasn't a *soul* in sight. [=there wasn't anyone in sight] • He didn't tell a *soul* [=*anyone*] that he was leaving. • a village of barely a hundred *souls*
4 [*noncount*] : a quality that gives emotional force and effectiveness to a performance, a work of art, etc. • He's a skillful performer, but his music lacks *soul*.
5 [*noncount*] : SOUL MUSIC • My favorite types of music are jazz and *soul*.
6 [*singular*] : a person who has a lot of a particular quality — + *of* • He is the *soul of* integrity. [=he is a very honest person] • I promise I'll be ***the soul of discretion***. [=I'll be very discreet]
7 [*singular*] : the central or most important part of something that makes it effective, valuable, etc. — usually + *of* • Honesty is the very *soul of* any good relationship. • Our employees are the ***heart and soul of*** our company.
bless my soul see BLESS
body and soul see BODY
keep body and soul together see BODY
pour your soul out see POUR
sell your soul (to the devil) see [1]SELL

soul brother *noun, pl* ~ **-thers** [*count*] *US, informal + old-fashioned* : a black man or boy — called also *brother*

soul–destroying *adj* [*more* ~; *most* ~] : causing a person to feel very unhappy or depressed • the *soul-destroying* confinement of city life • Rejection is *soul-destroying*.

soul food *noun* [*noncount*] : the type of food traditionally eaten by African-Americans in the southern U.S.

soul·ful /ˈsoʊlfəl/ *adj* [*more* ~; *most* ~] : full of or expressing feeling or emotion • *soulful* music • a *soulful* perfomer • a handsome actor with *soulful* eyes
– soul·ful·ly *adv* • She sang *soulfully*. **– soul·ful·ness** *noun* [*noncount*]

soul·less /ˈsoʊlləs/ *adj*
1 : not having or showing any of the qualities and feelings (such as sympathy and kindness) that make people appealing • a government run by *soulless* bureaucrats • These companies are heartless, *soulless*, money-making machines.
2 : having or showing no special or interesting qualities • The houses in the new development are completely *soulless*.
– soul·less·ly *adv* **– soul·less·ness** *noun* [*noncount*]

soul mate *noun, pl* ~ **mates** [*count*]
1 : a close friend who completely understands you • a husband and wife who are perfect *soul mates*
2 : a person who has the same beliefs and opinons as another person • They are ideological *soul mates*.

soul music *noun* [*noncount*] : a popular style of music expressing deep emotion that was created by African-Americans

soul–search·ing /ˈsoʊlˌsɚʧɪŋ/ *noun* [*noncount*] : the activity of thinking seriously about your feelings and beliefs in order to make a decision or to understand the reasons for your own behavior • I decided to take the job after a lot of *soul-searching*.

[1]**sound** /ˈsaʊnd/ *noun, pl* **sounds**
1 : something that is heard [*count*] the *sound* of footsteps/thunder • the *sounds* of laughter • I heard a loud, buzzing *sound*. [=*noise*] • I didn't hear a *sound*. [=I didn't hear anything] • They never made a *sound*. • speech *sounds* [=the sounds people make when they speak words] • the *sound* of "th" in "this" [*noncount*] devices used to record *sound* • measuring the speed of *sound* [=the speed at which the vibrations that create sounds move through the air]
2 [*noncount*] : the speech, music, etc., that is heard as part of a broadcast, film, or recording • The film was good, but the *sound* was poor. • digital *sound* • "Can you turn up the *sound*? [=*volume*] I can't hear what they're saying."
3 [*count*] : the particular musical style of an individual, a group, or an area — usually singular • the Nashville *sound* • I like the band's *sound*.
4 [*noncount*] : the idea that is suggested when something is said or described • "The doctor says my case is unusual." "I ***don't like the sound of that***." [=I don't like the way that sounds; that sounds bad/serious] • ***By/from the sound of it***, you may have poison ivy.
sound and fury : loud and angry words that attract a lot of attention but do nothing useful • The town meeting created lots of *sound and fury*, but no resolution.
— compare [5]SOUND

[2]**sound** *verb* **sounds; sound·ed; sound·ing**
1 a [+ *obj*] : to cause (something) to make a sound or be heard • *sound* a trumpet • *sound* a horn/buzzer — sometimes used figuratively • He *sounded* a confident note [=he expressed confidence] when he talked about the company's future plans. **b** [+ *obj*] : to make (something) known by making a sound • They *sounded* the alarm. • The clock *sounded* noon. **c** [*no obj*] : to make a sound • The game was over when the buzzer *sounded*. • A ringing noise kept *sounding* in his ears.
2 [*linking verb*] : to seem to be something when heard • You *sound* tired. You should get some rest. : to seem to be something when heard about • Their plan *sounds* good to me. • Her story *sounds* false. • It *sounded* too good to be true. • I'll plan to pick you up at noon. How does that *sound*? [=do you think that is a good/acceptable plan?] • His new job *sounds* exciting. • A picnic *sounds* lovely. — often used in the phrases ***sound as if, sound as though***, and ***sound like*** • It *sounds* to

S

me *as if* they won't be coming. ▪ The movie *sounds as though* it might be good. [=the things I have heard about the movie suggest that it might be good] ▪ It *sounds like* the weather may be bad tomorrow. [=I have heard that the weather may be bad tomorrow] ▪ You *sound like* you're tired. ▪ That *sounds like* a good idea. = (*Brit*) That *sounds* a good idea. — see also SOUND LIKE (below)
3 [+ *obj*] **:** to make the sound of (a word or letter) with your voice **:** PRONOUNCE ▪ He *sounded* each syllable clearly. ▪ The "k" in "know" is not *sounded*.
sound like **1 :** to have a voice that is like the voice of (someone else) ▪ I knew he must be your brother. He *sounds* just *like* you. **2 :** to say something that is like what is commonly said by (someone else) ▪ You *sound* just *like* your mother when you say that.
sound off [*phrasal verb*] **1 :** to say your opinions in a very direct and often angry way ▪ She *sounded off* about the unequal pay raises. **2** *US* **:** to count out loud the steps you take while marching ▪ The troops were *sounding off* during their exercises.
– compare [6]SOUND

[3]sound *adj* **sound·er; -est** [*also more* ~; *most* ~]
1 a : in good condition **:** solid and strong ▪ a building of *sound* construction ▪ The bridge is structurally *sound*. **b :** in good health **:** HEALTHY ▪ a *sound* mind in a *sound* body ▪ The tests show that his heart is *sound*. ▪ My health is *sound*. [=I am healthy] ▪ (*law*) He was found to be ***of sound mind*** [=*sane*] when he committed the murder.
2 : free from mistakes **:** showing good judgment ▪ a *sound* argument ▪ She used *sound* reasoning in making the decision. ▪ She gave us some *sound* advice. ▪ a *sound* investment
3 *always used before a noun* **:** complete or thorough ▪ She has a *sound* understanding of the system's structure. ▪ The stock market has made a *sound* recovery. ▪ They gave us a *sound* beating in yesterday's game. [=they beat/defeated us easily by a large amount]
4 *of sleep* **:** deep and restful ▪ She fell into a *sound* sleep. ▪ I was never a ***sound sleeper***. [=someone who sleeps deeply]
(as) sound as a bell *informal* **:** in excellent condition ▪ There's nothing wrong with your health. You're *as sound as a bell*. ▪ The car's engine is *as sound as a bell*.
– sound·ly /ˈsaʊndli/ *adv* ▪ I slept more *soundly* last night than I have in a while. ▪ an argument *soundly* based on logic ▪ We were *soundly* beaten/defeated in yesterday's game.
– sound·ness /ˈsaʊndnəs/ *noun* [*noncount*]

[4]sound *adv, of sleep* **:** deeply and completely ▪ He was *sound* asleep. ▪ She slept *sound*. [=(more commonly) *soundly*]

[5]sound *noun, pl* **sounds** [*count*] **:** a long and narrow area of water that connects two larger areas — often used in names ▪ Long Island *Sound* — compare [1]SOUND

[6]sound *verb* **sounds; sounded; sounding** [+ *obj*] *technical* **:** to measure the depth of the water in a lake, ocean, etc.
sound out [*phrasal verb*] ***sound (someone or something) out or sound out (someone or something)*** **:** to try to find out the opinions of someone by asking questions ▪ They *sounded* me *out* on the idea. [=they asked me what I thought about the idea] ▪ polls that *sound out* public opinion
– compare [2]SOUND

sound barrier *noun*
the sound barrier **:** the large increase in air resistance that occurs as an aircraft nears the speed of sound ▪ a plane that is able to ***break the sound barrier*** [=to travel faster than the speed of sound]

sound bite *noun, pl* ~ **bites** [*count*] **:** a short recorded statement that is broadcast on a television or radio news program ▪ His campaign relies on catchy *sound bites*.

sound card *noun, pl* ~ **cards** [*count*] *computers* **:** a device in a computer system designed to produce or reproduce sound

sound·ing /ˈsaʊndɪŋ/ *noun, pl* **-ings** [*count*]
1 : a measurement of the depth of water ▪ The sailors were taking *soundings* as the ship approached the coast.
2 : something that is done to find out what people think about something — usually plural ▪ They took *soundings* on his chances of winning. [=they talked to and questioned people about his chances of winning]

sounding board *noun, pl* ~ **boards** [*count*] **:** a person or group with whom you discuss ideas to see if the ideas are good ▪ My friend is my *sounding board* for new ideas.

sound·less /ˈsaʊndləs/ *adj* **:** making no sound **:** SILENT ▪ Her footsteps were *soundless*. ▪ the almost *soundless* approach of the boat
– sound·less·ly *adv* ▪ The cat moved *soundlessly* through the room.

[1]sound·proof /ˈsaʊndˌpruːf/ *adj* [*more* ~; *most* ~] **:** not allowing sound to enter or leave ▪ a *soundproof* room/studio ▪ *soundproof* walls

[2]soundproof *verb* **-proofs; -proofed; -proof·ing** [+ *obj*] **:** to make (something) soundproof ▪ *soundproof* a room ▪ The studio is *soundproofed*.

sound system *noun, pl* ~ **-tems** [*count*] **:** equipment that is used to play music through speakers

sound·track /ˈsaʊndˌtræk/ *noun, pl* **-tracks** [*count*] **:** the sounds and especially the music recorded for a movie ▪ The movie's *soundtrack* is now available on CD.

sound wave *noun, pl* ~ **waves** [*count*] **:** a wave that is formed when a sound is made and that moves through the air and carries the sound to your ear

[1]soup /ˈsuːp/ *noun, pl* **soups :** a food made by cooking vegetables, meat, or fish in a large amount of liquid [*count*] a delicious chicken *soup* [*noncount*] a bowl of *soup* ▪ a *soup* spoon — see also PEA SOUP
in the soup *informal + old-fashioned* **:** in a bad situation **:** in trouble ▪ That stunt landed her *in the soup*.
soup to nuts *US, informal* **1 :** covering every detail or part of something ▪ The book provides a *soup to nuts* look at the current political scene. **2** ***from soup to nuts*** **:** in every detail or part ▪ The entire procedure *from soup to nuts* is changing.

[2]soup *verb* **soups; souped; soup·ing**
soup up [*phrasal verb*] ***soup (something) up or soup up (something)*** *informal* **:** to increase the power of (something, such as an engine) ▪ *soup up* a car's engine ▪ His hobby was *souping up* older cars. — see also SOUPED-UP

soup·çon /ˈsuːpˌsɑːn/ *noun, pl* **-çons** [*count*] **:** a small amount of something **:** TRACE ▪ Add just a *soupçon* of salt.

souped–up /ˈsuːptˈʌp/ *adj* **:** made greater in power or appeal ▪ *souped-up* cars ▪ My computer is a *souped-up* version of the standard machines. — see also *soup up* at [2]SOUP

soup kitchen *noun, pl* ~ **-chens** [*count*] **:** a place that gives food (such as soup and bread) to poor people

soupy /ˈsuːpi/ *adj* **soup·i·er; -est**
1 : resembling soup ▪ The gravy/sauce was too *soupy*.
2 *informal* **:** very foggy or cloudy ▪ *soupy* weather

[1]sour /ˈsawɚ/ *adj* **sour·er; -est** [*also more* ~; *most* ~]
1 : having an acid taste that is like the taste of a lemon **:** TART ▪ *sour* pickles ▪ a *sour* apple ▪ a slightly *sour* taste — see also SWEET-AND-SOUR
2 : having the unpleasant taste or smell of food that is no longer fresh ▪ The milk had turned/gone *sour*. ▪ The cream smells *sour*. ▪ a *sour* odor ▪ *sour* [=*bad*] breath
3 : unpleasant or unfriendly ▪ a *sour*, cynical person ▪ He made a *sour* face. ▪ Their relationship ended ***on a sour note***. [=ended unpleasantly]
4 *informal* **:** bad or wrong ▪ Their relationship had turned/gone *sour*. ▪ All their investments went *sour*.
sour on *informal* **:** having a bad opinion of (something) ▪ She was *sour on* politics in general.
– sour·ly *adv* ▪ She noted *sourly* that something was wrong.
– sour·ness *noun* [*noncount*] ▪ The dish gets its *sourness* from lemons.

[2]sour *noun, pl* **sours** [*count*] **:** an alcoholic drink that has a sour taste ▪ a whiskey *sour*

[3]sour *verb* **sours; soured; sour·ing**
1 [*no obj*] *of food* **:** to lose freshness and get an unpleasant taste or smell **:** to become sour ▪ The milk *soured* quickly.
2 a [*no obj*] **:** to become unpleasant or unfriendly ▪ Her disposition has *soured* in recent years. ▪ Their friendship has *soured*. [=they are no longer friends] **b** [+ *obj*] **:** to make (someone or something) unpleasant or unfriendly ▪ Jealousy has *soured* their relationship. ▪ His experiences have *soured* him.
3 [+ *obj*] **:** to make (something good) less pleasant or enjoyable ▪ The team's victory was *soured* by an injury to one of their best players.
sour on [*phrasal verb*] ***sour on (something) or sour (someone) on (something)*** *US* **:** to stop liking or being interested in (something) or to cause (someone) to stop liking or being interested in (something) ▪ Investors have *soured on* (buying) the company's stock. ▪ Many fans have *soured on* the team after years of losing. ▪ The disappointing result of the election *soured* her *on* politics.

source /ˈsoɚs/ *noun, pl* **sourc·es** [*count*]

1 : someone or something that provides what is wanted or needed • The college had its own power *source.* • a water *source* = a *source* of water • She has been a great *source* of strength to me. • His job is the family's main *source* of income.
2 : the cause of something (such as a problem) — usually + *of* • The delays are a *source of* concern. • The team's bad play has been a *source of* disappointment.
3 : a person, book, etc., that gives information • A government *source* spoke to the press today. • The reporter has refused to reveal his *sources.* • According to one *source,* the program will not cost a lot. • information from various intelligence *sources* • print *sources* • a reference *source*
4 : the beginning of a stream or river of water • the *source* of the Nile

sour cream *noun [noncount]* : a thick cream that has a sour flavor • He put *sour cream* on his baked potato. — called also *(Brit)* *soured cream*

sour·dough /ˈsawɚˌdoʊ/ *noun [noncount]* : a type of dough that is allowed to ferment before it is baked and that has a slightly sour taste • *sourdough* bread

sour grapes *noun [plural] informal* : unfair criticism that comes from someone who is disappointed about not getting something • His remarks are nothing but *sour grapes.*

sour·puss /ˈsawɚˌpʊs/ *noun, pl* **-puss·es** *[count] informal* : a person who complains frequently or constantly and looks unhappy • He's just an old *sourpuss.*

soused /ˈsaʊst/ *adj*
1 : completely covered by a liquid • cucumbers *soused* in vinegar
2 *informal* : very drunk • He sat at the bar quietly getting *soused.*

[1]**south** /ˈsaʊθ/ *noun*
1 *[noncount]* : the direction that is to your right when you are facing the rising sun : the direction that is the opposite of north • The nearest town is 20 miles to the *south* (of here). • The wind blew from the *south.* • Which way is *south?*
2 ***the south or the South*** : regions or countries south of a certain point • The birds migrate from *the South.*; *especially* : the southern part of the U.S. • Parts of *the South* were hit hard by the storm. • I grew up in *the South.* • The American Civil War was between the North and *the South.*

[2]**south** *adj*
1 : located in or toward the south • the *south* entrance • *South* America
2 : coming from the south • a *south* wind

[3]**south** *adv*
1 : to or toward the south • Turn *south* onto Elm Street. • It's a mile *south* of here. • The birds fly/go *south* in the winter.
2 *US, informal* : into a worse state or condition • The company's profits have ***gone south*** in recent months. • The TV show's ratings have been ***heading south.***
down south informal : in or to the southern part of a country or region • She spent a few years *down south.* • We'll be heading *down south* for the winter. — compare *up north* at [3]NORTH

south·bound /ˈsaʊθˌbaʊnd/ *adj* : going or heading south • a *southbound* train • The *southbound* lanes are closed to traffic.

[1]**south·east** /saʊθˈiːst/ *noun*
1 *[noncount]* : the direction between south and east
2 ***the southeast or the Southeast*** : the southeastern part of a country or region • A mountain range is in *the southeast* of the country.; *especially* : the southeastern part of the U.S. • Rain is moving into *the Southeast.* • He grew up in *the Southeast.*

[2]**southeast** *adj*
1 : located in or toward the southeast • *southeast* Europe • My office is in the *southeast* corner of the building.
2 : coming from the southeast • a *southeast* wind

[3]**south·east** *adv* : to or toward the southeast • It's a few miles *southeast* of here. • We headed *southeast.*

south·east·er /saʊθˈiːstɚ/ *noun, pl* **-ers** *[count]*
1 : a strong wind that blows from the southeast
2 : a storm with winds that blow from the southeast

south·east·er·ly /saʊθˈiːstɚli/ *adj*
1 : located in or moving toward the southeast • They sailed in a *southeasterly* direction.
2 : blowing from the southeast • *southeasterly* winds

south·east·ern /saʊθˈiːstɚn/ *adj*
1 : located in or toward the southeast • the *southeastern* corner of the state
2 : of or relating to the southeast • a *southeastern* bird

south·east·ern·er *or* **South·east·ern·er** /saʊθˈiːstɚnɚ/ *noun, pl* **-ers** *[count]* : a person born, raised, or living in the southeast; *especially* : a person born, raised, or living in the southeastern U.S.

south·east·ward /saʊθˈiːstwɚd/ *also chiefly Brit* **south·east·wards** /saʊθˈiːstwɚdz/ *adv* : toward the southeast • The storm is moving *southeastward.*
– southeastward *adj* • The storm followed a *southeastward* course.

south·er·ly /ˈsʌðɚli/ *adj [more ~; most ~]*
1 : located in or moving toward the south • *southerly* latitudes • We sailed in a *southerly* direction.
2 : blowing from the south • a *southerly* wind
– southerly *adv* • We sailed *southerly* around the island. • The storm is headed *southerly.*

south·ern /ˈsʌðɚn/ *adj*
1 *[more ~; most ~]* : located in or toward the south • *southern* U.S. • the *southern* part of the state • the *southern* shore of the lake
2 **a** : of or relating to the south • a *southern* species • *southern* cities **b** ***Southern*** : of or relating to the people born, raised, or living in the southeastern U.S. • a *Southern* accent • *Southern* hospitality/cooking

south·ern·er *or* **South·ern·er** /ˈsʌðɚnɚ/ *noun, pl* **-ers** *[count]* : a person born, raised, or living in the south; *especially* : a person born, raised, or living in the southern U.S. — compare NORTHERNER

Southern Lights *noun*
the Southern Lights : large areas of green, red, blue, or yellow light that sometimes appear in the night sky in far southern regions — called also *aurora australis*

south·ern·most /ˈsʌðɚnˌmoʊst/ *adj* : furthest to the south • the *southernmost* tip of the island

south·paw /ˈsaʊθˌpɑː/ *noun, pl* **-paws** *[count] informal* : someone who is left-handed; *especially* : a left-handed baseball pitcher or boxer

South Pole *noun*
the South Pole : the most southern point on the surface of the earth

south·ward /ˈsaʊθˌwɚd/ *also chiefly Brit* **south·wards** /ˈsaʊθˌwɚdz/ *adv* : toward the south • birds flying *southward*
– southward *adj* • a *southward* course/expansion

[1]**south·west** /saʊθˈwɛst/ *noun*
1 *[noncount]* : the direction between south and west
2 ***the southwest or the Southwest*** : the southwestern part of a country or region • A mountain range is in *the southwest* of the country.; *especially* : the southwestern part of the U.S. • These plants grow in *the Southwest.*

[2]**southwest** *adj*
1 : located in the southwest • the *southwest* corner of the building • *southwest* France
2 : blowing from the southwest • a *southwest* wind

[3]**southwest** *adv* : to or toward the southwest • It's about 80 miles *southwest* of here. • traveling *southwest*

south·west·er·ly /saʊθˈwɛstɚli/ *adj*
1 : located in or moving toward the southwest • The storm is headed in a *southwesterly* direction.
2 : blowing from the southwest • a *southwesterly* wind
– southwesterly *adv* • We sailed *southwesterly.*

south·west·ern /saʊθˈwɛstɚn/ *adj*
1 : in, toward, or from the southwest • *southwestern* Arizona • the *southwestern* border
2 : of or relating to the southwest • a *southwestern* bird

south·west·ern·er *or* **South·west·ern·er** /saʊθˈwɛstɚnɚ/ *noun, pl* **-ers** *[count]* : a person born, raised, or living in the southwest; *especially* : a person born, raised, or living in the southwestern U.S.

south·west·ward /saʊθˈwɛstwɚd/ *also chiefly Brit* **south·west·wards** /saʊθˈwɛstwɚdz/ *adv* : toward the southwest • The storm is moving *southwestward.*
– southwestward *adj* • The storm will follow a *southwestward* course.

sou·ve·nir /ˌsuːvəˈniɚ/ *noun, pl* **-nirs** *[count]* : something that is kept as a reminder of a place you have visited, an event you have been to, etc. • When I went to the Super Bowl, I kept my ticket stub as a *souvenir.* • a ***souvenir shop*** [=a shop that sells souvenirs] — often + *of* • This coffee mug is a *souvenir of* our trip to Hawaii.

sou'·west·er /saʊˈwɛstɚ/ *noun, pl* **-ers** *[count]*
1 : a hat that is worn when it rains and that is longer in the

S

back than in the front and ties under the chin
2 : a long coat worn by sailors that keeps them dry during stormy weather

[1]**sov·er·eign** /ˈsɑːvrən/ *noun, pl* **-eigns** [*count*]
1 *formal* **:** a king or queen ▪ a Spanish *sovereign*
2 : a British gold coin that was used in the past

[2]**sovereign** *adj, formal*
1 a : having unlimited power or authority ▪ a *sovereign* prince **b :** not limited ▪ the *sovereign* power of a king
2 : having independent authority and the right to govern itself ▪ a *sovereign* state/nation
3 *US* **:** highest and most important ▪ The government's *sovereign* duty is to protect the rights of its citizens.

sov·er·eign·ty /ˈsɑːvrənti/ *noun* [*noncount*]
1 : unlimited power over a country — often + *over* ▪ He claimed *sovereignty over* the nation.
2 : a country's independent authority and the right to govern itself ▪ national *sovereignty* ▪ a claim of/to *sovereignty*

so·vi·et /ˈsouviˌɛt/ *noun, pl* **-ets**
1 [*count*] **:** an elected council in the former U.S.S.R.
2 ***Soviets*** [*plural*] *chiefly US* **:** the people and especially the political and military leaders of the former U.S.S.R. ▪ disputes between Americans and *Soviets* ▪ The plan was opposed by ***the Soviets***.

Soviet *adj* **:** of or relating to the former U.S.S.R. or its people ▪ the *Soviet* government

[1]**sow** /ˈsou/ *verb* **sows; sowed; sown** /ˈsoun/ *or* **sowed; sow·ing**
1 : to plant seeds in an area of ground [*+ obj*] Every year we *sow* corn. ▪ Farmers *sowed* the fields with corn. [*no obj*] We'll *sow* in the early spring.
2 [*+ obj*] **:** to cause (fear, doubt, etc.) to affect many people ▪ Threats of war have *sown* fear in the region. [=have made many people in the region afraid] ▪ They have been deliberately attempting to *sow* discord. [=to cause people to disagree and argue with each other]
reap what you sow see REAP
sow the seeds of **:** to create a situation in which (something) is likely or certain to happen or develop ▪ Opponents have succeeded in *sowing the seeds of* suspicion/doubt. [=have succeeded in making people have suspicions/doubts] ▪ They have *sowed the seeds of* their own destruction. [=they have done something that will lead to their own destruction]
sow your (wild) oats **:** to have many sexual relationships particularly when you are young ▪ He *sowed his wild oats* in his younger years, but he's married now and has a family.
— sow·er /ˈsowɚ/ *noun, pl* **-ers** [*count*]

[2]**sow** /ˈsau/ *noun, pl* **sows** [*count*] **:** a fully grown female pig

soy /ˈsoɪ/ *noun* [*noncount*] *US*
1 : soybeans and the food products that are made from soybeans ▪ His book promotes the health benefits of *soy*. — often used before another noun ▪ *soy* flour ▪ *soy* milk [=a drink that resembles cow's milk but that is made from soybeans]
2 : SOY SAUCE ▪ The recipe calls for two tablespoons of *soy*.

soya /ˈsojə/ *noun* [*noncount*] *Brit* **:** soybeans and the food products that are made from soybeans **:** SOY

soy·bean /ˈsoɪˌbiːn/ *noun, pl* **-beans** [*count*] *US* **:** the bean of an Asian plant that contains a large amount of protein and that is used as a food — called also (*Brit*) *soya bean*

soy sauce *noun* [*noncount*] **:** a brown sauce that is made from soybeans and used especially in Chinese and Japanese cooking — called also (*Brit*) *soya sauce*

soz·zled /ˈsɑːzəld/ *adj, slang* **:** very drunk ▪ He got *sozzled* at the party last night.

spa /ˈspɑː/ *noun, pl* **spas** [*count*]
1 a : a place where water that has many minerals in it comes up naturally from the ground and where people go to improve their health by swimming in, bathing in, or drinking the water **b :** a place where people go to improve their health and appearance by exercising, relaxing, etc. — called also *health spa*, (*chiefly Brit*) *health farm*
2 *US* **:** a bathtub in which a pump causes hot water and air bubbles to move around your body ▪ Their property includes a swimming pool and *spa*.

[1]**space** /ˈspeɪs/ *noun, pl* **spac·es**
1 a [*noncount*] **:** the amount of an area, room, surface, etc., that is empty or available for use ▪ There's still some *space* for a bookshelf. ▪ the *space* behind/above/near the couch ▪ Is there *space* in the cabinet for these dishes? ▪ There's not much empty/clear *space*. ▪ He moved the books to create more *space* on his desk. ▪ Those old boxes take up a lot of *space*. ▪ There should be plenty of *space* [=*room*] on the disk to save the files. — see also *a waste of space* at [1]WASTE **b :** an area that is used or available for a specific purpose [*count*] a parking *space* ▪ She needs a *space* [=*place*] where she can do her homework. [*noncount*] floor *space* ▪ storage *space* ▪ The magazine devotes a lot of *space* to advertising.
2 a : an empty area between things [*count*] She has a *space* between her front teeth. [*noncount*] There isn't much *space* between our houses. ▪ Is there enough *space* [=*room*] for me to park there? **b :** an area of land with no buildings on it [*plural*] the ***wide open spaces*** of the western U.S. [*noncount*] They live in an area where there's a lot of ***open space***.
3 [*noncount*] **:** the region beyond the Earth's atmosphere in which there are stars and planets **:** OUTER SPACE ▪ sent the satellite into *space* — often used before another noun ▪ *space* exploration/travel ▪ the *space* program [=the program devoted to exploring space]
4 [*noncount*] **:** the limitless area in which all things exist and move ▪ the movement of sound waves through *space* ▪ exploring the relationship between time and *space*
5 [*count*] **:** a period of time — usually singular ▪ a ***short space of time*** [=a short time] ▪ They finished ***in/within the space of*** an hour. [=within an hour]
6 a : a blank area separating written or printed words or lines [*count*] There should be a *space* after the comma. [*noncount*] Let's leave more *space* between the paragraphs. **b :** a blank part or section on a document where something can be written [*count*] There's a *space* for your name and address. [*noncount*] There is *space* at the bottom for your name and address.
7 [*noncount*] **a :** the freedom and time to behave and think as you want to without being controlled or influenced by someone else ▪ I need more *space* in our relationship. **b :** PERSONAL SPACE ▪ You're invading my *space*. [=you're too close to me]
8 [*count*] **:** an available seat on a bus, train, etc. ▪ There are no *spaces* left on the bus.
stare/gaze (off) into space **:** to look straight ahead without looking at anything specific ▪ He wouldn't even look at me. He just sat there, *staring into space*.

[2]**space** *verb* **spaces; spaced; spac·ing** [*+ obj*]
1 : to place or arrange (things) so that there is a particular amount of space between them ▪ widely/closely *spaced* posts ▪ *Space* the seedlings about six inches apart. — often + *out* ▪ Try to *space out* the poles evenly.
2 : to separate (things) by particular periods of time ▪ He *spaces* his albums so that he puts one out every two to three years. ▪ They *spaced* the births of their three children two years apart. — often + *out* ▪ They *spaced out* the births of their three children.
space out [*phrasal verb*] *informal* **:** to stop paying attention **:** to become unaware of what is happening around you ▪ I *spaced out* for a minute and didn't hear what she said. ▪ I *spaced out* halfway through the lecture.

space–age /ˈspeɪsˈeɪʤ/ *adj, informal* **:** very modern ▪ a *space-age* machine/design

space bar *noun, pl* **~ bars** [*count*] **:** the wide key at the bottom of a computer keyboard or typewriter that is used to make a space

space cadet *noun, pl* **~ -dets** [*count*] *informal* **:** a person who does not pay attention or who tends to forget things ▪ Don't be such a *space cadet*.

space·craft /ˈspeɪsˌkræft, *Brit* ˈspeɪsˌkrɑːft/ *noun, pl* **spacecraft** [*count*] **:** a vehicle that is used for travel in outer space

spaced /ˈspeɪst/ *adj* [*more* ~; *most* ~] *US, informal* **:** SPACED OUT ▪ He was too *spaced* on drugs to know what he was doing.

spaced out *adj, informal* **:** unable to think clearly or to pay attention to what is going on around you ▪ He looked like he was *spaced out* on drugs. ▪ I was tired and feeling pretty *spaced out*. ▪ She had a *spaced out* look on her face.

space·flight /ˈspeɪsˌflaɪt/ *noun, pl* **-flights :** flight into outer space in a spacecraft [*count*] the first manned *spaceflight* [*noncount*] a history of human *spaceflight*

space heater *noun, pl* **~ -ers** [*count*] *US* **:** a small device that is used for heating a room

space·man /ˈspeɪsˌmæn/ *noun, pl* **-men** /-ˌmɛn/ [*count*]
1 *informal* **:** a person (especially a man) who travels in a spacecraft into outer space **:** ASTRONAUT
2 *in stories* **:** a visitor to Earth from outer space ▪ *spacemen* from Mars

space probe *noun, pl* ~ **probes** [*count*] : a device that is used to obtain information from outer space and send it back to Earth

space·ship /ˈspeɪs,ʃɪp/ *noun, pl* **-ships** [*count*] : SPACECRAFT

space shuttle *noun, pl* ~ **shuttles** [*count*] : a spacecraft that can be used more than once and that carries people into outer space and back to Earth

space station *noun, pl* ~ **-tions** [*count*] : a large spacecraft in which people live for long periods of time in order to do research and experiments

space suit *noun, pl* ~ **suits** [*count*] : a special suit that is designed to keep astronauts alive in outer space

space walk *noun, pl* ~ **walks** [*count*] : an activity in which an astronaut moves around and does work outside a spacecraft while it is in outer space

spac·ey /ˈspeɪsi/ *adj* **spac·i·er**; **-est** [*also more* ~; *most* ~] : SPACED OUT ▪ I'm a little *spacey* today.

spac·ing /ˈspeɪsɪŋ/ *noun* [*noncount*] : the amount of space between letters, words, or lines on a printed page ▪ The *spacing* between characters should be even.

spa·cious /ˈspeɪʃəs/ *adj* [*more* ~; *most* ~] : having a large amount of space ▪ a *spacious* room/office/house ▪ The dining room is *spacious* [=*roomy*] enough to seat our whole family and several guests.
– **spa·cious·ly** *adv* ▪ a *spaciously* arranged room – **spa·cious·ness** *noun* [*noncount*]

spade /ˈspeɪd/ *noun, pl* **spades**
1 [*count*] : a tool with a heavy metal blade attached to a handle that is used for digging — see picture at GARDENING
2 [*count*] : a playing card that is marked with a black shape that looks like a pointed leaf ▪ two hearts, one club, and three *spades* — see picture at PLAYING CARD
3 ***spades*** [*plural*] : the suit in a deck of playing cards that consists of spades ▪ the queen of *spades*
call a spade a spade : to speak in an honest and direct way ▪ Why don't you just *call a spade a spade* and say that he's a liar?
in spades : to a great degree : in large amounts ▪ We've been having problems *in spades*. ▪ His hard work and dedication were rewarded *in spades*.

spade·work /ˈspeɪd,wɚk/ *noun* [*noncount*] : difficult work that is done especially to prepare for something ▪ She had her assistants do the *spadework* in preparation for the trial.

spa·ghet·ti /spəˈgɛti/ *noun* [*noncount*] : pasta in the shape of long, thin strings — see picture at PASTA

spaghetti strap *noun, pl* ~ **straps** [*count*] : a very thin piece of material that is worn over the shoulder and that holds up a piece of clothing (such as a dress) — see color picture on page C15

spaghetti western *noun, pl* ~ **-erns** [*count*] : a movie about the old American West that is produced in Italy ▪ I'm a fan of *spaghetti westerns* of the 1960s.

spake /ˈspeɪk/ *archaic past tense of* SPEAK

[1]**spam** /ˈspæm/ *noun* [*noncount*] *informal* : e-mail that is not wanted : e-mail that is sent to large numbers of people and that consists mostly of advertising ▪ tips to reduce *spam* ▪ a ***spam filter*** [=software that identifies and blocks spam]

[2]**spam** *verb* **spams**; **spammed**; **spam·ming** [+ *obj*] : to send unwanted e-mail to (someone) ▪ That company keeps *spamming* me. [=keeps sending me spam]
– **spam·mer** *noun, pl* **-mers** [*count*]

Spam /ˈspæm/ *trademark* — used for a type of meat that is sold in cans

[1]**span** /ˈspæn/ *noun, pl* **spans** [*count*]
1 : the period of time between two dates or events ▪ a 25-year *span* ▪ a brief ***time span*** — often + *of* ▪ a brief *span of* time ▪ The symphonies were composed over a *span of* eight years. ▪ I received two job offers within the *span of* a week. — see also ATTENTION SPAN, LIFE SPAN
2 : the part of a bridge or other structure that goes across a space from one support to another
3 : the width of something from one side to the other — often + *of* ▪ the *span of* his shoulders ▪ It's a *span of* a few hundred miles to cross the state. — see also WINGSPAN
— see also SPIC-AND-SPAN

[2]**span** *verb* **spans**; **spanned**; **span·ning** [+ *obj*]
1 : to continue throughout (a period of time) ▪ His career as a singer *spanned* three decades.
2 : to cover or include (a wide area, a large number of things, etc.) ▪ Their empire once *spanned* several continents. ▪ Her academic interests *span* a wide variety of topics.
3 : to cross over (something) ▪ A bridge *spans* the river.

span·dex /ˈspæn,dɛks/ *noun* [*noncount*] : a material that stretches easily and is used especially to make sports clothing; *also* : clothing made of this material

[1]**span·gle** /ˈspæŋgəl/ *verb* **span·gles**; **span·gled**; **span·gling** [+ *obj*] : to decorate or cover (something) with many small, shiny objects — usually used as *(be) spangled* ▪ *spangled* pants/gloves — often used figuratively ▪ a night sky *spangled* with stars

[2]**spangle** *noun, pl* **spangles** [*count*] : a small, shiny piece of metal or plastic that is used to decorate clothing ▪ showgirls dressed in costumes with gold *spangles*

Span·glish /ˈspæŋglɪʃ/ *noun* [*noncount*] *chiefly US* : Spanish that includes the use of English words

Span·iard /ˈspænjɚd/ *noun, pl* **-iards** [*count*] : a person born, raised, or living in Spain : a Spanish person

span·iel /ˈspænjəl/ *noun, pl* **-iels** [*count*] : a type of small dog that has long ears and a soft coat

Span·ish /ˈspænɪʃ/ *noun*
1 [*noncount*] : the language of Spain, Mexico, and many countries in Latin America
2 ***the Spanish*** : the people of Spain : Spanish people
– **Spanish** *adj* ▪ *Spanish* art/cooking/culture/territories ▪ She has a *Spanish* accent.

Spanish American *noun, pl* ~ **-cans** [*count*] : a person living in the U.S. whose native language is Spanish
– **Spanish–American** *adj* ▪ *Spanish-American* culture

Spanish moss *noun* [*noncount*] : a type of American plant that has long gray strands and that hangs down from the branches of trees

Spanish rice *noun* [*noncount*] *US* : rice cooked with onions, green peppers, and tomatoes

spank /ˈspæŋk/ *verb* **spanks**; **spanked**; **spank·ing** [+ *obj*] : to hit (someone) on the buttocks with your hand as a form of punishment ▪ Parents shouldn't *spank* their children.
– **spanking** *noun, pl* **-ings** [*count*] ▪ If you don't stop jumping on the couch, you're going to ***get a spanking***. [=get spanked] ▪ She ***gave him a spanking***. [=spanked him]

spank·ing /ˈspæŋkɪŋ/ *adv, informal* : VERY ▪ ***spanking new*** [=*brand-new*] sneakers ▪ He keeps his apartment ***spanking clean***.

span·ner /ˈspænɚ/ *noun, pl* **-ners** [*count*] *Brit* : [1]WRENCH 1
put/throw a spanner in the works *informal* : to cause something to not go as planned ▪ We were ready to start the project when the bank *threw a spanner in the works* by denying the loan.

[1]**spar** /ˈspaɚ/ *verb* **spars**; **sparred**; **spar·ring** [*no obj*]
1 : to box with someone as a form of training or practice ▪ He's been *sparring* with his trainer.
2 : to argue with someone in a friendly way ▪ They *sparred* playfully over whose team was better. — see also SPARRING PARTNER

[2]**spar** *noun, pl* **spars** [*count*] : a thick pole or similar structure that supports something (such as the sails of a ship or the wing of an aircraft)

[1]**spare** /ˈspeɚ/ *adj* **spar·er**; **spar·est**
1 *always used before a noun* **a** : kept as something extra that can be used if it is needed ▪ a *spare* pair of gloves ▪ *spare* parts ▪ I keep a *spare* set of keys in my desk. ▪ a *spare* bedroom [=an extra bedroom where guests can sleep] — see also SPARE TIRE **b** : available to be used in whatever way you want ▪ He likes to ski in his ***spare time***. [=his free time; the time when he is not working] **c** : not needed by you and available to be shared or given to someone else ▪ Do you have any *spare* cash/change? [=any extra cash/change that you could give to me]
2 : somewhat thin ▪ He has a *spare* frame. ▪ He was tall and *spare*.
3 : simple or plain ▪ I like her *spare* style of writing.
going spare *Brit, informal* : not being used : available for someone to use ▪ land that is *going spare*
go spare *Brit, informal* : to become very angry or upset ▪ My dad *went spare* when he found out what I'd done.
– **spare·ly** *adv* ▪ a *sparely* decorated room – **spare·ness** *noun* [*noncount*] ▪ the *spareness* of her writing

[2]**spare** *verb* **spares**; **spared**; **spar·ing** [+ *obj*]
1 **a** : to choose not to punish or harm (someone) ▪ No one knows why the gunman shot some people and *spared* others. ▪ No one knows why he ***spared their lives***. [=why he didn't kill them] **b** : to not destroy or harm (something) ▪ Some-

S

how the storm *spared* our house while nearby buildings were destroyed.

2 : **to prevent (someone or something) from experiencing or being affected by something unpleasant, harmful, etc.** • She was *spared* from having to answer any more questions. • He wanted to *spare* his family from the stress he had endured. • Our church was *spared* the fate of many others that have been closed. [=our church was not closed] • I could have *spared* myself the trouble. • He *spared* them the embarrassment of a public apology.

3 : **to give (something, such as time, money, etc.) to someone** • Can you *spare* (me) a few minutes? [=can you spend a few minutes with me?] • I can't *spare* the time to see you today. [=I don't have enough time to see you today] • If you could *spare* a cup of sugar, it would save me a trip to the store. • You should ***spare a thought for*** [=think about] those who are less fortunate than you.

4 : **to not do or provide (something)** • Nothing was *spared* by the hotel [=the hotel provided everything possible] to make its guests relaxed and comfortable. • We will ***spare no effort*** [=we will do everything we can] to ensure the safety of the tunnels. • When they go on vacation, they ***spare no expense***. [=they do not worry about spending too much money; they spend a lot of money] • He said that he would *spare no expense* [=he would spend as much money as necessary] to make the restaurant successful.

5 : **to use or give out (something) in small amounts — usually used in negative statements** • More pancakes, please, and don't *spare* the syrup. [=give me a lot of syrup]

spare someone's blushes *Brit, informal* **:** to prevent someone from being embarrassed • The manager spoke up to *spare the blushes* of his young employee.

spare someone's feelings **:** to avoid doing or saying something that will hurt someone emotionally **:** to avoid upsetting someone • He admitted that he hadn't told me the whole story because he wanted to *spare my feelings*.

spare (someone) the details **:** to not tell someone all the unpleasant or boring details about something • "I drank too much last night and got sick." "Please, *spare me the details*."

to spare ✧ If you have money, time, energy, etc., *to spare*, you have more than enough money, time, energy, etc. • He seems to have energy *to spare*. [=he seems to have a lot of energy] • We have very little time *to spare*. [=we do not have a lot of time] • I have no money *to spare* [=I do not have enough money] for such things. • He got there ***with (only) minutes/seconds to spare***. [=he got there only minutes/seconds before he needed to; he got there just in time] • He got there ***with time to spare***. [=he got there early; he got there in plenty of time]

[3]**spare** *noun, pl* **spares** [*count*]

1 : **something extra that is kept to be used if it is needed** • "I've lost the key." "You'll find a *spare* in the drawer." • If that one breaks, I've got a *spare*.; *especially* **:** SPARE TIRE 1 • Most cars come with *spares*.

2 *bowling* **:** **the achievement of knocking down all 10 pins with the first two balls** • He got a strike and two *spares*. • He ***made/bowled a spare***. — compare [2]STRIKE 6

spare·rib /ˈspeɚˌrɪb/ *noun, pl* **-ribs** [*count*] **:** a piece of meat from a pig that includes a rib — usually plural • barbecued *spareribs*

spare tire (*US*) *or Brit* **spare tyre** *noun, pl* ~ **tires** [*count*]

1 : an extra tire for a car

2 *informal* **:** a roll of fat around your waist • I have to go on a diet and try to lose this *spare tire*.

spar·ing /ˈsperɪŋ/ *adj* **:** not using or giving a lot of something • an artist who is *sparing* in her use of color [=who does not use much color] • He has been *sparing* with details about his personal life. [=he has not talked much about his personal life]

– spar·ing·ly /ˈsperɪŋli/ *adv* • He used the funds only *sparingly*.

[1]**spark** /ˈspɑɚk/ *noun, pl* **sparks**

1 [*count*] **a :** a small piece of burning material that comes from a fire or is produced by rubbing or hitting two hard objects together • A *spark* from the fireplace set the rug on fire. • The car's tailpipe made *sparks* as it scraped the road. **b :** a short, bright flash of electricity between two points • A *spark* ignites the stove's burner.

2 [*noncount*] **:** a quality that makes someone or something enjoyable, interesting, successful, etc. • In its fourth year, the TV series has lost its *spark*. • She's a talented gymnast but she doesn't have the *spark* of some of her competitors.

3 [*count*] **:** a small amount of something • A *spark* of hope remains. • Sometimes there were surprising *sparks* of humor in his letters. • occasional *sparks* of insight

4 [*count*] **:** an action, occurrence, etc., that causes something larger to happen • His death was the *spark* that ignited the revolution. • Her suggestion was the *spark* for the entire renovation project.

bright spark *Brit, informal + disapproving* **:** a person who says or does something that seems intelligent but is really not • Who's the *bright spark* who came up with this rotten idea?

sparks fly ✧ When *sparks fly*, it means that two people are either having an argument with each other or are sexually attracted to each other. • The *sparks flew* [=they had an angry argument] when he arrived late for her special dinner. • *Sparks flew* when they met for the first time.

[2]**spark** *verb* **sparks; spark·ing; sparked**

1 [+ *obj*] **:** to cause (something) to start or happen • The question *sparked* a debate. • Her fifth-grade teacher *sparked* her interest in history. — sometimes + *off* • The arrests *sparked off* [=*touched off*] a riot. • His hit *sparked off* [=*started*] a rally that brought in four runs.

2 [*no obj*] **:** to produce sparks • The fire *sparked* and crackled. • The wires made contact and *sparked*.

3 [+ *obj*] **:** to add interest, liveliness, or flavor to (something) • prose *sparked* with humor — often + *up* • *spark up* an otherwise bland sauce

[1]**spar·kle** /ˈspɑɚkəl/ *verb* **spar·kles; spar·kled; spar·kling** [*no obj*]

1 : to produce small flashes of light • The diamond *sparkled*.

2 : to perform very well • The dancers *sparkled* on stage.

3 : to be or become bright and lively • The conversation *sparkled*. • Her eyes *sparkled* with pride. — see also SPARKLING

[2]**sparkle** *noun, pl* **sparkles**

1 : a small flash of bright light [*count*] The sun reflected off the water in bright *sparkles* of light. [*noncount*] He caught the *sparkle* of her diamond out of the corner of his eye.

2 [*noncount*] **:** a lively quality • a performance full of *sparkle* and originality • the *sparkle* in her eyes

spar·kler /ˈspɑɚklɚ/ *noun, pl* **-klers** [*count*] **:** a type of firework that you hold in your hand and that throws off very bright sparks as it burns

sparkling *adj* [*more* ~; *most* ~]

1 : shining with or reflecting bright points of light • the *sparkling* blue sea • *sparkling* jewels

2 : bright and clever • *sparkling* wit

3 : of the best quality **:** excellent or outstanding • a *sparkling* performance • The building is a *sparkling* example of modern architecture at its best. • (*Brit*) athletes in *sparkling* [=*superb, brilliant*] form

4 *always used before a noun* **:** containing bubbles • *sparkling* wine • *sparkling* grape juice

spark plug *noun, pl* ~ **plugs** [*count*] **:** a part of an engine that produces a spark that makes the fuel burn — see picture at ENGINE

sparky /ˈspɑɚki/ *adj* **spark·i·er; -est** *chiefly Brit, informal* **:** lively and energetic • *sparky* youngsters • a *sparky* heroine • *sparky* conversation

sparring partner *noun, pl* ~ **-ners** [*count*]

1 : someone who helps a boxer practice **:** someone a boxer spars with for training

2 : a person that you have serious but friendly arguments with • They have been political *sparring partners* for years.

spar·row /ˈsperoʊ/ *noun, pl* **-rows** [*count*] **:** a common type of small bird that usually has brown or gray feathers — see color picture on page C9

sparse /ˈspɑɚs/ *adj* **spars·er; -est :** present only in small amounts **:** less than necessary or normal • Reliable data is *sparse*.; *especially* **:** thinly covering an area **:** not thick or full • *sparse* vegetation • a *sparse* beard ***synonyms*** see MEAGER

– sparse·ly *adv* • a *sparsely* populated area • The room was *sparsely* furnished. **– sparse·ness** *noun* [*noncount*]

spar·tan *also* **Spar·tan** /ˈspɑɚtn̩/ *adj* [*more* ~; *most* ~] **:** very bare and simple **:** lacking the things that make life comfortable or more pleasant • They lived in *spartan* conditions.

spasm /ˈspæzəm/ *noun, pl* **spasms** [*count*]

1 : a sudden uncontrolled and often painful tightening of a muscle • violent back *spasms* • a disease that causes muscle *spasms*

2 : a sudden and usually brief occurrence of something you cannot control • He was racked with coughing *spasms.* • She was suffering *spasms* of guilt. • *spasms* of joy/rage

spas·mod·ic /spæzˈmɑːdɪk/ *adj*
1 : relating to or caused by a spasm • *spasmodic* movements/jerks
2 : happening suddenly and briefly at different times in a way that is not regular • He made only *spasmodic* attempts to lose weight. • *spasmodic* [=*intermittent*] activity
– **spas·mod·i·cal·ly** /spæzˈmɑːdɪkli/ *adv* • His neck was jerking *spasmodically.* • Outbursts of violence continued *spasmodically* after the war ended.

spas·tic /ˈspæstɪk/ *adj*
1 *medical* **a** : relating to or affected with spasms • a *spastic* colon • *spastic* paralysis **b** *old-fashioned* : suffering from cerebral palsy or a similar disease that causes uncontrolled movements • a *spastic* child
2 [*more* ~; *most* ~] *informal* : having movements like spasms : clumsy or awkward • *spastic* fingers • *spastic* dancing
– **spastic** *noun, pl* **-tics** [*count*]

[1]**spat** *past tense and past participle of* [1]SPIT

[2]**spat** /ˈspæt/ *noun, pl* **spats** [*count*] : a short argument about something that is not important • The newlyweds were having another *spat.* — compare [4]SPAT

[3]**spat** *verb* **spats; spat·ted; spat·ting** [*no obj*] *somewhat old-fashioned* : to argue or fight : to have a spat • They were typical sisters, *spatting* one minute, playing together the next.

[4]**spat** *noun, pl* **spats** [*count*] : a cloth or leather covering for the ankle and foot that men wore over their shoes in the past — usually plural • a pair of *spats* — compare [2]SPAT

spate /ˈspeɪt/ *noun, pl* **spates** [*count*] : a large number of things that appear or happen in a short period of time • A *spate* of books on the subject have come out recently. • the recent *spate* [=*rash*] *of* forest fires • There was a *spate* of corporate mergers in the 1980s.
in spate *chiefly Brit, of a river, stream, etc.* : very full : filled with water flowing very fast • The river was *in spate* due to heavy rains.

spa·tial /ˈspeɪʃəl/ *adj* [*more* ~; *most* ~] *technical* : of or relating to space and the relationship of objects within it • the *spatial* dimensions of a room • tests of *spatial* ability
– **spa·tial·ly** *adv*

[1]**spat·ter** /ˈspætɚ/ *verb* **-ters; -tered; -ter·ing** : to cause drops of a liquid to be thrown forcefully in different directions [+ *obj*] A passing car *spattered* [=*splattered*] mud all over her new coat. • The dog jumped in the pool and *spattered* us with water. • His clothes were *spattered* with paint. [*no obj*] When you cook bacon, the grease *spatters* everywhere. • He showed me how to use the paintbrush so the paint wouldn't *spatter.*

[2]**spatter** *noun, pl* **-ters** : a mark made when something wet hits a surface [*count*] There were grease *spatters* all over the wall. • The floor was covered with *spatters* of paint. [*noncount*] There was a lot of paint *spatter* on the floor. • (*US*) He cleaned the bug *spatter* off the windshield.

spat·u·la /ˈspætʃələ/ *noun, pl* **-las** [*count*]
1 *US* **a** : a kitchen tool that has a handle which is bent upward and a wide, thin blade used for lifting and turning foods on a hot surface — called also (*Brit*) *fish slice*; see picture at KITCHEN **b** : a kitchen tool that has a long handle and short, soft blade and that is used especially for mixing, spreading, etc.
2 : a kitchen tool similar to a knife that has a flexible blade and that is used for mixing, spreading, etc. — called also (*Brit*) *palette knife*
3 *Brit* : TONGUE DEPRESSOR

[1]**spawn** /ˈspɑːn/ *verb* **spawns; spawned; spawn·ing**
1 [*no obj*] : to produce or lay eggs in water — used of animals such as fish or frogs • Salmon *spawn* in late summer or fall.
2 [+ *obj*] : to cause (something) to develop or begin : to produce or create (something) • The health-food craze *spawned* a multimillion-dollar industry. • the incident that *spawned* a generation of student protests • a TV show that *spawned* a host of imitations

[2]**spawn** *noun* [*noncount*] : the eggs of a fish or frog • Pacific salmon return to Alaskan streams to deposit their *spawn.*

spawning ground *noun, pl* ~ **grounds** [*count*]
1 : a place where animals (such as fish or frogs) go to lay eggs • Pacific salmon swim to their *spawning grounds* in Alaskan rivers.
2 : a place where something is created or produced often in large numbers • The country is a *spawning ground* for terrorists.

spay /ˈspeɪ/ *verb* **spays; spayed; spay·ing** [+ *obj*] : to remove the sex organs of (a female animal) : to make (a female animal) unable to have babies • Our cat has been *spayed.* — compare NEUTER

spaz /ˈspæz/ *noun, pl* **spaz·zes** [*count*] *US slang* : a person who is very clumsy or awkward : KLUTZ • I'm a real *spaz* on the ski slopes.

speak /ˈspiːk/ *verb* **speaks; spoke** /ˈspoʊk/; **spo·ken** /ˈspoʊkən/; **speak·ing**
1 **a** [*no obj*] : to say words in order to express your thoughts, feelings, opinions, etc., to someone : to talk to someone • Have you two *spoken* since yesterday? • She and I *spoke* this morning. • He never *speaks* at the meetings. • Without *speaking*, she walked from the room. • They were *speaking* in Japanese. — often + *to* • We need to *speak to* our son's teacher about his grades. • He *spoke to* the police through an interpreter. • They *spoke to* each other in a whisper. — often + *with* in U.S. English • The coach refused to *speak with* the reporters. • May I *speak with* you privately? • I *spoke with* him on the phone yesterday. — often used at the beginning of telephone conversations • "Hello. May I *speak* to Noah?" "*Speaking.*" [=I am Noah] • "Hello. This is Noah *speaking.*" **b** [*no obj*] : to talk about a particular subject or person — often + *about* or *of* • She *spoke* intelligently *about* the current political situation. • He still *speaks of* his ex-wife with affection. • The company is doing very well, ***financially speaking***. [=is doing very well financially] **c** [*no obj*] : to say words to express yourself in a particular way • When I said you were my best friend, I was *speaking* sincerely. • *Speaking* personally, I don't think you should take the job. [=my personal opinion is that you should not take the job] • ***Generally speaking***, people like her as a leader. [=people in general like her as a leader] • The restaurant isn't too expensive, ***comparatively/relatively speaking***. [=when compared to other restaurants] • ***Speaking as*** a student (myself), I'm concerned about the alarming increase in school violence. **d** [+ *obj*] : to say (something) to someone • She must be *speaking* the truth. • Not a word was *spoken* between them the whole time. • Don't be afraid to ***speak your mind***. [=say what you think] • Do not ***speak a word*** of this to anyone else. [=do not tell anyone else anything about this]
2 : to use your voice to say words [*no obj*] He has laryngitis and can't *speak.* • You're *speaking* too fast/loudly. • She *speaks* with a Southern accent. • I was so surprised I could hardly *speak.* • She got a ***speaking part/role*** in the play. [=she got a part/role for which she says words] • He has a very deep ***speaking voice***. [=his voice is very deep when he speaks] [+ *obj*] The singer *speaks* the last verse instead of singing it.
3 [*no obj*] : to be willing to talk to someone after having a disagreement, fight, etc. • They haven't *spoken* since the argument two years ago. • Are they still not *speaking*? • He apologized, so I'm *speaking* with/to him again. • They're not ***on speaking terms***. [=they're not friendly and do not speak to each other]
4 [+ *obj*] : to use (a particular language) to talk to someone • He can *speak* German and French. • English is widely *spoken* in many parts of the world. • We didn't know what language they were *speaking.* • the Spanish-*speaking* population/world • I can't ***speak a word*** of French. [=I do not know any French]
5 [*no obj*] : to talk about something formally to a group of people : to make or give a speech • She was asked to *speak* at the conference. • He has a talent for *speaking* to large audiences. • While most of the senators *spoke* against tax increases, one senator *spoke* in favor of them. • I have a *speaking* engagement [=I will be giving a speech] this evening. — see also PUBLIC SPEAKING
actions speak louder than words see ACTION
in a manner of speaking see MANNER
so to speak — used to indicate that you are using words in an unusual or figurative way rather than a literal way • We need to be all on the same wavelength, *so to speak.*
speak for [*phrasal verb*] **1** ***speak for (someone)*** : to express the thoughts or opinions of (someone) • They chose him to *speak for* the group. • *Speaking* only *for* myself, I'm against the plan. [=I'm only expressing my own opinion when I say that I'm against the plan] • "We don't want any dessert." "***Speak for yourself***. I want some." — often used figuratively • I have nothing more to say. The facts ***speak for themselves***. [=the facts clearly show what is true] **2** ***speak***

S

for (something or someone) *chiefly US* : to show that (something or someone) does or does not deserve to be praised, admired, etc. • It ***speaks well for*** [=*says a lot for*] the company that it donates so much money to local charities. • Her calm reaction to the crisis *speaks well for* her ability to perform under pressure. • The test results ***speak poorly for*** our school system. **3** ***be spoken for*** : to not be available because of already being claimed by someone else or in a relationship with someone else • I'm sorry. This seat *is spoken for*. • I can't go out with you; I'*m* already *spoken for*.

speak of [*phrasal verb*] **1** ***speak of (someone or something)*** : to talk or write about (someone or something) : to mention (a subject) in speech or writing • *Speaking of* Jill, where is she? • It was the first time she *spoke of* going to law school. • She never *speaks of* her suffering during the war. • In the letter, he *spoke of* feeling ill. **2** ***speak of (something)*** : to indicate or suggest (something) • His diaries *speak of* a troubled mind. [=they show that he had a troubled mind] **3** ***speak of (someone or something)*** **a** : to talk about (someone or something) in a specified way • He *spoke* well/highly/favorably *of* both job candidates. **b** *chiefly US* : to show that (someone or something) does or does not deserve to be praised, admired, etc. • The continued success of the business ***speaks well of*** their judgment. [=shows that their judgment is good] • Her bad behavior ***speaks poorly of*** her upbringing.

speak of the devil see DEVIL

speak out [*phrasal verb*] : to speak freely and confidently about something : to express an opinion in an open way • She is never afraid to *speak out* on controversial issues. — often + *against* • Protesters *spoke out against* the decision.

speak the same language see LANGUAGE

speak up [*phrasal verb*] **1** : to speak loudly and clearly • "*Speak up*. I can't hear you." **2** : to speak at a meeting, in a class, etc. • Seeing that no one was going to answer the teacher's question, he decided to *speak up*. **3** : to speak freely and confidently about something : to express an opinion openly • Several of us decided to *speak up* about our working conditions. — often + *for* • She is always ready to *speak up for* animal rights.

speak volumes see VOLUME

speak your mind see [1]MIND

to speak of : worth mentioning or noticing • There was no progress *to speak of*.

> ***synonyms*** SPEAK and TALK mean to express yourself by saying words. SPEAK refers to anything that is said, whether it is understood or not and whether it is heard or not. • What language are they *speaking*? • She *spoke* to the class. TALK suggests that there is a listener who understands what is said and often that both people do some speaking. • Do you have time to *talk*? • We *talked* about school.

-speak /ˌspiːk/ *noun combining form* — used to form words that refer to the special languages or words used for particular activities or by particular groups • computer*speak* [=the language used by people talking about computers] • California*speak* [=the type of language used by people in California]

speak·easy /ˈspiːkˌiːzi/ *noun, pl* **-eas·ies** [*count*] : a place where alcoholic drinks were sold illegally in the U.S. during the 1920s

speak·er /ˈspiːkɚ/ *noun, pl* **-ers**

1 [*count*] : someone who speaks a particular language • fluent *speakers* of French = fluent French *speakers* — see also NATIVE SPEAKER

2 [*count*] : someone who talks about something to a group of people • I disagree with the last *speaker*. • He is an excellent public *speaker*. • She was invited to be a ***guest speaker*** [=to give a speech] at the conference.

3 ***the Speaker*** : the person who controls the discussions in a legislature • She became ***the Speaker of the House*** (of Representatives).

4 [*count*] : someone who is speaking • improper grammar used by a writer or *speaker* • The word "take" often indicates movement away from the *speaker*, while "bring" indicates movement toward the *speaker*.

5 [*count*] : the part of a radio, television, computer, etc., that changes electric signals into sound • I bought new *speakers* for my stereo system. — see picture at LIVING ROOM; see also LOUDSPEAKER

speak·er·phone /ˈspiːkɚˌfoun/ *noun, pl* **-phones** *chiefly US* : a feature on a telephone that allows you to talk and listen to someone without holding the receiver to your head [*count*] We used the *speakerphone* for the call so that everyone could hear what was said. [*noncount*] He put her ***on speakerphone*** so that everyone could hear what she said.

[1]**spear** /ˈspiɚ/ *noun, pl* **spears** [*count*]

1 : a weapon that has a long straight handle and a sharp point • The hunters used *spears*.

2 : a new part of a plant that is thin and pointed : a shoot or sprout of a plant • *spears* of grass • asparagus *spears*

[2]**spear** *verb* **spears; speared; spear·ing** [+ *obj*] : to push a spear or other pointed object into (something) • *spear* a fish • She *speared* an olive with a toothpick.

[1]**spear·head** /ˈspiɚˌhɛd/ *noun, pl* **-heads** [*count*] : a person, thing, or group that organizes or leads something (such as a movement or attack) • Her book was the *spearhead* of the clean water movement.

[2]**spearhead** *verb* **-heads; -head·ed; -head·ing** [+ *obj*] : to be the leader of (something, such as a political movement) • She *spearheaded* the campaign for better schools. • The movement was *spearheaded* by the teachers' union.

spear·mint /ˈspiɚˌmɪnt/ *noun* [*noncount*] : a plant that has a strong and pleasant flavor and smell and that is grown especially for its oil

spec /ˈspɛk/ *noun, pl* **specs** : a detailed description of work to be done or materials to be used in a project : SPECIFICATION [*count*] — usually plural • technical/design *specs* • products that conform to *specs* [*noncount*] (*US*) • parts built according to *spec*

on spec **1** : without having a definite buyer or customer but with the hope or expectation of finding one when work is completed • He built the house *on spec*. • She wrote the script *on spec*. **2** *chiefly Brit* : without being sure of success but with the hope of success • He wrote to the company *on spec*, hoping for a job.

— see also SPECS

[1]**spe·cial** /ˈspɛʃəl/ *adj*

1 [*more* ~; *most* ~] : different from what is normal or usual • This is a *special* case and I want you to handle it personally. • Only under *special* circumstances will you be allowed to retake the test. • Is there any *special* [=*particular*] reason why you're not coming?; *especially* : unusual in a good way : better or more important than others • Your many years of service put you in a *special* category. • Why should you receive any *special* treatment? • It takes a *special* quality to do what he did. • This is a very *special* occasion. • Are you doing anything *special* over the holidays? • The movie was nothing *special*. [=was not particularly good] • We have a *special* guest tonight—the mayor.

2 [*more* ~; *most* ~] : especially important or loved • a *special* friend • No one is more *special* to me than my wife. • He always made her feel *special*. • He holds a *special* place in her heart.

3 *always used before a noun* **a** : more than is usual • Pay *special* attention to the last paragraph. • Take *special* care on the way down the stairs. • They showed *special* concern for the children. • The report places *special* emphasis on new technology. **b** : additional or extra • a *special* edition of a newspaper • He won't tell us the *special* ingredient in his salad dressing. • This camera has a *special* feature that lets you take panoramic views.

4 *always used before a noun* : relating to or intended for a particular purpose • a *special* diet • He was on *special* assignment for the government. • *special* election coverage • I was given *special* orders not to let you in. • To clean the oven, I had to wear *special* gloves. [=a particular kind of glove] • Do you have any *special* instructions for the babysitter? • a *special* correspondent/prosecutor

[2]**special** *noun, pl* **-cials** [*count*]

1 : a television or radio program that is not part of a regular series • a one-hour *special* on whales • an after-school *special*

2 : a meal that is not on a restaurant's usual menu • Today's lunch *special* is chili. • The *specials* are on the board.

3 : SALE 2 • They were having a *special* on paper towels so I stocked up.

handyman's special see HANDYMAN

on special *US* : selling at a price that is lower than usual : on sale • Pork chops are *on special* [=(*Brit*) *on special offer*] this week.

special agent *noun, pl* ~ **agents** [*count*] : an agent who works for the FBI

Special Air Service *noun* [*noncount*] : SAS

Special Branch *noun* [*noncount*] : the department of the British police force that deals with political crimes and terrorism • Officers from *Special Branch* are investigating the case.

special character *noun, pl* ~ **-ters** [*count*] : a symbol used in writing, typing, etc., that represents something other than a letter or number • The symbol § is a *special character*.

special delivery *noun* [*noncount*] : a special service that delivers mail more quickly than usual for an extra fee • She sent him a letter by *special delivery*.

special education *noun* [*noncount*] : classes for children who have special needs because of physical or learning problems — called also *special ed*

special effect *noun, pl* ~ **-fects** [*count*] : an image or sound that is created in television, radio, or movies to represent something real (such as an explosion) or imaginary (such as a monster) — usually plural • The movie is worth seeing just for the spectacular *special effects*.

special forces *noun* [*plural*] : a part of an army made up of soldiers specially trained to fight against enemies (such as guerrilla forces or terrorists) who do not belong to a regular army

special interest *noun, pl* ~ **-ests** [*count*] *chiefly US* : a group that tries to influence the people who run a government in order to help a particular business, cause, industry, etc. — often plural • The congressmen were accused of selling out to *special interests*. • contributions made by *special interests* — often used before another noun • *special interest* money/politics • the influence of ***special interest groups***

spe•cial•ism /ˈspɛʃəˌlɪzəm/ *noun, pl* **-isms** [*count*] *Brit* : a particular subject or area of study or practice • The professor's *specialism* [=*specialty*] is labor law. — often + *in* • a doctor whose *specialism* [=*specialty, specialization*] is *in* blood disorders [=a doctor who specializes in blood disorders] • an accounting firm with a *specialism in* corporate mergers

spe•cial•ist /ˈspɛʃəlɪst/ *noun, pl* **-ists** [*count*]
1 a : a person who has special knowledge and skill relating to a particular job, area of study, etc. : EXPERT • She consulted a marketing *specialist* when she decided to go into business. • child development *specialists* • He's a *specialist* in international law. [=he specializes in international law] — compare GENERALIST **b** : a doctor who deals with health problems that relate to a specific area of medicine • He saw a *specialist* for his foot problem. • a leading *cancer* specialist • a *skin* specialist — compare GENERAL PRACTITIONER
2 : a rank in the U.S. Army that is above the rank of private and below the rank of corporal
– specialist *adj, always used before a noun* • *specialist* publications

specialist shop *noun, pl* ~ **shops** [*count*] *Brit* : SPECIALTY SHOP

spe•ci•al•i•ty /ˌspɛʃiˈæləti/ *noun, pl* **-ties** [*count*] *chiefly Brit* : SPECIALTY

spe•cial•ize *also Brit* **spe•cial•ise** /ˈspɛʃəˌlaɪz/ *verb* **-iz•es; -ized; -iz•ing** [*no obj*] : to limit your business or area of study to one specific subject • Some carpenters do a wide range of jobs, while others *specialize*. — usually + *in* • My mechanic *specializes* in repairing foreign cars.
– spe•cial•i•za•tion *also Brit* **spe•cial•i•sa•tion** /ˌspɛʃələˈzeɪʃən, *Brit* ˌspɛʃəˌlaɪˈzeɪʃən/ *noun, pl* **-tions** [*noncount*] a law firm whose area of *specialization* is family law [*count*] She studies government with a *specialization* in foreign policy.

specialized *also Brit* **specialised** *adj* [*more* ~; *most* ~] : made or used for one particular purpose, job, place, etc. • *specialized* regions of the brain • *specialized* gear for deep-sea fishing • a *specialized* habitat • *specialized* knowledge/skills

spe•cial•ly /ˈspɛʃəli/ *adv*
1 : for a special purpose : SPECIFICALLY • dresses made *specially* for a wedding • The speech was written *specially* for the occasion. • The room was *specially* designed to be used as a library. • *specially* trained troops
2 : to a special or unusual degree : particularly or especially • I was *specially* pleased with your gift. • people who are not *specially* gifted
3 [*more* ~; *most* ~] : in a special manner • I don't want to be treated *specially*.

special needs *noun* [*plural*] : mental, emotional, or physical problems in a child that require a special setting for education • a child with *special needs* — often used before another noun • *special-needs* students • a *special-needs* teacher [=a teacher who teaches children with special needs] • a *special-needs* classroom

special offer *noun, pl* ~ **-fers** [*count*] : a product that is being sold for less than its usual price or the act of selling something for less than the usual price • Shoppers will be able to take advantage of *special offers* after the holidays. • (*Brit*) Fresh turkeys are ***on special offer*** [=(*US*) *on special*] this week.

special school *noun, pl* ~ **schools** [*count*] : a school for children who have physical or mental problems

spe•cial•ty /ˈspɛʃəlti/ *noun, pl* **-ties** [*count*] *US*
1 : something that a person or place is known for making or producing very well • Eggs are my dad's *specialty*. [=(*Brit*) *speciality*] • Buttermilk pie is a Southern *specialty*.
2 : an area of study or business that a person specializes in or has special knowledge of • a doctor whose *specialty* [=(*Brit*) *speciality*] is skin problems

specialty shop *noun, pl* ~ **shops** [*count*] *US* : a shop that sells one type of thing • a cheese *specialty shop*

spe•cies /ˈspiːʃiz/ *noun, pl* **species** [*count*]
1 *biology* : a group of animals or plants that are similar and can produce young animals or plants : a group of related animals or plants that is smaller than a genus • There are approximately 8,000 *species* of ants. • All European domestic cattle belong to the same *species*. • laws that protect endangered/threatened *species* — see also SUBSPECIES
2 : a particular group of things or people that belong together or have some shared quality • the different *species* [=*kinds, types*] of criminals

spe•cif•ic /spɪˈsɪfɪk/ *adj* [*more* ~; *most* ~]
1 *always used before a noun* : special or particular • Is there anything *specific* you want for dinner? • There is a *specific* word for this kind of feeling. • a bird species that requires a *specific* environment • We were each given a *specific* topic to talk about.
2 : clearly and exactly presented or stated : precise or exact • The doctor gave the patient *specific* instructions on how to care for the wound. • Can you be more *specific*? What exactly did the policeman say? • He gave her a ring—or, to be more *specific*, he gave her an engagement ring. • She was very *specific*—you have to use a certain kind of tomato in the sauce. • Give *specific* examples. • Do you have a *specific* [=*certain*] date in mind for your party?
3 a : relating *to* a particular person, situation, etc. • an education plan *specific to* each student's interests and abilities • problems *specific to* this one housing project • a tax regulation *specific to* this kind of business **b** *technical* : having a particular function or effect • highly *specific* antibodies • an antibiotic that is *specific* to/for the organism that causes the disease — see also SPECIFICS

spe•cif•i•cal•ly /spɪˈsɪfɪkli/ *adv* [*more* ~; *most* ~]
1 : in a definite and exact way • The report *specifically* names two companies that were involved. • I *specifically* told her not to bother you. • Knead the bread dough for several minutes, or, more *specifically*, until it forms a smooth ball.
2 — used to indicate the exact purpose or use of something • The show is aimed *specifically* at a female audience. • The new rules apply *specifically* to situations like this. • furniture designed *specifically* for outdoor use

spec•i•fi•ca•tion /ˌspɛsəfəˈkeɪʃən/ *noun, pl* **-tions** [*count*] : a detailed description of work to be done or materials to be used in a project : an instruction that says exactly how to do or make something — usually plural • the architect's *specifications* for a new building • The equipment will be manufactured to your *specifications*.

specific gravity *noun* [*noncount*] *technical* : a measurement that indicates how dense a substance is by comparing it to the density of water • determining the *specific gravity* of a mineral

spec•i•fic•i•ty /ˌspɛsəˈfɪsəti/ *noun* [*noncount*] *formal* : the quality of being specific • I was impressed by the *specificity* of her instructions.

spe•cif•ics /spɪˈsɪfɪks/ *noun* [*plural*] : the specific facts or details that relate to something • While avoiding *specifics*, he made it pretty clear that the presentation was full of flaws. • I'd like to know the *specifics* [=*particulars*] of your plan. • Let's get down to *specifics*.

spec•i•fy /ˈspɛsəˌfaɪ/ *verb* **-fies; -fied; -fy•ing** [+ *obj*] : to name or mention (someone or something) exactly and clearly : to be specific about (something) • Can you *specify* the cause of the argument? • *Specify* the color and quantity when you order. • He clearly *specified* California wine. • The instructions do not *specify* what kind of screws to use. • All subscriptions are for one year unless otherwise *specified*. • At

S

the *specified* time, we rang the bell. ▪ She agreed to the terms *specified* in the contract.

spec·i·men /ˈspɛsəmən/ *noun, pl* **-mens** [*count*]
1 a : something (such as an animal or plant) collected as an example of a particular kind of thing ▪ a museum *specimen* **b :** a small amount or piece of something that can be tested or examined ▪ a urine/blood *specimen* [=*sample*]
2 a : a notable example of something ▪ The church is a magnificent *specimen* of baroque architecture. **b** *humorous* **:** an example of a type of person ▪ Her dance partner is a superb physical *specimen*. ▪ fine *specimens* of manhood

spe·cious /ˈspiːʃəs/ *adj* [*more* ~; *most* ~] *formal* **:** falsely appearing to be fair, just, or right **:** appearing to be true but actually false ▪ a *specious* argument ▪ He justified his actions with *specious* reasoning.
– spe·cious·ly *adv, formal* **– spe·cious·ness** *noun* [*noncount*] *formal* ▪ the *speciousness* of his reasoning

speck /ˈspɛk/ *noun, pl* **specks** [*count*]
1 : a very small piece or spot ▪ There was not a *speck* of dust anywhere. ▪ Soon the balloon was only a *speck* in the sky.
2 : a very small amount **:** BIT ▪ She writes without a *speck* of humor.

specked /ˈspɛkt/ *adj* **:** marked with many small spots ▪ bread *specked* with black pepper ▪ paint-*specked* pants

speck·le /ˈspɛkəl/ *noun, pl* **speck·les** [*count*] **:** a small mark of color ▪ a ripe banana with lots of brown *speckles*

speck·led /ˈspɛkəld/ *adj* [*more* ~; *most* ~] **:** covered with many small marks ▪ *speckled* trout ▪ a gold-*speckled* scarf

specs /ˈspɛks/ *noun* [*plural*] *informal* **:** glasses or spectacles ▪ I have to wear my *specs* when I drive. — see also SPEC

spec·ta·cle /ˈspɛktɪkəl/ *noun, pl* **-ta·cles**
1 [*count*] **:** a very impressive show ▪ a giant film *spectacle* ▪ a Broadway *spectacle*
2 [*count*] **:** something that attracts attention because it is very unusual or very shocking — usually singular ▪ The photo exhibit was quite a *spectacle*. ▪ She hoped the situation would not become a *spectacle*.
3 ***spectacles*** [*plural*] *old-fashioned* **:** GLASSES ▪ He peered through his *spectacles*.
make a spectacle of yourself **:** to do something in front of other people that is very embarrassing ▪ You *made a spectacle of yourself* at the party.
rose-colored spectacles see ROSE-COLORED

spec·ta·cled /ˈspɛktɪkəld/ *adj* **:** wearing glasses ▪ The *spectacled* [=*bespectacled*] clerks bent over their account books.

spec·tac·u·lar /spɛkˈtækjələ/ *adj* [*more* ~; *most* ~] **:** causing wonder and admiration **:** very impressive ▪ a *spectacular* sunset ▪ a *spectacular* play in a football game ▪ The stock market has made a *spectacular* [=*sensational*] recovery. ▪ *spectacular* [=*thrilling*] aerial photography ▪ The autumn foliage was *spectacular*.
– spec·tac·u·lar·ly *adv* ▪ He played *spectacularly*. ▪ a *spectacularly* successful novel ▪ The new system failed *spectacularly*. [=it was a complete failure]

spec·tate /ˈspɛkˌteɪt/ *verb* **-tates; -tat·ed; -tat·ing** [*no obj*] **:** to watch something (such as a sports event) ▪ She no longer participates in sports but merely *spectates*. [=she is is just a spectator]

spec·ta·tor /ˈspɛkˌteɪtə/ *noun, pl* **-tors** [*count*] **:** a person who watches an event, show, game, activity, etc., often as part of an audience ▪ The *spectators* lining the road cheered the racers on. ▪ The accident attracted a large crowd of *spectators*. ▪ I wasn't a participant in the preparations, merely a *spectator*.

spectator sport *noun, pl* ~ **sports** [*count*]
1 : a sport (such as football, baseball, ice hockey, etc.) that many people watch ▪ People generally don't think of sailboat racing as a *spectator sport*.
2 : something that people watch other people do without becoming involved themselves ▪ For many, politics has become a *spectator sport*.

spec·ter (*US*) *or chiefly Brit* **spec·tre** /ˈspɛktə/ *noun, pl* **-ters** [*count*] *literary* **:** a ghost or spirit of a dead person ▪ "Ghost of the Future," he exclaimed, "I fear you more than any *spectre* I have seen . . ." —Charles Dickens, *A Christmas Carol* (1867)
the specter of (something) **:** something bad that might happen in the future ▪ a nation alarmed/haunted by *the specter of* famine/war ▪ News of the disease ***raised the specter of*** [=made people worry about] a possible plague.

spectra *plural of* SPECTRUM

spec·tral /ˈspɛktrəl/ *adj*
1 *literary* **:** of, relating to, or suggesting a ghost **:** GHOSTLY ▪ a *spectral* figure
2 *technical* **:** of, relating to, or made by a spectrum ▪ *spectral* lines

spec·tro·scope /ˈspɛktrəˌskoʊp/ *noun, pl* **-scopes** [*count*] *technical* **:** a device that is used to measure the properties of light
– spec·tro·scop·ic /ˌspɛktrəˈskɑːpɪk/ *adj* ▪ *spectroscopic* analysis **– spec·tros·co·py** /spɛkˈtrɑːskəpi/ *noun, pl* **-pies** [*count*] ▪ infrared/laser *spectroscopy*

spec·trum /ˈspɛktrəm/ *noun, pl* **spec·tra** /ˈspɛktrə/ *or* **spec·trums** [*count*]
1 a : the group of colors that a ray of light can be separated into including red, orange, yellow, green, blue, indigo, and violet **:** the colors that can be seen in a rainbow ▪ beautiful scarves in all the colors of the *spectrum* **b** *technical* **:** an entire range of light waves, radio waves, etc.
2 : a complete range of different opinions, people, etc. ▪ reaching voters across the political *spectrum* [=voters with all the different political beliefs that people have] — often + *of* ▪ the whole *spectrum of* emotions ▪ The city's populations represent a broad/wide *spectrum of* society.

spec·u·late /ˈspɛkjəˌleɪt/ *verb* **-lates; -lat·ed; -lat·ing**
1 : to think about something and make guesses about it **:** to form ideas or theories about something usually when there are many things not known about it [*no obj*] She could only *speculate* about/on her friend's motives. ▪ He *speculated* as to whether she would come. ▪ We don't know what happened—we can only *speculate*. [+ *obj*] — + *that* ▪ Scientists *speculate that* the illness is caused by a virus.
2 [*no obj*] **:** to invest money in ways that could produce a large profit but that also involve a lot of risk ▪ *speculating* on the stock market
– spec·u·la·tor /ˈspɛkjəˌleɪtə/ *noun, pl* **-tors** [*count*] ▪ a land *speculator* ▪ a Wall Street *speculator*

spec·u·la·tion /ˌspɛkjəˈleɪʃən/ *noun, pl* **-tions**
1 : ideas or guesses about something that is not known [*noncount*] He dismissed their theories as mere *speculation*. ▪ The book is just a lot of idle *speculation* about the future. ▪ There is *speculation* that he will run for president again. [=some people think that he might run for president again] [*count*] Her *speculations* leave many questions unanswered.
2 [*noncount*] **:** activity in which someone buys and sells things (such as stocks or pieces of property) in the hope of making a large profit but with the risk of a large loss ▪ He lost everything in foolish land *speculation*.

spec·u·la·tive /ˈspɛkjələtɪv/ *adj*
1 a : based on guesses or ideas about what might happen or be true rather than on facts ▪ His conclusions are highly/purely *speculative*. **b :** tending to think about what might happen or be true **:** tending to speculate ▪ a writer with a *speculative* mind **c :** showing curiosity or uncertainty ▪ She gave him a *speculative* glance. [=she looked at him in a way that showed she was thinking/wondering about him]
2 : involving financial risk **:** of or relating to financial activity that could result in either a large profit or a large loss ▪ a *speculative* boom in housing construction ▪ *speculative* deals
– spec·u·la·tive·ly *adv* ▪ The question can only be answered *speculatively*. ▪ She eyed him *speculatively*.

sped *past tense and past participle of* ²SPEED

speech /ˈspiːtʃ/ *noun, pl* **speech·es**
1 [*count*] **:** a spoken expression of ideas, opinions, etc., that is made by someone who is speaking in front of a group of people ▪ She has to make/give/deliver a *speech* at the convention. ▪ a graduation *speech* about/on embracing future challenges ▪ He kept revising his *speech* [=the words that he had written for his speech] right up until the last minute. ▪ She thanked us in her ***acceptance speech***. [=a speech given by someone receiving an award or prize] — see also STUMP SPEECH
2 [*noncount*] **:** the ability to speak ▪ I was so flustered that I momentarily lost the ***power of speech***. ▪ She has a mild ***speech impediment***. [=a condition that makes it difficult to speak normally] ▪ They fought for ***freedom of speech***. = They fought for the right to/of ***free speech***. [=they fought for the legal right to express their opinions freely]
3 [*noncount*] **:** spoken language ▪ Slang is used mostly in informal/casual *speech*. ▪ Many words are more common in *speech* than in writing.
4 [*noncount*] **:** the manner or style of speaking that is used by a particular person or group ▪ His *speech* was slurred. ▪ local/regional *speech* patterns

5 [*count*] : a group of lines spoken by a character in a play ▪ I get to perform one of the best *speeches* in the play.
— see also FIGURE OF SPEECH, PART OF SPEECH

speech day *noun, pl* ~ **days** [*count*] *Brit* : an event held once a year in some British schools at which prizes are awarded to students and speeches are given

speech·ify /ˈspiːʧəˌfaɪ/ *verb* **-ifies; -ified; -ify·ing** [*no obj*] *informal + disapproving* : to make a speech especially in a way that is boring, annoying, etc. ▪ We had to listen to him *speechify* about what a wonderful governor he would be.
— **speechifying** *noun* [*noncount*] ▪ The political *speechifying* has begun.

speech·less /ˈspiːʧləs/ *adj* : unable to speak because of anger, surprise, etc. ▪ I was *speechless* with shock/anger. ▪ Your story ***left me speechless.***

speech therapy *noun* [*noncount*] : treatment or therapy to help people who have speech problems learn to pronounce words correctly
— **speech therapist** *noun, pl* ~ **-pists** [*count*]

speech·writ·er /ˈspiːʧˌraɪtɚ/ *noun, pl* **-ers** [*count*] : a person whose job is to write speeches that are given by someone else (such as a politician) ▪ She is the President's principal *speechwriter.*

[1]**speed** /ˈspiːd/ *noun, pl* **speeds**
1 : the rate at which someone or something moves or travels [*noncount*] The trucks gain/gather *speed* as they drive down the hill. = The trucks pick up *speed* as they drive down the hill. [=the trucks go faster as they drive down the hill] ▪ This instrument measures wind *speed.* ▪ He was running ***at full/top speed.*** [=as fast as possible] ▪ The machine was operating ***at high/medium/low speed.*** ▪ traveling at nearly the ***speed of light/sound*** [*count*] Under the right conditions the car can reach *speeds* over 200 miles an hour. ▪ The vehicle maintained a *speed* of 40 miles per hour.
2 : the rate at which something happens or is done [*noncount*] The work was done with remarkable *speed.* ▪ They ate their lunch ***at lightning speed.*** [=extremely quickly] [*count*] This computer works at a much faster processing *speed* than my old one. ▪ He types at a *speed* of about 50 words per minute. = His typing *speed* is about 50 words per minute.
3 [*noncount*] : the quality of being quick ▪ The machine chops up tree branches and leaves with *speed* and ease.
4 [*count*] *photography* **a** : a measurement that indicates how quickly film reacts to light and that is expressed as a number (such as 100 or 200) ▪ 200 *speed* film **b** : the time during which a camera's shutter is open ▪ faster/slower ***shutter speeds***
5 [*count*] : a gear in a vehicle or bicycle ▪ a three-*speed* bicycle ▪ Her old car has four *speeds.*
6 [*noncount*] *informal* : an illegal drug that makes a person feel more excited and full of energy ▪ He was high on *speed.*
at speed *chiefly Brit* : very quickly : at a fast speed ▪ He ran *at speed* out of the room.
full speed ahead see [1]FULL
up to speed : having the latest information about something ▪ Everyone here is *up to speed.* ▪ Let me ***bring you up to speed*** on our plans. [=let me tell you about the changes in our plans] : having the knowledge that is needed to do or understand something ▪ It will take some time for the new secretary to ***get up to speed.*** [=to learn the job]

[2]**speed** *verb* **speeds; sped** /ˈspɛd/ *or* **speed·ed; speed·ing**
1 *always followed by an adverb or preposition* [*no obj*] : to move fast ▪ A group of kids *sped* past us on their bikes. ▪ They jumped in the car and *sped/speeded* away. ▪ A car was *speeding* down/up the street.
2 *always followed by an adverb or preposition* [+ *obj*] : to move (someone or something) somewhere very quickly ▪ An ambulance *sped* her to the hospital.
3 [*no obj*] : to drive faster than the legal speed limit ▪ I got pulled over twice last month because I was *speeding* on the highway. ▪ Don't *speed.*
4 [+ *obj*] *somewhat formal* : to cause (an action, movement, process, etc.) to happen faster ▪ We kept the plants under artificial lights at night to *speed* their growth. ▪ Is there anything we can do to *speed* the process (along)?
speed up [*phrasal verb*] ***speed up or speed up (something or someone) or speed (something or someone) up*** : to become faster or to make (something or someone) faster ▪ I hate it when cars *speed up* [=*accelerate*] while you're trying to pass them. ▪ The work has been slow so far but it should *speed up* soon. ▪ They add another chemical to the photo developer to *speed up* the process. ▪ I'm afraid there's nothing you can do to *speed* things *up.* ▪ They're working too slowly. How can we *speed* them *up*? — see also SPEEDUP

speed·boat /ˈspiːdˌboʊt/ *noun, pl* **-boats** [*count*] : a motorboat that can go very fast

speed bump *noun, pl* ~ **bumps** [*count*] : a low raised ridge across a road or parking lot that causes people to drive more slowly — called also (*Brit*) *speed hump*

speed demon *noun, pl* ~ **-mons** [*count*] *chiefly US, informal* : someone or something that moves or works very fast ▪ The new cook is a regular *speed demon.* ▪ This computer is a real *speed demon* compared with/to my old computer.

speed dial *noun* [*noncount*] *chiefly US* : a feature on some telephones that allows a person to call certain phone numbers quickly by pressing only one button ▪ a phone with *speed dial* ▪ I have you on *speed dial.* = I have your number on *speed dial.*
— **speed–dial** *verb* **-dials; -dialed; -dialing** [+ *obj*] *chiefly US* ▪ I've added your number to my phone so I can *speed-dial* you now.

speed·er /ˈspiːdɚ/ *noun, pl* **-ers** [*count*] : someone who drives faster than the legal speed limit ▪ The cops were out ticketing *speeders* yesterday.

speed hump *noun, pl* ~ **humps** [*count*] *Brit* : SPEED BUMP

speeding *noun* [*noncount*] : the offense of driving faster than the legal speed limit ▪ I got a ticket for *speeding.*

speeding ticket *noun, pl* ~ **-ets** [*count*] : a piece of paper that a police officer gives to someone who was driving too fast and that indicates a fine that the driver will have to pay ▪ I got a *speeding ticket* and a $150 fine.

speed limit *noun, pl* ~ **-its** [*count*] : the highest speed at which you are allowed to drive on a particular road ▪ The *speed limit* here is 55 mph. ▪ She got a ticket for breaking/exceeding the *speed limit.*

speed·om·e·ter /spɪˈdɑːmətɚ/ *noun, pl* **-ters** [*count*] : an instrument in a car, truck, etc., that indicates how fast the vehicle is going — called also (*Brit*) *speedo* /ˈspiːdoʊ/; see picture at CAR; compare ODOMETER, TACHOMETER

speed–read·ing /ˈspiːdˌriːdɪŋ/ *noun* [*noncount*] : a method of reading something very quickly
— **speed–read** *verb* **-reads; -read; -reading** [+ *obj*] ▪ I *speed-read* the book in one night.

speed skating *noun* [*noncount*] : the sport of racing on ice skates
— **speed skater** *noun, pl* ~ **-ers** [*count*]

speed·ster /ˈspiːdstɚ/ *noun, pl* **-sters** [*count*] : someone or something that moves or works very fast ▪ She drives a sporty little *speedster.* ▪ The team has a couple of talented *speedsters.*

speed trap *noun, pl* ~ **traps** [*count*] : an area of road where police hide from drivers and use special equipment to catch people who are driving too fast

speed·up /ˈspiːdˌʌp/ *noun, pl* **-ups** : an increase in the speed or rate of something [*count*] — usually singular ▪ Economists are worried about a possible *speedup* in/of inflation. [*noncount*] I'd like to see some *speedup* in the selection process. — see also *speed up* at [2]SPEED

speed·way /ˈspiːdˌweɪ/ *noun, pl* **-ways**
1 [*count*] *chiefly US* : a track where cars or motorcycles race
2 [*noncount*] *Brit* : the sport of racing motorcycles on a special track

speedy /ˈspiːdi/ *adj* **speed·i·er; -est**
1 : moving or able to move quickly : fast or quick ▪ a *speedy* car/boat
2 : happening quickly ▪ a *speedy* process ▪ They wished her a *speedy* recovery.
— **speed·i·ly** /ˈspiːdəli/ *adv* ▪ They worked *speedily* and efficiently. ▪ We must move *speedily* to address the problem.
— **speed·i·ness** /ˈspiːdinəs/ *noun* [*noncount*]

[1]**spell** /ˈspɛl/ *verb* **spells; spelled** *or chiefly Brit* **spelt** /ˈspɛlt/; **spell·ing** *chiefly US*
1 a : to say, write, or print the letters of (a word or name) [+ *obj*] How do you *spell* your last name? ▪ You *spelled* "catastrophe" wrong. ▪ "Foggy" is *spelled* with two g's. — sometimes + *out* ▪ Please *spell out* your full name. [*no obj*] He doesn't *spell* very well. **b** [+ *obj*] — used to indicate the letters that form a particular word ▪ S-O-N *spells* "son."
2 [+ *obj*] : to have or lead to (a particular result or effect) ▪ Her boss's resignation *spelled* the end to her troubles. [=her troubles ended when her boss resigned] ▪ The amount of

S

planning you do could *spell* [=*mean*] the difference between success and failure. ▪ Their carelessness could ***spell trouble/disaster*** for all of us.

spell out [*phrasal verb*] ***spell (something) out or spell out (something)*** **1 :** to explain the details of (something) clearly ▪ The contract *spelled out* the terms of his employment. ▪ She didn't get the hint, so he had to *spell* it *out* for her. **2 :** to write out (something) in complete words instead of using a number, an abbreviation, etc. ▪ When addressing the invitations, *spell out* "street," "road," etc. ▪ On this line you need to *spell out* the dollar amount. — see also [1]SPELL 1 (above)

– compare [3]SPELL

[2]spell *noun, pl* **spells**

1 [*count*] **a :** a group of secret words that are believed to have magic power ▪ He said a ***magic spell*** of protection. **b :** magic that is performed by saying a group of secret words ▪ In the story, the witch ***casts a spell on/over*** the children. ▪ Drinking the potion will ***break the spell***. [=end the magic] ▪ She felt like she was ***under a spell***. [=affected by magic]

2 [*singular*] **:** a quality that attracts or influences someone or something in a powerful or seemingly magical way ▪ The sound of the phone ringing broke the *spell* of the music. ▪ Many people think she has ***fallen under his spell***, but I think she knows what she's doing.

– compare [4]SPELL

[3]spell *verb* **spells; spelled; spell•ing** [+ *obj*] *chiefly US* **:** to take the place of (another person who has been working or doing something for a period of time) **:** to take over for (someone) ▪ When they're taking care of their grandson, they *spell* [=*relieve*] each other throughout the day. — compare [1]SPELL

[4]spell *noun, pl* **spells** [*count*]

1 : a short period of time usually marked by a particular activity or condition ▪ a dizzy/fainting *spell* ▪ I'm tired and need to sit down for a *spell*. ▪ It looks like we're in for a *spell* of rainy weather. ▪ The flowers died during a ***dry/cold spell***. [=a period of dry/cold weather]

2 : a period spent doing a job or duty ▪ After a *spell* as an editor she went back to teaching.

– compare [2]SPELL

spell•bind•ing /ˈspɛlˌbaɪndɪŋ/ *adj* **:** holding your attention completely **:** extremely interesting, entertaining, etc. ▪ I found her performance *spellbinding*. [=*fascinating, riveting*] ▪ He's a *spellbinding* speaker.

spell•bound /ˈspɛlˌbaʊnd/ *adj* **:** giving all of your attention and interest to something or someone ▪ The children were *spellbound* by the puppet show. ▪ She's a storyteller that will hold/keep you *spellbound*.

spell–check /ˈspɛlˌʧɛk/ *verb* **-checks; -checked; -check•ing** [+ *obj*] **:** to use a computer program (called a spell-checker) to find and correct spelling errors in (something you have written) ▪ I *spell-checked* my homework.

spell–check•er /ˈspɛlˌʧɛkɚ/ *noun, pl* **-ers** [*count*] **:** a computer program that finds and corrects misspelled words in documents, e-mail, etc. — called also *spell-check, spelling checker*

spell•er /ˈspɛlɚ/ *noun, pl* **-ers** [*count*] **:** a person who spells words in a particular way ▪ She is a ***bad/good speller***. [=she is bad/good at spelling words]

spell•ing /ˈspɛlɪŋ/ *noun, pl* **-ings**

1 [*noncount*] **:** the act of forming of words from letters ▪ He's very good at *spelling*. = His *spelling* is very good. [=he spells words correctly] — often used before another noun ▪ Make sure there are no ***spelling mistakes/errors*** in the application. ▪ The students have a ***spelling test*** every Friday.

2 [*count*] **:** the way in which a word is correctly spelled ▪ The American *spelling* is "color" while the British *spelling* is "colour." ▪ The words "made" and "maid" sound alike but have different *spellings*.

spelling bee *noun, pl* **~ bees** [*count*] *chiefly US* **:** a contest in which contestants spell words aloud and are removed from the contest when they spell a word wrong

spelling checker *noun, pl* **~ -ers** [*count*] **:** SPELL-CHECKER

spelt *chiefly Brit past tense and past participle of* [1]SPELL

spe•lunk•er /spɪˈlʌŋkɚ/ *noun, pl* **-ers** [*count*] *US* **:** a person who explores and studies caves as a hobby — called also *caver*

spe•lunk•ing /spɪˈlʌŋkɪŋ/ *noun* [*noncount*] *US* **:** the sport or practice of exploring or studying caves ▪ Her hobbies include hiking, biking, and *spelunking*. ▪ They love to ***go spelunking***. — called also *caving*

spend /ˈspɛnd/ *verb* **spends; spent** /ˈspɛnt/; **spend•ing**

1 : to use (money) to pay for something [+ *obj*] I *spent* $30 on his birthday gift. ▪ They *spend* a lot on clothes and cars. ▪ I want to buy a new car, but I don't have much money to *spend*. ▪ This computer wasn't cheap, but it was money ***well spent***. [=it was worth its price] [*no obj*] Her willingness to *spend* freely made her popular among her friends. ▪ He *spends* lavishly on vacations.

2 [+ *obj*] **:** to allow (time) to pass in a particular place or while doing a particular activity ▪ I *spent* my summer at the beach. ▪ She *spent* eight months living in New York City. ▪ Relaxing with friends is a great way to *spend* a weekend. ▪ Our cat *spends* most of his time sleeping. ▪ Too much of my time is *spent* arguing with customers.

3 [+ *obj*] **:** to use (energy or effort) to do something ▪ She *spends* far too much energy worrying about her daughter. ▪ I wish he *spent* as much (of his) effort/energy on studying as he does on video games. ▪ Our energy/effort(s) would ***be better spent*** (in) solving the problem rather than just complaining about it.

spend the night ◇ If you sleep at a place for a night, you *spend the night* there. ▪ After the party she was too drunk to drive so she *spent the night*. ▪ They *spent the night* at her brother's. If you ***spend the night with*** someone, or if you and someone else ***spend the night together***, you stay with someone overnight and have sex with that person. ▪ We *spent the night together*. ▪ I *spent the night with* her/him.

spend•er /ˈspɛndɚ/ *noun, pl* **-ers** [*count*] **:** a person who spends money ▪ The restaurant gives the ***big spenders*** [=people who spend lots of money] special treatment.

spending *noun* [*noncount*] **:** the money that is spent especially by a government or organization ▪ government/federal/public *spending* ▪ They have proposed cuts in military/defense *spending*.

spending money *noun* [*noncount*] **:** extra money that you can spend on whatever you want ▪ She earned *spending money* at an after-school job.

spend•thrift /ˈspɛndˌθrɪft/ *noun, pl* **-thrifts** [*count*] **:** a person who spends money in a careless or wasteful way

– spendthrift *adj* ▪ their *spendthrift* way of life

spent /ˈspɛnt/ *adj*

1 : used up and no longer useful ▪ *spent* nuclear fuel ▪ (*chiefly Brit*) He was once one of the most powerful men in the government, but now he's largely ***a spent force***. [=he no longer has the power or influence he once had]

2 *somewhat formal* **:** tired and drained of energy ▪ By the end of the race I was completely *spent*. [=*exhausted*]

sperm /ˈspɚm/ *noun, pl* **sperm** *also* **sperms** *biology*

1 [*count*] **:** a cell that is produced by the male sexual organs and that combines with the female's egg in reproduction ▪ The *sperm* fertilizes the egg. ▪ a man with a low ***sperm count*** [=a man whose body produces few active sperm] — called also *spermatozoon, sperm cell*

2 [*noncount*] **:** fluid that is produced by the male sexual organs which contains sperm cells **:** SEMEN

sper•ma•to•zo•on /spɚˌmætəˈzoʊˌɑːn/ *noun, pl* **-zoa** /-ˈzowə/ [*count*] *biology* **:** SPERM 1

sperm bank *noun, pl* **~ banks** [*count*] **:** a place where sperm are collected, stored, and then used to help women become pregnant

sperm cell *noun, pl* **~ cells** [*count*] *biology* **:** SPERM 1

sperm donor *noun, pl* **~ -nors** [*count*] **:** a man who gives his sperm usually to a sperm bank so that it can be used to help women get pregnant

sper•mi•cide /ˈspɚməˌsaɪd/ *noun, pl* **-cides** [*count, noncount*] **:** a substance that is used to kill sperm in order to prevent pregnancy

– sper•mi•cid•al /ˌspɚməˈsaɪdəl/ *adj* ▪ a *spermicidal* gel

sperm whale *noun, pl* **~ whales** [*count*] **:** a type of whale that has a very large head and is hunted for its fat and oil

spew /ˈspjuː/ *verb* **spews; spewed; spew•ing**

1 a *always followed by an adverb or preposition* [*no obj*] **:** to flow out of something in a fast and forceful way ▪ Exhaust *spewed* out of the car. ▪ Smoke and ashes *spewed* from the volcano. **b** [+ *obj*] **:** to cause (something) to flow out in a fast and forceful way ▪ The volcano *spewed* hot ash. ▪ The faucet started *spewing* dirty water. — often used figuratively ▪ They *spewed* (out) an endless stream of questions. ▪ He *spewed* insults at his critics.

2 *informal* **:** [1]VOMIT [*no obj*] The dog *spewed* (up) all over

S

the rug. [+ obj] The dog *spewed* vomit on the rug.

SPF /ˌɛsˌpiːˈɛf/ *noun* : a number that indicates how well a cream, lotion, etc., protects your skin from the sun [*singular*] a sunscreen with an *SPF* of 15 [*noncount*] a sunscreen with *SPF* 15 — called also *sun protection factor*

sphag·num /ˈsfægnəm/ *noun* [*noncount*] : PEAT MOSS

sphere /ˈsfiɚ/ *noun, pl* **spheres** [*count*]

1 a : a round object : GLOBE ▪ a glass *sphere* **b** *geometry* : a three-dimensional shape that looks like a ball ▪ All points on a *sphere* are the same distance from the center. — see picture at GEOMETRY

2 *somewhat formal* : an area of influence or activity ▪ Women at that time were confined to the domestic *sphere*. ▪ They recognize that jobs in the ***public/private sphere*** are valuable. ▪ The region has moved back and forth between Spanish and Portuguese ***spheres of influence***. [=has been under the control or influence of Spain and Portugal at different times]

spher·i·cal /ˈsfirɪkəl, ˈsfɛrɪkəl/ *adj* : having the shape of a sphere : ROUND ▪ a *spherical* object

spher·oid /ˈsfiɚˌoɪd, ˈsfeɚˌoɪd/ *noun, pl* **-oids** [*count*] *technical* : an object that is somewhat round but not perfectly round

sphinc·ter /ˈsfɪŋktɚ/ *noun, pl* **-ters** [*count*] *medical* : a ring-shaped muscle that surrounds a body opening and that can tighten to close the opening

sphinx *or* **Sphinx** /ˈsfɪŋks/ *noun, pl* **sphinx·es** *or* **Sphinx·es** [*count*] *in ancient Greek and Egyptian stories* : a creature with the body of a lion and the head of a person ▪ a statue of ***the Sphinx***; *also* : something (such as a statue) in the shape of a sphinx ▪ *the* (Great) *Sphinx* of Giza

spic *also* **spick** /ˈspɪk/ *noun, pl* **spics** *also* **spicks** [*count*] *US, informal + offensive* : a person who is a native Spanish-speaker or whose family is from a Spanish-speaking country ✧ The word *spic* is very offensive. Do not use this word.

spic–and–span *or* **spick–and–span** (*chiefly US*) *also chiefly Brit* **spick and span** *or* **spic and span** /ˌspɪkənˈspæn/ *adj* : very clean and neat ▪ He keeps the house *spic-and-span*.

[1]**spice** /ˈspaɪs/ *noun, pl* **spic·es**

1 : a substance (such as pepper or nutmeg) that is used in cooking to add flavor to food and that comes from a dried plant and is usually a powder or seed [*count*] herbs and *spices* [*noncount*] The soup needs a little more *spice*. — often used before another noun ▪ a *spice* mix/blend ▪ a *spice* cake ▪ a ***spice rack*** [=a shelf, cabinet, etc., used to hold small containers of spices]

2 [*noncount*] : something that adds interest or excitement ▪ The elaborate costumes added a little *spice* [=*interest*] to the performance. ▪ ***Variety is the spice of life***. [=variety makes life more interesting]

[2]**spice** *verb* **spices; spiced; spic·ing** [+ *obj*]

1 *not used in progressive tenses* : to flavor (food) with spices ▪ I *spiced* the chicken with ginger. ▪ a highly/heavily/lightly/mildly *spiced* dish

2 : to add interest or excitement to (something) — usually + *up* ▪ They looked for advice on how to *spice up* their living room. ▪ We need to *spice up* our relationship. ▪ We tried to ***spice things up*** by putting on some lively music.

spicy /ˈspaɪsi/ *adj* **spic·i·er; -est**

1 *of food* : flavored with or containing strong spices and especially ones that cause a burning feeling in your mouth ▪ This salsa is too *spicy* [=*hot*] for me.

2 : exciting and somewhat shocking ▪ a *spicy* sex scandal ▪ a *spicy* story/tale

– spic·i·ness /ˈspaɪsinəs/ *noun* [*noncount*]

spi·der /ˈspaɪdɚ/ *noun, pl* **-ders** [*count*] : a small creature that has eight legs and usually creates a web of sticky threads in which it catches insects for food ▪ We watched the *spider* spin its web. — see color picture on page C10

spider monkey *noun, pl* ~ **-keys** [*count*] : a monkey of Central and South America that has long, thin arms and legs and a very long tail

spider plant *noun, pl* ~ **plants** [*count*] : a plant that is often grown in people's houses and that has long narrow leaves and stems which produce smaller plants at the end

spi·der web /ˈspaɪdɚˌwɛb/ *noun, pl* ~ **webs** [*count*] *US* : a network of sticky threads made by a spider and used as a resting place and a trap for food — called also *spider's web, web*; see color picture on page C10; compare COBWEB

spi·dery /ˈspaɪdəri/ *adj* : long and thin like the legs of a spider ▪ *spidery* arms and legs ▪ *spidery* handwriting [=writing that is long, uneven, and often difficult to read]

spiel /ˈspiːl/ *noun, pl* **spiels** [*count*] *informal* : a fast speech that someone has often said before and that is usually intended to persuade people to buy something, agree to something, etc. ▪ I listened to the salesman's *spiel* but still refused to buy anything. ▪ He gave me a long *spiel* about the benefits of joining the club.

spiff /ˈspɪf/ *verb* **spiffs; spiffed; spiff·ing**

spiff up [*phrasal verb*] ***spiff (someone or something) up*** *or* ***spiff up (someone or something)*** *US, informal* : to make (someone or something) neater or more attractive ▪ She wants to *spiff up* her wardrobe. ▪ A fresh coat of paint would really *spiff* the place *up*. ▪ The company is trying to *spiff up* [=*improve*] its image.

spiffy /ˈspɪfi/ *adj* **spiff·i·er; -est** *chiefly US, informal* : neat, stylish, and attractive ▪ a *spiffy* new uniform ▪ She looked very *spiffy* in her new dress.

spig·ot /ˈspɪgət/ *noun, pl* **-ots** [*count*]

1 : a device that controls the flow of liquid from a large container ▪ the *spigot* on a beer keg — called also *tap*

2 *US* : FAUCET; *especially* : an outdoor faucet ▪ Hook the hose up to the *spigot* behind the house.

[1]**spike** /ˈspaɪk/ *noun, pl* **spikes**

1 [*count*] : a long, thin rod that ends in a point and is often made of metal ▪ There are *spikes* on top of the fence. ▪ The climbers drove metal *spikes* into the ice. ▪ a railroad *spike* [=a large nail used to attach rails to railroad ties]

2 [*count*] : a sudden, rapid increase in something ▪ There's been a *spike* in traffic since the new grocery store opened. ▪ a price *spike*

3 a [*count*] : a metal point attached to the bottom of shoes worn by athletes in some sports — usually plural ▪ I need to replace the *spikes* on my golf shoes. **b** ***spikes*** [*plural*] : shoes with metal points attached to the bottom ▪ Baseball players usually wear *spikes*. ▪ a pair of *spikes* **c** ***spikes*** [*plural*] : women's shoes with high, thin heels ▪ She wore (a pair of) *spikes*. [=*spike heels*]

4 [*count*] : a long, narrow group of flowers that grow on one stem ▪ a *spike* of flowers = a flower *spike*

[2]**spike** *verb* **spikes; spiked; spik·ing**

1 [+ *obj*] **a** : to add alcohol or drugs to (food or drink) ▪ Someone *spiked* the punch at the party. — often + *with* ▪ They *spiked* the punch *with* tequila. ▪ The brownies were *spiked with* marijuana. **b** : to add something that gives flavor or interest to (something) — usually + *with* ▪ She *spiked* the sauce *with* vinegar. ▪ Her writing is *spiked with* sarcasm.

2 [*no obj*] *chiefly US* : to increase greatly in a short period of time ▪ The medication caused his blood pressure to *spike*. ▪ Oil and gas prices have *spiked* (upward) again.

3 [+ *obj*] *sports* **a** : to hit (a volleyball) sharply downward towards the ground ▪ She *spiked* the ball and scored the winning point. **b** *US* : to throw (a ball) sharply downward ▪ After he scored a touchdown he *spiked* the ball in the end zone.

4 [+ *obj*] : to form (something, such as hair) into spikes or points ▪ She *spikes* her hair.

5 [+ *obj*] : to pierce or cut (someone or something) with a sharp point or spike ▪ The second baseman was *spiked* by the runner. [=injured by the spikes on the runner's shoes]

6 [+ *obj*] : to prevent (something, such as a story or rumor) from being published or becoming known by many people ▪ The newspaper's editors *spiked* the article.

spike someone's guns *Brit* : to ruin an opponent's plans

spiked /ˈspaɪkt/ *adj* : having sharp points : formed into points ▪ *spiked* [=*spiky*] hair ▪ a lizard with a *spiked* tail

spike heel *noun, pl* ~ **heels** *chiefly US*

1 [*count*] : a very tall and thin heel on women's shoes — called also *spiked heel*

2 ***spike heels*** [*plural*] : shoes with tall, thin heels ▪ She wore (a pair of) *spike heels*. [=*spikes*]

spiky /ˈspaɪki/ *adj* **spik·i·er; -est**

1 : having sharp points : formed into points ▪ He has short, *spiky* [=*spiked*] hair. ▪ a plant with *spiky* leaves

2 *Brit, informal* : tending to become angry or annoyed easily ▪ He has a *spiky* personality.

[1]**spill** /ˈspɪl/ *verb* **spills;** *chiefly US* **spilled** /ˈspɪld/ *or chiefly Brit* **spilt** /ˈspɪlt/; **spill·ing**

1 a [+ *obj*] : to cause or allow (something) to fall, flow, or run over the edge of a container usually in an accidental way ▪ I accidentally *spilled* coffee all over my new suit. ▪ Clean up the flour you *spilled* on the floor. ▪ a puddle of *spilled* water ▪ She opened her purse and *spilled* its contents (out) onto the table. ▪ The bag ripped open and *spilled* (out) its contents all

S

over the floor. — sometimes used figuratively • He *spilled* his thoughts out to her. [=he told her his thoughts in a very free and open way] **b** [*no obj*] **:** to fall or flow over the edge of a container • Milk *spilled* (out) onto the table. • Water *spilled* over the dam. • The bag ripped open and the flour *spilled* (out) onto the floor. — sometimes used figuratively • Her hair *spilled* down her back. • All his thoughts suddenly came ***spilling out*** [=he suddenly began to express all his thoughts]
2 [*no obj*] **:** to move or spread out into a wider place or area • After the movie the crowd *spilled* (out) into/onto the street. • She opened the door and light *spilled* into the room.
3 [*+ obj*] *US, informal* **:** to tell (a secret) to someone • an interviewer who gets celebrities to *spill* their secrets • Come on, *spill* it. Who gave you the money?
cry over spilled/spilt milk see [1]CRY
spill blood see BLOOD
spill over [*phrasal verb*] **1 :** to be completely covered or filled with something **:** to be overflowing with something • The platter was *spilling over* with grapes and melon slices and cheeses. • They were *spilling over* with happiness. [=they were very happy] **2 :** to spread and begin to affect other people, areas, etc. • The stress at work began to *spill over* into other aspects of his life. — see also SPILLOVER
spill the beans see BEAN
spill your guts see [1]GUT

[2]**spill** *noun, pl* **spills** [*count*]
1 : an accident in which liquid is spilled or an amount of liquid that is spilled • Please clean up the *spill* on the kitchen floor. • The coastline was seriously damaged by an ***oil spill***.
2 : an accidental act of falling • She was injured in a *spill* the last time she went riding. • He ***took a spill*** [=he fell] while skiing and broke his leg.

spill·age /ˈspɪlɪʤ/ *noun, pl* **-ag·es** *formal* **:** an occurrence in which something is spilled accidentally [*noncount*] The design of this travel mug helps prevent/reduce/avoid *spillage*. [*count*] an oil *spillage* • small leaks and *spillages*

spill·over /ˈspɪlˌoʊvɚ/ *noun, pl* **-overs :** something that flows out of or spreads beyond a container, space, area, etc. [*count*] Put a pan under the pie to catch any *spillovers*. • We have benefited from a *spillover* of prosperity from neighboring states. [=the prosperity of neighboring states has spread to our state] [*noncount*] Nearby stores were getting some *spillover* from the festival. [=some people who went to the festival also visited the stores] • New technology has a positive ***spillover effect*** into countless fields. — see also *spill over* at [1]SPILL

[1]**spin** /ˈspɪn/ *verb* **spins; spun** /ˈspʌn/; **spin·ning**
1 : to turn or cause someone or something to turn around repeatedly [*no obj*] The Earth *spins* [=*rotates*] on its axis once a day. • The car hit a patch of ice and *spun* into the wall. • a *spinning* propeller • He ***spun around*** [=turned around quickly] and looked at me in surprise. [*+ obj*] The children were *spinning* a top. • He grabbed her and ***spun her around***. [=he grabbed her and turned her around quickly]
2 [*no obj*] **:** to seem to be moving around in a way that makes you feel dizzy or sick • I tried to stand up but the room was *spinning*. • After the night of drinking, ***my head was spinning***. [=I was dizzy] • All of that information ***made my head spin***. [=made me feel confused or dizzy]
3 : to draw out and twist fibers of cotton, wool, silk, etc., into yarn or thread [*+ obj*] She *spun* the silk into thread. • They *spun* the wool into yarn. [*no obj*] tools used for *spinning* — see also SPINNING WHEEL
4 [*+ obj*] *of insects* **:** to form (something) by producing a fluid that quickly hardens into a thread • a spider *spinning* its web • worms *spinning* silk
5 [*+ obj*] **:** to tell (a story, especially a story that you create by using your imagination) • He was ***spinning yarns*** [=telling stories] about his adventures in the navy. • She ***spun a tale*** [=made up a story] about her car breaking down to explain why she was late.
6 *always followed by an adverb or preposition* [*no obj*] **:** to move very quickly on wheels or in a vehicle • The motorcycles *spun* [=*sped*] along the country road.
7 [*+ obj*] **:** to describe (something, such as an event) in a certain way in order to influence what people think about it • Both parties tried to *spin* the debate as a victory for their candidate. • He accused the companies of *spinning* the results of their studies to their own benefit.
8 [*+ obj*] *chiefly US, informal* **:** to play recorded music at a party or nightclub • We hired my favorite DJ to ***spin records/tunes/discs*** at the party.
spinning in his/her grave see [1]GRAVE
spin off [*phrasal verb*] ***spin off*** *or* ***spin (something) off*** *or* ***spin off (something)*** **:** to create something new (such as a new television show or company) by basing it on or taking it from something that already exists • The show was so popular that it *spun off* a new series. [=a new series was created based on the show] • The cartoon has *spun off* dolls and other merchandise. • They *spun off* their specialty foods line into a separate company. • The auto parts manufacturer *spun off* from another company. — see also SPIN-OFF
spin on your heel see [1]HEEL
spin out [*phrasal verb*] **1** *US, of a vehicle* **:** to slide and turn around quickly in an uncontrolled way • The truck *spun out* on a patch of ice. • He took a sharp corner too fast and *spun out*. **2** ***spin (something) out*** *or* ***spin out (something)*** *chiefly Brit* **:** to make (something) last for a very long time • They're deliberately trying to *spin out* the debate. **3** ***spin out of control*** **a :** to move in a way that is not controlled • The rocket *spun out of control* and crashed. **b :** to keep getting worse in a way that is hard to stop or fix • Her drinking problem is *spinning out of control*.
spin your wheels *US, informal* **:** to stay in the same condition or position without making progress • I need to look for a new job. I feel like I'm just *spinning my wheels* here.

[2]**spin** *noun, pl* **spins**
1 a : the act of turning around and around **:** an act of spinning [*noncount*] the direction of the Earth's *spin* [*count*] The ice-skater executed graceful jumps and *spins*. **b :** a rapid turning motion given to a ball by someone who throws or hits it [*noncount*] A baseball thrown with *spin* is harder to hit. • She put *spin* on the ball/shot. [*count*] The bowler put a sideways *spin* on the ball. — see also BACKSPIN, TOPSPIN
2 : a certain way of describing or talking about something that is meant to influence other people's opinion of it [*singular*] Each author puts a new/different *spin* on the story. • a positive/favorable *spin* [*noncount*] They claim to report the news with no *spin*. — see also SPIN CONTROL, SPIN DOCTOR
3 [*count*] *informal* **:** a short trip in a vehicle • He took me for a *spin* in his new car. • Would you like to go for a *spin*?
4 [*count*] **:** a condition in which an airplane is falling rapidly while turning around and around • The plane went into a *spin*. [=*tailspin*] — sometimes used figuratively • The news of her death sent him into a *spin*. [=caused him to become very unhappy, to lose control of his life, etc.]
5 [*singular*] **:** a state of being mentally confused or anxious • Her head was all ***in a spin***. [=her head was spinning; she was very confused]

spi·na bi·fi·da /ˌspaɪnəˈbɪfədə/ *noun* [*noncount*] *medical* **:** a condition in which a person's spine does not develop completely before birth and does not completely cover the spinal cord

spin·ach /ˈspɪnɪʧ/ *noun* [*noncount*] **:** a plant with dark green leaves that are eaten as a vegetable — see color picture on page C4

spi·nal /ˈspaɪnl/ *adj* **:** of, relating to, or affecting the spine • a *spinal* injury

spinal column *noun, pl* **~ -umns** [*count*] *technical* **:** BACKBONE — see picture at HUMAN

spinal cord *noun, pl* **~ cords** [*count*] **:** the large group of nerves which runs through the center of the spine and carries messages between the brain and the rest of the body

spinal tap *noun, pl* **~ taps** [*count*] *medical* **:** a procedure in which a needle is inserted into the spinal cord in order to take out fluid or inject medicine

spin bowler *noun, pl* **~ -ers** [*count*] *cricket* **:** SPINNER 3

spin control *noun* [*noncount*] **:** the activity of trying to control the way something (such as an important event) is described to the public in order to influence what people think about it • political *spin control* • When the defective part was recalled, the company had to do some clever *spin control*.

spin·dle /ˈspɪndl/ *noun, pl* **spin·dles** [*count*]
1 a : a thin rod or stick with pointed ends that is used in making yarn **b :** the long, thin pin on a spinning wheel that is used to make thread
2 : something shaped like a long, thin rod; *especially* **:** a long, thin part of a machine which turns around something or around which something turns

spin·dly /ˈspɪndli/ *adj* **spin·dli·er; -est** [*also more ~; most ~*] **:** long and thin and usually weak • *spindly* legs

spin doctor *noun, pl* **~ -tors** [*count*] *informal* **:** a person (such as a political aide) whose job involves trying to control the way something (such as an important event) is described

S

to the public in order to influence what people think about it • The *spin doctors* from both sides were already declaring victory for their candidates as soon as the debate ended. — called also *spinner*

spin–dryer *also* **spin–drier** *noun, pl* **-ers** [*count*] *chiefly Brit* : a machine that partly dries washed clothes by spinning them very fast

– spin–dry *verb* **-dries**; **-dried**; **-dry·ing** [+ *obj*] • The clothes were washed and *spin-dried*.

spine /ˈspaɪn/ *noun, pl* **spines**

1 [*count*] : the row of connected bones down the middle of the back : BACKBONE • This X-ray shows her *spine*. — see picture at HUMAN

2 [*count*] : a sharp, pointed part on an animal or plant • Hedgehogs are covered with *spines*. • cactus *spines*

3 [*noncount*] *informal* : courage or strength of character • They lack the *spine* to do what needs to be done.

4 [*count*] : the part of a book to which the pages are attached • Stack the books so that all the *spines* are facing the same way. ✧ A book's spine often has the title and author's name printed on it.

up/down your spine ✧ If something ***sends a chill/shiver up/down your spine*** or if ***a chill/shiver runs up/down your spine***, you become frightened, thrilled, etc. • Her performance of the national anthem *sent a chill up my spine*. [=her performance was thrilling and emotional] • The very thought of what those people did *sends a shiver down my spine*. [=scares me] • A (cold) *shiver ran down my spine* when I heard his voice.

spine–chill·ing /ˈspaɪn,ʧɪlɪŋ/ *adj* [*more* ~; *most* ~] : very exciting, thrilling, or frightening : SPINE-TINGLING • a *spine-chilling* scream • *spine-chilling* musical moments

spine·less /ˈspaɪnləs/ *adj*

1 [*more* ~; *most* ~] *disapproving* : lacking courage or strength • a *spineless* coward • *spineless* displays of cowardice

2 : having no spine or spines • Jellyfish are *spineless*. • a *spineless* cactus

– spine·less·ness *noun* [*noncount*]

spin·et /ˈspɪnət/ *noun, pl* **-ets** [*count*]

1 *US* **a** : a small piano **b** : a small electric organ

2 : a small harpsichord

spine–tingling *adj* [*more* ~; *most* ~] : very exciting, thrilling, or frightening • *spine-tingling* suspense • a *spine-tingling* performance

spin·na·ker /ˈspɪnɪkɚ/ *noun, pl* **-kers** [*count*] : a large triangular sail on a boat that is used when the wind is blowing from behind

spin·ner /ˈspɪnɚ/ *noun, pl* **-ners** [*count*]

1 : someone or something that spins yarn or thread

2 : a small device that spins and that is used by fishermen to attract fish

3 *cricket* : a bowler who throws the ball so that it spins — called also *spin bowler*

4 : SPIN DOCTOR

spin·ney /ˈspɪni/ *noun, pl* **-neys** [*count*] *Brit* : a small group of trees

spinning wheel *noun, pl* ~ **wheels** [*count*] : a machine that was used in the past for making yarn or thread

spin–off /ˈspɪn,ɑːf/ *noun, pl* **-offs** [*count*]

1 : a television program, movie, book, etc., that is based on characters from another television program, movie, book, etc. • a *spin-off* of a hit TV show • The comic book is a *spin-off* of the movie.

2 : a new company created by a large company • companies that are *spin-offs* of large corporations

3 : something useful that results from work done to produce something else • *spin-offs* [=*by-products*] of space research — see also *spin off* at [1]SPIN

spin·ster /ˈspɪnstɚ/ *noun, pl* **-sters** [*count*] *old-fashioned* + *often disapproving* : an unmarried woman who is past the usual age for marrying and is considered unlikely to marry — now often considered an insulting word • She was afraid of becoming a *spinster*. • my *spinster* aunts

– spin·ster·hood /ˈspɪnstɚ,hʊd/ *noun* [*noncount*]

spiny /ˈspaɪni/ *adj* **spin·i·er**; **-est** : having or covered with many sharp, pointed parts • a *spiny* fish • *spiny* underbrush/fish

[1]**spi·ral** /ˈspaɪrəl/ *noun, pl* **-rals** [*count*]

1 : a circular curving line that goes around a central point while getting closer to or farther away from it • The glider flew in a wide *spiral* over the field.

2 : a situation in which something continuously increases, decreases, or gets worse — usually singular • an inflationary *spiral* [=a continuous increase in prices] • a *spiral* of problems • Gas prices continued their dizzying ***upward spiral***. [=gas prices got higher] • His drug use drove him into a ***downward spiral***. [=his condition became worse and worse]

3 *American football* : a kick or throw in which the ball spins while moving through the air • The quarterback threw a tight *spiral* to the receiver.

[2]**spiral** *verb* **-rals**; *US* **-raled** *or Brit* **-ralled**; *US* **-ral·ing** *or Brit* **-ral·ling** [*no obj*]

1 *always followed by an adverb or preposition* : to move in a circle around a central point while getting closer to or farther away from it : to move in a spiral • Smoke *spiraled* up from the chimney. • Vultures *spiraled* [=*circled*] overhead. • The airplane *spiraled* to the ground and crashed.

2 : to greatly increase, decrease, or get worse in a continuous and usually fast and uncontrolled way • The unemployment rate has been *spiraling* upward. • The stock market is *spiraling* downward. • *spiraling* [=rapidly increasing] costs • Let's deal with this crisis before it ***spirals out of control***.

[3]**spiral** *adj, always used before a noun* : winding or circling around a central point and usually getting closer to or farther away from it : shaped or moving like a spiral • a *spiral* seashell • a *spiral* driveway

spi·ral–bound /ˈspaɪrəl,baʊnd/ *adj, of a book* : having pages held together along one edge by a continuous piece of wire or plastic that passes through holes in the pages • a *spiral-bound* notebook

spiral staircase *noun, pl* ~ **-cases** [*count*] : a set of stairs that winds around a central post or column

spire /ˈspajɚ/ *noun, pl* **spires** [*count*] : a tall, narrow, pointed structure on the top of a building • church *spires*

– spired /ˈspajɚd/ *adj* • a twin-*spired* cathedral

[1]**spir·it** /ˈspirət/ *noun, pl* **-its**

1 a : the force within a person that is believed to give the body life, energy, and power [*count*] the *spirits* of my ancestors • Some religions believe that the same *spirit* is reincarnated many times in different bodies. [*noncount*] Yoga is very healthy for both body and *spirit*. • I'm sorry I can't make it to your wedding, but I'll be there ***in spirit***. [=I will be thinking about you] **b** [*count*] : the inner quality or nature of a person • He still has a curious and youthful *spirit*. [=he is still a curious and youthful person] • We will all miss her generous *spirit*.

2 [*count*] : a person • My father was a proud *spirit*. • They are ***kindred spirits***. [=people with similar interests or concerns] — see also FREE SPIRIT

3 a [*count*] : GHOST • evil *spirits* **b** ***the Spirit*** : HOLY SPIRIT

4 a : a desire or determination to do something [*count*] His many disappointments never broke his *spirit*. [=never took away his desire to succeed] • He has a strong ***fighting spirit***. [*noncount*] She's a good athlete with a lot of skill and *spirit*. **b** [*noncount*] : enthusiastic loyalty • The students showed their school *spirit* by having a rally to support the football team.

5 [*singular*] **a** : the attitude or feeling that a person has about a particular job, activity, etc. • He didn't approach the work in/with the right *spirit*. **b** : a shared attitude or feeling that relates to a particular time, place, activity, etc. — often + *of* • the *spirit of* the times • a new *spirit of* cooperation • the *spirit of* competition • We all ***got/entered into the spirit of*** the holidays. • You'd have more fun if you'd just relax and *get into the spirit of* things.

6 ***spirits*** [*plural*] : feelings of happiness or unhappiness • *Spirits* were low [=people were unhappy] after our team lost again. • We need to do something to ***lift your spirits***. [=to make you feel better/happier] • It's hard work, but try to ***keep your spirits up***. [=keep a happy and positive attitude] • We were all ***in high spirits*** [=*happy, cheerful*] after the game. • She was ***in low spirits***. [=she was unhappy] • He's still in the hospital, but he's ***in good spirits***. [=happy and positive] — see also HIGH-SPIRITED, LOW-SPIRITED

7 [*noncount*] : the real meaning or intention of something (such as a law) • They seem to be more concerned with obeying the letter of the law than with understanding ***the spirit of the law***. [=what was intended by the law when it was written]

8 ***spirits*** [*plural*] : strong alcoholic drinks : LIQUOR • The store sells wines and *spirits*.

as/when the spirit moves you : when you feel like it : when the time is right • I'll write *when the spirit moves me*.

moving spirit see MOVING

that's the spirit *informal* — used to express approval of

S

someone's attitude • "I know I can do it if I keep trying." "Yeah, *that's the spirit!*" [=that's the right attitude to have]

the spirit is willing but the flesh is weak — used to say that you want to do something but you cannot because you do not have the strength or energy; often used humorously • I try to get up early and exercise, though sometimes *the spirit is willing but the flesh is weak.*

– see also SURGICAL SPIRIT, WHITE SPIRIT

[2]**spirit** *verb, always followed by an adverb or preposition* **-its; -it·ed; -it·ing** [+ *obj*] : to carry (someone or something) away secretly • The singer was *spirited* away in a limousine after the show. • Some of the funds had been *spirited away* to other accounts.

spir·it·ed /ˈspirətəd/ *adj* [*more* ~; *most* ~] : full of courage or energy : very lively or determined • We had a *spirited* [=*lively*] discussion. • The team put up a *spirited* defense. • She's a very *spirited* young lady. — see also HIGH-SPIRITED, LOW-SPIRITED, MEAN-SPIRITED, PUBLIC-SPIRITED

– spir·it·ed·ly *adv*

spir·it·less /ˈspirətləs/ *adj* [*more* ~; *most* ~] : lacking courage, energy, or cheerfulness • a *spiritless* performance

spirit level *noun, pl* **~ -vels** [*count*] *chiefly Brit* : [1]LEVEL 5

[1]**spir·i·tu·al** /ˈspirɪʧəwəl/ *adj* [*more* ~; *most* ~]

1 : of or relating to a person's spirit • Doctors must consider the emotional and *spiritual* needs of their patients. • I'm working on my *spiritual* growth/development. [=the growth of my mind and spirit]

2 : of or relating to religion or religious beliefs • I regularly consult our pastor about *spiritual* matters. • an influential *spiritual* leader

3 : having similar values and ideas : related or joined in spirit • The Romantic composers saw Beethoven as a *spiritual* ancestor. • France will always be the ***spiritual home*** of wine lovers.

– spir·i·tu·al·ly *adv* • She was physically and *spiritually* exhausted. • a *spiritually* uplifting performance

[2]**spiritual** *noun, pl* **-als** [*count*] : a religious folk song that was sung originally by African-Americans in the southern U.S. • The congregation sang hymns and *spirituals.*

spir·i·tu·al·ism /ˈspirɪʧəwəˌlɪzəm/ *noun* [*noncount*] : a belief that the spirits of dead people can communicate with living people

– spir·i·tu·al·ist /ˈspirɪʧəwəlɪst/ *noun, pl* **-ists** [*count*]

spir·i·tu·al·i·ty /ˌspirɪʧəˈwæləti/ *noun* [*noncount*] : the quality or state of being concerned with religion or religious matters : the quality or state of being spiritual • a man of deep *spirituality* [=a very religious man] • We studied Eastern traditions of *spirituality.*

[1]**spit** /ˈspɪt/ *verb* **spits; spat** /ˈspæt/ *or chiefly US* **spit; spit·ting**

1 a [*no obj*] : to force saliva from your mouth • She saw him *spit* on the sidewalk. • I scolded the child for *spitting* at another student. • He *spit/spat* in my face. **b** [+ *obj*] : to force (something, such as food or liquid) from your mouth — often + *out* • He took a taste of the soup and quickly *spat/spit* it *out.* • She *spit out* her gum before class. — sometimes used figuratively • Our manager was ***spitting blood/venom*** [=was extremely angry] when he found out what had happened. • I'm so angry, I could ***spit nails!***

2 [+ *obj*] : to say (something) in a quick and angry way • She *spat* a few nasty remarks at him as he left. • "You make me sick!" he *spat.*

3 [*no obj*] : to throw off or send out something (such as sparks or drops of fat) especially while burning or cooking • The meat was *spitting* in the pan. • The wet wood hissed and *spat* in the fireplace.

4 *informal* : to rain or snow lightly [*no obj*] Take your umbrella, ***it's spitting.*** • a cold, *spitting* rain [+ *obj*] The sky briefly *spat* rain.

spit it out *informal* — used to tell someone to say something that he or she does not want to say or is having a hard time saying. • "Come on, *spit it out!* What happened?"

spit up [*phrasal verb*] ***spit up or spit (something) up or spit up (something)*** *US, informal, of babies* : to vomit or throw up a usually small amount of food or liquid • The baby *spit up* all over my blouse. • The baby *spat up* his breakfast.

[2]**spit** *noun* [*noncount*]

1 : the liquid produced in your mouth : SALIVA • I wiped the *spit* [=*drool, spittle*] off the baby's chin.

2 : someone who looks very much like someone else : SPITTING IMAGE • She's the ***spit and image of*** her mother. = (*Brit*) She's the ***(dead) spit of*** her mother.

spit and vinegar *US, informal* : strength and energy • She's 80 years old but still full of *spit and vinegar.*

– compare [3]SPIT

[3]**spit** *noun, pl* **spits** [*count*]

1 : a thin pointed rod or stick that is used for holding meat over a fire to cook it

2 : a narrow piece of land that goes out into a body of water • a narrow *spit* of land

– compare [2]SPIT

spit and polish *noun* [*noncount*] *informal* : careful attention to making something clean and polished • All the car needs is some *spit and polish.*

spit·ball /ˈspɪtˌbɑːl/ *noun, pl* **-balls** [*count*] *US*

1 : a small piece of paper that is chewed and rolled into a ball so that it can be thrown or shot at someone • The kids were shooting *spitballs* at each other.

2 *baseball* : an illegal pitch in which the ball is made wet with saliva or sweat

[1]**spite** /ˈspaɪt/ *noun* [*noncount*] : a desire to harm, anger, or defeat another person especially because you feel that you have been treated wrongly in some way • He is jealous and full of *spite.* • an act of *spite* • You only denied his request ***out of (pure) spite.***

in spite of : without being prevented by (something) : DESPITE — used to say that something happens or is true even though there is something that might prevent it from happening or being true • He failed the test *in spite of* all his studying. • She went ahead *in spite of* the snow. • They made it on time ***in spite of the fact*** that they got a flat tire.

in spite of yourself : even though you do not want to or expect to • I ended up having a good time *in spite of myself.*

[2]**spite** *verb* **spites; spit·ed; spit·ing** [+ *obj*] : to deliberately annoy, upset, or hurt (someone) • He only did it to *spite* me.

cut off your nose to spite your face see [1]NOSE

spite·ful /ˈspaɪtfəl/ *adj* [*more* ~; *most* ~] : having or showing a desire to harm, anger, or defeat someone : having or showing spite • She's just being *spiteful.* • a *spiteful* remark

– spite·ful·ly *adv* • She *spitefully* refused my request.

– spite·ful·ness *noun* [*noncount*]

spitting distance *noun* [*noncount*] *informal* : a short distance • Our house is ***within spitting distance*** of the park.

spitting image *noun, pl* **~ -ages** [*count*] : someone who looks very much like someone else — usually singular • She is ***the spitting image of*** her mother.

spit·tle /ˈspɪtl/ *noun* [*noncount*] : the liquid produced in your mouth : saliva or spit • *Spittle* sprayed from his lips as he shouted at them.

spit·toon /spɪˈtuːn/ *noun, pl* **-toons** [*count*] : a container that people spit into ✧ Spittoons were common in the past but are now rare. — called also (*chiefly US*) *cuspidor*

spit–up *noun* [*noncount*] *US, informal* : a small amount of vomit from a baby • She wiped the *spit-up* off the baby's chin.

spiv /ˈspɪv/ *noun, pl* **spivs** [*count*] *Brit slang, old-fashioned* : a man who makes money dishonestly • a smooth-talking *spiv*

[1]**splash** /ˈsplæʃ/ *verb* **splash·es; splashed; splash·ing**

1 *always followed by an adverb or preposition* [*no obj*] *of a liquid* : to move, fall, or hit something in a noisy or messy way • Water/Mud *splashed* everywhere. • He dropped the bottle and bleach *splashed* onto the floor. • We could hear the waves *splashing* against the side of the boat.

2 [+ *obj*] **a :** to cause (water or another liquid) to move in a noisy way or messy way • The baby *splashed* the water. • Don't *splash* water at your brother. • I accidentally *splashed* some water on the floor. • She *splashed* cold water on her face. **b :** to make (someone or something) wet with large drops of water or another liquid • Don't *splash* your brother. • We were *splashed* by a passing car. • She *splashed* her face with cold water.

3 [*no obj*] : to move through water in a noisy and messy way • The kids love *splashing* (around) in the pool. • The dog was *splashing* through the waves.

4 [+ *obj*] : to mark (something) with patches of color or light • The sunset *splashed* the sky with red. — often used as *(be) splashed with* • The canvas *was splashed with* bold colors.

splash across/over [*phrasal verb*] ***splash (something) across/over (something)*** : to put (something, such as a photograph or news headline) in a place or position where it will be easily seen by many people • The scandal was *splashed across* the front page. • Her picture was *splashed* (all) *over* the news.

splash down [*phrasal verb*] *of a spacecraft* **:** to land in the ocean ▪ The space capsule *splashed down* in the Gulf of Mexico. — see also SPLASHDOWN

splash out [*phrasal verb*] ***splash out*** *or* ***splash out (something)*** *or* ***splash (something) out*** *Brit, informal* **:** to spend a lot of money ▪ If you really want to *splash out* [=*splurge*], let's go to dinner and a show in town. ▪ We can't afford to *splash out* that much money for luxuries.

²splash *noun, pl* **splash·es**
1 [*count*] **a :** the sound made when someone or something hits liquid or when liquid hits something — usually singular ▪ He listened to the gentle *splash* of the waves against the boat. ▪ We heard a *splash* from the pool. ▪ The bird dived into the pond with a *splash*. **b :** the movement of liquid when something hits it — usually singular ▪ There was barely a *splash* when the diver hit the water. ▪ I was hit by the *splash* when a truck drove through the puddle.
2 [*count*] **:** a mark or spot made when a liquid is splashed on something — often + *of* ▪ You've got *splashes of* mud on your pants.
3 [*count*] **:** a small area of bright color or light — + *of* ▪ a *splash of* color ▪ *splashes of* light on the floor
4 [*singular*] *informal* **:** a small amount of liquid added to a drink — usually + *of* ▪ coffee with just a *splash of* cream
make a splash *informal* **:** to attract a lot of attention in an exciting way ▪ The young director is *making* (quite) *a splash* in Hollywood. ▪ The news of her arrest *made a* huge *splash*.

splash·down /ˈsplæʃˌdaʊn/ *noun, pl* **-downs** [*count, noncount*] **:** the landing of a spacecraft in the ocean — see also *splash down* at ¹SPLASH

splash guard *noun, pl* **~ guards** [*count*] *US* **:** MUD FLAP

splashy /ˈsplæʃi/ *adj* **splash·i·er; -est** [*also more ~; most ~*] **:** having a bright or exciting quality that attracts attention or is meant to attract attention ▪ bright *splashy* colors ▪ big, *splashy* movie musicals ▪ a *splashy* ad

splat /ˈsplæt/ *noun, pl* **splats** [*singular*] *informal* **:** the sound made when something wet hits a surface ▪ The water balloon hit the ground and broke with a *splat*.
– splat *verb* **splats; splat·ted; splat·ting** [*no obj*] *informal* ▪ A bug *splatted* on the windshield.

¹splat·ter /ˈsplætɚ/ *verb* **-ters; -tered; -ter·ing**
1 [*no obj*] **a** *of a liquid* **:** to move, fall, or hit something in large drops ▪ Mud *splattered* everywhere when the wet dog shook himself. ▪ Rain *splattered* against the windows. **b** *of something that contains liquid* **:** to hit something and break apart ▪ A big bug *splattered* against the windshield of the car. ▪ The egg *splattered* on the floor.
2 [+ *obj*] **a :** to cause (a liquid) to move or fall in large drops ▪ You're *splattering* paint everywhere. **b :** to make (something) wet or dirty with large drops of liquid ▪ The paint *splattered* my clothes. — often used as *(be) splattered with* ▪ My clothes *were splattered with* paint.

²splatter *noun, pl* **-ters :** a mark or spot made by a large drop of liquid [*count*] I had paint *splatters* on my jeans. ▪ There were mud *splatters* all over the carpet. [*noncount*] Blood *splatter* was found at the crime scene.

splay /ˈspleɪ/ *verb* **splays; splayed; splay·ing :** to move (things, especially your legs, fingers, etc.) out and apart from each other [+ *obj*] He sat with his legs *splayed* apart. ▪ Her son was *splayed out* [=*spread out, stretched out*] on the couch watching TV. ▪ She *splayed* her fingers to show off her manicure. [*no obj*] His fingers *splayed* out over the table as he steadied himself.

spleen /ˈspliːn/ *noun, pl* **spleens**
1 [*count*] **:** an organ located near your stomach that destroys worn-out red blood cells and produces white blood cells ▪ a ruptured *spleen* — see picture at HUMAN
2 [*noncount*] *literary* **:** feelings of anger ▪ I listened patiently while she ***vented her spleen***. [=while she expressed her angry feelings]

splen·did /ˈsplɛndəd/ *adj* [*more ~; most ~*]
1 : very impressive and beautiful ▪ The balcony gave us a *splendid* [=*magnificent*] view of the river.
2 *somewhat old-fashioned* **:** very good **:** EXCELLENT ▪ We have a *splendid* opportunity to do something really useful. ▪ I have some *splendid* news. ▪ "We'll be coming out to visit over the summer." "Oh, *splendid*!"
– splen·did·ly *adv* ▪ She performed *splendidly*.

splen·dor (*US*) *or Brit* **splen·dour** /ˈsplɛndɚ/ *noun, pl* **-dors**
1 [*noncount*] **:** great and impressive beauty ▪ The palace had lost much of its original *splendor*. ▪ the *splendor* of nature
2 *US* **splendors** *or Brit* **splendours** [*plural*] **:** things that are very beautiful or impressive ▪ architectural *splendors* — often + *of* ▪ the *splendors of* the countryside

sple·net·ic /splɪˈnɛtɪk/ *adj* [*more ~; most ~*] *chiefly Brit, formal* **:** very angry and annoyed ▪ *splenetic* political commentators ▪ a *splenetic* rant

¹splice /ˈsplaɪs/ *verb* **splic·es; spliced; splic·ing** [+ *obj*]
1 : to join ropes, wires, etc., by weaving or twisting them together
2 : to join (pieces of film, magnetic tape, etc.) by connecting their ends together
get spliced *Brit, informal* **:** to get married ▪ So, when are you two *getting spliced*?
– splic·er /ˈsplaɪsɚ/ *noun, pl* **-ers** [*count*]

²splice *noun, pl* **splic·es** [*count*] **:** the place where two things (such as two pieces of rope or film) have been joined by being spliced together

splice

spliff /ˈsplɪf/ *noun, pl* **spliffs** [*count*] *Brit slang* **:** a marijuana cigarette **:** JOINT

splint /ˈsplɪnt/ *noun, pl* **splints** [*count*] **:** a piece of wood, metal, plastic, etc., that is used to hold a broken bone in the correct position while it heals ▪ His leg was in a *splint*. ▪ a wrist *splint*

splint

¹splin·ter /ˈsplɪntɚ/ *noun, pl* **-ters** [*count*] **:** a thin, sharp piece of something (such as wood, glass, etc.) that has broken off a larger piece **:** SLIVER ▪ I got a *splinter* in my finger. ▪ There were *splinters* of glass everywhere.
– splin·tery /ˈsplɪntəri/ *adj* [*more ~; most ~*] ▪ planks of *splintery* wood

²splinter *verb* **-ters; -tered; -ter·ing**
1 : to break (something) into small pieces or splinters [*no obj*] The board *splintered* under his weight. [+ *obj*] The impact of the crash *splintered* the glass.
2 : to divide or split a group of people into smaller groups [*no obj*] groups that have *splintered* off to form new political movements [+ *obj*] a political party that has been *splintered* by disagreements
– splintered *adj* ▪ a *splintered* tree stump

splinter group *noun, pl* **~ groups** [*count*] **:** a group of people that has separated from a larger group (such as a political party)

¹split /ˈsplɪt/ *verb* **splits; split; split·ting**
1 : to break apart or into pieces especially along a straight line [*no obj*] The board *split* in two. ▪ The floorboards are starting to warp and *split* (up). ▪ The hull of the ship *split* apart on the rocks. ▪ A large chunk of ice *split* off/away from the iceberg and crashed into the water. [+ *obj*] *split* (up) a log ▪ She *split* the muffin and gave me half.
2 a : to separate or divide into parts or groups [*no obj*] The class *split* into several small groups. ▪ Two of the band members *split* off to form their own band. — often + *up* ▪ Let's *split up* and look for the lost dog. [+ *obj*] The teacher *split* the class into groups. ▪ The river *splits* the town in two. — often + *up* ▪ Families were often *split up* during the war. **b :** to separate or divide into groups that disagree [*no obj*] The party is *split* over/on the issue of taxes. ▪ The church *split* into moderate and conservative factions. [+ *obj*] The budget issue has *split* (up) the town. ▪ Opinion is *split* on the wording of the new law.
3 [+ *obj*] **:** to divide (something, such as money or food) among two or more people or things ▪ We should *split* [=*share*] the costs. ▪ Why don't we just *split* a pizza for dinner? ▪ She *splits* her time between Boston and New York. [=she spends time in both Boston and New York] ▪ The prize money should be *split* (up) evenly.
4 : to cut, rip, or tear (something) especially along a straight line [+ *obj*] I *split* my lip when I fell. ▪ He bent over and *split* the seat of his pants. [*no obj*] His pants *split* when he bent over.
5 *informal* **:** to end or cause the end of a relationship [*no obj*] My parents *split* when I was little. — usually + *up* ▪ The band *split up* just after they released their new album. [+ *obj*] — + *up* ▪ Creative differences eventually *split up* the band.
6 [*no obj*] *informal* + *somewhat old-fashioned* **:** to leave

S

quickly • "Let's *split*!" [=let's get out of here]

split hairs see HAIR

split on [*phrasal verb*] ***split on (someone)*** *Brit, informal* : to give information about the secret or criminal activity of (someone) to the police • He would never *split on* [=(*US*) *inform on*] his chums.

split the difference : to agree to an amount that is halfway between two given amounts • He thought I should pay $40 and I thought I should pay $30, so we decided to *split the difference* at $35.

split the ticket *US* : to vote for candidates from more than one political party — see also SPLIT TICKET

split your sides (laughing) *informal* : to laugh very hard • The movie was hilarious. I (almost) *split my sides laughing.*

²split *noun, pl* **splits**
1 [*count*] : a narrow break, tear, or crack • There's a *split* down the back of your jacket.
2 [*count*] : a division or separation in a group that is caused by a disagreement • The new policy has caused a *split* in the organization. • a *split* between liberals and conservatives
3 [*count*] : a clear separation or difference between two or more things • a wide *split* of opinions
4 [*singular*] **a** : a part of something that has been divided • Here's your *split* [=*portion, share*] of the proceeds. **b** : the act of dividing something among two or more people or things • We agreed to a fifty-fifty *split* of the profit. [=we agreed to divide the profits equally]
5 [*count*] : a position in which you are sitting on the floor with your legs extended in a straight line and in opposite directions • The ballerina did a *split*. = The ballerina did ***the splits***.
— see also BANANA SPLIT

split ends *noun* [*plural*] : hairs that have become dry or damaged and have split apart at the end • She has *split ends*. • You should trim off your *split ends*.

split–fingered fastball *noun, pl* ~ **-balls** [*count*] *baseball* : a fast pitch that drops quickly as it nears the batter — called also *split-finger, splitter*

split infinitive *noun, pl* ~ **-tives** [*count*] *grammar* : an English phrase in which an adverb or other word is placed between *to* and a verb • "To really start" is an example of a *split infinitive*. ✧ Some people feel that the use of split infinitives should be avoided, but they are common in both speech and writing.

split–lev·el /ˈsplɪtˈlɛvəl/ *adj* : divided so that the floor in one part is about halfway between two floors in the other part • a *split-level* house
— **split–lev·el** /ˈsplɪtˌlɛvəl/ *noun, pl* **-levels** [*count*] *US* • They bought a nice *split-level* in a quiet neighborhood.

split pea *noun, pl* ~ **peas** [*count*] : a dried pea that has had the outer skin removed and that is split into two parts • *split pea* soup

split personality *noun, pl* ~ **-ties** [*count*] : a condition in which a person behaves in two very different ways at different times — sometimes used figuratively • a city with a *split personality*

split second *noun* [*singular*] : a very short period of time • In a *split second*, it was all over.

split–second *adj, always used before a noun*
1 : done very quickly • a *split-second* decision
2 : very accurate or precise • *split-second* timing

split·ter /ˈsplɪtɚ/ *noun, pl* **-ters** [*count*]
1 : a device that divides or splits something (such as wood or electronic signals) • a log *splitter* • a three-way phone line *splitter*
2 *baseball* : SPLIT-FINGERED FASTBALL

split ticket *noun, pl* ~ **-ets** [*count*] *US* : a ballot on which a voter votes for candidates from more than one political party

splitting headache *noun, pl* ~ **-aches** [*count*] : a very bad headache

splodge /ˈsplɑːʤ/ *noun, pl* **splodg·es** [*count*] *Brit, informal* : SPLOTCH • a *splodge* of ink

splotch /ˈsplɑːʧ/ *noun, pl* **splotch·es** [*count*] *chiefly US* : a large spot or mark of dirt, paint, etc. • There's an ink *splotch* [=(*Brit*) *splodge*] on your shirt. • *splotches* of ink/rust
— **splotched** /ˈsplɑːʧt/ *adj* • Her pants were *splotched* with paint. [=there were splotches of paint on her pants]
— **splotchy** /ˈsplɑːʧi/ *adj* **splotch·i·er; -est** • *splotchy* skin

splurge /ˈsplɚʤ/ *verb* **splurg·es; splurged; splurg·ing** [*no obj*] *informal* : to spend more money than usual on something for yourself • You should let yourself *splurge* once in a while. — often + *on* • We decided to *splurge on* a bottle of good wine for dinner.
— **splurge** *noun, pl* **splurges** [*count*] *informal* — usually singular • She went on a shopping *splurge*. [=*spree*] • This year's big *splurge* [=expensive purchase] was a new car.

splut·ter /ˈsplʌtɚ/ *verb* **-ters; -tered; -ter·ing**
1 [*no obj*] : to make a series of short, loud noises like the noises of someone who is struggling to breathe • She coughed and *spluttered* as she climbed out of the icy water. • The old lawn mower *spluttered* [=*sputtered*] to life. [=noisily started working]
2 : to say (something) in short, confused phrases [*no obj*] When I demanded an explanation, he just stood there *spluttering*. [+ *obj*] She *spluttered* an excuse. • "Th-that's simply not true," he *spluttered*.
— **splutter** *noun, pl* **-ters** [*count*]

¹spoil /ˈspojəl/ *verb* **spoils; spoiled** *or chiefly Brit* **spoilt** /ˈspojəlt/; **spoil·ing**
1 [+ *obj*] : to have a bad effect on (something) : to damage or ruin (something) • The fight *spoiled* the party. • The camping trip was *spoiled* by bad weather. • Don't let one mistake *spoil* your day. • He always *spoils* everything. • Don't *spoil* your appetite by snacking too much. • Exposure to air will *spoil* the wine. • I *spoiled* the sauce by adding too much garlic.
2 [*no obj*] : to decay or lose freshness especially because of being kept too long • The milk/fruit was beginning to *spoil*.
synonyms see ¹DECAY
3 [+ *obj*] *disapproving* **a** : to give (someone, such as a child) everything that he or she wants : to have a bad effect on (someone) by allowing too many things or by not correcting bad behavior • Her grandparents *spoil* her. — often used as *(be) spoiled* • He *was spoiled* by his parents. • a *spoiled* brat • That child is ***spoiled rotten***. [=very spoiled] — sometimes used figuratively • We've *been spoiled* lately by/with this beautiful weather. [=we've had so much beautiful weather that we expect the weather always to be beautiful] • (*Brit*) Customers are ***spoiled/spoilt for choice*** [=customers have a lot of choices] when buying a new car. **b** : to treat (someone) very well • The hotel *spoils* their guests with fine dining and excellent service. • She always *spoils* me on my birthday. • You should *spoil* yourself with a day at the spa.

(be) spoiling for : to have a strong desire for (something, such as a fight) • They *are spoiling for* a fight/argument. • The team *is spoiling for* a rematch.

²spoil *noun, pl* **spoils** [*count*] *formal*
1 : something stolen or taken by thieves, soldiers, etc. — usually plural; usually used with *the* • The pirates divided *the spoils* among themselves. • ***the spoils of war***
2 : something valuable or desirable that someone gets by working or trying hard — usually plural; usually used with *the* • We shared *the spoils* of victory. • *the spoils* of success

spoil·age /ˈspoɪlɪʤ/ *noun* [*noncount*] *technical* : the process or result of decaying • food *spoilage* • The milk should be refrigerated to prevent *spoilage*.

spoil·er /ˈspoɪlɚ/ *noun, pl* **-ers** [*count*]
1 : a person or thing that spoils something: such as **a** : a political candidate who cannot win but who prevents another candidate from winning by taking away votes **b** *chiefly US* : a person or team that surprisingly defeats a competitor that is expected to win • They played (the role of) the *spoiler* and ruined our chance to play in the finals. **c** : information about the things that happen in a movie, book, etc., that spoils the surprise or suspense for someone who has not seen it or read it yet • The review contains a few *spoilers*, so don't read it if you haven't seen the movie.
2 **a** : a long narrow part on the back of an automobile that prevents it from lifting off the road at high speeds **b** : a part of an airplane's wing that may be raised to control the amount of lift produced by the wing

spoil·sport /ˈspojəlˌspoɚt/ *noun, pl* **-sports** [*count*] *informal* : someone who spoils other people's fun or enjoyment • Oh, don't be a *spoilsport*. Let them try it. • Dad's a *spoilsport*. He won't let us play football.

spoilt *chiefly Brit spelling of* ¹SPOIL

¹spoke *past tense of* SPEAK

²spoke *noun, pl* **spokes** [*count*] : one of the bars that connect the center of a wheel to the rim • The stick got caught in the wheel's *spokes*. — see picture at BICYCLE

¹spo·ken /ˈspoʊkən/ *past participle of* SPEAK

²spoken *adj*
1 : using speech and not writing • a *spoken* statement • the *spoken* word/language

2 : speaking in a specified manner — used in combination • She is soft-*spoken*. • a plain*spoken* man [=a man who speaks plainly] — see also WELL-SPOKEN

spokes•man /ˈspoʊksmən/ *noun, pl* **-men** /ˈspoʊksmən/ [*count*] : someone who speaks for or represents a person, company, etc. • A White House *spokesman* answered questions from the reporters. — often + *for* • a *spokesman for* the musician/company • The success of his books has made him a *spokesman for* his generation. • a *spokesman for* AIDS awareness

spokes•per•son /ˈspoʊksˌpɚsn̩/ *noun, pl* **spokes•peo•ple** /ˈspoʊksˌpi:pəl/ [*count*] : a man or woman who speaks for or represents someone or something • a statement from the company's *spokesperson*

spokes•wom•an /ˈspoʊksˌwʊmən/ *noun, pl* **-wom•en** /ˈspoʊksˌwɪmən/ [*count*] : a woman who speaks for or represents someone or something • The company's *spokeswoman* addressed the reporters.

[1]sponge /ˈspʌnʤ/ *noun, pl* **spong•es**

1 [*count*] : a piece of light natural or artificial material that becomes soft when it is wet, is able to take in and hold liquid, and is used for washing or cleaning • a kitchen *sponge* — sometimes used figuratively • His mind is (like) a *sponge*. [=he remembers a lot of information easily] — see picture at KITCHEN

2 [*count*] : a type of sea animal from which natural sponges are made

3 [*count, noncount*] *Brit* : SPONGE CAKE • a slice of *sponge*

4 [*count*] *informal + disapproving* : someone who gets something from someone else without doing or paying anything in return : SPONGER • He's a lazy *sponge*.

5 [*count*] : a device like a sponge that is used by women to prevent pregnancy • a contraceptive *sponge*

[2]sponge *verb* **sponges; sponged; spong•ing**

1 [+ *obj*] **a** : to clean or wipe (something) with a sponge • He *sponged* the table. • She *sponged* up the spilt milk. • He *sponged* off his face. • She *sponged* the dirt off her shirt. **b** : to put (paint) on a surface with a sponge • She *sponged* the paint on the walls. = She *sponged* the walls.

2 *informal + disapproving* : to get money, food, etc., from (someone) without doing or paying anything in return [+ *obj*] She always *sponges* meals from us. [*no obj*] — often + *off* • She lives at home and *sponges off* her parents.

sponge bath *noun, pl* ~ **baths** [*count*] *US* : a bath in which someone or something is not placed in water but is cleaned with a wet, soapy sponge or cloth • The nurse gave him a *sponge bath*.

sponge cake *noun, pl* ~ **cakes** : a very light cake made with flour, eggs, and sugar [*count*] a lemon *sponge cake* [*noncount*] layers of *sponge cake*

spong•er /ˈspʌnʤɚ/ *noun, pl* **-ers** [*count*] *informal + disapproving* : someone who gets money, food, etc., from someone else without doing or paying anything in return • Her brother's a lazy *sponger*.

spongy /ˈspʌnʤi/ *adj* **spong•i•er; -est** [*also more* ~; *most* ~] : soft and full of holes or water : resembling a sponge • *spongy* bread • The ground was *spongy*.

— **spong•i•ness** *noun* [*noncount*]

[1]spon•sor /ˈspɑ:nsɚ/ *noun, pl* **-sors** [*count*]

1 a : a person or organization that pays the cost of an activity or event (such as a radio or television program, sports event, concert, etc.) in return for the right to advertise during the activity or event • Our company is a *sponsor* of the race. • corporate *sponsors* **b** : a person or organization that gives someone money for participating in a charity event (such as a walk or race) • I have over 50 *sponsors* for next week's race. **c** : an organization that gives money to an athlete for training, clothes, equipment, etc., in return for the right to use the athlete for advertising • Her *sponsors* include a major sneaker company.

2 a : someone who takes the responsibility for someone or something • He agreed to be my *sponsor* so that I could join the club. • The senator is a *sponsor* of the proposed bill. **b** : a person who teaches and guides someone in religious or spiritual matters • She was my *sponsor* at my confirmation. [=she helped to prepare me for my confirmation]

[2]sponsor *verb* **-sors; -sored; -sor•ing** [+ *obj*] : to be a sponsor for (something or someone) • The radio station *sponsored* the concert. • The tournament is *sponsored* by local businesses. • Will you *sponsor* me for the charity race? • He *sponsored* me at my confirmation. • She *sponsored* the new tax bill. • *sponsored* events — sometimes used in combination • a state-*sponsored* study • government-*sponsored* programs

spon•sor•ship /ˈspɑ:nsɚˌʃɪp/ *noun, pl* **-ships**

1 : an arrangement in which a sponsor agrees to give money to someone or something [*noncount*] You cannot race without *sponsorship*. • He receives millions of dollars in *sponsorship*. • *sponsorship* deals [*count*] She has a *sponsorship* from the sneaker company. • corporate *sponsorships*

2 [*noncount*] : the act of sponsoring someone or something — often + *of* • The group protested the tobacco company's *sponsorship of* the tournament.

spon•ta•ne•i•ty /ˌspɑ:ntəˈnejəti/ *noun* [*noncount*] : the quality or state of being spontaneous • the *spontaneity* of their behavior • She liked his *spontaneity*.

spon•ta•ne•ous /spɑnˈteɪnijəs/ *adj*

1 : done or said in a natural and often sudden way and without a lot of thought or planning • *spontaneous* laughter • a *spontaneous* kiss/decision • The comment was completely *spontaneous*.

2 [*more* ~; *most* ~] : doing things that have not been planned but that seem enjoyable and worth doing at a particular time • He's a guy who's *spontaneous* and fun.

— **spon•ta•ne•ous•ly** *adv* • He laughed *spontaneously*. • She acted *spontaneously*. • They *spontaneously* decided to go to the beach.

spontaneous combustion *noun* [*noncount*] *technical* : burning that is caused by chemical actions inside of something rather than by heat from the outside

spoof /ˈspu:f/ *noun, pl* **spoofs** [*count*] : a humorous movie, book, play, etc., that copies something in a silly and exaggerated way • a Shakespearean *spoof* — often + *of* or *on* • a *spoof of* horror films • a *spoof on* Shakespeare's play

— **spoof** *verb* **spoofs; spoofed; spoof•ing** [+ *obj*] • The movie *spoofs* horror films.

[1]spook /ˈspu:k/ *noun, pl* **spooks** [*count*] *informal*

1 : [1]GHOST 1 • scary *spooks*

2 *chiefly US* : [1]SPY 1 • a CIA *spook*

[2]spook *verb* **spooks; spooked; spook•ing** *chiefly US, informal*

1 [+ *obj*] : to scare or frighten (a person or animal) • The noise *spooked* the cat. • The little girl was *spooked* by scary masks.

2 [*no obj*] : to become frightened • She doesn't *spook* easily. — usually used of an animal • The horse *spooked* and ran away.

spooky /ˈspu:ki/ *adj* **spook•i•er; -est** [*also more* ~; *most* ~] : strange and frightening • a *spooky* movie • The music was pretty *spooky*. • a *spooky* old house • He looks *spooky*. = He's *spooky* looking. • a *spooky* coincidence [=a very strange coincidence that makes you feel uneasy]

spool /ˈspu:l/ *noun, pl* **spools** [*count*] : a round object that is made to have something (such as thread, wire, or tape) wrapped around it • a *spool* of film • (*US*) a *spool* of thread [=(*Brit*) a cotton reel] — see picture at SEWING

[1]spoon /ˈspu:n/ *noun, pl* **spoons** [*count*]

1 : an eating or cooking tool that has a small shallow bowl attached to a handle • a wooden *spoon* — see picture at PLACE SETTING; see also TABLESPOON, TEASPOON

2 : SPOONFUL — often + *of* • two *spoons of* sugar

born with a silver spoon in your mouth see BORN

— see also GREASY SPOON

[2]spoon *verb, always followed by an adverb or preposition* **spoons; spooned; spoon•ing** [+ *obj*] : to move or pick up (food) with a spoon • She *spooned* the gravy onto her potatoes. • He *spooned* the ice cream into a bowl.

spoo•ner•ism /ˈspu:nəˌrɪzəm/ *noun, pl* **-isms** [*count*] : a humorous mistake in which a speaker switches the first sounds of two or more words • the *spoonerism* "tons of soil" for "sons of toil"

spoon–feed /ˈspu:nˌfi:d/ *verb* **-feeds; -fed** /-ˌfɛd/; **-feed•ing** [+ *obj*]

1 : to feed (someone) with a spoon • She *spoon-fed* the baby.

2 *disapproving* : to give someone information in a way that requires or allows no further thinking or effort • The material was *spoon-fed* to the students. • The students are being *spoon-fed* facts and dates without having any opportunity for discussion. • Misleading facts about the war are being *spoon-fed* to the public.

spoon•ful /ˈspu:nˌfʊl/ *noun, pl* **-fuls** [*count*] : as much as a spoon can hold — often + *of* • one *spoonful of* sugar

spo•rad•ic /spəˈrædɪk/ *adj* : happening often but not regu-

S

larly : not constant or steady • *Sporadic* cases of the disease were reported. • *sporadic* [=*intermittent*] gunfire/fighting
– spo·rad·i·cal·ly /spəˈrædɪkli/ *adv* • The gunfire was heard *sporadically*. [=*intermittently*] • Occurrences of the disease were *sporadically* reported.

spore /ˈspoɚ/ *noun, pl* **spores** [*count*] *biology* : a cell made by some plants that is like a seed and can produce a new plant • mold *spores*

¹sport /ˈspoɚt/ *noun, pl* **sports**
1 a [*count*] : a contest or game in which people do certain physical activities according to a specific set of rules and compete against each other • My favorite (competitive) *sports* are tennis and volleyball. • the *sport* of boxing • Do you play a *sport*? = Do you play any *sports*? • Baseball is a ***team sport*** [=a sport played by teams] — often used in the plural especially in U.S. English to refer to sports in a general way • My brother likes *sports*. [=he enjoys playing and/or watching games such as football, baseball, basketball, golf, etc.] • I like watching *sports* on TV. • She likes to ***play sports*** — see also SPECTATOR SPORT, WINTER SPORT **b** [*noncount*] *Brit* : sports in general • He's not interested in *sport*. [=(*US*) *sports*] • She likes to ***play sport***
2 : a physical activity (such as hunting, fishing, running, swimming, etc.) that is done for enjoyment [*count*] Ice-skating with friends is my favorite *sport*. [*noncount*] He hunts and fishes ***for sport*** [=he hunts and fishes because he enjoys it and not as a job or because he needs food for survival] — see also BLOOD SPORT
3 [*count*] **a** — used with *good, bad*, etc., to say if someone has behaved politely or not after losing a game or contest • He lost but he was a ***good sport*** about it. [=he was not rude or angry about losing] • Don't be a ***poor/bad sport*** [=don't be angry or rude if you lose] **b** *informal + old-fashioned* : someone who is kind or generous • ***Be a (good) sport*** and let him play with you. **c** *informal + old-fashioned* — used as a friendly way to address someone (especially a man) • See you later, *sport*. • Hey, *sport* [=*buddy*]. Can you tell me where the nearest gas station is?
in sport *somewhat formal + old-fashioned* : in a joking way : in a way that is not serious • Don't take offense. I was only saying it *in sport*. [=*in fun*]
make sport of *somewhat formal + old-fashioned* : to laugh at and make jokes about (someone or something) in an unkind way • They *made sport of* [=*made fun of*] the way he talked.

²sport *adj, always used before a noun*
1 : done for enjoyment rather than as a job or for food for survival • *sport* fishing/hunting
2 *chiefly US* : participating in an activity (such as hunting or fishing) for enjoyment rather than as a job or for food for survival • a *sport* fisherman — compare SPORTS

³sport *verb* **sports; sport·ed; sport·ing**
1 [+ *obj*] : to wear (something) in a way that attracts attention • She showed up at the party *sporting* a bright red hat.
2 [*no obj*] *literary* : to play in a happy and lively way • The lambs *sported* [=*frolicked*] in the meadow.

sport coat *noun, pl* **~ coats** [*count*] *US* : a man's coat that is like the top part of a suit but is less formal — called also *sports coat, sports jacket*, (*US*) *sport jacket*; see color picture on page C15

sport·ing /ˈspoɚtɪŋ/ *adj, always used before a noun*
1 : of, relating to, or used in sports • *sporting* events • *sporting* dogs • (*US*) a store that sells ***sporting goods*** = a ***sporting goods store***
2 : fairly good — used in the phrase ***a sporting chance*** • There is *a sporting chance* that your plan will work. • He may not win, but he should at least be given *a sporting chance* [=a fair chance] to succeed.
3 [*more ~; most ~*] *chiefly Brit* : done or behaving in a way that treats the other people in a sport or competition fairly • It wasn't very *sporting* of you to trip him. • a *sporting* gesture [=a gesture that shows good sportsmanship] — opposite UNSPORTING

sport of kings *noun*
the sport of kings *somewhat old-fashioned* : the sport of racing horses : HORSERACING

sports /ˈspoɚts/ *adj, always used before a noun* : of, relating to, or suitable for sports • a *sports* team/fan • a *sports* center • the *sports* section/pages of the newspaper • *sports* equipment/facilities • a *sports* bra — compare ²SPORT

sports bar *noun, pl* **~ bars** [*count*] *US* : a bar that has televisions for watching sports and is decorated with sports items

sports car *noun, pl* **~ cars** [*count*] : a low, small car that seats two people and that is made for fast driving — see picture at CAR

sports·cast /ˈspoɚtsˌkæst, *Brit* ˈspɔːtsˌkɑːst/ *noun, pl* **-casts** [*count*] *US* : a television or radio broadcast of a sports event or of news about sports

sports·cast·er /ˈspoɚtsˌkæstɚ, *Brit* ˈspɔːtsˌkɑːstə/ *noun, pl* **-ers** [*count*] *US* : someone who describes the action of a sports event or gives news about sports during a sportscast

sports coat *noun, pl* **~ coats** [*count*] : SPORT COAT

sports day *noun, pl* **~ days** [*count*] *Brit* : FIELD DAY

sport shirt *noun, pl* **~ shirts** [*count*] *US* : an informal shirt; *especially* : POLO SHIRT — called also *sports shirt*

sports jacket *noun, pl* **~ -ets** [*count*] : SPORT COAT

sports·man /ˈspoɚtsmən/ *noun, pl* **sports·men** /ˈspoɚtsmən/ [*count*]
1 *US* : a man who participates in outdoor activities like hunting and fishing
2 *chiefly Brit* : a man who participates in sports • a champion *sportsman* [=*athlete*] • He was a keen *sportsman* all his life.

sports·man·like /ˈspoɚtsmənˌlaɪk/ *adj* : fair, respectful, and polite toward other players when participating in a sport : showing sportsmanship • She is always *sportsmanlike* when she plays. • *sportsmanlike* behavior — opposite UNSPORTSMANLIKE

sports·man·ship /ˈspoɚtsmənˌʃɪp/ *noun* [*noncount*] : fair play, respect for opponents, and polite behavior by someone who is competing in a sport or other competition • He's a great player who's also admired for his *sportsmanship*. • She showed good/bad/poor *sportsmanship*.

sports medicine *noun* [*noncount*] : a field of medicine that relates to the prevention and treatment of injuries and other health problems that affect people who play sports

sports shirt *noun, pl* **~ shirts** [*count*] : SPORT SHIRT

sports·wear /ˈspoɚtsˌweɚ/ *noun* [*noncount*]
1 : clothes that people wear for playing sports
2 *chiefly US* : comfortable clothes that people wear for informal activities

sports·wom·an /ˈspoɚtsˌwʊmən/ *noun, pl* **-wom·en** /-ˌwɪmən/ [*count*] : a woman who participates in sports • a champion *sportswoman*

sports·writ·er /ˈspoɚtsˌraɪtɚ/ *noun, pl* **-ers** [*count*] : someone who writes about sports for a newspaper, magazine, etc.

sport–util·i·ty vehicle /ˈspoɚtjuˈtɪləti-/ *noun, pl* **~ -hicles** [*count*] : SUV

sporty /ˈspoɚti/ *adj* **sport·i·er; -est** [*also more ~; most ~*]
1 *of clothing* : attractive and suitable for informal wear • a *sporty* jacket/shirt
2 *of a car* : having the qualities or appearance of a sports car • a *sporty* red convertible
3 *chiefly Brit* : liking sports : active in and good at sports : ATHLETIC • *sporty* children

¹spot /ˈspɑːt/ *noun, pl* **spots** [*count*]
1 a : a small area of a surface that is different from other areas • The wood still has some rough *spots*. • The chair's original paint is still visible in *spots*. • He fell through a weak *spot* in the ice. — often + *on* • The dog is black with a white *spot on* its chest. • There are wet *spots on* the floor. • a sore *spot on* his hand • He tries to cover up the bald *spot on* his head. • a bruised *spot on* the apple — see also BEAUTY SPOT, SUNSPOT **b** : a small amount of a substance that is on something • The tablecloth had a couple of *spots*. • There were mud *spots* on the back of his pants. • rust *spots* on the metal — often + *of* • a *spot of* grease • There was a tiny *spot of* ketchup at the corner of her mouth. • There wasn't a *spot of* dust anywhere. **c** : a small mark or lump on your skin, on the surface of a plant, etc. • I noticed some red *spots* on my arms. • *spots* of rot on the leaf **d** *Brit* : PIMPLE • a teenager with *spots* on his face
2 : a particular space or area : PLACE • This looks like a good *spot* for a picnic. • a sunny/shady *spot* • a quiet *spot* by the river • our family's favorite vacation *spot* • We had trouble finding a parking *spot*. [=*space*] • The battle happened exactly on/at this *spot* over 150 years ago. • There are *spots* in the essay where the writer drifts from his argument. • This is a good *spot* to stop the movie. — see also BLACK SPOT, HOT SPOT, NIGHTSPOT, TROUBLE SPOT, *bright spot* at BRIGHT
3 : a particular position in a competition, organization, program, etc. • The teams are battling for the last play-off *spot*. •

S

The band deserves a better *spot* in the festival's lineup. ▪ The talk show has been moved to a daytime *spot*. ▪ He's trying out for a *spot* on the team. ▪ With such a large lead, the team is in a comfortable *spot*.

4 : an appearance on a television or radio program ▪ The host has several guest *spots* lined up tonight.

5 : a short announcement or advertisement on television or radio ▪ advertising *spots*

6 : a difficult or embarrassing position or situation — usually singular ▪ When the truth came out, they found themselves in an awful *spot*. [=*fix, mess, predicament*] ▪ You put me ***in a (tight) spot***

7 *Brit* **:** a small amount *of* something ▪ I had a *spot of* [=*bit of*] trouble putting the bicycle together. ▪ How about a *spot of* tennis before lunch? ▪ a *spot of* lunch ▪ Just a *spot of* brandy, please. ▪ They had a ***spot of bother*** with the Inland Revenue.

a leopard can't change its spots see LEOPARD

hit the spot *informal, of food or drink* **:** to be very enjoyable or satisfying ▪ That dinner really *hit the spot*. [=I enjoyed that dinner very much]

knock spots off *Brit, informal* **:** to be much better than (someone or something) ▪ They *knock spots off* the competition.

on the spot **1 :** right away at the place that has been mentioned **:** IMMEDIATELY ▪ I offered him the job when he came for an interview, and he accepted the offer *on the spot*. ▪ When the boss saw him stealing, he was fired *on the spot*. **2 :** at the place where something is happening ▪ She was *on the spot* reporting on the fire soon after the alarm was sounded. **3 :** in a difficult or dangerous position or situation ▪ The question put me ***on the spot*** **4** *Brit* **:** in the same location without moving forward or backward ▪ running/jogging *on the spot* [=(*US*) *in place*]

— see also BLIND SPOT, SOFT SPOT

²spot *verb* **spots; spot·ted; spot·ting** [+ *obj*]

1 *not used in progressive tenses* **:** to see or notice (someone or something that is difficult to see or find) ▪ She *spotted* a deer in the woods. ▪ He *spotted* a typo. ▪ Can you *spot* [=*recognize*] the difference between the pictures? ▪ The band's lead singer was recently *spotted* with a well-known actress.

2 *US* **a :** to give (an opponent) a specified advantage at the beginning of a race, game, etc., in order to make a competition more even ▪ They *spotted* us five points, and we still lost. ▪ (*golf*) He *spotted* him two strokes a hole. **b** *informal* **:** to lend (someone) a small amount of money ▪ I'm a little short of cash. Can you *spot* me five bucks?

3 *American football* **:** to put (the football) at the appropriate place on the field in preparation for the next play ▪ The official *spotted* the ball at the 10-yard line.

4 : to mark (something) with spots ▪ A trail of blood *spotted* the snow. — usually used as *(be) spotted with* ▪ His pants *were spotted with* mud. [=there were spots of mud on his pants]

³spot *adj, always used before a noun, finance* **:** relating to goods or shares that are paid for and delivered immediately instead of at a future time ▪ the difference between futures and *spot* commodities ▪ the *spot* price of wheat/oil ▪ the *spot* market ▪ *spot* cash [=cash paid immediately for something]

spot check *noun, pl* ~ **checks** [*count*] **:** an act of looking at a few things or people in a group in order to find possible problems ▪ Police carried out *spot checks* of/on cars at the border.

spot–check /ˈspɑːtˌtʃɛk/ *verb* **-checks; -checked; -check·ing :** to check (something) quickly for problems especially by looking at a few things or people in a group [+ *obj*] He *spot-checked* the data for errors. ▪ Police *spot-checked* cars at the border. [*no obj*] — often + *for* ▪ She *spot-checked for* errors.

spot·less /ˈspɑːtləs/ *adj* **:** perfectly clean ▪ a *spotless* kitchen ▪ She keeps her room *spotless*. — often used figuratively ▪ He has a *spotless* record/reputation.

– spot·less·ly *adv* ▪ The house is ***spotlessly clean***

¹spot·light /ˈspɑːtˌlaɪt/ *noun, pl* **-lights**

1 [*count*] **a :** a device that directs a narrow, bright beam of light on a small area ▪ They aimed the *spotlight* at the center of the stage. **b :** the area of light created by a spotlight ▪ A *spotlight* moved across the stage. ▪ The actor stood in the *spotlight*. ▪ performing under the *spotlights*

2 ***the spotlight*** **:** public attention or notice ▪ a baseball star who hates *the spotlight* ▪ They're always ***in the spotlight*** ▪ School violence is once again ***under the*** media ***spotlight*** [=getting a lot of attention from the media] ▪ The news article ***turned/put the spotlight on*** the city's financial problems.

²spotlight *verb* **-lights; -light·ed** *or* **-lit; -light·ing** [+ *obj*]

1 : to shine a spotlight on (someone or something) ▪ She was *spotlighted* as she sang her solo. ▪ a *spotlit* area

2 : to give special attention to (something) ▪ The news *spotlighted* the city's financial problems.

spot–on /ˈspɑːtˈɑːn/ *adj, chiefly Brit, informal* **:** exactly correct **:** completely accurate ▪ The weather forecast was *spot-on*. ▪ a *spot-on* impersonation

spot·ted /ˈspɑːtəd/ *adj* **:** marked with spots ▪ a *spotted* cat

spotted dick *noun, pl* ~ **dicks** [*count, noncount*] *Brit* **:** a hot dessert that is like a moist cake made with suet and currants or raisins

spot·ter /ˈspɑːtɚ/ *noun, pl* **-ters** [*count*]

1 : someone who looks for a particular type of person or thing ▪ a *trend* spotter ▪ plane *spotters* — see also TRAINSPOTTER

2 : a person who watches and helps someone who is exercising in order to help prevent injuries ▪ When you lift weights, you should always have a *spotter*.

spot·ty /ˈspɑːti/ *adj* **spot·ti·er; -est**

1 *chiefly US* **:** not always good **:** good in some parts or at some times but not others ▪ Her work has been *spotty*. ▪ The service at that restaurant is a little *spotty*. ▪ students with *spotty* attendance records ▪ *spotty* [=*inconsistent*] data/results

2 : marked with spots ▪ The photograph was *spotty*. ▪ (*Brit*) a *spotty* [=*pimply*] youth

spouse /ˈspaʊs/ *noun, pl* **spous·es** [*count*] **:** someone who is married **:** a husband or wife ▪ my brothers and sisters and their *spouses*

– spou·sal /ˈspaʊzəl/ *adj, always used before a noun* ▪ *spousal* abuse/consent/support

¹spout /ˈspaʊt/ *verb* **spouts; spout·ed; spout·ing**

1 a [+ *obj*] **:** to shoot out (a liquid) with force ▪ The well was *spouting* oil. ▪ The volcano *spouted* lava. **b** [*no obj*] **:** to flow out with force ▪ Blood *spouted* [=*spurted*] (out) from the wound.

2 : to say or talk about (something) in a way that is boring or annoying [+ *obj*] He started *spouting* poetry. — often + *off* ▪ He *spouted off* a long list of statistics to prove his point. [*no obj*] She kept *spouting* on and on about politics. — often + *off* ▪ I'm tired of hearing him *spout off* about his adventures.

²spout *noun, pl* **spouts** [*count*]

1 : a tube, pipe, or hole out of which a liquid flows ▪ Water was flowing from/down the *spout*. ▪ the *spout* of a tea kettle — see also DOWNSPOUT, WATERSPOUT

2 : a sudden strong stream of liquid ▪ a *spout* of water/blood

up the spout *Brit, informal* — used to describe something that has completely failed, been ruined, etc. ▪ The economy's *up the spout*. ▪ His marriage is going *up the spout*. [=*down the drain*]

sprain /ˈspreɪn/ *verb* **sprains; sprained; sprain·ing** [+ *obj*] **:** to injure (a joint) by twisting it in a sudden and painful way ▪ I fell and *sprained* [=*twisted*] my ankle/wrist. ▪ a *sprained* ankle — compare STRAIN

– sprain *noun, pl* **sprains** [*count*] ▪ My wrist isn't broken. It's just a bad *sprain*.

sprang *past tense of* ²SPRING

sprat /ˈspræt/ *noun, pl* **sprats** [*count, noncount*] **:** a small fish that is used for food

¹sprawl /ˈsprɑːl/ *verb, always followed by an adverb or preposition* **sprawls; sprawled; sprawl·ing** [*no obj*]

1 : to lie or sit with your arms and legs spread wide apart ▪ The kids *sprawled* on the floor to watch TV. ▪ He *sprawled* (out) on the couch. ▪ One punch ***sent him sprawling*** to the floor. [=caused him to fall to the floor in a violent and uncontrolled way] ▪ She tripped and ***went sprawling*** into the table.

2 : to spread or develop in an uneven or uncontrolled way ▪ The city *sprawls* along the coastline. ▪ The bushes were *sprawling* along the road.

– sprawled *adj* ▪ He saw her *sprawled* across the bed. ▪ He was *sprawled* (out) in his chair. **– sprawling** *adj* ▪ a *sprawling* city ▪ It was hard to follow the *sprawling* plot of the novel.

²sprawl *noun*

1 [*singular*] **:** a group of things (such as buildings) that cover an area in an uneven and ugly way — often + *of* ▪ a *sprawl of* stores and restaurants

2 [*noncount*] **:** URBAN SPRAWL ▪ efforts to stop/prevent *sprawl*

¹spray /ˈspreɪ/ *noun, pl* **sprays**

1 a [*count*] **:** liquid that is forced out of a container in a

stream of very small drops • The paint was applied in a fine *spray*. **b** : a liquid substance that is used or applied by being forced out of a container in a stream of very small drops [*count*] A nasal/nose *spray* should help you breathe better. • Hand me the bug *spray*. [*noncount*] a can of hair *spray* — see also PEPPER SPRAY **c** [*count*] : the act of putting a liquid on something in a stream of small drops : the act of spraying something • Give your hair one more *spray* to be sure it stays in place. • a quick *spray* of perfume
2 [*noncount*] : very small drops of water moving through the air • sea *spray*
3 [*count*] : a stream of liquid in the form of very small drops — often + *of* • a *spray of* water/blood • The car splashed a *spray of* mud on me. — sometimes used figuratively • a *spray of* bullets [=a number of bullets that are shot quickly] • A *spray of* gravel hit the car.
– compare ³SPRAY

²spray *verb* **sprays; sprayed; spray·ing**
1 [+ *obj*] **a** : to put a stream of small drops of liquid on (someone or something) • She *sprayed* herself with perfume. • I *sprayed* the plants (with a pesticide). • The crops are *sprayed* monthly. • We were *sprayed* by water from the crashing waves. **b** : to put (something) on a surface or into the air using a special container that produces a stream of small drops of liquid • The boys *sprayed* graffiti on the wall. • He *sprayed* the paint evenly over the surface. • She *sprayed* some perfume into the air.
2 [*no obj*] : to flow out in a stream of very small drops • The soda *sprayed* from the bottle. • The blood *sprayed* onto the wall.
3 [+ *obj*] : to shoot many bullets at someone or something • The gunmen *sprayed* the house with bullets. = The gunmen *sprayed* bullets into the house. • They *sprayed* the crowd with bullets.
4 a [*no obj*] *of a cat* : to wet something (such as a bush) with urine • Cats may *spray* to mark their territory. **b** [+ *obj*] *of a skunk* : to wet (an animal or person) with a liquid that has a very bad smell • He was *sprayed* by a skunk. • The skunk *sprayed* the dog.

³spray *noun, pl* **sprays** [*count*]
1 : a branch of a plant that usually has flowers and is used as a decoration — often + *of* • a *spray* [=*sprig*] *of* apple blossoms
2 : an attractive arrangement of flowers — often + *of* • a *spray of* roses
– compare ¹SPRAY

spray can *noun, pl* ~ **cans** [*count*] : a can that contains a liquid (such as paint) that can be sprayed

spray·er /ˈsprejɚ/ *noun, pl* **-ers** [*count*] : a device that is used for spraying a liquid on or into something • a paint *sprayer*

spray paint *noun, pl* ~ **paints** : paint that is sprayed onto a surface from a can that you can hold in one hand [*noncount*] a can of *spray paint* • I used *spray paint* on the table. [*count*] *Spray paints* cannot be sold to children.
– spray–paint *verb* **-paints; -paint·ed; -paint·ing** [+ *obj*] • I'm going to *spray-paint* the table. • Graffiti was *spray-painted* on the wall.

¹spread /ˈsprɛd/ *verb* **spreads; spread; spread·ing**
1 [+ *obj*] **a** : to open, arrange, or place (something) over a large area • The newspaper was *spread* across his lap. • Her notes were *spread* all over the desk. • Help me *spread* the cloth on the table. — often + *out* • He *spread out* the map on the table. = He *spread* the map *out* on the table. • The cards were *spread out* across the table. • The city is *spread out* over a wide area. [=the city covers a wide area] **b** : to place (things) over a large area • We *spread* fertilizer on our yard. • The seeds are *spread* by wind, birds, and animals.
2 a [*no obj*] : to become larger or to affect a larger area : to move into more places • The fire *spread* quickly through the building. • The cancer has *spread* to her throat. • The use of computer technology has *spread* into all fields of work. • The odor *spread* throughout the room. • The plant will *spread*. [=the plant will produce more plants in the area around it] • The fashion quickly *spread* from France to England. **b** [+ *obj*] : to cause (something) to be present in more places throughout a large area • Flies *spread* diseases. • Missionaries were sent to the colonies to *spread* Christianity. • The religion was *spread* through/over much of Europe.
3 a [*no obj*] : to pass from person to person • Her determination and desire to win *spread* to the other players. **b** [*no obj*] : to become known by many people • The rumor *spread* quickly. • The news ***spread like wildfire***. [=the news became known very quickly] **c** [+ *obj*] : to cause (something) to become known by many people • He was *spreading* lies/gossip/rumors about her. • People are ***spreading the word*** [=telling others] about his book.
4 : to move (parts of your body) outward or away from each other [+ *obj*] She *spread* [=*stretched*] her arms wide and hugged him. • The bird *spreads* its wings. • *Spread* your fingers wide apart. — often + *out* • *Spread out* your toes. = *Spread* your toes *out*. • There's no room on the couch to *spread* yourself *out*. • *Spread* your arms *out*. [*no obj*] — + *out* • There's no room on the couch to *spread out*. [=*stretch out*]
5 [*no obj*] *of a smile or other facial expression* : to appear and slowly grow more apparent • A smile slowly *spread* across her face. • A look of disbelief *spread* across/over their faces.
6 [+ *obj*] : to put a layer of (something) on top of something else • He *spread* butter on the bread. = He *spread* the bread with butter. • She carefully *spread* the plaster over the hole. • *Spread* the glue evenly on the paper.
7 [+ *obj*] : to divide up (something) over a period of time or among members of a group • The payments are *spread* over a period of six years. • You should ***spread the wealth***. [=share your money or good fortune with others] — often + *out* • I plan to *spread* the work *out* over the next couple of weeks. • The course is *spread out* over two semesters.
spread out [*phrasal verb*] : to move apart from the other members of a group especially to search an area • The police *spread out* [=*fanned out*] to search the area faster. — see also ¹SPREAD 1a, 4, 7 (above)
spread your net wide see ¹NET
spread your wings see ¹WING

²spread *noun, pl* **spreads**
1 [*noncount*] : growth or increase that causes something to cover a larger area, affect a larger number of people, etc. — often + *of* • We need to slow the *spread of* the disease/virus. • the *spread of* infection • the *spread of* new technology • the *spread of* drugs in the city • the *spread of* civilization/religion/peace
2 : a soft food that is spread on bread, crackers, etc. [*count*] She offered crackers and a cheese *spread*. [*noncount*] He uses low-fat *spread* on his toast.
3 [*count*] : the total distance between the two outer edges of something — usually singular; often + *of* • the *spread of* a bird's wings • The plant has a *spread of* three feet.
4 [*count*] *informal* : a large meal — usually singular • We always have a huge *spread* for Thanksgiving.
5 [*count*] : something (such as an advertisement or a series of photos) that covers two or more pages in a newspaper or magazine • a two-page *spread*
6 [*count*] *US* : BEDSPREAD
7 [*count*] *US* : a large farm or ranch — usually singular • He bought a *spread* of 100 acres. • They have quite a *spread*.
8 [*count*] : a variety or range of things or people — usually singular; often + *of* • The poll showed a large *spread of* opinions.

spread–ea·gled /ˈsprɛdˌiːgəld/ *adj* : with arms and legs spread wide apart • He lay *spread-eagled* on the bed. • a *spread-eagled* position

spread·er /ˈsprɛdɚ/ *noun, pl* **-ers** [*count*] : a person or thing that spreads something • Mosquito are *spreaders* of disease. • a manure/seed *spreader* • a *spreader* of gossip/lies

spread·sheet /ˈsprɛdˌʃiːt/ *noun, pl* **-sheets** [*count*]
1 : a computer program that calculates numbers and organizes information in columns and rows
2 : a document that has columns and rows which are used to calculate numbers and organize information

spree /ˈspriː/ *noun, pl* **sprees** [*count*] : a short period of time when you do a lot of something • a buying/shopping/spending *spree* [=*binge*] • They went on a killing/crime *spree*.

sprig /ˈsprɪg/ *noun, pl* **sprigs** [*count*] : a small twig or stem that has leaves or flowers on it • a *sprig* of parsley

spright·ly /ˈspraɪtli/ *adj* **spright·li·er; -est** : full of life and energy — used especially to describe an older person • a *sprightly* old woman of 80
– spright·li·ness *noun* [*noncount*]

¹spring /ˈsprɪŋ/ *noun, pl* **springs**
1 : the season between winter and summer : the season when plants and trees begin to grow [*count*] We'll plant the seeds next *spring*. • We've had a rainy *spring*. • the *spring* of 1984 [*noncount*] a beautiful day in early/late *spring* • The first few weeks of *spring* were unusually warm. — often used before another noun • our *spring* catalog • a new *spring* wardrobe • *spring* colors/flowers

2 a [*count*] : a twisted or coiled piece of metal that returns to its original shape when it is pressed down or stretched ▪ The mattress is old and some of the *springs* are broken. — see also BOX SPRING **b** [*noncount*] : the ability of something to return to its original shape when it is pressed down, stretched, twisted, etc. ▪ The cushion has lost its *spring*.
3 [*count*] : a source of water coming up from the ground ▪ a mineral *spring* — see also HOT SPRING
4 [*singular*] : a lively and energetic quality ▪ She had a *spring* in her step.
5 [*singular*] : a quick sudden leap up or forward ▪ The deer gave a *spring* and was gone. — see also HANDSPRING

[2]**spring** *verb* **springs; sprang** /ˈspræŋ/ *or* **sprung** /ˈsprʌŋ/; **sprung; spring·ing**
1 [*no obj*] **a** : to move or leap suddenly forward or upward ▪ The lion was waiting to *spring*. ▪ The deer *sprang* up the path. ▪ I *sprang* to my feet. ▪ He *sprang* out of his seat and ran to the door. **b** *always followed by an adverb or preposition* : to move quickly to a different position ▪ The lid *sprang* open/shut. ▪ The branch *sprang* back and hit her. ▪ The rope stretches and *springs* back into shape. [=returns to its original shape]
2 [+ *obj*] *informal* : to help (someone) to get out of or escape from jail, prison, etc. ▪ He tried to *spring* his accomplice. ▪ His lawyer managed to get him *sprung* from prison.
spring a leak : to start to leak : to suddenly let water in or out through a crack or break ▪ The boat/pipe *sprang a leak*.
spring a surprise : to do, ask, or say something that is not expected ▪ Everyone knows she's not likely to *spring a surprise*. ▪ The teacher *sprang a surprise* on us and gave a quiz.
spring a trap : to capture someone or something (such as an animal or criminal) with a trap — often + *on* ▪ Police *sprang a trap on* the drug smugglers.
spring for [*phrasal verb*] ***spring for (something)*** *US, informal* : to pay for (something) : to spend money on (something) ▪ She refuses to *spring for* a new coat. ▪ I'll *spring for* dinner.
spring from [*phrasal verb*] ***spring from (something)*** *informal* : to start from or be caused by (something) ▪ The idea *sprang from* [=*came from*] a dream I had.
spring from the loins see LOIN
spring into/to action/life : to become suddenly very active and energetic ▪ They *sprang into action* as soon as they received their orders. ▪ The crowd *sprang to life* after the first goal was scored.
spring on [*phrasal verb*] ***spring (something) on (someone)*** : to surprise (someone) with (something, such as a request or announcement) ▪ You should try to prepare them for your decision instead of just *springing* it *on* them suddenly.
spring to mind see [1]MIND
spring up [*phrasal verb*] : to grow or appear suddenly ▪ The weeds *sprang up* overnight. ▪ New housing developments are *springing up* all over the state.
tears spring to your eyes ✧ If *tears spring to your eyes*, you suddenly start to cry. ▪ *Tears sprang to his eyes* when he read about the accident.

spring·board /ˈsprɪŋˌboɚd/ *noun, pl* **-boards** [*count*]
1 : a strong, flexible board that is used for jumping very high in gymnastics or diving
2 : something that helps you start an activity or process ▪ The news served as a *springboard* for a class discussion.

spring·bok /ˈsprɪŋˌbɑːk/ *noun, pl* **springbok** *or* **spring·boks** [*count*] : a small, very fast deer that lives in Africa

spring break *noun, pl* ~ **breaks** *US* : a vacation from classes at a school usually for a week in the spring; *especially* : such a vacation at a college or university [*noncount*] Many students go to Florida for/on *spring break*. [*count*] How was your *spring break*?

spring chicken *noun, pl* ~ **-ens** [*count*] *informal + humorous* : a young person — usually used in negative statements to say that someone is not young ▪ She's ***no spring chicken***, that's for sure.

spring–clean *verb* **-cleans; -cleaned; -cleaning** [+ *obj*] : to clean (a place) thoroughly in the spring ▪ It's time to *spring-clean* the house and air out the place.
– spring–clean *noun* [*singular*] *Brit* ▪ It's time to give the house a *spring-clean*. **– spring–cleaning** *noun* [*noncount*] ▪ We were busy with *spring-cleaning*.

spring fever *noun* [*noncount*] : a feeling of wanting to go outdoors and do things because spring is coming and the weather is getting warmer ▪ The children all have *spring fever*.

spring–loaded *adj* : containing a metal spring that presses one part against another ▪ a *spring-loaded* mousetrap

spring onion *noun, pl* ~ **-ions** [*count*] *chiefly Brit* : GREEN ONION

spring peeper *noun, pl* ~ **-ers** [*count*] : PEEPER

spring roll *noun, pl* ~ **rolls** [*count*] : EGG ROLL

spring tide *noun, pl* ~ **tides** [*count*] : a tide in which the sea rises and falls more than usual ✧ Spring tides happen when the moon, earth, and sun are aligned with each other.

spring·time /ˈsprɪŋˌtaɪm/ *noun* [*noncount*] : the season of spring ▪ *Springtime* is her favorite time of year. ▪ It's beautiful here ***in (the) springtime***. [=in the spring]

spring training *noun* [*noncount*] *US* : the time in the spring when baseball teams prepare for the regular season by playing practice games

springy /ˈsprɪŋi/ *adj* **spring·i·er; -est**
1 : returning to an original shape when pressed down, twisted, stretched, etc. ▪ a *springy* bed ▪ *springy* vines
2 : having or showing lively and energetic movement ▪ He walks with a *springy* step.
– spring·i·ness /ˈsprɪŋinəs/ *noun* [*noncount*] ▪ The cushion has lost its *springiness*.

[1]**sprin·kle** /ˈsprɪŋkəl/ *verb* **sprin·kles; sprin·kled; sprin·kling**
1 [+ *obj*] **a** : to drop or spread small pieces or amounts of something over something ▪ He *sprinkled* water on the plants. ▪ I *sprinkled* grass seed over the soil. ▪ She *sprinkled* grated cheese on the pasta. = She *sprinkled* the pasta with grated cheese. — often used figuratively ▪ The essay is *sprinkled* with quotations. [=there are quotations in different parts of the essay] **b** : to put small drops of liquid on (someone or something) ▪ She *sprinkled* the clothes before ironing them.
2 [*no obj*] *US* : to rain lightly ▪ "Is it raining?" "It's just *sprinkling* a little."

[2]**sprinkle** *noun*
1 [*singular*] : a light rain ▪ a *sprinkle* of rain ▪ It rained last night, but it was just a *sprinkle*.
2 [*singular*] : a small amount that is sprinkled on something ▪ She topped the pasta with a *sprinkle* of parsley. — sometimes used figuratively ▪ We've received a *sprinkle* [=a very small number] of complaints.
3 ***sprinkles*** [*plural*] *US* : tiny candies that are put on top of a sweet food (such as ice cream) ▪ chocolate *sprinkles*

sprin·kler /ˈsprɪŋklɚ/ *noun, pl* **-klers** [*count*]
1 : a device that is used to spray water on plants or soil — see picture at GARDENING
2 : a device in a building that sprays water if there a is fire

sprin·kling /ˈsprɪŋklɪŋ/ *noun* [*singular*] : a small amount that is sprinkled on something ▪ She put a *sprinkling* of parsley on the pasta. [=she sprinkled a small amount of parsley on the pasta] — often used figuratively ▪ We received only a *sprinkling* of suggestions. [=only a few suggestions]

[1]**sprint** /ˈsprɪnt/ *verb* **sprints; sprint·ed; sprint·ing** [*no obj*] : to run or go very fast for a short distance ▪ He *sprinted* to class. ▪ The bicycle racers *sprinted* for the finish line.
– sprint·er *noun, pl* **-ers** [*count*]

[2]**sprint** *noun, pl* **sprints**
1 [*count*] : a race over a short distance at a very fast speed
2 [*singular*] : a short period of running or going very fast ▪ He made a *sprint* for the finish line.

sprite /ˈspraɪt/ *noun, pl* **sprites** [*count*] *in stories* : a small creature that has magical powers : an elf or fairy ▪ a water *sprite*

spritz /ˈsprɪts/ *verb* **spritz·es; spritzed; spritz·ing** [+ *obj*] *US* : to spray (something) quickly with a small amount of liquid ▪ Make sure to *spritz* the plants with water every day. ▪ She *spritzed* her hair with hairspray.
– spritz *noun, pl* **spritzes** [*count*] ▪ a *spritz* of water

spritz·er /ˈsprɪtsɚ/ *noun, pl* **-ers** [*count*] : a drink made of wine mixed with soda water ▪ a white wine *spritzer*

sprock·et /ˈsprɑːkət/ *noun, pl* **-ets** [*count*] : a wheel that has a row of teeth around its edge which fit into the holes of something (such as a bicycle chain or a piece of film) and cause it to turn when the wheel turns; *also* : any one of the teeth on such a wheel

sprog /ˈsprɑːg/ *noun, pl* **sprogs** [*count*] *Brit, informal* : a child or baby ▪ a cute little *sprog*

[1]**sprout** /ˈspraʊt/ *verb* **sprouts; sprout·ed; sprout·ing**
1 : to produce new leaves, buds, etc. [*no obj*] seeds *sprouting* in the spring ▪ Potatoes will *sprout* in the bag if kept in a

S

warm place. [+ *obj*] The garden is *sprouting* weeds. ▪ The tree is already *sprouting* leaves.

2 : to grow or develop (something) [+ *obj*] He *sprouted* a beard since the last time I saw him. ▪ She dreamed that her boss had *sprouted* horns. [*no obj*] Hair *sprouted* on his face.

3 [*no obj*] **:** to appear suddenly and in large numbers — often + *up* ▪ Dozens of new restaurants have been *sprouting up* [=*popping up*] around the city.

²sprout *noun, pl* **sprouts**

1 [*count*] **:** a new part (such as a leaf or bud) that is growing on a plant

2 ***sprouts*** [*plural*] *chiefly US* **:** very young plants that come from alfalfa or bean seeds and that are used as a vegetable

3 [*count*] *chiefly Brit* **:** BRUSSELS SPROUT

¹spruce /ˈspru:s/ *noun, pl* **spruc·es** *also* **spruce**

1 [*count*] **:** a type of tree that has long, thin needles instead of leaves and that stays green throughout the year

2 [*noncount*] **:** the wood of a spruce tree

²spruce *verb* **spruces; spruced; spruc·ing**

spruce up [*phrasal verb*] ***spruce (someone or something) up or spruce up (someone or something)*** **:** to make (someone or something) look cleaner, neater, or more attractive ▪ We *spruced up* the room with a fresh coat of paint. ▪ I need to *spruce* myself *up* a bit before we go out to dinner.

³spruce *adj* **spruc·er; -est** *somewhat old-fashioned* **:** neat, clean, or stylish in appearance ▪ He looked very *spruce* in his new suit.

– spruce·ly *adv* ▪ a *sprucely* decorated room

sprung *past tense and past participle of* ²SPRING

spry /ˈspraɪ/ *adj* **spri·er** *or* **spry·er** /ˈsprajɚ/; **spri·est** *or* **spry·est** /ˈsprajəst/ **:** full of life and energy — used especially to describe an older person ▪ She's 64 and still as *spry* as she was at 30.

– spry·ly *adv* **– spry·ness** *noun* [*noncount*]

spud /ˈspʌd/ *noun, pl* **spuds** [*count*] *informal* **:** POTATO 1

spume /ˈspju:m/ *noun* [*noncount*] *literary* **:** bubbles that form on ocean waves **:** FOAM

spun *past tense and past participle of* ¹SPIN

spun glass *noun* [*noncount*] **:** FIBERGLASS

spunk /ˈspʌŋk/ *noun* [*noncount*]

1 *informal* **:** spirit, courage, and determination ▪ That little girl has a lot of *spunk*.

2 *Brit slang, impolite* **:** SEMEN

spunky /ˈspʌŋki/ *adj* **spunk·i·er; -est** *informal* **:** full of spirit, courage, and determination ▪ a *spunky* little girl

– spunk·i·ness /ˈspʌŋkinəs/ *noun* [*noncount*]

¹spur /ˈspɚ/ *noun, pl* **spurs**

1 [*count*] **:** a sharp pointed object that is attached to the heel of a horse rider's boot and that is pressed into the horse's side to make the horse go faster

spur

2 [*singular*] **:** something that makes you want to do something or that causes something to happen **:** INCENTIVE — often + *to* ▪ The reward was offered as a *spur to* greater work/achievement. ▪ a *spur to* the imagination

3 [*count*] **:** a mass of sharp rock on the side of a mountain

4 [*count*] **:** a short section of railway track that leads from the main line

on/at the spur of the moment ✧ If something is done *on/at the spur of the moment*, it is done immediately without planning. ▪ We decided *on the spur of the moment* to go to the beach. — see also SPUR-OF-THE-MOMENT

win/earn your spurs **:** to do something which shows that you deserve to be respected or noticed ▪ He *earned/won his spurs* by doubling the company's profits in the past year.

²spur *verb* **spurs; spurred; spur·ring** [+ *obj*]

1 : to encourage (someone) to do or achieve something ▪ The reward *spurred* them to work harder. — often + *on* ▪ His encouragement *spurred* them *on* to finish the project.

2 : to cause (something) to happen or to happen more quickly ▪ Lower interest rates should *spur* economic growth.

3 : to urge (a horse) to go faster by pushing spurs into its sides ▪ He *spurred* the horse onward.

spu·ri·ous /ˈspjɚrijəs/ *adj*

1 : not genuine, sincere, or authentic ▪ *spurious* [=*fake*] gems ▪ *spurious* [=*insincere*] kindness

2 : based on false ideas or bad reasoning ▪ *spurious* claims/justifications

– spu·ri·ous·ly *adv* **– spu·ri·ous·ness** *noun* [*noncount*]

spurn /ˈspɚn/ *verb* **spurns; spurned; spurn·ing** [+ *obj*] *literary* **:** to refuse to accept (someone or something that you do not think deserves your respect, attention, affection, etc.) ▪ She *spurned* [=*rejected*] their offer. ▪ a *spurned* lover

spur–of–the–moment *adj, always used before a noun* **:** done suddenly and without planning ▪ They made a *spur-of-the-moment* decision to go the movies. — see also *on/at the spur of the moment* at ¹SPUR

¹spurt /ˈspɚt/ *verb* **spurts; spurt·ed; spurt·ing**

1 : to pour out or come out quickly and suddenly [*no obj*] Water *spurted* from the broken pipe. ▪ Blood was *spurting* out of his nose. ▪ Flames *spurted* from the open window. [+ *obj*] His nose *spurted* blood.

2 [*no obj*] **:** to move at a fast speed for a short distance ▪ He *spurted* [=*sprinted*] for the finish line.

²spurt *noun, pl* **spurts** [*count*]

1 : an amount of liquid, flame, etc., that comes out of something suddenly ▪ a *spurt* of water/blood ▪ a *spurt* of venom

2 : a short period of greatly increased effort, activity, or development ▪ a *spurt* of hard work ▪ When he was 11 he had a ***growth spurt***. [=he grew quickly and suddenly in a short period of time] ▪ They worked on the house ***in spurts***, whenever they had time.

3 *US* **:** a short period of time ▪ They played well for a brief *spurt* but then started losing again.

sput·ter /ˈspʌtɚ/ *verb* **-ters; -tered; -ter·ing**

1 [*no obj*] **:** to make loud sounds like explosions ▪ The motor *sputtered* and died.

2 : to speak quickly or in a confused way because you are upset, surprised, etc. [*no obj*] He was *sputtering* with rage. [+ *obj*] She *sputtered* an angry protest. ▪ "You, you have to be kidding!" he *sputtered*.

– sputter *noun, pl* **-ters** [*count*] ▪ The motor gave a *sputter* and died.

spu·tum /ˈspju:təm/ *noun* [*noncount*] *medical* **:** a thick liquid that comes up from your lungs when you are sick

¹spy /ˈspaɪ/ *noun, pl* **spies** [*count*]

1 : a person who tries secretly to get information about a country or organization for another country or organization ▪ He was a *spy* for the CIA. ▪ a Cold War *spy* — often used before another noun ▪ a *spy* novel/thriller [=a novel/thriller about spies] ▪ a *spy* camera/plane [=a camera/plane used for spying]

2 : someone who secretly watches the movement or actions of other people ▪ My coworker is a *spy* for the boss. ▪ the neighborhood *spy*

²spy *verb* **spies; spied; spy·ing**

1 [*no obj*] **:** to try secretly to get information about a country, organization, etc. **:** to act as a spy ▪ They were accused of *spying* for a foreign government. — often + *on* ▪ They were accused of *spying on* a rival company.

2 [+ *obj*] **:** to see or notice (someone or something) ▪ She *spied* [=*caught sight of*] a friend in the crowd.

spy on [*phrasal verb*] ***spy on (someone or something)*** **:** to watch (someone) secretly ▪ He *spies on* his neighbors. ▪ Have you been *spying on* me? — see also ²SPY 1 (above)

spy out [*phrasal verb*] **1** ***spy (something) out or spy out (something)*** **:** to notice, find, or learn about (something) by looking often in a secret way ▪ They were trying to *spy out* the enemy's position. **2** ***spy out the land*** *chiefly Brit* **:** to find or get more information about a situation secretly and before making a decision

spy·glass /ˈspaɪˌglæs, *Brit* ˈspaɪˈglɑ:s/ *noun, pl* **-glass·es** [*count*] **:** a small telescope used by sailors in the past

spy·ware /ˈspaɪˌweɚ/ *noun* [*noncount*] **:** computer software that secretly records information about the way you use your computer

sq. *abbr* square

squab·ble /ˈskwɑ:bəl/ *verb* **squab·bles; squab·bled; squab·bling** [*no obj*] **:** to argue loudly about things that are not important ▪ The children were *squabbling* over the toys.

– squabble *noun, pl* **squabbles** [*count*] ▪ A *squabble* broke out among the children.

squad /ˈskwɑ:d/ *noun, pl* **squads** [*count*]

1 : a part of a police force that deals with a specific type of crime ▪ the bomb/fraud/vice *squad*

2 : a small organized group of soldiers ▪ an elite infantry *squad* ▪ the *squad* leader

3 : a group of people who are involved in a particular activity ▪ a rescue *squad* ▪ the cheerleading *squad* ▪ a *squad* of searchers

4 *sports* **:** a group of people from which a team is chosen • the Olympic gymnastics *squad*
– see also FIRING SQUAD

squad car *noun, pl* ~ **cars** [*count*] **:** POLICE CAR

squad·die *or* **squad·dy** /ˈskwɑːdi/ *noun, pl* **squad·dies** [*count*] *Brit slang* **:** a soldier of low rank **:** a soldier who is not an officer

squad·ron /ˈskwɑːdrən/ *noun, pl* **-rons** [*count*] **:** a military unit consisting of soldiers, ships, or aircraft • a bomber/reconnaissance *squadron*

squadron leader *noun, pl* ~ **-ers** [*count*] **:** a high-ranking officer in the British air force

squal·id /ˈskwɑːləd/ *adj* [*more* ~; *most* ~]
1 : very dirty and unpleasant • The family lived in *squalid* conditions. • a *squalid* [=*run-down*] apartment building
2 : immoral or dishonest • a *squalid* affair • *squalid* behavior
– squal·id·ness *noun* [*noncount*]

¹squall /ˈskwɑːl/ *verb* **squalls; squalled; squall·ing** [*no obj*] **:** to cry loudly • a *squalling* baby

²squall *noun, pl* **squalls** [*count*] **:** a loud cry • The baby gave a sudden *squall* of hunger. — compare ³SQUALL

³squall *noun, pl* **squalls** [*count*] **:** a sudden violent wind often with rain or snow • a snow *squall* — compare ²SQUALL
– squally /ˈskwɑːli/ *adj* **squall·i·er; -est** • a *squally* day

squa·lor /ˈskwɑːlɚ/ *noun* [*noncount*] **:** very bad and dirty conditions • The family was living in *squalor*. • I was shocked by the *squalor* of their surroundings.

squan·der /ˈskwɑːndɚ/ *verb* **-ders; -dered; -der·ing** [+ *obj*] **:** to use (something) in a foolish or wasteful way • She *squandered* her inheritance/allowance. • He vowed not to *squander* this opportunity. • The government *squandered* [=*wasted*] the money on failed programs.
– squan·der·er /ˈskwɑːndərɚ/ *noun, pl* **-ers** [*count*]

¹square /ˈskweɚ/ *noun, pl* **squares** [*count*]
1 : a four-sided shape that is made up of four straight sides that are the same length and that has four right angles • The fabric is decorated with circles and *squares*. • Cut the brownies into *squares*. — often + *of* • a *square of* tile/cloth — see picture at GEOMETRY; compare RECTANGLE
2 : any of the squares on a board for playing games (such as chess and checkers) • The board has red and black *squares*. — see picture at CHESS
3 *mathematics* **:** the number that results from multiplying a number by itself • The *square* of 2 [=2^2] is 4. [=2 x 2 = 4] — compare ¹CUBE 2
4 : an open area in a village, city, etc., where two or more streets meet • The bank is located at the main *square*. • the market/town *square*
5 *somewhat old-fashioned, informal + disapproving* **:** someone who does not like or try unusual things that other people consider exciting, interesting, etc. • Don't be such a *square*. Let's try something different for a change.
6 *technical* **:** a flat tool that is used to mark or check angles • a carpenter's *square* — see picture at CARPENTRY; compare T SQUARE
7 *chiefly US, informal* **:** SQUARE MEAL • I try to have three *squares* a day.

²square *adj* **squar·er; squar·est** [*also more* ~; *most* ~]
1 a : shaped like a square **:** having four straight sides that are the same length and four right angles at each corner • The room is *square*. • a *square* box **b :** forming a right angle • The room has four *square* corners. • Make sure the post is *square* to the floor. [=make sure that there is a right angle where the post and the floor meet]
2 — used to describe a measurement that is produced by multiplying something's length and width • a tile measuring one *square* foot [=a tile that is one foot long and one foot wide] • a *square* inch/meter/mile — compare CUBIC
3 : shaped more like a right angle than a curve • a *square* jaw • *square* shoulders ◇ This sense of *square* often suggests strength and toughness.
4 *somewhat old-fashioned* **:** honest and fair • a *square* deal • She is *square* in all her dealings. — see also *fair and square* at ¹FAIR
5 *somewhat old-fashioned, informal + disapproving* — used to describe someone who does not like or try unusual things that other people consider exciting, interesting, etc. • He's nice but he's kind of *square*.
6 a *informal* **:** having nothing owed by either side **:** EVEN • Here's the rest of the money. Now we're *square*. [=now we don't owe each other anything] **b** *not used before a noun* **:** having the same number of points **:** TIED • The teams were *all square* after the first half.

a square peg in a round hole see ¹PEG

³square *verb* **squares; squared; squar·ing** [+ *obj*]
1 : to make (something) square **:** to give (something) straight edges, flat surfaces, or sharp, even corners • The machine *squares* the wood into flat boards. — often + *off* • I still need to *square off* the end of the board.
2 *mathematics* **:** to multiply (a number) by itself • If you *square* 3, you get 9. — usually used as *(be) squared* • 3 *squared* is/equals 9. [=3 x 3 = 9] — compare ²CUBE 2
3 : to pay money that is owed for (something) • We *squared* [=*settled*] our accounts. — often + *up* • Is this enough money to *square up* my part of the bill?
4 : to make the score of (something, such as a game or series) the same **:** TIE • The goal *squared* the game 2–2. • Their win *squares* the series at three games apiece.

square away [*phrasal verb*] ***square (something) away*** *or* ***square away (something)*** *US* **:** to put (something) in an organized and proper state or condition — often used as *(be/get) squared away* • I need to *get* my work *squared away* [=*taken care of*] before I leave for vacation. • I can finally relax since everything *is squared away*.

square off [*phrasal verb*] **1 a :** to prepare to fight **:** to get into the position of two people who are going to fight each other • The two men *squared off*, but no punches were thrown. **b :** to fight or argue — often + *against* • They *squared off against* each other in a heated debate. **2 :** to compete in a contest • The two teams will *square off* again tomorrow. — often + *against* • They *squared off against* each other in the election. — see also ³SQUARE 1 (above)

square up [*phrasal verb*] **1 :** to turn so that you are facing something or someone directly • She *squared up* (with/to the basket) for a three-point shot. • They *squared up* for a fight. [=they faced each other and prepared to fight] — see also ³SQUARE 3 (above) **2** ***square up to (someone or something)*** **:** to begin to deal with (a difficult person or situation) in a direct way • We need to *square up to* this problem. • He's finally *squaring up to* his critics.

square with [*phrasal verb*] **1** ***square with (something)*** **:** to agree with (something) • Your story doesn't *square with* the facts. **2** ***square (something) with (something)*** **:** to make (something) agree with (something) • How can they *square* what they've done *with* what they've said? **3** ***square (something) with (someone)*** **:** to get agreement about or approval of (something) from (someone) • I'll go on the trip if I can ***square it with*** my parents. [=if my parents will agree to let me go]

square yourself **:** to turn so that you are facing something or someone directly • He *squared himself* and prepared for the hit.

square your shoulders **:** to stand with your shoulders pulled back in a straight line in a way that shows you are ready to do or deal with something directly • She stood up straight and *squared her shoulders*.

⁴square *adv* **:** in a direct way • She ran *square* [=*directly, right*] into me. • Look (at) me *square* in the eye and tell me you're not lying.

square bracket *noun, pl* ~ **-ets** [*count*] **:** ¹BRACKET 3a

square dance *noun, pl* ~ **dances** [*count*] **:** a dance for four couples that begins with each couple facing one of the other couples so that the four couples form a square
– square dancer *noun, pl* ~ **-ers** [*count*] **– square dancing** *noun* [*noncount*] • We enjoy *square dancing*. = We like to ***go square dancing***.

square knot *noun, pl* ~ **knots** [*count*] *US* **:** a strong and simple type of knot — called also (*chiefly Brit*) *reef knot*

square·ly /ˈskweɚli/ *adv*
1 : in a direct and honest way • We must face these problems/issues *squarely*. • It's time to deal *squarely* with the facts.
2 : in the exact location or position that is mentioned **:** EXACTLY, RIGHT • literature that is *squarely* in/within the American tradition • Their marketing campaign is aimed *squarely* at adolescents. • The dart hit the board *squarely* in the middle/center. • Look me *squarely* in the eye and tell me you're not lying.
3 : in a way that makes direct contact • He hit the ball *squarely*. • Her feet were *squarely* planted.
4 : in a way that is not limited in any way **:** COMPLETELY • The responsibility lies *squarely* with us.

square meal *noun, pl* ~ **meals** [*count*] **:** a full or complete meal • Inmates receive three *square meals* a day.

square one *noun [noncount]* : the beginning stage or starting point ▪ His idea didn't work, so he had to ***go back to square one.*** [=he had to start over] ▪ They lost everything and found themselves ***back at square one.***

square root *noun, pl* ~ **roots** *[count] mathematics* : a number that produces a specified number when it is multiplied by itself ▪ The *square root* of 9 is 3. — compare CUBE ROOT

squar·ish /ˈskwerɪʃ/ *adj* : having a shape that is almost like a square ▪ a *squarish* face ▪ The dog's nose is *squarish.*

[1]**squash** /ˈskwɑːʃ/ *verb* **squash·es; squashed; squash·ing**

1 *[+ obj]* : to press (something) into a flat or flatter shape ▪ She *squashed* the bug. ▪ He *squashed* his nose against the window. ▪ The tomatoes got *squashed.*

2 *[+ obj]* : to stop (something) from continuing by doing or saying something ▪ She tried to *squash* [=*quash*] the rumors. ▪ His poor performance *squashed* any hope he had of a promotion. ▪ The boss *squashed* my idea immediately.

3 *always followed by an adverb or preposition* : to move into a space that is very tight or crowded *[no obj]* Four of us *squashed* [=*squeezed*] into the backseat. ▪ *(Brit)* ***Squash up*** [=move closer together] to make room for one more person. *[+ obj]* Someone had *squashed* all the ribbons together in one box. — often used as *(be) squashed* ▪ We *were squashed* between the table and wall. ▪ The ribbons had all *been squashed* together into one box.

[2]**squash** *noun, pl* **squashes**

1 *[noncount]* : a game played by two people with rackets and a rubber ball in a court with four walls ▪ We play *squash* [=*(Brit) squash rackets*] once a week. ▪ a *squash* court/racket — see picture at RACKET

2 *[count, noncount] Brit* : a drink made with fruit juice, sugar, and water ▪ a glass of lemon *squash*

3 *[singular] Brit* : a situation in which people or things are pushed into a space that is too small or crowded ▪ It's a real *squash* with six people in the car.

– compare [3]SQUASH

[3]**squash** *noun, pl* **squash** *or* **squashes** : a type of vegetable (such as a pumpkin) that has a usually hard skin and that is eaten cooked *[noncount]* Would you like some *squash*? *[count]* I cooked two *squashes.* — see color picture on page C4; see also BUTTERNUT SQUASH, SUMMER SQUASH, WINTER SQUASH — compare [2]SQUASH

squashy /ˈskwɑːʃi/ *adj* **squash·i·er; -est** *[also more* ~; *most* ~*] chiefly Brit* : soft and easy to press into a different shape ▪ *squashy* [=*squishy*] cushions/pillows ▪ a *squashy* sofa

[1]**squat** /ˈskwɑːt/ *verb* **squats; squat·ted; squat·ting** *[no obj]*

1 : to bend your knees and lower your body so that you are close to your heels or sitting on your heels ▪ He *squatted* behind the bush to avoid being seen. ▪ a *squatting* position [=a position in which you are squatting] — often + *down* ▪ She *squatted down* to pick up the paper.

2 : to live in a building or on land without the owner's permission and without paying ▪ A family has been *squatting* in that house for months.

[2]**squat** *noun, pl* **squats**

1 *[count]* : a position in which your knees are bent and your body lowered so that you are close to your heels or sitting on your heels

2 *[noncount] US slang* : the least amount : anything at all ▪ I don't know *squat* [=*diddly-squat*] about baseball. ▪ He didn't do *squat* all day. ▪ The car is worth *squat.* [=nothing at all]

3 *[count] chiefly Brit* : an empty building that squatters live in ▪ She lives in a *squat.*

[3]**squat** *adj* **squat·ter; squat·test** : short and thick ▪ a *squat* man = a man with a *squat* body ▪ a *squat* tower

squat·ter /ˈskwɑːtɚ/ *noun, pl* **-ters** *[count]* : someone who lives in a building or on land without the permission of the owner and without paying : someone who squats

squaw /ˈskwɑː/ *noun, pl* **squaws** *[count] often offensive* : a Native American woman

squawk /ˈskwɑːk/ *verb* **squawks; squawked; squawk·ing** *[no obj]*

1 *of a bird* : to make a short, harsh cry ▪ The crow *squawked* loudly.

2 : to complain or protest loudly or with strong feeling ▪ The customers *squawked* about the high prices. ▪ Opponents of the project have been *squawking.*

– squawk *noun, pl* **squawks** *[count]* ▪ The bird gave a *squawk.* ▪ *squawks* from customers

[1]**squeak** /ˈskwiːk/ *verb* **squeaks; squeaked; squeak·ing**

1 *[no obj]* : to make a short, high-pitched cry or noise ▪ I could hear the mouse *squeaking.* ▪ She *squeaked* when I pinched her. ▪ My shoes *squeak* when I walk. ▪ The wheel *squeaks* when it turns. ▪ a *squeaking* sound/wheel

2 *always followed by an adverb or preposition [no obj]* : to barely succeed at doing something : to almost lose or fail but to finally succeed, win, etc. ▪ The team *squeaked* into the finals. [=the team almost did not get into the finals] ▪ She *squeaked* out a 5–4 win. [=she won narrowly by getting 5 points while her opponent got 4] ▪ The bill *squeaked* through the Senate. [=it barely got enough votes to be accepted] ▪ He *squeaked* into office by fewer than 2,000 votes.

3 *[+ obj]* : to say (something) in a high-pitched voice especially because you are nervous or excited ▪ "I can't believe it!" she *squeaked.*

[2]**squeak** *noun, pl* **squeaks** *[count]* : a sharp, high-pitched cry or sound ▪ She gave/let out a *squeak.*

squeak·er /ˈskwiːkɚ/ *noun, pl* **-ers** *[count] informal* : a contest (such as a game or an election) that is won by only a small amount ▪ The election was a *squeaker.* [=the election was very close] ▪ They won in a 10–9 *squeaker.*

squeaky /ˈskwiːki/ *adj* **squeak·i·er; -est** *[also more* ~; *most* ~*]* : making or likely to make a sharp, high-pitched sound ▪ a *squeaky* door ▪ Her voice is *squeaky.*

a/the squeaky wheel gets the grease/oil see [1]WHEEL

– squeak·i·ly /ˈskwiːkəli/ *adv* **– squeak·i·ness** /ˈskwiːkinəs/ *noun [noncount]*

squeaky–clean *adj*

1 : completely clean ▪ The glass is *squeaky-clean.* ▪ *squeaky-clean* hair

2 : not connected with or involving anything morally wrong ▪ He has a *squeaky-clean* reputation/image.

[1]**squeal** /ˈskwiːl/ *verb* **squeals; squealed; squeal·ing**

1 : to make or cause (something) to make a long, high-pitched cry or noise *[no obj]* The pigs were *squealing.* ▪ The car ***squealed to a stop.*** — often + *with* or *in* ▪ The children *squealed with/in* delight when they saw the clown. *[+ obj]* He ***squealed the tires*** and drove off.

2 *[no obj] informal + disapproving* : to tell someone in authority (such as the police or a teacher) about something wrong that someone has done ▪ She *squealed* to the teacher. ▪ "How did they find out?" "Someone must have *squealed.*" [=*snitched*] ▪ He ***squealed on*** [=*informed on*] his friend.

3 *[+ obj]* : to say (something) in a high and excited voice ▪ "Let me go," she *squealed.*

– squeal·er *noun, pl* **-ers** *[count] informal + disapproving* ▪ I won't tell anyone what you did. I'm no *squealer.*

[2]**squeal** *noun, pl* **squeals** *[count]* : a long, high-pitched cry or noise ▪ She heard the pig's *squeals.* — often + *of* ▪ a *squeal of* delight ▪ We heard the *squeal of* the brakes.

squea·mish /ˈskwiːmɪʃ/ *adj [more* ~; *most* ~*]*

1 a : afraid to deal with or do things that might hurt or offend people — often used in negative statements ▪ Journalists can't be *squeamish.* ▪ My parents are not *squeamish* about talking about sex. ▪ As a supervisor, you can't be *squeamish* about firing people. **b** : having an unpleasantly nervous or doubtful feeling ▪ I used to be *squeamish* about eating raw fish.

2 : easily shocked, offended, or disgusted by unpleasant things ▪ I'm too *squeamish* to watch horror movies.

3 : having a sick feeling in the stomach : suffering from nausea ▪ She gets *squeamish* [=*queasy*] at the sight of blood.

the squeamish : squeamish people : people who are easily shocked or offended by unpleasant things ▪ The movie is ***not for the squeamish.***

– squea·mish·ness *noun [noncount]* ▪ You'll have to get over your *squeamishness* about firing people.

squee·gee /ˈskwiːˌʤiː/ *noun, pl* **-gees** *[count]* : a tool that has a blade of rubber attached to a handle and that is used for spreading or wiping liquid on, across, or off a surface (such as a window or floor)

– squeegee *verb* **-gees; -geed; -gee·ing** *[+ obj]* ▪ He *squeegeed* the water into the drain.

squeez·able /ˈskwiːzəbəl/ *adj* : having parts or sides that can be pressed together ▪ a *squeezable* bottle of ketchup ▪ *squeezable* toys

[1]**squeeze** /ˈskwiːz/ *verb* **squeez·es; squeezed; squeez·ing**

1 : to press together the parts and especially the opposite sides of (something) *[+ obj]* *Squeeze* the bottle/tube. ▪ He lightly *squeezed* her hand and smiled. ▪ Gently *squeeze* the fruit to see if it's ripe. • She ***squeezed her eyes shut.*** [=she closed her eyes very tightly] [*no obj*] Hold it securely but don't *squeeze* too hard.

2 *always followed by an adverb or preposition* [+ *obj*] : to get or remove (something) by squeezing something • He *squeezed* the juice from the orange. • She *squeezed* out some ketchup. = She *squeezed* some ketchup out. • freshly *squeezed* orange juice — sometimes used figuratively • They can't *squeeze* much more money out of the business.

3 [+ *obj*] : to pull back on (a gun's trigger) with your finger • He took aim and *squeezed* [=*pulled*] the trigger. — see also SQUEEZE OFF (below)

4 *always followed by an adverb or preposition* : to move into or through a small or crowded space [*no obj*] We had to *squeeze* past/by the people in the aisles. • trying to *squeeze* into tight jeans • The cat *squeezed* through the opening. • We all *squeezed* into the elevator. • (*Brit*) ***Squeeze up*** [=move closer together], please. We need to make room for one more person. [+ *obj*] We can *squeeze* one more person in the back seat. • The instructor *squeezed* a lot of information into one week. • We were all *squeezed* [=*squashed*] into the elevator.

5 [+ *obj*] : to barely succeed at getting or doing (something) • The police *squeezed* a confession from her. — often + *out* • The team *squeezed out* a victory. • The police *squeezed* a confession *out* of her.

6 [+ *obj*] **a** : to decrease the amount of (something, such as money) • Rising costs have *squeezed* profits. **b** : to cause financial problems for (a business or organization) • The availability of music on the Internet has *squeezed* the record industry. **c** *informal* : to force (someone) to give you something or to do something by using threats or pressure • The banks are *squeezing* them for more money. • She tried to *squeeze* me for $100.

squeeze in [*phrasal verb*] ***squeeze (someone or something) in or squeeze in (someone or something)*** : to find time for (someone or something) • I can try to *squeeze* you *in* after my one o'clock appointment. • The teacher tried to *squeeze in* a few more lessons before school vacation.

squeeze off [*phrasal verb*] ***squeeze off (a round)*** : to fire (a shot) by squeezing the trigger of a gun • He quickly *squeezed off* four rounds.

squeeze out [*phrasal verb*] ***squeeze out (someone or something) or squeeze (someone or something) out*** : to force (someone or something) out of a position, place, etc. • The city's low-income residents have been *squeezed out* [=have been forced to leave their homes] by rising real estate prices. • These big stores have *squeezed out* a lot of the smaller locally owned shops.

²squeeze *noun, pl* **squeezes**

1 [*singular*] : a situation in which people or things are crowded together • Fifty guests will be a bit of a *squeeze.* • It'll be a ***tight squeeze***, but we can all fit.

2 [*count*] : an act of squeezing something — usually singular • He gave the bottle a good *squeeze.* • She gave his hand a *squeeze.* [=she squeezed his hand]

3 [*count*] : a small amount that is gotten or removed from something (such as a piece of fruit) by squeezing it — often + *of* • a *squeeze of* lemon/lime

4 a [*count*] : a situation in which there is not enough of something — usually singular • There is a serious housing *squeeze* [=*shortage*] in the city. [=there are not enough houses, apartments, etc., available] • a credit *squeeze* [=a situation in which it is difficult for people, companies, etc., to get credit] **b** ***the squeeze*** *informal* : a situation that causes feelings of stress and pressure • We are really ***feeling the squeeze*** since I lost my job. • The government is ***putting the squeeze on*** tax evaders.

5 [*noncount*] *chiefly US slang* : a romantic partner : a boyfriend or girlfriend • So who's your current *squeeze*? • She's my ***main squeeze.***

squeeze bottle *noun, pl* ~ **-tles** [*count*] : a plastic bottle that forces out its contents when it is squeezed : a squeezable bottle

squelch /ˈskwɛltʃ/ *verb* **squelch·es; squelched; squelch·ing** [+ *obj*] *US* : to stop (something) from continuing by doing or saying something • A statement was made to *squelch* [=*squash, scotch, quash*] the rumors. • Police *squelched* [=*quelled*] the protest. = The protest was *squelched* by police.

squib /ˈskwɪb/ *noun, pl* **squibs** [*count*] : a small firecracker

damp squib *Brit* : something that is disappointing because it is not as exciting or effective as expected • The stock turned out to be something of a *damp squib.*

squib kick *noun, pl* ~ **kicks** [*count*] *American football* : a kickoff in which the ball is kicked so that it bounces along the ground

squid /ˈskwɪd/ *noun, pl* **squid** *or* **squids** [*count*] : a sea animal that has a long, thin, soft body and 10 long arms

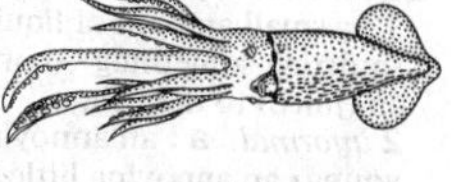
squid

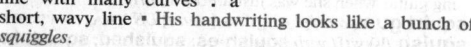

squig·gle /ˈskwɪgəl/ *noun, pl* **squig·gles** [*count*] : a short line with many curves : a short, wavy line • His handwriting looks like a bunch of *squiggles.*

— **squig·gly** /ˈskwɪgli/ *adj* **squig·gli·er; -est** • *squiggly* lines

¹squint /ˈskwɪnt/ *verb* **squints; squint·ed; squint·ing**

1 [*no obj*] : to look at something with your eyes partly closed • She had to *squint* to read the small print. • They were *squinting* into the sun. [=looking toward the sun with their eyes partly closed] • He *squinted* through the haze of smoke.

2 [+ *obj*] : to cause (your eyes) to partly close • I had to *squint* my eyes to focus on the tiny letters.

3 [*no obj*] *chiefly Brit* : to have a medical condition that makes your eyes unable to look in the same direction • I noticed that he *squints.*

²squint *noun, pl* **squints**

1 [*singular*] : a condition in which you are looking at something with your eyes partly closed : an act of squinting • Her gaze narrowed into a *squint.*

2 [*count*] *chiefly Brit* : a medical condition in which your eyes are unable to look in the same direction — usually singular • She was born with a *squint.*

3 [*singular*] *Brit, informal* : a quick look — + *at* • He took a *squint at* the document. • Have a *squint at* this.

squinty /ˈskwɪnti/ *adj* **squint·i·er; -est** *of the eyes* : partly closed or seeming to be partly closed • He looked at me with *squinty* eyes. • a *squinty*-eyed scowl

squire /ˈskwajɚ/ *noun, pl* **squires** [*count*]

1 : a young man in the Middle Ages who helped a knight before eventually becoming a knight himself

2 : a man in the past in England who owned most of the land in a village or district in the country

3 *Brit, informal + old-fashioned* — used to address a man whose name is unknown • "Where to, *squire*?" asked the taxi driver.

squirm /ˈskwɚm/ *verb* **squirms; squirmed; squirm·ing** [*no obj*] : to make a lot of twisting movements because you are nervous, uncomfortable, bored, etc. • The baby *squirmed* a lot when I tried to hold him. • She *squirmed* under her father's angry stare. • The children *squirmed* with delight. • He tried to hold onto her but she *squirmed* free. • The frog *squirmed* out of his hands. • The gory details of the story had me *squirming* in my seat. — sometimes used figuratively • a Congressional investigation that is making the industry *squirm* [=making people in the industry very nervous and uncomfortable]

— **squirmy** /ˈskwɚmi/ *adj* **squirm·i·er; -est** • an audience of *squirmy* kids

¹squir·rel /ˈskwɚrəl, *Brit* ˈskwɪrəl/ *noun, pl* **squir·rels** *also* **squirrel** [*count*] : a small animal with a long tail and soft fur that lives in trees — see picture at RODENT

²squirrel *verb* **-rels;** *US* **-reled** *or Brit* **-relled;** *US* **-rel·ing** *or Brit* **-rel·ling**

squirrel away [*phrasal verb*] ***squirrel away (something) or squirrel (something) away*** : to put (something) in a safe or secret place especially so that it can be kept for future use • She's *squirreled* a lot of money *away* in a secret bank account. • Most of his money is *squirreled away* somewhere.

squir·rel·ly *also* **squir·rely** /ˈskwɚrəli, *Brit* ˈskwɪrəli/ *adj* [*more* ~; *most* ~] *US, informal*

1 : tending to move around a lot : RESTLESS • It was the end of the school year, when all the kids get a little *squirrelly.*

2 : very odd, silly, or foolish • *squirrelly* behavior

¹squirt /ˈskwɚt/ *verb* **squirts; squirt·ed; squirt·ing**

1 a [+ *obj*] : to suddenly force (a liquid) out through a small opening • He *squirted* some oil on the door hinge. • She *squirted* ketchup all over her fries. • Some snakes can *squirt* venom from their mouths. **b** [*no obj*] *of a liquid* : to suddenly be forced out through a small opening • Water *squirted* out from/of a hole in the pipe. • Juice from the lemon *squirted* into my eye.

2 [+ *obj*] : to make (someone or something) wet with a

S

stream of liquid — often + *with* ▪ My brother *squirted* me *with* the hose. [=made me wet with water from the hose] ▪ He *squirted* the door hinge *with* oil.

²squirt *noun, pl* **squirts** [*count*]
1 : a small amount of liquid that is produced by squeezing or squirting something — often + *of* ▪ He added a *squirt of* lemon (juice) to the fish.
2 *informal* **a :** an annoying person who is small and usually young ▪ an annoying little *squirt* who kept pestering me ▪ Listen *squirt*, I'm in charge here. **b :** CHILD ▪ She started playing guitar when she was just a little *squirt*.

squirt gun *noun, pl* **~ guns** [*count*] *US* **:** WATER PISTOL

squish /ˈskwɪʃ/ *verb* **squish·es; squished; squish·ing**
1 [+ *obj*] **:** to press (something) into a flatter shape **:** SQUASH ▪ She *squished* the bug. ▪ The cake accidentally got *squished*.
2 : to move into a space that is tight or crowded **:** SQUASH [*no obj*] We *squished* together to make more room. [+ *obj*] We managed to *squish* four people in the backseat of the car. — often used as *(be) squished* ▪ Four of us *were squished* together in the backseat.
3 [*no obj*] **:** to make the sound that is made when something very wet is pressed, stepped on, etc. ▪ His wet shoes *squished* when he walked.

squishy /ˈskwɪʃi/ *adj* **squish·i·er; -est** [*also more ~; most ~*] **:** soft and often wet ▪ The ground was wet and *squishy*. ▪ *squishy* cushions

Sr. (*chiefly US*) *or Brit* **Sr** *abbr* **1** senior **2** sister

SS *abbr* **1** saints **2** Social Security **3** steamship

SSN *abbr* Social Security number

st *abbr, Brit* stone ▪ She weighs 7*st* 5lbs. [=7 stone and 5 pounds]

St. (*chiefly US*) *or Brit* **St** *abbr* **1** saint **2** street

-st *symbol* — used in writing after the number 1 for the word *first* ▪ He's in the 1*st* [=*first*] grade. ▪ It is her 21*st* birthday.

¹stab /ˈstæb/ *noun, pl* **stabs** [*count*]
1 : a wound made by a pointed weapon (such as a knife) ▪ He died from a *stab* to the heart. [=died from being stabbed in the heart] ▪ a *stab* wound/victim
2 : a sudden, strong feeling of physical or emotional pain — + *of* ▪ a *stab of* pain/regret/doubt/fear
3 *informal* **:** an attempt to do something successfully — often + *at* ▪ She ***took/made a stab at*** solving the problem. [=she made an attempt to solve the problem] ▪ Let me ***give it a stab***. = Let me ***have a stab at it*** [=let me try to do it]
a stab in the back **:** an action or way of behaving that hurts someone who trusts you **:** an act of betrayal ▪ I can't believe that someone I had helped and supported would steal from me. It's *a real stab in the back*.
a stab in the dark **1 :** a guess that is based on very little or no information or evidence ▪ They don't really know how much the work will cost. They're just taking *a stab* [=*shot*] *in the dark*. **2 :** an attempt that is not likely to succeed ▪ It's *a stab* [=*shot*] *in the dark*, but we should try anyway.

²stab *verb* **stabs; stabbed; stab·bing**
1 [+ *obj*] **:** to wound (someone or something) with a pointed weapon (such as a knife) ▪ He *stabbed* her with a dagger. ▪ The victim was *stabbed* in the chest five times.
2 : to quickly or suddenly push a pointed object into or toward someone or something [+ *obj*] He *stabbed* the piece of meat with a fork. = He *stabbed* the fork into the piece of meat. ▪ She *stabbed* [=*jabbed*] the air with her pen as she spoke. [*no obj*] — often + *at* ▪ She *stabbed at* the dead animal with a stick.
stab (someone) in the back **:** to hurt (someone who trusts you) by not giving help or by doing something morally wrong **:** to betray (someone) ▪ He's the kind of person who gets you to trust him but then *stabs you in the back*.

¹stab·bing /ˈstæbɪŋ/ *noun, pl* **-bings** [*count*] **:** an attack in which someone is wounded with a pointed weapon (such as a knife) ▪ a fatal *stabbing*

²stabbing *adj, always used before a noun*
1 : of or relating to a stabbing ▪ a *stabbing* victim [=a person who has been stabbed] ▪ a *stabbing* death
2 : felt very suddenly in part of your body **:** very sharp and sudden ▪ She felt a *stabbing* pain in her back.

sta·bil·i·ty /stəˈbɪləti/ *noun* [*noncount*] **:** the quality or state of being stable: such as **a :** the quality or state of something that is not easily changed or likely to change ▪ the country's political and economic *stability* **b :** the quality or state of something that is not easily moved ▪ Test the platform for *stability* before using it. **c :** the quality or state of someone who is emotionally or mentally healthy ▪ There are some questions about the applicant's mental *stability*.

sta·bi·lize *also Brit* **sta·bi·lise** /ˈsteɪbəˌlaɪz/ *verb* **-liz·es; -lized; -liz·ing**
1 : to become stable or to make (something) stable: such as **a :** to stop quickly changing, increasing, getting worse, etc. [*no obj*] The country's population has *stabilized* at 3.2 million. ▪ Prices have *stabilized*. [+ *obj*] The government's efforts to *stabilize* prices have not succeeded. ▪ Even the administration's most vocal critics agree that the President has succeeded in *stabilizing* the economy. — opposite DESTABILIZE **b** [+ *obj*] **:** to make (something) less easily moved ▪ We'll use ropes to *stabilize* the platform. **c** [+ *obj*] *technical* **:** to give (something) a chemical structure or to put (something) into a physical state that does not change easily ▪ a process that *stabilizes* the vaccine
2 [+ *obj*] **:** to make (something) steady ▪ drugs that *stabilize* a patient's heartbeat ▪ The pilots were able to *stabilize* the airplane and land safely.
– sta·bi·li·za·tion *also Brit* **sta·bi·li·sa·tion** /ˌsteɪbələˈzeɪʃən, *Brit* ˌsteɪbəˌlaɪˈzeɪʃən/ *noun* [*noncount*] ▪ political/economic *stabilization*

sta·bi·liz·er *also Brit* **sta·bi·lis·er** /ˈsteɪbəˌlaɪzɚ/ *noun, pl* **-ers**
1 [*count*] **:** a device or substance that is used to make something stable or steady: such as **a :** a device that is used to keep a ship steady in rough seas **b :** the part of an airplane's tail that cannot be moved **c :** a substance that is added to something (such as a food mixture) to keep it in a desired condition
2 ***stabilisers*** [*plural*] *Brit* **:** TRAINING WHEELS

¹sta·ble /ˈsteɪbəl/ *adj* **sta·bler; sta·blest** [*also more ~; most ~*]
1 a : in a good state or condition that is not easily changed or likely to change ▪ a *stable* community/government ▪ They have a *stable* relationship. ▪ Children need to be raised in a *stable* environment. ▪ a *stable* income ▪ The economy is *stable*. **b** *medical* **:** not getting worse or likely to get worse ▪ The patient is *stable*. ▪ (*US*) She is ***in stable condition*** after suffering multiple injuries. = (*Brit*) She is ***in a stable condition*** after suffering multiple injuries.
2 : not easily moved ▪ Make sure the platform is *stable*. ▪ The ladder doesn't seem very *stable*. [=*secure*]
3 : emotionally or mentally healthy **:** calm and reasonable ▪ a mentally/emotionally *stable* person
4 *technical* **:** having a chemical structure or physical state that does not change easily ▪ a *stable* compound/element

²stable *noun, pl* **stables** [*count*]
1 : a building in which horses are kept, fed, and cared for ▪ She rode the horse back to the *stable*. ▪ a horse *stable* — sometimes used in the plural form ***stables*** especially to mean a place where horses are kept for riding lessons ▪ She rode the horse back to the *stables*. ▪ riding *stables*
2 a : the group of racehorses that belong to the same owner ▪ There have been three winners from his *stable* this season. **b :** a group of people (such as athletes, writers, or performers) who work for or are trained by the same person, organization, or business ▪ a *stable* of actors/writers **c :** a group of products that are made by the same company ▪ A new model will be added to the car company's *stable* of sedans.

³stable *verb* **sta·bles; sta·bled; sta·bling** [+ *obj*] **:** to put or keep (a horse) in a stable ▪ She *stabled* the horse. ▪ Where do you *stable* your horses?

sta·ble·mate /ˈsteɪbəlˌmeɪt/ *noun, pl* **-mates** [*count*] **:** a horse, person, product, etc., that belongs to the same stable as another horse, person, product, etc. ▪ horses that are *stablemates* ▪ a new car model and its *stablemates*

stac·ca·to /stəˈkɑːtoʊ/ *adj*
1 *music* **:** short and not sounding connected ▪ *staccato* notes/chords ▪ the *staccato* blasts of a horn — compare LEGATO
2 : sudden and brief ▪ the dialogue's *staccato* sentences ▪ *staccato* movements
– staccato *adv* ▪ playing/singing *staccato*

¹stack /ˈstæk/ *noun, pl* **stacks**
1 [*count*] **:** a usually neat pile **:** a group of things that are put one on top of the other ▪ He had arranged the letters in *stacks*. ▪ She took a magazine from near the top of the *stack*. — often + *of* ▪ a *stack of* dishes/papers — see also HAYSTACK
2 [*count*] **:** a large amount of something — usually + *of* ▪ There is a *stack of* evidence against her. ▪ They have *stacks of* money.
3 [*count*] **:** a tall chimney on a factory, ship, etc., for carrying smoke away **:** SMOKESTACK

4 the stacks **:** the rows of shelves where books are stored in a library • I couldn't find the book in *the stacks.*
blow your stack see [1]BLOW

[2]stack *verb* **stacks; stacked; stack·ing**
1 : to arrange (things) in a stack **:** to put (things) in a usually neat pile [+ *obj*] She spent the afternoon splitting and *stacking* firewood. • She *stacked* the plates in the cupboard. • He *stacked* the books on the table. — often + *up* • She *stacked* the wood *up* against the fence. [*no obj*] The chairs don't *stack.* [=the chairs cannot be put in a stack; the chairs cannot be stacked]
2 [+ *obj*] **a :** to cheat at a card game by arranging (a deck of cards) in a special way • The other players accused him of ***stacking the deck*** **b** — used to describe a situation in which one person, team, etc., is given an advantage over others often in a way that is unfair • In many ways, the ***cards are stacked against*** immigrants. [=immigrants face unfair and difficult circumstances] • There are things you can do to ***stack the odds*** in your favor. [=to make it more likely for you to win, succeed, etc.] • The ***odds are stacked against*** you. [=the odds are against you; you do not have a good or fair chance of winning, succeeding, etc.]
stack up [*phrasal verb*] **1 :** to increase in number or amount to a total that is difficult to deal with • Cars quickly *stacked up* behind the bus. • My bills are *stacking up.* [=*piling up*] **2 :** to be good enough or equally good • The camera doesn't *stack up* [=*measure up*] when it comes to performance. • This model *stacks up* well when compared with other cameras. [=the camera is as good as or better than others] **3** ***stack up against (something or someone) or stack (something or someone) up against (something or someone)*** **:** to compare (something or someone) with others of the same kind • How does this computer *stack up against* other models? [=how good is it compared to other models?] • How does he *stack up against* the other candidates? • The camera does pretty well when you *stack* it *up against* the competition.

stack·able /ˈstækəbəl/ *adj* **:** able to be arranged in a stack • The chairs are *stackable.* • *stackable* plastic crates

stacked /ˈstækt/ *adj, informal + impolite, of a woman* **:** having large breasts

sta·di·um /ˈsteɪdijəm/ *noun, pl* **-ums** [*count*] **:** a very large usually roofless building that has a large open area surrounded by many rows of seats and that is used for sports events, concerts, etc.

[1]staff /ˈstæf, *Brit* ˈstɑːf/ *noun, pl* **staffs** *or* **staves** /ˈsteɪvz/
1 *pl* ***staffs*** **a :** a group of people who work for an organization or business [*count*] The entire *staff* has done a great job this year. • The *staff* is at a meeting. • a teaching/sales/editorial/coaching/pitching *staff* • the hospital/library/kitchen *staff* • The department has a *staff* of 40 (people). • She's a new member of the *staff.* • He has been ***on the staff*** [=a member of the staff] for 25 years. [*noncount*] (*US*) There are 100 people ***on staff*** [=working as members of the staff] • (*Brit*) She's a new ***member of staff*** • a *staff* member/director/writer/meeting — see also WAITSTAFF **b** [*count*] **:** a group of military officers who help a commanding officer but who do not take part in active fighting • The general's *staff* is planning the army's next move. — see also CHIEF OF STAFF, JOINT CHIEFS OF STAFF

> ***usage*** *Staff* may be used as a plural noun to mean the members of a staff. • The company employs 20 full-time *staff.* • The *staff* are at a meeting.

2 *pl* ***staves*** [*count*] **a** *old-fashioned* **:** a long stick that you carry in your hand for support while walking **b :** a long stick that is carried as a symbol of authority • a bishop's *staff*
3 *pl* ***staves*** [*count*] *music* **:** the five horizontal lines and the spaces between them on which music is written — called also *stave*
staff of life *literary* **:** a basic food; *especially* **:** BREAD

[2]staff *verb* **staffs; staffed; staff·ing** [+ *obj*]
1 : to supply (an organization or business) with workers • We'll need 300 workers to properly *staff* the hotel. — often used as *(be) staffed* • The department *is staffed* with an equal number of men and women. • The office *is* fully *staffed.* — see also OVERSTAFFED, SHORT-STAFFED, UNDERSTAFFED
2 : to work for (an organization or business) as a member of a staff • the 300 workers who *staff* the hotel — often used as *(be) staffed* • The organization *is staffed* by volunteers.
– staffing *adj* • *staffing* needs/problems/levels

staff·er /ˈstæfɚ/ *noun, pl* **-ers** [*count*] *US* **:** a member of a staff • newspaper *staffers* • a congressional *staffer* [=a person who is a member of a congressman's or congresswoman's staff]

staff nurse *noun, pl* **~ nurses** [*count*] **:** a nurse who is on the staff of a hospital — compare CHARGE NURSE

staff officer *noun, pl* **~ -cers** [*count*] **:** an officer who is a member of a military commander's staff

staff sergeant *noun, pl* **~ -geants** [*count*] **:** an officer in the army, air force, or marines with a rank above a sergeant

stag /ˈstæg/ *noun, pl* **stags** *or* **stag** [*count*] **:** an adult male deer
go stag *US* **:** to go to a party or other social event by yourself • He's *going stag* [=going alone] to the party. — see also STAG PARTY

[1]stage /ˈsteɪʤ/ *noun*
1 [*count*] **:** a particular point or period in the growth or development of something • an early/late *stage* of the disease • children at the same *stage* of development • the first/last *stage* [=*phase*] of the plan
2 a : a raised platform in a theater, auditorium, etc., where the performers stand [*count*] The actors walked out onto the *stage.* • She has ***shared a stage with*** [=performed with] many great actors. • The band ***took the stage*** [=walked onto the stage] and the concert began. [*noncount*] He was ***on stage*** for the entire show. • an actor with a commanding ***stage presence*** [=an actor with a powerful quality that attracts attention on the stage] — see picture at THEATER; see also BACKSTAGE, CENTER STAGE, OFFSTAGE **b** [*noncount*] **:** the art or profession of acting and especially of acting in theaters • He is a star of *stage* [=*theater*], screen, and television. • She ***went on the stage*** [=became an actor] at age 15. • a *stage* actor/play
3 [*singular*] **:** a place or area of activity in which the things that happen are watched with great interest by many people • She has become an important figure on the national political *stage.* [=an important figure in national politics] • He has no intention of leaving the political *stage.* • The company wants to compete on the world *stage.*
4 [*count*] **:** a section of a rocket that has its own fuel and engine • a three-*stage* missile
in stages **:** in a series of separate steps rather than all at one time • The changes will be made *in stages.* • The new law will be implemented *in stages.*
set the stage (for something) **:** to make (something) possible or likely • His discoveries *set the stage for* a revolution in medical research. • Her early training *set the stage for* her later success.

[2]stage *verb* **stag·es; staged; stag·ing** [+ *obj*]
1 : to produce (a play, performance, etc.) on a stage • The school *stages* two plays each year.
2 a : to organize and produce (a public event) • The students *staged* a protest/demonstration. • The school is *staging* a track meet. **b :** to arrange or do (something that is intended to get a lot of public attention) • The prisoners are *staging* a hunger strike. • The photograph of the two leaders shaking hands was deliberately *staged.*
3 : to succeed in doing or making (something) • His career as a singer appeared to be over, but then he ***staged a comeback*** • The company has ***staged a (remarkable) recovery*** in the past two years.

stage·coach /ˈsteɪʤˌkoʊʧ/ *noun, pl* **-coach·es** [*count*] **:** a large carriage pulled by horses that was used in the past to carry passengers and mail along a regular route

stage direction *noun, pl* **~ -tions** [*count*] **:** a written instruction in a play telling an actor what to do

stage door *noun, pl* **~ doors** [*count*] **:** the door at the back of a theater that is used by actors and the people who work in the theater

stage fright *noun* [*noncount*] **:** a nervous feeling felt by someone who is going to appear in front of an audience • She got over her *stage fright* by the second act. • I get *stage fright* whenever I have to speak in front of a large group of people.

stage·hand /ˈsteɪʤˌhænd/ *noun, pl* **-hands** [*count*] **:** someone who prepares the scenery, lights, etc., for a performance on a stage

stage left *adv* **:** on the left side of a stage when you are on the stage and facing the audience • The actor exited *stage left.*

stage–man·age /ˈsteɪʤˌmænɪʤ/ *verb* **-ag·es; -aged; -ag·ing**
1 : to organize the details of (a performance in a theater) [+ *obj*] She *stage-managed* last year's production of the school

play. [*no obj*] She was hired to *stage-manage* for the show. [=to be the show's stage manager]

2 [+ *obj*] **:** to carefully plan and arrange (something) in order to achieve a desired effect • The press conference was carefully *stage-managed*, and only approved questions were allowed. • He *stage-managed* his son's tennis career.

stage manager *noun, pl* **~ -ers** [*count*] **:** a person who is in charge of the stage, scenery, lighting, etc., for a performance in a theater

stage name *noun, pl* **~ names** [*count*] **:** a name used by an actor instead of the actor's real name

stage right *adv* **:** on the right side of a stage when you are on the stage and facing the audience • The actor exited *stage right*.

stage·struck /ˈsteɪʤˌstrʌk/ *adj* **:** very interested in the theater; *especially* **:** having an eager desire to become an actor • He was a *stagestruck* young man with dreams of stardom.

stage whisper *noun, pl* **~ -pers** [*count*]

1 : a loud whisper by an actor that can be heard by the audience but which the other actors on the stage pretend not to hear

2 : a loud whisper that is intended to be heard by everyone • "I've had more than I can stand," she complained in a *stage whisper*.

stagey *variant spelling of* STAGY

stag·fla·tion /ˌstægˈfleɪʃən/ *noun* [*noncount*] **:** an economic situation in which prices of goods and services continually increase, many people do not have jobs, and businesses are not very successful

¹stag·ger /ˈstægɚ/ *verb* **-gers; -gered; -ger·ing**

1 : to move or cause (someone) to move unsteadily from side to side [*no obj*] The drunk *staggered* away/off. • She *staggered* over to the sofa. [+ *obj*] A hard slap on the back *staggered* him.

2 [+ *obj*] **:** to shock or surprise (someone) very much • Their indifference *staggers* me. • It *staggers* me to see how much money they've spent on this project.

3 [+ *obj*] **:** to arrange (things) in a series of different positions or times • They *staggered* the runners' starting positions. • *stagger* work shifts — see also STAGGERED

²stagger *noun, pl* **-ers** [*count*] **:** an unsteady movement while walking or standing • He walked with a slight *stagger*.

staggered *adj*

1 : extremely shocked or surprised • I'm just *staggered* at/by her attitude.

2 : arranged so that things are positioned at different places or happen at different times • *staggered* finish lines • *staggered* conference dates

stag·ger·ing /ˈstægərɪŋ/ *adj* [*more ~; most ~*] **:** very large, shocking, or surprising • *staggering* medical bills • The storm caused a *staggering* amount of damage.

– stag·ger·ing·ly *adv* • The bills are *staggeringly* large.

stag·ing /ˈsteɪʤɪŋ/ *noun, pl* **-ings**

1 : the performance of a play on a stage [*count*] She has acted in several *stagings* [=*productions*] of the play. [*noncount*] The *staging* of the play was more difficult than expected.

2 [*noncount*] **:** a temporary raised platform that a person can sit or stand on while working • Once the *staging* [=*scaffolding*] is in place we can start painting the ceiling.

staging area *noun, pl* **~ areas** [*count*] **:** a place where soldiers gather and military equipment is prepared before a mission

staging post *noun, pl* **~ posts** [*count*] **:** a place where people can stop for rest, supplies, etc., during a long journey

stag·nant /ˈstægnənt/ *adj*

1 : not flowing • a *stagnant* puddle • *stagnant* water/air

2 : not active, changing, or progressing • a *stagnant* economy • *stagnant* wages [=wages that are not increasing]

stag·nate /ˈstægˌneɪt/ *verb* **-nates; -nat·ed; -nat·ing** [*no obj*] **:** to stop developing, progressing, moving, etc. **:** to be or become stagnant • Wages have *stagnated* recently. • Their relationship is *stagnating*. • a puddle of *stagnating* water

– stag·na·tion /stægˈneɪʃən/ *noun* [*noncount*]

stag party *noun, pl* **~ -ties** [*count*] **:** a party for men only that is usually on the night before a man's wedding — called also (*Brit*) *stag night*

stagy *or* **stag·ey** /ˈsteɪʤi/ *adj* **stag·i·er; -est :** looking or seeming like something from a performance on a stage rather than something natural • an artificial and *stagy* manner • a *stagy* gesture • The movie looks *stagy*.

staid /ˈsteɪd/ *adj* [*more ~; most ~*] **:** serious, boring, or old-fashioned • a *staid* and solemn businessman • a *staid* demeanor/manner

– staid·ness *noun* [*noncount*]

¹stain /ˈsteɪn/ *verb* **stains; stained; stain·ing**

1 a : to leave a mark on something [+ *obj*] The red wine *stained* the carpet. • a wine-*stained* carpet [*no obj*] Be careful—grape juice *stains*. **b** [*no obj*] **:** to be marked or damaged by a stain • This fabric *stains* easily.

2 [+ *obj*] **:** to use a special liquid to change the color of (something) • He *stained* the wood a dark cherry color.

3 [+ *obj*] **:** to damage or spoil (something, such as someone's reputation) • The accusations *stained* his reputation.

– stain·er /ˈsteɪnɚ/ *noun, pl* **-ers** [*count*]

²stain *noun, pl* **stains** [*count*]

1 : a mark made on a surface, a piece of clothing, etc., that is very hard or impossible to remove • There's a juice/wine *stain* on the floor. • She has a *stain* on her shirt. • Will those grass *stains* wash out? — see also BLOODSTAIN

2 : a special liquid that is used to change the color of something (such as wood or cloth)

3 : something that causes people to have less respect for someone **:** something that damages a person's reputation — usually singular • The accusation left a *stain* that followed him the rest of his life. • a *stain* on her honor/reputation

– stain·less /ˈsteɪnləs/ *adj* • He has a *stainless* reputation.

stained glass *noun* [*noncount*] **:** colored glass that is used to make pictures and patterns in windows • a cathedral with beautiful *stained glass* windows

stainless steel *noun* [*noncount*] **:** a type of steel that does not rust

stair /ˈsteɚ/ *noun, pl* **stairs**

1 ***stairs*** [*plural*] **:** a series of steps that go from one level or floor to another • She ran down the *stairs*. • He waited at the foot/bottom of the *stairs*. • She slipped and fell down the *stairs*. • The *stairs* lead to the roof. • We had to climb another ***flight/set of stairs*** to get to the roof.

2 [*count*] **:** one of the steps in a set of stairs • a squeaky *stair* • He tripped on the bottom *stair* and almost fell.

3 [*singular*] *literary* **:** STAIRCASE • climbing the *stair*

stair·case /ˈsteɚˌkeɪs/ *noun, pl* **-cas·es** [*count*] **:** a set of stairs and its supporting structures • a wooden *staircase* — see also MOVING STAIRCASE, SPIRAL STAIRCASE

stair–climb·er /ˈsteɚˈklaɪmɚ/ *noun, pl* **-ers** [*count*] *US* **:** an exercise machine on which you make a continuous series of upward steps like someone who is climbing stairs — see picture at GYM

stair·way /ˈsteɚˌweɪ/ *noun, pl* **-ways** [*count*] **:** a set of stairs that go from one level or floor to another • He took the *stairway* up to the third floor. [=he went to the third floor by walking up the stairs]

stair·well /ˈsteɚˌwɛl/ *noun, pl* **-wells** [*count*] **:** a space in a building where stairs are located

¹stake /ˈsteɪk/ *noun, pl* **stakes**

1 [*count*] **:** a pointed stick or post that is pushed into the ground especially to mark a place or to support something

2 ***the stake*** **:** a post that a person was tied to and burned on in the past as a form of punishment • Joan of Arc was burned at *the stake*.

3 ***stakes*** [*plural*] **:** something (such as money) that you could win or lose in a game, contest, etc. • a poker game with high *stakes* • The *stakes* are too high/low/big.

4 [*count*] **a :** an interest or share in a business • They have a *stake* in the company. [=they own part of the company] • a majority *stake* **b :** an interest or degree of involvement in something • We all have a *stake* in the health of our economy. [=the health of our economy affects us all]

at stake **:** in a position to be lost or gained • Millions of dollars are *at stake* in the battle over his inheritance. • Thousands of jobs are *at stake*. • Many lives are *at stake*. • My reputation is *at stake* if this project fails. [=my reputation will be lost/damaged if this project fails]

go to the stake for/over *Brit* **:** to defend (something or someone) even though your actions or statements may cause you trouble or harm • She's willing to *go to the stake for* her beliefs.

pull up stakes *US, informal* **:** to leave your job or home • Her career was going nowhere, so she decided it was time to *pull up stakes*.

²stake *verb* **stakes; staked; stak·ing** [+ *obj*]

1 : to risk the loss of (something, such as money) — usually + *on* • She *staked* [=*bet, wagered*] all her money *on* the race. • He *staked* [=*risked*] his reputation *on* the success of the new plan. ▪ The corporation *staked* billions of dollars *on* the deal. ▪ She *staked* everything *on* one last attempt. ▪ That's the man who robbed the bank. ***I would stake my life on it.*** [=I am absolutely sure]

2 : to support (something, such as a plant) with stakes ▪ She *staked* the tomatoes to keep them from falling over.

stake out [*phrasal verb*] ***stake (something) out*** *or* ***stake out (something)*** **1 :** to mark the limits of (an area) with stakes ▪ *stake out* a mining area ▪ We *staked out* the area where the pool will be installed. **2 :** to watch (a place) secretly especially because you are looking for illegal activity ▪ The police *staked out* the building until they caught the vandals. — see also STAKEOUT **3 :** to state (your opinion) in a very clear and definite way ▪ He *staked out* his position on this issue in a speech he gave last month.

***stake (out) a/your claim* :** to say or show that you believe you should have something or that you deserve something ▪ They *staked their claim* to the land. ▪ With her strong showing in the early rounds of the tournament, she has *staked her claim* to be considered one of the favorites.

stake·hold·er /ˈsteɪkˌhoʊldɚ/ *noun, pl* **-ers** [*count*]

1 : a person or business that has invested money in something (such as a company) ▪ corporate *stakeholders*

2 : a person who holds the money that people have bet on something and then gives it to the winner

stake·out /ˈsteɪkˌaʊt/ *noun, pl* **-outs** [*count*] **:** a situation in which the police secretly watch a place in order to look for illegal activity ▪ The drug deal was witnessed during a *stakeout* of the building. ▪ The police were ***on a stakeout***. — see also *stake out* at [2]STAKE

sta·lac·tite /stəˈlækˌtaɪt, *Brit* ˈstæləkˌtaɪt/ *noun, pl* **-tites** [*count*] **:** a pointed piece of rock that hangs down from the roof of a cave and that is formed by dripping water which contains minerals

sta·lag·mite /stəˈlægˌmaɪt, *Brit* ˈstæləgˌmaɪt/ *noun, pl* **-mites** [*count*] **:** a pointed piece of rock that sticks up from the floor of a cave and that is formed by dripping water which contains minerals

stalactite and stalagmite

stale /ˈsteɪl/ *adj* **stal·er; -est** [*more* ~; *most* ~]

1 a *of food* **:** no longer good or appealing **:** no longer fresh ▪ *stale* food ▪ *stale* bread **b :** not clean, clear, or pure **:** having an unpleasant taste or smell ▪ *stale* air/water ▪ a room filled with *stale* smoke

2 : not interesting or new **:** boring or unoriginal ▪ *stale* news/jokes ▪ Their relationship ***went stale***. [=became dull or predictable]

3 : not as strong, effective, or energetic as before ▪ She felt *stale* [=*bored*] in her job.

stale·mate /ˈsteɪlˌmeɪt/ *noun, pl* **-mates**

1 : a contest, dispute, competition, etc., in which neither side can gain an advantage or win [*count*] The budget debate ended in a *stalemate*. ▪ The new agreement could break the *stalemate*. [*noncount*] The budget debate ended in *stalemate*.

2 [*count, noncount*] **:** a situation in chess in which a player cannot successfully move any of the pieces and neither player can win ▪ The game ended in (a) *stalemate*. — compare CHECKMATE

– stalemate *verb* **-mates; -mat·ed; -mat·ing** [+ *obj*] ▪ He was *stalemated* by the opposition.

[1]**stalk** /ˈstɑːk/ *noun, pl* **stalks** [*count*]

1 : a thick or tall stem of a plant ▪ a flower *stalk* ▪ celery *stalks* — see color pictures on pages C4 and C6; see also CORNSTALK

2 : a thin, upright object or part that supports or connects something ▪ the *stalk* of a goblet

[2]**stalk** *verb* **stalks; stalked; stalk·ing**

1 [+ *obj*] **a :** to follow (an animal or person that you are hunting or trying to capture) by moving slowly and quietly ▪ Lions *stalked* the herd. ▪ a movie about a detective being *stalked* by a killer **b :** to go through (a place or area) while hunting ▪ This is the time of year when hunters are *stalking* the woods for deer. — often used figuratively ▪ A killer *stalks* the streets of the city. [=there is a killer somewhere in the city] ▪ a city that is *stalked* by fear [=a city where people are in a constant state of fear]

2 [+ *obj*] **:** to follow, watch, and bother (someone) constantly in a way that is frightening, dangerous, etc. ▪ She called the police because her ex-boyfriend was *stalking* her.

3 *always followed by an adverb or a preposition* [*no obj*] **:** to walk in a stiff or proud manner ▪ She angrily *stalked* out of the room.

– stalk·ing /ˈstɑːkɪŋ/ *noun* [*noncount*] ▪ He was arrested and charged with *stalking*.

stalk·er /ˈstɑːkɚ/ *noun, pl* **-ers** [*count*]

1 : a person who closely follows and watches another person for a long period of time in a way that is threatening, dangerous, etc. ▪ a famous actress who is being threatened by a *stalker* ▪ She has a *stalker*. [=someone is stalking her]

2 : a person who slowly and quietly hunts an animal ▪ a deer *stalker*

stalking horse *noun, pl* ~ **horses** [*count*] **:** someone or something that is used to hide a true purpose; *especially* **:** a candidate for a political office or position who has no real chance of winning but is being used by a political party to weaken the support for an opposing party, to find out if another candidate might be successful, etc.

[1]**stall** /ˈstɑːl/ *noun, pl* **stalls**

1 [*count*] **:** a small open counter or partially enclosed structure where things are displayed for sale ▪ food *stalls* ▪ a souvenir *stall* ▪ a market *stall* ▪ She set up a *stall* selling jewelry in the marketplace.

2 [*count*] **:** an enclosed area in a building where a farm animal (such as a horse or cow) is kept ▪ She cleaned the horses' *stalls*.

3 [*count*] **:** a seat in a church that is wholly or partly enclosed ▪ choir *stalls*

4 [*count*] *chiefly US* **:** a small, enclosed area with room for one person in a bathroom ▪ shower *stalls*; *especially* **:** a small, enclosed area with a toilet ▪ All the (bathroom) *stalls* were occupied.

5 ***the stalls*** *Brit* **:** the seats on the main level of a theater in front of the stage ▪ Our tickets are for seats in *the stalls*. [=(*US*) *the orchestra*]

– compare [3]STALL

[2]**stall** *verb* **stalls; stalled; stall·ing**

1 *of an engine* **:** to stop suddenly because of a problem [*no obj*] The engine suddenly *stalled*. [+ *obj*] Stopping too quickly can *stall* the engine.

2 *of an airplane* **:** to stop flying suddenly and begin to fall because the wings cannot produce enough lift [*no obj*] The airspeed got very low and the plane nearly *stalled*. [+ *obj*] The pilot almost *stalled* the airplane.

3 [+ *obj*] **:** to put or keep (an animal) in a stall ▪ They *stalled* the horses for the night.

– compare [4]STALL

[3]**stall** *noun* [*singular*] **:** a situation in which an engine suddenly stops or an airplane suddenly stops flying ▪ an engine *stall* ▪ The airplane went into a *stall*. — compare [1]STALL

[4]**stall** *verb* **stalls; stalled; stalling**

1 : to avoid doing something or to delay someone in a deliberate way because you need more time, do not want to do something, etc. [*no obj*] Please stop *stalling* and answer the question. [+ *obj*] Try to *stall* them until I get the place cleaned up.

2 : to stop progressing or developing [*no obj*] The economic recovery has *stalled*. ▪ His career has *stalled* in recent years. [+ *obj*] Budget problems have *stalled* the project.

– compare [2]STALL

stall·hold·er /ˈstɑːlˌhoʊldɚ/ *noun, pl* **-ers** [*count*] *Brit* **:** someone who manages a stall at which goods are sold

stal·lion /ˈstæljən/ *noun, pl* **-lions** [*count*] **:** an adult male horse and especially one that is used for breeding — compare GELDING

[1]**stal·wart** /ˈstɑːlwɚt/ *adj* [*more* ~; *most* ~] *formal*

1 : very loyal and dedicated ▪ *stalwart* fans/supporters

2 : physically strong ▪ their strong and *stalwart* son ▪ *stalwart* fortifications

– stal·wart·ly *adv*

[2]**stalwart** *noun, pl* **-warts** [*count*] *formal* **:** a loyal supporter ▪ party *stalwarts* [=people who support a political party very loyally]

sta·men /ˈsteɪmən/ *noun, pl* **-mens** [*count*] *botany* **:** the part of a flower that produces pollen — see picture at FLOWER; compare PISTIL

stam·i·na /ˈstæmənə/ *noun* [*noncount*] **:** great physical or mental strength that allows you to continue doing something for a long time ▪ Do you have the/enough *stamina* to finish the job?

stam·mer /ˈstæmɚ/ *verb* **-mers; -mered; -mer·ing :** to speak with many pauses and repetitions because you have a speech problem or because you are very nervous, frightened, etc. [*no obj*] He *stammers* [=*stutters*] when he's nervous. [+ *obj*] "I d-don't know what you're talking about!" she *stammered*. ▪ He *stammered* an excuse and fled.

– **stammer** *noun* [*singular*] ▪ He develops a *stammer* [=*stutter*] when he's nervous. – **stam·mer·er** /ˈstæmərə/ *noun, pl* **-ers** [*count*]

[1]**stamp** /ˈstæmp/ *noun, pl* **stamps**

1 [*count*] **a** : a small piece of paper that you buy and then stick to an envelope or package to pay the cost of mailing it ▪ a 39-cent *stamp* — called also *postage stamp*; see picture at MAIL **b** : a small piece of paper that is attached to something and that shows that a tax or fee has been paid — see also FOOD STAMP

2 [*count*] **a** : a device or tool that is used to mark something (such as a piece of paper) with a design, pattern, word, etc., by being pushed against a surface : a device or tool used for stamping something — see also RUBBER STAMP **b** : the mark made by a stamp ▪ There was a *stamp* on the letter showing the date when it was received.

3 a [*singular*] : a sign of a special or specific quality — usually + *of* ▪ Her poetry bears the *stamp of* genius. ▪ His quiet manner gives/lends his words the *stamp of* authority. [=makes his words seem authoritative] **b** [*count*] : an indication of something — usually singular ▪ She gave the plan her ***stamp of approval***. [=she approved the plan] **c** [*singular*] : an important or lasting effect ▪ He ***put/left his stamp*** on the process. [=he affected/changed the process in some important way]

4 [*singular*] *literary* : a particular kind or type ▪ He was a man of a different *stamp*. [=he was a different sort of man]

5 [*count*] : the act of bringing your foot down heavily and noisily ▪ an angry *stamp* of his foot

[2]**stamp** *verb* **stamps; stamped; stamp·ing**

1 [+ *obj*] : to bring (your foot) down heavily and noisily ▪ He *stamped* his foot in anger. ▪ The fans cheered and *stamped* [=*stomped*] their feet as the team took the lead.

2 *always followed by an adverb or preposition* [*no obj*] : to walk heavily and noisily ▪ She *stamped* [=*stomped*] off in a huff. ▪ He *stamped* out of the room.

3 [+ *obj*] **a** : to use a special device (called a stamp) to put a design, word, etc., on something : to create a mark by pressing a special tool against a surface ▪ She *stamped* the bill "paid." ▪ He *stamped* the date on the letter. = He *stamped* the letter with the date. **b** [+ *obj*] : to form (something) with a device that presses down on a material and cuts out shapes ▪ newly *stamped* coins

4 [+ *obj*] : to cause (something) to stay in your mind or memory ▪ The event is *stamped* [=*imprinted*] in her mind.

5 [+ *obj*] : to attach a postage stamp to (something) ▪ *stamp* a letter ▪ a *stamped* envelope

stamp as [*phrasal verb*] ***stamp (someone) as (something)*** : to show that (someone) is (a particular type of person) ▪ The decision *stamped* him *as* a man of honor.

stamp on [*phrasal verb*] ***stamp on (something)*** **1** : to step heavily on (something) with your foot ▪ She accidentally *stamped on* my toe. **2** : to end (something) in a forceful way ▪ The city council *stamped on* any efforts to build a liquor store.

stamp out [*phrasal verb*] ***stamp (something) out*** *or* ***stamp out (something)*** **1** : to stop or destroy (something bad) ▪ *stamp out* smallpox/corruption **2** : to stop (something) from burning by stepping on it forcefully with your feet ▪ *stamp out* a fire ▪ She *stamped* the cigarette *out*. [=she put out the cigarette by stepping on it]

– **stamp·er** *noun, pl* **-ers** [*count*]

stamp collecting *noun* [*noncount*] : the hobby of collecting postage stamps

– **stamp collector** *noun, pl* **~ -tors** [*count*]

[1]**stam·pede** /stæmˈpiːd/ *noun, pl* **-pedes** [*count*]

1 : an occurrence in which a large group of frightened or excited animals or people run together in a wild and uncontrolled way to escape from something, get out of a place, etc. ▪ a buffalo *stampede* ▪ a *stampede* to the exits

2 : a situation in which a lot of people try to do the same thing at the same time ▪ a *stampede* to buy the stock ▪ a *stampede* of new applicants

[2]**stampede** *verb* **-pedes; -ped·ed; -ped·ing**

1 a [*no obj*] : to run away in a large group from something especially because of fear ▪ The cattle *stampeded*. ▪ People *stampeded* to the exits. **b** [+ *obj*] : to cause (animals) to run away in a large group ▪ The gunshot *stampeded* the cattle.

2 [+ *obj*] : to cause (a person or a group of people) to do something suddenly and without proper thought — often used as *(be) stampeded into* ▪ Don't let yourself *be stampeded into* doing something you don't really agree with.

stamping ground *noun, pl* **~ grounds** [*count*] *Brit* : STOMPING GROUND

stance /ˈstæns, *Brit* ˈstɑːns/ *noun, pl* **stanc·es** [*count*]

1 : a publicly stated opinion — usually singular ▪ He changed his *stance* after new evidence was discovered. ▪ She has maintained a neutral *stance* [=*position*] during the negotiations. ▪ She was criticized for her antiwar *stance*.

2 : a way of standing — usually singular ▪ She adopted a casual/relaxed *stance*. ▪ a batting *stance* [=the way someone stands to bat in baseball]

stanch (*chiefly US*) *or* **staunch** /ˈstɑːntʃ/ *verb* **stanch·es** *or* **staunch·es; stanched** *or* **staunched; stanch·ing** *or* **staunch·ing** [+ *obj*] : to stop something (especially blood) from flowing ▪ He used a towel to try to *stanch* the (flow of) blood. ▪ I applied pressure to *stanch* the wound. [=to stop the flow of blood from the wound]

stan·chion /ˈstæntʃən/ *noun, pl* **-chions** [*count*] : a strong, upright pole that is used to support something

[1]**stand** /ˈstænd/ *verb* **stands; stood** /ˈstʊd/; **stand·ing**

1 [*no obj*] **a** : to be in an upright position with all of your weight on your feet ▪ She was *standing* near the window. ▪ He was *standing* next to me. ▪ All of the seats on the bus were taken so we had to *stand*. ▪ Don't just *stand* there (doing nothing)—do something! ▪ He can *stand* using a cane. ▪ You're *standing* on my foot. [=you're standing with your foot on top of my foot] ▪ He was *standing* in a puddle of water. ▪ The deer ***stood still***, listening for danger. ▪ The soldiers ***stood (up) straight***. ▪ We had to ***stand in line*** for over an hour. ▪ People were just ***standing around*** [=standing without doing anything], waiting to get inside the theater. **b** : to move onto your feet from a sitting or low position ▪ Please *stand* [=(more formally) *rise*] for the national anthem. — often + *up* ▪ He *stood up* to greet her. ▪ She was crouching down to look at something, but she *stood up* when she saw me.

2 a [*no obj*] : to be in an upright position ▪ Two bowling pins were left *standing*. ▪ A shovel and rake *stood* in the corner. ▪ The house she grew up in is no longer *standing*. [=the house has been destroyed or knocked down; the house no longer exists] **b** [+ *obj*] : to put (something or someone) in an upright position ▪ She *stood* the ladder against the house. — often + *up* ▪ He *stood* the boy *up* on a chair. ▪ Could you *stand* the picture frame back *up*?

3 [*no obj*] **a** *always followed by an adverb or preposition* : to be in a particular place or position ▪ A clock *stood* on the mantelpiece. ▪ The mansion *stands* on a hill. ▪ A row of trees *stands* between the two houses. — often used figuratively ▪ A single putt ***stands between*** her and the title. [=if she makes the putt, she will win the title] ▪ Go ahead and leave. I won't ***stand in your way***. [=I won't try to stop you] ▪ We won't let anyone or anything ***stand in the way*** of our happiness. [=prevent us from being happy] **b** : to remain in a place or position without moving or being moved ▪ The plane *stood* on the runway ready for takeoff. ▪ The machine *stood* idle. ▪ rainwater *standing* in stagnant pools ▪ Add the water and let the mixture *stand* for three minutes.

4 *not used in progressive tenses* [*no obj*] : to be a specified height ▪ He *stands* six feet two (inches tall). ▪ The tower *stands* over 1,000 feet high.

5 [*no obj*] : to be in a particular state or situation ▪ Where do we *stand* financially? [=what is our financial condition?] ▪ She ***stands accused of*** murder. [=she has been accused of murder]

6 [*no obj*] : to have a particular belief or opinion about something ▪ Where do you *stand* on the death penalty? Do you think it should be used or not? ▪ We still don't know where he *stands* on this issue. ▪ They *stand* divided [=they disagree] on this issue. ▪ She *stands* for/against the new regulations. [=she supports/opposes the new regulations] ▪ We ask you to *stand* (with us) in support of this proposal. [=we ask you to support this proposal] ▪ ***From where I stand***, I think we have to do it.

7 *always followed by an adverb or preposition* [*no obj*] : to have a particular rank or position within a group ▪ The team still *stands* [=*ranks*] first in the division. ▪ She is currently *standing* in second place. ▪ (*chiefly Brit*) He ***stands high/low*** with the voters. [=the voters have a good/bad opinion of him]

8 [*no obj*] : to continue to be at a specified number or

S

amount — often + *at* ▪ Interest rates *stand at* 13 percent. ▪ The home run record *stands at* 73.

9 [*no obj*] **:** to not be changed **:** to remain valid or effective ▪ The decision still *stands*. ▪ The record she set seems likely to *stand* for many years.

10 [*no obj*] **:** to exist at the present time ▪ You must take or leave our offer as it *stands*. ▪ That is how the situation *stands* at present. ▪ ***As things stand***, we will not be able to meet your deadline.

11 [*no obj*] **:** to be in a position in which you are likely to gain or lose something — followed by *to + verb* ▪ We *stand to make* a sizable profit from the sale. ▪ They *stand to lose* their home if they can't find a way to pay their bills.

12 [+ *obj*] **a :** to be willing or able to accept (something or someone unpleasant) without complaint — usually used with *can, can't, cannot, could,* and *couldn't* ▪ *Can* you *stand* [=*tolerate, put up with*] waiting a few more minutes? = *Can* you *stand* to wait a few more minutes? ▪ How *can* you *stand* her friends? ▪ He *couldn't stand* [=*bear, endure*] the pain. ▪ I *can* only *stand* so much of your nonsense. ▪ His behavior was ***more than I could stand***. ▪ I ***couldn't stand the thought/idea*** of having to move again. **b** — used to say that someone strongly dislikes a person or thing ▪ I ***can't stand*** him. [=I hate him] ▪ She *can't stand* cooking. = She *can't stand* to cook. ▪ They *can't stand* being apart. ▪ I *can't stand* it when people behave like that!

13 [+ *obj*] **:** to not be harmed by (something) **:** WITHSTAND ▪ I need a frying pan that can *stand* being placed in the oven. ▪ These plants can *stand* [=*endure*] very cold temperatures. ▪ His plays have ***stood the test of time***. [=his plays are still read by many people today]

14 [+ *obj*] — used to say that someone or something should have or do something or would be helped by something; usually used after *could* ▪ You look like you *could stand* some sleep. [=you look very tired; you look like you need some sleep] ▪ He *could stand* losing a few pounds. = He *could stand* to lose a few pounds. ▪ That bush *could stand* to be trimmed. [=that bush needs to be trimmed]

15 [*no obj*] *Brit* **:** to be a candidate in an election for a particular office — often + *for* ▪ He is *standing* [=*(US) running*] *for* a seat in Parliament.

16 [+ *obj*] *Brit, informal* **:** to pay for (a meal or drink) ▪ I'll *stand* a meal for you. = I'll *stand* you a meal. ▪ He *stood* drinks for the table.

(as) sure as I'm standing here US, informal — used to say that you believe that something is certainly true, will happen, etc. ▪ They may claim that this was a surprise to them, but *as sure as I'm standing here*, they planned it all along.

I stand corrected see ²CORRECT

make your hair stand on end see HAIR

not have a leg to stand on see ¹LEG

stand a chance see ¹CHANCE

stand alone **1 :** to be in a position or situation in which you are not helped or supported by others ▪ She *stood alone* in her opposition to the proposal. **2** — used to say that someone or something is better than all others ▪ For great sound quality, this system *stands alone*.

stand aside [*phrasal verb*] **1 :** move to the left or right with one or a few small steps ▪ Please *stand aside* and let me pass. **2 :** to allow something to happen **:** to not try to stop someone from doing something ▪ I'm not going to *stand aside* [=*stand by*] and watch you ruin your life.

stand back [*phrasal verb*] **1 :** to take a few steps backwards ▪ The paramedics told the crowd to *stand back*. **2 :** to stop doing something or being actively involved in something for a time so that you can think about it and make decisions in a calm and reasonable way ▪ It's time to *stand back* [=*step back*] and take a long hard look at your problems.

stand behind [*phrasal verb*] ***stand behind (someone or something)*** **:** to support (someone or something) ▪ I'll *stand behind* you no matter what you decide to do. ▪ I'll *stand behind* your decision 100 percent.

stand by [*phrasal verb*] **1 :** to stand or be present without taking any action while something is happening ▪ A group of students *stood by* and watched the boys fight. ▪ How can you *stand by* and do nothing? **2 :** to be ready or available for use ▪ An ambulance was *standing by* in case anyone got seriously injured. ▪ Operators are *standing by* (to take your calls). — see also STANDBY **3** ***stand by (something)*** **a :** to support or defend (something) ▪ He said that he was *standing by* what he said earlier. ▪ I *stand by* my actions and have no regrets. **b :** to act in the way that is required by (something, such as belief or promise) ▪ She *stood by* her promise. **4** ***stand by (someone)*** **:** to remain loyal to (someone) **:** to continue to support (someone) ▪ They promised to *stand by* each other until the end. ▪ She *stood by* her husband throughout the trial.

stand down [*phrasal verb*] *Brit* **1 :** to leave the witness stand in a court of law ▪ The judge thanked the witness and allowed her to *stand down*. **2 :** to leave a job or official position ▪ He *stood down* [=*stepped down*] (from his office) as Lord Mayor. ▪ She *stood down* in favour of a more popular candidate.

stand firm **:** to refuse to change your decision, position, etc. ▪ The judge *stood firm* in her ruling.

stand for [*phrasal verb*] ***stand for (something)*** **1 :** to have (a specified meaning) ▪ "FYI" *stands for* "for your information." ▪ The sign @ *stands for* "at." ▪ The color white often *stands for* [=*represents*] innocence and purity. **2 :** to support (something) ▪ The political party has always *stood for* reform. **3 :** to allow (something) to continue to happen — usually used in negative statements ▪ I will not *stand for* [=*put up with*] any more of this nonsense. — see also ¹STAND 15 (above)

stand guard/watch **:** to stand in a position and guard or watch someone or something in order to look for possible danger, threats, etc. ▪ A soldier *stood guard* by the door.

stand in [*phrasal verb*] **:** to take the place of (someone who is away for a time) ▪ He can't be here today, so he asked me to *stand in*. [=*fill in*] — often + *for* ▪ He asked me to *stand in for* him while he was away. — see also STAND-IN

stand on ceremony see CEREMONY

stand on your head/hands **:** to be in a position in which your legs and feet are straight up in the air and your weight is supported by your head or hands ▪ She can *stand on her head/hands*. [=she can do a headstand/handstand]

stand on your own two feet see ¹FOOT

stand or fall — used to say that the future or success of someone or something depends on another person or thing ▪ We (will) *stand or fall* by their decision. [=their decision will control what happens to us] ▪ Our company will *stand or fall* on our ability to make better products than our competitors. [=our success or failure depends on our ability to make better products than our competitors]

stand out [*phrasal verb*] **1 :** to be easily seen or noticed ▪ His bright tie made him *stand out* (in the crowd). ▪ The trees' red leaves *stood out* against the gray sky. **2 :** to be better or more important than the other people or things in a group in a way that is easily seen or noticed ▪ As a student, she *stood out* above/from the rest. ▪ Only one contestant really *stands out* [=*sticks out*] in my mind. ▪ Two facts *stand out* from her testimony. ▪ His performance really *stood out*. **3 :** to stick out from a surface ▪ The hat made her ears *stand out*. — see also STANDOUT

stand out like a sore thumb see ¹SORE

stand pat see ³PAT

stand someone/something in good stead see STEAD

stand tall **:** to stand with your body very straight — often used figuratively in U.S. English ▪ We can *stand tall* and take pride in what we've accomplished. ▪ Despite the criticism, he has continued to *stand tall*.

stand to reason see ¹REASON

stand trial **:** to be on trial in a court of law ▪ He is *standing trial* for the murder of his wife.

stand up [*phrasal verb*] **1 :** to remain valid or acceptable when tested or examined ▪ We need evidence that will *stand up* in court. **2** ***stand (someone) up informal*** **:** to fail to meet or keep an appointment with (someone) ▪ You *stood* me *up* yesterday. ▪ I got *stood up* by my date. **3** ***stand up for (someone or something)*** **:** to defend (someone or something) against attack or criticism ▪ He *stood up for* his friend. ▪ You have to *stand up for* yourself. ▪ They were *standing up for* their rights. **4** ***stand up to (someone)*** **:** to refuse to accept bad treatment from (someone) ▪ She finally *stood up to* the girl who had been teasing her at school. **5** ***stand up to (something)*** **:** to remain in good condition despite (something) ▪ These boots have *stood up to* [=*withstood*] a lot of abuse. **6** ***stand up and be counted*** **:** to make your opinions or beliefs publicly known especially when such action may cause trouble ▪ It's time for everyone who cares about this issue to *stand up and be counted*. — see also ¹STAND 1b, 2b (above), STAND-UP

stand your ground see ¹GROUND

²stand *noun, pl* **stands**

1 [*count*] **:** a strongly held opinion about something — usually singular ▪ The senator ***took a firm/strong stand*** against

S

higher taxes. — often + *on* ▪ What is your *stand on* this issue?
2 [*count*] : a strong effort to defend yourself or oppose something ▪ The team insured their victory with an impressive goal-line *stand.* ▪ The army is preparing to ***make a stand against*** the enemy. ▪ students *making a stand against* the war
3 [*count*] : a partially enclosed structure where things are sold or displayed ▪ a hot-dog/ice-cream/vegetable *stand* ▪ He set up a *stand* [=*booth*] at the fair. ▪ We have display *stands* in many bookstores. ▪ concession *stands* ▪ a roadside *stand* — see also NEWSSTAND
4 [*count*] : a device or piece of furniture that holds an object in an upright position ▪ an umbrella *stand* ▪ a bicycle/microphone *stand* — see also NIGHTSTAND, WASHSTAND
5 [*count*] : a raised platform for people (such as performers or hunters) to stand on
6 ***the stands*** : the rows of seats in a stadium that people sit in when they are watching a sports event, concert, etc. ▪ The ball was hit into *the stands.* — see also GRANDSTAND
7 ***the stand*** : the place where a witness testifies in court : WITNESS STAND ▪ She lied while ***on the stand.*** ▪ The witness was asked to ***take the stand.***
8 [*count*] *chiefly US* : a series of performances, games, etc., that are at a particular place for a period of time ▪ The magician was booked for a three-night *stand.* ▪ (*baseball*) The team has a six-game *stand* at home. = The team has a 6-game ***home stand.*** — see also ONE-NIGHT STAND
9 [*count*] : a group of plants growing close together ▪ a *stand* of pines
— see also HANDSTAND, HEADSTAND, TAXI STAND

stand–alone /ˈstændəˈloʊn/ *adj* : able to operate without control from another system, company, etc. ▪ *stand-alone* computers ▪ *stand-alone* businesses

[1]**stan·dard** /ˈstændəd/ *noun, pl* **-dards**
1 a : a level of quality, achievement, etc., that is considered acceptable or desirable [*count*] high/low *standards* of quality ▪ His work is not up to our *standards.* [=is not as good as we require it to be] ▪ By modern/today's *standards,* the house is just too small. ▪ industry *standards* ▪ Their *standards* are slipping. [*noncount*] His work is not ***up to standard.*** = His work is ***below standard.*** [=his work is not good enough] — see also DOUBLE STANDARD, STANDARD OF LIVING **b** ***standards*** [*plural*] : ideas about morally correct and acceptable behavior ▪ She has high moral *standards.* [=*principles*]
2 [*count*] : something that is very good and that is used to make judgments about the quality of other things ▪ This book is the *standard* by which all others must be judged.
3 [*count*] : a fixed official unit of measurement ▪ a *standard* of weight — see also GOLD STANDARD
4 [*count*] : a flag that is used in official ceremonies
5 [*count*] : a song that has been sung by many different artists ▪ an old *standard*

[2]**standard** *adj*
1 : regularly and widely used, seen, or accepted : not unusual or special ▪ a *standard* approach/treatment ▪ the *standard* features/colors ▪ a *standard* medical procedure ▪ *standard* weight ▪ a window of *standard* width ▪ The movie was a pretty *standard* romantic comedy.
2 : generally accepted and used because of high quality or excellence ▪ *standard* reference works
3 : accepted and used by most of the educated speakers and writers of a language ▪ *standard* spelling/English ▪ The word is considered *standard.* — opposite NONSTANDARD; compare SUBSTANDARD

stan·dard–bear·er /ˈstændədˌberə/ *noun, pl* **-ers** [*count*] *formal*
1 : the leader of an organization, movement, or political party
2 : someone who carries a flag or banner

stan·dard–is·sue /ˈstændədˌɪˌʃuː/ *adj* : of the common or usual type ▪ a *standard-issue* [=*typical*] action movie ▪ a *standard-issue* blue suit

stan·dard·ize *also Brit* **stan·dard·ise** /ˈstændəˌdaɪz/ *verb* **-iz·es; -ized; -iz·ing** [+ *obj*] : to change (things) so that they are similar and consistent and agree with rules about what is proper and acceptable ▪ He *standardized* procedures for the industry. ▪ *standardized* tests
— **stan·dard·i·za·tion** *also Brit* **stan·dard·i·sa·tion** /ˌstændədəˈzeɪʃən, *Brit* ˌstændəˌdaɪˈzeɪʃən/ *noun* [*noncount*]

standard lamp *noun, pl* ~ **lamps** [*count*] *Brit* : FLOOR LAMP

standard of living *noun* [*singular*] : the amount of wealth, comfort, and possessions that a person or group has ▪ People in that area enjoy a high *standard of living.* [=they have a lot of money and are able to live very comfortably] ▪ raising/lowering/improving our *standard of living*

standard time *noun* [*noncount*] : the official time of a particular region or country

[1]**stand·by** /ˈstændˌbaɪ/ *noun, pl* **stand·bys** /ˈstændˌbaɪz/ [*count*] : a person or thing that is available especially in emergencies ▪ More police officers were sent as *standbys.* ▪ We bought an electric generator as a *standby.* — see also *stand by* at [1]STAND
on standby **1** : ready or available for immediate action or use ▪ The police officers were ***put on standby.*** **2** : ready to travel if a ticket becomes available ▪ We're ***on standby*** for the next flight to Washington, D.C.

[2]**standby** *adj, always used before a noun* : relating to or traveling by an airline service in which the passenger must wait for an available seat ▪ *standby* tickets/passengers — see also *stand by* at [1]STAND

stand·ee /stænˈdiː/ *noun, pl* **-ees** [*count*] *chiefly US* : a person who is standing when other people are sitting ▪ The audience of 3,000 included several hundred *standees.*

stand–in /ˈstændˌɪn/ *noun, pl* **-ins** [*count*] : a person or thing that takes the place of someone or something else for a period of time ▪ He was the boss's *stand-in* during her illness. — see also *stand in* at [1]STAND

[1]**stand·ing** /ˈstændɪŋ/ *adj, always used before a noun*
1 a : used in or for standing ▪ Start the exercise in a *standing* position. **b** : done while in a standing position ▪ a *standing* jump
2 : not flowing : STAGNANT ▪ *standing* water
3 : remaining at the same level or amount until canceled ▪ The *standing* offer for the computer system is $1,499.
4 : continuing to exist or be used for an unlimited period of time : PERMANENT ▪ *standing* armies/committees ▪ She has a *standing* invitation to use the university's research laboratory. ▪ a *standing* tradition ▪ It's a ***standing joke*** at the office. [=it's something that often happens or is said or done and that the people in the office think is funny] — see also FREE-STANDING, LONG-STANDING

[2]**standing** *noun, pl* **-ings**
1 [*count*] : the position or rank of someone in a group ▪ He's trying to improve his *standing* with the voters. [=trying to get the voters to rank him more highly] ▪ a lawyer of high *standing* ▪ (*chiefly US*) a member in/of good *standing* [=*status*]
2 ***standings*** [*plural*] *US, sports* : a list that shows the positions of the players or teams that are competing against each other ▪ They've won five games in a row and are starting to move up in the *standings.* ▪ They're in first place in the current *standings.*
3 [*noncount*] : length of existence : DURATION ▪ a marriage of many years' *standing*

standing order *noun, pl* ~ **-ders** [*count, noncount*] : an order or procedure that continues to be followed until it is changed or canceled ▪ She placed a *standing order* for fresh flowers every week. ▪ They were ***on standing orders*** never to leave the prisoner unattended.

standing ovation *noun, pl* ~ **-tions** [*count*] : an occurrence in which the people at a play, speech, sporting event, etc., stand up and applaud to show enthusiastic approval or appreciation ▪ The crowd gave her a *standing ovation.* — called also (*US, informal*) *standing O*

standing room *noun* [*noncount*] : space available for people to stand after all seats are filled ▪ There was ***standing room only*** at the concert. [=all the seats for the concert had been sold]

stand·off /ˈstændˌɑːf/ *noun, pl* **-offs** [*count*] : an argument, contest, etc., in which there is no winner ▪ The two governments are currently in a *standoff* over who has rights to the land. ▪ They played to a 3–3 *standoff.* [=*tie*]

stand·off·ish /ˌstændˈɑːfɪʃ/ *adj* [*more* ~; *most* ~] : not friendly toward other people ▪ She tends to be a bit *standoffish* with strangers.

stand·out /ˈstændˌaʊt/ *noun, pl* **-outs** [*count*] *US* : a person or thing that is better or more important than the others in a group ▪ She is a *standout* among the available candidates. ▪ All the cameras we tested were good, but there was no real *standout.* — often used before another noun ▪ a *standout* candidate/performance — see also *stand out* at [1]STAND

stand·point /ˈstændˌpɔɪnt/ *noun, pl* **-points** [*count*] : a way in which something is thought about or considered

S

: POINT OF VIEW • From an economic *standpoint*, the policy is sound.

stand·still /ˈstændˌstɪl/ *noun* [*singular*] : a state in which all activity or motion is stopped • Production is at a *standstill*. [=production has stopped completely] • The accident brought traffic to a *standstill*.

¹stand–up /ˈstændˌʌp/ *adj, always used before a noun*
1 a : done by a performer who is standing alone on a stage • *stand-up* comedy • a *stand-up* act/routine **b :** performing stand-up comedy • a *stand-up* comedian/comic
2 : done in or requiring a standing position • a *stand-up* lunch/bar
3 : designed to stand upright • a *stand-up* collar
4 *US, informal* **:** able to be trusted and respected : very good, loyal, etc. • His friends say he's a real *stand-up* (kind of) guy.
5 *Brit* **:** involving very angry or violent behavior • a *stand-up* fight/argument — see also *stand up* at ¹STAND

²stand–up *noun, pl* **-ups**
1 [*noncount*] **:** stand-up comedy • I've always wanted to try *stand-up*.
2 [*count*] **:** a performer who does stand-up comedy : a stand-up comedian • a talented *stand-up*

stank *past tense of* ¹STINK

stan·za /ˈstænzə/ *noun, pl* **-zas** [*count*] : a group of lines in a poem : VERSE

staph /ˈstæf/ *noun* [*noncount*] *medical* : a group of bacteria that cause many common illnesses (such as skin infections and food poisoning) • a resistant strain of *staph* • a *staph* infection

¹sta·ple /ˈsteɪpəl/ *noun, pl* **sta·ples** [*count*] : a piece of metal or wire in the shape of a U that is used for attaching things: such as **a :** a short, thin wire that goes through papers and is bent over at the ends to hold the papers together or that goes through a piece of paper, a photograph, etc., to attach it to a surface • Please fasten the pages (together) with paper clips rather than *staples*. • The notice was attached to the wall with *staples*. — see also STAPLER **b :** a piece of metal or thick wire that is pushed into a surface to hold or attach something (such as rope or wire) — see also STAPLE GUN
– compare ³STAPLE

²staple *verb* **staples; sta·pled; sta·pling** [+ *obj*] : to attach (something) with staples • I *stapled* the pages in the upper left corner. — often + *to* or *together* • I *stapled* the check *to* the form. • The notice had been *stapled to* the wall. • I *stapled* the pages *together*.

³staple *noun, pl* **staples** [*count*]
1 : an important food that is eaten very often • I need to buy some *staples*, like bread and milk. • Rice is the *staple* of their diet.
2 : the main product of a country, area, company, etc. • Technology has replaced steel as the region's *staple*.
3 : something that is used widely and often • Rock music was a *staple* when I was growing up. — often + *of* • His writings are a *staple of* [=a basic part of] economic theory.
– compare ¹STAPLE

⁴staple *adj, always used before a noun*
1 : used, needed, or enjoyed constantly by many people • such *staple* items as flour and sugar • That's a *staple* plot in mystery novels. — see also STAPLE DIET
2 : produced regularly or in large quantities • *staple* crops like wheat, rice, or sugarcane

staple diet *noun* [*singular*] : the food or foods that a person or animal eats most often • Environmental changes are depriving the birds of the insects that form their *staple diet*. — often used figuratively • I grew up on a *staple diet* of cartoons and comic books.

staple gun *noun, pl* **~ guns** [*count*] : a tool used for putting large staples into walls, wood, etc.

sta·pler /ˈsteɪplə/ *noun, pl* **-plers** [*count*] : a device that you use to put staples into something (such as paper) — see picture at OFFICE

¹star /ˈstaə/ *noun, pl* **stars** [*count*]
1 : any one of the objects in space that are made of burning gas and that look like points of light in the night sky • They gazed up at the *stars*. • There are billions of *stars* in the universe. • bright *star* clusters • a distant *star* system • The ***stars are out*** [=are not hidden by clouds] tonight. • I'm glad we didn't use the tent. It's so much nicer to sleep outside ***under the stars***. — see also EVENING STAR, MORNING STAR, NORTH STAR, POLE STAR, SHOOTING STAR
2 : a star or planet especially in a certain position that is believed in astrology to influence people's lives • I was born under a lucky *star*. [=I was born lucky] — usually plural • (*Brit*) Did you read your *stars* [=*horoscope*] today? • I guess romance just isn't ***in the stars*** for me right now. [=romance isn't going to happen for me right now] • You can ***thank your lucky stars*** [=you are lucky] that no one was hurt. — see also STAR-CROSSED
3 a : something (such as a symbol or medal) with five or more points that represents or suggests a star • The teacher gives out gold *stars* [=gold stickers in the shape of stars] for good behavior. • I put *stars* [=*asterisks*] next to the most important items in the list. — see also BRONZE STAR, SILVER STAR, STARS AND STRIPES **b :** a symbol that is shaped like a star and that is used as part of a rating system to show how good something is • The restaurant was awarded four *stars* for excellence. • Critics give the movie three *stars*. — see also FIVE-STAR, FOUR-STAR

star

4 a : the most important and well-known performer in a movie, play, etc. • She's the ***star of the show***. **b :** an extremely famous and successful performer or athlete • His performance in that film made him a *star*. • She always dreamed of being a movie *star*. • baseball/football/track *stars* • a rock/pop *star* • He's made a name for himself as the hair stylist ***to the stars***. [=for famous people] — often used before another noun • *star* athletes • the ***star system*** [=the practice of using famous actors in movies, etc., in order to attract a bigger audience] • The producers are looking for someone with ***star quality***. [=the talent, looks, etc., needed to become a star] **c :** a person who is very successful, important, etc. • There were many talented students in the class, but she was clearly the *star*. [=the most talented one] • He is ***a rising star*** [=a person who is becoming more popular and successful] in the world of politics. — often used before another noun • a *star* student • our *star* trumpeter • She was the *star* witness at the trial. • The pandas are the zoo's ***star attraction***. [=they are the most popular attraction at the zoo] — see also MEGASTAR, SUPERSTAR
5 *Brit, informal* **:** someone who is good or helpful • "Thank you. You're a *star*!"

(have) stars in your eyes ✧ If you *have stars in your eyes* you are very hopeful and excited about something and think that it will be much better or more enjoyable than it actually is. • When she left home she *had stars in her eyes*.

promise (someone) the stars see ²PROMISE

reach for the stars **:** to try to do something that is very difficult and impressive • She always encouraged her children to *reach for the stars*.

see stars **:** to see flashes of light usually because you have been hit on the head • I bumped into the wall so hard that I *saw stars*.

– **star·less** /ˈstaələs/ *adj* • a cloudy, *starless* sky – **star·like** /ˈstaəˌlaɪk/ *adj* • a *starlike* pattern • white *starlike* flowers

²star *verb* **stars; starred; star·ring**
1 a [*no obj*] **:** to play the most important role in a movie, play, etc. — usually + *in* • an actor who has *starred in* many films • The couple will *star* together *in* a new play. • She had the ***starring role*** [=she was the star] *in* her last three films. **b** [+ *obj*] **:** to have (someone) as the most important performer • The new television series *stars* a famous movie actress. • a concert *starring* some of the biggest names in the business
2 [*no obj*] **:** to perform extremely well • He *starred* in both baseball and football when he was in college. • She *starred* for/with the basketball team last year.
3 [+ *obj*] **:** to mark (something) with a star or other symbol • This restaurant is *starred* in the guidebook.
– see also ILL-STARRED

star anise *noun* [*noncount*] : a small brown star-shaped fruit that is dried and used as a spice especially in Chinese cooking

star·board /ˈstaəbəd/ *noun* [*noncount*] : the side of a ship or aircraft that is on the right when you are looking toward the front • The ship turned ***to starboard***. — compare PORT
– **starboard** *adj* • the *starboard* side/engine

star·burst /ˈstaəˌbəst/ *noun, pl* **-bursts** [*count*] : something (such as a pattern) that looks like rays of light spreading out from a center • a *starburst* of color • a *starburst* design

¹starch /ˈstaətʃ/ *noun, pl* **starch·es**
1 : a substance that is found in certain foods (such as bread, rice, and potatoes) [*noncount*] the *starch* in pasta • They tried to limit *starch* [=starchy foods] in their diet. [*count*]

S

The body breaks down *starches* [=*carbohydrates*] into sugars. — see also CORNSTARCH

2 [*noncount*] **:** a powder or liquid that contains starch and is used to make clothing stiff

take the starch out of *US, informal + old-fashioned* **:** to make (someone) weak or unsure **:** to cause (someone) to lose energy or confidence ▪ When he lost the second game, it seemed to *take the starch out of* him.

²starch *verb* **starches; starched; starch·ing** [+ *obj*] **:** to make (clothing) stiff by using starch ▪ He *starches* the collars of his shirts. ▪ a *starched* collar ▪ a *starched* white uniform

starchy /ˈstɑɚʧi/ *adj* **starch·i·er; -est**

1 : containing, consisting of, or resembling starch ▪ a *starchy* diet ▪ *starchy* foods

2 : very formal and serious in behavior ▪ a *starchy* traditionalist

— starch·i·ness /ˈstɑɚʧinəs/ *noun* [*noncount*]

star–crossed /ˈstɑɚˌkrɑːst/ *adj* **:** not lucky **:** having bad luck ▪ *star-crossed* lovers

star·dom /ˈstɑɚdəm/ *noun* [*noncount*] **:** the state of being a very famous performer ▪ an actress who has achieved movie *stardom* ▪ When he went to Hollywood he had dreams of *stardom*. [=dreams of becoming a star] ▪ the path to *stardom*

¹stare /ˈsteɚ/ *verb* **stares; stared; star·ing** [*no obj*] **:** to look at someone or something for a long time often with your eyes wide open ▪ She was *staring* straight ahead. = Her eyes were *staring* straight ahead. ▪ She *stared* out the window. ▪ His mother told him not to *stare*. — often + *at* ▪ We just sat and *stared at* each other. ▪ They *stared* in disbelief *at* the accident scene. ▪ I spend a lot of my time *staring at* a computer screen. — often used figuratively ▪ The solution was ***staring right at me*** but I didn't see it. [=the solution was obvious but I failed to see it] ***synonyms*** see ¹GAZE

stare daggers (at someone) see DAGGER

stare down (*US*) *or Brit* ***stare out*** [*phrasal verb*] ***stare (someone) down/out*** *or* ***stare down/out (someone)*** **:** to look directly into someone's eyes without fear until he or she becomes uncomfortable and looks away ▪ The batter tried to *stare down* the pitcher. — often used figuratively ▪ They had *stared down* danger more than once.

stare (off) into space see ¹SPACE

stare (someone) in the face *also chiefly US* ***stare (someone) in the eye(s)*** **:** to look directly into the eyes of (someone) ▪ She *stared me in the face* and told me to leave. — usually used figuratively ▪ The solution was *staring me in the face*. [=the solution was obvious but I failed to see it] ▪ Failure was *staring him in the face*. [=he was very close to failing; he was almost certain to fail] ▪ They *stared death in the face/eye* [=they came very close to death; they did something that was very dangerous and that could have caused their death] and didn't flinch.

²stare *noun, pl* **stares** [*count*] **:** the act of looking directly at someone or something for a long time **:** the act of staring ▪ They looked at me with accusing *stares*. ▪ I asked him about it, but my question only drew/got a ***blank stare***. [=he looked at me in a way that showed he did not understand or know the answer to my question]

fix (someone) with a stare see ¹FIX

star·fish /ˈstɑɚˌfɪʃ/ *noun, pl* **-fish** *also* **-fish·es** [*count*] **:** a sea animal that has five arms and that looks like a star

starfish

star·gaz·er /ˈstɑɚˌgeɪzɚ/ *noun, pl* **-ers** [*count*] **:** a person who looks at the stars **:** a person who studies astronomy or astrology

star·gaz·ing /ˈstɑɚˌgeɪzɪŋ/ *noun* [*noncount*] **:** the act or practice of looking at or studying the stars ▪ We left the city after dark to do some *stargazing*.

¹stark /ˈstɑɚk/ *adj* **stark·er; -est**

1 : having a very plain and often cold or empty appearance ▪ a *stark* white room ▪ a *stark* landscape ▪ a *stark* winter day ▪ The room was decorated with *stark* simplicity.

2 : unpleasant and difficult to accept or experience ▪ the *stark* reality of death ▪ She gave the facts of the case in *stark* [=*harsh*] and sobering detail. ▪ This tragedy serves as a *stark* reminder of the dangers of drunk driving.

3 : very obvious **:** very plain and easily seen ▪ There is a *stark* difference between them. ▪ His criticism of the movie stands in *stark* contrast to the praise it has received from others.

— stark·ly *adv* [*more* ~; *most* ~] ▪ a *starkly* modern building

— stark·ness *noun* [*noncount*] ▪ the *starkness* of black and white

²stark *adv* **:** completely or fully ▪ He was standing there ***stark naked***. [=he was wearing no clothes at all] ▪ That noise is going to drive me ***stark raving mad***. = (*Brit*) That noise is going to drive me ***stark staring mad***. [=completely insane]

stark·ers /ˈstɑɚkɚz/ *adj, chiefly Brit, informal* **:** completely naked ▪ He was standing there *starkers*.

star·let /ˈstɑɚlət/ *noun, pl* **-lets** [*count*] **:** a young movie actress ▪ She was a *starlet* in the 1940s.

star·light /ˈstɑɚˌlaɪt/ *noun* [*noncount*] **:** the light produced by stars ▪ We had to find our way by *starlight*.

star·ling /ˈstɑɚlɪŋ/ *noun, pl* **-lings** [*count*] **:** a dark brown or black bird that is common in Europe and the U.S. — see color picture on page C9

star·lit /ˈstɑɚˌlɪt/ *adj* **:** lighted by the stars ▪ We slept outdoors under a *starlit* sky.

Star of Da·vid /-ˈdeɪvəd/ *noun, pl* **Stars of David** [*count*] **:** a six-pointed star that is used as a symbol of Judaism and of Israel — usually singular

star·ry /ˈstɑri/ *adj* **star·ri·er; -est** [*also more* ~; *most* ~]

1 : full of stars ▪ the *starry* heavens ▪ a *starry* sky

2 : having a shape like a star ▪ *starry* flowers

3 : including many famous actors, athletes, etc. ▪ a *starry* [=*star-studded*] cast

4 : shining brightly ▪ She gazed at him with *starry* eyes.

star·ry–eyed /ˈstɑriˌaɪd/ *adj* [*more* ~; *most* ~] **:** having hopes and desires that are not realistic or practical ▪ *starry-eyed* lovers ▪ She was too *starry-eyed* about her future.

Stars and Stripes *noun*

the Stars and Stripes **:** the flag of the United States

star sign *noun, pl* ~ **signs** [*count*] **:** one of the 12 symbols of the zodiac ▪ What is your *star sign*? — called also *sign*

star·struck /ˈstɑɚˌstrʌk/ *adj* **:** feeling or showing great interest in and admiration for famous people ▪ *starstruck* fans ▪ She stared at him in *starstruck* awe. ▪ I know she's famous, but try not to act *starstruck* when you meet her.

star–stud·ded /ˈstɑɚˌstʌdəd/ *adj* **:** having many famous actors, athletes, etc. ▪ The play featured a *star-studded* cast.

¹start /ˈstɑɚt/ *verb* **starts; start·ed; start·ing**

1 a : to do the first part of something **:** to begin doing something [+ *obj*] They *started* clearing land for the new housing development. ▪ He *started* the speech (out) with a joke. ▪ He *started* studying music at the age of five. ▪ She saw her divorce as an opportunity to *start* a new life. = She saw her divorce as an opportunity to *start* life anew/afresh/over. [*no obj*] As soon as you're ready to play, we'll *start*. ▪ Let's *start* with some warm-up exercises. ▪ He deleted what he wrote and *started* fresh/again/over. ▪ Nothing like this had ever been done before, so we had to ***start from scratch***. [=we had to begin from a point at which nothing had been done yet] ▪ Olympic athletes ***start young*** and train hard. ▪ The tire tracks at the scene of the crime were a ***starting point*** for investigators. [=investigators used the tire tracks to start their investigation] **b** [+ *obj*] **:** to begin to work on, produce, or give attention to (something) ▪ I *started* the quilt last month. ▪ Have you *started* your book report? ▪ Did you *start* (reading) the book yet? **c** [+ *obj*] **:** to cause (something) to begin ▪ We *started* the meeting at 6:30. **:** to cause (something) to begin in a specified way ▪ She started the meeting with a brief review of the previous meeting. ▪ He *starts* every day with a cup of coffee. **d** [+ *obj*] **:** to begin to have a feeling, thought, etc. — usually followed by *to + verb* ▪ She *started to feel* dizzy soon after the accident. ▪ I'm *starting to think* the oversight was intentional. — sometimes + *-ing verb* ▪ She *started feeling* dizzy soon after the accident. ▪ He *started having* chest pains. **e :** to begin working at a new job or going to school [+ *obj*] I *start* my new job next Monday. ▪ When does she *start* school? [*no obj*] I just got a new job. I *start* next week.

2 a : to begin to happen, to exist, to be done, etc. [*no obj*] The fire *started* in the cellar. ▪ The rain will *start* soon and should end sometime this evening. ▪ The game *started* late. ▪ *Starting* next week, all employees will be required to wear ID tags. ▪ The movie just *started*. ▪ What is the movie's *starting* time? ▪ When does school *start*? ▪ The game was just *starting* when it began to rain. [+ *obj*] — often followed by *to + verb* ▪ It *started to rain*. ▪ The leaves are *starting to change* colors. — often + *-ing verb* ▪ It *started raining*. **b** [+ *obj*] **:** to cause (something) to exist or happen ▪ He *started* a scholarship

fund. ▪ The tradition was *started* many years ago. ▪ "Stop fighting, you two!" "He *started* it." [=he did something to cause the fight] ▪ She's always *starting* arguments. ▪ They want to **start a family** [=begin to have children] soon.
3 a [*no obj*] **: to begin to function or operate** ▪ The car/engine won't *start*. **b** [+ *obj*] **: to cause (something) to begin to function or operate** ▪ She *started* the car and drove away.
4 [+ *obj*] **: to begin the use of (something)** ▪ You'll have to *start* a new roll of tape. This one's empty.
5 *always followed by an adverb or preposition* [*no obj*] **a : to have a particular beginning : to begin at a specified place or in a specified way** ▪ The English alphabet *starts* with A and ends with Z. ▪ The first word in a sentence should *start* with a capital letter. ▪ The parade *starts* at the intersection of First and Main. ▪ The path/trail *starts* here and ends at the lake. **b : to have a specified quality, identity, job, etc., at the beginning** — often + *as* ▪ What *started* (off) *as* a simple idea has become an expensive and complicated project. ▪ She *started* (out) *as* a sales assistant but is now the marketing director.
6 *always followed by an adverb or preposition* [*no obj*] **: to begin to move toward a particular place or in a particular direction** ▪ We'll *start* for home soon. ▪ We should *start* back to the camp before it gets dark. ▪ He *started* toward the door. ▪ The dog *started* after the squirrel.
7 [*no obj*] — used to indicate the beginning of a range, series, etc.; often + *at* ▪ The rates *start at* $10 per hour. ▪ At his company, salaries *start at* around $30,000. [=$30,000 is the lowest salary] ▪ Interest rates for CDs were *starting at* 3.9 percent. ▪ What is the ***starting salary*** for the job? [=what is the salary people are paid when they start the job?] ▪ The ***starting price*** [=the basic price when nothing extra has been added] for the car is $18,000.
8 a : to participate in a game or contest at its beginning [*no obj*] Despite his injury, he'll *start* in center field today. ▪ The manager removed the ***starting pitcher*** [=the pitcher who was playing at the beginning of the game] in the third inning. ▪ He's in the ***starting lineup***. [=a list of the players who will be playing when the game begins] — often + *for* ▪ Who's *starting for* the home team? [+ *obj*] He'll *start* today's game in center field. ▪ a pitcher who has *started* five games so far this year ▪ She *started* the race but wasn't able to finish. **b** [+ *obj*] **: to put (someone or something) into a game or contest at its beginning** ▪ The coach is *starting* him at quarterback for the next game. ▪ He plans to *start* [=*enter*] the horse in only a few races this year.
9 [+ *obj*] **a : to cause (someone) to begin doing something** ▪ Her questions *started* me thinking. **: to cause (someone) to begin a job or activity in a particular way, at a particular level, etc.** ▪ The company *started* him at the same salary he had been getting at his previous job. **b : to cause (someone) to begin talking about a particular subject** ▪ "What do you think of the new boss?" "***Don't get me started***. I can't stand him." — often + *on* ▪ ***Don't get him started on*** the war: he'll never stop!
10 [*no obj*] **: to move suddenly and quickly because you are surprised or frightened** ▪ The loud noise made him *start*. [=*jump*] ▪ The horse *started* when the shot rang out.
11 [*no obj*] *informal* **: to begin complaining, arguing, etc.** ▪ He ***started with me***, so I hit him. ▪ ***Don't (you) start (with me)***. I made a mistake—that's the end of it.
get started **: to begin doing or working on something** ▪ You (had) better *get started* if you want to finish on time. ▪ newlyweds who are just *getting started* [=who are just starting their lives together]
start in [*phrasal verb*] *chiefly US, informal* **1 : to start doing a particular activity or action** ▪ He took a break from painting to eat lunch, then *started in* again. — often + *on* ▪ She *started in on* another book. **2 *start in on (someone)* : to criticize (someone) about something** ▪ My dad *started in on* me about not having a job.
start off [*phrasal verb*] **1 *start off or start (something) off or start off (something)* : to start or cause (something) to start in a specified way** ▪ He *started off* by introducing himself. ▪ She *started off* (her run) at a slow jog. ▪ The performance *started off* badly. — often + *with* ▪ I *started off* my speech *with* a joke. ▪ We *started off* the meal *with* shrimp cocktails. ▪ The team *started* the season *off with* a 10-game winning streak. **2 : to have a specified quality, identity, job, etc., at the start** ▪ She *started off* as a sales assistant but is now the marketing director. **3 : to begin an important period in your life or career** ▪ The house is perfect for a couple just *starting off*. **4 : to begin to move toward a particular place or in a particular direction** ▪ She ate breakfast before *starting off* for work. **5 *start (someone) off or start off (someone)* : to cause (someone) to begin doing a particular activity or action** ▪ He *started* his daughter *off* on the piano. ▪ The game-show host *started* her *off* with some easy questions.
start on [*phrasal verb*] **1 *start on (something)* : to begin doing (something)** ▪ Did you *start on* your homework yet? **2 *start (someone) on (something)* : to cause (someone) to start doing or using (something)** ▪ The doctor *started* him *on* [=made him start taking] antibiotics. ▪ When should we *start* the baby *on* solid food? [=start feeding the baby solid food] **3 *start on at (someone)*** *chiefly Brit, informal* **: to criticize (someone) about something** ▪ Don't *start on at* me again about spending money!
start out [*phrasal verb*] **1 : to begin in a specified way** ▪ He *started out* by introducing himself. ▪ She *started out* at a slow jog. ▪ The day *started out* hot and humid. ▪ The story *started out* good, but I didn't like the ending. ▪ She *started out* wanting to be a doctor but became a midwife instead. — often + *with* ▪ I *started out with* $100 but I have only $10 left. ▪ Let's *start out with* some warm-up exercises. **2 : to have a specified quality, identity, job, etc., at the start** ▪ What *started out* as a simple idea has become an expensive and complicated project. ▪ He *started out* in teaching before becoming a lawyer. **3 : to begin an important period in your life or career** ▪ The couple is just *starting out*. ▪ She *started out* on a career in teaching. **4 : to begin to travel** ▪ They *started out* in the early morning. **5 : to have a particular place as a beginning point** ▪ The parade *starts out* at the intersection of First and Main.
start over [*phrasal verb*] *chiefly US* **1 *start over or start (something) over* : to begin doing something again** ▪ I'm sorry, but you'll have to *start over*. = I'm sorry, but you'll have to ***start (all) over again***. ▪ She saw her divorce as an opportunity to *start* (her life) *over*. **2 : to begin to happen again** ▪ In the spring, the eggs hatch, and the cycle *starts over*. = The cycle ***starts (all) over again***.
start something *also* ***start anything*** *informal* **: to do something that causes trouble** ▪ She is always trying to *start something*. ▪ Don't *start anything*.
start the ball rolling see [1]BALL
start up [*phrasal verb*] **1 : to begin to happen or exist** ▪ New businesses are *starting up* all over the state. ▪ The rain *started up* again. **2 *start up or start (something) up or start up (something)* : to begin to function or to make (something) begin to function** ▪ The car/engine won't *start up*. ▪ He *started* the lawn mower *up*.
to start with **1** — used to introduce a statement that is the first in a series of statements ▪ "I don't think we should buy the car." "Why not?" "*To start with*, I'm not sure we can afford it." **2 : at the beginning : before the current time or situation** ▪ She has lost a lot of weight, and she wasn't very heavy *to start with*. ▪ He didn't like his job *to start with* [=*at first, initially*], but he got used to it eventually.

[2]start *noun, pl* starts

1 [*count*] **: the time at which something begins** — usually singular ▪ At the season's *start*, the team didn't play well. ▪ It was clear ***from the (very) start*** that she would eventually succeed. ▪ The game was close ***from start to finish***. — often + *of* ▪ The *start of* the race was delayed.
2 [*count*] **: the first part of an activity, development, event, etc.** — usually singular ▪ The restaurant is off to a promising/shaky *start*. ▪ His parents gave him a good *start* in life. ▪ Their marriage ***got off to a good/bad start***. [=was good/bad at the beginning] — often + *of* ▪ We missed the *start of* the game. ▪ Their discovery could be the *start of* something big. — see also FLYING START, RUNNING START, *a slow start* at [1]SLOW
3 [*count*] **: the first opportunity to begin a career** — usually singular ▪ the company where he got his *start* [=where he started his career] — often + *in* ▪ She got her *start in* an off-Broadway play. ▪ She gave him his *start in* the business.
4 [*count*] **: the act of starting something** ▪ ***Housing starts*** [=the number of new houses that people started to build] declined in September. — usually singular ▪ Despite his late *start*, he managed to take the lead in the race. ▪ She got an early *start* working in the garden the next morning. ▪ We didn't get as much done as we'd hoped, but it's a *start*. ▪ Her divorce gave her an opportunity to ***make a fresh/new start***. [=to start a new life] ▪ He ***made a start on*** dinner. [=he started dinner] — see also FALSE START
5 [*singular*] **: a brief, sudden action or movement** ▪ She ***gave a start*** [=*started, jumped*] when he tapped her on the shoulder. ▪ He woke ***with a start***.

S

6 ***the start*** : the place where a race begins ▪ The runners lined up at *the start*.
7 [*count*] *sports* **a** : a game in which someone (such as a baseball pitcher) is playing at the beginning ▪ He's undefeated in six *starts* this year. [=he has started six games and has won them all] ▪ He pitched poorly in his last *start*. **b** : a race in which a person, horse, etc., participates as a competitor ▪ The horse has had 10 *starts* this season.
8 [*count*] : HEAD START
by/in fits and starts see [4]FIT
for a start — used to introduce a statement that is the first in a series of statements ▪ "What was the restaurant like?" "Well, *for a start* [=*for starters*], the food was fantastic."

[1]**start·er** /ˈstɑɚtɚ/ *noun, pl* **-ers** [*count*]
1 : a player, horse, etc., that is in a game or race at its beginning ▪ The team is playing only five regular *starters*.
2 : someone who gives the signal for a race to start
3 : a device that is used for starting an engine ▪ The car's *starter* needs to be replaced.
4 : someone or something that starts an activity, process, etc. ▪ He was a late *starter* in school. [=he started school later than most children] ▪ The question was a good conversation *starter*. ▪ He bought a ***starter kit*** for building a model airplane. — see also SELF-STARTER
5 *chiefly Brit* : APPETIZER
for starters — used to introduce a statement that is the first in a series of statements ▪ "Why don't you like him?" "Well, *for starters* [=*first of all*], he was rude to my parents."

[2]**starter** *adj, always used before a noun* — used to describe something small or basic that you get when you are doing something for the first time ▪ She bought a *starter* piano for her daughter. ▪ This small house would make a great ***starter home/house*** [=a first home] for a young couple.

starting block *noun, pl* ~ **blocks** [*count*] : a device that has two blocks for runners to put their feet on and push against at the start of a race — sometimes used figuratively ▪ He came charging out of the *starting blocks* to take an early lead in the campaign.

starting gate *noun, pl* ~ **gates** [*count*] : a gate or set of gates that opens at the start of a horse or dog race to let the animals begin racing

starting gun *noun, pl* ~ **guns** [*count*] : a special gun used to signal the beginning of a race ▪ The official fired the *starting gun* and the runners were off.; *also* : the signal made by a starting gun ▪ As soon as she heard the *starting gun*, she took off running.

starting line *noun, pl* ~ **lines** [*count*] : a line that marks the beginning of a race

star·tle /ˈstɑɚtl̩/ *verb* **star·tles; star·tled; star·tling**
1 [+ *obj*] : to surprise or frighten (someone) suddenly and usually not seriously ▪ The noise *startled* me. ▪ I'm sorry that I *startled* you. — often used as *(be) startled* ▪ I *was startled* by the noise. ▪ He *was startled* to discover he knew the answer. ▪ She *was startled* into wakefulness by a loud noise.
2 [*no obj*] : to move or jump suddenly because something surprises you or frightens you ▪ The cat *startles* easily.

star·tling /ˈstɑɚtlɪŋ/ *adj* [*more* ~; *most* ~] : very surprising, shocking, or frightening ▪ *Startling* new evidence/facts came to light during the trial. ▪ He made a *startling* discovery/revelation. ▪ It is a city of *startling* contrasts.
— **star·tling·ly** *adv* ▪ *startlingly* loud noises ▪ The prediction was *startlingly* accurate.

S

start–up /ˈstɑɚtˌʌp/ *noun, pl* **-ups** [*count*] : a new business ▪ They were looking for money to fund/launch a *start-up*. — often used before another noun ▪ small *start-up* businesses/companies ▪ *start-up* funds/money

star turn *noun, pl* ~ **turns** [*count*]
1 : a performance or role in a movie, play, etc., that is done by a star or that makes someone become a star ▪ She was nominated for an Oscar for her *star turn* as a single mother raising three children alone. ▪ do a *star turn*
2 *Brit* : the most important or successful person or thing in a group (such as a sports team) : STAR ▪ She was the *star turn* in yesterday's game.

star·va·tion /stɑɚˈveɪʃən/ *noun* [*noncount*] : suffering or death caused by having nothing to eat or not enough to eat : the condition of someone who is starving ▪ The famine brought mass *starvation*. ▪ Millions of people face *starvation* every day. ▪ They died from/of *starvation*.

starvation diet *noun, pl* ~ **diets** [*count*] : a diet that does not provide a person with enough food to be healthy

starvation wages *noun* [*plural*] : money paid to workers that is not enough to pay for the things (such as food and shelter) that are needed to live

starve /ˈstɑɚv/ *verb* **starves; starved; starv·ing**
1 [*no obj*] : to suffer or die from lack of food : to suffer extreme hunger ▪ Without food they would *starve*. ▪ They left him to *starve* out in the desert. ▪ Those people are *starving*. ▪ providing food for *starving* children ▪ The famine caused many to ***starve to death***. [=to die from lack of food]
2 [+ *obj*] : to cause (a person or animal) to suffer or die because of lack of food ▪ They tried to *starve* their enemies into submission. ▪ It was clear that the dog had been *starved*. ▪ You don't have to *starve* yourself to lose weight.
3 a [*no obj*] *chiefly US* : to want or need something very much — usually used as *(be) starving for* ▪ Those children *are starving for* attention. [=they badly need to be given more attention] ▪ After being alone for so long, I *was starving for* conversation. ▪ a government program that *is starving for* funds **b** [+ *obj*] : to not give (someone or something) enough of something that is wanted or needed ▪ Those children have been ***starved of*** attention. [=they have not been given enough attention] ▪ (*chiefly US*) Those children are ***starved for*** attention. [=they badly need to be given more attention] — sometimes used in combination ▪ a cash-*starved* company
be starving *or* ***be starved*** *chiefly US, informal* : to be very hungry ▪ I skipped lunch, so by dinnertime I *was starving*. ▪ When are we eating? *I'm starved*!

[1]**stash** /ˈstæʃ/ *verb* **stash·es; stashed; stash·ing** [+ *obj*] *informal* : to put (something) in a secret or hidden place ▪ The police found where he had *stashed* the drugs. ▪ The gifts were *stashed* in the closet. ▪ He *stashed* the equipment under the bed. ▪ We wondered what they had *stashed* in their backpacks. — often + *away* ▪ She kept her money *stashed* safely *away*. ▪ The papers were *stashed away* in a box.

[2]**stash** *noun, pl* **stashes** [*count*] *informal* : an amount of something that is stored or hidden ▪ a drug *stash* — often + *of* ▪ a *stash of* guns ▪ She kept a *stash of* money for emergencies. ▪ We found her *stash of* candy.

sta·sis /ˈsteɪsəs/ *noun* [*noncount*] *formal* : a state or condition in which things do not change, move, or progress ▪ The country is in economic *stasis*. ▪ His art was characterized by bursts of creativity followed by long periods of *stasis*.

[1]**stat** /ˈstæt/ *noun, pl* **stats** [*count*] *US, informal* : STATISTIC ▪ an interesting *stat* ▪ baseball *stats* ▪ a ***stat sheet*** [=a list of statistics]

[2]**stat** *adv* : without delay : IMMEDIATELY — used chiefly in medicine ▪ Get this patient to the operating room, *stat*! ✧ *Stat* comes from the Latin word *statim*, which means "immediately."

[1]**state** /ˈsteɪt/ *noun, pl* **states**
1 [*count*] **a** : a way of living or existing ▪ Happiness is the *state* or condition of being happy. ▪ We must keep our armed forces in a constant *state* of readiness. ▪ She meditates to achieve a higher ***state of being***. **b** : the overall physical condition of something : the ability of something to be used, enjoyed, etc. ▪ The museum restored the painting to its original *state*. [=*condition*] ▪ The building is in such a sorry *state* that it's hardly worth fixing. ▪ The car is in a ***good/bad state of repair***. [=the car is in good/bad condition] **c** : the things that affect the way you think or feel : your physical or mental condition ▪ her mental/emotional *state* ▪ By the time I arrived, he was in quite a *state*. [=he was very upset, worried, angry, etc.] — often + *of* ▪ They were in a *state of* shock/confusion. [=they were shocked/confused] ▪ I'm worried about the *state of* her health. ▪ The drug creates an altered *state of* consciousness. ▪ an unhappy ***state of mind*** ▪ She was ***in no (fit) state*** [=*in no condition*] to drive. [=she was too sick, drunk, etc., to drive] **d** : the things that affect the way something is or happens : the characteristics of a situation ▪ What is the company's financial *state*? [=*condition*] — often + *of* ▪ the current/present *state of* the economy ▪ Her life is in a *state of* complete chaos. ▪ The empire fell into a ***state of decline***. ▪ The country is in a ***state of war***. [=the country is at war] ▪ Tonight the President will give the ***State of the Union address***. [=an annual speech given to the U.S. Congress by the President to report on the state of the country] — see also STATE-OF-THE-ART, *state of emergency* at EMERGENCY
2 [*count*] : the fact of being a liquid, solid, or gas ▪ water in a gaseous *state* ▪ the solid and liquid *states*
3 [*count*] **a** : a politically organized group of people usually occupying a definite territory : NATION ▪ African/Arabic *states* ▪ the member *states* of the United Nations Security Council — see also CITY-STATE, NATION-STATE **b** : a par-

ticular kind of government or politically organized society — see also POLICE STATE, SLAVE STATE, WELFARE STATE
4 a [*count*] : a region of a country that is controlled by the country's central government but that has the authority to make its own laws about certain things • the 50 *states* of the U.S. • Chihuahua is a *state* in northern Mexico. • Vermont was the only New England *state* to pass the law. • the *state* legislature • *state* and federal laws • *state* lines/borders • This matter falls under *state* jurisdiction. • Today is a ***state holiday*** here. [=it is an official holiday in this state but not nationally] — often used in combination • a *state*-run program • *state*-funded scholarships • This land is *state*-owned. — see also DOWNSTATE, UPSTATE **b *the States informal*** : the United States of America • My cousin from England is coming to visit me in *the States*. • The band plans to tour *the States*.
5 [*noncount*] : the government of a country • matters of *state* [=government business] • the separation of church and *state* • a crown worn only on *state* occasions • The President will make a *state* visit to China. • the (U.S.) ***Department of State*** = the ***State Department*** [=the part of the U.S. government that is responsible for how the U.S. deals with other countries] — see also STATE'S EVIDENCE
lie in state ✧ When the body of a famous leader (such as a former U.S. president or the pope) *lies in state*, it is displayed in a coffin in a public place so that people can view it and show respect.

[2]**state** *verb* **states; stat•ed; stat•ing** [+ *obj*]
1 : to express (something) formally in speech or writing • The lawyer will *state* the facts of the case. • He *stated* his name in full. • I was merely *stating* an opinion. • "This is a difficult situation," he *stated* simply. • Please *state* the purpose of your visit. • I'd like to *state* for the record that I disagree with the board's decision. • For the reasons *stated* above, I hereby withdraw from the competition. • She accused me of ***stating the obvious***. [=telling people things they already know]
2 : to give (specific information, instructions, rules, etc.) in writing • The rules clearly *state* that you can only draw one card. — often used as *(be) stated* • The rules of the contest *are stated* at the bottom of the page. • You must comply with the terms as *stated* [=*written, specified*] in the contract.

state attorney *noun, pl* **~ -neys** [*count*] *US, law* : a government official (such as a district attorney) who represents a U.S. state in court cases within a district — called also *state's attorney*

state college *noun, pl* **~ -leges** [*count*] : a college that is owned and run by one of the states of the U.S. as part of the state's public educational system

state•craft /ˈsteɪtˌkræft, *Brit* ˈsteɪtˌkrɑːft/ *noun* [*noncount*] *formal* : the art or skill of conducting government affairs • The treaty was a triumph of *statecraft*. [=*statesmanship*]

stated *adj* : expressed formally or officially • The board shall meet at the *stated* [=*indicated*] times. • Their *stated* [=*declared*] intention/goal is to settle the dispute quickly.

state•hood /ˈsteɪtˌhʊd/ *noun* [*noncount*] : the condition of being a state; *especially* : the condition or status of being one of the states of the U.S. • Alaska and Hawaii achieved *statehood* in 1959. [=they officially became U.S. states in 1959]

state•house /ˈsteɪtˌhaʊs/ *noun, pl* **-hous•es** [*count*] : the building in which the legislature of a U.S. state meets and works

state•less /ˈsteɪtləs/ *adj* : not belonging to a nation : not a citizen of any country • a *stateless* refugee

state•ly /ˈsteɪtli/ *adj* **state•li•er; -est** [*or more ~; most ~*] : very impressive in appearance, manner, or size • *stately* pine trees • a *stately* building • a slow *stately* rhythm
– state•li•ness *noun* [*noncount*] • the *stateliness* of the building

stately home *noun, pl* **~ homes** [*count*] *Brit* : a large and impressive old home that has an interesting history and that can usually be visited by the public

state•ment /ˈsteɪtmənt/ *noun, pl* **-ments**
1 [*count*] : something that you say or write in a formal or official way : something that is stated • His office issued/released an official *statement* concerning his departure. • This is his first public *statement* about the investigation. • I disagree with your earlier *statement* about my record on this issue. • The advertisement included misleading/false *statements* about the product. • The police took the witness's *statement*. • We have a signed *statement* from a witness. • a ***sworn statement*** [=a statement that someone makes under oath and swears to be true] — often used in the phrase ***make a statement*** • He *made a statement* to the police. • We can't *make a* definitive *statement* on the matter until all the facts are in. — see also MISSION STATEMENT
2 [*count*] : an opinion, attitude, etc., that you express through the things you do, the way you dress, etc. • The boycott was intended as a political *statement*. — often used in the phrase ***make a statement*** • The government *made a statement* [=sent a message] by setting stiff punishments for repeat offenders. • The painting *makes a* strong/clear *statement*. • The way you dress can *make a statement* about you. • She thinks she's ***making a fashion statement*** [=being fashionable in a bold way], but I think she looks ridiculous.
3 [*count*] : a document which shows amounts of money that you have received, spent, etc. : a brief record of a financial account • a *statement* of expenses • a monthly ***bank statement*** • We'll need to review your recent ***financial statements***.
4 [*count*] : a line of information in a computer program
5 : the act or process of stating something in speech or writing [*noncount*] His writing shows great eloquence and precision of *statement*. [*singular*] She began her speech with a *statement* of her beliefs.

state–of–the–art *adj* : using or having the most modern methods, knowledge, or technology • *state-of-the-art* surgical procedures • His stereo system is *state-of-the-art*.

state park *noun, pl* **~ parks** [*count*] : an area of land that is owned and protected by a U.S. state because of its natural beauty or its importance in history

state•room /ˈsteɪtˌruːm/ *noun, pl* **-rooms** [*count*]
1 : a private room on a ship or on a railroad car
2 *Brit* : a large room in a palace or home that is used for special occasions

state's attorney *noun, pl* **~ -neys** [*count*] *US* : STATE ATTORNEY

state's evidence *noun*
turn state's evidence *US, law* ✧ If you are charged with a crime and you *turn state's evidence*, you agree to give information (such as the names of other criminals) to the court in order to reduce your own punishment. • One of the gang members *turned state's evidence* [=(*Brit*) *turned King's/Queen's evidence*] and testified against the other members.

state•side *or* **State•side** /ˈsteɪtˌsaɪd/ *adv* : in or to the U.S. • It's a car model that will be sold *stateside* for the first time next year. • He's been living in England for several years but he's returning *stateside* next month.
– stateside *or* **Stateside** *adj* • It was the band's first *stateside* tour.

states•man /ˈsteɪtsmən/ *noun, pl* **-men** /-mən/ [*count*] : a usually wise, skilled, and respected government leader • He was a soldier and *statesman*. • a great/eminent *statesman* — see also ELDER STATESMAN
– states•man•like /ˈsteɪtsmənˌlaɪk/ *adj* [*more ~; most ~*] • a politician with a gift for sounding *statesmanlike*
– states•man•ship /ˈsteɪtsmənˌʃɪp/ *noun* [*noncount*]

states•wo•man /ˈsteɪtsˌwʊmən/ *noun, pl* **-wo•men** /-ˌwɪmən/ [*count*] : a woman who is a wise, skilled, and respected government leader • a great *stateswoman*

state university *noun, pl* **~ -ties** [*count*] : a university that is owned and run by one of the states of the U.S. as part of the state's public educational system

state•wide /ˈsteɪtˈwaɪd/ *adj* : including all parts of a U.S. state • a *statewide* survey of voters • a *statewide* election • She is running for *statewide* [=*state*] office. [=she is trying to get elected as an official in the state government]
– statewide *adv* • The big game will be televised *statewide*.

[1]**stat•ic** /ˈstætɪk/ *adj*
1 : showing little or no change, action, or progress • a *static* population • Culture is not *static*. • The computer program can turn *static* [=*still*] images into movies.
2 : of, relating to, or producing static electricity • a *static* charge • Use a fabric softener to prevent ***static cling***. [=a condition in which clothes stick to one another because of static electricity]

[2]**static** *noun* [*noncount*]
1 : unwanted noise caused in a radio or television receiver by electricity or by conditions in the atmosphere • There was so much *static* on the radio we couldn't hear the broadcast.
2 : STATIC ELECTRICITY
3 *US, informal* : criticism or complaints • He was getting a lot of *static* about his decision.

static electricity *noun* [*noncount*] : electricity that collects on the surface of something and does not flow as a current and can cause a mild shock if you touch it • In dry

S

weather, *static electricity* can cause clothes to cling.

stat·ics /ˈstætɪks/ *noun* [*noncount*] *technical* **:** the science that studies the relationship between forces that keep objects in balance

[1]**sta·tion** /ˈsteɪʃən/ *noun, pl* **-tions** [*count*]

1 : a place where buses, trains, etc., regularly stop so that passengers can get on and off ▪ They drove him to the bus/train *station*. ▪ a subway *station* — see also WAY STATION

2 : a place where someone does a job or waits for a task ▪ The waiters were at their *stations* in the dining room. ▪ a nurse's/nursing *station* [=an office area for the nurses working in a hospital] ▪ The sailors were ordered to man their battle *stations*. ▪ After joining the army, he spent five years at his first *station*. [=*post*]

3 *old-fashioned* **:** a person's social or official position in relation to others **:** RANK ▪ He had married above his *station*. ▪ They were aware of her *station* in life.

4 : a building, area, etc., where a certain kind of work or activity is done ▪ a research/space/weather *station* ▪ a computer *station* ▪ a feeding *station* for livestock

5 : a place that provides a certain kind of service to the public ▪ A firefighter led the children on a tour of the *station*. [=*fire station*] ▪ She stopped for gas at the first *station* [=(*US*) *gas station*, (*Brit*) *petrol station*] she saw. ▪ Officers brought him to the *station* [=*police station*] for questioning.

6 : a company that makes radio or television broadcasts ▪ He turned to his favorite sports *station*. ▪ What *station* is the game on?; *also* **:** the building from which radio or television broadcasts are made ▪ Our offices are located next door to a TV *station*.

7 : a farm or ranch in Australia or New Zealand ▪ a sheep *station*

[2]**station** *verb* **-tions; -tioned; -tion·ing** [+ *obj*]

1 : to assign (someone) to a station or position **:** POST ▪ He *stationed* the guards around the camp. ▪ They *stationed* troops at the border. — often used as *(be) stationed* ▪ She has *been stationed* at the base for a few years. ▪ They *were stationed* in the region of the fighting.

2 : to put (yourself) in a place and stay there for a period of time ▪ He *stationed* himself by the door to greet the guests.

sta·tion·ary /ˈsteɪʃəˌneri, *Brit* ˈsteɪʃənri/ *adj*

1 : not moving **:** staying in one place or position ▪ *stationary* machinery ▪ shooting at *stationary* objects/targets ▪ The weather front has remained *stationary* over the Southeast.

2 : not changing ▪ a *stationary* [=*stable*] population

Do not confuse *stationary* with *stationery*.

stationary bike *noun, pl* ~ **bikes** [*count*] *US* **:** an exercise machine that you pedal like a bicycle but that stays in one place — called also *exercise bike, stationary bicycle*; see picture at GYM

station break *noun, pl* ~ **breaks** [*count*] *US* **:** a pause in a broadcast during which a radio or TV station announces its name or runs an advertisement

sta·tio·ner /ˈsteɪʃənɚ/ *noun, pl* **-ners** [*count*] **:** a business or person that sells stationery

sta·tio·nery /ˈsteɪʃəˌneri, *Brit* ˈsteɪʃənri/ *noun* [*noncount*]

1 : materials (such as paper, pens, and ink) that are used for writing or typing ▪ a store that sells *stationery* = a *stationery* store ▪ *stationery* items/supplies

2 : paper that is used for writing letters and that usually has matching envelopes ▪ business *stationery*

Do not confuse *stationery* with *stationary*.

S

station house *noun, pl* ~ **houses** [*count*] **:** a house or building that is part of a station; *especially, US* **:** POLICE STATION

sta·tion·mas·ter /ˈsteɪʃənˌmæstɚ, *Brit* ˈsteɪʃənˌmɑːstə/ *noun, pl* **-ters** [*count*] **:** an official who is in charge of the operation of a railroad station

Stations of the Cross *noun* [*plural*] **:** a series of usually 14 pictures in some Christian churches that show the sufferings and death of Jesus Christ

station wagon *noun, pl* ~ **-ons** [*count*] *US* **:** a car that has a large open area behind the back seat instead of a trunk and that has a door at the back for loading and unloading things — called also (*US*) *wagon*, (*Brit*) *estate car*; see picture at CAR

sta·tis·tic /stəˈtɪstɪk/ *noun, pl* **-tics**

1 [*count*] **:** a number that represents a piece of information (such as information about how often something is done, how common something is, etc.) ▪ One *statistic* that stuck out is that 40 percent of those surveyed did not have college degrees. — often plural ▪ The *statistics* show that teenagers are involved in a high percentage of traffic accidents. ▪ Her speech included some revealing *statistics* about unemployment rates in rural areas. ▪ basketball *statistics* — sometimes used figuratively ▪ I may be just another *statistic* to my employer, but I am a human being and have feelings. — called also (*US, informal*) *stat*

2 ***statistics*** [*noncount*] **:** a type of mathematics that deals with the study of statistics

– sta·tis·ti·cal /stəˈtɪstɪkəl/ *adj* ▪ *Statistical* evidence indicates smokers are more likely to get lung cancer than nonsmokers. **– sta·tis·ti·cal·ly** /stəˈtɪstɪkli/ *adv*

stat·is·ti·cian /ˌstætəˈstɪʃən/ *noun, pl* **-cians** [*count*] **:** a person who collects and studies statistics

stat·u·ary /ˈstæʧəˌweri/ *noun* [*noncount*] *formal* **:** a collection of statues ▪ a fine example of late Renaissance *statuary*

stat·ue /ˈstæˌʧuː/ *noun, pl* **stat·ues** [*count*] **:** a figure usually of a person or animal that is made from stone, metal, etc. ▪ bronze *statues* — compare SCULPTURE

stat·u·esque /ˌstæʧəˈwɛsk/ *adj* [*more* ~; *most* ~] **:** tall and beautiful ▪ a *statuesque* young woman

stat·u·ette /ˌstæʧəˈwɛt/ *noun, pl* **-ettes** [*count*] **:** a small statue

stat·ure /ˈstæʧɚ/ *noun* [*noncount*]

1 : the level of respect that people have for a successful person, organization, etc. ▪ We are honored to be working with a writer of his *stature*. [=a writer who is so highly respected] ▪ The university has grown/gained in *stature* during her time as president.

2 *somewhat formal* **:** a person's height ▪ a woman of rather short *stature* [=a rather short woman]

sta·tus /ˈsteɪtəs, ˈstætəs/ *noun, pl* **-tus·es**

1 a : the position or rank of someone or something when compared to others in a society, organization, group, etc. [*noncount*] He likes his job and the high (social) *status* that comes with it. ▪ She has achieved celebrity *status*. [=she has become a celebrity] ▪ They want to maintain the city's *status* as a major tourist attraction. ▪ The book quickly achieved best-seller *status*. [=became a best seller] [*count*] He wants to improve his *status* in the community. ▪ people of different social and economic *statuses* **b** [*noncount*] **:** high position or rank in society ▪ She married a man of *status* and wealth. ▪ This job brings with it a measure of *status*.

2 : the official position of a person or thing according to the law [*noncount*] They sought asylum and were given refugee *status* by the government. [*count*] They are still considered refugees. Their *statuses* have not changed. — see also MARITAL STATUS

3 [*count*] **:** the current state of someone or something — usually singular ▪ What is the *status* of the project? ▪ What is their financial *status*? ▪ The boss asked for a *status* report.

status quo /-ˈkwoʊ/ *noun* [*singular*] **:** the current situation **:** the way things are now ▪ He is content with the *status quo* and does not like change. ▪ She wants to maintain the *status quo*. [=to keep the situation as it is now]

status symbol *noun, pl* ~ **-bols** [*count*] **:** something (such as an expensive car) that you own and that shows that you are wealthy or have a high social status

stat·ute /ˈstæˌʧuːt/ *noun, pl* **-utes**

1 : a written law that is formally created by a government [*count*] The state legislature passed the *statute* by an overwhelming margin. [*noncount*] business practices that are prohibited/protected by *statute* ***synonyms*** see LAW

2 [*count*] **:** a written rule or regulation ▪ college/university *statutes*

statute book *noun*

the statute book — used to refer to the written laws that have been formally and officially approved by a government ▪ a law that is now on the *statute book(s)* [=a law that has now been officially approved]

statute of limitations *noun, pl* **statutes of limitations** [*count*] *law* **:** a law that states the amount of time that must pass before a crime can no longer be punished or a right can no longer be given

stat·u·to·ry /ˈstæʧəˌtori, *Brit* ˈstæʧətri/ *adj, law*

1 : of or relating to formal laws or statutes ▪ *statutory* acts

2 : controlled or determined by a law or rule ▪ He had reached the *statutory* age of retirement. [=the age at which retirement was required by law]

statutory rape *noun, pl* ~ **rapes** [*count, noncount*] *law* **:** the crime of having sex with someone who is younger than an age that is specified by law

[1]staunch *variant spelling of* STANCH

[2]staunch /ˈstɑːntʃ/ *adj, always used before a noun* **staunch·er; -est** [*also more ~; most ~*] **:** very devoted or loyal to a person, belief, or cause ▪ She is a *staunch* advocate of women's rights. ▪ He's a *staunch* believer in the value of regular exercise. ▪ I'm one of his *staunchest* supporters.
– **staunch·ly** *adv* ▪ She is *staunchly* opposed to the death penalty.

[1]stave /ˈsteɪv/ *noun, pl* **staves** [*count*]
1 : one of the narrow strips of wood that form the sides of a barrel
2 : a long wooden stick **:** STAFF
3 *chiefly Brit* **:** [1]STAFF 3

[2]stave *verb* **staves; staved** *also* **stove** /ˈstoʊv/; **stav·ing**
stave in [*phrasal verb*] ***stave in*** *or* ***stave (something) in*** *or* ***stave in (something)*** **:** to be broken or crushed inward or to break or crush (something) inward ▪ The hull of the boat *stove in* when it hit the rocks. ▪ The rocks *stove in* the hull of the boat.
stave off [*phrasal verb*] ***stave (someone or something) off*** *or* ***stave off (someone or something)*** **:** to keep (someone or something) away usually for a short time ▪ He's trying to *stave off* his creditors. ▪ Our company cannot *stave* bankruptcy *off* any longer. ▪ She ate a few crackers to *stave off* hunger. [=to prevent herself from getting too hungry]

staves *plural of* [1]STAFF

[1]stay /ˈsteɪ/ *verb* **stays; stayed; stay·ing**
1 a [*no obj*] **:** to continue to be in the same place or with the same person or group for a period of time **:** REMAIN ▪ Please *stay* in the auditorium. ▪ I *stayed* in my seat until I was dismissed. ▪ He decided to *stay* with the team. ▪ I decided to *stay* in Montreal for a couple more days. ▪ We *stayed* home last night and watched TV. ▪ Go to your room and *stay* there. ▪ I'll ***stay around*** for a few more minutes. ▪ I need a man who will *stay around.* [=remain in the relationship and not leave suddenly] ▪ You can go on ahead. I'll ***stay behind*** [=not leave yet] to help clean up. **b :** to continue to be in a specified state, condition, or position **:** REMAIN [*no obj*] Please *stay* seated through the entire show. ▪ She *stayed* angry all night. ▪ Can you *stay* awake through the whole show? ▪ The guard urged everyone to *stay* calm. ▪ The store will *stay* open until midnight tonight. ▪ We have *stayed* in touch/contact over the years. ▪ He *stayed* in the game although he was injured. [*linking verb*] They ***stayed friends*** [=continued to be friends] throughout their lives.
2 [*no obj*] **:** to live in a place as a guest for a short period of time ▪ I will be *staying* in a hotel this weekend. ▪ Do you want to *stay* [=*sleep*] at my place tonight? ▪ I *stayed* overnight at his house. ▪ Is he *staying* (with us) all week?
3 [+ *obj*] **:** to give a legal order that stops or delays (something) ▪ The judge agreed to *stay* [=*halt*] the execution.
here to stay see [1]HERE
stay away [*phrasal verb*] **:** to not go near someone or something ▪ I know I shouldn't go there, but it's hard to *stay away.* — usually + *from* ▪ *Stay away from* my girlfriend! ▪ He usually *stays away from* [=*avoids*] large crowds. ▪ I try to *stay away from* [=*avoid*] caffeine.
stay in [*phrasal verb*] **:** to stay inside or at home instead of going out ▪ We went to a movie last night, but tonight we're *staying in.*
stay off [*phrasal verb*] ***stay off (something)*** **1 :** to avoid (something) ▪ She's doing a good job of *staying off* drugs. [=of not taking drugs] ▪ Let's *stay off* the subject of politics. **2 :** to not go on (something) ▪ Please *stay off* [=*keep off*] the grass.
stay on [*phrasal verb*] **1 :** to continue to work at a job ▪ She thought about retiring, but she finally decided to *stay on* for a few more years. ▪ After she graduated, she *stayed on* at the college, working in the alumnae office. **2** ***stay on (something)*** **:** to continue taking (a medication, drug, etc.) ▪ I have to *stay on* the antibiotics for a full two weeks.
stay out [*phrasal verb*] **1 a :** to avoid going into (a place) ▪ They kicked us out of the bar and told us to *stay out.* — often + *of* ▪ I told her to *stay out of* my room. **b** ***stay out of (something)*** **:** to avoid becoming involved in (something) ▪ Please try to *stay out of* trouble. ▪ This is not your business, so *stay out of* it. **2 :** to spend time away from home ▪ She *stayed out* dancing all night.
stay over [*phrasal verb*] **:** to sleep at another person's house for the night ▪ Can she *stay over* tonight?
stay put see [3]PUT
stay the course **:** to continue with a process, effort, etc., even though it is difficult ▪ We'll succeed in the end if we just *stay the course.*
stay the night **:** to sleep at another person's house for the night ▪ After the party she was too drunk to drive so she *stayed the night.* [=*stayed over, spent the night*] ▪ They *stayed the night* at her brother's.
stay tuned see [2]TUNE
stay up [*phrasal verb*] **:** to continue to be awake past the time when you usually go to bed ▪ Don't *stay up* past your bedtime. ▪ She *stayed up* to watch the late movie. ▪ I can't *stay up* that late.
stay with [*phrasal verb*] **1** ***stay with (someone)*** ◊ If something from the past *stays with* you, you remember it and it continues to influence or affect you in some way. ▪ The memory of that tragic day has *stayed with* her ever since. ▪ That is an image that has *stayed with* me. **2** ***stay with (something)*** **:** to continue using or doing (something) ▪ *Stay with* the medication for a couple more days and see if the rash clears up. ▪ I know the work is hard, but if you just *stay with* it for a while longer, it'll be done. **3** ***stay with (someone)*** **:** to go or make progress at the same rate as (someone) **:** to keep even with (someone) in a race, competition, etc. ▪ The other runners struggled to *stay with* the leader.

[2]stay *noun, pl* **stays** [*count*]
1 : an occasion in which you spend time at a place as a guest or visitor ▪ I hope you have a pleasant *stay.* [=*visit*] ▪ Our *stay* in the country was a short one. — see also SHORT-STAY
2 : a legal order that stops or delays something ▪ The court issued a ***stay of execution***. [=an order that temporarily stops an execution]
– compare [3]STAY

[3]stay *noun, pl* **stays** [*count*]
1 : a rope or wire that supports a pole, a ship's mast, etc. ▪ The men tightened the *stays* on the circus tent.
2 : a piece of stiff plastic, bone, etc., that provides shape to a piece of clothing ▪ a corset *stay* ▪ a collar *stay*
– compare [2]STAY

stay–at–home /ˈstejətˈhoʊm/ *adj, always used before a noun* **:** staying at home to take care of a child instead of working somewhere else ▪ a *stay-at-home* mom/dad

staying power *noun* [*noncount*] **:** the quality or ability that allows someone or something to continue to be effective, successful, popular, etc., for a long period of time ▪ a long-distance runner with a lot of *staying power* ▪ a song with *staying power* ▪ Her *staying power* as a pop icon is remarkable.

std. *abbr* standard

STD /ˌɛsˌtiːˈdiː/ *noun, pl* **STDs** [*count*] **:** any one of various diseases that you can get by having sex with a person who has the disease ▪ a discussion of AIDS and other *STDs* ◊ *STD* is an abbreviation for "sexually transmitted disease."

stead /ˈstɛd/ *noun*
in someone's/something's stead *formal* **:** in the place of someone or something ▪ She conducted the meeting *in his stead.* ▪ One empire died, and another arose *in its stead.*
stand someone/something in good stead *formal* **:** to be useful or helpful to someone or something ▪ His language skills will *stand him in good stead* when he is traveling.

stead·fast /ˈstɛdˌfæst, *Brit* ˈstɛdˌfɑːst/ *adj* [*more ~; most ~*] **:** very devoted or loyal to a person, belief, or cause **:** not changing ▪ They were *steadfast* friends. ▪ He was *steadfast* in his support of the governor's policies. ▪ a *steadfast* refusal
– **stead·fast·ly** *adv* ▪ She *steadfastly* held to her views.
– **stead·fast·ness** /ˈstɛdˌfæstnəs, *Brit* ˈstɛdˌfɑːstnəs/ *noun* [*noncount*]

[1]steady /ˈstɛdi/ *adj* **stead·i·er; -est** [*also more ~; most ~*]
1 : not shaking or moving **:** held firmly in one place or position ▪ She used a tripod to keep the camera *steady.* ▪ Painting takes a *steady* hand and a good eye. ▪ a *steady* gaze ▪ He was drunk and wasn't very *steady* on his feet. [=his balance was not good; he looked like he might fall]
2 : not changing as time passes: such as **a :** not increasing or decreasing ▪ Prices have remained *steady* over the last month. ▪ a *steady* heart rate **b :** lasting or continuing for a long period of time in a dependable way ▪ He finally has a *steady* job. ▪ They do a *steady* business at the restaurant. **c** — used to describe a romantic relationship with one person that lasts for a long time ▪ He's never really had a *steady* relationship with one woman. ▪ a ***steady boyfriend/girlfriend***
3 : happening or developing in a continuous and usually gradual way ▪ There has been a *steady* increase in prices. ▪ I am making *steady* progress on refinishing the basement. ▪

S

There was a *steady* rain all day. ▪ We've received a ***steady stream*** of donations.
4 : not nervous or excited ▪ *steady* nerves ▪ Her voice was calm and *steady.*
5 : dependable or reliable ▪ She has been a *steady* friend to me. ▪ He's a very *steady* worker.
at a steady clip see [3]CLIP
ready, steady, go see [1]READY
steady on *Brit, informal* — used to tell someone to be calmer, to stop thinking or saying foolish or unreasonable things, etc. ▪ "Everything's going wrong!" "*Steady on,* now. It's not as bad as that."
– steadi·ly /ˈstɛdəli/ *adv* [*more* ~; *most* ~] ▪ He held the camera *steadily.* ▪ Wages have *steadily* increased. **– steadi·ness** /ˈstɛdinəs/ *noun* [*noncount*]

[2]**steady** *verb* **stead·ies; stead·ied; steady·ing :** to make (something or someone) steady or to become steady: such as **a** [+ *obj*] **:** to keep (something or someone) from moving, shaking, falling, etc. ▪ He *steadied* the gun and fired. ▪ She used a tripod to *steady* the camera. ▪ He held the rail to ***steady himself.*** [=to keep himself balanced] **b :** to cause (something) to stop changing, increasing, decreasing, etc. [+ *obj*] The doctor gave her medication to help *steady* her heart rate. [*no obj*] Her heart rate had been erratic but eventually *steadied.* ▪ Prices have *steadied* in recent months.
steady your nerves **:** to make yourself calm or calmer ▪ She took a drink to try to *steady her nerves.*

[3]**steady** *adv* **:** in a steady way ▪ Hold the camera *steady.*
go steady *informal + old-fashioned* **:** to have a lasting romantic relationship with one person and no one else ▪ He asked me after the dance if I wanted to *go steady.* ▪ We *went steady* for over a year before we got engaged.

[4]**steady** *noun, pl* **stead·ies** [*count*] *US, informal + old-fashioned* **:** the only person you are having a romantic relationship with **:** the person you are going steady with ▪ He's my *steady.* [=my steady boyfriend]

steak /ˈsteɪk/ *noun, pl* **steaks**
1 : a thick, flat piece of meat and especially beef [*count*] I grilled a *steak* for dinner. ▪ ham *steaks* [*noncount*] We had *steak* and potatoes for dinner. ▪ a slice of *steak*
2 [*count*] **:** a thick, flat piece of fish ▪ a tuna/swordfish *steak*
3 [*noncount*] *Brit* **:** beef that is cut into small pieces and used for stews, casseroles, etc. ▪ *steak* and kidney pie

steak house *noun, pl* ~ **houses** [*count*] **:** a restaurant that serves mostly steaks — compare CHOP HOUSE

steak knife *noun, pl* ~ **knives** [*count*] **:** a very sharp knife that is used for cutting meat

[1]**steal** /ˈsti:l/ *verb* **steals; stole** /ˈstoul/; **sto·len** /ˈstoulən/; **steal·ing**
1 a : to take (something that does not belong to you) in a way that is wrong or illegal [+ *obj*] They *stole* thousands of dollars' worth of jewelry from the store. ▪ Someone *stole* my bicycle. ▪ He discovered that his car had been *stolen.* ▪ a *stolen* watch [*no obj*] The store manager accused the boy of *stealing.* **b** [+ *obj*] **:** to take (something that you are not supposed to have) without asking for permission ▪ I *stole* a cookie from the cookie jar. **c** [+ *obj*] **:** to wrongly take and use (another person's idea, words, etc.) ▪ He *stole* my idea. **d** [+ *obj*] **:** to persuade (someone who has been with someone else) to be with you especially by doing things that are unfair or dishonest ▪ He *stole* my girlfriend. ▪ They *stole* our best pitcher away from our team.
2 [+ *obj*] **:** to get (something that is difficult to get) in usually a quick and often secret way ▪ I *stole* a nap this afternoon. [=I managed to take a brief nap this afternoon] ▪ He ***stole a peek/look*** [=took a quick peek/look] at the birthday cake. ▪ He ***stole a glance*** at her [=glanced at her quickly] before riding away. ▪ She ***stole a kiss*** from him [=kissed him in a quick and sudden way] and ran away.
3 [+ *obj*] **:** to get more attention than others during (a performance, scene, etc.) ▪ Her impassioned acting *stole* the scene. [=everyone in the audience watched her during the scene because of her impassioned acting] ▪ His outstanding performance ***stole the show.***
4 a *baseball* **:** to reach (a base) safely by running to it from the previous base when the ball has not been hit by a batter [+ *obj*] He reached first base on a single and then *stole* second (base). [*no obj*] She tried to *steal* but got thrown out. ▪ He leads the league in *stealing.* **b** [+ *obj*] *sports* **:** to take (the ball, puck, etc.) from another player ▪ (*basketball*) He *stole* the ball and took it down the court for two points. ▪ He *stole* the pass.
5 [*no obj*] **:** to come or go quietly or secretly ▪ They *stole* out of the room. ▪ She *stole* away silently.
beg, borrow, or/and steal see BEG
steal a march on see [2]MARCH
steal someone's thunder see [1]THUNDER

[2]**steal** *noun, pl* **steals** [*count*]
1 *informal* **:** something that is being sold at a low price ▪ This car is a *steal* at only $5,000.
2 a *baseball* **:** the act of stealing a base ▪ He has 40 *steals* this season. **b** *sports* **:** the act of taking the ball, puck, etc., from another player ▪ a nifty *steal* by the defender

[1]**stealth** /ˈstɛlθ/ *noun* [*noncount*] **:** a secret, quiet, and clever way of moving or behaving ▪ The fox uses *stealth* and cunning to hunt its prey.

[2]**stealth** *adj, always used before a noun*
1 *technical* — used to describe military aircraft that are designed so that they cannot be easily seen by radar ▪ a *stealth* bomber/fighter
2 *chiefly US* **:** done or happening in a secret or quiet way that does not attract attention ▪ He says his political enemies have been conducting a *stealth* [=*secret*] campaign to block his nomination.

stealthy /ˈstɛlθi/ *adj* **stealth·i·er; -est** [*also more* ~; *most* ~] **:** quiet and secret in order to avoid being noticed ▪ the *stealthy* movements of the crocodile ▪ a *stealthy* burglar
– stealth·i·ly /ˈstɛlθəli/ *adv* ▪ She moved *stealthily* from room to room.

[1]**steam** /ˈsti:m/ *noun* [*noncount*]
1 a : the hot gas that is created when water is boiled ▪ Careful, the *steam* from the pot is hot. **b :** steam that is created by a machine and kept under pressure to provide power ▪ *Steam* drives the turbines. ▪ a *steam*-powered engine ▪ The boat runs on *steam.* — often used before another noun ▪ a *steam* engine/train
2 : very small drops of water that form on a surface when warm air that contains a lot of water is cooled down ▪ He wiped the *steam* from the mirrors.
3 *informal* **:** the strength, force, or energy that allows something or someone to continue, to go faster, etc. ▪ Sales have ***lost steam*** [=have slowed down] in recent weeks. ▪ The campaign quickly ***gained/gathered steam.*** [=became more popular and successful] ▪ He was afraid he would ***run out of steam*** before the end of the race. ▪ I was making good progress this morning, but now I'm starting to *run out of steam.* ▪ The project is slowly ***picking up steam.*** [=slowly beginning to move ahead in a faster and more effective way]
full head of steam see [1]HEAD
full steam ahead see [1]FULL
let/blow off (some) steam *informal* **:** to calm down and get rid of energy or anger by doing something active ▪ I play racquetball every evening just to *let off some steam.* ▪ Tell him to go *blow off some steam* and then we can talk.
under its own steam *of a ship, boat, etc.* **:** by using its own power ▪ The ship was damaged but was able to return to port *under its own steam.* — often used figuratively ▪ He got there *under his own steam.* [=by himself; by his own efforts]

[2]**steam** *verb* **steams; steamed; steam·ing**
1 [*no obj*] **:** to produce steam ▪ a *steaming* bowl of soup
2 [+ *obj*] **:** to cook, heat, or treat (something) with steam ▪ She prefers to *steam* carrots rather than boil them. ▪ *steamed* vegetables
3 : to cause (something, such as a piece of glass) to become covered with small drops of water [+ *obj*] Their breath *steamed* the windows. — usually + *up* ▪ Try not to *steam up* your glasses. ▪ The windows *were* all *steamed up.* [*no obj*] My glasses *steamed up* [=*fogged up*] when I came indoors from the cold.
4 *always followed by an adverb or preposition* [*no obj*] **a :** to move by using power produced by steam ▪ The ship *steamed* into port. ▪ We *steamed* up the river. [=we went up the river on a ship powered by steam] **b :** to move forward in a quick and forceful way ▪ He *steamed* into the room and began shouting orders. — sometimes used figuratively ▪ Our plans are *steaming* ahead. — see also STEAMED, STEAMING

steam·boat /ˈsti:mˌbout/ *noun, pl* **-boats** [*count*] **:** a boat that is powered by steam

steam clean *verb* ~ **cleans;** ~ **cleaned;** ~ **cleaning** [+ *obj*] *chiefly US* **:** to clean (something) with a machine that produces hot steam ▪ I *steam cleaned* the carpets.

steamed /ˈsti:md/ *adj, not used before a noun* [*more* ~; *most* ~] *chiefly US, informal* **:** angry or irritated ▪ I am so *steamed*! — often + *up* ▪ What are you getting *steamed up* about?

steam·er /ˈstiːmɚ/ *noun, pl* **-ers** [*count*]
1 : a container in which food is cooked with steam
2 : a boat or ship that is powered by steam ▪ We rode a *steamer* down the Mississippi.
3 *US* **:** a type of clam that has a thin shell and that is often cooked by being steamed

steaming *adj, informal*
1 : very hot ▪ *steaming* weather ▪ The weather has been ***steaming hot***.
2 : very angry ▪ *steaming* drivers stuck in traffic ▪ His wife was *steaming* when he finally got home. ▪ She was ***steaming mad***.

steam·roll /ˈstiːmˌroʊl/ *verb* **-rolls; -rolled; -roll·ing** *US, informal*
1 *always followed by an adverb or preposition* **:** to go forward or make progress in a forceful and steady way [*no obj*] The project *steamrolled on*. ▪ The bill *steamrolled* through Congress. [+ *obj*] The bill *steamrolled* its way through Congress.
2 [+ *obj*] **:** to defeat (someone or something) in a very forceful and complete way ▪ Our team got *steamrolled* in last year's game. The final score was something like 54–7.

[1]**steam·roll·er** /ˈstiːmˌroʊlɚ/ *noun, pl* **-ers** [*count*] **:** a large, heavy machine that is used for making a road or other surface flat

[2]**steamroller** *verb* **-ers; -ered; -er·ing** [+ *obj*] *informal* **:** STEAMROLL 2

steam·ship /ˈstiːmˌʃɪp/ *noun, pl* **-ships** [*count*] **:** a ship that is powered by steam

steam shovel *noun, pl* **~ -els** [*count*] *US* **:** a large machine that is powered by steam and that is used for digging large holes — called also *excavator*

steamy /ˈstiːmi/ *adj* **steam·i·er; -est** [*also more ~; most ~*]
1 : full of steam or warm, moist air ▪ a *steamy* bathroom ▪ It is 92 degrees in *steamy* Miami this afternoon. ▪ *steamy* [=hot and humid] weather
2 : showing or relating to sex **:** sexually exciting ▪ a *steamy* love scene

steed /ˈstiːd/ *noun, pl* **steeds** [*count*] *literary* **:** a horse that a person rides ▪ a brave knight and his noble *steed*

[1]**steel** /ˈstiːl/ *noun, pl* **steels**
1 [*noncount*] **a :** a strong, hard metal made of iron and carbon ▪ The beams are made of *steel*. — often used before another noun ▪ *steel* bars ▪ a *steel* mill [=a mill/factory where steel is made] — see also STAINLESS STEEL **b :** the industry that makes steel ▪ *Steel* is an important industry in this area. ▪ She came from a ***steel town*** [=a town where steel is made] in Pennsylvania. ▪ ***Big Steel*** [=the steel industry] is lobbying Congress for new legislation.
2 a [*noncount*] *literary* **:** things (such as weapons) that are made of steel ▪ The invaders were driven back by *steel*. ▪ the clash of *steel* **b** [*singular*] **:** the part of something that is made of steel ▪ the *steel* of a knife **c** [*count*] **:** a device or tool that is made of steel ▪ a sharpening *steel* [=a steel rod that has a rough surface and is used for sharpening knives] — see also PEDAL STEEL
3 — used to describe something or someone that is very strong ▪ He had a grip ***of steel***. = He had a grip ***like steel***. [=he had a very powerful grip] ▪ a ***man of steel*** [=a very strong man] — see also *nerves of steel* at NERVE

[2]**steel** *verb* **steels; steeled; steel·ing**
steel yourself **:** to make (yourself) ready for something difficult or unpleasant **:** to fill (yourself) with determination and courage ▪ *Steel yourself* [=*brace yourself*]—I have bad news. ▪ He *steeled himself* for the interview.

steel band *noun, pl* **~ bands** [*count*] **:** a group of musicians who play steel drums

steel drum *noun, pl* **~ drums** [*count*] **:** a metal drum shaped like a bowl or barrel that makes different sounds when it is hit at different places

steel guitar *noun, pl* **~ -tars** [*count*] **:** PEDAL STEEL

steel wool *noun* [*noncount*] **:** long threads of metal that are wound together to form a rough pad which is used for cleaning and polishing things

steel·work·er /ˈstiːlˌwɚkɚ/ *noun, pl* **-ers** [*count*] *US* **:** a person who works at a place where steel is made

steely /ˈstiːli/ *adj* **steel·i·er; -est**
1 : very strong and determined often in a cold or unfriendly way ▪ a thief with *steely* nerves ▪ He had a *steely* determination to succeed. ▪ She gave him a *steely* gaze.
2 : resembling steel especially in color ▪ a sky filled with *steely* gray clouds ▪ the judge's *steely* blue eyes

[1]**steep** /ˈstiːp/ *adj* **steep·er; -est** [*also more ~; most ~*]
1 : almost straight up and down **:** rising or falling very sharply ▪ a *steep* slope/hillside ▪ The stairs are very *steep*.
2 : going up or down very quickly ▪ a *steep* drop/increase in prices
3 : very high ▪ The store's prices are too *steep* for me. ▪ Their rates are pretty *steep*.
pay a steep price see [1]PAY
– steep·ly *adv* [*more ~; most ~*] ▪ The hill rose *steeply*. ▪ Stock prices rose/fell *steeply* today. **– steep·ness** *noun* [*noncount*]

[2]**steep** *verb* **steeps; steeped; steep·ing :** to put (something) in a liquid for a period of time [+ *obj*] *Steep* the tea for three minutes. [*no obj*] The tea *steeped* for five minutes.
steep in [*phrasal verb*] **1** ***steep (someone) in (something)*** **:** to make (someone) know and understand a lot about (something) ▪ Prior to his trip, he spent a few weeks ***steeping himself in*** the language. [=learning a lot about the language] — often used as *(be) steeped in* ▪ She *was steeped in* the classics. [=she had learned a lot about the classics] **2** — used as *(be) steeped in* to say that there is a lot of something in a place, time, etc. ▪ an area *steeped in* history [=an area where many important historical events occurred] ▪ It was a time in the nation's history that *was steeped in* bloodshed. [=a time when there was a lot of bloodshed]

steep·en /ˈstiːpən/ *verb* **-ens; -ened; -en·ing :** to become steep or steeper or to make (something) steep or steeper [*no obj*] The path *steepened* as we approached the summit. [+ *obj*] A large glacier *steepened* the side of the mountain.

stee·ple /ˈstiːpəl/ *noun, pl* **stee·ples** [*count*] **:** a tall, pointed tower on a church
– stee·pled /ˈstiːpəld/ *adj* ▪ a *steepled* church

stee·ple·chase /ˈstiːpəlˌʧeɪs/ *noun, pl* **-chas·es** [*count*]
1 : a race in which people riding horses jump over fences, water, etc.
2 : a race in which runners jump over fences and water

stee·ple·chas·er /ˈstiːpəlˌʧeɪsɚ/ *noun, pl* **-ers** [*count*] **:** a person or horse that takes part in a steeplechase

stee·ple·jack /ˈstiːpəlˌʤæk/ *noun, pl* **-jacks** [*count*] *old-fashioned* **:** a person who repairs chimneys, towers, etc.

[1]**steer** /ˈstiɚ/ *verb* **steers; steered; steer·ing**
1 a : to control the direction in which something (such as a ship, car, or airplane) moves [+ *obj*] She *steered* the ship through the strait. ▪ He *steered* his car carefully into the parking space. ▪ He *steered* the wheelchair through the aisles. [*no obj*] Skillful navigators can *steer* by the positions of the stars. **b** [*no obj*] — used to describe how easy or difficult it is to steer a vehicle ▪ The car *steers* well.
2 [*no obj*] **:** to be moved or guided in a particular direction or along a particular course ▪ The car was *steering* right at us. ▪ The boat *steered* out to sea.
3 [+ *obj*] **a :** to direct or guide the movement or progress of (something) ▪ He tried to *steer* the conversation away from his recent problems. ▪ She skillfully *steered* the bill through the legislature. ▪ He *steered* the team to another championship last year. **b :** to cause (someone) to act in a particular way ▪ The high recent returns on stocks have *steered* many investors away from bonds. ▪ You should listen to me. I won't ***steer you wrong***. [=I won't give you bad advice]
steer clear *US* **:** to keep away from someone or something completely ▪ He's in a bad mood. You'd better *steer clear* [=avoid him] if you don't want trouble. — usually + *of* ▪ You'd better *steer clear of* him. ▪ I try to *steer clear of* the subject of politics when I talk to him.

[2]**steer** *noun, pl* **steers** [*count*] **:** a male cow that has had its sex organs removed and is raised for meat

steer·age /ˈstirɪʤ/ *noun* [*noncount*] **:** the section on a passenger ship in the past where passengers who had the cheapest tickets would stay

steering *noun* [*noncount*] **:** the mechanical parts of a car, boat, etc., that are used to control its direction ▪ The *steering* on this car is a little stiff. ▪ There's a problem with the boat's *steering*.

steering column *noun, pl* **~ -umns** [*count*] **:** the thick post in a car that holds the steering wheel

steering committee *noun, pl* **~ -tees** [*count*] **:** a group of people who are in charge of managing or directing something ▪ The CEO consulted with the project's *steering committee* and asked for a status report. — called also *(chiefly Brit) steering group*

S

steering wheel *noun, pl* ~ **wheels** [*count*] : a wheel in a vehicle that the driver turns to steer the vehicle — see picture at CAR

stein /ˈstaɪn/ *noun, pl* **steins** [*count*] : a large mug for beer

stel·lar /ˈstɛlɚ/ *adj*
1 *technical* : of or relating to the stars • *stellar* light • the rate of *stellar* expansion
2 [*more* ~; *most* ~] : very good : EXCELLENT • The movie has a *stellar* cast. • a *stellar* performance

[1]stem /ˈstɛm/ *noun, pl* **stems** [*count*]
1 a : the main long and thin part of a plant that rises above the soil and supports the leaves and flowers • He cut the plant off at the base of the *stem*. — see color picture on page C6 **b** : the long, thin part of a fruit, leaf, flower, etc., that connects it to its plant • Hold the cherry by the *stem*.
2 : a long and thin part: such as **a** : the long, thin piece that supports the bowl of a wine glass **b** : the long, thin part of a tobacco pipe
3 *grammar* : the main part of a word that does not change when endings are added to it • The *stem* of "winded" is "wind."
from stem to stern : from one end of a ship or boat to the other • We scrubbed her down *from stem to stern*. [=we cleaned the entire ship/boat] — often used figuratively • We cleaned the house *from stem to stern*.
– stem·less /ˈstɛmləs/ *adj* • *stemless* cherries

[2]stem *verb* **stems; stemmed; stem·ming** [+ *obj*] : to remove the stem from (a fruit, leaf, flower, etc.) • She *stemmed* and quartered the figs. • The strawberries need to be *stemmed*.
stem from [*phrasal verb*] ***stem from (something or someone)*** : to be caused by (something or someone) : to come from (something or someone) • Most of her health problems *stem from* an accident she had when she was younger. • His love of the outdoors *stems from* his father.
— compare [3]STEM

[3]stem *verb* **stems; stemmed; stem·ming** [+ *obj*] : to stop the progress or spread of (something) • efforts to *stem* the dramatic decline of an endangered species • The doctor ***stemmed the flow*** of blood by applying pressure to the wound. • Voters hope that the proposition will ***stem the tide*** of illegal immigration. — compare [2]STEM

stem cell *noun, pl* ~ **cells** [*count*] *technical* : a simple cell in the body that is able to develop into any one of various kinds of cells (such as blood cells, skin cells, etc.)

stemmed *adj* : having a stem — usually used in combination • long-*stemmed* roses

stem·ware /ˈstɛmˌweɚ/ *noun* [*noncount*] : drinking glasses that have a long stem between the bowl and the base • crystal *stemware*

stench /ˈstɛntʃ/ *noun* [*singular*] : a very bad smell : STINK • the *stench* of rotting meat — sometimes used figuratively • the *stench* of corruption/fear

[1]sten·cil /ˈstɛnsəl/ *noun, pl* **-cils** [*count*]
1 : a piece of paper, metal, etc., that has a design, letter, etc., cut out of it ✧ You use a stencil by putting it on a flat surface and painting over it so that the design appears on the surface • letter/number/floral *stencils*
2 : a design or a print that is made with a stencil • The walls of the living room had a delicate vine *stencil* drawn on them.

[2]stencil *verb* **-cils**; *US* **-ciled** *or Brit* **-cilled**; *US* **-cil·ing** *or Brit* **-cil·ling** [+ *obj*] : to make a design on something with a stencil : to use a stencil on (something) • We *stenciled* our mailbox with our house number. = We *stenciled* our house number on the mailbox. • We *stenciled* the room's walls.

S

steno /ˈstɛnoʊ/ *noun, pl* **sten·os** *US, informal*
1 [*count*] : STENOGRAPHER
2 [*noncount*] : STENOGRAPHY — often used before another noun • a ***steno pad*** [=a pad of paper used for stenography]

ste·nog·ra·pher /stəˈnɑːgrəfɚ/ *noun, pl* **-phers** [*count*] : a person whose job is to write down the words that someone says by using a special type of writing (called shorthand) • a courtroom *stenographer*

ste·nog·ra·phy /stəˈnɑːgrəfi/ *noun* [*noncount*] : a method used for writing down the words that someone says very quickly by using a special type of writing (called shorthand) • Secretaries must be able to do *stenography*.
– steno·graph·ic /ˌstɛnəˈgræfɪk/ *adj* • *stenographic* notes

stent /ˈstɛnt/ *noun, pl* **stents** [*count*] *medical* : a metal or plastic tube that is put in a blood vessel to keep it open

sten·to·ri·an /stɛnˈtorijən/ *adj* [*more* ~; *most* ~] *literary* : very loud • a *stentorian* voice

[1]step /ˈstɛp/ *noun, pl* **steps**
1 [*count*] **a** : a movement made by lifting your foot and putting it down in a different place • counting our *steps* • She ***took*** one ***step*** forward/backward. • The baby *took* her first *steps* today. • He had to ***retrace his steps*** [=go back along the way he had come] to find his keys. **b** : the sound of a foot making a step : FOOTSTEP • I heard *steps* on the stairs. **c** : the distance covered in one step • The edge of the cliff was only about three *steps* to my left.; *also* : a short distance • The cottage is just *steps* from the beach. **d** : a mark left by a foot or shoe : FOOTPRINT • *steps* in the sand
2 [*singular*] : the way that someone walks • He walks with a spring in his *step*. • She walked down the hall with a quick/light *step*. — see also GOOSE STEP, LOCKSTEP
3 [*count*] : one of a series of actions that are done to achieve something • a major/important *step* towards independence • We are ***taking steps*** to correct the situation. • The court's decision is a ***step backward/forward*** for the reform movement. [=it is something that will hurt/help the reform movement] • Exercise won't solve all your health problems, but it's ***a step in the right direction***. [=it will improve your health] • They're taking ***baby steps***. [=they're doing minor things that produce only a small amount of progress toward achieving something]
4 [*count*] : a stage in a process • We're in the first/intermediate/last *steps* of the negotations. • She's one *step* nearer/closer to graduation. • I want to take it a *step* further. [=I want to move to the next stage in the process] • He was criticized at every *step*. = He was criticized ***every step of the way***. • We'll guide you through the process ***step by step***. • Let's take this ***one step at a time***.
5 [*count*] : a level or rank in a scale • a *step* above/below average • a *step* beyond what was expected • The new job is ***a step up/down*** for her. [=the new job is more/less important, challenging, etc., than the job she had before]
6 [*count*] : the flat piece of wood, stone, etc., that forms one of the levels of a staircase • They sat on the *steps* in front of the house. • The top *step* [=*stair*] squeaks when you step on it. — see picture at HOUSE; see also DOORSTEP
7 [*count*] : a movement or pattern of movements made by someone who is dancing • a ballet *step* • dance *steps*
8 *US, music* : the distance from one tone of a musical scale to the next [*count*] The melody moves up/down a *step*. [*noncount*] The melody moves upward ***by step*** [=in a series of steps] from D to C. — see also HALF STEP, WHOLE STEP
9 [*count*] : a piece of exercise equipment consisting of a small platform that you use by stepping on and off it • Working out with a *step* can be very rigorous. — see also STEP AEROBICS
10 *steps* [*plural*] *Brit* : STEPLADDER
a/one step ahead of **1** : better prepared than (someone or something) • The teacher really has to work to keep *one step ahead of* the class. • She always seems to be *one step ahead of* me. **2** : able to avoid being caught or found by (someone or something) • So far the killer has managed to stay *one step ahead of* the police/law. [=managed to avoid being caught by the police]
break step : to stop walking or marching with the same rhythm as another person or group of people • The soldier was startled and *broke step*.
fall into step : to begin walking or marching with the same rhythm as another person or group of people • He *fell into step beside* her and struck up a conversation.
in step **1** : with the same rhythm as someone or something • They walked *in step* down the avenue. — usually + *with* • We danced *in step with* the music. **2** : matching or agreeing *with* someone or something • She's *in step with* people her age. [=she has the same ideas, problems, etc., as other people her age] • The practice is not *in step with* modern morality.
mind/watch your step **1** : to walk carefully • It's slippery, so *watch your step*. **2** : to speak or behave carefully • You'd better *watch your step* with me, young lady.
out of step **1** : not moving with the same rhythm as someone or something • One of the dancers was *out of step*. **2** : not matching or agreeing with someone or something • Her fashion sense is completely *out of step*. — often + *with* • She's *out of step with* current fashion. • Critics say the rule is ***out of step with the times***. [=the rule does not agree with the ideas that are popular or important now]
– step·like /ˈstɛpˌlaɪk/ *adj* **– stepped** /ˈstɛpt/ *adj* • a *stepped* pyramid [=a pyramid with sides made of steps]

[2]step *verb, always followed by an adverb or preposition* **steps; stepped; step·ping** [*no obj*]
1 : to move in a specified direction by lifting your foot and putting it down in a different place ▪ The sailor *stepped* ashore. ▪ She *stepped* onto/off the bus. ▪ They *stepped* aside/forward/backward to let her pass. ▪ Please *step* away from the door. **:** to move somewhere by walking ▪ He *stepped* outside for a moment. ▪ *Step* in/into my office for a minute.
2 : to put your foot down — usually + *in* or *on* ▪ He accidentally *stepped on* a nail. ▪ She *stepped in* a puddle.
step aside/down [*phrasal verb*] **:** to leave a job or official position ▪ He *stepped down* [=*resigned*] as president. ▪ She'll *step aside* after her replacement is appointed.
step back [*phrasal verb*] **:** to stop doing something or being actively involved in something for a time so that you can think about it and make decisions in a calm and reasonable way ▪ You need to *step back* and give yourself some time to work through this.
step forward [*phrasal verb*] **:** to give or offer help, information, etc. ▪ A witness *stepped forward* to identify the robber.
step in [*phrasal verb*] **:** to become involved in an activity, discussion, etc., in order to prevent trouble or provide help ▪ He *stepped in* and took charge. ▪ She *stepped in* before a fight could start.
step into [*phrasal verb*] ***step into (something)*:** to take a particular role or do a particular task ▪ She *stepped into* the role/position of director. ▪ She's retiring, and it won't be easy to find someone who can ***step into her shoes***. [=*fill her shoes*; who can do her job]
step lively see LIVELY
step on it *or US* ***step on the gas*** *informal* **:** to drive faster ▪ *Step on it*, they're getting away!
step on someone's toes see [1]TOE
step out [*phrasal verb*] *US* **:** to briefly leave a place ▪ I need to *step out* [=*pop out*] for a moment. ▪ She just *stepped out* to get some milk.
step out of line *informal* **:** to disobey rules or behave badly ▪ If you *step out of line*, you'll get kicked off the bus.
step right up *chiefly US* — used to invite people to gather around to see a show or to buy things ▪ *Step right up* [=(*Brit*) *roll up, roll up*] and see the world's greatest magic show!
step up [*phrasal verb*] **1 :** to increase in amount or speed ▪ Production has *stepped up* in recent months. **2 a :** to say openly or publicly that you are the person who should get something or who can do something **:** to come forward ▪ No one yet has *stepped up* to claim responsibility. **b :** to do better **:** to succeed in providing what is needed by making a greater effort, improving your performance, etc. ▪ The team's best player is injured, so someone else needs to *step up*. **3** ***step (something) up*** *or* ***step up (something)*** **a :** to increase the amount or speed of (something) ▪ The company has *stepped up* production. **b :** to improve (something) ▪ The other players need to *step up* their performance. — see also STEP-UP
step up to the plate see [1]PLATE
– step·per /ˈstɛpɚ/ *noun, pl* **-ers** [*count*]

step- *combining form* — used to describe family relationships that are created when a person who already has a child marries someone who is not the child's parent ▪ *step*sister ▪ *step*son ▪ *step*mother ▪ *step*father

step aerobics *noun* [*noncount*] **:** a system of exercise that involves repeatedly stepping on and off a raised platform often while music is playing ▪ a class in *step aerobics* = a *step aerobics* class; *also* [*plural*] **:** exercises in this system ▪ I do *step aerobics* twice a week.

step·broth·er /ˈstɛpˌbrʌðɚ/ *noun, pl* **-ers** [*count*] **:** the son of your stepmother or stepfather

step–by–step /ˌstɛpˌbaɪˈstɛp/ *adj*
1 : showing or explaining each stage in a process ▪ *step-by-step* directions/procedures
2 : happening or done in a series of steps or stages **:** GRADUAL ▪ the *step-by-step* approach to the problem
– step by step *adv* ▪ We're moving ahead with the project slowly, taking it *step by step*. [=*one step at a time*]

step change *noun* [*singular*] *chiefly Brit* **:** an important change in something ▪ There has been a *step change* [=*sea change*] in our understanding of the problem.

step·child /ˈstɛpˌʧajəld/ *noun, pl* **-chil·dren** [*count*]
1 : your wife's or husband's child by a past marriage or relationship **:** a stepson or stepdaughter
2 : someone or something that does not receive enough care or attention ▪ The school has long been the forgotten *stepchild* of the state university system.

step·daugh·ter /ˈstɛpˌdɑːtɚ/ *noun, pl* **-ters** [*count*] **:** your wife's or husband's daughter by a past marriage or relationship

step·fa·ther /ˈstɛpˌfɑːðɚ/ *noun, pl* **-thers** [*count*] **:** a man that your mother marries after her marriage to or relationship with your father has ended

step·lad·der /ˈstɛpˌlædɚ/ *noun, pl* **-ders** [*count*] **:** a ladder that has wide, flat steps and two pairs of legs which are connected at the top and that opens at the bottom so that it can stand without being attached to or supported by something else

stepladder

step·moth·er /ˈstɛpˌmʌðɚ/ *noun, pl* **-ers** [*count*] **:** a woman that your father marries after his marriage to or relationship with your mother has ended

step·par·ent /ˈstɛpˌperənt/ *noun, pl* **-ents** [*count*] **:** someone that your mother or father marries after the marriage to or relationship with your other parent has ended

steppe /ˈstɛp/ *noun, pl* **steppes** [*count*] **:** a large, flat area of land with grass and very few trees especially in eastern Europe and Asia

step·ping–stone /ˈstɛpɪŋˌstoun/ *noun, pl* **-stones** [*count*]
1 : a large, flat stone that you step on to cross a stream
2 : something that helps you get or achieve something ▪ He regarded his first job as a *stepping-stone* to a better career.

step·sis·ter /ˈstɛpˌsɪstɚ/ *noun, pl* **-ters** [*count*] **:** the daughter of your stepmother or stepfather

step·son /ˈstɛpˌsʌn/ *noun, pl* **-sons** [*count*] **:** your wife's or husband's son by a past marriage or relationship

step stool *noun, pl* **~ stools** [*count*] **:** a usually short stool with one or two steps

step–up /ˈstɛpˌʌp/ *noun, pl* **-ups** [*count*] **:** an increase in size or amount ▪ a *step-up* in production — see also ***step up*** at [2]STEP

-ster /stɚ/ *noun combining form*
1 : someone who does or handles or operates something ▪ team*ster*
2 : someone who makes or uses something ▪ song*ster* ▪ prank*ster*
3 : someone who is associated with or participates in something ▪ gang*ster*
4 : someone who has a specified quality ▪ young*ster*

[1]ste·reo /ˈsterijou/ *noun, pl* **-reos**
1 [*count*] **:** a piece of electronic equipment that plays the radio, CDs, etc., and that uses two speakers for the sound — see picture at LIVING ROOM
2 [*noncount*] **:** a way of recording and playing back sound so that the sound comes from two directions ▪ broadcasting ***in stereo*** — compare MONO

[2]stereo *adj* **:** of or relating to a system that directs sound through two speakers ▪ *stereo* headphones/equipment

ste·reo·phon·ic /ˌsterijəˈfɑːnɪk/ *adj* **:** [2]STEREO ▪ *stereophonic* sound

ste·reo·scope /ˈsterijəˌskoup/ *noun, pl* **-scopes** [*count*] **:** a device that is used for viewing stereoscopic images

ster·eo·scop·ic /ˌsterijəˈskɑːpɪk/ *adj*
1 — used to describe an image that appears to have depth and solidness and that is created by using a special device (called a stereoscope) to look at two slightly different photographs of something at the same time ▪ *stereoscopic* images/photographs
2 *technical* **:** able to see depth and solidness ▪ normal *stereoscopic* vision

[1]ste·reo·type /ˈsterijəˌtaɪp/ *noun, pl* **-types** [*count*] **:** an often unfair and untrue belief that many people have about all people or things with a particular characteristic ▪ racial/cultural *stereotypes* ▪ the *stereotype* of the absentminded professor
– ste·reo·typ·i·cal /ˌsterijəˈtɪpɪkəl/ *adj* [*more ~; most ~*] ▪ a *stereotypical* representation/idea/approach ▪ He's the *stereotypical* absentminded professor. [=he's a professor who is absentminded in the way that people often think of professors as being] **– ste·reo·typ·i·cal·ly** /ˌsterijəˈtɪpɪkli/ *adv*

S

[2]**stereotype** *verb* **-types; -typed; -typ·ing** [+ *obj*] : to believe unfairly that all people or things with a particular characteristic are the same • It's not fair to *stereotype* a whole group of people based on one person you don't like.
– **stereotyped** /ˈsterijəˌtaɪpt/ *adj* • a *stereotyped* representation/approach/character • *stereotyped* roles
– **stereotyping** *noun* [*noncount*] • ethnic/gender *stereotyping*

ster·ile /ˈsterəl, *Brit* ˈstɛˌrajəl/ *adj* [*more* ~; *most* ~]
1 : not able to produce crops or plants • *sterile* soil/fields
2 a : not able to produce children, young animals, etc. • Mules are *sterile*. • *sterile* offspring **b** : not able to grow or develop • *sterile* eggs
3 : clean and free of bacteria and germs • a *sterile* dressing for a wound • *sterile* needles
4 : not producing or containing new ideas, useful results, etc. • a *sterile* debate/subject
5 : very plain and not interesting or attractive • a *sterile* building/room
– **ste·ril·i·ty** /stəˈrɪləti/ *noun* [*noncount*] • a disease that causes *sterility* • emotional/creative *sterility*

ster·il·ize *also Brit* **ster·il·ise** /ˈsterəˌlaɪz/ *verb* **-iz·es; -ized; -iz·ing** [+ *obj*]
1 : to clean (something) by destroying germs or bacteria • *sterilize* the dental instruments
2 : to make (someone or something) unable to produce children, young animals, etc. • The organization encourages people to *sterilize* their cats and dogs.
– **ster·il·i·za·tion** *also Brit* **ster·il·i·sa·tion** /ˌsterələˈzeɪʃən, *Brit* ˌstɛrəˌlaɪˈzeɪʃən/ *noun, pl* **-tions** [*count, noncount*]
– **ster·il·iz·er** *also Brit* **ster·il·is·er** /ˈsterəˌlaɪzə/ *noun, pl* **-ers** [*count*]

[1]**ster·ling** /ˈstəlɪŋ/ *noun* [*noncount*]
1 : silver that is 92 percent pure — called also *sterling silver*
2 : British money • a drop in the value of *sterling* — see also POUND STERLING

[2]**sterling** *adj*
1 : made of silver that is 92 percent pure • a *sterling* bracelet
2 *always used before a noun* : very good : EXCELLENT • *sterling* ideas/work • a *sterling* example of democracy at work

[1]**stern** /ˈstən/ *adj* **stern·er; -est**
1 a : very serious especially in an unfriendly way • a *stern* judge • a *stern* warning **b** : expressing strong disapproval or criticism • He gave me a *stern* look.
2 : not likely to change or become weaker • *stern* determination/resolve
be made of sterner stuff : to be an emotionally and morally strong person with more determination than other people • Another woman would have broken down, but she *is made of sterner stuff*.
– **stern·ly** *adv* • "No running in the house," he said *sternly*.
– **stern·ness** /ˈstənnəs/ *noun* [*noncount*]

[2]**stern** *noun, pl* **sterns** [*count*] : the back part of a boat or ship — see picture at BOAT; opposite [3]BOW
from stem to stern see [1]STEM

ster·num /ˈstənəm/ *noun, pl* **-nums** [*count*] *technical* : BREASTBONE

ste·roid /ˈstɛˌroɪd/ *noun, pl* **-roids** [*count*]
1 : a natural substance that is produced in the body
2 : ANABOLIC STEROID • a *steroid* user/abuser • He was accused of taking/using *steroids*.
on steroids 1 : using anabolic steroids • There were many rumors that she was *on steroids*. 2 *US, informal + humorous* : very large or impressive • a cookie *on steroids* [=a very large cookie]

stetho·scope /ˈstɛθəˌskoup/ *noun, pl* **-scopes** [*count*] *medical* : an instrument that is used for listening to someone's heart or lungs

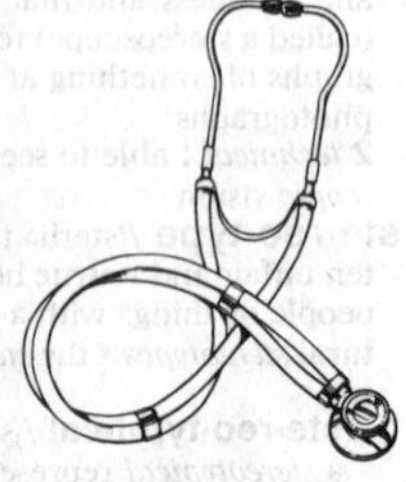
stethoscope

Stet·son /ˈstetsən/ *trademark* — used for a somewhat tall hat with a wide brim

ste·ve·dore /ˈstiːvəˌdoə/ *noun, pl* **-dores** [*count*] : a person whose job is to load and unload ships at a port : LONGSHOREMAN

[1]**stew** /ˈstuː, *Brit* ˈstjuː/ *noun, pl* **stews** : a dish of vegetables and usually meat cooked in hot liquid for a long time [*count*] I cooked/made a *stew* for dinner. [*noncount*] Would you like some *stew*?
in a stew *informal* : excited, worried, or confused • He got himself *in a stew* over nothing. • She's been *in a stew* for days.

[2]**stew** *verb* **stews; stewed; stew·ing**
1 : to cook (something) slowly in hot liquid [+ *obj*] *stewing* the meat [*no obj*] The meat still needs to *stew*. • a can of *stewed* tomatoes
2 [*no obj*] : to be upset or worried • She's been *stewing* over/about what he said for days.
stew in your own juice/juices *informal* : to worry and suffer because of something that you did • Let him *stew in his own juices* for a while.

stew·ard /ˈstuːwəd, *Brit* ˈstjuːwəd/ *noun, pl* **-ards** [*count*]
1 : a person and especially a man whose job is to serve meals and take care of passengers on a train, airplane, or ship — compare FLIGHT ATTENDANT
2 a : someone who protects or is responsible for money, property, etc. • the *steward* of their investments • teaching our children to be good *stewards* of the land **b** : a person whose job is to manage the land and property of another person • the *steward* of the estate — called also (*Brit*) *bailiff*
3 *chiefly Brit* : someone who is in charge of a race, contest, or other public event • The race *stewards* are reviewing the results.
– see also SHOP STEWARD, WINE STEWARD

stew·ard·ess /ˈstuːwədəs, *Brit* ˈstjuːwədəs/ *noun, pl* **-ess·es** [*count*] *somewhat old-fashioned* : a woman whose job is to serve meals and take care of passengers on a train, airplane, or ship — compare FLIGHT ATTENDANT

stew·ard·ship /ˈstuːwədˌʃɪp, *Brit* ˈstjuːwədˌʃɪp/ *noun* [*noncount*] : the activity or job of protecting and being responsible for something — usually + *of* • the *stewardship of* their investments/estate • the *stewardship of* our natural resources

[1]**stick** /ˈstɪk/ *noun, pl* **sticks**
1 [*count*] : a cut or broken branch or twig • They collected dry *sticks* for the campfire. • a pile of *sticks*
2 [*count*] **a** : a long, thin piece of wood, metal, plastic, etc., that is used for a particular purpose • He served pieces of fruit on *sticks*. • a candied apple on a *stick* • a measuring/hiking *stick* — see also BROOMSTICK, CHOPSTICK, DIPSTICK, DRUMSTICK, WALKING STICK, YARDSTICK **b** : a long, thin object that is used for hitting or moving a ball or puck in a game • a hockey/lacrosse *stick* **c** : a stick that is used as a weapon • You know the old saying: "*Sticks* and stones may break my bones, but words/names can/will never hurt me." — often used figuratively in British English • The minister's inappropriate comments gave his opponents a new *stick* with which to beat him. — see also NIGHTSTICK
3 [*count*] **a** : something that is long and thin like a stick • He has *sticks* for legs. • cinnamon/carrot/celery *sticks* — often + *of* • a *stick of* dynamite — see also FISH STICK, MATCHSTICK, POGO STICK **b** : a long piece *of* something that is usually wrapped in paper, plastic, etc. • a *stick of* gum/butter **c** : a solid substance that is sold in a tall container which is open at the top • a glue *stick* • a *stick* of deodorant — see also LIPSTICK
4 [*count*] **a** : JOYSTICK • The pilot pulled back on the *stick*. **b** : STICK SHIFT • Does your car have a *stick*?
5 ***the sticks*** *informal* : an area in the country that is far away from towns and cities • We live way out in *the sticks*. [=*the boonies, the boondocks*]
6 [*count*] *informal* : punishment or the threat of punishment that is used to try to persuade someone to do something ✧ This sense of *stick* is often contrasted with *carrot*, which refers to the reward or advantage someone will get if they do something. • She'll have to choose between the *carrot* and the *stick*. • They say that a *carrot* works better than a *stick*. • The administration was criticized for its ***carrot-and-stick*** approach to foreign policy.
7 [*noncount*] *Brit, informal* : CRITICISM • I gave him a lot of *stick* [=*flak*] for his mistake.
get on the stick *US, informal* : to start working hard at something that you have been avoiding doing • You'd better *get on the stick* with those college applications!
more than you can shake a stick at see [1]SHAKE
stick to beat someone with or ***stick with which to beat someone*** *Brit, informal* : something that is used to attack or punish someone or to make an attack or punishment seem reasonable or right • The fee is just another *stick with which to beat the unions*. • These charges have given her opponents a new *stick to beat her with*.
the short end of the stick *chiefly US, informal* : unfair or

unfavorable treatment • She got *the short end of the stick* in the deal.

the wrong end of the stick *chiefly Brit, informal* : an incorrect understanding of something • You've got (hold of) *the wrong end of the stick.* He didn't push me; I fell.

up sticks *Brit, informal* : to pack up your belongings and move to a different place • They *upped sticks* and left for London.

— see also BIG STICK, CANDLESTICK, SLAPSTICK

[2]**stick** *verb* **sticks; stuck** /ˈstʌk/; **stick·ing**

1 *always followed by an adverb or preposition* **a** [+ *obj*] : to push (something usually sharp or pointed) into something • He *stuck* a toothpick in/into the sandwich. • The jacket was too thick to *stick* a pin through. • The nurse *stuck* the needle into the patient's leg. • *Stick* these candles in the birthday cake. **b** [*no obj*] *of something usually sharp or pointed* : to go partly into something • The thorn *stuck* in the dog's paw. • The spears *stuck* into the ground. : to have a part that has been pushed into something : to be partly inside something • The victim was found with a knife *sticking* out of her back. • darts *sticking* out of the wall • I saw a letter *sticking* (out) from his pocket. = I saw a letter *sticking* out of his pocket.

2 *always followed by an adverb or preposition* [+ *obj*] *informal* : to put (something or someone) in a specified place • He *stuck* [=*tucked*] the pencil behind his ear. • The dog *stuck* its head out the window. • She *stuck* [=*pushed*] the letter under the door. • She *stuck* [=*reached*] her hand into the box and pulled out a piece of paper. • The librarian *stuck* [=*put*] the book back on its shelf. • The little girl *stuck* her fingers in the batter. • The photographer *stuck* the shorter people in the front row. • The deer *stuck* its nose up in the air. • He pointed the gun at me and said "***stick 'em up***." [=put your hands up in the air]

3 a *always used before an adverb or preposition* [+ *obj*] *informal* : to attach (something) to a surface with glue, tape, pins, etc. • She *stuck* two stamps on the letter. • He *stuck* a note (up) on the door. • She *stuck* the pieces of wood together with glue. **b** [*no obj*] : to become attached to the surface of something • The suction cup wouldn't *stick.* • Several pages had *stuck* together. • Spray the pan with oil to keep the biscuits from *sticking.* — often + *to* • The peanut butter *stuck to* the knife. • Magnets *stick to* steel. • The glue had *stuck to* her fingers.

4 [*no obj*] : to become difficult or impossible to move from a place or position • The door's handle has a tendency to *stick.* • That door always *sticks.* • Her foot *stuck* in the mud. • A piece of food *stuck* [=*lodged*] in her throat. — often used figuratively • His words ***stuck in my mind***. [=I remembered his words] • One of the kids called him "Stretch," and ***the name stuck***. [=everyone started calling him "Stretch"] • You can charge them with fraud, but you'll need more evidence if you want to ***make it stick***. [=if you want them to be legally punished for fraud]

5 [+ *obj*] *Brit, informal* : to deal with or accept (an unpleasant situation, experience, person, etc.) : STAND — usually used in questions and negative statements with *can, can't, cannot, could*, and *couldn't* • He *couldn't stick* the new job. • How *can* you *stick* being there all the time? • She *can't stick* his friends. [=she strongly dislikes his friends]

stick around [*phrasal verb*] *informal* : to stay somewhere especially in order to wait for something or someone • *Stick around.* The band should start playing soon. • If you *stick around*, you can meet my girlfriend.

stick at it *Brit, informal* : to continue doing or trying to do something • If you *stick at it* [=*keep at it*] long enough, you'll succeed.

stick at nothing *Brit, informal* : to be willing to do anything in order to get or achieve something • She'll *stick at nothing* [=*stop at nothing*] to get what she wants.

stick a toe in the water see [1]TOE

stick by [*phrasal verb*] ***stick by (someone or something)*** : to continue to support or be loyal to (someone or something) • The troops *stuck by* [=*stood by*] their general to the end. • She *stuck by* [=*stood by*] her husband throughout the trial. • I *stick by* my promise. [=I still will do what I promised] • He *stuck by* what he said earlier.

stick in your craw see CRAW

stick it to (someone) *US, informal* : to treat (someone) harshly or unfairly especially in order to get something for yourself (such as revenge or money) • Her political rivals used the scandal as an opportunity to *stick it to* her. • businesses that *stick it to* consumers by charging high fees • The government is really *sticking it to* the taxpayers.

stick like glue *informal* **1** : to stay very firmly attached to something • Wash the egg off before it dries, or it will *stick like glue.* — often used figuratively • One of the kids called him "Stretch," and the nickname *stuck* (to him) *like glue.* [=everyone started calling him by that nickname] **2** : to stay very close to someone • Her dog always *stuck* to her *like glue.* • The two friends *stick* (together) *like glue.*

stick out [*phrasal verb*] **1** : to extend outward beyond an edge or surface • His ears *stick out.* [=they extend outward more than most people's ears] • A peninsula *sticks out* from the shore into the bay. **2** ***stick out (something) or stick (something) out*** : to extend (something, such as a body part) outward • She said "hello," and *stuck* her hand *out.* • He *stuck out* his chest and walked away. • She was sitting with her feet *stuck out* in the aisle. • *Stick out* your tongue and say "ah." **3** : to be easily seen or recognized • You will certainly *stick out* [=*stand out*] with that orange hat. **4** : to be better or more important than the other people or things in a group in a way that is easily seen or noticed • Only one contestant really *sticks out* [=*stands out*] in my mind. • Two facts *stick out* from her testimony. **5** ***stick out (something) or stick (something) out informal*** : to continue doing (something unpleasant or difficult) • She *stuck* the job *out* for the remainder of the summer. • Though the home team was down by 20 points, a few fans ***stuck it out*** [=stayed and watched the game] until the very end. **6** ***stick out for (something)*** *Brit, informal* : to refuse to accept or agree to something in order to get (something) • The strikers are *sticking out for* [=*holding out for*] higher pay.

stick out like a sore thumb see [1]SORE

stick to [*phrasal verb*] ***stick to (something)*** : to continue doing or using (something) especially when it is difficult to do so • She *stuck to* her story about the money already being missing when she got there. • Please *stick to* the script/subject/rules. • *Stick to* the marked trails. • If you want to succeed, you've got to ***stick to it***! [=keep trying, working, etc.] : to not change (a decision, belief, etc.) • I intend to *stick to* my promise/word. • She's *sticking to* her decision to retire.

stick together *informal* : to continue to support each other • Families need to *stick together.*

stick to your guns see [1]GUN

stick two fingers up at see [1]FINGER

stick up [*phrasal verb*] **1** : to extend upward above a surface • The baby's hair *sticks* (straight) *up.* • A large rock was *sticking up* in the middle of the river. **2** ***stick up for (someone)*** *informal* : to defend (someone) against attack or criticism • He *stuck up for* his friend. • She *stuck up for* herself. — see also STICKUP

stick with [*phrasal verb*] *informal* **1** ***stick with (something)*** : to continue using or doing (something) • You need to find a job and *stick with* it. • I'll *stick with* my usual brand. : to not change (a decision, belief, etc.) • The company is *sticking with* its decision to close the store. **2** ***stick (someone) with (something or someone)*** : to force (someone) to deal with (something or someone unpleasant) • They always *stick* me *with* the bill. [=make me pay the bill] • The teacher always *sticks* me *with* Tom. — often used as ***(be/get) stuck with*** • I *was stuck with* washing dishes. • I *got stuck with* Tom again. **3** ***stick with (someone)*** **a** : to stay close to (someone) in a race or competition • The challenger *stuck with* the champion until the very last round. **b** : to stay near (someone) in order to gain knowledge, protection, etc. • *Stick with* me, kid, and you'll learn something! **c** : to be remembered by someone for a very long time • The lessons she learned from that experience *stuck with* her.

stick your head above the parapet see PARAPET

stick your neck out see [1]NECK

stick your nose in/into see [1]NOSE

stick your oar in see OAR

— see also STUCK

stick·ball /ˈstɪkˌbɑːl/ *noun* [*noncount*] *US* : a game like baseball that is played on the street or in a small area with a stick (such as a broomstick) and ball

stick·er /ˈstɪkɚ/ *noun, pl* **-ers** [*count*] : a piece of paper with a picture or writing on it and a sticky substance on its back that is used to attach it to a surface — see also BUMPER STICKER

sticker price *noun, pl* **~ prices** [*count*] *US* : the price of a vehicle that is suggested by the manufacturer and that is shown on a sticker which is attached to the vehicle • We managed to negotiate 15 percent off the *sticker price*; *also* : the stated price of something • The speakers are excellent and well worth the *sticker price.*

S

sticker shock *noun* [*noncount*] *US* : a feeling of surprise and disappointment caused by learning that something you want to buy is very expensive • We left the store suffering severe *sticker shock*.

stick figure *noun, pl* ~ **-ures** [*count*] : a drawing that shows the head of a person or animal as a circle and all other parts as usually straight lines

stick·han·dling /ˈstɪkˌhændlɪŋ/ *noun* [*noncount*] *sports* : the use of a stick to control a puck or ball • a hockey player who is skilled at *stickhandling*

sticking plaster *noun, pl* ~ **-ters** [*count*] *Brit* : a piece of material that is put on your skin over a small cut or wound : PLASTER

sticking point *noun, pl* ~ **points** [*count*] : something that people disagree about and that prevents progress from being made in discussions • The length of the contract has become a *sticking point* in the negotiations.

stick insect *noun, pl* ~ **-sects** [*count*] : an insect with a long, thin body that looks like a stick — called also (*US*) *walking stick*

stick–in–the–mud /ˈstɪkənðəˌmʌd/ *noun, pl* **stick–in–the–muds** [*count*] *informal* + *disapproving* : someone who has old-fashioned ideas or who does not like trying new or exciting things • He's just an old *stick-in-the-mud*.

stick·ler /ˈstɪkələ/ *noun, pl* **-lers** [*count*] : a person who believes that something is very important and should be done or followed all the time • an etiquette *stickler* — usually + *for* • a *stickler for* proper etiquette • He's a *stickler for* the rules.

stick–on *adj, always used before a noun* : having a sticky substance on one side for attaching to something • *stick-on* labels

stick·pin /ˈstɪkˌpɪn/ *noun, pl* **-pins** [*count*] *US* : a decorative pin that is worn on a jacket or used to hold the ends of a necktie in place

stick shift *noun, pl* ~ **shifts** [*count*] *US*
1 : a device in a car that you move into different positions in order to change the car's gears — called also *stick*; compare GEARSHIFT
2 : a car that has a stick shift : MANUAL • Do you know how to drive a *stick shift*? — called also *stick*

stick–to–it·ive·ness /stɪkˈtuːwətɪvnəs/ *noun* [*noncount*] *US, informal* : the quality that allows someone to continue trying to do something even though it is difficult or unpleasant • I admire her *stick-to-itiveness*. [=*perseverance, tenacity*]

stick·up /ˈstɪkˌʌp/ *noun, pl* **-ups** [*count*] *US, informal* : a robbery that is done using a gun : HOLDUP • He pulled out a gun and shouted, "This is a *stickup*!" — see also *stick up* at [2]STICK

stick·work /ˈstɪkˌwək/ *noun* [*noncount*] *sports* : the use of a stick to control a puck or ball • a hockey player who's known for his skillful/fancy *stickwork*

sticky /ˈstɪki/ *adj* **stick·i·er; -est**
1 : having a substance (such as glue or honey) on it that things easily attach to : covered in a substance that things stick to • My fingers are *sticky*. • *sticky* hands • The floor is *sticky*.
2 *of a substance* : tending to have things attach to it : tending to have things stick to it • The sap is very *sticky*. • There is a *sticky* substance on the table. • The paint was still *sticky*.
3 *informal* : unpleasantly warm and humid • It's *sticky* outside. • a *sticky* summer afternoon • The weather was ***hot and sticky***.
4 *informal* : difficult or unpleasant • It's a *sticky* [=*tricky*] situation.
– stick·i·ness /ˈstɪkinəs/ *noun* [*noncount*] • The tape has lost its *stickiness*.

sticky bun *noun, pl* ~ **buns** [*count*] *chiefly US* : a usually round sweet cake made with cinnamon and topped with melted brown sugar and butter

sticky fingers *noun* [*noncount*] *informal* : a tendency to steal things • people with *sticky fingers* • She's known for having *sticky fingers*.

sticky note *noun, pl* ~ **notes** [*count*] : a small piece of paper that has a strip of a sticky substance on the back so that it can be attached to a surface — see picture at OFFICE

sticky–sweet *adj, chiefly US, informal* : extremely sweet : too sweet • *sticky-sweet* caramel • a *sticky-sweet* smell • a love song full of *sticky-sweet* sentiment

sticky tape *noun* [*noncount*] *Brit* : a type of clear tape that is used for sticking things (such as pieces of paper) together : clear adhesive tape • a roll of *sticky tape*

sticky wicket *noun* [*singular*] *Brit, informal* : a difficult situation • It's a bit of a *sticky wicket*. • She was ***on a sticky wicket*** when she saw her friend steal the fund-raiser money.

[1]**stiff** /ˈstɪf/ *adj* **stiff·er; -est** [*also more* ~; *most* ~]
1 a : difficult to bend or move • *stiff* valves/cardboard/fabric • *stiff* hairs/bristles • The brush was ***as stiff as a board***. [=very stiff] **b** : painful to move or use • *stiff* muscles • a *stiff* back/neck • When I got out of bed this morning my back was *stiff as a board*.; *also* : showing pain in movement or use • a *stiff* walk
2 : thick and difficult to stir or pour • Beat the egg whites until they are *stiff*. • *stiff* batter
3 : difficult, strict, or severe • a *stiff* [=*heavy*] penalty/fine • a *stiff* task/challenge • *stiff* competition
4 : not graceful, relaxed, or friendly • Our host seemed somewhat *stiff*. • a *stiff* manner : too formal • *stiff* writing/dialogue
5 : very expensive • a *stiff* price
6 : strong and forceful • a *stiff* wind/breeze • The troops encountered *stiff* resistance.
7 : containing a lot of alcohol • a *stiff* drink/cocktail
stiff upper lip : a calm and determined attitude in a difficult situation • She managed to ***keep a stiff upper lip*** even as everything fell apart.
– stiff·ly *adv* • "Excuse me," he said *stiffly*. **– stiff·ness** *noun* [*noncount*]

[2]**stiff** *adv, informal* : very much : to an extreme degree • She was ***scared/bored stiff***.
frozen stiff **1** : completely stiff because of being wet and frozen • The shirt was *frozen stiff*. **2** *informal* : extremely cold • We were *frozen stiff* by the time we got indoors.

[3]**stiff** *noun, pl* **stiffs** [*count*] *informal*
1 : the body of a dead person
2 *US* **a** : a person who you think is lucky, unlucky, etc. • You lucky *stiff*! • That poor *stiff* never gets a break. **b** : an ordinary or dull person • (*disapproving*) He's OK but his friends are a bunch of *stiffs*. • They have the kind of luxuries the average ***working stiff*** can't afford.

[4]**stiff** *verb* **stiffs; stiffed; stiff·ing** [+ *obj*] *US, informal* : to not give as much money as you should give to (someone) • He *stiffed* the waiter on the tip. [=he didn't give the waiter a tip or he gave a tip that was too small]

stiff–arm /ˈstɪfˌɑəm/ *noun, pl* **-arms** [*count*] *American football* : STRAIGHT-ARM
– stiff–arm *verb* **-arms; -armed; -arm·ing** [+ *obj*] • The ball-carrier *stiff-armed* the tackler.

stiff·en /ˈstɪfən/ *verb* **-ens; -ened; -en·ing**
1 [*no obj*] : to stop moving and become completely still especially because of fear, anger, etc. • She *stiffened* when he grabbed her shoulder. • The dogs *stiffened* in alarm.
2 [*no obj*] : to become painful to move or use — often + *up* • My muscles *stiffened up* the next day.
3 : to become more severe or strong or to make (something) more severe or strong [*no obj*] The wind *stiffened*. • His resolve has *stiffened*. [+ *obj*] He *stiffened* his resolve. • The law would *stiffen* penalties for tax evasion.
4 [+ *obj*] : to make (something, such as cloth) difficult to bend or move • *stiffen* a shirt with starch
– stiff·en·er /ˈstɪfənə/ *noun, pl* **-ers** [*count*]

stiff–necked /ˈstɪfˈnɛkt/ *adj* [*more* ~; *most* ~] *disapproving* : very proud and formal • a *stiff-necked* military man • *stiff-necked* arrogance • She's too *stiff-necked* to ask for help.

sti·fle /ˈstaɪfəl/ *verb* **sti·fles; stifled; sti·fling**
1 [+ *obj*] **a** : to not allow yourself to do or express (something) • trying to *stifle* a cry/yawn • I had to *stifle* the desire/urge to yell "Stop!" **b** : to stop (someone) from doing or expressing something • Students at the school are *stifled* by the pressure to score high on tests.
2 [+ *obj*] : to make (something) difficult or impossible • Too many regulations *stifle* innovation. • something that *stifles* the growth of the plant/economy
3 a [*no obj*] : to be unable to breathe easily • I wish we could go outside instead of *stifling* in this tiny room. **b** [+ *obj*] : to make (someone) unable to breathe or unable to breathe easily • He was almost *stifled* by the smoke.

stifling *adj* [*more* ~; *most* ~]
1 : making it difficult to breathe • The heat was *stifling*. : very hot and humid • a *stifling* day
2 : not allowing something to be done or expressed • *stifling* rules/regulations/requirements • a *stifling* relationship [=a relationship that prevents someone from behaving freely, expressing emotion, etc.]

– stifling *adv* ▪ The weather was ***stifling hot***. [=very hot] **– sti·fling·ly** *adv* ▪ *stiflingly* hot

stig·ma /ˈstɪgmə/ *noun, pl* **-mas**
1 [*singular*] **:** a set of negative and often unfair beliefs that a society or group of people have about something ▪ the *stigma* associated with mental illness = the *stigma* of mental illness ▪ the *stigma* of being poor = the *stigma* of poverty ▪ There's a ***social stigma*** attached to receiving welfare.
2 [*count*] *botany* **:** the top part in the center of a flower which receives the pollen

stig·ma·ta /stɪgˈmɑːtə/ *noun* [*plural*] **:** marks on someone's hands and feet which resemble Jesus Christ's wounds from being nailed on the cross

stig·ma·tize *also Brit* **stig·ma·tise** /ˈstɪgməˌtaɪz/ *verb* **-tiz·es; -tized; -tiz·ing** [+ *obj*] *usually disapproving* **:** to describe or regard (something, such as a characteristic or group of people) in a way that shows strong disapproval ▪ Society *stigmatizes* welfare recipients. ▪ a legal system that *stigmatizes* juveniles as criminals
– stig·ma·ti·za·tion *also Brit* **stig·ma·ti·sa·tion** /ˌstɪgmətəˈzeɪʃən, *Brit* ˌstɪgməˌtaɪˈzeɪʃən/ *noun* [*noncount*]

stile /ˈstajəl/ *noun, pl* **stiles** [*count*] **:** a set of steps to help people climb over a fence or wall

sti·let·to /stəˈlɛtoʊ/ *noun, pl* **-tos** *or* **-toes** [*count*]
1 a : a woman's shoe with a very high, thin heel ▪ a pair of *stilettos* [=*spikes, spike heels*] **b :** the heel of a stiletto — called also *spike heel*
2 : a knife with a thin, pointed blade

[1]still /ˈstɪl/ *adv*
1 : happening or existing before now and continuing into the present — used to say that an action or condition continues ▪ He *still* lives there. [=he continues to live there] ▪ It's *still* early/cold/Tuesday. ▪ She's *still* mad about what happened yesterday. ▪ Eat your soup while it's *still* hot. [=while it continues to be hot; before it cools]
2 : in spite of that — used to say that something happens or is true even though there is something that might prevent it from happening or being true ▪ Careful people can *still* make mistakes. ▪ I tried again and *still* I failed.
3 : without moving **:** without motion ▪ Sit *still*. It'll just take a minute. ▪ She stood very *still*.
4 : to a greater extent or degree — used to add force to words like *more, better, bigger,* etc. ▪ a *still* more difficult problem = a problem that is more difficult *still* ▪ *still* bigger/better/longer
5 : in addition — used for emphasis ▪ He won *still* [=*yet*] another tournament. ▪ *still* more complications
jury is still out see JURY
still less see [2]LESS

[2]still *adj*
1 a : not moving ▪ *still* water ▪ The cat twitched slightly, and then was *still*. — see also STOCK-STILL **b :** lacking motion or activity ▪ Everyone had left, and the house was finally *still*. ▪ a hot, *still* day [=a day without wind]
2 *photography* **a** — used to describe an ordinary photograph that does not show movement as compared to a movie ▪ *still* photographs **b :** relating to or used for still photographs ▪ a class in *still* photography ▪ a *still* camera
3 *chiefly Brit, of a liquid* **:** not having bubbles ▪ They had *still* and fizzy drinks. ▪ *still* wine
still waters run deep — used to say that people who are quiet or shy are often very intelligent and interesting
– still·ness *noun* [*noncount*]

[3]still *verb* **stills; stilled; still·ing** *literary*
1 [+ *obj*] **:** to make (something) less severe or strong ▪ Her reassuring words *stilled* our fears/apprehensions.
2 : to become still or to make (something) still **:** to stop moving or to cause (something) to stop moving [*no obj*] The water *stilled* at last. [+ *obj*] river waters *stilled* by dams
3 [+ *obj*] **:** to stop (something) from continuing ▪ The report has not *stilled* debate about whether the procedure is safe.

[4]still *noun, pl* **stills**
1 [*noncount*] *literary* **:** quiet or silence ▪ the *still* of late evening ▪ the *still* of the deep woods
2 [*count*] **:** PHOTOGRAPH; *specifically* **:** a photograph of actors or scenes from a movie ▪ a series of *stills* from the movie
the still of the night *literary* **:** the time late at night when it is very quiet and dark
– compare [5]STILL

[5]still *noun, pl* **stills** [*count*] **:** a piece of equipment that is used for making strong alcoholic drinks ▪ a whisky *still* — compare [4]STILL

still·birth /ˈstɪlˌbɚθ/ *noun, pl* **-births** [*count*] **:** the birth of a dead baby

still·born /ˈstɪlˈboən/ *adj*
1 *of a baby* **:** dead at birth
2 : never able to begin operating or proceeding ▪ The plan was *stillborn*. [=the plan had failed even before it had begun to be used]

still life *noun, pl* **~ lifes** [*count*] **:** a painting, drawing, etc., of a carefully arranged group of objects (such as flowers and fruit) ▪ an exhibit of *still lifes*; *also* [*noncount*] **:** the art or activity of making still lifes ▪ She prefers portraiture to *still life*.

stilt /ˈstɪlt/ *noun, pl* **stilts** [*count*]
1 : one of a set of upright posts that are used to hold a building up above water or the ground
2 : one of a pair of long poles with platforms for your feet that you can stand on to walk high above the ground ▪ a circus performer walking on *stilts*

stilts

stilt·ed /ˈstɪltəd/ *adj* **:** awkward especially because of being too formal ▪ a *stilted* speech ▪ *stilted* dialogue/language

stim·u·lant /ˈstɪmjələnt/ *noun, pl* **-lants** [*count*]
1 : something (such as a drug) that makes you more active or gives you more energy ▪ Caffeine is a *stimulant*.
2 : something that causes more activity **:** STIMULUS ▪ The movie was a *stimulant* to discussion.

stim·u·late /ˈstɪmjəˌleɪt/ *verb* **-lates; -lat·ed; -lat·ing** [+ *obj*]
1 : to make (something) more active ▪ Caffeine *stimulates* the heart. **:** to cause or encourage (something) to happen or develop ▪ A raise in employee wages might *stimulate* production. ▪ The economy was not *stimulated* by the tax cuts. ▪ a hormone that *stimulates* the growth of muscle tissue
2 : to make (a person) excited or interested in something ▪ Their discussion *stimulated* him to research the subject more. ▪ He was *stimulated* by their discussion.
– stim·u·la·tion /ˌstɪmjəˈleɪʃən/ *noun* [*noncount*] ▪ physical/intellectual/sexual *stimulation*

stimulating *adj* [*more ~; most ~*]
1 : exciting or interesting ▪ a *stimulating* conversation ▪ a *stimulating* environment for studying
2 : causing someone to become more energetic or alert ▪ the *stimulating* effects of caffeine

stim·u·lus /ˈstɪmjələs/ *noun, pl* **stim·u·li** /ˈstɪmjəˌlaɪ/ [*count*]
1 : something that causes something else to happen, develop, or become more active ▪ The pay raise was a *stimulus* for production. ▪ an economic *stimulus* plan
2 : something that causes a change or a reaction ▪ Heat and light are physical *stimuli*. ▪ The dog responded to the *stimulus* of the ringing bell.

[1]sting /ˈstɪŋ/ *verb* **stings; stung** /ˈstʌŋ/; **sting·ing**
1 *of an insect, plant, or animal* **:** to hurt (someone) by piercing the skin with a sharp, pointed part that usually contains poison [+ *obj*] I got *stung* by a bee. ▪ The jellyfish *stung* the swimmer. [*no obj*] The bees will *sting* if you bother them.
2 : to cause a quick, sharp pain [*no obj*] The iodine will *sting* for a few minutes. [+ *obj*] The cold rain *stung* my eyes.
3 a [*no obj*] **:** to feel a quick sharp pain ▪ The smoke made our eyes *sting*. **b** *not used in progressive tenses* **:** to cause (someone) to feel emotional or mental pain [+ *obj*] She was *stung* by their harsh criticism. ▪ His words *stung* her. [*no obj*] Your comment *stung*.
4 [+ *obj*] *informal* **:** to treat (someone) unfairly in a business deal — usually used as *(be/get) stung* ▪ He *got stung* on that deal.
sting for [*phrasal verb*] ***sting (someone) for (something)*** *Brit, informal* **:** to ask (someone) to give or lend you (something) ▪ Can I *sting* you *for* some gum?
– stinging *adj* ▪ *stinging* tentacles ▪ a *stinging* feeling ▪ She gave him a *stinging* rebuke.

[2]sting *noun, pl* **stings**
1 [*singular*] **:** a quick, sharp pain ▪ When you get the shot, you'll feel a little *sting*.— often used figuratively ▪ He'll eventually overcome the *sting* of being rejected. ▪ His smile took the *sting* out of his words. [=his smile showed that his words were not meant to be hurtful]
2 [*count*] **:** an injury caused when an insect or animal stings

S

you • His arm was covered with bee *stings*.

3 [*count*] : a complicated and clever plan that is meant to deceive someone especially in order to catch criminals • They were caught in a drug *sting*. • a *sting* operation by police

4 [*count*] *Brit* : STINGER

sting·er /ˈstɪŋɚ/ *noun, pl* **-ers** [*count*] *chiefly US* : a pointed part on an insect and animal that is used to sting someone • the *stinger* of a bee — called also (*Brit*) *sting*

sting·ray /ˈstɪŋˌreɪ/ *noun, pl* **-rays** [*count*] : a type of fish that has a large, flat body and a long tail with spines on it that are used to sting other animals

stin·gy /ˈstɪnʤi/ *adj* **sting·i·er; -est** [*also more ~; most ~*] *disapproving*

1 : not liking or wanting to give or spend money • a *stingy* old miser • The company was too *stingy* to raise salaries. : not generous • He is *stingy* with compliments. [=he doesn't give many compliments]

2 : small in size or amount • *stingy* portions of food

– stin·gi·ly /ˈstɪnʤəli/ *adv* **– stin·gi·ness** /ˈstɪnʤinəs/ *noun* [*noncount*] • He is known for his *stinginess*.

¹stink /ˈstɪŋk/ *verb* **stinks; stank** /ˈstæŋk/ *or* **stunk** /ˈstʌŋk/; **stunk; stink·ing** [*no obj*]

1 : to have a very bad smell • These dirty clothes *stink*. • Something *stinks* in here. — often + *of* • His clothes *stank of* dead fish. — sometimes used figuratively • Something *stinks* about his story. [=something about his story does not seem true or honest] • The whole project *stinks of* corruption.

2 *informal* **a** : to do something very poorly • I *stink* at golf. [=I'm a very bad golfer] **b** : to be very low in quality • The movie *stunk*. [=the movie was very bad] • The food is good at that restaurant, but the service *stinks*. **c** : to be very unpleasant, unfair, etc. • Having a root canal *stinks*. • It *stinks* that you can't stay longer. [=I'm very sorry/disappointed that you can't stay longer]

stink up (*US*) *or Brit* ***stink out*** [*phrasal verb*] ***stink (something) up/out*** *or* ***stink up/out (something)*** : to give a very bad smell to (something) • His cigars *stink up* the house.

stink up the joint see ¹JOINT

²stink *noun* [*singular*]

1 : a very bad smell • the *stink* of garbage

2 *informal* : a situation in which someone complains in a very angry and often public way • She ***caused (quite) a stink*** when her request was refused. • People ***raised a stink*** about the new law. • He ***kicked up a stink*** about the way he'd been treated.

stink bomb *noun, pl* **~ bombs** [*count*] : a small device that produces a very bad smell when it is broken, burned, etc. • Someone set off a *stink bomb* at the school.

stink·er /ˈstɪŋkɚ/ *noun, pl* **-ers** [*count*] *informal*

1 *somewhat old-fashioned* : a person or thing that is disliked • He is a dirty little *stinker*.

2 : something (such as a book or film) that is very bad • Her last movie was pretty good, but this one's a *stinker*. [=this one stinks] • a real *stinker* of a performance

¹stink·ing /ˈstɪŋkɪŋ/ *adj*

1 : having a very bad smell • Put out that *stinking* cigar.

2 *always used before a noun, informal* — used for emphasis when you are angry • I hate this *stinking* job.

²stinking *adv, informal* : very or extremely • They're ***stinking rich***. [=*filthy rich*] • He was ***stinking drunk***.

stinky /ˈstɪŋki/ *adj* **stink·i·er; -est** *informal* : having a very bad smell • Move your *stinky* feet!

¹stint /ˈstɪnt/ *noun, pl* **stints** [*count*] : a period of time spent doing a certain job or activity • He had a brief *stint* as a mail carrier. • a four-year *stint* in the army

²stint *verb* **stints; stint·ed; stint·ing** [*no obj*] : to use or give something in limited amounts — usually + *on* or *with* • She doesn't *stint on* spices in her cooking. [=she uses a lot of spices] • He can be *stinting with* praise. [=he tends not to praise people very often]

sti·pend /ˈstaɪˌpɛnd/ *noun, pl* **-pends** [*count*] : a usually small amount of money that is paid regularly to someone • He receives a small *stipend* for his work as a research fellow. • a weekly *stipend*

stip·ple /ˈstɪpəl/ *verb* **stip·ples; stip·pled; stip·pling** [+ *obj*] : to draw or paint small dots on (something) — usually used as *(be) stippled* • The paper was *stippled* with paint.

– stippled *adj* • a *stippled* background **– stippling** *noun* [*noncount*] • The pages were decorated with *stippling*.

stip·u·late /ˈstɪpjəˌleɪt/ *verb* **-lates; -lat·ed; -lat·ing** [+ *obj*] : to demand or require (something) as part of an agreement • The cease-fire was *stipulated* by the treaty. • The rules *stipulate* that players must wear uniforms.

stip·u·la·tion /ˌstɪpjəˈleɪʃən/ *noun, pl* **-tions** : something that is required as part of an agreement [*count*] contract *stipulations* • We agreed to the deal with the *stipulation* that she pay the expenses herself. [*noncount*] *stipulation* of requirements

¹stir /ˈstɚ/ *verb* **stirs; stirred; stir·ring**

1 [+ *obj*] : to mix (something) by making circular movements in it with a spoon or similar object • She *stirred* her coffee. • The cake batter must be *stirred* for 10 minutes. • *Stir* one cup of sugar into the batter.

2 : to move or cause (someone or something) to move after being still [*no obj*] She heard him *stir* (in bed). [=heard him begin to move in bed as he woke up] • He never *stirred* from the couch [=he stayed on the couch] all afternoon. [+ *obj*] She was *stirred* from her sleep by the noise. • The breeze *stirred* the leaves on the tree.

3 a [*no obj*] : to be active or busy • We could see people *stirring* inside the shop. • "Not a creature was *stirring*" —Clement Moore, "A Visit from Saint Nicholas" (1822) **b** [+ *obj*] : to cause (someone or something) to be active • A good book can *stir* the imagination. • He ***stirred himself*** to action. [=he began to take action]

4 [+ *obj*] : to cause (an emotion or reaction) • The bad economic news has *stirred* anxiety among investors. [=has caused investors to worry] — usually + *up* • The bad news has *stirred up* a lot of anxiety. • The story *stirred up* some deep emotions within him.

stir up [*phrasal verb*] **1** ***stir up (someone)*** *or* ***stir (someone) up*** : to cause (someone) to feel a strong emotion and a desire to do something • The speech *stirred up* the crowd. **2** ***stir (something) up*** *or* ***stir up (something)*** **a** : to cause (something) to move up into and through the air or water • The workers *stirred up* a lot of dust. **b** : to cause (something, usually something bad or unpleasant) to happen • They're trying to *stir up* trouble. • *stirring up* racial hatred • His comments certainly ***stirred things up***. [=caused a lot of excitement, anger, etc.] — see also ¹STIR 4 (above)

²stir *noun* [*singular*]

1 : a state of excitement, anger, or surprise among a group of people • His comments have caused quite a *stir*.

2 : a small movement • the *stir* of the leaves in the breeze

3 : the act of stirring something with a spoon or similar object • She gave the sauce a *stir*. [=she stirred the sauce]

4 *chiefly US slang, old-fashioned* : PRISON • He spent five years in *stir*.

stir–cra·zy /ˈstɚˈkreɪzi/ *adj, not used before a noun* : unhappy and upset because you have been in a place for a long time and want to get out • I was ***going stir-crazy*** after being stuck in the house all week.

¹stir–fry /ˈstɚˌfraɪ/ *noun, pl* **-fries** [*count, noncount*] : a dish made of foods (such as meat or vegetables) that are fried quickly over high heat while being stirred constantly • We had (a) chicken *stir-fry* for dinner last night.

²stir–fry /ˈstɚˈfraɪ/ *verb* **-fries; -fried; -fry·ing** [+ *obj*] : to fry (something) quickly over high heat while stirring it constantly • *Stir-fry* the pork for four minutes. • *stir-fried* chicken

stir·rer /ˈstɚrɚ/ *noun, pl* **-rers** [*count*]

1 : something that is used to stir liquids • a coffee/paint *stirrer*

2 *Brit, informal* : a person who causes trouble

¹stir·ring /ˈstɚrɪŋ/ *adj* [*more ~; most ~*] : causing strong feelings • She gave a *stirring* [=*moving*] speech at the awards banquet. • a *stirring* rendition of the national anthem

²stirring *noun, pl* **-rings** [*count*] : the beginning of a motion, activity, feeling, idea, etc. — + *of* • We felt the first *stirrings of* hope when we heard the news.

stir·rup /ˈstɚrəp, *Brit* ˈstɪrəp/ *noun, pl* **-rups** [*count*] : one of two loops that are attached to a saddle for the rider's feet — see picture at HORSE

stirrup pants *noun* [*plural*] *US* : a pair of women's pants that have a strip of fabric on the bottom of each leg that goes underneath the foot

¹stitch /ˈstɪʧ/ *noun, pl* **stitch·es**

1 [*count*] : a piece of thread that is passed through a piece of material with a needle • the *stitches* on a baseball • She pulled out the *stitches*. — see also CROSS-STITCH

2 [*count*] *medical* : a special piece of thread that is used to hold a large cut or wound closed • His cut required six *stitches*. • She gets her *stitches* removed tomorrow.

3 a [*count*] : a single loop of thread or yarn that is wrapped around a tool (such as a knitting needle) and is linked to oth-

S

er loops to make fabric • After knitting another row she realized she had ***dropped a stitch***. [=let a loop fall off a knitting needle] **b** : a particular type or style of stitch used in sewing, knitting, crocheting, etc. [*count*] The book teaches a variety of *stitches*. [*noncount*] a scarf worked in knit/purl *stitch*
4 [*count*] : a sudden sharp pain in your side — usually singular • I've got a *stitch* (in my side).
a stitch *informal* ✧ If you ***are not wearing a stitch, do not have a stitch on***, etc., you are naked. • She *wasn't wearing a stitch* (of clothes/clothing).
a stitch in time (saves nine) ✧ The phrase *a stitch in time (saves nine)* means that it is better to fix a problem when it is small than to wait and let it become a bigger problem.
in stitches *informal* : laughing very hard • His jokes had us all *in stitches*.

²stitch *verb* **stitches; stitched; stitch·ing** [+ *obj*]
1 : to use a needle and thread to make or repair (something, such as a piece of clothing) : to join (something, such as a piece of fabric or a button) to something else with stitches : SEW • He *stitched* a patch onto his coat.
2 : to make (something, such as a design) out of stitches • Her initials were *stitched* on the pillowcase. • He *stitched* a design along the border of the tablecloth.
stitch together [*phrasal verb*] ***stitch (something) together*** *or* ***stitch together (something)*** : to make (something) out of many different things • I *stitched together* a novel from several stories I had written earlier.
stitch up [*phrasal verb*] **1** ***stitch (someone or something) up or stitch up (someone or something)*** : to use a needle and thread to close a large cut or wound on someone • The doctor *stitched* him *up*. = The doctor *stitched up* his wound. **2** ***stitch (someone) up or stitch up (someone)*** *Brit, informal* : to make (an innocent person) appear to be guilty of a crime : FRAME • They *stitched* him *up* for murder. **3** ***stitch (something) up or stitch up (something)*** *Brit, informal* : to do the final things that are needed to complete (something) in a successful way : to finish or do (something) successfully • The mayor *stitched up* a deal with the union. • We thought that we had the game *stitched up*. [=*sewn up*; we thought we were definitely going to win the game]
– stitch·er *noun, pl* **-ers** [*count*]

stitching *noun* [*noncount*] : a series of stitches or the type of stitches that are used in something • He admired the *stitching* on the quilt.

stoat /ˈstoʊt/ *noun, pl* **stoats** [*count*] *chiefly Brit* : a small animal that has a long body and brown fur that turns white in winter; *especially* : this animal when its fur is brown — compare ERMINE

¹stock /ˈstɑːk/ *noun, pl* **stocks**
1 : the supply of goods available for sale in a store [*noncount*] That camera is ***out of stock***. • Do you have any more light bulbs ***in stock***? [*singular*] They carry ***a large/small stock*** of computer software.
2 : a supply of something that is available for use [*count*] We built up an ample *stock* of food before the storm. • She always seems to have a fresh *stock* of funny jokes. [*noncount*] There was a decrease in available ***housing stock*** [=houses and apartment buildings] last year.
3 : a share of the value of a company which can be bought, sold, or traded as an investment [*count*] The value of his *stocks* has soared. • Most of her money is invested in *stocks*. [*noncount*] Do you own any *stock*? — often used before another noun • *stock* prices • a *stock* certificate
4 [*count*] : the part of a gun that is held against your shoulder • the *stock* of a rifle — see picture at GUN
5 [*noncount*] : the country or group of people that a person comes from • He is of Irish *stock*. [=his family comes originally from Ireland]
6 [*noncount*] : farm animals (such as cattle) from which meat, wool and other products are obtained : LIVESTOCK
7 [*noncount*] : liquid in which meat, fish, or vegetables have been cooked and then removed and which is used to make soups, sauces, etc. • The recipe calls for one cup of chicken/beef *stock*.
8 [*noncount*] *US* : confidence or faith in someone or something • He ***placed/put a lot of stock*** in her ability to get the job done. [=he had a lot of trust in her ability to get the job done] • I don't ***put much stock in*** the rumors. [=I don't think the rumors are believable; I doubt the rumors]
9 [*noncount*] — used to describe how popular or unpopular someone or something is at a particular time • The mayor's *stock* with voters is high/low right now. [=the mayor is popular/unpopular with voters right now]
10 ***stocks*** [*plural*] : a wooden frame with holes in it for a person's feet, hands, or head that was used in the past as a form of punishment • He was sent to the *stocks*.
lock, stock, and barrel see ¹LOCK
take stock : to carefully think about something in order to make a decision about what to do next • We need to *take stock* and formulate a plan. — often + *of* • We should *take stock of* our finances.

²stock *verb* **stocks; stocked; stock·ing** [+ *obj*]
1 : to have a supply of (something) in a store for sale • Our store *stocks* only the finest goods. • Do you *stock* this item?
2 : to fill (something, such as a room or a building) with a supply of food, drinks, etc. • The bar is *stocked* with beer, wine and liquor. • a well-*stocked* kitchen • They *stocked* the shelves in the store with a variety of imported foods.
stock up [*phrasal verb*] : to get a large quantity of something so that you will have it for later use • I need to head to the store to *stock up*. — often + *on* • We made sure to *stock up on* food before the storm hit.

³stock *adj, always used before a noun*
1 a : regularly used or included with something : STANDARD • Here are the *stock* patterns you can choose from. **b** : commonly used and not original or interesting • She gave a *stock* answer to the reporter's question. • a dull narrative with *stock* characters
2 : usually available for sale in a store • That item is a *stock* model. • *stock* sizes

stock·ade /stɑˈkeɪd/ *noun, pl* **-ades** [*count*] : a line of tall posts that are set in the ground and used as a barrier to protect or defend a place • a fort *stockade*

stock·bro·ker /ˈstɑːkˌbroʊkɚ/ *noun, pl* **-kers** [*count*] : someone whose job is to buy and sell shares of stock for other people

stock car *noun, pl* **~ cars** [*count*] : a car used for racing that has the same basic structure as a car normally sold to the public but has a more powerful engine, a stronger frame, etc. — often used before another noun • *stock car* racing

stock company *noun, pl* **~ -nies** [*count*] *US*
1 : a company whose ownership is divided into shares that can be bought and sold
2 : a theater group made up of actors who perform together

stock cube *noun, pl* **~ cubes** [*count*] *Brit* : BOUILLON CUBE

stock·er /ˈstɑːkɚ/ *noun, pl* **-ers** [*count*] *US* : a person whose job is to put products on a store's shelves, in a store's cases, etc. • He works as a produce *stocker* at the grocery store.

stock exchange *noun, pl* **~ -changes** [*count*] : a system or place where shares of various companies are bought and sold • domestic and international *stock exchanges* • Shares of the company were trading at $20 on the New York *Stock Exchange*. • He works as a stockbroker on the floor of the New York *Stock Exchange*.

stock·hold·er /ˈstɑːkˌhoʊldɚ/ *noun, pl* **-ers** [*count*] *US* : someone who owns stock in a company : SHAREHOLDER

stock·ing /ˈstɑːkɪŋ/ *noun, pl* **-ings** [*count*]
1 : a close-fitting usually long covering for the foot and leg • a pair of wool *stockings*
2 : a covering for the foot and ankle : SOCK
3 : a decorative pouch shaped like a large sock that is used for holding gifts at Christmas • The children hung their (Christmas) *stockings* on the mantel.
in your stockinged/stocking feet : wearing socks but not shoes • Don't go outside ***in your stocking feet!***

stocking cap *noun, pl* **~ caps** [*count*] *US* : a knitted close-fitting cap that sometimes has a decorative part (called a tassel or pom-pom) at the top

stocking stuffer *noun, pl* **~ -fers** [*count*] *US* : a small gift that is usually placed in a Christmas stocking • Small toys make great *stocking stuffers*. — called also (*Brit*) *stocking filler*

stock–in–trade /ˌstɑːkənˈtreɪd/ *noun* [*noncount*] : something that someone or something does or makes very well and often • Ballads were her *stock-in-trade*. • Sitcoms are the *stock-in-trade* of the major networks.

stock·ist /ˈstɑːkɪst/ *noun, pl* **-ists** [*count*] *Brit* : a person or store that sells a particular kind of product • a *stockist* of medical supplies

stockman /ˈstɑːkmən/ *noun, pl* **-men** /-mən/ [*count*] : a person who raises cattle, sheep, etc.

stock market *noun, pl* **~ -kets**

S

1 [*noncount*] : the business or activity of buying and selling stocks ▪ We lost money in the *stock market*. ▪ He made a lot of money ***playing the stock market***. [=buying and selling stocks]
2 [*count*] : a system for buying and selling stocks or a place where stocks are bought and sold ▪ International *stock markets* saw declines at the end of the trading day. ▪ The *stock market* [=the total value of stocks traded on the stock market] dropped 15 points today.

stock option *noun, pl* ~ **-tions** [*count*] *US* : a right that is given by a company to an employee that lets the employee purchase stock in the company usually for a price that is lower than the normal price — usually plural ▪ He decided to ***exercise his stock options***. [=he decided to buy stock in the company that he works for] — called also (*Brit*) *share option*

[1]**stock·pile** /ˈstɑːkˌpajəl/ *noun, pl* **-piles** [*count*] : a large supply of something that is kept for future use ▪ a *stockpile* of ammunition/weapons ▪ a *stockpile* of medical supplies

[2]**stockpile** *verb* **-piles; -piled; -pil·ing** [+ *obj*] : to get and keep a large supply of (something) for future use ▪ The government *stockpiled* vaccines to prepare for a flu epidemic.

stock·pot /ˈstɑːkˌpɑːt/ *noun, pl* **-pots** [*count*] : a large pot for making stock, soups, stews, etc.

stock·room /ˈstɑːkˌruːm/ *noun, pl* **-rooms** [*count*] : a storage area for the supplies and goods that are used or sold in a business

stock–still /ˈstɑːkˈstɪl/ *adj, not used before a noun* : very still : not moving at all ▪ He stood/stayed *stock-still*.

stock·tak·ing /ˈstɑːkˈteɪkɪŋ/ *noun*
1 *chiefly Brit* : the activity or process of thinking about a problem or situation in order to decide what to do [*noncount*] It is time for some *stocktaking*. [=it's time to take stock of the situation] [*singular*] It is time for a *stocktaking*.
2 [*noncount*] *Brit* : the act or process of making a complete list of the items or things that are in a place : INVENTORY

stocky /ˈstɑːki/ *adj* **stock·i·er; -est** : short and heavy or broad ▪ a short, *stocky* man ▪ That outfit makes you look *stocky*.
– **stock·i·ly** /ˈstɑːkəli/ *adv* ▪ He is *stockily* built.

stock·yard /ˈstɑːkˌjɑɚd/ *noun, pl* **-yards** [*count*] *chiefly US* : an enclosed area where farms animals (such as cattle) are kept so they can be slaughtered, sold, or shipped

stodge /ˈstɑːʤ/ *noun* [*noncount*] *Brit* : heavy food that makes you feel very full ▪ We filled up on *stodge* at the banquet.

stodgy /ˈstɑːʤi/ *adj* **stodg·i·er; -est** *disapproving*
1 **a** : having very old-fashioned opinions, attitudes, etc. ▪ a *stodgy* old man **b** : too plain or dull to be interesting ▪ *stodgy* clothes
2 *Brit, of food* : unpleasantly heavy and causing you to feel very full ▪ a *stodgy* meal
– **stodg·i·ness** /ˈstɑːʤinəs/ *noun* [*noncount*]

sto·gie *or* **sto·gy** /ˈstoʊgi/ *noun, pl* **sto·gies** [*count*] *US, informal* : CIGAR ▪ He was smoking a *stogie*.

[1]**sto·ic** /ˈstowɪk/ *or* **sto·i·cal** /ˈstowɪkəl/ *adj* [*more* ~; *most* ~] : showing no emotion especially when something bad is happening ▪ She remained *stoic* [=she did not complain or become upset] even as he continued to insult her. ▪ He had a *stoic* expression on his face.
– **sto·ical·ly** /ˈstowɪkli/ *adv* ▪ He accepted the punishment *stoically*.

[2]**stoic** *noun, pl* **-ics** [*count*] : a person who accepts what happens without complaining or showing emotion

S

sto·i·cism /ˈstowəˌsɪzəm/ *noun* [*noncount*] : the quality or behavior of a person who accepts what happens without complaining or showing emotion ▪ She endured his criticism with her usual *stoicism*.

stoke /ˈstoʊk/ *verb* **stokes; stoked; stok·ing** [+ *obj*]
1 : to stir or add fuel to (something that is burning) ▪ *stoke* a fire ▪ The engineer *stoked* the coals. ▪ He *stoked* the furnace. [=he added more fuel to the furnace to make the fire hotter] ▪ *stoke* the flames
2 : to increase the amount or strength of (something) ▪ The new ad campaign has helped to *stoke* sales. ▪ Poor revenue figures have *stoked* concerns about possible layoffs.
– **stok·er** /ˈstoʊkɚ/ *noun, pl* **-ers** [*count*] *chiefly Brit* ▪ He worked as a coal *stoker* for the railroad.

stoked *adj, not used before a noun* [*more* ~; *most* ~] *US slang* : very excited ▪ He was *stoked* to see her.

[1]**stole** *past tense of* [1]STEAL

[2]**stole** /ˈstoʊl/ *noun, pl* **stoles** [*count*] : a long, wide piece of clothing that is usually worn across the shoulders ▪ a mink *stole*

stolen *past participle of* [1]STEAL

stol·id /ˈstɑːləd/ *adj* [*more* ~; *most* ~] : showing little or no emotion : not easily excited or upset ▪ She remained *stolid* during the trial. ▪ a *stolid* face
– **stol·id·ly** *adv* ▪ The guard stood *stolidly* at his post.

[1]**stom·ach** /ˈstʌmək/ *noun, pl* **-achs**
1 [*count*] **a** : the organ in your body where food goes and begins to be digested after you swallow it ▪ She has problems with her *stomach*. ▪ I've had enough to eat. My *stomach* is full. ▪ His *stomach* was growling. — often used before another noun ▪ a *stomach* ulcer ▪ *stomach* gas — see picture at HUMAN **b** : the part of your body that contains the stomach ▪ She punched him in the *stomach*. [=*belly*] ▪ He was lying on his *stomach*.
2 [*noncount*] : the desire, courage, etc., that is needed to do or accept something difficult or unpleasant — usually used in negative statements ▪ She didn't have the *stomach* to confront him. ▪ He has no *stomach* for controversy.
a strong/weak stomach ✧ If you have *a strong stomach*, you are not bothered by things that many people find disgusting, shocking, or offensive. ▪ You need *a strong stomach* to watch that movie. If you have *a weak stomach*, you are easily bothered by disgusting, shocking, or offensive things. ▪ It's a very violent movie. Don't watch it if you have *a weak stomach*.
on a full stomach : after eating a lot of food ▪ Don't try to go swimming *on a full stomach*.
on an empty stomach : with nothing in your stomach ▪ Take this medication *on an empty stomach*. [=when your stomach is empty because you have not eaten for a time]
sick to your stomach see [1]SICK
turn your stomach ✧ Something that ***turns your stomach*** or ***makes your stomach turn*** makes you feel ill or uncomfortable usually because it is offensive or disgusting. ▪ The violence in his movies really *turns my stomach*.
your eyes are bigger than your stomach see [1]EYE

[2]**stomach** *verb* **stom·achs; stom·ached; stom·ach·ing** [+ *obj*]
1 : to accept or experience (something unpleasant) without becoming sick, upset, etc. ▪ I could barely *stomach* the smell. ▪ His behavior is very hard to *stomach* [=*tolerate*] sometimes.
2 : to eat (something) without getting a sick or unpleasant feeling in your stomach ▪ I can't *stomach* raw onions.

stom·ach·ache /ˈstʌməkˌeɪk/ *noun, pl* **-aches** : pain in or near your stomach [*count*] Eating too much food will give you a *stomachache*. [*noncount*] Side effects include gas, bloating, and *stomachache*.

stomp /ˈstɑːmp/ *verb* **stomps; stomped; stomp·ing**
1 *always followed by an adverb or preposition* [*no obj*] : to walk or move with very heavy or noisy steps ▪ He *stomped* angrily out of the room. ▪ She *stomped* [=*stamped*] around the yard in her muddy boots.
2 [+ *obj*] *chiefly US* : to put (your foot) down forcefully and noisily ▪ He angrily *stomped* [=*stamped*] his foot. ▪ The fans were *stomping* their feet and shouting.
stomp on [*phrasal verb*] ***stomp on (someone or something)*** : to step on (something or someone) very forcefully ▪ He *stomped on* the bug. ▪ The elephant almost *stomped on* them. ▪ I *stomped on* the brakes.
stomp out [*phrasal verb*] ***stomp out (something)*** **1** : to stop or destroy (something bad) ▪ They are determined to *stomp out* [=*stamp out*] corruption. **2** : to stop (something) from burning by stepping on it forcefully with your feet ▪ She *stomped out* her cigarette.

stomp·er /ˈstɑːmpɚ/ *noun, pl* **-ers** [*count*] *informal* : a piece of music that is very lively and makes you want to dance ▪ a jazzy *stomper*

stomping ground *noun, pl* ~ **grounds** [*count*] *US* : a place where someone likes to go or often goes ▪ The mall was their *stomping ground*. — usually plural ▪ We enjoyed going back home and visiting our old *stomping grounds*. — called also (*Brit*) *stamping ground*

[1]**stone** /ˈstoʊn/ *noun, pl* **stones**
1 [*noncount*] : a hard substance that comes from the ground and is used for building, carving, etc. ▪ The pedestal is made of *stone*. — often used before another noun ▪ *stone* buildings ▪ a *stone* wall
2 [*count*] **a** : a small piece of rock ▪ We threw *stones* [=(*US*) *rocks*] at the sign. **b** : a piece of rock used for a particular

purpose • His birthdate and date of death were carved on the *stone*.— see also HEADSTONE
3 [*count*] : a jewel • precious *stones* [=*gemstones*]
4 [*count*] : a small, hard object that sometimes forms in a part of the body (such as the kidney) • She had *stones* in her bladder.— see also GALLSTONE, KIDNEY STONE
5 [*count*] *chiefly Brit* : a large, hard seed found in the center of some fruits (such as plums and peaches) : PIT
6 *pl* **stone** [*count*] *Brit* : a British unit of weight equal to 14 pounds (6.35 kilograms) • He weighs 12 *stone*.— abbr. *st*
a stone's throw : a short distance • The high school is just *a stone's throw* from his house. • She lives just *a stone's throw* away from the beach.
carved/etched/set/written in stone : permanent or not able to be changed • These new rules are not *carved in stone*; if they don't work, we'll change them.
kill two birds with one stone see [1]KILL
leave no stone unturned : to make every possible effort to find someone or something • Their lawyer said that he would *leave no stone unturned* in trying to find more evidence. • The researchers *left no stone unturned* in their search for the original documents.
sink like a stone see [1]SINK

[2]**stone** *verb* **stones; stoned; ston·ing** [+ *obj*]
1 : to throw stones at (someone or something) • Rioters *stoned* the building.
2 : to kill (someone) by throwing stones • He was *stoned* to death for his crimes.
3 *Brit* : to remove the hard, large seed of (a fruit) : PIT • *Stone* the peaches before serving.
stone the crows *Brit, informal + somewhat old-fashioned* — used to express surprise • "He's won the lottery!" "Well, *stone the crows*!"

[3]**stone** *adv* : totally or completely • (*US*) They sat there, *stone* silent. • The soup was ***stone cold***. • He was ***stone broke***. [=he had no money at all] • ***stone dead*** — sometimes used in combination • I thought I had gone ***stone-deaf***. — see also STONE-COLD

Stone Age *noun*
the Stone Age : the oldest period in which human beings are known to have existed : the age during which humans made and used stone tools • It was a skill developed during *the Stone Age*. • *Stone Age* weapons — often used figuratively • His political ideas are from *the Stone Age*. [=are from the distant past; are very out of date] • I'm still using a *Stone Age* computer. [=an outdated/obsolete computer] — compare BRONZE AGE, IRON AGE

stone–cold /ˈstounˈkould/ *adv, chiefly US, informal* : completely or totally • He's ***stone-cold sober***.

stone·cut·ter /ˈstounˌkʌtɚ/ *noun, pl* **-ters** [*count*] *US* : a person who cuts or carves stone

stoned /ˈstound/ *adj* [*more ~; most ~*] *informal* : intoxicated by a drug (such as marijuana) • He was *stoned* on pot. • They ***got stoned*** at the party.

stone–faced /ˈstounˌfeɪst/ *also* **stony–faced** /ˈstouniˌfeɪst/ *adj* [*more ~; most ~*] : showing no emotion • He stood there *stone-faced* while the verdict was announced. • a *stone-faced* judge

stone–ground /ˈstounˈgraund/ *adj* : ground by being crushed between two large stones (called millstones) • *stone-ground* flour

stone·ma·son /ˈstounˌmeɪsn̩/ *noun, pl* **-sons** [*count*] : a person who cuts, prepares, and builds with stone

ston·er /ˈstounɚ/ *noun, pl* **-ers** [*count*] *US, informal* : a person who uses drugs frequently : a person who is often stoned on drugs (such as marijuana) • The movie's a comedy about a couple of *stoners*.— often used before another noun • a *stoner* comedy

stone·wall /ˈstounˌwɑːl/ *verb* **-walls; -walled; -wall·ing** : to refuse or fail to answer questions, to do what has been requested, etc., especially in order to delay or prevent something [*no obj*] They *stonewalled* until they could come up with a response. • They were just *stonewalling* for time. [+ *obj*] (*chiefly US*) • They're trying to *stonewall* the media/investigation. • We're trying to get the information, but we're being *stonewalled*.

stone·ware /ˈstounˌweɚ/ *noun* [*noncount*] : objects made of a special baked clay — often used before another noun • a set of *stoneware* dishes

stone·washed /ˈstounˌwɑːʃt/ *adj* — used to describe clothes (such as jeans) that are made lighter in color and softer by being washed with small stones • She was wearing *stonewashed* jeans, a sweater, and cowboy boots.

stone·work /ˈstounˌwɚk/ *noun* [*noncount*] : a structure or part of a structure that is built of stone • The *stonework* on this house is over 100 years old.
– stone·work·er /ˈstounˌwɚkɚ/ *noun, pl* **-ers** [*count*]

[1]**stonk·ing** /ˈstɑːŋkɪŋ/ *adj, Brit slang*
1 : very large • We spent a *stonking* sum on the tickets. • *stonking* amounts of money
2 : very good • We had a *stonking* time.

[2]**stonking** *adv, Brit slang* : very or extremely • a *stonking* good book • a *stonking* great victory

stony /ˈstouni/ *adj* **ston·i·er; -est**
1 : full of stones • *stony* [=*rocky*] soil • a *stony* beach
2 : made of stone or hard like stone • a smooth, *stony* surface • a *stony* material
3 : showing no emotion or friendliness • She gave him a *stony* stare. • *stony* silence
– ston·i·ly /ˈstounəli/ *adv* • He remained *stonily* silent.

stood *past tense and past participle of* [1]STAND

stooge /ˈstuːʤ/ *noun, pl* **stoog·es** [*count*]
1 *disapproving* : a weak or unimportant person who is controlled by a powerful person, organization, etc. • a gangster and his *stooges* • He's just a *stooge* for the oil industry. • a government *stooge*
2 : a performer in a show who says and does foolish things that other performers make jokes about

stool /ˈstuːl/ *noun, pl* **stools** [*count*]
1 a : a seat that fits one person and that has no back or arms • She sat on a *stool*. • a bar *stool* • a piano *stool* **b** : a piece of furniture that supports the feet of a person who is sitting : FOOTSTOOL
2 *medical* : a piece of solid waste that is released from the body • The patient had bloody/loose/hard *stools*. • a *stool* sample • *stool* softener [=a medicine that makes it easier to discharge bodily waste]

stool

stool·ie /ˈstuːli/ *noun, pl* **-ies** [*count*] *US, informal + old-fashioned* : STOOL PIGEON

stool pigeon *noun, pl* **~ -geons** [*count*] *chiefly US, informal* : a criminal who gives the police information about other criminals

[1]**stoop** /ˈstuːp/ *verb* **stoops; stooped; stoop·ing** [*no obj*]
1 : to bend down or over • She *stooped* down to hug the child. • He had to *stoop* to pick it up.
2 : to walk or stand with your head and shoulders bent forward • He tends to *stoop* as he walks.
3 : to do something that is not honest, fair, etc. • She would never *stoop* to lying. [=she would never lie; she is too good a person to lie] • He really did that? I didn't think he could *stoop* so low.
stoop to someone's level see [1]LEVEL

[2]**stoop** *noun* [*singular*] : a bend or curve forward of your back and shoulders • He walks with a slight *stoop*.— compare [3]STOOP
– stooped *adj* • His shoulders are *stooped*. [=his shoulders are bent forward]

[3]**stoop** *noun, pl* **stoops** [*count*] *US* : a raised area (such as a porch, platform, or stairway) at the entrance to a house or building • I found a package on the (front/back) *stoop*. — compare [2]STOOP

[1]**stop** /ˈstɑːp/ *verb* **stops; stopped; stop·ping**
1 a [*no obj*] : to not move, walk, etc., after doing so before • She was walking toward me, and then she suddenly *stopped*. • The bus *stopped* at the corner. • He *stopped* to watch the sun set. • She had to *stop* to catch her breath. = She had to *stop* and catch her breath. • He *stopped* to pick up a penny. • The car was going so fast that it couldn't *stop* in time. • The traffic light turned red, so she had to *stop*. • *Stop*. [=*halt*] Who goes there? • I ***stopped (dead) in my tracks*** [=stopped suddenly] when I saw the bear. **b** [+ *obj*] : to cause (someone or something) to not move, walk, etc., after doing so before • *Stop* that man! He stole my wallet. • They *stopped* us at the border to check our passports. • She *stopped* the car and turned back. • He was *stopped* by the police for speeding. • The goalie *stopped* [=*blocked*] the ball/shot. • The sight of the bear ***stopped me (dead) in my tracks***.
2 a : to not do something that you have been doing before : to not continue doing something [*no obj*] He constantly teases her and never knows when to *stop*. • We've been working all morning. It's time to *stop* and take a break. • The boss

said that he was unhappy with some of his employees, but he ***stopped short of*** naming which ones. [=but he did not say which ones] ▪ Did you ever ***stop*** [=*pause*] ***to think*** about the risk you took? ▪ She never ***stopped to consider*** how her decision might affect others. [+ *obj*] Can you please *stop* what you are doing to help me? ▪ I *stop* work at 5 o'clock. ▪ The phone *stopped* ringing. ▪ *Stop* arguing/talking/running. ▪ She *stopped* [=*quit*] smoking last year. ▪ The patient suddenly *stopped* breathing. ▪ His heart *stopped* beating. ▪ ***Stop it/that*** or I'll tell Mom. **b** [+ *obj*] **: to make (someone or something) no longer do something : to keep (someone or something) from continuing to do something** ▪ I'm leaving and you can't *stop* me. ▪ *Stop* me if you've heard this joke before. ▪ It's too late. There's no *stopping* them now. [=they can't be stopped now] ▪ (*Brit*) I couldn't *stop* him crying. — often + *from* in U.S. English ▪ I couldn't *stop* him *from* crying. ▪ He *stopped* [=*restrained*] himself *from* laughing out loud. ▪ Nothing can *stop* me *from* leaving. ▪ Environmentalists tried to *stop* them *from* cutting down the trees. ▪ There is nothing to *stop* you *from* going. ▪ We need to *stop* the disease *from* spreading.

3 [+ *obj*] **a : to cause (something) to end : to end (something)** ▪ The teacher *stopped* the fight. ▪ We need to *stop* the violence in our city. ▪ They tried to *stop* the bleeding. **b : to cause (a recording) to not play** ▪ She *stopped* the CD because it was skipping. ▪ We *stopped* [=*paused*] the movie to grab some snacks.

4 [*no obj*] **: to no longer happen or exist : to end** ▪ The music suddenly *stopped*. ▪ The path *stops* about halfway up the mountain. ▪ The rain had *stopped* by the time we left. [=it was not raining anymore when we left]

5 [*no obj*] **: to suddenly not work or function** ▪ The engine just *stopped*. ▪ His heart *stopped*.

6 [*no obj*] **a : to not travel during a journey for a short period of time in order to rest, eat, etc.** — + *for* ▪ We *stopped for* lunch. ▪ We need to *stop for* gas. [=we need to get gas] ▪ We *stopped for* a night in Atlanta. [=we stayed in Atlanta for a night] **b : to go to a place during a journey** ▪ I'll *stop* for a short visit. ▪ The tour *stops* in several cities. **c : to make a brief social visit** ▪ I'm not *stopping*. [=*staying*] I just wanted to drop this off. — see also STOP BY, STOP IN, STOP OFF, STOP OVER (below)

7 [+ *obj*] **: to close, block, or fill (a hole)** ▪ He *stopped* his ears with his fingers. [=he put his fingertips in his ears so that he couldn't hear] — usually + *up* ▪ She *stopped up* the cracks with plaster. ▪ The sink is *stopped up* [=*blocked*] with food.

8 [+ *obj*] **a : to tell your bank not to pay a check** ▪ I called to *stop* payment on the check. = I called to *stop* the check. **b** *chiefly Brit* **: to take (money) from something** — often + *from* ▪ £200 will be *stopped* [=*withheld*] *from* your wages next week.

9 *always followed by an adverb or preposition* [*no obj*] *Brit, informal* **: to stay or remain** ▪ I am *stopping* at home. — see also STOP IN, STOP OUT, STOP UP (below)

stop and smell the roses see ²ROSE

stop at nothing — used to say that someone will do anything to achieve a goal or purpose ▪ She will *stop at nothing* to get what she wants.

stop by [*phrasal verb*] *informal* **: to visit someone briefly** ▪ Feel free to *stop by* [=*drop by, drop in*] anytime. ▪ I'll *stop by* for a short visit.

stop in [*phrasal verb*] *informal* **1 : to visit someone briefly** ▪ You should *stop in* [=*stop by*] for tea sometime. **2** *Brit* **: to stay at home** ▪ I'm *stopping* [=*staying*] *in* tonight.

stop off [*phrasal verb*] *informal* **: to go or stay somewhere briefly while traveling to another place** ▪ I'll *stop off* (at the store) to pick up some milk. ▪ She is *stopping off* in Miami to visit a friend. ▪ Could you *stop off* at the house to water the plants?

stop out [*phrasal verb*] *Brit, informal* **: to stay out at night** ▪ He doesn't normally *stop out* late.

stop over [*phrasal verb*] *informal* **: to go to or stay in a place while traveling to another place** ▪ The plane *stops over* in Chicago before going on to Seattle. ▪ She *stopped over* at a friend's house for a couple of days.

stop up [*phrasal verb*] *Brit, informal* **: to stay up at night** ▪ She *stopped up* late last night. — see also ¹STOP 7 (above)

the buck stops here see ¹BUCK

²stop *noun, pl* **stops** [*count*]

1 : an act of stopping or a state of being stopped: such as a : a state in which someone or something is no longer moving — usually singular ▪ The car skidded/slowed ***to a stop***. [=to a halt] ▪ The ball rolled *to a stop*. ▪ The train ***came to a stop***. ▪ He slowly ***brought the car to a stop***. — see also FULL STOP **b : a state in which no further activity happens** — usually singular ▪ Production was ***brought to a stop*** [=was stopped] by the strike. ▪ Negotiations ***brought a stop to*** [=*ended*] the conflict. ▪ Work on the project ***came to a stop*** [=work on the project stopped] because of a lack of funding. ▪ The fighting *came to a* sudden *stop*. ▪ We need to ***put a stop to*** [=*end*] these practices. ▪ She wanted to *put a stop to* the rumors. **c** *sports* **: a play that stops an opponent from scoring a goal** ▪ The goalie made a great *stop*. [=*save*]

2 a : a place that you visit or go to for a short period of time during a journey ▪ His first *stop* will be Washington, D.C. ▪ Our first *stop* has to be the gas station. — see also PIT STOP, REST STOP, TRUCK STOP, WHISTLE-STOP **b : a short period of time during which you stop or stay at a place during a journey** ▪ The trip includes an overnight *stop* [=*stay*] in Paris. ▪ We'll ***make a stop*** [=*stop, rest*] when we get to the top of this hill. ▪ We should *make a stop* at the museum. [=we should visit the museum] ▪ I need to *make a stop* at the grocery store on the way home.

3 a : the place where a bus or train regularly stops on a route to let passengers get on and off ▪ a bus *stop* ▪ The next *stop* is Main Street and Tower Square. ▪ I'm getting off at the next *stop*. ▪ What is your *stop*? **b** *US* **: a place on a road (such as an intersection) where traffic must stop** ▪ a four-way *stop* ▪ Slow down as you approach the *stop*. ▪ a ***stop sign*** [=a sign telling drivers to stop and wait until they can continue safely] — see also STOPLIGHT

4 : an order that tells a bank not to pay a check — usually singular ▪ I ***put a stop on*** the check.

5 *music* **a : a set of organ pipes that produce a similar sound b :** STOP KNOB

6 *linguistics* **: a sound (such as the "p" of "apt" or the "g" of "tiger") that is made by stopping the flow of air completely and then suddenly letting air out** — see also GLOTTAL STOP

pull out all the stops informal **: to do everything possible in order to do or achieve something** ▪ The company *pulled out all the stops* to advertise their new product. = The company *pulled out all the stops* in advertising their new product. ▪ When he throws a party, he really *pulls out all the stops*.

— see also DOORSTOP, SHORTSTOP

stop–action /ˈstɑːpˈækʃən/ *noun* [*noncount*] **:** STOP-MOTION

stop–and–go /ˌstɑːpənˈgoʊ/ *adj, chiefly US* **: making or having many stops : stopping and starting again and again** ▪ *stop-and-go* driving/traffic ▪ It was *stop-and-go* on the highway.

stop·cock /ˈstɑːpˌkɑːk/ *noun, pl* **-cocks** [*count*] **: a device used for controlling or stopping the flow of a liquid or gas through a pipe**

stop·gap /ˈstɑːpˌgæp/ *noun, pl* **-gaps** [*count*] **: someone or something that is intended to be used for a short time and then replaced by someone or something better : a temporary substitute** ▪ The new law is intended only as a *stopgap*. — often used before another noun ▪ a *stopgap* solution

stop–go *adj, Brit* **: having inactive periods followed by active periods** ▪ a *stop-go* economy/policy

stop knob *noun, pl* **~ knobs** [*count*] *music* **: any one of the handles that an organ player pushes in or pulls out to stop or allow sound from certain pipes**

stop·light /ˈstɑːpˌlaɪt/ *noun, pl* **-lights** [*count*] *US* **:** TRAFFIC LIGHT

stop–mo·tion /ˈstɑːpˈmoʊʃən/ *noun* [*noncount*] **: a filming technique in which objects (such as clay models) are photographed in a series of slightly different positions so that the objects seem to move** ▪ The show was filmed with *stop-motion*. — often used before another noun ▪ *stop-motion* films/animation

stop·over /ˈstɑːpˌoʊvɚ/ *noun, pl* **-overs** [*count*] **: a brief period of time when you stop at a place during a journey** ▪ We have a six-hour *stopover* [=*layover*] in Puerto Rico.; *also* **: a place where a stopover occurs** ▪ The city is a favorite *stopover* for tourists.

stop·page /ˈstɑːpɪʤ/ *noun, pl* **-pag·es** [*count*]

1 : the act of stopping something ▪ the *stoppage* of payments

2 : a situation in which workers stop working for a period of time as a protest ▪ Workers threatened a *stoppage* [=*strike*] if their wages were not increased. ▪ work *stoppages*

3 *sports* **: an occurrence in which play is stopped during a game** ▪ The penalty caused a *stoppage* in play. ▪ There have been more than 10 minutes in *stoppages*. ▪ 10 minutes of *stoppage* time

¹stop·per /ˈstɑːpɚ/ *noun, pl* **-pers** [*count*]

1 : someone or something that stops something • crime *stoppers* • His comment was a conversation *stopper*. — see also SHOWSTOPPER
2 : something that is used to block an opening • a plastic bottle *stopper* • a wine *stopper*

²stopper *verb* **-pers; -pered; -per·ing** [+ *obj*] **:** to close (something) with a stopper • Please *stopper* the bottle. • a *stoppered* bottle

stopping distance *noun, pl* ~ **-tances** [*count, noncount*] **:** the distance that a driver needs in order to safely bring a vehicle to a complete stop

stop·watch /ˈstɑːpˌwɑːʧ/ *noun, pl* **-watch·es** [*count*] **:** a watch that can be started and stopped very quickly and that is used for measuring the amount of time that is taken to do something (such as to run a race)

stor·age /ˈstorɪʤ/ *noun* [*noncount*]
1 a : space where you put things when they are not being used • The house has plenty of *storage*. [=the house has plenty of space in its closets, cabinets, etc.] • Her new house is much smaller, so she had to rent additional *storage*. **b :** the state of being kept in a place when not being used **:** the state of being stored somewhere • We need to get our furniture out of *storage*. • He kept his belongings ***in storage*** [=he stored his belongings] until he found an apartment. **c :** the act of putting something that is not being used in a place where it is available, where it can be kept safely, etc. **:** the act of storing something • the body's *storage* of fat • the *storage* of nuclear waste • The table folds down ***for storage***. [=when you want to store it; when you are not using it] • The cellar is used *for* (food/wine) *storage*.
2 *computers* **a :** space for placing information • a computer with 64 megabytes of *storage* [=*memory*] • disk *storage* **b :** the act of placing information in a computer memory • data *storage*
– storage *adj, always used before a noun* • There is plenty of *storage* space in the attic. • a *storage* room/area • a rental/rented *storage* unit • *storage* costs • a *storage* capacity of 64 megabytes • an internal/external *storage* device

storage battery *noun, pl* ~ **-teries** [*count*] **:** a type of battery that can be given a new charge by passing an electric current through it — called also *storage cell*

¹store /ˈstoɚ/ *verb* **stores; stored; stor·ing** [+ *obj*]
1 a : to put (something that is not being used) in a place where it is available, where it can be kept safely, etc. • I *stored* my furniture until I found a new apartment. • She *stores* her jewels in a safe. • The wine should be *stored* at room temperature. — often + *away* • The grain was *stored away* for the winter. • We *stored away* her old toys in the attic. **b :** to collect and put (something) into one location for future use • The body *stores* fat. • The solar panels *store* energy. — often + *up* • The squirrels are *storing up* nuts for the winter. • Plants *store up* the sun's energy. • (*Brit*) If you get yourself into debt, you're only ***storing up trouble/problems*** for the future.
2 : to place (information) in a person's memory or a computer's memory • They're studying how our brains *store* memories. — often + *away* • He *stored away* his childhood memories. • The file is *stored away* on the backup drive.

²store *noun, pl* **stores**
1 [*count*] **a :** a building or room where things are sold • a grocery/furniture/pet/candy *store* • I'm going to the *store* to buy groceries. • The *stores* are always crowded around the holiday season. — see also BOOKSTORE, CHAIN STORE, CONVENIENCE STORE, DEPARTMENT STORE, DIME STORE, DRUGSTORE, GENERAL STORE, PACKAGE STORE, SUPERSTORE, VARIETY STORE ***usage*** see ¹SHOP 1a **b :** a large building in which something is kept for future use • a grain/weapons *store*
2 [*count*] **:** a large amount or supply of something that is kept for future use • the body's fat *stores* — often + *of* • a *store of* wood/information
3 stores [*plural*] **:** things that are collected and kept for future use • medical/military *stores*
4 [*noncount*] — used to say that something is regarded as having a lot of value or importance • Our family ***sets/lays great store by*** tradition. [=our family values tradition very highly] • He ***puts considerable store in/by*** her opinions. [=he feels her opinions are very important and valuable]
in store **:** in a state of being ready or prepared to happen or be done • We have a big surprise *in store* [=*ready, prepared*] for you. — used to talk about what will happen to someone in the future • I wonder what the future ***holds in store*** for us. = I wonder what ***lies in store*** for us in the future. [=I wonder what will happen to us in the future]
mind the store see ²MIND

store–bought /ˈstoɚˌbɑːt/ *adj, US* **:** bought at a store or shop and not made at home • *store-bought* cookies

store brand *noun, pl* ~ **brands** [*count*] **:** a product that is made for a store and has the store's name on it — compare NAME BRAND
– store–brand *adj, always used before a noun* • *store-brand* products

store card *noun, pl* ~ **cards** [*count*] **:** a credit card that is given out by a store and that can be used to buy goods at that store

store·front /ˈstoɚˌfrʌnt/ *noun, pl* **-fronts** [*count*] *US*
1 : the front side of a store • The *storefront* [=*shop front*] was decorated for the holidays.
2 : a room or group of rooms in the front part of a store building • He rented a *storefront* on Main Street.
– storefront *adj, always used before a noun* • a *storefront* window/office

store·house /ˈstoɚˌhaus/ *noun, pl* **-hous·es** [*count*]
1 : a building where goods are kept for future use **:** WAREHOUSE
2 : a large amount or supply of something • a *storehouse* of information/knowledge/ideas

store·keep·er /ˈstoɚˌkiːpɚ/ *noun, pl* **-ers** [*count*] *US* **:** someone who owns or manages a store or shop **:** SHOPKEEPER

store·room /ˈstoɚˌruːm/ *noun, pl* **-rooms** [*count*] **:** a room or space where things are stored

store·wide /ˈstoɚˈwaɪd/ *adj, US* **:** including all or most of the things that are being sold in a store • a *storewide* sale/clearance

storey *chiefly Brit spelling of* ²STORY

¹sto·ried /ˈstorid/ *adj, always used before a noun* **:** having an interesting history • a *storied* castle/player/leader **:** interesting because of stories that relate to it • She has a *storied* past/career. — compare ²STORIED

²storied (*US*) *or Brit* **sto·reyed** /ˈstorid/ *adj* **:** having a specified number of stories — used in combination • a two-*storied* house • a 50-*storied* building — compare ¹STORIED

stork /ˈstoɚk/ *noun, pl* **storks** [*count*] **:** a large bird that has long legs and a long bill and neck

¹storm /ˈstoɚm/ *noun, pl* **storms** [*count*]
1 : an occurrence of bad weather in which there is a lot of rain, snow, etc., and often strong winds • The sky got dark and it looked like a *storm* was coming. • A ***storm was brewing***. • We made it home before the ***storm struck/broke***. [=before the *storm* began] • I went out for a walk and got ***caught in a storm***. [=I was outside when the storm began] — see also DUST STORM, ELECTRICAL STORM, ELECTRIC STORM, FIRESTORM, HAILSTORM, ICE STORM, RAINSTORM, SANDSTORM, SNOWSTORM, THUNDERSTORM, TROPICAL STORM, WINDSTORM
2 a : a sudden occurrence of something in large amounts — usually singular; often + *of* • a *storm of* publicity • The speaker was greeted with a *storm of* applause. • a *storm of* punches — see also BRAINSTORM **b :** a situation in which many people are angry, upset, etc. — usually singular • His racial comments ***kicked/whipped/stirred up a storm*** in the newspapers. [=newspapers criticized his racial comments very strongly] — often + *of* • a *storm of* controversy/protest
any port in a storm see ¹PORT
a storm in a teacup *Brit* **:** a situation in which people are very angry or upset about something that is not important • The whole controversy turned out to be *a storm in a teacup*. [=(*US*) *a tempest in a teapot*]
take (something) by storm **1 :** to quickly become very successful or popular in (a particular place) or among (a particular group) • The writer has *taken* the literary world *by storm*. • The new fashion has *taken* London *by storm*. **2 :** to attack and capture (a place) suddenly by using a lot of force or a large number of people • The soldiers *took* the castle *by storm*.
the calm/lull before the storm **:** a period of quiet that comes before a time of activity, excitement, violence, etc. • The college was quiet that morning, but it was *the calm before the storm*. Thousands of students would arrive later.
up a storm *informal* — used to say that something is being done with a lot of energy or enthusiasm • They danced/sang *up a storm*. • He was cooking *up a storm*.
weather the storm *or* ***ride out the storm*** **:** to deal with a

difficult situation without being harmed or damaged too much • Newspapers have *weathered the storm* of online information by providing news online themselves. • It was a difficult time but they managed to *ride out the storm.*

[2]**storm** *verb* **storms; stormed; storm·ing**
1 [*no obj*] — used with *it* to say that a storm (sense 1) is happening • *It stormed* all night.
2 : to attack (something) suddenly with a lot of force or with a large number of people [+ *obj*] Soldiers *stormed* the fort. • Police *stormed* the building. [*no obj*] The army *stormed* ashore.
3 *always followed by an adverb or preposition* [*no obj*] **:** to go quickly and in an angry, loud way • The mob *stormed* through the streets. • She yelled at us and *stormed* off. • He *stormed* out of the room. • She *stormed* into the office.
4 : to shout loudly and angrily [*no obj*] — often + *at* • She *stormed at* her parents and ran to her room. [+ *obj*] "Do you know who I am?" he *stormed.*

storm cloud *noun, pl* ~ **clouds** [*count*] **:** a dark cloud which shows that a storm is coming — sometimes used figuratively • Economic *storm clouds* loom on the horizon.

storm door *noun, pl* ~ **doors** [*count*] *US* **:** a second door that is placed outside the usual outside door of a building for protection against cold and bad weather

storm drain *noun, pl* ~ **drains** [*count*] **:** a drain that carries water (such as rainwater) away from a street, parking lot, etc.

storm trooper *noun, pl* ~ **-ers** [*count*] **:** a member of a group of specially trained and violent soldiers especially in Nazi Germany during World War II

storm window *noun, pl* ~ **-dows** [*count*] *US* **:** a second window that covers the usual outside window of a building for protection against cold and bad weather

stormy /ˈstoɚmi/ *adj* **storm·i·er; -est** [*also more* ~; *most* ~]
1 : relating to or affected by a storm • a dark, *stormy* sky • a *stormy* sea • The weather/day was cold and *stormy.*
2 : full of anger, shouting, etc. • a *stormy* meeting • Their relationship was very *stormy.* • a *stormy* family life
– storm·i·ness /ˈstoɚminəs/ *noun* [*noncount*]

[1]**sto·ry** /ˈstori/ *noun, pl* **-ries**
1 [*count*] **:** a description of how something happened • The movie is based on a true *story.* • What is the *story* behind (the making of) this painting? • That's not the whole *story.* [=there are more details to be told] • Many years later they met again, but that's another *story.* • He said he wasn't at the scene of the crime, but the fingerprints ***tell a different story.*** [=the fingerprints show that he was there] • "Why are you late?" "It's ***a long story.*** [=it is too complicated to explain] I'll tell you later." • (*US*) They were having a lot of problems. ***To make a long story short,*** she decided to leave him. = (*Brit*) ***To cut a long story short,*** she decided to leave him. • (*informal*) He yelled at me, and I left. ***End of story.*** [=there is nothing more to say about it] — often + *about* or *of* • We're still waiting to hear the full *story* [=all of the details] *of* what happened. • She's told us the *story of* the great snowstorm of 1977 many times. • He told all sorts of *stories* [=*anecdotes*] *about* his childhood. • Tell them the *story about* that time you got stuck in the elevator. ✧ The phrase ***the story goes*** is used to say that you are telling a story that you heard from other people. • *The story goes* [=people say] that after he died, he haunted the house. • *The story goes* like this: He was walking through the woods when he spotted a huge bear. • She was very depressed or ***so the story goes.*** [=or so people say] — see also HORROR STORY, SOB STORY, SUCCESS STORY, WAR STORY
2 [*count*] **a :** a description of imaginary events that is told as a form of entertainment • Don't be scared. It's only a *story.* • The *story* (of the book) is about growing up in Harlem during the 1920s. • The movie is a *story* of three single women looking for true love. • a horror/detective *story* • She read the child a ***bedtime story.*** [=a story that you read or tell a child at bedtime] — see also GHOST STORY, SHAGGY-DOG STORY, SHORT STORY **b :** the series of events that happen in a story • The *story* [=*plot*] is the same in all her books/movies/plays.
3 [*count*] **:** something that is reported in a newspaper, on television, etc. **:** a news article or broadcast • a news *story* [=*report*] • The lead *story* in the news today is about the earthquake. • His death was one of the biggest *stories* of the year. • The *story* about the fire made the front page of the newspaper. = The front-page *story* was about the fire. • The magazine ***ran a story*** [=printed an article] about the scandal. — see also COVER STORY
4 [*count*] **:** a description of the most important events in someone's life • the Princess Diana *story* = the *story* of Princess Diana • The biography is a *story* of courage. • She told her ***life story*** to him. [=she told him about the things that had happened in her life] — sometimes used figuratively • Having bad luck with men is ***the story of my life.*** [=I have often had bad luck with men] • Gaining and losing weight is *the story of her life.*
5 a [*count*] **:** a condition or set of conditions that affects someone or something **:** SITUATION • We lost power, and it's the same *story* throughout the city. [=people throughout the city also lost power] • Living on your own is a whole different *story* [=*matter*] from living with your parents. • She got good grades in math, but English was ***another story.*** [=she did not do well in English] • The restaurant has great desserts, but that's only/just ***half the story.*** [=part of the story] It also has wonderful entertainment. • It's ***the same old story*** [=things have not changed] with her—she just can't or won't keep a job. **b *the story*** *somewhat informal* **:** basic information about someone or something • I'm still trying to find out *the story* [=the reason] behind this new policy. • What's *the story* [=*the deal*] with that guy? [=what can you tell me about that guy?]
6 [*count*] **a :** a lie that someone tells **:** a false story • You shouldn't tell *stories.* — see also COCK-AND-BULL STORY, FISH STORY **b :** an explanation or excuse and especially one that is not true • The police don't believe his *story.* — often + *about* • She made up some *story about* getting stuck in traffic.
a likely story see [1]LIKELY
– compare [2]STORY

[2]**story** *also chiefly Brit* **sto·rey** /ˈstori/ *noun, pl* **stories** [*count*] **:** a group of rooms or an area that forms one floor level of a building • She lives/works on the second floor of a five-*story* building. [=a building that has five stories/floors] • The building is 20 *stories* high. — see also MULTISTORY
— compare [1]STORY

sto·ry·board /ˈstoriˌboɚd/ *noun, pl* **-boards** [*count*] **:** a series of drawings or pictures that show the changes of scenes and actions for a movie, television show, etc.
– storyboard *verb* **-boards; -board·ed; -board·ing** [+ *obj*] • He *storyboarded* the fight scene.

[1]**sto·ry·book** /ˈstoriˌbʊk/ *noun, pl* **-books** [*count*] **:** a book of stories for children

[2]**storybook** *adj, always used before a noun* **:** like something described in a storybook • a *storybook* [=*fairy-tale*] ending/romance

story line *noun, pl* ~ **lines** [*count*] **:** the series of events that happen in a story **:** PLOT

sto·ry·tell·er /ˈstoriˌtɛlɚ/ *noun, pl* **-ers** [*count*] **:** someone who tells or writes stories • She's a good/master *storyteller.*
– sto·ry·tell·ing /ˈstoriˌtɛlɪŋ/ *noun* [*noncount*] • She is good at *storytelling.*

stoup /ˈstuːp/ *noun, pl* **stoups** [*count*] **:** a container for holy water at the entrance of a church

[1]**stout** /ˈstaʊt/ *adj* **stout·er; -est** [*also more* ~; *most* ~]
1 : thick and strong • The plant has a *stout* [=*sturdy*] stem. • *stout* legs • a *stout* neck
2 : having a large body that is wide with fat or muscles • a short, *stout* [=*stocky*] man
3 a *literary* **:** brave and strong • a *stout* leader • He has a *stout* heart. **b** *formal* **:** forceful and determined • His lawyer put up a *stout* defense in court.
– stout·ly *adv* • a *stoutly* built man • She *stoutly* defended him.

[2]**stout** *noun, pl* **stouts** [*count, noncount*] **:** a very dark, heavy beer

stout·heart·ed /ˈstaʊtˌhɑɚtəd/ *adj, literary* **:** brave and determined • a *stouthearted* soldier

[1]**stove** /ˈstoʊv/ *noun, pl* **stoves** [*count*]
1 *chiefly US* **:** a flat piece of kitchen equipment for cooking that usually has four devices (called burners) which become hot when they are turned on and that often is attached to an oven • Is the *stove* on/off? • She put the pan on the *stove* over medium heat. • I cooked the burgers on the *stove.* — called also (*Brit*) *cooker*; compare COOKTOP; see also COOKSTOVE
2 : a device that burns fuel for heating or cooking • a wood-burning/gas *stove* — see also POTBELLIED STOVE
3 : an oven or furnace that is used for hardening, burning, or drying something (such as pottery) **:** KILN

[2]**stove** *past tense and past participle of* [2]STAVE

S

stove•pipe /ˈstoʊv,paɪp/ *noun, pl* **-pipes** [*count*]
1 : a metal pipe used for carrying away smoke from a stove
2 : a very tall silk hat ▪ a *stovepipe* hat

stove•top /ˈstoʊv,tɑ:p/ *noun, pl* **-tops** [*count*] *US* **:** the top of a stove — compare COOKTOP

stow /ˈstoʊ/ *verb* **stows; stowed; stow•ing** [+ *obj*] **:** to put (something that is not being used) in a place where it is available, where it can be kept safely, etc. **:** STORE ▪ He *stowed* his gear in a locker. ▪ Luggage may be *stowed* under the seat. — often + *away* ▪ The supplies were *stowed away* below deck.
stow away [*phrasal verb*] **:** to hide on a ship, airplane, etc., in order to travel without paying or being seen ▪ When he was a young boy he *stowed away* on a merchant ship headed for China. — see also STOWAWAY

stow•age /ˈstowɪʤ/ *noun* [*noncount*] **:** space especially on a ship or airplane for stowing things ▪ There's a lot of *stowage* below deck.

stow•away /ˈstowə,weɪ/ *noun, pl* **-aways** [*count*] **:** someone who hides on a ship, airplane, etc., in order to travel without paying or being seen ▪ A *stowaway* was discovered on the ship. — see also *stow away* at STOW

strad•dle /ˈstrædl/ *verb* **strad•dles; strad•dled; strad•dling** [+ *obj*]
1 : to sit or ride with a leg on either side of (something) ▪ He *straddled* the stool. ▪ She *straddled* the horse.
2 a : to be on both sides of (something) ▪ Campsites *straddled* the river. — often used figuratively ▪ Their music *straddles* the line between rock and jazz. **b :** to have parts that are in (different places, regions, etc.) ▪ Turkey *straddles* Asia and Europe. — often used figuratively ▪ The movie *straddles* too many genres.
3 : to agree with or seem to agree with two opposite sides of (something) ▪ She *straddled* the issue.

strafe /ˈstreɪf/ *verb* **strafes; strafed; straf•ing** [+ *obj*] **:** to attack (something) with machine guns from low-flying airplanes ▪ The planes *strafed* the town/battleship.

strag•gle /ˈstrægəl/ *verb, always followed by an adverb or preposition* **strag•gles; strag•gled; strag•gling** [*no obj*]
1 : to walk slowly into or from a place in a way that is not continuous or organized ▪ The children *straggled* in from outside. ▪ People *straggled* off the train.
2 : to move away or spread out from others in a disorganized way ▪ She *straggled* behind the rest of the group. ▪ Branches *straggled* out and blocked the path.

strag•gler /ˈstræglɚ/ *noun, pl* **-glers** [*count*] **:** a person or animal that moves slower than others and becomes separated from them ▪ People waited for the *stragglers* to finish the race. ▪ The cowboy had to round up a few *stragglers*.

strag•gly /ˈstrægli/ *adj* **strag•gli•er; -est** [*also more* ~; *most* ~] **:** growing or hanging in an untidy way **:** SCRAGGLY ▪ *straggly* hair ▪ His beard is *straggly*.

¹straight /ˈstreɪt/ *adj* **straight•er; -est** [*also more* ~; *most* ~]
1 : not having curves, bends, or angles ▪ a *straight* line/edge ▪ She has long, *straight* hair. ▪ Keep your back *straight*.
2 : vertical or level ▪ The flagpole is perfectly *straight*. ▪ The picture isn't quite *straight*.
3 *always used before a noun* **:** following one after the other in order ▪ He has won three *straight* [=*consecutive*] tournaments. **:** following each other without interruption ▪ We sat in the airport for five *straight* hours.
4 : honest and direct ▪ They wouldn't give me a *straight* answer. ▪ He's known for his *straight* dealing. ▪ They're not being *straight* with you. ▪ What we want is some ***straight talk***.
5 *always used before a noun* **a :** including only two people or things ▪ It was a *straight* choice: accept the offer or don't. ▪ a *straight* exchange/swap **b :** not including any things or parts of a different kind ▪ a *straight* romance novel ▪ The band plays *straight* blues. ▪ (*US*) He always votes a *straight* Democratic ticket. [=he always votes for Democratic candidates] ▪ (*US*) She got *straight* A's in all her classes last year. [=she got an A in every class] ▪ (*US*) a ***straight-A*** student
6 *not used before a noun* **:** with everything in its proper place ▪ After supper, the kids helped ***set/put*** the kitchen ***straight***. [=tidy up the kitchen]
7 *not used before a noun* **:** agreeing with what is true or what is stated to be true ▪ We have to have our stories *straight* or else the police will get suspicious. ▪ Let me ***get this straight*** [=I am surprised/confused by what you are saying and I want to be sure that I understand you correctly]: You want me to lend you $2,000? ▪ You need to ***get your facts straight***. [=you need to get your facts correct] ▪ He ***set/put her straight about/on*** what happened. [=he corrected her and explained to her what actually happened] — see also *set/put the record straight* at ¹RECORD
8 *not used before a noun, informal* **:** having nothing owed by either side ▪ You pay for my ticket, and I'll consider us *straight*. [=*even*]
9 : behaving in a way that is socially correct and acceptable ▪ (*disapproving*) She's too *straight* [=*conventional*] and needs to lighten up. ▪ (*informal*) He left the gang and promised himself that he would ***go straight***. [=stop being a criminal]
10 *informal* **:** HETEROSEXUAL ▪ He's gay but he has a lot of *straight* friends.
11 : not using drugs or alcohol ▪ She has been *straight* for two years now.
12 *US, of alcoholic drinks* **:** not mixed with anything **:** without ice or water added ▪ I like my bourbon/whiskey *straight*. [=*neat*] ▪ I'll have a martini ***straight up***.
13 : not joking or funny **:** SERIOUS ▪ a *straight* actor ▪ *straight* theatrical drama — see also STRAIGHT MAN
– straight•ness *noun* [*noncount*]

²straight *adv*
1 : in a straight or direct way ▪ She looked him *straight* [=*right, directly*] in the eye and told him to leave. ▪ She walked *straight* up to him and slapped him in the face. ▪ The tunnel goes *straight* through the mountain. ▪ The library is *straight* ahead. ▪ This road will take you *straight* [=*directly*] to the next town. ▪ He was so drunk he couldn't walk *straight*. ▪ She sat with her legs *straight* out. ▪ The tree fell *straight* down. ▪ The car went *straight* off the road. ▪ She told him ***straight to his face*** that she hated him.
2 : in or into a vertical position ▪ Pine trees stood *straight* along the path. ▪ Sit up *straight* and don't slouch.
3 a : without any delay **:** directly or immediately ▪ She came *straight* [=*right*] home from school. ▪ The company hires many people *straight* [=*right*] out of college. ▪ He went *straight* to bed when he came home. ▪ Let me ***get/come straight to the point***: I think we should break up. **b :** without interruption ▪ The rescue crew has been working for three days *straight*. ▪ The baby slept *straight* through the night. ▪ Since no one objected to her plan, she went ***straight on*** to talk about how to begin.
4 : in an honest and direct way ▪ Tell me *straight*: did you do it or didn't you? ▪ Are you ***dealing/playing straight*** with me? [=are you being honest with me?] ▪ (*informal*) ***Straight up***, what did you really pay for the tickets?
5 : in the usual, normal, or correct way ▪ She was so drunk she couldn't ***see straight***. ▪ Can you please be quiet? I can't ***think straight***.
ramrod straight see RAMROD
straight off *US, informal* **:** without delay or hesitation **:** IMMEDIATELY ▪ I told him *straight off* that I wouldn't help him. ▪ I knew *straight off* [=*right away*] that she was lying.
straight out *informal* **:** in a very direct way ▪ I asked him *straight out* if he was doing drugs.

³straight *noun, pl* **straights** [*count*]
1 *informal* **:** HETEROSEXUAL — usually plural ▪ gays and *straights*
2 : a straight part of a racecourse **:** STRAIGHTAWAY — usually singular ▪ He overtook them on the *straight*.
3 : a hand of playing cards in poker that contains five cards in sequence (such as a five, a six, a seven, an eight, and a nine)
the straight and narrow *informal* **:** the way of living that is honest and morally proper ▪ His wife keeps him ***on the straight and narrow***.

straight–arm /ˈstreɪt,ɑɚm/ *noun, pl* **-arms** [*count*] *American football* **:** the act of pushing another player away from you with the palm of your hand while your arm is fully extended — called also *stiff-arm*
– straight–arm *verb* **-arms; -armed; -arm•ing** [+ *obj*] ▪ The ball-carrier *straight-armed* the tackler.

straight arrow *noun, pl* ~ **-rows** [*count*] *US, informal* **:** a person who is very honest and morally proper ▪ He doesn't drink or smoke. He's a real *straight arrow*.

¹straight•away /,streɪtəˈweɪ/ *adv* **:** without any delay **:** IMMEDIATELY ▪ He found the information *straightaway*.

²straight•away /ˈstreɪtə,weɪ/ *noun, pl* **-aways** [*count*] *chiefly US* **:** a straight part of a racecourse — usually singular ▪ He overtook them on the *straightaway*.

straight•edge /ˈstreɪt,ɛʤ/ *noun, pl* **-edg•es** [*count*] **:** a piece of wood, metal, plastic, etc., with a straight edge that you use to make sure something (such as a line or surface) is straight or to make straight lines or cuts

straight·en /ˈstreɪtn̩/ *verb* **-ens; -ened; -en·ing**

1 : to make (something) straight or to become straight [+ *obj*] He *straightened* the bent antenna. • *Straighten* your legs. — often + *out* • You need to *straighten out* your legs for this stretch. [*no obj*] The drooping flowers *straightened* in the rain. — often + *out* • The river curves and then *straightens out* again.

2 [+ *obj*] **:** to make (something) organized or tidy **:** to put (something) in order — usually + *out* or *up* • He took time to *straighten out* the papers on his desk. • They *straightened up* the house after the party.

straighten out [*phrasal verb*] **1** ***straighten out (something) or straighten (something) out* :** to deal with (something) successfully • I need more time to *straighten out* my problems. **2 a** ***straighten out*** *or* ***straighten out (something) or straighten (something) out* :** to improve in behavior or condition • He *straightened out* after joining the army. • The problem will not *straighten out* on its own. • You need to *straighten* your life *out*. **b** ***straighten (someone) out*** *or* ***straighten out (someone)* :** to improve the behavior of (someone) • Her parents sent her to boarding school to *straighten* her *out*.

straighten up [*phrasal verb*] **1 :** to move your body to an upright position • *Straighten up*. There's no excuse for slouching. **2** *US* **:** to improve in behavior • You need to *straighten up*, young man.

– straight·en·er /ˈstreɪtnɚ/ *noun, pl* **-ers** [*count*] She uses a *straightener* to make her hair straight. [*noncount*] a bottle of hair *straightener*

straight face *noun, pl* **~ faces** [*count*] **:** a face that shows no emotion and especially no amusement • She lied with a *straight face*. • It was hard to ***keep a straight face***. [=to not laugh or smile] • The students quickly ***put on straight faces*** as the teacher walked into the room.

– straight–faced /ˈstreɪtˈfeɪst/ *adj* • *straight-faced* lawyers • He told the story *straight-faced*. [=with a straight face]

straight flush *noun, pl* **~ flushes** [*count*] **:** a hand of playing cards in poker that contains five cards of the same suit in sequence (such as a five, a six, a seven, an eight, and a nine of clubs) — compare ROYAL FLUSH

straight·for·ward /ˌstreɪtˈfoɚwɚd/ *adj* [*more ~; most ~*]

1 : easy to do or understand **:** not complicated • Using the computer program is fairly *straightforward*. • The instructions are *straightforward*.

2 : honest and open • He was very *straightforward* with us. • She gave a *straightforward* account of what happened.

– straight·for·ward·ly *adv* • She spoke *straightforwardly* about what had happened. **– straight·for·ward·ness** *noun* [*noncount*]

straightjacket *variant spelling of* STRAITJACKET

straightlaced *variant spelling of* STRAITLACED

straight man *noun, pl* **~ men** [*count*] **:** a member of a comedy team who says things that allow a partner to make jokes

straight–out /ˈstreɪtˈaʊt/ *adj* **:** very clear and direct • Her answer was a *straight-out* no.

straight razor *noun, pl* **~ -zors** [*count*] *chiefly US* **:** a razor that is enclosed in a case which forms a handle when the razor is pulled out for use — called also *(Brit) cut-throat razor*

straight shooter *noun, pl* **~ -ers** [*count*] *US, informal* **:** a person who is very honest • He's a *straight shooter* who says what he thinks.

straight·way /ˈstreɪtˈweɪ/ *adv, old-fashioned* **:** STRAIGHTAWAY, IMMEDIATELY • I spotted them *straightway*.

[1]strain /ˈstreɪn/ *noun, pl* **strains**

1 : a feeling of stress and worry that you have because you are trying to do too much, are dealing with a difficult problem, etc. [*count*] The work has been a *strain* on me. [=it has been stressful for me] • The *strain* of working and going to school full-time was too much for her. • He talked about the ***stresses and strains*** of owning a business. • The long hours at work have ***put/placed a strain on*** me. • She has been ***under a strain*** lately. [*noncount*] Help from other workers took some of the *strain* [=*pressure*] off me. • She has been ***under (a lot of) strain*** lately. • He is holding up ***under the strain***. [=he is able to deal with the pressure] • He ***cracked/collapsed/buckled under the strain***. [=he was not able to deal with the pressure]

2 : something that is very difficult to deal with and that causes harm or trouble [*count*] There are *strains* [=*problems*] in their relationship. • Being deeply in debt has been a *strain* [=*burden*] on our marriage. • The disagreement has ***put/placed a strain on*** their friendship. • Sending their children to college has *put/placed a strain on* their finances. [*noncount*] Being in debt has been a source of *strain* on our marriage. • Their friendship is ***under strain***.

3 : a force that pulls or stretches something **:** STRESS [*count*] The cable is designed to withstand *strains* of more than four tons. — usually singular • The *strain* on the cables supporting the bridge is enormous. • The cables could not take the *strain* of the extra weight. [*noncount*] If there is too much *strain* on the cables they will snap. • Moving the piano will ***put/place too much strain*** on our back muscles. • The cable broke ***under the strain***.

4 : an injury to a body part or muscle that is caused by too much tension, effort, or use [*count*] a leg/muscle *strain* [*noncount*] Long hours of study can cause eye *strain*. • Heavy lifting is a cause of muscle *strain*.

– compare [3]STRAIN

[2]strain *verb* **strains; strained; strain·ing**

1 [+ *obj*] **:** to injure (a body part or muscle) by too much tension, use, or effort • I *strained* my back trying to lift the couch. • Too much computer work *strains* the eyes. • He *strained* a muscle in his leg. — compare SPRAIN

2 : to try very hard to do or get something [*no obj*] — often + *for* • He was *straining for* air. [=he was struggling to breathe] — often followed by *to + verb* • He *strained to open* the jar. • She *strained to sing* the high notes. • The people in the back of the room *strained to hear* the speaker. [+ *obj*] I ***strained my ears*** to hear [=I tried very hard to hear] what they were whispering. • I ***strained my eyes*** [=I tried very hard to see] in the darkness.

3 a : to be pulled or stretched in a forceful way [*no obj*] His muscles *strained* under the heavy weight. [+ *obj*] People were ***straining their necks*** [=were lifting their heads as high as they could by stretching their necks] to see the fight. — sometimes used figuratively • You are *straining* (the limits of) my patience with your nagging. **b** [*no obj*] **:** to pull hard on or push hard against something — + *at* or *against* • The dog *strained at* its leash. • His belly *strained against* the buttons of the shirt. — sometimes used figuratively • The kids were ***straining at the leash*** to get going. [=were very eager to get going]

4 [+ *obj*] **:** to cause problems or trouble for (something) • The disagreement *strained* their relationship. • The rent has *strained* our finances. • The company is financially *strained*.

5 [+ *obj*] **:** to separate a liquid from solid pieces by using a special device (called a strainer) • He *strained* the pasta. = He *strained* the water from the pasta. • She *strained* the gravy. = She *strained* the lumps out of the gravy.

strain yourself **1 :** to injure yourself by making your muscles do too much work • Don't *strain yourself* trying to move the couch. **2 :** to put a lot of physical or mental effort into doing something • Don't *strain yourself* trying to think of the answer. I can tell you what it is.

[3]strain *noun, pl* **strains**

1 [*count*] **:** a group of closely related plants or animals **:** VARIETY — often + *of* • a strong *strain of* wheat • a new *strain of* bacteria • This *strain of* mice is resistant to the disease.

2 [*count*] *literary + somewhat old-fashioned* **:** a usually bad quality that someone or something has — usually singular; usually + *of* • There is a *strain of* snobbery in her. • There is a *strain of* madness in that family.

3 [*singular*] *formal + literary* **:** a small amount of something • There was a *strain* [=*touch, trace*] of sadness in his voice.

4 [*count*] **:** a kind or sort of something — usually + *of* • a different *strain of* philosophy • a new *strain of* pop music

5 ***strains*** [*plural*] *formal* **:** the musical sounds *of* someone or something • We relaxed to the *strains of* Chopin. • the *strains of* a harp

– compare [1]STRAIN

strained /ˈstreɪnd/ *adj*

1 : feeling or showing the effect of too much work, use, effort, etc. • Her voice sounded *strained*. • a *strained* face

2 : not natural and sincere **:** FORCED • a *strained* smile • He made a *strained* attempt at being polite. • His apology seemed *strained*.

3 : not friendly and relaxed • Their relationship was *strained*.

strain·er /ˈstreɪnɚ/ *noun, pl* **-ers** [*count*] **:** a kitchen device that has many small holes and that is used to hold back solid pieces while a liquid passes through **:** SIEVE

strait /ˈstreɪt/ *noun, pl* **straits**

1 [*count*] **:** a narrow passage of water that connects two large bodies of water • the Bering *Strait* — often plural • the *Straits* of Gibraltar

2 straits *[plural]* : a very difficult situation • Her campaign is in desperate *straits*. • The company is in desperate financial *straits*. • The economy is in ***dire straits***.

strait·ened /ˈstreɪtn̩d/ *adj, always used before a noun, formal* : not having enough money : having less money than before • They live ***in straitened circumstances***.

strait·jack·et *also* **straight·jack·et** /ˈstreɪtˌʤækət/ *noun, pl* **-ets** *[count]* : a jacket that has long arms which can be tied together behind someone's back and that is used to control the movements of a violent prisoner or patient — sometimes used figuratively • He struggled to free himself from the *straitjacket* of debt.

strait·laced *or* **straight·laced** /ˈstreɪtˈleɪst/ *adj [more ~; most ~]* : very proper in manners, morals, or opinion • She is very *straitlaced*.

[1]**strand** /ˈstrænd/ *noun, pl* **strands** *[count]*

1 : a thin piece of thread, wire, hair, etc. • The *strands* were twisted together. — often + *of* • a *strand of* thread • The police found a single *strand of* hair at the crime scene.

2 : something that is long like a string — often + *of* • a *strand of* pearls • a *strand of* DNA

3 : one of the parts of something that is very complicated — often + *of* • All the *strands of* the story's plot are woven together in the final chapter. • The police are slowly putting the *strands of* evidence together.

– compare [3]STRAND

[2]**strand** *verb* **strands; strand·ed; strand·ing** *[+ obj]*

1 : to leave (a person or animal) in a place without a way of leaving it — usually used as *(be) stranded* • She *was stranded* in a foreign city with no money. • They *were stranded* on a deserted island. • His car broke down, and he *was stranded* in the middle of nowhere. • Her flight was canceled, so she was ***left stranded*** at the airport.

2 : to cause (something, such as a boat or a sea animal) to become stuck on land — usually used as *(be) stranded* • The ship *was stranded* on the sandbank. • a *stranded* [=*beached*] whale

3 *baseball* **:** to leave (a base runner) on base at the end of an inning • The team *stranded* 10 runners during the game. • Two base runners were ***left stranded*** at the end of the inning.

[3]**strand** *noun, pl* **strands** *[count]* : the land along the edge of a sea, lake, etc. : a shore or beach • We walked along the *strand*. — compare [1]STRAND

strange /ˈstreɪnʤ/ *adj* **strang·er; strang·est** *[also more ~; most ~]*

1 : different from what is usual, normal, or expected : ODD • Does his behavior seem *strange* to you? • Truth is sometimes *stranger* than fiction. • That is one of the *strangest* creatures I have ever seen. • What a *strange*-looking animal. • There was something *strange* [=*peculiar*] about his new friend. • She got a *strange* [=*weird*] feeling when the phone rang. • He gave me a *strange* look. • *Strange* as it may seem, I don't like walking barefoot on the grass. • It's *strange* that nobody told me about this before. • It's *strange* [=*surprising*] how quickly a person's opinion can change. • It is *strange* (that) he would leave town and not tell anybody. • That's *strange*. He was here a minute ago. • The *strange* thing is that nobody saw him enter or leave the building. • A *strange* [=*funny*] thing happened to me on my way home. • ***For some strange reason***, we thought you weren't coming. [=it is strange that we thought you weren't coming] • ***Strange to say*** [=*strangely*], I was thinking the same thing.

2 : not known, heard, or seen before : UNFAMILIAR • Children are taught not to talk to *strange* people. • The language was *strange* to me. • a *strange* city/country

3 *not used before a noun* **:** not entirely comfortable or well • He ***felt strange*** being the boss of people who were as old as his parents. • My stomach *feels* a little *strange*. • I began to *feel strange*, and then I fainted.

– **strange·ness** /ˈstreɪnʤnəs/ *noun [noncount]* • The *strangeness* of the dream puzzled me.

strange·ly /ˈstreɪnʤli/ *adv*

1 *[more ~; most ~]* **:** in a strange way • He has been acting very *strangely* lately. • She had never been there before, but the place seemed *strangely* [=*oddly*] familiar to her.

2 — used to say that something is strange or surprising • *Strangely*, my dad never asked me why I needed to borrow the car. • ***Strangely enough***, he wasn't disappointed that he didn't get the job.

strang·er /ˈstreɪnʤɚ/ *noun, pl* **-ers** *[count]*

1 : someone who you have not met before or do not know • Children are taught not to talk to *strangers*. • He is a complete/total/perfect *stranger* to me.

2 : someone who has not experienced something — + *to* • He is a *stranger to* losing. [=he does not know what losing is like] — usually used in negative statements • She is ***no stranger to*** controversy. [=she has been involved in controversy before]

3 : someone who is in a new and unfamiliar place • "Excuse me. Do you know where the library is?" "I'm sorry. I'm a *stranger* here myself." • I'm a *stranger* to the area.

4 *informal* **a —** used to greet someone you have not seen in a long time • Hello, *stranger*. I haven't seen you in ages. **b —** used to say that you hope to see someone again soon • ***Don't be a stranger***, now. Come back real soon.

stran·gle /ˈstræŋgəl/ *verb* **stran·gles; stran·gled; stran·gling** *[+ obj]*

1 : to kill (a person or animal) by squeezing the throat • He used a rope to *strangle* her (to death). = He *strangled* her (to death) with a rope.

2 : to stop (something) from growing or developing • The weeds are *strangling* the plant. • The company is trying to *strangle* the smaller competition.

– **stran·gler** /ˈstræŋglɚ/ *noun, pl* **-glers** *[count]* • She was the first victim killed by the *strangler*.

strangled *adj* — used to describe a cry or other sound that stops suddenly or that seems strained because of tightness in the throat • She let out a *strangled* cry/sob. • He spoke in a *strangled* voice.

stran·gle·hold /ˈstræŋgəlˌhould/ *noun, pl* **-holds** *[count]*

1 : an illegal hold in wrestling by which your opponent is choked

2 : a force or influence that stops something from growing or developing — usually singular • He finally broke free from the *stranglehold* of his domineering parents. — often + *on* • The state has a *stranglehold on* the city's finances.

stran·gu·la·tion /ˌstræŋgjəˈleɪʃən/ *noun [noncount]* : the act of killing someone by squeezing the throat : the act of strangling someone • The cause of death was *strangulation*.

[1]**strap** /ˈstræp/ *noun, pl* **straps** *[count]* : a narrow and usually flat piece of a material that is used for fastening, holding together, or wrapping something • a bra/leather *strap* • a watch *strap* — see pictures at BAG, SHOE; see also BOOTSTRAPS, JOCKSTRAP, SHOULDER STRAP, SPAGHETTI STRAP

[2]**strap** *verb* **straps; strapped; strap·ping** *[+ obj]*

1 *always followed by an adverb or preposition* **:** to fasten (someone or something) by using a strap • We *strapped* our snowshoes on. • She climbed the mountain with a 40-pound pack *strapped* to her back. • She ***strapped*** the children ***in*** [=fastened the children's seat belts] and drove away. • She made sure that both children were ***strapped in***.

2 *chiefly Brit* **:** to wrap (an injured or broken part of the body) with bandages — often + *up* • His broken leg will be *strapped up* for a long time.

strap on the feedbag see FEEDBAG

strap·less /ˈstræpləs/ *adj* : made or worn without straps over the shoulders • a *strapless* evening gown

strapped *adj, informal* : not having enough money : lacking money • The company is financially *strapped* and is expected to file for bankruptcy. • I can't go out tonight. I'm ***strapped for cash***.

strapping *adj, always used before a noun, of a person* : tall, strong, and healthy • a *strapping* young man

strap·py /ˈstræpi/ *adj, always used before a noun* : having straps • *strappy* sandals/shoes

strata *plural of* STRATUM

strat·a·gem /ˈstrætəʤəm/ *noun, pl* **-gems** *[count] formal* : a trick or plan for deceiving an enemy or for achieving a goal • a clever *stratagem*

stra·te·gic /strəˈtiːʤɪk/ *also* **stra·te·gi·cal** /strəˈtiːʤɪkəl/ *adj*

1 : of or relating to a general plan that is created to achieve a goal in war, politics, etc., usually over a long period of time • *strategic* planning/warfare • The bridges have great *strategic* value. • *strategic* maneuvers [=maneuvers that are done as part of a general strategy] • *strategic* bombing • a *strategic* retreat [=a retreat that is done in order to help accomplish a general plan] • *strategic* nuclear weapons [=powerful nuclear weapons that are designed to be used against targets that are chosen as part of a general plan to defeat an enemy rather than in an attempt to win a specific battle]

2 : useful or important in achieving a plan or strategy • The hill is located at a *strategic* position. • a *strategic* location

S

– stra·te·gi·cal·ly /strəˈtiːʤɪkli/ *adv* ▪ *strategically* placed armies ▪ The road is *strategically* located.

strat·e·gist /ˈstrætəʤɪst/ *noun, pl* **-gists** [*count*] : a person who is skilled in making plans for achieving a goal : someone who is good at forming strategies ▪ military/political/campaign *strategists*

strat·e·gize /ˈstrætəˌʤaɪz/ *verb* **-giz·es; -gized; -giz·ing** [*no obj*] *US* : to make a plan for achieving a goal and especially a military or political goal : to form a strategy ▪ The organization *strategizes* for Republican candidates.

strat·e·gy /ˈstrætəʤi/ *noun, pl* **-gies**
1 [*count*] : a careful plan or method for achieving a particular goal usually over a long period of time ▪ They are proposing a new *strategy* for treating the disease with a combination of medications. ▪ The government is developing innovative *strategies* to help people without insurance get medical care. ▪ marketing/business/investment/defense *strategies*
2 [*noncount*] : the skill of making or carrying out plans to achieve a goal ▪ a specialist in campaign/military *strategy*

strat·i·fi·ca·tion /ˌstrætəfəˈkeɪʃən/ *noun, pl* **-tions**
1 [*count, noncount*] : the state of being divided into social classes ▪ social *stratification/stratifications*
2 [*noncount*] *technical* : the state of having many layers ▪ the *stratification* of the Earth's crust

strat·i·fied /ˈstrætəˌfaɪd/ *adj*
1 : arranged or formed in layers ▪ *stratified* rock
2 [*more ~; most ~*] : divided into social classes ▪ *stratified* societies

strato·sphere /ˈstrætəˌsfiə/ *noun*
the stratosphere **1** : the upper layer of the Earth's atmosphere that begins about 7 miles (11 kilometers) above the Earth's surface and ends about 30 miles (50 kilometers) above the Earth's surface **2** : a very high position, level, or amount ▪ Tuition at many colleges has soared into *the stratosphere.* [=has become extremely expensive] ▪ His career is clearly headed for *the stratosphere.*

stra·tum /ˈstreɪtəm, *Brit* ˈstrɑːtəm/ *noun, pl* **stra·ta** /ˈstreɪtə, *Brit* ˈstrɑːtə/ [*count*]
1 : one of usually many layers of a substance (such as rock) ▪ a rock *stratum* ▪ a *stratum* of earth
2 : a level of society made up of people of the same rank or position ▪ Drug abuse is a problem in every *stratum* of society. = Drug abuse is a problem in all social *strata.*

straw /ˈstrɑː/ *noun, pl* **straws**
1 a [*noncount*] : the dry stems of wheat and other grain plants ▪ a bed/pile of *straw* — often used before another noun ▪ a *straw* hat/mat **b** [*count*] : a single dry stem of a grain plant ▪ He was chewing on a *straw.*
2 [*count*] : a thin tube used for sucking up a drink ▪ He asked for a *straw* for his iced tea. ▪ She drank the juice through a *straw.*
clutch/grasp at straws : to try to solve a problem by doing things that probably will not help ▪ I asked her for a loan. I didn't think she'd agree, but at that point I was *grasping at straws.*
draw straws see [1]DRAW
straw in the wind : a sign of what might come in the future ▪ A few *straws in the wind*—such as increased tourism and shopping—suggest that the economy is improving.
the final/last straw *or* ***the straw that breaks/broke the camel's back*** : the last in a series of bad things that happen to make someone very upset, angry, etc. ▪ It had been a difficult week, so when the car broke down, it was *the last straw.*

straw·ber·ry /ˈstrɑːˌbɛri, *Brit* ˈstrɔːbri/ *noun, pl* **-ries** [*count*] : a soft, juicy red fruit that grows on a low plant with white flowers ▪ We picked *strawberries.* — often used before another noun ▪ a *strawberry* plant ▪ *strawberry* jam/preserves/sauce — see color picture on page C5

strawberry blonde *or* **strawberry blond** *noun, pl* **~ blondes** *or* **~ blonds** [*count*] : a person who has reddish-blond hair
– strawberry blonde *or* **strawberry blond** *adj* ▪ *strawberry blonde* hair

strawberry mark *noun, pl* **~ marks** [*count*] : a red mark on a person's skin : a red birthmark

straw–colored (*US*) *or Brit* **straw–coloured** *adj* : light yellow in color : like the color of straw ▪ *straw-colored* hair

straw man *noun, pl* **~ men** [*count*] *US* : a weak or imaginary argument or opponent that is set up to be easily defeated — called also (*chiefly Brit*) *man of straw*

straw poll *noun, pl* **~ polls** [*count*] : an informal and unofficial poll or vote that is done to get information about what people think about something — called also (*US*) *straw vote*

[1]stray /ˈstreɪ/ *verb* **strays; strayed; stray·ing** [*no obj*] : to go in a direction that is away from a group or from the place where you should be ▪ Two cows *strayed* [=*wandered*] into the woods. ▪ The airplane *strayed* off course. — often + *from* ▪ She *strayed from* the group and got lost. ▪ Her eyes *strayed from* her computer to the window. [=she stopped looking at her computer and began looking at/out the window] — often used figuratively ▪ She never *strayed* [=*deviated*] *from* the path her parents envisioned for her. ▪ The menu at their house rarely *strays* (too) far *from* meat and potatoes. ▪ The class discussion *strayed* [=*deviated*] *from* the original topic. ▪ a *straying* husband [=a husband who has sexual relations with a woman who is not his wife]

[2]stray *adj, always used before a noun*
1 *of an animal* : lost or having no home ▪ a *stray* cat/dog
2 : separated from another or others of the same kind ▪ a *stray* sock
3 : not in or going in the proper or intended place ▪ a few *stray* hairs ▪ He was hit by a *stray* bullet. [=a bullet that was supposed to go somewhere else]

[3]stray *noun, pl* **strays** [*count*]
1 : an animal (such as a cat or dog) that is lost or has no home ▪ Both of her cats were *strays* that she found wandering in the neighborhood.
2 : a person or thing that is separated from a group ▪ I matched up the socks in the laundry but I was left with one *stray.* [=one extra sock]

[1]streak /ˈstriːk/ *noun, pl* **streaks** [*count*]
1 : a long, thin mark that is a different color from its background ▪ He left *streaks* where he wiped the glass. ▪ The miners had *streaks* of coal dust on their faces.
2 : a quality that is noticeable especially because it is different from a person's other qualities — usually singular ▪ a *streak* of stubbornness = a stubborn *streak* ▪ She has an adventurous/competitive *streak* in her. ▪ He has a ***mean streak.*** [=a tendency to be mean]
3 : a period of repeated success or failure ▪ a lucky *streak* ▪ a *streak* of 11 straight victories ▪ a ***winning/losing streak*** [=a series of wins/losses] ▪ The team has recently been on a ***hot streak.*** [=the team has been winning a lot of games recently]
4 : a long, narrow area or flash *of* light ▪ a *streak of* lightning/light

[2]streak *verb* **streaks; streaked; streak·ing**
1 [+ *obj*] : to make long lines of a different color on or in (something) ▪ Tears *streaked* her face. — often used as *(be) streaked with* ▪ Her face *was streaked with* tears. ▪ Her hair *is streaked with* gray.
2 *always followed by an adverb or preposition* [*no obj*] : to go or move very quickly ▪ A shooting star *streaked* across the sky. ▪ A skateboarder *streaked* past us.
3 [*no obj*] : to run through a public place naked in order to get attention
streak·er /ˈstriːkə/ *noun, pl* **-ers** [*count*] : a person who runs through a public place naked in order to get attention ▪ The ceremony was interrupted when a *streaker* ran across the stage.
streaky /ˈstriːki/ *adj* **streak·i·er; -est** [*also more ~; most ~*]
1 : having or showing streaks ▪ *streaky* windows
2 *chiefly US* : good or successful at some times and bad or unsuccessful at others : not reliably or consistently good ▪ a *streaky* player/golfer ▪ The team's play has been very *streaky* this year. [=the team has played very well at times and very badly at other times]

[1]stream /ˈstriːm/ *noun, pl* **streams** [*count*]
1 : a natural flow of water that is smaller than a river ▪ a mountain *stream* ▪ A *stream* flows/runs through the field. — compare RIVER
2 : any flow of liquid or gas — often + *of* ▪ a *stream of* urine ▪ A *stream of* cold air came in through the crack. — see also BLOODSTREAM, JET STREAM, SLIPSTREAM
3 : a continuous flow of people or things — usually + *of* ▪ a *stream of* words ▪ The island is visited by a continuous/constant/steady *stream of* tourists. ▪ an endless *stream of* traffic
4 *Brit* : [1]TRACK 8
on stream *chiefly Brit* : in or into a working or functioning state : in or into operation ▪ This week the new factory came *on stream.* [=*on line*]

[2]stream *verb* **streams; streamed; stream·ing**
1 *always followed by an adverb or preposition* [*no obj*] : to

move in a steady flow • Tears *streamed* down his cheeks. • I could feel the cold air *streaming* in through the crack in the window. • Sunlight was *streaming* in through the window. • rays of light *streaming* through the clouds

2 *of the body or a body part* **a :** to produce a liquid continuously and often in large amounts [*no obj*] — usually + *with* • Her eyes were *streaming with tears.* [+ *obj*] Her eyes *streamed* tears. **b** [*no obj*] **:** to be or become wet *with* a liquid • His face *streamed with* sweat.

3 *always followed by an adverb or preposition* [*no obj*] **:** to come or flow continuously to a place in large numbers • People *streamed* into the hall. • Immigrants *streamed* into the country. • Hundreds of letters *streamed* in from listeners.

4 [*no obj*] **:** to move freely in one direction especially in wind or water • Her long hair *streamed* behind her as she ran.

5 [+ *obj*] *Brit* **:** to group students in a particular grade according to their abilities and needs **:** TRACK • Children were *streamed* according to ability.

stream•er /ˈstriːmɚ/ *noun, pl* **-ers** [*count*]

1 : a long, narrow piece of colored paper or plastic that is used as a decoration

2 : a long, narrow flag

stream•ing /ˈstriːmɪŋ/ *adj, computers* **:** playing continuously as data is sent to a computer over the Internet • *streaming* audio/media/video

stream•line /ˈstriːmˌlaɪn/ *verb* **-lines; -lined; -lin•ing** [+ *obj*]

1 : to design or make (something, such as a boat or car) with a smooth shape which makes motion through water or air easier • The manufacturer has *streamlined* the car's design.

2 : to make (something) simpler, more effective, or more productive • The business is looking for ways to *streamline* production/operations.

– stream•lined /ˈstriːmˌlaɪnd/ *adj* [*more ~; most ~*] • a very *streamlined* car/design

stream of consciousness *noun* [*noncount*] **:** the continuous series of thoughts that occur in someone's mind especially when they are expressed in writing as a constant flow of words • the narrator's *stream of consciousness*

¹street /ˈstriːt/ *noun, pl* **streets** [*count*]

1 : a road in a city or town that has houses or other buildings on one or both sides • They live on a busy/residential *street.* • a deserted *street* • a dead-end/one-way *street* • You should look both ways before crossing the *street.* • Trash littered the *streets.* • The police car cruised up/down the *street.* • People don't feel safe ***walking the streets*** (of the city) at night. [=don't feel safe walking outside in the city at night] • our neighbor ***down the street*** [=our neighbor who lives farther down on our street] • They live ***across the street*** (from us). [=they live across from us on the other side of the street] • Many of our customers walk in ***off the street*** without having heard of us before. • Angry citizens ***took to the streets*** [=went outside on the streets] to protest the war. • He lost his job and eventually was living ***on the street(s)***. [=was homeless] — often used in names • The store is at 84th *Street* and 35th Avenue. • My address is 156 Elm *Street.* — sometimes used figuratively • Word ***on the street*** is that the company is going out of business. [=people are saying that the company is going out of business] — see also EASY STREET, FLEET STREET, HIGH STREET, MAIN STREET, WALL STREET

2 *informal* **:** a poor part of a city where there is a lot of crime — usually plural • He is from the *streets.* • the raw language of the *streets*

hit the streets see ¹HIT

pound the streets see ²POUND

streets ahead of *Brit, informal* **:** much better than (other people or things) • She is *streets ahead of* the other students.

the man in the street see ¹MAN

up someone's street *Brit, informal* **:** suited to someone's tastes or abilities • The job is ***right up his street***. [=the job suits him very well] • Working with animals is *right up her street.* [=(*chiefly US*) *right up her alley*]

²street *adj, always used before a noun*

1 : of or relating to streets • a *street* map • the store's *street* address • poor *street* lighting • I saw him standing on the ***street corner*** [=the area of the sidewalk where two streets meet] waiting for the bus. • Our apartment is at ***street level***. [=our apartment is on the ground floor of the building]

2 : occurring, performing, working, or living on a street or sidewalk • *street* fighting/musicians/vendors • a *street* fair/demonstration • ***street people*** [=homeless people]

3 : of, relating to, or characteristic of a poor part of a city where there is a lot of crime • *street* drugs/crime/culture/gangs/slang

street•car /ˈstriːtˌkɑɚ/ *noun, pl* **-cars** [*count*] *US* **:** a vehicle that travels on streets on metal tracks and that is used for carrying passengers — called also (*chiefly Brit*) *tram*

street clothes *noun* [*noncount*] **:** the ordinary clothes that people wear in public • She changed out of her uniform and into her *street clothes.*

street cred *noun* [*noncount*] *informal* **:** the acceptance and respect of people who live in poor city neighborhoods • the tough neighborhood where he earned his *street cred*

street hockey *noun* [*noncount*] *chiefly US* **:** a game like ice hockey that is played on a hard surface using hockey sticks and a small ball

street•light /ˈstriːtˌlaɪt/ *noun, pl* **-lights** [*count*] **:** a light on a tall pole next to a public road — called also *street lamp*; see picture at STREET

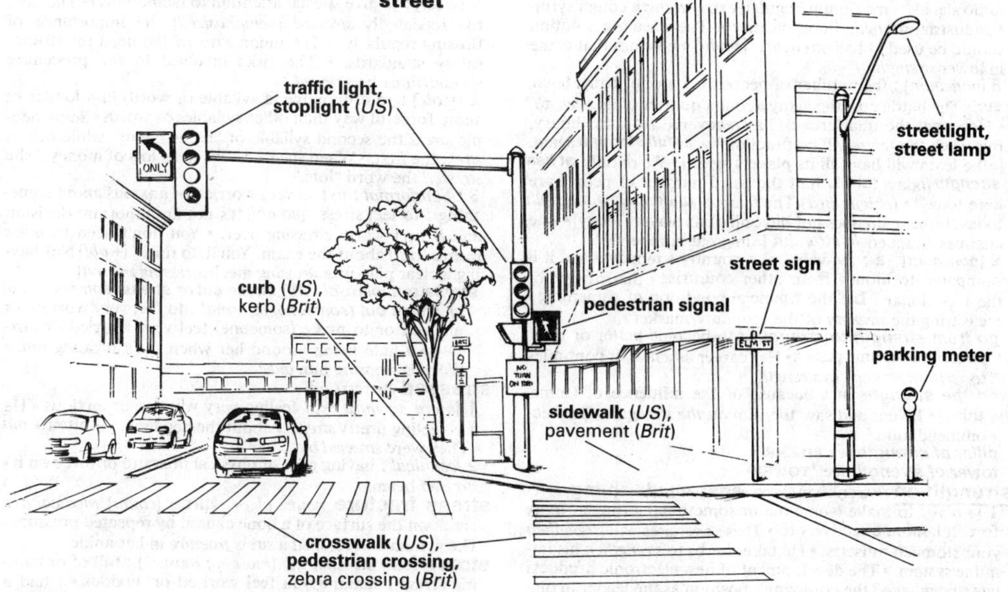

street–smart /ˈstriːtˌsmɑɚt/ *adj* [*more* ~; *most* ~] *chiefly US* : STREETWISE • *street-smart* teenagers

street smarts *noun* [*plural*] *chiefly US* : the knowledge needed to survive in difficult and dangerous places or situations in a city

street·walk·er /ˈstriːtˌwɑːkɚ/ *noun, pl* **-ers** [*count*] : a prostitute who finds customers by walking around in the streets

street·wise /ˈstriːtˌwaɪz/ *adj* [*more* ~; *most* ~] : having the knowledge needed to survive in difficult and dangerous places or situations in a city • a smart, *streetwise* cop

strength /ˈstrɛŋkθ/ *noun, pl* **strengths**

1 [*noncount*] : the quality or state of being physically strong • I don't have enough *strength* [=I'm not strong enough] to lift the box by myself. • I was impressed by his *strength*. • She's doing exercises to build up the *strength* in her legs. • Don't work too hard. You need to conserve/save your *strength* for tomorrow. • Pull-ups increase upper body *strength*. • muscular *strength* • Working on a farm requires a lot of ***physical strength***. • He didn't mean to knock you down; he just ***doesn't know his own strength***. [=doesn't realize how strong he really is] • She hit the ball ***with all her strength***. [=she hit the ball as hard as she could] • She goes to the gym for ***strength training***. [=activities that make muscles stronger]

2 [*noncount*] : the ability to resist being moved or broken by a force • the *strength* and durability of the material • bone *strength*

3 [*noncount*] : the quality that allows someone to deal with problems in a determined and effective way • I pray that I'll have the *strength* to do what I have to do. • moral *strength* • His determination shows real ***strength of character***. • Her ***inner strength*** is an inspiration to us all.

4 [*count*] : a quality or feature that makes someone or something effective or useful • Her greatest *strength* is her keen attention to details. • We talked about the *strengths* and weaknesses [=the good parts and bad parts] of the movie. — opposite WEAKNESS

5 [*noncount*] : the power or influence of a group, organization, etc. • The antiwar movement is gathering/gaining *strength*. [=is becoming stronger and more effective] • The country has great military/economic *strength*. • There is ***strength in numbers***. [=a group of people has more influence or power than one person] • We are negotiating from a ***position of strength***. [=from a strong position; from a position that gives us an advantage] • The strike was intended as a ***show of strength*** by the union's leaders.

6 [*noncount*] — used to describe how strong or deeply held an emotion or opinion is • The *strength* of their feelings inspired us all. = Their *strength* of feeling inspired us all. • I was impressed by the *strength* of her convictions.

7 — used to describe how powerful something is [*noncount*] the *strength* of the wind • This device measures the *strength* of radio signals. • maximum/regular/extra *strength* cough syrup • industrial-*strength* floor cleaner • The cleaning solution should be used at half-*strength*. [*count*] medicines that come in lower *strengths*

8 [*noncount*] : the number of people in a group, army, team, etc. • The battle cost the army about a quarter of its *strength*. • Now that the quarterback has recovered from his injury, this week the team will be functioning ***at full strength*** again. [=the team will have all its players again] • We're only ***at half strength*** today. [=only half the usual number of people are here today] • (*chiefly Brit*) The team is ***under/below strength*** today. [=the team does not have all of its players today] • The enemies attacked ***in strength***. [=in great numbers]

9 [*noncount*] **a** : the value of a country's money when it is compared to money from other countries • the *strength* of the U.S. dollar **b** : the financial condition of something • measuring the *strength* of the economy/market

go from strength to strength : to become better or more successful as time passes • Her career as a lawyer continues to *go from strength to strength*.

on the strength of : because of the influence of (something) • I went and saw the film *on the strength of* his recommendation.

pillar of strength see PILLAR

tower of strength see [1]TOWER

strength·en /ˈstrɛŋkθən/ *verb* **-ens**; **-ened**; **-en·ing**

1 [+ *obj*] : to make (someone or something) stronger, more forceful, more effective, etc. • These exercises will *strengthen* your stomach muscles. • He takes herbs to *strengthen* his immune system. • The development of new electronic products has *strengthened* the company's position as the leader in digital technology. • Holidays often serve to *strengthen* bonds between family members. • Their financial situation *strengthened* her determination to find a new career. • The team has been *strengthened* by the addition of several new players.

2 [*no obj*] : to become stronger, more forceful, more effective, etc. • The winds are expected to *strengthen*. • The storm is continuing to *strengthen* [=to become more powerful] as it approaches land. • Her determination has *strengthened*. • The economy is slowly *strengthening*.

3 *of money* : to increase in value when compared to money from other countries [*no obj*] The Canadian dollar is ***strengthening against*** the U.S. dollar. [+ *obj*] The trade restrictions will *strengthen* the pound. — opposite WEAKEN

stren·u·ous /ˈstrɛnjəwəs/ *adj* [*more* ~; *most* ~] : requiring or showing great energy and effort • Avoid all *strenuous* exercise until the sprain heals. • a *strenuous* climb • Today has been a very *strenuous* day. • *strenuous* efforts • The proposal has faced *strenuous* opposition.

– **stren·u·ous·ly** *adv*

strep throat /ˈstrɛp-/ *noun* [*noncount*] *US, medical* : a painful infection of the throat caused by streptococcus bacteria • He has *strep throat*. — called also *strep*

strep·to·coc·cus /ˌstrɛptəˈkɑːkəs/ *noun, pl* **-coc·ci** /-ˈkɑːˌkaɪ/ [*count*] *medical* : a type of bacteria that causes diseases in people and animals

[1]**stress** /ˈstrɛs/ *noun, pl* **stress·es**

1 a [*noncount*] : a state of mental tension and worry caused by problems in your life, work, etc. • She uses meditation as a way of reducing/relieving *stress*. • Hormones are released into the body in response to emotional *stress*. • He needs help with ***stress management***. [=ways to deal with stress] **b** : something that causes strong feelings of worry or anxiety [*noncount*] I'm sorry for being grumpy. I've been ***under*** (a lot of) ***stress*** at work lately. [*count*] She is dealing with the *stresses* of working full-time and going to school. • He talked about the ***stresses and strains*** of owning a business.

2 : physical force or pressure [*noncount*] Carrying a heavy backpack around all day puts a lot of *stress* on your shoulders and back. • To reduce the amount of *stress* on your back, bend your knees when you lift something heavy. • The ship's mast snapped ***under the stress*** of high winds. [*count*] measuring the effects of *stresses* on the material

3 [*noncount*] : special importance or attention that is given to something • The teacher ***laid/put stress on*** [=*emphasized*] the need for good study habits.

4 : greater loudness or force given to a syllable of a word in speech or to a beat in music [*noncount*] *Stress* falls on the first syllable of the word "language." [*count*] *Stresses* fall on different beats in different parts of the song. • The *stress* [=*accent*] is on the first syllable.

[2]**stress** *verb* **stresses**; **stressed**; **stress·ing**

1 [+ *obj*] : to give special attention to (something) • The dentist repeatedly *stressed* [=*emphasized*] the importance of flossing regularly. • The union *stressed* the need for stricter safety standards. • The risks involved in the procedure should/must be *stressed*.

2 [+ *obj*] : to pronounce (a syllable or word) in a louder or more forceful way than other syllables or words • Some people *stress* the second syllable of "harassment," while others *stress* the first. • When she said, "We need lots of money," she *stressed* the word "lots."

3 *US, informal* : to feel very worried or anxious about something : to feel stress [*no obj*] It's not an important decision and it isn't worth *stressing* over. • You don't need to *stress* [=*stress out*] about the exam. You'll do fine. [+ *obj*] Not having a clear plan was *stressing* me. [=*stressing me out*]

stress out [*phrasal verb*] ***stress out*** *or* ***stress (someone) out*** *or* ***stress out (someone)*** *informal* : to feel very worried or anxious or to make (someone) feel very worried or anxious • I hate being around her when she's *stressing out*. • Work is *stressing* him *out*.

stressed /ˈstrɛst/ *adj*

1 [*more* ~; *most* ~] : feeling very worried or anxious • He was feeling pretty *stressed* about the deadline. — often + *out* • They were *stressed out*.

2 *technical* : having a lot of physical pressure or force on it • *stressed* beams

stress fracture *noun, pl* ~ **-tures** [*count*] *medical* : a crack on the surface of a bone caused by repeated pressure • The gymnast developed a *stress fracture* in her ankle.

stress·ful /ˈstrɛsfəl/ *adj* [*more* ~; *most* ~] : full of or causing stress : making you feel worried or anxious • I had a

S

stressful day at work today. • a *stressful* situation/event/job

stress mark *noun, pl* ~ **marks** [*count*] : a mark (such as ˈ or ˌ) used to show the part of a word that should be given greater stress when it is spoken

stress·or /ˈstrɛsɚ/ *noun, pl* **-ors** [*count*] : something that makes you worried or anxious : a source of stress • Credit card debt is a major *stressor* in her life.

stress test *noun, pl* ~ **tests** [*count*] : a test to show how strong something is; *especially* : a medical test to show how strong and healthy your heart is during a period of exercise

¹stretch /ˈstrɛʧ/ *verb* **stretch·es; stretched; stretch·ing**

1 a [+ *obj*] : to make (something) wider or longer by pulling it • Don't yank on my sweater. You'll *stretch* it. • I'm trying to *stretch* (out) the wool hat that shrank in the wash. • Carefully *stretch* the dough. **b** [*no obj*] : to become longer or wider when pulled • The elastic waistband of my pants won't *stretch* any more. • jeans/pants that *stretch* • The material/fabric *stretches*.

2 a : to put your arms, legs, etc., in positions that make the muscles long and tight [*no obj*] It's important to *stretch* before you exercise. • The baby *stretched* and yawned. [+ *obj*] She woke up and *stretched* her arms above her head. • These exercises *stretch* (the muscles of) your lower back. **b** *always followed by an adverb or preposition* : to extend your arm, leg, etc., in order to reach something [*no obj*] She *stretched* over us to open the window. — often + *out* • Her hand *stretched out* toward him. [=she reached toward him with her hand] [+ *obj*] She *stretched* her hand toward him. — often + *out* • She *stretched out* her hand.

3 *always followed by an adverb or preposition* [+ *obj*] : to pull (something) so that it becomes flat and smooth and goes across a surface or area • She *stretched* the canvas over the wooden frame. • The T-shirt was *stretched* tight over his belly. • A big banner was *stretched* across the doorway.

4 *always followed by an adverb or preposition* [*no obj*] **a** : to continue for a specified distance : to extend over an area • The cornfields *stretch* as far as the eye can see. • The restaurant chain began in Chicago but now *stretches* to the West Coast. — used to describe how long something is • The horse's tail *stretches* three and a half feet from base to end. **b** : to continue over a period of time • Her interest in art *stretches* back to her childhood. [=she has been interested in art since she was a child] • Construction that began in late April *stretched* [=*continued*] into June.

5 [+ *obj*] : to say something that is not exactly true • He was ***stretching the truth*** [=*exaggerating*] to make the story more interesting. • Although it may be ***stretching a point*** [=exaggerating slightly] to say that this was his best win ever, it was nevertheless impressive. • (*informal*) She's a good musician but comparing her to the legends is ***stretching it***. [=she's good but she can't really be compared to the legends] • (*informal*) It's ***stretching things*** to say that she enjoys his visits. [=she doesn't really enjoy his visits]

6 [+ *obj*] **a** : to cause or force (something) to be used for a longer time or for more purposes than originally planned or expected • They were forced to *stretch* their food supplies. • The unexpected expenses have *stretched* their budget to the breaking point. • The country is *stretching* its military forces to the limit. — often + *out* • They were forced to *stretch out* their food supplies for another week. **b** : to cause (something, such as a rule) to have a meaning or purpose that is different from what was originally intended • He is clearly *stretching* the rules in his favor. [=he is doing something that is not really allowed by the rules] • The clause was *stretched* beyond its original meaning. **c** — used figuratively in various phrases • Her bad behavior is ***stretching my patience*** (to the limit). [=is causing me to lose patience] • His explanation ***stretches credulity***. [=is hard to believe]

7 [+ *obj*] : to require (someone) to use a lot of effort, ability, skill, etc., in order to succeed • The work doesn't *stretch* me intellectually. [=the work is too easy for me; the work is not intellectually challenging]

stretch out [*phrasal verb*] ***stretch out or stretch (yourself) out*** : to extend your body in a flat position : to spread out in a relaxed position • She *stretched out* on the bed. • He *stretched himself out* on the couch. — often used as *(be) stretched out* • He *was* (lying) *stretched out* on the couch. — see also ¹STRETCH 2b, 6a (above)

stretch your legs *informal* : to stand up and walk especially after sitting for a long period of time

– stretch·able /ˈstrɛʧəbəl/ *adj* • a *stretchable* fabric

²stretch *noun, pl* **stretches**

1 [*count*] : a continuous area or length of land or water • a 60-mile *stretch* of beach • an open *stretch* of highway/road

2 [*count*] **a** : a continuous period of time • We sat silently for a long/short/brief *stretch* (of time). • She can sit and read for hours ***at a stretch***. [=at one time without stopping] **b** *informal* : a period of time spent in prison — usually singular • He just got out of prison after a six-year *stretch*.

3 : an act of stretching your body or part of your body [*count*] These are good *stretches* for your leg muscles. • I always spend a few minutes doing *stretches* before I exercise. [*noncount*] I can feel the *stretch* in the back of my legs.

4 ***the stretch*** : the final straight part of a racecourse before the finish line • the horses are in *the* (final) *stretch* — often used figuratively • They won some crucial games down *the stretch*. [=in the last part of the season] • She's in *the* final *stretch*. The baby's due next month. — see also HOMESTRETCH

5 [*noncount*] : the ability to be stretched without breaking or being torn • material with a lot of *stretch*

6 [*singular*] *chiefly US* **a** : something that requires a special effort to be done : something that is beyond a person's usual abilities • Portraying a famous actress was not much of a *stretch* [=*challenge*] for the popular movie star. **b** : a statement, description, etc., that is not strictly true or accurate • Some people think it's a *stretch* to call fishing a sport.

at full stretch *Brit, informal* : with as much effort as possible • The medical team worked *at full stretch*.

by any/no stretch of the imagination — used to emphasize that something is not true, does not happen, etc. • They're not wealthy *by any stretch of the imagination*. [=they're not wealthy at all] • *By no stretch of the imagination* does the factory operate efficiently. [=the factory does not operate at all efficiently]

the seventh-inning stretch *baseball* : the time between the two halves of the seventh inning when the people watching a game traditionally stand up and stretch their legs

³stretch *adj, always used before a noun* : made to stretch easily and then return to the original shape and size • *stretch* socks/pants

¹stretch·er /ˈstrɛʧɚ/ *noun, pl* **-ers** [*count*] : a device that is made of a long piece of thick cloth stretched between two poles and that is used for carrying an injured or dead person • They carried her out to the ambulance on a *stretcher*.

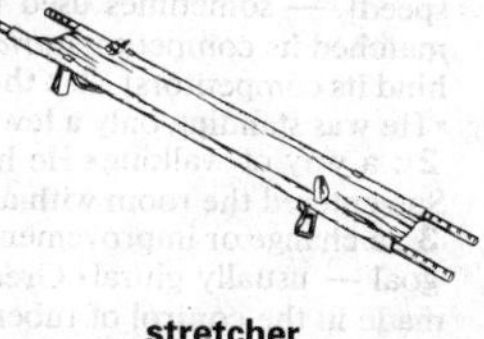
stretcher

²stretcher *verb* **-ers; -ered; -er·ing** [+ *obj*] *Brit* : to carry (someone) on a stretcher — often used as *(be) stretchered* • The injured player *was stretchered* off the field.

stretch limo *noun, pl* ~ **lim·os** [*count*] : a very large and fancy car that is longer than standard cars and that is driven by a professional driver • The chauffeur drove her to the wedding in a *stretch limo*. — called also *stretch limousine*

stretch marks *noun* [*plural*] : long marks on the skin left after the skin has been stretched especially by pregnancy

stretchy /ˈstrɛʧi/ *adj* **stretch·i·er; -est** [*also more* ~; *most* ~] : able to stretch and then return to the original size and shape • a tight *stretchy* shirt • The fabric is very *stretchy*.

strew /ˈstru:/ *verb* **strews; strewed; strewed** *or* **strewn** /ˈstru:n/; **strew·ing** [+ *obj*]

1 : to spread or scatter things over or on the ground or some other surface • She *strewed* the birdseed on the ground. • He *strewed* fresh hay on the floors of the stable. = He *strewed* the floors of the stable with fresh hay. — often used as *(be) strewed/strewn* • The children's toys *were strewed* [=*scattered*] all around the room. [=were lying in different places all around the room] • The park *was strewn* with litter. [=there was litter scattered throughout the park] — often used figuratively • Her stories *are strewn* with clichés. [=her stories have many clichés]

2 *literary* : to lie on or cover (something) • Leaves *strewed* the ground.

stri·at·ed /ˈstraɪˌeɪtəd/ *adj, technical* : having lines, bands, or grooves • *striated* muscle tissue

– stri·a·tion /straɪˈeɪʃən/ *noun, pl* **-tions** [*count, noncount*]

strick·en /ˈstrɪkən/ *adj* : powerfully affected by disease, trouble, sorrow, etc. • I saw her *stricken* face looking up at us. — often + *by* or *with* • He was too *stricken by* embarrassment to speak. ▪ a nation *stricken with* grief ▪ She had been *stricken with* polio as a child. — often used in combination ▪ disease-*stricken* villages — see also GRIEF-STRICKEN, PANIC-STRICKEN, POVERTY-STRICKEN, [1]STRIKE

strict /ˈstrɪkt/ *adj* **strict•er; -est** [*also more ~; most ~*]
1 — used to describe a command, rule, etc., that must be obeyed ▪ *strict* rules/laws/regulations ▪ They want to impose *strict* limits on government spending. ▪ We are ***under strict orders*** not to leave the prisoner alone.
2 : demanding that people obey rules or behave in a certain way ▪ a *strict* teacher ▪ Her parents aren't very *strict*.
3 a : carefully obeying the rules or principles of a religion or a particular way of life ▪ a *strict* Hindu ▪ a *strict* vegetarian **b :** complete or thorough ▪ This project requires *strict* [=*absolute*] secrecy. ▪ He insists on *strict* adherence to the rules.
4 : completely correct **:** exact or precise ▪ He's not a volunteer ***in the strict/strictest sense (of the word)*** [=he is not really a volunteer] because he receives a small stipend.
– strict•ly /ˈstrɪktli/ *adv* ▪ The speed limit is *strictly* enforced. ▪ Smoking is *strictly* forbidden/prohibited. ▪ From a *strictly* practical perspective, this is the best way of doing things. ▪ She follows a *strictly* vegetarian diet. ▪ All personal information is kept *strictly* confidential. ▪ ***Strictly speaking*** the book is not a novel but a series of short stories.
– strict•ness /ˈstrɪktnəs/ *noun* [*noncount*]

stric•ture /ˈstrɪktʃɚ/ *noun, pl* **-tures** [*count*] *formal*
1 : a law or rule that limits or controls something **:** RESTRICTION ▪ moral *strictures* — often + *against* or *on* ▪ *strictures on/against* the sale and possession of weapons
2 : a strong criticism — usually plural ▪ I don't agree with all of her *strictures* on the state of contemporary literature.

[1]**stride** /ˈstraɪd/ *verb, always followed by an adverb or preposition* **strides; strode** /ˈstroʊd/; **strid•den** /ˈstrɪdn̩/; **strid•ing** /ˈstraɪdɪŋ/ [*no obj*] **:** to walk with very long steps ▪ She *strode* across the room towards me.

[2]**stride** *noun, pl* **strides** [*count*]
1 a : a long step ▪ She crossed the room in only a few *strides*. ▪ As he ran down the field, the defender kept up with him ***stride for stride*** [=the defender ran next to him at the same speed] — sometimes used figuratively ▪ The company has matched its competitors *stride for stride*. [=has not fallen behind its competitors] **b :** the distance covered by a long step ▪ He was standing only a few *strides* away from me.
2 : a way of walking ▪ He has a distinctive bouncy *stride*. ▪ She entered the room with a confident *stride*.
3 : a change or improvement that brings someone closer to a goal — usually plural ▪ Great *strides* [=*advances*] have been made in the control of tuberculosis. ▪ The patient is making *strides* toward a complete recovery.
break (your) stride *chiefly US* **:** to stop walking or running in a regular and steady way ▪ He caught the ball and passed it to a teammate without *breaking stride*. — often used figuratively ▪ She graduated from college, went to law school, and without *breaking stride* joined a successful law firm.
hit your stride (*US*) *or Brit* ***get into your stride*** **:** to begin to do something in a confident and effective way after starting slowly ▪ Both teams seem to have *hit their stride* in the second half.
off stride ✧ If you are walking or running and someone or something (*chiefly US*) ***throws/knocks you off (your) stride*** or (*chiefly Brit*) ***puts you off your stride***, you are unable to continue walking or running steadily. ▪ Another runner bumped into him and *threw/knocked him off his stride*. These phrases are often used figuratively. ▪ She was surprised and *thrown off stride* [=*thrown off balance*] by the unexpected question. ▪ He was working steadily until an interruption *put him off his stride*.
take (something) in stride (*US*) *or Brit* ***take (something) in your stride*** **:** to deal with (something difficult or upsetting) in a calm way ▪ I thought she'd be upset, but she has *taken* the news *in stride*.

stri•dent /ˈstraɪdn̩t/ *adj* [*more ~; most ~*]
1 : sounding harsh and unpleasant ▪ The *strident* tone in his voice revealed his anger. ▪ a *strident* voice
2 : expressing opinions or criticism in a very forceful and often annoying or unpleasant way ▪ *strident* critics/slogans
– stri•den•cy /ˈstraɪdn̩si/ *noun* [*noncount*] **– stri•dent•ly** *adv*

strife /ˈstraɪf/ *noun* [*noncount*] *formal* **:** very angry or violent disagreement between two or more people or groups ▪ political/religious *strife* ▪ civil *strife*

[1]**strike** /ˈstraɪk/ *verb* **strikes; struck** /ˈstrʌk/; **struck** *also* **strick•en** /ˈstrɪkən/; **strik•ing** /ˈstraɪkɪŋ/
1 [+ *obj*] **a :** to hit (someone or something) in a forceful way ▪ The ship *struck* an iceberg. ▪ The car *struck* the tree. ▪ The bullet *struck* him in the leg. ▪ The cyclist was *struck* by a car. ▪ The tree was *struck* by lightning. ▪ He fell and his head *struck* the pavement. ▪ I could hear the rain *striking* the rooftop. **b :** to cause (something) to hit something in a forceful way ▪ I *struck* [=*banged, bumped*] my knee against the leg of the table. ▪ She *struck* the cymbals together. **c :** to hit (someone or something) with your hand, a weapon, etc. ▪ The killer *struck* him with a blunt object. ▪ She accidentally *struck* another player in the face.
2 [*no obj*] **:** to attack someone or something suddenly ▪ The snake was about to *strike*. ▪ Police say that the killer may *strike* again. — often + *at* ▪ The snake *struck at* the mouse. ▪ He *struck at* her with a knife. — often used figuratively ▪ He hurt her feelings by *striking at* [=*attacking, criticizing*] her personal beliefs. ▪ The proposed law *strikes at* the foundations of our democracy.
3 *not used in progressive tenses* **:** to affect (someone or something) suddenly in a bad way **:** to cause damage, harm, illness, etc., to (someone or something) [+ *obj*] The flu *strikes* millions of people each year. [=millions of people get sick with the flu each year] ▪ A hurricane *struck* the island. ▪ The city has been *struck* by a powerful earthquake. — often used as *(be) stricken* ▪ He *was stricken* with a high fever. [*no obj*] The hurricane is expected to *strike* tomorrow. ▪ When disaster *strikes*, will you be prepared? — often used figuratively ▪ The home team *struck* [=*scored*] first on the opening drive.
4 *not used in progressive tenses* [+ *obj*] **:** to cause (someone) to be in a certain condition suddenly — usually used as *(be) struck* ▪ They *were struck* speechless with surprise. ▪ He ***was struck deaf/blind*** [=he became deaf/blind] at an early age. ▪ I was ***struck dumb*** [=*dumbstruck*] by the news.
5 [+ *obj*] **a :** to cause someone to feel (a strong emotion) suddenly — often + *in* or *into* ▪ Their war cries *struck* terror *in* (the hearts of) their enemies. ▪ Her words ***struck fear into the hearts*** of her listeners. **b :** to affect (someone) *with* a strong emotion ▪ He was *struck with* horror at the sight. = The sight *struck* him *with* horror.
6 [+ *obj*] **:** to cause (something) to happen or exist **:** to do or achieve (something) ▪ He needs to ***strike a*** better ***balance*** between his work life and his family life. [=he needs to spend less time at work and more time with his family] ▪ They ***struck a blow*** for freedom and against tyranny. [=they did something that helped freedom and opposed tyranny] ▪ Fate has *struck a* heavy *blow* against us. = Fate has *struck* us *a* heavy *blow*.
7 *not used in progressive tenses* [+ *obj*] **:** to be thought of by (someone) suddenly **:** to occur to (someone) ▪ It suddenly *struck* me [=I realized suddenly] that I would never see her again. ▪ The answer just *struck* me. ▪ ***It strikes me*** [=I realize] that there is a larger issue at stake.
8 *not used in progressive tenses* [+ *obj*] **:** to cause (someone) to think about someone or something in a particular way ▪ What really *struck* me was their enthusiasm. [=I especially noticed their enthusiasm] ▪ ***It strikes me*** [=it surprises me] that so few of them were willing to help. — often + *as* ▪ Her comment *struck* me *as* odd. [=her comment seemed odd to me] ▪ She *strikes* us *as* a very qualified candidate. [=we think she is a very qualified candidate]
9 [*no obj*] *of a group of workers* **:** to stop work in order to force an employer to agree to demands **:** to refuse to work until your employer does what you want ▪ The teachers are threatening to *strike*. [=*go on strike*] ▪ *striking* workers — often + *for* ▪ The workers are *striking for* an increase in pay.
10 *of a clock* **:** to make the time known by making a sound [*no obj*] The clock *struck* as they entered the room. [+ *obj*] The clock *struck* one.
11 [+ *obj*] **:** to cause (a match) to start burning by rubbing it against a surface ▪ She *struck* a match and lit the candle.
12 [+ *obj*] **:** to make (an agreement) ▪ The two parties have finally ***struck a bargain/deal***
13 [+ *obj*] **:** to remove (something) *from* (something) ▪ She *struck* the song *from* the album at the last minute. ▪ He *struck* [=*deleted*] the sentence *from* the paragraph. ▪ The clause has been *stricken from* the contract.
14 *not used in progressive tenses* [+ *obj*] **:** to find or discover (something) especially by digging ▪ They are hoping to *strike* oil/gold. — see also STRIKE GOLD (below)
15 [+ *obj*] **:** to place yourself in (a particular position, posture, etc.) ▪ She *struck* [=*assumed, took on*] a dramatic pose. ▪ He *struck* a defensive attitude.

S

16 [+ *obj*] : to play (a note, chord, etc.) on a musical instrument by using your fingers on keys or strings ▪ Fans cheered when he *struck* the song's opening chords. — often used figuratively ▪ She *struck* the right note/tone with her speech. [=she said things in a way that appealed to her audience]
17 *always followed by an adverb or preposition* [*no obj*] : to begin to walk or go in a particular direction — usually + *off* or *out* ▪ He *struck off* through the woods. ▪ The men *struck out* for/toward their campsite when they saw the storm clouds moving in. — see also STRIKE OUT 4 (below)
18 [+ *obj*] : to make (a coin, medal, etc.) by pressing an image into a piece of metal ▪ The coins were *struck* in 1789.
be struck by *informal* : to be very impressed by or pleased with (something or someone) ▪ Visitors *are* always *struck by* the beauty of the landscape.
lightning never strikes (the same place) twice see [1]LIGHTNING
strike a chord see [2]CHORD
strike a nerve see NERVE
strike back [*phrasal verb*] : to try to hurt someone who has hurt you or treated you badly ▪ When he called her lazy, she immediately *struck back* by calling him fat. — often + *at* ▪ He angrily *struck back at* his critics.
strike down [*phrasal verb*] **1** ***strike (someone) down*** **a** : to make (someone) unable to work, act, or function in the usual way — usually used as *(be) struck down* ▪ She *was struck down* by an injury at the height of her athletic career. **b** : to cause (someone) to die suddenly — usually used as *(be) struck down* ▪ He *was struck down* by a heart attack at age 55. **2** ***strike (something) down*** *or* ***strike down (something)*** *chiefly US, law* : to say officially that (something) is no longer legally valid ▪ The board *struck down* the appointment. ▪ The Supreme Court *struck down* the law.
strike gold : to have great success with something ▪ The studio *struck gold* with their latest film. — see also [1]STRIKE 14 (above)
strike home see [2]HOME
strike it rich *informal* : to become rich suddenly ▪ Her family *struck it rich* when they won the lottery.
strike off [*phrasal verb*] **1** ***strike off (something)*** *or* ***strike (something) off*** : to draw a line through (a name or item on a list) ▪ The teacher *struck off* [=*crossed out*] the names as he called them out. **2** ***strike off (something)*** *or* ***strike (something) off*** : to remove (something) by hitting it with a tool in a forceful way ▪ He *struck off* the top of the coconut with a machete. **3** ***strike off (someone)*** *or* ***strike (someone) off*** *Brit* : to remove the name of (someone, such as a doctor or lawyer) from an official register — usually used as *(be) struck off* ▪ The doctor *was struck off* for unethical practices. [=the doctor is no longer allowed to practice] — see also [1]STRIKE 17 (above)
strike on/upon [*phrasal verb*] **1** ***strike on/upon (something)*** *not used in progressive tenses* : to find or discover (something) especially suddenly ▪ He *struck on* an idea for his novel. ▪ They *struck upon* a salt mine. **2** ***be struck on*** *Brit, informal* : to like or be impressed by (someone or something) very much ▪ He *was* quite *struck on* her. ▪ She seems to *be* very ***struck on herself***. [=*stuck on herself*]
strike out [*phrasal verb*] **1** *baseball* **a** ***strike (someone) out*** *or* ***strike out (someone)*** *of a pitcher* : to cause (a batter) to be out by pitching three strikes ▪ The pitcher *struck* him *out* with a curve. ▪ The pitcher *struck out* the first two batters. **b** *of a batter* : to make an out by getting three strikes ▪ The first two batters *struck out*. — see also STRIKEOUT **2** ***strike (something) out*** *or* ***strike out (something)*** : to remove (something) from a document : DELETE ▪ The editor *struck out* the last paragraph. **3** *US, informal* : to be unsuccessful : FAIL ▪ "Did you get her phone number?" "No, I *struck out*." **4** : to begin a course of action ▪ She ***struck out on her own*** after graduation. — see also [1]STRIKE 17 (above) **5** : to try to hit someone or something suddenly ▪ He *struck out* wildly with his arms. — often + *at* ▪ He *struck out* wildly *at* the police officers. **6** : to make a sudden and angry attack against someone — often + *at* ▪ Both candidates *struck out at* their critics.
strike pay dirt see PAY DIRT
strike (someone) dead : to kill (someone) in a quick and unexpected way ▪ A bolt of lightning *struck him dead*.
strike up [*phrasal verb*] **1** ***strike up (something)*** **a** : to begin to play (a piece of music) ▪ The orchestra *struck up* a waltz. **b** : to cause (an orchestra, a band, etc.) to begin playing ▪ The conductor *struck up* the band. **2** ***strike up (something)*** *also* ***strike (something) up*** : to begin (something) ▪ I *struck up* a conversation with him at the party. ▪ The two boys *struck up* a friendship.
strike while the iron is hot : to do something immediately while you still have a good chance to do it ▪ We may not have a chance like this again. We need to *strike while the iron is hot*.
— see also STRIKING DISTANCE

[2]**strike** *noun, pl* **strikes**
1 : a period of time when workers stop work in order to force an employer to agree to their demands [*count*] a teachers' *strike* ▪ a *strike* by airline pilots [*noncount*] The workers are ***on strike***. ▪ Workers are threatening to ***go (out) on strike***. = (*Brit*) Workers are threatening to ***come out on strike***. ▪ Workers threatened to take ***strike action***. — see also HUNGER STRIKE, LIGHTNING STRIKE
2 [*count*] : a military attack ▪ The allies have launched several *strikes*. ▪ an ***air strike*** [=an attack by aircraft] — see also FIRST STRIKE, SURGICAL STRIKE
3 [*count*] : the act of hitting something with force ▪ The forest fire was caused by a ***lightning strike***. [=was caused when something on the ground was hit/struck by lightning]
4 [*count*] **a** *baseball* : a pitch that passes through a certain area over home plate without being hit and that counts against the batter ▪ The first pitch was a ball but the next two pitches were *strikes*. ▪ That's *strike* two. One more *strike* and he's out. — see also STRIKE ZONE **b** *US* : a perfectly thrown ball or pass ▪ The quarterback threw a *strike* to the receiver.
5 [*count*] *chiefly US* : something that makes someone or something less likely to be accepted, approved, successful, etc. ▪ Her poor attendance was a ***strike against*** her. [=her poor attendance counted against her] ▪ He has a criminal record, so that's one *strike against* him. ▪ I want the job, but I'm young and I don't have much experience, so I feel like I already have two *strikes against* me.
6 [*count*] *bowling* : the achievement of knocking down all 10 pins with the first ball ▪ She ***made/bowled a strike***. — compare [3]SPARE 2
7 [*count*] : a discovery of something valuable (such as oil) — usually singular ▪ an oil *strike*

strike·break·er /ˈstraɪkˌbreɪkɚ/ *noun, pl* **-ers** [*count*] : a person who is hired to replace a worker who is on strike or who continues to work during a strike
— **strike·break·ing** /ˈstraɪkˌbreɪkɪŋ/ *noun* [*noncount*]

strike force *noun, pl* ~ **forces** [*count*]
1 : a military force that is ready to attack
2 *US* : a team of federal agents assigned to investigate organized crime in a specific area

strike·out /ˈstraɪkˌaʊt/ *noun, pl* **-outs** [*count*] *baseball* : an out in baseball that occurs when a batter gets three strikes ▪ The pitcher had 10 *strikeouts* in the game. [=the pitcher struck out 10 batters] — see also *strike out* at [1]STRIKE

strik·er /ˈstraɪkɚ/ *noun, pl* **-ers** [*count*]
1 : a worker who is on strike
2 : a forward in soccer

strike zone *noun*
the strike zone *baseball* : the area over home plate where the baseball must pass after it is pitched in order to be called a strike

strik·ing /ˈstraɪkɪŋ/ *adj* [*more* ~; *most* ~]
1 : unusual or extreme in a way that attracts attention ▪ a place of *striking* [=*remarkable*] beauty ▪ The poverty of the city is *striking*. ▪ There is a *striking* resemblance between the girls. ▪ The building's modern style is/stands ***in striking contrast to*** the surrounding neighborhood. [=is very different from the surrounding neighborhood]
2 : very attractive especially in an unusual or interesting way ▪ a *striking* young man ▪ an actress known for her *striking* good looks
— **strik·ing·ly** *adv* ▪ a *strikingly* beautiful woman ▪ The two islands are *strikingly* different.

striking distance *noun* [*noncount*] : the distance from which something can be easily reached ▪ The snake was ***within striking distance***. ▪ They live *within striking distance* of the city. [=they live close to the city] — often used figuratively ▪ They were almost *within striking distance* of their goal. = Their goal was almost *within striking distance*. [=they were close to achieving their goal]

[1]**string** /ˈstrɪŋ/ *noun, pl* **strings**
1 : a long, thin piece of twisted thread that you use to attach things, tie things together, or hang things [*count*] She tied a *string* around the boxes. [*noncount*] a piece/loop/ball of

string ▪ He tied the packages together with *string*. — see also APRON STRING, DRAWSTRING, G-STRING, SHOESTRING

2 [*count*] **:** a group of objects that are connected with a string, wire, chain, etc. — + *of* ▪ She was wearing a *string of* pearls. ▪ We used four *strings of* Christmas lights to decorate the tree.

3 [*count*] **a :** a series of similar things — + *of* ▪ He owns a *string of* movie theaters. ▪ a long/whole *string of* names/numbers **b :** a series of events which follow each other in time — + *of* ▪ a *string of* robberies ▪ The band had a *string of* hits in the 1990s. **c** *technical* **:** a group of letters, words, or numbers which is treated as a single unit in a computer program ▪ a character *string*

4 [*count*] **:** a long, thin piece of tightly stretched wire or other material (such as nylon) that is used to produce sounds in a musical instrument (such as a violin or piano) ▪ guitar/piano *strings* — see also THE STRINGS (below)

5 [*noncount*] *chiefly US* **:** a group of players on a team that play together because they have similar abilities ▪ the first/second *string* of a football team ▪ He was demoted to the second *string*. — see also FIRST-STRING, SECOND-STRING

6 ***strings*** [*plural*] **:** requirements that are connected with something **:** things that you have to do, give, etc., if you accept something (such as a gift or an offer) ▪ She won't accept the gift if there are *strings*. [=if she is expected to do something in return for it] ▪ They offered her the job ***with no strings attached***. [=with no conditions] ▪ He's generous, but there are always ***strings attached***. [=he always expects something in return for what he gives to people]

7 [*count*] **:** a long, thin piece of nylon or other material that is stretched tightly across a tennis racket or similar object

have more than one string to your bow *Brit* **:** to have more than one idea, skill, plan, etc., that you can use if it is needed ▪ That didn't fix the problem, but I have *more than one string to my bow*.

have (someone) on a string *informal* **:** to be able to make (someone) do anything you want ▪ He *has* his girlfriend *on a string*.

how long is a piece of string *Brit, informal* — used as a reply to a question when the answer is not known ▪ "How long will you be staying?" "*How long is a piece of string?*"

pull strings **:** to use the influence that you have with important people to get or achieve something ▪ His father had to *pull* (some) *strings* to get him the job.

pull the strings **:** to control someone or something often in a secret way ▪ It turned out that his brother was the person *pulling the strings* behind the operation.

purse strings see [1]PURSE

the strings *or* ***the string section*** **:** the instruments of an orchestra (such as the cello, violin, or piano) that have strings or the musicians who play them ▪ The concert was excellent, especially *the strings*. ▪ *The* orchestra's *string section* is excellent.

[2]**string** *verb* **strings; strung** /ˈstrʌŋ/; **string·ing** [+ *obj*]

1 : to put (things) together on a string, thread, chain, etc. ▪ *string* beads ▪ We *strung* popcorn garlands for the Christmas tree.

2 : to place or hang (things) in a line or series ▪ They *strung* wires from tree to tree. ▪ We *strung* [=*hung*] Christmas lights along the railing. ▪ Scouts *strung* lanterns along the trail.

3 : to tie, hang, or fasten (something) with string ▪ She *strung* the key around her neck.

4 : to attach strings to (something, such as a musical instrument or tennis racket) ▪ You'll have to *string* your guitar/racket before you can play.

string along [*phrasal verb*] **1** ***string (someone) along*** **:** to continue to deceive or trick (someone) for a long time ▪ He was just *stringing* us *along* with false promises. ▪ He really loved her but she was just *stringing* him *along*. [=making him think that she loved him so she could use him] **2** ***string along with (someone or something)*** *Brit, informal* **:** to go with or follow (someone or something) ▪ She *strung along with* them to the museum.

string out [*phrasal verb*] ***string (something) out*** *or* ***string out (something)*** **:** to make (something) take longer than it should ▪ You're just *stringing* this *out* to avoid having to leave. — see also STRUNG OUT

string together [*phrasal verb*] ***string (something) together*** *or* ***string together (something)*** **:** to combine (different things) into something that is complete, useful, etc. ▪ See if you can *string* the theories *together* into something that makes sense. ▪ The filmmaker *strung together* interviews with a number of experts on the subject. **:** to create (something) by putting different things together ▪ She was finding it hard to *string together* a coherent argument.

string up [*phrasal verb*] ***string (someone) up*** *or* ***string up (someone)*** *informal* **:** to hang (someone) by the neck **:** to kill (someone) by hanging ▪ They threatened to *string* him *up* in a tree.

string bean *noun, pl* **~ beans** [*count*] *chiefly US*

1 : a type of long, thin green bean

2 *informal* **:** a very tall thin person ▪ Her boyfriend's a real *string bean*.

string cheese *noun* [*noncount*] *chiefly US* **:** cheese that can be pulled apart in narrow strips

stringed instrument /ˈstrɪnd-/ *noun, pl* **~ -ment** [*count*] **:** a musical instrument (such as a guitar, violin, or piano) that has strings and that produces sound when the strings are touched or struck

strin·gent /ˈstrɪnʤənt/ *adj* [*more ~; most ~*] **:** very strict or severe ▪ *stringent* training ▪ *stringent* budgetary constraints — used to describe a command, rule, etc., that must be obeyed ▪ *stringent* rules/requirements/restrictions/standards

— **strin·gen·cy** /ˈstrɪnʤənsi/ *noun* [*noncount*] — **strin·gent·ly** *adv* ▪ The rule is *stringently* applied/enforced.

string·er /ˈstrɪŋə/ *noun, pl* **-ers** [*count*] **:** a journalist who is not on the regular staff of a newspaper but who writes stories for that newspaper

stringy /ˈstrɪŋi/ *adj* **string·i·er; -est**

1 : containing long, thin pieces that are like string and that are hard to chew ▪ *stringy* vegetables ▪ a tough, *stringy* piece of meat

2 *of hair* **:** long, thin, and dirty ▪ a *stringy* beard

3 : having long, thin muscles ▪ *stringy* arms ▪ a *stringy* woman

— **string·i·ness** *noun* [*noncount*]

[1]**strip** *noun, pl* **strips**

1 [*count*] **:** a long, narrow piece of something ▪ *strips* of bacon ▪ a small *strip* of cloth/paper

2 [*count*] **:** a long, narrow piece of land ▪ a *strip* of land ▪ *strips* of forest/coastline ▪ the half-mile *strip* of road — see also DRAG STRIP, MEDIAN STRIP, RUMBLE STRIP

3 [*count*] *US* **:** a road that has a lot of shops, restaurants, etc., along it ▪ driving along the *strip* ▪ the Las Vegas *strip*

4 [*count*] **:** AIRSTRIP

5 [*count*] **:** COMIC STRIP ▪ *Peanuts* has always been one of my favorite *strips*.

6 [*singular*] *Brit* **:** the uniform worn by a sports team ▪ the team's ***away strip*** [=the uniform that the team wears when it is not playing at its home field, stadium, etc.]

7 [*count*] *Brit* : the act of taking your clothes off in a sexually exciting way while someone is watching • She ***did a strip*** [=*striptease*] for her husband.

tear (someone) off a strip or ***tear a strip off (someone)*** *Brit, informal* : to talk angrily to (someone who has done something wrong) • His dad *tore him off a strip* for denting the car.

— see also POWER STRIP

²strip /ˈstrɪp/ *verb* **strips; stripped; strip·ping**

1 a : to remove your clothing [*no obj*] I *stripped* for bed. • He ***stripped to the waist.*** [=he took off all the clothes on his upper body] • The prisoners were told to ***strip naked.*** [=remove all their clothes] — often + *down* • He *stripped down* to his underwear. [=he took all his clothes off except for his underwear] [+ *obj*] He *stripped* himself *down* to his underwear. **b** [+ *obj*] : to take the clothes off (someone) • The prisoners were *stripped naked.* **c** [*no obj*] : to remove your clothing in a sexually exciting way while someone is watching • She gets paid to dance and *strip* at the club.

2 [+ *obj*] : to remove an outer covering or surface from something • *strip* the bark from a tree = *strip* a tree of its bark • We are going to *strip* [=*remove*] the old wallpaper. • They *stripped* the table and refinished it. • Please ***strip your bed*** [=remove all the sheets] so I can wash the sheets.

3 [+ *obj*] : to remove everything (such as furniture or equipment) from (a room, building, car, etc.) • They *stripped* the room when they left. • The building had been completely *stripped* of its original woodwork.

4 [+ *obj*] : to separate (a machine or piece of equipment) into parts for cleaning or repair • *strip* a rifle — often + *down* • They *stripped down* the engine.

5 [+ *obj*] : to take (something) away from someone in a forceful way — + *of* • They *stripped* the slaves *of* their dignity. — often + *away* • Their rights were *stripped away.* — often used as *(be) stripped* • The pageant winner *was stripped of* her crown/title after the scandal. [=she was forced to give up her crown/title after the scandal]

6 [+ *obj*] : to damage part of a screw or gear so that it does not work properly • Pushing too hard will *strip* the screw.

strip away [*phrasal verb*] ***strip (something) away*** or ***strip away (something)*** **1** : to remove (something that covers a surface) : to pull pieces of a covering away from a surface • *strip away* the bark of a tree **2** : to remove (unimportant material) from something • The editor *stripped away* repetitive sections of the essay. — see also ²STRIP 5 (above)

strip cartoon *noun, pl* ~ **-toons** [*count*] *Brit* : COMIC STRIP

strip club *noun, pl* ~ **clubs** [*count*] *informal* : a place where people go to watch performers take their clothes off in a sexually exciting way : a nightclub with performances by strippers — called also (*US*) *strip joint*

stripe /ˈstraɪp/ *noun, pl* **stripes** [*count*]

1 : a long, narrow line of color • light gray *stripes* on a black background • a zebra's *stripes* — see also PINSTRIPE, STARS AND STRIPES

2 : a piece of material worn on the arm of a military uniform to show the rank of the person wearing the uniform • He finally got his sergeant's *stripes.*

3 : a particular type of person or thing • classes for artists ***of all stripes*** [=for all kinds of artists] • activists ***of any/every stripe***

earn your stripes : to do something which shows that you deserve to be accepted and respected by the other people in a field or profession • She has yet to *earn her stripes* as a reporter.

striped /ˈstraɪpt/ *adj* : having stripes or bands of color • a *striped* shirt — see color picture on page C12

stripey *variant spelling of* STRIPY

strip lighting *noun* [*noncount*] *Brit* : a type of lighting that uses long white tubes • The bright *strip lighting* in the office was not very flattering.

— **strip light** *noun, pl* ~ **lights** [*count*]

strip·ling /ˈstrɪplɪŋ/ *noun, pl* **-lings** [*count*] *old-fashioned + humorous* : a boy or young man • I've known him since he was a mere *stripling.* [=since he was very young]

strip mall *noun, pl* ~ **malls** [*count*] *US* : a long building that is divided into separate shops which usually have outside entrances and which share a parking lot

strip mine *noun, pl* ~ **mines** [*count*] : a mine that is dug by removing the surface of a large piece of land one section at a time

— **strip–mine** *verb* **-mines; -mined; -min·ing** [+ *obj*] • a region where coal is *strip-mined*

strip·per /ˈstrɪpɚ/ *noun, pl* **-pers**

1 [*count*] : a performer who removes his or her clothing in a sexually exciting way : a dancer who does a striptease • She worked as a *stripper* for a few years.

2 a [*count*] : a tool that you use to remove something (such as paint) from a surface **b** [*count, noncount*] : a liquid chemical that you use to remove something (such as paint) from a surface • a can of paint *stripper*

strip search *noun, pl* ~ **searches** [*count*] : an act of removing someone's clothing to see if that person is hiding illegal drugs, weapons, etc. • The administrators ordered random *strip searches* of all prisoners.

— **strip–search** *verb* **-search·es; -searched; -search·ing** [+ *obj*] • They were *strip-searched* at the airport.

strip·tease /ˈstrɪpˌtiːz/ *noun, pl* **-teas·es** [*count*] : a performance in which someone removes clothing in a sexually exciting way

stripy or **strip·ey** /ˈstraɪpi/ *adj* **strip·i·er; -est** *Brit, informal* : STRIPED • *stripy* shirts

strive /ˈstraɪv/ *verb* **strives; strove** /ˈstroʊv/ *also* **strived; striv·en** /ˈstraɪvən/ *or* **strived; striv·ing** [*no obj*] *formal* : to try very hard to do or achieve something • We must all *strive* to do better. • She always *strives* for perfection. • They *strove* for success. = They *strove* to succeed. • They continue to *strive* toward their goals. • *striving* against injustice [=working hard to fight injustice] ***synonyms*** see ¹ATTEMPT

— **striv·er** /ˈstraɪvɚ/ *noun, pl* **-ers** [*count*]

strobe light /ˈstroʊb-/ *noun, pl* ~ **lights** [*count*] : a bright light that flashes on and off very quickly

strode *past tense of* ¹STRIDE

¹stroke /ˈstroʊk/ *noun, pl* **strokes**

1 [*count*] *medical* : a serious illness caused when a blood vessel in your brain suddenly breaks or is blocked • He had/suffered a *stroke* last winter. • a *stroke* patient/victim — see also SUNSTROKE

2 [*count*] **a** : an act of hitting a ball or the movement made to hit a ball during a game • She has a strong backhand *stroke.* • a forceful *stroke* — see also GROUND STROKE **b** *golf* : an act of hitting the ball that is counted as part of a player's score • He is ahead by two *strokes.*

3 [*count*] **a** : one of a series of repeated movements of your arms in swimming or rowing that you make to move yourself or the boat through the water • She swims with long, smooth *strokes.* • the *stroke* of an oar **b** : a style of swimming • She knows the four basic *strokes.* — see also BACKSTROKE, BREASTSTROKE

4 [*count*] : one of a series of repeated movements by something that goes up and down or back and forth • The bird soared higher with each *stroke* of its wings. • the *stroke* of a piston

5 [*count*] : an act of hitting someone or something with a stick, whip, etc. • a *stroke* of the whip

6 [*count*] : a gentle movement of your hand over or along something • She gave the cat a *stroke.* [=she stroked the cat]

7 [*count*] : a single act of moving a pen or brush when it is being used to write or paint • He writes with smooth *strokes.* • You can see the *strokes* of the painter's brush throughout the painting. • (*figurative*) He has the power to end this policy ***with a (single) stroke of a/the/his pen.*** [=by signing a law, order, etc., which ends it]; *also* : a line or mark made by a pen or brush • A few *strokes* (of paint) form the basic shape of the horse. — see also BRUSHSTROKE, KEYSTROKE

8 a [*count*] : one of the sounds made by a clock or bell to indicate a particular time • the first *stroke* of the clock at midnight **b** [*singular*] : an exact time • They arrived ***at the stroke of*** midnight. [=exactly at midnight]

9 [*count*] : a single decisive action • She solved all our problems with a single, brilliant/bold *stroke.* • We can resolve this at/by/in/with one *stroke.*

10 [*count*] : something good, lucky, etc., that happens or is thought of suddenly — usually singular • Her idea for the design for the interior was a ***stroke of inspiration.*** • It was only by a ***stroke of luck*** that we found a parking spot. • It was a ***lucky stroke.*** • Deciding to relocate the company was ***a stroke of genius.*** [=a brilliant idea]

11 [*count*] : a bright flash of lightning • a *stroke* of lightning

a stroke of work *informal* : any work at all • They haven't done *a stroke of work* all day.

S

put (someone) off their stroke *Brit* : to cause someone to hesitate or be confused • The last-minute change of plans *put me off my stroke.*

[2]**stroke** *verb* **strokes; stroked; strok·ing** [+ *obj*]
1 : to move your hand over (someone or something) gently and in one direction • She was *stroking* the cat's fur.
2 *always followed by an adverb or preposition* **a :** to move (something) gently in one direction • He *stroked* the pen lightly over the paper. **b :** to hit or kick (a ball) with a smooth movement • She *stroked* the ball toward the hole.
3 *chiefly US, informal* **:** to say nice things to (someone) in order to get approval, agreement, etc. • You're just *stroking* me so I'll go along with you. • She works with celebrities and spends half her time ***stroking their egos.***
– strok·er *noun, pl* **-ers** [*count*]

stroll /ˈstroʊl/ *verb* **strolls; strolled; stroll·ing :** to walk slowly in usually a pleasant and relaxed way [*no obj*] They *strolled* along/down/across the street looking in the store windows. [+ *obj*] We *strolled* the streets of the village.
– stroll *noun, pl* **strolls** [*count*] • He went for a *stroll* in/through the park.

stroll·er /ˈstroʊlɚ/ *noun, pl* **-ers** [*count*]
1 *US* **:** a small carriage with four wheels that a baby or small child can ride in while someone pushes it — called also (*Brit*) *pushchair*
2 : someone who is walking in a slow and relaxed way **:** someone who is strolling • I met a few *strollers* on the beach.

strong /ˈstrɑːŋ/ *adj* **strong·er** /ˈstrɑːŋgɚ/; **strong·est** /ˈstrɑːŋgəst/
1 : having great physical power and ability **:** having a lot of strength • a big *strong* kid • an athlete with *strong* muscles/legs • He's ***as strong as an ox.*** — opposite WEAK
2 : not easy to break or damage • The table should be *strong* enough to survive the trip. • The builder added supports to make the walls *stronger.*
3 : not sick or injured **:** HEALTHY • He'll return to work when he's feeling a little *stronger.*
4 : very noticeable • He speaks with a *strong* accent. • She has *strong* features like her father. • He bears a *strong* resemblance to his father.
5 : having great power or force • a *strong* breeze/wind • a good *strong* kick
6 a : very powerful in action or effect • Morphine is a *strong* drug. • a *strong* detergent • He needs *strong* glasses for reading. **b :** having a powerful and sometimes unpleasant taste or smell • *strong* cheese • The spices are too *strong* for me. • a *strong* perfume • A *strong* smell came from the basement.
7 : containing a large amount of an important ingredient (such as alcohol) • I could use a *strong* drink. • She drank nothing *stronger* than iced tea. • a *strong* cup of coffee
8 : having a lot of power or influence • a *strong* leader/government
9 : likely to persuade or convince people that something is true, real, correct, etc. • He made a *strong* [=*compelling, persuasive*] argument/case for keeping the center open. • *strong* evidence
10 : very confident and able to deal with difficult situations • a *strong* character/personality • I don't think I'm *strong* enough to handle this by myself. • Her spirit remained *strong* throughout her illness.
11 : felt, believed, or expressed in a very definite and powerful way • an especially *strong* conviction/commitment • She is a woman of *strong* and independent opinions. • a *strong* desire/liking/hatred • He has a *strong* sense of responsibility. • I had a *strong* desire/temptation/urge to call him. • He has a *strong* need for control. • The proposal has faced *strong* opposition. • He thanked them for their *strong* support.
12 : powerful and effective in supporting something, opposing something, etc. • She is a *strong* advocate for child welfare. • a *strong* opponent of the proposal
13 : well established and likely to continue • *strong* traditions • *strong* friendships/relationships/ties
14 : likely to succeed or to happen • a *strong* candidate/contender • There is a *strong* [=very good] possibility/chance that he will be promoted.
15 a : great in number • There was a *strong* turnout for the election. [=a large number of people voted in the election] **b** — used to indicate the number of people in a large group • The army was ten thousand *strong.* [=there were 10,000 soldiers in the army]
16 a : having a value that is great or that is increasing • The dollar has been *strong.* **b :** in a good financial condition **:** doing well • The business remains *strong* despite the setbacks. • The economy is *strong.*
17 : very forceful and sometimes obscene or offensive • The movie contains some ***strong language.*** [=*swearing*]
18 : very bright • She likes *strong* colors. • a *strong* light
a bit strong *Brit, informal* **:** unfair or too critical • Weren't you *a bit strong* on him?
a strong stomach see [1]STOMACH
come on strong see [1]COME
going strong **:** very active, healthy, or successful • The company has been *going strong* for nearly a century. • He's 92 years old and still *going strong.*
strong on **1 :** very good at (something) • She's *strong on* vocabulary but not grammar. • The author is not *strong on* characterization. **2 :** containing a lot of (something) • The explanation was *strong on* detail.
– strong·ly /ˈstrɑːŋli/ *adv* [*more* ~; *most* ~] • I feel very *strongly* about this. • She spoke *strongly* against the idea. • I *strongly* agree/disagree with her. • I *strongly* advise you to see a doctor. • The kitchen smelled *strongly* of baking. • *strongly* flavored • a *strongly* worded letter of complaint

[1]**strong–arm** /ˈstrɑːŋˈɑɚm/ *adj, always used before a noun* **:** using force or threats to make someone do what is wanted • They accused the government of using *strong-arm* tactics to silence its opponents.

[2]**strong–arm** *verb* **-arms; -armed; -arm·ing** [+ *obj*] **:** to use force or threats to make (someone) do what is wanted • She *strong-armed* us into cooperating.

strong·box /ˈstrɑːŋˌbɑːks/ *noun, pl* **-box·es** [*count*] **:** a box that is usually made of metal, that can be locked, and that is used to keep money or valuable things **:** SAFE

strong·hold /ˈstrɑːŋˌhoʊld/ *noun, pl* **-holds** [*count*]
1 : an area where most people have the same beliefs, values, etc. **:** an area dominated by a particular group • The area/district/state is a Republican *stronghold.*
2 : a protected place where the members of a military group stay and can defend themselves against attacks • The rebels retreated to their mountain *stronghold.*
3 : an area where a particular type of uncommon animal can still be found • the last *stronghold* of the endangered deer

strong·man /ˈstrɑːŋˌmæn/ *noun, pl* **-men** /-ˌmɛn/ [*count*]
1 : a politician or leader who uses violence or threats
2 : a man who performs in a circus and who is very strong

strong–mind·ed /ˈstrɑːŋˈmaɪndəd/ *adj* [*more* ~; *most* ~] **:** having very strong and definite beliefs and opinions **:** not easily influenced • a *strong-minded* woman • He is the most *strong-minded* child I have ever known.
– strong–mind·ed·ly *adv* **– strong–mind·ed·ness** *noun* [*noncount*]

strong room *noun, pl* ~ **rooms** [*count*] **:** a special room in a bank where money and other valuable things can be kept safe

strong suit *noun* [*singular*] **:** something that a person does well — often used in negative statements • Irony is not my *strong suit.* • Swimming has never been his *strong suit.*

strong–willed *adj* [*more* ~; *most* ~] **:** very determined to do something even if other people say it should not be done • two *strong-willed* children

stron·tium /ˈstrɑːnʃijəm/ *noun* [*noncount*] **:** a soft silver-white metal that is used in color TV tubes and red fireworks

strop /ˈstrɑːp/ *noun, pl* **strops**
1 [*count*] **:** a narrow piece of leather that is used for sharpening a razor
2 [*singular*] *Brit, informal* **:** a bad mood • He ***gets in a strop*** if he has to wait for someone.

strop·py /ˈstrɑːpi/ *adj* **strop·pi·er; -est** *Brit, informal* **:** easily annoyed and difficult to deal with • There's no need to get *stroppy* with me.
– strop·pi·ness *noun* [*noncount*]

strove *past tense of* STRIVE

struck *past tense and past participle of* [1]STRIKE

struc·tur·al /ˈstrʌktʃərəl/ *adj, always used before a noun* **:** relating to the way something is built or organized **:** relating to the structure of something • The house suffered no *structural* damage. • *structural* defects/weaknesses
– struc·tur·al·ly *adv* • The building is *structurally* sound.

[1]**struc·ture** /ˈstrʌktʃɚ/ *noun, pl* **-tures**
1 [*count*] **a :** the way that something is built, arranged, or organized • They studied the compound's molecular *structure.* • The film had a simple narrative *structure.* • the *structure* of a plant **b :** the way that a group of people are organized • a solid family *structure* • the social *structure* of a

S

college campus • changes to the company's power *structure*
2 [*count*] **: something (such as a house, tower, bridge, etc.) that is built by putting parts together and that usually stands on its own** • a brick/steel *structure* • The *structure* was damaged by fire. • a 12-story *structure*
3 [*noncount*] **: the quality of something that is carefully planned, organized, and controlled** • The novel lacks *structure*. • Children need a lot of *structure* in their lives.

²structure *verb* **-tures; -tured; -tur·ing** [+ *obj*] **: to arrange or organize (something) in a particular way** • She *structured* the essay chronologically. • The story is *structured* [=*built*] around several main themes.

stru·del /ˈstruːdl/ *noun, pl* **-dels** [*count, noncount*] **: a German pastry made of thin dough rolled up with fruit filling and baked** • apple *strudel*

¹strug·gle /ˈstrʌgəl/ *verb* **strug·gles; strug·gled; strug·gling** [*no obj*]
1 : to try very hard to do, achieve, or deal with something that is difficult or that causes problems • He has been *struggling* with the problem of how to keep good workers from leaving. • They *struggled* for the right to vote. • She is *struggling* with her health. [=she is having problems with her health] • They *struggled* against injustice. • I had to *struggle* against the impulse to laugh. [=I had to make a strong effort to keep myself from laughing] — **often followed by** *to + verb* • She's *struggling to survive*. • He was *struggling to breathe*. • They have been *struggling to pay* their bills.
2 a : to move with difficulty or with great effort • She *struggled* up the hill through the snow. **b : to try to move yourself, an object, etc., by making a lot of effort** • She *struggled* to lift the package by herself, but it was too heavy. • He *struggled* to get free of the wreckage. • She was *struggling* with the door. [=trying to open the door] **c : to fight with someone in order to get something** • They *struggled* (with each other) for/over the gun. [=they fought with each other as they each tried to get the gun]
3 : to be failing : to be doing something without success • He's been *struggling* in math class for most of the year. • The team has continued to *struggle* in recent weeks. • He was living as a *struggling* artist in the city.
struggle on [*phrasal verb*] **: to continue doing something that is difficult or tiring** • I suppose all we can do now is *struggle on*.
– strug·gler /ˈstrʌglɚ/ *noun, pl* **-ers** [*count*]

²struggle *noun, pl* **struggles**
1 [*count*] **: a long effort to do, achieve, or deal with something that is difficult or that causes problems** • a *struggle* to succeed • a *struggle* against injustice [=an effort to stop injustice] • the *struggle* for civil rights/freedom/survival • She talked about her *struggles* with depression. [=the problems she has had because of her depression; her attempts to find a cure for her depression] • The ***power struggle*** [=the fight for control] between the two owners destroyed the company.
2 [*count*] **: a physical fight between usually two people** • There was a *struggle* for/over the gun. • There was no sign of a *struggle*.
3 [*singular*] **: something that is difficult to do or achieve** • The work is a real *struggle* for me. [=the work is very difficult] • It was a *struggle* getting out of bed this morning.

strum /ˈstrʌm/ *verb* **strums; strummed; strum·ming** [+ *obj*]
1 : to play (a guitar or similar instrument) by moving your fingers across the strings • She *strummed* the guitar/banjo.
2 : to play (music) on a guitar, banjo, etc., by moving your fingers over the strings • He *strummed* a tune on the guitar.
– strum·mer *noun, pl* **-ers** [*count*]

strum·pet /ˈstrʌmpət/ *noun, pl* **-pets** [*count*] *old-fashioned + offensive* **: a woman who has sex with men for money or who has sex with many men**

strung *past tense and past participle of* ²STRING

strung out *adj*
1 [*more* ~; *most* ~] *informal* **: strongly affected by an illegal drug** — **often +** *on* • They were *strung out on* heroin.
2 : spread out with spaces between • stars *strung out* across the galaxy

strung up *adj* [*more* ~; *most* ~] *Brit, informal* **: very nervous, excited, or worried** • Don't get so *strung up* about everything.

¹strut /ˈstrʌt/ *verb* **struts; strut·ted; strut·ting** [*no obj*] **: to walk in a confident and proud way** • She *strutted* across the stage.
strut your stuff *informal* **: to proudly show your abilities** • The audition gave aspiring actors a chance to *strut their stuff*.
– strut·ter *noun, pl* **-ers** [*count*]

²strut *noun, pl* **struts**
1 [*count*] **: a long, thin piece of wood or metal used for support in a building, vehicle, etc.**
2 [*singular*] **: a proud and confident walk** • the *strut* of a supermodel

strych·nine /ˈstrɪkˌnaɪn/ *noun* [*noncount*] **: a poisonous substance that can be used in very small amounts as a medicine**

¹stub /ˈstʌb/ *noun, pl* **stubs** [*count*]
1 : a short part left after a larger part has been broken off or used up • a pencil *stub*
2 : a part of a ticket that is kept by the person who uses the ticket • Hold onto your ticket *stub* in case you leave the theater and want to come back in again.
3 : a piece of paper that is attached to a check and has information (such as the amount and the date) printed on it • a check *stub* — see also PAY STUB

²stub *verb* **stubs; stubbed; stub·bing** [+ *obj*] **: to put out (a cigarette) by pressing it down against something** — **usually +** *out* • He *stubbed* his cigarette *out* in/on the ashtray.
stub your toe **: to hurt your toe by hitting it against something** • She *stubbed her toe* against/on the leg of the chair.

stub·ble /ˈstʌbəl/ *noun* [*noncount*]
1 : short hairs growing from the face of a man who has not shaved very recently • He ran his hand over his *stubble*. — see picture at BEARD
2 : the short ends of crops left in the ground after the crops have been cut down
– stub·bled /ˈstʌbəld/ *adj* • his *stubbled* chin • We drove past *stubbled* fields. **– stub·bly** /ˈstʌbəli/ *adj* • a *stubbly* beard

stub·born /ˈstʌbɚn/ *adj* [*more* ~; *most* ~]
1 : refusing to change your ideas or to stop doing something • She's wrong, but she's too *stubborn* to admit it. • I admire his *stubborn* refusal to quit. • She ***has a stubborn streak***. [=she is often stubborn] • He's ***(as) stubborn as a mule***. [=he's very/extremely stubborn]
2 : difficult to deal with, remove, etc. • *stubborn* hair • trying to treat a *stubborn* infection • a *stubborn* stain
– stub·born·ly *adv* • She *stubbornly* refused to move. • The fever persisted *stubbornly*. **– stub·born·ness** /ˈstʌbɚnnəs/ *noun* [*noncount*]

stub·by /ˈstʌbi/ *adj* **stub·bi·er; -est : short and thick** • hands with thick *stubby* fingers • My dog has a short *stubby* tail. • *stubby* legs

stuc·co /ˈstʌkoʊ/ *noun* [*noncount*] **: a type of plaster used for decoration or to cover the outside walls of houses**
– stuc·coed /ˈstʌkoʊd/ *adj* • *stuccoed* buildings/ceilings/walls

¹stuck /ˈstʌk/ *adj, not used before a noun*
1 a : difficult or impossible to move from a position • The ring is *stuck* on my finger. • The zipper is *stuck*. • The door keeps ***getting stuck***. • The elevator *got stuck* on the fifth floor. — **sometimes used figuratively** • He's an old man and ***stuck in his ways***. [=completely unwilling to change his ways of doing or thinking about things] • The song is ***stuck in my head***. [=I keep hearing the song over and over again in my head] **b : in a place or situation that is difficult or impossible to get out of** • The car was *stuck* in the mud. • We were *stuck* there for three days because of bad weather. • She was *stuck* in an awful marriage. • I was *stuck* at the office all day. • *stuck* at home with nothing to do • I ***got stuck*** in traffic. **c : forced to keep or deal with someone or something unpleasant** • We're *stuck* with this old sofa that nobody wants. • I was *stuck* washing dishes. = I ***got stuck*** washing dishes. — see also *stick with* at ²STICK
2 *informal* **: unable to think of a solution, an idea, etc.** • I'm *stuck*. Can you help me? • I'm ***stuck on*** this math problem. • I ***got stuck on*** the very first problem. • If you're ***stuck for*** ideas, I can help. • (*chiefly Brit*) She's never ***stuck for words***. [=*lost for words*]
get stuck in/into *Brit, informal* **: to start doing something with a lot of energy** • Grab a plate and *get stuck in*.
stuck on *informal* **: loving or admiring someone foolishly or too much** • He was *stuck on* her for a while in high school. • She is ***stuck on herself***. [=*stuck-up*]

²stuck *past tense and past participle of* ²STICK

stuck–up /ˈstʌkˈʌp/ *adj* [*more* ~; *most* ~] *informal* **: acting unfriendly towards other people because you think you are**

S

better than they are : CONCEITED • They're just *stuck-up* people with too much money.

¹stud /ˈstʌd/ *noun, pl* **studs**
1 : a male animal (such as a horse) kept for breeding [*count*] retired racehorses being used as *studs* [*noncount*] retired racehorses ***at stud*** • a horse that has been ***put out to stud***
2 [*count*] *informal* **:** a very attractive and masculine man : a man who has sexual relations with many women • She left her husband and ran off with some young *stud*.
— compare ²STUD

²stud *noun, pl* **studs** [*count*]
1 *US* **:** one of the upright pieces of wood that are used to build the frame of a wall
2 : a small metal knob that is used for decoration • a belt decorated with silver *studs*
3 : a small metal object used as a clothing fastener or for decoration • shirt *studs*
4 : a small piece of jewelry that is attached through a hole in part of a person's body (such as an ear) • She was wearing diamond *studs*. — see color picture on page C11
5 : one of the short pieces of metal or rubber on the surface of a snow tire
— compare ¹STUD

³stud *verb* **studs; stud·ded; stud·ding** [+ *obj*] **:** to decorate or cover (something) with many small items • Beads *stud* the surface of the gown. — often used figuratively • Bright stars *studded* the sky.

studded *adj* **:** covered or decorated with many small parts or pieces • a *studded* tire • a gown *studded* with jewels — often used figuratively • a sky *studded* with stars • a career *studded* with honors — sometimes used in combination • celebrity-*studded* shows [=shows that have many celebrities]

stu·dent /ˈstuːdn̩t, *Brit* ˈstjuːdn̩t/ *noun, pl* **-dents** [*count*]
1 : a person who attends a school, college, or university • a high school *student* • a group of college *students* • She is a *student* at Georgetown University. • She is a *student* [=*pupil*] at our local elementary school. — often used before another noun • *student* athletes/groups/leaders/loans/trips — see also MATURE STUDENT
2 : a person who studies something — + *of* • She is a *student of* human nature.

student body *noun, pl* **~ -ies** [*count*] **:** the students at a school • The school has a large *student body*. [=a large number of students attend the school]

student council *noun, pl* **~ -cils** [*count*] **:** a group of students who are elected to help plan activities and to organize and manage life at school for other students

student driver *noun, pl* **~ -ers** [*count*] *US* **:** someone who is learning to drive a car — called also (*Brit*) *learner*, (*Brit*) *learner driver*

student government *noun, pl* **~ -ments :** a group of students in a school who are elected to help plan activities and to organize and manage life at school for other students [*count*] She was president of the *student government*. [*noncount*] He is active in *student government*.

student teacher *noun, pl* **~ -ers** [*count*] **:** a student who is learning how to teach and practicing teaching for the first time
— **student teaching** *noun* [*noncount*] • Where did you do your *student teaching*?

student union (*chiefly US*) *or Brit* **students' union** *noun, pl* **~ unions** [*count*]
1 : a building at a college or university that is used for students' social activities
2 *Brit* **:** an association of students at a college or university

stud·ied /ˈstʌdid/ *adj*
1 : carefully thought out or prepared : THOUGHTFUL • She gave a *studied* response.
2 : done deliberately • a *studied* insult • He viewed us with a *studied* indifference.

stu·dio /ˈstuːdiˌoʊ, *Brit* ˈstjuːdiˌəʊ/ *noun, pl* **-dios** [*count*]
1 : the building or room where an artist works
2 : a place where people go to learn, practice, or study an art (such as singing, dancing, or acting)
3 a : a place where movies are made **b :** a company that makes movies • the president of a major Hollywood *studio*
4 : a place where radio or television programs are broadcast
5 : a place where music is recorded
6 : STUDIO APARTMENT • I rented a *studio* in the city.

studio apartment *noun, pl* **~ -ments** [*count*] *US* **:** a small apartment that has a main room, a very small kitchen, and a bathroom — called also *studio*, (*Brit*) *studio flat*

stu·di·ous /ˈstuːdijəs, *Brit* ˈstjuːdiəs/ *adj* [*more ~; most ~*]
1 : very serious about studying, reading, learning, etc. • a *studious* child • *studious* habits
2 : very careful and serious • He made a *studious* effort to obey the rules. • *studious* avoidance of trouble
— **stu·di·ous·ly** *adv* • They did the homework assignment *studiously*. • She has been *studiously* avoiding/ignoring me.
— **stu·di·ous·ness** *noun* [*noncount*] • The teacher complimented the student on her *studiousness*.

stud·ly /ˈstʌdli/ *adj* **stud·li·er; -est** *US slang, of a man* **:** very attractive and masculine • a *studly* [=*hunky*] actor

¹study /ˈstʌdi/ *noun, pl* **stud·ies**
1 : the activity or process of learning about something by reading, memorizing facts, attending school, etc. [*noncount*] Becoming a doctor requires years of *study*. • You can improve your knowledge of the natural world by *study* and observation. • She is engaged in the *study* of law. [=she is studying law] • You can design your own ***course of study***. [=you can choose the subjects you will study] [*plural*] She will return to her *studies* after vacation. • He left the service to pursue his *studies*.
2 a [*count*] **:** an area of learning taught in a school : SUBJECT — usually plural • literary/American/women's *studies* — see also SOCIAL STUDIES **b** [*singular*] **:** something that a person studies or gives attention to • Their habits make an interesting *study*. [=it is interesting to study their habits] • She has ***made a study of*** the problem. [=she has studied the problem]
3 [*count*] **a :** an organized experiment in which many things are looked at, measured, recorded, etc., in order to learn more about something • The agency conducted an environmental *study*. • He took part in a *study* of childhood obesity. **b :** a report or publication based on a study • The *study* of the new drug will be published next year.
4 [*count*] **:** a quiet room in someone's home for reading, writing, etc. • She spent the evening reading in her/the *study*.
5 [*singular*] *US* **:** a person who learns or memorizes something • He's a ***fast/quick study***. [=he learns things quickly] • When it comes to computers, I'm a ***slow study***.
6 [*singular*] **:** something or someone that clearly has or shows a particular quality or feature • The evening was a *study* in contrasts. [=some parts of the evening were very different from other parts] • He was a *study* in concentration as he gazed at the computer screen.
7 [*count*] *art* **:** an artistic work that deals with a particular subject and that is done especially to prepare for a larger work
8 [*count*] *music* **:** a musical composition that is created for the practice of a particular technique
under study **:** being thought about and considered so that a decision can be made : being studied • The proposal is *under study*.

²study *verb* **studies; stud·ied; study·ing**
1 : to read, memorize facts, attend school, etc., in order to learn about a subject [*no obj*] She *studied* hard. • Did you *study* for the test? • She's *studying* to be a teacher. [+ *obj*] He is *studying* music.
2 [+ *obj*] **a :** to give careful attention to (something) • I *studied* the request carefully. • She was *studying* his face for a reaction. • The proposal was *studied* in great detail. **b :** to conduct an organized experiment in order to learn more about (something) • The effects of the drug have never been thoroughly *studied*.

study hall *noun, pl* **~ halls** *US* **:** a time during the school day when a student is expected to go to a particular room in the school to study or to complete work assigned in other classes [*noncount*] I have *study hall* next period. • She got in trouble for talking in/during *study hall*. [*count*] a required *study hall* • My *study hall* starts at 11:04.

¹stuff /ˈstʌf/ *noun* [*noncount*]
1 *informal* **a :** materials, supplies, or equipment • She got out the cooking *stuff* to bake some cookies. • computers, word processors, and *stuff* like that • I need a place to store my *stuff*. **b :** a group or pile of things that are not specifically described • Pick that *stuff* up off the floor.
2 *informal* — used to refer to something when you do not need to name exactly what it is • They sold tons of the *stuff*. • Trust me. This *stuff* works. • That *stuff's* expensive. • She wears cool *stuff*. • They're giving away free *stuff* at the door. • I didn't like her early books, but her recent *stuff* is very good. • The *stuff* he says about me is just not true. • I drink wine and beer occasionally, but I never touch ***the hard stuff***.

[=hard liquor; alcoholic drinks like whiskey, vodka, etc.] — see also HOT STUFF, KID STUFF

3 *informal* — used to speak in a general way about something that is talked about, written about, etc. ▪ There's some fascinating *stuff* in this book. ▪ I can't believe the *stuff* teenagers talk about.

4 *informal* — used to describe the quality of a performance, experience, etc. ▪ The presentation of facts in history can be pretty dull *stuff*. [=can be pretty dull] ▪ This is great *stuff* [=is very enjoyable] for music fans.

5 *informal* : actions or behavior of a particular kind ▪ How do they get away with such *stuff*? ▪ Don't try any funny *stuff*. ▪ There's all this crazy *stuff* going on. ▪ He does *stuff* that bugs his parents.

6 : personality or character ▪ He's a coward but his brother is ***made of sterner/tougher stuff***. [=his brother is a stronger/tougher person] ▪ A person who has ***the right stuff*** [=who has the necessary personal qualities] will do well here.

7 : the material that something is made of ▪ The floor tiles are made of very tough *stuff*. — often used figuratively ▪ He has ***the stuff of greatness***. [=he has the qualities that can make a person great] ▪ Her partying became ***the stuff of legend***. [=became very famous or legendary]

8 *baseball* : the ability to throw pitches that are hard to hit ▪ a pitcher with good *stuff*

and stuff *informal* — used in speech to refer to things that are similar to the thing just mentioned ▪ They asked me about my plans for the future *and stuff*. ▪ The store sells TVs and stereos *and stuff* (like that).

do your stuff *informal* : to do the things that you are able to do well : to do things that you are known for doing ▪ You'll succeed if you just get out there and *do your stuff*.

know your stuff *informal* : to be an expert at something ▪ When it comes to gardening, she really *knows her stuff*. [=she knows a lot about gardening]

show your stuff *informal* : to show what you are able to do : to show your skills ▪ The competition gives young performers a chance to *show their stuff*.

strut your stuff see [1]STRUT

[2]stuff *verb* **stuffs; stuffed; stuff·ing** *[+ obj]*

1 : to fill (something) so that there is no room for anything else ▪ The boy *stuffed* his pockets with candy. ▪ She *stuffed* the laundry bag full. — often used figuratively ▪ The book is *stuffed* [=*filled*] with information. ▪ The students were ***stuffing their heads*** with facts.

2 : to push (something) quickly and carelessly into a small space — usually + *into* ▪ The boy *stuffed* the candy *into* his pockets. ▪ He tried to *stuff* [=*cram*] all his clothes *into* one suitcase.

3 : to put a seasoned mixture of food into (something that is being cooked) ▪ *stuff* a turkey ▪ *stuff* a pepper

4 : to fill the skin of (a dead animal) so that it looks the way it did when it was alive — often used as *(be) stuffed* ▪ He had the deer's head *stuffed*.

stuff it *informal* — used as an angry and rude way to say that you do not want something or are not interested in something ▪ When they offered me the job I told them they could *stuff it*.

stuff the ballot box see BALLOT BOX

stuff yourself or ***stuff your face*** *informal + often disapproving* : to eat a large amount of food ▪ They *stuffed themselves* with pizza.

stuffed *adj*

1 *not used before a noun* : filled with food : not hungry any more ▪ "Would you like another piece of pie?" "No, thanks. I'm *stuffed*."

2 : filled with mucus because of illness ▪ My nose is *stuffed* (up). = I'm (all) ***stuffed up***. ▪ a *stuffed* (up) nose

get stuffed *chiefly Brit, informal* — used as an angry and rude way to tell someone to go away or to leave you alone ▪ When they refused to consider him for the promotion he told them they could *get stuffed*.

stuffed animal *noun, pl* ~ **-mals** *[count] US* : a toy in the shape of an animal that usually has fake fur and is filled with soft material — called also *(Brit) soft toy*

stuffed shirt *noun, pl* ~ **shirts** *[count] informal + disapproving* : a person who behaves in a very formal way and expects to be treated as someone very important

stuff·ing /ˈstʌfɪŋ/ *noun, pl* **-ings**

1 *[noncount]* : soft material that is used to fill a pillow, cushion, etc.

2 : a seasoned mixture of food that is put inside another food and cooked *[noncount]* Would you like more *stuffing*? *[count]* a delicious bread *stuffing*

knock the stuffing out of *informal* : to cause (someone) to lose energy and confidence : to make (someone) feel weak or overwhelmed ▪ When he found out that he didn't get the job, it really *knocked the stuffing out of* him.

stuffy /ˈstʌfi/ *adj* **stuff·i·er; -est**

1 : lacking fresh air ▪ a *stuffy* attic/room ▪ It's very *stuffy* in here.

2 : filled with mucus because of illness : STUFFED ▪ She had a *stuffy* nose. ▪ I had a *stuffy* feeling in my head.

3 *informal + disapproving* : very formal, serious, or old-fashioned ▪ the *stuffiest* members of that exclusive club ▪ a *stuffy* old judge

– stuff·i·ly /ˈstʌfəli/ *adv* ▪ *stuffily* respectable people **– stuff·i·ness** /ˈstʌfinəs/ *noun [noncount]*

stul·ti·fy /ˈstʌltəˌfaɪ/ *verb* **-fies; -fied; -fy·ing** *[+ obj] formal* : to cause (someone or something) to become dull, slow, etc. ▪ The government has been *stultified* by bureaucracy.

– stultifying *adj [more ~; most ~]* ▪ *stultifying* boredom

stum·ble /ˈstʌmbəl/ *verb* **stum·bles; stum·bled; stum·bling** *[no obj]*

1 : to hit your foot on something when you are walking or running so that you fall or almost fall : TRIP ▪ I *stumbled* on the uneven pavement. ▪ The horse *stumbled* and almost fell.

2 *always followed by an adverb or preposition* : to walk in an awkward way ▪ He *stumbled* drunkenly across the room. ▪ He *stumbled* over to the table. ▪ She usually ***stumbles out of bed*** [=gets out of bed] around 7:00 am.

3 a : to speak or act in an awkward way ▪ I heard him *stumble* over the unfamiliar words. ▪ She *stumbled* through an apology. **b** : to begin to have problems after a time of success ▪ The economy has *stumbled* in recent months.

4 *always followed by an adverb or preposition* : to find or learn about something unexpectedly ▪ I ***stumbled across/on/upon*** [=*found*] this book by chance. ▪ He ***stumbled onto*** [=*found out*] the truth. ▪ We *stumbled onto/across* the ruins of an old fort. ▪ They *stumbled on/upon* [=*discovered*] a bizarre plot.

– stumble *noun, pl* **stumbles** *[count]* ▪ After a few *stumbles*, the economy was back on track. **– stum·bler** /ˈstʌmbələ/ *noun, pl* **-blers** *[count]*

stum·ble·bum /ˈstʌmbəlˌbʌm/ *noun, pl* **-bums** *[count] US, informal* : a clumsy and stupid person ▪ His political opponents have portrayed him as an inept *stumblebum*.

stumbling block *noun, pl* ~ **blocks** *[count]* : something that stops you from doing what you want to do ▪ Lack of funds is a major *stumbling block* to the project. ▪ My plans hit a *stumbling block*.

[1]stump /ˈstʌmp/ *noun, pl* **stumps** *[count]*

1 : a part that remains after something has been broken off, removed, worn down, etc. ▪ the *stump* of a pipe/tooth

2 : the part of a tree that remains in the ground after the tree is cut down ▪ a tree *stump*

3 : the part of an arm or leg that remains after most of it has been cut off

4 *cricket* : one of the three sticks that form a wicket

on the stump : traveling around and giving speeches during a campaign for election to a political office ▪ candidates who give the same speech over and over when they're *on the stump* — see also STUMP SPEECH

[2]stump *verb* **stumps; stumped; stump·ing**

1 *[+ obj]* : to be too difficult for (someone) to answer ▪ The question completely *stumped* the contestant. [=the contestant did not know the answer to the question] ▪ This problem ***has me stumped***. [=I do not know the solution to this problem]

2 *US* : to go to different places and make speeches during a political campaign *[no obj]* She will be *stumping* in our district this week. *[+ obj]* Several candidates have been *stumping* the state for the past month.

3 *[+ obj] cricket* : to cause (a batsman who is away from the hitting area) to be out by touching the wicket with the ball

stump up *[phrasal verb]* ***stump up*** or ***stump up (something)*** also ***stump (something) up*** *Brit, informal* : to pay (an amount of money) especially when you do not want to ▪ He may be required to *stump up* for the repairs. ▪ If she can't pay, I'll have to *stump up* [=*cough up*] the money.

stump·er /ˈstʌmpə/ *noun, pl* **-ers** *[count] US, informal* : a very difficult question ▪ Some of the questions on the test were real *stumpers*.

S

stump speech *noun, pl* ~ **speeches** [*count*] *US* : a speech that is made many times by a politician who is traveling to different places during a campaign for election

stumpy /ˈstʌmpi/ *adj* **stump·i·er; -est** : short and thick ▪ a dog with a *stumpy* [=*stubby*] tail ▪ *stumpy* legs

stun /ˈstʌn/ *verb* **stuns; stunned; stun·ning** [+ *obj*]
1 : to surprise or upset (someone) very much ▪ a theft that *stunned* [=*shocked*] the art world ▪ The angry criticism *stunned* them. ▪ They were *stunned* by the news. = The news *stunned* them. ▪ His old friends were *stunned* at his success. ▪ She sat in *stunned* disbelief/silence. ▪ There was a *stunned* expression on her face.
2 : to cause (someone) to suddenly become very confused, very dizzy, or unconscious ▪ weapons that can *stun* people temporarily

stung *past tense and past participle of* [1]STING

stun gun *noun, pl* ~ **guns** [*count*] : a gun that produces an electric shock which makes someone unconscious or stops someone from moving

stunk *past tense and past participle of* [1]STINK

stun·ner /ˈstʌnɚ/ *noun, pl* **-ners** [*count*] *informal*
1 : a very attractive person ▪ His wife is a real *stunner*.
2 : something that amazes or shocks people ▪ The jury's decision was a *stunner*.

stunning *adj* [*more* ~; *most* ~]
1 : very surprising or shocking ▪ Researchers have made a *stunning* discovery. ▪ *stunning* news ▪ a *stunning* decision
2 : very beautiful or pleasing ▪ Our room had a *stunning* view of the lake. ▪ a *stunning* gown ▪ a *stunning* young woman
— **stun·ning·ly** *adv* ▪ a *stunningly* beautiful woman ▪ a *stunningly* clear/sharp picture ▪ a *stunningly* rude remark

[1]**stunt** /ˈstʌnt/ *verb* **stunts; stunt·ed; stunt·ing** [+ *obj*] : to stop (someone or something) from growing or developing ▪ Poor soil can *stunt* a plant's growth. ▪ Too many restrictions have *stunted* the economy.

[2]**stunt** *noun, pl* **stunts** [*count*]
1 : something that is done to get attention or publicity ▪ Some people say that the announcement of his retirement was just a *stunt*. ▪ a promotional/publicity *stunt*
2 : a difficult and often dangerous action ▪ a pilot doing loops and other dangerous *stunts*; *especially* : a difficult action or scene that is done by actors in a movie ▪ a star actor who does/performs his own *stunts*
pull a stunt *informal* : to do something foolish or dangerous ▪ Don't ever *pull a stunt* like that again!

stunt double *noun, pl* ~ **doubles** [*count*] : a person who takes an actor's place during the filming of stunts and dangerous scenes for a movie or TV show

stunt·man /ˈstʌntˌmæn/ *noun, pl* **-men** /-ˌmɛn/ [*count*] : a man who takes an actor's place during the filming of stunts and dangerous scenes for a movie or TV show ▪ a Hollywood *stuntman*

stunt·wom·an /ˈstʌntˌwʊmən/ *noun, pl* **-wom·en** /-ˌwɪmən/ [*count*] : a woman who takes an actor's place during the filming of stunts and dangerous scenes for a movie or TV show ▪ a Hollywood *stuntwoman*

stu·pe·fy /ˈstu:pəˌfaɪ, *Brit* ˈstju:pəˌfaɪ/ *verb* **-fies; -fied; -fy·ing** [+ *obj*] : to shock or surprise (someone) very much : to cause (someone) to become confused or unable to think clearly — usually used as *(be) stupefied* ▪ I *was stupified* by their decision.
— **stu·pe·fac·tion** /ˌstu:pəˈfækʃən, *Brit* ˌstju:pəˈfækʃən/ *noun* [*noncount*] ▪ They looked at her in *stupefaction*. — **stupefied** *adj* [*more* ~; *most* ~] ▪ They looked at her with *stupefied* expressions on their faces. — **stupefying** *adj* [*more* ~; *most* ~] ▪ a *stupefying* display of arrogance ▪ *stupefying* boredom — **stu·pe·fy·ing·ly** /ˈstu:pəˌfajɪŋli, *Brit* ˈstju:pəˌfajɪŋli/ *adv* ▪ a chore that's *stupefyingly* boring

stu·pen·dous /stʊˈpɛndəs, *Brit* stjʊˈpɛndəs/ *adj* [*more* ~; *most* ~] : so large or great that it amazes you ▪ a *stupendous* [=*magnificent*] fireworks display ▪ a person with *stupendous* wealth
— **stu·pen·dous·ly** *adv* ▪ a *stupendously* wealthy person

stu·pid /ˈstu:pəd, *Brit* ˈstju:pəd/ *adj* **stu·pid·er; -est** [*also more* ~; *most* ~]
1 : not intelligent : having or showing a lack of ability to learn and understand things ▪ She angrily described her boss as a *stupid* old man. ▪ He had a *stupid* expression on his face. ▪ I'm not *stupid* enough to fall for that trick.
2 : not sensible or logical : FOOLISH ▪ Why are you being so *stupid*? ▪ It was *stupid* of me to try to hide this from you. ▪ We were *stupid* to wait so long before we made a decision. ▪ I did some pretty *stupid* things when I was young. ▪ a *stupid* movie ▪ a silly, *stupid* song ▪ a *stupid* decision/mistake
3 : not able to think normally because you are drunk, tired, etc. ▪ Two glasses of wine are enough to make me *stupid*. ▪ I was *stupid* with fatigue.
4 *informal* — used to refer to something in an angry or irritated way ▪ The *stupid* car won't start. ▪ Where did I put those *stupid* keys?
— **stu·pid·ly** *adv* ▪ He's been acting *stupidly*. ▪ I *stupidly* thought it was a good idea. ▪ She was staring *stupidly* out the window.

stu·pid·i·ty /stʊˈpɪdəti, *Brit* stjʊˈpɪdəti/ *noun, pl* **-ties**
1 [*noncount*] : the state of being foolish or unintelligent : the condition of being stupid ▪ I was shocked by the *stupidity* of their decision/behavior.
2 [*count*] : a stupid idea or action — usually plural ▪ the *stupidities* of war

stu·por /ˈstu:pɚ, *Brit* ˈstju:pɚ/ *noun, pl* **-pors** [*count*] : a condition in which someone is not able to think normally because of being drunk, drugged, tired, etc. ▪ He fell into a drunken *stupor*. ▪ drug-induced *stupors* ▪ in a *stupor* of fatigue

stur·dy /ˈstɚdi/ *adj* **stur·di·er; -est** [*also more* ~; *most* ~]
1 : strongly made ▪ a *sturdy* ship ▪ *sturdy* furniture
2 : strong and healthy ▪ *sturdy*, muscular legs ▪ a *sturdy* athlete ▪ a dog with a strong *sturdy* build
3 : having or showing mental or emotional strength ▪ *sturdy* common sense ▪ *sturdy* self-reliance
— **stur·di·ly** /ˈstɚdəli/ *adj* ▪ *sturdily* made furniture — **stur·di·ness** /ˈstɚdinəs/ *noun* [*noncount*] ▪ the *sturdiness* of the furniture ▪ the bank's financial *sturdiness* [=*strength*]

stur·geon /ˈstɚʤən/ *noun, pl* **-geons** [*count, noncount*] : a type of large fish that is eaten as food ✧ The eggs of the sturgeon are eaten as caviar.

[1]**stut·ter** /ˈstʌtɚ/ *verb* **-ters; -tered; -ter·ing** : to have a speech problem that causes you to repeat the beginning sound of some words [*no obj*] I used to *stutter* when I was a child. ▪ She *stutters* when she gets excited. [+ *obj*] He *stuttered* [=*stammered*] something that I didn't understand.
— **stut·ter·er** /ˈstʌtərɚ/ *noun, pl* **-ers** [*count*] ▪ I was a *stutterer* as a child. — **stuttering** *noun* [*noncount*] ▪ He had speech therapy for his *stuttering*.

[2]**stutter** *noun* [*singular*] : a speech problem that causes someone to repeat the beginning sounds of some words ▪ He has a *stutter*. = He speaks with a *stutter*. [=he stutters]

[1]**sty** /ˈstaɪ/ *noun, pl* **sties** *also* **styes** [*count*]
1 : a place where pigs are kept : PIGSTY
2 *informal* : a dirty or messy place : PIGSTY ▪ His room was a *sty*.
— compare [2]STY

[2]**sty** *or* **stye** /ˈstaɪ/ *noun, pl* **sties** *or* **styes** [*count*] *medical* : a painful, swollen red area on the edge of an eyelid — compare [1]STY

[1]**style** /ˈstajəl/ *noun, pl* **styles**
1 : a particular way in which something is done, created, or performed [*count*] I don't like the flowery *style* of his writing. ▪ She has a unique *style* of singing. ▪ a baseball pitcher with an unusual *style* [*noncount*] She writes with more attention to *style* than to content. ▪ The room was decorated in modern *style*.
2 [*count*] : a particular form or design of something ▪ The car is available in several different *styles*. ▪ a new dress *style* ▪ the Greek *style* of architecture ▪ The range of clothing *styles* has become more varied. ▪ Victorian-*style* drapes
3 [*count*] : a way of behaving or of doing things ▪ His management *style* is abrasive. ▪ Openly criticizing a fellow worker is just ***not my style*** [=I would never openly criticize a fellow worker] ▪ You're a good negotiator. I ***like your style*** [=I like the way you do things]
4 [*noncount*] : a particular way of living ▪ He has been living ***in high style*** [=he has been living the way rich people live] — see also LIFESTYLE
5 [*noncount*] : the quality that makes things attractive, fashionable, etc. ▪ He has a real sense of *style*. ▪ She's a woman ***of style*** [=she's a stylish woman]
6 [*noncount*] : an easy and graceful manner ▪ It was an awkward moment but she handled it with *style*.
7 [*count*] : the way that written words are spelled, capitalized, etc. ▪ Each newspaper had its own *style*. ▪ a *style* guide
cramp your style see [2]CRAMP
in style **1** : popular or fashionable ▪ clothes that are always *in style* [=*in fashion*] **2** : in a way that is impressive or admired because it shows talent, good taste, etc. : in a stylish

S

way ▪ When she travels she likes to do it *in style.* ▪ He finished the tournament *in style* by winning his last match very quickly and easily.

out of style : not popular or fashionable : not stylish ▪ a fad that has fallen/gone *out of style*

[2]**style** *verb* **styles; styled; styl•ing** [+ *obj*]

1 *formal* : to give (yourself) a name or title even if you do not really deserve it ▪ She *styles* [=*calls*] herself a "spiritual adviser." — often + *as* ▪ He *styles* himself *as* an expert in international politics. — see also SELF-STYLED

2 : to give a particular shape to (someone's hair) ▪ She cuts and *styles* hair. ▪ She's having her hair *styled* tomorrow.

3 : to design (something) for a particular purpose ▪ clothing *styled* for teenagers ▪ a book *styled* for a general audience

[1]**styling** *noun* [*noncount*] : the way in which something is designed ▪ a car with sleek new *styling* ▪ clothing with classic *styling*

[2]**styling** *adj, always used before a noun* : used for creating a hair style ▪ *styling* products/salons

styl•ish /ˈstaɪlɪʃ/ *adj* [*more* ~; *most* ~] : following the popular style : FASHIONABLE ▪ She wears *stylish* clothes. = She's a *stylish* dresser. ▪ a *stylish* apartment/house

– **styl•ish•ly** *adv* ▪ a *stylishly* dressed person – **styl•ish•ness** *noun* [*noncount*]

styl•ist /ˈstaɪlɪst/ *noun, pl* **-ists** [*count*]

1 : a person whose job is to make something (such as a person's hair) look attractive ▪ a hair *stylist* ▪ a fashion/food *stylist*

2 : a person known for writing, singing, etc., in a particular style ▪ She is a fine literary/prose/song *stylist.*

sty•lis•tic /staɪˈlɪstɪk/ *adj* : of or relating to style ▪ There are a number of *stylistic* changes in the new car. ▪ *stylistic* differences among various writers

– **sty•lis•ti•cal•ly** /staɪˈlɪstɪkli/ *adv* ▪ *stylistically* different writers ▪ *Stylistically*, the movie resembles a documentary.

styl•ized *also Brit* **styl•ised** /ˈstajəˌlaɪzd/ *adj* [*more* ~; *most* ~] : made to look like a style or pattern rather than the way it would really look in nature ▪ *stylized* floral/flower motifs ▪ fabric with highly *stylized* animal prints

sty•lus /ˈstaɪləs/ *noun, pl* **sty•li** /ˈstaɪˌlaɪ/ *also* **sty•lus•es** /ˈstaɪləsəs/ [*count*]

1 : a very small, pointed piece of metal that touches a record and produces sound when the record is played : NEEDLE

2 : a tool used long ago for writing on clay or wax tablets

3 : a small tool that is used to write or touch buttons on a computer

sty•mie /ˈstaɪmi/ *verb* **-mies; -mied; -mie•ing** [+ *obj*] : to stop (someone) from doing something or to stop (something) from happening ▪ The bad weather has *stymied* [=*thwarted*] the police in their investigations. ▪ Progress on the project has been *stymied* by lack of money.

Sty•ro•foam /ˈstaɪrəˌfoʊm/ *trademark* — used for a type of light and usually white plastic

suave /ˈswɑːv/ *adj* **suav•er; -est** [*or more* ~; *most* ~] : behaving in a relaxed, confident, and pleasant way in social situations ▪ a *suave* and sophisticated businessman

– **suave•ly** *adv* – **suave•ness** *noun* [*noncount*] – **sua•vi•ty** /ˈswɑːvəti/ *noun* [*noncount*]

[1]**sub** /ˈsʌb/ *noun, pl* **subs** [*count*] *informal*

1 : someone who does the job of another person when that person is not able to do it : SUBSTITUTE ▪ The team's *subs* need to be versatile. ▪ (*US*) We had a *sub* [=*substitute teacher*] in English class all week.

2 *Brit* : SUBEDITOR

– compare [3]SUB

[2]**sub** *verb* **subs; subbed; sub•bing**

1 : to take the place of another person : to act as a substitute [*no obj*] Smith *subbed* for Jones at halftime. ▪ *subbing* in a Broadway play ▪ Mr. Johnson will be *subbing* [=working as a substitute teacher] at the high school. [+ *obj*] (*chiefly Brit*) ▪ Smith *subbed* Jones at halftime. — usually used as (*be/get*) *subbed* ▪ Jones *was subbed* (by Smith) at halftime.

2 [+ *obj*] : SUBCONTRACT ▪ The company *subs* (out) some of its jobs.

[3]**sub** *noun, pl* **subs** [*count*] *informal*

1 : SUBMARINE ▪ a nuclear *sub*

2 *US* : SUBMARINE SANDWICH ▪ I had a *sub* for lunch.

– compare [1]SUB

sub- *prefix*

1 : under : beneath : below ▪ *sub*soil ▪ *sub*freezing

2 a : at a lower rank or secondary level ▪ *sub*station **b** : division or smaller part of ▪ *sub*committee ▪ *sub*topic

sub•al•tern /səˈbɑːltən, *Brit* ˈsʌbəltən/ *noun, pl* **-terns** [*count*] : a junior officer in the British army

sub–aq•ua /ˌsʌbˈækwə/ *adj, always used before a noun, Brit* : relating to activities done under water : UNDERWATER ▪ *sub-aqua* diving ▪ joined a *sub-aqua* club

sub•atom•ic /ˌsʌbəˈtɑːmɪk/ *adj*

1 : smaller than an atom ▪ *subatomic* particles

2 : of or relating to the inside of an atom ▪ studied *subatomic* physics

sub•com•mit•tee /ˈsʌbkəˌmɪti/ *noun, pl* **-tees** [*count*] : a part of a committee that is organized for a certain purpose ▪ The Senate has formed a *subcommittee* to set up an investigation.

sub•com•pact /ˈsʌbˈkɑːmˌpækt/ *noun, pl* **-pacts** [*count*] *US* : a very small car

[1]**sub•con•scious** /ˌsʌbˈkɑːnʃəs/ *adj* : existing in the part of the mind that a person is not aware of : existing in the mind but not consciously known or felt ▪ *subconscious* desires/motives ▪ the *subconscious* mind

– **sub•con•scious•ly** *adv* ▪ Things can influence us *subconsciously.* ▪ Perhaps I *subconsciously* wanted it to happen.

[2]**subconscious** *noun* [*noncount*] : the part of a person's mind that has ideas, feelings, etc., that the person is not aware of ▪ A person's behavior can be influenced by urges that exist only in the *subconscious.* ▪ Those feelings had been hidden in her *subconscious.* — compare UNCONSCIOUS

sub•con•ti•nent /ˌsʌbˈkɑːntənənt/ *noun, pl* **-nents** [*count*] : a large area of land that is a part of a continent — used especially to refer to the area that includes India, Pakistan, and Bangladesh ▪ the Indian *subcontinent*

– **sub•con•ti•nen•tal** /ˌsʌbˌkɑːntəˈnɛntl̩/ *adj*

[1]**sub•con•tract** /ˌsʌbˈkɑːnˌtrækt/ *verb* **-tracts; -tract•ed; -tract•ing** : to hire another person or company to do part of a job that you have been hired to do [+ *obj*] Parts of the project were *subcontracted* (out) to specialists. = Specialists were *subcontracted* for parts of the project. [*no obj*] The large firm *subcontracted* with a smaller company.

– **sub•con•trac•tor** /ˌsʌbˈkɑːnˌtræktə/ *noun, pl* **-tors** [*count*] ▪ There are several *subcontractors* working at the new building site. ▪ He has good relationships with all the *subcontractors* he hires.

[2]**subcontract** *noun, pl* **-tracts** [*count*] : a legal agreement by which you hire another person or company to do part of a job you have been hired to do

sub•cul•ture /ˈsʌbˌkʌlʧə/ *noun, pl* **-tures** [*count*] : a group that has beliefs and behaviors that are different from the main groups within a culture or society ▪ a *subculture* of local painters/writers ▪ a *subculture* of poverty and crime

– **sub•cul•tur•al** /ˌsʌbˈkʌlʧərəl/ *adj* ▪ *subcultural* groups ▪ *subcultural* differences

sub•cu•ta•ne•ous /ˌsʌbkjuˈteɪnijəs/ *adj, medical* : under the skin ▪ *subcutaneous* tissues ▪ a *subcutaneous* injection

– **sub•cu•ta•ne•ous•ly** *adv*

sub•di•vide /ˌsʌbdəˈvaɪd/ *verb* **-vides; -vid•ed; -vid•ing** [+ *obj*]

1 : to divide (something) into several or many smaller parts ▪ The house is being *subdivided* into several apartments. ▪ The people who attend the conference can be *subdivided* into three distinct groups.

2 *US* : to divide (a piece of land) into smaller areas on which houses will be built ▪ He plans to *subdivide* his property. ▪ The land will be *subdivided* into building lots.

sub•di•vi•sion /ˈsʌbdəˌvɪʒən/ *noun, pl* **-sions**

1 [*count*] : one of the parts into which something is divided ▪ a political *subdivision* of the state

2 [*noncount*] : the act or process of dividing something into smaller parts ▪ The plan calls for (the) *subdivision* of the property into several building lots.

3 [*count*] *US* : an area of land that has been divided into smaller areas on which houses are built ▪ She lives in a new *subdivision* [=*development*] out in the suburbs.

sub•due /səbˈduː, *Brit* səbˈdjuː/ *verb* **-dues; -dued; -du•ing** [+ *obj*]

1 : to get control of (a violent or dangerous person or group) by using force, punishment, etc. ▪ The troops were finally able to *subdue* the rebel forces after many days of fighting. ▪ He was injured while trying to *subdue* a violent drunk.

2 : to get control of (something, such as a strong emotion) ▪ She struggled to *subdue* her fears.

sub•dued /səbˈduːd, *Brit* səbˈdjuːd/ *adj* [*more* ~; *most* ~] : not strong, loud, intense, etc. ▪ She spoke in a *subdued* voice. ▪ a *subdued* manner ▪ The color/lighting in the lobby is *subdued.*

sub·ed·i·tor /ˌsʌbˈɛdətɚ/ *noun, pl* **-tors** [*count*] *Brit* : a person whose job is to prepare a book, newspaper, etc., for printing by making sure the words are correct : COPY EDITOR

– **sub·ed·it** /ˌsʌbˈɛdət/ *verb* **-its**; **-it·ed**; **-it·ing** [+ *obj*]

sub·freez·ing /ˌsʌbˈfri:zɪŋ/ *adj, chiefly US* : colder than the temperature at which water freezes : colder than 32°F or 0°C ▪ *subfreezing* temperatures/weather

sub·head /ˈsʌbˌhɛd/ *noun, pl* **-heads** [*count*] : SUBHEADING

sub·head·ing /ˈsʌbˌhɛdɪŋ/ *noun, pl* **-ings** [*count*]

1 : an additional headline or title that comes immediately after the main headline or title ▪ The newspaper headline read "House burns down on Elm Street" with the *subheading* "Arson suspected."

2 : a title given to one of the parts or divisions of a piece of writing ▪ You can find the chart in the "Financial Matters" chapter under the *subheading* "Mortgages and Loans."

sub·hu·man /ˌsʌbˈhju:mən/ *adj*

1 : not having or showing the level of kindness, intelligence, etc., that is expected of normal human beings ▪ The prisoners suffered *subhuman* treatment. ▪ *subhuman* murderers

2 : not suitable for human beings ▪ *subhuman* living conditions — compare INHUMAN, NONHUMAN

[1]**sub·ject** /ˈsʌbʤɪkt/ *noun, pl* **-jects** [*count*]

1 : the person or thing that is being discussed or described : TOPIC ▪ The new museum is the *subject* of an article in today's paper. ▪ Death is a difficult *subject* that few people like to talk about. ▪ I need to break the news to her, but I'm not sure how to bring up the *subject.* ▪ If you're interested in linguistics, I know an excellent book on the/that *subject.* ▪ an excellent book ***on the subject of*** linguistics ▪ While we're *on the subject of* [=talking about] work, have you met the new boss? ▪ Every time I talk to her, we seem to ***get on/onto the subject of*** work. [=we start talking about work] ▪ These meetings would be much shorter if we could keep him from ***getting off the subject.*** ▪ I didn't want to talk about work, so I ***changed the subject.*** [=started a new topic of conversation] ▪ When he started getting upset, I ***dropped the subject.*** [=stopped talking about that topic] ▪ The morality of capital punishment is a frequent ***subject of/for debate.***

2 : an area of knowledge that is studied in school ▪ Chemistry was my favorite *subject* in high school. ▪ The classes cover a variety of ***subject areas***, including mathematics and English.

3 : a person or thing that is being dealt with in a particular way — + *of* ▪ He was the *subject of* a criminal investigation. [=he was investigated to find out if he had committed a crime] ▪ She was the *subject of* a lawsuit.

4 : someone or something that is shown in a photograph, painting, etc. ▪ Love between a mother and child is the *subject* of many of her paintings. ▪ The photographer's principal *subjects* were poor immigrant workers. ▪ What kind of exposure should I use for a dark *subject* on a light background?

5 : a person or animal that is used in an experiment, study, etc. ▪ Each *subject* was asked to fill out a questionnaire. ▪ The hospital is recruiting ***test subjects*** for the study.

6 *grammar* : a noun, noun phrase, or pronoun that performs the action of a verb in a sentence ▪ In English, the *subject* goes before the verb and the object comes after. ▪ "He" is the *subject* (of the verb "kissed") in the sentence "He kissed me." — compare OBJECT

7 : a person who lives in a country that is ruled by a king or queen : a citizen of a monarchy ▪ British *subjects*

[2]**sub·ject** /ˈsʌbʤɪkt/ *adj* : under the control of a ruler ▪ *subject* peoples — often + *to* ▪ They were *subject to* the emperor.

subject to **1** : affected by or possibly affected by (something) ▪ Clothing purchases over $200 are *subject to* tax. [=tax must be paid on clothing purchases over $200] ▪ Anyone caught trespassing is *subject to* a $500 fine. [=anyone caught trespassing will have to pay a $500 fine] ▪ The firm is *subject to* state law. ▪ The schedule is tentative and ***subject to change.*** [=the schedule may be changed at a later date] **2** : likely to do, have, or suffer from (something) : PRONE ▪ My cousin is *subject to* panic attacks. ▪ I'd rather not live in an area that is *subject to* flooding. [=an area where floods occur] **3** : dependent on something else to happen or be true ▪ The sale of the property is *subject to* approval by the city council. [=the property cannot be sold unless the city council approves the sale] ▪ All rooms are just $100 a night, *subject to* availability.

[3]**sub·ject** /səbˈʤɛkt/ *verb* **-jects**; **-ject·ed**; **-ject·ing**

subject to [*phrasal verb*] ***subject (someone or something) to (something)*** **1** : to cause or force (someone or something) to experience (something harmful, unpleasant, etc.) ▪ They are suspected of *subjecting* their children *to* abuse. [=of abusing their children] ▪ The test involved *subjecting* the sample *to* intense heat. — often used as *(be) subjected to* ▪ The prisoners *were subjected to* torture. ▪ During the hurricane, many buildings *were subjected to* [=many buildings experienced] 100 mile-per-hour winds. ▪ No one should have to *be subjected to* my uncle's bad jokes. ▪ His argument *was subjected to* careful analysis. [=was carefully analyzed] **2** : to bring (someone or something) under (your control or rule) ▪ He *subjected* her *to* his will. [=he forced her to do what he wanted her to do] ▪ Alexander the Great *subjected* much of Europe and Asia *to* his rule.

– **sub·jec·tion** /səbˈʤɛkʃən/ *noun* [*noncount*] *formal* ▪ the prisoners' *subjection* to torture ▪ The tyrant kept the people ***in subjection.***

sub·jec·tive /səbˈʤɛktɪv/ *adj*

1 *philosophy* : relating to the way a person experiences things in his or her own mind ▪ *subjective* reality ▪ Dreaming is a *subjective* experience. ▪ a person's *subjective* perception of the world

2 [*more* ~; *most* ~] : based on feelings or opinions rather than facts ▪ a *subjective* judgment/decision ▪ Personal taste in clothing is very *subjective.* ▪ In reviewing applicants, we consider both objective criteria, such as test scores, and *subjective* criteria, such as leadership ability. ▪ Law can be maddeningly *subjective.* So much is left up to your own interpretation. — opposite OBJECTIVE

3 *grammar* : relating to nouns, noun phrases, or pronouns that are the subjects of verbs ▪ The pronoun "we" is in the *subjective* [=*nominative*] case in the sentence "We saw her." — compare OBJECTIVE

– **sub·jec·tive·ly** *adv* ▪ Contest entries are *subjectively* evaluated. – **sub·jec·tiv·i·ty** /səbˌʤɛkˈtɪvəti/ *noun* [*noncount*] ▪ the *subjectivity* of opinions and judgments

subject matter *noun* [*noncount*] : the information or ideas that are discussed or dealt with in a book, movie, etc. : what something is about ▪ I found the film's *subject matter* to be quite disturbing. ▪ The magazine's editors care more about style than about *subject matter.* [=*content*] ▪ She disapproves of the artist's choice of *subject matter.*

sub·ju·gate /ˈsʌbʤɪˌgeɪt/ *verb* **-gates**; **-gat·ed**; **-gat·ing** [+ *obj*] *formal* : to defeat and gain control of (someone or something) by the use of force : to conquer and gain the obedience of (a group of people, a country, etc.) ▪ The emperor's armies *subjugated* the surrounding lands. ▪ a people *subjugated* by invaders — often used figuratively ▪ a legal system that *subjugates* [=*oppresses*] women

– **sub·ju·ga·tion** /ˌsʌbʤɪˈgeɪʃən/ *noun* [*noncount*]

[1]**sub·junc·tive** /səbˈʤʌŋktɪv/ *adj, grammar* : of or relating to the verb form that is used to express suggestions, wishes, uncertainty, possibility, etc. ▪ In "I wish it were Friday," the verb "were" is in the *subjunctive* mood. ▪ a *subjunctive* verb form — compare INDICATIVE

[2]**subjunctive** *noun, pl* **-tives** *grammar*

1 ***the subjunctive*** : the form that a verb or sentence has when it is expressing a suggestion, wish, uncertainty, possibility, etc. ▪ "I wish it were not so" is in the *subjunctive.*

2 [*count*] : a subjunctive verb or sentence ▪ *Subjunctives* can be used to express doubt.

[1]**sub·lease** /ˈsʌbˌli:s/ *noun, pl* **-leas·es** [*count*] *US* : a legal agreement by which someone who is renting an apartment, house, etc., is allowed to rent it to someone else for a period of time

[2]**sublease** /ˈsʌbˈli:s/ *verb* **-leas·es**; **-leased**; **-leas·ing** [+ *obj*] *US* : [1]SUBLET ▪ She *subleased* her apartment to a student for the summer. ▪ The agency *subleases* office space from a law firm.

[1]**sub·let** /ˈsʌbˈlɛt/ *verb* **-lets**; **-let**; **-let·ting**

1 : to allow someone to use (an apartment, house, etc., that you are renting) for a period of time in return for payment [+ *obj*] She *sublet* her apartment to a student for the summer. [*no obj*] He asked his landlord if he could *sublet.*

2 : to use (an apartment, house, etc., that is rented by someone) in return for payment [+ *obj*] The agency *sublets* office space from a law firm in the building. ▪ I need someone to *sublet* my apartment for the summer. [*no obj*] She agreed to *sublet.*

S

²sublet /ˈsʌbˌlɛt/ *noun, pl* **-lets** [*count*] : an apartment, house, etc., that you sublet from someone • I'm looking for a *sublet* since I'm only going to be here for the summer.

sub·li·mate /ˈsʌbləˌmeɪt/ *verb* **-mates; -mat·ed; -mat·ing** [+ *obj*] *psychology* : to express a desire or feeling by changing it into a form that is socially acceptable • She *sublimated* her erotic feelings into a series of paintings. • I *sublimated* my grief at the death of my mother by throwing myself into my work.
– sub·li·ma·tion /ˌsʌbləˈmeɪʃən/ *noun* [*noncount*]

sub·lime /səˈblaɪm/ *adj* [*more* ~; *most* ~]
1 : very beautiful or good : causing strong feelings of admiration or wonder • Her paintings are *sublime.* • He composed some of the most *sublime* symphonies in existence. • the *sublime* beauty of the canyon
2 : complete or extreme : UTTER • *sublime* ignorance/stupidity
the sublime : something that is very beautiful or good • writings on *the sublime* • They have brought ordinary food to the level of *the sublime.* [=they have made ordinary food extraordinary] • The movies shown at the festival ranged ***from the sublime to the ridiculous.***
– sub·lime·ly *adv* • a *sublimely* stunning landscape **– sub·lim·i·ty** /səˈblɪməti/ *noun* [*noncount*] • I've never heard anyone who could match the *sublimity* of her playing.

sub·lim·i·nal /səˈblɪmənl/ *adj* : relating to things that influence your mind in a way that you do not notice • The studio denied the existence of ***subliminal messages*** in the movie. • I am skeptical that ***subliminal advertising*** actually works.
– sub·lim·i·nal·ly *adv*

sub·ma·chine gun /ˌsʌbməˈʃiːn-/ *noun, pl* ~ **guns** [*count*] : a small, light machine gun

¹sub·ma·rine /ˈsʌbməˌriːn/ *noun, pl* **-rines** [*count*]
1 : a ship that can operate underwater • nuclear *submarines*
2 *US* : SUBMARINE SANDWICH

²submarine *adj, always used before a noun, technical* : located below the surface of the water : UNDERWATER, UNDERSEA • a *submarine* canyon

sub·ma·ri·ner /ˌsʌbməˈriːnɚ, *Brit* ˌsʌbˈmærənə/ *noun, pl* **-ners** [*count*] : someone who is a member of a submarine crew

submarine sandwich *noun, pl* ~ **-wiches** [*count*] *US* : a sandwich that is made by splitting a long roll and filling it with meat, cheese, etc. — called also *grinder, hero, hoagie, po'boy, sub, submarine*

sub·menu /ˈsʌbˌmɛnˌjuː/ *noun, pl* **-men·us** [*count*] *computers* : a menu in a computer program that you reach by going through another menu first • Selecting "Options" from the main menu brings up a *submenu.*

sub·merge /səbˈmɚʤ/ *verb* **-merg·es; -merged; -merg·ing**
1 [+ *obj*] : to make (someone or something) go under the surface of water or some other liquid : to cover (someone or something) with a liquid • After boiling the broccoli, *submerge* it in ice water to stop the cooking process. • The town was *submerged* by the flood.
2 [*no obj*] : to go underwater • We watched as the divers prepared to *submerge.*
3 [+ *obj*] : to make (yourself) fully involved in an activity or interest • After his sister died, he *submerged* [=*immersed*] himself in his work. • She's a marvelous actress who *submerges* herself totally in her roles.
4 [+ *obj*] : to keep (emotions, opinions, etc.) from being openly shown or expressed • It's a job where you'll have to *submerge* [=*suppress*] your ego and do what you're told. • The passion is there in the music, though it's often *submerged.*
– submerged *adj* • Some seals can stay *submerged* for an hour. • tales of a *submerged* city in the Mediterranean Sea

¹sub·mers·ible /səbˈmɚsəbəl/ *adj* : able to be used underwater • a *submersible* pump

²submersible *noun, pl* **-ibles** [*count*] : a small vehicle that can operate underwater and that is used especially for research

sub·mis·sion /səbˈmɪʃən/ *noun, pl* **-sions**
1 a : an act of giving a document, proposal, piece of writing, etc., to someone so that it can be considered or approved : an act of submitting something [*noncount*] I'm preparing the results of my study for *submission* to a medical journal. • the electronic *submission* of tax returns [*count*] The deadline for *submissions* is January 31st. **b** [*count*] : something that is submitted • We cannot accept *submissions* longer than 2,000 words. • Over 5,000 *submissions* were received.
2 [*noncount*] : the state of being obedient : the act of accepting the authority or control of someone else • a religion that preaches *submission* to God's will • The prisoners were beaten ***into submission.***

sub·mis·sive /səbˈmɪsɪv/ *adj* [*more* ~; *most* ~] : willing to obey someone else • a *submissive* person • *submissive* behavior
– sub·mis·sive·ly *adv* • He behaved *submissively.* **– sub·mis·sive·ness** *noun* [*noncount*]

sub·mit /səbˈmɪt/ *verb* **-mits; -mit·ted; -mit·ting**
1 [+ *obj*] : to give (a document, proposal, piece of writing, etc.) to someone so that it can be considered or approved • Candidates interested in the position should *submit* their résumés to the Office of Human Resources. • *Submit* your application no later than January 31st. • Requests must be *submitted* in writing. • Photographs *submitted* for publication will not be returned.
2 [*no obj*] : to stop trying to fight or resist something : to agree to do or accept something that you have been resisting or opposing • He vowed that he would never *submit.* [=*give in*] — often + *to* • He refused to *submit to* their demands. • We will not *submit to* you without a fight. • Public outcry caused him to *submit to* an investigation of his finances.
3 [+ *obj*] *formal* : to offer (something) as an opinion or suggestion — often + *that* • I *submit that* his guilt has not been proven.

sub·nor·mal /ˌsʌbˈnoɚməl/ *adj, technical*
1 : lower or smaller than normal • *subnormal* body temperature • *subnormal* levels of vitamin C • *subnormal* intelligence
2 : having less of something than is normal • people who are *subnormal* in insulin production • mentally *subnormal* people

sub·op·ti·mal /ˌsʌbˈɑːptəməl/ *adj, formal* : less than the best or most desirable • working under *suboptimal* conditions

¹sub·or·di·nate /səˈboɚdənət/ *adj*
1 : in a position of less power or authority than someone else • a *subordinate* officer/commander — often + *to* • The priests are *subordinate to* the bishops.
2 : less important than someone or something else • a *subordinate* concern — often + *to* • In some cultures, the welfare of the individual is *subordinate to* the welfare of the group.

²subordinate *noun, pl* **-nates** [*count*] : someone who has less power or authority than someone else : someone who is subordinate to someone else • She leaves the day-to-day running of the firm to her *subordinates.*

³sub·or·di·nate /səˈboɚdəˌneɪt/ *verb* **-nates; -nat·ed; -nat·ing** [+ *obj*] *formal* : to think of or treat (someone or something) as less important than someone or something else — usually + *to* • The company is guilty of *subordinating* safety *to* profit. • His personal life has been *subordinated to* his career.
– sub·or·di·na·tion /səˌboɚdəˈneɪʃən/ *noun* [*noncount*]

subordinate clause *noun, pl* ~ **clauses** [*count*] *grammar* : a clause that does not form a simple sentence by itself and that is connected to the main clause of a sentence • In the sentence "I went home because I felt ill," "because I felt ill" is a *subordinate clause.* — called also *dependent clause;* compare COORDINATE CLAUSE, MAIN CLAUSE

subordinating conjunction *noun, pl* ~ **-tions** [*count*] *grammar* : a conjunction that joins a main clause and a clause which does not form a complete sentence by itself

sub·orn /səˈboɚn/ *verb* **-orns; -orned; -orn·ing** [+ *obj*] *law*
1 : to persuade (someone) to do something illegal (such as to lie in a court of law) • He's accused of *suborning* a witness.
2 : to get (false testimony) from a witness • The lawyer *suborned* (false) testimony. • *suborn* perjury

sub·par /ˈsʌbˌpɑɚ/ *adj, US* : below a usual or normal level • a *subpar* performance

sub·plot /ˈsʌbˌplɑːt/ *noun, pl* **-plots** [*count*] : a plot that is related to but less important than the main plot of a story

¹sub·poe·na /səˈpiːnə/ *noun, pl* **-nas** [*count*] *law* : a written order that commands someone to appear in court to give evidence — compare SUMMONS

²subpoena *verb* **-nas; -naed; -na·ing** [+ *obj*] *law* : to order someone to appear in court to give evidence : to issue a subpoena to (someone) or for (something) • He was *subpoenaed* to testify in a hearing. • The prosecutor *subpoenaed* the defendant's financial records.

sub·rou·tine /ˈsʌbˌruːˌtiːn/ *noun, pl* **-tines** [*count*] *computers* : a set of computer instructions that performs a particu-

S

lar task, that is part of a larger computer program, and that can be used repeatedly

sub·scribe /səbˈskraɪb/ *verb* **-scribes; -scribed; -scrib·ing** [*no obj*]

1 : to pay money to get a publication or service regularly ▪ *Subscribe* today and get your first issue free! ▪ You'll receive a user name and password when you *subscribe*. — often + *to* ▪ I *subscribe to* several newspapers/magazines. ▪ He's thinking of *subscribing to* satellite TV.

2 : to agree to buy shares in a company — usually + *for* ▪ She *subscribed for* 100 shares.

3 *Brit* **:** to belong to or support something (such as an organization) by paying money regularly — usually + *to* ▪ *subscribe to* a charity

subscribe to [*phrasal verb*] ***subscribe to (something)*** **:** to agree with or support (an opinion, theory, etc.) ▪ I *subscribe to* the idea that voting is my civic duty. ▪ She *subscribes to* the theory that some dinosaurs were warm-blooded and others were cold-blooded.

– sub·scrib·er *noun, pl* **-ers** [*count*] ▪ cable TV *subscribers* ▪ The magazine has about a million *subscribers*.

sub·scrip·tion /səbˈskrɪpʃən/ *noun, pl* **-tions**

1 : an agreement that you make with a company to get a publication or service regularly and that you usually pay for in advance [*count*] a magazine/newspaper *subscription* = a *subscription* to a magazine/newspaper ▪ Annual/monthly *subscriptions* cost $20. ▪ She bought a *subscription*. = She took out a *subscription*. ▪ online *subscription* services ▪ I'm going to ***renew/cancel my subscription*** [*noncount*] You won't find this magazine at newsstands. It's sold only by *subscription*.

2 [*count, noncount*] *Brit* **:** a fee that you pay regularly to belong to or support an organization

sub·sec·tion /ˈsʌbˌsɛkʃən/ *noun, pl* **-tions** [*count*] **:** a part of a section especially of a legal document ▪ as provided/stated in *Subsection* (b)

sub·se·quent /ˈsʌbsəkwənt/ *adj, formal* **:** happening or coming after something else ▪ The rate of population growth reached a peak in 1999 and declined in *subsequent* years. ▪ Her work had a great influence on *subsequent* generations. ▪ *Subsequent* studies confirmed their findings. ▪ his arrest and *subsequent* conviction — often + *to* ▪ events *subsequent to* [=*after*] the war

– sub·se·quent·ly /ˈsʌbsəˌkwɛntli/ *adv, formal* ▪ She graduated from college and *subsequently* [=*afterward*] moved to New York. ▪ *Subsequently*, the drug was found to cause cancer.

sub·ser·vi·ent /səbˈsɚvijənt/ *adj* [*more ~; most ~*]

1 : very willing or too willing to obey someone else ▪ She left her first husband because he wanted a *subservient* [=*submissive*] wife. ▪ She refused to take/accept/play a *subservient* role in their marriage. — often + *to* ▪ She refused to be *subservient to* her husband.

2 *formal* **:** less important than something or someone else — usually + *to* ▪ He believes that rights of individuals should be *subservient to* the rights of society as a whole.

– sub·ser·vi·ence /səbˈsɚvijəns/ *noun* [*noncount*]

sub·set /ˈsʌbˌsɛt/ *noun, pl* **-sets** [*count*] *technical* **:** a group of things, people, etc., that is part of a larger group ▪ The set {1,2,3} is a *subset* of the set {1,2,3,4,5}. ▪ Only a small *subset* of the patients in the study experienced these side effects.

sub·side /səbˈsaɪd/ *verb* **-sides; -sid·ed; -sid·ing** [*no obj*]

1 : to become less strong or intense ▪ The pain/swelling will *subside* in a couple of hours. ▪ After his anger had *subsided*, he was able to look at things rationally. ▪ We'll have to wait until the wind/storm/rain *subsides*.

2 : to move down to a lower level ▪ The road will remain closed until the water/flood/river *subsides*. ▪ a place where the ground has *subsided* [=*sunk, settled*]

sub·si·dence /səbˈsaɪdn̩s/ *noun* [*noncount*] *technical* **:** movement of the ground to a lower level ▪ *Subsidence* can cause a building's collapse.

[1]**sub·sid·iary** /səbˈsɪdiˌeri, *Brit* səbˈsɪdiəri/ *adj*

1 : not as important as something else ▪ a *subsidiary* issue ▪ *subsidiary* streams ▪ *subsidiary* details

2 : owned or controlled by another company ▪ a *subsidiary* corporation

[2]**subsidiary** *noun, pl* **-iar·ies** [*count*] **:** a company that is owned or controlled by another company ▪ one of the company's foreign *subsidiaries*

sub·si·dize *also Brit* **sub·si·dise** /ˈsʌbsəˌdaɪz/ *verb* **-diz·es; -dized; -diz·ing** [+ *obj*] **:** to help someone or something pay for the costs of (something) ▪ The state *subsidizes* housing for low-income families. ▪ She feels that private businesses should not be *subsidized* by taxpayers. ▪ The company *subsidizes* health insurance for its employees. ▪ *subsidized* agriculture/housing

– sub·si·di·za·tion *also Brit* **sub·si·di·sa·tion** /ˌsʌbsədəˈzeɪʃən, *Brit* ˌsʌbsəˌdaɪˈzeɪʃən/ *noun* [*noncount*] ▪ the government's *subsidization* of agriculture

sub·si·dy /ˈsʌbsədi/ *noun, pl* **-dies** [*count*] **:** money that is paid usually by a government to keep the price of a product or service low or to help a business or organization to continue to function ▪ The city is increasing *subsidies* for public transit. ▪ housing/farm *subsidies*

sub·sist /səbˈsɪst/ *verb* **-sists; -sist·ed; -sist·ing** [*no obj*] *formal* **:** to exist or continue to exist ▪ The author's right to royalties shall *subsist* for the term of the copyright.

subsist on [*phrasal verb*] ***subsist on (something)*** **:** to use (something) as a way to stay alive **:** to live on (something) ▪ poor people *subsisting on* just one or two dollars a day ▪ The villagers *subsist* almost entirely *on* rice and fish. ▪ (*humorous*) My brother *subsists on* [=eats a lot of] pizza.

sub·sis·tence /səbˈsɪstəns/ *noun* [*noncount*] **:** the amount of food, money, etc., that is needed to stay alive ▪ They depended on hunting and fishing for *subsistence*. ▪ Farming is their means of *subsistence*. ▪ ***subsistence farming/agriculture*** [=farming that provides enough food to live on but not enough food to sell to other people] ▪ More than a quarter of the population lives below (the) ***subsistence level*** [=a level of income that provides only enough money for basic needs]

sub·soil /ˈsʌbˌsojəl/ *noun* [*noncount*] **:** the layer of soil that is under the top layer — compare TOPSOIL

sub·son·ic /ˌsʌbˈsɑːnɪk/ *adj* **:** slower than the speed of sound ▪ *subsonic* aircraft ▪ *subsonic* speeds

sub·spe·cies /ˈsʌbˌspiːʃiz/ *noun, pl* **subspecies** [*count*] **:** a group of related plants or animals that is smaller than a species **:** a division of a species ▪ There are two *subspecies* of bison in North America.

sub·stance /ˈsʌbstəns/ *noun, pl* **-stanc·es**

1 [*count*] **a :** a material of a particular kind ▪ chemical/toxic/hazardous/dangerous *substances* ▪ The pancreas secretes a *substance* called insulin. ▪ The floor was covered with a white, powdery *substance* that turned out to be flour. **b :** a drug that is considered harmful and whose use is controlled by law or made illegal ▪ heroin and other illegal *substances* ▪ He had a history of ***substance abuse*** ▪ Codeine is a ***controlled substance*** [=a drug that you need permission from a doctor to use]

2 [*noncount*] **a :** the quality of being meaningful, useful, or important ▪ matters of *substance* ▪ When has he ever said anything of *substance*? ▪ The book lacks *substance*. **b :** the quality of being true or believable ▪ These rumors have no *substance*. = These rumors are ***without substance*** [=these rumors are not true] ▪ The results of the study ***give substance*** to their theory.

3 [*noncount*] **:** the most basic or necessary part or quality of something **:** ESSENCE ▪ the *substance* of my argument ▪ These two books differ in both style and *substance*. [=*content*] ▪ He stated, ***in substance*** [=*in essence, essentially*], that it is not his fault and he will not pay for damages.

a man/woman/person of substance *literary* **:** a person who is rich and powerful ▪ She married *a man of substance*.

sum and substance see [1]SUM

sub·stan·dard /ˌsʌbˈstændɚd/ *adj* **:** below what is considered standard, normal, or acceptable ▪ a *substandard* performance ▪ *substandard* housing — compare NONSTANDARD

sub·stan·tial /səbˈstænʃəl/ *adj* [*more ~; most ~*]

1 : large in amount, size, or number ▪ A *substantial* number of people commute to work each day. ▪ This will save us a *substantial* [=*considerable*] amount of money/time. ▪ Activities like that pose a *substantial* risk of injury. ▪ She purchased her tickets at a *substantial* discount.

2 : strongly made **:** STURDY ▪ a *substantial* house ▪ Only the buildings that were constructed of more *substantial* materials survived the earthquake.

3 *of food* **:** enough to satisfy hunger ▪ I was hoping that they would serve us something more *substantial* than wine and cheese. ▪ a *substantial* [=*filling*] meal

sub·stan·tial·ly /səbˈstænʃəli/ *adv*

1 : very much **:** a lot ▪ It's *substantially* [=*considerably*] less expensive to buy a used car than a new car. ▪ A new car costs *substantially* more than a used car. ▪ Costs have increased *substantially* [=*significantly*] in recent years.

2 a : in a general or basic way ▪ The methods are *substantially* [=*essentially*] the same. **b** : almost completely : MOSTLY ▪ There are still a few details to wrap up, but the project is *substantially* complete.

sub·stan·ti·ate /səbˈstænʃiˌeɪt/ *verb* **-ates; -at·ed; -at·ing** [+ *obj*] *formal* : to prove the truth of (something) ▪ He offered no evidence to *substantiate* [=*support*] his claim.
– **sub·stan·ti·a·tion** /səbˌstænʃiˈeɪʃən/ *noun* [*noncount*]

[1]**sub·stan·tive** /ˈsʌbstəntɪv/ *adj* [*more* ~; *most* ~] *formal*
1 : important, real, or meaningful ▪ *substantive* issues/matters ▪ These changes are more symbolic than *substantive*. ▪ No *substantive* changes were made to the document.
2 : supported by facts or logic ▪ *substantive* arguments ▪ There is no *substantive* reason to change the law.
– **sub·stan·tive·ly** *adv*

[2]**substantive** *noun, pl* **-tives** [*count*] *grammar* : NOUN

sub·sta·tion /ˈsʌbˌsteɪʃən/ *noun, pl* **-tions** [*count*]
1 : a place where the strength of electricity is changed as the electricity passes through on its way from the power plant to homes and businesses
2 : a police station that serves a particular area

[1]**sub·sti·tute** /ˈsʌbstəˌtu:t, *Brit* ˈsʌbstəˌtju:t/ *noun, pl* **-tutes** [*count*]
1 : a person or thing that takes the place of someone or something else ▪ a fat/sugar/meat *substitute* — often + *for* ▪ Carob is used as a *substitute for* chocolate. ▪ When learning a language, there is no *substitute for* living among native speakers. ▪ Watching the movie is a poor *substitute for* reading the book.
2 *sports* : a player who takes the place of another player during a game ▪ Gonzales came on as a *substitute* [=*replacement*] during the second half.
3 *US* : SUBSTITUTE TEACHER
– **substitute** *adj, always used before a noun* ▪ a *substitute* mother/father ▪ *substitute* players

[2]**substitute** *verb* **-tutes; -tut·ed; -tut·ing**
1 [+ *obj*] : to put or use (someone or something) in place of someone or something else ▪ If cream is unavailable, you can *substitute* milk. [=you can use milk instead of cream] — often + *for* ▪ You can sometimes *substitute* applesauce *for* vegetable oil in cake recipes. ▪ The coach *substituted* Jones *for* Smith in the last few minutes of the game.
2 [*no obj*] : to do the job of someone else or serve the function of something else ▪ One of our teachers is sick, so we need someone to *substitute*. — often + *for* ▪ She'll be *substituting for* the regular teacher today. ▪ Applesauce can *substitute for* vegetable oil in this recipe.
3 [+ *obj*] : to replace (one person or thing) with another ▪ They *substituted* real candles with electric ones. — often used as *(be) substituted* ▪ Real candles *were substituted* by/with electric ones. ▪ (*chiefly Brit*) Smith *was substituted* by Jones in the last few minutes of the game.

substitute teacher *noun, pl* ~ **-ers** [*count*] *US* : a teacher who teaches a class when the usual teacher is not available — called also (*US*) *sub*, (*US*) *substitute*, (*Brit*) *supply teacher*

sub·sti·tu·tion /ˌsʌbstəˈtu:ʃən, *Brit* ˌsʌbstəˈtju:ʃən/ *noun, pl* **-tions**
1 : the act of substituting or replacing one person or thing with another [*count*] The coach made three *substitutions* in the second half of the game. ▪ I'd prefer rice with my steak instead of potatoes, but the menu says "no *substitutions*." [*noncount*] *Substitution* of applesauce for oil is one way of reducing the fat in recipes.
2 [*count*] : someone or something that is or can be substituted for another ▪ The cookbook has a long list of *substitutions* for ingredients that may be hard to find.

sub·stra·tum /ˈsʌbˌstreɪtəm/ *noun, pl* **-stra·ta** /-ˌstreɪtə/ [*count*] : a layer of something (such as soil or rock) that is under another layer ▪ drilled into the bedrock *substratum* — often used figuratively ▪ the city's social *substrata*

sub·struc·ture /ˈsʌbˌstrʌktʃə/ *noun, pl* **-tures** [*count*] : a supporting part or structure that is below something ▪ The bridge's *substructure* was damaged. — often used figuratively ▪ political/economic *substructures* — compare SUPERSTRUCTURE

sub·ter·fuge /ˈsʌbtəˌfju:ʤ/ *noun, pl* **-fug·es** *formal* : the use of tricks especially to hide, avoid, or get something [*noncount*] They obtained the documents by/through *subterfuge*. [*count*] a clever *subterfuge*

sub·ter·ra·nean /ˌsʌbtəˈreɪnijən/ *adj, formal*
1 : located or living under the surface of the ground ▪ *subterranean* caverns/termites
2 : existing or working in secret ▪ the *subterranean* [=*underground*] world of organized crime

sub·ti·tle /ˈsʌbˌtaɪtl/ *noun, pl* **-ti·tles** [*count*]
1 : words that appear on the screen during a movie, video, or television show and that are translations of what the actors are saying — usually plural ▪ The film is in Chinese with English *subtitles*.
2 : a title that comes after the main title of a book and that often gives more information about the contents of the book
– **subtitle** *verb* **-titles; -ti·tled; -ti·tling** [+ *obj*] ▪ It takes a lot of work to *subtitle* a film. – **subtitled** *adj* ▪ a *subtitled* movie

sub·tle /ˈsʌtl/ *adj* **sub·tler; sub·tlest** [*or more* ~; *most* ~]
1 : hard to notice or see : not obvious ▪ a *subtle* difference in meaning between the words ▪ *subtle* changes/variations ▪ the *subtlest* details ▪ Racial discrimination still exists, only now it's *subtler* than it once was. ▪ *subtle* flavors
2 : clever and indirect : not showing your real purpose ▪ When it comes to giving criticism, sometimes it's best to take a *subtle* approach. ▪ He didn't seem to understand my *subtle* hints. ▪ It was her *subtle* way of telling me to mind my own business.
3 : having or showing skill at recognizing and understanding things that are not obvious : PERCEPTIVE ▪ She has a *subtle* mind. ▪ a *subtle* analysis
– **sub·tly** /ˈsʌtli/ *adv* ▪ *subtly* different shades of red

sub·tle·ty /ˈsʌtlti/ *noun, pl* **-ties**
1 [*noncount*] : the quality or state of being subtle ▪ The pianist performed with *subtlety* and passion. ▪ The movie lacks *subtlety*.
2 [*count*] : a small detail that is usually important but not obvious — usually plural ▪ the *subtleties* of social interaction

sub·top·ic /ˈsʌbˌtɑ:pɪk/ *noun, pl* **-ics** [*count*] : a topic that is one of the parts or divisions of the main topic of a piece of writing ▪ Each chapter is broken down into *subtopics*.

sub·to·tal /ˈsʌbˌtoutl/ *noun, pl* **-tals** [*count*] : the sum of a set of numbers that is then added to another number or set of numbers ▪ Your *subtotal* is $14, and with tax, that will be $14.70.

sub·tract /səbˈtrækt/ *verb* **-tracts; -tract·ed; -tract·ing** : to take (a number or amount) from another number or amount [+ *obj*] — usually + *from* ▪ If we *subtract* 5 *from* 9, we get 4. ▪ *Subtract* the expenses *from* your income. [*no obj*] The children are learning how to add and *subtract*. [=to perform subtraction] — opposite ADD

sub·trac·tion /səbˈtrækʃən/ *noun* [*noncount*] *mathematics* : the act or process of subtracting one number from another ▪ The children are learning addition and *subtraction*.

sub·trop·i·cal /ˌsʌbˈtrɑ:pɪkəl/ *adj* [*more* ~; *most* ~] : relating to or living in an area that is close to tropical parts of the world ▪ a *subtropical* [=*semitropical*] region ▪ *subtropical* vegetation ▪ a *subtropical* bird

sub·trop·ics /ˌsʌbˈtrɑ:pɪks/ *noun*
the subtropics : parts of the world that are close to the tropics : subtropical regions

sub·urb /ˈsʌˌbəb/ *noun, pl* **-urbs** [*count*] : a town or other area where people live in houses near a larger city ▪ She left the city and moved to ***the suburbs***. [=one of the suburbs near that city] — often + *of* ▪ the *suburbs of* Chicago ▪ I grew up in a *suburb of* Denver.

sub·ur·ban /səˈbəbən/ *adj* : living in or relating to a suburb or to suburbs in general ▪ a *suburban* mother of two ▪ typical *suburban* houses ▪ *suburban* Denver [=the suburbs near Denver]

sub·ur·ban·ite /səˈbəbəˌnaɪt/ *noun, pl* **-ites** [*count*] : a person who lives in a suburb

sub·ur·bia /səˈbəbijə/ *noun* [*noncount*] : suburbs in general ▪ a problem that is common in *suburbia* ▪ the percentage of the country's population living in *suburbia*; *also* : people who live in suburbs ▪ The film is an interesting critique of *suburbia*. ▪ the values of *suburbia*

sub·ven·tion /səbˈvenʃən/ *noun, pl* **-tions** [*count*] *chiefly Brit* : an amount of money that is given to a person or group by a government or organization ▪ government *subventions* [=*subsidies*]

sub·ver·sive /səbˈvəsɪv/ *adj* [*more* ~; *most* ~]
1 : secretly trying to ruin or destroy a government, political system, etc. ▪ *subversive* groups/activities ▪ The government blamed a *subversive* organization for the riots.
2 : criticizing something in a clever and indirect way in order to make it weaker or less effective ▪ I enjoy her *subversive* sense of humor. ▪ the author's *subversive* attitude toward pop

culture • ideas that are *subversive* of society/authority
– subversive *noun, pl* **-sives** [*count*] • The government claims that the riots were incited by *subversives*. **– sub·ver·sive·ly** *adv* **– sub·ver·sive·ness** *noun* [*noncount*]

sub·vert /səbˈvɚt/ *verb* **-verts; -vert·ed; -vert·ing** [+ *obj*] *formal*
1 : to secretly try to ruin or destroy a government, political system, etc. • They conspired to *subvert* the government.
2 : to make (something) weaker or less effective • *subvert* [=*undermine*] the rule of law • trying to *subvert* the electoral process
– sub·ver·sion /səbˈvɚʒən/ *noun, pl* **-sions** [*count, noncount*] • They were charged with *subversion*. • a *subversion* of the rule of law **– sub·vert·er** *noun, pl* **-ers** [*count*] • *subverters* of democracy

sub·way /ˈsʌbˌweɪ/ *noun, pl* **-ways** [*count*]
1 *chiefly US* **:** a system of underground trains in a city • I took/rode the *subway* to midtown. • No one on the *subway* seemed to mind how crowded it was. • I've been on both the New York *subway* and the Underground in London. — often used before another noun • a *subway* car/station • the *subway* platform
2 *Brit* **:** a road or passage for walking under a road, set of railroad tracks, etc. **:** UNDERPASS

sub·woof·er /ˈsʌbˈwʊfɚ/ *noun, pl* **-ers** [*count*] *technical* **:** a speaker (sense 5) that produces very low sounds — compare TWEETER, WOOFER

sub·ze·ro /ˌsʌbˈziroʊ/ *adj* **:** below zero degrees **:** extremely cold • *subzero* temperatures/weather

suc·ceed /səkˈsiːd/ *verb* **-ceeds; -ceed·ed; -ceed·ing**
1 [*no obj*] **a :** to do what you are trying to do **:** to achieve the correct or desired result • You can *succeed* where others failed. • She hopes to *succeed* [=to do well] at her job. — often + *in* • He will never *succeed in* this business. [=he will never be successful in this business] • Our team *succeeded in* stopping their offensive momentum. • She finally *succeeded in* persuading me to go. • I tried to apologize but ***only succeeded in*** making her angrier. [=all I did was make her angrier when I tried to apologize] **b :** to happen in the planned or desired way • The plan just might *succeed*. • Their attempt seemed unlikely to *succeed*.
2 a [+ *obj*] **:** to come after (something) in a series • The new model will *succeed* [=*replace*] the current one next spring. **b :** to get a particular job, position, or title after the person who had it before you has retired, died, etc. [+ *obj*] Both of them have ambitions to *succeed* the prime minister. • She will *succeed* him as chair of the committee. • The Queen died and was *succeeded* by James I. [*no obj*] James I ***succeeded to the throne*** upon the Queen's death in 1603.
nothing succeeds like success — used to say that one success often results in another success

succeeding *adj, always used before a noun* **:** coming after something **:** coming or happening at a later time • now and for *succeeding* decades • The trait is apparent in *succeeding* generations.

suc·cess /səkˈsɛs/ *noun, pl* **-cess·es**
1 [*noncount*] **a :** the fact of getting or achieving wealth, respect, or fame • *Success* came easily to him. • With *success* comes responsibility. • ***the secret of my success*** [=why I am successful] **b :** the correct or desired result of an attempt • Did you ***have any/much success*** in finding the dog? [=did you find the dog?] • The project ***met with little success*** [=was not successful] • He tried to repair the engine but ***without success*** [=he was not able to repair the engine]
2 [*count*] **:** someone or something that is successful **:** a person or thing that succeeds • The play was an immediate *success*. [=it was immediately popular] • one of her many *successes* [=one of many things she has done successfully] • She is country music's most recent *success*. • The growth of the tourism industry is one of the city's great *successes*.

suc·cess·ful /səkˈsɛsfəl/ *adj* [*more* ~; *most* ~]
1 : having the correct or desired result **:** ending in success • a *successful* attempt • The treatment was *successful*. • a *successful* movie [=a movie that makes a large profit] • Our search was *successful*. [=we found what we were searching for]
2 : having gotten or achieved wealth, respect, or fame • a *successful* businesswoman
– suc·cess·ful·ly *adv* • We have *successfully* finished the project. • The infection was treated *successfully*.

suc·ces·sion /səkˈsɛʃən/ *noun, pl* **-sions**
1 [*noncount*] **:** the act of getting a title or right after the person who had that title or right before you has died or is no longer able or allowed to have it • His *succession* to the throne occurred in 1603. [=he became king in 1603]; *also* **:** the process by which this happens • royal *succession* • As third in ***the line/order of succession***, she would only become queen if her brothers both died or became ineligible.
2 [*count*] **:** a series of people or things that come one after the other — usually singular; usually + *of* • The exhibit has attracted a *succession of* visitors. • We hired a *succession of* temporary workers.
in succession **:** following one after the other • The guests arrived *in succession*. • He won the championship twice *in succession*. [=*in a row*] • She listed the names ***in quick/rapid succession***.

suc·ces·sive /səkˈsɛsɪv/ *adj, always used before a noun* **:** following one after the other in a series **:** following each other without interruption • It snowed for three *successive* [=*consecutive*] days. • the third *successive* day • a trait found in *successive* generations • their fourth *successive* [=*consecutive*] victory
– suc·ces·sive·ly *adv* • He has owned a series of *successively* larger boats. [=a series of boats in which each boat is larger than the one before it]

suc·ces·sor /səkˈsɛsɚ/ *noun, pl* **-sors** [*count*] **:** a person who has a job, position, or title after someone else **:** someone who succeeds another person • The CEO's *successor* used to be the vice president here. • the *successor* to the throne — opposite PREDECESSOR

success story *noun, pl* ~ **stories** [*count*] **:** a successful person or thing: such as **a :** someone or something that has achieved a goal • I am one of the diet clinic's *success stories*. [=the diet clinic was able to help me] **b :** someone or something that has achieved wealth, respect, or fame • That company is one of this area's biggest *success stories*.

suc·cinct /səkˈsɪŋkt/ *adj* [*more* ~; *most* ~] **:** using few words to state or express an idea • He gave a *succinct* overview of the expansion project. • a *succinct* description
synonyms see CONCISE
– suc·cinct·ly *adv* • Tell me as *succinctly* as you can what happened.

suc·cor (*US*) *or Brit* **suc·cour** /ˈsʌkɚ/ *noun* [*noncount*] *literary* **:** something that you do or give to help someone who is suffering or in a difficult situation • We see it as our duty to give *succor* to those in need.
– succor (*US*) *or Brit* **succour** *verb* **-cors; -cored; -cor·ing** [+ *obj*] • It is our duty to *succor* those in need.

suc·co·tash /ˈsʌkəˌtæʃ/ *noun* [*noncount*] *US* **:** a dish consisting of corn and lima beans that are cooked together

¹suc·cu·lent /ˈsʌkjələnt/ *adj* [*more* ~; *most* ~]
1 : full of juice • a *succulent* steak • *succulent* [=*juicy*] oranges
2 *of plants* **:** having thick, heavy leaves or stems that store water • Cacti are *succulent* plants.
– suc·cu·lence /ˈsʌkjələns/ *noun* [*noncount*] • the *succulence* of these oranges

²succulent *noun, pl* **-lents** [*count*] **:** a plant that stores water in its leaves or stems **:** a succulent plant • cacti and other *succulents*

suc·cumb /səˈkʌm/ *verb* **-cumbs; -cumbed; -cumb·ing** [*no obj*] *somewhat formal*
1 : to stop trying to resist something • They will pressure you, and you must try not to *succumb*. — often + *to* • Try not to *succumb to* the pressure. • It's easy to *succumb* [=*give in*] to the temptation to oversimplify this kind of problem.
2 : to die • The patient eventually *succumbed*. — usually + *to* • He *succumbed to* his injuries. [=he died because of his injuries] • She fought a good fight but finally *succumbed to* cancer.

¹such /ˈsʌʧ/ *adj*
1 *always used before a noun* — used to say that something is great in degree, quality, or number • I've been *such* a fool! [=I've been very foolish] • How could you believe *such* nonsense? • I've never seen *such* a (large) crowd here before. • Where are you off to in *such* a rush? • The building had deteriorated ***to such a degree*** [=*so much*] that they had to tear it down. • I was surprised that the town had changed ***to such an extent*** [=*so much*]
2 *not used before a noun* — used to say that something has a quality that results in something specified • The evidence is ***such as to*** leave no doubt of his guilt. = The evidence is ***such that*** there can be no doubt of his guilt. • Her excitement was *such that* she could hardly contain herself. [=she was so excited that she could hardly contain herself]
3 *always used before a noun* **:** of the kind specified • The gun

had his fingerprints on it. *Such* evidence [=evidence of that kind] leaves little doubt of his guilt. ▪ She has published her first sci-fi novel and hopes to write more *such* novels. ▪ No *such* agreement was made. ▪ I know it was an accident, but *such* people [=people like that] should not be allowed to drive. ▪ "Can I talk to Mary?" "I'm sorry. There is no *such* person here." [=there is no one named Mary here] ▪ In *such* a situation (as this), it is important to remain calm. ▪ The magazine publishes articles about *such* varied subjects as astronomy, politics, and gardening. ▪ It will be documented in *such* a way/manner as to prevent misunderstanding. = It will be documented in *such* a way/manner that there can be no misunderstanding. [=it will be documented in a way that prevents misunderstanding] ▪ I've never heard of ***such a thing***! ▪ "You will apologize at once!" "I'll do ***no such thing***!" [=I will not apologize] ▪ There is **no such thing as** having too many friends. [=you cannot have too many friends] ▪ She said she was too busy ***or some such*** nonsense. [=or something similar]

²such *pronoun, somewhat formal*

1 : that kind or type of person or thing ▪ She has a plan, if it may be called *such*. [=if it deserves to be called a plan; if it is good/practical enough to be referred to as a plan] ▪ He was not only a politician but also an inventor and well-known ***as such***. [=well-known as an inventor] ▪ It is a serious problem and should be treated *as such*. — see also AS SUCH (below)
2 : something previously stated or specified ▪ If *such* is the decision, nothing further should be done. ▪ We were outnumbered and surrounded. *Such* being the case [=since that was the case], we had to surrender. ▪ If you retained a receipt, please enclose a copy of *such*. [=please enclose a copy of the receipt]

and such **:** and things of that kind ▪ Pens, pencils, markers, *and such* are in this drawer.

as such **1 :** of the usual or expected kind **:** in the usual sense ▪ I have no boss *as such* [=there is no one who is actually my boss], but I do have to answer to my clients. **2 :** by, of, or in itself — used to indicate that something is being considered by itself and not along with other things ▪ There's nothing wrong with gambling *as such* [=*per se*], but it's best to do it in moderation. — see also ²SUCH 1 (above)

such is life **:** life is like that and cannot be changed ▪ We've had our share of problems, but *such is life*.

³such *adv*

1 *somewhat informal* — used to make a description more forceful ▪ The team has *such* tall players. [=the team's players are very tall] ▪ She wears *such* stylish clothes. [=her clothes are very stylish] ▪ She hasn't been in *such* good spirits lately. ▪ We had *such* a good time [=a very good time] at the party! ▪ It is *such* a long trip. ▪ It was *such* an awkward moment. ▪ Today was *such* a nice/beautiful day! ▪ I don't think that's *such* a good/great idea. [=I don't think that's a good idea]
2 : to the degree that is specified or understood ▪ *Such* violent movies (as these) are not suitable for children. ▪ We've never had *such* a cold winter (as this). ▪ I have never seen *such* a large cat! ▪ I had *such* a bad headache that I couldn't think straight.

ever such see EVER

such as **1** — used to introduce an example or series of examples ▪ You will need some form of identification, *such as* [=*like*] a driver's license. ▪ "I have my reasons for not wanting to go." "*Such as*?" [=give me an example] **2 :** of the specified kind ▪ In cases *such as* [=*like*] this (one), it's best to be cautious. ▪ Questions *such as* the one you've asked are difficult to answer.

such as it is — used to say that something is not very good in quality or condition ▪ The meal, *such as it was*, was served quickly. [=the meal, which was not very good, was served quickly] ▪ Welcome to my humble home—*such as it is*.

¹such and such *adj, always used before a noun* **:** not named or specified ▪ people from *such and such* areas ▪ If you were born in ***such and such a*** year . . .

²such and such *pronoun* **:** something that is not specified ▪ If you earn *such and such* per year, then . . .

¹such·like /ˈsʌtʃˌlaɪk/ *adj, always used before a noun, chiefly Brit* **:** sharing qualities or characteristics **:** SIMILAR ▪ rakes, shovels, and *suchlike* things

²suchlike *pronoun*

and suchlike *chiefly Brit* **:** and things of that kind ▪ Pens, pencils, markers, *and suchlike* are in this drawer.

¹suck /ˈsʌk/ *verb* **sucks; sucked; suck·ing**

1 a [+ *obj*] **:** to pull (liquid, air, etc.) into your mouth especially while your lips are forming a small hole ▪ *sucking* milk through a straw **b :** to pull on (something in your mouth) with the muscles of your lips and mouth [+ *obj*] a toddler *sucking* his thumb ▪ She just *sucked* her teeth and stared. [*no obj*] She *sucked* on an orange slice. **c :** to let (something, such as candy or medicine) stay in your mouth as it melts [+ *obj*] I *sucked* a cough drop. [*no obj*] *sucking* on a lollipop
2 *always followed by an adverb or preposition* [+ *obj*] **a :** to pull (something) with the force of moving water, air, etc. ▪ The tide almost *sucked* us out to sea. ▪ The boat was *sucked* under the water in the storm. **b :** to remove (something) from an area or substance by pulling it with the force of moving water, air, etc. ▪ These plants *suck* moisture from the soil. ▪ The fan *sucks* smoke from the air. ▪ a vacuum cleaner that **sucks up** water as well as dirt — sometimes used figuratively ▪ She just seems to *suck* the joy out of the room. ▪ This heat has *sucked* every ounce of energy out of me.
3 [+ *obj*] **:** to make (part of your body) flatter or tighter by pulling your muscles inward — + *in* ▪ He was *sucking in* his gut. [=pulling in his stomach to make himself seem thinner] ▪ It looked like she had *sucked* her cheeks *in* for the picture.
4 [+ *obj*] **:** to cause (someone) to become involved or interested in something — + *in* or *into* ▪ Their lifestyle seemed exciting, and I admit it really *sucked* me *in*. — often used as *(be/get) sucked in/into* ▪ Hundreds of people *got sucked into* the scheme and many lost their entire life savings.
5 *not used in progressive tenses* [*no obj*] *informal + sometimes impolite* **a :** to be very bad or unpleasant ▪ You lost your job? That *sucks*. ▪ People who went to the party said it *sucked*. **b :** to do something very badly ▪ He sang a few songs, and man, he *sucks*. [=he sings badly] — often + *at* ▪ I *suck at* golf. [=I play golf badly]

suck it and see *Brit, informal* **:** to try something in order to find out if it is good, effective, etc. ▪ We don't know if it will work. We'll have to just *suck it and see*. [=try it and see] ▪ a *suck-it-and-see* approach/situation

suck (someone or something) dry see ¹DRY

suck up [*phrasal verb*] **1** *informal + disapproving* **:** to try to get the approval of someone in authority by saying and doing helpful and friendly things that are not sincere ▪ There he goes, *sucking up* again. — usually + *to* ▪ She's always *sucking up to* [=*kissing up to*] the boss. — see also SUCK-UP **2** ***suck it up*** *US, informal* **:** to do or deal with something unpleasant by making a special effort ▪ I know you don't want to see him, but you'll just have to *suck it up* and be polite. ▪ I had to *suck it up* and play with an injured finger. — see also ¹SUCK 2b (above)

²suck *noun, pl* **sucks** [*count*] **:** an act of sucking ▪ He took a *suck* on his pipe.

¹suck·er /ˈsʌkɚ/ *noun, pl* **-ers** [*count*]

1 *informal* **:** a person who is easily tricked or deceived ▪ He's just a con artist looking for another *sucker*. ▪ There's a *sucker* born every minute. [=there are many people who are easily tricked or deceived]
2 *informal* **:** a person who is very strongly attracted to a particular type of thing or person — + *for* ▪ She's a *sucker for* mystery novels. [=she likes mystery novels very much] ▪ He's a *sucker for* women with dark hair.
3 *chiefly US, informal* **:** an annoying person or thing ▪ That kid is a mean little *sucker*. ▪ I got the other window open, but I just can't seem to get this *sucker* [=this window] to budge.
4 : a person who sucks something specified — usually used in combination ▪ She's a thumb-*sucker*.
5 : a part of an animal's body that is used for sucking or for attaching to things ▪ the *suckers* on an octopus's arms
6 : a new branch that grows from the base of a plant ▪ Cut off any *suckers* growing at the base of the bush.
7 *US, informal* **:** LOLLIPOP
8 *Brit* **:** SUCTION CUP

²sucker *verb* **-ers; -ered; -er·ing**

sucker into [*phrasal verb*] ***sucker (someone) into (something)*** *US, informal* **:** to deceive or trick (someone) in order to make that person do (something) ▪ I was *suckered into* volunteering at the cookout. ▪ She *suckered* me *into* paying for her meal. ▪ How did I get *suckered into* (doing) this?

sucker punch *verb* **~ punches; ~ punched; ~ punch·ing** [+ *obj*] *US* **:** to hit (a person) suddenly and usually without any obvious reason ▪ One of them *sucker punched* me. — sometimes used figuratively ▪ a series of bad storms that have *sucker punched* the island

— **sucker punch** *noun, pl* **~ punches** [*count*] ▪ He hit me with a *sucker punch*.

S

suck·le /ˈsʌkəl/ *verb* **suck·les; suck·led; suck·ling** [+ *obj*] : to give (a baby or young animal) milk from a breast or from an udder ▪ a mother *suckling* [=*breast-feeding*] her baby ▪ a cat *suckling* her kittens

suck·ling pig /ˈsʌklɪŋ-/ *noun, pl* ~ **pigs** [*count, noncount*] : a young pig that is roasted and served at a meal

suck–up /ˈsʌk,ʌp/ *noun, pl* **-ups** [*count*] *US, informal + disapproving* : a person who tries to get the approval of someone in authority by saying and doing helpful and friendly things that are not sincere ▪ I don't think you can give your professor a gift without being considered a *suck-up*. — see also *suck up* at [1]SUCK

su·crose /ˈsuː,krous/ *noun* [*noncount*] *technical* : a type of sugar that is found in most plants ✧ Sucrose is the kind of sugar commonly used for cooking and baking.

[1]**suc·tion** /ˈsʌkʃən/ *noun* [*noncount*] : the act or process of removing the air, water, etc., from a space in order to pull something into that space or in order to cause something to stick to a surface ▪ The vacuum cleaner picks up dirt by *suction*. ▪ The octopus grasps things using *suction*.; *also* : the force with which the air, water, etc., in a space is removed ▪ a vacuum cleaner with enough *suction* to pick up the heaviest particles of dirt ▪ strong *suction*

[2]**suction** *verb* **-tions; -tioned; -tion·ing** [+ *obj*] *technical* : to remove (something) by pulling it with the force of moving water, air, etc. : to remove (something) by using suction ▪ The surgeon will *suction* blood out of the area.

suction cup *noun, pl* ~ **cups** [*count*] : a round, shallow cup made of a flexible material (such as rubber) that you attach to a surface by pressing the cup against the surface until the air between the cup and surface is removed ▪ The device is held to the wall with two *suction cups*.

sud·den /ˈsʌdn̩/ *adj* [*more* ~; *most* ~] : happening, coming, or done very quickly in a way that is usually not expected ▪ a *sudden* change/rise in temperature ▪ *Sudden* fame/success can be difficult to deal with. ▪ She had a *sudden* urge to be outside. ▪ His death was very *sudden*. ▪ a *sudden* turn in the road ▪ I was surprised by her *sudden* decision to quit. ▪ The director's *sudden* departure leaves the organization's future uncertain.

all of a sudden : SUDDENLY ▪ I was walking down the street when, *all of a sudden*, it started raining. ▪ *All of a sudden*, I saw what he was looking at.

– sud·den·ness /ˈsʌdn̩nəs/ *noun* [*noncount*] ▪ the *suddenness* of the attack ▪ I was surprised by the *suddenness* of her decision.

sudden death *noun* [*noncount*]

1 *sports* : a period of extra play that is added when teams or players are tied at the end of normal play and that ends as soon as one team or player scores a point or gains the lead ▪ We won 27–24 in *sudden death*. — often used before another noun ▪ a *sudden-death* play-off in golf

2 *medical* : quick and unexpected death from any cause other than violence ▪ a serious heart condition that can result in *sudden death*

sudden infant death syndrome *noun* [*noncount*] *technical* : the death of a healthy baby that happens for no known reason while the baby is sleeping — called also *crib death*, (*Brit*) *cot death*, *SIDS*

sud·den·ly /ˈsʌdn̩li/ *adv* : very quickly in usually an unexpected way : in a sudden way ▪ *Suddenly* the lights went out. ▪ I was *suddenly* very nervous. ▪ There were no instances of the disease here until it *suddenly* appeared last year. ▪ She *suddenly* decided to quit her job. ▪ He died *suddenly* of a heart attack.

suds /ˈsʌdz/ *noun*

1 [*plural*] : bubbles that form on top of water that contains soap — called also *soapsuds*

2 [*noncount*] *US, informal* : BEER ▪ a bottle of *suds*

– sudsy /ˈsʌdzi/ *adj* **suds·i·er; -est** [*also more* ~; *most* ~] ▪ *sudsy* water

sue /ˈsuː, *Brit* ˈsjuː/ *verb* **sues; sued; su·ing** : to use a legal process by which you try to get a court of law to force a person, company, or organization that has treated you unfairly or hurt you in some way to give you something or to do something : to bring a lawsuit against someone or something [*no obj*] Some people *sue* over the most minor things. ▪ People injured in accidents caused by the defective tire have threatened to *sue*. — often + *for* ▪ They're ***suing for damages***. [=suing to get money for the unfair treatment, damage, etc., that they have suffered] ▪ His wife is ***suing for divorce***. [=his wife has begun a legal process in order to get a divorce] [+ *obj*] They've threatened to *sue* the company. ▪ He is *suing* the doctor who performed the unnecessary surgery. — often + *for* ▪ They're *suing* the company *for damages*. ▪ She's *suing* her husband *for divorce*.

sue for peace formal : to officially ask for an end to fighting ▪ a decisive battle after which the rebels *sued for peace*

suede /ˈsweɪd/ *noun* [*noncount*] : soft leather that has been rubbed on one side to make a surface that looks and feels like velvet ▪ The gloves are *suede*. — often used before another noun ▪ a *suede* jacket

su·et /ˈsuːwət/ *noun* [*noncount*] : a type of hard fat that is found in cows and sheep ▪ beef *suet*

suf·fer /ˈsʌfɚ/ *verb* **-fers; -fered; -fer·ing**

1 : to experience pain, illness, or injury [*no obj*] Before the surgery it was clear that she was really *suffering*. [=was in pain] ▪ He died instantly and did not *suffer*. — often + *from* ▪ She *suffers from* arthritis. ▪ This patient is clearly *suffering from* shock. [+ *obj*] He *suffered* a heart attack and died instantly. ▪ She *suffered* an injury during the game.

2 : to experience something unpleasant (such as defeat, loss, or damage) [*no obj*] We *suffered* a great deal during the war. ▪ I hate to see a child *suffer*. ▪ She *suffered* through another one of their long visits. [+ *obj*] The team ***suffered a defeat*** in the play-offs. ▪ He broke the law, so he has to ***suffer the consequences***. [=he has to be punished for what he has done]

3 [*no obj*] : to become worse because of being badly affected by something ▪ Their relationship *suffered* because of her work. ▪ He was working so hard that his health began to *suffer*. [=he began to have health problems] ▪ His parents told him he could play football as long as his grades didn't *suffer* (as a result).

suffer fools gladly : to be kind to and patient with people who annoy or bother you — usually used in negative statements ▪ My mother was a woman who did not *suffer fools gladly*.

suf·fer·ance /ˈsʌfərəns/ *noun*

on sufferance Brit, formal ✧ If you are allowed to do something *on sufferance*, you are allowed to do it by someone who does not want you to do it. ▪ She was allowed in only *on sufferance*.

suf·fer·er /ˈsʌfərɚ/ *noun, pl* **-ers** [*count*] : a person who has a particular illness or condition ▪ asthma *sufferers*

suf·fer·ing /ˈsʌfərɪŋ/ *noun, pl* **-ings**

1 [*noncount*] : pain that is caused by injury, illness, loss, etc. : physical, mental, or emotional pain ▪ ways to alleviate human *suffering* ▪ They hope these new drugs will help to bring an end to the *suffering* of arthritis patients. ▪ His lawsuit seeks damages for ***pain and suffering***.

2 ***sufferings*** [*plural*] : feelings of pain ▪ the *sufferings* of the dying

suf·fice /səˈfaɪs/ *verb* **-fic·es; -ficed; -fic·ing** [*no obj*] : to be or provide as much as is needed : to be sufficient ▪ No, you don't need to write a letter. A phone call will *suffice*. ▪ Her example alone should *suffice* to show that anything is possible.

suffice (it) to say — used to say that you could give more information about something but that the statement that follows is enough ▪ First, the car wouldn't start, and then I got stuck in traffic—*suffice it to say*, there was no way I could get here on time. ▪ *Suffice to say*, she has a lot on her hands with four children.

suf·fi·cient /səˈfɪʃənt/ *adj* [*more* ~; *most* ~] *somewhat formal* : having or providing as much as is needed : ENOUGH ▪ A brisk walk is *sufficient* to raise your heart rate. ▪ A 15 percent tip is *sufficient*. [=*adequate*] ▪ There must be *sufficient* funds in your bank account to cover the check. ▪ *sufficient* savings ▪ Her explanation was not *sufficient* to satisfy the police. — see also SELF-SUFFICIENT

– suf·fi·cien·cy /səˈfɪʃənsi/ *noun, pl* **-cies** [*count, noncount*] ▪ challenging the *sufficiency* of the evidence/proof

– suf·fi·cient·ly *adv* ▪ He was *sufficiently* bothered by the noise to complain to the manager. ▪ Her health has improved *sufficiently* to allow her to return to work. ▪ Make sure that the temperature is *sufficiently* cool.

suf·fix /ˈsʌfɪks/ *noun, pl* **-fix·es** [*count*] : a letter or a group of letters that is added to the end of a word to change its meaning or to form a different word ▪ The adjective "smokeless" is formed by adding the *suffix* "-less" to the noun "smoke." ▪ The adverb "sadly" is formed by adding the *suffix* "-ly" to the adjective "sad." — compare AFFIX, PREFIX

suf·fo·cate /ˈsʌfə,keɪt/ *verb* **-cates; -cat·ed; -cat·ing**

1 a [*no obj*] : to die because you are unable to breathe ▪

S

Don't put that pillow over her face—she could *suffocate*. • The poor dog could *suffocate* in the car on a hot day like this. — sometimes used figuratively • I'm *suffocating* in this job. [=I can't express myself, act freely, etc., in this job] **b** [+ *obj*] : to kill (someone) by making breathing impossible • She was afraid that thick pillows and blankets could *suffocate* [=*smother*] the baby. • The victims were found *suffocated*. — sometimes used figuratively • Anger and resentment slowly *suffocated* their marriage. • Critics say that the new tax will *suffocate* local businesses.

2 [*no obj*] : to be uncomfortable because there is not enough fresh air — usually used as *(be) suffocating* • We *were suffocating* in the stuffy boardroom.

– suf·fo·ca·tion /ˌsʌfəˈkeɪʃən/ *noun* [*noncount*] • The victims died of *suffocation*.

suffocating *adj* [*more* ~; *most* ~]

1 : very unpleasant or uncomfortable because there is not enough fresh air • *suffocating* heat • a *suffocating* room

2 — used to describe something that makes it difficult to act freely • a *suffocating* bureaucracy/relationship

3 — used to describe something that makes you very uncomfortable • a *suffocating* silence

– suffocatingly *adj* • a *suffocatingly* hot day • a *suffocatingly* close relationship

suf·frage /ˈsʌfrɪʤ/ *noun* [*noncount*] : the right to vote in an election • women who fought for *suffrage* • ***universal suffrage*** [=the right of all adult citizens to vote in an election]

suf·frag·ette /ˌsʌfrɪˈʤɛt/ *noun, pl* **-ettes** [*count*] : a woman who worked to get voting rights for women in the past when women were not allowed to vote

suf·frag·ist /ˈsʌfrɪʤɪst/ *noun, pl* **-ists** [*count*] : a person in the past who worked to get voting rights for people who did not have them

suf·fuse /səˈfjuːz/ *verb* **-fus·es**; **-fused**; **-fus·ing** [+ *obj*] *literary* : to spread over or fill (something) • Morning light *suffused* the room. — usually used as *(be) suffused* • The room *was suffused* with morning light.

Su·fi /ˈsuːfi/ *noun, pl* **-fis** [*count*] : a member of a Muslim group of people who try to experience God directly especially by praying and meditating

– Su·fism /ˈsuːˌfɪzəm/ *noun* [*noncount*]

¹sug·ar /ˈʃʊgɚ/ *noun, pl* **-ars**

1 a [*noncount*] : a sweet substance usually in the form of white or brown crystals or white powder that comes from plants and is used to make foods sweeter • Would you pass the *sugar*, please? • Do you take *sugar* in your coffee? • a lump/cube/packet of *sugar* — see also BROWN SUGAR, CANE SUGAR, CONFECTIONERS' SUGAR, MAPLE SUGAR, POWDERED SUGAR **b** [*count*] : the amount of sugar in one spoonful, lump, packet, etc. • Coffee with two *sugars* and milk, please.

2 [*count*] *technical* : any one of various substances that are found in plants and that your body uses or stores for energy — usually plural • Everyone's body metabolizes *sugars* differently. • Simple *sugars* are easier to digest than complex *sugars*.

3 [*noncount*] *informal* : the amount of sugar present in a person's blood at a particular time • Her *sugar* (level) is very high. — called also *blood sugar*

4 *chiefly US, informal* — used to address someone you like or love • "Hey, *sugar* [=*honey*], how are you doing?"

²sugar *verb* **sugars**; **sug·ared**; **sug·ar·ing**

1 [+ *obj*] : to put sugar on or in (something) • The clean fruit is then dried and *sugared*. • She *sugared* her coffee.

2 [*no obj*] *US* : to make maple syrup or maple sugar by boiling sap from maple trees • They've been *sugaring* since they were children.

sugar the pill see ¹PILL

– sugared *adj* • heavily *sugared* coffee/tea [=coffee/tea with a lot of sugar added to it] • *sugared* almonds

sugar beet *noun, pl* ~ **beets** [*count*] : a white beet that is grown for the sugar in its root

sug·ar·cane /ˈʃʊgɚˌkeɪn/ *noun* [*noncount*] : a tall grass that is grown in warm places as a source of sugar

sug·ar·coat /ˈʃʊgɚˌkoʊt/ *verb* **-coats**; **-coat·ed**; **-coat·ing** [+ *obj*] : to talk about or describe (something) in a way that makes it seem more pleasant or acceptable than it is • textbooks that *sugarcoat* history • She has very strong opinions, and she doesn't try to *sugarcoat* them.

sugar–coated *adj*

1 : covered in sugar • *sugar-coated* cereal

2 [*more* ~; *most* ~] *disapproving* : made to seem more pleasant or acceptable than it is • a *sugar-coated* version of history

sugar cube *noun, pl* ~ **cubes** [*count*] : a small cube of sugar that is put in coffee or tea to make it sweet — called also *(Brit) sugar lump*

sugar daddy *noun, pl* ~ **-dies** [*count*] *informal* : a rich, older man who gives money, gifts, etc., to someone (such as a young woman) in exchange for sex, friendship, etc. • She's on the lookout for a new *sugar daddy*. — sometimes used figuratively in U.S. English • politicians getting money from their corporate *sugar daddies*

sugar–free *adj* : not containing sugar : containing an artificial sweetening substance instead of sugar • *sugar-free* gum

sug·ar·less /ˈʃʊgɚləs/ *adj* : SUGAR-FREE • *sugarless* gum

sugar maple *noun, pl* ~ **-ples** [*count*] *chiefly US* : a kind of maple tree that grows in eastern North America and that has sweet sap that is used to make maple syrup and maple sugar

sugar pill *noun, pl* ~ **pills** [*count*] : a pill that is given to a patient like a drug but that has no medicine in it : PLACEBO • Half the patients were given the medication and the other half received a *sugar pill*.

sug·ar·plum /ˈʃʊgɚˌplʌm/ *noun, pl* **-plums** [*count*] *US, old-fashioned* : a small, sweet candy that is usually shaped like a ball

sugar snap pea *noun, pl* ~ **peas** [*count*] : a type of pea whose thick outer part and seeds can be eaten — called also *snap pea*

sug·ary /ˈʃʊgəri/ *adj* [*more* ~; *most* ~]

1 : tasting like sugar or containing a lot of sugar • *sugary* breakfast cereals

2 *disapproving* : showing or expressing a pleasant emotion in a way that seems excessive and false : too sweet • a *sugary* ballad • *sugary* cheerfulness/sentiment

sug·gest /səˈʤɛst/ *verb* **-gests**; **-gest·ed**; **-gest·ing** [+ *obj*]

1 : to mention (something) as a possible thing to be done, used, thought about, etc. • I *suggest* (that) you call the store. • We *suggested* to the committee that they review the case again. • It was *suggested* that we leave early. • He *suggested* several different ways of dealing with the problem. • She *suggested* a stroll after dinner. = She *suggested* that we go for a stroll after dinner.

2 : to say that (someone or something) is good or deserves to be chosen : RECOMMEND • Who would you *suggest* for the job? • They *suggested* a restaurant we might want to try. • I *suggest* caution in a situation like this.

3 : to show that (something) is likely or true : to indicate (something) usually without showing it in a direct or certain way • The evidence *suggests* arson as the cause of the fire. • There is nothing to *suggest* that the two events are connected. • As the name *suggests*, a yarn winder is a device used to wind balls of yarn.

4 : to say (something) in an indirect way • Are you *suggesting* [=*implying*] (that) he deliberately cheated? • I think he's *suggesting* that we shouldn't have helped them.

suggest itself *somewhat formal, of an idea, plan, etc.* : to be thought of : to seem or become obvious • No good solution *suggested itself*. [=I was unable to think of a good solution]

sug·gest·ible /səˈʤɛstəbəl/ *adj* [*more* ~; *most* ~] : likely to believe that what someone says is true or may be true : easily influenced • The patient/child was highly *suggestible*.

sug·ges·tion /səˈʤɛsʧən/ *noun, pl* **-tions**

1 [*count*] **a** : an idea about what someone should do or how someone should behave • Do you have any *suggestions*? • Please send comments and *suggestions* to our post office box. • I have a *suggestion*: call the store and ask them about it. • I'd like to offer/make a *suggestion*. • I am always ***open to suggestions***. [=ready to hear new ideas] **b** : something that is said in an indirect way • I'm shocked at the *suggestion* that he deliberately cheated. = The very *suggestion* that he deliberately cheated is shocking (to me). • I reject his *suggestion* that we shouldn't have helped them.

2 a : an action, quality, appearance, etc., that seems to indicate the presence or existence of something [*count*] — usually singular • There was a *suggestion* of boredom in his tone of voice. [*noncount*] They were careful to avoid any *suggestion* of impropriety. [=avoid doing anything that could be seen as improper] • There was some *suggestion* of swelling around his ankle. [=his ankle appeared to be slightly swollen] **b** [*count*] : a very small amount of something — usually singular • a flavor of chocolate with a (slight) *suggestion* [=*hint*] of pepper

3 [*noncount*] **:** the process by which you make people think or feel something by saying, expressing, or showing something that is related only indirectly ▪ trying to influence people's thoughts by using *suggestion* ▪ The director relies on the ***power of suggestion*** rather than explicitly showing the murder.

at/on someone's suggestion **:** because someone said that you should ▪ *On his suggestion,* I applied for the job. [=I applied for the job because he suggested that I should] ▪ She went to Germany *at my suggestion.*

sug·ges·tive /sə'ʤɛstɪv/ *adj* [*more* ~; *most* ~]
1 a : bringing thoughts, memories, or feelings into the mind — + *of* ▪ music *suggestive* [=*evocative*] *of* a past era **b :** showing or seeming to show something — + *of* ▪ symptoms *suggestive of* AIDS
2 : causing or tending to cause sexual feelings or excitement ▪ a *suggestive* [=*revealing*] nightgown ▪ *suggestive* [=*provocative*] song lyrics
– sug·ges·tive·ly *adv* ▪ The dancers moved *suggestively.*

sui·cid·al /ˌsuːwə'saɪdl̩/ *adj* [*more* ~; *most* ~]
1 : wanting to kill yourself ▪ psychiatrists working with *suicidal* patients ▪ Her friends are worried that she might be *suicidal.* [=that she might want to kill herself] **:** showing a desire to kill yourself ▪ She had *suicidal* thoughts/tendencies.
2 : extremely dangerous **:** likely to cause your death ▪ The mission is *suicidal.* ▪ a *suicidal* rescue attempt **:** likely to cause great harm to yourself ▪ He knows that supporting a tax increase would be politically *suicidal.*

[1]sui·cide /'suːwəˌsaɪd/ *noun, pl* **-cides**
1 a : the act of killing yourself because you do not want to continue living [*noncount*] She had thoughts of *suicide.* ▪ He ***committed suicide.*** [=he killed himself] ▪ He ***attempted suicide.*** [=he tried to kill himself] [*count*] Authorities have officially ruled the death a *suicide.* ▪ There were two *suicides* last year at the university. — see also ASSISTED SUICIDE, PHYSICIAN-ASSISTED SUICIDE **b** [*count*] **:** a person who commits suicide ▪ Her father was a *suicide.* [=her father killed himself]
2 [*noncount*] **:** an action that ruins or destroys your career, social position, etc. ▪ Accepting that kind of support is political *suicide.* [=it will cause the end of your career in politics] ▪ It would be *suicide* for the company to try to expand too quickly. [=the company would fail if it tried to expand too quickly]

[2]suicide *adj, always used before a noun* **:** of or relating to suicide ▪ a *suicide* attempt ▪ Did he leave a ***suicide note***? [=a note/letter explaining why he killed himself] — used especially to describe something that is done by a person who plans and expects to be killed while doing it ▪ a ***suicide mission/bombing*** ▪ a ***suicide bomber*** [=a person who commits suicide by exploding a bomb in order to kill other people]

suicide pact *noun, pl* ~ **pacts** [*count*] **:** an agreement between two or more people to kill themselves at the same time ▪ The two friends died in what appeared to be a *suicide pact.*

sui ge·ner·is /ˌsuːˌaɪ'ʤɛnərəs/ *adj, formal* **:** in a class or group of its own **:** not like anything else ▪ As a scholar, she is *sui generis.* [=*unique*]

[1]suit /'suːt/ *noun, pl* **suits**
1 [*count*] **:** a set of clothes that usually consists of a jacket and a skirt or pair of pants that are made out of the same material ▪ a tweed/wool *suit* ▪ He wore his gray *suit* to the job interview. — see color picture on page C15; see also BUSINESS SUIT, LEISURE SUIT, LOUNGE SUIT, PANTSUIT, SAILOR SUIT, SHELL SUIT, THREE-PIECE SUIT, TROUSER SUIT, TWO-PIECE SUIT, ZOOT SUIT
2 [*count*] **:** a set of clothes or protective covering that is worn for a special purpose or under particular conditions ▪ a gym *suit* ▪ a *suit* of armor — see also BATHING SUIT, BODYSUIT, CATSUIT, JUMPSUIT, SNOWSUIT, SPACE SUIT, SWEAT SUIT, SWIMSUIT, UNION SUIT, WET SUIT
3 : a process by which a court of law makes a decision to settle a disagreement or problem between people or organizations **:** LAWSUIT [*count*] a civil/criminal *suit* ▪ divorce/custody/paternity *suits* ▪ He ***filed/brought a suit*** [=started legal proceedings] against her. [*noncount*] He ***filed/brought suit*** [=started legal proceedings] against her.
4 [*count*] **:** all the cards that have the same symbol in a pack of playing cards ▪ The trump *suit* is hearts/clubs/diamonds/spades.
5 [*count*] *informal* + *disapproving* **:** a person who has an important job in an office and who wears a suit **:** a business executive ▪ She described her boss as "an ***empty suit.***" [=a stupid and ineffective businessman] — usually plural ▪ Get back to work. The *suits* just walked in.

birthday suit see BIRTHDAY
follow suit see [1]FOLLOW
– see also LONG SUIT, STRONG SUIT

[2]suit *verb* **suits; suit·ed; suit·ing** [+ *obj*]
1 a : to provide what is required or wanted by or for (someone or something) ▪ This program should *suit* [=*satisfy*] your needs. ▪ The restaurant offers meals to *suit* [=*please*] all tastes. ▪ I can schedule the meeting for tomorrow. Does that *suit* you? [=is that convenient for you?] ▪ That *suits* me fine. ▪ He only helps out when it *suits* him. [=when he wants to; when it is convenient for him to help out] **b :** to be proper or suitable for (someone or something) ▪ This kind of behavior hardly *suits* a person of your age. ▪ She gave a serious speech that *suited* the occasion. ▪ The formal furniture really *suited* the style of the house. ▪ The job *suits* her very well. ▪ (*Brit*) This kind of work ***suits me down to the ground.*** [=suits me perfectly; I like/enjoy this kind of work very much]
2 : to be attractive on (someone) — not used in passive constructions ▪ Your new hairstyle *suits* [=*becomes*] you. ▪ That dress doesn't really *suit* her.

suit someone's book *Brit, informal* **:** to be suitable or satisfactory to someone ▪ The changes should *suit your book.*

suit up [*phrasal verb*] *US* **:** to put on a uniform or special clothing ▪ The players are *suiting up* for the game. ▪ The divers *suited up.*

suit yourself *informal* **:** to do what you want to do — used especially to tell people that they can do what they want even though you do not think it is what they should do ▪ "I don't want to go." "*Suit yourself.* [=do what you want] We'll go without you."

suit·able /'suːtəbəl/ *adj* [*more* ~; *most* ~] **:** having the qualities that are right, needed, or appropriate for something ▪ The dress was a *suitable* choice. ▪ We upgraded the computer to make it *suitable* to our needs. — often + *for* ▪ Is this shirt *suitable for* work? ▪ Her experience makes her more *suitable for* the job. ▪ What is a *suitable* time/place *for* us to meet? ▪ The movie is not *suitable for* children. [=children should not watch it] — opposite UNSUITABLE
– suit·abil·i·ty /ˌsuːtə'bɪləti/ *noun* [*noncount*] ▪ No one questioned her *suitability* for the job. **– suit·ably** /'suːtəbli/ *adv* ▪ They were *suitably* dressed for the occasion. ▪ The old house was a *suitably* spooky place for a Halloween party.

suit·case /'suːtˌkeɪs/ *noun, pl* **-cas·es** [*count*] **:** a large case that you use to carry your clothing and belongings when you are traveling ▪ She packed her *suitcases* the night before she left.

suite /'swiːt/ *noun, pl* **suites** [*count*]
1 a : a group of rooms that is used for one purpose ▪ a *suite* of offices on the fifth floor ▪ The executive *suite* is on the top floor. **b :** a group of rooms in a hotel that is used by one person, couple, family, etc. ▪ She checked into a *suite.* ▪ We stayed in the hotel's honeymoon/bridal *suite.* — see also EN SUITE
2 : a piece of music that is made up of many short pieces that are taken from a larger work (such as a ballet) ▪ The orchestra will be performing a *suite.* ▪ the Nutcracker *Suite*
3 *chiefly Brit* **:** a set of matching pieces of furniture for a room ▪ a bedroom/bathroom *suite* ▪ We bought a three-piece *suite* [=a couch and two chairs] for the living room.
4 : a set of computer programs that are designed to work together ▪ a *suite* of business software

suit·ed /'suːtəd/ *adj* [*more* ~; *most* ~] **:** having the qualities that are right, needed, or appropriate for something — + *for* or *to* ▪ The land is well *suited for* farming. ▪ We will hire the person who is best/most *suited to* the job. ▪ The plant is *suited to* (living in) tropical climates.

suit·ing /'suːtɪŋ/ *noun* [*noncount*] **:** cloth that is used in making suits

suit·or /'suːtɚ/ *noun, pl* **-ors** [*count*]
1 *old-fashioned* **:** a man who wants to marry a particular woman ▪ He was her most persistent *suitor,* and she eventually agreed to marry him.
2 *technical* **:** a company that wants to take over another company ▪ An unwanted *suitor* is buying up the company's stock.

sul·fate (*US*) *or chiefly Brit* **sul·phate** /'sʌlˌfeɪt/ *noun, pl* **-fates** [*count, noncount*] *chemistry* **:** a salt that is formed when sulfuric acid reacts with another chemical element ▪ copper *sulfate*

S

sul·fide (*US*) *or chiefly Brit* **sul·phide** /ˈsʌlˌfaɪd/ *noun, pl* **-fides** [*count, noncount*] *chemistry* : a compound that contains sulfur and one or more other chemical elements

sul·fur (*US*) *or chiefly Brit* **sul·phur** /ˈsʌlfɚ/ *noun* [*noncount*] *chemistry* : a yellow chemical element that has a strong, unpleasant odor when it is burned and that is used in making paper, gunpowder, medicine, etc.

> ***usage*** In U.S. English, the spelling *sulfur* is chiefly used in technical writing, while both *sulfur* and *sulphur* are common in general writing.

sulfur dioxide (*US*) *or chiefly Brit* **sulphur dioxide** *noun* [*noncount*] *chemistry* : a gas that has a strong smell, that is used in many industries, and that contributes to air pollution

sul·fu·ric acid (*US*) *or chiefly Brit* **sul·phu·ric acid** /sʌlˈfjɚrɪk-/ *noun* [*noncount*] *chemistry* : a very strong type of acid

sul·fu·rous (*US*) *or chiefly Brit* **sul·phu·rous** /ˈsʌlfərəs/ *adj, chemistry* : of, relating to, or containing sulfur • *sulfurous* compounds/gas • a *sulfurous* odor

¹sulk /ˈsʌlk/ *verb* **sulks**; **sulked**; **sulk·ing** [*no obj*] : to be angry or upset about something and to refuse to discuss it with other people • He went to *sulk* in his room. • She has been *sulking* all day.

²sulk *noun, pl* **sulks** [*count*] : a period of time when someone is angry or upset and refuses to speak • tantrums and *sulks* • He was ***in a sulk***. [=he was sulking] • She has a case of ***the sulks***. [=she's sulking]

sulky /ˈsʌlki/ *adj* **sulk·i·er**; **-est** [*also more ~; most ~*]
1 : angry or upset about something and refusing to discuss it with others • She is very *sulky* today. • She's in a *sulky* mood.
2 : often quiet and angry or upset • a *sulky* [=*moody*] child
— **sulk·i·ly** /ˈsʌlkəli/ *adv* • He sat *sulkily* in the chair. — **sulk·i·ness** /ˈsʌlkinəs/ *noun* [*noncount*]

sul·len /ˈsʌlən/ *adj* [*more ~; most ~*]
1 — used to describe an angry or unhappy person who does not want to talk, smile, etc. • *sullen* teenagers • He's in a *sullen* mood. • She sat in *sullen* silence. • His face was *sullen*. = He had a *sullen* expression on his face.
2 *literary* : gray and dark • a *sullen* [=*gloomy*] sky/morning
— **sul·len·ly** *adv* • He stared *sullenly* out the window. — **sul·len·ness** /ˈsʌlənnəs/ *noun* [*noncount*]

sul·ly /ˈsʌli/ *verb* **sul·lies**; **sul·lied**; **sul·ly·ing** [+ *obj*] *formal* : to damage or ruin the good quality of (something) • The scandal *sullied* [=*tarnished*] her reputation.

sulphate, sulphide, sulphur, sulphur dioxide, sulphuric acid, sulphurous *chiefly Brit spellings of* SULFATE, SULFIDE, SULFUR, SULFUR DIOXIDE, SULFURIC ACID, SULFUROUS

sul·tan /ˈsʌltn̩/ *noun, pl* **-tans** [*count*] : a king or ruler of a Muslim state or country

sul·ta·na /ˌsʌlˈtænə, *Brit* ˌsʌlˈtɑːnə/ *noun, pl* **-nas** [*count*]
1 : the wife, mother, sister, or daughter of a sultan
2 *chiefly Brit* : GOLDEN RAISIN

sul·tan·ate /ˈsʌltəˌneɪt/ *noun, pl* **-ates** [*count*]
1 : a state or country that is ruled by a sultan
2 : the position of a sultan or the period of time when a sultan rules • His *sultanate* ended in 1923.

sul·try /ˈsʌltri/ *adj* **sul·tri·er**; **-est** [*also more ~; most ~*]
1 : very hot and humid • a *sultry* day • *sultry* air/weather
2 : attractive in a way that suggests or causes feelings of sexual desire • She looked at him with a *sultry* glance. • a *sultry* woman/dress • an actress with a *sultry* voice
— **sul·tri·ness** /ˈsʌltrinəs/ *noun* [*noncount*] • the *sultriness* of her voice

¹sum /ˈsʌm/ *noun, pl* **sums**
1 [*count*] : an amount of money • They spent large/considerable *sums* (of money) repairing the house. • We donated a small *sum* (of money) to the charity. • The sellers were asking for a modest *sum*. • I paid the *sum* of $500. — see also LUMP SUM
2 [*count*] **a** : the result of adding two or more numbers together • The *sum* of 5 and 7 is 12. **b** : a simple problem in mathematics — usually plural • schoolchildren doing *sums*
3 [*singular*] : the whole amount of something • Working odd summer jobs has been ***the sum of*** my experience so far. [=has been all the experience I've had so far] — see also SUM TOTAL
in sum **1** : as a brief statement of the most important information in a piece of writing or speech • *In sum* [=*in summary*], we need a better public health-care system. **2** : in a few words • The movie was, *in sum* [=*in short*], entertaining as well as educational.
sum and substance : the general or basic meaning of something said or written • What is the *sum and substance* [=*gist*] of the argument?
sum of its parts ✧ Something that is ***greater/better/more than the sum of its parts*** is better or more effective as a team, combination, etc., than you would expect it to be when you look at the different parts that form it. • The team lacks standout players, but it has proved to be *greater than the sum of its parts*.
— see also ZERO-SUM GAME

²sum *verb* **sums**; **summed**; **sum·ming**
sum up [*phrasal verb*] **1** ***sum up or sum up (something) or sum (something) up*** : to tell (information) again using fewer words : to give a summary of (statements, facts, etc.) : SUMMARIZE • I would like to take a moment to *sum up* the facts that I presented earlier. • She *sums up* the main arguments of the essay in the final paragraph. • The judge *summed up* the evidence in his speech to the jury. • ***To sum up***, we need a better public health-care system. **2** ***sum up (someone or something) or sum (someone or something) up*** **a** : to describe or show the most important parts or qualities of (someone or something) in a brief or simple way • The article nicely *sums up* her career. • That picture *sums* him *up* perfectly. [=that picture perfectly shows what kind of person he is] **b** : to describe (someone or something) using few words • The solution to the landfill problem can be *summed up* in one word: recycling. • The word "lazy" *sums* him *up* pretty well. • "So, you don't want to go because you think it will be boring?" "That just about ***sums it up***." — see also SUMMING-UP

su·mac /ˈʃuˌmæk, ˈsuːˌmæk/ *noun, pl* **-macs** [*count, noncount*] : a type of tree, bush, or vine that has many small leaves and produces red or white berries — see also POISON SUMAC

sum·ma cum lau·de /ˌsʌməˌkʌmˈlɑːdə/ *adv, formal* : with highest honor — used in the U.S. to indicate that a student has graduated from a college or university at the highest of three special levels of achievement • She graduated *summa cum laude*. — compare CUM LAUDE, MAGNA CUM LAUDE

sum·ma·rize (*US*) *also Brit* **sum·ma·rise** /ˈsʌməˌraɪz/ *verb* **-riz·es**; **-rized**; **-riz·ing** : to tell (information) again using fewer words [+ *obj*] I would like to take a moment to *summarize* the facts that I presented earlier. • She *summarizes* the essay's main arguments in the final paragraph. = She *summarizes* the essay in the final paragraph. [*no obj*] He *summarized* by saying we needed better planning and implementation. • ***To summarize***, we need better schools.
— **sum·ma·ri·za·tion** *also Brit* **sum·ma·ri·sa·tion** /ˌsʌmərəˈzeɪʃən, *Brit* ˌsʌməˌraɪˈzeɪʃən/ *noun, pl* **-tions** [*count, noncount*] • A *summarization* [=*summary*] of the study's results can be found at the end of the report.

¹sum·ma·ry /ˈsʌməri/ *noun, pl* **-ries** [*count*] : a brief statement that gives the most important information about something • He concluded the report with a brief *summary*. • a chapter/plot *summary* • They gave a *summary* of their progress in building the bridge.
in summary : as a brief statement of the most important information in a piece of writing or speech • *In summary* [=*in conclusion, in sum*], we need a better public health-care system.

²summary *adj, always used before a noun*
1 : using few words to give the most important information about something • a *summary* account of the accident • a *summary* report
2 *formal* : done quickly in a way that does not follow the normal process • a *summary* dismissal/execution/judgment • a *summary* court proceeding
— **sum·mar·i·ly** /səˈmerəli/ *adv, formal* • He was *summarily* dismissed/executed.

sum·ma·tion /səˈmeɪʃən/ *noun, pl* **-tions** [*count*]
1 *formal* : a brief description of the most important information about something • A *summation* can be found at the end of the report. • We gave a *summation* of our discovery.
2 *US, law* : a final speech made by a lawyer in a court of law to give a summary of the main arguments in a case • The defense attorneys and prosecutors are set to make their final *summations* today.

¹sum·mer /ˈsʌmɚ/ *noun, pl* **-mers** : the warmest season of the year that is after spring and before autumn [*count*] What are your plans for this *summer*? • the *summer* of 2005 • We visited them two *summers* ago. [*noncount*] in early/late *summer* ▪ the first day of *summer* — often used before another noun ▪ the *summer* months ▪ a hot *summer* day ▪ the company's *summer* catalog ▪ *summer* clothes ▪ a *summer* job ▪ *summer* vacation ▪ The children have fond memories of *summer* camp. — see also INDIAN SUMMER

[2]**summer** *verb* **-mers; -mered; -mer·ing** [*no obj*] **:** to spend the summer in a particular place ▪ We *summer* (at our house) in Virginia.

sum·mer·house /ˈsʌmɚˌhaʊs/ *noun, pl* **-hous·es** [*count*]
1 *chiefly Brit* **:** a covered structure in a garden or park that is used as a resting place in summer
2 ***summer house*** **:** a house that someone lives in during the summer ▪ They have a *summer house* on the lake. — called also *summer home*

summer school *noun, pl* **~ schools** [*count, noncount*] **:** special classes that are taught at a school during the summer

summer squash *noun* [*count, noncount*] *US* **:** a long, usually yellow vegetable that is a type of squash and that has soft skin which can be eaten — see color picture on page C4; compare WINTER SQUASH

sum·mer·time /ˈsʌmɚˌtaɪm/ *noun* [*noncount*]
1 : the season of summer ▪ We go there to pick strawberries in the *summertime*.
2 ***Summer Time*** *Brit* **:** BRITISH SUMMER TIME

sum·mery /ˈsʌməri/ *adj* [*more ~; most ~*] **:** suitable for or typical of summer ▪ a *summery* dress ▪ *summery* afternoons

sum·ming–up /ˌsʌmɪŋˈʌp/ *noun, pl* **sum·mings–up** /ˌsʌmɪŋzˈʌp/ [*count*]
1 : the act of telling information again using fewer words ▪ a *summing-up* of the results
2 *law* **:** a final speech made by a lawyer or judge in a court of law to give a summary of the arguments and evidence in a case — see also *sum up* at [2]SUM

sum·mit /ˈsʌmət/ *noun, pl* **-mits** [*count*]
1 a : the highest point of a mountain **:** the top of a mountain ▪ The mountain range has *summits* over 10,000 feet high. ▪ the *summit* [=*peak*] of Mount Everest ▪ The climbers failed to reach the *summit*. **b :** the highest level ▪ He reached the *summit* [=*peak*] of his career three years ago.
2 : a meeting or series of meetings between the leaders of two or more governments ▪ Leaders of several nations attended the economic *summit*. ▪ A *summit* on global warming was held that year. ▪ a *summit* meeting/conference

sum·mon /ˈsʌmən/ *verb* **-mons; -moned; -mon·ing** [+ *obj*] *formal*
1 a : to order (someone) to come to a place ▪ The queen *summoned* him back to the palace. **b :** to order (someone) to appear in a court of law — often used as *(be) summoned* ▪ She *was summoned* to (appear in) court. ▪ She *was summoned* (to appear) before a judge.
2 : to ask for (someone or something) to come **:** to send or call for (someone or something) ▪ She *summoned* a doctor. ▪ The boy *summoned* help.
3 : to get (the courage, energy, strength, etc., that you need to do something) by making a special effort ▪ She couldn't *summon* [=*muster*] the strength/energy to finish the race.— often + *up* ▪ He finally *summoned up* the courage to ask her out on a date.
4 : to ask or order a group of people to come together for (a meeting) ▪ The president *summoned* [=*convened*] a meeting/conference.
summon up [*phrasal verb*] ***summon up (something)*** **:** to bring (a memory, feeling, image, etc.) into the mind ▪ Visiting his old house *summoned up* memories of his childhood. — see also SUMMON 3 (above)

[1]**sum·mons** /ˈsʌmənz/ *noun, pl* **-mons·es**
1 *law* **:** an official order to appear in a court of law [*count*] The judge issued a *summons*. ▪ He was served with a *summons* (to appear in court). [*noncount*] a writ/service of *summons* — compare SUBPOENA
2 [*count*] **:** an official order to appear at a particular place ▪ He received a royal *summons*.

[2]**summons** *verb* **-monses; -monsed; -mons·ing** [+ *obj*] *law* **:** to order (someone) to appear in a court of law **:** SUMMON — usually used as *(be) summonsed* ▪ She *was summonsed* to (appear in) court as a witness.

su·mo /ˈsuːmoʊ/ *noun* [*noncount*] **:** a Japanese form of wrestling that is performed by very large men ▪ *sumo* wrestlers

sump /ˈsʌmp/ *noun, pl* **sumps** [*count*]
1 : a low part or area where liquid collects when it drains from something ▪ *sump* pits/trenches
2 *chiefly Brit* **:** OIL PAN

sump pump *noun, pl* **~ pumps** [*count*] *US* **:** a pump that removes water from underneath a house or building

sump·tu·ous /ˈsʌmpʃəwəs/ *adj* [*more ~; most ~*] **:** very expensive, rich, or impressive ▪ a *sumptuous* banquet/dinner/feast ▪ *sumptuous* [=*luxurious*] hotels
– sump·tu·ous·ly *adv* ▪ a *sumptuously* furnished house
– sump·tu·ous·ness *noun* [*noncount*] ▪ the *sumptuousness* of the dessert

sum total *noun*
the sum total **:** the whole amount **:** the entire total of something — usually + *of* ▪ *The sum total of* the payments will be $28,000. ▪ That's *the sum total of* what I know about cars. [=that's all I know about cars]

[1]**sun** /ˈsʌn/ *noun, pl* **suns**
1 a ***the sun*** *also* ***the Sun*** **:** the star that the Earth moves around and that gives the Earth heat and light ▪ The rain has stopped and *the sun* is shining. ▪ *The sun* rises in the east and sets in the west. ▪ *the* rising/setting *sun* ▪ the warmth of *the sun's* rays **b** [*count*] **:** any star that has planets which move around it ▪ They dream of traveling to distant *suns*.
2 [*noncount*] **:** the heat or light produced by the sun **:** sunshine or sunlight ▪ The plant needs full *sun*. [=it should not be in the shade] ▪ Try to keep out of the *sun*. ▪ The cat lay basking in the *sun*. ▪ I couldn't see because ***the sun was in my eyes***. [=the bright light of the sun was shining directly in my eyes] ▪ We went to the beach to ***get/catch some sun***. [=to spend time in the sunlight]
in the sun ✧ If someone or something has a ***day/moment/time, etc., in the sun***, that person or thing is popular or gets a lot of attention during a period of time. ▪ Organic foods are having their *moment in the sun*. ▪ The singer is still waiting for his *day in the sun*.
make hay (while the sun shines) see HAY
place in the sun **:** a very good, successful, or desirable position ▪ After years of struggling as an unknown actor, he has finally found his/a *place in the sun*.
under the sun **:** in the world — used to emphasize the large number of things that are being mentioned ▪ There is nothing *under the sun* [=nothing at all] that we cannot do. ▪ We talked about everything *under the sun*. ▪ She called me every name *under the sun*.

[2]**sun** *verb* **suns; sunned; sun·ning :** to sit or lie in the light of the sun especially in order to make your skin darker [*no obj*] He is *sunning* [=*sunbathing*] by the pool. [+ *obj*] People *sunned* themselves on the hillside.

Sun. *abbr* Sunday

sun–baked *adj*
1 : made very hard and dry by the heat of the sun ▪ bricks made out of *sun-baked* mud
2 : receiving a lot of heat and light from the sun ▪ sandy, *sun-baked* beaches

sun·bathe /ˈsʌnˌbeɪð/ *verb* **-bathes; -bathed; -bath·ing** [*no obj*] **:** to sit or lie in the light of the sun especially in order to make your skin darker ▪ She *sunbathes* every afternoon. ▪ People were *sunbathing* on the beach.
– sun·bath·er /ˈsʌnˌbeɪðɚ/ *noun, pl* **-ers** [*count*]

sun·beam /ˈsʌnˌbiːm/ *noun, pl* **-beams** [*count*] **:** a ray of sunlight

sun·bed /ˈsʌnˌbɛd/ *noun, pl* **-beds** [*count*]
1 *chiefly Brit* **:** TANNING BED
2 *Brit* **:** CHAISE LONGUE

Sun·belt /ˈsʌnˌbɛlt/ *noun*
the Sunbelt **:** the southern and southwestern states of the U.S. ▪ She moved to *the Sunbelt*.

sun·block /ˈsʌnˌblɑːk/ *noun, pl* **-blocks** [*count, noncount*] **:** a lotion that you put on your skin to prevent sunburn by completely blocking out the sun's rays — compare SUNSCREEN

sun·burn /ˈsʌnˌbɚn/ *noun, pl* **-burns :** a condition in which your skin becomes sore and red from too much sunlight [*count*] He has a bad *sunburn*. [*noncount*] Use sunscreen to prevent *sunburn*.
– sunburn *verb* **-burns; -burned** /-ˌbɚnd/ *or* **-burnt** /-ˌbɚnt/; **-burn·ing** [*no obj*] *chiefly US* ▪ Her skin *sunburns* [=*burns*] easily. = She *sunburns* easily.

sunburned *also* **sunburnt** *adj*
1 : sore and red from too much sunlight **:** having a sunburn ▪ Her skin is badly *sunburned*. ▪ a *sunburned* nose
2 *Brit* **:** having attractive skin that has been turned darker by being in the sun ▪ a handsome, *sunburned* [=*tanned*] surfer

S

sun cream *noun, pl* ~ **creams** [*count, noncount*] *chiefly Brit* : a cream or lotion that you put on your skin to prevent sunburn

sun·dae /ˈsʌnˌdeɪ/ *noun, pl* **-daes** [*count*] : a dessert of ice cream that is topped with a sweet sauce, nuts, whipped cream, etc. ▪ a hot-fudge *sundae*

sundae

Sun·day /ˈsʌnˌdeɪ/ *noun, pl* **-days** : the day of the week between Saturday and Monday [*count*] She visited me last *Sunday*. ▪ What are you doing this/next *Sunday*? = What are you doing this coming *Sunday*? ▪ We go to church on *Sundays*. [=every Sunday] ▪ My birthday falls on a *Sunday* this year. ▪ (*Brit*) Next week I'll arrive on the Monday and leave on the *Sunday*. [*noncount*] Next week I'll arrive on Monday and leave on *Sunday*. ▪ I will leave on *Sunday* morning. ▪ the *Sunday* newspaper ▪ a *Sunday* brunch — abbr. *Sun.*

a month of Sundays see MONTH

– **Sundays** *adv* ▪ He works *Sundays*. [=he works every Sunday]

Sunday best *noun* [*noncount*] : your best clothing that you wear to church or on special occasions ▪ All the people at the concert were wearing their *Sunday best*.

Sunday school *noun* [*count, noncount*] : a school especially for children that is held on Sunday for religious education

sun·deck /ˈsʌnˌdɛk/ *noun, pl* **-decks** [*count*] : a deck on a ship or an outside area on a building where people can sit in the sun

sun·der /ˈsʌndɚ/ *verb* **-ders**; **-dered**; **-der·ing** [+ *obj*] *formal + literary* : to split apart (an organization, two people, etc.) especially in a violent way ▪ a family *sundered* by scandal — see also ASUNDER

sun·di·al /ˈsʌnˌdajəl/ *noun, pl* **-als** [*count*] : a device that is used to show the time of day by the position of the sun and that consists of a plate with markings like a clock and an object with a straight edge that casts a shadow onto the plate

sun·down /ˈsʌnˌdaʊn/ *noun* [*noncount*] *chiefly US* : the time when the sun goes below the horizon : SUNSET ▪ Passover ends tomorrow at *sundown*.

sun–drenched *adj, always used before a noun* : receiving a lot of heat and light from the sun ▪ *sun-drenched* beaches/islands

sun·dress /ˈsʌnˌdrɛs/ *noun, pl* **-dress·es** [*count*] : a dress that is worn in warm weather and that does not cover the arms, shoulders, or neck

sun–dried *adj, always used before a noun* : dried by the heat of the sun ▪ *sun-dried* tomatoes

sun·dries /ˈsʌndriz/ *noun* [*plural*] *formal* : various small things that are not mentioned specifically ▪ pins, needles, and other *sundries*

sun·dry /ˈsʌndri/ *adj, always used before a noun, formal* : made up of different things ▪ *sundry* [=*various*] items ▪ for *sundry* reasons

all and sundry *formal* : every person ▪ It was clear to *all and sundry* [=*everyone, everybody*] that something was wrong.

sun·fish /ˈsʌnˌfɪʃ/ *noun, pl* **-fish** [*count*] : a large fish with a round body that lives in the sea — see color picture on page C8

sun·flow·er /ˈsʌnˌflawɚ/ *noun, pl* **-ers** [*count*] : a tall plant that has very large yellow flowers and that produces seeds which can be eaten ▪ a row of *sunflowers* ▪ *sunflower* seeds/oil — see color picture on page C6

sung *past tense and past participle of* SING

sun·glass·es /ˈsʌnˌglæsəz, *Brit* ˈsʌnˌglɑːsəz/ *noun* [*plural*] : glasses with dark lenses that protect the eyes from the sun ▪ a pair of *sunglasses* — called also (*informal*) *shades*

sun god *noun, pl* ~ **gods** [*count*] : a god that represents the sun in various religions

sun hat *noun, pl* ~ **hats** [*count*] : a hat that you wear to protect your head and neck from the sun

sunk *past tense and past participle of* [1]SINK

sunk·en /ˈsʌŋkən/ *adj*

1 *always used before a noun* : completely covered with water : lying at the bottom of a sea, lake, etc. ▪ a *sunken* ship ▪ *sunken* treasure

2 : curving inward because of illness, age, etc. ▪ *sunken* [=*hollow*] cheeks ▪ Her eyes were *sunken* and lifeless.

3 *always used before a noun* : lying or built at a lower level than the surrounding area ▪ a *sunken* garden ▪ a *sunken* living room ▪ a *sunken* tub

sun–kissed *adj*

1 : SUNNY ▪ the *sun-kissed* beaches/shores of the Caribbean

2 *of a person's skin* : having an attractive color because of having been in the sun ▪ *sun-kissed* skin/faces ▪ a *sun-kissed* glow

sun·lamp /ˈsʌnˌlæmp/ *noun, pl* **-lamps** [*count*] : a special lamp that produces light similar to sunlight and that is used to make your skin darker or to treat illness

sun·less /ˈsʌnləs/ *adj* : having little light from the sun : not sunny ▪ a *sunless* room/day

sun·light /ˈsʌnˌlaɪt/ *noun* [*noncount*] : the light of the sun : SUNSHINE ▪ the early morning *sunlight* ▪ *Sunlight* streamed through the windows. ▪ Avoid exposure to (bright/direct) *sunlight*.

sun·lit /ˈsʌnˌlɪt/ *adj* : lighted by the sun ▪ a *sunlit* room

sun lounge *noun, pl* ~ **lounges** [*count*] *Brit* : SUNROOM

sun lounger *noun, pl* ~ **-ers** [*count*] *Brit* : a long chair that is used for sitting or lying outdoors

Sun·ni /ˈsuni/ *noun, pl* **-nis** *or* **-ni**

1 [*noncount*] : one of the two main branches of Islam — compare SHIA

2 [*count*] : a Muslim who is a member of the Sunni branch of Islam — compare SHIITE

– **Sunni** *adj, always used before a noun* ▪ the *Sunni* faith/tradition ▪ *Sunni* Muslims/Arabs

sun·ny /ˈsʌni/ *adj* **sun·ni·er**; **-est**

1 : having plenty of bright sunlight ▪ a *sunny* room/day ▪ *sunny* weather ▪ the *sunniest* parts of the country ▪ We found a *sunny* place/spot to have lunch. ▪ If it's *sunny* later, we can go to the park.

2 : cheerful and happy ▪ a *sunny* smile/disposition

sun·ny–side up /ˌsʌniˌsaɪdˈʌp/ *adj, chiefly US, of an egg* : fried on one side only ▪ "I'd like my eggs *sunny-side up*."

sun protection factor *noun* [*noncount*] : SPF

sun·rise /ˈsʌnˌraɪz/ *noun, pl* **-rises**

1 [*noncount*] : the time when the sun appears above the horizon in the morning : dawn or daybreak ▪ We were up before/at *sunrise*. ▪ We worked ***from sunrise to sunset***

2 : the colors that are in the sky when the sun slowly appears above the horizon [*count*] a beautiful *sunrise* ▪ We watched the *sunrise* from the beach. [*noncount*] the pink light of *sunrise*

sun·roof /ˈsʌnˌruːf/ *noun, pl* **-roofs** [*count*] : a part of the roof of a car or truck that can be opened to let air and light in — see picture at CAR; compare MOONROOF

sun·room /ˈsʌnˌruːm/ *noun, pl* **-rooms** [*count*] *US* : a room in a house that has a lot of windows and glass to let sunlight in — called also (*Brit*) *sun lounge*

sun·screen /ˈsʌnˌskriːn/ *noun, pl* **-screens** [*count, noncount*] : a lotion that you put on your skin to prevent sunburn by blocking out some of the sun's rays — compare SUNBLOCK

sun·set /ˈsʌnˌsɛt/ *noun, pl* **-sets**

1 [*noncount*] : the time when the sun goes below the horizon in the evening ▪ We arrived just before *sunset*. [=(*chiefly US*) *sundown*] ▪ Prayers begin at *sunset*. ▪ We worked ***from sunrise to sunset***

2 : the colors that are in the sky when the sun slowly goes below the horizon [*count*] a beautiful *sunset* [*noncount*] the golden light of *sunset*

sun·shade /ˈsʌnˌʃeɪd/ *noun, pl* **-shades** [*count*] : something (such as a parasol or awning) that blocks sunlight

sun·shine /ˈsʌnˌʃaɪn/ *noun* [*noncount*]

1 : the sun's light or rays : warmth and light from the sun ▪ Today's forecast calls for *sunshine*. ▪ Let's go out and enjoy the *sunshine*!

2 *informal* : a feeling of happiness ▪ She was the kind of person who brought *sunshine* into people's lives. ▪ She was a ***ray of sunshine*** for her patients. [=she made her patients feel happier and more cheerful]

3 *Brit, informal* — used as a form of address that can be either friendly or rude ▪ "Hey, *sunshine*. What are you doing?"

sun·shiny /ˈsʌnˌʃaɪni/ *adj, US*

1 : bright with the sun's rays ▪ a *sunshiny* [=*sunny*] day

2 : full of happiness ▪ *sunshiny* songs ▪ the children's *sunshiny* [=*happy*] faces

sun·spot /ˈsʌnˌspɑːt/ *noun, pl* **-spots** [*count*] *astronomy* : a dark spot that sometimes appears on the surface of the sun

S

sun·stroke /ˈsʌn,stroʊk/ *noun* [*noncount*] *medical* **:** a serious condition that happens when someone has been in the sun too long and that causes a person to stop sweating, have a very high body temperature, and become exhausted or unconscious — compare HEATSTROKE

sun·tan /ˈsʌn,tæn/ *noun, pl* **-tans** [*count*] **:** a browning of the skin that is caused by the sun's rays ▪ She has a nice *suntan.* [=*tan*] ▪ *suntan* lotion
– **sun·tanned** /ˈsʌn,tænd/ *adj* [*more* ~; *most* ~] ▪ *suntanned* bodies/faces – **sun·tan·ning** /ˈsʌn,tænɪŋ/ *noun* [*noncount*]

sun·up /ˈsʌn,ʌp/ *noun* [*noncount*] *chiefly US* **:** SUNRISE ▪ We will meet at *sunup.*

sun worshipper *noun, pl* ~ **-pers** [*count*] *informal* **:** someone who enjoys lying in the sun to get a suntan

[1]**sup** /ˈsʌp/ *verb* **sups; supped; sup·ping** [*no obj*] *old-fashioned + literary* **:** to eat dinner **:** DINE ▪ journalists *supping* with politicians ▪ They *supped* on local delicacies. — compare [2]SUP

[2]**sup** *verb* **sups; supped; supping** [+ *obj*] *Brit* **:** to drink (a liquid) especially in small amounts ▪ He *supped* [=*sipped*] a glass of wine while waiting for his meal. — compare [1]SUP

[1]**su·per** /ˈsuːpɚ/ *adj, informal* **:** extremely good ▪ She's a *super* cook. ▪ We had a *super* time. ▪ The party was *super.* ▪ "Yes, I'd love to come." "*Super!* I'll see you later."

[2]**super** *adv, US, informal* **:** very or extremely ▪ She's *super* nice/rich/smart. ▪ a *super* fast car

[3]**super** *noun, pl* **-pers** [*count*] *US, informal* **:** SUPERINTENDENT 3

super- *prefix*
1 : bigger, better, or more important than others of the same kind ▪ *super*human
2 : superior in position or rank ▪ a military *super*power

su·per·abun·dance /,suːpɚrəˈbʌndəns/ *noun* [*singular*] *formal* **:** a great or excessive amount *of* something ▪ a *superabundance of* wealth
– **su·per·abun·dant** /,suːpɚrəˈbʌndənt/ *adj* ▪ a *superabundant* supply

su·per·an·nu·at·ed /,suːpɚˈænjə,weɪtəd/ *adj, formal* **:** old and therefore no longer very effective or useful ▪ a *superannuated* opera star ▪ *superannuated* [=*outdated*] software

su·per·an·nu·a·tion /,suːpɚ,ænjəˈweɪʃən/ *noun* [*noncount*] *Brit* **:** a type of pension that both the employee and the employer pay for ▪ an improved *superannuation* scheme

su·perb /sʊˈpɚb/ *adj* **:** extremely good **:** excellent or brilliant in a very noticeable way ▪ a *superb* example ▪ wines of *superb* quality ▪ They've done a *superb* job. ▪ The performance was absolutely *superb.*
– **su·perb·ly** *adv* ▪ a *superbly* gifted writer ▪ The defense played *superbly.*

Super Bowl *service mark* — used for the annual championship game of the National Football League

su·per·charged /ˈsuːpɚ,ʧɑɚʤd/ *adj*
1 : supplied with air or fuel at a higher pressure than normal to increase power ▪ a *supercharged* engine
2 *informal* **:** filled with energy, tension, or emotion ▪ a *supercharged* atmosphere

su·per·cil·ious /,suːpɚˈsɪlijəs/ *adj* [*more* ~; *most* ~] *formal + disapproving* **:** having or showing the proud and unpleasant attitude of people who think that they are better or more important than other people ▪ a *supercilious* professor ▪ a *supercilious* tone/attitude ▪ *supercilious* behavior
– **su·per·cil·ious·ly** *adv* ▪ He glanced at her and smiled *superciliously.* – **su·per·cil·ious·ness** *noun* [*noncount*]

su·per·com·put·er /ˈsuːpɚkəm,pjuːtɚ/ *noun, pl* **-ers** [*count*] **:** a large and very fast computer

su·per·con·duc·tiv·i·ty /,suːpɚ,kɑː,n,dʌkˈtɪvəti/ *noun* [*noncount*] *technical* **:** the ability of something (such as a metal) to allow electricity to flow through it easily especially at very low temperatures

su·per·con·duc·tor /,suːpɚkənˈdʌktɚ/ *noun, pl* **-tors** [*count*] *technical* **:** a material or object that allows electricity to flow through it easily at very low temperatures

su·per·ego /,suːpɚˈiːgoʊ/ *noun, pl* **-egos** [*count*] *psychology* **:** a part of a person's mind that relates to attitudes about what is right and wrong and to feelings of guilt — compare EGO, ID

su·per·fi·cial /,suːpɚˈfɪʃəl/ *adj* [*more* ~; *most* ~]
1 : concerned only with what is obvious or apparent **:** not thorough or complete ▪ a *superficial* analysis of the results/data ▪ They had a *superficial* knowledge/understanding of the topic. ▪ These *superficial* changes/solutions don't address the underlying problem.
2 a : affecting only the outer part or surface of something **:** not deep or serious ▪ *superficial* wounds/cuts ▪ The storm only caused *superficial* damage to the building. **b :** lying close to the surface ▪ *superficial* veins
3 — used to describe a quality, characteristic, etc., that can be seen in the outward appearance or manner of something or someone but that is not deep or genuine ▪ Despite a *superficial* resemblance, the paintings are by two different artists. ▪ These similarities/differences are only *superficial.* ▪ Don't be deceived by his *superficial* charm. ▪ ***On a superficial level***, his theory works, but the facts don't support it.
4 *disapproving* **:** not caring about or involving important matters or deep emotions ▪ He thinks she's vain and *superficial.* [=*shallow*] ▪ I'm not interested in *superficial* relationships.
– **su·per·fi·ci·al·i·ty** /,suːpɚ,fɪʃiˈæləti/ *noun* [*noncount*] ▪ the *superficiality* of pop culture – **su·per·fi·cial·ly** /,suːpɚˈfɪʃəli/ *adv* ▪ *Superficially*, at least, the two paintings are similar.

su·per·fine /,suːpɚˈfaɪn/ *adj, chiefly US* **:** extremely fine: such as **a :** extremely thin ▪ *superfine* wire **b :** made up of extremely small pieces ▪ *superfine* sugar **c :** of very high quality ▪ *superfine* wool

su·per·flu·i·ty /,suːpɚˈfluːwəti/ *noun* [*singular*] *formal* **:** more of something than is needed ▪ a *superfluity* of volunteers

su·per·flu·ous /sʊˈpɚfluwəs/ *adj* [*more* ~; *most* ~] *formal* **:** beyond what is needed **:** not necessary ▪ a *superfluous* word/detail ▪ Further discussion seemed *superfluous.*
– **su·per·flu·ous·ly** *adv*

su·per·glue /ˈsuːpɚ,gluː/ *noun* [*noncount*] **:** a very strong glue

su·per·grass /ˈsuːpɚ,græs, *Brit* ˈsuːpə,grɑːs/ *noun, pl* **-grass·es** [*count*] *Brit, informal* **:** a criminal who gives information to the police about a large number of other criminals

su·per·he·ro /ˈsuːpɚ,hiroʊ/ *noun, pl* **-roes** [*count*]
1 : a fictional character who has amazing powers (such as the ability to fly) ▪ comic-book *superheroes*
2 : a very heroic person ▪ The people who do this dangerous work are real-life *superheroes* who deserve our gratitude.

su·per·high·way /,suːpɚˈhaɪ,weɪ/ *noun, pl* **-ways** [*count*] *US* **:** a large and wide highway used for traveling at high speeds over long distances

su·per·hu·man /,suːpɚˈhjuːmən/ *adj* **:** greater than normal human power, size, or ability ▪ The character in the film acquires *superhuman* powers. ▪ *superhuman* strength/courage ▪ tales of *superhuman* feats ▪ It will take a *superhuman* effort for them to win the championship.

su·per·im·pose /,suːpɚrɪmˈpoʊz/ *verb* **-pos·es; -posed; -pos·ing** [+ *obj*] **:** to place or lay (something) over something else ▪ A triangle *superimposed* on an inverted triangle forms a six-pointed star. ▪ *superimposed* images — often used figuratively ▪ a Shakespearean play *superimposed* upon a modern setting ▪ We should not try to *superimpose* our values on other cultures. [=should not try to make other cultures accept/adopt our values]
– **su·per·im·po·si·tion** /,suːpɚ,ɪmpəˈzɪʃən/ *noun* [*noncount*] ▪ the *superimposition* of two images

su·per·in·tend /,suːpɚrɪnˈtɛnd/ *verb* **-tends; -tend·ed; -tend·ing** [+ *obj*] *formal* **:** to direct or manage (something, such as a project or activity) ▪ A licensed contractor will *superintend* [=*supervise*] the work.
– **su·per·in·ten·dence** /,suːpɚnˈtɛndəns/ *noun* [*noncount*] ▪ Decisions will be made under the *superintendence* [=*supervision*] of the board of directors.

su·per·in·ten·dent /,suːpɚnˈtɛndənt/ *noun, pl* **-dents** [*count*]
1 : a person who directs or manages a place, department, organization, etc. ▪ (*US*) Our district *superintendent* (of schools) is retiring soon. ▪ a park *superintendent*
2 : a high rank in a police department or a person who has this rank
3 *US* **:** a person who is in charge of cleaning, maintaining, and repairing a building — called also (*informal*) *super*

[1]**su·pe·ri·or** /sʊˈpirijɚ/ *adj*
1 a : of high quality **:** high or higher in quality ▪ *superior* products/results ▪ a *superior* wine = a wine of *superior* quality ▪ This new model offers *superior* performance. — often + *to* ▪ The new model is (vastly/far) *superior to* the old one. **b**

: great or greater in amount, number, or degree • her *superior* strength/intelligence • The small army was overwhelmed by *superior* numbers.

2 *disapproving* **a :** better than other people • He only helps us because it makes him feel *superior*. — often + *to* • He thinks he's *superior to* everyone else. **b :** having or showing the attitude of people who think that they are better or more important than other people : ARROGANT • a *superior* manner/tone

3 *always used before a noun* : high or higher in rank • Report to your *superior* officer. • The verdict was reversed by a *superior* court. — compare SUBORDINATE

²superior *noun, pl* **-ors** [*count*] : a person of higher rank or status than another • His *superior* gave him an excellent evaluation. • You should report any problems to your ***immediate superior***. — compare SUBORDINATE; see also MOTHER SUPERIOR

su·pe·ri·or·i·ty /sʊˌpiriˈorəti/ *noun* [*noncount*]

1 : the quality or state of being high or higher in quality — often + *of* or *over* • The *superiority of* our product is obvious. • one product's *superiority over* another

2 : the belief that you are better than other people • His success has given him a false sense of *superiority*. • an irritating ***air of superiority*** [=an arrogant way of behaving]

3 : the quality or state of being larger, stronger, etc., than others • the country's technological/economic *superiority* • To win this war, we must achieve ***air superiority***. [=we must have a larger/better air force than our enemies]

¹su·per·la·tive /sʊˈpɚlətɪv/ *adj*

1 *grammar* : of or relating to the form of an adjective or adverb that is used to indicate the greatest degree of a particular quality • The *superlative* form of "nice" is "nicest"; the *superlative* form of "bad" is "worst"; the *superlative* form of "interesting" is "most interesting." — compare COMPARATIVE

2 *somewhat formal* : of very high quality • *superlative* [=*excellent*] work • a *superlative* performance

— **su·per·la·tive·ly** *adv* • He's *superlatively* qualified. • They performed *superlatively* (well).

²superlative *noun, pl* **-tives** [*count*] *grammar* : the form of an adjective or adverb that is used to indicate the greatest degree of a particular quality : the superlative form of an adjective or adverb • "Simplest" is the *superlative* of "simple." — compare COMPARATIVE

su·per·man /ˈsuːpɚˌmæn/ *noun, pl* **-men** /-ˌmɛn/ [*count*] : a man who is very strong, successful, etc. — compare SUPERWOMAN

su·per·mar·ket /ˈsuːpɚˌmɑɚkət/ *noun, pl* **-kets** [*count*] : a store where customers can buy a variety of foods and usually household items • I made a quick trip to the *supermarket*. [=(*chiefly US*) *grocery store*] • a *supermarket* chain • *supermarket* coupons — compare SUPERSTORE

su·per·mod·el /ˈsuːpɚˌmɑːdl/ *noun, pl* **-els** [*count*] : a very famous and successful fashion model

su·per·mom /ˈsuːpɚˌmɑːm/ *noun, pl* **-moms** [*count*] *US, informal* : a woman who raises a child and takes care of a home while also having a full-time job

su·per·nat·u·ral /ˌsuːpɚˈnætʃərəl/ *adj* : unable to be explained by science or the laws of nature : of, relating to, or seeming to come from magic, a god, etc. • *supernatural* powers/phenomena/beings

the supernatural : things that cannot be explained by science and seem to involve ghosts, spirits, magic, etc. • their belief in *the supernatural*

su·per·no·va /ˌsuːpɚˈnoʊvə/ *noun, pl* **-vas** *or* **-vae** /-ˈnoʊvi/ [*count*] *astronomy* : the explosion of a star that causes the star to become extremely bright

su·per·pow·er /ˈsuːpɚˌpawɚ/ *noun, pl* **-ers** [*count*] : an extremely powerful nation • economic/military *superpowers*

su·per·script /ˈsuːpɚˌskrɪpt/ *noun, pl* **-scripts** [*count*] : a symbol (such as a number or letter) written above and immediately to the left or right of another character

— **superscript** *adj* • *superscript* characters/letters

su·per·sede /ˌsuːpɚˈsiːd/ *verb* **-sedes; -sed·ed; -sed·ing** [+ *obj*] : to take the place of (someone or something that is old, no longer useful, etc.) : to replace (someone or something) • This edition *supersedes* the previous one. • Former stars were being *superseded* by younger actors.

su·per·size /ˈsuːpɚˌsaɪz/ *verb* **-siz·es; -sized; -siz·ing** [+ *obj*] : to make (something, such as a serving of food in a fast food restaurant) very large • "I'll have the combo meal." "Would you like to *supersize* it?"

— **supersize** *or* **supersized** *adj, always used before a noun* • a *supersize* meal/drink • *supersized* houses/cars

su·per·son·ic /ˌsuːpɚˈsɑːnɪk/ *adj* : faster than the speed of sound • a *supersonic* airplane

— **su·per·son·i·cal·ly** /ˌsuːpɚˈsɑːnɪkli/ *adv*

su·per·star /ˈsuːpɚˌstɑɚ/ *noun, pl* **-stars** [*count*] : an extremely famous and successful performer, athlete, etc. • a Hollywood *superstar* • a football *superstar*

su·per·sti·tion /ˌsuːpɚˈstɪʃən/ *noun, pl* **-tions** : a belief or way of behaving that is based on fear of the unknown and faith in magic or luck : a belief that certain events or things will bring good or bad luck [*count*] It is a common *superstition* that a black cat crossing your path is bad luck. [*noncount*] tales of *superstition*, witchcraft, and magic

su·per·sti·tious /ˌsuːpɚˈstɪʃəs/ *adj* [*more* ~; *most* ~] : of, relating to, or influenced by superstition • *superstitious* practices/beliefs • He's very *superstitious* and won't pitch without his lucky mitt.

— **su·per·sti·tious·ly** *adv*

su·per·store /ˈsuːpɚˌstoɚ/ *noun, pl* **-stores** [*count*] : a very large store that sells a wide variety of goods • an electronics *superstore* [=*megastore*] — compare SUPERMARKET

su·per·struc·ture /ˈsuːpɚˌstrʌktʃɚ/ *noun, pl* **-tures** [*count*] : the part of a structure (such as a ship or bridge) that is above the lowest part — compare SUBSTRUCTURE

su·per·tank·er /ˈsuːpɚˌtæŋkɚ/ *noun, pl* **-ers** [*count*] : a very large ship that has tanks for carrying large amounts of liquid • an oil *supertanker*

su·per·vene /ˌsuːpɚˈviːn/ *verb* **-venes; -vened; -ven·ing** [*no obj*] *formal* : to happen unexpectedly in a way that interrupts, stops, or greatly changes an existing situation • a *supervening* event • They had a quiet, happy life until the war *supervened*.

su·per·vise /ˈsuːpɚˌvaɪz/ *verb* **-vis·es; -vised; -vis·ing** [+ *obj*] : to be in charge of (someone or something) : to watch and direct (someone or something) • The builder *supervised* the construction of the house. • She *supervises* a staff of 30 workers. • a *supervised* study period

su·per·vi·sion /ˌsuːpɚˈvɪʒən/ *noun* [*noncount*] : the action or process of watching and directing what someone does or how something is done : the action or process of supervising someone or something • Young children need constant *supervision*. • Parental *supervision* is recommended. • She's responsible for the *supervision* of a large staff. • The medication should be taken ***under*** a doctor's ***supervision***. = The medication should be taken ***under the supervision of*** a doctor.

su·per·vi·sor /ˈsuːpɚˌvaɪzɚ/ *noun, pl* **-sors** [*count*] : a person who supervises someone or something • The *supervisor* fired him after he showed up at work drunk. • If you have a problem, go to your *supervisor*. • an office/plant *supervisor*

— **su·per·vi·so·ry** /ˌsuːpɚˈvaɪzəri/ *adj* • He took on a *supervisory* role in the company. • *supervisory* personnel • candidates with *supervisory* experience

su·per·wom·an /ˈsuːpɚˌwʊmən/ *noun, pl* **-wom·en** /-ˌwɪmən/ [*count*] : a woman who is very strong, successful, etc.; *especially* : a woman who has both a successful career and a family — compare SUPERMAN

su·pine /ˈsuːˌpaɪn/ *adj, formal*

1 : lying on your back with your face upward • a *supine* position • He was lying *supine* on the couch. — compare PRONE

2 *disapproving* : willing to be controlled by others : weak or passive • a *supine* attitude • a *supine* legislature that is afraid to take action

sup·per /ˈsʌpɚ/ *noun, pl* **-pers**

1 : the evening meal — used especially to refer to an informal meal that you eat at home [*count*] I always enjoyed our Sunday night *suppers*. [*noncount*] It's almost time for *supper*. • We had *supper* together. • We took a walk after *supper*. • I had too much wine at *supper*. • He didn't come home for *supper*.

2 [*count*] *chiefly US* : a social event especially for raising money that takes place in the evening and includes a meal • a church *supper*

3 [*count, noncount*] *chiefly Brit* : a light meal or snack that is eaten late in the evening

sup·per·time /ˈsʌpɚˌtaɪm/ *noun, pl* **-times** : the usual time for supper [*noncount*] The doorbell rang right at *suppertime*. [*count*] When is your *suppertime*?

sup·plant /səˈplænt/ *verb* **-plants; -plant·ed; -plant·ing** [+ *obj*] : to take the place of (someone or something that is old or no longer used or accepted) • DVDs have *supplanted* videos. — often used as *(be) supplanted* • Videos have *been* *supplanted* by DVDs. • Older workers are *being supplanted* by recent college graduates.

sup·ple /ˈsʌpəl/ *adj* **sup·pler** /ˈsʌpəlɚ/; **-plest** /-pələst/ [*also more ~; most ~*]
1 *of a body or body part* **:** able to bend or twist easily • a *supple* body • her long, *supple* limbs • Stretching helped to keep him *supple.* [=*limber*]
2 : soft and able to bend or fold easily • *supple* leather/skin — opposite STIFF
– sup·ple·ness /ˈsʌpəlnəs/ *noun* [*noncount*]

¹sup·ple·ment /ˈsʌpləmənt/ *noun, pl* **-ments** [*count*]
1 : something that is added to something else in order to make it complete • dietary/vitamin *supplements*
2 : an extra part that is added to a book or newspaper • an advertising/literary *supplement* • the *supplement* to the encyclopedia
3 *Brit* **:** an amount of money that must be paid in addition to the regular price • First-class accommodation is available for a *supplement.*

²sup·ple·ment /ˈsʌpləˌmɛnt/ *verb* **-ments; -ment·ed; -ment·ing** [+ *obj*] **:** to add something to (something) in order to make it complete • He sells his paintings to *supplement* his income. = He *supplements* his income by selling his paintings. • She began *supplementing* her diet with vitamins.
– sup·ple·men·ta·tion /ˌsʌpləˌmɛnˈteɪʃən/ *noun* [*noncount*]

sup·ple·men·tal /ˌsʌpləˈmɛntl/ *adj, chiefly US* **:** added to something else to make it complete • She receives a *supplemental* income every month from the government. • *supplemental* information

sup·ple·men·ta·ry /ˌsʌpləˈmɛntəri/ *adj* **:** SUPPLEMENTAL • a list of *supplementary* material/readings for the class

sup·pli·ant /ˈsʌplijənt/ *noun, pl* **-ants** [*count*] *formal* **:** SUPPLICANT
– suppliant *adj* [*more ~; most ~*] • a *suppliant* tone

sup·pli·cant /ˈsʌplɪkənt/ *noun, pl* **-cants** [*count*] *formal* **:** a person who asks for something in a respectful way from a powerful person or God • a humble *supplicant*

sup·pli·ca·tion /ˌsʌpləˈkeɪʃən/ *noun, pl* **-tions** *formal* **:** an act of asking for something in a respectful way [*count*] their prayers and *supplications* to God [*noncount*] They knelt ***in supplication*** before the king.

sup·pli·er /səˈplajɚ/ *noun, pl* **-ers** [*count*] **:** a person or company that supplies goods or services • food/drug/paper *suppliers* • They are the biggest *supplier* of books in the area.

¹sup·ply /səˈplaɪ/ *noun, pl* **-plies**
1 : the amount of something that is available to be used [*count*] the nation's food/oil *supply* • adequate/sufficient *supplies* of fresh water • He bought a month's *supply* of cigarettes. [*noncount*] Doctors are ***in short supply.*** [=there are not enough doctors] — see also MONEY SUPPLY
2 ***supplies*** [*plural*] **:** things (such as food, equipment, fuel, etc.) that are needed for a particular purpose and that will be used by a particular person or group • They took a month's worth of *supplies* on the camping trip. • The town is in need of basic medical *supplies.* • a store that sells art/office/cleaning *supplies*
3 [*noncount*] **:** the process or system by which something is provided to a person, place, etc. • The state is trying to disrupt the *supply* of illegal drugs. • The storm interrupted the town's electricity *supply.*
4 [*noncount*] **:** the quantities of goods or services that are offered for sale at a particular time or at one price • When demand increases, will *supply* increase, too? — see also SUPPLY AND DEMAND

²supply *verb* **-plies; -plied; -ply·ing** [+ *obj*] **:** to make (something) available to be used **:** to provide someone or something with (something that is needed or wanted) • The company *supplied* the necessary money. • You'll have to *supply* your own food. — often + *to* • He *supplied* the information *to* us. — often + *with* • The company *supplied* us *with* the necessary money. • He kept us *supplied with* the latest news.

supply and demand *noun* [*noncount*] **:** the amount of goods and services that are available for people to buy compared to the amount of goods and services that people want to buy • If the company produces less of a product than the public wants, the ***law of supply and demand*** says that the company can charge more for the product.

supply line *noun, pl* **~ lines** [*count*] **:** the route that is used to deliver food, equipment, etc., to soldiers during a war • enemy *supply lines*

supply–side economics *noun* [*noncount*] *economics* **:** a theory that reducing taxes especially for rich people will lead to an improved economy

supply teacher *noun, pl* **~ -ers** [*count*] *Brit* **:** SUBSTITUTE TEACHER

¹sup·port /səˈpoɚt/ *verb* **-ports; -port·ed; -port·ing** [+ *obj*]
1 a : to agree with or approve of (someone or something) • I completely *support* your decision to stay. • She no longer *supports* the war. • The senator says that he *supports* the proposed legislation. • Which presidential candidate do you *support?* • The study is *supported* by the American Medical Association. **b :** to show that you approve of (someone or something) by doing something • The country's citizens were asked to *support* the war effort. • Her friends *supported* her by signing her petition.
2 a : to give help or assistance to (someone or something) • The charity *supports* needy families. • Bombers were called in to *support* the ground troops. **b :** to provide what is needed by (someone or something) • The planet's atmosphere cannot *support* human life. • This computer does not *support* that software. [=you cannot use that software on this computer] **c :** to provide the money that is needed by or for (someone or something) • He works two jobs to *support* his family. • She has two children to *support.* • We *support* the charity by making annual donations. • The foundation *supports* cancer research. • The theater is *supported* by donations. • She sold illegal drugs to *support* her own drug habit.
3 : to hold (something or someone) up **:** to stop (something or someone) from falling down • Thick cables help *support* the bridge. • The roof is *supported* by thick wooden pillars throughout the house. • She *supported* herself on my arm as we walked together. • He *supports* himself with a cane.
4 : to provide evidence for (something) **:** to help show that (something) is true • His alibi is *supported* by his neighbors. • The results of the study *support* her theory. • Their claims are not *supported* by the evidence.
5 *chiefly Brit* **:** to be a fan of (a sports team) • She *supports* both teams.

²support *noun, pl* **-ports**
1 [*noncount*] **:** the act of showing that you believe that someone or something is good or acceptable **:** approval of someone or something • The proposal has had little public *support.* [=few people have supported the proposal] • The team gets a lot of *support* from its fans. • The candidate is gaining *support* among young voters. [=many more young voters say they will vote for the candidate] — often + *for* • There isn't much *support for* the proposal. • You can show your *support for* our cause by wearing one of these red ribbons.
2 [*noncount*] **a :** the act of helping someone by giving love, encouragement, etc. • I'd like to thank my parents for all of their love and *support* over the years. • He depended on his wife for emotional *support.* • We all came along to give her ***moral support.*** [=to give her encouragement] **b :** help that is given in the form of money or other valuable things • He applied for financial *support* from the state. • They had no ***means of support*** [=source of income] after they lost their farm. — see also CHILD SUPPORT **c :** the act of helping someone by giving information or services • She was having trouble connecting to the Internet, so she called ***technical/tech support*** [=a department or person that helps people with computer problems] for assistance. • the company's friendly ***support staff***
3 a [*count*] **:** something that holds a person or thing up and stops that person or thing from falling down • Inspectors found that some of the bridge's *supports* were weak. • She used my arm as a *support* and limped to the chair. **b** [*noncount*] **:** the act of holding something up • These sneakers are designed to give your feet extra *support.* — often used after *for* • He grabbed the railing *for support.*
4 [*noncount*] **:** evidence which shows that something is true • The results of the study give further *support* to the hypothesis. • The police continue to gather *support* for their case.
in support of **1 :** in a way that shows approval of (something) **:** in favor of (something) • A majority voted *in support of* the bill. **2 :** in order to support (something) • He presented evidence *in support of* his hypothesis. [=evidence that helps to prove his hypothesis] • The band is touring *in support of* their latest album. [=to help promote their latest album]
– see also LIFE SUPPORT

sup·port·er /səˈpoɚtɚ/ *noun, pl* **-ers** [*count*]
1 : a person who supports an idea, a politician, a cause, etc. • the proposal's *supporters* • the President's *supporters* • a *supporter* of the Independent party

S

2 : a fan of a sports team ▪ the team's loyal *supporters* – see also ATHLETIC SUPPORTER

support group *noun, pl* ~ **groups** [*count*] **:** a group of people who have similar experiences and concerns and who meet in order to provide emotional help, advice, and encouragement for one another ▪ He joined an alcoholics' *support group*.

supporting *adj, always used before a noun*
1 : having a less important part than the main actor or actress ▪ She won the award for best *supporting* actress. ▪ He has a *supporting* role in the movie.
2 : holding something up **:** keeping something from falling down ▪ the house's *supporting* beams/walls
3 : showing that something is true ▪ There is no *supporting* evidence for her claim. [=there is no evidence that supports her claim]
– see also SELF-SUPPORTING

sup·port·ive /sə'poətɪv/ *adj* [*more* ~; *most* ~] **:** giving help or encouragement to someone ▪ She has very *supportive* parents. ▪ Try to be more *supportive* of your teammates.

support system *noun, pl* ~ **-tems** [*count*] **:** a group of people who give someone help, money, encouragement, etc. ▪ students who have good *support systems* at home

sup·pose /sə'poʊz/ *verb* **-pos·es; -posed; -pos·ing** [+ *obj*]
1 : to think of (something) as happening or being true in order to imagine what might happen ▪ *Suppose* a fire broke out. How would we escape? ▪ Just *suppose* for a moment that you agreed with me. ▪ *Supposing* he refuses to help, what do we do then?
2 a : to believe (something) to be true ▪ The renovations will cost much more than we originally *supposed*. ▪ Who do you *suppose* [=*think*] will win? **b :** to believe (something) to be possible — usually used following the pronoun *I* ▪ *I suppose* [=(*chiefly US*) *I guess*] you're right. ▪ *I suppose* that could happen, but it's not likely. ▪ You could say, *I suppose*, that he was not ready for marriage. ▪ "Do you *suppose* it's true?" "Yes, *I suppose* it is." ✧ In responding to a question, the phrase ***I suppose (so)*** is used as a way of agreeing or saying "yes" when you are not certain or not very excited or interested. ▪ "The pink one is prettier, isn't it?" "*I suppose*." ▪ "Do you want to come along?" "*I suppose so*." ✧ The phrase ***I suppose not*** is used as an informal way of agreeing with a negative statement or of saying "no." ▪ "That wasn't a very smart thing to do, was it?" "*I suppose not*."
3 — used to ask a question in a polite way ▪ Do you *suppose* you could help me make dinner? = ***I don't suppose*** you could help me make dinner? [=could you help me make dinner?] ▪ *I don't suppose* you found the keys, did you? [=did you find the keys?]
be supposed **1 a :** to be expected *to do* something ▪ They *are supposed to arrive* tomorrow. ▪ She *was supposed to be* here an hour ago. ▪ The movie *was supposed to earn* a lot of money at the box office, but it didn't. **b :** to be intended or expected *to be* (something) ▪ The party *was supposed to be* a surprise. **c** — used to show that you are angry or offended by something; followed by *to* + *verb* ▪ *Was* that *supposed to be* funny? I thought it was quite rude. ▪ "Well, you've done it again." "***What's that supposed to mean***?" [=what do you mean by that comment?] **2 a** — used to say what someone should do; followed by *to* + *verb* ▪ You *are supposed to listen* to your parents. ▪ I'*m supposed to clean* my room before I go outside. ▪ What *are we supposed to do* [=what should/can we do] in a situation like this? ▪ Do what you'*re supposed to*. **b** — used to say what someone is allowed to do; followed by *to* + *verb* ▪ We *were* not *supposed to leave* the room. ▪ *Are* you *supposed to be* here after the building has closed? **3** — used to indicate what people say about someone or something; followed by *to* + *verb* ▪ She *is supposed to be* the best doctor in town. [=people say that she's the best doctor in town] ▪ That breed of dog *is supposed to be* good with kids. ▪ The word *is supposed to be* derived from Latin.

sup·posed /sə'poʊzəd/ *adj, always used before a noun* **:** claimed to be true or real — used to say that a particular description is probably not true or real even though many people believe that it is ▪ a *supposed* cure for cancer ▪ *supposed* experts

sup·pos·ed·ly /sə'poʊzədli/ *adv* **:** according to what someone has said or what is generally believed to be true or real ▪ These detergents are *supposedly* better for the environment. ▪ He has *supposedly* changed since then, but I'm doubtful that he really has. ▪ *Supposedly*, she left a message on my answering machine. I never actually got it.

sup·po·si·tion /ˌsʌpə'zɪʃən/ *noun, pl* **-tions :** an idea or theory that you believe is true even though you do not have proof [*count*] an idle *supposition* [=*assumption*] ▪ a *supposition* that proved correct ▪ Her decision was made ***on the supposition that*** we would all agree. [=when she made her decision she supposed/assumed that we would all agree] [*noncount*] This is just idle *supposition*.

sup·pos·i·to·ry /sə'pɑːzəˌtori, *Brit* sə'pɒzətri/ *noun, pl* **-ries** [*count*] *medical* **:** a small piece of solid medicine that is placed in the rectum or vagina and left there to dissolve

sup·press /sə'prɛs/ *verb* **-press·es; -pressed; -press·ing** [+ *obj*]
1 : to end or stop (something) by force ▪ Political dissent was brutally *suppressed*. ▪ *suppressing* a rebellion
2 : to keep (something) secret **:** to not allow people to know about or see (something) ▪ The governor tried to *suppress* the news. ▪ The judge may decide to *suppress* the evidence. [=to not allow the evidence to be used at a trial] ▪ She ordered the magazine (to be) *suppressed*.
3 a : to not allow yourself to feel, show, or be affected by (an emotion) ▪ He struggled to *suppress* his feelings of jealousy. ▪ She could not *suppress* her anger. ▪ I had to *suppress* an urge to tell him what I really thought. **b :** to stop yourself from doing something (such as smiling, coughing, or laughing) that might bother other people ▪ I found it hard to *suppress* a smile [=to keep myself from smiling] when he told me about what happened. ▪ She tried to *suppress* a cough/laugh. [=she tried not to cough/laugh]
4 : to slow or stop the growth, development, or normal functioning of (something) ▪ a drug that *suppresses* the immune system ▪ The pill works by *suppressing* your appetite.
– sup·pres·sion /sə'prɛʃən/ *noun* [*noncount*] ▪ political *suppression* ▪ the *suppression* of evidence ▪ the *suppression* of your emotions ▪ appetite *suppression*

sup·pres·sant /sə'prɛsn̩t/ *noun, pl* **-sants** [*count*] **:** a drug that prevents or controls something ▪ cough *suppressants* ▪ an appetite *suppressant*

su·pra·na·tion·al /ˌsuːprə'næʃənl/ *adj, formal* **:** involving more than one country ▪ a *supranational* treaty

su·prem·a·cist /sə'prɛməsɪst/ *noun, pl* **-cists** [*count*] **:** a person who believes that one group of people is better than all other groups and should have control over them ▪ racial/religious/cultural *supremacists* ▪ a *supremacist* group/organization — see also WHITE SUPREMACIST

su·prem·a·cy /sə'prɛməsi/ *noun* [*noncount*] **:** the quality or state of having more power, authority, or status than anyone else **:** the state of being supreme ▪ military/economic *supremacy* ▪ a battle/struggle for *supremacy*

su·preme /sə'priːm/ *adj*
1 : highest in rank or authority ▪ NATO's *supreme* commander ▪ She ***reigns supreme*** [=is the best] in the world of tennis.
2 : highest in degree or quality **:** greatest or highest possible ▪ The board has *supreme* authority over such issues. ▪ She has an air of *supreme* confidence about her. ▪ the *supreme* example of what not to do ▪ a problem of *supreme* importance ▪ It's a matter of *supreme* indifference to her. ▪ He made ***the supreme sacrifice*** [=he died] for his country.
– su·preme·ly *adv* ▪ *supremely* [=*extremely*] confident/indifferent/imaginative ▪ *supremely* boring/unimportant

Supreme Being *noun*
the Supreme Being *literary* **:** GOD 1

supreme court *or* **Supreme Court** *noun* [*singular*] **:** the highest court of law in a country or U.S. state ▪ *Supreme Court* justices/decisions ▪ The case went all the way to ***the (U.S.) Supreme Court***.

su·pre·mo /sə'priːmoʊ/ *noun, pl* **-mos** [*count*] *Brit, informal* **:** a person who has the most authority or power in a particular activity ▪ drug *supremos* ▪ a banking *supremo*

Supt. (*US*) *or chiefly Brit* **Supt** *abbr* superintendent

sur·charge /'sɚˌʧɑɚʤ/ *noun, pl* **-charg·es** [*count*] **:** an amount of money that must be paid in addition to the regular price ▪ The airline has added a $20 fuel *surcharge* on all international flights.

[1]sure /'ʃɚ, *Brit* 'ʃɔː/ *adj* **sur·er; -est** [*also more* ~; *most* ~]
1 *not used before a noun* **:** not having any doubt about something **:** convinced or certain ▪ I am *sure* (that) everything will be fine. ▪ We are quite/completely *sure* (that) we will be finished on time. ▪ She's not *sure* who will be there. ▪ Are you *sure* you want to go? ▪ Are you *sure* about that? ▪ She'll be there, I'm *sure* of it. ▪ Are you *sure* of the results?

2 : not allowing any doubt or possibility of failure ▪ The return of the robins is a *sure* sign of spring. ▪ The letter is a *sure* indication that she cares. ▪ Pizza is a *sure* crowd pleaser. ▪ The *surest* way to lose weight is with diet and exercise. ▪ One *sure* way to improve your health is to stop smoking. ▪ He's a ***sure bet*** to receive the award. [=he's sure/certain to receive the award] ▪ It's a ***sure thing*** that they'll win. [=it is certain that they'll win] ▪ Flowers and chocolates are always *sure things* [=people always like to be given flowers and chocolates], but consider giving your wife something different this year. — see also SURE THING (below)

3 — used to say that something will definitely happen or that someone will definitely do something; usually followed by *to + verb* ▪ It's *sure to be* a great party. ▪ I'll be *sure to call* when I get home. ▪ They are *sure to win*. ▪ Her latest movie is *sure to make* you laugh. ▪ Whatever you say, he's *sure to disagree* with you.

4 : known to be true or correct ▪ What is *sure* [=*definite, indisputable*] is that they have a problem, and we have the means to fix it. ▪ Nothing else is *sure*. ▪ ***One thing is (for) sure***, we'll never eat there again. [=we certainly will never eat there again]

5 a : firm or solid ▪ a *sure* hold/grip ▪ a hiking boot that provides *sure* footing [=that helps to keep your foot from slipping] — often used figuratively ▪ He lacks a *sure* grasp of the issue. [=he does not understand the issue well] ▪ She has a *sure* command of the French language. **b :** calm, steady, and confident ▪ the *sure* hands of a surgeon

be sure — used to tell someone not to forget *to do* something ▪ *Be sure to lock* the door when you leave.

for sure **:** without a doubt : definitely or certainly ▪ No one knows *for sure* [=*for certain*] what happened. ▪ That was a mistake *for sure*. = That *for sure* was a mistake. ▪ (*US, informal*) "Do you want to come to the party?" "*For sure*." [=I certainly do] ▪ "We don't want that to happen again." "***That's for sure!***" [=that is certainly true]

make sure **:** to find out or do something so that you have no doubt about whether something is true, correct, will happen, etc. ▪ *Make sure* (that) you turn the oven off. ▪ Remember to *make sure* (that) all the doors are locked. ▪ They *made sure* everyone knew where they were supposed to be. ▪ *Make sure* it doesn't happen again.

sure of yourself **1 :** confident in your abilities ▪ He was never very *sure of himself* as a comedian. **2** *somewhat disapproving* **:** overly confident or arrogant ▪ They seem awfully *sure of themselves*.

sure thing *informal* — used to say "yes" or to agree to a request or suggestion ▪ "Can you be here in five minutes?" "*Sure thing*." — see also [1]SURE 2 (above)

to be sure *formal* — used to say that you admit that something is true ▪ It will be challenging, *to be sure*, but I am confident that we will succeed.

[2]**sure** *adv, informal*

1 a — used to say "yes" or to agree to a request or suggestion ▪ "Can you help me with this?" "*Sure*." [=*certainly*] **b** — used to disagree with a negative statement or suggestion ▪ "I don't think he's coming." "*Sure* he is. He's just a little late." ▪ "Don't you like popcorn?" "*Sure* I like popcorn. I just don't want any right now."

2 — used to emphasize that you agree with the first part of the statement that you are about to make ▪ *Sure*, she's very talented, but other factors could limit her success.

3 *US* — used as an informal way to accept someone's thanks ▪ "Thank you for your help." "*Sure*." [=*you're welcome*]

4 *US* — used for emphasis ▪ I *sure* am tired. ▪ This *sure* beats working. ▪ "Do you want to come?" "I *sure* do!" ▪ (*impolite*) I ***sure as hell*** hope you know what you're doing!

sure enough — used to say that what happened was not surprising or unexpected ▪ We were finally ready to go outside, and *sure enough*, it started to rain.

sure·fire /ˈʃɚˈfajɚ, *Brit* ˈʃɔːˈfajə/ *adj, always used before a noun, informal* **:** certain not to fail : sure to be successful ▪ *surefire* solutions ▪ The movie is a *surefire* hit/success with teenagers. ▪ There is no *surefire* way to predict the outcome.

sure·foot·ed /ˈʃɚˈfʊtəd, *Brit* ˈʃɔːˈfʊtəd/ *adj* [*more* ~; *most* ~] **:** not likely to slip or fall when walking, climbing, or running ▪ a *surefooted* athlete ▪ as *surefooted* as a mountain goat — often used figuratively ▪ a *surefooted* leader [=a confident leader who is not likely to make mistakes] ▪ *surefooted* leadership

– sure·foot·ed·ly *adv* ▪ He *surefootedly* made his way through the difficult terrain. **– sure·foot·ed·ness** *noun* [*noncount*]

sure–hand·ed /ˈʃɚˈhændəd, *Brit* ˈʃɔːˈhændəd/ *adj* [*more* ~; *most* ~] *US* **:** not likely to drop something (such as a ball) that you are holding or catching ▪ a *sure-handed* ball player — often used figuratively ▪ a confident and *sure-handed* director [=a director who is not likely to make mistakes] ▪ *sure-handed* leadership

– sure–hand·ed·ly *adv* **– sure–hand·ed·ness** *noun* [*noncount*]

sure·ly /ˈʃɚli, *Brit* ˈʃɔːli/ *adv*

1 : in a confident way ▪ She answered quickly and *surely*.

2 *formal* **a :** without a doubt : CERTAINLY ▪ He will *surely* be missed. ▪ This is *surely* the best dessert you have ever made. ▪ *Surely* you must admit that it was a good decision. **b** — used in negative statements to show surprise that something could be true ▪ "Are they going to get away with it?" "*Surely* not." ▪ *Surely* you don't think that we are responsible for this! ▪ *Surely* you haven't forgotten my name!

slowly but surely see SLOWLY

sure·ness /ˈʃɚnəs, *Brit* ˈʃɔːnəs/ *noun* **:** a feeling that you know what you want to do and that you are able to do it [*singular*] He spoke with a newfound *sureness* [=*confidence*] in his voice. [*noncount*] She performs with the *sureness* of a veteran actress. ▪ the artist's *sureness* of touch/technique/hand

sure·ty /ˈʃɚrəti, *Brit* ˈʃɔːrəti/ *noun, pl* **-ties**

1 [*count*] *law* **:** money that you give as a guarantee that you will do what you are legally required to do (such as to appear in court) ▪ a *surety* of $10,000 = a $10,000 ***surety bond***

2 *law* **:** someone who agrees to be legally responsible if another person fails to pay a debt or to perform a duty [*count*] As *sureties*, they will be liable in his place. [*noncount*] She will ***stand surety*** for him. [=she agrees to be legally responsible if he fails to do what he promised]

3 [*noncount*] *formal* **:** the state of being or feeling sure or certain ▪ She answered with *surety*. [=*certainty*]

[1]**surf** /ˈsɚf/ *verb* **surfs; surfed; surf·ing**

1 [*no obj*] **:** to ride on ocean waves using a special board (called a surfboard) ▪ He learned to *surf* when he was living in California. — see also WINDSURF

2 : to look for information or other interesting things on the Internet [+ *obj*] *surfing* the Internet/Web [*no obj*] *surfing* on the Internet/Web — see also CHANNEL SURFING, SURFING

– surf·er *noun, pl* **-ers** [*count*]

[2]**surf** *noun* [*noncount*] **:** large waves that fall on the shore and the white foam and sound that they produce ▪ We could hear the roar of the *surf*. — see color picture on page C7

[1]**sur·face** /ˈsɚfəs/ *noun, pl* **-fac·es**

1 [*count*] **:** an outside part or layer of something ▪ The painting's *surface* is covered with fine cracks. ▪ The bowl has a shiny *surface*. ▪ The *surface* of wood was rough. ▪ Be careful of icy *surfaces* on the roads. ▪ a textured *surface*

2 [*count*] **:** the upper layer of an area of land or water — usually singular ▪ Hot lava bubbled up to the Earth's *surface*. ▪ exploring the *surface* of Mars ▪ The pipes are buried deep below the *surface*. ▪ The pond's *surface* was covered with leaves. ▪ bubbles rose/floated to the *surface* (of the water)

3 [*count*] **:** the flat, top part of something (such as a table or desk) that you can work on ▪ kitchen work *surfaces*

4 *the surface* **:** the part of someone or something that is easy to see or notice : the outer quality or appearance of someone or something that may not show true or hidden problems, feelings, etc. ▪ ***On the surface*** the plan seems simple. ▪ She seemed fine *on the surface*, but underneath, she was suffering. ▪ Their relationship has a lot of problems simmering ***below/beneath/under the surface***. ▪ His true feelings ***lie close to the surface***. [=they are easy to see] ▪ The tension between them is beginning to ***rise to the surface***. [=it is becoming easy to see]

5 [*count*] **:** a flat or curved side of an object ▪ Each *surface* of the die is marked with one to six black dots.

scratch the surface see [1]SCRATCH

[2]**surface** *verb* **-faces; -faced; -fac·ing**

1 [*no obj*] **:** to rise to the surface of water ▪ The whale *surfaced* and then dove back down. ▪ The submarine *surfaced*.

2 [*no obj*] **:** to appear or become obvious after being hidden or not seen ▪ The information *surfaced* many years later. ▪ After several years, the actress *surfaced* in a comedy. ▪ Suspicions eventually *surfaced*.

3 [+ *obj*] **:** to put a surface on (something, such as a road) ▪ The road needs to be *surfaced* again.

4 [*no obj*] *chiefly Brit, informal* **:** to wake up and get out of bed ▪ She hasn't *surfaced* yet.

S

[3]**surface** *adj, always used before a noun*
1 : involving only the parts that are easy to see or notice **:** SUPERFICIAL ▪ *surface* friendships ▪ Despite the *surface* differences between the two candidates, they are very similar in most ways.
2 : involving the removal of the surface of a large area of land to get at coal or other material that is near to the surface ▪ *surface* mining ▪ a *surface* mine

surface area *noun [singular]* **:** the amount of area covered by the surface of something ▪ The lake has roughly the same *surface area* as 10 football fields.

surface mail *noun [noncount]* **:** mail that is carried on land rather than by air or by sea

surface tension *noun [noncount] technical* **:** the force that causes the molecules on the surface of a liquid to be pushed together and form a layer

surface–to–air missile *noun, pl* ~ **-siles** *[count]* **:** a missile that is fired from the ground or a ship and directed at an airplane

surface–to–surface missile *noun, pl* ~ **-siles** *[count]* **:** a missile that is fired from the ground or a ship and directed at a target on the ground

surf and turf *noun [noncount] chiefly US* **:** seafood and steak served together as a meal at a restaurant ▪ We both ordered the *surf and turf.*

surf•board /ˈsəfˌboəd/ *noun, pl* **-boards** *[count]* **:** a long, light, narrow board that is used for surfing

surfboard

sur•feit /ˈsəfət/ *noun [singular] formal* **:** an amount that is too much or more than you need — + *of* ▪ a *surfeit of* choices

surf•ing /ˈsəfɪŋ/ *noun [noncount]*
1 : the activity or sport of riding ocean waves on a special board (called a surfboard) ▪ Her hobbies include diving and *surfing.* ▪ We ***went surfing*** yesterday.
2 : the activity of looking for information or interesting things on the Internet ▪ Web *surfing* — see also CHANNEL SURFING

[1]**surge** /ˈsəʤ/ *verb* **surg•es; surged; surg•ing** *[no obj]*
1 *always followed by an adverb or preposition* **:** to move very quickly and suddenly in a particular direction ▪ We all *surged* toward the door. ▪ She *surged* past the other runners. ▪ Thoughts of what could happen were *surging* through his mind. ▪ She has been *surging* in the polls. [=she is quickly becoming more popular as a candidate]
2 : to suddenly increase to an unusually high level ▪ Housing prices have *surged* in recent months. ▪ Interest in the sport has been *surging.*
– surging *adj* ▪ *surging* oil costs ▪ *surging* demand/growth ▪ the country's *surging* population ▪ a *surging* interest in the sport

[2]**surge** *noun, pl* **surges** *[count]*
1 : a sudden, large increase ▪ The sport is enjoying a *surge* in popularity. ▪ a *surge* of support for the candidate ▪ a *surge* of excitement — see also UPSURGE
2 : a sudden movement of many people ▪ There was a sudden *surge* toward the door. ▪ There has been a *surge* of immigrants into the city.
3 : a large wave of water ▪ an ocean *surge*
4 : a sudden increase in the amount of electricity that is flowing through an electrical circuit ▪ an electrical/power *surge*

sur•geon /ˈsəʤən/ *noun, pl* **-geons** *[count]* **:** a doctor who performs operations that involve cutting into someone's body in order to repair or remove damaged or diseased parts **:** a doctor who performs surgery ▪ a brain/heart *surgeon* — see also PLASTIC SURGEON

surgeon general *noun, pl* **surgeons general** *or* **surgeon generals** *[count]* **:** the chief medical officer of a branch of the military or of a public health service ▪ a health warning from the (U.S.) *Surgeon General*

surge protector *noun, pl* ~ **-tors** *[count]* **:** a device that prevents an electrical surge from damaging electronic equipment

sur•gery /ˈsəʤəri/ *noun, pl* **-ger•ies**
1 : medical treatment in which a doctor cuts into someone's body in order to repair or remove damaged or diseased parts *[noncount]* He's a specialist in brain *surgery.* ▪ The doctor has recommended *surgery.* ▪ He has recently undergone *surgery* on his shoulder. ▪ The patient is still ***in surgery.*** [=still being operated on] ▪ The doctor has been *in surgery* [=performing an operation] for two hours. *[count] (chiefly US)* ▪ She is now recovering from her *surgery.* [=*operation*] ▪ a doctor who has performed many *surgeries* — see also PLASTIC SURGERY
2 *[noncount] chiefly US* **:** the area in a hospital where surgery is performed ▪ The patient was taken directly to *surgery.* — compare OPERATING ROOM
3 *[count] Brit* **:** a place where a doctor or dentist treats people ▪ I was waiting in the doctor's *surgery.* [=*(US) office*]
4 *[noncount] Brit* **:** OFFICE HOURS 3
5 *[count] Brit* **:** a special period of time when people can visit a member of the British Parliament to ask questions

sur•gi•cal /ˈsəʤɪkəl/ *adj, always used before a noun*
1 a : of or relating to the process of performing a medical operation **:** of or relating to surgery ▪ a simple *surgical* procedure/treatment **b :** used during surgery ▪ *surgical* instruments/gloves/masks/tape **c :** resulting from a surgery ▪ a *surgical* scar/fever
2 : very careful and accurate ▪ The work was done with *surgical* precision/exactness. ▪ a ***surgical strike*** [=a carefully planned military attack that does not damage the surrounding area]
– sur•gi•cal•ly /ˈsəʤɪkli/ *adv* ▪ The tumor will have to be *surgically* removed.

surgical spirit *noun [noncount] Brit* **:** RUBBING ALCOHOL

sur•ly /ˈsəli/ *adj* **sur•li•er; -est :** rude and unfriendly ▪ *surly* customers
– sur•li•ness /ˈsəlinəs/ *noun [noncount]*

sur•mise /səˈmaɪz/ *verb* **-mis•es; -mised; -mis•ing** *[+ obj] formal* **:** to form an opinion about something without definitely knowing the truth **:** GUESS ▪ We can only *surmise* what happened. ▪ He must have *surmised* that I was not interested.
– surmise *noun, pl* **-mises** *[count, noncount]* ▪ This is no more than a *surmise.* [=*guess*]

sur•mount /səˈmaʊnt/ *verb* **-mounts; -mount•ed; -mount•ing** *[+ obj] formal*
1 : to deal with (a problem or a difficult situation) successfully ▪ Women often have to *surmount* [=*overcome*] social barriers to advance their careers. ▪ *surmounting* obstacles
2 : to be placed at the top of (something) — usually used as *(be) surmounted* ▪ a chain-link fence that *is surmounted* [=*topped*] by barbed wire
– sur•mount•able /səˈmaʊntəbəl/ *adj [more ~; most ~]* ▪ These setbacks are *surmountable.*

sur•name /ˈsəˌneɪm/ *noun, pl* **-names** *[count]* **:** the name that is shared by the people in a family ✧ In English, your surname comes after your first name and middle name. ▪ She took her husband's *surname* when they got married. — called also FAMILY NAME; compare LAST NAME

sur•pass /səˈpæs, *Brit* səˈpɑːs/ *verb* **-pass•es; -passed; -pass•ing** *[+ obj]* **:** to be better or greater than (someone or something) ▪ She soon *surpassed* [=*exceeded*] her teacher in skill and proficiency. ▪ Attendance is expected to *surpass* last year's record. ▪ Last quarter, sales *surpassed* two million. ▪ His work regularly *surpasses* all expectations.

sur•pass•ing /səˈpæsɪŋ, *Brit* səˈpɑːsɪŋ/ *adj, always used before a noun, formal* **:** very great **:** to a much greater degree than others ▪ a woman of *surpassing* grace and beauty
– sur•pass•ing•ly *adv* ▪ *surpassingly* difficult

sur•plice /ˈsəpləs/ *noun, pl* **-plic•es** *[count]* **:** a loose, white piece of clothing that is worn by priests or singers at church services

[1]**sur•plus** /ˈsəpləs/ *noun, pl* **-plus•es :** an amount (such as an amount of money) that is more than the amount that is needed *[noncount]* If there is any *surplus,* it will be divided equally. *[count]* crop *surpluses* ▪ There is a *surplus* of workers and not enough jobs. ▪ The state currently has a $3 million ***budget surplus.*** [=has $3 million more than it needs to pay for all of its planned expenses] — opposite DEFICIT; see also TRADE SURPLUS

[2]**surplus** *adj* **:** more than the amount that is needed ▪ *surplus* food/cloth/equipment ▪ The government bought the *surplus* grain to help growers.
surplus to requirements *Brit, formal* **:** no longer needed ▪ His services had become *surplus to requirements.*

[1]**sur•prise** /səˈpraɪz/ *noun, pl* **-pris•es**

S

1 [*count*] **a :** an unexpected event, piece of information, etc. ▪ What a pleasant *surprise* to see you! ▪ It's no *surprise* that he doesn't want to go. ▪ Is it any *surprise* that she should feel disappointed? ▪ The news ***came as a (complete/total) surprise*** to everyone. [=everyone was surprised by the news] ▪ It ***came as no surprise*** to me. [=I was not surprised by it] ▪ The teacher ***sprang a surprise*** on us and gave a pop quiz. ▪ They are ***in for a (big/real) surprise*** [=they are going to be very surprised] when they come home. **b :** an unexpected gift, party, etc. ▪ I have a special *surprise* for the children. ▪ The trip was a *surprise* for her birthday. ▪ Is the party a *surprise*?
2 [*noncount*] **:** the feeling caused by something that is unexpected or unusual ▪ She expressed *surprise* at their decision. [=she said that she was surprised by their decision] ▪ Imagine our *surprise* when they sold their house and moved to the Bahamas. ▪ ***Much to our surprise***, she refused. [=we were very surprised when she refused] ▪ He stared at her ***in surprise***. ▪ The attackers were relying on the ***element of surprise***. [=they were relying on their attack being unexpected]
3 — used as an interjection ▪ *Surprise*! Happy Birthday!
catch/take (someone or something) by surprise **1 :** to happen to (someone or something) unexpectedly **:** to surprise (someone or something) ▪ The question *caught* him *by surprise*. ▪ The organization was *taken* completely *by surprise* by the announcement. **2 :** to attack, capture, or approach (someone or something) without warning ▪ The enemy troops *took* us completely *by surprise*. ▪ Photographers *caught* the couple *by surprise* as they were leaving a restaurant.
surprise, surprise *informal* — used to say in a joking or ironic way that something is not surprising at all ▪ "She's going to be late again." "*Surprise, surprise*."

[2]**surprise** *verb* **-prises; -prised; -pris·ing** [+ *obj*]
1 : to cause (someone) to feel surprised ▪ The results will *surprise* you. ▪ Nothing you could say would *surprise* me. ▪ They *surprised* everyone by moving to the Bahamas. ▪ He *surprised* her at work with a vase of flowers. [=he unexpectedly gave her a vase of flowers while she was at work]
2 : to find, attack, or meet (someone or something) unexpectedly ▪ A police officer *surprised* the burglars. ▪ The troops were *surprised* by an attack from the north.

[3]**surprise** *adj, always used before a noun* **:** not expected **:** causing a feeling of surprise ▪ a *surprise* best seller/success ▪ She made a *surprise* announcement/appearance at the concert. ▪ I got a *surprise* call/visit from the governor. ▪ We threw him a ***surprise party***. [=we secretly planned a party for him and did not tell him about it until he arrived]

surprised *adj* [*more ~; most ~*] **:** having or showing the feeling that people get when something unexpected or unusual happens **:** feeling or showing surprise ▪ She had a *surprised* expression on her face. ▪ Are you *surprised* that they aren't going? ▪ I'm not *surprised*. I always thought he would do it. — often followed by *to + verb* ▪ I am *surprised to hear* about the changes. ▪ They seemed very *surprised to see* us. — often + *at* or *by* ▪ I wasn't at all *surprised by* the news. ▪ You would be *surprised at* how much things have changed.

surprising *adj* [*more ~; most ~*] **:** unexpected or unusual **:** causing surprise ▪ *surprising* results ▪ It's not *surprising* that he doesn't want to go. ▪ The changes to the campus were *surprising*. ▪ He shows a *surprising* lack of concern for others. ▪ A *surprising* number of people were laid off at the factory.
– sur·pris·ing·ly /sɚˈpraɪzɪŋli/ *adv* ▪ Not *surprisingly*, he agreed. ▪ She earns a *surprisingly* low salary. ▪ The event went *surprisingly* well, considering the bad weather.

sur·re·al /səˈriːl/ *adj* [*more ~; most ~*] **:** very strange or unusual **:** having the quality of a dream ▪ a *surreal* atmosphere/experience ▪ The whole thing was completely *surreal*.

sur·re·al·ism /səˈriːjəˌlɪzəm/ *noun* [*noncount*] **:** a 20th-century art form in which an artist or writer combines unrelated images or events in a very strange and dreamlike way
– sur·re·al·ist /səˈriːjəlɪst/ *noun, pl* **-ists** [*count*]
– surrealist *adj* ▪ a *surrealist* painting

sur·re·al·is·tic /səˌriːjəˈlɪstɪk/ *adj*
1 : very strange **:** SURREAL ▪ It was a *surrealistic* experience.
2 : of or relating to surrealism ▪ a *surrealistic* painter/painting

[1]**sur·ren·der** /səˈrɛndɚ/ *verb* **-ders; -dered; -der·ing**
1 : to agree to stop fighting, hiding, resisting, etc., because you know that you will not win or succeed [*no obj*] The enemy finally *surrendered* after three days of fighting. ▪ The gunman *surrendered* and was taken into custody. — often + *to* ▪ After a short chase, the suspect *surrendered to* the police. [+ *obj*] The suspect ***surrendered himself*** (to the police).
2 [+ *obj*] **:** to give the control or use of (something) to someone else ▪ The troops were forced to *surrender* the fort. ▪ He *surrendered* [=*handed over*] his weapon to the police. ▪ They were required to *surrender* their passports. ▪ They *surrendered* their rights. ▪ the *surrendering* of land to the government
3 : to allow something (such as a habit or desire) to influence or control you — often + *to* [*no obj*] She *surrendered* [=*gave in*] *to* temptation and ordered dessert. ▪ He refused to *surrender to* despair. [+ *obj*] He refused to ***surrender himself to*** despair.

[2]**surrender** *noun* [*singular*]
1 : an agreement to stop fighting, hiding, resisting, etc., because you know that you will not win or succeed **:** an act of surrendering ▪ Their *surrender* was formalized in a treaty. ▪ They demanded an unconditional *surrender*.
2 : the act of giving the control or use of something to someone else ▪ the *surrender* of territory
3 : the act of allowing yourself to be influenced or controlled by someone or something ▪ a *surrender* to desire

sur·rep·ti·tious /ˌsɚəpˈtɪʃəs/ *adj* **:** done in a secret way ▪ She had a *surreptitious* relationship with her employee. ▪ a *surreptitious* glance
– sur·rep·ti·tious·ly *adv* ▪ He contacted her *surreptitiously*.
– sur·rep·ti·tious·ness *noun* [*noncount*]

sur·rey /ˈsɚri/ *noun, pl* **-reys** [*count*] *US* **:** a light, old-fashioned carriage that has two wide seats and four wheels and that is pulled by a horse

sur·ro·ga·cy /ˈsɚrəgəsi/ *noun* [*noncount*] **:** the practice by which a woman (called a surrogate mother) becomes pregnant and gives birth to a baby in order to give it to someone who cannot have children ▪ choosing between adoption and *surrogacy*

sur·ro·gate /ˈsɚrəgət/ *noun, pl* **-gates** [*count*]
1 : a person or thing that takes the place or performs the duties of someone or something else ▪ He could not attend the meeting, so he sent his *surrogate*. ▪ The governor and her *surrogates* asked the public to support the change.
2 : SURROGATE MOTHER ▪ They had their baby through a *surrogate*.
– surrogate *adj, always used before a noun* ▪ She considered them her *surrogate* family.

surrogate mother *noun, pl* **~ -ers** [*count*] **:** a woman who agrees to become pregnant in order to give the baby to someone who cannot have children

[1]**sur·round** /səˈraʊnd/ *verb* **-rounds; -round·ed; -round·ing** [+ *obj*]
1 : to be on every side of (someone or something) ▪ A wall *surrounds* the old city. — often used as *(be) surrounded* ▪ The lake *is surrounded* by cottages.
2 : to move close to (someone or something) on all sides often in order to stop a person from escaping ▪ Police *surrounded* the house. ▪ They had the suspect *surrounded*. ▪ She was suddenly *surrounded* by a crowd of excited fans.
3 : to be closely related or connected to (something) ▪ There's a lot of uncertainty *surrounding* the decision. ▪ His departure was *surrounded* by secrecy.
4 *of a family, group, etc.* **:** to always be near (someone) — often + *with* ▪ Her family *surrounded* her *with* love and attention. [=her family gave her a lot of love and attention] — often used as *(be) surrounded* ▪ As a child she *was surrounded* by her large, loving family.
surround yourself with (someone or something) **:** to cause (certain types of people or things) to be near you ▪ He *surrounds himself with* very talented people. ▪ They *surround themselves with* luxuries. [=they have many luxuries]

[2]**surround** *noun, pl* **-rounds** [*count*] **:** a border or an area that is around the outside edge of something ▪ a fireplace/bathtub *surround* ▪ the park's urban *surrounds*

surrounding *adj, always used before a noun* **:** near or around someone or something ▪ the *surrounding* area/neighborhood/land

sur·round·ings /səˈraʊndɪŋz/ *noun* [*plural*] **:** the places, conditions, or objects that are around you **:** ENVIRONMENT ▪ They will need some time to become familiar with their new *surroundings*.

sur·tax /ˈsɚˌtæks/ *noun, pl* **-tax·es** [*count*] **:** a tax that is charged on income which is more than a certain amount and that is charged in addition to the normal income tax

sur·veil·lance /sɚˈveɪləns/ *noun* [*noncount*] **:** the act of carefully watching someone or something especially in order to prevent or detect a crime • government *surveillance* of suspected terrorists • The bank robbery was recorded by *surveillance* video cameras. • ***electronic surveillance*** [=the act of using electronic devices to watch people or things] • The police ***kept*** her ***under surveillance***. [=watched her closely]

[1]sur·vey /ˈsɚˌveɪ/ *noun, pl* **-veys** [*count*]

1 : an activity in which many people are asked a question or a series of questions in order to gather information about what most people do or think about something : POLL • The *survey* found/revealed some surprising tendencies among the population. • We conducted an opinion *survey* on the issue and found that most people agree. • a *survey* on American drinking habits

2 : an act of studying something in order to make a judgment about it • *Surveys* of each department were conducted earlier this year. • A *survey* of recent corporate layoffs reveals a new trend in business management.

3 : an act of measuring and examining an area of land • A new land *survey* changed the borders of their property.

4 : a general description of or report about a subject or situation • a *survey* [=*overview*] of current events • *surveys* of English literature

5 *Brit* **:** a close examination of a building to see if it is in good condition • A *survey* [=(*US*) *inspection*] must be done before the house can be sold.

[2]sur·vey /sɚˈveɪ/ *verb* **-veys; -veyed; -vey·ing** [+ *obj*]

1 : to ask (many people) a question or a series of questions in order to gather information about what most people do or think about something • A total of 250 city residents were *surveyed* about the project. • 64 percent of the people *surveyed* said that the economy was doing well. • The magazine *surveyed* its readers on their romantic relationships. [=the magazine took/conducted a survey of its readers to find out about their romantic relationships]

2 : to look at and examine all parts of (something) • The teacher *surveyed* the room. • People were *surveying* the damage after the storm.

3 : to measure and examine (an area of land) • Engineers *surveyed* the property to see what could be built on it.

4 : to give a general description or report of (something, such as a subject or a situation) • The class *surveys* American history before the Civil War.

5 *Brit* **:** to examine (a building) to make sure it is in good condition • The house must be *surveyed* [=(*US*) *inspected*] before it can be sold.

survey course *noun, pl* ~ **courses** [*count*] *US* **:** a class at a college or university that gives general information about a subject for students who have not studied it before : an introductory course at a college or university

sur·vey·or /sɚˈvejɚ/ *noun, pl* **-ors** [*count*]

1 : someone whose job is to measure and examine an area of land • a land *surveyor*

2 *Brit* **:** someone whose job is to examine buildings • *Surveyors* [=(*US*) *inspectors*] condemned the building. — see also QUANTITY SURVEYOR

sur·viv·al /sɚˈvaɪvəl/ *noun, pl* **-als**

1 [*noncount*] **:** the state or fact of continuing to live or exist especially in spite of difficult conditions • The refugees depend on foreign aid for their *survival*. • Small businesses are fighting/struggling for *survival*. • the *survival* of an old folktale • The doctor said her ***chance of survival*** [=chance that she would get better and continue to live] was about 50 percent. — often used before another noun • The scouts learned basic *survival* skills/techniques. • Patients have a high *survival* rate if the cancer is detected early. • an animal's ***survival instinct*** [=an animal's ability to know what to do to stay alive] • He uses his wits as a ***survival mechanism***. [=as a way of protecting himself from being hurt by other people]

2 [*count*] **:** something from an earlier period that still exists or is done — usually singular • The holiday custom is a *survival* from colonial times.

survival of the fittest **1 :** NATURAL SELECTION **2** — used to refer to a situation in which only the people or things that are strongest, most skillful, etc., are able to succeed or to continue to exist • In the business world, it's *survival of the fittest*.

sur·viv·al·ist /sɚˈvaɪvəlɪst/ *noun, pl* **-ists** [*count*] **:** a person who believes that government and society will soon fail completely and who stores food, weapons, etc., in order to be prepared to survive when that happens

– **survivalist** *adj* • *survivalist* techniques

sur·vive /sɚˈvaɪv/ *verb* **-vives; -vived; -viv·ing**

1 [*no obj*] **a :** to remain alive : to continue to live • I don't see how any creature can *survive* under those conditions. • bacteria that *survive* in extreme temperatures • (*humorous*) He didn't think he could *survive* without golf. — often + *on* • The plant *survives on* very little water. • They managed to *survive on* his small salary. • (*humorous*) I mainly *survived on* peanut butter and jelly sandwiches when I was in college. **b :** to continue to exist • Only a few written records *survive* from those times. • These ancient practices still *survive* in some regions. • Some of the original bridges *survive*. • Many businesses are struggling to *survive* in today's economy.

2 [+ *obj*] **:** to remain alive after the death of (someone) : OUTLIVE • Only his son *survived* him. • She *survived* her husband by only a few years. — often used as *(be) survived* • She *is survived* by her three children.

3 [+ *obj*] **a :** to continue to be alive or to exist after (something) • They *survived* the crash/flood. • The fruit trees didn't *survive* [=*live through*] the harsh winter. • This type of plant cannot *survive* [=*withstand*] temperatures below freezing. **b :** to continue to function, succeed, etc., in spite of (something) • He *survived* a political scandal and was elected to the state legislature. • The company *survived* the recession. • helpful hints for *surviving* the holidays

– **sur·viv·able** /sɚˈvaɪvəbəl/ *adj* [*more* ~; *most* ~] • This form of cancer is *survivable* if it's detected early.

– **surviving** *adj* • one of the few *surviving* traditions • His son is his sole *surviving* heir.

sur·vi·vor /sɚˈvaɪvɚ/ *noun, pl* **-vors** [*count*]

1 a : a person who continues to live after an accident, illness, war, etc. • She interviewed *survivors* of the flood. • a Holocaust/cancer *survivor* • The plane crashed and there were no *survivors*. • There was only one *survivor* of the accident. **b :** a member of a group who continues to live after other members have died • Most of the people I went to school with are gone now. I'm one of the few *survivors*. **c :** a family member who remains alive after another person's death • He died without any *survivors*.

2 : someone or something that continues to exist, function, compete, etc. • The *survivors* of the first round of competition will be meeting today in the second round. • This newspaper is the only *survivor* of six newspapers that were founded in the city in the 19th century.

3 : someone who is able to keep living or succeeding despite a lot of problems • There's no question about it—Aunt Annie's a *survivor*.

sus·cep·ti·bil·i·ty /səˌsɛptəˈbɪləti/ *noun, pl* **-ties**

1 : the state of being easily affected, influenced, or harmed by something — usually + *to* [*count*] — usually singular • They are concerned about the city's *susceptibility to* attack. • A weak immune system increases your *susceptibility to* disease. [*noncount*] A weak immune system causes increased *susceptibility to* disease.

2 ***susceptibilities*** [*plural*] *chiefly Brit, formal* **:** a person's feelings • We do not want to offend their *susceptibilities*. [=we do not want to offend them]

sus·cep·ti·ble /səˈsɛptəbəl/ *adj* [*more* ~; *most* ~]

1 : easily affected, influenced, or harmed by something • The virus can infect *susceptible* individuals. — often + *to* • He is very *susceptible to* colds. [=he catches colds easily] • a surface highly *susceptible to* scratches • He is *susceptible to* flattery.

2 *formal* **:** capable of being affected by a specified action or process — + *of* • a contract that is *susceptible of* modification [=a contract that can be modified]

su·shi /ˈsuːʃi/ *noun* [*noncount*] **:** a Japanese dish of cold cooked rice shaped in small cakes and topped or wrapped with other ingredients (such as pieces of raw fish)

[1]sus·pect /səˈspɛkt/ *verb* **-pects; -pect·ed; -pect·ing** [+ *obj*]

1 a : to think that (someone) is possibly guilty of a crime or of doing something wrong • He's *suspected* in four burglaries. — often + *of* • The police *suspect* him *of* murder. • No one *suspects* you *of* cheating. **b :** to think that (something) is possibly the cause of something bad — usually + *of* • The pesticide is *suspected of* causing cancer. **c :** to think that (a crime) has possibly been committed • The police do not *suspect* murder in this case. • The fire chief *suspects* arson.

2 : to think that (something, especially something bad) possibly exists, is true, will happen, etc. • We *suspected* a trap. • I *suspect* it will rain. • Call the doctor immediately if you *suspect* you've been infected. • The latest research confirms what scientists have long *suspected*. • I *suspect* she's not who she says she is. • "We haven't done our homework." "I *suspected* as much."

3 : to have feelings of doubt about (something) **:** to be suspicious about (something) ▪ I *suspected* his motives in giving me the money. ▪ I have reason to *suspect* her sincerity when she makes promises like that.

– suspected /sə'spɛktəd/ *adj, always used before a noun* ▪ a *suspected* arsonist ▪ The pesticide is a *suspected* carcinogen. ▪ a *suspected* case of smallpox

²sus·pect /'sʌˌspɛkt/ *noun, pl* **-pects** *[count]*

1 : a person who is believed to be possibly guilty of committing a crime ▪ a murder *suspect* ▪ One *suspect* has been arrested. ▪ She is a possible/prime *suspect* in connection with the kidnapping.

2 : a thing that is thought of as a possible cause of something bad ▪ The prime *suspect* for the food poisoning is the potato salad.

the usual suspects **:** the usual people or things that are suspected or thought of in a particular situation — often used humorously ▪ The breakfast menu had all *the usual suspects* [=the usual things]—eggs, pancakes, waffles, and French toast.

³sus·pect /'sʌˌspɛkt/ *adj [more ~; most ~]* **:** not able to be trusted **:** causing feelings of doubt or suspicion ▪ The *suspect* [=*suspicious*] vehicle was reported to the police. ▪ The witness's claim was *suspect*. [=*dubious, questionable*] ▪ The room had a *suspect* odor.

sus·pend /sə'spɛnd/ *verb* **-pends; -pend·ed; -pend·ing** *[+ obj]*

1 : to force (someone) to leave a job, position, or place for a usually short period of time as a form of punishment ▪ He was *suspended* from the team for missing too many practices. ▪ The police officers were *suspended* without pay for their conduct. ▪ The principal *suspended* the student from school for fighting.

2 a : to stop (something) for a usually short period of time ▪ The city *suspended* bus service during the storm. ▪ The company was forced to *suspend* operations. ▪ They have *suspended* the peace talks. ▪ The plot is ridiculous, but if you can ***suspend (your) disbelief*** [=allow yourself to believe that something is true even though it seems impossible], it's an enjoyable movie. **b :** to make (something) happen later **:** to delay (something) ▪ The judge *suspended* [=*postponed*] the hearing for one week. ▪ I advise *suspending* judgment until the investigation is over. **c :** to make (something) invalid or ineffective for a usually short period of time ▪ Her license to practice law was *suspended*. ▪ We can *suspend* the rules just this once. ▪ He's driving with a *suspended* license.

3 a : to hang something so that it is free on all sides except at the point of support ▪ They *suspended* the lantern from the ceiling. ▪ A pot of stew was *suspended* over the fire. ▪ a wire ***suspended between*** two poles [=hung so that it is attached at each end to a pole] **b :** to prevent (something) from falling or sinking by some invisible support — usually used as *(be) suspended* ▪ Dust *was suspended* [=was floating] in the air. ▪ The structure appears to *be suspended* in space.

suspended animation *noun [noncount]* **:** a state in which the processes of the body (such as blood circulation) stop or become very slow for a period of time while a person or animal is unconscious ▪ animals that sleep through the winter in a state of *suspended animation* — often used figuratively ▪ The project has been in (a state of) *suspended animation* for over 15 years.

suspended sentence *noun, pl* **~ -tences** *[count] law* **:** a legal arrangement in which a person who has been found guilty of a crime is not sentenced to jail but may be sentenced for that crime at a future time if he or she commits another crime during a specified period ▪ The judge handed down a *suspended sentence* to the first-time offender.

sus·pend·er /sə'spɛndɚ/ *noun, pl* **-ers**

1 ***suspenders*** *[plural] US* **:** straps that are used for holding up pants and that go over a person's shoulders — called also *(Brit)* braces; see color picture on page C14

2 *[count] Brit* **:** GARTER 2

suspender belt *noun, pl* **~ belts** *[count] Brit* **:** GARTER BELT

sus·pense /sə'spɛns/ *noun [noncount]* **:** a feeling or state of nervousness or excitement caused by wondering what will happen ▪ I can't bear/stand the *suspense*. ▪ The *suspense* builds as the story progresses. ▪ a novel of *suspense* ▪ Alfred Hitchcock was a master of *suspense*. ▪ The movie is a *suspense* thriller. ▪ I don't know who won and ***the suspense is killing me***. [=I am very anxious to know who won] ▪ She kept him ***in suspense*** [=waiting anxiously] for two whole days before she agreed to marry him.

– sus·pense·ful /sə'spɛnsfəl/ *adj [more ~; most ~]* ▪ a *suspenseful* story/situation/movie

sus·pen·sion /sə'spɛnʃən/ *noun, pl* **-sions**

1 : the act of forcing someone to leave a job, position, or place for a usually short period of time as a form of punishment **:** the act of suspending someone *[count]* He was angry about his *suspension* from the team. ▪ His record shows several *suspensions* from school. *[noncount]* He's ***under suspension*** for breaking the rules.

2 *[singular, noncount]* **:** the act of stopping or delaying something for a usually short period of time ▪ (a) *suspension* of peace talks

3 : the act of making something invalid or ineffective for a usually short period of time *[count]* a 30-day license *suspension* ▪ a *suspension* of the rules *[noncount]* She was punished by *suspension* of her driver's license.

4 *[count] technical* **:** a substance (usually a liquid) that has very small pieces of a solid material mixed throughout it

5 *[noncount] technical* **:** the parts of a vehicle that connect the body to the tires and allow the vehicle to move more smoothly over uneven surfaces ▪ the car's front/rear *suspension*

suspension bridge *noun, pl* **~ bridges** *[count]* **:** a bridge that is hung from two or more cables that are held up by towers

sus·pi·cion /sə'spɪʃən/ *noun, pl* **-cions**

1 *[noncount]* **:** a feeling that someone is possibly guilty of a crime or of doing something wrong ▪ Her strange behavior has aroused *suspicion*. [=has made people think that she is doing something wrong] ▪ He is ***under suspicion of*** [=suspected of] selling illegal drugs. ▪ He was arrested ***on suspicion of*** robbery. [=he was arrested because the police suspect that he committed a robbery] ▪ They are not ***above/beyond suspicion***. [=they are not considered to be obviously or certainly innocent and unable to be suspected]

2 *[count]* **:** a feeling that something bad is likely or true ▪ There has long been a *suspicion* that the painting is a fake. ▪ There was not the slightest *suspicion* of a trap. [=no one suspected a trap] ▪ I thought the water might be making us sick, and my *suspicions* were confirmed by the lab tests. ▪ The note aroused her *suspicions* that he was having an affair. ▪ I have a ***sneaking suspicion*** that those cookies aren't really homemade.

3 : a feeling of doubt *[noncount]* The new policies are regarded by many with *suspicion*. ▪ His story has raised some *suspicion*. *[count]* I have my *suspicions* about his motives.

4 *[singular]* **:** a very small amount *of* something **:** TRACE ▪ a *suspicion of* garlic

the finger of suspicion see ¹FINGER

sus·pi·cious /sə'spɪʃəs/ *adj [more ~; most ~]*

1 : causing a feeling that something is wrong or that someone is behaving wrongly **:** causing suspicion ▪ We were instructed to report any *suspicious* activity/behavior in the neighborhood. ▪ The *suspicious* vehicle was reported to police. ▪ He died under *suspicious* circumstances. [=under circumstances that suggest a crime may have been committed] ▪ *Suspicious* characters were seen hanging around the bank. ▪ He found a *suspicious* lump on his back and was afraid it might be cancer.

2 : having or showing a feeling that something is wrong or that someone is behaving wrongly **:** feeling or showing suspicion ▪ Officials are *suspicious* about her death. ▪ His manner made me *suspicious*. — often + *of* ▪ She became *suspicious of* his behavior. ▪ The dog is *suspicious of* strangers. [=the dog does not trust strangers] ▪ We noticed the *suspicious* stare of the security guard.

– sus·pi·cious·ly *adv* ▪ "Is there someone in the bedroom?" he asked *suspiciously*. ▪ The security guard stared at us *suspiciously*. ▪ He was acting/behaving *suspiciously*. ▪ The answers on the two students' tests are *suspiciously* alike. ▪ This sounds *suspiciously* like an excuse to get out of work.

suss /'sʌs/ *verb* **suss·es; sussed; suss·ing** *[+ obj] Brit, informal*

1 : to find or discover (something) by thinking — usually + *out* ▪ They had to *suss out* [=*figure out*] whether he was telling the truth. ▪ I think I've ***got him sussed out***. [=I understand what kind of person he is]

2 : to inspect or investigate (something) in order to gain more knowledge — usually + *out* ▪ He carefully *sussed out* the situation.

sus·tain /sə'steɪn/ *verb* **-tains; -tained; -tain·ing** *[+ obj]*

S

1 : to provide what is needed for (something or someone) to exist, continue, etc. • There is not enough oxygen to *sustain* [=*support*] life at very high altitudes. • Hope *sustained* us during that difficult time. • The movie *sustained* our interest [=kept us interested] from beginning to end. • The country is enjoying a period of *sustained* [=*continuing*] economic growth. • a *sustained* discussion/effort

2 *formal* **:** to hold up the weight of (something) • The roof, unable to *sustain* the weight of all the snow, collapsed.

3 *formal* **:** to deal with or experience (something bad or unpleasant) **:** SUFFER • The army *sustained* heavy losses. • He *sustained* serious injuries in the accident.

4 *law* **:** to decide or state that (something) is proper, legal, or fair • The judge *sustained* the motion. • The lawyer's objection was *sustained*.

5 *formal* **:** to show that (something) is true or correct **:** to confirm or prove (something) • The report *sustains* their story/claims. • The evidence does not *sustain* a guilty verdict.

sus·tain·able /sə'steɪnəbəl/ *adj* [*more ~; most ~*]

1 : able to be used without being completely used up or destroyed • *sustainable* energy resources • a *sustainable* water supply

2 : involving methods that do not completely use up or destroy natural resources • *sustainable* agriculture/farming/techniques

3 : able to last or continue for a long time • *sustainable* development/growth

– sus·tain·abil·i·ty /səˌsteɪnə'bɪləti/ *noun* [*noncount*]

– sus·tain·ably /sə'steɪnəbli/ *adv*

sus·te·nance /'sʌstənəns/ *noun* [*noncount*] *formal*

1 : something (such as food) that keeps someone or something alive • Tree bark provides deer with *sustenance* in periods of drought. • The village depends on the sea for *sustenance*.

2 : something that gives support, help, or strength • She draws spiritual *sustenance* from daily church attendance. • reading for intellectual *sustenance*

[1]su·ture /'su:ʧɚ/ *noun, pl* **-tures** [*count*] *medical* **:** a stitch or a series of stitches used to close a cut or wound

[2]suture *verb* **-tures; -tured; -tur·ing** [+ *obj*] *medical* **:** to sew together (a cut, wound, etc.) **:** to close (something) with a suture • The surgeon *sutured* the incision.

SUV /ˌɛsˌju:'vi:/ *noun, pl* **SUVs** [*count*] **:** a large vehicle that is designed to be used on rough surfaces but that is often used on city roads or highways — called also *sport-utility vehicle*; see picture at CAR

svelte /'svɛlt/ *adj* [*more ~; most ~*] **:** thin in an attractive or graceful way **:** SLENDER • She has a *svelte* figure. • a *svelte* young actor • a *svelte* aircraft

SW *abbr* southwest, southwestern

[1]swab /'swɑ:b/ *noun, pl* **swabs** [*count*]

1 : a small piece of soft material sometimes on the end of a small stick that is used for applying medicine, cleaning a wound, etc. • Use a cotton *swab* dipped in alcohol to disinfect the area.

2 : a small amount of material taken with a swab as a sample from a person's body • The doctor took a throat *swab* and sent it to the lab.

[2]swab *verb* **swabs; swabbed; swab·bing** [+ *obj*]

1 : to wipe or clean (something, such as a wound) with a swab • The nurse *swabbed* the cut with a disinfectant.

2 : [2]MOP 1 • sailors *swabbing* the decks

swad·dle /'swɑ:dl/ *verb* **swad·dles; swad·dled; swad·dling** [+ *obj*] **:** to wrap (someone, especially a baby) tightly with a blanket, pieces of cloth, etc. • He *swaddled* the baby in a blanket.

swaddling clothes *noun* [*plural*] **:** narrow strips of cloth that were wrapped around babies in the past • an infant wrapped in *swaddling clothes*

swag /'swæg/ *noun* [*noncount*] *informal + old-fashioned* **:** stolen property **:** LOOT • The robbers divided the *swag*.

[1]swag·ger /'swægɚ/ *noun, pl* **-gers** [*count*] **:** a way of walking or behaving that shows you have a lot of confidence • He has a *swagger* that annoys some of his teammates.

[2]swagger *verb* **-gers; -gered; -ger·ing** [*no obj*] **:** to walk in a very confident way **:** to walk with a swagger • He *swaggered* [=*strutted*] into the shop like he owned the place.

Swa·hi·li /swɑ'hi:li/ *noun* [*noncount*] **:** a language widely used in East Africa and the Congo region

swain /'sweɪn/ *noun, pl* **swains** [*count*] *old-fashioned + humorous* **:** a man who is a woman's lover • a fair maiden and her *swain*

[1]swal·low /'swɑ:loʊ/ *verb* **-lows; -lowed; -low·ing**

1 a : to take (something) into your stomach through your mouth and throat [+ *obj*] He *swallowed* the grape whole. [*no obj*] Chew your food well before you *swallow*. **b** [*no obj*] **:** to move the muscles in your throat as if you are swallowing something often because you are nervous • I *swallowed* before answering. • The boss said, "Come in." I ***swallowed hard*** and walked in. — sometimes used figuratively • If she insults you, just *swallow hard* [=make an effort to control yourself] and don't say anything.

2 [+ *obj*] **a :** to flow over and cover (something) completely — often + *up* • The wave *swallowed up* the small vessel. — often used figuratively • More small companies are being *swallowed (up)* [=*taken over, absorbed*] by giant conglomerates. • We watched as he was *swallowed up* by the crowd. [=as he disappeared into the crowd] **b :** to use up (an amount of money) — usually + *up* • The cost of childcare *swallows up* most of her income.

3 [+ *obj*] *informal* **:** to accept or believe (something) • Her story is pretty hard to *swallow*. • I can usually take criticism, but this is more than I can *swallow*.

4 [+ *obj*] **:** to not allow yourself to show or be affected by (an emotion) • We have to *swallow* our disappointment/anger about the election and keep trying to make things better. • She had to ***swallow her pride*** and ask for help.

(a) bitter pill to swallow see [1]PILL

[2]swallow *noun, pl* **-lows** [*count*] **:** an amount that is swallowed at one time • She took a *swallow* of water to wash down the pill. **:** the act of swallowing something • He drank the water in/with one *swallow*. — compare [3]SWALLOW

[3]swallow *noun, pl* **-lows** [*count*] **:** a small bird that has long wings and a deeply forked tail — compare [2]SWALLOW

swam *past tense of* [1]SWIM

swa·mi /'swɑ:mi/ *noun, pl* **-mis** [*count*] **:** a Hindu priest or religious teacher

[1]swamp /'swɑ:mp/ *noun, pl* **swamps :** land that is always wet and often partly covered with water [*noncount*] The area is mostly *swamp*. [=*swampland*] [*count*] Alligators live in the lowland *swamps*.

– swampy /'swɑ:mpi/ *adj* **swamp·i·er; -est** [*also more ~; most ~*] • *swampy* land

[2]swamp *verb* **swamps; swamped; swamp·ing** [+ *obj*]

1 : to cover (something) with water • The sea level rose and *swamped* the coastal villages. • The boat sank after it was *swamped* by waves.

2 : to cause (someone or something) to have to deal with a very large amount of things or people at the same time — usually used as *(be) swamped* • The agency has *been swamped* by requests for assistance. • I'*m swamped* with work right now. [=I'm extremely busy right now] • Because of the new laws, we *were swamped* with paperwork. • In the summer, the town *is swamped* with/by tourists.

swamp·land /'swɑ:mpˌlænd/ *noun, pl* **-lands :** wet land that is partly covered with water **:** SWAMP [*noncount*] attempting to build on *swampland* [*plural*] the ecology of the coastal *swamplands*

[1]swan /'swɑ:n/ *noun, pl* **swans** *also* **swan** [*count*] **:** a large usually white bird that lives on or near water and that has a very long and graceful neck

swan

[2]swan *verb, always followed by an adverb or preposition* **swans; swanned; swan·ning** [*no obj*] *chiefly Brit, informal + disapproving* **:** to go to or move about a place in a very relaxed and aimless way for your own pleasure • She's always *swanning* off to some exotic locale. • He's been *swanning* around foreign countries for the last six months.

[1]swank /'swæŋk/ *adj* **swank·er; -est** *chiefly US* **:** very fashionable and expensive **:** SWANKY • a *swank* club/hotel/restaurant

[2]swank *verb* **swanks; swanked; swank·ing** [*no obj*] *Brit, informal + disapproving* **:** to behave in a way that is intended to impress people • rich people *swanking* around in their expensive cars

swanky /'swæŋki/ *adj* **swank·i·er; -est** *informal* **:** very fashionable and expensive • a *swanky* club/hotel/restaurant

swan song *noun, pl* **~ songs** [*count*] **:** the last performance or piece of work by an actor, athlete, writer, etc. • She has announced that this tournament will be her *swan song*.

S

[=this will be her last tournament]

[1]**swap** *also Brit* **swop** /ˈswɑ:p/ *verb* **swaps; swapped; swap·ping** *informal*

1 : to give something to someone and receive something in return **:** to trade or exchange (things) [+ *obj*] He *swapped* his cupcake for a candy bar. • He *swapped* desserts with his brother. = He and his brother *swapped* desserts. • I'll *swap* my sandwich for your popcorn. = I'll *swap* you my sandwich for your popcorn. • I *swapped* seats with my sister so she could see the stage better. • We often get together and *swap* [=*exchange*] recipes. • We spent some time ***swapping stories*** about our college days. [=telling each other stories about our college days] [*no obj*] I liked her blue notebook and she liked my red one, so we *swapped*. • He wanted the window seat so we *swapped*. = (*Brit*) He wanted the window seat so we ***swapped over***.

2 : to replace (something) with something else [+ *obj*] He *swapped* (out) his hard drive for a bigger one. • The nurse *swapped* [=*switched*] the patients' charts by mistake. [*no obj*] (*Brit*) Our company decided to ***swap over*** to a new supplier.

[2]**swap** *noun, pl* **swaps** [*count*] **:** an act of giving or taking one thing in return for another thing **:** a trade or exchange • They made the *swap* in secret. • an even *swap*

swap meet *noun, pl* **~ meets** [*count*] *US* **:** an event at which people can buy, sell, or trade used items

sward /ˈswoɚd/ *noun, pl* **swards** [*count, noncount*] *literary* **:** an area of land covered with grass

[1]**swarm** /ˈswoɚm/ *noun, pl* **swarms** [*count*] **:** a very large number of insects moving together • a *swarm* of bees/mosquitoes/ants/locusts — often used figuratively • The tourists arrived in *swarms*.

[2]**swarm** *verb* **swarms; swarmed; swarm·ing**

1 [*no obj*] **:** to move in a large group • Bees were *swarming* near the hive. • Spectators *swarmed* into the stadium.

2 a [*no obj*] **:** to be surrounded or filled *with* a large group of insects, people, etc., moving together • The hive was *swarming with* bees. • The island was *swarming with* tourists. **b** [+ *obj*] **:** to surround (something or someone) with a large group • Police *swarmed* the smuggler's hideout. • The movie star was *swarmed* by adoring fans. • Enemy soldiers *swarmed* the castle.

swar·thy /ˈswoɚði/ *adj* **swar·thi·er; -est** [*also more ~; most ~*] **:** having dark skin • a *swarthy* man/complexion

swash·buck·ler /ˈswɑ:ʃˌbʌklɚ/ *noun, pl* **-lers** [*count*] **:** a person or a character in a movie, book, etc., who is very brave and has many exciting adventures

– swash·buck·ling /ˈswɑ:ʃˌbʌkəlɪŋ/ *adj* [*more~; most~*] • *swashbuckling* heroes • a *swashbuckling* tale/adventure

swas·ti·ka /ˈswɑ:stɪkə/ *noun, pl* **-kas** [*count*] **:** a symbol in the form of a cross with its ends bent at right angles all in the same direction ✧ The swastika was used as a symbol of the German Nazi Party.

swat /ˈswɑ:t/ *verb* **swats; swat·ted; swat·ting** [+ *obj*] **:** to hit (someone or something) with a quick motion • She *swatted* the fly with a magazine. • The cat was *swatting* the injured mouse with its paw. • He *swatted* the tennis ball out of bounds.

– swat *noun, pl* **swats** [*count*] • He took a *swat* at the ball but missed. • She gave the ball a *swat*. [=she swatted the ball]

SWAT /ˈswɑ:t/ *noun* [*noncount*] *chiefly US* **:** a police or military unit that is specially trained to handle very dangerous situations — usually used before another noun • a *SWAT* team ✧ *SWAT* is an abbreviation of "special weapons and tactics."

S

swatch /ˈswɑ:ʧ/ *noun, pl* **swatch·es** [*count*] **:** a small piece of cloth that is used as a sample for choosing colors, fabrics, etc. • She looked at fabric *swatches* to select material for the drapes.

swath /ˈswɑ:θ/ *or* **swathe** /ˈswɑ:ð/ *noun, pl* **swaths** *or* **swathes** [*count*]

1 : a long, wide strip of land • An aerial view of the countryside shows wide *swathes* of green.

2 : an area of grass or grain that has been cut or mowed • He ***cut a swath through*** the field with his scythe. — often used figuratively • The tornado *cut a swath through* the county.

swathe /ˈswɑ:ð/ *verb* **swathes; swathed; swath·ing** [+ *obj*] *literary* **:** to wrap or cover (someone or something) • The nurse *swathed* the wounded soldier's leg in bandages. • Her neck was *swathed* in jewels. • mountains *swathed* in mist

[1]**sway** /ˈsweɪ/ *verb* **sways; swayed; sway·ing**

1 [*no obj*] **:** to move slowly back and forth • branches *swaying* in the breeze • He *swayed* a moment before he fainted.

2 [+ *obj*] **:** to cause (someone) to agree with you or to share your opinion • The lawyer tried to *sway* the jury. • She persisted in her argument, but I wouldn't let her *sway* me. — often used as *(be) swayed* • He can *be* easily *swayed*.

[2]**sway** *noun* [*noncount*]

1 : a slow movement back and forth • the *sway* of the ship • the sexy *sway* of her hips

2 : a controlling force or influence • He has them ***under his sway***. [=he controls them] • He has come/fallen *under the sway* of terrorists. • The ancient Romans ***held sway*** over most of Europe. • The theory still *holds sway* today. [=still influences people today]

[1]**swear** /ˈsweɚ/ *verb* **swears; swore** /ˈswoɚ/; **sworn** /ˈswoɚn/; **swear·ing**

1 a : to state (something) very strongly and sincerely [+ *obj*] I *swear* (that) I was there. [=I was definitely there; I am telling you the truth when I say that I was there] • Her English is so good that you would *swear* she has been studying it for years. [=you would really think that she has been studying it for years, even though she has not] • You'd *swear* (that) the jewels are real. [=the jewels look very real even though they are not] • I ***could have sworn*** that I left my keys on the counter. [=I'm very surprised that my keys are not on the counter because I definitely remember putting them there] • (*US*) She ***swore up and down*** [=*insisted*] (that) she didn't do it. • (*Brit*) He ***swore blind*** [=*insisted*] (that) he was innocent. [*no obj*] I didn't do anything wrong. ***I swear (on my mother's grave)***. [=I am being absolutely honest when I say that I didn't do anything wrong] • I wouldn't ***swear to it*** [=I'm not absolutely sure about it], but I think he's written three books so far. **b :** to promise very strongly and sincerely to do or not do something [+ *obj*] He *swore* [=*vowed*] to seek revenge. • He *swore* revenge on the killers. • I *swear* (that) I'll never do that again. [*no obj*] I ***swear to God***, I'll kill him if he comes back. • I'll never do that again. *Swear to God*. [=I promise you that I'll never do that again]

2 [*no obj*] **:** to use offensive words when you speak • Don't *swear* in front of the children. — often + *at* • The other driver *swore at* me and drove away.

3 : to make a formal or official promise especially in a court of law [+ *obj*] I do solemnly *swear* to tell the whole truth. • They *swore* (an oath of) allegiance to the United States of America. [=they formally promised that they would be loyal to the United States of America] [*no obj*] Witnesses are required to ***swear on the Bible*** [=to put a hand on the Bible and make a formal promise to tell the truth] before they testify.

4 [+ *obj*] **:** to cause (someone) to make a promise • He ***swore us to secrecy/silence***. [=he made us promise not to tell anyone his secret] — often used as *(be) sworn* • Witnesses *are sworn* to tell the truth.

I swear *informal* — used for emphasis • *I swear*, every time I see her she's got a new boyfriend. • *I swear*, if I had a nickel for every time you did that, I'd be rich.

swear by [*phrasal verb*] ***swear by (something)*** **:** to have or express a lot of confidence in (something) **:** to say that (something) is very good or useful • She *swears by* this diet. • His method sounds pretty strange, but he *swears by* it.

swear in [*phrasal verb*] ***swear (someone) in*** *or* ***swear in (someone)*** **:** to place (someone) in a new office or position by having an official ceremony in which that person makes a formal promise to do the work properly, to be honest and loyal, etc. • When do they *swear* him *in*? — often used as *(be) sworn in* • The new president will *be sworn in* tomorrow. — see also SWEARING-IN

swear off [*phrasal verb*] ***swear off (something)*** *chiefly US* **:** to stop doing, having, or being involved in (something) • He was so disgusted by the election results that he *swore off* politics for good. • She tried to *swear off* chocolate, but she couldn't do it.

– see also SWORN

[2]**swear** *noun, pl* **swears** [*count*] *US, informal* **:** SWEARWORD • I heard him say a *swear*.

swearing–in *noun, pl* **swearings–in** [*count*] **:** an occasion or ceremony in which someone begins a new official job or position by making a formal promise to do the work properly, to be honest and loyal, etc. — see also *swear in* at [1]SWEAR

swear·word /ˈsweɚˌwɚd/ *noun, pl* **-words** [*count*] **:** an offensive word • a movie filled with violent images and rough *swearwords*

[1]sweat /ˈswɛt/ *verb* **sweats**; **sweat** *or* **sweat·ed**; **sweat·ing**

1 [*no obj*] **:** to produce a clear liquid from your skin when you are hot or nervous ▪ He *sweats* a lot when he exercises. ▪ The dancers were *sweating* [=(more formally) *perspiring*] profusely. ▪ (*informal*) He was **sweating like a pig**. [=sweating a lot]

2 [*no obj*] *informal* **:** to work very hard ▪ They *sweated* and saved so their children could go to college. — often + *over* ▪ She was *sweating over* her law books all afternoon. ▪ He *sweated over* the wording of his speech for several days.

3 *informal* **a :** to feel worried or nervous about something [*no obj*] We'll let them *sweat* a while longer. — often + *over* ▪ After they took the test, they were *sweating over* [=worrying about] their scores. [+ *obj*] We'll let them **sweat it out** for a while longer. **b** [*no obj*] **:** to go through an experience that causes a lot of emotional stress or worry — usually + *through* ▪ The cops made him *sweat through* 15 minutes of intense questioning before they let him go. ▪ I *sweated* [=*struggled*] *through* geometry in high school. **c** [+ *obj*] *US* **:** to worry or be nervous about (something) ▪ "The car won't start—what are we going to do?" "Don't **sweat it**. I know all about fixing cars." ▪ Don't **sweat the small stuff**. [=don't worry about minor things]

4 [*no obj*] **:** to produce small drops of liquid on the surface ▪ Cheese *sweats* during ripening. ▪ A pitcher of ice water *sweats* on a hot day.

5 [+ *obj*] *chiefly Brit* **:** to cook (something) slowly in a covered pan with a little fat ▪ *Sweat* sliced onions in a little olive oil until they are soft.

sweat blood see BLOOD

sweat bullets *US, informal* **:** to be very nervous or worried ▪ I was *sweating bullets* while I waited to talk to my boss.

sweat off [*phrasal verb*] ***sweat off (something)*** *or* ***sweat (something) off*** **:** to lose (an amount of weight) by sweating (especially by exercising a lot) ▪ He's trying to *sweat off* a few more pounds.

sweat out [*phrasal verb*] ***sweat out (something)*** *or* ***sweat (something) out*** *informal* **1 :** to wait nervously until the end of (something) ▪ It was a close game, and the fans were really **sweating it out** at the end. **2** *US* **a :** to work hard at (something) ▪ She was **sweating it out** on the treadmill. [=she was exercising and sweating on the treadmill] **b :** to get or achieve (something, such as a victory) by working very hard ▪ He managed to *sweat out* a narrow victory in the semifinals. **3 :** to end (an illness) by exercising and sweating ▪ He's trying to *sweat out* his cold at the gym.

[2]sweat *noun*

1 [*noncount*] **:** the clear liquid that forms on your skin when you are hot or nervous **:** PERSPIRATION ▪ We were drenched/bathed in *sweat* after the workout. ▪ The runners were dripping with *sweat*. ▪ Her forehead was covered with beads of *sweat*.

2 [*count*] **:** the state or condition of someone who is sweating ▪ nervous *sweats* — usually singular ▪ After a few minutes of exercise, we had **worked up a sweat**. [=we were sweating] ▪ I **broke into a sweat** as I struggled up the hill. = I **broke out in a sweat** as I struggled up the hill. [=I began to sweat as I struggled up the hill] — see also COLD SWEAT

3 [*noncount*] **:** hard work ▪ It took a lot of *sweat* and toil to build the house. ▪ We helped them not with money but with our blood and *sweat*.

4 [*noncount*] **:** moisture that forms in drops on a surface ▪ He wiped the *sweat* [=*condensation*] off the bottle.

break a sweat (*US*) *or Brit* ***break sweat*** **:** to begin to sweat ▪ He started running and soon *broke a sweat*. ▪ He loaded all five boxes without *breaking a sweat*. — often used figuratively to say that something is not hard for someone to do ▪ He gave a perfect performance and didn't *break a sweat*. ▪ She rattled off the answers without *breaking a sweat*. [=she gave the answers very easily]

by the sweat of your brow **:** by doing hard, physical work ▪ He earned his money *by the sweat of his brow*.

in a sweat *informal* **:** very nervous or worried about something ▪ He's *in a sweat* about his exams. ▪ There's no need to **get in a sweat** about minor details.

no sweat *informal* **:** with little or no difficulty **:** EASILY ▪ I can do that *no sweat*. ▪ "Can you move that big board for me?" "Sure, *no sweat*." ▪ "Thanks a lot for your help." "*No sweat*." [=helping was not difficult and I was glad to do it]

sweat·band /ˈswɛtˌbænd/ *noun, pl* **-bands** [*count*]

1 : a band of material that you wear around your head or wrist to absorb sweat while you are exercising

2 : a band of material along the inner edge of a hat or cap to absorb sweat

sweated labour *noun* [*noncount*] *Brit* **:** people who work hard and in poor conditions for low pay ▪ goods made cheaply by *sweated labour*; *also* **:** the type of work done by such people

sweat equity *noun* [*noncount*] *US* **:** value in a property, business, etc., that results from the work that a person does to improve it ▪ He's built up a lot of *sweat equity* in his house.; *also* **:** the work itself ▪ He put countless hours of *sweat equity* into that old house.

sweat·er /ˈswɛtɚ/ *noun, pl* **-ers** [*count*] **:** a warm usually knitted piece of clothing for the upper part of your body: such as **a :** one that is put on by pulling it over your head **:** PULLOVER — called also (*Brit*) *jumper*; see color picture on page C15 **b** *US* **:** one that opens like a jacket and that is fastened in the front with buttons or a zipper — called also *cardigan*

sweater vest *noun, pl* **~ vests** [*count*] *US* **:** a sleeveless sweater worn over a shirt — called also (*Brit*) *tank top*

sweat·pants /ˈswɛtˌpænts/ *noun* [*plural*] *chiefly US* **:** pants made from a thick, soft material that are worn mostly when you are exercising — see color picture on page C14

sweats /ˈswɛts/ *noun* [*plural*] *US, informal*

1 : SWEATPANTS

2 : SWEAT SUIT

sweat·shirt /ˈswɛtˌʃɚt/ *noun, pl* **-shirts** [*count*] **:** a piece of clothing for the upper part of your body that is made from a thick, soft material — see color picture on page C14

sweat·shop /ˈswɛtˌʃɑːp/ *noun, pl* **-shops** [*count*] **:** a place where people work long hours for low pay in poor conditions ▪ clothing made in *sweatshops* ▪ *sweatshop* conditions/labor/workers

sweat suit *noun, pl* **~ suits** [*count*] *US* **:** clothing that consists of a matching sweatshirt and sweatpants

sweaty /ˈswɛti/ *adj* **sweat·i·er**; **-est** [*also more ~; most ~*]

1 : causing you to sweat ▪ *sweaty* work ▪ a hot and *sweaty* afternoon

2 : wet with sweat ▪ We were hot and *sweaty* after playing basketball. ▪ *sweaty* palms ▪ My clothes are all *sweaty* from my workout.

swede /ˈswiːd/ *noun, pl* **swedes** [*count, noncount*] *Brit* **:** RUTABAGA

Swede /ˈswiːd/ *noun, pl* **Swedes** [*count*] **:** a person born, raised in, or living in Sweden

[1]sweep /ˈswiːp/ *verb* **sweeps**; **swept** /ˈswɛpt/; **sweep·ing**

1 a *always followed by an adverb or preposition* [+ *obj*] **:** to remove (something, such as dust or dirt) from a surface with a broom or brush or with a quick movement of your hand, fingers, etc. ▪ He *swept* the dirt off the driveway. ▪ He *swept* the crumbs from the table. **b :** to remove dust, dirt, etc., from (something) with a broom or brush [+ *obj*] She *swept* the floor. ▪ I need to *sweep* the kitchen. ▪ Are you finished *sweeping* the porch? [*no obj*] Have you *swept* yet? — see also SWEEP OUT (below), SWEEP UP (below)

2 *always followed by an adverb or preposition* **a** [*no obj*] **:** to move or pass quickly, forcefully, or smoothly ▪ A storm *swept* across the plains. ▪ Fires *swept* through the forest. — often used figuratively ▪ She **swept to victory** on a wave of popularity. **b** [*no obj*] **:** to move or walk in a smooth, quick, and impressive way ▪ She proudly *swept* into the room. ▪ The limo *swept* up to the door. **c** [+ *obj*] **:** to push or move (something) quickly or forcefully ▪ He *swept* the curtains aside. ▪ She *swept* the books off the desk. **d** [+ *obj*] **:** to push, carry, or lift (someone or something) with great force ▪ The debris was *swept* [=*carried*] out to sea by the tide. ▪ She was *swept* toward the door by the crowd. ▪ He *swept* her into his arms. — often used figuratively ▪ We were *swept* along/away by her enthusiasm. ▪ The party was **swept into power** in the last election.

3 *always followed by an adverb or preposition* [*no obj*] *of a feeling or emotion* **:** to be felt suddenly ▪ Fear *swept* over/through her. [=she suddenly felt afraid] ▪ A feeling of relief *swept* over him.

4 *always followed by an adverb or preposition* [+ *obj*] **:** to move (your hand, arm, etc.) in a wide, curving motion ▪ He *swept* his arm across the table.

5 [+ *obj*] **:** to pass over (all of an area or place) in a continuous motion ▪ The teacher's gaze *swept* the classroom. ▪ A searchlight *swept* the area. ▪ Strong winds *sweep* the mountainside.

6 [+ *obj*] **:** to become very popular or common suddenly in (a

particular place) ▪ It's the latest craze *sweeping* the nation.
7 [+ *obj*] : to win everything that can be won in (something, such as an election) in an easy or impressive way ▪ The opposition party *swept* the election.
8 [+ *obj*] *US, sports* : to win all of the games in a series of games against another team ▪ They *swept* their rivals in a three-game series. ▪ They *swept* the series/doubleheader. ▪ They were *swept* in the play-offs last year.
9 *always followed by an adverb or preposition* [+ *obj*] : to brush or pull (your hair) away from your face ▪ She *swept* her hair up/back and clipped it in place.
10 *always followed by an adverb or preposition* [*no obj*] : to form a long, smooth curve ▪ The property *sweeps* down to the water's edge.
sweep aside [*phrasal verb*] ***sweep (something) aside*** *or* ***sweep aside (something)*** : to treat (something) as not important : to ignore (something) ▪ He *swept aside* [=*brushed aside*] questions about his son's arrest. ▪ He *swept aside* [=*dismissed*] their objections, refusing to change his plans.
sweep away [*phrasal verb*] ***sweep (something) away*** *or* ***sweep away (something)*** : to destroy or remove (something) completely ▪ Floods *swept away* several houses. ▪ an ancient civilization *swept away* by war ▪ His performance today *swept away* any doubts about his ability to play.
sweep out [*phrasal verb*] ***sweep (something) out*** *or* ***sweep out (something)*** : to remove dust, dirt, etc., from (something) by using a broom or brush ▪ Please *sweep out* the room when you're done working.
sweep (someone) off his/her feet : to make (someone) suddenly become very attracted to you in a romantic way ▪ She says that he *swept* her *off her feet*, and they were married six months later.
sweep (something) under the rug (*US*) *or chiefly Brit* ***sweep (something) under the carpet*** : to hide (something that is illegal, embarrassing, or wrong) ▪ He tried to *sweep* his past mistakes *under the rug*. ▪ This is not something we can just *sweep under the rug*.
sweep the board *chiefly Brit* : to win everything that can be won in a competition ▪ She *swept the board* at the awards ceremony.
sweep up [*phrasal verb*] **1** ***sweep up*** *or* ***sweep (something) up*** *or* ***sweep up (something)*** **a** : to remove dust, dirt, etc., from (something) by using a broom or brush ▪ When I was *sweeping up*, I found an earring that I had lost. ▪ Can you please *sweep up* the porch? **b** ***sweep (something) up*** *or* ***sweep up (something)*** : to remove (something, such as dust, dirt, etc.) from a surface by using a broom or brush ▪ She *swept up* the broken glass. **2** ***sweep (someone or something) up*** *or* ***sweep up (someone or something)*** : to pick up (someone or something) in one quick, continuous motion ▪ She *swept* the baby *up* and carried her to the crib.

[2]**sweep** *noun, pl* **sweeps**
1 [*count*] : an act of cleaning an area with a broom or brush — usually singular ▪ He gave the floor/room a quick *sweep*. [=he swept the floor/room quickly]
2 [*count*] : a long, smooth movement often in a wide curve — often + *of* ▪ He brushed the crumbs away with a *sweep of* his hand.
3 [*count*] : a large area of land often forming a wide curve — + *of*; usually singular ▪ the *sweep of* the coastline
4 [*singular*] : everything that is included in something : the full range or extent of something — + *of* ▪ The book attempts to cover the whole *sweep of* American history.
5 [*count*] : a search for something over a large area — usually singular ▪ The search party made a *sweep* of the forest.
6 [*count*] *US, sports* : an occurrence in which one team wins all the games in a series of games against another team ▪ They won the series in a *sweep*. ▪ a World Series *sweep* — see also *clean sweep* at [1]CLEAN
7 ***sweeps*** [*plural*] *US* : a time during the year when television stations try to see which shows are the most popular in order to decide how much can be charged for advertising ▪ The network is trying to increase ratings during (the) *sweeps*. ▪ *sweeps* week/month
8 [*count*] : CHIMNEY SWEEP

sweep·er /ˈswiːpɚ/ *noun, pl* **-ers** [*count*]
1 : a person or machine that sweeps something — see also MINESWEEPER
2 *soccer* : a player whose position is behind other defending players

[1]**sweeping** *adj* [*more* ~; *most* ~]
1 : including or involving many things : wide in range or amount ▪ *sweeping* changes/reforms ▪ a *sweeping* view of the valley ▪ The election was a ***sweeping victory*** [=a victory that is won by a large margin] for the party.
2 *disapproving* : too general : including or involving too many things or people ▪ *sweeping* claims/generalizations ▪ a *sweeping* condemnation
3 *always used before a noun* : having a curving form : forming a curve ▪ a *sweeping* coastline ▪ He dismissed the idea with a *sweeping* motion of his arm.

[2]**sweeping** *noun* [*singular*] : an act of cleaning an area with a broom or brush ▪ The porch needs a good *sweeping*.

sweep·stakes /ˈswiːpˌsteɪks/ *noun* [*plural*] : a race or contest in which the winner receives all the prize money

[1]**sweet** /ˈswiːt/ *adj* **sweet·er; -est** [*also more* ~; *most* ~]
1 : containing a lot of sugar ▪ *sweet* dishes/foods ▪ *sweet* desserts ▪ She likes her coffee *sweet*. ▪ a *sweet* wine ▪ That candy is too *sweet*.
2 : very gentle, kind, or friendly ▪ a *sweet* elderly couple ▪ He's a really *sweet* guy. ▪ She has a *sweet* smile. ▪ It was *sweet* of her to take care of them.
3 *chiefly Brit* : very pretty or cute ▪ The baby looks *sweet* [=*adorable*] in her bonnet.
4 a : having a very pleasant smell, sound, or appearance ▪ the *sweet* fragrance/scent of spring flowers ▪ *sweet* music/voices ▪ a *sweet*-smelling perfume **b** : clean and fresh ▪ The spring air was *sweet*. ▪ The water from the well is *sweet*. **c** *US* : not salty or salted ▪ *sweet* butter
5 : making you feel happy or pleased ▪ Victory/success/revenge is *sweet*. : very pleasant ▪ "Good night and ***sweet dreams***." [=I hope you will sleep well and have pleasant dreams]
6 *chiefly US, informal* : very good or impressive ▪ Prosecutors offered him a *sweet* deal if he'd testify. ▪ a *sweet* job offer ▪ This video game is pretty *sweet*. [=*cool*] ▪ "I got backstage passes." "*Sweet!*"
be sweet on *old-fashioned + informal* : to be in love with (someone) ▪ He's *been sweet on* her since they were kids.
home sweet home see [1]HOME
keep someone sweet *Brit, informal* : to be kind and friendly so that someone will do something for you later
short and sweet see [1]SHORT
sweet nothings see [3]NOTHING
your own sweet time see [1]TIME

[2]**sweet** *noun, pl* **sweets**
1 a [*count*] : a food that contains a lot of sugar : a sweet food ▪ I'm trying to cut down on *sweets*. **b** [*count*] *Brit* : a piece of candy ▪ a bag of *sweets* **c** [*count, noncount*] *Brit* : a sweet food served at the end of a meal : DESSERT
2 [*noncount*] *old-fashioned* — used to address someone you love ▪ Good morning, ***my sweet***

sweet–and–sour /ˌswiːtnˈsawɚ/ *adj, always used before a noun* : having a flavor that is both sweet and sour ▪ *sweet-and-sour* chicken/pork

sweet·bread /ˈswiːtˌbrɛd/ *noun* [*count, noncount*] : a part (called the pancreas) of a young cow or sheep that is eaten as food — usually plural

sweet corn *noun* [*noncount*]
1 *US* : a kind of corn (sense 1) that contains a lot of sugar
2 *sweetcorn Brit* : [1]CORN 1b

sweet·en /ˈswiːtn/ *verb* **-ens; -ened; -en·ing** [+ *obj*]
1 : to make (something) sweet or sweeter in taste ▪ She *sweetened* her coffee. ▪ He *sweetened* his cereal a little.
2 : to make (something) more valuable or attractive ▪ He *sweetened* the deal with a large signing bonus.
sweeten the pill see [1]PILL
sweeten up [*phrasal verb*] ***sweeten up (someone)*** *or* ***sweeten (someone) up*** *informal* : to be very nice to (someone) in order to get something ▪ He's been trying to *sweeten* his mother *up* so she'll lend him the car.
– sweet·en·er /ˈswiːtnɚ/ *noun, pl* **-ers** [*count*] ▪ She used an artificial *sweetener* in the pie instead of sugar.

sweet FA /-ˈɛfˈeɪ/ *also* **sweet Fan·ny Ad·ams** /-ˈfæniˈædəmz/ *noun* [*noncount*] *Brit slang* : nothing at all ▪ You've done *sweet FA* to help me and I'm angry! ▪ Don't listen to him. He knows *sweet FA* about this.

sweet·heart /ˈswiːtˌhɑɚt/ *noun, pl* **-hearts**
1 a [*count*] *somewhat old-fashioned* : a person you love very much ▪ childhood/college *sweethearts* **b** — used to address someone you love ▪ How was your day, *sweetheart*? [=*darling, dear*] ▪ *Sweetheart*, what's the matter?
2 [*count*] : a kind or helpful person : someone who is very nice ▪ Be a *sweetheart* and help your grandmother. ▪ She is such a little *sweetheart*.

S

sweetheart deal *noun, pl* ~ **deals** [*count*] *chiefly US* : an unusually good arrangement or agreement that helps someone who has a lot of influence or who knows someone important ▪ He got a *sweetheart deal* on the new job/car because he knows the manager.

sweet·ie /ˈswi:ti/ *noun, pl* **-ies** *informal*
1 a [*count*] : a person you love very much ▪ My *sweetie* and I will be at the party. **b** — used to address someone you love ▪ "How are you feeling, *sweetie*?"
2 [*count*] : a kind or helpful person : someone who is very nice ▪ She's a total/real *sweetie*.
3 [*count*] *Brit* : a candy or sweet — used especially by children or when speaking to children ▪ a jar of *sweeties*

sweetie pie *noun, pl* ~ **pies** *informal*
1 [*count*] : a person you love very much ▪ my *sweetie pie*
2 — used to address someone you love ▪ "*Sweetie pie*, what's wrong?"

sweet·ish /ˈswi:tɪʃ/ *adj* : slightly or somewhat sweet in taste or smell ▪ a *sweetish* red wine

sweet·ly /ˈswi:tli/ *adv*
1 : in a kind or loving way ▪ He asked *sweetly* if she was all right. ▪ She smiled *sweetly* at him.
2 : smelling or tasting sweet ▪ a *sweetly* scented candle ▪ *sweetly* flavored dishes
3 : in a pleasant or appealing way ▪ *sweetly* melodious music

sweet·meat /ˈswi:tˌmi:t/ *noun, pl* **-meats** [*count*] *old-fashioned* : a piece of candy or a piece of fruit covered with sugar

sweet·ness /ˈswi:tnəs/ *noun* [*noncount*]
1 : the quality of tasting or smelling sweet ▪ I like the *sweetness* of the sauce.
2 : the quality of being kind or loving ▪ the *sweetness* of his nature ▪ I'll never forget the *sweetness* of her smile.
3 : the quality of being pleasant or appealing ▪ the *sweetness* of the melody
sweetness and light : pleasant and enjoyable ▪ Life is not all *sweetness and light*. ▪ She was yelling at us all morning, but when the guests arrived, she was all *sweetness and light*.

sweet pea *noun, pl* ~ **peas** [*count*] : a climbing plant with flowers that have a sweet smell

sweet pepper *noun, pl* ~ **-pers** [*count*] : a type of hollow vegetable (called a pepper) that is usually red, green, or yellow, that has a mild flavor, and that can be eaten raw or cooked ▪ a red/green *sweet pepper*

sweet potato *noun, pl* ~ **-toes** [*count, noncount*] : a large root of a tropical plant that has orange skin and orange flesh, that is eaten as a vegetable, and that tastes sweet — see color picture on page C4; compare YAM

sweet–talk /ˈswi:tˌtɑ:k/ *verb* **-talks; -talked; -talk·ing** [+ *obj*] : to say nice things to (someone) in order to persuade that person to do something — often + *into* ▪ He tried to *sweet-talk* her *into* doing his work for him.
– sweet talk *noun* [*noncount*] ▪ Don't fall for his *sweet talk*.

sweet tooth *noun* [*singular*] *informal* : a liking for sweet foods ▪ He's always ***had a sweet tooth.*** [=he has always liked sweets]

[1]swell /ˈswɛl/ *verb* **swells; swelled; swelled** *or* **swol·len** /ˈswoʊlən/; **swell·ing**
1 [*no obj*] : to become larger than normal ▪ Her broken ankle *swelled* badly. — often + *up* ▪ The bee sting made my whole arm *swell up*.
2 [+ *obj*] : to make (something, such as a river) larger or more full than normal ▪ Heavy rains *swelled* the river.
3 : to increase in size or number [*no obj*] The population has *swelled/swollen* in recent years. ▪ The economy is *swelling* at an annual rate of five percent. [+ *obj*] Immigrants have *swelled* the population.
4 [*no obj*] : to become louder ▪ The music *swelled*.
5 : to cause (something, such as a sail) to stretch outward and become full [+ *obj*] The breeze *swelled* (out) the sails. [*no obj*] The sails *swelled* (out) in the breeze.
6 [*no obj*] : to feel an emotion strongly — + *with* ▪ His heart *swelled with* pride. [=he felt very proud]
a swelled head see [1]HEAD
– swollen *adj* ▪ a *swollen* ankle/gland ▪ a *swollen* river

[2]swell *noun, pl* **swells**
1 [*count*] : an upward and downward movement of the water in the sea ▪ The storm has brought high winds and heavy *swells* along the coast.
2 [*noncount*] : the curved or rounded shape of something ▪ the *swell* of a pregnant woman's belly
3 [*singular*] **a** : an increase in size or number ▪ a *swell* in the population **b** : an increase in loudness ▪ the *swell* of the music **c** : an increase in the strength of an emotion ▪ a *swell* of enthusiasm/fear/hope — see also GROUNDSWELL
4 [*count*] *informal + old-fashioned* : a socially important or fashionable person ▪ a party for a bunch of *swells*

[3]swell *adj, US, informal + old-fashioned* : very good : EXCELLENT ▪ That was a *swell* party. ▪ He's a *swell* guy.

swell·ing /ˈswɛlɪŋ/ *noun, pl* **-ings**
1 [*count*] : an area on someone's body that is larger than normal because of an illness or injury ▪ There was a *swelling* above her eye.
2 [*noncount*] : the condition of being larger than normal ▪ The *swelling* around her eye should subside in a few days.

swel·ter /ˈswɛltɚ/ *verb* **-ters; -tered; -ter·ing** [*no obj*] : to be very hot and uncomfortable ▪ We were *sweltering* in the summer heat.

swel·ter·ing /ˈswɛltərɪŋ/ *adj* : very hot ▪ a *sweltering* summer day

swept *past tense and past participle of* [1]SWEEP

swerve /ˈswɚv/ *verb* **swerves; swerved; swerv·ing** [*no obj*] : to change direction suddenly especially to avoid hitting someone or something ▪ The car *swerved* [=*turned*] sharply to avoid hitting the deer. ▪ He lost control of the car and *swerved* toward a tree.

[1]swift /ˈswɪft/ *adj* **swift·er; -est** [*also more* ~; *most* ~]
1 : happening or done quickly or immediately ▪ a *swift* and accurate response ▪ a *swift* kick
2 : moving or able to move very fast ▪ a *swift* horse/runner ▪ a *swift* river current
3 *US, informal* : smart or intelligent — usually used in negative statements ▪ She's a nice kid, but she's not too *swift*. ▪ "I locked myself out of my car." "That wasn't very *swift*."
– swift·ly *adv* [*more* ~; *most* ~] ▪ He answered *swiftly*.
– swift·ness /ˈswɪftnəs/ *noun* [*noncount*]

[2]swift *noun, pl* **swifts** [*count*] : a small bird that has long, narrow wings

swig /ˈswɪg/ *verb* **swigs; swigged; swig·ging** [+ *obj*] *informal* : to drink (something) quickly and in large amounts : to swallow a lot of (a drink) ▪ She was *swigging* [=*gulping*] water from a bottle after her workout.
– swig *noun, pl* **swigs** [*count*] ▪ He took a *swig* of whisky.

[1]swill /ˈswɪl/ *verb* **swills; swilled; swill·ing**
1 [+ *obj*] *informal* : to drink (something) quickly in large amounts ▪ They were *swilling* (down) beer and playing cards.
2 a [*no obj*] *of a liquid* : to move around in a container ▪ She watched the water *swill* around in the bucket. **b** [+ *obj*] : to cause (a liquid) to move around in a container ▪ He *swilled* the water around in the pot.
3 [+ *obj*] *chiefly Brit* : to clean (something) by pouring water on it ▪ He *swilled* the floor with buckets of water.

[2]swill *noun* [*noncount*]
1 : food for animals (such as pigs) made from scraps of food and water
2 *informal* : food or drink that is very bad or unappealing ▪ I refuse to eat this *swill*. [=*garbage*]

[1]swim /ˈswɪm/ *verb* **swims; swam** /ˈswæm/; **swum** /ˈswʌm/; **swim·ming**
1 a [*no obj*] : to move through water by moving your arms and legs ▪ He's teaching the children to *swim*. ▪ She *swam* across the pool. ▪ I can't *swim*. ▪ He *swam* (for) almost a mile. — see also SWIMMING **b** [+ *obj*] : to move through or across (an area of water) by swimming ▪ He *swam* the English Channel. **c** [+ *obj*] : to swim by using (a specified method) ▪ The racers must *swim* the backstroke. **d** [*no obj*] *of a fish, bird, etc.* : to move through or over water ▪ We watched the fish *swimming* in the river. ▪ Ducks *swam* in/on the pond.
2 [*no obj*] : to be completely covered with a liquid — usually used as *(be) swimming in* ▪ The potatoes *were swimming in* butter/gravy.
3 [*no obj*] **a** : to feel dizzy or unable to think clearly because you are sick, confused, etc. ▪ I felt weak and my ***head was swimming.*** ▪ All the facts and figures he was reciting were starting to make my *head swim*. [=starting to make me feel confused, unable to think clearly, etc.] **b** *of something you are looking at* : to seem to be moving around because you are tired, sick, etc. ▪ The room *swam* before my eyes.
sink or swim see [1]SINK
swim with/against the tide see [1]TIDE

[2]swim *noun, pl* **swims** [*count*] : an act or period of swimming — usually singular ▪ We have time for a quick *swim* before dinner. ▪ Would you like to ***go for a swim***? ▪ The schools competed in a ***swim meet***. [=a swimming competition with many races]

in/into the swim (of things) *informal* : involved in an activity or informed about a situation ▪ She likes to be *in the swim of things*. ▪ When he gets *into the swim of things*, he'll be much happier.

swim·mer /ˈswɪmɚ/ *noun, pl* **-mers** [*count*] : a person who swims ▪ She's a good/strong/fast *swimmer*. : a person who is swimming ▪ There were a few *swimmers* at the lake this morning.

swimming *noun* [*noncount*] : the sport or activity of moving through water by moving your arms and legs ▪ *Swimming* keeps her fit. ▪ I am ***going swimming*** later today. — see also SYNCHRONIZED SWIMMING

swimming bath *noun, pl* ~ **baths** [*count*] *Brit* : a public swimming pool that is usually indoors

swimming cap *noun, pl* ~ **caps** [*count*] *chiefly Brit* : a tight rubber cap that you wear while you swim to keep your hair dry

swimming costume *noun, pl* ~ **-tumes** [*count*] *Brit* : SWIMSUIT

swimming hole *noun, pl* ~ **holes** [*count*] *US* : a place in a river, pond, etc., where people swim ▪ The boys cooled off at the *swimming hole*.

swim·ming·ly /ˈswɪmɪŋli/ *adv, informal* : very well ▪ We expect everything to ***go swimmingly***.

swimming pool *noun, pl* ~ **pools** [*count*] : a large structure that is filled with water and that is used for swimming ▪ Our neighbors have a *swimming pool* in their backyard. ▪ a public *swimming pool*

swimming trunks *noun* [*plural*] : special shorts that men and boys wear for swimming — called also *trunks*; see color picture on page C13

swim·suit /ˈswɪmˌsuːt/ *noun, pl* **-suits** [*count*] : special clothing that women and girls wear for swimming — called also (*chiefly US*) *bathing suit*, (*Brit*) *swimming costume*; see color picture on page C13

swim·wear /ˈswɪmˌweɚ/ *noun* [*noncount*] : special clothing worn for swimming

swin·dle /ˈswɪndl̩/ *verb* **swin·dles**; **swin·dled**; **swin·dling** [+ *obj*] : to take money or property from (someone) by using lies or tricks : CHEAT — usually + *out of* ▪ He *swindled* elderly women *out of* their savings.

— **swindle** *noun, pl* **swindles** [*count*] ▪ an insurance *swindle* ▪ bank *swindles* — **swin·dler** /ˈswɪndlɚ/ *noun, pl* **-dlers** [*count*]

swine /ˈswaɪn/ *noun, pl* **swine** [*count*]

1 : PIG 1 ▪ methods of raising *swine* ▪ a herd of *swine*

2 *informal* : a very bad person ▪ He's such a *swine*! ▪ He's a filthy *swine*.

cast/throw pearls before swine see [1]PEARL

swine·herd /ˈswaɪnˌhɚd/ *noun, pl* **-herds** [*count*] *old-fashioned* : a person whose job is to take care of pigs

[1]**swing** /ˈswɪŋ/ *verb* **swings**; **swung** /ˈswʌŋ/; **swing·ing**

1 : to move backward and forward or from side to side while hanging from something [*no obj*] The sheets *swung* on the clothesline. ▪ The clock's pendulum stopped *swinging*. [+ *obj*] She sat on the edge of the table, *swinging* her legs. ▪ She *swung* the bag by the handle. [=she held the handle of the bag and made the bag swing]

2 *always followed by an adverb, adjective, or preposition* : to move with a smooth, curving motion [*no obj*] The monkeys were *swinging* from branch to branch high up in the trees. ▪ The door *swung* open/shut. [+ *obj*] He *swung* himself (up) into the truck. ▪ I *swung* my suitcase into the backseat of the car. ▪ She sat on the counter and *swung* her legs over to the other side. ▪ She *swung* the door open.

3 : to move (your arm, a tool, etc.) with a quick, curving motion especially to try to hit something [+ *obj*] Be careful how you *swing* that ax. ▪ She *swung* the bat but missed the ball. ▪ She *swung* her purse at me. [*no obj*] She *swung* (at the ball) but missed. ▪ He ***swung at me*** [=tried to hit me with his fist] for no reason.

4 [*no obj*] : to move back and forth on a special type of seat (called a swing) ▪ a playground where kids go to *swing*

5 *always followed by an adverb or preposition* : to turn or move quickly in a particular direction [*no obj*] The road *swings* to the left sharply after a few miles. — often + *around* ▪ He *swung around* to look at the clock. [+ *obj*] She *swung* the car into the driveway. ▪ He *swung* the flashlight toward the noise.

6 a *always followed by an adverb or preposition* [*no obj*] : to change suddenly from one state or condition to another ▪ Sales *swung* up sharply at the end of the year. ▪ The game suddenly *swung* in favor of the home team. ▪ His mood can *swing* wildly from cheerful to angry. ▪ They have to be ready to ***swing into action*** [=to start doing something quickly] at a moment's notice. **b** [+ *obj*] : to change or influence (something) in an important way ▪ His strong performance in the second half *swung* the game in our favor. ▪ Her promise to lower taxes may have *swung* [=changed the outcome of] the presidential election. ▪ They may still *swing* their votes to the other candidate.

7 [+ *obj*] *informal* : to do or manage (something) successfully ▪ Do you think you can *swing* the job? ▪ She isn't able to *swing* [=*afford*] a new car on her income. ▪ If he can ***swing it***, he'll visit next month.

8 [*no obj*] *informal + somewhat old-fashioned* : to be lively or exciting ▪ The bar really *swings* on weekends. ▪ The party was *swinging*.

9 [*no obj*] *old-fashioned* : to die by hanging ▪ He *swung* for his crimes.

swing both ways *informal* : to be bisexual

swing by *also* ***swing over*** [*phrasal verb*] *US, informal* : to make a brief visit ▪ I'll *swing by* [=*stop by*] after work to drop off the paperwork.

swing the balance : to change a situation so that one person, group, etc., is more able or likely to succeed than another ▪ Both candidates are qualified, but her experience could *swing the balance* in her favor.

[2]**swing** *noun, pl* **swings**

1 [*count*] **a** : an act of moving something with a quick, sweeping motion : an act of swinging a bat, fist, etc. ▪ One *swing* of the hammer was all it took to drive the nail through the board. ▪ She needs to work on her (golf) *swing*. [=she needs to practice the way she swings a golf club] ▪ He ***took a swing*** at the pitch. [=he swung at the pitch; tried to hit the ball with his bat] ▪ Some drunk *took a swing* at me. [=tried to hit me] **b** : the movement of something that swings backward and forward or from side to side ▪ the *swing* of a pendulum

2 [*count*] : a usually sudden change from one state or condition to another ▪ upward/downward *swings* in the stock market ▪ She couldn't deal with his unpredictable ***mood swings***. [=changes in his mood]

3 [*count*] : a seat that hangs from ropes or chains and that moves back and forth ▪ The kids were playing on the *swings*. ▪ We sat on the porch *swing* and watched the neighbors. — see picture at PLAYGROUND

4 [*noncount*] : a style of jazz music that has a lively rhythm and that is played mostly for dancing

go with a swing *Brit, informal* : to be lively and enjoyable ▪ What a great party! It really *went with a swing*!

in full swing : at the highest level of activity ▪ Work on the project is *in full swing*. ▪ The party was *in full swing* by the time we arrived.

in/into the swing of *informal* : fully involved and comfortable with (a regular activity, process, etc.) ▪ After a while, she ***got into the swing of*** her job. [=she got used to her job and was able to do it well] ▪ I've been away on vacation but I should ***be (back) in the swing of things*** in a few days.

swings and roundabouts *Brit, informal* — used to say that two choices or situations are basically the same because they have an equal number of advantages and disadvantages ▪ It is a case of *swings and roundabouts*.

[3]**swing** *adj, always used before a noun*

1 : of or relating to the style of jazz music called swing ▪ a *swing* band ▪ *swing* music/dancing

2 : not certain to vote for a particular candidate or party in an election and therefore often able to decide the result of the election ▪ *swing* voters/states

swing bridge *noun, pl* ~ **bridges** [*count*] : a bridge that can be moved or raised so that tall boats can pass under it

swinge·ing /ˈswɪnʤɪŋ/ *adj, Brit*

1 : very large and difficult to deal with ▪ Homeowners now face *swingeing* increases in their bills. ▪ *swingeing* fines/penalties/taxes ▪ *swingeing* cuts in pay

2 : very critical or severe ▪ a *swingeing* criticism of the government's policies

swing·er /ˈswɪŋɚ/ *noun, pl* **-ers** [*count*]

1 *informal + old-fashioned* : someone who is lively, entertaining, and fashionable

2 : someone who has sex with many people ▪ She and her husband are *swingers*. [=they have a relationship in which each of them is allowed to have sex with many other people]

swing·ing /ˈswɪŋɪŋ/ *adj* [*more* ~; *most* ~] *informal* + *old-fashioned* : lively or exciting ▪ This music is really *swinging*. ▪ a *swinging* party

swinging door *noun, pl* ~ **doors** [*count*] *US* : a door that can be pushed open from either side and that swings shut when it is released — called also (*Brit*) *swing door*

swing set *noun, pl* ~ **sets** [*count*] *US* : a wooden or metal structure that has swings hanging from it and that may have a slide or other things attached to it for children to play on

swing shift *noun, pl* ~ **shifts** [*count*] *US* : a scheduled period of work that begins in the afternoon and ends at night ▪ He works the *swing shift*.

[1]**swipe** /ˈswaɪp/ *verb* **swipes**; **swiped**; **swip·ing**
1 : to reach toward and try to hit (something) with a swinging motion [+ *obj*] The cat *swiped* the dog across the nose. [*no obj*] — usually + *at* ▪ The cat *swiped at* the dog.
2 [+ *obj*] *informal* : to steal (something) ▪ They *swiped* some candy from the store. ▪ She *swiped* my idea.
3 [+ *obj*] : to pass (a credit card, ATM card, etc.) through a machine that reads information from it ▪ The cashier *swiped* the credit card and gave it back to me.

[2]**swipe** *noun, pl* **swipes** [*count*]
1 *informal* : a criticism or insult that is directed toward a particular person or group ▪ She ***took a swipe at*** her former company in her latest column.
2 : a swinging movement of a person's hand, an animal's paw, etc., that is done in an attempt to hit something ▪ a *swipe* of the cat's paw ▪ He ***took a swipe at*** the ball. [=he swung at the ball and tried to hit it]

swipe card *noun, pl* ~ **cards** [*count*] : a special plastic card with a magnetic strip that has information which can be read by special machines

[1]**swirl** /ˈswɚl/ *verb* **swirls**; **swirled**; **swirl·ing** : to move in circles or to cause (something) to move in circles [+ *obj*] She *swirled* the drink (around) in her glass. [*no obj*] The water *swirled* around/down the drain. ▪ strong *swirling* winds — often used figuratively ▪ Rumors are *swirling* about/around the team. [=there are a lot of rumors about the team]

[2]**swirl** *noun, pl* **swirls** [*count*]
1 : a twisting or swirling movement, form, or object ▪ A *swirl* of smoke rose from the chimney. ▪ He painted *swirls* of color on the canvas. ▪ ice cream with chocolate *swirls*
2 : a state of busy movement or activity — usually + *of* ▪ She was caught up in the *swirl of* events.

[1]**swish** /ˈswɪʃ/ *verb* **swish·es**; **swished**; **swish·ing** : to move with or cause (something) to move with a soft sweeping or brushing sound [*no obj*] He watched as the windshield wipers *swished* back and forth. ▪ The horse's tail *swished* back and forth. [+ *obj*] The horse *swished* its tail back and forth.
— **swish** *noun* [*singular*] ▪ The horse shooed the flies away with a *swish* of its tail.

[2]**swish** *adj*, *Brit*, *informal* : fashionable and expensive : SWANKY ▪ a *swish* hotel

[1]**Swiss** /ˈswɪs/ *adj* : of or relating to Switzerland or its people ▪ *Swiss* history ▪ the *Swiss* ski team

[2]**Swiss** *noun*
the Swiss : the people of Switzerland ▪ the traditions of *the Swiss*

Swiss chard *noun* [*noncount*] : CHARD

Swiss cheese *noun* [*noncount*] : a type of cheese that is hard and pale yellow and that has many large holes

Swiss roll *noun, pl* ~ **rolls** [*count, noncount*] *Brit* : JELLY ROLL

[1]**switch** /ˈswɪʧ/ *noun, pl* **switch·es** [*count*]
1 : a small device that starts or stops the flow of electricity to something (such as a lamp or a machine) when it is pressed or moved up and down ▪ She flicked a *switch* and turned the lamp/lights on. ▪ a light/dimmer *switch* ▪ He threw the *switch* to stop the machine. — see also DIP SWITCH, TOGGLE SWITCH
2 : a sudden change from one thing to another — usually singular ▪ a *switch* from the old way of doing things ▪ There has been a *switch* in plans. [=the plans have changed] ▪ If you're not happy in your current job, maybe it's time to ***make a switch*** (to another job). ▪ "He says he'll do it himself." "Well, ***that's a switch.***" [=that's something unusual] — see also BAIT AND SWITCH

switch

3 *US* : a device for moving the rails of a track so that a train may be turned from one track to another
4 : a thin stick that can be easily bent

[2]**switch** *verb* **switches**; **switched**; **switch·ing**
1 : to make a change from one thing to another : to start doing or using something that is different [*no obj*] I *switched* to a new doctor. ▪ He kept *switching* back and forth between topics. ▪ She *switched* back to/from her original insurance company. ▪ We *switched* over to a different telephone service. [+ *obj*] Why did you *switch* jobs?
2 : to make a change from one thing to another by turning or pushing a button or moving a switch, lever, etc. [*no obj*] He *switched* (over) to a different channel. [+ *obj*] Stop *switching* channels.
3 [+ *obj*] : to change or replace (something) with another thing ▪ They *switched* places/positions/roles/sides. ▪ He *switched* (around) his last two appointments. ▪ (*US*) He is going to ***switch (shifts) with*** me Monday. [=he will work my shift and I will work his shift on Monday]
switch gears see [1]GEAR
switch off [*phrasal verb*] **1** ***switch (something) off*** or ***switch off (something)*** : to turn off (something) by turning or pushing a button or moving a switch, lever, etc. ▪ He *switched off* the light/lamp. **2** *informal* : to stop paying attention ▪ When the topic turned to the stock market, he *switched off*. [=*tuned out*]
switch on [*phrasal verb*] ***switch (something) on*** or ***switch on (something)*** : to turn on (something) by turning or pushing a button or moving a switch, lever, etc. ▪ I *switched on* the TV and watched the news.

switch·back /ˈswɪʧˌbæk/ *noun, pl* **-backs** [*count*] : a road, trail, or section of railroad tracks that has many sharp turns for climbing a steep hill

switch·blade /ˈswɪʧˌbleɪd/ *noun, pl* **-blades** [*count*] *chiefly US* : a knife that has a blade inside the handle which springs out when a button is pressed — called also (*Brit*) *flick-knife*

switch·board /ˈswɪʧˌboɚd/ *noun, pl* **-boards** [*count*] : a system used to connect telephone calls with many separate phone lines in a building ▪ She used to work as a *switchboard* operator. ▪ Angry callers flooded/jammed the company's *switchboard*. [=made telephone calls to the company]

switch·er·oo /ˌswɪʧəˈruː/ *noun, pl* **-oos** [*count*] *US, informal* : an unexpected or secret change ▪ They changed to a different system without telling anyone that they had ***pulled a switcheroo***.

switch–hit·ter /ˈswɪʧˈhɪtɚ/ *noun, pl* **-ters** [*count*] *baseball* : a batter who bats right-handed against a left-handed pitcher and left-handed against a right-handed pitcher
— **switch–hit** /ˈswɪʧˈhɪt/ *verb* **-hits**; **-hit**; **-hit·ting** [*no obj*] ▪ His father taught him how to *switch-hit* when he was a kid.

[1]**swiv·el** /ˈswɪvəl/ *noun, pl* **-els** [*count*] : a device that joins two parts so that one of the parts can turn or spin while the other part does not move ▪ a ***swivel chair*** [=a chair with the seat mounted on a swivel so that it turns freely]

[2]**swivel** *verb* **-els**; *US* **-eled** or *Brit* **-elled**; *US* **-el·ing** or *Brit* **-el·ling** : to turn around [*no obj*] He *swiveled* [=*spun*] around to see who was calling him. ▪ She *swiveled* in her seat to check the time. [+ *obj*] The owl *swiveled* [=*twisted*] its head around. ▪ She *swiveled* the chair around to face us.

swollen see [1]SWELL

swoon /ˈswuːn/ *verb* **swoons**; **swooned**; **swoon·ing** [*no obj*]
1 : to become very excited about someone or something — usually + *over* ▪ Teenage girls *swooned over* the band's lead singer.
2 *old-fashioned* : to suddenly become unconscious : FAINT ▪ She almost *swooned* from fright.
— **swoon** *noun* [*singular*] *old-fashioned* ▪ She fell into a *swoon*. [=she swooned]

swoop /ˈswuːp/ *verb* **swoops**; **swooped**; **swoop·ing** [*no obj*]
1 : to fly down through the air suddenly — usually + *down* ▪ A hawk *swooped down* and caught a rabbit in the field.
2 *always followed by an adverb or preposition* : to arrive at a place suddenly and unexpectedly ▪ The police *swooped* in and captured the criminals.
in/at one fell swoop see [3]FELL
— **swoop** *noun, pl* **swoops** [*count*] ▪ the *swoop* of a hawk

swoosh /ˈswuːʃ/ *verb* **swoosh·es**; **swooshed**; **swoosh·ing** [*no obj*] : to make sound by moving quickly through the air ▪ The ball *swooshed* by/past my head.
— **swoosh** *noun, pl* **swooshes** [*count*] ▪ I heard a loud

S

swoosh as the ball flew past my head.

swop *Brit spelling of* SWAP

sword /ˈsoɚd/ *noun, pl* **swords** [*count*] : a weapon with a long metal blade that has a sharp point and edge

beat/turn swords into plowshares *literary* : to stop fighting wars and begin to live peacefully

cross swords see ²CROSS

put (someone) to the sword *literary* : to kill (someone) with a sword

sword of Dam·o·cles /-ˈdæməˌkliːz/ : something bad and frightening that might happen at any time • a threat that hangs over us like a/the *sword of Damocles*

sword·fish /ˈsoɚdˌfɪʃ/ *noun, pl* **-fish** [*count*] : a very large fish that lives in the ocean, that has a long, pointed upper jaw which looks like a sword, and that is eaten as food

sword·play /ˈsoɚdˌpleɪ/ *noun* [*noncount*] : the art or skill of fighting with a sword

swords·man /ˈsoɚdzmən/ *noun, pl* **-men** /-mən/ [*count*] : a person who fights with a sword • a skilled *swordsman*

swore *past tense of* ¹SWEAR

¹**sworn** *past participle of* ¹SWEAR

²**sworn** /ˈswoɚn/ *adj, always used before a noun*

1 — used to describe people who have openly stated their feelings, opinions, etc. • He's a *sworn* conservative. • They are ***sworn enemies/friends***.

2 : made or given by someone who has made a formal promise to tell the truth • *sworn* testimony/statements

¹**swot** /ˈswɑːt/ *noun, pl* **swots** [*count*] *Brit, informal + disapproving* : a person who works or studies too much • At university he had a reputation as a *swot*. [=(*US*) *grind*]

²**swot** *verb* **swots**; **swotted**; **swotting** [*no obj*] *Brit, informal* : to study very hard for an exam — + *for* • He's been *swotting for* the French exam.

swot up [*phrasal verb*] ***swot up or swot (something) up or swot up (something)*** : to study (something) very hard • She *swotted up* for the French exam. = She *swotted up* French for the exam. — often + *on* • He needs to *swot up on* French verbs.

swum *past participle of* ¹SWIM

swung *past tense and past participle of* ¹SWING

syb·a·rit·ic /ˌsɪbəˈrɪtɪk/ *adj* [*more ~; most ~*] *literary* : relating to, desiring, or involving expensive comforts and pleasures • *sybaritic* desires/pleasures/entertainments/excesses • a *sybaritic* lifestyle

syc·a·more /ˈsɪkəˌmoɚ/ *noun, pl* **-mores** [*count*]

1 : a tree of the eastern and central U.S. that has light-brown bark that peels off in thin flakes

2 : a type of European maple tree with five-pointed leaves

sy·co·phant /ˈsɪkəfənt/ *noun, pl* **-phants** [*count*] *formal + disapproving* : a person who praises powerful people in order to get their approval

– **sy·co·phan·cy** /ˈsɪkəfənsi/ *noun* [*noncount*] • Her praise was obvious *sycophancy*. – **sy·co·phan·tic** /ˌsɪkəˈfæntɪk/ *adj* [*more ~; most ~*] • *sycophantic* praise/flattery

syl·lab·ic /səˈlæbɪk/ *adj, linguistics* : of or relating to syllables • *syllabic* accent/stress

syl·la·ble /ˈsɪləbəl/ *noun, pl* **-la·bles** [*count*] : any one of the parts into which a word is naturally divided when it is pronounced • The word "doctor" has two *syllables*. • "Doctor" is a two-*syllable* word. • The first *syllable* of the word "doctor" is given stress.

in words of one syllable see ¹WORD

S

syl·la·bus /ˈsɪləbəs/ *noun, pl* **-bi** /-ˌbaɪ/ *or* **-bus·es** [*count*] : a list of the topics or books that will be studied in a course

syl·lo·gism /ˈsɪləˌʤɪzəm/ *noun, pl* **-gisms** [*count*] *formal* : a formal argument in logic that is formed by two statements and a conclusion which must be true if the two statements are true • An example of a *syllogism* is: "All men are human; all humans are mortal; therefore all men are mortal."

sylph /ˈsɪlf/ *noun, pl* **sylphs** [*count*] *literary* : a thin and graceful woman or girl

– **sylph·like** /ˈsɪlfˌlaɪk/ *adj* • a *sylphlike* young woman

syl·van /ˈsɪlvən/ *adj, literary* : having a lot of woods or trees • a *sylvan* setting • *sylvan* surroundings

sym·bi·o·sis /ˌsɪmbiˈoʊsəs/ *noun, pl* **-o·ses** /-ˈoʊˌsiːz/

1 *biology* : the relationship between two different kinds of living things that live together and depend on each other [*count*] — usually singular • The bacteria exist in a *symbiosis* with the plant's roots. [*noncount*] The bird lives in *symbiosis* with the hippopotamus.

2 *formal* : a relationship between two people or groups that work with and depend on each other [*count*] — usually singular • There is a *symbiosis* between celebrities and the media. [*noncount*] Their professional association was one of *symbiosis*.

– **sym·bi·ot·ic** /ˌsɪmbiˈɑːtɪk/ *adj* • a *symbiotic* relationship – **sym·bi·ot·i·cal·ly** /ˌsɪmbiˈɑːtɪkli/ *adv*

sym·bol /ˈsɪmbəl/ *noun, pl* **-bols** [*count*]

1 : an action, object, event, etc., that expresses or represents a particular idea or quality — often + *of* • The wearing of black clothing is often a *symbol of* mourning in Western cultures. • The lion is a *symbol of* courage. • The flag is a *symbol of* our country. — see also SEX SYMBOL, STATUS SYMBOL

2 : a letter, group of letters, character, or picture that is used instead of a word or group of words • The company's *symbol* [=*logo*] is a red umbrella. — usually + *for* • "K" is the *symbol for* a strikeout in baseball. • "Cl" is the chemical *symbol for* chlorine. • "+" is the *symbol for* addition.

sym·bol·ic /sɪmˈbɑːlɪk/ *also* **sym·bol·i·cal** /sɪmˈbɑːlɪkəl/ *adj*

1 [*more ~; most ~*] : expressing or representing an idea or quality without using words • The lighting of the candles is *symbolic*. • a purely *symbolic* act/gesture [=an act/gesture that is intended as a symbol of something but that does not have any real effect] — often + *of* • Wedding rings are *symbolic of* eternal love. • The dove is *symbolic of* peace.

2 [*more ~; most ~*] : relating to or being used as a symbol • The number 7 has *symbolic* significance/importance [=has significance/importance as a symbol] in their religion. • The sharing of the wine has *symbolic* meaning.

3 : using symbols • *symbolic* writing

– **sym·bol·i·cal·ly** /sɪmˈbɑːlɪkli/ *adv* • *Symbolically*, the color green represents envy. • The storm is *symbolically* important in the story.

sym·bol·ism /ˈsɪmbəˌlɪzəm/ *noun* [*noncount*]

1 : the use of symbols to express or represent ideas or qualities in literature, art, etc. • The story was filled with religious *symbolism*.

2 : the particular idea or quality that is expressed by a symbol • What is the *symbolism* of the lion in the picture? [=what does the lion symbolize in the picture?]

sym·bol·ize *also Brit* **sym·bol·ise** /ˈsɪmbəˌlaɪz/ *verb* **-izes**; **-ized**; **-iz·ing** [+ *obj*] : to be a symbol of (something) • The lion *symbolizes* [=*represents*] courage. • She came to *symbolize* the women's movement in America.

sym·met·ri·cal /səˈmɛtrɪkəl/ *also* **sym·met·ric** /səˈmɛtrɪk/ *adj* [*more ~; most ~*] : having sides or halves that are the same : having or showing symmetry • The human body is *symmetrical*. • a *symmetrical* design/pattern — opposite ASYMMETRICAL

– **sym·met·ri·cal·ly** /səˈmɛtrɪkli/ *adv* • *symmetrically* arranged/divided

sym·me·try /ˈsɪmətri/ *noun* [*noncount*] : the quality of something that has two sides or halves that are the same or very close in size, shape, and position : the quality of having symmetrical parts • the *symmetry* of the human body • The building has perfect *symmetry*.

sym·pa·thet·ic /ˌsɪmpəˈθɛtɪk/ *adj* [*more ~; most ~*]

1 : feeling or showing concern about someone who is in a bad situation : having or showing feelings of sympathy • He received much help from *sympathetic* friends. — often + *to* or *toward* • She is very *sympathetic to/toward* the poor.

2 *not used before a noun* : having or showing support for or approval of something — often + *to* or *toward* • He was not *sympathetic to/toward* their cause. [=he did not support their cause]

3 : having pleasant or appealing qualities : causing feelings of sympathy • The book doesn't really have any *sympathetic* [=*likable*] characters. • I didn't find the hero in the movie very *sympathetic*.

– **sym·pa·thet·i·cal·ly** /ˌsɪmpəˈθɛtɪkli/ *adv* • She *sympathetically* asked how she could help. • The character was treated *sympathetically*.

sym·pa·thize *also Brit* **sym·pa·thise** /ˈsɪmpəˌθaɪz/ *verb* **-thiz·es**; **-thized**; **-thiz·ing** [*no obj*]

1 : to feel sorry for someone who is in a bad situation : to feel sympathy for someone because you understand that person's problems • I *sympathize* but how can I help? — often + *with* • I *sympathize with* you. — compare EMPATHIZE

2 : to feel or show support for or approval of something — + *with* • She *sympathized with* their cause.

– **sym·pa·thiz·er** *also Brit* **sym·pa·this·er** *noun, pl* **-ers** [*count*] ▪ The group has many *sympathizers.* [=*supporters*]

sym·pa·thy /ˈsɪmpəθi/ *noun, pl* **-thies**
1 : the feeling that you care about and are sorry about someone else's trouble, grief, misfortune, etc. **:** a sympathetic feeling [*noncount*] She went to her best friend for *sympathy.* ▪ Letters of *sympathy* were sent to the families of the victims. — often + *for* ▪ There is a lot of *sympathy for* the families of the victims. ▪ I have no *sympathy for* her. [*count*] My deepest *sympathies* go out to the families of the victims. ▪ Our *sympathies* are with them. — often + *for* ▪ She has/feels a deep *sympathy for* the families of the victims. — compare EMPATHY; see also TEA AND SYMPATHY
2 : a feeling of support for something [*noncount*] — often + *for* ▪ He expressed *sympathy for* the rebels. [*plural*] She has liberal/conservative *sympathies.* — often + *with* ▪ Her *sympathies* are/lie *with* the rebels.
3 [*noncount*] **:** a state in which different people share the same interests, opinions, goals, etc. ▪ There was no *sympathy* between them. — often + *with* ▪ He's not ***in sympathy with*** the other members of the group. = He's ***out of sympathy with*** the other members. ▪ He seems to be *in sympathy with* our views. [=to agree with and support our views]

sym·phon·ic /sɪmˈfɑːnɪk/ *adj* **:** of or relating to a symphony or symphony orchestra ▪ *symphonic* music

sym·pho·ny /ˈsɪmfəni/ *noun, pl* **-nies** [*count*]
1 : a long piece of music that is usually in four large, separate sections and that is performed by an orchestra
2 : SYMPHONY ORCHESTRA

symphony orchestra *noun, pl* ~ **-tras** [*count*] **:** a large orchestra of musicians who play classical music together and are led by a conductor ▪ She's a member of the Chicago *Symphony Orchestra.*

sym·po·sium /sɪmˈpoʊzijəm/ *noun, pl* **-sia** /-zijə/ *or* **-siums** [*count*] *formal*
1 : a formal meeting at which experts discuss a particular topic ▪ Professors and graduate students attended the *symposium.* — often + *on* ▪ a *symposium on* cloning
2 : a collection of articles on a particular subject — often + *on* ▪ The organization will be publishing a *symposium on* genetic research.

symp·tom /ˈsɪmptəm/ *noun, pl* **-toms** [*count*]
1 : a change in the body or mind which indicates that a disease is present ▪ cold/flu *symptoms* — often + *of* ▪ *symptoms of* heart disease ▪ a *symptom of* depression
2 : a change which shows that something bad exists **:** a sign of something bad — often + *of* ▪ Layoffs and salary freezes are *symptoms of* a company in financial trouble.

symp·tom·at·ic /ˌsɪmptəˈmætɪk/ *adj*
1 *medical* **a :** showing that a particular disease is present — usually + *of* ▪ A fever and runny nose are *symptomatic of* the flu. [=are symptoms of the flu] **b :** relating to or showing symptoms of a disease ▪ *symptomatic* relief/improvement/treatments ▪ The patient was not *symptomatic.* [=the patient did not have any symptoms] — opposite ASYMPTOMATIC
2 *formal* **:** showing the existence of a particular problem — usually + *of* ▪ The child's behavior is *symptomatic of* an unstable home life. ▪ Poor sales are *symptomatic* [=*characteristic*] *of* a poor economy.
– **symp·tom·at·i·cal·ly** /ˌsɪmptəˈmætɪkli/ *adv*

syn·a·gogue /ˈsɪnəˌgɑːg/ *noun, pl* **-gogues** [*count*] **:** a building that is used for Jewish religious services

syn·apse /ˈsɪˌnæps/ *noun, pl* **-aps·es** [*count*] *biology* **:** the place where a signal passes from one nerve cell to another
– **syn·ap·tic** /səˈnæptɪk/ *adj* ▪ *synaptic* connections

sync *also* **synch** /ˈsɪŋk/ *noun*
in sync **1 :** in a state in which two or more people or things move or happen together at the same time and speed ▪ The dancers moved *in sync.* ▪ The film's sound and picture need to be *in sync.* — often + *with* ▪ She moved *in sync with* her partner. **2 :** in a state in which two or more people or things agree with or match one another and work together properly ▪ Our ideas are *in sync.* — often + *with* ▪ The quarterback was *in sync with* his receivers. ▪ The President is not *in sync with* [=the President does not understand] the interests and concerns of the people. ▪ Her views are *in sync with* [=her views agree with] our own.
out of sync **1 :** in a state in which two or more people or things do not move or happen together at the same time and speed ▪ Some of the soldiers were marching *out of sync.* ▪ The soundtrack was *out of sync* so they stopped the film. — often + *with* ▪ She was *out of sync with* the other dancers. **2 :** in a state in which two or more people or things do not agree with or match one another ▪ All the clocks in the office are *out of sync.* [=all the clocks show different times] — often + *with* ▪ His actions are completely *out of sync with* our goals.
— see also LIP-SYNCH

syn·chro·nize *also Brit* **syn·chro·nise** /ˈsɪŋkrəˌnaɪz/ *verb* **-niz·es; -nized; -niz·ing**
1 [+ *obj*] **:** to cause (things) to agree in time or to make (things) happen at the same time and speed ▪ They *synchronized* their watches. [=they adjusted their watches so that they all showed the same time] ▪ The dancers practiced until they *synchronized* their movements.
2 [*no obj*] **:** to happen at the same time and speed ▪ The sound and picture have to *synchronize* perfectly. — often + *with* ▪ The sound has to *synchronize with* the picture.
– **syn·chro·ni·za·tion** *also Brit* **syn·chro·ni·sa·tion** /ˌsɪŋkrənəˈzeɪʃən/ *noun* [*noncount*] ▪ the *synchronization* of sound and action ▪ The dancers moved in perfect *synchronization.*

synchronized swimming *noun* [*noncount*] **:** a sport in which swimmers move together in patterns to music
– **synchronized swimmer** *noun, pl* ~ **-mers** [*count*]

syn·chro·nous /ˈsɪŋkrənəs/ *adj, formal* + *technical* **:** happening, moving, or existing at the same time ▪ *synchronous* developments/movements

syn·chro·ny /ˈsɪŋkrəni/ *noun* [*noncount*] *formal* + *technical* **:** a state in which things happen, move, or exist at the same time ▪ The objects moved ***in synchrony with*** each other. [=at the same time]

syn·co·pat·ed /ˈsɪŋkəˌpeɪtəd/ *adj, of music* **:** of, relating to, or having a rhythm that stresses the weak beats instead of the strong beats ▪ *syncopated* beats ▪ a *syncopated* melody/rhythm

syn·co·pa·tion /ˌsɪŋkəˈpeɪʃən/ *noun* [*noncount*] *music* **:** musical rhythm in which stress is given to the weak beats instead of the strong beats

[1]**syn·di·cate** /ˈsɪndɪkət/ *noun, pl* **-cates** [*count*]
1 a : a group of people or businesses that work together ▪ A *syndicate* owns the company. — often + *of* ▪ The company is owned by a *syndicate of* investors. ▪ The money for the project was provided by a *syndicate of* banks. **b :** a group of people who are involved in organized crime ▪ a crime *syndicate*
2 : a business that sells something (such as a piece of writing, comic strip, or photograph) to several different newspapers or magazines for publication at the same time **:** a business that syndicates something
3 : a group of newspapers that are managed by one company ▪ a newspaper *syndicate*

[2]**syn·di·cate** /ˈsɪndəˌkeɪt/ *verb* **-cates; -cat·ed; -cat·ing** [+ *obj*]
1 : to sell (something, such as a piece of writing, comic strip, or photograph) to many different newspapers or magazines for publication at the same time ▪ The company *syndicates* her work. — often used as *(be) syndicated* ▪ His column *is syndicated* in all the major newspapers. ▪ a *syndicated* column/columnist
2 : to sell (a series of television or radio programs) to many different stations at the same time ▪ The company *syndicated* the show to local stations. — often used as *(be) syndicated* ▪ The program has *been syndicated* nationally. ▪ a *syndicated* program
– **syn·di·ca·tion** /ˌsɪndəˈkeɪʃən/ *noun* [*noncount*] ▪ The television show's *syndication* begins next fall. ▪ The show is now ***in syndication*** [=reruns of the show are being shown on different stations that have paid to show them]

syn·drome /ˈsɪnˌdroʊm/ *noun, pl* **-dromes** [*count*] **:** a disease or disorder that involves a particular group of signs and symptoms ▪ a rare *syndrome* ▪ psychological *syndromes* — see also CARPAL TUNNEL SYNDROME, DOWN SYNDROME, PREMENSTRUAL SYNDROME, SUDDEN INFANT DEATH SYNDROME, TOURETTE'S SYNDROME, TOXIC SHOCK SYNDROME

syn·er·gy /ˈsɪnəʤi/ *noun, pl* **-gies** *technical* **:** the increased effectiveness that results when two or more people or businesses work together [*count*] A *synergy* has developed among the different groups working on this project. [*noncount*] two companies that have found *synergy*

syn·od /ˈsɪnəd/ *noun, pl* **-ods** [*count*]
1 : a formal meeting of church leaders
2 : a group of church leaders who are in charge of making

S

decisions and laws related to the church

syn·o·nym /ˈsɪnəˌnɪm/ *noun, pl* **-nyms** [*count*]
1 : a word that has the same meaning as another word in the same language ▪ "Small" and "little" are *synonyms.* — often + *for* or *of* ▪ Can you think of a *synonym for* "original"? ▪ "Small" is a *synonym of* "little." — opposite ANTONYM
2 : a word, name, or phrase that very strongly suggests a particular idea, quality, etc. — + *for* ▪ He is a tyrant whose name has become a *synonym for* oppression.

syn·on·y·mous /səˈnɑːnəməs/ *adj*
1 : having the same meaning ▪ "Small" and "little" are *synonymous.* [=are synonyms] ▪ *synonymous* words — often + *with* ▪ "Small" is *synonymous with* "little."
2 *not used before a noun* **:** strongly suggesting a particular idea, quality, etc. **:** very strongly associated with something — + *with* ▪ The company's name is *synonymous with* quality.
– syn·on·y·mous·ly *adv* ▪ two words that are used *synonymously*

syn·op·sis /səˈnɑːpsəs/ *noun, pl* **syn·op·ses** /səˈnɑːpˌsiːz/ [*count*] *formal* **:** a short description of the most important information about something **:** a summary or outline ▪ a plot *synopsis* — often + *of* ▪ She gave us a brief *synopsis of* the report/story.
– syn·op·tic /səˈnɑːptɪk/ *adj* ▪ He gave a *synoptic* overview of the project.

syn·tac·tic /sɪnˈtæktɪk/ *or* **syn·tac·ti·cal** /sɪnˈtæktɪkəl/ *adj, linguistics* **:** of or relating to syntax ▪ *syntactic* rules/structures
– syn·tac·ti·cal·ly /sɪnˈtæktɪkli/ *adv* ▪ The sentence is *syntactically* incorrect.

syn·tax /ˈsɪnˌtæks/ *noun* [*noncount*] *linguistics* **:** the way in which words are put together to form phrases, clauses, or sentences ▪ "I saw that she a cookie ate" is an example of incorrect *syntax.*

syn·the·sis /ˈsɪnθəsəs/ *noun, pl* **-the·ses** /-θəˌsiːz/
1 [*count*] *formal* **:** something that is made by combining different things (such as ideas, styles, etc.) — often + *of* ▪ The band's sound is a *synthesis of* jazz and rock music. ▪ His theory is actually a *synthesis of* several other theories.
2 *technical* **:** the production of a substance by combining simpler substances through a chemical process [*count*] — usually singular; often + *of* ▪ the *synthesis of* water from hydrogen and oxygen [*noncount*] protein *synthesis* — see also PHOTOSYNTHESIS
3 [*noncount*] **:** the production of sounds or speech by using electronic equipment ▪ voice/speech *synthesis*

syn·the·size *also Brit* **syn·the·sise** /ˈsɪnθəˌsaɪz/ *verb* **-siz·es; -sized; -siz·ing** [+ *obj*]
1 *formal* **a :** to make (something) by combining different things ▪ She *synthesized* the treatment from traditional and modern philosophies of medicine. **b :** to combine (things) in order to make something new ▪ He *synthesized* old and new ideas to form his theory.
2 *technical* **:** to make (something) from simpler substances through a chemical process ▪ Scientists *synthesize* new drugs. ▪ Glands *synthesize* the enzymes. ▪ Amino acid is *synthesized* in the body.
3 : to produce (sounds, speech, etc.) by using electronic equipment ▪ He *synthesized* the drumbeat. [=he created the drumbeat by using a synthesizer]
– synthesized *also Brit* **synthesised** *adj* ▪ *synthesized* proteins/drugs ▪ *synthesized* music ▪ a *synthesized* voice ▪ The drumbeat is *synthesized.*

syn·the·siz·er *also Brit* **syn·the·sis·er** /ˈsɪnθəˌsaɪzɚ/ *noun, pl* **-ers** [*count*] **:** an electronic machine that produces and controls sound and is used especially in music and for reproducing speech ▪ The band used a *synthesizer* for the drumbeat.

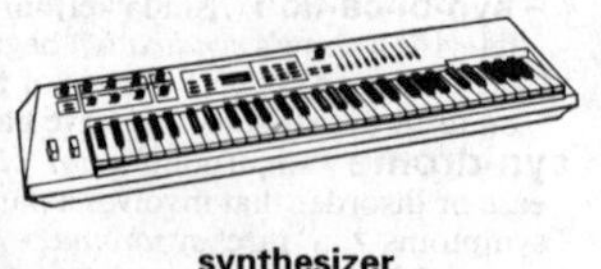
synthesizer

¹syn·thet·ic /sɪnˈθɛtɪk/ *adj* **:** made by combining different substances **:** not natural ▪ *synthetic* drugs/chemicals/rubber ▪ The material is *synthetic.* [=man-made]
– syn·thet·i·cal·ly /sɪnˈθɛtɪkli/ *adv* ▪ The fibers are *synthetically* produced.

²synthetic *noun, pl* **-ics** [*count*] **:** something made by combining different artificial substances ▪ The drug is a *synthetic.* — usually plural ▪ The fabric is made of *synthetics.*

syph·i·lis /ˈsɪfələs/ *noun* [*noncount*] *medical* **:** a very serious disease that is spread through sexual intercourse
– syph·i·lit·ic /ˌsɪfəˈlɪtɪk/ *adj* ▪ *syphilitic* symptoms/patients

syphon *variant spelling of* SIPHON

sy·ringe /səˈrɪnʤ/ *noun, pl* **-ring·es** [*count*] **:** a device made of a hollow tube and a needle that is used to force fluids into or take fluids out of the body

syr·up /ˈsirəp/ *noun, pl* **-ups**
1 [*noncount*] **:** a sweet, thick liquid made of sugar and water with flavoring or medicine added to it ▪ a medicinal *syrup* ▪ ice cream and chocolate *syrup* — see also COUGH SYRUP
2 [*count, noncount*] **:** a sweet, thick liquid made from the juice of a fruit or plant ▪ She poured *syrup* all over her pancakes. ▪ fruit *syrups* — see also CORN SYRUP, MAPLE SYRUP

syr·upy /ˈsirəpi/ *adj* [*more* ~; *most* ~]
1 : thick and sweet like syrup ▪ a *syrupy* liquid ▪ ice cream topped with a *syrupy* fruit sauce
2 *disapproving* **:** too romantic or emotional ▪ a *syrupy* [=*sappy*] love song

sys·tem /ˈsɪstəm/ *noun, pl* **-tems**
1 [*count*] **:** a group of related parts that move or work together ▪ a *system* of rivers ▪ railroad *systems* ▪ a security/telephone/heating *system* ▪ an alarm *system* ▪ a stereo/computer *system* — see also ECOSYSTEM, PA SYSTEM, PUBLIC ADDRESS SYSTEM, SOLAR SYSTEM, SOUND SYSTEM
2 [*count*] **a :** a body of a person or animal thought of as an entire group of parts that work together — usually singular ▪ The disease affected her entire *system.* ▪ Greasy foods are not good for your *system.* ▪ No drugs were found in his *system.* **b :** a group of organs that work together to perform an important function of the body ▪ the digestive/reproductive/respiratory *system* — see also CENTRAL NERVOUS SYSTEM, IMMUNE SYSTEM, NERVOUS SYSTEM
3 [*count*] **:** a way of managing, controlling, organizing, or doing something that follows a set of rules or a plan ▪ the legal *system* ▪ The players like the coach's *system.* ▪ Under the new *system,* students will have to pass an exam to graduate. ▪ She devised a new filing *system.* ▪ We need a better *system* for handling incoming e-mail. — often + *of* ▪ the state's *system of* education ▪ a democratic *system of* government ▪ Every religion has its own *system of* beliefs and practices. — see also HONOR SYSTEM, METRIC SYSTEM, OPERATING SYSTEM
4 ***the system*** *disapproving* **:** a powerful government or social organization that controls people's lives ▪ You can't beat *the system.* ▪ We spent our youth rebelling against *the system.*
all systems (are) go see ²GO
a shock to the/your system see ¹SHOCK
get it out of your system *informal* **1 :** to do something that you have been wanting to do so that you no longer feel a strong desire to do it ▪ You keep talking about making a cross-country trip. I think you just need to do it and *get it out of your system.* **2 :** to get rid of a strong emotion (such as anger) by doing something ▪ He really angered her, so she went for a walk to *get it out of her system.*
the buddy system see ¹BUDDY

sys·tem·at·ic /ˌsɪstəˈmætɪk/ *adj* **:** using a careful system or method **:** done according to a system ▪ We used a *systematic* approach to solve the problem. ▪ She made a *systematic* study of the evidence. ▪ He is very *systematic* [=*methodical*] in his work. ▪ the *systematic* production of cars
– sys·tem·at·i·cal·ly /ˌsɪstəˈmætɪkli/ *adv* ▪ We approached the problem *systematically.*

sys·tem·a·tize *also Brit* **sys·tem·a·tise** /ˈsɪstəməˌtaɪz/ *verb* **-tiz·es; -tized; -tiz·ing** [+ *obj*] *formal*
1 : to make (something) into a system ▪ The country is *systematizing* yearly exams for high-school students.
2 : to organize (something) by using a system ▪ The computer program *systematizes* the data and enters it into a table.

sys·tem·ic /sɪˈstɛmɪk/ *adj*
1 *formal* **:** of or relating to an entire system ▪ The company made some *systemic* changes to the way it operated. ▪ The problem seems to be *systemic.*
2 *medical* **:** of, relating to, or affecting the entire body ▪ a *systemic* disease

systems analysis *noun, pl* **~ -y·ses** [*count*] **:** the process of studying a procedure or business in order to identify its goals and purposes and create systems and procedures that will achieve them in an efficient way
– systems analyst *noun, pl* **~ -lysts** [*count*]

T

[1]t *or* **T** /ˈtiː/ *noun, pl* **t's** *or* **ts** *or* **T's** *or* **Ts** /ˈtiːz/ **:** the 20th letter of the English alphabet [*count*] a word that begins with a *t* [*noncount*] a word that begins with *t*

to a T *informal* **:** in a perfect or exact way ▪ Her new car fits/suits her *to a T.* [=*to a tee*] ▪ That's him *to a T.* [=that is a perfect description of him]

[2]t *abbr* **1** temperature **2** time **3** ton

ta /ˈtɑː/ *interj, Brit, informal* — used to say "thank you"

TA *abbr* **1** *US* teaching assistant **2** *Brit* Territorial Army

[1]tab /ˈtæb/ *noun, pl* **tabs** [*count*]

1 a : a small, flat piece on a box, envelope, etc., that can be put into a hole in order to hold two parts together ▪ Insert the *tab* into this slot to close the box. **b :** a small, flat piece that sticks out from the edge of something (such as a folder) and allows you to identify and find it easily ▪ a notebook with index *tabs* **c** *US* **:** a small piece of metal, plastic, etc., that is pulled in order to open or close something ▪ The *tab* on the zipper is broken. ▪ the *tab* [=*(US) pull tab, (Brit) ring pull*] on a can of soda

2 *US, informal* **:** a record of the things (such as drinks at a bar) that a customer has ordered and will pay for later ▪ He ran up a $200 bar *tab.* ▪ The final *tab* [=*bill*] came to $200. ▪ He put the drinks on his *tab.* ▪ She offered to ***pick up the tab.*** [=pay the bill] for the meal.

3 : TAB KEY ▪ You can move to the next column in a table by pressing *tab.* [=by pressing the tab key]

4 *informal* **:** a small pill of an illegal drug ▪ a *tab* of Ecstasy

keep tabs on *informal* **:** to carefully watch (someone or something) in order to learn what that person or thing is doing ▪ We are *keeping tabs on* their movements. ▪ The magazine *keeps tabs on* the latest fashion trends.

[2]tab *verb* **tabs; tabbed; tab·bing**

1 [*+ obj*] **:** to put a small, identifying label (called a tab) on something — often used as *(be) tabbed* ▪ a *tabbed* notebook [=a notebook with index tabs]

2 [*+ obj*] *US, informal* **:** to say that (someone or something) will do something or have a particular role or purpose — often used as *(be) tabbed* ▪ She *was tabbed* (as) the favorite to win. ▪ an amount of money *tabbed* for maintenance

3 [*no obj*] **:** to hit the tab key on a computer or typewriter ▪ After you type your name in the first box, you can move to the next box by *tabbing.*

Ta·bas·co /təˈbæskoʊ/ *trademark* — used for a spicy sauce made from hot peppers

tab·by /ˈtæbi/ *noun, pl* **-bies** [*count*] **:** a cat that has dark and light stripes or spots on its fur

tab·er·na·cle /ˈtæbɚˌnækəl/ *noun, pl* **-na·cles**

1 [*count*] **:** a place of worship that is used by some Christian groups ▪ a Mormon/Baptist *tabernacle*

2 [*count*] **:** a box in which the holy bread and wine are kept in a Catholic church

3 ***the Tabernacle*** **:** a small, movable tent that was used as a place of worship by the ancient Israelites

tab key *noun, pl* **~ keys** [*count*] **:** a key on the keyboard of a typewriter or computer that is used to move several spaces at a time or to move to a particular position in a document

[1]ta·ble /ˈteɪbəl/ *noun, pl* **tables** [*count*]

1 a : a piece of furniture that has a flat top and one or more legs ▪ They were sitting at/around the dining/dinner *table.* ▪ She reserved a *table* for two at the restaurant. ▪ Please set the *table* for dinner. [=place plates, silverware, etc., on the table] — see also COFFEE TABLE, END TABLE **b :** a piece of furniture with a flat surface that is designed to be used for a particular purpose ▪ a billiard/poker *table* — see also CARD TABLE, DRAWING TABLE, NEGOTIATING TABLE, OPERATING TABLE

2 : a group of people who are sitting at a table ▪ He had the attention of the entire *table.*

3 : a collection of information that is arranged in rows and columns ▪ The *table* shows the salary of each employee. — see also MULTIPLICATION TABLE, PERIODIC TABLE, TIMES TABLE

at table *Brit* **:** sitting at a table and eating a meal ▪ The whole family was *at table.*

lay/put (all/all of) your cards on the table see [1]CARD

on the table **:** able to be considered or discussed ▪ All options are *on the table.* ▪ A new contract offer is *on the table.*

run the table *chiefly US* **1** *pool, billiards, etc.* **:** to hit all the remaining balls into pockets without missing **2** *informal* **:** to win all the remaining games, points, etc. ▪ The team could *run the table* to win the league championship.

table of contents see [1]CONTENT

turn the tables **:** to change a situation completely so that you have an advantage over someone who previously had an advantage over you — often *+ on* ▪ He *turned the tables on* his attacker and pinned him to the ground.

under the table **1** — used to describe a situation in which a worker is being paid in a secret and illegal way in order to avoid paying taxes ▪ They were paying her *under the table.* ▪ He's working *under the table.* **2** *informal* ✧ To ***drink someone under the table*** means to drink more alcohol than someone else without becoming extremely drunk, unconscious, etc. ▪ He tried to *drink me under the table.*

— see also WATER TABLE

table

title — PLANETS; header, heading — Diameter (mi), Diameter (km); row — Earth; cell — 120,536; column

PLANETS	Diameter (mi)	Diameter (km)
Mercury	3,033	4,879
Mars	4,222	6,794
Venus	7,522	12,104
Earth	7,928	12,756
Neptune	30,782	49,528
Uranus	31,770	51,118
Saturn	74,914	120,536
Jupiter	88,865	142,984

[2]table *verb* **tables; ta·bled; ta·bling** [*+ obj*]

1 *US* **:** to decide not to discuss (something) until a later time ▪ The committee *tabled* the issue until the next meeting.

2 *Brit* **:** to formally present (something) for discussion ▪ She plans to *table* a motion for debate in Parliament.

tab·leau /ˈtæˌbloʊ/ *noun, pl* **tab·leaux** *also* **tab·leaus** /ˈtæˌbloʊz/ [*count*]

1 : a view or sight that looks like a picture **:** SCENE ▪ The houses are grouped together in a charming *tableau.* ▪ a stunning *tableau*

2 : a scene that typically shows an event in history or literature and that is created on a stage by a group of people who are dressed in costumes and who do not speak or move ▪ historical *tableaux*

ta·ble·cloth /ˈteɪbəlˌklɑːθ/ *noun, pl* **-cloths** [*count*] **:** a cloth that is placed on a table before other objects are placed on it — see picture at PLACE SETTING

table football *noun* [*noncount*] *Brit* **:** FOOSBALL

ta·ble·land /ˈteɪbəlˌlænd/ *noun, pl* **-lands** [*count, noncount*] **:** an area of high flat land **:** PLATEAU

table linen *noun, pl* **~ linens** [*count*] **:** cloths (such as tablecloths and napkins) that are used during a meal

table manners *noun* [*plural*] **:** behavior while eating a meal at a table ▪ He needs to learn good *table manners.*

table mat *noun, pl* **~ mats** [*count*] *Brit* **:** a piece of cloth or wood that is placed underneath a hot dish or pot in order to protect the surface of a table

ta·ble·mate /ˈteɪbəlˌmeɪt/ *noun, pl* **-mates** [*count*] *US* **:** a person who is sitting with you at a table ▪ He was loudly arguing with one of his *tablemates.*

table salt *noun* [*noncount*] **:** the type of salt that is usually on a table for people to use while they are dining

table soccer *noun* [*noncount*] *US* **:** FOOSBALL

ta·ble·spoon /ˈteɪbəlˌspuːn/ *noun, pl* **-spoons** [*count*]

1 a : a spoon that is used by cooks for measuring dry and liquid ingredients and that holds an amount equal to ½ fluid ounce or three teaspoons ▪ She carefully measured the flour with a *tablespoon.* **b :** the amount that a tablespoon will hold **:** TABLESPOONFUL ▪ Add two *tablespoons* of flour. ▪ The recipe calls for four *tablespoons* of milk. — abbr. *tb., tbs., tbsp.*

T

2 : a fairly large spoon that is used for serving or eating food — compare TEASPOON

ta·ble·spoon·ful /ˈteɪbəlˌspuːnˌfʊl/ *noun, pl* **-spoon·fuls** /-ˌspuːnˌfʊlz/ *or* **-spoons·ful** /-ˌspuːnzˌfʊl/ [*count*] **:** the amount that a tablespoon will hold ▪ Add two *tablespoonfuls* [=*tablespoons*] of flour. — abbr. *tb., tbs., tbsp.*

tab·let /ˈtæblət/ *noun, pl* **-lets** [*count*]
1 : a flat piece of stone, clay, or wood that has writing on it ▪ an ancient stone *tablet*
2 : a small usually round piece of medicine ▪ aspirin/vitamin *tablets*
3 *chiefly US* **:** a set of paper sheets for writing or drawing that are glued or fastened at one edge **:** PAD ▪ a writing *tablet*

table talk *noun* [*noncount*] **:** informal conversation at a table or during a meal

table tennis *noun* [*noncount*] **:** a game in which players stand at opposite ends of a table and use wooden paddles to hit a small plastic ball to each other across a net — compare PING-PONG

ta·ble·top /ˈteɪbəlˌtɑːp/ *noun, pl* **-tops** [*count*] **:** the surface of a table
– tabletop *adj, always used before a noun* ▪ a *tabletop* game

ta·ble·ware /ˈteɪbəlˌweɚ/ *noun* [*noncount*] *formal* **:** dishes, glasses, knives, forks, etc., that are used for serving and eating food at a table

table wine *noun, pl* **~ wines** [*count, noncount*] **:** a wine that is not very expensive and that is used for ordinary meals

tab·loid /ˈtæˌblɔɪd/ *noun, pl* **-loids** [*count*] **:** a newspaper that has pages about half the size of an ordinary newspaper and that typically contains many photographs and stories about famous people and other less serious news items ▪ She is used to seeing her name in the *tabloids*. — compare BROADSHEET
– tabloid *adj, always used before a noun* ▪ *tabloid* journalism/reporters

[1]**ta·boo** /təˈbuː/ *adj* [*more ~; most ~*] **:** not acceptable to talk about or do ▪ Sex is a *taboo* subject for many people. ▪ In this company, dating a coworker is considered *taboo*.

[2]**taboo** *noun, pl* **-boos** [*count*]
1 : a rule against doing or saying something in a particular culture or religion ▪ religious/social *taboos* against drinking alcohol
2 : something that is not acceptable to talk about or do **:** something that is taboo ▪ Marrying a close relative is a *taboo* in many cultures.

tab·u·lar /ˈtæbjəlɚ/ *adj* **:** arranged in rows or columns in a table ▪ data displayed in *tabular* form [=data displayed in a table]

tab·u·late /ˈtæbjəˌleɪt/ *verb* **-lates; -lat·ed; -lat·ing** [*+ obj*] **:** to arrange information in an organized way so that it can be studied, recorded, etc. ▪ Officials *tabulated* the scores. ▪ A machine is used to *tabulate* the votes.
– tab·u·la·tion /ˌtæbjəˈleɪʃən/ *noun* [*noncount*]

tach·o·graph /ˈtækəˌgræf/ *noun, pl* **-graphs** [*count*] *Brit* **:** a device in a truck or similar vehicle that records the speed of the vehicle and the times when it is moving and not moving

ta·chom·e·ter /tæˈkɑːmətɚ/ *noun, pl* **-ters** [*count*] *technical* **:** a device that measures how fast something (such as a wheel) is turning — see picture at CAR; compare ODOMETER, SPEEDOMETER

tac·it /ˈtæsət/ *adj, formal* **:** expressed or understood without being directly stated ▪ She felt that she had her parents' *tacit* approval to borrow the car. ▪ There was a *tacit* agreement that he would pay off the loan.
– tac·it·ly *adv* ▪ They felt that he had *tacitly* agreed to their proposal by not objecting to it.

tac·i·turn /ˈtæsəˌtɚn/ *adj* [*more ~; most ~*] *formal* **:** tending to be quiet **:** not speaking frequently ▪ a somewhat *taciturn* young man
– tac·i·tur·ni·ty /ˌtæsəˈtɚnəti/ *noun* [*noncount*]

[1]**tack** /ˈtæk/ *noun, pl* **tacks**
1 [*count*] **a :** a small, sharp nail usually with a wide, flat head ▪ carpet *tacks* **b** *US* **:** THUMBTACK
2 *sailing* **a** [*count, noncount*] **:** the direction that a ship or boat is sailing in as it moves at an angle to the direction of the wind ▪ We were sailing on (a/the) port *tack*. [=with the wind coming from our port/left side] ▪ the starboard *tack* **b** [*count*] **:** a change from one direction to another direction while sailing ▪ a *tack* from port to starboard **c** [*count*] **:** the distance traveled while sailing in a particular direction ▪ a long *tack*
3 : a way in which you do something or try to do something [*singular*] He thought he should try a new/different *tack*. [*noncount*] The company decided to change *tack*. [=to try using a different method/approach]
4 [*count*] **:** a loose stitch that is used to hold pieces of cloth together before sewing them tightly together
get down to brass tacks see BRASS
— compare [3]TACK

[2]**tack** *verb* **tacks; tacked; tack·ing**
1 *always followed by an adverb or preposition* [*+ obj*] **:** to fasten or attach (something) with tacks ▪ She *tacked* a poster on the wall. ▪ A message was *tacked* to the board.
2 [*+ obj*] **:** to add on or attach (something) in a quick or careless way — usually *+ on* or *onto* ▪ They *tacked* one more provision *onto* the deal. ▪ The porch looked like it was just *tacked on/onto* the house.
3 [*no obj*] *sailing* **:** to turn a ship or boat so that the wind is coming at it from the opposite side ▪ We had to *tack* repeatedly as we sailed toward the harbor.

[3]**tack** *noun* [*noncount*] **:** the equipment (such as a saddle and a bridle) that is used for riding a horse — compare [1]TACK

[1]**tack·le** /ˈtækəl/ *noun, pl* **tack·les**
1 [*noncount*] **:** equipment that is used for a particular activity (especially fishing) ▪ a box for fishing *tackle* ▪ a *tackle* shop [=a shop that sells fishing equipment]
2 [*count*] *sports* **:** the act of tackling another player: such as **a** *American football or rugby* **:** the act of forcing the player who has the ball to fall to the ground ▪ He made two *tackles* in the first half. ▪ He missed the *tackle*. [=he failed to make the tackle] **b** *soccer, field hockey, etc.* **:** the act of trying to get the ball from an opposing player
3 [*count*] *American football* **a :** either one of two players on the offensive team who play in positions on the line of scrimmage next to the guards **b :** either one of two players on the defensive team who play in positions near the center of the line of scrimmage — see also NOSE TACKLE
4 [*count, noncount*] **:** an arrangement of ropes and wheels used for lifting or pulling something heavy — see also BLOCK AND TACKLE
5 [*noncount*] *Brit, informal* **:** a man's sexual organs

[2]**tackle** *verb* **tackles; tack·led; tack·ling** [*+ obj*]
1 a : to forcefully seize (someone) and cause that person to fall to the ground ▪ The police officer *tackled* him as he tried to escape. **b** *American football or rugby* **:** to force (the player with the ball) to fall to the ground ▪ He was *tackled* at the line of scrimmage. **c** *soccer, field hockey, etc.* **:** to try to get the ball from (an opposing player who has it)
2 : to deal with (something difficult) ▪ I'll *tackle* my homework later. ▪ We found new ways to *tackle* the problem.
– tack·ler /ˈtækəlɚ/ *noun, pl* **-lers** [*count*]

tacky /ˈtæki/ *adj* **tack·i·er; -est** [*also more ~; most ~*]
1 : slightly wet and sticky ▪ The paint is still a little *tacky*.
2 *informal* **a :** having a cheap and ugly appearance **:** not tasteful or stylish ▪ We got rid of that *tacky* old furniture/wallpaper. ▪ bright, *tacky* clothes ▪ *tacky* souvenirs **b** *chiefly US* **:** not socially proper or acceptable ▪ *tacky* behavior ▪ a very *tacky* comment
– tack·i·ness /ˈtækinəs/ *noun* [*noncount*] ▪ the *tackiness* of the newly painted walls ▪ the *tackiness* of his bright clothes

ta·co /ˈtɑːkoʊ/ *noun, pl* **-cos** [*count*] **:** a Mexican food that consists of a folded and usually fried piece of thin bread (called a tortilla) that is filled with meat, cheese, lettuce, etc.

tact /ˈtækt/ *noun* [*noncount*] **:** the ability to do or say things without offending or upsetting other people ▪ The peace talks required great *tact* on the part of both leaders. ▪ I was surprised by his lack of *tact*.

tact·ful /ˈtæktfəl/ *adj* [*more ~; most ~*] **:** careful not to offend or upset other people **:** having or showing tact ▪ He gave a *tactful* critique of her story. ▪ It was *tactful* of her not to criticize me in front of my boss.
– tact·ful·ly /ˈtæktfəli/ *adv* ▪ *tactfully* worded comments
– tact·ful·ness *noun* [*noncount*]

tac·tic /ˈtæktɪk/ *noun, pl* **-tics**
1 [*count*] **:** an action or method that is planned and used to achieve a particular goal ▪ an effective *tactic* for solving crimes ▪ political *tactics* ▪ We may need to change *tactics*. — see also DELAYING TACTIC
2 ***tactics*** [*plural*] **:** the activity or skill of organizing and moving soldiers and equipment in a military battle ▪ a specialist in naval *tactics*

T

tac·ti·cal /ˈtæktɪkəl/ *adj* : of, relating to, or used for a specific plan that is created to achieve a particular goal in war, politics, etc. ▪ a *tactical* maneuver/procedure [=a maneuver/procedure that is done to produce a particular result] ▪ They gained a *tactical* advantage by joining with one of their competitors. ▪ He made a serious *tactical* error. ▪ *tactical* decisions/skills ▪ The planes provided *tactical* air support for the soldiers on the ground. ▪ *tactical* missiles/weapons [=missiles/weapons that are designed to be used over a short distance in a military battle]
– **tac·ti·cal·ly** /ˈtæktɪkli/ *adv*

tac·ti·cian /tækˈtɪʃən/ *noun, pl* **-cians** [*count*] : someone who is good at making plans in order to achieve particular goals ▪ a brilliant political/military *tactician*

tac·tile /ˈtæktl, *Brit* ˈtækˌtaɪl/ *adj* [*more ~; most ~*] *formal* : relating to the sense of touch ▪ The thick brushstrokes give the painting a *tactile* quality. ▪ visual and *tactile* experiences

tact·less /ˈtæktləs/ *adj* [*more ~; most ~*] : tending to offend or upset people : not showing or having tact ▪ a *tactless* question/comment ▪ a rude, *tactless* man
– **tact·less·ly** *adv* ▪ He *tactlessly* asked her how old she was.
– **tact·less·ness** *noun* [*noncount*]

tad /ˈtæd/ *noun*
a tad *informal* **1** : a small amount ▪ Move it *a tad* [=*a bit*] to the right. **2** : very slightly ▪ I'm just *a tad* nervous. ▪ He's *a tad* taller than I am.

tad·pole /ˈtædˌpoʊl/ *noun, pl* **-poles** [*count*] : a small creature that becomes an adult frog or toad, that has a rounded body and a long tail, and that lives in water — called also (*US*) *polliwog*

tae kwon do *or* **Tae Kwon Do** /ˈtaɪˈkwɑːnˈdoʊ/ *noun* [*noncount*] : a style of fighting that originated in Korea and that uses kicks and punches but no weapons

taf·fe·ta /ˈtæfətə/ *noun* [*noncount*] : a stiff, shiny type of cloth that is used especially to make dresses

taf·fy /ˈtæfi/ *noun, pl* **taf·fies** [*count, noncount*] *US* : a type of soft and chewy candy ▪ saltwater *taffy*

[1]tag /ˈtæg/ *noun, pl* **tags**
1 [*count*] : a small piece of cloth, paper, metal, etc., that is attached to something and that has information written on it ▪ a dog's identification/ID *tags* ▪ luggage *tags* ▪ According to the *tag*, the shirt needs to be washed in cold water. — see also DOG TAG, NAME TAG, PRICE TAG
2 [*count*] : a name or phrase that is used to describe someone or something ▪ They started calling her "rich girl," and the *tag* stayed with her until graduation.
3 *tags* [*plural*] *US* **a** : a vehicle's license plates ▪ The policeman checked the car's *tags*. **b** : small stickers on a vehicle's license plates which show that the vehicle can legally be driven until a particular date
4 [*count*] *computers* : a piece of computer code that is used to identify a particular type of text so that the text can be arranged or shown in a certain way ▪ HTML *tags*
5 [*count*] : TAG QUESTION
– compare [3]TAG

[2]tag *verb* **tags; tagged; tag·ging** [+ *obj*]
1 : to put a tag on (something) ▪ The items were *tagged* for the sale.
2 : to name or describe (someone or something) in a specified way : LABEL ▪ He was *tagged* (as) a miser for his careful spending.
3 *US, informal* : to damage (someone else's property) by illegally writing or painting something (such as your name) on it : to write graffiti on (something) ▪ Someone *tagged* the walls of the school.
– compare [4]TAG
– **tag·ger** /ˈtægɚ/ *noun, pl* **-gers** [*count*]

[3]tag *noun, pl* **tags**
1 [*noncount*] : a children's game in which one player is called "it" and chases the other players to try to touch one of them and make that player "it" ▪ Do you want to play *tag*? — see also PHONE TAG
2 [*count*] *baseball* : the act of causing a base runner to be out by touching the runner with the ball : the act of tagging a runner ▪ The catcher applied/made the *tag* for the last out of the game.
– compare [1]TAG

[4]tag *verb* **tags; tagged; tagging** [+ *obj*]
1 : to touch (a player) in a game of tag ▪ *Tag*! You're it!
2 *baseball* **a** : to cause (a base runner) to be out by touching him or her with the ball ▪ She was *tagged* out by the catcher. **b** : to put your foot on a base and stay there until a fly ball is caught before you begin to run to try to reach the next base ▪ The runner at third *tagged* and tried to score on a fly ball to left field. — often + *up* ▪ The runner *tagged up* and tried to score.
tag along [*phrasal verb*] *informal* : to go somewhere with someone ▪ "I'm going to the store." "Would you mind if I *tagged along* with you?"
– compare [2]TAG

tag·along /ˈtægəˌlɑːŋ/ *noun, pl* **-alongs** [*count*] *US* : a person who follows or goes somewhere with another person or group often in an annoying way ▪ His little sister was sometimes a *tagalong* on his outings with his friends. — see also *tag along* at [4]TAG

tag·line /ˈtægˌlaɪn/ *noun, pl* **-lines** [*count*]
1 : a memorable phrase or sentence that is closely associated with a particular person, product, movie, etc. ▪ the movie's famous *tagline*
2 : the words at the end of a joke, story, etc. : PUNCH LINE

tag question *noun, pl* **~ -tions** [*count*] *grammar* : a brief question (such as "don't you?" in "You know him, don't you?") that comes at the end of a statement usually to ask if the statement is correct

tag sale *noun, pl* **~ sales** [*count*] *US* : GARAGE SALE

tag team *noun, pl* **~ teams** [*count*] : a team of two or more professional wrestlers who take turns fighting during a match — often used figuratively ▪ a political *tag team*

tai chi *or* **t'ai chi** *or* **Tai Chi** *or* **T'ai Chi** /ˈtaɪˈʧiː/ *noun* [*noncount*] : a Chinese form of exercise that uses very slow and controlled movements

[1]tail /ˈteɪl/ *noun, pl* **tails**
1 [*count*] : the part of an animal's body that extends from the animal's back end ▪ a monkey with a long *tail* — see pictures at BIRD, HORSE
2 [*count*] **a** : a long piece that extends from the back end or bottom of something ▪ the *tail* of a kite ▪ a comet's *tail* — see also PIGTAILS, PONYTAIL, SHIRTTAIL **b** : the back end of an airplane, helicopter, etc. — see picture at AIRPLANE
3 *tails* [*plural*] : the back side of a coin : the side of a coin that is opposite the side which shows a picture of a person's head — usually used to refer to one of the two choices you can make when a coin is thrown in the air to decide something ▪ I call *tails*. ▪ Is it heads or *tails*? [=did the coin land with heads or tails facing up?] — compare [1]HEAD 5
4 *tails* [*plural*] : TAILCOAT ▪ He wore a top hat and *tails*.
5 [*singular*] *informal* : a person (such as a detective) who follows or watches someone ▪ They ***put a tail on*** the suspect. [=they had someone follow the suspect]
bright-eyed and bushy-tailed see BRIGHT
not make head or/nor tail of see [1]HEAD
on someone's tail *informal* : following closely behind someone ▪ The sheriff was hot *on their tails*.
the tail wagging the dog *informal* — used to describe a situation in which an important or powerful person, organization, etc., is being controlled by someone or something that is much less important or powerful
turn tail *informal* : to turn around and run away from danger, trouble, etc. ▪ He *turned tail* and ran from the fight. ▪ You can't just *turn tail* and run from your problems.
with your tail between your legs : with a feeling of being embarrassed or ashamed especially because you have been defeated ▪ He lost the fight and went home *with his tail between his legs*.
– **tail·less** /ˈteɪlləs/ *adj* ▪ *tailless* cats

[2]tail *verb* **tails; tailed; tail·ing**
1 [+ *obj*] *informal* : to follow (someone) closely ▪ The police had been *tailing* the suspect for several miles. ▪ She is constantly *tailed* by the press.
2 *always followed by an adverb or preposition* [*no obj*] : to move in a line that is not straight ▪ The pitch *tailed* away from the batter.
tail back [*phrasal verb*] *Brit, of vehicles* : to form a line that moves slowly or not at all because of heavy traffic, an accident, etc. ▪ Traffic *tailed back* [=*backed up*] for miles. — see also TAILBACK 2
tail off [*phrasal verb*] : to become smaller or quieter in a gradual way ▪ Our productivity *tailed off* last year. ▪ She started to ask a question and then her voice *tailed off*. [=*trailed off*]

tail·back /ˈteɪlˌbæk/ *noun, pl* **-backs** [*count*]
1 *American football* : a player on offense who runs with the ball and blocks : HALFBACK
2 *Brit* : a situation in which the flow of traffic is blocked and

T

a long line of vehicles forms ▪ a traffic *tailback* [=(*US*) *backup*] — see also *tail back* at [2]TAIL

tail·bone /ˈteɪlˌboʊn/ *noun, pl* **-bones** [*count*] : the small bone at the end of the spine : COCCYX

tail·coat /ˈteɪlˌkoʊt/ *noun, pl* **-coats** [*count*] : a formal jacket that is worn by a man and that has a short front and a long back which divides into two pieces

tailed /ˈteɪld/ *adj* : having a tail of a specified type — used in combination ▪ a white-*tailed* deer ▪ long-*tailed* monkeys

tail end *noun*
the tail end : the last part of something ▪ I came late to the meeting and only caught the *tail end*. ▪ the *tail end* of summer ▪ She is at the *tail end of* her career.

tail fin *noun, pl* **~ fins** [*count*]
1 : a fin at the back end of a fish, whale, etc.
2 : a decorative part on the back of a car that is shaped like a fish's fin

[1]**tail·gate** /ˈteɪlˌgeɪt/ *noun, pl* **-gates** [*count*] *chiefly US* : a door at the back of a vehicle (such as a station wagon or pickup truck) that opens downward and that can be lowered or removed to make it easier to load things into the vehicle — see also TAILGATE PARTY

[2]**tailgate** *verb* **-gates; -gat·ed; -gat·ing**
1 : to drive too closely behind another vehicle [*no obj*] He hit the car in front of him because he was *tailgating*. [+ *obj*] Someone was *tailgating* me.
2 [*no obj*] *US* : to have a tailgate party ▪ They started *tailgating* at 10 o'clock.

tailgate party *noun, pl* **~ -ties** [*count*] *US* : a party in which people serve food and drinks from the back end of their vehicles usually in a parking lot before or after a major public event (such as a football game, a concert, etc.)

tail·light /ˈteɪlˌlaɪt/ *noun, pl* **-lights** [*count*] : a red light at the back of a vehicle — see picture at CAR

[1]**tai·lor** /ˈteɪlɚ/ *noun, pl* **-lors** [*count*] : a person who makes men's clothes (such as suits and jackets) that are measured to fit a particular person

[2]**tailor** *verb* **-lors; -lored; -lor·ing** [+ *obj*]
1 : to make (clothing that is measured to fit a particular person) ▪ I had my suit *tailored*.
2 : to make or change (something) so that it meets a special need or purpose ▪ They *tailored* the show for/to younger audiences.
– tai·lored /ˈteɪlɚd/ *adj* ▪ He wore a nicely *tailored* suit.
– tail·or·ing /ˈteɪlərɪŋ/ *noun* [*noncount*] ▪ The store offers free *tailoring*.

tai·lor–made /ˌteɪlɚˈmeɪd/ *adj*
1 : made by a tailor ▪ a *tailor-made* suit
2 : made or seeming to have been made for a particular person or purpose ▪ The job is *tailor-made* [=*perfect*] for him.

tail·pipe /ˈteɪlˌpaɪp/ *noun, pl* **-pipes** [*count*] *chiefly US* : [2]EXHAUST 2

tail·spin /ˈteɪlˌspɪn/ *noun* [*singular*]
1 : a condition in which an airplane is falling rapidly while turning around and around ▪ The plane went into a *tailspin*. [=*spin*]
2 : a state in which something quickly becomes much worse ▪ Stock prices are ***in a tailspin***. ▪ The team went ***into a tailspin*** and lost six straight games. ▪ The news of his death sent her *into a tailspin*. [=caused her to become very unhappy, to lose control of her life, etc.]

tail·wind /ˈteɪlˌwɪnd/ *noun, pl* **-winds** [*count*] : a wind that blows in the same direction as something (such as a ship or an airplane) that is moving forward — compare HEADWIND

[1]**taint** /ˈteɪnt/ *verb* **taints; taint·ed; taint·ing** [+ *obj*]
1 : to hurt or damage the good condition of (something) — often used as *(be) tainted* ▪ The reputation of the university has *been tainted* [=*blemished, marred*] by athletic scandals. ▪ Their relationship *was tainted* with/by suspicion.
2 : to make (something) dangerous or dirty especially by adding something harmful or undesirable to it ▪ Bacteria had *tainted* [=*contaminated, spoiled*] the meat. — often used as *(be) tainted* ▪ The water had *been tainted* by pesticides.
– tainted *adj* ▪ *tainted* food

[2]**taint** *noun* [*singular*] : something that causes a person or thing to be thought of as bad, dishonest, etc. — usually + *of* ▪ a political career damaged by the *taint of* scandal

[1]**take** /ˈteɪk/ *verb* **took** /ˈtʊk/; **tak·en** /ˈteɪkən/; **tak·ing**
1 [+ *obj*] **a :** to carry or move (something) to a place ▪ She *took* her things to her room. ▪ It looks like rain. You had better *take* an umbrella with you. **b :** to carry and give (something) to a person ▪ *Take* this note to your teacher, please. = *Take* your teacher this note, please. **c :** to carry, move, or lead (someone) to a place ▪ This bus *takes* you downtown. ▪ Her office is down that hallway. I can *take* you there, if you want me to. ▪ He was *taken* to the hospital by ambulance. ▪ If you're going to the store, would you mind *taking* me (along) with you? ▪ She *took* us for a ride in her new car. ▪ He's not the kind of guy you can *take* home to meet your parents. ▪ I ***took him aside*** [=to a place that is away from other people] and told him what had happened. ▪ She ***took*** her child ***to one/the side*** and scolded him. — sometimes used figuratively ▪ She *took* her team [=she helped her team go] to the state finals. ▪ Her landlord threatened to ***take her to court***. [=to start a lawsuit against her; to sue her] ▪ He ***took me to the cleaners***. [=he got most of my money in an unfair way]

> ***usage*** The verbs *bring* and *take* are sometimes used in a way that shows that they have opposite meanings. When this is true, *bring* suggests that something is moving toward someone or something, and *take* suggests that something is moving away. ▪ Here, I *brought* you some flowers. ▪ May I *take* your luggage to your room for you?

2 [+ *obj*] : to begin to hold (someone or something) with your fingers, arms, etc. ▪ I *took* the pen and signed my name. ▪ *Take* the pan by the handle. ▪ He *took* her by the hand. ▪ He *took* her hand and looked into her eyes. ▪ She *took* her son in her arms. [=she put her arms around him] ▪ Please, *take* a free sample.
3 [+ *obj*] : to remove (something) from a place, a person's hand, etc. — often + *from* ▪ She *took* the letter (*from* him) and read it aloud. ▪ He *took* a beer *from* the fridge. ▪ We'll have to *take* some blood *from* your arm.
4 [+ *obj*] **a :** to get (something) : to gain possession of (something) ▪ Thieves *took* [=*stole*] the painting from the museum several years ago. ▪ That man *took* my purse! ▪ We will *take* [=*seize, capture*] the city at dawn. ▪ Their land had been *taken* by force. ▪ She *took* [=*borrowed*] her dad's car without his permission. ▪ I accidentally *took* your jacket instead of mine. ▪ Military leaders ***took control of*** the government in 2002. ▪ I have my pride, and no one can ***take that (away) from me***. [=no one can cause me to lose my pride] ▪ I did all the work, and she ***took the credit***. [=she allowed people to believe that she did the work] **b :** to claim (someone or something) as your own — usually used as *(be) taken* ▪ "Excuse me. Is this chair free?" "No, I'm sorry. It's *taken*." [=someone else is planning to sit in the chair] ▪ (*somewhat old-fashioned*) She can't be your girlfriend because she's already *taken*. [=she is already someone else's girlfriend]
5 [+ *obj*] : to cause (someone) to be your prisoner ▪ They *took* us as hostages. = They ***took us hostage***. ▪ Three soldiers were ***taken prisoner/captive***.
6 [+ *obj*] : to cause (someone) to die ▪ She was *taken* [=she died] in her prime. **:** to cause (someone's life) to end ▪ The plane crash ***took the lives of*** all the people on board. ▪ He ***took his own life***. [=he killed himself]
7 [+ *obj*] **a :** to borrow or use (a phrase, an idea, etc., that was created by a different person or used in a different place) — usually + *from* ▪ a quotation *taken from* Shakespeare ▪ The album's title is *taken from* [=it is the same as] a line in the album's first song. ▪ The builders *took* their inspiration *from* [=the builders were inspired by] the Acropolis in Athens. **b :** to begin to have (a particular shape or form) ▪ The college *took* its present form after World War II. ▪ The plan is finally starting to ***take form/shape***. [=to have a definite arrangement]
8 [+ *obj*] : to choose to have (something) ▪ He'll have the fish and I'll *take* the chicken. ▪ Do you *take* cream in your coffee? ▪ You can have either one. ***Take your pick***. [=choose whichever one you want]
9 [+ *obj*] **a :** to accept or receive (something) as payment or as a response ▪ Do you *take* credit cards? ▪ an elected official accused of *taking* bribes ▪ (*Brit*) The restaurant *took* [=(*US*) *took in*] an enormous amount of money in its first week of business. ▪ I was hoping they would pay me more, but at this point I'll ***take what I can get***. ▪ I insist that you come to my party, and I ***won't take no for an answer***! **b :** to accept (something, such as blame, credit, or responsibility) ▪ I *take* full responsibility for what happened. ▪ No one else was willing to *take* the blame/rap (for what happened). ▪ I did the work and he *took* all the credit.
10 [+ *obj*] : to allow (someone) to join a club, to attend a school, to become part of a relationship, etc. ▪ The school *takes* [=*admits*] just 20 students a year. ▪ The doctor's office is

not *taking* [=*accepting*] any new patients. • (*old-fashioned*) It is time for you to ***take a wife/husband***. [=to get married] — see also TAKE ON (below)

11 [+ *obj*] **: to be able to hold (a number of people or things) : to have enough room for (something)** • I think the elevator will *take* a few more people.

12 [+ *obj*] **a : to need or require (something)** • What size shoe do you *take*? • It *took* four people to move the couch. • What would it *take* to get you to buy this car? • It will *take* several years to finish the bridge. = The bridge will *take* several years to finish. • Do you ***have what it takes*** [=do you have the skills and personality] to do this job? • The new color is nice, but ***it'll take some getting used to***. [=I will need to get used to it] • Be patient. These things ***take (a lot of) time***. [=a lot of time needs to pass before they happen or are finished] • Keeping everyone happy does ***take a lot of doing***. = It ***takes some doing***. [=it requires a lot of work] **b** ✧ The phrases ***it takes two*** and ***it takes two to tango*** are used to say that two people or groups are needed in order to do something. • Both of you should be punished for fighting. *It takes two*, you know. • We'd like to continue negotiating, but *it takes two to tango*—we can't solve this problem by ourselves.

13 [+ *obj*] **: to do or perform (something)** • Let's *take* a walk. [=let's walk] • He's *taking* a shower [=he's showering] upstairs. • *Take* a look/peek/gander at this. • How old do you think I am? *Take* a guess. • The kids *take* their naps around one o'clock. • He *took* a bite of his sandwich. • *Take* a deep breath and try to calm down. • We are *taking* a tour of the building tomorrow. • They *took* a pledge never to tell anyone their secret. • It's time for you to ***take a stand*** [=to express your opinion] and tell them that things need to change.

14 [+ *obj*] **: to get (a drug, pill, etc.) into your body by swallowing it, breathing it in, etc.** • *Take* one of these pills in the morning and one before bedtime. • She refuses to *take* her medicine. • She stopped ***taking drugs*** [=she stopped using illegal drugs] years ago.

15 [+ *obj*] **: to sit or stand in (a particular place) : to move into position on (a stage, field, etc.)** • Please *take* a seat. [=please sit down] • I *took* my place next to her at the table. • The actors *took* their places on the stage. • They *took* the stage for their final bow. • The home team is now *taking* the field. • Will the next witness please *take* the stand? • She *took* the witness stand. • The senator from Nevada would now like to ***take the floor***. [=to begin speaking at a public meeting]

16 [+ *obj*] **: to create or record (a picture or image)** • She *took* our picture in front of the waterfall. • Our new camera *takes* beautiful pictures. • The doctor wants to *take* an X-ray of your leg. • They arrested him and *took* his fingerprints.

17 [+ *obj*] **a : to find out (a person's temperature, height, etc.)** • The last time we *took* his temperature, it was 102 degrees. • The nurse weighed me and *took* my blood pressure. • Before the seamstress can make your dress, she has to *take* your measurements. **b : to find out and write down (information)** • He *took* my name and number and said he would call me back. **c : to create (a list or a record of information)** • I can't come to class today. Would you mind *taking* notes for me? • The census we *took* last year shows that our population is growing very rapidly. • We *took* an inventory at the store yesterday to find out what we need to order.

18 [+ *obj*] **a : to travel using (a road, vehicle, etc.)** • We *took* the highway into the city. • She had to *take* a different route home. • He *takes* the subway to work. **b : to turn toward (a particular direction)** • *Take* a right [=turn right] at the next stop light. • *Take* your first left and go straight for a mile. • We ***took a wrong turn*** [=went the wrong way; turned in the wrong direction] and got lost.

19 [+ *obj*] **: to move on or over (something) in a particular way** • He *took* the stairs [=went up/down the stairs] two at a time. • She *took* the curve too fast and the car skidded.

20 [+ *obj*] **a : to agree to do or have (a job, role, etc.)** • He *took* a job as a janitor at the high school. • She hasn't decided if she is going to *take* the position or not. • I *took* a few overtime shifts this month. • He *took* the role of Romeo in the play. • She says that parents should be *taking* a more active role in their children's education. [=should be more actively involved in their children's education] • The former governor ***took office*** [=became governor] in 1998. • She was the first woman to ***take her seat*** [=to begin her official duties as a member] in Parliament. **b** *Brit* **: to teach (a person or class) or lead (a religious service)** • The new teacher *took* us for English. • She *took* a class of eight children. • The vicar won't be able to *take* the early service.

21 [+ *obj*] **: to study (a subject) or participate in (a class) as a student** • Her parents made her *take* piano lessons when she was 10. • He *takes* both French and Spanish. • I *took* five classes last semester. • I'm *taking* a course on world history.

22 [+ *obj*] **: to complete (a test or exam)** • If you fail the first time, you have to *take* the test again.

23 [+ *obj*] *of a machine* **: to use or need (something) in order to work** • What size batteries does the flashlight *take*? • a car that *takes* diesel

24 [+ *obj*] **: to use (something) for a particular purpose** • The team's coaches decided to *take* another approach. • Let me *take* this opportunity to thank everyone for coming. • Harsh measures were *taken* to reduce crime in the city. • I suggest you *take* his advice. • They never ***took the time*** [=*bothered*] to get to know her.

25 [+ *obj*] **: to accept (the power to deal with something) : to accept control of (something)** • She was chosen to ***take charge/control of*** the organization. • I'll get you started, and you ***take it*** [=*take over*] from there. • Citizens are discouraged from ***taking the law into their own hands***. [=punishing people for breaking laws even though they have no right to punish them]

26 [+ *obj*] *Brit* **: to make (a decision) with authority** • The committee will *take* [=*make*] their decision next week.

27 [+ *obj*] **: to deal with or consider (something)** • The governor will give a statement and then *take* questions from reporters. • Will you *take* this call? • Cases will be *taken* in order of importance. • Let's ***take first things first***. • We'll see what happens and ***take it as it comes***. • I'll need a long time to recover, so I'm just ***taking (it) one day at a time***.

28 [+ *obj*] **a : to understand or think about (something or someone) in a certain way** • I don't quite know how to *take* that comment. • He said that I was full-figured, and I *took* it as a compliment. • No one *took* her literally/seriously when she said that she was going to quit. • He *takes* himself too seriously. • He says unkind things to everyone. Try not to ***take it personally***. [=to be offended or upset by what he said] • ***Don't take this the wrong way*** [=do not be offended by this], but I think you could find a better boyfriend. • When it started to rain, we ***took it as a sign*** [=we believed that the rain was a sign] that we should go home. • Can't you ***take a hint***? [=understand that I am trying to give you a hint?] • I ***take it*** [=(more formally) *assume, suppose*] that you didn't get my message. • So, you're staying here, I *take it*. • I know it's just gossip, so I ***take it for what it's worth***. [=I do not strongly believe that it is true or important] **b : to react to (someone or something) in a certain way** • I was surprised by how well she *took* the news. • He *took* it pretty badly/hard [=he was very upset] when his dog died. • She doesn't *take* such things lightly. [=she acts as though such things are very important]

29 [+ *obj*] **: to think about (something or someone) as an example** • They just want attention. For instance, *take* the way they wear their hair. • *Take* last year's record high temperatures, for example. • The system isn't working properly. *Take* the case of Jane Smith.

30 [+ *obj*] **: to think of (someone or something) as a particular type of person or thing — usually + *for*** • Oh, you're not Jill. Excuse me. I *took* you *for* [=mistakenly thought you were] an old friend of mine. • Of course we know how to do it. ***Do you take us for*** idiots? [=do you think we are idiots?] • "Can you finish everything in two hours?" "Two hours?! ***Who do you take me for***? Superman?" [=do you think I'm Superman?]

31 [+ *obj*] **: to believe (something that someone tells you)** • ***Take it from me***. [=believe me] He would love to go to the concert with you. • Okay, I'll ***take your word for it***. [=I will believe that what you say is true] • You don't have to *take my word for it*. Ask him yourself. • She ***can't take a compliment***. [=she does not believe that the nice things said about her are true]

32 [+ *obj*] **a : to begin to have (an opinion, interest, etc.)** • She has yet to *take* a position on the issue. • The program inspires young people to *take* an interest [=become interested] in current events. • They ***take a dim view*** [=have a negative opinion] of the country's current foreign policy. • She *took a dim view* of his behavior. **b : to ask people to make choices or give opinions in (a vote, poll, etc.)** • They *took* a survey of shoppers to find out which brands people liked best. • I think we should *take* a vote [=should vote] about what to do.

33 a [+ *obj*] **: to feel or experience (an emotion)** • Please don't *take* offense. [=please don't be offended] • Investors ***took fright*** [=suddenly became afraid] at the news and pulled their money. **— often + *in* or *to*** • His grandparents *took* special pleasure *in* [=were very pleased by] seeing him graduate from college. • It's important to *take* pride *in* your work. • I *take* comfort/solace *in* the fact that others have had to go through the same thing. • She *takes* an instant dislike *to* [=she instantly dislikes] anyone who tries to sell her something. **b** ✧ If you ***are taken ill/sick*** or (*US*) ***take ill/sick***, you suddenly become ill. • He and I both *took ill* after eating the fish. • Several other customers also *were taken ill/sick*.

34 [+ *obj*] **a :** to experience or be affected by (something unpleasant) • Everyone will have to *take* a pay cut. • She had to *take* a two-stroke penalty. • The ship sunk after *taking* [=*sustaining*] a direct hit. • He *took* several punches to the head. • He *took* quite a beating. • "*Take* that," she said as she slapped him in the face. **b :** to experience (something bad or unpleasant) without being seriously harmed • These shoes have *taken* [=*withstood*] a lot of punishment. — often used in negative statements • These plants can't *take* [=*tolerate*] the cold. • You no longer have to *take* [=*endure*] the pain of arthritis. — sometimes used in an exaggerated way • What happens next? I can't *take* the suspense. • I can't *take* this noise anymore! **c :** to accept the difficulty or unpleasantness of (something or someone) without complaining or making changes • I wouldn't *take* [=*tolerate*] that kind of rudeness from anyone. • I'm not going to *take* it anymore! • Are you just going to sit there and *take* it? • Don't ***take it lying down***. Do something about it. • I thought she would be upset, but she's ***taking it in stride***. [=not upset about it] • Stop crying and ***take it like a man***. • I wasn't being serious. Can't you ***take a joke***? [=can't you laugh at a joke that is about you?] • He's a little ***hard to take*** sometimes. [=he is sometimes a little rude, annoying, etc.]

35 [+ *obj*] **:** to become known by (someone) in a certain way • Her reaction ***took me by surprise***. [=surprised me] • The latest band ***taking the country by storm*** [=quickly becoming very popular throughout the country] is a Swedish group.

36 [+ *obj*] **:** to be liked or enjoyed by (someone) **:** to delight (someone) — used as *(be) taken*; usually + *with* or *by* • He *was* quite *taken with* her at their first meeting. • None of us *was* completely *taken with* the idea of staying there for an entire month. • The critic *was* so *taken by* the restaurant that she gave it four stars out of a possible five.

37 [+ *obj*] **:** to be the cause of (damage, suffering, etc.) • She vowed to *take* (her) revenge against him. • She swore that she would *take* vengeance on him. • The storm *took* its toll. [=the storm did a lot of damage] • A war could *take* a terrible toll on the economy.

38 [+ *obj*] **a :** to win or get (something) in a game, contest, etc. • She sang well enough to *take* first prize in her high school's talent contest. • He *took* second place behind last year's winner. • They *took* an 8–6 lead in the seventh inning. • The number 20 car *took* the lead with one lap to go. • They ***took home*** the championship for the third year in a row. • Let's play one more round. ***Winner takes all***. [=the winner of this round will win the whole contest] **b :** to beat or defeat (someone) in a game, fight, etc. • She *took* her opponent in the second round. • He's not that big. I think I can *take* him.

39 [+ *obj*] **:** to cause (someone or something) to move to a particular level or area of activity • They decided to *take* the company public. • Are you ready to *take* your business to the next level? • When *taken* to extremes, their philosophy can have negative consequences.

40 [+ *obj*] **:** to go to a safe or calm place for (shelter, cover, etc.) • If it rains, we can *take* shelter in the clubhouse. • Here come the bombers! *Take* cover! • a quiet place to *take* refuge

41 [*no obj*] **:** to be effective or become established • Clearly, the lesson he had tried to teach them didn't *take*. [=they didn't learn the lesson] • We are waiting to see if the heart transplant *takes*.

42 [+ *obj*] **:** to be able to have (something) when treated in a particular way • a surface that *takes* a fine/high polish

43 [+ *obj*] *grammar* **:** to appear or be used with (something) • Transitive verbs *take* an object while intransitive verbs do not. • Most words that end in "sh," such as "brush" and "wish," *take* "es" in their plural forms.

44 [+ *obj*] *mathematics* **:** SUBTRACT — often + *away* • When you *take* two (*away*) from five you get three.

> In addition to the phrases shown below, *take* occurs in many idioms that are shown at appropriate entries throughout the dictionary. For example, *take a backseat* can be found at BACKSEAT and *take the cake* can be found at [1]CAKE.

take aback [*phrasal verb*] ***take (someone) aback*** **:** to surprise or shock (someone) — usually used as *(be) taken aback* • When I told him my answer, he seemed *taken aback*. [=*shocked*] — often + *by* • He *was taken aback by* her answer.

take action **:** to do something **:** to act in order to get a particular result • The committee is ready to *take action*. • If we fail to *take action* [=fail to act], many innocent people could be hurt. • She is threatening to *take* legal *action* against the company. [=threatening to sue the company]

take after [*phrasal verb*] ***take after (someone)*** **:** to be like (someone, such as a parent) **:** to resemble (someone) • He *takes after* his father in height and build. • "She's such a sweet child." "Yes. She *takes after* her mother."

take against [*phrasal verb*] ***take against (someone or something)*** *Brit, somewhat old-fashioned* **:** to begin to dislike (someone or something) • They *took against* her for no apparent reason.

take a lot out of you ✧ If something *takes a lot out of you* or (*Brit*) ***takes it out of you***, it requires a lot of work or energy and causes you to feel physically or emotionally tired. • That interview really *took a lot out of me*.

take apart [*phrasal verb*] **1** ***take apart (something) or take (something) apart*** **:** to remove or separate the parts of (something) • They practiced *taking apart* [=*disassembling*] their rifles and putting them back together again. • Help me *take* this puzzle *apart*. **2** ***take apart (something) or take (something) apart*** **:** to talk about the different parts of (an idea, story, etc.) often in order to criticize it • He *takes apart* the theory and shows its weaknesses. **3** ***take apart (someone) or take (someone) apart*** *chiefly Brit* **:** to badly beat (a person or team) in a game or contest • The champion really *took* the challenger *apart* in the second round.

take away [*phrasal verb*] **1** ***take away (someone or something) or take (someone or something) away*** **:** to remove (someone or something) **:** to cause (someone or something) to go away, to no longer exist, to no longer be held, etc. • "*Take* him *away*!" said the queen. • He was trying to *take* the ball *away* from the dog. • A new store would *take* business *away* from existing stores in the area. • Her parents threatened to *take away* her driving privileges. • If you *take away* [=if you do not consider] his fancy clothes, he's a rather ordinary person. • The beautiful new theater ***took my breath away***. [=it made me feel surprised and excited] **2** ***take away (something) or take (something) away*** **a :** to remember (something) for possible use in the future — usually + *from* • What lesson can we *take away from* this? **b** *Brit* **:** to buy (food that is cooked in a restaurant) and carry it to another place • We sell hot food to *take away*. [=(*US*) we sell hot food for takeout] **3** ***take it away*** *informal* **:** to start playing or singing music • *Take it away*, Annie! **4** ***take away from*** [*phrasal verb*] ***take away from (something)*** **:** to reduce the value or importance of (something) • The ugly door *takes away from* [=detracts from] the beauty of the house. • She made a few mistakes during her speech, but that didn't *take away from* her overall message. — see also [1]TAKE 44 (above)

take back [*phrasal verb*] **1** ***take back (someone or something) or take (someone or something) back*** **a :** to return (something or someone) • If you bought any of these toys, *take* them *back* to the store for a full refund. • Waiter, this soup is terrible. Please *take* it *back*. [=return it to the kitchen] • I *took* him *back* to his apartment. **b :** to accept or receive (someone or something) again • They wouldn't *take back* the dress because I didn't have the receipt. • His wife left him but he decided to *take* her *back*. **2** ***take (someone) back*** **:** to cause (someone) to remember a time or event — usually + *to* • This meal *takes* me *back to* [=it makes me remember] our vacation in Mexico. • a song that *takes* you *back to* your childhood **3** ***take back (something) or take (something) back*** **:** to say that you did not really mean (something that you said) • My mom is not fat! *Take* it *back*! • He refused to *take back* what he said.

take down [*phrasal verb*] ***take down (something) or take (something) down*** **1 :** to remove (something) from the place where it is hanging or standing • She *took* the books *down* from the shelf. • I need to *take down* those curtains and bring them to the dry cleaner's. • *Take down* that terrible picture of me. • Please, *take* it *down*. • He *took down* the old shed and built a new one. **2 :** to lower but not remove (something) • The doctor asked him to *take down* [=*pull down*] his pants. **3 :** to write (something) • He *took* her phone number *down* on a napkin. • Did you *take down* the car's license number?

take in [*phrasal verb*] **1** ***take in (someone) or take (some-***

one) in **a** : to allow (a person or animal) to stay in your house, hotel, etc. • The family started *taking in* boarders to make ends meet. • The homeless shelter *takes in* women and children. • They agreed to *take* him *in* for the summer. • *taking in* stray cats **b** : to take (someone) to a police station • The police *took* him *in* for driving while drunk. • The suspects were *taken in* for questioning. **c** : to trick or deceive (someone) — often used as *(be) taken in* • He *was taken in* by a man who said he was collecting money for a charity. **2** ***take in (something) or take (something) in*** **a** : to make (a piece of clothing) smaller or shorter • I lost weight and had to *take in* my pants. • I had to *take* them *in* at the waist. — opposite *let out* at [1]LET **b** *US* : to receive (something) as payment or earnings • The restaurant has been *taking in* [=(*Brit*) *taking*] thousands of dollars a night. • They couldn't *take* enough money *in* to stay in business. **c** : to allow (water, air, etc.) to enter your body • She stood on the shore *taking in* the salty sea air. **d** : to look at and think about (something) • We spent the hour talking and *taking in* the view. • You'll have plenty of time to *take in* all the sights. **e** : to learn about and try to understand (something) • We paused to *take in* the situation. • It's hard to *take* all this information *in* at once. • We need to *take in* all the options before making a decision. **f** : to watch (a show, game, etc.) • If we have time after dinner, I thought maybe we could *take in* a movie. **g** : to include (a place) among the places that you go to • Our trip to New York City will *take in* several museums. = We will *take in* [=*visit*] several museums on our trip to New York City.

take it or leave it **1** — used to say that you will not make a better offer than the one you have made • I'll give you $500 for the camera, but that's my final offer. *Take it or leave it.* **2** — used to say that you do not care about or are not excited about something • "Do you like lobster?" "I can *take it or leave it.*" [=I neither strongly like nor dislike lobster]

take it upon/on yourself : to do something that needs to be done even though no one has asked you to do it • Thank you for *taking it upon yourself* to organize the meeting.

take long : to require or use a long amount of time • It didn't *take long* to realize that something was wrong. • Hurry up. You're *taking* too *long*. • What's *taking* so *long*?

take note *or* ***take notice*** : to notice or pay attention to something • The news made them ***sit up and take notice***. [=suddenly give full attention to something] — often + *of* • She *took note of* [=*noted*] the exact time. • No one remembers *taking notice of* her [=no one remembers noticing her] at the party.

take off [*phrasal verb*] **1 a** : to suddenly go somewhere • She *took off* without even saying goodbye. • Where did you *take off to*? [=where did you go?] **b** ***take off after (someone or something)*** *US* : to start to move quickly in order to catch (someone or something) • If my dog sees a cat, she'll *take off after* [=*chase*] it. • He jumped in his car and *took off after* them. **2** : to begin to fly • Please sit down. The plane's about to *take off*. • They *took off* and landed safely. **3** : to quickly become very successful or popular • Her career *took off* after she won an Oscar for best supporting actress. • Our business is really starting to *take off*. **4** ***take off (something) or take (something) off*** **a** : to remove (something) • I *took* my boots *off* and put on some slippers. • Always *take off* your makeup before going to bed. • *Take* that smile *off* your face! [=stop smiling] • This new diet will *take* inches *off* your waist and hips. • Please ***take your hands off*** me. [=stop touching or holding me] • I can't ***take my eyes off*** [=I cannot stop looking at] that beautiful ring of yours! • Hiring more teachers would help ***take the pressure off*** [=reduce the amount of stress felt by] our staff. • Her show was ***taken off the air*** [=it was no longer shown on TV] after three seasons. • The toy was ***taken off the market*** [=it was stopped from being sold] for safety reasons. **b** : to reduce the price of something by (a specified amount) • You can *take* 20 percent *off* everything in the store. • They *took* $3,000 *off* the original price of the car. **c** : to spend (an amount of time) away from a job or activity • He *took* the day *off* and went to the beach. • I *took* two weeks *off* (work) to visit my family. • I haven't *taken* any time *off* yet this year. **5** ***take (someone) off (something)*** **a** : to tell (someone) to stop using (something, such as a medicine) • The doctor *took* her *off* the drug and put her on a new one. • He *took* himself *off* his medication. [=he stopped using it] • *taking* a patient *off* a ventilator **b** : to tell (someone) to no longer work on (something) • The newspaper's editor *took* her *off* the story. • He was *taken off* the project. **6** ***take off (someone) or take (someone) off*** *Brit* : to copy (someone) usually in order to make other people laugh • He can *take off* [=*mimic*, *imitate*] our teacher perfectly. — see also TAKEOFF

take on [*phrasal verb*] **1** ***take on (something) or take (something) on*** **a** : to begin to deal with (something, such as a job or responsibility) • I don't have time to *take on* any new responsibilities right now. • We are depending on you to *take on* this important assignment. • Her willingness to *take on* new challenges is admirable. **b** : to begin to have (a particular quality or appearance) • Her writings *took on* new meaning after her death. • In the evening, the plaza *takes on* a different air/aura. • stories in which animals *take on* human attributes • The story was broadcast throughout the world and began to ***take on a life of its own***. [=to become very large, important, and hard to control] • The story has ***taken on mythic proportions***. [=it has become very famous or important] **2** ***take on (someone or something) or take (someone or something) on*** **a** : to fight or struggle with (someone or something) • Police have been *taking on* the neighborhood's drug dealers. • She's not afraid to *take on* her critics/detractors directly. • They will need lots of money and resources to *take on* the tobacco companies. : to criticize or argue against (someone or something) • She *takes on* the country's current foreign policy in her new book. • *taking on* sexism in the music industry **b** : to compete against (a person, team, etc.) • The Yankees are set to *take on* the Red Sox at Yankee Stadium tonight. • She *took* him *on* in a game of tennis. **c** : to allow (someone or something) to enter • The train *took on* a few more passengers before leaving the city. • The ship sprung a leak and began to *take on* water. [=water began getting into the ship] **3** ***take on (someone) or take (someone) on*** : to accept (someone) as an employee, client, etc. • I'm sorry, but the doctor isn't *taking on* [=*taking*] any new patients. • She agreed to *take* him *on* as an assistant.

take out [*phrasal verb*] **1** ***take (something) out or take out (something)*** **a** : to remove (something) from a thing, place, or person • She had her tonsils *taken out* when she was ten years old. • Remove the board and *take out* all the nails. : to move (something) from the place that held, enclosed, or hid it • Please *take out* a pencil and begin the test. • Please *take* your homework *out*. • I forgot to *take out* the garbage [=to bring it outside] this morning. **b** : to get (something, such as insurance, a loan, etc.) by a standard process or series of steps : to make the arrangements, payments, etc., that are required for (something) • All drivers in the state must *take out* insurance on their vehicles. • They had to *take out* a second mortgage on their home. • They *took out* ads in several magazines and newspapers. **c** : to borrow or rent (something) from a store, library, etc. • She *took out* a couple of books from the library. **d** : to destroy (something) • Our mission is to *take out* two enemy targets. • She swerved off the road and *took out* a telephone pole. **2** ***take (someone) out or take out (someone)*** **a** : to go with (someone you have invited) to a restaurant, party, etc. • Can I *take* you *out* sometime? • teenagers *taking* each other *out* on dates • They *took* us *out* for/to lunch. **b** : to cause (a person or team) to no longer be part of a competition • He *took* his opponent *out* in the first 60 seconds of the match. • Our team was *taken out* in the second round of competition. **3** ***take (something) out on (someone)*** ✧ If you ***take your anger, frustration, etc., out on someone***, you treat someone badly because you feel angry, frustrated, etc. • workers who go home and *take* their frustration *out* on their families • I'm sorry you didn't get the job, but don't *take* it *out* on me. [=don't treat me badly because you are disappointed] — see also TAKEOUT

take over [*phrasal verb*] ***take over or take over (something) or take (something) over*** **1** : to start doing (something that someone has stopped doing) • Here, you *take over* stirring the soup while I start making the salad. • *Take over* for me for a while. **2** : to become the person who has control of (something) • Since she has *taken over* the company, productivity and profits have soared. • Military leaders *took over* the government in 2002. • They *took over* in 2002. — see also TAKEOVER

take sides *or* ***take someone's side*** : to agree with or support one person or group and not another • She refuses to *take sides* on the issue. • When my sister and I fight, our dad always *takes her side*. • Why do you always *take her side*? • The government responded by *taking the side of* the consumer.

T

take through [*phrasal verb*] ***take (someone) through (something)*** **: to tell (someone) how (something) happens or is done by explaining the details of each step** ▪ I asked him to *take* [=*lead, walk*] me *through* his daily exercise regimen. ▪ *Take* me *through* that day hour by hour. [=tell me what happened each hour of that day]

take to [*phrasal verb*] **1** ***take to (something)*** **: to go to or into (a place)** ▪ They grabbed their weapons and *took to* the hills. ▪ Thousands of people *took to* the streets in protest. [=went out into the streets to protest] ▪ He ***took to the airwaves*** [=he spoke on the radio] with his message. **2** ***take to (someone or something)*** **: to begin to like (someone or something)** ▪ I *took to* her as soon as she smiled at me. ▪ Many students have not *taken* well *to* the new school uniforms. ▪ He tried skiing and *took to* it immediately. [=he quickly learned how to ski and liked doing it] ▪ She *took to* horseback riding like a duck (takes) to water. [=she learned it in a very easy and natural way] ▪ (*informal*) They don't ***take kindly to*** strangers [=they don't like strangers] around here. **3** ***take to (doing something)*** **: to begin (doing something) as a habit** ▪ He *took to* drinking after he lost his job. ▪ She had *taken to* sleeping on the floor. ▪ We've *taken to* calling him "Mr. Dependable." **4** ***take (something) to (someone or something)*** **: to use (something) to do something to (someone or something)** ▪ Someone needs to *take* a mop *to* this floor. [=someone needs to mop this floor] ▪ I *took* an ax *to* the dead tree in front of my house. [=I cut down the dead tree with an ax] ▪ He was criticized for *taking* a belt *to* his children. [=hitting his children with a belt]

take up [*phrasal verb*] **1** ***take up or take up (something) or take (something) up*** **: to begin (something) again : to continue (something) after you or another person stops** ▪ She *took up* [=*picked up*] the story where he left off. ▪ He is hoping that he and his ex-girlfriend can *take up* [=that they can continue their relationship] where they left off. **2** ***take up (something)*** **: to fill (an area, amount of time, etc.) completely or almost completely** ▪ The new couch *takes up* half of the room. ▪ I don't want to *take up* too much of your time, but I do have a few questions. ▪ The entire day was *taken up* by/with meetings. ▪ We don't use this table for anything. It's just *taking up* space. **3** ***take up (something) or take (something) up*** **a : to begin studying or practicing (an activity, subject, instrument, etc.) usually as a hobby** ▪ I was thinking about *taking up* skiing/dancing/photography. ▪ She *took up* the guitar at age 11. ▪ *taking up* art lessons **b : to begin to deal with (a problem, an issue, etc.)** ▪ The cause of global warming has been *taken up* by many celebrities recently. ▪ The court *took up* the question of how to deal with companies that break the law. ▪ He seemed willing to *take up* [=*take on*] the challenge. **c : to begin to have (a new job, home, etc.)** ▪ He will *take up* his post [=begin working at his new post/job] at the beginning of the year. ▪ She went to France and *took up* residence in Paris. [=became a resident of Paris; began living in Paris] ▪ She *took up* [=she began to lead] the life of an artist. = She *took up* life as an artist. ▪ Two men with guns had *taken up* (their) positions on the roof. **d** *somewhat old-fashioned* **: to begin to use (something)** ▪ They *took up* hammers and nails and went to work building the house. ▪ Once again, they ***took up arms*** [=picked up weapons and became ready to fight] to defend their country. **e : to make (something, such as a piece of clothing) shorter** ▪ Can you *take* the legs of these pants *up* two inches? **f : to lift and remove (something)** ▪ We *took up* the carpet in the living room and replaced it with hardwood flooring. **g : to gather (money, clothes, etc.) from many different people or places** ▪ They are *taking up* a collection for the homeless shelter. **4** ***take (someone) up on (something)*** **: to make an agreement with (someone) to accept (an offer)** ▪ "Can I buy you a drink?" "Sure, I'll *take* you *up on* that." ▪ We *took* the company *up on* its offer to replace the computer for free. **5** ***take (something) up with (someone)*** **: to talk about (something, such as a problem) with (someone)** ▪ If you have a problem, please *take* it *up with* one of our managers. ▪ Have you *taken* this *up with* your mother yet? **6** ***take up with (someone)*** **: to begin a friendly or romantic relationship with (someone)** ▪ After her divorce, she *took up with* a younger man. — see also TAKE-UP

– see also GIVE-AND-TAKE

[2]take *noun, pl* **takes** [*count*]

1 a : the way that a particular person thinks about or understands something : a distinct point of view — often + *on* ▪ What's your *take on* what happened? [=what do you think about what happened?] ▪ I had a different *take on* the experience. ▪ She has an unusual *take on* life. **b : a particular way of dealing with or treating something — usually + *on*** ▪ Audiences seem to be enjoying the film's modern *take on* Dickens' famous story. ▪ a new *take on* an old problem

2 : a scene that is filmed or a song that is recorded at one time without stopping ▪ It took us 20 *takes* to get the scene right. ▪ She nailed it on the first *take*.

3 *informal* **a : the amount of money that is earned or received** ▪ He stands to earn 10 percent of the company's $1 million *take* on the deal. **b : a share or percentage of an amount of money** ▪ She was expecting a bigger *take*.

on the take *informal* **: illegally taking money for doing favors for someone : illegally accepting bribes** ▪ We've heard rumors that the senator is *on the take*.

– see also DOUBLE TAKE

take·away /ˈteɪkəˌweɪ/ *noun, pl* **-aways**

1 *Brit* **a** [*noncount*] **:** TAKEOUT 1 ▪ We ordered some Chinese *takeaway*. **b** [*count*] **:** TAKEOUT 2 ▪ She works in a Chinese *takeaway*.

2 [*count*] *sports* **: an act of taking the ball or puck from a player on the other team** ▪ He leads the league in *takeaways*.

– takeaway *adj, always used before a noun, Brit* ▪ *takeaway* food ▪ a *takeaway* restaurant

take–charge /ˈteɪkˈʧɑɚʤ/ *adj, always used before a noun, chiefly US, informal* **: having the qualities of a forceful leader : able to make decisions in a confident way and then act on them** ▪ a *take-charge* attitude ▪ a *take-charge* guy/woman

take–home pay /ˈteɪkˌhoʊm-/ *noun* [*noncount*] **: the amount of money that a person earns after taxes and other amounts have been subtracted** ▪ She grosses $40,000 a year but her *take-home pay* is about $25,000.

taken *past participle of* [1]TAKE

take–no–prisoners *adj, always used before a noun, US, informal* **: very tough and aggressive** ▪ *take-no-prisoners* politics ▪ a journalist with a *take-no-prisoners* style — see also *take no prisoners* at PRISONER

take·off /ˈteɪkˌɑːf/ *noun, pl* **-offs**

1 : the moment when an airplane, helicopter, etc., leaves the ground and begins to fly [*noncount*] Please remain seated during *takeoff*. ▪ Air Force One, you're ready for *takeoff*. [*count*] perfect *takeoffs* and landings

2 [*count*] **: the beginning of a jump** ▪ All the high jumpers had flawless *takeoffs*.

3 [*count*] **: a sudden increase in size, activity, or popularity** ▪ the country's economic *takeoff*

4 [*count*] **: a new or unusual way of making or doing something** ▪ an interesting *takeoff* on traditional lasagna

5 [*count*] **a : a performance in which someone copies the way another person speaks, moves, etc., in usually a humorous way** ▪ He did a perfect *takeoff* [=*imitation, impression*] of our teacher. **b** *chiefly US* **: a piece of writing, music, etc., that imitates the style of someone or something else in an amusing way :** PARODY ▪ They did a funny *takeoff* on/of a quiz show.

– see also *take off* at [1]TAKE

take·out /ˈteɪkˌaʊt/ *noun, pl* **-outs** *US*

1 [*noncount*] **: food that is cooked in a restaurant and taken by a customer to be eaten in another place** ▪ We ordered some Chinese *takeout*. — called also (*chiefly US*) *carryout*, (*Brit*) *takeaway*

2 [*count*] **: a restaurant that sells takeout** ▪ She works in a Chinese *takeout*. — called also (*chiefly US*) *carryout*, (*Brit*) *takeaway*

– take–out *adj, always used before a noun, US* ▪ *take-out* food ▪ a *take-out* restaurant

take·over /ˈteɪkˌoʊvɚ/ *noun, pl* **-overs** [*count*] **: an occurrence in which a person, company, etc., takes control of something** ▪ The government experienced a military *takeover* in 2002. ▪ *takeover* bids ▪ The company was trying to protect itself from a ***hostile takeover***. [=an attempt to buy a company when the people who own the company do not want to sell it] — see also *take over* at [1]TAKE

tak·er /ˈteɪkɚ/ *noun, pl* **-ers** [*count*]

1 : a person who takes something ▪ He's more of a giver than a *taker*. [=he likes to give rather than receive things] ▪ She's not much of a risk *taker*. [=she does not like to take risks] ▪ I'm a terrible test *taker*. ▪ a poll *taker* ▪ ticket *takers*

2 *informal* **: a person who accepts something that is offered** ▪ The class had no *takers*. [=no one took the class] ▪ I have two tickets for sale. Any *takers*?

take–up /ˈteɪkˌʌp/ *noun* [*singular*] *Brit* **:** the rate at which something offered is accepted by people ▪ Fewer French classes are being offered due to low *take-up*. ▪ *Take-up* of our products has been high. — see also *take up* at ¹TAKE

tak·ings /ˈteɪkɪŋz/ *noun* [*plural*] *chiefly Brit* **:** the amount of money that is earned **:** TAKE ▪ They will donate half of the *takings* to charity. ▪ box office *takings*

talc /ˈtælk/ *noun* [*noncount*] **:** TALCUM POWDER

tal·cum powder /ˈtælkəm-/ *noun* [*noncount*] **:** a soft, white powder that is used to make your skin feel dry and smooth

tale /ˈteɪl/ *noun, pl* **tales** [*count*]

1 : a story about imaginary events **:** an exciting or dramatic story ▪ The movie is a stirring *tale* of courage. ▪ *tales* about ghosts — see also FAIRY TALE, FOLKTALE

2 a : a story about someone's actual experiences ▪ We listened to his familiar ***tale of woe/misfortune*** as he talked again about the failure of his marriage. **b :** an exciting story that may not be completely true ▪ He told us thrilling *tales* about his adventures as a pilot in the war. — see also TALL TALE

3 : a false story that is told to deceive someone ▪ Are you telling *tales* again? Or is that the truth?

dead men tell no tales — used to say that someone who has been killed cannot reveal secret information

thereby hangs a tale see ¹HANG

– see also OLD WIVES' TALE

tal·ent /ˈtælənt/ *noun, pl* **-ents**

1 : a special ability that allows someone to do something well [*noncount*] a singer with an enormous amount of *talent* ▪ I have no musical *talent*. ▪ Her artistic/creative *talent* has been obvious ever since she was a child. ▪ athletic *talent* ▪ a person of *talent* = a person who has *talent* ▪ They sang a duet in the ***talent show/contest***. [*count*] She has a job that makes the most of her *talents*. ▪ His experience, skills, and *talents* make him perfectly suited for the job. ▪ He has many *talents*. = He's a man of many *talents*. ▪ He seems to have a *talent* for getting into trouble. [=he often gets into trouble]

2 : a person or group of people with a special ability to do something well **:** a talented person or group [*count*] There are many good players on the team, but she's a special *talent*. [*noncount*] The company has hired some expensive legal *talent* for the trial. ▪ The team has recruited some of the best *talent* around. ▪ The company is doing a ***talent search*** to find the right person for the job.

3 [*noncount*] *Brit slang* **:** people who are sexually attractive ▪ checking out the local *talent*

tal·ent·ed /ˈtæləntəd/ *adj* [*more* ~; *most* ~] **:** having a special ability to do something well **:** having talent ▪ a very/highly *talented* actor/musician/singer/athlete ▪ As a writer, she is enormously *talented*.

tal·ent·less /ˈtæləntləs/ *adj* **:** lacking talent **:** not at all talented ▪ a *talentless* singer/athlete

talent scout *noun, pl* ~ **scouts** [*count*] **:** a person whose job is to find talented performers, athletes, etc. — called also (*Brit*) *talent spotter*

tal·is·man /ˈtæləsmən/ *noun, pl* **-mans** [*count*] **:** an object (such as a ring or stone) that is believed to have magic powers and to cause good things to happen to the person who has it

¹talk /ˈtɑːk/ *verb* **talks; talked; talk·ing**

1 a : to say words in order to express your thoughts, feelings, opinions, etc., to someone [*no obj*] She never *talks* at the meetings. ▪ He did most of the *talking* during dinner. ▪ He loves to hear himself *talk*. — often + *to* ▪ You shouldn't *talk to* your mother that way. — often + *about* ▪ She still *talks about* your wedding and how perfect it was. [+ *obj*] I think she's *talking* a lot of nonsense/rubbish/drivel. ▪ You should listen to her; she's *talking* (good) sense. [=she's saying sensible things] **b** [*no obj*] **:** to have a conversation or discussion with someone ▪ We need to *talk*. ▪ I can't *talk* right now. I'm running late. ▪ They were *talking* in Spanish. ▪ We *talked* on the phone until midnight. ▪ Both sides in the dispute are now willing to *talk*. — often + *to* ▪ They *talked to* each other in a whisper. ▪ Who were you *talking to* on the phone? ▪ I could hear her *talking to* herself as she studied. — often + *with* ▪ The coach refused to *talk with* the reporters. ▪ May I *talk with* you privately? — often + *about* ▪ You might feel better if you *talked to* someone *about* your problems. ▪ The teacher *talked with* him *about* his poor grades. ▪ When they get together, all they do is *talk about* sports. **c** [+ *obj*] **:** to have a conversation about (something) ▪ They are in the conference room *talking* business. ▪ They were *talking* baseball/politics. ▪ They like to ***talk shop*** [=to talk about work] during lunch. ***synonyms*** see SPEAK

2 [*no obj*] **:** to use your voice to say words **:** SPEAK ▪ She had laryngitis and couldn't *talk*. ▪ I can't understand you. You're *talking* too fast. ▪ No *talking* during the performance, please! ▪ Would you please stop *talking*. I'm trying to watch the movie. ▪ She *talks* very loud. ▪ He is teaching the parrot to *talk*. ▪ She started *talking* when she was only eight months old.

3 [*no obj*] **:** to be willing to talk to someone after having an argument, disagreement, fight, etc., with that person — always used as *(be) talking* ▪ It's been two weeks and they*'re* still not *talking* (to each other).

4 [*no obj*] **:** to talk about the personal lives of other people ▪ It's rude to *talk* [=*gossip*] about people behind their back(s). ▪ If you continue behaving like that, people are bound to *talk*.

5 [*no obj*] **:** to tell secret information to someone ▪ The police forced him to *talk*.

6 [*no obj*] **:** to give information without speaking **:** to communicate with signs, numbers, etc. ▪ They were *talking* to each other in sign language. ▪ When she gets excited, she *talks* with her hands. [=she moves her hands when she talks] ▪ The computer is *talking* to the printer.

7 *always followed by an adverb or preposition* [+ *obj*] **:** to talk until (someone or something) is in a specified state ▪ He *talked* himself hoarse. [=he talked so much that his voice became hoarse] ▪ She *talked* herself into a corner. [=she put herself in a bad position by talking too much] ▪ We *talked* the night away. [=we talked throughout the night] — see also SWEET-TALK

8 [*no obj*] **:** to criticize someone ✧ This sense of *talk* is often used in phrases like ***look who's talking, you're one to talk***, and ***you should talk*** to say that someone should not criticize another person because he or she has the same faults as that other person. ▪ "She's way too skinny." "*You're one to talk*. You need to gain some weight, too."

9 [+ *obj*] *informal* — used to describe or suggest the size or amount of something; always used as *(be) talking* ▪ To fix the car, you*'re talking* at least $500. [=it will cost at least $500 to fix the car] ▪ The heat was awful. I*'m talking* 100-degree weather and no air-conditioning.

know what you are talking about see ¹KNOW

money talks see MONEY

now you're talking *informal* — used to say that someone has said or suggested something that you think is good, worth doing, etc. ▪ "You don't want hamburgers. Well, how about steak?" "Yeah, *now you're talking*."

talk a blue streak see ¹BLUE

talk about **1** ✧ The phrase ***what are you talking about?*** can be used to show that you are confused, worried, upset, etc., about something that someone has just said. ▪ *What are you talking about*? I did what you told me to do. **2** *informal* — used to emphasize the size, amount, or extent of something ▪ *Talk about* rain! I've never seen it rain like this in my entire life! ▪ *Talk about* having a bad day. I had the worst day ever! ▪ *Talk about* short. She's only four feet tall! — see also ¹TALK 1a, b (above)

talk a good game *informal* **:** to say things that make people believe that you can do something or that something is true about you even though it is not true ▪ They *talk a good game*, but they're not really ready for the championship. ▪ She *talks a good game* about protecting the environment, but she doesn't even recycle.

talk around *also chiefly Brit* ***talk round*** [*phrasal verb*] **1** ***talk around/round (something)*** **:** to avoid talking about (a particular subject) especially because it is difficult, unpleasant, or embarrassing ▪ They've been *talking around* the real issue rather than addressing it directly. **2** ***talk (someone) around/round*** **:** to cause (someone) to accept and support something (such as an idea) after opposing it ▪ She says she doesn't agree with it, but we'll *talk* her *around* eventually. [=we'll eventually convince/persuade her to support it] — often + *to* ▪ We can *talk* her *round to* our way of thinking.

talk at [*phrasal verb*] *informal* ***talk at (someone)*** **:** to speak to (someone) without listening to what he or she says to you in reply ▪ My dad is always *talking at* me. ▪ You need to talk to your children, not *talk at* them.

talk back [*phrasal verb*] **:** to answer (someone) in a rude way that does not show proper respect ▪ Don't *talk back*! — often + *to* ▪ She was punished for *talking back to* her parents.

talk down [*phrasal verb*] **1** ***talk down to (someone)*** **:** to talk to (someone) in an overly simple way which suggests that he or she is not intelligent ▪ Many politicians are guilty of

T

talking down to voters. ▪ Don't *talk down to* me. I'm not stupid. **2** ***talk down (something or someone) or talk (something or someone) down*** **a** : to describe (something or someone) as unimportant ▪ He *talked down* [=*downplayed*] his accomplishments. **b** : to cause (the price of something) to be lower by talking to someone ▪ She managed to *talk down* his asking price for the car. : to convince (someone) to lower the price of something ▪ She *talked* him *down* 500 dollars. **3** ***talk (someone) down*** : to convince (someone who is standing on a high place and threatening to jump) to come down and not to commit suicide ▪ He tried to *talk* her *down* from the ledge. [=to convince her to not jump from the ledge] — sometimes used figuratively ▪ He was about to quit his job in anger, but she managed to *talk* him *down*. [=to convince him not to do it]

talk into [*phrasal verb*] ***talk (someone) into (something)*** : to get (someone) to do something by talking about the good reasons for doing it : to convince or persuade (someone) to do something ▪ The salesman *talked* us *into* buying the car. ▪ Her friends couldn't *talk* her *into* going on the trip.

talk nineteen to the dozen *Brit, informal* : to speak rapidly and without stopping ▪ He showed us around the house while *talking nineteen to the dozen*. [=(*US*) *talking a blue streak*]

talk of [*phrasal verb*] ***talk of (someone or something)*** : to speak or write about (someone or something) : to mention (a subject) in speech or writing ▪ It was the first time she *talked of* going to law school. ▪ She never *talks of* [=*talks about, speaks of*] her suffering during the war. ▪ In the letter, he *talked of* feeling ill. ▪ (*Brit*) *Talking of* [=*speaking of*] Jill, where is she?

talk of the devil see DEVIL

talk out [*phrasal verb*] ***talk out (something) or talk (something) out*** : to talk about (something) in order to find a solution ▪ The teacher told him to *talk out* the problem.

talk out of [*phrasal verb*] **1** ***talk (someone) out of (something)*** : to prevent (someone) from doing (something) by talking about the good reasons for not doing it : to persuade or convince (someone) not to do (something) ▪ He *talked* her *out of* quitting school. **2** ***talk (yourself) out of (something) or talk your way out of (something)*** : to avoid (something unpleasant or undesirable) by saying things to make other people forgive or excuse you ▪ She *talked* herself *out of* trouble. = She *talked her way out of* trouble. [=she got herself out of trouble by talking] ▪ He *talked his way out of* staying to clean up after the party.

talk over [*phrasal verb*] ***talk (something) over or talk over (something)*** : to discuss (something) with someone in order to make a decision or reach an agreement ▪ We need some time to *talk over* the offer. — usually + *with* ▪ I need to *talk* it *over with* my wife, first.

talk someone's ear off *US, informal* : to talk to someone for a very long period of time ▪ He *talks my ear off* every time I call him.

talk (some) sense into/to see [1]SENSE

talk the hind leg(s) off a donkey *Brit, informal* : to talk for a long time ▪ She rarely spoke, but her brother could *talk the hind legs off a donkey*. [=he was very talkative]

talk the same language see LANGUAGE

talk the talk : to say that you will do things ▪ Sure, she *talks the talk*, but can she walk the walk? [=she says that she will do things, but will she actually do them?]

talk through [*phrasal verb*] **1** ***talk (someone) through (something)*** : to help (someone) understand or do something by explaining its steps in a careful way ▪ The woman on the phone *talked* me *through* the procedure. **2** ***talk (something) through*** : to discuss (something) with someone in order to make a decision or reach an agreement ▪ Have you *talked* this *through* with your family? **3** *informal + old-fashioned* ✧ If you are ***talking through your hat***, you are saying incorrect, foolish, or illogical things. ▪ If he says that there's no problem, he's *talking through his hat*.

talk tough : to say that you will act in a forceful and aggressive way ▪ When the subject is national security, all the candidates *talk tough*. [=they say that they will act aggressively to support national security] — often + *on* ▪ The new mayor *talks tough on* crime.

talk trash see [1]TRASH

talk turkey see TURKEY

talk up [*phrasal verb*] ***talk up (someone or something) or talk (someone or something) up*** : to describe (someone or something) in a favorable way ▪ The salesperson *talked up* the car's safety features. ▪ He's being *talked up* as the next big pop star.

[2]talk *noun, pl* **talks**

1 [*count*] : an occurrence in which one person talks about something with another person : a conversation or discussion — often + *about* ▪ After a long *talk about* our relationship, we decided to get married. — often + *with* ▪ The boss would like to ***have a talk with*** you. — see also PEP TALK

2 [*count*] : the act of talking formally about something before a group of people : a speech or lecture — often + *on* ▪ He gave a *talk on* organic farming. ▪ She is preparing a *talk on* Christianity in the 21st century.

3 [*count*] : a formal discussion between two or more groups that are trying to reach an agreement about something — usually plural ▪ The country refuses to participate in *talks* on nuclear disarmament. ▪ a round of trade *talks*

4 [*noncount*] : a particular way of speaking ▪ I will not allow that kind of *talk* in my house. ▪ The movie has plenty of action and tough *talk*. ▪ ***street talk*** [=a way of speaking that is associated with people who live in a poor part of a city] ▪ ***straight talk*** [=speech that is very honest and direct] — see also SHOPTALK

5 [*noncount*] **a** : discussion about what might happen ▪ There has been some *talk* of further delays. [=some people have been saying that there will/may be further delays] ▪ I've been hearing *talk* that she plans to run for president. **b** : the act of talking about a subject with another person or group : discussion or conversation ▪ When they get together, the *talk* always turns to [=they always talk about] their years together in high school.

6 [*noncount*] : the things people say about what they want to do or are going to do ▪ It's not just *talk*. I'm serious about moving out. ▪ If we're ever going to solve these problems, we need less *talk* and more action. ▪ The town's last mayor was ***all talk*** (and no action). [=the mayor talked about doing things but never actually did them] ▪ ***Talk is cheap***. [=it is easy to say that you will do something] I need to see results.

talk the talk see [1]TALK

the talk of the town : a person or thing that many people in a town, city, etc., are talking about in an interested or excited way ▪ Last year at this time no one had ever heard of him, but now he's *the talk of the town*. ▪ The new restaurant is *the talk of the town*.

— see also BABY TALK, DOUBLE-TALK, PILLOW TALK, SMALL TALK

talk·a·tive /ˈtɑːkətɪv/ *adj* [*more ~; most ~*] : tending to talk a lot or to enjoy having conversations with people ▪ Their little boy is very *talkative*. ▪ She was in a *talkative* mood.

talk·er /ˈtɑːkɚ/ *noun, pl* **-ers** [*count*] : a person who talks in a particular way or who talks a lot ▪ That little girl is quite a *talker*. I don't think she's stopped talking since she got in the car. ▪ He's not much of a *talker*. ▪ He's more of a *talker* than a doer. [=he often talks about doing things without actually doing them] ▪ She is a great/fast/loud *talker*. ▪ a ***smooth talker*** [=a person who tends to flatter people]

talk·ie /ˈtɑːki/ *noun, pl* **-ies** [*count*] *old-fashioned* : a movie with sound — often plural ▪ The era of silent movies ended when *talkies* were introduced. — see also WALKIE-TALKIE

talking head *noun, pl* **~ heads** [*count*] : a person who gives information or opinions on a television show and whose head and shoulders are shown on the television screen ▪ The debate was followed by hours of *talking heads* analyzing the candidates' performances.

talking point *noun, pl* **~ points** [*count*] : a particular subject, idea, etc., that is part of a discussion ▪ We have several *talking points* we need to cover. ▪ I have a list of *talking points* here that support my case.

talking shop *noun, pl* **~ shops** [*count*] *Brit* : a place where people talk about doing things but do not actually achieve anything — usually singular ▪ She complained that Parliament had come to be an ineffective *talking shop*.

talk·ing–to /ˈtɑːkɪŋˌtuː/ *noun* [*singular*] *informal* : an angry or serious conversation in which you criticize someone's behavior ▪ We gave our daughter a good/stern *talking-to* about her poor grades.

talk radio *noun* [*noncount*] *chiefly US* : radio programs in which people talk about politics, sports, etc., and listeners can make phone calls to give their opinions ▪ He listens to business/sports *talk radio* in the car.

talk show *noun, pl* **~ shows** [*count*] : a radio or television program in which usually well-known people talk about something or are interviewed ▪ She asked the actor to appear on her *talk show.* • a famous *talk-show* host — called also (*Brit*) *chat show*

talky /ˈtɑːki/ *adj* **talk·i·er; -est** *somewhat informal*
1 : tending or wanting to talk **:** TALKATIVE • She was in a *talky* mood.
2 : having a lot of talking • a *talky* movie [=a movie in which people do a lot of talking]

tall /ˈtɑːl/ *adj* **tall·er; -est**
1 : greater in height than the average person, building, etc. • All the children in my family grew up to be very *tall.* • My mother is short but my father is fairly *tall.* • The giraffe is the *tallest* animal. • *tall* trees • the *tallest* [=*highest*] mountain • the world's *tallest* building • The drinks were served in *tall* glasses. — opposite SHORT ***synonyms*** see [1]HIGH
2 *always used after a noun* **:** having a specified height • She is five feet *tall.* • The building is six stories *tall.* [=*high*]
stand tall see [1]STAND
walk tall see [1]WALK

tall order *noun* [*singular*] *informal* **:** something that is very difficult to do • Getting the project done on schedule is going to be a *tall order.* • That's a (pretty/very) *tall order.* = That's a ***tall order to fill.***

tal·low /ˈtæloʊ/ *noun* [*noncount*] **:** fat from cattle and sheep that is used chiefly to make candles and soap

tall ship *noun, pl* **~ ships** [*count*] **:** a very large sailing ship with at least two masts

tall tale *noun, pl* **~ tales** [*count*] **:** a story that is very difficult to believe **:** a greatly exaggerated story • They sat around the campfire telling *tall tales* about their hunting adventures. — called also *tall story*

[1]**tal·ly** /ˈtæli/ *noun, pl* **-lies** [*count*]
1 a : a recorded count of scores, votes, etc. • What is the final *tally*? **b :** a record of money that has been paid and money that has been received • He kept a daily/running *tally* [=*account*] of his expenses.
2 *US, informal* **:** a score or point made in a game or sport • Her second goal turned out to be the game-winning *tally.*

[2]**tally** *verb* **tal·lies; tal·lied; tal·ly·ing**
1 [+ *obj*] **:** to record and count or calculate (something) • He *tallied* his expenses every day. — often + *up* • They carefully *tallied up* the cost of the repairs. • They *tallied up* the results of the vote.
2 [*no obj*] **:** to agree or match • The numbers on the old list and the new list don't *tally.* — usually + *with* • The old numbers don't *tally with* the new numbers.
3 [+ *obj*] *US, informal* **:** to score (a goal, point, etc.) in a game or sport • She *tallied* [=*scored*] her second goal just before the end of the period.

Tal·mud /ˈtɑːlˌmʊd/ *noun*
the Talmud **:** the writings that declare Jewish law and tradition • They consulted *the Talmud.* — compare TORAH
– Tal·mu·dic /tælˈmuːdɪk/ *adj* • *Talmudic* scholars

tal·on /ˈtælən/ *noun, pl* **-ons** [*count*] **:** one of the sharp claws on the feet of some birds • The hawk gripped the mouse in its *talons.* • the owl's *talons*

ta·ma·le /təˈmɑːli/ *noun, pl* **-les** [*count*] **:** a Mexican food that consists of seasoned ground meat or beans rolled in cornmeal, wrapped in a corn husk, and steamed

tam·bou·rine /ˌtæmbəˈriːn/ *noun, pl* **-rines** [*count*] **:** a small musical instrument that is held in one hand and played by shaking or hitting it with the other hand — see picture at PERCUSSION

[1]**tame** /ˈteɪm/ *adj* **tam·er; -est** [*also more ~; most ~*]
1 a : not wild **:** trained to obey people • a *tame* elephant **b :** not afraid of people • The island's birds are quite *tame.*
2 : not exciting or interesting **:** DULL • They ran a pretty/quite/rather *tame* campaign. • Some people were shocked by the movie, but I found the story pretty *tame.*
3 : gentle and obedient • Members of the audience were too *tame* to interrupt the speaker.
– tame·ly *adv* **– tame·ness** *noun* [*noncount*]

[2]**tame** *verb* **tames; tamed; tam·ing** [+ *obj*]
1 : to make (an animal) tame • It took a while to *tame* the horse.
2 : to make (something) less wild or difficult to control **:** to bring (something) under control • the people who *tamed* the Wild West • He struggled to *tame* his temper. • The government needs to do something to *tame* inflation.
– tamed *adj* • a *tamed* animal **– tam·er** *noun, pl* **-ers** [*count*] • a lion/tiger *tamer*

tamp /ˈtæmp/ *verb* **tamps; tamped; tamp·ing** [+ *obj*] **:** to press (something) down by hitting it lightly — often + *down* • He *tamped down* the soil with his foot. — sometimes used figuratively • She tried to *tamp down* the rumors.

tam·per /ˈtæmpɚ/ *verb* **-pers; -pered; -per·ing**
tamper with [*phrasal verb*] ***tamper with (something)*** **:** to change or touch (something) especially in a way that causes damage or harm • Someone *tampered with* the lock. • The evidence has been *tampered with.*

tam·per·proof /ˈtæmpɚˌpruːf/ *adj* **:** designed so that tampering cannot occur • pills that come in *tamperproof* packaging

tam·pon /ˈtæmˌpɑːn/ *noun, pl* **-pons** [*count*] **:** a piece of soft material (such as cotton) that is placed in the vagina to absorb the blood that occurs during menstruation — compare SANITARY NAPKIN

[1]**tan** /ˈtæn/ *noun, pl* **tans**
1 [*count*] **:** a browning of the skin that is caused by the sun's rays • She has a nice *tan.* [=*suntan*] • I ***got a tan*** on my vacation.
2 [*count, noncount*] **:** a light brown color — see color picture on page C3

[2]**tan** *verb* **tans; tanned; tan·ning**
1 a [+ *obj*] **:** to cause (skin) to become darker especially from being exposed to the sun's rays • The sun *tanned* her skin. [=the sun made her skin tan] **b** [*no obj*] **:** to become darker especially from being exposed to the sun's rays • My skin *tans* easily. = I *tan* easily. — see also TANNED, TANNING
2 [+ *obj*] **:** to change (the skin of an animal) into leather by a chemical process • *tan* the hides
3 [+ *obj*] *informal + old-fashioned* **:** to beat or whip (someone) very badly • He threatened to ***tan my hide*** if I didn't do what he told me to do.

[3]**tan** *adj* [*more ~; most ~*]
1 : having skin that has been made darker by being exposed to the sun's rays • I can't believe how *tan* she is!
2 : having a light brown color • a *tan* coat • a horse with *tan* markings

tan·dem /ˈtændəm/ *noun, pl* **-dems** [*count*]
1 : TANDEM BICYCLE
2 *chiefly US* **:** a group of two people or things that work together or are associated with each other • The team has a *tandem* of talented guards. • He and his partner make/form quite a *tandem.* [=*duo*]
in tandem *of two people, groups, or things* **:** working or happening together or at the same time • They moved *in tandem.* • The two products can be used alone or *in tandem.* • They're working ***in tandem with*** scientists from England to find a cure.

tandem bicycle *noun, pl* **~ -cycles** [*count*] **:** a bicycle built for two riders with one sitting behind the other

tan·doori /tɑnˈduri/ *adj, always used before a noun* **:** of or relating to an Indian method of cooking meat over charcoal in a clay oven • *tandoori* chicken • a *tandoori* oven

tang /ˈtæŋ/ *noun* [*singular*] **:** a strong, sharp taste or smell • the salt *tang* in the air • a dish with a *tang* of citrus
– tangy /ˈtæŋi/ *adj* **tang·i·er; -est** • *tangy* salt air • a *tangy* flavor/sauce

tan·gent /ˈtænʤənt/ *noun, pl* **-gents** [*count*] *geometry* **:** a line that touches a sphere or circle at only one point
go off on a tangent (*US*) *or Brit* ***go off at a tangent*** **:** to start talking about something that is only slightly or indirectly related to the original subject • She *went off on a tangent* about what happened to her last summer.

tan·gen·tial /tænˈʤɛnʃəl/ *adj*
1 *formal* **:** slightly or indirectly related to something **:** not closely connected to something • Their romance is *tangential* to the book's main plot. • a *tangential* point
2 *geometry* **:** relating to a tangent **:** in or along a tangent • *tangential* force
– tan·gen·tial·ly *adv* • *tangentially* related/involved

tan·ger·ine /ˈtænʤəˌriːn/ *noun, pl* **-ines**
1 [*count*] **:** a small, sweet fruit that is like an orange with a loose skin which is easy to remove
2 [*noncount*] **:** a deep orange-yellow color — see color picture on page C3
– tangerine *adj* • a room with *tangerine* walls

tan·gi·ble /ˈtænʤəbəl/ *adj*
1 : easily seen or recognized • *tangible* benefits/results • There is no *tangible* evidence to support her claim.
2 : able to be touched or felt • *tangible* objects • the company's *tangible* assets [=its buildings, equipment, etc.] • Their sense of relief was ***almost tangible.*** — opposite INTANGIBLE

T

– **tan·gi·bil·i·ty** /ˌtænʤəˈbɪləti/ *noun* [*noncount*] – **tan·gi·bly** /ˈtænʤəbli/ *adv* • *tangibly* real

[1]tan·gle /ˈtæŋgəl/ *verb* **tan·gles; tan·gled; tan·gling** : to become or cause (something) to become twisted together [+ *obj*] Don't *tangle* the yarn. • Her foot was *tangled* (up) in the cord. — often used figuratively • He got *tangled* up in legal problems. [*no obj*] This fishing line *tangles* easily. — see also TANGLED

tangle with [*phrasal verb*] ***tangle with (someone or something) informal*** : to fight or argue with (someone or something) • He's not someone I would want to *tangle with.*

[2]tangle *noun, pl* **tangles** [*count*]

1 : a twisted knot of hair, thread, etc. : SNARL • a *tangle* of string/vines • She brushed the *tangles* out of her hair.

2 : a state of disorder or confusion • They got caught in a legal/financial *tangle*.

3 *informal* : a fight or disagreement • He got into a *tangle* with police.

tangled *adj*

1 : twisted together into a knot • *tangled* yarn/hair

2 : complicated or confusing • a *tangled* plot • their *tangled* finances

[1]tan·go /ˈtæŋgoʊ/ *noun, pl* **-gos** [*count*] : a Latin-American dance in which couples make long pauses in difficult positions • We danced a/the *tango*.; *also* : the music used for this dance • The band played a *tango*.

[2]tango *verb* **-gos; -goed; -go·ing** [*no obj*] : to dance the tango • He's trying to learn how to *tango*.

it takes two to tango see [1]TAKE 12

[1]tank /ˈtæŋk/ *noun, pl* **tanks** [*count*]

1 a : a container for holding a liquid or gas • a water/oil/fuel *tank* • fish *tanks* • I filled the (gas) *tank* before I left for Maine. — see pictures at CAR, SCUBA DIVING; see also SEPTIC TANK, THINK TANK **b** : the amount that a tank will hold • We went through a *tank* [=*tankful*] of gas on the trip.

2 : a military vehicle that moves on two large metal belts with wheels inside them and that is covered in heavy armor

in/into the tank *US, informal* : in or into a very bad state or condition • The economy is *in the tank* right now. • The team ***went into the tank*** [=got much worse; became very unsuccessful] last season.

tank

– **tank·ful** /ˈtæŋkˌfʊl/ *noun, pl* **-fuls** [*count*] • a *tankful* of gas

[2]tank *verb* **tanks; tanked; tank·ing** *US, informal*

1 [*no obj*] : to be very unsuccessful : to fail completely • The movie *tanked*.

2 : to make no effort to win a contest (such as a tennis match) : to deliberately lose a game, match, etc. [+ *obj*] Some people say she deliberately *tanked* the match. [*no obj*] Some people have accused her of *tanking*.

tank up [*phrasal verb*] *US, informal* : to fill a vehicle with fuel • We should *tank up* [=*fill up*] before we leave.

– see also TANKED

tan·kard /ˈtæŋkɚd/ *noun, pl* **-kards** [*count*] : a large, metal cup for drinking beer that has a handle and often an attached lid • a *tankard* of ale

tanked (*US*) /ˈtæŋkt/ *or chiefly Brit* **tanked up** *adj, not used before a noun, informal* : very drunk • He got *tanked* at the party.

tank·er /ˈtæŋkɚ/ *noun, pl* **-ers** [*count*] : a vehicle (such as a ship, truck, or airplane) that is designed to carry liquids — see pictures at SHIP, TRUCK; see also OIL TANKER, SUPERTANKER

tank top *noun, pl* ~ **tops** [*count*]

1 *US* : a shirt that has no sleeves or collar and usually has wide shoulder straps — see color picture on page C14

2 *Brit* : SWEATER VEST

tanned /ˈtænd/ *adj* : having skin that has been made darker by the sun • He's *tanned* and rested after his vacation.

tan·ner /ˈtænɚ/ *noun, pl* **-ners** [*count*] : a person who tans animal skins to make leather

tan·nery /ˈtænəri/ *noun, pl* **-ner·ies** [*count*] : a place where animal skins are tanned and made into leather

tan·nic acid /ˈtænɪk-/ *noun* [*noncount*] : TANNIN

tan·nin /ˈtænən/ *noun, pl* **-nins** [*count, noncount*] : a reddish acid that comes from plants, is used in making ink and leather, and occurs in various foods and drinks (such as wine) — called also *tannic acid*

tan·ning /ˈtænɪŋ/ *noun* [*noncount*] : the act or process of darkening your skin by exposing it to the bright light of the sun or a special type of lamp • indoor *tanning* • *tanning* oils/lotions

tanning bed *noun, pl* ~ **beds** [*count*] *US* : a machine that people lie in while being exposed to bright light in order to darken their skin — called also (*chiefly Brit*) *sunbed*

tanning booth *noun, pl* ~ **booths** [*count*] *chiefly US* : a machine that people stand in while being exposed to bright light in order to darken their skin

tan·ta·lize *also Brit* **tan·ta·lise** /ˈtæntəˌlaɪz/ *verb* **-liz·es; -lized; -liz·ing** [+ *obj*] : to cause (someone) to feel interest or excitement about something that is very attractive, appealing, etc. • She was *tantalized* by the possibility of earning a lot of money quickly.

– **tan·ta·liz·ing** *also Brit* **tan·ta·lis·ing** *adj* [*more* ~; *most* ~] • the *tantalizing* aroma of baking bread • a *tantalizing* glimpse into their lives – **tan·ta·liz·ing·ly** *also Brit* **tan·ta·lis·ing·ly** *adv* • I came *tantalizingly* close to victory.

tan·ta·mount /ˈtæntəˌmaʊnt/ *adj* : equal *to* something in value, meaning, or effect • His statement was *tantamount to* an admission of guilt. • They see any criticism of the President as *tantamount to* treason.

tan·trum /ˈtæntrəm/ *noun, pl* **-trums** [*count*] : an uncontrolled expression of childish anger : an angry outburst by a child or by someone who is behaving like a child • When he doesn't get his way, he ***has/throws a tantrum***. [=he gets very angry and upset and behaves like a child] • a ***temper tantrum***

Tao /ˈdaʊ/ *noun* [*noncount*] : the source and guiding principle of all reality according to Taoism

Tao·ism /ˈdaʊˌɪzəm/ *noun* [*noncount*] : a Chinese philosophy based on the writings of Lao-tzu that stresses living simply and honestly and in harmony with nature

– **Tao·ist** /ˈdawɪst/ *noun, pl* **-ists** [*count*]

[1]tap /ˈtæp/ *verb* **taps; tapped; tap·ping**

1 : to hit (someone or something) lightly especially with a small sound [+ *obj*] He was *tapping* the desk with a pencil. • He *tapped* her (on the) shoulder to get her attention. [*no obj*] Go *tap* on a window and see if anyone is home.

2 : to hit (your fingers, feet, etc.) against something lightly [+ *obj*] He was *tapping* a pencil on the desk. • She *tapped* her foot to (the beat of) the music. [*no obj*] Her foot was *tapping* to the music.

3 [+ *obj*] *chiefly US* : to choose (someone) for a particular job, honor, etc. — often + *for* • She was *tapped for* police commissioner. — often followed by *to* + *verb* • She was *tapped to be* police commissioner.

tap in/into [*phrasal verb*] ***tap (something) in*** *or* ***tap in (something) or tap (something) in/into (something)*** : to put (information) into a machine (such as a computer or telephone) by pushing buttons • She *tapped in* my name and found my account records. • He *tapped* the numbers *into* the calculator.

tap out [*phrasal verb*] ***tap (something) out or tap out (something)*** **1** : to follow the pattern of (something, such as a rhythm) by tapping on a surface • She *tapped out* the beat with her feet. **2** : to press buttons on a computer or typewriter to write (something) • He quickly *tapped out* a memo.

– compare [4]TAP

[2]tap *noun, pl* **taps** [*count*]

1 : a light hit or touch or the sound that it makes • There was a *tap* at the door. • I felt a *tap* on my shoulder. [=someone tapped my shoulder]

2 : a small metal plate on the sole or heel of a shoe used for tap dancing

– compare [3]TAP

[3]tap *noun, pl* **taps** [*count*]

1 : a device for controlling the flow of a liquid or gas from a pipe or container: such as **a** : FAUCET • turn on/off the *tap* • the hot/cold *tap* • a bathroom/kitchen *tap* ✧ In British English, *tap* is the usual word for this device. In U.S. English, *tap* is also commonly used in this way, but *faucet* is more common. — see pictures at BATHROOM, KITCHEN; see also TAP WATER **b** : SPIGOT 1 • the *tap* on a beer keg

2 : a device that allows someone to secretly listen to phone conversations • There was a *tap* on her phone. — called also *wiretap*

on tap **1** : served from a barrel • beer *on tap* **2** : available

whenever you need it ▪ The hotel has Internet service *on tap*. **3** *US* : planned or scheduled to happen ▪ I called to find out what's *on tap* for the weekend.
– compare ²TAP; see also SPINAL TAP

⁴tap *verb* **taps; tapped; tapping**
1 : to take or use money, knowledge, etc., from a source [+ *obj*] *tap* the nation's resources [*no obj*] We need to ***tap into*** new markets. — often used figuratively ▪ The story *taps into* powerful emotions.
2 [+ *obj*] : to make liquid flow from something by attaching a special device (called a spigot or tap), making or opening a hole, etc. ▪ *tap* a keg ▪ *tapping* maple trees for their sap = *tapping* sap from maple trees
3 [+ *obj*] : to place a device on (someone's phone) in order to secretly listen to telephone calls ▪ The FBI *tapped* her phone.
4 [+ *obj*] : to get something useful or valuable from (someone) — usually + *for* ▪ He tried to *tap* me *for* a loan. [=tried to get me to give him a loan]
– compare ¹TAP

tap dance *noun, pl* ~ **dances** [*count*] : a kind of dance in which you wear special shoes with metal plates on the heels and toes and make tapping sounds with your feet
– **tap–dance** *verb* **-dances; -danced; -dancing** [*no obj*] – **tap dancer** *noun, pl* ~ **-ers** [*count*] – **tap dancing** *noun* [*noncount*]

¹tape /ˈteɪp/ *noun, pl* **tapes**
1 [*noncount*] : a long, narrow piece of material that is sticky on one side and that is used to stick things together or to cover or repair something ▪ adhesive/packing *tape* ▪ a piece of *tape* ▪ His eyeglasses are held together with *tape*. — see also DUCT TAPE, MASKING TAPE
2 a [*noncount*] : a thin piece of plastic that is coated with magnetic material on which information (such as sound or television images) may be stored ▪ The show was recorded ***on tape***. — called also *magnetic tape* **b** [*count*] : something recorded on tape ▪ We watched a *tape* [=*recording*] of a program/concert. ▪ I was listening to a *tape* in the car. — called also *tape recording* **c** [*count*] : a thin case that contains a long piece of magnetic tape on which something is recorded : CASSETTE ▪ an audio *tape* ▪ She stuck a *tape* in the VCR. — see also VIDEOTAPE
3 ***the tape*** : a long, thin piece of material that is stretched across the finish line of a race ▪ She ***broke the tape*** [=she finished first in the race] in record time.
4 [*count*] : TAPE MEASURE
5 [*noncount*] : a long, thin piece of plastic, paper, or cloth ▪ The crime scene was marked off with yellow ***police tape***.
– see also RED TAPE, TICKER TAPE

²tape *verb* **tapes; taped; tap·ing** [+ *obj*]
1 : to attach (something) using sticky tape ▪ She *taped* a note to/on the refrigerator.
2 : to fasten, tie, or cover (something) with tape ▪ I *taped* the box shut. ▪ He *taped* (up) the ends of the wire.
3 : to record (something) on magnetic tape ▪ The show is *taped* before a live audience. ▪ a *taped* interview
4 *chiefly US* : to wrap (an injured body part) tightly with long pieces of special cloth ▪ The doctor *taped* (up) her ankle.
have (someone) taped *Brit, informal* : to completely understand (someone) : to know how to deal with (someone) ▪ She *has* him *taped*. = She's *got* him *taped*.

tape deck *noun, pl* ~ **decks** [*count*] : a machine that plays and records sounds on magnetic tape ▪ a stereo system that includes a *tape deck*

tape measure *noun, pl* ~ **-sures** [*count*] : a long, thin piece of plastic, cloth, or metal that is marked with units of length (such as inches or centimeters) and that is used for measuring things — called also *measuring tape*; see pictures at CARPENTRY, SEWING

tape player *noun, pl* ~ **-ers** [*count*] : a machine that is used to play sound that has been recorded on magnetic tapes

¹ta·per /ˈteɪpɚ/ *verb* **-pers; -pered; -per·ing** [*no obj*] : to become gradually smaller toward one end ▪ leaves that *taper* to a point ▪ Her slacks *taper* [=become narrower] at the ankle.
taper off [*phrasal verb*] : to become gradually less and less : to decrease slowly ▪ Production has been *tapering off*.
– **tapered** *adj* [*more* ~; *most* ~] ▪ *tapered* slacks

²taper *noun, pl* **-pers**
1 [*count*] **a** : a piece of string covered with wax that is used for lighting lamps, candles, etc. **b** : a long, thin candle
2 [*singular*] : the shape of something that becomes gradually smaller toward one end ▪ The *taper* of her slacks is not flattering.

tape–re·cord /ˌteɪprɪˈkoɚd/ *verb* **-cords; -cord·ed; -cord·ing** [+ *obj*] : to make a recording of (something) on magnetic tape ▪ *tape-record* a concert

tape recorder *noun, pl* ~ **-ders** [*count*] : a machine used to record and play sound on magnetic tape

tape recording *noun, pl* ~ **-dings** [*count*] : ¹TAPE 2b ▪ a *tape recording* of the concert

tap·es·try /ˈtæpəstri/ *noun, pl* **-tries** [*count*]
1 : a heavy cloth that has designs or pictures woven into it and that is used for wall hangings, curtains, etc. ▪ an ancient/medieval *tapestry*
2 : something made up of different things, people, colors, etc. — often + *of* ▪ a *tapestry of* ideas ▪ the rich *tapestry* of life in the city ▪ (*chiefly Brit*) Whether you win or lose, it's all part of ***life's rich tapestry***.
– **tap·es·tried** /ˈtæpəstrid/ *adj* ▪ *tapestried* halls

tape·worm /ˈteɪpˌwɚm/ *noun, pl* **-worms** [*count*] : a long, flat worm that lives in the intestines of people and animals

tap·i·o·ca /ˌtæpiˈoʊkə/ *noun* [*noncount*]
1 : the small, white grains of the cassava plant
2 : a dessert made by cooking tapioca grains usually with milk, eggs, and sugar — called also *tapioca pudding*

ta·pir /ˈteɪpɚ/ *noun, pl* **tapir** *or* **ta·pirs** [*count*] : an animal that is like a pig with a long nose and short legs and that lives in tropical America and Southeast Asia

tap·root /ˈtæpˌruːt/ *noun, pl* **-roots** [*count*] : the large main root of a plant from which smaller roots grow

taps /ˈtæps/ *noun* [*plural*] *US, military* : a song played on a bugle at military funerals and at night as a signal for soldiers to go to bed

tap water *noun* [*noncount*] : water that comes through pipes from the public water system

¹tar /ˈtɑɚ/ *noun, pl* **tars** [*count, noncount*]
1 : a very thick, black, sticky liquid made from coal that becomes hard when it cools and that is used especially for road surfaces — see also COAL TAR
2 : a sticky substance that is formed by burning tobacco ▪ low-*tar* cigarettes

²tar *verb* **tars; tarred; tar·ring** [+ *obj*] : to cover (something) with tar ▪ *tar* a roadway
tar and feather (someone) **1** : to cover (someone) with tar and then with feathers as an old-fashioned punishment **2** *informal* : to punish (someone) very severely ▪ If I don't get home in time, Mom will *tar and feather* me.
tar (someone) with the same brush : to think that (someone) has the same bad qualities and deserves the same blame or criticism as another person because of being connected or associated with that person in some way ▪ It's a shame that when a few people get caught cheating everyone else gets *tarred with the same brush*.

ta·ran·tu·la /təˈrænʧələ/ *noun, pl* **-las** [*count*] : a large, hairy spider that lives in warm regions — see color picture on page C10

tar·dy /ˈtɑɚdi/ *adj* **tar·di·er; -est** *formal*
1 : slow in moving, acting, or happening ▪ *tardy* progress
2 a : done or happening late ▪ a *tardy* payment/arrival **b** : arriving or doing something late ▪ *tardy* students ▪ She was *tardy* to/for work. ▪ They were *tardy* in filing the application.
– **tar·di·ly** /ˈtɑɚdəli/ *adv* ▪ arrived/responded *tardily* – **tar·di·ness** /ˈtɑɚdinəs/ *noun* [*noncount*] ▪ Please excuse my *tardiness*.

¹tar·get /ˈtɑɚgət/ *noun, pl* **-gets** [*count*]
1 : something that you are trying to do or achieve ▪ We failed to meet/reach this month's sales *targets*. [=goals] ▪ Our ***target amount*** for the fund-raiser is $2,500. ▪ They set a ***target date*** of May 31.
2 : a place, thing, or person at which an attack is aimed ▪ Planes struck at key military *targets*. ▪ He was a favorite *target* of the media. [=the media often attacked/criticized him] ▪ Her policies have been a *target* for/of criticism. [=criticism has been aimed/directed at her policies] ▪ Tourists are often ***easy targets*** for thieves. ▪ The bullet ***found its target***. [=the bullet hit the target it was aimed at]— often used figuratively ▪ Men in this age group are ***prime targets*** for heart disease. [=are more likely than most other people to be affected by heart disease]
3 : the person or group that someone is trying to influence, sell something to, etc. — often used before another noun ▪ Their ***target audience/market*** is teenagers.
4 : something (such as a round board with circles on it) that you try to hit with arrows, bullets, etc. ▪ I aimed at the *target* and fired. ▪ a moving *target* ▪ *target* shooting/practice

T

off target **1 :** not correct or accurate • Her accusations are way *off target*. **2 :** not likely to reach a goal • We are *off target* in terms of sales this quarter.
on target **1 :** correct or accurate • His predictions are always *on target*. **2 :** likely to reach a goal • We are *on target* to meet this month's sales goals.

²target *verb* **-gets; -get·ed; -get·ing** [+ *obj*]
1 : to aim an attack at someone or something • The missile attacks *targeted* [=were aimed at] major cities. = The missiles were *targeted* [=*aimed*] at major cities. • Thieves often *target* tourists. • drugs that *target* cancer cells • He has frequently been *targeted* by the media. [=he has been the target of frequent attacks by the media]
2 : to direct an action, message, etc., at someone or something • The commercial is *targeted* [=*aimed*] at children. • government programs that are *targeted* at low-income areas = government programs that *target* low-income areas

tar·iff /ˈterəf/ *noun, pl* **-iffs** [*count*]
1 : a tax on goods coming into or leaving a country
2 *chiefly Brit* **:** a list of prices charged by a hotel or restaurant for meals, rooms, etc., or by a public company for gas, electricity, etc.

tar·mac /ˈtɑɚˌmæk/ *noun*
the tarmac **:** the area covered by pavement at an airport • airplanes parked on *the tarmac*

Tar·mac /ˈtɑɚˌmæk/ *trademark* — used for a paving material made of layers of crushed stone covered with tar

tarn /ˈtɑɚn/ *noun, pl* **tarns** [*count*] **:** a small lake among mountains

¹tar·nish /ˈtɑɚnɪʃ/ *verb* **-nish·es; -nished; -nish·ing**
1 : to become or cause (metal) to become dull and not shiny [*no obj*] Silver *tarnishes* easily. [+ *obj*] Some foods will *tarnish* silver.
2 [+ *obj*] **:** to damage or ruin the good quality of (something, such as a person's reputation, image, etc.) • His actions *tarnished* [=*sullied*] the family's good name. • The scandal *tarnished* his reputation.
– tarnished *adj* • *tarnished* silverware • the company's *tarnished* image

²tarnish *noun* [*singular, noncount*] **:** a thin layer on the surface of metal which makes the metal look dull • a polish that removes *tarnish*

ta·ro /ˈtɑroʊ, ˈteroʊ/ *noun, pl* **-ros** [*count, noncount*] **:** a tropical plant with a thick root that can be boiled and eaten

tar·ot /ˈteroʊ/ *noun* [*singular*] **:** a set of 78 cards with pictures and symbols that is used to see what will happen in the future • reading the *tarot* • *tarot* cards

tarp /ˈtɑɚp/ *noun, pl* **tarps** [*count*] *US* **:** TARPAULIN

tar paper *noun* [*noncount*] *US* **:** a heavy type of paper covered with tar that is used especially in roofs

tar·pau·lin /tɑɚˈpɑːlən/ *noun, pl* **-lins** [*count*] **:** a large piece of waterproof material (such as plastic or canvas) that is used to cover things and keep them dry

tar·ra·gon /ˈterəˌgɑːn/ *noun* [*noncount*] **:** a small European herb that is used to flavor food

¹tar·ry /ˈteri/ *verb* **-ries; -ried; -ry·ing** [*no obj*] *literary* **:** to be slow in going **:** to stay somewhere **:** LINGER • He *tarried* over breakfast. • *Tarry* with us a while.

²tar·ry /ˈtɑri/ *adj*
1 : covered with tar • a *tarry* surface
2 : dark or thick like tar • a *tarry* substance

tar·sus /ˈtɑɚsəs/ *noun, pl* **tar·si** /ˈtɑɚˌsaɪ/ [*count*] *technical* **:** the ankle or one of the seven small bones in the ankle
– tar·sal /ˈtɑɚsəl/ *adj*

¹tart /ˈtɑɚt/ *noun, pl* **tarts** [*count*]
1 : an open pie that usually has a sweet filling (such as fruit or custard) • an apple *tart*
2 *informal + disapproving* **a :** a woman who wears very sexy clothing and has sex with many men **b :** PROSTITUTE

²tart *adj* **tart·er; -est** [*also more ~; most ~*]
1 : having a sharp or sour taste • a *tart* apple/cherry • The wine is rather *tart*.
2 : having a sharp and unkind quality • a *tart* reply • *tart* criticism
– tart·ly *adv* • "Be quiet," she told him *tartly*. **– tart·ness** *noun* [*noncount*]

³tart *verb* **tarts; tart·ed; tart·ing**
tart up [*phrasal verb*] ***tart (someone) up*** *informal* **:** to try to make (yourself or someone else) attractive by wearing fancy clothes, makeup, etc. • She ***tarted herself up*** for the party. = She got *tarted up* for the party. — often used figuratively in British English • old ideas *tarted up* to look new

tar·tan /ˈtɑɚtn̩/ *noun, pl* **-tans**
1 [*count*] **:** a traditional Scottish cloth pattern of stripes in different colors and widths that cross each other to form squares • a kilt in the clan's *tartan*
2 [*count, noncount*] **:** fabric with a tartan pattern

¹tar·tar /ˈtɑɚtɚ/ *noun* [*noncount*] **:** a hard substance that forms on teeth — compare ²TARTAR; see also CREAM OF TARTAR

²tartar *noun, pl* **-tars** [*count*] *informal + old-fashioned* **:** a person who is often angry or violent • Her husband sounds like a real *tartar*. — compare ¹TARTAR

tar·tar sauce (*US*) *or Brit* **tar·tare sauce** /ˈtɑɚtɚ-/ *noun* [*noncount*] **:** a sauce that is made of mayonnaise and chopped pickles and that is often served with fish

tarty /ˈtɑɚti/ *adj* **tart·i·er; -est** *informal + disapproving* **:** trying to appear sexy in an improper or offensive way • a *tarty* outfit

¹task /ˈtæsk/ *noun, pl* **tasks** [*count*] **:** a piece of work that has been given to someone **:** a job for someone to do • a daunting/difficult/impossible *task* • complete/accomplish a *task* • performing simple/routine *tasks* • Our first/main *task* is to review the budget. • This is not an easy *task*. = This is ***no easy task*** • I need to concentrate on ***the task at hand*** [=the work I'm doing right now] — see also MULTITASKING
take (someone) to task **:** to criticize (someone) harshly • The boss *took* me *to task* for wasting time.

> ***synonyms*** TASK, DUTY, JOB, and CHORE mean a piece of work that has to be done. TASK suggests work given to you by someone who has authority. • The boss used to give me all the hard *tasks*. DUTY stresses that someone is responsible for doing the work. • The *duty* of the police is to protect the people. JOB may suggest that the work is necessary, hard, or important. • We all have to do our *jobs*. CHORE suggests a small, ordinary piece of work that is done regularly. • Taking out the garbage is a daily *chore*.

²task *verb* **tasks; tasked; task·ing** [+ *obj*] **:** to assign (someone) a piece of work **:** to give (someone) a job to do — usually used as *(be) tasked with* • She *was tasked with* proofreading the manuscript.

task·bar *noun, pl* **-bars** [*count*] *computers* **:** a narrow band across the bottom of a computer screen that shows which programs are running and which documents are open — see picture at COMPUTER; compare TOOLBAR

task force *noun, pl* **~ forces** [*count*]
1 : a group of people who deal with a specific problem • a crime-fighting *task force* • They appointed a *task force* to review the situation.
2 : a military force that is sent to a particular place to deal with a problem

task·mas·ter /ˈtæskˌmæstɚ, *Brit* ˈtɑːskˌmɑːstə/ *noun, pl* **-ters** [*count*] **:** a person who assigns work to other people • He's a hard/tough/stern *taskmaster*.

tas·sel /ˈtæsəl/ *noun, pl* **-sels** [*count*]
1 : a decoration made of a bunch of strings fastened at one end • shoes with *tassels*
2 : a flower or group of flowers at the top of a cornstalk
– tas·seled (*chiefly US*) *or chiefly Brit* **tas·selled** /ˈtæsəld/ *adj* • *tasseled* loafers/pillows/shoes

tassel

¹taste /ˈteɪst/ *noun, pl* **tastes**
1 [*count*] **:** the sweet, sour, bitter, or salty quality of a thing that you can sense when it is in your mouth **:** the flavor that you can taste when you eat or drink something • The wine had a slightly bitter *taste*. • She likes the *taste* of apples and cinnamon. • I detected a strong *taste* of ginger in the sauce. — sometimes used figuratively • The experience ***left a bad taste in my mouth*** [=the experience made me feel bad, disgusted, etc.]
2 [*noncount*] **:** the ability to notice or recognize flavors when you eat or drink **:** the ability to taste things • The food was very pleasing to the *taste*. [=the food tasted very good] • The illness affected her sense of *taste*.
3 [*count*] **:** a small amount of food or drink that you have in order to see how it tastes — usually singular • May I have a *taste* of your ice cream?
4 [*singular*] **:** something (such as a brief experience) that gives you some knowledge about what something is like — usually + *of* • It was her first *taste of* success. • That first

storm was just a ***taste of things to come***. [=that storm was followed by many other storms]

5 : the feelings that each person has about what is appealing, attractive, etc. : the feelings that cause someone to like or not like something [*noncount*] He has no/little *taste* for gossip. [=he does not like gossip] • The movie was not ***to their taste***. [=they did not like the movie] • The movie is intended to appeal to ***popular taste***. [=to be liked by many or most people] • Whether you like the music or not is purely a ***matter of taste***. [=a matter of opinion] [*count*] She has developed/acquired a *taste* for Italian wine. • Different people have different *tastes*. • They have expensive *tastes*. [=they like expensive things] • The store has something to suit all *tastes*. • The music is too loud ***for my taste***. [=the music is louder than I prefer it to be] — see also *acquired taste* at ACQUIRE

6 [*noncount*] **a :** the ability to choose what is appealing, attractive, appropriate, or enjoyable • She is a person of *taste*. • The way he dresses shows that he has no *taste*. • She has good/poor *taste* in music. • The room was decorated with *taste*. [=the room was tastefully decorated] **b** — used in phrases to say that something (such as a person's speech or behavior) is or is not proper and acceptable • I think the joke he told was ***in (very) bad/poor taste***. [=was offensive] • Some people felt that her behavior wasn't ***in good taste***.

a taste of your own medicine see MEDICINE

to taste : in an amount that results in the taste that you want — used in recipes to indicate how much salt, pepper, etc., should be added to food • Salt the stew *to taste*.

²taste *verb* **tastes; tast·ed; tast·ing**

1 *not used in progressive tenses* [*linking verb*] : to have a particular taste • This milk *tastes* sour. • The pie *tasted* too sweet. • The wine *tastes* like vinegar. • This sauce *tastes* good/bad. • a sweet-*tasting* fruit — sometimes + *of* • The salad *tastes of* garlic.

2 [+ *obj*] **a :** to sense the flavor of (something that you are eating or drinking) • She said there was garlic in the sauce, but I couldn't really *taste* it. • Have you ever *tasted* anything so delicious? **b :** to put a small amount of (food or drink) in your mouth in order to find out what its flavor is • I *tasted* the tea and put more sugar in it. • She offered to *taste* the wine. • He *tasted* the tea to see if it was sweet enough. **c** *not used in progressive tenses* : EAT • This is the first food I've *tasted* since yesterday.

3 [+ *obj*] : to experience (something) • She talked about the day when she first *tasted* the joy of flying. • He has *tasted* the frustration of defeat. • The team has yet to *taste* victory/defeat.

taste blood see BLOOD

taste bud *noun, pl* ~ **buds** [*count*] : one of many small spots on your tongue that give you the ability to taste things

taste·ful /ˈteɪstfəl/ *adj* [*more* ~; *most* ~] : done or chosen with a knowledge of what is appealing, attractive, appropriate, or enjoyable : having or showing good taste • a *tasteful* and attractive design • *tasteful* decorations

– taste·ful·ly *adv* • The room was *tastefully* decorated. **– taste·ful·ness** *noun* [*noncount*]

taste·less /ˈteɪstləs/ *adj*

1 : not having much flavor • a nearly *tasteless* broth • *tasteless* vegetables

2 [*more* ~; *most* ~] : not having or showing good taste : not tasteful • a very *tasteless* joke • a vulgar and *tasteless* publicity stunt

– taste·less·ly *adv* • a *tastelessly* furnished room **– taste·less·ness** *noun* [*noncount*]

taste·mak·er /ˈteɪstˌmeɪkɚ/ *noun, pl* **-ers** [*count*] : a person whose judgments about what is good, fashionable, etc., are accepted and followed by many other people • She is one of the most powerful *tastemakers* in the fashion world.

tast·er /ˈteɪstɚ/ *noun, pl* **-ers** [*count*]

1 : a person who tastes foods or drinks to test their quality • a food/wine *taster*

2 *Brit, informal* : a small amount or sample of something that you can try to see if you like it • The magazine printed a *taster* of the author's new novel.

tasting *noun, pl* **-ings** [*count*] : a social event at which something (such as food or wine) is sampled and tasted • a menu/wine *tasting*

tasty /ˈteɪsti/ *adj* **tast·i·er; -est** [*also more* ~; *most* ~]

1 : having a good flavor : pleasing to the taste • That was a very *tasty* [=*delicious*] meal.

2 *informal* **a :** very appealing or interesting • a *tasty* [=*juicy*] bit of gossip **b** *Brit* : very attractive • a *tasty* young woman/man

– tast·i·ly /ˈteɪstəli/ *adv* **– tast·i·ness** /ˈteɪstinəs/ *noun* [*noncount*]

tat /ˈtæt/ *noun* [*noncount*] *Brit, informal* : items that are cheap and poorly made • shops full of *tat* [=*junk*] — see also TIT FOR TAT

ta–ta /ˌtæˈtɑː/ *interj, chiefly Brit, informal* : GOODBYE

ta·ter /ˈteɪtɚ/ *noun, pl* **-ters** [*count*] *informal*

1 : POTATO

2 *baseball* : HOME RUN

tat·tered /ˈtætɚd/ *adj* : old and torn : RAGGED • a *tattered* flag • a pile of old *tattered* books • Her jeans were *tattered*. — often used figuratively • He was left trying to restore his *tattered* image/pride. • the *tattered* remains of her reputation

tat·ters /ˈtætɚz/ *noun* [*plural*] : clothes that are old and badly torn • Her clothes were reduced to *tatters*. • They were dressed ***in tatters***. [=*in rags*] — often used figuratively • After the war, the economy was *in tatters*. [=was in a state of ruin] • Her hopes lay *in tatters*.

tat·tie /ˈtæti/ *noun, pl* **-ties** [*count*] *chiefly Scotland* : POTATO

tat·tle /ˈtætl̩/ *verb* **tat·les; tat·tled; tat·tling** [*no obj*] *chiefly US, informal* : to tell a parent, teacher, etc., about something bad or wrong that another child has done • He saw his sister take a cookie and threatened to *tattle* (to their mother). — usually + *on* • He *tattled on* her. — see also TITTLE-TATTLE

– tat·tler /ˈtætl̩ɚ/ *noun, pl* **tat·tlers** [*count*] • She's a crybaby and a *tattler*! [=*tattletale*]

tat·tle·tale /ˈtætl̩ˌteɪl/ *noun, pl* **-tales** [*count*] *chiefly US, informal + disapproving* : a child who tells a parent, teacher, etc., about something bad or wrong that another child has done : a child who tattles on another child • No one likes a *tattletale*. [=(*Brit*) *telltale*]

¹tat·too /tæˈtuː/ *noun, pl* **-toos** [*count*] : a picture, word, etc., that is drawn on a person's skin by using a needle and ink • He had a *tattoo* of a heart on his shoulder. • a ***tattoo parlor*** [=a place where people go to get tattoos] — compare ³TATTOO

²tattoo *verb* **-toos; -tooed; -too·ing** [+ *obj*] : to draw or write (a picture, word, etc.) on a part of someone's body by using a needle and ink • A heart was *tattooed* on his arm. [=he had a tattoo of a heart on his arm]

³tattoo *noun, pl* **-toos**

1 [*singular*] : a rapid rhythmic beat • The rain was ***beating a tattoo*** on the roof.

2 [*count*] *Brit* : an outdoor performance in the evening with music and marching by members of the military

— compare ¹TATTOO

tat·too·ist /tæˈtuːwɪst/ *noun, pl* **-ists** [*count*] : a person whose job is to draw tattoos on people's bodies — called also *tattoo artist*

tat·ty /ˈtæti/ *adj* **tat·ti·er; -est** *informal* : old and in poor condition : SHABBY • a *tatty* old shirt/sweater

taught *past tense and past participle tense of* TEACH

taunt /ˈtɑːnt/ *verb* **taunts; taunt·ed; taunt·ing** [+ *obj*] : to say insulting things to (someone) in order to make that person angry • The boys continually *taunted* each other.

– taunt *noun, pl* **taunts** [*count*] • He suffered the *taunts* of the other children. **– taunt·er** *noun, pl* **-ers** [*count*] **– taunt·ing·ly** /ˈtɑːntɪŋli/ *adv*

taupe /ˈtoʊp/ *noun, pl* **taupes** [*count, noncount*] : a brownish-gray color — see color picture on page C2

Tau·rus /ˈtorəs/ *noun, pl* **-rus·es**

1 [*noncount*] : the second sign of the zodiac that comes between Aries and Gemini and has a bull as its symbol — see picture at ZODIAC

2 [*count*] : a person born under the sign of Taurus : a person born between April 20 and May 20 • My friend is an Aries while I'm a *Taurus*.

taut /ˈtɑːt/ *adj* **taut·er; -est** [*also more* ~; *most* ~]

1 : very tight from being pulled or stretched : not loose or slack • The rope was drawn/pulled/stretched *taut*.

2 : firm and strong : not loose or flabby • *taut* muscles

3 : very tense • *taut* nerves • The book is a *taut* thriller.

– taut·ly *adv* • a rope pulled *tautly* **– taut·ness** *noun* [*noncount*] • check the wire's *tautness*

taut·en /ˈtɑːtn̩/ *verb* **-ens; -ened; -en·ing** : to make (something) tight or taut or to become tight or taut [+ *obj*] They *tautened* the rope. [*no obj*] The wire *tautened* as they pulled on it.

tau·tol·o·gy /tɑˈtɑːləʤi/ *noun, pl* **-gies** : a statement in

which you repeat a word, idea, etc., in a way that is not necessary [*count*] "A beginner who has just started" is a *tautology*. [*noncount*] trying to avoid *tautology*
– **tau·to·log·i·cal** /ˌtɑːtəˈlɑːʤɪkəl/ *adj* ▪ a *tautological* statement

tav·ern /ˈtævɚn/ *noun, pl* **-erns** [*count*]
1 : a place where alcoholic drinks are served : BAR
2 *old-fashioned* : a building that provides lodging and food for people who are traveling : INN

taw·dry /ˈtɑːdri/ *adj* **taw·dri·er; -est** *disapproving*
1 : having a cheap and ugly appearance ▪ *tawdry* [=*tacky*] decorations
2 : morally low or bad ▪ The scandal was a *tawdry* affair.
– **taw·dri·ness** /ˈtɑːdrinəs/ *noun* [*noncount*]

taw·ny /ˈtɑːni/ *adj* : having a brownish-orange color ▪ *tawny* fur

[1]**tax** /ˈtæks/ *noun, pl* **taxes** : an amount of money that a government requires people to pay according to their income, the value of their property, etc., and that is used to pay for the things done by the government [*count*] The decision was made to raise/cut *taxes*. ▪ He was accused of evading *taxes*. ▪ What was your income before/after *taxes*? — often + *on* ▪ a *tax on* tobacco products [*noncount*] What is the amount of *tax* to be paid? ▪ What was your income before/after *tax*? ▪ *tax* deductions/laws/rates — see also INCOME TAX, POLL TAX, PRETAX, SALES TAX, SURTAX, VALUE-ADDED TAX, WITHHOLDING TAX

[2]**tax** *verb* **tax·es; taxed; tax·ing** [+ *obj*]
1 a : to require (someone) to pay a tax ▪ He believes in *taxing* the rich to give to the poor. ▪ You are *taxed* according to your income. **b** : to require someone to pay a tax on (something) — often used as *(be) taxed* ▪ All income/property *is taxed*. ▪ The sale of wine *is taxed* in this state.
2 : to require a lot from (something or someone) : to put demands on (something or someone) ▪ That job really *taxed* our strength. [=required us to use a lot of physical effort] ▪ All this waiting is *taxing* my patience. [=is making me lose my patience] ▪ puzzles that *tax* your brain ▪ You can have an enjoyable vacation without *taxing* your budget. [=without having to spend a lot of money]
tax with [*phrasal verb*] ***tax (someone) with (something)*** *formal* : to accuse (someone) of (something) ▪ She *taxed* them *with* carelessness.
– **tax·er** *noun, pl* **-ers** [*count*]

tax·able /ˈtæksəbəl/ *adj* : able to be taxed ▪ The sale of wine is *taxable* in this state. ▪ *taxable* income/property [=income/property that you are required to pay a tax on]

tax·a·tion /tækˈseɪʃən/ *noun* [*noncount*] : the action, process, or system of taxing people or things ▪ the federal right of *taxation* ▪ The company is trying to shield its profits from *taxation*. [=to prevent its profits from being taxed] ▪ They favor reduced *taxation* on capital gains. [=they think that capital gains should be taxed at a reduced rate]

tax base *noun* [*noncount*] : the amount of money or property that can be taxed within an area ▪ an area with a large *tax base*

tax–deductible *adj* : allowed to be subtracted from the total amount of your income before you calculate the tax you are required to pay : allowable as a deduction from taxes ▪ Your donation is *tax-deductible*.

tax–deferred *adj, US* : not taxed until sometime in the future ▪ a *tax-deferred* savings plan

tax disc *noun, pl* ~ **discs** [*count*] *Brit* : a small, round sticker placed on the window of a vehicle showing that a tax has been paid so that the vehicle may be used on roads

tax–exempt *adj* : not taxed : exempted from a tax ▪ a *tax-exempt* organization ▪ *tax-exempt* bonds/funds

tax exile *noun, pl* ~ **-iles** [*count*] *chiefly Brit* : a person who has moved from one country to another country in order to avoid paying taxes

tax–free *adj* : not taxed : TAX-EXEMPT ▪ *tax-free* medical benefits

tax haven *noun, pl* ~ **-vens** [*count*] : a place where people go to live and companies go to operate in order to avoid paying high taxes

[1]**taxi** /ˈtæksi/ *noun, pl* **tax·is** /ˈtæksiz/ : a car that carries passengers to a place for an amount of money that is based on the distance traveled [*count*] We caught/took/got a *taxi* to the restaurant. ▪ She went outside and ***hailed a taxi*** [=waved or called for a taxi to pull over and stop] [*noncount*] We went to the restaurant ***by taxi*** — often used before another noun ▪ a *taxi* driver/company/service — called also *cab, taxicab*

[2]**taxi** *verb* **taxis** *or* **tax·ies; tax·ied; taxi·ing**
1 [*no obj*] *of an airplane* : to move on wheels along the ground ▪ The plane *taxied* slowly to the runway.
2 : to direct an airplane as it moves on wheels along the ground [*no obj*] The pilot *taxied* out to the runway. [+ *obj*] The pilot *taxied* the plane out to the runway.

taxi·cab /ˈtæksiˌkæb/ *noun, pl* **-cabs** : [1]TAXI [*count*] He drives a *taxicab*. [*noncount*] They arrived by *taxicab*.

taxi·der·my /ˈtæksəˌdɚmi/ *noun* [*noncount*] : the skill, activity, or job of preparing, stuffing, and mounting the skins of dead animals so that they look like they did when they were alive
– **taxi·der·mist** /ˈtæksəˌdɚmɪst/ *noun, pl* **-mists** [*count*]

tax·ing /ˈtæksɪŋ/ *adj* [*more* ~; *most* ~] : requiring a lot of effort, energy, etc. ▪ a *taxing* job/chore ▪ The journey proved to be very *taxing*.

taxi stand *noun, pl* ~ **stands** [*count*] *US* : a place where taxis park while waiting to be hired — called also *(Brit) taxi rank*

tax·man /ˈtæksˌmæn/ *noun, pl* **-men** /-ˌmɛn/
1 [*count*] : a person who collects taxes
2 ***the taxman*** *informal* : the department of the government that collects taxes ▪ One-third of her salary goes to *the taxman*.

tax·on·o·my /tækˈsɑːnəmi/ *noun, pl* **-mies** *technical* : the process or system of describing the way in which different living things are related by putting them in groups [*noncount*] plant *taxonomy* [*count*] the *taxonomies* of various plant groups
– **tax·o·nom·ic** /ˌtæksəˈnɑːmɪk/ *adj* ▪ *taxonomic* relationships – **tax·o·nom·i·cal·ly** /ˌtæksəˈnɑːmɪkli/ *adv* ▪ *taxonomically* related species – **tax·on·o·mist** /tækˈsɑːnəmɪst/ *noun, pl* **-mists** [*count*]

tax·pay·er /ˈtæksˌpejɚ/ *noun, pl* **-ers** [*count*] : a person who pays taxes

tax shelter *noun, pl* ~ **-ters** [*count*] : a way of investing money that reduces the amount of tax that has to be paid

tb. *abbr* tablespoon; tablespoonful

TB /ˌtiːˈbiː/ *noun* [*noncount*] : TUBERCULOSIS

TBA *abbr* to be announced — used to indicate that the time or place of something has not yet been decided and will be announced at a later time ▪ The meeting will be next Wednesday at 2:00, location *TBA*.

T–ball /ˈtiːˌbɑːl/ *noun* [*noncount*] *sports* : a form of baseball for young children in which the ball is hit off a support (called a tee) rather than pitched

T–bar /ˈtiːˌbɑɚ/ *noun, pl* **-bars** [*count*] : a machine that is used to pull skiers up a mountain and that has a series of T-shaped bars each of which pulls two skiers — called also *T-bar lift*

TBD *abbr, US* to be determined — used to indicate that the time or place of something has not yet been decided and will be announced at a later time ▪ The game has been postponed until next week, time *TBD*.

T–bone /ˈtiːˌboun/ *noun, pl* **-bones** [*count*] : a thick piece of beef that contains a T-shaped bone — called also *T-bone steak*

tbs. *or* **tbsp.** *abbr* tablespoon; tablespoonful

TD /ˈtiːˈdiː/ *noun, pl* **TDs** [*count*] *American football, informal* : TOUCHDOWN

tea /ˈtiː/ *noun, pl* **teas**
1 [*count, noncount*] **a** : a drink that is made by soaking the dried leaves of an Asian plant in hot water ▪ a cup of *tea* **b** : a similar drink that is made by using the dried leaves of another kind of plant ▪ herbal/mint *tea* — see also GREEN TEA
2 [*noncount*] : the dried leaves that are used in making tea ▪ a bag of *tea*
3 *Brit* **a** : a light meal or snack that usually includes tea with sandwiches, cookies, or cakes and that is served in the late afternoon [*noncount*] Let's meet for *tea* tomorrow. [*count*] That shop does a great afternoon *tea*. **b** [*count, noncount*] : a cooked meal that is served in the early evening — see also CREAM TEA, HIGH TEA
not for all the tea in China *informal + old-fashioned* : not for any reason ▪ I would never invite him to my house again—*not for all the tea in China*.
not your cup of tea see [1]CUP

tea and sympathy *noun* [*noncount*] *chiefly Brit, old-fashioned* : kind treatment and care that is given to someone

T

who is upset • She could use some *tea and sympathy*.

tea bag *noun, pl* ~ **bags** [*count*] : a small bag of dried tea leaves that is soaked in hot water to make tea

tea break *noun, pl* ~ **breaks** [*count*] *chiefly Brit* : a short period of time in which a worker stops to rest and have tea, coffee, etc. : COFFEE BREAK

tea cake *noun, pl* ~ **cakes** [*count*] : a small, flat cake that usually has raisins and is eaten with tea

teach /ˈtiːʧ/ *verb* **teach•es; taught** /ˈtɑːt/; **teach•ing**
1 a : to cause or help (someone) to learn about a subject by giving lessons [+ *obj*] He enjoys *teaching* his students about history. [*no obj*] She no longer *teaches*. • He wants to *teach*. [=to be a teacher] **b** [+ *obj*] : to give lessons about (a particular subject) to a person or group • She *taught* English for many years at the high school. • He *teaches* music/science. **c** [+ *obj*] : to cause or help (a person or animal) to learn how to do something by giving lessons, showing how it is done, etc. • She is *teaching* us (how to use) sign language. — often followed by *to + verb* • *teach* a child *to read/swim* • I *taught* my dog *to retrieve* sticks. • She *taught* me (how) *to ride* a bike.
2 [+ *obj*] : to show someone how to behave, think, etc. • The church *teaches* compassion and forgiveness. • Someone needs to *teach* her right and wrong. • The experience *taught* us that money doesn't mean everything.
3 [+ *obj*] *informal* : to cause (someone) to know the unpleasant results of something • Her injury will *teach* her not to be so careless with a knife. • He got the punishment he deserved. That'll *teach* him to lie to me. [=show him that he should not to lie to me again] • That will ***teach her a lesson***. [=that will show her not to do something again]
you can't teach an old dog new tricks see [1]DOG

teach•able /ˈtiːʧəbəl/ *adj* [*more* ~; *most* ~]
1 : able and willing to learn : capable of being taught • students who are *teachable* and eager to learn
2 : allowing something to be taught or learned easily • The book's style makes it very *teachable*. • (*US*) choosing a ***teachable moment*** [=a time that is favorable for teaching something, such as proper behavior]

teach•er /ˈtiːʧɚ/ *noun, pl* **-ers** [*count*] : a person or thing that teaches something • Experience is a good *teacher*.; *especially* : a person whose job is to teach students about certain subjects • She is a first-grade *teacher*. • a language/math/science *teacher* • a *teacher* of driver's education — see also SCHOOLTEACHER, STUDENT TEACHER, SUBSTITUTE TEACHER

teachers college *noun, pl* ~ **-leges** [*count, noncount*] *US* : a college for the training of teachers

teacher's pet *noun* [*singular*] *informal + disapproving* : a student in a class who is liked by the teacher and who is treated better than other students

teach–in /ˈtiːʧˌɪn/ *noun, pl* **-ins** [*count*] *US* : a meeting usually held on a college campus for people to talk about and learn about something (such as a social or political issue) • The group held a *teach-in* to discuss discrimination.

[1]**teaching** *noun, pl* **-ings**
1 [*noncount*] : the job or profession of a teacher • He went into *teaching* after college.
2 [*count*] : something that is taught : the ideas and beliefs that are taught by a person, religion, etc. — usually plural; often + *of* • the *teachings of* Confucius • the *teachings* [=*lessons*] *of* the Bible

[2]**teaching** *adj, always used before a noun* : of, relating to, or used for teaching someone or something • the *teaching* profession • a *teaching* aid

teaching assistant *noun, pl* ~ **-tants** [*count*] *US* : a graduate student who teaches classes at a college or university — abbr. *TA*

teaching hospital *noun, pl* ~ **-tals** [*count*] : a hospital where people who are training to become doctors work and learn

tea cloth *noun, pl* ~ **cloths** [*count*] *Brit* : DISH TOWEL

tea•cup /ˈtiːˌkʌp/ *noun, pl* **-cups** [*count*] : a small cup used for drinking tea
a storm in a teacup see [1]STORM

tea garden *noun, pl* ~ **-dens** [*count*]
1 : a public garden where tea and other refreshments are served
2 : an area of land where tea is grown

tea•house /ˈtiːˌhaʊs/ *noun, pl* **-houses** [*count*] : a restaurant where tea and other refreshments are served

teak /ˈtiːk/ *noun* [*noncount*] : the strong, hard, yellowish-brown wood of a tree that grows in southeast Asia and that is used especially for making furniture and ships — called also *teakwood*

tea•ket•tle /ˈtiːˌkɛtl/ *noun, pl* **-ket•tles** [*count*] *US* : a covered container that is used for boiling water and that has a handle and a spout — called also *kettle*

teal /ˈtiːl/ *noun, pl* **teal** *or* **teals**
1 [*count*] : a small duck found in Europe and America
2 [*noncount*] : a dark greenish-blue color — called also *teal blue*; see color picture on page C2

[1]**team** /ˈtiːm/ *noun, pl* **teams** [*count*]
1 : a group of people who compete in a sport, game, etc., against another group • a doubles *team* in tennis • a basketball/gymnastics/bowling *team* • He is the best player on his *team*. • They are the worst *team* in baseball. • Our *team* is losing. = (*Brit*) Our *team* are losing. • (*US*) He is ***on a team***. = (*Brit*) He is ***in a team***. — often used before another noun • She is the *team* captain. • Baseball is a ***team sport***. [=a sport played by teams] — see also TAG TEAM
2 : a group of people who work together • To get the job done more quickly, we split up into *teams*. • We worked as a *team* to put out the fire. • The company hired a *team* of lawyers to advise them. • a search and rescue *team* — often used before another noun • The project was a *team* effort. • corporate efforts to build *team* spirit [=the desire to work well as a team]
3 : a group of two or more animals used to pull a wagon, cart, etc. • a *team* of horses • A dog *team* pulled the sled.

[2]**team** *verb* **teams; teamed; team•ing** [+ *obj*] : to bring together (two people or things) • a show that *teams* two of television's funniest comedians — often used as *(be) teamed with* • The fish *was teamed with* roasted potatoes and a salad.
team up [*phrasal verb*] : to join with someone to work together • They *teamed up* to get the work done quickly. — often + *with* • Several organizations have *teamed up with* one another in the relief effort. • The movie is about a young policeman who is *teamed up with* an experienced detective.

team•mate /ˈtiːmˌmeɪt/ *noun, pl* **-mates** [*count*] : a person who is on the same team as someone else • They have been *teammates* for several years. • She's very popular among her *teammates*.

team player *noun, pl* ~ **-ers** [*count*] : someone who cares more about helping a group or team to succeed than about his or her individual success • The other people on the staff don't like him because he's not a *team player*.

team•ster /ˈtiːmstɚ/ *noun, pl* **-sters** [*count*] *US* : someone who drives a truck as a job

team•work /ˈtiːmˌwɚk/ *noun* [*noncount*] : the work done by people who work together as a team to do something • They credit good *teamwork* for their success.

tea party *noun, pl* ~ **-ties** [*count*] : an afternoon social gathering at which tea is served

tea•pot /ˈtiːˌpɑːt/ *noun, pl* **-pots** [*count*] : a pot that is used for making and serving tea and that has a spout and handle
a tempest in a teapot see TEMPEST

[1]**tear** /ˈteɚ/ *verb* **tears; tore** /ˈtoɚ/; **torn** /ˈtoɚn/; **tear•ing**
1 *always followed by an adverb or preposition* : to separate (something) into parts by pulling it, cutting it, etc. : to rip, split, or open (something) quickly or violently [+ *obj*] He *tore* the letter in half. • They began *tearing* their presents open. • He ***tore apart*** the two tickets and handed one to me. • The dog ***tore*** the pillow ***to pieces/shreds***. [*no obj*] *Tear* along the dotted line.
2 a : to make (a hole or opening) in a piece of clothing, a piece of paper, etc., usually by cutting it on something sharp [+ *obj*] She *tore* a hole in her sock when she jumped over the fence. [*no obj*] His coat got caught on a nail and *tore*. • His pants *tore* at the seam. **b** [+ *obj*] : to make (a hole, a path) in a violent or forceful way • The explosion *tore* a hole in the side of the building. — sometimes used figuratively • The new evidence could *tear* a hole in their theory. [=it could show that their theory is not correct]
3 [+ *obj*] : to cut or injure (skin, a muscle, etc.) • He *tore* a ligament in his left knee during football practice. • a *torn* leg muscle • When she fell, she *tore* the skin on her elbow.
4 *always followed by an adverb or preposition* [+ *obj*] : to remove (something) quickly or violently • The curtains had been *torn* from the windows. • She *tore* the book out of my hands. • They decided to *tear* out the kitchen's old cabinets. • He *tore* the page out of the magazine. • I wanted to *tear* her head off! • He *tore* off a piece of bread and ate it. • She *tore* a

corner off of a sheet of paper and wrote her number on it. ▪ Open up or we'll *tear* down this door! ▪ The police officer grabbed him, but he managed to ***tear himself loose/free.*** [=to pull himself away from the police officer]

5 *always followed by an adverb or preposition* [*no obj*] **:** to go or move very quickly ▪ The kids *tore* into the house and up the stairs. ▪ We watched the cars *tear* around the track. ▪ He went *tearing* down the street on his bicycle. ▪ The fire *tore* through the forest. ▪ An epidemic was *tearing* through the region. ▪ The bullet *tore* through his leg.

6 [+ *obj*] **:** to damage or harm (something, such as a country) very badly — usually used as *(be) torn* ▪ The region has *been torn* [=*ravaged*] by disease and hunger for the last 50 years. ▪ a country *torn* by violence ▪ a war-*torn* country

7 [+ *obj*] **:** to cause (someone) to feel confused, upset, etc., especially about making a choice or decision — often + *apart* or *up* ▪ I can't decide, and it's *tearing* me *apart*! ▪ It's *tearing* me *up* (inside). — usually used as *(be) torn* ▪ I've been trying to decide, but I'*m* still *torn*. [=I'm still unable to decide] ▪ She *was torn* by conflicting loyalties. — often + *between* ▪ He *is torn between* his career and his responsibilities as a father. ▪ a person *torn between* two lovers

tear apart [*phrasal verb*] **1** ***tear (something) apart*** *or* ***tear apart (something)*** **:** to completely destroy (something) by tearing it into pieces ▪ I couldn't open the box nicely, so I just *tore* it *apart*. — often used figuratively ▪ The robbers *tore apart* the house [=they made a mess in the house] looking for the money. ▪ We *tore* the other team *apart* [=we easily beat the other team] in yesterday's game. ▪ Civil war threatened to *tear apart* the country. ▪ We can't agree, and it's *tearing* our family *apart*. **2** ***tear (someone or something) apart*** *or* ***tear apart (someone or something)*** **:** to criticize (someone or something) in a very harsh or angry way especially by describing weaknesses, flaws, etc. ▪ The article *tears apart* the government's handling of the situation. ▪ I thought it was a good movie, but she *tore* it *apart*. ▪ They *tore* him *apart* when he left. — see also ¹TEAR 1, 7 (above)

tear at [*phrasal verb*] ***tear at (someone or something)*** **:** to attack and pull pieces from (something) in a violent way ▪ The cat *tore at* my pants with its claws. ▪ wolves *tearing at* a dead deer — often used figuratively ▪ Those two are always *tearing at* each other's throats. [=always arguing with and harshly criticizing each other] ▪ Her sadness *tore at* his heart. [=made him very upset/unhappy]

tear away [*phrasal verb*] ***tear (someone or something) away*** **:** to cause (someone) to leave or move away from something ▪ I needed to leave the party, but I couldn't *tear* myself *away*. ▪ She couldn't *tear* him *away* from the TV. ▪ He couldn't ***tear his eyes away*** from the TV. [=he could not stop watching the TV] — see also TEARAWAY

tear down [*phrasal verb*] ***tear down (something)*** *or* ***tear (something) down*** **:** to completely destroy (something, such as a building or wall) ▪ They *tore down* the old hospital and built a new one. ▪ We're planning to *tear down* the wall between the kitchen and the dining room. — often used figuratively ▪ *tearing down* walls of injustice ▪ They're trying to *tear* his reputation *down*.

tear into [*phrasal verb*] *informal* **1** ***tear into (something)*** **:** to begin doing (something) in a very quick or forceful way ▪ The kids *tore into* the pizza. [=quickly began eating the pizza] ▪ The band *tore into* the next song with a lot of energy. **2** ***tear into (someone or something)*** **:** to criticize (someone or something) in a very harsh or angry way ▪ My father *tore into* me for coming home an hour late. ▪ The critics *tore into* her performance in the movie.

tear (someone) limb from limb see LIMB

tear (someone) off a strip see ¹STRIP

tear (someone or something) to pieces/shreds **:** to criticize (someone or something) in a very harsh or angry way ▪ They *tore* my idea *to pieces*. ▪ The actress was *torn to shreds* in the press. — see also ¹TEAR 1 (above)

tear up [*phrasal verb*] ***tear up (something)*** *or* ***tear (something) up*** **1 :** to completely destroy (something) by tearing it into pieces ▪ I *tore* the letter *up* and threw it away. — often used figuratively ▪ They offered to *tear up* his old contract [=get rid of his old contract] and give him a new one. ▪ The burglars *tore* the house *up*. [=made a mess in the house] **2 :** to break apart and remove pieces of (something) ▪ The city *tore* the street *up* to fix a broken water main. ▪ They *tore up* 20 acres of forest and built a new shopping mall. **3** *chiefly US, informal* **:** to perform very well on or in (something) ▪ They were *tearing up* the dance floor. [=they were dancing in very skillful, energetic, and impressive way] ▪ He *tore up* the league last season.

tear your hair out see HAIR

that's torn it *Brit, informal* — used to say that something is no longer possible ▪ Well, *that's torn it*. Now everyone knows my little secret. ▪ *That's torn it*: the deal's off!

– compare ⁴TEAR

²tear *noun, pl* **tears** [*count*] **:** a hole or opening in something (such as a piece of paper or cloth) that is made by cutting it or tearing it ▪ The nail left a *tear* in his jacket. ▪ She had a *tear* in her stockings. ▪ She suffered a partial *tear* of the ligament in her right knee.

on a tear *US, informal* **:** having great success over a period of time ▪ The team has been *on a tear* in recent weeks. [=has been playing very well, has been winning a lot of games] ▪ The economy is *on a tear*, but can it last?

wear and tear see ²WEAR

– compare ³TEAR

³tear /ˈtiɚ/ *noun, pl* **tears** [*count*] **:** a drop of liquid that comes from your eyes especially when you cry **:** TEARDROP ▪ A single *tear* ran down his cheek. ▪ She wiped the *tears* from her eyes. ▪ Let me wipe away your *tears*. ▪ She was crying/weeping *tears* of anger/frustration/shame. ▪ *tear*-filled eyes ▪ That song ***brings a tear to my eye*** [=makes me cry a little] every time I hear it. ▪ She suddenly ***burst into tears.*** [=started to cry] ▪ He looked like he was ***close to tears.*** [=going to cry soon] ▪ Come now. ***Dry your tears*** [=stop crying] and try to be happy. ▪ I tried to ***fight back the tears.*** [=I tried not to cry] ▪ I couldn't ***hold back my tears.*** [=I could not stop myself from crying] ▪ The memory brought on a sudden ***flood of tears.*** ▪ We were laughing so hard that we were ***in tears.*** [=tears were coming out of our eyes] ▪ Everyone in the audience was ***moved to tears*** by their performance. [=their performance made everyone cry] ▪ His hateful words ***reduced me to tears.*** [=they made me cry]

blink back/away tears see ¹BLINK

bore you to tears see ¹BORE

dissolve in/into tears see DISSOLVE

end in tears **:** to have an ending in which people are crying or unhappy ▪ In our family, discussions about money always seem to *end in tears*.

shed tears **:** to cry or weep ▪ They *shed tears* of joy/gratitude when they heard the news. ▪ I never saw my father *shed* a single *tear*, even when my mother died.

– compare ²TEAR; see also CROCODILE TEARS

⁴tear *verb* **tears; teared; tear·ing** [*no obj*] **:** to fill with tears ▪ Why do your eyes *tear* when you cut onions? — often + *up* ▪ His eyes started *tearing up*. = He started *tearing up*. — compare ¹TEAR

tear·away /ˈterəˌweɪ/ *noun, pl* **-aways** [*count*] *Brit, informal* **:** a young person who behaves badly and who does dangerous, foolish, or illegal things ▪ a gang of teenage *tearaways* — see also *tear away* at ¹TEAR

tear·drop /ˈtiɚˌdrɑːp/ *noun, pl* **-drops** [*count*]

1 : ³TEAR

2 : something that is pointed at the top and round at the bottom **:** something that is shaped like a falling tear ▪ diamond *teardrop* earrings

tear·ful /ˈtiɚfəl/ *adj* [*more ~; most ~*]

1 : filled with tears ▪ He looked up at me with his *tearful* eyes and asked for help.

2 : happening with tears ▪ a *tearful* plea for help [=a plea for help by someone who is crying] ▪ a *tearful* goodbye ▪ the *tearful* parting of two lovers

– **tear·ful·ly** *adv* ▪ He pleaded *tearfully* for help. – **tear·ful·ness** *noun* [*noncount*] ▪ The scene quickly changed from *tearfulness* to laughter.

tear gas *noun* [*noncount*] **:** a gas that makes people unable to see by causing their eyes to be filled with tears and that is used especially by the police or military to separate large groups of people

– **tear·gas** /ˈtiɚˌgæs/ *verb* **-gas·ses; -gassed; -gas·sing** [+ *obj*] ▪ The protesters were *teargassed* by the police.

tear·jerk·er /ˈtiɚˌʤɚkɚ/ *noun, pl* **-ers** [*count*] *informal* **:** a story, song, movie, etc., that makes you cry or feel very sad ▪ I'm not in the mood to see a *tearjerker*. Let's watch something funny instead.

– **tear–jerk·ing** /ˈtiɚˌʤɚkɪŋ/ *adj* [*more ~; most ~*] ▪ a *tearjerking* love song

tea·room /ˈtiːˌruːm/ *noun, pl* **-rooms** [*count*] **:** a small restaurant that serves light meals — called also *tea shop*

teary /ˈtiri/ *adj* **tear·i·er; -est** [*also more ~; most ~*] **:** filled with tears or happening with tears **:** TEARFUL ▪ There were many *teary* eyes/faces among those in the audience. ▪ He made a *teary* farewell to the fans.

teary–eyed *adj* [*more* ~; *most* ~] **:** having eyes that are wet with tears ▪ I got a little *teary-eyed* at the end of the movie. [=I shed a few tears at the end of the movie] ▪ She said goodbye to her *teary-eyed* mother.

[1]**tease** /ˈtiːz/ *verb* **teas·es; teased; teas·ing**

1 : to laugh at and criticize (someone) in a way that is either friendly and playful or cruel and unkind [+ *obj*] He and his wife enjoy *teasing* each other about their different tastes in music. ▪ The other children *teased* her because she was wearing braces. ▪ He was always *teased* by his brother about being short. [*no obj*] Oh, don't get so angry. I was just/only *teasing*! ▪ Stop your *teasing*!

2 [+ *obj*] **:** to annoy or bother (an animal) ▪ The boy's mother told him to stop *teasing* the dog.

3 [+ *obj*] *US* **:** to make (hair) look fuller or bigger by combing it in a special way ▪ She *teases* [=(*chiefly Brit*) *backcombs*] her hair.

4 : to make (someone) feel excitement or interest about something you might do or say without actually doing it or saying it [+ *obj*] Stop *teasing* us and tell us who your surprise guest is. [*no obj*] She likes to *tease*.

5 [+ *obj*] **:** to remove or separate (thin pieces of something) slowly and carefully ▪ The twisted strands of the rope were gently *teased* apart. — often + *out* ▪ They described the techniques used to *tease out* [=*extract*] genetic material from DNA. ▪ She carefully *teased* the roots of the young plant *out* of the soil. — often used figuratively ▪ Reporters are still trying to *tease out* [=*find out*] the details of the accident. ▪ It won't be easy to *tease out* the meaning of these statistics.

– teas·ing *adj* ▪ a *teasing* tone of voice **– teasing** *noun* [*noncount*] ▪ There was some affectionate *teasing* about the way he was dressed. **– teas·ing·ly** /ˈtiːzɪŋli/ *adv* ▪ They *teasingly* remarked about the way he was dressed.

[2]**tease** *noun, pl* **teases** [*count*]

1 : a person who teases other people — usually singular ▪ He's just a *tease*.; *especially* **:** a person who seems to be sexually interested in someone but who is not serious about having sexual relations ▪ a pretty girl who has the reputation of being a bit of a *tease*

2 : a joking remark that criticizes someone in a friendly way **:** a teasing remark — usually singular ▪ Don't take what he said seriously. It was just a *tease*.

3 *US* **:** TEASER 2 ▪ The lower rate is just a *tease* to attract new customers.

teas·er /ˈtiːzɚ/ *noun, pl* **-ers** [*count*]

1 : a person who teases other people **:** TEASE

2 : something that is done, offered, or shown to make people want something or want to see something that will be offered or shown at a later time ▪ A *teaser* for the sequel appeared at the end of the movie. ▪ credit cards offering *teaser* rates to get people to sign up

3 *Brit* **:** a difficult problem or puzzle **:** BRAINTEASER

tea service *noun, pl* ~ **-vices** [*count*] **:** TEA SET

tea set *noun, pl* ~ **sets** [*count*] **:** a matching set of cups and dishes that are used for serving tea

tea shop *noun, pl* ~ **shops** [*count*] **:** TEAROOM

tea·spoon /ˈtiːˌspuːn/ *noun, pl* **-spoons** [*count*]

1 : a small spoon that is used especially for eating soft foods and stirring drinks ▪ She stirred her coffee with a *teaspoon*. — compare TABLESPOON

2 a : a spoon that is used by cooks for measuring dry and liquid ingredients and that holds an amount equal to ⅙ fluid ounce or ⅓ tablespoon ▪ He measured the salt with a *teaspoon*. **b :** the amount that a teaspoon will hold **:** TEASPOONFUL ▪ She put a *teaspoon* of sugar in her coffee. — abbr. *tsp*.

tea·spoon·ful /ˈtiːˌspuːnˌfʊl/ *noun, pl* **-spoon·fuls** /-ˌspuːnˌfʊlz/ *or* **-spoons·ful** /-ˌspuːnzˌfʊl/ [*count*] **:** the amount that a teaspoon will hold ▪ The recipe calls for a *teaspoonful* [=*teaspoon*] of salt. — abbr. *tsp*.

teat /ˈtɪt, ˈtiːt/ *noun, pl* **teats** [*count*]

1 : the part of a female animal (such as a cow) through which a young animal receives milk

2 *Brit* **:** NIPPLE 2

tea·time /ˈtiːˌtaɪm/ *noun* [*noncount*] *Brit* **:** the usual time for the afternoon meal known as tea **:** late afternoon or early evening ▪ It was nearing *teatime*.

tea towel *noun, pl* ~ **-els** [*count*] *chiefly Brit* **:** DISH TOWEL

tea tray *noun, pl* ~ **trays** [*count*] **:** a tray for holding a tea set

tech /ˈtɛk/ *noun, pl* **techs**

1 [*count*] *informal* **:** TECHNICIAN ▪ lab/computer *techs*

2 [*noncount*] *informal* **:** TECHNOLOGY — often used before another noun ▪ *tech* companies ▪ He's a *tech* geek.

3 [*noncount*] **:** a technical school — used in the shortened forms of names of technical schools ▪ Georgia *Tech*

tech·ie /ˈtɛki/ *noun, pl* **-ies** [*count*] *informal* **:** someone who knows a lot about technology ▪ computer *techies*

tech·ni·cal /ˈtɛknɪkəl/ *adj*

1 a : relating to the practical use of machines or science in industry, medicine, etc. ▪ *technical* training/knowledge/skills ▪ the latest *technical* [=(more commonly) *technological*] advances in aircraft design ▪ If you have any problems with your new computer, we offer 24-hour ***technical support***. ▪ I missed the first 10 minutes of the show because the network was experiencing ***technical difficulties/problems***. **b :** teaching practical skills rather than ideas about literature, art, etc. ▪ a *technical* school/college

2 [*more* ~; *most* ~] **a :** having special knowledge especially of how machines work or of how a particular kind of work is done ▪ *Technical* experts analyzed the data. ▪ The film's director hired a real police officer as a *technical* consultant/adviser. **b :** relating to the special skills or techniques needed to do a particular job or activity ▪ a pianist/painter with good *technical* skills ▪ Her ice-skating routine had the highest level of *technical* difficulty. = Her routine was very *technical*.

3 [*more* ~; *most* ~] **:** involving special knowledge, language, etc., that is used or understood by experts but usually not by others ▪ *technical* writing ▪ The essay is too *technical* for me. ▪ the more *technical* details/aspects of their research ▪ "Cartography" is the *technical* name/term/word for the making of maps. ▪ He is using the word in its *technical* sense/meaning.

4 : according to a very strict explanation of a rule, fact, etc. ▪ a *technical* violation of the law ▪ They were arguing over a minor ***technical point*** [=*technicality*] ▪ (*informal*) I'm not really 18 years old until tomorrow, if you want to ***get technical*** about it. [=if you want to be very exact or precise about it]

technical foul *noun, pl* ~ **fouls** [*count*] *basketball* **:** a foul that involves improper behavior or language rather than physical contact with an opponent — compare PERSONAL FOUL

tech·ni·cal·i·ty /ˌtɛknəˈkæləti/ *noun, pl* **-ties** [*count*]

1 : a small detail in a rule, law, etc., and especially one that forces an unwanted or unexpected result ▪ These cases were dropped because of legal *technicalities*. ▪ She lost the contest because of a *technicality*. = She lost the contest ***on a technicality***.

2 : something that is understood by experts but usually not by other people — usually plural; often + *of* ▪ I don't want to get into the *technicalities of* genetic cloning.

technical knockout *noun, pl* ~ **-outs :** an occurrence in which a fighter wins a boxing match when an opponent is unable to continue to fight usually because of injuries [*count*] He has 10 knockouts and 6 *technical knockouts*. [*noncount*] He won by *technical knockout*. — called also *TKO*

tech·ni·cal·ly /ˈtɛknɪkli/ *adv*

1 a : according to a very strict explanation of a rule, fact, etc. ▪ The computer took a minute to download the file. Well, *technically* it took 53 seconds. ▪ The use of the drug is *technically* illegal but difficult to prosecute. ▪ *Technically*, a tomato is a fruit, not a vegetable. = ***Technically speaking***, a tomato is a fruit, not a vegetable. **b** [*more* ~; *most* ~] **:** according to or among experts ▪ A map maker is (more) *technically* known as a cartographer.

2 [*more* ~; *most* ~] **:** in a way that relates to the use of special techniques or skills ▪ Her newest ice-skating routine is more *technically* difficult. ▪ *Technically*, the pianist was perfect, but the performance was uninspired.

3 [*more* ~; *most* ~] **:** in a way that relates to the use of machines or science in industry, medicine, etc. ▪ We live in a *technically* [=(more commonly) *technologically*] advanced society. ▪ This kind of surgery is now *technically* possible, but it is still risky.

tech·ni·cian /tɛkˈnɪʃən/ *noun, pl* **-cians** [*count*]

1 : a person whose job relates to the practical use of machines or science in industry, medicine, etc. ▪ medical/X-ray/laboratory *technicians* ▪ They hired a *technician* to help maintain the office's computers. ▪ She is the lighting/sound *technician* for the play. — see also EMERGENCY MEDICAL TECHNICIAN

2 *somewhat formal* **:** someone who has mastered the basic

T

techniques or skills in a sport, an art, etc. ▪ As a painter, he was more than just a *technician*; he was a creative genius.

Tech•ni•col•or /ˈtɛknɪˌkʌlɚ/ *trademark* — used for a process of color photography in movies

tech•nique /tɛkˈniːk/ *noun, pl* **-niques**
1 [*count*] : a way of doing something by using special knowledge or skill ▪ We learned some *techniques* for relieving stress. ▪ I used a special *technique* to make the bread.
2 [*noncount*] : the way that a person performs basic physical movements or skills ▪ The players need to practice in order to improve their *technique*. ▪ a dancer with excellent *technique* ▪ The ice-skaters will be judged on *technique* and creativity.

tech•no /ˈtɛkˌnoʊ/ *noun* [*noncount*] : a type of electronic dance music that has a fast beat ▪ The club plays only *techno*. ▪ *techno* music

techno- *combining form* : technical ▪ *techno*crat : technological ▪ *techno*phobe

tech•noc•ra•cy /tɛkˈnɑːkrəsi/ *noun, pl* **-cies** [*count, noncount*] *formal* : a system in which people with a lot of knowledge about science or technology control a society

tech•no•crat /ˈtɛknəˌkræt/ *noun, pl* **-crats** [*count*] : a scientist or technical expert who has a lot of power in politics or industry

tech•no•crat•ic /ˌtɛknəˈkrætɪk/ *adj* : of, relating to, or similar to a technocrat or technocracy ▪ a *technocratic* leader/society ▪ a *technocratic* approach

tech•nol•o•gist /tɛkˈnɑːləʤɪst/ *noun, pl* **-gists** [*count*] : someone who is an expert in technology

tech•nol•o•gy /tɛkˈnɑːləʤi/ *noun, pl* **-gies**
1 [*noncount*] : the use of science in industry, engineering, etc., to invent useful things or to solve problems ▪ Recent advances in medical *technology* have saved countless lives. ▪ The company is on the cutting edge of *technology*.
2 : a machine, piece of equipment, method, etc., that is created by technology [*count*] The government is developing innovative/advanced *technologies* to improve the safety of its soldiers. ▪ How can we apply this new *technology* to our everyday lives? [*noncount*] The car has the latest in fuel-saving *technology*.
– **tech•no•log•i•cal** /ˌtɛknəˈlɑːʤɪkəl/ *also US* **tech•no•log•ic** /ˌtɛknəˈlɑːʤɪk/ *adj* ▪ Many *technological* advances/developments/changes in medicine have taken place over the past decade. – **tech•no•log•i•cal•ly** /ˌtɛknəˈlɑːʤɪkli/ *adv* ▪ a *technologically* advanced society ▪ *technologically* savvy consumers

technology park *noun, pl* **~ parks** [*count*] : RESEARCH PARK

tech•no•phile /ˈtɛknəˌfajəl/ *noun, pl* **-philes** [*count*] : someone who likes and enjoys technology and modern machines (such as computers)

tech•no•phobe /ˈtɛknəˌfoʊb/ *noun, pl* **-phobes** [*count*] : someone who fears or dislikes modern machines (such as computers) ▪ My father is a *technophobe*.
– **tech•no•pho•bia** /ˌtɛknəˈfoʊbijə/ *noun* [*noncount*] ▪ He finally overcame his *technophobia* and bought a computer.
– **tech•no•pho•bic** /ˌtɛknəˈfoʊbɪk/ *adj* [*more* ~; *most* ~] ▪ *technophobic* people

tec•ton•ic /tɛkˈtɑːnɪk/ *adj, always used before a noun*
1 *geology* : of or relating to changes in the structure of the Earth's surface ▪ *tectonic* plates/forces
2 : having a large and important effect ▪ There has been a recent *tectonic* shift/change in voting patterns.

tec•ton•ics /tɛkˈtɑːnɪks/ *noun* [*noncount*] *geology* : the structure of the Earth's surface and the ways in which it changes shape over time ▪ Scientists are studying the *tectonics* of the ocean floor. — see also PLATE TECTONICS

ted•dy /ˈtɛdi/ *noun, pl* **-dies** [*count*] *chiefly US* : a piece of light clothing that is worn by women as underwear or in bed

teddy bear *noun, pl* **~ bears** [*count*] : a soft toy bear

te•dious /ˈtiːdijəs/ *adj* [*more* ~; *most* ~] : boring and too slow or long ▪ He made a *tedious* 45-minute speech. ▪ The work is *tedious*, but it needs to get done.
– **te•dious•ly** *adv* ▪ a *tediously* long speech – **te•dious•ness** *noun* [*noncount*]

te•di•um /ˈtiːdijəm/ *noun* [*noncount*] *somewhat formal* : the quality or state of being tedious or boring ▪ The movie was three hours of *tedium*. ▪ I took a day off to relieve the *tedium* of work.

¹tee /ˈtiː/ *noun, pl* **tees** [*count*]
1 a : a small peg on which a golf ball is placed so that it can be hit **b** : an object that is used for holding a football in position so that it can be kicked **c** *chiefly US* : a post on which a baseball is placed so that a child can hit the ball with a bat in T-ball ▪ a batting *tee*
2 : the area from which a golf ball is first hit to start play on a hole ▪ She hit an excellent drive from the first *tee*. ▪ a ***tee shot*** [=a first shot that is taken on a hole] ▪ We have an 8 a.m. ***tee time***. [=we start playing golf at 8 a.m.]
to a tee : in a perfect or exact way ▪ Her new car fits/suits her *to a tee*. [=*to a T*] ▪ That's him *to a tee*. [=that is a perfect description of him]

²tee *verb* **tees; teed; tee•ing**
tee off [*phrasal verb*] **1** : to hit a golf ball for the first time on a hole or in a round ▪ We *teed off* at 8 a.m. ▪ We watched her *tee off* at the ninth hole. **2** ***tee off (someone) or tee (someone) off*** *US, informal* : to make (someone) angry ▪ That guy really *tees* me *off*. — see also TEED OFF **3** ***tee off on (someone or something)*** *US, informal* : to speak about (someone or something) in an angry way ▪ The coach *teed off on* his players to the media.
tee up [*phrasal verb*] ***tee up or tee (a ball) up or tee up (a ball)*** : to place (a ball) on a tee ▪ It's time to *tee up*. ▪ He *teed up* the ball. = He *teed* the ball *up*.

teed off *adj* [*more* ~; *most* ~] *US, informal* : angry or annoyed ▪ She was very *teed off*. ▪ a *teed off* customer — see also *tee off* at ²TEE

¹teem /ˈtiːm/ *verb* **teems; teemed; teem•ing**
teem with [*phrasal verb*] ***teem with (something)*** : to be full of (life and activity) : to have many (people or animals) moving around inside ▪ The river *teems* [=*abounds*] *with* fish. — usually used as *(be) teeming with* ▪ The river *was teeming with* fish. ▪ streets *teeming with* shoppers — sometimes used figuratively ▪ My mind *is teeming with* ideas. — compare ²TEEM
– **teeming** *adj* ▪ the city's *teeming* [=*bustling*] streets

²teem *verb* **teems; teemed; teeming** [*no obj*] *of rain* : to come down heavily : POUR ▪ They continued to play as the rain ***teemed down***. ▪ She waited in the ***teeming rain***. ▪ (*chiefly Brit*) It has been ***teeming down*** [=raining heavily] all day. = It has been ***teeming with rain*** all day. — compare ¹TEEM

teen /ˈtiːn/ *noun, pl* **teens** [*count*] : someone who is between 13 and 19 years old : TEENAGER
– **teen** *adj, always used before a noun* ▪ He was a *teen* idol. ▪ a *teen* magazine/movie ▪ *teen* [=*teenage*] pregnancy — see also PRETEEN

teen•age /ˈtiːnˌeɪʤ/ *adj, always used before a noun*
1 *or* ***teen•aged*** /ˈtiːnˌeɪʤd/ : between 13 and 19 years old ▪ the *teenage* population ▪ *teenage* boys/girls
2 : relating to people who are between 13 and 19 years old ▪ *teenage* [=*teen*] pregnancy/rebellion ▪ the *teenage* years

teen•ag•er /ˈtiːnˌeɪʤɚ/ *noun, pl* **-ers** [*count*] : someone who is between 13 and 19 years old ▪ Their daughter is a *teenager*. ▪ The show is very popular among *teenagers*.

teens /ˈtiːnz/ *noun* [*plural*] : the numbers 13 through 19 ▪ The temperature will be in the *teens* today.; *especially* : the years 13 through 19 in a century or a person's lifetime ▪ Both of my children are in their *teens* now. [=are teenagers now]

teen•sy /ˈtiːnsi/ *adj* **teen•si•er; -est** [*also more* ~; *most* ~] *informal* : very small : TEENY

teen•sy–ween•sy /ˌtiːnsiˈwiːnsi/ *adj* **-ween•si•er; -est** [*also more* ~; *most* ~] *informal* : very small : TEENY-WEENY

tee•ny /ˈtiːni/ *adj* **tee•ni•er; -est** [*also more* ~; *most* ~] *informal* : very small : TINY ▪ I'll just have a *teeny* piece of cake. ▪ I'm a ***teeny bit*** upset/nervous. ▪ a ***teeny little*** house ▪ a ***teeny tiny*** bug

teeny•bop•per /ˈtiːniˌbɑːpɚ/ *noun, pl* **-pers** [*count*] *informal* + *old-fashioned* : a girl who is about 11 to 13 years old and who listens to popular music and likes current fashions

tee•ny–wee•ny /ˌtiːniˈwiːni/ *adj* **-ween•i•er; -est** [*also more* ~; *most* ~] *informal* : very small : TINY ▪ I'll just have a *teeny-weeny* piece of cake. ▪ Aren't you even a ***teeny-weeny bit*** jealous? ▪ a ***teeny-weeny little*** house/bug ▪ (*humorous*) I like the car, too, but there's just one *teeny-weeny little* problem: we can't afford it!

teepee *variant spelling of* TEPEE

tee shirt *variant spelling of* T-SHIRT

tee•ter /ˈtiːtɚ/ *verb* **-ters; -tered; -ter•ing** [*no obj*] : to move in an unsteady way back and forth or from side to side ▪ The pile of books *teetered* and fell to the floor. ▪ She *teetered* down the street in her high heels. — often used figuratively ▪ Our relationship *teeters* between friendship and romance. ▪ The bird is ***teetering on the edge of*** extinction. [=the bird is almost extinct] ▪ The countries are ***teetering on the brink of*** war. [=the countries are close to going to war]

tee·ter–tot·ter /ˈtiːtɚˌtɑːtɚ/ *noun, pl* **-ters** [*count*] *US* : [1]SEESAW 1

teeth *plural of* TOOTH

teethe /ˈtiːð/ *verb* **teethes; teethed; teeth·ing** [*no obj*]
1 : to have the first set of teeth begin to grow ▪ The baby is starting to *teethe.* ▪ She is still *teething.*
2 : to bite on something in order to relieve pain caused by teething — usually + *on* ▪ Give her something cold to *teethe on.*

teething ring *noun, pl* **~ rings** [*count*] : a rubber or plastic ring for a baby to bite on when teething

teething troubles *noun* [*plural*] *Brit* : small problems that happen when a business, project, system, etc., is first started or used ▪ There were some *teething troubles* [=*growing pains*] when we began our business. — called also *teething problems*

tee·to·tal·er (*chiefly US*) *or chiefly Brit* **tee·to·tal·ler** /ˈtiːˈtoʊtlɚ/ *noun, pl* **-ers** [*count*] : someone who never drinks alcohol
– tee·to·tal /ˈtiːˈtoʊtl̩/ *adj, Brit* ▪ a *teetotal* store owner ▪ He is *teetotal.*

TEFL /ˈtɛfəl/ *abbr, chiefly Brit* teaching English as a foreign language

Tef·lon /ˈtɛˌflɑːn/ *trademark* — used for a substance that is used especially for nonstick coatings on cooking pans

Te·ja·no /teɪˈhɑːnoʊ/ *noun* [*noncount*] : a type of popular music from Texas and northern Mexico — often used before another noun ▪ *Tejano* music/singers

tel *abbr* telephone; telephone number

tele- *combining form*
1 : at or over a long distance ▪ *tele*gram ▪ *tele*scope ▪ *tele*communications ▪ *tele*vision
2 : television ▪ *tele*cast
3 : using a telephone ▪ *tele*marketing

tele·cast /ˈtɛlɪˌkæst, *Brit* ˈtɛlɪˌkɑːst/ *verb* **-casts; -cast; -cast·ing** [+ *obj*] : to broadcast (a program) by television ▪ The network will *telecast* [=*televise*] the game live. — often used as *(be) telecast* ▪ The game will *be telecast* live.
– telecast *noun, pl* **-casts** [*count*] ▪ a live *telecast* of the concert **– tele·cast·er** *noun, pl* **-ers** [*count*]

tel·e·com /ˈtɛlɪˌkɑːm/ *noun, pl* **-coms** *somewhat technical*
1 [*count*] : a telecommunications company ▪ a major *telecom*
2 [*noncount*] : the telecommunications industry ▪ investments in *telecom* — often used before another noun ▪ *telecom* companies/equipment/services ▪ the *telecom* industry

tele·com·mu·ni·ca·tions /ˌtɛlɪkəˌmjuːnəˈkeɪʃənz/ *noun* [*plural*] : the technology of sending and receiving signals, images, etc., over long distances by telephone, television, satellite, etc. — often used before another noun ▪ *telecommunications* companies/equipment ▪ the *telecommunications* industry

tele·com·mute /ˈtɛlɪkəˌmjuːt/ *verb* **-mutes; -mut·ed; -mut·ing** [*no obj*] : to work at home by using a computer connection to a company's main office ▪ The company now allows some of its employees to *telecommute.*
– tele·com·mut·er *noun, pl* **-ers** [*count*]

tele·con·fer·enc·ing /ˈtɛlɪˌkɑːnfrənsɪŋ/ *noun* [*noncount*] : the use of telephones and video equipment to have a meeting with people who are in different places ▪ The manager talked to her employees via/by (video) *teleconferencing.*
– tele·con·fer·ence /ˈtɛlɪˌkɑːnfrəns/ *noun, pl* **-enc·es** [*count*] ▪ We had three *teleconferences* in one day.

tele·ge·nic /ˌtɛləˈʤɛnɪk/ *adj* [*more ~; most ~*] : tending to look good or seem likable on television ▪ She is very *telegenic.* ▪ a *telegenic* politician — compare PHOTOGENIC

tele·gram /ˈtɛləˌgræm/ *noun, pl* **-grams** [*count*] : a message that is sent by telegraph — called also *wire*

[1]tele·graph /ˈtɛləˌgræf, *Brit* ˈtɛlɪˌgrɑːf/ *noun, pl* **-graphs**
1 [*noncount*] : an old-fashioned system of sending messages over long distances by using wires and electrical signals ▪ I sent the message by *telegraph.*
2 [*count*] : a device used for sending or receiving messages by telegraph

[2]telegraph *verb* **-graphs; -graphed; -graph·ing**
1 a : to send (a message) by telegraph [+ *obj*] He *telegraphed* a message to her. [*no obj*] Please *telegraph* when you get there. **b** [+ *obj*] **:** to send a telegram to (someone) ▪ Please *telegraph* me when you get there.
2 [+ *obj*] : to make (something that you are about to do or say) obvious or apparent by the way you move, look, etc. ▪ The look on her face *telegraphed* bad news. ▪ He lost the boxing match because he was *telegraphing* his punches.

telegraph pole *noun, pl* **~ poles** [*count*] *Brit* : TELEPHONE POLE

tele·mar·ket·ing /ˌtɛləˈmɑɚkətɪŋ/ *noun* [*noncount*] *chiefly US* : the activity or job of selling goods or services by calling people on the telephone ▪ He has a job in *telemarketing.* [=(*chiefly Brit*) *telesales*]
– tele·mar·ket·er /ˌtɛləˈmɑɚkətɚ/ *noun, pl* **-ers** [*count*]

te·lem·e·try /təˈlɛmətri/ *noun* [*noncount*] *technical* : the process of using special equipment to take measurements of something (such as pressure, speed, or temperature) and send them by radio to another place

tele·path·ic /ˌtɛləˈpæθɪk/ *adj*
1 : of or relating to telepathy ▪ *telepathic* communication/powers
2 : having the ability to know another person's thoughts without being told what they are : able to read minds ▪ You need to tell me what you're thinking. I'm not *telepathic.*
– tele·path·i·cal·ly /ˌtɛləˈpæθɪkli/ *adv* ▪ The twins seem to communicate *telepathically.*

te·lep·a·thy /təˈlɛpəθi/ *noun* [*noncount*] : a way of communicating thoughts directly from one person's mind to another person's mind without using words or signals

[1]tele·phone /ˈtɛləˌfoʊn/ *noun, pl* **-phones**
1 [*noncount*] : a system that uses wires and radio signals to send sounds (such as people's voices) over long distances : PHONE ▪ We spoke *by telephone.* ▪ a *telephone* line/company/operator ▪ I just have to make a quick ***telephone call*** before we leave. ▪ You can order the cake ***over the telephone.*** ▪ (*Brit*) He screamed at me ***down the telephone.*** [=through the telephone]
2 [*count*] : a device that is connected to a telephone system and that you use to listen or speak to someone who is somewhere else : PHONE ▪ The *telephone* has been ringing all morning! ▪ She picked up the *telephone* and dialed the number. ▪ He slammed/put down the *telephone.* ▪ They hired someone to answer the *telephones.* ▪ All our *telephones* are cordless. ▪ I left the *telephone* off the hook. ▪ a public *telephone* ▪ a ***cellular telephone*** [=*cell phone*]
on the telephone **1 :** using a telephone to talk to someone ▪ She is always (talking) *on the telephone.* [=*on the phone*] ▪ He came to the door while I was *on the telephone.* **2** *Brit* **:** connected to a telephone system ▪ the percentage of households *on the telephone* [=*on the phone*]

telephone

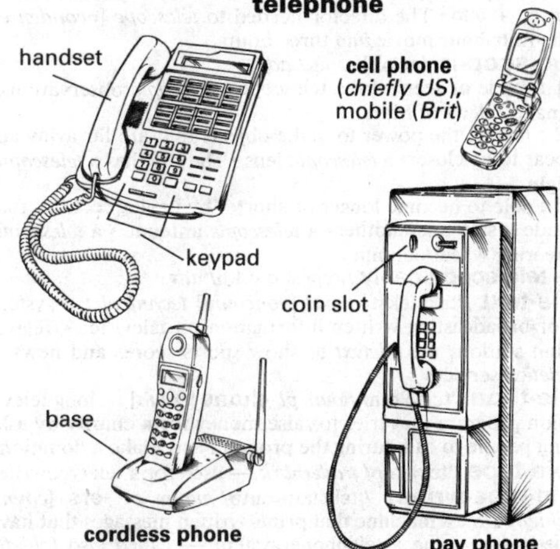

[2]telephone *verb* **-phones; -phoned; -phon·ing :** to speak or try to speak to (someone) using a telephone : to call or phone (someone) [+ *obj*] He *telephoned* me to say that he was going to be late. ▪ I'll *telephone* the police. [*no obj*] He *telephoned* to say that he was going to be late. ▪ You never write or *telephone.*

telephone book *noun, pl* **~ books** [*count*] : PHONE BOOK

telephone booth *noun, pl* **~ booths** [*count*] *chiefly US* : PHONE BOOTH

telephone box *noun, pl* **~ boxes** [*count*] *Brit* : PHONE BOOTH

telephone directory *noun, pl* **~ -ries** [*count*] : PHONE BOOK

telephone number *noun, pl* **~ -bers** [*count*] : a number that you dial on a telephone to reach a particular person, business, etc. : PHONE NUMBER

telephone pole *noun, pl* **~ poles** [*count*] *chiefly US* : a tall wooden pole that supports the wires of a telephone system — called also (*Brit*) *telegraph pole*

telephone tag *noun* [*noncount*] *chiefly US* : a situation in which two people keep trying to call each other on the telephone but are unable to reach each other • We've been playing *telephone tag*—she's always out when I call, and vice versa. — called also (*US, informal*) *phone tag*

te·le·pho·nist /tə'lɛfənɪst/ *noun, pl* **-nists** [*count*] *Brit* : OPERATOR 2

te·le·pho·ny /tə'lɛfəni/ *noun* [*noncount*] *technical* : the use of a telephone system to send and receive sounds over long distances

tele·pho·to lens /ˌtɛlə'foʊtoʊ-/ *noun, pl* **~ lenses** [*count*] : a lens for a camera that makes things that are far away appear to be closer — compare ZOOM LENS

tele·print·er /'tɛləˌprɪntə/ *noun, pl* **-ers** [*count*] *chiefly Brit* : TELETYPEWRITER

tele·prompt·er /'tɛləˌprɑːmptə/ *noun, pl* **-ers** [*count*] *chiefly US* : a machine that helps someone who is speaking to an audience or on television by showing the words that need to be said

tele·sales /'tɛləˌseɪlz/ *noun* [*noncount*] *chiefly Brit* : TELEMARKETING

[1]**tele·scope** /'tɛləˌskoʊp/ *noun, pl* **-scopes** [*count*] : a device shaped like a long tube that you look through in order to see things that are far away • The rings of Saturn can be seen ***through a telescope*** — see also RADIO TELESCOPE

telescope

[2]**telescope** *verb* **-scopes; -scoped; -scop·ing**

1 [*no obj*] : to become shorter by having one section slide inside another somewhat larger section • The radio antenna *telescopes.*

2 [+ *obj*] : to make (something) shorter in length or time — often + *into* • The director needed to *telescope* [=*condense*] the four-hour movie *into* three hours.

tele·scop·ic /ˌtɛlə'skɑːpɪk/ *adj*

1 : made or seen with a telescope • *telescopic* observations/images/views of Mars

2 : having the power to make objects that are far away appear to be closer • a *telescopic* lens • The rifle has a *telescopic* sight.

3 : able to become longer or shorter by having sections that slide inside one another • a *telescopic* antenna • a *telescopic* steering wheel/column

— **tele·scop·i·cal·ly** /ˌtɛlə'skɑːpɪkli/ *adv*

tele·text /'tɛləˌtɛkst/ *noun* [*noncount*] *technical* : a system for broadcasting written information on television • Television stations use *teletext* to show sports scores and news. • *teletext* services

tele·thon /'tɛləˌθɑːn/ *noun, pl* **-thons** [*count*] : a long television program that tries to raise money for a charity by asking people to call during the program and make a donation

Tele·type /'tɛləˌtaɪp/ *trademark* — used for a teletypewriter

tele·type·writ·er /ˌtɛlə'taɪpˌraɪtə/ *noun, pl* **-ers** [*count*] *chiefly US* : a machine that prints written messages that have been sent using a telephone system — called also (*chiefly Brit*) *tele·prin·ter* /'tɛləˌprɪntə/

tel·evan·ge·list /ˌtɛlɪ'vænʤəlɪst/ *noun, pl* **-lists** [*count*] : a person and especially a preacher who appears on television in order to teach about Christianity and try to persuade people to become Christians

— **tel·evan·ge·lism** /ˌtɛlɪ'vænʤəˌlɪzəm/ *noun* [*noncount*]

tele·vise /'tɛləˌvaɪz/ *verb* **-vis·es; -vised; -vis·ing** [+ *obj*] : to broadcast (something) by television • The same network will *televise* the tournament next year. — often used as *(be) televised* • The speech will *be televised* live. • *televised* baseball games • a *televised* debate

tele·vi·sion /'tɛləˌvɪʒən/ *noun, pl* **-sions**

1 [*noncount*] : an electronic system of sending images and sounds by a wire or through space • Do you have satellite or cable *television*? [=*TV*]

2 [*count*] : a piece of equipment with a screen that receives images and sounds sent by television • Can you turn on/off the *television*? [=*TV*, (*chiefly Brit*) *telly*] • Please turn up/down the *television*. [=make the television louder/quieter] • wide-screen *televisions* — see picture at LIVING ROOM

3 [*noncount*] : programs that are broadcast by television • We don't watch much *television*. [=*TV*, (*chiefly Brit*) *telly*] • a *television* [=*TV*] program/show/series

4 [*noncount*] : the television broadcasting industry • She works in *television*. • He's a star of stage, screen, and *television*. • a *television* [=*TV*] producer/reporter/company

on (the) television : broadcast by television : being shown by television • What is *on the television* [=*on TV*, (*chiefly Brit*) *on (the) telly*] tonight? • There's nothing *on television* right now. [=there are no programs that I would like to watch now] • The movie will be *on television* next month. • I recognize your face. Are you *on television*? [=do you appear in a television program?]

television set *noun, pl* **~ sets** [*count*] : TELEVISION 2

tele·work·ing /'tɛləˌwəkɪŋ/ *noun* [*noncount*] *chiefly Brit* : the activity of working at home and communicating with customers or other workers by using a computer, telephone, etc.

— **tele·work·er** /'tɛləˌwəkə/ *noun, pl* **-ers** [*count*]

tel·ex /'tɛˌlɛks/ *noun, pl* **-ex·es**

1 [*noncount*] : a system of communication in which messages are sent over long distances by using a telephone system and are printed by using a special machine (called a teletypewriter) • The message was sent by *telex*.

2 [*count*] : a message sent by telex • We received a *telex* from New York.

— **telex** *verb* **-exes; -exed; -ex·ing** [+ *obj*] • He *telexed* her a message.

tell /'tɛl/ *verb* **tells; told** /'toʊld/; **tell·ing**

1 [+ *obj*] **a** : to say or write (something) to (someone) • He *told* us the story. • Has she *told* you the good news, yet? • Please *tell* us your name and occupation. • She looked at the palm of my hand and *told* me my fortune. • I promise not to *tell* anyone your secret. = I promise not to *tell* your secret to anyone. — often + *about* • You can *tell* me all *about* your trip at dinner. — often + *that* • If you see her, *tell* her (*that*) we miss her. • People *tell* me (*that*) Paris is nice this time of year. • I keep *telling* myself (*that*) everything will be OK. • My husband *tells/told* me (*that*) you play golf. — often + *what, where*, etc. • He *told* us *what* happened. • Can you *tell* them *how* to play the game while I get the cards? • ***I can't tell you how*** pleased we are [=we are very pleased] that you could join us. ✧ This sense of *tell* is often used informally to emphasize a statement. • You are wrong, ***I tell you*** • ***I can tell you***—it's not worth the hassle. • ***I'm telling you***, I don't know anyone by that name. • ***I'll tell you one thing***: she was awfully arrogant. • ***I'll tell you something/this***: I would never have bought that car. • ***Let me tell you (something)***: he may be old, but he can still win baseball games. • ***To tell you the truth***, I didn't really like the movie. • "The car turned out to be a lemon!" "***What did I tell you?***" [=you should have listened to me; you should have followed my advice] **b** : to say (a word or words) to (someone) • I didn't get a chance to *tell* him goodbye. [=to say goodbye to him] • If you see her, *tell* her hello for me. • "I feel sick," he *told* his mom.

2 **a** : to give information to (someone) by speaking or writing [+ *obj*] "What is his name?" "I don't know. He didn't *tell* me." • Be sure to *tell* me when they get here. = When they get here, be sure to *tell* me (so). • "I know the answer." "***Don't tell me*** [=don't say what the answer is] I want to guess." • "Do you know where the library is?" "I'm sorry. ***I couldn't tell you***" [=I don't know] [*no obj*] "Who is the letter from?" "I'm not *telling*." **b** : to let (someone) know a secret [+ *obj*] I promise not to *tell* anyone. • I can't *tell* you because it's a secret. [*no obj*] Your secret is safe with me: I'll never *tell*.

3 [+ *obj*] : to express (something) by speaking • He loves *telling* stories/jokes. • You shouldn't *tell* [=*reveal*] other people's secrets. • She got in trouble for *telling* a lie. • I'm *telling* the truth. • I didn't really like the movie, ***to tell the truth*** [=to say what I really think] • ***Truth be told*** [=to say what the truth is], the food was pretty bad.

4 [+ *obj*] : to give (someone) an instruction or command • Be quiet and do what I *tell* you. = Be quiet and ***do as you're told*** — usually followed by *to* + *verb* • The police officer *told* him

to stop. • I was *told to stay* here. • I'll *tell* them *to meet* us there at 6 o'clock. • I *told* myself *to pick up* some milk on the way home, but I forgot to do it. • You can't *tell* me what *to do.*
5 : to inform others that someone has done something wrong or behaved badly — used especially by children [*no obj*] If you do that, I'll *tell.* [+ *obj*] I'm *telling* Mom. — see also TELL ON 1 (below)
6 [+ *obj*] : to give information to (someone or something) by doing a particular action or making a particular sound • When the dog scratches at the door, she is *telling* you that she wants to go outside. • The oven will beep to *tell* you when it is preheated.
7 [+ *obj*] : to make (something) known to (someone) • The expressions on their faces *told* me everything I needed to know. • The evidence *tells* us that there were two robbers. • The signs will *tell* you what exit to take off the highway.
8 *not used in progressive tenses* [+ *obj*] : to see or understand the differences between two people or things • I can definitely ***tell a/the difference between*** the two sauces. • They look exactly the same. How can you ***tell which is which***? • I can't ***tell who is who*** with their uniforms on. • He is old enough to ***tell right from wrong***. [=to know what things are good and what things are bad]
9 *not used in progressive tenses* : to see or know (something) with certainty [+ *obj*] It was easy to *tell* that the bill was counterfeit. • It's hard to *tell* if she's kidding or not. — usually used after *can* or *could* • "He's lying." "Really? How *can* you *tell*?" • I *could tell* (by/from the look on his face) that he was lying. • You *can tell* a lot about a person by the kind of car they drive. • ***No one can tell*** for sure whether it will happen. • ***Who can tell*** [=who can predict] what will happen next season? • ***You can never tell*** what type of mood he will be in. • ***You never can tell*** how he'll be feeling. [*no obj*] You might win the raffle—*you never can tell.* • ***As far/near as I can tell***, he is happy at his new job. [=he seems to me to be happy in his new job]
all told see ²ALL
don't tell me informal **1** — used to show that you already know what someone is going to say especially because he or she often says such things • "I have a favor to ask of you." "*Don't tell me*—I bet you need to borrow more money, don't you?" **2** — used to express surprise and disappointment • "*Don't tell me* the concert tickets were all sold out?!" "No, I bought the last two tickets."
I/I'll tell you what *also* ***tell you what*** *informal* — used to introduce a suggestion or to emphasize a statement • *(I'll) Tell you what*—I'll let you borrow the car if you fill it up with gas. • *I tell you what,* I wouldn't pay that much for a pair of shoes.
I told you (so) *informal* — used to say to someone that you were right about something especially when that person disagreed with you • "You were right after all." "See. *I told you so!*"
tell against [*phrasal verb*] ***tell against (someone)*** *Brit, formal* : to be a disadvantage to (someone) • His unkempt appearance is bound to *tell against* him in court.
tell apart [*phrasal verb*] ***tell (someone or something) apart*** : to see what the differences are between (people or things) : to identify (people or things that look similar to each other) • They look so much alike that I can barely/hardly/scarcely *tell* them *apart.* • It is hard *telling* the twins *apart.*
tell it like it is *US, informal* : to say what the facts are : to speak about unpleasant things in an honest way • I don't want to offend anyone; I'm just *telling it like it is.* • You can always count on John to *tell it like it is.*
tell me — used in speech to introduce a question • *Tell me,* is there a subway nearby? • So *tell me,* what did you think of the movie?
tell me about it *informal* — used to say that you understand what someone is talking about because you have had the same or a similar experience • "Something is wrong with that computer." "Yeah, *tell me about it.* I can never get it to work properly."
tell of [*phrasal verb*] *formal + literary* **1** ***tell of (something)*** **a** : to be evidence of (something) : INDICATE • Her smile *told of* her good news. • His rough hands *tell of* a hard life. **b** : to describe (something) : to make the details of (something) known • The article *tells of* her Arctic journey. • The explorer's journals *tell of* a vast unexplored wilderness. **2** ***tell (someone) of (something)*** : to talk to (someone) about (something) • He *told* us *of* his plans to move to the city.
tell off [*phrasal verb*] ***tell (someone) off or tell off (someone)*** *informal* **1** *US* : to yell at or insult (someone who did or said something that made you angry) • He wished that he could *tell* his boss *off.* — often + *for* • She *told* him *off for* spreading rumors about her. **2** *Brit* : to criticize (someone) in an angry way from a position of authority — often + *for* • The teacher *told* the girl *off for* talking during class.
tell on [*phrasal verb*] **1** ***tell on (someone)*** *informal* : to tell someone in authority about the bad behavior or actions of (someone) • Please don't *tell on* me. **2** ***tell on (someone or something)*** *not used in progressive tenses* : to have a noticeable effect on (someone or something) • The stress began to *tell on* her face/health.
tell time or tell the time see ¹TIME
there's no telling — used to say that it is impossible to know something with certainty • *There's no telling* how long the strike will last.
you're telling me informal — used to say that you already know and completely agree with something that was just said • "This hot weather is brutal." "*You're telling me.*"

tell–all /ˈtɛlˈɑːl/ *noun, pl* **-alls** [*count*] : a book that contains new and usually shocking information about someone or something — often used before another noun • a *tell-all* biography

tell·er /ˈtɛlɚ/ *noun, pl* **-ers** [*count*]
1 : a person who tells something (such as a story) to someone else • a *teller* of tales— see also FORTUNE-TELLER, STORYTELLER
2 : a person who works in a bank and whose job is to receive money from customers and pay out money to customers
3 : a person whose job is to count votes

tell·ing /ˈtɛlɪŋ/ *adj* [*more ~; most ~*]
1 : producing a strong or important effect • Her experience is/provides a *telling* example of why the nation's educational system needs to be changed. • The most *telling* moment in the case was when the victim took the stand.
2 : giving information about someone or something without intending to • Her response to the question was very *telling.* [=it showed how she really felt; it revealed something about her character] • a *telling* comment/remark
– tell·ing·ly *adv* • *Tellingly,* she chose not to reply.

¹tell·tale /ˈtɛlˌteɪl/ *adj, always used before a noun* : indicating that something exists or has occurred • The sauce had the *telltale* odor of garlic. • He had the ***telltale signs*** of smallpox. • Slurred speech is usually a *telltale sign* of intoxication.

²telltale *noun, pl* **-tales** [*count*] *Brit, informal* : TATTLETALE

tel·ly /ˈtɛli/ *noun, pl* **tel·lies** *chiefly Brit, informal* : TELEVISION [*count*] Please turn off the *telly.* [*noncount*] I just want to relax and watch the/some *telly.*
on (the) telly : being shown by television • What's *on telly* tonight?

tem·blor /ˈtɛmblɚ, *Brit* tɛmˈblɔː/ *noun, pl* **-blors** [*count*] *chiefly US, somewhat formal* : EARTHQUAKE • a minor *temblor*

te·mer·i·ty /təˈmerəti/ *noun* [*noncount*] *formal* : the quality of being confident and unafraid of danger or punishment especially in a way that seems rude or foolish • No one has the *temerity* [=*audacity*] to disagree with her. • He was punished for his *temerity.*

¹temp /ˈtɛmp/ *noun, pl* **temps** [*count*]
1 *chiefly US, informal* : TEMPERATURE • What's the *temp* outside? • Is he ***running a temp***? = Does he ***have a temp***?
2 : someone who works at a place for a limited and usually short period of time : a temporary worker • We had to hire a *temp* to fill in for her.

²temp *verb* **temps; temped; temp·ing** [*no obj*] : to work as a temporary worker • I *temped* [=worked as a temp] in a doctor's office for a couple of months.

tem·peh /ˈtɛmˌpeɪ/ *noun* [*noncount*] : an Asian food that is made from fermented soybeans

¹tem·per /ˈtɛmpɚ/ *noun, pl* **-pers**
1 a [*count*] : the tendency of someone to become angry • She has a bad/hot/quick/terrible/violent *temper.* • That boy has quite a *temper.* • He needs to learn to ***control his temper***. • ***Tempers flared*** [=people became angry] and a fight broke out. • After months of delays, ***tempers began to fray***. [=people began to get angry] — see also SHORT TEMPER **b** : a state of being angry [*noncount*] She hit him in a fit of *temper.* [*singular*] He slammed the door and left ***in a temper***.
2 [*count*] : calmness of mind : COMPOSURE • I ***lost my temper*** [=got angry] (with him) and yelled at him. • It's often difficult for parents not to *lose their tempers.* • He was upset but ***kept his temper***. [=remained calm; did not become angry, begin shouting, etc.]

T

3 [*singular*] **a :** the way that a person is feeling at a particular time : MOOD • He is ***in a pleasant/foul temper.*** **b :** the usual attitude, mood, or behavior of a person or animal • a dog with a good/bad *temper* [=*temperament, disposition*] • She has an even *temper.* [=she does not easily become angry, upset, etc.] — see also TEMPERED

4 [*noncount*] *formal* **:** the ideas, attitudes, etc., that a group of people have especially during a particular period of time • Her novels capture the ***temper of the times.***

[2]**temper** *verb* **-pers; -pered; -per·ing** [+ *obj*]

1 *formal* **:** to make (something) less severe or extreme • Higher interest rates have *tempered* [=*lessened*] the demand for new houses. — often + *with* or *by* • He *tempered* his criticism *with* a few words of encouragement. = He *tempered* his criticism *by* adding a few words of encouragement. — often used as *(be) tempered* • He believes in justice *tempered with* mercy.

2 *technical* **:** to cause (something, such as steel or glass) to become hard or strong by heating it and cooling it • The steel/glass must be properly *tempered.* — see also TEMPERED

tem·pera /ˈtɛmpərə/ *noun* [*noncount*] **:** a kind of paint in which the color is mixed with water and usually egg • He paints in/with *tempera.*

tem·per·a·ment /ˈtɛmprəmənt/ *noun, pl* **-ments :** the usual attitude, mood, or behavior of a person or animal [*count*] She has a nervous *temperament.* [=she is a nervous person] • The dogs have excellent *temperaments.* [=*dispositions, tempers*] • people with artistic/poetic *temperaments* [*noncount*] The two women were opposite in *temperament.*

tem·per·a·men·tal /ˌtɛmprəˈmɛntl/ *adj*

1 [*more* ~; *most* ~] **a :** likely to become upset or angry • a *temperamental* child • The actor is known for being *temperamental.* **b :** unpredictable in behavior or performance • a *temperamental* horse • The old computer is *temperamental.*

2 : of or relating to someone's usual attitude, mood, or behavior • They divorced due to *temperamental* differences.

– tem·per·a·men·tal·ly *adv* • *Temperamentally,* he's not suited for the job. • The twins are *temperamentally* different.

tem·per·ance /ˈtɛmprəns/ *noun* [*noncount*]

1 *old-fashioned* **:** the practice of drinking little or no alcohol • The minister preached about *temperance.*

2 *formal* **:** the practice of always controlling your actions, thoughts, or feelings so that you do not eat or drink too much, become too angry, etc. • His lifestyle was marked by *temperance.* [=*moderation*]

tem·per·ate /ˈtɛmprət/ *adj*

1 : having temperatures that are not too hot or too cold • *temperate* climates/forests/regions/zones

2 *formal* **:** emotionally calm and controlled • They had a *temperate* discussion. • He is a *temperate* man.

3 *old-fashioned* **:** avoiding behavior that goes beyond what is normal, healthy, or acceptable • a *temperate* [=*moderate*] drinker — opposite INTEMPERATE

tem·per·a·ture /ˈtɛmprəˌʧuɚ/ *noun, pl* **-tures**

1 : a measurement that indicates how hot or cold something is **:** a measurement in degrees showing the heat of something (such as air or water) [*count*] The water *temperature* has risen (by) two degrees. [=the water has become two degrees warmer] • Water boils at a *temperature* of 212°F. • The samples are kept/maintained at a constant *temperature.* • The weatherman predicted unusually low/high *temperatures* for the area. • There was a sudden fall/drop in *temperature.* [=it got colder] • a change in *temperature* = a *temperature* change [*noncount*] Keep the wine at ***room temperature.*** [=the temperature of a room that is comfortable]

2 a [*singular*] **:** a measurement of the heat in a person's body • the normal body *temperature* of 98.6°F • Did you ***take his temperature?*** [=did you use a thermometer to find out if he had a fever?] **b** [*count*] **:** a level of heat that is above what is normal for the human body : FEVER • I ***have a temperature.*** = I am ***running a temperature.***

3 [*count*] *formal* **:** the level of anger, excitement, etc., in a situation • The governor's speech ***raised/lowered the*** political ***temperature.*** [=it made people more/less angry about the political situation] • The love affair *raised the temperature* of the story. [=it made the story more exciting]

tem·pered /ˈtɛmpəd/ *adj, always used before a noun* **:** brought to the desired hardness or strength by heating and cooling • *tempered* steel/glass — see also BAD-TEMPERED, GOOD-TEMPERED, ILL-TEMPERED, QUICK-TEMPERED, SHORT-TEMPERED

tem·pest /ˈtɛmpəst/ *noun, pl* **-pests** [*count*] *literary* **:** a violent storm — often used figuratively • A *tempest* is brewing over the new tax laws. • a *tempest* of controversy/emotions

a tempest in a teapot *US* **:** a situation in which people are upset or angry about something that is not very important • The whole problem/controversy turned out to be *a tempest in a teapot.* [=(*Brit*) *a storm in a teacup*]

tem·pes·tu·ous /tɛmˈpɛsʧəwəs/ *adj* [*more* ~; *most* ~]

1 *literary* **:** affected by a tempest : STORMY • a *tempestuous* sea • *tempestuous* weather

2 : full of strong emotions (such as anger or excitement) : STORMY • a *tempestuous* romance/relationship/debate

tem·plate /ˈtɛmplət/ *noun, pl* **-plates** [*count*]

1 : a shape or pattern that is cut out of a hard material (such as metal or plastic) and used to make the same shape and pattern in other pieces of material

2 *computers* **:** a computer document that has the basic format of something (such as a business letter, chart, graph, etc.) and that can be used many different times • The software includes *templates* for common marketing documents like pamphlets and flyers.

3 : something that is used as an example of how to do, make, or achieve something — often + *for* • The bridge's design became a *template for* other bridges. • Her career was my *template for* success in the publishing industry. [=I followed her example of how to succeed in the publishing industry]

[1]**tem·ple** /ˈtɛmpəl/ *noun, pl* **tem·ples**

1 a [*count*] **:** a building for worship • Buddhist/Hindu/Jewish/Mormon *temples* • ancient Greek *temples* — compare CHURCH, MOSQUE, SYNAGOGUE **b** [*noncount*] *chiefly US* **:** religious services held in a temple • Friday evenings we ***go to temple.*** [=attend services] • He is ***at temple.***

2 [*count*] **:** a meeting place for the members of a local group that is part of a larger organization • a Masonic *temple*

– compare [2]TEMPLE

[2]**temple** *noun, pl* **temples** [*count*] **:** the small, flat area on each side of your forehead — see picture at FACE — compare [1]TEMPLE

tem·po /ˈtɛmpoʊ/ *noun*

1 *pl* ***tem·pos*** *also* ***tem·pi*** /ˈtɛmpi/ **:** the speed at which a musical piece is played or sung [*count*] The song has a slow/fast/upbeat *tempo.* [*noncount*] The composition has many changes of *tempo.* — compare RHYTHM; see also UP-TEMPO

2 *pl* ***tempos*** **:** the speed at which something moves or happens : PACE [*count*] We walked at a fast *tempo.* • The *tempo* of the game slowed down. [*noncount*] The dance starts out fast and then switches *tempo.*

[1]**tem·po·ral** /ˈtɛmpərəl/ *adj*

1 *formal* **:** of or relating to life on the earth and not spiritual life • the *temporal* [=*secular*] and spiritual worlds

2 *technical* **:** of or relating to time • They are studying the spatial and *temporal* patterns of weather systems.

– compare [2]TEMPORAL

[2]**temporal** *adj, always used before a noun* **:** located near the temples at the sides of the forehead • the *temporal* bone/lobe — compare [1]TEMPORAL

tem·po·rary /ˈtɛmpəˌreri/ *adj*

1 : continuing for a limited amount of time : not permanent • The drug will give you *temporary* relief from the pain. • a *temporary* job • The delay is only *temporary.*

2 : intended to be used for a limited amount of time • *temporary* workers • The settlers built *temporary* shelters. • a *temporary* solution

– tem·po·rari·ly /ˌtɛmpəˈrerəli/ *adv* • We lost power *temporarily.* • The store is *temporarily* closed for renovations.

tem·po·rize *also Brit* **tem·po·rise** /ˈtɛmpəˌraɪz/ *verb* **-rizes; -rized; -riz·ing** [*no obj*] *formal* **:** to avoid making a decision or giving a definite answer in order to have more time • Pressured by voters on both sides of the issue, the congressmen *temporized.*

tempt /ˈtɛmpt/ *verb* **tempts; tempt·ed; tempt·ing** [+ *obj*] **:** to cause (someone) to do or want to do something even though it may be wrong, bad, or unwise • The smell of the pie *tempted* me, but I resisted. [=I wanted some pie but did not eat any] • He *tempted* [=*enticed*] me with the offer of more money. — often + *into* • The smell of the pie *tempted* me *into* having a piece. [=it caused me to eat a piece of pie] • The saleswoman tried to *tempt us into* buying a more expensive model. — often followed by *to* + *verb* • The saleswoman tried to *tempt* us *to buy* a more expensive model. — often

T

used as *(be) tempted* ▪ "Would you like some more pie?" "I'm *tempted*, but no thank you." ▪ Students may *be tempted to cheat* on the test. [=they may consider cheating on the test] ▪ I *was* sorely *tempted to say* [=I very much wanted to say] something rude to her, but I didn't. ▪ She *was tempted to quit* and find a new job. ▪ *I'm tempted* [=I'm inclined] *to say* yes, but I'm not completely sure.

tempt fate : to do something that is very risky or dangerous ▪ He felt it would be *tempting fate* if he invested all his money in one company. ▪ Race car drivers *tempt fate* every time they race.

temp·ta·tion /tɛmpˈteɪʃən/ *noun, pl* **-tions**
1 : a strong urge or desire to have or do something [*count*] — often followed by *to + verb* ▪ I resisted the *temptation to buy* the shoes. ▪ He could not resist the *temptation to show off* his new car. ▪ Don't give in to the *temptation to snack* between meals. ▪ There is always a/the *temptation to procrastinate*. [*noncount*] She gave in to *temptation*. = She succumbed to *temptation*.
2 [*count*] : something that causes a strong urge or desire to have or do something and especially something that is bad, wrong, or unwise ▪ Money/power is always a *temptation*. ▪ The dessert menu has a lot of delicious *temptations*. ▪ the *temptations* of the city

tempt·ing /ˈtɛmptɪŋ/ *adj* [*more* ~; *most* ~] : causing an urge or desire to have or do something ▪ The desserts look very *tempting*. ▪ It is *tempting* to think of him as the next American president. ▪ It was a *tempting* [=*enticing*] offer.
– tempt·ing·ly *adv* ▪ It is *temptingly* easy to cheat on taxes. ▪ The desserts were *temptingly* [=*enticingly*] displayed.

tempt·ress /ˈtɛmptrəs/ *noun, pl* **-ress·es** [*count*] : a woman who makes a man want to have sex with her : a very attractive woman ▪ a seductive *temptress*

tem·pu·ra /tɛmˈpurə/ *noun* [*noncount*] : a Japanese dish that is made of seafood or vegetables that are covered in batter and fried

ten /ˈtɛn/ *noun, pl* **tens**
1 [*count*] : the number 10
2 [*count*] : the tenth in a set or series ▪ the *ten* of spades ▪ page *ten*
3 [*noncount*] : ten o'clock ▪ "What time is it" "It's *ten*."
4 [*count*] **a** *US* : a ten-dollar bill ▪ The total cost was $7.83 and she gave him a *ten*. ▪ Do you have any fives or *tens*? **b** *Brit* : a ten-pound note
5 [*singular*] **a** : something that is the best ▪ The food at the restaurant is a (perfect) *ten*. **b** : a very attractive person ▪ She's a *ten*.

ten a penny *Brit, informal* : very common ▪ Thrillers are *ten a penny* [=*(US) a dime a dozen*] these days.

ten out of ten — used to say that something was done very well ▪ I'll give them *ten out of ten* for creativity.

ten to one *informal* : very likely ▪ *Ten to one* they'll lose. [=I think they'll almost certainly lose]

– ten *adj* ▪ *ten* cars/guests/choices **– ten** *pronoun* ▪ *Ten* (of them) passed the test.

ten·a·ble /ˈtɛnəbəl/ *adj* [*more* ~; *most* ~] *formal* : capable of being defended against attack or criticism ▪ The theory is no longer *tenable*. [=*defensible*] ▪ a *tenable* argument

te·na·cious /təˈneɪʃəs/ *adj* [*more* ~; *most* ~]
1 a : not easily stopped or pulled apart : firm or strong ▪ The company has a *tenacious* hold on the market. ▪ a *tenacious* grip **b** : continuing for a long time ▪ *tenacious* myths/traditions ▪ a *tenacious* effort/battle
2 : very determined to do something ▪ He is a *tenacious* [=*persistent*] negotiator/competitor. ▪ She is quite *tenacious*.
– te·na·cious·ly *adv* ▪ She clung *tenaciously* to her beliefs. ▪ He fought *tenaciously*. **– te·nac·i·ty** /təˈnæsəti/ *noun* [*noncount*] ▪ I am impressed by their *tenacity*. ▪ She fought with great *tenacity*.

ten·an·cy /ˈtɛnənsi/ *noun, pl* **-cies** *formal*
1 a [*noncount*] : the right to use another person's property (such as land, a house, etc.) for a short period of time ▪ He was granted *tenancy* of the farm. **b** [*count*] : the amount of time during which you are allowed to use another person's property ▪ a 12-month *tenancy* ▪ During his *tenancy*, he tried to make as many improvements as he could.
2 [*noncount*] : the state or fact of owning property (such as land, a house, etc.) ▪ They had joint *tenancy* of the building. [=they owned the building together/jointly]

ten·ant /ˈtɛnənt/ *noun, pl* **-ants** [*count*] : a person, business, group, etc., that pays to use another person's property : someone who rents or leases a house, apartment, etc., from a landlord ▪ A *tenant* is now leasing the apartment.

tenant farmer *noun, pl* ~ **-mers** [*count*] : a farmer who raises crops on land that is rented from someone else

tend /ˈtɛnd/ *verb* **tends; tend·ed; tend·ing**
1 [*no obj*] **a** — used to describe what often happens or what someone often does or is likely to do; followed by *to + verb* ▪ He *tends to slouch*. ▪ I have to be careful about what I eat because I *tend to gain* weight easily. ▪ People in my family *tend to be* tall. [=a lot of people in my family are tall] ▪ The store *tends to get* busy [=the store is often/usually busy] on weekends. ▪ I *tend* not *to trust* politicians. [=I often/usually don't trust politicians] **b** — used to describe a quality that someone or something often has or is likely to have; + *toward* or *towards* ▪ He *tends towards* perfectionism. [=he tends to be a perfectionist] ▪ Her decorating style *tends toward* the informal. [=tends to be informal]
2 : to give your attention to and take care of (something or someone) [+ *obj*] Please *tend* [=*mind*] the store while I'm away. ▪ She *tends* her garden daily. ▪ well-*tended* gardens ▪ He *tended* his ailing mother. [*no obj*] — + *to* ▪ I have to *tend to* (the) business. ▪ The nurse *tended to* their wounds.

tend bar see [1]BAR

ten·den·cy /ˈtɛndənsi/ *noun, pl* **-cies** [*count*]
1 : a quality that makes something likely to happen or that makes someone likely to think or behave in a particular way ▪ The door has a *tendency* to get stuck. [=the door often gets stuck] ▪ She has a *tendency* to overreact. = She has a *tendency* toward/towards overreacting. [=she tends to overreact; she often overreacts] ▪ She displayed criminal *tendencies* [=she behaved in ways that suggested she was going to become a criminal] even when she was very young.
2 : a way of behaving, proceeding, etc., that is developing and becoming more common ▪ There is a growing *tendency* among young people to continue living with their parents after college. [=more and more young people are continuing to live with their parents after college] ▪ The economy has shown a general *tendency* toward inflation.

ten·den·tious /tɛnˈdɛnʃəs/ *adj* [*more* ~; *most* ~] *formal* + *disapproving* : strongly favoring a particular point of view in a way that may cause argument : expressing a strong opinion ▪ He made some extremely *tendentious* remarks.
– ten·den·tious·ly *adv* **– ten·den·tious·ness** *noun* [*noncount*]

[1]**ten·der** /ˈtɛndɚ/ *adj* **-der·er; -est** [*or more* ~; *most* ~]
1 : very loving and gentle : showing affection and love for someone or something ▪ He gave her a *tender* look. ▪ She was *tender* and loving with her new child. ▪ *tender* words ▪ a *tender* love song
2 *of food* : easy to chew or bite : not tough ▪ a *tender*, juicy steak ▪ Cook the pasta until it is just *tender*.
3 : painful when touched : SORE ▪ Her wrist was swollen and *tender*.
4 : easily damaged : delicate and weak ▪ *tender* young plants — sometimes used figuratively ▪ He has a *tender* [=*sensitive*] ego. ▪ *tender* pride

tender loving care : extra attention to make someone or something look or feel better ▪ You need a little *tender loving care*. [=*TLC*] ▪ an antique chair that needs some *tender loving care*

tender (young) age : a very young age ▪ She left home at the *tender young age* of 14. ▪ He was playing the piano at a *tender age*.

– ten·der·ly *adv* [*more* ~; *most* ~] ▪ He kissed her *tenderly*. ▪ She will be *tenderly* cared for. **– ten·der·ness** *noun* [*noncount*]

[2]**tender** *verb* **-ders; -dered; -der·ing**
1 [+ *obj*] *formal* : to give or offer (something, such as a payment or a letter) ▪ The defendant must *tender* full payment. ▪ I *tendered* my resignation today.
2 [*no obj*] *Brit* : to offer to do work or to provide goods for a particular price : to make a bid for something — + *for* ▪ We *tendered for* [=*(US) bid for*] the job/contract.

[3]**tender** *noun, pl* **-ders** [*count*] *US, informal* : a small piece of chicken meat that is usually cooked by being breaded and fried ▪ Can I have an order of chicken *tenders*? — compare [4]TENDER

[4]**tender** *noun, pl* **-ders** [*count*]
1 : a ship that carries passengers or cargo between the shore and a larger ship ▪ a submarine *tender*
2 : a car that is attached to a train and that carries fuel and water ▪ a coal *tender*
– compare [3]TENDER; see also LEGAL TENDER

ten·der·foot /ˈtɛndɚˌfʊt/ *noun, pl* **-feet** /-ˌfiːt/ *also* **-foots** /-ˌfʊts/ [*count*] *US, informal*
1 : someone who has just started doing something **:** BEGINNER ▪ a political *tenderfoot*
2 : a person who is not used to living in rough conditions or outdoors

ten·der–heart·ed /ˈtɛndɚˌhɑɚtəd/ *adj* [*more* ~; *most* ~] **:** very gentle and kind **:** showing love, kindness, or pity ▪ She is a *tender-hearted* [=*compassionate*] mother. ▪ a *tender-hearted* pet owner

ten·der·ize *also Brit* **ten·der·ise** /ˈtɛndəˌraɪz/ *verb* **-iz·es; -ized; -iz·ing** [+ *obj*] **:** to make (meat) softer before cooking it so that it is easier to cut and eat ▪ The marinade helps to *tenderize* the meat.
– ten·der·i·za·tion *also Brit* **ten·der·i·sa·tion** /ˌtɛndərəˈzeɪʃən, *Brit* ˌtɛndəˌraɪˈzeɪʃən/ *noun* [*noncount*] **– ten·der·iz·er** *also Brit* **ten·der·is·er** /ˈtɛndəˌraɪzɚ/ *noun, pl* **-ers** [*count, noncount*]

ten·der·loin /ˈtɛdɚˌlɔɪn/ *noun, pl* **-loins** [*count, noncount*] **:** a piece of very tender meat from the back of a cow or pig ▪ beef/pork *tenderloin*

tender offer *noun, pl* ~ **-fers** [*count*] *business* **:** an offer to buy a certain number of stock shares of a company for a set price in order to gain control of the company

ten·di·ni·tis *also* **ten·do·ni·tis** /ˌtɛndəˈnaɪtəs/ *noun* [*noncount*] *medical* **:** a painful condition in which a tendon in your arm, leg, etc., becomes inflamed ▪ She was diagnosed with *tendinitis* of the elbow. ▪ I have *tendinitis* in my knee.

ten·don /ˈtɛndən/ *noun, pl* **-dons** [*count*] **:** a tough piece of tissue in your body that connects a muscle to a bone — compare LIGAMENT

ten·dril /ˈtɛndrəl/ *noun, pl* **-drils** [*count*]
1 : the thin stem of a climbing plant that attaches to walls, fences, etc.
2 : something that is thin and curly ▪ A few *tendrils* of hair framed her face. ▪ *tendrils* of smoke

ten·e·ment /ˈtɛnəmənt/ *noun, pl* **-ments** [*count*] **:** a large building that has apartments or rooms for rent and that is usually in a poorer part of a city ▪ inner-city *tenements* ▪ a *tenement* building/apartment — called also *tenement house*

te·net /ˈtɛnət/ *noun, pl* **-nets** [*count*] *formal* **:** a belief or idea that is very important to a group ▪ the central *tenets* of a religion ▪ one of the basic *tenets* of the fashion industry

ten·fold /ˈtɛnˌfoʊld/ *adj* **:** ten times as much or as many ▪ a *tenfold* increase in sales
– ten·fold /ˈtɛnˈfoʊld/ *adv* ▪ Online sales increased *tenfold*.

ten–gallon hat *noun, pl* ~ **hats** [*count*] *US* **:** COWBOY HAT

Tenn. *abbr* Tennessee

ten·ner /ˈtɛnɚ/ *noun, pl* **-ners** [*count*] *Brit, informal* **:** a ten-pound note

ten·nies /ˈtɛniz/ *noun* [*plural*] *US, informal* **:** TENNIS SHOES ▪ a pair of *tennies*

ten·nis /ˈtɛnəs/ *noun* [*noncount*] **:** a game that is played by two people or two pairs of people on a special court (called a tennis court) where they hit a small ball back and forth over a net using rackets ▪ a game of *tennis* = a *tennis* game ▪ a *tennis* racket/ball — see pictures at BALL, RACKET; see also LAWN TENNIS, TABLE TENNIS

tennis court *noun, pl* ~ **courts** [*count*] **:** a large rectangular area that you play tennis on

tennis elbow *noun* [*noncount*] **:** a condition in which you have pain on the outer side of your elbow that is caused by twisting or straining your lower arm

tennis shoe *noun, pl* ~ **shoes** [*count*] **:** a low shoe that is worn while playing sports (such as tennis) or exercising **:** SNEAKER

T

ten·on /ˈtɛnən/ *noun, pl* **-ons** [*count*] *technical* **:** an end of a piece of wood that is cut into a special shape to fit into a hole (called a mortise) in another piece of wood and form a strong joint

[1]**ten·or** /ˈtɛnɚ/ *noun, pl* **-ors**
1 [*count*] **:** the highest adult male singing voice ▪ He has a high, lilting *tenor*.; *also* **:** a singer who has such a voice ▪ She asked the *tenors* to sing the line again. — compare ALTO, BASS, SOPRANO
2 [*singular*] **:** the general or basic quality or meaning of something ▪ I was surprised by the angry *tenor* [=*tone*] of her letter. ▪ The *tenor* of his remarks is clear.

[2]**tenor** *adj, used before a noun* **:** having a range that is lower than an alto and higher than a baritone ▪ Verdi wrote some difficult *tenor* parts. ▪ She plays the *tenor* sax/saxophone.

ten·pin /ˈtɛnˌpɪn/ *noun, pl* **-pins**
1 [*count*] **:** one of the large bottle-shaped pieces that is knocked down with a ball in the game of tenpin bowling
2 ***tenpins*** [*plural*] *US* **:** TENPIN BOWLING ▪ a game of *tenpins*

tenpin bowling *noun* [*noncount*] **:** a game in which players try to knock down 10 pins by rolling a large ball towards them

[1]**tense** /ˈtɛns/ *adj* **tens·er; -est**
1 : nervous and not able to relax ▪ She was feeling pretty *tense*. ▪ Why are you so *tense*?
2 : showing or causing nervousness ▪ a *tense* situation ▪ We sat quietly for a few *tense* moments. ▪ It was a *tense* meeting. ▪ a *tense* thriller
3 : not relaxed but hard and tight ▪ My calf muscles are really *tense*. ▪ *tense* muscles
– tense·ly *adv* ▪ She looked at him *tensely*. ▪ We sat *tensely*.
– tense·ness *noun* [*noncount*]

[2]**tense** *verb* **tens·es; tensed; tens·ing**
1 : to make (a muscle) hard and tight [+ *obj*] She *tensed* her shoulders. [*no obj*] Her shoulders *tensed* (up).
2 [*no obj*] **:** to become nervous or tense ▪ She *tensed* as he walked toward her. ▪ He ***tensed up*** and missed the putt.
– tensed *adj* [*more* ~; *most* ~] ▪ I was feeling *tensed*. [=*tense*] — often + *up* ▪ feeling *tensed up*

[3]**tense** *noun, pl* **tenses** *grammar* **:** a form of a verb that is used to show when an action happened [*count*] The sentence will read better if you change the *tense* of the verb. [*noncount*] You should avoid changing *tense* in the middle of a paragraph. — see also FUTURE TENSE, PAST TENSE, PERFECT TENSE, PRESENT TENSE

ten·sile /ˈtɛnsəl, *Brit* ˈtɛnˌsajəl/ *adj, technical* **:** relating to the amount that something (such as a wire) can stretch or be stretched without breaking ▪ the *tensile* strength of steel cable

ten·sion /ˈtɛnʃən/ *noun, pl* **-sions**
1 [*noncount*] **a :** a feeling of nervousness that makes you unable to relax ▪ You can see she is just filled with *tension* about her job. **b :** a feeling of nervousness, excitement, or fear that is created in a movie, book, etc. ▪ The dramatic *tension* was very satisfying. ▪ The author resolves the *tension* too soon.
2 : a state in which people, groups, countries, etc., disagree with and feel anger toward each other [*count*] Political *tensions* in the region make it unstable. [*noncount*] Do you sense the *tension* between those two? ▪ There was a lot of *tension* at the meeting. ▪ The book describes the *tension*-filled days before the war.
3 : a difficult situation caused by the opposite needs or effects of two different ideas, desires, etc. [*count*] He felt a *tension* between duty and love. [*noncount*] There will always be some *tension* between the desire to reduce risk and the desire to make as much money as possible.
4 [*noncount*] **:** the degree to which something is stretched **:** the amount that something is stretched ▪ I don't like the *tension* on this tennis racket. ▪ muscle *tension* [=*tightness*] ▪ She has a lot of *tension* in her shoulders.
– see also HIGH-TENSION, SURFACE TENSION

tent /ˈtɛnt/ *noun, pl* **tents** [*count*] **:** a portable shelter that is used outdoors, is made of cloth (such as canvas or nylon), and is held up with poles and ropes ▪ We will ***pitch the tent*** [=put our tent up, set our tent up] here. — see picture at CAMPING; see also OXYGEN TENT
– tent·like /ˈtɛntˌlaɪk/ *adj* [*more* ~; *most* ~] ▪ a *tentlike* structure

ten·ta·cle /ˈtɛntɪkəl/ *noun, pl* **-ta·cles**
1 [*count*] **:** one of the long, flexible arms of an animal (such as an octopus) that are used for grabbing things and moving
2 ***tentacles*** [*plural*] *often disapproving* **:** power or influence that reaches into many areas ▪ The corporation's *tentacles* are felt in every sector of the industry. ▪ the *tentacles* of organized crime

ten·ta·tive /ˈtɛntətɪv/ *adj* [*more* ~; *most* ~]
1 : not done with confidence **:** uncertain and hesitant ▪ a *tentative* smile ▪ the baby's first *tentative* steps
2 : not definite **:** still able to be changed ▪ We have *tentative* plans for the weekend. ▪ *tentative* approval
– ten·ta·tive·ly *adv* ▪ We have *tentatively* made plans for the weekend. ▪ The meeting is *tentatively* scheduled for Friday.
– ten·ta·tive·ness *noun* [*noncount*]

tent·ed /ˈtɛntəd/ *adj* [*more* ~; *most* ~]
1 : made up of or filled with tents ▪ a *tented* village

2 : having a peak like a tent : shaped like the inside of a tent • a high *tented* ceiling/room

ten·ter·hooks /ˈtɛntɚˌhʊks/ *noun*

on tenterhooks : waiting nervously for something to happen : in a state of nervousness or excitement caused by wondering what will happen • She keeps her readers *on tenterhooks* throughout the book. • I've been *on tenterhooks* since I applied for the job.

[1]**tenth** /ˈtɛnθ/ *noun, pl* **tenths**

1 [*singular*] : the number 10 in a series • the *tenth* of February • He was *tenth* in line.

2 [*count*] : one of 10 equal parts of something • He traded stocks for one *tenth* their face value. • I only paid a *tenth* of what you did for that jacket.

[2]**tenth** *adj* : occupying the number ten position in a series • This year is our *tenth* wedding anniversary. • the *tenth* grade

– **tenth** *adv* • the world's *tenth* largest country

ten·u·ous /ˈtɛnjəwəs/ *adj* [*more ~; most ~*]

1 : not certain, definite, or strong : flimsy, weak, or uncertain • He has a *tenuous* grasp/grip/hold on reality. • a *tenuous* hypothesis/relationship • The local theater has had a *tenuous* existence in recent years. • He could demonstrate only a *tenuous* claim to ownership. • The connection between his absence and the robbery is *tenuous* [=*shaky*] at best.

2 *literary* : very thin • the silkworm's *tenuous* threads

– **ten·u·ous·ly** *adv* • He was *tenuously* linked to the crime.

ten·ure /ˈtɛnjɚ/ *noun, pl* **-ures**

1 [*count*] : the amount of time that a person holds a job, office, or title • During his *tenure* as head coach, the team won the championship twice. • her 12-year *tenure* with the company • His *tenure* in office will end with the next election.

2 [*noncount*] : the right to keep a job (especially the job of being a professor at a college or university) for as long as you want to have it • After seven years I was finally granted *tenure*. • He hopes to get *tenure* next year.

3 [*noncount*] *law* : the right to use property • The defendant did not have *tenure* on the land. • land *tenure* in Anglo-Saxon Britain

– **ten·ured** /ˈtɛnjɚd/ *adj, US* • She became a *tenured* professor. • *tenured* faculty members

tenure–track *adj, US* : relating to or having a teaching job that may lead to tenure (sense 2) • This is a *tenure-track* position. • *tenure-track* faculty

te·pee *or* **tee·pee** *also* **ti·pi** /ˈtiːpi/ *noun, pl* **-pees** *or* **-pis** [*count*] : a tent that is shaped like a cone and that was used in the past by some Native Americans as a house

tepee

wigwam

tep·id /ˈtɛpəd/ *adj* [*more ~; most ~*]

1 : not hot and not cold : WARM • a *tepid* [=*lukewarm*] bath

2 : not energetic or excited • He gave a *tepid* performance. • My suggestion was given a *tepid* response.

te·qui·la /təˈkiːlə/ *noun, pl* **-las** [*count, noncount*] : a strong, clear alcoholic drink from Mexico

ter·i·ya·ki /ˌteriˈjɑːki/ *noun* [*noncount*]

1 : a sauce used in some Asian cooking • Marinate the meat in *teriyaki* (sauce).

2 : a dish that is flavored with teriyaki • chicken *teriyaki* = *teriyaki* chicken

[1]**term** /ˈtɚm/ *noun, pl* **terms**

1 a [*count*] : a word or phrase that has an exact meaning • "I had the feeling that I had been there before." "The *term* for that is 'déjà vu.'" • That's an outdated *term* that no one uses anymore. • scientific/technical *terms* **b terms** [*plural*] : the particular kinds of words used to describe someone or something • He spoke about them in glowing *terms*. • The law had been understood in broad *terms*. • in economic *terms* • He expressed his disapproval ***in no uncertain terms***. [=in very strong and clear language]

2 [*count*] **a** : the length of time during which a person has an official or political office • The governor will run for a second *term*. • He is currently serving his third *term* in the U.S. Senate. • She made many changes during her ***term of/in office***. [=during the time when she was in office] • He is in favor of ***term limits*** for members of Congress. [=he believes that members of Congress should only be allowed to serve for a specified number of terms] **b** : the length of time during which someone is in a prison, jail, etc. • He was sentenced to a ten-year *term* in the state penitentiary. • a long jail/prison *term* • a *term* of imprisonment **c** : the length of time during which something (such as a contract) continues • The *term* of the contract is 60 months. — see also LONG TERM, MEDIUM-TERM, SHORT TERM

3 [*count*] : one of the parts of the school year • His grades have improved since last *term*. • English 122 is not offered this *term*.

4 ***terms*** [*plural*] : the conditions or rules that limit something (such as an agreement or a contract) : the things that must be agreed upon in order for something to happen or continue • They would not agree to our *terms*. • She objected to the *terms* of the contract. • Early payment is not permitted under the *terms* of our agreement.

5 ***terms*** [*plural*] — used to describe the kind of relationship that people have with each other • He was ***on good terms*** with his ex-wife. [=he and his ex-wife were friendly with each other] • He left the team ***on bad terms***. • They are no longer ***on speaking terms***. [=they are no longer speaking to each other] • (*Brit*) He is on ***first-name terms*** with his staff.

6 [*noncount*] *medical* : the time at which a pregnancy of normal length ends • She carried the baby ***to term***. = She carried the baby ***full term***. [=to the natural end of the pregnancy]

come to terms **1** : to reach an agreement • The two sides have not been able to *come to terms*. — often + *with* • The company has *come to terms with* the union. **2** : to learn how to accept or live with something that is difficult or painful — + *with* • It took him a long time to *come to terms with* the end of his marriage. • She has found it hard to *come to terms with* the demands of her job.

contradiction in terms see CONTRADICTION

in terms of — used to indicate the specific thing that is being described, thought of, etc. • The car is great *in terms of* gas mileage [=the car's gas mileage is great], but it's not very comfortable. • He thinks of everything *in terms of* money. [=his judgments/opinions about everything are based on thoughts about money]

on your (own) terms : according to your own wishes : in your own way • She wants to succeed *on her own terms*. • If I agree to help, it will only be *on my terms*.

term of address see [2]ADDRESS

term of endearment see ENDEARMENT

terms of reference *Brit* : a description of what must be dealt with and considered when something is being done, studied, etc. • The *terms of reference* for the committee are narrow and specific.

[2]**term** *verb* **terms; termed; term·ing** [+ *obj*] : to give a particular name or description to (something) : to call (something) by a particular name or to describe (something) in a particular way • They *termed* the structure a "double helix." • The project was *termed* a success.

ter·mi·na·ble /ˈtɚmənəbəl/ *adj* [*more ~; most ~*] *formal* : able to be ended • His employment was *terminable* at the will of his employer. • The contract will be *terminable* by either party.

[1]**ter·mi·nal** /ˈtɚmənl/ *adj*

1 a : causing death eventually : leading finally to death • She was diagnosed with *terminal* cancer. • a *terminal* [=*fatal*] illness/disease **b** : having an illness that cannot be cured and that will soon lead to death • a *terminal* patient **c** : of or relating to patients who have a terminal illness • *terminal* care

2 *informal* : very bad or severe • I was suffering from *terminal* boredom. • another person with *terminal* stupidity

3 : at the end : forming or coming at the end of something • branches that end in a *terminal* bud • We're on the *terminal* [=*final*] leg of our trip. • The *terminal* [=*last*] stop for this line is Boston.

in terminal decline *Brit* : getting worse without any chance to improve • The business is *in terminal decline*.

– **ter·mi·nal·ly** *adv* • He is ***terminally ill***. [=he has a disease that cannot be cured and will cause his death]

[2]**terminal** *noun, pl* **-nals** [*count*]

1 a : a building where buses or trains regularly stop so that passengers can get on and off : STATION • I will meet you outside the bus *terminal*. **b** : a building at an airport where people get on and off airplanes • Flight 1584 is now departing from Gate 6 in *Terminal* A. • You are not allowed in the *terminal* without a ticket.

T

2 : a computer or a combination of a keyboard and a video display that is connected to a system and used for entering or receiving data ▪ Ten *terminals* are connected to this server.
3 : a part on a piece of electrical equipment (such as a car battery) where you make an electrical connection ▪ You will need to clean the corrosion off the battery *terminals*.

ter·mi·nate /ˈtəməˌneɪt/ *verb* **-nates; -nat·ed; -nat·ing** *formal*
1 [*no obj*] **:** to end in a particular way or at a particular place ▪ The branches of that tree *terminate* in flower clusters. ▪ The rail line *terminates* in Boston.
2 [+ *obj*] **:** to cause (something) to end ▪ *terminate* a pregnancy ▪ You have to *terminate* the program before the computer will shut down properly. ▪ His contract was *terminated* last month. ▪ They *terminated* their agreement.
3 [+ *obj*] *US* **:** to take a job away from (someone) **:** FIRE ▪ He was *terminated* last month. ▪ Plans are being made to *terminate* unproductive employees.

ter·mi·na·tion /ˌtəməˈneɪʃən/ *noun, pl* **-tions** *formal*
1 : an act of ending something [*noncount*] The law protects against unfair contract *termination*. ▪ the *termination* of a lease [*count*] an early *termination* of the contract
2 *US* **:** the act of making a person leave a job **:** the act of firing or dismissing someone [*count*] The company noted over 300 *terminations* last quarter. [*noncount*] Are there plans for the *termination* of unproductive employees?
3 [*count, noncount*] **:** an operation to end a pregnancy before the mother would have given birth **:** ABORTION

termini *plural of* TERMINUS 2

ter·mi·nol·o·gy /ˌtəməˈnɑːləʤi/ *noun, pl* **-gies :** the special words or phrases that are used in a particular field [*noncount*] legal/medical *terminology* [*count*] a lexicon covering the *terminologies* of several scientific fields
– ter·mi·no·log·i·cal /ˌtəmənəˈlɑːʤɪkəl/ *adj*

term insurance *noun* [*noncount*] **:** a type of insurance that is provided for a specified period of time

ter·mi·nus /ˈtəmənəs/ *noun* [*count*]
1 *pl* ***ter·mi·nus·es*** **:** the end of a travel route (such as a rail or bus line) or the station at the end of a travel route ▪ Stockholm is the *terminus* for the southbound train. ▪ a bus *terminus*
2 *pl* ***ter·mi·ni*** /ˈtəməˌnaɪ/ *technical* **:** the end of something ▪ Geologists took samples from the *terminus* of the glacier. ▪ the *terminus* of the DNA strand

ter·mite /ˈtəˌmaɪt/ *noun, pl* **-mites** [*count*] **:** a kind of soft, white insect that lives in groups, eats wood, and causes a lot of damage to wooden structures ▪ *termite* colonies ▪ The house has a lot of *termite* damage. — see color picture on page C10

term paper *noun, pl* **~ -pers** [*count*] *US* **:** a long essay that usually requires research and that is written by a student as part of a course or class ▪ I have a *term paper* due next week.

term time *noun* [*noncount*] *Brit* **:** the part of the year in which schools and universities are holding classes ▪ He's in Cambridge during *term time*.

tern /ˈtən/ *noun, pl* **terns** [*count*] **:** a kind of bird that lives near the ocean, is usually black and white, and has long wings and a tail with two points

ter·race /ˈterəs/ *noun, pl* **-rac·es**
1 [*count*] **:** a flat area created on the side of a hill and used especially for growing crops ▪ rice growing in/on hillside *terraces*
2 [*count*] **:** a flat area next to a building where people can sit and relax ▪ For sale: large three-bedroom house with adjoining *terrace* and garden.
3 [*count*] *Brit* **:** a row of houses that are joined together **:** a group of row houses
4 ***the terraces*** *Brit* **:** a section of a stadium with wide steps where people stand to watch soccer matches
– ter·raced /ˈterəst/ *adj* ▪ a *terraced* hillside ▪ *terraced* gardens **– ter·rac·ing** /ˈterəsɪŋ/ *noun* [*noncount*] ▪ hillside *terracing*

terraced house *noun, pl* **~ houses** [*count*] *Brit* **:** ROW HOUSE

ter·ra–cot·ta /ˌterəˈkɑːtə/ *noun, pl* **-tas**
1 a [*noncount*] **:** a reddish clay that is used for pottery and tiles ▪ planters/jars made of *terra-cotta* **b** [*count*] **:** things (such as tiles, pottery, or statues) that are made from terra-cotta — often used before another noun ▪ *terra-cotta* jars from ancient Greece ▪ *terra-cotta* tiles
2 [*noncount*] **:** a brownish-orange color — see color picture on page C3

ter·ra fir·ma /ˌterəˈfəmə/ *noun* [*noncount*] **:** dry and solid ground as compared to air or water ▪ We were glad to be back on *terra firma* [=back on the ground] after our bumpy flight.

ter·rain /təˈreɪn/ *noun, pl* **-rains :** land of a particular kind [*noncount*] We had to drive over some rough *terrain*. [*count*] We hiked through a variety of *terrains*. — see also ALL-TERRAIN VEHICLE

ter·ra in·cog·ni·ta /ˈterəˌɪnˌkɑːgˈniːtə/ *noun, pl* **ter·rae in·cog·ni·tae** /ˈterˌaɪˌɪnˌkɑːgˈniːˌtaɪ/ [*count*] *formal* **:** a place that has not been discovered or that is unknown ▪ the *terra incognita* beyond those mountains — often used figuratively ▪ This subject is *terra incognita* for/to me. [=I don't know anything about this subject]

ter·ra·pin /ˈterəpən/ *noun, pl* **-pins** [*count*] **:** a kind of small turtle that lives in water

ter·rar·i·um /təˈrerijəm/ *noun, pl* **-ums** [*count*] **:** a glass or plastic box that is used for growing plants or keeping small animals indoors

ter·res·tri·al /təˈrɛstrijəl/ *adj* [*more ~; most ~*]
1 : relating to or occurring on the earth ▪ *terrestrial* life forms
2 *technical* **:** living or growing on land instead of in water or air ▪ The toad has *terrestrial* habits, spending most of its time on shore. ▪ *terrestrial* birds
3 : sending a broadcast signal from the Earth ▪ *terrestrial* wireless networks ▪ a *terrestrial* radio station

ter·ri·ble /ˈterəbəl/ *adj* [*more ~; most ~*]
1 : very shocking and upsetting ▪ a *terrible* [=*horrible*] disaster/crime ▪ Traffic was held up by a *terrible* accident. ▪ We just got some *terrible* [=*dreadful*] news.
2 : very bad or unpleasant ▪ *terrible* music/food ▪ The garbage smells really *terrible*. [=*awful*] ▪ I have a *terrible* cold. ▪ What a *terrible* [=*horrible*] thing to say! ▪ a *terrible* mistake ▪ The service at that restaurant is *terrible*. ▪ I'm a *terrible* chess player. = I'm *terrible* at chess. [=I play chess very badly] ▪ I woke up this morning feeling *terrible*. [=very sick] ▪ She feels *terrible* [=very sorry] that she hurt your feelings.
– see also ENFANT TERRIBLE

ter·ri·bly /ˈterəbli/ *adv* [*more ~; most ~*]
1 : very or extremely ▪ The movie made me feel *terribly* sad. ▪ It is *terribly* important that the package be delivered tomorrow. ▪ They don't know each other *terribly* well. ▪ Something has gone *terribly* wrong. ▪ I miss you *terribly*. [=very much]
2 : in a very bad or unpleasant way ▪ I like tennis, but I play *terribly*. [=very badly]

ter·ri·er /ˈterijɚ/ *noun, pl* **-ers** [*count*] **:** a type of small dog originally used for hunting

ter·rif·ic /təˈrɪfɪk/ *adj*
1 *informal* **:** extremely good **:** EXCELLENT ▪ He makes *terrific* chili. ▪ She's given me some *terrific* ideas. ▪ Your test scores were *terrific*. ▪ They did a *terrific* job painting the house. ▪ I had a *terrific* time. ▪ I've recovered completely. In fact, I feel *terrific*.
2 : causing a feeling of surprise or wonder ▪ an athlete with *terrific* [=*astounding, amazing*] speed ▪ We were hit by a *terrific* snowstorm last week.
– ter·rif·i·cal·ly /təˈrɪfɪkli/ *adv* ▪ The news is *terrifically* exciting. ▪ The band is *terrifically* popular in Japan.

terrified *adj* [*more ~; most ~*] **:** extremely afraid ▪ *terrified* onlookers ▪ I was/felt *terrified* and just wanted to go home. ▪ The thought of losing his job has him *terrified*. ▪ She was *terrified* that she was going to die alone. = She was *terrified* of dying alone.

ter·ri·fy /ˈterəˌfaɪ/ *verb* **-fies; -fied; -fy·ing** [+ *obj*] **:** to cause (someone) to be extremely afraid **:** to frighten (someone) very much ▪ Big dogs *terrify* me. ▪ The thought of dying alone *terrifies* her.

terrifying *adj* [*more ~; most ~*] **:** causing great fear ▪ The thought of dying alone was *terrifying*. ▪ a *terrifying* ordeal
– ter·ri·fy·ing·ly *adv* ▪ We came *terrifyingly* close to dying on that mountain.

ter·rine /təˈriːn/ *noun, pl* **-rines** [*count, noncount*] **:** liver or meat that has been chopped into very small pieces and cooked in a special dish

ter·ri·to·ri·al /ˌterəˈtorijəl/ *adj*
1 : of or relating to land or water that is owned or controlled by a government ▪ *territorial* boundaries ▪ *territorial* claims by settlers ▪ a *territorial* government ▪ The two countries are in a ***territorial dispute***. [=a disagreement about which one controls a particular territory]
2 [*more ~; most ~*] — used to describe animals or people that try to keep others away from an area that they use or

T

control • The neighbor's dog is extremely *territorial* and barks if you come close to the yard. • the human tendency to be *territorial*

– ter·ri·to·ri·al·ly *adv* • The region was *territorially* important to the empire.

Territorial Army *noun*

the Territorial Army **: a part of the military forces of Britain that is made up of people who are not professional soldiers but are given military training for a period of time each year** — abbr. *TA*

ter·ri·to·ri·al·i·ty /ˌterəˌtoriˈæləti/ *noun* [*noncount*] **: the behavior of animals or people that try to keep others away from an area that they use or control** • a scientific study of *territoriality* in bears/mice

territorial waters *noun* [*plural*] **: the part of the ocean near a country's coast that is legally controlled by that country**

ter·ri·to·ry /ˈterəˌtori, *Brit* ˈtɛrətri/ *noun, pl* **-ries**

1 a : an area of land that belongs to or is controlled by a government [*noncount*] Those mountains are in Mexican *territory*. • We're entering ***enemy territory***. [=an area of land that belongs to or is controlled by our enemy] [*count*] disputed *territories* **b** [*count*] **: one of the parts of the United States that is not a state** • Guam is a U.S. *territory*. **c** [*count*] **: any one of the large parts that some countries are divided into** • Canada's Yukon *Territory*

2 : an area that an animal or group of animals uses and defends [*count*] The birds are busy establishing *territories* and building nests. [*noncount*] Male cats spray to mark *territory*.

3 [*noncount*] **: an area of land or water** • We've covered a lot of *territory* today. [=we have traveled a long distance] • The goal of the expedition is to map ***unexplored/uncharted territory***. — sometimes used figuratively • an area of study that was *unexplored/uncharted territory* at the time • Let's get the meeting started. We have a lot of *territory* to cover today. [=a lot to talk about, decide, etc.] • Dealing with our cars and the mechanic is her *territory*. [=something she is in charge of] • As the conversation turned to politics, I knew we were heading into ***dangerous territory***.

4 [*count*] **: an area that someone is responsible for when doing a job** • a salesman whose *territory* includes New England and upstate New York

5 [*count*] *sports* **: the area on a playing field (such as a football field) that is defended by a particular team** • They started deep in their own *territory* and went all the way down the field to score a touchdown.

come/go with the territory **: to be a natural part of a particular situation, position, or area of work** • Of course players get injured sometimes. It *comes with the territory*.

ter·ror /ˈterɚ/ *noun*

1 : a very strong feeling of fear [*noncount*] The sound of guns being fired fills me with *terror*. • There was a look of (sheer) *terror* on her face. • Many civilians fled ***in terror***. • They lived *in terror* of being discovered. = They lived *in terror* that they would be discovered. • Until recently, the mere mention of the disease ***struck terror in (the hearts of)*** people. [*singular*] someone with a *terror* of water [=someone who is extremely afraid of being in water] • a *terror* that is still fresh in her memory

2 : something that causes very strong feelings of fear : something that is terrifying [*count*] the *terrors* of war • the *terrors* of life in the jungle [*noncount*] tales of *terror*

3 [*noncount*] **: violence that is committed by a person, group, or government in order to frighten people and achieve a political goal** • a regime that rules by *terror* • bombings and other acts of *terror* • These people have been living with *terror* and the threat of *terror* for many years. • a war on *terror* [=*terrorism*] • a campaign of *terror* against ethnic minority groups — see also REIGN OF TERROR

4 [*count*] *informal* **: a child who behaves very badly** • My nephew is a little *terror*. [=*brat*] • Their kids are ***holy terrors***. [=their kids behave very badly]

hold no terror or ***hold no terrors*** ✧ If something *holds no terror/terrors* for you, you are not afraid of it. • Death *holds no terror* for them. • She's done it enough times that it *holds no terrors* now.

ter·ror·ism /ˈterɚˌɪzəm/ *noun* [*noncount*] **: the use of violent acts to frighten the people in an area as a way of trying to achieve a political goal** • They have been arrested for acts of *terrorism*. • international *terrorism* • the fight/struggle/war against *terrorism* • ***state terrorism*** [=terrorism by a government] — see also COUNTERTERRORISM

ter·ror·ist /ˈterɚrɪst/ *noun, pl* **-ists** [*count*] **: a person who uses or supports the use of terrorism** • A number of people were deported for being suspected *terrorists*.

– terrorist *adj, always used before a noun* • *terrorist* activities/attacks/bombings/threats • a *terrorist* organization/group/network

ter·ror·ize *also Brit* **ter·ror·ise** /ˈterəˌraɪz/ *verb* **-iz·es; -ized; -iz·ing** [+ *obj*]

1 : to cause (someone) to be extremely afraid • As a child she *terrorized* her younger siblings. • She was *terrorized* by nightmares. • neighborhoods *terrorized* by gangs

2 : to force (someone) to do something by using threats or violence • Employees were *terrorized* into accepting abysmal working conditions.

ter·ry cloth /ˈteri-/ *noun* [*noncount*] **: a type of soft, thick cloth with many tiny loops on its surface that is often used to make towels** • a *terry cloth* robe/towel — called also *terry*, (*Brit*) *towelling*

terse /ˈtɚs/ *adj* **: brief and direct in a way that may seem rude or unfriendly** • a *terse* statement/sentence/summary • She gave me a few *terse* instructions and promptly left the room. ***synonyms*** see CONCISE

– terse·ly *adv* • a *tersely* worded reply **– terse·ness** *noun* [*noncount*]

ter·ti·ary /ˈtɚʃiˌeri, *Brit* ˈtɜːʃəri/ *adj, formal* **: third in order, importance, or value** • Headaches often occur during the *tertiary* stage of the illness. • our *tertiary* goals • (*chiefly Brit*) ***tertiary education*** [=education at the college or university level] — compare PRIMARY, SECONDARY

TESL /ˈtɛsəl/ *abbr, chiefly US* **teaching English as a second language**

TESOL /ˈtiːsɔl/ *abbr* **1** *US* **Teachers of English to Speakers of Other Languages 2 teaching English to speakers of other languages**

[1]test /ˈtɛst/ *noun, pl* **tests** [*count*]

1 : a set of questions or problems that are designed to measure a person's knowledge, skills, or abilities • She is studying for her math/spelling/history *test*. • I passed/failed/flunked my biology *test*. • The teacher sat at his desk grading *tests*. • a driver's/driving *test* [=a test that is used to see if someone is able to safely drive a car] • an IQ *test* • *test* questions • The *test* will be on [=the questions on the test will be about] the first three chapters of the book. • We ***took/had a test*** on European capitals. = (*Brit*) We ***did a test*** on European capitals. • The college relies on ***test scores*** in its admissions process. — see also INTELLIGENCE TEST, RORSCHACH TEST, SCREEN TEST

2 a : a careful study of a part of the body or of a substance taken from the body • The *test* showed/revealed a problem with your liver function. • a vision/hearing *test* [=a test that shows how well you see/hear] • a urine *test* [=a test that examines a person's urine for evidence of disease or illegal drugs] • allergy *tests* [=tests that show what you are allergic to] • All applicants must pass a ***drug test***. [=a test that examines a person's blood or urine for evidence of illegal drugs] • The doctor will call you with the ***test results***. • They went to the drug store to buy a ***pregnancy test***. [=a device that reacts to a woman's urine in a way that shows whether or not she is pregnant] • a ***DNA test*** [=a test that examines DNA and that is used to identify someone or to show that people are relatives] — see also BLOOD TEST, BREATH TEST, STRESS TEST **b : a careful study of a small amount of water, soil, air, etc., in order to see if its quality is good, to find out if it contains a dangerous substance, etc.** • The *test* indicated high levels of lead in the soil. • routine water *tests*

3 : a planned and usually controlled act or series of acts that is done to learn something, to see if something works properly, etc. • lab/laboratory *tests* • underground nuclear *tests* • a *test* of a new vaccine • ***Taste tests*** revealed that people prefer this brand of cola over that one. — often used before another noun • As participants in the sleep study, ***test subjects*** will be kept awake for 18 hours. • The effects of the drug were clear when the ***test group*** was compared with the control group. — see also ROAD TEST

4 : something (such as a difficult situation or task) that shows how strong or skilled someone or something is • a *test* of will/strength/character • The real/true *test* of your ability as a skier is whether you can ski well on very hard snow. — see also ACID TEST, LITMUS TEST

5 *Brit, sports* **: TEST MATCH**

put (someone or something) to the test **: to cause (someone or something) to be in a situation that shows how strong, good, etc., that person or thing really is** • The team

T

has been playing well so far, but tomorrow's game will really *put them to the test.* [=will really test them] • A trip through the desert will *put* the truck *to the test.* • We decided to *put* the idea/theory *to the test* [=to test the theory] with a little experiment.

stand the test of time : to continue to be important, respected, etc., for a long period of time • Great art/literature/music can *stand the test of time.*

test of (your) character see CHARACTER

– see also HIGH-TEST, MEANS TEST

²test *verb* **tests; test·ed; test·ing**

1 [+ *obj*] : to use a set of questions or problems to measure someone's skills, knowledge, or abilities • Weekly quizzes will *test* your understanding of the material. • The students will all be *tested* again at the end of the school year. — often + *on* • The exam will *test* you *on* your understanding of basic grammar rules.

2 : to examine a part of the body or a substance taken from the body [+ *obj*] The school nurse will be *testing* students' hearing next week. — often + *for* • They *tested* the campers *for* Lyme disease. • Blood samples from the animals are being *tested for* the presence of the virus. • Athletes competing in the tournament will be *tested for* illegal drugs. [*no obj*] The athletes knew that tournament officials would be *testing for* (the presence of) illegal drugs. • She ***tested positive/negative*** *for* AIDS.

3 : to examine a small amount of water, soil, air, etc., in order to see if its quality is good, if it contains a dangerous substance, etc. [+ *obj*] The water gets *tested* regularly. — often + *for* • They will *test* the soil *for* traces of lead. [*no obj*] — + *for* • They will *test for* the presence of lead in the soil.

4 [+ *obj*] : to use (something) in a planned and usually controlled way in order to see if it works properly • Only one of the vehicles they *tested* performed well in wet conditions. • Researchers are currently *testing* (the safety of) the vaccine. • The vaccine has not been *tested* on humans yet. • We designed a series of experiments to *test* our hypothesis. — see also FIELD-TEST

5 [+ *obj*] : to show how strong, good, etc., someone or something is in a difficult situation • The stress is *testing* the strength of our relationship. • The scandal is *testing* the country's faith in its leadership. • Life's ordeals *test* us. • You're *testing* my patience. [=you are starting to make me annoyed or upset] — see also TIME-TESTED

test the waters *also* ***test the water*** : to do something to find out if people like or approve a possible plan, product, etc., so that you can make a decision about it • The company is *testing the waters* with a new online version of the product. • She's *testing the waters* for a presidential bid.

– test·able /ˈtɛstəbəl/ *adj* • a *testable* hypothesis

tes·ta·ment /ˈtɛstəmənt/ *noun, pl* **-ments**

1 : proof or evidence that something exists or is true [*count*] The success of the album, which is only available online, is a ***testament to*** the power/strength of the Internet. [*noncount*] The event is *testament to* [=*evidence of*] what a small group of determined people can do.

2 [*count*] *law* : the legal instructions in which you say who should receive your property, possessions, etc., after you die : WILL • a person's ***last will and testament***

– see also NEW TESTAMENT, OLD TESTAMENT

– tes·ta·men·ta·ry /ˌtɛstəˈmɛntəri/ *adj, law*

test ban *noun, pl* **~ bans** [*count*] : an official agreement between countries with nuclear weapons to not test those weapons • a nuclear *test ban* treaty

test case *noun, pl* **~ cases** [*count*] *law* : a legal case that will be used as an example when other similar cases are decided in the future

test drive *noun, pl* **~ drives** [*count*] : an occurrence in which you drive a car that you do not own to see if you like it and would like to buy it • Would you like to take the car for a *test drive*?

– test–drive *verb* **-drives; -drove; -driv·en; -driv·ing** [+ *obj*] • She *test-drove* four or five different cars before deciding on one.

test·er /ˈtɛstə/ *noun, pl* **-ers** [*count*]

1 : a person or device that tests something • She works as a video game *tester.*

2 : a container of perfume, lotion, etc., in a store that customers can use to try the product

testes *plural of* TESTIS

tes·ti·cle /ˈtɛstɪkəl/ *noun, pl* **-ti·cles** [*count*] : one of two small organs that are located in a sack of skin (called the scrotum) in men and male animals and that produce sperm and male hormones

– tes·tic·u·lar /tɛˈstɪkjələ/ *adj, always used before a noun* • *testicular* cancer

tes·ti·fy /ˈtɛstəˌfaɪ/ *verb* **-fies; -fied; -fy·ing**

1 a : to talk and answer questions about something especially in a court of law while formally promising that what you are saying is true [*no obj*] She refused to *testify* about who had given her the information. • Three witnesses were called/summoned to *testify* at (the) trial. • She *testified* before Congress today. • He agreed to ***testify against*** his drug dealer. • They will ***testify for*** the defense/prosecution. [=they will testify because the defense/prosecution has asked them to] [+ *obj*] He *testified* that he'd seen two people leave the building on the night of the murder. **b** : to talk about or say (something) in an honest and confident way [+ *obj*] I can (personally) *testify* that the food at that diner is excellent. [*no obj*] — + *to* • Many of her former employees came forward to *testify to* her generosity. [=to say that she is a generous person]

2 : to show that something is true or real : to give proof of something [*no obj*] — + *to* • These statistics *testify to* the fact that the program is working. [=show that the program is working] • The fact that doctors were able to catch the disease before it had spread *testifies to* the importance of medical screenings. [+ *obj*] These statistics *testify* that the program is working.

3 [*no obj*] *US* : to talk to a group of people about your belief in God especially as part of a church service • Several people *testified* during the revival meeting.

¹tes·ti·mo·ni·al /ˌtɛstəˈmounijəl/ *noun, pl* **-als** [*count*]

1 a : a written or spoken statement in which you say that you used a product or service and liked it ✧ Testimonials are often used to sell the products or services they are about. • The Web site is full of *testimonials* from satisfied customers. **b** : a written or spoken statement that praises someone's work, skill, character, etc. • He received a glowing *testimonial* from his former employer.

2 : an event at which someone is honored • They have planned a *testimonial* [=*tribute*] in her honor. — often used before another noun • She is being honored at a *testimonial* dinner next week.

3 : TESTAMENT 1 — + *to* • The book's popularity is a *testimonial to* its timeliness.

²testimonial *adj* : relating to testimony and especially to legal testimony • *testimonial* evidence

tes·ti·mo·ny /ˈtɛstəˌmouni/ *noun, pl* **-nies**

1 : something that someone says especially in a court of law while formally promising to tell the truth [*noncount*] The jury heard 10 days of *testimony.* [*count*] There were contradictions in her *testimony.* • the personal/oral/written/eyewitness *testimonies* of survivors of the war

2 : proof or evidence that something exists or is true : TESTAMENT — + *to* [*noncount*] It is *testimony to* her courage and persistence that she worked for so long in the face of such adversity. [*count*] The popularity of diet fads is a *testimony to* the fact that people want a quick fix for their health and weight problems.

test·ing /ˈtɛstɪŋ/ *adj* [*more* ~; *most* ~] : difficult to deal with • It's been a *testing* [=*trying*] time for all of us.

testing ground *noun, pl* **~ grounds** [*count*]

1 : a place where machines, vehicles, etc., are tested to see if they are working correctly • a *testing ground* for weapons

2 : a place or situation in which new ideas, methods, etc., can be tried • Her class served as a *testing ground* [=*proving ground*] for new teaching methods.

tes·tis /ˈtɛstəs/ *noun, pl* **tes·tes** /ˈtɛˌsti:z/ [*count*] *technical* : TESTICLE

test match *noun, pl* **~ matches** [*count*] *chiefly Brit, sports* : a game or series of games of cricket or rugby played by teams from different countries

tes·tos·ter·one /tɛˈstɑ:stəˌroun/ *noun* [*noncount*]

1 *medical* : a substance (called a hormone) that occurs naturally in men and male animals ✧ Testosterone causes the development of the male reproductive system and characteristics of the adult male body.

2 *informal* + *often disapproving* : qualities (such as noticeable strength and aggressiveness) that agree with traditional ideas about what men are like • a *testosterone*-fueled television show

test pilot *noun, pl* **~ -lots** [*count*] : a pilot who flies new aircraft in order to see how well they work

test run *noun, pl* **~ runs** [*count*] : an occurrence in which a product or procedure is tried in order to see if it works correctly : TRIAL RUN • They did a *test run* of the new software.

test tube *noun, pl* ~ **tubes** [*count*] : a glass container that is shaped like a tube which is closed at one end and that is used especially in science experiments

test–tube baby *noun, pl* ~ **-bies** [*count*] : a child produced from an egg that was fertilized outside of a woman's body and then put back into the woman's body to finish developing

tes·ty /ˈtɛsti/ *adj* **tes·ti·er; -est** : becoming angry or annoyed easily • She grew a little *testy* [=*irritable*, (*chiefly Brit*) *tetchy*] as the afternoon wore on.

– **tes·ti·ly** /ˈtɛstəli/ *adv* • He replied *testily* that, no, he did not want any help. – **tes·ti·ness** /ˈtɛstinəs/ *noun* [*noncount*]

tet·a·nus /ˈtɛtnəs/ *noun* [*noncount*] *medical* : a dangerous disease that is caused by bacteria that usually enter the body through a cut or wound ✧ Tetanus causes muscles and especially muscles in the jaw to become stiff. — called also (*informal*) *lockjaw*

tetchy /ˈtɛʧi/ *adj* **tetch·i·er; -est** *chiefly Brit* : becoming angry or annoyed easily • *tetchy* [=*irritable*] children • She was in a *tetchy* [=*testy*] mood.

– **tetch·i·ly** /ˈtɛʧəli/ *adv* – **tetch·i·ness** /ˈtɛʧinəs/ *noun* [*noncount*]

tête–à–tête /ˌtɛtəˈtɛt/ *noun, pl* **tête-à-têtes** [*count*] : a private conversation between two people • They had a quiet *tête-à-tête* over dinner last night. ✧ *Tête-à-tête* in French literally means "head-to-head."

[1]**teth·er** /ˈtɛðɚ/ *noun, pl* **-ers** [*count*] : a rope or chain that is used to tie an animal to a post, wall, etc., so that it will stay in a particular area

the end of your tether see [1]END

[2]**tether** *verb* **-ers; -ered; -er·ing** [+ *obj*] : to use a rope or chain to tie (an animal) to something in order to keep it in a particular area • They *tethered* the horses in the shade. • The dog was *tethered* to the fence.— often used figuratively • She can't stand being *tethered* to her desk all day. [=having to stay at her desk all day]

Teu·ton·ic /tuˈtɑːnɪk, *Brit* tjuˈtɒnɪk/ *adj*

1 : thought to be typical of German people • a *Teutonic* commitment to hard work

2 a : relating to Germany, Germans, or the German language • the *Teutonic* wilderness • a *Teutonic* [=*Germanic*] scholar/word **b** : relating to an ancient people who lived in northern Europe • *Teutonic* legends

Tex. *abbr* Texas

Tex–Mex /ˈtɛksˈmɛks/ *adj, always used before a noun* : relating to Mexican-American culture, music, or food of the kind that exists especially in southern Texas • a *Tex-Mex* restaurant

[1]**text** /ˈtɛkst/ *noun, pl* **texts**

1 [*noncount*] : the original words of a piece of writing or a speech • A good critic will refer back to the *text* often. • You can find the full *text* of his speech on his Web site. • the *text* of the Constitution

2 [*noncount*] : the words that make up the main part of a book, magazine, newspaper, Web site, etc. • The book is mostly photographs—it has very little *text*. • At this point the Web site is only *text*. Graphics will be added later.

3 [*count*] **a** : a book or other piece of writing; *especially* : one that is studied • an ancient religious *text* • Students will read and discuss various ***literary texts***. • (*Brit*) Shakespearean plays are ***set texts*** [=pieces of writing that must be studied in schools] in many secondary schools. **b** *US* : TEXTBOOK • a psychology *text*

4 a [*noncount*] : data handled by a computer, cell phone, etc., that is mostly in the form of words • I typed 32 pages of *text*. • a *text* file **b** [*count*] : TEXT MESSAGE • He sends hundreds of *texts* a month.

5 [*count*] : a short section of the Bible that is read aloud especially during a religious service

[2]**text** *verb* **texts; text·ed; text·ing** : to send someone a text message [+ *obj*] I *texted* her a little while ago. • I *texted* a message to her. • She just *texted* me back. [*no obj*] She just *texted* back.

– **texting** *noun* [*noncount*] • *Texting* [=*text messaging*] is a major preoccupation for many teens.

[1]**text·book** /ˈtɛkstˌbʊk/ *noun, pl* **-books** [*count*] : a book about a particular subject that is used in the study of that subject especially in a school • an algebra *textbook*

[2]**textbook** *adj, always used before a noun* : very typical • The scandal is a ***textbook*** [=*classic, perfect*] ***case/example*** of corporate greed.

tex·tile /ˈtɛkˌstajəl, ˈtɛkstl̩/ *noun, pl* **-tiles**

1 [*count*] : FABRIC, CLOTH; *especially* : a fabric that is woven or knit • They import fine silk *textiles* from China. • a factory where *textiles* are made = a *textile* factory

2 ***textiles*** [*noncount*] : the businesses that make textiles • She made her fortune in *textiles*. [=the textile industry]

text message *noun, pl* ~ **-sag·es** [*count*] : a short message that is sent electronically to a cell phone or other device • She sent me a *text message* saying that she'll be late. — called also *text*

– **text messaging** *noun* [*noncount*] • I use my cell phone for *text messaging*. [=for sending text messages]

tex·tu·al /ˈtɛksʧəwəl/ *adj* : relating to or based on a piece of writing (such as a book or magazine) • *textual* analysis/criticism • *textual* evidence [=evidence expressed in writing]

tex·ture /ˈtɛksʧɚ/ *noun, pl* **-tures**

1 : the way that something feels when you touch it [*count*] wood with a rough *texture* • the smooth *texture* of silk [*noncount*] The plant's leaves are almost leathery in *texture*. • Mixing sand into the paint will add *texture*. [=will give the paint a rough texture when it dries]

2 : the way that a food or drink feels in your mouth [*count*] a crunchy/rich/silky *texture* • foods with very different *textures* [*noncount*] The custard should be smooth and creamy in *texture*. • Next I added some flour to the sauce for *texture*. [=to give it the right texture]

3 : the various parts of a song, poem, movie, etc., and the way they fit together [*count*] a song with layered *textures* • I liked the raw, gritty *texture* of the film. [*noncount*] The movies are similar in *texture*.

– **tex·tur·al** /ˈtɛksʧərəl/ *adj* • *textural* contrast

tex·tured /ˈtɛksʧɚd/ *adj* : having a surface that was designed so that it is not smooth • *textured* fabrics • The invitations were printed on handmade *textured* paper.

TGIF *abbr, US* thank God/goodness it's Friday

Th. *abbr* Thursday

-th *or* **-eth** *adj suffix* — used in writing after numbers other than 1, 2, and 3 • 100*th* = hundred*th* • Fortie*th* Street = 40*th* Street • a 5*th*-grade teacher • the eigh*th* of April

Thai /ˈtaɪ/ *noun, pl* **Thai** *or* **Thais**

1 [*count*] **a** : a person born, raised, or living in Thailand **b** : a person whose family is from Thailand

2 [*noncount*] : the language of Thailand

– **Thai** *adj* • *Thai* food/curry • *Thai* people

[1]**than** /ˈðæn, ðən/ *conj*

1 — used to introduce the second or last of two or more things or people that are being compared; used with the comparative form of an adjective or adverb • Ten is less *than* 20. • She is younger *than* I am. = (*somewhat formal*) She is younger *than* I. • He can run more quickly *than* his father (can). • Both recipes use more salt *than* mine (does). • The situation will improve sooner *than* you think (it will). • The meeting will end no later *than* noon. [=it will end at noon or some time before noon] • Losing weight is easier said *than* done. [=is difficult to do] • I would rather go out to dinner *than* cook at home tonight. • Your hair looks better (when it's) brown *than* (when it's) blond. • She would rather/sooner work four jobs *than* move out of Manhattan to live somewhere cheaper.— see also *other than* at [1]OTHER, *rather than* at RATHER

2 — used to say that something happens immediately after something else • ***Hardly/scarcely*** had the sun come up ***than*** dark clouds began to roll in. • ***No sooner*** had I spoken ***than*** he appeared. [=he appeared immediately after I spoke]

[2]**than** *prep* : when compared to — used with pronouns in the objective case (*me, her, him, them*, and *us*) in the same way that the conjunction *than* is used with pronouns in the subjective case (*I, she, he, they*, and *we*) • She is younger *than me*. [=she is younger than I (am)] • I'm taller *than* him. [=I'm taller than he (is)]

> ***usage*** Some people consider the use of *than* as a preposition to be incorrect. It is very common, however, especially in the phrase ***than me***.

none other than see [1]NONE

thank /ˈθæŋk/ *verb* **thanks; thanked; thank·ing** [+ *obj*] : to tell (someone) that you are grateful for something that he or she has done or given • I *thanked* her for (giving me) the present. • I want to *thank* everyone who helped today. • There's no need to *thank* me. Anyone would have done the same. ▪ He *thanked* his grandmother with a big hug. [=he thanked her by hugging her]

have (someone or something) to thank for (something) — used to say that someone or something is responsible for something ▪ The television show *has* young audiences *to thank for* its success. [=the show is successful because it is popular with young audiences] ▪ The city *has* the mayor *to thank* [=*to blame*] *for* its current fiscal problems.

thank God/goodness/heaven(s)/the Lord — used to express happiness or relief that something did or did not happen ▪ *Thank God* you got here when you did. ▪ *Thank goodness* it turned out to be a false alarm.

thank you **1** — used to thank someone ▪ "Here's your change." "*Thank you.*" "You're welcome." ▪ *Thank you* from the bottom of my heart. = (more formally) I *thank you* from the bottom of my heart. — often + *for* ▪ *Thank you* (very much) *for* helping me. = *Thank you* (very much) *for* your help. **2** — used to politely accept or refuse an offer ▪ "Can I carry that for you?" "*Thank you* (very much)." ▪ "Would you like another one?" "***Yes, thank you***" [=*yes, please*] ▪ "Can I carry that for you?" "***No, thank you*** I'll do it myself." **3** — used to tell someone in a somewhat annoyed way that you do not want help or advice ▪ I'm perfectly capable of doing it by myself, *thank you* (very much).

thank·ful /ˈθæŋkfəl/ *adj* [*more* ~; *most* ~]

1 : glad that something has happened or not happened, that something or someone exists, etc. ▪ I'm *thankful* (that) we were not on the boat when the storm hit. ▪ Everyone was *thankful* to hear the good news. — often + *for* ▪ We have so much to be *thankful for*. ▪ I'm very *thankful* [=*grateful*] *for* all the help they've given me. ▪ I'm so *thankful for* my family.

2 : of, relating to, or expressing thanks ▪ a *thankful* feeling ▪ *thankful* words

— thank·ful·ness *noun* [*noncount*] ▪ a feeling of *thankfulness*

thank·ful·ly /ˈθæŋkfəli/ *adv*

1 : in a way that makes you feel thankful ▪ I knew I could call her if there was an emergency but *thankfully* [=*fortunately*] it wasn't necessary. ▪ *Thankfully*, no one was hurt. [=I am glad/thankful that no one was hurt] ▪ The instructions were *thankfully* simple.

2 *old-fashioned* **:** with a feeling of thanks ▪ I always receive your calls *thankfully*.

thank·less /ˈθæŋkləs/ *adj*

1 : difficult and not valued by other people ▪ a *thankless* task/job

2 : not showing or feeling thanks ▪ *thankless* people

thanks /ˈθæŋks/ *noun* [*plural*]

1 : a good feeling that you have towards someone who has helped you, given something to you, etc. ▪ I brought you a gift as a way of showing my *thanks* for all you've done. ▪ I want express my *thanks* [=*gratitude*] (to you) for your kindness and generosity.

2 : something done or said to express thanks ▪ A simple bouquet of flowers can be a nice way to say *thanks*. ▪ We should ***give thanks*** (to God) for all the good things in our lives.

3 — used as a less formal way to say "thank you" ▪ "Here's your change." "*Thanks.*" "You're welcome." ▪ *Thanks*! I appreciate it. ▪ "How's your mother doing?" "She's doing well, *thanks.*" [=thank you for asking] — often + *for* ▪ *Thanks for* coming. ▪ *Thanks* so much *for* your kind letter. = Many *thanks for* the kind letter.

4 — used like "thank you" as a polite way of accepting or refusing an offer ▪ "Do you want another one?" "*Thanks.*" [=*yes, please*] ▪ "Do you want another one?" "***Yes, thanks***" [=*yes, please*] ▪ "Do you want another one?" "***No, thanks***" ▪ "Can I help you find something?" "*No thanks*, I'm just looking." ▪ "Would you like a ride?" "***Thanks, but no thanks*** I'll walk."

no thanks to **:** without the help of (someone or something) **:** despite (someone or something) ▪ The vote passed, *no thanks to* the mayor. [=the vote passed even though the mayor did not help or want it to pass]

owe a debt of thanks to see DEBT

thanks a bunch/lot/million *informal* **:** thank you very much ▪ Wow, this is great! *Thanks a million*! — often used in an ironic way to say that you are not pleased that someone has done or said something ▪ "I'm boring? *Thanks a lot*!" ▪ *Thanks a million* for leaving the door open. There are flies everywhere now.

thanks to **:** with the help of (someone or something) **:** because of (someone or something) ▪ I'm a lot happier these days *thanks to* my new girlfriend. ▪ *Thanks to* a new technique, patients typically recover from the surgery in only a few days. — often used in an ironic way ▪ *Thanks to* you we have to do the whole thing over again.

thanks·giv·ing /θæŋksˈgɪvɪŋ/ *noun* [*noncount*]

1 ***Thanksgiving*** **:** the fourth Thursday in November in the U.S. or the second Monday in October in Canada celebrated as a legal holiday for people to be thankful for what they have ✧ People traditionally eat a large meal with family or friends on Thanksgiving. ▪ Are you going home for *Thanksgiving*? ▪ *Thanksgiving* dinner — called also *Thanksgiving Day*

2 *formal* **:** a prayer that expresses thanks to God ▪ They sang a hymn of *thanksgiving*.

thank–you /ˈθæŋkˌjuː/ *noun, pl* **-yous** [*count*] **:** something that you give or do to show thanks **:** a polite expression of thanks — usually singular ▪ They threw him a big party as a *thank-you* for his work at the community center. ▪ Have you sent out the *thank-yous* [=notes/cards/letters thanking people for their gifts, help, etc.] yet? — often used before another noun ▪ a ***thank-you note/letter/gift***

[1]that /ˈðæt, ðət/ *pronoun, pl* **those** /ˈðoʊz/

1 a — used to indicate which person, thing, fact, or idea is being shown, pointed to, or mentioned ▪ *That* is my book. ▪ *Those* are my shoes. ▪ *That* is where I went to school. ▪ "What kind of tree is *that*?" "*That* is a maple." ▪ Who was *that*? ▪ Is *that* your boyfriend (standing) over there? ▪ *Those* are my sisters. ▪ Well, look at *that*. The baby can crawl now. ▪ "It will be difficult." "*That*'s true." ▪ You are the first person in our family to graduate from college, and *that* makes me proud. ▪ "Why did you quit?" "Because I felt like it. *That*'s why." ▪ "The meeting is canceled." "Who told you *that*?" ▪ "It was the worst movie I've ever seen." "Come on—it couldn't have been as bad as *that*." ▪ It may cost as much as $30, but no more than *that*. ***usage*** see [1]THIS **b** — used to refer to a time, action, or event that was just mentioned ▪ You quit? Why did you do *that*? ▪ I brushed my teeth, and after *that* I went to bed. ▪ He won't be there until six o'clock, but I expect to arrive before *that*. [=before then; before six o'clock] ▪ "I hate you!" she screamed. And ***with that*** [=after saying that] she stormed out of the room. **c** — used to refer to the one that is farther away or less familiar ▪ This is my hat and *that* is yours. ▪ *Those* are nice, but I like these better. ▪ Do you want this one or *that* (one)? ▪ Don't do it like *that*. Do it like this.

2 *somewhat formal* **a :** the kind or thing described or identified ▪ The aluminum parts are much lighter than *those* made from steel. [=much lighter than the parts made from steel] — often + *of* ▪ We know of no other planet with an atmosphere like *that of* the Earth. [=an atmosphere like the Earth's atmosphere] **b :** the kind or thing stated previously — usually singular ▪ "There is the matter of your raise (to discuss)." "Yes, there is *that*." — sometimes used to stress the truth of a statement ▪ "Is she capable?" "She is *that*." [=(more commonly) *she certainly is*] ▪ "He told us more than we needed to know, but at least he answered our question." "Oh, yes. *That* he did." [=he certainly did do that] — see also *that's . . . for you* at [1]FOR

3 ***those*** *somewhat formal* **:** a particular group of people ▪ Let's take a vote. All *those* in favor, say "aye." ▪ There are ***those who*** think she should resign.

4 *formal + literary* **:** the one **:** the thing **:** the kind — used to introduce a clause ▪ What is *that* you say? [=what did you say?]

all that **1** *informal* **a :** everything of the kind stated or suggested ▪ She had money, fame, ***and all that*** — see also FOR ALL THAT (below) **b :** more things of the same kind ▪ The store sells computers, cell phones, ***and all that*** [=and other such things] **2 :** the stated or suggested degree, amount, etc. — usually used in negative statements ▪ The movie couldn't have been as bad as *all that*. [=the movie must have been better than you say it was] — see also *all that* at [2]ALL

and that **1** *somewhat formal* — used to refer to an idea just mentioned ▪ He was helpful, *and that* to an unusual degree. [=he was unusually helpful] **2** *chiefly Brit, informal* **:** and more things of the same kind ▪ She spends her money drinking, gambling, *and that*. [=*and so forth*]

at that **1** — used when giving more information about something or someone that was just mentioned ▪ It's a fancy new car, and a sports car *at that*. — usually used in the phrase ***and a bad/good (etc.) one at that*** ▪ The band did a remake of the song, *and a bad one at that*. ▪ She is a lawyer, *and a very talented one at that*. **2 :** without adding or doing anything more • Let's just say that I got in a little trouble with the police, and ***leave it at that.*** = Let's ***let it go at that.*** [=I do not want to say anything more about it] • They offered him the salary that he asked for, but he couldn't *leave it at that.* [=he asked them for something else/more]

for all that : in spite of something just mentioned • She sacrificed many nights to study for the exam, but *for all that* she still failed.

that does it see [1]DO

that is or ***that is to say*** **1** — used when giving more accurate or specific information about someone or something that was just mentioned • We—*that is to say* my wife and I—will be attending the wedding. **2** — used when giving information that affects something previously mentioned • We plan on going to the concert—*that is,* if tickets are still available.

that is all or ***that's all*** **1** — used to say that something is finished or completed • "Do you need anything else?" "No, thanks, *that's all.*" • They're (just) different, *that's all.* [=I am not saying anything more than that they are different] **2** — used to say that something is all that is needed or wanted • I went there to visit friends and *that's all.* [=that is all I wanted to do there]

that is that or ***that's that*** — used to say that a decision or situation cannot be changed • I won't sell it for less than 50 dollars and *that is that.* • I'm not going and *that's that.*

that's a good boy/girl/dog (etc.) — used to praise a child or animal for obeying you • Please pick up your toys. *That's a good girl.* • Sit. *That's a good dog.*

that should/will do (it) see [1]DO

that's it see [1]IT

that's life — used to say that something unpleasant or difficult is a normal part of life • Sometimes you try your hardest and still don't succeed. *That's life.*

– compare [4]THAT

[2]**that** *conj*

1 — used to introduce a clause that is the subject or object of a verb • *That* he said no is not surprising. • I never said *that* I was afraid. • Mom said *that* we could go to the park. • The reason for his absence is *that* he is ill.

2 — used to introduce a clause that completes or explains the meaning of a previous noun or adjective or of the pronoun *it* • There is a chance *that* it might rain. • I am certain *that* it is true. • It's not surprising *that* he said no. • It is unlikely *that* she'll be in. • He made it clear *that* he needed our help. • It's not *that* they said no—that's not why I'm upset; it's *that* they were so rude about it. • (*formal*) The power of the wind was such *that* trees were uprooted.

3 — used to introduce a clause that states a reason or purpose • I'm glad *that* you're here. • I am sorry *that* you lost your dog. • (*literary*) Rejoice *that* the war is over! • (*literary*) "The Lord only gives us our worldly goods *that* we may do justice and mercy . . . " —Harriet Beecher Stowe, *Uncle Tom's Cabin* (1852) • She was saving money ***so that*** she could buy a car. • Carry it with both hands *so that* you don't drop it.

4 — used especially after a phrase beginning with *so* or *such* to introduce a clause that states a result • She was *so* dizzy *that* she fell down. • He was in *such* a rush *that* he forgot to take his hat.

> ***usage*** *That* in senses 1, 2, 3 and 4 is often omitted in informal English, except when it is used at the beginning of a sentence. • I never said (*that*) I was afraid. • There is a chance (*that*) it might rain. • I am certain (*that*) it's true. • I'm glad (*that*) you're here. • Carry it with both hands so (*that*) you don't drop it. • She was so dizzy (*that*) she fell down. • He was in such a rush (*that*) he forgot to take his hat.

5 *literary* — used to introduce a clause expressing surprise, sorrow, anger, desire, etc. • Oh, *that* he would come back! [=I wish that he would come back] • *That* it should come to this! [=I am very shocked, disappointed, etc., by this result]

in that see [2]IN

not that — used to say that something that may seem true is not true • She ignored my suggestion—*not that* I care. [=I do not care that she ignored my suggestion] • *Not that* it matters much [=it does not matter much], but is the artist a man or a woman? • Some people lie to get out of jury duty. *Not that* I ever would, of course. [=I would never lie to get out of jury duty]

[3]**that** *adj, always used before a noun, pl* **those**

1 — used to indicate which person, thing, or idea is being shown, pointed to, or mentioned • *That* boy hit me. • *Those* books are mine. • *Those* shoes are nice. • *That* sister of yours ruined my shirt. • Can you hand me *that* wrench over there? • I like *that* idea. • Go *that* way. • *That* kind of behavior will not be tolerated in the classroom. • I was not at home on *that* day. • I left her a message, and she called me later *that* afternoon. • By *that* point in the trip, everyone was getting tired. • At *that* moment, the answer finally dawned on me. • "I can't seem to reach him at home." "***In that case*** [=if that is true], you'd better call his cell phone." • He's skilled at writing dialogue, and ***in that regard/respect*** his new novel is excellent.

2 — used to indicate the one that is farther away or less familiar • Do you want this one or *that* one? • I'd like *that* one. • Are you talking about these shoes, or *those* shoes over there? • I'll try going this way, and you try going *that* way.

3 : the other • She twisted it this way and *that* way.

that way **1** : in the manner described or suggested • What makes her act *that way*? **2** : in or into the condition described or suggested • He is a very successful man and it is easy to see how he got *that way.*

[4]**that** *pronoun* — used to introduce a group of words that limits the meaning of a noun especially to a specific person, place, or thing • The person *that* [=*who*] won the race also won last year. • I'm no longer the man *that* I used to be. • Is it me *that* you are looking for? • Can you describe the person *that* [=*who,* (*formal*) *whom*] you saw? • children *that* learn to talk early • The movie *that* we watched was a drama. • The restaurant *that* I like is closing. • You should open the wine *that* our guests brought. • You were born the same year *that* I was. • I just want to be treated with the same respect *that* others are treated with. • The fact *that* you are here shows how much you care about me. • There is nothing *that* you can do about it now.

> ***usage*** *That* in this sense is often omitted in informal English. • You were born the same year (*that*) I was. • You should open the wine (*that*) our guests brought. When it is the subject of a verb, however, it is always included. • The person *that* won the race also won last year. • children *that* learn to talk early

– compare [1]THAT

[5]**that** /ˈðæt/ *adv*

1 a : to the degree that is stated or suggested • "It was the worst movie that I have ever seen." "Was it really *that* bad?" "Yes, it was *that* bad." • What would you do with *that* much money? • I don't think I'd ever been *that* sad. [=as sad as I was then] • "Don't go over the speed limit." "Does the car even go *that* fast?" • I didn't realize the book was *that* long. • (*Brit, informal*) They were *that* [=*so*] poor they couldn't buy food. — often used in negative statements • I can't believe (that) a cup of coffee costs *that* much. • Come closer—I can't throw the ball *that* far. • We rarely see snow. It doesn't usually get *that* cold here. **b** : to the degree or extent indicated by a gesture • He is about *that* [=*this, so*] tall. • I need a nail about *that* long.

2 *informal* : to a great degree : VERY — usually used in negative statements • She didn't take his comments *that* seriously. • "How cold is it outside?" "It's not *that* cold." • "When did it happen?" "Not *that* long ago." — see also *all that* at [2]ALL

[1]**thatch** /ˈθætʃ/ *noun*

1 a [*noncount*] : dried plant material (such as straw or leaves) that is used to make the roof of a building • Mice were living in the *thatch* of the roof. **b** [*count*] : a roof made of thatch : a thatched roof • We ate lunch in the shade under the *thatch* of a beachfront restaurant.

2 [*singular*] : a thick mass of hair on a person's head • her *thatch* of dark brown hair

[2]**thatch** *verb* **thatch·es; thatched; thatch·ing** [+ *obj*] : to make (a roof) with dried plant material (called thatch) • *thatch* a roof

– **thatched** *adj* • a *thatched* roof • *thatched* cottages/huts [=cottages/huts that have roofs made of thatch]

[1]**thaw** /ˈθɑː/ *verb* **thaws; thawed; thaw·ing**

1 : to stop being frozen or to cause (something) to stop being frozen [*no obj*] The ice on the pond is beginning to *thaw.* [=*melt*] • Plant the seeds in early spring as soon as the ground *thaws.* — often + *out* • The meat will have to *thaw out* before you can use it. [+ *obj*] The sun will soon *thaw* the snow and ice. — often + *out* • You'll have to *thaw* the meat *out* before you can use it.

2 [*no obj*] *of weather* : to become warm enough that snow and ice melt • The weather is beginning to *thaw.*

3 : to return to a normal temperature after being very cold

T

[*no obj*] Our cold fingers and toes eventually *thawed.* — often + *out* • We sat in front of the fire and let our feet *thaw out.* [+ *obj*] She held the coffee cup tightly, trying to *thaw* her frozen fingers.

4 : to become more friendly and less angry [*no obj*] Relations between the countries have *thawed* since the trade embargo was lifted. [+ *obj*] Efforts to *thaw* relations between the two countries have failed.

²thaw *noun, pl* **thaws** [*count*]

1 : a period of weather that is warm enough to melt ice and snow • flooding from the spring *thaw*

2 : a situation in which a relationship becomes more friendly and less angry • a *thaw* in international relations

the /ðə *before consonant sounds,* ði *before vowel sounds,* ˈði: *when said with emphasis*/ *definite article*

1 — used to indicate a person or thing that has already been mentioned or seen or is clearly understood from the situation • He bought a house, but this is not *the* house he bought. • This is *the* restaurant I was telling you about. • I'll take *the* red one. • Put *the* cat outside. • *The* teacher gave a quiz. • She's *the* boss. • I am telling *the* truth. • What is *the* matter/problem? • I'm no fool; you're *the* fool for believing him.

2 a — used to refer to things or people that are common in daily life • We talked on *the* telephone for an hour. • Turn on *the* television. • She opened *the* windows. • You need to go to *the* doctor. • He said he put the letter in *the* mail yesterday. • My suit is still at *the* dry cleaner. **b** — used to refer to things that occur in nature • *The* sky is getting dark. • A strong wind was blowing from *the* east. • The planets revolve around *the* sun. • Our daughter has *the* flu. • They talked for a while about *the* weather.

3 a — used to refer to a particular unit or period of time • She is out of the office at *the* moment. • *The* time has come for us to make peace. • It is the best movie of *the* year. • We are usually not home during *the* day. • during *the* winter • in *the* future/past/present • The style was popular during *the* 1980s. **b** *Brit* — used to indicate the day on which something happened or will happen • He left five days later, on *the* Sunday. [=(*US*) on Sunday]

4 — used before the name of a specific person, place, event, work of art, etc. • *the* President of *the* United States of America • *the* White House • *the* New York Yankees • *the* Department of Transportation • *the* Mississippi River • *the* American Civil War • *the* Renaissance • *the* Mona Lisa • *the* Bible

5 — used to indicate which person or thing you are referring to or discussing • She gave *the* correct answer. • He is competing against *the* best of *the* best. • *the* fastest runner • I took *the* last piece of pizza. • I never have *the* time to read. • He doesn't have *the* patience to paint the house. • *the* English language • *the* poet William Wordsworth • *the* right to vote • *the* London of Victorian times • He plays *the* hero of the play. • She is from *the* west coast of Africa. • *the* beginning/arrival of spring • *the* announcement of his candidacy

6 — used in titles after a person's name • Alexander *the* Great • Elizabeth *the* Second • Jack *the* Ripper • William *the* Conqueror

7 — used before an ordinal number • This is *the* first time he has been late. • Payment is due on *the* fifth of each month. • Friday *the* 13th • *the* Fourth of July

8 a — used before a singular noun to refer in a general way to people or things of a particular kind • This book gives some useful tips for *the* beginner. [=for beginners] • *The* cobra is a poisonous snake. [=cobras are poisonous snakes] **b** — used to indicate the type of musical instrument someone plays • She plays *the* guitar. **c** — used before an adjective that is being used as a noun to refer to all of the people or things that have a particular quality • *the* rich • *the* homeless • *the* British • *the* living and *the* dead **d** — used before a plural noun to indicate that every person or thing of the kind specified is included • *the* Greeks and *the* Romans • *The* newspapers covered the story. **e** — used before the plural form of a person's last name to indicate that all the members of the family are included • *the* Smiths

9 a — used to indicate that a person or thing is the best of its kind • This is *the* life. [=this is the way I want to live; this is a very enjoyable way to live, spend time, etc.] • I think he's *the* one (for me), and I want to marry him. • He is *the* person [=the right person] for the job. • This seems to be *the* place to be. **b** — used to indicate the most famous person having a particular name ✧ This sense of *the* is emphasized in speech. • "I saw Julia Roberts when I was in L.A." "You saw *the* Julia Roberts, the famous actress?"

10 — used to refer in a general way to a specific type of activity • *the* law • *the* arts and sciences • *the* publishing industry • I love *the* opera. • *the* cinema • He competes in *the* long jump. • *the* backstroke • The cat was on *the* prowl. • The soldiers were on *the* move.

11 a — used to refer to a part of your body or clothing • How's *the* [=*your*] arm feeling today? • He grabbed me by *the* [=*my*] sleeve. • She led him by *the* [=*his*] hand. **b** *informal* — used before a noun that refers to a person's family, job, health, etc. • How is *the* [=*your*] family? • I have to talk the offer over with *the* [=*my*] wife. • Is *the* job going well? • How's *the* headache?

the·ater (*US*) *or chiefly Brit* **the·atre** /ˈθijətə/ *noun, pl* **-aters**

1 [*count*] **a :** a building where plays, shows, etc., are performed on a stage • the oldest *theater* in the city • a *theater* performance • the *theater* district in New York City — see also DINNER THEATER **b** *US* **:** a building or room in which movies are shown • The film is now showing in *theaters.* • a movie *theater* • a home *theater*

2 [*noncount*] **a :** plays in general or as a form of entertainment • We enjoyed a weekend of music, dance, and *theater.* • He was very fond of the *theater* and had purchased tickets for several performances. • Her interests include *theater* and poetry. • the *theater* of 16th-century England • a *theater* critic **b :** the art or activity of performing in or producing plays on a stage • She majored in *theater* in college. • a course in American *theater* • His monologues made for good *theater.* • The play makes lively *theater.* • a *theater* troupe/company — see also COMMUNITY THEATER

3 [*count*] **a :** a place where important events or actions occur — usually singular • the *theater* of health-care reform **b :** a large area where there is a war • He fought in the Pacific *theater* (of operations) in World War II.

4 [*count*] *Brit* **:** OPERATING ROOM

the·ater·go·er (*US*) *or chiefly Brit* **the·atre·go·er**

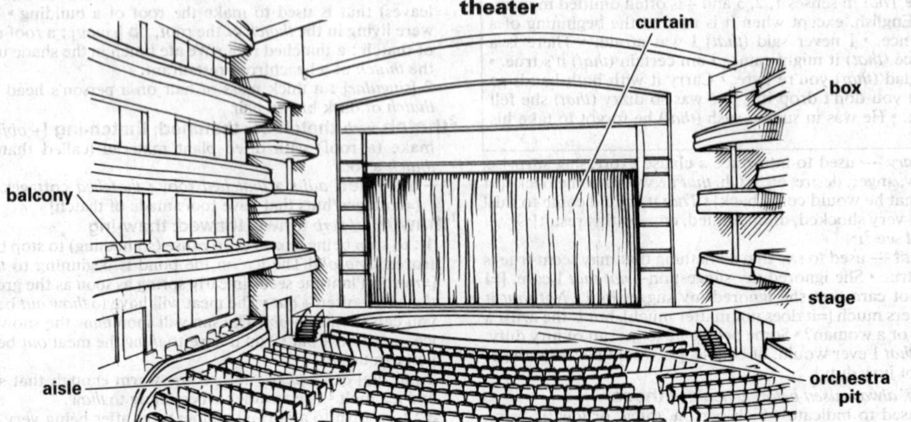

/ˈθijətəˌgowɚ/ *noun, pl* **-ers** [*count*] **:** a person who often goes to the theater to see plays
– the·ater·go·ing (*US*) *or chiefly Brit* **the·atre–go·ing** /ˈθijətəˌgowɪŋ/ *adj* ▪ the *theatergoing* public

the·at·ri·cal /θiˈætrɪkəl/ *adj*
1 : of or relating to the theater ▪ *theatrical* costumes/ambitions
2 [*more ~; most ~*] **:** behaving or done in a way that is meant to attract attention and that is often not genuine or sincere ▪ a *theatrical* gesture/bow ▪ *theatrical* behavior ▪ a politician who has a highly/very *theatrical* manner of speaking
– the·at·ri·cal·i·ty /θiˌætrəˈkæləti/ *noun* [*noncount*] **– the·at·ri·cal·ly** /θiˈætrɪkli/ *adv*

the·at·ri·cals /θiˈætrɪkəlz/ *noun* [*plural*]
1 : the performance of plays on a stage ▪ amateur *theatricals*
2 *Brit* **:** THEATRICS 1

the·at·rics /θiˈætrɪks/ *noun* [*plural*] *chiefly US*
1 *often disapproving* **:** ways of behaving and speaking that are like a performance on a stage and are intended to attract attention ▪ courtroom *theatrics* ▪ the *theatrics* of politicians
2 : THEATRICALS 1 ▪ amateur *theatrics*

thee /ˈðiː/ *pronoun, old-fashioned + literary* **—** used as a singular form of "you" when it is the object of a verb or preposition. ▪ "I take *thee* at thy word . . ." —Shakespeare, *Romeo and Juliet* (1594–95) ▪ "Sweet land of liberty, of *thee* I sing . . ." —Samuel Francis Smith, "My Country, 'Tis of Thee" (1831)

theft /ˈθɛft/ *noun, pl* **thefts :** the act or crime of stealing [*count*] car *thefts* ▪ The *theft* of the jewelry and other valuables was immediately reported to the police. [*noncount*] He was found guilty of *theft*. **—** see also GRAND THEFT, PETIT THEFT, PETTY THEFT

their /ˈðeɚ, ðɚ/ *adj, always used before a noun, possessive form of* THEY
1 : relating to or belonging to certain people, animals, or things ▪ All the furniture in *their* house is brand-new. ▪ They are on friendly terms with *their* neighbors. ▪ The students are seeking to exercise *their* rights. ▪ The birds have left *their* nest. ▪ The trees have all shed *their* leaves. **:** made or done by certain people, animals, or things ▪ *Their* artwork is on display at the museum. ▪ They did *their* best. ▪ *Their* conversation went well. ▪ He was angry because of *their* arriving/being late.
2 : his or her **:** his **:** her **:** its **—** used to refer to a single person whose sex is not known or specified ▪ Anyone in *their* right mind would find it unjust. ▪ Each person reacts to *their* environment differently.

Do not confuse *their* with *there* or *they're*.

theirs /ˈðeɚz/ *pronoun*
1 : that which belongs to or is connected with them **:** their one **:** their ones ▪ The computer is *theirs*. [=the computer belongs to them; it is their computer] ▪ He bought his car on the same day his parents bought *theirs*. ▪ She is a friend ***of theirs***. [=she is their friend] ▪ That dog *of theirs* [=their dog] is always barking.
2 : his or hers **—** used to refer to a single person whose sex is not known or specified ▪ I will do my part if everybody else does *theirs*.

the·ism /ˈθiːˌɪzəm/ *noun* [*noncount*] **:** the belief that God exists or that many gods exist **—** compare MONOTHEISM, POLYTHEISM
– the·ist /ˈθiːjɪst/ *noun, pl* **-ists** [*count*]

them /ˈðɛm, ðəm/ *pronoun, objective form of* THEY
1 — used to refer to certain people, animals, or things as the objects of a verb or preposition ▪ Their mother drove *them* to soccer practice. ▪ I haven't met *them* yet. ▪ You can ask any of *them* for help. ▪ I played basketball with *them* yesterday.
2 : him or her **—** used to refer to a single person whose sex is not known or specified ▪ The teacher said that if anyone came forward and admitted to the prank, she wouldn't punish *them*. [=she wouldn't punish that person]
3 *informal + humorous* **:** those **—** used in nonstandard speech ▪ *Them*'s fighting words. [=those are words that are likely to cause a fight]

the·mat·ic /θɪˈmætɪk/ *adj* **:** of or relating to a theme ▪ *thematic* writing ▪ the *thematic* development in the story
– the·mat·i·cal·ly /θɪˈmætɪkli/ *adv* ▪ The poems are grouped *thematically*.

theme /ˈθiːm/ *noun, pl* **themes** [*count*]
1 : the main subject that is being discussed or described in a piece of writing, a movie, etc. ▪ The quest for power is the underlying *theme* of the film. ▪ A constant *theme* in his novels is religion. ▪ The playwright skillfully brings together various *themes*. ▪ The album focuses on *themes* of love and loss. ▪ Adventures are popular *themes* in children's books.
2 a : a particular subject or issue that is discussed often or repeatedly ▪ The growing deficit was a dominant *theme* in the election. **b :** the particular subject or idea on which the style of something (such as a party or room) is based ▪ The party had a Hawaiian luau *theme*. ▪ The *theme* of the baby's room was zoo animals. [=the baby's bedroom was decorated with pictures of zoo animals] ▪ a *theme* party
3 *music* **a :** the main melody that is repeated in a piece of music **b :** THEME SONG ▪ They played the *theme* from/to the movie "Rocky."
4 *US* **:** a short piece of writing by a student on a particular subject **:** ESSAY ▪ The students were assigned to write a *theme* on the person they admired most.
– themed /ˈθiːmd/ *adj, always used before a noun* ▪ *themed* restaurants/events ▪ a sports-*themed* restaurant ▪ a Hawaiian-*themed* party

theme park *noun, pl* **~ parks** [*count*] **:** an amusement park where the rides and attractions are based on a particular theme (sense 2b)

theme song *noun, pl* **~ songs** [*count*] **:** a song that is played at the beginning and end of a television show, movie, etc. ▪ He was playing the *theme song* from/to "The Godfather."

them·selves /ðɛmˈsɛlvz/ *pronoun*
1 : those same people, animals, or things: **a —** used as the object of a verb or preposition to refer to people, animals, or things that have already been mentioned ▪ They are getting *themselves* ready. ▪ They did most of the painting *themselves*. ▪ nations that govern *themselves* ▪ They were dedicated to helping those less fortunate than *themselves*. ▪ people who are unable to care ***for themselves*** ▪ They enjoyed working *for themselves*. ▪ They kept their plans ***to themselves***. [=they kept their plans secret] ▪ She had the house ***all to herself***. [=she was alone in the house] **b —** used for emphasis to refer again to people, animals, or things that have already been mentioned ▪ They were young once *themselves*. ▪ They *themselves* were quite surprised when they won the game.
2 : himself or herself **—** used to refer to a single person whose sex is not known or specified ▪ Nobody should blame *themselves*.
3 : their normal or healthy selves ▪ They were *themselves* again after a night's rest. ▪ They didn't feel like *themselves* for a while after the long flight.
by themselves **1 :** without any help from other people ▪ The students solved the math problem *by themselves*. **2 :** with nobody else **:** ALONE ▪ They toured the city *by themselves* instead of traveling with a guide.

[1]then /ˈðɛn/ *adv*
1 : at that time **:** at the time mentioned ▪ It was *then* believed (that) the Earth was flat. ▪ She lived in the Soviet Union, as it *then* was called. ▪ Just *then* he walked in. ▪ Back *then*, he was living in New York.
2 a — used to indicate what happened or happens next ▪ He walked down the street, *then* turned the corner. ▪ First the clowns come out, (and) *then* the elephants and lions (come out). **b —** used to indicate what should be done next ▪ "Take your first right, (and) *then* turn left at the light," he said. ▪ Bring the soup to a boil, *then* turn down the heat and let it simmer for half an hour. **c —** used to indicate something more that must be done or thought of ▪ We need to choose the menu, rent a banquet hall, and *then* there are the invitations to send.
3 a — used to indicate what must be true or what must or should happen if something else is true or happens ▪ If you were there, *then* you must have seen him. ▪ If it rains, *then* we can't go. ▪ "It's raining." "*Then* we can't go." ▪ "He confessed." "The case is closed, *then*." ▪ If you want it, *then* take it. = Take it, *then*, if you want it. ▪ Hurry, *then*, if you want to catch the bus. ▪ What if there should be a fire? ***What then***? [=what will happen then?] ✧ *Then* is often omitted following *if*. ▪ If it rains, (*then*) we can't go. **b —** used to say or ask about what appears to be true based on what has happened or been said ▪ You did go, *then*, after all. ▪ Your mind is made up, *then*? **c —** used to say what has been agreed to or decided ▪ OK, *then*, I'll see you at seven o'clock. **d** *somewhat formal* **—** used to make a final statement that refers back to the things that have just been mentioned or described ▪ These, *then*, are the things you must do. ▪ All of us, *then*, must accept some blame for these problems.

4 — used after words like *all right* and *OK* at the beginning of a statement ▪ All right, *then*, let's get started.
and then some see [2]SOME
but then see [1]BUT
even then see [2]EVEN
(every) now and then see [1]NOW
then and there** or chiefly Brit* ***there and then : immediately at that place ▪ I decided (right) *then and there* that I would accept the offer. ▪ I made up my mind *then and there*.

[2]**then** *noun [singular]* : that time ▪ Since *then*, I've been more careful. ▪ He advised me to wait until *then*. ▪ They'll announce their decision next week. Until *then*, she'll just have to hope for the best. ▪ We should get there before *then*. ▪ They were friends from *then* on. ▪ Nothing like that had ever happened up to *then*.

[3]**then** *adj, always used before a noun* : existing at or belonging to the time mentioned ▪ She was appointed to the position by Connecticut's *then* governor. [=by the person who was Connecticut's governor at that time]

thence /ˈðɛns/ *adv, formal* : from that place : from there ▪ Their travels took them to the Bahamas, *thence* south to Venezuela.

thence·forth /ˈðɛnsˌfoɚθ/ *adv, formal* : from that time forward : starting then ▪ He was determined *thenceforth* to dedicate himself to his studies. ▪ *Thenceforth*, she decided, she would deal with the media herself.

the·oc·ra·cy /θiˈɑːkrəsi/ *noun, pl* **-cies**
1 *[noncount]* : a form of government in which a country is ruled by religious leaders
2 *[count]* : a country that is ruled by religious leaders
— **theo·crat·ic** /ˌθiːjəˈkrætɪk/ *adj* ▪ a *theocratic* government/regime

theo·lo·gian /ˌθiːjəˈloʊʤən/ *noun, pl* **-gians** *[count]* : a person who is an expert on theology

the·ol·o·gy /θiˈɑːləʤi/ *noun, pl* **-gies**
1 *[noncount]* : the study of religious faith, practice, and experience : the study of God and God's relation to the world ▪ He has an interest in *theology* and pastoral work.
2 *[count]* : a system of religious beliefs or ideas ▪ Christian/Muslim/Jewish *theology* ▪ The bishop was opposed to the group's *theology*.
— **theo·log·i·cal** /ˌθiːjəˈlɑːʤɪkəl/ *adj* ▪ *theological* studies/arguments — **theo·log·i·cal·ly** /ˌθiːjəˈlɑːʤɪkli/ *adv*

the·o·rem /ˈθiːjərəm/ *noun, pl* **-rems** *[count] technical* : a formula or statement that can be proved from other formulas or statements ▪ mathematical *theorems*

the·o·ret·i·cal /ˌθiːjəˈrɛtɪkəl/ *also* **the·o·ret·ic** /ˌθiːjəˈrɛtɪk/ *adj*
1 : relating to what is possible or imagined rather than to what is known to be true or real ▪ On a *theoretical* level, hiring more people seems logical. ▪ The idea is purely *theoretical* at this point. ▪ a *theoretical* argument ▪ The teacher gave us a *theoretical* [=*hypothetical*] situation as an example. ▪ The danger is more than just a *theoretical* possibility. ▪ I was speaking ***in theoretical terms***. [=*theoretically*]
2 : relating to the general principles or ideas of a subject rather than the practical uses of those ideas ▪ *theoretical* physics
— **the·o·ret·i·cal·ly** /ˌθiːjəˈrɛtɪkli/ *adv* ▪ *Theoretically*, the value of the funds could triple in the next few months. ▪ It is *theoretically* possible but unlikely to happen. ▪ He argued *theoretically*.

the·o·re·ti·cian /ˌθiːjərəˈtɪʃən/ *noun, pl* **-cians** *[count]* : THEORIST

the·o·rist /ˈθiːjərɪst/ *noun, pl* **-rists** *[count]* : a person who forms theories about something ▪ political *theorists*

the·o·rize *also Brit* **the·o·rise** /ˈθiːjəˌraɪz/ *verb* **-riz·es; -rized; -riz·ing** : to think of or suggest ideas about what is possibly true or real : to form or suggest a theory about something *[no obj]* Many scientists have *theorized* about/on the possibility of life on other planets. *[+ obj]* — usually + *that* ▪ The police *theorized that* the same person was responsible for both murders.

the·o·ry /ˈθiːjəri/ *noun, pl* **-ries**
1 : an idea or set of ideas that is intended to explain facts or events *[count]* a widely accepted scientific *theory* ▪ Einstein's *theory* of relativity ▪ *theories* on/about evolution *[noncount]* according to atomic/economic *theory*
2 *[count]* : an idea that is suggested or presented as possibly true but that is not known or proven to be true ▪ Her method is based on the *theory* that all children want to learn. ▪ There are a number of different *theories* about the cause of the disease. ▪ She proposed a *theory* of her own. ▪ Investigators rejected the *theory* that the death was accidental. ▪ There is no evidence to support such a *theory*.
3 *[noncount]* : the general principles or ideas that relate to a particular subject ▪ He is a specialist in film *theory* and criticism. ▪ music *theory*
in theory 1 — used to say what should happen or be true if a theory is correct ▪ *In theory*, the reading skills of the students should improve. 2 — used to say that something seems to be true or possible as an idea but may not actually be true or possible ▪ I agree with you *in theory*, but realistically I don't think we have the time to do that.

ther·a·peu·tic /ˌθerəˈpjuːtɪk/ *adj*
1 *[more ~; most ~]* : producing good effects on your body or mind ▪ the *therapeutic* benefits of yoga ▪ Gardening can be very *therapeutic*.
2 : of or relating to the treatment of illness ▪ a *therapeutic* diet ▪ the *therapeutic* effects of radiation

ther·a·peu·tics /ˌθerəˈpjuːtɪks/ *noun [noncount] medical* : a branch of medicine that deals with the ways to treat illnesses

ther·a·pist /ˈθerəpɪst/ *noun, pl* **-pists** *[count]*
1 : a person trained in methods of treating illnesses especially without the use of drugs or surgery ▪ He works with a *therapist* to improve his speech. — see also OCCUPATIONAL THERAPIST, PHYSICAL THERAPIST, PHYSIOTHERAPIST
2 : a person who helps people deal with mental or emotional problems by talking about those problems : a person trained in psychotherapy ▪ He saw his *therapist* [=*psychotherapist*] regularly when he was going through his divorce. ▪ a family *therapist*

ther·a·py /ˈθerəpi/ *noun, pl* **-pies**
1 : the treatment of physical or mental illnesses *[noncount]* He is undergoing cancer *therapy*. *[count]* new drug *therapies* — see also CHEMOTHERAPY, GENE THERAPY, GROUP THERAPY, HORMONE REPLACEMENT THERAPY, OCCUPATIONAL THERAPY, PHYSICAL THERAPY, SHOCK THERAPY, SPEECH THERAPY
2 *[noncount]* : PSYCHOTHERAPY

[1]**there** /ˈðeɚ/ *adv*
1 a : in that place : at that location ▪ Put the package *there* on the table. ▪ Go to your room and stay *there*. ▪ Turn *there* at the church. ▪ She was sitting *there* a minute ago. ▪ Hello. Is Pat *there*? ▪ They have lived *there* for 30 years. ▪ When will you be *there*? ▪ Please stand over *there*. ▪ I used to live near/around *there*. ▪ What do you see out/down/up/in *there*? ▪ At last we're *there*! [=we have arrived at the place we were traveling to] ▪ The opportunity to score was *there* [=was available], so I took the shot. — used in speech when something is found ▪ So *there* you are. I've been looking for you. ▪ Ah, *there*'s the book I've been looking for. **b** : to or into that place ▪ If we leave now, we should get *there* by noon. ▪ I drove the kids *there*. ▪ He drove *there* and back in one day. ▪ Can we walk *there*? ▪ We go *there* every year.
2 a : at that point in a process, activity, story, etc. ▪ Stop right *there*, before you say something you'll regret. ▪ *There* the story takes a surprising turn. **b** : in that particular matter ▪ *There* is where I disagree with you.
3 a — used with the verb *be* at the beginning of a sentence that makes a statement about a situation or asks about a situation ▪ *There is* no way to know when he'll be home. ▪ *There's* no point in arguing about it. ▪ *There's* still a lot for us to do. ▪ *There are* many things to be considered. ▪ *There is* a person waiting to see you. [=a person is waiting to see you] ▪ *Is there* a gas station nearby? **b** — used to introduce a sentence in which the subject comes after the verb ▪ *There* will come a time [=a time will come] when I will need your help. ▪ *There* used to be a school here. ▪ Once upon a time, *there* lived a beautiful princess named Snow White.
4 — used in speech after a noun to emphasize which person, thing, etc., you are referring to ▪ That clock *there* once belonged to my great-grandmother. ▪ I just saw that boy *there* stealing a piece of candy. ▪ You *there*! What are you doing?!
5 *informal* — used to address a person or animal ▪ Well, hello *there*. ▪ Say *there*, do you have the time?
6 — used to introduce a sentence in which the subject comes after the verb ▪ *There* was your chance [=that was your chance] to ask her out on a date. ▪ *There*'s still a lot for us to do. ▪ Eat your vegetables. *There*'s a good girl. [=you're a good girl if you eat your vegetables]

Do not confuse *there* with *their* or *they're*.

been there, done that see BE 8

T

have been there — used to say that you have experienced the same thing that someone else has experienced • I know how you feel. I*'ve been there* (before) myself.
here and there see [1]HERE
here, there, and everywhere see [1]HERE
neither here nor there see [1]HERE
***out there** informal* — used to say in a general way that someone or something exists • I'm not surprised that he lied about it. There are a lot of people like him *out there*. [=there are a lot of other people who would have lied] • Be careful when you drive. There are a lot of crazy drivers *out there*. • She's been searching for the right car to buy. It's *out there* somewhere. — see also OUT-THERE
then and there** or **there and then see [1]THEN
there go/goes see [1]GO
there's . . . for you see [1]FOR
***there you are** or **there you go** informal* **1** — used to tell someone that you have given them what they asked for • *There you are*, sir. That will be $3 for the coffees. • "Could you pass the salt?" "Sure, *there you go*." **2** — used to indicate that something is completed or done in a satisfactory way • You just plug it in, push this button, and *there you are*. • *There you are*, then. You got what you wanted. • Wait, I want to fix your tie. *There you go*.
***there you have it** informal* — used to indicate that something is completed or done in a satisfactory way • You just plug it in, push this button, and *there you have it*. • *There you have it*. The mystery is solved.
you have me there** or **there you have me see HAVE

[2]there *adj, not used before a noun* **:** capable of being relied on for support or help • My dad has always been *there* for me. [=has always helped me when I needed his help] • She is *there* to answer any questions you might have.
not all there see [2]ALL

[3]there *interj*
1 — used to attract attention • *There*, look at that. • *There*, you've gone and broken it!
2 — used to show satisfaction, approval, or encouragement • *There*, it's finished at last. • *There*, I told you so.
***so there** informal* — used to say in a somewhat rude, angry, or childish way that you have stated your opinion or decision and will not change it • Well, I don't want to be your friend, either. *So there*! • I'm going no matter what you say. *So there*!
there, there — used to tell someone not to be worried or unhappy • *There, there* [=*now, now*], don't cry. Everything will be OK.

[4]there *noun* [*noncount*]
1 : that place • Get away ***from there***.
2 : that point • I'll get everything ready, and you ***take it from there***.

there·abouts /ˌðerəˈbaʊts/ *also US* **there·about** /ˌðerəˈbaʊt/ *adv* **:** near or around that place, time, number, amount, etc. • He lives on Maple Street ***or thereabouts***. • It happened in 1977 *or thereabouts*. • There were 50 people *or thereabouts*. — compare HEREABOUTS

there·af·ter /ðeəˈæftɚ, *Brit* ðerˈɑːftə/ *adv, formal* **:** after that • *Thereafter*, the two companies operated in full partnership. • She returned shortly *thereafter*.

there·by /ðeəˈbaɪ/ *adv, formal* **:** by means of that act, those words, that document, etc. • He signed the contract, *thereby* forfeiting his right to the property.
thereby hangs a tale see [1]HANG

there'd /ˈðeəd/ — used as a contraction of *there had* or *there would* • *There'd* [=*there had*] never been a case like it before. • I knew *there'd* [=*there would*] be trouble.

there·fore /ˈðeəˌfoə/ *adv, somewhat formal* **:** for that reason **:** because of that • The cell phone is thin and light and *therefore* very convenient to carry around. • Payment was received two weeks after it was due; *therefore*, you will be charged a late fee.

there·in /ðeəˈɪn/ *adv, formal*
1 : in or into that place or thing • The insurance covers the apartment and all the property *therein*. • His name was mentioned in the article, although he was incorrectly described *therein* as a medical doctor.
2 : in that statement, fact, or detail • They have to make a decision soon. ***Therein lies*** the problem. [=that is why there is a problem] If they act too quickly, they run the risk of choosing the wrong plan.

there·of /ðeəˈʌv/ *adv, formal* **:** of the thing that has been mentioned • The professor explained the problem and solution *thereof*. [=the problem and the solution of the problem] • A will or any part *thereof* [=any part of a will] may be revoked by a subsequent will. • The problem is money, or (a/the) ***lack thereof***. [=the problem is a lack of money]

there·on /ðeəˈɑːn/ *adv, formal* **:** on the thing that has been mentioned • The highway and structures *thereon* are being repaired. • a text with a commentary *thereon*

there's /ˈðeəz, ðəz/ — used as a contraction of *there is* or *there has* • *There's* [=*there is*] a lot more to do. • *There's* [=*there has*] never been any reason to doubt him.

there·to /ðeəˈtuː/ *adv, formal* **:** to the thing that has been mentioned • The bill and amendments *thereto* are being considered.

there·un·der /ðeəˈʌndɚ/ *adv, formal* **:** under the thing that has been mentioned • the statute and regulations *thereunder*

there·up·on /ˈðerəˌpɑːn/ *adv, formal*
1 : immediately after that • The committee reviewed the documents and *thereupon* decided to accept the proposal.
2 : on the thing that has been mentioned • The jurors discussed the evidence and made/based their decision *thereupon*.

[1]ther·mal /ˈθɚməl/ *adj*
1 : of, relating to, or caused by heat • *thermal* energy • *thermal* insulation/stress
2 : designed to keep you warm by preventing heat from leaving your body • *thermal* clothing/underwear
3 : having hot water flowing out of the ground • *thermal* springs/waters
– ther·mal·ly *adv*

[2]thermal *noun, pl* **-mals**
1 [*count*] **:** a rising current of warm air that is produced when the sun heats an area of the ground
2 ***thermals*** [*plural*] *Brit* **:** thermal clothing or underwear

ther·mo·dy·nam·ics /ˌθɚmoʊˌdaɪˈnæmɪks/ *noun* [*noncount*] *technical* **:** a science that deals with the action of heat and related forms of energy
– ther·mo·dy·nam·ic /ˌθɚmoʊˌdaɪˈnæmɪk/ *adj* **– ther·mo·dy·nam·i·cal·ly** /ˌθɚmoʊˌdaɪˈnæmɪkli/ *adv*

ther·mom·e·ter /θɚˈmɑːmətɚ/ *noun, pl* **-ters** [*count*] **:** an instrument used for measuring temperature • The *thermomemeter* says it's almost 80 degrees outside, but it doesn't feel that hot. • a digital/meat *thermometer*

thermometer

ther·mo·nu·cle·ar /ˌθɚmoʊˈnuːklijɚ, *Brit* ˌθɜːməʊˈnjuːkliə/ *adj, technical* **:** of or relating to the changes in the nucleus of atoms that happen at extremely high temperatures • a *thermonuclear* reaction/explosion • Hydrogen bombs are *thermonuclear* weapons/devices.

ther·mos /ˈθɚməs/ *noun, pl* **-mos·es** [*count*] **:** a container that keeps liquids hot or cold for long periods of time — called also *(US) thermos bottle, (Brit) flask, (Brit) vacuum flask*

ther·mo·stat /ˈθɚməˌstæt/ *noun, pl* **-stats** [*count*] **:** a device that automatically adjusts the temperature in a room temperature to a desired level • I set the *thermostat* to 68 degrees.; *also* **:** a similar device used for adjusting the temperature of a machine or system

thermostat

the·sau·rus /θɪˈsorəs/ *noun, pl* **-sau·ri** /-ˈsoəˌaɪ/ *or* **-sau·rus·es** /-ˈsorəsəz/ [*count*] **:** a book in which words that have the same or similar meanings are grouped together

these *plural of* THIS

the·sis /ˈθiːsəs/ *noun, pl* **the·ses** /ˈθiːˌsiːz/ [*count*]
1 : a long piece of writing on a particular subject that is done to earn a degree at a university • She wrote her *thesis* on Renaissance Nativity scenes. • a master's/doctoral *thesis* on the effects of global warming
2 *formal* **:** a statement that someone wants to discuss or prove • New evidence supports his *thesis*. • We disagreed with the basic *thesis* of the report. • The book's central *thesis* is that propaganda influences the masses in important ways.

thes·pi·an /ˈθɛspijən/ *noun, pl* **-ans** [*count*] *formal + sometimes humorous* **:** ACTOR • a renowned *thespian* and director

T

they /ˈðeɪ/ *pronoun*
1 : those people, animals, or things ▪ *They* dance very well. ▪ *They* both played on the football team. ▪ *They* are thinking of getting a pet. ▪ What are *they* doing?
2 — used to refer to people in a general way or to a group of people who are not specified ▪ You know what *they* say: you only live once. ▪ *They* say it will be a mild winter. [=people who predict the weather say that it will be a mild winter] ▪ She's as hardworking as *they* come. [=she's extremely hardworking] ▪ *They* will be holding the graduation outdoors if the weather permits. ▪ *They* took away his license.
3 : he or she — used to refer to a single person whose sex is not known or specified ▪ Everyone can go if *they* want to.

they'd /ˈðeɪd/ — used as a contraction of *they had* or *they would* ▪ They admitted that *they'd* [=*they had*] been foolish. ▪ *They'd* [=*they would*] love to go but won't be able to.

they'll /ˈðeɪl, ðɛl/ — used as a contraction of *they will* ▪ *They'll* be arriving soon.

they're /ˈðeɚ, ðɚ/ — used as a contraction of *they are* ▪ It all depends on whether *they're* available or not.

Do not confuse *they're* with *their* or *there*.

they've /ˈðeɪv/ — used as a contraction of *they have* ▪ I don't think *they've* made up their minds yet.

thi•a•mine *or* **thi•a•min** /ˈθajəmən/ *noun* [*noncount*] **:** a natural substance (called a vitamin) that is found in certain foods and that helps your body to be healthy — called also *vitamin* B_1

[1]**thick** /ˈθɪk/ *adj* **thick•er; -est** [*also more ~; most ~*]
1 a : having a large distance between the top and bottom or front and back surfaces **:** not thin ▪ a *thick* book/board ▪ *thick* walls ▪ a *thick* layer of ice ▪ He wore *thick* glasses. [=glasses with thick lenses] ▪ a *thick* cigar ▪ a *thick* slice of ham/bread/cake ▪ a *thick*, juicy steak ▪ pizza with a *thick* crust ▪ a *thick* wool sweater ▪ a bodybuilder with a *thick*, short body ▪ He was a man in his fifties, a little ***thick around the middle***. [=fat around his waist] **b :** having a specified distance from one surface to the opposite surface **:** having a specified thickness ▪ The planks were two inches *thick*. ▪ The log was 12 inches *thick*. ▪ The recipe calls for one cup of mushrooms sliced ¼ inch *thick*.
2 a : having parts that are close together ▪ a *thick* [=*dense*] forest ▪ *thick* woods **b :** growing closely together and in a large amount ▪ a dog/cat with *thick* fur ▪ She has *thick*, curly hair.
3 : difficult to see through **:** DENSE ▪ *thick* black smoke ▪ The fog/haze was *thick* this morning. ▪ a *thick* blanket of fog
4 *of a liquid* **:** not flowing easily ▪ The stew/chili was very *thick*. ▪ *thick* gravy/sauce/syrup ▪ a *thick* milkshake ▪ The batter was too *thick*.
5 a *of speech or the voice* **:** difficult to understand ▪ His speech was *thick* and slurred. — often + *with* ▪ Her voice was *thick with* emotion when she talked about her divorce. **b** *of a person's accent* **:** very easy to notice ▪ He spoke with a *thick* [=*heavy*] accent.
6 *informal* **:** STUPID 1 ▪ They were just too *thick* to understand what I was saying. ▪ Why can't he get it through his ***thick head*** that I don't like him? [=why can't he understand that I don't like him?]
7 *not used before a noun* **a** *chiefly US* **:** existing in great numbers or large amounts ▪ The mosquitoes were *thick* [=there were a lot of mosquitoes] near the lake. ▪ Tension was *thick* in the office. [=there was a lot of tension in the office] **b :** having great numbers or a large amount of something — + *with* ▪ The air was *thick with* mosquitoes. ▪ The atmosphere was *thick with* anticipation as we waited for the results.
8 *not used before a noun, informal* **:** having a close and friendly relationship ▪ Those two are really *thick*. [=*close*] ▪ They were (as) ***thick as thieves*** [=very close and secretive] for weeks, which made us wonder what they were doing. — often + *with* ▪ He was very *thick with* his pastor.
a thick ear *Brit, informal* **:** the punishment of being hit on the side of the head ▪ He threatened to ***give him a thick ear***. [=(*US*) to slap him upside the head]
(a) thick skin see [1]SKIN
blood is thicker than water see BLOOD
thick on the ground **:** existing or occurring in large amounts ▪ Hotels and restaurants are *thick on the ground* along the strip. ▪ Presidential candidates are *thick on the ground* this year. [=there are a lot of presidential candidates this year]

[2]**thick** *adv* **thick•er; -est** [*also more ~; most ~*]
1 : in a way that makes thick pieces, layers, etc. ▪ Slice the roast *thick*.
2 : in great numbers ▪ Apples hung *thick* on the trees. ▪ Suggestions were coming in ***thick and fast***. [=large numbers of suggestions were coming in quickly]
lay it on thick see [1]LAY

[3]**thick** *noun*
in the thick of **:** in the most active or intense part of (something) ▪ a soldier *in the thick of* (the) battle ▪ He found himself *in the thick of* the action. ▪ We're really *in the thick of* things now.
through thick and thin **:** through many difficult times over a long period ▪ She stood by me *through thick and thin*.

thick•en /ˈθɪkən/ *verb* **-ens; -ened; -en•ing :** to make (something) thick or thicker or to become thick or thicker [+ *obj*] I *thickened* the gravy with flour. [*no obj*] When the mixture *thickens*, add the remaining ingredients. ▪ The fog *thickened* when night fell.
the plot thickens see [1]PLOT
— thick•en•er /ˈθɪkənɚ/ *noun, pl* **-ers** [*count*] ▪ Flour/cornstarch is used as a *thickener* in sauces.

thick•et /ˈθɪkət/ *noun, pl* **-ets** [*count*] **:** a group of bushes or small trees that grow close together ▪ a dense *thicket* of rosebushes — often used figuratively ▪ A *thicket* of reporters blocked the entrance to city hall. ▪ a tangled *thicket* of laws

thick–head•ed /ˈθɪkˌhɛdəd/ *adj* [*more ~; most ~*] *informal* **:** not intelligent or sensible **:** STUPID ▪ He's a stubborn and *thick-headed* old fool. ▪ a *thick-headed* decision

thick•ly /ˈθɪkli/ *adv* [*more ~; most ~*]
1 : in a way that makes thick pieces, layers, etc. ▪ *thickly* sliced mushrooms ▪ *thickly* padded cushions ▪ He buttered the bread *thickly*.
2 : with a lot of people, trees, etc., close together ▪ a *thickly* settled neighborhood ▪ a *thickly* wooded area
3 *of speech or the voice* **:** in a way that is difficult to understand ▪ *thickly* accented speech

thick•ness /ˈθɪknəs/ *noun*
1 a : the distance between the top and bottom or front and back surfaces of something **:** a measurement of how thick something is [*noncount*] The plank measures two inches in *thickness*. [*count*] the length, circumference, and *thickness* of the log ▪ Plywood is available in various *thicknesses*. ▪ Cooking time will vary depending on the *thickness* of the steak/chops. **b** [*noncount*] **:** the quality of being thick ▪ I added flour to increase the gravy's *thickness*. ▪ I was surprised by the *thickness* of his accent.
2 [*count*] **:** a layer or sheet of some material — usually + *of* ▪ a single *thickness of* canvas/foil/cloth

thick•set /ˈθɪkˌsɛt/ *adj* [*more ~; most ~*] **:** having a short, thick body ▪ a *thickset* man

thick–skinned /ˈθɪkˌskɪnd/ *adj* [*more ~; most ~*]
1 : having a thick skin ▪ a *thick-skinned* orange
2 : not easily bothered by criticism or insults **:** not sensitive ▪ You need to be *thick-skinned* if you are going to work in politics. — opposite THIN-SKINNED

thief /ˈθiːf/ *noun, pl* **thieves** /ˈθiːvz/ [*count*] **:** a person who steals something ▪ a car *thief* ▪ A *thief* took my purse.

thiev•ery /ˈθiːvəri/ *noun* [*noncount*] *formal* **:** the act of stealing ▪ They accused him of *thievery*. [=they accused him of stealing something] ▪ a case of suspected *thievery*

thiev•ing /ˈθiːvɪŋ/ *noun* [*noncount*] *somewhat old-fashioned* **:** the act or activity of stealing ▪ They finally found out about his *thieving*.
— thieving *adj, always used before a noun* ▪ You *thieving* liar!

thigh /ˈθaɪ/ *noun, pl* **thighs** [*count*]
1 : the part of your leg that is above the knee — see picture at HUMAN
2 : the side part of the leg of a bird ▪ boneless chicken *thighs*

thigh•bone /ˈθaɪˌboʊn/ *noun, pl* **-bones** [*count*] **:** the long bone in the upper part of the leg **:** FEMUR — see picture at HUMAN

thim•ble /ˈθɪmbəl/ *noun, pl* **thim•bles** [*count*] **:** a small metal or plastic cap used in sewing to protect the finger that pushes the needle — see picture at SEWING

[1]**thin** /ˈθɪn/ *adj* **thin•ner; -nest** [*also more ~; most ~*]
1 : having a small distance between the top and bottom or front and back surfaces **:** not thick ▪ *thin* paper/walls ▪ a *thin* band/line/stripe ▪ a *thin* coating/layer of dust ▪ pizza with a *thin* crust ▪ a *thin* slice of ham
2 : not having a lot of extra flesh on the body **:** not fat ▪ a *thin* child ▪ She is very/too *thin*. ▪ *thin* legs ***synonyms*** see [2]LEAN

3 a : not growing closely together • a *thin* stand of trees **:** not growing in a large amount • *thin* hair • His hair is a little *thin* on top. = He's a little *thin* on top. [=he does not have a lot of hair on the top of his head] **b :** having less than the usual, original, or needed number or amount • Attendance at the carnival was a bit *thin*. [=*low*] • My patience was ***wearing/running thin***. [=I was becoming less patient]
4 *of a liquid* **:** flowing very easily **:** containing a lot of water • *thin* broth/gravy/soup
5 : having less oxygen than normal • *thin* air • a *thin* atmosphere
6 : easy to see through • The fog was relatively *thin*. • a *thin* mist
7 : not large or impressive • a *thin* [=very small] margin of victory • She has a *thin* [=*narrow*] lead in the polls.
8 : not very good, useful, etc. **:** WEAK • *thin* arguments/explanations • That excuse is pretty *thin*. • The story's plot is pretty *thin*. • His argument quickly ***wore thin***. • a ***thin smile*** [=a weak smile that does not seem sincere]
9 *of a voice* **:** weak and high • a high, *thin* voice
(a) thin skin see [1]SKIN
disappear/vanish into thin air **:** to disappear completely in a way that is mysterious • The papers seem to have *vanished into thin air*.
have a thin time (of it) *Brit* **:** to be in a difficult situation especially because you do not have enough money • He was *having a thin time of it* until his novel started selling.
on thin ice see [1]ICE
out of thin air — used to say that someone or something appears in a sudden and unexpected way • He appeared *out of thin air*. [=*out of nowhere*]
the thin end of the wedge *Brit* **:** the beginning of something that will become more serious, unpleasant, etc. • The bank's decision to raise rates could be *the thin end of the wedge*. [=many other banks may also decide to raise rates]
thin on the ground *Brit* **:** existing or occurring in very small amounts • Useful suggestions have been *thin on the ground* lately. [=there have been very few useful suggestions lately]
through thick and thin see [3]THICK
– thin•ness /ˈθɪnnəs/ *noun* [*noncount*]

[2]thin *verb* **thins; thinned; thin•ning :** to make (something or someone) thin or thinner or to become thin or thinner: such as **a :** to become less crowded, close together, or full [*no obj*] The crowd gradually *thinned* [=grew smaller] as the night went on. • The trees *thinned* as we climbed higher. [=there were fewer trees as we climbed higher] [*+ obj*] The bad weather *thinned* (out) the crowd a little. • He plans to *thin* (out) the young carrots in the garden. [=to remove some of them so that there is more room between the remaining carrots] **b** [*+ obj*] **:** to make (a liquid) less thick by adding water or some other liquid to it • He added a little more water to *thin* the gravy. **c** [*no obj*] *of a person's hair* **:** to become less thick as more hairs fall out over time • His hair is *thinning*. = He has *thinning* hair. **d** [*no obj*] *of fog, smoke, etc.* **:** to become easier to see through **:** to become less thick or dense • The haze *thinned* in the late afternoon. **e :** to become less fat or to make (someone) less fat [*no obj*] — usually *+ down* • She's *thinned down* a lot in the past year. [*+ obj*] His face has been *thinned* by illness.

[3]thin *adv* **thin•ner; -nest** [*also more* ~; *most* ~] **:** in a way that makes thin pieces, layers, etc. • She sliced the cheese *thin*.

[1]thine /ˈðaɪn/ *pronoun, old-fashioned + literary* **:** YOURS • May God's blessings be *thine*.

[2]thine *adj, old-fashioned + literary* **:** YOUR — used before words beginning with a vowel or an "h" • "Give every man *thine* ear, but few thy voice . . ." —Shakespeare, *Hamlet* (1600)

thing /ˈθɪŋ/ *noun, pl* **things**
1 [*count*] **a :** an object whose name is not known or stated • What is that *thing* on the floor? • That *thing* is loud. • He is good at making *things* out of clay. **b :** an object, animal, quality, etc., of any kind • My doctor told me to avoid fatty *things* like donuts and potato chips. • We must respect all living *things*. • She loves all *things* chocolate. [=she loves anything made out of chocolate] • Her voice is a *thing* of great beauty. [=her voice is very beautiful] • The disease is said to be ***a thing of the past*** [=the disease no longer exists] • The drawer has pens, paper clips, ***and things (like that)***. **c :** a particular event, occurrence, or situation • Birth is a miraculous *thing*. • It was the worst *thing* that could have happened. • That sunset was the most beautiful *thing* I have ever seen. • Let's just forget about the whole *thing* and move on. • The one *thing* I hate most is being lied to. • It's ***a good thing*** (that) no one was injured. • Becoming friends with your boss is ***not a bad thing***. = Becoming friends with your boss is ***no bad thing***. [=becoming friends with your boss could have good results]
2 *things* [*plural*] **:** objects that belong to a person **:** personal possessions or belongings • Are all your *things* packed? • I need a place to store my *things*. • The children's *things* are always lying around on the floor. • When she realized she was late for work, she quickly put on her *things* [=she put on her clothes, shoes, etc.] and left.
3 *things* [*plural*] **:** objects that are used for a particular activity • Put the cleaning *things* away when you are done. • She got out the cooking *things* to bake some cookies.
4 [*count*] **:** an action that is done, that will be done, or that needs to be done • I have many *things* to do today. = I have lots of *things* that need to get done today. • There are a few *things* we still have to deal with. • There is actually one *thing* you can do to help. • Let's get this *thing* over with quickly. • That was a mean/cruel/kind/generous/thoughtful *thing* to do. • They expect great *things* from her. [=they expect her to be very successful] • The boy did ***the right thing*** and gave back the toy he took. • It's ***no easy thing*** [=it's not easy] to raise three children by yourself. • Cathy and I hit it off on our first date. ***One thing led to another***, and pretty soon we were engaged. — sometimes used to say that one action is more serious, difficult, or important than another. • It is one *thing* to say you're sorry but (it is) another (*thing*) to actually mean it. • Planning a project is one *thing*; doing it is another.
5 [*count*] **a :** an activity • What *things* do you like to do in your spare time? • I like hiking, biking—that sort of *thing*. • The students are allowed to ***do their own thing***. [=do the activities that they want to do] • Just ***do your thing*** [=do what you usually do] and pretend I'm not here. **b** *informal* **:** an activity that is done by a particular group of people • They spent the evening doing guy *things*. [=doing the kind of things that guys/men tend to like doing] • You wouldn't understand, Dad. It's a girl *thing*. **c** *US, informal* **:** an activity and everything that is related to it — usually singular • He tried the college *thing* [=he tried going to college] but dropped out after the first semester. • She's done with the whole rebellious teenager *thing*. [=she's done being a rebellious teenager] **d** *informal* **:** an activity that someone enjoys or does well — usually singular • Ballroom dancing is his *thing*, not mine. • It's not really my (kind of) *thing*.
6 *things* [*plural*] **:** the conditions that exist at a particular time and in a particular place • *Things* are improving. [=the situation is improving] • How are *things* with the new baby? • You're just making *things* more difficult for yourself. • As *things* stand now [=in the current situation], we can't afford a new car. • An apology would not change *things* between us. • ***All things considered*** [=*overall*; when you think about everything that happened], the party went very well.
7 [*count*] **:** a fact or piece of information about something or someone • He checks every little *thing*. [=*detail*] • There are a lot of *things* you don't know about us. • The *thing* I don't understand is why the car costs so much. • When buying a car, price and performance are important *things* to consider. • There is one more *thing* I'd like to ask you. • Several *things* were discussed at the meeting. • I'll give you a couple of days to ***think things over***. [=to think about the situation and make a decision] • We are always arguing, but ***the (funny) thing is***, I think I love him. • ***The thing is*** that [=it is important to understand that] you can never predict who will win. • I make excellent chili. *The thing is* to pick the right peppers. [=to make excellent chili, you need to pick the right peppers] • ***The thing with/about*** him [=an important characteristic to know about him] is that he is not reliable.
8 [*count*] **:** a thought, idea, or opinion • He just says the first *thing* that pops into his mind. • Don't say *things* you might regret later. • That was a terrible *thing* to say. • He had some interesting *things* to suggest. • She always knows the right *thing* to say.
9 [*singular*] **:** a reason for something • I can't stand being around him. ***For one thing***, he smokes. For another, he's rude. • OK, ***here's the thing***. I don't have enough money to go to college. • I'm sorry I didn't call you. ***The thing is***, I've been really busy with work and school. • ***The thing is that*** I haven't had time to call you.
10 [*singular*] **a :** a goal or purpose • The *thing* is to get well, and then you can think about playing again. **b :** a way of reaching or achieving a goal • There is only one *thing* left for

T

us to do: fight back! ▪ (*Brit*) ***There's only one thing for it***: we must fight.

11 [*count*] *informal* — used for a person, animal, or object that causes strong feelings of affection or dislike in you ▪ You poor *thing*, you must be freezing. ▪ She's a pretty little *thing*, isn't she! ▪ Get that dirty *thing* out of my house!

12 [*count*] *informal* **:** a strong feeling of liking or disliking something or someone — usually singular; used with *have* ▪ She *has* a *thing* about snakes. [=she's afraid of snakes] ▪ He has always *had* this *thing* with flying. ▪ My teacher *had* this/a *thing* against me. [=my teacher disliked me for some unknown reason] ▪ He *has* a *thing* for [=he likes] women with red hair.

13 *the thing* **a :** the item that is the most fashionable or popular ▪ Long skirts are *the thing* to wear this season. ▪ It's *the* newest/latest *thing* in fashion. **b :** the fashionable or proper way of behaving, talking, or dressing ▪ It's *the thing* this year to buy products made from recycled materials. ▪ Wearing athletic shoes with a suit is not quite *the thing*.

all/other things being equal *formal* — used to say what should happen or be true if two situations, products, etc., are different in a specified way but not in other ways ▪ *All things being equal*, a person with a PhD should be getting a higher salary than someone with only a Master's degree.

all things to all people/men **:** a person or thing that makes all people happy by giving them what they want or need ▪ It was clear that the senator was trying to be *all things to all people* in her campaign. ▪ The museum is *all things to all people*, young and old.

amount to the same thing ✧ If two or more things *amount to the same thing*, there is very little difference between them. ▪ "Lying and cheating *amount to the same thing*," she said.

a thing **:** ANYTHING — used in negative statements ▪ I can't see *a thing* [=I can see nothing] without my glasses on. ▪ The guests will be here soon, and I don't have *a thing* (that is appropriate) to wear. ▪ Don't worry about *a thing*. I'll take care of everything. ▪ I can't do *a thing* to stop them! ▪ I got there early so I wouldn't miss *a thing*. ▪ The police couldn't get *a thing* out of him. ▪ She refused to tell me *a thing* about it. ▪ I haven't heard *a thing* from him since graduation. ▪ We haven't had *a thing* to eat all day. ▪ Forget what he said—***it doesn't mean a thing***. [=it has no meaning or importance; it's not true] ▪ None of this will *mean a thing* if we lose. ▪ She doesn't look ***a thing like*** [=*anything like*] her older sister. ▪ His new album doesn't sound *a thing like* his last one. [=his new album sounds nothing like his old one]

a thing or two *informal* **:** some useful information ▪ I know *a thing or two* about cars. ▪ When it comes to cooking, she could teach you *a thing or two*.

at the center of things see [1]CENTER

be hearing things see HEAR

chance would be a fine thing see [1]CHANCE

first thing see [1]FIRST

first things first see [1]FIRST

have another thing coming *informal* — used to say that someone is wrong or mistaken ▪ If he thinks he can fool me, he *has another thing coming*.

just the thing **:** the thing that is most likely to be helpful ▪ Chicken soup is *just the thing* for a cold. ▪ I know *just the thing* to cheer you up—ice cream! ▪ He always does/says ***just the right thing*** to make me feel better.

last thing see [2]LAST

make a big thing *informal* ✧ If you *make a big thing (out) of (something)* or *make a big thing about (something)*, you act as if something is very important or serious when it is not. ▪ It was a minor error, but she *made a big thing out of* it. ▪ Don't *make* such *a big thing about* missing the bus: there'll be another one along in a minute.

no such thing **1** — used to say that a particular person, object, etc., does not really exist ▪ A perfect person? There's *no such thing*. — often + *as* ▪ There is *no such thing as* a unicorn. ▪ There is *no such thing as* bad publicity. All publicity is good. **2** — used to say that you did not say or do something that someone believes or says you did ▪ "Why did you invite her?" "I did *no such thing*. She just showed up." ▪ "He said that you're not going with us." "I said *no such thing*."

of all things — used to emphasize that the thing you are referring to is the thing you would least expect ▪ The coach is making the entire football team take, *of all things*, ballet classes.

one of those things *informal* — used to refer to a bad or unfortunate experience that happened and to say that such experiences happen to everyone ▪ I missed the train and had to take a later one. It was just *one of those things*, I guess.

one thing after another — used to complain about the large number of bad or unfortunate events that happen to someone ▪ It's *one thing after another* with him. Now he's in jail for drunk driving. ▪ First I locked my keys in the car, and then I spilled coffee all over myself. It was just *one thing after another* today!

push things see [1]PUSH

see things see [1]SEE

sure thing see [1]SURE

the real thing **:** something that is genuine and not a copy or imitation **:** something that is truly valuable or important ▪ The diamond turned out to be *the real thing*. ▪ a substitute for *the real thing* ▪ You've done very well in your training. Let's just hope you're ready for *the real thing*.

(what) with one thing and another *informal* — used to say that you have been very busy doing or dealing with many things ▪ *What with one thing and another*, I have very little free time.

thing·am·a·bob /ˈθɪŋəməˌbɑːb/ *noun, pl* **-bobs** [*count*] *informal* **:** THINGAMAJIG

thing·am·a·jig *or* **thing·um·a·jig** /ˈθɪŋəməˌʤɪg/ *noun, pl* **-jigs** [*count*] *informal* **:** something whose name you have forgotten or do not know ▪ It's one of those *thingamajigs* that can give you driving directions.

thing·um·my /ˈθɪŋəmi/ *noun, pl* **-mies** [*count*] *chiefly Brit, informal* **:** THINGAMAJIG

thingy /ˈθɪŋi/ *noun, pl* **thing·ies** [*count*] *informal* **:** THINGAMAJIG ▪ She was wearing one of those hair *thingies*.

[1]**think** /ˈθɪŋk/ *verb* **thinks; thought** /ˈθɑːt/; **think·ing**

1 : to believe that something is true, that a particular situation exists, that something will happen, etc. [+ *obj*] — often + *that* ▪ I *thought* (*that*) I heard your voice. ▪ She *thinks* (*that*) she knows the answer. ▪ I *think* (*that*) you can do it. ▪ We didn't *think* [=*expect*] (*that*) we would have any trouble. ▪ Did you really/honestly *think* (*that*) I would agree with you? ▪ I never *thought* (*that*) I would become a teacher. ▪ Who would have *thought* (*that*) we would meet each other here? ▪ He never *thought* (*that*) she would leave him. ▪ I hate to *think* (*that*) we will never see each other again. ▪ It was once *thought* (*that*) the Earth was flat. = The Earth was once *thought* to be flat. ▪ He is *thought* to have drowned. ▪ "Has she accepted the job?" "***I (don't) think so***." ▪ Am I right ***in thinking*** (*that*) you used to work there? ▪ "I can beat you." "***That's what you think***." [=you might believe that you can beat me, but you're wrong] ▪ "Where is he?" "He's still at home." "***I thought as much***." [=I thought he was still at home] ▪ Well, yes. ***I should think*** so. ▪ You ***would think*** (*that*) the school would have dictionaries in the classrooms. [=the school should have dictionaries in the classroom] ▪ $50 is enough, I ***would have thought***. [*no obj*] It's going to be much more difficult than they *think*. [=*suspect, expect*] ▪ We may finish sooner than you *think*.

2 : to have an opinion about someone or something [+ *obj*] It's hot in here, don't you *think*? [=don't you agree?] ▪ People *think* he is one of the greatest jazz musicians of all time. = He is *thought* to be one of the greatest jazz musicians of all time. ▪ I *think* he should apologize. = I ***should/would think*** he would apologize. ▪ Is this a good use of our tax dollars? ***I think not/so***. [=I don't/do believe that it is] ▪ You should ***think yourself*** [=*consider yourself*] lucky/fortunate to have gotten off with only a warning! — often + *that* ▪ I *thought* (*that*) the movie was excellent. ▪ He *thinks* (*that*) he is a good writer. ▪ Where do you *think* (*that*) we should eat? ▪ Do you *think* (*that*) we should buy the house? ▪ They *think* (*that*) it is unfair to have a rule like that. = They *think* it unfair to have a rule like that. [*no obj*] — + *about* or *of* ▪ What did you *think about/of* the movie? [=did you like or dislike the movie?] ▪ I told him exactly what I *thought of* him!

3 : to form or have (a particular thought) in your mind [+ *obj*] "He's handsome," she *thought* (to herself). ▪ You should relax and try to *think* pleasant thoughts. ▪ I was just *thinking* what it would be like to be a doctor. ▪ I dread to *think* how he will react. ▪ Why do you always ***think the worst***? ▪ ***Just think*** how nice it would be to live here. [*no obj*] *Just think*—in two days we'll be on vacation, lying on the beach. — usually + *about* or *of* ▪ I was just *thinking about* you. ▪ I was *thinking of* the time we rented that cabin in the mountains. ▪ Just *think*

about how much money we'll save.
4 a : to use your mind to understand or decide something [*no obj*] *Think* before you answer the question. • The game teaches students how to *think*. • Let me *think*. Where did I see your car keys? • We *thought* long and hard about it before we reached our decision. • Don't disturb him: he's *thinking*. • You have to ***think positive/positively*** if you want to succeed. — often + *about* • The lecture gave the students a lot to *think about*. • I have *thought* very deeply *about* this problem, trying to find an answer. • *Think about* the offer. You might change your mind. • Do you ever *think about* what you are going to do after you graduate? • If/When you *think about* it, the argument does make sense. [+ *obj*] Give me a minute to *think* what to do. • He couldn't *think* where they would have gone. • You're awfully quiet. What are you *thinking*? • I can't believe he did that! What was he *thinking*? **b** [+ *obj*] **:** to have thoughts about (something) • She talks and *thinks* business all the time. • He is always *thinking* [=thinking about] money.
5 [+ *obj*] **:** to remember (something) • Can you *think* where you put it? • She was trying to *think* where she had heard that name before. — often followed by *to + verb* • Neither of us *thought to close* the garage door. • She never *thinks to call* home. • He never *thought to ask* how we are doing.
6 [+ *obj*] **:** to have thoughts about possibly doing (something) **:** to have the intention of doing (something) • I *think* I'll give him a call today.
7 [+ *obj*] **a** — used to make a statement or suggestion less definite • They used to live here, I *think*. [=I believe that they used to live here, although I'm not sure] • I *thought* maybe we could go for a walk in the park. • I was *thinking* we might have dinner together some time. **b** — used to politely ask someone to do something or give you something • ***Do you think (that)*** you could give me a ride to the airport? [=could you give me a ride to the airport?] • *Do you think* I could borrow the car tonight, Dad? **c** — used in questions that show anger or surprise about what someone has done or is doing • What do you *think* you're doing? I just said you couldn't have one. • Where do you *think* you're going? [=where are you going?] No one gave you permission to leave. • Who do you *think* you are, barging in here like that?

come to think of it see [1]COME

don't even think about (doing) it informal — used to tell someone in a forceful way that something is not allowed • It's illegal to park here. *Don't even think about it!*

not think anything of **:** to not think of (something) as being important or unusual • I *didn't think anything of* it at the time—but it turned out to be the clue that would solve the case. • I *didn't think anything of* his wearing a long coat since it was cold outside.

not think much of **:** to not like (someone or something) very much • They *didn't think much of* my idea. • Though the singer was very popular, she *didn't think much of* him.

think again informal — used to say that what someone believes, expects, etc., is not true or will not happen • If you think you can get away with this, *think again*. [=you are wrong]

think ahead **:** to prepare for a future event or situation by thinking about what might happen • We should have *thought ahead* and brought an umbrella.

think aloud or think out loud **:** to say your thoughts so that other people can hear them • No, I wasn't talking to you. I was just *thinking out loud*.

think back [*phrasal verb*] **:** to think about something that happened in the past — often + *to* • *Thinking back to* my childhood, I remember summers at the beach. • *Think back to* that night. What were you doing?

think better of **:** to decide not to do (something) after thinking further about it • She was going to make a comment but *thought better of* it.

think big see [2]BIG

think fit see [1]FIT

think for yourself **:** to form opinions and make decisions without help from other people • Don't let others tell you what to believe. You need to learn to *think for yourself*.

think less of **:** to not respect (someone) as much as you did before **:** to have a worse opinion of (someone) • I hope you don't *think* (any) *less of* me now that you know about the trouble I got into when I was younger.

think nothing of **1 :** to not hesitate at all about (doing something that other people think is very difficult or dangerous) • She *thinks nothing of* running 10 miles. **2** ***think nothing of it*** — used as a polite response when someone has apologized to you or thanked you • "Thanks for the ride." "*Think nothing of it*—I was going in this direction anyway." • "I'm so sorry." "It's all right. *Think nothing of it*."

think of [*phrasal verb*] **1** ***think of (something)*** **a :** to have thoughts about possibly doing (something) • She is *thinking of* applying to grad school. • He *thought of* sending an e-mail but decided against it. • She couldn't *think of* ever leaving her children. **b :** to use your mind to form or invent (something) • The best plan they could *think of* was to leave. • "Can you give me an example?" "I'll *think of* something." • I can't *think of* one reason why you shouldn't do it. • Cell phones that can access the Internet and take pictures—what will they *think of* next? **c :** to remember (something) • I can *think of* plenty of other times when you were wrong. • I can't *think of* her name at the moment. • I just *thought of* a good joke. • She *thought of* her old home when she saw the picture. **2** ***think of (someone or something)*** **a :** to have a particular kind of opinion about (someone or something) • The hiring committee ***thought highly of*** her. [=had a high opinion of her] • She ***thinks a great deal of*** her doctor. [=she likes/respects her doctor very much] • I wouldn't want you to ***think badly of*** me. • He ***thinks the world of*** his family. [=his family is very important to him] **b :** to form or have an idea about (someone or something) • People are *thinking of* her for president. [=are thinking that she should be the president] • Are you *thinking of* any place in particular? • I am *thinking of* a number between 1 and 10. • I'll be *thinking of* you in my prayers. • He *thinks of* them with great affection. **c :** to be concerned about (someone or something) when you make decisions about what to do • I must *think* first *of* my family. • You should *think of* your job security. • She is always *thinking of* the welfare of others. **3** ***think of (someone or something) as (someone or something)*** **:** to believe that (someone or something) is (a particular type of person or thing) or has (a particular quality) • He *thinks of* himself *as* a good writer. [=he thinks/believes that he is a good writer] • I *think of* you guys *as* my family. • Play can be *thought of as* a child's work since it is through play that children learn.

think out [*phrasal verb*] ***think out (something) or think (something) out*** **:** to think about (something, such as a problem) for a period of time in an effort to find a solution, make a decision, etc. • He spent hours *thinking out* the solution to the physics problem. • I need time to *think* things *out*. • The details of the contract have been carefully *thought out*. • Your argument is well *thought out*.

think outside the box see [1]BOX

think over [*phrasal verb*] ***think (something) over or think over (something)*** **:** to think about (something) for a period of time especially in an effort to understand or make a decision about it • I'll give you time to *think* the matter *over*. • *Think* it *over*, and let me know what you decide. • I've *thought over* what you said, and you're right.

think through [*phrasal verb*] ***think (something) through or think through (something)*** **:** to think about all the different parts or effects of (something) for a period of time especially in an effort to understand or make a decision about it • I need time to *think* this *through*. • We have *thought through* the matter and have come to a decision.

think twice informal **:** to think seriously about whether you really want to do something before you do it • I'd *think twice* about/before doing that if I were you.

think up [*phrasal verb*] ***think up (something) or think (something) up informal*** **:** to use your mind to form or invent (something) • Quick! We have to *think up* an excuse. • They *thought up* a new way of raising money for charity.

to think — used to express surprise or shock • *To think* (that) he lied to you! • *To think*, all we needed to do was to wait a few more days.

[2]think *noun* [*singular*] *chiefly Brit, informal* **:** an act of thinking about something • I'd ***have another think about*** doing that if I were you. • Feel free to *have a* good *think about* it before you say yes.

have another think coming informal — used to say that somone is wrong or mistaken • If he thinks he can fool me, he ***has another think coming***. [=he's wrong; he can't fool me]

think·able /ˈθɪŋkəbəl/ *adj, not used before a noun* **:** capable of being thought about and done • They divorced during a time when that was barely *thinkable*. — opposite UNTHINKABLE

think·er /ˈθɪŋkɚ/ *noun, pl* **-ers** [*count*]

1 : a person who thinks in a specified way • an original/quick *thinker*
2 : a person who studies ideas about knowledge, truth, etc. : PHILOSOPHER • He was one of the great *thinkers* of his time.

[1]thinking /ˈθɪŋkɪŋ/ *noun [noncount]*
1 : the action of using your mind to produce ideas, decisions, memories, etc. : the activity of thinking about something • Form your own opinions: don't let others do your *thinking* for you! • I've been doing some *thinking* about this, and I don't think you're right after all. • The school's curriculum encourages independent *thinking*. • A piece of quick *thinking* got us out of trouble. • What was the *thinking* [=*reasoning*] behind their decision? — see also LATERAL THINKING, WISHFUL THINKING
2 : opinion or judgment • It is, to my (way of) *thinking*, complete nonsense. • I'd like to know your *thinking* on this.
3 : a way of thinking that is characteristic of a particular group, time period, etc. • What is the current *thinking* on the subject? • Western/Eastern *thinking*

[2]thinking *adj, always used before a noun* : able to think intelligently about complicated things • *thinking* citizens • Chess is a *thinking* man's game.

thinking cap *noun, pl* ~ **caps** *[count] informal* — used to refer to the act of trying to solve a problem by thinking carefully about it • The students weren't wearing their *thinking caps* this morning. [=they weren't thinking very well] • It's time to ***put your thinking cap on.*** [=it's time to start trying to think of what should be done]

think tank *noun, pl* ~ **tanks** *[count]* : an organization that consists of a group of people who think of new ideas on a particular subject or who give advice about what should be done — called also (*US*) *think factory*

thin·ly /ˈθɪnli/ *adv [more ~; most ~]*
1 : in a way that makes thin pieces, layers, etc. • *thinly* sliced carrots • The table was *thinly* coated/covered/layered in dust.
2 : with very few people or things close together • a *thinly* populated area • a area *thinly* planted with trees
3 : in a weak way that does not seem sincere • He smiled *thinly*.
4 : in a way that does not completely hide something • The book is a *thinly* disguised autobiography. • *thinly* veiled criticism

thin·ner /ˈθɪnɚ/ *noun, pl* **-ners** *[count]* : a liquid (such as turpentine) that is added to paint to make it thinner and able to flow more easily

thin–skinned /ˈθɪnˌskɪnd/ *adj [more ~; most ~]*
1 : having a thin skin • a *thin-skinned* fruit
2 : easily bothered by criticism or insults : very sensitive • He's too *thin-skinned* for a career in show business. — opposite THICK-SKINNED

[1]third /ˈθɚd/ *adj, always used before a noun*
1 **a** : occupying the number three position in a series • We sat in the *third* row. • the *third* house on the left • the author's *third* novel • C is the *third* letter in the alphabet. • That's the *third* time I've seen him today. • The office is on the *third* floor. **b** : next to the second in importance or rank • I won *third* prize. • Do you have a *third* choice?
2 : equal in size, value, amount, etc., to one third of something • a *third* share in the profits • a *third* pound of cheese
3 : used to refer to the third forward gear or speed of a vehicle • shift into *third* gear
the third time is the charm (*US*) or *Brit* ***third time lucky*** — used to say that two efforts at something have already failed but perhaps the third will be successful
– **third** *adv* • She finished *third* in the race. • the *third* highest mountain

[2]third *noun, pl* **thirds**
1 *[singular]* : something that is third : the third thing in a series • We arrived on the *third* of October. [=on October 3] • The win was his *third* of the year.
2 *[count]* : one of three equal parts of something • a *third* of the pie • Rent costs two-*thirds* of my paycheck. • She divided the cookie into *thirds*.
3 *[noncount]* : the third forward gear or speed of a vehicle • He shifted to/into *third*.
4 *[noncount] baseball* : THIRD BASE • He stole *third*. • There's a runner on *third*.
5 *[count] Brit* : an undergraduate degree of the lowest level from a British university • He took/received a *third* in history.

third base *noun [singular] baseball* : the base that must be touched third by a base runner • a runner on *third base*; *also* : the position of the player who defends the area near third base • She plays *third base*. — compare FIRST BASE, HOME PLATE, SECOND BASE

third baseman *noun, pl* ~ **-men** *[count] baseball* : the player who defends the area near third base : the fielder who plays third base

third class *noun*
1 *[noncount]* **a** : the level of service on a train, ship, etc., that is the cheapest • seats in *third class* **b** : a class of mail in the U.S. that includes advertisements
2 *[singular] Brit* : an undergraduate degree of the lowest level given by a British university • She got a *third class* in English.

third–class *adj* : of or relating to third class • We'll be traveling in the *third-class* cabin. • (*US*) *third-class* mail
– **third–class** *adv* • travel *third-class*

third degree *noun*
the third degree *informal* : a long and intense period of questioning • The police ***gave him the third degree.*** [=they questioned him intensely] • He ***got the third degree.*** • Mom ***gave me the third degree*** when I got home late.

third–degree *adj, always used before a noun*
1 *US, of a crime* : of the least serious level : deserving the mildest punishment • *third-degree* murder/theft/arson
2 : causing severe injury • He suffered *third-degree* burns and may not survive. — compare FIRST-DEGREE, SECOND-DEGREE

third·ly /ˈθɚdli/ *adv* — used to introduce a statement that is the third statement in a series • *Thirdly*, a dictionary provides examples of usage. — compare FIRSTLY, SECONDLY

third party *noun, pl* ~ **-ties** *[count] law* : someone who is not one of the two main people involved in a legal agreement but who is still affected by it in some way

third–party *adj, always used before a noun, law* : of, relating to, or involving insurance that pays money to someone who is harmed by your actions • a *third-party* policy • *third-party* insurance

third person *noun [noncount]*
1 *grammar* : a set of words or forms (such as pronouns or verb forms) that refer to people or things that the speaker or writer is not addressing directly — often used before another noun • "He," "she," and "it" are *third person* pronouns.
2 : a writing style that uses third person pronouns and verbs • a story written in the *third person* — compare FIRST PERSON, SECOND PERSON

third rail *noun [singular]*
1 : a metal rail on a train track that carries electric current to the train's motor
2 : a difficult issue that politicians try to avoid talking about • Social Security is the *third rail* of American politics.

third–rate *adj* : of very low quality • a *third-rate* writer • *third-rate* work • The meal was *third-rate*.

third world or **Third World** *noun [singular] sometimes offensive* : the countries of the world that are very poor and that have very few industries : the poor nations of the world — often used before another noun • *Third World* nations — compare FIRST WORLD

[1]thirst /ˈθɚst/ *noun*
1 **a** : an uncomfortable feeling that is caused by the need for something to drink *[noncount]* He quenched his *thirst*. [=he had a drink] *[singular]* a powerful *thirst* **b** *[noncount]* : a very great need for something to drink • He ***died of/from thirst***. [=he died because he did not have enough fluids in his body]
2 *[singular] literary* : a strong desire *for* something • a *thirst for* fame/knowledge/success — compare HUNGER

[2]thirst *verb* **thirsts; thirst·ed; thirst·ing** *[no obj] literary* : to have or feel a strong desire — usually + *after* or *for* • She *thirsts for/after* justice. — compare HUNGER

thirsty /ˈθɚsti/ *adj* **thirst·i·er; -est**
1 **a** : having an uncomfortable feeling because you need something to drink : feeling thirst • a *thirsty* child • The salty food was making her *thirsty*. **b** : needing water • *thirsty* land/plants
2 *not used before a noun, literary* : feeling a strong desire or need *for* something • *thirsty for* knowledge
– **thirst·i·ly** /ˈθɚstəli/ *adv* • She drank *thirstily*.

thir·teen /ˌθɚˈtiːn/ *noun, pl* **-teens** *[count]* : the number 13
– **thirteen** *adj* • *thirteen* students – **thirteen** *pronoun* • All *thirteen* (of them) passed the exam. – **thir·teenth**

T

/ˌθɚˈtiːnθ/ *noun, pl* **-teenths** [*count*] ▪ the *thirteenth* of October ▪ one *thirteenth* of the budget – **thirteenth** *adj* ▪ the *thirteenth* caller – **thirteenth** *adv* ▪ She finished *thirteenth.* ▪ the nation's *thirteenth* largest city

thir·ty /ˈθɚti/ *noun, pl* **-ties**

1 [*count*] **:** the number 30

2 ***thirties*** [*plural*] **a :** the numbers ranging from 30 to 39 ▪ The temperature outside is in the high *thirties.* **b :** a set of years ending in digits ranging from 30 to 39 ▪ He is in his *thirties.* ▪ old photographs from the *thirties* [=from 1930–1939]

– **thir·ti·eth** /ˈθɚtijəθ/ *noun, pl* **-tieths** [*count*] ▪ the *thirtieth* of November ▪ seven *thirtieths* of a degree – **thirtieth** *adj* ▪ her *thirtieth* birthday – **thirty** *adj* ▪ *thirty* days/dollars – **thirty** *pronoun* ▪ *thirty* of his classmates – **thir·ty·ish** /ˈθɚtijɪʃ/ *adj* ▪ He was tall, *thirtyish* [=about 30 years old], and had glasses and brown hair.

thir·ty·some·thing /ˈθɚtiˌsʌmθɪŋ/ *noun, pl* **-things** [*count*] *informal* **:** a person who is between 30 and 39 years old ▪ a TV show about a group of *thirtysomethings*

– **thirtysomething** *adj* ▪ *thirtysomething* parents

[1]**this** /ˈðɪs, ðəs/ *pronoun, pl* **these** /ˈðiːz/

1 [*count*] **:** the person, thing, or idea that is present or near in place, time, or thought or that has just been mentioned ▪ *This* is my favorite T-shirt. ▪ *These* are my friends. ▪ Anything would be better than *this.* ▪ "What's *this* right/over here?" "It's a very rare gold coin." ▪ Would you take a look at *this,* please? ▪ All of *this* is mine. ▪ *This* is the most fun I've had in years! ▪ "It will be difficult." "*This* is true." ▪ What is the meaning of *this?*

> ***usage*** When asking who you are speaking to on the phone, you use the pronouns *this* in U.S. English and *that* in British English. ▪ (*US*) Hello. Is *this* John? = (*Brit*) Hello. Is *that* John?

2 [*count*] **:** the thing that is closest to you or that is being shown to you ▪ *This* is silver and that is gold. ▪ *This* is my jacket and that's yours. ▪ Those sunglasses are nice, but I like *these* better. ▪ *This* is how you're supposed to do it.

3 [*singular*] **:** the present time ▪ We expected you to return before *this.* ▪ *This* is your last chance to ask questions before the test.

4 [*singular*] **:** the following idea **:** what is stated in the following sentence or phrase ▪ I can only say *this:* it wasn't here yesterday. ▪ How about *this:* you stay here while I go to the store? ▪ It's as easy as *this:* turn left at the first intersection and go straight. ▪ If you think that's funny, wait until you hear *this!* [=I will tell you another thing that is even funnier] ▪ ***What's this*** I hear about you getting engaged? [=I heard that you got engaged. Is it true?] ▪ ***What's*** all ***this*** about the Earth getting warmer?

like this see [3]LIKE

this and that *also chiefly Brit* ***this, that, and the other*** *informal* **:** several different things ▪ We started talking about *this and that,* and before we knew it, it had gotten late. ▪ "What have you been doing all day?" "Oh, a little bit of *this and that.*"

this is it — used to say that a very important thing is about to be done, a very important event is about to happen, etc. ▪ *This is it,* men. Let's take home the championship! ▪ As the car skidded out of control, I thought, "*This is it.* I'm going to die."

[2]**this** *adj, always used before a noun pl* **these**

1 — used to indicate the person, thing, or idea that is present or near in place, time, or thought or that has just been mentioned ▪ Out of all my T-shirts, *this* one is my favorite. ▪ *This* cake is delicious. ▪ *These* books are hers. ▪ How much does *this* necklace cost? ▪ Do you take *this* man to be your lawfully wedded husband? ▪ I'm not sure I understand *this* theory of yours. ▪ Who's *this* Mrs. Jones on your list? ▪ *These* dogs require a lot of exercise. ▪ *This* kind of behavior will not be tolerated in the classroom. ▪ Let's try to do a better job *this* time. ▪ By *this* point in the trip, everyone was getting tired. ▪ It's happening at *this* very moment. ▪ While her earlier poems are light and optimistic, *these* ones are sad and depressing. ▪ Get back here ***this instant/minute/second!*** [=*immediately, now*] ▪ ***To this day*** [=*still*] no one knows what really happened. ▪ The problem usually goes away on its own, but ***in this case*** you may need to see a doctor. ▪ ***In this regard/respect,*** the two books are very similar.

2 — used to indicate the thing that is closest to you or that is being shown to you ▪ *This* jacket's mine and that's yours. ▪ Would you prefer *this* one or that one? ▪ I like *these* sunglasses better than those (over there). ▪ Don't do it that way. Do it *this* way. ▪ They said to go that way, but I think we should go *this* way. ▪ Step *this* way, ladies and gentlemen: the show is about to begin. ▪ She twisted it *this* way and that way.

3 — used to indicate the present period of time or a period of time that is near the present time ▪ How are you feeling *this* morning? ▪ Not much has been happening in the news *this* week. ▪ We're planning to take a trip to New York *this* summer. ▪ Is she coming home *this* week or next (week)? ▪ The snow started early *this* morning. ▪ *These* years have been particularly difficult for our family. ▪ You're just friends with him? ***All this time*** I thought you were dating him. ▪ She'll return ***this coming*** Friday. = She'll return *this* Friday. [=she'll return on the Friday of this week] ▪ She left ***this past*** [=*last*] Monday. ▪ I spoke to him on the phone just *this past* weekend. [=the weekend that just took place] ▪ It's hard to find good help ***these days.***

4 : stated in the following sentence or phrase ▪ How about *this* idea: you stay here while I go to the store? ▪ What's *this* nonsense (I hear) about you quitting?

5 — used to introduce someone or something that has not been mentioned yet ▪ We both had *this* sudden urge to go shopping. ✧ This sense of *this* is often used to produce excitement when telling a story. ▪ I was walking down the street when *this* dog starts chasing me. [=when a dog started chasing me] ▪ Then *these* two guys come/came in and start asking her questions.

[3]**this** /ˈðɪs/ *adv*

1 : to the degree or extent that is suggested in the present situation ▪ We've waited *this* long for the pizza, we might as well stay until it's ready. — often used in negative statements ▪ I haven't had *this* much fun in ages! ▪ They didn't expect *this* many people to come to the party. ▪ She's never been *this* far away from home.

2 : to the degree or extent indicated by a gesture ▪ He's about *this* tall. ▪ I need a nail about *this* long.

this·tle /ˈθɪsəl/ *noun, pl* **this·tles** [*count*] **:** a wild plant that has sharp points on its leaves and purple, yellow, or white flowers

this·tle·down /ˈθɪsəlˌdaʊn/ *noun* [*noncount*] **:** the light parts of thistle flowers that contain the seeds and that blow away in the wind

thith·er /ˈθɪðɚ/ *adv, old-fashioned + literary* **:** to that place **:** THERE ▪ traveling/wandering/running ***hither and thither*** [=here and there]

thong /ˈθɑːŋ/ *noun, pl* **thongs** [*count*]

1 : a long thin strip of material (such as leather) that is used to attach something

2 : a kind of women's underpants that has only a thin strip of material in the back

3 *US* **:** [1]FLIP-FLOP 1

tho·rax /ˈθoɚˌæks/ *noun, pl* **tho·rax·es** *or* **tho·ra·ces** /ˈθorəˌsiːz/ [*count*] *technical*

1 : the part of an animal's body between the neck and the waist

2 : the middle section of an insect's body

– **tho·rac·ic** /θəˈræsɪk/ *adj* ▪ the *thoracic* cavity

thorn /ˈθoɚn/ *noun, pl* **thorns** [*count*]

1 : a sharp point on the stem of some plants (such as roses) — see color picture on page C6

2 *Brit* **:** a tree or bush that has thorns

a thorn in the/your flesh/side **:** a person or thing that repeatedly annoys you or causes problems for you ▪ He's been *a thorn in my side* for years. ▪ ***a thorn in the side*** of the industry

– **thorned** /ˈθoɚnd/ *adj* – **thorn·less** /ˈθoɚnləs/ *adj*

thorny /ˈθoɚni/ *adj* **thorn·i·er; -est** [*also more ~; most ~*]

1 : having a lot of thorns ▪ *thorny* bushes

2 : very difficult or complicated ▪ a *thorny* issue/problem/question

– **thorn·i·ness** *noun* [*noncount*]

thor·ough /ˈθɚroʊ/ *adj* [*more ~; most ~*]

1 : including every possible part or detail ▪ a *thorough* investigation/search ▪ a *thorough* [=*complete*] examination ▪ a *thorough* understanding of the rules and regulations

2 : careful about doing something in an accurate and exact way **:** METICULOUS ▪ a *thorough* worker ▪ The investigator will have to be *thorough.*

3 *always used before a noun, chiefly Brit* **:** complete or absolute ▪ a *thorough* disgrace ▪ a *thorough* mess/nuisance

– **thor·ough·ly** *adv* [*more ~; most ~*] ▪ You've *thoroughly* [=*completely*] messed things up. ▪ I *thoroughly* enjoyed the performance. ▪ He studied the proposal very *thoroughly.* ▪

T

That's been *thoroughly* documented/proven. **– thor·ough·ness** *noun [noncount]*

thor·ough·bred /ˈθɚrəˌbrɛd/ *noun, pl* **-breds** *[count]*
1 : an animal (especially a horse) whose parents are from the same breed
2 ***Thoroughbred*** **:** a type of fast horse used mainly for racing
– thoroughbred *adj* • *thoroughbred* [=*purebred*] dogs • *Thoroughbred* horses

thor·ough·fare /ˈθɚrəˌfeə/ *noun, pl* **-fares** *[count]* **:** a main road

thor·ough·go·ing /ˌθɚrəˈgowɪŋ/ *adj [more ~; most ~]* **:** including every possible detail **:** very thorough or complete • a *thoroughgoing* analysis • *thoroughgoing* changes

those *plural of* THAT

[1]thou /ˈðaʊ/ *pronoun, old-fashioned + literary* — used as a singular form of "you" when it is the subject of a verb • "*Thou* shalt have no other gods before me." —Exodus 20:3 (KJV)

[2]thou /ˈθaʊ/ *noun, pl* **thou** *[count] US, informal* **:** a thousand dollars • She earns more than a hundred *thou* a year.

[1]though /ˈðoʊ/ *conj* **:** ALTHOUGH • *Though* it was raining, we went hiking • She seemed healthy, *though* (she is) thin. • That's possible, *though* (it is) not likely.
as though see [2]AS
even though see [2]EVEN

[2]though *adv* — used when you are saying something that is different from or contrasts with a previous statement • She was happy. Not for long, *though.* [=*however*] • Inevitably, *though*, something will go wrong.

[1]thought *past tense and past participle of* [1]THINK

[2]thought /ˈθɑːt/ *noun, pl* **thoughts**
1 *[count]* **:** an idea, plan, opinion, picture, etc., that is formed in your mind **:** something that you think of • My first *thought* was that something must have changed. • She had a sudden *thought.* = A sudden *thought* occurred to her. • The *thought* of leaving never crossed my mind. • Do you have any *thoughts* about/on the subject? • She abandoned all *thoughts* of going home. • It was just a *thought.* • That's a good *thought.* — see also SECOND THOUGHT
2 a *[noncount]* **:** the act or process of thinking • She was lost/deep in *thought.* • She abandoned all *thought* of going home. • ***thought patterns/processes*** [=the way you think about things] **b** *[noncount]* **:** the act of carefully thinking about the details of something • I'll give the idea some *thought.* [=*consideration*] • They should have put more *thought* into the proposal. **c** *[singular]* **:** the act of thinking about the feelings or situations of other people • While you're enjoying the holidays, you should spare a *thought* for those who are less fortunate. • He has no *thought* for anyone but himself.
3 *[noncount]* **:** a way of thinking that is characteristic of a particular group, time period, etc. • Western *thought* • the mainstream *thought* on the subject • modern economic *thought* • There are two main ***schools of thought*** [=systems of thinking] on the topic.
(a) penny for your thoughts see PENNY
food for thought see FOOD
perish the thought see PERISH

thought·ful /ˈθɑːtfəl/ *adj [more ~; most ~]*
1 : serious and quiet because you are thinking • She looked at me with a *thoughtful* expression. • He looked *thoughtful* for a moment.
2 : done or made after careful thinking • a *thoughtful* book/gift • pages of *thoughtful* criticism
3 : showing concern for the needs or feelings of other people **:** CONSIDERATE • a *thoughtful* gesture • Her husband is always *thoughtful.* • That's very *thoughtful* of you. — opposite THOUGHTLESS
– thought·ful·ly /ˈθɑːtfəli/ *adv* • *thoughtfully* prepared • He looked at me *thoughtfully.* **– thought·ful·ness** *noun [noncount]*

thought·less /ˈθɑːtləs/ *adj [more ~; most ~]* **:** not showing concern for the needs or feelings of other people **:** INCONSIDERATE • *thoughtless* behavior • *thoughtless* comments • a selfish and *thoughtless* person — opposite THOUGHTFUL
– thought·less·ly *adv* • "That's stupid," he said *thoughtlessly.* **– thought·less·ness** *noun [noncount]*

thought–provoking *adj [more ~; most ~]* **:** causing people to think seriously about something • a *thought-provoking* article/book/film

thou·sand /ˈθaʊzənd/ *noun, pl* **-sands**
1 *pl* ***thousand*** *[count]* **:** the number 1,000 • a/one *thousand* (of them) • a *thousand* and one = one *thousand* and one = (*chiefly US*) a *thousand* one [=1,001] • two *thousand* (of them)
2 ***thousands*** *[plural]* **:** an amount that is more than 2,000 • *Thousands* (and *thousands*) of people visited the shrine.
3 *[count]* **:** a very large number — usually plural • I've done this *thousands* of times. [=many times]
a picture is worth a thousand words see [1]WORTH
bat a thousand see [2]BAT
never/not in a thousand years see YEAR
– thousand *adj, always used before a noun* • a *thousand* miles [=1,000 miles] • a *thousand* dollars/years/times
– thousands *pronoun* • *Thousands* protested the convention. **– thou·sandth** /ˈθaʊzəndθ/ *noun, pl* **-sandths** *[count]* • a/one *thousandth* of a second = one one-*thousandths* of a second [=1/1000 second] **– thousandth** *adj* • the *thousandth* person to join

thousand island dressing *noun [noncount] chiefly US* **:** a creamy salad dressing that contains a mixture of finely chopped vegetables (such as pickles, peppers, and onions)

thrall /ˈθrɑːl/ *noun*
in thrall literary **:** in a state of being controlled or strongly influenced by someone or something • He was completely *in thrall* to her. = He was completely *in* her *thrall.*

[1]thrash /ˈθræʃ/ *verb* **thrash·es; thrashed; thrash·ing**
1 *[+ obj]* **:** to hit (someone or something) very hard with a stick, whip, etc. • He *thrashed* me with his belt.
2 *[+ obj] informal* **:** to defeat (someone or something) very easily or completely • The team *thrashed* them last week.
3 *[no obj]* **:** to move about violently • Something was *thrashing* wildly in the water. • She *thrashed* around/about in her sleep.
thrash out *[phrasal verb]* ***thrash (something) out*** *or* ***thrash out (something)*** **:** to talk about (something) in order to make a decision, find a solution, etc. • They had a meeting to *thrash out* their problems. **:** to produce (something, such as an agreement or plan) by a lot of discussion • *thrash out* a plan
– thrashing /ˈθræʃɪŋ/ *noun, pl* **-ings** *[count]* • He gave the prisoner a *thrashing.* • (*informal*) Last week's game was a complete *thrashing.*

[2]thrash *noun, pl* **thrashes**
1 *[noncount]* **:** a type of rock music that is very fast and loud
2 *[singular]* **:** a violent movement • The shark swam away with a *thrash* of its tail.
3 *[count] Brit, informal + old-fashioned* **:** a party with loud music and dancing

[1]thread /ˈθrɛd/ *noun, pl* **threads**
1 : a long, thin piece of cotton, silk, etc., used for sewing *[noncount]* a spool of *thread* *[count]* A *thread* was hanging from the hem of her coat. — see picture at SEWING
2 *[count] literary* **:** a long, thin line of something — usually + *of* • A slender *thread of* smoke rose up from the chimney.
3 *[count]* **:** the raised line that winds around a screw
4 *[singular]* **:** an idea, feeling, etc., that connects the different parts of something (such as a story) • The stories share a common *thread.* • A *thread* of self-pity runs through his autobiography. • I lost the *thread* of the plot long before the story ended. • I found it hard to follow the *thread* of the conversation.
5 *[count] computers* **:** a series of related messages that are written on an Internet message board • If you want to discuss a different subject, you should start a new *thread.*
6 ***threads*** *[plural] US, informal + old-fashioned* **:** CLOTHES • nice *threads*
hang by a thread see [1]HANG
pick up the threads informal **:** to begin something again after a long time • I'm hoping to *pick up the threads* of our relationship.
– thread·like /ˈθrɛdˌlaɪk/ *adj* • a *threadlike* worm

[2]thread *verb* **threads; thread·ed; thread·ing**
1 *[+ obj]* **:** to put a thread, string, rope, etc., through a hole in something • *thread* a needle • She *threaded* her shoelace through the holes. • *thread* a pipe with wire = *thread* a wire through a pipe
2 *[+ obj]* **:** to put (film or tape) into a movie camera, tape recorder, etc., so that it is ready to be used • *thread* film through a camera
3 : to move forward by turning and going through narrow spaces *[+ obj]* They had to ***thread their way*** through the crowd. *[no obj]* Waiters *threaded* through the crowd. • a river that *threads* through narrow valleys
4 *[+ obj]* **:** to put (something) on a thread **:** STRING • *thread* beads

T

– **thread•er** *noun, pl* **-ers** [*count*]

thread•bare /ˈθrɛdˌbeɚ/ *adj* [*more* ~; *most* ~]
1 : very thin and in bad condition from too much use : SHABBY • a *threadbare* carpet/suit
2 : not very effective, interesting, etc., because of being used too often • a *threadbare* joke • the story's *threadbare* plot

threat /ˈθrɛt/ *noun, pl* **threats**
1 : a statement saying you will be harmed if you do not do what someone wants you to do [*count*] He was willing to use violence and *threats* to get what he wanted. • She ignored their *threats* and continued to do what she felt was right. • bomb/death *threats* • He carried out his *threat*. [=he did the thing that he threatened to do] • She said she would leave him, but he knew it was an ***idle/empty threat***. [=he knew that she did not mean it] [*noncount*] an action done ***under threat*** [=done by someone who has been threatened with harm]
2 a [*count*] : someone or something that could cause trouble, harm, etc. — usually singular • The country is a great/major/serious *threat* to world peace. • He perceived the question as a *threat* to his authority. • These people are not a *threat* to the social order. • Their financial problems are a *threat* to their marriage. **b** : the possibility that something bad or harmful could happen [*count*] — usually singular • We can't ignore the *threat* posed by nuclear weapons. • The weather forecast calls for cloudy skies with a *threat* of rain. • There is a real *threat* of civil war. [*noncount*] a country ***under threat*** of civil war

threat•en /ˈθrɛtn̩/ *verb* **-ens; -ened; -en•ing**
1 [+ *obj*] : to say that you will harm someone or do something unpleasant or unwanted especially in order to make someone do what you want • The mugger *threatened* him with a gun. • He *threatened* to tell their boss. = He *threatened* that he would tell their boss. • She *threatened* to quit if they didn't give her a raise, but no one believed her. • He tried to get what he wanted by *threatening* people (with violence). • The workers have *threatened* to strike if their demands are not met. = The workers have *threatened* a strike if their demands are not met. • The kidnapper *threatened* to kill her. = The kidnapper ***threatened her life***.
2 a : to be something that is likely to cause harm to (someone or something) : to be a threat to (someone or something) [+ *obj*] Civil war has been *threatening* the country for years. • a marriage *threatened* by financial problems • Overfishing *threatens* the survival of certain fish species. • She felt (emotionally) *threatened* by his friendships with female coworkers. [*no obj*] Disaster *threatens*. **b** — used to say that something bad or harmful appears likely or possible [+ *obj*] The clouds were *threatening* rain. [=the clouds made it appear that it was likely to rain] • The latest news *threatens* trouble for the economy. [*no obj*] It looks like it's *threatening* to rain. [=it looks like it may rain]
– **threat•en•ing** /ˈθrɛtnɪŋ/ *adj* [*more* ~; *most* ~] • a *threatening* comment • *threatening* clouds • I find your competitiveness a little *threatening*. – **threat•en•ing•ly** /ˈθrɛtnɪŋli/ *adv* • The sky darkened *threateningly*.

three /ˈθriː/ *noun, pl* **threes**
1 [*count*] : the number 3
2 [*count*] : the third in a set or series • the *three* of hearts
3 [*noncount*] : three o'clock • "What time is it?" "It's *three*." • I leave each day at *three*.
in threes : in groups of three • You'll be working *in threes*.
three sheets to the wind see ²SHEET
two's company, three's a crowd see COMPANY
– **three** *adj* • *three* feet/dollars/weeks – **three** *pronoun* • I'll take *three*, please. • Seven students passed the test and *three* failed.

three–cornered *adj*
1 : having three corners • a *three-cornered* hat
2 : involving three people or groups • a *three-cornered* agreement

3–D /ˈθriːˈdiː/ *noun*
in 3-D : made in a way that causes an image to appear to be three-dimensional • The movie is *in 3-D*.
– **3–D** *adj* • a *3-D* painting

three–dimensional *adj*
1 : having or seeming to have length, width, and depth • a *three-dimensional* sculpture • a *three-dimensional* image
2 [*more* ~; *most* ~] : having different qualities that are like the qualities of a real person • The characters in the novel are very *three-dimensional*.

three•fold /ˈθriːˌfoʊld/ *adj*
1 : having three parts • a *threefold* purpose
2 : three times as great or as many • a *threefold* increase
– **three•fold** /ˈθriːˈfoʊld/ *adv* • Problems have increased *threefold*.

three–leg•ged race /ˈθriːˈlɛgəd-/ *noun, pl* ~ **races** [*count*] : a race in which two people run together with one person's left leg tied to the other person's right leg

three•pence /ˈθrɛpəns/ *noun, pl* **threepence** *or* **three•penc•es** *Brit, old-fashioned*
1 [*count*] : a coin worth three pennies
2 [*noncount*] : the sum of three British pennies

three•pen•ny /ˈθrɛpəni/ *adj, always used before a noun, Brit, old-fashioned* : worth three British pennies • a *threepenny* bit/piece

three–piece suit *noun, pl* ~ **suits** [*count*] : a suit in which the jacket, vest, and pants are made of the same material — compare TWO-PIECE SUIT

three–piece suite *noun, pl* ~ **suites** [*count*] *Brit* : a set of furniture that consists of a sofa and two chairs covered in the same material

three–ply *adj* : having three layers or threads • *three-ply* paper

three–point line *noun* [*singular*] *basketball* : a curved line on a basketball court that is a set distance (such as 22 feet) from the basket and beyond which successful shots count for three points

three–point turn *noun, pl* ~ **turns** [*count*] : a way of turning a vehicle around in a small space by driving forward, then back, then forward again

three–quarter *adj, always used before a noun* : three-quarters of the full amount, length, size, etc., of something • *three-quarter* sleeves

three–quarters *noun* [*plural*] : an amount equal to three of the four parts which make up something : seventy-five percent • *Three-quarters* of the class will be going on the trip. • *three-quarters* of an hour [=45 minutes]

three–ring circus *noun, pl* ~ **-cuses** [*count*]
1 : a circus that has three separate areas where performances occur at the same time
2 *US, informal* : a place with a lot of busy and confusing activity • When the kids come home from school, my house is a *three-ring circus*.

three R's *noun*
the three R's : the basic subjects of reading, writing, and arithmetic that are taught in school to young children

three•score /ˈθriːˈskoɚ/ *adj, old-fashioned* : SIXTY • *threescore* years [=60 years]

three•some /ˈθriːsəm/ *noun, pl* **-somes** [*count*] : a group of three people or things • a *threesome* of reporters • a golfing *threesome*

three–way *adj, always used before a noun*
1 : involving three people or groups • a *three-way* conversation/deal/partnership — compare ONE-WAY, TWO-WAY
2 : allowing movement in any one of three directions • a *three-way* intersection — compare ONE-WAY, TWO-WAY

thren•o•dy /ˈθrɛnədi/ *noun, pl* **-dies** [*count*] *literary* : a song or poem that expresses sorrow for someone who is dead

thresh /ˈθrɛʃ/ *verb* **thresh•es; threshed; thresh•ing** : to separate the seeds of corn, wheat, etc., from the plant by using a special machine or tool [+ *obj*] *thresh* wheat [*no obj*] *threshing* and harvesting at the same time
– **thresh•er** /ˈθrɛʃɚ/ *noun, pl* **-ers** [*count*]

thresh•old /ˈθrɛʃˌhoʊld/ *noun, pl* **-olds** [*count*]
1 : a piece of wood, metal, or stone that forms the bottom of a door and that you walk over as you enter a room or building • He stepped across the *threshold*. • When they were married he ***carried her over the threshold***. [=he picked her up and carried her into their home when they entered it together for the first time]
2 : the point or level at which something begins or changes • If your income rises above a certain *threshold*, your tax rate also rises. • sounds that are above/below the *threshold* of hearing [=sounds that are too high/low to be heard] • I have a low *threshold* for boredom. [=I get bored easily] • He has a high ***pain threshold***. [=he does not feel pain as easily as other people]
on/at the threshold : at the beginning of something or very close to something (such as a new condition, an important discovery, etc.) — usually + *of* • young people *on the threshold of* adulthood • We are (standing) *at the threshold of* a great adventure.

threw *past tense of* ¹THROW

thrice /ˈθraɪs/ *adv, old-fashioned* : three times ▪ She was *thrice* married.

thrift /ˈθrɪft/ *noun [noncount]*
1 *old-fashioned* : careful use of money so that it is not wasted ▪ Through hard work and *thrift* they sent all of their children to college.
2 *US* : a business like a bank that is used for saving money : a savings bank or a savings and loan association — called also *thrift institution*

thrift shop *noun, pl* **~ shops** *[count] US* : a store that sells used goods and especially used clothes and that is often run by a charity — called also *thrift store*; compare CHARITY SHOP

thrifty /ˈθrɪfti/ *adj* **thrift·i·er; -est** : managing or using money in a careful or wise way ▪ a *thrifty* family/shopper ▪ She has *thrifty* habits.
– **thrift·i·ness** /ˈθrɪftinəs/ *noun [noncount]* ▪ a man known for his *thriftiness*

[1]**thrill** /ˈθrɪl/ *verb* **thrills; thrilled; thrill·ing**
1 *[+ obj]* : to cause (someone) to feel very excited or happy ▪ Circus performers still *thrill* audiences today. ▪ I was *thrilled* by their decision.
2 *[no obj]* : to feel very excited or happy about something — usually + *at* or *to* ▪ Crowds *thrilled to* the sights and sounds of the circus. ▪ She *thrilled at* the thought of meeting him.
— see also THRILLED

[2]**thrill** *noun, pl* **thrills** *[count]*
1 : a feeling of great excitement or happiness ▪ The *thrill* is gone from our marriage. ▪ He felt a *thrill* of pride/pleasure/anticipation. ▪ the *thrill* of discovery/victory ▪ He gets a big *thrill* out of seeing his grandchildren. [=seeing his grandchildren makes him very happy] ▪ He had a great career and gave the fans a lot of *thrills.* ▪ What do people do for *thrills* [=*excitement*] around here? ▪ She got the ***thrill of her life*** from seeing the Queen. [=seeing the Queen was very exciting] ▪ They ***get their thrills from*** drag racing. [=they drag race because it is exciting]
2 : a very exciting or enjoyable event or experience ▪ It's a real *thrill* for me to be here tonight. ▪ What a *thrill* it was to see the Queen! ▪ (*US*) a movie with a lot of ***thrills and chills*** [=exciting and scary parts] ▪ the ***thrills and spills*** of car racing

thrilled *adj, not used before a noun [more ~; most ~]* : very excited and happy ▪ I'm so *thrilled* to see you. ▪ "Will you come to dinner at my house tomorrow?" "Certainly. I'd be *thrilled.*" ▪ I'm not *thrilled* about/with her decision. ▪ (*US*) He was ***thrilled to death/pieces*** [=very excited and pleased] about the baby. = (*chiefly Brit*) He was ***thrilled to bits*** about the baby. ▪ I'm ***less than thrilled*** [=not happy] with her decision. ▪ He was ***none/not too thrilled*** [=not pleased] by the idea.

thril·ler /ˈθrɪlɚ/ *noun, pl* **-lers** *[count]* : a novel, movie, etc., that is very exciting : a story full of exciting action, mystery, adventure, or suspense ▪ His latest novel is a political *thriller.*

thrilling *adj [more ~; most ~]* : very exciting ▪ I can't imagine a more *thrilling* experience. ▪ a *thrilling* discovery ▪ It was *thrilling* to see her win the race.
– **thrill·ing·ly** /ˈθrɪlɪŋli/ *adv*

thrill ride *noun, pl* **~ rides** *[count]* : a very exciting ride (such as a roller coaster) at an amusement park — often used figuratively ▪ The campaign has been a *thrill ride* from the beginning. [=the campaign has been very exciting]

thrive /ˈθraɪv/ *verb* **thrives; thrived** *or old-fashioned* **throve** /ˈθroʊv/; **thrived** *also old-fashioned* **thriv·en** /ˈθrɪvən/; **thriv·ing** /ˈθraɪvɪŋ/ *[no obj]* : to grow or develop successfully : to flourish or succeed ▪ Business is *thriving.* [=*booming*] ▪ The region *thrived* [=*prospered*] under his rule. ▪ plants that *thrive* [=grow well] in the desert
thrive on *[phrasal verb]* ***thrive on (something)*** : to do well in a situation in which you are given (a particular type of treatment) ▪ She *thrives on* attention. : to benefit from (something, especially something that others might find difficult or unpleasant) ▪ These plants seem to *thrive on* neglect. ▪ He actually *thrives on* stress.
– **thriving** *adj* ▪ a *thriving* economy ▪ a *thriving* port

throat /ˈθroʊt/ *noun, pl* **throats** *[count]*
1 : the tube inside the neck that leads to the stomach and lungs ▪ My *throat* was dry so I took a sip of water. ▪ His *throat* was sore. ▪ He ***cleared his throat*** [=made a noise in his throat in order to get attention or to prepare to speak] and began to speak. — see also STREP THROAT
2 : the front part of the neck ▪ He held a knife to her *throat.* ▪ His shirt was open at the *throat.* ▪ He grabbed her by the *throat.*
a frog in your throat see FROG
a lump in your throat see [1]LUMP
at each other's throats : very angry with each other : having a serious fight or argument ▪ Workers and management have been *at each other's throats.*
cut your own throat : to do something that is bad for you : to act in a way that will cause you harm ▪ They ended up *cutting their own throats* when they raised prices because their customers went elsewhere.
force/ram/shove (something) down someone's throat *informal* : to force someone to accept or like (something, such as your ideas or beliefs) ▪ She was always *forcing* her opinions *down his throat.*
jump down someone's throat *informal* : to respond angrily to someone ▪ He *jumped down my throat* when I suggested a different plan.

throat·ed /ˈθroʊtəd/ *adj*
1 : making a certain kind of sound from the throat — used in combination ▪ a full-*throated* cry ▪ the bullfrog's deep-*throated* call
2 : having a throat of a certain kind or color — used in combination ▪ a white-*throated* sparrow

throaty /ˈθroʊti/ *adj* **throat·i·er; -est** *of a sound* : deep or rough : made in the back of the throat ▪ a *throaty* laugh
– **throat·i·ly** /ˈθroʊtəli/ *adv* ▪ He chuckled *throatily.*

[1]**throb** /ˈθrɑːb/ *verb* **throbs; throbbed; throb·bing** *[no obj]*
1 : to feel a pain that starts and stops quickly and repeatedly ▪ Her finger *throbbed* with pain. ▪ My head is *throbbing.*
2 : to beat with a strong, steady rhythm ▪ He could hear his heart *throbbing.* [=*pounding*] ▪ The music *throbs* with a Caribbean beat. ▪ drums *throbbing* in the distance — sometimes used figuratively ▪ a soul *throbbing* with loneliness [=a very lonely soul] ▪ a tiny stream *throbbing* with life [=full of life]
– **throbbing** *adj* ▪ He had a *throbbing* pain in his shoulder. ▪ I have a *throbbing* [=*pounding*] headache.

[2]**throb** *noun [singular]*
1 : a strong, steady beat ▪ the *throb* of the drums
2 : pain that starts and stops quickly and repeatedly ▪ The pain has changed to a dull *throb.*
– see also HEARTTHROB

throes /ˈθroʊz/ *noun [plural]* : painful emotions, sensations, or feelings ▪ She was suffering the *throes* [=*pangs*] of remorse. ▪ the *throes* of childbirth ▪ death *throes*
in the throes of : experiencing (something painful) ▪ She met him while he was *in the throes of* a messy divorce.

throm·bo·sis /θrɑmˈboʊsəs/ *noun, pl* **-bo·ses** /-ˈboʊˌsiːz/ *[count, noncount] medical* : a serious condition caused when a blood clot blocks the flow of blood in a blood vessel ▪ coronary *thrombosis*

throne /ˈθroʊn/ *noun, pl* **thrones**
1 *[count]* : the special chair for a king, queen, or other powerful person ▪ The king sat on his *throne.*
2 ***the throne*** : the position of king or queen ▪ He is next in line for *the throne.* ▪ the heir to *the throne* ▪ He ***ascended the throne*** [=became king] after the death of his father.
the power behind the throne see [1]POWER

[1]**throng** /ˈθrɑːŋ/ *noun, pl* **throngs** *[count]* : a large group of people — often + *of* ▪ There were *throngs of* shoppers in the mall. ▪ A *throng of* fans was waiting for the players to arrive.

[2]**throng** *verb* **throngs; thronged; throng·ing**
1 *[+ obj]* : to go to (a place) in a large group or in large numbers ▪ Shoppers *thronged* the mall for the sales. ▪ The island was *thronged* with tourists. = Tourists *thronged* the island. ▪ People *thronged* [=*filled*] the streets.
2 *[no obj]* : to gather in a crowd or in great numbers — + *around* or *to* ▪ Fans *thronged around* him. ▪ Shoppers *thronged to* the mall.

[1]**throt·tle** /ˈθrɑːtl/ *noun, pl* **throt·tles** *[count] technical* : a device that controls the flow of fuel to an engine ▪ When you press a car's accelerator, it opens the *throttle,* and the car goes faster.
at full throttle : as fast as possible ▪ She drove *at full throttle.* ▪ The project is proceeding *at full throttle.*

[2]**throttle** *verb* **throttles; throt·tled; throt·tling** *[+ obj]*
1 : to choke or strangle (someone) ▪ He *throttled* her in a fit of jealous rage. ▪ I'm so mad I could *throttle* her!
2 *US, informal* : to defeat (someone or something) easily or completely ▪ The home team *throttled* [=*clobbered*] the opposition last night.

3 : to not allow (something) to grow or develop ▪ policies that *throttle* creativity

throttle back [*phrasal verb*] **throttle back or throttle back (something) or throttle (something) back :** to reduce the amount of fuel flowing to an engine by adjusting the throttle ▪ He *throttled back* to 45 mph. — sometimes used figuratively ▪ You need to *throttle back* your anger. [=you need to stop being so angry]

¹through /ˈθruː/ *prep*

1 : into one side and out the other side of (something) ▪ He hit the nail *through* the wood. ▪ She looked *through* the binoculars. ▪ The bullet had gone *through* his hand.

2 : from one side or end to another side or end of (something) ▪ He just walked *through* the door. ▪ The security guards pushed their way *through* the crowd. ▪ She could see a figure *through* the fog. ▪ I looked *through* the window.

3 — used to describe movement within a place or an area of land, air, etc. ▪ They spent a couple of hours walking *through* the mall. [=walking to various places in the mall] ▪ We rode our mountain bikes *through* the woods. ▪ The snake slithered *through* the grass. ▪ birds gliding *through* the air

4 — used to indicate the path that is followed to get somewhere or the path that someone or something moves along ▪ The bathroom is *through* that hallway on the left. ▪ Cold air was getting in *through* a crack in the wall. ▪ People usually come in *through* the side door.

5 : without stopping for (a traffic signal, a stop sign, etc.) ▪ He got caught driving *through* a red light.

6 a : by using (someone or something) ▪ The leaders communicated *through* interpreters. ▪ I learned of the job opening *through* her. [=she told me about the job opening] ▪ They ruled the country *through* fear. [=by making people afraid] **b :** by doing (something) ▪ He learned to cook *through* [=*by*] watching his mother in the kitchen. **c :** because of (something) ▪ The company's profits increased *through* improved sales. ▪ We will succeed only *through* [=*by means of*] hard work. ▪ knowledge that is gained *through* life experience

7 : over all the parts of (something) **:** THROUGHOUT ▪ The illness swept *through* the town. ▪ The students were given time to go *through* their notes before the exam.

8 : from the beginning to the end of (something) ▪ He slept *through* the movie. ▪ Many students work *through* the summer. ▪ All *through* [=*throughout*] her life, she dreamed of going up into outer space. ▪ We left ***halfway through*** [=in the middle of] the lecture.

9 *US* — used to indicate the numbers, days, etc., that are included in a range ▪ The store is open Monday *through* Friday. [=is open Monday, Tuesday, Wednesday, Thursday, and Friday] ▪ Read chapters 2 *through* 5 for homework.

10 — used to say that you have survived or completed something ▪ We're *through* the worst part of the storm. [=the worst part of the storm has ended] ▪ I think she'll be more comfortable at college now that she's *through* her first semester. [=now that she has completed her first semester]

11 : to a state of official acceptance or approval by (an organization) ▪ The vote got the bill *through* the legislature.

²through *adv*

1 : from one side or end to the other ▪ Let these people go *through*, please. ▪ The nail went completely *through*.

2 : over the whole distance ▪ It snowed heavily, but we made it *through*. ▪ We'll never get *through*—the mud is too deep. ▪ The package was shipped *through* to New Orleans.

3 : from the beginning to the end ▪ Read the essay *through* and tell me what you think. ▪ The teacher stopped the movie ***halfway through***. [=when it was half finished]

4 : without stopping ▪ The light was red, but he drove straight *through*.

5 : to the end of an action, process, or activity **:** until something is completed or achieved ▪ I need time to ***think*** this problem ***through***. [=to think about it until I understand it completely or have made a decision] ▪ He intended to ***see*** the project ***through***. [=to continue working until the project was finished]

6 : in or to every part **:** completely or thoroughly ▪ Her clothes were wet *through*. ▪ He heated the casserole *through*. ▪ You are your mother's child ***through and through***. [=you are like your mother in every way] ▪ He is a gentleman *through and through*.

7 *of a phone call* **:** in connection with the person you are calling ▪ The operator ***put me through*** to him. ▪ I called, but I couldn't ***get through***.

³through *adj*

1 *not used before a noun, chiefly US* **a :** having reached the end of an activity, job, etc. **:** FINISHED ▪ I'm not *through* yet. I have one more topic to discuss. ▪ If you're *through* using the phone, I'd like to use it next. — often + *with* ▪ She is almost *through with* law school. [=she has almost finished law school] ▪ He says he's *through with* gambling. [=he will not gamble anymore] ▪ I left when the movie was about ***halfway through***. **b :** no longer in a romantic relationship ▪ Lisa and I are *through*. [=*finished*] — often + *with* ▪ I'm *through with* him. **c :** no longer able to continue in a role, activity, etc. ▪ After this scandal, he could be *through* [=*finished*] as a politician. ▪ His career is *through*.

2 *always used before a noun* **a :** allowing passage from one end to the other ▪ Is this a *through* road/street? **b :** going the whole distance without stopping ▪ The left lane is for *through* traffic only.

¹through·out /θruˈaʊt/ *prep*

1 : in or to every part of (something) ▪ The company has stores *throughout* the United States and Canada. ▪ She has traveled *throughout* the world.

2 : during an entire (situation or period of time) ▪ His supporters remained loyal *throughout* his difficulties. ▪ *Throughout* her life, she has suffered with the disease. ▪ It rained *throughout* the day.

²throughout *adv*

1 : in or to every part ▪ The house is painted white *throughout*. ▪ The house has wood floors *throughout*.

2 : from the beginning to the end **:** during the whole time or situation ▪ He had a difficult year, but his supporters remained loyal *throughout*.

through·put /ˈθruːˌpʊt/ *noun, pl* **-puts** *technical* **:** the amount of material, data, etc., that enters and goes through something (such as a machine or system) [*count*] The network can handle large *throughputs*. [*noncount*] finding ways to increase *throughput*

throughway *variant spelling of* THRUWAY

throve *old-fashioned past tense of* THRIVE

¹throw /ˈθroʊ/ *verb* **throws; threw** /ˈθruː/; **thrown** /ˈθroʊn/; **throw·ing**

1 : to cause (something) to move out of your hand and through the air by quickly moving your arm forward [+ *obj*] She *threw* the ball to first base. ▪ We *threw* our hats in the air at the end of the ceremony. ▪ *Throw* me the car keys. = *Throw* the car keys to me. ▪ a poorly *thrown* ball [*no obj*] Let's see how far you can *throw*. ▪ You *throw* like a wimp. ▪ He hurt his *throwing* arm/hand. [=the arm/hand that he uses to throw a baseball, football, etc.]

2 *always followed by an adverb or preposition* [+ *obj*] **:** to put (something) in a particular place in a careless or forceful way ▪ She *threw* her coat on the bed. ▪ Don't *throw* your trash on the ground. *Throw* it in the trash can. ▪ He *threw* (down) the newspaper on the table in disgust. — sometimes used figuratively ▪ *Throwing* all his inhibitions aside/overboard, he took off his clothes and went skinny-dipping.

3 *always followed by an adverb or preposition* [+ *obj*] **:** to cause (someone or something) to move suddenly or forcefully to or away from a particular place ▪ The wrestler *threw* his opponent to the mat. ▪ The crash *threw* the driver from the car. ▪ She was *thrown* from the horse. ▪ The storm *threw* the boat against a reef.

4 [+ *obj*] *sports* **:** to perform an action that involves throwing a ball ▪ (*American football*) The quarterback *threw* a pass. ▪ (*American football*) The quarterback *threw* a touchdown/interception. [=threw a pass that resulted in a touchdown/interception] ▪ (*baseball*) The pitcher *threw* a curve to him. = The pitcher *threw* him a curve. ▪ (*baseball*) He *threw* [=*pitched*] the first three innings of the game. ▪ (*baseball*) In her last game, she *threw* [=*pitched*] a no-hitter/shutout.

5 a : to send (something) from your hand in a way that causes it to move forward and turn over many times along a surface [+ *obj*] She shook the dice and *threw* [=*rolled*] them on the table. ▪ He *threw* the bowling ball. [*no obj*] It's your turn to *throw*. **b** [+ *obj*] **:** to get (a number or score) by throwing dice or a bowling ball ▪ She *threw* a six/spare.

6 *always followed by an adverb or preposition* [+ *obj*] **:** to cause or force (someone or something) to suddenly be in a particular state, condition, or position ▪ The discovery *threw* the previous theory into (a state of) doubt. ▪ They arrested him and *threw* him in/into prison. [=put him in prison] ▪ The government *threw* the territory open to settlers. — often used as *(be) thrown* ▪ The crowd *was thrown* into confusion. [=the crowd suddenly became very confused] ▪ He *was thrown* into prison. ▪ She *was thrown* into a very difficult situ-

ation. ▪ When the factory closed, the workers *were thrown* out of their jobs. [=the workers lost their jobs]
7 [+ *obj*] **a** *always followed by an adverb or preposition* **:** to forcefully move (yourself or a part of your body) in a particular direction ▪ They *threw* their arms around each other. ▪ She *threw* herself into his arms. ▪ She *threw* back her head in laughter. ▪ He *threw* his shoulders back and stuck out his chest. ▪ He *threw* himself onto the couch. ▪ She *threw* her leg over the arm of the chair. **b :** to swing your arm and try to hit someone with your fist ▪ The boxer *threw* a quick left jab. ▪ I broke up the argument before they started ***throwing punches***. [=trying to hit each other]
8 [+ *obj*] **a** *always followed by an adverb or preposition* **:** to move (something) to an open or closed position in a forceful and sudden way ▪ She *threw* open the window to get some air. ▪ He *threw* the door shut. **b :** to move (a switch) to an on or off position ▪ She *threw* the switch.
9 [+ *obj*] **:** to organize and hold (a party) ▪ Let's *throw* a party to celebrate. ▪ Her friends are *throwing* her a baby shower. = They are *throwing* a baby shower for her.
10 [+ *obj*] **:** to lose (a game or contest) in a deliberate way ▪ He was suspected of *throwing* the boxing match.
11 [+ *obj*] **:** to express strong emotions in an uncontrolled way ▪ The child was ***throwing a (temper) tantrum*** in the middle of the store. ▪ Dad will ***throw a fit*** [=he will be extremely angry] if he finds out.
12 [+ *obj*] **:** to use (your effort, influence, money, etc.) in order to accomplish something ▪ Lobbyists are ***throwing their weight/influence behind*** the legislation. [=they are using their influence to support the legislation] — often + *into* ▪ She *threw* all her efforts *into* the boy's defense. [=she worked as hard as she could for the boy's defense] ▪ They've been *throwing* all their money *into* (repairing) the house. ▪ She *threw* everything she had *into* winning the match. [=she tried as hard as she could to win the match]
13 [+ *obj*] **:** to direct (something, such as a question or look) at someone ▪ She *threw* him an evil look. — often + *at* ▪ She *threw* an evil look *at* him. ▪ He ***threw*** the question ***back at*** me. [=he asked me the same question that I asked him]
14 [+ *obj*] *informal* **:** to cause (someone) to feel confused or surprised ▪ The tricky wording of the contract didn't *throw* her. ▪ The announcement that he was resigning really *threw* me. — see also *throw (someone) for a loop* at [1]LOOP, *throw (someone) for a loss* at LOSS
15 [+ *obj*] **:** to cause (something, such as a shadow) to appear on a surface ▪ The tree *threw* a shadow across the lawn. ▪ The setting sun *threw* long shadows on the buildings. — sometimes used figuratively ▪ His alleged steroid use *threw* a shadow on his record.
16 [+ *obj*] **:** to put (a vehicle) *into* a different gear especially in a quick and sudden way ▪ He *threw* the car *into* reverse.
17 [+ *obj*] **:** to make (your voice) sound as if it is coming from another person or place ▪ Ventriloquists can *throw* their voices so that their dummies appear to speak.
18 [+ *obj*] *US, informal* **:** to do (something that requires special skill) successfully ▪ Kids were *throwing* [=*performing*] stunts/tricks on skateboards at the park.
19 [+ *obj*] *technical* **:** to form or shape (something, such as clay or a pot) on a special wheel ▪ She enjoys *throwing* pottery.

> In addition to the phrases shown below, *throw* occurs in many idioms that are shown at appropriate entries throughout the dictionary. For example, *throw down the gauntlet* can be found at [2]GAUNTLET and *throw light on* can be found at [1]LIGHT.

throw away [*phrasal verb*] ***throw away (something) or throw (something) away*** **1 :** to put (something that is no longer useful or wanted) in a trash can, garbage can, rubbish bin, etc. ▪ We *threw away* [=*threw out*] a lot of old junk that was in the basement. ▪ *Throw* that candy wrapper *away*, please. — see also THROWAWAY **2 a :** to use (something) in a foolish or wasteful way ▪ He *threw away* [=*squandered*] his life savings. ▪ He *threw* all of his money *away* on gambling. ▪ Don't *throw* your life *away*. **b :** to foolishly fail to use (something, such as a chance) ▪ She *threw away* [=*wasted*] an opportunity. ▪ You had a chance to do something great, and you *threw* it *away*.
throw in [*phrasal verb*] ***throw in (something) or throw (something) in*** **1 :** to add (something) to what you are selling without asking for more money ▪ If you buy two, we'll *throw in* a third (for free)! **2 :** to add (something) to the effort or activity of a group ▪ He *threw in* a guitar solo toward the end of the song. ▪ She *threw in* a suggestion or two during the meeting.
throw off [*phrasal verb*] **1** ***throw off (something) or throw (something) off*** **a :** to quickly remove (a piece of clothing) ▪ He *threw* his robe *off* and jumped into the shower. **b :** to get rid of (something you do not want, such as a quality or a condition) ▪ She tried to *throw off* her reputation as being difficult to work with. ▪ He *threw off* his inhibitions and went skinny-dipping. ▪ *throwing off* all restraint **c :** to cause (something) to be incorrect ▪ A decimal point in the wrong place *threw* his calculations *off*. ▪ The dropped ball *threw off* the quarterback's timing. **d :** to send (light, smoke, etc.) out from a source ▪ The woodstove *throws off* [=*gives off*] a lot of heat. **2** ***throw off (someone) or throw (someone) off*** **a :** to cause (someone) to be confused or uncertain about where to go, what to do, etc. ▪ The professor was *thrown off* [=*distracted*] during her lecture by a ringing cell phone. ▪ I'm sorry about getting the date wrong. I was *thrown off* by the fact that yesterday was a holiday. **b :** to get away from (someone who is trying to catch you) ▪ He managed to *throw off* [=escape from] his pursuers by swimming across the river.
throw on [*phrasal verb*] ***throw on (something) or throw (something) on*** **1 :** to quickly put on (a piece of clothing) ▪ She *threw on* her coat and ran out the door. ▪ Let me *throw* some shoes *on*. **2 :** to cause (something) to work by moving a switch ▪ He *threw on* [=*switched on*] the lights.
throw out [*phrasal verb*] **1** ***throw out (something) or throw (something) out*** **a :** to put (something that is no longer useful or wanted) in a trash can, garbage can, rubbish bin, etc. ▪ She *threw out* [=*threw away*] a pair of old shoes. **b :** to refuse to accept or consider (something) ▪ The committee *threw out* [=*rejected*] the proposal. ▪ His testimony was *thrown out* by the judge. **c :** to mention (something) as a possible thing to be done, thought about, etc. **:** SUGGEST ▪ She *threw out* a couple of ideas for improving the company's Web site. ▪ He *threw out* some hints, but nobody could guess the surprise. **d :** to send (light, smoke, etc.) out from a source ▪ The campfire started *throwing out* sparks. ▪ The woodstove *throws out* a lot of heat. **e :** to injure (a part of your body) ▪ I *threw out* my back lifting a chair. **2** ***throw (someone) out or throw out (someone)*** **a :** to force (someone) to leave a place, game, etc. ▪ The referee *threw out* two players for fighting. ▪ His parents threatened to *throw* him *out* (of the house) if he didn't start behaving better. ▪ She got *thrown out* of school for cheating. **b** *baseball* **:** to cause (a player) to be out by throwing the ball to the base that the player is running to ▪ The shortstop *threw* the runner *out* at second.
throw together [*phrasal verb*] **1** ***throw together (something) or throw (something) together*** **:** to make (something) by joining or combining things in a quick and usually careless way ▪ He *threw* some dinner *together* for his friends. ▪ They *threw together* the bookshelf in less than an hour. **2** ***throw together (people) or throw (people) together*** **:** to bring (people) together usually in an unexpected way ▪ People of different occupations were *thrown together* for the jury.
throw up [*phrasal verb*] **1** ***throw up or throw up (something) or throw (something) up informal*** **:** to have the food, liquid, etc., that is in your stomach come out through your mouth **:** VOMIT ▪ She said she felt sick and then *threw up*. ▪ The patient was *throwing up* blood. **2** ***throw up (something) or throw (something) up*** **a :** to raise or lift (something) quickly or suddenly ▪ He *threw up* the window and yelled down to her. ▪ Her car's tires *threw up* dust as she sped away. **b :** to build (something) quickly ▪ The house was *thrown up* almost overnight. **c** *chiefly Brit* **:** to leave (your job, home, etc.) ▪ She *threw up* [=*quit*] her job to devote time to painting. **d** *Brit* **:** to cause (something) to be known ▪ A lot of information has been *thrown up* from the investigation. ▪ The study has *thrown up* some surprising results. **3** ***throw up your hands or throw your hands up (in the air)*** **:** to stop an activity or effort and admit that you cannot do anything to make a situation better ▪ He tried to convince her not to go, but in the end he had to *throw up his hands* in despair. ▪ She *threw her hands up* in disgust.
throw yourself at (someone) *informal* **:** to try too hard to attract the attention of (someone you are sexually attracted to) ▪ Stop *throwing yourself at* him. You'll look desperate.
throw yourself into **:** to begin doing or working on (something) with great energy and determination ▪ He *threw him-*

T

self into (composing/performing) his music. ▪ She *threw herself into* the assignment with a lot of enthusiasm.

²throw *noun, pl* **throws** [*count*]
1 a : an act of throwing something (such as a ball) ▪ The quarterback made a perfect *throw*. — see also FREE THROW, HAMMER THROW **b :** an act of rolling dice ▪ He lost all his winnings on his last *throw*.
2 : the distance over which something is thrown or could be thrown ▪ a discus *throw* of 200 feet ▪ It's a long *throw* from center field to home plate.
3 : a loose blanket or cloth that is put on a sofa, chair, etc.
a stone's throw see ¹STONE
a throw *Brit, informal* **:** for each one **:** APIECE ▪ Tickets cost £25 *a throw*.

throw·away /ˈθrowəˌweɪ/ *adj, always used before a noun*
1 : made to be thrown away after use **:** DISPOSABLE ▪ *throwaway* containers
2 : made or said with very little thought ▪ a *throwaway* remark
3 : tending to throw things away instead of keeping them and using them again **:** very wasteful ▪ a *throwaway* culture/society

throw·back /ˈθroʊˌbæk/ *noun, pl* **-backs** [*count*] **:** a person or thing that is similar to someone or something from the past or that is suited to an earlier time — usually singular; usually + *to* ▪ She's a *throwback to* the actresses of the 1950s. ▪ The band's music is a *throwback to* the 1980s.

throw·er /ˈθrowɚ/ *noun, pl* **-ers** [*count*] **:** a person or thing that throws something ▪ discus *throwers* — see also FLAMETHROWER, SNOW THROWER

throw–in /ˈθroʊˌɪn/ *noun, pl* **-ins** [*count*] *sports* **:** an act of throwing a ball into a playing area or to another player: such as **a :** a throw made in soccer or rugby to put the ball back in play after it has gone out of the playing area **b :** a throw from a player in the outfield to a player in the infield in baseball

thrown *past participle of* ¹THROW

throw pillow *noun, pl* **~ -lows** [*count*] *chiefly US* **:** a small pillow that is used especially for decoration — called also (*Brit*) *scatter cushion*; see picture at LIVING ROOM

throw rug *noun, pl* **~ rugs** [*count*] *chiefly US* **:** a small rug that can be easily moved — called also *scatter rug*

thrum /ˈθrʌm/ *verb* **thrums; thrummed; thrum·ming** [*no obj*] **:** to make a low, steady sound ▪ The engine *thrummed*.
– thrum *noun* [*singular*] ▪ the *thrum* of the engine

¹thrush /ˈθrʌʃ/ *noun, pl* **thrushes** [*count*] **:** a type of bird that is brown with a spotted breast — compare ²THRUSH

²thrush *noun* [*noncount*] *medical*
1 : a disease that occurs mostly in babies and children, that is caused by a fungus, and that produces white patches in the mouth and throat
2 *chiefly Brit* **:** YEAST INFECTION
– compare ¹THRUSH

¹thrust /ˈθrʌst/ *verb* **thrusts; thrust; thrust·ing**
1 *always followed by an adverb or preposition* [+ *obj*] **:** to push (someone or something) with force **:** SHOVE ▪ He *thrust* his hands into his pockets. ▪ He *thrust* his fist into the air. ▪ She *thrust* him aside [=pushed him to the side] and walked past him. ▪ He *thrust* his way through the crowd. [=he went through the crowd by pushing people aside] — sometimes used figuratively ▪ Her best-selling book suddenly *thrust* her into the spotlight. ▪ He *thrust* all caution aside. ▪ She's unable to *thrust* aside [=to forget] those memories.
2 [+ *obj*] **:** to cause (something sharp) to enter or go through something else by pushing ▪ The doctor *thrust* the needle into the patient's arm.
3 [*no obj*] **:** to make a sudden, strong, forward movement *at* someone or something with a weapon ▪ He *thrust at* me with his sword.
thrust on/upon [*phrasal verb*] ***thrust (something) on/upon (someone)*** **:** to force (someone) to have or accept (something) ▪ Fame was *thrust upon* her. [=she became famous even though she did not try or want to be famous]

²thrust *noun, pl* **thrusts**
1 [*count*] **:** a forward or upward push ▪ With one last *thrust* he broke through the barrier. ▪ a *thrust* of the hip = a hip *thrust* ▪ a single *thrust* of his sword
2 [*singular*] **a :** the main point or meaning of something ▪ I agreed with the (main) *thrust* of the argument/theory/article. **b :** the main concern or purpose of something ▪ The major *thrust* of their research [=the main reason they are doing their research] will be to find practical applications.
3 [*noncount*] *technical* **:** the force produced by an engine that causes an aircraft, rocket, etc., to move forward ▪ forward *thrust*
cut and thrust see ²CUT

thru·way *also* **through·way** /ˈθruːˌweɪ/ *noun, pl* **-ways** [*count*] *US* **:** a large highway that can be entered and left only at certain places ▪ the New York State *Thruway*

¹thud /ˈθʌd/ *verb* **thuds; thud·ded; thud·ding** [*no obj*]
1 : to hit something with a loud, dull sound ▪ The ball *thudded* against the side of the house.
2 : to beat forcefully ▪ Her heart was *thudding* [=*thumping, pounding*] against her rib cage.

²thud *noun, pl* **thuds** [*count*] **:** a loud, dull sound made especially when a heavy object hits something **:** THUMP ▪ The book hit the floor with a *thud*. ▪ The ball landed with a *thud*. ▪ I heard a heavy *thud* on the roof.

thug /ˈθʌg/ *noun, pl* **thugs** [*count*] **:** a violent criminal ▪ a gang of *thugs* ▪ He was beaten and robbed by street *thugs*.
– thug·gish /ˈθʌgɪʃ/ *adj* [*more ~; most ~*] ▪ *thuggish* violence/behavior ▪ a *thuggish* regime

thug·gery /ˈθʌgəri/ *noun* [*noncount*] *formal* **:** behavior that is violent and illegal **:** the behavior of thugs ▪ political corruption and *thuggery* ▪ protection from street *thuggery*

¹thumb /ˈθʌm/ *noun, pl* **thumbs** [*count*]
1 : the short, thick finger on the side of your hand ▪ a little girl sucking her *thumb* ▪ I accidentally cut my *thumb*. — see picture at HAND; see also GREEN THUMB
2 : the part of a glove or mitten that covers a thumb ▪ My mitten has a hole in the *thumb*.
all thumbs (*US*) *or Brit* ***all fingers and thumbs*** **:** extremely awkward or clumsy ▪ I'm *all thumbs* when it comes to wrapping packages.
rule of thumb see ¹RULE
stick out like a sore thumb see ¹SORE
twiddle your thumbs see TWIDDLE
under someone's thumb **:** under someone's control or influence ▪ He kept the employees *under his thumb*.

²thumb *verb* **thumbs; thumbed; thumb·ing** *informal* **:** to ask for or get a ride in a passing vehicle by sticking out your arm with your thumb up as you stand on the side of the road **:** HITCHHIKE [+ *obj*] I *thumbed* a ride/lift to school. ▪ He *thumbed* his way to New York. [*no obj*] He *thumbed* across the country.
thumb through [*phrasal verb*] ***thumb through (something)*** **:** to turn the pages of (a book, magazine, etc.) quickly ▪ I *thumbed through* a magazine while I waited.
thumb your nose at **:** to show very clearly that you do not like or care about (something) ▪ She *thumbed her nose at* my suggestions. ▪ They *thumb their nose at* the rules. [=they ignore the rules]
– thumbed *adj* — used in combination ▪ a well-*thumbed* book [=a book that has been used/read a lot] ▪ a much-*thumbed* copy of the rules

thumb index *noun, pl* **~ -dexes** [*count*] **:** a series of small cuts in the edge of the pages in a large book that are labeled and that make it easier to open the book to a particular section ▪ a dictionary that has a *thumb index*
– thumb–indexed *adj* ▪ a *thumb-indexed* dictionary

¹thumb·nail /ˈθʌmˌneɪl/ *noun, pl* **-nails** [*count*]
1 : the hard covering at the end of a thumb **:** the fingernail of a thumb — see picture at HAND
2 *computers* **:** a very small copy of a larger picture on a computer ▪ You can see a larger version of the picture by clicking on the *thumbnail*.

²thumbnail *adj* **:** very short or brief ▪ a *thumbnail* history ▪ He included a ***thumbnail sketch*** [=a short description] of the poet.

thumb·print /ˈθʌmˌprɪnt/ *noun, pl* **-prints** [*count*] **:** the pattern of marks made by pressing your thumb on a surface **:** a fingerprint made by a thumb ▪ He left a dirty *thumbprint* on the page. — sometimes used figuratively ▪ Her *thumbprints* are all over this project. [=it is obvious that she was very involved in this project]

thumb·screw /ˈθʌmˌskruː/ *noun, pl* **-screws** [*count*]
1 : a device used in the past to torture people by crushing their thumbs — sometimes used figuratively ▪ The government is ***tightening/putting the thumbscrews on*** dissenters. [=the government is putting a lot of pressure on dissenters to stop; the government is treating dissenters very harshly]
2 : a type of screw with a flat-sided head that can be held and turned with your thumb and fingers

thumbs–down /ˈθʌmzˈdaʊn/ *noun* [*singular*] **:** a gesture in

T

which you hold your hand out with your thumb pointed down in order to say no, to show disapproval, etc. ▪ When I asked him if they won, he just shook his head and gave me a/the *thumbs-down.* — often used figuratively ▪ Our proposal got a/the *thumbs-down.* [=our proposal was rejected] ▪ The show got a big *thumbs-down* from critics. [=critics did not like the show]

thumbs–up /ˈθʌmzˈʌp/ *noun [singular]* : a gesture in which you hold your hand out with your thumb pointed up in order to say yes, to show approval, etc. ▪ The coach gave me a/the *thumbs-up* after I scored the goal. — often used figuratively ▪ Our proposal got a/the *thumbs-up.* [=our proposal was approved] ▪ The movie got a *thumbs-up* from most critics. [=most critics liked the movie]

thumb·tack /ˈθʌmˌtæk/ *noun, pl* **-tacks** *[count] US* : a short pin that has a large, flat head and that is used to attach papers, pictures, etc., to a wall or bulletin board — called also *(Brit) drawing pin*; see picture at OFFICE

¹thump /ˈθʌmp/ *verb* **thumps; thumped; thump·ing**
1 : to hit or beat something or someone and make a loud, deep sound *[no obj]* Someone was *thumping* [=*pounding*] loudly on the door. ▪ The boat *thumped* against the side of the pier. *[+ obj]* gorillas *thumping* their chests ▪ I *thumped* [=*pounded*] him on the back. ▪ I was so angry I wanted to *thump* him (one).
2 *[no obj]* : to beat forcefully ▪ I could feel my heart *thumping* [=*pounding*] inside my chest.
3 *always followed by an adverb or preposition [no obj]* : to walk or run with loud, heavy steps ▪ She *thumped* [=*clumped*] up the stairs.

²thump *noun, pl* **thumps** *[count]*
1 : a loud, deep sound made especially when a heavy object hits something ▪ The ball landed with a *thump.*
2 : an act of hitting someone or something ▪ I gave him a (good) *thump* on the back. [=I thumped him on the back]

¹thump·ing /ˈθʌmpɪŋ/ *adj, chiefly Brit, informal* : very large, great, etc. ▪ She won the election by a *thumping* [=*whopping*] 79 percent. ▪ He told a *thumping* lie.

²thumping *adv, Brit, informal* : VERY, EXTREMELY ▪ That was a *thumping* great story she told. ▪ We had a *thumping* good time.

¹thun·der /ˈθʌndɚ/ *noun*
1 *[noncount]* : the very loud sound that comes from the sky during a storm : the sound that follows a flash of lightning ▪ Her dog is afraid of *thunder.* ▪ Lightning flashed and *thunder* boomed/crashed. ▪ Suddenly there was a loud clap of *thunder.* ▪ We could hear the rumble of *thunder* in the distance.
2 *[singular]* : a loud noise that sounds like thunder ▪ the *thunder* of horses' hooves ▪ the distant *thunder* of cannon fire ▪ She accepted the award to a *thunder* of applause.
a face like thunder *Brit* : a face that looks very angry ▪ He burst into the room with *a face like thunder.*
steal someone's thunder : to prevent someone from having success or getting a lot of attention, praise, etc., by doing or saying whatever that person was planning to do or say ▪ I didn't mean to *steal your thunder,* but I just had to tell your mom about your promotion.

²thunder *verb* **-ders; -dered; -der·ing**
1 *[no obj]* : to produce thunder ▪ The sky *thundered* and the rain poured down. ▪ It was raining and *thundering* all night.
2 *[no obj]* **a** : to make a loud sound like the sound of thunder ▪ Guns *thundered* in the distance. ▪ a *thundering* waterfall **b** *always followed by an adverb or preposition* : to move in a way that makes a very loud sound ▪ Horses *thundered* down the road. ▪ Jets *thundered* overhead. ▪ Trucks *thundered* past on the highway.
3 *[+ obj]* : to shout (something) very loudly ▪ The crowd *thundered* [=*roared*] its approval. ▪ "How dare you come into my house!" he *thundered.*

thun·der·bolt /ˈθʌndɚˌboʊlt/ *noun, pl* **-bolts** *[count]* : a flash of lightning that makes a loud sound of thunder and that hits someone or something ▪ He was struck dead by a *thunderbolt.* — sometimes used figuratively ▪ The news hit them like a *thunderbolt.* [=the news was very shocking or surprising]

thun·der·clap /ˈθʌndɚˌklæp/ *noun, pl* **-claps** *[count]* : a very loud, sharp sound of thunder ▪ I was awakened by a *thunderclap.*

thun·der·cloud /ˈθʌndɚˌklaʊd/ *noun, pl* **-clouds** *[count]* : a large, dark cloud that produces lightning and thunder ▪ We watched the gathering *thunderclouds.* — compare STORM CLOUD

thun·der·head /ˈθʌndɚˌhɛd/ *noun, pl* **-heads** *[count] chiefly US* : a very large cloud appearing before a thunderstorm ▪ A *thunderhead* was forming to the west.

thun·der·ous /ˈθʌndərəs/ *adj* : making a loud noise like the sound of thunder : very loud ▪ The audience responded with *thunderous* applause.
— **thun·der·ous·ly** *adv* ▪ It was *thunderously* loud.

thun·der·show·er /ˈθʌndɚˌʃawɚ/ *noun, pl* **-ers** *[count] US* : a brief storm with lightning and thunder : a brief thunderstorm ▪ *Thundershowers* are forecast for tomorrow.

thun·der·storm /ˈθʌndɚˌstoɚm/ *noun, pl* **-storms** *[count]* : a storm with lightning and thunder ▪ There are *thunderstorms* in the forecast. ▪ The weather service has issued a severe *thunderstorm* warning.

thun·der·struck /ˈθʌndɚˌstrʌk/ *adj* : feeling sudden and great surprise or shock ▪ She was *thunderstruck* when her parents told her she was adopted.

thun·dery /ˈθʌndəri/ *adj [more ~; most ~] Brit* : producing or likely to produce thunder ▪ *thundery* showers ▪ *thundery* [=*stormy*] weather

thunk /ˈθʌŋk/ *noun [singular] chiefly US* : a dull, hollow sound made especially when a heavy object hits something ▪ The book landed on the floor with a *thunk.*

Thurs. *or* **Thur.** *abbr* Thursday

Thurs·day /ˈθɚzˌdeɪ/ *noun, pl* **-days** : the day between Wednesday and Friday *[count]* He was late last *Thursday.* ▪ *(Brit)* We went on the *Thursday* and returned on the Saturday. ▪ The class meets on *Thursdays.* [=every Thursday] *[noncount]* We went on *Thursday* and returned on Saturday. ▪ She will arrive on *Thursday.* = *(US)* She will arrive *Thursday.* — abbr. *Thurs.* or *Thur.* or *Th.*
— **Thurs·days** /ˈθɚzˌdeɪz/ *adv* ▪ The class meets *Thursdays.* [=every Thursday]

thus /ˈðʌs/ *adv, formal*
1 a : in this way or manner : like this ▪ The judge expressed it *thus*: "Our obligation is to discover the truth." **b** : by so doing ▪ I took her shift, *thus* enabling her to have the night off. [=I enabled her to have the night off by taking her shift]
2 : because of this : THEREFORE ▪ This detergent is highly concentrated and *thus* you will need to dilute it. ▪ *Thus,* we conclude . . .
thus far see ¹FAR

thwack /ˈθwæk/ *verb* **thwacks; thwacked; thwack·ing** *[+ obj]* : to hit (someone or something) hard with a loud sound ▪ A book fell off the shelf and *thwacked* me on the head.
— **thwack** *noun, pl* **thwacks** *[count]* ▪ I gave the ball a good *thwack.* [=I hit the ball hard] ▪ The book hit the floor with a loud *thwack.*

thwart /ˈθwoɚt/ *verb* **thwarts; thwart·ed; thwart·ing** *[+ obj]* : to prevent (someone) from doing something or to stop (something) from happening ▪ She did all she could to *thwart* his plans. ▪ The army *thwarted* the attempt at a coup. — often used as *(be) thwarted* ▪ The plot *was thwarted.* ▪ He *was thwarted* in his evil plans. ▪ *thwarted* ambition/hopes

thy /ˈðaɪ/ *adj, old-fashioned + literary* : YOUR — used when speaking to a single person ▪ ". . . thou shalt love *thy* neighbor as thyself." —Leviticus 19:18 (KJV)

thyme /ˈtaɪm/ *noun [noncount]* : a sweet-smelling herb with small leaves that is used in cooking — see color picture on page C6

thy·roid /ˈθaɪˌroɪd/ *noun, pl* **-roids** *[count] medical* : a small gland in the neck that affects growth ▪ an overactive/underactive *thyroid* ▪ a *thyroid* condition — called also *thyroid gland*

thy·self /ðaɪˈsɛlf/ *pronoun, old-fashioned + literary* : YOURSELF — used when speaking to a single person ▪ ". . . Physician, heal *thyself* . . ." —Luke 4:23 (KJV) ▪ Know *thyself.*

ti /ˈtiː/ *noun [noncount]* : the seventh note of a musical scale ▪ do, re, mi, fa, sol, la, *ti*

ti·ara /tiˈerə, *Brit* tiˈɑːrə/ *noun, pl* **-aras** *[count]*
1 : a crown worn by the pope
2 : a small crown that is decorated with jewels and that is worn by women or girls on special occasions ▪ a diamond *tiara*

tib·ia /ˈtɪbijə/ *noun, pl* **tib·i·ae** /ˈtɪbiˌiː/ *or* **tib·i·as** *[count] medical* : the bone that forms the front part of the leg between the knee and the ankle — called also *shinbone*; see picture at HUMAN

tic /ˈtɪk/ *noun, pl* **tics** *[count]*
1 : a small repeated movement of a muscle especially in the

T

face that cannot be controlled • a facial *tic*
2 : a word or phrase that someone frequently says or an action that someone frequently does without intending to • a nervous *tic* • The verbal *tic* "you know" often occurs in her speech.

¹tick /ˈtɪk/ *noun*
1 [*singular*] : a small, quick sound that is made by a machine (such as a clock) and that often occurs in a series to produce a rhythm • the *tick* of a clock
2 [*count*] *chiefly Brit* : the time that it takes a clock to make one tick : a very short period of time • I'll be there in a *tick*. [=*second*] • Give me two *ticks* to get ready.
3 [*count*] *chiefly Brit* : a mark ✓ that is used to show that something (such as an item on a list) has been noted, done, etc. : CHECK • Put a *tick* next to your name.
– compare ³TICK, ⁴TICK

²tick *verb* **ticks; ticked; tick·ing**
1 [*no obj*] : to make a small, quick, and often rhythmic tapping sound • I could hear the clock *tick/ticking*.
2 [*no obj*] : to continue to work or function in a normal way : RUN • His old heart is still *ticking*.
3 [+ *obj*] *chiefly Brit* : to mark (something) with a written tick (✓) : CHECK • *Tick* the box next to your choice. — often + *off* • *Tick off* your choice below. • You're coming? Okay, I'll *tick* you *off* (on my list). [=I'll put a tick/check next to your name on my list]
4 [+ *obj*] : to touch (something) quickly or lightly • The bat *ticked* the ball.
tick away/by/past [*phrasal verb*] *of time* : to pass or go by • Time is *ticking away*. • She became impatient as the hours *ticked by*.
tick off [*phrasal verb*] **1** ***tick (someone) off or tick off (someone)*** **a** *US, informal* : to make (someone) angry • He really *ticks* me *off* sometimes. • She was *ticked off* by the rude salesclerk. **b** *Brit* : to criticize (someone) strongly : to tell (someone) in an angry way that he or she did something wrong • His mother *ticked* him *off* for his behavior. **2** ***tick (someone or something) off or tick off (someone or something)*** **a** *US* : to say the name of (someone or something) as part of a list • Her parents *ticked off* [=*listed*] all the reasons she should not have stayed out late. **b** : to count or mark things as they pass • We are *ticking off* the days until vacation. — see also ²TICK 3 (above)
tick over [*phrasal verb*] **1** *chiefly Brit, of a vehicle's engine* : to run at a very low speed **2** *Brit* : to run or proceed in a steady but slow way • "How's business?" "Oh, just *ticking over*."
what makes someone tick *informal* : the things that cause someone to behave a certain way : the feelings, opinions, concerns, etc., that are parts of someone's personality • I've always wondered *what makes* people like that *tick*. • It's hard to say *what makes him tick*.

³tick *noun, pl* **ticks** [*count*] : a very small insect that attaches itself to the skin of larger animals or people and drinks their blood — see also DEER TICK — compare ¹TICK, ⁴TICK

tick

⁴tick *noun* [*noncount*] *Brit, old-fashioned* : an agreement to pay for something after a period of time : CREDIT • She bought her supplies *on tick*. [=she promised to pay for the supplies later] — compare ¹TICK, ³TICK

ticked /ˈtɪkt/ *or* **ticked off** *adj, not used before a noun, US, informal* : very angry or upset • I was so *ticked*. • She was pretty *ticked off* about what he said. — often + *at* • I was so *ticked off at* him.

tick·er /ˈtɪkɚ/ *noun, pl* **-ers** [*count*]
1 a : a machine that receives and prints out stock prices and other news on long, thin pieces of paper • The news came over the *ticker*. **b** : a narrow area that shows information across the top or bottom of a television or computer screen
2 *informal* : HEART • Exercise is good for your/the *ticker*.

ticker tape *noun* [*noncount*] : long, thin pieces of paper on which news and stock prices are printed by a special machine (called a ticker)

ticker–tape parade *noun, pl* **~ -rades** [*count*] *US* : a parade in which small pieces of paper are thrown into the air to celebrate something, welcome someone, etc. • The astronauts were given a *ticker-tape parade* through the streets of New York.

¹tick·et /ˈtɪkət/ *noun, pl* **-ets**
1 [*count*] : a piece of paper that allows you to see a show, participate in an event, travel on a vehicle, etc. • May I see your *tickets*, please? = *Tickets*, please. • We bought *tickets* for/to the opera. • a movie/concert *ticket* • a bus/train *ticket* • She bought a ***one-way ticket*** to New York. [=a ticket that allows her to travel to New York] • (*US*) a ***round-trip ticket*** = (*Brit*) a ***return ticket*** [=a ticket that allows you to travel to one place and then return back to the place you left] — see also SEASON TICKET
2 [*count*] : a card or piece of paper that shows that you are participating in a contest, raffle, etc. • a winning lottery *ticket* — see also SCRATCH TICKET
3 [*count*] : a piece of paper that officially tells you that you have driven or parked your car improperly and that you will have to pay a fine • I got a *ticket* for speeding. — see also PARKING TICKET, SPEEDING TICKET
4 [*count*] *Brit* : a piece of paper that is attached to an item in a store and that gives information about its price, size, etc. • a price *ticket* [=*tag*]
5 [*singular*] *chiefly US* : a list of the candidates supported by a political party in an election • The senator heads her party's *ticket*. [=she is the leader of her party in the election] • the Republican/Democratic *ticket* — see also SPLIT TICKET, *split the ticket* at ¹SPLIT
6 [*singular*] : something that makes it possible to get or achieve something that you want • She believed that education was the/her *ticket* to a good job. • He expected the novel to be his *ticket* to fame and fortune. • This job could be their *ticket* out of poverty. — see also MEAL TICKET
7 ***the ticket*** *informal + somewhat old-fashioned* : the correct or most desirable thing : the thing that is needed or wanted • Compromise, now ***that's the ticket***. [=that's what we need] — often used in the phrase ***just the ticket*** • For a romantic dinner, candles are *just the ticket*.
write your own ticket see WRITE
– see also HOT TICKET

²ticket *verb* **-ets; -et·ed; -et·ing** [+ *obj*]
1 *chiefly US* : to give (a driver) a ticket for driving or parking improperly • He was *ticketed* for speeding.
2 : to give or sell a ticket to (someone) • methods used for *ticketing* airline passengers
3 *US* : to give (someone or something) a specific purpose or destination — usually used as *(be) ticketed* • The building has *been ticketed* [=*designated*] for renovations. • a baseball player *ticketed* for the minor leagues [=a baseball player who is being sent to the minor leagues]
– ticketing *noun* [*noncount*] • Most airlines now allow electronic *ticketing*.

ticket office *noun, pl* **~ -fices** [*count*] : a place where you can buy tickets to travel on a bus, to see a play, to go to a concert, etc.

ticket tout *noun, pl* **~ touts** [*count*] *Brit* : a person who buys tickets for an event and resells them at a much higher price : SCALPER

tick·ing /ˈtɪkɪŋ/ *noun* [*noncount*] : a strong type of cloth that is often used as a covering for mattresses and pillows

tick·le /ˈtɪkəl/ *verb* **tick·les; tick·led; tick·ling**
1 [+ *obj*] : to try to make (someone) laugh by lightly touching a very sensitive part of the body with your fingers, a feather, etc. • Her little brother screamed with laughter as she *tickled* him.
2 : to have or cause a slightly uncomfortable feeling on a part of your body [+ *obj*] The tag on the sweater *tickled* his neck. [*no obj*] My nose started to *tickle*. • Don't touch me there; it *tickles*.
3 [+ *obj*] : to please or amuse (someone or something) • The food will *tickle* your taste buds. [=you'll enjoy the taste of the food] • We were *tickled* by the invitation. • The idea of going to the party *tickled* her.
tickled pink *informal* : very happy or amused • I was *tickled pink* to see her.
tickle the ivories see IVORY
tickle your fancy *informal* : to interest or attract you • Do you see anything on the menu that *tickles your fancy*?
tickle your funny bone see FUNNY BONE
– tickle *noun, pl* **tickles** [*count*] • He gave her neck a *tickle*. [=he tickled her neck] • He felt a *tickle* in his throat. **– tick·ler** /ˈtɪkəlɚ/ *noun, pl* **-lers** [*count*]

tick·lish /ˈtɪklɪʃ/ *adj* [*more ~; most ~*]
1 : sensitive and easily tickled • My feet are very *ticklish*. • I'm very *ticklish*.

T

2 : difficult to deal with : requiring special care • Religion can be a very *ticklish* [=*sensitive, touchy*] subject.

tic–tac–toe *or* **tick–tack–toe** /ˌtɪkˌtækˈtoʊ/ *noun* [*noncount*] *US* : a game in which one player draws Xs and another player draws Os inside a set of nine squares and each player tries to be the first to fill a row of squares with either Xs or Os — called also (*Brit*) *noughts and crosses*

tid·al /ˈtaɪdl̩/ *adj* : of or relating to tides : rising and falling at regular times • *tidal* currents

tidal wave *noun, pl* ~ **waves** [*count*]
1 : a very high, large wave in the ocean that is often caused by strong winds or an earthquake : TSUNAMI
2 : a very large amount of something • a *tidal wave* of emotion/tourists

tid·bit (*US*) /ˈtɪdˌbɪt/ *or Brit* **tit·bit** /ˈtɪtˌbɪt/ *noun, pl* **-bits** [*count*]
1 : a small piece of food • tasty *tidbits*
2 : a small piece of news or interesting information • I just heard a juicy *tidbit* about your brother. • *tidbits* of gossip

tid·dler /ˈtɪdlɚ/ *noun, pl* **tid·dlers** [*count*] *Brit, informal*
1 : a small fish
2 : a small and unimportant person or thing • The company is no *tiddler*.

tid·dly·winks /ˈtɪdliˌwɪŋks/ *also US* **tid·dle·dy·winks** /ˈtɪdl̩diˌwɪŋks/ *noun* [*noncount*] : a children's game in which players make small discs jump into a small container by pressing on them with another disc

¹tide /ˈtaɪd/ *noun, pl* **tides**
1 a [*count*] : the regular upward and downward movement of the level of the ocean that is caused by the pull of the Sun and the Moon on the Earth • a chart of the *tides* • Is the *tide* coming in or going out? = Is the *tide* rising or falling? — see also EBB TIDE, FLOOD TIDE, HIGH TIDE, LOW TIDE, RIPTIDE **b** [*singular*] : the flow of the ocean's water as the tide rises or falls • The boat got swept away in/by the *tide*.
2 [*singular*] : the way in which something is changing or developing • We tried to gauge the *tide* of public opinion. [=to find out how public opinion was changing] • the *tide* of history • The team was on a losing streak, but then ***the tide turned*** [=their luck changed] and they went on to win the championship.
3 [*singular*] : something that increases over time — + *of* • The government is dealing with a rising/swelling/growing *tide of* criticism over its foreign policy. • They are concerned about the rising *tide of* crime [=the increasing amount of crime] in the city. • We have to do something to ***stem the tide*** of violence. [=to stop the violence from continuing and increasing]
go/swim with/against the tide ✧ If you *go/swim with/against the tide*, you think or behave in a way that agrees/disagrees with how most other people think or behave. • Politically, she tends to *go against the tide* on her college campus. [=she tends to have different political opinions than most people on her college campus]

²tide *verb* **tides; tid·ed; tid·ing**
tide over [*phrasal verb*] ***tide (someone) over*** : to give (someone) what is needed to get through a short period of time • My parents lent us some money to *tide* us *over* for a while. • He had a snack to *tide* himself *over* until dinner.

tide·mark /ˈtaɪdˌmɑɚk/ *noun, pl* **-marks** [*count*]
1 *chiefly Brit* : a mark on the beach that shows how far the water came in toward the shore when the tide was high
2 *Brit, informal* : a mark left by dirty water in a bathtub

tide pool *noun, pl* ~ **pools** [*count*] *US* : an area of water that is left on a beach after the tide has fallen

tide·wa·ter /ˈtaɪdˌwɑːtɚ/ *noun, pl* **-ters**
1 [*noncount*] : water that flows over land during high tide
2 [*count*] *US* : an area of land along the coast

T

tid·ings /ˈtaɪdɪŋz/ *noun* [*plural*] *old-fashioned* : NEWS • good/glad *tidings*

¹ti·dy /ˈtaɪdi/ *adj* **ti·di·er; -est** [*also more* ~; *most* ~]
1 : clean and organized : not messy • She keeps her desk *tidy*. [=*neat*] • a *tidy* kitchen • The house is ***neat and tidy.*** [=clean and organized]
2 : keeping things clean and organized • He has always been a *tidy* person.
3 *informal, of an amount of money* : fairly large • She earns a *tidy* salary. • They paid a *tidy* sum for the house.

²tidy *verb* **-dies; -died; -dy·ing** : to make (something) tidy : to make (something) clean and organized [+ *obj*] I *tidied* the house before they arrived. — usually + *up* • We need to *tidy up* the house. [*no obj*] — + *up* • I didn't have time to *tidy up*. • I'm tired of always ***tidying up after*** you. [=cleaning up your messes]
tidy away [*phrasal verb*] ***tidy (something) away or tidy away (something)*** *Brit* : to put (something) in its proper place in order to make a place tidy • I *tidied* all the loose papers *away* before the guests arrived.

³tidy *noun, pl* **-dies** [*count*] *Brit* : a container for storing small items • a desk/sink/car *tidy*

¹tie /ˈtaɪ/ *verb* **ties; tied; ty·ing** /ˈtajɪŋ/
1 a [+ *obj*] : to attach (someone or something) *to* something with a string, rope, etc. • His kidnappers *tied* him *to* a chair. • She *tied* (up) the dog *to* a post and went into the store. **b** [+ *obj*] : to pass (something, such as a string, ribbon, or rope) around itself in a way that attaches it to something or holds it in place : to make a knot or bow in (something) • He *tied* (up) his shoelaces/necktie. • She *tied* a scarf around her neck. • He *tied* the ropes together. [=he attached the ropes to each other by tying a knot] • She wrapped a ribbon around the box and ***tied a bow***. [=made a bow] • She ***tied knots*** in the rope. — often + *to* • He *tied* the rope *to* a tree branch. • I *tied* the dog's leash *to* a post and went into the store. — sometimes used figuratively • At the end of the book, she *ties* together the separate plots of the story. **c** : to close or hold (something) with a string, rope, etc., that is attached to it or wrapped around it [+ *obj*] You need to *tie* your shoe. • The butcher *tied* (up) the package with string. • His hands and feet had been *tied* together. • *Tie* your hair back (in a ponytail) so it won't fall in your face. • She *tied* the apron loosely around her waist. [*no obj*] The apron *ties* (up) in the back. — see also *hands are tied* at ¹HAND
2 a : to make the score of a game or contest equal [+ *obj*] She *tied* (up) the score with a late goal. • He can *tie* (up) the game with a home run. [*no obj*] The team still has a chance to *tie*. **b** [*no obj*] : to end a game, race, etc., with the same score or in the same position as another person or team • He *tied* for first/second place. [=he and another competitor both finished with the same score in first/second place] **c** [+ *obj*] : to achieve the same score, time, etc., as (a person, a record, etc.) • I had the lead but he *tied* me by making a birdie on the last hole. • Her time *tied* the world record. • He *tied* the school's record in the high jump.
3 [+ *obj*] : to connect (someone or something) *to* another person or thing — usually used as *(be) tied to* • He argues that poverty *is* closely *tied to* poor health. [=that poverty and poor health are closely related/connected] • The rise in crime has *been tied* [=*linked*] *to* drug dealing. • The rate of production *is tied to* consumer demand. [=the rate of production depends on consumer demand] • The prices of Web ads *are tied to* the number of visitors the sites have.
4 [+ *obj*] : to cause or require (someone) to be somewhere, do something, etc. • He has responsibilities that *tie* him to this area. [=that prevent him from leaving this area] — often used as *(be) tied to* • She was tired of *being tied to* the same routine. [=of always having the same routine] • He *was tied to* his desk all day. [=he had to work at his desk all day] • I didn't want to *be tied to* driving her to work every day.
fit to be tied see ¹FIT
tie down [*phrasal verb*] **1** ***tie (something or someone) down or tie down (something or someone)*** : to attach (something or someone) especially to a flat surface by using string, rope, etc. • A storm was coming, so the captain ordered us to *tie* everything *down*. • She *tied down* the flaps of the tent. • They had him *tied down* on a stretcher. **2** ***tie (someone) down or tie down (someone)*** : to limit the freedom of (someone) • Having a family *ties* people *down*. • She doesn't want to *tie* herself *down* to a schedule. — often used as *(be) tied down* • You're too young to *be tied down* with so much responsibility.
tie in [*phrasal verb*] **1** : to be related or connected to something — + *to* or *with* • The book's illustrations *tie in to/with* the story very well. **2** ***tie in (something) or tie (something) in*** : to connect (something) to something else — + *to* or *with* • The teacher *tied in* what we learned last week *with* today's lesson. • The publication of the senator's book was *tied in to* his announcement that he will run for president. — see also TIE-IN
tie off [*phrasal verb*] ***tie off (something) or tie (something) off***
1 : to fasten or hold (something) by tying a knot or bow at its end • I finished knitting the last row and *tied off* the yarn. **2** : to close (something) with string, thread, etc. • The surgeon *tied off* the vein.
tie one on *US, informal + old-fashioned* : to become drunk • He really *tied one on* last night.

tie on the feedbag see FEEDBAG
tie the knot see [1]KNOT
tie up *[phrasal verb]* **1** ***tie up or tie (something) up or tie up (something)*** **:** to become attached or to attach (something) to a fixed object with a string, rope, etc. ▪ They *tied* (the boat) *up* and jumped out. ▪ The ferry *ties up* at the south slip. **2** ***tie (something) up or tie up (something)*** **a :** to deal with (something) in order to complete something ▪ The project is almost finished, but we still have a few final details to *tie up*. = We still have to ***tie up some loose ends***. ▪ The writer *ties up all the loose ends* at the end of the story. **b** *US* **:** to prevent the use or progress of (something) ▪ He *tied up* the phone for an hour. [=he used the phone for an hour and other people could not use it] ▪ Traffic was *tied up* [=*backed up*] for hours/miles. **3** ***tie up (money) in (something) or tie (money) up in (something)*** **:** to invest (money) in (something) in a way that prevents it from being used for some other purpose ▪ They *tied up* all of their money *in* their new business. — usually used as *(be) tied up in* ▪ The money *was tied up in* stocks. **4** ***tie up with (something) or be tied up with (something)*** **:** to be connected or related to (something) ▪ Today's lesson *tied up with* what was taught yesterday. ▪ My life *is tied up with* hers. **5** ***tie (someone) up or tie up (someone)*** **a :** to tie rope, tape, etc., around the body, arms, or legs of (someone) in order to keep that person from moving or escaping ▪ The robbers *tied up* the clerk. **b :** to prevent (someone) from doing other things or from going to a particular place ▪ Meetings *tied* me *up* for most of the afternoon. — usually used as *(be) tied up* ▪ She *was tied up* in traffic. ▪ I'd like to help but I'*m* a bit *tied up* at the moment. — see also [1]TIE 1, 2 (above), TIE-UP
tie yourself (up) in knots see [1]KNOT

[2]tie *noun, pl* **ties** *[count]*
1 : NECKTIE ▪ He was wearing a suit and *tie*. ▪ You have a spot on your *tie*. — see also BOW TIE
2 : a piece of string, ribbon, cord, etc., that is used for fastening, joining, or closing something ▪ The pants have a *tie* at the top. — see also TWIST TIE
3 a : something (such as an idea, interest, experience, or feeling) that is shared by people or groups and that forms a connection between them — usually plural ▪ family *ties* ▪ political/economic/cultural *ties* ▪ the *ties* of friendship ▪ The company has close *ties* to conservative groups. ▪ Recent events have strengthened/cemented the *ties* between our two countries. ▪ She has severed all *ties* with the company. ▪ The experience loosened the *ties* that bind (us together). **b :** a responsibility that limits a person's freedom to do other things ▪ He was not ready to accept the *ties* of family life.
4 a : the final result of a game, contest, etc., in which two or more people or teams finish with the same number of points, votes, etc. — usually singular ▪ The game ended in a *tie*. = The game was a *tie*. [=both teams/players had the same score at the end of the game] ▪ They played to a 3–3 *tie*. [=each team/player had 3 points when the game ended] ▪ There was a *tie* for second place. **b :** a situation in which two or more people or teams have the same number of points, votes, etc., in a game or contest — usually singular ▪ She broke the *tie* with a goal in the final seconds of the match. ▪ a *tie* score
5 *US* **:** one of the heavy pieces of wood to which the rails of a railroad are fastened — called also *(Brit) sleeper*
6 *Brit, sports* **:** a match in a sports competition (such as a soccer or tennis tournament) in which the loser is eliminated ▪ They won the *tie* in the first round and went on to win the cup.

tie·back /ˈtaɪˌbæk/ *noun, pl* **-backs** *[count]* **:** a cord or piece of cloth, metal, etc., that is used for holding a curtain to the side of a window

tie–break *noun, pl* **-breaks** *[count] sports* **:** a tiebreaker in tennis ▪ She won the *tie-break*.

tie·break·er /ˈtaɪˌbreɪkɚ/ *noun, pl* **-ers** *[count]* **:** something (such as an extra period of play or an extra question) that is used to decide a winner when a game, contest, etc., has ended with a tied score

tied /ˈtaɪd/ *adj* **:** having an equal number of points in a contest ▪ The teams were *tied* 7–7 at the end of the first quarter. ▪ The candidates are presently *tied* in the polls. **:** having an equal number of points for each side ▪ The score was *tied* (at) 7–7. ▪ It was a *tied* [=*tie*] game at the end of the first half.

tie–dye /ˈtaɪˌdaɪ/ *verb* **-dye; -dyed; -dyeing** *[+ obj]* **:** to decorate (fabric or clothing) by tying parts of the fabric with knots, strings, etc., and soaking it in often several different colors of dye ▪ We *tie-dyed* our T-shirts.
– tie–dyed *adj* ▪ a *tie-dyed* shirt **– tie–dye·ing** /ˈtaɪˌdajɪŋ/ *noun [noncount]*

tie–in /ˈtaɪˌɪn/ *noun, pl* **-ins** *[count]* **:** a product (such as a toy) that is connected with a movie, television show, etc. — see also *tie in* at [1]TIE

tie·pin /ˈtaɪˌpɪn/ *noun, pl* **-pins** *[count]* **:** a decorative pin that is used to hold the ends of a necktie in place

tier /ˈtiɚ/ *noun, pl* **tiers** *[count]*
1 : a row or layer of things that is above another row or layer ▪ We were seated in the theater's top *tier*.
2 : a particular level in a group, organization, etc. ▪ top *tier* colleges [=the best or most expensive colleges] ▪ the lowest *tier* of management

tiered /ˈtiɚd/ *adj* **:** arranged in layers or tiers ▪ The hors d'oeuvres were served on *tiered* platters. — usually used in combination ▪ a three-*tiered* cake ▪ a two-*tiered* justice system that treats poor and wealthy people differently

tie tack *noun, pl* **~ tacks** *[count] US* **:** a short pin with a separate back or clasp that fastens behind a necktie

tie–up /ˈtaɪˌʌp/ *noun, pl* **-ups** *[count]*
1 *chiefly US* **:** a situation in which something (such as traffic) becomes very slow or stops because of a problem, accident, etc. ▪ An overturned truck caused a traffic *tie-up* for miles.
2 *chiefly Brit* **a :** a close connection between people or things ▪ the *tie-up* [=*link*] between poverty and poor health **b :** an agreement to do business together ▪ There are rumors of a proposed *tie-up* between the two companies. — see also *tie up* at [1]TIE

tiff /ˈtɪf/ *noun, pl* **tiffs** *[count]* **:** a small fight or argument about something that is not important ▪ She got into a *tiff* [=*quarrel*] with her boyfriend. ▪ a *tiff* over money

ti·ger /ˈtaɪgɚ/ *noun, pl* **-gers** *[count]*
1 a : a large, wild cat that has a coat of usually yellow or orange fur and black stripes and that lives in Asia — see picture at CAT **b :** a striped cat that lives with people — called also *tiger cat*
2 : a person who is very fierce or aggressive ▪ He was a *tiger* on the basketball court. — see also PAPER TIGER
– ti·ger·ish /ˈtaɪgərɪʃ/ *adj [more ~; most ~]*

[1]tight /ˈtaɪt/ *adj* **tight·er; -est**
1 : difficult to move **:** fastened, attached, or held in a position that is not easy to move ▪ The lid is too *tight*. I can't loosen it. ▪ She made a *tight* knot in the rope. ▪ Keep a *tight* grip/hold on his hand when you cross the street. — opposite LOOSE
2 : fitting very close to your body ▪ *tight* [=*snug*] T-shirts ▪ a *tight* pair of jeans = a pair of *tight* jeans ▪ These shoes are too *tight*. [=they are too small] ▪ a *tight* bandage — opposite LOOSE; see also SKINTIGHT
3 : flat or firm from being pulled or stretched ▪ a *tight* wire/string ▪ Pull the ribbon *tight* and make a bow. — opposite LOOSE
4 : tense or stiff **:** not relaxed ▪ Her muscles were *tight*. ▪ His throat/chest felt *tight*. ▪ a *tight* smile ▪ She answered in a *tight* voice. — opposite LOOSE
5 : hard and muscular ▪ an athlete with a *tight* stomach/body ▪ He has *tight* abs.
6 : having parts that are very close together ▪ The cat was curled into a *tight* ball. ▪ a fabric with a *tight* weave ▪ The swimming goggles should create a *tight* seal around your eyes. — see also AIRTIGHT, WATERTIGHT
7 : not having or allowing much room ▪ Space was *tight* at their first home. [=their first home was small; they did not have much room] ▪ There's a *tight* space you can crawl through underneath the house. ▪ The tunnel gets pretty *tight* up ahead. ▪ We got everything into the suitcase, but it was a ***tight squeeze***. [=the suitcase was very full/packed]
8 : not having or allowing much time ▪ We are on a *tight* schedule. ▪ The project has a very *tight* deadline. ▪ Time was *tight*, so we couldn't stay long.
9 : close or equal in score, progress, or ability ▪ It was a very *tight* race/game. ▪ It was one of the *tightest* presidential elections in history. ▪ The teams play in a *tight* division.
10 : not allowing much freedom **:** strict about controlling what happens ▪ She kept a *tight* hand on the business. [=she controlled the business in a very strict way] ▪ The mayor put *tighter* security in place for the concert. ▪ He has people working for him, but he ***has/keeps a tight rein*** on every part of the process.
11 : difficult or awkward ▪ You've put me in a *tight* spot. [=a difficult position] ▪ They were in a *tight* spot financially.

T

[=they did not have much money; they were having financial problems]
12 a : low in supply : not easily available ▪ We can't afford a vacation right now because money is *tight*. [=*scarce*] ▪ Jobs are *tight* right now. [=there are not many jobs available right now] **b** — used to describe a situation that is difficult because there is not enough of something ▪ Things have been a little *tight* [=money has been scarce] since I lost my job. ▪ a *tight* job market [=a situation in which there are few jobs]
13 *informal + usually disapproving* **:** not giving or spending money freely : stingy or cheap ▪ He's pretty *tight* with his money.
14 : having a close personal or professional relationship ▪ We've been *tight* [=very friendly] for a long time. ▪ a *tight* group of friends — often + *with* ▪ She's *tight with* the boss.
15 : curving or changing direction suddenly ▪ There is a *tight* [=*sharp*] bend in the road up ahead. ▪ Make a *tight* right turn at the traffic light.
16 *informal + old-fashioned* **:** very drunk ▪ getting *tight* at a bar
run a tight ship see [1]SHIP
– tight·ly *adv* ▪ The shirt fits too *tightly* around the arms. ▪ The luggage was secured *tightly* to the top of the car. ▪ Hold on *tightly* to the railing. ▪ shelves packed *tightly* with books ▪ a *tightly* knit [=*tight-knit*] family **– tight·ness** *noun* [*noncount*] ▪ He felt some muscle *tightness* in his back.

[2]**tight** *adv* **:** in a tight way ▪ Hold on *tight*. ▪ Is the door shut *tight*? ▪ She screwed the cap on *tight*. ▪ Don't close the lid so *tight*. ▪ We were packed as *tight* as sardines on the bus.
hang tight see [1]HANG
sit tight see SIT
sleep tight see [1]SLEEP

tight·en /ˈtaɪtn̩/ *verb* **-ens; -ened; -en·ing :** to make (something) tight or tighter or to become tight or tighter [+ *obj*] I'll *tighten* the screw. ▪ She *tightened* her hold on the handle. [*no obj*] His jaw muscles *tightened*.
tighten the noose see NOOSE
tighten the screws see [1]SCREW
tighten up [*phrasal verb*] ***tighten up or tighten (something) up or tighten up (something)*** **:** to become more strict or effective or to make (something) more strict or effective ▪ Security around the building has *tightened up* recently. ▪ They *tightened up* security around the building. ▪ We installed new machines to *tighten up* the assembly line.
tighten your belt see [1]BELT

tight end *noun, pl* **~ ends** [*count*] *American football* **:** a player on the offensive team who plays in a position on the line of scrimmage and who blocks and sometimes catches passes

tight·fist·ed /ˈtaɪtˈfɪstəd/ *adj* [*more ~; most ~*] *disapproving* **:** not wanting to give or spend money : stingy or cheap ▪ The company's *tightfisted* owner won't raise the workers' salaries.

tight–knit /ˈtaɪtˈnɪt/ *adj* [*more ~; most ~*] — used to describe a group of people who care about each other and who are very friendly with each other ▪ We are a *tight-knit* [=*close-knit*] family/community.

tight–lipped /ˈtaɪtˈlɪpt/ *adj* [*more ~; most ~*]
1 : not willing to speak about something ▪ He remained *tight-lipped* about his plans. ▪ *tight-lipped* witnesses
2 : having your lips pressed tightly together because you are thinking hard, angry, etc. ▪ He was *tight-lipped* in concentration.

tight·rope /ˈtaɪtˌroʊp/ *noun, pl* **-ropes** [*count*] **:** a tightly stretched rope or wire high above the ground that a performer walks on, does tricks on, etc., especially in a circus ▪ a *tightrope* walker — often used figuratively to describe a dangerous or uncertain situation in which you have to be very careful not to make mistakes ▪ As soldiers during the war, we ***walked a tightrope*** between life and death every day. ▪ The writer manages to *walk a tightrope* between good humor and poor taste.

tights /ˈtaɪts/ *noun* [*plural*]
1 : a piece of clothing that is worn especially by girls, women, and dancers, that fits closely over the feet, legs, and waist, and that is made of a thicker material than pantyhose — see color picture on page C13
2 *Brit* **:** PANTYHOSE

tight·wad /ˈtaɪtˌwɑːd/ *noun, pl* **-wads** [*count*] *informal + disapproving* **:** a person who does not like to spend or give money ▪ Her husband's such a *tightwad* that he never wants to go out to dinner.

ti·gress /ˈtaɪgrəs/ *noun, pl* **-gress·es** [*count*] **:** a female tiger

tike *variant spelling of* TYKE

ti·ki bar /ˈtiːki-/ *noun, pl* **~ bars** [*count*] *US* **:** a bar or restaurant that is decorated in a Polynesian style

'til *or* **til** *variant spellings of* [1]TILL, [2]TILL

til·de /ˈtɪldə/ *noun, pl* **-des** [*count*] **:** a mark **~** used in some languages (such as Spanish and Portuguese) to show that the letter *n* is pronounced /nj/ or that a vowel is pronounced in a different way

[1]**tile** /ˈtajəl/ *noun, pl* **tiles**
1 a : a usually flat piece of hard clay, stone, or other material that is used for covering walls, floors, etc. [*count*] decorative ceramic *tiles* [*noncount*] We installed new *tile* in the kitchen. **b** [*count, noncount*] **:** a curved piece of hard clay that is used for covering roofs
2 [*count*] **:** a small, flat piece that is used in some board games
on the tiles *Brit, informal* **:** drinking, dancing, etc., until late at night ▪ She came back late after a night *on the tiles*.

[2]**tile** *verb* **tiles; tiled; til·ing** [+ *obj*] **:** to cover (something) with tiles ▪ We hired him to *tile* the bathroom floor.
– tiled *adj* ▪ a *tiled* roof **– til·er** *noun, pl* **-ers** [*count*] ▪ He's a professional carpenter and *tiler*.

[1]**till** *or* **'til** *also* **til** /ˈtɪl, təl/ *prep* **:** UNTIL ▪ We won't finish *till* next week. ▪ Wait *till* next year. ▪ The event doesn't start *till* tomorrow.

[2]**till** *or* **'til** *also* **til** *conj* **:** UNTIL ▪ They kept playing *till* it got dark. ▪ He spun around *till* he was dizzy.

[3]**till** /ˈtɪl/ *verb* **tills; tilled; till·ing** [+ *obj*] **:** to prepare (soil, a piece of land, etc.) for growing crops ▪ The farmers are *tilling* the soil.
– till·able /ˈtɪləbəl/ *adj* [*more ~; most ~*] ▪ This land is not *tillable*. [=not suitable for growing crops]

[4]**till** *noun, pl* **tills** [*count*]
1 : a drawer for keeping money in a store or bank
2 *Brit* **:** CASH REGISTER
in the till ✧ To ***have/put your hand(s) in the till*** is to steal money from the place where you work. ▪ He was accused of *putting his hand in the till*. ▪ She was ***caught with her hands in the till***.

till·age /ˈtɪlɪʤ/ *noun* [*noncount*] **:** the activity or process of preparing land for growing crops ▪ *tillage* tools/equipment/methods

[1]**till·er** /ˈtɪlɚ/ *noun, pl* **-ers** [*count*]
1 : a person who tills land
2 : a tool used for preparing land for growing crops — compare [2]TILLER

[2]**til·ler** /ˈtɪlɚ/ *noun, pl* **-lers** [*count*] **:** a handle that is used to steer a boat by turning the rudder — compare [1]TILLER

[1]**tilt** /ˈtɪlt/ *verb* **tilts; tilt·ed; tilt·ing**
1 a : to lift or move (something) so that one side is higher than another side [+ *obj*] *Tilt* the glass as you pour in the beer. ▪ The picture on the wall was *tilted*. [=it was not straight or level] [*no obj*] The steering wheel can *tilt* downward. **b** [+ *obj*] **:** to move (your head, chin, etc.) up, down, or to one side ▪ *Tilt* your head back. ▪ *Tilt* your chin up. ▪ She *tilted* her head and looked questioningly at him. ▪ Her head was *tilted* to the side.
2 : to influence (something) or to change so that a particular result or occurrence is more likely, a particular group is favored, etc. [+ *obj*] Rising inflation could *tilt* the economy into/toward a recession. ▪ The quarterback's injury could *tilt* (the outcome of) the game in the other team's favor. [=could make it more likely that the other team will win] ▪ His election *tilted* the city council to the left/right. [=made the city council more liberal/conservative] ▪ The law ***tilts the balance of power*** towards corporations. [=the law gives corporations more power] [*no obj*] The economy could be *tilting* into/toward a recession.
tilt at [*phrasal verb*] **1** ***tilt at (someone or something)*** *Brit* **:** to attack (someone or something) in writing or speech ▪ critics *tilting at* [=*criticizing*] the established system **2** ***tilt at windmills*** **:** to use time and energy to attack an enemy or problem that is not real or important

[2]**tilt** *noun, pl* **tilts** [*count*]
1 : the state of having one side higher than the other ▪ The picture is at a slight *tilt*. [=is slightly tilted] ▪ He gave a *tilt* of his head. [=he tilted his head]
2 a : the state of favoring one person, belief, etc., over another ▪ She criticized the media's *tilt* [=*bias*] toward one of the candidates. ▪ a politician with a socialist *tilt* [=who tends

T

to have socialist ideas] **b :** a change of the actions or opinions of a person or group in a particular direction ▪ If he were elected, there would be a *tilt* [=*shift*] in the political balance of the city council. [=the city council would become more liberal or conservative]
3 *US, informal* **:** a game or competition between two people, teams, etc. ▪ The teams were tied in the standings heading into last night's *tilt*.
4 *Brit* **a :** an attempt to win something — + *at* ▪ The team wants a *tilt at* the championship. **b :** a written or spoken attack on someone or something — + *at* ▪ a *tilt at* the government
(at) full tilt **:** as fast as possible **:** at high speed ▪ The heater has been going *full tilt* all morning. ▪ He ran away *at full tilt*.

tim·ber /ˈtɪmbɚ/ *noun, pl* **-bers**
1 [*noncount*] **a :** trees that are grown in order to produce wood **b** — used as an interjection to warn people nearby that a cut tree is about to fall ▪ They shouted "*Timber*!" as the tree began to fall.
2 [*count*] **:** a large piece of wood that is used to form a part of a building ▪ the roof's oak *timbers*
3 [*noncount*] *chiefly Brit* **:** wood that is used to make something ▪ a chair made of sturdy *timber* [=(*US*) *lumber*]
– timber *adj* ▪ The house has a *timber* frame. ▪ the *timber* industry

tim·ber·land /ˈtɪmbɚˌlænd/ *noun, pl* **-lands** [*count, noncount*] *US* **:** land that is covered with trees that are grown in order to produce wood ▪ 40 acres of *timberland*

tim·ber·line /ˈtɪmbɚˌlaɪn/ *noun, pl* **-lines** [*singular*] **:** an imaginary line on a mountain or high area of land that marks the level above which trees do not grow — called also *tree line*

timber yard *noun, pl* **~ yards** [*count*] *Brit* **:** LUMBERYARD

tim·bre /ˈtæmbɚ/ *noun, pl* **-bres :** the quality of the sound made by a particular voice or musical instrument [*count*] the *timbre* of his voice [*noncount*] subtle differences in *timbre*

¹time /ˈtaɪm/ *noun, pl* **times**
1 [*noncount*] **:** the thing that is measured as seconds, minutes, hours, days, years, etc. ▪ The *time* passed slowly/quickly. ▪ The two events were separated by *time* and space. ▪ The poem is a reflection on the passage/passing of *time*. ▪ What was happening at that particular moment in *time*? ▪ At this point in *time*, we have not made a decision. [=we have not yet made a decision] ▪ It has been that way since the beginning of *time*. ▪ If only I could travel back in *time* and do things differently. ▪ They were given a relatively short ***amount of time*** to finish the job. ▪ The situation has been getting more complicated ***as time goes by/on***. ▪ ***In the course of time*** [=as time passed], people learned to accept the changes. ▪ The medicine is released in small amounts ***over time***. [=it is released slowly] ▪ Her condition should improve ***with time***. [=it should become better as time passes] ▪ happening for an extended ***period of time*** ▪ The study took place over a ***time span*** of 20 years. [=the study continued for 20 years]
2 a [*singular*] **:** a particular minute or hour shown by a clock ▪ What *time* is it? = (*chiefly Brit*) What's the *time*? ▪ The *time* is 6:15. [=it is 6:15] ▪ I'll see you tomorrow, same *time*, same place. = I'll see you here this *time* tomorrow. ▪ Would you prefer the meeting to be at an earlier *time*? ▪ Feel free to call me at any *time*, day or night. ▪ What *time* did you leave work? [=when did you leave work?] ▪ They arrived at the appointed/agreed-on *time*. [=*hour*] ▪ Do you know the *time*? = (*chiefly US*) Do you ***have the time***? = (*chiefly Brit*) Have you ***got the time***? ▪ (*US*) ***What time do you have***? = (*Brit*) ***What time do you make it***? [=what time is it?] ▪ "***Look at the time***! We have to go." **b** [*noncount*] **:** the time in a particular area or part of the world ▪ We'll be arriving at 9:00 a.m. local *time*. ▪ It's 2:00 p.m. Tokyo *time*. — see also BRITISH SUMMER TIME, DAYLIGHT SAVING TIME, GREENWICH MEAN TIME, LOCAL TIME, STANDARD TIME
3 a : the part of a day, week, month, or year when something usually happens or is scheduled to happen [*noncount*] My kids love bath *time*. ▪ It's party *time*! ▪ Test *time* is at 8:00. [=the test will begin at 8:00] ▪ I did some work on my house during my vacation *time*. [*count*] She gave the family some advice on how to make breakfast *times* less hectic. — see also BEDTIME, DINNERTIME, DRIVE TIME, LUNCHTIME, MEALTIME, PLAYTIME, PRIME TIME, TEATIME **b** [*count*] **:** a particular part of a day, week, month, or year ▪ He has to go to the classes at certain *times* of the month. ▪ There was snow on the ground at this *time* last year. ▪ It's unusually hot for this ***time of year***. [=*season*] ▪ My favorite *times of year* are spring and fall. — see also CHRISTMASTIME, DAYTIME, NIGHTTIME, NOONTIME, SPRINGTIME, SUMMERTIME, WINTERTIME
4 [*count*] **:** an occurrence of an action or event **:** an instance of something happening or of someone doing something ▪ She's already seen the movie several *times*. ▪ He told us the story about the *time* he bought his first car. ▪ Do you remember the *time* we got lost in Washington, D.C.? ▪ Take one pill two *times* daily [=take one pill twice each day] for seven days. ▪ This is my first *time* on an airplane. [=I have never been on an airplane before] ▪ He ran for governor for the second *time* in 1980. ▪ I cry ***each/every time*** [=*whenever*] I hear that song. ▪ Remember to buckle up your seatbelt ***each and every time*** you ride in a car. ▪ I'll come by the ***next time*** I'm in town. ▪ The ***last time*** I saw him [=the most recent time that I saw him] was at his wedding. ▪ Okay, I'll do it again ***one last time***. ▪ ***For the last time***, please stop! = This is the last *time* I'm going to tell you: please stop! ▪ Would you please do it ***one more time***? [=*again, once more*] ▪ ***How many times*** do I have to tell you? I don't know where it is! ▪ I've told you ***many times*** not to do that. = I've told you ***a hundred/thousand/million times*** not to do that. ▪ Don't worry about it. We've all made that same mistake ***many a time***. = ***Many's the time*** we have made that same mistake. ▪ "***This time*** you've gone too far!" he said. ▪ She beats me at chess ***nine times out of ten***. [=for every ten games we play, she beats me nine times] ▪ They may have lost their last championship game, but they're determined to win ***the next time around/round***. ▪ We're going to win ***this time out***. ▪ ***One time*** [=*once*, (more formally) *on one occasion*] I came home two hours late and nobody noticed.
5 a [*singular*] **:** the period of time when something happens ▪ I had lived in 12 different cities ***by the time*** I turned 18. [=when I was 18 years old, I had already lived in 12 different cities] ▪ She had known that she wanted to be President ***from the time*** [=*since*] she was seven years old. ▪ ***Since that time***, the government has done much to fix the problem. — often used after *at* ▪ If you're busy now, perhaps we can get together *at* another *time*. ▪ ***At no time*** did the defendant ask for a lawyer. [=the defendant never asked for a lawyer] ▪ It was raining ***at the time*** of the accident. [=it was raining when the accident happened] ▪ This information was correct *at the time* of publication. ▪ He was elected pope in 1978, ***at which time*** he took the name John Paul. — see also AT THE SAME TIME (below), AT TIMES (below) **b** [*count*] **:** the exact moment when a particular event happens or is scheduled to happen ▪ ***Curtain time*** is at 7:30 p.m. [=the performance begins at 7:30 p.m.] ▪ What is the movie's ***starting time***? [=when does the movie start?] ▪ The patient's ***time of death*** was 2:15 a.m. ▪ He called to give me his flights' ***departure/arrival times***. [=the times when his flights are scheduled to depart/arrive] ▪ The network moved my favorite television show to a different ***time slot***. — see also CLOSING TIME, SHOWTIME
6 : a period of time when a situation or set of conditions exists **:** a period of minutes, hours, days, weeks, etc., when something is happening or someone is doing something [*count*] I can't remember a *time* that/when I've been happier. ▪ She helped me in my *time* of need. [=she helped me when I needed help] ▪ He is someone you can depend on in *times* of crisis. ▪ He sat down to rest, and after a *time* [=*while*] he continued on his way. ▪ She served in the military ***for a time*** in her early twenties. ▪ No one spoke to us the ***entire/whole time*** we were there. ▪ We will be able to stay here only a ***short time***. ▪ I haven't seen you in such a ***long time***! ▪ It took them a *long time* to find out what was causing the problem. ▪ His promotion was ***a long time coming***. [=he waited a long time to be promoted] ▪ It happened ***a long time ago***. — often + *when* ▪ There was a *time when* I thought he would never graduate from college. — often used after *at* ▪ She was calm *at* a *time when* everyone else was panicking. ▪ Sometimes this helps, while *at* other *times* it makes things worse. ▪ No more than five people should ride in the car ***at any one time***. ▪ There are between 200 and 300 patients in the hospital ***at any given time***. ▪ How could you think about food ***at a time like this***? ▪ ***At one time*** [=during one period of time in the past], 20 people lived together in this house. ▪ Everyone has experienced this feeling ***at one time or another***. ▪ ***At the present time*** [=*presently, right now*], we don't know why it happened. = We don't know why it happened ***at this time***. [*noncount*] ***Some time ago*** [=at some point in the past], I read that the restaurant had closed. ▪ She has been living there ***for (quite) some time***. [=for a somewhat long time] ▪ I get sick if I sit in

the back seat of a car ***for any length of time***. [=for more than a very small amount of time]
7 [*noncount*] **: the number of minutes, days, years, etc., before something happens : the amount of time it takes for something to happen — usually used after *in*** • The movie is coming out *in* two months' *time*. [=it is coming out two months from now] • They expect the system to be completely replaced *in* a few years' *time*. • This machine can have the job finished *in* half the *time* (it would take you to do it by hand). • It can do the job *in* a fraction of the *time*. [=it can do the job much more quickly] • It's just ***a matter of time*** before someone gets hurt. [=someone will get hurt eventually] • The police will catch him. It's only ***a question of time***. [=the police will catch him at some point in the future]
8 [*noncount*] **: the amount of time that is used, needed, available, or allowed for a particular activity or for someone to do something** • You must complete the project within the *time* allotted. • I'll try not to take up too much of your *time*. • Thank you for your *time*. [=thank you for listening to me] • It's not worth your *time* and energy. • Is there (enough) *time* to stop for lunch? • What do you do in your ***free/spare time***? [=when you are not working] • We played games to ***pass/kill the time*** on the bus. [=we played games to cause time to seem to go by more quickly] • How much more *time* do we have (left)? = How are we ***doing on/for time***? • We're ***pressed for time***. [=we don't have much time left to do what we need to do] • We ***ran out of time*** and didn't finish the project. [=we had no more time to work on the project] • ***Time's up***. [=the allowed period of time has ended] Please put down your pencils and hand in your tests. • They finished ***with time to spare***. [=they finished early] • We're using up ***valuable/precious time*** talking when we could be getting started. • The candidates will receive ***equal time*** to answer questions during the debate. • Her teammates were complaining about their lack of ***playing time***. [=the amount of time that they were allowed to play during a game] • Sometimes she would drop by to ***pass the time of day***. [=to have a friendly and informal conversation] • She's had a lot of ***time on her hands*** [=time when she was not busy] lately. • He can't manage to ***find (the) time*** to exercise. **— often used with *save*** • This new system will *save time* [=take less time, be faster] and money. • We can *save* a lot of *time* by using this shortcut. **— often used with *lose*** • They *lost* a lot of *time* getting started. • You'll just have to ***make up for lost time*** by working harder now. [=you'll have to work faster because you have less time to finish the work] **— often used with *spend*** • He *spends* all his *time* watching TV. • I'm looking forward to *spending* more *time* at home [=being at home more] with my family. **— often used with *waste*** • Stop *wasting time* [=doing nothing or doing something that is not useful] and get to work! • They ***wasted no time*** in decorating their new apartment. [=they started decorating it immediately] • That class was a (big) ***waste of time***. [=the class was not good] I didn't learn a thing. **— often followed by *to + verb*** • If we leave now, there's just (enough) *time to catch* the last show. • There's no *time to explain*. I'll have to tell you why later. • In the *time* it takes you *to read* one chapter, she can read the entire book. • We will have plenty of *time to buy* souvenirs later. • I haven't had much *time to think* about it. • We have to hurry. ***There's no time to lose***. [=we have little time, so we cannot waste any of it]
9 : the right moment to do something or for something to happen [*count*] This is no *time* for jokes. • The *time* for talking has passed. We must take action now. • There is a *time* and a place for everything. • Am I calling at a ***bad time***? [=are you too busy to talk to me?] • Is this a ***good time*** for you? • This is ***as good a time as any***. • "Should we do it now?" "Sure. ***There's no time like the present***." [=let's do it now] **— often followed by *to + verb*** • Now is the perfect *time to buy* a new car. • Now's not the *time to discuss* such things. **— often used with *come*** • We feel that the *time* has *come* for a decision to be made. • When the *time comes* to move out of their apartment, they will have saved up enough money to buy a house. • ***There comes a time*** when children leave their parents and start families of their own. • an idea whose ***time has come*** [=an idea that is ready to be used] [*noncount*] It's *time to go*. • It is *time* for us *to consider* an alternative.
10 [*count*] **: the quality of a person's experience on a particular occasion or during a particular period** • We all had a ***good/great/lovely time*** at the concert. [=we enjoyed the concert very much] • Did you have a *good time*? • A *good time* was had by all. • Try to remember the *good times* you had together rather than the ***bad times***. • Their music helped me get through some ***difficult/hard/rough/tough times*** in my life. • He looked like he was ***having the time of his life***. [=enjoying himself very much; having a lot of fun] • They've been ***having a hard time*** finding an apartment in the city.
11 [*count*] **: a specific period in the past** • It happens more now than at any other *time* in history. • The writings date back to the *time* of Shakespeare. [=the period of time when Shakespeare was alive] • Like most families at/of/during that *time*, they had only one car. • There was a *time* when people could let their children play outside without worrying about their safety. • He was a famous comedian of the/that *time*. • The bridge was built around the *time* of World War I. • It was the most important book of its *time*. • He is one of the greatest actors of ***our time***. [=of the present day] • Life was very different ***at that time***. [=*then*] • People have been creating art since ***time immemorial***. [=for a very long time] **— often used after *in*** • Things were very different *in* your grandparents' *time*. [=*day*] • I've seen a lot of crazy things ***in my time***. [=during my life] • She was ***a legend in her own time***. [=she was someone who was very famous and admired while she was still alive] • The tools were known to be in use ***in medieval/ancient/prehistoric times***. • ***In earlier times***, this road was an important trade route. • farming methods used ***in times past*** [=in the past] **— often used in the titles of books, newspapers, etc.** • She was reading the latest issue of the *New York Times*. • The biography was titled *The Life and Times of Napoleon*.
12 *times* [*plural*] **a : the conditions experienced by a group of people now or during a particular period in the past** • The country is facing some difficult/trying *times*. • Those were lean *times*, and our family couldn't afford new clothes. • Life can be difficult even at/in the best of *times*. **b : the styles, events, or ideas that are popular or important in a culture now or at a particular period in the past** • Companies must change/evolve/move with the *times* or risk losing their customers. • In this business, you have to ***keep up with the times***. [=stay current; change as conditions change] • ***Times have changed*** since then. • Come on. ***Get with the times***. [=understand and change to fit what is now happening and accepted in the culture] • Their methods are ***behind the times***. [=*outdated*]
13 a [*count*] **: a period or stage in a person's life** • I'm at a *time* in my life when I don't care much about my appearance. • at various *times* of her life **b** [*singular*] **: the time when a woman gives birth to a child** • Her *time* is drawing near. **c** [*singular*] **: the time when someone dies** • "Why did he have to die?" "It was just his *time*."
14 a [*singular*] **: the number of months, years, etc., that a person spends at a particular place or in a particular group or organization** • I learned a great deal during my *time* at Harvard. • She used her *time* in the Senate to fight for the environment. **b** [*singular*] **: the number of months or years that an active member of the military is required to stay in the military** • She plans on going to college after she ***serves her time*** in the army. = She plans on going to college after she ***puts in her time*** in the army. • He was an ex-soldier who ***did his time*** in Vietnam. [=he fought in Vietnam while he was a soldier] **c** [*noncount*] *informal* **: the number of days, months, or years that a person must stay in prison** • She's now ***doing time*** for armed robbery. • (*US*) He could be facing ***hard time*** [=a long or difficult prison sentence] for his crimes.
15 [*count*] **: the seconds, minutes, etc., it takes to do something (such as finish a race)** • She ran the mile in a *time* of 5 minutes and 15 seconds. • What was my *time*? [=how long did it take me to do it?] • He finished ***in record time***. [=in the least amount of time ever]
16 [*noncount*] **: the minutes, hours, or days that a person works or is required to work for a company : the time during which a company is paying a worker** • She has been putting in a lot of *time* [=she has been working a lot] at the office. • I'll ask my supervisor if I can ***take time off (work)*** to go to the dentist. • She ***took time out*** from her career to raise her children. [=she stopped working while she raised her children] • (*US*) Employees need to make personal calls ***on their own time***. = (*Brit*) Employees need to make personal calls ***in their own time***. [=when their employer is not paying them to work] • (*US*) Please do not make personal calls (when you are) ***on company time***. = (*Brit*) Please do not make personal calls (when you are) ***in company time***. [=when your employer is paying you to work] — see also DOUBLE TIME, FLEXTIME, FULL-TIME, OVERTIME, PART-TIME, SHORT TIME, TIME AND A HALF
17 *times* [*plural*] **— used to say how much bigger, smaller,**

faster, etc., something is than something else ▪ Her salary is five *times* greater than mine. = She earns five *times* as much money as I do. ▪ The area received three *times* the amount of rain it got last year. ▪ You would have to spend ***two times*** [=*twice*] as much at a regular department store. ▪ Their original investment has paid for itself ***many times over***. — see also TIMES

18 [*noncount*] *music* **a** : the rate of speed at which a piece of music is performed ▪ We clapped ***in time to*** [=in a way that matched the speed of] the music. ▪ March *in time*. — see also KEEP TIME 2 (below) **b** : the way that beats are grouped together in a piece of music ▪ the use of 6/8 *time* in certain styles of music — often used after *in* ▪ If a song is *in 3/4 time*, that means that there are three beats per bar/measure and that each of those beats is a quarter note. ▪ a dance performed *in 4/4 time* with a quick tempo

against time ✧ If you are ***racing/working (etc.) against time*** or are in ***a race against time***, you are doing something quickly because you have only a small amount of time. ▪ We're *working against time* to finish this book. ▪ They *raced against time* to get her to the hospital. ▪ It was *a race against time* to find a cure for the disease.

ahead of time : before something happens : earlier than a time or event ▪ He called the restaurant *ahead of time* to make a dinner reservation. ▪ She read the report *ahead of time* to prepare for the meeting.

ahead of your/its time ✧ If you are *ahead of your time* or if your ideas, creations, etc., are *ahead of their time*, you are too advanced or modern to be understood or appreciated during the time when you live or work. ▪ As a director, he was *ahead of his time*. His movies are now regarded as classics, but they were unpopular when he made them.

(all) in good time : when the appropriate moment arrives : when the time is right ▪ I'll let him know *in good time*. ▪ It will happen *all in good time*.

all (of) the time **1** : ALWAYS ▪ You can't be right *all of the time*. **2** *informal* : very often or frequently ▪ "Do you ever take the subway to work?" "Yeah, *all the time*." ▪ My sisters and I used to fight *all of the time*. **3** *usually* **all the time** : since something began ▪ We thought that he disliked her, while *all the time* [=(more commonly) *all along, the whole time*] he was in love with her. ▪ I knew the truth *all the time*. ▪ The police knew *all the time* who was guilty.

(and) not before time (too) *chiefly Brit* — used to say that something should have happened sooner ▪ They're finally going to change things, *and not before time, too*. [=*and it's about time*]

any time (now) : very soon ▪ The train should be arriving *any time now*.

a sign of the times see ¹SIGN

a stitch in time (saves nine) see ¹STITCH

at all times : without stopping or changing at any time : ALWAYS ▪ The system is kept running *at all times*. ▪ Keep your hands inside the vehicle *at all times*.

at a time **1** : during one particular moment ▪ I can only do one thing *at a time*. [=*at once*] ▪ Please speak ***one at a time***. [=so that only one person is speaking at any time] ▪ We carried the boxes *two at a time* up the stairs. [=we carried two boxes each time we went up the stairs] **2** : during one period of time without stopping ▪ She can sit and read for hours *at a time*. [=*at a stretch*] **3** ✧ If you ***take one day at a time*** or ***take it/things one day at a time***, you make progress in a slow and careful way by dealing with each day as it comes. ▪ We got through the ordeal by *taking one day at a time*. [=*taking it day by day*]

at the same time **1** : during the same moment ▪ She was driving, eating, and talking on the phone all *at the same time*. ▪ She tries to appear to be both glamorous and modest *at the same time*. ▪ As a parent, he is ***at one and the same time*** strict and loving. [=he is both strict and loving] **2** — used to introduce a statement that adds to and differs from a preceding statement ▪ The new regulations will help the environment. *At the same time* [=*on the other hand*], they may be a burden to businesses. ▪ She wants more respect, but *at the same time* she does nothing to earn it. = She wants more respect, while *at the same time* doing nothing to earn it.

at times : SOMETIMES ▪ He is an intelligent person, but he can be quite stubborn *at times*. [=*from time to time*] ▪ *At times*, I wondered if we were doing the right thing.

before your time **1** — used to say that something happened before you were born or before you were involved in some activity ▪ You wouldn't know about that. It was *before your time*. **2** ✧ If you become ***old before your time***, you look and feel older than you are. ▪ Such experiences make people *old before their time*. **3** ✧ If you ***die before your time***, you die at a younger age than you should. ▪ Mozart *died before his time*.

behind the times : not having or showing knowledge of current ideas or styles : OUTDATED ▪ The entire country is *behind the times* when it comes to protecting the environment. ▪ Our professor is surprisingly *behind the times*. [=*old-fashioned*]

be living on borrowed time see BORROW

better luck next time see ¹LUCK

bide your time see BIDE

buy time see ¹BUY

call time **1** *US, sports* : to ask for a time-out ▪ The coach *called time*. : to give the order for a time-out ▪ The referee *called time*. **2** *Brit* **a** : to announce that it is time for a bar or pub to close **b** : to say or decide that something has ended : to end something — usually + *on* ▪ an athlete who has *called time on* his career

for the time being : during the present time but possibly not in the future ▪ I think we should stay here *for the time being*. [=*for now*] ▪ *For the time being*, this car suits all of our family's needs.

from time to time : SOMETIMES ▪ Such things are bound to happen *from time to time*. [=*at times*] ▪ *From time to time* [=*occasionally, once in a while*], it's nice to let someone else make the decisions.

give (someone) a hard time see ¹HARD

half the time *informal* : very often ▪ *Half the time* I have no idea what my professor is talking about.

hard times see ¹HARD

have a thin time (of it) see ¹THIN

have time **1** : to be able to use an amount of time for a particular purpose ▪ "Can you go to the store for me?" "I'm sorry, but I don't *have time*." [=I'm too busy] ▪ Unfortunately, I ***haven't got*** (the) ***time***. ▪ We're on a deadline, but he acts like we ***have all the time in the world***! — often followed by *to + verb* ▪ I didn't *have time to read* the whole book. ▪ Do you *have time to look* this over for me? ▪ We haven't *had* any *time to talk* about it yet. — often + *for* ▪ We don't *have time for* this nonsense! ▪ I don't *have* the *time* or the patience *for* this. ▪ Do we *have* enough *time for* another drink? ▪ We*'ve got time for* a few more questions. **2** : to like or be willing to spend time dealing with (something or someone) — usually + *for* ▪ I *have* no *time for* liars. ▪ (*Brit*) We *have* a lot of *time for* her.

in no time : very quickly or soon ▪ We'll be there *in no time*. ▪ Don't worry. It'll all be over *in no time*.

in the nick of time see ¹NICK

in time **1** : before something happens : early enough ▪ Do you think we'll get there *in time*? — often followed by *to + verb* ▪ They arrived just *in time to catch* the last train out of town. — often + *for* ▪ I'll try to make it home *in time for* dinner. ▪ The CD will be released just *in time for* Christmas. **2** : when an amount of time has passed ▪ *In time*, she forgave him. ▪ Things will get better *in time*. [=*eventually*]

in your own (good) time : at the time that is right or appropriate for you and not sooner ▪ He'll make a decision *in his own good time*. ▪ Everything happens *in its own time*.

it's about time *informal* — used to say often in an annoyed way that something should have happened sooner ▪ *It's about time* you got here. I've been waiting for over an hour! ▪ "They're getting married." "Well, *it's about time*!"

it's high time see ¹HIGH

keep time **1** *of a watch or clock* : to show the correct time ▪ My watch *keeps* good/perfect *time*. [=it shows the correct time; it works well] **2** *music* : to perform music at the correct speed ▪ Among other things, the conductor helps the orchestra *keep time* (to the music).

make good time : to travel somewhere quickly ▪ They *made good time* on their trip. ▪ We're *making good time*. We've already traveled a hundred miles today.

make time : to cause an amount of time to be available for an activity ▪ I'll have to *make* (the) *time* to get it done. — often + *for* ▪ She has trouble *making time* in her busy schedule *for* exercise. ▪ No matter how busy he was, Grandpa always *made time for* us.

mark time see ²MARK

most of the time or ***most times*** : on most occasions : USUALLY ▪ Sometimes I go out for lunch, but *most of the time* I bring my own lunch to work. ▪ *Most times*, this method works just fine.

ninety/ninety-nine (etc.) percent of the time : on most occasions : USUALLY • I hate to admit it, but he's right *ninety percent of the time.* [=*most of the time*]

not give someone the time of day ✧ If you do *not give someone the time of day*, you do not give that person any attention or help. • I asked them for directions, but they *wouldn't give me the time of day.*

of all time : that has ever lived or existed • In my opinion, he is still the greatest basketball player *of all time.* — see also ALL-TIME

once upon a time see [1]ONCE

(only) time will tell — used to say that the results of a situation will be known only after a certain amount of time has passed • "Will he be OK?" "I don't know. *Only time will tell.*"

on time : at or before the correct moment : at a time that is not late • Try to be there *on time.* • I paid all of my bills *on time* [=when they were due] this month. • Please hand in your homework *on time.* • We arrived ***right on time.*** [=exactly at the right time]

play for time see [1]PLAY

stand the test of time see [1]TEST

take (the) time to do something : to use an amount of time in order to do something important • They never *took the time to get* to know her. • *Take (the) time to think* about it before you make a decision. • I *took* some *time to think* about it, and my answer is still "no."

take time ✧ People say that something ***takes some/no (etc.) time*** to describe how much time is needed for something to happen or be done. • You have to be patient. Things like this *take time.* [=things like this cannot be done quickly] • It may *take some time* for the medication to wear off. • The meeting won't *take too much time.* [=the meeting will be short] • This project will *take a lot of time.* • It'll ***take no time at all.*** = It will *take very little time.*

take your time : to do something slowly or without hurrying • I need to *take my time* and think about it for a while. • There's no need to hurry. *Take your time.* [=take all the time you need] • Please *take your time* filling out the form.

tell time (*US*) *or Brit* ***tell the time*** : to be able to know what time it is by looking at a clock • My son is just learning to *tell time.*

the end of time see [1]END

the whole time **1** : since something began : during the entire period of time • We thought that he disliked her, while *the whole time* [=*all along, all the time*] he was in love with her. • I knew the truth *the whole time.* • The police knew *the whole time* who was guilty. **2** *Brit* : ALWAYS • You can't be right *the whole time.* [=*all (of) the time*] **3** *Brit, informal* : very often • My sisters and I used to fight *the whole time.* [=*all (of) the time*]

time after time *or* ***time and again*** *or* ***time and time again*** : on many occasions : very often or frequently • *Time after time,* we see this happen with our patients. • I've told you *time and again* [=*repeatedly*] not to do that.

time flies — used to say that time passes quickly • As they say, "*Time flies* when you're having fun." • Your son is in high school already? My, how *time flies!*

time heals all wounds *or chiefly Brit* ***time is a/the great healer*** — used to say that feelings of sadness, disappointment, etc., gradually go away as time passes • I thought I would never be able to love again, but, as they say, *time heals all wounds.*

time is money see MONEY

time is (not) on your side ✧ If *time is on your side,* you have a good chance of success because you can wait until a situation improves. If *time is not on your side,* your chance of success is less because you have to do something very soon. • House prices are all dropping, and in the case of home buyers, *time is on their side.* [=the houses that people want to buy will become cheaper as more time passes] • If we wait too long to buy the tickets, the concert may be sold out: *time is not on our side.* [=all the tickets may be sold if we wait too long to buy them]

time marches on : time continues to pass • I was very disappointed when it happened. But *time marches on,* and I've learned to accept it now.

time was (when) *old-fashioned* — used to say that something was true in the past and usually to express annoyance that it is no longer true • *Time was,* you could buy a candy bar for a nickel. • *Time was when* people respected their elders. [=people used to respect their elders in the past]

until such time as *formal* : until the time when : UNTIL • He will be suspended from work *until such time as* this matter has been resolved.

your (own) sweet time *chiefly US, informal* ✧ If you do something ***in your (own) sweet time*** or you ***take your (own) sweet time*** about doing something, you do it slowly even though other people want you to do it more quickly. • She's *taking her own sweet time* about finishing the work.

[2]time *verb* **times; timed; tim·ing** [+ *obj*]

1 : to choose the hour, day, month, etc., when (something) will happen : to schedule (something, such as an event) to happen at a particular time • They *timed* their vacation to coincide with the jazz festival. — often used as *(be) timed* • The ceremony *was timed* to coincide with the President's visit. • It was a poorly *timed* visit. [=the visit happened at an unfortunate or inconvenient time] — see also ILL-TIMED, WELL-TIMED

2 *sports* : to cause (something, such as a throw or pass) to happen at a certain moment • He *timed* it so that he made the shot just before the clock ran out. • She *timed* the shot perfectly.

3 : to measure the amount of time needed by someone to do something (such as to finish a race) • The runners are *timed* with special watches. • He *timed* the students as they completed their tests. • *timing* a horse race

time and a half *noun* [*noncount*] : a rate of pay that is equal to what a worker usually earns for an hour plus half of that amount • If they make you work during holidays, they pay you *time and a half.* • We get paid 20 dollars an hour for 40 hours and *time and a half* for overtime.

time bomb *noun, pl* ~ **bombs** [*count*]

1 : a bomb that is set to explode at a particular moment

2 : a person or situation that will probably become dangerous or harmful in the future • He's a *time bomb* getting ready to explode. • If we don't do something about the pollution problem, we'll be sitting on a ***ticking time bomb.***

time capsule *noun, pl* ~ **-sules** [*count*] : a container that is filled with things (such as newspapers or clothing) from the present time and that is meant to be opened by people at some time in the future

time card *noun, pl* ~ **cards** [*count*] : a piece of paper or cardboard that is put into a special clock in order to record the times when an employee starts and stops working • Don't forget to punch your *time card* on your way out.

time clock *noun, pl* ~ **clocks** [*count*] : a special clock that is used to record the times when an employee starts and stops working

time–con·sum·ing /ˈtaɪmkənˌsuːmɪŋ, *Brit* ˈtaɪmkənˈsjuːmɪŋ/ *adj* [*more* ~; *most* ~] : using or needing a large amount of time • *time-consuming* chores • a very expensive and *time-consuming* process • Can we try to make this less *time-consuming?*

time frame *noun, pl* ~ **frames** [*count*] : a period of time that is used or planned for a particular action or project • They were not able to finish the project within the established *time frame.*

time–hon·ored (*US*) *or Brit* **time–hon·oured** /ˈtaɪmˌɑːnəd/ *adj, always used before a noun* : existing and respected for a long time • *time-honored* traditions/institutions

time·keep·er /ˈtaɪmˌkiːpə/ *noun, pl* **-ers** [*count*]

1 : a person who controls or records official times during a contest (such as a race or game) • The *timekeeper* forgot to stop the clock during the team's last time-out.

2 *Brit* — used in the phrases ***good timekeeper*** and ***bad/poor timekeeper*** to say that someone is or is not good about arriving at the correct or expected time • We expect our employees to be *good timekeepers.*

— **time·keep·ing** /ˈtaɪmˌkiːpɪŋ/ *noun* [*noncount*]

time lag *noun* [*singular*] : a period of time between two related actions (such as a cause and its effect) • There's a *time lag* between when you see a stop sign and when your foot steps on the brake.

time–lapse /ˈtaɪmˌlæps/ *adj, always used before a noun* — used to describe a way of filming something in which many photographs are taken over a long period of time and are shown quickly in a series so that a slow action (such as the opening of a flower bud) appears to happen quickly • *time-lapse* photography

time·less /ˈtaɪmləs/ *adj*

1 : staying beautiful or fashionable as time passes • The dresses that she designs are elegant and *timeless.* • the *timeless* beauty of the sea

2 : lasting forever • *timeless* [=*ageless*] truths/wisdom

– **time·less·ly** *adv* – **time·less·ness** *noun* [*noncount*]

time limit *noun, pl* ~ **-its** [*count*] : an amount of time in which something must be done or completed • My boss gave me a three-hour *time limit* to finish the job.

time·line /ˈtaɪm͵laɪn/ *noun, pl* **-lines** [*count*]

1 : a plan which shows the order of events that will happen, things that will be done, etc. • She drew up a *timeline* [=*timetable*] for the project.

2 : a line that includes marks showing when particular events happened in the past • The *timeline* shows the important events in American history.

time·ly /ˈtaɪmli/ *adj* **time·li·er; -est** [*or more* ~; *most* ~] : happening at the correct or most useful time : not happening too late • Her very *timely* book examines the effects of global warming on the world's climates. • a *timely* decision/warning • She always responds to my requests ***in a timely fashion/manner.*** — opposite UNTIMELY

– **time·li·ness** *noun* [*noncount*] • the *timeliness* of the warning

time machine *noun, pl* ~ **-chines** [*count*] *in stories* : a machine that allows people to travel to a time in the past or future

time–out /ˈtaɪmˈaʊt/ *noun, pl* **-outs**

1 : a short period of time during a sports event when the game stops and the players rest or talk to their coach [*count*] The coach asked for a *time-out* to talk to her players. • The coach called a *time-out.* [*noncount*] The quarterback ***called time-out*** [=asked for a time-out] with 20 seconds remaining.

2 : a short period of time when you stop doing something so that you can rest or do something else [*count*] We've been working all morning. Let's take a *time-out* and get some coffee. [*noncount*] Let's take *time-out* for a few minutes.

3 *US* : a short period of time when a child must sit quietly as punishment for behaving badly [*count*] The book talks about the proper way to use *time-outs.* • If you do that again, you're getting a *time-out*! = If you do that again, I'm giving you a *time-out*! [*noncount*] There's no talking during *time-out.*

time·piece /ˈtaɪm͵piːs/ *noun, pl* **-piec·es** [*count*] *formal* : a clock or watch • an expensive German *timepiece*

tim·er /ˈtaɪmɚ/ *noun, pl* **-ers** [*count*]

1 : a special watch that is used to measure the amount of time that is taken to finish a race, a test, etc. : STOPWATCH; *also* : a person who uses such a watch to time someone or something • He was the official *timer* for the race.

2 a : a device that makes a sound when a certain amount of time has passed • She set the *timer* on the oven for one hour. • The *timer* is set to go off in 15 minutes. **b** : a device that can be set to turn something (such as a light) on or off at a certain time — often used after *on* • The sprinkler is *on a timer.* [=(*Brit*) *time switch*] • We put the house lights *on timers* before going on vacation.

— see also OLD-TIMER, TWO-TIMER

time–re·lease /ˈtaɪmrɪˈliːs/ *adj* : releasing a drug slowly over a period of time instead of all at once • *time-release* capsules/tablets

times /ˈtaɪmz/ *prep* : multiplied by • Two *times* two is/equals four. — see also [1]TIME 17

time–sav·ing /ˈtaɪm͵seɪvɪŋ/ *adj* : making it possible to do something quickly : causing something to happen or end faster • microwaves, washing machines, and other *time-saving* devices of the 20th century • The company implemented new *time-saving* measures to increase productivity.

– **time–sav·er** /ˈtaɪm͵seɪvɚ/ *noun, pl* **-ers** [*count*] • This new shortcut is a real *time-saver.*

time·scale /ˈtaɪm͵skeɪl/ *noun, pl* **-scales** [*count*]

1 : a period of time whose size can be compared to other periods of time • When considered on the 4.6 billion year *timescale* of the Earth, our lives can seem insignificant.

2 *chiefly Brit* : TIME FRAME • What is the *timescale* for completion of the work?

time–share /ˈtaɪm͵ʃeɚ/ *noun, pl* **-shares** [*count*] : a vacation home that is owned or rented by several people who use it at different times of the year • They own a *time-share* in Florida.

– **time–shar·ing** /ˈtaɪm͵ʃerɪŋ/ *noun* [*noncount*]

time sheet *noun, pl* ~ **sheets** [*count*] : a piece of paper that you use to record the hours that you worked each day

time signature *noun, pl* ~ **-tures** [*count*] : a number that is written at the beginning of a piece of music and that shows the number and length of the beats in each measure

times sign *noun, pl* ~ **signs** [*count*] : the symbol × that is used to show that two numbers are to be multiplied

times table *noun, pl* ~ **tables** [*count*] : MULTIPLICATION TABLE

time switch *noun, pl* ~ **switches** [*count*] *Brit* : TIMER 2b

time·ta·ble /ˈtaɪm͵teɪbəl/ *noun, pl* **-ta·bles** [*count*]

1 : a plan of things that need to be done and the times they will be done — often + *for* • In planning for the project, you should include a list of goals and a *timetable* [=*schedule*] *for* achieving those goals. • The agency set a strict/rigid/tight *timetable for* completing the work.

2 *chiefly Brit* : a list of the times when something (such as a bus, train, or airplane) is expected to leave or arrive • a bus *timetable* [=(*US*) *schedule*]

3 *Brit* : a written or printed list of activities and the times when they will be done • There have been a few changes to the class *timetable.* [=(*US*) *schedule*]

– **time–table** *verb* **-tables; -tabled; -tabling** [+ *obj*] *chiefly Brit* • The meeting is *timetabled* [=*scheduled*] for 10 a.m. = The meeting is *timetabled* to begin at 10 a.m.

time–test·ed /ˈtaɪm͵testəd/ *adj, chiefly US* : done or used for a long time and proved to be effective • These *time-tested* methods have worked for farmers for hundreds of years.

time trial *noun, pl* ~ **trials** [*count*] : a race in which competitors are timed as they race over a course and the one who completes the course in the least amount of time is the winner • He posted the second best lap in the *time trials.*

time warp *noun, pl* ~ **warps** [*count*] : a feeling, state, or place in which time seems to stop, go backward, etc. • Walking into the castle was like entering a *time warp.* • She dresses like someone caught/stuck/trapped in a 1950s *time warp.* [=she dresses in styles from the 1950s]

time·worn /ˈtaɪm͵woɚn/ *adj* [*more* ~; *most* ~]

1 : in bad condition because of age • a *timeworn* sweater with holes in the sleeves • The houses on the street are all *timeworn* and badly in need of repair.

2 : no longer interesting or effective because of being old or used too often • a *timeworn* joke/excuse • He gave us the same *timeworn* speech about the need to work hard.

time zone *noun, pl* ~ **zones** [*count*] : any one of the world's 24 divisions that has its own time ✧ Each time zone is one hour earlier than the time zone directly to the east. • We flew west and landed in a different *time zone.*

tim·id /ˈtɪməd/ *adj* [*more* ~; *most* ~] : feeling or showing a lack of courage or confidence • She's very *timid* and shy when meeting strangers. • He gave her a *timid* smile.

– **ti·mid·i·ty** /təˈmɪdəti/ *noun* [*noncount*] – **tim·id·ly** /ˈtɪmədli/ *adv* • She *timidly* entered the room.

tim·ing /ˈtaɪmɪŋ/ *noun* [*noncount*]

1 : the time when something happens or is done especially when it is thought of as having a good or bad effect on the result • The *timing* of the sale could not have been better.

2 : the ability to choose the best moment for some action, movement, etc. • Her *timing* was a little off and she missed the shot. • an athlete with impeccable *timing*

tim·o·rous /ˈtɪmərəs/ *adj* [*more* ~; *most* ~] *formal* : easily frightened : FEARFUL • a shy and *timorous* teenager • He spoke with a *timorous* voice.

– **tim·o·rous·ly** *adv* • She *timorously* approached the teacher. – **tim·o·rous·ness** *noun* [*noncount*]

tim·pa·ni /ˈtɪmpəni/ *noun* [*plural*] *music* : a set of two or three large drums (called kettledrums) that are played by one performer in an orchestra — see picture at PERCUSSION

– **tim·pa·nist** /ˈtɪmpənɪst/ *noun, pl* **-nists** [*count*]

tin /ˈtɪn/ *noun, pl* **tins**

1 [*noncount*] : a soft, shiny, bluish-white metal that has many different uses

2 [*count*] **a** : a container or plate made of metal • a pie *tin* **b** : a decorative metal box with a cover or lid • a *tin* of biscuits/tobacco **c** *chiefly Brit* : [2]CAN 1a • a *tin* of tomatoes • sardine *tins* **d** *Brit* : [1]PAN 1a • a roasting *tin*

– **tin** *adj* • a *tin* kettle/roof

tinc·ture /ˈtɪŋkʧɚ/ *noun, pl* **-tures** [*count*] *technical* : a medicine that is made of a drug mixed with alcohol • a *tincture* of iodine • medicinal *tinctures*

tin·der /ˈtɪndɚ/ *noun* [*noncount*] : dry material (such as wood or grass) that burns easily and can be used to start a fire : KINDLING

T

tin·der·box /ˈtɪndɚˌbɑːks/ *noun, pl* **-box·es** [*count*]
1 : a box that holds material that can be used to start a fire easily **:** a container for tinder
2 a : a structure that would burn very quickly if it caught on fire ▪ That old house is really a *tinderbox*. **b :** a place or situation that could suddenly become very violent ▪ The campus was a *tinderbox* [=*powder keg*] on the verge of a riot.

tine /ˈtaɪn/ *noun, pl* **tines** [*count*] **:** one of the thin, pointed parts on a fork **:** PRONG ▪ One of the fork's *tines* was bent.

tin ear *noun, pl* ~ **ears** [*count*] *chiefly US* **:** a lack of ability to hear something (such as music or speech) in an accurate and sensitive way ▪ My wife is a talented musician, but I have a *tin ear*. ▪ a writer with a *tin ear* for dialogue [=who writes dialogue that does not sound real]

tin·foil /ˈtɪnˌfojəl/ *noun* [*noncount*] **:** a thin sheet of shiny metal that is used especially for cooking or storing food ▪ Wrap the leftover food in *tinfoil*. ▪ a piece of *tinfoil*

¹tinge /ˈtɪnʤ/ *noun, pl* **ting·es** [*count*] **:** a slight color, flavor, or quality ▪ showing a *tinge* of color ▪ dark hair with reddish *tinges* ▪ a *tinge* [=*hint*] of mystery/regret

²tinge *verb* **tinges; tinged; tinge·ing** [+ *obj*]
1 : to give a small amount of color to (something) ▪ The ink *tinged* his fingers blue. — often used as *(be) tinged* ▪ The sky *was tinged* with red. ▪ trees *tinged* in yellow and orange
2 : to give a small amount of some quality to (something) — usually used as *(be) tinged with* ▪ Her days *were tinged with* sadness. ▪ a comment *tinged with* sarcasm [=a somewhat sarcastic comment]

tin·gle /ˈtɪŋgəl/ *verb* **tin·gles; tin·gled; tin·gling** [*no obj*]
1 : to have a feeling like the feeling of many small sharp points pressing into your skin ▪ My arm/leg was numb and *tingling*.
2 : to feel an emotion (such as excitement) very strongly ▪ Everyone was ***tingling with excitement***. [=everyone was very excited] — see also SPINE-TINGLING
– tingle *noun, pl* **tingles** [*count*] ▪ The music sent *tingles* up and down my spine. **– tingling** *noun* [*noncount*] ▪ The patient felt numbness, *tingling*, and pain in her left leg. **– tin·gly** /ˈtɪŋgəli/ *adj* **tin·gli·er; -est** ▪ a *tingly* sensation

tin·horn /ˈtɪnˌhoɚn/ *noun, pl* **-horns** [*count*] *US, informal + disapproving* **:** a person who talks and acts like someone who is strong and powerful but who is really weak, unimportant, etc. — usually used before another noun ▪ a *tinhorn* dictator/tyrant

¹tin·ker /ˈtɪŋkɚ/ *verb* **-kers; -kered; -ker·ing** [*no obj*] **:** to try to repair or improve something (such as a machine) by making small changes or adjustments to it ▪ He was *tinkering* in the garage. — often + *with* ▪ The car wouldn't start, but my brother *tinkered with* the engine a little and got it going again. ▪ They are still *tinkering* (around) *with* the details of the plan.
– tin·ker·er /ˈtɪŋkərɚ/ *noun, pl* **-ers** [*count*]

²tinker *noun, pl* **-kers** [*count*] **:** a person who in the past traveled to different places and made money by selling or repairing small items (such as pots and pans)

tink·er's damn *also* **tink·er's dam** /ˈtɪŋkɚzˈdæm/ *noun* [*singular*] *US, informal* **:** the smallest possible amount — used like *damn* in negative statements ▪ He obviously doesn't ***give a tinker's damn*** [=doesn't care at all] about what happens. ▪ If you ask me, his opinions aren't ***worth a tinker's damn***. [=aren't worth anything]

Tin·ker·toy /ˈtɪŋkɚˌtoɪ/ *trademark* — used for a construction toy with parts that fit together

¹tin·kle /ˈtɪŋkəl/ *verb* **tin·kles; tin·kled; tin·kling**
1 : to make sounds like the sounds of a small bell [*no obj*] The ice *tinkled* in the glass. ▪ A piano was *tinkling* in the background. [+ *obj*] He *tinkled* a small bell.
2 [*no obj*] *informal* **:** to pass urine from the body **:** URINATE — used especially by small children ▪ The little boy said he had to *tinkle*.

²tinkle *noun, pl* **tinkles**
1 [*count*] **:** the sound produced by a small bell or a similar sound ▪ the *tinkle* of wineglasses
2 [*singular*] *Brit, informal* **:** a telephone call ▪ ***Give me a tinkle*** [=*call me*] when you have the time.
3 [*singular*] *informal* **:** the act of passing urine from the body — used especially by small children ▪ The little boy said he had to ***have/take a tinkle***. [=he had to urinate/pee]
– tin·kly /ˈtɪŋkəli/ *adj* ▪ a *tinkly* sound

tinned /ˈtɪnd/ *adj, Brit* **:** preserved in a metal or glass container **:** CANNED ▪ *tinned* ham/peaches/tuna

tin·ni·tus /ˈtɪnətəs, təˈnaɪtəs/ *noun* [*noncount*] *medical* **:** a condition that causes you to hear ringing or roaring sounds that only you can hear

tin·ny /ˈtɪni/ *adj* **tin·ni·er; -est :** having a high and unpleasant sound ▪ a *tinny* voice ▪ The music sounded *tinny*.

tin opener *noun, pl* ~ **-ers** [*count*] *Brit* **:** CAN OPENER

Tin Pan Alley *noun* [*noncount*] **:** an area in a city where people who write and produce popular music live and work

tin–pot /ˈtɪnˈpɑːt/ *adj, always used before a noun, informal + disapproving* **:** of little worth or importance **:** TWO-BIT ▪ a *tinpot* dictator/tyrant

tin·sel /ˈtɪnsəl/ *noun* [*noncount*]
1 : thin strips of shiny metal or paper that are used as decoration ▪ I like to decorate the Christmas tree with *tinsel*.
2 : something that seems attractive or appealing but is of little worth ▪ He's not attracted to the *tinsel* and glitter of Hollywood.

Tin·sel·town /ˈtɪnsəlˌtaʊn/ *noun, informal* — used as a name for Hollywood, California ▪ young actors seduced by *Tinseltown* — often used before another noun ▪ *Tinseltown* films/stars

¹tint /ˈtɪnt/ *noun, pl* **tints**
1 [*count*] **:** a small amount of color ▪ a photo with a sepia *tint* ▪ green with a yellowish *tint*
2 a [*count, noncount*] **:** dye used to change the color of hair **b** [*singular*] **:** an act of changing the color of hair by using dye ▪ She got a red *tint* at the salon.

²tint *verb* **tints; tint·ed; tint·ing** [+ *obj*] **:** to give a small amount of color to (something) ▪ They *tinted* the water with blue dye. ▪ She wanted to have her hair *tinted*. [=*dyed*]
– tinted *adj* ▪ *tinted* glasses/lenses/windows

tin·tin·nab·u·la·tion /ˌtɪntəˌnæbjəˈleɪʃən/ *noun, pl* **-tions** [*count*] *literary* **:** the sound of ringing bells

tin·type /ˈtɪnˌtaɪp/ *noun, pl* **-types** [*count*] *US* **:** an old type of photograph that was made on a piece of metal

ti·ny /ˈtaɪni/ *adj* **ti·ni·er; -est :** very small ▪ a *tiny* baby bird ▪ The computer chips were *tiny*. ▪ He's from a *tiny* town that you've probably never heard of. ▪ the *tiniest* of openings ▪ There's just one *tiny* little problem. ▪ Aren't you even a *tiny* bit scared?

¹tip /ˈtɪp/ *verb* **tips; tipped; tip·ping**
1 : to turn or move something so that it is not straight or level **:** to cause something to lean or slant **:** TILT [+ *obj*] She *tipped* her head to the left. ▪ He *tipped* his glass and spilled some water. ▪ He *tipped* his chair back and fell over. [*no obj*] The glass *tipped* slightly and some of the water spilled out.
2 [+ *obj*] *chiefly Brit* **:** to cause (something) to move or fall from a place, container, etc. ▪ She *tipped* [=*poured*] the batter into a large bowl.
tip over [*phrasal verb*] ***tip over*** *or* ***tip (something) over*** *or* ***tip over (something)*** **:** to fall over or to cause (something) to fall over ▪ The glass nearly *tipped over*. ▪ He accidentally *tipped* the lamp *over* and broke it.
tip the scales **1** *or* ***tip the balance*** **:** to change a situation so that one person, group, etc., is more able or likely to succeed **:** to give an advantage to someone or something ▪ Both candidates are qualified, but her experience *tips the scales* in her favor. **2** ***tip the scales at*** **:** to have (a specified weight) ▪ He *tips the scales at* 285 pounds. [=he weighs 285 pounds]
tip up [*phrasal verb*] ***tip (something) up*** *or* ***tip up (something)*** **:** to move or cause (something) to move so that one end is lifted up ▪ She *tipped up* the lid of the box and looked inside.
tip your cap/hat **1 :** to touch your hat or cap or to lift it off your head as a way of greeting or saying goodbye to someone ▪ He *tipped his hat* to her as she walked past. **2** — used informally to say that you admire or respect someone ▪ I really have to *tip my hat* to those people for all their hard work.
tip your hand **:** to show what you are planning to do ▪ The company wants to avoid *tipping its hand* about its decision until next month.
– compare ⁴TIP, ⁶TIP, ⁸TIP

²tip *noun, pl* **tips**
1 [*singular*] **:** the act of touching your hat or cap or lifting it off your head as a way of greeting or saying goodbye to someone **:** the act of tipping your hat ▪ With a *tip* of his hat, he said goodbye and headed out the door.
2 [*count*] *Brit* **a :** a place where rubbish is left **:** DUMP **b** *informal* **:** a very messy place **:** DUMP ▪ This place is a real *tip*!
– compare ³TIP, ⁵TIP, ⁷TIP, ⁹TIP

T

[3]tip *noun, pl* **tips** [*count*] : the end of something that is usually long and thin • a pencil *tip* • the *tips* of her fingers • the *tip* of a ski • The village is located at the southern *tip* of the island.

on the tip of your tongue **1** ✧ If a word, name, etc., is *on the tip of your tongue*, you know it but cannot remember it. • His name is (right) *on the tip of my tongue.* **2** ✧ If a statement is *on the tip of your tongue*, you nearly say it but decide not to say it. • A sarcastic reply was *on the tip of her tongue.*

the tip of the iceberg see ICEBERG

– compare [2]TIP, [5]TIP, [7]TIP, [9]TIP

[4]tip *verb* **tips; tipped; tip•ping** [+ *obj*] *sports* : to hit or push (a moving ball or hockey puck) lightly so that it changes direction • The hockey player *tipped* the puck into the net. — see also TIP-IN

tip off [*phrasal verb*] *of a basketball game* : [2]START • The game is scheduled to *tip off* at 7:00 o'clock tonight. — see also [2]TIP-OFF

– compare [1]TIP, [6]TIP, [8]TIP

[5]tip *noun, pl* **tips** [*count*] *sports* : an act of lightly pushing or hitting a moving ball or hockey puck to make it change direction • a foul *tip* — compare [2]TIP, [3]TIP, [7]TIP, [9]TIP

[6]tip *verb* **tips; tipped; tipping** [+ *obj*]

1 : to give useful or secret information to (someone) • Someone *tipped* [=*told*] the police about their plans. — see also TIP OFF (below)

2 *Brit* : to say that someone or something is likely to succeed, win, etc. • The new book is being *tipped* [=*touted*] as a probable best seller.

tip off [*phrasal verb*] ***tip (someone) off or tip off (someone)*** : to give useful or secret information to (someone) • Someone *tipped off* the police about the robbery. • Someone *tipped* them *off* that there would be a robbery. — see also [1]TIP-OFF

tip (someone) the wink *Brit, informal* : to give secret information to (someone) • How could he have known about the plan? Someone must have *tipped* him *the wink.*

– compare [1]TIP, [4]TIP, [8]TIP

[7]tip *noun, pl* **tips** [*count*]

1 : a piece of advice or useful information • She got a *tip* on how to prepare for the test. • *tips* for saving money • The book provides some good household cleaning *tips.*

2 : a piece of secret information given by a person who has special knowledge about something • an insider's *tip* on when to sell the stock • The police got a *tip* about the suspect from an informer. • I got a ***hot tip*** about a great new restaurant.

– compare [2]TIP, [3]TIP, [5]TIP, [9]TIP

[8]tip *verb* **tips; tipped; tipping** : to give an extra amount of money to someone who performs a service for you : to give a tip to (someone) [+ *obj*] Did you remember to *tip* the waiter/waitress? • How much should I *tip* for a haircut? [*no obj*] She always *tips* generously. — compare [1]TIP, [4]TIP, [6]TIP

– tip•per /ˈtɪpɚ/ *noun, pl* **-pers** [*count*] • She is a generous *tipper.*

[9]tip *noun, pl* **tips** [*count*] : an extra amount of money that you give to someone (such as a waitress or waiter) who performs a service for you • I left/gave the waitress a good/generous *tip.* • The doorman earned a lot in *tips* over the holiday season. — compare [2]TIP, [3]TIP, [5]TIP, [7]TIP

tipi *variant spelling of* TEPEE

tip–in /ˈtɪpˌɪn/ *noun, pl* **-ins** [*count*] *US, sports* : a goal that is scored by lightly pushing or touching a moving ball or hockey puck so that it goes into the basket or net from a short distance away • She scored the winning basket/goal on a *tip-in.*

[1]tip–off /ˈtɪpˌɑːf/ *noun, pl* **-offs** [*count*]

1 : a warning that something (such as a crime) is going to happen • The police received a *tip-off* about the robbery from an informer. — see also *tip off* at [6]TIP

2 : a clear sign or indication of something • The worried expression on his face was a *tip-off* that something had gone wrong.

– compare [2]TIP-OFF

[2]tip–off *noun, pl* **-offs** [*count*] *basketball* : the start of a game when the ball is thrown in the air and a player from each team jumps up and tries to get the ball • We arrived at the arena just a few minutes before *tip-off.* — compare [1]TIP-OFF; see also *tip off* at [4]TIP

tipped /ˈtɪpt/ *adj* : having a specified color or material on the end or tip • red flowers *tipped* with yellow — often used in combination • silver-*tipped* hair • a diamond-*tipped* drill bit

[1]tip•ple /ˈtɪpəl/ *verb* **tip•ples; tip•pled; tip•pling** [*no obj*] *informal* : to drink alcohol • He gave up *tippling.*

– tip•pler /ˈtɪpəlɚ/ *noun, pl* **tip•plers** [*count*] • a heavy *tippler* [=a person who drinks a lot of alcohol]

[2]tipple *noun, pl* **tipples** [*count*] *informal* : an alcoholic drink • His preferred/favorite *tipple* is whiskey.

tip•ster /ˈtɪpstɚ/ *noun, pl* **-sters** [*count*] : a person who gives useful information to someone • An anonymous *tipster* reported the crime.

tip•sy /ˈtɪpsi/ *adj* **tip•si•er; -est** [*or more* ~; *most* ~] *informal* : unsteady or foolish from drinking : slightly drunk • I got a little *tipsy* at the party last night.

[1]tip•toe /ˈtɪpˌtoʊ/ *noun*

on tiptoe *or* ***on (your) tiptoes*** : with your toes touching the ground and your heels raised up • She had to stand *on tiptoe* to reach the shelf. • He stood *on his tiptoes* trying to see over the crowd. • He walked *on tiptoe* to avoid waking the children.

[2]tiptoe *verb* **-toes; -toed; -toe•ing** [*no obj*] : to walk with your heels raised up and only your toes touching the ground • She *tiptoed* through the puddle. • He *tiptoed* quietly around the house to avoid waking the children.

tiptoe around [*phrasal verb*] ***tiptoe around (something)*** : to avoid talking about (something) : to talk about (something) only in an indirect way • They *tiptoed around* the subject of her poor health.

[3]tiptoe *adv* : with your toes touching the ground and your heels raised up • She had to stand *tiptoe* to reach the shelf.

[1]tip–top /ˈtɪpˈtɑːp/ *noun, pl* **-tops** [*count*] *informal* : the highest point of something • the very *tip-top* of the mountain

[2]tip–top *adj, informal* : very good : excellent or great • The car is in *tip-top* shape/condition.

ti•rade /ˈtaɪˌreɪd/ *noun, pl* **-rades** [*count*] : a long and angry speech • He went into a *tirade* about the failures of the government. • The coach directed a *tirade* at the team after the loss.

[1]tire /ˈtajɚ/ *verb* **tires; tired; tir•ing**

1 [*no obj*] : to lose energy and begin to feel that you need to rest : to become tired • I *tired* long before the race was over. • The pitcher seems to be *tiring.*

2 [+ *obj*] : to cause (someone) to lose energy : to make (someone) tired • The long hike *tired* the younger children. — often + *out* • Shoveling snow *tires* me *out.*

tire of [*phrasal verb*] ***tire of (something)*** : to become bored by (something) : to stop being interested in (something) • He soon *tired of* doing the same work every day. • They eventually *tired of* life on the road. • She never *tires of* listening to music.

[2]tire (*US*) *or Brit* **tyre** /ˈtajɚ/ *noun, pl* **tires** [*count*] : a rubber ring that usually contains air and that fits around the wheel of a car, bicycle, etc. • bicycle/automobile *tires* • a flat *tire* — see pictures at BICYCLE, CAR; see also SNOW TIRE, SPARE TIRE

tired *adj* [*more* ~; *most* ~]

1 : feeling a need to rest or sleep : WEARY • I was really *tired* after the long trip. • She's too *tired* to go out tonight. • *tired* muscles • The children were *tired* after the hike. — see also DOG-TIRED

2 : bored or annoyed by something because you have heard it, seen it, done it, etc., for a long time — + *of* • He's *tired of* working for other people. • Are you *tired of* your job? • I got *tired of* listening to her. • She never gets *tired of* their music. • I'm ***sick and tired of*** [=very tired of] your complaining.

3 *disapproving* : used over and over again • We had to listen to the same old *tired* excuses again. • a *tired* joke

4 : worn down by long use : RUN-DOWN • a neighborhood of *tired* houses • a *tired* old town

– tired•ly *adv* • She *tiredly* leaned her head back. **– tired•ness** *noun* [*noncount*]

tire•less /ˈtajɚləs/ *adj* : working very hard with a lot of energy for a long time : never seeming to get tired • He's a *tireless* worker. • She has been a *tireless* advocate for reform.

– tire•less•ly *adv* • She has worked *tirelessly* to help the homeless.

tire•some /ˈtajɚsəm/ *adj* [*more* ~; *most* ~] : causing you to feel bored, annoyed, or impatient • a *tiresome* [=*boring*] lecture • All those stories about his childhood can become *tiresome* after a while.

– tire•some•ly *adv*

tiring *adj* [*more* ~; *most* ~] : causing you to feel tired • The work was very *tiring.*

'tis /ˈtɪz, təz/ *old-fashioned + literary* — used as a contraction of "it is" • *'Tis* the season to be jolly.

tis•sue /ˈtɪʃu/ *noun, pl* **-sues**
1 [*count*] : a piece of soft and very thin paper that is used especially for cleaning ▪ a box of *tissues* ▪ She wiped her nose with a *tissue*. ▪ a facial *tissue*
2 : the material that forms the parts in a plant or animal [*noncount*] a sample of brain/lung/muscle *tissue* ▪ a *tissue* sample [*plural*] The drug can damage the body's *tissues*.
3 [*noncount*] : TISSUE PAPER ▪ a box wrapped in *tissue*
a tissue of lies chiefly Brit : a story or report that is completely false : a story that is full of lies ▪ The article was nothing but *a tissue of lies*.

tissue paper *noun* [*noncount*] : thin paper used especially for covering or wrapping something

[1]**tit** /ˈtɪt/ *noun, pl* **tits** [*count*] *informal + often offensive* : a woman's breast — usually plural — compare [2]TIT

[2]**tit** *noun, pl* **tits** [*count*] : a small European bird — compare [1]TIT

ti•tan /ˈtaɪtn̩/ *noun, pl* **-tans** [*count*]
1 ***Titan*** : one of a family of giants in Greek mythology
2 : an extremely large and powerful person, company, etc. ▪ media *titans* ▪ a *titan* of industry ▪ multinational *titans*

ti•tan•ic /taɪˈtænɪk/ *adj* [*more ~; most ~*] : very great in size, force, or power : GIGANTIC ▪ They put up a *titanic* struggle. ▪ The batter hit a *titanic* home run. ▪ a *titanic* explosion

ti•ta•ni•um /taɪˈteɪnijəm/ *noun* [*noncount*] : a very strong and light silvery metal

titbit *Brit spelling of* TIDBIT

tit•fer /ˈtɪtfɚ/ *noun, pl* **-fers** [*count*] *Brit, informal* : HAT

tit for tat /ˌtɪtfɚˈtæt/ *noun* [*noncount*] : a situation in which you do something to harm someone who has done something harmful to you ▪ a *tit for tat* between two rival politicians
– tit–for–tat *adj* ▪ *tit-for-tat* bombings

tithe /ˈtaɪð/ *noun, pl* **tithes** [*count*] : an amount of money that a person gives to a church which is usually equal to 1/10 of that person's income

tit•il•late /ˈtɪtəˌleɪt/ *verb* **-lates**; **-lat•ed**; **-lat•ing** : to interest or excite (someone) in an enjoyable and often sexual way [*+ obj*] a film made to *titillate* the audience [*no obj*] writing that *titillates* and provokes
– titillating *adj* [*more ~; most ~*] ▪ *titillating* gossip ▪ an intentionally *titillating* movie **– tit•il•la•tion** /ˌtɪtəˈleɪʃən/ *noun* [*noncount*] ▪ sexual *titillation*

[1]**ti•tle** /ˈtaɪtl̩/ *noun, pl* **ti•tles**
1 [*count*] : the name given to something (such as a book, song, or movie) to identify or describe it ▪ What was the *title* of that book you were reading last week? ▪ The *title* of the first chapter is "Getting Started." — see also SUBTITLE
2 [*count*] : a published book ▪ The company published 25 new *titles* last year. ▪ This is one of our best-selling *titles*.
3 [*count*] : a word or name that describes a person's job in a company or organization ▪ Her *title* is Vice President of Marketing. ▪ He has an impressive job *title*.
4 [*count*] : a word (such as *Sir* or *Doctor*) or an abbreviation (such as *Mr.* or *Dr.*) that is used with someone's name to show that person's rank, profession, or marital status
5 [*count*] : the status or position of being the champion in a sport or other competition ▪ He won the batting *title* [=*championship*] last year. ▪ He currently holds the heavyweight *title*. ▪ The school has won six basketball *titles*.
6 *law* **a** [*noncount*] : a legal right to the ownership of property ▪ The court ruled that he had *title* to the land. **b** [*count*] : a document which shows that someone owns property ▪ Did he find the *title* to his car?
rejoice in the title of see REJOICE

[2]**title** *verb* **titles**; **ti•tled**; **ti•tling** [*+ obj*] : to give a name or title to (something) : to call (a book, song, movie, etc.) by a title ▪ She *titled* the book *The Story of My Life*. ▪ a movie *titled Gone With the Wind*

[3]**title** *adj, always used before a noun*
1 : having the same name as a movie, play, etc. ▪ He played the *title* role in *Hamlet*. [=he played the role of Hamlet in the play *Hamlet*] ▪ the *title* song/track on the CD
2 : of, relating to, or involving a championship ▪ The *title* game/match [=the game/match that decides who wins the championship] will be played tonight.

titled *adj* : having a title (such as "Lord" or "Lady") : belonging to the highest social class ▪ a *titled* British family ▪ a member of the *titled* ranks

ti•tle•hold•er /ˈtaɪtl̩ˌhouldɚ/ *noun, pl* **-ers** [*count*]
1 : a person who has won a championship title in a sport : CHAMPION ▪ the heavyweight boxing *titleholder*
2 *law* : a person, company, etc., that owns property

title page *noun, pl* **~ pages** [*count*] : a page in the front of a book that includes the book's title

ti•tlist /ˈtaɪtlɪst/ *noun, pl* **-tlists** [*count*] *US* : a person who holds a title as champion : CHAMPION ▪ the heavyweight *titlist*

tit•mouse /ˈtɪtˌmaus/ *noun, pl* **tit•mice** /ˈtɪtˌmaɪs/ [*count*] : a small American bird

tit•ter /ˈtɪtɚ/ *verb* **-ters**; **-tered**; **-ter•ing** [*no obj*] : to laugh in a quiet and nervous way ▪ Some people in the audience *tittered* nervously during an awkward pause in the speech.
– titter *noun, pl* **-ters** [*count*] ▪ There were a few *titters* in the classroom.

tit•tle–tat•tle /ˈtɪtl̩ˌtætl̩/ *noun* [*noncount*] *chiefly Brit, informal* : talk about things that are not important or interesting ▪ gossipy *tittle-tattle* about celebrities

tit•ty /ˈtɪti/ *noun, pl* **-ties** [*count*] *informal + offensive* : a woman's breast — usually plural

tit•u•lar /ˈtɪʧəlɚ/ *adj*
1 : having an important or impressive title but not having the power or duties that usually go with it ▪ Although retired, he remains the *titular* chairman of the company. ▪ the country's *titular* head/ruler/monarch
2 : having the name of the character that is featured in the title of a movie, play, etc. ▪ He played the *titular* [=*title*] role in *Hamlet*. [=he played the role of Hamlet in the play *Hamlet*]

tix /ˈtɪks/ *noun* [*plural*] *US, informal* : tickets ▪ concert *tix* for sale

tiz•zy /ˈtɪzi/ *noun* [*singular*] *informal* : a state in which you feel very worried, upset, and confused ▪ She's always ***getting in/into a tizzy*** over minor things. — called also (*Brit*) **tizz** /ˈtɪz/

TKO /ˌtiːˌkeɪˈoʊ/ *noun, pl* **TKOs** [*count*] : TECHNICAL KNOCKOUT

TLC /ˌtiːˌɛlˈsiː/ *noun* [*noncount*] *informal* : care and attention that is given to make someone feel better, to improve the bad condition of something, etc. ▪ He just needed some rest and a little *TLC*. ▪ It's an old house that needs some *TLC*. ✧ *TLC* is an abbreviation of "tender loving care."

TM *abbr* trademark

TN *abbr* Tennessee

TNT /ˌtiːˌɛnˈtiː/ *noun* [*noncount*] : a very powerful explosive

[1]**to** /ˈtuː, tə/ *prep*
1 — used to indicate that the following verb is in the infinitive form ▪ I like *to* swim. ▪ "*To* be, or not *to* be—that is the question . . . " —Shakespeare, *Hamlet* (1600) ▪ That's a tough question *to* answer. ▪ I have an appointment *to* keep. ▪ The soup is too hot *to* eat. ▪ Do you need *to* use this? ▪ I have *to* go now. ▪ *To* look at him, you'd never think he was 80! ▪ I didn't really like the movie, *to* be honest. — often used by itself in place of an infinitive verb when the verb is understood ▪ You can go if you want *to*. [=you can go if you want to go] ▪ "You left the door unlocked." "I didn't mean *to*."
2 a — used to indicate the place, person, or thing that someone or something moves toward ▪ We are flying *to* London tomorrow. ▪ They climbed *to* the top of the mountain. ▪ I sent the e-mail *to* the wrong address. ▪ He was sent *to* the principal. ▪ The little girl ran *to* her mother. **b** — used to indicate the place where someone participates in a particular activity ▪ Where do you go *to* school? ▪ She wore her new red dress *to* the party. ▪ We went *to* lunch together. ▪ This is the child's first visit *to* the dentist.
3 — used to indicate the direction of something ▪ There is a lake a mile *to* the south of here. ▪ She had her back *to* me. [=her back was facing me] ▪ The roads are parallel *to* each other.
4 — used to indicate the limit or range of something ▪ The water was up *to* my waist. ▪ The temperature outside rose *to* 100 degrees. ▪ The word dates (back) *to* 1639. ▪ The show's audience is mainly men from 18 *to* 30 years of age. ▪ The band plays all kinds of music from country *to* hard rock. ▪ The shirt is a light *to* medium pink. ▪ The wines we tasted ranged from very poor *to* good *to* excellent. ▪ *To* my knowledge, she has never visited Paris. [=I do not know of any time when she visited Paris] ▪ I'll do it *to* the best of my ability. [=as well as I can]
5 a — used to indicate a particular result or end ▪ The school was converted *to* an apartment building. ▪ The vase was smashed *to* pieces. ▪ The promotion increased her salary *to* $50,000. ▪ He was sentenced *to* death. ▪ *To* their surprise, the train left on time. ▪ A firefighter came *to* her rescue. [=a

firefighter rescued her] • It's 100 miles (from here) *to* the nearest town. **b : according to (something)** • The wedding gown was made *to* her specifications. [=was made in the way that she specified] • Add salt *to* taste. [=add as much salt as you want according to your taste]

6 a — used to indicate the end of a particular period of time • He works from nine *to* [=*until, till*] five. • Up *to* now, no one has beaten the record. • The movie keeps your attention from beginning *to* end. **b : before the start of (something, such as an hour or event)** • It is ten *to* six. [=it is 10 minutes before 6 o'clock] • She arrived at a quarter *to* five. • I can't believe there are only five days *to* the wedding. • How long *to* kickoff?

7 a — used to indicate the person or thing that receives an object or action • Give the letter *to* me. [=give me the letter] • The teacher spoke *to* his parents. • She showed a picture of her kids *to* me. • Refer *to* the dictionary. • Let me introduce you *to* my sister. • She was very rude *to* [=*toward*] him. • "He's smart," she thought *to* herself. **b : in honor of (someone or something)** • Let us drink *to* the bride and groom. • The people built temples *to* their gods. • The book is dedicated *to* her husband and children.

8 a — used to indicate how people or things are related, connected, etc. • She is married *to* my cousin. • He is related *to* me. • He is the assistant *to* the dean. • You have always been a good friend *to* me. • I can't find the key (that goes) *to* this door. • He owns the title *to* the property. **b : in response to (something)** • There wasn't much I could say *to* that. • The answer *to* your question is no. • What would you say *to* a drink? [=would you like a drink?] • Her dog comes *to* her call. [=comes when she calls]

9 — used to indicate the thing that causes something to happen • She lost her mother *to* cancer. [=her mother died of cancer]

10 — used when one person or thing is being compared to another • He prefers a good book *to* a movie. • I have a pair of shoes similar *to* those. • His followers compared/likened him *to* a god. • This problem is nothing *to* [=is nothing when compared to] the ones we previously had. • We won the game ten *to* six. [=we won the game because we had ten points while the other team had only six] • Their odds of winning are ten *to* one.

11 — used to indicate that something is attached to or touches something else • He tied the dog's leash *to* the post. • She put her hand *to* [=*on, against*] her heart. • He gently touched the bow *to* the violin's strings.

12 — used to indicate the thing that contains or includes a certain number or amount of something • The pencils come ten *to* a box. [=there are ten pencils in each box] • There are two pints *to* a quart.

13 — used to indicate the sound that people hear while they do something or while something happens • Children were dancing *to* the music. • He woke *to* the sound of pouring rain.

14 a : in the opinion of (someone) • The plan is agreeable *to* all of us. • Her excuse sounded suspicious *to* me. • *To* him, the work seemed unnecessary. **b : from the point of view of (someone)** • Their marriage is news *to* me. [=I did not know about their marriage] • Your problems are of no concern *to* me! [=I don't care about your problems]

to yourself — used with *have* to say that you are the only one who is using something or who is in a place • I finally *had* the computer (all) *to myself*. • We *had* the whole house *to ourselves*. [=we were the only ones in the house]

Do not confuse *to* with *too* or *two*.

[2]**to** /ˈtuː/ *adv*

1 : into a state of being awake or conscious • He ***brought her to*** [=woke her up; made her conscious again] with smelling salts. • He ***came to*** [=he became conscious] an hour after the accident.

2 *chiefly Brit* **: into a position that is closed or almost closed** • The wind blew the door *to*.

to and fro **: forward and backward** • The baby rocked *to and fro* in the swing. **: from one place to another** • The small boat was tossed *to and fro* by the waves.

toad /ˈtoud/ *noun, pl* **toads** [*count*]

1 : a small animal that looks like a frog but has dry skin and lives on land — see picture at FROG

2 *informal* **: an unpleasant person** • He's such a mean little *toad*.

toad–in–the–hole *noun* [*noncount*] *Brit* **: a dish made of sausages cooked in batter**

toad·stool /ˈtoudˌstuːl/ *noun, pl* **-stools** [*count*] **: a kind of fungus that is similar to a mushroom, that consists of a round cap on a short stem, and that is often poisonous**

[1]**toady** /ˈtoudi/ *noun, pl* **toad·ies** [*count*] *informal + disapproving* **: a person who praises and helps powerful people in order to get their approval** • She's a real *toady* to the boss.

[2]**toady** *verb* **toadies; toad·ied; toady·ing** [*no obj*] *informal + disapproving* **: to try to get the approval of someone powerful by saying and doing helpful and friendly things that are not sincere : to be a toady** • He's always *toadying* to the boss.

[1]**toast** /ˈtoust/ *noun* [*noncount*] **: bread that has been sliced and then made crisp and brown by heat** • a piece of *toast* • I had *toast* for breakfast. — see also FRENCH TOAST

(as) warm as toast see [1]WARM

be toast *informal* **: to be in a lot of trouble** • If anyone finds out about this, we*'re toast*. **: to be completely ruined, defeated, etc.** • His career *is toast*. [=is finished/ruined]

— compare [3]TOAST

[2]**toast** *verb* **toasts; toast·ed; toast·ing** [*+ obj*]

1 : to make (food, such as bread) crisp and brown by heat • He *toasted* the bread in the oven. • (*Brit*) a *toasted* cheese sandwich [=(*US*) a grilled cheese sandwich]

2 : to warm (yourself or part of your body) by being close to a fire or some other source of heat • He was *toasting* his feet by the fire.

— compare [4]TOAST

[3]**toast** *noun, pl* **toasts** [*count*] **: an occurrence in which words are said that honor someone, express good wishes, etc., and people take a drink to show that they agree with what has been said** • He made/proposed a *toast* to the bride and groom. • Everyone ***drank a toast*** to the bride and groom.

the toast of **: a person who is very popular in (a particular place) or among (a particular group of people)** • After she won the championship, she was *the toast of* the town. • He's *the toast of* society.

— compare [1]TOAST

[4]**toast** *verb* **toasts; toasted; toasting** [*+ obj*] **: to drink a toast to (someone)** • Everyone *toasted* the bride and groom. — compare [2]TOAST

toast·er /ˈtoustɚ/ *noun, pl* **-ers** [*count*] **: an electrical device used for toasting bread — see picture at** KITCHEN

toaster oven *noun, pl* **~ -ens** [*count*] *US* **: a small oven in which food is toasted, heated, or cooked — see picture at** KITCHEN

toast·mas·ter /ˈtoustˌmæstɚ, *Brit* ˈtəustˌmɑːstə/ *noun, pl* **-ters** [*count*] **: a person who introduces the speakers at a formal occasion (such as a banquet)**

toasty /ˈtousti/ *adj* **toast·i·er; -est** *US, informal* **: comfortably warm** • The room was nice and *toasty*.

to·bac·co /təˈbækou/ *noun* [*noncount*]

1 : a plant that produces leaves which are smoked in cigarettes, pipes, etc. • a farm that grows *tobacco*

2 : the leaves of the tobacco plant used for smoking or chewing • chewing/pipe *tobacco*

3 : products (such as cigars or cigarettes) that are made from tobacco • a state tax on *tobacco* • the *tobacco* industry

to·bac·co·nist /təˈbækənɪst/ *noun, pl* **-nists**

1 [*count*] **: a person who sells tobacco and tobacco products (such as cigarettes)**

2 ***the tobacconist*** *or* ***the tobacconist's*** **: a store where tobacco and tobacco products are sold** • He bought some cigars at *the tobacconist's*.

to–be /təˈbiː/ *adj* **— used to indicate what someone will be at a future time; used in combination** • his bride-*to-be* [=his future bride] • the father-*to-be*

[1]**to·bog·gan** /təˈbɑːgən/ *noun, pl* **-gans** [*count*] **: a long, light sled that has a curved front and that is used for sliding over snow and ice**

toboggan

[2]**toboggan** *verb* **-gans; -ganed; -gan·ing** [*no obj*] **: to ride on a toboggan especially down a hill** • The kids *tobogganed* down the hill.

toc·ca·ta /təˈkɑːtə/ *noun, pl* **-tas** [*count*] *music* **: a piece of music for the piano or a similar instrument that is played very quickly**

[1]**to·day** /təˈdeɪ/ *noun* [*noncount*]

1 : this day ▪ Is *today* a holiday? ▪ Have you read *today's* newspaper? ▪ The sale ends ***a week from today***. [=in one week]
2 : the present time ▪ the computers of *today* = *today's* computers

²today *adv*
1 : on, during, or for this day ▪ We have to finish *today*. ▪ Earlier *today* I saw my cousin. ▪ I have an appointment later *today*. ▪ They announced *today* that he'll be promoted.
2 : at the present time **:** NOWADAYS ▪ I worry about children *today*. ▪ *Today*, more than a million people live there. ▪ Cars aren't built *today* like they were 30 years ago.

tod·dle /ˈtɑːdl̩/ *verb* **tod·dles; tod·dled; tod·dling** [*no obj*]
1 *of a young child* **:** to walk with short, unsteady steps ▪ The little boy *toddled* across the room.
2 *always followed by an adverb or preposition* **:** to walk along in a slow and relaxed way ▪ I *toddled* off/down to the pub for a pint. ▪ She *toddled* off to bed.

tod·dler /ˈtɑːdlɚ/ *noun, pl* **tod·dlers** [*count*] **:** a young child who is just learning to walk
– tod·dler·hood /ˈtɑːdlɚˌhʊd/ *noun* [*noncount*]

tod·dy /ˈtɑːdi/ *noun, pl* **-dies** [*count*] **:** a hot drink made with whisky, sugar, and water ▪ a hot *toddy*

to–do /təˈduː/ *noun* [*singular*] *informal* **:** excited or angry activity that is usually not necessary or wanted ▪ He made a big *to-do* [=*fuss*] about her birthday. ▪ They're making a big *to-do* about nothing.

¹toe /ˈtoʊ/ *noun, pl* **toes** [*count*]
1 : one of the five separate parts at the end of your foot ▪ He felt the sand/grass between his *toes*. ▪ I accidentally stepped on her *toe*. ▪ I ***stubbed my toe*** on the table's leg. — see picture at FOOT; compare FINGER; see also BIG TOE
2 : the part of a shoe or sock that covers the front part of your foot ▪ My sock has a hole in the *toe*. ▪ boots with steel *toes* ▪ the *toe* of her boot — see picture at SHOE
3 : something that is shaped like a toe ▪ the *toe* of the peninsula
dip/put/stick a toe in the water *informal* **:** to try an activity briefly to see if you like it ▪ I'm not sure I want to join, but I'd like to *dip a toe in the water*.
from top to toe see ¹TOP
keep (someone) on their toes *informal* **:** to cause someone to be alert and prepared to deal with problems ▪ Taking care of three kids really *keeps* me *on my toes*. ▪ The boss made regular inspections in order *to keep* employees *on their toes*.
make your toes curl *informal* **:** to cause you to have a very strong and usually unpleasant feeling (such as a feeling of being embarrassed, annoyed, etc.) ▪ Just thinking about my old boyfriend *makes my toes curl*.
point your toes see ²POINT
step on someone's toes (*US*) or *Brit* ***tread on someone's toes*** *informal* **:** to do something that upsets or offends someone ▪ You might *step on the toes of* some important people with this project. ▪ I don't want to *step on* anyone's *toes*.

²toe *verb* **toes; toed; toe·ing** [+ *obj*] *chiefly US* **:** to touch, reach, or kick (something) with your toe or with the end of your foot ▪ She *toed* off her shoes. ▪ The pitcher *toed* the rubber.
toe the line **:** to do what you are told or required to do even though you do not want to do it ▪ We expect you to *toe the line* if you want to stay here. ▪ He has to *toe the* company *line* to keep his job.

-toed /ˈtoʊd/ *adj* **:** having a toe or toes of a specified kind or number — used in combination ▪ a three-*toed* sloth ▪ steel-*toed* shoes

T

TOEFL /ˈtoʊfəl/ *trademark* — used for a test of the language skills of people who have learned English as a foreign language

toe·hold /ˈtoʊˌhoʊld/ *noun, pl* **-holds** [*count*]
1 : a place where your toes may be placed when you are climbing a cliff, a mountain, etc.
2 : a position that makes it possible to begin an activity or effort ▪ His father helped him get a *toehold* [=*foothold*] in show business. ▪ American companies looking for *toeholds* in foreign markets

toe·nail /ˈtoʊˌneɪl/ *noun, pl* **-nails** [*count*] **:** the hard covering at the end of a toe — see picture at FOOT

toe·rag /ˈtoʊˌræg/ *noun, pl* **-rags** [*count*] *Brit slang, offensive* **:** a person you strongly dislike

toe–to–toe *adv, informal* — used to describe a fight in which two people stand close together facing each other ▪ They fought each other *toe-to-toe*. ▪ He ***went toe-to-toe*** (in a fight) with the schoolyard bully. — sometimes used figuratively ▪ They *went toe-to-toe* [=competed against each other in a very exciting way] for 18 holes of golf.
– toe–to–toe *adj* ▪ a *toe-to-toe* competition

toff /ˈtɑːf/ *noun, pl* **toffs** [*count*] *Brit, informal + disapproving* **:** a person who belongs to a high social class

tof·fee /ˈtɑːfi/ *noun* [*noncount*] **:** a hard, sticky candy made by boiling sugar and butter together

tof·fee–nosed /ˈtɑːfiˌnoʊzd/ *adj* [*more ~; most ~*] *Brit, informal + disapproving* **:** having or showing the attitude of people who think they are better than other people **:** SNOBBISH ▪ *toffee-nosed* art critics

to·fu /ˈtoʊˌfuː/ *noun* [*noncount*] **:** a soft, white food made from soybeans and often used in vegetarian cooking instead of meat — called also *bean curd*

tog /ˈtɑːg/ *verb* **togs; togged; tog·ging**
be/get togged up/out *Brit, informal* **:** to be or get dressed in special clothes for a particular occasion or activity ▪ He *got* (himself) *togged up* for the meeting.

to·ga /ˈtoʊgə/ *noun, pl* **-gas** [*count*] **:** a long, loose piece of clothing that was worn by people in ancient Rome

¹to·geth·er /təˈgɛðɚ/ *adv*
1 : with each other ▪ They went to the party *together*. ▪ They have been living *together* for eight years. ▪ We enjoy spending time *together*. ▪ The old friends were *together* again after many long years apart. ▪ The partners have been in business *together* since 1971. ▪ lie/sit down *together*
2 : in or into one group, mixture, piece, etc. ▪ They gathered *together* to celebrate. ▪ The presentation binds/joins/lumps/ties *together* several concepts. ▪ Blend/Combine/Mix the ingredients *together*. ▪ The old fence was held *together* by chicken wire. ▪ two sticks of dynamite bound *together* by tape
3 : in a close relationship ▪ She got back *together* with her old boyfriend. ▪ How long have you two been going *together*? ▪ They've been *together* for almost five years.
4 : so that two or more people or things touch ▪ The doors banged *together*. ▪ He knocked the sticks *together*.
5 : at the same time ▪ They all cheered *together*.
6 a : to each other ▪ Add the numbers *together* to get the total. **b :** considered as a whole ▪ All *together* there were 15 of us. ▪ He earns more than all of us *together*. [=*combined*]
usage see ALTOGETHER
come together see ¹COME
get together, get your act together see GET
hang together see ¹HANG
hold together see ¹HOLD
pull together see ¹PULL
throw together see ¹THROW
together with **:** in addition to (someone or something) ▪ *Together with* myself and my husband, four people will be attending. ▪ The comment, *together with* [=*along with*] her expression, suggested that she was very upset. ▪ The fingerprint *together with* the other evidence was enough to prove that he was there.

²together *adj* [*more ~; most ~*] *informal* **:** confident, organized, and able to deal with problems in a calm and skillful way ▪ She's always so *together*. ▪ He's a very *together* person.

to·geth·er·ness /təˈgɛðɚnəs/ *noun* [*noncount*] **:** a state or feeling of closeness and happiness among people who are together as friends, family members, etc. ▪ family *togetherness* ▪ trying to encourage a sense of *togetherness* among the people in the community

¹tog·gle /ˈtɑːgəl/ *noun, pl* **tog·gles** [*count*]
1 : a small piece of wood, plastic, metal, etc., that is pushed through a loop or hole to fasten one part of something to another part ▪ Instead of buttons, the jacket has *toggles*.
2 *computers* **:** a setting that can be switched between two different options by pressing a single key, making a single choice from a menu, etc.

²toggle *verb* **toggles; tog·gled; tog·gling** [*no obj*] *computers* **:** to switch between two options by pressing a single key, making a single choice from a menu, etc. ▪ The progam lets you *toggle* easily between two different views.

toggle switch *noun, pl* **~ switches** [*count*] **:** a switch that turns the flow of electricity to a machine on and off

togs /ˈtɑːgz/ *noun* [*plural*] *Brit, informal* **:** CLOTHES ▪ fancy *togs*

¹toil /ˈtojəl/ *noun* [*noncount*] *formal + literary* **:** work that is difficult and unpleasant and that lasts for a long time **:** long, hard labor • days of *toil* and sweat

²toil *verb* **toils; toiled; toil•ing** [*no obj*] *formal + literary*
1 : to work very hard for a long time • He's been *toiling* (away) in his workshop. • workers *toiling* in the fields
2 : to move slowly and with a lot of effort • They were *toiling* up a steep hill.
– toil•er /ˈtoɪlɚ/ *noun, pl* **-ers** [*count*]

toi•let /ˈtoɪlət/ *noun, pl* **-lets** [*count*]
1 : a large bowl attached to a pipe that is used for getting rid of bodily waste and then flushed with water • flush the *toilet* • One of the kids needed to use the *toilet*. • a *toilet* brush/seat/bowl • (*Brit*) The little boy told his mother that he had to ***go to the toilet***. [=use the toilet; (*US*) *go to the bathroom*] — see picture at BATHROOM
2 *chiefly Brit* **:** BATHROOM • a public *toilet* [=*restroom*] • He's in the *toilet*. [=*loo*]
3 *old-fashioned* **:** the act or process of washing and dressing yourself • a painting of a woman at her *toilet*
flush something down the toilet see ²FLUSH

toilet bag *noun, pl* **~ bags** [*count*] *Brit* **:** a small bag that you use to carry a toothbrush, soap, etc., while traveling

toilet paper *noun* [*noncount*] **:** thin, soft paper used to clean yourself after you have used the toilet — called also *toilet tissue*, (*Brit*) *lavatory paper*; see picture at BATHROOM

toi•let•ries /ˈtoɪlətriz/ *noun* [*plural*] **:** things (such as soap, lotions, etc.) that are used to clean yourself and make yourself look neat

toilet roll *noun, pl* **~ rolls** [*count*] *chiefly Brit* **:** a roll of toilet paper

toilet training *noun* [*noncount*] **:** the process of teaching a small child to use the toilet — called also *potty training*
– toilet train *verb* **~ trains; ~ trained; ~ training** [*+ obj*] • We're planning to *toilet train* him next summer. **– toilet–trained** *adj* • The twins are *toilet-trained* now.

toilet water *noun* [*noncount*] **:** a liquid that has a light, pleasant smell and that people put on their skin **:** a kind of perfume that consists mostly of water and does not have a strong scent

toke /ˈtoʊk/ *verb* **tokes; toked; tok•ing** *informal* **:** to inhale marijuana smoke [*no obj*] *toke* on a joint [*+ obj*] *toke* a joint
– toke *noun, pl* **tokes** [*count*] • He took a *toke* off the joint.

¹to•ken /ˈtoʊkən/ *noun, pl* **-kens** [*count*]
1 : a round piece of metal or plastic that is used instead of money in some machines **:** an object that looks like a coin and is used in place of a coin • a bus/subway *token*
2 : something that is a symbol of a feeling, event, etc. — usually + *of* • Consider this gift a *token of* my affection/gratitude. • a *token of* our friendship
3 *Brit* **:** GIFT CERTIFICATE • a book/record/gift *token*
by the same token **:** for the same reason **:** in the same way — used to introduce a statement that says something more and often something different about the same situation referred to by a previous statement • The result was disappointing, but *by the same token*, it could have been much worse.

²token *adj, always used before a noun, disapproving*
1 — used to describe something that is done with very little effort and only to give the appearance that an effort is being made • The government has made only a *token* effort to end homelessness. • *token* resistance • a *token* gesture
2 : included in a group only to prevent criticism that people of a particular kind are being unfairly left out • All the people who work there are men except for a couple of *token* women. • The ad campaign features a few *token* minorities.

to•ken•ism /ˈtoʊkəˌnɪzəm/ *noun* [*noncount*] **:** the practice of doing something (such as hiring a person who belongs to a minority group) only to prevent criticism and give the appearance that people are being treated fairly • Did the company choose her for her merits, or merely as an act of *tokenism*?

told *past tense and past participle of* TELL

tol•er•able /ˈtɑːlərəbəl/ *adj* [*more ~; most ~*]
1 : unpleasant but able to be accepted or tolerated • The heat was *tolerable* for only a short time. • a *tolerable* [=*bearable*] level of pain • This kind of behavior is not *tolerable*. [=*acceptable*] — opposite INTOLERABLE
2 : good enough to be accepted but not very good • a *tolerable* effort
– tol•er•ably /ˈtɑːlərəbli/ *adv* • He did *tolerably* well.

tol•er•ance /ˈtɑːlərəns/ *noun*
1 : willingness to accept feelings, habits, or beliefs that are different from your own [*noncount*] religious *tolerance* [*singular*] a *tolerance* for/of other lifestyles — see also ZERO TOLERANCE
2 : the ability to accept, experience, or survive something harmful or unpleasant [*count*] The plants have a high/low *tolerance* for/of heat. [*noncount*] I don't have much *tolerance* for cold weather. [=I dislike cold weather; cold weather makes me uncomfortable] • I have no *tolerance* for such behavior. [=I cannot accept/tolerate such behavior]
3 *medical* **:** your body's ability to become adjusted to something (such as a drug) so that its effects are experienced less strongly [*count*] Some patients gradually develop a *tolerance* for the drug and need to be given a larger dose. [*noncount*] Some patients develop greater *tolerance* for the drug's effects.

tol•er•ant /ˈtɑːlərənt/ *adj* [*more ~; most ~*]
1 : willing to accept feelings, habits, or beliefs that are different from your own • a *tolerant* society/community • *tolerant* attitudes/opinions/views — often + *of* • The people in the community are *tolerant of* each other's differences.
2 : able to allow or accept something that is harmful, unpleasant, etc. — often + *of* • These plants are *tolerant of* hot climates. [=are able to live and grow in hot climates] • Our teacher is not *tolerant of* bad grammar. [=will not tolerate/accept bad grammar]
– tol•er•ant•ly *adv*

tol•er•ate /ˈtɑːləˌreɪt/ *verb* **-ates; -at•ed; -ating** [*+ obj*]
1 : to allow (something that is bad, unpleasant, etc.) to exist, happen, or be done • Our teacher will not *tolerate* bad grammar. • Racist or sexist behavior will not be *tolerated*. • I can't *tolerate* that noise. • The government cannot *tolerate* lawlessness. • How can you *tolerate* such laziness?
2 : to experience (something harmful or unpleasant) without being harmed • These plants *tolerate* drought well.
3 : to accept the feelings, behavior, or beliefs of (someone) • I don't like my boss, but I *tolerate* him.
– tol•er•a•tion /ˌtɑːləˈreɪʃən/ *noun* [*noncount*] • religious *toleration*

¹toll /ˈtoʊl/ *noun, pl* **tolls** [*count*]
1 a : an amount of money that you are required to pay for the use of a road or bridge • We had to stop to pay the *toll*. • a *toll* road/bridge [=a road/bridge that you can use only if you pay a toll] **b** *chiefly US* **:** an amount of money paid for a long-distance telephone call — see also TOLL CALL, TOLL-FREE
2 : the number of people who are killed or injured in an accident, disaster, war, etc. — usually singular • The full/final *toll* of the disaster is not yet known. — see also DEATH TOLL
take a toll *or* ***take its toll*** **:** to have a serious, bad effect on someone or something **:** to cause harm or damage • If you keep working so hard, the stress will eventually *take its toll*. [=your health will be harmed] — often + *on* • The stress will *take its toll on* you. • Too much sunlight can *take a* (heavy) *toll on* your skin. [=can harm your skin] • Her illness has *taken a toll on* her marriage.
– compare ³TOLL

²toll *verb* **tolls; tolled; toll•ing**
1 : to ring slowly [*no obj*] Church bells *tolled* as people gathered for the service. [*+ obj*] The bells were *tolled* for the service.
2 [*+ obj*] **:** to make (something) known by ringing • The church bells *tolled* the hour.

³toll *noun, pl* **tolls** [*count*]
1 : the sound of bells being rung slowly • The *toll* of the bells sounded throughout the village.
2 : a single sound made by a ringing bell • He counted the *tolls* of the bell.
– compare ¹TOLL

toll•booth /ˈtoʊlˌbuːθ/ *noun, pl* **-booths** [*count*] **:** a small building where you pay a toll to use a road or bridge

toll call *noun, pl* **~ calls** [*count*] *US* **:** a long-distance telephone call for which you must pay an extra amount of money — called also (*Brit*) *trunk call*

toll–free /ˈtoʊlˈfriː/ *adj, US* **:** allowing you to make a long-distance telephone call without having to pay a toll • a *toll-free* call/number
– toll–free *adv* • call *toll-free*

toll•gate /ˈtoʊlˌgeɪt/ *noun, pl* **-gates** [*count*] **:** a place where the driver of a vehicle must pay a toll to go through a gate that blocks a road

toll•house /ˈtoʊlˌhaʊs/ *noun, pl* **-hous•es** [*count*] **:** a building where you pay a toll to use a road or bridge

toll plaza *noun, pl* **~ -zas** [*count*] **:** PLAZA 3b

T

tom /ˈtɑːm/ *noun, pl* **toms** [*count*]
1 : TOMCAT
2 : a male turkey

tom·a·hawk /ˈtɑːmɪˌhɑːk/ *noun, pl* **-hawks** [*count*] : a small ax used as a weapon by Native Americans

to·ma·to /təˈmeɪtoʊ, *Brit* təˈmɑːtəʊ/ *noun, pl* **-toes** [*count*] : a round, soft, red fruit that is eaten raw or cooked and that is often used in salads, sandwiches, sauces, etc. ▪ crushed *tomatoes* — often used before another noun ▪ *tomato* soup/sauce/paste/juice — see color picture on page C4; see also CHERRY TOMATO, PLUM TOMATO

tomato ketchup *noun* [*noncount*] : KETCHUP

tomb /ˈtuːm/ *noun, pl* **tombs** [*count*] : a building or chamber above or below the ground in which a dead body is kept ▪ the *tomb* of Alexander the Great

tom·bo·la /ˈtɑːmbələ, *Brit* tɒmˈbəʊlə/ *noun, pl* **-las** [*count*] *Brit* : [1]RAFFLE

tom·boy /ˈtɑːmˌbɔɪ/ *noun, pl* **-boys** [*count*] : a girl who enjoys things that people think are more suited to boys
– **tom·boy·ish** /ˈtɑːmˌbojɪʃ/ *adj* [*more ~; most ~*] ▪ *tomboyish* behavior/clothing

tomb·stone /ˈtuːmˌstoʊn/ *noun, pl* **-stones** [*count*] : GRAVESTONE

tom·cat /ˈtɑːmˌkæt/ *noun, pl* **-cats** [*count*] : a male cat — called also *tom*

Tom, Dick, and Har·ry /ˌtɑːmˌdɪkəndˈheri/ *noun*
any/every Tom, Dick, and Harry *informal* : any person : ANYONE ▪ We don't just hand out jobs to *every Tom, Dick, and Harry* who walks in here.

tome /ˈtoʊm/ *noun, pl* **tomes** [*count*] *formal* : a very large, thick book ▪ a long *tome* on European history

tom·fool·ery /ˌtɑːmˈfuːləri/ *noun* [*noncount*] *old-fashioned* : playful or silly behavior ▪ There was a lot of *tomfoolery* going on behind the scenes.

[1]**to·mor·row** /təˈmɑroʊ/ *noun*
1 [*noncount*] : the day after today ▪ *Tomorrow* is a school day. ▪ She is giving a presentation at *tomorrow's* meeting.
2 : the future [*noncount*] Who knows what *tomorrow* may bring? ▪ designing the car of *tomorrow* ▪ Today's children are *tomorrow*'s leaders. [*singular*] All we can do is hope for a better *tomorrow*.
like there's no tomorrow : in a quick and careless way without any thought about the future ▪ He's spending money *like there's no tomorrow*. [=he is spending a lot of money now and not saving any for the future]

[2]**tomorrow** *adv* : on, during, or for the day after today ▪ I'll finish the housework *tomorrow*. ▪ Is it supposed to rain *tomorrow*? ▪ He has an interview *tomorrow*. ▪ *Tomorrow* we're going fishing.

tom–tom /ˈtɑːmˌtɑːm/ *noun, pl* **-toms** [*count*] : a tall, narrow drum that is usually played with the hands

ton /ˈtʌn/ *noun, pl* **tons** [*count*]
1 *pl also* **ton** **a** *US* : a unit for measuring weight that equals 2,000 pounds (907 kilograms) **b** *Brit* : a unit for measuring weight that equals 2,240 pounds (1,016 kilograms) — see also MEGATON, METRIC TON
2 *informal* : a large amount ▪ I still have a *ton* to do before the guests arrive. ▪ Her purse ***weighs a ton***. [=is very heavy] — often + *of* ▪ He earns a *ton of* money. ▪ I've got *tons of* homework to do.
like a ton of bricks see [1]BRICK

ton·al /ˈtoʊnl/ *adj*
1 *technical* : of or relating to musical or color tones ▪ *tonal* variations
2 *music* : having or based in a particular key ▪ traditional *tonal* music — opposite ATONAL
– **to·nal·i·ty** /toʊˈnæləti/ *noun, pl* **-ties** [*count, noncount*] ▪ the *tonality* of a piece of music – **ton·al·ly** *adv*

[1]**tone** /ˈtoʊn/ *noun, pl* **tones**
1 [*count*] **a** : the quality of a person's voice ▪ She spoke in a sharp *tone*. [=he spoke sharply] ▪ He replied in a friendly *tone*. ▪ They spoke in hushed/conspiratorial *tones*. ▪ Don't use that rude ***tone of voice*** with me. **b** : the quality of a sound produced by a musical instrument or singing voice ▪ the low *tones* of an organ
2 [*count*] **a** : a quality, feeling, or attitude expressed by the words that someone uses in speaking or writing ▪ The speech had religious *tones* to it. ▪ The author's *tone* shows her attitude toward the subject. ▪ The professor's condescending *tone* irritated some students. **b** : the general quality of a place, situation, etc. ▪ the city's upbeat *tone* ▪ The seriousness of his opening statement ***set the tone*** for/of the meeting. [=his opening statement established that the meeting would be serious]
3 [*count*] **a** : a shade of color ▪ a bright, dark, or light *tone* of blue ▪ the soft *tones* of the painting — see also EARTH TONE **b** : a small amount of a color ▪ gray with a slightly bluish *tone* [=*tint*]
4 [*noncount*] : strength and firmness of the muscles or skin ▪ These exercises help build muscle *tone*.
5 [*noncount*] : the highness or lowness of a spoken syllable ▪ a rising/falling *tone* — see also TONE LANGUAGE
6 [*count*] : a sound made as a signal by a machine (such as a telephone or answering machine) ▪ Please leave a message after the *tone*. ▪ (*Brit*) I keep getting the ***engaged tone***. [=(*US*) *busy signal*; the sound which indicates that the telephone line is already being used] — see also DIAL TONE, RINGTONE
7 [*count*] *music* **a** : a sound of a particular pitch and vibration ▪ the different *tones* [=*notes*] of a musical scale **b** *chiefly Brit* : WHOLE STEP

[2]**tone** *verb* **tones; toned; ton·ing** [+ *obj*] : to give strength and firmness to (something, such as muscles or skin) ▪ These exercises are a good way to *tone* (up) your stomach muscles.
tone down [*phrasal verb*] ***tone (something) down or tone down (something)*** **1** : to make (something) less forceful, offensive, or harsh ▪ People will be more likely to listen to you if you *tone down* your language a little. **2** : to make (something) less bright or colorful ▪ She *toned down* her wardrobe.
tone in [*phrasal verb*] ***tone in with (something)*** *Brit* : to match the color of (something) ▪ That tie *tones in* well *with* your suit.

toned *adj*
1 : having or showing strength or firmness ▪ *toned* muscles ▪ his *toned* body
2 : having a certain type of tone or color — used in combination ▪ olive-*toned* skin ▪ sepia-*toned* photographs

tone–deaf /ˈtoʊnˌdɛf/ *adj* : unable to hear the difference between musical notes or sing the right musical notes

tone language *noun, pl* **~ -guages** [*count*] : a language (such as Chinese) in which changes in the tone of words indicate different meanings

ton·er /ˈtoʊnɚ/ *noun, pl* **-ers**
1 [*noncount*] : a dark powder that is used like ink in machines that print and copy documents ▪ The copier needs *toner*.
2 [*count, noncount*] : a liquid that is used to clean and tighten the skin

tongs /ˈtɑːŋz/ *noun* [*plural*] : a tool used for lifting or holding objects that is made of two long pieces connected at one end or in the middle ▪ ice/salad *tongs* ▪ a pair of *tongs*
hammer and tongs see [1]HAMMER

[1]**tongue** /ˈtʌŋ/ *noun, pl* **tongues**
1 **a** [*count*] : the soft, movable part in the mouth that is used for tasting and eating food and in human beings for speaking ▪ The cow ran its *tongue* over its lips. ▪ The taste of the spice was still on her *tongue*. ▪ The little girl stuck her *tongue* out at me. ▪ My mom shook her head and ***clicked her tongue*** [=made a noise with her tongue] in disapproval. — see picture at MOUTH **b** [*count, noncount*] : the tongue of an animal (such as an ox or sheep) that is eaten as food
2 [*count*] : LANGUAGE ▪ He spoke in a foreign *tongue*. ▪ English is my native *tongue*. ▪ They speak the same *tongue*. — see also MOTHER TONGUE
3 [*count*] : a particular way or quality of speaking ▪ His sharp/quick *tongue* is going to get him into trouble someday. ▪ Although she was angry, she ***kept a civil tongue***. [=she was polite] ▪ ***Watch your tongue***, young man! [=don't say rude or offensive things] — see also TONGUED
4 [*count*] : something that is shaped like a tongue — + *of* ▪ *tongues of* fire/flame
5 [*count*] : a long flap that is under the laces or buckles of a shoe — see picture at SHOE
6 [*count*] : a long, raised part at the end of a board that extends out and fits into a long cut (called a groove) in another board — see also TONGUE-AND-GROOVE
a slip of the tongue see [2]SLIP
bite your tongue see [1]BITE
Cat got your tongue? see CAT
get your tongue around *informal* ✧ If you cannot *get your tongue around* a word or phrase, you have difficulty saying it. ▪ I can't *get my tongue around* his last name.
hold your tongue see [1]HOLD

loosen someone's tongue see LOOSEN
on the tip of your tongue see [3]TIP
roll/trip off the tongue : to be easy to say or pronounce • The name just *rolls off the tongue.*
speak in tongues ✧ Someone who is *speaking in tongues* is saying strange words that no one can understand, especially as part of a religious experience.
speak/talk with (a) forked tongue see FORKED
tongues (are) wagging ✧ If something ***sets/gets tongues wagging*** or if ***tongues are wagging***, people are talking a lot about something. • The news of their engagement *set tongues wagging.* = *Tongues were wagging* over their engagement.
with (your) tongue in (your) cheek : TONGUE IN CHEEK • He was talking *with his tongue in his cheek.*

[2]**tongue** *verb* **tongues; tongued; tongu·ing**
1 : to produce separate notes when you are blowing air through a musical instrument (such as a trumpet) by using your tongue to briefly stop the flow of air [+ *obj*] learning how to *tongue* notes on the clarinet [*no obj*] notes produced by *tonguing*
2 [+ *obj*] : to touch or lick something with your tongue • *tongue* a cigarette

tongue–and–groove *adj* : joining pieces of wood together by having a long, raised part (called a tongue) on the edge of one board that fits into a long cut (called a groove) on the edge of another board • *tongue-and-groove* flooring

tongued /ˈtʌŋd/ *adj* : having a particular way or quality of speaking — used in combination • smooth-*tongued* — see also SHARP-TONGUED, SILVER-TONGUED

tongue depressor *noun, pl* **~ -sors** [*count*] *US* : a thin piece of wood that is rounded at both ends and that a doctor uses to press down on a patient's tongue when looking in the patient's throat — called also (*Brit*) *spatula*

tongue in cheek *adv* : in a way that is not serious and that is meant to be funny • The whole interview was done *tongue in cheek.*
– **tongue–in–cheek** *adj* • a *tongue-in-cheek* comment • The movie is half serious and half *tongue-in-cheek.*

tongue–lash·ing *noun, pl* **-ings** [*count*] *informal* : an occurrence in which someone speaks in a very angry and critical way to someone who has done something wrong : a severe scolding • She gave him quite a *tongue-lashing* when he failed to file the papers on time.

tongue–tied /ˈtʌŋˌtaɪd/ *adj* : unable to speak because you are nervous or shy • She became *tongue-tied* whenever he was around.

tongue twister *noun, pl* **~ -ers** [*count*] : a word, name, phrase, or sentence that is hard to say • Her last name is a real *tongue twister.*

ton·ic /ˈtɑːnɪk/ *noun, pl* **-ics**
1 [*count, noncount*] : a type of water that has bubbles in it, has a bitter taste, and is often used in alcoholic drinks • gin and *tonic* — called also *tonic water*
2 [*count*] **a** : something that makes you feel healthier and more relaxed — usually singular • A weekend in the mountains was always a *tonic* for him. • To her, classical music is a *tonic.* **b** : a medicine that brings you back to a normal physical or mental condition • an herbal *tonic* **c** *somewhat old-fashioned* : a liquid that is used on your hair to make it healthier • a hair *tonic*
3 [*count*] *music* : the main note of a musical key

[1]**to·night** /təˈnaɪt/ *noun* [*noncount*] : this night or the night following this day • *Tonight* will be rainy. • *Tonight's* party should be fun. • He is staying until *tonight.*

[2]**tonight** *adv* : on this night or on the night following this day • It is cold *tonight.* • This afternoon I'm busy, but *tonight* I'm free. • He's leaving *tonight.*

ton·nage /ˈtʌnɪʤ/ *noun, pl* **-nag·es** [*count, noncount*]
1 : the size of a ship or the total weight that it carries in tons
2 : the total weight or amount of something in tons

tonne /ˈtʌn/ *noun, pl* **tonnes** [*count*] : METRIC TON

ton·sil /ˈtɑːnsəl/ *noun, pl* **-sils** [*count*] : either one of the pair of round, soft parts on the inside of your throat • He ***had his tonsils out*** [=had an operation to remove his tonsils] when he was 10.

ton·sil·lec·to·my /ˌtɑːnsəˈlɛktəmi/ *noun, pl* **-mies** [*count*] *medical* : an operation to remove a person's tonsils • The surgeon performed a *tonsillectomy.*

ton·sil·li·tis /ˌtɑːnsəˈlaɪtɪs/ *noun* [*noncount*] *medical* : a condition in which a person's tonsils are painful and swollen

ton·sure /ˈtɑːnʃɚ/ *noun, pl* **-sures** [*count*] : a round, shaved area on the top of a priest's or monk's head
– **ton·sured** /ˈtɑːnʃɚd/ *adj* • a *tonsured* monk

tony /ˈtoʊni/ *adj* **ton·i·er; -est** [*also more ~; most ~*] *US, informal* : very expensive and fashionable • *tony* private schools • a *tony* restaurant/hotel

To·ny /ˈtoʊni/ *noun, pl* **-nys** [*count*] : an award given every year in New York City for the best plays, actors, directors, etc., in the theater • She won a *Tony* (award) for her performance in the play.

too /ˈtuː/ *adv*
1 *usually used at the end of a sentence or clause* : in addition : ALSO • We are selling the house and the furniture *too.* • He saw something, and she saw it *too.* • "I'm hungry." "Me *too.*" • I want to go *too!* • My new girlfriend is funny and pretty—and rich *too.* [=*besides*] — often used for emphasis • He lost his job—and right after he bought a house *too.* • We decided not to go out that night. And it was a good thing *too*, because we had a big snowstorm. • He finally proposed to her. It's about time *too.*
2 *always used before an adjective or adverb* : more than what is wanted, needed, acceptable, possible, etc. • The soup is *too* hot. • The offer was *too* good to refuse. • This shirt is way/much *too* big for me. • I'm *too* old for rock concerts. = I'm *too* old to go to rock concerts. • She is much/far *too* young to be watching this movie. • Thank you for your donation. You are *too* kind. [=you are very kind] • You gave me *too* many cards. • I have *too* much to do. • He works much *too* hard. • You work *too* slowly. • Slow down. You're talking *too* fast. • Don't stay *too* long. • It's *too* late to do anything about it now. • Her efforts to improve her grade were ***too little, too late.*** [=her efforts were not enough and not soon enough to make a difference] • She knew ***all/only too*** well [=unfortunately, she knew very well] what the punishment would be. • This kind of mistake happens *all too* often. [=happens more often than it should] — see also *too bad* at [1]BAD, *too much* at [1]MUCH
3 *always used before an adjective or adverb* : to a high degree or extent : very or extremely — used in negative statements • I'm not *too* [=*so*] sure that he's right. [=I think he may be wrong] • The climb up the mountain was not *too* hard. • The students didn't seem *too* interested. • She's not doing *too* well. • He doesn't seem *too* upset. • It is not *too* cold outside. • He was ***none too pleased*** [=he was not pleased] to hear that I didn't do what he asked.
4 *chiefly US, informal* : most certainly • "You're not strong enough to lift that box." "I am *too.*" [=I am so; yes, I am] • "I didn't do it." "You did *too.*" [=yes, you did (do it)]

Do not confuse *too* with *to* or *two.*

took *past tense of* [1]TAKE

[1]**tool** /ˈtuːl/ *noun, pl* **tools** [*count*]
1 : something (such as a hammer, saw, shovel, etc.) that you hold in your hand and use for a particular task • carpentry/garden *tools* • power *tools* [=tools that use electricity] • I don't have the right *tools* to fix the engine. — see also HAND TOOL, MACHINE TOOL ***synonyms*** see [1]IMPLEMENT
2 **a** : something that is used to do a job or activity • Words are a writer's *tools.* **b** : something that helps to get or achieve something • Words are *tools* for communication. • A book's cover can be a great marketing *tool.* • The Internet has become an important research *tool.* • He has the *tools* [=natural skills] to be a great pitcher.
3 *disapproving* **a** : someone or something that is used or controlled by another person or group — often + *of* • a politician who is just a *tool of* special interests • He claims the government has become a *tool of* giant corporations. **b** *informal* : a foolish person who can easily be used or tricked by others • He's such a *tool.*
4 *informal + impolite* : a man's penis
tools of the/your trade see [1]TRADE

[2]**tool** *verb* **tools; tooled; tool·ing**
1 *always followed by an adverb or preposition* [*no obj*] *US, informal* : to drive or ride in a vehicle • We *tooled* along/up/down the highway. • I *tooled* around (town) all day.
2 [+ *obj*] : to shape, form, or finish (something) with a tool • He *tooled* a design on the leather belt. • a belt made of *tooled* leather
tool up [*phrasal verb*] ***tool (something) up or tool up (something)*** : to provide (a factory) with machines and tools for producing something • The factory was not *tooled up* for this type of production.

tool·bar /ˈtuːlˌbɑɚ/ *noun, pl* **-bars** [*count*] : a row of icons on a computer screen that allow you to do various things when you are using a particular program — see picture at COMPUTER; compare TASKBAR

tool·box /ˈtuːlˌbɑːks/ *noun, pl* **-box·es** [*count*] : a box for storing or carrying tools — see picture at CARPENTRY

tool kit *noun, pl* **~ kits** [*count*] : a set of tools ▪ A pair of pliers is a good thing to have in your *tool kit.*

tool·mak·er /ˈtuːlˌmeɪkɚ/ *noun, pl* **-ers** [*count*] : a person or company that makes tools ▪ The company is a leading *toolmaker.*
– **tool·mak·ing** /ˈtuːlˌmeɪkɪŋ/ *noun* [*noncount*]

tool·shed /ˈtuːlˌʃɛd/ *noun, pl* **-sheds** [*count*] : a small building for storing tools — see picture at GARDENING

toon·ie /ˈtuːni/ *noun, pl* **-nies** [*count*] *Canada* : a coin that is worth two Canadian dollars

toot /ˈtuːt/ *verb* **toots; toot·ed; toot·ing**
1 [*no obj*] : to make a short, high sound with a horn or whistle ▪ She *tooted* [=*honked*] at me as she drove past. ▪ The horn *tooted.*
2 [+ *obj*] : to cause (a horn or whistle) to make a short high sound ▪ The driver *tooted* [=*honked*] his horn angrily. ▪ The referee *tooted* [=*blew*] his whistle.
toot your own horn see [1]HORN
– **toot** *noun, pl* **toots** [*count*] ▪ I heard the *toot* of a horn. ▪ She gave the horn a *toot.* [=she tooted the horn]

tooth /ˈtuːθ/ *noun, pl* **teeth** /ˈtiːθ/
1 [*count*] : one of the hard white objects inside the mouth that are used for biting and chewing ▪ The dentist will have to pull that *tooth.* ▪ You should brush/clean your *teeth* every morning and night. ▪ She clenched her *teeth* in anger. ▪ He has a set of false *teeth.* ▪ a loose *tooth* ▪ *tooth* decay ▪ She ***sank her teeth into*** [=*bit*] the apple. — see picture at MOUTH; see also BABY TOOTH, BUCK TEETH, EYETOOTH, MILK TOOTH, SWEET TOOTH, WISDOM TOOTH
2 [*count*] : a sharp or pointed object that sticks out of something and is part of a row of similar objects ▪ the *teeth* of a saw/comb
3 ***teeth*** [*plural*] : the power that makes something effective ▪ drug laws with *teeth* ▪ The labor union showed that it ***has teeth.***
a kick in the teeth see [2]KICK
an eye for an eye and a tooth for a tooth see [1]EYE
by the skin of your teeth see [1]SKIN
cut a tooth, cut your teeth see [1]CUT
fly in the teeth of see [1]FLY
get/take the bit between your teeth see [2]BIT
get your teeth into or *chiefly US* ***sink your teeth into*** : to become fully involved in (something, such as a new activity) : to do or deal with (something) with a lot of energy, interest, etc. ▪ He finally has a project he can *get his teeth into.*
grit your teeth see [2]GRIT
in the teeth of **1** *or* ***into the teeth of*** : directly against (a strong wind, storm, etc.) ▪ They sailed *in/into the teeth of* the wind. **2** : despite (something) ▪ A shopping mall was built *in the teeth of* fierce opposition.
like pulling teeth — used to say that something is very difficult and frustrating ▪ Getting him to make a decision is *like pulling teeth.* [=it is very hard to get him to make a decision]
long in the tooth *informal* : no longer young : OLD ▪ Isn't she a little *long in the tooth* for those kinds of antics?
set your teeth on edge ✧ If a sound, taste, etc., *sets your teeth on edge,* it makes your body feel tense or uncomfortable. ▪ That awful squeaking is enough to *set my teeth on edge!*
tooth and nail : with a lot of effort and determination ▪ They fought *tooth and nail.*
to the teeth : fully or completely ▪ The men were ***armed to the teeth.*** [=the men had a lot of weapons]

tooth·ache /ˈtuːθˌeɪk/ *noun, pl* **-aches** : pain in or near a tooth [*count*] He has a *toothache.* [*noncount*] (*Brit*) He's got *toothache.*

tooth·brush /ˈtuːθˌbrʌʃ/ *noun, pl* **-brush·es** [*count*] : a brush for cleaning your teeth — see picture at GROOMING

toothed /ˈtuːθt/ *adj* : having teeth ▪ a *toothed* whale : having teeth of a specified kind — often used in combination ▪ buck-*toothed* ▪ gap-*toothed*

tooth fairy *noun*
the tooth fairy : an imaginary creature who is supposed to leave money for children while they sleep in exchange for a tooth that has come out

tooth·less /ˈtuːθləs/ *adj*
1 : having or showing no teeth ▪ a *toothless* whale ▪ a *toothless* smile ▪ He is completely *toothless.*
2 : not effective or powerful ▪ *toothless* legislation

tooth·paste /ˈtuːθˌpeɪst/ *noun* [*noncount*] : a substance that is used for cleaning teeth ▪ a tube of *toothpaste* — see picture at GROOMING

tooth·pick /ˈtuːθˌpɪk/ *noun, pl* **-picks** [*count*] : a short, pointed stick used for removing small pieces of food from between your teeth

tooth·some /ˈtuːθsəm/ *adj* [*more* ~; *most* ~] : having a pleasing taste ▪ *toothsome* [=(more commonly) *tasty, delicious*] pies

toothy /ˈtuːθi/ *adj* **tooth·i·er; -est** : having or showing many teeth ▪ a *toothy* mouth/grin/smile
– **tooth·i·ly** /ˈtuːθəli/ *adv* ▪ She smiled *toothily.*

too·tle /ˈtuːtl/ *verb* **too·tles; too·tled; too·tling** *Brit, informal*
1 *always followed by an adverb or preposition* [*no obj*] : to drive or move slowly ▪ We *tootled* along the highway. ▪ I *tootled* around (town) all day.
2 : to play a series of notes on a flute, horn, etc., by blowing into it [*no obj*] He *tootled* on the flute. [+ *obj*] He *tootled* his flute.

toots /ˈtʊts/ *noun* [*noncount*] *US slang, old-fashioned* — used to address a woman or girl ▪ How are you, *toots*? ▪ (*impolite*) Hey, *toots*—get out of the way! ✧ *Toots* is often used in a joking way but may be considered offensive when you use it to address a woman you do not know well.

toot·sy *also* **toot·sie** /ˈtʊtsi/ *noun, pl* **-sies** [*count*] *informal* : FOOT ▪ She was using a blanket to keep her *tootsies* warm.

[1]**top** /ˈtɑːp/ *noun, pl* **tops**
1 [*count*] : the highest part, point, or level of something ▪ The *tops* of the walls are painted and the bottoms are covered in wood paneling. — usually singular ▪ He was calling down from the *top* of the stairs. ▪ Please write your name on the *top* of the page. ▪ She climbed to the *top* of the mountain. ▪ She had a scratch on the *top* of her foot. ▪ He filled the glass to the *top.*
2 [*count*] : an upper surface or edge of something ▪ a table with a glass *top* — see also COOKTOP, COUNTERTOP, DESKTOP, TABLETOP
3 [*count*] : something that covers the upper part or opening of something ▪ I'm looking for a pen with a red *top.* [=*cap*] ▪ She took the *top* [=*lid*] off the jar. ▪ The box's *top* had been removed. ▪ I hate it when you leave the *top* off the toothpaste!
4 [*noncount*] : the highest position in rank, success, or importance ▪ He is at the *top* of his profession. ▪ The company's new CEO started at the bottom and worked her way to the *top.* ▪ employees at the *top* of the pay scale ▪ The team is at the *top* of the league. ▪ He graduated ***at the top of his/the class.*** [=his grades were among the highest in his class] ▪ The order came ***straight from the top.*** [=from the person with the most authority or power] ▪ Studying for the test is on the ***top of my list.*** [=it is the first and most important thing that I need to do]
5 [*count*] : a piece of clothing that is worn on the upper part of your body ▪ She was wearing a blue silk *top* and black pants. ▪ a bikini *top* — see also TANK TOP
6 [*noncount*] *informal* : the beginning ▪ We'll have another news update for you at the *top* of the hour. [=at the start of the next hour] ▪ Let's rehearse the scene ***from the top.*** ▪ OK, everybody. Let's ***take it from the top.*** [=start from the beginning of a scene, song, etc.]
7 [*noncount*] : the first half of an inning in baseball ▪ the *top* of the sixth inning
8 [*noncount*] *chiefly Brit* : the part of something (such as a street) that is farthest away ▪ Try the shop at the *top* of the road.
9 [*noncount*] *chiefly Brit* : the highest gear of a vehicle ▪ She shifted into *top* once she got on the highway.
at the top of the heap see [1]HEAP
at the top of the pile see [1]PILE
at the top of your voice/lungs : in the loudest way possible ▪ She sang *at the top of her voice.* ▪ They were shouting *at the top of their lungs.*
blow your top see [1]BLOW
come out on top : to win a competition, argument, etc. ▪ He's confident that he'll *come out on top* when all the votes have been counted.
from top to bottom : in a very thorough way ▪ We cleaned/searched the house *from top to bottom.*

T

from top to toe : from your head to your feet ▪ They were covered *from top to toe* [=(more commonly) *from head to toe*] in mud.
off the top of your head *informal* : immediately by thinking quickly about something ▪ *Off the top of my head*, I can think of three people who might be interested. ▪ I can't remember her name *off the top of my head*.
on top **1** : on the highest part or surface of something ▪ He gave us vanilla ice cream with chocolate sauce *on top*. ▪ We finished decorating our Christmas tree by putting a star *on top*. ▪ She picked the card *on top*. **2** *chiefly Brit* : winning a game or competition ▪ The team was *on top* [=*in front, ahead*] after the first half. — see also COME OUT ON TOP (above)
on top of **1** : on the highest or upper part of (something or someone) ▪ The house sits *on top of* a hill. ▪ Put the card back *on top of* the deck. ▪ Books and papers were piled *on top of* each other. ▪ I fell to the ground and the dog jumped *on top of* me. **2** : in control of (something) : doing the things that are needed to deal with (something) ▪ You can count on them to be *on top of* things when problems develop. ▪ "Can you get this done by next week?" "Don't worry. I'm *on top of* it." ▪ She's not **on top of her game** this morning. [=she is not performing well this morning] **3** : aware of what is happening in (a particular area of activity) ▪ She tries to keep/stay *on top of* current events. **4** : very close to or near (someone or something) ▪ The deadline was *on top of* them before they knew it. ▪ The houses are built right *on top of* each other. **5** : in addition to (something) ▪ You owe me $20, and that's *on top of* the $40 you owe me from earlier. ▪ *On top of* everything else, he lost his job. **6** ◊ In British English, if something ***gets on top of you***, it becomes too difficult for you to handle or deal with. ▪ Planning their wedding was starting to *get on top of them*.
on top of the world *informal* : in a very successful or happy state ▪ I had just gotten married and felt like I was *on top of the world*.
over the top *informal* : beyond what is expected, usual, normal, or appropriate : very wild or strange often in an amusing way ▪ His performances are always *over the top*. [=(*Brit*) *OTT*]
top of the tree *Brit, informal* : the most powerful or most successful position in a profession, organization, etc. ▪ She is still (at/on the) *top of the tree* in her field. [=she's still at the top in her field]
— compare [3]TOP; see also BIG TOP

[2]top *adj, usually used before a noun*
1 : located at the highest part or position ▪ the *top* drawer/shelf ▪ They live on the *top* floor of the building. ▪ That's my husband in the *top* [=*upper*] right-hand corner of the picture.
2 : highest in rank, success, or importance ▪ the *top* news story of the day ▪ the country's *top* three car manufacturers ▪ He is among the *top* pitchers of the league. ▪ She is the *top* student in her class. = (*chiefly Brit*) She is *top* in her class. ▪ Safety is our *top* concern/priority.
3 : highest in quality, amount, or degree ▪ The winner showed *top* form. ▪ Houses are selling at *top* prices. ▪ What is the car's *top* speed?

[3]top *noun, pl* **tops** [*count*] : a child's toy that can be made to spin very quickly ▪ spinning like a *top* — compare [1]TOP

[4]top *verb* **tops; topped; top·ping** [+ *obj*]
1 : to be or become more than (a particular amount) ▪ Album sales have already *topped* [=*exceeded*] 500,000. ▪ Donations are expected to *top* $1,000,000 by the end of the month.
2 : to be in the highest position on (a list) because of success ▪ The song has *topped* the charts for seven weeks. ▪ Who *tops* the list this year for Hollywood's highest-paid actor? [=who is the highest-paid actor in Hollywood this year?]
3 : to do or be better than (someone or something) ▪ He *topped* [=*surpassed*] his previous record. ▪ They *topped* the other company's offer. ▪ She *tops* everyone else on the team. ▪ Being at the beach sure *tops* [=*beats*] working in the office. ▪ I've seen some pretty weird things in my life—but that *tops* everything!
4 : to cover or form the top of (something) ▪ A fresh layer of snow *topped* the mountains. — often + *with* ▪ She *topped* the pizza *with* cheese and mushrooms. — often used as *(be) topped* ▪ a cup of hot chocolate *topped* (off) *with* whip cream ▪ The cathedral *was topped* (off/out) *with* a spire.
5 : to cut off the top of (something) ▪ He *topped* the tree/carrots.
6 *literary* : to reach the top of (something) ▪ When we *topped* the hill, we saw a small village in the valley.

top off [*phrasal verb*] **top off (something)** *or* **top (something) off** **1** : to end (something) usually in an exciting or impressive way ▪ We *topped off* dinner with dessert and coffee. ▪ The band *topped off* the show with an extended version of their classic hit. ▪ The victory *tops off* the coach's extremely successful career. **2** *US* : to fill (something) completely with a liquid ▪ I added a little more coffee to *top off* the mug. ▪ He stopped at the gas station to *top off* [=(*Brit*) *top up*] the car's tank. [=to fill the car's tank with gas]
top out [*phrasal verb*] : to reach the highest amount or level and stop increasing — often + *at* ▪ Interest rates are expected to *top out at* 15 percent.
top up [*phrasal verb*] **top up (something)** *or* **top (something) up** *Brit* **1** : to fill (something) completely with a liquid ▪ He *topped up* [=(*US*) *topped off*] (the glasses of) his guests. **2** : to bring (something) to the full or desired amount ▪ The store keeps its fruits and vegetables *topped up*. ▪ She works part-time to *top up* her income. — see also TOP-UP
top yourself *Brit, informal* : to kill yourself
to top it (all) off (*US*) *or chiefly Brit* **to top it all** — used to indicate a final thing that happened that was even better, worse, etc., than what happened before ▪ The car was filthy when she returned it to me, and *to top it (all) off*, there was almost no gas left in the tank.

to·paz /ˈtoʊˌpæz/ *noun, pl* **-paz·es** [*count, noncount*] : a clear yellow to brownish-yellow stone that is used as a jewel — see color picture on page C11

top banana *noun, pl* ~ **-nanas** [*count*] *informal* : the most important or powerful person in a group or organization ▪ He's the mob's *top banana*.

top brass *noun* [*noncount*] *informal* : BRASS 4 ▪ Navy *top brass* met earlier today. — often used with *the* ▪ *The* (company) *top brass* have/has decided that no action is necessary.

top·coat /ˈtɑːpˌkoʊt/ *noun, pl* **-coats** [*count*]
1 *somewhat old-fashioned* : a long coat the is worn in cold weather : OVERCOAT
2 : the last layer of paint that is put on a surface

top dog *noun, pl* ~ **dogs** [*count*] *informal* : a person or group that has the most power or success ▪ the industry's *top dogs*

top dollar *noun* [*noncount*] : the highest amount of money that something costs or that someone earns — often + *for* ▪ She paid *top dollar for* the tickets. [=she paid a lot of money for the tickets] ▪ They charge/get *top dollar for* their services.

top–down /ˈtɑːpˈdaʊn/ *adj, always used before a noun*
1 : controlled or directed from the highest levels ▪ *top-down* management — opposite BOTTOM-UP
2 : starting with a general idea and having details gradually added ▪ *top-down* programming/design

to·pee *or* **to·pi** /toʊˈpiː, *Brit* ˈtəʊˌpiː/ *noun, pl* **-pees** *or* **-pis** [*count*] : a hard, light hat that is worn in hot countries to protect your head from the sun

top–end /ˈtɑːpˈɛnd/ *adj, chiefly Brit* : of the highest price and quality ▪ *top-end* [=(*US*) *high-end*] homes/restaurants

top·flight /ˈtɑːpˈflaɪt/ *adj, always used before a noun* : of the highest quality : EXCELLENT ▪ a *topflight* staff/performance

Top 40 *noun* [*plural*] : the forty best-selling music recordings for a particular period of time ▪ She never had a song in the *Top 40*.
— **Top 40** *adj* ▪ a *Top 40* record

top gear *noun* [*noncount*] *Brit*
1 : a vehicle's highest gear ▪ She got to the highway and shifted into *top gear*. [=(*US*) *high gear*]
2 : a state of great or intense activity ▪ The project is now in *top gear*. [=(*US*) *high gear*] ▪ The party **hit top gear** when the guest of honour arrived.

top gun *noun, pl* ~ **guns** [*count*] *US, informal*
1 : a person who is the best at a particular activity ▪ He's the team's *top gun*. ▪ The company has its *top guns* handling the lawsuit.
2 : a powerful or important person

top hat *noun, pl* ~ **hats** [*count*] : a tall, usually black hat that is worn by men on very formal occasions ▪ He wore a *top hat* and tails.

top–heavy /ˈtɑːpˌhɛvi/ *adj*
1 : likely to fall over because the top part is too large and heavy for the bottom part ▪ a *top-heavy* truck
2 : having too many people whose job is to manage workers and not enough ordinary workers ▪ a *top-heavy* corporation

topi *variant spelling of* TOPEE

to·pi·ary /ˈtoʊpiˌeri, *Brit* ˈtəʊpiəri/ *noun, pl* **-ar·ies**

1 [*noncount*] : plants (such as trees and bushes) that are cut or grown into decorative shapes ▪ a *topiary* garden; *also* : the art of shaping plants in this way
2 [*count*] : a plant that is cut or grown into a decorative shape ▪ a garden featuring *topiaries* and fountains

top·ic /ˈtɑːpɪk/ *noun, pl* **-ics** [*count*] : someone or something that people talk or write about : SUBJECT ▪ He is comfortable discussing a wide range of *topics*. ▪ a popular/hot *topic* ▪ *topics* such as health and fitness — often + *of* ▪ What is the *topic of* your speech? ▪ a book on the *topic of* language ▪ a *topic of* debate/discussion ▪ The new boss has been the main *topic of* conversation. — see also SUBTOPIC

top·i·cal /ˈtɑːpɪkəl/ *adj*
1 [*more ~; most ~*] : relating to current news or events : dealing with things that are important, popular, etc., right now ▪ *topical* issues/themes ▪ a *topical* reference ▪ *topical* humor
2 *medical* : made to be put on the skin ▪ *topical* lotions/creams ▪ a *topical* drug/treatment
– top·i·cal·ly /ˈtɑːpɪkli/ *adv* ▪ Apply the medicine *topically*. **– top·i·cal·i·ty** /ˌtɑːpəˈkæləti/ *noun* [*noncount*] ▪ the *topicality* of his humor

top·less /ˈtɑːpləs/ *adj*
1 *of a woman* : wearing no clothing on the upper body ▪ *topless* dancers ▪ She likes to ***go topless*** on the beach.
2 : done while not wearing any clothing on the upper body ▪ *topless* sunbathing
3 : having or allowing topless women ▪ a *topless* beach ▪ *topless* bars [=bars with topless waitresses, dancers, etc.]
– topless *adv* ▪ pose/dance/sunbathe *topless*

top–level *adj, always used before a noun*
1 : highest in level, position, or rank ▪ *top-level* executives
2 : involving people of the highest level, position, or rank ▪ a *top-level* competition/meeting

top·most /ˈtɑːpˌmoust/ *adj, always used before a noun* : highest in position or importance ▪ He was standing on the *topmost* step. ▪ the country's *topmost* leaders

top–notch /ˈtɑːpˈnɑːʧ/ *adj, informal* : of the best quality ▪ The hotel offers *top-notch* service. ▪ Their food is *top-notch*. [=*excellent*]

top–of–the–line (*US*) *or Brit* **top–of–the–range** *adj* : of the best quality ▪ *top-of-the-line* cameras

to·pog·ra·phy /təˈpɑːgrəfi/ *noun* [*noncount*] *technical*
1 : the art or science of making maps that show the height, shape, etc., of the land in a particular area
2 : the features (such as mountains and rivers) in an area of land — often + *of* ▪ The map shows the *topography of* the island.
– to·pog·ra·pher /təˈpɑːgrəfɚ/ *noun, pl* **-phers** [*count*] **– to·po·graph·ic** /ˌtɑːpəˈgræfɪk/ *or* **to·po·graph·i·cal** /ˌtɑːpəˈgræfɪkəl/ *adj* ▪ a *topographic* map **– to·po·graph·i·cal·ly** /ˌtɑːpəˈgræfɪkli/ *adv* ▪ *topographically* similar areas

top·per /ˈtɑːpɚ/ *noun, pl* **-pers** *informal*
1 [*count*] : something that is placed on top of something else ▪ a Christmas tree *topper* ▪ (*chiefly US*) salad/ice-cream/pizza *toppers* [=*toppings*]
2 [*count*] : TOP HAT
3 [*count*] : something that is highest on a list ▪ Their new song soon became a ***chart topper***.
4 ***the topper US*** : the thing that is better, worse, etc., than everything before it ▪ The whole day was bad, but the *topper* came when our car broke down.

top·ping /ˈtɑːpɪŋ/ *noun, pl* **-pings** : a food that is added to the top of another food [*count*] What *toppings* do you want on the pizza? [*noncount*] an ice-cream sundae with whipped-cream *topping*

top·ple /ˈtɑːpəl/ *verb* **top·ples; top·pled; top·pling**
1 : to cause (something) to become unsteady and fall [+ *obj*] The strong winds *toppled* many trees. ▪ The earthquake *toppled* the buildings. [*no obj*] The tree *toppled* into the river. — often + *over* ▪ The pile of books *toppled over*.
2 [+ *obj*] **a** : to remove (a government or a leader) from power : OVERTHROW ▪ The rebels tried to *topple* the dictator. **b** *US* : to win a victory over (someone or something) in a war, contest, etc. ▪ The team was *toppled* [=*beaten, defeated*] in the first round. ▪ The phone company has *toppled* its local competition.

top–ranking *adj, always used before a noun* : having the highest rank : most important, powerful, or successful ▪ *top-ranking* officials/students ▪ It's one of the *top-ranking* schools in the country.

[1]tops /ˈtɑːps/ *adj, not used before a noun, informal* : highest in quality, ability, popularity, or importance ▪ He is *tops* in his field. ▪ You're *tops* in my book!

[2]tops *adv, informal* : at the very most ▪ It should only cost $50, *tops*. [=the most it should cost is $50] ▪ It takes me 15 minutes *tops* to do the dishes.

top secret *adj* : kept completely secret by high government officials ▪ *top secret* weapons/documents ▪ The mission is *top secret*.

top–shelf /ˈtɑːpˈʃɛlf/ *adj* : of the best quality ▪ *top-shelf* liquors ▪ a *top-shelf* player

top·side /ˈtɑːpˈsaɪd/ *adv* : on or onto the deck of a ship ▪ Let's ***go topside***.

top·soil /ˈtɑːpˌsojəl/ *noun* [*noncount*] : the upper layer of soil in which plants have most of their roots ▪ rich, well-fertilized *topsoil*

top·spin /ˈtɑːpˌspɪn/ *noun* [*noncount*] : a forward spinning motion of a ball ▪ (*tennis*) She puts a lot of *topspin* on her serves to make them harder to return.

top·sy–tur·vy /ˌtɑːpsiˈtɚvi/ *adv* : in or into great disorder or confusion ▪ Her life was ***turned topsy-turvy*** when her husband left her.
– topsy–turvy *adj* ▪ this *topsy-turvy* world we live in

top–up /ˈtɑːpˌʌp/ *noun, pl* **-ups** [*count*] *Brit*
1 : an amount of liquid that is added to make something full
2 : a payment that is made to bring an amount of money to a certain level ▪ He got a *top-up* on his pension.

tor /ˈtoɚ/ *noun, pl* **tors** [*count*] *chiefly Brit* : a high, rocky hill

To·rah /ˈtorə/ *noun*
the Torah **1** : the wisdom and law contained in Jewish sacred writings and oral tradition **2** : the first five books of the Jewish Bible that are used in a synagogue for religious services — compare TALMUD

[1]torch /ˈtoɚʧ/ *noun, pl* **torch·es** [*count*]
1 : a long stick with material at one end that burns brightly ▪ the Olympic *torch* — often used figuratively ▪ the *torch* of truth/hope
2 : BLOWTORCH
3 *Brit* : FLASHLIGHT
carry a torch : to continue to have romantic feelings for someone who does not love you — usually + *for* ▪ Is she still *carrying a torch for* him after all this time?
carry the torch : to support or promote a cause in an enthusiastic way ▪ His children continue to *carry the torch* [=*crusade*] for justice.
pass the torch *chiefly US* ◊ If you ***pass the torch (on)*** *or* ***pass on the torch***, you give your job, duties, etc., to another person. ▪ He is retiring and *passing the torch on* to his successor. ▪ She says she's ready to *pass the torch*.

[2]torch *verb* **torches; torched; torch·ing** [+ *obj*] : to set fire to (something, such as a building) deliberately : to cause (something) to burn ▪ An arsonist *torched* the building.

torch·bear·er /ˈtoɚʧˌberɚ/ *noun, pl* **-ers** [*count*]
1 : someone who carries a torch at the head of a group of people
2 : someone who leads a campaign, movement, etc. ▪ He became the *torchbearer* for civil rights.

torch·light /ˈtoɚʧˌlaɪt/ *noun* [*noncount*]
1 : the light from a burning torch ▪ The men worked by *torchlight*. ▪ a *torchlight* parade/procession
2 *Brit* : the light from a flashlight

torch singer *noun, pl* **~ -ers** [*count*] : a singer of torch songs

torch song *noun, pl* **~ songs** [*count*] : a very sad or sentimental song about love and romance

tore *past tense of* [1]TEAR

to·re·a·dor /ˈtorijəˌdoɚ/ *noun, pl* **-dors** [*count*] : someone who fights bulls in a bullfight : BULLFIGHTER

to·re·ro /təˈrerou/ *noun, pl* **-ros** [*count*] : TOREADOR

[1]tor·ment /ˈtoɚˌmɛnt/ *noun, pl* **-ments**
1 [*noncount*] : extreme physical or mental pain ▪ She lived in *torment* [=*anguish*] for the rest of her life. ▪ No one could understand his inner *torment*. ▪ After years of *torment*, she left her husband.
2 [*count*] : something that causes extreme physical or mental pain ▪ The mosquitoes were a constant *torment*.

[2]tor·ment /toɚˈmɛnt/ *verb* **-ments; -ment·ed; -ment·ing** [+ *obj*] : to cause (someone or something) to feel extreme physical or mental pain ▪ Flies *tormented* the cattle. ▪ Not knowing where she was *tormented* him. ▪ Stop *tormenting* [=*annoying, teasing*] your sister! — often used as *(be) tor-*

mented by ▪ He *was tormented by* thoughts of death. ▪ She *was tormented by* her classmates.
– **tor·men·tor** /toɚˈmɛntɚ/ *noun, pl* **-tors** [*count*] ▪ She tried to avoid her *tormentors*.

torn *past participle of* [1]TEAR

tor·na·do /toɚˈneɪdoʊ/ *noun, pl* **-does** *or* **-dos** [*count*] : a violent and destructive storm in which powerful winds move around a central point ▪ in the path of a *tornado* ▪ a *tornado* warning

tornado

[1]**tor·pe·do** /toɚˈpiːdoʊ/ *noun, pl* **-does** [*count*] : a bomb that is shaped like a tube and that is fired underwater ▪ The battleship was sunk by a *torpedo* fired by a submarine.

[2]**torpedo** *verb* **-does; -doed; -do·ing** [+ *obj*]
1 : to hit or sink (a ship) with a torpedo ▪ The submarine *torpedoed* the battleship.
2 *somewhat informal* : to destroy or stop (something) completely ▪ Her injury *torpedoed* her goal of competing in the Olympics. ▪ He *torpedoed* the plan.

tor·pid /ˈtoɚpəd/ *adj* [*more* ~; *most* ~] *formal* : having or showing very little energy or movement : not active ▪ In winter, the frogs go into a *torpid* state. = The frogs become *torpid*. ▪ a *torpid* economy

tor·por /ˈtoɚpɚ/ *noun* [*singular*] *formal* : a state of not being active and having very little energy ▪ The news aroused him from his *torpor*. ▪ fall/sink into (a state of) *torpor*

torque /ˈtoɚk/ *noun* [*noncount*] *technical* : a force that causes something to rotate ▪ An automobile engine delivers *torque* to the driveshaft.

tor·rent /ˈtorənt/ *noun, pl* **-rents** [*count*]
1 : a large amount of water that moves very quickly in one direction ▪ The storm turned the stream into a raging *torrent*. ▪ *torrents* of rain ▪ The rain came down ***in torrents***.
2 : a large amount of something that is released suddenly — usually + *of* ▪ He responded with a *torrent of* criticism/abuse. ▪ The company receives *torrents of* e-mail every day.

tor·ren·tial /təˈrɛnʃəl/ *adj, always used before a noun* : coming in a large, fast stream ▪ *torrential* rains ▪ a *torrential* downpour ▪ The rain caused *torrential* flooding.

tor·rid /ˈtorəd/ *adj*
1 : very hot and usually dry ▪ a *torrid* summer ▪ *torrid* weather
2 : showing or expressing very strong feelings especially of sexual or romantic desire ▪ a *torrid* [=*passionate*] love affair
3 *Brit* : very difficult, uncomfortable, or unpleasant ▪ The team had a *torrid* time trying to score.

tor·sion /ˈtoɚʃən/ *noun* [*noncount*] *technical* : the twisting of something (such as a piece of metal)

tor·so /ˈtoɚsoʊ/ *noun, pl* **-sos** [*count*] : the main part of the human body not including the head, arms, and legs : TRUNK ▪ exercises that strengthen the/your *torso*

tort /ˈtoɚt/ *noun, pl* **torts** [*count*] *law* : an action that wrongly causes harm to someone but that is not a crime and that is dealt with in a civil court

torte /ˈtoɚt/ *noun, pl* **tortes** [*count*] : a type of cake that is made with many eggs and often nuts ▪ a chocolate *torte*

tor·tel·li·ni /ˌtoɚtəˈliːni/ *noun, pl* **tortellini** *also* **tor·tel·li·nis** [*count*] : pasta in the form of small, ring-shaped cases containing meat, cheese, etc. — see picture at PASTA

tor·ti·lla /toɚˈtiːjə/ *noun, pl* **-llas** [*count*] : a round, thin Mexican bread that is usually eaten hot with a filling of meat, cheese, etc.

tortilla chip *noun, pl* ~ **chips** [*count*] : a thin, hard piece of food (called a chip) that is made from corn and usually salted ▪ We had salsa and *tortilla chips* as an appetizer.

tor·toise /ˈtoɚtəs/ *noun, pl* **-tois·es** [*count*] : a kind of turtle that lives on land

tor·toise·shell /ˈtoɚtəˌʃɛl/ *noun, pl* **-shells**
1 [*count, noncount*] : the usually brown and yellow shell of a turtle that is used to make decorations
2 [*count*] : a cat with yellow, orange, white, and black fur
3 [*count*] : a usually brown and orange butterfly
– **tortoiseshell** *adj* ▪ *tortoiseshell* glasses ▪ a *tortoiseshell* comb ▪ a *tortoiseshell* cat/butterfly

tor·tu·ous /ˈtoɚʧəwəs/ *adj* [*more* ~; *most* ~]
1 : having many twists and turns ▪ a *tortuous* path/route up the mountain
2 : complicated, long, and confusing ▪ a *tortuous* argument/explanation
– **tor·tu·ous·ly** *adv* ▪ The road winds *tortuously* up the mountain.

[1]**tor·ture** /ˈtoɚʧɚ/ *noun* [*noncount*]
1 : the act of causing severe physical pain as a form of punishment or as a way to force someone to do or say something ▪ the *torture* of prisoners ▪ a *torture* chamber/device
2 : something that causes mental or physical suffering : a very painful or unpleasant experience ▪ Waiting is just *torture* for me. ▪ Listening to him can be *torture*.

[2]**torture** *verb* **-tures; -tured; -tur·ing** [+ *obj*]
1 : to cause (someone) to experience severe physical pain especially as a form of punishment or to force that person to do or say something ▪ The report revealed that prisoners had been repeatedly *tortured*.
2 : to cause (someone) to feel very worried, unhappy, etc. ▪ Don't *torture* yourself over the mistake.
– **tor·tur·er** /ˈtoɚʧərɚ/ *noun, pl* **-ers** [*count*]

tor·tur·ous /ˈtoɚʧərəs/ *adj* [*more* ~; *most* ~] : causing great pain or suffering ▪ *torturous* hardships ▪ a *torturous* workout
– **tor·tur·ous·ly** *adv*

To·ry /ˈtori/ *noun, pl* **-ries** [*count*] *informal* : a member of the British Conservative Party ▪ He's a *Tory*.
– **Tory** *adj* ▪ the *Tory* Party

tosh /ˈtɑːʃ/ *noun* [*noncount*] *Brit, informal* : NONSENSE ▪ What a lot/load of *tosh*.

[1]**toss** /ˈtɑːs/ *verb* **toss·es; tossed; toss·ing**
1 [+ *obj*] : to throw (something) with a quick, light motion ▪ I *tossed* the ball to him. = I *tossed* him the ball. ▪ She *tossed* the ball high in/into the air. ▪ She *tossed* the paper at/into the recycling bin. ▪ He *tossed* his dirty socks onto the floor.
2 [+ *obj*] : to move or lift (something, such as a part of your body) quickly or suddenly ▪ He *tossed* his head back. ▪ She *tossed* her hair and smiled.
3 : to move (something) back and forth or up and down [+ *obj*] Waves *tossed* the ship about. [*no obj*] The ship *tossed* on the waves.
4 [+ *obj*] : to stir or mix (something) lightly ▪ Gently *toss* the salad. ▪ *Toss* the vegetables with olive oil.
5 : to cause (something) to turn over by throwing it into the air [+ *obj*] *toss* a coin ▪ *toss* [=*flip*] a pancake [*no obj*] "Who's going to put out the trash?" "Let's *toss* for it." [=let's toss a coin to decide]
toss and turn : to move about and turn over in bed because you are unable to sleep ▪ She was *tossing and turning* all night.
toss back [*phrasal verb*] ***toss back (something) or toss (something) back informal*** : to drink (something) quickly ▪ He *tossed back* a shot of whiskey.
toss in [*phrasal verb*] ***toss in (something) or toss (something) in*** : to add (something) to what you are selling without asking for more money ▪ I'll even *toss in* [=*throw in*] an upgrade for free.
toss off [*phrasal verb*] **1** ***toss (something) off or toss off (something) informal*** **a** : to produce (something) quickly and without much effort ▪ He *tossed off* a few lines of poetry. **b** : to drink (something) quickly ▪ He *tossed off* a shot of whiskey. **2** ***toss (someone) off Brit, informal + impolite*** : MASTURBATE
toss out [*phrasal verb*] *US* **1** ***toss (something) out or toss out (something)*** **a** : to put (something that is no longer useful or wanted) in a trash can, garbage can, etc. : to throw (something) out ▪ It's time to *toss out* those bananas. ▪ Did you *toss* the newspapers *out* already? **b** : to refuse to accept or consider (something) ▪ His testimony was *tossed out* by the judge. **c** : to mention (something) as a possible thing to be done, thought about, etc. : SUGGEST ▪ She *tossed out* a couple of ideas for improving the company's Web site. **2** ***toss (someone) out or toss out (someone)*** : to force (someone) to leave a place ▪ They *tossed* him *out* [=threw him out] of the bar after he started a fight.
toss your hat in/into the ring see HAT

[2]**toss** *noun, pl* **tosses** [*count*]
1 : the act of throwing or tossing something with a quick, light motion ▪ a bouquet *toss* ▪ He gave the salad a quick *toss*. [=he tossed the salad]— see also RING TOSS
2 : the act of throwing a coin up into the air in order to make a decision about something based on which side of the coin is shown after it lands ▪ They decided what to do by a

coin *toss*. ▪ the *toss* of a coin ▪ She won the *toss*.

3 : the act of moving your head suddenly upward and backward ▪ She threw her hair back with a *toss* of her head.

argue the toss *chiefly Brit, informal* **:** to argue or disagree about something that is not important, that cannot be changed, etc.

not give a toss *Brit, informal* **:** to not care at all about something ▪ He does*n't give a toss* about our problems.

toss·er /ˈtɑːsɚ/ *noun, pl* **-ers** [*count*] *Brit slang* **:** a stupid or unpleasant person

toss–up /ˈtɑːsˌʌp/ *noun* [*singular*] **:** a situation in which there is no clear right choice or in which what will happen is not known ▪ The election is a *toss-up*.

¹tot /ˈtɑːt/ *noun, pl* **tots** [*count*]

1 *informal* **:** a young child ▪ cute little *tots*

2 *Brit* **:** a small amount of a strong alcoholic drink ▪ a *tot* of rum

²tot *verb* **tots; tot·ted; tot·ting**

tot up [*phrasal verb*] ***tot (something) up*** *or* ***tot up (something)*** *Brit, informal* **:** to add numbers together to find out the total ▪ He *totted up* [=*totaled*] the bill.

¹to·tal /ˈtoʊtl̩/ *adj*

1 : complete or absolute ▪ *total* [=*utter, sheer*] chaos/destruction/ruin ▪ *total* darkness/freedom ▪ It's a *total* loss. ▪ a *total* lack of support/sympathy/understanding ▪ a *total* eclipse of the sun ▪ He demanded *total* control of/over the project. ▪ a *total* stranger

2 : after everything or everyone is counted ▪ What was the *total* amount of the bill? ▪ the *total* annual budget/cost/sales ▪ the *total* number of words ▪ The country has a *total* population of about 100 million.

²total *noun, pl* **-tals** [*count*] **:** the number or amount of everything counted **:** SUM ▪ The *total* is 64. ▪ a *total* of 25 square miles — see also GRAND TOTAL, SUBTOTAL, SUM TOTAL

³total *verb* **-tals;** *US* **-taled** *or Brit* **-talled;** *US* **-tal·ing** *or Brit* **-tal·ling** [+ *obj*]

1 a : to produce (a total) when added together ▪ Donations *totaled* $120. **b :** to add numbers together to find out the total ▪ He carefully *totaled* the bill. — often + *up* ▪ He *totaled up* the bill.

2 *US* **:** to damage (something, such as a car) so badly that it is not worth repairing ▪ He *totaled* the car.

to·tal·i·tar·i·an /toʊˌtæləˈterijən/ *adj* **:** controlling the people of a country in a very strict way with complete power that cannot be opposed ▪ a *totalitarian* regime/state

– to·tal·i·tar·i·an·ism /toʊˌtæləˈterijəˌnɪzəm/ *noun* [*noncount*]

to·tal·i·ty /toʊˈtæləti/ *noun* [*noncount*] **:** the whole or entire amount of something ▪ the *totality* of human knowledge

in its/their totality **:** with nothing left out ▪ The exhibit must be viewed *in its totality* to be properly understood.

to·tal·ly /ˈtoʊtl̩i/ *adv* **:** completely or entirely ▪ I'm *totally* against it. ▪ He was *totally* naked. ▪ *totally* committed/free/surprised ▪ That's a *totally* different issue. ▪ He's *totally* in control. ▪ a *totally* new method

tote /ˈtoʊt/ *verb* **totes; tot·ed; tot·ing** [+ *obj*] **:** to carry (something) ▪ She's been *toting* that bag all day. ▪ a book-*toting* professor — often + *around* ▪ He's always *toting* tools *around*.

– tot·er /ˈtoʊtɚ/ *noun, pl* **-ers** [*count*] ▪ gun-*toters*

tote bag *noun, pl* **~ bags** [*count*] **:** a large bag used for carrying things — see picture at BAG

tote board /ˈtoʊtˌboɚd/ *noun, pl* **~ boards** [*count*] *US* **:** a large, electrically operated board at a racetrack that shows the odds for a race, the results of a race, etc.

to·tem /ˈtoʊtəm/ *noun, pl* **-tems** [*count*]

1 a : something (such as an animal or plant) that is the symbol for a family, tribe, etc., especially among Native Americans **b :** a usually carved or painted figure that represents such a symbol

2 : a person or thing that represents an idea ▪ Private jets are a *totem* of success among extremely wealthy people.

– to·tem·ic /toʊˈtɛmɪk/ *adj* ▪ *totemic* images

totem pole *noun, pl* **~ poles** [*count*]

1 : a tall usually wooden pole that is carved and painted with symbols, figures, or masks which represent different Native American tribes

2 *US, informal* — used to describe someone's position or level in a company or organization ▪ She's rather low on the company's *totem pole*. [=she does not have an important position in the company] ▪ He knows that he is (the) ***low man on the totem pole*** [=he has the lowest rank; he is the least important/powerful person]

tot·ter /ˈtɑːtɚ/ *verb* **-ters; -tered; -ter·ing** [*no obj*]

1 *always followed by an adverb or preposition* **:** to move or walk in a slow and unsteady way ▪ The child *tottered* across the room. ▪ He *tottered* away/off to bed.

2 : to become weak and likely to fail or collapse ▪ The economy is *tottering*. ▪ a *tottering* company

tou·can /ˈtuːˌkæn/ *noun, pl* **-cans** [*count*] **:** a tropical American bird that has bright feathers and a very large beak

¹touch /ˈtʌʧ/ *verb* **touch·es; touched; touch·ing**

1 : to put your hand, fingers, etc., on someone or something [+ *obj*] Please do not *touch* the statue. ▪ Slowly bend forward and try to *touch* your toes. ▪ Stop *touching* your sister. ▪ He tried to *touch* the snake with a stick. [*no obj*] — usually used in negative statements ▪ You can look (at the statue) but don't *touch*!

2 : to be in contact with (something) — used to say that one thing is directly against another thing with no space between [+ *obj*] The top of the Christmas tree almost *touches* the ceiling. ▪ Sparks flew when the wires *touched* each other. [*no obj*] They were standing side-by-side with their shoulders *touching*. ▪ Sparks flew when the wires *touched*.

3 [+ *obj*] **a :** to change or move (something) — usually used in negative statements ▪ Don't *touch* anything before the police come. ▪ Your things haven't been *touched* while you were away. ▪ This room hasn't been *touched* in 20 years. **b :** to harm (someone or something) ▪ Their house burned to the ground, but the house next door wasn't *touched* by the fire. ▪ I won't let anyone *touch* you. = I won't let anyone ***touch a hair on your head***

4 [+ *obj*] **a :** to deal with or work on (something) ▪ I haven't *touched* my essay all week, and it's due this Friday! **b :** to become involved with (someone or something) ▪ He's a good player, but since he failed the drug test, no team will *touch* him. ▪ Everything she *touches* turns to gold. [=everything she is involved with becomes successful]

5 [+ *obj*] **:** to use (something) — usually used in negative statements ▪ She never *touches* [=*drinks*] alcohol. ▪ The dog hasn't *touched* [=*eaten*] its food. ▪ We haven't *touched* the money in our savings account. ▪ Alcohol? I never ***touch the stuff***

6 [+ *obj*] **a :** to affect or involve (someone) ▪ Air pollution is a matter that *touches* [=*concerns*] everyone. **b :** to affect the feelings of (someone) **:** to cause (someone) to feel an emotion (such as sympathy or gratitude) ▪ His neighbors' acts of kindness *touched* him deeply. ▪ She wants to *touch* her audience through her music. ▪ The story seemed to ***touch the hearts*** of the students. — see also TOUCHING

7 [+ *obj*] **:** to influence (something) ▪ As a teacher, she ***touched the lives*** of many young people.

8 [+ *obj*] **:** to be as good as (someone or something) — usually used in negative statements ▪ No one can *touch* her when it comes to songwriting. [=she is much better than everyone else as a songwriter] ▪ You can't *touch* her songwriting ability.

9 [+ *obj*] *chiefly Brit* **:** to reach (a particular level or amount) ▪ The temperature outside was *touching* 38 degrees Celsius.

10 [+ *obj*] *baseball* **:** to get a hit off or score a run against (a pitcher) — usually + *for* ▪ He was *touched for* a run in the first inning. [=they scored a run off him in the first inning]

11 [+ *obj*] *literary* **:** to appear on (something) ▪ A smile *touched* her lips. [=she smiled slightly]

not touch (someone or something) with a ten-foot pole (*US*) *or Brit* ***not touch (someone or something) with a bargepole*** *informal* **:** to refuse to go near or become involved with (someone or something) ▪ That investment is too risky. I would*n't touch it with a ten-foot pole*.

touch a chord see ²CHORD

touch all the bases *or* ***touch every base*** see ¹BASE

touch a nerve see NERVE

touch base see ¹BASE

touch down [*phrasal verb*] **1 :** to return to the ground or another surface after a flight **:** LAND ▪ The plane *touched down* at 3:15. **2** ***touch (the ball) down*** *or* ***touch down (the ball)*** *rugby* **:** to score by putting (the ball) on the ground behind an opponent's goal line ▪ He *touched* the ball *down* under the posts. — see also TOUCHDOWN

touch for [*phrasal verb*] ***touch (someone) for (something)*** *informal Brit* **:** to persuade (someone) to give or lend you (an amount of money) ▪ He *touched* me *for* a tenner. — see also ¹TOUCH 10 (above)

touch off [*phrasal verb*] ***touch off (something)*** *or* ***touch (something) off*** **:** to cause (something) to start suddenly ▪

What *touched off* the fire? ▪ The judge's verdict *touched off* riots throughout the city.

touch on/upon [*phrasal verb*] ***touch on/upon (something)*** **1** : to briefly talk or write about (something) : to mention (something) briefly ▪ The reports *touched on* many important points. ▪ She *touches upon* the issue in the article but never fully explains it. **2** : to come close to (something) : to almost be (something) ▪ Your actions *touch on* [=*verge on*] treason.

touch up [*phrasal verb*] **1** ***touch up (something)*** *or* ***touch (something) up*** : to improve (something) by making small changes or additions ▪ She *touched up* the photographs on the computer. **2** ***touch (someone) up*** *or* ***touch up (someone)*** *Brit, informal* : to touch (someone) in a sexual way ▪ He tried to *touch* her *up* [=feel her up] at the party.

touch wood see [1]WOOD

touch your forelock see FORELOCK

[2]touch *noun, pl* **touches**

1 [*count*] : the act of touching someone or something — usually singular ▪ He felt a gentle *touch* on his shoulder. ▪ Fax machines allow you to send a document with/at the *touch* [=*push*] of a button. [=by touching/pushing a button]

2 [*noncount*] : the ability to be aware of something physical by touching it : the sense that allows you to feel physical things ▪ Blind since birth, she relies on her sense of *touch* to read braille. ▪ Sand the wood until it is smooth ***to the touch***. [=until it feels smooth when you touch it] ▪ The plate was hot *to the touch*.

3 [*singular*] : the quality of a thing that is experienced by feeling or touching it ▪ the smooth *touch* [=*feel*] of silk

4 [*count*] : a small detail that is added to improve or complete something — usually + *to* ▪ He added the final *touches to* the letter and mailed it. ▪ The candles and light jazz music added a nice *touch to* their dinner together.

5 [*singular*] : a quality that can be seen in the way something is done ▪ The painting showed the *touch* of a master. ▪ Here at our hotel, we strive to provide service with a personal *touch*. ▪ This room needs a ***woman's/feminine touch***. [=it needs a woman to help decorate it] ▪ He has a ***magic touch*** with animals. [=he is able to calm and control animals with unusual ease] — see also MIDAS TOUCH

6 [*count*] : an act of handling or controlling the ball in a sport (such as basketball, soccer, or American football) ▪ That was her first *touch* of the game.

7 [*noncount*] : the area outside of the lines that mark the long edges of the playing area in soccer or rugby ▪ The ball went into *touch*. ▪ The ball was thrown in by a player standing in *touch*.

a touch : to a small extent : SLIGHTLY ▪ She aimed *a touch* [=*a bit, a little*] too low and missed. ▪ Can you turn up the radio *a touch* more?

a touch of : a small amount of (something) : a hint or trace of (something) ▪ She noticed *a touch of* garlic in the sauce. ▪ I think I have *a touch of* the flu.

finishing touch see [1]FINISH

in touch **1** : in a state in which people communicate with each other especially by calling or writing to each other ▪ We kept/stayed *in touch* after college. — often + *with* ▪ I'll be *in touch with* you [=I will call you, e-mail you, etc.] later this week. ▪ I have been trying to get *in touch with* her all day. **2 a** : the state of being aware of what is happening, how a particular group of people feels, etc. — usually + *with* ▪ As a professor of biology, it is important to keep/stay *in touch with* the latest research. ▪ She is *in touch with* the voters and their needs. **b** : the state of being aware of a particular part of your character that is not easily noticed — usually + *with* ▪ He is *in touch with* his sensitive side. ▪ She meditates to get *in touch with* her inner self.

lose touch **1** : to stop communicating with each other : to no longer know what is happening in each other's lives ▪ They were friends in college, but then they moved to different cities and *lost touch*. — often + *with* ▪ She *lost touch with* her college roommate after graduation. **2** : to stop knowing what is happening, how a particular group of people feels, etc. — usually + *with* ▪ I read the newspaper every morning so that I don't completely *lose touch with* what's happening in the world. ▪ She seems to have ***lost touch with reality*** [=she believes things that are not true] and thinks that she can have everything she wants.

lose your touch : to no longer have the ability to do things that you were able to do successfully in the past ▪ His last album flopped; he seems to be *losing his touch*. ▪ I must have *lost my touch*; I can't get this camera to work anymore.

out of touch **1** : not communicating with each other ▪ I don't know if he still lives there. We've been *out of touch* for some time. **2** : in a state of not knowing what is happening, how a particular group of people feels, etc. ▪ I've been away from the business for several years and feel quite *out of touch*. — usually + *with* ▪ He is *out of touch with* the younger generation.

— see also COMMON TOUCH, SOFT TOUCH

touch and go *adj, informal* — used to describe a situation in which no one is sure what will happen and there is a chance that the result will be bad ▪ It was *touch and go* there for a while, but the patient survived.

touch·back /ˈtʌʧˌbæk/ *noun, pl* **-backs** [*count*] *American football* : a situation in which the ball is put out of play behind the goal line after a kick or interception ✧ After a touchback, the team with the ball begins play on its own 20-yard line.

touch·down /ˈtʌʧˌdaʊn/ *noun, pl* **-downs**

1 [*count*] *American football* : a score that is made by carrying the ball over the opponent's goal line or by catching the ball while standing in the end zone ▪ He scored a *touchdown*. ▪ The quarterback threw a *touchdown* (pass) to the wide receiver. ▪ They won the game by a *touchdown*. [=by seven points] ✧ A touchdown is worth six points and is usually followed by a kick that is worth another point.

2 [*count*] *rugby* : the act of scoring points by putting the ball on the ground behind an opponent's goal line

3 [*count, noncount*] : the moment when an airplane or spacecraft touches the ground at the end of a flight ▪ What was the plane's speed at *touchdown*?

— see also *touch down* at [1]TOUCH

tou·ché /tuˈʃeɪ/ *interj* — used to admit that someone has made a clever or effective point in an argument

touched /ˈtʌʧt/ *adj, not used before a noun*

1 : having a small amount of something — usually + *with* ▪ His hair was *touched with* gray.

2 [*more ~; most ~*] : having emotional feelings because you are grateful or pleased by what someone has done or said ▪ She was *touched* that he had come only to see her. ▪ We were very *touched* by their story.

3 *informal + old-fashioned* : slightly crazy ▪ He's a bit *touched* (in the head).

touch football *noun* [*noncount*] : a form of American football in which the player with the ball is not tackled but instead must stop when touched by an opponent

touch·ing /ˈtʌʧɪŋ/ *adj* [*more ~; most ~*] : having a strong emotional effect : causing feelings of sadness or sympathy ▪ Their story was deeply/very *touching*. [=*moving*]

— **touch·ing·ly** *adv*

touch·line /ˈtʌʧˌlaɪn/ *noun, pl* **-lines** [*count*] : either one of the lines that mark the long sides of the playing field in rugby or soccer

touch pad *noun, pl* **~ pads** [*count*] : a flat surface on an electronic device (such as a microwave oven) that is divided into several differently marked areas which you can touch to choose options ▪ Press the start button on the *touch pad*.

touch screen *noun, pl* **~ screens** [*count*] *computers* : a type of screen on a computer which shows options that you can choose by touching the screen

touch·stone /ˈtʌʧˌstoʊn/ *noun, pl* **-stones** [*count*] : something that is used to make judgments about the quality of other things ▪ Good service is one *touchstone* of a first-class restaurant.

touch–tone /ˈtʌʧˈtoʊn/ *adj, always used before a noun* : having numbered buttons that produce different sounds when they are pushed ▪ a *touch-tone* phone

touch–type /ˈtʌʧˌtaɪp/ *verb* **-types; -typed; -typ·ing** [*no obj*] : to type without looking at the keyboard ▪ The class taught him how to *touch-type*.

touchy /ˈtʌʧi/ *adj* **touch·i·er; -est** [*also more ~; most ~*]

1 : easily hurt or upset by the things that people think or say about you : SENSITIVE ▪ Don't be so *touchy*. I was just kidding. — often + *about* ▪ He's a little *touchy about* his weight. [=he tends to get upset if you say anything about his weight]

2 : likely to cause people to become upset ▪ a *touchy* subject

— **touch·i·ness** /ˈtʌʧinəs/ *noun* [*noncount*]

touchy–feely /ˌtʌʧiˈfiːli/ *adj* [*more ~; most ~*] *informal + usually disapproving* : very emotional and personal : tending to show emotions very openly ▪ Some teachers get all *touchy-feely* with their students. ▪ *touchy-feely* people

[1]tough /ˈtʌf/ *adj* **tough·er; tough·est**

1 : very difficult to do or deal with ▪ a *tough* [=*hard*] assignment/problem ▪ *tough* choices ▪ She had a *tough* time in college. ▪ It's been a *tough* year for our family. = This year has been ***tough on*** [=*hard on*] our family. — often followed by *to* + *verb* ▪ It was *tough to quit* smoking. ▪ The problem was *tough to solve*.

2 a : physically and emotionally strong : able to do hard work, to deal with harsh conditions, etc. ▪ *tough* soldiers ▪ Are you *tough* enough for the job? **b :** physically strong and violent ▪ *tough* criminals ▪ He's been hanging around with a bunch of *tough* guys.

3 a : strong and not easily broken or damaged ▪ *tough* fibers ▪ The rug is made of *tough* material. **b :** difficult to cut or chew ▪ *tough* meat

4 : very strict ▪ a *tough* law/policy ▪ He's a *tough* boss/teacher, but fair. ▪ The candidates both vow to ***get tough on*** crime. [=to deal harshly with criminals]

5 : having a lot of crime or danger ▪ a *tough* neighborhood

6 : hard to influence or persuade ▪ She's a *tough* bargainer/negotiator.

7 *informal* **:** unfortunate in a way that seems unfair ▪ It's *tough* that he lost that job. — often used in an ironic way to show that you do not feel sympathy for someone ▪ "He failed the test." "Well, that's *tough*. Maybe if he'd studied a little he would have passed." ▪ He failed the test? *Tough*! [=*too bad*] He should have studied more than he did. — see also *tough luck* at [1]LUCK

(as) tough as nails see [1]NAIL

(as) tough as old boots *Brit, informal* **:** very tough ▪ This steak is *as tough as old boots*. ▪ Don't worry about her—she's *as tough as old boots*.

a tough act to follow see FOLLOW

a tough nut (to crack) see NUT

a tough row to hoe see [1]ROW

hang tough see [1]HANG

– tough·ly *adv* **– tough·ness** *noun* [*noncount*]

[2]tough *verb* **toughs; toughed; tough·ing**

tough it out *informal* **:** to deal with a difficult situation by being determined and refusing to quit ▪ She hated her job, but she *toughed it out* until she found a better one. ▪ Can you *tough it out* until the end of the game?

[3]tough *noun, pl* **toughs** [*count*] *informal + old-fashioned* **:** a tough and violent person ▪ a gang of *toughs*

[4]tough *adv* **:** in a way that shows that you are strong or tough ▪ play *tough* ▪ He talks *tough* but he's not really dangerous.

tough·en /ˈtʌfən/ *verb* **-ens; -ened; -en·ing**

1 : to make (something) stricter or to become stricter [+ *obj*] The government is *toughening* antidrug laws. — often + *up* ▪ The antidrug laws have been *toughened up* recently. [*no obj*] — usually + *up* ▪ The antidrug laws have *toughened up* recently.

2 : to make (someone) physically or emotionally stronger or to become physically or emotionally stronger [+ *obj*] The experience *toughened* him. — often + *up* ▪ The experience *toughened* him *up*. [*no obj*] — usually + *up* ▪ You need to *toughen up* if you want to succeed in this business.

tough·ie /ˈtʌfi/ *noun, pl* **-ies** [*count*] *informal*

1 : a difficult problem or question ▪ The last question on the test was a *toughie*.

2 : a tough person : a strong person who is not afraid ▪ He thinks he's a real *toughie*.

tough love *noun* [*noncount*] **:** love or concern that is expressed in a strict way especially to make someone behave responsibly

tou·pee /tuˈpeɪ/ *noun, pl* **-pees** [*count*] **:** a small wig that is worn by a man to cover a bald spot on his head

[1]tour /ˈtuɚ/ *noun, pl* **tours**

1 [*count*] **a :** a journey through the different parts of a country, region, etc. ▪ We went on a *tour* of Italy. ▪ They went on a driving *tour* of New England. ▪ a sightseeing *tour* ▪ We hired a ***tour guide***. [=a person who takes people on trips through an area and explains the interesting details about it] **b :** an activity in which you go through a place (such as a building or city) in order to see and learn about the different parts of it ▪ They went on a *tour* of the city. ▪ We were taken on a *tour* of/through the school. ▪ We went on a guided *tour* of the museum. ▪ They gave us a *tour* of their new house. ▪ We made a *tour* of the garden. [=we walked around the garden] ▪ a ***tour of inspection*** [=an activity in which someone goes through a place in order to see if things are in the proper condition] — see also GRAND TOUR

2 : a series of related performances, appearances, competitions, etc., that occur at different places over a period of time [*count*] a golf/book/concert *tour* [*noncount*] The band will be ***on tour*** [=traveling on a tour] for the next month.

3 [*count*] **:** a period of time during which someone (such as a soldier) is on duty or in a certain place ▪ during his *tour* in Vietnam ▪ He served a ***tour of duty*** in Germany.

[2]tour *verb* **tours; toured; tour·ing**

1 : to make a journey or trip through an area or place : to make a tour of (something) [+ *obj*] We *toured* London. ▪ We'll *tour* the museum tomorrow. [*no obj*] We *toured* around for several weeks last summer. ▪ "Are you here to study?" "No, I'm just *touring*."

2 : to travel from place to place to perform, give speeches, etc. [*no obj*] Is the band *touring* this year? [+ *obj*] The show has *toured* the country.

tour de force /ˌtuɚdəˈfoɚs/ *noun* [*singular*] **:** a very skillful and successful effort or performance ▪ The book/film is a *tour de force*. ▪ Her performance in the play was a real *tour de force*.

Tou·rette's syndrome /tʊˈrɛts-/ *noun* [*noncount*] *medical* **:** a disorder that causes someone to move and speak in an uncontrolled way

tour·ism /ˈtuɚˌɪzəm/ *noun* [*noncount*]

1 : the activity of traveling to a place for pleasure ▪ The city developed the riverfront to encourage/promote *tourism*.

2 : the business of providing hotels, restaurants, entertainment, etc., for people who are traveling ▪ the *tourism* industry ▪ She has a job in *tourism*.

tour·ist /ˈturɪst/ *noun, pl* **-ists** [*count*]

1 : a person who travels to a place for pleasure ▪ The museums attract a lot of *tourists*. ▪ In the summer the town is filled with *tourists*.

2 *Brit* **:** a member of a sports team that is playing a series of official games in a foreign country ▪ The *tourists* defeated the home side.

– tourist *adj, always used before a noun* ▪ The museum is a big *tourist* attraction/destination. ▪ She has a job in the *tourist* industry.

tourist class *noun* [*noncount*] **:** the cheapest seats on an airplane or the cheapest rooms on a ship or in a hotel ▪ *Tourist class* is all we could afford.

– tourist class *adv* ▪ We traveled *tourist class* on the ship.

tourist trap *noun, pl* **~ traps** [*count*] *disapproving* **:** a place that attracts many tourists and that charges high prices ▪ The street market is a *tourist trap* that mostly sells cheap souvenirs. ▪ That hotel is just a *tourist trap*.

touristy /ˈturəsti/ *adj* [*more ~; most ~*] *informal + often disapproving* **:** attracting or appealing to tourists ▪ *touristy* souvenirs ▪ *touristy* activities/restaurants ▪ When we travel we usually try to avoid the *touristy* areas. [=the areas where there are a lot of tourists]

tour·na·ment /ˈtuɚnəmənt/ *noun, pl* **-ments** [*count*]

1 : a sports competition or series of contests that involves many players or teams and that usually continues for at least several days ▪ a basketball/golf *tournament* ▪ She's an excellent tennis player who has won many *tournaments*.

2 : a contest of skill and courage between soldiers or knights in the Middle Ages

tour·ney /ˈtuɚni/ *noun, pl* **-neys** [*count*] *chiefly US, informal* **:** TOURNAMENT 1 ▪ a tennis *tourney*

tour·ni·quet /ˈtuɚnɪkət/ *noun, pl* **-quets** [*count*] **:** a bandage, strip of cloth, etc., that is tied tightly around an injured arm or leg to stop or slow the bleeding from a wound

tou·sle /ˈtaʊzəl/ *verb* **tou·sles; tou·sled; tou·sling** [+ *obj*] **:** to make (someone's hair) untidy ▪ She *tousled* the little boy's hair.

[1]tout /ˈtaʊt/ *verb* **touts; tout·ed; tout·ing**

1 [+ *obj*] **:** to talk about (something or someone) as being very good, effective, skillful, etc. ▪ The company is running advertisements *touting* the drug's effectiveness. ▪ The company's stock is being *touted* by many financial advisers. ▪ the college's much *touted* [=*praised*] women's studies program — often + *as* ▪ The company is *touting* the drug *as* a miracle cure. ▪ She is being *touted* [=*promoted*] *as* a likely candidate for the Senate.

2 *Brit* **:** to try to persuade people to buy your goods or services [*no obj*] — + *for* ▪ They *touted for* business/customers everywhere but had few takers. [+ *obj*] vendors *touting* their wares

3 *Brit* **:** to buy tickets for an event and resell them at a much higher price **:** SCALP [+ *obj*] People were *touting* tickets outside the stadium. [no obj] People were *touting* outside the stadium.

²tout *noun, pl* **touts** [*count*]
1 *US* : a person who sells information about which horses are likely to win the races at a racetrack
2 *Brit* : a person who buys tickets for an event and resells them at a much higher price • ticket *touts* [=(*US*) *scalpers*]

¹tow /ˈtou/ *verb* **tows; towed; tow•ing** [+ *obj*] : to pull (a vehicle) behind another vehicle with a rope or chain • The car was *towed* to the nearest garage after the accident. • The police *towed* my car because it was parked illegally.

²tow *noun, pl* **tows** [*count*] : the act of pulling a vehicle behind another vehicle with a rope or chain — usually singular • He called for a *tow* to the nearest garage.
in tow **1** *or* ***under tow*** *or Brit* ***on tow*** — used to describe a situation in which one vehicle, boat, etc., is being pulled by another • a car with a boat *in tow* • The damaged ship was brought into the harbor *under tow.* ✧ If a ship or boat is ***taken in tow***, it is tied to and pulled by another boat or ship. This phrase is often used figuratively. • The tourists were *taken in tow* by a friendly guide. **2** *informal* — used to describe a situation in which someone is going somewhere with another person or group • a woman with seven children *in tow*

to•ward /ˈtowəd, ˈtoəd/ *or* **to•wards** /ˈtowədz, ˈtoədz/ *prep*
1 a : in the direction of (something or someone) • The bus is heading *toward* town. • She took a step *toward* the door. • He leaned *towards* me. **b** — used to indicate the direction faced by something • Turn the chair *toward* the window. • The mirrors are pointed *toward* each other.
2 a : near (a particular place) • They live out *towards* the edge of town. **b** : not long before (a particular time) • It was (getting) *toward* noon when they arrived. • We're thinking of taking a vacation *towards* the end of the month.
3 : in a process that is intended to produce or achieve (something) • Efforts *toward* peace have been largely unsuccessful. • a step/trend *towards* democracy
4 : in regard to (something or someone) • He has a generally positive attitude *toward* [=*about*] life. • She's been very kind *towards* them. [=she has treated them very kindly]
5 : as part of the payment for (something) • We put $100 *toward* a new sofa.

tow•away zone /ˈtowə,weɪ-/ *noun, pl* ~ **zones** [*count*] *US* : an area where parking is not allowed and where a parked car will be towed

tow bar *noun, pl* ~ **bars** [*count*] : a metal bar on the back of a vehicle that is used for towing something (such as a vehicle or trailer)

¹tow•el /ˈtawəl/ *noun, pl* **-els** [*count*] : a piece of cloth used for drying things • She dried her hair with a *towel.* • Here's a *towel* to wipe up the spill. — see also BEACH TOWEL, DISH TOWEL, HAND TOWEL, PAPER TOWEL
throw in the towel *informal* : to stop an activity or effort : to admit that you cannot do something and stop trying : QUIT • I *threw in the towel* a long time ago. • He couldn't seem to win, but he wasn't ready to *throw in the towel.*

²towel *verb* **-els**; *US* **-eled** *or Brit* **-elled**; *US* **-el•ing** *or Brit* **-el•ling** : to dry (something) with a towel [+ *obj*] He *toweled* (off) his hair. [*no obj*] — + *off* or *down* • She climbed out of the tub and quickly *toweled off.* [=dried herself with a towel]

tow•el•ling /ˈtawəlɪŋ/ *noun* [*noncount*] *Brit* : TERRY CLOTH

towel rack *noun, pl* ~ **racks** [*count*] *US* : a bar on which a towel is hung in a bathroom — called also (*US*) *towel bar,* (*chiefly Brit*) *towel rail*; see picture at BATHROOM

¹tow•er /ˈtawə/ *noun, pl* **-ers** [*count*]
1 : a tall, narrow building or structure that may stand apart from or be attached to another building or structure • a bell/clock/radio *tower* • the church *tower* • a cell phone *tower* — see also IVORY TOWER, WATCHTOWER, WATER TOWER
2 : a tall piece of furniture used to store something • a CD/DVD *tower*
3 *computers* : a personal computer that stands in an upright position — see picture at COMPUTER
tower of strength : an emotionally strong person who gives a lot of support or help during difficult times • She's been a/my *tower of strength* during my illness.

²tower *verb* **-ers; -ered; -er•ing**
tower above/over [*phrasal verb*] ***tower over/above (someone or something)*** **1** : to be much taller than (someone or something) • He *towers over* his sister. • The two skyscrapers *tower above* the other buildings of the city. **2** : to be much better or more important than (someone or something) • Her intellect *towers above/over* ours.

tower block *noun, pl* ~ **blocks** [*count*] *Brit* : a very tall building that contains apartments or offices

tow•er•ing /ˈtawərɪŋ/ *adj, always used before a noun*
1 : very tall • *towering* mountain peaks • *towering* skyscrapers
2 : very powerful or intense • He flew into a *towering* rage.
3 : very great or impressive • a *towering* performance

tow•head /ˈtou,hɛd/ *noun, pl* **-heads** [*count*] *US, informal* + *old-fashioned* : a person with very light blond hair
– tow•head•ed /ˈtou,hɛdəd/ *adj* • a *towheaded* child

tow•line /ˈtou,laɪn/ *noun, pl* **-lines** [*count*] : a rope or chain used for towing vehicles

town /ˈtaun/ *noun, pl* **towns**
1 [*count*] : a place where people live that is larger than a village but smaller than a city • a *town* in Georgia • a mining *town* • the *town* of Jackson, Florida • The nearest shopping mall is two *towns* away. • *town* officials — see also COUNTY TOWN, GHOST TOWN, SHANTYTOWN, TWIN TOWN
2 a [*count*] : the people in a town — usually singular • I think the entire *town* has heard the news by now. • The whole *town* was at the parade. **b** ***the town*** : the government of a town • *The town* plans to increase property taxes.
3 [*noncount*] : the business and shopping center of a town • We're heading to *town* later on. — see also DOWNTOWN, UPTOWN
4 : the town where someone lives [*noncount*] He left *town* when he was 16. • The circus is coming to *town.* • the *town* parade • This is the best restaurant ***in town.*** [=in this town] • Let's get together. I'll be *in town* next week. [=I'll be in your town next week] • She's from ***out of town.*** [=from a different town] [*singular*] My *town* has changed a lot over the years. — see also HOMETOWN
go to town *informal* : to do something in a very thorough and enthusiastic way • When they throw a party, they really *go to town.* [=they spend a lot of money and have a big party] — often + *on* • She really *went to town on* the decorations for the party.
hit the town *informal* : to spend time in the area of a city or town where there are a lot of restaurants, bars, etc. • We're planning to *hit the town* tomorrow.
(out) on the town *informal* : going to the restaurants, bars, etc., of a city or town for entertainment • We spent the night *out on the town.*
paint the town (red) see ²PAINT
the talk of the town see ²TALK

town centre *noun, pl* ~ **centres** [*count*] *Brit* : the main or central part of a town — compare CITY CENTRE, DOWNTOWN

town crier *noun, pl* ~ **-ers** [*count*] *old-fashioned* : an official who made public announcements in past times

town hall *noun, pl* ~ **halls** [*count*] : a town government's main building — usually singular

town house *noun, pl* ~ **houses** [*count*]
1 *US* : a house that has two or three levels and that is attached to a similar house by a shared wall
2 : a house in a city or town; *especially* : a house in a town or city owned by someone who also has a house in the country

town•ie /ˈtauni/ *noun, pl* **-ies** [*count*] *informal*
1 : a person who lives in a town or city
2 *US* : a person who lives in a town that has a college or university but does not work at or attend the school • fights between *townies* and college kids

town meeting *noun, pl* ~ **-ings** [*count*] : a meeting of the people who live in a town to pass laws for the town or to discuss town problems, issues, etc.

town•scape /ˈtaun,skeɪp/ *noun, pl* **-scapes**
1 [*noncount*] : the area where a town is and the way it looks
2 [*count*] : a picture that shows part or all of a town • historic *townscapes*

towns•folk /ˈtaunz,fouk/ *noun* [*plural*] : the people who live in a town : TOWNSPEOPLE

town•ship /ˈtaun,ʃɪp/ *noun, pl* **-ships** [*count*] : a unit of local government in the U.S.

towns•peo•ple /ˈtaunz,pi:pəl/ *noun* [*plural*] : the people who live in a town or city

tow•path /ˈtou,pæθ, *Brit* ˈtəu,pɑ:θ/ *noun, pl* **-paths** [*count*] *old-fashioned* : a path along a river or canal used by people or horses for towing boats

tow•rope *noun, pl* **-ropes** [*count*] : a rope or chain used for towing vehicles

tow truck *noun, pl* ~ **trucks** [*count*] : a truck with special equipment on the back of it to tow away vehicles — called also (*Brit*) *breakdown truck*; see picture at TRUCK

tox·e·mia (*US*) *or Brit* **tox·ae·mia** /tɑkˈsiːmijə/ *noun* [*noncount*] *medical*
1 : PREECLAMPSIA
2 : an infection that is caused by harmful bacteria in the blood

tox·ic /ˈtɑːksɪk/ *adj* [*more ~; most ~*] : containing poisonous substances : POISONOUS • a *toxic* substance/compound • The fumes from that chemical are highly *toxic*. • Tests will be run to determine if the landfill is *toxic*. — sometimes used figuratively • a *toxic* [=very unpleasant] work environment — see also TOXIC SHOCK SYNDROME, TOXIC WASTE

tox·ic·i·ty /tɑkˈsɪsəti/ *noun, pl* **-ties** [*count, noncount*] *technical* : the state of being poisonous or the degree to which something (such as a drug) is poisonous • a pesticide with low *toxicity* to humans

tox·i·col·o·gy /ˌtɑːksəˈkɑːləʤi/ *noun* [*noncount*] *technical* : the study of poisonous chemicals, drugs, etc., and how a person or other living thing reacts to them — often used before another noun • *Toxicology* reports indicate he died from a drug overdose.
– tox·i·col·o·gist /ˌtɑːksəˈkɑːləʤɪst/ *noun, pl* **-gists** [*count*]

toxic shock syndrome *noun* [*noncount*] *medical* : a serious illness that is caused by bacteria and occurs especially in women who use tampons — abbr. *TSS*; called also *toxic shock*

toxic waste *noun, pl* ~ **wastes** : unwanted chemicals that are the result of manufacturing or industry and that are poisonous to living things [*noncount*] The company was fined for dumping *toxic waste* into the river. • *toxic waste* dumps/sites [*count*] *Toxic wastes* were detected in the soil samples.

tox·in /ˈtɑːksən/ *noun, pl* **-ins** [*count*] : a poisonous substance and especially one that is produced by a living thing • the *toxin* in scorpion venom • Scientists are studying how exposure to ***environmental toxins*** [=small amounts of poisons found in air, water, food, etc.] may affect our health.

[1]**toy** /ˈtoɪ/ *noun, pl* **toys** [*count*]
1 : something a child plays with • Please put away your *toys*. • a plastic/wooden/plush/stuffed *toy* — see also CHEW TOY, SOFT TOY, TINKERTOY
2 *sometimes disapproving* : something that an adult buys or uses for enjoyment or entertainment • He bought a new TV and a few other *toys*. • Her latest *toy* is a sports car.
3 : something that is very small • Your car is just a *toy* compared to this truck.
4 : a person who is controlled or used by someone else • She's just his *toy*. • (*US*) a ***boy toy*** = (*Brit*) a ***toy boy*** [=a young man who is having a romantic or sexual relationship with an older woman]
– toy·like /ˈtoɪˌlaɪk/ *adj* • a tiny *toylike* device

[2]**toy** *verb* **toys; toyed; toy·ing**
toy with [*phrasal verb*] **1** ***toy with (something)*** **a** : to think about (something) briefly and not very seriously • I *toyed with* the idea of moving to France but ended up staying here. **b** : to move or touch (something) with your fingers often without thinking • She *toyed* [=*played*] *with* her hair while she talked on the phone. **2** ***toy with (someone or something)*** : to deal with or control (someone or something) in a clever and usually unfair or selfish way • Don't *toy with* my emotions. • Do you really love me, or are you just *toying with* me?

[3]**toy** *adj, always used before a noun*
1 a : of, for, or relating to toys • a *toy* store • Put your toys back in the ***toy box/chest***. **b** : of a kind that is meant for a child to play with • *toy* cars/trains • *toy* soldiers [=small figures shaped like soldiers]
2 — used to describe an animal (such as a dog) that is the smallest kind of a particular breed • a *toy* poodle

[1]**trace** /ˈtreɪs/ *noun, pl* **trac·es** [*count*]
1 : a very small amount of something • He could detect a *trace* [=*hint*] of cinnamon in the cookies. • She spoke without a *trace* of irony. — sometimes used before another noun • *Trace* amounts of the pesticide were found in many foods. — see also TRACE ELEMENT
2 : something (such as a mark or an object) which shows that someone or something was in a particular place • The scientists found *traces* of human activity in the area. • The thieves left no *trace* of evidence behind. • He disappeared/vanished ***without a trace***. [=without leaving any signs to show where he went]
3 *technical* : a line drawn by a machine to record how something (such as a heartbeat or an earthquake) changes or happens over time

[2]**trace** *verb* **traces; traced; trac·ing**
1 [+ *obj*] **a** : to draw the outline of (something) • The children *traced* their hands onto the sidewalk with chalk.; *especially* : to copy (a design or picture) by putting a thin piece of paper that you can see through over it and drawing on top of it • You can put a piece of paper over the pattern and *trace* it. **b** : to draw (something, such as letters or a picture) especially in a careful way • She *traced* the letters of her name. • I *traced* a circle in the air/sand (with my finger). — often + *out* • She *traced* the letters *out* on a sheet of paper.
2 [+ *obj*] : to follow the path or line of (something) • We will need to *trace* the electrical wires through the walls. • She *traced* the edge of the book with her finger. [=she moved her finger along the edge of the book]
3 : to follow (something) back to its cause, beginning, or origin : to find out where something came from [+ *obj*] — usually + *to* • The noise was *traced to* a loose bolt in the car's engine. • The police *traced* the call *to* a payphone. — often + *back* • He can *trace* his family history all the way *back to* the Pilgrims. • The word "amiable" can be *traced back to* the Latin word for "friend." [*no obj*] The word "amiable" *traces back to* the Latin word for "friend." • a tradition that *traces back to* [=*goes back to*] the time of the ancient Romans
4 [+ *obj*] : to describe or study the way (something) happened over time • Her book *traces* the development of art through the ages.
5 [+ *obj*] : to try to find (someone or something) by collecting and studying evidence • The detective is in charge of *tracing* [=(more commonly) *tracking down*] missing persons.
– trace·able /ˈtreɪsəbəl/ *adj* [*more ~; most ~*] • The word "amiable" is *traceable* to the Latin word for "friend." • This phone call is *traceable*.

trace element *noun, pl* ~ **-ments** [*count*] *technical*
1 : a chemical element that is present only in very small amounts
2 : a chemical or element that a living thing needs in very small amounts in order to live

trac·er /ˈtreɪsɚ/ *noun, pl* **-ers** [*count*]
1 : a type of bullet that shows its path by creating smoke or light as it moves through the air • The enemy fired *tracers* at the aircraft carrier. • *tracer* fire/rounds/bullets
2 *medical* : a substance that is put in a patient's body so that doctors can watch a biological process (such as digestion) or see how a condition (such as cancer) is progressing • They injected her with a radioactive *tracer* and tracked it via X-rays.

trac·ery /ˈtreɪsəri/ *noun* [*noncount*]
1 : decorative patterns made in stone in some church windows • This window is an example of Gothic *tracery*.
2 : lines that cross each other in a complicated and attractive pattern • the delicate *tracery* of a butterfly's wing

tra·chea /ˈtreɪkijə, *Brit* trəˈkiːjə/ *noun, pl* **-che·ae** /-kiˌiː, *Brit* -ˈkiːji/ *or* **-che·as** [*count*] *medical* : a long tube in your neck and chest that carries air into and out of your lungs — called also *windpipe*
– tra·che·al /ˈtreɪkijəl/ *adj*

tra·che·o·to·my /ˌtreɪkiˈɑːtəmi/ *noun, pl* **-mies** [*count*] *medical* : an emergency operation in which a cut is made in the trachea so that a person can breathe

trac·ing /ˈtreɪsɪŋ/ *noun, pl* **-ings** [*count*] : a copy of a picture, map, etc., that is made by tracing the original

tracing paper *noun, pl* ~ **-pers** [*count, noncount*] : a very thin kind of paper that you can see through and use to trace a design, picture, etc.

[1]**track** /ˈtræk/ *noun, pl* **tracks**
1 [*count*] : a mark left on the ground by a moving animal, person, or vehicle — usually plural • moose/tire *tracks* • Dinosaur *tracks* were found in the canyon.
2 [*count*] : a path or trail that is made by people or animals walking through a field, forest, etc. • Follow the *track* into the forest.
3 [*count*] **a** : a pair of metal bars that a train, trolley, or subway car rides along • The train went off the *track*. = The train jumped the *track*. — usually plural • We were walking beside the train/railroad *tracks*. **b** *US* : a set of tracks at a train or subway station • The train to Chicago will leave *track* 3.
4 [*count*] : an often circular path or road that is used for racing • She ran a few laps around the *track* before the race. • a dog/horse *track* [=a track where dog/horse races are held] — see also RACETRACK

5 [*noncount*] *US* : TRACK AND FIELD • He ran *track* in high school. — often used before another noun • a *track* star • our *track* team • a *track* event/meet — see also TRACKSUIT
6 [*count*] : a rod or bar that is used to hold something (such as a curtain or sliding door) — see also TRACK LIGHTING
7 [*count*] : the course along which someone or something moves or proceeds • the *track* of a storm/bullet • His brother and sister went to college, but he chose a different *track*. [=he chose to do something different] — see also FAST TRACK, INSIDE TRACK, TENURE-TRACK
8 [*count*] *US* : a course of study followed by students who have particular abilities, needs, and goals • students on the *college* track — called also (*Brit*) *stream*
9 [*count*] **a** : a song on a record, CD, etc. • *Tracks* 6 and 11 are particularly good. • The ***title track*** [=the song with the same title as the album] is a hit. — see also SOUNDTRACK **b** : a separate recording of each instrument or voice in a song • Increase the volume on the drum/vocal *track*. — see also LAUGH TRACK, SOUNDTRACK

cover your tracks : to hide anything that shows where you have been or what you have done so that no one can find or catch you • The culprits *covered their tracks* well and left little evidence at the crime scene.

in your tracks : ✧ If you stop or are stopped *in your tracks*, you stop doing something suddenly or immediately. • He stopped/froze *in his tracks*, turned, and came back. • Her comment ***stopped me (dead) in my tracks***. [=it surprised me very much; it caused me to stop and think]

keep track : to be aware of how something is changing, what someone is doing, etc. • There's so much going on that it's hard to *keep track*. — usually + *of* • It's hard to *keep track of* what's going on. • *Keep track of* your little brother for me, will you? • It's her job to *keep track of* how the money is spent. • I watch the news to *keep track of* current events.

lose track : to stop being aware of how something is changing, what someone is doing, etc. • With so much going on, it's easy to *lose track*. — usually + *of* • It's easy to *lose track of* what's going on. • I'm sorry I'm late. I *lost track of* the time. • We *lost track of* each other after high school.

make tracks *informal* : to leave a place quickly • Here comes your mom—I'd better *make tracks*.

off the beaten track see BEATEN

off track : away from the main point, thought, etc. • Let's not get *off track*. • He kept the discussion from going too far *off track*.

on the right/wrong track : following a course that will lead to success/failure • Although their research is far from complete, the scientists are convinced that they are *on the right track*. • She believes that our current foreign policy is *on the wrong track*.

on track : happening the way that you expect or want things to happen : following a schedule, routine, etc. • Are we *on track* with the project? • The project is *on track*. • I had to get my life ***back on track*** after the accident.

the wrong side of the tracks : the part of a town, city, etc., where poor people live • She fell in love with a boy from *the wrong side of the tracks*.

— **track·less** /ˈtrækləs/ *adj* • a *trackless* wilderness/desert/expanse

[2]track *verb* **tracks; tracked; track·ing**
1 [+ *obj*] **a** : to follow and try to find (an animal) by looking for its tracks and other signs that show where it has gone • He *tracked* the deer for a mile. **b** : to follow and find (someone or something) especially by looking at evidence • The detectives *tracked* the killer to Arizona. — often + *down* • They *tracked* him *down* in Arizona. • Scientists *tracked down* the cause of the disease to a particular gene. • If I manage to *track down* [=*find*] those photos, I'll let you know.
2 [+ *obj*] **a** : to follow or watch the path of (something) • The ship can *track* incoming missiles with radar. • Meteorologists are *tracking* the storm. • an electronic *tracking* device/system **b** : to watch or follow the progress of (someone or something) • You should start *tracking* [=*keeping track of*] your living expenses. • The study *tracked* the patients over the course of five years.
3 [*no obj*] *US* : to move in a certain way or in a certain direction • The boat *tracks* well. • The squadron will *track* north by northeast for 40 miles.
4 [+ *obj*] *US* : to make marks by bringing (dirt, mud, etc.) indoors on the bottom of your feet • Don't you *track* mud into this clean kitchen! • The dog *tracked* dirt all over the floor.
5 *US* : to place young students in certain classes according to their abilities and needs [*no obj*] This school does not *track*. [+ *obj*] The school *tracks* [=(*Brit*) *streams*] students into "remedial," "average," and "gifted" classes.
6 [*no obj*] *of a movie camera or video camera* : to move in a particular direction especially in a straight line • At the start of the movie, the camera *tracks* along the street to the house's front door.

— **track·er** *noun, pl* **-ers** [*count*] • He is a skilled animal *tracker*. • The automatic flight *tracker* will tell you when her plane will be landing.

track and field *noun* [*noncount*] *US* : a sport in which athletes participate in different running, jumping, and throwing contests (such as the hurdles, long jump, and shot put) — called also *track*, (*Brit*) *athletics*

— **track–and–field** /ˌtrækənˈfiːld/ *adj* • She is on the *track-and-field* team. • *track-and-field* events

track·ball /ˈtrækˌbɑːl/ *noun, pl* **-balls** [*count*] *computers* : a device which consists of a small ball that you roll with your fingers to control the movement of a pointer on a computer screen

track lighting *noun* [*noncount*] *US* : lights that are spaced along a bar or rod placed on a ceiling or wall • We installed some *track lighting* in the kitchen. — called also *track lights*; see picture at LIGHTING

track record *noun, pl* **~ -cords** [*count*] : the things that someone or something has done or achieved in the past regarded especially as a way to judge what that person or thing is likely to do in the future • The Senator has a good *track record* on these issues. [=the Senator has dealt with these issues in a proper/effective way in the past] • These stocks have a ***proven track record***.

track·suit /ˈtrækˌsuːt/ *noun, pl* **-suits** [*count*] : a pair of loose pants and a matching jacket that are worn especially during exercise

[1]tract /ˈtrækt/ *noun, pl* **tracts** [*count*]
1 : a system of body parts or organs that has a particular purpose • the digestive/urinary/respiratory *tract*
2 : an area of land • She bought a 200-acre *tract* out in the country. • large/huge/vast ***tracts of land***
— compare [2]TRACT

[2]tract *noun, pl* **tracts** [*count*] : a small, thin book that typically expresses a group's political or religious ideas • religious *tracts* — compare [1]TRACT

trac·ta·ble /ˈtræktəbəl/ *adj* [*more ~; most ~*] *formal*
1 : easily managed or controlled • This new approach should make the problem more *tractable*. — opposite INTRACTABLE
2 : willing to learn or be guided by another • He's a very *tractable* child. • a *tractable* horse

tract house *noun, pl* **~ houses** [*count*] *US* : a house that is one of many similar houses built on an area of land

trac·tion /ˈtrækʃən/ *noun* [*noncount*]
1 **a** : the force that causes a moving thing to stick against the surface it is moving along • These tires get good *traction* on wet roads. • A patch of ice caused the car to lose *traction*. **b** : the power that is used to pull something • steam *traction*
2 *medical* : a way of treating broken bones in which a device gently pulls the bones back into place • She was ***in traction*** for three weeks after she broke her hip.
3 *informal* : the support, interest, etc., that is needed for something to succeed or make progress • The bill failed to ***gain traction*** in the Senate. • We didn't ***get traction*** on this idea until the board took interest.

trac·tor /ˈtræktɚ/ *noun, pl* **-tors** [*count*]
1 : a large vehicle that has two large back wheels and two smaller front wheels and that is used to pull farm equipment
2 *US* : a short, heavy truck that is designed to pull a large trailer

tractor

tractor–trailer *noun, pl* **-ers** [*count*] *US* : SEMITRAILER 2

trad /ˈtræd/ *adj* [*more ~; most ~*] *chiefly Brit* : TRADITIONAL • ***trad jazz***

trad·able *also* **trade·able** /ˈtreɪdəbəl/ *adj* : able to be bought or sold • *tradable* stocks • Those company shares are not *tradable*.

[1]trade /ˈtreɪd/ *noun, pl* **trades**
1 **a** [*noncount*] : the activity or process of buying, selling, or exchanging goods or services : COMMERCE • foreign/inter-

national *trade* ▪ the *trade* between the two countries ▪ The tariff is a barrier to *trade*. = The tariff is a *trade* barrier. ▪ *trade* agreements ▪ a *trade* route [=a route used for transporting goods] — see also FREE TRADE, TRADE DEFICIT, TRADE SURPLUS **b :** the amount of things or services that are bought and sold **:** the money made by buying and selling things or services [*noncount*] *Trade* accounts for half of our gross national product. [*singular*] The store does a brisk/lucrative *trade* in T-shirts. [=the store sells a lot of T-shirts]

2 [*count*] **a :** the act of exchanging one thing for another ▪ My cupcake for your brownie is a fair/good *trade*. [=*swap*] **b** *US, sports* **:** the act of giving one of your players to another team and getting one of their players in return ▪ The Tigers made a few good *trades* this season and picked up some promising players.

3 : a job; *especially* **:** a job that requires special training and skills and that is done by using your hands [*count*] Are you interested in learning a new *trade*? [=learning the skills that are needed to perform a different job] ▪ She entered the *trade* [=she began working in her profession] just after graduating from high school. [*noncount*] I am a carpenter/electrician/beautician **by trade** [=I work as a carpenter/electrician/beautician] — see also JACK-OF-ALL-TRADES

4 [*count*] **:** a certain kind of business or industry ▪ the drug *trade* ▪ The tourist *trade* is our main source of state revenue. ▪ a *trade* group/association ▪ *trade* publications — see also RAG TRADE

tools of the/your trade **:** a set of tools or skills that are necessary for a particular kind of job or work ▪ She showed me her paints, brushes, and the other *tools of her trade*. ▪ When you work with young children, patience and consistency are *tools of the trade*.

trick of the/your trade **:** a quick or clever way of doing something that you have learned usually as part of your job ▪ Let me show you a little *trick of the trade*. ▪ a mystery writer who knows all the *tricks of his trade*

— see also STOCK-IN-TRADE

²trade *verb* **trades; trad•ed; trad•ing**

1 a : to give something to someone and receive something in return **:** to give something in exchange for something else [*no obj*] Do you want to *trade*? [=*swap*] ▪ If you don't like your seat, I'll *trade* with you. [+ *obj*] We *traded* [=*switched*] seats halfway through the show. ▪ I'll *trade* my chips for your popcorn. = I'll *trade* you my chips for your popcorn. ▪ I *traded* seats with her halfway through the show. ▪ The boys are on the phone *trading* jokes/secrets. [=telling each other jokes/secrets] ▪ I got tired of listening to them ***trade insults***. [=insult each other] ▪ I would love to ***trade places with*** him. [=I would love to be in his situation] **b** [+ *obj*] *US, sports* **:** to give (one of your players) to another team in exchange for one of their players ▪ He was *traded* to the Yankees. ▪ They *traded* him to the Broncos.

2 [+ *obj*] **:** to stop using (one thing) and start using another ▪ I *traded* my pen for a pencil and kept writing.

3 a [*no obj*] **:** to buy, sell, or exchange goods or services — often + *with* or *in* ▪ The two countries continue to *trade with* each other. ▪ They are suspected of *trading in* illegal weapons. ▪ China is one of our biggest *trading* partners. **b :** to buy and sell stocks, bonds, etc. [+ *obj*] Their firm specializes in *trading* bonds. [*no obj*] She mostly *trades* in stocks. ▪ The stock is *trading* at [=is being sold for] $71 a share.

4 [*no obj*] *chiefly Brit* **:** to exist as a company or business ▪ Our company *trades* [=does business] under the name Smith & Sons.

trade down [*phrasal verb*] **:** to sell something you own and buy a similar thing that costs less money ▪ They *traded down* to a smaller house after their children had grown up and moved away.

trade in [*phrasal verb*] ***trade (something) in** or **trade in (something)*** **:** to sell (something) back to a business as part of your payment for something else ▪ We *traded* our car *in* for a newer model. ▪ *Trade in* your car and get $3,000 towards a new car! — see also TRADE-IN

trade off [*phrasal verb*] **1 *trade off** or **trade off (something)*** *US* — used to describe a situation in which one person does something, then another person does it, and so on ▪ When you get tired of driving, I'll *trade off* with you. = When you get tired of driving, we can *trade off*. [=when you get tired, I will drive for a while] ▪ They *trade off* [=*take turns*] babysitting each other's kids. ▪ Two of the band members *traded off* guitar solos. [=they took turns playing guitar solos] **2 *trade off (something)*** **:** to give up (something that you want) in order to have something else — usually + *for* ▪ The car's designers *traded off* some power *for* greater fuel efficiency. — see also TRADE-OFF

trade on [*phrasal verb*] ***trade on (someone or something)*** **:** to use (something) in a way that helps you **:** to get an advantage from (something) ▪ He wants to succeed by working hard instead of just *trading on* his good looks.

trade up [*phrasal verb*] **:** to sell something you own and buy a similar thing that is more expensive ▪ They keep *trading up*, buying larger and larger houses.

trade book *noun, pl* **~ books** [*count*] **:** a book that is published for and sold to the general public

trade deficit *noun, pl* **~ -cits** [*count*] *finance* **:** a situation in which a country buys more from other countries than it sells to other countries **:** the amount of money by which a country's imports are greater than its exports ▪ We have an annual *trade deficit* of $6.2 billion. — called also *(Brit) trade gap*; opposite TRADE SURPLUS

trade fair *noun, pl* **~ fairs** [*count*] **:** TRADE SHOW

trade–in /ˈtreɪdˌɪn/ *noun, pl* **-ins** [*count*] **:** something (such as a used car) that you sell to a business as part of your payment for something new ▪ Bring in your *trade-in* and receive $3,000 towards any new car on the lot. — see also *trade in* at ²TRADE

trade•mark /ˈtreɪdˌmɑɚk/ *noun, pl* **-marks** [*count*]

1 : something (such as a word) that identifies a particular company's product and cannot be used by another company without permission ▪ "Kleenex" is a registered *trademark*. — abbr. *TM*

2 : a quality or way of behaving, speaking, etc., that is very typical of a particular person, group, or organization ▪ Outspokenness has always been his *trademark*. ▪ Courtesy is the company's *trademark*. — often used before another noun ▪ She greeted us with her *trademark* smile.

– trade•marked /ˈtreɪdˌmɑɚkt/ *adj* ▪ That name is *trademarked*. = That is a *trademarked* name.

trade name *noun, pl* **~ names** [*count*]

1 : BRAND NAME ▪ Ibuprofen is sold under several *trade names*.

2 : the name of a business

trade–off /ˈtreɪdˌɑːf/ *noun, pl* **-offs** [*count*]

1 : a situation in which you must choose between or balance two things that are opposite or cannot be had at the same time — often + *between* ▪ There's often a *trade-off between* the need for safety and the desire to work quickly.

2 *US* **:** something that you do not want but must accept in order to have something that you want ▪ The job pays well. The biggest *trade-off* is that you have to work long hours. — see also *trade off* at ²TRADE

trad•er /ˈtreɪdɚ/ *noun, pl* **-ers** [*count*] **:** a person who buys, sells, or exchanges goods ▪ She is a stock/bond/commodities *trader*. ▪ early explorers and fur *traders*

trade school *noun, pl* **~ schools** [*count*] *US* **:** a school in which people learn how to do a job that requires special skills ▪ an automotive *trade school*

trade secret *noun, pl* **~ -crets** [*count*] **:** something (such as a special way of doing or making something) that is known only by the company that uses it and is protected from competitors

trade show *noun, pl* **~ shows** [*count*] **:** a large gathering in which different companies in a particular field or industry show their products to possible customers ▪ The company unveiled a new product at the annual *trade show* this week. — called also *trade fair*

trades•man /ˈtreɪdzmən/ *noun, pl* **-men** /-mən/ [*count*]

1 : a person who works in a job that requires special skill or training ▪ electricians, plumbers, and other *tradesmen* ▪ He joined the *tradesmen's* union.

2 *chiefly Brit* **:** someone who sells or delivers goods; *especially* **:** SHOPKEEPER

trades•peo•ple /ˈtreɪdzˌpiːpəl/ *noun* [*plural*]

1 : people who work in a trade **:** people whose professions require special skills and work that is done with the hands ▪ Local *tradespeople* like plumbers and electricians have raised their rates.

2 *Brit* **:** people who own and run shops **:** shopkeepers or merchants

trade surplus *noun, pl* **~ -pluses** [*count*] *finance* **:** a situation in which a country sells more to other countries than it buys from other countries **:** the amount of money by which a country's exports are greater than its imports ▪ The country's *trade surplus* increased last year. ▪ a trade surplus of almost $10 billion — opposite TRADE DEFICIT

trade union *noun, pl* ~ **unions** [*count*] *Brit* : LABOR UNION
– **trade unionist** *noun, pl* ~ **-ists** [*count*] *Brit*

trade wind *noun, pl* ~ **winds** [*count*] : a wind that blows almost constantly to the west and towards the equator — usually plural • sailors who followed the *trade winds*

trading *noun* [*noncount*] : the act or practice of buying and selling something (such as stocks or bonds) • *Trading* was slow at the stock market today. • He's accused of ***insider trading***. [=illegally using a company's secret information to buy and sell that company's stocks]— often used before another noun • a major *trading* center of Europe • a *trading* company/partner

trading card *noun, pl* ~ **cards** [*count*] : a card that usually has pictures of and information about someone (such as an athlete) and that is part of a set which you collect by exchanging cards with other people • He had a complete set of his favorite baseball team's *trading cards*.

trading post *noun, pl* ~ **posts** [*count*] : a place (such as a store, a town, or a fort) that is far from other towns and is used as a center for buying, selling, and trading goods and services • The French set up a *trading post* on the coast. • The town was first established as a *trading post*.

tra·di·tion /trəˈdɪʃən/ *noun, pl* **-tions**
1 : a way of thinking, behaving, or doing something that has been used by the people in a particular group, family, society, etc., for a long time [*count*] cultural *traditions* • an ancient/old *tradition* • One of our town's time-honored *traditions* is to have an Easter egg hunt the week before Easter. • It is their *tradition* to give thanks before they start eating. • There's an office *tradition* of wearing casual clothes on Fridays. • Our company has a long *tradition* [=*history*] of excellence in our field. • My dad and granddad were both carpenters, and my brother is ***carrying on the tradition***. [=my brother is also a carpenter] • They no longer ***follow the traditions*** of their ancestors. [*noncount*] The cheese is made according to *tradition*. [=made in way that has been used for many years; made in the traditional way] • We ***broke with tradition*** and had goose for Thanksgiving instead of turkey. • ***By tradition***, the celebration begins at midnight. • They no longer ***follow tradition***. • a ceremony ***steeped in tradition*** [=having many traditional parts]
2 [*noncount*] : the stories, beliefs, etc., that have been part of the culture of a group of people for a long time • According to *tradition*, the goddess lies sleeping beneath the mountain. • He studied the Anglo-Saxon ***oral tradition***. [=the stories, beliefs, etc., that a group of people shared by telling stories and talking to each other]
3 [*singular*] — used to say that someone has qualities which are like the qualities of another well-known person or group of people from the past • He's a politician in the best liberal *tradition*. [=a politician like other liberal politicians of the past] • a politician ***in the (great/grand) tradition of*** Franklin Delano Roosevelt

tra·di·tion·al /trəˈdɪʃənl/ *adj* [*more* ~; *most* ~]
1 a : based on a way of thinking, behaving, or doing something that has been used by the people in a particular group, family, society, etc., for a long time : following the tradition of a certain group or culture • It is *traditional* to eat turkey and cranberry sauce on Thanksgiving. • We often cook *traditional* Mexican meals for our guests. • She wore a *traditional* Japanese kimono. • a *traditional* Russian fairy tale **b** : typical or normal for something or someone : having the qualities, beliefs, etc., that are usual or expected in a particular type of person or thing • She is a *traditional* liberal politician. • We got a *traditional* bank loan with a fixed interest rate.
2 : based on old-fashioned ideas : not new, different, or modern • I prefer a more *traditional* style of furniture. • His views on marriage are quite *traditional*. He says that the wife should stay home with the children while the husband works. • *traditional* beliefs/values
– **tra·di·tion·al·ly** *adv* • *Traditionally*, guests are served first. • She thinks too *traditionally* for my taste.

tra·di·tion·al·ist /trəˈdɪʃənəlɪst/ *noun, pl* **-ists** [*count*] : a person who believes that older ways of doing or thinking about things are better than newer ways : a person who follows a particular and established tradition • She is a *traditionalist* when it comes to men's and women's roles. • conservative/religious *traditionalists* • a *traditionalist* view
– **tra·di·tion·al·ism** /trəˈdɪʃənəˌlɪzəm/ *noun* [*noncount*] • religious *traditionalism*

tra·duce /trəˈduːs, *Brit* trəˈdjuːs/ *verb* **-duc·es**; **-duced**; **-duc·ing** [+ *obj*] *formal* : to tell lies about (someone) : SLANDER • He was *traduced* in the press.

¹traf·fic /ˈtræfɪk/ *noun* [*noncount*]
1 : all the vehicles driving along a certain road or in a certain area • Let's leave early to avoid rush hour *traffic*. • *Traffic* is backed up to the bridge. • *traffic* congestion • a *traffic* accident
2 : the movement of airplanes, ships, etc., along routes • air *traffic* • Barge *traffic* was halted because of flooding.
3 : the amount of people who pass through a certain place or travel in a certain way • Airlines saw a decrease in passenger *traffic* this year. • There is a walkway along the bridge for ***pedestrian/foot traffic***. [=people who are walking] • We get a lot of *foot traffic* [=people who walk by and stop to look] in our shop.
4 *computers* : the number of people who visit a Web site or use a system • We're trying to increase *traffic* to our site. • Internet/network *traffic* can cause slower response times during peak hours.
5 : the buying and selling of illegal goods or services especially between countries • Drug *traffic* across the border has increased.

²traffic *verb* **-fics**; **-ficked**; **-fick·ing** [*no obj*] : to buy or sell something especially illegally — usually + *in* • a gang that *traffics in* drugs — sometimes used figuratively • It is a play that *traffics in* bawdy humor. • I don't *traffic in* sarcasm.

traffic circle *noun, pl* ~ **circles** [*count*] *US* : a circular area where two or more roads meet and on which all vehicles must go in the same direction called also (*US*) *rotary*, (*Brit*) *roundabout*

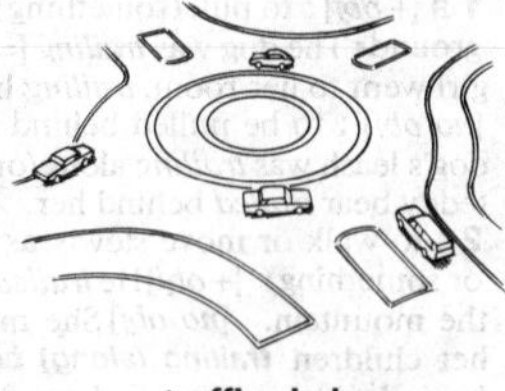
traffic circle

traffic cone *noun, pl* ~ **cones** [*count*] : a brightly colored plastic cone that is placed on a road to warn drivers not to drive too close to an area where work is being done, an accident has occurred, etc.

traffic cop *noun, pl* ~ **cops** [*count*] : a police officer who directs traffic or gives fines to people who break traffic laws • A *traffic cop* pulled me over and gave me a speeding ticket.

traffic court *noun, pl* ~ **courts** [*count, noncount*] *US* : a court of law where drivers who have broken traffic laws are punished • She has to be in *traffic court* this morning.

traffic island *noun, pl* ~ **-lands** [*count*] *US* : ISLAND 2a

traffic jam *noun, pl* ~ **jams** [*count*] : a situation in which a long line of vehicles on a road have stopped moving or are moving very slowly • I'm stuck in a *traffic jam*, so I'll be late.

traf·ficked /ˈtræfɪkt/ *adj* [*more* ~; *most* ~] : having a certain amount of traffic • That is a heavily *trafficked* [=*used*] bridge. • It's one of the most *trafficked* [=the most often visited] sites on the Web.

traf·fick·er /ˈtræfɪkə/ *noun, pl* **-ers** [*count*] : a person who buys and sells something that is illegal • a drug *trafficker*

trafficking *noun* [*noncount*] : the act or business of illegally buying something and selling it especially in another country • She was convicted of drug *trafficking*.

traffic light *noun, pl* ~ **lights** [*count*] : an electric lamp that usually has a red, a green, and a yellow light and that is used to control traffic • Take a left at the *traffic light*.— often plural — called also *light, traffic signal*, (*US*) *stoplight*; see picture at STREET

traffic ticket *noun, pl* ~ **-ets** [*count*] : ¹TICKET 3 • I got a *traffic ticket* for speeding.

traffic warden *noun, pl* ~ **-dens** [*count*] *Brit* : someone whose job is to check for cars that are parked illegally

tra·ge·di·an /trəˈʤiːdijən/ *noun, pl* **-ans** [*count*]
1 : a person who writes tragedies
2 : an actor who often plays tragic roles

trag·e·dy /ˈtræʤədi/ *noun, pl* **-dies**
1 a : a very bad event that causes great sadness and often involves someone's death [*count*] Her son's death was a terrible *tragedy*. [*noncount*] The situation ended in *tragedy* when the gunman shot and killed two students. **b** [*count*] : a very sad, unfortunate, or upsetting situation : something that causes strong feelings of sadness or regret • It is a *tragedy* [=*pity, shame*] that so many victims are afraid to report the abuse. • The biggest *tragedy* here is that the accident could have easily been prevented.

T

2 a [*count*] : a play, movie, etc., that is serious and has a sad ending (such as the death of the main character) • "Hamlet" is one of Shakespeare's best-known *tragedies*. • a Greek *tragedy* **b** [*noncount*] : plays, movies, etc., that are tragedies • The students are studying Greek *tragedy*. • an actor who is drawn to *tragedy*

trag·ic /ˈtræʤɪk/ *adj* [*more* ~; *most* ~]

1 : causing strong feelings of sadness usually because someone has died in a way that seems very shocking, unfair, etc. • Their deaths were *tragic* and untimely. • They both died in a *tragic* car accident. • Romeo and Juliet's *tragic* love affair • Pride was his ***tragic flaw*** [=a bad quality that causes someone to fail, die, etc.] — sometimes used in an exaggerated way to describe something that is very bad, unfortunate, etc. • She has a *tragic* lack of imagination.

2 : involving very sad or serious topics • We saw a *tragic* play about a man with AIDS. : of or relating to tragedy • the *tragic* characters of her novel

– trag·i·cal·ly /ˈtræʤɪkli/ *adv* • He died *tragically*. • *Tragically*, she could not afford treatment for her cancer.

tragi·com·e·dy /ˌtræʤɪˈkɑːmədi/ *noun, pl* **-dies** [*count*] : a play, movie, situation, etc., that is both sad and funny • The play is a *tragicomedy* about a man's search for love.

– tragi·com·ic /ˌtræʤɪˈkɑːmɪk/ *also* **tragi·com·i·cal** /ˌtræʤɪˈkɑːmɪkəl/ *adj* • a *tragicomic* view of life

[1]trail /ˈtreɪl/ *verb* **trails; trailed; trail·ing**

1 a [+ *obj*] : to pull (something) behind you especially on the ground • The dog was *trailing* [=*dragging*] its leash. • The little girl went to her room, *trailing* her teddy bear behind her. **b** [*no obj*] : to be pulled behind someone or something • The dog's leash was *trailing* along/on the ground. • The little girl's teddy bear *trailed* behind her.

2 : to walk or move slowly as you follow behind (someone or something) [+ *obj*] He *trailed* us as we worked our way up the mountain. [*no obj*] She marched down the street with her children ***trailing (along) behind/after*** (her). • He *trailed behind* (us) as we worked our way up the mountain.

3 : to be behind in a race or competition [*no obj*] The President is *trailing* in the polls as the election approaches. • We were *trailing* by 3 runs at the end of the 6th inning. [+ *obj*] Our team *trailed* their team at the end of the 6th inning.

4 [+ *obj*] : to follow and watch or try to catch (someone or something) • The dogs were *trailing* a fox. • Police *trailed* the suspect for six blocks.

5 *always followed by an adverb or preposition* [*no obj*] : to move, flow, or extend slowly in a thin line • Smoke *trailed* (away) from the chimney. • A tear *trailed* down her cheek.

6 [*no obj*] : to hang down to the ground • The curtains *trailed* onto the floor. — see also TRAILING

trail away/off [*phrasal verb*] — used to say that someone's voice becomes softer and softer and then stops • She started asking him a question, but then her voice *trailed off*. • "Do you think you could . . . " she said before *trailing off*.

[2]trail *noun, pl* **trails** [*count*]

1 : a path through a forest, field, etc. • Stay on the *trail* if we get separated. • a bike/ski *trail* — see also NATURE TRAIL

2 : the marks, signs, smells, etc., that are left behind by someone or something and that can often be followed • He left (behind) a *trail* of blood. • The car left a *trail* of smoke as it sped off. • The storm left a *trail* of destruction in its wake. [=the storm caused a lot of destruction as it moved across the land] • The dogs were following her *trail*. = The dogs were ***on her trail*** • When we got to the river, the ***trail went cold*** [=it could no longer be found or followed] • The police are ***hot on the trail of*** the escaped convicts. [=are chasing the escaped convicts and are close to catching them] — sometimes used figuratively • As he gained more political power, he left a *trail* of bitterness behind him. [=he treated people badly and made them feel bitter] — see also PAPER TRAIL, VAPOR TRAIL

3 : a route that someone follows to go somewhere or achieve something • following the *trail* to success • The candidates talked about the people they met on the ***campaign trail*** [=the people they met while going to different places during the campaign]

blaze a trail see [4]BLAZE

hit the trail *chiefly US* : to begin a journey • We should be ready to *hit the trail* by 8:00. • The candidates will soon be *hitting the* campaign *trail*.

trail·blaz·er /ˈtreɪlˌbleɪzɚ/ *noun, pl* **-ers** [*count*]

1 : a person who makes, does, or discovers something new and makes it acceptable or popular • one of the *trailblazers* [=*pioneers*] of rock and roll • technological *trailblazers*

2 : a person who marks or prepares a trail through a forest or field for other people to follow

– trail·blaz·ing /ˈtreɪlˌbleɪzɪŋ/ *adj* [*more* ~; *most* ~] • *trailblazing* architectural designs

trail·er /ˈtreɪlɚ/ *noun, pl* **-ers** [*count*]

1 : a long platform or box with wheels that is pulled behind a truck or car and used to transport things • We helped them load the furniture onto the *trailer*. • a horse/boat *trailer* — see also TRACTOR-TRAILER

2 *chiefly US* **a :** a vehicle that can be pulled by a truck or car and that can be parked and used as an office, vacation home, etc. • We parked our *trailer* [=(*Brit*) *caravan*] next to the lake for the summer. **b :** MOBILE HOME

3 : a selected group of scenes that are shown to advertise a movie : PREVIEW • a theatrical *trailer*

trailer park *noun, pl* ~ **parks** [*count*] *chiefly US* : a large piece of land where trailers (sense 2a) can be parked and connected to electricity and water supplies

trailer trash *noun* [*noncount*] *US, informal* + *offensive* : poor people who live in trailers • They called her *trailer trash*.

trail·head /ˈtreɪlˌhɛd/ *noun, pl* **-heads** [*count*] *chiefly US* : the beginning of a trail through a forest • The hikers met at the *trailhead* at 8 a.m.

trailing *adj* [*more* ~; *most* ~]

1 : having stems that hang downward or rest on the ground • *trailing* flowers/plants/vines • *trailing* rosemary

2 : forming the back or last part of something • the ***trailing edge*** of the airplane's wing [=the edge of the wing that is not facing forward]

trail mix *noun* [*noncount*] *chiefly US* : a mixture of nuts, seeds, dried fruits, and sometimes chocolate that is eaten as a snack

[1]train /ˈtreɪn/ *noun, pl* **trains**

1 : a group of vehicles that travel on a track and are connected to each other and usually to an engine : a connected group of railroad cars [*count*] The *train* pulled into the station. • You can get off/on the *train* in Atlanta. • I took a *train* to Madrid. • We caught the last *train*. • We slept on the *train*. • a ***passenger train*** [=a train that people use for traveling] • a ***commuter train*** [=a train that people use to get to and from work] • an ***express train*** [=a train that has very few stops] • a ***subway train*** [=an underground train] • (*US*) a ***freight train*** = (*Brit*) a ***goods train*** [=a train carrying cargo] [*noncount*] We traveled ***by train*** through Europe. — often used before another noun • a *train* [=*railroad*] station • *train* tracks • a *train* schedule/signal/ticket • a *train* crash = (*US*) a *train* wreck

2 [*count*] *old-fashioned* : a group of people, vehicles, or animals that are moving in a line • a funeral *train* • a mule *train* — see also WAGON TRAIN

3 [*count*] : an orderly series of events, actions, or ideas • a *train* of events • I lost my ***train of thought*** [=I forgot what I was thinking about] when you interrupted me.

4 [*count*] *technical* : a series of moving machine parts (such as gears) for controlling motion • There's a problem with the car's drive *train*. • the gear *train*

5 [*count*] : a part of a long dress that trails behind the woman who is wearing it • the bride's *train* — see color picture on page C16

in train *Brit, formal* : in an active state or condition • a process that had been *in train* for decades • The plans have been ***set in train*** [=*set in motion*]

— see also GRAVY TRAIN

[2]train *verb* **trains; trained; train·ing**

1 a [+ *obj*] : to teach (someone) the skills needed to do something (such as a job) : to give instruction to (someone) • He was never formally *trained* as a chef. • I've been *trained* in first aid. • I'm *training* her to take over my job when I retire. • My boss is *training* me on the new equipment. • We need to *train* more nurses. • They are ***highly trained*** professionals. **b** [*no obj*] : to be taught the skills needed to do something (such as a job) • I'm *training* to be/become a nurse. • I *trained* at that hospital. • He's *training* as a chef.

2 [+ *obj*] : to cause (someone or something) to develop an ability or skill • She had to *train* her mind to think scientifically. • You can *train* yourself to relax. • A *trained* [=*practiced*] eye can detect the slightest imperfection. • Only a *trained* ear could hear the difference.

3 a [*no obj*] : to try to make yourself stronger, faster, or better at doing something before competing in an event or competition • The team *trains* five hours a day. • He is *training* for

the Olympics. **b** [+ *obj*] : to help (someone) to prepare for an event or competition : to coach (an athlete) ▪ He *trained* several generations of track-and-field athletes.
4 [+ *obj*] : to teach (an animal) to obey commands ▪ She *trained* her dog to sit. ▪ The police use *trained* dogs to sniff out drugs. ▪ The dog was never properly *trained.* [=taught to obey] — see also HOUSE-TRAIN
5 [+ *obj*] : to make (a plant) grow in a particular direction usually by bending, cutting, or tying it ▪ You can *train* this vine to climb up a wall.
6 [+ *obj*] : to aim or point (something) toward something or in a particular direction ▪ He *trained* the flashlight into the hole. ▪ We *trained* our eyes on the horizon. [=we looked toward the horizon]
– train·able /ˈtreɪnəbəl/ *adj* [*more* ~; *most* ~] ▪ a very *trainable* dog

train·ee /treɪˈniː/ *noun, pl* **-ees** [*count*] : a person who is being trained for a job ▪ on-the-job *trainees* ▪ management *trainees* ▪ a *trainee* cook

train·er /ˈtreɪnɚ/ *noun, pl* **-ers** [*count*]
1 : a person who teaches or coaches athletes or animals : a person who trains athletes or animals ▪ the boxer and his *trainer* ▪ a horse *trainer* ▪ She hired a personal *trainer*.
2 *US* : a person who treats the injuries of the members of a sports team ▪ an athletic *trainer* ▪ the team *trainer*
3 *Brit* : SNEAKER

train·ing /ˈtreɪnɪŋ/ *noun* [*noncount*]
1 : a process by which someone is taught the skills that are needed for an art, profession, or job ▪ The job requires special *training.* ▪ She owes her flexibility to her early *training* as a dancer. ▪ He received *training* in first aid. ▪ combat/flight *training* ▪ *training* programs ▪ ***on-the-job training*** [=training that you are given while you are doing a job and getting paid] ▪ She's ***in training*** to be an astronaut. [=she is being trained to be an astronaut] ▪ a young doctor who's still *in training* ▪ a ***training manual*** [=a book of instructions for a job or task] — see also BASIC TRAINING, TOILET TRAINING
2 : the process by which an athlete prepares for competition by exercising, practicing, etc. ▪ She's ***in training*** for the Olympics. — see also SPRING TRAINING

training college *noun, pl* ~ **-leges** [*count*] *Brit* : a college that prepares people for a particular job; *especially* : a college for the training of teachers

training shoe *noun, pl* ~ **shoes** [*count*] *chiefly Brit* : SNEAKER

training wheels *noun* [*plural*] *US* : a small pair of extra wheels that are added to a child's bicycle so that the bicycle can be balanced more easily while the child is learning to ride it — called also (*Brit*) *stabilisers*

train set *noun, pl* ~ **sets** [*count*] : a toy train with its tracks, buildings, etc.

train·spot·ter /ˈtreɪn͵spɑːtɚ/ *noun, pl* **-ters** [*count*] *Brit* : a person who is interested in trains and who writes down the numbers of passing trains as a hobby
– train·spot·ting /ˈtreɪn͵spɑːtɪŋ/ *noun* [*noncount*]

traipse /ˈtreɪps/ *verb* **traips·es; traipsed; traips·ing** [*no obj*] *informal* : to walk or go somewhere ▪ I *traipsed* all over town looking for the right dress. ▪ I'm too old to go *traipsing* around Europe.

trait /ˈtreɪt, *Brit* ˈtreɪ/ *noun, pl* **traits** [*count*] *formal* : a quality that makes one person or thing different from another ▪ Humility is an admirable *trait.* [=*quality*] ▪ This dog breed has a number of desirable *traits.* ▪ feminine/masculine *traits* ▪ inherited and acquired *traits*

trai·tor /ˈtreɪtɚ/ *noun, pl* **-tors** [*count*] : a person who is not loyal to his or her own country, friends, etc. : a person who betrays a country or group of people by helping or supporting an enemy ▪ She has been called a *traitor* to the liberal party's cause. ▪ He was a *traitor* who betrayed his country by selling military secrets to the enemy. ▪ He ***turned traitor.*** [=he became a traitor; he betrayed his country/friends]
– trai·tor·ous /ˈtreɪtərəs/ *adj* [*more* ~; *most* ~] ▪ *traitorous* acts

tra·jec·to·ry /trəˈʤɛktəri/ *noun, pl* **-ries** [*count*] : the curved path along which something (such as a rocket) moves through the air or through space ▪ the *trajectory* of the missile — often used figuratively to describe a process of change or development that leads toward a particular result ▪ Her early education put her on a *trajectory* toward a distinguished career. ▪ his political *trajectory* from local activist to world leader

tram /ˈtræm/ *noun, pl* **trams** [*count*]
1 *US* : a vehicle that runs on a track or on rails and that is usually used to carry groups of people for a short distance ▪ Take the *tram* to the departure terminal.
2 *chiefly Brit* : STREETCAR

tram·car /ˈtræm͵kɑɚ/ *noun, pl* **-cars** [*count*] *chiefly Brit* : STREETCAR

tram·line /ˈtræm͵laɪn/ *noun, pl* **-lines** [*count*] *Brit* : the metal tracks on a street that a streetcar moves along

tram·mel /ˈtræməl/ *verb* **-mels;** *US* **-meled** *or Brit* **-melled;** *US* **-mel·ing** *or Brit* **-mel·ling** [+ *obj*] *formal* : to limit or restrict (something or someone) unfairly ▪ laws that *trammel* our rights as citizens

[1]tramp /ˈtræmp/ *verb* **tramps; tramped; tramp·ing**
1 [*no obj*] : to walk or step heavily ▪ Workmen were *tramping* [=(*US*) *tromping*] through the house all day.
2 : to walk for a long distance or time [*no obj*] We spent the day *tramping* through the woods. [+ *obj*] He *tramped* the streets looking for his dog.

[2]tramp *noun, pl* **tramps**
1 [*count*] : a person who travels from place to place and does not have a home or much money ▪ *tramps* [=*hobos, vagrants*] sleeping under a bridge
2 [*count*] *chiefly US, disapproving + somewhat old-fashioned* : a woman who has sex with many different
3 [*count*] *somewhat old-fashioned* : a walking trip : HIKE ▪ a *tramp* through the woods
4 [*singular*] : the sound made by someone walking heavily ▪ I could hear the *tramp* of boots on the path ahead.

tram·ple /ˈtræmpəl/ *verb* **tram·ples; tram·pled; tram·pling**
1 : to cause damage or pain by walking or stepping heavily on something or someone [*no obj*] The workmen *trampled* on my flower bed. [+ *obj*] Her glasses were *trampled* underfoot by the crowd. ▪ Many people were *trampled* to death trying to escape the burning building.
2 : to treat other people's rights, wishes, or feelings as if they are worthless or not important [*no obj*] They are *trampling* on our rights. [+ *obj*] They are *trampling* our rights. ▪ Their most cherished traditions have been *trampled.*

tram·po·line /͵træmpəˈliːn/ *noun, pl* **-lines** [*count*] : a piece of equipment that has a sheet of strong cloth attached by springs to a metal frame and that is used for jumping up and down for exercise or as a sport

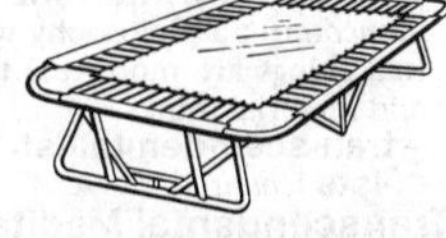
trampoline

trance /ˈtræns/ *noun, pl* **tranc·es** [*count*]
1 : a state that is like being asleep except that you can move and respond to questions and commands like a person who is awake ▪ The hypnotist put him in a (hypnotic) *trance.* ▪ The spiritual healer ***fell/went into a trance.***
2 : a state in which you are not aware of what is happening around you because you are thinking of something else ▪ He was staring out the window ***in a trance.***

tran·ny /ˈtræni/ *noun, pl* **-nies** [*count*] *informal*
1 : a transsexual or a transvestite
2 *US* : TRANSMISSION 3 ▪ He fixed the car's *tranny.*

tran·quil /ˈtræŋkwəl/ *adj* [*more* ~; *most* ~] : quiet and peaceful ▪ a *tranquil* life/sea/village
– tran·quil·ly *adverb*

tran·quil·i·ty (*US*) *or chiefly Brit* **tran·quil·li·ty** /trænˈkwɪləti/ *noun* [*noncount*] : the quality or state of being quiet and peaceful ▪ the *tranquility* of the quiet countryside ▪ peace and *tranquility*

tran·quil·ize *also Brit* **tran·quil·lise** /ˈtræŋkwə͵laɪz/ *verb* **-iz·es; -ized; -iz·ing** [+ *obj*] : to use a drug to cause (a person or animal) to become very relaxed and calm ▪ They *tranquilized* the bear with a dart so that it could be safely moved to a different area.

tran·quil·iz·er *also Brit* **tran·quil·lis·er** /ˈtræŋkwə͵laɪzɚ/ *noun, pl* **-iz·ers** [*count*] : a drug that causes a person or animal to become very relaxed and calm ▪ a patient who is on/taking *tranquilizers* ▪ They shot the bear with a *tranquilizer* gun. [=a gun that shoots a dart which contains a drug that causes a wild animal to become very relaxed and unable to move]

trans- *prefix*
1 : on or to the other side of : across or beyond ▪ *trans*atlantic

2 : so as to change in form or position • *trans*literate • *trans*plant

trans·act /træn'zækt/ *verb* **-acts; -act·ed; -act·ing** [+ *obj*] *somewhat formal* : to do (business) with another person, company, etc. • We had some important business to *transact* with our distributors. • I prefer not to *transact* [=*conduct*] business over the phone. • *transact* a real estate deal

trans·ac·tion /træn'zækʃən/ *noun, pl* **-tions**

1 [*count*] : a business deal : an occurrence in which goods, services, or money are passed from one person, account, etc., to another • business/commercial *transactions* • The entire *transaction* took place over the phone. • a real estate *transaction* • a record of your recent banking *transactions* • electronic *transactions*

2 [*noncount*] : the act or process of doing business with another person, company, etc. : the act or process of transacting business • the *transaction* of business over the phone

trans·at·lan·tic /ˌtrænsət'læntɪk/ *adj*

1 : going across the Atlantic Ocean • a *transatlantic* cable • a *transatlantic* voyage

2 : located on or coming from the other side of the Atlantic Ocean • our *transatlantic* friends

3 : involving people or countries on both sides of the Atlantic Ocean • a *transatlantic* conspiracy

trans·ceiv·er /træn'si:və/ *noun, pl* **-ers** [*count*] : a radio that can send and receive messages

tran·scend /træn'sɛnd/ *verb* **-scends; -scend·ed; -scend·ing** [+ *obj*] *formal* : to rise above or go beyond the normal limits of (something) • music that *transcends* cultural boundaries • She was able to *transcend* her own suffering and help others. • Her concerns *transcended* local issues.

tran·scen·dent /træn'sɛndənt/ *adj, formal*

1 : going beyond the limits of ordinary experience • *transcendent* beings • *transcendent* truths • a *transcendent* [=*transcendental*] experience

2 : far better or greater than what is usual : EXTRAORDINARY • *transcendent* beauty • a *transcendent* performance

– tran·scen·dence /træn'sɛndəns/ *noun* [*noncount*]

tran·scen·den·tal /ˌtrænˌsɛn'dɛntl/ *adj* : TRANSCENDENT 1 • *transcendental* truths/experiences

tran·scen·den·tal·ism /ˌtrænˌsɛn'dɛntəˌlɪzəm/ *noun* [*noncount*] : a philosophy which says that thought and spiritual things are more real than ordinary human experience and material things

– tran·scen·den·tal·ist /ˌtrænˌsɛn'dɛntəlɪst/ *noun, pl* **-ists** [*count*]

Transcendental Meditation *service mark* — used for a method of meditating in which you close your eyes and repeatedly think of a simple sound, word, or phrase (called a mantra)

trans·con·ti·nen·tal /ˌtrænsˌkɑ:ntə'nɛntl/ *adj* : going across a continent • the *transcontinental* railroad • a six-hour *transcontinental* flight • *transcontinental* shipping

tran·scribe /træn'skraɪb/ *verb* **-scribes; -scribed; -scrib·ing** [+ *obj*]

1 a : to make a written copy of (something) • He *transcribed* all of his great-grandfather's letters. **b** : to write down (something that is spoken) • The senator's speech was *transcribed.*

2 : to rewrite (a piece of music) so that it can be performed by a different instrument or voice • a Mozart string quartet *transcribed* for piano

3 *technical* : to represent (speech sounds) with written symbols • a system that allows linguists to *transcribe* the sounds of any language

4 : to change (something written) into a different language • *transcribe* textbooks into braille

– tran·scrib·er *noun, pl* **-ers** [*count*]

T

tran·script /'trænˌskrɪpt/ *noun, pl* **-scripts** [*count*]

1 : a written, printed, or typed copy of words that have been spoken • a *transcript* of a radio program • a full *transcript* of the court proceedings • a *transcript* of the senator's speech

2 *US* : an official record of a student's grades • You must submit your college *transcript* with your job application.

tran·scrip·tion /træn'skrɪpʃən/ *noun, pl* **-tions**

1 [*noncount*] : the act or process of making a written, printed, or typed copy of words that have been spoken • an error in *transcription* • *Transcription* of the tapes took weeks.

2 [*count*] : a written, printed, or typed copy of words that have been spoken • a *transcription* [=*transcript*] of the tape recordings

trans·du·cer /træns'du:sə, *Brit* træns'dju:sə/ *noun, pl* **-ers** [*count*] *technical* : a device that changes power from one system into another form for another system

tran·sept /'trænˌsɛpt/ *noun, pl* **-septs** [*count*] : the shorter area that goes across and sticks out from the long part of a church and that gives the church the shape of a cross when it is viewed from above — compare NAVE

trans fat /'træns-, 'trænz-/ *noun* [*count, noncount*] *technical* : a type of fat that is found especially in some vegetable oils and that is bad for your health

[1]**trans·fer** /træns'fə/ *verb* **-fers; -ferred; -fer·ring**

1 [+ *obj*] : to move (someone or something) from one place to another • We *transferred* the baby's car seat to the other car. • The patient was *transferred* to a different hospital.

2 [+ *obj*] : to cause (something) to move from one person, place, or thing to another: such as **a** : to move (data, money, etc.) from one place to another electronically • *transfer* data on the hard drive to a disk • *transfer* funds electronically • He *transferred* my call to another line. **b** : to cause (a disease, virus, etc.) to move from one living thing to another : TRANSMIT • The virus is *transferred* by mosquitoes. **c** *technical* : to give (property or rights) to another person • He *transferred* control of the company to his son. • *transfer* property by deed

3 a [+ *obj*] : to use (something, such as an idea, a skill, etc.) for a new or different purpose • She was able to *transfer* her organizational skills to her new job. **b** [*no obj*] : to be used for a new or different purpose • Her skills *transferred* well to her new job.

4 a [*no obj*] : to stop going to one school and begin going to another • She *transferred* from another high school last year. • He *transferred* to Stanford. • (*Brit*) My son will *transfer* to secondary school [=will begin going to secondary school] next year. **b** : to move to a different place or job for the same employer [*no obj*] I asked to *transfer* to the sales department. [+ *obj*] He was *transferred* to the Los Angeles office last year. • She was *transferred* to a different department. • The army *transferred* him to Germany.

5 [+ *obj*] *chiefly US* : to use (credits earned at one school) at a different school • I was able to *transfer* my credits from summer school.

6 *Brit, sports* : to move (a player) to another team in exchange for money [+ *obj*] He was *transferred* [=(*US*) *sold*] to Arsenal. [*no obj*] He *transferred* to Arsenal.

7 : to change from one plane, bus, train, etc., to another while traveling [*no obj*] We *transferred* in Chicago. [+ *obj*] We had to *transfer* [=*change*] planes in Chicago. • The passengers were *transferred* to another plane.

[2]**trans·fer** /'trænsˌfə/ *noun, pl* **-fers**

1 a : an act or process of moving someone or something from one place to another [*count*] We switched to another car, and the *transfer* only took a few minutes. • They arranged for a *transfer* of the prisoner to a different prison. • a *transfer* of funds [*noncount*] a material that reduces heat *transfer* • speeding up data *transfer* between computers **b** [*count*] : a process by which one method, system, etc., is replaced by another • We are doing everything possible to ensure a smooth *transfer* to the new system.

2 [*count*] : the act or process of giving the property or rights of one person to another person • a *transfer* by deed or will • a *transfer* of power/ownership/wealth

3 [*count*] : an act of moving from one job or location to another for the same company • a *transfer* to the home office • My overseas *transfer* has been approved.

4 [*count*] *US* : a student who has moved from one school to another • The school accepts only a few *transfers* each year. • She's a *transfer* from the junior college. • He's a ***transfer student.***

5 [*count*] *chiefly Brit* : a picture or label that is made on special paper so that it sticks to a surface : DECAL • The lettering was put on the sign by using *transfers.*

6 [*count*] *chiefly US* : a ticket that allows a passenger on a bus or train to continue traveling on another bus or train

trans·fer·able *also* **trans·fer·ra·ble** /træns'fərəbəl/ *adj* [*more* ~; *most* ~]

1 : capable of being moved or transferred from one place or situation to another • *transferable* skills • *transferable* college credits

2 : capable of being given or sold to another person • These plane tickets are not *transferable.* • a *transferable* life insurance policy

trans·fer·ence /træns'fərəns, 'trænsˌfərəns/ *noun* [*noncount*]

1 *technical* : the act of moving something from one place to another • *transference* of energy • heat *transference*
2 *psychology* : a process by which the feelings that you had for someone (such as a parent) when you were a child become directed to someone else (such as a psychoanalyst)

trans•fig•ure /trænsˈfɪgjɚ, *Brit* trænsˈfɪgə/ *verb* **-ures; -ured; -ur•ing** [+ *obj*] *literary* : to change the appearance of something or someone • Her face seemed *transfigured* by happiness.

trans•fix /trænsˈfɪks/ *verb* **-fix•es; -fixed; -fix•ing** [+ *obj*] *formal* : to cause someone to sit or stand without moving because of surprise, shock, interest, etc. — usually used as *(be) transfixed* • He stood *transfixed* by her gaze. • The children sat *transfixed* in front of the TV.

trans•form /trænsˈfoɚm/ *verb* **-forms; -formed; -form•ing** [+ *obj*] : to change (something) completely and usually in a good way • The new paint completely *transformed* [=changed the appearance of] the room. • A little creativity can *transform* an ordinary meal into a special event. • The old factory has been *transformed* into an art gallery. • The Internet has completely *transformed* [=changed the nature of] many retail businesses.

trans•for•ma•tion /ˌtrænsfɚˈmeɪʃən/ *noun, pl* **-tions** : a complete or major change in someone's or something's appearance, form, etc. [*count*] His appearance has undergone a complete *transformation.* [=his appearance has changed completely] • The building underwent various *transformations* over the years. • the character's inner *transformation* [*noncount*] an agent of *transformation*

trans•for•ma•tive /trænsˈfoɚmətɪv/ *adj, formal* : causing or able to cause a change; *especially* : causing someone's life to be different or better in some important way • a *transformative* experience • the *transformative* power of love • a *transformative* force

trans•form•er /trænsˈfoɚmɚ/ *noun, pl* **-ers** [*count*] *technical* : a device that changes the voltage of an electric current

trans•fuse /trænsˈfjuːz/ *verb* **-fus•es; -fused; -fus•ing** [+ *obj*] *medical* : to take (blood) from one person or animal and put it into another • The hospital staff *transfuses* more than 8,000 units of blood annually.

trans•fu•sion /trænsˈfjuːʒən/ *noun, pl* **-sions** : BLOOD TRANSFUSION [*noncount*] the *transfusion* of blood [*count*] Without a *transfusion* her chances of survival were slim. — often used figuratively • The project has received a much-needed *transfusion of* funds. [=has received a new supply of funds/money]

trans•gen•der /trænsˈʤɛndɚ/ *adj* : of or relating to people who have a sexual identity that is not clearly male or clearly female • the *transgender* community • *transgender* issues
– **trans•gen•dered** /trænsˈʤɛndɚd/ *adj* • transgendered people

trans•gress /trænsˈgrɛs/ *verb* **-gress•es; -gressed; -gress•ing** *formal* : to do something that is not allowed : to disobey a command or law [*no obj*] He who *transgresses* must seek forgiveness. [+ *obj*] There are legal consequences for companies that *transgress* the rules.
– **trans•gres•sion** /trænsˈgrɛʃən/ *noun, pl* **-sions** [*count*] • a minor *transgression* – **trans•gres•sor** /trænsˈgrɛsɚ/ *noun, pl* **-sors** [*count*]

[1]**tran•sient** /ˈtrænzijənt/ *adj* [*more* ~; *most* ~] *formal*
1 : not lasting long • *transient* joys
2 : staying somewhere only a short time • a *transient* population • *transient* guests
– **tran•sience** /ˈtrænzijəns/ *noun* [*noncount*] • the *transience* of fame/joy – **transiently** *adv*

[2]**transient** *noun, pl* **-sients** [*count*] *chiefly US* : a person who does not have a permanent home and who stays in a place for only a short time before going somewhere else

tran•sis•tor /trænˈzɪstɚ/ *noun, pl* **-tors** [*count*]
1 : a small device that is used to control the flow of electricity in radios, computers, etc.
2 *somewhat old-fashioned* : TRANSISTOR RADIO

transistor radio *noun, pl* ~ **-dios** [*count*] *somewhat old-fashioned* : a small radio that has transistors

tran•sit /ˈtrænsət/ *noun* [*noncount*]
1 : the act of moving people or things from one place to another • Some of the goods were lost ***in transit.*** [=in the process of being transported]
2 *US* : MASS TRANSIT • the problems of urban *transit* — often used before another noun • a proposal for a new rail *transit* route — see also RAPID TRANSIT

transit camp *noun* ~ **camps** [*count*] *chiefly Brit* : a place for refugees to stay for a short period of time

[1]**tran•si•tion** /trænˈzɪʃən/ *noun, pl* **-tions** : a change from one state or condition to another [*count*] We want to have a smooth *transition* when the new owners take control of the company. • the sometimes difficult *transition* from childhood to adulthood • The country made/underwent a peaceful *transition* from dictatorship to democracy. [*noncount*] The industry is undergoing *transition.* [=is changing in some important way] • The company is ***in transition*** [=is changing] as it adapts to the new management team.
– **tran•si•tion•al** /trænˈzɪʃənəl/ *adj* • a *transitional* government • a *transitional* phase/period/stage

[2]**transition** *verb* **-tions; -tioned; -tion•ing** [*no obj*] *chiefly US* : to make a change from one state, place, or condition to another : to make a transition • The company has *transitioned* to new management in the past year. • a student who is *transitioning* to a new school

tran•si•tive /ˈtrænsətɪv/ *adj, grammar, of a verb* : having or taking a direct object • a *transitive* verb • In "I like pie" and "She makes hats," the verbs "like" and "makes" are *transitive.* — compare INTRANSITIVE
– **tran•si•tive•ly** *adv* • The verb is being used *transitively.*

tran•si•to•ry /ˈtrænsəˌtori, *Brit* ˈtrænzətri/ *adj* : lasting only for a short time : TEMPORARY • the *transitory* nature of earthly pleasures • a *transitory* phase

transit visa *noun, pl* ~ **visas** [*count*] : a document (called a visa) that allows a person to go through one country while traveling to another country

trans•late /trænsˈleɪt, ˈtrænzˌleɪt/ *verb* **-lates; -lat•ed; -lat•ing**
1 : to change words from one language into another language [*no obj*] My client speaks only Spanish. Will you *translate* for me? • The French word "bonjour" *translates* as "hello" in English. [+ *obj*] We need someone who can *translate* Japanese into English. • We have *translated* the report. • The book has been *translated* into 37 languages. — compare INTERPRET
2 [+ *obj*] : to explain (something) in a way that is easier to understand • Can you *translate* this technical jargon?
3 [*no obj*] : to have the same meaning • To teenagers, "middle-aged" *translates* as "boring." [=teenagers think middle-aged people are boring] • Seventy million Americans—that *translates* into one American out of every four—are under the age of 24.
4 : to change (something) into a different form [+ *obj*] His job is to *translate* the decision into a working program. • She needs to *translate* her ideas into action. [*no obj*] The play *translated* quite successfully to the big screen.
translate into [*phrasal verb*] ***translate into (something)*** : to lead to (something) as a result • Competition often *translates into* [=results in] lower costs to the consumer. • Artistic success doesn't always *translate into* financial success. • The new design *translates into* more space inside the car.
– **trans•lat•able** /trænsˈleɪtəbəl/ *adj* [*more* ~; *most* ~] • The phrase isn't easily *translatable.*

trans•la•tion /trænsˈleɪʃən/ *noun, pl* **-tions**
1 a : words that have been changed from one language into a different language : words that have been translated [*count*] She is working on a *translation* of the novel. • a new *translation* of the *Iliad* • an accurate *translation* • a literal *translation* • a rough/loose *translation* • There were English *translations* on the menu. [*noncount*] I have only read Dostoevsky ***in translation.*** [=in translated form] **b** [*noncount*] : the act or process of translating something into a different language • Some things defy *translation.* [=are impossible to translate] • The quote loses something ***in translation.*** [=the quote does not have the same meaning or effectiveness when it is translated into another language] • Something must have gotten ***lost in translation*** [=lost when changed from one language into another] because the joke isn't funny in English.
2 [*noncount*] *formal* : the act or process of changing something from one form to another : TRANSFORMATION • the *translation* of economic power into political strength

trans•la•tor /trænsˈleɪtɚ, ˈtrænzˌleɪtɚ/ *noun, pl* **-tors** [*count*] : a person who changes words written in one language into a different language • a well-known *translator* of ancient Greek • She works as a *translator* for the government. — compare INTERPRETER

trans•lit•er•ate /trænsˈlɪtəˌreɪt/ *verb* **-ates; -at•ed; -at•ing** [+ *obj*] : to write words or letters in the characters of another alphabet • The Russian letter я is usually *transliterated* in English as *ya* or *ia.*

T

– **trans·lit·er·a·tion** /trænsˌlɪtəˈreɪʃən/ *noun, pl* **-tions** [*count, noncount*]

trans·lu·cent /trænsˈluːsn̩t/ *adj* [*more ~; most ~*] **:** not completely clear or transparent but clear enough to allow light to pass through ▪ Frosted glass is *translucent.* ▪ *translucent* gemstones — compare OPAQUE

– **trans·lu·cence** /trænsˈluːsn̩s/ *or* **trans·lu·cen·cy** /trænsˈluːsn̩si/ *noun* [*noncount*] ▪ Quartz has a high degree of *translucency.*

trans·mi·gra·tion /ˌtrænsˌmaɪˈgreɪʃən/ *noun* [*noncount*] **:** the movement of a soul into another body after death ▪ a belief in *transmigration*

trans·mis·si·ble /trænsˈmɪsəbəl/ *adj* [*more ~; most ~*] **:** able to be spread to other people, animals, etc. **:** capable of being transmitted ▪ *transmissible* diseases/infections ▪ The virus is highly *transmissible* to/among humans.

trans·mis·sion /trænsˈmɪʃən/ *noun, pl* **-sions**

1 a [*noncount*] **:** the act or process of sending electrical signals to a radio, television, computer, etc. ▪ The equipment is used for the *transmission* of television signals. ▪ data *transmission* **b** [*count*] **:** something (such as a message or broadcast) that is transmitted to a radio, television, etc. ▪ a fax *transmission* ▪ We are receiving a live *transmission* from the scene of the accident.

2 [*noncount*] **:** the act or process by which something is spread or passed from one person or thing to another ▪ the *transmission* of disease ▪ the *transmission* of knowledge from one generation to the next

3 : the part of a vehicle that uses the power produced by the engine to turn the wheels [*count*] My car has a manual *transmission.* [*noncount*] This car comes with automatic *transmission.* — see picture at CAR

trans·mit /trænsˈmɪt/ *verb* **-mits; -mit·ted; -mit·ting**

1 : to send (information, sound, etc.) in the form of electrical signals to a radio, television, computer, etc. [+ *obj*] The technology allows data to be *transmitted* by cellular phones. ▪ *transmitting* and receiving radio signals [*no obj*] The radio *transmits* on two different frequencies.

2 [+ *obj*] **:** to give or pass (information, values, etc.) from one person to another ▪ the different ways that people *transmit* their values/opinions/knowledge

3 [+ *obj*] **:** to cause (a virus, disease, etc.) to be given to others ▪ insects that *transmit* diseases ▪ The disease is *transmitted* by sexual contact.

4 [+ *obj*] **:** to allow (light, heat, etc.) to pass through ▪ Glass *transmits* light.

– **trans·mit·ta·ble** /trænsˈmɪtəbəl/ *adj* [*more ~; most ~*] ▪ *transmittable* [=*transmissible*] diseases

trans·mit·ter /trænsˈmɪtɚ, ˈtrænzˌmɪtɚ/ *noun, pl* **-ters** [*count*]

1 : a device that sends out radio or television signals

2 : a person or thing that causes something to be spread or transmitted to others ▪ Mosquitoes are the main *transmitters* of the disease. ▪ a *transmitter* of tradition

trans·mute /trænsˈmjuːt/ *verb* **-mutes; -mut·ed; -mut·ing** *formal* **:** to completely change the form, appearance, or nature of (someone or something) — usually + *into* [+ *obj*] Her art *transmutes* [=*transforms*] trash *into* a thing of beauty. ▪ The stories of their lives were *transmuted into* works of fiction. [*no obj*] The former criminal had *transmuted into* a national hero.

– **trans·mu·ta·tion** /ˌtrænsmjuˈteɪʃən/ *noun, pl* **-tions** [*count, noncount*]

trans·na·tion·al /ˌtrænsˈnæʃənl/ *adj* **:** operating in or involving more than one country ▪ *transnational* corporations ▪ *transnational* crime

trans·oce·an·ic /ˌtrænsˌoʊʃiˈænɪk/ *adj* **:** crossing the ocean ▪ *transoceanic* flights — compare TRANSATLANTIC, TRANSPACIFIC

tran·som /ˈtrænsəm/ *noun, pl* **-soms** [*count*]

1 *US* **:** a small window that is above a door or larger window — called also (*Brit*) *fan light*

2 : a stone or wooden bar that goes across the top of a door or window

over the transom *US* **:** without being asked for or expected — used especially to describe a book, story, etc., that is sent to a publisher ▪ The manuscript arrived *over the transom.*

trans·pa·cif·ic /ˌtrænspəˈsɪfɪk/ *adj*

1 : crossing the Pacific Ocean ▪ *transpacific* ocean liners

2 : of, relating to, or involving countries on both sides of the Pacific Ocean ▪ *transpacific* trade

trans·par·en·cy /trænsˈperənsi/ *noun, pl* **-cies**

1 [*noncount*] **:** the quality of being transparent: such as **a :** the quality that makes it possible to see through something ▪ the *transparency* of a piece of glass **b :** the quality that makes something obvious or easy to understand ▪ the *transparency* of their motives ▪ He says that there needs to be more *transparency* in the way the government operates.

2 [*count*] **:** a piece of thin, clear plastic with pictures or words printed on it that can be viewed on a large screen by shining light through it ▪ The professor used *transparencies* and an overhead projector during her lectures.

trans·par·ent /trænsˈperənt/ *adj* [*more ~; most ~*]

1 : able to be seen through ▪ *transparent* plastic bags ▪ *transparent* [=*clear*] glass

2 a : easy to notice or understand **:** OBVIOUS ▪ a *transparent* lie/falsehood ▪ Their motives were *transparent.* **b :** honest and open **:** not secretive ▪ The company's business dealings need to be more *transparent.* [=information about the company needs to be more available for people to see]

– **trans·par·ent·ly** *adv* ▪ a *transparently* silly excuse

tran·spire /trænˈspajɚ/ *verb* **-spires; -spired; -spir·ing**

1 [*no obj*] *formal* **:** to happen ▪ They wouldn't say what had *transpired* [=*taken place*] at the meeting. ▪ No one will soon forget the historic events that *transpired* on that day.

2 [*no obj*] *formal* **:** to become known — usually used with *it* ▪ Her name, *it transpired,* was false. [=(less formally) it turned out that her name was false] ▪ *It transpired* that they had met previously. [=we found out that they had met previously]

3 *technical, of a plant* **:** to have water evaporate from the surface of leaves [*no obj*] A plant *transpires* more freely on a hot dry day. [+ *obj*] Trees *transpire* water at a rapid rate.

[1]**trans·plant** /ˌtrænsˈplænt/ *verb* **-plants; -plant·ed; -plant·ing**

1 : to remove (a plant) from the ground or from a pot and move it to another place [+ *obj*] She carefully *transplanted* the seedlings. ▪ The bush was *transplanted* to a different part of the garden. [*no obj*] This plant does not *transplant* well. [=this plant does not grow well if you transplant it]

2 [+ *obj*] *medical* **:** to perform a medical operation in which an organ or other part that has been removed from the body of one person is put it into the body of another person ▪ Doctors *transplanted* one of his kidneys into his sister. ▪ a recipient of a *transplanted* heart

3 : to move (a person or animal) to a new home **:** RELOCATE [+ *obj*] The group *transplanted* the beavers to another part of the state. [*no obj*] She is a New Yorker who recently *transplanted* to the West Coast.

– **trans·plan·ta·tion** /ˌtrænsˌplænˈteɪʃən/ *noun, pl* **-tions** [*count, noncount*]

[2]**trans·plant** /ˈtrænsˌplænt/ *noun, pl* **-plants**

1 *medical* **a :** a medical operation in which an organ or other part is removed from the body of one person and put into the body of another person [*count*] The heart *transplant* was successful. ▪ He is going to need a liver *transplant.* [*noncount*] The doctors are trying to keep him alive until a liver can be found for *transplant.* ▪ *transplant* patients/recipients **b** [*count*] **:** an organ, piece of skin, etc., that is transplanted ▪ The patient's body rejected the *transplant.* ▪ She received a bone marrow *transplant* from an unknown donor.

2 [*count*] **:** a person who has moved to a new home especially in a different region or country ▪ She's a Southern *transplant* who now lives in New York.

trans·pon·der /trænˈspɑːndɚ/ *noun, pl* **-ders** [*count*] *technical* **:** a device that receives a radio signal and sends out a signal in response and that is used especially to show the location of something (such as an airplane)

[1]**trans·port** /ˌtrænsˈpoɚt/ *verb* **-ports; -port·ed; -port·ing** [+ *obj*]

1 : to carry (someone or something) from one place to another ▪ A van at the hotel *transports* guests to and from the airport. ▪ the cost of producing and *transporting* goods ▪ The melons are *transported* in large wooden crates. ▪ The illness was first *transported* across the ocean by European explorers.

2 a : to cause (someone) to imagine that he or she is in a different place or time ▪ The movie *transports* us to a world of stunning beauty. ▪ While reading, I was *transported* back to the year 1492. **b** *literary* **:** to cause (someone) to feel very happy, interested, or excited — usually used as *(be) transported* ▪ We *were transported* by the music.

3 *in the past* **:** to send (a criminal) to live in a distant country as a form of punishment ▪ He was *transported* for stealing.

– **trans·port·able** /ˌtræns'poɚtəbəl/ *adj* [*more* ~; *most* ~] ▪ easily *transportable* goods

[2]**trans·port** /'trænsˌpoɚt/ *noun, pl* **-ports**
1 [*noncount*] **:** the act or process of moving people or things from one place to another **:** TRANSPORTATION ▪ the *transport* of manufactured goods
2 [*count*] **a :** a ship that is made for carrying soldiers or military equipment ▪ a troop *transport* **b :** an airplane that is used to carry people or goods ▪ an executive jet *transport* ▪ supersonic *transports*
3 [*noncount*] *chiefly Brit* **:** TRANSPORTATION 2 ▪ I was left without *transport* when the car broke down. ▪ She relies on public *transport*.
4 [*count*] *literary* **:** a strong or extremely pleasant emotion — usually plural ▪ The news sent them into *transports* of joy. [=the news made them extremely happy]

trans·por·ta·tion /ˌtrænspɚ'teɪʃən/ *noun* [*noncount*]
1 *chiefly US* **:** the act or process of moving people or things from one place to another ▪ the *transportation* of troops overseas ▪ She arranged for the *transportation* of her furniture to her new apartment.
2 *chiefly US* **a :** a way of traveling from one place to another place ▪ I was left without *transportation* [=(*chiefly Brit*) *transport*] when the car broke down. ▪ modern ***air transportation*** [=travel in airplanes, helicopters, etc.] ▪ The hotel offers free ***ground transportation*** to and from the airport. [=the hotel has vehicles that will take you to and from the airport for free] **b :** a system for moving passengers or goods from one place to another ▪ high speed rail *transportation* ▪ He was the U.S. Secretary of *Transportation* under President Reagan. ▪ You can go almost anywhere in New York City using ***public transportation***. [=a system of trains, buses, etc., that is paid for or run by the government]
3 : a method of punishment used in the past especially in Britain in which criminals were sent to live in a distant country

transport café *noun, pl* ~ **cafés** [*count*] *Brit* **:** TRUCK STOP

trans·port·er /træns'poɚtɚ/ *noun, pl* **-ers** [*count*] **:** something that is used to move or transport people or things; *especially, chiefly Brit* **:** a vehicle for carrying large and heavy loads ▪ a car *transporter*

trans·pose /træns'pouz/ *verb* **-pos·es; -posed; -pos·ing** [+ *obj*]
1 : to change the position or order of (two things) ▪ I must have accidentally *transposed* the numbers when I dialed his phone number.
2 : to change (something) by giving it a different form, using it in a different place or situation, etc. ▪ a story originally set in London that has been *transposed* to Paris for this film
3 *music* **:** to write or perform (a piece of music) in a different key ▪ a melody *transposed* to the key of C
– **trans·po·si·tion** /ˌtrænspə'zɪʃən/ *noun, pl* **-tions** [*count, noncount*]

trans·sex·u·al /træn'sɛkʃəwəl/ *noun, pl* **-als** [*count*] **:** a person who tries to look, dress, and act like a member of the opposite sex; *especially* **:** someone who medically changes himself or herself into a member of the opposite sex — compare TRANSVESTITE
– **transsexual** *adj* ▪ *transsexual* issues – **trans·sex·u·al·ism** /træn'sɛkʃəwəˌlɪzəm/ *noun* [*noncount*]

tran·sub·stan·ti·a·tion /ˌtrænsəbˌstænʃi'eɪʃən/ *noun* [*noncount*] **:** the belief in some Christian religions that the bread and wine given at Communion become the body and blood of Jesus Christ when they are blessed

trans·verse /træns'vɚs/ *adj, technical* **:** lying or made across something ▪ The surgeon made a *transverse* incision across her abdomen.
– **trans·verse·ly** *adv* ▪ cut *transversely* into sections

trans·ves·tite /træns'vɛˌstaɪt/ *noun, pl* **-tites** [*count*] **:** a person who likes to dress like a person of the opposite sex ▪ *transvestites* dressed in drag — compare TRANSSEXUAL
– **trans·ves·tism** /træns'vɛˌstɪzəm/ *noun* [*noncount*]
– **transvestite** *adj* ▪ a *transvestite* magazine/show

[1]**trap** /'træp/ *noun, pl* **traps** [*count*]
1 : a device that is used for catching animals ▪ They set *traps* to catch the mice. ▪ a bear/lobster *trap* ▪ She has a mind like a steel *trap*. [=she remembers everything] — see also MOUSETRAP
2 a : something that is used or done to stop or capture someone (such as a criminal) ▪ The police are laying/setting a *trap* to catch him. ▪ The soldiers had walked/stumbled into a *trap*. **b :** a situation in which someone is tricked into doing or saying something ▪ Credit card companies were accused of laying/setting *traps* for consumers. [=tricking consumers] — see also SPEED TRAP **c :** a bad position or situation from which it is difficult to escape ▪ a mental/theoretical *trap* ▪ Many new businesses fail because they try to expand too quickly, but we have so far managed to avoid that *trap*. ▪ They tended to view marriage as a *trap*. ▪ Don't ***fall into the trap of*** believing that technology can solve all our problems. — see also POVERTY TRAP
3 *US, golf* **:** SAND TRAP
4 *slang* **:** MOUTH ▪ Can he ***keep his trap shut*** about it? [=can he be trusted not to tell anyone about it?] ▪ ***Shut your trap***! I've heard enough!
5 *US, technical* **:** a bend in a pipe that contains water and that prevents gas from passing through the pipe ▪ a plumbing *trap* — called also (*Brit*) *U-bend*; see picture at PLUMBING
6 : a light carriage that is usually pulled by one horse ▪ a horse and *trap*
spring a trap see [2]SPRING
– see also BOOBY TRAP, DEATH TRAP, TOURIST TRAP

[2]**trap** *verb* **traps; trapped; trap·ping** [+ *obj*]
1 : to catch (an animal) in a trap ▪ *trapping* mice ▪ They *trapped* the bear and relocated it to another forest.
2 : to force (a person or animal) into a place or position from which escape is very difficult or impossible ▪ The police *trapped* [=*cornered*] the robber in an alley.
3 a : to cause (a person or animal) to be unable to move or escape from a dangerous place ▪ A tree fell in front of the door and *trapped* the people inside. — usually used as (*be*) *trapped* ▪ They *were trapped* and couldn't get out. ▪ She *was trapped* in the elevator for more than an hour. **b :** to force (someone) to stay in a bad or unpleasant situation — + *in* ▪ He felt *trapped in* his marriage. ▪ people *trapped in* low-paying jobs
4 : to fool or trick (someone) into doing or saying something ▪ The lawyer tried to *trap* the witness into admitting that she had lied.
5 : to stop (something) from escaping or being lost ▪ Greenhouse gases *trap* heat inside the Earth's atmosphere.
6 *Brit* **:** to cause (something, such as a part of your body) to become stuck and unable to move ▪ She *trapped* [=(*US*) *caught, pinched*] her finger in the door.
7 *baseball* **:** to catch (the ball) immediately after it bounces off the ground ▪ The outfielder *trapped* the ball.

trap·door /'træp'doɚ/ *noun, pl* **-doors** [*count*] **:** a door that covers or hides an opening in a floor or ceiling

tra·peze /træ'piːz/ *noun, pl* **-pez·es** [*count*] **:** a short bar that is hung high above the ground by two ropes and that is held by circus performers who perform athletic tricks on it ▪ performing tricks on the *trapeze* ▪ a *trapeze* artist/act

tra·pe·zi·um /trə'piːzijəm/ *noun, pl* **-zi·ums** *or* **-zia** /-zijə/ [*count*] *geometry*
1 *US* **:** a four-sided shape that has no parallel sides — called also (*Brit*) *trapezoid*
2 *Brit* **:** TRAPEZOID 1

trap·e·zoid /'træpəˌzoɪd/ *noun, pl* **-zoids** [*count*] *geometry*
1 *US* **:** a four-sided shape that has two sides that are parallel and two sides that are not parallel — called also (*Brit*) *trapezium*
2 *Brit* **:** TRAPEZIUM 1
– **trap·e·zoi·dal** /ˌtræpə'zoɪdl/ *adj* ▪ a *trapezoidal* shape

trap·per /'træpɚ/ *noun, pl* **-pers** [*count*] **:** someone who catches animals in traps; *especially* **:** someone who catches wild animals in traps and kills them for their fur ▪ 18th-century Canadian fur *trappers*

trap·pings /'træpɪŋz/ *noun* [*plural*] **:** the objects, activities, etc., that are associated with a particular condition, situation, or position in life **:** the visible signs of something ▪ Despite its democratic *trappings*, the country's government was a dictatorship. — often + *of* ▪ She had lots of money and enjoyed all the *trappings of* success/wealth.

[1]**trash** /'træʃ/ *noun* [*noncount*]
1 *US* **a :** things that are no longer useful or wanted and that have been thrown away ▪ *Trash* [=*rubbish*] was strewn throughout the yard. ▪ Take out the *trash*, please. ▪ Raccoons were going through our *trash*. [=*garbage*] **b :** a container where people put things that are being thrown away ▪ I put/threw the dirty diaper in the *trash*.
2 *informal* **:** something that is very low in quality ▪ There's nothing but *trash* [=*rubbish*] on TV these days. ▪ I can't believe you're reading that *trash*.

T

3 *chiefly US, informal + disapproving* **:** someone who has very low social status or who is not respected ▪ She thinks that they're all *trash.* ▪ They treated him like *trash.* [=treated him very badly] — see also TRAILER TRASH, WHITE TRASH

talk trash *US, informal* **:** to say insulting things especially to an opponent in a contest, game, etc. ▪ Players on both teams were *talking trash.* — see also TRASH TALK

[2]**trash** *verb* **trash·es; trashed; trash·ing** [+ *obj*] *informal*

1 *US* **:** to throw away (something) ▪ a computer program that *trashes* useless files ▪ The vacuum cleaner couldn't be fixed, so I *trashed* it.

2 : to cause great damage to (something) ▪ The apartment had been *trashed.* ▪ He says that the government's policies are *trashing* the environment.

3 : to criticize (someone or something) very harshly ▪ The critics *trashed* [=(*Brit*) *rubbished*] the new film.

trash can *noun, pl* ~ **cans** [*count*] *US* **:** a container that holds materials that have been thrown away — called also (*Brit*) *dustbin,* (*Brit*) *litter bin*

trashed *adj* [*more* ~; *most* ~] *US, informal* **:** very drunk ▪ By the end of the party he was completely *trashed.*

trashman *noun, pl* **-men** [*count*] *US* **:** a person who collects and removes trash

trash talk *noun* [*noncount*] *US, informal* **:** insulting comments that are made especially to an opponent in a contest, game, etc. ▪ He had to listen to a lot of *trash talk* from the other players. — see also *talk trash* at [1]TRASH

– trash–talk /ˈtræʃˌtɑːk/ *verb* **-talks; -talked; -talk·ing** [*no obj*] They *trash-talked* throughout the game. [+ *obj*] He's always *trash-talking* the other players. **– trash–talk·er** /ˈtræʃˌtɑːkɚ/ *noun, pl* **-ers** [*count*] **– trash–talking** *noun* [*noncount*] ▪ There was a lot of *trash-talking* going on throughout the game.

trashy /ˈtræʃi/ *adj* **trash·i·er; -est** *informal + disapproving*

1 : not decent or respectable **:** involving improper behavior ▪ *trashy* films/novels ▪ *trashy* women ▪ Her outfit was a bit *trashy.*

2 : very low in quality ▪ *trashy* television programs ▪ a *trashy* amusement park

– trash·i·ness *noun* [*noncount*]

trau·ma /ˈtrɑːmə/ *noun, pl* **-mas**

1 : a very difficult or unpleasant experience that causes someone to have mental or emotional problems usually for a long time [*count*] She never fully recovered from the *traumas* she suffered during her childhood. [*noncount*] She never fully recovered from the *trauma* of her experiences.

2 *medical* **:** a serious injury to a person's body [*noncount*] an accident victim with severe head *trauma* ▪ repeated *trauma* to a knee [*count*] The accident victim sustained multiple *traumas.* — see also *blunt trauma* at [1]BLUNT

trauma center (*US*) *or Brit* **trauma centre** *noun, pl* ~ **-ters** [*count*] **:** a part of a hospital that is specially prepared to perform emergency surgery on people with severe injuries

trau·mat·ic /trəˈmætɪk/ *adj* [*more* ~; *most* ~]

1 : causing someone to become very upset in a way that can lead to serious mental and emotional problems ▪ She had a *traumatic* childhood. ▪ a *traumatic* event/experience ▪ Losing your job can be very *traumatic.* — see also POST-TRAUMATIC STRESS DISORDER

2 *medical* **:** related to or caused by a severe injury to your body ▪ He suffered a *traumatic* brain injury in the accident.

– trau·mat·i·cal·ly /trəˈmætɪkli/ *adv*

trau·ma·tize *also Brit* **trau·ma·tise** /ˈtrɑːməˌtaɪz/ *verb* **-tiz·es; -tized; -tiz·ing** [+ *obj*] **:** to cause (someone) to become very upset in a way that often leads to serious emotional problems **:** to cause (someone) to suffer emotional trauma ▪ He was *traumatized* by the experience.

T

tra·vail /trəˈveɪl/ *noun, pl* **-vails**

1 [*count*] *formal* **:** a difficult experience or situation — usually plural ▪ The book describes the political *travails* of the President during his first year in office.

2 [*noncount*] *literary* **:** painful or difficult work or effort ▪ They finally succeeded after many months of *travail.*

[1]**trav·el** /ˈtrævəl/ *verb* **-els;** *US* **-eled** *or Brit* **-elled;** *US* **-el·ing** *or Brit* **-el·ling**

1 a [*no obj*] **:** to go on a trip or journey **:** to go to a place and especially one that is far away ▪ The birds are *traveling* south for the winter. ▪ His job requires him to *travel* frequently. ▪ She enjoys *traveling* around Europe. ▪ *traveling* by bus/car/plane/train ▪ They *traveled* cross-country from New York to California. ▪ I prefer to ***travel light*** [=to travel with very little baggage] — often used figuratively ▪ My mind *traveled* back to my childhood. [=I began thinking about my childhood] **b** [+ *obj*] **:** to go through or over (a place) during a trip or journey ▪ They *traveled* the countryside.

2 [*no obj*] **a :** to move from one place to another ▪ The car was *traveling* at a very high (rate of) speed. ▪ The pain *traveled* down his back. ▪ the way that sound *travels* in an empty room ▪ Her eyes *traveled* around the room. [=she looked around the room] **b** *informal* **:** to go fast ▪ That car was really *traveling* when it passed us.

3 [*no obj*] **:** to be brought from one place to another ▪ The order/shipment is *traveling* by plane. ▪ a dish that *travels* well [=that is easily moved and does not break, make messes, etc.]

4 [*no obj*] **:** to spread or be passed from one place or person to another ▪ The news of his death *traveled* fast.

5 [*no obj*] **:** to spend time with a particular group or kind of people ▪ She *travels* in conservative political circles. ▪ He *traveled* with a sophisticated crowd.

6 [*no obj*] *basketball* **:** to take more steps while holding a basketball than the rules allow ▪ I saw him *travel.* ▪ The referee called her for *traveling.*

[2]**travel** *noun, pl* **-els**

1 [*noncount*] **:** the act or activity of traveling ▪ She doesn't enjoy foreign *travel.* ▪ Air *travel* was affected by the storm. ▪ train/rail *travel* ▪ The book discusses the future of *travel* in outer space. — often used before another noun ▪ *travel* books ▪ *travel* costs/expenses ▪ a *travel* bag/mug [=a bag/mug that is designed to be used while you are traveling]

2 ***travels*** [*plural*] **:** trips or journeys to distant places ▪ We extended our *travels* for another week. ▪ *travels* in foreign lands

travel agency *noun, pl* ~ **-cies** [*count*] **:** a business that helps to make arrangements for people who want to travel

travel agent *noun, pl* ~ **agents** [*count*] **:** a person whose job is to help people who want to travel by buying plane tickets, making hotel reservations, etc.

trav·eled (*US*) *or Brit* **trav·elled** /ˈtrævəld/ *adj* [*more* ~; *most* ~]

1 : having traveled to many different places ▪ a well/widely *traveled* journalist

2 : used by travelers ▪ a well *traveled* road [=a busy road, a road on which there is a lot of traffic] ▪ less *traveled* streets

trav·el·er (*US*) *or Brit* **trav·el·ler** /ˈtrævəlɚ/ *noun, pl* **-ers** [*count*]

1 : someone who is traveling or who travels often ▪ Groups of *travelers* were everywhere that summer. ▪ The airport can handle large numbers of *travelers.* ▪ a seasoned *traveler*

2 *Brit* **:** a person who moves around from place to place instead of living in one place for a long time

traveler's check (*US*) *or Brit* **traveller's cheque** *noun, pl* ~ **checks** [*count*] **:** a check that is paid for in advance and that may be exchanged for or used like cash

trav·el·ing (*US*) *or Brit* **trav·el·ling** /ˈtrævəlɪŋ/ *adj, always used before a noun*

1 : going to different places instead of staying in one place ▪ a troupe of *traveling* actors ▪ a *traveling* circus ▪ a *traveling* exhibit

2 a : relating to the activity of traveling ▪ *traveling* expenses **b :** designed to be used by someone who is traveling ▪ a *traveling* alarm clock **c :** going with someone who is traveling ▪ a ***traveling companion*** [=a person who goes with you when you travel somewhere]

traveling salesman (*US*) *or Brit* **travelling salesman** *noun, pl* ~ **-men** [*count*] **:** a person whose job is to travel to different places in a particular area and to sell products or get orders from customers

trav·el·ogue *also US* **trav·el·og** /ˈtrævəˌlɑːg/ *noun, pl* **-ogues** *also* **-ogs** [*count*] **:** a speech, movie, or piece of writing about someone's experiences while traveling

travel sickness *noun* [*noncount*] *Brit* **:** MOTION SICKNESS

– travel–sick *adj*

tra·verse /trəˈvɚs/ *verb* **-vers·es; -versed; -vers·ing** [+ *obj*] *somewhat formal* **:** to move across (an area) ▪ The candidates *traversed* the state throughout the campaign. ▪ ships *traversing* the ocean ▪ The river *traverses* the county.

– tra·verse /ˈtrævɚs, trəˈvɚs/ *noun, pl* **-vers·es** [*count*] ▪ The climbers made a dangerous *traverse* across the glacier.

trav·er·tine /ˈtrævɚˌtiːn/ *noun* [*noncount*] **:** a light-colored type of rock that is used especially in buildings ▪ *travertine* tile/floors

trav·es·ty /ˈtrævəsti/ *noun, pl* **-ties** [*count*] **:** something that is shocking, upsetting, or ridiculous because it is not what it is supposed to be ▪ It is a *travesty* and a tragedy that so many people would be denied the right to vote. ▪ The investigation into the causes of the accident was a complete *travesty*. [=*sham*] • The trial was ***a travesty of justice***.

[1]**trawl** /ˈtrɑːl/ *noun, pl* **trawls** [*count*] : a large net that a boat pulls along the bottom of the ocean to catch fish

[2]**trawl** *verb* **trawls; trawled; trawl·ing**
1 : to catch fish with a large net (called a trawl) [*no obj*] The boat *trawled* far out at sea. [+ *obj*] a fishing boat *trawling* the ocean floor
2 : to search through (something) in order to find someone or something [+ *obj*] He *trawled* the Internet looking for Web sites on growing grapes. [*no obj*] She was *trawling* through old letters for information about her family.

trawl·er /ˈtrɑːlɚ/ *noun, pl* **-ers** [*count*] : a boat that is used for catching fish with a large net (called a trawl)

tray /ˈtreɪ/ *noun, pl* **trays** [*count*]
1 : a thin, flat, and often rectangular piece of plastic, metal, wood, etc., that has a low rim and that is used for carrying things • She carried the *tray* of food to our table. — see also TEA TRAY
2 : a container that has low sides and usually no top and that is used to hold something • a car with several storage *trays* • (*Brit*) a litter *tray* [=(*US*) box; a container for holding litter for a cat] • an ice cube *tray* [=a container used to make ice cubes] • a seedling *tray* [=a container in which young plants are grown] — see also ASHTRAY, IN TRAY, OUT TRAY

treach·er·ous /ˈtrɛtʃərəs/ *adj* [*more* ~; *most* ~]
1 : not able to be trusted • a *treacherous* ally/enemy : showing that someone cannot be trusted • a *treacherous* act of betrayal • *treacherous* misdeeds
2 : very dangerous and difficult to deal with • sailing through *treacherous* waters • They were not prepared to hike over such *treacherous* terrain. • The snow made their hike all the more *treacherous*. • Discussions about money can lead couples into *treacherous* territory.
– treach·er·ous·ly *adv*

treach·ery /ˈtrɛtʃəri/ *noun, pl* **-er·ies**
1 [*noncount*] : harmful things that are done usually secretly to a friend, your own country, etc. • a tale of *treachery* and revenge
2 [*count*] : an act of harming someone who trusts you • She was deeply hurt by her husband's *treacheries*. [=her husband's treacherous acts]

trea·cle /ˈtriːkəl/ *noun* [*noncount*]
1 *Brit* **a :** MOLASSES **b :** a blend of molasses, sugar, and corn syrup
2 : something that is annoying because it is too sentimental • The book is ruined by all the *treacle* about his childhood.
– trea·cly /ˈtriːkəli/ *adj* **trea·cli·er; -est** [*also more* ~; *most* ~] • dark, *treacly* syrup • a *treacly* greeting card

[1]**tread** /ˈtrɛd/ *verb* **treads; trod** /ˈtrɑːd/ *also* **tread·ed; trod·den** /ˈtrɑːdn̩/ *or* **trod; tread·ing**
1 [*no obj*] : to walk • They slowly *trod* back to the camp. • Don't *tread* on the grass. — often used figuratively • He has gone ***where others fear to tread***. [=he has done things that other people are afraid to do] • If you're thinking about asking for a raise, I advise you to ***tread lightly***. [=to proceed carefully]
2 [+ *obj*] : to walk on or along (something) • *treading* the halls of the Senate — often used figuratively • The company is *treading* a fine line between tradition and innovation.
3 [+ *obj*] : to form (a path) by walking • Countless footsteps have *trodden* a path to their door.
4 [+ *obj*] : to crush or press (something) with your feet • Don't *tread* dirt into the carpet. • *treading* grapes for wine
tread on someone's toes see [1]TOE
tread the boards *old-fashioned* : to perform on a stage as an actor • It's been many years since he first *trod the boards* on Broadway.
tread water **1 :** to float upright in deep water by moving your legs and usually your arms forward and backward **2 :** to stay in a situation without making any progress • I'm just *treading water* financially right now.

[2]**tread** *noun, pl* **treads** [*count*]
1 a : the part of a tire that touches the ground : the pattern of raised lines on the surface of a tire • The *treads* of the tires were badly worn. **b :** a mark made by a tire when it rolls over the ground • The police found tire *treads* [=*tracks*] in the mud. — see also RETREAD
2 : the part of a shoe or boot that touches the ground : the pattern of raised lines on the bottom of a shoe or boot • running shoes with good *treads*
3 : the part of a stair that you step on
4 : the way that someone walks or the sound made by walking • a light/heavy *tread* [=*step*]

trea·dle /ˈtrɛdl̩/ *noun, pl* **trea·dles** [*count*] : a small, flat bar that you press with your foot to operate a machine (such as a pump or sewing machine)

tread·mill /ˈtrɛd,mɪl/ *noun, pl* **-mills**
1 [*count*] : an exercise machine which has a large belt that moves around while a person walks or runs on it — see picture at GYM
2 [*singular*] : a boring or tiring activity, job, etc., in which you repeatedly do the same things • the office *treadmill* • the *treadmill* of exhausting family schedules

trea·son /ˈtriːzn̩/ *noun* [*noncount*] : the crime of trying to overthrow your country's government or of helping your country's enemies during war • He is guilty of *treason*. — called also *high treason*
– trea·son·able /ˈtriːzənəbəl/ *adj* • *treasonable* acts **– trea·son·ous** /ˈtriːzənəs/ *adj* • *treasonous* [=*traitorous*] behavior

[1]**trea·sure** /ˈtrɛʒɚ/ *noun, pl* **-sures**
1 [*noncount*] : something valuable (such as money, jewels, gold, or silver) that is hidden or kept in a safe place • a legend about the pirates' buried/sunken/hidden *treasure* • the royal *treasure*
2 [*count*] : something that is very special, important, or valuable • childhood *treasures* [=things that are important to you because you had them when you were a child] • Central Park is one of New York City's many *treasures*. • The panda is considered one of China's ***national treasures***. [=something that is greatly valued by the people of China]
3 [*singular*] : a person who is greatly loved or valued especially because of being very helpful • Grandmother's nurse has been a real *treasure*.

[2]**treasure** *verb* **treasures; trea·sured; trea·sur·ing** [+ *obj*] : to value (something) very much • I *treasure* our friendship. • He *treasures* that autographed baseball. • My grandmother's ring is my most *treasured* possession. ***synonyms*** see APPRECIATE

treasure chest *noun, pl* ~ **chests** [*count*] : a large box that is filled with gold, silver, jewels, etc. — often used figuratively • The house is a *treasure chest* filled with artifacts from a bygone era.

treasure house *noun, pl* ~ **houses** [*count*] : a place where there are many valuable things — often + *of* • The city is a *treasure house of* art. [=there are many works of art in the city] • Books are *treasure houses of* knowledge.

treasure hunt *noun, pl* ~ **hunts** [*count*]
1 : an act of searching for treasure • The adventurers set sail on a *treasure hunt*. — sometimes used figuratively • a *treasure hunt* at one of the city's flea markets
2 : a game in which each player or team tries to be the first to find an object or group of objects that have been hidden
– treasure hunter *noun, pl* ~ **-ers** [*count*]

trea·sur·er /ˈtrɛʒərɚ/ *noun, pl* **-ers** [*count*] : someone who is officially in charge of the money that is taken in and paid out by a government, business, organization, etc. • She is *treasurer* of the college/museum/company.

treasure trove *noun, pl* ~ **troves** [*count*]
1 : a collection of valuable things (such as gold and silver coins or jewels) found in a place where it was hidden, buried, etc. • Divers found a *treasure trove* of gold and silver in the wreckage of a ship that sank hundreds of years ago.
2 : a source or collection of valuable things — usually + *of* • The area is a *treasure trove of* fossils. [=the area has a very large number of fossils] • The book is a *treasure trove of* useful information.

trea·sury /ˈtrɛʒəri/ *noun, pl* **-sur·ies** [*count*]
1 : the place where the money of a government, club, etc., is kept • A government official has been accused of stealing from the nation's *treasury*. • The fees are deposited into the state's *treasury*. • How much (money) is in the club's *treasury*?; *also* : the money itself • A part of the nation's *treasury* is spent on space exploration.
2 : a place in a church, castle, palace, etc., where money and valuable objects are kept
3 : a group of valuable things that are related in some way • a *treasury* of ideas • The author has collected a *treasury* of facts and lore about horses. — used especially in the titles of books • The Horse Lover's *Treasury*
the Treasury : the government department that is in charge of handling a country's money • the U.S. Secretary of *the Treasury* — often used as ***Treasury*** before another noun •

T

Treasury bills/bonds/securities ▪ *Treasury* officials ▪ the *Treasury* Secretary — called also *the Treasury Department*

[1]treat /ˈtri:t/ *verb* **treats; treat·ed; treat·ing**

1 *always followed by an adverb or preposition* [+ *obj*] **:** to deal with or think about (something) especially in a particular way ▪ The author *treats* this issue in the next chapter. ▪ You should *treat* [=*consider, regard*] this information as top secret. ▪ He *treats* [=*regards*] everything I say as a joke. ▪ This situation must be *treated* with great care.

2 *always followed by an adverb or preposition* [+ *obj*] **:** to think of and act toward (someone or something) in a specified way ▪ I try to *treat* everyone equally. ▪ She *treats* the horse cruelly. ▪ They *treated* me like a member of their family. ▪ I was *treated* like a queen/criminal. ▪ My parents still *treat* me like a child. ▪ Try to *treat* everyone as an equal. ▪ Young people should always *treat* their elders with respect. ▪ He ***treated me like dirt*** [=he was very rude, disrespectful, or unkind to me]

3 a : to pay for someone's food, drink, or entertainment [*no obj*] Let's go out to dinner. I'll *treat*. [+ *obj*] — usually + *to* ▪ They *treated* us *to* lunch. **b** [+ *obj*] **:** to provide (someone) with something pleasant or amusing — + *to* ▪ At the end of the concert, the band *treated* their fans *to* a new song. — often used as *(be) treated* ▪ The people on the tour *were treated to* a rare glimpse of the bird. [=the people on the tour had the rare and enjoyable experience of seeing the bird] **c** [+ *obj*] **:** to buy or get something special and enjoyable for (yourself) — + *to* ▪ He *treated* himself *to* some ice cream. ▪ She *treated* herself *to* a massage.

4 [+ *obj*] **a :** to give medical care to (a person or animal) ▪ Doctors immediately *treated* the patient. ▪ She was *treated* for dehydration. **b :** to deal with (a disease, infection, etc.) in order to make someone feel better or become healthy again ▪ She is taking medication to *treat* the condition. ▪ The infection can be *treated* with antibiotics.

5 [+ *obj*] **:** to put a chemical or other substance on or in (something) in order to protect it, preserve it, clean it, etc. — often + *with* ▪ He *treated* the wood *with* a waterproof sealant. — often used as *(be) treated* ▪ The crops *were treated with* a pesticide. ▪ Has the water *been treated*?

[2]treat *noun, pl* **treats** [*count*]

1 : an occurrence in which you pay for someone's food, drink, or entertainment ▪ Let's go out to dinner. It'll be my *treat*. [=I will pay for our dinners] — see also DUTCH TREAT, TRICK OR TREAT

2 : something pleasant or amusing that is unusual or unexpected ▪ Seeing her again was a real *treat*. = It was a real *treat* to see her again. ▪ We took the kids to the water park as a special *treat*.

3 *US* **:** something that tastes good and that is not eaten often ▪ freshly baked *treats* [=*goodies*] ▪ cookies and other tasty *treats* ▪ She rewarded the dog with a *treat*.

a treat *Brit, informal* **:** very well ▪ The plan ***worked a treat*** ▪ The food ***went down a treat*** [=tasted very good] **:** very good ▪ He ***looks a treat*** [=he is handsome, attractive, etc.] in his new suit.

treat·able /ˈtri:təbəl/ *adj, medical* **:** capable of being improved or cured with medical care ▪ Her condition is *treatable*. ▪ a *treatable* disease ▪ The infection is *treatable* with antibiotics.

trea·tise /ˈtri:təs/ *noun, pl* **-tis·es** [*count*] **:** a book, article, etc., that discusses a subject carefully and thoroughly — often + *on* ▪ a *treatise on* higher education

treat·ment /ˈtri:tmənt/ *noun, pl* **-ments**

1 [*noncount*] **:** the way that you think of and act toward someone or something ▪ We don't deserve such rude *treatment*. [=we don't deserve to be treated so rudely] ▪ The principal's daughter received special/preferential *treatment* from teachers. [=teachers were kinder to and less strict with the principal's daughter than with other students] ▪ We want to ensure equal *treatment* for everyone. ▪ The law requires humane *treatment* of prisoners. — see also SILENT TREATMENT

2 a [*noncount*] **:** the way that you deal with or discuss a subject ▪ It's a complicated issue that requires careful *treatment*. ▪ A five-minute news report on the subject does not allow for depth of *treatment*. [=does not allow the subject to be dealt with in a way that is complete, thorough, etc.] ▪ The book's *treatment* of this important issue is unimpressive. **b** [*count*] **:** something that deals with or discusses a subject ▪ Previous *treatments* of this topic have ignored some key issues. ▪ an interesting *treatment*

3 : something that deals with a disease, injury, etc., in order to make someone feel better or become healthy again **:** medical care [*noncount*] The patient required immediate medical *treatment*. ▪ She is receiving *treatment* for cancer. ▪ a *treatment* facility [=a place where you can get medical care] [*count*] The drug has been approved as a *treatment* for AIDS. ▪ cancer *treatments*

4 [*count*] **:** something that you use or do to feel and look healthy or attractive ▪ Mud is sometimes used as a skin *treatment*. ▪ She went to a spa for a beauty *treatment*.

5 : a process in which a chemical or other substance is put on or in something in order to protect it, preserve it, clean it, etc. [*count*] A special *treatment* is used to kill bacteria in water. ▪ This *treatment* will protect the wood from rotting. [*noncount*] The instruments are sterilized by *treatment* with alcohol. ▪ a waste/sewage *treatment* plant

trea·ty /ˈtri:ti/ *noun, pl* **-ties** [*count*] **:** an official agreement that is made between two or more countries or groups ▪ the *Treaty* of Paris ▪ a nuclear test ban *treaty* ▪ The country's warring factions have signed a ***peace treaty***. [=an agreement to stop fighting a war]

[1]tre·ble /ˈtrɛbəl/ *noun, pl* **tre·bles** *music*

1 : the highest range of sounds used in music [*noncount*] Turn down the *treble* on the radio and turn up the bass. [*count*] a shrill *treble* — compare BASS

2 [*count*] **:** a voice or instrument that has the highest range of sound ▪ The part is sung by a boy *treble*.

[2]treble *adj*

1 *always used before a noun, music* **:** having or indicating a high sound or range ▪ the *treble* clef ▪ a *treble* voice/instrument

2 *chiefly Brit* **:** [3]TRIPLE

[3]treble *verb* **trebles; tre·bled; tre·bling** *chiefly Brit*

1 [+ *obj*] **:** to cause (something) to become three times as great or as many **:** TRIPLE ▪ She *trebled* her earnings in only two years.

2 [*no obj*] **:** to become three times as great or as many **:** TRIPLE ▪ Prices have *trebled* in only two years.

tree /ˈtri:/ *noun, pl* **trees** [*count*]

1 : a usually tall plant that has a thick, wooden stem and many large branches ▪ pine/oak/apple *trees* ▪ He chopped/cut down the *tree*. — see color picture on page C6; see also CHRISTMAS TREE, GUM TREE

2 : a drawing that connects things with lines to show how they are related to each other ▪ a *tree* (diagram) that shows the relationships between different languages — see also FAMILY TREE

barking up the wrong tree see [1]BARK

grow on trees see GROW

not see the forest for the trees (*US*) *or* ***US miss the forest for the trees*** *or Brit* ***not see the wood for the trees*** **:** to not understand or appreciate a larger situation, problem, etc., because you are considering only a few parts of it ▪ This investment would be good for the company, but he's so concerned about saving money that he *can't see the forest for the trees*.

out of your tree *informal* **:** CRAZY ▪ That guy is completely *out of his tree*. [=(more commonly) *out of his mind*]

top of the tree see [1]TOP

— see also SHOE TREE

– treed *adj* ▪ a heavily *treed* [=*wooded*] area [=an area in which there are many trees] **– tree·less** /ˈtri:ləs/ *adj* ▪ a *treeless* plain **– tree·like** /ˈtri:ˌlaɪk/ *adj* ▪ a *treelike* structure

tree house *noun, pl* **~ houses** [*count*] **:** a small house that is built among the branches of a tree for children to play in

tree hug·ger /-ˈhʌgɚ/ *noun, pl* **~ -gers** [*count*] *disapproving* **:** someone who is regarded as foolish or annoying because of being too concerned about protecting trees, animals, and other parts of the natural world from pollution and other threats

tree line *noun* [*singular*] **:** TIMBERLINE ▪ The hikers had reached the *tree line* by noon.

tree–lined *adj* **:** having trees on both sides ▪ a *tree-lined* street

tree·top /ˈtri:ˌtɑ:p/ *noun, pl* **-tops** [*count*] **:** the highest part of a tree ▪ a view from the highest *treetop* — usually plural ▪ Monkeys swung through the *treetops*.

tre·foil /ˈtri:ˌfojəl/ *noun, pl* **-foils** [*count*]

1 : a plant (such as a clover) that has three leaves on each stem

2 : a decorative object or design that is shaped like a leaf with three parts

[1]trek /ˈtrɛk/ *verb* **treks; trekked; trek·king** [*no obj*]

1 : to walk usually for a long distance ▪ We had to *trek* up six flights of stairs with our groceries.

2 : to travel by walking through an area with many mountains, rivers, etc., for pleasure and adventure ▪ On their vacation last year they went *trekking* in the Himalayas.

3 : to go on a long and often difficult journey ▪ We *trekked* across the country in her old car.

²**trek** *noun, pl* **treks** [*count*] : a long and difficult journey that is made especially by walking ▪ Our car broke down and we had a long *trek* back to town. ▪ a *trek* across the country

trel·lis /ˈtrɛləs/ *noun, pl* **-lis·es** [*count*] : a frame with long pieces of wood that cross each other that is used as a support for climbing plants

trem·ble /ˈtrɛmbəl/ *verb* **trem·bles**; **trem·bled**; **trem·bling** [*no obj*]

1 : to shake slightly because you are afraid, nervous, excited, etc. ▪ His arms and legs began to *tremble*. ▪ My voice *trembled* as I began to speak. ▪ I opened the letter with *trembling* hands. — often + *with* ▪ She was *trembling with* fear/excitement.

2 : to shake slightly because of some force ▪ The house *trembled* as the big truck drove by.

3 *somewhat formal* : to be afraid or nervous ▪ I *tremble* to think of what could happen. = I *tremble* at the thought of what could happen.

– **tremble** *noun, pl* **trembles** [*count*] — usually singular ▪ I felt a *tremble* as the truck drove by. ▪ I could hear a *tremble* in her voice. — often + *of* ▪ He felt a *tremble of* nervousness.

tre·men·dous /trɪˈmɛndəs/ *adj* [*more* ~; *most* ~]

1 : very large or great ▪ He has a *tremendous* amount of energy. ▪ a *tremendous* problem ▪ The engine's power is *tremendous*. ▪ She is a writer of *tremendous* talent.

2 : very good or excellent : WONDERFUL ▪ That performance was *tremendous*! ▪ We had a *tremendous* time.

– **tre·men·dous·ly** *adv* ▪ The two cars vary *tremendously*. ▪ He became *tremendously* successful.

trem·o·lo /ˈtrɛməˌloʊ/ *noun, pl* **-los** [*count*] *music* : a musical sound made by a voice or instrument that seems to shake

trem·or /ˈtrɛmɚ/ *noun, pl* **-ors** [*count*]

1 : a shaking movement of the ground before or after an earthquake ▪ Small *tremors* were still being felt several days after the earthquake.

2 : a slight shaking movement or sound that is caused especially by nervousness, weakness, or illness ▪ I heard a *tremor* in her voice. ▪ His *tremors* were caused by the disease.

trem·u·lous /ˈtrɛmjələs/ *adj, formal + literary*

1 : shaking slightly especially because of nervousness, weakness, or illness ▪ She opened the letter with *tremulous* hands. ▪ He spoke with a *tremulous* voice.

2 [*more* ~; *most* ~] : feeling or showing a lack of confidence or courage ▪ He is a shy, *tremulous* [=*timid*] person. ▪ a *tremulous* smile

– **trem·u·lous·ly** *adv*

trench /ˈtrɛntʃ/ *noun, pl* **trench·es** [*count*]

1 a : a long, narrow hole that is dug in the ground : DITCH **b** : a deep, narrow hole in the ground that is used as protection for soldiers — usually plural ▪ a brave soldier who fought in the *trenches* in World War I ▪ ***trench warfare*** [=military fighting by soldiers in trenches]

2 : a long, narrow hole in the ocean floor

the trenches : a place or situation in which people do very difficult work ▪ These people are working every day down ***in the trenches*** to improve the lives of refugees.

tren·chant /ˈtrɛntʃənt/ *adj* [*more* ~; *most* ~] *formal* : very strong, clear, and effective ▪ a *trenchant* analysis/essay ▪ a writer with a *trenchant* wit

– **tren·chant·ly** *adv* ▪ a *trenchantly* funny critique

trench coat *noun, pl* ~ **coats** [*count*] : a usually long raincoat with deep pockets and a belt

trend /ˈtrɛnd/ *noun, pl* **trends** [*count*]

1 : a general direction of change : a way of behaving, proceeding, etc., that is developing and becoming more common ▪ the downward/upward *trend* of the stock market ▪ Digital technology is the latest/current *trend* in television. ▪ Teachers are trying to reverse the general *trend* [=*tendency*] of lower test scores. ▪ There is a disturbing/growing *trend* toward obesity in children. ▪ *trends* in fashion ▪ The director has ***set/started a (new) trend*** in moviemaking. [=other directors are copying the director's way of making movies]

2 : something that is currently popular or fashionable ▪ fashion *trends*

trend·set·ter /ˈtrɛndˌsɛtɚ/ *noun, pl* **-ters** [*count*] : someone who starts a new fashion, style, etc., or helps to make it popular

– **trend·set·ting** /ˈtrɛndˌsɛtɪŋ/ *adj, always used before a noun* ▪ a *trendsetting* fashion designer

¹**trendy** /ˈtrɛndi/ *adj* **trend·i·er**; **-est** [*also more* ~; *most* ~]

1 *sometimes disapproving* : currently popular or fashionable ▪ *trendy* fashions/clothes/restaurants

2 *often disapproving* : liking or tending to like whatever is currently popular or fashionable : influenced by trends ▪ a group of *trendy* young professionals

– **trend·i·ly** /ˈtrɛndəli/ *adv* ▪ She dresses very *trendily*. – **trend·i·ness** /ˈtrɛndinəs/ *noun* [*noncount*] ▪ He tries to avoid *trendiness* when he buys new clothes.

²**trendy** *noun, pl* **tren·dies** [*count*] *Brit, informal + disapproving* : someone who likes whatever is fashionable : a trendy person ▪ Only young *trendies* go to that pub.

trep·i·da·tion /ˌtrɛpəˈdeɪʃən/ *noun* [*noncount*] *formal* : a feeling of fear that causes you to hesitate because you think something bad or unpleasant is going to happen ▪ He had/felt some *trepidation* about agreeing to their proposal.

¹**tres·pass** /ˈtrɛˌspæs, *Brit* ˈtrɛspəs/ *verb* **-pass·es**; **-passed**; **-pass·ing** [*no obj*]

1 : to go on someone's land without permission ▪ He told me I was *trespassing*. ▪ The sign said "No *Trespassing*." — often + *on* ▪ The hunters *trespassed on* the farmer's land.

2 *old-fashioned* : to do something that hurts or offends someone — usually + *against* ▪ We must try to forgive those who *trespass against* us.

3 *formal* : to treat someone unfairly especially by asking for or expecting more than is fair or reasonable — often + *on* or *upon* ▪ I hope I am not *trespassing on/upon* your time. [=I hope I am not using too much of your time]

– **tres·pass·er** *noun, pl* **-ers** [*count*]

²**tres·pass** /ˈtrɛspəs/ *noun, pl* **-pass·es**

1 *law* : the crime of going on someone's land without permission [*noncount*] He was arrested for *trespass*. [*count*] They committed a *trespass*.

2 [*count*] *old-fashioned* : a sin or other wrong or improper act ▪ Forgive us our *trespasses*.

tress·es /ˈtrɛsəz/ *noun* [*plural*] *literary* : a woman's long hair ▪ She combed her long, golden *tresses*.

tres·tle /ˈtrɛsəl/ *noun, pl* **tres·tles** [*count*]

1 : a frame that is made of a horizontal piece between two vertical pieces and that is used to support something (such as the top of a table)

2 : a complex structure that is used especially for supporting railroad tracks over a valley, river, etc.

T. rex /ˈtiːˈrɛks/ *noun, pl* ~ **rexes** [*count*] : TYRANNOSAURUS

trey /ˈtreɪ/ *noun, pl* **treys** [*count*]

1 *basketball, informal* : a shot that is worth three points

2 : a playing card with the number 3 or a symbol repeated three times on it

tri- *prefix* : three : having three parts ▪ *tri*angle ▪ *tri*cycle

tri·ad /ˈtraɪˌæd/ *noun, pl* **-ads** [*count*]

1 : a group of three usually related people or things — often + *of* ▪ Sufferers experience a *triad of* symptoms: headache, fever, and sore throat.

2 : a secret Chinese criminal organization

tri·age /ˈtriːˌɑːʒ/ *noun* [*noncount*] *medical* : the process of deciding which patients should be treated first based on how sick or seriously injured they are ▪ Nurses do *triage* in the emergency room.

¹**tri·al** /ˈtrajəl/ *noun, pl* **-als**

1 : a formal meeting in a court in which evidence about crimes, disagreements, etc., is presented to a judge and often a jury so that decisions can be made according to the law [*count*] civil/criminal *trials* ▪ a murder *trial* ▪ He did not get/have/receive a fair *trial*. ▪ a *trial* by jury = a jury *trial* ▪ He testified at the *trial*. [*noncount*] He testified at *trial*. ▪ She is awaiting *trial* on charges of assault. ▪ She will ***stand/face trial*** [=*be tried*] for murder. [=there will be a trial to decide if she is guilty of murder] ▪ He was arrested but not ***brought to trial***. [=*tried*; there was never a trial to decide if he was guilty or innocent] ▪ The case never ***came to trial***. [=there was never a trial to make a decision about the case]

2 [*count*] **a** : a test of the quality, value, or usefulness of something ▪ Early *trials* have shown that the treatment has some serious side effects. ▪ a ***clinical trial*** [=a test in which scientists study how a drug, medical device, etc., affects a group of people in order to see if it is safe and effective] **b** : a test

of someone's ability to do something that is used to see if he or she should join a team, perform in a play, etc. • the Olympic *trials* • (*Brit*) He was cut from the team after the first *trial*. [=(*US*) tryout]
3 [*count*] **a** : something (such as a difficult situation or task) that shows how patient, strong, or trusting you are • Recovering from her injury was a real *trial* of strength. **b** : something or someone that is difficult to deal with : an annoying or unpleasant thing or person • I know I was a bit of a *trial* to my parents when I was a teenager. • Cold winters can be a *trial* for older people. • The book describes the ***trials and tribulations*** [=difficult experiences, problems, etc.] of the colony's earliest settlers.
4 [*count*] : an event at which animals compete and perform • a horse/dog *trial*
on trial : in a situation in which evidence against you is presented in a court to a judge and often a jury to decide if you are guilty of a crime • He is *on trial* [=being tried] for murder. • She was *on trial* on charges of drug possession. = She ***went on trial*** for possession of drugs. — sometimes used figuratively • The controversial case has put the entire health-care system *on trial*. [=has caused people to think about the health-care system in a critical way]
trial and error : a process in which you find out the best way to solve a problem, do something, etc., by trying different ways until one is successful • We often learn by/through *trial and error*.

[2]**trial** *adj, always used before a noun* : relating to or used in a test that is done for a period of time to see if something is worth buying, using, etc. • *trial* use of the product • If you choose to use the software beyond the 30-day free ***trial period***, you are required to pay for it. • I'm using the product ***on a trial basis***. [=for a short period of time]

[3]**trial** *verb* **-als; -alled; -al·ling** [+ *obj*] *Brit* : to test the quality, value, or usefulness of (something) • Companies are *trialling* the new accounting software.

trial balloon *noun, pl* **~ -loons** [*count*] : something that you do or say in order to find out what people think about an idea, plan, etc. • She's been floating *trial balloons* about a possible run for Congress.

trial run *noun, pl* **~ runs** [*count*] : a test in which a product or procedure is tried in order to see if it works correctly : TEST RUN • They will put the software through many *trial runs* before putting it on the market. • We will have to give the machine a *trial run*.

tri·an·gle /ˈtraɪˌæŋgəl/ *noun, pl* **-an·gles** [*count*]
1 : a shape that is made up of three lines and three angles — see picture at GEOMETRY; see also EQUILATERAL TRIANGLE, ISOSCELES TRIANGLE, RIGHT TRIANGLE
2 : something that is shaped like a triangle • She cut the sandwiches into *triangles*. • a *triangle* of land
3 : a musical instrument that is made of a steel rod bent into the shape of a triangle and that you play by hitting with a metal rod
4 : a situation in which one member of a couple is involved in a romantic or sexual relationship with another person • a love *triangle*
5 *US* : a usually plastic or metal device that is shaped like a triangle and used for drawing straight lines and angles — called also (*Brit*) *set square*

tri·an·gu·lar /traɪˈæŋgjələ/ *adj*
1 : shaped like a triangle • a *triangular* table
2 : involving three people, groups, or things • a *triangular* agreement

tri·an·gu·la·tion /traɪˌæŋgjəˈleɪʃən/ *noun* [*noncount*] *technical* : a method of finding a distance or location by measuring the distance between two points whose exact location is known and then measuring the angles between each point and a third unknown point
– tri·an·gu·late /traɪˈæŋgjəˌleɪt/ *verb* **-lates; -lat·ed; -lat·ing** [+ *obj*] • Using the device we were able to *triangulate* the building's precise location.

tri·ath·lon /traɪˈæθlən/ *noun, pl* **-lons** [*count*] *sports* : a long-distance race that has three parts (such as swimming, bicycling, and running) • the Olympic *triathlon*
– tri·ath·lete /traɪˈæθˌliːt/ *noun, pl* **-letes** [*count*]

trib·al /ˈtraɪbəl/ *adj* : of or relating to a tribe or tribes • *tribal* art/customs/groups/people • a *tribal* chief • Their society is *tribal*.
– trib·al·ly *adv* • The land is *tribally* owned.

trib·al·ism /ˈtraɪbəˌlɪzəm/ *noun* [*noncount*] *often disapproving* : loyalty to a tribe or other social group especially when combined with strong negative feelings for people outside the group • *Tribalism* within the group is strong. • the corrupting influence of *tribalism*

tribe /ˈtraɪb/ *noun, pl* **tribes** [*count*]
1 a : a group of people that includes many families and relatives who have the same language, customs, and beliefs • Native American *tribes* • nomadic *tribes* **b** *informal + humorous* : a large family — usually singular • The whole *tribe* came to the party.
2 *humorous + sometimes disapproving* : a group of people who have the same job or interest • a *tribe* of artists with wild hair and casual manners
3 *biology* : a group of related plants or animals • the rose/cat *tribe*

tribes·man /ˈtraɪbzmən/ *noun, pl* **-men** /-mən/ [*count*] : someone (especially a man) who is a member of a tribe

tribes·peo·ple /ˈtraɪbzˌpiːpəl/ *noun* [*plural*] : members of a tribe

tribes·wom·an /ˈtraɪbzˌwʊmən/ *noun, pl* **-wom·en** /-ˌwɪmən/ [*count*] : a woman who is a member of a tribe

trib·u·la·tion /ˌtrɪbjəˈleɪʃən/ *noun, pl* **-tions** *formal*
1 [*noncount*] : unhappiness, pain, or suffering • Her son's illness has been a source of great *tribulation*.
2 [*count*] : an experience that causes someone to suffer • The play is about the *tribulations* of a family of immigrants in New York. • the ***trials and tribulations*** [=difficult experiences, problems, etc.] of starting a new business

tri·bu·nal /traɪˈbjuːnl̩/ *noun, pl* **-nals** [*count*] : a kind of court that has authority in a specific area • An international *tribunal* was formed to deal with war crimes.

tri·bune /ˈtrɪˌbjuːn/ *noun, pl* **-bunes** [*count*]
1 : an official in ancient Rome whose job was to protect the rights of citizens
2 *formal* : someone who defends the rights of people • They've become *tribunes* of the people.

trib·u·tary /ˈtrɪbjəˌteri, *Brit* ˈtrɪbjətri/ *noun, pl* **-tar·ies** [*count*] : a stream that flows into a larger stream or river or into a lake • one of the river's *tributaries* • This stream is a *tributary* of the Ohio River. — often used before another noun • a *tributary* stream

trib·ute /ˈtrɪˌbjuːt/ *noun, pl* **-utes**
1 [*count*] : something that you say, give, or do to show respect or affection for someone • The concert was a *tribute* to the musician. • Yellow ribbons were tied on trees as a *tribute* to the soldiers at war. • ***floral tributes*** [=flowers that people send to a funeral or leave at a grave] • a ***tribute album*** [=a recording of a set of songs that another musician or musical group is known for performing] • an event at which artists and musicians ***paid tribute*** to the famous composer
2 [*singular*] : something that proves the good quality or effectiveness of something — + *to* • The pyramids are a *tribute to* Egyptian ingenuity. • It's a *tribute to* her skills as a writer that she can make such a convincing case so efficiently.
3 : money or goods that a ruler or country gives to another ruler or country especially for protection [*noncount*] The country was forced to ***pay tribute***. [*count*] The ruler *paid* a *tribute* every year.

trice /ˈtraɪs/ *noun*
in a trice *chiefly Brit* : in a small amount of time : QUICKLY • He set the table *in a trice*. • She should be here *in a trice*. [=in a moment]

tri·cep /ˈtraɪˌsɛp/ *noun, pl* **-ceps** [*count*] : TRICEPS • an injured *tricep*

tri·ceps /ˈtraɪˌsɛps/ *noun, pl* **triceps** [*count*] : a large muscle along the back of the upper arm • He felt a pain in his right *triceps*. — usually plural • This exercise machine works the *triceps*. • My *triceps* are sore. — compare BICEPS

tri·cer·a·tops /traɪˈserəˌtɑːps/ *noun, pl* **triceratops** [*count*] : a large dinosaur that had three horns on its head and that ate plants

[1]**trick** /ˈtrɪk/ *noun, pl* **tricks** [*count*]
1 : an action that is meant to deceive someone • It was a *trick* to persuade her to give him money. • That was a ***dirty/mean/rotten trick***. [=an unkind or unfair thing to do] — see also DIRTY TRICKS
2 : something done to surprise or confuse someone and to make other people laugh • He ***played a trick on*** me. [=he tricked me] • She enjoys *playing tricks* on her friends.
3 : a clever and skillful action that someone performs to entertain or amuse people • For his last *trick*, the magician made a rabbit disappear. • magic/card/circus *tricks*
4 : a clever and effective way of doing something • I know a

T

good *trick* for removing stains from clothes. • He knows a lot of useful programming *tricks*. • a handy *trick* for remembering names • He has a lot of experience with gardening, so he should be able to ***show/teach us a trick or two***. [=he should be able to give us good advice about gardening]

5 : something that causes confusion or that makes something seem different from what it actually is • He was so tired ***his mind was playing tricks on him***. [=he could not think clearly] • The paint looked blue, but it was just a ***trick of the light***. [=the light made the paint appear blue even though it was a different color]

6 : the cards that are played in one round of a card game • She has won the last three *tricks*.

7 *US, informal* : a sex act performed by a prostitute • She was living on the street and ***turning tricks*** [=taking money for sex] to survive.

do the trick *informal* : to produce a desired result : to solve a problem • One small adjustment will *do the trick*.

every trick in the book ✧ If you try *every trick in the book*, you do everything you can to achieve something. • They'll use *every trick in the book* to get you to buy their products. • He tried *every trick in the book* [=he tried every method he knew] to get the car started, but nothing worked.

never/not miss a trick *informal* : to notice everything : to always know what is happening • He *never misses a trick*.

trick of the/your trade see ¹TRADE

up to your (old) tricks *informal* ✧ If you are *up to your (old) tricks*, you are doing the kind of dishonest things that you have done in the past.

you can't teach an old dog new tricks see ¹DOG

— see also HAT TRICK, TRICK OR TREAT

²trick *verb* **tricks; tricked; trick·ing** [+ *obj*] : to deceive (someone) • He *tricked* her by wearing a disguise.

trick into [*phrasal verb*] ***trick (someone or something) into (something)*** : to use a trick to make (someone or something) do (something) • He was *tricked into* buying the car. [=he bought the car because he was deceived]

trick out [*phrasal verb*] **1** ***trick (someone) out*** : to dress (someone or yourself) in an unusual way — usually + *in* • She was *tricked out in* a horrible, brightly colored costume. **2** ***trick (something) out or trick out (something)*** : to decorate (something) — usually + *with* • The room was *tricked out with* ribbons and streamers.

trick out of [*phrasal verb*] ***trick (someone) out of (something)*** : to use a trick to get (something) from (someone) • She was *tricked out of* [=*cheated out of*] her savings.

³trick *adj, always used before a noun*

1 : using methods that are meant to deceive someone • ***trick photography*** [=photography that uses special methods to make things that are not real seem to be real] • a ***trick question*** [=a deceptive question that is intended to make you give an answer that is not correct or that causes trouble for you]

2 : done in a clever or entertaining way • a *trick* shot in pool

3 *US* : weak and tending to fail suddenly • He has a ***trick knee***.

trick·ery /ˈtrɪkəri/ *noun* [*noncount*] : the use of tricks to deceive or cheat someone • He resorted to *trickery* to get what he wanted. • an act of *trickery*

¹trick·le /ˈtrɪkəl/ *verb* **trick·les; trick·led; trick·ling** [*no obj*]

1 : to flow or fall in drops • Tears *trickled* down her cheeks. • Water was *trickling* out of the gutter.

2 *always followed by an adverb or preposition* : to move or go slowly in small numbers or amounts • People *trickled* into the theater. • Donations have been *trickling* in.

trickle down [*phrasal verb*] : to spread from the upper levels of a society, organization, etc., to the lower levels — used especially to describe the movement of money through an economic system • They believe that the benefits of the tax cut for corporations should eventually *trickle down* to the average consumer. — see also TRICKLE-DOWN

²trickle *noun* [*singular*]

1 : a slow, thin flow of water • We heard the *trickle* of water from the roof. • The flow of water slowed to a *trickle*.

2 : a slow movement of people or things in small numbers or amounts • Sales have slowed to a *trickle* in recent weeks. • A slow/steady *trickle* of customers came into the store throughout the day.

trickle–down *adj, always used before a noun* — used to describe an economic theory which says that financial benefits and advantages given to wealthy people, corporations, etc., will improve the economy and eventually help the poorer people in a society • *trickle-down* theory • *trickle-down* economics — see also *trickle down* at ¹TRICKLE

trick or treat *noun* [*noncount*] : a custom on Halloween in which children knock on people's doors and say "trick or treat" when the doors are opened to ask for candy • We got all dressed up for *trick or treat*. • When the door opened the kids all shouted "*Trick or treat!*"

— trick–or–treat·er *noun, pl* **-ers** [*count*] • We had a lot of *trick-or-treaters* at our house this year. **— trick–or–treat·ing** *noun* [*noncount*] • The kids ***went trick-or-treating***.

trick·ster /ˈtrɪkstɚ/ *noun, pl* **-sters** [*count*] : someone who tricks or deceives people especially in order to get something • a sly *trickster* — see also CONFIDENCE TRICKSTER

tricky /ˈtrɪki/ *adj* **trick·i·er; -est** [*also more* ~; *most* ~]

1 : using or likely to use dishonest tricks • a *tricky* salesman

2 : requiring skill or caution : difficult to do or deal with • a *tricky* subject/question • a *tricky* intersection • The lock is *tricky* to open.

— trick·i·ness /ˈtrɪkinəs/ *noun* [*noncount*]

¹tri·col·or (*US*) *or Brit* **tri·col·our** /ˈtraɪˌkʌlɚ, *Brit* ˈtrɪkələ/ *noun, pl* **-ors** [*count*] : a flag (such as the national flag of France) that has three equal bands of different colors

²tricolor (*US*) *or Brit* **tricolour** *or US* **tri·col·ored** *or Brit* **tri·col·oured** /ˈtraɪˈkʌlɚd/ *adj* : having or using three colors • a *tricolor* flag • a *tricolored* cat

tri·cy·cle /ˈtraɪsəkəl/ *noun, pl* **-cy·cles** [*count*] : a three-wheeled vehicle that a person rides by pushing on foot pedals ✧ Tricycles are usually ridden by young children. • He likes to ride his *tricycle*. [=(*informal*) *trike*] — compare BICYCLE, UNICYCLE

tricycle

tri·dent /ˈtraɪdənt/ *noun, pl* **-dents** [*count*] : a spear that has three points and that looks like a large fork

¹tried *past tense and past participle of* ¹TRY

²tried /ˈtraɪd/ *adj* : found to be good or effective through use or testing • a *tried* (and tested) recipe • a *tried* and trusted friend

tried–and–true *adj, chiefly US* : known to be good or effective : known to be reliable • *tried-and-true* recipes • a *tried-and-true* remedy for colds

tri·er /ˈtrajɚ/ *noun, pl* **-ers** [*count*] : someone who tries very hard to do something • Even if she fails she's a real *trier*.

¹tri·fle /ˈtraɪfəl/ *noun, pl* **tri·fles**

1 [*count*] : something that does not have much value or importance • There's no reason to argue over such *trifles*. • The money is a mere *trifle* to me.

2 [*count, noncount*] : a dessert made of layers of cake, jam or jelly, and custard and topped with whipped cream

a trifle : to a small degree : SLIGHTLY • The music is just *a trifle* [=*a bit, a tad*] too loud.

²trifle *verb* **trifles; tri·fled; tri·fling**

trifle with [*phrasal verb*] ***trifle with (someone or something)*** : to treat or deal with (someone or something) in a way that shows a lack of proper respect or seriousness • You shouldn't *trifle with* their feelings. • Crime is not a subject to be *trifled with*. • She is not someone to be *trifled with*. [=she should be treated with respect]

tri·fling /ˈtraɪfəlɪŋ/ *adj* [*more* ~; *most* ~] : having little value or importance • *trifling* details • a *trifling* sum of money

trig /ˈtrɪg/ *noun* [*noncount*] *US, informal* : TRIGONOMETRY

¹trig·ger /ˈtrɪgɚ/ *noun, pl* **-gers** [*count*]

1 : a lever on a gun that you pull to fire the gun • He pulled/squeezed the *trigger*. • Police officers are trained to not be too ***quick on the trigger***. [=eager to fire a gun] — see picture at GUN

2 : something that causes something else to happen — often + *for* • The faulty wire was the *trigger for* the explosion.

²trigger *verb* **-gers; -gered; -ger·ing** [+ *obj*]

1 a : to cause (something, such as an alarm) to start functioning • Smoke *triggered* the fire alarm. **b** : to cause (a bomb) to explode • The timer was set to *trigger* the bomb in exactly one hour.

2 : to cause (something) to start or happen • His remarks *triggered* a public outcry. • Certain foods *trigger* his headaches. • The power outage was *triggered* by heavy rains.

T

trig·ger–hap·py /ˈtrɪgɚˌhæpi/ *adj* [*more* ~; *most* ~] *informal + disapproving* : eager to fire a gun ▪ *trigger-happy* hunters

trig·o·nom·e·try /ˌtrɪgəˈnɑːmətri/ *noun* [*noncount*] : a branch of mathematics that deals with relationships between the sides and angles of triangles
– **trig·o·no·met·ric** /ˌtrɪgənəˈmɛtrɪk/ *also* **trig·o·no·met·ri·cal** /ˌtrɪgənəˈmɛtrɪkəl/ *adj* ▪ a *trigonometric* function
– **trig·o·no·met·ri·cal·ly** /ˌtrɪgənəˈmɛtrɪkli/ *adv*

trike /ˈtraɪk/ *noun, pl* **trikes** [*count*] *informal* : TRICYCLE

tri·lat·er·al /traɪˈlætərəl/ *adj* : involving three groups or countries ▪ a *trilateral* peace agreement

tril·by /ˈtrɪlbi/ *noun, pl* **-bies** [*count*] *chiefly Brit* : a soft hat with part of the top pushed in — called also *trilby hat*

[1]trill /ˈtrɪl/ *noun, pl* **trills** [*count*]
1 : the sound of going quickly back and forth many times between two musical notes that are close to each other
2 : a quick high sound that is repeated ▪ She pronounces her r's with a *trill*. ▪ the *trill* of the bird

[2]trill *verb* **trills; trilled; trill·ing**
1 [+ *obj*] : to say (something) with a trill ▪ He *trills* [=*rolls*] his r's when he speaks.
2 [*no obj*] : to make a series of quick high sounds ▪ The phone *trilled* on her desk.

tril·lion /ˈtrɪljən/ *noun, pl* **trillion** *or* **tril·lions** [*count*]
1 : the number 1,000,000,000,000 : one thousand billion ▪ a/one/two *trillion* (of them) ▪ a hundred *trillion* = 100 *trillion* ▪ several *trillion* (of them) = (less commonly) several *trillions* (of them) ▪ hundreds of *trillions* (of them) ▪ a *trillion* and one [=1,000,000,000,001] ▪ a *trillion* and a half = 1.5 *trillion* [=1,500,000,000,000] ▪ a *trillion* dollars
2 : a very large amount or number ▪ I've heard that excuse a *trillion* times before. [=many, many times before] — often plural ▪ We could see *trillions* of stars in the sky. ▪ ***trillions and trillions*** of cells
3 *Brit, old-fashioned* : the number 1,000,000,000,000,000,000 : one million million million
– **tril·lionth** /ˈtrɪljənθ/ *adj* ▪ This is the *trillionth* time I've seen this show. – **trillionth** *noun, pl* **-lionths** [*count*] ▪ one *trillionth* [=one of a trillion equal parts] of a second

tril·o·gy /ˈtrɪləʤi/ *noun, pl* **-gies** [*count*] : a series of three novels, movies, etc., that are closely related and involve the same characters or themes ▪ the last book in the *trilogy* ▪ a science-fiction *trilogy*

[1]trim /ˈtrɪm/ *verb* **trims; trimmed; trim·ming** [+ *obj*]
1 a : to cut (something) off something else : to remove (something) by cutting — often + *away, from,* or *off* ▪ She *trimmed away* the dead branches. ▪ She *trimmed* the fat *from/off* the meat. **b** : to make (something) neat by cutting it ▪ He *trimmed* his mustache. ▪ The hedges need to be *trimmed*.
2 : to make the size, amount, or extent of (something) smaller ▪ They are looking for ways to *trim* the budget.
3 : to decorate (something) especially around the edges with ribbons, ornaments, etc. ▪ We *trimmed* the Christmas tree. ▪ a pillow *trimmed* in/with lace
4 : to adjust (a boat's sails) in order to move faster ▪ The sailors *trimmed* the sails.
trim down [*phrasal verb*] : to become thinner : to lose weight ▪ He *trimmed down* over the summer.
– **trim·mer** /ˈtrɪmɚ/ *noun, pl* **-mers** [*count*] ▪ a mustache *trimmer*

[2]trim *adj* **trim·mer; trim·mest**
1 : neat and orderly ▪ a *trim* lawn
2 : slim and healthy ▪ She has a *trim* figure. ▪ He keeps fit and *trim* by biking.
– **trim·ly** *adv*

[3]trim *noun, pl* **trims**
1 [*count*] : an act of trimming something (such as hair) — usually singular ▪ He went to the barber for a *trim*. ▪ The lawn needs a *trim*.
2 : material (such as ribbons, lace, etc.) that is used for decorating something especially around its edges [*noncount*] a skirt with lace *trim* ▪ The house is gray with black *trim*. [=the pieces of wood around the doors, windows, etc., are painted black] [*count*] — usually singular ▪ The fabric has a gold *trim*.
in trim : in good condition ▪ He's been exercising to get *in trim* for the season.

tri·ma·ran /ˈtraɪməˌræn/ *noun, pl* **-rans** [*count*] : a boat that has three hulls

tri·mes·ter /traɪˈmɛstɚ/ *noun, pl* **-ters** [*count*]
1 : a period of three months; *especially* : one of three periods into which a woman's pregnancy is often divided ▪ development in the first/second/third *trimester*
2 *US* : one of three periods into which an academic year is sometimes divided — compare QUARTER, SEMESTER, TERM

trim·mings /ˈtrɪmɪŋz/ *noun* [*plural*]
1 : something that is added to complete a dish or meal ▪ a feast with turkey and ***all the trimmings*** [=all the other foods that are typically served with turkey]
2 : pieces removed from something by trimming it ▪ hedge/meat *trimmings*
3 *US* : something added as a decoration especially around the edges ▪ a hat with leather *trimmings*

trin·i·ty /ˈtrɪnəti/ *noun, pl* **-ties**
1 ***the Trinity*** *Christianity* : the Father, the Son, and the Holy Spirit existing as one God — called also *the Holy Trinity*
2 [*count*] : a group of three people or things ▪ a *trinity* of goals ▪ an unholy *trinity* of criminal organizations

trin·ket /ˈtrɪŋkət/ *noun, pl* **-kets** [*count*] : a piece of jewelry or an ornament that has little value

trio /ˈtriːjoʊ/ *noun, pl* **tri·os** [*count*]
1 : a group of three singers or musicians who perform together ▪ He plays in a jazz *trio*.; *also* : a piece of music for such a group ▪ a piano *trio*
2 : a group or three people or things ▪ a *trio* of novels

[1]trip /ˈtrɪp/ *noun, pl* **trips**
1 [*count*] **a** : a journey to a place ▪ They got back from their *trip* yesterday. ▪ a *trip* around the world ▪ How was your *trip*? ▪ a ***day trip*** [=a journey in which you go to visit a place and then return to your home on the same day] ▪ She is away on a ***business trip***. [=she is traveling as part of her work] — often + *to* ▪ She took a *trip to* Europe. — see also FIELD TRIP, ROAD TRIP, ROUND TRIP **b** : a short journey to a store, business, office, etc., for a particular purpose — usually + *to* ▪ He made a *trip to* the dentist. ▪ I need to make a quick *trip to* the store for milk and eggs.
2 [*count*] *informal* : the experience of strange mental effects (such as seeing things that are not real) that is produced by taking a very powerful drug (such as LSD) ▪ He was on an acid *trip*.
3 [*count*] : an act of falling or nearly falling that is caused by accidentally hitting your foot on something as you are walking or running ▪ an ankle injury caused by a *trip*
4 [*singular*] *US, informal + somewhat old-fashioned* : an exciting or unusual experience or person ▪ The party was quite a *trip*. ▪ His mother is a *trip*.
5 [*count*] : an experience or activity that is like a journey ▪ He's on a nostalgia *trip*. [=he is thinking about the past a lot] — see also EGO TRIP, GUILT TRIP, POWER TRIP

[2]trip *verb* **trips; tripped; trip·ping**
1 a [*no obj*] : to hit your foot against something while you are walking or running so that you fall or almost fall ▪ Be careful. Don't *trip*. — often + *on* or *over* ▪ He *tripped* [=*stumbled*] *over* the curb. ▪ She *tripped on* the stairs and almost fell. **b** [+ *obj*] : to cause (someone who is walking or running) to fall or almost fall ▪ He deliberately tried to *trip* me. — often + *up* ▪ He got *tripped up* by the wires on the floor.
2 *always followed by an adverb or preposition* [*no obj*] *literary* : to dance or walk with light, quick steps ▪ The dancers *tripped* off the stage.
3 [+ *obj*] : to cause (something, such as an alarm or a switch) to be turned on often in an accidental way ▪ Burglars smashed in the window and *tripped* [=*set off*] the alarm. ▪ She *tripped* [=*threw*] the switch.
4 [*no obj*] *informal* : to experience strange mental effects (such as seeing things that are not real) after taking a very powerful drug (such as LSD) — often + *on* ▪ They were *tripping on* acid.
trip off the tongue see [1]TONGUE
trip the light fantastic *informal + old-fashioned* : DANCE ▪ They were *tripping the light fantastic* all night.
trip up [*phrasal verb*] ***trip up (someone) or trip (someone) up*** : to cause (someone) to make a mistake ▪ He tried to *trip up* the cashier as she counted his change. — see also [2]TRIP 1b (above)

tri·par·tite /traɪˈpɑɚˌtaɪt/ *adj, formal* : involving three people, groups, or parts ▪ a *tripartite* treaty

tripe /ˈtraɪp/ *noun* [*noncount*]
1 : the stomach of an animal (such as a cow or ox) that is eaten as food
2 : something that is worthless, unimportant, or of poor quality ▪ How can you watch this *tripe*? [=*rubbish*] ▪ That's just a load of *tripe*.

T

[1]tri·ple /ˈtrɪpəl/ *verb* **tri·ples; tri·pled; tri·pling**
1 a [+ *obj*] : to cause (something) to become three times as great or as many ▪ He *tripled* his winnings at the track. **b** [*no obj*] : to become three times as great or as many ▪ The town's population has *tripled* in size.
2 [*no obj*] *baseball* : to hit a triple : to hit the ball so that you can reach third base ▪ He *tripled* to right field.

[2]triple *noun, pl* **triples** [*count*] *baseball* : a hit that allows the batter to reach third base — compare DOUBLE, HOME RUN, SINGLE

[3]triple *adj*
1 : three times bigger in size or amount ▪ She got a new job with *triple* the salary of her old one. ▪ He ordered a *triple* espresso.
2 *always used before a noun* : having three parts or including three people or things ▪ *triple* bypass surgery [=surgery on three blood vessels surrounding the heart] ▪ a *triple* murder [=a murder of three people]
– **tri·ply** /ˈtrɪpli/ *adv*

triple bond *noun, pl* **~ bonds** [*count*] *technical* : a chemical bond in which three atoms in a molecule share three pairs of electrons — compare DOUBLE BOND, SINGLE BOND

Triple Crown *noun* [*singular*]
1 : an occurrence in which a horse wins a series of three major races ▪ a horse that won the first leg of the *Triple Crown*
2 *baseball* : the achievement of a baseball player who at the end of a season leads the league in batting average, home runs, and runs batted in ▪ Who was the last player to win the *Triple Crown* in the American League?
3 *or* ***triple crown*** : a set of three major awards, wins, or achievements in a particular field

tri·ple–deck·er /ˌtrɪpəlˈdɛkɚ/ *noun, pl* **-ers** [*count*] : something that has three levels or layers ▪ The bus we rode on was a *triple-decker*. — usually used before another noun ▪ We took a tour of London on a *triple-decker* bus. ▪ a *triple-decker* sandwich — compare DOUBLE-DECKER, SINGLE-DECKER

tri·ple–dou·ble /ˈtrɪpəlˈdʌbəl/ *noun, pl* **-dou·bles** [*count*] *basketball* : the achievement of a player who gets 10 or more points, assists, and rebounds in one game

tri·ple–head·er /ˈtrɪpəlˈhɛdɚ/ *noun, pl* **-ers** [*count*] *US* : three games played one after another on the same day ▪ a basketball *triple-header*

triple jump *noun*
the triple jump : an athletic event in which people compete by making three jumps one after another

triple play *noun, pl* **~ plays** [*count*] *baseball* : a play in which the team in the field causes three runners to be put out ▪ The batter hit into a *triple play*. ▪ They ***turned a triple play*** in the first inning. — compare DOUBLE PLAY

trip·let /ˈtrɪplət/ *noun, pl* **-lets** [*count*]
1 : one of three babies that are born at the same time to the same mother — usually plural ▪ She had *triplets*. [=she gave birth to three babies] — compare QUADRUPLET, QUINTUPLET, SEXTUPLET, TWIN
2 : a combination, set, or group of three things ▪ a *triplet* of colors

tri·plex /ˈtrɪˌplɛks/ *noun, pl* **-plex·es** [*count*] *US* : a building that is divided into three separate homes

[1]trip·li·cate /ˈtrɪplɪkət/ *noun*
in triplicate : in three copies ▪ File the forms *in triplicate*.

[2]triplicate *adj, always used before a noun* : having or existing in three copies ▪ a *triplicate* invoice

tri·pod /ˈtraɪˌpɑːd/ *noun, pl* **-pods** [*count*] : a support or stand for a camera, telescope, etc., that has three legs

tripod

trip·per /ˈtrɪpɚ/ *noun, pl* **-pers** [*count*] *chiefly Brit* : a person who takes a short trip to visit an interesting place ▪ a ***day tripper*** [=a person who goes on a short trip that lasts for less than a full day]

trip·py /ˈtrɪpi/ *adj* **-pi·er; -est** *informal* : relating to or like the strange mental effects experienced by someone who has taken a powerful drug (such as LSD) ▪ The movie was full of *trippy* images. ▪ *trippy* music

trip·tych /ˈtrɪpˌtɪk/ *noun, pl* **-tychs** [*count*] : a picture (such as a painting) that has three panels placed next to each other

trip·wire /ˈtrɪpˌwajɚ/ *noun, pl* **-wires** [*count*] : a wire placed close to the ground which trips people, sets off an alarm, or causes an explosion when it is touched

trite /ˈtraɪt/ *adj* **trit·er; -est** [*or more* ~; *most* ~] : not interesting or effective because of being used too often : not fresh or original ▪ That argument has become *trite*. ▪ *trite* clichés
– **trite·ly** *adv* ▪ *tritely* obvious remarks – **trite·ness** *noun* [*noncount*]

[1]tri·umph /ˈtrajəmf/ *noun, pl* **-umphs**
1 [*count*] **a** : a great or important victory ▪ They earned/gained a magnificent *triumph* over the invading army. ▪ They celebrated their *triumph* with a parade through the steets of the city. ▪ They were able to achieve an important *triumph* against their chief rivals. **b** : a great success or achievement ▪ Quitting smoking was a personal *triumph* for her. ▪ The party was a *triumph*. ▪ The bridge is an engineering *triumph*.
2 [*noncount*] : the very happy and joyful feeling that comes from victory or success ▪ They had a feeling of *triumph* after finishing the project. ▪ shouts of *triumph* ▪ They stood atop the mountain in *triumph*.
3 [*count*] : something good that is an excellent example of a particular method, quality, etc. ▪ The design is a *triumph* of simplicity. [=the design is very good and simple]

[2]triumph *verb* **-umphs; -umphed; -umph·ing** [*no obj*] : to achieve victory especially in a long or difficult contest ▪ She likes stories where good *triumphs* [=*prevails*] over evil. ▪ His favorite team *triumphed* in the championship game.

tri·um·phal /traɪˈʌmfəl/ *adj* : of, relating to, or honoring a triumph : celebrating a victory or success ▪ a *triumphal* procession ▪ a *triumphal* arch

tri·um·phant /traɪˈʌmfənt/ *adj*
1 : resulting in victory or success ▪ The boxer made a *triumphant* return to the ring. [=the boxer won when he returned to the ring to fight again]
2 : celebrating victory or success ▪ a *triumphant* shout
– **tri·um·phant·ly** *adv* ▪ The fans cheered *triumphantly*.

tri·um·vi·rate /traɪˈʌmvərət/ *noun, pl* **-rates** [*count*] : a group of three people who share a position of authority or power

triv·et /ˈtrɪvət/ *noun, pl* **-ets** [*count*] : a short metal stand used for holding a hot dish

triv·ia /ˈtrɪvijə/ *noun* [*noncount*]
1 : unimportant facts or details ▪ She doesn't pay attention to such *trivia*.
2 : facts about people, events, etc., that are not well-known ▪ He is an expert on baseball *trivia*. ▪ *trivia* questions

triv·i·al /ˈtrɪvijəl/ *adj* [*more* ~; *most* ~] : not important ▪ statistics and other *trivial* matters ▪ a *trivial* sum of money ▪ Compared to her problems, our problems seem *trivial*.

triv·i·al·i·ty /ˌtrɪviˈæləti/ *noun, pl* **-ties**
1 [*count*] : something that is not important : TRIFLE ▪ We shouldn't spend time on such *trivialities*.
2 [*noncount*] : the quality or state of being trivial ▪ the *triviality* of the problem

triv·i·al·ize *also Brit* **triv·i·al·ise** /ˈtrɪvijəˌlaɪz/ *verb* **-iz·es; -ized; -iz·ing** [+ *obj*] *usually disapproving* : to make (something) seem less important or serious than it actually is ▪ The news story *trivialized* the problem. ▪ He is *trivializing* the situation.
– **triv·i·al·i·za·tion** *also Brit* **triv·i·al·i·sa·tion** /ˌtrɪvijələˈzeɪʃən, *Brit* ˌtrɪviəˌlaɪˈzeɪʃən/ *noun, pl* **-tions** [*noncount*] the *trivialization* of their efforts [*count*] The movie was a *trivialization* of an important era in American history.

trod *past tense and past participle of* [1]TREAD

trodden *past participle of* [1]TREAD

trog·lo·dyte /ˈtrɑːgləˌdaɪt/ *noun, pl* **-dytes** [*count*] : a person who lived in a cave in prehistoric times

troi·ka /ˈtroɪkə/ *noun, pl* **-kas** [*count*] : a group of three people, things, countries, etc. ▪ a *troika* of judges ▪ A *troika* of countries signed the agreement.

Tro·jan /ˈtroʊʤən/ *noun, pl* **-jans** [*count*] : a person who was born or who lived in the ancient city of Troy
work like a Trojan *chiefly Brit, old-fashioned* : to work very hard ▪ He's been *working like a Trojan* on this project.
– **Trojan** *adj*

Trojan horse *noun, pl* **~ horses** [*count*]
1 : someone or something that is used to hide what is true or real in order to trick or harm an enemy ▪ They may be using the other corporation as a *Trojan horse*.
2 *computers* : a seemingly useful computer program that is actually designed to harm your computer (such as by destroying data files) if you use it

[1]troll /ˈtroʊl/ *noun, pl* **trolls** [*count*]
1 *in stories* : a creature that looks like a very large or very small ugly person

2 *computers* **:** a person who tries to cause problems on an Internet message board by posting messages that cause other people to argue, become angry, etc.

[2]**troll** *verb* **trolls; trolled; troll·ing**

1 : to fish with a hook and line that you pull through the water [+ *obj*] They were *trolling* the ocean floor. [*no obj*] — often + *for* ▪ They *trolled for* fish.

2 a [*no obj*] **:** to search for or try to get (something) — often + *for* ▪ *troll for* answers/comments/responses ▪ politicians *trolling for* votes **b** [+ *obj*] **:** to search through (something) ▪ She loves to *troll* flea markets looking for bargains.

– troll·er *noun, pl* **-ers** [*count*]

trol·ley /ˈtrɑːli/ *noun, pl* **-leys** [*count*]

1 a *US* **:** an electric vehicle that runs along the street on tracks — called also *streetcar, (US) trolley car, (chiefly Brit) tram* **b :** a vehicle that is pulled along tracks on the ground by a moving cable or that hangs from a moving cable — called also *(US) trolley car*

2 *chiefly Brit* **a :** a metal basket on wheels used to hold groceries while you are shopping ▪ a shopping *trolley* [=(*US*) *cart*] **b :** a table with wheels used especially for serving food ▪ a dessert *trolley* [=(*US*) *cart*]

***off your trolley** Brit, informal* **:** CRAZY ▪ If you think I'm going to do that you're *off your trolley.* [=(*US*) *off your rocker*]

trol·lop /ˈtrɑːləp/ *noun, pl* **-lops** [*count*] *old-fashioned + offensive* **:** a woman who has sex with many different men

trom·bone /trɑmˈboʊn/ *noun, pl* **-bones** [*count*] **:** a large brass musical instrument that you blow into and that has a tube that you slide in and out to play different notes — see picture at BRASS INSTRUMENT

– trom·bon·ist /trɑmˈboʊnɪst/ *noun, pl* **-ists** [*count*]

tromp /ˈtrɑːmp/ *verb, always followed by an adverb or preposition* **tromps; tromped; tromp·ing** [*no obj*] *US, informal* **:** [1]TRAMP 1 ▪ We *tromped* over/through the grass. ▪ Workmen were *tromping* through the building all day.

trompe l'oeil /ˌtrɑːmpˈlɔɪ/ *noun* [*noncount*] **:** a style of painting in which things are painted in a way that makes them look like real objects ✧ In French, *trompe l'oeil* means "deceives the eye."

[1]**troop** /ˈtruːp/ *noun, pl* **troops**

1 a [*count*] **:** a group of soldiers ▪ Where is his *troop* heading? **b troops** [*plural*] **:** soldiers in a group ▪ American *troops* fighting overseas ▪ enemy *troops* ▪ a plan to withdraw *troops* — see also SHOCK TROOPS

2 [*count*] **:** a group of people or things ▪ a *troop* of enthusiastic children ▪ a *troop* of monkeys

3 [*count*] **:** a group of Boy Scouts or Girl Scouts

> Do not confuse *troop* with *troupe.*

[2]**troop** *verb, always followed by an adverb or preposition* **troops; trooped; troop·ing** [*no obj*] **:** to walk somewhere in a group ▪ We all *trooped* back inside. ▪ The kids *trooped* off to school.

troop·er /ˈtruːpɚ/ *noun, pl* **-ers** [*count*]

1 : a low-ranking soldier — see also PARATROOPER, STORM TROOPER

2 *US* **:** a state police officer ▪ a state *trooper*

> Do not confuse *trooper* with *trouper.*

troop·ship /ˈtruːpˌʃɪp/ *noun, pl* **-ships** [*count*] **:** a ship used to transport soldiers

trope /ˈtroʊp/ *noun, pl* **tropes** [*count*] *technical* **:** a word, phrase, or image used in a new and different way in order to create an artistic effect ▪ a literary *trope*

tro·phy /ˈtroʊfi/ *noun, pl* **-phies** [*count*]

1 : an object (such as a large cup or sculpture) that is given as a prize for winning a competition ▪ a golf/bowling *trophy* ▪ a *trophy* case/room

2 : something that you keep or take to show that you were successful in hunting, war, etc. ▪ hunting *trophies*

trophy wife *noun, pl* **~ wives** [*count*] *informal + disapproving* **:** an attractive young woman who is married to an older successful man ▪ a millionaire and his young *trophy wife*

trop·ic /ˈtrɑːpɪk/ *noun, pl* **-ics**

1 [*singular*] **:** either one of the two imaginary lines that circle the Earth to the north and south of the equator ✧ ***The Tropic of Cancer*** is 23½ degrees north of the equator and ***the Tropic of Capricorn*** is 23½ degrees south of the equator.

2 *the tropics* : the part of the world that is near the equator where the weather is very warm ▪ a vacation in *the tropics*

trop·i·cal /ˈtrɑːpɪkəl/ *adj* **:** of, relating to, occurring in, or used in the tropics ▪ a *tropical* climate/country/region ▪ *tropical* forests/plants — see also SUBTROPICAL

– trop·i·cal·ly /ˈtrɑːpɪkli/ *adv*

tropical fish *noun, pl* **~ fish** [*count*] **:** a small, brightly colored fish that lives in warm water in tropical areas

tropical rain forest *noun, pl* **~ -ests** [*count*] **:** RAIN FOREST

tropical storm *noun, pl* **~ storms** [*count*] **:** a powerful storm that begins in the tropics and that has winds which are not as strong as those of a hurricane

[1]**trot** /ˈtrɑːt/ *verb* **trots; trot·ted; trot·ting** [*no obj*]

1 *of a horse* **:** to move at a speed faster than walking by stepping with each front leg at the same time as the opposite back leg ▪ A horse *trotted* past us.

2 *always followed by an adverb or preposition* **a :** to run at a slow, steady pace ▪ The batter *trotted* around the bases after hitting a home run. **b :** to move quickly **:** HURRY ▪ She *trotted* off to help. ▪ The little boy *trotted* along after his mother.

hot to trot see [1]HOT

trot out [*phrasal verb*] ***trot (something) out or trot out (something)*** *informal* **1** *disapproving* **:** to say (something that has been said before) as an excuse, explanation, etc. ▪ Don't *trot out* that old excuse again. **2 :** to bring (something) out to be displayed ▪ Designers *trotted out* their latest designs at the fashion show.

[2]**trot** *noun, pl* **trots**

1 [*singular*] **:** a horse's way of moving that is faster than a walk but slower than a gallop ▪ The horse went into a slow *trot.* — compare [1]CANTER, [1]GALLOP

2 [*singular*] **:** a person's way of running slowly ▪ He set off at a *trot.*

3 *the trots* *informal* **:** DIARRHEA ▪ Something I ate gave me *the trots.*

***on the trot** Brit, informal* **1 :** following one after another ▪ He won the race three times *on the trot.* [=*in a row*] **2 :** busy all the time ▪ Working full-time and raising children keeps her *on the trot* [=*on the go*] from morning till night.

– see also FOX-TROT

troth /ˈtrɑːθ/ *noun*

plight your troth see [2]PLIGHT

trot·ter /ˈtrɑːtɚ/ *noun, pl* **-ters** [*count*]

1 : a horse that has been trained to trot in races

2 : a pig's foot cooked and used as food

– see also GLOBE-TROTTER

trou·ba·dour /ˈtruːbəˌdoɚ/ *noun, pl* **-dours** [*count*] **:** a writer and performer of songs or poetry in the Middle Ages

[1]**trou·ble** /ˈtrʌbəl/ *noun, pl* **trou·bles**

1 : problems or difficulties [*noncount*] The new system is giving me *trouble.* ▪ He was having *trouble* with his homework. ▪ I had a little *trouble* finding the place. ▪ He had no *trouble* finding a new job. ▪ This decision could ***spell trouble*** [=cause problems] for all of us. ▪ So far, the trip has been ***trouble free*** [=so far, there have been no problems on the trip] ▪ gangs looking to ***make/cause trouble*** [*count*] — usually plural ▪ She told me all her personal *troubles.* ▪ Your *troubles* are over now that he's out of your life. ▪ I have my own *troubles* to worry about. ▪ They've had some financial *troubles* since he lost his job.

2 [*noncount*] **a :** a situation that is difficult or has a lot of problems ▪ When the new CEO arrived, the company was ***in trouble.*** ▪ She's *in* big/deep financial *trouble.* [=she has serious problems with her money] ▪ She got ***into trouble*** with her credit cards. ▪ Can anyone help get the company ***out of trouble?*** [=solve the company's problems] **b :** a situation that occurs if you do something wrong or break a rule and which will make someone angry or cause you to be punished ▪ He's always ***getting in/into trouble*** at school. ▪ He promised to ***keep/stay out of trouble.*** [=behave well, not do anything bad] — often + *with* ▪ She was *in trouble with* the police. ▪ He will be *in trouble with* his mom if he's late.

3 [*noncount*] **:** a physical pain or illness ▪ heart/stomach *trouble* ▪ She has been having *trouble* with her knee.

4 [*noncount*] **:** a situation in which a machine does not work correctly ▪ He's been having car/engine/computer *trouble.* ▪ She was having *trouble* with her computer.

5 [*singular*] **:** a bad feature, characteristic, quality, etc. ▪ His *trouble* is that he's lazy and unreliable. — often + *with* ▪ The *trouble with* driving into the city is finding a place to park.

6 [*noncount*] **:** extra effort or work ▪ You didn't have to ***go to all that trouble*** for me. [=you didn't have to do all the extra work for me] ▪ Thank you for ***taking the trouble*** [=making the effort] to write. ▪ They didn't even *take the trouble* to call and let me know they'd be late. ▪ I decided that upgrading

T

the software was ***more trouble than it's worth.*** ▪ It's ***not worth the trouble.*** ▪ If it's ***no trouble*** [=if it is not too difficult or inconvenient], could you bring us some more coffee? ▪ "I'm sorry to bother you." "It's *no trouble.* I'm happy to help."
ask for trouble see ASK
look for trouble see [1]LOOK

[2]**trouble** *verb* **troubles; trou•bled; trou•bling** [+ *obj*]
1 : to make (someone) feel worried or upset : WORRY ▪ The accusations *troubled* him deeply. ▪ I'm *troubled* by his strange behavior.
2 *formal* **:** to disturb or bother (someone) ▪ I don't mean to *trouble* you, but I have a question. ▪ Could I *trouble* you for the time? [=can you tell me what time it is?] ▪ ***Don't trouble yourself*** [=I don't need your help], I can handle it.
3 : to cause (someone) to feel pain ▪ My back has been *troubling* [=*bothering*] me again.
4 : to make an effort *to do* something ▪ I wish you'd at least *troubled* [=*bothered*] *to call.*

troubled *adj* [*more* ~; *most* ~]
1 : worried or anxious ▪ a *troubled* expression/look ▪ She seemed *troubled* about something.
2 : having many problems ▪ a *troubled* child/student ▪ These have been *troubled* times. ▪ a *troubled* marriage/relationship
***troubled waters* :** a difficult or confusing situation ▪ He entered the *troubled waters* of the college application process.

trou•ble•mak•er /ˈtrʌbəlˌmeɪkɚ/ *noun, pl* **-ers** [*count*] **:** a person who causes trouble : a person who creates problems or difficulties involving other people ▪ He had the reputation of being a *troublemaker* in high school.

trou•ble•shoot•er /ˈtrʌbəlˌʃuːtɚ/ *noun, pl* **-ers** [*count*]
1 : a person who finds and fixes problems in machinery and technical equipment (such as computers)
2 : a person who tries to find solutions to problems or end disagreements ▪ a financial *troubleshooter*
– trou•ble•shoot•ing /ˈtrʌbəlˌʃuːtɪŋ/ *noun* [*noncount*] ▪ *troubleshooting* tips

trou•ble•some /ˈtrʌbəlsəm/ *adj* [*more* ~; *most* ~] **:** causing problems or worry : causing trouble ▪ a *troublesome* infection ▪ *troublesome* children
– trou•ble•some•ly *adv* **– trou•ble•some•ness** *noun* [*noncount*]

trouble spot *noun, pl* ~ **spots** [*count*] **:** a place where violence or war often happens ▪ one of the world's *trouble spots*

trou•bling /ˈtrʌbəlɪŋ/ *adj* [*more* ~; *most* ~] **:** causing feelings of worry : disturbing or upsetting ▪ *troubling* events/news/questions

trough /ˈtrɑːf/ *noun, pl* **troughs** [*count*]
1 : a long, shallow container from which animals (such as cows, pigs, horses, etc.) eat or drink ▪ a water *trough*
2 : a period in which there is little economic activity and prices are usually low ▪ The economy/business is in a *trough* right now.
3 : a long, low area between waves or hills
4 *weather* **:** a long, narrow area of low air pressure between two areas of higher pressure — compare RIDGE 4
have/get your nose/snout in the trough *Brit, disapproving* **:** to be in or get into a situation in which you are getting or trying to get a lot of money

trounce /ˈtraʊns/ *verb* **trounc•es; trounced; trounc•ing** [+ *obj*] **:** to defeat (someone or something) easily and thoroughly ▪ Their opponents *trounced* them in the final game. [=their opponents won by a large amount]

troupe /ˈtruːp/ *noun, pl* **troupes** [*count*] **:** a group of actors, singers, etc., who work together ▪ an acting/singing/dance *troupe*

Do not confuse *troupe* with *troop.*

troup•er /ˈtruːpɚ/ *noun, pl* **-ers** [*count*] *informal*
1 : an actor or other performer who is very experienced and reliable
2 : someone who works very hard, is very reliable, and does not complain when there are problems ▪ She's been a real *trouper* about the whole thing.

Do not confuse *trouper* with *trooper.*

trou•sers /ˈtraʊzɚz/ *noun* [*plural*] **:** PANTS 1
all mouth and no trousers see [1]MOUTH
wear the trousers see [1]WEAR
with your trousers down *Brit, informal* **:** in an embarrassing situation ▪ another CEO caught *with his trousers down* [=(*US*) *with his pants down*]
– trou•ser /ˈtraʊzɚ/ *adj, always used before a noun* ▪ a *trouser* leg

trouser suit *noun, pl* ~ **suits** [*count*] *Brit* **:** PANTSUIT

trous•seau /ˈtruːˌsoʊ/ *noun, pl* **trous•seaux** *or* **trous•seaus** /ˈtruːˌsoʊz/ [*count*] *old-fashioned* **:** the clothes and personal possessions that a woman collects when she is about to get married

trout /ˈtraʊt/ *noun, pl* **trout** *also* **trouts**
1 [*count, noncount*] **:** a common fish that lives in rivers and lakes and is often used as food — see color picture on page C8
2 *pl* **trouts** [*count*] *Brit, informal* **:** an unpleasant old woman — usually used in the phrase ***old trout***

trove /ˈtroʊv/ *noun, pl* **troves** [*count*] see TREASURE TROVE

trow•el /ˈtrawəl/ *noun, pl* **-els** [*count*]
1 : a small tool with a curved blade that is used by gardeners for digging holes — see picture at GARDENING
2 : a small tool with a flat blade that is used for spreading and smoothing mortar or plaster

tru•ant /ˈtruːwənt/ *noun, pl* **-ants** [*count*] **:** a student who misses school without permission ▪ an increasing number of *truants* ▪ a ***truant officer*** [=a person who looks for students who are not in school]
play truant *Brit, informal* **:** to miss school without permission ▪ He's been *playing truant* [=(*US*) *playing hooky,* (*Brit*) *skiving off*] with his friends.
– tru•an•cy /ˈtruːwənsi/ *noun, pl* **-cies** [*noncount*] What can we do about the problem of *truancy* in our schools? [*count*] How can we reduce *truancies* in our schools?
– truant *adj* ▪ He's been *truant* twice this week.

truce /ˈtruːs/ *noun, pl* **truc•es** [*count*] **:** an agreement between enemies or opponents to stop fighting, arguing, etc., for a certain period of time ▪ They called/proposed a *truce.* ▪ There's been an uneasy *truce* between her and her parents for the past several months. ▪ They ***broke the truce.*** [=they began fighting when there was an agreement not to fight]

[1]**truck** /ˈtrʌk/ *noun, pl* **trucks** [*count*]
1 : a vehicle that carries things: such as **a :** a very large, heavy vehicle that is used to move large or numerous objects ▪ a flatbed/tanker *truck* ▪ a delivery *truck* — called also (*Brit*) *lorry;* see picture on next page; see also DUMP TRUCK, FIRE TRUCK, TOW TRUCK **b :** a vehicle that is larger than a car and that has an open back with low sides : PICKUP — see also PANEL TRUCK
2 : a piece of equipment that has wheels and handles and that you push or pull to move heavy objects ▪ He loaded the boxes onto the *truck* and wheeled them into the building.
3 *Brit* **:** a railroad car that is open at the top ▪ a cattle *truck*
have/hold/want no truck with **:** to refuse to be involved with (someone or something) ▪ I'll *have no truck* with such nonsense.

[2]**truck** *verb* **trucks; trucked; truck•ing** *US*
1 [+ *obj*] **:** to transport (something) in a truck ▪ They *trucked* food to the market. — often + *in* ▪ Produce is *trucked in* from local farms.
2 *always followed by an adverb or preposition* [*no obj*] *informal* **:** to move or go especially in an easy, steady, or relaxed way ▪ Everyone *trucked* on over to our house after the game. ▪ The economy has been doing poorly, but somehow our company manages to keep *trucking* along.

truck•er /ˈtrʌkɚ/ *noun, pl* **-ers** [*count*] *US* **:** a person whose job is to drive a truck

truck farm *noun, pl* ~ **farms** [*count*] *US* **:** a farm where people grow vegetables that will be sold in markets — called also (*Brit*) *market garden*
– truck farmer *noun, pl* ~ **-ers** [*count*]

truck•ing /ˈtrʌkɪŋ/ *noun* [*noncount*] **:** the business of transporting things in trucks — often used before another noun ▪ *trucking* companies

truck•load /ˈtrʌkˈloʊd/ *noun, pl* **-loads** [*count*]
1 : a load that fills a truck ▪ a *truckload* of sand
2 *informal* **:** a large amount of something ▪ He borrowed a *truckload* [=*a lot*] of money to start the business.

truck stop *noun, pl* ~ **stops** [*count*] *US* **:** a restaurant that is near a highway and that is used especially by truck drivers — called also (*Brit*) *transport café*

tru•cu•lent /ˈtrʌkjələnt/ *adj* [*more* ~; *most* ~] **:** easily annoyed or angered and likely to argue ▪ a *truculent* person
– truc•u•lence /ˈtrʌkjələns/ *noun* [*noncount*] **– tru•cu•lent•ly** *adv*

[1]**trudge** /ˈtrʌʤ/ *verb, always followed by an adverb or preposition* **trudg•es; trudged; trudg•ing** [*no obj*] **:** to walk slow-

T

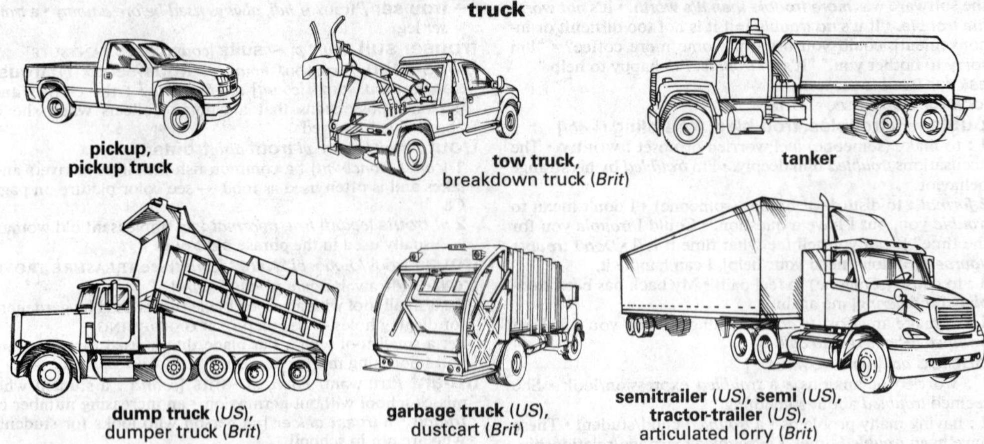

ly and heavily because you are tired or working very hard • I was *trudging* through the snow. • She *trudged* up the hill.

²trudge *noun* [*singular*] : a long, slow walk that makes you tired • a *trudge* across the snow

¹true /ˈtruː/ *adj* **tru·er; -est** [*also more* ~; *most* ~]

1 : agreeing with the facts : not false • a *true* description/statement • Indicate whether each of the following statements is *true* or false. • Their fears proved (to be) *true*. [=turned out to be valid] • If their predictions are *true*, we'll be in for a long winter. • Is it *true* that you were planning to go without me? • Jobs are scarce, and that is especially *true* for managers. • He can be stubborn, but that is *true* of many people. [=many people can be stubborn] • This is a ***true story***. [=an account of something that really happened] • The same ***holds true*** [=is valid] for/in all similar situations.

2 *always used before a noun* **:** real or genuine • The *true* cost proved to be much higher than they said it would be. • His *true* character/nature was revealed. • the *true* meaning of the term • She let him know her ***true feelings***. [=the way she really felt]

3 : having all the expected or necessary qualities of a specifed type of person or thing • He's a *true* artist/expert. [=he is truly an artist/expert] • a *true* gentleman • From the moment they met they knew it was ***true love***. [=knew that their love was strong and lasting]

4 : completely loyal or faithful • I am your *true* servant. • *true* friends — often + *to* • He's always been *true to* his wife.

5 : placed or done correctly or perfectly : without error • His aim was *true*. [=he hit the target]

6 *always used before a noun* **:** rightful, legal, or official • She is the car's *true* [=*lawful, legitimate*] owner.

7 : exact and accurate : FAITHFUL • The story is a *true* depiction of life in a small town. — often + *to* • The movie is *true to* the book. [=the story told in the movie closely matches the story told in the book]

8 — used to admit that something is correct or true • *True*, prices are rising, but I'm not convinced that the economy is failing. • "It would cost a lot less if we did it ourselves." "(That's) *True*."

9 *not used before a noun, technical* **:** in a position that is exactly straight, flat, even, etc. • If the cabinet doors are *true*, they will close tightly.

come true **:** to become real : to happen in the way that you wished or dreamed • Everything we hoped for *came true*. • Their prediction seems to be *coming true*. • The trip abroad was a ***dream come true*** for her. [=it was something that she really wanted to do and that actually happened]

show your true colors see ¹COLOR

too good to be true see ¹GOOD

true believer **:** someone who is completely and often foolishly loyal to a person or an idea • She is a *true believer* in the cause.

true to form see ¹FORM

true to life **:** realistic and natural • The author presents the characters in a way that feels very *true to life*.

true to yourself **:** acting in a way that agrees with your beliefs or values • He's always *true to himself*. [=he always does what he thinks is right]

true to your word **:** doing what you said you would do : keeping your promise • He said he would help, and he was *true to his word*.

— see also TRIED-AND-TRUE

²true *adv* **:** in a straight line • The bullet traveled straight and *true*.

³true *noun* [*noncount*] **:** the quality or state of being straight, flat, even, etc. • The door is slightly ***out of true***. [=is not in its correct position]

true–blue *adj*

1 *US* **:** completely faithful and loyal to a person or an idea • a *true-blue* patriot

2 *Brit, informal* **:** loyal to the ideas of the British Conservative party • *true-blue* Tories

true–life /ˈtruːˈlaɪf/ *adj, always used before a noun* **:** based on a real story and not imaginary • a *true-life* adventure/movie/story

true north *noun* [*noncount*] **:** north that is calculated by using an imaginary line through the Earth rather than by using a compass : the direction that leads to the North Pole — compare MAGNETIC NORTH

truf·fle /ˈtrʌfəl/ *noun, pl* **truf·fles** [*count*]

1 : a type of fungus that grows under the ground and that is used in cooking

2 : a kind of chocolate candy with a soft center

tru·ism /ˈtruːˌɪzəm/ *noun, pl* **-isms** [*count*] **:** a true statement that is very commonly heard : a common statement that is obviously true

tru·ly /ˈtruːli/ *adv* [*more* ~; *most* ~]

1 : in an honest manner : SINCERELY • I *truly* believe they can do it. • She's *truly* sorry. • He *truly* enjoyed the concert.

2 : in truth : actually or really • This is *truly* a different situation. • A country is not *truly* democratic until all of its citizens can vote freely. • Is this poll *truly* representative of the voters' intentions?

3 : without question or doubt — used to make a statement more definite or forceful • It's *truly* hot out today. • *truly* amazing/awful/weird

yours truly **1** — used at the end of a letter and before the writer's signature **2** *humorous* — used to refer to yourself • "Who is in charge here?" "*Yours truly*." [=I am]

¹trump /ˈtrʌmp/ *noun, pl* **trumps**

1 [*count*] **:** a card from the suit that has been chosen as the most valuable for a particular card game • I won the trick by playing a *trump*. — called also *trump card*

2 ***trumps*** [*plural*] **:** the suit whose cards are the most valuable for a particular card game • Diamonds are *trumps*.

come/turn up trumps *Brit, informal* **:** to do or provide what is necessary in order to succeed • The team *turned up trumps* in the final game and won the championship.

²trump *verb* **trumps; trumped; trump·ing** [+ *obj*]

1 : to beat (another card) by playing a card from the suit that beats the other suits : to play a trump card to beat (another card) • She *trumped* my ace to win the trick.

2 a : to do better than (someone or something) in a contest, competition, etc. • Their offer for the house was *trumped* by a higher bid. **b :** to be more important than (something) • The need for blood donors *trumps* all other concerns.

trump up [*phrasal verb*] ***trump up (something)*** **:** to create or make up (something false) in order to cause problems for someone, connect someone to a crime, etc. • She *trumped up* some excuse to fire him. • *trump up* an accusation — see also TRUMPED-UP

trump card *noun, pl* **~ cards** [*count*]
1 : [1]TRUMP 1
2 : something that gives you an advantage • The prosecution's *trump card* is the evidence linking the defendant to the murder weapon. • He ***played/used his trump card*** during the negotiations.

trumped–up /ˈtrʌmptˈʌp/ *adj* **:** deliberately done or created to make someone appear to be guilty of a crime • She was arrested on *trumped-up* charges. • *trumped-up* evidence

[1]**trum•pet** /ˈtrʌmpət/ *noun, pl* **-pets** [*count*]
1 : a brass musical instrument that you blow into that has three buttons which you press to play different notes — see picture at BRASS INSTRUMENT
2 : something shaped like a trumpet • the *trumpet* of a flower
blow your own trumpet *Brit, informal* **:** to talk about yourself or your achievements especially in a way that shows that you are proud or too proud • He had a very successful year and has every right to *blow his own trumpet.* [=(*US*) *blow/toot his own horn*]

[2]**trumpet** *verb* **-pets; -pet•ed; -pet•ing**
1 [+ *obj*] **:** to praise (something) loudly and publicly especially in a way that is annoying • He likes to *trumpet* his own achievements. • The law was *trumpeted* as a solution to everything.
2 [*no obj*] **:** to make a sound like a trumpet • The elephant *trumpeted* loudly.

trum•pet•er /ˈtrʌmpətɚ/ *noun, pl* **-ers** [*count*] **:** a person who plays a trumpet

trun•cate /ˈtrʌŋˌkeɪt/ *verb* **-cates; -cat•ed; -cat•ing** [+ *obj*] *formal* **:** to make (something) shorter — often used as *(be) truncated* • The essay *was truncated* before it was published. • a *truncated* discussion
– trun•ca•tion /trʌŋˈkeɪʃən/ *noun* [*noncount*]

trun•cheon /ˈtrʌnʃən/ *noun, pl* **-cheons** [*count*] *Brit* **:** NIGHTSTICK

trun•dle /ˈtrʌndəl/ *verb, always followed by an adverb or preposition* **trun•dles; trun•dled; trun•dling**
1 a [+ *obj*] **:** to roll (something) on wheels slowly and noisily • She *trundled* her suitcase into the room. **b** [*no obj*] **:** to move noisily on wheels • Trucks *trundled* through town.
2 [*no obj*] **:** to walk slowly and heavily • The children *trundled* off to bed.
trundle out [*phrasal verb*] ***trundle (something) out*** *or* ***trundle out (something)*** *Brit, informal* + *disapproving* **:** to say (something that has been said before) as an excuse, explanation, etc. • He *trundled out* [=*trotted out*] another excuse.

trunk /ˈtrʌŋk/ *noun, pl* **trunks**
1 [*count*] **:** the thick main stem of a tree — see color picture on page C6
2 [*count*] **:** the main part of the human body not including the head, arms, and legs **:** TORSO
3 [*count*] **:** the main or central part of something • the *trunk* of an artery
4 [*count*] *US* **:** the enclosed space in the back of a car for carrying things • He keeps a jack and spare tire in the *trunk.* — called also (*Brit*) *boot*; see picture at CAR
5 [*count*] **:** a large, strong box used for holding clothes or other things especially for traveling • a *trunk* full of clothes
6 [*count*] **:** the long, flexible nose of an elephant
7 ***trunks*** [*plural*] **a :** SWIMMING TRUNKS **b :** shorts worn by a boxer

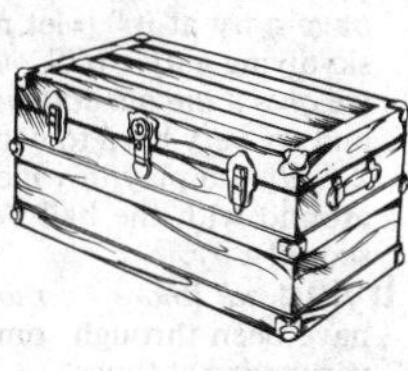
trunk

trunk call *noun, pl* **~ calls** [*count*] *Brit, old-fashioned* **:** TOLL CALL

trunk road *noun, pl* **~ roads** [*count*] *Brit* **:** a main road

[1]**truss** /ˈtrʌs/ *verb* **truss•es; trussed; truss•ing** [+ *obj*]
1 : to tie up (someone) tightly to prevent movement • The thieves *trussed* [=*bound*] the guards and stole several paintings. — usually + *up* • The guards were *trussed up* with ropes.
2 : to tie together the wings or legs of (a turkey, chicken, etc.) for cooking • She stuffed and *trussed* the duck.

[2]**truss** *noun, pl* **trusses** [*count*]
1 : a strong frame of beams, bars, or rods that supports a roof or bridge
2 : a special belt that is worn by someone who has a hernia

[1]**trust** /ˈtrʌst/ *noun, pl* **trusts**
1 [*noncount*] **:** belief that someone or something is reliable, good, honest, effective, etc. • Our relationship is founded on mutual love and *trust.* • His lies and deception shattered my *trust* in him. • She has no *trust* in the security of online banking. • He ***placed/put his trust in*** [=*trusted*] his closest friends and few others. • She ***betrayed my trust.***
2 a : an arrangement in which someone's property or money is legally held or managed by someone else or by an organization (such as a bank) for usually a set period of time [*count*] He created a *trust* for his children. [*noncount*] The property will be ***held in trust*** until her 18th birthday. — see also TRUST FUND, UNIT TRUST **b** [*count*] **:** an organization that results from the creation of a trust • a charitable *trust*
3 [*count*] *chiefly US* **:** a group of companies that work together to try to control an industry by reducing competition • laws limiting the formation of *trusts*
4 [*noncount*] **:** responsibility for the safety and care of someone or something • The child was committed to his *trust.* • We left our pets ***in the trust of*** [=in the care of] our neighbor while we were gone. • She has been placed in a ***position of trust.*** [=she has been given a job/position in which she has a lot of responsibility and power]
take something on trust **:** to believe that something you have been told is true or correct even though you do not have proof of it • I don't know anything about cars so I had to *take* the mechanic's recommendations *on trust.*
– see also BRAIN TRUST

[2]**trust** *verb* **trusts; trust•ed; trust•ing** [+ *obj*]
1 a : to believe that someone or something is reliable, good, honest, effective, etc. **:** to have confidence in (someone or something) • Working together is going to be difficult if you don't *trust* each other. • "Are you sure this will work?" "*Trust* me. I know what I'm doing." • I *trust* him to do the right thing. [=I believe that he will do the right thing because I trust him] • If you have a problem, tell your parent, teacher, or someone else you *trust.* • I should never have *trusted* him. • Their company is a *trusted* name in quality appliances. • I don't *trust* that ladder. [=I don't think that ladder is safe] • She got her cast taken off, but she doesn't quite *trust* her leg yet. [=she doesn't feel confident that her leg is completely strong/healthy yet] **b :** to believe that something is true or correct • Don't *trust* everything you read. • You can't *trust* the rumors. • You should *trust* your instincts/judgment and do what you think is right. • You can *trust* her word. [=you can believe that she will do what she says she will do and that what she says is true]
2 *somewhat formal* **:** to hope or expect that something is true or will happen — often used to politely tell someone what you think they should do • ***I trust*** that you'll pay me for the broken window. • All of this will be cleaned up by the time I get back, *I trust.*
trust in [*phrasal verb*] ***trust in (someone or something)*** *formal* **:** to have a strong belief in the goodness or ability of (someone or something) **:** to have trust in (someone or something) • They *trust in* God. • It is important that they *trust in* themselves and their abilities.
trust to [*phrasal verb*] **1** ***trust to (something)*** **:** to rely on (something you have no control over, such as luck or chance) to get what you want or need • We can't control what happens. All we can do at this point is hope for the best and *trust to* luck. • You're more likely to make friends if you seek them out rather than simply *trusting to* chance.
2 ***trust (something) to (someone)*** **:** to give the responsibility of doing (something) to (someone) • They *trusted* the care of their daughter *to* her grandparents while they were on vacation.
trust with [*phrasal verb*] ***trust (someone) with (something)*** **:** to allow (someone) to have or use (something valuable) • They *trusted* their son *with* the family car. • I *trusted* the reporter *with* my story.

trust•ee /ˌtrʌˈstiː/ *noun, pl* **-ees** [*count*]
1 : a person or organization that has been given responsibility for managing someone else's property or money through a trust • They were named as *trustees* to the child's estate.
2 : a member of a group that manages the money of an organization • the museum's/school's ***board of trustees***

trust•ee•ship /ˌtrʌˈstiːˌʃɪp/ *noun, pl* **-ships**
1 [*count, noncount*] **:** the position or job of a trustee
2 [*noncount*] **:** control over an area of land given to a country or countries by the United Nations

T

trust fund *noun, pl* **~ funds** [*count*] : money that belongs to one person but is legally held or managed by another person or by an organization • She paid for college out of a *trust fund* set up for her by her grandfather.

trust·ing /ˈtrʌstɪŋ/ *adj* [*more ~; most ~*] : tending to believe that other people are honest, good, etc. • He is too naive and *trusting* and often lets people take advantage of him.

trust·wor·thy /ˈtrʌstˌwɚði/ *adj* [*more ~; most ~*] : able to be relied on to do or provide what is needed or right : deserving of trust • *trustworthy* friends • a *trustworthy* [=*dependable*] news source
– **trust·wor·thi·ness** *noun* [*noncount*]

[1]**trusty** /ˈtrʌsti/ *adj, always used before a noun* **trust·i·er; -est** [*also more ~; most ~*] : able to be depended on — used especially to describe a useful too, device, etc., that you have had and used for a long time • I never go anywhere without my *trusty* pocketknife.

[2]**trusty** *noun, pl* **trust·ies** [*count*] *US* : a prisoner who is trusted and given special privileges because of good behavior

truth /ˈtru:θ/ *noun, pl* **truths** /ˈtru:ðz, ˈtru:θs/
1 ***the truth*** : the real facts about something : the things that are true • Are you telling (me) *the truth*? • At some point you have to face *the* simple/hard/honest/plain/naked *truth* that we failed. • Their explanation was simpler but came closer to *the truth*. • The article explains *the truth* about global warming. • A reporter soon discovered/revealed/uncovered *the truth*. • Do you swear to tell ***the whole truth*** and nothing but *the truth*? • I know you think I don't care, but ***nothing could be further from the truth***. [=that is absolutely not true] • ***The truth of the matter is (that)*** you failed the exam and it's going to be reflected in your final grade. • ***To tell (you) the truth***, I liked her first book better than this one. [=I am being honest when I say that I liked her first book better] • "When was the last time you went to New York?" "*To tell you the truth*, I don't remember." [=I have to admit that I don't remember] • I told her I liked the restaurant but *the truth* is that the food was pretty bad. = I told her I liked the restaurant but, ***truth be told/known***, the food was pretty bad.
2 [*noncount*] : the quality or state of being true • There's no *truth* in anything he says. [=nothing he says is true] • I doubt the *truth* of their accusations. [=I doubt that their accusations are true] • Her story contains ***a grain/kernel of truth*** but also lots of exaggeration.
3 [*count*] : a statement or idea that is true or accepted as true — usually plural • Her experience taught her some basic/fundamental/eternal/universal *truths* about human nature. • mathematical *truths* — see also HALF-TRUTH, HOME TRUTH, UNTRUTH
bend the truth see [1]BEND
in truth : in fact : actually or really • She said she was feeling fine, but *in truth* she was very ill.
moment of truth see MOMENT

truth·ful /ˈtru:θfəl/ *adj* [*more ~; most ~*]
1 : telling the truth : HONEST • She is a very *truthful* person. [=she says things that are true; she doesn't lie] • We were not entirely *truthful* with her about where we went last night. • I like keeping the house clean but, ***to be truthful***, I hate vacuuming.
2 : containing or expressing the truth • *truthful* remarks • *truthful* information • Why can't you give me a *truthful* [=*honest*] answer? • The documentary tries its hardest to be *truthful* to actual events. [=to show what actually happened]
– **truth·ful·ly** /ˈtru:θfəli/ *adv* • He told us *truthfully* [=*honestly*] that he had been in the hospital for mental illness. • *Truthfully*, she deserves most of the credit. [=I am being honest when I say that she deserves most of the credit]
– **truth·ful·ness** *noun* [*noncount*]

[1]**try** /ˈtraɪ/ *verb* **tries; tried; try·ing**
1 : to make an effort to do something : to attempt to accomplish or complete something [*no obj*] I don't know if I can do it, but I'll *try*. • Keep *trying*. You can do it. • You can do it if you *try* hard enough. • "He said he can beat you." "I'd like to see him *try*!" • I *tried*, but I just couldn't do it. • "She's not in the office now." "OK. I'll *try* again later." • If you don't succeed the first time, ***try, (and) try again***. • He still hasn't found a job, but ***it is not for lack/want of trying***. [=he has been trying to find a job but he has not found one] [+ *obj*] I ***tried my best/hardest*** [=I tried very hard, I did everything that I could do], but I just couldn't do it. — often followed by *to + verb* • He *tried to move* the sofa by himself. • Please *try* not *to make* any noise. • I was only *trying to help*! • You should *try to exercise* more. — often followed by *and + verb* • *Try and* relax. • *Try and* think of another example.
synonyms see [1]ATTEMPT
2 [+ *obj*] : to do or use (something) in order to see if it works or will be successful • I don't know where she is. *Try* calling her on her cell phone. • *Try* her cell phone. • He *tried* a few things to remove the stain, but nothing worked. • *Try* (pressing) that button. • Did you *try* restarting the computer? • If you want to lose weight, *try* exercising more. • She *tried* a karate move on him. • He *tried* the switch, and the lights flickered on. • I *tried* (opening) the door, but it was locked. • No, we don't sell those. *Try* the store across the street. • I *tried* several hotels, but there were no rooms available. — often + *out* • If you can't solve the problem, you should *try out* a different approach.
3 [+ *obj*] **a** : to do or use (something) in order to find out if you like it • He never wants to *try* anything new. • I *tried* skiing for the first time last winter. • Have you ever *tried* teaching? — often + *out* • He decided to *try* the car *out*. • She has *tried out* many different jobs but can't find one she likes. **b** : to taste (food or drink) to find out what it is like • You should *try* the cake. It's excellent. • "Would you like to *try* some caviar?" "Sure—I'll *try* anything once." • *Try* a little bite.
4 [+ *obj*] : to test how good, strong, etc., something or someone is • "These are the times that *try* men's souls." —Thomas Paine, "The Crisis" (1776) • "Oh, you probably don't know the answer!" "***Try me***." [=ask me the question] • You are ***trying my patience***. [=you are making me lose my patience and become angry]
5 [+ *obj*] **a** : to examine and make a decision about (a legal case) — usually used as *(be) tried* • The case *was tried* in a federal court. **b** : to have a trial to decide if someone is innocent or guilty — usually used as *(be) tried for* • He *was tried for* murder. [=he was put on trial for murder]
try for [*phrasal verb*] ***try for (something)*** : to make an attempt or effort to get (something) • You've already won $100. Do you want to *try for* more? • He *tried for* second place but finished third instead. • She *tried for* the job and got it. • They have been ***trying for a baby*** [=trying to have a baby] for several years.
try it on *Brit, informal* **1** : to behave badly so that someone becomes annoyed or angry — often + *with* • Don't take any notice of him—he's only *trying it on with* you. **2** : to try to start a sexual relationship with someone — often + *with* • He *tried it on with* a girl at the pub.
try on [*phrasal verb*] ***try on (something)*** or ***try (something) on*** : to put on (a piece of clothing, a pair of shoes, etc.) in order to see how it fits and looks • This is the fifth dress you've *tried on*. • ***Try*** this shoe ***on for size***. [=put on this shoe to see if it is the correct size]
try out [*phrasal verb*] *chiefly US* : to compete for a position on an athletic team or a part in a play • She *tried out* [=*auditioned*] and got the lead role. — often + *for* • He *tried out for* the golf team. — see also [1]TRY 2, 3 (above), TRYOUT
try your damnedest see DAMNEDEST
try your hand see [1]HAND
try your luck see [1]LUCK

[2]**try** *noun, pl* **tries** [*count*]
1 : an effort or attempt to do something — usually singular • I doubt it will work, but it's ***worth a try***. • ***Nice try***. I'm sure you'll do better next time. • "I can't open this jar." "Let me ***have a try*** at it." [=let me try to open it] • You should ***give*** skydiving ***a try***. • (*US, old-fashioned*) We can win this game if we ***give it the old college try***! [=if we give our very best effort and try very hard to win]
2 *rugby* : a play in which points are scored by touching the ground with the ball behind the opponent's goal line • He scored a *try*.

trying *adj* [*more ~; most ~*] : difficult to deal with • They have been through some *trying* times together. • He can be very *trying* at times.

try·out /ˈtraɪˌaʊt/ *noun, pl* **-outs** [*count*]
1 *US* : a test of someone's ability to do something that is used to see if he or she should join a team, perform in a play, etc. • She was cut from the team after the first *tryout*. [=(*Brit*) *trial*] • Open *tryouts* for the team are next Monday.
2 *chiefly Brit* : a test of the quality, value, or usefulness of something • The car did not do well in its *tryout*. [=*trial*] — often used before another noun • I have a 30-day free *tryout* period before I have to start paying for the service.
– see also *try out* at [1]TRY

tryst /ˈtrɪst/ *noun, pl* **trysts** [*count*] *literary* : a meeting by lovers at a secret time or place

tsar, tsarina, tsarist *variant spellings of* CZAR, CZARINA, CZARIST

tset·se fly /ˈsɛtsi-, ˈsiːtsi-/ *noun, pl* ~ **flies** [*count*] : a kind of fly found in Africa that bites people and animals, sucks their blood, and can spread a serious disease (called sleeping sickness) to humans — called also *tsetse*

T–shirt *also* **tee shirt** /ˈtiːˌʃɚt/ *noun, pl* **T–shirts** *also* **tee shirts** [*count*] : a shirt that has short sleeves and no collar and that is usually made of cotton — see color picture on page C14

tsk tsk /*a clicking sound, often read as* ˈtɪskˌtɪsk/ *interj* — used to show disapproval often in a humorous way • *Tsk tsk!* Who left the cap off the toothpaste?

tsp. *abbr* teaspoon, teaspoonful

T square *noun, pl* ~ **squares** [*count*] : a tool that is shaped like the letter T and that is used to draw parallel lines and right angles

TSS *abbr* toxic shock syndrome

tsu·na·mi /sʊˈnɑːmi/ *noun, pl* **-mis** [*count*] : a very high, large wave in the ocean that is usually caused by an earthquake under the sea and that can cause great destruction when it reaches land : TIDAL WAVE

Tu. *abbr* Tuesday

tub /ˈtʌb/ *noun, pl* **tubs** [*count*]

1 : a wide container used to hold something • a *tub* of margarine/butter • We let the pans soak overnight in a *tub* of soapy water. — see also WASHTUB

2 *US* : BATHTUB • The bathroom has a shower and *tub.* — see also HOT TUB

3 : the amount that a tub will hold • She ate the whole *tub* of ice cream.

tu·ba /ˈtuːbə, *Brit* ˈtjuːbə/ *noun, pl* **-bas** [*count*] : a large brass musical instrument that is played by blowing air into it and that produces low tones — see picture at BRASS INSTRUMENT

tub·by /ˈtʌbi/ *adj* **tub·bi·er; -est** *informal* : short and somewhat fat • a *tubby* little kid

tube /ˈtuːb, *Brit* ˈtjuːb/ *noun, pl* **tubes**

1 [*count*] **a** : a long, hollow object that is used especially to control the flow of a liquid or gas • She was breathing oxygen through a *tube.* • The nurse inserted a ***feeding tube.*** [=a tube used to deliver food to the stomach of a patient who cannot eat] **b** : an object shaped like a pipe • a *tube* of lipstick • a cardboard *tube* — see also INNER TUBE, TEST TUBE, VACUUM TUBE

2 [*count*] : a soft, long, narrow container that has a small opening at one end and that contains a soft material which can be pushed out by squeezing • a *tube* of paint/toothpaste

3 [*count*] : a thin, long, hollow part within an animal or plant • the bronchial *tubes* • a pollen *tube*

4 ***the tube*** *US, informal* : the television • They spent all afternoon sitting in front of *the tube.* [=(*Brit*) *the box*] • What's on *the tube* tonight? — see also BOOB TUBE, CATHODE-RAY TUBE

5 [*noncount*] *Brit* : the system of trains that run underground in London • It's easy to get around London on ***the tube.*** • There's a ***tube station*** a couple of blocks away from here. • She travels ***by tube*** to work every day.

go down the tubes *informal* **1** : to fail or become ruined • His health is *going down the tubes.* **2** : to be wasted or lost • All my hard work *went down the tubes.* [=*went down the drain*]

– **tube·like** /ˈtuːbˌlaɪk, *Brit* ˈtjuːbˌlaɪk/ *adj* • The plant produces *tubelike* flowers.

tu·ber /ˈtuːbɚ, *Brit* ˈtjuːbə/ *noun, pl* **-bers** [*count*] : a short, thick, round stem that is a part of certain plants (such as the potato), that grows underground, and that can produce a new plant

– **tu·ber·ous** /ˈtuːbərəs, *Brit* ˈtjuːbərəs/ *adj* • *tuberous* roots

tu·ber·cu·lo·sis /tʊˌbɚkjəˈlousəs, *Brit* tjʊˌbɜːkjəˈləʊsəs/ *noun* [*noncount*] *medical* : a serious disease that mainly affects the lungs — called also *TB,* (*old-fashioned*) *consumption*

– **tu·ber·cu·lar** /tʊˈbɚkjəlɚ, *Brit* tjʊˈbɜːkjələ/ *adj* • a *tubercular* infection/cough – **tu·ber·cu·lous** /tʊˈbɚkjələs, *Brit* tjʊˈbɜːkjələs/ *adj* • a *tuberculous* patient

tube sock *noun, pl* ~ **socks** [*count*] *US* : a long sock that is shaped like a tube without a place for your heel and that is often worn while playing sports

tube top *noun, pl* ~ **tops** [*count*] *US* : a piece of clothing for women and girls that is shaped like a tube and that covers the chest and back but not the shoulders or arms — called also (*Brit*) *boob tube*

tub·ing /ˈtuːbɪŋ, *Brit* ˈtjuːbɪŋ/ *noun* [*noncount*]

1 : material in the form of a tube : a series or system of tubes • The fluids travel through flexible plastic/rubber *tubing.*

2 : the activity of riding on an inner tube over snow, down a river, etc. • We ***go tubing*** on the river every summer.

tub–thumping *noun* [*noncount*] *chiefly Brit* : the activity of talking about someone or something that you support in a loud and forceful manner

– **tub–thump·er** /ˈtʌbˌθʌmpɚ/ *noun, pl* **-ers** [*count*] – **tub–thumping** *adj, always used before a noun* • *tub-thumping* radicals

tu·bu·lar /ˈtuːbjəlɚ, *Brit* ˈtjuːbjələ/ *adj*

1 : having the form of a tube • *tubular* flowers/pasta

2 : made of a tube or tubes • a *tubular* chair • a radiator of *tubular* construction

¹tuck /ˈtʌk/ *verb* **tucks; tucked; tuck·ing**

1 [+ *obj*] : to push the end of (something, such as a piece of cloth or paper) into or behind something in order to hold it in place, make it look neat, etc. • *Tuck* in your shirt. [=push the bottom of your shirt into the waist of your pants or skirt] • She hadn't sealed the envelope, but had simply *tucked* in the flap. • Instead of tying his shoes, he just *tucked* the laces inside. • The sheets were *tucked* tightly under the mattress.

2 [+ *obj*] **a** : to put (something) in a particular place usually to hide it, hold it, or make it safe • A bag was *tucked* under her arm. • She *tucked* her hair up under her hat. • The dog *tucked* its tail between its legs and slinked away. • The bird slept with its head *tucked* under its wing. — often + *away* • The apartment is tiny so he keeps the dog's bed *tucked away* all day until he brings it out at night. — sometimes used figuratively • They manage to *tuck away* [=*save*] a portion of their paychecks every month. **b** — used as *tucked* to indicate the quiet or hidden place where something is located • They live in a log cabin *tucked* among the trees. — often + *away* • The Vietnamese restaurant is *tucked away* on a quiet street. [=is located on a quiet street]

3 *Brit, informal* : to eat with pleasure [+ *obj*] — + *away* • He *tucked away* a big lunch. [*no obj*] — + *in* or *into* • We all *tucked in* [=started eating eagerly] as soon as the food was served. • We all *tucked into* the delicious food.

tuck in *or chiefly Brit* ***tuck up*** [*phrasal verb*] ***tuck (someone) in/up*** : to make (someone, such as a child) comfortable in bed by moving the blankets to the right positions • I *tucked* him *in* and kissed him good night. • The children are *tucked up* in bed for the night.

²tuck *noun, pl* **tucks** [*count*]

1 : a fold that is sewn into a piece of clothing or fabric • The skirt is bordered with satin *tucks.*

2 : an operation to remove extra skin or fat from a part of the body • a tummy *tuck*

– see also NIP AND TUCK

tuck·er /ˈtʌkɚ/ *verb* **-ers; -ered; -er·ing**

tucker out *US, informal* : to cause (someone) to become very tired • Raking all the leaves *tuckered* me *out.* — often used as *(be) tuckered out* • We *were* all *tuckered out* by the hard work.

Tu·dor /ˈtuːdɚ, *Brit* ˈtjuːdə/ *adj* : relating to the period of British history from 1485 to 1603 • *Tudor* England • the *Tudor* monarchs • a *Tudor* mansion

Tues. *or* **Tue.** *abbr* Tuesday

Tues·day /ˈtuːzˌdeɪ, *Brit* ˈtjuːzˌdeɪ/ *noun, pl* **-days** : the day of the week between Monday and Wednesday [*count*] I had lunch with her last *Tuesday.* • I'll be seeing her again next *Tuesday.* • The class meets on *Tuesdays.* [=every Tuesday] • My birthday falls on a *Tuesday* this year. • (*Brit*) Next week I'll arrive on the *Tuesday* and leave on the Friday. [*noncount*] Next week I'll arrive on *Tuesday* and leave on Friday. • The paper is due on *Tuesday.* = (*chiefly US*) The paper is due *Tuesday.* • I will arrive on *Tuesday* morning. — abbr. *Tues.*, *Tue.*, or *Tu.*; see also SHROVE TUESDAY

– **Tues·days** /ˈtuːzˌdeɪz, *Brit* ˈtjuːzˌdeɪz/ *adv* • He works late *Tuesdays.* [=he works late every Tuesday]

tuft /ˈtʌft/ *noun, pl* **tufts** [*count*] : a small bunch of feathers, hairs, grass, etc., that grow close together • *tufts* of grass • A *tuft* of hair stuck out from under his hat.

tuft·ed /ˈtʌftəd/ *adj* : having a tuft or tufts • The fox has large *tufted* ears.

¹tug /ˈtʌg/ *verb* **tugs; tugged; tug·ging** : to pull something with a quick, forceful movement [*no obj*] I felt someone *tug-*

ging on/at my sleeve. [+ *obj*] She *tugged* the cord until the plug came out of the wall socket.

tug your forelock see FORELOCK

[2]**tug** *noun, pl* **tugs** [*count*]

1 : an act of pulling on something : a quick pull • He felt a gentle *tug* on his sleeve. • She gave the rope a *tug*. [=she tugged the rope]

2 : a strong pulling force — usually singular • the *tug* of gravity — often used figuratively • The *tug* of urban life drew him from his country home and into the city.

3 : TUGBOAT

tug·boat /ˈtʌgˌbout/ *noun, pl* **-boats** [*count*] : a small, powerful boat that is used for pulling and pushing ships especially into harbors or up rivers — called also *tug*

tug–of–love *noun* [*singular*] *Brit* : a situation in which two divorced or separated parents are in a legal fight about who will take care of their child or children • a bitter *tug-of-love* [=*custody battle*]

tug–of–war /ˌtʌgəvˈwoɚ/ *noun, pl* **tugs–of–war**

1 [*singular*] : a contest in which two teams pull against each other at opposite ends of a rope

2 [*count*] : a struggle between two people or groups to win control or possession of something — usually singular • The two countries have been involved in a *tug-of-war* over control of the region.

tu·ition /təˈwɪʃən, *Brit* tjuˈɪʃən/ *noun* [*noncount*]

1 : money that is paid to a school for the right to study there • Her uncle agreed to pay part of her *tuition*. • There's going to be a *tuition* increase next year. • *tuition* fees

2 *formal* : teaching that is done especially for a single person or small group • Before the company transferred her to Mexico, they offered her private *tuition* in Spanish.

tu·lip /ˈtuːləp, *Brit* ˈtjuːləp/ *noun, pl* **-lips** [*count*] : a large, bright flower that is shaped like a cup and that grows in the spring — see color picture on page C6

tulle /ˈtuːl/ *noun* [*noncount*] : a light, thin type of cloth that is like a net and that is used for veils, evening dresses, etc.

tum /ˈtʌm/ *noun, pl* **tums** [*count*] *Brit, informal* : your stomach or belly • She pulled her shirt down over her *tum*. [=*tummy*]

[1]**tum·ble** /ˈtʌmbəl/ *verb* **tum·bles; tum·bled; tum·bling** [*no obj*]

1 a : to fall down suddenly and quickly • He tripped and *tumbled* to the ground. • The abandoned house finally *tumbled* [=*collapsed*] to the ground. • The statue ***came tumbling down*** during the riots. **b :** to fall forward while turning over • The satellite was *tumbling* out of control. • She slipped and *tumbled* down the hill/steps.

2 : to fall or drop suddenly in amount, value, etc. • Stock prices *tumbled* today.

3 *always followed by an adverb or preposition* : to move in a fast, confused, or uncontrolled way • Everyone came *tumbling* out of the bar at closing time. • He *tumbled* into bed and fell asleep. • Water *tumbled* over the rocks.

4 : to roll or turn your body across the ground or through the air while performing a series of athletic movements • *tumbling* acrobats/gymnasts

5 *of hair* : to fall or hang down loosely • Her long, curly hair *tumbled* down her back.

tumble to [*phrasal verb*] ***tumble to (something)*** *Brit, informal* : to understand or become aware of (something) • They didn't *tumble to* [=*realize*] the seriousness of the problem. • I thought you'd *tumble to* what I'd meant.

[2]**tumble** *noun, pl* **tumbles** [*count*]

1 : an act of falling or tumbling • She ***took a tumble*** down the stairs. [=she fell down the stairs] • The value of the stock has *taken a tumble* [=has gone down] in recent weeks. — see also ROUGH-AND-TUMBLE

2 : an athletic movement in which you roll or turn your body across the ground or through the air • gymnasts doing *tumbles*

tum·ble·down /ˈtʌmbəlˌdaun/ *adj, always used before a noun, of a building* : in bad condition : ready to fall down • a *tumbledown* [=*dilapidated*] shack

tumble dry *verb* ~ **dries;** ~ **dried;** ~ **drying** [+ *obj*] : to dry (clothes, sheets, etc.) in a machine • He *tumble dried* his clothes on high heat.

tumble dryer *or* **tumble drier** *noun, pl* **~-ers** [*count*] *Brit* : a machine used for drying clothes after they are washed • He dried his clothes in the *tumble dryer*. [=(*US*) *dryer*]

tum·bler /ˈtʌmblɚ/ *noun, pl* **tum·blers** [*count*]

1 a : a glass used for drinking that has a flat bottom and no stem or handle • a water *tumbler* **b :** the amount of liquid held in a tumbler • She drank a *tumbler* of water.

2 : a person who performs athletic movements that involve rolling or turning along the ground or through the air • circus *tumblers* [=*acrobats*] • a gymnast who's a skillful *tumbler*

tum·ble·weed /ˈtʌmbəlˌwiːd/ *noun, pl* **-weeds** [*count, noncount*] : a plant found especially in the North American desert that breaks away from its roots and is blown across the ground by the wind

tu·mes·cent /tuˈmɛsn̩t, *Brit* tjuˈmɛsn̩t/ *adj, technical* : somewhat swollen • *tumescent* tissue

– tu·mes·cence /tuˈmɛsn̩s, *Brit* tjuˈmɛsn̩s/ *noun* [*noncount*]

tum·my /ˈtʌmi/ *noun, pl* **-mies** [*count*] *informal* : your stomach or belly • His mother rubbed his *tummy* until he fell asleep. • She woke up with a *tummy* ache. [=a stomachache] — usually used by children or when speaking to children

tu·mor (*US*) *or Brit* **tu·mour** /ˈtuːmɚ, *Brit* ˈtjuːmə/ *noun, pl* **-mors** [*count*] : a mass of tissue found in or on the body that is made up of abnormal cells • a brain *tumor* • cancerous *tumors* • a benign/malignant *tumor*

tu·mult /ˈtuːˌmʌlt, *Brit* ˈtjuːˌmʌlt/ *noun, pl* **-mults** *formal*

1 : a state of noisy confusion or disorder [*count*] A great *tumult* [=*uproar, commotion*] arose in the street. • We had to shout to be heard over the *tumult*. [*noncount*] The country was in *tumult*.

2 : a state of great mental or emotional confusion [*noncount*] emotional *tumult* [=*turmoil*] [*count*] Her mind was in a *tumult* of emotions.

tu·mul·tu·ous /tuˈmʌlʧəwəs, *Brit* tjʊˈmʌlʧəwəs/ *adj* [*more ~; most ~*]

1 : loud, excited, and emotional • The returning astronauts were given a *tumultuous* welcome. • The room filled with *tumultuous* applause.

2 : involving a lot of violence, confusion, or disorder • the nation's *tumultuous* past

– tu·mul·tu·ous·ly *adv* **– tu·mul·tu·ous·ness** *noun* [*noncount*]

tu·na /ˈtuːnə, *Brit* ˈtjuːnə/ *noun, pl* **tuna** *also* **tunas**

1 [*count*] : a large fish that lives in the ocean and is eaten as food — see color picture on page C8

2 [*noncount*] : the meat of a tuna that is eaten as food • a can of *tuna* • We ordered grilled/blackened *tuna* for dinner. • canned/fresh *tuna* — often used before another noun • *tuna* steaks • a *tuna* casserole • *tuna* salad — called also *tuna fish*

tun·dra /ˈtʌndrə/ *noun, pl* **-dras** [*count, noncount*] : a large area of flat land in northern parts of the world where there are no trees and the ground is always frozen • the Canadian *tundra*

[1]**tune** /ˈtuːn, *Brit* ˈtjuːn/ *noun, pl* **tunes** [*count*] : a series of musical notes that produce a pleasing sound when played or sung • I can't get that *tune* [=*song*] out of my head. • an upbeat dance *tune* • He played a delightful little *tune* [=*melody*] on the piano. • The concert featured popular Broadway ***show tunes***. [=songs from musicals]

call the tune *informal* : to be in charge or control of something • She *called the tune* all through the meeting.

change your tune *or* ***sing a different tune*** *informal* : to change the way you talk about something : to have a different opinion about something • He bragged that the test was easy, but when he saw his grade he *changed his tune*. • Now he's *singing a different tune*. • They say they're not worried about money, but once they see how much the new equipment will cost, they'll be *singing a different tune*.

dance to someone's tune see [1]DANCE

in tune **1 :** in a state in which the correct musical sound is played or sung • The guitar was *in tune*. **2 a :** in a state in which people agree with or understand one another • The president and his followers were clearly *in tune*. — usually + *with* • They were clearly *in tune with* each other. • The speaker was very much *in tune with* our concerns. [=understood and shared our concerns] • The new supervisor is not *in tune with* the needs of the staff. [=does not understand/appreciate the needs of the staff] **b :** in a state in which one thing agrees with or matches another — usually + *with* • His formal clothing was *in tune with* the occasion.

out of tune **1 :** in a state in which the correct musical sound is not played or sung • The piano was *out of tune*. **2 a :** in a state in which people do not agree with or understand one another — usually + *with* • His speech was completely *out of tune with* our concerns. **b :** in a state in which one thing does not agree with or match another —

usually + *with* ▪ His values are *out of tune with* the times.
to the tune of **1 :** using the tune of (a particular song) ▪ Amusing lyrics were sung *to the tune of* [=to the music of the song] "New York, New York." **2** *informal* — used to emphasize a large amount of money ▪ A telecommunications company funded the event *to the tune of* [=at a cost of] several million dollars.

²tune *verb* **tunes; tuned; tun•ing**
1 [+ *obj*] **:** to adjust (a musical instrument) so that it makes the correct sound when played ▪ I *tuned* my guitar/violin. ▪ The piano needs to be *tuned*.
2 [+ *obj*] **:** to make small changes to (something) in order to make it work better ▪ We *tuned* our bikes before the road trip. ▪ The mechanic *tuned* the engine. — often + *up* ▪ The mechanic *tuned up* the engine. — see also FINE-TUNE, TUNE-UP
3 : to adjust (a radio or television) so that it receives a broadcast clearly [+ *obj*] The copilot *tuned* the radio to hear the message. — often used as *(be) tuned* ▪ The televisions in the store *were* all *tuned* (in) to the same channel. [*no obj*] — + *to* ▪ He *tuned* (in) *to* the news channel.
stay tuned **:** to keep watching a television show or listening to a radio broadcast ▪ *Stay tuned* for more after this word from our sponsors. ▪ *Stay tuned* for a news update. — often used figuratively ▪ *Stay tuned* for a new and improved version of the software. [=a new and improved version of the software will be available soon]
tune in [*phrasal verb*] **1 :** to watch a television show or listen to a radio broadcast ▪ *Tune in* next week for the conclusion. ▪ Millions of listeners/viewers *tuned in* for coverage of the presidential debate. ▪ We *tuned in* to hear the results of the election. **2** ***be tuned in*** **:** to understand and be aware of a situation, other people's needs, etc. — usually + *to* ▪ He *was* not *tuned in to* the needs of his staff.
tune out [*phrasal verb*] *informal* **1 :** to stop paying attention to what other people are saying or doing **:** to become unaware of what is happening around you ▪ I could tell he was *tuning out* because when I asked him for his opinion, he had no idea what I was talking about. **2** ***tune (someone or something) out*** or ***tune out (someone or something)*** **:** to ignore or not listen to (someone or something) ▪ She *tuned out* the noise and concentrated on her work. ▪ There was a loud group at the restaurant, but we were able to *tune* them *out*.

tune•ful /ˈtu:nfəl, *Brit* ˈtju:nfəl/ *adj* [*more* ~; *most* ~] **:** having a pleasant musical sound ▪ a *tuneful* song/melody/ballad
— **tune•ful•ly** *adv* — **tune•ful•ness** *noun* [*noncount*]

tune•less /ˈtu:nləs, *Brit* ˈtju:nləs/ *adj* **:** not having a pleasant musical sound **:** not tuneful ▪ *tuneless* humming
— **tune•less•ly** *adv* — **tune•less•ness** *noun* [*noncount*]

tun•er /ˈtu:nɚ, *Brit* ˈtju:nə/ *noun, pl* **-ers** [*count*]
1 : a person who tunes musical instruments ▪ a piano *tuner*
2 : an electronic device that changes radio signals into sounds or images ▪ an AM-FM *tuner* ▪ televisions with digital *tuners*

tune–up /ˈtu:nˌʌp, *Brit* ˈtju:nˌʌp/ *noun, pl* **-ups** [*count*] *chiefly US*
1 : a process in which small changes are made to something (such as an engine) in order to make it work better ▪ Regular *tune-ups* kept the car running smoothly. ▪ My car needs a *tune-up*.
2 : an event or activity that helps you practice or prepare for a more important event or activity ▪ Preseason games are *tune-ups* for the regular season.

tung•sten /ˈtʌŋstən/ *noun* [*noncount*] **:** a hard metal that is used to make the thin wire in light bulbs and to harden other metals (such as steel)

tu•nic /ˈtu:nɪk, *Brit* ˈtju:nɪk/ *noun, pl* **-nics** [*count*]
1 : a loose piece of clothing usually without sleeves that reaches to the knees and that was worn by men and women in ancient Greece and Rome
2 : a long shirt worn by women that reaches to or just below the hips
3 : a long jacket with a high collar worn by soldiers, police officers, etc.

tuning fork *noun, pl* ~ **forks** [*count*] **:** a metal device that has two long points, that produces a particular note when it is hit, and that is used to tune musical instruments

tuning peg *noun, pl* ~ **pegs** [*count*] **:** ¹PEG 2

¹tun•nel /ˈtʌnl/ *noun, pl* **-nels** [*count*] **:** a passage that goes under the ground, through a hill, etc. ▪ an underground *tunnel* ▪ The train goes through a *tunnel* in the mountain. ▪ The moles dug *tunnels* in the yard.
a light at the end of the tunnel see ¹LIGHT
— see also CARPAL TUNNEL SYNDROME, WIND TUNNEL

²tunnel *verb* **-nels;** *US* **-neled** *or Brit* **-nelled;** *US* **-nel•ing** *or Brit* **-nel•ling :** to make a tunnel [*no obj*] Workers are *tunneling* through the hill. ▪ Insects had *tunneled* into the tree. [+ *obj*] The prisoners tried to *tunnel* their way out. [=tried to escape by digging a tunnel]

tunnel vision *noun* [*noncount*]
1 *medical* **:** a condition in which you can see things that are straight ahead of you but not to the side
2 *often disapproving* **:** a tendency to think only about one thing and to ignore everything else ▪ His *tunnel vision* made sensible discussions on political issues nearly impossible.

tun•ny /ˈtʌni/ *noun, pl* **tunny** [*count, noncount*] *Brit* **:** TUNA

tup•pence /ˈtʌpəns/ *noun* [*noncount*] *Brit* **:** TWOPENCE

tur•ban /ˈtɚbən/ *noun, pl* **-bans** [*count*] **:** a head covering that is worn especially by men in some parts of the Middle East and in southern Asia and that is made of a long cloth wrapped around the head
— **tur•baned** /ˈtɚbənd/ *adj* ▪ a *turbaned* cleric

tur•bid /ˈtɚbəd/ *adj* [*more* ~; *most* ~] *formal, of a liquid* **:** not clean or clear **:** cloudy or muddy ▪ *turbid* waters ▪ a *turbid* stream
— **tur•bid•i•ty** /ˌtɚˈbɪdəti/ *noun* [*noncount*]

tur•bine /ˈtɚbən/ *noun, pl* **-bines** [*count*] **:** an engine that has a part with blades that are caused to spin by pressure from water, steam, or air — see also WIND TURBINE

tur•bo /ˈtɚboʊ/ *noun, pl* **-bos** [*count*] **:** TURBOCHARGER

tur•bo•charged /ˈtɚboʊˌʧɑɚʤd/ *adj* **:** having a turbocharger ▪ *turbocharged* engines

tur•bo•charg•er /ˈtɚboʊˌʧɑɚʤɚ/ *noun, pl* **-ers** [*count*] **:** a device that supplies air to an engine at a higher pressure than normal to increase the engine's power

tur•bo•jet /ˈtɚboʊˌʤɛt/ *noun, pl* **-jets** [*count*] **:** an airplane that has a turbojet engine

turbojet engine *noun, pl* ~ **-gines** [*count*] **:** a type of powerful jet engine

tur•bo•prop /ˈtɚboʊˌprɑ:p/ *noun, pl* **-props** [*count*] **:** an airplane that has a turboprop engine

turboprop engine *noun, pl* ~ **-gines** [*count*] **:** a type of powerful engine that has a turbine which spins a propeller

tur•bot /ˈtɚbət/ *noun, pl* **turbot** *also* **tur•bots** [*count, noncount*] **:** a large European fish that is eaten as food

tur•bu•lence /ˈtɚbjələns/ *noun* [*noncount*]
1 : sudden, violent movements of air or water ▪ The plane hit quite a bit of *turbulence* during our flight.
2 : a state of confusion, violence, or disorder ▪ A period of *turbulence* preceded the riots. ▪ political/economic/emotional *turbulence*

tur•bu•lent /ˈtɚbjələnt/ *adj* [*more* ~; *most* ~]
1 : moving in an irregular or violent way ▪ *Turbulent* waters caused the boat to capsize.
2 : full of confusion, violence, or disorder **:** not stable or steady ▪ The sixties were a *turbulent* period in American history. ▪ a *turbulent* relationship
— **tur•bu•lent•ly** *adv*

turd /ˈtɚd/ *noun, pl* **turds** [*count*] *informal + impolite*
1 : a piece of solid waste passed out of the body
2 : someone who is very unpleasant and not liked ▪ He's an obnoxious little *turd*.

tu•reen /təˈri:n, *Brit* tjʊˈri:n/ *noun, pl* **-reens** [*count*] **:** a deep bowl with a cover that is used for serving food (such as soup)

¹turf /ˈtɚf/ *noun, pl* **turfs** *also Brit* **turves** /ˈtɚvz/
1 a [*noncount*] **:** the upper layer of ground that is made up of grass and plant roots ▪ a piece of *turf* **b** *Brit* **:** a square piece of turf cut out of the ground that is used for making lawns [*count*] a lawn made by laying *turfs* [*noncount*] a lawn made by laying *turf* [=(*US*) *sod*]
2 : a material that looks like grass and that is used especially to cover athletic fields [*noncount*] Synthetic *turf* was installed in the playing field instead of grass. [*count*] playing fields with artificial *turfs*
3 : an area or a place that you control or that feels like your home [*count*] gangs defending/protecting their *turfs* ▪ The team beat us on our own *turf*. [=we were defeated at home] [*noncount*] gangs defending/protecting their *turf* ▪ The team played on ***home turf***. ▪ ***turf wars*** between gangs — often used figuratively ▪ In chapter two, the author is on unfamiliar *turf*. [=is dealing with an unfamiliar subject]
4 ***the turf*** **:** the sport or business of horse racing — often

T

used as *turf* before another noun • *turf* writers/races
– see also SURF AND TURF

²turf *verb* **turfs; turfed; turf·ing**

turf out** also **turf off [*phrasal verb*] ***turf (someone) out/off** or **turf out/off (someone)** Brit, informal* : to force (someone) to leave a place or position • She *turfed* him *out* of the house. • He got *turfed off* the bus.

turf accountant *noun, pl* **~ -tants** [*count*] *Brit* : BOOKMAKER

tur·gid /ˈtɚʤəd/ *adj* [*more ~; most ~*] *formal*
1 *disapproving* : very complicated and difficult to understand • *turgid* prose/language
2 : larger or fuller than normal because of swelling • *turgid* [=*swollen*] limbs

Turk /ˈtɚk/ *noun, pl* **Turks** [*count*] : a person born, raised, or living in Turkey

tur·key /ˈtɚki/ *noun, pl* **-keys**
1 a [*count*] *pl also* ***turkey*** : a large American bird that is related to the chicken and that is hunted or raised by people for its meat — see color picture on page C9 **b** [*noncount*] : the meat of the turkey used as food • roasted/smoked *turkey* — often used before another noun • *turkey* sandwiches/burgers • We had a traditional *turkey* dinner on Thanksgiving.
2 [*count*] *US, informal* **a** : something (such as a play or movie) that has failed • The new play was a *turkey*. [=*flop*] **b** : a stupid or foolish person • He was acting like a complete *turkey*.

***talk turkey** chiefly US, informal* : to speak with someone in a plain, clear, or honest way • It's time to *talk turkey* about the problems in our relationship.
– see also COLD TURKEY

turkey vulture *noun, pl* **~ -tures** [*count*] : a large American bird that eats dead animals — called also *turkey buzzard*

¹Turk·ish /ˈtɚkɪʃ/ *noun* [*noncount*] : the language of the Turks

²Turkish *adj* : of or relating to Turkey, Turks, or Turkish • *Turkish* culture/politics • He is from Ankara, the *Turkish* capital.

Turkish bath *noun, pl* **~ baths** [*count*] : a bath in which a person passes through a series of rooms that are increasingly hot and then has a massage and takes a cold shower

Turkish coffee *noun, pl* **~ -fees** [*count, noncount*] : a strong black coffee that is sweetened and served in small cups

Turkish delight *noun* [*noncount*] : a type of candy made of thick jelly that is cut into pieces and covered with sugar

tur·moil /ˈtɚˌmojəl/ *noun* : a state of confusion or disorder [*noncount*] The country has been in *turmoil* for the past 10 years. • a period of political/economic *turmoil* • emotional *turmoil* [*singular*] His life has been in a constant *turmoil*.

¹turn /ˈtɚn/ *verb* **turns; turned; turn·ing**
1 : to move around a central point [*no obj*] The Earth *turns* [=*rotates, revolves*] on its axis. — often + *around* • We spun the top and watched it *turn around* in circles. [+ *obj*] He *turned* the key and opened the door. • She slowly *turned* the doorknob. • *Turn* the steering wheel all the way to the left. • Someone *turned* the switch and the lights came on.
2 a : to cause your body or a part of your body to face a different direction [*no obj*] They *turned* and walked away. • She *turned* to leave—but stopped. • She *turned* (around) to look at me. • They *turned* (away) from the gruesome sight. • He *turned* aside/sideways to let me pass. • The patient *turned* onto his side. • The photographer asked her to *turn* slightly to her/the left. [+ *obj*] He *turned* himself around to see the back of his shirt in the mirror. • She *turned* her face away from the camera. **b** : to cause (something or a side of something) to face an opposite or different direction [+ *obj*] *Turn* the picture (around) so that I can see it. • I think you should *turn* [=*flip*] the pancakes now. • *Turn* the page (over). • The tag says to *turn* the shirt inside out before washing it. • He *turned* up/down the collar of his jacket. • Before planting the seeds, she *turned* the soil. [=brought lower levels of soil to the surface by digging] [*no obj*] The plant's leaves had *turned* toward the window.
3 a : to move in a particular direction and especially toward the left or right [*no obj*] A car *turned* into the driveway. • He ran down the street and *turned* toward the park. • *Turn* left at the next intersection. • *Turn* right onto Main Street. • *Turn* here. [+ *obj*] He *turned* the light in the direction of the noise. • She *turned* the car into the driveway. • The bicyclists *turned* the corner [=they rode around the corner] at full speed. **b** [*no obj*] : to begin to go in a different direction • The road *turns* sharply to the right up ahead. • The river *turns* east for a few miles and then continues south. **c** [*no obj*] *of a tide* : to begin to move in the opposite direction • We're waiting for the tide to *turn*.
4 : to change into a different state or form [*no obj*] The leaves *turn* [=they change color] in the fall. • The milk has *turned*. [=it has become sour] • His luck *turned*, and he lost all his winnings. — often + *into* or *to* • The argument quickly *turned into* a fistfight. • The sofa can *turn into* a bed. • He has seen his little girl *turn into* a bright, beautiful woman. • Water *turns to* ice at 32 degrees Fahrenheit. • Her cereal had *turned to* mush. [+ *obj*] — often + *into* or *to* • The witch *turned* the prince *into* a frog. • The studio plans to *turn* the book *into* a movie. • There are plans to *turn* the old school *into* an apartment building. • The cold weather *turned* the water *to* ice. • Her stare, it was said, could *turn* men *to* stone.
5 a [*linking verb*] : to change to a different state, condition, etc. : BECOME • The milk has *turned* sour. • The weather *turned* cold overnight. • His hair was beginning to *turn* gray. • She *turned* red with embarrassment. • It was beginning to *turn* dark outside. • an actress *turned* director [=an actress who became a director] • Two of his teammates have decided to ***turn pro*** [=to become professional athletes] • She was a spy who ***turned traitor*** [=became a traitor] and gave secret information to the enemy. **b** [+ *obj*] : to cause (someone or something) to change in a specified way • A drought would *turn* things from bad to worse for the farmers. • The events of his life had *turned* [=*made*] him bitter. • The sun *turned* her skin (a) golden brown. **c** [*linking verb*] : to reach a particular age • She *turned* two years old last week. • He moved away from home when he *turned* 20.
6 [+ *obj*] : to change the volume, temperature, channel, etc., of (something) by pressing a button, moving a switch, etc. • *Turn* the TV to channel 4. • He *turned* the oven to 400 degrees. • The lights in the room had been *turned* low. — see also TURN DOWN (below), TURN UP (below)
7 [+ *obj*] : to direct (your thoughts, attention, etc.) toward or away from something : to start or stop thinking about or paying attention to someone or something • He *turned* his thoughts to home. [=he began to think of home] • She *turned* her attention to the child. • I could not *turn* my mind away from the idea. • Their efforts were *turned* to defending the country's borders.
8 [+ *obj*] : to earn (a profit) • He *turned* a quick profit. • (*chiefly Brit*) people looking to *turn* a penny or two [=to earn a profit]
9 [+ *obj*] : to perform (a particular action) • The team *turned* a double play to end the inning. • She learned how to *turn* a cartwheel. • They were living on the streets and ***turning tricks*** [=taking money for sex] to survive.
10 [+ *obj*] : to form (a sentence, phrase, etc.) in a particular way • perfectly *turned* phrases • He knows how to *turn* a sentence.
11 [+ *obj*] : to injure (your ankle) by moving it in an unnatural way • She *turned* [=*twisted*] her ankle during the game.
12 [+ *obj*] : to create or shape (something) from a piece of wood or metal by using a special machine (called a lathe) • *turn* a set of table legs

> In addition to the phrases shown below, *turn* occurs in many idioms that are shown at appropriate entries throughout the dictionary. For example, *turn a blind eye* can be found at ¹BLIND and *turn the tables* can be found at ¹TABLE.

turn against [*phrasal verb*] **1 a** ***turn against (someone or something)*** : to stop supporting or being friendly to (someone or something) • The senator eventually *turned against* the war. • She *turned against* her best friend. **b** ***turn (someone) against (someone)*** : to cause (someone) to stop being friendly toward (someone) • He tried to *turn* our friends *against* us. **2** ***turn (something) against (someone)*** : to use (something) in a way that harms (someone) • She started *turning* my argument *against* me. • He tried to *turn* her many years of experience in Washington *against* her. [=tried to persuade people that her experience was not a good thing]

turn around** or chiefly Brit **turn round [*phrasal verb*] **1** ***turn around** or **turn around (something)** or **turn (something) around*** : to cause a vehicle to travel in the opposite direction • We *turned around* in someone's driveway. • She *turned* the car *around* and drove back home. **2 a** : to change and become better or more successful • Recently, the company has *turned around*, and it should have a profitable year. ▪ The economy should *turn around* soon. **b** ***turn around (something) or turn (something) around*** : to change (something) in a way that makes it better or more successful ▪ The new CEO has really *turned* the company *around* in the past year. ▪ You need to *turn* your life *around* before it's too late. **3** ***turn around and (do something) informal*** : to act in an unexpected or surprising way by doing (something specified) ▪ He just *turned around and* left school. [=he just suddenly left school] ▪ You can't *turn around and* say that you don't want to go. I already bought the tickets! — see also TURNAROUND

turn away [*phrasal verb*] ***turn away (someone) or turn (someone) away*** : to refuse to allow (someone) to enter a place ▪ All the seats were sold and a large crowd had to be *turned away*. ▪ The homeless shelter will not *turn away* people in need. ▪ We *turn away* hundreds of applicants each year.

turn back [*phrasal verb*] **1 a** : to move in the opposite direction in order to return to a place ▪ The sun is setting. It's time to *turn back*. ▪ It's too late to *turn back*. We have to keep going. **b** : to return to an earlier place or time ▪ *Turn back* to the first page. ▪ Once you start the process, ***there's no turning back*** [=you must continue the process] **2** ***turn back (someone or something) or turn (someone or something) back*** **a** : to force (someone or something) to move in an opposite direction ▪ They fought to *turn back* the enemy. ▪ If I could ***turn back (the hands of) time***[=return to a condition that existed in the past], I would. **b** : to force (someone or something) to return to a place ▪ The refugees were *turned back* at the border.

turn down [*phrasal verb*] **1** ***turn down (something) or turn (something) down*** : to lower the volume, temperature, etc., of something by pressing a button, moving a switch, etc. ▪ Please *turn down* the heat. ▪ The lights in the restaurant were *turned down* low. ▪ He *turned* the volume *down* on the TV. = He *turned down* the TV. ▪ *Turn* the oven *down* to 325 degrees. — see also [1]TURN 6 (above) **2** ***turn down (something) or turn (something) down*** : to fold (something) down or back ▪ She *turned down* the bedsheets. ▪ He *turned down* the corner of the page. **3** ***turn down (someone or something) or turn (someone or something) down*** : to say no to (someone or something) especially in a polite way ▪ She *turned* the offer *down*. ▪ They *turned down* our invitation. ▪ I asked her out, but she *turned me down*.

turn in [*phrasal verb*] **1** : to enter a place by turning from a road or path ▪ Here's the house. You can *turn in* up there. **2** : to go to bed ▪ It's time to *turn in*. **3** ***turn (something) in or turn in (something)*** **a** *chiefly US* : to give (something) to a person who will review or accept it ▪ He *turned in* [=*handed in*] his application/resignation yesterday. ▪ Students should *turn* their papers *in* on Thursday. **b** : to return (something that you have borrowed, found, etc.) ▪ Please *turn in* [=*return*] the art supplies when you are finished with them. ▪ She found a set of keys and *turned* them *in* to the secretary at the front desk. ▪ Has anyone *turned in* a wallet recently? ▪ The suspended officer was asked to *turn in* his badge and gun. **c** : to perform or produce (something) ▪ She *turned in* [=*gave*] a fine performance. ▪ The company has *turned in* a healthy profit for the third year running. **4** ***turn (someone) in*** **a** : to give control of (someone) to the police or some other authority ▪ His own parents brought him to the police station and *turned* him *in*. ▪ The escaped prisoner ***turned himself in***(to the police). [=he went to the police and allowed himself to be arrested] **b** : to give information about the location of (someone who has committed a crime) to the police or some other authority ▪ His girlfriend threatened to *turn* him *in*.

turn loose see *let loose* at [1]LOOSE

turn off [*phrasal verb*] **1** : to go in a direction that moves you away from a straight course or main road ▪ They *turned off* onto the wrong road. ▪ *Turn off* at the next exit. **2** ***turn off (something) or turn (something) off*** : to stop the operation or flow of (something) by pressing a button, moving a switch, etc. ▪ She *turned off* the alarm/heat/lights/water. ▪ Should I leave the TV on or *turn* it *off*? **3** ***turn (someone) off or turn off (someone) informal*** : to cause a strong feeling of dislike in (someone) : to be unappealing to (someone) ▪ People who smoke *turn* me *off*. — see also TURNOFF

turn on [*phrasal verb*] **1** ***turn on (something) or turn (something) on*** : to cause (something) to work or flow by pressing a button, moving a switch, etc. ▪ She *turned on* the lights/computer/radio/water. ▪ We *turned on* the heat in the house. — often used figuratively ▪ He really knows how to *turn on* the charm. [=knows how to be charming] ▪ She *turned* the tears *on* [=she started crying] to get their sympathy. **2** ***turn (someone) on or turn on (someone) informal*** : to cause (someone) to feel excitement or enjoyment : to be appealing to (someone) ▪ What kind of music *turns* you *on*? — see also TURN-ON **3** ***turn (someone) on to (something)*** : to cause (someone) to use or become interested in (something) for the first time ▪ She *turned* him *on to* water-skiing. ▪ He was *turned on to* cocaine by an acquaintance. **4** ***turn on (someone or something)*** : to attack or criticize (someone or something) in a sudden or unexpected way ▪ The dog suddenly *turned on* its owner. ▪ The rock star's fans began to *turn on* him. **5** ***turn on/upon (something)*** **a** : to be determined or decided by (something) ▪ The outcome of the election *turns on* [=*depends on*] how well the candidates perform in the next debate. **b** : to have (something) as a main subject or interest ▪ The discussion *turned on* the question of how the money should be spent. **6** ***turn (something) on (someone or something)*** : to use (something, such as a weapon) to harm, stop, or kill (someone or something) ▪ Fire hoses were *turned on* the protesters. ▪ He killed three people before *turning* the gun *on* himself. [=before shooting himself]

turn out [*phrasal verb*] **1** : to leave your home in order to participate in or do something ▪ Few people *turned out* for the election. ▪ Few people *turned out* to vote. — see also TURNOUT 1 **2 a** : to happen, end, or develop in a particular way ▪ Despite some initial difficulties, everything *turned out* well. ▪ Things don't always *turn out* the way you want them to. ▪ As it/things *turned out*, I didn't need an umbrella after all. **b** ***turn out to be (something)*** — used to say that something or someone eventually becomes something or is found to have a particular identity, quality, ability, etc. ▪ The play *turned out to be* a success. ▪ The animal in the bushes *turned out to be* a cat. ▪ I hope I *turn out to be* right. **c** ***turn out like (someone or something)*** : to become like (someone or something) ▪ He didn't want to *turn out like* his father. ▪ Nobody thought it would ever *turn out like* this. **3** ***turn out (something) or turn (something) out*** **a** : to cause (something) to face or point outward ▪ She *turned* her feet *out* and bent down. ▪ He stood with his feet *turned out*. **b** : to cause (a lamp, flashlight, etc.) to no longer produce light by pushing a button, moving a switch, etc. ▪ Who *turned out* the lights? **c** : to produce (something) ▪ The factory *turns out* parts for car engines. ▪ They *turn out* a new CD almost every year. **d** : to cause (something, such as a pocket) to become inside out ▪ He *turned out* his pockets to show that they were empty. **e** : to empty the contents of (something) especially for cleaning or organizing ▪ She *turned out* the drawer. ▪ He *turned out* the closet in search of his baseball glove. **4** ***turn (someone) out or turn out (someone)*** **a** : to force (someone) to leave a place or position ▪ The landlord *turned* them *out* from/of the apartment for not paying the rent. ▪ Voters are unhappy with the governor and want to *turn* her *out*. **b** : to dress (yourself or someone else) in a careful or fancy way — usually (*be*) *turned out* ▪ a handsomely *turned out* gentleman ▪ She *was turned out* in a beautiful blue gown.

turn over [*phrasal verb*] **1 a** : to move and face the opposite direction ▪ She *turned over* (in bed) to see what time it was. ▪ The kayak *turned over* in the rapids. — sometimes used figuratively ▪ (*Brit*) The boat ride *turned over* my stomach. **b** ***turn over (someone or something) or turn (someone or something) over*** : to cause (someone or something) to face the opposite direction ▪ If you *turn* the paper *over*, you will find more math problems. ▪ He *turned over* the baby onto her back. **2** *of an engine* : to start to work ▪ The engine would not *turn over*. **3** ***turn over (something) or turn (something) over*** **a** : to earn (a particular amount of money) ▪ The store has been *turning over* $1,000 a week. **b** *US, sports* : to allow the other team to get possession of (a ball) ▪ The quarterback has *turned* the ball *over* three times. — see also TURNOVER 4 **4** ***turn (someone or something) over to (someone) or turn over (someone or something) to (someone)*** : to give the control or responsibility of (someone or something) to (someone) ▪ I am *turning* the job *over to* you. [=I am giving you the job] ▪ He *turned* the property *over to* his niece. ▪ The case has been *turned over to* the district attorney. ▪ The suspect was *turned over to* the police on Wednesday. **5** ***turn (something) over to (something) or turn over (something) to (something)*** : to change the use of (something, such as

T

land or a building) • She plans to *turn over* the land *to* growing wheat and barley. **6** ***turn over (something) in your mind or turn (something) over in your mind*** : to think about (something) in order to understand it or make a decision • She kept *turning over* the problem *in her mind*, trying to find a solution. **7** *chiefly Brit* : to change the channel on a television set • *Turn over* to channel 7. **8** ***turn over (a place) or turn (a place) over*** *Brit slang* : to make a mess of (a place) while robbing it • The shop has been *turned over* three times in the last year.

turn to [*phrasal verb*] **1** ***turn to (someone or something)*** : to go to (someone or something) for support, information, etc. • I was all alone and had no one to *turn to*. • She became depressed and *turned to* drugs. [=began using drugs] — often + *for* • She *turned to* a friend *for* help. • He *turned to* the employment agency *for* support. • *Turn to* [=*refer to*] the handout *for* the exact figures. **2** ***turn to (something)*** **a** : to become involved in or with (something) • He *turned to* a life of crime. • She sang rock music before *turning to* the blues. **b** : to begin to deal with (something different) as a topic • The conversation eventually *turned to* politics. • We should *turn to* the next item on the list. **c** : to turn the pages of a book, magazine, etc., until you have reached the desired or specified page • She *turned* ahead *to* the third chapter. • Please *turn* (over) *to* page 22 of your textbook.

turn up [*phrasal verb*] **1 a** : to be found usually unexpectedly • I'm sure your ring will *turn up* somewhere. • New evidence has *turned up*. **b** : to be found to be in a specified condition • The missing person eventually *turned up* dead. • He ***turned up missing*** at roll call. [=he was not present at roll call] **c** ***turn up (something) or turn (something) up*** : to find or discover (something) • I'll let you know if I *turn up* anything interesting. **2** : to happen unexpectedly • Something is always *turning up* to prevent us from getting together. **3 a** : to arrive at a place • And who should *turn up* at the ceremony but John! • Things were looking bad, but he was sure someone would *turn up* to save him. **b** : to appear in a place • Her name is always *turning up* in the newspapers. **4** ***turn up (something) or turn (something) up*** **a** : to increase the volume, temperature, etc., of something by pressing a button, moving a switch, etc. • I *turned up* the heat. • Please *turn* the volume *up* on the TV. = Please *turn* the TV *up*. • The oven was *turned up* to 400 degrees. **b** : to make (a skirt, a pair of pants, etc.) shorter • These pants need to be *turned up* a little. — opposite *let down* at [1]LET

[2]**turn** *noun, pl* **turns** [*count*]

1 : an opportunity or responsibility to do or use something before or after other people • You have to wait your *turn* in line. • Is it my *turn* yet? • Can I please have/take a *turn* on your bike? [=can I have a chance to use your bike?] — often followed by *to + verb* • Whose *turn* is it *to do* the dishes? • It's her *turn to bat*. • You've made me suffer in the past, so now it's your *turn to suffer*!

2 : an act of turning something around a central point • Give the wheel another *turn*. • He tightened the screw with one last *turn*. • With a *turn* of the switch, the lights came back on.

3 : an act of changing the direction that someone or something is facing or moving in • Take a left-hand *turn* at the next intersection. • I made a right *turn* [=I turned right] onto Main Street. • a quick *turn* of her head — see also THREE-POINT TURN, U-TURN

4 : a change in the state or condition of something — usually used with *take* • The stock market *took* a sharp downward *turn* today. • The conversation suddenly *took* an unexpected *turn* when he announced that he was getting married. • Business ***took a turn for the worse/better***. [=it became worse/better] • There has been a dramatic ***turn of events***. [=something important and surprising has happened] • It's hard to follow all the ***twists and turns*** [=the surprising changes] of the plot.

5 a *US* : a place where a road connects to another road that goes in a different direction • I think we took a wrong *turn*. [=(*Brit*) *turning*] **b** : a place where a road, path, etc., changes direction • There is a dangerous *turn* up ahead. • The runners are coming down the straightaway and heading into the *turn*. • The road through the mountains has many ***twists and turns***. [=curves and frequent changes of direction]

6 : an act that affects someone in a particular way • He did me a nasty *turn*. • You have done me a few good *turns*, so now let me help you. • ***One good turn deserves another***. [=if someone does something nice for you, you should do something nice for that person]

7 : a public appearance or performance • The actor makes frequent guest *turns* on the show. — see also STAR TURN

8 *old-fashioned* : a short walk or ride — usually singular • They ***took a turn*** [=went for a stroll] through the park.

9 *old-fashioned* : a sudden feeling of being frightened — usually singular • He startled me and ***gave me quite a turn***.

10 *Brit, old-fashioned* : a sudden, short period of feeling slightly ill, faint, or dizzy — usually singular • He ***had a turn*** and had to lie down.

at every turn : in a constant or continuous way : each time a person tries to do something • They opposed her *at every turn*.

by turns — used to describe different things that happen one after another • The book was praised and criticized *by turns*. • The stories in the collection are, *by turns*, curious, tragic, disturbing, and heartening.

done to a turn *Brit* : cooked, performed, etc., in a perfect way : done to perfection • The chicken was *done to a turn*.

in turn **1** : following one after another in a particular order • Each witness *in turn* gave his or her version of what happened. • The algae feeds the fish, which *in turn* become food for larger sea animals. **2** : as a result • I supported him and expected that he, *in turn*, would support me.

on the turn *Brit* : about to start changing • The political situation in the country is *on the turn*.

out of turn **1** : not at the time you are expected to do something according to a set order • She rolled the dice *out of turn*. [=when it was not her turn] **2** : at a wrong or improper time or place • Excuse me for speaking *out of turn* [=for speaking when it is not proper for me to speak], but I don't believe you are treating him fairly.

take turns *also Brit* ***take it in turns*** ◇ If people *take turns* doing or using something or *take it in turns* to do or use something, they do or use it one after another in order to share the responsibility or opportunity of doing or using it. • We *take turns* washing the dishes. • The kids *took turns* on the swing.

the turn of the century : the beginning of a new century • We were discussing how Americans lived at *the turn of the* 19th/last *century*.

turn of mind : a way of thinking • He has a philosophical/inquiring *turn of mind*. • Her *turns of mind* are revealed in her journals.

turn of phrase : a way of saying or describing something • a nice *turn of phrase*

turn of speed *Brit* : an increase in speed or progress • The horse gave an impressive *turn of speed*.

turn·about /ˈtɚnəˌbaʊt/ *noun, pl* **-abouts** [*count*] : TURNAROUND 2 — usually singular; often + *in* • There was a sharp *turnabout in* oil prices. • a *turnabout in* the country's foreign policy

turnabout is fair play *US* — used to say that if someone does something to harm you it is fair for you to do something to harm that person • She did it to me, so I'm going to do it to her. *Turnabout is fair play*.

turn·around /ˈtɚnəˌraʊnd/ *also Brit* **turn·round** /ˈtɚnˌraʊnd/ *noun, pl* **-arounds** [*count*]

1 a : the time it takes someone to receive, deal with, and return something • The *turnaround* for most orders is/takes 24 hours. • There is a 24-hour *turnaround* time on most orders. **b** : the process of making something (such as an airplane) ready for use again after it has arrived at a place • a quick *turnaround* between flights

2 : a complete change from a bad situation to a good situation, from one way of thinking to an opposite way of thinking, etc. • The team needs a big *turnaround* after their loss last week. • The company has achieved a remarkable *turnaround* in the past year. • The latest news has caused a *turnaround* in public opinion. — see also *turn around* at [1]TURN

turn·coat /ˈtɚnˌkoʊt/ *noun, pl* **-coats** [*count*] *disapproving* : a person who stops being a member of a group in order to join another group that opposes it : TRAITOR • a political *turncoat*

turn·ing /ˈtɚnɪŋ/ *noun, pl* **-ings** [*count*] *Brit* : [2]TURN 5a

turning point *noun, pl* **~ points** [*count*] : a time when an important change happens • Winning that game was the *turning point* of the team's season. • That job was a major *turning point* in her career.

tur·nip /ˈtɚnəp/ *noun, pl* **-nips** [*count, noncount*] : a round, light-colored root of a plant that is eaten as a vegetable; *also* : the plant that produces such a root — see color picture on page C4

T

turn·key /ˈtɚn͵kiː/ *adj, always used before a noun* : complete and ready to be used ▪ a *turnkey* computer system

turn·off /ˈtɚn͵ɑːf/ *noun, pl* **-offs** [*count*]
1 : a road that allows vehicles to leave a highway
2 *informal* : something that you dislike or that causes you to stop being interested in or attracted to someone or something ▪ His strong cologne was a real *turnoff*. ▪ What are your *turnoffs*? — see also *turn off* at ¹TURN

turn–on /ˈtɚn͵ɑːn/ *noun, pl* **-ons** [*count*] : something that you like or that causes you to be interested and excited ▪ Classical music is one of his biggest *turn-ons*. ▪ sexual *turn-ons* — see also *turn on* at ¹TURN

turn·out /ˈtɚn͵aʊt/ *noun, pl* **-outs** [*count*]
1 : the number of people who go to or participate in something ▪ There was a good/large *turnout* at the town meeting. [=a large number of people attended the town meeting] ▪ The opening game of the season brought only a small *turnout*. ▪ a 50 percent voter *turnout* ▪ heavy voter *turnouts* — see also *turn out* 1 at ¹TURN
2 *US* : an area next to a road where vehicles can stop — called also (*Brit*) *lay-by*

turn·over /ˈtɚn͵oʊvɚ/ *noun, pl* **-overs**
1 : the amount of money that is received in sales by a store or company [*count*] — usually singular ▪ an annual *turnover* of one million dollars [*noncount*] The company had an increase in *turnover* this quarter.
2 : the rate at which people leave a place, company, etc., and are replaced by others [*noncount*] The company has experienced a lot of *turnover* (of personnel) in the past year. [=a lot of people have left the company and been replaced by new employees] ▪ The company has a high *turnover* rate. [*count*] — usually singular ▪ The store has a high employee *turnover*.
3 : the rate at which the goods in a store are sold and replaced by other goods [*count*] — usually singular ▪ a rapid *turnover* of inventory [*noncount*] We want to find ways to speed up inventory *turnover*.
4 [*count*] *US, sports* : an occurrence in which the team that has the ball loses it to the other team because of an error or a minor violation of the rules ▪ The team committed/had two *turnovers* in the first quarter. ▪ He forced a *turnover*. [=he caused the other team to lose possession of the ball]
5 [*count*] : a type of small pie that has one half of the crust folded over the other half and that is filled with fruit, meat, or a vegetable ▪ an apple/chicken/potato *turnover*
– see also *turn over* at ¹TURN

turn·pike /ˈtɚn͵paɪk/ *noun, pl* **-pikes** [*count*] *US* : a major road that you must pay to use ▪ the Massachusetts *Turnpike*

turn·round /ˈtɚn͵raʊnd/ *noun, pl* **-rounds** [*count*] *Brit* : TURNAROUND 1

turn signal *noun, pl* ~ **-nals** [*count*] *US* : one of the lights on a vehicle that flash to indicate that the vehicle is turning left or right — called also (*US*) *blinker*, (*Brit*) *indicator*; see picture at CAR

turn·stile /ˈtɚn͵stajəl/ *noun, pl* **-stiles** [*count*] : a gate at an entrance that has arms which turn around and that allows only one person at a time to pass through

turnstile

turn·ta·ble /ˈtɚn͵teɪbəl/ *noun, pl* **-ta·bles** [*count*]
1 : the part of a record player that turns the record
2 : a platform that is used to turn vehicles (such as railroad cars) around

turn–up /ˈtɚn͵ʌp/ *noun, pl* **-ups** *Brit*
1 [*count*] : ¹CUFF 2
2 [*singular*] *informal* : an unexpected or surprising event ▪ It was a real ***turn-up for the books*** when he won the election!

tur·pen·tine /ˈtɚpən͵taɪn/ *noun* [*noncount*] : a type of oil with a strong smell that is used to make paint thinner and to clean paint brushes

tur·pi·tude /ˈtɚpə͵tuːd, *Brit* ˈtɜːpə͵tjuːd/ *noun* [*noncount*] *formal* : a very evil quality or way of behaving ▪ moral *turpitude*

turps /ˈtɚps/ *noun* [*noncount*] *Brit, informal* : TURPENTINE

tur·quoise /ˈtɚ͵kɔɪz, ˈtɚ͵kwɔɪz/ *noun* [*noncount*]
1 : a bluish-green stone used in jewelry — see color picture on page C11
2 : a bluish-green color — see color picture on page C2
– **turquoise** *adj* ▪ a *turquoise* dress/bracelet

tur·ret /ˈtɚrət/ *noun, pl* **-rets** [*count*]
1 : a small tower on a building ▪ a castle with *turrets*
2 : the part on a military tank, airplane, or ship from which guns are fired
– **tur·ret·ed** /ˈtɚrətəd/ *adj* ▪ a *turreted* castle

tur·tle /ˈtɚtl/ *noun, pl* **tur·tles** [*count*] : a reptile that lives mostly in water and that has a hard shell which covers its body — see also SEA TURTLE, SNAPPING TURTLE

turtle

turn turtle *chiefly Brit, of a boat* : to turn upside down ▪ Their boat *turned turtle* during the storm.

tur·tle·dove /ˈtɚtl͵dʌv/ *noun, pl* **-doves** [*count*] : a type of bird that makes a soft pleasant sound ✧ Turtledoves are sometimes used as symbols of love and lovers.

tur·tle·neck /ˈtɚtl͵nɛk/ *noun, pl* **-necks** [*count*]
1 *US* : a high collar that covers most of your neck even when the collar is folded over itself; *also* : a knit shirt or sweater with this kind of collar ▪ She wore a *turtleneck* under her jacket. — called also (*Brit*) *polo neck*; see color picture on page C15
2 *Brit* : MOCK TURTLENECK

turves *Brit plural of* ¹TURF

tush /ˈtʊʃ/ *noun, pl* **tush·es** [*count*] *US, informal + humorous* : the part of the body that you sit on : BUTTOCKS ▪ He fell on his *tush*.

tusk /ˈtʌsk/ *noun, pl* **tusks** [*count*] : a very long, large tooth that sticks out of the mouth of an animal (such as an elephant, walrus, or boar)
– **tusked** /ˈtʌskt/ *adj* ▪ a *tusked* boar

¹**tus·sle** /ˈtʌsəl/ *verb* **tus·sles; tus·sled; tus·sling** [*no obj*]
1 : to fight or struggle with (someone) by grabbing or pushing ▪ The two basketball players *tussled* for the ball. ▪ Some guy *tussled* [=*scuffled*] with a security guard for a few minutes before he was arrested.
2 : to argue or compete with (someone) ▪ The residents of the neighborhood *tussled* with city hall for years about the broken parking meters.

²**tussle** *noun, pl* **tussles** [*count*]
1 : a short fight or struggle ▪ The suspect was arrested after a *tussle* with a security guard.
2 : an argument or a dispute ▪ a *tussle* for control of the company ▪ The President is in for another *tussle* with Congress.

tus·sock /ˈtʌsək/ *noun, pl* **-socks** [*count*] : a small area that is covered with long thick grass ▪ There were grassy *tussocks* throughout the marsh.

¹**tut** /*a clicking sound, often read as* ˈtʌt/ *interj* : ¹TUT-TUT

²**tut** /ˈtʌt/ *noun, pl* **tuts** [*count*] : ²TUT-TUT

³**tut** /ˈtʌt/ *verb* **tuts; tut·ted; tut·ting** [*no obj*] : ³TUT-TUT

tu·te·lage /ˈtuːtəlɪʤ, *Brit* ˈtjuːtəlɪʤ/ *noun* [*noncount*] *formal*
1 : the teaching of an individual student by a teacher ▪ He studied music ***under the tutelage of*** his father. = He studied music ***under his father's tutelage***. [=he was taught music by his father]
2 : an act of guarding or protecting something ▪ an African nation formerly under British *tutelage* [=*guardianship*]
3 : helpful influence or guidance ▪ The company is relying on the *tutelage* of its new CEO to increase profits.

¹**tu·tor** /ˈtuːtɚ, *Brit* ˈtjuːtə/ *noun, pl* **-tors** [*count*]
1 : a teacher who works with one student ▪ I got a *tutor* to help me with my homework. ▪ a private *tutor*
2 *Brit* : a teacher at a British university who works with one student or a small group of students ▪ He is a *tutor* in European history.

²**tutor** *verb* **-tors; -tored; -tor·ing** : to teach a single student : to teach someone as a tutor [*no obj*] She earned extra money *tutoring* in the evening. [+ *obj*] She spent her evenings *tutoring* her son in math. [=helping her son study math] ▪ Some teachers stay after school to *tutor* [=*coach*] struggling students.

¹**tu·to·ri·al** /tuˈtorijəl, *Brit* tjuˈtɔːriəl/ *noun, pl* **-als** [*count*]
1 : a book, computer program, etc., that teaches someone how to do something by explaining each stage of a process ▪ a helpful programming *tutorial* ▪ An online *tutorial* gives basic instructions for those who have never made reservations on the Web.
2 : a class taught by a tutor for one student or for a small

group of students • The professor was offering a *tutorial* in her office a week before the exam.

²tutorial *adj* **:** of or relating to a tutor • We offer *tutorial* instruction for test preparation.

tut·ti–frut·ti /ˌtuːtiˈfruːti/ *noun* [*noncount*] **:** a kind of ice cream that contains small pieces of nuts and fruit

¹tut–tut /*two clicking sounds, often read as* ˈtʌtˈtʌt/ *interj* — used to show disapproval • *Tut-tut* [=*tsk-tsk*], this time you've gone too far.

²tut–tut /ˈtʌtˈtʌt/ *noun, pl* **-tuts** [*count*] **:** a sound made to show disapproval • There were a few inevitable *tut-tuts* from the older folks in the crowd.

³tut–tut /ˈtʌtˈtʌt/ *verb* **-tuts; -tut·ted; -tut·ting** [*no obj*] **:** to show disapproval by making a sound (such as "tut-tut") • Some people may *tut-tut* disapprovingly about obscenities on television. **:** to say something that expresses disapproval • Political commentators have been *tut-tutting* over the latest scandal in Washington.

tu·tu /ˈtuːˌtuː/ *noun, pl* **-tus** [*count*] **:** a short skirt that is made of many layers of material and that is worn by a ballerina

tutu

tux /ˈtʌks/ *noun, pl* **tux·es** [*count*] *chiefly US, informal* **:** TUXEDO

tux·e·do /ˌtʌkˈsiːdoʊ/ *noun, pl* **-dos** *or* **-does** [*count*] *chiefly US* **:** a formal suit for a man; *especially* **:** a formal black suit worn with a white shirt and a black bow tie — called also (*Brit*) *dinner suit*; see color picture on page C16; compare DINNER JACKET

TV /ˈtiːˈviː/ *noun, pl* **TVs :** TELEVISION [*count*] unplug the *TV* • We need a new *TV*. [*noncount*] Do you want to watch some *TV* before bed? • She works in *TV*. — often used before another noun • a *TV* host/set/show

on TV **:** broadcast by television **:** being shown by television • There's nothing (good) *on TV* [=*on television*] tonight.

TV dinner *noun, pl* **~ -ners** [*count*] **:** a cooked meal that is frozen and packaged and that needs only to be heated before it is eaten

twad·dle /ˈtwɑːdl̩/ *noun* [*noncount*] *informal + old-fashioned* **:** foolish words or ideas **:** NONSENSE • We don't believe that *twaddle* anymore.

twain /ˈtweɪn/ *noun* [*noncount*] *old-fashioned* **:** TWO

never the twain shall meet — used to say that two things, places, etc., are very different and can never be brought together or made similar • As far as he's concerned, work is work, family life is family life, and *never the twain shall meet*.

¹twang /ˈtwæŋ/ *noun, pl* **twangs** [*count*]

1 : the typical sound of the speech of people from a certain place; *especially* **:** a sound that seems to be produced through the nose as well as the mouth • an Australian *twang* • I noticed a slight Southern *twang* in her voice. • He always has a nasal *twang* when he sings.

2 : a harsh, quick sound made by pulling something (such as a wire) tight and then letting it go • The clothesline snapped with a *twang*. • We heard the *twang* of an electric guitar coming from the basement.

²twang *verb* **twangs; twanged; twang·ing :** to make a harsh, quick sound [*no obj*] The rope *twanged* when it snapped. [*+ obj*] He was *twanging* the strings of the guitar.

'twas /ˈtwʌz/ *old-fashioned + literary* — used as a contraction of "it was" • *'Twas* a day like no other.

twat /ˈtwɑːt/ *noun, pl* **twats** [*count*] *offensive*

1 *Brit* **:** a stupid or annoying person

2 : a woman's sexual organs ✧ *Twat* is an extremely offensive word in all of its uses and should be avoided.

¹tweak /ˈtwiːk/ *verb* **tweaks; tweaked; tweak·ing** [*+ obj*]

1 : to change (something) slightly in order to improve it **:** to make small adjustments to (something) • The company may have to *tweak* [=*adjust*] its image. • Our software developers are *tweaking* [=*fine-tuning*] the program. • We just wanted to *tweak* his original idea a bit.

2 : to injure (a part of your body) slightly • He *tweaked* his ankle playing soccer.

3 : to pinch and pull (something) with a sudden movement • My brother hates it when our grandmother *tweaks* his cheek.

4 *chiefly US* **:** to criticize or make fun of (someone or something) • His friends *tweaked* [=*teased*] him for gaining weight.

²tweak *noun, pl* **tweaks** [*count*]

1 : a small change made in order to improve something • Our software developer decided that the program needed a few *tweaks*. [=small improvements]

2 : a sudden pull or twist that causes a slight injury • He gave his knee a *tweak* [=he tweaked his knee] playing racquetball.

3 : an act of pinching or pulling something • She gave his cheek a *tweak*.

twee /ˈtwiː/ *adj* [*more ~; most ~*] *chiefly Brit, informal + disapproving* **:** sweet or cute in a way that is silly or sentimental • The movie was a bit *twee* for my taste.

tweed /ˈtwiːd/ *noun, pl* **tweeds**

1 [*count, noncount*] **:** a rough, woolen cloth that is woven with different colored threads • a skirt made of *tweed* — often used before another noun • a *tweed* jacket/suit

2 ***tweeds*** [*plural*] **:** tweed clothing (such as a suit) • The elderly professor was always seen in his *tweeds*.

tweedy /ˈtwiːdi/ *adj* **tweed·i·er; -est** [*also more ~; most ~*]

1 : made of tweed or resembling tweed • The fabric is a *tweedy* blend of wool and mohair. • a *tweedy* jacket

2 *informal* **:** wearing tweed clothing or tending to wear tweed clothing — used to describe members of the British upper class, college professors, etc. • The new laws banning fox hunting caused outrage in *tweedy* circles. • a *tweedy* English gentleman • a *tweedy* professor

¹tween /ˈtwiːn/ *prep, literary* **:** BETWEEN

²tween *noun, pl* **tweens** [*count*] *US* **:** a boy or girl who is 11 or 12 years old **:** PRETEEN • a movie that appeals to *tweens*

tweet /ˈtwiːt/ *verb* **tweets; tweet·ed; tweet·ing** [*no obj*] **:** to make a short, high sound • A few birds were *tweeting* in the trees.

– tweet *noun, pl* **tweets** [*count*] • the *tweets* of the birds • The *tweet* of the referee's whistle stopped the game.

tweet·er /ˈtwiːtɚ/ *noun, pl* **-ers** [*count*] *technical* **:** a speaker (sense 5) that produces high sounds — compare SUBWOOFER, WOOFER

twee·zers /ˈtwiːzɚz/ *noun* [*plural*] **:** a small tool that is made of two narrow pieces of metal which are joined at one end and that is used to hold, move, or pull very small objects • He used (a pair of) *tweezers* to take a splinter out of his finger. — see picture at GROOMING

¹twelfth /ˈtwɛlfθ/ *noun, pl* **twelfths**

1 [*singular*] **:** number 12 in a series • I come home on the *twelfth*. [=the twelfth day of the month]

2 [*count*] **:** one of 12 equal parts of something • a *twelfth* of the population

²twelfth *adj* **:** occupying the number 12 position in a series • the *twelfth* day in a row • finished in *twelfth* place

– twelfth *adv* • Our son finished *twelfth* in the race. • the *twelfth* best-selling book

twelve /ˈtwɛlv/ *noun, pl* **twelves**

1 [*count*] **:** the number 12

2 [*count*] **:** the 12th in a set or series • question number *twelve*

3 [*noncount*] **:** twelve o'clock • "What time is it?" "It's *twelve*." • I have lunch at *twelve*.

4 ***the Twelve*** **:** the twelve original disciples of Jesus Christ

– twelve *adj* • It was a *twelve*-hour flight. • *twelve* days later **– twelve** *pronoun* • All *twelve* (of them) came to the party.

twen·ty /ˈtwɛnti/ *noun, pl* **-ties**

1 [*count*] **:** the number 20

2 [*count*] **:** the 20th in a set or series • item/question *twenty*

3 ***twenties*** [*plural*] **a :** the numbers ranging from 20 to 29 • Tomorrow the temperature will be in the low *twenties*. **b :** a set of years ending in digits ranging from 20 to 29 • She's in her *twenties*. • the gangsters of the *twenties* [=of the 1920s]

4 [*count*] **a** *US* **:** a twenty-dollar bill • All I have is a *twenty*. **b** *Brit* **:** a twenty-pound note

– twen·ti·eth /ˈtwɛntijəθ/ *noun, pl* **-eths** [*count*] • What are you doing on the *twentieth*? [=the twentieth day of the month] • a *twentieth* of the population **– twentieth** *adj* • their *twentieth* anniversary **– twenty** *adj* • It was a *twenty*-hour flight. • *twenty* days later **– twenty** *pronoun* • Only *twenty* showed up for the review session. • We spent forty dollars and had *twenty* left.

twen·ty–four seven *or* **24–7** *or* **24/7** /ˈtwɛntiˈfoɚˈsɛvən/ *adv, informal* **:** all the time **:** twenty-four hours a day and seven days a week • She worries about you *24/7*. • The store is open *24/7*.

twen·ty–one /ˌtwɛntiˈwʌn/ *noun* [*noncount*] *US* **:** BLACKJACK 1

twen·ty·some·thing /ˈtwɛntiˌsʌmθɪŋ/ *noun, pl* **-things**

[*count*] *informal* : a person who is between 20 and 29 years old ▪ The magazine is aimed primarily at *twentysomethings*.
– twentysomething *adj* ▪ a *twentysomething* customer

twen·ty–twen·ty *or* **20/20** /ˈtwɛntiˈtwɛnti/ *adj* : having good vision and able to see without glasses ▪ My mother has *20/20* vision.
twenty-twenty hindsight *or* ***20/20 hindsight*** : the full knowledge and complete understanding that you have about an event only after it has happened ▪ With *20/20 hindsight* we now see where our strategy went wrong.

twen·ty–two *or* **.22** /ˈtwɛntiˈtu:/ *noun, pl* **twenty-twos** *or* **.22s** [*count*] : a gun that fires small bullets ▪ My uncle used a *.22* to shoot rabbits. — often used before another noun ▪ a *.22* caliber handgun ▪ a *.22* rifle

twerp /ˈtwɚp/ *noun, pl* **twerps** [*count*] *informal* : someone who is stupid or annoying ▪ Some little *twerp* took her seat. ▪ Her boyfriend's just a pretentious *twerp*.

twice /ˈtwaɪs/ *adv*
1 : two times : on two occasions ▪ I only wore it *twice*. ▪ I called you *twice*. ▪ He has rehearsals *twice* a month. ▪ He *twice* lost to younger opponents. ▪ We visited them *twice* in 10 years. ▪ The dictionary has been *twice* updated since 1993. ▪ I've been there at least *twice*. ▪ We've eaten at that restaurant ***once or twice***. [=one or two times] ▪ We go to Europe ***twice a year***. [=two times every year] ▪ The mail is delivered ***twice a day***. [=two times every day]
2 : doubled in amount or degree ▪ The new house is *twice* [=two times] as large as our old one. ▪ He must be *twice* her age. ▪ The population is *twice* that of Canada. ▪ The new one costs about *twice* as much. ▪ He could earn *twice* his present salary at the new job. ▪ *Twice* two is four. [=two times two is/equals four]
think twice see [1]THINK

twid·dle /ˈtwɪdl/ *verb* **twid·dles; twid·dled; twid·dling** : to turn (something) back and forth slightly [+ *obj*] Just *twiddle* the dial on the radio a bit for better reception. ▪ *Twiddle* the knob on the telescope until things are in focus. ▪ She *twiddled* her pen while she talked on the phone. [*no obj*] She *twiddled* with her pen while she talked on the phone.
twiddle your thumbs *informal* : to do nothing : to waste time while you wait for something to happen ▪ I was just *twiddling my thumbs* until the phone rang.
– twiddle *noun, pl* **twiddles** [*count*] *Brit* ▪ Give the knob a *twiddle*.

[1]**twig** /ˈtwɪg/ *noun, pl* **twigs** [*count*] : a small branch of a tree or bush ▪ We should gather up small *twigs* for the campfire. — see color picture on page C6
– twig·gy /ˈtwɪgi/ *adj* **twig·gi·er; -est** ▪ big *twiggy* birds' nests ▪ *twiggy* trees [=trees that have many small branches]

[2]**twig** *verb* **twigs; twigged; twig·ging** *Brit, informal* : to understand (something) suddenly [+ *obj*] He seemed confused until he *twigged* that something was going on. [*no obj*] I had to explain it to him three times but he finally *twigged*.

twi·light /ˈtwaɪˌlaɪt/ *noun*
1 [*noncount*] **a** : the light from the sky at the end of the day when night is just beginning ▪ The sun set and *twilight* fell. ▪ in the autumn *twilight* **b** : the period when day is ending and night is beginning ▪ We had to stop working at *twilight*. [=*dusk*] — often used before another noun ▪ a *twilight* baseball game [=a game played at twilight] ▪ We heard the birds chirping in the *twilight* hours.
2 [*singular*] : a period when something is ending ▪ He's in the *twilight* of his career. [=the last part of his career] — often used before another noun ▪ He became less radical in his *twilight* years.

twilight world *noun* [*singular*] : a mysterious or secret world ▪ the *twilight world* of informants and spies

twilight zone *noun* [*singular*]
1 : a situation or an idea that is unclear or confusing ▪ a legal *twilight zone* [=a legal situation that is hard to understand] ▪ a *twilight zone* between war and peace
2 : a world of fantasy where things are not real ▪ He gets lost in the *twilight zone* of video games.

twi·lit /ˈtwaɪˌlɪt/ *adj* : lighted by twilight ▪ a *twilit* garden

twill /ˈtwɪl/ *noun* [*noncount*] : cloth that is made in a way that produces a pattern of diagonal lines ▪ cotton *twill* pants

[1]**twin** /ˈtwɪn/ *noun, pl* **twins** [*count*]
1 : either one of two babies that are born at the same time to the same mother ▪ She's the mother of *twins*. ▪ The *twins* went swimming after lunch. ▪ My sister just had *twins*. ▪ Sarah and her brother are *twins*. ▪ I didn't know she had a *twin*. [=a sister/brother who is her twin] — compare QUADRUPLET, QUINTUPLET, SEXTUPLET, TRIPLET; see also CONJOINED TWIN, FRATERNAL TWIN, IDENTICAL TWIN
2 : either one of two similar things that form a pair ▪ I found one glove but I can't find its *twin*. [=I can't find the other glove]

[2]**twin** *adj, always used before a noun*
1 — used to describe children who are twins ▪ my *twin* brother [=my brother who is my twin] ▪ They had *twin* girls.
2 : made up of two similar things that are used together ▪ a *twin*-engine airplane [=an airplane that has two engines]
3 : forming one of a pair of related or connected ideas or places ▪ the *twin* goals of reducing oil dependence and protecting the environment

[3]**twin** *verb* **twins; twinned; twin·ning** [+ *obj*]
1 : to bring (two things) together in close association — usually used as *(be) twinned* ▪ Research *is twinned* [=*coupled*] with technology. ▪ They will *be twinned* [=*paired*] in the pages of history. ▪ two cultures with a *twinned* destiny
2 *Brit* : to form a relationship between (two towns in two countries) — usually used as *(be) twinned* ▪ Our town *is twinned* with a town of roughly the same size in France.

twin bed *noun, pl* **~ beds** [*count*]
1 : either one of a pair of single beds that match ▪ Do you want a room with a double bed or *twin beds*?
2 *US* : a bed that is big enough for only one person : a single bed — see picture at BED
– twin–bed·ded *adj, Brit* ▪ a *twin-bedded* hotel room

[1]**twine** /ˈtwaɪn/ *noun* [*noncount*] : a string made of two or more threads twisted together ▪ The package was wrapped in brown paper and tied with *twine*. ▪ a strong piece of *twine*

[2]**twine** *verb* **twines; twined; twin·ing** : to twist or wrap around (someone or something) [+ *obj*] She *twined* her arms around him. ▪ The tree was *twining* its branches around the chimney. [=the branches were growing around the chimney] [*no obj*] Ivy *twines* around the columns.

twinge /ˈtwɪnʤ/ *noun, pl* **twing·es** [*count*]
1 : a sudden and usually slight pain ▪ He felt a *twinge* of arthritis when he stood up. ▪ I still feel an occasional *twinge* in my leg from the accident.
2 : a sudden slight feeling or emotion ▪ I felt a *twinge* of guilt/jealousy. ▪ I must admit to a *twinge* of envy. ▪ a *twinge* of sadness

[1]**twin·kle** /ˈtwɪŋkəl/ *noun* [*singular*] : a quick flash of light : a sparkle or flicker of light ▪ We saw the *twinkle* of a candle in the window.
a twinkle in your eye : a friendly or happy expression in your eyes ▪ He always talks about his children with *a twinkle in his eye*. ▪ Her grandchildren put *a twinkle in her eye*. [=made her happy]
in the twinkle of an eye *informal* : very quickly : in a very short time ▪ He was back *in the twinkle of an eye*.
– twin·kly /ˈtwɪŋkəli/ *adj* **-kli·er; -est** [*also more* ~; *most* ~] ▪ *twinkly* lights

[2]**twinkle** *verb* **twin·kles; twin·kled; twin·kling** [*no obj*]
1 : to shine with an unsteady light : to produce small flashes of light ▪ The lights of the city *twinkled* in the distance. ▪ Stars *twinkle* in the night sky. ▪ *twinkling* Christmas lights
2 *of the eyes* : to have a friendly or happy expression ▪ Her eyes *twinkled* with excitement/joy/pride.

twin·kling /ˈtwɪŋkəlɪŋ/ *noun*
in a twinkling *or* ***in the twinkling of an eye*** : very quickly : in a very short time ▪ He was back *in a twinkling*.

twin·set /ˈtwɪnˈsɛt/ *noun, pl* **-sets** [*count*] : a woman's pullover sweater and buttoned outer sweater that match and are worn together

twin–size /ˈtwɪnˈsaɪz/ *adj, US, of a bed* : having a size of 39 inches by 75 inches (about 1.0 by 1.9 meters) — compare FULL-SIZE, KING-SIZE, QUEEN-SIZE

twin town *noun, pl* **~ towns** [*count*] *Brit* : SISTER CITY

[1]**twirl** /ˈtwɚl/ *verb* **twirls; twirled; twirl·ing**
1 [+ *obj*] : to turn (something) around and around quickly ▪ *twirl* a baton
2 [*no obj*] : to turn or spin around and around ▪ They *twirled* past us on the dance floor. ▪ The cheerleaders jumped and *twirled*. ▪ The kite twisted and *twirled* in the wind.
3 [+ *obj*] : to twist or wrap (something) around something ▪ He was nervously *twirling* his hair. [=turning a lock of his hair over and over again with his finger] ▪ The chef *twirled* the noodles around his fork.
– twirl·er /ˈtwɚlɚ/ *noun, pl* **-ers** [*count*] ▪ The baton *twirlers* preceded the marching band in the parade.

[2]**twirl** *noun, pl* **twirls** [*count*] : an act of turning or spinning

T

around quickly ▪ The dancers executed perfect *twirls*.

[1]twist /ˈtwɪst/ *verb* **twists; twist·ed; twist·ing**

1 [+ *obj*] **a :** to bend or turn (something) in order to change its shape ▪ The toy can be *twisted* into different shapes. ▪ She *twisted* balloons into the shapes of different animals. **b :** to bend or turn (something) into a shape or position that is not normal or natural ▪ The antenna was *twisted* out of shape. ▪ The car was a heap of *twisted* metal after the accident. ▪ She *twisted* [=*contorted*] her face as if she was about to cry. ▪ He *twists* his lip into an odd expression when he's thinking.

2 : to turn (something) in a circular motion with your hand [+ *obj*] *twist* the dials on the radio [*no obj*] The bottle cap *twists* off.

3 [+ *obj*] **:** to pull off or break (something) by turning it — often + *off* ▪ He *twisted* a small branch *off* the tree.

4 [*no obj*] **:** to turn a part of your body around **:** to change your position ▪ Everyone in the audience *twisted* in their seats to see what made the noise. ▪ He *twisted* around to face me.

5 [+ *obj*] **:** to hurt (your ankle, knee, wrist, etc.) by turning it too far ▪ I *twisted* my ankle playing softball.

6 [+ *obj*] **:** to combine several threads or wires by wrapping them around one another ▪ *Twist* the wire ends together to make an electrical connection. ▪ Rope is made by *twisting* many threads together.

7 : to wrap or wind (something) around something [+ *obj*] I like the way she *twists* [=*coils, wraps*] that scarf around her neck. [*no obj*] Ivy *twisted* [=*wound*] around the columns of the porch.

8 [+ *obj*] **:** to change the meaning of (something, such as a word) unfairly ▪ He was accused of *twisting* [=*distorting*] the facts. ▪ He ***twisted my words*** [=he repeated what I said in a way that had a different meaning] and made it seem like I was angry.

9 [*no obj*] **:** to curve or change direction suddenly ▪ Be careful, the road *twists* up ahead. ▪ a *twisting* path

twist and turn **1 :** to curve or change direction often ▪ The road along the coast *twists and turns*. **2 :** to move with twisting motions **:** to be restless and to change position often ▪ A little boy was *twisting and turning* [=moving a lot] in the seat behind me.

twist someone's arm **1 :** to grab someone's arm and bend it in order to cause pain ▪ He *twisted my arm* behind my back and forced me into the car. **2** *informal* **:** to try to force someone to do something ▪ My wife really had to *twist my arm* to get me to apologize to my boss. — see also ARM-TWISTING

twist the knife (in the wound) see [1]KNIFE

[2]twist *noun, pl* **twists** [*count*]

1 : an act of turning or twisting ▪ a simple *twist* of the wrist ▪ The jar should open with a *twist* of the lid.

2 : a turn, curve, or bend in a road, river, etc. ▪ The road has some nasty *twists*. ▪ The coastal road had many ***twists and turns***.

3 a : an unexpected or strange occurrence ▪ The plot has many *twists*. [=*surprises*] ▪ It was a film noir with some clever *twists*. ▪ In an unusual *twist*, the police arrested one of their own. ▪ They were brought together by a strange ***twist of fate***. **b :** something new created by changing something slightly ▪ It's a new *twist* [=*variation*] on an old recipe.

4 : a small piece of lemon or lime peel used to flavor a drink ▪ a diet cola with a *twist* of lemon

5 ***the twist*** **:** a lively dance from the 1960s in which dancers twist their bodies quickly from side to side ▪ We did *the twist*.

get your knickers in a twist see KNICKERS

round the twist *Brit, informal* **:** CRAZY ▪ Her constant complaining is driving me *round the twist*. [=(*US*) *around the bend*]

twist·ed /ˈtwɪstəd/ *adj* [*more* ~; *most* ~] **:** strange and unpleasant **:** not normal ▪ He has a *twisted* [=*sick*] sense of humor.

twist·er /ˈtwɪstɚ/ *noun, pl* **-ers** [*count*] *US, somewhat informal* **:** TORNADO — see also TONGUE TWISTER

twist tie *noun, pl* **~ ties** [*count*] *US* **:** a small piece of wire that you use to close something (such as a plastic bag) by twisting the ends together

twit /ˈtwɪt/ *noun, pl* **twits** [*count*] *informal* **:** a stupid or foolish person ▪ Only a complete *twit* would insult his hosts.

[1]twitch /ˈtwɪʧ/ *verb* **twitch·es; twitched; twitch·ing**

1 [*no obj*] **:** to make a slight, sudden movement that is not controlled or deliberate ▪ His left leg *twitched*. ▪ Her mouth was *twitching* as she began to cry.

2 [+ *obj*] **:** to move or pull (something) with a sudden motion ▪ The rabbit *twitched* its ears.

[2]twitch *noun, pl* **twitches** [*count*]

1 : a slight, sudden movement of a muscle or body part that you do not control ▪ sudden muscle *twitches* ▪ a *twitch* of pain

2 : a sudden and quick movement or change ▪ Economists are studying every *twitch* and hiccup of the business cycle.

– twitchy /ˈtwɪʧi/ *adj* **twitch·i·er; twitch·i·est** [*also more* ~; *most* ~]

twitch·er /ˈtwɪʧɚ/ *noun, pl* **-ers** [*count*] *Brit, informal* **:** BIRD-WATCHER

[1]twit·ter /ˈtwɪtɚ/ *verb* **-ters; -tered; -ter·ing**

1 : to make fast and usually high sounds [*no obj*] The birds were *twittering* in the trees. [+ *obj*] A robin *twittered* its morning song.

2 [*no obj*] **:** to talk in a quick and informal way about unimportant things ▪ What are those people *twittering* about?

[2]twitter *noun, pl* **-ters** [*count*]

1 : the short, high sounds that birds make ▪ The *twitter* of songbirds filled the air.

2 : a light, silly laugh ▪ The teacher heard *twitters* [=*giggles*] coming from the back of the classroom.

in a twitter *informal* **:** very nervous or excited about something. ▪ She was all *in a twitter* about the birthday party. — see also ATWITTER

twittering *noun, pl* **-ings** [*count*] **:** [2]TWITTER ▪ the *twittering* of the birds

two /ˈtu:/ *noun, pl* **twos**

1 [*count*] **:** the number 2

2 [*count*] **:** the second in a set or series ▪ page *two*

3 [*noncount*] **:** two o'clock ▪ It was *two* in the morning.

a bird in the hand is worth two in the bush see BIRD

a thing or two see THING

in two **:** into two equal parts **:** in half ▪ He cut the apple *in two*.

in twos **:** in groups of two ▪ You will be working *in twos*. [=*in pairs*]

in two shakes see [2]SHAKE

it takes two, it takes two to tango see [1]TAKE

of two minds, in two minds see [1]MIND

put two and two together **:** to make a correct guess based on what you have seen or heard **:** to figure something out ▪ You weren't home so I *put two and two together* and went back to your office to find you.

put/stick two fingers up at someone see [1]FINGER

serve two masters see [1]SERVE

two by two **:** in groups of two **:** in pairs ▪ The children lined up *two by two*.

two cents see CENT

two left feet see [1]FOOT

two's company, three's a crowd see COMPANY

two sides of the same coin see [1]COIN

– two *adj* ▪ a *two*-hour test ▪ I had met him just *two* days earlier. **– two** *pronoun* ▪ There are only *two* left. ▪ Come back in a week or *two*. [=come back sometime between one and two weeks from now]

Do not confuse *two* with *to* or *too*.

two–bit /ˈtu:ˈbɪt/ *adj, always used before a noun, informal* **:** not very important or valuable ▪ a *two-bit* thief/town/opinion

two bits *noun* [*plural*] *US, old-fashioned* **:** twenty-five cents ▪ I remember when you could buy a cup of coffee for *two bits*.

two–by–four /ˌtu:baɪˈfoɚ/ *noun, pl* **-fours** [*count*] *US* **:** a piece of wood that has been cut to be long and straight so that it can be used for building things and that is about 2 inches thick and 4 inches wide ▪ We used *two-by-fours* to build the porch.

two–dimensional *adj*

1 : having only two dimensions (such as length and width) ▪ a *two-dimensional* [=*flat*] map/image

2 [*more* ~; *most* ~] *disapproving* **:** not having qualities that are like the qualities of a real person ▪ The characters in this novel are *two-dimensional* and the story is shallow.

two–edged *adj*

1 : having a blade that is sharp on both sides **:** having two sharp edges ▪ a *two-edged* knife

2 : able to be understood in two different ways **:** having two different meanings ▪ There was a *two-edged* message in the speech. ▪ Fame is a ***two-edged sword***. [=there are both good and bad parts of fame]

two–faced /ˈtu:ˈfeɪst/ *adj* [*more* ~; *most* ~] *informal* + *dis-*

approving : not honest or sincere : saying different things to different people in order to get their approval instead of speaking and behaving honestly ▪ *two-faced* [=*hypocritical*] politicians ▪ He's a *two-faced* liar.

two·fold /ˈtuːˌfoʊld/ *adj*
1 : twice as much or as many ▪ a *twofold* increase in spending
2 : having two parts ▪ The aims of the study are *twofold*.
– **two·fold** /ˈtuːˈfoʊld/ *adv* ▪ Our funding increased *twofold* last year.

two–hand·ed /ˈtuːˈhændəd/ *adj*
1 : using or needing both hands ▪ a *two-handed* sword ▪ She scored a point with a *two-handed* backhand. ▪ He made a *two-handed* catch.
2 : needing two people ▪ a *two-handed* saw

two–hand·er /ˈtuːˈhændɚ/ *noun, pl* **-ers** [*count*]
1 : something that is done with both hands ▪ She hit a *two-hander* [=a two-handed tennis shot] down the line.
2 : a play that is written to be performed by two actors

two·pence /ˈtʌpəns/ *noun* [*noncount*] *Brit* : the sum of two pence — called also *tup·pence* /ˈtʌpəns/

two–piece suit *noun, pl* ∼ **suits** [*count*] : a suit consisting of a jacket with matching pants or a jacket with a matching skirt — compare THREE-PIECE SUIT

two–ply /ˈtuːˈplaɪ/ *adj* : having two layers of material ▪ *two-ply* cotton underwear ▪ *two-ply* toilet paper

two–seater *noun, pl* **-ers** [*count*] : a car, airplane, or piece of furniture that only has enough seating space for two people ▪ His new car is a little *two-seater*.

two·some /ˈtuːsəm/ *noun, pl* **-somes** [*count*] : a group of two people or things ▪ They became a *twosome* [=*couple*] after their second year of college. ▪ We were the first *twosome* out on the golf course this morning.

two–time /ˈtuːˌtaɪm/ *verb* **-times**; **-timed**; **-tim·ing** *informal* : to be unfaithful to (your husband, wife, partner, etc.) by having a sexual relationship with someone else [+ *obj*] He *two-timed* [=*cheated on*] his girlfriend with her best friend. [*no obj*] She finally dumped her *two-timing* [=*unfaithful*] husband.
– **two–tim·er** *noun, pl* **-ers** [*count*]

two–tone /ˈtuːˈtoʊn/ *adj, always used before a noun* : having two colors or two shades of one color ▪ a *two-tone* paint job ▪ *two-tone* shoes

two–way *adj*
1 : moving or allowing movement in both directions ▪ *two-way* traffic ▪ a *two-way* street — compare ONE-WAY, THREE-WAY
2 : involving two people or groups ▪ Communication is a *two-way* process. ▪ Trust between two people is a ***two-way street*** [=trust requires effort from both people] — compare ONE-WAY, THREE-WAY
3 : made to send and receive messages ▪ a *two-way* radio — compare ONE-WAY

two–way mirror *noun, pl* ∼ **-rors** [*count*] : ONE-WAY MIRROR

TX *abbr* Texas

ty·coon /taɪˈkuːn/ *noun, pl* **-coons** [*count*] : a very wealthy and powerful business person ▪ a business/media/oil/shipping *tycoon*

tying *present participle of* [2]TIE

tyke *also* **tike** /ˈtaɪk/ *noun, pl* **tykes** *also* **tikes** [*count*] *informal*
1 : a small child ▪ an active *tyke*
2 *Brit* : a person from Yorkshire

tympani *variant spelling of* TIMPANI

tym·pa·num /ˈtɪmpənəm/ *noun, pl* **-na** /-nə/ *also* **-nums** [*count*] *technical* : EARDRUM

[1]**type** /ˈtaɪp/ *noun, pl* **types**
1 [*count*] : a particular kind or group of things or people ▪ What *type* [=*sort*] of food do you like? ▪ We were not prepared to face this *type* of crisis. ▪ We studied various *types* of trees. ▪ a seedless *type* of orange ▪ Allergies of this *type* [=*kind*] are common. ▪ He only likes two *types* of music. ▪ She likes all *types* of books. — see also BLOOD TYPE
2 [*singular*] : a particular kind of person ▪ She's a real outdoors *type*. [=she loves hiking, camping, etc., in the outdoors] ▪ The dinner guests were mostly urban *types*. [=people who lived in the city] ▪ He's ***not her type***. [=he is not the kind of man she is attracted to] ▪ Her mother is ***not the type*** to complain. [=she does not often complain]
3 [*noncount*] **a** : printed letters ▪ italic *type* **b** : small metal blocks that are used for printing letters and numbers on paper ▪ lead *type*
revert to type see REVERT

[2]**type** *verb* **types**; **typed**; **typ·ing**
1 : to write with a computer keyboard or typewriter [*no obj*] How fast can you *type*? ▪ I never learned how to *type*. [+ *obj*] *Type* your name here. ▪ She asked her secretary to *type* a memo. — sometimes + *up* ▪ Can you *type* this *up* for me?
2 [+ *obj*] *technical* : to find out what group something is in ▪ The lab will *type* this blood sample. [=the lab will determine what type of blood the sample is]
– **typing** *noun* [*noncount*] ▪ genetic *typing*

type·cast /ˈtaɪpˌkæst, *Brit* ˈtaɪpˌkɑːst/ *verb* **-cast**; **-cast**; **-cast·ing** [+ *obj*] : to always give (an actor or actress) the same kind of role : to cause people to think that (an actor or actress) should always play the same kind of role ▪ Her television work *typecast* her as a helpless victim. — often used as *(be) typecast* ▪ He feared *being typecast* as a criminal.

type·face /ˈtaɪpˌfeɪs/ *noun, pl* **-fac·es** [*count*] : a set of letters, numbers, etc., that are all in the same style and that are used in printing : FONT ▪ The book's *typeface* is very elegant.

type·set·ting /ˈtaɪpˌsɛtɪŋ/ *noun* [*noncount*] : the process or job of arranging type for printing ▪ a *typesetting* system
– **type·set** /ˈtaɪpˌsɛt/ *verb* [+ *obj*] ▪ *typeset* a magazine article
– **type·set·ter** /ˈtaɪpˌsɛtɚ/ *noun, pl* **-ters** [*count*] ▪ The manuscript has been sent to the typesetter.

type·writ·er /ˈtaɪpˌraɪtɚ/ *noun, pl* **-ers** [*count*] : a machine that prints letters or figures on a sheet of paper when a person pushes its keys

type·writ·ing /ˈtaɪpˌraɪtɪŋ/ *noun* [*noncount*]
1 : the use of a typewriter
2 : writing done with a typewriter

type·writ·ten /ˈtaɪpˌrɪtn̩/ *adj* : written by using a typewriter or a computer ▪ five *typewritten* [=*typed*] pages

ty·phoid /ˈtaɪˌfoɪd/ *noun* [*noncount*] *medical* : a serious disease that is passed from one person to another in dirty food or water — called also *typhoid fever*

ty·phoon /taɪˈfuːn/ *noun, pl* **-phoons** [*count*] : an extremely large, powerful, and destructive storm that occurs especially in the region of the Philippines or the China Sea

ty·phus /ˈtaɪfəs/ *noun* [*noncount*] *medical* : a serious disease that is carried by small insects that live on the bodies of people and animals and that causes high fever, headache, and a dark red rash — called also *typhus fever*

typ·i·cal /ˈtɪpɪkəl/ *adj* [*more* ∼; *most* ∼]
1 : normal for a person, thing, or group : average or usual ▪ We had a *typical* [=*normal*] New England winter. ▪ a *typical* example ▪ It was his *typical* response. ▪ It was *typical* of her to be late. [=she's often late]
2 : happening in the usual way ▪ It was a *typical* Saturday night for us. ▪ a *typical* scenario ▪ We wanted him to have the *typical* college experience of living on campus.

typ·i·cal·ly /ˈtɪpɪkli/ *adv* [*more* ∼; *most* ∼]
1 : generally or normally — used to say what normally happens ▪ *Typically*, the members of our staff receive little recognition. ▪ We *typically* go for coffee after our walk. ▪ These recitals *typically* [=*usually*] last one hour. ▪ I *typically* order the steak when I eat there.
2 : in the usual way — used to describe what is normal or expected of a certain place, person, situation, etc. ▪ *Typically*, she was late. [=she was late, as she often/usually is] ▪ I tried to get him to talk, but he was *typically* reluctant to say anything. ▪ They serve *typically* American food. [=the kind of food that is usual/typical in America]

typ·i·fy /ˈtɪpəˌfaɪ/ *verb* **-fies**; **-fied**; **-fy·ing** [+ *obj*]
1 : to represent what is normal for (something) : to be a good or typical example of (something) ▪ His heroic actions *typified* the courage of all the firefighters at the scene. ▪ The decor *typifies* the elegance of royal residences. ▪ He *typifies* what a professional athlete should be.
2 : to have the usual characteristics of (something) : to be a typical part or feature of (something) ▪ Gothic architecture is *typified* by soaring rooflines and stained glass.

typ·ist /ˈtaɪpɪst/ *noun, pl* **-ists** [*count*]
1 : a person who uses a typewriter or a computer keyboard ▪ She's a good/poor *typist*. [=she types well/badly]
2 : a person who works in an office and whose main job is typing letters, memos, etc.

ty·po /ˈtaɪpoʊ/ *noun, pl* **-pos** [*count*] *informal* : a mistake (such as a misspelled word) in typed or printed text ▪ I spotted three *typos* on the menu.

ty·pog·ra·pher /taɪˈpɑːgrəfɚ/ *noun, pl* **-ers** [*count*] : a person whose job is to choose the style, arrangement, or appearance of printed letters on a page : a person who is skilled in typography

ty·pog·ra·phy /taɪˈpɑːgrəfi/ *noun [noncount]*
1 : the work of producing printed pages from written material
2 : the style, arrangement, or appearance of printed letters on a page
– ty·po·graph·i·cal /ˌtaɪpəˈgræfɪkəl/ *also* **ty·po·graph·ic** /ˌtaɪpəˈgræfɪk/ *adj* ▪ The book contains a number of *typographical errors.* [=(*informal*) *typos*] **– ty·po·graph·i·cal·ly** /ˌtaɪpəˈgræfɪkli/ *adv*

ty·pol·o·gy /taɪˈpɑːləʤi/ *noun, pl* **-gies** *[count, noncount] formal* : a system used for putting things into groups according to how they are similar : the study of how things can be divided into different types
– ty·po·log·i·cal /ˌtaɪpəˈlɑːʤɪkəl/ *adj*

ty·ran·ni·cal /təˈrænɪkəl/ *adj [more ~; most ~]* : using power over people in a way that is cruel and unfair ▪ a *tyrannical* dictatorship ▪ Everyone was afraid of their overbearing and *tyrannical* boss.
– ty·ran·ni·cal·ly /təˈrænɪkli/ *adv*

tyr·an·nize *also Brit* **tyr·an·nise** /ˈtirəˌnaɪz/ *verb* **-niz·es; -nized; -niz·ing** : to use power to treat (people) in a cruel and unfair way [+ *obj*] a government that *tyrannizes* its own people ▪ The owner of the company is nothing but a bully who *tyrannizes* his employees. [=who behaves like a tyrant toward his employees] [*no obj*] — + *over* ▪ He *tyrannizes over* his employees.

ty·ran·no·sau·rus /təˌrænəˈsorəs/ *noun, pl* **-rus·es** *[count]* : a very large meat-eating dinosaur — called also *T. rex, tyrannosaurus rex* /-ˈrɛks/

tyr·an·nous /ˈtirənəs/ *adj, old-fashioned* : TYRANNICAL ▪ *tyrannous* dictators

tyr·an·ny /ˈtirəni/ *noun, pl* **-nies**
1 : cruel and unfair treatment by people with power over others *[noncount]* The refugees were fleeing *tyranny.* ▪ He was dedicated to ending the *tyranny* of slavery. ▪ a nation ruled by *tyranny* ▪ the ***tyranny of the majority*** [=a situation in which a group of people are treated unfairly because their situation is different from the situation of most of the people in a democratic country] *[count]* She felt lost in the bureaucratic *tyrannies* of the university system. — sometimes used figuratively ▪ the *tyrannies* of fashion
2 *[count]* : a government in which all power belongs to one person : the rule or authority of a tyrant ▪ The king sought an absolute *tyranny* over the colonies.

ty·rant /ˈtaɪrənt/ *noun, pl* **-rants** *[count]*
1 : a ruler who has complete power over a country and who is cruel and unfair ▪ The country was ruled by a corrupt *tyrant* [=*despot*] for decades.
2 : someone who uses power in a cruel and unfair way ▪ Our boss is a real *tyrant.*

tyre *Brit spelling of* [2]TIRE

ty·ro /ˈtaɪˌroʊ/ *noun, pl* **-ros** *[count]* : a person who has just started learning or doing something : a beginner or novice ▪ Most of the people in the class were *tyros* like me.

tzar, tzarina, tzarist *variant spellings of* CZAR, CZARINA, CZARIST

U

u *or* **U** /ˈjuː/ *noun, pl* **u's** *or* **U's** /ˈjuːz/
1 : the 21st letter of the English alphabet *[count]* There are three *u's* in "unusual." *[noncount]* a word that starts with *u*
2 *[count] Brit* : a grade given to a student whose work is judged as not satisfactory

U. *abbr* university

U–bend *noun, pl* **-bends** *[count] Brit, technical* : [1]TRAP 5

über- *also* **uber-** /ˈuːbɚ/ *prefix, informal*
1 — used to indicate that someone is a great or extreme example of a particular kind of person ▪ an *über*celebrity
2 : better, larger, or greater than : SUPER- ▪ He is *über*cool. ▪ an *über*expensive diamond ring

ubiq·ui·tous /juˈbɪkwətəs/ *adj [more ~; most ~]* : seeming to be seen everywhere ▪ *ubiquitous* celebrities ▪ The company's advertisements are *ubiquitous.*
– ubiq·ui·tous·ly *adv* **– ubiq·ui·tous·ness** *noun [noncount]* **– ubiq·ui·ty** /juˈbɪkwəti/ *noun [noncount] formal* ▪ the *ubiquity* of the company's ads

U–boat /ˈjuːˌboʊt/ *noun, pl* **-boats** *[count]* : a German submarine

ud·der /ˈʌdɚ/ *noun, pl* **-ders** *[count]* : the bag-shaped part of a cow, goat, etc., that hangs below the belly and produces milk

UFO /ˌjuːˌɛfˈoʊ/ *noun, pl* **UFO's** *or* **UFOs** /ˌjuːˌɛfˈoʊz/ *[count]* : a flying object in the sky that some people believe could be a spaceship from another planet ▪ a *UFO* sighting ✧ *UFO* is an abbreviation of "unidentified flying object."

ugh /ˈʌg/ *interj, informal* — used to show that you are annoyed, disgusted, or upset about something ▪ *Ugh,* I can't stand that movie.

ug·ly /ˈʌgli/ *adj* **ug·li·er; -est** [*also more ~; most ~*]
1 a : unpleasant to look at : not pretty or attractive ▪ That house is *ugly.* ▪ an *ugly* person ▪ an *ugly* shade of green ▪ (*informal*) That dog of yours is ***(as) ugly as sin.*** [=very ugly] **b** : unpleasant to hear ▪ an *ugly* sound/voice
2 : offensive or disgusting ▪ *ugly* habits ▪ an *ugly* racial slur
3 : very bad or unpleasant ▪ They avoided what could have been an *ugly* situation. ▪ Things could get/turn *ugly.* [=*nasty*] ▪ He has an *ugly* disposition/temper.
rear its ugly head see [1]HEAD
– ug·li·ness /ˈʌglinəs/ *noun [noncount]*

ugly duckling *noun, pl* **~ -lings** *[count]* : a person or thing that is not attractive or successful but that is likely to become attractive or successful in the future ▪ The house is an *ugly duckling,* but it has a lot of potential. ▪ an *ugly duckling* that has become a beautiful swan [=an ugly/unsuccessful person or thing that has become beautiful/successful]

uh /ˈʌ/ *interj, chiefly US, informal* — used when you hesitate because you are not sure about what to say ▪ "What time is it?" "*Uh,* I'm not sure." ▪ Do you want to, *uh,* go out sometime?

UHF *abbr* ultra high frequency ✧ Ultra high frequency radio waves are used for broadcasting television and some types of radio signals. ▪ *UHF* television stations

uh–huh /ˌʌˈhʌ *but spoken nasally/ interj, informal* — used to show that you agree or understand ▪ "Is that your dog?" "*Uh-huh.*" [=*yeah, yes*] ▪ "Do you know what I mean?" "*Uh-huh.* I sure do." — sometimes used to encourage someone to continue talking ▪ "I'm still kind of worried about tomorrow." "*Uh-huh.*"

uh–oh /ˈʌˌoʊ *with a stop between the vowels/ interj, chiefly US, informal* — used when you realize that you are in a bad situation, that you have made a mistake, etc. ▪ *Uh-oh,* we're in trouble! ▪ *Uh-oh.* What happened?

uh–uh /ˈʌˌʌ *but spoken nasally/ interj, chiefly US, informal* — used to say no or to emphasize a negative answer to a question, request, or offer ▪ "Are you going to the party?" "*Uh-uh.* I have to study." ▪ I won't do it. *Uh-uh.*

UK *also* **U.K.** *abbr* United Kingdom

uku·le·le /ˌjuːkəˈleɪli/ *noun, pl* **-les** *[count]* : a musical instrument that is like a small guitar with four strings

ul·cer /ˈʌlsɚ/ *noun, pl* **-cers** *[count] medical* : a painful, sore area inside or outside the body ▪ a stomach *ulcer* ▪ a skin *ulcer* — see also PEPTIC ULCER

ul·cer·ate /ˈʌlsəˌreɪt/ *verb* **-ates; -at·ed; -at·ing** *[no obj] medical* : to form an ulcer ▪ The wound began to *ulcerate.*
– ulcerated *adj* ▪ an *ulcerated* wound [=a wound that has formed an ulcer or many ulcers] ▪ an *ulcerated* stomach/throat **– ul·cer·a·tion** /ˌʌlsəˈreɪʃən/ *noun, pl* **-tions** *[count, noncount]*

U

ul·na /ˈʌlnə/ *noun, pl* **-nae** *or* **-nas** [*count*] *medical* **:** the bone in the lower part of your arm on the side that is opposite to your thumb — see picture at HUMAN

ul·te·ri·or /ˌʌlˈtirijɚ/ *adj* **:** kept hidden in order to get a particular result • I think she has an ***ulterior motive*** for helping us. [=she has a secret reason for wanting to help us]

[1]**ul·ti·mate** /ˈʌltəmət/ *adj, always used before a noun*
1 : happening or coming at the end of a process, series of events, etc. • Their *ultimate* [=*final*] destination was Paris. • What was the *ultimate* [=*final, eventual*] outcome/result? • Their *ultimate* fate has not yet been decided. • I never doubted their *ultimate* success. [=I never doubted that they would eventually succeed] • The president has *ultimate* [=*final*] authority/control/responsibility over the decision. • Our ***ultimate aim/goal/purpose*** is to increase production.
2 : greatest or most extreme — used to say that something or someone is the greatest or most extreme example of a particular type of thing or person • He says that dying for your country is the *ultimate* act of patriotism. • the *ultimate* expression of love • the *ultimate* betrayal/challenge • He was the *ultimate* hero.
3 — used to refer to the original or basic source or cause of something • They traced the river back to its *ultimate* source. • Lack of money is the *ultimate* cause of our problems.
4 : most distant in space or time • the *ultimate* [=*farthest*] reaches of the universe

[2]**ultimate** *noun*
the ultimate in **:** the greatest or most extreme form or example of (something) • This car is *the ultimate in* safety. [=this car is as safe as a car can be] • They provide their customers with *the ultimate in* service. [=with the best possible service]

ul·ti·mate·ly /ˈʌltəmətli/ *adv*
1 : at the end of a process, period of time, etc. • He *ultimately* [=*finally, eventually*] agreed to the deal. • I have confidence that the plan will *ultimately* succeed. [=will succeed in the end] • The changes *ultimately* proved to be unnecessary.
2 : at the most basic level **:** in the central or most important way • *Ultimately*, it's a question of who is more popular.

ul·ti·ma·tum /ˌʌltəˈmeɪtəm/ *noun, pl* **-tums** *or* **-ta** /-tə/ [*count*] **:** a final threat **:** a promise that force or punishment will be used if someone does not do what is wanted • She was given an *ultimatum*—work harder or lose her job.

ul·tra- /ˌʌltrə/ *prefix*
1 : beyond **:** extremely **:** more than is usual • *ultra*modern • *ultra*serious
2 *technical* **:** beyond the range or limits of • *ultra*violet • *ultra*sonic

ul·tra·ma·rine /ˌʌltrəməˈriːn/ *noun* [*noncount*] **:** a very bright blue color
– ultramarine *adj*

ul·tra·son·ic /ˌʌltrəˈsɑːnɪk/ *adj* — used to describe sounds that are too high for humans to hear • *ultrasonic* frequencies

ul·tra·sound /ˈʌltrəˌsaʊnd/ *noun, pl* **-sounds**
1 [*noncount*] **:** a type of sound that is too high for humans to hear
2 *medical* **:** a method of producing images of the inside of the body by using a machine that produces sound waves which are too high to be heard [*noncount*] They used *ultrasound* to examine his heart. • She had an *ultrasound* exam/examination this morning. [*count*] She had an *ultrasound* this morning.
3 [*count*] **:** an image that is made using ultrasound • She showed me an *ultrasound* of her unborn baby.

ul·tra·vi·o·let /ˌʌltrəˈvajələt/ *adj, technical* — used to describe rays of light that cannot be seen and that are slightly shorter than the rays of violet light • *ultraviolet* light/radiation

ul·u·late /ˈʌljəˌleɪt, ˈjuːljəˌleɪt/ *verb* **-lates; -lat·ed; -lat·ing** [*no obj*] *literary* **:** to cry loudly • a widow *ululating* in sorrow
– ul·u·la·tion /ˌʌljəˈleɪʃən, ˌjuːljəˈleɪʃən/ *noun, pl* **-tions** [*count, noncount*]

um /ˈʌm *or a prolonged* m *sound*/ *interj* — used when you hesitate because you are not sure about what to say • "Are you coming to the party?" "*Um*, I think so."

um·ber /ˈʌmbɚ/ *noun* [*noncount*] **:** a dark, yellowish brown color
– umber *adj*

um·bil·i·cal cord /ˌʌmˈbɪlɪkəl-/ *noun, pl* **~ cords** [*count*] **:** a long, narrow tube that connects an unborn baby to the placenta of its mother — sometimes used figuratively • The time has come to ***cut/sever the umbilical cord*** that keeps us dependent on foreign aid.

um·brage /ˈʌmbrɪʤ/ *noun* [*noncount*] *formal* **:** a feeling of being offended by what someone has said or done — usually used in the phrase ***take umbrage*** • I imagine some people will *take umbrage* [=will be offended] when they hear the quote. — often + *at* • I *take umbrage at* [=I am offended by] that remark.

um·brel·la /ˌʌmˈbrɛlə/ *noun, pl* **-las** [*count*]
1 : a device that is used for protection from the rain and sun ✧ An umbrella consists of a circle of fabric attached to a folding frame that is connected to a central pole or handle. • You shouldn't go out in the rain without an *umbrella*. • a beach *umbrella*

umbrella

2 : a group or organization that includes many smaller groups — often used before another noun • an *umbrella* corporation
3 : something that includes several or many different things • The store sells Indian, Asian, and Middle Eastern foods under the *umbrella* of international cuisine. — often used before another noun • I used the heading "Odds and Ends" as an ***umbrella term*** for items that did not fit anywhere else. • I bought an ***umbrella policy*** that insures my car, jewelry, and house.

um·laut /ˈuːmˌlaʊt/ *noun, pl* **-lauts** [*count*] **:** a mark ¨ placed over a vowel (such as a *u* in German) to indicate a specific pronunciation

[1]**um·pire** /ˈʌmˌpajɚ/ *noun, pl* **-pires** [*count*] **:** a person who controls play and makes sure that players act according to the rules in a sports event (such as a baseball game or a cricket or tennis match)

[2]**umpire** *verb* **-pires; -pired; -pir·ing :** to be an umpire in a sports event (such as a baseball game) [+ *obj*] Who *umpired* the game? [*no obj*] Who *umpired*?

ump·teen /ˈʌmpˌtiːn/ *adj, informal* **:** very many • I have *umpteen* things to do today. [=I have a lot of things to do today]
– ump·teenth /ˈʌmpˌtiːnθ/ *adj* • That's the *umpteenth* time you've said that.

UN *also* **U.N.** *abbr* United Nations

un- /ˌʌn/ *prefix*
1 : not • *un*happy • *un*pleasant • *un*lawful • *un*skilled • *un*breakable • *un*wise
2 : opposite of **:** contrary to • *un*ethical • *un*constitutional • *un*godly • *un*orthodox
3 : do the opposite of **:** reverse (a specified action) • *un*tie • *un*dress • *un*screw • *un*fold
4 : remove (a specified thing) from • *un*cork a wine bottle • *un*cover • *un*leash

un·abashed /ˌʌnəˈbæʃt/ *adj* [*more* ~; *most* ~] **:** not embarrassed or ashamed about openly expressing strong feelings or opinions • She is an *unabashed* supporter/admirer of the president's policies.
– un·abash·ed·ly /ˌʌnəˈbæʃədli/ *adv* • They're *unabashedly* proud of their son's accomplishments.

un·abat·ed /ˌʌnəˈbeɪtəd/ *adj* **:** continuing at full strength or force without becoming weaker • The rain continued *unabated*. • Her popularity remains *unabated*.

un·able /ˌʌnˈeɪbəl/ *adj, not used before a noun* **:** not able to do something • I was *unable* to afford the trip. • He was *unable* to play tennis after the injury.

un·abridged /ˌʌnəˈbrɪʤd/ *adj* **:** not shortened by leaving out some parts **:** not abridged • an *unabridged* reprint of a novel • an *unabridged* dictionary

un·ac·cept·able /ˌʌnɪkˈsɛptəbəl/ *adj* **:** not pleasing or welcome **:** not acceptable • socially *unacceptable* behavior • a word that is *unacceptable* in formal English • Some of her ideas were *unacceptable* to other people.
– un·ac·cept·ably /ˌʌnɪkˈsɛptəbli/ *adv* • The unemployment rate is *unacceptably* high.

un·ac·com·pa·nied /ˌʌnəˈkʌmpənid/ *adj*
1 a : without another person **:** ALONE • He attended the party *unaccompanied*. • *Unaccompanied* children are not allowed in the store. • She arrived at the party ***unaccompanied by*** [=*without*] her husband. **b :** not together with something specified • All we've had from him is a lot of talk *unaccom-*

panied by any real effort to solve the problem.

2 *music* : played or sung without another musical instrument or singer ▪ a piece written for an *unaccompanied* cello ▪ an *unaccompanied* solo

un·ac·count·able /ˌʌnəˈkaʊntəbəl/ *adj, formal*

1 : not able to be explained : strange or mysterious ▪ She has shown an *unaccountable* reluctance to accept their offer.

2 a : not required to explain actions or decisions — usually + *to* ▪ judges who are not elected and so are *unaccountable to* the public ▪ He remains *unaccountable to* the voters. **b** : not required to be responsible for something — usually + *for* ▪ Despite all the problems he has caused, he remains *unaccountable for* his mistakes.

un·ac·count·ably /ˌʌnəˈkaʊntəbli/ *adv, formal* : in a way that is difficult to explain or understand ▪ She was looking *unaccountably* upset. : for reasons that are hard to understand ▪ *Unaccountably*, the problem was ignored.

un·ac·count·ed /ˌʌnəˈkaʊntəd/ *adj*

unaccounted for — used to say that what happened to someone or something is not known ▪ Many people were *unaccounted for* after the disaster. ▪ A great deal of money remains *unaccounted for*. [=no one knows what happened to the money]

un·ac·cus·tomed /ˌʌnəˈkʌstəmd/ *adj, formal*

1 : not usual or common : not customary ▪ They responded to our request with *unaccustomed* speed.

2 : not familiar with something so that it does not seem normal or usual : not used to something — + *to* ▪ Her pets are *unaccustomed to* travel/traveling. ▪ She was *unaccustomed to* fame.

un·ac·knowl·edged /ˌʌnɪkˈnɑːlɪʤd/ *adj* : not recognized, accepted, or admitted : not acknowledged ▪ He had a powerful and largely *unacknowledged* effect on the outcome of the election.

un·ac·quaint·ed /ˌʌnəˈkweɪntəd/ *adj*

1 : not having knowledge about something : not having seen or experienced something — often + *with* ▪ I am *unacquainted with* her books. [=I have never read or heard about her books]

2 : not having met : not knowing each other in a personal or social way ▪ *unacquainted* cousins — often + *with* ▪ Although they both lived in the same small town, my friend was *unacquainted with* my brother.

un·adorned /ˌʌnəˈdoənd/ *adj* : not decorated or fancy : not adorned ▪ The room is *unadorned* and very plain. ▪ I like her *unadorned* [=*simple, plain*] writing style.

un·adul·ter·at·ed /ˌʌnəˈdʌltəˌreɪtəd/ *adj*

1 : not having anything added : not adulterated : PURE ▪ *unadulterated* foods

2 : complete and total ▪ They felt *unadulterated* happiness. ▪ *unadulterated* nonsense

un·ad·ven·tur·ous /ˌʌnədˈvenʧərəs/ *adj [more ~; most ~]*

1 : afraid to do or try new and dangerous or exciting things ▪ an *unadventurous* eater/cook ▪ When it comes to travel, she's very *unadventurous*.

2 : not exciting or unusual ▪ an *unadventurous* film/menu ▪ I've lived a pretty *unadventurous* life.

un·af·fect·ed /ˌʌnəˈfɛktəd/ *adj*

1 : not influenced or changed mentally, physically, or chemically ▪ They shortened the book when they made the movie, but the basic story remained *unaffected*. — often + *by* ▪ Her concentration was *unaffected* [=was not affected] *by* the constant noise.

2 : genuine, sincere, or natural ▪ He has a friendly and *unaffected* manner.

un·af·fil·i·at·ed /ˌʌnəˈfɪliˌeɪtəd/ *adj* : not connected with something (such as a program or organization) as a member or partner ▪ Two of the candidates are *unaffiliated* with any political party. ▪ *Unaffiliated* voters cannot vote in a party's primary election.

U

un·afraid /ˌʌnəˈfreɪd/ *adj, not used before a noun* : not frightened or fearful : not afraid ▪ He is *unafraid* of failure. ▪ They were *unafraid* to take a chance.

un·aid·ed /ˌʌnˈeɪdəd/ *adj* : without help : not aided ▪ patients who can get out of bed *unaided* [=*unassisted*] ▪ The stars are visible to the *unaided* eye. [=the stars can be seen without using a telescope or binoculars]

un·alien·able /ˌʌnˈeɪlijənəbəl/ *adj, chiefly US, formal* : impossible to take away or give up : INALIENABLE ▪ *unalienable* rights

un·aligned /ˌʌnəˈlaɪnd/ *adj* : not associated with other groups, nations, etc. : not aligned ▪ candidates *unaligned* with any party ▪ *unaligned* nations

un·al·loyed /ˌʌnəˈlɔɪd/ *adj* : not mixed with something else : PURE ▪ (*technical*) *unalloyed* metals ▪ (*literary*) *unalloyed* happiness

un·al·ter·able /ˌʌnˈɑːltərəbəl/ *adj* : not capable of being changed or altered ▪ *unalterable* conditions

— **un·al·ter·ably** /ˌʌnˈɑːltərəbli/ *adv* ▪ They are *unalterably* opposed to any increase in taxes.

un·al·tered /ˌʌnˈɑːltəd/ *adj* : not changed or altered : remaining in an original state ▪ *unaltered* photographs ▪ an *unaltered* landscape

un·am·big·u·ous /ˌʌnæmˈbɪgjəwəs/ *adj [more ~; most ~]* : clearly expressed or understood : not ambiguous ▪ She gave a clear, *unambiguous* answer. ▪ *unambiguous* evidence

— **un·am·big·u·ous·ly** *adv*

un·am·bi·tious /ˌʌnæmˈbɪʃəs/ *adj [more ~; most ~]* : feeling or showing a lack of ambition ▪ an *unambitious* worker/movie

un–Amer·i·can /ˌʌnəˈmerɪkən/ *adj* : not agreeing with American values, principles, or traditions ▪ If you ask me, failing to vote is downright *un-American*. ▪ They were accused of *un-American* activities.

unan·i·mous /juˈnænəməs/ *adj*

1 : agreed to by everyone ▪ a *unanimous* vote ▪ The judges made a *unanimous* ruling.

2 *not used before a noun* : having the same opinion — often + *in* ▪ The councillors were *unanimous in* their approval of the report. [=they all approved the report]

— **una·nim·i·ty** /ˌjuːnəˈnɪməti/ *noun [noncount]* ▪ I was surprised by the *unanimity* of their decision. — **unan·i·mous·ly** *adv* ▪ They voted *unanimously*.

un·an·nounced /ˌʌnəˈnaʊnst/ *adj* : surprising and unexpected : not having been announced or spoken about before ▪ The teacher gave the students an *unannounced* test. ▪ They arrived *unannounced* at my door.

un·an·swer·able /ˌʌnˈænsərəbəl/ *adj*

1 : not capable of being answered ▪ an *unanswerable* question

2 : impossible to prove wrong ▪ The argument is *unanswerable*. [=*irrefutable*]

un·an·swered /ˌʌnˈænsəd/ *adj*

1 : without a reply : not answered ▪ Our questions went *unanswered*. [=our questions were not answered]

2 *US, sports* : scored during a time when an opponent fails to score ▪ The team scored 20 *unanswered* points in the third quarter. [=the team scored 20 points and the opposing team did not score any]

un·an·tic·i·pat·ed /ˌʌnænˈtɪsəpeɪtəd/ *adj [more ~; most ~]* : not expected or anticipated : not thought of as a possibility ▪ The new policy has had some *unanticipated* side effects. ▪ *unanticipated* problems

un·apol·o·get·ic /ˌʌnəˌpɑːləˈʤɛtɪk/ *adj* : not feeling or showing regret or shame : not apologetic ▪ She was *unapologetic* about her remarks. ▪ He's an *unapologetic* liberal/conservative.

— **un·apol·o·get·i·cal·ly** /ˌʌnəˌpɑːləˈʤɛtɪkli/ *adv* ▪ an *unapologetically* old-fashioned person

un·ap·peal·ing /ˌʌnəˈpiːlɪŋ/ *adj [more ~; most ~]* : not attractive or appealing ▪ The decorations were *unappealing*. ▪ an *unappealing* choice ▪ an *unappealing* color/taste

un·ap·pe·tiz·ing *also Brit* **un·ap·pe·tis·ing** /ˌʌnˈæpəˌtaɪzɪŋ/ *adj [more ~; most ~]* : not appealing to a person's taste : not attractive or appetizing ▪ The food looked *unappetizing*. ▪ an *unappetizing* book title

un·ap·pre·ci·at·ed /ˌʌnəˈpriːʃiˌeɪtəd/ *adj [more ~; most ~]* : not given the respect or thanks that is deserved : not appreciated ▪ I feel *unappreciated* at work. ▪ She was an *unappreciated* genius. ▪ Her efforts/talents were *unappreciated*.

un·ap·proach·able /ˌʌnəˈproʊʧəbəl/ *adj [more ~; most ~]* : not easy to talk to or deal with : having an unfriendly manner : not approachable ▪ a cold and *unapproachable* person

un·ar·gu·able /ˌʌnˈɑəgjəwəbəl/ *adj, formal* : certain or clearly true : not open to doubt or argument : INARGUABLE ▪ *unarguable* evidence/proof

— **un·ar·gu·ably** /ˌʌnˈɑəgjəwəbli/ *adv*

un·armed /ˌʌnˈɑəmd/ *adj*

1 : not having a weapon : not armed ▪ an *unarmed* security guard

2 : not using or involving a weapon ▪ *unarmed* robbery/combat

un·ashamed /ˌʌnəˈʃeɪmd/ *adj* **:** not feeling or showing shame or guilt **:** not ashamed ▪ He is *unashamed* of his patriotism. ▪ She was *unashamed* to tell the truth.
– **un·asham·ed·ly** /ˌʌnəˈʃeɪmədli/ *adv* ▪ He *unashamedly* began to cry.

un·asked /ˌʌnˈæskt, *Brit* ˌʌnˈɑːskt/ *adj* **:** not asked ▪ He felt that there were many *unasked* questions after his demonstration.
unasked for **:** not requested **:** not asked for ▪ *unasked for* advice ▪ What they did was unwanted and *unasked for.*

un·as·sail·able /ˌʌnəˈseɪləbəl/ *adj, formal* **:** not able to be doubted, attacked, or questioned ▪ an *unassailable* [=*undeniable, indisputable*] fact/truth
– **un·as·sail·ably** /ˌʌnəˈseɪləbli/ *adv*

un·as·ser·tive /ˌʌnəˈsɚtɪv/ *adj* [*more* ~; *most* ~] **:** not talking or behaving in a loud and confident way **:** not assertive ▪ a modest, *unassertive* person ▪ an *unassertive* manner

un·as·sist·ed /ˌʌnəˈsɪstəd/ *adj*
1 : without help or assistance ▪ He is unable to walk *unassisted.* [=*unaided*]
2 *sports* **:** done without help from another player ▪ an *unassisted* double play ▪ The goal was *unassisted.*

un·as·sum·ing /ˌʌnəˈsuːmɪŋ, *Brit* ˌʌnəˈsjuːmɪŋ/ *adj* [*more* ~; *most* ~] *approving* **:** not having or showing a desire to be noticed, praised, etc. **:** MODEST ▪ He's just an *unassuming* guy. ▪ They lived in an *unassuming* home/neighborhood.
– **un·as·sum·ing·ly** *adv*

un·at·tached /ˌʌnəˈtætʃt/ *adj*
1 : not married, engaged, or in a serious romantic relationship ▪ My brother is currently *unattached.*
2 : not joined to another building ▪ an *unattached* [=*detached*] garage

un·at·tend·ed /ˌʌnəˈtɛndəd/ *adj* **:** not cared for or watched ▪ Do not leave your child *unattended.* ▪ *Unattended* luggage will be confiscated. ▪ Her health problems have gone *unattended* for too long. [=she has ignored her health problems for too long] ▪ an *unattended* lighthouse ▪ The campfire was left *unattended.*

un·at·trac·tive /ˌʌnəˈtræktɪv/ *adj* [*more* ~; *most* ~] **:** not beautiful, interesting, or pleasing **:** not attractive ▪ an *unattractive* man/woman ▪ *unattractive* ideas
– **un·at·trac·tive·ly** *adv* ▪ *unattractively* decorated/dressed/presented

un·au·tho·rized *also Brit* **un·au·tho·rised** /ˌʌnˈɑːθəˌraɪzd/ *adj* **:** without permission **:** not authorized ▪ an *unauthorized* use of government vehicles ▪ *Unauthorized* personnel are not allowed in the building. ▪ an *unauthorized* biography [=a biography that is written without the permission of the subject]

un·avail·able /ˌʌnəˈveɪləbəl/ *adj* **:** not available: such as **a :** not possible to get or use ▪ The shoes are *unavailable* in certain sizes. ▪ The Internet provides many resources that were previously *unavailable* (to us). **b :** not able or willing to do something — often + *for* ▪ Officials were *unavailable for* comment. — often followed by *to* + *verb* ▪ The witness is *unavailable to testify.* ▪ She's *unavailable to teach* the course next semester.
– **un·avail·abil·i·ty** /ˌʌnəˌveɪləˈbɪləti/ *noun* [*noncount*]

un·avail·ing /ˌʌnəˈveɪlɪŋ/ *adj, formal* **:** not useful or successful **:** FUTILE ▪ *unavailing* arguments/efforts
– **un·avail·ing·ly** /ˌʌnəˈveɪlɪŋli/ *adv* ▪ He argued *unavailingly* against the proposed changes.

un·avoid·able /ˌʌnəˈvoɪdəbəl/ *adj* **:** not able to be prevented or avoided ▪ The accident was *unavoidable.* ▪ an *unavoidable* fact
– **un·avoid·ably** /ˌʌnəˈvoɪdəbli/ *adv* ▪ They were *unavoidably* delayed.

un·aware /ˌʌnəˈweɚ/ *adj* [*more* ~; *most* ~] **:** not having knowledge about something **:** not aware — often + *that* ▪ They were *unaware that* they were being watched. — often + *of* ▪ We were *unaware of* the problem. ▪ She seemed *unaware of* what was going on.
– **un·aware·ness** *noun* [*singular, noncount*] ▪ He claimed *unawareness* of the problem.

un·awares /ˌʌnəˈweɚz/ *adv* **:** without warning — used to describe something that happens without being expected ▪ The rainstorm ***caught us unawares.*** [=we were not expecting the storm] ▪ She was ***taken unawares*** [=*taken by surprise*] by the sudden change in plans.

un·bal·ance /ˌʌnˈbæləns/ *verb* **-anc·es; -anced; -anc·ing** [+ *obj*] **:** to cause (something or someone) to stop being balanced, steady, stable, etc. ▪ If too many people stand up, it will *unbalance* the boat. ▪ The tax cuts have *unbalanced* the budget. ▪ His experiences in the war *unbalanced* his mind. [=made him slightly crazy]

un·bal·anced /ˌʌnˈbælənst/ *adj*
1 : not in a state of balance **:** not balanced: such as **a :** not having equal weight on all sides ▪ an *unbalanced* load ▪ The weight was *unbalanced.* **b :** not having good or equal amounts of all the necessary parts of something ▪ He's been eating an *unbalanced* diet.
2 : not completely sane ▪ mentally *unbalanced* people

un·bear·able /ˌʌnˈberəbəl/ *adj* [*more* ~; *most* ~] **:** too bad, harsh, or extreme to be accepted or endured **:** not bearable ▪ *unbearable* [=*intolerable, unendurable*] pain ▪ We were in an almost *unbearable* state of excitement.
– **un·bear·ably** /ˌʌnˈberəbli/ *adv* ▪ an *unbearably* harsh climate ▪ an *unbearably* painful condition

un·beat·able /ˌʌnˈbiːtəbəl/ *adj*
1 : not capable of being defeated ▪ an *unbeatable* team
2 : very good or excellent ▪ a restaurant with *unbeatable* food ▪ The store has *unbeatable* prices.

un·beat·en /ˌʌnˈbiːtn̩/ *adj* **:** not defeated **:** not beaten ▪ The team is *unbeaten* so far this season. ▪ He remains *unbeaten* in his career.

un·be·com·ing /ˌʌnbɪˈkʌmɪŋ/ *adj* [*more* ~; *most* ~]
1 : not attractive **:** not becoming ▪ an *unbecoming* dress ▪ That color is very *unbecoming* on her.
2 *formal* **:** not appropriate or acceptable for a person in a particular job or position ▪ conduct *unbecoming* an officer [=conduct/behavior that is not appropriate for an officer] — often + *of* or *to* ▪ behavior *unbecoming of/to* a public official

un·be·knownst /ˌʌnbɪˈnoʊnst/ *or* **un·be·known** /ˌʌnbɪˈnoʊn/ *adj*
unbeknownst/unbeknown to **:** without being known about by (someone) ▪ *Unbeknownst to* the students, the teacher had entered the room. [=the students did not know/realize that the teacher had entered the room] ✧ In U.S. English *unbeknownst* is more common than *unbeknown.* In British English, *unbeknown* is more common.

un·be·lief /ˌʌnbəˈliːf/ *noun* [*noncount*] *formal* **:** lack of religious belief ▪ living in an age of *unbelief* — compare DISBELIEF

un·be·liev·able /ˌʌnbəˈliːvəbəl/ *adj* [*more* ~; *most* ~]
1 : difficult or impossible to believe ▪ His story/explanation is *unbelievable.*
2 — used to describe something that is so good, bad, etc., that it is difficult to believe ▪ The destruction was *unbelievable.* ▪ He made an *unbelievable* catch in center field.
– **un·be·liev·ably** /ˌʌnbəˈliːvəbli/ *adv* ▪ an *unbelievably* bizarre story ▪ He's an *unbelievably* [=*amazingly*] fast runner.

un·be·liev·er /ˌʌnbəˈliːvɚ/ *noun, pl* **-ers** [*count*] **:** a person who does not believe something; *especially* **:** a person who does not believe in a particular religious faith

un·be·liev·ing /ˌʌnbəˈliːvɪŋ/ *adj* **:** feeling or showing that you do not believe something ▪ She had an *unbelieving* look on her face.
– **un·be·liev·ing·ly** *adv* ▪ He stared at the destruction *unbelievingly.*

un·bend /ˌʌnˈbɛnd/ *verb* **-bends; -bent** /-ˌbɛnt/; **-bend·ing**
1 : to make (something) straight or to become straight [+ *obj*] He was bending and *unbending* his fingers. [*no obj*] His fingers were bending and *unbending.*
2 [*no obj*] **:** to stop being serious or tense **:** RELAX ▪ He *unbent* a little at the party.

un·bend·ing /ˌʌnˈbɛndɪŋ/ *adj* [*more* ~; *most* ~] *sometimes disapproving* **:** not willing to change an opinion, decision, etc. ▪ She was *unbending* [=*inflexible*] in her decision. ▪ He has an *unbending* will. ▪ *unbending* determination

un·bi·ased /ˌʌnˈbajəst/ *adj* **:** not having or showing an unfair tendency to believe that some people, ideas, etc., are better than others **:** not biased ▪ an *unbiased* [=*impartial*] judge ▪ Let me offer an *unbiased* opinion.

un·bid·den /ˌʌnˈbɪdn̩/ *adj, formal* **:** not asked for or invited ▪ He appeared *unbidden* [=*uninvited*] at my door. ▪ thoughts that come to the mind *unbidden*

un·bind /ˌʌnˈbaɪnd/ *verb* **-binds; -bound** /ˌʌnˈbaʊnd/; **-bind·ing** [+ *obj*] **:** UNTIE ▪ She managed to *unbind* her hands. ▪ *Unbind* the prisoner.

un·blem·ished /ˌʌnˈblɛmɪʃt/ *adj* **:** not blemished: such as **a :** not having any unwanted marks or blemishes ▪ *unblemished* skin **b :** not harmed or damaged in any way ▪ She has an *unblemished* reputation for honesty.

un·blink·ing /ˌʌnˈblɪŋkɪŋ/ *adj*
1 : not blinking ▪ *unblinking* eyes
2 : looking at or describing something in a very honest and accurate way ▪ The book provides an *unblinking* view of the causes of the war. ▪ *unblinking* honesty
— un·blink·ing·ly *adv* ▪ She stared at me *unblinkingly.* [=without blinking] ▪ an *unblinkingly* honest person

un·block /ˌʌnˈblɑːk/ *verb* **-blocks; -blocked; -block·ing** [+ *obj*] **:** to stop (something) from being blocked ▪ A procedure was done to *unblock* his arteries. ▪ *unblock* [=*unclog*] a drain

un·born /ˌʌnˈboən/ *adj* **:** not yet born ▪ her *unborn* child ▪ *unborn* generations

[1]**unbound** *past tense and past participle of* UNBIND

[2]**un·bound** /ˌʌnˈbaʊnd/ *adj* **:** not bound: such as **a :** not controlled or influenced by something ▪ He dresses however he likes and feels *unbound* by convention. **b :** not tied together with something (such as string or rope) ▪ *unbound* stacks of newspapers ▪ long, *unbound* hair **c :** not having a cover or binding ▪ *unbound* pages/copies **d** *technical* **:** not held by chemical or physical forces ▪ a test to determine the amount of *unbound* iron in the blood ▪ *unbound* energy

un·bound·ed /ˌʌnˈbaʊndəd/ *adj* **:** not limited in any way ▪ *unbounded* enthusiasm/joy

un·bowed /ˌʌnˈbaʊd/ *adj, literary* **:** not defeated or willing to admit defeat ▪ He was *unbowed* by failure.

un·break·able /ˌʌnˈbreɪkəbəl/ *adj* **:** not able to be broken **:** not breakable ▪ The two of them had an *unbreakable* bond of friendship. ▪ The plastic is virtually *unbreakable.*

un·bridge·able /ˌʌnˈbrɪʤəbəl/ *adj* — used to say that two people, groups, or things are too widely separated or different from each other to ever be brought together, made to agree, etc. ▪ He says that there is an ***unbridgeable gulf/gap*** between the rich and the poor in this country.

un·bri·dled /ˌʌnˈbraɪdl̩d/ *adj, formal + literary* **:** not controlled or limited **:** done, felt, or expressed in a free and uncontrolled way ▪ The crowd was swept with *unbridled* enthusiasm. ▪ (*chiefly US*) They live in an area of *unbridled* development. [=an area where many houses and other buildings are being built without much control by the government]

un·bro·ken /ˌʌnˈbroʊkən/ *adj*
1 : not damaged or broken ▪ *unbroken* eggs ▪ His spirit remains *unbroken.*
2 : not interrupted **:** CONTINUOUS ▪ an *unbroken* row of trees ▪ eight hours of *unbroken* sleep ▪ The band has had an *unbroken* string of hits.
3 *of a record* **:** not beaten or improved upon **:** not surpassed ▪ The Olympic record he set is still *unbroken.*

un·buck·le /ˌʌnˈbʌkəl/ *verb* **-buck·les; -buck·led; -buck·ling** [+ *obj*] **:** to open the buckle of (something, such as a belt) ▪ She *unbuckled* her seat belt.

un·bur·den /ˌʌnˈbədn̩/ *verb* **-dens; -dened; -den·ing** [+ *obj*] **:** to take a problem or burden away from (someone or something) ▪ They tried to *unburden* her of her worries/troubles. [=tried to take away her worries/troubles]
unburden yourself **:** to talk about something that is causing you to feel worried, guilty, etc. ▪ When she asked what was bothering him, he welcomed the opportunity to *unburden himself.*
— un·bur·dened /ˌʌnˈbədn̩d/ *adj* ▪ She felt *unburdened* [=not burdened] by the expectations of other people. ▪ The book is *unburdened* by academic language and statistics.

un·but·ton /ˌʌnˈbʌtn̩/ *verb* **-tons; -toned; -ton·ing** [+ *obj*] **:** to open the buttons of (something) ▪ He *unbuttoned* his coat/shirt.

un·called–for /ˌʌnˈkɑːldˌfoə/ *adj* **:** not necessary or appropriate **:** not called for ▪ His jealousy is completely *uncalled-for.* ▪ *uncalled-for* insults

un·can·ny /ˌʌnˈkæni/ *adj* [*more* ~; *most* ~] **:** strange or unusual in a way that is surprising or difficult to understand ▪ She had an *uncanny* resemblance to someone I had seen before. ▪ She has an *uncanny* sense of direction. ▪ an *uncanny* ability to predict the weather
— un·can·ni·ly /ˌʌnˈkænəli/ *adv* ▪ He looks *uncannily* like a friend of mine. ▪ an *uncannily* realistic painting

un·cared for /ˌʌnˈkeəd-/ *adj* **:** not given attention or care ▪ The garden looked *uncared for.* [=*neglected*]

un·car·ing /ˌʌnˈkerɪŋ/ *adj* [*more* ~; *most* ~] **:** not feeling or showing concern for someone or something ▪ She has an *uncaring* attitude toward her schoolwork. ▪ He is a cold and *uncaring* man.

un·ceas·ing /ˌʌnˈsiːsɪŋ/ *adj* **:** never stopping **:** not ceasing ▪ *unceasing* efforts ▪ *unceasing* vigilance
— un·ceas·ing·ly /ˌʌnˈsiːsɪŋli/ *adv* ▪ They worked *unceasingly* [=*endlessly*] for peace.

un·cen·sored /ˌʌnˈsɛnsəd/ *adj* **:** expressed openly without removal of words or opinions that may shock or offend people **:** not censored ▪ The book reveals his *uncensored* thoughts about his political rivals. ▪ *uncensored* news reports

un·cer·e·mo·ni·ous /ˌʌnˌserəˈmoʊnijəs/ *adj* **:** happening or done very suddenly and quickly with no effort to be careful or polite ▪ His *unceremonious* dismissal by the new boss surprised everybody.
— un·cer·e·mo·ni·ous·ly *adv* ▪ The team *unceremoniously* dumped him at the end of the season.

un·cer·tain /ˌʌnˈsətn̩/ *adj* [*more* ~; *most* ~] **:** not certain: such as **a :** not exactly known or decided **:** not definite or fixed ▪ an *uncertain* quantity ▪ The time of departure is still *uncertain.* **b :** not sure **:** having some doubt about something ▪ We are still *uncertain* of the truth. ▪ She remains *uncertain* about her plans. ▪ I'm *uncertain* about how to respond. **c :** not definitely known ▪ an *uncertain* claim ▪ The cause of the fire is *uncertain.* **d :** likely to change **:** not constant or dependable ▪ *uncertain* weather ▪ He has an *uncertain* temper. ▪ They face a financially *uncertain* future.
in no uncertain terms **:** in a very clear and direct way ▪ My mother told me *in no uncertain terms* to never say that word again!
— un·cer·tain·ly *adv* ▪ "Should I leave?" I asked *uncertainly.* ▪ A drunk guy staggered *uncertainly* along the street.

un·cer·tain·ty /ˌʌnˈsətn̩ti/ *noun, pl* **-ties**
1 [*noncount*] **:** the quality or state of being uncertain **:** DOUBT ▪ There is some *uncertainty* about the company's future. ▪ He accepted the position without hesitation or *uncertainty.*
2 [*count*] **:** something that is doubtful or unknown **:** something that is uncertain — usually plural ▪ Life is full of *uncertainties.*

un·chal·lenged /ˌʌnˈʧæləndʒd/ *adj* **:** not questioned or doubted **:** not challenged ▪ His remark went *unchallenged* by the interviewer. ▪ She is the *unchallenged* authority in the field.

un·change·able /ˌʌnˈʧeɪndʒəbəl/ *adj* **:** not able to change or be changed ▪ The past is *unchangeable.* ▪ an *unchangeable* deadline

un·changed /ˌʌnˈʧeɪndʒd/ *adj* **:** not changed ▪ Their plans remain *unchanged.* ▪ My old neighborhood is still pretty much *unchanged.*

un·chang·ing /ˌʌnˈʧeɪndʒɪŋ/ *adj* **:** not changing **:** staying the same ▪ an *unchanging* truth ▪ *unchanging* traditions

un·char·ac·ter·is·tic /ˌʌnˌkerəktəˈrɪstɪk/ *adj* **:** not typical or usual **:** not characteristic ▪ It was an *uncharacteristic* outburst of temper. ▪ Her *uncharacteristic* silence bothered me.
— un·char·ac·ter·is·ti·cal·ly /ˌʌnˌkerəktəˈrɪstɪkli/ *adv* ▪ She was *uncharacteristically* irritable/quiet/tense.

un·char·i·ta·ble /ˌʌnˈʧerətəbəl/ *adj* [*more* ~; *most* ~] **:** very harsh in judging others **:** not charitable ▪ an *uncharitable* critic ▪ *uncharitable* comments
— un·char·i·ta·bly /ˌʌnˈʧerətəbli/ *adv* ▪ an *uncharitably* harsh review

un·chart·ed /ˌʌnˈʧɑətəd/ *adj* **:** not recorded or located on a map, chart, or plan ▪ an *uncharted* island — often used figuratively ▪ The discussion moved into ***uncharted territory/waters.*** [=moved into a new and unknown area]

un·checked /ˌʌnˈʧɛkt/ *adj* **:** not stopped, slowed, or controlled **:** not checked ▪ *unchecked* power ▪ The disease is often fatal if left *unchecked.* ▪ The rabbit population has grown/gone *unchecked.*

un·civ·il /ˌʌnˈsɪvəl/ *adj* [*more* ~; *most* ~] *formal* **:** rude or impolite ▪ *uncivil* behavior ▪ *uncivil* remarks
— un·civ·il·ly *adv*

un·civ·i·lized *also Brit* **un·civ·i·lised** /ˌʌnˈsɪvəˌlaɪzd/ *adj* [*more* ~; *most* ~] **:** not civilized: such as **a :** not polite, reasonable, or respectful ▪ *uncivilized* [=*rude*] behavior ▪ He was awakened at an *uncivilized* hour. **b :** showing no concern for the well-being of people or for the proper way to behave toward people ▪ They believe that capital punishment is *uncivilized.* **c** *old-fashioned* **:** not having the kinds of social systems, technologies, etc., that are seen in most modern societies ▪ *uncivilized* [=*primitive*] cultures

un·claimed /ˌʌnˈkleɪmd/ *adj* **:** not asked for or taken by an

U

owner : not claimed ▪ *unclaimed* property

un·clas·si·fied /ˌʌnˈklæsəˌfaɪd/ *adj* : not kept secret by the government ▪ *unclassified* documents ▪ *unclassified* information

un·cle /ˈʌŋkəl/ *noun, pl* **un·cles**

1 [*count*] : the brother of your father or mother or the husband of your aunt ▪ I have three *uncles* and two aunts. ▪ My *Uncle* David is visiting next week.

2 *US, informal* — used as a word that you say when you are being hurt in a fight to show that you admit being defeated and do not want to continue fighting ▪ He was forced to ***cry/say uncle***. [=forced to surrender]

and Bob's your uncle see BOB

un·clean /ˌʌnˈkliːn/ *adj*

1 : not clean : dirty ▪ Many of their health problems were caused by *unclean* living conditions.

2 : not innocent and good : morally impure ▪ *unclean* thoughts/desires

3 : not allowed to be used by religious law ▪ *unclean* meat

un·clear /ˌʌnˈkliə/ *adj* [*more* ~; *most* ~]

1 : difficult to understand ▪ Their directions were *unclear*. ▪ The cause of the disease remains *unclear*.

2 : confused or uncertain about something — often + *about* ▪ I'm a little *unclear about* what to do. ▪ She was *unclear about* whether she would attend.

un·clench /ˌʌnˈklɛntʃ/ *verb* **-clench·es; -clenched; -clench·ing** : to move (something) out of a tightly closed position and make it less tense [+ *obj*] He *unclenched* his jaw and took deep breaths. ▪ He *unclenched* his fist. [*no obj*] I could feel my jaw *unclenching* as the pain subsided.

Un·cle Sam /ˌʌŋkəlˈsæm/ *noun* [*noncount*] *informal* : the American government, nation, or people pictured or thought of as a person ▪ *Uncle Sam* wants you to join the Army!

Uncle Tom /ˌʌŋkəlˈtɑːm/ *noun, pl* **~ Toms** [*count*] *disapproving* : a black person who is eager to win the approval of white people and willing to cooperate with them

un·clog /ˌʌnˈklɑːg/ *verb* **-clogs; -clogged; -clog·ging** [+ *obj*] : to open (something) so things can pass or flow through ▪ He *unclogged* the drain/sink/toilet. ▪ He had a procedure done to *unclog* his arteries. ▪ finding ways to *unclog* busy roads

un·clothed /ˌʌnˈkloʊðd/ *adj, formal* : not wearing clothes : NAKED ▪ Police found the victim's *unclothed* body in the woods.

un·clut·tered /ˌʌnˈklʌtəd/ *adj* : not filled or covered with unnecessary things : not cluttered ▪ Her desk is always neat and *uncluttered*.

un·coil /ˌʌnˈkojəl/ *verb* **-coils; -coiled; -coil·ing** : to make (something that is curled or coiled) straight [+ *obj*] He *uncoiled* the rope. [*no obj*] The spring began to *uncoil*.

un·com·fort·able /ˌʌnˈkʌmfətəbəl/ *adj* [*more* ~; *most* ~]

1 a : causing a feeling of physical discomfort ▪ a very *uncomfortable* chair **b** : feeling physical discomfort ▪ You look *uncomfortable* in that chair. Would you like to sit here instead?

2 a : causing a feeling of being embarrassed or uneasy ▪ The silence went on so long that it became very *uncomfortable*. ▪ We were in the *uncomfortable* position of asking for money. **b** : feeling embarrassed or uneasy ▪ I was *uncomfortable* about talking to them. ▪ She's *uncomfortable* being in the spotlight.

– un·com·fort·ably /ˌʌnˈkʌmfətəbli/ *adv* ▪ The room was *uncomfortably* hot. ▪ They came *uncomfortably* close to having an accident.

un·com·mit·ted /ˌʌnkəˈmɪtəd/ *adj* : not yet supporting a particular person, belief, etc. : not committed ▪ *uncommitted* voters

un·com·mon /ˌʌnˈkɑːmən/ *adj* [*more* ~; *most* ~]

1 : not often found, seen, or experienced : UNUSUAL ▪ It is not *uncommon* for people to become depressed after they retire. ▪ *uncommon* plants/birds/animals

2 : not ordinary : remarkable or exceptional ▪ an athlete with *uncommon* ability ▪ a soldier of *uncommon* courage ▪ She is an *uncommon* woman.

– un·com·mon·ly *adv* ▪ He is *uncommonly* smart. ▪ an *uncommonly* cold winter ▪ an *uncommonly* good book

un·com·mu·ni·ca·tive /ˌʌnkəˈmjuːnəˌkeɪtɪv, ˌʌnkəˈmjuːnəkətɪv/ *adj* [*more* ~; *most* ~] : not tending or liking to talk or give out information ▪ a silent, *uncommunicative* [=*reserved*] person ▪ They have been *uncommunicative* with us about their plans. [=they have not told us about their plans]

un·com·pet·i·tive /ˌʌnkəmˈpɛtətɪv/ *adj* : not good enough to compete successfully with others : not competitive ▪ As long as the school system keeps offering *uncompetitive* wages, people looking for jobs will apply elsewhere.

un·com·plain·ing /ˌʌnkəmˈpleɪnɪŋ/ *adj* [*more* ~; *most* ~] *approving* : accepting, doing, or dealing with something difficult or unpleasant without complaining ▪ an *uncomplaining* worker

– un·com·plain·ing·ly /ˌʌnkəmˈpleɪnɪŋli/ *adv* ▪ She worked *uncomplainingly* in very difficult conditions.

un·com·plet·ed /ˌʌnkəmˈpliːtəd/ *adj* : not finished : not completed ▪ an *uncompleted* [=*unfinished*] building/memoir/play

un·com·pli·cat·ed /ˌʌnˈkɑːmpləˌkeɪtəd/ *adj* [*more* ~; *most* ~] : easy to understand, do, or use : not complicated ▪ The plot was *uncomplicated* and easy to follow. ▪ *uncomplicated* machinery ▪ He's an *uncomplicated*, straightforward person.

un·com·pli·men·ta·ry /ˌʌnˌkɑːmpləˈmɛntəri/ *adj* [*more* ~; *most* ~] : expressing a low opinion of someone or something : not complimentary ▪ an *uncomplimentary* comment/remark

un·com·pre·hend·ing /ˌʌnˌkɑːmprɪˈhɛndɪŋ/ *adj* : not understanding what is happening, being referred to, etc. ▪ They were *uncomprehending* of what was going on. : showing a lack of understanding or knowledge ▪ He gave me an *uncomprehending* look when I mentioned her name.

– un·com·pre·hend·ing·ly *adv* ▪ He looked at me *uncomprehendingly*.

un·com·pro·mis·ing /ˌʌnˈkɑːmprəˌmaɪzɪŋ/ *adj* [*more* ~; *most* ~] : not willing to change a decision, opinion, method, etc. : not willing to make or accept a compromise ▪ They were *uncompromising* in their demands. ▪ *uncompromising* standards of excellence

– un·com·pro·mis·ing·ly *adv*

un·con·cern /ˌʌnkənˈsən/ *noun* [*noncount*] : lack of care about or interest in something : INDIFFERENCE ▪ He has shown a surprising *unconcern* for his own safety.

un·con·cerned /ˌʌnkənˈsənd/ *adj* : not worried or upset : not concerned ▪ She's *unconcerned* about/with that issue. ▪ The economy seems to be slowing down, but many investors remain *unconcerned*.

– un·con·cern·ed·ly /ˌʌnkənˈsənədli/ *adv*

un·con·di·tion·al /ˌʌnkənˈdɪʃənl/ *adj* : not limited in any way : complete and absolute ▪ They demanded an *unconditional* surrender. ▪ He had an *unconditional* loyalty to his family. ▪ their *unconditional* love of their children

– un·con·di·tion·al·ly *adv* ▪ He loved her *unconditionally*.

un·con·firmed /ˌʌnkənˈfəmd/ *adj* : not supported by evidence : not confirmed ▪ an *unconfirmed* rumor/report

un·con·ge·nial /ˌʌnkənˈdʒiːnijəl/ *adj* [*more* ~; *most* ~] *formal*

1 : not pleasant or enjoyable ▪ an *uncongenial* task

2 : not proper or suited to a particular situation, person, etc. ▪ He was being asked to support a policy that was *uncongenial* to him.

un·con·nect·ed /ˌʌnkəˈnɛktəd/ *adj* : not related or connected ▪ The question is completely *unconnected* with/to the discussion. ▪ two *unconnected* murders ▪ The computer is *unconnected* to the network. ▪ The movie is about four seemingly *unconnected* people.

un·con·quer·able /ˌʌnˈkɑːŋkərəbəl/ *adj*

1 : not able to be conquered or defeated ▪ She has an *unconquerable* [=*indomitable*] spirit/will.

2 : not able to be dealt with successfully ▪ seemingly *unconquerable* [=*insurmountable*] difficulties/problems

un·con·scio·na·ble /ˌʌnˈkɑːnʃənəbəl/ *adj, formal*

1 : extremely bad, unfair, or wrong ▪ *unconscionable* cruelty

2 : going far beyond what is usual or proper ▪ They have had to endure *unconscionable* delays.

– un·con·scio·na·bly /ˌʌnˈkɑːnʃənəbli/ *adv* ▪ an *unconscionably* cruel nature ▪ an *unconscionably* long delay

[1]un·con·scious /ˌʌnˈkɑːnʃəs/ *adj* : not conscious: such as **a** : not awake especially because of an injury, drug, etc. ▪ He was knocked *unconscious* by a fall. ▪ She was *unconscious* for three days after the accident. **b** : not aware of something — usually + *of* ▪ He is *unconscious of* his mistake. ▪ She was *unconscious of* being watched. **c** : not intended or planned : not consciously done ▪ an *unconscious* mistake ▪ an *unconscious* bias

– un·con·scious·ly *adv* ▪ People constantly make decisions, consciously or *unconsciously*. **– un·con·scious-**

U

ness *noun [noncount]* ▪ He drifted into *unconsciousness.*

²unconscious *noun [noncount]* : the part of the mind that a person is not aware of but that is often a powerful force in controlling behavior — compare SUBCONSCIOUS

un·con·sid·ered /ˌʌnkənˈsɪdɚd/ *adj*
1 *formal* : not formed from careful thought ▪ *unconsidered* opinions/remarks
2 : not thought about ▪ a previously *unconsidered* strategy ▪ *unconsidered* trifles

un·con·sti·tu·tion·al /ˌʌnˌkɑːnstəˈtuːʃənl̩, ˌʌnˌkɒnstəˈtjuːʃənl̩/ *adj* : not allowed by the constitution of a country or government : not constitutional ▪ an *unconstitutional* infringement of rights ▪ The law may be *unconstitutional.*
– **un·con·sti·tu·tion·al·i·ty** /ˌʌnˌkɑːnstəˌtuːʃəˈnæləti, *Brit* ˌʌnˌkɒnstəˌtjuːʃəˈnæləti/ *noun [noncount]* – **un·con·sti·tu·tion·al·ly** *adv*

un·con·test·ed /ˌʌnkənˈtestəd/ *adj* : not having or involving disagreement, argument, or opposition ▪ an *uncontested* divorce [=a divorce which both people agree to] ▪ The Fifth Congressional District seat was *uncontested.* [=only one person ran in the election for the Fifth Congressional District seat] ▪ She ran *uncontested* for class treasurer.

un·con·trol·la·ble /ˌʌnkənˈtroʊləbəl/ *adj* : not able to be controlled ▪ *uncontrollable* anger ▪ an *uncontrollable* urge ▪ *uncontrollable* children
– **un·con·trol·la·bly** /ˌʌnkənˈtroʊləbli/ *adv* ▪ He was laughing *uncontrollably.*

un·con·trolled /ˌʌnkənˈtroʊld/ *adj* : happening or done without being stopped, slowed, or controlled ▪ the government's *uncontrolled* spending ▪ *uncontrolled* bleeding ▪ *uncontrolled* growth

un·con·ven·tion·al /ˌʌnkənˈvɛnʃənl̩/ *adj [more ~; most ~]* : very different from the things that are used or accepted by most people : not traditional or usual : not conventional ▪ an *unconventional* wardrobe ▪ Her lifestyle is rather *unconventional.* ▪ In his lectures, he encourages *unconventional* thinking. [=he encourages people to think in new and different ways]
– **un·con·ven·tion·al·i·ty** /ˌʌnkənˌvɛnʃəˈnæləti/ *noun [noncount]* – **un·con·ven·tion·al·ly** *adv* ▪ The class was encouraged to think *unconventionally.*

un·con·vinced /ˌʌnkənˈvɪnst/ *adj, not used before a noun [more ~; most ~]* : not completely sure or certain about something : not convinced ▪ The jury was *unconvinced* that the defendant was guilty.

un·con·vinc·ing /ˌʌnkənˈvɪnsɪŋ/ *adj [more ~; most ~]* : not able to make you believe that something is true, real, or acceptable : not convincing ▪ His arguments for changing the rules were *unconvincing.* ▪ a novel with *unconvincing* characters

un·cooked /ˌʌnˈkʊkt/ *adj* : not cooked : RAW ▪ *uncooked* meat

un·cool /ˌʌnˈkuːl/ *adj [more ~; most ~] informal*
1 : not popular or fashionable ▪ Her parents' car is totally *uncool.* ▪ *uncool* music
2 : not respectable or acceptable ▪ It's *uncool* to lie to your friends.

un·co·op·er·a·tive /ˌʌnkoʊˈɑːprətɪv/ *adj [more ~; most ~]* : not willing to do what someone wants or asks for : not cooperative ▪ *uncooperative* children ▪ an *uncooperative* witness [=a witness who will not talk to the police] ▪ We planned a picnic, but the weather was *uncooperative.* [=the weather was too bad for us to have a picnic]

un·co·or·di·nat·ed /ˌʌnkoʊˈoɚdəˌneɪtəd/ *adj [more ~; most ~]*
1 : not able to move different parts of your body together well or easily ▪ I'm too *uncoordinated* to be a good dancer.
2 : not well organized : not working together effectively ▪ Their efforts to manage the event were *uncoordinated.*

un·cork /ˌʌnˈkoɚk/ *verb* **-corks; -corked; -cork·ing** *[+ obj]*
1 : to remove a cork from (a bottle) ▪ *uncork* a bottle of wine
2 *informal* : to allow (something that was contained or controlled) to come out, escape, etc. ▪ The incident *uncorked* years of pent-up anger and frustration.

un·cor·rect·ed /ˌʌnkəˈrɛktəd/ *adj* : having errors or flaws ▪ an *uncorrected* manuscript : not corrected ▪ The problem remains *uncorrected.*

un·cor·rob·o·rat·ed /ˌʌnkəˈrɑːbəˌreɪtəd/ *adj* : not supported or proved by evidence ▪ *uncorroborated* evidence/testimony

un·count·able /ˌʌnˈkaʊntəbəl/ *adj* : too many to be counted : not countable ▪ an *uncountable* number of insects

un·count·ed /ˌʌnˈkaʊntəd/ *adj*
1 : not counted ▪ Their votes went *uncounted.*
2 : too many to be counted ▪ They spent *uncounted* hours on the project.

un·cou·ple /ˌʌnˈkʌpəl/ *verb* **-cou·ples; -cou·pled; -cou·pling** *[+ obj]* : to separate or disconnect (something) from something else ▪ They *uncoupled* the railroad cars.

un·couth /ˌʌnˈkuːθ/ *adj [more ~; most ~]* : behaving in a rude way : not polite or socially acceptable ▪ People thought he was *uncouth* and uncivilized. ▪ *uncouth* language/behavior

un·cov·er /ˌʌnˈkʌvɚ/ *verb* **-ers; -ered; -er·ing** *[+ obj]*
1 : to remove a cover from (something) ▪ *Uncover* the pot.
2 : to find or become aware of (something that was hidden or secret) ▪ Police *uncovered* a criminal plot. ▪ We are still trying to *uncover* (the truth about) what happened.
3 : to allow (something) to be seen by removing a covering ▪ Archaeologists *uncovered* the ruins of an ancient city.
– **un·cov·ered** /ˌʌnˈkʌvɚd/ *adj* ▪ She left the pot *uncovered* so the soup could cool.

un·cred·it·ed /ˌʌnˈkrɛdɪtəd/ *adj* : not named or listed as one of the people who created or performed in something (such as a movie) ▪ He was an *uncredited* actor in the movie. ▪ She had a small, *uncredited* role.

un·crit·i·cal /ˌʌnˈkrɪtɪkəl/ *adj [more ~; most ~] usually disapproving* : not expressing or willing to express appropriate criticism or disapproval : not critical ▪ The senator's *uncritical* support for the measure reflects his poor judgment. ▪ an *uncritical* newspaper article
– **un·crit·i·cal·ly** /ˌʌnˈkrɪtɪkli/ *adv*

un·cross /ˌʌnˈkrɑːs/ *verb* **-cross·es; -crossed; -cross·ing** *[+ obj]* : to move one arm, leg, etc., so that it is no longer over the other ▪ She *uncrossed* her legs.

un·crowd·ed /ˌʌnˈkraʊdəd/ *adj* : not containing a lot of people : not crowded ▪ an *uncrowded* beach ▪ The train was *uncrowded.*

un·crowned /ˌʌnˈkraʊnd/ *adj* : not having or wearing a crown : not officially recognized as a king or queen ▪ an *uncrowned* king — often used figuratively to describe someone who is considered the best or most successful person in a particular field or group ▪ He is the *uncrowned* king of comedy.

unc·tu·ous /ˈʌŋkʧəwəs/ *adj [more ~; most ~] formal + disapproving* — used to describe someone who speaks and behaves in a way that is meant to seem friendly and polite but that is unpleasant because it is obviously not sincere ▪ an *unctuous* hostess
– **unc·tu·ous·ly** *adv* – **unc·tu·ous·ness** *noun [noncount]*

un·cul·ti·vat·ed /ˌʌnˈkʌltəˌveɪtəd/ *adj* : not prepared or used for growing crops or plants : not cultivated ▪ *uncultivated* land

un·cul·tured /ˌʌnˈkʌlʧɚd/ *adj [more ~; most ~]* : not having or showing good education, tastes, and manners ▪ *uncultured* people

un·curl /ˌʌnˈkɚl/ *verb* **-curls; -curled; -curl·ing** : to make (something that is curled or coiled) straight *[+ obj]* *Uncurl* your toes. *[no obj]* The snake *uncurled* and slithered off.

un·cut /ˌʌnˈkʌt/ *adj* : not cut: such as **a** : allowed to continue growing ▪ an *uncut* forest/lawn ▪ His hair was *uncut* but neat. **b** : not cut into a different shape ▪ a raw, *uncut* diamond **c** : not shortened or edited ▪ the *uncut* version of the film

un·dam·aged /ˌʌnˈdæmɪʤd/ *adj* : not harmed or damaged in any way ▪ The stolen painting was returned *undamaged.*

un·dat·ed /ˌʌnˈdeɪtəd/ *adj* : not having a date written or printed on it ▪ *undated* letters/documents/photos

un·daunt·ed /ˌʌnˈdɑːntəd/ *adj [more ~; most ~]* : not afraid to continue doing something or trying to do something even though there are problems, dangers, etc. ▪ The firefighters were *undaunted* by the dangerous conditions they faced. ▪ *Undaunted,* they continued on their journey. ▪ *undaunted* firefighters
– **un·daunt·ed·ly** *adv*

un·de·cid·ed /ˌʌndɪˈsaɪdəd/ *adj*
1 : not having made a decision ▪ *undecided* voters — often + *about* ▪ She was *undecided about* what to do.
2 : not having an answer or result : not yet settled or resolved ▪ The question is still *undecided.* ▪ Much remains *undecided* about his future.

U

un·de·clared /ˌʌndɪˈkleɚd/ *adj* : not stated or decided in an official way : not declared ▪ The government has been waging an *undeclared* war against them for decades. ▪ an *undeclared* candidate ▪ a college student with an *undeclared* major ▪ *undeclared* income [=income not reported on a tax form]

un·dec·o·rat·ed /ˌʌnˈdɛkəˌreɪtəd/ *adj* : not having decorations ▪ an *undecorated* cake/wall

un·de·feat·ed /ˌʌndɪˈfiːtəd/ *adj* : not having or including any losses or defeats ▪ They were *undefeated* in their first nine games. [=they won their first nine games] ▪ an *undefeated* team/season

un·de·fend·ed /ˌʌndɪˈfɛndəd/ *adj* : not protected or defended ▪ There are hundreds of miles of *undefended* border between the two countries. ▪ She scored a point when the goal was left *undefended.*

un·de·fined /ˌʌndɪˈfaɪnd/ *adj* : not shown or described clearly ▪ The rules are still largely *undefined.* ▪ the department's *undefined* roles/powers ▪ an *undefined* amount of money

un·de·mand·ing /ˌʌndɪˈmændɪŋ, *Brit* ˌʌndɪˈmɑːndɪŋ/ *adj* [*more* ~; *most* ~] : not demanding: such as **a** : not requiring much time, attention, or effort ▪ an *undemanding* job **b** *of a person* : not expecting much time, attention, effort, etc., from other people : not difficult to satisfy ▪ He is an enjoyable, *undemanding* guest.

un·dem·o·crat·ic /ˌʌnˌdɛməˈkrætɪk/ *adj* [*more* ~; *most* ~] : not agreeing with democratic practices or ideals : not democratic ▪ an *undemocratic* government ▪ The proposed law is fundamentally *undemocratic.*

un·de·mon·stra·tive /ˌʌndɪˈmɑːnstrətɪv/ *adj* [*more* ~; *most* ~] : not showing emotion or feelings in a free and open way : not demonstrative ▪ His father was distant and *undemonstrative.*

un·de·ni·able /ˌʌndɪˈnajəbəl/ *adj* [*more* ~; *most* ~] : clearly true : impossible to deny ▪ an *undeniable* fact ▪ The band's popularity is *undeniable.*

— **un·de·ni·ably** /ˌʌndɪˈnajəbli/ *adv* ▪ She is *undeniably* [=*certainly*] the best tennis player of her time.

un·de·pend·able /ˌʌndɪˈpɛndəbəl/ *adj* [*more* ~; *most* ~] : not able to be trusted or relied on : not dependable ▪ an *undependable* car/employee

[1]**un·der** /ˈʌndɚ/ *prep*

1 : in or to a lower place than (something) : below or beneath (something) : UNDERNEATH ▪ They couldn't climb over the wall, so they dug a hole *under* it. ▪ Draw a line *under* each word you don't know. ▪ We sat *under* a tree and rested a while. ▪ I'm wearing a sweater *under* my jacket. ▪ The ball rolled *under* the car. ▪ He had a mechanic check *under* the hood (of the car). ▪ How long can you hold your breath *under* water? ▪ There were 12 of us living ***under one roof.*** [=in one place]

2 : guided or managed by (a person or group) ▪ The cafe is *under* new management. ▪ The army captured three forts while *under* the general's command. ▪ She has 12 employees (working) *under* her.

3 : controlled or affected by (something) ▪ He has been *under* a lot of pressure/stress at work lately. ▪ The roof collapsed *under* the weight of the snow. [=the weight of the snow on the roof caused it to collapse] ▪ The work was done *under* the direction/guidance/supervision of an architect. [=an architect directed/guided/supervised the work] ▪ She was not *under* a doctor's care [=she did not have a doctor] at the time of the accident. ▪ Driving while *under* the influence of alcohol [=driving while drunk] is dangerous and illegal. ▪ You will be *under* anesthesia during the operation. ▪ I can't work *under* these conditions! ▪ I would never, *under* any circumstances, agree to do such a thing. ▪ The company was *under* no obligation [=was not obligated/required] to release the information. ▪ I was ***under the impression*** [=I thought] that admission was free.

4 : in a particular state or condition : affected by a particular process ▪ The police put her ***under arrest.*** [=the police arrested her] ▪ The house is ***under construction.*** [=is now being built] ▪ The incident is currently ***under investigation.*** [=is being investigated] ▪ His suggestion is still ***under discussion/consideration/review*** [=is still being discussed/considered/reviewed] by the committee.

5 : according to (something) ▪ *Under* the terms of the lease, rent will be due on the first of each month. ▪ They have fulfilled all their obligations *under* the treaty.

6 : within the group that has (a particular title or label) ▪ The purchase is listed *under* "debits." ▪ Many of these foods would come *under* the heading (of) "delicacies" in certain parts of the world.

7 — used to say that a particular name is used to indicate something ▪ The table is reserved *under* my last name.

8 : less or lower than (a certain age, amount of money, etc.) ▪ All the children in the class are *under* the age of 14. ▪ We arrived in *under* an hour. ▪ You get all three items for *under* $10.

9 : hidden below (an outward appearance) ▪ *Under* that rough exterior, he is a kind and gentle man.

[2]**under** *adv*

1 a : in or into a position that is below or beneath something ▪ Pull the bed sheets tight then fold the ends *under.* ▪ He turned *under* his shirt's collar.; ***especially*** : in a position that is below the surface of water ▪ The whale surfaced briefly then dove *under* again. **b** : in a forward direction that passes below something ▪ The bridge was too low for the ship to sail *under.*

2 : less than an expected or stated number or amount ▪ A score of 60 is needed to pass; anything *under* is failing. ▪ Children aged five ***and under*** [=children who are five years old and younger] may enter the park for free. ▪ Most of the restaurant's entrees are $10 ***or under.*** [=they cost $10 or less than $10]

3 : into an unconscious state ▪ They had to put me *under* for surgery.

go under see [1]GO

under- *prefix*

1 : below ▪ *under*current ▪ *under*side ▪ *under*lying ▪ *under*shirt

2 : less than an expected or correct number or amount ▪ *under*appreciated ▪ *under*paid ▪ *under*estimate ▪ *under*age ▪ *under*charge ▪ *under*achieve ▪ *under*cook ▪ *under*developed ▪ *under*dressed

un·der·achiev·er /ˌʌndərəˈʧiːvɚ/ *noun, pl* **-ers** [*count*] : someone (such as a student or athlete) who does not perform as well or work as hard as he or she can — opposite OVERACHIEVER

— **un·der·achieve** /ˌʌndərəˈʧiːv/ *verb* **-achieves; -achieved; -achiev·ing** [*no obj*] ▪ Many students *underachieve* during their senior year. — **un·der·achieve·ment** /ˌʌndərəˈʧiːv/ *noun* [*noncount*]

un·der·ac·tive /ˌʌndɚˈæktɪv/ *adj* : not active enough ▪ an *underactive* thyroid

un·der·age /ˌʌndɚˈeɪʤ/ *adj* : too young to do something legally ▪ They were not allowed into the club because they were *underage.* ▪ *underage* drinking ▪ an *underage* driver — opposite OVERAGE

un·der·ap·pre·ci·at·ed /ˌʌndərəˈpriːʃiˌeɪtəd/ *adj* [*more* ~; *most* ~] : not appreciated or valued enough ▪ Her work is *underappreciated* by the critics. ▪ an *underappreciated* talent

[1]**un·der·arm** /ˈʌndɚˈɑɚm/ *adj*

1 *always used before a noun* : placed on or along the armpit ▪ *underarm* deodorant ▪ an *underarm* seam

2 *Brit* : [1]UNDERHAND 1 ▪ an *underarm* throw

[2]**un·der·arm** /ˌʌndɚˈɑɚm/ *adv, Brit* : [2]UNDERHAND ▪ He threw the ball *underarm.*

[3]**un·der·arm** /ˈʌndɚˌɑɚm/ *noun, pl* **-arms** [*count*] : ARMPIT

un·der·bel·ly /ˈʌndɚˌbɛli/ *noun, pl* **-lies**

1 [*count*] : the bottom part of an object or an animal's body — usually singular ▪ the *underbelly* of an airplane ▪ a whale's *underbelly*

2 [*singular*] : an area that is easy to attack or criticize ▪ the army's *underbelly* ▪ They exposed the *underbelly* of the nation's economic policy.

3 [*singular*] : a part of society, an organization, etc., that is hidden and usually unpleasant ▪ the sordid *underbelly* of city life ▪ the industry's dark *underbelly*

un·der·bid /ˌʌndɚˈbɪd/ *verb* **-bids; -bid; -bid·ding** [+ *obj*] : to offer to do work for less money than (another person or group) : to bid less than (someone else) ▪ We were *underbid* by another company [=another company offered to do a job for less money than we did] and we lost the contract.

un·der·brush /ˈʌndɚˌbrʌʃ/ *noun* [*noncount*] *chiefly US* : plants, bushes, and small trees growing under larger trees in a forest : UNDERGROWTH ▪ We made our way through the thick *underbrush.*

un·der·car·riage /ˈʌndɚˌkerɪʤ/ *noun, pl* **-riag·es** [*count*]

1 *chiefly US* : the supporting structures of a car, truck, etc.

2 : LANDING GEAR ▪ There was a problem with the plane's *undercarriage.*

un·der·charge /ˌʌndɚˈʧɑɚʤ/ *verb* **-charg·es; -charged;**

-charg·ing [+ *obj*] : to charge (someone) too little for something : to ask (someone) to pay too little money for something • They *undercharged* him for the book by $5. — opposite OVERCHARGE

un·der·class /ˈʌndɚˌklæs, *Brit* ˈʌndəˌklɑːs/ *noun, pl* **-class·es** [*count*] : a social class made up of people who are very poor and have very little power or chance to improve their lives : the lowest social class — usually singular • the suffering of the *underclass*

un·der·class·man /ˌʌndɚˈklæsmən, *Brit* ˌʌndəˈklɑːsmən/ *noun, pl* **-men** /-mən/ [*count*] *US* : a student in the first or second year of high school or college — compare UPPERCLASSMAN

un·der·clothes /ˈʌndɚˌklouz/ *or* **un·der·cloth·ing** /ˈʌndɚˌklouðɪŋ/ *noun* [*plural*] *formal* : UNDERWEAR

un·der·coat /ˈʌndɚˌkout/ *noun, pl* **-coats** [*count*] : a coat of paint that is put on a surface to prepare it for another coat of paint

un·der·cook /ˌʌndɚˈkʊk/ *verb* **-cooks; -cooked; -cook·ing** [+ *obj*] : to not cook (food) enough — usually used as *(be) undercooked* • The chicken *was undercooked*. [=*underdone*] — opposite OVERCOOK

un·der·cov·er /ˌʌndɚˈkʌvɚ/ *adj* : done or working in a secret way in order to catch criminals or collect information • an *undercover* investigation • *undercover* officers/agents

– **undercover** *adv* • He went *undercover* as a drug dealer. • The agent has worked *undercover* in several countries.

un·der·cur·rent /ˈʌndɚˌkɚrənt/ *noun, pl* **-rents** [*count*]

1 : a flow of water that moves below the surface of the ocean or a river • You could be pulled under water by the dangerous *undercurrents*.

2 : a hidden feeling or tendency that is usually different from the one that is easy to see or understand — usually + *of* • Despite the losing streak, there is an *undercurrent of* hope within the team. • *undercurrents of* resentment

un·der·cut /ˌʌndɚˈkʌt/ *verb* **-cuts; -cut; -cut·ting** [+ *obj*]

1 : to offer to sell things or work for a lower cost than (another person or company) • They *undercut* the competing store by 10 percent.

2 : to make (something) weaker or less effective : UNDERMINE • a law that *undercuts* the Constitution • Her behavior *undercuts* her own credibility.

un·der·de·vel·oped /ˌʌndɚdɪˈvɛləpt/ *adj* [*more* ~; *most* ~]

1 : not developed to a normal size or strength • The baby was born with *underdeveloped* lungs.

2 *of a country, society, etc.* : having many poor people and few industries • *underdeveloped* nations

un·der·dog /ˈʌndɚˌdɑːg/ *noun, pl* **-dogs** [*count*]

1 : a person, team, etc., that is expected to lose a contest or battle • I always root for the *underdog* instead of the favorite.

2 : a less powerful person or thing that struggles against a more powerful person or thing (such as a corporation) • As a lawyer, she consistently represented the *underdog*.

un·der·done /ˌʌndɚˈdʌn/ *adj* : not cooked enough • The chicken was *underdone*. [=*undercooked*] : not cooked completely • She likes her steak *underdone*. [=*rare*] — compare WELL-DONE

un·der·dress /ˌʌndɚˈdrɛs/ *verb* **-dress·es; -dressed; -dress·ing** [*no obj*] : to dress in clothes that are too informal or not warm enough for an occasion • I don't want to *underdress* for the party. — opposite OVERDRESS

– **underdressed** *adj* • They were *underdressed* for the wedding. • I was *underdressed* for the weather.

un·der·em·ployed /ˌʌndɚrɪmˈplɔɪd/ *adj* : having a job that does not use your skills • *underemployed* college graduates

– **un·der·em·ploy·ment** /ˌʌndɚɪmˈplɔɪmənt/ *noun* [*noncount*]

un·der·es·ti·mate /ˌʌndɚˈɛstəˌmeɪt/ *verb* **-mates; -mat·ed; -mat·ing** [+ *obj*]

1 : to estimate (something) as being less than the actual size, quantity, or number • The city *underestimated* the cost of the new building. • The number of people in the crowd was *underestimated* by 5,000.

2 : to think of (someone or something) as being lower in ability, influence, or value than that person or thing actually is • Never *underestimate* the importance of a good education. • Her talent has always been *underestimated*. — opposite OVERESTIMATE

– **un·der·es·ti·mate** /ˌʌndɚˈɛstəmət/ *noun, pl* **-mates** [*count*] • an *underestimate* of the cost • That number might be an *underestimate*. – **un·der·es·ti·ma·tion** /ˌʌndɚˌɛstəˈmeɪʃən/ *noun, pl* **-tions** [*count, noncount*]

un·der·ex·pose /ˌʌndɚɪkˈspouz/ *verb* **-pos·es; -posed; -pos·ing** [+ *obj*] : to allow too little light to fall on (film in a camera) when you are taking a photograph • The film was *underexposed* and the pictures came out too dark. • *underexposed* negatives/pictures

– **un·der·ex·po·sure** /ˌʌndɚɪkˈspouʒɚ/ *noun* [*noncount*]

un·der·fed /ˌʌndɚˈfɛd/ *adj* [*more* ~; *most* ~] : not given enough food to eat • The cat looked *underfed*.

un·der·floor heating /ˈʌndəˌflɔə-/ *noun* [*noncount*] *chiefly Brit* : a heating system that is placed under the floor of a building • The kitchen was updated with *underfloor heating*.

un·der·foot /ˌʌndɚˈfʊt/ *adv*

1 : below your feet • The ground was slippery *underfoot*. • We walked with dried leaves crunching *underfoot*.

2 : near your feet so as to make movement difficult — often used figuratively • It can be hard to clean the house with five children *underfoot*.

un·der·fund·ed /ˌʌndɚˈfʌndəd/ *adj* [*more* ~; *most* ~] : not having enough money to do what is needed • The city's school system is badly *underfunded*.

un·der·gar·ment /ˈʌndɚˌgɑɚmənt/ *noun, pl* **-ments** [*count*] *somewhat old-fashioned* : a piece of underwear

un·der·gird /ˌʌndɚˈgɚd/ *verb* **-girds; -gird·ed; -gird·ing** [+ *obj*] *chiefly US* : to strengthen or support (something) from below — usually used figuratively • Their way of life is *undergirded* by religious faith.

un·der·go /ˌʌndɚˈgou/ *verb* **-goes; -went** /-ˈwɛnt/; **-gone** /-ˈgɑːn/; **-go·ing** [+ *obj*] : to experience or endure (something) • She will have to *undergo* an operation. • He *underwent* a personal transformation [=he became a different sort of person] after his heart attack.

un·der·grad /ˈʌndɚˌgræd/ *noun, pl* **-grads** [*count*] *chiefly US* : UNDERGRADUATE

un·der·grad·u·ate /ˌʌndɚˈgrædʒəwət/ *noun, pl* **-ates** [*count*] : a student at a college or university who has not yet earned a degree • a group of college *undergraduates* — often used before another noun • an *undergraduate* program • *undergraduate* classes

[1]**un·der·ground** /ˈʌndɚˌgraund/ *adj*

1 : located or occurring below the surface of the earth • *underground* parking garages • an *underground* explosion — compare ABOVEGROUND, INGROUND

2 *always used before a noun* : secret and usually illegal • an *underground* deal • The drugs are supplied through an *underground* network.

3 *always used before a noun* : of, relating to, or produced in a social and artistic world that is different and separate from the main part of society • She loves the city's *underground* music scene. • *underground* newspapers/movies

[2]**un·der·ground** /ˌʌndɚˈgraund/ *adv*

1 : below the surface of the earth • The wires run *underground*. • animals that live *underground*

2 : in or into a place that is hidden or secret : out of the view of the public • They had been living *underground* as fugitives. • The political party ***went underground*** [=started working in secret] after the new government took power.

[3]**un·der·ground** /ˈʌndɚˌgraund/ *noun*

1 *Brit* : a system of trains that run below the ground in a large city : SUBWAY [*singular*] I've ridden on the New York subway, the Paris Metro, and the London *Underground*. [*noncount*] She commutes by *underground*.

2 ***the underground*** : a group of people who secretly work to oppose or overthrow a government

un·der·growth /ˈʌndɚˌgrouθ/ *noun* [*noncount*] : UNDERBRUSH

[1]**un·der·hand** /ˈʌndɚˌhænd/ *adj*

1 *US* : made with the hand brought forward and upward from below the shoulder • an *underhand* [=(*US*) *underhanded*, (*Brit*) *underarm*] throw — compare OVERHAND

2 [*more* ~; *most* ~] *chiefly Brit* : UNDERHANDED 1 • an *underhand* deal/tactic

[2]**underhand** *adv, US* : with an underhand motion • Throw the ball *underhand*.

un·der·hand·ed /ˌʌndɚˈhændəd/ *adj*

1 [*more* ~; *most* ~] *chiefly US* : done in a secret and dishonest way : intended to deceive or trick someone • People resented the *underhanded* [=(*chiefly Brit*) *underhand*] way that he came to power. • *underhanded* tactics/methods

2 *US* : [1]UNDERHAND 1 ▪ an *underhanded* throw
– **underhanded** *adv, US* ▪ She threw the ball *underhanded*.

un·der·lay /ˌʌndɚˈleɪ/ *noun, pl* **-lays** [*count*] : a layer of material that is placed under something else (such as a carpet)

un·der·lie /ˌʌndɚˈlaɪ/ *verb* **-lies; -lay** /-ˈleɪ/; **-lain** /-ˈleɪn/; **-ly·ing** [+ *obj*]
1 : to lie or be located under (something) ▪ A tile floor *underlies* the rug. ▪ The river is *underlain* by limestone.
2 : to form the basis or foundation of (an idea, a process, etc.) ▪ We discussed the principles that *underlay* their methods. ▪ A theme of revenge *underlies* much of her writing.

un·der·line /ˈʌndɚˌlaɪn/ *verb* **-lines; -lined; -lin·ing** [+ *obj*]
1 : to draw a line under (something) ▪ His name was *underlined* in the book.
2 : to emphasize (something) : to show the importance of (something) ▪ The accident *underlines* our need for better safety procedures.

un·der·ling /ˈʌndɚlɪŋ/ *noun, pl* **-lings** [*count*] *disapproving* : a person of low rank who works for a more powerful person : SUBORDINATE ▪ He takes all the credit, but most of the hard work is done by his *underlings*.

un·der·ly·ing /ˌʌndɚˈlajɪŋ/ *adj*
1 — used to identify the idea, cause, problem, etc., that forms the basis of something ▪ The argument relies on the *underlying* assumption that all criminals are dangerous. ▪ an *underlying* cause of the accident ▪ They're dealing with the symptoms but they haven't done anything about the *underlying* problem/disease.
2 : lying under or below something ▪ the ocean and the *underlying* rock

un·der·manned /ˌʌndɚˈmænd/ *adj* [*more* ~; *most* ~] : not having enough workers : UNDERSTAFFED ▪ *undermanned* construction crews

un·der·mine /ˌʌndɚˈmaɪn/ *verb* **-mines; -mined; -min·ing** [+ *obj*] : to make (someone or something) weaker or less effective usually in a secret or gradual way ▪ She tried to *undermine* my authority by complaining about me to my boss. ▪ The events of the past year have *undermined* people's confidence in the government.

[1]**un·der·neath** /ˌʌndɚˈni:θ/ *prep*
1 : below or beneath (something) : UNDER ▪ He hid the envelope *underneath* his coat. ▪ She slipped a note *underneath* the door. ▪ The ball rolled *underneath* the car. ▪ He lives in the apartment *underneath* mine.
2 : on the bottom of (something) ▪ There was gum stuck *underneath* the table.
3 : hidden below (an outward appearance) ▪ *Underneath* her calm exterior was a nervous woman with a hot temper. ▪ They actually had a lot in common *underneath* their obvious differences. ▪ He might seem unkind, but ***underneath it all*** [=*actually*], he's a very caring person.

[2]**underneath** *adv*
1 : below or beneath ▪ He wore a white sweater with a red shirt *underneath*. ▪ She lifted up the rock and found ants crawling *underneath*.
2 : on the lower side ▪ The car had rust *underneath*.

[3]**underneath** *noun*
the underneath *chiefly Brit* : the bottom surface of something : UNDERSIDE ▪ The plate had a name stamped on *the underneath*.

un·der·nour·ished /ˌʌndɚˈnɚrɪʃt/ *adj* [*more* ~; *most* ~] : not getting enough food or not getting enough healthy food for good health and growth ▪ *undernourished* children
– **un·der·nour·ish·ment** /ˌʌndɚˈnɚrɪʃmənt/ *noun* [*noncount*]

underpaid *past tense of* UNDERPAY

un·der·pants /ˈʌndɚˌpænts/ *noun* [*plural*]
1 *US* : underwear that people wear on the lower part of their bodies
2 *Brit* : underpants for men and boys

un·der·pass /ˈʌndɚˌpæs, *Brit* ˈʌndəˌpɑ:s/ *noun, pl* **-pass·es** [*count*] : a place where a road or railroad crosses under another road or railroad ▪ We stood on the bridge and looked down at the *underpass*. — compare OVERPASS

un·der·pay /ˌʌndɚˈpeɪ/ *verb* **-pays; -paid** /-ˈpeɪd/; **-pay·ing** : to pay too little for something [*no obj*] She *underpaid* for her meal. [+ *obj*] He realized that he had *underpaid* the cashier. ▪ The company *underpays* its workers. ▪ They are *underpaid* for the work they do. ▪ *underpaid* workers — opposite OVERPAY
– **un·der·pay·ment** *noun, pl* **-ments** [*count, noncount*]

un·der·per·form /ˌʌndɚpɚˈfoɚm/ *verb* **-forms; -formed; -form·ing** [*no obj*] : to be less successful than expected or required ▪ The report shows which schools are *underperforming*. ▪ *underperforming* stocks

un·der·pin /ˌʌndɚˈpɪn/ *verb* **-pins; -pinned; -pin·ning** [+ *obj*] : to strengthen or support (something) from below ▪ a wall *underpinned* by metal beams — usually used figuratively ▪ a report *underpinned* by ample research
– **un·der·pin·ning** /ˈʌndɚˌpɪnɪŋ/ *noun, pl* **-nings** [*count, noncount*] ▪ the moral *underpinnings* [=*basis*] of the administration's policies

un·der·play /ˌʌndɚˈpleɪ/ *verb* **-plays; -played; -play·ing** [+ *obj*]
1 : to make (something) seem less important than it actually is : to give too little attention to (something) ▪ Don't *underplay* the importance of exercise. ▪ She often *underplays* [=*downplays*] her abilities. — opposite OVERPLAY
2 *disapproving* : to show too little emotion when acting in a play, movie, etc. ▪ I thought she *underplayed* her character.

un·der·priv·i·leged /ˌʌndɚˈprɪvəlɪʤd/ *adj* [*more* ~; *most* ~] : having less money, education, etc., than the other people in a society : having fewer advantages, privileges, and opportunities than most people : poor or disadvantaged ▪ *underprivileged* students
the underprivileged : underprivileged people ▪ We have to find ways to help *the underprivileged*.

un·der·rate /ˌʌndɚˈreɪt/ *verb* **-rates; -rat·ed; -rat·ing** [+ *obj*] : to rate or value (someone or something) too low ▪ She *underrated* her student's ability.
– **underrated** *adj* [*more* ~; *most* ~] ▪ He is the most *underrated* player in the league. ▪ an *underrated* restaurant

un·der·score /ˈʌndɚˌskoɚ/ *verb* **-scores; -scored; -scor·ing** [+ *obj*]
1 : to emphasize (something) or show the importance of (something) ▪ These failures *underscore* the difficulty of what we're attempting to do. ▪ The President's visit *underscores* the administration's commitment to free trade.
2 : to draw a line under (something) : UNDERLINE ▪ She *underscored* the most important points.

un·der·sea /ˌʌndɚˈsi:/ *adj, always used before a noun* : found, done, or used below the surface of the sea ▪ an *undersea* volcano ▪ They are conducting *undersea* research. ▪ *undersea* cables/vessels

un·der·sec·re·tary /ˌʌndɚˈsɛkrəˌteri, *Brit* ˌʌndəˈsɛkrətri/ *noun, pl* **-tar·ies** [*count*] : a high-ranking government official who serves under a department secretary or other high official ▪ the U.S. *Undersecretary* of Defense

un·der·sell /ˌʌndɚˈsɛl/ *verb* **-sells; -sold** /-ˈsoʊld/; **-sell·ing** [+ *obj*]
1 : to sell goods for a lower price than (another person or company) ▪ They promised to *undersell* their competitors. ▪ We will not be *undersold*.
2 : to be sold at a lower price than (something else) ▪ imported cars that *undersell* domestic models

un·der·shirt /ˈʌndɚˌʃɚt/ *noun* **-shirts** [*count*] *US* : a shirt that has no collar and sometimes no sleeves and that is worn as underwear — see color pictures on page C13; compare VEST

un·der·shorts /ˈʌndɚˌʃoɚts/ *noun* [*plural*] : underpants for men or boys

un·der·side /ˈʌndɚˌsaɪd/ *noun, pl* **-sides**
1 [*count*] : the bottom side or part of something ▪ the *underside* of the table
2 [*singular*] : a part of life, a city, etc., that is hidden and usually unpleasant ▪ The book explores the *underside* of human nature. ▪ Hollywood's dark *underside*

un·der·signed /ˈʌndɚˌsaɪnd/ *noun*
the undersigned *formal* : the person whose name is signed or the people whose names are signed at the end of a document ▪ *The undersigned* agrees to pay all debts to the bank. ▪ We, *the undersigned*, object to the recent rulings.

un·der·sized /ˌʌndɚˈsaɪzd/ *adj* [*more* ~; *most* ~] : smaller than the usual size ▪ He is *undersized* for a basketball player. ▪ the bird's *undersized* wings

un·der·staffed /ˌʌndɚˈstæft, *Brit* ˌʌndəˈstɑ:ft/ *adj* [*more* ~; *most* ~] : not having enough workers : having a staff that is too small ▪ The office was *understaffed*. ▪ an *understaffed* hospital

un·der·stand /ˌʌndɚˈstænd/ *verb* **-stands; -stood** /-ˈstʊd/; **-stand·ing**
1 : to know the meaning of (something, such as the words that someone is saying or a language) : COMPREHEND [+

obj] Do you *understand* English? • "Did you *understand* what he said?" "Not a word (of it)." • I can't *understand* a word you're saying. • I don't *understand* these directions. • I didn't *understand* what you told me. = I didn't *understand* you. • If I *understand* you correctly [=if I understand what you are saying correctly], this needs to be changed. [*no obj*] I want you to stay away from her. Do you *understand*? • The work has to be finished today. *Understand*? [=do you understand what I am telling you?]

2 [+ *obj*] **: to know how (something) works or happens** • They *understand* local politics. • I don't *understand* how this is supposed to work. • He doesn't really *understand* the situation. • You should read the book in order to *understand* more about the subject. • I can't *understand* why she would do such a thing. • She's beginning to *understand* what's going on. • You have to *understand* that I had no other choice. • We still don't fully *understand* the causes of the disease. = The causes of the disease are still not fully *understood*.

3 a [+ *obj*] **: to know how (someone) thinks, feels, or behaves** • I *understand* [=*know*] him well enough to know that he won't want to go. • She *understands* children. • At first we didn't get along, but I think we *understand* each other now. **b : to feel sympathy for someone's feelings or situation** [+ *obj*] She had a similar experience, so she *understands* what I'm going through. • I can *understand* your/you feeling annoyed. [=I think you have good reason for feeling annoyed] [*no obj*] They will *understand* if you need some time off. • My cousin doesn't *understand* about these things.

4 [+ *obj*] **a : to think or believe (something)** • She was ***given to understand*** [=she was led to believe] that the job was hers. **— used to say what you believe to be true based on what you have heard, read, etc.** • I *understand* that they will arrive today. • As I *understand* it, this has been a problem for several years. • I *understand* that some doctors disagree. • He *understood* that he would be paid for the work. **b — used to say that something is agreed to or accepted and does not need to be discussed; usually used as *(be) understood*** • It's *understood* that more time will be needed. [=we all know/accept that more time will be needed] • He believed it *was understood* [=believed that everyone had agreed] that he would be paid for the work.

5 [+ *obj*] **: to think that (something) has a particular meaning : INTERPRET** • I *understood* the letter to be a refusal.

6 [+ *obj*] **— used to say that a word or phrase is thought of as having been said even though it is not actually said; usually used as *(be) understood*** • When people say "they're engaged," the phrase "to be married" *is understood*. [="they're engaged" is understood to mean "they're engaged to be married"]

make yourself understood see [1]MAKE

un·der·stand·able /ˌʌndɚˈstændəbəl/ *adj* [*more* ~; *most* ~]

1 : normal and reasonable for a particular situation • an *understandable* feeling/reaction • She made an *understandable* error. • It's perfectly *understandable* that you would feel sad.

2 : able to be understood • He can make scientific concepts *understandable* [=*comprehensible*] to the general public.

— un·der·stand·ably /ˌʌndɚˈstændəbli/ *adv* • She was *understandably* alarmed/upset/worried.

[1]**un·der·stand·ing** /ˌʌndɚˈstændɪŋ/ *noun*

1 : the knowledge and ability to judge a particular situation or subject — usually + *of* [*singular*] He has a thorough/full *understanding of* the subject. • She has a basic/better/deep *understanding of* the process. • I hope to get/gain a clearer *understanding of* the issues involved. [*noncount*] He seems to have little *understanding of* our situation.

2 [*singular*] **: an informal agreement** • We have an *understanding* that whoever cooks doesn't have to do the dishes. • After a long discussion they finally ***achieved/reached an understanding***. = After a long discussion they finally ***came to an understanding***. [=they finally agreed]

3 [*noncount*] **: a willingness to understand people's behavior and forgive them** • She treats them with kindness and *understanding*. • a relationship based on mutual *understanding*

4 [*singular*] **: your belief about something based on what you have heard, read, etc.** • My *understanding* was that you were going to help. = ***It was my understanding*** that you were going to help. [=I thought that you were going to help]

***on the understanding that* — used to say that something is done, accepted, etc., because you have been told that something else will happen or is true** • She agreed to do the work *on the understanding that* she would be paid now.

[2]**understanding** *adj* [*more* ~; *most* ~] **: showing sympathy and kindness : tolerant or sympathetic** • an *understanding* husband/wife • You've been very *understanding* [=*patient*] about his recent problems.

un·der·state /ˌʌndɚˈsteɪt/ *verb* **-states; -stat·ed; -stat·ing** [+ *obj*] **: to say that (something) is smaller, less important, etc., than it really is** • He *understated* his taxable income. • She's trying to *understate* the issue/problem.

un·der·stat·ed /ˌʌndɚˈsteɪtəd/ *adj* **: expressed or done in a quiet or simple way** • an *understated* style • an *understated* performance • *understated* elegance

un·der·state·ment /ˌʌndɚˈsteɪtmənt/ *noun, pl* **-ments**

1 [*count*] **: a statement that makes something seem smaller, less important, etc., than it really is** • To say that I didn't like the book is an *understatement*. [=I hated the book] • "I may have overreacted a little." "That's ***the understatement of the year!***" [=you overreacted very badly]

2 [*noncount*] **: the practice of describing things in a way that makes them seem smaller, less important, etc., than they really are** • He has a knack for *understatement*. • a masterpiece of *understatement*

understood *past tense and past participle of* UNDERSTAND

un·der·study /ˈʌndɚˌstʌdi/ *noun, pl* **-stud·ies** [*count*] **: an actor who prepares to take the part of another actor if that actor is unable to perform**

— understudy *verb* **-studies; -stud·ied; -study·ing** [*no obj*]

un·der·take /ˌʌndɚˈteɪk/ *verb* **-takes; -took** /-ˈtʊk/; **-tak·en** /-ˈteɪkən/; **-tak·ing** [+ *obj*] *formal*

1 : to begin or attempt (something) • *undertake* a task/journey • He's *undertaking* a thorough search. • The researchers *undertook* a series of studies.

2 : to agree or promise to do (something) — usually followed by *to + verb* • He *undertook to raise* his sister's child. • The company *undertook to end* the strike.

un·der·tak·er /ˈʌndɚˌteɪkɚ/ *noun, pl* **-ers** [*count*] **: a person whose job is to arrange and manage funerals : FUNERAL DIRECTOR**

un·der·tak·ing /ˈʌndɚˌteɪkɪŋ/ *noun, pl* **-ings**

1 [*count*] **: an important or difficult task or project** • The restoration of the old theater is a huge/major/massive *undertaking*. • He advised us against such a risky/dangerous *undertaking*. • a new creative *undertaking*

2 [*noncount*] **: the business of an undertaker** • a career in *undertaking*

3 [*count*] *Brit, formal* **: a promise or agreement to do or not do something** • The newspaper ***gave an undertaking*** [=*promised*] not to disclose his identity.

un·der·tone /ˈʌndɚˌtoʊn/ *noun, pl* **-tones** [*count*]

1 : a low or quiet voice • She commented in an *undertone* that the music was really not very good.

2 : a quality, meaning, etc., that is present but not clear or obvious • The play is a comedy with dark *undertones*. **— often + *of*** • There was an *undertone* [=*hint, undercurrent*] *of* fear throughout the city.

3 : a color that you can see in small amounts • The fabric is a rich brown color with *undertones of* red.

undertook *past tense and past participle of* UNDERTAKE

un·der·tow /ˈʌndɚˌtoʊ/ *noun, pl* **-tows** [*count*] **: a current in the sea or ocean that is below the surface and that moves away from the shore** • Don't get caught in the *undertow*.

un·der·used /ˌʌndɚˈjuːzd/ *adj* **: not used enough : not fully used** • *underused* land • Her talent is *underused*.

un·der·val·ue /ˌʌndɚˈvælju/ *verb* **-val·ues; -val·ued; -val·u·ing** [+ *obj*]

1 : to place too low a value on (something) • Experts *undervalued* the stock.

2 : to fail to give enough importance to (something) • Her contribution to the project was *undervalued*.

un·der·wa·ter /ˌʌndɚˈwɑːtɚ/ *adj* **: located, used, done, or happening below the surface of water** • *underwater* caves/volcanoes • *underwater* photography • an *underwater* camera

— underwater *adv* • swimming *underwater*

under way *or* **un·der·way** /ˌʌndɚˌweɪ/ *adv*

1 : in or into motion • The train has had to stop briefly, but it should be *under way* again soon. • The ship finally got *under way*. [=began sailing]

2 : happening now • Preparations for their arrival are already *under way*. • A search is *under way*. [=*in progress*]

un·der·wear /ˈʌndɚˌweɚ/ *noun* [*noncount*] **: clothing that is worn next to your skin and under other clothing** • He answered the door ***in his underwear***. [=while wearing only underwear] • You should pack a ***change of underwear***. [=addi-

U

tional underwear that you can wear at another time] ▪ ***long/ thermal underwear*** [=winter underwear that covers your arms and legs]

un·der·weight /ˌʌndɚˈweɪt/ *adj* [*more* ~; *most* ~] : weighing less than the normal or expected amount : too light ▪ He is slightly *underweight.* ▪ She had become dangerously *underweight.* [=*thin*]

underwent *past tense of* UNDERGO

un·der·whelm /ˌʌndɚˈwɛlm/ *verb* **-whelms; -whelmed; -whelm·ing** [+ *obj*] *somewhat humorous* : to fail to impress (someone) ▪ I was *underwhelmed* by the evidence/performance. [=the evidence/performance was not very good and did not impress me]
– **underwhelming** *adj* ▪ The evidence is *underwhelming.* [=not very good or convincing] ▪ an *underwhelming* performance

un·der·wire /ˈʌndɚˌwajɚ/ *noun, pl* **-wires** [*count, noncount*] *chiefly US* : wire running through the bottom edge of a brassiere to provide support for a woman's breasts
– **underwire** (*chiefly US*) *or Brit* **un·der·wired** /ˈʌndɚˌwajɚd/ *adj* ▪ an *underwire* bra

un·der·world /ˈʌndɚˌwɚld/ *noun* [*singular*]
1 : the world of crime and criminals ▪ the criminal *underworld* ▪ an *underworld* spy
2 ***the underworld*** : the place where dead people go in Greek myths

un·der·write /ˈʌndɚˌraɪt/ *verb* **-writes; -wrote** /-ˌroʊt/; **-writ·ten** /-ˌrɪtn/; **-writ·ing** [+ *obj*]
1 *formal* : to give money to support (something, such as a new business) and agree to be responsible for any losses if it fails ▪ *underwrite* an expedition/project
2 *technical* : to agree to pay for a certain kind of loss or damage by offering (an insurance policy) ▪ *underwrite* a homeowner's policy
3 *technical* : to agree to buy (shares) that are not bought by investors when the shares are first offered for sale
– **un·der·writ·er** /ˈʌndɚˌraɪtɚ/ *noun, pl* **-ers** [*count*] ▪ an insurance *underwriter*

un·de·served /ˌʌndɪˈzɚvd/ *adj* : not earned or deserved : unfair or unjustified ▪ She was given *undeserved* credit for the idea. ▪ an *undeserved* reputation ▪ Her promotion wasn't entirely *undeserved.*

un·de·serv·ing /ˌʌndɪˈzɚvɪŋ/ *adj* [*more* ~; *most* ~]
1 : not having qualities that deserve praise, support, etc. ▪ The article is written well but the author chose an *undeserving* subject. ▪ He left all his money to his *undeserving* children. ▪ (*old-fashioned*) the ***undeserving poor*** [=poor people who have bad moral character and do not deserve to be helped]
2 *not used before a noun* — used to say that someone should not have or be given something; + *of* ▪ He is *undeserving of* the criticism he has received. [=he does not deserve the criticism he has received]

un·de·sir·able /ˌʌndɪˈzaɪrəbəl/ *adj* [*more* ~; *most* ~] : bad, harmful, or unpleasant ▪ an *undesirable* behavior/habit ▪ The drug has some *undesirable* side effects. ▪ This may have *undesirable* consequences. : not worth having or getting : not desirable ▪ Frankly, it's an *undesirable* and unpleasant job.
– **un·de·sir·abil·i·ty** /ˌʌndɪˌzaɪrəˈbɪləti/ *noun* [*noncount*]
– **un·de·sir·ably** /ˌʌndɪˈzaɪrəbli/ *adv* ▪ costs are *undesirably* high

un·de·sir·ables /ˌʌndɪˈzaɪrəbəlz/ *noun* [*plural*] : people who are considered to be dangerous or immoral ▪ That bar seems to attract a lot of *undesirables.*

un·de·sired /ˌʌndɪˈzajɚd/ *adj* [*more* ~; *most* ~] : UNWANTED ▪ *undesired* behaviors ▪ an *undesired* outcome

un·de·tect·able /ˌʌndɪˈtɛktəbəl/ *adj* : impossible to discover or notice : not detectable ▪ problems which are *undetectable* by modern medicine

un·de·tect·ed /ˌʌndɪˈtɛktəd/ *adj* : not noticed by anyone : not detected ▪ The tumor was/went/remained *undetected* for years. ▪ No one can slip by the guards *undetected.*

un·de·terred /ˌʌndɪˈtɚd/ *adj* : not discouraged or stopped by problems, criticism, etc. ▪ Despite the opposition to their proposal, they remain *undeterred.* ▪ The team was *undeterred* by their recent losses.

un·de·vel·oped /ˌʌndɪˈvɛləpt/ *adj* [*more* ~; *most* ~]
1 *of land* : not used for building, farming, industry, etc. ▪ *undeveloped* areas
2 *of a country, society, etc.* : having many poor people and a low level of industrial production : not developed ▪ an *undeveloped* nation
3 : not fully grown or developed ▪ *undeveloped* skills

un·dies /ˈʌndiz/ *noun* [*plural*] *informal* : UNDERWEAR; *especially* : underpants or panties ▪ a pair of *undies* ▪ wearing *undies* and a bra

un·dif·fer·en·ti·at·ed /ˌʌnˌdɪfəˈrɛnʃiˌeɪtəd/ *adj* : not divided or able to be divided into different parts ▪ an *undifferentiated* mass

un·dig·ni·fied /ˌʌnˈdɪgnəˌfaɪd/ *adj* [*more* ~; *most* ~] : not serious or formal : not dignified ▪ Some people thought her behavior was *undignified.* [=*silly, embarrassing*] ▪ There was an *undignified* rush to the door as soon as the meeting ended.

un·di·lut·ed /ˌʌnˌdaɪˈluːtəd/ *adj*
1 *literary, of emotions* : very strong : not mixed with other emotions ▪ *undiluted* joy/pleasure
2 *of a liquid* : not mixed with water ▪ *undiluted* [=*pure*] whiskey

un·di·min·ished /ˌʌndəˈmɪnɪʃt/ *adj* : not less, smaller, or weaker ▪ She continued to work with *undiminished* enthusiasm. ▪ His interest in the project remains *undiminished.*

un·dis·charged /ˌʌndɪsˈʧɑɚʤd/ *adj, Brit* — used to describe a person who has been declared bankrupt by a court of law but who is still required to pay back money that is owed ▪ an ***undischarged bankrupt***

un·dis·ci·plined /ˌʌnˈdɪsəplənd/ *adj* [*more* ~; *most* ~] : behaving in a way that is not properly controlled, organized, serious, etc. : lacking discipline ▪ He has been very *undisciplined* about studying. ▪ *undisciplined* children

un·dis·closed /ˌʌndɪˈsklouzd/ *adj* : not made known to the public : not named or identified ▪ an *undisclosed* sale of stock ▪ They settled out of court for an *undisclosed* amount.

un·dis·cov·ered /ˌʌndɪˈskʌvɚd/ *adj* : not having been found or noticed : not discovered ▪ *undiscovered* territory

un·dis·crim·i·nat·ing /ˌʌndɪˈskrɪməˌneɪtɪŋ/ *adj* [*more* ~; *most* ~] : unable to notice the differences between things that are of good quality and those that are not ▪ *undiscriminating* tastes

un·dis·guised /ˌʌndəˈskaɪzd/ *adj, of a feeling* : not concealed or hidden ▪ *undisguised* [=*obvious*] fear/hatred

un·dis·mayed /ˌʌndɪˈsmeɪd/ *adj* : not worried or upset ▪ He was *undismayed* [=*untroubled*] by the setbacks.

un·dis·put·ed /ˌʌndɪˈspjuːtəd/ *adj*
1 : definitely true : not doubted or questioned ▪ the *undisputed* facts of the case ▪ It is *undisputed* that he knew the defendant.
2 : accepted by everyone ▪ the *undisputed* leader/champion

un·dis·turbed /ˌʌndɪˈstɚbd/ *adj*
1 : not moved, changed, touched, etc., by anyone or anything ▪ an *undisturbed* forest/tomb ▪ an area *undisturbed* by industrialization ▪ I'd like to work *undisturbed* for a while. [=I'd like to work without being disturbed/interrupted for a while] ▪ The nest should be ***left undisturbed.*** [=*left alone*]
2 : not upset or affected by something ▪ She was *undisturbed* by the changes.

un·di·vid·ed /ˌʌndəˈvaɪdəd/ *adj*
1 : complete or total ▪ You have my *undivided* [=*full*] attention.
2 : not separated into smaller parts ▪ an *undivided* property

un·do /ˌʌnˈduː/ *verb* **-does; -did** /-ˈdɪd/; **-done** /-ˈdʌn/; **-do·ing** [+ *obj*]
1 : to open or release (something) : to unfasten or loosen (something) ▪ *undo* a belt/button/zipper ▪ She *undid* [=*unbuttoned*] her blouse. ▪ I can't *undo* [=*untie*] this knot.
2 : to change or stop the effect of (something) : REVERSE ▪ You can't *undo* the past. ▪ The damage cannot be *undone.* ▪ (*computers*) Will the program let me *undo* a change if I make a mistake?
3 *formal* : to cause the failure of (someone or something) ▪ He was *undone* by greed.
— see also UNDONE

un·doc·u·ment·ed /ˌʌnˈdɑːkjəˌmɛntəd/ *adj*
1 : not having the official documents that are needed to enter, live in, or work in a country legally ▪ *undocumented* workers/aliens/immigrants
2 : not supported by evidence that consists of documents : not having written proof ▪ The company cannot reimburse you for *undocumented* travel expenses.

un·do·ing /ˌʌnˈduːwɪŋ/ *noun* [*singular*]
1 : something that causes someone's failure, ruin, etc. ▪ My quick temper ***was my undoing.***
2 : a state of failure, ruin, etc. ▪ His quick temper helped lead to his *undoing.* ▪ The incident resulted in her *undoing.*

un·done /ˌʌnˈdʌn/ *adj, not used before a noun*
1 : not fastened or tied ▪ My shoelace is *undone.* = My shoelace has ***come undone.***
2 : not done : unfinished ▪ There were still some tasks ***left undone.***
3 *old-fashioned* : defeated or destroyed ▪ "... I am spoil'd, *undone* by villains!" —Shakespeare, *Othello* (1603–05)

un·doubt·ed /ˌʌnˈdaʊtəd/ *adj* : definitely true or existing : not doubted ▪ an *undoubted* [=*undisputed*] truth/fact ▪ his *undoubted* [=*undeniable*] charm
— **un·doubt·ed·ly** *adv* ▪ She was *undoubtedly* [=*without a doubt*] one of the best athletes in the school.

un·dreamed of /ˌʌnˈdri:md-/ *also chiefly Brit* **un·dreamt of** /ˌʌnˈdrɛmt-/ *adj* : much more or better than you thought was possible ▪ opportunities *undreamed of* 10 years ago — usually used as *undreamed–of* or *undreamt–of* before a noun ▪ an *undreamed-of* opportunity

¹un·dress /ˌʌnˈdrɛs/ *verb* **-dress·es**; **-dressed**; **-dress·ing**
1 [*no obj*] : to take your clothes off ▪ She *undressed* and climbed into bed.
2 [+ *obj*] : to remove the clothes of (someone) ▪ She *undressed* the children for bed.

²undress *noun* [*noncount*] *formal* : a state of wearing no clothing or of not being fully dressed ▪ partial *undress* ▪ She was in a ***state of undress.*** [=she was not dressed]

un·dressed /ˌʌnˈdrɛst/ *adj*
1 *not used before a noun* : wearing no clothing : not dressed ▪ I was *undressed* when the fire alarm went off. ▪ She ***got undressed*** [=took off her clothes] and went to bed.
2 : not cared for or covered ▪ an *undressed* wound
3 *technical* : not finished : not prepared for use ▪ *undressed* hides/stones

un·drink·able /ˌʌnˈdrɪŋkəbəl/ *adj* : unhealthy or unpleasant to drink ▪ The water was *undrinkable* and had to be boiled. ▪ an *undrinkable* wine

un·due /ˌʌnˈdu:, *Brit* ˌʌnˈdju:/ *adj, always used before a noun, formal* : more than is reasonable or necessary : EXCESSIVE ▪ *undue* pressure/influence ▪ These requirements shouldn't cause you any *undue* hardship/burden. ▪ His writing is elegant without calling *undue* attention to itself.

un·du·late /ˈʌnʤəˌleɪt, *Brit* ˈʌndjəˌleɪt/ *verb* **-lates**; **-lat·ed**; **-lat·ing** [*no obj*] *formal* : to move or be shaped like waves ▪ *undulating* hills ▪ an *undulating* surface
— **un·du·la·tion** /ˌʌnʤəˈleɪʃən, *Brit* ˌʌndjəˈleɪʃən/ *noun, pl* **-tions** [*count*]

un·du·ly /ˌʌnˈdu:li, *Brit* ˌʌnˈdju:li/ *adv, formal* : to an extreme, unreasonable, or unnecessary degree : EXCESSIVELY ▪ He wasn't *unduly* troubled/concerned. ▪ taxes that *unduly* burden homeowners ▪ The punishment was *unduly* harsh.

un·dy·ing /ˌʌnˈdajɪŋ/ *adj, always used before a noun* : lasting forever : never ending ▪ *undying* gratitude/love ▪ He swore his *undying* devotion to her.

un·earned /ˌʌnˈənd/ *adj* : not earned by working ▪ Bank interest is regarded as *unearned* income.

un·earth /ˌʌnˈəθ/ *verb* **-earths**; **-earthed**; **-earth·ing** [+ *obj*]
1 : to find (something) that was buried in the earth ▪ *unearth* [=*dig up*] buried treasure
2 : to find or discover (something) that was hidden or lost ▪ *unearth* a secret ▪ An old document was *unearthed* from the files. ▪ They *unearthed* evidence that he had accepted bribes.

un·earth·ly /ˌʌnˈəθli/ *adj*
1 : very strange, unnatural, and frightening ▪ an *unearthly* scream
2 *Brit* : unreasonably early or late ▪ She was up at an/some ***unearthly hour.*** [=*ungodly hour*] ▪ We left at the ***unearthly time*** of 5:00 a.m.

un·ease /ˌʌnˈi:z/ *noun* [*noncount*] : a feeling of worry or unhappiness ▪ A feeling of *unease* came over her. ▪ They noticed increasing signs of *unease* among the workers. — often + *about* ▪ I couldn't shake a sense of *unease about* what he told me. ▪ He had a feeling of *unease about* the future.

un·easy /ˌʌnˈi:zi/ *adj* [*more ~; most ~*]
1 : worried or unhappy about something ▪ Rain made the crew *uneasy.* ▪ I'm (feeling) *uneasy* about/with the change.
2 : likely to change or end : not secure or settled ▪ an *uneasy* truce/alliance ▪ He has an *uneasy* relationship with his father.
3 : awkward and uncomfortable : not relaxed ▪ an *uneasy* silence ▪ She's *uneasy* among strangers. ▪ We spent an *uneasy* night waiting for news.
— **un·eas·i·ly** /ˌʌnˈi:zəli/ *adv* ▪ She looked around *uneasily.*
— **un·eas·i·ness** *noun* [*noncount*]

un·eat·en /ˌʌnˈi:tn̩/ *adj* : not eaten ▪ A lot of *uneaten* food remained after the banquet ended. ▪ Most of her meal was left *uneaten.*

un·eco·nom·ic /ˌʌnˌɛkəˈnɑ:mɪk/ *adj*
1 : not making a profit ▪ an *uneconomic* business
2 : UNECONOMICAL ▪ an *uneconomic* car

un·eco·nom·i·cal /ˌʌnˌɛkəˈnɑ:mɪkəl/ *adj* [*more ~; most ~*] : not using money, resources, etc., in a careful way : not economical ▪ an *uneconomical* car ▪ It is *uneconomical* [=too expensive] to keep the factory running.

un·ed·i·fy·ing /ˌʌnˈɛdəˌfajɪŋ/ *adj* [*more ~; most ~*] *formal* : unpleasant and offensive : causing embarrassment ▪ an *unedifying* sight/spectacle

un·ed·u·cat·ed /ˌʌnˈɛʤəˌkeɪtəd/ *adj* [*more ~; most ~*] : having or showing little or no formal schooling : not educated ▪ an *uneducated* man ▪ *uneducated* speech

un·emo·tion·al /ˌʌnɪˈmoʊʃənl/ *adj* [*more ~; most ~*] : not emotional : not showing emotion ▪ an *unemotional* voice/manner ▪ He was a cold and *unemotional* person.

un·em·ploy·able /ˌʌnɪmˈplojəbəl/ *adj* : lacking the skills, abilities, or qualities that are necessary to get or keep a job : not employable ▪ His drug addiction has made him *unemployable.*

un·em·ployed /ˌʌnɪmˈplɔɪd/ *adj* : having no job : not employed ▪ *unemployed* workers ▪ I'm currently *unemployed.*
the unemployed : people who have no jobs ▪ centers for *the unemployed* ▪ Many of *the* city's *unemployed* are former factory workers.

un·em·ploy·ment /ˌʌnɪmˈplɔɪmənt/ *noun* [*noncount*]
1 : the state of not having a job ▪ My *unemployment* lasted about six months. ▪ workers facing *unemployment*
2 : the total number of people who do not have jobs in a particular place or area ▪ high/low *unemployment* ▪ the level of *unemployment* ▪ *Unemployment* has been increasing/rising for months. ▪ The current ***unemployment rate*** is six percent.
3 *US* : money paid by the government to someone who does not have a job ▪ She was ***on unemployment*** for a few months. = She was receiving/collecting *unemployment* for a few months. — called also *unemployment benefits,* (*Brit*) *unemployment benefit,* (*US*) *unemployment compensation*

un·end·ing /ˌʌnˈɛndɪŋ/ *adj* : lasting forever ▪ an *unending* [=*endless, never-ending*] quest/supply

un·en·dur·able /ˌʌnɪnˈdərəbəl, *Brit* ˌʌnɪnˈdjuərəbəl/ *adj* : too unpleasant, painful, etc., to accept or endure ▪ *unendurable* [=*unbearable*] pain/stress/suffering

un·en·light·ened /ˌʌnɪnˈlaɪtn̩d/ *adj* [*more ~; most ~*] : not having or showing a good understanding of how people should be treated ▪ *unenlightened* people/comments ▪ his *unenlightened* [=*ignorant*] attitude about women's rights

un·en·thu·si·as·tic /ˌʌnɪnˌθu:ziˈæstɪk, *Brit* ˌʌnɪnˌθju:ziˈæstɪk/ *adj* [*more ~; most ~*] : having or showing a lack of excitement or interest : not enthusiastic ▪ She seemed *unenthusiastic* about the idea. ▪ an *unenthusiastic* response

un·en·vi·able /ˌʌnˈɛnvijəbəl/ *adj* [*more ~; most ~*] : very bad or unpleasant ▪ I was given the *unenviable* task of cleaning the toilets. ▪ He found himself in the *unenviable* position of having to admit he'd lied.

un·equal /ˌʌnˈi:kwəl/ *adj*
1 : not the same in a way that is unfair : giving more advantages, power, etc., to some people and less to other people for unfair reasons ▪ *unequal* academic standards for male and female students ▪ *unequal* justice/treatment based on race ▪ an *unequal* contest/fight ▪ the *unequal* [=*uneven*] distribution of wealth/resources
2 : different in number, degree, quality, size, etc. ▪ *unequal* amounts ▪ The two boards are ***unequal in*** length/size. = The two boards are ***of unequal*** length/size.
3 *not used before a noun* : not able to do what is needed — + *to* ▪ She felt *unequal to* the job. [=she felt that she could not do the job]
— **un·equal·ly** *adv* ▪ He treats them *unequally.*

un·equaled *also chiefly Brit* **un·equalled** /ˌʌnˈi:kwəld/ *adj* : better than all others : UNPARALLELED ▪ an *unequaled* achievement/talent

un·equiv·o·cal /ˌʌnɪˈkwɪvəkəl/ *adj, formal* : very strong and clear : not showing or allowing any doubt : not equivocal ▪ *unequivocal* evidence ▪ Her answer was an *unequivocal* yes/no. ▪ He told them in ***(clear and) unequivocal terms*** what was expected of them.

– un·equiv·o·cal·ly /ˌʌnɪˈkwɪvəkli/ *adv* ▪ She refused *unequivocally.*

un·err·ing /ˌʌnˈɛrɪŋ, ˌʌnˈərɪŋ/ *adj, formal* : always right and accurate : making no errors ▪ She has an *unerring* instinct for language. ▪ He has an *unerring* sense of good taste.
– un·err·ing·ly *adv*

un·eth·i·cal /ˌʌnˈɛθɪkəl/ *adj [more ~; most ~]* : morally bad : not ethical ▪ *unethical* behavior/methods ▪ a medical procedure that she considers *unethical*
– un·eth·i·cal·ly /ˌʌnˈɛθɪkli/ *adj*

un·even /ˌʌnˈiːvən/ *adj* : not even: such as **a** *[more ~; most ~]* : not level, flat, or smooth ▪ large *uneven* teeth ▪ *uneven* handwriting ▪ an *uneven* surface/texture **b** *[more ~; most ~]* : not straight or parallel ▪ *uneven* edges **c** *[more ~; most ~]* : not following a regular pattern : not the same in all parts or at all times : IRREGULAR ▪ *uneven* heating/drying ▪ His breathing was shallow and *uneven.* ▪ You should check your car's tires often for signs of *uneven* wear. **d** *[more ~; most ~]* : better in some parts than in others : not consistently good ▪ an *uneven* performance **e** *[more ~; most ~]* : unequal or unfair : giving an advantage to one side or group ▪ an *uneven* distribution of wealth/resources **f** *[more ~; most ~]* : more likely to be won easily by one side than the other : having competitors with an unequal chance of winning ▪ an *uneven* match **g** : ODD 5a ▪ We have an *uneven* number of players, so we'll have to rotate.
– un·even·ly *adv* ▪ *unevenly* cooked food ▪ *unevenly* matched teams ▪ The money was distributed *unevenly.*
– un·even·ness /ˌʌnˈiːvənnəs/ *noun [noncount]*

uneven bars *noun [plural] sports* : a pair of long bars that are supported by a base, are parallel to each other at different heights, and are used in gymnastics — called also *uneven parallel bars*; compare PARALLEL BARS

un·event·ful /ˌʌnɪˈvɛntfəl/ *adj [more ~; most ~]* : having nothing exciting, interesting, or unusual happening : not eventful ▪ an *uneventful* vacation/day/life ▪ The flight home was *uneventful.*
– un·event·ful·ly *adv* ▪ The day began *uneventfully.*

un·ex·cep·tion·able /ˌʌnɪkˈsɛpʃənəbəl/ *adj, formal* : not likely to cause objection or offense — usually used to describe something that is good but not outstanding or excellent ▪ Her work was *unexceptionable.*

un·ex·cep·tion·al /ˌʌnɪkˈsɛpʃənəl/ *adj [more ~; most ~]* : not unusually good, interesting, etc. : not exceptional ▪ an *unexceptional* [=*unremarkable*] student/writer ▪ As an actor he was *unexceptional*, but he had a beautiful singing voice.

un·ex·pect·ed /ˌʌnɪkˈspɛktəd/ *adj* : not expected ▪ *unexpected* consequences/results ▪ *unexpected* guests ▪ an *unexpected* turn of events ▪ The story is full of *unexpected* [=*surprising*] twists. ▪ I'm sad that she's leaving, but it was not *unexpected.* ▪ Drivers must always be prepared to deal with ***the unexpected***. [=things that happen unexpectedly]
– un·ex·pect·ed·ly *adv* ▪ Guests arrived *unexpectedly.* ▪ Sales were *unexpectedly* high this month.

un·ex·plained /ˌʌnɪkˈspleɪnd/ *adj* : having no known reason or cause : not explained ▪ an *unexplained* death/illness ▪ For some *unexplained* reason, the plane went off course.

un·ex·plod·ed /ˌʌnɪkˈsploʊdəd/ *adj, of a bomb* : not yet exploded : LIVE ▪ *unexploded* bombs/mines ▪ an *unexploded* shell

un·ex·plored /ˌʌnɪkˈsploəd/ *adj*
1 : not yet investigated or explored ▪ *unexplored* territory
2 : not yet studied or discussed thoroughly ▪ The subject is still *unexplored.*

un·ex·pur·gat·ed /ˌʌnˈɛkspəˌgeɪtəd/ *adj, formal, of a book, play, etc.* : with all the parts that might offend people still included ▪ She had read an *unexpurgated* version of the text.

un·fail·ing /ˌʌnˈfeɪlɪŋ/ *adj* : not failing or likely to fail: such as **a** : never changing or becoming weaker even in difficult times ▪ *unfailing* loyalty/support ▪ She is known for her *unfailing* optimism. **b** : always providing enough of what is needed ▪ an *unfailing* [=*inexhaustible*] supply
– un·fail·ing·ly *adv* ▪ He is *unfailingly* [=*always*] punctual/polite.

un·fair /ˌʌnˈfeə/ *adj [more ~; most ~]* : treating people in a way that favors some over others : not fair, honest, or just ▪ an *unfair* trial ▪ *unfair* advantages ▪ It's *unfair* for them to be allowed to leave early if we can't. ▪ It seems *unfair* to single her out for criticism. ▪ Don't you think you're being a little *unfair* (to her)? ▪ Life is often *unfair.* ▪ The company has been accused of *unfair* labor practices.
– un·fair·ly *adv* ▪ They treated her *unfairly.* **– un·fair·ness** *noun [noncount]*

un·faith·ful /ˌʌnˈfeɪθfəl/ *adj*
1 : having a sexual relationship with someone who is not your wife, husband, or partner ▪ an *unfaithful* husband — often + *to* ▪ She has been *unfaithful to* him over the years. [=she has had sex with other people]
2 : not accurate ▪ an *unfaithful* translation — often + *to* ▪ The movie was *unfaithful to* the book. [=the movie did not tell the story the way it was written in the book]
– un·faith·ful·ness *noun [noncount]*

un·fa·mil·iar /ˌʌnfəˈmɪljə/ *adj [more ~; most ~]* : not frequently seen, heard, or experienced ▪ He gets nervous when he is in *unfamiliar* surroundings. ▪ an *unfamiliar* face/place ▪ The book is full of *unfamiliar* words. — often + *to* ▪ The language is *unfamiliar to* him. [=he does not know the language at all]
unfamiliar with (something) : not having any knowledge of something ▪ I'm *unfamiliar with* that subject/language.
– un·fa·mil·iar·i·ty /ˌʌnfəˌmɪlˈjerəti/ *noun [noncount]* ▪ His *unfamiliarity* with the language made the trip very challenging.

un·fash·ion·able /ˌʌnˈfæʃənəbəl/ *adj [more ~; most ~]* : not currently popular or stylish : not fashionable ▪ *unfashionable* shoes

un·fas·ten /ˌʌnˈfæsn̩, *Brit* ˌʌnˈfɑːsən/ *verb* **-tens; -tened; -ten·ing** *[+ obj]* : to make (something) loose : UNDO ▪ *unfasten* a belt/buckle/button

un·fath·om·able /ˌʌnˈfæðəməbəl/ *adj, literary* : impossible to understand ▪ *unfathomable* reasons/motives ▪ His behavior is completely *unfathomable.*

un·fa·vor·able *(US) or Brit* **un·fa·vour·able** /ˌʌnˈfeɪvərəbəl/ *adj [more ~; most ~]*
1 : likely to cause problems or difficulties ▪ *unfavorable* [=*bad*] weather for a camping trip
2 : expressing disapproval ▪ *unfavorable* [=*critical*] comments ▪ The movie has gotten some *unfavorable* [=*bad*] reviews. ▪ She formed an *unfavorable* impression of him. ▪ The article cast/put him ***in an unfavorable light***. [=the article made him look bad]
– un·fa·vor·ably *(US) or Brit* **un·fa·vour·ably** /ˌʌnˈfeɪvərəbli/ *adv*

un·fazed /ˌʌnˈfeɪzd/ *adj* : not confused, worried, or shocked by something that has happened ▪ She was *unfazed* by the delay.

un·feel·ing /ˌʌnˈfiːlɪŋ/ *adj [more ~; most ~]* : not kind or sympathetic toward other people ▪ She says the most *unfeeling* things. ▪ How can you be so cold and *unfeeling*?
– un·feel·ing·ly *adv*

un·feigned /ˌʌnˈfeɪnd/ *adj* : not false or pretended : GENUINE ▪ an *unfeigned* [=*real*] interest in people ▪ She looked at him with *unfeigned* admiration.

un·fet·tered /ˌʌnˈfɛtəd/ *adj, formal* : not controlled or restricted ▪ *unfettered* [=*free*] access ▪ an *unfettered* market

un·filled /ˌʌnˈfɪld/ *adj* : not filled: such as **a** : available because no one has been chosen to take it ▪ The job/position is still *unfilled.* **b** : requested but not yet prepared or given ▪ an *unfilled* order ▪ *unfilled* prescriptions

un·fin·ished /ˌʌnˈfɪnɪʃt/ *adj* : not completed : not finished ▪ an *unfinished* building/play/sentence ▪ *unfinished* furniture [=furniture made of wood that has not yet been stained or varnished]
unfinished business : something that you need to deal with or work on : something that has not yet been done, dealt with, or completed ▪ You and I still have some *unfinished business* together.

un·fit /ˌʌnˈfɪt/ *adj*
1 : not proper, suitable, or acceptable — often + *for* ▪ The movie is *unfit for* children. [=children should not watch the movie] ▪ The land is *unfit for* human habitation. — often followed by *to* + *verb* ▪ The food was *unfit to eat.*
2 : not having the necessary qualities, skills, mental health, etc., to do something ▪ an *unfit* parent [=a person who cannot care for a child properly] — often + *for* ▪ He's clearly *unfit for* the position. ▪ He's *unfit for* army service. ▪ The defendant was declared *unfit for* trial. — sometimes followed by *to* + *verb* ▪ The defendant is *unfit to stand* trial.
3 : not physically healthy : not in good physical condition ▪ Her sisters are overweight and *unfit.* [=*out of shape*]
– un·fit·ness *noun [noncount]*

un·flag·ging /ˌʌnˈflægɪŋ/ *adj* : not decreasing or becoming

U

weaker : remaining strong • her *unflagging* energy/enthusiasm

un·flap·pa·ble /ˌʌnˈflæpəbəl/ *adj* [*more* ~; *most* ~] : not easily upset : unusually calm in difficult situations • He has a reputation for being *unflappable*.

un·flat·ter·ing /ˌʌnˈflætərɪŋ/ *adj* [*more* ~; *most* ~] : making someone or something look or seem worse or less attractive : not flattering • She was wearing the most *unflattering* outfit. • an *unflattering* color • *unflattering* news coverage

un·flinch·ing /ˌʌnˈflɪnʧɪŋ/ *adj* [*more* ~; *most* ~]
1 : staying strong and determined even when things are difficult • *unflinching* dedication
2 : looking at or describing something or someone in a very direct way • his *unflinching* gaze • The movie takes an *unflinching* look at the war. [=it tells the truth about the war, even the unpleasant parts]
— un·flinch·ing·ly *adv*

un·fo·cused *or Brit* **un·fo·cussed** /ˌʌnˈfoukəst/ *adj* : not focused: such as **a :** not relating to or directed toward one specific thing (such as a particular goal or task) • an *unfocused* approach to studying • Your essay seems *unfocused* and unclear. • He seemed a little *unfocused* [=*distracted*] today. • She has lots of *unfocused* energy/anger. **b :** not looking at anything specific • an *unfocused* gaze • Her eyes were *unfocused*.

un·fold /ˌʌnˈfould/ *verb* **-folds; -fold·ed; -fold·ing**
1 : to spread or cause (something) to spread or straighten out from a folded position [+ *obj*] *unfold* a map/newspaper [*no obj*] The couch *unfolds* to form a bed.
2 [*no obj*] **:** to happen as time passes • We'll have more news as events *unfold*. • We watched the drama *unfold* on live television.
3 [*no obj*] **:** to be told or made known • As the story *unfolds*, we learn that the boy became an orphan when he was one year old.

un·forced /ˌʌnˈfoəst/ *adj*
1 : not caused by someone else : caused by your own poor play, performance, etc. • an *unforced* error
2 : natural and done without effort • an *unforced* smile/style

un·fore·see·able /ˌʌnˌfoəˈsiːjəbəl/ *adj* : impossible to predict or expect • *unforeseeable* problems

un·fore·seen /ˌʌnˌfoəˈsiːn/ *adj* : not predicted or expected : UNEXPECTED • *unforeseen* consequences • cancellations due to illness and other *unforeseen* circumstances • Barring any *unforeseen* problems, we should finish on time.

un·for·get·ta·ble /ˌʌnfəˈgɛtəbəl/ *adj* [*more* ~; *most* ~] : very special, unusual, beautiful, etc., and therefore difficult or impossible to forget • It was an *unforgettable* [=*memorable*] experience/night.
— un·for·get·ta·bly /ˌʌnfəˈgɛtəbli/ *adv*

un·for·giv·able /ˌʌnfəˈgɪvəbəl/ *adj* [*more* ~; *most* ~] : so bad that it can never be forgiven • an *unforgivable* crime/sin • His comment was *unforgivable*. [=*inexcusable*]
— un·for·giv·ably /ˌʌnfəˈgɪvəbli/ *adv*

un·for·giv·ing /ˌʌnfəˈgɪvɪŋ/ *adj* [*more* ~; *most* ~]
1 : not willing to forgive other people • an *unforgiving* person/attitude • They are *unforgiving* of the smallest mistake.
2 : very harsh or difficult : not allowing weakness, error, etc. • an *unforgiving* climate/environment • the *unforgiving* world of politics

un·formed /ˌʌnˈfoəmd/ *adj* : not fully or completely developed • an *unformed* thought/idea • *unformed* young minds

¹un·for·tu·nate /ˌʌnˈfoəʧənət/ *adj* [*more* ~; *most* ~]
1 : not fortunate: such as **a :** having bad luck : UNLUCKY • She was *unfortunate* enough to have been chosen as an example. • the *unfortunate* victim • some *unfortunate* person **b :** coming or happening by bad luck • an *unfortunate* experience/result • an *unfortunate* chain of events • *unfortunate* investments • It's *unfortunate* that he couldn't be here for your birthday.
2 : not appropriate or desirable • He has an *unfortunate* tendency to show up late. • an *unfortunate* choice of words

²unfortunate *noun, pl* **-nates** [*count*] *literary* : an unfortunate person • a group of poor *unfortunates*

un·for·tu·nate·ly /ˌʌnˈfoəʧənətli/ *adv* [*more* ~; *most* ~] — used to say that something bad or unlucky has happened • *Unfortunately*, we didn't finish on time. • *Unfortunately* for us, the car broke down. • That, *unfortunately*, cannot be guaranteed. • "Would you like to have dinner with us?" "I can't, *unfortunately*. I have to work." • The show was great, but *unfortunately* we had very bad seats. — opposite FORTUNATELY

un·found·ed /ˌʌnˈfaundəd/ *adj, formal* : not based on facts or proof : GROUNDLESS • *unfounded* claims/rumors • His fears are *unfounded*.

un·freeze /ˌʌnˈfriːz/ *verb* **-freez·es; -froze** /-ˈfrouz/; **-froz·en** /-ˈfrouzn/; **-freez·ing**
1 : to stop being frozen or to cause (something) to stop being frozen : THAW [*no obj*] We can't wait until the ground *unfreezes* so we can start gardening. [+ *obj*] The warm weather *unfroze* the lake.
2 [+ *obj*] **:** to allow (money or property) to be used, spent, etc. • The Justice Department agreed to *unfreeze* the company's assets.
3 : to start working properly again [*no obj*] I had to wait for my computer to *unfreeze* before I could read my e-mail. [+ *obj*] He helped me to *unfreeze* my computer.
— unfrozen *adj* • an *unfrozen* lake • The computer is *unfrozen*.

un·friend·ly /ˌʌnˈfrɛndli/ *adj* **un·friend·li·er; -est** : not friendly: such as **a :** not kind or helpful • *unfriendly* people • They were very *unfriendly* to/towards us. **b :** not showing kind or friendly feelings • an *unfriendly* greeting/stare **c :** harmful or unpleasant • an *unfriendly* environment **d** — used to describe a country, government, etc., that opposes yours • *unfriendly* nations
— un·friend·li·ness /ˌʌnˈfrɛndlinəs/ *noun* [*noncount*]

un·ful·filled /ˌʌnˌfʊlˈfɪld/ *adj*
1 : not yet achieved • an *unfulfilled* dream/promise
2 : not feeling happy and satisfied about life : feeling that your abilities and talents are not being fully used • She's bored and *unfulfilled* at her job.

un·ful·fill·ing /ˌʌnfʊlˈfɪlɪŋ/ *adj* [*more* ~; *most* ~] : not providing happiness or satisfaction : not fulfilling • an *unfulfilling* job/relationship

un·fun·ny /ˌʌnˈfʌni/ *adj, disapproving* : not funny • He told some *unfunny* jokes that made us all uncomfortable.

un·furl /ˌʌnˈfəl/ *verb* **-furls; -furled; -furl·ing :** to cause (something that is folded or rolled up) to open [+ *obj*] They *unfurled* the sails. • *unfurl* a flag/banner [*no obj*] The flowers/leaves are starting to *unfurl*. [=*open*]

un·fur·nished /ˌʌnˈfənɪʃt/ *adj* : without furniture : not furnished • She rented an *unfurnished* apartment.

un·gain·ly /ˌʌnˈgeɪnli/ *adj* [*more* ~; *most* ~] : moving in an awkward or clumsy way : not graceful • a large, *ungainly* animal • He was tall and *ungainly*.
— un·gain·li·ness *noun* [*noncount*]

un·glued /ˌʌnˈgluːd/ *adj*
come unglued *US, informal* **1 :** to become extremely upset or angry • She *came unglued* when they refused her request. **2 :** to fail suddenly or completely • Their marriage *came unglued* [=(*Brit*) *came unstuck*] soon after the baby was born.

un·god·ly /ˌʌnˈgɑːdli/ *adj* **un·god·li·er; -est** [*or more* ~; *most* ~]
1 *somewhat old-fashioned* **a :** not believing in or respecting God • *ungodly* people **b :** immoral or evil • *ungodly* behavior
2 *always used before a noun* **:** very bad or shocking : outrageous or unacceptable • They need an *ungodly* [=extremely large] amount of money to complete the project. • What an *ungodly* racket they're making! • Who would call at this ***ungodly hour***? [=who would call so late/early?]
— un·god·li·ness /ˌʌnˈgɑːdlinəs/ *noun* [*noncount*]

un·gov·ern·able /ˌʌnˈgʌvənəbəl/ *adj, formal*
1 : impossible to govern • The people there seemed almost *ungovernable*.
2 : impossible to control • an *ungovernable* temper

un·gra·cious /ˌʌnˈgreɪʃəs/ *adj* [*more* ~; *most* ~] *formal* : not polite or respectful : not gracious : RUDE • There's no need to be *ungracious* about it. • an *ungracious* response
— un·gra·cious·ly *adv* **— un·gra·cious·ness** *noun* [*noncount*]

un·gram·mat·i·cal /ˌʌngrəˈmætɪkəl/ *adj* : not following the rules of grammar : not grammatical • an *ungrammatical* sentence

un·grate·ful /ˌʌnˈgreɪtfəl/ *adj* [*more* ~; *most* ~] : not feeling or showing thanks for favors, gifts, etc. : not grateful • an *ungrateful* child • I don't mean to seem *ungrateful*.
— un·grate·ful·ly *adv* **— un·grate·ful·ness** *noun* [*noncount*]

un·ground·ed /ˌʌnˈgraundəd/ *adj* : not based on facts : GROUNDLESS • *ungrounded* accusations

un·guard·ed /ˌʌnˈgɑədəd/ *adj*

1 : speaking carelessly without thinking about what you are saying **:** direct and honest especially when you should be cautious ▪ an *unguarded* remark ▪ I let the secret about the surprise party spill out ***in an unguarded moment***
2 : not protected or watched over ▪ an *unguarded* border

un·guent /ˈʌŋgwənt/ *noun, pl* **-guents** [*count*] *old-fashioned* **:** an oily substance that is put on the skin or a wound

un·guid·ed /ˌʌnˈgaɪdəd/ *adj* **:** not controlled or led by anyone or anything **:** not guided ▪ an *unguided* tour ▪ *unguided* missiles

un·ham·pered /ˌʌnˈhæmpɚd/ *adj* **:** allowed to move, progress, or happen without difficulties or obstacles ▪ *unhampered* freedom — usually + *by* ▪ She enjoyed a season *unhampered by* injury.

un·hap·pi·ly /ˌʌnˈhæpəli/ *adv*
1 : without happiness **:** in an unhappy manner ▪ They were *unhappily* married for two years.
2 : in a way that is unfortunate or unlucky ▪ *Unhappily* [=*unfortunately*], many of the passengers got seasick on the tour.

un·hap·py /ˌʌnˈhæpi/ *adj* **un·hap·pi·er; -est** [*or more ~; most ~*]
1 : sad, depressed, or disappointed **:** not happy ▪ I can see that he's *unhappy*, but I don't know why. ▪ I've never seen her looking so *unhappy*. ▪ I left the store an *unhappy* [=*unsatisfied*] customer. — often + *with* ▪ He was *unhappy with* the quality of the food. — often + *about* ▪ The children were all *unhappy about* going back to school. — often + *that* ▪ She was *unhappy that* her favorite television show was canceled.
2 : causing or involving feelings of sadness **:** not pleasant or joyful ▪ an *unhappy* childhood/marriage ▪ For three *unhappy* days we were all stuck in the house because of the blizzard.
3 : not appropriate or lucky ▪ an *unhappy* choice of career/words ▪ The movie's hero meets an *unhappy* fate.
— **un·hap·pi·ness** *noun* [*noncount*] ▪ His *unhappiness* was clear from the expression on his face.

un·harmed /ˌʌnˈhɑɚmd/ *adj, not used before a noun* **:** safe or unhurt **:** not harmed ▪ They escaped from the fire *unharmed*.

un·healthy /ˌʌnˈhɛlθi/ *adj* **un·health·i·er; -est** [*or more ~; most ~*] **:** not healthy: such as **a :** not having or showing good health ▪ an *unhealthy* liver ▪ *unhealthy* workers ▪ Her skin looks blotchy and *unhealthy*. **b :** harmful to your health **:** likely to make you sick ▪ *unhealthy* eating habits ▪ Tests revealed an *unhealthy* level of lead in the water. ▪ Eating honey can be *unhealthy* for babies. **c :** not doing well **:** not successful ▪ an *unhealthy* economy ▪ a financially *unhealthy* company **d :** involving or causing feelings and thoughts that are not normal and healthy ▪ He was stuck in an *unhealthy* relationship. ▪ She has an *unhealthy* interest in natural disasters.
— **un·health·i·ly** /ˌʌnˈhɛlθəli/ *adv*

un·heard /ˌʌnˈhɚd/ *adj*
1 : not given attention ▪ The students' concerns ***went unheard*** [=were ignored] by the school's administration.
2 : not heard or listened to ▪ Their cries for help were *unheard*. ▪ a previously *unheard* recording

un·heard–of /ˌʌnˈhɚdˌʌv/ *adj* **:** not known to have existed or happened before **:** very unusual ▪ In those days, indoor plumbing was almost *unheard-of*. [=very few people had indoor plumbing] ▪ He was hired for an *unheard-of* salary of more than a million dollars. ▪ It's not *unheard-of* for a patient's condition to improve this quickly.

un·heat·ed /ˌʌnˈhiːtəd/ *adj* **:** not having a system that provides warmth **:** not heated ▪ an *unheated* room/home

un·heed·ed /ˌʌnˈhiːdəd/ *adj* **:** heard or noticed but then ignored or not followed ▪ *unheeded* warnings ▪ The panel's recommendations ***went unheeded*** [=were ignored]

un·help·ful /ˌʌnˈhɛlpfəl/ *adj* [*more ~; most ~*] **:** giving no help **:** not helpful or useful ▪ His advice was well-intended but *unhelpful*.
— **un·help·ful·ly** *adv* — **un·help·ful·ness** *noun* [*noncount*]

un·her·ald·ed /ˌʌnˈherəldəd/ *adj, formal*
1 : not getting the praise or appreciation that is deserved ▪ Our goalie is one of the *unheralded* players on our team.
2 : happening without any warning ▪ an *unheralded* [=*unexpected*] visit

un·hes·i·tat·ing /ˌʌnˈhɛzəˌteɪtɪŋ/ *adj* **:** done, made, or shown quickly and immediately without waiting or hesitating ▪ an *unhesitating* reply ▪ They responded to the danger with *unhesitating* courage.
— **un·hes·i·tat·ing·ly** *adv* ▪ She *unhesitatingly* accepted their offer.

un·hin·dered /ˌʌnˈhɪndɚd/ *adj* **:** able or allowed to happen or continue without being slowed, stopped, or made more difficult ▪ a journey *unhindered* by rain ▪ She was given *unhindered* access to the files.

un·hinge /ˌʌnˈhɪnʤ/ *verb* **-hing·es; -hinged; -hing·ing** [+ *obj*] **:** to make (someone) very upset or mentally ill — usually used as *(be) unhinged* ▪ He *was unhinged* by grief.

un·hip /ˌʌnˈhɪp/ *adj* [*more ~; most ~*] *chiefly US* **:** not knowing about or following the newest styles, fashions, etc. **:** not hip ▪ The students thought that their teachers were hopelessly *unhip*.

un·hitch /ˌʌnˈhɪʧ/ *verb* **-hitch·es; -hitched; -hitch·ing** [+ *obj*] **:** to disconnect (something) that is attached to something else by a knot, hook, or hitch ▪ We *unhitched* the trailer from the car. ▪ They *unhitched* the horses.

un·ho·ly /ˌʌnˈhouli/ *adj*
1 : not showing respect for a god or a religion **:** not holy ▪ an *unholy* attitude
2 — used to describe people or groups that are working together for a bad purpose ▪ an ***unholy alliance*** between politicians and lobbyists
3 *always used before a noun, informal* **:** shockingly or surprisingly bad, large, etc. ▪ Our finances were an *unholy* mess. ▪ They have spent an *unholy* amount of money on the project.

un·hook /ˌʌnˈhʊk/ *verb* **-hooks; -hooked; -hook·ing** [+ *obj*]
1 : to remove (something) from a hook ▪ He *unhooked* the fish from the line.
2 : to open or remove (something that is attached with hooks) ▪ She reached behind her and *unhooked* her bra.

un·hur·ried /ˌʌnˈhɚrid/ *adj* **:** not happening or done quickly or too quickly **:** relaxed and calm ▪ We strolled along at an *unhurried* [=*leisurely*] pace.
— **un·hur·ried·ly** *adv*

un·hurt /ˌʌnˈhɚt/ *adj, not used before a noun* **:** not hurt ▪ They were *unhurt* [=*unharmed*] in the crash.

un·hy·gien·ic /ˌʌnˌhaɪˈʤɛnɪk/ *adj* **:** not clean and therefore likely to make you sick **:** not hygienic ▪ *unhygienic* conditions

uni /ˈjuːni/ *noun, pl* **unis** *informal*
1 [*count*] *US* **:** UNIFORM ▪ The players were wearing their new *unis*.
2 [*noncount*] *Brit* **:** UNIVERSITY ▪ She spent the first year after *uni* looking for a job.

uni- *prefix* **:** one **:** single ▪ *uni*lateral

uni·cam·er·al /ˌjuːnɪˈkæmərəl/ *adj, technical* **:** having only one part — used to describe a government in which the people who make laws are not divided into more than one group ▪ a *unicameral* parliament

UNICEF /ˈjuːnəˌsɛf/ *abbr* United Nations Children's Fund ✧ UNICEF is an organization created by the United Nations to help children in poor countries around the world.

uni·corn /ˈjuːnəˌkoɚn/ *noun, pl* **-corns** [*count*] **:** an imaginary animal that looks like a horse and has a straight horn growing from the middle of its forehead

uni·cy·cle /ˈjuːnɪˌsaɪkəl/ *noun, pl* **-cy·cles** [*count*] **:** a vehicle that is similar to a bicycle but has only one wheel — compare BICYCLE, TRICYCLE

un·iden·ti·fi·able /ˌʌnaɪˌdɛntəˈfajəbəl/ *adj* **:** impossible to identify ▪ Many of the bodies pulled out of the wreckage were *unidentifiable*. ▪ an *unindentifiable* substance

un·iden·ti·fied /ˌʌnaɪˈdɛntəˌfaɪd/ *adj* **:** not known or identified ▪ Police said that an *unidentified* person saved the boy from drowning. ▪ an ***unidentified flying object*** [=*UFO*]

[1]**uni·form** /ˈjuːnəˌfoɚm/ *noun, pl* **-forms :** a special kind of clothing that is worn by all the members of a group or organization (such as an army or team) [*count*] a school/police/baseball *uniform* [*noncount*] soldiers ***in (full) uniform*** [=wearing uniforms] — see color picture on page C16

[2]**uniform** *adj* [*more ~; most ~*] **:** not varying or changing **:** staying the same at all times, in all places, or for all parts or members ▪ The museum is kept at a *uniform* temperature to protect the artifacts. ▪ The cookies should be *uniform* in size. = The cookies should be of *uniform* size. ▪ All departments have *uniform* training standards.
— **uni·form·ly** *adv* ▪ The trees are *uniformly* [=*evenly*] spaced along the walkway. ▪ *uniformly* high standards

uni·formed /ˈjuːnəˌfoəmd/ *adj* : dressed in a uniform ▪ *uniformed* officers/police/soldiers

uni·for·mi·ty /ˌjuːnəˈfoəməti/ *noun* : the quality or state of being the same : the quality or state of being uniform or identical [*noncount*] There is little *uniformity* among the states in voting procedures. [=different states have different voting procedures] [*singular*] There is a *uniformity* of opinion among the students. [=they all have the same opinion]

uni·fy /ˈjuːnəˌfaɪ/ *verb* **-fies; -fied; -fy·ing** [+ *obj*] : to cause (people or things) to be joined or brought together : UNITE ▪ The creation of the national railroad system *unified* the country. ▪ two very different people *unified* by a common belief

– uni·fi·ca·tion /ˌjuːnəfəˈkeɪʃən/ *noun* [*noncount*] ▪ the *unification* of Germany

uni·lat·er·al /ˌjuːnɪˈlætərəl/ *adj* : involving only one group or country ▪ Our country is prepared to take *unilateral* action. ▪ a *unilateral* cease-fire — compare BILATERAL, MULTILATERAL, TRILATERAL

– uni·lat·er·al·ism /ˌjuːnɪˈlætərəˌlɪzəm/ *noun* [*noncount*] **– uni·lat·er·al·ly** *adv* ▪ We will act *unilaterally* to defend our interests.

un·imag·in·able /ˌʌnəˈmæʤənəbəl/ *adj* [*more* ~; *most* ~] : not possible to imagine : beyond what you would normally imagine ▪ the *unimaginable* horrors of war ▪ a disaster of almost *unimaginable* proportions ▪ This technology would have been *unimaginable* five years ago.

– un·imag·in·ably /ˌʌnəˈmæʤənəbli/ *adv* ▪ *unimaginably* large numbers

un·imag·i·na·tive /ˌʌnəˈmæʤənətɪv/ *adj* [*more* ~; *most* ~] : not having or showing an ability to think of new and interesting ideas : not imaginative ▪ a predictable and *unimaginative* writer/book ▪ The service is great but the menu is *unimaginative*.

– un·imag·i·na·tive·ly *adv*

un·imag·ined /ˌʌnəˈmæʤənd/ *adj* : not yet thought of : not imagined ▪ Space exploration holds *unimagined* possibilities.

un·im·paired /ˌʌnɪmˈpeəd/ *adj* : not made weaker or worse by illness, injury, etc. : not impaired ▪ He suffered some brain damage but his speech remained *unimpaired*. ▪ *unimpaired* drivers [=drivers who are not drunk, drugged, etc.]

un·im·peach·able /ˌʌnɪmˈpiːʧəbəl/ *adj, formal* : very reliable and trusted : not able to be doubted or questioned ▪ a person of *unimpeachable* integrity ▪ The information is from an *unimpeachable* source.

– un·im·peach·ably /ˌʌnɪmˈpiːʧəbli/ *adv* ▪ an *unimpeachably* honest person

un·im·ped·ed /ˌʌnɪmˈpiːdəd/ *adj* : not slowed, delayed, or blocked ▪ an *unimpeded* view of the ocean ▪ They had *unimpeded* access to the archives. ▪ He crossed the border *unimpeded* (by police).

un·im·por·tant /ˌʌnɪmˈpoətn̩t/ *adj* [*more* ~; *most* ~] : not important ▪ She played a relatively *unimportant* role in the movie. ▪ *unimportant* [=*trivial*] details/matters

– un·im·por·tance /ˌʌnɪmˈpoətn̩s/ *noun* [*noncount*] ▪ He doesn't waste time on issues of relative *unimportance*.

un·im·pressed /ˌʌnɪmˈprɛst/ *adj, not used before a noun* : not feeling that someone or something is very good or special : not impressed ▪ He was *unimpressed* by/with their arguments.

un·im·pres·sive /ˌʌnɪmˈprɛsɪv/ *adj* [*more* ~; *most* ~] : not deserving attention, admiration, or respect : not impressive ▪ Her work is good but *unimpressive*. ▪ an *unimpressive* performance

un·in·formed /ˌʌnɪnˈfoəmd/ *adj* [*more* ~; *most* ~] : not having knowledge or information about something : not informed ▪ Many Americans are sadly *uninformed* [=*ignorant*] about politics. ▪ *uninformed* readers ▪ an *uninformed* opinion

un·in·hab·it·able /ˌʌnɪnˈhæbətəbəl/ *adj* : not safe or suitable to be lived in ▪ an *uninhabitable* wasteland ▪ Flooding made the building *uninhabitable*.

un·in·hab·it·ed /ˌʌnɪnˈhæbətəd/ *adj, of a place* : not lived in by people ▪ a small *uninhabited* island

un·in·hib·it·ed /ˌʌnɪnˈhɪbətəd/ *adj* [*more* ~; *most* ~] : able to express thoughts and feelings freely : not inhibited ▪ She's very *uninhibited* and is always the life of the party.

un·ini·ti·at·ed /ˌʌnɪˈnɪʃiˌeɪtəd/ *noun*

the uninitiated : people who do not have knowledge of or experience with something ▪ For *the uninitiated*, let me explain how this device works.

– uninitiated *adj* ▪ An *uninitiated* observer might find his behavior strange.

un·in·jured /ˌʌnˈɪnʤəd/ *adj* : not hurt : not injured ▪ The driver of the car died but the passengers were *uninjured*.

un·in·spired /ˌʌnɪnˈspajəd/ *adj* [*more* ~; *most* ~] : not very good or clever : not inspired ▪ She gave an *uninspired* performance. ▪ The menu was *uninspired*.

un·in·spir·ing /ˌʌnɪnˈspaɪrɪŋ/ *adj* [*more* ~; *most* ~] : not causing people to want to do or create something : not inspiring ▪ an *uninspiring* public speaker ▪ The landscape was dreary and *uninspiring*.

un·in·sured /ˌʌnɪnˈʃəd/ *adj* : not having insurance : not insured ▪ *uninsured* drivers

the uninsured : people who do not have insurance

un·in·tel·li·gent /ˌʌnɪnˈtɛləʤənt/ *adj* [*more* ~; *most* ~] : not intelligent ▪ The radio show was full of *unintelligent* banter. ▪ *unintelligent* animals

un·in·tel·li·gi·ble /ˌʌnɪnˈtɛləʤəbəl/ *adj* : impossible to understand : not intelligible ▪ He left an *unintelligible* message on my voice mail. — often + *to* ▪ They have their own lingo that is *unintelligible to* outsiders.

– un·in·tel·li·gi·bly /ˌʌnɪnˈtɛləʤəbli/ *adv*

un·in·tend·ed /ˌʌnɪnˈtɛndəd/ *adj* : not planned as a purpose or goal : not intended ▪ an *unintended* pregnancy ▪ The proposed bill could have ***unintended consequences***.

un·in·ten·tion·al /ˌʌnɪnˈtɛnʃənl/ *adj* : not done in a way that is planned or intended : not intentional ▪ If I said something to offend you, I swear it was *unintentional*. ▪ an *unintentional* omission/error

– un·in·ten·tion·al·ly *adv* ▪ He *unintentionally* stepped on my foot.

un·in·ter·est·ed /ˌʌnˈɪntrəstəd/ *adj* : not wanting to learn more about something or become involved in something : not interested — often + *in* ▪ She seemed *uninterested in* our problems.

un·in·ter·est·ing /ˌʌnˈɪntrəstɪŋ/ *adj* [*more* ~; *most* ~] : dull and boring : not interesting ▪ a topic that is *uninteresting* to most readers ▪ The food was bland and *uninteresting*.

un·in·ter·rupt·ed /ˌʌnˌɪntəˈrʌptəd/ *adj* : not interrupted, stopped, or blocked ▪ She managed eight hours of *uninterrupted* [=*continuous*] sleep. ▪ a workday *uninterrupted* by distractions ▪ From the hotel window we had an *uninterrupted* view of the ocean.

– un·in·ter·rupt·ed·ly *adv*

un·in·vit·ed /ˌʌnɪnˈvaɪtəd/ *adj* : not asked or expected to come or to do something with others : not invited ▪ She showed up *uninvited*. ▪ I was annoyed that he brought two ***uninvited guests*** to my party.

un·in·vit·ing /ˌʌnɪnˈvaɪtɪŋ/ *adj* [*more* ~; *most* ~] : not appealing or attractive : not inviting ▪ He was facing the *uninviting* prospect of having to move again. ▪ The house was dark and *uninviting*.

un·in·volved /ˌʌnɪnˈvɑːlvd/ *adj* : not involved : not having a part in some activity ▪ He was *uninvolved* in the crime.

union /ˈjuːnjən/ *noun, pl* **unions**

1 [*count*] : an organization of workers formed to protect the rights and interests of its members ▪ She joined the teachers' *union*. ▪ *union* members/leaders/officials — called also (*US*) *labor union*, (*Brit*) *trade union*

2 [*noncount*] : an act of joining two or more things together ▪ An embryo is created through the *union* of sperm and egg. ▪ a perfect *union* of Eastern and Western music

3 [*singular*] : a group of states or nations that are ruled by one government or that agree to work together ▪ the former Soviet *Union* ▪ the European *Union*

4 ***the Union*** **a** : the United States ▪ Utah joined *the Union* in 1896. ✧ The ***State of the Union address*** is a yearly speech given by the U.S. President to Congress and the people to tell them about important things that are affecting the country. **b** : the group of northern states that supported the federal government during the American Civil War ▪ One brother fought for *the Union* and one for the Confederacy. — often used as *Union* before another noun ▪ *Union* soldiers

5 [*count*] : an organized group of people, businesses, etc., that have the same purpose or interest ▪ the American Civil Liberties *Union* ▪ the International Skating *Union* — see also STUDENT UNION

6 *formal* : the act of getting married or of causing two people to be married [*noncount*] the *union* of two people in marriage [*count*] They celebrated their *union* [=*marriage*]

with more than 200 friends and family members. — see also CIVIL UNION
7 [*count, noncount*] *formal* : the activity or an act of having sex ▪ sexual *union*

union·ist /ˈjuːnjənɪst/ *noun, pl* **-ists** [*count*]
1 : someone who supports labor unions
2 *Unionist* : a supporter of the Union (sense 4b) during the American Civil War
3 *Unionist* : a person who believes that Northern Ireland should remain a part of the United Kingdom
— **union·ism** /ˈjuːnjəˌnɪzəm/ *noun* [*noncount*]

union·ize *also Brit* **union·ise** /ˈjuːnjəˌnaɪz/ *verb* **-iz·es; -ized; -iz·ing**
1 [*no obj*] : to form or join a labor union ▪ Workers are fighting for the right to *unionize*.
2 [+ *obj*] : to help (people) form or join a labor union ▪ Organizers *unionized* the staff. ▪ *unionized* workers/industries
— **union·i·za·tion** *also Brit* **union·i·sa·tion** /ˌjuːnjənəˈzeɪʃən, *Brit* ˌjuːnjəˌnaɪˈzeɪʃən/ *noun* [*noncount*] ▪ the *unionization* of factory workers

Union Jack *noun*
the Union Jack : the national flag of the United Kingdom

union suit *noun, pl* ~ **suits** [*count*] *US* : underwear usually for men that covers the body, legs, and arms, and that has buttons down the front

unique /jʊˈniːk/ *adj*
1 — used to say that something or someone is unlike anything or anyone else ▪ The shape of each and every snowflake is *unique*. ▪ His talents make him truly *unique*.
2 [*more* ~; *most* ~] : very special or unusual ▪ a *unique* opportunity ▪ a *unique* feature/characteristic ▪ She's in the *unique* position of running for office against her husband. ▪ Humans are *unique* among mammals in several respects.
3 : belonging to or connected with only one particular thing, place, or person — + *to* ▪ a species *unique to* the region ▪ These problems are not *unique to* our city. [=these problems occur in other places and not only in our city]
— **unique·ly** *adv* ▪ a *uniquely* American tradition ▪ Her sense of humor is *uniquely* her own. ▪ He is *uniquely* suited to lead this company. — **unique·ness** *noun* [*noncount*]

uni·sex /ˈjuːnəˌsɛks/ *adj, always used before a noun* : designed for or used by both men and women ▪ *unisex* clothing ▪ a *unisex* hair salon

uni·son /ˈjuːnəsən/ *noun*
in unison ✧ If people do something *in unison*, they do it together at the same time. ▪ singing/playing *in unison* ▪ The children recited the alphabet *in unison*. If people ***work in unison***, they work together to achieve something. ▪ Local residents and police are *working in unison* to make the neighborhood safer.

unit /ˈjuːnət/ *noun, pl* **units** [*count*]
1 : a single thing, person, or group that is a part of something larger ▪ The family is the basic *unit* of society. ▪ The search party broke up into smaller *units*. ▪ Their army *unit* guarded the border.
2 : a part of a hospital where a particular type of care is provided ▪ the intensive care *unit* ▪ a trauma *unit*
3 : a particular amount of length, time, money, etc., that is used as a standard for counting or measuring ▪ Feet and meters are *units* of length. ▪ *units* of measurement ▪ The dollar is the principal *unit* of American currency.
4 : a part of a school course or textbook with a particular subject ▪ Our class is finishing up the *unit* on World War I.
5 *US, education* : an amount of work used for measuring a student's progress towards earning a degree in a school, college, etc. ▪ Each *unit* of credit represents 120 classroom hours.
6 *business* : an individual item of one of the products that a company makes and sells ▪ Last year the company sold 200,000 *units* of that particular model of car.
7 : a machine or part of a machine or system that has a particular use ▪ an air-conditioning *unit* ▪ a portable/handheld *unit* ▪ the computer's ***central processing unit***
8 : one of a number of apartments in a building ▪ The building is divided into eight *units*.
9 : a set of similar pieces of furniture (such as shelves or cabinets) that are grouped or attached together ▪ a built-in storage/wall *unit* ▪ (*chiefly Brit*) a ***kitchen unit*** [=a set of kitchen cabinets and appliances]

Uni·tar·i·an Uni·ver·sal·ist /ˌjuːnəˈterijən ˌjuːnəˈvəsəlɪst/ *noun, pl* ~ **-ists** [*count*] : a person who belongs to a religion that allows its members to freely choose their own religious beliefs and that supports liberal social action — abbr. *UU*
— **Unitarian Uni·ver·sal·ism** /-ˌjuːnəˈvəsəˌlɪzəm/ *noun* [*noncount*] — **Unitarian Universalist** *adj*

uni·tary /ˈjuːnəˌteri, *Brit* ˈjuːnətri/ *adj, formal* : relating to or forming a single unit ▪ the formation of a *unitary* state

unite /jʊˈnaɪt/ *verb* **unites; unit·ed; unit·ing**
1 : to join together to do or achieve something [*no obj*] Party members *united* in support of their candidate. ▪ Students *united* to protest the tuition increase. ▪ *uniting* against a common enemy [+ *obj*] The struggle to end slavery *united* rich and poor. — often used as *(be) united* ▪ We *were* all *united* by a common purpose.
2 a [+ *obj*] : to cause (two or more people or things) to be joined together and become one thing ▪ A treaty *united* the independent nations. ▪ They were *united* in marriage [=they were married] on Sunday, August 24. **b** [*no obj*] : to become joined together as one thing ▪ The sperm and egg *unite* to form an embryo.

united *adj*
1 : involving people or groups working together to achieve something ▪ a *united* campaign against drug abuse
2 : made up of members who share the same purpose, interest, etc. ▪ a *united* Europe ▪ a *united* family ▪ The party must present a ***united front*** on these issues. [=all party members must show agreement about these issues] — often used in the names of countries and organizations ▪ the *United* States of America ▪ the *United* Methodist Church

United Nations *noun*
the United Nations : an international organization that helps to solve world conflicts peacefully — abbr. *UN* or *U.N.*

unit trust *noun, pl* ~ **trusts** [*count*] *Brit* : MUTUAL FUND

uni·ty /ˈjuːnəti/ *noun*
1 : the state of being in full agreement : HARMONY [*noncount*] political *unity* ▪ a sense of national *unity* [*singular*] They have dealt with this issue with an impressive *unity* of purpose. [=they have joined together and shared the same purpose in dealing with this issue]
2 [*noncount*] : a way of combining the parts in a work of art or literature so that they seem to belong together ▪ His paintings lack *unity*.

Univ. *abbr* University

uni·ver·sal /ˌjuːnəˈvəsəl/ *adj* [*more* ~; *most* ~]
1 : done or experienced by everyone ▪ *universal* human emotions ▪ an idea with *universal* appeal/acceptance : existing or available for everyone ▪ *universal* health care ▪ ***universal suffrage*** [=the right for all adults in a country to vote]
2 : existing or true at all times or in all places ▪ *universal* truths/laws ▪ a pattern that is *universal* across all cultures
— **uni·ver·sal·i·ty** /ˌjuːnəvəˈsæləti/ *noun* [*noncount*] — **uni·ver·sal·ly** *adv* ▪ a *universally* recognized/accepted truth

uni·verse /ˈjuːnəˌvəs/ *noun, pl* **-verses**
1 ***the universe*** : all of space and everything in it including stars, planets, galaxies, etc. ▪ How many stars are there in *the universe*? ▪ It means more to me than anything else in *the* entire/whole *universe*.
2 [*count*] : an area of space or a world that is similar to but separate from the one that we live in ▪ She is convinced that parallel/alternate *universes* exist. ▪ He creates his own *universe* in his novels.
3 [*singular*] : the people, places, experiences, etc., that are associated with a particular person, place, or thing ▪ The college campus is its own little *universe*. [=*world*] ▪ Her young son is the ***center of her universe***. [=the most important part of her life] ▪ New York City is the *center of the* publishing *universe*.

uni·ver·si·ty /ˌjuːnəˈvəsəti/ *noun, pl* **-ties** : a school that offers courses leading to a degree (such as a bachelor's, master's, or doctoral degree) and where research is done [*count*] I applied to several public/private *universities*. ▪ the *University* of Michigan ▪ Harvard *University* ▪ He lives near the *university*. [*noncount*] *university* students/professors ▪ (*Brit*) Did she go ***to university***? [=did she study at a university?] ▪ (*Brit*) She studied chemistry ***at university***. — abbr. *U., Univ.*; compare COLLEGE; see also STATE UNIVERSITY

un·just /ˌʌnˈʤʌst/ *adj* [*more* ~; *most* ~] *formal* : not fair or deserved : not just ▪ The convict received an *unjust* sentence.
— **un·just·ly** *adv* ▪ She was *unjustly* accused of fraud.

un·jus·ti·fi·able /ˌʌnˈʤʌstəˌfajəbəl/ *adj* [*more* ~; *most* ~] : not able to be defended, excused, or accepted : not justifiable ▪ an *unjustifiable* expense ▪ Their actions were *unjustifiable.*

– un·jus·ti·fi·ably /ˌʌnˈʤʌstəˌfajəbli/ *adv* ▪ *unjustifiably* high prices

un·jus·ti·fied /ˌʌnˈʤʌstəˌfaɪd/ *adj [more ~; most ~]* **:** unnecessary and not right or fair **:** not justified ▪ The shooting of the unarmed suspect was *unjustified.*

un·kempt /ˌʌnˈkɛmpt/ *adj* **:** not neat or orderly **:** messy or untidy ▪ an *unkempt* lawn ▪ She wore rumpled clothing and her hair was *unkempt.*

un·kind /ˌʌnˈkaɪnd/ *adj* **un·kind·er; -est** *[also more ~; most ~]* **:** not friendly, pleasant, helpful, etc. **:** not kind ▪ an *unkind* remark ▪ *unkind* treatment ▪ It was *unkind* of you not to invite her. ▪ How could you be so *unkind*? — often + *to* ▪ He was *unkind to* her. [=he treated her harshly/badly] ▪ Fate was *unkind to* them. [=they were unlucky]

– un·kind·ly *adv* ▪ He was treated *unkindly.* ▪ Judges tend to ***look unkindly on/upon*** [=disapprove of] repeat offenders. ▪ She said, ***not unkindly***, that I might benefit from some lessons. **– un·kind·ness** /ˌʌnˈkaɪndnəs/ *noun [noncount]*

un·know·able /ˌʌnˈnowəbəl/ *adj* **:** not able to be known **:** not knowable ▪ a God whose nature is unknown and *unknowable*

un·know·ing /ˌʌnˈnowɪŋ/ *adj, always used before a noun* **:** not aware of what is really happening ▪ She became an *unknowing* [=*unwitting*] accomplice to the crime.

– un·know·ing·ly /ˌʌnˈnowɪŋli/ *adv* ▪ He had *unknowingly* infected others with the virus.

[1]**un·known** /ˌʌnˈnoʊn/ *adj*

1 : not known ▪ a disease of *unknown* cause/origin ▪ Much remains *unknown* about his early life. ▪ Her music was previously *unknown* outside of Asia. ▪ An *unknown* number of cases go unreported. ▪ The victim's attacker was *unknown* to her. ▪ ***For some unknown reason***, my computer crashed.

2 : not well-known **:** not famous ▪ an *unknown* artist/writer ▪ a book of *unknown* poems

unknown quantity see QUANTITY

unknown to **:** without being known about by (someone) ▪ *Unknown to* me, my partner was organizing a surprise party for my birthday.

[2]**unknown** *noun, pl* **-knowns**

1 ***the unknown*** **:** a place, situation, or thing that you do not know about or understand ▪ explorers venturing off into *the unknown* ▪ A ***fear of the unknown*** kept her from changing jobs.

2 *[count]* **:** a person who is not famous or well-known ▪ The director cast an *unknown* in the lead role.

3 *[count]* **:** something that is not known or not yet discovered ▪ We're facing too many *unknowns.* ▪ (*chiefly US*) The ***big unknown*** [=the important thing that everyone would like to know] is how investors will react.

4 *[count] mathematics* **:** a quantity that is not known and that is usually shown in equations as a letter (such as *x, y,* or *z*)

un·lace /ˌʌnˈleɪs/ *verb* **-lac·es; -laced; -lac·ing** *[+ obj]* **:** to loosen or pull out the laces of (a shoe, boot, etc.) ▪ She *unlaced* her boots.

un·latch /ˌʌnˈlæʧ/ *verb* **-latch·es; -latched; -latch·ing** *[+ obj]* **:** to open or loosen (something, such as a door) by lifting a latch ▪ I *unlatched* the gate.

un·law·ful /ˌʌnˈlɑːfəl/ *adj, formal* **:** not allowed by the law **:** ILLEGAL ▪ The sale of alcohol to minors is *unlawful.* ▪ an *unlawful* search

– un·law·ful·ly *adv*

un·lead·ed /ˌʌnˈlɛdəd/ *adj* **:** not containing lead ▪ *unleaded* gasoline — opposite LEADED

un·learn /ˌʌnˈlən/ *verb* **-learns; -learned; -learn·ing** *[+ obj]* **:** to forget and stop doing (something, such as a habit) in a deliberate way because it is bad or incorrect ▪ It is hard to *unlearn* bad habits.

un·learned *adj*

1 /ˌʌnˈlənd/ — used to describe a type of behavior that is natural and does not have to be learned ▪ Breathing is *unlearned* behavior.

2 /ˌʌnˈlənəd/ *formal* **:** having or showing very little learning, education, or knowledge ▪ the *unlearned* masses

un·leash /ˌʌnˈliːʃ/ *verb* **-leash·es; -leashed; -leash·ing** *[+ obj]*

1 : to allow or cause (something very powerful) to happen suddenly ▪ The storm *unleashed* its fury. ▪ The editorial *unleashed* a torrent/flood of angry responses.

2 : to remove a leash from (an animal) so that it can freely run, attack someone, etc. ▪ They *unleashed* the hounds.

un·leav·ened /ˌʌnˈlɛvənd/ *adj, of bread* **:** flat because of being made without yeast, baking powder, etc. **:** not leavened ▪ *unleavened* bread

un·less /ənˈlɛs/ *conj* — used to say what will happen, be done, or be true if something else does not happen, is not done, or is not true ▪ He will fail the course *unless* he gets a 90 on the exam. ▪ *Unless* something is done, the species will become extinct. ▪ I won't have an operation *unless* surgery is absolutely necessary. [=I will only have an operation if surgery is absolutely necessary] ▪ "Will I have to pay?" "***Not unless*** [=only if] you want to."

un·let·tered /ˌʌnˈlɛtəd/ *adj, formal + literary* **:** unable to read or write **:** ILLITERATE ▪ *unlettered* peasants

un·li·censed /ˌʌnˈlaɪsnst/ *adj* **:** not having an official document giving you permission to do, own, or make something ▪ *unlicensed* drivers ▪ *unlicensed* software [=a copy of a computer program made without getting permission from the original producer of the software]

un·lik·able (*chiefly US*) *or chiefly Brit* **un·like·able** /ˌʌnˈlaɪkəbəl/ *adj [more ~; most ~]* **:** not easy to like **:** not having pleasant or appealing qualities **:** not likable ▪ He's an arrogant, *unlikable* man.

[1]**un·like** /ˌʌnˈlaɪk/ *prep*

1 : different from (something or someone) ▪ The plants that grow here are *unlike* the plants that grow where I live. ▪ She's *unlike* anyone I've ever met. ▪ Its texture is ***not unlike*** [=similar to] that of oatmeal.

2 : not typical of (someone) **:** not normal for (someone) ▪ It was *unlike* her to be late. [=it was unusual for her to be late] ▪ That's *unlike* him.

3 — used to indicate how someone or something is different from other people or things ▪ *Unlike* most mammals, the platypus lays eggs. ▪ A cold, *unlike* strep throat, is caused by a virus.

[2]**unlike** *adj, somewhat formal* **:** not similar **:** DIFFERENT ▪ a comparison of *unlike* things

un·like·li·hood /ˌʌnˈlaɪkliˌhʊd/ *noun [noncount]* **:** the chance that something will not happen or not be true **:** the quality or state of being unlikely ▪ Given the *unlikelihood* of a tax increase, these programs will probably run out of funding next year.

un·like·ly /ˌʌnˈlaɪkli/ *adj* **un·like·li·er; -est** *[or more ~; most ~]*

1 : not likely — used to say that something probably will not happen or is not true ▪ It is *unlikely* that the company will survive more than another year. ▪ That explanation is *unlikely* to be true. ▪ an *unlikely* story [=a story that is hard to believe] ▪ Her recovery is *unlikely.* = It is *unlikely* that she will recover. = She is *unlikely* to recover. ▪ In the ***unlikely event that*** I win the lottery, I will pay off the mortgage.

2 *always used before a noun* **:** not seeming to be right or suited for a purpose ▪ He was an *unlikely* candidate for the position. ▪ A big city seems like an *unlikely* place to find wildlife. ▪ I received support from an *unlikely* ally. ▪ an *unlikely* combination

un·lim·it·ed /ˌʌnˈlɪmətəd/ *adj*

1 : without any limits or restrictions ▪ Membership gives you *unlimited* access to the facilities. ▪ A ruler who is granted *unlimited* [=*limitless*] power is sure to abuse it. ▪ This ticket is good for *unlimited* travel on all trains.

2 : not limited in number or amount ▪ This plan allows you to make an *unlimited* number of phone calls to anywhere in the U.S. ▪ Her funds seem to be *unlimited.*

un·lined /ˌʌnˈlaɪnd/ *adj*

1 : not marked with lines ▪ *unlined* paper ▪ his smooth, *unlined* face

2 : not having a lining ▪ an *unlined* jacket

un·list·ed /ˌʌnˈlɪstəd/ *adj*

1 : not appearing on an official list ▪ There's an *unlisted* bonus track on the CD.; *especially, chiefly US* **:** not appearing in a telephone book ▪ She has an *unlisted* [=(*Brit*) *ex-directory*] phone number.

2 : not included in the list of companies whose stocks are sold on a particular stock exchange ▪ He is buying shares in an *unlisted* company.

un·lis·ten·able /ˌʌnˈlɪsn̩əbəl/ *adj [more ~; most ~]* **:** impossible to listen to and enjoy ▪ I find his music (to be) *unlistenable.*

un·lit /ˌʌnˈlɪt/ *adj*

1 : not having any light shining so you can see ▪ an *unlit* [=*dark*] room

2 : not burning : not lit • an *unlit* cigarette • an *unlit* burner
3 : not turned on to provide light • an *unlit* neon sign

un·load /ˌʌnˈloʊd/ *verb* **-loads; -load·ed; -load·ing**
1 : to remove something (such as cargo) from a truck, ship, etc. [+ *obj*] It took four hours to *unload* the truck. • Could you help me *unload* the car? • After the ship docked, they *unloaded* its cargo. • I have to *unload* the groceries. [*no obj*] Most ships *unload* at another dock now.
2 [+ *obj*] : to allow (someone) to leave a train, ship, etc. • The train made several stops to *unload* passengers.
3 [+ *obj*] *informal* : to get rid of (something or someone) quickly • He's trying to *unload* [=*sell*] his old car. • Rumor has it that the manager wants to *unload* him. Maybe he'll be traded to another team. • She *unloaded* a huge amount of stock when prices fell.
4 [+ *obj*] **a** : to take something out of a device • Could you show me how to *unload* film (from the camera)? • *unload* a camera [=take film out of a camera] • *unload* a gun [=remove the bullets from a gun] • He *unloaded* the dishwasher and put away the dishes. **b** *informal* : to fire (bullets) from a weapon • He *unloaded* [=*shot*] several rounds from the gun.
5 [*no obj*] *informal* : to talk about something that has been bothering or troubling you • I really need to *unload*. Do you have a few minutes?
6 [*no obj*] *US, informal* **a** : to express a strong feeling (such as anger) in a very forceful way — + *on* • The coach really *unloaded on* [=*yelled at*] the players after the game. **b** : to hit someone or something very forcefully — usually + *on* • He *unloaded on* the pitch and drove it over the right field wall.

un·lock /ˌʌnˈlɑːk/ *verb* **-locks; -locked; -lock·ing** [+ *obj*]
1 : to open the lock on (something) • Could you *unlock* the door for me? • He *unlocked* the car.
2 : to find out about (something that was secret or unknown) : REVEAL • geneticists *unlocking* the secrets of DNA • The material's potential was *unlocked* only through extensive testing.
3 : to make (something) available for use • How can I *unlock* my computer if I've forgotten the password? • This class will *unlock* your creativity.
– **unlocked** *adj* • Is the car *unlocked*? • Leave the door *unlocked*.

un·looked–for /ˌʌnˈlʊktˌfoɚ/ *adj, formal* : not expected • an *unlooked-for* bonus

un·loose /ˌʌnˈluːs/ *verb* **-loos·es; -loosed; -loos·ing** [+ *obj*] *literary*
1 : to untie or release (something) • He *unloosed* the bonds that held her.
2 : to allow or cause (something powerful) to happen or be expressed • The court's decision has *unloosed* [=*let loose*] a flood of criticism.

un·loos·en /ˌʌnˈluːsn̩/ *verb* **-ens; -ened; -en·ing** [+ *obj*] : to make (something) loose : to untie (something) • He *unloosened* [=*loosened*] his tie.

un·lov·able /ˌʌnˈlʌvəbəl/ *adj* [*more* ~; *most* ~] : not having attractive or appealing qualities : not lovable • She was totally *unlovable*. • an *unlovable* character

un·loved /ˌʌnˈlʌvd/ *adj* : not loved by anyone • She is alone and *unloved*.

un·love·ly /ˌʌnˈlʌvli/ *adj* **un·love·li·er; -est** [*or more* ~; *most* ~] *literary* : not attractive : UGLY • an *unlovely* name

un·lov·ing /ˌʌnˈlʌvɪŋ/ *adj* [*more* ~; *most* ~] : not feeling or showing love • *unloving* parents

un·luck·i·ly /ˌʌnˈlʌkəli/ *adv* : UNFORTUNATELY • *Unluckily* for her, it rained that day.

un·lucky /ˌʌnˈlʌki/ *adj* **un·luck·i·er; -est** [*also more* ~; *most* ~]
1 : having bad luck • She was *unlucky* enough to get a flat tire on the way to her job interview. • He's been **unlucky in love**. [=he has had a series of bad romantic relationships]
2 : causing bad luck • Some people think that 13 is an *unlucky* number. • He thinks it's *unlucky* to have a black cat cross your path.
3 : resulting from bad luck • an *unlucky* accident

un·made /ˌʌnˈmeɪd/ *adj*
1 — used to describe a bed that looks untidy because it has been slept in and its blankets and sheets have not been neatly arranged to cover the mattress • an *unmade* bed
2 *Brit* : not covered with a hard, smooth surface • an *unmade* [=(*US*) *unpaved*] road

un·man·age·able /ˌʌnˈmænɪʤəbəl/ *adj* [*more* ~; *most* ~] : difficult to deal with or control • *unmanageable* children • *unmanageable* hair • His debt has become *unmanageable*.
– **un·man·age·ably** /ˌʌnˈmænɪʤəbli/ *adv* • an *unmanageably* large mortgage

un·man·ly /ˌʌnˈmænli/ *adj* [*more* ~; *most* ~] *disapproving* : not typical of a man or suitable for a man : not manly • He felt *unmanly* because he wasn't interested in sports. • I disagree that dancing is an *unmanly* pursuit. • My father told me that it's *unmanly* to cry.

un·manned /ˌʌnˈmænd/ *adj* : not carrying or done by a person • an *unmanned* spacecraft • *unmanned* missions to Venus • *unmanned* flights/stations

un·marked /ˌʌnˈmaɚkt/ *adj* : not having any marks or signs that show what something is • *unmarked* police cars • He is buried in an *unmarked* grave.

un·mar·ried /ˌʌnˈmerid/ *adj* : not married • an *unmarried* couple who are living together • an *unmarried* [=*single*] man/woman

un·mask /ˌʌnˈmæsk, *Brit* ˌʌnˈmɑːsk/ *verb* **-masks; -masked; -mask·ing** [+ *obj*] : to reveal the true identity or nature of (someone or something) • He was *unmasked* as a spy.

un·matched /ˌʌnˈmæʧd/ *adj*
1 : better than all others • The company has a level of expertise that is *unmatched* (anywhere) in the industry. • *unmatched* quality • Her talents are *unmatched* [=not matched] by any other player.
2 *chiefly US* : not properly matched with something else • He was wearing *unmatched* socks. [=socks that were not the same type, color, etc.]

un·mem·o·ra·ble /ˌʌnˈmɛmərəbəl/ *adj* [*more* ~; *most* ~] : plain or ordinary : not memorable • It's been an *unmemorable* year. • The food was decent, but *unmemorable*.

un·men·tion·able /ˌʌnˈmɛnʃənəbl/ *adj* : too offensive, shocking, or embarrassing to talk about or mention • There are certain topics that are considered to be *unmentionable*. • *unmentionable* words

un·men·tion·ables /ˌʌnˈmɛnʃənəblz/ *noun* [*plural*] *somewhat old-fashioned + humorous* : UNDERWEAR • I won't hang my *unmentionables* out on the clothesline to dry!

un·mer·ci·ful /ˌʌnˈmɚsɪfəl/ *adj* [*more* ~; *most* ~] : not having or showing any mercy : very harsh or cruel : MERCILESS • an *unmerciful* attack • *unmerciful* critics
– **un·mer·ci·ful·ly** /ˌʌnˈmɚsɪfli/ *adv* • They taunted him *unmercifully*.

un·met /ˌʌnˈmɛt/ *adj* : not satisfied or fulfilled • *unmet* expectations • Her needs went *unmet* for years.

un·mind·ful /ˌʌnˈmaɪndfəl/ *adj* : not aware of something that might be important — often + *of* or *that* • He was *unmindful of* the possible consequences of his decision. • He complained loudly about his boss, *unmindful that* she was standing nearby.

un·mis·tak·able /ˌʌnməˈsteɪkəbəl/ *adj* : not capable of being mistaken or misunderstood • The evidence is *unmistakable*. • an *unmistakable* odor
– **un·mis·tak·ably** /ˌʌnməˈsteɪkəbli/ *adv* • Her art is *unmistakably* modern.

un·mit·i·gat·ed /ˌʌnˈmɪtəˌgeɪtəd/ *adj, always used before a noun* : complete and total — usually used to describe something bad • The party was an *unmitigated* disaster. • She had the *unmitigated* gall to suggest that it was all my fault.

un·mo·ti·vat·ed /ˌʌnˈmoʊtəˌveɪtəd/ *adj* [*more* ~; *most* ~] : having no desire to do or succeed at something : not motivated • How can I get *unmotivated* students to do their homework? • I am/feel totally *unmotivated* to work today.

un·moved /ˌʌnˈmuːvd/ *adj* : not feeling pity, sympathy, or admiration for someone or something : not emotionally affected by something • He was *unmoved* by their pleas.

un·named /ˌʌnˈneɪmd/ *adj*
1 — used to indicate that a person's name is not mentioned or known • The article quoted an *unnamed* source/official. • She is believed to be one of the three *unnamed* candidates being considered for the position.
2 : not having a name • The map shows an *unnamed* stream flowing down the side of the hill.

un·nat·u·ral /ˌʌnˈnæʧərəl/ *adj* [*more* ~; *most* ~] : not natural: such as **a** : different from how things usually are in the physical world or in nature • It seems *unnatural* to keep the bird in a cage. • an *unnatural* color • deaths from **unnatural causes** [=deaths caused by things other than old age or disease] **b** : different from what is normal in a way that is seen as wrong, disturbing, etc. • He thought that it was *unnatural*

[=*abnormal*] for a boy to enjoy ballet. ▪ She has an *unnatural* obsession with money. **c :** not real ▪ Her smile looked forced and *unnatural*. ▪ The movie's dialogue sounded so *unnatural* [=*fake*] to me.
– un·nat·u·ral·ly *adv* ▪ *unnaturally* high levels of cholesterol ▪ grew to an *unnaturally* large size

un·nec·es·sary /ˌʌnˈnɛsəˌseri, *Brit* ˌʌnˈnɛsəsri/ *adj* [*more* ~; *most* ~] **:** not needed or necessary ▪ In this city, owning a car is *unnecessary*. ▪ an *unnecessary* delay ▪ Let's not take any *unnecessary* risks.
– un·nec·es·sar·i·ly /ˌʌnˌnɛsəˈserəli, *Brit* ˌʌnˈnɛsəsrəli/ *adv* ▪ I think the punishment you gave her was *unnecessarily* harsh. ▪ These new rules are *unnecessarily* complex.

un·nerve /ˌʌnˈnɚv/ *verb* **-nerves; -nerved; -nerv·ing** [+ *obj*] *somewhat formal* **:** to make (someone) feel afraid or upset and unable to think clearly ▪ Seeing the police in there *unnerved* me. ▪ She was *unnerved* by his strange manner.
– unnerving *adj* [*more* ~; *most* ~] ▪ I had an *unnerving* encounter with her yesterday. ▪ The news of my brother's accident was *unnerving*. **– un·nerv·ing·ly** /ˌʌnˈnɚvɪŋli/ *adv* ▪ The neighborhood was *unnervingly* quiet.

un·no·ticed /ˌʌnˈnoʊtəst/ *adj* **:** not seen or noticed ▪ He walked into the restaurant *unnoticed*. ▪ His efforts **went** (largely) ***unnoticed***.

un·num·bered /ˌʌnˈnʌmbɚd/ *adj* **:** not identified with a number ▪ an *unnumbered* page ▪ That highway has *unnumbered* exits. ▪ driving along *unnumbered* roads

un·ob·jec·tion·able /ˌʌnəbˈʤɛkʃənəbəl/ *adj* [*more* ~; *most* ~] **:** not likely to bother or offend anyone **:** not objectionable ▪ The practice is seen as perfectly *unobjectionable*.

un·ob·served /ˌʌnəbˈzɚvd/ *adj* **:** not seen or noticed ▪ The fire went *unobserved* for several minutes. ▪ an *unobserved* problem

un·ob·tain·able /ˌʌnəbˈteɪnəbəl/ *adj* [*more* ~; *most* ~] **:** not possible to get or achieve ▪ an *unobtainable* outcome ▪ The championship seemed *unobtainable*.

un·ob·tru·sive /ˌʌnəbˈtruːsɪv/ *adj* **:** not attracting attention in a way that bothers you ▪ an *unobtrusive* waiter ▪ *unobtrusive* advertising
– un·ob·tru·sive·ly *adv* ▪ He was sitting *unobtrusively* in a corner.

un·oc·cu·pied /ˌʌnˈɑːkjəˌpaɪd/ *adj* **:** not being used, filled up, or lived in **:** EMPTY ▪ an *unoccupied* house ▪ About half of the seats were *unoccupied* when the concert started. ▪ A third of the beds at the hospital were *unoccupied*.

un·of·fi·cial /ˌʌnəˈfɪʃəl/ *adj* **:** not official: such as **a :** not formally chosen by an official decision or vote ▪ The song is the college's *unofficial* anthem. ▪ She was the group's *unofficial* leader. **b :** not done or made in a formal way by someone in a position of authority ▪ *Unofficial* estimates of the number of people killed in the earthquake range from 3,000 to 5,000. ▪ I am including an *unofficial* translation of the speech. **c :** not having the authority to make a statement, decision, etc. ▪ According to *unofficial* sources, the decision will be appealed. **d :** not done in a public and formal way as part of someone's job ▪ The mayor paid an *unofficial* visit to the hospital.
– un·of·fi·cial·ly *adv* ▪ His name is Bob, but he's *unofficially* known as "Doc."

un·opened /ˌʌnˈoʊpənd/ *adj* **:** not opened ▪ There was a pile of *unopened* mail on the table. ▪ The letter was *unopened*.

un·op·posed /ˌʌnəˈpoʊzd/ *adj* **:** not having any competition in an election, contest, etc. **:** not opposed ▪ The mayor is running *unopposed* for reelection.

un·or·ga·nized *also Brit* **un·or·ga·nised** /ˌʌnˈoɚgəˌnaɪzd/ *adj*
1 : not arranged in an orderly way ▪ boxes of *unorganized* photos
2 : not part of a formal organization (such as a labor union) ▪ These industries usually employ *unorganized* workers.

un·orig·i·nal /ˌʌnəˈrɪʤənl/ *adj* [*more* ~; *most* ~] **:** not new or different ▪ an *unoriginal* idea ▪ The movie was completely *unoriginal*. **:** not able to think of or make new and creative things ▪ an *unoriginal* thinker
– un·orig·i·nal·i·ty /ˌʌnəˌrɪʤəˈnæləti/ *noun* [*noncount*] ▪ I was disappointed by the *unoriginality* of the book's plot.

un·or·tho·dox /ˌʌnˈoɚθəˌdɑːks/ *adj* [*more* ~; *most* ~] **:** different from what is usually done or accepted ▪ She's known for using *unorthodox* [=*unconventional*] methods to achieve her goals. ▪ *unorthodox* views/opinions/beliefs

un·pack /ˌʌnˈpæk/ *verb* **-packs; -packed; -pack·ing**
1 : to take something out of a suitcase, box, etc. [+ *obj*] It's been a year since I moved here and I still haven't *unpacked* all of my books. ▪ I *unpacked* my suitcase as soon as I arrived home. ▪ I *unpacked* all my clothes (from my suitcase) as soon as I arrived home. [*no obj*] By the time we got to the hotel, I was too tired to *unpack*.
2 [+ *obj*] **:** to make (something) easier to understand by breaking it up into smaller parts that can be examined separately ▪ She's good at *unpacking* complex concepts.

un·paid /ˌʌnˈpeɪd/ *adj*
1 : needing to be paid ▪ I have a pile of *unpaid* bills sitting on my desk. ▪ The city is trying to collect *unpaid* taxes. ▪ debts left *unpaid*
2 : done or taken without payment ▪ She took three months of *unpaid* leave from her job.
3 : not receiving money for work that is done ▪ I served as an *unpaid* consultant on the project. ▪ *unpaid* labor

un·par·al·leled /ˌʌnˈperəˌlɛld/ *adj, formal*
1 : not found elsewhere **:** never seen or experienced before **:** UNIQUE ▪ War crimes of this type are *unparalleled* in history. ▪ The new telescope offers an *unparalleled* opportunity to conduct research.
2 : having no equal **:** better or greater than anyone or anything else ▪ Her knowledge of the subject is *unparalleled*.

un·par·don·able /ˌʌnˈpɑɚdnəbəl/ *adj* [*more* ~; *most* ~] *formal* **:** too bad to be forgiven ▪ *unpardonable* offenses ▪ an *unpardonable* sin

un·pa·tri·ot·ic /ˌʌnˌpeɪtriˈɑːtɪk, *Brit* ˌʌnˌpætriˈɒtɪk/ *adj* [*more* ~; *most* ~] **:** not having or showing love and support for your country **:** not patriotic ▪ Her actions were seen as *unpatriotic*.

un·paved /ˌʌnˈpeɪvd/ *adj, chiefly US* **:** not covered with a hard, smooth surface **:** not paved ▪ *unpaved* roads/streets/highways

un·per·sua·sive /ˌʌnpɚˈsweɪsɪv/ *adj* [*more* ~; *most* ~] **:** not able to make you agree that something is true, real, or acceptable **:** not persuasive ▪ I find your reasoning to be *unpersuasive*. ▪ an *unpersuasive* argument
– un·per·sua·sive·ly *adv*

un·per·turbed /ˌʌnpɚˈtɚbd/ *adj* **:** calm and relaxed **:** not upset or worried ▪ She was *unperturbed* by the sudden change in plan.

un·planned /ˌʌnˈplænd/ *adj* **:** not planned or expected ▪ an *unplanned* pregnancy ▪ *unplanned* purchases

un·play·able /ˌʌnˈplejəbəl/ *adj* **:** not able to be played, played on, or played with ▪ The game was canceled due to *unplayable* conditions on the field. ▪ A broken string made the guitar *unplayable*. ▪ an *unplayable* DVD ▪ The golf ball was in an *unplayable* lie.

un·pleas·ant /ˌʌnˈplɛznt/ *adj* [*more* ~; *most* ~]
1 : not pleasant or enjoyable **:** causing discomfort or pain ▪ I stopped taking the drug because of its *unpleasant* side effects. ▪ There was an *unpleasant* smell/odor coming from the basement. ▪ The weather is so *unpleasant* here.
2 : not friendly ▪ I like the shop, but the staff are so *unpleasant*.
– un·pleas·ant·ly *adv* ▪ I was *unpleasantly* surprised to discover that I couldn't find my keys. ▪ The juice was *unpleasantly* sour. ▪ Our vacation started *unpleasantly* with long delays and bad weather. **– un·pleas·ant·ness** *noun* [*noncount*] ▪ I left because I wanted to avoid any potential *unpleasantness*.

un·plug /ˌʌnˈplʌg/ *verb* **-plugs; -plugged; -plug·ging** [+ *obj*] **:** to disconnect (something, such as a lamp or television) from an electrical source or another device by removing its plug ▪ *Unplug* the iron. ▪ I forgot to *unplug* my guitar from the amp.

un·plugged /ˌʌnˈplʌgd/ *adj, informal* **:** sung or performed without electrical instruments ▪ The band's latest album was *unplugged*. ▪ He did an *unplugged* [=*acoustic*] number for the encore.

un·pol·lut·ed /ˌʌnpəˈluːtəd/ *adj* **:** clean and safe for use **:** not polluted ▪ *unpolluted* streams and lakes

un·pop·u·lar /ˌʌnˈpɑːpjəlɚ/ *adj* [*more* ~; *most* ~]
1 : not liked by many people **:** not popular ▪ I was *unpopular* in high school. ▪ Her third album has been *unpopular* with fans. ▪ Recent conflicts have made him *unpopular* among the staff.
2 : not shared by most people ▪ He has *unpopular* opinions/views.
– un·pop·u·lar·i·ty /ˌʌnˌpɑːpjəˈlerəti/ *noun* [*noncount*]

un·prec·e·dent·ed /ˌʌnˈprɛsəˌdɛntəd/ *adj* **:** not done or experienced before ▪ The team has enjoyed *unprecedented* success this year. ▪ This level of growth is *unprecedented*. ▪ An *unprecedented* number of students are taking the class.

un·pre·dict·able /ˌʌnprɪˈdɪktəbəl/ *adj* [*more* ~; *most* ~] : not predictable: such as **a** : not capable of being known before happening or being done ▪ The weather has been completely *unpredictable* lately. ▪ *unpredictable* results/behavior **b** : not always behaving in a way that is expected ▪ He's very *unpredictable*. We never know what he'll do next.
– un·pre·dict·abil·i·ty /ˌʌnprɪˌdɪktəˈbɪləti/ *noun* [*noncount*] ▪ the *unpredictability* of the stock market **– un·pre·dict·ably** /ˌʌnprɪˈdɪktəbli/ *adv* ▪ Illness can cause people to behave *unpredictably*.

un·prej·u·diced /ˌʌnˈprɛʤədəst/ *adj* [*more* ~; *most* ~] : not having or showing an unfair feeling of dislike for a particular person, group, etc. : not prejudiced ▪ an *unprejudiced* jury ▪ an *unprejudiced* [=*unbiased*] analysis of the problem

un·pre·pared /ˌʌnprɪˈpeəd/ *adj* [*more* ~; *most* ~] : not ready to deal with something : not prepared ▪ She was *unprepared* for the test. ▪ This will teach you how to avoid being caught *unprepared*. ▪ We were *unprepared* to handle the crowds.
– un·pre·pared·ness /ˌʌnprɪˈperədnəs/ *noun* [*noncount*]

un·pre·ten·tious /ˌʌnprɪˈtɛnʃəs/ *adj* [*more* ~; *most* ~] : not having or showing the unpleasant quality of people who want to be regarded as more impressive, successful, or important than they really are : not pretentious ▪ He's easygoing and *unpretentious*. ▪ a casual and *unpretentious* restaurant
– un·pre·ten·tious·ly *adv* **– un·pre·ten·tious·ness** *noun* [*noncount*] ▪ I found her *unpretentiousness* to be refreshing.

un·prin·ci·pled /ˌʌnˈprɪnsəpəld/ *adj* [*more* ~; *most* ~] : not having or showing concern for what is right ▪ an *unprincipled* politician ▪ a dishonest and *unprincipled* attack on his reputation

un·print·able /ˌʌnˈprɪntəbəl/ *adj*
1 : too offensive or shocking to be printed or published ▪ *unprintable* words ▪ I can't tell you what he said because it's *unprintable*.
2 : unable to be printed ▪ Does the file contain any *unprintable* characters?

un·pro·duc·tive /ˌʌnprəˈdʌktɪv/ *adj* [*more* ~; *most* ~] : not giving good, steady, or useful results : not productive ▪ The talks were *unproductive*. ▪ It's *unproductive* to waste time arguing.
– un·pro·duc·tive·ly *adv* ▪ Our time was spent *unproductively*.

un·pro·fes·sion·al /ˌʌnprəˈfɛʃənl/ *adj* [*more* ~; *most* ~] : not having or showing the experience, skill, etc., that is expected or appropriate in a person who is trained to do a job well ▪ She was accused of *unprofessional* conduct. ▪ He ran the firm in an *unprofessional* manner. ▪ Typos look very *unprofessional*.
– un·pro·fes·sion·al·ism /ˌʌnprəˈfɛʃənəˌlɪzəm/ *noun* [*noncount*] ▪ He was criticized for his *unprofessionalism*. **– un·pro·fes·sion·al·ly** /ˌʌnprəˈfɛʃənəli/ *adv* ▪ She acted *unprofessionally*.

un·prof·it·able /ˌʌnˈprɑːfətəbəl/ *adj* [*more* ~; *most* ~]
1 : not making money ▪ an *unprofitable* company
2 : not producing good or helpful results or effects ▪ an *unprofitable* discussion

un·prom·is·ing /ˌʌnˈprɑːməsɪŋ/ *adj* [*more* ~; *most* ~] : not likely to be successful or good ▪ Things got off to an *unpromising* start. ▪ She can do a lot with *unpromising* material.

un·promp·ted /ˌʌnˈprɑːmptəd/ *adj* : done or said by someone who has not been asked or reminded to do or say anything ▪ He gave her an *unprompted* offer to help. ▪ His answers were *unprompted*.

un·pro·nounce·able /ˌʌnprəˈnaʊnsəbəl/ *adj* : impossible or very difficult to say ▪ She has an *unpronounceable* name.

un·pro·tect·ed /ˌʌnprəˈtɛktəd/ *adj*
1 : not guarded or kept from something that can cause harm or damage ▪ They're planning to build roads over thousands of acres of *unprotected* land/wilderness. ▪ If your computer is *unprotected*, you're likely to get a virus.
2 *of sexual activity* : done without using anything (such as a condom) that can prevent unwanted pregnancy or the spread of disease (such as AIDS) ▪ They had *unprotected* [=*unsafe*] sex.

un·prov·able /ˌʌnˈpruːvəbəl/ *adj* : not able to be proved or shown to be true ▪ Your theory is *unprovable*. ▪ an *unprovable* claim/assertion

un·proved /ˌʌnˈpruːvd/ *adj* : UNPROVEN ▪ His abilities are still *unproved*.

un·prov·en /ˌʌnˈpruːvən/ *adj* : not tested and shown to be true, good, or useful ▪ scientifically *unproven* treatments/therapies ▪ So much in science still remains *unproven*. ▪ He's an *unproven* rookie. [=a rookie who has not yet shown that he can perform well]

un·pub·lished /ˌʌnˈpʌblɪʃt/ *adj*
1 : not prepared, printed, and sold as or as part of a book, magazine, newspaper, etc. ▪ an *unpublished* manuscript ▪ An anthology of his *unpublished* plays is scheduled to be released next year.
2 — used to describe a writer whose works have not yet been published ▪ an *unpublished* poet/author/playwright

un·pun·ished /ˌʌnˈpʌnɪʃt/ *adj* : not punished ▪ Their crime must not be allowed to ***go unpunished***.

un·qual·i·fied /ˌʌnˈkwɑːləˌfaɪd/ *adj*
1 [*more* ~; *most* ~] : not having the skills, knowledge, or experience needed to do a particular job or activity ▪ He is clearly *unqualified* for the job. ▪ an *unqualified* candidate ▪ It's a judgment that you are *unqualified* to make.
2 : complete or total ▪ You have my *unqualified* support. ▪ The operation was an *unqualified* success. [=it was successful in every way]

un·ques·tion·able /ˌʌnˈkwɛsʧənəbəl/ *adj* : not able to be questioned or doubted ▪ a person of *unquestionable* integrity ▪ His influence on modern art is *unquestionable*.

un·ques·tion·ably /ˌʌnˈkwɛsʧənəbli/ *adv*
1 : in a way that is certain and not able to be doubted : CERTAINLY ▪ This book is *unquestionably* a masterpiece. ▪ She is *unquestionably* one of the finest writers who has ever lived. ▪ His strong views have *unquestionably* influenced others.
2 — used to emphasize that something is definitely true ▪ "Global warming is one of the great challenges of the 21st century." "*Unquestionably*." [=I agree]

un·ques·tioned /ˌʌnˈkwɛsʧənd/ *adj* : not doubted or questioned ▪ Her honesty is *unquestioned*. [=everyone knows that she is honest]

un·ques·tion·ing /ˌʌnˈkwɛsʧənɪŋ/ *adj* : given completely and without asking questions or expressing doubt ▪ I am truly disturbed by her *unquestioning* acceptance of authority. ▪ He demanded *unquestioning* obedience. ▪ *unquestioning* loyalty
– un·ques·tion·ing·ly *adv* ▪ She accepted his explanation *unquestioningly*.

un·qui·et /ˌʌnˈkwajət/ *adj* [*more* ~; *most* ~] *literary* : not peaceful and calm : TROUBLED ▪ *unquiet* sleep ▪ an *unquiet* mind ▪ We live in *unquiet* times.

un·quote /ˈʌnˌkwoʊt/ *noun* — used in speech with *quote* to show that you are exactly repeating someone else's words ▪ She said that she didn't feel prepared to deal with *quote*, "the real world," *unquote*. ▪ He called me a ***quote, unquote*** "dirty, rotten liar."

un·rat·ed /ˌʌnˈreɪtəd/ *adj, US* : not having a special mark (such as PG or R) which shows that a movie is appropriate for a specific audience ▪ an *unrated* film

un·rav·el /ˌʌnˈrævəl/ *verb* **-els**; *US* **-eled** *or Brit* **-elled**; *US* **-el·ing** *or Brit* **-el·ling**
1 : to cause the separate threads of something to come apart [+ *obj*] *unravel* the yarn ▪ *unravel* a rope [*no obj*] This will keep the ends of the rope from *unraveling*. [=*fraying*]
2 [+ *obj*] : to find the correct explanation for (something that is difficult to understand) ▪ Scientists are still *unraveling* the secrets/mysteries of DNA.
3 [*no obj*] : to fail or begin to fail ▪ Their plans *unraveled* when she lost her job. ▪ His frequent absences from home caused his marriage to *unravel*. ▪ I feel like my life is *unraveling*.

un·reach·able /ˌʌnˈriːʧəbəl/ *adj* : not reachable: such as **a** : not able to be arrived at ▪ The island was *unreachable* by air. **b** : not able to be achieved ▪ an *unreachable* goal **c** : not able to be found or spoken to ▪ He was *unreachable* for weeks.

un·read /ˌʌnˈrɛd/ *adj* : not read ▪ an *unread* book ▪ On her desk was a pile of magazines that had been left *unread* for months.

un·read·able /ˌʌnˈriːdəbəl/ *adj* [*more* ~; *most* ~]
1 : unable to be read or understood ▪ Your handwriting is *unreadable*. [=*illegible*] ▪ The computer file is *unreadable*. ▪ She had an *unreadable* expression on her face.

2 : too difficult, badly written, etc., to be worth reading ▪ an *unreadable* novel ▪ This physics textbook is *unreadable*.

un·ready /ˌʌnˈrɛdi/ *adj* [*more* ~; *most* ~] : not prepared for something : not ready ▪ Many people graduate from high school *unready* to enter college.
— **un·read·i·ness** *noun* [*noncount*] ▪ a state of *unreadiness*

un·re·al /ˌʌnˈriːjəl/ *adj* [*more* ~; *most* ~]
1 : not real : artificial or fake ▪ The town seemed as *unreal* as a movie set. ▪ The fashion model looked *unreal*, like a doll.
2 *informal* : very strange or unusual ▪ I think it's *unreal* that he survived the accident. ▪ Some of the things I've seen around here are pretty *unreal*. [=*bizarre*]
3 *informal* — used to describe something that is so good, bad, etc., that it is difficult to believe ▪ The detail in the graphics is *unreal*. [=*superb*] ▪ It's *unreal* that I can access so much information on the Internet. ▪ The pain was *unreal*.
— **un·re·al·i·ty** /ˌʌnriˈæləti/ *noun* [*noncount*] *formal* ▪ There was an air of *unreality* about the place. [=the place seemed unreal]

un·re·al·is·tic /ˌʌnˌriːjəˈlɪstɪk/ *adj* [*more* ~; *most* ~] : not realistic: such as **a** : not able to see things as they really are ▪ an *unrealistic* person **b** : based on what is wanted or hoped for rather than on what is possible or likely : not sensible and appropriate ▪ *unrealistic* expectations/demands ▪ It's *unrealistic* to expect so much. **c** : not showing people and things as they are in real life ▪ The dialogue in the movie was *unrealistic*. ▪ an *unrealistic* scenario
— **un·re·al·is·tic·al·ly** /ˌʌnˌriːjəˈlɪstɪkli/ *adv* ▪ You're being *unrealistically* optimistic.

un·rea·son·able /ˌʌnˈriːznəbəl/ *adj* [*more* ~; *most* ~] : not fair, sensible, or appropriate : not reasonable ▪ I told him that I wouldn't pay unless he sent me a replacement. Am I being *unreasonable*? ▪ You are entitled to compensation for *unreasonable* delays. ▪ *unreasonable* demands/expectations ▪ The prices were not *unreasonable*. [=were not too high]
— **un·rea·son·ably** /ˌʌnˈriːznəbli/ *adv* ▪ *unreasonably* high standards ▪ In my opinion, you acted *unreasonably*.

un·rea·son·ing /ˌʌnˈriːznɪŋ/ *adj*, *formal* : not based on or controlled by reason ▪ an *unreasoning* hatred of the government ▪ his *unreasoning* devotion to a cause

un·re·cep·tive /ˌʌnrɪˈsɛptɪv/ *adj* [*more* ~; *most* ~] : not willing to listen to or accept ideas, suggestions, etc. ▪ She was *unreceptive* to my ideas.

un·rec·og·niz·able *also Brit* **un·rec·og·nis·able** /ˌʌnˈrɛkɪgˌnaɪzəbəl/ *adj* [*more* ~; *most* ~] : not able to be identified or recognized ▪ After the accident, the car was completely *unrecognizable*.

un·rec·og·nized /ˌʌnˈrɛkɪgˌnaɪzd/ *adj* : not recognized: such as **a** : not given deserved attention or notice ▪ The artist's work went *unrecognized* in his lifetime. **b** : not known about ▪ a previously *unrecognized* problem

un·re·cord·ed /ˌʌnrɪˈkoɚdəd/ *adj*
1 : not written down ▪ The motion was passed by an *unrecorded* vote.
2 : not recorded on a record, CD, etc. ▪ a local *unrecorded* musician

un·re·con·struct·ed /ˌʌnˌriːkənˈstrʌktəd/ *adj* — used to describe someone who has strongly held opinions and beliefs that have not changed even though they have been criticized or have become unpopular ▪ He describes himself as an *unreconstructed* liberal.

un·re·fined /ˌʌnrɪˈfaɪnd/ *adj*
1 : still in the natural and original state or form : not yet refined ▪ *unrefined* oils ▪ *unrefined* sugar ▪ *unrefined* metal
2 [*more* ~; *most* ~] *disapproving* : not having or showing good education and manners ▪ a crass, *unrefined* fellow ▪ Your accent makes you sound *unrefined*.
3 [*more* ~; *most* ~] : not smooth, fine, or precise ▪ The dashboard controls feel clunky and *unrefined*.

un·reg·is·tered /ˌʌnˈrɛʤəstɚd/ *adj* : not entered on an official list or in a system of public records : not registered ▪ She was charged with driving an *unregistered* vehicle. ▪ owning an *unregistered* firearm

un·reg·u·lated /ˌʌnˈrɛgjəˌleɪtəd/ *adj* : not subject to laws passed by the government about how something is done, made, processed, sold, etc. ▪ an *unregulated* utility ▪ Herbal supplements are *unregulated* in the U.S.

un·re·hearsed /ˌʌnrɪˈhɚst/ *adj*, *chiefly US* : not practiced or prepared in advance ▪ an *unrehearsed* performance ▪ The speech was natural and *unrehearsed*.

un·re·lat·ed /ˌʌnrɪˈleɪtəd/ *adj* : not related: such as **a** : not part of the same family : not having any shared ancestors ▪ We have the same last name, but we're *unrelated*. **b** : not connected in any way to someone or something else ▪ His recent travel is *unrelated* to his job. ▪ The two incidents are entirely *unrelated*.

un·re·lent·ing /ˌʌnrɪˈlɛntɪŋ/ *adj*
1 : not slowing down, stopping, or growing weaker ▪ *unrelenting* pressure ▪ The pain is *unrelenting*. [=the pain never stops] ▪ She has endured *unrelenting* [=*relentless*] criticism.
2 — used to describe someone who does something in a constant and determined way without stopping or becoming less forceful ▪ an *unrelenting* taskmaster ▪ She was *unrelenting* in her demands for justice.
— **un·re·lent·ing·ly** *adv* ▪ I found the movie to be *unrelentingly* bleak.

un·re·li·able /ˌʌnrɪˈlajəbəl/ *adj* [*more* ~; *most* ~]
1 : not able to be trusted to do or provide what is needed or promised ▪ Public transportation here is *unreliable*. The buses never come on time. ▪ an *unreliable* car [=a car that breaks down often]
2 : not believable or trustworthy ▪ an *unreliable* witness ▪ That report is *unreliable*.
— **un·re·li·abil·i·ty** /ˌʌnrɪˌlajəˈbɪləti/ *noun* [*noncount*] — **un·re·li·ably** /ˌʌnrɪˈlajəbli/ *adv* ▪ The equipment performs *unreliably*.

un·re·lieved /ˌʌnrɪˈliːvd/ *adj*
1 *of something unpleasant* : continuing without stopping or changing : CONSTANT ▪ *unrelieved* pain/hostility/gloom
2 : not including anything that provides a desirable change ▪ windowless walls *unrelieved* by even a single doorway ▪ a grim novel *unrelieved* by any humorous touches

un·re·mark·able /ˌʌnrɪˈmɑɚkəbəl/ *adj* [*more* ~; *most* ~] : not worthy of special attention or notice : ORDINARY ▪ I've led an *unremarkable* life. ▪ The food was *unremarkable*.
— **un·re·mark·ably** /ˌʌnrɪˈmɑɚkəbli/ *adv* ▪ The day began *unremarkably*.

un·re·mit·ting /ˌʌnrɪˈmɪtɪŋ/ *adj*, *formal* : not stopping or growing weaker ▪ She was recognized for her *unremitting* efforts to improve the lives of people in her city. ▪ *unremitting* hostility/pain
— **un·re·mit·ting·ly** *adv*

un·re·peat·able /ˌʌnrɪˈpiːtəbəl/ *adj*
1 : not able to be done or made again ▪ *unrepeatable* results
2 : too rude or offensive to be said again ▪ He made some *unrepeatable* remarks about sex.

un·re·pen·tant /ˌʌnrɪˈpɛntn̩t/ *adj* [*more* ~; *most* ~] : not sorry for something wrong that you have done ▪ an *unrepentant* sinner
— **un·re·pen·tant·ly** *adv*

un·re·port·ed /ˌʌnrɪˈpoɚtəd/ *adj* : not told to someone in authority : not reported ▪ *unreported* income ▪ Many cases of abuse go *unreported* each year.

un·rep·re·sen·ta·tive /ˌʌnˌrɛprɪˈzɛntətɪv/ *adj* [*more* ~; *most* ~] : not showing what a group of people or things is truly like : not representative ▪ The people who live here are *unrepresentative* of the population as a whole. ▪ an *unrepresentative* sample/minority

un·re·quit·ed /ˌʌnrɪˈkwaɪtəd/ *adj* : not shared or returned by someone else ▪ a song about *unrequited* love ▪ *unrequited* passion/longing

un·re·served /ˌʌnrɪˈzɚvd/ *adj*
1 : not kept for use only by a particular person or group ▪ Seating at the concert will be *unreserved*. ▪ *unreserved* seating ▪ *unreserved* funds
2 : not limited in any way ▪ I have nothing but *unreserved* admiration for him. ▪ (*chiefly Brit*) He offered me an *unreserved* apology.
— **un·re·serv·ed·ly** /ˌʌnrɪˈzɚvədli/ *adv*

un·re·solv·able /ˌʌnrɪˈzɑːlvəbəl/ *adj* : not able to be answered or ended in a satisfying way ▪ an *unresolvable* conflict

un·re·solved /ˌʌnrɪˈzɑːlvd/ *adj* : still needing an answer, a solution, or an ending ▪ *unresolved* issues ▪ *unresolved* conflict

un·re·spon·sive /ˌʌnrɪˈspɑːnsɪv/ *adj* [*more* ~; *most* ~]
1 : not replying or reacting to someone's question, request, demand, etc. ▪ The mayor has been *unresponsive* to the concerns of the community. ▪ an *unresponsive* bureaucracy
2 *medical* : not reacting or able to react in a normal way when touched, spoken to, etc. ▪ The victim was *unresponsive* when police arrived.
— **un·re·spon·sive·ness** *noun* [*noncount*]

un·rest /ˌʌnˈrɛst/ *noun* [*noncount*] : a situation in which many of the people in a country are angry and hold protests or act violently • The country has experienced years of civil/social/political *unrest*.

un·re·strained /ˌʌnrɪˈstreɪnd/ *adj*
1 : not held in place by a belt, seat, device, etc. • The child in the car accident was *unrestrained*. • She was fined for driving with an *unrestrained* infant.
2 : not controlled or limited • *unrestrained* spending • *unrestrained* growth • Their enthusiasm was *unrestrained*.

un·re·strict·ed /ˌʌnrɪˈstrɪktəd/ *adj* **:** not controlled or limited in any way **:** not restricted • I was granted *unrestricted* access to the documents. • I bought an *unrestricted* ticket allowing me to travel at any time. • We had an *unrestricted* view of the stage.

un·re·ward·ing /ˌʌnrɪˈwoədɪŋ/ *adj [more ~; most ~]* **:** not giving you a good feeling that you have done something valuable, important, etc. **:** not rewarding • an *unrewarding* task • I find the work dull and *unrewarding*.

un·ripe /ˌʌnˈraɪp/ *adj, of food* **:** not fully grown or developed **:** not yet ready to eat **:** not ripe • *unripe* fruit • Bananas are green when *unripe*.

un·ri·valed *(US) or Brit* **un·ri·valled** /ˌʌnˈraɪvəld/ *adj* **:** better than anyone or anything else • a palace of *unrivaled* magnificence • Her athletic records are *unrivaled*.

un·roll /ˌʌnˈroʊl/ *verb* **-rolls; -rolled; -roll·ing**
1 : to make (something that has been rolled) flat **:** to smooth out (something that is rolled up) [+ *obj*] He carefully *unrolled* the ancient scroll. • I *unrolled* the new carpet. • When we arrived at the cabin, we *unrolled* our sleeping bags. [*no obj*] The hose will *unroll* if you pull on it.
2 a [+ *obj*] **:** to make (something) known in a public or formal way • Last week, the government *unrolled* a new vaccination campaign. **b** [*no obj*] **:** to happen as time passes **:** UNFOLD • The scandal *unrolled* over the course of several weeks.

un·ro·man·tic /ˌʌnroʊˈmæntɪk/ *adj [more ~; most ~]* **:** not romantic: such as **a :** not suitable for romance or for creating romantic feelings • an *unromantic* setting **b :** not doing and saying things to show that you love someone • My wife is so *unromantic*. **c :** describing or thinking about something in a realistic way • His books offer an *unromantic* view of war.

un·ruf·fled /ˌʌnˈrʌfəld/ *adj* **:** not upset or disturbed • She remained *unruffled* despite the delays.

un·ruly /ˌʌnˈruːli/ *adj [more ~; most ~] disapproving* **:** difficult to control • *unruly* children • The bus driver called in the police to deal with an *unruly* [=*disruptive*] passenger. • his *unruly* hair
– un·rul·i·ness *noun [noncount]*

un·sad·dle /ˌʌnˈsædl/ *verb* **-sad·dles; -sad·dled; -sad·dling**
1 [+ *obj*] **:** to remove the saddle from (a horse) • She *unsaddled* her horse.
2 [*no obj*] **:** to get off a horse, bicycle, etc. • The riders *unsaddled* after the race.

un·safe /ˌʌnˈseɪf/ *adj* **un·saf·er; -est** [*or more ~; most ~*] **:** not safe: such as
1 a : able or likely to cause harm, damage, or loss • It's *unsafe* to send cash through the mail. • The water is *unsafe* for drinking. = It is *unsafe* to drink the water. • Driving while talking on a cell phone is *unsafe*. • He was fired for operating the machinery in an *unsafe* manner. **b :** not giving protection from danger, harm, or loss • This intersection is *unsafe* for pedestrians. • That country is an *unsafe* place to visit. • working under *unsafe* conditions • *unsafe* sex [=sex done without using anything (such as a condom) that can prevent unwanted pregnancy or the spread of disease] **c :** not protected from danger, harm, or loss • Incidents at the school have made students feel *unsafe*. **d :** likely to take risks **:** not careful • The police should be doing more to get *unsafe* drivers off the road.
2 *Brit, law* — used to describe a decision, judgment, etc., that is based on evidence which is not considered to be good enough • an *unsafe* conviction
– un·safe·ly *adv* • She was arrested for driving *unsafely*.

un·said /ˌʌnˈsɛd/ *adj* **:** thought but not spoken out loud or discussed • I think that some things are better left *unsaid*.

un·salt·ed /ˌʌnˈsɑːltəd/ *adj* **:** not salted or containing extra salt • *unsalted* butter

un·san·i·tary /ˌʌnˈsænəˌteri, *Brit* ˌʌnˈsænətri/ *adj [more ~; most ~]* **:** dirty and likely to cause disease **:** not sanitary • working under *unsanitary* conditions • The bathroom facilities were *unsanitary*.

un·sat·is·fac·to·ry /ˌʌnˌsætəsˈfæktəri/ *adj [more ~; most ~]* **:** not good enough **:** not satisfactory • He was fired for *unsatisfactory* performance. • The repairs were *unsatisfactory*.
– un·sat·is·fac·to·ri·ly /ˌʌnˌsætəsˈfæktərəli/ *adv*

un·sat·is·fied /ˌʌnˈsætəsˌfaɪd/ *adj [more ~; most ~]*
1 : not dealt with in a way that provides what is needed or wanted • an *unsatisfied* curiosity/hunger/need
2 : not pleased or happy about what has happened or been done **:** DISSATISFIED • an *unsatisfied* [=*unhappy*] customer • I'm very *unsatisfied* with the result.

un·sat·is·fy·ing /ˌʌnˈsætəsˌfajɪŋ/ *adj [more ~; most ~]* **:** not providing what is needed or wanted **:** not satisfying • The meal was expensive and *unsatisfying*.

un·sat·u·rat·ed /ˌʌnˈsætʃəˌreɪtəd/ *adj* — used to describe a type of oil or fat that is found in foods and that is better for your health than other types • *unsaturated* fats • *unsaturated* fatty acids — compare MONOUNSATURATED, POLYUNSATURATED, SATURATED

un·sa·vory *(US) or Brit* **un·sa·voury** /ˌʌnˈseɪvəri/ *adj [more ~; most ~]* **:** unpleasant or offensive • He is an *unsavory* character. • She lives in an *unsavory* [=*dangerous, bad*] neighborhood.

un·scathed /ˌʌnˈskeɪðd/ *adj, not used before a noun* **:** not hurt, harmed, or damaged • She escaped/emerged from the wreckage *unscathed*. • The administration was left relatively *unscathed* by the scandal.

un·scent·ed /ˌʌnˈsɛntəd/ *adj* **:** not having any added smell from perfumes, chemicals, etc. • *unscented* candles

un·sched·uled /ˌʌnˈskɛˌʤuːld, *Brit* ˌʌnˈʃɛˌdjuːld/ *adj* **:** not planned for a certain time **:** not scheduled • an *unscheduled* departure

un·schooled /ˌʌnˈskuːld/ *adj, formal + old-fashioned* **:** not formally taught or trained • These things look the same to my *unschooled* eye. • sculptures made by *unschooled* artists • Their children were *unschooled*. [=their children did not go to school]

un·sci·en·tif·ic /ˌʌnˌsajənˈtɪfɪk/ *adj* **:** not done in a way that agrees with the methods of science **:** not scientific • I conducted an *unscientific* survey/poll. • an *unscientific* theory
– un·sci·en·tif·i·cal·ly /ˌʌnˌsajənˈtɪfɪkli/ *adv* • a poll conducted *unscientifically*

un·scram·ble /ˌʌnˈskræmbəl/ *verb* **-scram·bles; -scram·bled; -scram·bling** [+ *obj*] **:** to change (something, such as a message or an electronic signal) from a form that cannot be understood to a form that can be properly displayed, heard, read, etc. • We weren't able to *unscramble* the satellite signal. • Detectives worked to *unscramble* [=*decode*] the messages. • *Unscramble* the letters ALCEDNRA to spell "CALENDAR."

un·screw /ˌʌnˈskruː/ *verb* **-screws; -screwed; -screw·ing**
1 : to loosen and remove (something) by turning it [+ *obj*] *unscrew* a light bulb • I *unscrewed* the jar lid. [*no obj*] The lid *unscrews* easily.
2 [+ *obj*] **:** to remove the screws from (something) • You'll need to *unscrew* the cover before you remove it.

un·script·ed /ˌʌnˈskrɪptəd/ *adj* **:** not written or planned at an earlier time • *unscripted* comments • Her reaction was completely *unscripted*.

un·scru·pu·lous /ˌʌnˈskruːpjələs/ *adj [more ~; most ~]* **:** not honest or fair **:** doing things that are wrong, dishonest, or illegal • an *unscrupulous* businessman
– un·scru·pu·lous·ly *adv* **– un·scru·pu·lous·ness** *noun [noncount]*

un·seal /ˌʌnˈsiːl/ *verb* **-seals; -sealed; -seal·ing** [+ *obj*] **:** to open (something) by breaking or removing a seal • She *unsealed* the envelope. • The court *unsealed* the documents in the Douglas trial today.
– unsealed *adj* • an *unsealed* envelope [=an envelope that is not sealed]

un·sea·son·able /ˌʌnˈsiːzn̩əbəl/ *adj [more ~; most ~] of weather* **:** not normal for a certain time of year **:** not seasonable • *unseasonable* weather • Temperatures have been *unseasonable*.
– un·sea·son·ably /ˌʌnˈsiːzn̩əbli/ *adv* • The weather has been *unseasonably* cool.

un·sea·soned /ˌʌnˈsiːzn̩d/ *adj*
1 : not having a lot of experience in a particular job or activity • an *unseasoned* actor/writer/rookie
2 *of food* **:** not having added spices, herbs, salt, pepper, etc. • The dish can be left *unseasoned*. • *unseasoned* hamburger

un·seat /ˌʌnˈsiːt/ *verb* **-seats; -seat·ed; -seat·ing** [+ *obj*]
1 : to remove (someone or something) from a position of power or authority ▪ He *unseated* an incumbent senator.
2 : to cause (someone) to fall from a seat or saddle ▪ The horse bucked and *unseated* its rider.

un·se·cured /ˌʌnsɪˈkjɚd/ *adj* **:** not protected against risk or loss **:** not secure ▪ *unsecured* debt ▪ an *unsecured* loan

un·seed·ed /ˌʌnˈsiːdəd/ *adj* **:** not ranked as one of the best players in a sports competition (such as a tennis tournament) **:** not seeded ▪ An *unseeded* player defeated the fourth-seeded player.

un·see·ing /ˌʌnˈsiːjɪŋ/ *adj, formal + literary* — used to describe someone whose eyes are open but who is not looking at or noticing anything ▪ He stared out the window with *unseeing* eyes.

un·seem·ly /ˌʌnˈsiːmli/ *adj* [*more* ~; *most* ~] *formal* **:** not proper or appropriate for the situation **:** not seemly ▪ rude and *unseemly* behavior ▪ He spent *unseemly* amounts of money on himself.
— un·seem·li·ness /ˌʌnˈsiːmlinəs/ *noun* [*noncount*]

un·seen /ˌʌnˈsiːn/ *adj* **:** not seen or able to be seen ▪ *unseen* dangers ▪ an *unseen* sniper ▪ He escaped *unseen*.
sight unseen see [1]SIGHT

un·self·con·scious /ˌʌnˌsɛlfˈkɑːnʃəs/ *adj* [*more* ~; *most* ~] **:** confident and comfortable **:** not self-conscious ▪ He sang with *unselfconscious* ease.
— un·self·con·scious·ly *adv*

un·self·ish /ˌʌnˈsɛlfɪʃ/ *adj* [*more* ~; *most* ~] **:** having or showing more concern for other people than for yourself **:** not selfish ▪ *unselfish* behavior ▪ She's a very *unselfish* young woman.
— un·self·ish·ly *adv* ▪ She *unselfishly* gave of her time.
— un·self·ish·ness *noun* [*noncount*]

un·sen·ti·men·tal /ˌʌnˌsɛntəˈmɛntl/ *adj* [*more* ~; *most* ~] **:** based on, influenced by, or resulting from reason or thought rather than feelings or emotions **:** not sentimental ▪ an *unsentimental* decision ▪ She's completely *unsentimental* about holidays. ▪ a tough, *unsentimental* man

un·set·tle /ˌʌnˈsɛtl/ *verb* **-set·tles; -set·tled; -set·tling** [+ *obj*] **:** to make (someone) nervous, worried, or upset ▪ Such a sudden change will *unsettle* her.

un·set·tled /ˌʌnˈsɛtld/ *adj* [*more* ~; *most* ~]
1 : feeling nervous, upset, or worried **:** not comfortable ▪ *unsettled* investors ▪ an *unsettled* stomach
2 : not lived in by people **:** not inhabited or populated ▪ This region of the country is still largely *unsettled*. [=not settled]
3 : not yet finally decided or dealt with ▪ an *unsettled* question ▪ We have some *unsettled* business to attend to.
4 : likely to change **:** not calm or stable ▪ *unsettled* weather ▪ an *unsettled* political climate
5 : not yet paid ▪ *unsettled* debts

un·set·tling /ˌʌnˈsɛtlɪŋ/ *adj* [*more* ~; *most* ~] **:** making you upset, nervous, worried, etc. ▪ *unsettling* news ▪ *unsettling* images

un·shack·le /ˌʌnˈʃækəl/ *verb* **-shack·les; -shack·led; -shack·ling** [+ *obj*] **:** to take shackles or handcuffs off (someone) ▪ He *unshackled* the prisoner. — often used figuratively ▪ We need to *unshackle* our creativity.

un·shak·able *or* **un·shake·able** /ˌʌnˈʃeɪkəbəl/ *adj* [*more* ~; *most* ~] **:** too strong to be changed, weakened, or destroyed ▪ Their love was *unshakable*. ▪ our *unshakable* belief in equal treatment ▪ an *unshakable* faith ▪ He had the *unshakable* feeling that something was wrong.
— un·shak·ably *adv*

un·shak·en /ˌʌnˈʃeɪkən/ *adj* [*more* ~; *most* ~] *formal* **:** not changed or weakened ▪ Her faith was *unshaken*. ▪ He remained *unshaken* [=*firm*] in his beliefs. ▪ *unshaken* confidence

un·shav·en /ˌʌnˈʃeɪvən/ *adj* **:** not shaved or not recently shaved ▪ Her legs were *unshaven*. ▪ He was scruffy and *unshaven*.

un·sight·ly /ˌʌnˈsaɪtli/ *adj* [*more* ~; *most* ~] **:** not pleasant to look at **:** UGLY ▪ an *unsightly* scar ▪ The cracks in the wall are *unsightly*.

un·signed /ˌʌnˈsaɪnd/ *adj*
1 a : not having a signature ▪ an *unsigned* note **b :** published without the name of the writer ▪ an *unsigned* editorial
2 : not having a contract with a professional sports team, music company, etc. ▪ *unsigned* draft picks ▪ an *unsigned* pitcher ▪ Their band is still *unsigned*.

un·skilled /ˌʌnˈskɪld/ *adj*
1 : not having special skills **:** without training or education ▪ *unskilled* laborers
2 : not requiring special skills or training ▪ *unskilled* jobs — opposite SKILLED

un·smil·ing /ˌʌnˈsmaɪlɪŋ/ *adj* [*more* ~; *most* ~] *somewhat formal* **:** not smiling **:** serious and unfriendly ▪ The soldiers were tense and *unsmiling*. ▪ an *unsmiling* woman

un·so·cia·ble /ˌʌnˈsoʊʃəbəl/ *adj* [*more* ~; *most* ~]
1 : not liking to be with other people **:** not sociable ▪ an *unsociable* man
2 *Brit* **:** UNSOCIAL ▪ a job with *unsociable* hours

un·so·cial /ˌʌnˈsoʊʃəl/ *adj* [*more* ~; *most* ~] *Brit* **:** occurring at times that prevent you from being with your friends and family ▪ a job with ***unsocial hours*** [=a job that requires you to work at unusual hours when other people are spending time together]

un·sold /ˌʌnˈsoʊld/ *adj* **:** not sold **:** not bought by someone ▪ The books went *unsold*. ▪ *unsold* inventory

un·so·lic·it·ed /ˌʌnsəˈlɪsətəd/ *adj* **:** not asked for **:** given or received without being requested ▪ *unsolicited* e-mail ▪ That comment was *unsolicited* and rude.

un·solved /ˌʌnˈsɑːlvd/ *adj* **:** not yet solved **:** never solved ▪ an *unsolved* crime ▪ one of science's great *unsolved* problems ▪ The case remains *unsolved*.
— un·solv·able /ˌʌnˈsɑːlvəbəl/ *adj* ▪ The problem is not *unsolvable*.

un·so·phis·ti·cat·ed /ˌʌnsəˈfɪstəˌkeɪtəd/ *adj* [*more* ~; *most* ~] **:** not sophisticated: such as **a :** not having or showing a lot of experience and knowledge about the world and about culture, art, literature, etc. ▪ She was innocent and *unsophisticated* when she left for college. ▪ He has *unsophisticated* tastes. **b :** not highly developed or complex ▪ *unsophisticated* weapons

un·sound /ˌʌnˈsaʊnd/ *adj* [*more* ~; *most* ~]
1 : not based on truth or logic **:** not showing good judgment ▪ *unsound* [=*faulty*] arguments ▪ *unsound* business practices
2 : poorly built or in bad condition ▪ an *unsound* [=*unsafe*] building ▪ The roof is structurally *unsound*.
of unsound mind *law* **:** mentally ill **:** not sane ▪ He was found to be *of unsound mind* when he committed the murder.

un·spar·ing /ˌʌnˈsperɪŋ/ *adj* [*more* ~; *most* ~] *formal* **:** very harsh or severe ▪ *unsparing* criticism ▪ an *unsparing* critic
— un·spar·ing·ly *adv* ▪ She was *unsparingly* frank.

un·speak·able /ˌʌnˈspiːkəbəl/ *adj* [*more* ~; *most* ~]
1 : very bad or evil ▪ the *unspeakable* horror of war ▪ *unspeakable* crimes
2 : impossible to describe in words ▪ an *unspeakable* loss ▪ moments of *unspeakable* beauty
— un·speak·ably /ˌʌnˈspiːkəbli/ *adv* ▪ She was *unspeakably* cruel.

un·spec·i·fied /ˌʌnˈspɛsəˌfaɪd/ *adj* **:** not named or mentioned **:** not specified ▪ an *unspecified* amount of money

un·spec·tac·u·lar /ˌʌnspɛkˈtækjəlɚ/ *adj* [*more* ~; *most* ~] **:** not spectacular or special **:** ORDINARY ▪ The team has had an *unspectacular* season. ▪ The company's stock has shown consistent if *unspectacular* growth.

un·spoiled /ˌʌnˈspojəld/ *or chiefly Brit* **un·spoilt** /ˌʌnˈspojəlt/ *adj* [*more* ~; *most* ~]
1 : still wild and not changed by people **:** not spoiled ▪ *unspoiled* beaches/countryside
2 : not affected by the special attention you are receiving because of fame or success ▪ He's completely *unspoiled* by success.

un·spo·ken /ˌʌnˈspoʊkən/ *adj* **:** expressed or understood without being directly stated ▪ an *unspoken* [=*unstated*] agreement

un·sport·ing /ˌʌnˈspoɚtɪŋ/ *adj* [*more* ~; *most* ~] *chiefly Brit* **:** not done or behaving in a way that treats the other people in a sport or competition fairly **:** not sporting ▪ It was very *unsporting* of you to trip him. ▪ *unsporting* behavior

un·sports·man·like /ˌʌnˈspoɚtsmənˌlaɪk/ *adj* **:** not fair, respectful, and polite toward other players when participating in a sport **:** not sportsmanlike ▪ *Unsportsmanlike* conduct will not be tolerated.

un·sta·ble /ˌʌnˈsteɪbəl/ *adj* [*more* ~; *most* ~] **:** not stable: such as **a :** likely to change ▪ *unstable* prices ▪ *unstable* weather **b :** not emotionally or mentally healthy ▪ She is emotionally/mentally *unstable*. **c :** not held in a secure position **:** likely to move or fall ▪ an *unstable* tower/ladder **d** *technical* **:** having a chemical structure or physical state that changes easily ▪ an *unstable* nuclear reactor core ▪ an *unstable* element

un·stat·ed /ˌʌnˈsteɪtəd/ *adj, somewhat formal* : expressed or understood without being directly stated ▪ an *unstated* conclusion/policy

un·steady /ˌʌnˈstɛdi/ *adj* [*more* ~; *most* ~] : not steady: such as **a** : not standing or moving in a steady and balanced way ▪ The stool/ladder is *unsteady*. ▪ He was a little *unsteady* on his feet. ▪ The horse walked with an *unsteady* gait. **b** : shaking or moving because of nervousness, weakness, etc. ▪ He signed his name with an *unsteady* hand. ▪ Her voice was *unsteady*. **c** : not happening or proceeding in a smooth and constant way ▪ The progress of the work has been *unsteady*. ▪ a period of *unsteady* growth

– un·stead·i·ly /ˌʌnˈstɛdəli/ *adv* **– un·stead·i·ness** /ˌʌnˈstɛdinəs/ *noun* [*noncount*]

un·stint·ing /ˌʌnˈstɪntɪŋ/ *adj* [*more* ~; *most* ~] *formal* — used to say that someone gives something (such as praise or support) in a very strong and generous way ▪ He was *unstinting* in his praise of her efforts. [=he praised her efforts very highly] ▪ *unstinting* support

– un·stint·ing·ly *adv* ▪ She gave *unstintingly* of her time.

un·stop·pa·ble /ˌʌnˈstɑːpəbəl/ *adj* [*more* ~; *most* ~] : not able to be stopped ▪ *unstoppable* momentum ▪ At this point in the campaign, he appears to be *unstoppable*.

un·stressed /ˌʌnˈstrest/ *adj* : not having an accent or a stress ▪ The second syllable of the word "random" is *unstressed*.

un·struc·tured /ˌʌnˈstrʌkʧəd/ *adj* [*more* ~; *most* ~] : not happening according to a plan : not organized or planned in a formal way ▪ *Unstructured* play time is important for children. ▪ Her life is very *unstructured*.

un·stuck /ˌʌnˈstʌk/ *adj* : able to move freely : no longer stuck ▪ We couldn't get the steering wheel *unstuck*.

become/come unstuck **1** : to stop being stuck to something ▪ The suction cup *came unstuck* from the wall. ▪ The photograph was *becoming unstuck*. **2** *Brit, informal* : to fail ▪ Their marriage *came unstuck* [=(*US*) *came unglued*] last summer.

un·stud·ied /ˌʌnˈstʌdid/ *adj*

1 [*more* ~; *most* ~] : not planned or done in a deliberate way : sincere and natural ▪ She moved with an *unstudied* grace.

2 : not studied by scientists before ▪ a previously *unstudied* species

un·styl·ish /ˌʌnˈstaɪlɪʃ/ *adj* : not stylish or fashionable ▪ *unstylish* clothes

un·sub·stan·ti·at·ed /ˌʌnsəbˈstænʃiˌeɪtəd/ *adj, formal* : not proven to be true ▪ *unsubstantiated* claims/rumors

un·suc·cess·ful /ˌʌnsəkˈsɛsfəl/ *adj* [*more* ~; *most* ~] : not having or producing success : not successful ▪ The operation was *unsuccessful*. ▪ an *unsuccessful* musician ▪ His last novel was *unsuccessful*. ▪ an *unsuccessful* attempt

– un·suc·cess·ful·ly *adv* ▪ They tried *unsuccessfully* to change his mind.

un·suit·able /ˌʌnˈsuːtəbəl/ *adj* [*more* ~; *most* ~] : not having the qualities that are right, needed, or appropriate for something : not suitable ▪ She is an *unsuitable* candidate for the job. ▪ The movie is *unsuitable* for children.

– un·suit·abil·i·ty /ˌʌnˌsuːtəˈbɪləti/ *noun* [*noncount*] ▪ Her *unsuitability* for the job became evident. **– un·suit·ably** /ˌʌnˈsuːtəbli/ *adv* ▪ They were *unsuitably* dressed for a dinner party.

un·suit·ed /ˌʌnˈsuːtəd/ *adj* [*more* ~; *most* ~] : not having the qualities that are right, needed, or appropriate for something or someone : not suited — *+ for* or *to* ▪ She is completely *unsuited for* the job. ▪ He is *unsuited to* academic life.

un·sul·lied /ˌʌnˈsʌlid/ *adj, formal + literary* : not harmed or damaged in any way ▪ an *unsullied* reputation

un·sung /ˌʌnˈsʌŋ/ *adj* [*more* ~; *most* ~] : not given attention and praise that is deserved for doing good things ▪ the *unsung* men and women who keep the streets safe ▪ He is one of the ***unsung heroes*** of the civil rights movement.

un·su·per·vised /ˌʌnˈsuːpəˌvaɪzd/ *adj* : not watched and directed by someone who has authority : not supervised ▪ The kids were left *unsupervised* while their parents were out. ▪ *Unsupervised* visits are not allowed at the prison.

un·sup·port·ed /ˌʌnsəˈpoətəd/ *adj*

1 : not having physical support ▪ Removing the posts left part of the roof *unsupported*.

2 : not having evidence showing that something is true ▪ an *unsupported* claim/theory ▪ *unsupported* allegations ▪ Their claims are *unsupported* by evidence.

un·sure /ˌʌnˈʃə/ *adj* [*more* ~; *most* ~] : not certain about something : not sure ▪ He was *unsure* whether she had reserved a room or not. ▪ I'm *unsure* about the offer. ▪ He seemed *unsure* of what to say. ▪ We're *unsure* (of) how to proceed.

unsure of yourself : not confident about what to do or say ▪ She was *unsure of herself* as a child. ▪ I felt a little *unsure of myself* when I started the job, but things are better now.

un·sur·passed /ˌʌnsəˈpæst, *Brit* ˌʌnsəˈpɑːst/ *adj, somewhat formal* : better or greater than anyone or anything else ▪ The region is *unsurpassed* in beauty. ▪ *unsurpassed* craftsmanship

un·sur·prised /ˌʌnsəˈpraɪzd/ *adj* : not surprised by something because you expected it ▪ I was *unsurprised* to find he would not be coming. ▪ Readers will be *unsurprised* by her revelations.

un·sur·pris·ing /ˌʌnsəˈpraɪzɪŋ/ *adj* [*more* ~; *most* ~] : not causing surprise because you expected it : not surprising ▪ His anger is *unsurprising*. ▪ an *unsurprising* fact

– un·sur·pris·ing·ly *adv* ▪ They decided, *unsurprisingly*, to stay with their original plan.

un·sus·pect·ed /ˌʌnsəˈspɛktəd/ *adj* : not known to exist ▪ He died suddenly of an *unsuspected* heart condition. : not suspected ▪ His real intentions were *unsuspected* by his friends.

un·sus·pect·ing /ˌʌnsəˈspɛktɪŋ/ *adj* [*more* ~; *most* ~] : not knowing about or expecting something bad that is going to happen or that could happen ▪ *unsuspecting* victims ▪ *Unsuspecting* tourists are the prey of pickpockets.

un·sus·tain·able /ˌʌnsəˈsteɪnəbəl/ *adj* : not able to last or continue for a long time : not sustainable ▪ *unsustainable* logging/fishing ▪ The current rate of economic growth is *unsustainable*.

un·swayed /ˌʌnˈsweɪd/ *adj* — used to say that someone's opinion has not changed despite efforts to change it ▪ I tried to convince him, but he remained *unswayed*.

un·sweet·ened /ˌʌnˈswiːtnd/ *adj* : not having sugar added : not sweetened ▪ *unsweetened* iced tea

un·swerv·ing /ˌʌnˈswəvɪŋ/ *adj* : not changing or becoming weaker : always staying strong ▪ his *unswerving* devotion to duty ▪ *unswerving* loyalty

un·sym·pa·thet·ic /ˌʌnˌsɪmpəˈθɛtɪk/ *adj* [*more* ~; *most* ~] : not sympathetic: such as **a** : not feeling or showing concern about someone who is in a bad situation ▪ an *unsympathetic* judge ▪ The magazine article was *unsympathetic*. — often *+ to* or *toward* ▪ She is very *unsympathetic to/toward* the poor. **b** *not used before a noun* : not having or showing support for or approval of something — often *+ to* or *toward* ▪ He was *unsympathetic to/toward* their cause. [=he did not support their cause] **c** : not having pleasant or appealing qualities ▪ The hero in the movie is an *unsympathetic* character.

un·taint·ed /ˌʌnˈteɪntəd/ *adj, formal* : not damaged or spoiled in any way : not tainted ▪ a woman of *untainted* character ▪ He was *untainted* by corruption.

un·tamed /ˌʌnˈteɪmd/ *adj* [*more* ~; *most* ~] : wild and not controlled by people : not tamed ▪ the wild and *untamed* beauty of the mountains ▪ *untamed* animals

un·tan·gle /ˌʌnˈtæŋgəl/ *verb* **-tan·gles; -tan·gled; -tan·gling** [*+ obj*] : to separate (things that are twisted together) ▪ He *untangled* the ropes. : to remove the twists or knots in (something) ▪ She carefully *untangled* the child's hair. ▪ He *untangled* the garden hose. — often used figuratively ▪ She *untangled* [=*solved*] the mystery. ▪ They're still trying to *untangle* the financial mess that they've gotten themselves into.

un·tapped /ˌʌnˈtæpt/ *adj* : available but not used ▪ *untapped* resources

un·ten·a·ble /ˌʌnˈtɛnəbəl/ *adj* [*more* ~; *most* ~] *formal* : not capable of being defended against attack or criticism : not tenable ▪ an *untenable* argument ▪ The theory is *untenable*.

un·tend·ed /ˌʌnˈtɛndəd/ *adj* : not watched and taken care of ▪ The garden was left *untended* while they were away. ▪ Three *untended* horses grazed in the field.

un·test·ed /ˌʌnˈtɛstəd/ *adj* : not yet shown to be good, strong, etc., by being used, placed in a difficult situation, etc. ▪ *untested* troops [=troops that have not yet fought in a battle] ▪ an *untested* theory

un·think·able /ˌʌnˈθɪŋkəbəl/ *adj* [*more* ~; *most* ~] : impossible to imagine or believe ▪ It was *unthinkable* [=*inconceiv-*

able] that he was leaving. **: too bad or shocking to be thought of** ▪ *unthinkable* [=*unimaginable*] cruelty

the unthinkable **:** something that you cannot accept, believe, or imagine; *especially* **:** something that is so bad that you do not want to think about it ▪ And then, *the unthinkable* happened: the car skidded out of control and crashed.

un·think·ing /ˌʌnˈθɪŋkɪŋ/ *adj* [*more* ~; *most* ~] **: done or said in a foolish or careless way without thinking about the possible effects** ▪ *unthinking* remarks ▪ His *unthinking* agreement made me uneasy. **: behaving in a foolish or careless way without careful thought** ▪ *unthinking* consumers

— **un·think·ing·ly** *adv* ▪ She agreed to go *unthinkingly*. ▪ I *unthinkingly* put my purse on the roof of the car.

un·ti·dy /ˌʌnˈtaɪdi/ *adj* [*more* ~; *most* ~]

1 a : not neat or clean ▪ His room was *untidy*. ▪ an *untidy* desk **b : not having neat or clean habits** ▪ *untidy* roommates

2 : not done in an organized and pleasant way ▪ an *untidy* [=*messy*] divorce

— **un·ti·di·ness** /ˌʌnˈtaɪdinəs/ *noun* [*noncount*]

un·tie /ˌʌnˈtaɪ/ *verb* **-ties; -tied; -ty·ing**

1 : to undo the knots in or of (something) [+ *obj*] She *untied* her shoelaces/shoes. ▪ He *untied* the package and opened it. ▪ *untie* a rope ▪ Your shoelaces are *untied*. [*no obj*] The knot *untied* easily.

2 [+ *obj*] **: to remove the rope, string, etc., that attaches (something or someone) to something** ▪ She *untied* the horse from the post.

[1]un·til /ənˈtɪl/ *prep*

1 : up to (a particular time) — used to indicate the time when a particular situation, activity, or period ends ▪ I stayed *until* morning. ▪ He was in prison from 1850 *until* the 1854 revolt. ▪ She will be out of the office *until* next week. ▪ The coupon is good *until* the end of March. ▪ ***Until then***, I had never known happiness. ▪ I will keep working ***up until*** dinnertime.

2 — used to indicate the time when something will happen, become true, etc. ▪ We don't open *until* ten. ▪ The car won't be ready *until* tomorrow.

[2]until *conj* **: up to the time or point that** ▪ We played *until* it got dark. ▪ Wait *until* I call. ▪ Keep going *until* I tell you to stop. ▪ I ran *until* I was breathless. ▪ Stay here *until* the danger has passed. ▪ Stir the dough *until* it forms a ball. ▪ You cannot go outside *until* you finish your homework. = ***Not until*** you finish your homework can you go outside. [=when you finish your homework you can go outside, but not before then]

un·time·ly /ˌʌnˈtaɪmli/ *adj* [*more* ~; *most* ~]

1 : happening or done sooner than you expect : occurring before the proper or right time ▪ the tragedy of her *untimely* [=*premature*] death

2 : happening or done at a time that is not suitable or appropriate ▪ an *untimely* comment/interruption/error

un·tir·ing /ˌʌnˈtaɪrɪŋ/ *adj* [*more* ~; *most* ~] **: working very hard with a lot of energy for a long time : never seeming to get tired** ▪ the rescuers' *untiring* efforts ▪ She is an *untiring* [=*tireless*] advocate for the poor.

un·ti·tled /ˌʌnˈtaɪtl̩d/ *adj* **: not named : not having a title** ▪ an *untitled* poem ▪ This work is *untitled*.

un·to /ˈʌntu/ *prep, old-fashioned* **— used in the past like "to"** ▪ I will search *unto* the ends of the earth for thee. ▪ I will be with you *unto* [=*until*] the end of time.

un·told /ˌʌnˈtoʊld/ *adj*

1 : not told or made public ▪ *untold* secrets ▪ His is a story yet *untold*.

2 : too many to count or too much to measure ▪ *untold* riches ▪ stars in *untold* numbers

[1]un·touch·able /ˌʌnˈtʌʧəbəl/ *adj* [*more* ~; *most* ~] **: not able to be touched: such as a : too powerful or important to be punished, criticized, etc.** ▪ The mayor believed that he was *untouchable* and not subject to the same laws as the rest of us. **b : too good to be equaled by anyone else** ▪ The team's record was *untouchable*.

[2]untouchable *noun, pl* **-ables** [*count*] **: a member of the lowest social class in India**

un·touched /ˌʌnˈtʌʧt/ *adj* **: not touched: such as a : not handled or used** ▪ The piano was *untouched* for years. **b** [*more* ~; *most* ~] **: not changed : still in the original state or condition** ▪ *untouched* wilderness ▪ The original agreement remains *untouched*. **c : not eaten or drunk : not tasted** ▪ He left his food *untouched*. **d : not emotionally affected by something** ▪ She was *untouched* [=*unmoved*] by his declarations of love. **e : not dealt with** ▪ The artist's biographer left a few important events of his life *untouched*.

un·to·ward /ˌʌnˈtowəd, ˌʌnˈtoəd/ *adj, formal*

1 : bad or unfavorable : not good ▪ *untoward* side effects ▪ disadvantages and *untoward* circumstances

2 : not proper or appropriate ▪ There was nothing *untoward* about his appearance.

un·trained /ˌʌnˈtreɪnd/ *adj* [*more* ~; *most* ~] **: without formal training** ▪ *untrained* employees ▪ an *untrained* singing voice ▪ To the *untrained* eye, it looks like the magician really is sawing the woman in half. ▪ His *untrained* ear could not pick out the wrong notes.

un·tram·meled (*US*) *or Brit* **un·tram·melled** /ˌʌnˈtræməld/ *adj, formal* **: not limited or restricted** ▪ *untrammeled* greed ▪ They lived as they pleased, *untrammeled* by convention.

un·treat·ed /ˌʌnˈtriːtəd/ *adj*

1 : not getting medical care : without medical treatment ▪ an *untreated* disease ▪ The patient remains *untreated*.

2 : not made better or safer by being treated with a chemical or other substance ▪ *untreated* sewage ▪ *untreated* wood

— **un·treat·able** /ˌʌnˈtriːtəbəl/ *adj* ▪ an *untreatable* disease

un·tried /ˌʌnˈtraɪd/ *adj* **: not yet shown to be good, strong, etc., by being used, placed in a difficult situation, etc. : not tested or tried** ▪ *untried* technology ▪ an *untried* remedy

un·true /ˌʌnˈtruː/ *adj* [*more* ~; *most* ~]

1 : not true : FALSE ▪ The allegations are *untrue*. ▪ He made *untrue* statements to the press.

2 *literary + old-fashioned* **: not loyal to someone or something : not honest** ▪ Her lover had been *untrue*.

un·trust·wor·thy /ˌʌnˈtrʌstˌwəði/ *adj* [*more* ~; *most* ~] **: not able to be trusted : not trustworthy** ▪ an *untrustworthy* person ▪ He has proven himself *untrustworthy*.

un·truth /ˌʌnˈtruːθ/ *noun, pl* **-truths** *formal*

1 [*count*] **: a statement that is not true : LIE** ▪ a blatant *untruth* ▪ the *untruths* he has uttered

2 [*noncount*] **: the state of being false or a lie** ▪ The *untruth* [=*falseness*] of that statement is apparent.

un·truth·ful /ˌʌnˈtruːθfəl/ *adj* [*more* ~; *most* ~] **: not telling the truth : not truthful** ▪ *untruthful* reports ▪ an *untruthful* witness

— **un·truth·ful·ly** *adv*

un·tucked /ˌʌnˈtʌkt/ *adj, chiefly US* **: not tucked into something (such as your pants)** ▪ Your shirt is *untucked*.

un·turned /ˌʌnˈtənd/ *adj*

leave no stone unturned see [1]STONE

un·tu·tored /ˌʌnˈtuːtəd, *Brit* ˌʌnˈtjuːtəd/ *adj* [*more* ~; *most* ~] *formal* **: not having been formally taught something** ▪ an *untutored* artist

un·typ·i·cal /ˌʌnˈtɪpɪkəl/ *adj* [*more* ~; *most* ~] **: not usual or normal : not typical** ▪ His behavior was *untypical*. [=*atypical*] ▪ Marrying at such a young age was not *untypical* of the time.

un·us·able /ˌʌnˈjuːzəbəl/ *adj* [*more* ~; *most* ~] **: not good enough to be used : not usable** ▪ The tools were rusty and *unusable*. ▪ *unusable* land

un·used /ˌʌnˈjuːzd/ *adj* [*more* ~; *most* ~]

1 : not being used : not having been used before ▪ *unused* airline tickets ▪ *unused* disk space ▪ The library has been *unused* for 10 years.

2 : available for use in the future ▪ I have four days of *unused* vacation time left.

un·used to /ˌʌnˈjuːst-/ **: not familiar or comfortable with (something) : not used to (something)** ▪ He is *unused to* large crowds. ▪ I was *unused to* being awake so late at night.

un·usu·al /ˌʌnˈjuːʒəwəl/ *adj* [*more* ~; *most* ~]

1 : not normal or usual ▪ *unusual* occurrences/behavior ▪ It's not *unusual* for him to stay late at work. ▪ a scene of *unusual* beauty ▪ cruel and *unusual* punishment

2 : different or strange in a way that attracts attention ▪ an *unusual* car/design

3 : not commonly seen, heard, etc. ▪ She saw an *unusual* [=*rare*] flower while hiking. ▪ She has an *unusual* name.

un·usu·al·ly /ˌʌnˈjuːʒəwəli/ *adv* [*more* ~; *most* ~]

1 : to a great degree : VERY ▪ an *unusually* large dog

2 : in a way that is not normal or usual ▪ My friend, most *unusually*, decided not to go with me. ▪ You're *unusually* quiet this morning.

un·ut·ter·able /ˌʌnˈʌtərəbəl/ *adj, always used before a noun* [*more* ~; *most* ~] *formal* **: too strong or great to be expressed or described** ▪ *unutterable* joy/pain

— **un·ut·ter·ably** /ˌʌnˈʌtərəbli/ *adv*

un·var·nished /ˌʌnˈvaənɪʃt/ *adj* [*more* ~; *most* ~]

1 : plain and direct : HONEST ▪ the *unvarnished* truth ▪ If you

U

want my *unvarnished* opinion, the movie stinks.
2 : not covered with varnish ▪ *unvarnished* wood

un·vary·ing /ˌʌnˈverijɪŋ/ *adj* : always the same : never changing or varying ▪ She follows the same, *unvarying* routine every morning.

un·veil /ˌʌnˈveɪl/ *verb* **-veils**; **-veiled**; **-veil·ing** [+ *obj*]
1 : to show or reveal (something) to others for the first time ▪ The developer *unveiled* plans for a new housing complex. ▪ The company will *unveil* its newest product today.
2 : to remove a cover from (something) so that people can see it ▪ *unveil* a statue
— **un·veiling** *noun, pl* **-ings** [*count*] ▪ Many people were present for the *unveiling* of the statue.

un·voiced /ˌʌnˈvɔɪst/ *adj*
1 : not expressed in spoken words ▪ They nodded their *unvoiced* [=*unspoken*] agreement.
2 *linguistics, of a speech sound* : made without vibrating your vocal cords ▪ The "th" in the word "thing" is *unvoiced*.

un·waged /ˌʌnˈweɪʤd/ *adj, Brit* : not earning or paying wages ▪ *unwaged* students ▪ *unwaged* work

un·want·ed /ˌʌnˈwɑːntəd/ *adj* [*more* ~; *most* ~] : not wanted or needed ▪ *unwanted* attention ▪ an *unwanted* pregnancy

un·war·rant·ed /ˌʌnˈworəntəd/ *adj* [*more* ~; *most* ~] *formal* : not necessary or appropriate : not warranted ▪ Your anger is *unwarranted*. ▪ an *unwarranted* assumption

un·wary /ˌʌnˈweri/ *adj* [*more* ~; *most* ~] : easily fooled or surprised : not aware of and careful about possible problems, dangers, etc. ▪ *unwary* buyers ▪ The fast-moving tide sometimes surprises *unwary* swimmers.

un·washed /ˌʌnˈwɑːʃt/ *adj* : not clean : not washed ▪ a sink full of *unwashed* dishes ▪ *unwashed* hair
the (great) unwashed *old-fashioned + humorous* : ordinary or common people who do not have a lot of money, power, or social status ▪ I'm just a member of *the great unwashed*.

un·wa·ver·ing /ˌʌnˈweɪvərɪŋ/ *adj* [*more* ~; *most* ~] : continuing in a strong and steady way : not changing or wavering ▪ He has my *unwavering* support. ▪ *unwavering* loyalty/bravery
— **un·wa·ver·ing·ly** *adv*

un·wed /ˌʌnˈwed/ *adj* : not married ▪ an *unwed* mother

un·wel·come /ˌʌnˈwɛlkəm/ *adj* [*more* ~; *most* ~] : not wanted or welcome ▪ *unwelcome* news ▪ He made me feel *unwelcome*.

un·wel·com·ing /ˌʌnˈwɛlkəmɪŋ/ *adj* [*more* ~; *most* ~] : not making you feel comfortable and welcome ▪ The hotel staff was *unwelcoming*. ▪ The restaurant was dark and *unwelcoming*.

un·well /ˌʌnˈwɛl/ *adj* [*more* ~; *most* ~] *formal* : not feeling well : SICK ▪ Miss Bennett, are you *unwell*? ▪ I am sorry she is feeling *unwell*.

un·whole·some /ˌʌnˈhoulsəm/ *adj* [*more* ~; *most* ~]
1 : not good for your health ▪ an *unwholesome* diet ▪ *unwholesome* foods
2 : not mentally or morally good and normal ▪ He has an *unwholesome* fascination with death. ▪ *unwholesome* thoughts ▪ The company has engaged in *unwholesome* [=*improper*] business practices.

un·wieldy /ˌʌnˈwiːldi/ *adj* [*more* ~; *most* ~] : difficult to handle, control, or deal with because of being large, heavy, or complex ▪ a large, *unwieldy* box ▪ The system is outdated and *unwieldy*. ▪ *unwieldy* [=*awkward*] prose
— **un·wield·i·ness** /ˌʌnˈwiːldinəs/ *noun* [*noncount*]

un·will·ing /ˌʌnˈwɪlɪŋ/ *adj* [*more* ~; *most* ~] : not willing: such as **a** : not wanting to do something — usually followed by *to + verb* ▪ The witness was *unwilling to cooperate*. ▪ He is *unwilling to help*. **b** *always used before a noun* : made to do something that you do not want to do ▪ He was an *unwilling* participant in the demonstration.
— **un·will·ing·ly** *adv* ▪ I took his money most *unwillingly*.
— **un·will·ing·ness** *noun* [*noncount*] ▪ Your *unwillingness* to do extra work cost you a promotion.

un·wind /ˌʌnˈwaɪnd/ *verb* **-winds**; **-wound** /-ˈwaund/; **-wind·ing**
1 : to move the end of something (such as a piece of string) that is wound in a roll, coil, etc., so that it becomes straight [+ *obj*] She *unwound* some thread from the spool. [*no obj*] The fishing line *unwound* quickly.
2 [*no obj*] : to relax and stop thinking about work, problems, etc. ▪ I wanted to *unwind* after a hard day.

un·wise /ˌʌnˈwaɪz/ *adj* [*more* ~; *most* ~] : not intelligent or wise ▪ an *unwise* decision ▪ It would be *unwise* to buy a house now.
— **un·wise·ly** *adv* ▪ You chose *unwisely*.

un·wit·ting /ˌʌnˈwɪtɪŋ/ *adj, always used before a noun* [*more* ~; *most* ~]
1 : not aware of what is really happening ▪ He kept the truth from his *unwitting* friends. ▪ an *unwitting* victim of fraud
2 : not intended or planned ▪ an *unwitting* mistake
— **un·wit·ting·ly** *adv* ▪ She *unwittingly* offended the hostess.

un·wont·ed /ˌʌnˈwɑːntəd, *Brit* ˌʌnˈwəuntəd/ *adj* [*more* ~; *most* ~] *formal* : not normal, usual, or expected ▪ He was surprised by her *unwonted* cheerfulness.

un·work·able /ˌʌnˈwɚkəbəl/ *adj* [*more* ~; *most* ~] : not able to be done well or successfully : not practical or workable ▪ It's an interesting idea, but completely *unworkable*. ▪ an *unworkable* plan

un·world·ly /ˌʌnˈwɚldli/ *adj* [*more* ~; *most* ~]
1 : having or showing a lack of experience or knowledge of the world ▪ an *unworldly* young man
2 : having an unusual quality that does not seem to be of this world ▪ the *unworldly* beauty of the Grand Canyon ▪ an *unworldly* landscape

un·wor·ried /ˌʌnˈwɚrid/ *adj* [*more* ~; *most* ~] : calm and relaxed : not worried ▪ She appeared *unworried* about/by the poll results.

un·wor·thy /ˌʌnˈwɚði/ *adj* **un·wor·thi·er**; **-est** [*also more* ~; *most* ~] *formal*
1 : not good enough to deserve something or someone : not worthy ▪ I am *unworthy*. — usually + *of* ▪ She thought he was *unworthy of* his promotion. ▪ He is *unworthy of* her.
2 : not appropriate or acceptable for a good or respected person ▪ *unworthy* thoughts/feelings — usually + *of* ▪ Those thoughts are *unworthy of* you. [=you are too good a person for those thoughts] ▪ actions *unworthy of* a gentleman
— **un·wor·thi·ness** /ˌʌnˈwɚðinəs/ *noun* [*noncount*]

unwound *past tense and past participle of* UNWIND

un·wrap /ˌʌnˈræp/ *verb* **-wraps**; **-wrapped**; **-wrap·ping** [+ *obj*] : to remove the covering that is around something ▪ He *unwrapped* the gift. ▪ *Unwrap* the bandages so I can see the wound.

un·writ·ten /ˌʌnˈrɪtn̩/ *adj* : spoken or understood without being written ▪ They had an *unwritten* agreement. ▪ an *unwritten* rule

un·yield·ing /ˌʌnˈjiːldɪŋ/ *adj* [*more* ~; *most* ~]
1 : not changing or stopping ▪ her *unyielding* [=*firm*] belief in his innocence ▪ *unyielding* opposition/devotion
2 : not flexible or soft ▪ the hard, *unyielding* ground
— **un·yield·ing·ly** *adv*

un·zip /ˌʌnˈzɪp/ *verb* **-zips**; **-zipped**; **-zip·ping** [+ *obj*]
1 : to open (something) by using a zipper ▪ He *unzipped* his jacket. ▪ She *unzipped* the tent flap.
2 *computers* : to cause (a file that has been reduced in size) to return to its original size by using special software ▪ *unzip* a compressed file

[1]up /ˈʌp/ *adv*
1 a : from a lower to a higher place or position ▪ The land rises *up* from the valley. ▪ Pull *up* your pants/socks. = Pull your pants/socks *up*. ▪ I'll come *up* [=*upstairs*] in a minute. ▪ She stood beneath the window and called *up* to her friend. ▪ Please pick your clothes *up* off the floor. ▪ We watched the sun come *up*. **b** : in a high position or place ▪ Keep your head *up*. ▪ He held *up* his hand. ▪ We stored the boxes *up* in the attic. ▪ She stuck a notice *up* on the wall. ▪ What's going on *up* there?
2 : toward the sky or ceiling ▪ He looked *up* at the stars. ▪ The cards were on the table facing *up*.
3 : from beneath the ground or water to the surface ▪ The dolphin came *up* for air. ▪ She was in the garden pulling *up* weeds.
4 a : to or toward the north ▪ She flew *up* from Florida. ▪ They drove *up* to Canada. ▪ The weather is much colder **up north**. **b** *informal* : to or toward a place that is thought of as above or away from another place ▪ She went *up* to the cabin for the weekend. ▪ How long will it take to drive *up* (to their house) and back? ▪ Come on *up* and see us sometime. **c** *chiefly Brit* : to or at a more important place (such as a large city or university) ▪ He went *up* to London. ▪ Their daughter is *up* at Oxford.
5 a : to or toward a place that is close to someone or something ▪ I walked *up* to her and said "hello." ▪ Please pull *up* a chair. ▪ He lay down and pulled the covers *up*. **b** : to or toward a more forward position ▪ We moved *up* to the front of

the line. ▪ I'll bring these *up* to the checkout for you.

6 : **in or into a vertical or upright position** ▪ Please stand *up* for the national anthem. ▪ Sit *up*. Don't slouch. ▪ He helped the man *up* (from his seat). ▪ She turned the box *up* on its end.

7 : **out of bed** ▪ What time did you get *up* this morning? ▪ I stayed *up* late last night. [=I went to sleep late last night]

8 a : **with greater force** ▪ Please speak *up*. I can't hear you. **b :** **at a higher or greater important position in a list or series** ▪ Supporting public education doesn't seem to be very ***high/far up*** on the government's agenda. ▪ Spending time with family ranks pretty *high up* on my list. [=I think it is important to spend time with family] — **opposite** DOWN **c :** **to a higher or greater level, amount, or rate** ▪ Could you turn the volume/heat *up*, please? ▪ It takes this car a long time to warm *up*. ▪ The price of oil went *up*. ▪ They ran *up* a big bill. ▪ The car sped *up* and then slowed down. ▪ The author is good at building *up* suspense. ▪ The game is for children 12 years old and *up*. [=and older] ▪ Students will be tested from fifth grade *up*. — **opposite** DOWN

9 : **into a better or more advanced position or state** ▪ She worked herself *up* in the company. ▪ He grew *up* on a farm.

10 : **so as to appear or be present** ▪ The missing ring turned *up*. [=the missing ring was found] ▪ They never showed *up*. ▪ Houses were going *up* quickly.

11 : **in or into a working or usable state** ▪ He set *up* his new computer. ▪ We should put the tents *up* first.

12 : **to someone's attention especially for discussion or consideration** ▪ He brought *up* the issue at the meeting. ▪ Her contract has come *up* for negotiation.

13 : **so as to be done or completed** ▪ He filled *up* the gas tank. ▪ She gathered *up* her belongings and left. ▪ I still have some work to finish *up*. ▪ She used *up* all the tape. ▪ They cleaned *up* the kitchen after supper. ▪ He summed *up* the results of the study. ▪ She added *up* all the numbers.

14 : **so as to be closed** ▪ He sealed *up* the package. ▪ She zipped *up* her son's jacket.

15 : **into pieces or parts** ▪ She tore/cut *up* the paper. ▪ Each group had a leader who divided *up* the work.

16 : **into a state of activity or excitement** ▪ She stirred *up* the fire/crowd. ▪ He worked himself *up* over nothing.

17 : **to a stop** ▪ He pulled the car *up* at the curb.

18 : **for each player or team :** APIECE ▪ The score is two *up*.

up and down **1 :** **forward and backward several or many times : repeatedly in one direction and then the opposite direction** ▪ He paced *up and down* in the waiting room. **2 :** **from a lower position to a higher position several times** ▪ The children were jumping *up and down*. ▪ Her father ***looked me up and down*** [=looked at me carefully to decide what he thought of me] before inviting me in.

up close see [3]CLOSE

[2]**up** *adj*

1 ***not used before a noun*** **a :** **in a high place or position** ▪ The candy is *up* on the top shelf. **b :** **raised so as to be opened** ▪ The window is already *up*. **c :** **risen above the horizon** ▪ The sun is *up*. **d :** **risen from beneath the ground or water to the surface** ▪ The tulips are *up*. **e :** **in a forward place or position** ▪ Your package is *up* at the front desk. ▪ We were *up* near the stage.

2 ***not used before a noun*** **a :** **out of bed** ▪ Are the kids *up* yet? ▪ We are *up* every morning at six. **b :** AWAKE ▪ I was *up* all night studying for the test. — **see also** UP AND ABOUT **(below)**

3 ***not used before a noun*** **:** **higher than usual** ▪ Gas prices are *up* again. ▪ The river is *up*. ▪ Attendance has been *up*. ▪ The interest rate is *up* (by) three percent. ▪ Profits are ***up on*** last year. [=profits are higher than they were last year]

4 ***always used before a noun*** **:** **moving or going to a higher level** ▪ the *up* escalator

5 ***not used before a noun, informal*** **:** **happening : going on** ▪ I could tell something was *up* by the look on her face. ▪ Your order should have arrived. Let me find out ***what's up***. ▪ "Can I talk to you for a minute?" "Sure. *What's up*?" [=what do you want to talk to me about?] ▪ (*US*) "Hi, Jim. *What's up*?" [=what's new?] "Not much." — **often + *with*** ▪ Something's *up with* her. She looks upset. ▪ Let me find out *what's up with* your order. ▪ *What's up with* you? Why are you so grumpy? ▪ "Did you hear that he quit his job?" "Yeah. ***What's up with that***?" [=why did he quit his job?]

6 ***not used before a noun*** **:** **having more points than an opponent : ahead of an opponent** ▪ The team was 10 points *up* [=it had a lead of 10 points] in the third quarter. ▪ The team was *up* (by) two runs.

7 ***not used before a noun*** **:** **operating or functioning** ▪ The system/network is *up* again. = The system/network is ***up and running*** again.

8 ***not used before a noun*** **:** **beginning your turn in an activity** ▪ Get ready. You're *up* next.

9 ***not used before a noun, of time*** **:** **at an end** ▪ Put your pencils down. Time is *up*. [=the time during which you are allowed to work on the test has ended] ▪ His term as president is nearly *up*. [=has nearly ended]

10 ***not used before a noun*** **[*more* ~; *most* ~] :** **happy or excited** ▪ She was feeling down, but now she's *up* again.

11 ***informal*** **:** **having a lot of knowledge about something** ▪ She's always ***up on*** the latest fashions.

12 ***chiefly Brit, of a road*** **:** **having the surface broken because repairs are being done** ▪ They've had the road *up* for weeks.

up against **1 :** **placed so as to be touching (something)** ▪ The bed was *up against* the wall. — **see also** ***up against a/the wall*** at [1]WALL **2 :** **confronted with** ▪ The problem we are *up against* [=the problem that we have to deal with] is a difficult one.

up against it ***informal*** **:** **in a difficult situation** ▪ With hardly any money or time left, we are really *up against it*!

up and about *or chiefly US* ***up and around*** **:** **out of bed and doing things** ▪ She recently had surgery, but now she's *up and about* again. ▪ I didn't expect you to be *up and around* this early.

up and down ***informal*** **:** **sometimes good and sometimes bad** ▪ Her relationship with him is *up and down*. ▪ They have an *up and down* relationship.

up for **1** ***informal*** **:** **wanting to have or do (something)** ▪ I'm *up for* some Chinese food. ▪ Are you *up for* watching a movie? ▪ We're going out dancing tonight. Are you *up for* it? [=are you interested in joining us?] **2 a — used to say that someone or something is or will be involved in a particular process and especially one that leads to a decision** ▪ His proposal is *up for* consideration. [=is being considered] ▪ The budget is *up for* discussion in today's meeting. ▪ She is *up for* reelection next year. [=she will be trying to get reelected next year] ▪ He'll be *up for* parole in two more years. **b — used to say that something is available to be bought** ▪ Our house is ***up for sale***. [=our house is being sold] ▪ items that are ***up for auction*** **3 :** **appearing in a court of law because of being accused of (a crime)** ▪ He was *up for* armed robbery.

up to **1 a :** **capable of performing or dealing with (something)** ▪ She feels she is *up to* her role in the play. ▪ She feels *up to* the challenge. ▪ The patient is now *up to* seeing visitors. [=is now healthy enough to see visitors] **b :** **good enough for (something)** ▪ Her performance wasn't *up to* her usual standards. [=wasn't as good as it usually is] ▪ The hotel wasn't *up to* our expectations. [=wasn't as good as we expected it to be] ▪ (*Brit*) My Spanish ***isn't up to much***. [=my Spanish is not very good] **2 :** **doing something especially in a way that is secret and with intentions that are bad** ▪ What are they *up to*? ▪ I know they're *up to* something, but I don't know what. ▪ I'm sure he is ***up to no good***. **3 — used to say who is responsible for making a choice or decision** ▪ "Do you want Chinese food tonight or Italian?" "It doesn't matter to me, so it's *up to* you." ▪ The amount of your donation is entirely *up to* you. ▪ It is *up to* you to decide. **4 a — used to indicate the place or level that is reached by something** ▪ The water was *up to* our knees. = We were in water *up to* our knees. **b :** **to or at (a specified amount, level, etc.)** ▪ Estimates for repairing the car ran from $500 *up to* $1,000. ▪ The lottery is *up to* five million dollars. **c :** **as many or as much as (a specified number or amount)** ▪ *Up to* eight people can play the game. ▪ The car holds *up to* six people. ▪ The ship can carry *up to* 10 tons. **5 :** **during the time or period before** ▪ *Up to* this point, we have been discussing our long-term goals. ▪ *Up to* [=*until*] that time they had been fairly successful.

up to here ***informal*** **— used to show that you have too much of something to deal with or that you are very annoyed by something and will not accept any more of it** ▪ I have work *up to here* to do. [=I have a lot of work to do] ▪ ***I've had it up to here with*** your nonsense! [=I am sick of your nonsense]

up to par see PAR

up to snuff see [2]SNUFF

up to speed see [1]SPEED

up to your ears see [1]EAR

up to your eyeballs see [1]EYEBALL

[3]**up** *prep*

1 : to, toward, or at a higher point on (something) ▪ He climbed *up* the ladder. ▪ She had to walk her bike *up* the hill. ▪ The bathroom is *up* the stairs.
2 : along the course or path of (something) ▪ Go *up* the street/road and turn left. ▪ We walked *up* the street to meet them. ▪ They live just *up* the block from us. ▪ I paddled the canoe *up* the river. ▪ The ship sailed *up* the coast. ▪ Her office is all the way *up* the hall on the right. ▪ He paced ***up and down*** the hall, waiting for news about his wife's operation.
up the creek (without a paddle) see CREEK
up the wazoo see WAZOO
up until *or* ***up till*** : during the time or period before ▪ *Up until* now, everything has gone very well.
up yours *slang, offensive* — used as a rude reply to someone who has annoyed or angered you

[4]up *noun, pl* **ups** [*count*] : a period or state of success, happiness, etc. — usually plural ▪ The company has had more *ups* than downs this year. ▪ We have had our ***ups and downs***.
on the up *chiefly Brit* : moving toward an improved or better state ▪ After a slow period, sales are *on the up*. [=sales are increasing]
on the up and up *informal* **1** *US* : honest and legal ▪ The deal seems to be *on the up and up*. ▪ I don't want to do anything dishonest. Let's keep everything *on the up and up*. **2** *Brit* : becoming more successful ▪ He recently got a promotion and is *on the up and up*.

[5]up *verb* **ups; upped** /ˈʌpt/; **up·ping** [+ *obj*] : to make (something) higher ▪ The restaurant *upped* [=*increased*] its prices.
up and *informal* : to do something specified in a sudden and unexpected way ▪ One day, he just *upped and* left home. ▪ Then she *ups and* marries some guy she'd just met. ✧ In U.S. English, *up and* is often used instead of *ups and* or *upped and*. ▪ One day, he just *up and* left home. [=he just suddenly left home] ▪ Then she *up and* marries some guy she'd just met.
up sticks see [1]STICK
up the ante see [1]ANTE

up–and–com·ing /ˌʌpəndˈkʌmɪŋ/ *adj* [*more* ~; *most* ~] : becoming more successful, important, and well known ▪ an *up-and-coming* young actor ▪ an *up-and-coming* new technology

up·beat /ˈʌpˌbiːt/ *adj* [*more* ~; *most* ~] : positive and cheerful : happy and hopeful ▪ I like a story with an *upbeat* ending. ▪ I tried to stay *upbeat* about losing the election. — opposite DOWNBEAT

up·braid /ˌʌpˈbreɪd/ *verb* **-braids; -braid·ed; -braid·ing** [+ *obj*] *formal* : to speak in an angry or critical way to (someone who has done something wrong) ▪ She *upbraided* [=*scolded*] him for not offering to help his grandfather.

up·bring·ing /ˈʌpˌbrɪŋɪŋ/ *noun, pl* **-ings** [*count*] : the way a child is raised : the care and teaching given to a child by parents or other people — usually singular ▪ My wife had a very sheltered *upbringing*. ▪ a religious/privileged *upbringing* ▪ His grandmother saw to his *upbringing*.

up·chuck /ˈʌpˌtʃʌk/ *verb* **-chucks; -chucked; -chuck·ing** *US, informal* : VOMIT [+ *obj*] The dog *upchucked* the food. [*no obj*] I felt like I was about to *upchuck*.

up·com·ing /ˈʌpˌkʌmɪŋ/ *adj, usually used before a noun* : happening or appearing soon ▪ the *upcoming* [=*approaching*] election/holiday ▪ the symphony's *upcoming* season ▪ *Upcoming* events are posted on our Web site.

up–coun·try /ˈʌpˌkʌntri/ *adj, old-fashioned* : of or relating to an area of land that is toward the middle of a country, north of a country, or outside of a particular region ▪ *up-country* cooking ▪ *up-country* farms ▪ an *up-country* accent
– up–coun·try /ˈʌpˈkʌntri/ *adv* ▪ He hitchhiked *up-country* in search of work. ▪ She lives *up-country*.

[1]up·date /ˌʌpˈdeɪt/ *verb* **-dates; -dat·ed; -dat·ing** [+ *obj*]
1 a : to change (something) by including the most recent information ▪ I need to *update* my address book. ▪ *update* all the population figures **b** : to make (something) more modern ▪ She wants to *update* her wardrobe. ▪ an *updated* [=*modern, up-to-date*] version of a classic story
2 : to give (someone) the most recent information about something — usually + *on* ▪ He *updated* us *on* his mother's health.

[2]up·date /ˈʌpˌdeɪt/ *noun, pl* **-dates** [*count*]
1 : a report that includes the most recent information about something ▪ I haven't heard the latest weather *update*. — often + *on* ▪ We receive daily *updates on* homes for sale in the area.
2 : a change or addition to computer software that includes the most recent information ▪ You can download *updates* for free.

up·draft /ˈʌpˌdræft, *Brit* ˈʌpˌdrɑːft/ *noun, pl* **-drafts** [*count*] *technical* : an upward flow of air ▪ hawks soaring on *updrafts*

up·end /ˌʌpˈɛnd/ *verb* **-ends; -end·ed; -end·ing** [+ *obj*]
1 : to cause (something) to be upside down : to turn (something) over ▪ He *upended* the bicycle to fix its flat tire. ▪ I *upended* the bucket to use as a stool. ▪ The security inspector *upended* my bag and dumped everything out.
2 : to cause (someone) to fall down or be turned over ▪ A giant wave *upended* the surfers. ▪ The midfielder was *upended* before he got the ball. — sometimes used figuratively especially in U.S. English ▪ The new regulations could *upend* the entire industry. ▪ The team was *upended* [=*defeated*] in the second round of the play-offs.

up–front /ˌʌpˈfrʌnt/ *adj*
1 [*more* ~; *most* ~] : not keeping anything secret or hidden : honest and direct ▪ I have been very *up-front* with you. ▪ They were *up-front* about their financial position.
2 — used to refer to money that is paid in advance ▪ The deal requires more *up-front* cash than I can come up with. ▪ *up-front* fees — see also *up front* at [1]FRONT

[1]up·grade /ˌʌpˈgreɪd/ *verb* **-grades; -grad·ed; -grad·ing**
1 a [+ *obj*] : to make (something) better by including the most recent information or improvements ▪ This course will help you to *upgrade* your computer skills. ▪ Airports have *upgraded* security. ▪ They've *upgraded* the quality of their service. ▪ The city is *upgrading* the sewage treatment plant. ▪ The office is *upgrading* the telephone system. ▪ They *upgraded* the hotel to attract more business patrons. **b** [*no obj*] : to choose to have or use something more modern, useful, etc. — often + *to* ▪ You might want to *upgrade to* a cable modem. ▪ We reserved a compact car, with the option of *upgrading to* a midsize car.
2 : to get something (such as a seat on an airplane or a room in a hotel) that is better than what you had originally — often + *to* [*no obj*] We were able to *upgrade to* first class. [+ *obj*] Our seats were *upgraded to* first class. [=we were given first-class seats] ▪ We had reserved a double room, but the hotel *upgraded* us *to* a suite.
3 [+ *obj*] : to give (someone or something) a higher rank or grade — often + *to* ▪ They *upgraded* my job classification *to* level four, which means I get a pay increase. ▪ The restaurant was *upgraded* from three *to* four stars. ▪ The storm has been *upgraded to* a hurricane. ▪ The doctors *upgraded* the patient's condition from "serious" *to* "good." — opposite DOWNGRADE
– up·grad·able *or* **up·grade·able** /ˌʌpˈgreɪdəbəl/ *adj* ▪ *upgradable* hardware

[2]up·grade /ˈʌpˌgreɪd/ *noun, pl* **-grades** [*count*]
1 : an area or surface that goes upward : an upward slope ▪ a slight *upgrade* in the roadway ▪ a gradual *upgrade*
2 : an occurrence in which one thing is replaced by something better, newer, more valuable, etc. ▪ software/system *upgrades* ▪ The hotel offered us a room *upgrade*. ▪ seat *upgrades*

up·heav·al /ˌʌpˈhiːvəl/ *noun, pl* **-als**
1 : a major change or period of change that causes a lot of conflict, confusion, anger, etc. [*noncount*] The civil rights movement marked a period of social *upheaval* in the U.S. ▪ the emotional *upheaval* of divorce [*count*] a period of cultural and social *upheavals*
2 *technical* : an occurrence in which a part of the Earth's surface moves up forcefully [*count*] The island was created by an *upheaval* of the ocean floor. [*noncount*] The lake was formed by geologic *upheaval*.

[1]up·hill /ˈʌpˈhɪl/ *adv* : toward the top of a hill or mountain ▪ It is easier to ride a bicycle downhill than *uphill*.

[2]up·hill /ˈʌpˌhɪl/ *adj*
1 : going or sloping up toward the top of a hill or mountain ▪ The path is *uphill*. ▪ an *uphill* climb
2 *always used before a noun* : not easy : difficult to do, deal with, etc. ▪ It has been an *uphill* battle/fight/struggle for her to get an education.

up·hold /ˌʌpˈhoʊld/ *verb* **-holds; -held** /-ˈhɛld/; **-hold·ing** [+ *obj*]
1 : to support or defend (something, such as a law) ▪ He took an oath to *uphold* the Constitution. ▪ They have a responsibility to *uphold* the law.
2 : to judge (a legal decision) to be correct : to decide not to change (a verdict) ▪ The Court of Appeals *upheld* his conviction.

U

– **up·hold·er** *noun, pl* **-ers** [*count*] ▪ *upholders* of democracy

up·hol·ster /ˌʌpˈhoʊlstɚ/ *verb* **-sters; -stered; -ster·ing** [+ *obj*] **:** to put a covering of cloth, leather, etc., on (a piece of furniture, such as a couch or chair) ▪ The couch was *upholstered* with a bright, floral fabric.

– **up·hol·stered** *adj* ▪ an *upholstered* chair – **up·hol·ster·er** /ˌʌpˈhoʊlstərɚ/ *noun, pl* **-ers** [*count*] ▪ We took the chair to an *upholsterer* to have it re-covered.

up·hol·stery /ˌʌpˈhoʊlstəri/ *noun* [*noncount*]
1 : the cloth, leather, etc., that covers a couch, chair, etc. ▪ an old chair that needs new *upholstery* ▪ a car with leather *upholstery* [=with seats that are covered in leather]
2 : the process or business of covering pieces of furniture with cloth, leather, etc. ▪ He learned *upholstery* from his father.

up·keep /ˈʌpˌkiːp/ *noun* [*noncount*] **:** the process of keeping something in good condition **:** the care or maintenance of buildings, equipment, etc. ▪ Who is responsible for the *upkeep* of these buildings? ▪ Once your car gets that old, the cost of *upkeep* can get very expensive. ▪ The yard requires very little *upkeep*. ▪ We sold our horse because we could no longer afford its *upkeep*.

up·land /ˈʌplənd/ *noun, pl* **-lands** [*count*] **:** a region of high land especially far from the sea — usually plural ▪ the *uplands* of eastern Turkey ▪ The sheep graze in the *uplands*.

– **upland** *adj, always used before a noun* ▪ an *upland* forest/species

[1]**up·lift** /ˌʌpˈlɪft/ *verb* **-lifts; -lift·ed; -lift·ing** [+ *obj*]
1 : to make (someone) happy or hopeful ▪ music that *uplifts* the soul
2 : to lift (something) up **:** to raise (something) to a higher position ▪ geologic forces that *uplifted* the mountains

[2]**up·lift** /ˈʌpˌlɪft/ *noun*
1 [*singular*] **:** an increase in amount or number **:** RISE ▪ an *uplift* in prices/sales
2 : an increase in happiness or hopefulness [*singular*] The beautiful spring day gave us a much-needed *uplift*. [=*lift*] [*noncount*] searching for spiritual *uplift*

uplifted *adj*
1 : raised or turned upward ▪ *uplifted* faces/hands
2 : made happier or more hopeful ▪ *uplifted* spirits ▪ We felt *uplifted* by the experience.

uplifting *adj* [*more* ~; *most* ~] **:** causing happy and hopeful feelings ▪ an *uplifting* sermon ▪ *uplifting* music

[1]**up·load** /ˌʌpˈloʊd/ *verb* **-loads; -load·ed; -load·ing** [+ *obj*] *computers* **:** to move or copy (a file, program, etc.) from a computer or device to a usually larger computer or computer network ▪ She *uploaded* the pictures from her digital camera to her computer. ▪ *upload* files to the Internet — compare DOWNLOAD

[2]**up·load** /ˈʌpˌloʊd/ *noun, pl* **-loads** [*count*] *computers* **:** a file, program, etc., that is uploaded ▪ a data *upload*

up·mar·ket /ˈʌpˈmɑɚkət/ *adj* [*more* ~; *most* ~] **:** made for or appealing to people who have a lot of money ▪ *upmarket* [=(*US*) *upscale*] restaurants/shops

– **upmarket** *adv* ▪ The brand is ***going/moving upmarket***. [=starting to sell products for people with more money]

up·on /əˈpɑːn/ *prep, formal*
1 : ON ▪ He carefully placed the vase *upon* the table. ▪ They built their city *upon* a cliff overlooking the sea. ▪ She was seated *upon* a throne. ▪ an assault *upon* traditional values ▪ She was admitted to his office immediately *upon* her arrival. ▪ That kind of behavior is frowned *upon*.
2 — used to say that someone or something is very close or has arrived ▪ The enemy was suddenly *upon* us. ▪ The holidays are nearly *upon* us. [=the holidays are nearly here; the holidays have nearly begun] ▪ Before we knew it, the date of the wedding was *upon* us.
3 — used to emphasize something that is repeated many times ▪ We removed layer *upon* layer [=many layers] of old paint from the paneling. ▪ She studied for hour *upon* hour. [=for many hours] ▪ thousands *upon* thousands of people

[1]**up·per** /ˈʌpɚ/ *adj, always used before a noun*
1 a : located above another or others of the same kind ▪ the tree's *upper* branches ▪ *upper* and lower front teeth ▪ the *upper* jaw ▪ her *upper* extremities/limbs [=her arms and hands] ▪ the wing's *upper* and lower surfaces ▪ the ship's *upper* and lower decks ▪ Who will sleep on the *upper* berth? ▪ The *upper* stories/floors are occupied by offices. ▪ the *upper* layer of the Earth's crust ▪ temperatures in the mid to *upper* 20s **b :** located at or near the top ▪ Write your name on the *upper* left-hand corner of the page. ▪ relief of *upper* back pain ▪ exercises to improve *upper* body strength [=strength in the arms, shoulders, neck, and back] ▪ the mountain's *upper* and lower slopes ▪ the *upper* atmosphere ▪ There is no *upper* age limit for participation. ▪ He's at the *upper* end of the pay scale. ▪ The *upper* two-thirds of the wall has been painted.
2 : located toward the north ▪ a restaurant in *upper* Manhattan ▪ an apartment on *upper* Fifth Avenue ▪ the *upper* Great Lakes region
3 : above another or others in position, rank, or order ▪ the *upper* echelons of society ▪ *upper*-level executives ▪ *upper* management ▪ the *upper* middle class
stiff upper lip see [1]STIFF

[2]**upper** *noun, pl* **-pers** [*count*]
1 : the parts of a shoe or boot above the sole ▪ leather *uppers*
2 *informal* **:** a drug that gives you more energy; *especially* **:** AMPHETAMINE ▪ He admitted he was on *uppers*. — compare DOWNER
on your uppers *Brit, old-fashioned + informal* **:** having very little money ▪ He'd come to me for money whenever he was *on his uppers*.

up·per·case /ˌʌpɚˈkeɪs/ *adj* **:** having as its typical form A, B, C rather than a, b, c **:** CAPITAL ▪ *uppercase* letters ▪ *uppercase* D — compare LOWERCASE

– **uppercase** *noun* [*noncount*] ▪ abbreviations written in *uppercase*

upper class *noun, pl* **~ classes** [*count*] **:** a social class that is above the middle class **:** the highest social class ▪ a popular pastime among the *upper classes* ▪ a member of the *upper class* — compare LOWER CLASS, MIDDLE CLASS, UNDERCLASS, WORKING CLASS

– **upper–class** *adj* ▪ *upper-class* families/neighborhoods

up·per·class·man /ˌʌpɚˈklæsmən, *Brit* ˌʌpəˈklɑːsmən/ *noun, pl* **-men** /-mən/ [*count*] *US* **:** a student in the third or fourth year of high school or college ▪ Only *upperclassmen* can go off-campus for lunch. — compare UNDERCLASSMAN

upper crust *noun*
the upper crust *informal* **:** the highest social class or group **:** UPPER CLASS ▪ *the upper crust* of American society ▪ the wealthy *upper crust*

– **upper–crust** *adj* ▪ *upper-crust* Americans/schools

up·per·cut /ˈʌpɚˌkʌt/ *noun, pl* **-cuts** [*count*] *boxing* **:** a punch directed upward with a bent arm ▪ He hit his opponent with an *uppercut* to the chin.

upper hand *noun*
the upper hand **:** the position of having power or being in control in a particular situation ▪ He always has to have *the upper hand*. — sometimes used figuratively ▪ The infection was gaining *the upper hand* [=was becoming worse] and the patient's condition was deteriorating.

up·per·most /ˈʌpɚˌmoʊst/ *adj* **:** highest in position or importance ▪ the *uppermost* [=*topmost*] branches of the tree ▪ Safety was *uppermost* in their minds. [=safety was the thing they were most concerned about]

– **uppermost** *adv*

upper school *noun, pl* **~ -schools** [*count, noncount*] **:** a school or part of a school for students between the ages of 14 and 18

up·pi·ty /ˈʌpəti/ *adj* [*more* ~; *most* ~] *informal + disapproving* **:** acting as if you are more important than you really are, do not have to do what you are told to do, etc. ▪ an *uppity* sales clerk ▪ Don't get *uppity* with me.

up·raised /ˌʌpˈreɪzd/ *adj* **:** raised or lifted up ▪ He danced with his arms *upraised*.

[1]**up·right** /ˈʌpˌraɪt/ *adj*
1 a : positioned to be straight up **:** VERTICAL ▪ an *upright* posture ▪ Put your seat back in the *upright* position. ▪ the fox's *upright* ears ▪ The container should be kept *upright* to prevent leaks. **b** — used to describe something that is tall rather than wide ▪ an *upright* freezer ▪ an *upright* vacuum cleaner ▪ an *upright* shrub
2 [*more* ~; *most* ~] **:** always behaving in an honest way **:** having high moral standards ▪ an *upright* citizen

– **upright** *adv* ▪ There wasn't enough room to stand *upright*, so we had to bend over. ▪ an early human ancestor that walked *upright* ▪ She ***sat bolt upright*** [=she sat up straight] in bed when I entered the room.

[2]**upright** *noun, pl* **-rights** [*count*]
1 : a board or pole placed in a vertical position to support something ▪ The *uprights* of the structure were embedded in concrete.
2 *American football* **:** GOALPOST — usually plural ▪ He

kicked the ball through the *uprights*.
3 : UPRIGHT PIANO
upright piano *noun, pl* ~ **-nos** [*count*] : a piano whose strings run from the top to the bottom — called also *upright*
up•ris•ing /ˈʌpˌraɪzɪŋ/ *noun, pl* **-ings** [*count*] : a usually violent effort by many people to change the government or leader of a country : REBELLION ▪ an armed *uprising* ▪ The government quickly put down the *uprising*.
up•riv•er /ˈʌpˈrɪvɚ/ *adv* : toward the start of a river ▪ The salmon swim *upriver* [=*upstream*] to spawn.
up•roar /ˈʌpˌroɚ/ *noun, pl* **-roars** : a situation in which many people are upset, angry, or disturbed by something [*noncount*] There was a lot of public *uproar* over the proposed jail. [*count*] There have been *uproars* in the past over similar proposals. ▪ The proposal caused an *uproar*. ▪ The town was ***in an uproar*** over the proposal to build a jail.
up•roar•i•ous /ˌʌpˈrorijəs/ *adj* [*more* ~; *most* ~]
1 : very noisy ▪ *uproarious* laughter
2 : extremely funny ▪ an *uproarious* comedy
– **up•roar•i•ous•ly** *adv* ▪ an *uproariously* funny comedy
up•root /ˌʌpˈruːt/ *verb* **-roots; -root•ed; -root•ing** [+ *obj*]
1 : to pull (a plant and its root) completely out of the ground ▪ *uproot* a vine ▪ Many trees were *uprooted* by the storm.
2 : to remove (something) completely ▪ Will we ever be able to *uproot* racial prejudice?
3 : to make (someone) leave home and move to a different place ▪ families *uprooted* by war ▪ Taking the job would mean *uprooting* my family.
[1]**up•scale** /ˈʌpˈskeɪl/ *adj* [*more* ~; *most* ~] *US* : relating to or appealing to people who have a lot of money ▪ *upscale* [=*upmarket*] restaurants/supermarkets ▪ an *upscale* neighborhood
– **upscale** *adv* ▪ The brand is ***going/moving upscale***. [=starting to sell products for people with more money]
[2]**upscale** *verb* **-scales; -scaled; -scal•ing** [+ *obj*] *US* : to make (something) more appealing to people who have a lot of money ▪ *upscaled* merchandise
[1]**up•set** /ˌʌpˈsɛt/ *adj* [*more* ~; *most* ~]
1 : angry or unhappy ▪ I was feeling *upset* by/about the whole experience. ▪ There's no point in getting all *upset* about it. ▪ I try not to let her make me *upset*. ▪ She was too *upset* to speak to him. ▪ I'm *upset* that you didn't call. ▪ I was so *upset* with him, I didn't call him for two weeks.
2 ✧ If you have an ***upset stomach***, you have an unpleasant feeling in your stomach because of illness or because of something you have eaten. ▪ I had an *upset stomach* after eating all those cookies. ▪ My stomach was *upset* and I felt like I might throw up.
[2]**up•set** /ˌʌpˈsɛt/ *verb* **-sets; -set; -set•ting** [+ *obj*]
1 : to make (someone) unhappy, worried, etc. ▪ That remark you made really *upset* me. ▪ Don't *upset* yourself over it. ▪ It *upsets* him that he can do nothing to help. ▪ A lot of people were *upset* by the court's decision. ▪ It *upsets* me to think I might never see him again.
2 : to cause an unpleasant feeling in (your stomach) ▪ Spicy food *upsets* my stomach.
3 : to cause (something) to be unable to continue in the expected way ▪ His sudden arrival *upset* [=*disrupted*] our plans.
4 : to defeat (someone who was expected to defeat you) ▪ The heavyweight challenger *upset* the reigning champion in the third round. ▪ She was *upset* in the primary.
5 : to cause (something) to fall ▪ He accidentally bumped the table and *upset* a lamp.
upset the apple cart *informal* : to do something that changes or spoils a plan, situation, system, etc. ▪ Let's not *upset the apple cart* by introducing new rules.
– **upsetting** *adj* [*more* ~; *most* ~] ▪ It was a very *upsetting* situation.
[3]**up•set** /ˈʌpˌsɛt/ *noun, pl* **-sets**
1 [*count*] : an occurrence in which a game, contest, etc., is won by a person or team that was expected to lose ▪ In a major *upset*, he took the gold medal. ▪ Her victory in the election was a big *upset*. ▪ an *upset* victory
2 : an unpleasant feeling of illness in your stomach [*noncount*] Spicy foods can cause stomach *upset*. [*count*] a minor stomach *upset*
3 : a period of worry and unhappiness caused by something that has happened [*count*] An emotional *upset* can affect your physical health. [*noncount*] a period of emotional *upset*
up•shift /ˈʌpˌʃɪft/ *verb* **-shifts; -shift•ed; -shift•ing** [*no obj*] : to put the engine of a vehicle into a higher gear ▪ She *upshifted* into fifth gear. — opposite DOWNSHIFT
– **upshift** *noun, pl* **-shifts** [*count*] ▪ an *upshift* into fifth gear
up•shot /ˈʌpˌʃɑːt/ *noun*
the upshot : the final result or outcome of a process, discussion, etc. ▪ *The upshot* is that we'll see him Thursday.— often + *of* ▪ *The upshot of* the decision is that the park will be closed.
[1]**up•side** /ˈʌpˌsaɪd/ *noun, pl* **-sides** [*count*] : a part of something that is good or desirable : an advantage or benefit ▪ One *upside* to the new house is its location. ▪ ***On the upside*** [=when you consider the good parts or advantages], the car does have a lot of trunk space. — often + *of* ▪ The *upside of* moving would be a shorter commute to work. — opposite DOWNSIDE
[2]**up•side** /ˈʌpˈsaɪd/ *prep, US, informal* : on or against the side of (something) ▪ She smacked him ***upside the head***. [=she hit/slapped him on the side of his head]
up•side down /ˌʌpˌsaɪdˈdaʊn/ *adv* : with the top at the bottom and the bottom at the top : placed so that the end that should be at the top is at the bottom ▪ You hung the picture *upside down*! ▪ To remove the plant, turn the pot *upside down* and tap gently on the bottom to loosen it. ▪ The baby was holding the book *upside down*.
turn (something) upside down *informal* : to make (something) very untidy ▪ I *turned* the room *upside down* looking for my car keys. ▪ The house was *turned upside down* while the renovations were under way.— often used figuratively ▪ His whole world was *turned upside down* when his mother died.
– **upside–down** *adj* ▪ The sculpture looked like an *upside-down* pyramid. ▪ That flag is *upside-down*.
upside–down cake *noun, pl* ~ **cakes** [*count, noncount*] *US* : a cake that is baked with a layer of fruit (such as pineapple) on the bottom and then turned over and served with the fruit side up
up•skill /ˌʌpˈskɪl/ *verb* **-skills; -skilled; -skill•ing** [+ *obj*] *Brit* : to improve the job skills of (someone) ▪ *upskilling* the workforce
up•slope /ˈʌpˈsloʊp/ *adv, US* : toward the top of a hill or mountain : up a slope ▪ The field extends *upslope* away from the water. ▪ moving *upslope*— opposite DOWNSLOPE
– **upslope** *adj* ▪ *upslope* winds – **upslope** *noun, pl* **-slopes** [*count*] ▪ We had to climb a long *upslope*.
[1]**up•stage** /ˈʌpˈsteɪʤ/ *adv* : toward the back part of a stage ▪ The actor moved *upstage*.
[2]**up•stage** /ˌʌpˈsteɪʤ/ *verb* **-stag•es; -staged; -stag•ing** [+ *obj*] : to take attention away from (someone or something else, such as another performer) ▪ The children *upstaged* the adult performers. [=people watched the children more than the adults] ▪ We don't want the flower girl *upstaging* the bride. ▪ My apple pie was *upstaged* by her chocolate cake.
[1]**up•stairs** /ˌʌpˈsteɚz/ *adv*
1 : on or to a higher floor of a building ▪ When you go *upstairs*, bring these towels with you. ▪ My in-laws live *upstairs*. ▪ She was on her way *upstairs* when she heard a car drive up.
2 *informal* : in the head : mentally or intellectually ▪ Some say he's a little slow *upstairs*. [=he's mentally slow; he's not intelligent]
kick (someone) upstairs see [1]KICK
[2]**up•stairs** /ˈʌpˈsteɚz/ *adj, always used before a noun* : located on a higher floor of a building ▪ You can use the *upstairs* bathroom.
[3]**up•stairs** /ˈʌpˈsteɚz/ *noun*
the upstairs : the upper floors of a building ▪ We've decided to rent out *the upstairs*. ▪ We're having *the upstairs* carpeted.
up•stand•ing /ˌʌpˈstændɪŋ/ *adj* [*more* ~; *most* ~]
1 : honest and respectable ▪ *upstanding* members of the community
2 : standing straight up ▪ a stiff, *upstanding* collar
be upstanding *Brit, formal* — used to tell the people in a place to stand up ▪ "Ladies and gentlemen, please *be upstanding* for the national anthem."
up•start /ˈʌpˌstɑɚt/ *noun, pl* **-starts** [*count*]
1 *disapproving* : a person who has recently begun an activity, become successful, etc., and who does not show proper respect for older and more experienced people ▪ a young *upstart* from Harvard who thinks he knows more than the boss
2 *chiefly US* : a newly successful person, business, etc. — often used before another noun ▪ *upstart* Internet companies
up•state /ˈʌpˌsteɪt/ *noun* [*noncount*] *US* : the northern part of a state ▪ She's from *upstate*.
– **up•state** /ˈʌpˈsteɪt/ *adj, always used before a noun* ▪ He

lives in *upstate* New York. **– up·state** /ˈʌpˈsteɪt/ *adv* ▪ They moved *upstate.*

up·stream /ˈʌpˈstriːm/ *adv* **:** in the direction opposite to the flow in a stream, river, etc. **:** toward the source of a stream, river, etc. ▪ salmon swimming *upstream* [=against the current] to spawn ▪ The canoe capsized *upstream* of the dam.
– upstream *adj* ▪ *upstream* farms

up·surge /ˈʌpˌsɚʤ/ *noun, pl* **-surg·es** [*count*] **:** a rapid or sudden increase or rise — usually + *in* or *of* ▪ a recent *upsurge in* crime ▪ an *upsurge of* popularity ▪ an *upsurge of* anger

up·swept /ˈʌpˌswɛpt/ *adj* **:** directed upward in a curved shape ▪ *upswept* hair ▪ *upswept* wings

up·swing /ˈʌpˌswɪŋ/ *noun, pl* **-swings** [*count*]
1 : a situation in which something is increasing or becoming better ▪ Business is ***on the upswing.*** [=*improving*] — often + *in* ▪ an *upswing in* profits
2 : an upward swing ▪ an *upswing* of the arms

up·take /ˈʌpˌteɪk/ *noun*
1 *technical* **:** the process by which something is taken in by the body, a plant, etc. [*noncount*] oxygen *uptake* by the body/tissue/cells ▪ the plant's *uptake* of water [*singular*] a rapid *uptake* of liquid
2 [*noncount*] *informal* **:** the ability to learn new things, to understand what is happening or being said, etc. ▪ Being ***slow on the uptake*** [=slow to comprehend], I didn't realize what was going on at first. ▪ She's pretty ***quick on the uptake.***

up–tem·po /ˈʌpˌtɛmpoʊ/ *adj* **:** played very fast **:** having a fast tempo ▪ *up-tempo* music ▪ an aggressive, *up-tempo* style of basketball

up·tick /ˈʌpˌtɪk/ *noun, pl* **-ticks** [*count*] *US* **:** a small increase or rise — often + *in* ▪ an *uptick in* sales/hiring

up·tight /ˈʌpˈtaɪt/ *adj* [*more* ~; *most* ~]
1 : nervous or worried and tending to become upset about something that does not make other people upset ▪ If our flight is delayed, there's nothing we can do. There's no reason to get so *uptight* about it.
2 : unable or unwilling to relax and express feelings openly **:** too concerned about behaving in a socially proper way ▪ I don't know why people are so *uptight* about sex. ▪ *uptight* conservatives

up·time /ˈʌpˌtaɪm/ *noun* [*noncount*] **:** time during which a computer or machine is working ▪ We need to maximize network *uptime.*

up–to–date *adj* [*more* ~; *most* ~]
1 : including the latest information ▪ *up-to-date* [=*current*] maps
2 : based on or using the newest information, methods, etc. ▪ *up-to-date* styles ▪ *up-to-date* [=*modern*] methods

up–to–the–minute *adj*
1 : including the very latest information ▪ *up-to-the-minute* news
2 : based on or using the newest information, methods, etc. ▪ *up-to-the-minute* equipment/information

[1]**up·town** /ˈʌpˌtaʊn/ *noun, pl* **-towns** [*count*] *chiefly US* **:** the upper part of a city or town **:** the part of a city or town that is away from the central part — usually singular ▪ They took a taxi from *uptown* to downtown. ▪ a fire in the city's *uptown* — compare DOWNTOWN

[2]**up·town** /ˈʌpˈtaʊn/ *adv, chiefly US* **:** to, toward, or in the upper part of a city or town ▪ We walked *uptown* to his apartment. ▪ He lives *uptown.*
– uptown *adj, always used before a noun* ▪ *uptown* Manhattan ▪ an *uptown* theater

up·turn /ˈʌpˌtɚn/ *noun, pl* **-turns** [*count*] **:** an increase or improvement — usually singular ▪ an *upturn* in the economy ▪ an *upturn* in sales

up·turned /ˈʌpˌtɚnd/ *adj*
1 : turned so that the bottom part is on top **:** turned upside down ▪ an *upturned* trash can ▪ an *upturned* boat
2 : turned or directed upward ▪ *upturned* faces ▪ a hat with *upturned* brim ▪ a bird with an *upturned* bill

[1]**up·ward** (*chiefly US*) /ˈʌpwɚd/ *or chiefly Brit* **up·wards** /ˈʌpwɚdz/ *adv*
1 : from a lower place or level to a higher place or level ▪ The road gradually rose *upward.* ▪ The temperature is heading *upward.* [=it is getting hotter]
2 : toward the ceiling, sky, etc. ▪ The hawk spiraled *upward.* ▪ He pointed *upward.* ▪ She directed my gaze *upward.*
3 : toward a higher or better condition or position ▪ They are moving *upward* socially and economically. ▪ moving *upward* in the corporate world
4 : to a larger amount **:** to a higher number ▪ Prices shot *upward.* ▪ The inflation rate was adjusted *upward.* ▪ Attendance figures have been heading *upward.*
onward and upward see [1]ONWARD
upwards of *also US* ***upward of*** **:** more than (an amount or number) ▪ *upwards of* half a million people ▪ He won *upwards of* $2,000.

[2]**upward** *adj, always used before a noun*
1 : moving or going from a lower place or level to a higher place or level ▪ *upward* movement/flow ▪ an *upward* curve ▪ in an *upward* direction
2 : moving or going toward the ceiling, sky, etc. ▪ the plant's *upward* growth
3 : changing to a larger amount or higher number ▪ an *upward* revision of the vote tally
– up·ward·ly *adv*

upwardly mobile *adj* [*more* ~; *most* ~] **:** moving or able to move into a higher social or economic position ▪ *upwardly mobile* professionals
– upward mobility *noun* [*noncount*] ▪ She wants a job with more *upward mobility.*

up·wind /ˈʌpˈwɪnd/ *adv* **:** in the direction that is opposite to the direction of the wind ▪ We sailed *upwind.* [=into the wind] — often + *of* ▪ We were standing *upwind of* the fire.
– upwind *adj* ▪ the *upwind* side of the fire

ura·ni·um /jʊˈreɪnijəm/ *noun* [*noncount*] **:** a radioactive element that is used to make nuclear energy and nuclear weapons

Ura·nus /ˈjərənəs, jʊˈreɪnəs/ *noun* [*singular*] **:** the planet that is seventh in order from the sun

ur·ban /ˈɚbən/ *adj* [*more* ~; *most* ~] **:** of or relating to cities and the people who live in them ▪ *urban* life/culture ▪ *urban* housing ▪ an *urban* neighborhood — opposite RURAL

ur·bane /ˌɚˈbeɪn/ *adj* [*more* ~; *most* ~]
1 : polite and confident ▪ an *urbane* diplomat ▪ The dialogue is witty and *urbane.*
2 : fashionable and somewhat formal ▪ the hotel's *urbane* sophistication
– ur·bane·ly *adv* ▪ a television show with *urbanely* witty dialogue **– ur·ban·i·ty** /ɚˈbænəti/ *noun* [*noncount*]

ur·ban·i·za·tion *also Brit* **ur·ban·i·sa·tion** /ˌɚbənəˈzeɪʃən/ *noun* [*noncount*] **:** the process by which towns and cities are formed and become larger as more and more people begin living and working in central areas ▪ rapid *urbanization* ▪ the effects/process of *urbanization*
– ur·ban·ize *also Brit* **ur·ban·ise** /ˈɚbəˌnaɪz/ *verb* **-iz·es; -ized; -iz·ing** [*no obj*] The country/region is rapidly *urbanizing.* [+ *obj*] farmland that is being *urbanized*
– urbanized *also Brit* **urbanised** *adj* [*more* ~; *most* ~] ▪ an *urbanized* area/society

urban legend *noun, pl* ~ **-ends** [*count*] **:** a story about an unusual event or occurrence that many people believe is true but that is not true — called also *urban myth*

urban renewal *noun* [*noncount*] **:** a process by which old buildings or buildings that are in bad condition in part of a city are replaced or repaired ▪ an area undergoing *urban renewal* — often used before another noun ▪ an *urban renewal* plan/project

urban sprawl *noun* [*noncount*] **:** a situation in which large stores, groups of houses, etc., are built in an area around a city that formerly had few people living in it ▪ efforts to stop/prevent *urban sprawl*

ur·chin /ˈɚʧən/ *noun, pl* **-chins** [*count*]
1 *old-fashioned* **:** a usually poor and dirty child who annoys people or causes minor trouble ▪ a street *urchin* [=an urchin who lives in a city]
2 : SEA URCHIN

Ur·du /ˈuədu, ˈɚdu/ *noun* [*noncount*] **:** the official language of Pakistan which is also used in parts of India

-ure *noun suffix*
1 : act **:** process ▪ expos*ure* ▪ fail*ure* ▪ clos*ure*
2 : a group of people who do a specified job or activity ▪ legislat*ure*

urea /jʊˈriːjə/ *noun* [*noncount*] *technical* **:** a substance that contains nitrogen, is found in the urine of mammals and some fish, and is used in some kinds of fertilizer

ure·thra /jʊˈriːθrə/ *noun, pl* **-thras** [*count*] *medical* **:** the tube through which urine moves from the bladder and out of the body and that in men and male animals is also the means by which semen leaves the body
– ure·thral /jʊˈriːθrəl/ *adj*

[1]**urge** /ˈɚʤ/ *verb* **urg·es; urged; urg·ing** [+ *obj*]

1 : to ask people to do or support (something) in a way that shows that you believe it is very important • He is continually *urging* reform. • The rescuers *urged* that we remain calm. • The group is *urging* a ban on the chemical. = The group is *urging* that the chemical be banned.

2 : to try to persuade (someone) in a serious way *to do* something • an editorial *urging* readers *to vote* • I *urge* you *to reconsider*.

3 *always followed by an adverb or preposition* : to use force or pressure to move (someone or something) in a particular direction or at a particular speed • A hand on her back *urged* her forward.

urge on [*phrasal verb*] ***urge (someone or something) on*** : to encourage (someone or something) to move ahead, to do something, etc. • riders *urging* their horses *on* • I wanted to quit but she *urged* me *on*.

[2]**urge** *noun, pl* **urges** [*count*] : a strong need or desire to have or do something • the *urge* for something sweet • He fought the *urge* to cry/laugh. • creative/sexual *urges*

ur·gent /ˈɚʤənt/ *adj* [*more ~; most ~*]

1 : very important and needing immediate attention • an *urgent* [=*pressing*] need for food/reform • We've come to deliver an *urgent* message. • an *urgent* appeal/request for assistance • an ***urgent care*** center/facility [=a place where people who are sick or injured can go for immediate treatment instead of a hospital emergency room]

2 : showing that something is very important and needs immediate attention • He addressed us in an *urgent* manner. • An *urgent* voice came over the intercom, telling us to leave the building immediately.

– ur·gen·cy /ˈɚʤənsi/ *noun* [*noncount*] • I'm not convinced of the *urgency* of the problem. [=I'm not convinced that the problem is urgent] **– ur·gent·ly** *adv* • Volunteers are *urgently* needed to help with the crisis. • speaking/calling *urgently*

urging *noun* [*noncount*] : the act of trying to persuade someone in a serious way to do something • At the *urging* of her teacher, she chose to pursue a career in journalism.

uri·nal /ˈjɚrənl, *Brit* juˈraɪnl/ *noun, pl* **-nals** [*count*] : a toilet that is attached to a wall especially in a public bathroom for men to urinate into

uri·nary /ˈjɚrəˌneri, *Brit* ˈjʊərənri/ *adj, always used before a noun, medical*

1 : relating to the parts of the body in which urine is produced and through which urine passes • the *urinary* bladder/tract • a *urinary* infection

2 : relating to or used for urine • a *urinary* catheter

uri·nate /ˈjɚrəˌneɪt/ *verb* **-nates; -nat·ed; -nat·ing** [*no obj*] *medical* : to send urine out of the body

– uri·na·tion /ˌjɚrəˈneɪʃən/ *noun* [*noncount*] • Symptoms include nausea and frequent *urination*.

urine /ˈjɚrən/ *noun* [*noncount*] *medical* : waste liquid that collects in the bladder before leaving the body

URL /ˌjuːˌɑɚˈɛl/ *noun* [*count*] *computers* : the letters and symbols (such as http://www.Merriam-Webster.com) that are the address of a Web site • What's the site's *URL*? ✧ *URL* is an abbreviation of "Uniform Resource Locator."

urn /ˈɚn/ *noun, pl* **urns** [*count*]

1 : a container that is often shaped like a vase with a closed top and that is used to hold the ashes of someone who has been cremated

2 : a closed container with a faucet near the bottom which is used to serve hot drinks • a coffee *urn*

Ur·sa Ma·jor /ˌɚsəˈmeɪʤɚ/ *noun* [*noncount*] : the group of stars in the northern sky that includes the stars that form the Big Dipper

Ur·sa Mi·nor /ˌɚsəˈmaɪnɚ/ *noun* [*noncount*] : the group of stars in the northern sky that includes the stars that form the Little Dipper

us /ˈʌs/ *pronoun, objective form of* WE

1 — used to refer to the speaker and another person or group of people as the indirect object or direct object of a verb • It was nice of you to invite *us*. • It's fine with *us* if you want to bring a friend. • There's nobody in here but *us* kids. • Someone please help *us*! • It's just the two of *us* for dinner. • They told *us* it would be a few minutes, so why don't we all wait outside? • ***All of us*** [=we all] will be affected by these changes. • It's an exciting time for *all of us*.

2 : people in general • Does God walk among *us*?

3 *Brit, informal* : ME • Give *us* a kiss.

U.S. *or* **US** *abbr* United States (of America)

U.S.A. *or* **USA** *abbr* United States of America

us·able /ˈjuːzəbəl/ *adj* : capable of being used : in good enough condition to be used • *usable* farmland • Is any of this junk *usable*?

USAF *abbr* United States Air Force

us·age /ˈjuːsɪʤ/ *noun*

1 [*noncount*] **a** : the act of using something • Seat belt *usage* in the state is now mandatory. • *Usage* [=*use*] of this exit is prohibited. • drug *usage* among college students **b** : the way that something is used • Restaurant dishes must be able to withstand rough *usage*. **c** : the amount of something that is used • efforts to reduce water/energy *usage* **d** : how often something is used • increasing *usage* of the nation's highways

2 : the way that words and phrases are used in a language [*noncount*] This word occurs in casual/common/popular *usage*. • differences between British and American *usage* • educated/formal *usage* • modern/current *usage* • a *usage* manual/guide/dictionary [*count*] I came across an uncommon *usage* I'd like to discuss with you.

USB /ˌjuːˌɛsˈbiː/ *noun* [*noncount*] *computers* : a system for connecting a computer to another device (such as a printer, keyboard, or mouse) by using a special kind of cord • a *USB* cable/port ✧ *USB* is an abbreviation of "Universal Serial Bus."

USDA *abbr* United States Department of Agriculture

[1]**use** /ˈjuːz/ *verb* **us·es; used; us·ing**

1 [+ *obj*] : to do something with (an object, machine, person, method, etc.) in order to accomplish a task, do an activity, etc. • I need to *use* the phone when you're done. • The machine is easy to *use*. • After the accident, she could no longer *use* her legs. • We *use* only organic fertilizers on our farm. • They make paper *using* traditional Japanese methods. • He *used* his time there well/wisely. • Don't *use* that kind of language with me! [=don't talk to me in that way] • Will you *use* [=*hire, employ*] a contractor or oversee the construction of the house yourself? • Which accountant/bank do you *use*? • Maybe if we ***use our heads*** [=think carefully], we can figure this out.— often followed by *to + verb* • *Use* this knife *to cut* the bread. • More and more people are *using* the Internet *to find/get* information.— often *+ for* • She *used* the money *for* college. — often *+ as* • We *use* that room *as* an office. • The word "place" can be *used as* a noun or verb.

2 [+ *obj*] : to take (something) from a supply in order to function or to do a task • a new kind of light bulb that *uses* very little electricity • Did you *use* all the eggs? • Who *used* the last match? • The car *uses* a lot of gas.— often *+ up* • Did you *use up* all the eggs?

3 [+ *obj*] — used to say that something is needed or to ask if something is needed or wanted; usually used with *can* or *could* • *Can* you *use* this lamp? I don't want it anymore. • The house *could use* [=it needs] a coat of paint. • You look like you *could use* some sleep. [=you look like you need to sleep; you look tired] • I sure *could use* some help.

4 **a** [+ *obj*] : to eat, drink, etc., (something) regularly • I don't *use* [=(more commonly) *take*] sugar in my tea. • She stopped *using* alcohol/drugs a year ago. **b** [*no obj*] *informal* : to take illegal drugs regularly • How long has he been *using*?

5 [+ *obj*] **a** : to treat (someone) well in order to get something for yourself • I realized that she was just *using* me (for my money). **b** : to treat (someone who is generous or helpful) unfairly • I'd been driving them all over the place, and I was beginning to feel *used*.

use up [*phrasal verb*] ***use up (something) or use (something) up*** : to take (all of something) from a supply • She quickly *used up* (all of) her inheritance. • Don't shower too long and *use up* (all) the hot water.— see also [1]USE 2 (above)

– see also USED, USED TO

[2]**use** /ˈjuːs/ *noun, pl* **us·es**

1 [*noncount*] **a** : the act of using something • The knife has become dull from constant *use*. [=from being used very often over a period of time] • Two players were suspended for illegal drug *use*.— often *+ of* • The law requires the *use of* seat belts. [=the law requires people to wear seat belts] • We talked about the author's *use of* irony in the novel. **b** : the state of being used • All of the computers are currently ***in use***. [=are currently being used] • When did the word first ***come into use***? [=when was the word first used?] • Typewriters have practically ***gone out of use***. [=almost no people use typewriters anymore]

2 **a** [*count*] : a way in which something is or can be used • This tool has many *uses*. [=you can do many things with this tool] • Doctors have found a new *use* for the drug. • According to the dictionary, the word has two *uses*. • The technique

has its uses[=the technique is useful in some ways], but better methods are available. **b** [*singular*] **: a way to use something or someone — usually + *for*** • I thought you might be able to find a *use for* this lamp. [=I thought that you might be able to use this lamp for some purpose] • Thanks for volunteering. I'm sure we'll be able to find a *use for* someone with your skills and experience. • Do you have a/any *use for* this old computer?

3 [*noncount*] **: the opportunity or right to use something** • She gave me the *use of* her car [=she allowed me to use her car] while she was away. • The pool is ***for the use of*** hotel guests only. [=only hotel guests are allowed to swim in the pool]

4 [*noncount*] **— used to say that something or someone is or is not helpful or useful** • It's too small to be of *use*. • I don't think that dreams are of much *use* in predicting the future. [=I don't think that dreams help people predict the future] • Go home and rest. You're no *use* to us if you're sick. [=you cannot help us if you're sick] • He's been of no *use* at all to me. [=he hasn't helped me at all] • I felt that I could be of some *use* to her. [=that I could help her in some way] • There's no *use* (in) worrying about the past. [=worrying about the past will not help, make anything better, etc.] • "You should talk to her." "***What's the use***? [=talking to her will not help] She's not going to change her mind." • *What's the use* of trying? It won't help.

5 [*noncount*] **: the ability or power to use something — + *of*** • He lost (the) *use of* his legs in a car accident.

have no use for *or* ***not have any use for*** **: to not like or value (someone or something)** • I *have no use for* such rude people. • I'm a logical person. I *have no use for* sentimentality.

it's no use **— used to say that something you have tried to do cannot be done** • *It's no use*—the door won't open. • We tried our hardest, but *it was no use*.

make use of **: to use (something)** • She *made use of* the money to pay for college. • He tried to ***make good/better use of*** his spare time. [=he tried to use it in a better and more productive way]

put (something) to (good) use **: to use (something) in an effective way** • I'm looking forward to *putting* my new skills *to use*. [=to using my new skills; to doing what I have just learned to do] • Thanks for the donation. We'll *put* it *to good use*. [=we'll do something good with it]

used /ˈjuːzd/ *adj*

1 : having been used before • a *used* tissue • a much-*used* excuse

2 : having had a previous owner • She bought a *used* [=*secondhand*] car. • The books on this shelf are *used*.

[1]**used to** /ˈjuːstə/ *adj* **: familiar with something so that it seems normal or usual** • I'm not *used to* driving this car yet. • He is *used to* criticism. = He is *used to* being criticized. • The dog will need a few days to become *used to* its new home. • I've been out of school for so long that I'm not *used to* studying anymore. • She quickly ***got used to*** the warm weather.

[2]**used to** *verb* [*modal verb*] **— used to say that something existed or repeatedly happened in the past but does not exist or happen now** • We *used to* go out more often. [=in the past we went out more often] • He never *used to* smoke. [=he never smoked in the past] • My grandmother said winters *used to* be harder here. • (*Brit, old-fashioned*) You ***used not to*** smoke, did you?

> ***usage*** *Used to* is usually used in the form *use to* when it occurs with ***did***. • *Did* you *use to* work there? [=did you work there in the past?] • It *didn't use to* be like that. • He *didn't use to* smoke.

use•ful /ˈjuːsfəl/ *adj* [*more ~; most ~*] **: helping to do or achieve something** • a *useful* invention/tool/skill • Does anyone have any *useful* suggestions/advice? • It can be *useful* to know CPR. • The Internet is *useful* for finding information quickly. • The therapy is *useful* as a treatment for diabetes. = The therapy is *useful* in treating diabetes. • She has become one of the team's most *useful* players. • Why don't you do something *useful* with your life? • The data could ***prove (to be) useful*** [=people may eventually find that the data is helpful] in identifying future problems. • I ***found*** this information ***(to be)*** quite ***useful*** • Her pocketknife ***came in useful*** [=(more commonly) *came in handy*] when we needed to cut the tangled fishing line. • I tried to ***make myself useful*** [=to be helpful; to do something helpful] by organizing his closet for him. • the ***useful life*** of a satellite [=the amount of time during which a satellite is in good enough condition to be used]

— use•ful•ly *adv* • The lessons learned from that experience can be *usefully* applied to the current situation. • She kept herself *usefully* employed. **— use•ful•ness** *noun* [*noncount*] • He questioned the *usefulness* of such a device.

use•less /ˈjuːsləs/ *adj* [*more ~; most ~*] **: not at all useful : not doing or able to do what is needed** • a dull, *useless* knife • The tent is *useless* in wet conditions. **: not producing or able to produce the effect you want** • I made a *useless* attempt at fixing the leak. • It's *useless* trying to change her mind. = It's *useless* to try to change her mind. • Drugs are *useless* in treating the condition.

— use•less•ly *adv* • The ship's sails flapped *uselessly*. **— use•less•ness** *noun* [*noncount*]

U.S. English *or* **US English** *noun* [*noncount*] **:** AMERICAN ENGLISH

us•er /ˈjuːzɚ/ *noun, pl* **-ers** [*count*]

1 : a person or thing that uses something • computer *users* • Please enter your ***user name*** [=the name or word that you use to identify yourself when you want to use a computer program or the Internet] — see also GRAPHICAL USER INTERFACE

2 : a person who frequently uses illegal drugs • I never knew she was a (drug) *user*.

us•er–friend•ly /ˌjuːzɚˈfrɛndli/ *adj* [*more ~; most ~*] **: easy to use or understand** • *user-friendly* software

— us•er–friend•li•ness *noun* [*noncount*]

[1]**ush•er** /ˈʌʃɚ/ *noun, pl* **-ers** [*count*] **: a person who leads people to their seats in a theater, at a wedding, etc.**

[2]**usher** *verb, always followed by an adverb or preposition* **-ers; -ered; -er•ing** [*+ obj*] **: to lead (someone) to a place** • He *ushered* them to their seats. • A nurse *ushered* us into the hospital room.

usher in [*phrasal verb*] ***usher in (something)*** *also* ***usher (something) in*** **1 : to happen at the beginning of (something, such as a period of activity) and usually to help cause it** • The book *ushered in* a new era of environmental consciousness. • a discovery that *ushered in* a period of change [=that marked the beginning of a period of change] **2 : to celebrate the beginning of (something)** • a celebration to *usher in* the New Year

USMC *abbr* United States Marine Corps

USO *abbr* United Service Organizations ✧ **The USO is a private organization that provides entertainment, social events, etc., for members of the U.S. military in countries around the world.**

USPS *abbr* United States Post Office

USS *abbr* United States ship — used in the names of U.S. naval vessels • (the) *USS Constitution*

U.S.S.R. *abbr* Union of Soviet Socialist Republics

[1]**usu•al** /ˈjuːʒəwəl/ *adj* [*more ~; most ~*] **: done, found, or used most of the time or in most cases : normal or regular** • She charges less than the *usual* fee. • He took his *usual* route to work. • the *usual* method for preparing chili • my *usual* activities • We've been working more than (is) *usual*. • She is not my *usual* doctor. • It's *usual* to charge a fee for delivery. • It's not *usual* for him to get home so late.

as usual **: in the way that happens or exists most of the time or in most cases** • We joked and laughed *as usual*. • The wait was twice as long *as usual*. • I was very tired at the end of the day, *as usual*. **— sometimes used with *per*** • He complained endlessly, *as per usual*. [=as he usually does]

be your usual self **: to behave in the way you usually do** • Is anything wrong? You*'re* not *your usual self* today.

business as usual see BUSINESS

the usual suspects see [2]SUSPECT

[2]**usual** *noun*

the usual *informal* **1 : what happens or is done most of the time** • "What have you been doing lately?" "Oh, you know. *The usual*." [=the things I usually do] **2 : what someone chooses to eat or drink most of the time — used especially in restaurants, bars, etc.** • "What'll it be, Joe?" "I'll have *the usual*, please."

usu•al•ly /ˈjuːʒəwəli/ *adv* **— used to describe what happens or exists most of the time or in most cases** • It's *usually* hotter than this in June. • The trip *usually* takes an hour. • I *usually* don't work on Saturdays. • *Usually*, there are no problems. • the way things are *usually* done

usu•rer /ˈjuːʒərɚ/ *noun, pl* **-ers** [*count*] *formal + disapproving* **: a person who lends money and requires the borrower to pay a high amount of interest**

U

usurp /jʊˈsɚp, *Brit* jʊˈzɜːp/ *verb* **usurps; usurp·ing; usurped** [+ *obj*] *formal* **:** to take and keep (something, such as power) in a forceful or violent way and especially without the right to do so ▪ Some people have accused city council members of trying to *usurp* the mayor's power. ▪ attempting to *usurp* the throne — sometimes used figuratively ▪ Have we allowed their lies to *usurp* the truth?
– usur·pa·tion /ˌjuːsɚˈpeɪʃən, *Brit* ˌjuːzɜːˈpeɪʃən/ *noun* [*noncount*] ▪ the *usurpation* of power/authority **– usurp·er** /jʊˈsɚpɚ, *Brit* jʊˈzɜːpə/ *noun, pl* **-ers** [*count*]

usu·ry /ˈjuːʒəri/ *noun* [*noncount*] *formal + disapproving* **:** the practice of lending money and requiring the borrower to pay a high amount of interest
– usu·ri·ous /jʊˈʒɚrijəs/ *adj* ▪ *usurious* interest rates

UT *abbr* Utah

uten·sil /jʊˈtɛnsəl/ *noun, pl* **-sils** [*count*] **:** a simple and useful device that is used for doing tasks in a person's home and especially in the kitchen ▪ cooking/kitchen *utensils*
synonyms see [1]IMPLEMENT

uter·us /ˈjuːtərəs/ *noun, pl* **uteri** /ˈjuːtəˌraɪ/ *also* **uter·us·es** [*count*] *medical* **:** the organ in women and some female animals in which babies develop before birth — called also *womb*
– uter·ine /ˈjuːtəˌraɪn, ˈjuːtərən/ *adj* ▪ the *uterine* lining ▪ *uterine* cancer

util·i·tar·i·an /jʊˌtɪləˈterijən/ *adj*
1 : made to be useful rather than to be decorative or comfortable ▪ *utilitarian* furniture/objects
2 *philosophy* **:** of or relating to utilitarianism ▪ a *utilitarian* argument/view

util·i·tar·i·an·ism /jʊˌtɪləˈterijəˌnɪzəm/ *noun* [*noncount*] *philosophy* **:** the belief that a morally good action is one that helps the greatest number of people

[1]**util·i·ty** /juˈtɪləti/ *noun, pl* **-ties**
1 [*noncount*] *formal* **:** the quality or state of being useful ▪ Some experts question the *utility* [=*usefulness*] of the procedure. ▪ a plan without much practical/economic *utility*
2 [*count*] **a :** a service (such as a supply of electricity or water) that is provided to the public — usually plural ▪ Many of these people are in danger of having their *utilities* shut off for nonpayment. [=of no longer getting electricity, water, etc., in their homes because they have not paid their bills] **b :** a company that provides electricity, water, etc. **:** PUBLIC UTILITY ▪ Notify the *utility* if there's an outage. — often used before another noun ▪ *utility* companies/industries
3 [*count*] *computers* **:** a computer program that does a specific task ▪ an antivirus *utility* [=a computer program that prevents/removes viruses] ▪ a *utility* program

[2]**utility** *adj, always used before a noun*
1 : designed for general use ▪ a *utility* bag ▪ a utility tool/truck — see also SPORT-UTILITY VEHICLE
2 *sports* **:** able to be used in several different positions or roles ▪ a *utility* infielder/player
3 : made to be useful rather than decorative ▪ *utility* shelves

utility knife *noun, pl* **~ knives** [*count*] **:** a knife designed for general use ▪ a chef's *utility knife*; *especially* **:** a cutting tool with a blade that can be pushed completely back into its handle — see picture at CARPENTRY

utility pole *noun, pl* **~ poles** [*count*] **:** a tall wooden pole that is used to support telephone wires, electrical wires, etc.

utility room *noun, pl* **~ rooms** [*count*] **:** a room in a home where equipment (such as furnaces and water heaters) or large appliances (such as washing machines) are kept

uti·lize *also Brit* **uti·lise** /ˈjuːtəˌlaɪz/ *verb* **-liz·es; -lized; -liz·ing** [+ *obj*] *formal* **:** to use (something) for a particular purpose ▪ The company will *utilize* [=*make use of, use*] available tax incentives to convert the factory to solar power. ▪ Many of the library's resources are not *utilized* by townspeople.
– uti·li·za·tion *also Brit* **uti·li·sa·tion** /ˌjuːtələˈzeɪʃən/ *noun* [*noncount*] ▪ the *utilization* of tax incentives

[1]**ut·most** /ˈʌtˌmoust/ *adj, always used before a noun*
1 : greatest or highest in degree, number, or amount ▪ This is a matter of the *utmost* importance/urgency. [=this is an extremely important/urgent matter] ▪ I have the *utmost* [=*greatest*] respect for the teachers here.
2 *formal* **:** farthest or most distant ▪ the *utmost* limit

[2]**utmost** *noun* [*singular*] **:** the highest point or degree that can be reached ▪ This new system represents the *utmost* in modern technology. ▪ It's designed to provide the *utmost* in comfort. ▪ We ***did our utmost*** to help. [=we did all the we could do to help] ▪ We had to push ourselves ***to the utmost*** to finish the job in time.

uto·pia *or* **Uto·pia** /jʊˈtoupijə/ *noun, pl* **-pias :** an imaginary place in which the government, laws, and social conditions are perfect [*count*] The town's founders wanted to create a Christian *utopia*. [*noncount*] It's a nice place to live, but it's no *Utopia*.
– uto·pi·an /jʊˈtoupijən/ *adj* [*more ~; most ~*] ▪ a *utopian* community/vision **– uto·pi·an·ism** /jʊˈtoupijəˌnɪzəm/ *noun* [*noncount*]

[1]**ut·ter** /ˈʌtɚ/ *adj, always used before a noun* **:** complete and total ▪ It's hard to believe that we were *utter* strangers just a few days ago. ▪ The situation descended into *utter* chaos. ▪ The children displayed an *utter* lack of interest in the performance. ▪ The movie was *utter* garbage. ▪ That argument is *utter* nonsense. ▪ The wedding was a ***complete and utter*** [=*absolute, total*] disaster.
– ut·ter·ly *adv* ▪ I was *utterly* convinced that she was wrong. ▪ The two cities are *utterly* different.

[2]**utter** *verb* **-ters; -tered; -ter·ing** [+ *obj*]
1 : to make (a particular sound) ▪ She *uttered* a cry of pleasure/pain.
2 : to say (something) ▪ He can hardly *utter* a sentence without swearing. ▪ Don't ***utter a word*** [=say anything] about this to anyone.

ut·ter·ance /ˈʌtərəns/ *noun, pl* **-anc·es** *formal*
1 [*count*] **:** something that a person says ▪ a politician's carefully crafted public *utterances* ▪ She hung on his every *utterance*. [=she paid careful attention to everything he said]
2 [*noncount*] **:** the act of saying something ▪ give *utterance* to an idea ▪ the ideas conveyed in the *utterance* of a simple sentence **:** the act of being said ▪ a word that by its very *utterance* tends to elicit strong emotion

ut·ter·most /ˈʌtɚˌmoust/ *adj, literary* **:** UTMOST 1 ▪ a matter of the *uttermost* importance
– uttermost *noun* [*singular*]

U–turn /ˈjuːˌtɚn/ *noun, pl* **-turns** [*count*]
1 : a turn that you make while driving a car, walking, etc., that causes you to begin going in the opposite direction **:** a 180-degree turn ▪ The driver ***made/did a*** quick ***U-turn*** and headed back north. ▪ It's illegal to *make a U-turn* at this intersection.
2 *informal* **:** a complete change of ideas, plans, etc. ▪ She ***did/made a U-turn*** when she found out how much the renovation would cost.

UU *abbr* Unitarian Universalist

UV *abbr* ultraviolet

uvu·la /ˈjuːvjələ/ *noun, pl* **-las** *or* **-lae** /-ˌliː/ [*count*] *medical* **:** a small, soft piece of flesh that hangs down from the back part of the roof of your mouth

V

[1]**v** *or* **V** /ˈviː/ *noun, pl* **v's** *or* **V's** /ˈviːz/
1 : the 22nd letter of the English alphabet [*count*] The word "vest" starts with a *v*. [*noncount*] The word "vest" starts with *v*.
2 [*count*] **:** the Roman numeral that means five ▪ XXV [=25]
3 [*count*] **:** something shaped like a V ▪ The birds flew in a *V*.

[2]**v** *abbr* **1** *or* **v.** versus — used between two names that are opposed in a contest or court case ▪ Brown *v.* Board of Education **2** *Brit, informal* very ▪ was *v* pleased **3** *V* volt ▪ a 60 *V* bulb **4** *V* volume

VA *abbr* **1** Veterans Administration **2** Veterans Affairs ▪ a *VA* hospital **3** Virginia

vac /ˈvæk/ *noun, pl* **vacs** [*count*] *Brit, informal* **:** a time when a university is closed **:** VACATION ▪ the summer *vac*

va·can·cy /ˈveɪkənsi/ *noun, pl* **-cies** [*count*]
1 *formal* **:** a job or position that is available to be taken ▪ School administrators are trying to fill *vacancies* before the beginning of the school year.
2 : a room in a hotel, motel, etc., that is available for use ▪ There were no *vacancies* at the hotel.

va·cant /ˈveɪkənt/ *adj*
1 : not filled, used, or lived in ▪ These lockers/seats are all *vacant*. ▪ There were no *vacant* apartments in the building. [=there were no empty apartments available to be rented] ▪ The children played in the ***vacant lot*** [=a piece of land that is not being used] between the two buildings.
2 *formal, of a job or position* **:** not occupied by a person **:** available to be taken by someone ▪ The seat/post/position was left *vacant* when the secretary resigned. ▪ The position will become *vacant* next year. = (*Brit*) The position will ***fall vacant*** next year. ▪ (*Brit*) I found my job through the ***situations vacant*** [=(*US*) *help wanted*] section of the newspaper.
3 : showing no indication of what someone is thinking, feeling, etc. ▪ He had a *vacant* expression on his face. ▪ a *vacant* stare/smile/look
– va·cant·ly *adv* ▪ She stared *vacantly* out the window.

vacant possession *noun* [*noncount*] *Brit* — used to describe a situation in which property (such as a house) is vacant when it is sold so that the new owner can move in immediately ▪ property sold with *vacant possession*

va·cate /ˈveɪˌkeɪt/ *verb* **-cates; -cat·ed; -cat·ing** [+ *obj*]
1 *formal* **:** to leave (a job or position) ▪ She refused to *vacate* her post even under increased pressure. ▪ The election will fill the congressional seat *vacated* by the retiring senator.
2 : to leave (a seat, hotel room, etc.) ▪ The police told everyone to *vacate* the premises. ▪ Students must *vacate* their rooms at the end of the semester.
3 *US, law* **:** to say officially that (a legal judgment) is no longer valid ▪ The court *vacated* the conviction.

[1]**va·ca·tion** /veɪˈkeɪʃən/ *noun, pl* **-tions**
1 *US* **:** a period of time that a person spends away from home, school, or business usually in order to relax or travel [*count*] We had a restful *vacation* [=(*Brit*) *holiday*] at the beach. ▪ Family *vacations* were a high point in my childhood. [*noncount*] — often used in the phrase ***on vacation*** ▪ I'll be *on vacation* [=(*Brit*) *on holiday*] next week. ▪ They're *on vacation* in Rome. — often used before another noun ▪ We had to cancel our *vacation* plans. ▪ a popular *vacation* spot [=a place where many people like to travel] ▪ His parents have a beautiful ***vacation home*** [=a house that someone lives in during vacations] by the lake.
2 [*noncount*] *chiefly US* **:** the number of days or hours per year for which an employer agrees to pay workers while they are not working ▪ When are you taking *vacation* this year? ▪ All employees are given three weeks *vacation*. [=they will be paid for 15 days that they do not work per year] ▪ Employees are entitled to 120 hours of ***paid vacation***. ▪ I don't have any ***vacation days*** left.
3 [*count*] **a** *US* **:** a time when schools, colleges, and universities are closed ▪ winter/spring/summer *vacation* ▪ We have a one-week *vacation* in February. ▪ The university will be closed for Christmas/Easter *vacation*. **b** *Brit* **:** a time when universities and courts of law are closed ▪ She spent most of her ***long vacations*** [=summer vacations] at her parents' house.

[2]**vacation** *verb* **-tions; -tioned; -tion·ing** [*no obj*] *US* **:** to go somewhere during a vacation ▪ He met her while he was *vacationing* [=(*Brit*) *holidaying*] abroad in Italy.

va·ca·tion·er /veɪˈkeɪʃənɚ/ *noun, pl* **-ers** [*count*] *US* **:** a person who takes a vacation somewhere **:** a person who is on vacation ▪ summer *vacationers* — called also (*Brit*) *holidaymaker*

vac·ci·nate /ˈvæksəˌneɪt/ *verb* **-nates; -nat·ed; -nat·ing** [+ *obj*] *medical* **:** to give (a person or an animal) a vaccine to prevent infection by a disease ▪ We *vaccinate* all the animals that come to our shelter. — often + *against* ▪ Children must be *vaccinated against* measles before attending school.
– vac·ci·na·tion /ˌvæksəˈneɪʃən/ *noun, pl* **-tions** [*count*] *vaccinations* against/for smallpox ▪ an oral *vaccination* [*noncount*] What are the side effects of *vaccination*?

vac·cine /vækˈsiːn/ *noun, pl* **-cines** *medical* **:** a substance that is usually injected into a person or animal to protect against a particular disease [*count*] the polio *vaccine* ▪ oral *vaccines* [*noncount*] a dose of *vaccine*

vac·il·late /ˈvæsəˌleɪt/ *verb* **-lates; -lat·ed; -lat·ing** [*no obj*] *formal* **:** to repeatedly change your opinions or desires ▪ She has *vacillated* on this issue. — often + *between* ▪ He *vacillates between* seeking attention from the public and avoiding the media altogether.
– vac·il·la·tion /ˌvæsəˈleɪʃən/ *noun, pl* **-tions** [*count, noncount*]

va·cu·i·ty /væˈkjuːwəti/ *noun* [*noncount*] *formal* **:** the state of lacking any real meaning, importance, or intelligence ▪ We tired of the *vacuity* of their conversation. ▪ intellectual/moral *vacuity* [=*emptiness*]

vac·u·ous /ˈvækjəwəs/ *adj* [*more* ~; *most* ~] *formal* **:** having or showing a lack of intelligence or serious thought **:** lacking meaning, importance, or substance ▪ a dull and *vacuous* movie ▪ *vacuous* comments/remarks ▪ He had a *vacuous* expression on his face.
– vac·u·ous·ly *adv* ▪ He smiled *vacuously* for the camera.
– vac·u·ous·ness *noun* [*noncount*]

[1]**vac·u·um** /ˈvæˌkjuːm/ *noun, pl* **vac·u·ums** [*count*]
1 : an empty space in which there is no air or other gas ▪ the *vacuum* of outer space **:** a space from which all or most of the air has been removed ▪ A pump was used to create a *vacuum* inside the bottle. ▪ a *vacuum* chamber
2 : VACUUM CLEANER
3 : a situation created when an important person or thing has gone and has not been replaced — usually singular ▪ Her death has ***caused/created/left a vacuum*** [=*void*] in our lives. ▪ A new leader is needed to ***fill the vacuum*** left by his retirement.
***in a vacuum* :** separated from outside events or influences ▪ The group was operating *in a vacuum*, cut off from the rest of the world. ▪ The city's riots did not happen *in a vacuum*. [=they were affected or caused by other events or influences]

[2]**vacuum** *verb* **vacuums; vac·u·umed; vac·u·uming** **:** to clean (something) with a vacuum cleaner [+ *obj*] I *vacuumed* [=(*Brit*) *hoovered*] the living room. — often + *up* ▪ *Vacuum up* the crumbs on the couch. [*no obj*] I just finished *vacuuming*.

vacuum cleaner *noun, pl* ~ **-ers** [*count*] **:** an electrical machine that cleans floors, rugs, etc., by sucking up dirt, dust, etc.

vacuum cleaner

vacuum flask *noun, pl* ~ **flasks** [*count*] *Brit* **:** THERMOS

vacuum–packed *adj* **:** packaged in a container that has had most of the air removed ▪ *vacuum-packed* meals/coffee

vacuum tube *noun, pl* ~ **tubes** [*count*] *US* **:** a glass tube that was used in the past in computers, televisions, etc., to control the flow of electricity — called also (*Brit*) *valve*

vag·a·bond /ˈvægəˌbɑːnd/ *noun, pl* **-bonds** [*count*] *old-fashioned + literary* **:** a person who travels from place to place and does not have a home or much money ▪ a solitary *vagabond*

va·ga·ries /ˈveɪgəriz/ *noun* [*plural*] *formal* **:** changes that are difficult to predict or control — usually + *of* ▪ Our plans are subject to the *vagaries of* the weather. ▪ the *vagaries of* the heart

va·gi·na /vəˈʤaɪnə/ *noun, pl* **-nas** [*count*] **:** the passage in a woman's or female animal's body that leads from the uterus to the outside of the body
– vag·i·nal /ˈvæʤənl/ *adj* ▪ *vaginal* intercourse

va·grant /ˈveɪgrənt/ *noun, pl* **-grants** [*count*] **:** a person who has no place to live and no job and who asks people for money ▪ a part of the city that attracts many *vagrants*
– va·gran·cy /ˈveɪgrənsi/ *noun* [*noncount*] ▪ Authorities are trying to address the problem of *vagrancy* in the city. ▪ He was arrested and charged with *vagrancy*.

vague /ˈveɪg/ *adj* **vagu·er; -est** [*also more* ~; *most* ~]
1 a : not clear in meaning **:** stated in a way that is general and not specific ▪ The instructions she left were *vague* and difficult to follow. ▪ He gave only a *vague* answer. ▪ The judges determined that the law was too *vague* to be fairly enforced. **b :** not thinking or expressing your thoughts clearly or precisely ▪ She has been *vague* about her plans for college. ▪ When I asked him what they talked about, he was rather *vague*. [=he did not tell me exactly what they talked about]
2 a : not completely formed or developed ▪ *vague* memories/recollections ▪ We had only a *vague* idea/notion of where we were. ▪ I think I have a *vague* understanding of how it works. ▪ He bore a *vague* resemblance to the famous actor. [=he looked a little like the famous actor] **b :** not able to be de-

V

scribed clearly : not clearly or strongly felt • He longed in some *vague* way for something different. • She felt a *vague* sense of uneasiness when she was around him. • I had the *vague* impression that they were withholding information. ***synonyms*** see [1]OBSCURE
3 : not able to be seen clearly • *vague* [=*indistinct*] figures in the distance • We could just barely make out the *vague* outline of a plane in the sky.

vague·ly /ˈveɪgli/ *adv* [*more* ~; *most* ~]
1 : somewhat or slightly • There was something *vaguely* [=*a little*] disturbing about the whole incident. • The landscape looked *vaguely* familiar. • He *vaguely* resembles a guy I knew in college. • We were *vaguely* aware of what was going on outside.
2 : in a way that is not clearly stated or expressed • *vaguely* defined concepts • They talked *vaguely* about the need for reform.
3 : in a way which shows that you are not paying attention • She only nodded *vaguely* in reply to my question.
– vague·ness *noun* [*noncount*]

vain /ˈveɪn/ *adj* **vain·er; -est**
1 [*also more* ~; *most* ~] **:** too proud of your own appearance, abilities, achievements, etc. **:** CONCEITED • She is very *vain* about her appearance. • He is the *vainest* man I know.
2 : having no success **:** not producing a desired result • They made a *vain* [=*unsuccessful*] attempt to escape. • A *vain* effort to quell the public's fears only made matters worse. • Volunteers searched the area in the *vain* hope of finding clues.
***in vain* :** without success **:** without producing a good or desired result • We searched *in vain* for the missing earring. [=we searched for the missing earring but did not find it] • He tried *in vain* to get the baby to sleep. • Her suffering will not be *in vain*. [=something good will happen because of her suffering]
***take someone's name in vain* :** to use (a name, especially the name of God) in a way that does not show proper respect • He *took God's name in vain*. • (*humorous*) I thought I heard someone *taking my name in vain*. [=saying my name]
– vain·ly *adv* • We tried *vainly* to get a taxi. • Volunteers *vainly* searched for clues.

vain·glo·ri·ous /ˌveɪnˈglorijəs/ *adj* [*more* ~; *most* ~] *literary* **:** having or showing too much pride in your abilities or achievements • a *vainglorious* celebrity • *vainglorious* words
– vain·glo·ry /ˈveɪnˌglori/ *noun* [*noncount*]

va·lance /ˈvæləns/ *noun, pl* **-lanc·es** [*count*]
1 *chiefly US* **:** a short piece of cloth or a wooden or metal frame that is placed across the top of a window for decoration — called also (*Brit*) *pelmet*; see picture at WINDOW
2 : a piece of material that hangs loosely from the frame of a bed or along a table or shelf for decoration

vale /ˈveɪl/ *noun, pl* **vales** [*count*] *literary* **:** VALLEY • hills and *vales*

val·e·dic·tion /ˌvæləˈdɪkʃən/ *noun, pl* **-tions** [*count*] *formal* **:** VALEDICTORY

val·e·dic·to·ri·an /ˌvæləˌdɪkˈtorijən/ *noun, pl* **-ans** [*count*] *US* **:** the student who has the highest grades in a graduating class and who gives a speech at graduation ceremonies • She was the *valedictorian* of her class in 1985. — compare SALUTATORIAN

val·e·dic·to·ry /ˌvæləˈdɪktəri/ *noun, pl* **-ries** [*count*] *formal* **:** a speech that expresses good wishes for someone who is leaving **:** the act of saying goodbye in a formal way • He received a very warm *valedictory* for his long career. — often used before another noun • a *valedictory* address/speech

va·lence /ˈveɪləns/ *also* **va·len·cy** /ˈveɪlənsi/ *noun, pl* **va·lenc·es** *also* **va·lenc·ies** [*count*] *chemistry* **:** the amount of power of an atom which is determined by the number of electrons the atom will lose, gain, or share when it forms compounds

val·en·tine /ˈvælənˌtaɪn/ *noun, pl* **-tines** [*count*]
1 : a card or gift that you give usually to someone you love on Valentine's Day
2 : a person you give a valentine to • Won't you be my *Valentine*?

Valentine's Day *noun* [*singular*] **:** February 14 observed as a time for sending valentines — called also *Saint Valentine's Day*

[1]**va·let** /ˈvæˌleɪ/ *noun, pl* **-lets** [*count*]
1 *US* **:** a person who parks cars for guests at a hotel, restaurant, etc. — see also VALET PARKING
2 : a man's personal male servant
3 *Brit* **:** someone who cleans the clothes of guests staying in a hotel

[2]**valet** *verb* **-lets; -let·ed; -let·ing** [+ *obj*] *Brit* **:** to clean (a person's car) very well • I had my car *valeted*. [=(*US*) *detailed*] • She runs her own *valeting* business.
– valeting *noun* [*noncount*]

valet parking *noun* [*noncount*] *US* **:** a service in which guests at a hotel, restaurant, etc., can have their cars parked by an employee — called also *valet service*

val·iant /ˈvæljənt/ *adj* [*more* ~; *most* ~] *somewhat formal* **:** having or showing courage **:** very brave or courageous • a *valiant* soldier • She died last year after a *valiant* battle with cancer. • Despite their *valiant* efforts, they lost the game. • She made a *valiant* attempt to fix the problem.
– val·iant·ly *adv* • They fought *valiantly*.

val·id /ˈvæləd/ *adj*
1 [*more* ~; *most* ~] **:** fair or reasonable • a *valid* argument • *valid* concerns • There is no *valid* reason to proceed with the change. • Her objections/conclusions were completely *valid*. • You make a *valid* point.
2 : acceptable according to the law • a *valid* contract/license/deed/title • You must present *valid* identification. • Their marriage is not legally *valid*. • The agreement is no longer *valid* under international law. • My passport is still *valid*. [=it has not expired yet] — opposite INVALID
– val·id·ly *adv*

val·i·date /ˈvæləˌdeɪt/ *verb* **-dates; -dat·ed; -dat·ing** [+ *obj*]
1 : to make (something) valid: such as **a :** to state or show that something is legal or official • The court *validated* the contract. • A judge still needs to *validate* the election. **b :** to put a mark on (something) to show that it has been checked and is official or accepted • Customs officers *validated* our passports. • They *validated* our parking ticket as soon as we arrived. [=they stamped the ticket so that we would not have to pay for parking]
2 : to show that something is real or correct • The claims cannot yet be *validated*. [=*confirmed*] • experiments that are designed to *validate* [=*prove*] a hypothesis
3 : to show that someone's feelings, opinions, etc., are fair and reasonable • The decline in sales only *validated* our concerns. — opposite INVALIDATE
– val·i·da·tion /ˌvæləˈdeɪʃən/ *noun* [*noncount*] • Further *validation* is needed before the findings are published. • the *validation* of our concerns • The restaurant provides parking *validation*.

va·lid·i·ty /vəˈlɪdəti/ *noun* [*noncount*]
1 : the state of being acceptable according to the law **:** the state of being valid • The *validity* of the contract/document is being questioned.
2 : the quality of being real or correct • Scientists questioned the *validity* of the findings.

va·lise /vəˈliːs/ *noun, pl* **-lis·es** [*count*] *old-fashioned* **:** a small suitcase

Val·ium /ˈvælijəm/ *trademark* — used for a drug that helps to reduce anxiety and stress

val·ley /ˈvæli/ *noun, pl* **-leys** [*count*]
1 : an area of low land between hills or mountains • the Shenandoah (River) *Valley* — see color picture on page C7; see also RIFT VALLEY
2 : a low period, point, or level • There are ***peaks and valleys*** [=high and low periods] in electricity usage throughout the year.

Valley girl *or* **Valley Girl** *noun, pl* ~ **girls** *or* **Girls** [*count*] *US* **:** a teenage girl from a wealthy family in southern California who speaks in a unique kind of slang and who cares about social status, personal appearance, shopping, etc., rather than about serious things • He said I talk like a *Valley girl*. And I said, "Like, whatever!"

val·or (*US*) *or Brit* **val·our** /ˈvælə/ *noun* [*noncount*] *literary* **:** courage or bravery • The soldiers received the nation's highest award for *valor*. • a woman of *valor*
discretion is the better part of valor see DISCRETION
– val·or·ous /ˈvælərəs/ *adj* [*more* ~; *most* ~] • *valorous* deeds

val·u·able /ˈvæljəbəl/ *adj* [*more* ~; *most* ~]
1 : worth a lot of money • *valuable* antiques/artwork • The watch is extremely *valuable*.
2 : very useful or helpful • A lot of *valuable* advice/information can be found in this book. • I learned a *valuable* lesson. • He made many *valuable* contributions to the field of science. • The volunteers provide a *valuable* service to the communi-

ty. • She is a *valuable* member of the staff. • He was named the league's ***most valuable player***. [=the player who contributes the most to his team's success]

3 : important and limited in amount • Clean air is a *valuable* natural resource that needs to be protected. • Please don't waste my time. My time is very *valuable*.

4 : important to someone in a personal way • *valuable* friendships • Her love and support are extremely *valuable* to me.

val·u·ables /ˈvæljəbəlz/ *noun [plural]* : small things that you own (such as items of jewelry, watches, etc.) that are worth a lot of money • You should not leave your *valuables* lying in your car where they can be seen by thieves.

val·u·a·tion /ˌvæljəˈweɪʃən/ *noun, pl* **-tions**

1 : the act or process of making a judgment about the price or value of something *[noncount]* methods/standards of property *valuation* *[count]* The total included a *valuation* of the company's assets.

2 *[count]* **:** the estimated value of something • The company was acquired at a high *valuation*. • Home *valuations* are at an all-time high.

[1]val·ue /ˈvælju/ *noun, pl* **val·ues**

1 : the amount of money that something is worth : the price or cost of something *[noncount]* The company's stock continues to decline/decrease/drop in *value*. • Real estate prices have doubled in *value* over the last decade. • The difference in *value* between the two currencies is not significant. • You may exchange the item for something of equal *value*. • We sold the home for less than its full *value*. • The reproductions of the paintings have little or no *value*. [=they are worth little or no money] • These antiques will acquire more *value* [=they will become more valuable/expensive] over time. *[count]* an increase in the *value* of the dollar • The home has a *value* of $1,000,000. • Property *values* tend to rise as interest rates fall. — see also BOOK VALUE, MARKET VALUE

2 : something that can be bought for a low or fair price *[count]* The store advertises great *values*. • They recommend the car as a good *value* (for the/your money). *[noncount]* (*Brit*) The new store offers ***value for money***. [=you can buy a lot with your money at the store]

3 a : usefulness or importance *[noncount]* No one can deny the *value* of a good education. • The broccoli adds color and nutritional *value* to the dish. • The program's educational *value* was questioned. • a document of great historical *value* *[count]* A lot of teenagers ***place a high value*** on being popular. [=they believe that being popular is very important] **b** *[noncount]* **:** importance or interest of a particular kind • Few sports have greater ***entertainment value*** [=few sports are more entertaining] than figure skating. • He uses offensive language for (its) ***shock value***. [=in order to shock people] • The picture has ***sentimental value*** for me. [=it reminds me of happy times in the past]

4 *[count]* **:** a strongly held belief about what is valuable, important, or acceptable — usually plural • cultural/moral/religious *values* • traditional/conservative/liberal *values* • Her *values* were very different from mine. • America was founded on the *values* of freedom and justice for all.

5 *[count] mathematics* **:** a mathematical quantity that is represented by a letter • If x + 3 = 5, what is the *value* of x?

of value **1 :** having value : worth a lot of money • The burglars stole everything *of value* in my apartment. • We lost a few possessions, but nothing *of* (real) *value*. **2 :** useful or important • They didn't have anything *of value* to say. [=what they were saying wasn't very important]

– see also FACE VALUE

[2]value *verb* **values; val·ued; valu·ing** *[+ obj]*

1 : to make a judgment about the amount of money that something is worth — usually + *at* • The agent/appraiser *valued* the estate *at* $3.4 million. — usually used as *(be) valued* • The necklace *was valued at* $250.

2 : to think that (someone or something) is important or useful • She *values* the time she spends with her family. • He *values* her advice/opinions. • The items/objects are highly *valued* by collectors. • The herbs are *valued* for their medicinal properties. ***synonyms*** see APPRECIATE

– valued *adj [more ~; most ~]* • She's a *valued* [=*valuable*] member of the staff. • We wish to thank our *valued* customers.

value–added tax *noun [noncount]* : a tax that is added to products at each stage of their production — called also *VAT*

value judgment *noun, pl* **~ -ments** *[count]* : a personal opinion about how good or bad someone or something is • I am not making *value judgments*, I am simply presenting the facts.

val·ue·less /ˈvæljuləs/ *adj, formal*

1 : worth no money or very little money • a *valueless* [=*worthless*] piece of land

2 : not useful or important • No one's life is *valueless*. [=*worthless*]

valve /ˈvælv/ *noun, pl* **valves** *[count]*

1 : a mechanical device that controls the flow of liquid, gas, etc., by opening and closing • They turned off the main water *valve* to the house. — see picture at PLUMBING; see also SAFETY VALVE

2 : a device in some musical instruments (such as trumpets) that you press to play different notes — see picture at BRASS INSTRUMENT

3 *medical* **:** a structure in the heart, stomach, etc., that temporarily stops the flow of fluid or that allows fluid to move in one direction only • a heart *valve*

4 *Brit* **:** VACUUM TUBE

vamp /ˈvæmp/ *noun, pl* **vamps** *[count] old-fashioned* : a woman who uses her sexual charm to make men do what she wants

vam·pire /ˈvæmˌpajə/ *noun, pl* **-pires** *[count] in stories* : a dead person who leaves the grave at night to bite and suck the blood of living people

vampire bat *noun, pl* **~ bats** *[count]* : a bat from Central and South America that sucks the blood of people and animals

van /ˈvæn/ *noun, pl* **vans** *[count]*

1 : a vehicle that is used for transporting goods and that is closed in on all sides • a delivery *van* — see also MOVING VAN

2 *US* **:** a vehicle that is larger than a car, that is shaped like a box, that has doors and windows at the back and sides, and that is used for transporting people or things — see also MINIVAN

3 *Brit* **:** a railroad car for carrying goods or baggage — see also GUARD'S VAN

van·dal /ˈvændl̩/ *noun, pl* **-dals** *[count]* : a person who deliberately destroys or damages property : a person who vandalizes something • *Vandals* defaced the school's walls.

van·dal·ism /ˈvændəˌlɪzəm/ *noun [noncount]* : the act of deliberately destroying or damaging property • acts of theft and *vandalism* • He was arrested for *vandalism*.

van·dal·ize *also Brit* **van·dal·ise** /ˈvændəˌlaɪz/ *verb* **-iz·es; -ized; -iz·ing** *[+ obj]* : to deliberately destroy or damage (property) • Our car was *vandalized* in the parking lot.

vane /ˈveɪn/ *noun, pl* **vanes** *[count]*

1 : WEATHER VANE

2 : a thin, flat or curved object that is attached to a wheel and that moves when air or water pushes it • the *vanes* of a windmill — see picture at WINDMILL

van·guard /ˈvænˌgaɚd/ *noun, pl* **-guards**

1 *[count]* **:** the group of people who are the leaders of an action or movement in society, politics, art, etc. — usually singular • a member of the feminist *vanguard* • They are ***at the vanguard*** of a revolution in medical research. [=they are leading a revolution in medical research] • She was ***in the vanguard*** of the feminist movement in the early seventies.

2 ***the vanguard*** **:** the soldiers, ships, etc., that are at the front of a fighting force that is moving forward

[1]va·nil·la /vəˈnɪlə/ *noun [noncount]* : a dark substance that is made from the beans of a tropical plant and that is used to flavor food • The frosting is flavored with *vanilla*. • *vanilla* flavoring/extract • (*chiefly US*) *vanilla* beans = (*Brit*) *vanilla* pods

[2]vanilla *adj*

1 : having the flavor of vanilla • *vanilla* ice cream

2 *chiefly US, informal* **:** not having any special features or qualities : PLAIN-VANILLA • The décor is pretty *vanilla*.

van·ish /ˈvænɪʃ/ *verb* **-ish·es; -ished; -ish·ing** *[no obj]*

1 : to disappear entirely without a clear explanation • My keys mysteriously *vanished*. • The missing girl *vanished* without a trace a year ago. • The papers seem to have ***vanished into thin air***.

2 : to stop existing • Dinosaurs *vanished* from the face of the earth millions of years ago. • The practice has all but *vanished*. [=the practice is very rare now]

vanishing act *noun [singular] informal* : an occurrence in which someone or something suddenly goes away or disappears • He ***pulled a vanishing act*** [=he disappeared] when the check for the meal arrived.

van·ish·ing·ly /ˈvænɪʃɪŋli/ *adv* — used to say that something is so small that it almost does not exist at all ▪ The difference is *vanishingly* small. [=there is almost no difference]

vanishing point *noun, pl* **~ points** [*count*] : a point where parallel lines appear to meet in the distance

van·i·ty /ˈvænəti/ *noun, pl* **-ties**
1 [*noncount*] : the quality of people who have too much pride in their own appearance, abilities, achievements, etc. : the quality of being vain ▪ The handsome actor's *vanity* was well-known. ▪ She described her accomplishments without exaggeration or *vanity*. ▪ personal *vanity*
2 [*count*] : something (such as a belief or a way of behaving) which shows that you have too much pride in yourself, your social status, etc. — usually plural ▪ the *vanities* of the wealthy and powerful
3 [*count*] *US* **a** : DRESSING TABLE **b** : a bathroom cabinet that is covered by a sink and a countertop
4 [*noncount*] *formal + literary* : the quality of being worthless or unimportant when compared to very serious things ▪ the *vanity* of human labors/wishes

vanity plate *noun, pl* **~ plates** [*count*] *US* : a license plate that has letters or numbers chosen by the owner of the vehicle

van·quish /ˈvæŋkwɪʃ/ *verb* **-quish·es; -quished; -quish·ing** [+ *obj*] *literary* : to defeat (someone) completely in a war, battle, etc. ▪ They were *vanquished* in battle. ▪ *vanquished* enemies/foes — sometimes used figuratively ▪ She sought to *vanquish* her desires.

van·tage point /ˈvæntɪʤ-/ *noun, pl* **~ points** [*count*] : a position from which something is viewed or considered ▪ You can see the whole valley from this *vantage point*. ▪ From our *vantage point* in the 21st century, it is difficult to imagine life without computers.

vap·id /ˈvæpəd/ *adj* [*more ~; most ~*] *formal* : not lively or interesting : dull or boring ▪ a song with *vapid* lyrics
– **va·pid·i·ty** /væˈpɪdəti/ *noun* [*noncount*] ▪ the *vapidity* of her writing – **vap·id·ly** *adv* ▪ *vapidly* sentimental

va·por (*US*) *or Brit* **va·pour** /ˈveɪpɚ/ *noun, pl* **-pors** [*count, noncount*] : a substance that is in the form of a gas or that consists of very small drops or particles mixed with the air ▪ water *vapor*

va·por·ize *also Brit* **va·por·ise** /ˈveɪpəˌraɪz/ *verb* **-iz·es; -ized; -iz·ing** : to change into a vapor or to cause (something) to change into a vapor [+ *obj*] Heat is used to *vaporize* the liquid. [*no obj*] Pressure causes the chemical to *vaporize*.
– **va·por·i·za·tion** *also Brit* **va·por·i·sa·tion** /ˌveɪpərəˈzeɪʃən, *Brit* ˌveɪpəˌraɪˈzeɪʃən/ *noun* [*noncount*] – **va·por·iz·er** *also Brit* **va·por·is·er** /ˈveɪpəˌraɪzɚ/ *noun, pl* **-ers** [*count*]

vapor trail (*US*) *or Brit* **vapour trail** *noun, pl* **~ trails** [*count*] : a visible stream of water or ice particles that is created in the sky by an airplane or rocket : CONTRAIL

[1]**var·i·able** /ˈverijəbəl/ *adj* [*more ~; most ~*] : able or likely to change or be changed : not always the same ▪ The winds were light and *variable*. ▪ a *variable* climate ▪ The loan has a *variable* interest rate. — opposite INVARIABLE
– **var·i·abil·i·ty** /ˌverijəˈbɪləti/ *noun* [*noncount*] ▪ the *variability* of the climate – **var·i·ably** /ˈverijəbli/ *adv* ▪ The term is used *variably* to mean different things.

[2]**variable** *noun, pl* **-ables** [*count*]
1 : something that changes or that can be changed : something that varies ▪ unemployment and other economic *variables*
2 *mathematics* : a quantity that can have any one of a set of values or a symbol that represents such a quantity

var·i·ance /ˈverijəns/ *noun, pl* **-anc·es**
1 *formal* : an amount of difference or change [*noncount*] There was some *variance* in the results. [*count*] We noticed a slight *variance* between/in the quality of the samples.
2 [*count*] *law* : an official decision or document that allows someone to do something that is not usually allowed by the rules ▪ He had to get a *variance* to add a garage on to his house.
at variance *formal* : not in agreement ▪ Their statements are *at variance*. — usually + *with* ▪ His current statements are completely *at variance with* his earlier position.

[1]**var·i·ant** /ˈverijənt/ *adj* : different in some way from others of the same kind ▪ *variant* strains of a disease ▪ *variant* points of view ▪ *variant* spellings [=different ways of spelling a word]

[2]**variant** *noun, pl* **-ants** [*count*]
1 : something that is different in some way from others of the same kind ▪ A new *variant* of the disease has appeared.
2 : one of two or more different ways to spell or pronounce a word ▪ regional *variants* in speech ▪ a spelling *variant*

var·i·a·tion /ˌveriˈeɪʃən/ *noun, pl* **-tions**
1 : a change in the form, position, condition, or amount of something [*count*] color/temperature *variations* — often + *in* ▪ extreme *variations in* temperature [*noncount*] He repeated the story without *variation*. [=without changing it] — often + *in* ▪ There's been a lot of *variation in* the weather lately. [=the weather has changed often lately] ▪ We need some *variation in* our routine. [=we need to change/vary our routine]
2 [*count*] : something that is similar to something else but different in some way — often + *on* ▪ His newest book is just a slight *variation on* a familiar theme. ▪ The meal she served us was an interesting *variation on* a traditional turkey dinner.
3 [*count*] *music* : a repeated version of a short piece of music with changes in its rhythm, tune, or harmony — often + *on* ▪ *variations on* a theme by Haydn

var·i·cose vein /ˈverəˌkous-/ *noun, pl* **~ veins** [*count*] *medical* : a vein that is abnormally swollen or made larger or wider ▪ He developed *varicose veins* on his legs in his old age.

var·ied /ˈverid/ *adj* [*more ~; most ~*] : having many forms or types : including many different things ▪ She has *varied* [=*diverse, various*] interests. ▪ We try to eat a more *varied* diet. ▪ My routine is *varied* enough so that I don't get bored. ▪ She studies subjects as *varied* as chemistry and sculpture.

var·ie·gat·ed /ˈverijəˌgeɪtəd/ *adj* [*more ~; most ~*]
1 : having patches, stripes, or marks of different colors ▪ *variegated* flowers/leaves
2 *formal* : including many different things : full of variety ▪ a *variegated* career

va·ri·ety /vəˈrajəti/ *noun, pl* **-et·ies**
1 [*singular*] : a number or collection of different things or people — usually + *of* ▪ The talks covered a wide/great *variety of* topics. [=the talks covered many different topics] ▪ The company sells a *variety of* gardening products. ▪ They broke up for a *variety of* reasons. ▪ The conference attracts a wide *variety of* people. ▪ He has a *variety of* health problems.
2 [*noncount*] : the quality or state of having or including many different things ▪ I was surprised by the *variety* of the choices that were available. ▪ Our diet lacks *variety*. ▪ My life needs more *variety*. ▪ You know what they say: ***variety is the spice of life***. [=life is more interesting and enjoyable when you do different things]
3 [*count*] : a particular kind of person or thing ▪ The museum has aircraft of every *variety*. [=*kind, sort*] ▪ people of all *varieties* ▪ different *varieties* of oranges ▪ exotic *varieties* of snakes
4 [*noncount*] : a type of entertainment that has many short performances (such as dances, skits, and songs) which follow one another and that are not related — usually used before another noun ▪ *variety* shows ▪ *variety* performers/theater
– see also GARDEN-VARIETY

variety store *noun, pl* **~ stores** [*count*] *US* : a store that sells many different kinds of products that are not expensive

var·i·ous /ˈverijəs/ *adj*
1 — used to refer to several different or many different things, people, etc. ▪ *Various* bands will be performing at the concert. ▪ The car is available in *various* colors. ▪ She has worked at *various* publishing companies. ▪ We stopped at *various* places along the way. ▪ The reasons for their decision were ***many and various***. [=they had many different reasons]
2 : different from each other ▪ He has lived in places as *various* as New York and Beijing.

var·i·ous·ly /ˈverijəsli/ *adv* : in several or many different ways : in various ways ▪ He has been *variously* described as a hero and a villain. ▪ The term is spelled *variously* in different places. ▪ The concept of freedom has been *variously* understood by different people.

var·mint /ˈvɑɚmənt/ *noun, pl* **-mints** [*count*] *chiefly US, old-fashioned + humorous*
1 : an animal that is considered a problem : PEST ▪ rats, mice, and other *varmints*
2 : a bad person ▪ The sheriff in the movie gets revenge on the dirty *varmint* who killed his brother.

[1]**var·nish** /ˈvɑɚnɪʃ/ *noun, pl* **-nish·es**
1 [*count, noncount*] : a liquid that is spread on a surface and that dries to form a hard, shiny coating ▪ floor *varnish* ▪ (*Brit*) ***nail varnish*** [=(*US*) *nail polish*]
2 [*noncount*] : the hard, shiny coating that is produced by varnish ▪ She accidentally scratched the *varnish*.

[2]**varnish** *verb* **-nishes; -nished; -nish·ing** [+ *obj*] : to cover (something) with varnish ▪ He *varnished* the table.

var·si·ty /ˈvɑɚsəti/ *noun, pl* **-ties** [*count, noncount*]

1 *US* : the main team of a college, school, or club in a particular sport ▪ She's trying to make (the) *varsity* this year. — often used before another noun ▪ *varsity* athletes ▪ Their son is on the high school's *varsity* baseball/football team. — compare JUNIOR VARSITY
2 *Brit, old-fashioned* : UNIVERSITY

vary /ˈveri/ *verb* **var·ies; var·ied; vary·ing**
1 [*no obj*] : to be different or to become different : CHANGE ▪ The terrain *varies* as you climb higher. ▪ The cost of a room at the hotel *varies* with the season. ▪ Their services *vary* depending on the customer. ▪ Opinions *vary* [=people have differing opinions] about the reasons for the company's failure. ▪ They've tried to improve their procedures, with *varying* degrees of success. ▪ The diamonds *vary* in size. ▪ Colors *vary* from light to dark.
2 [+ *obj*] : to make (something) different : to make changes to (something) so that it is not always the same ▪ I try to *vary* my diet by eating different kinds of foods.

vas·cu·lar /ˈvæskjələ/ *adj, medical* : of or relating to the veins, arteries, etc., that carry fluids (such as blood) through the body ▪ *vascular* diseases/tissue ▪ the *vascular* system

vase /ˈveɪs, *Brit* ˈvɑːz/ *noun, pl* **vas·es** [*count*] : a container that is used for holding flowers or for decoration ▪ a beautiful Chinese *vase* ▪ a *vase* of roses

va·sec·to·my /vəˈsɛktəmi/ *noun, pl* **-mies** [*count*] *medical* : an operation that makes a man unable to make a woman pregnant : a surgery that prevents a man from producing sperm when he has sex

Vas·e·line /ˌvæsəˈliːn/ *trademark* — used for a soft and thick substance (called petroleum jelly) that is used on a person's skin

vas·sal /ˈvæsəl/ *noun, pl* **-sals** [*count*] : a person in the past who received protection and land from a lord in return for loyalty and service — often used figuratively to describe a person, country, etc., that is controlled by someone or something more powerful ▪ The states became *vassals* of the empire.

vast /ˈvæst, *Brit* ˈvɑːst/ *adj* **vast·er; -est** [*more* ~; *most* ~] : very great in size, amount, or extent ▪ She has a *vast* amount of knowledge on this subject. ▪ *vast* quantities of information ▪ The policy is supported by the *vast* majority of citizens. ▪ a *vast* expanse of land
– **vast·ly** *adv* ▪ His background is *vastly* different from mine. ▪ They *vastly* increased spending. – **vast·ness** /ˈvæstnəs, *Brit* ˈvɑːstnəs/ *noun* [*noncount*] ▪ the *vastness* of the desert/ocean

vat /ˈvæt/ *noun, pl* **vats** [*count*] : a large container (such as a tub or barrel) used especially for holding liquids

VAT /ˌviːˌeɪˈtiː/ *noun* [*noncount*] : VALUE-ADDED TAX

Vat·i·can /ˈvætɪkən/ *noun*
the Vatican 1 : the place in Rome where the Pope lives and works ▪ I plan to visit *the Vatican* on my tour. 2 : the government of the Roman Catholic Church ▪ *The Vatican* has announced a new appointment. ▪ a *Vatican* official

vaude·ville /ˈvɑːdvəl/ *noun* [*noncount*] *US* : a type of entertainment that was popular in the U.S. in the late 19th and early 20th centuries and that had many different performers doing songs, dances, and comic acts ▪ She became a big star in/on *vaudeville*. ▪ a *vaudeville* performer/show
– **vaude·vil·lian** /ˌvɑːdˈvɪljən/ *noun, pl* **-lians** [*count*] ▪ an old *vaudevillian* [=performer in vaudeville]

[1]**vault** /ˈvɑːlt/ *noun, pl* **vaults** [*count*]
1 : an arched structure that forms a ceiling or roof ▪ They gazed up at the *vault* of the cathedral. — sometimes used figuratively to refer to the sky ▪ the *vault* of heaven
2 : a locked room where money or valuable things are kept ▪ a bank *vault*
3 : a room or chamber in which a dead person is buried
– compare [3]VAULT

[2]**vault** *verb* **vaults; vault·ed; vault·ing**
1 : to jump over (something) [+ *obj*] The dog *vaulted* the fence.; *especially* : to jump over (something) by using your hands or a pole to push yourself upward [+ *obj*] She *vaulted* the fence easily. [*no obj*] — often + *over* ▪ She put her hands on the top of the fence and *vaulted over* it easily.
2 *chiefly US* : to move suddenly and quickly into a better position [*no obj*] The team *vaulted* [=*jumped*] into the lead. ▪ She *vaulted* to fame [=she suddenly became famous] when her first movie was a hit. [+ *obj*] The success of the movie *vaulted* her to fame.
– **vault·er** /ˈvɑːltə/ *noun, pl* **-ers** [*count*] ▪ She's the first *vaulter* [=*pole-vaulter*] to clear that height.

[3]**vault** *noun* [*noncount*] : a jump that is made over something especially by using your hands or a pole to push yourself upward ▪ The gymnast performed a difficult *vault*. — see also POLE VAULT — compare [1]VAULT

vault·ed /ˈvɑːltəd/ *adj* : built in the form of an arch ▪ a *vaulted* ceiling/roof

vault·ing /ˈvɑːltɪŋ/ *adj, always used before a noun, literary* : rising or reaching very high — usually used in the phrase ***vaulting ambition*** ▪ He was a man of *vaulting ambition*. [=he was an extremely ambitious man]

vaunt·ed /ˈvɑːntəd/ *adj* : often spoken of or described as very good or great : often praised ▪ The team's *vaunted* defense faltered in the second half of the game.

VCR /ˌviːˌsiːˈɑə/ *noun, pl* **VCRs** [*count*] : a machine that is used to make and watch video recordings of television programs, movies, etc.

VD *abbr* venereal disease

've /v *after vowels*, əv *after consonants*/ — used as a contraction of *have* ▪ I've [=I have] been very busy.

veal /ˈviːl/ *noun* [*noncount*] : the meat of a young cow (called a calf) that is used for food ▪ cuts of *veal* ▪ *veal* chops/cutlets

vec·tor /ˈvɛktə/ *noun, pl* **-tors** [*count*]
1 *mathematics* : a quantity (such as velocity) that has size and direction
2 *technical* : the course or direction of an airplane
3 *biology* : an insect, animal, etc., that carries germs that cause disease ▪ a mosquito that is the principal *vector* of yellow fever

vee·jay /ˈviːˌdʒeɪ/ *noun, pl* **-jays** [*count*] : a person who introduces the music videos played on a television program — called also *VJ*

veep /ˈviːp/ *noun, pl* **veeps** [*count*] *US, informal* : VICE PRESIDENT; *especially* : the Vice President of the United States

veer /ˈviə/ *verb* **veers; veered; veer·ing** [*no obj*] : to change direction quickly or suddenly ▪ The ship *veered* away to the north. ▪ The car nearly *veered* off the road. ▪ The wind suddenly *veered* and began to blow from the east. ▪ The rocket ***veered off course***. [=began to go in the wrong direction] — often used figuratively ▪ The story *veers* toward the ridiculous at times. ▪ She *veered* into politics soon after college.

[1]**veg** /ˈvɛdʒ/ *verb* **veg·ges; vegged; veg·ging** [*no obj*] *informal* : to spend time doing something that does not require much thought or effort — usually + *out* ▪ We *vegged out* in front of the TV all afternoon. ▪ He's *vegging out* on the couch.

[2]**veg** *noun, pl* **veg** *chiefly Brit, informal* : VEGETABLE 1 [*count*] a delicious *veg* — usually plural ▪ a meal of meat and two *veg* [*noncount*] Would you like some *veg*? ▪ *veg* soup ▪ a *veg* sandwich

veg·an /ˈviːgən/ *noun, pl* **-ans** [*count*] : a person who does not eat any food that comes from animals and who often also does not use animal products (such as leather)

veg·e·ta·ble /ˈvɛdʒtəbəl/ *noun, pl* **-ta·bles** [*count*]
1 : a plant or plant part that is eaten as food ▪ The doctor said I should eat more fruits and *vegetables*. ▪ a bowl of *vegetable* soup ▪ a *vegetable* garden ▪ *vegetable* oil — see color picture on page C4; see also ROOT VEGETABLE
2 *sometimes offensive* : a person who is unable to talk, move, etc., because of severe brain damage ▪ The accident had left him a *vegetable*. — called also (*Brit, informal*) *cabbage*

veg·e·tar·i·an /ˌvɛdʒəˈterijən/ *noun, pl* **-ans** [*count*] : a person who does not eat meat
– **vegetarian** *adj* ▪ a *vegetarian* diet/meal/menu [=a diet/meal/menu that does not include meat] – **veg·e·tar·i·an·ism** /ˌvɛdʒəˈterijəˌnɪzəm/ *noun* [*noncount*]

veg·e·tate /ˈvɛdʒəˌteɪt/ *verb* **-tates; -tat·ed; -tat·ing** [*no obj*] : to spend time doing things that do not require much thought or effort : to be very lazy or inactive ▪ I just spent the weekend *vegetating* at home. ▪ I'm worried that after I retire I'll just sit at home, watch TV, and *vegetate*.

veg·e·ta·tion /ˌvɛdʒəˈteɪʃən/ *noun* [*noncount*] : plants in general : plants that cover a particular area ▪ the dense/lush *vegetation* of the jungle ▪ hills covered in/with *vegetation*

veg·e·ta·tive /ˈvɛdʒəˌteɪtɪv/ *adj* : of or relating to plants ▪ the area's *vegetative* cover ▪ *vegetative* growth — see also PERSISTENT VEGETATIVE STATE

veg·gie /ˈvɛdʒi/ *noun, pl* **-gies** [*count*] *informal*
1 *chiefly US* : VEGETABLE 1 ▪ Eat your *veggies*. ▪ fresh *veggies*
2 *chiefly Brit* : VEGETARIAN ▪ The restaurant is popular with *veggies*.

veggie burger *noun, pl* ~ **-gers** [*count*] : a food that looks like a hamburger but that is made with vegetables instead of meat

ve·he·ment /ˈviːjəmənt/ *adj* [*more* ~; *most* ~] **:** showing strong and often angry feelings **:** very emotional • He issued a *vehement* denial of the accusation. • The proposal has faced *vehement* opposition from many teachers. • She was *vehement* about the need for new safety measures.

– **ve·he·mence** /ˈviːjəməns/ *noun* [*noncount*] • She spoke with some *vehemence* about the need for new safety measures. – **ve·he·ment·ly** *adv* • He *vehemently* denied the accusation. • They argued *vehemently* against the proposal.

ve·hi·cle /ˈviːjəkəl/ *noun, pl* **-hi·cles** [*count*]

1 : a machine that is used to carry people or goods from one place to another • cars, trucks, and other *vehicles* • a stolen *vehicle* • The *vehicle's* driver was severely injured in the crash. • Have you seen his new car? It's a fine-looking *vehicle.* — see also MOTOR VEHICLE, RECREATIONAL VEHICLE, SPORT-UTILITY VEHICLE

2 : the thing that allows something to be passed along, expressed, achieved, or shown • an investment *vehicle* • Water and insects can be *vehicles* of infection. • art as a *vehicle* for self-expression • Words and pictures are *vehicles* of communication. • These big-budget movies are star *vehicles* for well-known actors.

ve·hic·u·lar /viˈhɪkjələ/ *adj*

1 : of, relating to, or designed for vehicles • The road was closed to *vehicular* traffic.

2 : caused by or resulting from the operation of a vehicle • *vehicular* homicide

[1]**veil** /ˈveɪl/ *noun, pl* **veils**

1 [*count*] **:** a piece of cloth or net worn usually by women over the head and shoulders and sometimes over the face • a bridal *veil*

2 [*count*] **:** something that covers or hides something else • *Veils* of moss draped the trees. • The *veil* of secrecy was lifted. [=the secret was made known]

take the veil *old-fashioned* **:** to become a nun

[2]**veil** *verb* **veils; veiled; veil·ing** [+ *obj*] **:** to cover (something) with a veil or with something that is like a veil **:** to hide or partly hide (something) • Her eyes were partially *veiled* by her long, dark hair. • Haze *veiled* the landscape. • The sun was *veiled* by clouds.

veiled /ˈveɪld/ *adj*

1 : having or wearing a veil • a *veiled* hat • *veiled* women

2 : able to be seen or understood but not openly shown or stated **:** expressed in a way that is not clear and direct • a thinly *veiled* threat • She looked at him with barely *veiled* contempt. • The report makes *veiled* references to his criminal activities.

vein /ˈveɪn/ *noun, pl* **veins**

1 [*count*] **:** any one of the tubes that carry blood from parts of the body back to the heart — compare ARTERY; see also VARICOSE VEIN

2 [*count*] **:** any one of the thin lines that can be seen on the surface of a leaf or on the wing of an insect

3 [*count*] **:** a long, narrow opening in rock filled with gold, silver, etc. • a *vein* of gold/ore

4 [*count*] **:** a thin line or streak of material that has a different color or texture from the material that surrounds it • white marble with greenish *veins* running through it

5 [*singular*] **:** a particular style, quality, etc. • Most of his stories are in the romantic *vein.* [=are romantic] • She introduced a welcome *vein* of humor. • We renewed discussion along the same *vein.*

ice water in your veins see ICE WATER

veined /ˈveɪnd/ *adj* **:** marked with thin lines **:** having veins or streaks • a *veined* leaf • *veined* cheese/marble

Vel·cro /ˈvɛlˌkroʊ/ *trademark* — used for a nylon fabric that can be fastened to itself

veld *or* **veldt** /ˈvɛlt/ *noun* [*noncount*] **:** an area of grassy land with few trees or shrubs especially in southern Africa

vel·lum /ˈvɛləm/ *noun* [*noncount*]

1 : a smooth material made from the skin of a young animal and used especially for covering books or for writing on

2 : a strong cream-colored paper

ve·loc·i·ty /vəˈlɑːsəti/ *noun, pl* **-ties :** quickness of motion **:** SPEED [*count*] particles moving at high *velocities* [*noncount*] measuring the *velocity* of sound • the *velocity* of a bullet • His pitches have great *velocity.* [=his pitches are very fast]

ve·lour /vəˈluə/ *noun* [*noncount*] **:** a type of cloth that resembles velvet

vel·vet /ˈvɛlvət/ *noun, pl* **-vets :** a soft type of cloth that has short raised fibers on one side [*noncount*] She was dressed in black *velvet.* [*count*] rich *velvets*

– **velvet** *adj* • a *velvet* sofa • a *velvet* dress/jacket

vel·ve·teen /ˌvɛlvəˈtiːn/ *noun* [*noncount*] **:** a fabric usually of cotton that resembles velvet • a dress made from *velveteen*

vel·vety /ˈvɛlvəti/ *adj* [*more* ~; *most* ~] **:** soft and smooth • *velvety* hair

ve·nal /ˈviːnəl/ *adj* [*more* ~; *most* ~] *formal* **:** willing to do dishonest things in return for money **:** CORRUPT • a *venal* court official

– **ve·nal·i·ty** /vɪˈnæləti/ *noun* [*noncount*]

ven·det·ta /vɛnˈdɛtə/ *noun, pl* **-tas** [*count*]

1 : a very long and violent fight between two families or groups **:** BLOOD FEUD

2 : a series of acts done by someone over a long period of time to cause harm to a disliked person or group • He waged a personal *vendetta* against his rivals in the Senate. • She claims that the police have a *vendetta* against her. [=that the police are deliberately and unfairly trying to cause trouble for her]

vending machine *noun, pl* ~ **-chines** [*count*] **:** a machine that you put money into in order to buy food, drinks, cigarettes, etc. — called also (*Brit*) *slot machine*

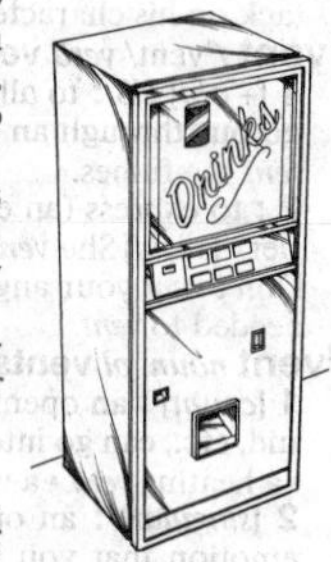

vending machine

ven·dor /ˈvɛndə/ *noun, pl* **-dors** [*count*]

1 : a person who sells things especially on the street • a hot dog *vendor*

2 : a business that sells a particular type of product • *vendors* of computer parts • software *vendors*

[1]**ve·neer** /vəˈniə/ *noun, pl* **-neers**

1 : a thin layer of wood or other material that is attached to the surface of something in order to make it look better [*count*] a wall with a stone *veneer* [*noncount*] a dresser with mahogany *veneer*

2 [*singular*] **:** a way of behaving or appearing that gives other people a false idea of your true feelings or situation — usually + *of* • She dropped her *veneer of* sophistication.

[2]**veneer** *verb* **-neers; -neered; -neer·ing** [+ *obj*] **:** to cover (something) with a veneer • The cabinet was *veneered* in oak.

ven·er·a·ble /ˈvɛnərəbəl/ *adj* [*more* ~; *most* ~] *formal* **:** old and respected **:** valued and respected because of old age, long use, etc. • a *venerable* tradition/institution • the family's *venerable* leader • a *venerable* old hotel

ven·er·ate /ˈvɛnəˌreɪt/ *verb* **-ates; -at·ed; -at·ing** [+ *obj*] *formal* **:** to feel or show deep respect for (someone or something that is considered great, holy, etc.) • a writer *venerated* by generations of admirers • She is *venerated* as a saint.

– **ven·er·a·tion** /ˌvɛnəˈreɪʃən/ *noun* [*noncount*] • The icon is an object of *veneration.*

ve·ne·re·al disease /vəˈnirijəl-/ *noun, pl* ~ **-eases** [*count, noncount*] *medical* **:** a disease (such as gonorrhea or syphilis) that is passed from one person to another through sexual intercourse — abbr. *VD*

ve·ne·tian blind /vəˈniːʃən-/ *noun, pl* ~ **blinds** [*count*] **:** a covering for a window made of strips of wood, plastic, or metal that can be turned to block out or let in light

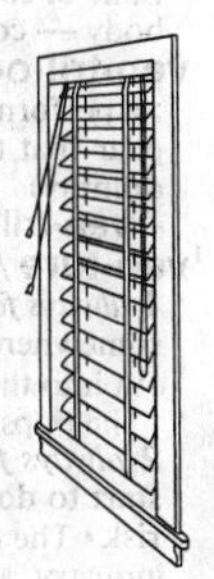
venetian blind

ven·geance /ˈvɛnʤəns/ *noun* [*noncount*] **:** the act of doing something to hurt someone because that person did something that hurt you or someone else • The fire was set as an act of *vengeance.* • He swore *vengeance* [=*revenge*] against his son's kidnapper. • Angry protesters wanted to inflict *vengeance* on the killer.

with a vengeance **:** with great force or effort • After losing the first three games, the team came back *with a vengeance* to win the next four. • She set to work *with a vengeance* and finished the job in two hours.

venge·ful /ˈvɛnʤfəl/ *adj* [*more* ~; *most* ~] **:** feeling or showing a desire to harm someone who has harmed you **:** feeling or showing a desire for vengeance • The robbery was committed by a *vengeful* former employee. • The fire was a *vengeful* act of destruction. • *vengeful* feelings

– **venge·ful·ly** *adv* • He glared *vengefully* at his accuser.

V

– **venge·ful·ness** *noun [noncount]*

ve·nial /ˈviːnijəl/ *adj [more ~; most ~]* : not serious : FORGIVABLE • a *venial* mistake

venial sin *noun, pl* **~ sins** *[count] in the Roman Catholic Church* : a sin (such as stealing something small) that is not very serious and will not result in punishment that lasts forever • commit a *venial sin* — compare MORTAL SIN

ven·i·son /ˈvɛnəsən/ *noun [noncount]* : the meat of a deer

ven·om /ˈvɛnəm/ *noun [noncount]*

1 : poison that is produced by an animal (such as a snake) and used to kill or injure another animal usually through biting or stinging

2 : a very strong feeling of anger or hatred • She spoke of him with *venom* in her voice. • He spewed *venom* against his rival.

ven·om·ous /ˈvɛnəməs/ *adj [more ~; most ~]*

1 a : capable of putting poison or venom into another animal's body usually by biting or stinging it • The cobra is a *venomous* snake. • a *venomous* spider **b** : containing venom • a *venomous* sting/bite

2 : expressing very strong hatred or anger • a *venomous* attack on his character • *venomous* comments

¹vent /ˈvɛnt/ *verb* **vents; vent·ed; vent·ing**

1 *[+ obj] US* : to allow (something, such as smoke or gas) to go out through an opening • Windows should be opened to *vent* the fumes.

2 : to express (an emotion) usually in a loud or angry manner *[+ obj]* She *vented* her frustrations by kicking the car. • Don't *vent* your anger on me. *[no obj]* I screamed because I needed to *vent*.

²vent *noun, pl* **vents**

1 *[count]* : an opening through which air, steam, smoke, liquid, etc., can go into or out of a room, machine, or container • a heating *vent* • a *vent* for the clothes dryer

2 *[singular]* : an opportunity or a way to express a strong emotion that you have not openly shown • She needed to find a *vent* for her frustration.

3 *[count]* : a thin opening at the bottom of a jacket or skirt where a seam ends

give vent to : to express (a strong emotion, such as anger) in a forceful and open way • He *gave vent to* his annoyance. • She didn't want to ***give full vent to*** her feelings. [=let her feelings out completely]

ven·ti·late /ˈvɛntəˌleɪt/ *verb* **-lates; -lat·ed; -lat·ing** *[+ obj]*

1 : to allow fresh air to enter and move through (a room, building, etc.) • She opened the windows to *ventilate* the room. • The room was adequately/poorly *ventilated*.

2 *formal* : to express or discuss (something) openly or publicly • *ventilate* feelings/opinions

– **ven·ti·la·tion** /ˌvɛntəˈleɪʃən/ *noun [noncount]* • The room has adequate/poor *ventilation*. • They installed a new *ventilation* system in the building.

ven·ti·la·tor /ˈvɛntəˌleɪtɚ/ *noun, pl* **-tors** *[count]*

1 : a device that lets fresh air enter and move through a room, building, etc.

2 *medical* : a device for helping a person to breathe : RESPIRATOR • The patient was put on a *ventilator*.

ven·tri·cle /ˈvɛntrəkəl/ *noun, pl* **-tri·cles** *[count] technical* : one of two sections of the heart that pump blood out to the body — compare ATRIUM

ven·tril·o·quist /vɛnˈtrɪləkwɪst/ *noun, pl* **-quists** *[count]* : a performer who is able to speak in a way that makes it appear that the words are being said by a large doll (called a dummy)

– **ven·tril·o·quism** /vɛnˈtrɪləˌkwɪzəm/ *noun [noncount]*

¹ven·ture /ˈvɛnʧɚ/ *verb* **-tures; -tured; -tur·ing**

1 *always followed by an adverb or preposition [no obj]* : to go somewhere that is unknown, dangerous, etc. • We *ventured* out into the woods. • He nervously *ventured* out onto the ice. • The pups never *ventured* far from home.

2 *always followed by an adverb or preposition [no obj]* : to start to do something new or different that usually involves risk • The company is ***venturing into*** the computer software industry. • a writer ***venturing on/upon*** a new project • The group's lead singer is now *venturing on* a solo career. • It's important to plan carefully before *venturing on* a long journey.

3 *[+ obj]* : to do, say, or offer something (such as a guess or an opinion) even though you are not sure about it • I'd like to *venture* [=*hazard*] a guess. — often followed by *to + verb* • He got angry at me when I *ventured to suggest* that things could have been worse.

nothing ventured, nothing gained — used to say that it is worth trying to do something because you might succeed even though success is not certain

²venture *noun, pl* **-tures** *[count]* : a new activity, project, business, etc., that typically involves risk • a *venture* into the unknown • a space *venture* • a joint business *venture* • *venture* partners

venture capital *noun [noncount]* : money that is used to start a new business

– **venture capitalist** *noun, pl* **~ -ists** *[count]*

ven·ture·some /ˈvɛnʧɚsəm/ *adj [more ~; most ~] formal*

1 : willing to take risks : DARING • a *venturesome* sea captain • a *venturesome* investor

2 : involving risk : DANGEROUS • a *venturesome* journey

ven·ue /ˈvɛnˌjuː/ *noun, pl* **-ues** *[count]* : the place where an event takes place • a sports *venue* • The *venue* of the trial has been changed. • The nightclub provided an intimate *venue* for her performance.

Ve·nus /ˈviːnəs/ *noun [singular]* : the planet that is second in order from the sun

Venus fly·trap /-ˈflaɪˌtræp/ *noun, pl* **~ -traps** *[count]* : a plant that has the tip of each leaf formed into a trap for capturing insects which it eats

ve·rac·i·ty /vəˈræsəti/ *noun [noncount] formal*

1 : truth or accuracy • We questioned the *veracity* of his statements.

2 : the quality of being truthful or honest • The jury did not doubt the *veracity* of the witness.

ve·ran·da *or* **ve·ran·dah** /vəˈrændə/ *noun, pl* **-das** *or* **-dahs** *[count]* : a long, open structure on the outside of a building that has a roof : PORCH

verb /ˈvɚb/ *noun, pl* **verbs** *[count] grammar* : a word (such as *jump, think, happen*, or *exist*) that is usually one of the main parts of a sentence and that expresses an action, an occurrence, or a state of being — see also ACTION VERB, AUXILIARY VERB, LINKING VERB, MODAL VERB, PHRASAL VERB

ver·bal /ˈvɚbəl/ *adj*

1 : relating to or consisting of words • The job requires someone with strong *verbal* skills. [=someone who is good at writing and speaking] • He scored well on the *verbal* section of the test. • *verbal* communication • She was a victim of ***verbal abuse***. [=harsh and insulting language]

2 : spoken rather than written • They had a *verbal* exchange. • a *verbal* agreement to finish the work • We gave only *verbal* instructions.

3 : relating to or formed from a verb • a *verbal* adjective

– **ver·bal·ly** *adv* • She was *verbally* abused. • They agreed *verbally* to the deal.

ver·bal·ize *also Brit* **ver·bal·ise** /ˈvɚbəˌlaɪz/ *verb* **-iz·es; -ized; -iz·ing** *[+ obj]* : to express (something) in words : to say (something) in speech or writing • She didn't know how to *verbalize* her feelings.

ver·ba·tim /vɚˈbeɪtəm/ *adj* : in exactly the same words • The court reporter recorded a *verbatim* account of the trial. [=recorded the exact words that were spoken at the trial]

– **verbatim** *adv* • She recited the poem *verbatim*. [=*word for word*]

ver·bi·age /ˈvɚbijɪʤ/ *noun [noncount]* : speech or writing that contains too many words or that uses words that are more difficult than necessary • The editor removed some of the excess *verbiage* from the article.

ver·bose /vɚˈbous/ *adj [more ~; most ~] formal* : using more words than are needed • He is a *verbose* speaker. • The teacher thought the essay was too *verbose*. [=*wordy*] • She has a *verbose* writing style.

– **ver·bose·ly** *adv* – **ver·bos·i·ty** /vɚˈbɑːsəti/ *noun [noncount]*

ver·dant /ˈvɚdn̩t/ *adj [more ~; most ~] literary* : green with growing plants • The fields were *verdant*. • a *verdant* forest

ver·dict /ˈvɚdɪkt/ *noun, pl* **-dicts** *[count]*

1 *law* : the decision made by a jury in a trial • The *verdict* was not guilty. • The jury reached a guilty *verdict*.

2 : a judgment or opinion about something • Do you want my *verdict* on the meal? • The critic's *verdict* about the show was positive.

¹verge /ˈvɚʤ/ *noun, pl* **verg·es** *[count] Brit* : an area along the edge of a road, path, etc. • a grassy *verge*

on the verge of *US + Brit* : at the point when (something) is about to happen or is very likely to happen • The company was *on the verge of* going bankrupt. [=was very close to go-

V

ing bankrupt] ▪ The child was *on the verge of* tears. [=was almost crying; was about to start crying] ▪ We were *on the verge of* divorce.

[2]**verge** *verb* **verges; verged; verg·ing**
verge on/upon [phrasal verb] ***verge on/upon (something)*** : to come near to being (something) ▪ comedy that *verges on* farce [=comedy that is almost farce] ▪ His accusations were *verging on* slander.

verg·er /ˈvɚʤɚ/ *noun, pl* **-ers** [*count*] *chiefly Brit* : someone who performs simple duties during church services

ver·i·fy /ˈverəˌfaɪ/ *verb* **-fies; -fied; -fy·ing** [+ *obj*] : to prove, show, find out, or state that (something) is true or correct ▪ We could not *verify* [=*confirm*] the rumor. ▪ She *verified* her flight number. ▪ He *verified* that the item was in stock. ▪ Can you *verify* whether I am scheduled to work or not?
– **ver·i·fi·able** /ˌverəˈfajəbəl/ *adj* ▪ a *verifiable* claim – **ver·i·fi·ca·tion** /ˌverəfəˈkeɪʃən/ *noun* [*noncount*] ▪ He received *verification* of the deposit from the bank.

ver·i·ly /ˈverəli/ *adv, old-fashioned* : certainly or truly ▪ I *verily* believe that these accusations are false.

veri·si·mil·i·tude /ˌverəsəˈmɪləˌtuːd, *Brit* ˌvɛrəsəˈmɪləˌtjuːd/ *noun* [*noncount*] *formal* : the quality of seeming real ▪ The novel lacks *verisimilitude*. [=the things that happen in the novel do not seem real]

ver·i·ta·ble /ˈverətəbəl/ *adj, always used before a noun, formal* : true or real — used to emphasize a description ▪ The island is a *veritable* paradise. ▪ The sale attracted a *veritable* mob of people.

ver·i·ty /ˈverəti/ *noun, pl* **-ties** [*count*] *formal* : something that is regarded as true — usually plural ▪ one of the eternal *verities* of life

ver·mi·cel·li /ˌvɚməˈʧɛli/ *noun* [*noncount*] : a type of pasta that is like spaghetti but thinner

ver·mil·ion *or* **ver·mil·lion** /vɚˈmɪljən/ *noun* [*noncount*] : a bright orange-red color — see color picture on page C3

ver·min /ˈvɚmən/ *noun* [*plural*]
1 : small insects and animals (such as fleas or mice) that are sometimes harmful to plants or other animals and that are difficult to get rid of ▪ The room was crawling with roaches and other *vermin*.
2 *informal* : very bad, unpleasant, or offensive people

ver·mouth /vɚˈmuːθ/ *noun* [*noncount*] : a type of wine that is flavored with herbs and spices and often mixed with other alcoholic drinks

[1]**ver·nac·u·lar** /vɚˈnækjəlɚ/ *noun, pl* **-lars** [*count*] : the language of ordinary speech rather than formal writing ▪ He spoke in the *vernacular* of an urban teenager. ▪ phrases that occur in the common *vernacular*

[2]**vernacular** *adj*
1 : of, relating to, or using the language of ordinary speech rather than formal writing ▪ *vernacular* phrases ▪ a speaker's *vernacular* style
2 : of or relating to the common style of a particular time, place, or group ▪ the *vernacular* architecture of the region

ver·nal /ˈvɚnl̩/ *adj, formal* : of, relating to, or occurring in the spring ▪ trees and flowers in *vernal* bloom ▪ *vernal* breezes ▪ the ***vernal equinox***

ver·sa·tile /ˈvɚsətl̩, *Brit* ˈvɜːsəˌtajəl/ *adj* [*more* ~; *most* ~]
1 : able to do many different things ▪ She is a *versatile* athlete who participates in many different sports.
2 : having many different uses ▪ A pocketknife is a *versatile* tool.
– **ver·sa·til·i·ty** /ˌvɚsəˈtɪləti/ *noun* [*noncount*]

verse /ˈvɚs/ *noun, pl* **vers·es**
1 [*noncount*] : writing in which words are arranged in a rhythmic pattern : POETRY ▪ The epic tale was written in *verse*. — see also BLANK VERSE, FREE VERSE
2 [*count*] : a part of a poem or song : STANZA ▪ The second *verse* is sung the same way as the first.
3 [*count*] : one of the parts of a chapter of the Bible
chapter and verse see CHAPTER

versed /ˈvɚst/ *adj* : having knowledge about something — + *in* ▪ He is well *versed in* French cooking. [=he knows a lot about French cooking] ▪ a writer *versed in* military history

ver·sion /ˈvɚʒən, *Brit* ˈvɜːʃən/ *noun, pl* **-sions** [*count*]
1 : a story or description that is different in some way from another person's story or description ▪ Let me tell you my *version* of what happened. ▪ We heard two different *versions* of the story.
2 : a form of something (such as a product) that is different in some way from other forms ▪ A new *version* of the word processing program should be available soon. ▪ I have an older *version* of the software. ▪ This new design is better than the first *version*. ▪ A film *version* of the novel is being made.
3 : a particular translation of the Bible ▪ the King James *Version* of the Bible

ver·sus /ˈvɚsəs, ˈvɚsəz/ *prep*
1 — used to indicate the two people, teams, etc., that are fighting or competing against each other or that are opposed to each other in a legal case ▪ It's Smith *versus* Jones in the title fight. ▪ In 1948, the U.S. presidential election was Dewey *versus* Truman. ▪ I sometimes feel like it's me *versus* [=*against*] the rest of the world. ▪ the State *versus* John Smith — abbr. *vs., v.*
2 — used to indicate two different things, choices, etc., that are being compared or considered ▪ We have a choice of going out *versus* staying home.

ver·te·bra /ˈvɚtəbrə/ *noun, pl* **-brae** /-ˌbreɪ/ *or* **-bras** [*count*] *technical* : one of the small bones that are linked together to form the backbone — see picture at HUMAN
– **ver·te·bral** /ˈvɚtəbrəl/ *adj, always used before a noun* ▪ the *vertebral* column

ver·te·brate /ˈvɚtəbrət/ *noun, pl* **-brates** [*count*] *biology* : an animal that has a backbone — compare INVERTEBRATE
– **vertebrate** *adj*

ver·tex /ˈvɚˌtɛks/ *noun, pl* **ver·ti·ces** /ˈvɚtəˌsiːz/ *also* **ver·tex·es** [*count*] *technical* : a point where two lines meet to form an angle; *especially* : the point on a triangle that is opposite to the base

ver·ti·cal /ˈvɚtɪkəl/ *adj*
1 : positioned up and down rather than from side to side : going straight up ▪ a *vertical* line ▪ a shirt with *vertical* stripes ▪ the *vertical* axis of a graph ▪ *vertical* cliffs — compare HORIZONTAL
2 : having a structure in which there are top, middle, and bottom levels ▪ a *vertical* social order
– **vertical** *noun, pl* **-cals** [*count*] The architect designs buildings with strong *verticals* [=vertical parts] and horizontals. [*noncount*] The post is several degrees off from (the) *vertical*. [=the post is not positioned straight up and down] – **ver·ti·cal·ly** /ˈvɚtɪkli/ *adv* ▪ The cliff rose *vertically* to the sky.

ver·tig·i·nous /vɚˈtɪʤənəs/ *adj, formal* : causing or likely to cause a feeling of dizziness especially because of great height ▪ a *vertiginous* drop ▪ *vertiginous* heights

ver·ti·go /ˈvɚtɪˌgoʊ/ *noun* [*noncount*] : a feeling of dizziness caused especially by being in a very high place ▪ Heights give me *vertigo*.

verve /ˈvɚv/ *noun* [*noncount*] : great energy and enthusiasm ▪ She played with skill and *verve*.

[1]**very** /ˈveri/ *adv*
1 : to a great degree : EXTREMELY — used for emphasis before adjectives and adverbs ▪ a *very* hot day ▪ *very* accurate results ▪ a *very* small/large number/amount ▪ *Very* few people attended. ▪ It was a *very* unusual/difficult situation. ▪ He talks *very* slowly. ▪ We checked *very* carefully. ▪ She did *very* well on the test. ▪ It was *very* nice of you to stop by. ▪ I'm *very* pleased to meet you. ▪ I'm *very* sorry. ▪ "Thank you *very* much." "You're *very* welcome." ▪ "Were you surprised?" "Yes, *very*." ▪ The building is *very* French. [=it looks like buildings in France] ▪ (*formal*) Any help you can provide would be *very* much appreciated. — often used in negative statements ▪ There weren't *very* many people there. ▪ She was never *very* popular. ▪ The food wasn't *very* good. ▪ I didn't like the food *very* much. ▪ "Was the food good?" "Not *very*." ▪ "Did you like the food?" "Not *very* much." ▪ "How's your dad?" "Not *very* well, I'm afraid." [=my dad is ill] ▪ She's not *very* happy with me right now. [=she's annoyed with me] ▪ They weren't *very* nice (to me). [=they didn't treat me well; they were mean to me]
2 — used to emphasize the exactness of a description ▪ the *very* best restaurants ▪ We left the *very* next day. ▪ I told the ***very same*** [=*exact same*, (*US*) *same exact*] story. ▪ Mom said I can have my ***very own*** room [=a bedroom that I do not have to share] in the new house!
very good see [1]GOOD
very much so — used to say "yes" or to say that you agree with something ▪ "Were you surprised?" "Yes, *very much so*."
very well **1** *somewhat old-fashioned* — used to say that you agree with something ▪ *Very well*, then. I'll see you tomor-

row. ▪ Oh, *very well.* Do as you please. — see also *all very well* at ²WELL **2 :** reasonably or properly ▪ I can't *very well* show up at the wedding uninvited. [=it would be improper for me to show up at the wedding uninvited]

²very *adj, always used before a noun*
1 — used to emphasize that you are talking about one specific thing or part and not another ▪ Those were his *very* [=*exact, precise, actual*] words. ▪ There's the *very* book I was looking for. ▪ the *very* heart [=the most central part] of the city ▪ the *very* [=*extreme*] beginning/end of the story ▪ I knew he was trouble right from the *very* start. ▪ That's the *very* [=*same*] car I saw yesterday. ▪ The President and the Prime Minister are meeting ***at this very moment.*** [=*right now*] ▪ ***At the very moment*** the meeting began, the lights went out. = The meeting began, and ***at that very moment,*** the lights went out.
2 : not having anything added or extra ▪ The *very* [=*mere*] idea/thought of making a speech terrified him. [=just thinking about making a speech terrified him] ▪ You could try to help, ***at the very least.*** [=the least you could do is to try to help; you could at least try to help]
3 — used to emphasize that something belongs to or is part of a particular person or thing ▪ He disappeared right before our *very* eyes! ▪ a room ***of my very own*** [=a room I do not have to share] ▪ Dogs are territorial ***by their very nature.***

ves·pers *or* **Ves·pers** /ˈvɛspɚz/ *noun [plural]* **:** an evening prayer service in some Christian churches

ves·sel /ˈvɛsəl/ *noun, pl* **-sels** *[count]*
1 *formal* **:** a ship or large boat ▪ a fishing/sailing *vessel*
2 *technical* **:** a vein or artery that carries blood through the body **:** BLOOD VESSEL
3 *somewhat old-fashioned* **:** a hollow container for holding liquids ▪ a drinking *vessel*

¹vest /ˈvɛst/ *noun, pl* **vests** *[count]*
1 *US* **a :** a sleeveless piece of clothing with buttons down the front that is worn over a shirt and under a suit jacket — called also (*chiefly Brit*) *waistcoat*; see color picture on page C15 **b :** SWEATER VEST
2 : a special piece of clothing that you wear on your upper body for protection or safety ▪ a bulletproof *vest* ▪ (*US*) a ***life vest*** [=*life jacket*]
3 *Brit* **:** a man's sleeveless undershirt
close to the vest see ²CLOSE

²vest *verb* **vests; vest·ed; vest·ing** *[+ obj] formal* **:** to give (someone) the legal right or power to do something or to own land or property ▪ Congress is *vested* with the power to declare war. = The power to declare war is *vested* in Congress. ▪ After five years, you'll be fully *vested* in the company pension plan. [=you will have earned the right to get a full pension when you retire]

vested interest *noun, pl* **~ -ests** *[count]* **:** a personal or private reason for wanting something to be done or to happen ▪ She has a *vested interest* in seeing the business sold, as she'll make a profit from the sale.

ves·ti·bule /ˈvɛstəˌbjuːl/ *noun, pl* **-bules** *[count] formal* **:** an entrance hall inside a building

ves·tige /ˈvɛstɪʤ/ *noun, pl* **-tig·es** *[count] formal*
1 : the last small part that remains of something that existed before **:** TRACE — *+ of* ▪ a *vestige of* an ancient tradition ▪ He is still clinging to ***the last vestiges of*** his power.
2 : the smallest possible amount of something — *+ of*; usually used in negative statements ▪ There's not a *vestige of* doubt that what she says is true.

ves·ti·gial /vɛˈstɪʤijəl/ *adj*
1 *technical, of a body part* **:** remaining in a form that is not fully developed or able to function ▪ Although it cannot fly, the bird still has *vestigial* wings.
2 *formal* **:** remaining as the last small part of something that existed before ▪ They uncovered *vestigial* traces of the home's original wallpaper. ▪ She has some *vestigial* doubts about investing in the company.

vest·ments /ˈvɛstmənts/ *noun [plural]* **:** the special clothing worn by a priest during church services

ves·try /ˈvɛstri/ *noun, pl* **-tries** *[count]* **:** a small room in a church where a priest dresses for the services and where holy items used during services are kept

V

¹vet /ˈvɛt/ *noun, pl* **vets** *[count]*
1 : VETERINARIAN ▪ I have to take my dog to the *vet.*
2 *US, informal* **:** VETERAN ▪ a World War II *vet*

²vet *verb* **vets; vet·ted; vet·ting** *[+ obj]*
1 : to investigate (someone) thoroughly to see if they should be approved or accepted for a job ▪ They *vetted* her thoroughly before offering her the job.
2 : to check (something) carefully to make sure it is acceptable ▪ The book was *vetted* by several different editors. ▪ He's already *vetted* the plan, so we can start right away.

vetch /ˈvɛʧ/ *noun [noncount]* **:** a plant that has small flowers and is used to feed farm animals

vet·er·an /ˈvɛtərən/ *noun, pl* **-ans** *[count]*
1 : someone who fought in a war as a soldier, sailor, etc. ▪ a Navy *veteran* — called also (*US, informal*) *vet*
2 : someone who has a lot of experience in a particular activity, job, etc. ▪ a *veteran* of the political scene ▪ a teaching *veteran* ▪ He's a 10-year *veteran* with/of the team.
– veteran *adj* ▪ a *veteran* politician ▪ *veteran* police officers

Veterans Day *noun [count, noncount]* **:** a holiday observed on November 11 in the U.S. to honor veterans of the armed forces

vet·er·i·nar·i·an /ˌvɛtərəˈnerijən/ *noun, pl* **-ans** *[count] chiefly US* **:** a person who is trained to give medical care and treatment to animals **:** an animal doctor — called also *vet,* (*Brit, formal*) *veterinary surgeon*

vet·er·i·nary /ˈvɛtərəˌneri, *Brit* ˈvɛtnri/ *adj* **:** relating to the medical care and treatment of animals ▪ *veterinary* medicine

veterinary surgeon *noun, pl* **~ -geons** *[count] Brit, formal* **:** VETERINARIAN

¹ve·to /ˈviːtoʊ/ *noun, pl* **-toes**
1 *[count]* **:** a decision by a person in authority to not allow or approve something (such as a new law) ▪ a legislative *veto* ▪ a *veto* of a bill ▪ Are there enough votes in Congress to override the President's *veto*?
2 *[noncount]* **:** the right or power of a person in authority to decide that something (such as a new law) will not be approved ▪ The President has the *veto* over new legislation. ▪ The President may choose to exercise his *veto.* ▪ *veto* power — see also LINE-ITEM VETO, POCKET VETO

²veto *verb* **-toes; -toed; -to·ing** *[+ obj]*
1 : to reject (a proposed law) officially **:** to refuse to allow (a bill) to become a law ▪ The President *vetoed* the bill.
2 : to refuse to allow or accept (something, such as a plan or suggestion) ▪ We wanted to do a cross-country trip, but our parents *vetoed* it. ▪ She *vetoed* several restaurants before we could agree on one.

vex /ˈvɛks/ *verb* **vex·es; vexed; vex·ing** *[+ obj] old-fashioned* **:** to annoy or worry (someone) ▪ This problem has *vexed* researchers for years. ▪ We were *vexed* by the delay.
– vexing *adj [more ~; most ~]* ▪ a *vexing* problem [=an irritating/annoying problem]

vex·a·tion /vɛkˈseɪʃən/ *noun, pl* **-tions** *old-fashioned*
1 *[noncount]* **:** the state of being worried or annoyed **:** irritation or annoyance ▪ He grumbled in *vexation.*
2 *[count]* **:** something that worries or annoys you ▪ the problems and *vexations* of everyday life
– vex·a·tious /vɛkˈseɪʃəs/ *adj [more ~; most ~]* ▪ a *vexatious* problem **– vex·a·tious·ly** *adv*

vexed /ˈvɛkst/ *adj [more ~; most ~]*
1 : difficult and frustrating to deal with ▪ a *vexed* question
2 *old-fashioned* **:** annoyed or worried ▪ She was feeling somewhat *vexed.*

VGA *abbr* video graphics array — used for a display system for computer monitors

VHF *abbr* very high frequency — used for a range of radio waves that is used in broadcasting, communications, and navigation

via /ˈvajə, ˈviːjə/ *prep*
1 : by going through (a particular place) **:** by way of (a particular place) ▪ She flew to Los Angeles *via* Chicago.
2 : by means of (a person, machine, etc.) **:** by using (something or someone) ▪ I'll let her know *via* one of our friends. ▪ He did some research *via* computer. ▪ tracking *via* satellite ▪ We went home *via* a shortcut.

vi·a·ble /ˈvajəbəl/ *adj*
1 *[more ~; most ~]* **a :** capable of being done or used **:** WORKABLE ▪ a *viable* solution to the problem ▪ He could not suggest a *viable* alternative/option. **b :** capable of succeeding ▪ Is she a *viable* candidate? ▪ a *viable* method
2 *technical* **:** capable of living or of developing into a living thing ▪ a *viable* human fetus ▪ *viable* seeds/eggs
– vi·a·bil·i·ty /ˌvajəˈbɪləti/ *noun [noncount]*

via·duct /ˈvajəˌdʌkt/ *noun, pl* **-ducts** *[count]* **:** a long, high bridge that carries a road or railroad over something (such as a valley)

Vi·ag·ra /vaɪˈægrə/ *trademark* — used for a drug that helps men to be able to have sex

vi·al /ˈvajəl/ *noun, pl* **-als** [*count*] **:** a very small glass or plastic container used for perfumes, medicines, etc. — called also (*Brit*) *phial*

vibe /ˈvaɪb/ *noun, pl* **vibes**
1 [*count*] *informal* **:** a feeling that someone or something gives you ▪ I got a weird *vibe* from her. — usually plural ▪ good/bad *vibes* [=*vibrations*]
2 *vibes* [*plural*] **:** VIBRAPHONE ▪ playing the *vibes*

vi·brant /ˈvaɪbrənt/ *adj* [*more* ~; *most* ~]
1 : having or showing great life, activity, and energy ▪ She has a *vibrant* personality. ▪ a *vibrant* city/culture
2 : very bright and strong ▪ *vibrant* colors ▪ We painted the room a *vibrant* blue.
3 *of a sound* **:** loud and powerful ▪ *vibrant* music
– vi·bran·cy /ˈvaɪbrənsi/ *noun* [*noncount*] **– vi·brant·ly** *adv* ▪ *vibrantly* colored paintings

vi·bra·phone /ˈvaɪbrəˌfoʊn/ *noun, pl* **-phones** [*count*] **:** an electronic musical instrument which has metal bars that you hit with small wooden hammers to play notes and which has a motor that makes the notes vibrate — compare XYLOPHONE

vi·brate /ˈvaɪˌbreɪt, *Brit* vaɪˈbreɪt/ *verb* **-brates; -brat·ed; -brat·ing :** to move back and forth or from side to side with very short, quick movements [*no obj*] The engine was *vibrating.* [=*shaking*] ▪ The car started to *vibrate.* [+ *obj*] When you blow into the instrument, the air *vibrates* the reed.
– vi·bra·to·ry /ˈvaɪbrəˌtori, *Brit* ˈvaɪbrətri/ *adj* ▪ *vibratory* motion

vi·bra·tion /vaɪˈbreɪʃən/ *noun, pl* **-tions**
1 : a continuous slight shaking movement **:** a series of small, fast movements back and forth or from side to side [*count*] *vibrations* from the engine [*noncount*] trying to reduce engine *vibration*
2 *vibrations* [*plural*] *informal* **:** a feeling that someone or something gives you ▪ The building gives off good/bad *vibrations.* [=*vibes*]

vi·bra·to /vɪˈbrɑːtoʊ/ *noun* [*noncount*] *music* **:** a way of making small, rapid changes in a musical note that you are singing or playing so that it seems to shake slightly

vi·bra·tor /ˈvaɪˌbreɪtɚ, *Brit* vaɪˈbreɪtə/ *noun, pl* **-tors** [*count*] **:** an electronic device that vibrates and that is used especially for massage or sexual pleasure

vic·ar /ˈvɪkɚ/ *noun, pl* **-ars** [*count*]
1 : a priest in the Church of England who is in charge of a particular church and the area around it
2 *US* **:** a pastor's assistant in an Episcopalian or Lutheran church

vic·ar·age /ˈvɪkərɪʤ/ *noun, pl* **-ag·es** [*count*] **:** a vicar's home

vi·car·i·ous /vaɪˈkerijəs/ *adj* **:** experienced or felt by watching, hearing about, or reading about someone else rather than by doing something yourself ▪ a *vicarious* experience ▪ *vicarious* joy/suffering ▪ a *vicarious* thrill
– vi·car·i·ous·ly *adv* ▪ She lived *vicariously* through her children. **– vi·car·i·ous·ness** *noun* [*noncount*]

[1]vice /ˈvaɪs/ *noun, pl* **vic·es**
1 a [*noncount*] **:** bad or immoral behavior or habits **:** WICKEDNESS ▪ Such men are prone to *vice.* **b** [*count*] **:** a moral flaw or weakness ▪ He thought gambling was a *vice.* ▪ the *vice* of greed
2 [*count*] **:** a minor bad habit ▪ Eating too much is my *vice.* ▪ a harmless *vice*
3 [*noncount*] **:** criminal activities that involve sex or drugs ▪ The city is a den of filth and *vice.* ▪ He was arrested by the ***vice squad***. [=police officers who investigate crimes involving sex or drugs]

[2]vice *Brit spelling of* VISE

vice admiral *noun, pl* **~ -rals** [*count*] **:** an officer in the navy with a rank just below that of admiral

vice–chan·cel·lor /ˌvaɪsˈʧænslɚ, *Brit* ˌvaɪsˈʧɑːnslə/ *noun, pl* **-lors** [*count*]
1 : a person who has a rank just below that of a chancellor
2 : the person who runs a British university

vice president *also* **vice–president** *noun, pl* **~ -dents** [*count*] **:** a person whose rank is just below that of the president of a country, business, etc. ▪ He became the *Vice President* of the United States. ▪ the company's executive *vice-president* of sales
– vice presidency *noun, pl* **~ -cies** [*count*]

vice·roy /ˈvaɪsˌrɔɪ/ *noun, pl* **-roys** [*count*] **:** a person sent by a king or queen to rule a colony in the past

vice ver·sa /ˌvaɪsˈvɚsə/ *adv* — used to say that the opposite of a statement is also true ▪ She ended up having a lot of influence on his career, and *vice versa.* [=and he also ended up having a lot of influence on her career] ▪ The camera can adjust for a light subject on a dark background, or *vice versa.* [=or a dark subject on a light background]

vi·cin·i·ty /vəˈsɪnəti/ *noun* [*singular*] **:** the area around or near a particular place ▪ She lives in Los Angeles, or somewhere in that/the *vicinity.* [=somewhere near there]
***in the vicinity of* 1 :** in the area that is close to (a place) ▪ He lives *in the* general/immediate *vicinity of* the school. **2 :** close to or around (an amount) ▪ His yearly salary is *in the vicinity of* [=*in the neighborhood of*] one million dollars.

vi·cious /ˈvɪʃəs/ *adj* [*more* ~; *most* ~]
1 : very violent and cruel ▪ a *vicious* attack/battle
2 : very dangerous ▪ a *vicious* dog
3 : having or showing very angry or cruel feelings ▪ *vicious* gossip ▪ a *vicious* tone of voice ▪ I know you're upset with her, but there's no need to be *vicious.*
4 *informal* **:** very bad or severe ▪ a *vicious* storm ▪ a *vicious* headache
– vi·cious·ly *adv* ▪ She was *viciously* attacked. ▪ He lashed out *viciously* at his critics. ▪ The dog snarled *viciously.* **– vi·cious·ness** *noun* [*noncount*]

vicious circle *noun* [*singular*] **:** a repeating situation or condition in which one problem causes another problem that makes the first problem worse ▪ We're trapped in a *vicious circle.* — called also *vicious cycle*

vi·cis·si·tudes /vəˈsɪsəˌtuːdz, *Brit* vəˈsɪsəˌtjuːdz/ *noun* [*plural*] *formal* **:** the many changes or problems that happen over time — often + *of* ▪ the *vicissitudes of* life

vic·tim /ˈvɪktəm/ *noun, pl* **-tims** [*count*]
1 : a person who has been attacked, injured, robbed, or killed by someone else ▪ a *victim* of abuse/violence ▪ a murder/rape *victim*
2 : a person who is cheated or fooled by someone else ▪ the *victims* of a hoax
3 : someone or something that is harmed by an unpleasant event (such as an illness or accident) ▪ a *victim* of fate/circumstance ▪ a tornado *victim* ▪ He was the *victim* of an error. ▪ an AIDS/cancer *victim* ▪ a ***fashion victim*** [=someone who wears fashionable clothes that make them look unattractive or silly]
4 : a person or animal that is offered as a gift to a god in a religious ritual ▪ sacrificial *victims*
***fall victim to* 1 :** to be attacked, injured, or killed by (someone or something) ▪ Police think she may have *fallen victim to* a serial killer. **2 :** to be affected badly by (something) ▪ She *fell victim to* the flu. ▪ He *fell victim to* a scam. ▪ schools *falling victim to* budget cuts

vic·tim·ize *also Brit* **vic·tim·ise** /ˈvɪktəˌmaɪz/ *verb* **-iz·es; -ized; -iz·ing** [+ *obj*]
1 : to treat (someone) cruelly or unfairly ▪ They were *victimized* because of their religion.
2 *chiefly US* **:** to make a victim of (someone) **:** to harm or commit a crime against (someone) ▪ people who have been *victimized* by thieves/theft [=people who are the victims of thieves; people who have been robbed] ▪ More than a dozen elderly women were *victimized* [=*swindled*] by the con artist.
– vic·tim·i·za·tion *also Brit* **vic·tim·i·sa·tion** /ˌvɪktəməˈzeɪʃən, *Brit* ˌvɪktəˌmaɪˈzeɪʃən/ *noun* [*noncount*]

victim mentality *noun* [*singular*] **:** the belief that you are always a victim **:** the idea that bad things will always happen to you ▪ He claims that our legal system promotes a *victim mentality.*

vic·tor /ˈvɪktɚ/ *noun, pl* **-tors** [*count*] *formal* **:** a person who defeats an enemy or opponent **:** WINNER ▪ the *victors* in the battle/game ▪ Who will ***emerge the victor*** [=be the winner] in this contest?

Vic·to·ri·an /vɪkˈtorijən/ *adj*
1 : relating to or typical of the period from 1837–1901 when Queen Victoria ruled England ▪ a *Victorian* house ▪ the *Victorian* period/age ▪ in *Victorian* times
2 [*more* ~; *most* ~] **:** similar to the old-fashioned moral values that were typical during the time of Queen Victoria ▪ My parents have very *Victorian* attitudes when it comes to sex.

vic·to·ri·ous /vɪkˈtorijəs/ *adj* **:** having won a victory or having ended in a victory ▪ the *victorious* army/side ▪ a *victorious* battle ▪ They were *victorious* over their enemies. ▪ Who will ***emerge victorious***? [=who will be the winner?]
– vic·to·ri·ous·ly *adv*

vic·to·ry /ˈvɪktəri/ *noun, pl* **-ries**

1 : success in defeating an opponent or enemy [*noncount*] The general led the troops to *victory*. ▪ They had never experienced the thrill of *victory*. ▪ a *victory* party/celebration/speech ▪ She was equally gracious ***in victory*** and in defeat. [=she was gracious when she won and when she lost] [*count*] The passage of the law was a tremendous *victory* for their cause. — opposite DEFEAT
2 [*count*] **:** the act of defeating an opponent or enemy ▪ an election *victory* ▪ Tonight's win is the team's fifth consecutive/straight *victory*. [=*win*] ▪ It was a decisive/great/major *victory* for the army. — see also PYRRHIC VICTORY, *moral victory* at [1]MORAL, *victory lap* at [3]LAP

vict·uals /ˈvɪtl̩z/ *noun* [*plural*] *old-fashioned* **:** food and drink

vi·cu·ña *or* **vi·cu·na** /vɪˈkuːnjə, *Brit* vɪˈkjuːnə/ *noun, pl* **-ñas** *or* **-nas** [*count*] **:** a large South American animal that produces wool which is used for clothing

[1]**vid·eo** /ˈvɪdijoʊ/ *noun, pl* **-eos**
1 [*count*] **:** a movie, television show, event, etc., that has been recorded onto a videocassette, DVD, etc., so that it can be watched on a television or computer screen ▪ We're going to rent a couple of *videos* to watch this weekend. ▪ She was talking about a popular *video* she saw on the Internet. ▪ The *video* of their wedding was made by a professional company. ▪ They showed us some of their ***home videos***. [=recordings that they had made using a video camera]
2 [*noncount*] **:** [1]VIDEOTAPE 1 ▪ The movie is available ***on video*** and DVD.
3 [*count*] **:** a recorded performance of a song in which visual images are shown together with the music ▪ a TV channel that plays *videos* all day ▪ Her latest ***music video*** was first released on the Internet.
4 [*noncount*] **:** the moving images that are seen in a recording or broadcast ▪ The audio is OK but there's a problem with the *video*.
5 [*count*] *Brit* **:** VCR

[2]**video** *adj, always used before a noun*
1 : of or relating to the pictures that are seen in a recording or broadcast ▪ The *video* portion of the broadcast was fine but the sound was poor.
2 : of, relating to, or involving videos that are shown on a television or computer screen ▪ a *video* terminal ▪ *video* equipment ▪ a short *video* clip ▪ The large *video* file took a while to upload on my computer.

[3]**video** *verb* **videos; vid·eoed; vid·eo·ing** [+ *obj*] *Brit* **:** VIDEOTAPE ▪ I *videoed* the program so I could watch it later.

video arcade *noun, pl* ~ **-cades** [*count*] *US* **:** a place with many video games **:** ARCADE 3

video camera *noun, pl* ~ **-eras** [*count*] **:** a camera that is used to create videos by recording moving images and sounds onto a videotape, computer disk, etc.

video card *noun, pl* ~ **cards** [*count*] *computers* **:** a device in a computer system that controls the images that are shown on the computer's screen

vid·eo·cas·sette /ˌvɪdijoʊkəˈsɛt/ *noun, pl* **-settes**
1 : a thin, plastic case that holds videotape and that is played using a VCR [*count*] a blank *videocassette* [*noncount*] That movie is now available ***on videocassette***.
2 [*count*] **:** [1]VIDEOTAPE 2 ▪ He has a large collection of *videocassettes*.

videocassette recorder *noun, pl* ~ **-ers** [*count*] **:** VCR

vid·eo·con·fer·enc·ing /ˌvɪdijoʊˈkɑːnfrənsɪŋ/ *noun* [*noncount*] **:** a method of holding meetings that allows people who are in different cities, countries, etc., to hear each other and see each other on computer or television screens
– vid·eo·con·fer·ence /ˌvɪdijoʊˈkɑːnfrəns/ *noun, pl* **-ences** [*count*]

vid·eo·disc *or* **vid·eo·disk** /ˈvɪdijoʊˌdɪsk/ *noun, pl* **-discs** *or* **-disks** [*count*] **:** a disk on which movies, television programs, etc., are recorded in order to be watched on a computer or television screen

video game *noun, pl* ~ **games** [*count*] **:** an electronic game in which players control images on a television or computer screen

vid·e·og·ra·pher /ˌvɪdiˈɑːgrəfɚ/ *noun, pl* **-ers** [*count*] **:** a person who records images or events using a video camera
– vid·e·og·ra·phy /ˌvɪdiˈɑːgrəfi/ *noun* [*noncount*]

video nasty *noun, pl* ~ **-ties** [*count*] *Brit, informal* **:** a very violent or offensive movie that is on video

vid·eo·phone /ˈvɪdijəˌfoʊn/ *noun, pl* **-phones** [*count*] **:** a telephone that can send and receive moving images so that users can see and hear each other

video recorder *noun, pl* ~ **-ers** [*count*] **:** VCR

[1]**vid·eo·tape** /ˈvɪdijoʊˌteɪp/ *noun, pl* **-tapes**
1 [*noncount*] **:** tape on which movies, television shows, etc., can be recorded ▪ I watched the movie ***on videotape***.
2 [*count*] **:** a movie, TV program, etc., that is recorded on videotape — compare AUDIOTAPE

[2]**videotape** *verb* **-tapes; -taped; -tap·ing** [+ *obj*] **:** to record (someone or something) on videotape ▪ They *videotaped* the baby's first steps.

videotape recorder *noun, pl* ~ **-ers** [*count*] **:** VCR

vie /ˈvaɪ/ *verb* **vies; vied; vy·ing** /ˈvajɪŋ/ [*no obj*] **:** to compete with others in an attempt to get or win something ▪ They are *vying* to win the championship for the third year in a row. — often + *for* or *with* ▪ Two young men were *vying for* her attention. ▪ They *vied with* each other *for* first place.

[1]**view** /ˈvjuː/ *noun, pl* **views**
1 [*count*] **:** an opinion or way of thinking about something ▪ What are your political *views*? = What are your *views* on/about politics? ▪ The *views* expressed herein are strictly those of the author. ▪ She has an old-fashioned *view* of women's roles in society. [=her ideas about women's roles are old-fashioned] ▪ There is no evidence to support that *view*. ▪ ***In my view*** the plan will fail. [=I think that the plan will fail] ▪ He ***takes the view*** [=he believes] that the economy will improve in the coming year. ▪ She ***takes a dim view of*** [=she disapproves of] their behavior. — see also POINT OF VIEW
2 [*count*] **:** the things that can be seen from a particular place ▪ The house has a *view* of the lake. [=you can see the lake when you are inside or near the house] ▪ a scenic/spectacular/beautiful *view* ▪ I asked for a room with a *view*. [=a room that allows you to see a beautiful or interesting scene from your window]
3 — used to say that something can or cannot be seen [*count*] I got a good *view* of the accident. [=I saw the accident clearly] ▪ You're blocking my *view*. ▪ Our *view* of the parade was obstructed. [=we could not see the parade because something was in front of us] [*noncount*] The ship slowly sailed ***out of view***. ▪ The ship disappeared ***from view***. ▪ Keep your hands ***in view*** [=keep them where they can be seen] at all times. ▪ The robbery was committed ***in (full) view of*** a group of tourists. ▪ Children, stay ***within view***. [=stay where I can see you] ▪ The museum is ***within view of*** our hotel. [=we can see the museum from our hotel]
4 [*count*] **:** a picture of a place ▪ The postcard shows an aerial *view* of the bay. [=it shows a picture of the bay taken from an aircraft] ▪ a panoramic *view* of the mountains
come in/into view see [1]COME
heave into view see [1]HEAVE
in plain view see [1]PLAIN
in view of *somewhat formal* **1 :** when thinking about or considering (something) ▪ His current support of the plan is surprising *in view of* [=*given*] his earlier opposition. **2 :** because of (something) ▪ *In view of* the fact that your payment is late, you'll have to pay a fine.
on view **:** available to be seen ▪ His paintings are now *on view* [=they are being displayed] at the local museum.
take the long view **:** to think about the things that might happen in the future rather than only about the things that are happening now ▪ Investors should *take the long view* when considering where to put their money.
with a view to *somewhat formal* **:** with the hope or goal of (doing something) ▪ They have reorganized the department *with a view to* making it more efficient. [=in order to make it more efficient]

[2]**view** *verb* **views; viewed; view·ing** [+ *obj*]
1 : to look at (something) carefully ▪ The building is most impressive when *viewed* from the front. ▪ A medical examiner is now *viewing* the evidence. ▪ The family came in to *view* the deceased. [=to look at the body of a dead person as part of a funeral or wake]
2 : to see or watch (a movie, a TV show, etc.) ▪ The program was *viewed* by millions of people.
3 : to think about (someone or something) in a particular way ▪ Different people *view* this problem in different ways. — often + *with* or *as* ▪ Students *viewed* [=*regarded*] the new rules *with* contempt. ▪ He doesn't *view* himself *as* a rebel. [=he doesn't believe that he is a rebel] ▪ I *view* this job *as* an opportunity to gain valuable work experience.
– view·ing /ˈvjuːwɪŋ/ *noun, pl* **-ings** [*count*] ▪ the first *viewing* of a film

view·er /ˈvjuːwɚ/ *noun, pl* **-ers** [*count*]
1 : a person who watches television ▪ The program attracts

V

millions of *viewers* every week. • She is a regular *viewer* of the evening news.

2 : a person who sees or looks at something • The exhibit was surrounded by a large crowd of *viewers*.

3 : a device that is used to look at photographs • a slide *viewer*

view·find·er /ˈvju:ˌfaɪndɚ/ *noun, pl* **-ers** [*count*] **:** a small hole or window on a camera that you look through to see what is being photographed — see picture at CAMERA

view·point /ˈvju:ˌpoɪnt/ *noun, pl* **-points** [*count*] **:** a way of looking at or thinking about something **:** POINT OF VIEW • The story is told from the *viewpoint* of someone who grew up during the Great Depression. • Her *viewpoint* is that of a person who has been in politics for decades. • They approached the issue from opposite *viewpoints*. [=*standpoints*]

vig·il /ˈvɪʤəl/ *noun, pl* **-ils :** an event or a period of time when a person or group stays in a place and quietly waits, prays, etc., especially at night [*count*] The night before he was scheduled to be executed, the group held a candlelight *vigil* for him outside the prison. [=they held candles and waited for him to be executed or pardoned] [*noncount*] She ***kept vigil*** at the bedside of her ailing son. [=she sat beside her son's bed when he was ill]

vig·i·lant /ˈvɪʤələnt/ *adj* [*more* ~; *most* ~] **:** carefully noticing problems or signs of danger • When traveling through the city, tourists should be extra *vigilant*. • They were *vigilant* about protecting their children. • We remain *vigilant* against theft. • a *vigilant* tourist/parent

– **vig·i·lance** /ˈvɪʤələns/ *noun* [*noncount*] • The situation requires constant *vigilance*. – **vig·i·lant·ly** *adv*

vig·i·lan·te /ˌvɪʤəˈlænti/ *noun, pl* **-tes** [*count*] **:** a person who is not a police officer but who tries to catch and punish criminals — often used before another noun • *vigilante* groups • *vigilante* justice

vi·gnette /vɪnˈjɛt/ *noun, pl* **-gnettes** [*count*]

1 : a short written description • The play's program features a little *vignette* about each member of the cast.

2 : a short scene in a movie or play • The film is a series of *vignettes* about living with cancer.

3 : a picture or engraving in a book

vig·or (*US*) *or Brit* **vig·our** /ˈvɪgɚ/ *noun* [*noncount*] **:** strength, energy, or determination • She defended her beliefs with great *vigor*.

vim and vigor see VIM

vig·or·ous /ˈvɪgərəs/ *adj* [*more* ~; *most* ~]

1 : healthy and strong • She remained *vigorous* into her nineties.

2 : done with great force and energy • His speech was met with *vigorous* applause. • She gave a *vigorous* defense of her beliefs. • a *vigorous* argument/debate • You should get 20 minutes of *vigorous* [=*strenuous*] exercise every day.

– **vig·or·ous·ly** *adv* • He scrubbed the dirty pan *vigorously*. • She *vigorously* defended her beliefs.

Vi·king /ˈvaɪkɪŋ/ *noun, pl* **-kings** [*count*] **:** a member of a group of Scandinavian people who attacked the coasts of Europe in the 8th to 10th centuries A.D. • a *Viking* invasion/ship

vile /ˈvajəl/ *adj* **vil·er; -est** [*also more* ~; *most* ~]

1 : evil or immoral • *vile* terrorist attacks • a *vile* and cowardly act

2 : very bad or unpleasant • What is that *vile* odor? • His comments were positively *vile*. • She has a *vile* temper. • (*chiefly Brit*) We've been having *vile* weather lately.

– **vile·ly** *adv* • They were treated *vilely*. – **vile·ness** *noun* [*noncount*] • the *vileness* of the crime

vil·i·fy /ˈvɪləˌfaɪ/ *verb* **-fies; -fied; -fy·ing** [+ *obj*] *formal* **:** to say or write very harsh and critical things about (someone or something) • He was *vilified* in the press for his comments.

– **vil·i·fi·ca·tion** /ˌvɪləfəˈkeɪʃən/ *noun* [*noncount*]

vil·la /ˈvɪlə/ *noun, pl* **-las** [*count*]

1 : a large house or estate that is usually located in the country

2 : a house that you can rent and live in when on vacation • They rented a seaside *villa* for two weeks.

3 *Brit* **:** a house in the city with a yard and garden

4 : a house or estate that was surrounded by farmland in ancient Rome

vil·lage /ˈvɪlɪʤ/ *noun, pl* **-lag·es** [*count*]

1 : a small town in the country • fishing/mining *villages* [=villages in which most people fish/mine as a job]

2 : the people who live in a village • Entire *villages* come to see the parade.

vil·lag·er /ˈvɪlɪʤɚ/ *noun, pl* **-ers** [*count*] **:** a person who lives in a village

vil·lain /ˈvɪlən/ *noun, pl* **-lains** [*count*]

1 : a character in a story, movie, etc., who does bad things • comic-book heroes and *villains* • He plays the *villain* in most of his movies.

2 *somewhat old-fashioned* **:** a person who does bad things • She describes her first husband as a *villain* who treated her terribly.

3 : someone or something that is blamed for a particular problem or difficulty • Don't try to make me the *villain*. It's your own fault that you're having these problems. • The article makes the government out to be the *villain*. = It portrays the government as ***the villain of the piece***.

4 *Brit, informal* **:** CRIMINAL

vil·lain·ous /ˈvɪlənəs/ *adj* [*more* ~; *most* ~] **:** very bad or evil **:** WICKED • a *villainous* attack • *villainous* criminals

– **vil·lain·ous·ly** *adv*

vil·lainy /ˈvɪləni/ *noun, pl* **-lain·ies** *formal* **:** evil behavior or actions [*noncount*] a story of *villainy* and betrayal [*count*] the gruesome *villainies* of war

vim /ˈvɪm/ *noun*

vim and vigor (*US*) *or Brit* ***vim and vigour*** **:** energy and enthusiasm • Though she's no longer young, she's still full of *vim and vigor*. [=*vitality*]

vin·ai·grette /ˌvɪnɪˈgrɛt/ *noun, pl* **-grettes** [*count, noncount*] **:** a mixture of oil, vinegar, and seasonings that is used especially as a salad dressing

vin·di·cate /ˈvɪndəˌkeɪt/ *verb* **-cates; -cat·ed; -cat·ing** [+ *obj*]

1 : to show that (someone) should not be blamed for a crime, mistake, etc. **:** to show that (someone) is not guilty • They have evidence that will *vindicate* [=*exonerate*] her. • She will be completely *vindicated* by the evidence.

2 : to show that (someone or something that has been criticized or doubted) is correct, true, or reasonable • These discoveries *vindicate* their theory. • Their approach to the problem has been *vindicated* by the positive results. • He ***felt vindicated*** when the truth became known.

– **vin·di·ca·tion** /ˌvɪndəˈkeɪʃən/ *noun* [*noncount*] She didn't need any further *vindication*. [*singular*] The positive results are a *vindication* of their approach.

vin·dic·tive /vɪnˈdɪktɪv/ *adj* [*more* ~; *most* ~] *disapproving* **:** having or showing a desire to hurt someone who has hurt or caused problems for you • He became bitter and *vindictive* [=*spiteful*, *vengeful*] after his divorce.

– **vin·dic·tive·ly** *adv* – **vin·dic·tive·ness** *noun* [*noncount*]

vine /ˈvaɪn/ *noun, pl* **vines** [*count*] **:** a plant that has very long stems and that grows along the ground or up and around something (such as a wall or tree) — see color picture on page C6; see also GRAPEVINE

die on the vine see [1]DIE

vin·e·gar /ˈvɪnɪgɚ/ *noun, pl* **-gars** [*count, noncount*] **:** a sour liquid that is used to flavor or preserve foods or to clean things — see also BALSAMIC VINEGAR, CIDER VINEGAR, WINE VINEGAR

piss and vinegar see [2]PISS

spit and vinegar see [2]SPIT

– **vin·e·gary** /ˈvɪnɪgəri/ *adj* [*more* ~; *most* ~] • a *vinegary* sauce

vine·yard /ˈvɪnjɚd/ *noun, pl* **-yards** [*count*] **:** a field where grapes are grown

vi·no /ˈvi:noʊ/ *noun* [*noncount*] *informal* **:** WINE • a glass of *vino*

[1]**vin·tage** /ˈvɪntɪʤ/ *adj, always used before a noun*

1 — used to describe a wine usually of high quality that was produced in a particular year which is identified on the bottle • The restaurant has a fine selection of *vintage* wines.

2 — used to describe something that is not new but that is valued because of its good condition, attractive design, etc. • a collection of *vintage* cars • *vintage* clothing shops

3 — used to describe something that has the best qualities or characteristics of the things made or done by a particular person, organization, etc. • *vintage* Elvis Presley songs • This painting is *vintage* Van Gogh.

vintage year **1 :** a year in which a vintage wine is produced • The date of the *vintage year* is marked on the bottle. **2 :** a very good or successful year • This has been a *vintage year* for independent films.

[2]**vintage** *noun, pl* **-tag·es**

1 [*count*] **:** the grapes or wine produced during one season

V

2 [*noncount*] : a period in which something was made or was begun • a piano of 1845 *vintage* • films of recent *vintage* [=films made recently]

vint·ner /ˈvɪntnɚ/ *noun, pl* **-ners** [*count*]
1 : a person who makes wine
2 : a person who sells wine

vi·nyl /ˈvaɪnl/ *noun* [*noncount*] : a plastic material that is used to make records, clothing, etc., and as a covering for floors, walls, furniture, etc. • I have that album ***on vinyl*** [=on a record made of vinyl] — often used before another noun • *vinyl* tablecloths • *vinyl* flooring • a house with *vinyl* siding

vi·ol /ˈvajəl/ *noun, pl* **-ols** [*count*] : a musical instrument used in the past that is similar to a violin

vi·o·la /viˈoʊlə/ *noun, pl* **-las** [*count*] : a stringed musical instrument that is like a violin but slightly larger and lower in pitch — see picture at STRINGED INSTRUMENT

vi·o·late /ˈvajəˌleɪt/ *verb* **-lates; -lat·ed; -lat·ing** [+ *obj*]
1 a : to do something that is not allowed by (a law, rule, etc.) • Students who *violate* [=*break*] the rules will be punished. • He was arrested for *violating* his parole. **b** : to take away, interfere with, or ignore (something, such as a person's rights or privacy) in an unfair or illegal way • He claims that his rights were *violated*. [=that he was treated unfairly] • The company *violated* its customers' privacy.
2 : to abuse or show disrespect for (something, such as a holy place) usually by damaging it • Vandals *violated* [=*desecrated*] the cemetery during the night.
3 *formal* : [1]RAPE • She was attacked and *violated* by an unknown intruder.
– vi·o·la·tor /ˈvajəˌleɪtɚ/ *noun, pl* **-tors** [*count*] • *Violators* (of the law) will be prosecuted.

vi·o·la·tion /ˌvajəˈleɪʃən/ *noun, pl* **-tions**
1 : the act of doing something that is not allowed by a law or rule [*count*] a serious *violation* of the law • A second *violation* was called on the basketball player. • a ***moving violation*** = a traffic *violation* [=the act of breaking a law while driving] [*noncount*] He was arrested for *violation* of his parole. • The evidence was seized ***in violation of*** the law. [=was seized in a way that was illegal]
2 : the act of ignoring or interfering with a person's rights [*count*] The group monitors human rights *violations*. [*noncount*] They protested the government's *violation* of human rights.
3 [*noncount*] : the act of showing disrespect for something (such as a holy place) usually by damaging it • They were responsible for the *violation* [=*desecration*] of the cemetery.

vi·o·lence /ˈvajələns/ *noun* [*noncount*]
1 : the use of physical force to harm someone, to damage property, etc. • an act of *violence* • They need to learn how to settle their arguments without resorting to *violence*. • They spoke out against (the use of) *violence* against women. • *Violence* erupted in the streets. [=people began fighting, setting fires, etc., in the streets] • movies filled with sex and *violence* • gun *violence* • ***domestic violence*** [=acts or threats of physical harm that happen in the home]
2 : great destructive force or energy • The *violence* of the storm caused great fear.
do violence to : to harm or weaken (something) : to make (something) less effective • They want to make a movie from the book without *doing violence to* the simplicity of the original story.

vi·o·lent /ˈvajələnt/ *adj* [*more* ~; *most* ~]
1 : using or involving the use of physical force to cause harm or damage to someone or something • They witnessed a *violent* struggle between police and protesters. • The peaceful protest suddenly turned *violent*. • The city has experienced an increase in *violent* crime in the past year. : showing violence • *violent* movies • The final scene was extremely *violent*.
2 : caused by physical force or violence • She suffered a *violent* death in a car accident.
3 a : trying to physically attack someone because of anger • The patient suddenly became *violent* and had to be restrained. **b** : likely to physically attack other people • *violent* criminals • He's not a particularly *violent* person. • He has a *violent* past. [=he has attacked people in the past]
4 : very forceful or intense • Her parents got into a *violent* argument. • a *violent* denial of guilt • The proposal has drawn *violent* criticism from many political commentators. • She went into *violent* spasms. • He suddenly felt a *violent* pain in his head. • *violent* [=extremely bright] colors
5 : very powerful and capable of causing damage • *violent* storms/winds
– vi·o·lent·ly *adv* • We were *violently* attacked. • They are *violently* opposed to the proposal. • She became ***violently ill*** [=she vomited]

vi·o·let /ˈvajələt/ *noun, pl* **-lets**
1 [*count*] : a plant that has small bluish-purple or white flowers — see also AFRICAN VIOLET
2 [*count, noncount*] : a bluish-purple color — see color picture on page C3
– see also SHRINKING VIOLET
– violet *adj* • She has *violet* eyes.

vi·o·lin /ˌvajəˈlɪn/ *noun, pl* **-lins** [*count*] : a musical instrument that has four strings and that you usually hold against your shoulder under your chin and play with a bow — called also (*informal*) *fiddle*; see picture at STRINGED INSTRUMENT

vi·o·lin·ist /ˌvajəˈlɪnɪst/ *noun, pl* **-ists** [*count*] : a person who plays the violin

VIP /ˌviːˌaɪˈpiː/ *noun, pl* **VIPs** /ˌviːˌaɪˈpiːz/ [*count*] *informal* : a person who is very important or famous • I was treated like a *VIP* at the reception. ✧ *VIP* is an abbreviation of the phrase "very important person."

vi·per /ˈvaɪpɚ/ *noun, pl* **-pers** [*count*] : a type of poisonous snake

vi·ra·go /vəˈrɑːgoʊ/ *noun, pl* **-goes** *or* **-gos** [*count*] *literary* + *disapproving* : an angry woman who often complains about and criticizes other people

vi·ral /ˈvaɪrəl/ *adj* : caused by a virus • *viral* diseases/infections

[1]vir·gin /ˈvɚʤən/ *noun, pl* **-gins** [*count*]
1 : a person who has not had sexual intercourse
2 : a person who does not have experience in a particular activity, job, etc. • a political *virgin*

[2]virgin *adj*
1 : never having had sexual intercourse • a *virgin* bride [=a bride who has never had sexual intercourse before her marriage]
2 : not changed from a natural or original condition : not affected by human activity • a *virgin* forest • *virgin* snow
3 *of olive oil* : obtained from the first light pressing of olives • extra *virgin* olive oil
4 : used or worked for the first time • *virgin* wool/wood/timber
virgin territory : an experience or situation that is new for someone • This is *virgin territory* for us. We've never faced a problem like this before. • We're headed into *virgin territory* with these new regulations.

vir·gin·al /ˈvɚʤənl/ *adj* [*more* ~; *most* ~]
1 : having a young, pure, and innocent quality • a *virginal* young girl • *virginal* innocence
2 : not changed from a natural or original condition • The land is still in its *virginal* state.

Vir·gin·ia creeper /vɚˈʤɪnjə-/ *noun, pl* ~ **-ers** [*count*] : a kind of vine that is often grown on walls

Virginia reel *noun* [*noncount*] : a traditional American dance in which two lines of people face each other and take turns doing a series of movements with the person they are facing

vir·gin·i·ty /vɚˈʤɪnəti/ *noun* [*noncount*] : the state of never having had sexual intercourse : the state of being a virgin • He ***lost his virginity*** [=he had sexual intercourse for the first time] when he was in college.

Virgin Mary *noun*
the Virgin Mary : the mother of Jesus Christ • They prayed to *the Virgin Mary*.

Vir·go /ˈvɚgoʊ/ *noun, pl* **-gos**
1 [*noncount*] : the sixth sign of the zodiac that comes between Leo and Libra and that has a virgin as its symbol — see picture at ZODIAC
2 [*count*] : a person born under the sign of Virgo : a person born between August 23 and September 22 • Are you a *Virgo* or a Libra?

vir·ile /ˈvirəl, *Brit* ˈvɪˌraɪl/ *adj* [*more* ~; *most* ~] : having or suggesting qualities (such as strength and sexual energy) that are associated with men and that are usually considered attractive in men • *virile* young athletes • a *virile* writing style
– vi·ril·i·ty /vəˈrɪləti/ *noun* [*noncount*] • an actor admired for his *virility*

vi·rol·o·gy /vaɪˈrɑːləʤi/ *noun* [*noncount*] *medical* : the study of viruses and the diseases they cause
– vi·rol·o·gist /vaɪˈrɑːləʤɪst/ *noun, pl* **-gists** [*count*]

vir·tu·al /ˈvɚʧəwəl/ *adj, always used before a noun*
1 : very close to being something without actually being it •

V

The country is ruled by a *virtual* dictator. [=by someone who is not officially a dictator but who is like a dictator in every important way] • Her victory is a *virtual* certainty. [=she almost certainly will win] • The species is nearing *virtual* extinction. [=it is almost extinct]

2 : existing or occurring on computers or on the Internet • a *virtual* library • *virtual* shopping • The Web site provides a *virtual* tour of the stadium.

vir·tu·al·ly /ˈvɚʧəwəli/ *adv* **:** very nearly **:** almost entirely • We spent *virtually* all day shopping. • The stadium was *virtually* empty by the time the game ended. • I remember *virtually* everything he said. • That illness is *virtually* unknown in this area. • She is *virtually* guaranteed to get the job. [=she almost certainly will get the job]

virtual reality *noun* [*noncount*] **:** an artificial world that consists of images and sounds created by a computer and that is affected by the actions of a person who is experiencing it

vir·tue /ˈvɚʧu/ *noun, pl* **-tues**

1 [*noncount*] **:** morally good behavior or character • I urge you all to lead lives of *virtue*. [=to live virtuously] • She says that *virtue* is its own reward. [=that if you do good things, you do not need to be rewarded with money, fame, etc.] • His supporters regard him as a model/paragon of *virtue*. [=as a person who has no moral faults]

2 [*count*] **:** a good and moral quality • Patience is a *virtue*.

3 [*noncount*] **:** the good result that comes from something • Her parents taught her the *virtue* of hard work. [=that hard work is important and valuable]

4 [*count*] **:** an advantage or benefit • The restaurant is inexpensive, and it has the added *virtue* of being close to our house. • One of the *virtues* of this job is the flexible hours.

by virtue of **:** because of (something) • She has the right to participate *by virtue of* her status as a former employee.

make a virtue (out) of necessity **:** to benefit from something that you are forced to do • When he lost his driver's license, he *made a virtue out of necessity* and got in shape by riding his bike to work.

vir·tu·os·i·ty /ˌvɚʧuˈɑːsəti/ *noun* [*noncount*] *formal* **:** great ability or skill shown by a musician, performer, etc. • Her *virtuosity* on the piano is amazing.

vir·tu·o·so /ˌvɚʧuˈousou/ *noun, pl* **-sos** *or* **-si** /-si/ [*count*] **:** a person who does something in a very skillful way • He's a real *virtuoso* in the kitchen.; *especially* **:** a very skillful musician • She's a piano *virtuoso*.

– virtuoso *adj, always used before a noun* • She gave a *virtuoso* performance.

vir·tu·ous /ˈvɚʧəwəs/ *adj* [*more ~; most ~*] **:** morally good **:** having or showing virtue • a *virtuous* man/woman • *virtuous* behavior/conduct • She felt that she had made a *virtuous* decision by donating the money to charity.

– vir·tu·ous·ly *adv* • He tried to live *virtuously*. **– vir·tu·ous·ness** *noun* [*noncount*] • I admire her *virtuousness*.

vir·u·lent /ˈvirələnt/ *adj* [*more ~; most ~*]

1 a : full of hate or anger • *virulent* racists/racism **b :** extremely or excessively harsh or strong • *virulent* criticism/remarks • The country seemed to be returning to the *virulent* nationalism of its past.

2 : extremely dangerous and deadly and usually spreading very quickly • a *virulent* disease/infection

– vir·u·lence /ˈvirələns/ *noun* [*noncount*] • the *virulence* of a particular strain of the disease • The *virulence* of the protest was surprising. **– vir·u·lent·ly** *adv* • a *virulently* racist comment • She *virulently* opposes the proposed new law.

vi·rus /ˈvairəs/ *noun, pl* **-rus·es** [*count*]

1 : an extremely small living thing that causes a disease and that spreads from one person or animal to another • the AIDS *virus* = the *virus* that causes AIDS • Is the illness caused by bacteria or a *virus*?

2 : a disease or illness caused by a virus **:** a viral disease • I think I have the *virus* that's going around this winter. • a stomach *virus*

3 *computers* **:** a program that is designed to harm a computer by deleting data, ruining files, etc., and that can be spread secretly from one computer to another • The software checks your hard drive for *viruses*.

vi·sa /ˈviːzə/ *noun, pl* **-sas** [*count*] **:** an official mark or stamp on a passport that allows someone to enter or leave a country usually for a particular reason • a work/student *visa* • ***exit visas*** [=visas that let you leave your own country]

vis·age /ˈvɪzɪʤ/ *noun, pl* **-ag·es** [*count*] *literary* **:** a person's face • his smiling *visage*

vis·cera /ˈvɪsərə/ *noun* [*plural*] *medical* **:** the organs (such as the heart, liver, and lungs) inside the main part of the body

vis·cer·al /ˈvɪsərəl/ *adj*

1 [*more ~; most ~*] *literary* **:** coming from strong emotions and not from logic or reason • *visceral* hatred • Her *visceral* reaction was to curse at the other driver.

2 *medical* **:** of or relating to the viscera • *visceral* tissues

– vis·cer·al·ly *adv* • They responded *viscerally* to the criticism.

vis·count /ˈvaɪˌkaʊnt/ *noun, pl* **-counts** [*count*] **:** a man who is a member of the British nobility and who ranks below an earl and above a baron

vis·count·ess /ˈvaɪˌkaʊntəs/ *noun, pl* **-ess·es** [*count*]

1 : the wife or widow of a viscount

2 : a woman who has the rank of a viscount

vis·cous /ˈvɪskəs/ *adj* [*more ~; most ~*] *of a liquid* **:** thick or sticky **:** not flowing easily • *viscous* liquids

– vis·cos·i·ty /vɪˈskɑːsəti/ *noun* [*noncount*] • a liquid with a high/low *viscosity*

vise (*US*) *or Brit* **vice** /ˈvaɪs/ *noun, pl* **vis·es** [*count*] **:** a tool that is usually attached to a table and that has two flat parts that can be opened and closed by a screw or lever in order to hold something (such as a piece of wood) very firmly — see picture at CARPENTRY

– vise·like (*US*) *or Brit* **vice·like** /ˈvaɪsˌlaɪk/ *adj* [*more ~; most ~*] • He had a *viselike* [=very firm] grip on my arm.

vis·i·bil·i·ty /ˌvɪzəˈbɪləti/ *noun* [*noncount*]

1 : the ability to see or be seen • Joggers should wear light-colored clothes to increase their *visibility*. [=to make it easier for people to see them] — used especially to describe how far you are able to see because of weather conditions, darkness, etc. • It was a clear day with good *visibility*. [=a day when you could see a long distance because the air was clear] • flying/driving under conditions of poor/low/reduced *visibility* • The fog was very heavy and *visibility* was down to a few feet.

2 : the quality or state of being known to the public • The extra publicity helped to increase the company's *visibility*.

vis·i·ble /ˈvɪzəbəl/ *adj* [*more ~; most ~*]

1 : able to be seen • The ship was not *visible* through the fog. • The ship was barely/clearly *visible*. • The patient showed no *visible* symptoms. • stars ***visible to the naked eye*** [=able to be seen without special equipment] — opposite INVISIBLE

2 : easily seen or understood **:** OBVIOUS • There was a *visible* change in his mood. • She has no ***visible means of support***. [=she had no obvious source of money, such as a job]

3 : known to or noticed by the public • They played a ***highly visible*** role in the negotiations. • a *highly visible* politician

– vis·i·bly /ˈvɪzəbli/ *adv* • He was *visibly* upset/excited.

vi·sion /ˈvɪʒən/ *noun, pl* **-sions**

1 [*noncount*] **:** the ability to see **:** sight or eyesight • She has good/poor *vision*. • She has normal *vision*. = She has 20/20 *vision*. • impaired/blurred *vision* • a *vision* test • *vision* problems • The pole was right in my ***line of vision***. [=the area in front of my eyes] — see also FIELD OF VISION, TUNNEL VISION

2 [*count*] **:** something that you imagine **:** a picture that you see in your mind • We had *visions* of fame and fortune. • the architect's *vision* for the new building • She had a clear *vision* of what she wanted to do.

3 [*count*] **:** something that you see or dream especially as part of a religious or supernatural experience • He had a *vision* of Christ. • The idea came to me ***in a vision***.

4 : a clear idea about what should happen or be done in the future [*noncount*] The job requires a leader with *vision*. [*count*] a leader with a *vision* of/for the future • They had two very different *visions* for the company.

5 [*count*] **:** a beautiful person or thing **:** a lovely sight — used especially of a woman • She was a *vision* in white. • a *vision* of beauty

6 [*noncount*] *Brit* **:** the picture that is shown on a television or in a film • technology that provides the very best in sound and *vision*

vision clears see [2]CLEAR

[1]**vi·sion·ary** /ˈvɪʒəˌneri, *Brit* ˈvɪʒənri/ *adj*

1 [*more ~; most ~*] **a :** having or showing clear ideas about what should happen or be done in the future • She is known as a *visionary* leader. • *visionary* leadership **b :** having or showing a powerful imagination • a *visionary* poet

2 : of or relating to something that is seen or imagined in a dream or vision (sense 3) • He had a *visionary* experience.

[2]**visionary** *noun, pl* **-ar·ies** [*count*]

1 a : a person who has clear ideas about what should happen or be done in the future ▪ She's a *visionary* in her field. ▪ a political *visionary* **b :** a person who has a powerful imagination ▪ an artistic *visionary*
2 : a person who sees visions (sense 3)

[1]vis·it /ˈvɪzət/ *verb* **-its; -it·ed; -it·ing**
1 a : to go somewhere to spend time with (someone, such as a friend or relative) [+ *obj*] She is *visiting* her aunt in New York. [*no obj*] When are you coming to *visit*? — often used + *with* in U.S. English ▪ She is *visiting with* her aunt in New York. **b** [+ *obj*] **:** to go somewhere to see and talk to (someone) in an official way or as part of your job ▪ He is *visiting* a client in Phoenix. **c** [+ *obj*] **:** to go to see (a doctor, dentist, etc.) ▪ She *visits* her doctor regularly.
2 [+ *obj*] **:** to go to (a place) for pleasure, as part of your job, etc. ▪ We *visited* the zoo. ▪ I would like to *visit* Rome someday. ▪ City officials *visited* the building site. ▪ Our town was once *visited* by the President.
3 [+ *obj*] **:** to go to (a Web site) on the Internet ▪ Be sure to *visit* our Web site.
visit on/upon [*phrasal verb*] ***visit (something) on/upon (someone)*** *formal + old-fashioned* **:** to punish (someone) with (something) ▪ The Lord *visited* a plague *upon* the city. ✧ The saying ***the sins of the fathers are visited upon the children*** means that children often suffer for the bad things their parents do.
visit with [*phrasal verb*] ***visit with (someone)*** *US* **:** to spend time talking informally with (someone) ▪ I had a chance to *visit with* her for a few minutes after the meeting. — see also [1]VISIT 1a (above)

[2]visit *noun, pl* **-its** [*count*]
1 : an occasion when someone goes to a place to see and talk to someone for usually a brief time ▪ We had a *visit* from the company president. ▪ Our son came home for a *visit*. ▪ He ***paid a visit*** to his parents. = He *paid* his parents *a visit*. [=he visited his parents]
2 a : an occasion when someone goes to a place for pleasure, as part of a job, to do something, etc. ▪ Have you been here before, or is this your first *visit*? — often + *to* ▪ Is this your first *visit to* the U.S.? ▪ The President will make a state *visit to* China. ▪ a recent *visit to* the doctor's office ▪ He made several *visits* [=*trips*] *to* the bathroom. **b :** an occasion when you are staying in a hotel, motel, etc. ▪ We hope you enjoy your *visit*. [=*stay*]
3 *US* **:** an occasion when you spend time talking informally with someone ▪ We had a nice *visit* after the meeting. — often + *with* ▪ I had a nice *visit with* her after the meeting.

vis·i·ta·tion /ˌvɪzəˈteɪʃən/ *noun, pl* **-tions**
1 [*noncount*] *law* **:** the act of visiting your children or the right to visit your children after you are divorced and while they are living with their other parent ▪ supervised *visitation* ▪ He has ***visitation rights*** on the weekends.
2 [*count, noncount*] *formal* **:** an official visit by an important person especially to look at or inspect something ▪ the *visitation* of a diocese by a bishop
3 [*count*] *US* **:** a time before a dead person is buried when people may view the body ▪ *Visitation* is from 8:00 to 10:00 a.m.
4 : an occurrence when something supernatural (such as a ghost or an angel) appears to someone [*count*] ghostly *visitations* [*noncount*] *visitation* by ghosts
5 [*count*] *formal + old-fashioned* **:** a bad thing that happens and is believed to be punishment from God ▪ a *visitation* of the plague upon the city

vis·it·ing /ˈvɪzətɪŋ/ *adj*
1 — used to describe someone (such as a teacher) who goes to work for a limited time at a different school, college, etc. ▪ a *visiting* teacher/professor
2 *sports* **:** playing on the field or court of an opponent ▪ the *visiting* team

visiting card *noun, pl* **~ cards** [*count*] *Brit* **:** CALLING CARD 2

vis·i·tor /ˈvɪzətɚ/ *noun, pl* **-tors** [*count*] **:** someone who visits a person or place ▪ We are expecting *visitors*. ▪ The museum gets *visitors* from all over the world. ▪ *Visitors* to the office must sign in at the desk. ▪ There's a *visitor* waiting for you in the lobby.

vi·sor /ˈvaɪzɚ/ *noun, pl* **-sors** [*count*]
1 : a piece on the front of a helmet that you can pull down to protect your face
2 *US* **:** the part of a hat or cap that sticks out in front to protect or shade your eyes — see picture at HAT
3 : a flat, stiff piece of material on the inside of a car above the windshield that you can pull down to keep sunlight from shining in your eyes — see picture at CAR

vis·ta /ˈvɪstə/ *noun, pl* **-tas** [*count*]
1 : a large and beautiful view of an area of land or water ▪ colorful mountain *vistas*
2 : a large number of things that may be possible in the future ▪ Computers have opened up (whole) new *vistas* for scientific research.

[1]vi·su·al /ˈvɪʒəwəl/ *adj* **:** relating to seeing or to the eyes ▪ a *visual* impairment ▪ *visual* perception ▪ color, shape, and other *visual* attributes ▪ She appreciates the *visual* arts such as painting and film. ▪ the movie's *visual* effects ▪ Maps are a *visual* tool for learning.
– vi·su·al·ly *adv* ▪ people who are ***visually impaired*** [=people who cannot see well]

[2]visual *noun, pl* **-als** [*count*] **:** something you look at (such as a picture, chart, or film) that is used to make something more appealing or easier to understand ▪ Should I include some *visuals* in my presentation? ▪ a film director known for his powerful/stunning *visuals*

visual aid *noun, pl* **~ aids** [*count*] **:** something you look at (such as a chart or film) that is used to make something easier to understand

visual field *noun, pl* **~ fields** [*count*] **:** FIELD OF VISION

vi·su·al·ize *also Brit* **vi·su·al·ise** /ˈvɪʒəwəˌlaɪz/ *verb* **-iz·es; -ized; -iz·ing** [+ *obj*] **:** to form a mental picture of (someone or something) **:** IMAGINE ▪ She tried to *visualize* the scene he was describing. ▪ I can't *visualize* him as a parent. = It's hard to *visualize* him as a parent. ▪ Before you swing, *visualize* yourself hitting the ball.
– vi·su·al·i·za·tion *also Brit* **vi·su·al·i·sa·tion** /ˌvɪʒəwələˈzeɪʃən, *Brit* ˌvɪʒəwəˌlaɪˈzeɪʃən/ *noun, pl* **-tions** [*count, noncount*]

vi·ta /ˈviːtə/ *noun, pl* **vi·tae** /ˈviːˌtaɪ/ [*count*] *US* **:** CURRICULUM VITAE

vi·tal /ˈvaɪtl̩/ *adj*
1 [*more ~; most ~*] **:** extremely important **:** CRUCIAL ▪ These matters are *vital* to national defense. ▪ He played a *vital* [=*key*] role in guiding the project. ▪ The sciences are a *vital* part of the school curriculum. ▪ ***It is vital*** that you follow all safety procedures. = It is ***of vital importance*** that you follow all safety procedures.
2 *always used before a noun* **:** needed by your body in order to keep living ▪ your heart, lungs, and other *vital* organs — see also VITAL SIGNS
3 [*more ~; most ~*] **:** very lively or energetic ▪ Exercise keeps her young and *vital*. ▪ Their music stills seems fresh and *vital* after all these years.
– vi·tal·ly *adv* ▪ A strong job market is *vitally* important to the economy.

vi·tal·i·ty /vaɪˈtæləti/ *noun* [*noncount*]
1 : a lively or energetic quality ▪ the *vitality* of youth ▪ A shopping district would bring new *vitality* [=*life*] to the downtown area. ▪ Her prose is full of *vitality*. ▪ His performance lacked *vitality*.
2 : the power or ability of something to continue to live, be successful, etc. ▪ These scandals could threaten the *vitality* of the sport. ▪ the economic *vitality* of our cities

vi·tal·ize /ˈvaɪtəˌlaɪz/ *verb* **-iz·es; -ized; -iz·ing** [+ *obj*] *chiefly US* **:** to give life or energy to (something) ▪ They believe that cutting taxes will *vitalize* [=*revitalize*] the economy.

vi·tals /ˈvaɪtl̩z/ *noun* [*plural*]
1 *old-fashioned* **:** the organs of the body (such as the heart, lungs, and liver) that are needed in order to keep living — sometimes used figuratively ▪ the corruption that is gnawing at the *vitals* of the government
2 *US, informal* **:** VITAL SIGNS ▪ The nurse checked the patient's *vitals*.

vital signs *noun* [*plural*] **:** important body functions (such as breathing and heartbeat) that are measured to see if someone is alive or healthy ▪ The patient's *vital signs* were normal.

vi·ta·min /ˈvaɪtəmən, *Brit* ˈvɪtəmən/ *noun, pl* **-mins** [*count*]
1 : a natural substance that is usually found in foods and that helps your body to be healthy ▪ This cereal contains essential *vitamins* and minerals. ▪ *vitamin* pills ✧ Most vitamins are named by letters. ▪ Oranges are a good source of ***vitamin C***. ▪ Milk contains ***vitamin D***.
2 : a pill containing vitamins ▪ Did you remember to take your *vitamin*?

vitamin B_1 /-ˈbiːˈwʌn/ *noun* [*noncount*] **:** THIAMIN

vitamin B_2 /-ˈbiːˈtuː/ *noun* [*noncount*] **:** RIBOFLAVIN

vi·ti·ate /ˈvɪʃiˌeɪt/ *verb* **-ates; -at·ed; -at·ing** [+ *obj*] *formal* : to make (something) less effective : to ruin or spoil (something) • The impact of the film was *vitiated* by poor acting.

vit·ri·ol /ˈvɪtrijəl/ *noun* [*noncount*] *formal* : harsh and angry words • His speech was full of political *vitriol*.
– **vit·ri·ol·ic** /ˌvɪtriˈɑːlɪk/ *adj* [*more* ~; *most* ~] • She launched a *vitriolic* attack against us. • a *vitriolic* debate

vit·tles /ˈvɪtl̩z/ *noun* [*plural*] *US, informal + humorous* : food and drink : VICTUALS • I'll cook up some *vittles*.

vi·tu·per·a·tion /vaɪˌtuːpəˈreɪʃən, *Brit* vaɪˌtjuːpəˈreɪʃən/ *noun* [*noncount*] *formal* : harsh and angry criticism • their *vituperation* against/of the president • Voters are tired of all the *vituperation* in this campaign.
– **vi·tu·per·a·tive** /vaɪˈtuːpərətɪv, *Brit* vaɪˈtjuːpərətɪv/ *adj* [*more* ~; *most* ~] • *vituperative* comments/remarks

[1]**vi·va** /ˈviːvə/ *interj* — used to show that you support or approve of someone or something • *Viva* America! ✧ *Viva* comes from Italian and Spanish, where it means "long live."

[2]**vi·va** /ˈvaɪvə/ *noun, pl* **vi·vas** [*count*] *Brit* : [2]VIVA VOCE

vi·va·cious /vəˈveɪʃəs/ *adj* [*more* ~; *most* ~] : happy and lively in a way that is attractive — used especially of a woman • She has a *vivacious* personality. • his *vivacious* wife
– **vi·va·cious·ly** *adv* • She greeted us *vivaciously*. – **vi·va·cious·ness** *noun* [*noncount*] – **vi·vac·i·ty** /vəˈvæsəti/ *noun* [*noncount*] • her natural *vivacity*

[1]**vi·va vo·ce** /ˌvaɪvəˈvoʊsi/ *adj* : spoken rather than written : ORAL • a *viva voce* examination
– **viva voce** *adv*

[2]**viva voce** *noun, pl* ~ **vo·ces** [*count*] *Brit* : an oral examination given at a British university — called also *viva*

viv·id /ˈvɪvəd/ *adj* [*more* ~; *most* ~]
1 *of a picture, memory, etc.* : seeming like real life because it is very clear, bright, or detailed • He gave a *vivid* description of the scene. • The book includes many *vivid* illustrations. • The dream was very *vivid*. • She could remember the dream ***in vivid detail***. ✧ If you have a ***vivid imagination***, you can imagine things that are not real very clearly and easily.
2 : very bright in color • The fabric was dyed a *vivid* red.
– **viv·id·ly** *adv* • I remember the incident *vividly*. • a *vividly* illustrated book – **viv·id·ness** *noun* [*noncount*]

viv·i·fy /ˈvɪvəˌfaɪ/ *verb* **-fies; -fied; -fy·ing** [+ *obj*] *chiefly US* : to make (someone or something) more lively or vivid • details that *vivify* the narrative

vivi·sec·tion /ˌvɪvəˈsɛkʃən/ *noun* [*noncount*] : the activity or practice of doing scientific or medical experiments on live animals

vix·en /ˈvɪksən/ *noun, pl* **-ens** [*count*]
1 : a female fox
2 *old-fashioned* : an angry and unpleasant woman : SHREW
3 *informal* : a sexually attractive woman • Hollywood *vixens*

viz /ˈvɪz/ *adv* — used before something that you are giving as an example • She limited her suggestions to the subjects she knows best, *viz* [=*namely*], layout and typography.

VJ /ˈviːˌʤeɪ/ *noun, pl* **VJs** [*count*] : VEEJAY

V–neck /ˈviːˌnɛk/ *noun, pl* **-necks** [*count*] : a shirt, sweater, etc., with a neck that has an opening shaped like the letter V • He wore a cotton *V-neck*. • a *V-neck* sweater; *also* : the neck opening itself • a sweater with a *V-neck*
– **V–necked** /ˈviːˌnɛkt/ *adj, always used before a noun* • a *V-necked* sweater

vo·cab·u·lary /voʊˈkæbjəˌleri, *Brit* vəʊˈkæbjələri/ *noun, pl* **-lar·ies**
1 [*count*] : the words that make up a language • the basic *vocabulary* of English
2 : all of the words known and used by a person [*noncount*] She has learned a lot of new *vocabulary*. [*count*] He has a large/wide *vocabulary*. [=he knows and uses many words] • He has a somewhat limited *vocabulary*. • Reading helped to expand/improve her *vocabulary*. • Our ***passive vocabulary*** [=the words we understand] is larger than our ***active vocabulary***. [=the words we use ourselves] — sometimes used in an exaggerated way to make a forceful statement • (The word) "Quit" ***is not in my vocabulary***. [=I will not quit; I refuse to quit]
3 [*count, noncount*] : words that are related to a particular subject • the *vocabulary* of the art world • The Internet has given us a whole new *vocabulary*.
4 [*count, noncount*] : a set of forms or elements that are used for expression in an art, in music, etc. • a rich musical *vocabulary* • architectural *vocabulary*

vo·cal /ˈvoʊkəl/ *adj*
1 : of, relating to, or produced by the voice • *vocal* sounds • the *vocal* organs [=the tongue, larynx, etc.] • *vocal* music [=music that is sung] • music with *vocal* and instrumental parts • *vocal* harmonies • a male *vocal* group [=a group of male singers]
2 [*more* ~; *most* ~] : expressing opinions in a public and forceful way : OUTSPOKEN • She is a *vocal* critic of the new law. • He was very *vocal* in his criticism/support of me.
– **vo·cal·ly** *adv* • She was *vocally* opposed to the new law.

vocal cords *noun* [*plural*] : the thin pieces of folded tissue in your throat that help you to make sounds with your voice

vo·cal·ist /ˈvoʊkəlɪst/ *noun, pl* **-ists** [*count*] : SINGER • a pop *vocalist*

vo·cal·ize *also Brit* **vo·cal·ise** /ˈvoʊkəˌlaɪz/ *verb* **-iz·es; -ized; -iz·ing** *formal*
1 [+ *obj*] : to express (something) by speaking words • *vocalizing* your thoughts/feelings
2 : to make a sound with the voice [*no obj*] The male bird *vocalizes* to attract a mate. [+ *obj*] a baby *vocalizing* sounds
– **vo·cal·i·za·tion** *also Brit* **vo·cal·i·sa·tion** /ˌvoʊkələˈzeɪʃən, *Brit* ˌvəʊkəˌlaɪˈzeɪʃən/ *noun* [*count, noncount*]

vocals /ˈvoʊkəlz/ *noun* [*plural*] : the parts of a piece of music that are sung • He played the guitar while I sang (the) *vocals*. • The album features my sister on *vocals*.

vo·ca·tion /voʊˈkeɪʃən/ *noun, pl* **-tions**
1 [*count*] : a strong desire to spend your life doing a certain kind of work (such as religious work) • It was her *vocation* [=*calling*] to be a teacher. • This isn't just a job for me; it's a *vocation*. • people who follow a religious *vocation* • He never felt a real ***sense of vocation***.
2 : the work that a person does or should be doing [*count*] his chosen *vocation* [=*occupation*] • She discovered architecture as her true *vocation* [=*calling*] while in college. • He feels he ***missed his vocation*** [=did not have the career he should have] by not becoming a doctor. [*noncount*] I'm a carpenter ***by vocation***, but my hobby is painting.

vo·ca·tion·al /voʊˈkeɪʃənl̩/ *adj* : relating to the special skills, training, etc., that you need for a particular job or occupation • *vocational* programs/courses • He went to a ***vocational school*** [=(*US*) *trade school*] to learn auto repair.

vo·cif·er·ous /voʊˈsɪfərəs/ *adj* [*more* ~; *most* ~] : expressing feelings or opinions in a very loud or forceful way • He is her most *vociferous* critic/opponent. • He was *vociferous* in his support of the proposal. • a *vociferous* debate : expressed in a very loud or forceful way • *vociferous* disagreement • The decision was made over their *vociferous* objections.
– **vo·cif·er·ous·ly** *adv* • They applauded/objected *vociferously*.

vod·ka /ˈvɑːdkə/ *noun, pl* **-kas** [*count, noncount*] : a strong, clear alcoholic drink that is originally from Russia

vogue /ˈvoʊg/ *noun, pl* **vogues** : something (such as a way of dressing or behaving) that is fashionable or popular in a particular time and place [*count*] the latest *vogues* • the new/current *vogue* for scarves • His art seems to be ***enjoying a vogue*** these days. [*noncount*] Short skirts are ***in vogue*** right now. = Short skirts are ***(all) the vogue*** right now. • When did Thai food come ***into vogue***? • That style went/fell ***out of vogue*** years ago.
– **vogue** *adj, always used before a noun* • a *vogue* word/phrase [=a word/phrase that is popular for a period of time]

[1]**voice** /ˈvoɪs/ *noun, pl* **voic·es**
1 : the sounds that you make with your mouth and throat when you are speaking, singing, etc. [*count*] He has a deep *voice*. • a loud/booming *voice* • a high/shrill *voice* • her small/timid *voice* • "Can we speak privately?" she said in a low/soft/quiet *voice*. • My teenage son's *voice* is beginning to change/break. [=it is beginning to sound deeper like a man's voice] • Her *voice* was breaking [=it was changing in sound because of emotion] as she said goodbye. • a *voice* on the radio • We heard *voices* coming from the next room. • She does the *voices* for several cartoon characters. • Please ***keep your voice down***. [=please speak quietly] • Please ***lower your voice***. [=please speak more quietly] • Father was stern, but he never ***raised his voice***. [=spoke loudly or harshly] • She was yelling ***at the top of her voice***. [=as loudly as she could] [*noncount*] I don't like your ***tone of voice***. [=the way you are speaking to me]
2 a [*noncount*] : the ability to speak • I shouted so much that I ***lost my voice***. **b** [*count*] : the ability to sing • She has a ter-

V

rific *voice*. ▪ He was ***in good voice*** [=able to sing well] for his recital.

3 a [*singular*] **:** a right or way to express your wishes, opinions, etc. ▪ The students complained that they had no *voice* [=*say*] in school affairs. ▪ Town meetings give people a *voice* in local politics. **b** [*count*] **:** a wish, opinion, etc., that you express openly or publicly ▪ Listen to the *voice* of the people. ▪ Please vote and make your *voices* heard! **c** [*count*] **:** a thought or feeling that comes to you especially when you do not expect it ▪ A little *voice* in my head told me not to trust him. ▪ You must learn to trust your ***inner voice***. **d** [*count*] **:** a person who expresses a wish, opinion, etc. ▪ A few *voices* in the crowd expressed displeasure. ▪ She was ***the voice of reason*** in our group. [=she stopped us from doing foolish things]

4 [*count*] *grammar* **:** a verb form that shows whether the subject of a sentence does or receives the action of the verb ✧ In the ***active voice***, the subject of the sentence does the action. ▪ "I found a quarter" is in the *active voice*. In the ***passive voice***, the subject of the sentence receives the action. ▪ "He was found by the police" is in the *passive voice*.

find your voice see [1]FIND

to give voice to *formal* **:** to express (a thought, feeling, etc.) to someone ▪ Therapy allowed her *to give voice to* her fears.

with one voice — used to say that all the people in a group say the same thing together, express the same opinion, etc. ▪ When asked if they wanted to help, they answered *with one voice* "Yes!" ▪ They spoke *with one voice* on the need to reduce taxes. [=they all agreed about the need to reduce taxes]

[2]**voice** *verb* **voices; voiced; voic·ing** [+ *obj*] **:** to express (something) in words ▪ He *voiced* concern about safety issues. [=he said that he felt concern about safety issues] ▪ The senator angrily *voiced* his objection to the bill.

voice box *noun, pl* ~ **boxes** [*count*] **:** the part of the throat that contains the vocal cords **:** LARYNX

voiced *adj*

1 : having a voice of a particular kind — used in combination ▪ A deep-*voiced* man answered the phone.

2 *technical, of a sound* **:** made by moving your vocal cords ▪ "M" is a *voiced* consonant. — opposite VOICELESS

voice·less /ˈvoɪsləs/ *adj*

1 : not large or powerful enough to be noticed by the government, the media, etc. ▪ a *voiceless* minority

2 *technical, of a sound* **:** made without moving your vocal cords ▪ "S" is a *voiceless* consonant. — opposite VOICED

voice mail *noun, pl* ~ **mails** [*noncount*] **:** a system in which callers can leave recorded messages for you over the telephone ▪ Just leave a message on my *voice mail*.; *also* [*count*] **:** a message left using this system ▪ I left her a *voice mail*. ▪ You have two new *voice mails*. ▪ a *voice-mail* message

voice–over /ˈvoɪsˌoʊvɚ/ *noun, pl* **-overs** [*count*] **:** words that are spoken in a movie or television program by a person who is not seen ▪ He does a lot of *voice-overs* [=*narration*] for commercials.

[1]**void** /ˈvoɪd/ *adj*

1 *law* **:** having no legal force or effect ▪ The contract is *void*. ▪ This sales offer is *void* where prohibited by law. — often used in the phrase ***null and void*** ▪ The law was declared *null and void*.

2 *formal* **:** not containing anything **:** EMPTY ▪ a *void* space

void of **:** not having (something that is expected or wanted) **:** completely lacking (something) ▪ a book *void of* [=*devoid of*] interest ▪ He is *void of* charm. [=he has no charm]

[2]**void** *noun, pl* **voids** [*count*] **:** a large empty space ▪ the great *voids* between galaxies — often used figuratively ▪ After she left, there was a *void* in my life. ▪ When he retires, it will be hard to find someone to ***fill the void***.

[3]**void** *verb* **voids; void·ed; void·ing** [+ *obj*] *law* **:** to make (something) invalid **:** to say that (something) is no longer in effect ▪ The judge *voided* the contract. ▪ Any unauthorized repairs will *void* the warranty.

— **void·able** /ˈvoɪdəbəl/ *adj, law* ▪ a *voidable* contract

voi·là *or* **voi·la** /vwɑˈlɑː/ *interj* — used when something is being presented or shown to someone ▪ "*Voilà*!" said the magician as he pulled a rabbit from the hat. ▪ Add a little oil and vinegar to the lettuce, and *voilà*—you have an easy salad.

voile /ˈvojəl/ *noun* [*noncount*] **:** a soft, light fabric that you can see through slightly and that is used for making curtains, summer clothes, etc.

vol. *abbr* volume — used in titles ▪ The Works of Shakespeare, *Vol.* I

[1]**vol·a·tile** /ˈvɑːlətəl, *Brit* ˈvɒləˌtajəl/ *adj* [*more* ~; *most* ~]

1 a : likely to change in a very sudden or extreme way ▪ The stock market can be very *volatile*. **b :** having or showing extreme or sudden changes of emotion ▪ She is a *volatile* woman. ▪ He has a very *volatile* temper. [=he gets angry very suddenly and violently]

2 : likely to become dangerous or out of control ▪ The protests are increasing, creating a *volatile* situation in the capital.

3 *technical* **:** easily becoming a gas at a fairly low temperature ▪ a *volatile* solvent ▪ highly *volatile* compounds

— **vol·a·til·i·ty** /ˌvɑːləˈtɪləti/ *noun* [*noncount*]

[2]**volatile** *noun, pl* **-tiles** [*count*] *technical* **:** a chemical or compound that changes into a gas easily

vol·ca·nic /vɑlˈkænɪk/ *adj*

1 : of, relating to, or produced by a volcano ▪ a *volcanic* eruption ▪ *volcanic* ash/rock ▪ *volcanic* activity

2 [*more* ~; *most* ~] *informal* **:** very angry or violent ▪ a *volcanic* temper ▪ *volcanic* emotions/rages

vol·ca·no /vɑlˈkeɪnoʊ/ *noun, pl* **-noes** *or* **-nos** [*count*] **:** a mountain with a hole in the top or side that sometimes sends out rocks, ash, lava, etc., in a sudden explosion (called an eruption) ▪ The *volcano* last erupted 25 years ago. ▪ an active *volcano* [=a volcano that could erupt at any time or that is erupting now] ▪ a dormant *volcano* [=a volcano that is not currently active] ▪ an extinct *volcano* [=a volcano that does not erupt anymore]

vole /ˈvoʊl/ *noun, pl* **voles** [*count*] **:** a small animal like a mouse that usually lives underground and that can be harmful to crops and gardens

vo·li·tion /voʊˈlɪʃən/ *noun* [*noncount*] *formal* **:** the power to make your own choices or decisions ▪ He left the company ***of his own volition***. [=*voluntarily, willingly*; he left because he wanted to, not because he was forced to]

— **vo·li·tion·al** /voʊˈlɪʃənl/ *adj* ▪ *volitional* acts

[1]**vol·ley** /ˈvɑːli/ *noun, pl* **-leys** [*count*]

1 *sports* **:** a shot or kick made by hitting a ball before it touches the ground ▪ (*tennis*) She won the point with a backhand *volley*. — compare GROUND STROKE

2 : a large number of bullets, arrows, stones, etc., that are shot or thrown at the same time ▪ The tank was hit by a *volley* of *bullets*. ▪ a *volley* of arrows

3 : a lot of comments, questions, etc., that are directed at a person very quickly ▪ She was overwhelmed by a *volley* of questions from the press. ▪ a *volley* of criticism

[2]**volley** *verb* **-leys; -leyed; -ley·ing** [+ *obj*] *sports* **:** to hit (a ball) while it is in the air and before it touches the ground ▪ She *volleyed* the shot over the net.

vol·ley·ball /ˈvɑːliˌbɑːl/ *noun, pl* **-balls**

1 [*noncount*] **:** a game in which two teams of players hit a large ball back and forth over a high net

2 [*count*] **:** the ball used to play volleyball — see picture at BALL

volt /ˈvoʊlt/ *noun, pl* **volts** [*count*] **:** a unit for measuring the force of an electrical current ▪ 15 *volts* of electricity ▪ a nine-*volt* battery — abbr. *V*

volt·age /ˈvoʊltɪʤ/ *noun, pl* **-ag·es :** the force of an electrical current that is measured in volts [*noncount*] We measured the change in *voltage* across the circuit. ▪ a high-*voltage* area [*count*] high *voltages*

volte–face /ˌvɑːltˈfɑːs/ *noun* [*singular*] *chiefly Brit, formal* **:** a complete change of attitude or opinion **:** ABOUT-FACE ▪ They did a sudden *volte-face*.

volt·me·ter /ˈvoʊltˌmiːtɚ/ *noun, pl* **-ters** [*count*] **:** a device that measures voltage

vol·u·ble /ˈvɑːljəbəl/ *adj* [*more* ~; *most* ~] *formal* **:** talking a lot in an energetic and rapid way ▪ a *voluble* host

— **vol·u·bly** /ˈvɑːljəbli/ *adv*

vol·ume /ˈvɑːlˌjuːm/ *noun, pl* **-umes**

1 a [*noncount*] **:** the amount of sound that is produced by a television, radio, stereo, etc. ▪ The *volume* is too loud. ▪ Can you turn the *volume* up/down? ▪ playing music at full/top/high/low *volume* ▪ This knob controls *volume*. **b** [*count*] **:** a knob, lever, etc., that controls the amount of sound something makes ▪ She fiddled with the *volume* on the stereo.

2 : an amount of something [*count*] a high/low/large/small *volume* of sales ▪ Huge *volumes* of park visitors come through every weekend. [*noncount*] an increase in traffic *volume*

3 : the amount of space that is filled by something [*count*] The box has a *volume* of three cubic meters. [*noncount*] We measure the items by weight, not ***by volume***.

4 [*count*] **a :** a book ▪ This thin little *volume* is a delightful

V

read. **b :** a book that is part of a series or set of books • a long novel that was published in three *volumes* • The first *volume* of the series was disappointing, but I hear the second *volume* is better. **c :** one of the magazines, newspapers, etc., in a series • The article appears in *volume* 19, number 4.

speak volumes **:** to provide a lot of information about something **:** to show something very clearly • The company's decision to ignore the problem *speaks volumes* [=says a lot] about its lack of leadership.

vo·lu·mi·nous /vəˈluːmənəs/ *adj* [*more* ~; *most* ~] *formal*
1 a : very large **:** containing a lot of space • a *voluminous* room • the building's high ceilings and *voluminous* spaces **b** *of clothing* **:** using large amounts of fabric **:** very full • a *voluminous* skirt
2 : having very many words or pages • They carried on a *voluminous* correspondence. [=they wrote many long letters to each other] • a *voluminous* report • a writer of *voluminous* output
– vo·lu·mi·nous·ly *adv* • He wrote *voluminously.*

vol·un·tary /ˈvɑːlənˌteri, *Brit* ˈvɒləntri/ *adj*
1 : done or given because you want to and not because you are forced to **:** done or given by choice • a *voluntary* agreement/decision • *voluntary* retirement • *voluntary* donations • Participation in the program is completely *voluntary.* • He was charged with *voluntary* manslaughter. — opposite INVOLUNTARY
2 a : provided or supported by people who do work without being paid • a *voluntary* [=*volunteer*] association/organization **b :** doing work without being paid • She works for the charity on a *voluntary* basis. [=she works as a volunteer for the charity] • (*chiefly Brit*) Several ***voluntary workers*** [=*volunteers*] help out at the nursing home.
3 : able to be controlled consciously • *voluntary* bodily movements • the *voluntary* muscles that control urination — opposite INVOLUNTARY
– vol·un·tari·ly /ˌvɑːlənˈterəli, *Brit* ˈvɒləntrəli/ *adv* • They *voluntarily* submitted to the testing. • Her confession was made *voluntarily.*

¹vol·un·teer /ˌvɑːlənˈtiə/ *noun, pl* **-teers** [*count*] **:** someone who does something without being forced to do it: such as **a :** a person who chooses to join the military **b :** a person who does work without getting paid to do it • *Volunteers* are needed to help with the bake sale. • The school was built by *volunteers.*

²volunteer *verb* **-teers; -teered; -teer·ing**
1 [*no obj*] **a :** to offer to do something without being forced to or without getting paid to do it • I *volunteered* to do the job. = I *volunteered* for the job. **b :** to choose to join the military • Our son *volunteered* for military service.
2 [+ *obj*] **:** to give (something) without being forced to or without getting paid for it • I *volunteered* my services. • He would not *volunteer* any information about her whereabouts.
3 [+ *obj*] **:** to say that someone will do something without asking if he or she wants to do it • I just found out that Mom *volunteered* me to babysit. [=that Mom said I would babysit without asking me if I wanted to]

³volunteer *adj, always used before a noun* **:** of, relating to, or done by volunteers • a *volunteer* army/organization • *volunteer* work

vo·lup·tu·ous /vəˈlʌptʃəwəs/ *adj* [*more* ~; *most* ~]
1 *of a woman* **:** very attractive because of having large hips and breasts • a *voluptuous* movie star
2 *literary* **:** giving pleasure to the senses • a *voluptuous* meal • *voluptuous* prose
– vo·lup·tuous·ly *adv* **– vo·lup·tu·ous·ness** *noun* [*noncount*]

¹vom·it /ˈvɑːmət/ *verb* **-its; -it·ed; -it·ing :** to have the food, liquid, etc., that is in your stomach come out through your mouth because you are sick [*no obj*] I feel like I am going to *vomit.* [=(less formally) *throw up*] • The dog *vomited* on the floor. [+ *obj*] The patient was *vomiting* blood.

²vomit *noun* [*noncount*] **:** the food, liquid, etc., that comes out of your body through your mouth when you vomit

¹voo·doo /ˈvuːˌduː/ *noun* [*noncount*] **:** a religion that is practiced chiefly in Haiti ✧ People often associate voodoo with magic and spells.

²voodoo *adj, always used before a noun*
1 : of or relating to voodoo • a *voodoo* priest • *voodoo* rituals
2 *chiefly US, disapproving* **:** not at all sensible or achievable **:** extremely unrealistic • *voodoo* economics

vo·ra·cious /vəˈreɪʃəs/ *adj* [*more* ~; *most* ~] **:** having or showing a tendency to eat very large amounts of food • a *voracious* eater/predator • He has a ***voracious appetite.*** — often used figuratively • I'm a *voracious* reader. • She has a *voracious appetite* for knowledge.
– vo·ra·cious·ly *adv* • She ate *voraciously.* **– vo·rac·i·ty** /vəˈræsəti/ *noun* [*noncount*]

vor·tex /ˈvoəˌtɛks/ *noun, pl* **vor·ti·ces** /ˈvoətəˌsiːz/ *also* **vor·tex·es** /ˈvoəˌtɛksəz/ [*count*] *technical* **:** a mass of spinning air, liquid, etc., that pulls things into its center — sometimes used figuratively • He was caught in a swirling *vortex* of terror.

vo·ta·ry /ˈvoutəri/ *noun, pl* **-ries** [*count*] *formal* + *old-fashioned* **:** a devoted follower of or believer in a religion, a cause, etc. • *votaries* of freedom

¹vote /ˈvout/ *verb* **votes; vot·ed; vot·ing**
1 [*no obj*] **:** to make an official choice for or against someone or something by casting a ballot, raising your hand, speaking your choice aloud, etc. • Citizens will *vote* today for their new governor. • Did you *vote* in the last election? • The committee hasn't yet *voted* on the matter. • She generally *votes* Republican/Democratic. • Congress *voted* 121 to 16 to pass the bill. • He ***voted against*** the proposal. • Most people ***voted for*** school reform. = Most people ***voted in favor of*** school reform.
2 [+ *obj*] **:** to make a decision about (someone or something) by voting: such as **a :** to make (something) legal by a vote • They *voted* the referendum into law. **b :** to choose (someone or something) for an award by voting — usually used as *(be) voted* • He *was voted* Bachelor of the Year. **c :** to officially agree to give (someone) something by voting • Senators *voted* themselves a pay raise despite the budget shortfall.
3 [+ *obj*] **:** to suggest (something) for others to agree or disagree with • We have to decide what to do about dinner. I *vote* that we get a pizza.

vote down [*phrasal verb*] ***vote (something) down*** *or* ***vote down (something)*** **:** to defeat or reject (something) by voting • The proposal was *voted down.*

vote in [*phrasal verb*] ***vote (someone) in*** *or* ***vote in (someone)*** **:** to elect (someone) to an office or position • She was *voted in* (as vice president) last year.

vote on/onto [*phrasal verb*] ***vote (someone) on/onto (something)*** **:** to decide by a vote that (someone) will be allowed to become a member of (a group, team, etc.) • You have been *voted onto* the team. • She was *voted on* the committee.

vote out [*phrasal verb*] ***vote (someone) out*** *or* ***vote out (someone)*** **:** to decide by a vote that (someone) will no longer have an office or position • She was *voted out* (of office) last year.

vote with your feet **:** to show your dislike of a particular place or situation by leaving and going somewhere else • When the restaurant changed its menu, many former customers *voted with their feet* and stopped coming.

vote with your wallet *or US* ***vote (with) your pocketbook***
1 : to vote in a way that helps you financially **2 :** to show what you like and dislike by choosing where to shop and what to buy • If our customers don't like our products, they will *vote with their wallets.* [=they will not buy our products]

– voting *noun* [*noncount*] • The polls will open for *voting* at 8:00. • *Voting* was heavy [=a lot of people voted] in the 5th Precinct.

²vote *noun, pl* **votes**
1 a [*count*] **:** the official choice that you make in an election, meeting, etc., by casting a ballot, raising your hand, speaking your choice aloud, etc. • They are counting/tallying the *votes* now. • There are 20 *votes* in favor and 12 against. • He got 56 percent of the *votes.* • She's campaigning hard to raise money and win *votes.* • People waited in line to ***cast their votes.*** • I *cast my vote* for the Republican/Democratic candidate. **b** [*singular*] **:** the result of voting • The *vote* was in her favor. • She won ***by a vote of*** 206 to 57.
2 ***the vote*** **a :** the legal right to vote • In 1920, American women won *the vote.* **b :** the whole group of people in an area who have the right to vote — usually used in the phrase ***get out the vote*** • Volunteers for his campaign helped *get out the vote* [=persuade people to go vote] on Election Day. **c :** the total number of votes made in an election • The candidate won only 10 percent of *the vote.* **d :** a particular group of people who have the right to vote • He tried to win *the* youth/Black/farm/business *vote.*
3 [*singular*] **:** an occurrence in which a group of people make a decision about something by voting • Let's take a *vote.* All those in favor say "aye." • The issue never ***came to a vote.*** •

The referendum will be *put to a vote.*

vote of confidence *noun, pl* **votes of confidence** [*count*]
1 : a formal process in which people (such as the members of a legislature) vote in order to indicate whether or not they support a leader, government, etc.
2 : a statement or action that shows continuing support and approval for someone ▪ Many people say the coach should be fired, but he was given a *vote of confidence* by the team president this week. [=the team president said that he supports and has confidence in the coach]

vote of no confidence *noun, pl* **votes of no confidence** [*count*] **:** a formal vote by which people (such as the members of a legislature) indicate that they do not support a leader, government, etc. ▪ He was forced to resign after a *vote of no confidence* by the board of directors.

vot·er /ˈvoʊtɚ/ *noun, pl* **-ers** [*count*] **:** a person who votes or who has the legal right to vote ▪ minority *voters* ▪ Less than 10 percent of (the) *voters* favor the measure. ▪ *voter* registration

voting booth *noun, pl* **~ booths** [*count*] *chiefly US* **:** a small, enclosed area in which a person stands while casting a vote — called also (*Brit*) *polling booth*

voting machine *noun, pl* **~ -chines** [*count*] **:** a machine that you use to cast a vote and that records and counts all of the votes made for each possible choice

vo·tive /ˈvoʊtɪv/ *adj, always used before a noun, formal* **:** consisting of or expressing a religious vow, wish, or desire ▪ a *votive* prayer **:** offered or performed as an expression of thanks or devotion to God ▪ *votive* offerings

votive candle *noun, pl* **~ -dles** [*count*] **:** a small candle that is sometimes used in religious ceremonies

vouch /ˈvaʊʧ/ *verb* **vouch·es; vouched; vouch·ing**
vouch for [*phrasal verb*] ***vouch for (someone or something)*** **:** to say that (someone or something) is honest, true, or good ▪ I can *vouch for* the authenticity of the document. ▪ We'll *vouch for* him. He's a good guy.

vouch·er /ˈvaʊʧɚ/ *noun, pl* **-ers** [*count*] **:** a document that gives you the right to get something (such as a product or service) without paying for it ▪ That item is out of stock, but we'll give you a *voucher* for 10 percent off any other item in the store. ▪ a travel *voucher*

vouch·safe /ˌvaʊʧˈseɪf/ *verb* **-safes; -safed; -saf·ing** [+ *obj*] *formal + old-fashioned* **:** to give (something) to someone as a promise or a privilege ▪ He *vouchsafed* the secret to only a few chosen disciples.

¹vow /ˈvaʊ/ *noun, pl* **vows** [*count*] **:** a serious promise to do something or to behave in a certain way ▪ The monks take a *vow* of silence/chastity/poverty. ▪ marriage/wedding *vows* ▪ The bride and groom exchanged *vows.* ▪ The mayor made a *vow* to reduce crime.

²vow *verb* **vows; vowed; vow·ing** [+ *obj*] **:** to make a serious promise to do something or to behave in a certain way — often followed by *to + verb* ▪ The mayor *vowed to reduce* crime. ▪ I *vow to honor* and *cherish* you all my days. — often + *that* ▪ I *vowed that* I would never lie to her again.

vow·el /ˈvawəl/ *noun, pl* **-els** [*count*]
1 : a speech sound made with your mouth open and your tongue in the middle of your mouth not touching your teeth, lips, etc.
2 : a letter (such as *a, e, i, o, u,* and sometimes *y* in English) that represents a vowel — compare CONSONANT

¹voy·age /ˈvojɪʤ/ *noun, pl* **-ag·es** [*count*] **:** a long journey to a distant or unknown place especially over water or through outer space ▪ The Titanic sank on her maiden *voyage.* ▪ He wrote about his many *voyages* into the South Seas. ▪ a manned *voyage* to Mars — often used figuratively ▪ a spiritual *voyage* ▪ a documentary on his *voyage* from rags to riches ▪ a *voyage* of self-discovery

²voyage *verb, always followed by an adverb or preposition* **-ages; -aged; -ag·ing** [*no obj*] **:** to take a long journey usually by ship or boat ▪ They *voyaged* to distant lands. ▪ He spent his youth *voyaging* around the globe.

voy·ag·er /ˈvojɪʤɚ/ *noun, pl* **-ers** [*count*] **:** a person who makes a long journey to a distant or unknown place especially by ship or boat ▪ Columbus and other *voyagers* who traveled to the New World

voy·eur /voɪˈɚ/ *noun, pl* **-eurs** [*count*]
1 : a person who gets sexual pleasure from secretly watching other people have sex
2 : a person who likes seeing and talking or writing about something that is considered to be private ▪ political *voyeurs*
– voy·eur·ism /voɪˈɚˌrɪzəm/ *noun* [*noncount*] ▪ the cheap *voyeurism* of reality television shows **– voy·eur·is·tic** /ˌvojəˈrɪstɪk/ *adj* [*more ~; most ~*] ▪ *voyeuristic* pleasures

VP *abbr* vice president

VR *abbr* virtual reality

vroom /ˈvru:m/ *noun* [*count*] *informal* **:** the sound made by the engine of a car, truck, etc., when it is running very fast ▪ the *vrooms* of engines being revved — often used as an interjection to imitate the sound of an engine ▪ *Vroom, vroom!*
– vroom *verb* **vrooms; vroomed; vroom·ing** [*no obj*] ▪ We heard him *vrooming* around town on his motorcycle.

vs *or* **vs.** *abbr* versus ▪ It'll be the Red Sox *vs.* the Yankees in tonight's game. ▪ Brown *vs.* Board of Education

V sign *noun, pl* **~ signs** [*count*]
1 : a sign that is made by holding your hand up with your palm facing out and your index and middle fingers in a "V" shape and that is used to mean "victory" or "peace"
2 *Brit* **:** a rude gesture that is made by holding your hand up with the palm facing you and the index and middle fingers in a "V" shape

vt *abbr* transitive verb

Vt *or* **VT** *abbr* Vermont

vul·ca·nized *also Brit* **vul·ca·nised** /ˈvʌlkəˌnaɪzd/ *adj, technical, of rubber* **:** treated with heat and chemicals to add strength and other useful qualities
– vul·ca·ni·za·tion *also Brit* **vul·ca·ni·sa·tion** /ˌvʌlkənəˈzeɪʃən ˌvʌlkəˌnaɪˈzeɪʃən/ *noun* [*noncount*] ▪ the *vulcanization* of rubber

vul·gar /ˈvʌlgɚ/ *adj* [*more ~; most ~*]
1 *disapproving* **:** not having or showing good manners, good taste, or politeness ▪ He was a *vulgar* man. ▪ She had a coarse, *vulgar* laugh. ▪ *vulgar* table manners ▪ a *vulgar* [=*tasteless*] display of wealth ▪ I will not tolerate such *vulgar* language in my home. ▪ *vulgar* jokes
2 : relating to the common people or the speech of common people ▪ *vulgar* Latin
– vul·gar·ly *adv* ▪ *vulgarly* sexual jokes

vul·gar·i·ty /ˌvʌlˈgerəti/ *noun, pl* **-ties**
1 [*noncount*] **:** the quality or state of not having good taste, manners, politeness, etc. ▪ a comedian known for her *vulgarity* ▪ I was shocked by the *vulgarity* of his language.
2 [*count*] **:** something (such as a word) that is offensive or rude ▪ He uttered a *vulgarity* and was silent. ▪ We have a policy against printing *vulgarities* in our magazine.

vul·gar·ize *also Brit* **vul·gar·ise** /ˈvʌlgəˌraɪz/ *verb* **-iz·es; -ized; -iz·ing** [+ *obj*] **:** to make (something) worse by making it less formal or more ordinary ▪ The movie is a *vulgarized* version of the original story.
– vul·gar·i·za·tion *also Brit* **vul·gar·i·sa·tion** /ˌvʌlgərəˈzeɪʃən, *Brit* ˌvʌlgəˌraɪˈzeɪʃən/ *noun* [*noncount*]

vul·ner·a·ble /ˈvʌlnərəbəl/ *adj* [*more ~; most ~*]
1 : easily hurt or harmed physically, mentally, or emotionally ▪ a *vulnerable* young woman ▪ He was very *vulnerable* after his divorce. — often + *to* ▪ The patient will be more/most *vulnerable to* infection immediately after surgery.
2 : open to attack, harm, or damage ▪ The troops were in a *vulnerable* position. ▪ The fort was undefended and *vulnerable.* — often + *to* ▪ Your computer is *vulnerable to* viruses.
– vul·ner·a·bil·i·ty /ˌvʌlnərəˈbɪləti/ *noun, pl* **-ties** [*count, noncount*]

vul·pine /ˈvʌlˌpaɪn/ *adj* [*more ~; most ~*] *formal* **:** of, relating to, or similar to a fox ▪ a *vulpine* smile

vul·ture /ˈvʌlʧɚ/ *noun, pl* **-tures** [*count*]
1 : any one of several large birds that eat dead animals and have a small and featherless head — see color picture on page C9; see also TURKEY VULTURE
2 *disapproving* **:** a person who tries to take advantage of someone who is in a very bad situation ▪ As soon as they learned of his arrest, the media *vultures* started circling.

vul·va /ˈvʌlvə/ *noun, pl* **vul·vas** *or* **vul·vae** /ˈvʌlˌvi:/ [*count*] **:** the parts of the female sexual organs that are on the outside of the body

vying *present participle of* VIE

V

1w *or* **W** /ˈdʌbəlˌju:/ *noun, pl* **w's** *or* **ws** *or* **W's** *or* **Ws** /ˈdʌbəlˌju:z/ **:** the 23rd letter of the English alphabet [*count*] a word that starts with a *w* [*noncount*] a word that starts with

2w *or* **W** *abbr* **1** watt ▪ a 60*W* light bulb **2** west, western ▪ Merge onto Rt. 9*W*. **3** width ▪ The area of a rectangle is L x *W*.

WA *abbr* Washington ✧ *WA* is an abbreviation for the U.S. state of Washington and is not used to refer to the city Washington, D.C.

wacko /ˈwækoʊ/ *noun, pl* **wack·os** [*count*] *US, informal* **:** a person who is crazy or very strange and unusual ▪ She's nice but her sister's a real *wacko*.
– **wacko** *adj* [*more* ~; *most* ~] ▪ They have some *wacko* ideas. ▪ His father's *wacko*. [=*wacky*]

wacky /ˈwæki/ *adj* **wack·i·er; -est** [*also more* ~; *most* ~] *informal* **:** amusing and very strange ▪ *wacky* ideas ▪ My *wacky* aunt takes a swim before the lake freezes every winter. ▪ the *wacky* world of his imagination
– **wack·i·ness** /ˈwækinəs/ *noun* [*noncount*]

1wad /ˈwɑ:d/ *noun, pl* **wads** [*count*]
1 : a small mass or ball of soft material — usually + *of* ▪ *Wads of* crumpled paper littered the floor. ▪ She spit a *wad of* gum into the trash. ▪ a *wad of* cotton
2 a : a thick roll or folded pile of paper money or papers — usually + *of* ▪ She pulled a *wad of* $20 bills out of her pocket. ▪ a *wad* of cash **b** *US, informal* **:** a large amount of money ▪ He spent a *wad* on clothes. ▪ They have *wads* of cash. [=lots of money]

2wad *verb* **wads; wad·ded; wad·ding** [+ *obj*] *chiefly US* **:** to crush or press (something, such as paper) into a small, tight ball — usually + *up* ▪ He *wadded up* the paper and threw it in the trash. ▪ The sweater was *wadded up* in the bottom of the backpack.

wad·ding /ˈwɑ:dɪŋ/ *noun* [*noncount*] **:** a soft mass or sheet of material used to fill a space, protect something, etc. ▪ cotton *wadding*

wad·dle /ˈwɑ:dl/ *verb* **wad·dles; wad·dled; wad·dling** [*no obj*] **:** to walk with short steps while moving from side to side like a duck ▪ He *waddled* down the hallway. ▪ A fat goose *waddled* across the yard.
– **waddle** *noun* [*singular*] ▪ She walked with a *waddle*.

wade /ˈweɪd/ *verb* **wades; wad·ed; wad·ing**
1 : to walk through water [*no obj*] We *waded* into the ocean. ▪ I jumped off the boat and *waded* back to shore. ▪ (*US*) They took off their sandals and *waded* [=(*Brit*) *paddled*] at the edge of the pond. [+ *obj*] They *waded* the river. [=they crossed the river by walking through the water]
2 a : to move or proceed with difficulty [*no obj*] Police *waded* into the crowd. ▪ We *waded* through the crowded bus station. ▪ It took several weeks to *wade* through all the evidence. [+ *obj*] We *waded* our way through the crowd. **b** [*no obj*] **:** to become involved in a discussion, situation, activity, etc., in a forceful, direct, or careless way — usually + *in* or *into* ▪ Most politicians would have tried to avoid the subject, but he *waded* right *in*. ▪ She *waded* right *into* their argument.

wad·er /ˈweɪdɚ/ *noun, pl* **-ers**
1 waders [*plural*] **:** high waterproof boots or pants worn for walking or standing in deep water especially while fishing — see picture at FISHING
2 [*count*] **:** WADING BIRD

wading bird *noun, pl* ~ **birds** [*count*] **:** a bird with long legs (such as a heron) that finds its food in water — called also *wader*

wading pool *noun, pl* ~ **pools** [*count*] *US* **:** a shallow pool for children to play in — called also (*Brit*) *paddling pool*

wa·fer /ˈweɪfɚ/ *noun, pl* **-fers** [*count*]
1 : a thin, crisp cracker
2 : a round, thin piece of bread eaten during the Christian Communion ceremony
3 : a small, round, thin object ▪ silicon *wafers*

wafer–thin *adj* **:** extremely thin and flat ▪ *wafer-thin* slices

1waf·fle /ˈwɑ:fəl/ *noun, pl* **waf·fles** [*count*] **:** a crisp cake with a pattern of deep squares on both sides that is made by cooking batter in a special device (called a waffle iron) ▪ He had *waffles* for breakfast. — compare 3WAFFLE

waffle

2waffle *verb* **waffles; waf·fled; waf·fling** [*no obj*] *informal*
1 *US* **:** to be unable or unwilling to make a clear decision about what to do — often + *on* ▪ Her opponent has accused her of *waffling on* the important issues.
2 *Brit* **:** to talk or write a lot without saying anything important or interesting — often + *on* ▪ His uncle was *waffling on* about politics.

3waffle *noun* [*noncount*] *Brit, informal* **:** foolish or dull talk or writing that continues for a long time ▪ The speech was a lot/load of *waffle* about politics. — compare 1WAFFLE

waffle iron *noun, pl* ~ **irons** [*count*] **:** a device used to cook waffles

waft /ˈwɑ:ft/ *verb, always followed by an adverb or preposition* **wafts; waft·ed; waft·ing :** to move lightly through the air [*no obj*] The smell of chicken soup *wafted* up to my bedroom. ▪ The sound of music *wafted* softly into the yard from our neighbor's house. [+ *obj*] A breeze *wafted* the scent of roses towards our table.
– **waft** *noun, pl* **wafts** [*count*] ▪ a *waft* of smoke/perfume

1wag /ˈwæg/ *verb* **wags; wagged; wag·ging :** to move something from side to side repeatedly [+ *obj*] The dog *wagged* its tail. ▪ She *wagged* her finger at the children as she scolded them. ▪ He *wagged* his head back and forth. [*no obj*] The dog's tail began to *wag* excitedly.
the tail wagging the dog see 1TAIL
tongues (are) wagging see 1TONGUE

2wag *noun, pl* **wags** [*count*] **:** a movement from side to side **:** a wagging movement ▪ He answered with a *wag* of his head/finger. ▪ the *wag* of a dog's tail — see also CHIN-WAG — compare 3WAG

3wag *noun, pl* **wags** [*count*] *old-fashioned* **:** a clever person who makes lots of jokes **:** JOKER ▪ He was known as quite a *wag*. — compare 2WAG

1wage /ˈweɪʤ/ *noun, pl* **wag·es** [*count*] **:** an amount of money that a worker is paid based on the number of hours, days, etc., that are worked ▪ a *wage* of $14 an hour = an hourly *wage* of $14 ▪ Both of them make decent *wages*. ▪ The table and chairs cost two weeks' *wages*. ▪ The company offers competitive *wages* and good benefits. ▪ The company gave workers a four percent *wage* increase this year. — compare SALARY; see also LIVING WAGE, MINIMUM WAGE, STARVATION WAGES

2wage *verb* **wages; waged; wag·ing** [+ *obj*] **:** to start and continue (a war, battle, etc.) in order to get or achieve something ▪ They *waged* a guerrilla war against the government. ▪ Local activists are *waging* a campaign to end homelessness in the region. ▪ They have *waged* [=*fought*] a battle against the proposed new law.

waged *adj, Brit* **:** earning or paying wages ▪ *waged* labor ▪ *waged* workers — opposite UNWAGED

wage earner *noun, pl* ~ **-ers** [*count*] **:** someone who works for wages or a salary ▪ Most *wage earners* were not affected by the income tax increase.

1wa·ger /ˈweɪʤɚ/ *noun, pl* **-gers** [*count*]
1 : an agreement in which people try to guess what will happen and the person who guesses wrong has to give something (such as money) to the person who guesses right **:** BET ▪ He has a *wager* on the game. ▪ a friendly *wager*
2 : the money or other valuable thing that you could win or lose in a bet ▪ I don't think the horse will win. What's your *wager*? ▪ I ***placed/made a wager*** on the horse. [=I bet money on the horse]

2wager *verb* **-gers; -gered; -ger·ing**
1 : to risk losing something (such as money) if your guess about what will happen is wrong **:** BET [+ *obj*] She *wagered* $50 on the game. [*no obj*] I wouldn't *wager* against them.
2 *informal* — used in the phrase ***I'll wager*** to indicate what you think will happen or what you believe is probably true ▪ He'll get promoted, *I'll wager*. [=I believe] ▪ *I'll wager* that

most people have never heard of him.

wag·gish /ˈwægɪʃ/ *adj* **:** silly and playful ▪ *waggish* pranks ▪ *waggish* humor ▪ a *waggish* writer

– wag·gish·ly *adv* **– wag·gish·ness** *noun* [*noncount*]

wag·gle /ˈwægəl/ *verb* **wag·gles; wag·gled; wag·gling**

: to move up and down or from side to side repeatedly [+ *obj*] He can *waggle* his ears. ▪ She *waggled* [=*wagged*] her finger at me. [*no obj*] He can make his ears *waggle*.

– waggle *noun* [*singular*]

wag·on /ˈwægən/ *noun, pl* **-ons** [*count*]

1 : a vehicle with four wheels that is used for carrying heavy loads or passengers and that is usually pulled by animals (such as horses) ▪ Pioneers crossed the American Midwest in *wagons*. — see also BANDWAGON, CHUCK WAGON, COVERED WAGON, PADDY WAGON, PATROL WAGON

2 : a small, low vehicle with four wheels that children play with ▪ He pulled his stuffed animals around in a little red *wagon*.

3 *US* **:** STATION WAGON

4 *Brit* **:** a railway car that carries goods

circle the/your wagons *chiefly US, informal* **:** to gather a group of people together in order to protect them from being attacked — usually used figuratively ▪ Reporters tend to *circle the wagons* [=tend to join together to defend themselves] whenever the media are attacked for bias.

hitch your wagon to *chiefly US, informal* **:** to rely on (someone or something) for success ▪ The team has *hitched its wagon to* its star pitcher.

on/off the wagon *informal* ✧ A person who is *on the wagon* has stopped drinking alcohol. ▪ He has been *on the wagon* since his child was born. A person who had stopped drinking alcohol but has started again has ***fallen off the wagon***. ▪ After a year of sobriety, she *fell off the wagon*.

wagon train *noun, pl* **~ trains** [*count*] **:** a long line of wagons traveling together over land; *especially* **:** a line of wagons traveling west in the U.S. during the 1800s

wag·tail /ˈwægˌteɪl/ *noun, pl* **-tails** [*count*] **:** a small European bird that has a long tail which regularly moves up and down

waif /ˈweɪf/ *noun, pl* **waifs** [*count*] **:** a young person who is thin and appears to have no home

waifs and strays *Brit* **:** people or animals that do not have a home

– waif·ish /ˈweɪfɪʃ/ *adj* ▪ The model has a bony, *waifish* look. **– waif·like** /ˈweɪfˌlaɪk/ *adj* ▪ a *waiflike* body

¹wail /ˈweɪl/ *verb* **wails; wailed; wail·ing**

1 [*no obj*] **:** to make a loud, long cry of sadness or pain ▪ The child started *wailing* after she stumbled and fell.

2 [*no obj*] **:** to make a long, high sound ▪ A saxophone *wailed* in the background. ▪ We could hear a siren *wailing*. = We could hear the *wailing* of a siren.

3 [+ *obj*] **:** to complain in a loud voice ▪ "No! I don't want to go!" he *wailed*. ▪ She *wailed* that the vacation was ruined.

²wail *noun, pl* **wails** [*count*]

1 : a long cry of sadness or pain ▪ a *wail* of sadness/despair

2 : a long, high sound ▪ the *wail* of a siren

wain·scot·ing /ˈweɪnˌskɑːtɪŋ/ *noun* [*noncount*]

1 *US* **:** wooden panels that cover the lower part of the walls of a room

2 *Brit, old-fashioned* **:** BASEBOARD

waist /ˈweɪst/ *noun, pl* **waists** [*count*]

1 : the middle part of your body between the hips and chest or upper back that is usually narrower than the areas above and below it ▪ He has a narrow *waist* and broad shoulders. ▪ He put his arm around her *waist*. ▪ They lay in the sun naked ***from the waist up*** = They lay in the sun ***stripped to the waist*** ▪ paralyzed ***from the waist down*** = paralyzed ***below the waist*** — see picture at HUMAN

2 : the part of a piece of clothing that fits around your waist ▪ These pants have an elastic *waist*. ▪ The waist of this *skirt* is too tight.

– waist·ed /ˈweɪstəd/ *adj* — usually used in combination ▪ high-*waisted* pants [=pants that have a high waist]

waist·band /ˈweɪstˌbænd/ *noun, pl* **-bands** [*count*] **:** the strip of fabric at the top of a piece of clothing that fits around your waist ▪ shorts with an elastic *waistband* — see color picture on page C13

W

waist·coat /ˈwɛskət/ *noun, pl* **-coats** [*count*] *chiefly Brit* **:** VEST

waist–high *adj* **:** reaching as high as your waist ▪ The corn is *waist-high* at this stage of growth.

waist·line /ˈweɪstˌlaɪn/ *noun, pl* **-lines** [*count*]

1 : the distance around the narrowest part of your waist ▪ The diet claims it will reduce your *waistline* in just four weeks. ▪ I'm watching my *waistline*. [=I'm trying not to eat too much so that I don't gain weight]

2 : the part of a piece of clothing that covers your waist ▪ The dress has a small *waistline* and a full skirt.

¹wait /ˈweɪt/ *verb* **waits; wait·ed; wait·ing**

1 [*no obj*] **:** to stay in a place until an expected event happens, until someone arrives, until it is your turn to do something, etc. ▪ I hate *waiting* in long lines. ▪ They *waited* at the train station together. ▪ You should have *waited* a little longer. He showed up right after you left. ▪ I don't have time to ***wait around*** If he's not here in five minutes, I'm leaving. ▪ She ***waited behind*** after class to talk to the professor. ▪ I'm sorry to have ***kept you waiting*** How may I help you? ▪ I ***waited and waited*** but he never showed up. — often followed by *to + verb* ▪ I'm *waiting to use* the bathroom. ▪ The taxi is *waiting to bring* us to the airport. ▪ Doctors are ***ready and waiting*** *to give* aid. — often + ***for*** ▪ She read the newspaper while *waiting for* the bus. ▪ *Wait for* me! I'll go with you. ▪ Take a seat and *wait for* your name to be called. ▪ It can take over an hour to be served at the restaurant, but the food is ***worth waiting for***.

2 : to not do something until something else happens [*no obj*] *Wait!* Don't start the engine yet. ▪ We *waited* for the sun to set before starting the fire. — often + ***until*** ▪ We'll *wait until* you come back to start the movie. [=we will not start the movie until you come back] [+ *obj*] You will have to ***wait your turn*** [=you cannot do something until it is your turn]

3 [*no obj*] **a :** to remain in a state in which you expect or hope that something will happen soon ▪ I know she was happy when I lost my job. She was *waiting* to see me fail. ▪ I have *waited* for this opportunity for a long time. **b :** to remain in a state in which you expect to learn or find out something soon ▪ You will have to *wait* two weeks for the test results. ▪ She *waited* for his answer. ▪ We are *waiting* to hear back from the doctor. ▪ He'll be a star some day—***just (you) wait*** [=I feel sure that he will be a star some day] ▪ I have to ***wait and see*** whether or not I got the job. ▪ "What are you making?" "*Wait and see*."

4 [*no obj*] **:** to be done or dealt with at a later time ▪ The other issues will just have to *wait* until our next meeting. ▪ "Can this *wait* until tomorrow?" "No, it can't *wait*."

5 [*no obj*] **:** to be in a place ready to be dealt with, taken, etc. — always used as *(be) waiting* ▪ It's time to come inside. Dinner *is waiting*. — often + ***for*** ▪ There *is* a package *waiting for* you at home. ▪ She had several messages *waiting for* her at the office.

accident waiting to happen see ACCIDENT

can't wait or can hardly wait ✧ If you *can't wait* or *can hardly wait*, you are very excited about doing something or eager for something to happen or begin. ▪ The concert is tomorrow, and we *can hardly wait!* ▪ The children *can hardly wait* for summer. ▪ I *can't wait* to try your apple pie.

hurry up and wait see ¹HURRY

wait a minute/moment/second **1** — used to tell someone to stop and wait briefly ▪ *Wait a minute*. I need to tie my shoe. ▪ Please *wait one moment* while I take this call. ▪ If you would just *wait a second*, I could explain what happened. **2** — used to interrupt someone or something because you have noticed, thought of, or remembered something ▪ *Wait a second*—that's not what she said. ▪ *Wait a minute*. I just remembered where I put the keys.

wait at table *Brit, formal* **:** to serve food or drinks as a waiter or waitress ▪ He *waited at table* for two years.

wait for it *chiefly Brit, informal* — used to emphasize that the following statement is foolish, surprising, funny, etc. ▪ He says he was fired because—*wait for it*—he refused to compromise his principles.

wait in [*phrasal verb*] *Brit* **:** to stay at home and wait for someone or something to arrive ▪ I can't go out. I've got to *wait in* for a delivery.

wait on *also* ***wait upon*** [*phrasal verb*] **1** ***wait on/upon (someone)*** **a :** to serve food or drinks as a waiter or waitress to (someone) ▪ The hostess *waits on* tables/people when the restaurant is crowded. **b :** to provide service to (a customer) **:** to help (a customer) make purchases ▪ He is busy *waiting on* customers at the moment. **c :** to act as a servant to (someone) ▪ He seems to expect his wife to *wait on* him. ▪ She ***waited on*** her children ***hand and foot*** [=she acted like a servant to her children; she provided her children with everything they needed or wanted] **2** ***wait on/upon (someone or something)*** *chiefly US* **:** to wait for (someone or something) to arrive or happen ▪ We *waited on* him, but he never came. ▪ The government's decision must *wait on* the committee's report. [=the government's decision will not be made until the committee has issued its report]

wait out [*phrasal verb*] **wait (something) out** *or* **wait out (something)** : to stay in one place until the end of (something) ▪ We *waited out* the storm in our hotel room.

wait tables *US* : to serve food or drinks as a waiter or waitress ▪ She has a job *waiting tables.*

wait until/till — used to emphasize that a future event is going to be very surprising, important, etc. ▪ *Wait till* you see their new house. It's just beautiful! ▪ You think you're in trouble now? **Just wait until** your father finds out what you did, young lady! [=your father will be very angry and will punish you when he finds out what you did]

wait up [*phrasal verb*] **1** : to delay going to bed while you wait for someone to arrive ▪ I'll be late; don't *wait up* (for me). **2** *chiefly US, informal* : to stop moving forward so that someone who is behind you can join you ▪ Hey, *wait up* (for me)! I'm going with you.

what are you waiting for? — used to say that someone should do something immediately ▪ *What are we waiting for?* Let's go inside and get something to eat. ▪ If you have so much work to do, then *what are you waiting for?*

²wait *noun, pl* **waits** [*count*] : a period of time when you must wait — usually singular ▪ There is never a *wait* at that restaurant. ▪ He had a long *wait* in line. ▪ The hostess said there would be a 45-minute *wait* before she could seat us. ▪ The dish takes a long time to prepare, but the results are **worth the wait.**

lie in wait : to hide and wait for the right moment to make an attack ▪ The killer may have been *lying in wait* for him. — sometimes used figuratively ▪ No one knows what *lies in wait for* us in the coming year. [=no one knows what will happen to us in the coming year]

wait·er /ˈweɪtɚ/ *noun, pl* **-ers** [*count*] : a man who serves food or drinks to people in a restaurant — see also DUMBWAITER, HEADWAITER

wait·ing game /ˈweɪtɪŋ-/ *noun* [*singular*] : a situation in which you wait to see what happens before you decide what to do ▪ Until they make their decision, we're just playing a *waiting game.*

waiting list *noun, pl* ~ **lists** [*count*] : a list that contains the names of people who are waiting for something ▪ The country club has a two-year *waiting list* to become a member. [=people have to wait two years before they can become a member] ▪ I'll put your name on the *waiting list.*

waiting room *noun, pl* ~ **rooms** [*count*] : a room in a hospital, doctor's office, train station, etc., where people can sit down and wait

wait·ress /ˈweɪtrəs/ *noun, pl* **-ress·es** [*count*] : a woman who serves food or drinks to people in a restaurant

– **waitress** *verb* **-resses; -ressed; -ress·ing** [*no obj*] ▪ She *waitressed* while going to college.

wait·staff /ˈweɪtˌstæf, *Brit* ˈweɪtˌstɑːf/ *noun, pl* **-staffs** [*count*] *US* : the group of waiters and waitresses who work at a restaurant ▪ a friendly *waitstaff* — often used with a plural verb ▪ The *waitstaff* were very helpful.

waive /ˈweɪv/ *verb* **waives; waived; waiv·ing** [+ *obj*] : to officially say that you will not use or require something that you are allowed to have or that is usually required ▪ She *waived* her right to a lawyer. ▪ The university *waives* the application fee for low-income students.

waiv·er /ˈweɪvɚ/ *noun, pl* **-ers** [*count*]

1 : the act of choosing not to use or require something that you are allowed to have or that is usually required ▪ a criminal defendant's *waiver* of a jury trial

2 : an official document indicating that someone has given up or waived a right or requirement ▪ The college got a special *waiver* from the town to exceed the building height limit. ▪ He signed an insurance *waiver* before surgery.

on waivers *baseball* — used to describe a process by which a player is removed from a team and is made available to be chosen by other teams ▪ He was placed *on waivers.*

¹wake /ˈweɪk/ *verb* **wakes; woke** /ˈwoʊk/ *also* **waked** /ˈweɪkt/; **wo·ken** /ˈwoʊkən/ *or* **waked** *also* **woke; wak·ing**

1 [+ *obj*] : to cause (a person or animal) to be awake after sleeping ▪ The sound of children shouting *woke* [=*awakened, wakened*] me. — often + *up* ▪ Don't hesitate to *wake* me *up* if you need anything at all.

2 [*no obj*] : to stop sleeping : to become awake after sleeping ▪ She can never remember her dreams upon *waking.* — usually + *up* ▪ I *woke up* late for work this morning. ▪ He had *woken up* with a headache.

wake up [*phrasal verb*] **1** : to become fully awake and energetic ▪ It takes a couple cups of coffee for me to really *wake up* in the morning. **2 wake up** *or* **wake (someone) up** : to become aware or to cause (someone) to become aware of something ▪ He finally started to *wake up* and take care of his health. — often + *to* ▪ Tourists are only now *waking up to* the fact [=are only now starting to realize] that this is a great place to visit. ▪ The study *woke* us *up to* the importance of regular exercise. [=made us realize the importance of regular exercise]

wake up and smell the coffee *also* **wake up and smell the roses** *US, informal* : to realize the truth about your situation : to become aware of what is really happening ▪ These problems are not going to fix themselves. Voters need to *wake up and smell the coffee* and elect someone who will get things done.

²wake *noun, pl* **wakes** [*count*] : a time before a dead person is buried when people gather to remember the person who has died and often to view the body — compare ³WAKE

³wake *noun, pl* **wakes** [*count*] : the track left by a boat moving through the water

in someone's or something's wake — used to say what is left behind by someone or something ▪ The dog climbed out of the pool, leaving a trail of water *in her wake.* ▪ He went from job to job, leaving a trail of broken promises *in his wake.*

in the wake of — used to say what happens after and often as a result of something ▪ Safety regulations were improved *in the wake of* the oil spill.

– compare ²WAKE

wake·ful /ˈweɪkfəl/ *adj* : not sleeping or not able to sleep ▪ an unusually *wakeful* baby ▪ *wakeful* [=*sleepless*] nights

– **wake·ful·ness** *noun* [*noncount*]

wak·en /ˈweɪkən/ *verb* **-ens; -ened; -en·ing** *formal* : to stop sleeping or to cause (someone) to stop sleeping [+ *obj*] She was *wakened* [=*woken, awoken*] by the telephone. [*no obj*] He *wakens* at sunrise.

wake–up call *noun, pl* ~ **calls** [*count*]

1 : a telephone call that a hotel makes to your room to wake you up

2 : something that makes you fully understand a problem, danger, or need ▪ His diagnosis of cancer was a *wake-up call* to all of us about the dangers of smoking.

waking *adj, always used before a noun, of time* : passing while you are awake and able to think and act ▪ I spent every **waking hour/moment** [=every hour/moment when I was awake] thinking about how to fix the problem.

¹walk /ˈwɑːk/ *verb* **walks; walked; walk·ing**

1 a [*no obj*] : to move with your legs at a speed that is slower than running ▪ Is your grandson *walking* yet? ▪ It's a lovely day—let's *walk* (instead of driving). ▪ He *walks* home from school every day. ▪ It's not far; you can *walk* there in five minutes. ▪ It was a while after the accident before she could *walk* again. ▪ He *walked* away without saying goodbye! ▪ She turned and *walked* away from him. ▪ The driver *walked* away from the accident unharmed. ▪ They *walk* around the neighborhood every morning for exercise. ▪ We *walked* around the city all day seeing the sights. ▪ He *walked* to the store. ▪ He *walked* with her to the library. ▪ We had to *walk* up five flights of stairs to his apartment. ▪ She *walked* up to the counter and ordered a coffee. ▪ You don't have to knock. Just *walk* right in. ▪ Her father *walked* in when they were kissing. = They were kissing when in *walked* her father. ▪ He *walked* into the room. [=he entered the room by walking] ▪ She wasn't paying attention and *walked* into the sign. [=she accidentally hit the sign while walking past it] ▪ We like to **go walking** [=go for walks; take walks] in the morning. — often used figuratively ▪ We can't let these big corporations just *walk* in and take over the town! — see also SLEEPWALK **b** [+ *obj*] : to go with (someone) to a place by walking : to walk with (someone) ▪ She *walks* her children home from school. ▪ The nurse *walked* the patient to the bathroom. ▪ I'll *walk* you to your car. **c** [+ *obj*] : to cause (an animal) to go for a walk with you : to take (an animal) for a walk ▪ He *walks* the dog at least three times a day. ▪ She *walked* the horse to the stable. **d** [+ *obj*] : to cause (something) to move with you while walking ▪ She *walked* her bike up the hill.

2 [+ *obj*] : to move (something) in a way that is like walking ▪ They *walked* the heavy bookcase over to the wall by moving

one end at a time. ▪ He *walked* his fingers along the baby's belly.

3 [+ *obj*] : to pass over, through, or along (something) by walking ▪ We *walked* four miles. ▪ We *walked* the whole trail. ▪ It is no longer safe to *walk* the streets at night. ▪ She slowly *walked* the tightrope. ▪ police officers ***walking the beat***

4 *baseball* **a** [*no obj*] *of a batter* : to get to first base by not swinging at four pitches that are balls ▪ She *walked* her first time at bat. **b** [+ *obj*] *of a pitcher* : to cause (a batter) to go to first base by throwing four pitches that are balls ▪ He *walked* the first two batters.

5 [*no obj*] : to be allowed to go free without being punished for a crime ▪ He *walked* on a technicality. ▪ Although there was evidence against her, she ***walked free*** because of an illegal search by the police.

walk away [*phrasal verb*] **1** : to decide not to do or be involved in something ▪ If you don't like the deal, you can just *walk away*. — often + *from* ▪ He *walked away from* a chance to play professional baseball to join the Peace Corps. ▪ You can't just *walk away from* your responsibilities! ▪ She is not one to *walk away from* a challenge. **2** ***walk away with (something)*** *informal* : to win (something) especially in a easy way ▪ She *walked away with* the election. ▪ He *walked away with* first place. ▪ She had the winning ticket and *walked away with* $50,000!

walk before you (can) run : to learn the basics before trying to do something more advanced ▪ Don't get ahead of yourself. You have to *walk before you can run*.

walk down the aisle see AISLE

walking on air see [1]AIR

walk in on [*phrasal verb*] ***walk in on (someone)*** : to enter a room and interrupt (someone or something) ▪ He *walked in on* me when I was getting dressed. ▪ She *walked in on* the meeting.

walk into [*phrasal verb*] ***walk into (something)*** **1** : to become involved in or fooled by (something) because you are not aware of what is really happening ▪ He *walked* right *into* our trap. ▪ "I can't believe you fell for that old joke!" "Yeah, I guess I ***walked right into that one***." **2** *chiefly Brit* : to get (a job) very easily ▪ After college, she *walked* straight *into* a job.

walk it *informal* **1** : to go to a place by walking ▪ "Should we take the car?" "It's not that far. Let's just *walk it*." **2** *Brit* : to do something successfully and easily ▪ It's an easy exam. You'll *walk it*.

walk off [*phrasal verb*] **1** : to leave somewhere suddenly especially as a way of showing disapproval ▪ She slapped him in the face and *walked off*. **2** ***walk off (something)*** *or* ***walk (something) off*** : to get rid of (something) by walking ▪ He *walked off* a cramp in his leg. ▪ That was a pretty big dinner. Let's *walk* some of it *off* in the park. **3** ***walk off with (something)*** *informal* **a** : to steal (something) ▪ He *walked off with* $500,000 worth of jewelry. **b** : to win (something) especially in an easy or impressive way ▪ They *walked off with* the state championship.

walk off the/your job *chiefly US, informal* : to stop working and go on strike ▪ Teachers *walked off the job* today.

walk on eggshells *or US* ***walk on eggs*** *informal* : to be very careful about what you say or do ▪ She is very touchy, so you have to *walk on eggshells* around her.

walk out [*phrasal verb*] **1 a** : to leave somewhere suddenly especially as a way of showing disapproval ▪ His racist remark caused many people in the audience to *walk out*. — often + *of* ▪ A whole group of angry parents *walked out of* the meeting. **b** : to go on strike ▪ The workers *walked out* over a wage dispute. **2** *informal* **a** ***walk out on (someone)*** : to leave (someone) suddenly and unexpectedly : to abandon or desert (someone) ▪ He *walked out on* his wife and children. **b** ***walk out on (something)*** : to leave before the completion of (something) ▪ The director has reportedly *walked out on* the movie.

walk over [*phrasal verb*] ***walk (all) over (someone)*** *informal* : to not consider the wishes or feelings of (someone) : to treat (someone) very badly ▪ Don't let people *walk all over* you! Stand up for yourself! ▪ They thought they could just *walk* right *over* us.

walk tall : to walk or behave in a way that shows you feel proud and confident ▪ After that winning performance, she can once again *walk tall*.

walk the plank : to be forced to walk along a board sticking out over the side of a ship and fall into the sea ▪ The traitor was forced to *walk the plank*.

walk the streets : to be a prostitute who finds customers by walking around in the streets ▪ young runaways forced to *walk the streets* — see also STREETWALKER

walk the walk *informal* : to do the things that you say you will do ▪ Don't talk the talk unless you can *walk the walk*! [=don't say that you can do something unless you can actually do it]

walk through [*phrasal verb*] **1** ***walk through (something)*** : to do (something) slowly or without much effort ▪ We *walked through* the whole dance routine once, then practiced each section. ▪ It's a shame to see such a talented actress just *walking through* her part. **2** ***walk (someone) through (something)*** : to help (someone) do (something) by going through its steps slowly ▪ He *walked* me *through* installing the software. — see also WALK-THROUGH

[2]**walk** *noun, pl* **walks**

1 [*count*] : an act of walking : an act of going somewhere by walking — usually singular ▪ It is a short/long *walk* to the restaurant. ▪ It is about a five-minute *walk* (from here). ▪ a quarter mile *walk* ▪ She finished her run and slowed to a *walk* to cool down. ▪ It's a nice day to ***go for a walk***. ▪ We ***took a walk*** along the beach. = (*Brit*) We ***had a walk*** along the beach. ▪ He ***took the dog for a walk***. — see also POWER WALK, SPACE WALK

2 [*count*] : a place or path for walking ▪ The cliff *walk* along the ocean is very popular. ▪ Many exotic plants can be found along the *walk*. ▪ (*US*) She raked the yard and swept off the front *walk*. [=*walkway*] — see picture at HOUSE; see also BOARDWALK, SIDEWALK

3 [*count*] *baseball* : BASE ON BALLS

4 [*count*] : an organized event in which people walk to raise money for a particular cause or group — often + *for* ▪ She is participating in the *walk for* breast cancer research.

5 [*count*] : a particular way of walking — usually singular ▪ His *walk* is just like his father's.

6 [*singular*] : a slow speed ▪ A shortage of raw materials slowed production to a *walk*.

all walks of life *or* ***every walk of life*** — used to refer to people who have many different jobs or positions in society; usually used with *from* ▪ People *from all walks of life* came to the carnival. ▪ Thousands of worshippers *from every walk of life* joined together in prayer. — sometimes used with *of* or *in* in U.S. English ▪ Children *of every walk of life* attend this school. ▪ people *in all walks of life*

cock of the walk see [1]COCK

walk in the park *US, informal* : something that is pleasant or easy ▪ Being a firefighter is no *walk in the park*. ▪ The test should be a *walk in the park* for her.

walk·able /ˈwɑːkəbəl/ *adj* : suitable for walking ▪ a very *walkable* city [=a city where you can easily walk to different places] ▪ The beach is within a *walkable* distance. [=is close enough so that you can walk there]

walk·about /ˈwɑːkəˌbaʊt/ *noun, pl* **-abouts** [*count*]

1 : an occasion in which an Australian Aborigine goes on a long walking journey on land that is far from towns and cities

2 *Brit* : an occasion in which a well-known person walks through a public place to meet and talk informally to people ▪ Many people gathered to meet the Queen during her *walkabout*.

go walkabout **1** : to go on a walkabout ▪ an Aborigine who has *gone walkabout* **2** *Brit, informal + humorous* — used to say that something or someone cannot be found ▪ My keys have *gone walkabout*. [=*gone missing*; I can't find my keys]

walk·a·thon /ˈwɑːkəˌθɑːn/ *noun, pl* **-thons** [*count*] *chiefly US* : an organized event in which people walk to raise money for a particular cause or group

walk·er /ˈwɑːkɚ/ *noun, pl* **-ers** [*count*]

1 a : someone who walks especially for exercise ▪ She joined a group of *walkers* in the neighborhood. **b** : someone who walks in a specified way ▪ He is a fast/slow *walker*. [=he walks at a fast/slow pace]

2 : a frame that is designed to support someone (such as a baby or an injured or elderly person) who needs help walking

walk·ies /ˈwɑːkiz/ *noun* [*noncount*] *Brit, informal* : the act of taking a dog for a walk ▪ It's time to ***go (for) walkies***!

walk·ie–talk·ie /ˌwɑːkiˈtɑːki/ *noun, pl* **-ies** [*count*] : a small radio for receiving and sending messages

[1]**walk–in** /ˈwɑːkˌɪn/ *adj, always used before a noun*

1 : large enough to be walked into ▪ a *walk-in* closet

2 a *of a place* : able to be visited without an appointment ▪ a *walk-in* clinic • a *walk-in* medical center **b** *of a person* : visiting a place without an appointment • *walk-in* customers/clients/patients

[2]walk–in *noun, pl* **-ins** [*count*] : a person who visits a place without an appointment • We get a lot of *walk-ins* at the clinic.

[1]walk·ing /ˈwɑːkɪŋ/ *noun* [*noncount*] : the activity of walking for exercise • *Walking* is good exercise. • She ***goes walking*** every day in the park.

[2]walking *adj, always used before a noun*
1 : suitable for walking • a good pair of *walking* shoes • They were going at a *walking* pace.
2 : capable of being easily walked • The store is ***within walking distance***. [=is close enough so that you can walk there]
3 *humorous* : in human form • He is a *walking* encyclopedia/dictionary. [=he knows so much that he's like a human encyclopedia/dictionary] • She is a *walking* disaster.
4 : done by walking : consisting of walking • a *walking* tour of the Lake District
5 : able to walk • the *walking* wounded [=wounded people who are able to walk]

walking papers *noun* [*plural*] *US, informal* — used to say that someone has been ordered to leave a place, job, etc. • His boss gave him his *walking papers*. [=(*Brit*) *marching orders*; his boss fired him]

walking stick *noun, pl* **~ sticks** [*count*]
1 : a stick that is used to help someone to walk
2 *US* : STICK INSECT

Walk·man /ˈwɑːkmən, ˈwɑːkˌmæn/ *trademark* — used for a small, portable audio player listened to by using headphones or earphones

walk–on /ˈwɑːkˌɑːn/ *noun, pl* **-ons** [*count*]
1 : a minor part in a play or movie • a *walk-on* part/role
2 *US* : a college athlete who tries to become a member of an athletic team without having been asked to join or given a scholarship

walk·out /ˈwɑːkˌaʊt/ *noun, pl* **-outs** [*count*]
1 : a strike by workers • Hundreds of workers staged a *walkout* to protest conditions in the factory.
2 : the act of leaving a meeting or organization as a way of showing disapproval — see also *walk out* at [1]WALK

walk·over /ˈwɑːkˌoʊvɚ/ *noun, pl* **-overs** [*count*] : an easy victory • She won the tournament in a *walkover*. [=she won very easily] • a *walkover* victory

walk–through /ˈwɑːkˌθruː/ *noun, pl* **-throughs** [*count*]
1 : an activity in which someone walks through an area, building, etc., in order to inspect it • We did a *walk-through* of the property.
2 a : the act of going slowly through the steps of a process, job, etc., in order to practice doing it or to help someone learn it • They gave us a *walk-through* of the new system. — see also *walk through* at [1]WALK **b :** an explanation or guide that tells you how to do something by explaining each of its parts or steps • video game *walk-throughs*

walk–up /ˈwɑːkˌʌp/ *noun, pl* **-ups** [*count*] *US* : a tall apartment or office building that does not have an elevator • Their offices are in the same *walk-up*.; *also* : an apartment or office in such a building • He rents a fifth-floor *walk-up*. • a *walk-up* apartment

walk·way /ˈwɑːkˌweɪ/ *noun, pl* **-ways** [*count*] : a passage or path for walking • a brick/wooden/concrete *walkway* • A covered *walkway* connects the two buildings.

[1]wall /ˈwɑːl/ *noun, pl* **walls** [*count*]
1 : a structure of brick, stone, etc., that surrounds an area or separates one area from another • A stone *wall* marks off their property. • the Great *Wall* of China • the *walls* of the ancient city — often used figuratively • The wave was like a *wall* of water. • The police formed a human *wall* around him. • His suggestion was met with a *wall* of silence. [=was met with complete silence] • a *wall* of sound • He built an emotional *wall* [=*barrier*] around himself. — see also CLIMBING WALL, FIRE WALL, RETAINING WALL, SEAWALL
2 : the structure that forms the side of a room or building • She hung posters on the *walls* of her room. • This apartment building has thin *walls*, and you can hear everything your neighbors say. • A lot has happened inside ***these four walls***. [=inside this room] • Lower your voice and be careful what you say. The ***walls have ears***. [=other people could be listening to what you say]
3 : the outer layer of something that is hollow (such as a part of the body or of a plant) • plant cell *walls* • Muscles in the abdominal *wall* help protect organs.

back is to/against the wall see [1]BACK
climbing the walls see [1]CLIMB
drive (someone) up a/the wall *informal* : to make (someone) irritated, angry, or crazy • Your constant tapping is *driving me up the wall*! • Her voice *drives me up a wall*. [=her voice is very annoying to me]
fly on the wall see [3]FLY
go to the wall *informal* **1** *US* : to make every possible effort to achieve something, to win, etc. • He's prepared to *go to the wall* to defend his beliefs. **2** *Brit* : to fail because of a lack of money • a company that has *gone to the wall*
hit a/the wall *informal* : to reach a point at which you find it very difficult or impossible to continue • He worked late every day and took frequent business trips for several years before he finally *hit the wall*. • They seem to have *hit the wall* in terms of new ideas. • Her tennis career *hit a wall* after the injury.
the writing/handwriting is on the wall *or* ***see/read the writing/handwriting on the wall*** — used to say that it is clear that something bad will probably happen soon • I haven't lost my job yet, but *the writing is on the wall*: my company just laid off 50 more people today. • No one told him he was going to be fired, but he could *see the writing on the wall*.
up against a/the wall *informal* : in a very bad position or situation • The team was *up against a wall* in the first half of the game.

[2]wall *verb* **walls; walled; wall·ing**
wall in [*phrasal verb*] ***wall (something) in*** *or* ***wall in (something)*** : to surround (something) with a wall or with something that is like a wall • The school grounds are *walled in*. • They *walled* the garden *in* with rows of thick shrubs.
wall off [*phrasal verb*] ***wall (something) off*** *or* ***wall off (something)*** : to separate (something) from the area around it with a wall • The school *walled off* the playground from the parking lot.
wall up [*phrasal verb*] **1** ***wall (something) up*** *or* ***wall up (something)*** : to close off (an opening) by filling it with stone, brick, etc. • They *walled up* the doorway of the abandoned house. **2** ***wall (someone) up*** *or* ***wall up (someone)*** : to keep (someone) as a prisoner in an enclosed space • He was *walled up* in the tower. [=was locked inside the tower]

wal·la·by /ˈwɑːləbi/ *noun, pl* **wal·la·bies** *also* **wallaby** [*count*] : an Australian animal that is like a small kangaroo

wall·board /ˈwɑːlˌboɚd/ *noun* [*noncount*] *US* : building material that is used for making walls and ceilings and that is made of large sheets of plaster covered with thick paper : DRYWALL

walled /ˈwɑːld/ *adj, always used before a noun* : surrounded by a wall • a *walled* city/garden

wal·let /ˈwɑːlət/ *noun, pl* **-lets** [*count*] : a small folding case that holds paper money, credit cards, etc. • She paid the bill and tucked her *wallet* back into her pocket/purse. • He pulled a few bills out of his *wallet*. — often used figuratively • High fuel prices are draining our *wallets*. [=we are spending a lot of money on high fuel prices] • The charity is asking people to open their *wallets* and make a donation. • Consumers are watching their *wallets*. [=are not spending a lot of money]

wallet

vote with your wallet see [1]VOTE

wall·eye /ˈwɑːlˌaɪ/ *noun, pl* **-eyes** [*count*] : a large North American fish that lives in fresh water and that has large eyes — called also *wall-eyed pike* /ˈwɑːlˌaɪd-/

wall·flow·er /ˈwɑːlˌflawɚ/ *noun, pl* **-ers** [*count*]
1 *informal* : a person who is shy or unpopular and who stands or sits apart from other people at a dance or party
2 : a garden plant grown for its bright, pleasant-smelling flowers

wall–mounted *adj* : attached to a wall • a *wall-mounted* television set

wal·lop /ˈwɑːləp/ *verb* **-lops; -loped; -lop·ing** [+ *obj*] *informal* : to hit (someone or something) very hard • She *walloped* the ball. • I was so angry I felt like *walloping* him. — often used figuratively • The city got *walloped* by a major blizzard. • He got *walloped* in the finals. [=he was easily defeated in the finals]

– wallop *noun* [*singular*] • She gave the ball a *wallop*. • He

took a *wallop* to his head. — sometimes used figuratively ▪ The comedy packs an unexpected emotional *wallop*.

wal·low /ˈwɑːloʊ/ *verb* **-lows; -lowed; -low·ing** [*no obj*]
1 : to spend time experiencing or enjoying something without making any effort to change your situation, feelings, etc. — usually + *in* ▪ *wallowing in* luxury ▪ (*disapproving*) I know she's hurt, but she should try to get on with her life instead of just *wallowing in* her misery/self-pity.
2 : to roll about in deep mud or water ▪ elephants *wallowing* in the river ▪ Buffalo *wallow* in mud to keep away flies.

wall painting *noun, pl* **~-ings** [*count*] **:** a painting done directly on a wall **:** MURAL

[1]**wall·pa·per** /ˈwɑːlˌpeɪpɚ/ *noun, pl* **-pers :** thick decorative paper used to cover the walls of a room [*noncount*] They hung *wallpaper* in the bedroom. = They put up *wallpaper* in the bedroom. ▪ The *wallpaper* began to peel. [*count*] flowery *wallpapers*

[2]**wallpaper** *verb* **-pers; -pered; -per·ing** [+ *obj*] **:** to put wallpaper on the walls of (a room) ▪ He *wallpapered* [=*papered*] the dining room.

Wall Street /ˈwɑːl-/ *noun* [*noncount*] **:** a street in New York City where the New York Stock Exchange and many major financial businesses are located ▪ Stocks rose on *Wall Street* today. [=stocks rose in the New York Stock Exchange] ▪ traders on *Wall Street* = *Wall Street* traders ▪ After college she got a job on *Wall Street*. — used to refer to the powerful people and businesses of Wall Street that play an important role in the U.S. economy ▪ The company's bankruptcy was extremely troubling to *Wall Street*.

wall–to–wall *adj*
1 : covering the entire floor of a room ▪ *wall-to-wall* carpeting
2 *informal* **:** filling an entire space or time **:** occurring or found everywhere or constantly ▪ The beach was *wall-to-wall* (with) sunbathers. [=there were sunbathers lying everywhere on the beach] ▪ Our schedule is *wall-to-wall* weddings from June through August. [=we're going to a lot of weddings from June through August]

wal·ly /ˈwɑːli/ *noun, pl* **-lies** [*count*] *Brit, informal* **:** a stupid or foolish person

wal·nut /ˈwɑːlˌnʌt/ *noun, pl* **-nuts**
1 [*count*] **:** a type of tree that produces large nuts which can be eaten — called also *walnut tree*
2 [*count*] **:** the nut of a walnut tree ▪ The banana bread has *walnuts* in it. ▪ The recipe calls for a cup of chopped *walnuts*. — see picture at NUT
3 [*noncount*] **:** the wood of a walnut tree ▪ a table made of *walnut* ▪ *walnut* cabinets

wal·rus /ˈwɑːlrəs/ *noun, pl* **walrus** *or* **wal·rus·es** [*count*] **:** a large animal that lives on land and in the sea in northern regions and that has flippers and long tusks

walrus

[1]**waltz** /ˈwɑːlts/ *noun, pl* **waltz·es** [*count*] **:** a dance in which a couple moves in a regular series of three steps ▪ They danced a *waltz* together.; *also* **:** the music used for this dance ▪ Johann Strauss wrote many beautiful *waltzes*.

[2]**waltz** *verb* **waltzes; waltzed; waltz·ing**
1 : to dance a waltz [*no obj*] He *waltzed* with his daughter at her wedding. [+ *obj*] He *waltzed* her around the dance floor.
2 *always followed by an adverb or preposition* [*no obj*] **:** to move or walk in a lively and confident manner ▪ He came *waltzing* into the room. ▪ She *waltzed* right up to him and introduced herself.
3 *always followed by an adverb or preposition* [*no obj*] **:** to succeed at something easily ▪ He *waltzed* [=*breezed*] through the tournament. ▪ The team *waltzed* to victory. [=the team won easily]
4 *always followed by an adverb or preposition* [+ *obj*] **:** to force (someone) to go ▪ She *waltzed* the child off to his room.
waltz off with [*phrasal verb*] ***waltz off with (something)*** **1** *chiefly US* **:** to take or get (something, such as a prize) easily ▪ The actress *waltzed off with* several awards. **2** *chiefly Brit* **:** to take (something) that belongs to someone else ▪ She *waltzed off with* my keys.

wam·pum /ˈwɑːmpəm/ *noun* [*noncount*] **:** beads, polished shells, etc., used in the past by Native Americans as money and decorations

wan /ˈwɑːn/ *adj*
1 : looking sick or pale ▪ a *wan* complexion
2 : having a weak quality **:** FEEBLE ▪ She gave a *wan* laugh/smile.
— **wan·ly** *adv* ▪ She smiled *wanly*.

wand /ˈwɑːnd/ *noun, pl* **wands** [*count*]
1 : a long, thin stick used by a magician or during magic tricks ▪ a magic *wand*
2 : a long, thin electronic device used to gather or enter information ▪ The cashier used a *wand* to scan the bar code. ▪ a security *wand*

wan·der /ˈwɑːndɚ/ *verb* **-ders; -dered; -der·ing**
1 : to move around or go to different places usually without having a particular purpose or direction [*no obj*] I was just *wandering* around the house. ▪ They *wandered* down the street. ▪ Don't let the children *wander* too far (off). [+ *obj*] Students were *wandering* the halls. ▪ She *wandered* the streets.
2 [*no obj*] **:** to follow a path with many turns ▪ The river *wanders* [=*meanders, winds*] through the valley.
3 [*no obj*] **:** to go away from a path, course, etc. ▪ He *wandered* away from the trail and got lost. — often used figuratively ▪ We are *wandering* from our original plan. ▪ The speech *wandered* off the subject. ▪ The speech was boring and my attention/mind began to *wander*. [=I began to think about other things besides the speech]
— **wander** *noun* [*singular*] *chiefly Brit* ▪ Let's ***have/take a wander***. = Let's ***go for a wander***. [=let's take a walk]
— **wan·der·er** /ˈwɑːndərɚ/ *noun, pl* **-ers** [*count*] ▪ a solitary *wanderer* ▪ restless *wanderers* — **wandering** *adj* ▪ *wandering* sailors ▪ a *wandering* stream/road ✧ If you have a ***wandering eye***, you look at and have sexual thoughts about other people even though you are already in a romantic relationship. ▪ Her husband has a *wandering eye*.
— **wandering** *noun, pl* **-ings** [*count*] ▪ The travel writer describes his *wanderings* in this book.

wan·der·lust /ˈwɑːndɚˌlʌst/ *noun* **:** a strong desire to travel [*singular*] an insatiable *wanderlust* [*noncount*] *Wanderlust* has led him to many different parts of the world.

[1]**wane** /ˈweɪn/ *verb* **wanes; waned; wan·ing** [*no obj*]
1 *of the moon* **:** to appear to become thinner or less full ▪ The moon waxes and then *wanes*.
2 : to become smaller or less **:** to decrease in size, amount, length, or quality ▪ The scandal caused her popularity to *wane*. ▪ Interest in this issue has continued to *wane*. ▪ the *waning* days of summer

[2]**wane** *noun*
on the wane **:** becoming smaller or less ▪ Her popularity was *on the wane*. [=she was becoming less popular]

wan·gle /ˈwæŋgəl/ *verb* **wan·gles; wan·gled; wan·gling** [+ *obj*] *informal* **:** to get (something) by clever methods or by persuading someone ▪ He *wangled* a free ticket to the show. ▪ He managed to *wangle* his way into the party.

wank /ˈwæŋk/ *verb* **wanks; wanked; wank·ing** *Brit slang, offensive* **:** MASTURBATE
— **wank** *noun* [*singular*]

wank·er /ˈwæŋkɚ/ *noun, pl* **-ers** [*count*] *Brit slang, offensive* **:** a stupid, foolish, or unpleasant person

wan·na /ˈwɑːnə/ — used in writing to represent the sound of the phrase *want to* when it is spoken ▪ I don't *wanna* go. ▪ They just *wanna* have fun. ✧ The pronunciation represented by *wanna* is common in informal speech. The written form should be avoided except when trying to represent such speech.

wan·na·be *also* **wan·na·bee** /ˈwɑːnəˌbiː/ *noun, pl* **-bes** *also* **-bees** [*count*] *informal* **:** a person who tries to look or act like someone else (such as a famous person) **:** a person who wants to be a particular person or type of person ▪ an actress *wannabe* ▪ a *wannabe* pop star

[1]**want** /ˈwɑːnt/ *verb* **wants; want·ed; want·ing**
1 [+ *obj*] **:** to desire or wish for (something) ▪ Do you *want* more coffee? ▪ He *wants* a bicycle for his birthday. ▪ I just *wanted* a chance to rest. ▪ She *wanted* more time to finish the test. ▪ Do you *want* anything from the store? ▪ What do you *want* for Christmas? ▪ You can choose whichever color you *want*. — often followed by *to* + *verb* ▪ She *wants to go* to college next year. ▪ I *want to be* alone. ▪ "How old are you?" "Well, if you really *want to know*, I'm 52." ▪ I'm supposed to work late tonight, but I really don't *want to* (*do* it). ▪ You can do whatever you *want to* (*do*). ▪ You can say what you *want* (*to say*) about his personality, but there's no denying that he

is efficient. ▪ I was so angry that I *wanted to scream.* [=that I felt like screaming]

2 [+ *obj*] **a** : to need (something) ▪ Our house *wants* painting. ▪ The motor *wants* a tune-up. **b** [+ *obj*] : to be without (something needed) : LACK ▪ Thousands of poor people still *want* food and shelter. ▪ He's not the most talented player, but he doesn't *want* self-confidence. [=he has a lot of self-confidence]

3 *not used in progressive tenses* [+ *obj*] **a** : to wish or demand to see or talk to (someone) ▪ Tell him that the teacher *wants* him. ▪ The police *want* him for questioning. ▪ You're *wanted* on the phone. [=someone wants to speak to you on the phone] **b** : to desire (someone) *to do* something ▪ Your mother *wants* you *to come* home. ▪ I just *want* him *to be* honest with me. ▪ Do you *want* me *to bring back* your book? — sometimes + *for* in informal U.S. English ▪ I *want for* you *to do* this. = What I *want* is *for* you *to do* this. **c** : to seek (someone) in order to make an arrest ▪ The police *want* him for murder. — usually used as *(be) wanted* ▪ The suspect *was wanted* for murder. ▪ one of the nation's most *wanted* criminals

4 *always followed by an adverb or preposition* [*no obj*] *informal* : to desire to move or be in or out of a place ▪ (*chiefly US*) The cat **wants in/out**. [=the cat wants to go inside/outside] — usually used figuratively ▪ At first she **wanted in on** the deal [=she wanted to be included in the deal], but now she **wants out of** it. [=she does not want to be included] ▪ He desperately **wanted (back) into** the game. [=wanted to get (back) into the game]

5 *not used in progressive tenses* [+ *obj*] *informal* — used to give advice about what someone should do or be; followed by *to* + *verb* ▪ You *want to be* very careful [=you should be very careful] when you pull out of the parking lot. ▪ We might *want to leave* a little early. [=maybe we should leave a little early]

6 *not used in progressive tenses* [+ *obj*] : to feel sexual desire for (someone) ▪ You can tell that he *wants* her.

want for [*phrasal verb*] ***want for (something or someone)*** : to be without (someone or something) : to lack (someone or something) ▪ She certainly will never *want for* friends. [=she will always have friends] — see also [1]WANT 3b (above)

want no part of/in see [1]PART

want nothing to do with see [1]DO

want rid of see RID

[2]**want** *noun, pl* **wants**

1 *formal* : the state or condition of not having any or enough of something : LACK [*singular*] His attitude shows a *want* of proper respect. [*noncount*] He is suffering from *want* of adequate sleep.

2 [*count*] : something that is desired or needed — usually plural ▪ We can supply all your *wants.* ▪ The company caters to the ***wants and needs*** of its customers.

3 [*noncount*] : the state or condition of being poor ▪ people who are living in *want*

for (the) want of : because of not having (something) : because (something) does not exist or is not available ▪ *For want of* a better name [=since we don't have a better name to use], let's call it "Operation One." ▪ People are dying *for want of* medical treatment. [=because they are not getting medical treatment] ▪ The project failed *for the want of* adequate funding.

in want of : in the condition of wanting or needing (something) ▪ The house is *in want of* repairs. [=the house needs to be repaired]

not for want of : not because of not having or doing (something) ▪ Her failure to get the information was *not for want of* trying. [=was not because she did not try]

want ad *noun, pl* ~ **ads** [*count*] *US* : a notice in a newspaper, magazine, etc., that lets people know about something that you want to buy or sell, a job that is available, etc. ▪ She checked the *want ads* to find a new job. — compare [2]CLASSIFIED

want·ing /ˈwɑːntɪŋ/ *adj* : not having all that is needed or expected : LACKING ▪ The plan was *wanting.* [=the plan was not good enough] — often + *in* ▪ They were *wanting in* common sense. [=they did not have much common sense] ▪ He was not *wanting in* confidence. [=he was very confident]

wan·ton /ˈwɑːntn/ *adj* [*more* ~; *most* ~]

1 : showing no thought or care for the rights, feelings, or safety of others ▪ Vandals were guilty of the *wanton* destruction of the school property. ▪ They were accused of *wanton* cruelty toward animals. ▪ He showed a *wanton* disregard for his friend's feelings.

2 : not limited or controlled ▪ a life of *wanton* luxury

3 *old-fashioned, of a woman* : having sex with many men ▪ a *wanton* woman

— **wan·ton·ly** *adv* ▪ They *wantonly* set fire to the cabin. — **wan·ton·ness** /ˈwɑːntnnəs/ *noun* [*noncount*]

wa·pi·ti /ˈwɑːpəti/ *noun, pl* **wapiti** *or* **wa·pi·tis** [*count*] : ELK 1

war /ˈwoə/ *noun, pl* **wars**

1 : a state or period of fighting between countries or groups [*count*] They fought a *war* over the disputed territory. ▪ A *war* broke out when the colonists demanded their independence. ▪ a nuclear *war* [=a war fought using nuclear weapons] [*noncount*] We need to resolve our conflicts without resorting to *war.* ▪ People behave differently during a time of *war.* ▪ *War* could break out soon. [=a war might start soon] ▪ The two countries were ***at war*** (with each other). ▪ The President decided against ***going to war***. [=starting a war with another country] ▪ The taking of American hostages was seen as an ***act of war*** by the United States. — often used before another noun ▪ *war* correspondents/reporters ▪ the *war* years ▪ his *war* service — see also CIVIL WAR, COLD WAR, HOLY WAR, PRISONER OF WAR, WORLD WAR

2 : a situation in which people or groups compete with or fight against each other [*count*] a class *war* ▪ countries conducting trade *wars* ▪ the budget *wars* in Washington [*noncount*] Local politicians were ***at war*** [=*fighting*] with one another over the vacant seat.

3 [*count*] : an organized effort by a government or other large organization to stop or defeat something that is viewed as dangerous or bad ▪ the *war* on/against cancer ▪ the *war* on drugs

all's fair in love and war see [1]FAIR

declare war see DECLARE

this means war — used to show you are offended by what someone has said or done and want to start a fight with that person ▪ He insulted my girlfriend, and as far as I'm concerned, *this means war.* ▪ (*humorous*) Make fun of my car, will you? *This means war*!

war of nerves see NERVE

war of words see [1]WORD

— see also TUG-OF-WAR

war·ble /ˈwoəbəl/ *verb* **war·bles; war·bled; war·bling**

1 [*no obj*] *of a bird* : to sing a song that has many different notes ▪ Birds were *warbling* in the trees.

2 [+ *obj*] *humorous* : to sing (something) especially with a high or shaky voice ▪ *warble* a tune ▪ He *warbled* his way through the song.

— **warble** *noun, pl* **warbles** [*count*] ▪ a canary's *warble*

war·bler /ˈwoəblə/ *noun, pl* **-blers** [*count*] : any one of many different kinds of small singing birds that live in America and Europe

war bride *noun, pl* ~ **brides** [*count*] : a woman who marries a soldier during a war ▪ My grandmother was a *war bride* during World War II.

war chest *noun, pl* ~ **chests** [*count*]

1 : an amount of money that can be used by a government to pay for a war

2 : an amount of money intended for a specific purpose, action, or campaign ▪ The candidate held fund-raising dinners to build up his *war chest.*

war crime *noun, pl* ~ **crimes** [*count*] : an act committed during a war that violates international law usually because it is cruel, unfair, etc. ▪ He was found guilty of torture and other *war crimes.*

— **war criminal** *noun, pl* ~ **-nals** [*count*]

war cry *noun, pl* ~ **cries** [*count*]

1 : a shouted word or sound used by fighters in battle to give each other courage or to frighten their enemy

2 : a phrase or saying that is used to make people support an idea, a cause, etc. : BATTLE CRY

[1]**ward** /ˈwoəd/ *noun, pl* **wards** [*count*]

1 a : a section in a hospital for patients needing a particular kind of care ▪ She works in the cancer/maternity/psychiatric *ward.* **b** *US* : a section in a prison ▪ a maximum security *ward*

2 : one of the sections into which a city or town is divided for the purposes of an election ▪ the council representative from *Ward* 22

3 : a person (such as a child) who is protected and cared for by a court or guardian ▪ They were *wards* of the state. ▪ (*US*) The boy was made a ***ward of the court***. = (*Brit*) The boy was made a ***ward of court***.

[2]**ward** *verb* **wards; ward·ed; ward·ing**
ward off *[phrasal verb]* ***ward (something) off or ward off (something)*** **:** to avoid being hit by (something) ▪ *ward off* a blow — often used figuratively ▪ I tried different remedies to *ward off* a cold.

[1]**-ward** /wɚd/ *also* **-wards** /wɚdz/ *adj suffix*
1 : that moves, tends, faces, or is directed toward ▪ wind*ward*
2 : that occurs or is located in the direction of ▪ left*ward* ▪ a rear*ward* movement of troops

[2]**-ward** *(chiefly US) or* **-wards** *adv suffix* **:** in or toward a (specified) direction ▪ up*ward* ▪ west*ward* ▪ looked sky*ward*

war dance *noun, pl* **~ dances** *[count]* **:** a dance performed in the past by Native Americans before a battle or to celebrate victory in battle

war·den /ˈwoɚdn/ *noun, pl* **-dens** *[count]*
1 : a person who is in charge of or takes care of something ▪ the *warden* of the cemetery ▪ a park/forest *warden* ▪ a ***game warden*** [=a person who makes sure that hunting and fishing laws are obeyed] — see also TRAFFIC WARDEN
2 *US* **:** an official who is in charge of a prison — called also *(Brit) governor*
3 *Brit* **:** any one of various officials at a British college

ward·er /ˈwoɚdɚ/ *noun, pl* **-ers** *[count] Brit* **:** a person who works as a guard in a prison

ward·robe /ˈwoɚˌdroʊb/ *noun, pl* **-robes** *[count]*
1 a : a collection of clothes that a person owns or wears ▪ She has a new summer *wardrobe*. ▪ She has quite an extensive *wardrobe*. [=she has a lot of clothes] **b :** the clothes worn by actors in films, plays, etc.; *also* **:** the department that keeps and takes care of the clothes for films, plays, etc. ▪ She went to *wardrobe* for her fitting.
2 : a room, closet, or chest where clothes are kept ▪ a walk-in *wardrobe*

ward·room /ˈwoɚˌdru:m/ *noun, pl* **-rooms** *[count]* **:** a room in a military ship where officers sleep and eat

ware /ˈweɚ/ *noun, pl* **wares**
1 *[noncount]* **:** things that are made from a particular material or that are designed for a particular use — usually used in combination ▪ cook*ware* ▪ glass*ware* ▪ table*ware*
2 ***wares*** *[plural]* **:** things that are being sold by someone ▪ She sold her *wares* at the market.

ware·house /ˈweɚˌhaʊs/ *noun, pl* **-hous·es** *[count]* **:** a large building used for storing goods

war·fare /ˈwoɚˌfeɚ/ *noun [noncount]*
1 : military fighting in a war ▪ guerrilla *warfare* ▪ nuclear *warfare* — see also BIOLOGICAL WARFARE, CHEMICAL WARFARE, *psychological warfare* at PSYCHOLOGICAL
2 : activity that is done as part of a struggle between competing groups, companies, etc. ▪ industrial *warfare* ▪ gang *warfare* ▪ economic *warfare*

war game *noun, pl* **~ games** *[count]* **:** a military training activity that is done to prepare for fighting in a war — usually plural

war·head /ˈwoɚˌhɛd/ *noun, pl* **-heads** *[count]* **:** the part of a missile that contains the explosive ▪ nuclear *warheads*

war·horse /ˈwoɚˌhoɚs/ *noun, pl* **-hors·es** *[count]*
1 : a person with a lot of experience in a field; *especially* **:** a soldier or politician who has served for a long time ▪ the Democratic *warhorse* in the Senate ▪ a general who describes himself as an old *warhorse*
2 : something (such as a work of art or musical composition) that has become very familiar because it has been played, shown, or seen many times ▪ a new production of an old *warhorse*
3 : a large horse used in war

war·like /ˈwoɚˌlaɪk/ *adj [more ~; most ~]*
1 : liking or tending to fight in wars or to start wars ▪ a *warlike* nation/tribe ▪ *warlike* people
2 : showing or suggesting that a country, group, etc., is ready or eager to fight a war ▪ The government has been criticized for its *warlike* attitude/statements.
3 : of, relating to, or useful in war ▪ *warlike* preparations

war·lock /ˈwoɚˌlɑ:k/ *noun, pl* **-locks** *[count]* **:** a man who has magical powers and practices witchcraft **:** a sorcerer or wizard

war·lord /ˈwoɚˌloɚd/ *noun, pl* **-lords** *[count]* **:** a leader of a military group who is not officially recognized and who fights against other leaders, groups, or governments

[1]**warm** /ˈwoɚm/ *adj* **warm·er; -est**
1 a : somewhat hot **:** not cool or cold ▪ Be sure to keep *warm* when you go outside. ▪ *warm* weather ▪ a *warm* fire/radiator ▪ I'm feeling *warm*. ▪ We sat by the fire to stay *warm*. ▪ It's too *warm* in here. We should open a window. **b :** causing or allowing you to feel warm ▪ This sweater is *warm*. ▪ *warm* clothing ▪ The sunshine was *warm* on my face.
2 : feeling or showing friendship and affection ▪ We were met with a *warm* welcome. ▪ She has a *warm* and friendly nature. ▪ The letter was signed, "*warmest* regards." ▪ She gave us each a long, *warm* hug.
3 : close to finding something, solving a puzzle, etc. ▪ Keep going; you're getting *warm*.
4 a : having a yellow, orange, or red color ▪ a room decorated in *warm* colors/shades **b** *of sound* **:** rich and full **:** not thin or harsh ▪ the *warm* sound of the cello
(as) warm as toast *informal* **:** comfortably or pleasantly warm ▪ The room was cold but I was *as warm as toast* lying under the covers in bed.
– warm·ness /ˈwoɚmnəs/ *noun [noncount]* ▪ the *warmness* of a summer's day ▪ She welcomed us with *warmness*.

[2]**warm** *verb* **warms; warmed; warm·ing :** to become warm or to make (someone or something) warm *[+ obj]* He *warmed* his hands in front of the fire. ▪ We *warmed* ourselves by the fire. ▪ I'm just going to *warm* (up) the leftovers. *[no obj]* Air rises when it *warms*.
like death warmed over/up see DEATH
warm the cockles of your heart see COCKLE
warm to *[phrasal verb]* **1** ***warm to (someone)*** **:** to begin to feel affection for (someone) ▪ She quickly *warmed to* her guests. **2** ***warm to (something)*** **:** to begin to be interested in or excited about (something) ▪ It took them a while to *warm to* the idea.
warm up *[phrasal verb]* **1 :** to become warmer ▪ After being outside too long, I'm slowly *warming up*. ▪ The days are starting to *warm up*. **2** ***warm up or warm (something) up or warm up (something)*** **:** to do exercises in order to prepare for some activity (such as a sport) ▪ You should always *warm up* for a few minutes before you begin to run. ▪ The singer *warmed up* her voice before the concert. — see also WARMUP **3 :** to start to do something that you will do in a more intense way later **:** to become more intense or enthusiastic ▪ He's just *warming up*; he's saving his best material for the end. ▪ The party finally *warmed up* [=*heated up*] after a couple of hours. **4** ***warm (someone) up or warm up (someone)*** **:** to entertain (people) before a show begins ▪ The comedian *warmed up* the audience before the concert. **5 a** *of a machine* **:** to become ready for use after being started or turned on ▪ I always let the car *warm up* for a couple of minutes in the winter before I start driving. **b** ***warm (a machine) up or warm up (a machine)*** **:** to cause or allow (a machine) to become ready for use after being started or turned on ▪ The engine needs to be *warmed up* for a couple of minutes.
warm your heart **:** to cause you to have pleasant feelings of happiness ▪ It *warms my heart* to see them together again.
– warming *noun [noncount]* ▪ The *warming* of air currents affects weather patterns. — see also GLOBAL WARMING

[3]**warm** *noun*
the warm *Brit* **:** a warm place ▪ come into *the warm*

warm–blood·ed /ˈwoɚmˈblʌdəd/ *adj, biology* **:** having blood that always remains warm **:** having a body temperature that does not change when the temperature of the environment changes ▪ *warm-blooded* animals — compare COLD-BLOODED

warmed–over /ˈwoɚmdˈoʊvɚ/ *adj, US*
1 *disapproving* **:** not fresh or new ▪ *warmed-over* ideas
2 : heated again ▪ *warmed-over* stew

warm·er /ˈwoɚmɚ/ *noun, pl* **-ers** *[count]* **:** something (such as a device or piece of clothing) that is used to keep something warm ▪ a bun *warmer* ▪ hand/leg *warmers*

warm front *noun, pl* **~ fronts** *[count]* **:** the front edge of a moving mass of warm air ▪ An approaching *warm front* often means that rain is coming. — compare COLD FRONT

warm fuz·zies /-ˈfʌziz/ *noun [plural] US, informal* **:** feelings of happiness and affection ▪ The movie gave her the *warm fuzzies*.

warm·heart·ed /ˈwoɚmˈhɑɚtəd/ *adj [more ~; most ~]* **:** having or showing kindness, sympathy, and affection ▪ a caring and *warmhearted* person ▪ a *warmhearted* gesture — opposite COLDHEARTED
– warm·heart·ed·ness *noun [noncount]*

warm·ly /ˈwoɚmli/ *adv [more ~; most ~]*
1 : in a very friendly way ▪ They greeted us *warmly*. ▪ The new official was *warmly* applauded/received.

W

2 : in a way that keeps you warm • It's cold out, so be sure to dress *warmly.*

war·mon·ger /ˈwoɚˌmʌŋgɚ, ˈwoɚˌmɑːŋgɚ/ *noun, pl* **-gers** [*count*] *disapproving* : a person who wants a war or tries to make other people want to start or fight a war • the *warmongers* in Congress
– **war·mon·ger·ing** /ˈwoɚˌmʌŋgərɪŋ, ˈwoɚˌmɑːŋgərɪŋ/ *noun* [*noncount*] • The press accused him of *warmongering.*
– **warmongering** *adj, always used before a noun* • a *warmongering* politician

warm spot *noun* [*singular*] *chiefly US* : a strong liking *for* someone or something • She has a *warm spot* [=*soft spot*] in her heart *for* her old classmates.

warmth /ˈwoɚmθ/ *noun* [*noncount*]
1 : the quality or state of being warm in temperature • I could feel the *warmth* of the fireplace. • She wore a sweater for extra *warmth.* [=so she would feel warmer]
2 : the quality or state of being kind or friendly • She enjoyed the *warmth* of their praise. • They possessed a graciousness and *warmth* that put their guests at ease.

warm·up /ˈwoɚmˌʌp/ *noun, pl* **-ups** *chiefly US*
1 [*count*] : an exercise or set of exercises done to prepare for a sport or other activity • She did a five-minute *warmup* before running. — often plural • He injured himself during *warmups.*
2 [*count*] : something done before something else to prepare an audience, a group, etc., for the next thing — usually singular • This presentation is just a *warmup* for the big session tomorrow. • Dinner is just a *warmup.* You should see what we're having for dessert! • He's just the *warmup* act.
3 warmups [*plural*] : comfortable clothing worn by athletes while they are preparing for competition — usually plural • The race was about to start, so the runners removed their *warmups.* — called also *warmup suit*
– see also *warm up* at ²WARM

warn /ˈwoɚn/ *verb* **warns; warned; warn·ing**
1 : to tell (someone) about possible danger or trouble [+ *obj*] I had been *warned* about the difficulties of the job. • She *warned* me that the stove was still hot. • The company has *warned* (investors) that its profits are likely to be lower in the coming year. • "This won't be easy," he *warned.* • Nobody *warned* me about the dangers. [*no obj*] — usually + *about* or *of* • The book *warns about/of* the dangers of not getting enough exercise.
2 : to tell (someone) to do or not to do something in order to avoid danger or trouble [+ *obj*] I *warned* him to be careful, but he didn't listen to me. • She *warned* us not to go too close to the fire. • We were *warned* against using [=warned not to use] the faulty light switch. [*no obj*] — usually + *against* • She *warns against* making changes too quickly.
warn off [*phrasal verb*] ***warn (someone) off*** or ***warn (someone) off (something)*** : to tell (someone) to go or stay away in order to avoid danger or trouble • The neighbors *warned* us *off* their land.

warn·ing /ˈwoɚnɪŋ/ *noun, pl* **-ings**
1 : something (such as an action or a statement) that tells someone about possible danger or trouble [*count*] She gave me a *warning* about the difficulties of the job. • There were storm *warnings* [=warnings that a storm was approaching] issued for the area. • She issued a stern *warning* against making changes too quickly. • Let that be a *warning* to you. [*noncount*] We had no *warning* of the dangers that were ahead of us. • Without any *warning* she turned around and ran. • The storm struck ***without warning.***
2 [*count*] : a statement that tells a person that bad or wrong behavior will be punished if it happens again • I was stopped for speeding, but the policeman just gave me a *warning.*
fair warning see ¹FAIR
– **warning** *adj, always used before a noun* • A *warning* bell rang before classes started. • The policeman fired a *warning* shot. • Falling prices may be a ***warning sign*** of a recession. [=may indicate that a recession is coming] • the *warning signs* of cancer

¹warp /ˈwoɚp/ *verb* **warps; warped; warp·ing**
1 : to twist or bend (something) into a different shape [+ *obj*] The wood was *warped* by moisture. [*no obj*] The heat caused the wood to *warp.*
2 [+ *obj*] *disapproving* : to cause (a person's opinions, thoughts, etc.) to be changed in a way that is wrong or unnatural • He held prejudices that *warped* his judgment.
– **warped** *adj* [*more ~; most ~*] • a *warped* vinyl record • a vicious criminal with a *warped* mind • They have a very *warped* view of human history.

²warp *noun, pl* **warps**
1 [*count*] : a twist or curve in something that is usually flat or straight • There's a *warp* in the floorboards. — see also TIME WARP
2 [*noncount*] *technical* : the threads that run up and down on a loom or in a woven fabric — compare WEFT

war paint *noun* [*noncount*]
1 : paint put on the face, the arms, etc., by Native Americans before going into battle • a picture of a chief dressed in a headdress and *war paint*
2 *informal + humorous* : MAKEUP • She piled on the *war paint.*

war·path /ˈwoɚˌpæθ, *Brit* ˈwɔːˌpɑːθ/ *noun*
on the warpath *informal* : angry and ready to fight with, criticize, or punish someone • The boss is *on the warpath* today because the project is behind schedule. • Her supporters ***went on the warpath*** in response to her opponent's accusations.

war·plane /ˈwoɚˌpleɪn/ *noun, pl* **-planes** [*count*] : a military airplane that has guns or missiles

¹war·rant /ˈworənt/ *noun, pl* **-rants**
1 [*count*] *law* : a document issued by a court that gives the police the power to do something • The police had a *warrant* for his arrest. — see also SEARCH WARRANT
2 [*noncount*] *formal* : a reason for thinking, deciding, or doing something • There was no *warrant* for such behavior.

²warrant *verb* **-rants; -rant·ed; -rant·ing** [+ *obj*]
1 : to require or deserve (something) • This report *warrants* careful study. [=this report should be given careful study] • The idea *warrants* [=*merits*] further consideration. • The writing was poor, but it hardly *warrants* that kind of insulting criticism. • The punishment he received was not *warranted.*
2 a : to make a legal promise that a statement is true • The seller *warrants* [=(more commonly) *guarantees*] that the car has no defects. **b** : to give a guarantee or warranty for (a product) — usually used as *(be) warranted* • The tires *are warranted* [=(more commonly) *guaranteed*] for 40,000 miles.
3 *old-fashioned* : to say (something) with certainty • ***I'll warrant*** (you) that they know the answer.

warrant officer *noun, pl* **~ -ers** [*count*] : an officer of middle rank in various branches of the armed forces

war·ran·ty /ˈworənti/ *noun, pl* **-ties** [*count*] : a written statement that promises the good condition of a product and states that the maker is responsible for repairing or replacing the product usually for a certain period of time after its purchase • The stereo came with a three-year *warranty.*

war·ren /ˈworən/ *noun, pl* **-rens** [*count*]
1 : a series of underground tunnels where rabbits live : RABBIT WARREN
2 : a building or place with many connected rooms, passages, etc., where you can get lost very easily • a *warren* of narrow hallways

war·ring /ˈworɪŋ/ *adj, always used before a noun* : involved in a war, conflict, or disagreement • *warring* nations • *warring* factions/parties

war·rior /ˈworijɚ/ *noun, pl* **-rior** [*count*] : a person who fights in battles and is known for having courage and skill • a proud and brave *warrior* — sometimes used figuratively • She has been a *warrior* against [=she has fought hard against] social injustice. — see also ROAD WARRIOR, WEEKEND WARRIOR

war room *noun, pl* **~ rooms** [*count*]
1 : a room where battles are planned that is equipped with maps, computers, etc.
2 : a room where people meet and exchange plans, ideas, information, etc., in an active way • the *war room* of the candidate's campaign headquarters

war·ship /ˈwoɚˌʃɪp/ *noun, pl* **-ships** [*count*] : a military ship that has many weapons and is used for fighting in wars

war story *noun, pl* **~ -ries** [*count*] : a story of a personal experience that usually involves danger, struggle, or adventure • He liked to tell *war stories* from his life as a sea captain. • We exchanged *war stories* about our time as interns at the same company.

wart /ˈwoɚt/ *noun, pl* **warts** [*count*]
1 : a small, hard lump on the skin caused by a virus
2 : a defect or fault • He was often selfish and thoughtless, but she loved him, ***warts and all.*** [=she loved him even though he had many faults]
– **warty** /ˈwoɚti/ *adj* • *warty* skin

wart·hog /ˈwoɚtˌhɑːg/ *noun, pl* **-hogs** [*count*] : a type of wild hog that lives in Africa

warthog

war·time /ˈwoɚˌtaɪm/ *noun* [*noncount*] : a time when a country is involved in a war ▪ Many goods were rationed during/in *wartime*. — often used before another noun ▪ *wartime* leaders/operations — opposite PEACETIME

war–torn *adj* : very badly harmed or damaged by war : torn apart by war ▪ a *war-torn* country

wary /ˈweri/ *adj* **war·i·er; -est** : not having or showing complete trust in someone or something that could be dangerous or cause trouble ▪ The store owner kept a *wary* eye on him. ▪ Investors are increasingly *wary* about putting money into stocks.— often + *of* ▪ They remain *wary of* the new plan.
– **war·i·ly** /ˈwerəli/ *adv* ▪ They looked at each other *warily*.
– **war·i·ness** /ˈwerinəs/ *noun* [*noncount*]

was *past tense of* BE

wa·sa·bi /ˈwɑːsəbi, wɑˈsɑːbi/ *noun* [*noncount*] : a Japanese food that has a strong, hot taste and that is often served with sushi

[1]**wash** /ˈwɑːʃ/ *verb* **wash·es; washed; wash·ing**
1 : to clean (something) with water and usually soap [+ *obj*] *wash* clothes ▪ *wash* the windows ▪ *wash* your hair ▪ We have to *wash* the dishes. ▪ Did you *wash* your hands? ▪ *Wash* [=*rinse*] the vegetables in the sink. [*no obj*] Tell the kids to please *wash* [=to wash their hands, faces, etc.] before eating. ▪ That shirt *washes* well. [=that shirt can be washed easily and without being damaged]
2 a [+ *obj*] : to carry (something) by the movement of water ▪ The flooding *washed* sand and silt all over the area. ▪ A sailor was ***washed overboard*** [=knocked off the ship and into the water] during the storm. ▪ A lot of debris was ***washed ashore*** [=brought onto the shore by waves] during the storm. ▪ The house is in danger of being ***washed out to sea***. [=being carried out to sea by the movement of the water] **b** [*no obj*] : to be carried by the movement of water ▪ The pollution *washes* into rivers from nearby factories.
3 [*no obj*] : to move by flowing ▪ Water *washed* over the deck of the ship. ▪ Waves *washed* up onto the beach.
4 [*no obj*] *informal* : to be believable or acceptable — usually used in negative statements ▪ That story won't *wash*. [=that story is not believable] ▪ These claims won't *wash*. [=these are not believable claims] ▪ Blaming her poor grades on the teacher just doesn't *wash*. [=is not acceptable]

wash away [*phrasal verb*] ***wash (something) away or wash away (something)*** **1** : to carry (something) away by the movement of water ▪ The waves at high tide *washed* our beach towels *away*. ▪ The footprints in the sand were *washed away*. ▪ The bridge was *washed away* by flooding last year. ▪ Heavy rain *washed away* the grass seed. **2** : to get rid of (something, such as unhappy or unpleasant thoughts) completely ▪ Take a vacation to *wash away* your troubles.

wash down [*phrasal verb*] ***wash (something) down or wash down (something)*** **1** : to clean (something) with water ▪ We'll have to *wash down* the walls before we paint them. **2** : to drink something after eating (food) ▪ The kids *washed down* their cookies with milk.

wash off [*phrasal verb*] **1** ***wash (something) off or wash off (something)*** : to clean (something) by using water ▪ *Wash* the mud *off* the bikes before you put them away. **2** : to be able to be removed or cleaned by washing ▪ This makeup *washes off* easily. ▪ Does that ink *wash off*?

wash out [*phrasal verb*] **1** : to be able to be removed or cleaned by washing ▪ The wine stain won't *wash out*. **2** ***wash (something) out or wash out (something)*** **a** : to clean the inside of (something, such as a cup or pot) with water ▪ Just *wash out* the coffee cups before you go. **b** : to damage or carry away (something) by the force of moving water ▪ The flooding river *washed out* the bridge. ▪ The flood *washed out* the road. **c** : to cause (something, such as a sports event) to be stopped or canceled because of rain ▪ Rain *washed out* Friday's game. ▪ This weekend's game was *washed out*. **3** *US, informal* : to fail to successfully complete a course of training because you do not have the necessary qualities, skills, or abilities ▪ This program is so tough, at least 30 percent of the students will *wash out* before the end of the first year.— see also WASHOUT

wash over [*phrasal verb*] ***wash over (someone or something)*** **1** : to affect or be felt by (someone) thoroughly and deeply ▪ A deep sadness suddenly *washed over* me. ▪ I felt relief *washing over* me. ▪ Just close your eyes and let the music *wash over* you. **2** : to appear on (a person's face) suddenly ▪ A look of surprise *washed over* his face.

wash up [*phrasal verb*] **1** : to be carried by the movement of water to the shore ▪ Trash *washed up* on the beach after the storm. **2** *US* : to wash your hands, face, etc. ▪ It will just take me a minute to *wash up* and then we can go. **3** *chiefly Brit* : to wash the dishes after a meal ▪ I cooked dinner and he *washed up* afterwards.

wash your hands of : to say or decide that you will no longer deal with or be responsible for (someone or something) because you are angry, disgusted, etc. : to refuse to be involved with (something or someone) anymore ▪ I've tried to help them and they won't listen to me, so I'm *washing my hands of* the whole mess.

[2]**wash** *noun, pl* **washes**
1 [*count*] : an act of cleaning something by using water and soap : an act of washing something — usually singular ▪ My car needs a *wash*. [=needs to be washed] ▪ (*Brit*) I'll ***have a quick wash*** [=(*US*) I'll wash up] before dinner.
2 [*singular*] : a group of clothes, towels, sheets, etc., that are being washed or that are going to be washed : LAUNDRY ▪ My jeans are ***in the wash***. ▪ (*Brit*) I'll ***put a wash on*** [=I'll put laundry in the washing machine] when I get home.
3 [*singular*] : the movement of water ▪ We could hear the *wash* of the waves against the rocks; *especially* : the waves made in the water after a moving boat passes by ▪ The *wash* from speedboats is dangerous for swimmers.
4 [*count*] : a thin layer of paint ▪ a thin *wash* of white paint — see also WHITEWASH
5 [*count*] **a** : a liquid used for cleaning ▪ They used a chemical *wash* to clean the bricks.— see also MOUTHWASH **b** : a soap or lotion for the skin ▪ an antibacterial skin *wash*
6 [*singular*] *US, informal* : a situation in which losses and gains balance each other ▪ You won the first game and I won the second, so ***it's a wash***. [=we are even] ▪ The price is less online than at the store, but once you add shipping costs, *it's a wash*. [=the two prices are about the same]

it will all come out in the wash *informal* **1** — used to say that a problem is not serious and will be solved in the future ▪ Don't worry about it. *It will all come out in the wash.* **2** — used to say that the truth will be known in the future ▪ No one knows who was responsible, but surely *it will all come out in the wash*.

wash·able /ˈwɑːʃəbəl/ *adj* [*more* ~; *most* ~]
1 : able to be washed without being damaged ▪ a *washable* silk ▪ Make sure your vacation clothes are ***machine washable***. [=able to be washed in a washing machine]
2 : able to be removed by washing ▪ *washable* ink
– **wash·abil·i·ty** /ˌwɑːʃəˈbɪləti/ *noun* [*noncount*]

wash–and–wear *adj, US* : made from a cloth that does not wrinkle so that clothes can be worn immediately after being washed ▪ *wash-and-wear* clothing

wash·bag /ˈwɑːʃˌbæg/ *noun, pl* **-bags** [*count*] *Brit* : TOILET BAG

wash·ba·sin /ˈwɑːʃˌbeɪsn/ *noun, pl* **-sins** [*count*]
1 : a large bowl for water that is used to wash your hands and face
2 *chiefly Brit* : a bathroom sink

wash·board /ˈwɑːʃˌboɚd/ *noun, pl* **-boards** [*count*]
1 : a board with ridges on its surface that was used in the past for washing clothes by rubbing wet clothes against it ✧ Washboards are also sometimes used as musical instruments in some types of folk and country music. ▪ The band featured a banjo and the rhythms of the *washboard*.
2 *US, informal* : a group of strong and well-shaped muscles that can be seen on a person's stomach — usually used before another noun ▪ a *washboard* stomach ▪ *washboard* abs

wash·cloth /ˈwɑːʃˌklɑːθ/ *noun, pl* **-cloths** [*count*] *US* : a small piece of cloth that you use to wash your face and body — called also *facecloth, (Brit) flannel, (US) washrag*; see picture at BATHROOM

wash·day /ˈwɑːʃˌdeɪ/ *noun, pl* **-days** [*count*] *old-fashioned* : the usual day of the week when clothes are washed

washed–out /ˈwɑːʃtˈaʊt/ *adj* [*more* ~; *most* ~]
1 *of a color* : not bright : very light or faded ▪ a very pale *washed-out* blue ▪ The colors look *washed-out* [=very faded] in these old photographs.
2 : very tired and without energy : EXHAUSTED ▪ I felt

W

washed-out after working all night.

washed–up /ˈwɑːʃtˈʌp/ *adj* [*more* ~; *most* ~] : no longer successful, popular, or needed • a *washed-up* actor/singer

wash·er /ˈwɑːʃɚ/ *noun, pl* **-ers** [*count*]
1 : a thin, flat ring that is made of metal, plastic, or rubber and that is used to make something (such as a bolt) fit tightly or to prevent rubbing — see picture at CARPENTRY
2 *informal* : WASHING MACHINE • the clothes *washer* • We bought a new *washer* and dryer.

wash·er·wom·an /ˈwɑːʃɚˌwʊmən/ *noun, pl* **-wom·en** /-ˌwɪmən/ [*count*] *old-fashioned* : a woman whose job is washing clothes

wash·ing /ˈwɑːʃɪŋ/ *noun, pl* **-ings**
1 [*count*] : an act of washing something with water and soap • These shirts will look great even after repeated *washings*.
2 [*noncount*] *Brit* : clothes, towels, sheets, etc., that need to be washed or that are being washed • His mother still does his *washing*. [=*laundry*] • She forgot to ***put the washing out***. [=to hang the laundry outside to dry]

washing machine *noun, pl* ~ **-chines** [*count*] : a machine used for washing clothes

washing powder *noun* [*noncount*] *Brit* : soap in the form of a powder that you use to wash clothes, towels, sheets, etc.

washing soda *noun* [*noncount*] : a chemical that is added to water to help clean very dirty clothes, towels, sheets, etc.

Washington's Birthday *noun* [*noncount*] : the third Monday in February celebrated in the U.S. as a holiday in honor of the birthday of George Washington ✧ The official name of this holiday is *Washington's Birthday*, but in most states it is now usually called *Presidents' Day* and is considered to be in honor of both George Washington and Abraham Lincoln.

washing–up *noun* [*noncount*] *Brit*
1 : the activity of washing dishes, pans, cups, etc. • She was in the kitchen ***doing the washing-up***. [=*doing the dishes*]
2 : dirty dishes, pans, cups, etc., that need to be washed • a pile of *washing-up*

washing–up liquid *noun* [*noncount*] *Brit* : DISH DETERGENT

wash·out /ˈwɑːʃˌaʊt/ *noun, pl* **-outs** [*count*] *informal*
1 : a complete failure • He was a *washout* as a professional golfer. • The team lost so many games that the season was a total *washout*.
2 : an event, game, etc., that is canceled because of rain • Yesterday's game was a *washout*.
– see also *wash out* at ¹WASH

wash·rag /ˈwɑːʃˌræg/ *noun, pl* **-rags** [*count*] *US* : WASHCLOTH

wash·room /ˈwɑːʃˌruːm/ *noun, pl* **-rooms** [*count*] *chiefly US* : a bathroom in a public building

wash·stand /ˈwɑːʃˌstænd/ *noun, pl* **-stands** [*count*] : a small table used especially in the past in a bedroom to hold the things you need for washing your face and hands

wash·tub /ˈwɑːʃˌtʌb/ *noun, pl* **-tubs** [*count*] : a tub used especially in the past for washing dirty clothes, towels, sheets, etc.

wasn't /ˈwʌznt/ — used as a contraction of *was not* • It *wasn't* important.

wasp /ˈwɑːsp/ *noun, pl* **wasps** [*count*] : a black-and-yellow flying insect that can sting — see color picture on page C10

WASP /ˈwɑːsp/ *or* **Wasp** *noun, pl* **WASPs** *or* **Wasps** *also* **WASPS** [*count*] *US, often disapproving* : an American whose family originally came from northern Europe and especially Britain and who is considered to be part of the most powerful group in society • Most of the members of the club are wealthy *WASPs*. • The college had been known as a bastion of *WASP* privilege. ✧ *WASP* is an abbreviation of "White Anglo-Saxon Protestant."

wasp·ish /ˈwɑːspɪʃ/ *adj* [*more* ~; *most* ~]
1 : easily annoyed • a *waspish* temper : showing annoyance • *waspish* comments
2 : very thin • her *waspish* waist
– wasp·ish·ly *adv*

was·sail /ˈwɑːsəl/ *noun* [*noncount*] *old-fashioned* : a hot alcoholic drink that is traditionally served in a large bowl especially at Christmastime

wast·age /ˈweɪstɪʤ/ *noun* [*noncount*] : wasteful use of something valuable : loss of something by using too much of it or using it in a way that is not necessary or effective • The current system results in a large amount of *wastage*. [=a lot of material is wasted because of the current system] • *wastage* of valuable resources • avoid food/water *wastage* — see also NATURAL WASTAGE

¹**waste** /ˈweɪst/ *noun, pl* **wastes**
1 a [*noncount*] : loss of something valuable that occurs because too much of it is being used or because it is being used in a way that is not necessary or effective • The current system causes a lot of *waste*. • We need to find ways to reduce/avoid unnecessary *waste*. **b** [*singular*] : an action or use that results in the unnecessary loss of something valuable • These old computers are still useful. It seems like such a *waste* to throw them away. • Any further investment would be a *waste* of valuable resources. • The show was a ***waste of money***. [=a bad use of money] • The lecture was a ***waste of time***. [=a bad use of time] **c** [*singular*] : a situation in which something valuable is not being used or is being used in a way that is not appropriate or effective • That role was a *waste* of her talents. [=a poor use of her talents]
2 : material that is left over or that is unwanted after something has been made, done, used, etc. [*noncount*] hazardous *waste* • disposal of industrial *waste* • *waste* removal • The city oversees *waste* disposal contracts. • household *waste* [=*trash, rubbish*] [*count*] hazardous *wastes* • household *wastes* — see also TOXIC WASTE
3 [*noncount*] : the solid and liquid substances that are produced by the body : feces and urine • liquid/solid *waste* • a *waste* treatment plant
4 ***wastes*** [*plural*] *literary* : a large and empty area of land : WASTELAND • the frozen *wastes* of the tundra
a waste of space *chiefly Brit, informal* : a worthless person or thing • He's *a* complete *waste of space*.
go to waste : to not be used : to be wasted • It's a shame to see all that food *go to waste*. • They don't let anything *go to waste* when they're camping.
haste makes waste see HASTE
lay waste to see ¹LAY

²**waste** *verb* **wastes**; **wast·ed**; **wast·ing** [+ *obj*]
1 : to use (something valuable) in a way that is not necessary or effective : to use more of (something) than is necessary • Don't *waste* water during the summer drought. • He always *wasted* his money on useless gadgets. • Turn off the lights so we don't *waste* electricity. • I think he's just *wasting* my time. • We can't afford to *waste* so much food.
2 : to use (something or someone) in a way that does not produce a valuable result or effect : to fail to use (something or someone) in an appropriate or effective way • We can't afford to *waste* this opportunity. • She's a good writer but she's *wasting* her talent. [=she's not using her talent to do the things that she should be doing] — often used as *(be) wasted* • My efforts *were wasted*. • He *was wasted* in that job. [=his talents/skills were not being used in the job]
3 *slang* : to kill or murder (someone) • Someone *wasted* him.
waste away [*phrasal verb*] : to become thinner and weaker because of illness or lack of food • The disease caused her to *waste away*.
waste no time : to do something quickly • We *wasted no time* getting our tickets. [=we hurried to get our tickets]
waste not, want not — used to say that if you never waste things you will always have what you need
waste your breath see BREATH

³**waste** *adj, always used before a noun* : of, relating to, or being material that is left over or unwanted after something has been made, done, used, etc. • *waste* material/water

waste·bas·ket /ˈweɪstˌbæskət, *Brit* ˈweɪstˌbɑːskət/ *noun, pl* **-kets** [*count*] *US* : a small container for trash • She tossed the wrapper into the *wastebasket*. — called also *wastepaper basket*; see pictures at BATHROOM, OFFICE

waste bin *noun, pl* ~ **bins** [*count*] *Brit* : DUSTBIN

wast·ed /ˈweɪstəd/ *adj*
1 : not used, spent, etc., in a good, useful, or effective way • a *wasted* effort/opportunity • *wasted* money
2 [*more* ~; *most* ~] : very thin because of sickness or lack of food • When she came home from the hospital her body was thin and *wasted*. [=*emaciated*]
3 [*more* ~; *most* ~] *informal* : very drunk or affected by drugs • I saw him before the party and he was already *wasted*.

waste disposal unit *noun, pl* ~ **units** [*count*] *Brit* : GARBAGE DISPOSAL

waste·ful /ˈweɪstfəl/ *adj* [*more* ~; *most* ~] : using more of something than is needed : causing something valuable to be wasted • a *wasteful* use of natural resources • a careless and *wasteful* person • It was a *wasteful* [=*unnecessary*] duplication of effort. • We must eliminate *wasteful* expenditures.

– **waste·ful·ly** *adv* – **waste·ful·ness** *noun [noncount]*

waste·land /ˈweɪstˌlænd/ *noun, pl* **-lands** *[count]*
1 : land where nothing can grow or be built : land that is not usable • a desert *wasteland*
2 : an ugly and often ruined place or area • The outskirts of the city became a grim industrial *wasteland*.
3 : something that is being compared to a large, empty area of land because it has no real value or interest • That part of the country is a cultural *wasteland*. • the vast *wasteland* of television

waste·pa·per /ˈweɪstˈpeɪpɚ/ *noun [noncount]* : paper that you throw away because it has been used or is not needed

wastepaper basket *noun, pl* ~ **-kets** *[count]* : WASTEBASKET

waste product *noun, pl* ~ **-ducts** *[count]* : useless material that is produced when making something else • a hazardous *waste product*

wast·er /ˈweɪstɚ/ *noun, pl* **-ers** *[count]*
1 : someone or something that uses too much of something or that uses something in a way that is not necessary or effective • He has been called a *waster* of taxpayers' money. • He thinks every meeting is a big time *waster*.
2 *Brit, informal* : a person who never succeeds : a person who is not successful, attractive, etc. • Her boyfriend's a real *waster*. [=*loser*]

wast·rel /ˈweɪstrəl/ *noun, pl* **-rels** *[count] literary* : a person who wastes time, money, etc. • a lazy *wastrel*

[1]**watch** /ˈwɑːtʃ/ *verb* **watch·es; watched; watch·ing**
1 a : to look at (someone or something) for an amount of time and pay attention to what is happening *[+ obj]* They have a rookie on the team who is fun to *watch*. • I fell asleep *watching* television. • What movie are you *watching*? • "Mom, *watch* me do a cartwheel!" • *Watch* us (do it) to see how it's done. • She sat and *watched* the children play. • He didn't know that he was ***being watched*** by the police. [=that the police were looking at what he was doing] *[no obj]* "Would you like to play, too?" "No, I'll just *watch*." • Just sit back and *watch*. • Keep *watching* to see what happens next. • "What happens next?" "***Watch and see***." **b** : to give your attention to (a situation, an event, etc.) *[+ obj]* People are *watching* this presidential race very carefully/closely. • Fans anxiously ***watched the clock*** [=they paid close attention to the time remaining on the clock] as the end of the game approached. *[no obj]* Investors *watched* with delight as stock prices rose.
2 *[+ obj]* : to care for (someone or something) for a period of time in order to make sure that nothing bad or unwanted happens • Will you *watch* my things (for me) until I get back? • He *watched* [=*took care of*] the baby while I made dinner. • Can you *watch* the dog for us this weekend? • ***Watch yourself*** [=be careful] up on the roof.
3 *[+ obj]* **a** : to try to control (something) • She tries to *watch* her weight. [=she tries not to gain weight] • The doctor told him that he has to *watch* what he eats. • We've been *watching* how much money we spend. **b** : to be careful about (something) — usually used in commands • *Watch* your step. These stairs are slippery. • *Watch* your head getting into the car. • *Watch* what you're doing! You almost hit me. • *Watch* what you say in front of him. He's very sensitive. • ***Watch your language/mouth/tongue***, young lady! [=don't say rude or inappropriate things]
4 *not used in progressive tenses [+ obj]* : to make sure that something bad or unwanted does not happen • You will want to *watch* that it doesn't happen again. — often used in commands • *Watch* (that) you don't fall! • *Watch* (that) the wind doesn't blow your papers away.

a watched pot never boils see [1]BOIL

watch for *[phrasal verb]* **1** ***watch for (someone or something)*** : to look for (someone or something that you expect to see) • Are you *watching for* your parents? They should be here any minute. • She *watches for* her school bus from inside her house. • The nurse *watched for* signs of the disease. • We need to *watch for* any sudden changes in his heartbeat. **2** ***watch for (something)*** : to look for (something that you want to get or use) • She is always *watching for* sales.

watch it *informal* — used to tell someone to be careful • *Watch it*! You nearly knocked over that lamp!

watch out *[phrasal verb]* : to be aware of something dangerous • If you don't *watch out* you could fall. • You'd better *watch out*. [=*be careful*] These stairs are slippery. — often + *for* • *Watch out for* that car! • There are many dangers that you need to *watch out for*.

watch over *[phrasal verb]* ***watch over (someone or something)*** : to take care of (someone or something) • The shepherds *watched over* their sheep. • She believed that angels were *watching over* her.

watch (someone or something) like a hawk see [1]HAWK

watch someone's back see [1]BACK

watch your back see [1]BACK

watch your p's and q's see [1]P

watch your step see [1]STEP

you watch *informal* — used to tell someone that you think something will probably happen • She'll change her mind again, *you watch*. [=I think she'll change her mind again]

[2]**watch** *noun, pl* **watches**
1 *[count]* : a device that shows what time it is and that you wear on your wrist or carry in a pocket • He glanced/looked at his *watch*. • digital *watches* — compare CLOCK; see also STOPWATCH, WRISTWATCH
2 a : the act of giving your attention to someone or something especially in order to make sure that nothing bad or unwanted happens *[singular]* — usually + *on* or *over* • He maintains a vigilant *watch over* his property. • The guards ***kept a close watch over*** the prisoner. [=the guards watched the prisoner closely] *[noncount]* We are continuing to ***keep watch on*** [=*monitor*] developments in the region. **b** *[singular]* : the act of looking for someone or something that you expect to see : the act of regularly checking to see if someone has arrived or if something has appeared or happened • She ***kept watch*** outside while the others robbed the bank. [=she watched to make sure that no one was coming while the others robbed the bank] • The police told residents to ***keep a watch out for*** a black van. [=to watch for a black van] • When you're driving in winter you should always ***be on the watch for*** ice on the roads. • I *am* always *on the watch for* a good bargain. [=always trying to find a good bargain] — see also WHALE WATCH
3 a : a period of time when a person or group is responsible for guarding or protecting someone or something *[count]* — usually singular • Who has first *watch*? • Everything was peaceful during his *watch*. • My *watch* ends in an hour. *[noncount]* Two guards were ***on watch***. = Two guards were ***standing watch***. **b** *[count]* : a group of people who guard or protect someone or something for a period of time — usually singular • A fresh group of soldiers relieved the morning/night *watch*. — see also NEIGHBORHOOD WATCH **c** *[count]* : the period of time during which someone is in charge of something — usually singular • The business increased its profits on her *watch*. [=the business increased its profits while she was running it] • "Will anything go wrong?" "Not on my *watch*!"
4 *[count] US* : a quick announcement from an official source which tells people that severe weather conditions could occur very soon — usually singular • The National Weather Service has issued a winter storm *watch*. • a tornado *watch*

watch·able /ˈwɑːtʃəbəl/ *adj [more ~; most ~]* : worth watching because of being interesting or entertaining • a minor but highly *watchable* film

watch·band /ˈwɑːtʃˌbænd/ *noun, pl* **-bands** *[count] US* : a strap or band that holds your watch on your wrist • a leather/metal *watchband*

watch·dog /ˈwɑːtʃˌdɑːg/ *noun, pl* **-dogs** *[count]*
1 : a dog that is trained to guard a place : GUARD DOG
2 : a person or organization that makes sure that companies, governments, etc., are not doing anything illegal or wrong • consumer/environmental *watchdogs* • *watchdog* groups

watch·er /ˈwɑːtʃɚ/ *noun, pl* **-ers** *[count]* : a person who watches someone or something regularly • a TV *watcher* — often used in combination • celebrity-*watchers* — see also BIRD-WATCHER

watch·ful /ˈwɑːtʃfəl/ *adj [more ~; most ~]* : always watching the actions of someone or something : paying careful attention to someone or something • We need to be more *watchful* of our children. • The supervisor ***keeps a watchful eye*** on the workers. [=the supervisor closely watches what the workers are doing] • The hotel is being built ***under the watchful eye of*** its architect.
– **watch·ful·ly** /ˈwɑːtʃfəli/ *adv* • Guards stood *watchfully* at the gate. – **watch·ful·ness** *noun [noncount]*

watching brief *noun [singular] Brit* : an act of watching the actions of a person or organization to make sure nothing illegal or wrong is being done • They have been ***keeping a watching brief*** on the company's financial dealings.

watch list *noun, pl* ~ **lists** *[count]* : a list of people or things that are being closely watched because they are likely to do or experience bad things in the future • The government has released its new terrorist *watch list*. • The animals are on a *watch list* of species that could become extinct soon.

watch·mak·er /ˈwɑːʧˌmeɪkɚ/ *noun, pl* **-ers** [*count*] : a person or company that makes or repairs watches or clocks
– **watch·mak·ing** /ˈwɑːʧˌmeɪkɪŋ/ *noun* [*noncount*]

watch·man /ˈwɑːʧmən/ *noun, pl* **-men** /-mən/ [*count*] : a person whose job is to watch and guard property at night or when the owners are away • A *watchman* stopped them at the gate. — see also NIGHT WATCHMAN

watch·tow·er /ˈwɑːʧˌtawɚ/ *noun, pl* **-ers** [*count*] : a tower that is used by a person who guards or watches a place

watch·word /ˈwɑːʧˌwɚd/ *noun, pl* **-words** [*count*] : a word or phrase that expresses a rule that a particular person or group follows : SLOGAN • "Safety" is our *watchword*. • The new *watchword* in his campaign is "It's time for change."

¹wa·ter /ˈwɑːtɚ/ *noun, pl* **-ters**
1 [*noncount*] : the clear liquid that has no color, taste, or smell, that falls from clouds as rain, that forms streams, lakes, and seas, and that is used for drinking, washing, etc. • Would you like a glass of *water*? • bottled/mineral/spring *water* • There's *water* dripping from the ceiling. • Drink some *water*. • ***drinking water*** [=water that is safe for drinking] • The house has hot and cold ***running water***. [=water carried by pipes inside a building] — see also BATHWATER, FRESHWATER, GROUNDWATER, HOLY WATER, ICE WATER, MINERAL WATER, RAINWATER, ROSE WATER, SALTWATER, SEAWATER, SODA WATER, TAP WATER, TOILET WATER, WHITE WATER
2 [*noncount*] : an area of water (such as a lake, river, or ocean) • deep/shallow *water* • The kids love playing in the *water*. • A stick was floating on/in the *water*. • They like to vacation near the *water*. — see also UNDERWATER
3 ***waters*** [*plural*] : a specific area of water; *especially* : an area of seawater • frigid northern *waters* • coastal/shallow *waters* • We are sailing in international *waters*. • They were fishing in Canadian *waters*. — often used figuratively • We are entering into ***dangerous waters*** [=a difficult or complicated situation] whenever we discuss religion in public. • He began studying the ***murky waters*** [=confusing details] of copyright law. • The company is moving into ***uncharted waters*** [=new and unknown areas] with its Internet marketing campaign. — see also HEADWATERS, TERRITORIAL WATERS
4 [*noncount*] : methods of travel that involve boats and ships • They came by *water*. [=by traveling on a boat or ship]
a fish out of water see ¹FISH
blood is thicker than water see BLOOD
come hell or high water see HELL
dead in the water see ¹DEAD
hold water *informal* : to be possible or believable — usually used in negative statements • Her argument doesn't *hold water*. [=does not make sense] • His theory cannot *hold water*. [=his theory is wrong]
in deep water see ¹DEEP
keep your head above water see ¹HEAD
like a duck to water see ¹DUCK
like water *informal* : in large amounts • He spends money *like water*.
muddy the waters see ²MUDDY
pass water *medical* : to send urine out of the body : URINATE • a patient who is finding it difficult to *pass water*
pour/throw cold water on : to say that you do not like (an idea, suggestion, etc.) in a way that stops other people from doing it or from feeling enthusiastic about it • He wanted to buy a new car, but I *poured/threw cold water on* that idea. [=I said he should not buy a new car]
still waters run deep see ²STILL
test the waters/water see ²TEST
tread water see ¹TREAD
troubled waters see TROUBLED
water breaks (*US*) *or Brit* ***waters break*** — used to describe what happens when fluid suddenly comes from a pregnant woman's body because her baby will be born soon • Her *water broke* early.
water off a duck's back *informal* ✧ If something, such as criticism, advice, etc., is (*like*) *water off a duck's back*, it has no effect on someone. • He tried to convince her to take the job, but his advice was *like water off a duck's back*. [=she completely ignored his advice]
water under the bridge — used to say that something happened in the past and is no longer important or worth arguing about • We had our differences in the past, but that's all *water under the bridge* now.

²water *verb* **-ters; -tered; -ter·ing**
1 [+ *obj*] : to pour water on (something, such as a plant) • We need to *water* the lawn/garden/plants.
2 [+ *obj*] : to give (an animal) water to drink • They fed and *watered* the horses in the barn.
3 [*no obj*] *of the eyes* : to produce tears • My eyes were *watering* as I chopped the onions.
4 [*no obj*] *of the mouth* : to become wet with saliva especially because you want to eat or taste something • Just smelling chocolate makes my mouth *water*. [=makes me want to taste or eat chocolate] — see also MOUTH-WATERING
5 [+ *obj*] *technical* : to supply water to (a region or city) — usually used as *(be) watered* • The vineyards are in a region *watered* by two rivers.
water down [*phrasal verb*] ***water (something) down*** *or* ***water down (something)*** **1** : to make (an alcoholic drink) weaker by adding water to it • Someone *watered down* [=*diluted*] the punch. **2** *disapproving* : to make (something) less effective, powerful, etc. • He had to *water down* [=*simplify*] the lecture for the younger students. • The movie *watered down* the lessons of the book. — see also WATERED-DOWN

water balloon *noun, pl* **~ -loons** [*count*] *chiefly US* : a balloon that is filled with water • The boys were throwing *water balloons* at each other.

water bed *noun, pl* **~ beds** [*count*] : a bed that has a mattress which is made of rubber or plastic and is filled with water

wa·ter·bird /ˈwɑːtɚˌbɚd/ *noun, pl* **-birds** [*count*] : a bird that swims and lives in or near water • gulls, ducks, and other *waterbirds*

wa·ter·borne /ˈwɑːtɚˌboɚn/ *adj* : spread or carried by water • *waterborne* diseases • *waterborne* commerce

water buffalo *noun, pl* **~ buffalo** *or* **~ buffaloes** [*count*] : a large animal like a cow with long horns that lives in Asia and is often used to pull plows

water buffalo

water bug *noun, pl* **~ bugs** [*count*] *US* : a small insect that lives in or near water

water butt *noun, pl* **~ butts** [*count*] *Brit* : a large container for collecting or storing a liquid (such as rainwater)

water cannon *noun, pl* **~ cannons** *or* **~ cannon** [*count*] : a machine that shoots a large, powerful stream of water and that is used by police to control violent crowds

water chestnut *noun, pl* **~ -nuts** [*count*] : the white root of a plant that grows in water and that is often used in Chinese cooking

water closet *noun, pl* **~ -ets** [*count*] *old-fashioned* : a room containing a toilet — abbr. *WC*

wa·ter·col·or (*US*) *or Brit* **wa·ter·col·our** /ˈwɑːtɚˌkʌlɚ/ *noun, pl* **-ors**
1 : a type of paint that is mixed with water [*noncount*] a landscape done in *watercolor* [*plural*] He only works in *watercolors*.
2 [*count*] : a picture painted with watercolors • We bought a *watercolor* of the shore. • an exhibition of *watercolors* • a *watercolor* landscape
– **wa·ter·col·or·ist** (*US*) *or Brit* **wa·ter·col·our·ist** /ˈwɑːtɚˌkʌlərɪst/ *noun, pl* **-ists** [*count*]

wa·ter cool·er /ˈwɑːtɚˌkuːlɚ/ *noun, pl* **~ -ers** [*count*] : a machine that cools and stores water for drinking and that is usually found in offices and public buildings — often used to refer to the kind of informal conversations that people have in an office when they are not doing work • We always talked baseball ***around the water cooler***. • He tried to avoid the ***water cooler gossip*** at the office.

wa·ter·course /ˈwɑːtɚˌkoɚs/ *noun, pl* **-cours·es** [*count*] *formal* : a river, stream, etc. • Pesticides are sometimes responsible for contamination of *watercourses*.

wa·ter·craft /ˈwɑːtɚˌkræft, *Brit* ˈwɔːtəˌkrɑːft/ *noun, pl* **-crafts** [*count, noncount*] : a ship or boat

wa·ter·cress /ˈwɑːtɚˌkrɛs/ *noun* [*noncount*] : a plant that grows in water and that has small, round leaves which are often used in salads

watered–down *adj* [*more ~; most ~*] : made to be less effective, powerful, etc. ▪ a *watered-down* compromise ▪ a *watered-down* version of the original proposal — see also *water down* at ²WATER

wa·ter·fall /ˈwɑːtɚˌfɑːl/ *noun, pl* **-falls** [*count*] : an area in a stream or river where running water falls down from a high place (such as over the side of a cliff) — see color picture on page C7

water fountain *noun, pl* ~ **-tains** [*count*]
 1 *chiefly US* : a machine that produces a small stream of water for drinking : DRINKING FOUNTAIN
 2 : FOUNTAIN 1 ▪ There is a beautiful *water fountain* in the park near the rose garden.

wa·ter·fowl /ˈwɑːtɚˌfawəl/ *noun, pl* **waterfowl** [*count*] : a duck or similar bird that swims and lives in or near water ▪ The lake is a refuge for migrating *waterfowl*.

wa·ter·front /ˈwɑːtɚˌfrʌnt/ *noun, pl* **-fronts** [*count*] : the land or the part of a town next to the water of an ocean, lake, etc. — usually singular ▪ They have evening concerts on the *waterfront*. — often used before another noun ▪ *waterfront* development

water glass *noun, pl* ~ **glasses** [*count*] : a drinking glass — see picture at PLACE SETTING

water gun *noun, pl* ~ **guns** [*count*] *US* : WATER PISTOL

water hole *noun, pl* ~ **holes** [*count*] : a small pool, pond, or lake used by animals for drinking — called also *watering hole*

water ice *noun, pl* ~ **ices** [*count, noncount*] *Brit* : SORBET

watering can *noun, pl* ~ **cans** [*count*] : a container that is used to pour water on plants — see picture at GARDENING

watering hole *noun, pl* ~ **holes** [*count*]
 1 *humorous* : a place (such as a bar) where people gather to drink ▪ We usually gathered at our favorite *watering hole* [=*bar*] downtown.
 2 : WATER HOLE

water jump *noun, pl* ~ **jumps** [*count*] : a pool or stream of water that horses or runners have to jump over in a race (such as a steeplechase)

wa·ter·less /ˈwɑːtɚləs/ *adj* [*more* ~; *most* ~] : without water ▪ a remote and *waterless* desert

water level *noun, pl* ~ **-els** [*count*] : the height of the surface of water in a lake, river, etc. ▪ Check the *water level* of the swimming pool. ▪ We should have good *water levels* through the summer after all this rain.

water lily *noun, pl* ~ **lilies** [*count*] : a plant that grows in water with round, floating leaves and large flowers

wa·ter·line /ˈwɑːtɚˌlaɪn/ *noun, pl* **-lines**
 1 *the waterline* : the level that water reaches on the side of a ship ▪ We repaired the hull below *the waterline*.
 2 [*count*] *US* : a horizontal mark on a wall or other surface that was made by water during a flood and that shows how high the water was

wa·ter·logged /ˈwɑːtɚˌlɑːgd/ *adj* [*more* ~; *most* ~] : filled or soaked with water ▪ a *waterlogged* boat ▪ *waterlogged* clothes/soil ▪ The ground was completely *waterlogged*.

Wa·ter·loo /ˌwɑːtɚˈluː/ *noun, pl* **-loos** [*count*] : a final defeat ▪ his political *Waterloo* ▪ The governor finally ***met his Waterloo*** [=was defeated] in the last election.

water main *noun, pl* ~ **mains** [*count*] : a large underground pipe that carries water ▪ The *water main* burst/broke and flooded the street.

wa·ter·mark /ˈwɑːtɚˌmaɚk/ *noun, pl* **-marks** [*count*] : a design or symbol (such as the maker's name) that is made in a piece of paper and that can be seen when the paper is held up to the light ✧ A watermark is usually found in expensive paper as a sign of quality.

water meadow *noun, pl* ~ **-ows** [*count*] *Brit* : a field near a river that is often flooded with water

wa·ter·mel·on /ˈwɑːtɚˌmɛlən/ *noun, pl* **-ons** [*count, noncount*] : a large, round fruit that has hard, green skin, sweet, red, juicy flesh, and black seeds — see color picture on page C5

water meter *noun, pl* ~ **-ters** [*count*] : a machine that measures how much water is used in a building

water mill *noun, pl* ~ **mills** [*count*] : a mill that uses power produced by moving water to run machinery

water moccasin *noun, pl* ~ **-sins** [*count*] : a poisonous snake found in the southern U.S. that lives on land and in water — called also *cottonmouth, cottonmouth moccasin*

water park *noun, pl* ~ **parks** [*count*] : an amusement park with rides that involve water and areas where people can play or swim in water

water pipe *noun, pl* ~ **pipes** [*count*]
 1 : a pipe that carries water ▪ The flooding was caused by a broken *water pipe*.
 2 : a device used for smoking tobacco, marijuana, etc., in which the smoke passes through water before it is inhaled

water pistol *noun, pl* ~ **-tols** [*count*] : a toy pistol that shoots a stream of water — called also (*US*) *water gun*, (*US*) *squirt gun*

water polo *noun* [*noncount*] : a game that is played in water by two teams of swimmers who try to score by throwing a ball into a goal

wa·ter·pow·er /ˈwɑːtɚˌpawɚ/ *noun* [*noncount*] : the power that comes from moving water and that is used to run machinery or make electricity ▪ *Waterpower* is a renewable source of energy.

¹wa·ter·proof /ˈwɑːtɚˌpruːf/ *adj*
 1 : designed to prevent water from entering or passing through ▪ *waterproof* boots ▪ The gaskets create a *waterproof* [=*watertight*] seal.
 2 : designed so that water alone will not remove it ▪ This suntan lotion is *waterproof*. ▪ *waterproof* mascara

²waterproof *noun, pl* **-proofs** [*count*] *chiefly Brit* : RAINCOAT

³waterproof *verb* **-proofs**; **-proofed**; **-proof·ing** [+ *obj*] : to put a substance on (something) in order to make it waterproof ▪ He *waterproofed* the deck by applying sealer to it.

wa·ter–re·pel·lent /ˌwɑːtɚrɪˈpɛlənt/ *adj* [*more* ~; *most* ~] : WATER-RESISTANT

wa·ter–re·sis·tant /ˌwɑːtɚrɪˈzɪstənt/ *adj* [*more* ~; *most* ~] : designed to not be easily harmed or affected by water or to not allow water to pass through easily ▪ a *water-resistant* watch ▪ *water-resistant* fabric

wa·ter·shed /ˈwɑːtɚˌʃɛd/ *noun, pl* **-sheds** [*count*]
 1 : a time when an important change happens — usually singular ▪ The protests mark a *watershed* [=*turning point*] in the history of the country. — often used before another noun ▪ a *watershed* moment/year/event
 2 a : a line of hills or mountains from which rivers drain : a ridge between two rivers **b** *chiefly US* : the area of land that includes a particular river or lake and all the rivers, streams, etc., that flow into it ▪ the Connecticut River *watershed*
 3 *Brit* : the time of day after which television programs not appropriate for children may be broadcast ▪ The show will not air until after the ***nine o'clock watershed***.

wa·ter·side /ˈwɑːtɚˌsaɪd/ *noun, pl* **-sides** [*count*] : the land next to a lake, river, etc. ▪ The trail winds along the *waterside*. — often used before another noun ▪ a *waterside* restaurant ▪ *waterside* plants

wa·ter–ski /ˈwɑːtɚˌskiː/ *verb* **-skis**; **-skied**; **-ski·ing** [*no obj*] : to ski on the surface of water while holding onto a rope that is attached to a motorboat moving at high speed ▪ They spent the day *water-skiing* at the lake.
 — **wa·ter–ski·er** /ˈwɑːtɚˌskiːjɚ/ *noun, pl* **-ers** [*count*] — **wa·ter·ski·ing** /ˈwɑːtɚˌskiːjɪŋ/ *noun* [*noncount*] ▪ Do you want to ***go waterskiing*** today?

water ski *noun, pl* ~ **skis** [*count*] : a ski that is used in water-skiing

water ski

wa·ter·slide /ˈwɑːtɚˌslaɪd/ *noun, pl* **-slides** [*count*] : a large slide usually at an amusement park that has water running down it and that is used for sliding down into a swimming pool

wa·ter·spout /ˈwɑːtɚˌspaʊt/ *noun, pl* **-spouts** [*count*]
 1 a : a pipe or tube for water to pass through **b** : an opening through which water flows
 2 : an area of rapidly spinning wind in the shape of a funnel or tube that forms between a cloud and the surface of an ocean or lake

water table *noun, pl* ~ **tables** [*count*] *technical* : the highest underground level at which the rocks and soil in a particular area are completely wet with water ▪ Heavy rainfall has caused the *water table* to rise.

wa·ter·tight /ˌwɑːtɚˈtaɪt/ *adj*
 1 : put or fit together so tightly that water cannot enter or pass through ▪ The doors/compartments are all *watertight*. ▪ a *watertight* seal

2 : too strong or effective to fail or to be defeated ▪ The evidence against the defendant was *watertight.* ▪ a *watertight* alibi/case

water tower *noun, pl* ~ **-ers** [*count*] : a tower with a large container for storing water that is usually supplied to buildings located near it

wa·ter·way /ˈwɑːtəˌweɪ/ *noun, pl* **-ways** [*count*] : a canal, river, etc., that is deep and wide enough for boats and ships to travel through

wa·ter·wheel /ˈwɑːtəˌwiːl/ *noun, pl* **-wheels** [*count*] : a usually large wooden or metal wheel that is turned by the force of water flowing against it

water wings *noun* [*plural*] : bands of plastic in the shape of a circle that are filled with air and worn on the arms to help people float when they are learning to swim ▪ a pair of *water wings*

wa·ter·works /ˈwɑːtəˌwəks/ *noun* [*plural*]

1 : a system for supplying water to a city or town that includes pipes, pumps, etc.

2 *Brit, informal + humorous* **:** the parts of the body that produce urine : the urinary system

turn on the waterworks *informal* **:** to start crying especially in order to get sympathy from someone ▪ kids who *turn on the waterworks* when they want attention

wa·tery /ˈwɑːtəri/ *adj* [*more* ~; *most* ~]

1 : containing or filled with water or a similar liquid ▪ The pollen caused her eyes to become *watery.* ▪ *watery* fields

2 a *of a liquid* **:** very thin and similar to water in appearance, taste, etc. ▪ The soup was *watery* and had no flavor. ▪ *watery* tomato juice **b :** pale and seeming to have little substance ▪ the *watery* light of winter ▪ the *watery* moon

a watery grave *literary* **:** death by drowning ▪ She was rescued from *a watery grave.*

watt /ˈwɑːt/ *noun, pl* **watts** [*count*] : a unit for measuring electrical power ▪ a 40-*watt* light bulb — abbr. *W*

watt·age /ˈwɑːtɪʤ/ *noun* [*noncount*] : the amount of electrical power measured in watts that something (such as a light bulb) uses ▪ Use a bulb with low *wattage.*

[1]**wat·tle** /ˈwɑːtl̩/ *noun* [*noncount*] : a structure that is made of upright poles and sticks, twigs, etc., that are woven with them and that is used for building fences, walls, etc. ▪ a framework of *wattle* ▪ huts built of ***wattle and daub*** [=wattle covered with clay] — compare [2]WATTLE

[2]**wattle** *noun, pl* **wat·tles** [*count*] : a piece of loose skin that hangs from the neck or head of some birds ▪ a turkey's *wattle* — compare [1]WATTLE

[1]**wave** /ˈweɪv/ *verb* **waves; waved; wav·ing**

1 : to move your hand or something held in your hand usually in a repeated motion in order to signal or greet someone [*no obj*] We *waved* to our friends through the window. ▪ They *waved* at us. ▪ She was *waving* in the direction of the bridge. [+ *obj*] We ***waved goodbye*** [=waved as a way of saying goodbye] to them and drove away. ▪ The traffic cop ***waved*** cars ***through.*** [=waved in a way that told drivers to continue driving through a particular area] ▪ We offered to help but he ***waved*** us ***off.*** [=he waved as a way of telling us that he did not want help] ▪ We tried to ***wave down*** a taxi. [=to get a taxi to stop for us by waving at its driver]

2 [*no obj*] **:** to float, shake, or move back and forth because of wind ▪ Flags were *waving* in the breeze. ▪ fields of *waving* grain

3 [+ *obj*] **:** to move (something) back and forth ▪ The magician *waved* his magic wand. ▪ The leader of the parade *waved* a flag. ▪ It was so hot that we were all *waving* our hands in front of our faces to cool off.

4 [+ *obj*] **:** to hold up and show (something) in a threatening way ▪ The robber *waved* a pistol at the clerk. ▪ a maniac *waving* [=*brandishing*] a knife

5 a [+ *obj*] **:** to make (someone's hair) curl slightly — usually used as *(be/get) waved* ▪ She *got* her hair *waved.* **b** [*no obj*] *of hair* **:** to curl slightly ▪ His hair *waves* naturally.

wave aside [*phrasal verb*] ***wave (something) aside*** *or* ***wave aside (something)*** **:** to refuse to consider or respond to (something) ▪ The officer *waved aside* my questions.

wave the flag see [1]FLAG

[2]**wave** *noun, pl* **waves**

1 [*count*] **:** an area of moving water that is raised above the main surface of an ocean, a lake, etc. ▪ The *waves* crashed onto the rocks. ▪ ocean *waves* ▪ The motion of the *waves* (under the boat) made us seasick. — see also TIDAL WAVE

2 [*count*] **:** something that has the shape or movement of a wave ▪ She has a *wave* in her hair. ▪ amber *waves* of grain ▪ *Waves* of warm air washed over us.

3 [*count*] **:** a usually repeated movement of your hand or of something held in your hand especially as a signal or greeting ▪ He gave me a *wave.* [=he waved to/at me] ▪ We got a *wave* from the Queen. ▪ The rabbit disappeared with a *wave* of the magician's wand. ▪ a kiss and a ***wave goodbye*** [=a wave that you use to say goodbye]

4 [*count*] **a :** a period of time in which a particular type of activity is being done commonly or repeatedly ▪ The tax cut triggered a *wave* of spending. ▪ a crime *wave* — see also HEAT WAVE **b :** a large number of people or things that do something together, are seen together, etc. ▪ a new *wave* of immigrants [=a large number of immigrants arriving at the same time] ▪ The attacks came in *waves.*

5 [*count*] **a :** a strong feeling that affects someone suddenly ▪ A *wave* of fatigue swept over me. [=I suddenly became very tired] ▪ He was overcome by *waves* of anger/fear. **b :** a strong feeling or attitude that is shared by many people at the same time ▪ The new school has triggered a *wave* of optimism [=has made many people feel optimistic] about the public school system. ▪ a *wave* of nostalgia ▪ At the age of 80, she's ***riding a/the wave of*** renewed interest in her work. [=she's experiencing a time when many people are interested in her work again] ▪ a time when the mayor was still *riding a wave of* public approval

6 [*count*] *technical* **:** an amount of energy (such as light) that moves in a shape resembling a wave from one point to another point ▪ light *waves* — see also AIRWAVES, RADIO WAVE, SHOCK WAVE, SHORTWAVE, SOUND WAVE

7 *the wave* : a movement made by a group of people especially in a stadium or arena in which individual people stand up and then sit down again according to where they are sitting in order to create the appearance of an ocean wave ▪ The crowd did *the wave* between innings. — called also *(Brit) the Mexican wave*

make waves *informal* **:** to do something that causes people to notice you ▪ He's *making waves* in the music industry.; *especially* **:** to cause trouble or annoy people by complaining ▪ I'm tempted to complain, but I don't want to *make waves.*

the wave of the future **:** an idea, product, way of thinking, etc., that will become very popular in the future ▪ These new video games are *the wave of the future.*

– see also NEW WAVE

– wave·like /ˈweɪvˌlaɪk/ *adj* [*more* ~; *most* ~] ▪ She made a *wavelike* motion with her arms.

wave·length /ˈweɪvˌlɛŋkθ/ *noun, pl* **-lengths** [*count*]

1 *technical* **:** the distance from one wave of energy to another as it is traveling from one point to another point ▪ Light and sound have different *wavelengths.* ▪ radio *wavelengths*

2 *informal* — used especially in the phrases ***on the same wavelength*** and ***on a different wavelength*** to say that people share or do not share a way of thinking ▪ We are usually *on the same wavelength.* [=we usually agree, think the same way about things, etc.] ▪ She is *on a different wavelength* than I am.

wave·let /ˈweɪvlət/ *noun, pl* **-lets** [*count*] *technical* **:** a small wave

wa·ver /ˈweɪvə/ *verb* **-vers; -vered; -ver·ing** [*no obj*]

1 : to go back and forth between choices or opinions : to be uncertain about what you think about something or someone ▪ people who are still *wavering* between the two candidates ▪ She *wavered* [=*vacillated*] over the decision for hours. ▪ They never *wavered* in their support for their leader. ▪ Despite the changes, he did not *waver* from his plan to retire.

2 : to move back and forth in an unsteady way ▪ The kite *wavered* in the wind.

3 : to become unsteady because of weakness, emotion, tiredness, etc. ▪ Her voice *wavered* [=*quavered*] as she told us about their argument. ▪ During a long lecture my attention will sometimes *waver.* [=*wander*; I will sometimes think about other things]

– wa·ver·er /ˈweɪvərə/ *noun, pl* **-ers** [*count*]

wavy /ˈweɪvi/ *adj* **wav·i·er; -est :** having the curving shape of a wave or of many waves ▪ She has *wavy* blond hair. ▪ *wavy* lines

– wav·i·ness /ˈweɪvinəs/ *noun* [*noncount*]

[1]**wax** /ˈwæks/ *noun, pl* **wax·es**

1 : a hard substance that becomes soft when it is heated and that is used to make various products (such as candles, crayons, or polish) [*count*] a variety of floor *waxes* [*noncount*] candles made of *wax* ▪ car *wax* [=a substance used to polish cars] — often used before another noun ▪ a *wax* candle/figurine — see also BEESWAX, SEALING WAX

2 [*noncount*] : a natural sticky substance that is produced inside the ear : EARWAX

– wax·like /ˈwæksˌlaɪk/ *adj* [*more* ~; *most* ~] ▪ a *waxlike* substance

²wax *verb* **waxes; waxed; wax·ing** [+ *obj*]

1 : to put a thin layer of wax on (something) : to treat or polish (something) by rubbing it with wax ▪ He *waxed* his car today. ▪ The floor has just been *waxed.*

2 : to remove hair from (a part of the body) by putting hot wax on it and then pulling the wax off ▪ She *waxes* her eyebrows/legs.

– compare ³WAX

³wax *verb* **waxes; waxed; waxing**

1 [*no obj*] *of the moon* : to appear to become larger or more full ▪ The moon *waxes* and then wanes.

2 [*no obj*] : to become larger or more : to increase in amount, size, etc. ▪ Interest in the story seems to *wax* and wane depending on other news.

3 *always followed by an adjective* [*linking verb*] : to talk or write about something in a way that shows that you are experiencing a specified mood or feeling ▪ He *waxed* nostalgic about his childhood. [=he talked/wrote nostalgically about his childhood] ▪ *waxing* poetic

– compare ²WAX

wax bean *noun, pl* ~ **beans** [*count*] *US* : a kind of bean whose long yellow seed cases are eaten as a vegetable — see color picture on page C4

wax·en /ˈwæksən/ *adj* [*more* ~; *most* ~] *literary*

1 : made of or covered in wax ▪ *waxen* figurines

2 : looking like something made of or covered in wax: such as **a** : very smooth and shiny ▪ flowers with *waxen* petals **b** : very pale especially in a way that suggests poor health ▪ a pale, *waxen* face

wax museum *noun, pl* ~ **-ums** [*count*] : a museum that has wax statues of famous people — called also (*Brit*) *waxworks*

wax paper *or* **waxed paper** *noun* [*noncount*] *US* : paper that is covered with wax in order to prevent water and other substances from passing through it and that is often used to wrap food — called also (*Brit*) *greaseproof paper*

wax·works /ˈwæksˌwɚks/ *noun, pl* **waxworks** [*count*] *Brit* : WAX MUSEUM

waxy /ˈwæksi/ *adj* **wax·i·er; -est** : seeming to be made of or covered in wax ▪ The polish left a *waxy* residue. ▪ a plant with *waxy* leaves ▪ a *waxy* surface/substance

¹way /ˈweɪ/ *noun, pl* **ways**

1 [*count*] **a** : how someone or something does something : how someone or something behaves, appears, feels, etc. — usually singular ▪ I like the *way* she looks/dresses/laughs. [=I like her appearance/clothing/laugh] ▪ The *way* he treats his mother is so sweet. ▪ The machine isn't working the *way* it's supposed to. ▪ It's strange the *way* things seem to happen for a reason. ▪ Do you really think that *way* about them? [=is that really your opinion of them?] ▪ The steak was rare, just the *way* I like it. ▪ Well, Your Honor, it happened this *way.* [=this is what happened] — often followed by *to + verb* ▪ That's no *way to talk* to your father. [=you should not talk to your father using those words, that tone of voice, etc.] ▪ There is no easy *way to say* this: you have to leave. — often used with *in* ▪ She explains things *in* a *way* that children can understand. ▪ He spoke *in* a calm and gentle *way.* [=*manner*] ▪ I said that she was quirky, but I meant it *in* a good/positive *way.* ▪ *In* a strange *way,* I've always known I would go back there. ▪ I try to be nice to everyone, and *in* the same *way,* I expect everyone to be nice to me. ▪ He wants to win ***in a big way.*** [=very much] ▪ ***In a small way*** [=to a small extent or degree], the experience helped me understand what it's like to be homeless. ▪ Their story is a tragedy ***in more ways than one.*** [=it is a tragedy for more than one reason] ▪ ***The way things are going*** [=if things continue to happen like this], I may lose my job. ▪ We were disappointed when we lost, but that's ***the way it/life goes.*** [=it is a fact that bad or disappointing things happen sometimes] ▪ Let's stop here. ***That/This way*** [=by doing that/this] we can look at the map before we get off the highway. **b** : a method or system that can be used to do something ▪ We'll try doing it your *way* first. ▪ Let me explain it this *way.* ▪ What are some (of the) *ways* that you deal with stress? ▪ You can pay for your purchase in one/either of two *ways*: by cash or by credit card. — often followed by *to + verb* ▪ I've tried lots of different *ways to lose* weight. ▪ That is a good *way to look* at the problem. ▪ There's no *way to know* what will happen next. — often + *of* ▪ There's no *way of* knowing what will happen. ▪ He uses art as a *way of* expressing his feelings. ▪ You have a funny *way of* showing that you like her. ▪ This gift is my *way of* saying thank you for all of your help. ▪ She will become famous ***one way or another***—if not by modeling, then by acting or singing. ▪ *One way or another,* it's going to happen. ▪ For months, he had been trying to find ***a way into/to her heart.*** [=to make her love him] ▪ ***Where there's a will, there's a way.*** [=if you have the desire and determination to do something, you can find a method for accomplishing it]

2 [*count*] : a person's usual habits, actions, qualities, etc. ▪ He has a charming *way* about him. [=he is charming; he behaves/talks in a charming way] ▪ Everyone is special in his or her own *way.* [=everyone has qualities that make him or her special] ▪ It is not his *way* to give up easily. [=he does not give up easily] ▪ She is familiar with Western *ways.* = She is familiar with the *ways* of Westerners. [=the typical habits, behaviors, etc., of people who live in the West] ▪ He is becoming older and more ***set in his ways.*** [=more unwilling to change his habits, behaviors, opinions, etc.]

3 [*count*] **a** : the series of roads, paths, etc., that can be used to go from one place to another — usually singular ▪ He asked the *way* to the museum. ▪ What's the quickest *way* to the library? ▪ We took the long *way* home. — often used figuratively to refer to a series of actions, procedures, etc., that can be used to achieve something ▪ One *way* around the problem of poor sales is to lower prices. ▪ He is a Broadway actor looking for a *way* into the movie industry. ▪ They ***smoothed the way*** for an end to the dispute. [=they made an end to the dispute easier and more likely] **b** : a road, path, etc. — usually singular ▪ We could not find the *way* that leads to the waterfall. ▪ The explorers hacked a *way* through the jungle. ▪ They live ***across the way*** from us. = (*Brit*) They live ***over the way*** from us. [=they live across from us on the other side of the street] ▪ There is another jewelry store *across the way.* — often used in names ▪ He lives at 121 Village *Way.* **c** : a door, opening, etc., that is used for going into or out of a place ▪ Which door is the *way* in? ▪ The back *way* was blocked. ▪ This door is the only *way* out of the room. — often used figuratively ▪ We're in trouble, and there is no (clear/simple) *way* out. [=no clear/simple way to get out of trouble] ▪ They're trying to ***take the easy way out.*** [=trying to find an easy way to avoid having to do something difficult] ◊ In British English a door or passage that leads outside or to an exit door is often marked ***Way Out,*** while in U.S. English it is marked ***Exit.***

4 [*count*] **a** : the route along which someone or something is moving or intends to move : the area in front of a moving person or thing ▪ A tree had fallen and was blocking our *way.* ▪ She used a flashlight to light her *way* to the shed. ▪ Please move—you're ***in my/the way.*** [=you are blocking my path] ▪ Get ***out of my/the way!*** ▪ He asked the children to stay/keep *out of his way* while he made dinner. ▪ "Can you give me a ride to the library if it's not *out of your way*?" [=if you do not have to take another route in order to do it] "Sure, I can give you a ride. The library is ***on my/the way*** home." [=I pass the library when I take my usual route home] ▪ I go past it *on my way* home. — see also IN THE WAY, ON THE WAY, OUT OF THE WAY (below) **b** — used with *her, his, their, its, your,* and *our* to describe someone or something that is moving forward, going somewhere, etc. ▪ Paramedics pushed *their way* through the crowd. ▪ The snail slowly inched *its way* toward the water. ▪ The river winds/snakes *its way* through the valley. ▪ He tried to ***buy his way*** into the prestigious college. [=he tried to use money to get himself accepted as a student at the college] ▪ She managed to ***talk her way*** past the guard. [=she was able to convince the guard to let her pass]

5 [*count*] **a** : a specified or indicated direction ▪ Face this *way* so I can take your picture. ▪ Try turning the key the other *way.* ▪ Which *way* should we go, left or right? ▪ They went that *way.* ▪ Look both *ways* before crossing the street. ▪ The exit is this *way,* ladies and gentlemen. ▪ She is coming/heading back this *way.* [=towards us] ▪ The rabbit ran ***this way and that*** [=in many different directions], trying not to get caught. **b** — used with *her, his, their, its, your,* and *our* to say that someone or something is moving toward or coming to a particular person or thing ▪ A storm is heading *our/their way.* [=towards us/them] ▪ A tax rebate may be coming *your way.* [=may be sent to you] ▪ A streak of bad luck had come *his way.* [=he was experiencing some bad luck]

6 [*singular*] : a distance ▪ They live a short *way* down the road. [=a short distance from here on the same road] ▪ He

grew up a long *way* from here. [=far from here] ▪ He talked ***the whole/entire way*** home. [=throughout the entire journey home] — often used figuratively ▪ If you want to run for the Senate, we'll support you ***every inch/step of the way.*** [=throughout the entire process] ▪ He still has ***a way to go*** [=a long time to wait] before the cast on his foot can be removed. — see also ALL THE WAY (below), WAYS

7 [*singular*] *informal* **:** the area or region where someone lives ▪ The weather has been rainy (out) our *way.* [=out where we live] ▪ I'll visit when I'm down your *way* again. ▪ They live out California *way.* [=in or near California]

8 [*count*] **a :** a particular part of something that is being thought about or discussed — used with *in* ▪ The new computer is superior to the other one ***in every way.*** [=it is completely superior; all parts of it are superior] ▪ ***In many ways,*** their stories are the same. [=their stories are the same to a great degree; many parts of their stories are the same] ▪ ***In some ways*** the movie is brilliant, but ***in other ways*** it is just horrible. ▪ Her statement is true, ***in a way.*** [=it is true to some extent; it is partly true] ▪ ***In no way*** am I like my father. [=I am not at all like him; no part of me is like him] **b :** a manner of thinking about or considering something ▪ The punishment was severe, but ***in a way*** it was appropriate. [=it was appropriate when you think about it from a certain point of view] ▪ I started looking at the problem *in a* different *way* than I had before. ▪ ***To my way of thinking*** [=in my opinion], this is the best strategy. = The ***way I see it,*** this is the best strategy.

9 [*singular*] **:** the situation that exists ▪ People are dying of hunger, and it doesn't have to ***be that way.*** [=the situation can be changed] ▪ Business is good, and we are doing everything we can to ***keep it that way.*** ▪ There's nothing we can do to help them. That's just ***the way things are.***

10 [*count*] **:** one of usually two possible decisions, actions, or results ▪ We thought she would vote against the bill, but surprisingly she voted/went the other *way.* [=she voted for the bill] ▪ I can't see how the election could have gone any other *way.* [=how it could have had a different result] ▪ I'm not sure if I will take the bus or train, but ***either way*** [=whether I take the bus or the train] I will be there tonight. ▪ It's all right with me *either way.* [=both possibilities are acceptable to me] ▪ You can have either lower taxes or better-funded public programs; you can't ***have it both ways.*** ▪ He ***wants it both ways.*** ▪ Yes or no? Give me an answer ***one way or the other.*** ▪ I don't have an opinion *one way or the other.* — see also GO EITHER WAY (below)

11 [*count*] **:** one of a specified number of usually equal parts into which something (such as an amount of money) is divided ▪ The money was divided three *ways.* [=it was divided into three amounts]

all the way **1 :** to the full or entire extent **:** as far as possible ▪ You have to pull the lever *all the way* back. ▪ We were seated *all the way* in the back. **2 :** throughout an entire process or period of time ▪ His family was with him *all the way* through his candidacy. ▪ They sang songs *all the way* home. [=throughout the journey home] **3 :** to the fullest and most complete extent ▪ I am with you *all the way.* = I support you *all the way.* [=I support every part of what you are doing] **4 :** over an entire distance ▪ She ran *all the way* there. ▪ You came ***all this way*** [=all the way to here] just to see me? — see also GO ALL THE WAY (below), [1]WAY 6 (above)

a long way see [1]LONG

by the way — used in speech to introduce a statement or question that may or may not relate to the current topic of conversation ▪ *By the way,* I really like your shoes. ▪ *By the way,* did you hear what happened today? ▪ When do you leave for college, *by the way?*

by way of **1 :** by traveling through (a place) **:** VIA ▪ She came here from China *by way of* England. **2 :** for the purpose of giving, making, or doing (something specified) ▪ She said that many people are finding ways to improve their diets, and she mentioned her own family *by way of* example. [=as an example; in order to give an example] ▪ This vase is slightly discolored. *By way of* comparison [=in order to make a comparison], examine the vase on the left.

change your ways **:** to improve your behavior, habits, or beliefs ▪ If you want to live a long life, you'd better *change your ways!* ▪ a former racist who has *changed her ways*

clear the way **1 :** to make the area through which someone or something is trying to pass open and able to be used ▪ *Clear the way,* please. [=move away from the area I am trying to pass through] ▪ She directed traffic to *clear the way* for the ambulance. **2 :** to allow something to happen or develop ▪ The truce would *clear the way* for further discussions between the two groups.

give way **1 :** to break apart and fall down ▪ The step feels like it will *give way* soon. ▪ The roof *gave way* [=*collapsed*] under heavy snow. **2** *formal* **:** to stop trying to fight or resist something **:** to agree to do or accept something that you have been resisting or opposing ▪ After several hours of debate, the opposition finally *gave way.* [=*gave in*] **3 :** to be replaced by something specified — often + *to* ▪ Our frustration soon *gave way to* anger. ▪ Much of the state's farmland has *given way to* shopping malls. ▪ time-honored traditions *giving way to* more modern methods **4** *Brit* **:** to allow another car or person to go ahead of you or in front of you — often + *to* ▪ Cars must *give way* [=(*US*) *yield*] *to* pedestrians.

go all the way *informal* **1** *sports* **:** to win a championship, title, etc. ▪ The team has the talent to *go all the way* this year. **2 :** to have sex with someone ▪ Did you *go all the way* (with him/her)?

go either way — used to say that either of two possible results is likely to occur and that neither is more likely than the other ▪ I don't know who's going to win. The game could *go either way.* [=either team could win]

go out of your way **:** to make a special effort to do something ▪ She frequently *goes out of her way* to help people in need. ▪ I hate to make you *go out of your way,* but yes, I could use your help.

go someone's way **1 :** to travel in the same direction as someone ▪ Let me walk with you—I'm *going your way.* **2 :** to happen in a way that helps someone ▪ Things haven't been *going our way* lately.

go your own way **:** to do the things that you want to do rather than doing the things that other people expect you to do ▪ She was the kind of woman who always *went her own way.*

go your separate ways see [1]SEPARATE

harm's way see [1]HARM

have a way of ✧ If someone or something *has a way of* being or doing something, the person or thing often has that characteristic or frequently does that thing. ▪ Remakes *have a way of* being [=remakes are often] worse than the original movies. ▪ She *has a way of* exaggerating [=she often exaggerates] when she tells stories. ▪ Life *has a way of* surprising us now and then.

have a way with **:** to be able to use (something) or to deal with (something or someone) well ▪ She *has a way with* kids/dogs. [=she is good at dealing with kids/dogs; kids/dogs like her and behave well when they are with her] ▪ He *has a way with* words. [=he is good with words; he uses words in a skillful and effective way]

have/get your (own) way **:** to get or do what you want to get or do despite the desires, plans, etc., of other people ▪ If I *had my way,* students at the school would all wear uniforms. — often disapproving ▪ He is a spoiled child who always *gets his (own) way.* ▪ All right. ***Have it your way.*** [=do what you want to do] I'm done arguing with you.

have your way with **:** to do exactly what you want to do to or with (something or someone); *especially* **:** to have sex with (someone, and especially someone over whom you have control, influence, etc.) ▪ He has *had his way with* many women.

in any way, shape, or form **:** under any circumstances or conditions ▪ That behavior is not acceptable *in any way, shape, or form.* [=is not at all acceptable] ▪ That is not *in any way, shape, or form* an acceptable or appropriate topic for class discussion.

in the way or ***in someone's or something's way*** **:** making it more difficult for a person to do something **:** preventing something from happening ▪ I left because I felt that I was just *in their way.* ▪ We have important issues to deal with, but these petty arguments keep ***getting in the way.*** ▪ We won't let anything ***stand in the way*** of progress! — see also [1]WAY 4a (above)

in the way of — used to indicate the type of thing that is being described, thought of, etc. ▪ His parents offered him little *in the way of* emotional support. [=they did not give him much emotional support] ▪ How much money has she received *in the way of* campaign contributions?

in the worst way see [1]WORST

lose your way **:** to become confused or uncertain about where you are **:** to become lost ▪ I *lost my way* [=*lost my bearings*] while hiking and ended up spending the night in

the woods. — often used figuratively • Some say that the political party has *lost its way* and really doesn't know how to connect with voters anymore.

make way : to create a path or open space so that someone or something can use it • Several houses were torn down to *make way* for the shopping center. • *Make way* for the paramedics. [=move aside so that the paramedics can pass through] • *Make way*! I'm coming through!

make your way : to move forward usually by following a path • When his name was called, he *made his way* to the stage. — often used figuratively • After college, she set out to *make her way* in the world as a lawyer.

mend your ways see [1]MEND

no two ways about it — used to say that something is definitely true • *No two ways about it*—that was the best performance she has ever given. [=that was definitely her best performance] • They were rude—(there are) *no two ways about it.*

no way** informal* **1** — used to say that you will definitely not do something • There is *no way* I'm going to swim with a shark. • "Do you want to try skydiving?" "*No way.*" • No, I'm not doing it. ***No way José. **2** *US* — used to show that you are very surprised by something or do not believe that something is true • "He's 40 years old." "*No way*! I would have guessed he was 25."

on the way** or **on someone's or something's way **1** : in a state of development : in progress • More layoffs are said to be *on the way*. [=more layoffs will happen soon] **2** : moving from one place to another place • The package should be *on its way*. • I'm afraid I must be *on my way*. [=I must leave now] • A funny thing happened to me *on my/the way* here. [=while I was traveling here] • You need help? I'm *on my way*. [=I am coming to help you now] • She stopped for gas *on the way* home. [=while she was traveling home] • I have to run a few errands *on my way* home. **3** : changing from one level or condition to another level or condition • House prices are *on their way* up. [=are increasing]

on the way out** or **on someone's or something's way out **1** : leaving a place or position • The phone rang while I was *on my way out*. [=while I was trying to leave] • Would you mind closing the door *on your way out*? • There are rumors that the superintendent of schools is *on the way out*. [=leaving his/her job] **2** : becoming no longer popular • Bell-bottom pants are, once again, *on their way out*. • He incorrectly predicted that the Internet would be *on its way out* within three years.

out of the way **1** : far from other places that are well-known • They rented a cottage that was quiet and *out of the way*. **2** : done or dealt with completely • She got her homework *out of the way* [=she finished her homework] so that she could watch TV. • Let's get these issues *out of the way* before we start working on any other issues. **3** : unusual or remarkable • There is nothing *out of the way* about the plan. — see also OUT-OF-THE-WAY, [1]WAY 4a (above)

parting of the ways see [1]PARTING

part ways see [2]PART

see your way (clear) to : to be willing to (do something) • I'd be very grateful if you could *see your way clear to* lend/lending me a few dollars. [=if you would lend me a few dollars]

the other way around** also chiefly Brit **the other way round **1** : in the opposite position, direction, or order • You put the fork on the right and the knife on the left. They should be *the other way around*. [=the fork should be on the left and the knife on the right] **2** — used to say that the opposite situation is true • Sometimes I cook and she does the dishes and sometimes it is *the other way around*. [=and sometimes she cooks and I do the dishes] • "I thought he wanted a divorce." "No, it was *the other way around*." [=she wanted a divorce]

***the way** informal* **1** — used to say what someone's way of speaking, behaving, etc., seems to suggest • You'd think she was rich, *the way* she spends money! [=she spends money like a rich person] • *The way* he talks, you would think he ran the company. [=he talks as if he were the person who runs the company] **2** — used to say that something happens or is done with the same attitude, at the same pace, etc., as something else • They replace their cars *the way* [=*like*] other people replace shoes.

the way/ways of the world : how things happen or how people behave • Success comes easier for some people. That's just *the way of the world*. • Because he was young and inexperienced in *the ways of the world*, people were able to take advantage of him.

way of life **1** : the habits, customs, and beliefs of a particular person or group of people • modern and traditional *ways of life* • Unhampered development is threatening these farmers' *way of life*. [=it could force them to stop farming] **2** : an important activity, job, etc., that affects all parts of someone's life • For me, tennis is not just a sport, it's a *way of life*.

***way to go** US, informal* — used to tell someone that he or she has done something well • Nice job, guys! *Way to go*!

work your way see [1]WORK

— see also MILKY WAY, UNDER WAY, WAYS AND MEANS

[2]way *adv, informal*

1 *always followed by an adverb or preposition* : to a great distance or extent : very far • He is *way* ahead of the other runners. • They live *way* out in the country. • We sat *way* back in the last row. • I missed a week of class and fell *way* behind. • Her political views are *way* to the left/right. [=they are very liberal/conservative]

2 : by a great amount • I ate *way* [=*far*] too much. • The car is *way* [=*much*] too expensive.

3 *always followed by an adjective, US* : VERY • Your parents are *way* cool. • We're *way* excited.

way back : from a time in the distant past • The group was popular *way back* in the 1960s. • They are friends ***from way back***. [=they have been friends for a long time]

way·far·er /ˈweɪˌferɚ/ *noun, pl* **-ers** *[count] literary* : a person who travels from place to place usually by walking

way·lay /ˈweɪˌleɪ/ *verb* **-lays**; **-laid** /-ˌleɪd/; **-lay·ing** *[+ obj]*

1 : to stop (someone who is going somewhere) — usually used as *(be) waylaid* • She *was waylaid* by reporters as she left the courthouse. — sometimes used figuratively • She *was waylaid* by the flu.

2 : to attack (someone or something) by surprise from a hidden place • Gangs sometimes *waylay* travelers on that road. • We were *waylaid* by a group of kids with water balloons.

way–out /ˈweɪˈaʊt/ *adj [more ~; most ~] informal* : very strange or unusual • an extremist with some *way-out* [=*far-out*] ideas

ways /ˈweɪz/ *noun [singular] US, informal* : a distance • We are a long *ways* [=*way*] from home. [=we are far from home] • We still have ***a ways to go***. [=a long way to go] — often used figuratively • We've done a lot of work, but we have a long *ways* [=*way*] to go. [=we still have a lot of work to do] • The wedding is still a long *ways* off. [=it is still far in the future] • She still has *a ways to go* [=she still has a long time to wait] before graduation.

ways and means *noun [noncount]*

1 *somewhat formal* : the methods and tools used for doing something • *ways and means* of increasing revenue

2 ***Ways and Means*** : a committee in the U.S. House of Representatives that is in charge of taxes, trade issues, government debt, etc.

way·side /ˈweɪˌsaɪd/ *noun, pl* **-sides** *[count]* : the land next to a road or path • Flowers grew along the *wayside*. — often used before another noun • a *wayside* inn/restaurant

by the wayside : into a state of no longer being considered, used, etc. • We were going to redo the kitchen this spring, but those plans have ***fallen/gone by the wayside***. [=we have dropped/abandoned those plans] • traditions that are *falling by the wayside*

way station *noun, pl* **~ -tions** *[count] US* : a place where people can stop for rest, supplies, etc., during a long journey — sometimes used figuratively • using the Senate as a *way station* to the presidency

way·ward /ˈweɪˌwɚd/ *adj [more ~; most ~]*

1 : tending to behave in ways that are not socially acceptable • parents of a *wayward* teenager

2 : not going or moving in the intended direction • a *wayward* throw • *wayward* rockets

— **way·ward·ly** *adv* — **way·ward·ness** *noun [noncount]*

wa·zoo /wɑˈzuː/ *noun, pl* **-zoos** *[count] US slang, humorous* : the part of the body you sit on : BUTTOCKS

***out/up the wazoo** US, informal* : in large amounts • We have bills *up the wazoo*. [=we have many bills] • a team with talent *out the wazoo* [=a team with a great amount of talent]

WC *abbr, chiefly Brit* water closet

we /ˈwiː/ *pronoun*

1 — used to refer to the speaker and another person or group of people as the subject of a verb • *We* had a party at work. • If you are ready, *we* can get started. • *We* would like a

W

table for two. ▪ What are *we* having for dinner? ▪ *We* are sharing a pizza. What are you having? ▪ Let us know where *we* should meet you. — compare I
2 a — used to refer to the company, business, organization, etc., that the speaker works for or is involved with ▪ *We* will publish the answers in next week's issue. ▪ *We* close for a week in July every year. ▪ *We* are only open until noon today. **b** *formal* — used like *I* by a king or queen ▪ "*We* welcome you," said the queen to her visitors. — see also *the royal "we"* at [1]ROYAL
3 : people in general ▪ *We* must learn to forgive those who hurt us.
4 : YOU — used in speech when trying to persuade or encourage someone to do or say something ▪ "How are *we* feeling today?," the nurse asked the patient. ▪ Be very quiet, children. *We* don't want to wake Daddy, do *we*? ▪ A little edgy, are *we*?

weak /ˈwi:k/ *adj* **weak·er; -est** [*also more* ~; *most* ~]
1 : having little physical power or ability **:** not strong ▪ He has a *weak* throwing arm. ▪ The illness left her too *weak* to stand up. ▪ The child was born with *weak* lungs. ▪ *weak* eyes/eyesight
2 : having little power or force ▪ The batter hit a *weak* ground ball. ▪ a *weak* punch ▪ *weak* winds ▪ She uttered her reply in a *weak* voice.
3 : likely to break or stop working properly **:** not able to handle weight, pressure, or strain ▪ The door's hinge is *weak*. ▪ a *weak* rope
4 *disapproving* **a :** having little power or influence ▪ He proved to be a *weak* and ineffectual leader. **b :** not able to make good decisions or deal with difficult situations ▪ Some see compromise as a sign of a *weak* character. ▪ In a ***weak moment*** [=during a brief time when I had bad judgment] I told them my secret.
5 a : lacking enough or the usual amount of an important ingredient ▪ This tea is *weak*. [=it has little tea flavor] ▪ *weak* cocktails [=cocktails that contain less than the usual amount of alcohol] ▪ a *weak* bleach solution [=a mixture of water and a small amount of bleach] **b :** not powerful in action or effect ▪ a *weak* drug ▪ a country with *weak* environmental laws ▪ a *weak* radio signal
6 : not likely to persuade or convince people that something is true, real, correct, etc. ▪ Her arguments in support of the theory were *weak*. ▪ He gave a *weak* excuse for being late. ▪ The prosecution has a *weak* case.
7 : not having enough skill or ability ▪ Many of the students are *weak* in math and science. ▪ The team is *weak* on defense.
8 : failing to produce the result that is wanted **:** not effective ▪ The pun was a *weak* attempt at humor. ▪ The novel's plot was *weak*. [=it did not make sense, did not seem realistic, etc.]
9 : showing little confidence or enthusiasm ▪ He gave only a *weak* smile.
10 a : having a value that is small or is not increasing **:** less valuable ▪ The dollar is *weak*. **b :** in a poor financial condition ▪ a *weak* economy ▪ a *weak* housing market [=a situation in which few people are buying houses]
11 : dull or pale ▪ The *weak* winter light shone through the window. ▪ *weak* colors
12 : smaller than the usual size ▪ a man with a *weak* chin
13 *grammar* **:** following the normal patterns by which the past tenses of verbs are usually formed **:** REGULAR ▪ Since "work" is a *weak* verb, its past tense is "worked."
a weak stomach see [1]STOMACH
the spirit is willing but the flesh is weak see [1]SPIRIT
the weak **:** weak people ▪ *the weak* and the powerful
weak at/in the knees **:** so nervous or powerfully affected that it is difficult for you to stand ▪ The announcement made me *weak at the knees*. ▪ She said hello to me and I went *weak in the knees*.
– weak·ly *adv* ▪ He smiled *weakly* at me.

> ***synonyms*** WEAK, FEEBLE, and FRAIL mean lacking strength. WEAK is a general word that can describe either a temporary or permanent lack of strength. ▪ He felt *weak* after his illness. ▪ I'm too *weak* to lift that heavy box by myself. FEEBLE stresses the kind of very great weakness that often makes other people feel pity or sympathy. ▪ *Feeble* with hunger, the dog was found wandering in the streets. FRAIL is usually used to describe a very weak person who is easily injured especially because of illness or age. ▪ a *frail* and sickly child ▪ She became very *frail* in her old age.

weak·en /ˈwi:kən/ *verb* **-ens; -ened; -en·ing**
1 [+ *obj*] **:** to make (something or someone) weaker, less forceful, less effective, etc. ▪ The disease *weakens* the immune system. ▪ people (whose bodies are) *weakened* by hunger ▪ Some are concerned that the increase in taxes will *weaken* the economy. ▪ The beams had been *weakened* by water damage. ▪ efforts to *weaken* environmental laws ▪ The recent setbacks have not *weakened* our resolve. ▪ These kinds of contradictions *weaken* your argument.
2 [*no obj*] **:** to become weaker, less forceful, less effective, etc. ▪ The disease causes the immune system to *weaken*. ▪ The housing market is *weakening*. [=fewer people are buying houses]
3 *of money* **:** to decrease in value when compared to money from other countries [*no obj*] The dollar has continued to ***weaken against*** the euro. [+ *obj*] Lower interest rates have *weakened* the dollar. — opposite STRENGTHEN
– weakening *noun* [*noncount*] ▪ the *weakening* of environmental laws

weak·ling /ˈwi:klɪŋ/ *noun, pl* **-lings** [*count*] *disapproving* **:** a weak person ▪ a 90-pound *weakling*

weak–mind·ed /ˈwi:kˈmaɪndəd/ *adj* [*more* ~; *most* ~] *disapproving* **:** having or showing a lack of good sense or judgment **:** FOOLISH ▪ the faulty logic of *weak-minded* individuals ▪ *weak-minded* rhetoric

weak·ness /ˈwi:knəs/ *noun, pl* **-ness·es**
1 [*noncount*] **:** the quality or state of being weak ▪ muscle *weakness* ▪ The *weakness* of her voice surprised me. ▪ The incident exposed his *weakness* as a leader. ▪ Some see compromise as a sign of *weakness*. ▪ moral *weakness* ▪ the *weakness* of a radio signal/Internet connection ▪ the *weakness* of the dollar/economy ▪ I told them my secret in a ***moment of weakness***
2 [*count*] **:** a quality or feature that prevents someone or something from being effective or useful ▪ The tutor assessed the student's strengths and *weaknesses*. ▪ The basketball team has few *weaknesses*.
3 [*count*] **a :** something that you like so much that you are often unable to resist it ▪ Chocolate is my greatest *weakness*. **b :** a strong feeling of desire *for* something ▪ He has a *weakness for* desserts.

weak sister *noun, pl* ~ **-ters** [*count*] *US* **:** a member of a group that is weak or unsuccessful in comparison to others in the group ▪ The company is no longer a/the *weak sister* among auto producers.

[1]**weal** /ˈwi:l/ *noun* [*noncount*] *old-fashioned* **:** a state of being happy, healthy, and successful **:** WELL-BEING ▪ work to improve the public/common *weal* — compare [2]WEAL

[2]**weal** *noun, pl* **weals** [*count*] **:** a usually reddish bump or bruise on the skin **:** WELT — compare [1]WEAL

wealth /ˈwɛlθ/ *noun*
1 [*noncount*] **a :** a large amount of money and possessions ▪ a nation/family that has acquired great *wealth* ▪ someone whose sole goal is the accumulation of *wealth* **b :** the value of all the property, possessions, and money that someone or something has ▪ Her personal *wealth* is estimated to be around $10 billion. ▪ What percentage of the national *wealth* is spent on health care?
2 [*singular*] **:** a large amount or number ▪ I was impressed by the *wealth* of choices. ▪ Libraries offer ***a wealth of*** information.
share/spread the wealth **:** to share your money, goods, etc., with other people ▪ If your garden is overflowing, be a good neighbor and *spread the wealth*. [=give some of what is growing in your garden to neighbors]

wealthy /ˈwɛlθi/ *adj* **wealth·i·er; -est :** having a lot of money and possessions **:** RICH ▪ He is a *wealthy* entrepreneur. ▪ the *wealthiest* nations in the world ▪ They live in a *wealthy* [=*well-to-do*] suburb. ▪ a *wealthy* [=*affluent*] neighborhood ▪ They were fabulously/very *wealthy*.
the wealthy **:** wealthy people ▪ policies to benefit *the wealthy* [=*the rich*]
– wealth·i·ness /ˈwɛlθinəs/ *noun* [*noncount*]

wean /ˈwi:n/ *verb* **weans; weaned; wean·ing** [+ *obj*] **:** to start feeding (a child or young animal) food other than its mother's milk ▪ The calves are *weaned* at an early age.
wean from/off [*phrasal verb*] ***wean (someone or something) from/off (something)*** **:** to make (someone or something) stop doing or using (something) ▪ efforts to *wean* the country *from* its dependence on foreign oil ▪ I'm gradually *weaning* myself *off* cigarettes.
wean on [*phrasal verb*] ***wean (someone) on (something)*** **:** to have (someone) see, use, or experience (something) often

especially from a young age — usually used as *(be) weaned on* • a generation of kids *weaned on* television [=a generation of kids who have watched television a lot since they were very young] • Although born in the 1970s, the singer says she *was weaned on* the music of the 1940s.

weap•on /ˈwɛpən/ *noun, pl* **-ons** *[count]*
1 : something (such as a gun, knife, club, or bomb) that is used for fighting or attacking someone or for defending yourself when someone is attacking you • assault with a deadly *weapon* • a concealed *weapon* • chemical/biological *weapons* [=weapons that use dangerous chemicals, germs, etc.] • ***weapons of mass destruction*** [=weapons that can destroy entire cities, regions, etc.] • The police never found the ***murder weapon***. [=the weapon used to commit murder]
2 : something (such as a skill, idea, or tool) that is used to win a contest or achieve something • The pitcher's slider is his most effective *weapon*. • a new *weapon* in the fight against cancer • The mayor's campaign unleashed its ***secret weapon***.

weap•on•ry /ˈwɛpənri/ *noun [noncount]* **:** WEAPONS • The army has developed some new high-tech *weaponry*.

[1]**wear** /ˈweɚ/ *verb* **wears; wore** /ˈwoɚ/; **worn** /ˈwoɚn/; **wear•ing** *[+ obj]*
1 a : to use or have (something) as clothing **:** to have (a shirt, pants, etc.) over part of your body • He was *wearing* blue jeans. • She *wore* a red blouse to work. • White coats are often *worn* by doctors. **b :** to use or have (something) on your body • I don't *wear* glasses. • He doesn't *wear* a watch. • Are you *wearing* perfume? • a badge *worn* by police officers • Were you *wearing* a seat belt? **c :** to grow or arrange (your hair) in a particular way • She *wears* her hair in a ponytail. • I used to *wear* my hair long. • He *wears* [=*has*] a beard now.
2 : to have or show (something, such as an emotion or facial expression) especially on your face • The teacher was *wearing* a frown/smile. • I guess I ***wear my heart on my sleeve***. [=show my emotions in an obvious way]
3 a : to cause (something) to become thinner, weaker, etc., because of continued use over time — used as *(be) worn* • The carpet *was* badly *worn* in some areas. **b :** to cause (something) to form gradually because of use • He *wore* a hole in his pants. • A path had been *worn* into the grass.
4 *somewhat formal* **:** to make (someone) very tired • soldiers *worn* by the strain of war

wear away *[phrasal verb]* ***wear away*** *or* ***wear (something) away*** *or* ***wear away (something)*** **:** to gradually disappear or to cause (something) to gradually disappear or become thinner, smaller, etc., because of use • The paint on the sign had *worn away*. • Even a trickle of water will eventually *wear* rock *away*. — often used as *(be) worn away* • The table's finish *was worn away*.

wear down *[phrasal verb]* ***wear (someone) down*** *or* ***wear down (someone)*** **1 :** to make (someone) tired or weak • The pressure at home and at work was *wearing* her *down*. **2 :** to convince (someone) to do what you want by trying again and again • She pleaded until she had *worn* her parents *down* and they agreed to let her go to the party.

wear many hats see HAT

wear off *[phrasal verb]* **:** to gradually decrease, disappear, or stop • The painkillers *wore off* [=stopped having an effect; stopped decreasing or removing pain] after a couple of hours. • The shine on the leather will *wear off* pretty quickly. [=the leather will no longer be shiny after a short time] • After you drive a new car for a while, ***the novelty wears off***. [=it is no longer exciting or new]

wear on *[phrasal verb]* **1** ***wear on (someone)*** **:** to annoy or bother (someone) • Their constant talking was *wearing on* me. **2 :** to continue in a way that seems slow • As their visit *wore on* [=*dragged on*] she started hinting that it was time to leave. • as the day *wore on*

wear out *[phrasal verb]* **1** ***wear (someone) out*** *or* ***wear out (someone)*** **:** to make (someone) tired • All that work in the yard yesterday really *wore me out*. • She was *worn out* [=*exhausted*] from exercising. **2** ***wear out*** *or* ***wear (something) out*** *or* ***wear out (something)*** **:** to become thinner, weaker, or no longer useful because of use or to cause (something) to become thinner, weaker, or no longer useful because of use • The tires *wore out* after 60,000 miles. • You'll *wear out* your shoes doing that. — often used as *(be) worn out* • The tape *is worn out*.

wear out your welcome see [4]WELCOME

wear the pants *(US) or Brit* ***wear the trousers*** **:** to be the leader **:** to make decisions for a group of people • She *wears the pants* [=she is in charge] in that family.

wear thin **1 :** to become weak or ineffective • I'd been waiting almost an hour, and my patience was *wearing thin*. [=I was losing patience; I was beginning to get annoyed/upset] **2 :** to become ineffective or uninteresting because of being too familiar or used too often • The comedy's plot relies on a case of mistaken identity, but the joke *wears thin*. • His charm is beginning to *wear thin*. **3 :** to become thin because of use • The rug by the door is *wearing thin* and needs to be replaced.

wear through *[phrasal verb]* ***wear through (something)*** *or* ***wear (something) through*** **:** to use (something) so much that a hole develops in it • I've *worn through* two pairs of work shoes since I started this job.

wear well **1 :** to remain in good condition after being used • The floor *wears well* even in high traffic areas. **2** *informal + humorous* **:** to look younger than you are • For 70, she's *wearing well*.

– wear•er *noun, pl* **-ers** *[count]* • Some clothes look good on some *wearers* but not others.

[2]**wear** *noun [noncount]*
1 a : the act of using something as clothing **:** the act of wearing something • shoes that are perfect for everyday *wear* **b :** the act of using something • The deck is built to withstand years of *wear*. • I got a lot of *wear* out of these boots.
2 : clothing that is designed for a specified kind of person, occasion, or use • children's *wear* • a new line of evening *wear* • active *wear* — see also FOOTWEAR, MENSWEAR, RAINWEAR, SPORTSWEAR, SWIMWEAR, UNDERWEAR
3 : damage that is caused by use • The carpet is showing signs of *wear*. • You should inspect the tires for *wear*.

wear and tear **:** damage that happens to something when it is used for a period of time • The apartment showed no damage other than normal *wear and tear*.

worse for wear ✧ Someone or something that is ***slightly/somewhat/much (etc.) (the) worse for wear*** looks worse after doing or experiencing something. • He came out of basic training only *slightly the worse for wear*. • The kids emerged from the woods looking ***none the worse for wear***. [=looking no worse than they had looked before]

wear•able /ˈwerəbəl/ *adj [more ~; most ~]* **:** capable of being worn **:** suitable to wear • *wearable* art • high-fashion clothes that are not really *wearable*
– wear•abil•i•ty /ˌwerəˈbɪləti/ *noun [noncount]*

wea•ri•some /ˈwirisəm/ *adj [more ~; most ~]* **:** causing you to feel bored, annoyed, or impatient **:** TIRESOME • We had to listen to the usual *wearisome* complaints. • Her stories can get a little *wearisome*.
– wea•ri•some•ly *adv* • a *wearisomely* familiar story

[1]**wea•ry** /ˈwiri/ *adj* **wear•i•er; -est** *[also more ~; most ~]*
1 : lacking strength, energy, or freshness because of a need for rest or sleep **:** TIRED • I need to rest my *weary* eyes. • The miners were *weary* after a long shift.
2 : bored or annoyed by something because you have seen it, heard it, done it, etc., many times or for a long time • She was *weary* from years of housework. • a *weary* sigh [=a sigh that shows that someone is weary] — often + *of* • I'm *weary of* fighting. Let's try to get along. • a professor who had ***grown weary of*** academia and wanted to try something different — sometimes used in combination • winter-*weary* travelers — see also WORLD-WEARY
3 *literary* **:** causing you to feel tired • the long, *weary* [=*tiring*] journey home
– wea•ri•ly /ˈwirəli/ *adv* • They trudged *wearily* down the trail. • "It's almost over," she said *wearily*. **– wea•ri•ness** /ˈwirinəs/ *noun [noncount]* • His *weariness* showed in his face.

[2]**weary** *verb* **-ries; -ried; -ry•ing** *[+ obj] somewhat formal* **:** to make (someone) very tired • The work *wearies* me sometimes.

weary of *[phrasal verb]* ***weary of (something)*** **:** to become bored by (something) **:** to stop being interested in (something) • She realized that she had *wearied of* [=*tired of*] the city. • He quickly *wearied of* answering their questions.

– wearying *adj [more ~; most ~]* • a *wearying* [=*tiring*] climb up the mountain **– wea•ry•ing•ly** *adv*

[1]**wea•sel** /ˈwi:zəl/ *noun, pl* **weasel** *or* **wea•sels** *[count]*
1 : a small animal that has a thin body and brown fur and that eats small birds and other animals
2 *informal* **:** a dishonest person who cannot be trusted • He's a lying *weasel*.

[2]**weasel** *verb* **weasels;** *US* **-seled** *or Brit* **-selled;** *US* **-sel•ing** *or Brit* **-sel•ling**

weasel into *[phrasal verb]* ***weasel into (something)*** *chiefly*

weasel

US, informal + usually disapproving : to get into (a place or situation) by being dishonest, by persuading someone in a clever way, etc. ▪ She *weaseled* (herself) *into* the position of manager. ▪ He managed to ***weasel his way into*** the restaurant even though he didn't have a reservation.
weasel out of [*phrasal verb*] ***weasel out of (something)*** *chiefly US, informal + usually disapproving* : to avoid doing (something) by being dishonest, by persuading someone in a clever way, etc. ▪ She *weaseled out of* our agreement. ▪ He ***weaseled his way out of*** helping me with the yard work.

wea·sel·ly *also* **wea·sely** /ˈwiːzəli/ *adj* [*more* ~; *most* ~] *informal + disapproving* : not direct and honest ▪ He's a *weaselly*, conniving thief. ▪ a *weaselly* response

weasel word *noun, pl* ~ **words** [*count*] *informal + disapproving* : a word used in order to avoid being clear or direct ▪ "Reorganization" is just a *weasel word* that the company is using to say that jobs are being eliminated.

[1]**weath·er** /ˈwɛðɚ/ *noun, pl* **-ers**
1 : the state of the air and atmosphere at a particular time and place : the temperature and other outside conditions (such as rain, cloudiness, etc.) at a particular time and place [*noncount*] How's the *weather*? ▪ The *weather* today will be hot and dry. ▪ severe/foul/mild/hot/cold *weather* ▪ a *weather* report/forecast ▪ The picnic will be outside, ***weather permitting***. [=if the weather is good enough to allow it] [*plural*] (*Brit*) She likes to ride her bike ***in all weathers***. [=in any kind of weather] — often used figuratively ▪ They have had their fair share of ***stormy weather*** [=they have had many problems] in their marriage.
2 [*noncount*] : bad or stormy weather ▪ The hikers sought protection from the *weather* under an overhang. ▪ It looks like we're in for some *weather* tomorrow.
3 ***the weather*** : a report or forecast about the weather ▪ We'll take a look at *the weather* right after this commercial break. ▪ Check *the weather* before you make plans.
keep a weather eye on *old-fashioned* : to watch (someone or something) very carefully ▪ She *kept a weather eye on* the stock report.
make heavy weather of see [1]HEAVY
under the weather : not feeling well : feeling sick ▪ She's (feeling) a little *under the weather* today, so she won't be joining us.
– see also FAIR-WEATHER

[2]**weather** *verb* **-ers; -ered; -er·ing**
1 [*no obj*] : to change in color, condition, etc., because of the effects of the sun, wind, rain, etc., over a long period of time ▪ The wood on the porch has *weathered* over the years.
2 [+ *obj*] : to deal with or experience (something dangerous or unpleasant) without being harmed or damaged too much ▪ They *weathered* a terrible storm while at sea. ▪ They had to *weather* [=*get through*] some difficult times in the early years of their marriage. ▪ He has *weathered* the criticism well. — see also *weather the storm* at [1]STORM
– weath·ered /ˈwɛðɚd/ *adj* ▪ the sailor's tanned and *weathered* face ▪ *weathered* cedar **– weathering** *noun* [*noncount*] ▪ The rocks have been worn down by *weathering*.

weath·er–beat·en /ˈwɛðɚˌbiːtn̩/ *adj* [*more* ~; *most* ~]
1 : toughened or colored by the effects of the sun, wind, rain, etc. ▪ their *weather-beaten* faces
2 : worn and damaged by the effects of the sun, wind, rain, etc. ▪ a *weather-beaten* barn

weath·er·board /ˈwɛðɚˌboɚd/ *noun, pl* **-boards** [*count, noncount*] *Brit* : CLAPBOARD
– weatherboard *adj* ▪ a *weatherboard* cottage

weath·er·ize /ˈwɛðəˌraɪz/ *verb* **-iz·es; -ized; -iz·ing** [+ *obj*] *US* : to make (a building, such as a house) better protected against winter weather ▪ We'll *weatherize* the cabin with insulation.

weath·er·man /ˈwɛðɚˌmæn/ *noun, pl* **-men** /-ˌmɛn/ [*count*] : a man who reports and forecasts the weather

weather map *noun, pl* ~ **maps** [*count*] : a map that shows what the current weather in an area is and what the weather in that area will be in the coming hours or days

weath·er·per·son /ˈwɛðɚˌpɚsn̩/ *noun, pl* **-peo·ple** /-ˌpiːpəl/ [*count*] : a person who reports and forecasts the weather

[1]**weath·er·proof** /ˈwɛðɚˌpruːf/ *adj*
1 : not able to be changed or damaged by the effects of the sun, wind, rain, etc. ▪ The material is *weatherproof* and will not rot from moisture. ▪ a *weatherproof* electrical outlet
2 : able to protect someone or something from the effects of the sun, wind, rain, etc. ▪ a *weatherproof* coat

[2]**weatherproof** *verb* **-proofs; -proofed; -proof·ing** [+ *obj*] : to make (something) protected against the effects of the sun, wind, rain, etc. : to make (something) weatherproof ▪ He *weatherproofed* his shoes. ▪ a *weatherproofed* cabin

weather station *noun, pl* ~ **-tions** [*count*] : a place where scientists record and study information about the weather

weather stripping *noun* [*noncount*] *US* : long, thin pieces of material that are used to seal a door or window around its edges so that wind, rain, snow, etc., cannot pass through
– weather strip *noun, pl* ~ **strips** [*count*] ▪ He put *weather strips* [=pieces of weather stripping] on the doors and windows. **– weather–strip** *verb* **-strips; -stripped; -strip·ping** [+ *obj*] ▪ He *weather-stripped* the doors and windows.

weath·er vane /ˈwɛðɚˌveɪn/ *noun, pl* ~ **vanes** [*count*] : an object that is usually put on the top of a roof and that has an arrow that turns as the wind blows to show the direction of the wind

[1]**weave** /ˈwiːv/ *verb* **weaves; wove** /ˈwoʊv/ *or* **weaved; wo·ven** /ˈwoʊvən/ *or* **weaved; weav·ing** ✧ *Wove* is the usual past tense and *woven* the usual past participle for senses 1, 2, and 4. *Weaved* is the usual past tense and past participle for sense 3.
1 : to make something (such as cloth) by crossing threads or other long pieces of material over and under each other [+ *obj*] She *weaves* cloth on her loom. ▪ He *wove* a basket (from the branches). = He *wove* the branches into a basket. [*no obj*] She spins and *weaves*.
2 [+ *obj*] : to create something (such as a story) by combining different things in usually a complicated way ▪ The author has *woven* an exciting tale of adventure and romance. ▪ She *wove* episodes from many sources into a single narrative. — often + *together* ▪ The musicians *wove together* a beautiful and complex melody. ▪ The story *weaves together* [=*combines*] the past and present in surprising ways.
3 : to move from side to side while going forward especially in order to avoid the people or things that are in front of you [*no obj*] The car was *weaving* in and out of traffic. ▪ She *weaved* through the defenders and scored a goal. [+ *obj*] He *weaved* his way through the crowd.
4 [+ *obj*] *of a spider* : to create (a web) : SPIN ▪ a spider *weaving* its web
– weav·er /ˈwiːvɚ/ *noun, pl* **-ers** [*count*] ▪ a basket *weaver* ▪ a *weaver* of blankets ▪ a *weaver* of tales

[2]**weave** *noun, pl* **weaves** [*count*] : a pattern in a woven cloth : a particular way of weaving cloth ▪ a twill/plain *weave* ▪ an open *weave*

web /ˈwɛb/ *noun, pl* **webs**
1 ***the Web*** : WORLD WIDE WEB ▪ I spent the afternoon surfing *the Web*. — often used before another noun ▪ a *Web* page ▪ *Web* browsers
2 [*count*] : a net made from silk threads woven together by a spider : SPIDER WEB ▪ The spider was spinning its *web*. — often used figuratively; often + *of* ▪ He was caught in a *web of* lies. ▪ a tangled *web of* deceit/deception
3 [*count*] : a complicated arrangement or pattern of things — usually + *of* ▪ a *web of* city streets ▪ a *web of* electrical cords ▪ a complex *web of* relationships
4 [*count*] : an area of skin that is between the fingers or toes of an animal or bird (such as a duck)
– web·like /ˈwɛbˌlaɪk/ *adj* ▪ a *weblike* network of wires

webbed /ˈwɛbd/ *adj* : having pieces of skin that connect all the toes on a foot ▪ the *webbed* feet of ducks

web·bing /ˈwɛbɪŋ/ *noun* [*noncount*] : strong and tightly woven material that is used in strips to support, catch, or hold things ▪ I need to replace the *webbing* on the lawn chair. ▪ the *webbing* of a baseball glove [=the part of a baseball glove between the thumb and fingers]

web·cam /ˈwɛbˌkæm/ *noun, pl* **-cams** [*count*] : a small video camera that is used to show live images on a Web site

web·cast /ˈwɛbˌkæst, *Brit* ˈwɛbˌkɑːst/ *verb* **-casts; -cast; -cast·ing** [+ *obj*] : to show or play (an event, a program, a musical performance, etc.) over the World Wide Web ▪ We'll be *webcasting* the concert live.
– webcast *noun, pl* **-casts** [*count*] ▪ We're watching a live *webcast* of the concert. **– web·cast·er** *noun, pl* **-ers** [*count*] **– webcasting** *noun* [*noncount*]

web·log /ˈwɛbˌlɑːg/ *noun, pl* **-logs** [*count*] : BLOG

Web•mas•ter /ˈwɛbˌmæstɚ, *Brit* ˈwɛbˌmɑːstə/ *noun, pl* **-ters** [*count*] : a person whose job is to create and maintain a Web site

Web page *noun, pl* ~ **pages** [*count*] : a page of words, pictures, etc., that is shown on a Web site

Web site *or* **web•site** /ˈwɛbˌsaɪt/ *noun, pl* **Web sites** *or* **web•sites** [*count*] : a place on the World Wide Web that contains information about a person, organization, etc., and that usually consists of many Web pages joined by hyperlinks • Visit our *Web site* at www.Merriam-Webster.com. • He posted pictures from his vacation on his *Web site*. • a corporate/news/sports *Web site*

wed /ˈwɛd/ *verb, not used in progressive tenses* **weds; wedded** *also* **wed; wed•ding**

1 *somewhat formal + old-fashioned* : MARRY [*no obj*] They will *wed* in the fall. [+ *obj*] The actress *wed* her fourth husband last year.

2 [+ *obj*] : to bring or join (two things) together • The novel *weds* tragedy and comedy. • His new writing job *wedded* his love of words and/to his eye for fashion.

we'd /ˈwiːd/ — used as a contraction of *we had* or *we would* • *We'd* [=we had] better be going. • We said *we'd* [=we would] try to do better.

Wed. *abbr* Wednesday

wedded *adj*

1 *formal* : MARRIED • Do you take this man as your lawfully *wedded* husband? • (*humorous*) ***wedded bliss*** [=the happiness experienced by people who are married]

2 : very closely involved and interested in something • He was *wedded to* his work. : supporting something very strongly • a program *wedded to* the ideals of justice for all peoples

wed•ding /ˈwɛdɪŋ/ *noun, pl* **-dings** [*count*] : a ceremony at which two people are married to each other • The *wedding* will be at 2:00 p.m. — often used before another noun • a *wedding* dress • a picture of the ***wedding party*** [=the bride, groom, and their attendants] • a ***wedding cake*** [=a large and fancy cake served at a wedding] — see color picture on page C16; see also WHITE WEDDING

hear wedding bells : to think that two people will get married to each other soon • The minute I saw your brother and my friend together, I *heard wedding bells*.

wedding rehearsal *noun, pl* ~ **-als** [*count*] : an event at which the people involved in a wedding ceremony practice what will be done at the ceremony ✧ A wedding rehearsal usually occurs on the day before the wedding.

wedding ring *noun, pl* ~ **rings** [*count*] : a ring that you wear as a sign that you are married — see color picture on page C11

[1]**wedge** /ˈwɛʤ/ *noun, pl* **wedg•es** [*count*]

1 : a piece of wood, metal, etc., with one pointed end and one thicker end that is used to split something, to fit into a space, to separate two things stuck together, etc. • He used a *wedge* to split the firewood. • A *wedge* held the door open.

wedge

2 : something that is shaped like a triangle or wedge • *wedges* of cheese • a lemon *wedge* • The battalion formed a *wedge* and marched toward the enemy.

3 : a golf club that is used for hitting short, high shots

drive a wedge between : to cause disagreement or anger between (people who had been friendly before) • A fight over their parents' estate *drove a wedge between* the brothers.

the thin end of the wedge see [1]THIN

[2]**wedge** *verb, always followed by an adverb or preposition* **wedges; wedged; wedg•ing** [+ *obj*]

1 : to force (someone or something) into a very small or narrow space • She *wedged* her foot into the crack. • The dog got *wedged* between the couch and the end table. • I *wedged* myself into the car's back seat. — sometimes used figuratively • The little shop was *wedged* between two larger stores. [=was located in the small space between two larger stores]

2 : to use a wedge or similar object to keep (something, such as a door or window) in an open or closed position • She *wedged* the door open.

wedge issue *noun, pl* ~ **-sues** [*count*] *US* : an issue about which a politician's supporters or the members of a political party disagree

wedg•ie /ˈwɛʤi/ *noun, pl* **-ies** [*count*] *chiefly US slang* : the act of pulling the back of someone's underpants quickly upward as a joke or prank • He gave me a *wedgie*.

wed•lock /ˈwɛdˌlɑːk/ *noun* [*noncount*] : the state of being married • Their child was born ***out of wedlock*** [=they were not married when their child was born]

Wednes•day /ˈwɛnzˌdeɪ/ *noun, pl* **-days** : the day of the week between Tuesday and Thursday [*count*] I had lunch with her last *Wednesday*. • I'll be seeing her again next *Wednesday*. • The class meets on *Wednesdays*. [=every Wednesday] • My birthday falls on a *Wednesday* this year. • (*Brit*) Next week I'll arrive on the *Wednesday* and leave on the Friday. [*noncount*] Next week I'll arrive on *Wednesday* and leave on Friday. • The paper is due on *Wednesday*. = (*chiefly US*) The paper is due *Wednesday*. • I will arrive on *Wednesday* morning. — abbr. *Wed.* or *Weds.*; see also ASH WEDNESDAY

— **Wednes•days** /ˈwɛnzˌdeɪz/ *adv* • He works late *Wednesdays*. [=he works late every Wednesday]

Weds. *abbr* Wednesday

wee /ˈwiː/ *adj, chiefly Scotland + Ireland* : very small or very young • He's just a *wee* lad.

a wee bit informal : by a very small amount or to a very small degree • She's *a wee bit* late. [=a little bit late] • I'm *a wee bit* confused.

wee hours see HOUR

[1]**weed** /ˈwiːd/ *noun, pl* **weeds**

1 [*count*] : a plant that grows very quickly where it is not wanted and covers or kills more desirable plants • We pulled *weeds* from the garden. • an invasive *weed* — see also MILKWEED, RAGWEED, SEAWEED, TUMBLEWEED

2 [*noncount*] *informal* : MARIJUANA • They were smoking *weed*.

3 ***the weed*** *chiefly Brit, informal* : cigarettes and other tobacco products • She's trying to give up *the weed*. [=trying to quit smoking]

grow like a weed *chiefly US, informal* : to grow very quickly • Their business is *growing like a weed*. • Look at you! You're *growing like a weed*!

[2]**weed** *verb* **weeds; weed•ed; weed•ing** [+ *obj*] : to remove weeds from (an area of land, such as a garden) • We need to *weed* the garden.

weed out [*phrasal verb*] ***weed (someone or something) out*** *or* ***weed out (someone or something)*** : to remove (people or things that are not wanted) from a group • They will review the applications to *weed out* the less qualified candidates. • He *weeded out* several unsuitable models before he found the right car.

weedy /ˈwiːdi/ *adj* **weed•i•er; -est**

1 : full of weeds • a *weedy* garden

2 *Brit, informal* : looking thin and weak • a *weedy* little man

week /ˈwiːk/ *noun, pl* **weeks**

1 : a period of seven days ✧ In the U.S., a week is usually considered to start on Sunday and end on Saturday, while in the U.K. a week is usually considered to start on Monday and end on Sunday. [*count*] the last *week* of the month • I can meet you sometime next *week*. • The menu changes each/every *week*. • I volunteer at the school once ***a week*** [=once every week] • You can never be sure what will happen ***from one week to the next*** [*noncount*] The menu changes ***from week to week*** • These problems have continued ***week after week*** [=for several or many weeks] — see also HOLY WEEK

2 [*count*] : any period of seven days in a row • The baby is two *weeks* old. [a two-*week*-old baby] • I'll be on vacation for two *weeks* starting this Tuesday. • That car rents for $200 a/per *week*. • We'll leave a *week* from today. [=seven days after today] • I arrived a *week* ago. • It took him two *weeks* to paint the house. • Sometimes he's away for *weeks* at a time. • The doctor said he wants to see me again in a *week*. = The doctor said he wants to see me again a *week* from now. = The doctor said he wants to see me again in ***a week's time***

3 [*count*] : the days from Monday through Friday when people usually work • We're open from 9 to 5 all *week*. • He earns $500 a *week* at his job. • I'll be working next *week*. • He has a 40-hour work *week*.

week in and week out *also* ***week in, week out*** : every week for many weeks : for a long time without stopping or changing • He has been working *week in and week out* with no vacation.

week•day /ˈwiːkˌdeɪ/ *noun, pl* **-days** [*count*] : any day of the week except Saturday and Sunday • The library is open on *weekdays* from 9:00 to 5:00.

– **week·days** /ˈwiːkˌdeɪz/ *adv, chiefly US* ▪ We're open *weekdays* from 9 to 5.

[1]**week·end** /ˈwiːkˌɛnd/ *noun, pl* **-ends** [*count*]
1 : Saturday and Sunday ▪ What are you doing this *weekend*? ▪ The office is closed on *weekends*. ▪ I'm going away for the *weekend*. ▪ (*US*) We're going to the city ***on the weekend***. = (*Brit*) We're going to the city ***at the weekend***.
2 : a trip or vacation that is taken on Saturday and Sunday ▪ She won a *weekend* in Cancun.
long weekend **:** a weekend that includes the Friday before, the Monday after, or both because you do not have to work or go to school on those days ▪ Next Friday is a holiday, so we'll have a *long weekend*.
– **week·ends** /ˈwiːkˌɛndz/ *adv* ▪ He travels *weekends*.

[2]**weekend** *verb, always followed by an adverb or preposition* **-ends; -end·ed; -end·ing** [*no obj*] **:** to spend the weekend at a specified place ▪ Her family *weekends* on the coast during the summer.

week·end·er /ˈwiːkˈɛndɚ/ *noun, pl* **-ers** [*count*] **:** a person who visits or stays in a place on the weekend ▪ The town is populated with *weekenders* from New York City.

weekend warrior *noun, pl* **~ -riors** [*count*] *US, informal*
1 : a member of the military reserves who trains on the weekends and for a few weeks every year
2 : a person who does a particular activity (such as a sport) only on the weekends

week·long /ˈwiːkˈlɑːŋ/ *adj* **:** lasting for a week ▪ We attended a *weeklong* training conference in Atlanta.

[1]**week·ly** /ˈwiːkli/ *adj*
1 : happening, done, or made every week ▪ I make *weekly* trips to the grocery store. ▪ Our meetings are *weekly*.
2 : published once every week ▪ a *weekly* newspaper column ▪ a *weekly* newsletter
3 : of or relating to one week ▪ a *weekly* paycheck [=the paycheck received every week] ▪ the *weekly* rental rate
– **weekly** *adv* ▪ We are paid *weekly*. [=once every week] ▪ The newsletter is published *weekly*.

[2]**weekly** *noun, pl* **-lies** [*count*] **:** a magazine or newspaper that is published once every week

week·night /ˈwiːkˌnaɪt/ *noun, pl* **-nights** [*count*] **:** the evenings of Monday through Friday **:** any evening except Saturday or Sunday evening ▪ The news is on every *weeknight* at 10 p.m. ▪ Her parents don't want her to be out that late on a *weeknight*.
– **week·nights** /ˈwiːkˌnaɪts/ *adv* ▪ We watch the news *weeknights* at 6 p.m.

wee·nie /ˈwiːni/ *noun, pl* **-nies** [*count*] *US*
1 *informal + disapproving* **:** a weak person who is easily frightened **:** WIMP ▪ Don't be such a *weenie*.
2 *informal* **:** HOT DOG ▪ a *weenie* roast
3 *slang* **:** PENIS

[1]**weep** /ˈwiːp/ *verb* **weeps; wept** /ˈwɛpt/; **weep·ing**
1 *somewhat formal* **:** to cry because you are very sad or are feeling some other strong emotion [*no obj*] He *wept* at the news of her death. ▪ She sat down and *wept*. ▪ He *wept* with joy/relief. [+ *obj*] He *wept* bitter tears of disappointment.
2 : to produce a liquid slowly [+ *obj*] The wound was *weeping* pus. [=pus was slowly coming out from the wound] [*no obj*] a *weeping* wound ▪ The meringue will *weep* if you put it in the fridge.

[2]**weep** *noun* [*singular*] *Brit* **:** an act of weeping or a period of time spent weeping ▪ She sat down and had a *weep*. [=*cry*]

weep·er /ˈwiːpɚ/ *noun, pl* **-ers** [*count*] *US, informal* **:** a sad movie, song, etc., that makes people cry ▪ The movie is a *weeper* about a single mother facing cancer.
finders keepers (losers weepers) see FINDER

weep·ie /ˈwiːpi/ *noun, pl* **-ies** [*count*] *US, informal* **:** a sad movie that makes people cry **:** TEARJERKER

weeping *adj, of a tree* **:** having thin branches that hang down toward the ground ▪ a *weeping* willow ▪ a *weeping* cherry tree

weepy /ˈwiːpi/ *adj* **weep·i·er; -est** *informal* **:** crying or likely to cry ▪ I was starting to feel *weepy*. [=to feel as if I was going to cry] ▪ She started getting *weepy* when she talked about her mother. **:** happening or done with tears ▪ He gave me a *weepy* [=*tearful*] apology.

wee·vil /ˈwiːvəl/ *noun, pl* **-vils** [*count*] **:** a small insect that eats grains and seeds and that can ruin crops — see also BOLL WEEVIL

wee–wee /ˈwiːˌwiː/ *verb* **-wees; -weed; -wee·ing** [*no obj*] *informal* **:** to pass urine from the body **:** URINATE — used especially by children or when talking to children ▪ The doggie *wee-weed* on the carpet.
– **wee–wee** *noun* [*noncount*] ▪ The dog ***went wee-wee*** on the carpet. [=the dog urinated on the carpet]

weft /ˈwɛft/ *noun* [*singular*] *technical* **:** the threads that run from side to side on a loom or in a woven fabric — called also *woof*; compare [2]WARP 2

weigh /ˈweɪ/ *verb* **weighs; weighed; weigh·ing**
1 a [+ *obj*] **:** to find how heavy (someone or something) is **:** to measure the weight of (someone or something) ▪ She *weighs* herself every morning. ▪ He used a scale to *weigh* the bananas. **b** *not used in progressive tenses* [*linking verb*] **:** to have a specified weight ▪ I *weigh* 180 pounds. ▪ The bananas *weigh* more than the apples. ▪ How much do you *weigh*? ▪ This box ***weighs a ton***. [=is very heavy]
2 [+ *obj*] **:** to think carefully about (something) in order to form an opinion or make a decision **:** CONSIDER ▪ You will need to *weigh* the pros and cons. ▪ He took time to *weigh* his options. ▪ You should ***weigh your words*** [=think carefully about what you are going to say] before you answer that question. — often + *up* ▪ She tried to *weigh up* [=*evaluate*] the pros and cons of staying at her current job. — see also WEIGH UP (below)
3 *always followed by an adverb or preposition* [*no obj*] **:** to be considered in a specified way when a person or thing is being judged ▪ The evidence *weighs* (heavily) against him. [=the evidence is not in his favor] ▪ Her previous experience *weighs* in her favor.
weigh down [*phrasal verb*] **1** ***weigh (someone or something) down or weigh down (someone or something)*** **:** to press down on (someone or something) **:** to make (someone or something) heavier and less able to move easily ▪ My heavy backpack *weighed* me *down*. ▪ The boat was *weighed down* by the extra cargo. **2** ***weigh (someone) down or weigh down (someone)*** **:** to cause (someone) to accept or deal with something difficult or unpleasant ▪ I don't want to *weigh* you *down* with my bad news. ▪ I'm feeling *weighed down* [=*burdened*] by all the work I have to do.
weigh in [*phrasal verb*] **1** ***weigh in or weigh (someone) in or weigh in (someone)*** **:** to be weighed or to weigh (someone) before competing in a fight, race, etc. ▪ When will the jockeys *weigh in*? ▪ The boxers were *weighed in* before the fight. — see also WEIGH-IN **2** ***weigh in*** **:** to have a specified weight — + *at* ▪ He *weighs in at* 240 pounds. [=he weighs 240 pounds] **3** ***weigh in informal*** **:** to give your opinion about something ▪ I think we're pretty much decided, unless you want to *weigh in*. — often + *with* ▪ Would you like to *weigh in with* your opinion? [=would you like to say what your opinion is?] — often + *on* in U.S. English ▪ Do you want to *weigh in on* our weekend plans? [=do you want to say your opinion about our weekend plans?]
weigh on [*phrasal verb*] ***weigh on (someone)*** **:** to make (someone or something) sad, depressed, or worried ▪ The bad news is really ***weighing on*** me. ▪ I can tell that something is ***weighing on his mind***. [=that he's worried about something]
weigh out [*phrasal verb*] ***weigh (something) out or weigh out (something)*** **:** to measure and remove a certain weight of (something) **:** to separate (a portion of something that weighs a certain amount) ▪ Would you *weigh out* 20 pounds of rice? ▪ I *weighed* the portions *out* and distributed them.
weigh up [*phrasal verb*] ***weigh (someone) up or weigh up (someone)*** **:** to look at and listen to (someone) in order to make a judgment about that person's character, abilities, etc. ▪ She was watching him closely as he spoke, *weighing him up*. [=*sizing him up*] — see also WEIGH 2 (above)

weigh–in /ˈweɪˌɪn/ *noun, pl* **-ins** [*count*] **:** an occurrence in which an athlete (such as a boxer or jockey) is weighed before an event ▪ The boxers arrived for the pre-fight *weigh-in*. — see also *weigh in* at WEIGH

[1]**weight** /ˈweɪt/ *noun, pl* **weights**
1 [*noncount*] **a :** a measurement that indicates how heavy a person or thing is ▪ Please indicate your height and *weight* on the form. ▪ Her *weight* is 105 pounds. **b :** the amount that a person or thing weighs **:** the heaviness of a person or thing ▪ The boat sank under the *weight* of the cargo. ▪ The doctor says you shouldn't put any *weight* on that foot for a week. [=you shouldn't stand on that foot for a week] ▪ Those columns have to be strong enough to support the *weight* of the roof. ▪ I'm trying to ***lose (some) weight***. [=to become less heavy or fat] ▪ He is trying to ***watch his weight***. [=to lose weight or to not gain weight] ▪ I think she has ***gained weight***.

[=become heavier] — see also DEAD WEIGHT, OVERWEIGHT, UNDERWEIGHT

2 [*count*] **a** : a heavy object that is lifted during exercising • a 10-pound *weight* • He stays in good shape by ***lifting weights.*** • She likes to exercise using ***free weights.*** [=weights (such as dumbbells and barbells) that are not attached to a piece of equipment] **b** : a heavy object that is used to press something down or to or hold something in place • I use pie *weights* to keep the pie crust from bubbling when I bake it. — see also COUNTERWEIGHT, PAPERWEIGHT

3 [*count*] : a unit of measurement (such as a pound, kilogram, etc.) used for showing how heavy someone or something is • *weights* and measures • a metric *weight*

4 [*singular*] **a** : something that causes worry or sadness • When I told her the truth I felt as if a *weight* had been lifted from my mind. • Well, that's a ***weight off my mind/shoulders.*** [=that's a relief] **b** : a difficult responsibility • I wish there were some way I could help lift this *weight* [=*load, burden*] from his shoulders. • He ***bore the weight*** of having to tell the family the bad news.

5 [*noncount*] **a** : the influence or power someone or something has over other people or things • He has a lot of *weight* in the company. • Several senators ***put/threw their weight behind*** the bill. [=used their influence to support the bill] • (*disapproving*) The new manager immediately started ***throwing her weight around,*** making changes to staff and policy. **b** : the power to influence the opinions of other people • Her opinion carries a lot of *weight* with me. [=her opinion is very important to me] • This new evidence gives added *weight* to his claims. [=makes his claims more believable]

pull your own weight : to do the things that you should be doing as part of a group of people who are working together • You have to *pull your own weight* around here if you want to stay.

worth your weight in gold see [1]GOLD

[2]**weight** *verb* **weights; weight·ed; weight·ing** [+ *obj*] : to put a weight on (something) to make it heavier or to keep it from moving • I *weighted* the fishing line with a lead sinker. — often + *down* • I *weighted* the papers *down* with a rock. — sometimes used figuratively • He was *weighted down* [=*weighed down*] with worry.

weight·ed /ˈweɪtəd/ *adj*

1 : held in place or made heavier by a weight • a *weighted* fishing line • The head of the golf club was *weighted.*

2 — used to say that something favors or does not favor a particular person, group, etc. • The ranking system is unfairly ***weighted in favor of*** the largest schools. • They feel that the system is ***weighted against*** them. • The new tax law is ***weighted toward*** people with higher incomes.

weighting *noun* [*noncount*] *Brit* : an amount added to your salary because you work in an area where things are expensive • The salary alone is not high, but you also get a London *weighting.*

weight·less /ˈweɪtləs/ *adj* : having no weight or seeming to have no weight • a light fabric that feels almost *weightless* • She floated in the pool, *weightless.* • The astronauts are living in a *weightless* environment. [=an environment in which people and things float because they are not affected in the usual way by gravity]

— **weight·less·ness** *noun* [*noncount*]

weight lifting *noun* [*noncount*] : the activity of lifting weights for exercise or in competition • I stay in shape by *weight lifting.*

— **weight lifter** *noun, pl* ~ **-ers** [*count*] • He had the physique of a *weight lifter.*

weight machine *noun, pl* ~ **-chines** [*count*] : a machine with weights attached that is used for exercise

weight room *noun, pl* ~ **rooms** [*count*] : a large room where people lift weights and exercise

weight training *noun* [*noncount*] : the activity of lifting weights regularly to strengthen your muscles

weighty /ˈweɪti/ *adj* **weight·i·er; -est** [*also more* ~; *most* ~]

1 : having a lot of weight : HEAVY • She grabbed a *weighty* book off the shelf.

2 : very important and serious • The film deals with some *weighty* issues.

3 : having the power to influence the opinions of other people • Those are *weighty* arguments in your favor. • He was a *weighty* figure in the art world.

— **weight·i·ness** /ˈweɪtinəs/ *noun* [*noncount*]

weir /ˈweɚ, ˈwiɚ/ *noun, pl* **weirs** [*count*] : a low wall or dam built across a stream or river to raise the level of the water or to change the direction of its flow

[1]**weird** /ˈwiɚd/ *adj* **weird·er; -est** [*also more* ~; *most* ~] : unusual or strange • She listens to some really *weird* [=*bizarre*] music. • My little brother acts *weird* sometimes. • I heard a *weird* noise. • That's *weird*—I put my book down right here just a few minutes ago and now it's gone. • a *weird*-looking creature

— **weird·ly** *adv* • Why are you behaving so *weirdly*? • a *weirdly* entertaining movie — **weird·ness** *noun* [*noncount*]

[2]**weird** *verb* **weirds; weird·ed; weird·ing**

weird out [*phrasal verb*] ***weird (someone) out*** or ***weird out (someone)*** *US, informal* : to make (someone) feel strange or uncomfortable • I don't mean to *weird* you *out.* • That movie totally *weirded* me *out.*

weirdo /ˈwiɚdoʊ/ *noun, pl* **weird·os** [*count*] *informal + disapproving* : a strange or unusual person • He's such a *weirdo.*

[1]**wel·come** /ˈwɛlkəm/ *interj* — used as a friendly greeting to someone who has arrived at a place • *Welcome* to America! • *Welcome* home! • *Welcome* back. We missed you.

welcome to the club see [1]CLUB

[2]**welcome** *adj* [*more* ~; *most* ~]

1 : giving someone happiness or pleasure • That is *welcome* news. • That will be a *welcome* change. • He was a *welcome* sight.

2 — used to say that you are happy to have someone come to and stay in a place (such as your home) • You're always *welcome* in our home. [=we are always glad to have you as a guest in our home] • They always made us feel very *welcome* when we visited them.

3 a — used to say that someone can have or take something because you do not want it yourself; + *to* • If you want that last cookie, you're *welcome to* it—I can't eat another bite. • If she really wants this old computer, she's *welcome to* it. **b** — used to say that someone can certainly do or use something if he or she wants to; followed by *to + verb* • Anyone is *welcome to use* the pool. [=anyone can use the pool] • You are *welcome to sleep* here if you want.

you're welcome — used as a response to someone who has thanked you • "Thanks for the ride." "*You're welcome.*"

[3]**welcome** *verb* **-comes; -comed; -com·ing** [+ *obj*]

1 : to greet (someone) in a warm and friendly manner • She *welcomed* the students into her home. • We *welcome* you to the show.

2 : to receive or accept (something) with happiness or pleasure • He's a bright student who *welcomes* a challenge. • We *welcome* your comments/suggestions. [=we will be glad to receive any comments/suggestions you may have] • I *welcome* this opportunity [=I am glad to have this opportunity] to explain what really happened.

[4]**welcome** *noun, pl* **-comes** [*count*] : the way in which someone is greeted • He extended a warm *welcome* to the new family in town. [=he greeted the new family warmly] • He was given a hero's *welcome* when he returned home after winning the race. • They gave us a cold *welcome.* [=they did not greet us in a friendly way] — sometimes used figuratively • Her suggestion was given a cold *welcome.* [=people did not like her suggestion]

outstay/overstay your welcome or ***wear out your welcome*** : to be no longer welcome to stay in a place because you have stayed too long, been impolite, etc. • After staying for a week, she felt she had *worn out her welcome.* • As much as he has contributed to the company, he has *outstayed his welcome* and needs to go.

welcome mat *noun, pl* ~ **mats** [*count*] *US* : a small rug that is placed by the door of a person's house, apartment, etc., for guests to wipe their feet on before entering

put/roll/throw out the welcome mat : to welcome someone in a warm and friendly way • The family *rolled out the welcome mat* for the new exchange student.

[1]**welcoming** *adj* [*more* ~; *most* ~] : friendly and pleasant : having qualities that make you feel welcome • The hotel staff is very *welcoming.* • a *welcoming* atmosphere/host

[2]**welcoming** *noun* [*singular*] : a friendly greeting : WELCOME • The college president gave the new students a warm *welcoming.*

[1]**weld** /ˈwɛld/ *verb* **welds; weld·ed; weld·ing**

1 : to join pieces of metal together by heating the edges until they begin to melt and then pressing them together [*no obj*] She learned how to *weld.* [+ *obj*] We *welded* the beams together.

2 [+ *obj*] : to join or bring (people or things) close together •

They were *welded* together in friendship. • His style of painting *welds* impressionism with surrealism.

[2]**weld** *noun, pl* **welds** [*count*] : a connection made by welding pieces of metal • That *weld* won't hold.

weld·er /ˈwɛldɚ/ *noun, pl* **-ers** [*count*] : a person whose job is to weld materials together

wel·fare /ˈwɛlˌfeɚ/ *noun* [*noncount*]
1 : a government program for poor or unemployed people that helps pay for their food, housing, medical costs, etc. • He wants to do away with *welfare*. • His family is ***on welfare***. [=receiving government assistance] — often used before another noun • *welfare* benefits/programs/payments/costs • ***welfare families*** [=families that receive welfare] — sometimes used figuratively • (*chiefly US*) ***corporate welfare*** [=money or aid given by the government to help a large company]
2 : the state of being happy, healthy, or successful : WELL-BEING • I have your *welfare* at heart. • The *welfare* of all the orphans was at stake. • She donates to organizations concerned about animal *welfare*.

welfare state *noun, pl* ~ **states** [*count, noncount*] : a social system in which a government is responsible for the economic and social welfare of its citizens and has policies to provide free health care, money for people without jobs, etc. • supporters/opponents of ***the welfare state***; *also* [*count*] : a country that has such a system

[1]**well** /ˈwɛl/ *adv* **bet·ter** /ˈbɛtɚ/; **best** /ˈbɛst/
1 a : in a successful way • "How did everything go?" "It went *well*, thank you." • The plan worked *well*. • She works *well* under pressure. • I did surprisingly *well* on my history test. • The company is doing *well*. • He has his own business and is ***doing well for*** himself. • You got a perfect score! ***Well done***. — see also *do well* at [1]DO **b :** in a skillful way • She sings and plays the guitar quite *well*. • The essay is *well* written. **c :** in a good, proper, or positive way • He doesn't smoke or drink, and he eats *well*. • She doesn't treat her boyfriend very *well*. • Did he take the news *well*? [=did he respond to the news in a positive way?] • The decision did not ***sit well with*** him. [=he was not happy about the decision] **d :** in a kind, friendly, or generous way • The novel was *well* received by the critics. • They always speak *well* of you. • I ***wish her well***. [=I hope she does well; I hope that she succeeds] • He ***means well*** [=he has good intentions], but he's not really helping anyone. • The company ***did well by*** me when I retired. [=the company treated me well when I retired]
2 : completely or fully • We are *well* aware of the problem. • The food at the restaurant is *well* worth the trip. • Their kitchen is *well* equipped. • Your promotion is *well* deserved. • The plane was *well* out of sight. • I can understand your dilemma very *well*. • She knows the area quite *well*. • I knew him *well* when we were in high school together. • I remember her ***well enough***. = I remember her ***fairly well***.
3 : to a great degree or extent • The group has sold *well* over a million albums. • The temperature will be *well* [=*far*] above average today. It will be *well* into the nineties. • He is *well* on his way to becoming a superstar. • I'm *well* into the book and should finish it soon. • She walked *well* ahead of the group.
4 a — used for emphasis to say that something is or is not proper, appropriate, etc. • She's angry, and *well* she should be. [=she has a good reason to be angry] — usually used with *can, could, may*, or *might* • I *cannot* very *well* refuse the invitation. [=it would be improper for me to refuse the invitation] • I *couldn't* very *well* just walk right in! • And what, one *might/may well* ask, makes this computer system worth its high price? • The decision *may well* be questioned. **b :** very possibly — usually used with *could, may*, or *might* • You *could* very *well* be right. [=it is very possible that you are right] • The concert *may well* be sold-out. [=it is possible/likely that the concert is sold-out] • It *may well* be true. **c :** without doubt or question • They can *well* afford to be generous. • As you ***well know***, I don't approve of this. = As you know very *well*, I don't approve of this. • You know ***perfectly well*** how to do it. • Their relationship is ***well and truly*** over.
5 a ✧ To ***live well*** is to live in the comfortable and enjoyable way of people who have a lot of money, possessions, etc. • He made a lot of money in real estate and was able to *live* very *well* after his retirement. **b** ✧ To ***marry well*** is to marry someone who has high social status, wealth, etc. • Their son/daughter married *well*.

as well **1** ***as well (as)*** : in addition to someone or something else • You bought a new car? I bought one *as well*. [=*also, too*] • He is loyal, and brave *as well*. = He is brave *as well as* loyal. [=he is brave and also loyal] • The coach, *as well as* the team, is ready. • She is good at softball *as well as* basketball. **2 a** — used in phrases like ***might as well*** and ***may as well*** to say that something should be done or accepted because it cannot be avoided or because there is no good reason not to do it • You *might as well* tell them the truth. • We *may as well* begin now. • They're not going to change their decision, so you *might (just) as well* get used to it. • (*informal*) "Should we start now?" "*Might as well*." **b** — used to say that something else could have been done with the same result • The party was so dull that I *might (just) as well* have stayed home. **3 :** in the same way • ***You know as well as I do*** [=you and I both know] that we can't afford that car.

[2]**well** *adj* **better**; **best**
1 : in good health : HEALTHY • The children are *well* again. • He is not *well*. = He is not a *well* man. • I don't feel very *well*. • You don't look so *well*. • I hope you ***get well soon***.
2 *not used before a noun* **:** in a good or satisfactory state • I hope all is *well* with you and your family. • We almost didn't make it here, but ***all's well that ends well***. [=we can forget about how unpleasant or difficult it was because everything ended in a good way] • I should have ***left/let well (enough) alone*** [=I should not have tried to make the situation better], but instead I tried to help and only made things worse.
3 *not used before a noun, formal* **:** wise, sensible, or reasonable • It might be *well* [=it might be a good idea] for you to leave now. • It would be ***as well*** for you to get some rest. [=you should get some rest]

alive and well see ALIVE

all very well *or* ***all well and good*** — used to say that something may seem proper, good, or reasonable by itself but that there are other things that also have to be considered • ***It's all very well*** your telling me to take it easy, but I have a deadline to meet! • They say we have to improve our schools. ***That's all very well***, but the question is, how can we find the money to do it? • It is *all well and good* that you have been enjoying yourself, but you have to start saving your money.

just as well see [2]JUST

very well see [1]VERY

[3]**well** *interj*
1 — used to show that you are unsure about something you are saying • They are, *well*, not quite what you'd expect. • "How old is he?" "*Well*, let me see now . . . " • "Can you explain how it works?" "*Well*, I can try." • *Well*, I suppose I could help you just this once.
2 — used to show that you accept something even though you are not happy about it • "I'm sorry about the mix-up." "*Well*, that's OK. These things happen." • Oh, ***very well***. I suppose we can finish this discussion tomorrow. • "We're busy this week." "***Oh, well***, maybe we can get together next week."
3 — used when you are trying to persuade someone or to make someone feel less upset, worried, etc. • *Well*, maybe it won't be that bad. • *Well*, you should at least consider their offer before you reject it.
4 — used when you are saying in a mild way that you disapprove of or disagree with something • *Well*, what if you're wrong? • *Well*, I still think my way is better.
5 — used to show that you are waiting for someone to say or do something • *Well*, what have you decided? • *Well*, don't just stand there—give me a hand!
6 — used to say that something has ended or to make a final statement about something • *Well*, we'd better get going. • *Well*, that's all of it. • *Well*, thanks for everything. • ***Well then***, it's all set. There's nothing more to do.
7 — used to begin a story or explanation or to continue one that was interrupted • *Well*, what happened was this. I fell asleep. • *Well*, as I was saying, I had never been there before. • You know Tom, don't you? *Well*, I ran into him yesterday. • "He speaks excellent Spanish." "*Well*, after all, he did study in Spain for a couple of years."
8 — used to express happiness or relief • "We're getting married." "*Well*, that's great news! Congratulations!" • "The doctor says it's nothing serious." "*Well*, thank goodness!"
9 — used to express surprise or annoyance • *Well, well*, what do we have here? • *Well*, hello! I wasn't expecting you so soon. • *Well*, if it isn't my old friend Tom! • Is that so? *Well*, I never would have guessed. • *Well*! It's about time you showed up!
10 — used when you want to correct a previous statement • Everyone—*well*, almost everyone—attended the meeting.

[4]**well** *noun, pl* **wells** [*count*]

1 : a deep hole made in the ground through which water can be removed — see also ARTESIAN WELL, WISHING WELL

2 : OIL WELL

3 : INKWELL, STAIRWELL

— see also INKWELL, STAIRWELL

[5]**well** *verb* **wells; welled; well·ing** *[no obj] of a liquid* : to rise to a surface and flow out — usually + *up* ▪ Tears of joy *welled up* in her eyes. [=her eyes filled with tears of joy] — often used figuratively ▪ He felt anger *welling up* inside him. [=he felt himself becoming angry]

we'll /ˈwiːl, ˈwɪl/ — used as a contraction of *we will* ▪ *We'll* be waiting.

well–ad·just·ed /ˌwɛləˈʤʌstəd/ *adj [more ~; most ~]* : able to deal with other people in a normal or healthy way ▪ He is now a happy, *well-adjusted* adult. — opposite MALADJUSTED

well–ad·vised /ˌwɛlədˈvaɪzd/ *adj [more ~; most ~]* : wise or sensible ▪ You would be *well-advised* to accept their offer. ▪ She made a *well-advised* decision. — opposite ILL-ADVISED

well–ap·point·ed /ˌwɛləˈpɔɪntəd/ *adj [more ~; most ~] formal* : having all the furniture, equipment, etc., that you need ▪ a *well-appointed* apartment

well–ba·lanced /ˌwɛlˈbælənst/ *adj [more ~; most ~]* : having good or equal amounts of all the necessary parts of something ▪ a *well-balanced* meal/diet ▪ a *well-balanced* account of the event

well–be·haved /ˌwɛlbɪˈheɪvd/ *adj [more ~; most ~]* : behaving in a polite or correct way ▪ a *well-behaved* dog ▪ Your children are very *well-behaved.*

well–be·ing /ˈwɛlˈbiːjɪŋ/ *noun [noncount]* : the state of being happy, healthy, or successful ▪ Meditation can increase a person's sense of *well-being.* — often + *of* ▪ The *well-being of* our families was at stake. ▪ the economic *well-being of* the state

well·born /ˈwɛlˈboən/ *adj, formal + old-fashioned* : coming from a noble, important, or wealthy family ▪ *wellborn* young ladies

well–bred /ˈwɛlˈbrɛd/ *adj [more ~; most ~] somewhat old-fashioned* : having or showing good manners : POLITE ▪ a *well-bred* child ▪ He was too *well-bred* to tell her that he didn't like her singing. — opposite ILL-BRED

well–built /ˈwɛlˈbɪlt/ *adj [more ~; most ~]*

1 : built to be strong or to work well ▪ a *well-built* house/car/system

2 : physically strong or attractive ▪ He's *well-built.*

well–con·nect·ed /ˌwɛlkəˈnɛktəd/ *adj [more ~; most ~]* : having important and powerful friends ▪ a *well-connected* lawyer

well–de·fined /ˌwɛldɪˈfaɪnd/ *adj [more ~; most ~]* : easy to see or understand ▪ a *well-defined* boundary ▪ *well-defined* policies — opposite ILL-DEFINED

well–de·vel·oped /ˌwɛldɪˈvɛləpt/ *adj [more ~; most ~]* : large, advanced, or complete : fully developed ▪ *well-developed* muscles ▪ She has a *well-developed* sense of humor. ▪ Their plan is *well-developed.*

well–dis·posed /ˌwɛldɪˈspoʊzd/ *adj [more ~; most ~] formal* : having a favorable or friendly feeling about someone or something — often + *toward* or *to* ▪ Many people remain *well-disposed toward* the government. ▪ They are not *well-disposed to* the idea. — opposite ILL-DISPOSED

well–doc·u·ment·ed /ˌwɛlˈdɑːkjəˌmɛntəd/ *adj [more ~; most ~]* — used to describe something that is known about or known to be true because there are many documents that describe it, prove it, etc. ▪ a *well-documented* account/case/fact ▪ That part of her life is not *well-documented.*

well–done /ˈwɛlˈdʌn/ *adj* : cooked completely ▪ a *well-done* steak — compare MEDIUM, RARE, UNDERDONE

well–dressed /ˌwɛlˈdrɛst/ *adj [more ~; most ~]* : wearing attractive or fashionable clothes ▪ He is a *well-dressed* man.

well–earned /ˈwɛlˈənd/ *adj [more ~; most ~]* : fully deserved ▪ a *well-earned* reputation/rest ▪ Her success is *well-earned.*

well–en·dowed /ˌwɛlɪnˈdaʊd/ *adj [more ~; most ~]*

1 *of a woman, informal* : having large breasts

2 *of a man, informal* : having a large penis

3 *of a school, museum, etc.* : having plenty of money : having a large endowment ▪ a *well-endowed* university

well–fed /ˈwɛlˈfɛd/ *adj [more ~; most ~]* : having plenty of food to eat ▪ *well-fed* pets ▪ The dinner they served wasn't fancy, but we went home *well-fed.*

well–found·ed /ˌwɛlˈfaʊndəd/ *adj [more ~; most ~]* : based on good reasoning, information, or judgment ▪ *well-founded* fears/advice

well–groomed /ˌwɛlˈgruːmd/ *adj [more ~; most ~]*

1 *of people* : having a clean, neat appearance ▪ The men were *well-groomed.*

2 *of things* : made very neat, tidy, and attractive ▪ *well-groomed* lawns

well–ground·ed /ˌwɛlˈgraʊndəd/ *adj [more ~; most ~]*

1 : having good training *in* a subject or activity ▪ She is *well-grounded in* Latin and Greek.

2 : WELL-FOUNDED ▪ *well-grounded* fears

well–heeled /ˌwɛlˈhiːld/ *adj [more ~; most ~] informal* : having plenty of money : WEALTHY ▪ *well-heeled* investors

wel·lie *or* **wel·ly** /ˈwɛli/ *noun, pl* **wel·lies** *[count] Brit, informal* : WELLINGTON

well–in·formed /ˌwɛlɪnˈfoəmd/ *adj [more ~; most ~]*

1 : having a lot of knowledge about current topics, a particular situation, etc. ▪ a *well-informed* doctor ▪ They kept me *well-informed* about her condition.

2 : based on facts ▪ a *well-informed* decision/opinion — opposite ILL-INFORMED

Wel·ling·ton /ˈwɛlɪŋtən/ *noun, pl* **-tons** *[count] Brit* : a tall boot made of rubber : RUBBER BOOT

well–in·ten·tioned /ˌwɛlɪnˈtɛnʃənd/ *adj* : WELL-MEANING ▪ She was *well-intentioned* but not very helpful. ▪ *well-intentioned* advice

well–kept /ˈwɛlˈkɛpt/ *adj [more ~; most ~]*

1 : always having a neat, tidy, and attractive appearance ▪ *well-kept* houses/lawns

2 : known by only a few people ▪ a ***well-kept secret***

well–known /ˈwɛlˈnoʊn/ *adj [more ~; most ~]* : known by many people ▪ a *well-known* writer/fact

well–liked /ˈwɛlˈlaɪkt/ *adj [more ~; most ~]* : liked by many people ▪ a *well-liked* restaurant ▪ He is *well-liked* by everyone.

well–made /ˈwɛlˈmeɪd/ *adj [more ~; most ~]* : made in an effective, strong, or skillful way ▪ *well-made* [=*well-built*] furniture ▪ a *well-made* wine ▪ a *well-made* movie

well–man·nered /ˌwɛlˈmænəd/ *adj [more ~; most ~] formal* : having good manners : POLITE ▪ a *well-mannered* child — opposite ILL-MANNERED

well–mean·ing /ˌwɛlˈmiːnɪŋ/ *adj [more ~; most ~]* : having or showing a desire to do something good but often producing bad results ▪ *well-meaning* but misguided politicians ▪ a *well-meaning* effort to improve the school system

well–meant /ˌwɛlˈmɛnt/ *adj [more ~; most ~]* : based on a desire to do something good but often producing bad results ▪ *well-meant* [=*well-meaning*] advice

well·ness /ˈwɛlnəs/ *noun [noncount] chiefly US* : the quality or state of being healthy ▪ Daily exercise is proven to promote *wellness.* — often used before another noun ▪ a *wellness* center/program [=a center/program that helps you become healthy]

well–nigh /ˈwɛlˈnaɪ/ *adv, formal* : almost or nearly ▪ *well-nigh* perfect ▪ It was *well-nigh* impossible to resist the temptation.

well–off /ˈwɛlˈɑːf/ *adj* **better off; best off** *[also more ~; most ~]*

1 : WEALTHY ▪ Her family is extremely *well-off.*

2 : in a good position or situation ▪ He ***doesn't know when he is well-off.*** [=he complains even when his situation is good] — usually used as ***better off*** ▪ You might be *better off* in a different career.

3 *Brit* : having a lot of something — + *for* ▪ She is *well-off for* money. ▪ Both teams are *well-off for* good players.

well–oiled /ˌwɛlˈojəld/ *adj [more ~; most ~]* : working in a proper and successful way ▪ Her campaign is a *well-oiled* political machine.

well–or·dered /ˌwɛlˈoədəd/ *adj [more ~; most ~]* : carefully organized or controlled ▪ a *well-ordered* household ▪ *well-ordered* lives

well–placed /ˌwɛlˈpleɪst/ *adj [more ~; most ~]* : directed or positioned in a way that is good or useful ▪ a *well-placed* piece of furniture ▪ She included a few *well-placed* jokes in her lecture. ▪ He has some *well-placed* friends in the government.

well–pre·served /ˌwɛlprɪˈzəvd/ *adj [more ~; most ~]* : kept in good condition over a long period of time ▪ *well-preserved* fossils ▪ (*humorous*) She just turned 60, but she's *well-preserved.* [=she looks younger than 60]

well–read /ˌwɛlˈrɛd/ *adj [more ~; most ~]* : having gained a lot of knowledge by reading ▪ a *well-read* scholar ▪ He is *well-read* in U.S. history.

well–round•ed /ˌwɛlˈraʊndəd/ *adj* [*more* ~; *most* ~]
1 : educated in many different subjects ▪ *well-rounded* students
2 : including many different things : having a lot of variety ▪ a *well-rounded* education/diet

well–run /ˈwɛlˈrʌn/ *adj* [*more* ~; *most* ~] **:** managed in a skillful way ▪ a *well-run* organization

well–spo•ken /ˌwɛlˈspoukən/ *adj* [*more* ~; *most* ~]
1 : speaking well, politely, or appropriately ▪ a *well-spoken* young woman
2 : spoken in an appropriate and proper way ▪ *well-spoken* words

well•spring /ˈwɛlˌsprɪŋ/ *noun, pl* **-springs** [*count*] **:** something or someone that provides a large amount of something : a good source *of* something ▪ The tour guide was a *well-spring of* information.

well–thought–of /wɛlˈθɑːtˌʌv/ *adj* [*more* ~; *most* ~] **:** having a good reputation ▪ a *well-thought-of* attorney ▪ She is very *well-thought-of.*

well–thought–out /ˈwɛlˈθɑːtˈaʊt/ *adj* [*more* ~; *most* ~] **:** carefully considered and formed ▪ a *well-thought-out* plan

well–timed /ˈwɛlˈtaɪmd/ *adj* [*more* ~; *most* ~] **:** done or happening at a good or suitable time : TIMELY ▪ a *well-timed* announcement ▪ The release of the book was *well-timed.* — opposite ILL-TIMED

well–to–do /ˌwɛltəˈduː/ *adj* [*more* ~; *most* ~] **:** having plenty of money and possessions : WEALTHY ▪ a *well-to-do* family

well–tried /ˈwɛlˈtraɪd/ *adj* [*more* ~; *most* ~] *chiefly Brit* **:** TRIED-AND-TRUE ▪ *well-tried* methods

well–trod•den /ˌwɛlˈtrɑːdn/ *adj* [*more* ~; *most* ~] **:** walked on by many people ▪ a *well-trodden* path — often used figuratively ▪ The book covers some *well-trodden* ground.

well–turned /ˈwɛlˈtənd/ *adj* [*more* ~; *most* ~] *formal* **:** expressed in a proper or skillful way ▪ a *well-turned* phrase

well–wish•er /ˈwɛlˌwɪʃɚ/ *noun, pl* **-ers** [*count*] **:** someone who wants another person to be happy, successful, etc. ▪ Dozens of *well-wishers* gathered to say goodbye to him.

well–worn /ˈwɛlˈwoɚn/ *adj* [*more* ~; *most* ~]
1 : having been used or worn a lot and no longer in good condition ▪ *well-worn* shoes
2 : not interesting or effective because of being used too often ▪ a *well-worn* quotation

welsh /ˈwɛlʃ/ *verb* **welsh•es; welshed; welsh•ing**
welsh/on [*phrasal verb*] ***welsh/on (something)*** *informal + disapproving* **:** to fail or refuse to do (something that you said you would do) ▪ She *welshes on* her promises. ▪ He *welshed on* his loan. [=he did not repay his loan]

Welsh /ˈwɛlʃ/ *noun*
1 [*noncount*] **:** the language of the Welsh people
2 ***the Welsh*** **:** the people of Wales
– Welsh *adj* ▪ *Welsh* literature

Welsh dresser *noun, pl* **~ -ers** [*count*] *Brit* **:** HUTCH 1

Welsh rare•bit /-ˈreɚbət/ *noun, pl* **~ -bits** [*count, noncount*] **:** melted cheese served on toast or crackers — called also *Welsh rabbit*

welt /ˈwɛlt/ *noun, pl* **welts** [*count*] **:** a usually large bump or red area that appears on your skin because of injury or illness

wel•ter /ˈwɛltɚ/ *noun* [*singular*] *formal* **:** a large and confusing number or amount — + *of* ▪ a *welter of* problems ▪ We need to sort through the *welter of* data we have collected.

wel•ter•weight /ˈwɛltɚˌweɪt/ *noun, pl* **-weights** [*count*] **:** a fighter in a class of boxers who weigh up to 147 pounds (67 kilograms) : a boxer who is heavier than a lightweight and lighter than a middleweight — often used before another noun ▪ the *welterweight* champion

wench /ˈwɛntʃ/ *noun, pl* **wench•es** [*count*] *old-fashioned + humorous* **:** a young woman; *especially* **:** a young woman who is a servant

wend /ˈwɛnd/ *verb* **wends; wend•ed; wend•ing** *literary* **:** to move from one place to another [*no obj*] We *wended* through the narrow streets. [+ *obj*] We ***wended our way*** through the narrow streets.

Wen•dy house /ˈwɛndi-/ *noun, pl* **~ hous•es** [*count*] *Brit* **:** PLAYHOUSE 2

went *past tense of* [1]GO

wept *past tense and past participle of* [1]WEEP

were see BE

we're /ˈwiɚ, wɚ/ — used as a contraction of *we are* ▪ *We're* here. ▪ We need to discuss the problems *we're* having.

weren't /ˈwɚənt/ — used as a contraction of *were not* ▪ We *weren't* expecting to win.

were•wolf /ˈweɚˌwulf/ *noun, pl* **-wolves** /-ˌwulvz/ [*count*] *in stories* **:** a person who sometimes changes into a wolf especially when the moon is full

[1]**west** /ˈwɛst/ *noun*
1 [*noncount*] **:** the direction where the sun sets : the direction that is the opposite of east ▪ There's a beautiful pond to the *west* of the trail. ▪ We will be traveling into the city from the *west.* ▪ If that way is east, then this way is *west.*
2 ***the west or the West*** **:** regions or countries west of a certain point: such as **a :** the western part of the U.S. ▪ Floods have caused extensive damage in *the West.* ▪ Come explore the natural wonders of *the American West.* — see also WILD WEST **b :** North America and Western Europe ▪ policies foreign to *the West*

[2]**west** *adj*
1 : located in or toward the west ▪ the *west* entrance ▪ cities on the *west* coast
2 : coming from the west ▪ a *west* wind

[3]**west** *adv* **:** to or toward the west ▪ They drove *west* after they got off the highway. ▪ They live just *west* of here.
out West or out west *US, informal* **:** in or to the western part of a country or region ▪ He headed *out west* after he graduated.

west•bound /ˈwɛstˌbaʊnd/ *adj* **:** going toward the west ▪ Traffic in the *westbound* lane is backing up. ▪ a *westbound* train

west•er•ly /ˈwɛstɚli/ *adj* [*more* ~; *most* ~]
1 : located or moving toward the west ▪ They sailed in a *westerly* direction. ▪ the lake's *westerly* shore
2 : blowing from the west ▪ strong *westerly* winds

[1]**west•ern** /ˈwɛstɚn/ *adj*
1 [*more* ~; *most* ~] **:** located in or toward the west ▪ the *western* part of the state ▪ the island's *western* shore ▪ the *western* U.S. ▪ *Western* Africa
2 ***Western*** **:** of or relating to the countries of North America and Western Europe ▪ *Western* culture ▪ *Western* values ▪ the *Western* world
3 : of or relating to the American West ▪ Old *western* movies are my favorites. — see also COUNTRY AND WESTERN
– west•ern•most /ˈwɛstɚnˌmoust/ *adj* ▪ the *westernmost* part of the state

[2]**western** *noun, pl* **-erns** [*count*] **:** a story, movie, or television show about life in the American West in the late 19th century; *especially* **:** a movie about cowboys

West•ern•er /ˈwɛstɚnɚ/ *noun, pl* **-ers** [*count*]
1 : a person born, raised, or living in North America or Western Europe ▪ *Westerners* tend to be unfamiliar with Asian customs.
2 : a person born, raised, or living in the western U.S. — compare EASTERNER

west•ern•ize *or* **West•ern•ize** *also Brit* **west•ern•ise** /ˈwɛstɚˌnaɪz/ *verb* **-iz•es; -ized; -iz•ing :** to cause (someone or something) to have the qualities or characteristics that are associated with Western Europe and North America [+ *obj*] *westernized* cities/countries ▪ He decided to *westernize* his name after moving from Japan to Canada. [*no obj*] The city has begun to *westernize.*
– west•ern•i•za•tion *or* **West•ern•i•za•tion** *also Brit* **west•ern•i•sa•tion** /ˌwɛstɚnəˈzeɪʃən, *Brit* ˌwɛstəˌnaɪˈzeɪʃən/ *noun* [*noncount*]

Western medicine *noun* [*noncount*] **:** the typical methods of healing or treating disease that are taught in Western medical schools

west•ward /ˈwɛstwɚd/ *also chiefly Brit* **west•wards** /ˈwɛstwɚdz/ *adv* **:** toward the west ▪ The settlers moved *westward.*
– westward *adj* ▪ the *westward* expansion of the country

[1]**wet** /ˈwɛt/ *adj* **wet•ter; wet•test**
1 : covered or soaked with water or another liquid : not dry ▪ a pile of *wet* clothes/towels/leaves ▪ Be careful not to slip on the *wet* floor. ▪ My hair is still *wet.* ▪ My shoes got *wet* when I stepped in the puddle. ▪ The grass was *wet* with dew. ▪ His clothes were ***dripping/soaking/sopping wet*** [=very wet] ▪ (*Brit*) His clothes were ***wet through*** [=completely/very wet]
2 : having a lot of rain : RAINY ▪ a cold, *wet* morning ▪ *wet* climates ▪ It has been a *wet* spring. [=it has rained a lot this spring]
3 *of paint, plaster, etc.* **:** not yet dry : still moist or sticky ▪ *wet* cement ▪ Don't touch the paint. It's still *wet.*

4 *US, informal* : allowing alcoholic beverages to be sold or drunk • a *wet* state/county
5 : soaked with urine • *wet* diapers : wearing a diaper that is soaked with urine • The baby is *wet*.
6 *Brit, informal + disapproving* : lacking strength and determination • The main character is so *wet* [=*weak*] that it's hard to feel sorry for him.
all wet *US, informal* : completely wrong : not correct • She told him that his argument was *all wet*. • He's *all wet*.
get your feet wet : to begin doing a new job, activity, etc., in usually a slow and simple way in order to become more familiar with it • She *got her feet wet* at her new job by doing some simple filing tasks.
wet behind the ears *informal* : young and not experienced • The young reporter was still *wet behind the ears*.
– wet·ly *adv* **– wet·ness** *noun* [*noncount*] • These plants will tolerate *wetness* and cold temperatures.

²wet *verb* **wets; wet** *or* **wet·ted; wet·ting** [+ *obj*]
1 : to cause (something) to become wet • I *wet/wetted* a sponge under the faucet. • Avoid *wetting* the leaves when you water the plant. • The morning dew had *wet/wetted* his shoes. — often + *down* • In the early evening, she *wets down* the grass with a hose.
2 : to make (a bed or your clothes) wet by urinating • The little boy accidentally ***wet his pants***. • Our daughter was still ***wetting the bed***. [=was still urinating while sleeping in bed] • I laughed so hard I almost ***wet myself***.
wet your whistle see ¹WHISTLE

³wet *noun, pl* **wets**
1 [*count*] *Brit, informal + disapproving* : a person who belongs to the Conservative Party and who has moderate or liberal ideas
2 ***the wet*** : rainy weather : RAIN • We stayed out in *the wet* all afternoon.

wet·back /ˈwɛtˌbæk/ *noun, pl* **-backs** [*count*] *US, offensive* : a Mexican who enters the U.S. illegally ◇ The word *wetback* is very offensive and should be avoided.

wet bar *noun, pl* ~ **bars** [*count*] *US* : a small counter in a house, hotel room, etc., that contains a sink and that is used for making alcoholic drinks

wet blanket *noun, pl* ~ **-kets** [*count*] *informal* : a person who makes it difficult for other people to enjoy themselves by complaining, by showing no enthusiasm, etc.

wet dream *noun, pl* ~ **dreams** [*count*] : a sexual dream that causes a boy or man to have an orgasm while sleeping

wet·land /ˈwɛtˌlænd/ *noun, pl* **-lands** [*count*] : an area of land (such as a marsh or swamp) that is covered with shallow water — usually plural • They want to protect the *wetlands* from developers.

wet nurse *noun, pl* ~ **nurses** [*count*] *old-fashioned* : a woman who cares for and breast-feeds other people's babies as a job

wet suit *noun, pl* ~ **suits** [*count*] : a piece of clothing that is made of rubber and that is worn by swimmers, divers, etc., when they are in cold water in order to keep their bodies warm — see picture at SCUBA DIVING

we've /ˈwiːv/ — used as a contraction of *we have* • *We've* got to go.

¹whack /ˈwæk/ *verb* **whacks; whacked; whack·ing**
1 *informal* : to hit (someone or something) with great force [+ *obj*] She *whacked* the piñata with a stick. • The old man lifted his cane and *whacked* the mugger on the head. [*no obj*] They were *whacking* through the jungle with their machetes.
2 [+ *obj*] *US, informal* : to reduce (something) by a large amount : SLASH • Congress *whacked* the budget by 1.5 billion dollars. = Congress *whacked* 1.5 billion dollars from the budget.
3 [+ *obj*] *US slang* : to murder or kill (someone) • He got *whacked* by mobsters.

²whack *noun, pl* **whacks** *informal*
1 [*count*] **a** : the act of hitting someone or something with great force • She gave him a *whack* on the head. [=she whacked him on the head] • He gave the ball a good *whack*. [=he hit the ball hard] **b** : the sound made when something is hit hard • The pile of books hit the floor with a *whack*.
2 [*noncount*] *Brit* : a share or portion of something • I ended up paying ***full whack*** [=*full price*] for items that went on sale the next day. • I paid ***top whack*** [=(*US*) *top dollar*] for these items. [=I paid the highest amount possible] • You need to pay your ***fair whack*** [=*fair share*] of the bill.
(all) in one whack *US, informal* : at one time : in a single amount • We borrowed $5,000 *all in one whack*.
have/take a whack at *US, informal* : to try to do (something) • She *took a whack at* solving the puzzle. • I can't open the jar. Do you want to *take a whack at* it? [=do you want to try to open it?]
out of whack *US, informal* : not working properly : not in good condition • He threw his knee *out of whack*. [=he injured his knee] • The garage door is still *out of whack*. • Their priorities are (all) *out of whack*. [=they do not understand what things are actually important]

W

whacked *adj* [*more* ~; *most* ~] *Brit, informal* : extremely tired : EXHAUSTED • I was/felt completely *whacked*.

whacked–out *also* **wacked–out** /ˈwæktˌaʊt/ *adj* [*more* ~; *most* ~] *US slang*
1 : unusual or different in usually an amusing way • a totally *whacked-out* [=*wacky*] world
2 : acting strangely because of the effects of drugs or alcohol • a *whacked-out* drug dealer — often + *on* • They were *whacked-out* [=*stoned*] on drugs.

whack·ing /ˈwækɪŋ/ *adj, Brit, informal* : very large • a *whacking* [=*whopping*] sum of money
– whacking *adv* • He told a *whacking* [=*very*] good story. • a *whacking* large income

¹whale /ˈweɪl/ *noun, pl* **whale** *or* **whales**
1 [*count*] : an often very large animal that lives in the ocean and that is a mammal rather than a fish — see also BLUE WHALE, HUMPBACK WHALE, KILLER WHALE, SPERM WHALE
2 [*singular*] *informal* : something that is very big, important, good, etc. — + *of* • It became one *whale of* a problem. [=a very big problem] • We had ***a whale of a time*** [=a great time] at the party.

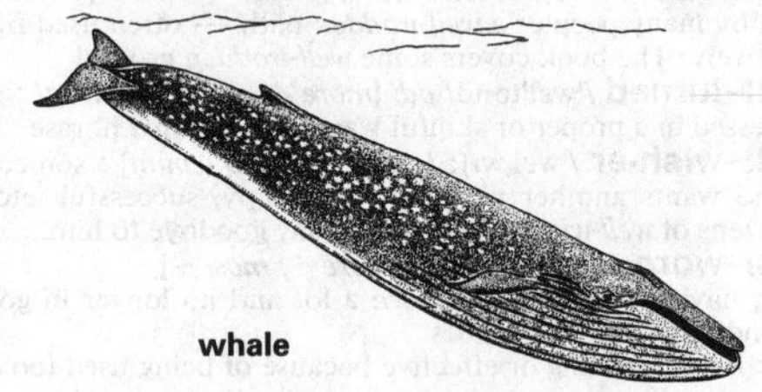
whale

²whale *verb* **whales; whaled; whal·ing** *US, informal*
1 [+ *obj*] : to hit (something) with great force and energy • He *whaled* the ball over the fence for a home run.
2 [*no obj*] : to attack or hit someone or something repeatedly — often + *at, into,* or *on* • She *whaled on* him [=she pounded him] with her fists. • The manager was *whaling into* his employees. [=was angrily criticizing his employees] — often + *away* • The candidates *whaled away at* each other.

whale·bone /ˈweɪlˌboʊn/ *noun* [*noncount*] : a hard substance that is found in the jaw of some types of whales

whal·er /ˈweɪlɚ/ *noun, pl* **-ers** [*count*]
1 : a person who hunts for whales
2 : a ship that is used for hunting whales

whale watch *noun, pl* ~ **watches** [*count*] : a trip that people take on a boat in order to see whales coming up to the surface of the water

whal·ing /ˈweɪlɪŋ/ *noun* [*noncount*] : the job or business of hunting whales • the *whaling* industry

wham /ˈwæm/ *interj* — used to imitate the sound of a loud, sudden noise or to say that something happened very quickly • *Wham*! The wind slammed the door shut. • Everything seemed fine and then—*wham*!—all hell broke loose.

wham·my /ˈwæmi/ *noun, pl* **-mies** [*count*] *informal* : something (such as a magical spell) that causes someone to have bad luck • Talking about his winning streak must have ***put the whammy on him*** [=caused him to have bad luck], because he lost the next day. — see also DOUBLE WHAMMY

wharf /ˈwoɚf/ *noun, pl* **wharves** /ˈwoɚvz/ *also* **wharfs** [*count*] : a flat structure that is built along the shore of a river, ocean, etc., so that ships can load and unload cargo or passengers

¹what /ˈwɑːt, ˈwʌt/ *pronoun*
1 a — used to ask for information about someone or something • *What* is your name? • *What* are those things on the table? • *What*'s your family like? • *What* happened? • *What* [=how much] does it cost? • "*What* did she say?" "She said yes." • *What* do you think of my idea? • *What* do you want to

do tonight? • "Dad!" "*What* (do you want)?" "You have a phone call." • *What* (on earth) are you doing?! • I finished dusting. Now *what* (should I do)? • *What* (should I do) next? • ***What else*** did he say? • You have money, fame, and a beautiful family. ***What more*** could you want? **b** — used to describe a question • Please ask them *what* they want for dinner. • They asked her *what* she knew about him. • I wonder *what* his motives were.

2 a — used to ask someone to say something again because you have not clearly heard or understood it • *What* did you say? = (*informal*) *What*? — often used to show surprise about the thing that someone has just said • "And then I said that he could go to hell." "You said *what*?!" • She did *what*?! • *What*? I don't believe it. You must be joking! **b** *informal* — used to express surprise, excitement, etc. • *What*, no breakfast? • "Have you heard? They won!" "*What*!? That's great!"

3 *informal* — used to ask what someone's last name is • "Her name's Kathy." "Kathy *what*?"

4 a : that which : the one or ones that • He has no income but *what* he gets from his writing. [=he has no income except for the income he gets from his writing] • "Do you have any other sizes?" "No, only *what* you see here." **b** : the kind that : the same as • The speech was very much *what* everyone expected. • My memory isn't ***what it used to be***. [=it is not as good as it used to be] **c** : something that • The dog is chewing on *what* appears to be a sock. • It was the beginning of *what* turned out to be a long and successful career. **d** : the thing or things that • *What* you need is a vacation. [=you need a vacation] • *What* made me angry was how he treated you. [=it was the way he treated you that made me angry] • *What* matters most is your safety. = Your safety is *what* matters most. • Romance novels are *what* she enjoys reading. • Do *what* you're told. • Tell me *what* you're looking for. • She is looking for something but I don't know *what*. • He knows *what* he should do. — often followed by *to + verb* • Stop telling me *what to do*. • I don't know *what to think/say/believe*. • She has (got) ***what it takes*** [=she has the skills and personality] to do the job. • I'll do *what it takes* to win. • You'll never ***guess what*** happened to me today. [=you'll be surprised by what happened to me today] ✧ *Guess what* is often used to tell someone that you have surprising news. • *Guess what* happened to me today! • "*Guess what*!" "What?" "I bought a new car." **e** : anything or everything that : WHATEVER • Say *what* you will, my opinion won't change. [=nothing you can say will change my opinion] • Take *what* you need. [=take anything that you need]

5 *informal* — used to direct attention to something that you are about to say • I'll tell you *what* I'm going to do: I'm going to let you have it for 30 percent off. • I'll tell you *what*. If he thinks I'm cleaning up this mess, he's wrong. • Tell you *what*—let's eat out tonight. • "It's not worth the money." "You know *what*—you're right."

or what *informal* **1** — used to ask about what is happening, being done, etc. • Is it snowing, raining, *or what*? • So are you ready to leave *or what*? **2** — used to ask if someone agrees with you • Is this exciting *or what*? [=isn't this exciting?; don't you agree that this is exciting?]

say what see [1]SAY

what about **1 a** : does that include (someone) : how about (someone) • "We're all going to the beach." "*What about* Kenny?" **b** : how does that affect (someone or something) : what should be done about (someone or something) • "I need to leave—something has come up." "*What about* the meeting?" "We can reschedule it." • "You can throw this one away." "*What about* the others?" "Those I want to keep." • (And/But) *What about* the people who can't afford health insurance? **2** — used to make a suggestion about what could be done • *What about* [=*how about*] coming with us? • *What about* driving to the coast for the weekend? • We'll need to talk about this again. *What about* (meeting) next week? • *What about* another game? [=would you like to play another game?] **3** — used to ask someone to tell you something in response to the thing that you have just said • I like skiing and hiking. ***What about you***? [=what sports do you like?] • Everyone else is coming. *What about you?* [=are you coming, too?]

what . . . for : for what purpose or reason • *What* did you do that *for*? [=why did you do that?] • *What* is this switch *for*? [=what does this switch do?] • "The principal wants to see you." "*What for*?" [=*why*?] — see also WHAT FOR

what have you *informal* : any of the other things that might also be mentioned • You can use the container to hold paper clips, pins, and/or *what have you*.

what if **1** : what would happen if • *What if* they find out? • *What if* it rains? **2** : what does it matter if — used to say that something is not important • "He's nice enough, I suppose. But he's poor." "*What if* he is poor? I love him!" • "They might find out." "***So what if*** they do? I don't care." — see also *so what* at [3]WHAT

what of **1** *formal* : how does that affect (someone or something) : what should be done about (someone or something) • *What of* [=*what about*] those who cannot afford health insurance? **2** : why does (something) matter • "Did you approve this request?" "Yes. ***What of it***?" [=*so what*?]

what's it to you? *informal* : why do you want to know — used to respond in a somewhat angry or annoyed way to a question that you do not want to answer • "How much do they pay you?" "Why? *What's it to you?*"

what's more : in addition : FURTHERMORE • Her boyfriend is intelligent and handsome; *what's more*, he respects her.

what's up? *US, informal* — used as a friendly greeting • "Hi, Jim. *What's up?*" "Not much."

what's what *informal* : the true state of things : the things that need to be known or understood in order to make good judgments, decisions, etc. • She knows *what's what* when it comes to fashion. [=she knows a lot about fashion] • We need to find out *what's what*.

what's with or ***what's up with*** *informal* **1** : what is the reason for (something) • (So) *what's with* the hat? [=why are you wearing that hat?] • He told me to go away. *What's up with* that? [=why did he do that?] **2** : what is wrong with (someone or something) • *What's with* him? • *What's up with* you? You look upset. • I can't figure out *what's up with* this computer.

[2]what *adj, always used before a noun*

1 — used to ask someone to indicate the identity or nature of someone or something • *What* fool told you that? • *What* book did you read? • *What* news have you heard from him? • In *what* way are these two stories the same? • We won the war, but ***at what price***? [=did we lose or give up too much in order to win the war?]

2 — used to say that someone or something is remarkable for having good or bad qualities • *What* a good idea! • *What* mountains! • Remember *what* fun we had? • *What* a horrible movie! • *What* a beautiful child.

3 — used to refer to an amount that someone has, uses, etc. • She gave *what* money she had [=she gave all the money she had] to the homeless man. • Give *what* excuses you will—it makes no difference. [=no excuses that you may give will make any difference] • He soon gambled away *what* (little) money he had left. • We spent *what* (little) time remained chatting.

[3]what *adv* : in what way • *What* [=*how*] does it matter? • *What* does she care? [=why is it important to her?]

so what *informal* — used to say that something said or done is not important • She has a glass of wine now and then—*so what*?

what with — used to introduce the part of a sentence that indicates the cause of something • *What with* the freezing temperatures, they nearly died. • *What with* school and sports, she's always busy. • Things have been difficult for him lately, *what with* his wife's illness and all.

what all *pronoun, informal* : WHATNOT

what·cha·ma·call·it /ˈwɑːtʃəməˌkɑːlət, ˈwʌtʃəməˌkɑːlət/ *noun, pl* **-its** [*count*] *US, informal* : something whose name you have forgotten or do not know : THINGAMAJIG • I can't find the *whatchamacallit* that holds the door open.

[1]what·ev·er /wɑtˈɛvɚ, wʌtˈɛvɚ/ *pronoun*

1 : anything or everything that • Say *whatever* you want, my opinion won't change. [=nothing you can say will change my opinion] • Take *whatever* you need.

2 : no matter what : regardless of what • *Whatever* he says, don't believe him. [=do not believe him at all] • "What's that smell?" "I don't know, but *whatever* it is, it's awful!" • ***Whatever you do***, don't press that button!

3 — used in questions that express surprise or confusion • *Whatever* made you do something as foolish as that? • *Whatever* did she mean (by that)?

4 *informal* : WHATNOT • I enjoy all kinds of sports—skiing, biking, (or) *whatever*.

[2]whatever *adj*

1 *always used before a noun* **a** : all the • Take *whatever* supplies you need. [=take any supplies that you need] **b** : any • She will buy the painting at *whatever* price. : any . . . that • We are willing to take *whatever* action is needed. [=to take

W

any action that is needed] **c** — used to refer to something that is not known ▪ For *whatever* reason, he refused to speak to us. [=he refused to speak to us for some reason that we don't know]

2 *not used before a noun* : of any kind or amount at all : WHATSOEVER ▪ There's no food *whatever*. ▪ There's no evidence *whatever* to support your theory.

³whatever *adv, informal* — used to show that something said or done is not important ▪ "Jen forgot to print out extra copies." "You mean Jean." "*Whatever*—you know who I mean." ▪ We could go see a movie, watch TV—*whatever*. [=it makes no difference to me what we do]

what for *noun* [*noncount*] *informal + somewhat old-fashioned* : harsh words or punishment ▪ Just wait until he gets home. I'll ***give him what for!*** — see also *what . . . for* at ¹WHAT

what–if /ˌwɑːtˈɪf, ˌwʌtˈɪf/ *noun, pl* **-ifs** [*count*] : a question that asks someone to imagine what might happen or what might have happened ▪ Life is full of *what-ifs*. ▪ He started thinking about the *what-ifs* of the game: What if we had thrown more passes? What if we hadn't missed that field goal?

what·not /ˈwɑːtˌnɑːt, ˈwʌtˌnɑːt/ *pronoun, informal* : any of the other things that might also be mentioned ▪ You can use the container to hold paper clips, pins, and/or *whatnot*.

what's–her–name *also US* **what's–her–face** *noun* [*singular*] *informal* : a woman whose name you have forgotten or do not know ▪ I just bumped into *what's-her-name* from the bank.

what's–his–name *also US* **what's–his–face** *noun* [*singular*] *informal* : a man whose name you have forgotten or do not know ▪ I think she's still dating *what's-his-name*.

what·sit /ˈwɑːtsət, ˈwʌtsət/ *also US* **what·sis** /ˈwɑːtsəs, ˈwʌtsəs/ *noun, pl* **-sits** *also US* **-sis·es** [*count*] *informal* : something whose name you have forgotten or do not know : THINGAMAJIG ▪ a little rubber *whatsit*

what·so·ev·er /ˌwɑːtsəˈwɛvɚ, ˌwʌtsəˈwɛvɚ/ *adj, not used before a noun* : of any kind or amount at all ▪ There's no evidence *whatsoever* [=*whatever*] to support your theory. ▪ She'll use any means *whatsoever* to achieve her goals. ▪ His remark had nothing *whatsoever* to do with you. ▪ "Is there any reason to wait?" "None *whatsoever*."

wheat /ˈwiːt/ *noun* [*noncount*]

1 : a kind of grain that is used to make flour for breads, cookies, etc. — see also SHREDDED WHEAT, WHOLE WHEAT

2 *US* : bread that is made from wheat flour ▪ a turkey sandwich on *wheat*

separate the wheat from the chaff see ²SEPARATE

wheat germ *noun* [*noncount*] : the center part of a grain of wheat which is eaten often as a source of vitamins and protein

whee /ˈwiː/ *interj* — used to express enjoyment especially by children ▪ The girl yelled "*Whee!*" as she went down the slide.

whee·dle /ˈwiːdl/ *verb* **whee·dles; whee·dled; whee·dling** *often disapproving* : to persuade someone to do something or to give you something by saying nice things [+ *obj*] He *wheedled* quite a bit of money from her. ▪ We managed to *wheedle* [=*coax*] the juicy details out of him. — often + *into* ▪ She tried to *wheedle* us *into* spending more money than we wanted. ▪ He *wheedled* his way *into* his current job. [*no obj*] She pleaded and *wheedled*, but I wouldn't be swayed.

¹wheel /ˈwiːl/ *noun, pl* **wheels**

1 [*count*] **a** : one of the round parts underneath a car, wagon, etc., that rolls and allows something to move ▪ The car's rear *wheels* started to spin on the icy road. ▪ the *wheels* of a train/airplane ▪ a bicycle *wheel* ▪ a suitcase with *wheels* on the bottom — see also TRAINING WHEELS **b** : a hard, round object that turns and causes machinery or a mechanical device to move — sometimes used figuratively ▪ You could almost see the *wheels* turning in his head. [=you could almost see him thinking about how to do something] — see also FLYWHEEL, PADDLE WHEEL, WATERWHEEL

2 [*count*] : STEERING WHEEL ▪ She fell asleep ***at the wheel*** [=she fell asleep while she was driving] ▪ He got ***behind the wheel*** [=he sat in the driver's seat] and sped off. ▪ I was nervous my first time *behind the wheel*. [=my first time driving a car] ▪ My sister offered to ***take the wheel*** [=offered to drive]

3 [*count*] : something that is round like a wheel or that turns like a wheel ▪ a *wheel* of cheddar cheese — see also CARTWHEEL, FERRIS WHEEL, PINWHEEL, POTTER'S WHEEL, PRAYER WHEEL, SPINNING WHEEL

4 [*count*] **a** : an essential or functioning part of an organization, process, etc. — usually plural ▪ the *wheels* of government ▪ They hoped that the tax cuts would ***grease the wheels*** of the economy. [=would help the economy work better] ▪ With today's announcement, she has ***set the wheels in motion*** for a run for the presidency. [=she has begun to run for president] **b** *informal* : an important person in an organization ▪ He's a ***big wheel*** [=*bigwig*] at the company.

5 ***wheels*** [*plural*] *slang* : CAR ▪ I couldn't get around easily without my *wheels*. ▪ She has a nice ***set of wheels***. [=she has a nice car]

a/the squeaky wheel gets the grease/oil — used to say that someone who complains or causes problems is more likely to receive attention or help than someone who stays quiet and does not cause problems

reinvent the wheel see REINVENT

spin your wheels see ¹SPIN

wheels come/fall off *informal* ◊ If the ***wheels come/fall off***, someone or something fails in a sudden or unexpected way. ▪ The pitcher was doing well for the first four innings, then *the wheels fell off* in the fifth.

wheels within wheels : a situation that is complex and difficult to deal with because it involves many different things ▪ The problem seems simple at first, but there are *wheels within wheels*.

²wheel *verb* **wheels; wheeled; wheel·ing**

1 [+ *obj*] **a** : to move (someone or something) on a vehicle that has wheels ▪ Doctors *wheeled* the patient into the operating room. — sometimes used figuratively ▪ Management *wheeled in* the experts [=management hired a group of experts] to study the matter further. **b** : to push (something) that has wheels on it ▪ He *wheeled* his motorcycle into the garage. ▪ Our waiter *wheeled* out a small dessert cart. — sometimes used figuratively ▪ She *wheeled out* [=*offered*] the same old excuse for being late.

2 [*no obj*] : to turn quickly and face a different direction ▪ She *wheeled* around in her chair when I entered the room.

3 [*no obj*] : to move in a circle or curve ▪ Seagulls *wheeled* overhead.

wheel and deal : to make deals or agreements in business or politics in a skillful and sometimes dishonest way ▪ There was a lot of *wheeling and dealing* going on at the convention. — see also WHEELER-DEALER

wheel·bar·row /ˈwiːlˌberoʊ/ *noun, pl* **-rows** [*count*] : a cart with two handles, a large bowl, and usually one wheel that is used for carrying heavy loads of dirt, rocks, etc. — called also *barrow*

wheel·chair /ˈwiːlˌʧeɚ/ *noun, pl* **-chairs** [*count*] : a chair with wheels that is used by people who cannot walk because they are disabled, sick, or injured ▪ He was in a *wheelchair* for several months after the accident. ▪ an entrance with *wheelchair* access [=an entrance that can be used by people in wheelchairs] — see picture at HOSPITAL

wheel clamp *noun, pl* **~ clamps** [*count*] *Brit* : DENVER BOOT

wheeled /ˈwiːld/ *adj*

1 : having wheels ▪ a *wheeled* vehicle

2 : having a specified number of wheels — used in combination ▪ a four-*wheeled* vehicle

wheel·er /ˈwiːlɚ/ *noun, pl* **-ers** [*count*] : a vehicle that has a specified number of wheels — used in combination ▪ an 18-*wheeler* [=a large truck with 18 wheels] ▪ a two-*wheeler* [=a bicycle that has two wheels]

wheel·er–deal·er /ˌwiːlɚˈdiːlɚ/ *noun, pl* **-ers** [*count*] *informal* : a person who makes deals in business or politics in a skillful and sometimes dishonest way ▪ a political *wheeler-dealer* — see also *wheel and deal* at ²WHEEL

wheel·house /ˈwiːlˌhaʊs/ *noun, pl* **-hous·es** [*count*] : an enclosed area on a boat or ship where a person stands to steer

wheel·ie /ˈwiːli/ *noun, pl* **wheel·ies** [*count*] : an action in which a bicycle, motorcycle, etc. is balanced for a short time on its rear wheel ▪ He did a *wheelie* on his bike.

wheelie bin *noun, pl* **~ bins** [*count*] *Brit* : a large container with wheels that is used for holding trash

¹wheeze /ˈwiːz/ *verb* **wheez·es; wheezed; wheez·ing** [*no obj*]

1 : to breathe loudly and with difficulty ▪ He was up all night hacking and *wheezing*.

2 : to make a sound like a person who is breathing with difficulty ▪ The car's motor *wheezed* and stalled.

²wheeze *noun, pl* **wheezes** [*count*]

1 : the sound made by a person who is having difficulty

W

breathing or a similar sound : the sound of wheezing • Between gasps and *wheezes*, he tried to explain what had happened. • the *wheeze* of an engine

2 *Brit, informal* : a clever idea or joke • We can count on him for a good *wheeze*.

– wheezy /ˈwiːzi/ *adj* **wheez·i·er; -est** • a *wheezy* cough

whelk /ˈwɛlk/ *noun, pl* **whelk** [*count*] : a large snail that lives in the ocean

[1]whelp /ˈwɛlp/ *noun, pl* **whelps** [*count*] *old-fashioned* : a young animal; *especially* : a young dog

[2]whelp *verb* **whelps; whelped; whelp·ing** [*no obj*] *of a female animal* : to give birth • The dog *whelped* in March.

[1]when /ˈwɛn/ *adv*

1 : at what time • *When* will you return? • *When* did the American Civil War begin? • The detective asked me *when* I last saw her. • *When* is the next performance? • (Do you) remember *when* that happened?

2 a : at, in, or during which • It was a time *when* people didn't have to lock their doors. • the happy days *when* we were together **b :** at or during which time • We're still waiting for the test results, *when* we'll decide our next move.

3 *informal* : at a former and usually less successful time • I can say I ***knew you when.*** [=I knew you before you were famous or successful]

[2]when *conj*

1 a : at or during the time that • We went fishing *when* [=*while*] we were on vacation. • I'll leave *when* you do. [=I'll leave at the same time as you] • *When* he finally showed up, he was drunk. • *When* I was in school, we didn't have computers. **b :** just after the time that • You can go *when* the bell rings. • Call me *when* you get home. • Things were better *when* he got a job. **c :** at any or every time that • I cry *when* [=*whenever*] I hear that song. • *When* he watches television, he falls asleep.

2 a — used to say what happens, is true, or can be done in a particular situation • *When* you have no family, you are really on your own. • We take the bus to school *when* it rains. • A contestant is disqualified *when* she disobeys the rules. • ***When and if*** he comes, you can ask him. = ***If and when*** he comes, you can ask him. **b** — used to ask why or how something is done in the situation that exists • Why buy a newspaper *when* you can read the news online for free? • How can he buy the house *when* he has no money? [=he has no money, so how can he buy the house?]

3 : in spite of the fact that : ALTHOUGH • She quit politics *when* she might have had a great career in it.

4 : the time or occasion at or in which • Tomorrow is *when* we must decide.

[3]when *pronoun* : what or which time • He retired in 1998, since *when* he has been devoting his time to gardening. • You need the report by *when*?

since when? see [1]SINCE

whence /ˈwɛns/ *adv, old-fashioned + literary* : from where • They returned to the land *whence* they came. • *Whence* the source of this tradition? [=where does this tradition come from?] — often + *from* • They returned to the land *from whence* they came.

[1]when·ev·er /wɛˈnɛvɚ/ *conj* : at any or every time that • You may leave *whenever* you wish. • *Whenever* he leaves the house he always takes an umbrella. • The teacher welcomes originality *whenever* it is shown. • We'll begin the meeting *whenever* the boss gets here.

[2]whenever *adv* : at any time : at whatever time • You can come tomorrow or *whenever*.

[1]where /ˈweɚ/ *adv*

1 a : at or in what place • *Where* are my keys? • *Where* did you meet her? • *Where* did you hear that? • *Where* can I find books about gardening? • *Where* are you from? • I don't know *where* that came from. — sometimes + *at* in very informal speech • *Where*'s the party *at*? **b :** to what place • *Where* are we going? • *Where* is she taking us? • Do you know *where* we're going? — often + *to* • *Where* are we going *to*? • ***Where to,*** Miss? [=what place do you want to go to?]

2 : when or at what point • *Where* does the story get interesting?

3 : how or in what way • *Where* am I wrong? • *Where* do the two candidates disagree on the issue?

4 : to what goal or result • *Where* will this course of action lead us?

where it's at *informal* **1 :** the best or most exciting or interesting place to be • Los Angeles, California, is *where it's at* if you want to get into the film industry. **2 :** a subject, field of interest, etc., that is very popular or important • Education is *where it's at* in politics.

where (someone) is at *informal* : someone's true position, state, or nature • I haven't quite figured out *where she's at* [=where she stands; what her opinions are] on that issue.

[2]where *conj*

1 a : at or in the place that • Please stay *where* you are. • We sat down *where* there was some shade. • He put the note *where* she could easily see it. **b :** to or in what place • He doesn't know *where* he is going. • It doesn't matter to me *where* we eat. — often followed by *to + verb* • She didn't know *where to go*. • He tells me *where to shop* for the best bargains. **c :** the place that • We could see the players very clearly from *where* we sat. • I know *where* their house is. **d :** that is the place in which • The town *where* we live is having an arts and crafts fair. • This is the room *where* the children sleep. • The store *where* we shop is closing.

2 : to or in whatever place : WHEREVER • I can go *where* I want, when I want. • People may sit *where* they like.

3 a — used to refer to a particular point in a story, process, etc. • My favorite part is toward the end of the book, *where* the heroine returns home. • The town has reached the size *where* traffic is a problem. • The project is at a point *where* the end is in sight. **b** — used to refer to a particular part of what is being discussed • That's *where* you're wrong. • *Where* the two candidates differ is in how to reform health care.

4 : in a situation in which • We must be especially careful *where* children are concerned. • *Where* most people saw a worthless investment, she saw opportunity.

[1]where·abouts /ˈwerəˌbaʊts/ *adv* : near what place • *Whereabouts* [=*where*] does he live? • *Whereabouts* did you park the car?

[2]whereabouts *noun* [*plural*] : the location of a person or thing • Do you know their *whereabouts*? — used with both singular and plural verbs • Her present *whereabouts* are/is unknown.

where·as /weɚˈæz/ *conj*

1 — used to make a statement that describes how two people, groups, etc., are different • Some of these species have flourished, *whereas* others have struggled. • *Whereas* many people have supported the proposal, others have opposed it very strongly. • He has brown eyes *whereas* his children have green eyes.

2 *law* : since it is true that — usually used at the beginning of a statement in an official document • *Whereas* the citizens of the state of Virginia have a right to know that . . .

where·by /weɚˈbaɪ/ *conj* : by which : according to which • They created a program *whereby* single parents could receive greater financial aid. [=a program that would allow single parents to receive greater financial aid]

where·fore /ˈweɚˌfoɚ/ *adv* — used in the past to mean "why" • "*Wherefore* art thou Romeo?" [=why are you Romeo?] —Shakespeare, *Romeo and Juliet* (1594–95)

the whys and (the) wherefores see [3]WHY

[1]where·in /weɚˈɪn/ *adv, formal* : in what way • *Wherein* was I wrong? : in what • *Wherein* lies the secret to the company's success?

[2]wherein *conj, formal*

1 a : in which : WHERE • the city *wherein* he lives **b :** during which • There was a period in her life *wherein* she took no active part in politics.

2 : in what way : HOW • He showed me *wherein* I was wrong.

where·of /weɚˈʌv, weɚˈɑːv/ *conj, formal + old-fashioned* : of what • I know *whereof* I speak. [=I know about the subject I'm speaking about]

where·up·on /ˈwerəˌpɑːn/ *conj, formal* : at which time — used to say that something happens directly after something else and often as a result of it • He graduated from high school in 1986, *whereupon* he immediately joined the navy.

[1]wher·ev·er /weɚˈɛvɚ/ *adv*

1 : in what place : WHERE — used in questions that express surprise or confusion • *Wherever* [=where on earth; where in the world] have you been? • *Wherever* did you get that hat? • *Wherever* did I put my keys?

2 : in, at, or to any place • "Where should I put this?" "Oh, just put it *wherever*." [=*anywhere*] • We can go to the park, the beach, (or) *wherever*.

[2]wherever *conj*

1 : at, in, or to any place that • We can have lunch *wherever* [=*anywhere*] you like. • Bodyguards follow the singer *wherever* [=*everywhere*] she goes.

2 : in any situation in which : at any time that • *Wherever*

W

[=*whenever*] (it is) possible, I try to help out.

wherever that may be** or **wherever that is — used to say that you do not know where a place is ▪ She's from Jefferson City, *wherever that may be*.

where·with·al /ˈweɚwɪˌðɑːl, ˈweɚwɪˌθɑːl/ *noun* [*noncount*] : the money, skill, etc., that is needed to get or do something ▪ A project as big as this requires a lot of financial *wherewithal*. ▪ He doesn't have the *wherewithal* to finish what he started.

whet /ˈwɛt/ *verb* **whets; whet·ted; whet·ting** [+ *obj*] : to make (something, such as a person's appetite or curiosity) sharper or stronger ▪ We had some wine to *whet* our appetites. ▪ You've *whetted* my curiosity. ▪ The ads are trying to *whet* booksellers' interest.

wheth·er /ˈwɛðɚ/ *conj*

1 a : if it is or was true that ▪ Did you ask *whether* [=*if*] they were going? ▪ I don't know *whether* they were invited. **b :** if it is or was better ▪ She was uncertain *whether* to go or stay.

2 — used to indicate choices or possibilities ▪ *Whether* we succeed or fail, we must try. ▪ It doesn't matter *whether* you pay by cash or check. ▪ We're going ***whether or not*** you decide to come along. = ***Whether or not*** you decide to come along, we're going. [=we're going if you decide to come with us and we're going if you decide not to come with us] ▪ I had to decide *whether or not* to respond to his letter. ▪ The police are investigating *whether* (*or not*) the death was a homicide. ▪ The game will be played *whether* it rains *or not*.

whet·stone /ˈwɛtˌstoʊn/ *noun, pl* **-stones** [*count*] : a stone used for sharpening knives, blades, etc.

whew /*a whistling sound, often read as* ˈhwuː, ˈhjuː/ *interj* — used to indicate that you are surprised, relieved, or hot ▪ "*Whew*! I'm glad that's over." ▪ "*Whew*! It's hot in here."

whey /ˈweɪ/ *noun* [*noncount*] : the watery part of milk that forms after the milk becomes thick and sour ▪ The curd has separated from the *whey*.

[1]**which** /ˈwɪʧ/ *adj* : what one or ones of a group : what particular one or ones — used to indicate what is being shown, pointed to, or mentioned ▪ He knew *which* people had paid and *which* hadn't. ▪ *Which* tie should I wear, the red one or the green one? ▪ *Which* way should we turn at the stoplight? ▪ Choose *which* style you like best.

every which way see EVERY

[2]**which** *pronoun*

1 : what one or ones out of a group — used to indicate or ask what is being shown, pointed to, or mentioned ▪ They are either swimming or canoeing, I don't know *which*. ▪ They could not decide *which* of the two roads to take. ▪ *Which* of those houses do you live in? ▪ *Which* of you want tea and *which* want lemonade?

2 a — used to introduce an additional statement about something that has already been mentioned ▪ She plays squash, *which* is a sport similar to racquetball. ▪ Our new car, *which* we bought last month, seats five people. **b** — used after a preposition to refer again to something that has already been mentioned ▪ She again demonstrated the qualities for *which* she is admired by so many people. ▪ The exhibit is on view here for three months, after *which* it travels to another city. **c** — used to introduce a group of words that limits the meaning of a noun to a specific place or thing ▪ This is a matter *which* [=*that*] requires further study.

which is which — used to say that you are unsure about the identity of each member of a group ▪ The two words sound alike, so it's hard to remember *which is which*. ▪ One of the twins is named John and the other William, but *which is which*?

[1]**which·ev·er** /wɪʧˈɛvɚ/ *pronoun* : whatever one or ones out of a group ▪ We can go on Tuesday or Friday, *whichever* you prefer. ▪ You may leave at 4:00 or when you've finished the job, *whichever* comes first.

[2]**whichever** *adj* : whatever one or ones out of a group ▪ Choose *whichever* one you want. ▪ It's the same distance *whichever* [=no matter which] way you go. ▪ He will support *whichever* candidate wins.

[1]**whiff** /ˈwɪf/ *noun, pl* **whiffs**

1 [*count*] : a slight smell of something : an odor that is weak ▪ I got/caught a *whiff* of new paint when I entered the room. ▪ a *whiff* of perfume

2 [*singular*] : a slight trace or indication ▪ The incident had a *whiff* [=*hint*] of scandal about it. ▪ I detected a *whiff* of sarcasm in her voice.

3 [*count*] *baseball, informal* : STRIKEOUT ▪ The pitcher had eight *whiffs* during the game.

[2]**whiff** *verb* **whiffs; whiffed; whiff·ing** *US, informal*

1 [+ *obj*] : to notice (a smell) ▪ He *whiffed* a strong odor of perfume.

2 *baseball* **a** [+ *obj*] *of a pitcher* : to cause (a batter) to be out by pitching three strikes ▪ The pitcher *whiffed* [=*struck out*] three batters in a row. **b** [*no obj*] *of a batter* : to make an out by getting three strikes ▪ The batter *whiffed* [=*struck out*] twice during the game.

3 : to fail to hit (something) [+ *obj*] The golfer nearly *whiffed* the shot. [*no obj*] The golfer nearly *whiffed* on the shot.

whif·fy /ˈwɪfi/ *adj* **whiff·i·er; -est** *Brit, informal* : having a bad smell ▪ Old cheese is often a bit *whiffy*. ▪ *whiffy* [=*smelly*] old socks

Whig /ˈwɪg/ *noun, pl* **Whigs** [*count*]

1 : a member or supporter of a British political group of the 18th and early 19th centuries that wanted to decrease royal power and to increase the power of the British Parliament

2 : an American who supported independence from Great Britain during the American Revolution

3 : a member or supporter of an American political party of the 19th century that was formed to oppose the Democrats

[1]**while** /ˈwajəl/ *conj*

1 : during the time that ▪ Someone called *while* you were out. ▪ You can get the photos developed *while* you wait. ▪ The phone rang *while* I was doing the dishes. ▪ They met *while* they were in college. ▪ We should enjoy this good weather *while* it lasts. = We should enjoy this good weather *while* we can. ▪ Can I get you anything *while* I'm at the store?

2 — used to make a statement that describes how two people, groups, etc., are different ▪ *While* some people think his comedy is funny, others find him offensive.

3 : in spite of the fact that : ALTHOUGH ▪ *While* (he is) respected, the mayor is not liked. ▪ He made a comment that, *while* well-intentioned, still hurt my feelings. ▪ *While* I think some parts of the plan are good, I don't think it's practical.

[2]**while** *noun* [*singular*] : a period of time ▪ It took them ***a while*** to find out what was causing the problem. ▪ Why don't we stay here (for) *a while*? ▪ It has been ***quite a while*** since I last saw her. = I haven't seen her ***for a (good) long while***. [=for a long time] ▪ He claimed that he was happy, but he was thinking ***all the while*** [=during that entire time] of quitting his job.

once in a while see [1]ONCE

worth your while : worth doing : interesting or rewarding ▪ If you help me I'll ***make it worth your while***. [=I'll make it worthwhile for you; I'll reward you for helping me] ▪ It would be *worth your while* to study the material again before the test. — see also WORTHWHILE

[3]**while** *verb* **whiles; whiled; whil·ing**

while away [*phrasal verb*] ***while away (time)** or **while (time) away*** : to spend (time) doing something pleasant and easy ▪ We *whiled away* the afternoon with a walk around the garden. ▪ They *whiled* the hours *away* telling jokes and stories.

whilst /ˈwajəlst/ *conj, chiefly Brit, formal* : [1]WHILE

whim /ˈwɪm/ *noun, pl* **whims** [*count*] : a sudden wish, desire, decision, etc. ▪ the *whims* of fashion ▪ It's hard to predict voters' *whims*. ▪ Her husband tries to ***satisfy her every whim***. [=make her happy by doing everything that she wants] ▪ He quit his job ***on a whim***. [=because of a sudden decision] ▪ The shop is only open ***at the whim*** of the owner. [=the shop is only open when the owner wants it to be open]

[1]**whim·per** /ˈwɪmpɚ/ *verb* **-pers; -pered; -per·ing**

1 [*no obj*] : to make a quiet crying sound ▪ I could hear the puppy *whimpering*.

2 : to complain in a weak or annoying way [*no obj*] She *whimpered* about having to get up early. [+ *obj*] "Where are you going?" she *whimpered*.

[2]**whimper** *noun, pl* **-pers** [*count*]

1 : a quiet crying sound ▪ I could hear the puppy's *whimpers*.

2 : a mild expression of complaint or protest ▪ The new law was passed, despite a few *whimpers* [=*objections*] from the opposition. ▪ She accepted their decision ***without a whimper***. [=without complaining]

whim·si·cal /ˈwɪmzɪkəl/ *adj* [*more* ~; *most* ~] : unusual in a playful or amusing way : not serious ▪ *whimsical* behavior ▪ *whimsical* decorations ▪ She has a *whimsical* sense of humor.

— **whim·si·cal·ly** /ˈwɪmzɪkli/ *adv* ▪ The streets in the village are *whimsically* named.

whim·sy *also US* **whim·sey** /ˈwɪmzi/ *noun* [*noncount*] : a playful or amusing quality : a sense of humor or playfulness ▪ The designer's new line showed a touch of *whimsy*. ▪ a bit of decorative *whimsy*

[1]**whine** /ˈwaɪn/ *verb* **whines; whined; whin·ing**

W

1 : to complain in an annoying way [*no obj*] He's always *whining* about the weather. ▪ Quit *whining* and finish your dinner. [+ *obj*] "I want to leave now," she *whined.* ▪ The workers were *whining* that the office was too cold/hot.
2 [*no obj*] **a** : to make a high, crying sound ▪ The dog was *whining* because it wanted to go out. **b** : to make a high and unpleasant sound that continues for a long time ▪ The electric saw *whined* as it cut through the wood.
– whin·er *noun, pl* **-ers** [*count*] ▪ They're all a bunch of *whiners.* **– whiny** *or* **whin·ey** /ˈwaɪni/ *adj* **whin·i·er; -est** [*also more* ~; *most* ~] ▪ a *whiny* child ▪ I'm sick of his *whiny* complaints. ▪ a *whiny* voice

²whine *noun, pl* **whines** [*count*] : a high and unpleasant sound that continues for a long time ▪ the *whine* of a jet engine

whinge /ˈwɪnʤ/ *verb* **whing·es; whinged; whing·ing** *or* **whinge·ing** [*no obj*] *Brit, informal* : to complain in an annoying way : WHINE ▪ Quit *whinging* and get on with the job. ▪ People were *whinging* about the lack of service.
– whing·er *noun, pl* **-gers** [*count*]

whin·ny /ˈwɪni/ *verb* **-nies; -nied; -ny·ing** [*no obj*] *of a horse* : to make a gentle, high sound ▪ I heard the horse *whinnying.* — compare NEIGH
– whinny *noun, pl* **-nies** [*count*] ▪ We heard a *whinny* come from the stable.

¹whip /ˈwɪp/ *noun, pl* **whips**
1 [*count*] : a long, thin piece of leather or similar material that is attached to a handle and that is used for hitting a person as punishment or to hit an animal (such as a horse) to make it move faster ▪ The rider cracked his *whip* and the horse began to run.
2 [*count*] : a member of a legislature (such as the U.S. Congress or the British Parliament) who is appointed by a political party to make sure that other members are present when votes are taken and that they do the things that they are expected to do ▪ the Republican/Democratic/Labour *whip*
3 [*count, noncount*] : a light dessert made by mixing together sweet ingredients ▪ a prune *whip*
a fair crack of the whip see ²CRACK
crack the whip see ¹CRACK

²whip *verb* **whips; whipped; whip·ping**
1 [+ *obj*] : to hit (a person or animal) with a whip or with something that is like a whip ▪ The sailor was *whipped* [=*flogged*] for disobeying orders. ▪ The jockey *whipped* his horse. — see also PISTOL-WHIP
2 *always followed by an adverb or preposition* [+ *obj*] : to move (something) to a different position or remove (something) from a place quickly and forcefully ▪ The riders were getting *whipped* around on the roller coaster. ▪ He suddenly *whipped* out a gun. ▪ He *whipped* off his jacket.
3 a *always followed by an adverb or preposition* [*no obj*] : to move quickly or forcefully ▪ The flag was *whipping* in the strong wind. ▪ A small branch *whipped* back and hit him. **b** [+ *obj*] : to cause (something) to move quickly or forcefully ▪ The wind *whipped* the ship's sails. **c** [+ *obj*] *sports* : to cause (something, such as a ball or puck) to go somewhere quickly and forcefully by throwing it, passing it, etc. ▪ The shortstop *whipped* the ball to first base. ▪ The winger *whipped* a pass toward the net.
4 [+ *obj*] **a** : to hit (something) forcefully ▪ Rain *whipped* the pavement. **b** : to cause (something) to hit something forcefully ▪ The wind *whipped* her hair across her face.
5 [+ *obj*] *informal* : to defeat (someone) easily ▪ He always *whips* me at tennis. ▪ The team got *whipped* in the play-offs.
6 [+ *obj*] : to mix or beat a food (such as cream or an egg) very quickly ▪ She *whipped* the cream. ▪ *whipped* butter/potatoes
7 *always followed by an adverb or preposition* [*no obj*] : to go very quickly ▪ The taxi *whipped* past me without stopping.
whip into [*phrasal verb*] ***whip (someone) into (something)*** : to cause (a group of people) to be in (a state of excitement, anger, etc.) ▪ The speaker *whipped* the crowd *into* a frenzy.
whip through [*phrasal verb*] ***whip through (something)*** *informal* : to do (something) very quickly ▪ She *whipped through* her chores.
whip together [*phrasal verb*] ***whip (something) together*** *or* ***whip together (something)*** *informal* : to produce or prepare (something) very quickly ▪ She *whipped together* a quick lunch. ▪ They had little time to *whip* a plan *together.*
whip up [*phrasal verb*] **1** ***whip (someone or something) up*** *or* ***whip up (someone or something)*** : to excite (someone or something) : to cause (someone or something) to feel strong emotions about something ▪ His speech *whipped up* the crowd. **2** ***whip (something) up*** *or* ***whip up (something)*** *informal* **a** : to cause or create (something) ▪ She was trying to *whip up* some enthusiasm. ▪ His remarks *whipped up* a controversy. **b** : to produce or prepare (a meal) very quickly ▪ I can *whip* a meal *up* in no time. ▪ Would you like me to *whip up* a snack?

whip hand *noun*
the whip hand : the position of having power or being in control in a particular situation ▪ The owners of the company ***had/held the whip hand*** in the negotiations.

whip·lash /ˈwɪpˌlæʃ/ *noun* [*noncount*] : an injury to the neck that is caused by a sudden backward movement of the head ▪ He got/suffered *whiplash* when his car was rear-ended.

whip·per·snap·per /ˈwɪpɚˌsnæpɚ/ *noun, pl* **-pers** [*count*] *informal + old-fashioned* : a young person who annoys older people by being very confident and acting like someone important ▪ a young *whippersnapper*

whip·pet /ˈwɪpət/ *noun, pl* **-pets** [*count*] : a small, fast dog that is used for racing

whipping *noun, pl* **-pings** [*count*] : the act of hitting someone with a whip ▪ They threatened to give him a *whipping.* [=they threatened to whip him]

whipping boy *noun, pl* **~ boys** [*count*] : someone or something that often is blamed for problems caused by other people ▪ The coach has become the *whipping boy* [=*scapegoat*] for all of the team's problems.

whipping cream *noun* [*noncount*] : a kind of cream that becomes thicker when it is stirred or beaten very quickly

whip–poor–will /ˈwɪpɚˌwɪl/ *noun, pl* **-wills** [*count*] : a bird of eastern North America that is active at night and has a loud call which sounds like its name

whip–round /ˈwɪpˌraʊnd/ *noun, pl* **-rounds** [*count*] *Brit, informal* : a collection of money from a group of people that is used to pay for something, buy a gift, make a donation, etc. ▪ We had a *whip-round* at the office to buy our secretary a retirement present.

whir *also* **whirr** /ˈwɚ/ *noun, pl* **whirs** *also* **whirrs** [*count*] : the sound made by something that is spinning very fast ▪ the *whir* of a fan
– whir *also* **whirr** *verb* **whirs** *also* **whirrs; whirred; whir·ring** [*no obj*] ▪ I could hear the engine *whirring.* ▪ The fan made a *whirring* sound.

¹whirl /ˈwɚəl/ *verb* **whirls; whirled; whirl·ing**
1 [*no obj*] : to move or go in a circle or curve especially with force or speed ▪ The cars were *whirling* around the track.
2 a : to turn rapidly in circles : SPIN [*no obj*] Clothes were *whirling* in the washing machine. ▪ *whirling* [=*swirling*] winds ▪ The water *whirled* around the drain. [+ *obj*] Her dance partner *whirled* her around. **b** [*no obj*] : to turn quickly and suddenly ▪ She *whirled* [=*wheeled*] around in surprise.
3 [*no obj*] : to be dizzy or confused ▪ My head was *whirling.* [=*reeling, spinning*]

²whirl *noun, pl* **whirls**
1 [*count*] **a** : a fast turning movement ▪ He give the crank a *whirl.* [=he turned the crank quickly] **b** : something that is turning quickly in circles ▪ a *whirl* of dust ▪ *whirls* of smoke
2 [*singular*] : a state of busy movement or activity ▪ a *whirl* [=*bustle*] of activity ▪ She's trying to avoid getting caught up in ***the social whirl*** [=busy social activity]
3 [*singular*] : a dizzy or confused mental state ▪ My head was ***in a whirl***
give (something) a whirl *informal* : to attempt or try (something) ▪ He thought he'd *give* acting *a whirl.* [=he thought he'd try acting; he thought he'd try to become an actor]

whirl·i·gig /ˈwɚlɪˌgɪg/ *noun, pl* **-gigs** [*count*] *old-fashioned*
1 : a child's toy that spins rapidly
2 : MERRY-GO-ROUND 1 — often used figuratively ▪ the *whirligig* of time ▪ The movie's ending is an emotional *whirligig.*

whirl·pool /ˈwɚəlˌpuːl/ *noun, pl* **-pools** [*count*]
1 : an area of water in a river, stream, etc., that moves very fast in a circle ▪ The swimmer was caught in a *whirlpool* and nearly drowned. — often used figuratively ▪ She has experienced a *whirlpool* of emotions. [=a confusing mixture of emotions]
2 : WHIRLPOOL BATH

whirlpool bath *noun, pl* **~ baths** [*count*] : a bath in which water moves around in strong currents to massage a person's body

[1]whirl•wind /ˈwərəlˌwɪnd/ *noun, pl* **-winds**
1 [*count*] : a very strong wind that moves in a spinning or swirling motion and that can damage buildings, trees, etc.
2 [*singular*] : something that involves many quickly changing events, feelings, etc. • My life has been a *whirlwind* lately. • He attended a *whirlwind* of meetings. • an emotional *whirlwind* = a *whirlwind* of emotions

[2]whirlwind *adj, always used before a noun* : happening or done very quickly • The band went on a *whirlwind* concert tour. • They were married after a *whirlwind* romance. • We continued on at a *whirlwind* pace.

whirly•bird /ˈwəliˌbəd/ *noun, pl* **-birds** [*count*] *US, informal* : HELICOPTER

[1]whisk /ˈwɪsk/ *noun, pl* **whisks** [*count*] : a cooking tool that is made of curved wire and that is used to stir or beat things (such as eggs, whipping cream, etc.) — see picture at KITCHEN

[2]whisk *verb* **whisks; whisked; whisk•ing** [+ *obj*]
1 : to stir or beat (eggs, sauces, etc.) with a whisk or fork • *Whisk* the eggs with the cream until the mixture thickens.
2 *always followed by an adverb or preposition* : to move or take (someone or something) to another place very quickly • She *whisked* the children off to bed. • The taxi *whisked* me to the airport. • The waitress *whisked* my plate away before I was finished eating.

whisk broom *noun, pl* ~ **brooms** [*count*] *US* : a small broom or brush with a short handle that you use especially to clean clothes

whis•ker /ˈwɪskɚ/ *noun, pl* **-kers**
1 [*count*] : a hair that grows on a man's face — usually plural • He's decided to shave off his *whiskers.*
2 [*count*] : any one of the long, stiff hairs that grow near the mouth of some animals — usually plural • a cat's *whiskers*
3 [*singular*] *informal* : a very small distance or amount • He won/lost the race ***by a whisker.*** • She came ***within a whisker*** of getting fired. [=she came very close to getting fired]
the cat's whiskers see CAT
– whis•kered /ˈwɪskɚd/ *adj* • a *whiskered* animal/chin

whis•key (*chiefly US* + *Ireland*) *or chiefly Brit* **whis•ky** /ˈwɪski/ *noun, pl* **whis•keys** *or* **whis•kies** [*count, noncount*] : a strong alcoholic drink made from a grain (such as rye, corn, or barley) • He ordered a *whiskey* and soda. [=whiskey mixed with soda water] • a glass of *whiskey* ✧ The usual spelling in the U.S. and Ireland is *whiskey*, but some writers use *whisky* when referring to the drink made in Scotland. In British and Canadian English, *whisky* is the usual spelling but *whiskey* is used for American and Irish whiskey. — compare BOURBON, SCOTCH

[1]whis•per /ˈwɪspɚ/ *verb* **-pers; -pered; -per•ing**
1 : to speak very softly or quietly [*no obj*] He *whispered* in/into my ear. • She leaned over and *whispered* to the girl next to her. • I couldn't hear what they were saying because they were *whispering.* [+ *obj*] She *whispered* his name. • She leaned over and *whispered* something to the girl next to her. • "I'll be right back," she *whispered.*
2 [*no obj*] : to produce a quiet sound • A soft breeze *whispered* through the trees.
– whis•per•er /ˈwɪspərɚ/ *noun, pl* **-ers** [*count*]

[2]whisper *noun, pl* **-pers** [*count*]
1 a : a very soft and quiet way of speaking • She spoke in a *whisper.* • I heard *whispers* downstairs. — see also STAGE WHISPER **b** : a soft and quiet sound • the *whisper* of the wind
2 : RUMOR • I've heard *whispers* that the company might go out of business.
3 a : a very small amount of something — usually singular • A *whisper* [=*trace*] of smoke was rising from the chimney. **b** : a small amount of information • I expected to hear back from them but I never heard a *whisper.* [=I never heard from them again]
– whis•pery /ˈwɪspəri/ *adj* • a *whispery* voice

whis•per•ing /ˈwɪspərɪŋ/ *noun, pl* **-ings** [*count*]
1 : something spoken in a very soft or quiet way — usually plural • I could hear faint *whisperings* coming from the other room.
2 : RUMOR — usually plural • There have been *whisperings* that the company might go out of business.

whispering campaign *noun, pl* ~ **-paigns** [*count*] : an effort to spread rumors about someone in order to hurt that person's reputation • He was the target of a *whispering campaign* started by his political rivals.

whist /ˈwɪst/ *noun* [*noncount*] : a type of card game for two teams of two players each

[1]whis•tle /ˈwɪsəl/ *noun, pl* **whis•tles** [*count*]
1 a : a small device that makes a very high and loud sound when a person blows air through it • The policeman blew his *whistle.* **b** : a device through which air or steam is forced to produce a very high and loud sound • a factory *whistle* • We could hear the train's *whistle.* — see also BELLS AND WHISTLES
2 : a high and loud sound made by forcing air through your lips or teeth • He gave a *whistle* [=he whistled] to catch my attention. — see also WOLF WHISTLE
3 : a sound made by blowing • We could hear the low *whistle* of the wind through the trees. • the *whistle* of the tea kettle
blow the whistle : to tell police, reporters, etc., about something (such as a crime) that has been kept secret — usually + *on* • He *blew the whistle on* the company's illegal hiring practices. — see also WHISTLE-BLOWER
clean as a whistle *informal* : very clean • We scrubbed the old boat until it was (as) *clean as a whistle.*
wet your whistle *US, informal* : to have a drink • Would you like to *wet your whistle*? [=would you like a drink?]

[2]whistle *verb* **whistles; whis•tled; whis•tling**
1 : to make a high sound by blowing air through your lips or teeth [*no obj*] He was *whistling* as he walked down the street. • He *whistled* for a cab. [+ *obj*] He *whistled* a happy tune.
2 [*no obj*] : to produce a high and loud sound by forcing air or steam through a device • The teakettle started to *whistle.*
3 *always followed by an adverb or preposition* [*no obj*] : to move, pass, or go very fast with a high sound • A bullet *whistled* past him.
whistle in the dark *or* ***whistle past the graveyard*** *informal* : to act or talk as if you are relaxed and not afraid when you are actually afraid or nervous • He shows a confident manner, but he may just be *whistling in the dark.*
– whistling *adj* • I heard a *whistling* noise/sound.

whis•tle–blow•er /ˈwɪsəlˌblowɚ/ *noun, pl* **-ers** [*count*] : a person who tells police, reporters, etc., about something (such as a crime) that has been kept secret • a corporate *whistle-blower* [=a person who works for a corporation and tells people about the corporation's illegal activities] — see also *blow the whistle* at [1]WHISTLE
– whis•tle–blow•ing /ˈwɪsəlˌblowɪŋ/ *noun* [*noncount*]

whis•tle–stop /ˈwɪsəlˌstɑːp/ *adj, always used before a noun, US* : relating to or involving a series of appearances by a politician in different communities during an election campaign • a *whistle-stop* speech • He went on a ***whistle-stop campaign/tour*** in the days leading up to the election.

whit /ˈwɪt/ *noun* [*singular*] *informal* + *old-fashioned* : a very small amount — usually used in negative statements • He didn't care a *whit* [=didn't care at all] about the money.

Whit /ˈwɪt/ *adj, always used before a noun, Brit* : at or near the time of the Christian holiday Pentecost • *Whit* Tuesday • ***Whit Sunday*** [=*Pentecost*]

[1]white /ˈwaɪt/ *adj* **whit•er; -est**
1 a : having the color of fresh snow or milk • He was wearing *white* sneakers. • a *white* T-shirt/blouse • *white* socks • *white* lilies • puffy *white* clouds • *white* hair • He had a long, *white* beard. • *white* rice **b** : light or pale in color • Her lips were *white* with fear. • He turned *white* when he heard the news. — see also SNOW-WHITE
2 : of or relating to a race of people who have light-colored skin and who come originally from Europe • The suspect was a *white* [=*Caucasian*] male. • He came from a *white* middle-class background. • His mother is Hispanic and his father is *white.*
3 *US* : not having anything written or printed on it • There was too much *white* [=*empty, blank*] space on the page.
4 *Brit* : served with cream or milk • *white* coffee/tea
a white Christmas : a Christmas when there is snow on the ground or when it is snowing • We were hoping for *a white Christmas.*
– white•ness /ˈwaɪtnəs/ *noun* [*noncount*] **– whit•ish** /ˈwaɪtɪʃ/ *adj* • *whitish* hair

[2]white *noun, pl* **whites**
1 [*count, noncount*] : the very light color of fresh snow or milk — see color picture on page C1
2 a [*noncount*] : white clothing • nurses dressed in *white* [=in white uniforms] • The bride looked beautiful in *white.* [=in her white dress] **b** ***whites*** [*plural*] : white clothes used to play sports • tennis *whites* [=white tennis clothes]

3 [*count*] : a white or light-colored thing or part: such as **a** : the white part of the eye • the *whites* of his eyes — see picture at EYE **b** : the clear or white liquid around the yolk of an egg • The cake recipe calls for four ***egg whites.***
4 [*count*] : a person belonging to a race of people who have light-colored skin : a white person : CAUCASIAN — usually plural • His policies are supported by both blacks and *whites.*

white·bait /ˈwaɪtˌbeɪt/ *noun* [*noncount*] : young fish that can be eaten whole

white blood cell *noun, pl* ~ **cells** [*count*] : a clear or colorless cell in the blood that protects the body from disease — called also *white cell, white blood corpuscle, white corpuscle*; compare RED BLOOD CELL

white·board /ˈwaɪtˌboɚd/ *noun, pl* **-boards** [*count*] : a large board with a smooth white surface that can be written on with special markers — compare BLACKBOARD, CHALKBOARD

white bread *noun* [*noncount*] : bread made with wheat flour that has been bleached so that it is white

white–bread /ˈwaɪtˈbrɛd/ *adj, always used before a noun, US, informal* : ordinary or traditional and associated with white, middle class people • *white-bread* values

white·caps /ˈwaɪtˌkæps/ *noun* [*plural*] *US* : waves that break into small white bubbles at their highest point • The blue sea was flecked with *whitecaps.* — called also (*Brit*) *white horses*

white cell *noun, pl* ~ **cells** [*count*] : WHITE BLOOD CELL

white chocolate *noun* [*noncount*] : a type of sweet chocolate that has a white color — compare DARK CHOCOLATE, MILK CHOCOLATE

white–col·lar /ˈwaɪtˈkɑːlɚ/ *adj* : of, relating to, or having the kind of jobs that are done in an office instead of a factory, warehouse, etc. • *white-collar* jobs/workers — compare BLUE-COLLAR, PINK-COLLAR
white-collar crime : crime that typically involves stealing money from a company and that is done by people who have important positions in the company : crime committed by white-collar workers • Embezzlement is a *white-collar crime.*

white corpuscle *noun, pl* ~ **-puscles** [*count*] : WHITE BLOOD CELL

white dwarf *noun, pl* ~ **dwarfs** [*count*] *astronomy* : a star that is at the end of its life and is very hot, small, and dense

white elephant *noun, pl* ~ **-phants** [*count*] : something that requires a lot of care and money and that gives little profit or enjoyment — usually singular • The run-down historic building has been the city's *white elephant.*

white flag *noun, pl* ~ **flags** [*count*] : a flag used to show that you want to stop fighting or to indicate defeat — usually singular • Ground troops ***waved the white flag*** after the battle. — often used figuratively • They ***raised the white flag*** [=admitted defeat] soon after the election results came in.

white flight *noun* [*noncount*] *US* : an occurrence in which many white people move out of a city as more and more people of other races move in

white flour *noun* [*noncount*] : a type of flour that is widely used in cooking, baking, etc., and that is made from wheat

white goods *noun* [*plural*] *chiefly Brit* : large pieces of household equipment (such as refrigerators and washing machines)

White·hall /ˈwaɪtˌhɑːl/ *noun* [*noncount*] *Brit* : a wide street in London where there are many government buildings — used to refer to the British government • *Whitehall* bureaucrats • There has been no response from *Whitehall* about the claims.

white horses *noun* [*plural*] *Brit* : WHITECAPS

white–hot /ˈwaɪtˈhɑːt/ *adj*
1 **a** : glowing white because of being very hot • *white-hot* metal **b** : extremely hot • a *white-hot* skillet
2 *informal* **a** : very intense or active • *white-hot* enthusiasm • The atmosphere was *white-hot.* **b** : very popular or successful • The band was *white-hot* after the release of their first album.

White House *noun*
the White House 1 : the place in Washington, D.C., where the U.S. President lives 2 : the executive branch of the U.S. government • The *White House* announced the new appointments to the Cabinet. • *White House* staffers

white knight *noun, pl* ~ **knights** [*count*] : someone or something that rescues or saves another person or thing from a bad situation; *especially* : a company that buys a second company in order to prevent it from being taken over by a third company

white–knuck·le /ˈwaɪtˈnʌkəl/ *also* **white–knuck·led** /ˈwaɪtˈnʌkəld/ *adj, always used before a noun* : showing, experiencing, or causing very strong feelings of fear, anxiety, etc. • a *white-knuckle* ride on a roller coaster • I'm a *white-knuckle* flier/traveler. [=flying/traveling is very stressful for me] • They rode their motorcycles at *white-knuckle* speeds.

white lie *noun, pl* ~ **lies** [*count*] : a lie about a small or unimportant matter that someone tells to avoid hurting another person • He told a (little) *white lie* as his excuse for missing the party.

white meat *noun* [*noncount*] : meat that comes from the breast or other thick parts of a chicken, turkey, etc., and that is lighter in color than the other parts when cooked; *also* : meat (such as pork) that is lighter in color than beef when cooked — compare DARK MEAT, RED MEAT

whit·en /ˈwaɪtn̩/ *verb* **-ens; -ened; -en·ing** : to make (something) white or whiter or to become white or whiter [*no obj*] His hair *whitened* as he aged. [+ *obj*] Bleach will *whiten* the linens. • The new toothpaste *whitens* teeth.

white noise *noun* [*noncount*] : a constant noise (such as that the noise from a television or radio that is turned on but is not receiving a clear signal) that is a mixture of many different sound waves

white·out /ˈwaɪtˌaʊt/ *noun, pl* **-outs** [*count*] : a type of snowstorm in which blowing or falling snow and clouds make it very difficult to see • We got caught in a *whiteout.* • *whiteout* conditions — compare BLACKOUT

white pages *noun*
the white pages or the White Pages US : the part of a phone book that lists the names, addresses, and phone numbers of people and businesses — compare YELLOW PAGES

White Paper *noun, pl* ~ **-pers** [*count*] *Brit* : a government document that provides information on a particular subject before a law is made — compare GREEN PAPER

white pepper *noun* [*noncount*] : a food seasoning that is made by grinding the dried berries of an Indian plant after removing the hard, black covers on the seeds — compare BLACK PEPPER

white sauce *noun* [*noncount*] : a light-colored sauce that is made with milk, cream, or broth and that is thickened with flour

white spirit *noun* [*noncount*] *Brit* : a liquid that is made from petroleum and that is used to make paint thinner

white supremacist *noun, pl* ~ **-cists** [*count*] : a person who believes that the white race is better than all other races and should have control over all other races • *White supremacists* were convicted of hate crimes.
– white supremacy *noun* [*noncount*]

white–tailed deer /ˈwaɪtˌteɪld-/ *noun, pl* **white–tailed deer** [*count*] : a common North American deer that has a tail which is white underneath — see picture at DEER

white–tie *adj* — used to describe a formal event at which men wear white ties and white formal coats and women wear formal gowns • a *white-tie* reception/event — compare BLACK-TIE

white trash *noun* [*noncount*] *US, informal + offensive* : poor white people who are not well educated

white·wall /ˈwaɪtˌwɑːl/ *noun, pl* **-walls** [*count*] *US* : a tire on a car that has a white band near the rim of the wheel • a set of *whitewalls*

[1]**white·wash** /ˈwaɪtˌwɑːʃ/ *noun, pl* **-wash·es**
1 [*noncount*] : a white liquid mixture used for making surfaces (such as walls or fences) whiter
2 [*count*] *disapproving* : a planned effort to hide a dishonest, immoral, or illegal act or situation : COVER-UP — usually singular • Many people believe that official report about the investigation was a *whitewash* written to conceal the truth.
3 [*count*] *chiefly Brit* : a defeat in a game or contest in which the loser does not score any points • a 10–0 *whitewash*

[2]**whitewash** *verb* **-washes; -washed; -wash·ing** [+ *obj*]
1 : to make (something) whiter by painting it with whitewash • They *whitewashed* the fence. • *whitewashed* walls/buildings
2 : to prevent people from learning the truth about (something bad, such as a dishonest, immoral, or illegal act or situation) • a book that tries to *whitewash* the country's past
3 *chiefly Brit* : to defeat (an opponent) easily by winning every game, point, etc. • She was *whitewashed* 8–0.

white water *noun [noncount]* : water in part of a river that looks white because it is moving very fast over rocks • The canoe got caught in *white water*.
– **white·wa·ter** /ˈwaɪtˌwɑːtɚ/ *adj* • *whitewater* rafting

white way *noun*
the Great White Way *US, informal + old-fashioned* : a street in New York City where there are many theaters : BROADWAY • Her show debuted on *the Great White Way*.

white wedding *noun, pl* ~ **-dings** *[count]* : a traditional wedding in which the bride wears a white dress

white wine *noun, pl* ~ **wines** *[count, noncount]* : wine that is light in color

whit·ey /ˈwaɪti/ *noun, pl* **whit·ies** *chiefly US slang, offensive*
1 *[count]* : a white person
2 *[noncount]* : white people as a group • The poet vented his rage against *whitey*.

whith·er /ˈwɪðɚ/ *adv, old-fashioned + literary* : to what place • He grew up in New York City *whither* his family had immigrated in the early 1920s. — sometimes used formally in questions to ask what the future of something will be • *Whither* stem-cell research? [=where is stem-cell research going?; what is the future of stem-cell research?]

whit·ing /ˈwaɪtɪŋ/ *noun, pl* **whiting** *[count]* : a small fish that lives in the sea and that is used for food

Whit·sun /ˈwɪtsən/ *noun [noncount] Brit* : the Christian holiday Pentecost and the days near it • the *Whitsun* holiday

whit·tle /ˈwɪtl/ *verb* **whit·tles; whit·tled; whit·tling** *[+ obj]* : to cut or shape (a piece of wood) by cutting small pieces from it • He was sitting on the porch, *whittling* a stick. : to make or shape (something) from a piece of wood by cutting small pieces from it • She *whittled* a walking stick from a maple tree branch.
whittle away *[phrasal verb]* ***whittle (something) away*** *or* ***whittle away (something)*** : to reduce or get rid of (something) slowly • I'm still trying to *whittle away* a few more pounds.
whittle down *[phrasal verb]* ***whittle (something) down*** *or* ***whittle down (something)*** : to gradually make (something) smaller by removing parts • We *whittled* the list *down* to four people.

[1]**whiz** *(chiefly US) or Brit* **whizz** /ˈwɪz/ *verb, always followed by an adverb or preposition* **whiz·zes; whizzed; whiz·zing** *[no obj] informal*
1 : to move quickly while making a buzzing or humming sound • The ball *whizzed* through the air. • Bullets *whizzed* overhead.
2 a : to pass by quickly • Cars *whizzed* by on the highway. • He *whizzed* past us on skates. **b** *chiefly Brit* : to accomplish or complete something easily • She *whizzed* through the exam.

[2]**whiz** *(chiefly US) or Brit* **whizz** *noun, pl* **whizzes** *[count]* : a humming or buzzing sound made by something moving quickly • We could hear the *whiz* of the ball as it sailed past us.
take a whiz *US, informal + impolite* : URINATE • He *took a whiz* right on the sidewalk.
– compare [3]WHIZ

[3]**whiz** *(chiefly US) or Brit* **whizz** *noun, pl* **whizzes** *[count] informal* : someone who is very good at something • a computer *whiz* • He's a *whiz* at math. — compare [2]WHIZ

whiz kid *(chiefly US) or Brit* **whizz kid** *noun, pl* ~ **kids** *[count]* : a person who is unusually intelligent or successful especially at an early age

who /ˈhuː/ *pronoun*
1 a : what or which person or people — used when you do not know the name or identity of a person or group of people that you are talking about or asking about • *Who* will be the next president? • *Who* is standing next to you in this photo? • I didn't know *who* he was. • Find out *who* they are. • I wonder *who* else signed up. • *Who* should walk in [=who do you think walked in] when we least expected it? My parents! • She isn't sure *who* she talked to. **b** — used to question a person's character or authority • *Who* are they to tell us what to do? [=what makes them think they can tell us what to do?] • *Who* do you think you are? [=what gives you the right to say or do this?] • *Who* do you think you're talking to? [=what gives you the right to speak to me in this (rude) manner?] **c** — used in questions that are meant to say that no one would or would not do something, know something, etc. • They may come or not. *Who* cares? [=no one cares; I don't care] • Of course I would love to win a million dollars. *Who* wouldn't? [=anyone would] • "Are they coming?" "*Who* knows?" [=no one knows; I don't know] • *Who* are we kidding? [=we aren't kidding/fooling anyone] ***usage*** see WHOM
2 — used after a noun or pronoun to show which group of people you are talking about • Subscribers *who* are interested in joining the discussion group should contact the secretary. • The people *who* conducted the study were extremely professional. • Someone *who* handles stress well will be more suited for the job. • I have a friend *who* my parents don't like.
3 — used to introduce an additional statement about someone who has already been mentioned • His patient, *who* was a well-known television personality, suffered a minor stroke. • The former president of the company, *who* is retired now, is credited with expanding and improving the product line. • Her uncle, *who* she's very fond of, lives next door.
who's who **1** *or* ***who is who*** : information about the people who make up a group • We had lived in this town long enough to know *who was who*. [=to know the names of the different people, what they did, etc.] • I'm still learning *who's who* around the office. **2 a** : a list of the names of the important and well-known people in a particular field • The guest list reads like a *who's who* of the publishing industry. **b** : the important and well-known people in a particular field • The convention was attended by a *who's who* of the publishing industry.

whoa /ˈwoʊ/ *interj*
1 — used to command a horse to stop moving
2 — used to tell someone to slow down or stop and think about something • *Whoa*. Take a deep breath and tell me what's wrong.
3 — used to show that you are surprised or impressed • *Whoa*, that's a cool car.

who'd /ˈhuːd/ — used as a contraction of *who would* or *who had* • *Who'd* [=who would] have thought he could do it? • We didn't know *who'd* [=who had] done it.

who·dun·it *(chiefly US) or Brit* **who·dun·nit** /huˈdʌnət/ *noun, pl* **-its** *[count] informal* : a novel, play, or movie about a murder where you do not know who committed the murder until the end

who·ev·er /huˈɛvɚ/ *pronoun*
1 : whatever person : any person at all • A prize will be given to *whoever* solves the riddle. • *Whoever* wants to come along is welcome to join us. • He's an honest man, *whoever* his friends might be. • *Whoever* did this will be held accountable.
2 — used in questions that express surprise or confusion • *Whoever* can that be?

[1]**whole** /ˈhoʊl/ *adj*
1 a *always used before a noun* : complete or full : not lacking or leaving out any part • The *whole* [=*entire*] family went on the trip. • The doctor assured me that the *whole* procedure would only take a few minutes. • The *whole* place was remodeled. It looks great now. • He was out sick for the *whole* [=*entire*] week. • It's been a *whole* week since I've seen him. • I spent the *whole* summer traveling through Europe. • The *whole* evening was a great success. • She read the *whole* book in one day. • I've been waiting my *whole* life for this. • I felt like the luckiest girl ***in the whole wide world*** [=*in the world*] that day. • They failed to tell us the ***whole story***. [=they failed to tell us everything; they only told us certain things] • It rained ***the whole time*** I was there. [=it rained continuously while I was there] • We decided to forget the ***whole thing***. **b** : having all the parts : not divided or cut into parts or pieces • a *whole* egg • *whole* strawberries [=strawberries that are not sliced or cut up] • We cooked a *whole* chicken. • *whole* grains • The recipe calls for two *whole* cloves. [=cloves that haven't been ground]
2 a : great or large in size, extent, etc. • The community center offers a *whole* range of programs. • The track team took part in a *whole* series of events. [=in a lot of events] • There's a *whole* set of criteria to consider. • She owns a *whole* collection of hats. [=she owns many different hats] **b** — used for emphasis before a noun • The *whole* idea is to make things better, not worse. • She missed the *whole* point of the story. • We weren't quite sure what to make of the *whole* situation. • He doesn't seem to have ***a whole lot of*** [=*much*] respect for other people's feelings. • Things are looking ***a whole lot*** [=*much*] brighter now.
go (the) whole hog see [1]HOG
out of whole cloth see CLOTH
the whole enchilada see ENCHILADA
the whole (kit and) caboodle see CABOODLE
the whole nine yards see [2]YARD
the whole shebang see SHEBANG

the whole shooting match see SHOOTING MATCH
whole nother see NOTHER
– whole•ness *noun [noncount]*

²whole *noun, pl* **wholes** *[count]* : something that is full or complete — usually singular ▪ The *whole* of my day was spent on the phone. [=I spent the entire day on the phone] ▪ the *whole* of creation [=all of creation] ▪ He felt he was part of ***a greater whole.*** [=that he was a part of something much larger and greater than himself]

as a whole : as a complete unit — used to make a statement that relates to all the parts of something ▪ Language *as a whole* is constantly evolving. ▪ The lecture was intended for the group *as a whole.* [=for everyone; not for just a few people] ▪ The company *as a whole* [=*overall*] is doing well.

in whole law : to the full or entire extent — used in the phrase ***in whole or in part*** ▪ The contract can be voided *in whole or in part* [=the entire contract can be voided or a part of the contract can be voided] ten days before the purchase date.

on the whole **1** — used to say what you think is true, what should be done, etc., when you consider a situation in a general way ▪ *On the whole*, it seemed best to cut the visit short. ▪ *On the whole*, I think we've made progress from last week. **2** : in general : in most cases ▪ *On the whole*, new parents reported that they were adapting very well to parenthood. ▪ He did a great job *on the whole*.

³whole *adv*
1 : entirely or completely ▪ He has a *whole* new way of looking at things now. [=he has a completely different attitude now]
2 : in one piece that has not been cut into parts ▪ We cooked the chicken *whole*. ▪ The frog swallowed the fly *whole*.

whole food *noun, pl* **~ foods** *[count, noncount]* : a food that is considered healthy because it is grown naturally, has not been processed, and contains no artificial ingredients

whole•heart•ed /ˈhoʊlˈhɑɚtəd/ *adj [more ~; most ~]* : having or showing no doubt or uncertainty about doing something, supporting someone, etc. ▪ *wholehearted* devotion/support ▪ a *wholehearted* effort ▪ The judges gave us their *wholehearted* approval.
– whole•heart•ed•ly *adv* ▪ I agreed *wholeheartedly* with his views. ▪ She threw herself *wholeheartedly* into the work.

whole life insurance *noun [noncount]* : a type of life insurance that costs the same as long as the insured person is alive and that pays benefits to survivors when the person has died

whole meal *adj, Brit* : WHOLE WHEAT ▪ *whole meal* bread

whole note *noun, pl* **~ notes** *[count] US* : a musical note equal in time to two half notes or four quarter notes — called also *(Brit) semibreve*

whole number *noun, pl* **~ -bers** *[count] mathematics* : a number (such as 0, 1, 2, 3, 4, 5, etc.) that is not a negative and is not a fraction

¹whole•sale /ˈhoʊlˌseɪl/ *noun [noncount]* : the business of selling things in large amounts to other businesses rather than to individual customers — compare RETAIL

²wholesale *adj*
1 : relating to the business of selling things in large amounts to other businesses rather than to individual customers ▪ a *wholesale* grocer/dealer/merchant ▪ *wholesale* prices ▪ The crops originated from *wholesale* growers. ▪ Is that price retail or *wholesale*?
2 : affecting large numbers of people or things ▪ The poor economy has caused *wholesale* layoffs [=has caused a large number of layoffs] in many industries.
– wholesale *adv* ▪ I can get the pet supplies *wholesale*. ▪ The fish sells for about $9 a pound *wholesale*.

³wholesale *verb* **-sales; -saled; -sal•ing**
1 *[+ obj]* : to sell (things) to other businesses rather than to individual customers ▪ The company *wholesales* clothing to boutiques in the area.
2 *[no obj]* : to be sold to other businesses for a specified price — usually + *at* or *for* ▪ a product that *wholesales at/for* $10 a pound

whole•sal•er /ˈhoʊlˌseɪlɚ/ *noun, pl* **-ers** *[count]* : a person or company that sells things to businesses and not to individuals ▪ a leading *wholesaler* in the book business

whole•some /ˈhoʊlsəm/ *adj [more ~; most ~]*
1 : helping to keep your body healthy : good for your health ▪ *wholesome* [=*healthy, nutritious*] meals/snacks ▪ a *wholesome* dish made with vegetables ▪ a *wholesome* diet
2 a : morally good ▪ *wholesome* family values ▪ less-than-*wholesome* entertainment that wasn't appropriate for children **b** : suggesting good health or behavior ▪ a young actor known for his *wholesome* good looks
– whole•some•ness *noun [noncount]*

whole step *noun, pl* **~ steps** *[count] US, music* : a difference in pitch that is equal to ⅙ of an octave — called also *(chiefly Brit) tone*

whole wheat *adj* : made from wheat from which no part (such as the bran) has been removed ▪ *whole wheat* bread

whol•ly /ˈhoʊlli/ *adv, formal* : completely or fully ▪ She is *wholly* devoted to her children. ▪ An infant is *wholly* dependent on its mother. ▪ The invention is *wholly* [=*entirely*] her own. ▪ The claim is *wholly* without merit.

whom /ˈhuːm/ *pronoun, objective case of* WHO — used in formal writing or speech ▪ To *whom* am I speaking? ▪ His brother, with *whom* he is very close, works for the same company. ▪ I was introduced to the artist, *whom* I was anxious to meet. ▪ an author *whom* I had never heard of

> ***usage*** *Whom* is a more formal word than *who* and is not commonly used in ordinary speech and writing, where it can seem awkward and unnatural. ▪ *(formal)* To *whom* did you speak? = *(formal) Whom* did you speak to? = (more commonly) *Who* did you speak to? ▪ *(formal)* We weren't sure *whom* to hire. = (more commonly) We weren't sure *who* to hire. ▪ *(formal)* The person to *whom* we spoke to was very helpful. = *(formal)* The person *whom* we spoke to was very helpful. = (more commonly) The person *who/that* we spoke to was very helpful. ▪ *(formal)* Her brother, *whom* I met last year, is an attorney. = (more commonly) Her brother, *who* I met last year, is an attorney.

to whom it may concern see ²CONCERN

whom•ev•er /huˈmɛvɚ/ *pronoun, objective case of* WHOEVER — used in formal writing or speech ▪ You can invite *whomever* you please.

¹whoop /ˈhuːp, ˈwuːp/ *verb* **whoops; whooped; whoop•ing** *[no obj] informal* : to shout loudly in an enthusiastic or excited way ▪ The children *whooped* with joy at the sight of all the presents.
whoop it up informal : to celebrate and have fun in a noisy way ▪ My pals and I *whooped it up* at the local bar after the concert. ▪ The band *whooped it up* for the sold-out crowd.

²whoop *noun, pl* **whoops** *[count]* : a high, loud sound expressing enthusiasm or excitement — usually singular ▪ The coach let out a big *whoop* when the team scored.
big whoop US, informal — used in an ironic way to say that something is not important or impressive ▪ "Their team is going to the play-offs." "*Big whoop*." [=*big deal*] ▪ It might look special but it's really ***no big whoop.*** [=*no big deal*; it's not very important]

whoop–de–do *or* **whoop–de–doo** /ˌwuːpdiˈduː, ˌwʊpdiˈduː/ *interj, US, informal* — used in an ironic way to say that something is not important or impressive ▪ "She can cook a five-course meal in an hour." "*Whoop-de-do*." [=so what?; who cares?]

¹whoop•ee /ˈwʊpi/ *interj* — used to express enthusiasm ▪ *Whoopee*! I passed the entrance exam! ▪ We did it! *Whoopee*!

²whoopee *noun*
make whoopee **1** *US, informal + old-fashioned* : to have sex ▪ They're *making whoopee*. **2** *Brit, informal + old-fashioned* : to have noisy fun

whoopee cushion *noun, pl* **~ -ions** *[count]* : a rubber bag filled with air that is used as a joke and that makes a loud, rude noise when someone sits on it

whoop•ing cough /ˈhuːpɪŋ-/ *noun [noncount] medical* : a disease that usually affects children and that causes severe coughing and difficult breathing

whoops *also* **woops** /ˈwʊps/ *interj* — used to express surprise or distress or to say in a mild way that you are sorry about having done or said something wrong ▪ *Whoops* [=*oops*], I slipped! ▪ *Woops*, I didn't mean to tell you.

¹whoosh /ˈwʊʃ/ *noun [count]*
1 : the sound made by something that is moving quickly — usually singular ▪ The ball flew by with a *whoosh*.
2 : a small amount of gas, liquid, etc., that comes from a place quickly — usually singular ▪ A *whoosh* of hot air escaped from the vent.

²whoosh *verb* **whoosh•es; whooshed; whoosh•ing** *[no obj]* : to move very quickly with the sound of quickly flowing air or water ▪ Cars *whooshed* along the highway. ▪ Water *whooshed* down the pipe.

whop•per /ˈwɑːpɚ/ *noun, pl* **-pers** *[count] informal*

W

1 : something that is very large and impressive ▪ That's a *whopper* of a diamond ring.

2 : a big lie ▪ He told us a real *whopper.*

whop·ping /ˈwɑːpɪŋ/ *adj, always used before a noun, informal* : very large, impressive, etc. ▪ The play was a *whopping* success. ▪ The car sped by at a *whopping* 110 miles per hour.

whore /ˈhoɚ/ *noun, pl* **whores** [*count*]

1 *somewhat old-fashioned* : a woman who has sex with people in exchange for money : PROSTITUTE

2 *informal + offensive* : a woman who has sex with a lot of people

whore·house /ˈhoɚˌhaʊs/ *noun, pl* **-hous·es** [*count*] *informal* : a place where prostitutes live and work : BROTHEL

whor·ing /ˈhorɪŋ/ *noun* [*noncount*] *old-fashioned* : the activity of having sex with a prostitute ▪ drinking and *whoring*

whorl /ˈwɚl, ˈworəl/ *noun, pl* **whorls** [*count*]

1 : something that turns or goes around in a circle ▪ a *whorl* of smoke ▪ the *whorls* and eddies of the river

2 : a pattern that is made by a series of circles that turn around a center point ▪ the *whorl* of a fingerprint

3 *technical* : an arrangement of leaves, petals, etc., that forms a circle around a stem

who's /ˈhuːz/ — used as a contraction of *who is* or *who has* ▪ *Who's* [=*who is*] in charge here? ▪ a student *who's* [=*who has*] always been interested in math

who's who see WHO

Do not confuse *who's* with *whose.*

[1]whose /ˈhuːz/ *adj*

1 — used in questions to ask who owns something, has something, etc. ▪ *Whose* bag is it? ▪ I wonder *whose* story was chosen. ▪ *Whose* side are you on anyway?

2 — used to show which person or thing you are talking about ▪ The gentleman *whose* cell phone was stolen was very upset. ▪ The prize will go to the writer *whose* story shows the most imagination. ▪ the book *whose* cover is torn

3 — used to give more information about a person or thing that has already been mentioned ▪ The curator, *whose* name I've since forgotten, put together an exceptional exhibit. ▪ My roommate, *whose* sister is an actress, gets lots of requests for autographs.

Do not confuse *whose* with *who's.*

[2]whose *pronoun* : that or those belonging to a person ▪ *Whose* are these? [=who is the owner of these?] ▪ Let him know *whose* you will choose.

Do not confuse *whose* with *who's.*

who·so·ev·er /ˌhuːsəˈwɛvɚ/ *pronoun, formal + literary* : WHOEVER

whup /ˈwʊp/ *verb* **whups**; **whupped**; **whup·ping** [*+ obj*] *US slang*

1 : to beat (someone or something) as a punishment ▪ His father *whupped* him for swearing.

2 : to defeat (someone or something) easily and completely ▪ Our team got *whupped* in last night's game. ▪ (*impolite*) We ***got our butts/asses whupped*** yesterday.

[1]why /ˈwaɪ/ *adv*

1 : for what reason or purpose ▪ *Why* did you quit your job? ▪ *Why* are you laughing? [=what are you laughing about?] ▪ *Why* is the sky blue? ▪ *Why* didn't you call me? ▪ *Why* didn't I think of that? ▪ "I can't go out tonight." "***Why not?***"

2 — used to offer a suggestion or to say that a course of action is not necessary ▪ If you don't want to go, *why* not just say so? ▪ Instead of calling, *why* not e-mail instead? ▪ *Why* should I care about that? ▪ *Why* don't you come over for dinner? [=we would like to have you over for dinner] ▪ You deserve the best treatment. *Why* settle for less? [=you shouldn't be happy with anything less] ▪ "I'll try calling again." "***Why bother?***" [=it's not worth the trouble]

3 — used to express irritation or annoyance ▪ *Why* can't you make up your mind? ▪ *Why* must I always repeat myself? ▪ *Why* would anyone say such a thing? ▪ ***Why oh why*** did I say something so stupid?

[2]why *conj*

1 : the cause, reason, or purpose for which ▪ I know *why* he did it. ▪ It's easy to see *why* she fell in love with him. ▪ He's a very good player. That's *why* he made the team.

2 : for which ▪ The reason *why* they succeeded is obvious. They worked really hard. ▪ Give me one good reason *why* I should stay.

[3]why *noun*

the whys and (the) wherefores : the reasons for something ▪ She explained *the whys and the wherefores* of the sudden price increase.

[4]why *interj, somewhat old-fashioned* — used at the beginning of a statement especially to express surprise ▪ *Why,* I can't imagine such a thing! ▪ "Do you know him?" "*Why,* yes! We know him quite well." ▪ "Would you like another drink?" "*Why,* yes. Thank you." ▪ If I want a drink, *why,* I'll just get it myself! ▪ *Why,* of course! That makes perfect sense.

WI *abbr* Wisconsin

Wic·ca /ˈwɪkə/ *noun* [*noncount*] : a religion that is characterized by belief in the existence of magical powers in nature
— **Wic·can** /ˈwɪkən/ *adj* ▪ *Wiccan* rituals ▪ My friend is *Wiccan.* — **Wiccan** *noun, pl* **-cans** [*count*] ▪ a group of *Wiccans*

[1]wick /ˈwɪk/ *noun, pl* **wicks** [*count*] : a string or piece of material in a candle or lamp that is lit for burning

get on someone's wick *Brit, informal* : to annoy someone ▪ His chatter was ***getting on my wick.*** [=*getting on my nerves*]

[2]wick *verb* **wicks**; **wicked**; **wicking** [*+ obj*] *US* : to cause (fluid or moisture) to be pulled away from a surface (such as your skin) — usually *+ away* ▪ a fabric that *wicks away* perspiration

[1]wick·ed /ˈwɪkəd/ *adj* **wick·ed·er**; **-est** [*also more ~; most ~*]

1 a : morally bad : EVIL ▪ a *wicked* act of cruelty ▪ She played the part of the *wicked* stepmother/witch in the play. **b** *informal* : having or showing slightly bad thoughts in a way that is funny or not serious ▪ She wore a *wicked* grin after her victory. ▪ *wicked* laughter ▪ She's known for having a *wicked* sense of humor.

2 *informal* : very bad or unpleasant ▪ She had a *wicked* case of food poisoning. ▪ A *wicked* odor was coming from the closet.

3 *informal* : very good ▪ He throws a *wicked* fastball.
— **wick·ed·ly** *adv* ▪ The chocolate cake looked *wickedly* tempting. ▪ He told a *wickedly* funny story. — **wick·ed·ness** *noun* [*noncount*] *old-fashioned*

[2]wicked *adv, US, informal* : very or extremely ▪ His car goes *wicked* fast. ▪ All his friends thought he was *wicked* cool. ▪ It's *wicked* funny! ▪ The tickets were *wicked* expensive.

wick·er /ˈwɪkɚ/ *noun* [*noncount*] : thin twigs or sticks that are woven together to make furniture and baskets — often used before another noun ▪ a *wicker* chair [=a chair made from wicker] ▪ *wicker* baskets

wick·er·work /ˈwɪkɚˌwɚk/ *noun* [*noncount*] : something (such as furniture) that is made from wicker ▪ We bought *wickerwork* for the screened porch. ▪ *wickerwork* baskets

wick·et /ˈwɪkət/ *noun, pl* **-ets** [*count*]

1 *US* : any one of the series of curved wires in the ground that the ball must be hit through in the game of croquet

2 *cricket* **a** : either of the two sets of three wooden sticks at which the ball is bowled **b** : the rectangular area of ground that is between the two wickets

— see also STICKY WICKET

wick·et·keep·er /ˈwɪkətˌkiːpɚ/ *noun, pl* **-ers** [*count*] *cricket* : the player who stands behind the wicket to catch the ball

[1]wide /ˈwaɪd/ *adj* **wid·er**; **wid·est**

1 a : extending a great distance from one side to the other : not narrow ▪ a *wide* [=*broad*] road ▪ the *widest* part of the river ▪ a *wide* smile — opposite NARROW **b** : measured from side to side : having a specified width ▪ The desk is three feet *wide.* ▪ How *wide* is the doorway?

2 : opened as far as possible ▪ Her eyes were *wide* with wonder.

3 : not limited in range or amount : EXTENSIVE ▪ We have a *wide* range of options. ▪ a job calling for *wide* experience ▪ The election received *wide* news coverage.

4 : including or involving a large number of people or things ▪ The dishes are available in a *wide* assortment of colors. [=in many colors] ▪ The book appealed to a *wide* audience. [=many people liked the book] ▪ That car dealership has the *widest* [=*largest*] selection around.

5 : extending throughout a specified area — usually used in combination ▪ Police conducted a neighborhood-*wide* search for the suspect. [=police searched for the suspect throughout the neighborhood] ▪ There has been an industry-*wide* decrease in production.

6 : away from a target — used to describe something that does not hit what you were aiming at ▪ His shot was *wide* and landed in the rough. — often *+ of* ▪ The shot was *wide of* the goal. [=the shot missed the goal] — see also *wide of the mark* at [1]MARK

give (someone or something) a wide berth see [1]BERTH
— **wide·ness** *noun* [*noncount*] ▪ the *wideness* of the beach

[2]**wide** *adv*
1 : at a great distance : FAR ▪ The poles were placed *wide* apart.
2 : to the side of something by a large distance ▪ The shot landed *wide*. — usually + *of* ▪ The arrow landed/went *wide of* the target. [=the arrow missed the target] ▪ He hit his shot *wide of* the green on the sixth hole.
3 : to the fullest extent : as fully as possible : COMPLETELY ▪ He opened his eyes/mouth *wide*. ▪ They spread the map out *wide*. ▪ ***wide open*** eyes ▪ His mouth was *wide open*. ▪ They like to hike through *wide open* spaces. ▪ It appears that the governor's race is still *wide open*. [=any of the candidates could win]
far and wide see [1]FAR

wide–angle lens *noun, pl* ~ **lenses** [*count*] : a camera lens that you use to take pictures that show a wider view than other lenses

wide awake *adj* : fully awake ▪ It was quite late, but the children were still *wide awake*. [=not tired at all]

wide boy *noun, pl* ~ **boys** [*count*] *Brit, informal + disapproving* : a man who earns a lot of money by doing things that are dishonest or illegal

wide–eyed /ˈwaɪdˈaɪd/ *adj*
1 : having your eyes wide open especially because of surprise or fear ▪ He stared at me, *wide-eyed* in astonishment.
2 : having or showing a lack of experience or knowledge ▪ *wide-eyed* [=*naive*] innocence

wide·ly /ˈwaɪdli/ *adv* [*more* ~; *most* ~]
1 : over or through a wide area : in or to many places ▪ They have traveled *widely*. ▪ *widely* scattered towns ▪ Their products are *widely* available.
2 : to a great extent : a lot ▪ The products differ *widely* [=*greatly*] in quality.
3 : by a large number of people ▪ a *widely* known political figure ▪ The books are *widely* read by adults as well as children. ▪ a *widely* [=*generally*] accepted belief
4 : over a wide range ▪ The students come from families with *widely* different incomes. [=from families with large incomes, small incomes, etc.] ▪ *widely* divergent viewpoints

wid·en /ˈwaɪdn̩/ *verb* **-ens; -ened; -en·ing**
1 [+ *obj*] **:** to make (something) wide or wider : BROADEN ▪ The city is going to *widen* the road. ▪ They plan to *widen* the investigation. ▪ The team *widened* [=*increased*] their lead in the fifth inning.
2 [*no obj*] **:** to become wide or wider ▪ Her eyes *widened* in surprise. ▪ They went swimming at a spot where the river *widens*. ▪ The *widening* [=*increasing*] gap between incomes was noted in the study. ▪ The scope of the investigation has *widened*.

wide·out /ˈwaɪdˌaʊt/ *noun, pl* **-outs** [*count*] *American football* : WIDE RECEIVER

wide–rang·ing /ˈwaɪdˌreɪnʤɪŋ/ *adj* [*more* ~; *most* ~] : including many different ideas, actions, or things ▪ She had *wide-ranging* interests. ▪ The implications of the investigation were *wide-ranging*.

wide receiver *noun, pl* ~ **-ers** [*count*] *American football* : a player on the offensive team who specializes in catching forward passes

wide–screen *adj* : having a screen that is wider than the screen of most televisions ▪ a *wide-screen* TV

wide·spread /ˈwaɪdˈsprɛd/ *adj* [*more* ~; *most* ~] : common over a wide area or among many people ▪ There is *widespread* public interest in the election. ▪ Trade partners had become more *widespread*. ▪ There was *widespread* opposition to the plan.

wid·get /ˈwɪʤət/ *noun, pl* **-gets** [*count*] *informal* : any small mechanical or electronic device : GADGET — often used to refer to an imaginary product that is being mentioned as an example in a discussion of business ▪ Could you make and sell *widgets* for less money than the competition?

wid·ow /ˈwɪdoʊ/ *noun, pl* **-ows** [*count*]
1 : a woman whose husband has died
2 *informal* **:** a woman whose husband often leaves her alone while he plays sports or is involved in other activities ▪ a football *widow* [=a woman whose husband spends a lot of time watching football] ▪ Everyone joked that she was a ***golf widow***. [=a woman whose husband is often away playing golf] — see also BLACK WIDOW
— **wid·ow·hood** /ˈwɪdoʊˌhʊd/ *noun* [*noncount*] ▪ She had a hard time during her first year of *widowhood*.

wid·owed /ˈwɪdoʊd/ *adj* — used to describe a woman whose husband has died or a man whose wife has died ▪ her *widowed* mother/father ▪ She ***was widowed*** by the war. [=her husband was killed in the war]

wid·ow·er /ˈwɪdəwɚ/ *noun, pl* **-ers** [*count*] : a man whose wife has died

width /ˈwɪdθ/ *noun, pl* **widths**
1 : the distance from one side of something to the other side : a measurement of how wide something is [*noncount*] What is the *width* of the table? ▪ She carefully measured the length and *width* of the room. ▪ The deck runs the full *width* of the house. [*count*] The carpet is available in several *widths*. ▪ We swam ten *widths* in the pool.
2 [*count*] **:** a measured and cut piece of material (such as cloth) ▪ I bought two *widths* of fabric.

wield /ˈwiːld/ *verb* **wields; wield·ed; wield·ing** [+ *obj*]
1 : to hold (something, such as a tool or weapon) in your hands so that you are ready to use it ▪ The man was *wielding* a gun/knife. ▪ Can he *wield* a hammer?
2 : to have and use (power, influence, etc.) ▪ He *wields* a great deal of influence over his students. ▪ *wield* clout/power
— **wield·er** *noun, pl* **-ers** [*count*] ▪ *wielders* of power

wie·ner /ˈwiːnɚ/ *noun, pl* **-ners** [*count*] *US, informal* : HOT DOG 1

wife /ˈwaɪf/ *noun, pl* **wives** /ˈwaɪvz/ [*count*] : a married woman : the woman someone is married to ▪ We met him and his *wife*. ▪ They were ***husband and wife*** [=a married couple] for almost 60 years. — compare HUSBAND; see also FISHWIFE, HOUSEWIFE, TROPHY WIFE

wife·ly /ˈwaɪfli/ *adj, old-fashioned* : of, relating to, or suitable for a wife ▪ *wifely* affection

[1]**wig** /ˈwɪg/ *noun, pl* **wigs** [*count*] : artificial hair that you wear on your head because you are bald or in order to change your appearance ▪ She was wearing a blonde *wig*. — compare HAIRPIECE, TOUPEE
flip your wig see [1]FLIP

[2]**wig** *verb* **wigs; wigged; wig·ging**
wig out [*phrasal verb*] ***wig out*** or ***wig (someone) out*** *US slang* **:** to become very upset or to cause (someone) to become very upset ▪ She *wigged out* [=*freaked out*] when the police arrived. ▪ The movie totally *wigged* me *out*.

wigging *noun* [*singular*] *Brit, old-fashioned* : an occurrence in which someone speaks in a very angry and critical way to someone who has done something wrong : a severe scolding ▪ He received a *wigging* for what he did.

wig·gle /ˈwɪgəl/ *verb* **wig·gles; wig·gled; wig·gling :** to move up and down or from side to side with short quick motions [+ *obj*] He *wiggled* his fingers/toes. ▪ She *wiggled* her hips. [*no obj*] His toes were *wiggling*. ▪ The puppy *wiggled* with excitement.
— **wiggle** *noun, pl* **wiggles** [*count*] ▪ She gave her hips a *wiggle*.

wiggle room *noun* [*noncount*] *US, somewhat informal* : the ability to make small changes in a plan, schedule, etc., if they are needed ▪ We should allow for some *wiggle room* [=*flexibility*] when we plan the schedule. ▪ The salesman has some *wiggle room* to reduce the price of the car.

wig·gly /ˈwɪgəli/ *adj* **wig·gli·er; -est**
1 : making many small movements : moving with a wiggle ▪ *wiggly* worms
2 : having many curves : not straight ▪ There were *wiggly* [=*wavy*] lines in the sand.

wig·wam /ˈwɪgˌwɑːm/ *noun, pl* **-wams** [*count*] : a round tent that was used in the past by Native Americans as a house or shelter — see picture at TEPEE

[1]**wild** /ˈwajəld/ *adj* **wild·er; -est**
1 a *of an animal* **:** living in nature without human control or care : not tame ▪ *wild* ducks/animals **b** *of a plant* **:** growing or produced in nature : not grown or farmed by people ▪ *wild* blueberries/grapes/honey — compare CULTIVATED **c** *of land* **:** not changed by people : not settled or developed ▪ *wild* places high in the mountains ▪ Few species can survive in this *wild* [=*savage*] landscape.
2 : uncontrolled and dangerous ▪ I felt a *wild* rage. ▪ He was *wild* with anger. ▪ He had a *wild* [=*crazy*] look in his eyes.
3 : very enthusiastic or excited ▪ *wild* laughter ▪ *wild* revelers ▪ The crowd ***went wild*** when the band took the stage.
4 : going far beyond what is normal or usual ▪ They painted the rooms with some *wild* colors. ▪ He has some pretty *wild* [=*strange*] ideas about raising children. ▪ He told us a *wild* story about their camping trip. ▪ The company was successful ***beyond my wildest dreams/fantasies***. [=much more suc-

cessful that I ever thought possible]

5 a : noisy and disorganized ▪ The party was getting kind of *wild* [=out of control] so we left. ▪ *wild* protests **b** : very enjoyable, lively, and exciting ▪ It was a *wild* party. ▪ He loves the city's *wild* nightclub scene.

6 : made without knowledge or information : not based on facts ▪ That's just a ***wild guess***.

7 *of a playing card* : able to represent any other playing card ▪ In this game, jokers are *wild*.

8 : done without accuracy or control ▪ The shortstop made a *wild* throw to first base. — see also WILD PITCH

9 : very stormy or violent ▪ It was a *wild* night of heavy snow and strong winds. ▪ a *wild* [=*rough, turbulent*] sea

be wild about : to like (someone or something) very much ▪ She's *wild about* [=*crazy about*] her new boyfriend. ▪ He *is* absolutely *wild about* baseball. ▪ She's not *wild about* the idea. [=she doesn't like the idea]

sow your (wild) oats see [1]SOW

wild and woolly see [1]WOOLLY

– wild·ness /ˈwajəldnəs/ *noun* [*noncount*] ▪ the *wildness* and beauty of the scenery

[2]**wild** *noun*

1 ***the wilds*** : a large area of land where people do not live and where plants, trees, etc., grow freely : WILDERNESS ▪ They hiked through *the wilds* of Maine.

2 ***the wild*** : a wild, free, or natural place, state, or existence ▪ The plants were collected from *the wild*. ▪ They will return the animal to *the wild* when it is healthy. ▪ Could these animals survive ***in the wild***? ▪ I've only seen that animal in a zoo, never *in the wild*.

[3]**wild** *adv* : without being controlled ▪ These plants ***grow wild*** on the roadside.

go hog wild see [1]HOG

run wild : to run, go, behave, etc., in a wild and uncontrolled way ▪ The mob was *running wild* in the streets. ▪ His imagination *ran wild*.

wild boar *noun, pl* **~ boars** [*count*] : BOAR 2

wild card *noun, pl* **~ cards** [*count*]

1 : a playing card that can represent any other card in a game ▪ The joker is a *wild card*.

2 : a person or thing that could affect a situation in a way that cannot be predicted : an unknown or unpredictable factor ▪ Taxes are the *wild card* in this election.

3 *sports* : a player or team chosen to fill a place in a competition after the regularly qualified players or teams have all been decided ▪ The team made it into the play-offs as the/a *wild card*.

4 *usually* ***wildcard*** : a symbol (such as ? or *) that is used in a computer search to represent any letter or number

wild·cat /ˈwajəldˌkæt/ *noun, pl* **-cats** [*count*] : a kind of cat that lives in the wilderness

wildcat strike *noun, pl* **~ strikes** [*count*] : a strike that is started by a group of workers without the approval of their union

wil·de·beest /ˈwɪldəˌbiːst/ *noun, pl* **wil·de·beests** *also* **wildebeest** [*count*] : a large African animal that has long curving horns — called also *gnu*

wil·der·ness /ˈwɪldɚnəs/ *noun, pl* **-ness·es** [*count*] : a wild and natural area in which few people live ▪ She enjoys hikes through the *wilderness*. — often used before another noun ▪ They liked to take *wilderness* excursions. ▪ *wilderness* conservation — often used figuratively ▪ a bureaucratic *wilderness*

wilderness area *noun, pl* **~ areas** [*count*] *US* : a large area of public land that is kept in its natural state

wild–eyed /ˈwajəldˈaɪd/ *adj*

1 : having a wild expression in the eyes : looking dangerous or out of control ▪ a *wild-eyed* criminal

2 : very extreme or wild ▪ *wild-eyed* schemes/theories

wild·fire /ˈwajəldˌfajɚ/ *noun, pl* **-fires** [*count*] : a fire in a wild area (such as a forest) that is not controlled and that can burn a large area very quickly ▪ The recent *wildfires* were made worse by the strong winds.

like wildfire *informal* : very quickly ▪ The new fad ***spread like wildfire***.

wild·flow·er /ˈwajəldˌflawɚ/ *noun, pl* **-ers** [*count*] : a flower that grows in natural places without being planted by people ▪ a field full of *wildflowers*

wild·fowl /ˈwajəldˌfawəl/ *noun* [*noncount*] : birds (such as ducks and geese) that live in the wild especially near water and are often hunted

wild goose chase *noun, pl* **~ chases** [*count*] : a difficult and long search for something that is not important or that cannot be found ▪ The boss sent me on a *wild goose chase* that wasted half the day.

wild·life /ˈwajəldˌlaɪf/ *noun* [*noncount*] : animals living in nature : wild animals ▪ an area with abundant *wildlife* — often used before another noun ▪ *wildlife* management/protection ▪ a *wildlife* preserve [=an area of land where wild animals are protected]

wild·ly /ˈwajəldli/ *adv* [*more ~; most ~*]

1 : in an uncontrolled or excited way : in a wild way ▪ He was waving his arms *wildly*.

2 : very or extremely ▪ a *wildly* popular restaurant ▪ *wildly* different cultures ▪ I'm not *wildly* enthusiastic about seeing them.

wild pitch *noun, pl* **~ pitches** [*count*] *baseball* : a pitch that cannot be caught by the catcher and that allows a runner to go to the next base

wild rice *noun* [*noncount*] : a kind of grain that is produced by a tall North American plant that grows in water

Wild West *noun*

the Wild West : the western United States in the past when there were many cowboys, outlaws, etc. ▪ stories about *the Wild West* — often used before another noun ▪ *Wild West* stories ▪ a Wild West show

wiles /ˈwajəlz/ *noun* [*plural*] : clever tricks that you use to get what you want ▪ She used her ***feminine wiles*** to entice him to give her the job.

[1]**will** /ˈwɪl, wəl/ *verb, past tense* **would** /ˈwʊd, wəd/; *present tense for both singular and plural* **will**; *negative* **will not** *or* **won't** /ˈwoʊnt/ [*modal verb*]

1 — used to say that something is expected to happen in the future ▪ We *will* [=we are going to] leave tomorrow. ▪ I *will* be there in fifteen minutes. ▪ Tomorrow *will* be partly cloudy and cool. ▪ What do you think *will* happen? ▪ Who do you think *will* win? ▪ He *will* be severely punished for this crime. ▪ We *will* continue our efforts, and we *will* succeed. [=we are determined to succeed]

2 a — used to say that you want something ▪ I *will* [=(more commonly) *I'll*] have a hamburger and fries. ▪ "*Will* you have another cup of tea?" "Yes, I *will*, thank you." **b** — used to say that you are willing to do something ▪ Yes, I *will* marry you. ▪ The doctor *will* see you now. ▪ "*Will* you help him?" "No, I most certainly *will* not!" ▪ No one *would* do it.

3 — used to ask someone to do something ▪ *Will* [=*would*] you please pass the salt? ▪ *Will* you help me with my homework? ▪ *Will* you please stop talking? ▪ Shut the window, *will* you? ▪ If you *will* follow me, ladies and gentlemen, I'll take you to the next gallery.

4 — used to give a command or to say what must happen or not happen ▪ You *will* do as I say. ▪ Everyone *will* leave immediately! ▪ I *will* not have my own children talking to me like that! ▪ No one *will* leave this room until a decision has been made.

5 a — used to say that something is likely or certain to be true ▪ That *will* be the babysitter at the door. ▪ The gray house on the left *will* be theirs. [=must be theirs] ▪ Try this soup—you *will* like it. [=(more commonly) *you'll* like it] ▪ Ask anyone and they *will* tell you the same thing. **b** — used to describe a situation that is continuing ▪ He *won't* stop bothering me. [=he keeps bothering me; he refuses to stop bothering me] ▪ The door *won't* open.

6 — used to say that something usually happens or that a person or thing usually does something ▪ The dog *will* growl if you get too close to it. ▪ She *will* wait until the last minute to finish her homework. ▪ People *will* talk if they see us together. ▪ Accidents *will* happen. [=accidents sometimes happen; it isn't possible to avoid all accidents] ✧ In British English, this sense is sometimes used to show that you are annoyed that someone does something often. ▪ He *will* leave his coat on the chair instead of hanging it up.

7 — used to say that something is able to do something or contain a certain amount ▪ The batteries *will* last a maximum of four hours. ▪ The back seat *will* [=*can*] hold three people. [=it is capable of holding three people] ▪ This *will* do if there is nothing better.

– compare [3]WILL, [4]WILL

[2]**will** /ˈwɪl/ *noun, pl* **wills**

1 [*count*] *law* : a legal document in which a person states who should receive his or her possessions after he or she dies ▪ In her *will*, she asked that her money be donated to the church. ▪ He ***made/prepared/wrote a will*** only days before his death. — see also LIVING WILL

2 : a strong desire or determination to do something *[count]* She has a strong *will.* = She has a ***will of iron.*** = She has an ***iron will.*** ▪ He won the ***battle/clash of wills*** with his wife. [=he got what he wanted] — often followed by *to + verb* ▪ During her illness, she never lost her *will to live/survive.* ▪ He has the *will to succeed.* [=he has a strong desire to succeed] *[noncount]* He has no *will* of his own. ▪ Does he have the ***strength of will*** [=is he willing to work extremely hard] to complete such demanding training? — see also FREE WILL, STRONG-WILLED

3 *[noncount]* : a person's choice or desire in a particular situation ▪ They were obedient to the king's *will.* [=they did what the king wanted them to do] ▪ a government that reflects the *will* of the people ▪ As a child, he was forced to play the violin ***against his will.*** [=even though he did not want to play it] ▪ She chose to ***go against her parents' will*** and marry him anyway. [=she chose to marry him even though her parents did not want her to marry him] ▪ She is always trying to ***impose her will*** on other people. [=trying to force other people to do what she wants]

at will : when you want or in a way that you want ▪ She is free to come and go *at will.* ▪ The document can be modified *at will.* ▪ The soldiers were told to fire *at will.*

where there's a will, there's a way — used to say that if you want to do something very much, you can find a way to do it ▪ "Do you think she can finish the project on time?" "She can if she really wants to. *Where there's a will, there's a way.*"

with a will : with a lot enthusiasm and energy ▪ She set about the work *with a will.*

with the best will in the world *Brit* : with the most sincere desire and effort to do something good or worthwhile — used especially to say that it is not possible to do something even if you want to do it very much ▪ Even *with the best will in the world,* the work cannot be done that quickly.

– see also GOODWILL, ILL WILL

³will /ˈwɪl/ *verb, present tense for both singular and plural* **will** *[+ obj]* : to want or desire (something) ✧ This verb is only used in the simple present tense. ▪ You can say ***what you will*** [=you can say whatever you want to say], but I will always love her. ▪ Call it *what you will,* it is still illegal. [=it is illegal no matter what you call it] ▪ Imagine, ***if you will,*** life without computers. ▪ Baseball is my love, my obsession *if you will.* [=if you want to call it that] — compare ¹WILL, ⁴WILL

⁴will /ˈwɪl/ *verb* **wills; willed; will·ing** *[+ obj]*

1 a : to cause or try to cause (something) to happen by using the power of your mind ▪ She was haunted by the thought that she had *willed* his death. [=that she had caused his death by wishing that he would die] **b** : to cause or try to cause (someone or something) *to do* something by using the power of your mind ▪ He *willed* himself *to stay* awake. ▪ As she neared the finish line she *willed* her legs *to keep* running.

2 : to want or intend (something) to happen ▪ It will happen if God *wills* it.

3 *law* : to state in a will that (your property) will be given to a particular person, organization, etc., after you die ▪ She *willed* her property to her children. ▪ He *willed* his entire estate to the church. = He *willed* the church his entire estate.

– compare ¹WILL, ³WILL

will·ful *or chiefly Brit* **wil·ful** /ˈwɪlfəl/ *adj, disapproving*

1 : refusing to change your ideas or opinions or to stop doing something ▪ a stubborn and *willful* child

2 : done deliberately : INTENTIONAL ▪ He has shown a *willful* disregard for other people's feelings. ▪ *willful* disobedience/murder

– **will·ful·ly** *adv* ▪ The press *willfully* ignored the facts of the case. – **will·ful·ness** *noun [noncount]*

wil·lies /ˈwɪliz/ *noun*

the willies *informal* : a nervous feeling ▪ Hearing noises at night gives me *the willies.* [=*the creeps*]

will·ing /ˈwɪlɪŋ/ *adj [more ~; most ~]*

1 : not refusing to do something : READY — followed by *to + verb* ▪ I'm perfectly *willing to try.* ▪ They are always *willing* and eager *to help.* ▪ We're ***ready and willing*** *to make* the trip.

2 : quick to act or respond : doing something or ready to do something without being persuaded ▪ He was a *willing* participant in the crime. ▪ *willing* workers ▪ She's lending a *willing* hand.

3 : done, made, or given by choice : VOLUNTARY ▪ *willing* obedience ▪ a *willing* sacrifice

God willing see GOD

the spirit is willing but the flesh is weak see ¹SPIRIT

– **will·ing·ly** /ˈwɪlɪŋli/ *adv* ▪ The student acted *willingly.* ▪ We *willingly* agreed to the proposal. – **will·ing·ness** *noun [noncount]* ▪ He appreciated her *willingness* to help.

will–o'–the–wisp /ˌwɪləðəˈwɪsp/ *noun [noncount]*

1 : a goal that cannot be reached ▪ the *will-o'-the-wisp* of world peace

2 : a light that sometimes appears at night over wet ground

wil·low /ˈwɪloʊ/ *noun, pl* **-lows** *[count]* : a tree that has long, narrow leaves and strong, thin branches that are used to make baskets — see also PUSSY WILLOW

wil·lowy /ˈwɪləwi/ *adj [more ~; most ~]* : tall, thin, and graceful ▪ a *willowy* young dancer ▪ Her figure is *willowy.*

will·pow·er /ˈwɪlˌpawɚ/ *noun [noncount]* : the ability to control yourself : strong determination that allows you to do something difficult (such as to lose weight or quit smoking) ▪ The dessert buffet tested my *willpower.* ▪ He conquered his drinking problem through sheer *willpower.*

wil·ly *also* **wil·lie** /ˈwɪli/ *noun, pl* **-lies** *[count] informal* : PENIS

wil·ly–nil·ly /ˌwɪliˈnɪli/ *adv*

1 : in a careless and unplanned way ▪ They decided *willy-nilly* to change the rules.

2 : in a way that does not allow any choices or planning ▪ We are being forced *willy-nilly* to accept whatever the government decides.

¹wilt /ˈwɪlt/ *verb* **wilts; wilt·ed; wilt·ing**

1 *of a plant* : to bend over because of not having enough water *[no obj]* The roses were *wilting.* *[+ obj]* The hot weather *wilted* the plants.

2 *[no obj]* **a** : to become weak and tired especially because of hot weather ▪ The crowd *wilted* in the heat. **b** : to lose energy, confidence, effectiveness, etc. ▪ He *wilted* under the pressure.

²wilt /ˈwɪlt/ *second person singular present tense of* WILL *old-fashioned* — used with "thou" ▪ Do what thou *wilt.* [=do what you will]

wily /ˈwaɪli/ *adj* **wil·i·er; -est** *[also more ~; most ~]* : full of clever tricks : very clever ▪ She turned out to be a *wily* negotiator. ▪ *wily* tactics

– **wil·i·ness** /ˈwaɪlinəs/ *noun [noncount]*

¹wimp /ˈwɪmp/ *noun, pl* **wimps** *[count] informal* : a weak person who lacks confidence, courage, etc. ▪ I was too much of a *wimp* [=*coward*] to confront him.

²wimp *verb*

wimp out *[phrasal verb] informal* : to fail to do something because you are too afraid, weak, etc. ▪ He wanted to ask her to the dance but he *wimped out.*

wim·ple /ˈwɪmpəl/ *noun, pl* **wim·ples** *[count]* : a cloth worn over the head and around the neck and chin by women in past times and by some nuns today

¹win /ˈwɪn/ *verb* **wins; won** /ˈwʌn/; **win·ning**

1 a : to achieve victory in a fight, contest, game, etc. *[+ obj]* The boxer *won* the match by knockout. ▪ They *won* the battle/war. ▪ She *won* the election. ▪ He won't give up until he's *won* the argument. ▪ Neither candidate *won* the debate. ▪ We tried our best, but ***you can't win them all.*** *[no obj]* They played well, but they didn't *win.* ▪ The chances of *winning* are 1 in 100,000. ▪ It's not about *winning* or losing. It's about having fun. ▪ Okay, ***you win.*** [=I agree to do what you want] We'll go to the movies. **b** *[+ obj]* : to get (something, such as a prize) by achieving victory in a fight, contest, game, etc. ▪ She *won* a tennis trophy. ▪ Her book *won* the Pulitzer Prize.

2 *[+ obj]* : to get (something) by effort ▪ She *won* praise for her hard work. ▪ His perseverance *won* him the job of his dreams. [=he got the job of his dreams because of his perseverance]

3 *[+ obj]* : to persuade (someone) to like you or to choose you ▪ She *won* the voters with her warm sense of humor. ▪ He broke up with his girlfriend but he's determined to *win* her back. [=to get her back; to persuade her to be his girlfriend again] ▪ He'll do anything to ***win her heart.*** [=to get her to fall in love with him]

can't win *informal* — used to say that success is not possible for someone in a particular situation ▪ I feel like I *can't win.* Nothing I do seems to make any difference. ▪ ***You can't win*** when you're dealing with someone so unreasonable.

win or lose : whether you succeed or fail ▪ *Win or lose,* we'll give it our best effort.

win out *also Brit* ***win through*** *[phrasal verb]* : to achieve victory or success after dealing with many difficulties ▪ It was a challenge, but we *won out* in the end.

W

win over [*phrasal verb*] ***win (someone) over*** : to persuade (someone) to accept and support something (such as an idea) after opposing it▪ They eventually *won* him *over* with some persuasive arguments.

²win *noun, pl* **wins** [*count*] : an act of achieving victory especially in a game or contest : VICTORY▪ a pitcher with 15 *wins* ▪ Their *win* over the first place team was unexpected. — opposite LOSS

wince /ˈwɪns/ *verb* **winc·es; winced; winc·ing** [*no obj*] : to have an expression on your face for a very short time which shows that you are embarrassed or in pain ▪ She *winced* [=*grimaced*] (in pain) when she hit her elbow. ▪ I *wince* [=*cringe*] with embarrassment whenever I think of that day.

– wince *noun, pl* **winces** [*count*]

winch /ˈwɪntʃ/ *noun, pl* **winch·es** [*count*] : a machine that has a rope or chain and that is used for pulling or lifting heavy things▪ a tow truck's *winch*

– winch *verb, always followed by an adverb or preposition* **winches; winched; winch·ing** [+ *obj*] ▪ They *winched* the car out of the lake.

¹wind /ˈwɪnd/ *noun, pl* **winds**

1 : a natural movement of air outside [*count*]The storm was accompanied by northerly *winds*. ▪ A gusty/light *wind* rustled the leaves. ▪ strong/hard *winds* [*noncount*]The *wind* is blowing hard. ▪ There isn't much *wind* today. — see also CROSSWIND, DOWNWIND, HEADWIND, TAILWIND, TRADE WIND, UPWIND, WHIRLWIND

2 [*count*] : something that has force or influence▪ the changing/shifting *winds* of political opinion ▪ The ***winds of change*** have begun to blow. [=change is going to happen; change is in the air] ▪ Her political opinions depend on ***which way the wind is blowing*** [=what opinions are popular at the time]

3 [*noncount*] : the ability to breathe normally▪ I needed to rest to get my *wind* back after the climb. [=to stop breathing hard and begin to breathe normally] ▪ The fall ***knocked the wind out of me*** [=knocked the air out of my lungs and made me unable to breathe normally for a brief time] — see also SECOND WIND

4 [*noncount*] *Brit* : gas in the stomach or intestines▪ Certain foods give me *wind*. [=(*US*) *gas*]

5 winds [*plural*] *music* : musical instruments (such as flutes and horns) that are played by blowing air into them : wind instruments

break wind : to pass gas out of the anus

catch/get wind of (something) : to hear about (something private or secret)▪ They *got wind of* our plans for a party. ▪ The police *caught wind of* the plot.

get/have the wind up *Brit, informal* : to become/be afraid or nervous▪ When they started questioning him, he *got the wind up*.

in the wind : about to happen▪ Change is *in the wind*.

like the wind : very fast▪ He grabbed the money and ***ran like the wind***

put the wind up (someone) *Brit, informal* : to make (someone) afraid or nervous▪ I tried to *put the wind up* him by threatening to call the police.

sail close to the wind see ¹SAIL

straw in the wind see STRAW

take the wind out of someone's sails : to cause someone to lose confidence or energy▪ The team's star player was injured and it really *took the wind out of their sails*.

three sheets to the wind see ²SHEET

throw/fling/cast caution to the wind see ¹CAUTION

²wind /ˈwaɪnd/ *verb* **winds; wound** /ˈwaʊnd/; **wind·ing**

1 *of a river, road, etc.* : to follow a series of curves and turns [*no obj*]The river *winds* through the valley. ▪ *winding* lanes/roads/streets [+ *obj*]The river *winds* its way through the valley.

2 [+ *obj*] : to wrap (something, such as a string) around something▪ He *wound* more twine around the box. ▪ *wind* thread on a spool ▪ She *wound* the scarf around her neck. ▪ The machine *winds* the tape from one reel to the other.

3 [+ *obj*] : to turn a knob, handle, etc., several times on something (such as a clock) so that it can work▪ *wind* a clock ▪ Her watch needs to be *wound* once a year. ▪ To start the old car, you have to *wind* the crank. — often + *up*▪ *wind up* a toy train

wind down [*phrasal verb*] **1 :** to end gradually▪ The party was *winding down*. **2 :** to relax and stop thinking about work, problems, etc. : UNWIND ▪ I intend to *wind down* with a good book this weekend.

wind up [*phrasal verb*] **1 :** to end▪ The meeting should be *winding up* soon. **2** ***wind (something) up or wind up (something)*** : to end or complete (something)▪ It's time to *wind up* the meeting. ▪ It's getting late so let's *wind* things *up*. **3 :** to reach or come to a place, situation, or condition that was not planned or expected▪ They *wound up* [=*ended up*] being millionaires. ▪ Although she studied art, she *wound up* [=*ended up*] working in publishing. ▪ After a wrong turn, we *wound up* in an unfamiliar neighborhood. — see also ²WIND 3 (above), WOUND UP

– wind·er /ˈwaɪndɚ/ *noun, pl* **-ers** [*count*]▪ a bobbin/clock *winder*

wind·bag /ˈwɪnd,bæg/ *noun, pl* **-bags** [*count*] *informal* + *disapproving* : a person who talks too much▪ a pompous old *windbag*

wind·blown /ˈwɪnd,bloʊn/ *adj*

1 : carried through the air by the wind▪ *windblown* pollen

2 : made messy by the wind▪ *windblown* hair

wind·break /ˈwɪnd,breɪk/ *noun, pl* **-breaks** [*count*] : something (such as a fence or group of trees) that protects an area from the wind

Wind·break·er /ˈwɪnd,breɪkɚ/ *trademark* — used for a light jacket that protects you from the wind

wind·burn /ˈwɪnd,bɚn/ *noun* [*noncount*] : a red and sore area on the skin that is caused by cold or very strong wind▪ His face was red from *windburn*.

– wind·burned /ˈwɪnd,bɚnd/ *adj*▪ *windburned* skin

wind·cheat·er /ˈwɪnd,ʧi:tɚ/ *noun, pl* **-ers** [*count*] *Brit* : a light jacket that protects you from the wind

wind·chill /ˈwɪnd,ʧɪl/ *noun, pl* **-chills** *chiefly US*

1 [*noncount*] : the effect that wind has of making air feel colder than it actually is▪ It's cold outside, and it feels even colder because of the *windchill*. — called also *windchill factor*

2 [*count*] : a temperature that shows how cold the air feels because of the wind▪ Expect *windchills* in the 20s tonight.

wind chime *noun, pl* **~ chimes** [*count*] : a collection of objects made from metal, glass, etc., that hang together from strings and touch each other to make a musical sound when they are blown by the wind — usually plural

wind·ed /ˈwɪndəd/ *adj* : unable to breathe easily or normally because you have been running, climbing, etc.▪ We were *winded* [=*out of breath*] after the long climb. — see also LONG-WINDED

wind·fall /ˈwɪnd,fɑ:l/ *noun, pl* **-falls** [*count*] : an unexpected amount of money that you get as a gift, prize, etc.▪ They received a *windfall* because of the tax cuts.

wind instrument *noun, pl* **~ -ments** [*count*] : a musical instrument (such as a flute, horn, or organ) that is played by blowing air through it — compare BRASS, WOODWIND

wind·jam·mer /ˈwɪnd,ʤæmɚ/ *noun, pl* **-mers** [*count*] : a sailing ship

wind·lass /ˈwɪndləs/ *noun, pl* **-lass·es** [*count*] : WINCH

wind·mill /ˈwɪnd,mɪl/ *noun, pl* **-mills** [*count*]

1 : a structure that has parts which are turned around by the wind and that is used to produce power, pump water, etc.

2 *Brit* : PINWHEEL 1

tilt at windmills see ¹TILT

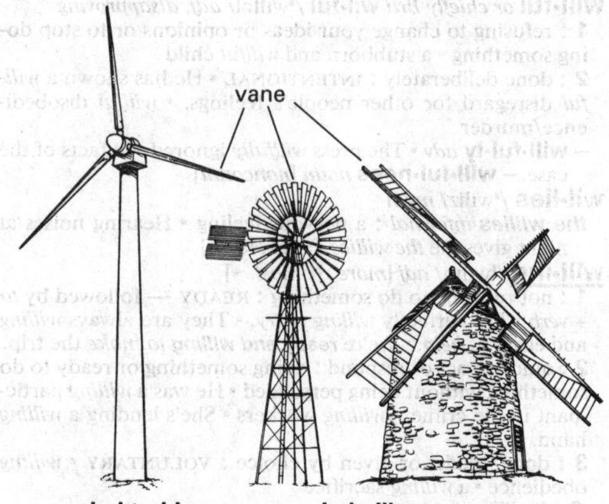

wind turbine **windmills**

N

win·dow /ˈwɪndoʊ/ *noun, pl* **-dows**
1 [*count*] **a :** an opening in a wall, door, etc., that usually contains a sheet of glass • She opened a *window* to let in some air. • I looked ***out the window*** and saw a deer. — see also BAY WINDOW, FRENCH WINDOW, PICTURE WINDOW, ROSE WINDOW, STORM WINDOW **b :** a sheet of glass that covers an opening in a building, vehicle, etc. • He used vinegar and water to wash the *windows*. • He accidentally broke a *window*. • Can you roll down the car *window*? **c :** a large window at the front of a store where goods are displayed so that they can be seen by people who are walking past • The *windows* along 5th Avenue were all decorated for Christmas. • I saw a beautiful dress ***in the window***. **d :** an opening in a wall through which business is conducted • He sits behind a *window* and sells movie tickets. • a ticket *window* • a bank teller's *window*
2 [*count*] **:** a part of something that you can see through • Make sure the address shows through the *window* in the envelope. • A *window* opened in the fog and we could finally see the ocean.
3 [*count*] **:** an area or box on a computer screen that shows a program that is currently running • Minimize that *window* and open a new one. • Close all the *windows* and restart the computer. — see picture at COMPUTER
4 [*singular*] **:** a period of time during which something can happen • The shuttle's launch has a *window* of only two days. [=it can only happen within two specific days] • The ***window of opportunity*** [=the time during which there is a chance to do something] has closed/ended.
a window into/on **:** something that makes it possible to see or understand something clearly • This knowledge opens *a window into* your opponent's mind. • The book gives the reader *a window on* war.
go out the window *informal* **:** to stop being used or thought about • By that point in the argument, reason had *gone out the window*.
throw (something) out the window *informal* **:** to stop using or thinking about (something) • We can *throw* that idea *out the window*.

window box *noun, pl* ~ **boxes** [*count*] **:** a long, thin box that is usually hung on the outside of a building beneath a window and that is used as a container for flowers and plants

window dresser *noun, pl* ~ **-ers** [*count*] **:** a person whose job is to decorate and arrange products to display in a store window

window dressing *noun* [*noncount*]
1 : the act of decorating and arranging products to display in a store window
2 *disapproving* **:** something that is intended to make a person or thing seem better or more attractive but that does not have any real importance or effect • These changes are being made for a good reason. They're not just *window dressing*.

win·dow·less /ˈwɪndoʊləs/ *adj* **:** not having a window • a *windowless* room

win·dow·pane /ˈwɪndoʊˌpeɪn/ *noun, pl* **-panes** [*count*] **:** a piece of glass that covers an opening in a window • Ice had formed on the *windowpane*. — see picture at WINDOW

window seat *noun, pl* ~ **seats** [*count*]
1 : a seat that is built or placed below a window
2 : the seat that is closest to the window on a plane, train, bus, etc.

window shade *noun, pl* ~ **shades** [*count*] *US* **:** a roll of cloth or plastic that is hung at the top of a window and that can be pulled down to cover the window — called also *blind*, *(US) shade*; see picture at WINDOW

win·dow–shop /ˈwɪndoʊˌʃɑːp/ *verb* **-shops; -shopped; -shop·ping** [*no obj*] **:** to walk in front of stores and look at the products displayed in the windows without buying anything • I like to *window-shop* when I'm in the city.
– **window shopper** *noun, pl* ~ **-pers** [*count*] – **window–shopping** *noun* [*noncount*] • We ***went window-shopping*** last weekend.

win·dow·sill /ˈwɪndoʊˌsɪl/ *noun, pl* **-sills** [*count*] **:** a narrow shelf that is attached to the bottom of a window — see picture at WINDOW

wind·pipe /ˈwɪndˌpaɪp/ *noun, pl* **-pipes** [*count*] **:** the tube in your neck and chest that carries air into and out of your lungs **:** TRACHEA • She got something stuck in her *windpipe*.

wind·proof /ˈwɪndˈpruːf/ *adj* [*more* ~; *most* ~] **:** not allowing wind to enter or move through • a *windproof* jacket

wind·screen /ˈwɪndˌskriːn/ *noun, pl* **-screens** [*count*] *Brit* **:** WINDSHIELD 1

windscreen wiper *noun, pl* ~ **-ers** [*count*] *Brit* **:** WINDSHIELD WIPER

wind·shield /ˈwɪndˌʃiːld/ *noun, pl* **-shields** [*count*]
1 *US* **:** the window at the front of a car, truck, etc., that protects the driver and passengers • The car had a damaged *windshield*. — called also **(*Brit*)** *windscreen*; see picture at CAR
2 : a piece of glass above the handlebars of a motorcycle that protects the rider

windshield wiper *noun, pl* ~ **-ers** [*count*] *US* **:** a long, thin piece of rubber on a metal frame that moves back and forth and pushes water, snow, etc., off the surface of a windshield — called also **(*Brit*)** *windscreen wiper*; see picture at CAR

wind·sock /ˈwɪndˌsɑːk/ *noun, pl* **-socks** [*count*] **:** a large fabric tube that is placed on a pole and used to show the direction of the wind

wind·storm /ˈwɪndˌstoɚm/ *noun, pl* **-storms** [*count*] **:** a storm that has very strong winds and usually very little rain or snow

wind·surf /ˈwɪndˌsɚf/ *verb* **-surfs; -surfed; -surf·ing** [*no obj*] **:** to ride along the surface of the water while standing on

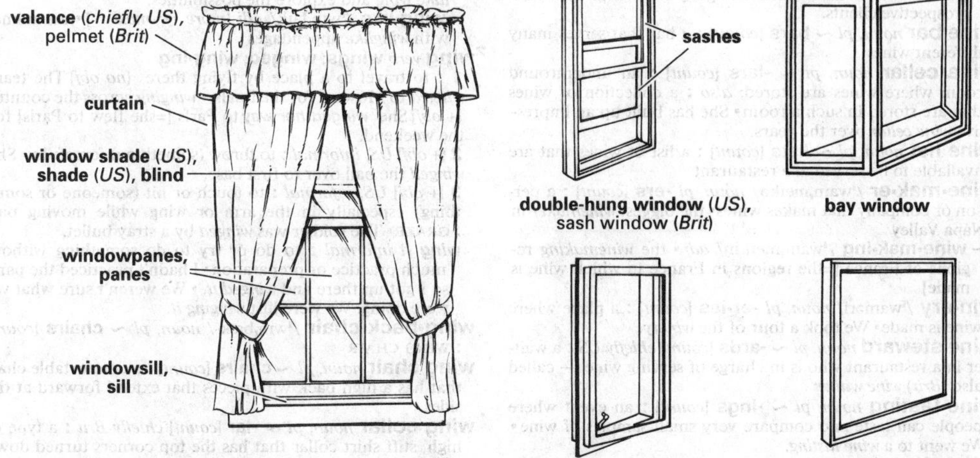

a long, narrow board that has a sail attached • He *windsurfed* in Hawaii last summer.

– **wind·surf·er** *noun, pl* **-ers** [*count*] • She is a talented *windsurfer.* [=*sailboarder*] – **wind·surf·ing** /ˈwɪndˌsɚfɪŋ/ *noun* [*noncount*] • We went *windsurfing* [=*sailboarding*] in Hawaii.

Wind·surf·er /ˈwɪndˌsɚfɚ/ *trademark* — used for a long, narrow board that has a sail attached and that is used for windsurfing

wind·swept /ˈwɪndˌswɛpt/ *adj* [*more* ~; *most* ~]
1 : exposed to strong winds • the treeless, *windswept* mountaintops
2 : made messy by the wind • *windswept* hair • The sailors looked *windswept* and tired.

wind tunnel *noun, pl* ~ **-nels** [*count*] : a long, narrow room through which air is blown in order to test the effects of wind on an airplane, car, etc.

wind turbine *noun, pl* ~ **-bines** [*count*] : a tall structure that has large blades attached to an engine and that is used to produce electricity — see picture at WINDMILL

[1]**wind-up** /ˈwaɪndˌʌp/ *noun* [*singular*]
1 : the things that are done at the end of something (such as an event or process) : the final part of something • the *wind-up* of the negotiations
2 *baseball* : the movements that a pitcher makes before the ball is thrown • He went into the/his *windup*, then threw the pitch. • a pitcher with an unusual *windup*
3 ***wind-up*** *Brit, informal* : something done or said in usually a joking way to make someone annoyed or upset • Her brother's act was just a *wind-up* to get her angry.
– see also *wind up* at [2]WIND

[2]**windup** *adj, always used before a noun* : having a motor that is given power when someone turns a handle • *windup* toys • She has an old *windup* record player in her attic.

[1]**wind·ward** /ˈwɪndwɚd/ *adj* : located on the side that is facing the direction that the wind is blowing from • The *windward* side of the mountain was rocky and treeless. — compare LEEWARD

[2]**windward** *noun* [*noncount*] : the side or direction that the wind is blowing from • sail to *windward* — compare LEEWARD

windy /ˈwɪndi/ *adj* **wind·i·er; -est**
1 : having a lot of wind • It's a *windy* day. • It's *windy* outside. • a *windy* part of the country
2 : using too many words • He gave a long, *windy* speech. • a *windy* politician

[1]**wine** /ˈwaɪn/ *noun, pl* **wines**
1 a : an alcoholic drink made from the juice of grapes [*count*] a dry/sweet *wine* [*noncount*] a glass/bottle of *wine* — see also BLUSH WINE, DESSERT WINE, RED WINE, TABLE WINE, WHITE WINE **b** : an alcoholic drink made from plants or fruits other than grapes [*noncount*] cooking with rice *wine* [*count*] apple, blueberry, and other fruit *wines*
2 [*noncount*] : a dark reddish-purple color

[2]**wine** *verb* **wines; wined; win·ing**
wine and dine : to entertain (someone) at a restaurant with good food, wine, etc. • The company *wined and dined* the prospective clients.

wine bar *noun, pl* ~ **bars** [*count*] : a bar that serves many different wines

wine cellar *noun, pl* ~ **-lars** [*count*] : an underground room where wines are stored; *also* : a collection of wines that are stored in such a room • She has built up an impressive *wine cellar* over the years.

wine list *noun, pl* ~ **lists** [*count*] : a list of wines that are available to be served at a restaurant

wine·mak·er /ˈwaɪnˌmeɪkɚ/ *noun, pl* **-ers** [*count*] : a person or company that makes wines • the biggest *winemaker* in Napa Valley
– **wine·mak·ing** /ˈwaɪnˌmeɪkɪŋ/ *adj* • the *winemaking* regions of France [=the regions in France in which wine is made]

win·ery /ˈwaɪnəri/ *noun, pl* **-er·ies** [*count*] : a place where wine is made • We took a tour of the *winery*.

wine steward *noun, pl* ~ **-ards** [*count*] *chiefly US* : a waiter in a restaurant who is in charge of serving wine — called also (*Brit*) *wine waiter*

wine tasting *noun, pl* ~ **-ings** [*count*] : an event where people can taste and compare very small samples of wine • We went to a *wine tasting*.

wine vinegar *noun, pl* ~ **-gars** [*count, noncount*] : a type of vinegar that is made from wine • red/white/rice *wine vinegar*

win·ey *or* **winy** /ˈwaɪni/ *adj* **win·i·er; -est** : made with wine or having the flavor of wine • beef in a *winey* sauce

[1]**wing** /ˈwɪŋ/ *noun, pl* **wings**
1 [*count*] **a** : a part of an animal's body that is used for flying or gliding • a bird's *wing* • bat/insect *wings* — see picture at BIRD **b** : the wing of a bird and especially a chicken eaten as food — often plural • We ordered some *wings.* — see also BUFFALO WING
2 [*count*] : one of usually two long, flat parts of an airplane that extend from the sides and make it possible for the airplane to fly — see picture at AIRPLANE; see also WATER WINGS
3 [*count*] : a particular section of a large building • In the library's north *wing*, you'll find the current periodicals. • She works in the pediatric *wing* of the hospital. • The guest room is in the east *wing*.
4 ***the wings*** : the areas on the sides of a stage where performers wait before going onto the stage • She was standing *in the wings*, waiting for her cue. — often used figuratively • The issue has been ***lurking/waiting in the wings*** [=it has been waiting to be dealt with] for several years.
5 [*count*] **a** : a particular part of a large organization or group • The conservative *wing* of the party opposed the legislation. • the political *wing* of the organization **b** : a group of military airplanes • the 107th Fighter *Wing*
6 [*count*] *sports* : a person who plays on the offense in a position that is towards the sides of the playing area in sports like hockey and soccer • The left/right *wing* passed the ball to the center. — called also *winger*
7 [*count*] *Brit* : FENDER 1
clip someone's wings : to limit someone's ability to do or say things • They *clipped* his *wings* by withholding funding for his projects.
get your wings *chiefly US, informal* **1** : to officially become a pilot : to receive the license that allows you to fly an airplane, helicopter, etc. • The pilots all *got their wings* at the end of training. **2** : to gain experience in something • He *got his wings* as a volunteer by doing work in a soup kitchen.
on a wing and a prayer *informal* : without much chance of success • She took the job *on a wing and a prayer*.
on the wing : in flight • The birds were *on the wing*. [=were flying]
spread your wings : to become more independent and confident : to try doing new things • He's known as a comic actor, but he's *spreading his wings* and trying a serious role in his new movie. • College gave her a chance to *spread her wings*.
take (someone) under your wing : to help, teach, or take care of (someone who is younger or has less experience than you) • He *took* the rookie pitcher *under his wing*. • She *took* me *under her wing* and showed me how things were done.
take wing : to begin to fly • The ducks *took wing* and flew away. — often used figuratively • Let your imagination *take wing* and explore the possibilities.
– **wing·like** /ˈwɪŋˌlaɪk/ *adj* [*more* ~; *most* ~] • an animal with *winglike* appendages

[2]**wing** *verb* **wings; winged; wing·ing**
1 : to travel to a place by flying there [*no obj*] The team *winged* to Moscow for the finals. • *winging* across the country [+ *obj*] She ***winged her way*** to Paris [=she flew to Paris] for the weekend.
2 [+ *obj*] *US, informal* : to throw (something) forcefully • She *winged* the ball over to first base.
3 [+ *obj*] *US, informal* : to touch or hit (someone or something) especially in the arm or wing while moving past : GRAZE • The soldier was *winged* by a stray bullet.
wing it *informal* : to do or try to do something without much practice or preparation • I hadn't practiced the part, so I got up there and *winged it*. • We weren't sure what we were doing. We were just *winging it*.

wing·back chair /ˈwɪŋˌbæk-/ *noun, pl* ~ **chairs** [*count*] : WING CHAIR

wing chair *noun, pl* ~ **chairs** [*count*] : a comfortable chair that has a high back with pieces that extend forward at the sides

wing collar *noun, pl* ~ **-lar** [*count*] *chiefly Brit* : a type of high, stiff shirt collar that has the top corners turned down and that is worn by a man on formal occasions

wing commander *noun, pl* ~ **-ers** [*count*] : a high-ranking officer in the British air force

winged /ˈwɪŋd/ *adj* : having wings ▪ birds and other *winged* creatures

wing·er /ˈwɪŋɚ/ *noun, pl* **-ers** [*count*] : [1]WING 6

wing·less /ˈwɪŋləs/ *adj* : having no wings ▪ a *wingless* insect

wing·man /ˈwɪŋmən/ *noun, pl* **wing·men** /-mən/ [*count*] : a pilot or airplane that flies behind and outside the leader of a group of airplanes in order to provide support or protection — often used figuratively ▪ She was my *wingman* [=she helped me] on the project.

wing mirror *noun, pl* ~ **-rors** [*count*] *Brit* : SIDE-VIEW MIRROR

wing nut *noun, pl* ~ **nuts** [*count*] : a piece of metal that has a hole in the center and two projecting parts and that you can screw onto a bolt by using your fingers

wing·span /ˈwɪŋˌspæn/ *noun, pl* **-spans** [*count*] : the distance from the tip of one wing of a bird or airplane to the tip of the other wing ▪ The hawk has a *wingspan* of about three feet. ▪ a plane with a 200-foot *wingspan*

wing·tip /ˈwɪŋˌtɪp/ *noun, pl* **-tips** [*count*]

1 : the pointed end of a wing ▪ a bird with a red head and black *wingtips* ▪ The *wingtip* of the plane almost touched the ground.

2 *US* : a type of usually leather shoe that is worn by a man and that has an extra piece of leather that covers the toe — see picture at SHOE

[1]**wink** /ˈwɪŋk/ *noun, pl* **winks** [*count*]

1 : an act of closing and opening one eye very quickly often as a way of giving a secret signal or private message to someone ▪ Her *wink* told me she was just kidding. ▪ "I knew you could do it," he said with a *wink*. ▪ He told her that he was working late, then ***gave me a wink***. [=winked at me]

2 *informal* : a very short amount of time ▪ It all disappeared ***in a wink***. [=in an instant] ▪ She said hello, and ***(as) quick as a wink*** [=*instantly*], she was gone. ▪ I ***didn't get a wink of sleep*** last night. = I ***didn't sleep a wink*** last night. [=I didn't sleep at all last night] — see also FORTY WINKS

tip (someone) the wink see [6]TIP

[2]**wink** *verb* **winks; winked; wink·ing**

1 a : to close and open one eye quickly as a signal to someone ▪ He *winked* and said that he understood. — often + *at* [*no obj*] She *winked at* me as she asked what I was doing tonight. [+ *obj*] She *winked* an eye *at* me. **b** [*no obj*] : to close and open your eyes quickly : BLINK ▪ The puppy was *winking* in the bright sun.

2 [*no obj*] **a** : to shine in an unsteady way : TWINKLE ▪ The stars *winked* in the night sky. **b** : to shine with a light that goes on and off : BLINK ▪ The airplane's landing lights *winked* on and off.

wink at [*phrasal verb*] ***wink at (someone or something)*** : to pretend that you have not seen or noticed (something) : IGNORE ▪ The city cops *wink at* the mayor's parking violations. — see also [2]WINK 1 (above)

win·kle /ˈwɪŋkəl/ *verb* **win·kles; win·kled; win·kling**

winkle out [*phrasal verb*] *Brit* **1** ***winkle out (something)*** *or* ***winkle (something) out of (someone)*** : to use a lot of effort to get (information) from a person ▪ It was hard to *winkle out* the facts. ▪ They *winkled* a confession *out of* him. **2** ***winkle (someone or something) out of (something)*** : to remove (someone or something) from (a place or position) by using a lot of effort ▪ They were *winkled out of* their hiding places.

win·na·ble /ˈwɪnəbəl/ *adj* [*more* ~; *most* ~] : able to be won ▪ The game is no longer *winnable*. ▪ We are fighting a *winnable* battle.

win·ner /ˈwɪnɚ/ *noun, pl* **-ners** [*count*]

1 : someone or something that wins a contest, prize, etc. ▪ The *winners* will receive their medals shortly. ▪ the *winners* and losers of the court case ▪ And the *winner* is . . . the blue team! ▪ You are the grand prize *winner*! [=the person who has won the grand prize]

2 *informal* : a very good or successful person or thing ▪ She's a real *winner*. ▪ That idea's a *winner*.

3 *sports* : the final goal, point, etc., that wins a game ▪ With seconds left on the clock, she scored the *winner*. — often used in combination ▪ She scored the game-*winner*.

winner's circle *noun, pl* ~ **circles** [*count*] : an area where the winner of a game, contest, etc., receives his or her award ▪ The jockey and horse approached the *winner's circle*. — sometimes used figuratively ▪ Neither golfer has been in the *winner's circle* [=neither golfer has won] for several years.

win·ning /ˈwɪnɪŋ/ *adj*

1 *always used before a noun* : relating to or producing a win ▪ the *winning* lottery ticket ▪ She scored the *winning* goal. ▪ The team is on a 12-game ***winning streak***. [=it has won 12 games in a row]

2 *always used before a noun* : successful at something ▪ They were a *winning* marketing team.

3 [*more* ~; *most* ~] : pleasing or attractive to other people ▪ a *winning* smile ▪ Chocolate and mint is a *winning* combination.

— **win·ning·ly** /ˈwɪnɪŋli/ *adv* ▪ He smiled *winningly*.

win·ning·est /ˈwɪnɪŋəst/ *adj, always used before a noun, US* : having the greatest number of wins : most successful ▪ She's the *winningest* coach in the conference. ▪ the *winningest* team in our school's history

winning post *noun* [*singular*] *Brit* : a post that marks the end of a race

win·nings /ˈwɪnɪŋz/ *noun* [*plural*] : money that is won in a game or contest ▪ The contestant's *winnings* totaled $25,000. ▪ Collect your *winnings* at the ticket booth.

win·now /ˈwɪnoʊ/ *verb* **-nows; -nowed; -now·ing** [+ *obj*]

1 : to remove (people or things that are less important, desirable, etc.) from a larger group or list ▪ The least qualified applicants were *winnowed* out of the initial pool. : to make (a list of possible choices) smaller by removing the less desirable choices ▪ The list of candidates has been *winnowed* [=*narrowed down, whittled down*] to five. — often + *down* ▪ He needs to *winnow down* his options.

2 : to remove (the unwanted coverings of seeds) from grain by throwing the grain up in the air and letting the wind blow the unwanted parts away ▪ Harvesters *winnowed* the chaff from the wheat.

wino /ˈwaɪnoʊ/ *noun, pl* **win·os** [*count*] *informal* + *disapproving* : a person who has no place to live and who is often drunk

win·some /ˈwɪnsəm/ *adj* [*more* ~; *most* ~] *formal* : cheerful, pleasant, and appealing ▪ He had a *winsome*, boyish smile.

— **win·some·ly** *adv* ▪ a *winsomely* written story — **win·some·ness** *noun* [*noncount*]

[1]**win·ter** /ˈwɪntɚ/ *noun, pl* **-ters** : the coldest season of the year that is after autumn and before spring [*count*] They spend *winters* in Florida. ▪ We're in for a cold *winter* this year, I hear. ▪ She traveled there two *winters* ago. [*noncount*] in early/late *winter* ▪ the last day of *winter* — often used before another noun ▪ the *winter* months ▪ a cold *winter* day ▪ the company's *winter* catalog ▪ *winter* clothes/coats/gloves ▪ *winter* storms/weather ▪ the *winter* holidays ▪ We went there during *winter* vacation. ▪ *winter* wheat [=a type of wheat that is planted in autumn and not harvested until the following spring or summer]

[2]**winter** *verb* **-ters; -tered; -ter·ing**

1 [*no obj*] : to spend the winter in a particular place ▪ The birds will *winter* in the southern part of the country. ▪ My family *winters* in Florida.

2 [+ *obj*] : to care for or manage (animals) during the winter ▪ The farm agreed to *winter* our horses for us.

win·ter·ize /ˈwɪntəˌraɪz/ *verb* **-iz·es; -ized; -iz·ing** [+ *obj*] *US* : to make (something) able to resist the effects of winter weather ▪ They are *winterizing* their cars by adding antifreeze and putting on snow tires.

winter sport *noun, pl* ~ **sports** [*count*] : a sport (such as ice hockey or skiing) that takes place in the winter on ice or snow

winter squash *noun, pl* ~ **squash** *or* ~ **squashes** [*count, noncount*] *US* : any one of several vegetables (such as acorn squashes and butternut squashes) that are grown until their shell and seeds are hard and that can be stored for several months — compare SUMMER SQUASH

win·ter·time /ˈwɪntəˌtaɪm/ *noun* [*noncount*] : the season of winter ▪ We enjoy skiing in the *wintertime*.

win·try /ˈwɪntri/ *also* **win·tery** /ˈwɪntəri/ *adj* **win·tri·er; -est** [*also more* ~; *most* ~]

1 : relating to, happening during, or typical of winter ▪ dark, *wintry* days ▪ a *wintry* mix of sleet and snow

2 *literary* : not cheerful or friendly ▪ She gave me a *wintry* welcome.

win–win /ˈwɪnˈwɪn/ *adj, always used before a noun* : providing a good result for everyone involved ▪ This is a *win-win* situation/deal.

winy *variant spelling of* WINEY

[1]**wipe** /ˈwaɪp/ *verb* **wipes; wiped; wip·ing** [+ *obj*]

1 : to clean or dry (something) by using a towel, your hand, etc. ▪ Would you *wipe* the dishes? ▪ She *wiped* her eyes with a tissue.
2 : to remove (something) by rubbing ▪ *Wipe* your tears. ▪ We were *wiping* the spots from the wine glasses. — often used figuratively ▪ She has *wiped* [=*erased*] the entire conversation from her mind. [=she has forgotten the entire conversation] ▪ The explosion ***wiped*** the island ***off the map.*** [=it completely destroyed the island] ▪ Their enemies have vowed to ***wipe*** them ***off the face of the earth.*** [=to destroy them completely; to annihilate them]
3 : to move (something) over a surface ▪ He *wiped* his hand across his forehead.
4 *chiefly Brit* : to completely remove recorded material from (a tape or disk) ▪ You can *wipe* [=*erase*] the tape/disk and use it again.
wipe away [*phrasal verb*] ***wipe (something) away*** *or* ***wipe away (something)*** : to remove (something) by rubbing ▪ *Wipe away* grease with our all-purpose cleaner. ▪ He *wiped* her tears *away*. — often used figuratively ▪ You cannot simply *wipe away* the history of this country.
wipe down [*phrasal verb*] ***wipe (something) down*** *or* ***wipe down (something)*** : to clean (a surface) by rubbing it with a cloth ▪ He *wiped down* the counters with a wet cloth. ▪ I *wiped* the car *down* with a towel.
wipe off [*phrasal verb*] **1** ***wipe (someone or something) off*** *or* ***wipe off (someone or something)*** : to clean (someone or something) by using a towel, your hand, etc. ▪ I *wiped off* the baby and took him out of the high chair. ▪ She *wiped* the counters *off*. **2** ***wipe (something) off*** *or* ***wipe off (something)*** : to remove (something) by rubbing ▪ I *wiped* the food *off* the baby's face. ▪ She *wiped off* the oil from the counter. — often used figuratively in British English ▪ More than a billion pounds have been *wiped off* share prices. [=the value of share prices has been reduced by more than a billion pounds]
wipe out [*phrasal verb*] **1** *US, informal* : to fall down violently especially when riding a bicycle, surfing, skiing, etc. ▪ The cyclist *wiped out* coming around the curve. — see also WIPEOUT **2** ***wipe (someone or something) out*** *or* ***wipe out (someone or something)*** : to kill or destroy (someone or something) completely ▪ Drought *wiped out* our crops this year. ▪ Doctors think they can *wipe out* the disease. ▪ One bad investment could *wipe out* your life savings. **3** ***wipe (someone) out*** : to make (someone) very tired ▪ That game completely *wiped me out*. — see also WIPED OUT
wipe (something) clean **1** : to clean (something) by wiping ▪ I *wiped* the table *clean*. **2** : to completely remove something from (something) : to remove everything from (something) — usually used as *(be) wiped clean* ▪ The computer's hard drive has *been wiped clean*. ▪ After the accident, his memory of the day *was wiped clean*. [=he could not remember anything about the day]
wipe that/the smile/smirk/grin off someone's face *informal* : to stop smiling or to make someone stop smiling or feeling happy ▪ She couldn't *wipe the smile off her face*. [=she couldn't stop smiling] ▪ He thinks he's won, but if I get my hands on him, I'll *wipe that smile off his face*! — often used to tell someone in an angry way to stop smiling ▪ *Wipe that smile off your face*! This isn't a joke!
wipe the floor with *informal* : to beat or defeat (someone or something) completely ▪ I thought I could beat him, but he *wiped the floor with* me.
wipe the slate clean : to forget all the things that have happened or been done and start doing something again : to start again from the very beginning ▪ She wishes she could *wipe the slate clean* and start over in a different career.
wipe up [*phrasal verb*] ***wipe (something) up*** *or* ***wipe up (something)*** : to use a cloth to remove (something) from a surface ▪ Will you *wipe up* that spill? ▪ I *wiped* the milk *up* off the floor.

[2]**wipe** *noun, pl* **wipes** [*count*]
1 : a small, wet cloth that is used for cleaning ▪ disposable *wipes* ▪ baby *wipes* [=wipes used to clean babies]
2 : an act of cleaning or drying something by using a towel, your hand, etc. ▪ With a *wipe*, the spill was gone. ▪ I gave the table a quick *wipe*. [=I quickly *wiped* the table]

wiped /ˈwaɪpt/ *adj* [*more ~; most ~*] *US, informal* : extremely tired : WIPED OUT ▪ After my workout, I was *wiped*.

wiped out *adj* [*more ~; most ~*] *informal* : extremely tired ▪ I am completely *wiped out*. — see also *wipe out* at [1]WIPE

wipe·out /ˈwaɪpˌaʊt/ *noun, pl* **-outs** [*count*] *US* : a sudden, violent fall by someone who is riding a bicycle, surfing, skiing, etc. ▪ The surfer had a nasty *wipeout*. — see also *wipe out* at [1]WIPE

wip·er /ˈwaɪpɚ/ *noun, pl* **-ers** [*count*] : WINDSHIELD WIPER

[1]**wire** /ˈwajɚ/ *noun, pl* **wires**
1 : a thin, flexible thread of metal [*noncount*] The flowers were bound together with thin *wire*. ▪ copper/aluminum *wire* ▪ a *wire* rack/fence ▪ *wire* brushes [*count*] There was a *wire* sticking out of the chair. — see also BARBED WIRE, BARBWIRE, CHICKEN WIRE, HIGH WIRE, TRIPWIRE, UNDERWIRE
2 [*count*] : a thread of metal that is covered with plastic, rubber, etc., and used to send or receive electricity or electrical signals ▪ A telephone *wire* had fallen on the road during the storm. ▪ A short black *wire* connects the computer's monitor to its keyboard. ▪ corroded *wires* — see also LIVE WIRE
3 [*singular*] *US* : a small microphone that is worn under clothing in order to secretly record a conversation ▪ The undercover officer wore a *wire* to her meeting with the drug dealer.
4 *chiefly US* **a** [*noncount*] : a service that sends news stories from one central office to many newspapers, magazines, television stations, etc. ▪ This story just came over the *wire*. [=*wire service*] **b** [*count*] : TELEGRAM ▪ They just received a *wire* from their daughter.
5 ***the wire*** *US* : a thin piece of string that the winner of a race breaks through at the end of the race ▪ She was ahead by two seconds at *the wire*. ▪ The marathon ended in a sprint to *the wire* by the two top runners. — often used figuratively ▪ Both candidates are prepared for a sprint to *the wire* as election day approaches. ▪ The committee was undecided ***right up to the wire.*** [=until the very end] ▪ We ***took them to the wire*** in last year's championship. [=we forced them to compete very hard against us until the end of the game] ▪ The election ***went/came (right) down to the wire.*** [=the election was not decided until the very end]
get/have your wires crossed *informal, of two people* : to fail to understand each other : to be confused because each person has a different idea about what is happening or being said ▪ We *got our wires crossed* for a minute there—I thought you were asking me something else. ▪ We must have *had our wires crossed*.
under the wire *chiefly US* : before something ends : at the end of the time when it is still possible to do something ▪ Her application got/came in ***just under the wire.*** [=*just in time*]
wire to wire *chiefly US, sports* : from the beginning of a race, game, etc., until the end ▪ He led the race (from) *wire to wire*. — see also WIRE-TO-WIRE
– **wire·like** /ˈwajɚˌlaɪk/ *adj* [*more ~; most ~*] ▪ the animal's stiff, *wirelike* hairs

[2]**wire** *verb* **wires; wired; wir·ing** [+ *obj*]
1 **a** : to provide (a building, room, etc.) with wires for a particular service or for electricity ▪ The house will be *wired* next week. ▪ My room is *wired* for cable. **b** : to connect (a device) to another device by using wires ▪ The microphone is *wired* to the speaker. ▪ You can *wire* the generator to a car battery. — see also HOT-WIRE
2 : to use wire to close or hold (something) ▪ Her jaw was *wired* shut after the accident.
3 **a** : to send (money) by using electronic methods ▪ She *wired* the money home to Canada. ▪ Can you *wire* me $300? **b** *chiefly US, old-fashioned* : to send a telegram to (someone) ▪ When you get in to town, *wire* me.

wire cutters *noun* [*plural*] : a tool that is used for cutting wire ▪ a pair of *wire cutters*

wired *adj*
1 [*more ~; most ~*] *chiefly US, informal* : very excited or full of nervous energy ▪ No more caffeine for me, I'm pretty *wired*. ▪ a group of *wired* teenagers ▪ She's a nice girl but she's ***wired (a little) too tight/tightly.*** [=she's too nervous or too energetic]
2 : connected to the Internet ▪ a *wired* classroom
3 — used to say that someone does or does not have a natural tendency to behave in a certain way, to like something, etc. ▪ I'm just not *wired* to like broccoli. ▪ Everyone's brain is *wired* differently. — see also HARDWIRED

wire fraud *noun* [*noncount*] : the crime of stealing money by using computers, telephones, etc. ▪ He was charged with *wire fraud*.

wire·haired /ˈwajɚˈheɚd/ *adj, of animals* : having an outer coat of hair that is very stiff like wire ▪ *wirehaired* dogs

[1]**wire·less** /ˈwajɚləs/ *adj*

1 : not using wires to send and receive electronic signals : sending and receiving electronic signals by using radio waves • The video game console comes with *wireless* controllers. • a *wireless* microphone

2 : of or relating to the use of radio waves to send and receive electronic signals • The café offers free *wireless* Internet access. • *wireless* communications • (*US*) I got a new cell phone from my ***wireless provider***. [=from the company that provides me with cell phone service]

[2]**wireless** *noun, pl* **-less•es** [*count*] *chiefly Brit, old-fashioned* : [1]RADIO • She listened to the *wireless* every Monday night.

wire service *noun, pl* **~ -vices** [*count*] : a news organization that sends news stories to many newspapers, magazines, etc. • The story was reported by several *wire services*.

[1]**wire•tap** /ˈwajɚˌtæp/ *noun, pl* **-taps** [*count*]

1 : a device that allows someone to secretly listen to phone conversations : TAP • Federal agents put a *wiretap* on his phone.

2 : a conversation that has been recorded using a wiretap • Investigators listened to the *wiretaps* for clues about the suspect's whereabouts.

[2]**wiretap** *verb* **-taps; -tapped; -tap•ping** [+ *obj*] : to place a device on (someone's phone) in order to secretly listen to telephone calls : TAP • The FBI *wiretapped* his phone.

– wire•tap•per /ˈwajɚˌtæpɚ/ *noun, pl* **-pers** [*count*] • *Wiretappers* bugged her phone.

wiretapping *noun* [*noncount*] : the act of secretly placing a microphone inside a telephone in order to hear and record private conversations • *Wiretapping* is illegal without a court order. — called also (*Brit*) *phone tapping*

wire–to–wire *adj, chiefly US, sports* — used to describe a race, game, etc., in which someone leads from the beginning until the end • He achieved a *wire-to-wire* win/victory in last year's race. • He was the *wire-to-wire* winner. — see also *wire to wire* at [1]WIRE

wire wool *noun* [*noncount*] *Brit* : STEEL WOOL

wiring *noun* [*noncount*] : the system of wires that carry electricity in a particular place, device, etc. • All the *wiring* in the house needs to be replaced. • He fixed the radio's *wiring*.

wiry /ˈwajəri/ *adj* **wir•i•er** /ˈwarijɚ/; **-est** [*or more ~; most ~*]

1 : very thin but strong and muscular • a man with long, *wiry* arms • She was lean and *wiry* from years of working out.

2 : stiff like wire • He has dark, *wiry* hair. • the dog's *wiry* coat/fur

Wis. *or* **Wisc.** *abbr* Wisconsin

wis•dom /ˈwɪzdəm/ *noun* [*noncount*]

1 **a** : knowledge that is gained by having many experiences in life • She has gained a lot of *wisdom* over the years. **b** : the natural ability to understand things that most other people cannot understand • a young person of great *wisdom* **c** : knowledge of what is proper or reasonable • He had the *wisdom* to stop before he said too much. : good sense or judgment • I fail to see the *wisdom* in doing that.

2 : advice or information given to a person • folk/divine *wisdom* • He shared a valuable bit of *wisdom* with his daughter. • These stories offer plenty of *wisdom* to readers. — see also CONVENTIONAL WISDOM

in someone's (infinite) wisdom — used in an ironic way to say that someone has made a foolish choice or decision • He decided, *in his infinite wisdom*, that it would be better to sell the house than to keep it.

pearls of wisdom see PEARL

wisdom tooth *noun, pl* **~ teeth** [*count*] : one of four large teeth in the back of your mouth that do not appear until you are an adult

[1]**wise** /ˈwaɪz/ *adj* **wis•er; -est**

1 : having or showing wisdom or knowledge usually from learning or experiencing many things • a *wise* old woman • a *wise* saying • I'm a little *wiser* now than I was back then. — see also PENNY-WISE, STREETWISE

2 : based on good reasoning or information : showing good sense or judgment • The *wisest* course of action would be to leave. • It was *wise* of you to ask permission first. = You were *wise* to ask permission first. • That was a *wise* choice. • Many have benefited from her *wise* counsel/advice.

3 *US, informal* : saying things that are rude or insulting • Don't you get *wise* [=*smart, fresh*] with me, young man!

a word to the wise see [1]WORD

crack wise see [1]CRACK

none the wiser *or* ***not any the wiser*** 1 : not knowing or understanding anything more about something • The investigation has been going on for months, and we're still *none the wiser* about the true cause of the accident. [=we still don't know anything more about the true cause] 2 *also* ***never the wiser*** — used to describe someone who is not at all aware of something that has happened • I borrowed his car and returned it, and he was *none the wiser*. [=he did not know that I had borrowed his car] • We left early, and *no one was any the wiser*. [=no one noticed that we had left]

wise in the ways of : having knowledge about or experience with (someone or something) • Don't worry. They're *wise in the ways of* finances. • She is *wise in the ways of* the world.

wise to *informal* : not fooled by (someone or something) • I'm *wise to* you. = I'm *wise to* what you're doing. [=I know what you're doing; I know that you are trying to do something dishonest] : aware of (something, especially something dishonest) • When she ***got wise to*** [=became aware of] his scheme, she left. • He told me I'd better *get wise to* what was happening. • (*chiefly US*) Let me ***put/make you wise to*** [=tell you about] their plans.

– wise•ly *adv* [*more ~; most ~*] • The witness *wisely* refused to answer the question. • If you invest *wisely*, you can make a lot of money. • Try to choose your words more *wisely*.

[2]**wise** *verb* **wis•es; wised; wis•ing**

wise up [*phrasal verb*] *informal* 1 : to become aware of what is really happening — often + *to* • They finally *wised up to* the fact that they were being cheated. 2 : to start to think and act in a more intelligent way • They could lose everything they have if they don't *wise up*. [=*smarten up*]

-wise /ˌwaɪz/ *combining form*

1 **a** : in the position or direction of • cross*wise* [=in a direction that goes across something] • length*wise* **b** : in the manner of • moving crab*wise* [=moving like a crab]

2 *informal* : with regard to : CONCERNING • She has made some bad choices career-*wise*. [=she has made some bad choices about her career] • Style-*wise*, their music is very different from mine. [=the style of their music is very different from mine] • Health-*wise*, I'm doing fine. [=my health is fine]

wise•acre /ˈwaɪzˌeɪkɚ/ *noun, pl* **-acres** [*count*] *chiefly US, informal + old-fashioned* : a person who says or does things that are funny but also annoying : SMART-ALECK • Quit being such a *wiseacre* and help your mother.

wise•ass /ˈwaɪzˌæs/ *noun, pl* **-ass•es** [*count*] *US, informal + impolite* : a person who says things that are funny but also rude or offensive — usually singular • You're such a *wiseass*. • His *wiseass* comments got him thrown out of class.

wise•crack /ˈwaɪzˌkræk/ *noun, pl* **-cracks** [*count*] *informal* : a funny and smart comment or joke • Someone in the theater was making *wisecracks* during the entire movie.

– wisecrack *verb* **-cracks; -cracked; -crack•ing** [*no obj*] • She's always *wisecracking* [=(*US*) *cracking wise*] in class. • a *wisecracking* waitress • Quit your *wisecracking*.

wise guy /ˈwaɪzˌgaɪ/ *noun, pl* **~ guys** [*count*] *informal*

1 *chiefly US* : a person who says or does things that are funny but also annoying or somewhat rude • Quit being a *wise guy*. • No more *wise-guy* remarks, got it?

2 *usually* ***wise•guy*** *US* : someone who is part of a secret organized group of criminals : MOBSTER • a movie about two *wiseguys*

[1]**wish** /ˈwɪʃ/ *verb* **wish•es; wished; wish•ing**

1 [+ *obj*] : to want (something) to be true or to happen • I *wish* (that) you were here. • I only *wish* (that) I knew what was going on. • He was *wishing* (that) she would leave him alone. • I *wish* (that) you would be quiet and listen to me.

2 [+ *obj*] *formal* : to want or ask to do (something) • You may use the telephone, if you *wish*. • You can ***do as you wish***. [=you can do whatever you want to do] — often followed by *to + verb* • Ms. Jones *wishes to see* you. • I *wish to speak* with your supervisor. • He *wished to be* left alone.

3 [+ *obj*] **a** : to want (someone) to be in a particular state • I *wish* him well. [=I hope that good things happen to him] • She *wished* him dead. • I *wish* you no harm. [=I don't want to harm you; I don't want you to be harmed] — see also WELL-WISHER **b** : to say that you hope someone will have happiness, health, etc. • I *wish* you both much happiness. = I *wish* great happiness for you both. [=I hope that you will both be very happy] • She *wished* them a happy New Year. • We *wish* you a Merry Christmas. • I ***wish you luck*** [=I hope you will have good luck]

4 [*no obj*] **a** : to think about something that you want and hope that you will get it or that it will happen in some magi-

cal way : to make a wish • Children *wished* upon a star [=made a wish while looking at a star] in the hopes that their dreams would come true. — usually + *for* • She closed her eyes, *wished for* a pony, and blew out the candles on her birthday cake. **b** : to hope for something that usually cannot be had — + *for* • He *wished for* a second chance. • We all *wish for* world peace. • I couldn't *wish for* a better friend than you. [=you are the best friend I could have]

(be) careful what you wish for — used to tell people to think before they say that they want something and to suggest that they may not actually want it • You think having twins would be fun? *Be careful what you wish for*, you may just get it.

I wish *or* ***don't I wish*** *informal* — used to say that you want something to happen but that you know it will probably not happen • "Did he ask you to the dance?" "*I wish*!" [=I wish he would ask me to the dance but he hasn't] • "Will you be getting the job?" "*Don't I wish*!"

wish away [*phrasal verb*] ***wish (something) away*** *or* ***wish away (something)*** : to cause (something) to stop or go away just by wanting it to stop or go away • You can't just *wish* your problems *away*.

wish on [*phrasal verb*] ***wish (someone or something) on (someone)*** : to want (someone) to have or be affected by (someone or something bad or unpleasant) • I wouldn't *wish* that terrible illness *on* anyone. [=I wouldn't want anyone to have that terrible illness] • I wouldn't *wish* it *on* my worst enemy. • I wouldn't *wish* that man *on* any woman.

you wish *or* ***don't you wish*** *informal* — used to tell people in a rude way that it is unlikely that they will get what they want • Give you a kiss? *You wish*. [=*dream on*] • You think she's going to ask you out? *Don't you wish*!

[2]**wish** *noun, pl* **wishes**

1 [*count*] : a desire for something to happen or be done : a feeling of wanting to do or have something • Please respect my *wishes* [=please do what I want you to do] and leave me alone. • It is my *wish* that my estate go to my granddaughter. [=I want my estate to go to my granddaughter] • He has a *wish* to be reunited with his son. • She has expressed a *wish* to retire [=has said she wants to retire] within the next two years. • I ***have no wish*** [=I do not want] to interfere in your plans. • It was her ***dying wish*** to see them married. [=it was the last thing she wanted before she died] • They did it ***against my wishes***. [=they did it even though they knew that I did not want them to do it] • They ***went against their parents' wishes*** and got married. [=they got married even though they knew that their parents did not want them to] — see also DEATH WISH

2 [*count*] : an act of thinking about something that you want and hoping that you will get it or that it will happen in some magical way • The genie will grant you three *wishes*. • Close your eyes and ***make a wish***. [=wish for something] • I ***got my wish***. = My ***wish came true***. [=I got what I wished for]

3 ***wishes*** [*plural*] : good thoughts or feelings directed toward a person • Send her my good/best *wishes*. • Best *wishes*!

pious wish see PIOUS

your wish is my command *humorous* — used to say that you will do what someone else wants you to do • "Could you put these dishes away for me?" "*Your wish is my command*."

wish•bone /ˈwɪʃˌboʊn/ *noun, pl* **-bones** [*count*] : a bone that is at the front of a bird's chest and that is shaped like a V ✧ When a chicken or turkey is eaten, its *wishbone* is traditionally dried and held by two people who each make a wish and pull the bone apart. The person who gets the bigger piece of the bone is supposed to get his or her wish.

wish•ful /ˈwɪʃfəl/ *adj* [*more* ~; *most* ~] : showing a belief that something will happen or succeed even though it is not likely to happen or succeed • her *wishful* attempts to change her husband's bad habits

wishful thinking *noun* [*noncount*] : an attitude or belief that something you want to happen will happen even though it is not likely or possible • The idea that the enemy will immediately surrender is nothing more than *wishful thinking*.

wishing well *noun, pl* ~ **wells** [*count*] : a well that people throw coins into while making a wish

wish list *noun, pl* ~ **lists** [*count*] : a list of things that someone would like to have • That book is on my *wish list*.

wishy–washy /ˈwɪʃiˌwɑːʃi/ *adj* **-wash•i•er**; **-est** [*also more* ~; *most* ~] *disapproving* : not having or showing strong ideas or beliefs about something : weak and not able or not willing to act • He gave me some *wishy-washy* answer. • *wishy-washy* politicians

wisp /ˈwɪsp/ *noun, pl* **wisps** [*count*]

1 : a thin streak of smoke, mist, etc. • *Wisps* of steam rose up from the teapot. • a *wisp* of smoke

2 : a thin thread or strand of something (such as hair) • A few *wisps* (of hair) framed the sides of her face. • *Wisps* of cotton candy clung to his mouth.

3 : a small amount of something • By the morning, there was just a *wisp* [=*bit*] of snow left on the ground. • There was a *wisp* of a smile [=a very slight smile] on her lips.

4 : a small and thin person • I met her when she was just ***a wisp of a girl***. [=a thin young girl]

– see also WILL-O'-THE-WISP

wispy /ˈwɪspi/ *adj* **wisp•i•er**; **-est**

1 : very thin and light • high *wispy* clouds • She wore a dress made from some *wispy* material.

2 *of hair* : not thick or full • soft *wispy* bangs • He had the *wispy* beginnings of a beard.

3 *of a voice* : very soft and quiet • a high, *wispy* voice

wis•te•ria /wɪˈstirijə/ *noun, pl* **-rias** [*count, noncount*] : a plant that grows as a thick vine with large bunches of purple or white flowers

wist•ful /ˈwɪstfəl/ *adj* [*more* ~; *most* ~] : having or showing sad thoughts and feelings about something that you want to have or do and especially about something that made you happy in the past • She was *wistful* for a moment, then asked, "Do you remember the old playground?" • He had a *wistful* look on his face.

– **wist•ful•ly** *adv* • He gazed at her *wistfully*. – **wist•ful•ness** *noun* [*noncount*]

wit /ˈwɪt/ *noun, pl* **wits**

1 [*noncount*] : an ability to say or write things that are clever and usually funny • She is full of *wit* and vivacity. • His latest book doesn't have the same *wit* as his earlier books. • The book is a collection of his ***wit and wisdom***.

2 [*count*] : a person who is known for making clever and funny remarks • She was a famous writer and *wit*. — see also HALF-WIT, NITWIT

3 a ***wits*** [*plural*] : the ability to think or reason • She's got the *wits* [=*intelligence*] to make it work. • He learned to ***live by his wits***. [=to survive by doing clever and sometimes dishonest things] • She can ***keep her wits about her*** [=remain calm and able to think clearly] in a crisis. • He needed a moment to ***gather/collect his wits*** [=to become calm and able to think clearly] after the collision. • (*chiefly US*) The chess champion will ***match wits*** [=*compete*] with a computer. = (*chiefly Brit*) He will ***pit his wits*** against a computer. — see also *battle of wits* at [1]BATTLE **b** ***the wit*** : the ability to make good decisions • She had *the wit* [=the good sense] to leave before the situation got any worse.

at (your) wit's end (*chiefly US*) *or* ***at (your) wits' end*** : not able to continue thinking or trying to solve a problem : upset and unable to think of what needs to be done • I've spent six hours trying to fix my computer, but now I'm *at my wit's end*. • She's *at her wit's end* trying to keep her brother out of trouble.

out of your wits *informal* — used for emphasis with verbs like *scare* and *frighten* • I was *scared out of my wits*! [=I was very scared; I was so scared that I couldn't think clearly]

to wit *formal* — used before stating the specific thing or example being discussed • This can only mean two things, *to wit*: that he lied, or that he is wrong.

witch /ˈwɪʧ/ *noun, pl* **witch•es** [*count*]

1 : a woman who is thought to have magic powers

2 : a person who practices magic as part of a religion (such as Wicca) • an herbalist and self-proclaimed *witch*

3 *informal* : a very unpleasant woman • Her mother-in-law is a bitter old *witch*.

– **witchy** /ˈwɪʧi/ *adj* **witch•i•er**; **-est** • She gave a *witchy* cackle. • His mother is a nasty, *witchy* old woman.

witch•craft /ˈwɪʧˌkræft, *Brit* ˈwɪʧˌkrɑːft/ *noun* [*noncount*] : magical things that are done by witches : the use of magical powers obtained especially from evil spirits • The villagers blamed their problems on *witchcraft*. [=*sorcery*]

witch doctor *noun, pl* ~ **-tors** [*count*] : a person in some cultures who is believed to have magic powers and to be able to cure illness and fight off evil spirits, curses, etc.

witches' brew *or* **witch's brew** *noun, pl* ~ **brews** [*count*] : a mixture of dangerous or unpleasant things • a *witches' brew* of hate and lies

witch hazel *noun* [*noncount*] : a lotion that is made from the bark of a plant and that is used to heal the skin

witch hunt *noun, pl* ~ **hunts** [*count*] *disapproving* : the act of unfairly looking for and punishing people who are accused of having opinions that are believed to be dangerous or evil • He was the victim of a congressional *witch hunt* against Communists.

witching hour *noun*

the witching hour **1** : the time late at night when the powers of a witch, magician, etc., are believed to be strongest **2** : MIDNIGHT • We arrived home shortly before *the witching hour*.

with /ˈwɪθ, ˈwɪð/ *prep*

1 — used to say that people or things are together in one place • Do you have your books *with* you? • I left the money in the car (along) *with* my keys. • The children are home *with* their father. • The doctor will be *with* you shortly. [=the doctor will come to see you soon] • We barely escaped ***with our lives***. [=we almost died while trying to escape]

2 — used to say that two or more people or things are doing something together or are involved in something • He went to the store *with* her. • Do you want to come *with* us? • I need to speak *with* you for a moment. • She was talking *with* a friend on the phone. • They usually study *with* me after class. • He works *with* his mother at the restaurant. • We are in competition for customers *with* a lot of other companies.

3 : having (a particular characteristic, possession, etc.) • a boy *with* green eyes [=a boy who has green eyes] • She's the one *with* (the) long hair and sunglasses. • He wants to marry someone *with* a lot of money. • You will be competing against people *with* more experience than you. • people *with* pets • She taught a class *with* [=that had] 20 students in it. • They graduated from college *with* honors.

4 : using (something specified) • She opened the door *with* her key. • He broke the window *with* a rock. • She walks *with* (the help of) a cane. • The sauce is made *with* milk and cheese. • He welcomed each of his guests *with* a handshake. • He entertained the crowd *with* a few jokes. • She ended her speech *with* a quote from Shakespeare. • *With* one kiss, the princess awoke and the spell was broken. • "*With* this ring, I thee wed."

5 — used to refer to the feeling, thought, quality, etc., that someone has or experiences when doing something • Please accept this gift *with* our thanks. • He spoke about his daughter *with* great pride. [=he spoke about his daughter very proudly] • She supports the idea, *with* reservations. [=she supports the idea but she has some concerns about it] • They accepted the offer *with* certain conditions. • You acted *with* great courage and skill. • They did it *with* no difficulty at all. [=they did it very easily]

6 — used to indicate the cause of something • His face was wet *with* [=because of] tears. • She was red *with* embarrassment. • They all wept *with* sorrow at the news of his death. • He was sick *with* the flu for a week.

7 — used to say that something fills something, covers something, etc. • The garage is filled *with* junk.

8 — used to indicate a related fact or situation • He stood there *with* [=*holding*] his hat in his hand. • It's hard to concentrate on my homework *with* the television on. [=while the television is on] • Our products have been designed *with* you in mind. [=especially for you] • They made it there *with* no time to spare. • The coach called time out *with* [=when there were] 10 seconds left on the clock. • *With* her on our team, there's no way we can lose. • *With* friends like that [=when you have such bad friends], who needs enemies?

9 — used to indicate the specific thing or person that is being referred to • Please be careful *with* those boxes. [=please handle those boxes carefully] • They are on friendly terms *with* their neighbors. • He's great *with* children. [=children like him and behave well for him] • I'm not very good *with* computers. [=I am not able to use computers well] • She no longer has any influence *with* [=*on, over*] them.

10 — used to say that someone has a relationship with a person, organization, etc. • He has been *with* the same woman for 35 years. • I plan to be *with* [=I plan to work for] the company until I retire.

11 — used to say that someone or something is the object of attention, behavior, or a feeling • I'm in love *with* you. • She is very angry *with* them. • He seems to be quite happy *with* his new job. • Were you satisfied *with* the way things turned out? • I don't want to get tough *with* you, but you have to learn to obey your mother. • What's going on *with* Jim? = What's happening *with* Jim?

12 : in the performance, condition, behavior, or quality of (something or someone) • What's the problem *with* your car? • The trouble *with* this computer is that it is too slow. • Is there a problem *with* your meal? • The doctors are trying to figure out what is wrong *with* him. • What's the matter *with* you? Are you upset about something? • (*informal*) ***What's with*** her? [=why is she acting so strangely?]

13 : in opposition to or against (someone) • The boys were fighting/arguing *with* each other. • We had a disagreement *with* our neighbors over the height of the new fence.

14 : so as to be separated from (someone or something) • She broke (ties) *with* her friends [=she no longer sees or talks to her friends] because of the incident. • They were my favorite books, and I hated to part *with* them.

15 a — used to say that you agree with or understand someone • "Do you see why I feel this way?" "Oh yes, I'm *with* you completely." • Are you still *with* me? [=are you still listening to me and understanding what I am saying?] **b** : supporting the beliefs or goals of (someone) : on the side of (someone) • If he's for helping the poor, I'm *with* him all the way! • You're either *with* [=*for*] us or against us. • Let's do it. Are you *with* me?

16 : in the opinion or judgment of (someone) • It's fine *with* [=*by*] us if you want to come, too. • That's okay *with* me.

17 : according to the experience or behavior of (someone) • It became a habit *with* them [=it became their habit] to read before going to bed. • As *with* many of her generation, she had lost interest in politics. • Promises are sacred *with* [=*for*] him. • *With* him, a promise is a promise.

18 : as successfully as (someone) • He can ski *with* the best of them. [=he can ski as well as the best skiers]

19 — used to say that things happen at the same time • The birds returned *with* the arrival of spring. • The book fell to the floor *with* a loud bang. • All of their games begin *with* the singing of the national anthem.

20 : in a way that changes according to (something) • The pressure varies *with* the depth. • Her health should improve *with* time. • The excitement grows *with* each passing day. [=there is more excitement each day]

21 : in the same direction as (something) • Sand the wood *with* the grain, not against it. • We were sailing *with* the wind.

22 — used to say that someone or something is included in a total number or amount • *With* [=*including*] my husband and me, there were 12 people at the party. • It costs $10.35 *with* tax.

23 : in spite of (something) • It's hard to believe that, *with* all her talent and hard work, she still didn't win the competition. • They love the team, *with* all its faults.

24 — used to indicate the object of an adverb in a type of command • Off *with* his head! [=cut off his head] • Away *with* her. [=take her away from here] • Down *with* injustice!

what with see [3]WHAT

with it *informal* **1** : in a state in which you are thinking clearly and aware of what is happening • I had just woken up and wasn't quite *with it* yet. • Come on, now. ***Get with it***. **2** : knowing a lot about current styles, ideas, or events • You have to be pretty *with it* if you want to talk to them about politics.

with that : immediately after doing or saying that • She said goodbye and closed the door behind her. And *with that*, she was gone.

with·draw /wɪðˈdrɑː, wɪθˈdrɑː/ *verb* **-draws; -drew** /-ˈdruː/; **-drawn** /-ˈdrɑːn/; **-draw·ing**

1 [+ *obj*] : to remove (money) from a bank account • She *withdrew* $200 from her checking account.

2 [+ *obj*] : to take (something) back so that it is no longer available • The pills were *withdrawn* [=*recalled*] from the market because they were unsafe.

3 [+ *obj*] *formal* : to take back (something that is spoken, offered, etc.) • The company *withdrew* [=*retracted*] the job offer. • The prosecutor *withdrew* her question to the witness. • They have *withdrawn* the charges. • *withdraw* support for a candidate

4 [*no obj*] : to stop participating in something • Students can *withdraw* from a class anytime until the last week of the semester. • The injury forced him to *withdraw* from [=*drop out of*] the tournament.

5 a *of soldiers* : to leave an area [*no obj*] The troops were forced to *withdraw*. • They *withdrew* from the battlefield. [+ *obj*] The troops were *withdrawn* [=*pulled back*] from the front line. **b** [*no obj*] *somewhat formal* + *old-fashioned* : to leave a room, area, etc., and go to another place — + *to* • He retired and *withdrew* [=*moved*] *to* the country. • After dinner, we *withdrew to* the library.

6 [*no obj*] : to stop spending time with other people : to spend more time alone and gradually stop talking to other people — often + *from* or *into* ▪ She *withdrew from* other people as she grew older. ▪ He *withdrew into* himself after his brother's death. — see also WITHDRAWN

7 [+ *obj*] : to take (something) back, away, or out ▪ He *withdrew* [=*removed*] his hand from the doorknob.

with·draw·al /wɪðˈdrɑːəl, wɪθˈdrɑːəl/ *noun, pl* **-als**

1 [*count*] **a** : an act of moving something away or taking something away ▪ The general authorized the *withdrawal* of troops from the fields. ▪ a *withdrawal* of support **b** : an act of ending your involvement in something ▪ He announced his *withdrawal* from the campaign. [=announced that he would no longer be involved in the campaign]

2 : the act of taking money out of a bank account [*count*] a *withdrawal* of $3,000 ▪ She ***made a withdrawal*** from her checking/savings account. [*noncount*] The bank charges you for the premature *withdrawal* of funds. [=for taking out money before you are supposed to] — opposite DEPOSIT

3 [*noncount*] **a** : the act or process of stopping the use of an addictive drug ▪ He underwent rehab to help him through his *withdrawal* from heroin. **b** : the physical and mental problems that occur for a period of time after a person stops using an addictive drug ▪ She experienced symptoms of nicotine *withdrawal* after she quit smoking.

with·drawn /wɪðˈdrɑːn, wɪθˈdrɑːn/ *adj* [*more ~; most ~*] : very quiet and usually shy : not talking much to other people ▪ He became more *withdrawn* after his brother's death. ▪ She was *withdrawn* as a child but is now more outgoing.

with·er /ˈwɪðɚ/ *verb* **-ers; -ered; -er·ing** [*no obj*] *of a plant* : to become dry and weak ▪ The plants *withered* and died. — often used figuratively ▪ The economy has *withered.* [=has become weaker] — often + *away* ▪ Our hopes have *withered away.* [=died away]

withered *adj* [*more ~; most ~*]

1 *of a plant* : dry and weak ▪ *withered* leaves

2 : thin and wrinkled because of illness, old age, etc. ▪ an old man with a *withered* face

with·er·ing /ˈwɪðərɪŋ/ *adj* [*more ~; most ~*] : very harsh, severe, or damaging ▪ The book has been the subject of *withering* criticism. ▪ She gave me a *withering* look.

with·ers /ˈwɪðɚz/ *noun* [*plural*] : the ridge between the shoulder bones of a horse ▪ The horse stands six feet high at the *withers.* — see picture at HORSE

with·hold /wɪθˈhoʊld, wɪðˈhoʊld/ *verb* **-holds; -held** /-ˈhɛld/; **-hold·ing** [+ *obj*]

1 : to hold (something) back ▪ You can *withhold* the fee until the work is complete. [=you can wait to pay the fee until after the work is complete] ▪ His letter was published in the newspaper but he asked that his name be *withheld.* [=that his name not be printed]

2 : to refuse to provide (something) ▪ She was accused of *withholding* evidence.

3 *US* : to take out (an amount of money for taxes) from someone's income ▪ She has $20 *withheld* from her paycheck every week.

withholding tax *noun, pl* **~ taxes** [*count*] *US* : money that is taken from a person's pay and given directly to the government as income tax — called also (*Brit*) *PAYE*

[1]**with·in** /wɪˈðɪn, wɪˈθɪn/ *prep*

1 **a** : inside (a certain area or space) ▪ They live *within* the city limits. ▪ *within* the country's borders ▪ The company's most important decisions are made *within* these four walls. [=inside this room] ▪ We could hear sounds coming from *within* his apartment. **b** : inside (a group, company, society, etc.) ▪ Reports from *within* the company indicate a change in policy. ▪ Divisions *within* the party [=disagreements between members of the party] are growing.

2 : before the end of (a particular period of time) ▪ Most students find a job *within* a year of graduating. ▪ Scientists predict that a cure will be found *within* (the next) five years. ▪ She made several friends *within* days of moving into her new apartment. ▪ He entered the house, and *within* seconds, he was surrounded by children. ▪ We should know the results of your test ***within the space of*** an hour. [=in an hour or less]

3 : less than (a particular distance) from something or someone ▪ Everything I need is *within* a few miles of my apartment. ▪ The school is *within* walking distance (of our house). ▪ Everything is ***within easy reach*** [=*nearby*] ▪ I keep my dictionary ***within reach*** [=close enough to reach] on my desk. ▪ The hotel is ***within sight*** of the ocean. [=you can see the ocean from the hotel]

4 : not beyond the limits of (something) ▪ They encourage living *within* your means/income and not using credit cards excessively. ▪ Let's try to stay *within* our/the budget. ▪ It is *within* the jurisdiction of the state to make such laws. ▪ Their actions fell *within* the guidelines [=they were acceptable according to the rules] set by the committee. ▪ It is *within* the realm of possibility [=it is possible], but it is not likely.

5 — used to say how close someone is or was to doing or achieving something ▪ She is currently *within* two hundred votes of being elected. ▪ Twice this season, they have come *within* five points of winning. [=they have lost by five or fewer points]

6 : in the thoughts or character of (someone) ▪ She searched *within* herself for the truth. ▪ The problem lies not with other people but *within* yourself. [=you are the problem]

[2]**within** *adv, formal*

1 : inside something ▪ We could hear sounds coming from *within.* ▪ The sign on the door says "Help Wanted: Inquire *Within.*"

2 : in someone's inner thoughts, feelings, etc. ▪ We all try to appear strong and attempt to hide the scared little child *within.* ▪ They were outwardly calm but nervous *within.* ▪ The truth lies *within.*

[1]**with·out** /wɪˈðaʊt, wɪˈθaʊt/ *prep*

1 : not having or including (something) ▪ Do you take your coffee with or *without* sugar? ▪ Don't leave home *without* your wallet. ▪ *Without* water, there would be no life on Earth. ▪ a world *without* war ▪ They were *without* electricity [=they did not have electricity] for a week after the storm. ▪ She's the one *without* the hat. [=the one who is not wearing a hat] ▪ I can't imagine life *without* a car. ▪ They fought *without* fear. [=they were not afraid when they fought] ▪ They managed to finish it *without* (experiencing) any difficulty. ▪ She survived the accident *without* serious injury. [=she was not seriously injured] ▪ It happened suddenly and *without* warning. ▪ He disappeared *without* a trace. [=there was no trace of him after he disappeared] ▪ We kept trying *without* success. [=we kept trying but we did not succeed] ▪ The prisoner will be held *without* bail until his trial. ▪ Applicants are considered ***without regard for*** age, race, religion, or sex. [=an applicant's age, race, religion, or sex are not important]

2 — used to say that someone is not with or is not involved with another person or group ▪ He went to the store *without* her. ▪ Please don't make a decision *without* me. ▪ I couldn't have done it *without* you. = I couldn't have done it *without* your help. ▪ We would have lost that game *without* her.

3 : not using (something specified) ▪ These cookies are made *without* flour. ▪ Try doing the math *without* a calculator. ▪ I can't see you *without* my glasses.

4 : not doing something specified ▪ They left *without* (even) saying goodbye. [=when they left they did not say goodbye] ▪ *Without* realizing it, he told them his secret. ▪ *Without* wishing to [=although I do not wish to] speak ill of the dead, he wasn't a very nice person. ▪ Even *without* studying, she answered all of the questions correctly. ▪ I can concentrate better *without* (having) the television on.

[2]**without** *adv* : not having something ▪ Do you take your coffee with sugar or *without?*

do without see [1]DO

go without see [1]GO

with·stand /wɪθˈstænd, wɪðˈstænd/ *verb* **-stands; -stood** /-ˈstʊd/; **-stand·ing** [+ *obj*]

1 : to not be harmed or affected by (something) ▪ cookware that can *withstand* high temperatures ▪ I couldn't *withstand* the rigors of army life.

2 : to deal with (something, such as an attack or criticism) successfully ▪ They *withstood* attacks from many critics.

wit·less /ˈwɪtləs/ *adj* [*more ~; most ~*]

1 : very foolish or stupid ▪ He committed a *witless* blunder. ▪ a *witless* fool

2 *not used before a noun, informal* : very much : very badly — used for emphasis ▪ We were bored *witless.* [=we were extremely bored] ▪ The ghost story had me scared *witless.* [=I was very scared]

— **wit·less·ly** *adv* — **wit·less·ness** *noun* [*noncount*]

[1]**wit·ness** /ˈwɪtnəs/ *noun, pl* **-ness·es**

1 [*count*] **a** : a person who sees something (such as a crime) happen ▪ a murder *witness* — often + *to* ▪ He was a *witness to* a robbery. — see also EYEWITNESS **b** *law* : a person who makes a statement in a court about what he or she knows or has seen ▪ The defense/prosecution called its first *witness* to the stand. ▪ a *witness* for the defense/prosecution ▪ a ***charac-***

W

ter witness [=a person who can say whether someone is honest, has a good character, etc.]
2 [*count*] **:** a person who is present at an event (such as a wedding) and can say that it happened ▪ His aunt and uncle were *witnesses* at his baptism. ▪ There must be two *witnesses* present when she signs the document.
3 [*noncount*] *US* **:** a statement of a person's religious beliefs ▪ They ***gave witness to*** their faith. [=declared their belief in a god or religion]
bear witness 1 **:** to show that something exists or is true — + *to* ▪ His success *bears witness to* the value of hard work. ▪ Rising ticket sales *bear witness to* the band's popularity. [=show that the band is popular] 2 *formal* **:** to make a statement saying that you saw or know something ▪ She was accused of ***bearing false witness***. [=saying that she saw something that she did not really see]
be witness to **:** to see (something) happen ▪ We have *been witness to* many changes in recent years. [=we have seen many changes in recent years]

[2]**witness** *verb* **-nesses; -nessed; -ness·ing**
1 [+ *obj*] **:** to see (something) happen ▪ Several people *witnessed* the accident. ▪ We are *witnessing* a historic moment.
2 [+ *obj*] *law* **:** to be present at (an event) in order to be able to say that it happened **:** to act as a legal witness of (something) ▪ He *witnessed* the signing of her will.
3 [+ *obj*] **:** to be the time or place when (something) happens ▪ The past decade has *witnessed* many new advances in medical research. [=many new advances have occurred in the past decade] ▪ The industry is *witnessing* a gradual decline in sales. [=sales are declining in the industry]
4 [+ *obj*] — used to say that something is an example of or is proof of something ▪ The economy is improving—*witness* the decrease in unemployment. [=the decrease in unemployment shows that the economy is improving]
5 [*no obj*] *US* **:** to make a public statement about your religious beliefs ▪ a chance to *witness* for the Lord ▪ speakers ***witnessing to*** their faith [=stating what they believe]
as witnessed by **:** as shown by ▪ The event was a success, *as witnessed by* the high turnout. [=the high turnout shows that the event was a success]

witness stand *noun, pl* ~ **stands** [*count*] *US* **:** the place in a court of law where a witness answers questions and promises to tell the truth **:** the place where a witness testifies in court — called also *the stand,* (*Brit*) *witness box*

wit·ter /ˈwɪtɚ/ *verb* **-ters; -tered; -ter·ing** [*no obj*] *Brit, informal* **:** to talk for a long time about something that is not important or interesting — often + *on* ▪ She *wittered on* [=*prattled on*] about her health problems.

wit·ti·cism /ˈwɪtəˌsɪzəm/ *noun, pl* **-cisms** [*count*] **:** a clever or funny remark ▪ a collection of famous *witticisms*

wit·ting·ly /ˈwɪtɪŋli/ *adv* **:** with knowledge or awareness of what you are doing ▪ I wasn't *wittingly* [=*consciously*] trying to hurt your feelings. ▪ Some parents, ***wittingly or not*** [=whether they mean to or not], don't spend enough time with their children. ▪ ***Wittingly or unwittingly*** [=knowingly or unknowingly], she hurt my feelings again.

wit·ty /ˈwɪti/ *adj* **wit·ti·er; -est :** funny and clever ▪ a *witty* talk show host ▪ a *witty* remark
– wit·ti·ly /ˈwɪtəli/ *adv* ▪ Her novel *wittily* portrays life in a small town. **– wit·ti·ness** /ˈwɪtinəs/ *noun* [*noncount*]

wives *plural of* WIFE

wiz /ˈwɪz/ *noun, pl* **wiz·zes** [*count*] *US, informal* **:** WIZARD ▪ She's a spelling *wiz.* [=she's very good at spelling]

wiz·ard /ˈwɪzɚd/ *noun, pl* **-ards** [*count*]
1 **:** a person who is skilled in magic or who has magical powers **:** a sorcerer or magician
2 **:** a person who is very good at something ▪ He is a *wizard* at math. ▪ a math *wizard*

wiz·ard·ry /ˈwɪzɚdri/ *noun* [*noncount*]
1 **:** the magical things done by a wizard **:** SORCERY ▪ *The Lord of the Rings* is a story of monsters, heroes, and *wizardry.*
2 **:** something that is very impressive in a way that seems magical ▪ the *wizardry* of modern technology ▪ She demonstrated her *wizardry* [=great skill] on the tennis court.

wiz·ened /ˈwɪzənd/ *adj* [*more* ~; *most* ~] **:** dry and wrinkled usually because of old age ▪ the old man's *wizened* face

wk *abbr* week

wkly *abbr* weekly

WMD *abbr* weapons of mass destruction

w/o *abbr* without

wob·ble /ˈwɑːbəl/ *verb* **wob·bles; wob·bled; wob·bling** [*no obj*]
1 **:** to move with an unsteady side-to-side motion ▪ The vase *wobbled* but didn't fall over. ▪ The boy was *wobbling* along on his bicycle. ▪ The table *wobbles* a little.
2 **:** to be or become unsteady or unsure ▪ They have been *wobbling* in their support of the president's policies.
– wobble *noun* [*singular*] ▪ The table has a slight *wobble.*

[1]**wob·bly** /ˈwɑːbəli/ *adj* **wob·bli·er; -est** [*more* ~; *most* ~]
1 **:** moving from side to side in an unsteady way ▪ The railing is *wobbly.* ▪ *wobbly* [=*shaky*] legs
2 **:** not strong or steady ▪ He replied in a *wobbly* [=*shaky*] voice. ▪ a *wobbly* [=*unstable*] housing market

[2]**wobbly** *noun*
throw a wobbly *Brit, informal* **:** to become very angry or upset ▪ He *threw a wobbly* [=*threw a fit*] when he found out his flight was delayed.

wodge /ˈwɑːʤ/ *noun, pl* **wodg·es** [*count*] *Brit, informal* **:** a large piece of something **:** a large amount of something — + *of* ▪ a *wodge of* cheese ▪ a *wodge of* cash

woe /ˈwoʊ/ *noun, pl* **woes**
1 [*noncount*] **:** a feeling of great pain or sadness ▪ She listened to his ***tale of woe***. [=his sad story]
2 ***woes*** [*plural*] **:** problems or troubles ▪ She may have found a remedy to her financial *woes.* [=her problems with money] ▪ The city's traffic *woes* are well-known.
woe is me — used in a humorous way to say that you are sad or upset about something ▪ Oh, *woe is me!*
woe to or ***woe betide*** *old-fashioned* — used as a warning that there will be trouble if someone does something specified ▪ *Woe betide* anyone who enters here! [=anyone who enters here will be harmed] ▪ *Woe to* any student who is late for her class. [=any student who is late for her class will be in trouble]

woe·be·gone /ˈwoʊbiˌgɑːn/ *adj* [*more* ~; *most* ~] **:** looking or feeling very sad ▪ His face had a *woebegone* expression. ▪ a *woebegone* town

woe·ful /ˈwoʊfəl/ *adj* [*more* ~; *most* ~]
1 **:** full of woe **:** very sad ▪ a *woeful* story ▪ The puppy had *woeful* eyes.
2 **:** very bad ▪ The student's grades were *woeful.* ▪ He was a *woeful* [=*pitiful*] excuse for a father.
– woe·ful·ly *adv* ▪ The teachers are *woefully* underpaid.

wok /ˈwɑːk/ *noun, pl* **woks** [*count*] **:** a pan that is shaped like a bowl and that is used especially for cooking Chinese food

woke *past tense and past participle of* [1]WAKE

woken *past participle of* [1]WAKE

wold /ˈwould/ *noun, pl* **wolds** [*count*] *Brit* **:** an area of hilly land in the country — usually used in names ▪ Yorkshire *Wolds*

[1]**wolf** /ˈwʊlf/ *noun, pl* **wolves** /ˈwʊlvz/ [*count*] **:** a large wild animal that is similar to a dog and that often hunts in groups ▪ a pack of *wolves* — compare COYOTE, JACKAL; see also LONE WOLF, WEREWOLF

coyote
wolf

a wolf in sheep's clothing **:** a person who appears to be friendly or helpful but who really is dangerous or dishonest ▪ He turned out to be *a wolf in sheep's clothing.*
cry wolf see [1]CRY
keep the wolf from the door *informal* **:** to have or earn enough money to afford things (such as food and clothing) that you need to live ▪ They make just enough to *keep the wolf from the door.*
throw someone to the wolves **:** to put someone in a position that allows them to be criticized or treated badly without any defense or protection ▪ He *threw his partner to the wolves* by exposing his involvement in the scandal.
– wolf·ish /ˈwʊlfɪʃ/ *adj* [*more* ~; *most* ~] ▪ The boy wore a *wolfish* grin.

[2]**wolf** *verb* **wolfs; wolfed; wolf·ing** [+ *obj*] **:** to eat (something) very quickly ▪ The kids were *wolfing* [=*devouring*] their food. — usually + *down* ▪ She *wolfed down* her breakfast.

wolf·hound /ˈwʊlfˌhaʊnd/ *noun, pl* **-hounds** [*count*] **:** a type of large dog that was used for hunting wolves and other large animals in the past

wolf whistle *noun, pl* ~ **whistles** [*count*] **:** a loud whistle made by men to indicate that a woman is attractive ✧ Some people consider wolf whistles to be offensive.

wol•ver•ine /ˌwʊlvəˈriːn/ *noun, pl* **-ines** [*count*] *US* : a strong animal with brown fur that lives in North America

wom•an /ˈwʊmən/ *noun, pl* **wom•en** /ˈwɪmən/

1 [*count*] : an adult female human being ▪ She was a shy and awkward girl who grew up to become a confident and beautiful *woman*. ▪ She is a grown *woman*. ▪ The store sells shoes for both men and *women*. ▪ *women*'s basketball — often used before another noun ▪ a survey of *women* doctors ▪ They hired a *woman* lawyer. ▪ the town's first *woman* mayor

2 [*count*] : a woman who has a specified job or position ▪ Do they have a cleaning *woman*? — usually used in combination ▪ She was named the committee chair*woman*. ▪ We asked the sales*woman* for assistance.

3 [*noncount*] : all women thought of as a group ▪ a celebration of *woman* [=*women*]

4 [*count*] *old-fashioned* : a female servant (such as a maid) ▪ My *woman* will bring your dinner.

5 [*count*] *informal* : the girlfriend, wife, or lover of a man ▪ Is there a new *woman* in your life? — see also LITTLE WOMAN, OTHER WOMAN

6 [*count*] : a woman who comes from or lives in a specified town, city, etc. — used chiefly by journalists ▪ One of the accident victims has been identified as a Boston *woman*.

7 [*count*] : a woman who likes something very much or who is known for some activity or interest ▪ I'm strictly a chocolate ice cream *woman*. [=I'm a woman who likes chocolate ice cream]

8 [*count*] *informal + old-fashioned* — used when you are talking to a woman in an angry way ▪ Don't bother me, *woman*!

woman of action see ACTION

woman of the hour see HOUR

wom•an•hood /ˈwʊmənˌhʊd/ *noun* [*noncount*]

1 : the state or condition of being an adult woman and no longer a girl ▪ a young girl on the verge of *womanhood* ▪ What is your view of *womanhood*?

2 : women in general ▪ The book is a celebration of *womanhood*.

wom•an•ish /ˈwʊmənɪʃ/ *adj* [*more ~; most ~*] : suitable for or typical of a woman rather than a man : not masculine ▪ He has a *womanish* [=*feminine*] voice. — compare WOMANLY

wom•an•iz•er *also Brit* **wom•an•is•er** /ˈwʊməˌnaɪzə/ *noun, pl* **-ers** [*count*] *disapproving* : a man who has sexual relationships with many women ▪ He has the reputation of being a *womanizer*. ▪ Her former husband was a *womanizer*.

– wom•an•ize *also Brit* **wom•an•ise** /ˈwʊməˌnaɪz/ *verb* **-iz•es; -ized; -iz•ing** [*no obj*] ▪ He has been accused of *womanizing*.

wom•an•kind /ˈwʊmənˌkaɪnd/ *noun* [*noncount*] : all women thought of as one group : WOMEN ▪ for the benefit of all *womankind* ▪ She vowed to wage a battle on behalf of *womankind*. — compare MANKIND

wom•an•ly /ˈwʊmənli/ *adj* [*more ~; most ~*] : having or showing qualities (such as beauty or gentleness) that are expected in a woman : FEMININE ▪ She gave off a *womanly* radiance. ▪ her *womanly* curves/figure

– wom•an•li•ness *noun* [*noncount*]

woman of letters *noun, pl* **women of letters** [*count*] : a woman who writes or who knows a lot about novels, poems, etc. : a literary woman

woman of the world *noun, pl* **women of the world** [*count*] : a woman who has had many experiences and who is not shocked by things that may be shocking to other people

womb /ˈwuːm/ *noun, pl* **wombs** [*count*] : UTERUS

wom•bat /ˈwɑːmˌbæt/ *noun, pl* **-bats** [*count*] : an Australian animal that looks like a small bear ✧ The female wombat has a pouch in which the young are carried.

wom•en•folk /ˈwɪmənˌfoʊk/ *noun* [*plural*] *old-fashioned + humorous* : the women of a family or community ▪ cowboys fighting to protect their *womenfolk*

women's rights *noun* [*plural*] : legal, political, and social rights for women that are equal to those of men ▪ She is an advocate of *women's rights*. ▪ the *women's rights* movement

women's room *noun, pl* ~ **rooms** [*count*] *US* : LADIES' ROOM

women's studies *noun* [*plural*] : the study of subjects relating to women, their roles in history, and their contributions to society ▪ a college with a *women's studies* program ▪ a major in *women's studies*

won *past tense and past participle of* [1]WIN

[1]**won•der** /ˈwʌndə/ *noun, pl* **-ders**

1 [*count*] : something or someone that is very surprising, beautiful, amazing, etc. ▪ The Grand Canyon is one of the natural *wonders* of the world. ▪ This new computer is a technological *wonder*. ▪ She's a *wonder* with a paintbrush. [=she is very good at painting] ▪ the *wonders* of science — see also NINE DAYS' WONDER, ONE-HIT WONDER

2 [*noncount*] : a feeling caused by seeing something that is very surprising, beautiful, amazing, etc. ▪ The child's eyes were filled with *wonder* during the trip to the circus. ▪ We watched the fireworks show with *wonder* and amazement. ▪ She gazed up at the tall buildings in *wonder*.

3 [*singular*] : something that is surprising or hard to believe ▪ It's a *wonder* we made it this far. [=it is surprising we made it this far] ▪ Is it any *wonder* why this movie is so popular?

do/work wonders : to help or improve something greatly ▪ A vacation will *do wonders* for your mood. ▪ The treatment *worked wonders* on my skin.

no wonder *or* ***small/little wonder*** — used to say that something is not surprising ▪ It's *no wonder* you're hungry; you didn't have any breakfast. ▪ *Small wonder* that we're lost, since we didn't ask for directions. ▪ They failed to realize how costly the work would be. *Little wonder*, then, that their plan was rejected.

wonders never cease *humorous* — used to say that you are happy and surprised by something good that has happened ▪ He was on time for work all week. *Wonders never cease*! ▪ My story is finally getting published! ***Will wonders never cease***? [=isn't that amazing/surprising?]

[2]**wonder** *verb* **-ders; -dered; -der•ing**

1 : to have interest in knowing or learning something : to think about something with curiosity [*+ obj*] Have you ever *wondered* why the sky is blue? ▪ I *wonder* [=I would like to know] if he's going to change jobs. ▪ I *wonder* where I put my keys. [=I'm not sure where I put my keys; I'm trying to remember where I put my keys] ▪ Who could that be at the door, I *wonder*? ▪ She *wondered* aloud what to do with the money. ▪ I *wonder* [=I am curious about] how they could afford that house. [*no obj*] I was *wondering* about that.

2 [*+ obj*] — used to ask a question or make a polite request ▪ I *wonder* if you could tell me where the post office is? ▪ We were *wondering* if you'd like to join us for dinner.

3 [*no obj*] : to feel surprise or amazement ▪ Sometimes his behavior makes me *wonder*. ▪ (*chiefly Brit*) The next class will be harder, ***I shouldn't wonder***. [=I won't be surprised if the next class is harder] — often *+ at* ▪ We stood and *wondered at* the impressive display of lights.

wonder drug *noun, pl* ~ **drugs** [*count*] : a very effective drug ▪ Scientists are developing a new *wonder drug* [=*miracle drug*] for treating arthritis.

won•der•ful /ˈwʌndəfəl/ *adj* [*more ~; most ~*] : extremely good ▪ The rooms were filled with *wonderful* works of art. ▪ It was a *wonderful* party. ▪ You did a *wonderful* job. ▪ We had a *wonderful* [=*great, terrific, fantastic*] meal. ▪ She came home with *wonderful* news. ▪ It's *wonderful* to finally meet you.

– won•der•ful•ly *adv* ▪ The story was *wonderfully* written.

won•der•land /ˈwʌndəˌlænd/ *noun, pl* **-lands** [*count*] : a place that is filled with things that are beautiful, impressive, or surprising ▪ The garden was a floral *wonderland*.

won•der•ment /ˈwʌndəmənt/ *noun* [*noncount*] : a feeling of being surprised or amazed ▪ He felt a sense of *wonderment*. ▪ They shook their heads in *wonderment*. [=*awe*]

won•drous /ˈwʌndrəs/ *adj* [*more ~; most ~*] : causing wonder or amazement : very beautiful or impressive ▪ The museum featured a display of *wondrous* tapestries. ▪ The artist can achieve *wondrous* [=*wonderful*] things with a paintbrush.

– won•drous•ly *adv* ▪ a *wondrously* lush forest

wonk /ˈwɑːŋk/ *noun, pl* **wonks** [*count*] *US, informal + sometimes disapproving* : a person who knows a lot about the details of a particular field (such as politics) and often talks a lot about that subject ▪ the ***policy wonks*** in the government

[1]**won•ky** /ˈwɑːŋki/ *adj* **won•ki•er; -est** *US, informal + sometimes disapproving*

1 : having or showing a lot of interest in and knowledge about the details of a particular subject : having the qualities of a wonk ▪ a *wonky* bureaucrat in the State Department

2 : very boring or complicated ▪ She enjoys reading about tax law and other *wonky* stuff.

— compare [2]WONKY

[2]**wonky** /ˈwɑːŋki/ *adj* **wonk•i•er; -est** *informal*

1 *Brit* : not straight or steady ▪ I was sitting on a *wonky* [=*shaky, wobbly*] chair. ▪ a *wonky* [=*loose*] tooth

W

2 : not working correctly : not reliable or stable ▪ He has a *wonky* knee.
– compare [1]WONKY

[1]**wont** /ˈwɑːnt, *Brit* ˈwəʊnt/ *adj, not used before a noun, formal* : likely *to do* something : having a tendency *to do* something ▪ Some people are *wont to blame* others [=some people have the habit of blaming others] for their faults. ▪ He played with his collar, as he is *wont to do* [=as he often does] when he is nervous.

[2]**wont** *noun* [*noncount*] *old-fashioned* : a usual habit or way of behaving ▪ He enjoyed a drink after work, ***as is his wont.*** [=as he usually or often does]

won't /ˈwoʊnt/ : will not ▪ I *won't* see him today.

won•ton /ˈwɑːnˌtɑːn/ *noun* [*noncount*] : a Chinese food made of dough that is filled with meat or vegetables and often served boiled in soup

woo /ˈwuː/ *verb* **woos; wooed; woo•ing** [+ *obj*]
1 *old-fashioned* : to try to make (someone) love you : to try to have a romantic relationship with (someone) ▪ He *wooed* [=*courted*] her with flowers and dinner. ▪ She was *wooed* [=*romanced*] by many boys when she was in school.
2 : to try to attract (someone, such as a customer, voter, worker, etc.) : to attempt to persuade (someone) to buy something from you, vote for you, work for you, etc. ▪ The store had a sale in an effort to *woo* new customers. ▪ The company must find creative ways to *woo* new employees.

[1]**wood** /ˈwʊd/ *noun, pl* **woods**
1 [*noncount*] : the hard substance that makes up the stems and branches of trees and shrubs ▪ a block of *wood* ▪ Some baseball bats are made out of *wood.* ▪ The *wood* on the deck has begun to rot. — see also DEADWOOD, DRIFTWOOD, HARDWOOD, PLYWOOD
2 a *or* **woods** [*count*] : an area of land covered with many trees ▪ Their house is near a small *wood.* ▪ A thick *woods* runs along the boundary of the estate. **b** ***woods*** : a thick growth of trees and bushes that covers a wide area : FOREST [*noncount*] The house is surrounded by *woods.* ▪ He went for a hike in the *woods.* [*plural*] The *woods* are a dangerous place for walking. [=the forest is a dangerous place for walking]
3 [*count*] : a golf club with a large head that was made of wood in the past but is now usually made of metal ▪ She hit a *wood* off the tee. ▪ a fairway *wood* [=a type of wood that is used to hit shots from the fairway] — compare [1]IRON 3
babe in the woods see BABE
knock on wood (*US*) *or chiefly Brit* ***touch wood*** ✧ People say *knock on wood* or *touch wood* and often hit or touch something made of wood as a way to prevent bad luck after they have just said that something good has happened, that they are in a good situation, etc. ▪ I've never broken a bone, *knock on wood.*
neck of the woods see [1]NECK
not see the wood for the trees see TREE
out of the wood/woods : in a position free from danger or difficulty ▪ Her health is getting better but she's not *out of the woods* yet. [=she is still sick; there is still a chance that her condition could get much worse]

[2]**wood** *adj*
1 : made of wood : WOODEN ▪ The walls had *wood* paneling. ▪ a *wood* floor
2 : used for cutting or working with wood ▪ a *wood* saw

wood•block /ˈwʊdˌblɑːk/ *noun, pl* **-blocks** [*count*] : a piece of wood that has a design cut into it and that is used for printing : WOODCUT ▪ She made a *woodblock* print.

wood carving *noun* [*noncount*] : the art of cutting designs into wood or carving objects out of wood
– wood–carv•er /ˈwʊdˌkɑɚvɚ/ *noun, pl* **-ers** [*count*]

wood•chuck /ˈwʊdˌʧʌk/ *noun, pl* **-chucks** [*count*] : a small, furry North American animal that lives in the ground — called also *groundhog*; see picture at RODENT

wood•cock /ˈwʊdˌkɑːk/ *noun, pl* **wood•cocks** *or* **wood•cock** [*count*] : a brown bird that has a short neck and long bill and that is often hunted

wood•cut /ˈwʊdˌkʌt/ *noun, pl* **-cuts** [*count*]
1 : WOODBLOCK
2 : a picture made from a woodcut ▪ a collection of fine *woodcuts*

wood•cut•ter /ˈwʊdˌkʌtɚ/ *noun, pl* **-ters** [*count*] *old-fashioned* : a person whose job is to chop down trees and cut wood

wood•ed /ˈwʊdəd/ *adj* [*more* ~; *most* ~] : covered with trees ▪ a *wooded* lot ▪ These sorts of birds live in more *wooded* areas.

wood•en /ˈwʊdn̩/ *adj*
1 : made of wood ▪ a *wooden* crate ▪ a *wooden* fence
2 [*more* ~; *most* ~] : awkward or stiff : not having or showing any emotion, energy, etc. ▪ The guest speaker was *wooden* and uninspiring. ▪ a movie with *wooden* dialogue
– wood•en•ly *adv* ▪ a *woodenly* acted movie **– wood•en•ness** /ˈwʊdn̩nəs/ *noun* [*noncount*]

wood•land /ˈwʊdlənd/ *noun, pl* **-lands** : land covered with trees and bushes : FOREST [*noncount*] The swamp was surrounded by dense *woodland.* — often used before another noun ▪ snakes, squirrels, and other *woodland* creatures ▪ a *woodland* habitat [*count*] a dense *woodland* — often plural ▪ The *woodlands* stretch for miles.

wood•lot /ˈwʊdˌlɑːt/ *noun, pl* **-lots** [*count*] : a small area of trees that can be used as fuel or to provide wood for building things

wood louse *noun, pl* ~ **lice** [*count*] : a small, gray insect that lives under stones and in other dark, wet places

wood•peck•er /ˈwʊdˌpɛkɚ/ *noun, pl* **-ers** [*count*] : a bird that has a very hard beak which it uses to make holes in trees to get insects for food — see color picture on page C9

wood•pile /ˈwʊdˌpajəl/ *noun, pl* **-piles** [*count*] : a pile of pieces of wood that will be used to make fires

wood•shed /ˈwʊdˌʃɛd/ *noun, pl* **-sheds** [*count*] : a small building used for storing firewood

woods•man /ˈwʊdzmən/ *noun, pl* **-men** /-mən/ [*count*] : a man who works in and knows many things about the forest ▪ an expert *woodsman*

woodsy /ˈwʊdzi/ *adj* **woods•i•er; -est** [*also more* ~; *most* ~] *US, informal*
1 : having many trees : covered with trees ▪ a *woodsy* area
2 : relating to or suggesting the forest ▪ a *woodsy* smell

wood•wind /ˈwʊdˌwɪnd/ *noun, pl* **-winds**
1 [*count*] : any one of the group of musical instruments that includes flutes, clarinets, oboes, bassoons, and saxophones ▪ He plays all the *woodwind* instruments very well. ▪ the ***woodwind section*** [=the group of musicians in an orchestra who play woodwinds] — see picture on next page; compare WIND INSTRUMENT
2 ***woodwinds*** [*plural*] : the section of a band or orchestra that plays woodwind instruments

wood•work /ˈwʊdˌwɚk/ *noun* [*noncount*]
1 : the parts of a room or house (such as window frames or stairs) that are made of wood ▪ decorative *woodwork* ▪ We painted the walls white and the *woodwork* red.
2 *Brit* : WOODWORKING
3 *Brit, informal* : the wooden frame of football or soccer goalposts ▪ The kick hit the *woodwork.*
come/crawl out of the woodwork *disapproving* ✧ If people *come/crawl out of the woodwork,* they appear suddenly, usually because they see an opportunity to get something for themselves. ▪ As soon as she won the lottery, people started *coming out of the woodwork,* asking for money.
into the woodwork — used in phrases like ***fade into the woodwork*** to describe someone or something that is not noticed or that seems to disappear ▪ He's so shy that he always seems to *fade into the woodwork* at parties.

wood•work•ing /ˈwʊdˌwɚkɪŋ/ *noun* [*noncount*] *US* : the skill or work of making things out of wood ▪ His favorite hobby was *woodworking.* ▪ *woodworking* projects/tools
– wood•work•er /ˈwʊdˌwɚkɚ/ *noun, pl* **-ers** [*count*]

woody /ˈwʊdi/ *adj* **wood•i•er; -est** [*also more* ~; *most* ~]
1 : having stems and branches that are made of wood ▪ *woody* plants : made of wood ▪ tall *woody* stems
2 : similar to wood ▪ a *woody* flavor/texture
3 *informal* : having many trees ▪ a *woody* piece of land

[1]**woof** /ˈwʊf/ *noun, pl* **woofs** [*count*] : the sound made by a dog : BARK — compare [2]WOOF
– woof *verb* **woofs; woofed; woof•ing** [*no obj*] ▪ The dog *woofed.*

[2]**woof** *noun, pl* **woofs** [*count*] *technical* : WEFT — compare [1]WOOF

woof•er /ˈwʊfɚ/ *noun, pl* **-ers** [*count*] : a loudspeaker (such as one connected to a stereo) that produces sounds of low pitch — compare SUBWOOFER, TWEETER

wool /ˈwʊl/ *noun* [*noncount*]
1 : the soft, thick hair of sheep and some other animals — see also LAMBSWOOL
2 : cloth or clothing made of wool ▪ She doesn't like *wool* because it can be itchy. ▪ virgin *wool* [=wool that is being used in fabric for the first time] — often used before another noun ▪ *wool* socks ▪ a *wool* blanket/sweater

woodwinds

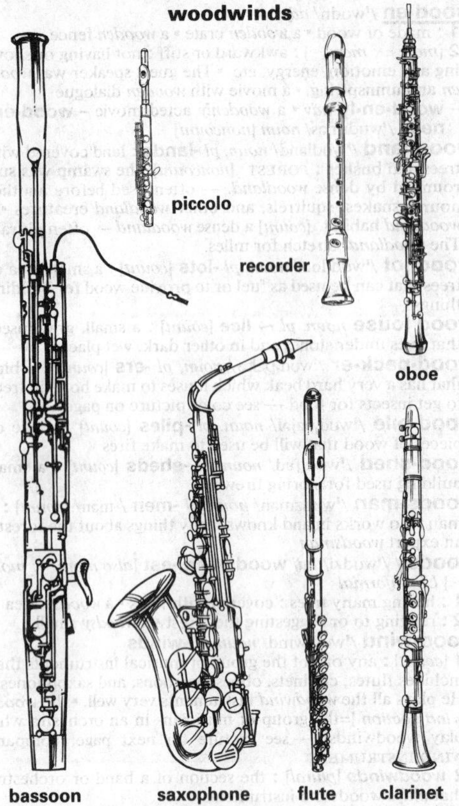

3 *chiefly Brit* : long, thick thread made of wool and used for knitting ▪ a ball of *wool* [=(US) yarn]

pull the wool over someone's eyes *informal* : to trick or deceive someone : to hide the truth from someone ▪ He was too clever to let them *pull the wool over his eyes*.

— see also COTTON WOOL, DYED-IN-THE-WOOL, STEEL WOOL, WIRE WOOL

wool·en *(US) or Brit* **wool·len** /ˈwʊlən/ *adj, always used before a noun*

1 : made of wool ▪ *woolen* blankets

2 : relating to the business of making cloth from wool ▪ the *woolen* industry

wool·ens *(US) or Brit* **wool·lens** /ˈwʊlənz/ *noun [plural] somewhat old-fashioned* : clothes made of wool ▪ He wore his best *woolens*.

[1]**wool·ly** *also* **wooly** /ˈwʊli/ *adj* **wool·li·er; -est** [*also more ~; most ~*]

1 : covered with wool ▪ a *woolly* animal

2 *chiefly Brit, informal* : made of wool or resembling wool : WOOLEN ▪ a *woolly* hat/jumper

3 *chiefly Brit* : confused and unclear ▪ *woolly* thinking ▪ a *woolly* argument

wild and woolly *chiefly US, informal* : very wild : without order or control ▪ His novels were about the *wild and woolly* Western frontier. ▪ a *wild and woolly* love affair

— **wool·li·ness** *noun [noncount]*

[2]**wool·ly** /ˈwʊli/ *noun, pl* **wool·lies** *[count] chiefly Brit, informal* : a warm piece of clothing (such as a sweater) made of knitted wool ▪ Get out your winter *woollies*.

woolly mammoth *noun, pl* ~ **-moths** *[count]* : [1]MAMMOTH 1

woops *variant spelling of* WHOOPS

woo·zy /ˈwuːzi/ *adj* **woo·zi·er; -est** [*also more ~; most ~*] : slightly dizzy, sick, or weak ▪ She was already feeling *woozy* after her first drink. ▪ *woozy* from fatigue

— **woo·zi·ness** *noun [noncount]*

wop /ˈwɑːp/ *noun, pl* **wops** *[count] informal + offensive* : an Italian person ✧ The word *wop* is very offensive and should be avoided.

[1]**word** /ˈwɚd/ *noun, pl* **words**

1 *[count]* : a sound or combination of sounds that has a meaning and is spoken or written ▪ How do you spell that *word*? ▪ "Please" is a useful *word*. ▪ Our teacher often used *words* I didn't know. ▪ What is the French *word* for car? ▪ She was a genius ***in every sense of the word***. [=she was truly a genius] ▪ You don't need to use ***big words*** [=difficult words used to try to impress people] to make your point. ▪ ***Words fail me***. [=I don't know what to say] — see also BUZZWORD, FOUR-LETTER WORD, FUNCTION WORD, PASSWORD, SWEARWORD, WATCHWORD, WEASEL WORD

2 *[count]* : a brief remark or conversation : something that a person says ▪ You can't believe a *word* (of what) she says. [=you can't believe anything she says] ▪ Describe the experience in your own *words*. ▪ The lawyer used Joe's *words* against him. ▪ Could I ***have a word with you***? [=could I talk with you briefly?] ▪ They gave me a ***word of warning*** [=they told me about] about the slippery roads. ▪ ***Don't say/breathe a word*** [=don't talk] about this to anyone. ▪ My grandfather was a ***man of few words***. [=a man who did not talk very much] ▪ I've been asked to ***say a few words*** [=make a short speech or statement] about the new play.

3 *[singular]* : an order or command ▪ She gave the *word* to begin. ▪ We will wait for your *word* before we serve dinner.

4 *[singular]* : news or information ▪ (Is there) Any *word* on how they are? ▪ If *word* of this gets out, we're all in trouble. ▪ What's the *word*? ▪ There is still no *word* from the hospital. ▪ ***Spread the word*** [=tell the others] that we're leaving in five minutes. ▪ They ***sent word*** [=sent a message] that they'd be late. ▪ ***Word has it*** [=I have heard] that the neighbors are moving next month. ▪ The police ***put/got the word out*** that they were looking for him. [=the police let people know that they were looking for him]

5 *[singular]* : a promise to do something ▪ I'll be there. I ***give you my word***. [=I promise] ▪ You'd better ***keep your word***. [=keep your promise to do something] ▪ He is a ***man of his word***. = ***His word is his bond***. [=he always keeps his promises] ▪ I told her I'd help. I can't ***go back on my word***. [=I can't break my promise] ▪ You'll have to ***take my word for it***. [=you'll have to believe me] ▪ She was ***true to her word***. [=she did what she said she would do] — see also WORD OF HONOR (below)

6 ***words*** *[plural]* : angry remarks ▪ *Words* were exchanged [=people said angry things to each other] and a fight broke out. ▪ He ***had words*** [=had an argument] with his boss.

7 ***the Word*** *religion* : stories and lessons of the Bible ▪ *the Word* of God

actions speak louder than words see ACTION

a picture is worth a thousand words see [1]WORTH

at a loss for words see LOSS

a word in someone's ear *chiefly Brit* : a remark that is made privately to someone ▪ May I ***have a word in your ear*** [=may I speak to you privately] before you leave?

a word to the wise — used to say that you are about to give someone advice or a warning ▪ *A word to the wise*: never sign a contract without reading it first.

by word of mouth : by being told by another person ▪ We found this hotel *by word of mouth*.

eat your words see EAT

from the word go *informal* : from the beginning ▪ The show was a success *from the word go*. ▪ We were in trouble (*right*) *from the word go*.

get a word in edgewise see EDGEWISE

good word : a favorable comment ▪ Please put in a *good word* for me [=say something good about me] when you talk to the boss. ▪ *(US, informal)* I haven't seen you in ages! ***What's the good word***? [=*how's it going?; how are you?*]

hang on someone's every word see [1]HANG

in a word : very briefly : in short — used to indicate that you are saying something by using only one word or by using as few words as possible ▪ Our answer, *in a word*, is no.

in other words — used to introduce a statement that repeats what has been said in a different and usually a simpler or more exact way ▪ "She said the movie was a bit predictable." "*In other words*, she didn't like it." ▪ So, *in other words*, you're saying that you forgot to do it.

in so many words *also* ***in as many words*** : in exactly those words or in exactly that way — usually used in negative statements ▪ "Did he say he wouldn't do it?" "***Not in so many words***, but that was the impression I got."

in words of one syllable : in clear and simple terms ▪ We explained our views to the press *in words of one syllable*.

lost for words see [2]LOST

mark my words see [2]MARK

mum's the word see [1]MUM

play with words see [1]PLAY

put words in/into someone's mouth : to suggest that someone said or meant something that he or she did not say or mean • Don't *put words in my mouth.* I wasn't defending his actions, despite what you may think.

say the word : to give an order • When you want to leave (just) *say the word.*

take the words right out of someone's mouth : to say exactly what someone was thinking • I agree! You *took the words right out of my mouth!*

the last/final word **1** : the final thing said in an argument or a discussion • Your mother's decision is *the final word* on the matter. • Why do you always have to ***have the last word***? [=to be the last person to speak] **2** : the power to make a final decision • The judge will have *the last word* [=*the final say*] on the divorce agreement. **3** *informal* : the most modern or best one of its kind • This is *the last word* in wireless phones. • The van's design is *the last word* in safety.

(upon) my word *somewhat old-fashioned* — used to express surprise • *My word,* what a beautiful dress!

war of words : an argument in which people or groups criticize and disagree with each other publicly and repeatedly for usually a long time • Rival groups have engaged in a *war of words* over the new law.

word for word : in the exact words • He gave the same speech *word for word* [=*verbatim*] yesterday.

word of honor ✧ Your *word of honor* is your promise that you will do something, that something is true, etc. • I give you my *word of honor* that I will pay the money back.

[2]**word** *verb* **words; word·ed; word·ing** [+ *obj*] : to say (something) in a particular way by choosing which words to use • They *worded* [=*phrased*] their request with great care. • Could we *word* the headline differently? — often used as *(be) worded* • Their request *was worded* very carefully. • a carefully *worded* statement

word·ing /ˈwɚdɪŋ/ *noun* [*noncount*] : the way in which something is said or written : the words that are used to say something • What's the exact *wording* of the agreement?

word·less /ˈwɚdləs/ *adj* : without using words : without speaking • a *wordless* agreement

– **word·less·ly** *adv*

word–perfect *adj, Brit* : correct in every detail : LETTER-PERFECT • All the actors should be congratulated on a *word-perfect* performance.

word·play /ˈwɚd,pleɪ/ *noun* [*noncount*] : playful or clever use of words • Oscar Wilde was famous for his witty *wordplay.*

word processing *noun* [*noncount*] : the production of printed pages of writing (such as business letters) that can be stored and printed by using computer equipment • These terminals are used mostly for *word processing.* • *word processing* software

word processor *noun, pl* ~ **-sors** [*count*]
1 : a computer used for creating, storing, and printing text : a computer used for word processing • At work she sits in front of her *word processor* all day.
2 : software used on a computer to perform word processing • She closed down her *word processor* and opened her e-mail program.

wordy /ˈwɚdi/ *adj* **word·i·er; -est** [*also more* ~; *most* ~] *disapproving* : using or containing too many words • The original script was too *wordy.* • His writing is very *wordy.* [=*verbose*]

– **word·i·ly** /ˈwɚdəli/ *adv* – **word·i·ness** /ˈwɚdinəs/ *noun* [*noncount*]

wore *past tense of* [1]WEAR

[1]**work** /ˈwɚk/ *verb* **works; worked; work·ing**

1 a : to have a job [*no obj*] I started *working* when I was sixteen. • Her husband doesn't *work.* • She *works* part-time at the restaurant. • She has always wanted to *work* in advertising. • She *works* with me. = She and I *work* together. [=she and I have jobs at the same place] • men and women who ***work outside the home*** [=who have jobs in factories, restaurants, office buildings, etc.] [+ *obj*] She has to *work* two jobs to support her family. • He *works* construction. [=he has a job in which he helps build things] **b** : to do things as part of your job [*no obj*] She *worked* through lunch to get the report done. • I'm not *working* tomorrow—the boss gave me the day off. • He *works* from home. [=his job allows him to stay home and do his work] • I *work* for him. [=I am his employee] • I *work* under her. [=she is my boss/supervisor] [+ *obj*] He *works* about 60 hours a week. • The job requires that you *work* some nights and weekends. • She is used to ***working long hours.*** **c** [+ *obj*] : to do work in, on, or at (an area, event, etc.) • She *works* the Northeast region of the state selling insurance. • He was hired as a sportscaster to *work* the games this season. • Crews *work* the quarry all day and night. • farmers *working* the fields • Our family has *worked* this land for centuries.

2 a [*no obj*] : to do something that involves physical or mental effort • She is *working* in the garden. • They *worked* all day (at) cleaning the house. • I can't *work* with all of this noise. • The principal *worked* hard to improve the school. • We're *working* toward a solution. • I enjoy *working* with my hands. [=using my hands to do or make things] • a sculptor who *works* in/with stone [=who makes things out of stone] **b** [+ *obj*] : to force (someone or something) to do something that involves physical or mental effort • The exercise is designed to *work* the muscles in your chest. • The coach *worked* her team hard during practice. • She ***worked us into the ground.*** [=she made us work very hard and become very tired]

3 [+ *obj*] : to use and control (something) • I don't know how to *work* your cell phone. • Who is *working* the machine? • The pump is *worked* by hand.

4 [*no obj*] : to perform or operate in the correct way • The computer isn't *working* (properly). • Is the elevator *working* again? • I can't get this thing to *work.*

5 [*no obj*] **a** : to have the intended effect or result • The medicine seems to be *working.* • Their plan *worked.* • The idea sounds good in theory, but it will never *work* in practice. • The commercial doesn't *work* for me. [=I don't like it; it doesn't affect me the way it is supposed to] • a dish detergent that ***works like magic*** [=that is very effective] **b** *always followed by an adverb or preposition* : to have a particular effect or result • You need to do what *works* best for you. • Red curtains would *work* well in this room. • I think you'll get the job. Being bilingual definitely ***works in your favor.*** [=it helps or benefits you] • Her lack of experience ***worked against her*** in the election. [=it made her less likely to win in the election]

6 [+ *obj*] : to cause (something) to happen • I'll do my best, but I can't ***work miracles.*** [=I can't make miracles happen] • He's a brilliant chef who ***works magic*** [=does special or remarkable things] with the most basic ingredients.

7 : to move (something) into or out of a particular position slowly or with difficulty [+ *obj*] She *worked* her foot into the shoe. • The screw had *worked* itself loose. [=the screw had become loose] [*no obj*] The glue would stop the knot from *working* loose. [=from becoming loose] — see also WORK YOUR WAY (below)

8 [+ *obj*] : to bring (something) into a desired shape or form by cutting it, pressing it, etc. • *Work* the dough with your hands until it is smooth. • a blacksmith *working* a piece of iron

9 [+ *obj*] : to talk to and try to gain the friendship or support of (the people in a group) • The singer *worked* the crowd throughout the whole concert. • He's a politician who really knows how to ***work a room.*** [=how to talk to the people in a room to get their support, approval, etc.]

work around *or chiefly Brit* ***work round*** [*phrasal verb*] **1** ***work around/round (something)*** : to organize things or proceed in a way that avoids (something, such as a problem) • We'll just have to find a way to *work around* the problem. **2** ***work around/round to (something)*** : to start talking or writing about (a subject, issue, etc.) after talking or writing about other things • He eventually *worked around to* the company's financial situation.

work at [*phrasal verb*] ***work at (something)*** : to make an effort to do (something) better • He needs to *work at* his handwriting. • She has been *working* (harder) *at* controlling her temper.

work in [*phrasal verb*] **1** ***work (something) in or work in (something)*** **a** : to add or include (something) in a conversation, essay, etc. • During the speech, he *worked in* a few jokes. • She *worked in* several important points in her article. **b** : to stir or mix (something) into something • *Work in* the blueberries. **2** ***work (someone or something) in US*** : to make an amount of time available for (someone or something) • My schedule is pretty full, but I think I can *work* you *in* [=fit you in] at 11:30.

work into [*phrasal verb*] **1** ***work (something) into (something)*** **a** : to add or include (something) in (something) • You should *work* more fresh fruit *into* your diet. • She tried to find a way of *working* her question *into* the conversation. **b** : to stir or mix (something) into (something) • *Work* the blueberries *into* the mixture. **2** ***work (someone) into (something)*** : to gradually cause (someone) to be in (an excited, angry, or frightened state) • The DJ *worked* the crowd *into* a frenzy. • He *worked* himself *into* a rage/panic.

***work it/things** informal* : to arrange your activities in a particular way so that it is possible for something to happen or be done • I'm supposed to be helping my sister that night, but I'll try to *work things* so that I can come to your party.

work off [*phrasal verb*] ***work off (something) or work (something) off*** **1** : to pay (a debt) by working • She *worked off* her loan. • His parents are making him *work off* the cost of the bike he ruined. **2** : to lose or get rid of (something) by physical activity • He walks every day to *work* the extra weight *off*. • Jogging is a great way to *work off* stress.

work on [*phrasal verb*] **1 a** ***work on (something)*** : to be in the process of making (something), doing (something), etc. • The director is *working on* a new movie. • I *worked on* this physics problem for three hours. • He is in the garage *working on* the car. • Scientists are beginning to *work on* a cure. **b** ***work on doing (something)*** : to make an effort to do (something) • They are currently *working on finding* a cure. [=trying to find a cure] • You have to *work on controlling* your temper. **2** ***work on (someone)*** : to try to influence or persuade (someone) to do something • She is *working on* them to change their votes.

work out [*phrasal verb*] **1** : to perform athletic exercises in order to improve your health or physical fitness • She *works out* at the gym twice a week. **2 a** : to happen, develop, or end in a desired or successful way • Our plan *worked out* perfectly. • We broke up because things didn't *work out* between us. **b** : to happen, develop, or end in a particular way or to have a particular result • Despite some difficulties, everything *worked out* well. • Things don't always *work out* the way you want them to. • I'm not sure how the story will *work out*. • How is your new roommate *working out*? [=how are things going with your new roommate?] • It will *work out* (to be) cheaper [=it will be cheaper] if we take the bus instead of the train. • With tax, it ***worked out at/to*** just over $115. [=the total amount was just over $115] **3** ***work out (something) or work (something) out*** **a** : to find or create (something, such as a solution or a plan) by thinking • I'm trying to *work out* [=*figure out*] a way to do it. • We *worked out* a plan to save money. • We'll *work* the details *out* later. • I don't know how you're going to get there. You have to *work* that *out* for yourself. **b** : to use mathematics to solve (something) • She *worked out* the problem on a piece of paper. **4** ***work (someone) out or work out (someone)*** *Brit* : to understand the behavior of (someone) • He does these crazy things, and I just can't *work* him *out*. [=figure him out]

work over [*phrasal verb*] ***work (someone) over*** *informal* : to hurt (someone) by hitting, kicking, etc. • He looked like someone had *worked* him *over* [=beat him up] pretty good.

work through [*phrasal verb*] : to deal with (something that is difficult or unpleasant) successfully • He saw a psychologist to help him *work through* his depression. • She *worked through* the pain without medication.

work to [*phrasal verb*] ***work to (something)*** *chiefly Brit* : to work within the limits of (something) • We have to *work to* a very tight budget.

work up [*phrasal verb*] **1** ***work (someone) up*** : to make (someone) feel very angry, excited, upset, etc. • Don't *work* yourself *up* again. — see also WORKED UP **2** ***work up (something) or work (something) up*** **a** : to produce (something) by physical or mental effort • I *worked up* a sweat at the gym. • He managed to *work up* the courage to ask her out on a date. **b** *chiefly Brit* : to improve your skill at (something) or increase your knowledge of (something) • I need to *work up* my French for the exam. **c** *chiefly Brit* : to develop or expand (something) — usually + *into* • He *worked up* the short story *into* a novel. **3** ***work up to (something)*** : to reach (something, such as a rate or level) by gradually increasing in speed, intensity, etc. • The ship gradually *worked up to* full speed. • The story starts slow but *works up to* a brilliant conclusion.

work wonders see [1]WONDER

work your fingers to the bone see [1]FINGER

work your magic see [1]MAGIC

work your way : to move yourself into or out of a particular position slowly or with difficulty • The prisoner somehow *worked his way* out of the handcuffs. • I *worked my way* to the center of the crowd. • They started *working their way* cautiously down the side of the mountain. — sometimes used figuratively • He had *worked his way* into her heart. • She is slowly *working her way* to the top of the company. ✧ If you ***work your way through college/school***, you have a job that helps you pay for your expenses while you go to college/school. • He is *working his way through college*.

[2]**work** *noun, pl* **works**

1 [*noncount*] **a** : a job or activity that you do regularly especially in order to earn money • How is *work* [=your job] going? • She is trying to find *work* in publishing. • How long have you been looking for *work*? • He started *work* as a car salesman. • I know him through *work*. • When do you get off *work*? [=when do you stop working for the day?] • She goes to the gym after *work*. [=after she has finished working] • full-time/part-time *work* • She plans to ***return to work*** [=start working her job again] in four months. • What ***line of work*** is your wife in? = What does your wife do for *work*? — see also LIFE'S WORK, SOCIAL WORK **b** : the place where you do your job • She didn't come to *work* today. • He left *work* a few minutes ago. • She's not here right now. She's at *work*. • We met at *work*. • She went out with her friends from *work*.

2 [*noncount*] **a** : the things that you do especially as part of your job • Can you describe your *work* to the class? • A large part of the *work* is responding to e-mails. • administrative/secretarial *work* • My brother did the electrical *work* on the house. • After you finish your *work*, you can go outside and play. • I have a lot of *work* to do. **b** : things (such as papers, files, etc.) that you use to do your job • His *work* cluttered his desk. • She brought some *work* home with her from the office. — see also DONKEY WORK, FIELDWORK, GROUNDWORK, HOMEWORK, HOUSEWORK, LEGWORK, PAPERWORK, PIECEWORK, SCHOOLWORK

3 [*noncount*] **a** : physical or mental effort that is used to perform a job or achieve a goal • Getting my PhD took a lot of *work*, but it was worth it. • Hard *work* is the key to success. • Careful police *work* led to the murderer's capture. • She hasn't done any *work* since she got here. **b** : the process or activity of working • He plans to start *work* on a new novel soon. • The rain forced the crew to stop *work* on the building. • *Work* on the project is already underway. [=people have started working on the project] • You need to ***get down to work*** [=start working] if you want to finish the assignment on time. • She ***set to work*** [=started working] on the project immediately. • She diligently ***went about her work***. [=did her work] • He was told to ***keep up the good work***. [=to continue doing good work] ✧ Phrases like ***good work, nice work***, etc., are used to tell people that they have done something very well. • "I finished the project ahead of schedule." "*Good work!*"

4 a [*noncount*] : something that is produced or done by someone • Some clever camera *work* gave the illusion that she was standing next to him. • The cabinets are the *work* of a skilled carpenter. [=the cabinets were made by a skilled carpenter] • The robberies were the *work* of [=were done by] the same gang. **b** : something (such as a book, song, or painting) that is produced by a writer, musician, artist, etc. [*noncount*] I love this painter's *work*. • the author's entire body of *work* [*count*] the complete/collected *works* of Charles Dickens • literary *works* • the painter's latest *work* • The painting is a ***work in progress***. [=it is not yet finished] — see also ARTWORK, HANDIWORK, HANDWORK

5 ***works*** [*plural*] : roads, bridges, dams, and similar structures : structures that are built by engineers • engineering *works* from the 19th century — see also PUBLIC WORKS, WATERWORKS

6 ***works*** : a place where industrial labor is done : a factory [*singular*] He got a job at a cement/lead/steel *works*. [*plural*] The local steel *works* have shut down. — see also GASWORKS

7 ***the works*** : the moving parts of a machine • *the works* of a clock — sometimes used figuratively • The office used to be very efficient, but the new regulations have ***gummed up the works***. [=made the work more difficult and slow]

8 ***the works*** *informal* : everything • They ordered a pizza with *the works*. [=with all the different toppings that were available] • When we went to New York, we visited the museums, did some shopping, saw some shows—***the whole works***.

9 [*noncount*] *physics* : the energy that is used when a force is applied over a given distance

at work **1 a** : actively doing work • He kept us hard *at work* but paid us well. • We're ***at work on*** the new project. **b** : doing your regular job • He has been out with a back injury, but he'll be back *at work* soon. **2** : having an effect or influence • She felt that a higher power was *at work*.

have your work cut out for you ✧ If you *have your work cut out for you*, the thing you need to do is very difficult, and you have to work very hard to achieve it. ▪ She knew she *had her work cut out for her*, but she was willing to do whatever it took to succeed.

in the works *informal* : in the process of being prepared, developed, or completed ▪ Her next movie is already *in the works*. ▪ Plans are *in the works* for building three new schools in the area.

in work *Brit* : having a regular job ▪ the percentage of people who are *in work* [=people who have jobs]

make short/quick/light work of **1** : to make it possible for (something) to be done quickly or easily ▪ This new snow shovel *makes short work of* clearing off the driveway. ✧ The expression ***many hands make light work*** means that people can do things more quickly and easily when they work together. **2** : to finish (something) or defeat (someone) quickly and easily ▪ She *made short work of* her opponents. ▪ The kids *made quick work of* the french fries. [=the kids ate the french fries quickly] ▪ He *made light work of* the problem. [=he solved the problem quickly and easily]

out of work : without a regular job ▪ The factory closed and left/put 5,000 people *out of work*. ▪ He has been *out of work* since January. [=he has not had a job since January]

put/throw a spanner in the works see SPANNER

throw a wrench into the works see [1]WRENCH

— see also PIECE OF WORK

[3]**work** *adj, always used before a noun*

1 : suitable to be worn while you are working ▪ *work* clothes/boots

2 : used for work ▪ a clean *work* surface/table

3 : of or relating to a person's job ▪ What does your *work* schedule look like this week? ▪ a 12-hour *work* shift ▪ There is a place to list your ***work experience*** [=the jobs that you have had] on the application. ▪ My parents both had a very strong ***work ethic***. [=a strong belief in the value and importance of work] ▪ She filed for a ***work permit***. [=an official document that shows that a person is allowed to work]

work·able /ˈwɚkəbəl/ *adj* [*more ~; most ~*]

1 : able to be used successfully ▪ a *workable* system/solution ▪ I think the plan is quite *workable*.

2 : able to be easily shaped or worked with ▪ *workable* plastic/wool ▪ Chill the cookie dough until it is more *workable*.

work·a·day /ˈwɚkəˌdeɪ/ *adj, always used before a noun* [*more ~; most ~*] : not unusual or interesting : ORDINARY ▪ Their vacation provided a welcome change from their *workaday* life. ▪ *workaday* jobs/activities ▪ the *workaday* struggles and concerns of the average person

work·a·hol·ic /ˌwɚkəˈhɑːlɪk/ *noun, pl* **-ics** [*count*] : a person who chooses to work a lot : a person who is always working, thinking about work, etc. ▪ My brother is a real *workaholic* who almost never takes time off.

work·bench /ˈwɚkˌbɛnʧ/ *noun, pl* **-bench·es** [*count*] : a long table that people use when they are working with tools

work·book /ˈwɚkˌbʊk/ *noun, pl* **-books** [*count*] : a book that contains problems or exercises and that students use to practice what they are learning in a class

work camp *noun, pl* **~ camps** [*count*] : PRISON CAMP

work·day /ˈwɚkˌdeɪ/ *noun, pl* **-days** [*count*] *chiefly US*

1 : a day on which you work at a job ▪ On *workdays* I usually wake up at six o'clock. ▪ my *workday* routine

2 : the period of time in a day during which you work at a job ▪ an 8-hour *workday*

worked up *adj, not used before a noun* [*more ~; most ~*] *informal* : very angry, excited, or upset about something ▪ What is she so *worked up* about? ▪ He got all *worked up* over the football game.

work·er /ˈwɚkɚ/ *noun, pl* **-ers** [*count*]

1 a : a person who does a particular job to earn money ▪ The company is planning to hire 200 *workers*. ▪ The average *worker* earned $1,000 more this year. ▪ office/factory/construction/postal *workers* ▪ skilled *workers* ▪ a migrant *worker* ▪ a full-time/part-time *worker* — see also GUEST WORKER, SOCIAL WORKER **b** : a person who is actively involved in a particular activity — often used in combination ▪ aid/rescue/research *workers*

2 : a person whose job does not involve managing other people ▪ If management doesn't make the changes, the *workers* will go on strike.

3 : a person who works in a particular way ▪ They are both hard/fast/good *workers*.

4 : a type of bee, ant, etc., that does most of the work in a colony of insects ▪ *worker* bees

workers' compensation *noun* [*noncount*] *US* : a system of insurance that pays an employee who cannot work because he or she has been injured while working — called also *workers' comp*

workfare /ˈwɚkˌfeɚ/ *noun* [*noncount*] : a program in which people must do work in order to receive money from the government for food, housing, medical costs, etc.

work·force /ˈwɚkˌfoɚs/ *noun* [*singular*]

1 : the group of people who work for a particular organization or business ▪ We have a *workforce* of 2,400 people.

2 : the number of people in a country or area who are available for work ▪ the nation's *workforce*

work·horse /ˈwɚkˌhoɚs/ *noun, pl* **-hors·es** [*count*]

1 : a dependable person who does a lot of work

2 : a dependable machine or vehicle that is used to do a lot of work

work·house /ˈwɚkˌhaʊs/ *noun, pl* **-hous·es** [*count*] *Brit* : POORHOUSE

work·ing /ˈwɚkɪŋ/ *adj, always used before a noun*

1 : having a job ▪ the *working* population ▪ *working* mothers [=mothers who also have paying jobs] ▪ a politician who is popular among *working* people [=among people who are not rich and powerful and who have jobs that usually do not pay a lot of money]

2 a : of or relating to a person's job ▪ poor *working* conditions ▪ regular/flexible *working* hours ▪ There is a good *working* relationship between the departments. ▪ She spent most of her *working* life/years [=most of the time when she was working] in politics. ▪ We had a *working* lunch. [=we discussed work while we ate lunch] **b** : suitable to be worn while working ▪ *working* clothes/boots

3 a : doing work ▪ the *working* parts of the machine ▪ a *working* farm **b** : relating to the work done by a machine, system, etc. ▪ She made sure that everything was ***in (good) working order/condition***. [=made sure that everything was working properly]

4 a : good enough to be used or useful although not perfect ▪ The person hired for this position should have at least a *working* knowledge of German. [=should be able to read and understand German fairly well] **b** : large enough to be effective ▪ The party has a ***working majority*** in the Senate.

5 — used to describe something that is used while work is being done on something (such as a project) and that may be changed later ▪ a *working* agreement/title/hypothesis

working capital *noun* [*noncount*] *business* : money that is available for use while running a business

working class *noun*

the working class *also Brit* ***the working classes*** : the class of people who earn money by doing usually physical work and who are not rich or powerful — compare LOWER CLASS, MIDDLE CLASS, UNDERCLASS, UPPER CLASS

— **working–class** *adj, always used before a noun* ▪ *working-class* virtues ▪ a *working-class* family

working day *noun, pl* **~ days** [*count*] *chiefly Brit* : WORKDAY

working girl *noun, pl* **~ girls** [*count*] *informal*

1 : a young woman who has a job

2 *chiefly Brit, somewhat old-fashioned* : PROSTITUTE

working papers *noun* [*plural*] *US* : official documents that allow a person who is younger than 16 years old or who was born in a different country to have a job in the U.S.

working party *noun, pl* **~ parties** [*count*] *Brit* : a group of people who investigate a particular problem and suggest ways of dealing with it — called also *working group*

work·ings /ˈwɚkɪŋz/ *noun* [*plural*]

1 : the moving parts that are inside a machine : the working parts of something ▪ There was a problem with the clock's inner *workings*.

2 : the ways in which something works — usually + *of* ▪ We learned about the inner *workings of* the government.

working week *noun, pl* **~ weeks** [*count*] *chiefly Brit* : WORKWEEK

work·load /ˈwɚkˌloʊd/ *noun, pl* **-loads** [*count*] : the amount of work that is expected to be done ▪ Students complained about the heavy *workload*.

work·man /ˈwɚkmən/ *noun, pl* **-men** /-mən/ [*count*] : a skilled worker (such as an electrician or carpenter)

work·man·like /ˈwɚkmənˌlaɪk/ *adj* : done with the skill expected of a good worker or performer but usually not in very exciting or impressive way ▪ He did a *workmanlike* job on the boat. • a *workmanlike* performance • She showed *workmanlike* thoroughness in everything she did.

work·man·ship /ˈwɚkmənˌʃɪp/ *noun* [*noncount*] : the quality of the work that is done by someone • He admires good *workmanship*. • The problems were caused by cheap materials and poor *workmanship*. • The excellent *workmanship* of the cabinets is remarkable.

work·mate /ˈwɚkˌmeɪt/ *noun, pl* **-mates** [*count*] *chiefly Brit* : a person who works with you : COWORKER

work of art *noun, pl* **works of art** [*count*]
1 : something that is made by an artist : a painting, sculpture, etc., that is created to be beautiful or to express an important idea or feeling • a beautiful *work of art*
2 : something that is attractive and skillfully made • The wedding cake was a real *work of art*.

work·out /ˈwɚkˌaʊt/ *noun, pl* **-outs** [*count*] : a period of physical exercise that you do in order to improve your fitness, ability, or performance • The team had a good *workout* at practice today. • Her *workout* includes running on the treadmill and lifting weights.

work·place /ˈwɚkˌpleɪs/ *noun, pl* **-plac·es** [*count*] : the office, factory, etc., where people work • a clean, comfortable *workplace* • Foul language will not be tolerated ***in the workplace***. • ***workplace romances*** [=romances between people who work together]

work release *noun* [*noncount*] *US* : the practice of allowing a prisoner to work outside of the prison during the day • a *work-release* program • prisoners ***on work release***

work·room /ˈwɚkˌruːm/ *noun, pl* **-rooms** [*count*] : a room used for doing work usually inside a store • There is a *workroom* at the back of the tailor's shop.

work·sheet /ˈwɚkˌʃiːt/ *noun, pl* **-sheets** [*count*]
1 : a piece of paper that contains printed exercises and problems to be done by a student
2 : a printed form that is used in planning or calculating something • a tax *worksheet*

work·shop /ˈwɚkˌʃɑːp/ *noun, pl* **-shops** [*count*]
1 : a place where things are made or repaired • He's in his *workshop* working on the lawnmower.
2 : a class or series of classes in which a small group of people learn the methods and skills used in doing something • a photography/music *workshop*

work–shy *adj* [*more ~; most ~*] *Brit, disapproving* : not willing to work : LAZY • *work-shy* layabouts

work·sta·tion /ˈwɚkˌsteɪʃən/ *noun, pl* **-tions** [*count*]
1 : an area that has the equipment needed for one person to do a particular job • Employees should keep their *workstations* neat and organized.
2 : a computer that is connected to a computer network

work–study program *noun, pl* **~ -grams** [*count*] *US* : a program that gives high school or college students the opportunity to work in a particular field in order to gain experience

work·top /ˈwɚkˌtɑːp/ *noun, pl* **-tops** [*count*] *Brit* : [1]COUNTER 2a

work–to–rule *noun* [*singular*] : the practice by workers of refusing to do any work that is not strictly required as a part of their jobs in order to protest something (such as unfair working conditions)

work·week /ˈwɚkˌwiːk/ *noun, pl* **-weeks** [*count*] *US* : the total amount of hours or days that you spend working at a job in one week • a 5-day/40-hour *workweek* • a shortened *workweek* — called also (*chiefly Brit*) *working week*

[1]**world** /ˈwɚld/ *noun, pl* **worlds**
1 a ***the world*** : the earth and all the people and things on it • the countries/people/languages of *the world* • He is famous throughout *the world*. • They sailed around *the world*. • people from (all) around/across *the world* = people from all over *the world* • the tallest building in *the* (whole/entire) *world* = *the world's* tallest building • It can be found anywhere/everywhere in *the world*. • The product is shipped ***halfway around/across the world***. • The problem occurs in many/other/different ***parts of the world***. • The island was cut off from ***the rest of the world***. • They want to ***see/travel the world***. **b** [*count*] : a part of the world and the people and things that exist there • the Eastern and Western *worlds* • the industrialized *world* • people living in the English-speaking *world* — see also FIRST WORLD, NEW WORLD, OLD WORLD, THIRD WORLD
2 [*count*] : human society • the history of the *world* • the ancient and modern *worlds* • I felt alone in the *world*. • She became depressed and withdrew from the *world*. • In an ideal/perfect *world*, no one would go hungry. • ambitious students who want to ***change the world*** • She seems ignorant of the ***ways of the world***. ✧ ***The real world*** is the world where everyone lives, works, and deals with everyday problems. • After college, she went out into *the real world* and got a job. • He seems out of touch with *the real world*.
3 ***the world*** : the people in the world • She felt that *the world* was against her. • We had no help or support. It was just us against *the world*. • They announced their discovery to *the world*. • He sat in a café watching *the world* go by. [=watching people go by] • *The world* watched as he attempted to break the Olympic record. • She felt ***the eyes of the world*** watching her. • It's a private matter. I wish you wouldn't tell ***the whole world*** about it! ✧ ***The outside world*** refers to the people who live outside of a particular place or who do not belong to a particular group. • The inmates have little contact with *the outside world*. • a local artist who was unknown to *the outside world*
4 [*count*] **a** : a particular kind of interest, activity, or social situation, or the people who are involved in it • the art/music/fashion *world* • the business and financial *worlds* • the *world* of the rich and famous — see also TWILIGHT WORLD **b** : a group of things of a particular type • the animal/plant/insect *world* **c** : a particular environment • the natural *world* • exploring the underwater *world* • Technology is forever changing our *world*.
5 [*count*] **a** : a particular part of human life and experience • the physical/material/spiritual *world* **b** : the life and experiences of a particular person • His (whole/entire) *world* fell apart when his wife left him. • She acts as if she doesn't ***have a care in the world***. [=she acts as if she has no worries at all]
6 [*count*] : a planet where there is life : a planet that is like Earth • stories about other *worlds* • a creature from another *world*
7 [*singular*] *informal* : a great amount *of* something • He's in a *world of* trouble. [=a lot of trouble] • The new mattress made a *world of* difference. • A vacation would do you a *world of* good.
8 ***the world*** : all that is important : EVERYTHING • I would give my children *the world* if I could. • She ***means the world to*** me. [=she is extremely important to me; I care about her very much] • It would *mean the world to* me if you came with me. • He ***thinks the world of*** you. [=he thinks very highly of you]

all the time in the world : a great deal of time to do something • Hurry up! We don't have *all the time in the world*!

a world away from : completely different from (something) • This small village is *a world away from* the hustle and bustle of the city.

come down in the world : to become less wealthy, successful, etc. • It is sad to see how he has *come down in the world*.

come into the world *formal + literary* : to be born • Their son *came into the world* at 10:32 p.m. on January 14, 2003.

dead to the world see [1]DEAD

for all the world : in every way : exactly • The copy looked *for all the world* like the original.

for the world *informal* : for any reason — used to make a statement more forceful • I wouldn't miss your wedding *for the world*.

in the world *informal* : among many possibilities — used to make a question or statement more forceful • What *in the world* [=*on earth*] are you talking about? • Where *in the world* were you? • How *in the world* could you do that to her? • This is the best apple pie *in the world*. • There is nothing *in the world* I would like better than to go to your wedding.

in your own world or ***in a world of your own*** ✧ If you ***are/live in a world of your own*** or ***are/live in your own (little) world***, you spend so much time thinking about something that you do not notice what is happening around you. • I tried to talk to him, but he *was in his own little world* and didn't seem to hear what I was saying.

(it's a) small world — used to show surprise when you meet someone you know at an unexpected place or find out that you share a friend, acquaintance, etc., with another person • You know him, too? Wow, *it's a small world*.

move up in the world : to become more wealthy, successful, etc. • He has really *moved up in the world*.

not long for this world : about to die soon • His grandfather is *not long for this world*.

not the end of the world see [1]END

on top of the world see [1]TOP

out of this world *informal* : very good : EXCELLENT • My

mom's apple pie is *out of this world.*

promise (someone) the world see ²PROMISE

set the world on fire *also chiefly Brit* ***set the world alight*** *informal* : to be very successful and attract a lot of attention • The company is doing all right, but they haven't exactly *set the world on fire.*

the best of all (possible) worlds : the best possible situation • The current economic situation is *the best of all possible worlds* for investors.

the best/worst of both worlds ✧ When you have *the best of both worlds*, you have all the advantages of two different situations and none of the disadvantages. • I have *the best of both worlds*—a wonderful family and a great job. When you have *the worst of both worlds*, you have all the disadvantages of two different situations and none of the advantages. • Living in the suburbs is *the worst of both worlds*—there's neither the excitement of the city nor the quiet of the country.

the (whole) world over : everywhere in the world • His books have entertained readers *the world over.*

the world is your oyster see OYSTER

world (is) coming to ✧ People say that they ***don't know what the world is coming to*** or they ask ***What is the world coming to?*** when they are shocked or disgusted by something that has happened. • I *don't know what the world is coming to* when so many poor children have to go to bed hungry every night.

world revolves around **1** ✧ If you think ***the world revolves around you***, you think that your own life, problems, etc., are more important than other people's. • I can't just drop everything to help you. *The world* doesn't *revolve around you*, you know. **2** ✧ If ***your world revolves around (someone or something)***, that person or thing is extremely important in your life. • *Their world revolves around* their children.

world(s) apart ✧ If something is ***a world apart from*** something else, or if two people or things are ***worlds apart***, they are completely different. • The place where she lives now is *a world apart from* the small town where she grew up. • They are *worlds apart* [=they disagree very much] on most issues.

— see also MAN OF THE WORLD, WOMAN OF THE WORLD

²**world** *adj, always used before a noun*

1 : of or relating to the whole world • *world* history/leaders • She broke the *world* record. • They won the *world* championship.

2 a : extending or found throughout the world : WORLDWIDE • *world* peace **b** : involving many parts of the world or the whole world • a *world* tour **c** : known or famous throughout the world • a *world* authority on gemstones

world–beat·er /ˈwɚld,biːtɚ/ *noun, pl* **-ers** [*count*] : someone or something that is better than all others of the same kind • He's a pretty good golfer, but he's no *world-beater.*

— **world–beat·ing** /ˈwɚld,biːtɪŋ/ *adj* • a *world-beating* athlete/car

world–class *adj* : among the best in the world • a *world-class* athlete

World Cup *noun, pl* ~ **Cups** [*count*] : an international competition in a sport (such as soccer or hockey) • they won the *World Cup* • the *World Cup* finals

world–famous *adj* : famous throughout the world • a *world-famous* scientist

world·ly /ˈwɚldli/ *adj*

1 *always used before a noun* : of or relating to the human world and ordinary life rather than to religious or spiritual matters • *worldly* goods/pleasures

2 [*more* ~; *most* ~] : having a lot of practical experience and knowledge about life and the world • She is more *worldly* than her younger sister.

— **world·li·ness** *noun* [*noncount*]

world·ly–wise /ˈwɚldli,waɪz/ *adj* [*more* ~; *most* ~] : having or showing a lot of experience and knowledge about life and the world : WORLDLY • He is very *wordly-wise* for someone so young.

world music *noun* [*noncount*] : popular music that is based on musical traditions from different parts of the world and that often has a rhythm that you can dance to

world power *noun, pl* ~ **-ers** [*count*] : a country that is powerful enough to affect the entire world by its influence or actions

world–renowned *adj* : known and admired throughout the world : WORLD-FAMOUS • a *world-renowned* authority on energy conservation

World Series *noun, pl* **World Series** [*count*]

1 *baseball* : the annual championship of the major leagues in the United States • the first game of the *World Series* • The team has played in three *World Series.*

2 *US* : a contest or event that is the most important one of its kind • This tournament is the *World Series* of poker.

world's fair *noun, pl* ~ **fairs** [*count*] *chiefly US* : a very large public event at which things from all over the world are displayed

world·view /ˈwɚld,vjuː/ *noun, pl* **-views** [*count*] : the way someone thinks about the world • a scientific/religious/cultural *worldview* • The two groups have very different *worldviews.*

world war *noun, pl* ~ **wars** : a war involving many nations of the world [*count*] the ***First World War*** = ***World War I*** [=the war that was fought mainly in Europe from 1914 to 1918] • the ***Second World War*** = ***World War II*** [=the war that was fought mainly in Europe and Asia from 1939 to 1945] • He fought in both *World Wars.* [*noncount*] The nations were prepared for *world war.*

world–wea·ry /ˈwɚld,wiri/ *adj* [*more* ~; *most* ~] : no longer having or showing excitement or interest in life • a *world-weary* young man • She spoke in a *world-weary* voice.

— **world–wea·ri·ness** *noun* [*noncount*]

world·wide /ˈwɚldˈwaɪd/ *adj* : happening or existing in all parts of the world • *worldwide* disarmament • a *worldwide* network • News of the attack attracted *worldwide* attention.

— **worldwide** *adv* • The disease affects millions of people *worldwide.*

World Wide Web *noun*

the World Wide Web : the part of the Internet that you can look at with a special program (called a browser) and that is made up of many documents which are linked together — abbr. *www* — called also *the Web*

¹**worm** /ˈwɚm/ *noun, pl* **worms**

1 [*count*] : a long, thin animal that has a soft body with no legs or bones and that often lives in the ground • I often see *worms* in the garden. • We always used *worms* as bait for fishing.— see also EARTHWORM

2 [*count*] : the young form of some insects that looks like a small worm — see also GLOWWORM, SILKWORM

3 [*count*] *informal* + *disapproving* : a person who is not liked or respected : a very bad person • I didn't think that she would go on a date with that *worm.* [=wretch]

4 *worms* [*plural*] : an infection or a disease caused by tiny worms that live inside the body of an animal or person • The veterinarian told us that our dog has *worms.* — see also ROUNDWORM, TAPEWORM

5 [*count*] *computers* : a computer virus that causes damage to computers connected to each other by a network

can of worms see ²CAN

the early bird catches/gets the worm see ²EARLY

the worm turns *informal* — used to talk about how a situation can suddenly change so that a person who has been weak, unlucky, unsuccessful, etc., can become strong, lucky, successful, etc. • *The worm turns* quickly in the world of politics. • Some investors believe that *the worm has turned*, and that the economy is getting better.

— **worm·like** /ˈwɚm,laɪk/ *adj* [*more* ~; *most* ~] • tiny *wormlike* creatures

²**worm** *verb* **worms; wormed; worm·ing**

1 *always followed by an adverb or preposition* : to move or proceed by twisting and turning [*no obj*] He slowly *wormed* through the crowd. [+ *obj*] He slowly *wormed* his way through the crowd.

2 [+ *obj*] : to give (an animal) medicine that destroys the small worms that live inside it and cause illness • *worm* a puppy • You should have the dog vaccinated and *wormed.*

worm into [*phrasal verb*] ***worm (your way or yourself) into (something)*** *informal* : to get (yourself) into (a desired position, situation, etc.) in a gradual and usually clever or dishonest way • I *wormed my way into* a job at the theater. • He somehow managed to *worm himself* back *into* her life.

worm out of [*phrasal verb*] *informal* **1** ***worm (something) out of (someone)*** : to get (information) from (someone) by asking many questions, by using clever methods of persuasion, etc. • We're still trying to *worm* it *out of* him. • She finally *wormed* the truth *out of* him. [=she finally got him to tell her the truth] **2** ***worm out of (something) or worm (your way) out of (something)*** : to avoid doing (something) in usually a clever or dishonest way ▪ He always managed to *worm his way out of* doing the dishes.

worm·hole /ˈwɚmˌhoul/ *noun, pl* **-holes** [*count*]
1 : a hole or passage made by a worm ▪ We found tiny *wormholes* in the potatoes.
2 *technical* **:** a hole or tunnel in outer space that some people believe connects two very distant places ▪ a *wormhole* in space

worm·wood /ˈwɚmˌwʊd/ *noun* [*noncount*] **:** a plant that has a bitter taste

wormy /ˈwɚmi/ *adj* **worm·i·er; -est** [*also more ~; most ~*]
1 : full of worms or damaged by worms ▪ *wormy* fruit
2 : resembling a worm ▪ *wormy* [=*wormlike*] creatures

worn *past participle of* [1]WEAR

worn–out /ˈwoɚnˈaʊt/ *adj* [*more ~; most ~*]
1 *of a thing* **:** too old or damaged from use to be used any longer ▪ My jeans were *worn-out* and I needed a new pair. ▪ *worn-out* seat cushions
2 : very tired **:** EXHAUSTED ▪ I'm *worn-out* after that hike. ▪ The horses are *worn-out* from the long ride.

wor·ried /ˈwɚrid/ *adj* [*more ~; most ~*] **:** feeling or showing fear and concern because you think that something bad has happened or could happen ▪ Her parents became *worried* when she didn't come home by dark. ▪ We were *worried* that we would arrive late. ▪ She's always *worried* about money. ▪ I'm not *worried* at all about the weather. ▪ She had a *worried* look on her face. ▪ I'm very *worried* about the test results. ▪ He has plenty to be *worried* about. ▪ We've been ***worried sick*** [=extremely worried] about you! ▪ You ***had me worried*** there for a moment—I thought that you really hurt yourself. ▪ Oh, I'm so glad you're not quitting! You really *had me worried.*
– wor·ried·ly /ˈwɚridli/ *adv*

wor·ri·er /ˈwɚrijɚ/ *noun, pl* **-ers** [*count*] **:** a person who worries too much or who worries about unimportant things ▪ She's a real *worrier.* ▪ He's such a *worrier.*

wor·ri·some /ˈwɚrisəm/ *adj* [*more ~; most ~*] *chiefly US* **:** causing people to worry ▪ *worrisome* [=*upsetting*] news ▪ There is the *worrisome* possibility of hurricane damage on the coast. ▪ a very *worrisome* situation

[1]**wor·ry** /ˈwɚri/ *verb* **-ries; -ried; -ry·ing**
1 : to think about problems or fears **:** to feel or show fear and concern because you think that something bad has happened or could happen [*no obj*] We didn't want you to *worry.* ▪ Don't *worry.* You'll be fine. ▪ Don't make your parents *worry.* ▪ When they didn't call after two hours, we began to *worry.* ▪ They were fine. We needn't have *worried.* — often + ***about*** ▪ Let the travel agent *worry about* the details. ▪ Haven't we got enough to *worry about*? ▪ We don't have to *worry about* choosing a restaurant. [=someone else will choose a restaurant] ▪ The nurse said her condition was ***nothing to worry about*** [=her condition was not serious] ▪ I'll take care of it. ***Don't worry about a thing.*** — sometimes + *over* ▪ She *worried over* her husband's health. [+ *obj*] — + *that* ▪ Medical experts *worry that* a new strain of the virus will be more difficult to contain. ▪ We *worry that* children don't get enough exercise. ▪ My parents *worry* [=*fear*] *that* I won't go to college.
2 [+ *obj*] **:** to make (someone) anxious or upset **:** to cause (someone) to worry ▪ His poor health *worries* me. ▪ What's *worrying* you? [=what is causing you to feel upset?] ▪ It doesn't seem to *worry* him that rain is in the forecast. ▪ We didn't tell you about the accident because we didn't want to *worry* you. ▪ ***Don't worry yourself.*** [=don't be upset or concerned] ▪ He ***worried himself sick*** [=he was extremely worried] before the exam.
not to worry *informal* — used to say that there is no cause for concern or worry ▪ "It looks like we're almost out of milk." "*Not to worry.* I'll get some more when I go to the store this afternoon."
worry at [*phrasal verb*] ***worry at (something)*** *chiefly Brit* **1 :** to pull, twist, or bite (something) repeatedly ▪ The dog was in the corner *worrying at* a bone. **2 :** to try to solve (a problem) by thinking about it for a long time ▪ She kept *worrying at* the problem all day.

[2]**worry** *noun, pl* **-ries**
1 [*noncount*] **:** a feeling of concern about something bad that might happen **:** the state or condition of worrying about something **:** ANXIETY ▪ His mother's health is a constant source of *worry.* [=*concern*] ▪ She finally ended months of *worry* over her credit card debt when she finished paying off her bill. ▪ His high blood pressure is cause for *worry.* ▪ Her parents have been ***sick with worry*** [=extremely worried] for days since the accident.
2 [*count*] **:** a problem or concern **:** something that causes you to be worried ▪ Our greatest *worry* is that she'll get lost. ▪ His only *worry* right now is getting to the airport on time. ▪ What's your *worry*? [=what are you worried about?] ▪ His money *worries* [=*difficulties*] are over. ▪ His mother's health is a ***constant worry.*** ▪ Her lost luggage was ***the least of her worries*** [=an unimportant problem] at the moment.
no worries *chiefly Australia + Brit, informal* — used to say that there is no reason to worry ▪ "What if we miss the bus?" "*No worries* [=*no problem*], there's another one in seven minutes."

worry beads *noun* [*plural*] **:** small beads on a string that people hold and move with their fingers in order to have something to do when they are nervous

wor·ry·wart /ˈwɚriˌwoɚt/ *noun, pl* **-warts** [*count*] *US, informal* **:** a person who worries too much or who worries about things that are not important ▪ My father is a real *worrywart.*

[1]**worse** /ˈwɚs/ *adj, comparative form of* [1]BAD
1 : lower in quality ▪ His schoolwork/grades got *worse* after his parents split up. ▪ Her second book was *worse* than her first one. ▪ Her first book was bad, but her second one is ***even worse.*** ▪ This one is ***no worse*** than that one.
2 : less pleasant, attractive, appealing, effective, useful, etc. ▪ Could the situation get any *worse*? ▪ You have even *worse* luck than I do. ▪ It turned out to be a *worse* idea than we originally thought. ▪ She ended up in *worse* shape than when she started. ▪ Things are bad for him now, but he was in a *worse* situation last week. ▪ Cheer up. ***Things could be worse,*** you know. ▪ I have ***even/still worse*** news for you. ▪ He broke the vase but ***what is worse,*** he lied to me about it. ▪ There's ***nothing worse than*** having wet socks. ▪ My car broke down, and ***to make matters worse,*** I can't afford to fix it. [=the situation is even worse because I can't afford to fix it]
3 : more serious or severe ▪ Her symptoms have gotten/grown *worse.* ▪ Don't scratch your rash or you'll make it *worse.* ▪ Lying will only get you into *worse* trouble. ▪ The rain got *worse* as the day went on.
4 a : in poorer health than before ▪ We thought she had recovered, but then she got/grew/became *worse.* ▪ I feel *worse* today than I felt yesterday. ▪ The medicine seems to have made the patient *worse.* **b :** less happy or pleased ▪ After we talked, I felt even *worse.* ▪ The more I dwelled on my mistakes, ***the worse*** I felt.
5 : less appropriate or acceptable ▪ There are *worse* ways to spend your money/time. ▪ You couldn't have picked a *worse* time to ask for a raise.
6 : less morally right or good ▪ It may be no *worse* to cheat than to steal. ▪ People have done *worse* things.
7 : less skillful ▪ He's a *worse* dancer than I am. ▪ I've gotten *worse* at golf.
from bad to worse see [1]BAD
worse for wear see [2]WEAR
your bark is worse than your bite see [2]BARK

[2]**worse** *adv, comparative form of* BADLY
1 : in a worse way ▪ I did much *worse* on my second try. ▪ You drive *worse* than he does. ▪ That isn't an excellent score, but you could have done *worse.* ▪ She was hurt *worse* than I was.
2 — used to say that what is going to be described is worse than what was mentioned before ▪ I got into an accident and suffered a cut on my arm. *Worse,* my car was totaled. ▪ I was scared that they were going to laugh at me—***or worse,*** beat me up. ▪ She found out that he was cheating on her. ***Even worse,*** her friends knew that he was and never told her.
could do worse — used to say that a particular choice, action, etc., is not a bad one ▪ You *could do worse* than to vote for her. [=voting for her would be a good idea]

[3]**worse** *noun* [*noncount*] **:** something that is worse ▪ I didn't want to tell her that *worse* was yet to come. ▪ Her accusations don't bother me. I've been accused of *worse.* ▪ The patient's condition ***took a turn for the worse*** [=became worse] overnight. ▪ When I lost my job, my life *took a turn for the worse.*
for better or (for) worse see [3]BETTER
if (the) worse comes to (the) worst, if worse comes to worse see [3]WORST

wors·en /ˈwɚsn̩/ *verb* **-ens; -ened; -en·ing :** to make (something) worse or to become worse [+ *obj*] Spending more money is only going to *worsen* the problem. [*no obj*] The situation has *worsened.* ▪ *worsening* conditions

worse off *adj*
1 : having less money and possessions **:** less wealthy ▪ He was *worse off* financially than he was before.

2 : in a worse position ▪ If you quit school, you will be *worse off.*

[1]wor·ship /ˈwɚʃəp/ *verb* **-ships; -shipped** *also US* **-shiped; -ship·ping** *also US* **-ship·ing**

1 [+ *obj*] **:** to honor or respect (someone or something) as a god ▪ Many ancient cultures *worshipped* the sun and moon.

2 : to show respect and love for God or for a god especially by praying, having religious services, etc. [*no obj*] They *worship* at this temple. [+ *obj*] I *worship* God in my own way.

3 : to love or honor (someone or something) very much or too much [+ *obj*] As a kid I *worshipped* [=*idolized*] my brother. ▪ Our society *worships* money. ▪ He ***worships the ground she walks on***. [=he admires/loves her very much] [*no obj*] My parents ***worship at the altar of*** money. [=my parents value money too much]

– wor·ship·per *also US* **wor·ship·er** *noun, pl* **-ship·pers** *also US* **-ship·ers** [*count*] ▪ *worshippers* of Buddha — see also SUN WORSHIPPER

[2]worship *noun*

1 [*noncount*] **:** the act of showing respect and love for a god especially by praying with other people who believe in the same god **:** the act of worshipping God or a god ▪ *worship* of gods and goddesses ▪ The ceremony will be held at our ***place/house of worship***. [=at our church, synagogue, etc.] ▪ *Worship* services are held daily.

2 [*noncount*] **:** excessive admiration for someone ▪ the media's *worship* of celebrities — see also HERO WORSHIP

3 ***Worship*** [*count*] *Brit* — used as a title when addressing or referring to certain officials (such as mayors and magistrates); used with *his, her, your,* or *their* ▪ Thank you, *your Worship*.

wor·ship·ful /ˈwɚʃəpfəl/ *adj* [*more* ~; *most* ~] **:** feeling or showing great admiration and love for someone or something ▪ She was greeted by thousands of *worshipful* fans.

[1]worst /ˈwɚst/ *adj, superlative form of* [1]BAD

1 a : worse than all others ▪ This is the *worst* car I've ever bought. ▪ In my opinion, it's her *worst* book. ▪ It was the *worst* movie I've ever seen. ▪ His *worst* quality is his impatience. ▪ This has got to be the *worst* day of my life. ▪ The *worst* part of working there is the long commute. ▪ My *worst* fears came true. ▪ I am my own *worst* critic. [=I criticize my work more harshly than anyone else] ▪ He lives in the *worst* area of the city. **b :** least skillful, talented, or successful ▪ He is the *worst* singer I've ever heard. ▪ They're the *worst* team ever.

2 : least appropriate, useful, or helpful ▪ That is the *worst* advice I've ever heard. ▪ I'm having the *worst* luck today. ▪ Leaving now is the *worst* thing you could do. ▪ He is the *worst* person to ask for advice. ▪ You've picked the *worst* time to come over. ▪ She called at the *worst* possible moment.

in the worst way *US, informal* **:** very much ▪ I want a new bike *in the worst way*.

worst of all — used to refer to the least pleasant or appealing part of something that has many bad parts ▪ I forgot my backpack, was late for class, and *worst of all*, I studied the wrong material for the test.

your own worst enemy see ENEMY

[2]worst *adv, superlative form of* BADLY **:** in the worst way **:** in a way that is worse than all others ▪ My sister was hurt *worst*. ▪ the areas *worst* hit by the drought ▪ She was voted the *worst*-dressed celebrity of 2005.

[3]worst *noun*

1 ***the worst*** **:** the worst person or thing ▪ What's *the worst* that can happen? ▪ When it comes to dancing, he is *the worst*. ▪ That movie was *the worst*! ▪ He is *the worst* of the bunch. ▪ They warned us to ***expect/fear the worst***. [=assume that something very bad would happen] ▪ Go ahead, ***do your worst*** [=hurt me as much as you can]! I'm not afraid of you! **:** the worst group of people or things ▪ This city's schools are *the worst* in the nation. = This city's schools are *the* nation's *worst*. ▪ He is one of *the worst* in the class. ▪ They are *the worst* of enemies. [=they dislike each other very much] **:** the worst part of something ▪ Even in *the worst* of times, she was hopeful. ▪ It's still raining, but *the worst* of the storm is over now. ▪ ***The worst of it is***, I don't even know how to contact her. ▪ The company was operating on high costs and low prices—***the worst of both worlds***.

2 [*singular*] **:** someone's or something's least effective or pleasant condition **:** someone's or something's worst condition — used in phrases like ***at your worst*** and ***at its worst*** ▪ This is politics *at its worst*. ▪ He's *at his worst* when he's drunk. ▪ She visited us when the house was *at its worst*.

at worst — used to refer to a result, condition, etc., that is the worst one possible ▪ *At worst*, you'll have to pay a fine, but you won't lose your license. ▪ He hoped that *at worst* he would suffer only a minor loss in the investment. ▪ At best the government is incompetent, and *at worst*, it is totally corrupt.

bring out the worst in ✧ If someone or something *brings out the worst in you*, that person or thing causes you to use or show your worst qualities. ▪ She seems to *bring out the worst in* him. ▪ I think competition *brings out the worst in* people. ▪ Drinking *brings out the worst in* him. [=makes him behave very badly]

get the worst of it **:** to lose a fight, argument, battle, etc. ▪ The bruises on his face after the fight showed that he'd *gotten the worst of it*.

if (the) worst comes to (the) worst *or* ***if (the) worse comes to (the) worst*** *also* ***if worse comes to worse*** **:** if the worst possible thing happens ▪ *If worst comes to worst*, you can always ask me for help.

wor·sted /ˈwustəd/ *noun* [*noncount*] **:** a type of cloth or yarn made from wool ▪ a suit made of *worsted*

[1]worth /ˈwɚθ/ *prep*

1 a — used to indicate the value of something ▪ a ruby *worth* five million dollars ▪ This painting is *worth* a fortune. ▪ You should be paid what your labor is *worth*. ▪ Each correct answer is *worth* five points. **b :** having money and possessions equal in value to (an amount) ▪ an actor *worth* several million dollars ▪ The corporation is *worth* billions of dollars.

2 : good, valuable, or important enough for (something) **:** deserving of (something) ▪ A carefully written cover letter and resume is *worth* the effort. ▪ It takes a long time to get a table at the restaurant, but the food is well *worth* the wait. ▪ The movie was good, but I didn't think it was *worth* all the fuss/hype. ▪ It's *worth* a try. = It's *worth* trying. ▪ Chicago is *worth* a visit. I think you'll really like it. ▪ Do you think the car is *worth* buying? ▪ It is *worth* noting/mentioning that his father and mother are also doctors. ▪ This book is not *worth* reading. ▪ an idea well *worth* consideration ▪ Going to college was ***worth every penny***. ▪ This contract ***isn't worth the paper it's written/printed on***. [=this contract has no real value; this contract is not legally valid] ▪ I promise that speaking with her will be ***worth your while***. [=speaking with her will be a good/useful thing for you to do] ▪ I had to sacrifice all of my free time to make this film, but in the end, it was all ***worth it***. ▪ The repairs cost a lot of money, but they were *worth it*. ▪ It's not *worth* fixing the car. = It's not *worth it* to fix the car. = The car is not *worth* fixing.

a bird in the hand is worth two in the bush see BIRD

a picture is worth a thousand words — used to say that it is often easier to show something in a picture than to describe it with words

for all something or someone is worth **:** to the fullest extent possible **:** as much as possible or with as much effort as possible ▪ They milked/exploited their advantage *for all it was worth*. [=they used their advantage to help themselves as much as they could] ▪ He was fighting *for all he was worth*. [=fighting as hard as he could] ▪ I ran *for all I was worth*. [=as fast as I could]

for what it's worth — used to say that you are not sure how helpful something you are about to say will be ▪ *For what it's worth*, I don't think your dad meant to insult you.

not worth the candle see CANDLE

worth your salt see [1]SALT

worth your weight in gold see [1]GOLD

[2]worth *noun* [*noncount*]

1 : an amount of something that has a specified value, that lasts for a specified length of time, etc. — + *of* ▪ He bought 40 dollars' *worth of* gas. [=an amount of gas that costs 40 dollars] ▪ We carried a week's *worth of* food [=an amount of food that will last for a week] on the hike. ▪ She has 15 years' *worth of* experience in advertising. [=she has worked in advertising for 15 years] ▪ 30 pounds' *worth of* rice [=an amount of rice weighing 30 pounds] ▪ She wrote a whole album's *worth of* songs. [=she wrote enough songs to make an album] ▪ A whole day's *worth of* work was erased when I deleted the file.

2 : the amount of money that something is worth **:** VALUE ▪ A diamond's *worth* is determined partly by its cut and clarity. ▪ The *worth* of the stocks has increased. ▪ The furniture was of little *worth* since it was in such bad condition. ▪ His ***personal worth*** is estimated at five million dollars. [=all of his money and possessions are worth about five million dollars]

3 : usefulness or importance **:** VALUE ▪ The painting is of little artistic *worth*. = The painting has little artistic *worth*. [=*merit*] ▪ He has ***proved his worth*** to the team. ▪ The book

has *proved its worth* by saving me hundreds of dollars.

your money's worth see MONEY

worth·less /ˈwɚθləs/ *adj* [*more ~; most ~*]
1 a : having no financial value ▪ *worthless* coins/stocks **b** : having no use, importance, or effect ▪ This land is *worthless* [=*useless*] for agriculture. ▪ The boots may be nice, but they're *worthless* if they don't fit you. ▪ a *worthless* guarantee ▪ an uninformed, *worthless* opinion
2 : having no good qualities ▪ a *worthless* coward ▪ She's depressed and believes that she's *worthless.*
– **worth·less·ness** *noun* [*noncount*] ▪ feelings of *worthlessness* ▪ the *worthlessness* of his argument

worth·while /ˈwɚθˌwajəl/ *adj* [*more ~; most ~*] : worth doing or getting : good enough, important enough, etc., to be worth spending time, effort, or money on ▪ a *worthwhile* investment ▪ The money is for a *worthwhile* cause/charity. ▪ The trip was *worthwhile.* ▪ Seeing my children's joy made building the tree house all *worthwhile.* ▪ Is it *worthwhile* to try to fix my computer?

[1]**wor·thy** /ˈwɚði/ *adj* **wor·thi·er; -est** [*or more ~; most ~*]
1 : good and deserving respect, praise, or attention ▪ Your donations will be going to a *worthy* cause. ▪ I consider him a *worthy* opponent. ▪ She is a *worthy* successor to the mayor.
2 : having enough good qualities to be considered important, useful, etc. — usually + *of* ▪ Your achievements are *worthy of* respect. [=your achievements deserve respect] ▪ The suggestion is *worthy of* consideration. ▪ Her latest book is *worthy of* mention. ▪ My girlfriend's parents felt that I wasn't *worthy of* her. [=felt that I was not good enough to be her boyfriend] — sometimes followed by *to + verb* ▪ The voters will decide if he is *worthy to become* governor.
worthy of : good enough to have been written, said, done, or created by (someone, especially someone famous) ▪ a symphony *worthy of* Mahler [=the kind of symphony that Mahler would write] — see also [1]WORTHY 2 (above)
– **wor·thi·ness** /ˈwɚðinəs/ *noun* [*noncount*] ▪ He must prove his *worthiness* to lead the country.

[2]**worthy** *noun, pl* **wor·thies** [*count*] : an important or respected person — often used in a joking or disapproving way to refer to people who think of themselves as important ▪ The party was attended by the mayor and a large group of local *worthies*.

would /ˈwʊd, wəd, əd/ *verb* [*modal verb*]
1 — used to indicate what someone said or thought about what was going to happen or be done ▪ She said she *would* be leaving soon. [=she said, "I will be leaving soon"] ▪ She said (that) she *would* help me with my project. ▪ He thought (that) the drive *would* take about two hours. ▪ I had no idea where the path *would* lead me. ▪ They knew (that) I *would* enjoy the trip. ▪ I never thought that she *would* lie to me.
2 — used to talk about a possible situation that has not happened or that you are imagining ▪ You *would* look good in a tuxedo. ▪ If I could leave work early, I *would.* ▪ It *would* be a shame to miss the party. ▪ What *would* you do if you won the lottery? ▪ You *would* be stupid to quit your job. = It *would* be stupid (of you) to quit your job. [=if you quit your job, you will be doing something stupid] ▪ Things *would* be different if I still had that job. ▪ If you lived closer, I *would* see you every day. ▪ If they were coming, they *would* be here by now.
3 — used with *have* to talk about something that did not happen or was not done ▪ She *would have* won the race if she hadn't tripped. ▪ I *would have* stopped by your house had I known you were home. ▪ If you had told me that you were coming, I *would have* picked you up at the airport.
4 — used to say what you think someone should do or to ask for someone's opinion about what to do ▪ If I were you, I *would* go to the hospital. [=I think that you should go to the hospital] ▪ I *would* take the train instead of driving into the city. ▪ I *would* turn back if I were you. ▪ What *would* you do in my situation?
5 — used to say that you want to do or have something ▪ We ***would like*** to help [=we want to help] in any way we can. ▪ I'*d like* to help, but I'm too busy. ▪ She *would like* to attend college, but she can't afford it right now. ▪ I ***would rather*** have ice cream than cheesecake. = (more commonly) I'*d rather* have ice cream than cheesecake. ▪ I'*d rather* not go out this evening. [=I don't want to go out this evening] ▪ I ***would sooner*** die than be enslaved. ▪ I'*d sooner* starve than eat that disgusting food.
6 — used to ask a polite question or to make a polite request, offer, invitation, etc. ▪ *Would* you please help us? ▪ *Would* you care for some tea? ▪ She asked if I *would* have dinner with her. ▪ *Would* you mind making a little less noise? = Please make a little less noise, *would* you? ▪ *Would* you come this way, please? [=please come this way] ▪ *Would* it be all right if we left a little early? ▪ I ***would like*** to see the wine list. ▪ *Would* you *like* to join me for dinner? ▪ *Would* anyone *like* more coffee?
7 a — used to say that you are willing to do something ▪ I *would* be glad/delighted to help. = I'*d* be glad/delighted to help. ▪ I *would* do anything to protect my children. **b** — used in negative statements to say that someone was not willing to do something ▪ He *would not* help us. = (more commonly) He *wouldn't* help us. [=he refused to help us]
8 — used to express a wish ▪ I wish that he *would* call me more often. = I wish he'*d* call me more often.
9 — used to express your opinion ▪ I *would* hate to have that job. ▪ I *would* love to be in her position.
10 — used to talk about something that always or often happened in the past ▪ When my friend still lived here, we *would* eat lunch together every day. ▪ She *would* always take the nine o'clock bus. = She'*d* always take the nine o'clock bus.
11 — used with *so (that)* to explain why something was done ▪ I packed the vase carefully *so that* it *would* survive the trip. ▪ We left early *so* we *would* be sure to arrive on time.
12 — used to say what you think is probably true ▪ I *would* say that he looks to be around sixty. [=he looks like he might be sixty years old, but I'm not sure] ▪ I *would* think/hope that he was telling the truth, but I really don't know. ▪ "How long will it take?" "I *would* imagine it will take about an hour."
13 — used to say that something is possible or likely ▪ I think my swimming pool *would* [=*could*] hold 20,000 gallons of water.
14 — used to express your displeasure with behavior that you think is typical of someone ▪ "He said that you were the one who made the mistake." "He *would* say that, *wouldn't* he? What a jerk."
15 *old-fashioned + literary* — used to say that you wish something was true, had happened, etc. ▪ I *would* [=*wish*] I were young again. — usually + *that* ▪ I *would* [=*wish*] *that* he had lived. = *Would that* he had lived.
how would I/we know — used to say that you do not know the answer to a question and are surprised that you were asked it ▪ "Where did they go?" "*How would I know*?"

would–be /ˈwʊdˈbi:/ *adj, always used before a noun* — used to describe someone who hopes to be a particular person or type of person ▪ a *would-be* poet/writer [=a person who wants to be a poet/writer] ▪ a *would-be* hero ▪ tips for *would-be* mothers

wouldn't /ˈwʊdn̩t/ — used as a contraction of *would not* ▪ I *wouldn't* call him if I were you. ▪ I knocked on his door, but he *wouldn't* answer.

would've /ˈwʊdəv/ — used as a contraction of *would have* ▪ I *would've* picked you up from the airport if I had known you were coming.

[1]**wound** /ˈwu:nd/ *noun, pl* **wounds** [*count*]
1 : an injury that is caused when a knife, bullet, etc., cuts or breaks the skin ▪ She suffered/received a knife/stab *wound* to/in her thigh. ▪ a gunshot/bullet *wound* — see also FLESH WOUND
2 : a feeling of sadness, anger, etc., that is caused by something bad that has happened to you ▪ Her mother's scorn left a *wound* that never healed. ▪ Talking about her divorce opened up some old *wounds.* [=caused her to again have old feelings of anger, sadness, etc.] ▪ emotional *wounds*
lick your wounds see [1]LICK
rub salt in/into someone's wounds see [1]RUB
time heals all wounds see [1]TIME
twist/turn the knife in the wound see [1]KNIFE

[2]**wound** *verb* **wounds; wound·ed; wound·ing** [+ *obj*]
1 : to injure (someone or something) by cutting or breaking the skin ▪ Four people were seriously/badly *wounded* in the explosion. ▪ The soldier's leg was *wounded* by a grenade.
2 : to cause (someone) to feel emotional pain ▪ I was *wounded* [=*hurt*] by her remarks. ▪ Losing the match ***wounded his pride/ego***.

[3]**wound** /ˈwaʊnd/ *past tense and past participle of* [2]WIND

wound·ed /ˈwu:ndəd/ *adj*
1 : injured by a weapon ▪ badly *wounded* soldiers
2 : feeling emotional pain ▪ *wounded* pride ▪ a *wounded* ego ▪ healing a *wounded* nation
the wounded : people who have been wounded ▪ They carried *the wounded* off the battlefield. ▪ help for ***the walking wounded*** [=people who are injured but still able to walk]

W

wound up *adj, not used before a noun* [*more ~; most ~*] *informal* : nervous or excited ▪ Don't get the kids all *wound up*. ▪ The crowd was *wound up* when the band came on stage.

wove *past tense of* [1]WEAVE

woven *past participle of* [1]WEAVE

[1]**wow** /ˈwaʊ/ *interj* — used to show that you are very surprised or pleased ▪ *Wow*! This is delicious! ▪ Oh, *wow*! I can't believe you came!

[2]**wow** *verb* **wows; wowed; wow·ing** [+ *obj*] *informal* : to impress or excite (someone) very much ▪ Her performance *wowed* the critics.

wpm *abbr* words per minute

wrack /ˈræk/ *verb* **wracks; wracked; wrack·ing** [+ *obj*] : to cause (someone or something) to suffer pain or damage : RACK — usually used as *(be) wracked* ▪ a neighborhood *wracked* by poverty ▪ a criminal who *is wracked* by/with guilt [=a criminal who feels very guilty]

wraith /ˈreɪθ/ *noun, pl* **wraiths** [*count*] : the spirit of a dead person : GHOST
– **wraith·like** /ˈreɪθˌlaɪk/ *adj* ▪ a *wraithlike* figure

[1]**wran·gle** /ˈræŋgəl/ *verb* **wran·gles; wran·gled; wran·gling**
1 [*no obj*] : to argue angrily with someone ▪ They were *wrangling* over/about money.
2 [+ *obj*] *US, informal* : to get (something) by clever methods or by persuading someone ▪ He managed to *wrangle* [=*wangle*] a couple of tickets to the concert.
3 [+ *obj*] *US* : to control and care for (horses, cattle, etc.) on a ranch ▪ He made a living *wrangling* horses.

[2]**wrangle** *noun, pl* **wrangles** [*count*] : a dispute that lasts for a long time ▪ They had a bitter *wrangle* over custody of their children. ▪ a salary *wrangle*

wran·gler /ˈræŋgələ/ *noun, pl* **-glers** [*count*] *US* : a person who takes care of horses on a ranch : COWBOY

[1]**wrap** /ˈræp/ *verb* **wraps; wrapped; wrap·ping**
1 [+ *obj*] **a** : to cover (something) by winding or folding a piece of material around it ▪ They were busy *wrapping* presents late on Christmas Eve. — often + *up, in*, or *with* ▪ Could you *wrap* this box *up* for me? = Could you *wrap up* this box for me? ▪ The nurse *wrapped* the baby *in* a blanket. ▪ She *wrapped* her hair *in* a towel. ▪ magazines *wrapped in* plastic ▪ The handle of the bat was *wrapped with* tape. **b** : to wind or fold (something) around something else ▪ Ribbons were *wrapped* around the dancers' arms. ▪ She *wrapped* a scarf around her neck. ▪ He *wrapped* tape around the bat's handle. **c** : to put (your arms, legs, etc.) around someone or something ▪ I *wrapped* my arms around her. ▪ She *wrapped* her legs around a pillow. ▪ He *wrapped* his hands around the trophy.
2 [*no obj*] : to go *around* something ▪ The line of people went out the door and *wrapped around* the corner.
3 : to finish filming a movie or television show or one of its scenes [*no obj*] After the movie *wraps* [=after the filming of the movie is completed], we'll hold a party for the cast and crew. [+ *obj*] Let's *wrap* this scene (up).
wrap (someone) around your (little) finger *informal* : to have complete control over (someone) ▪ She has him *wrapped around her little finger*. [=she controls him completely; he always does what she wants him to do]
wrap up [*phrasal verb*] **1** ***wrap (something) up*** *or* ***wrap up (something)*** *or* ***wrap up*** : to finish or end (something) ▪ Let's *wrap* this meeting *up*. ▪ The teacher quickly *wrapped up* her lecture toward the end of class. ▪ The meeting *wrapped up* [=*ended*] at four o'clock. — see also WRAP-UP **2** ***wrapped up in*** ✧ If you are *wrapped up in* something, you are fully involved or interested in it. ▪ I was (completely) *wrapped up in* my work, so I didn't hear you come in.
wrap your mind around *US, informal* : to find a way to understand or accept (something) ▪ I just couldn't *wrap my mind around* what had happened.

[2]**wrap** *noun, pl* **wraps**
1 [*noncount*] : material used for covering or wrapping something ▪ holiday ***gift wrap*** — see also PLASTIC WRAP, SHRINK-WRAP
2 [*count*] : a piece of clothing that is wrapped around a person's shoulders, waist, etc.
3 [*count*] : a thin piece of bread that is rolled around a filling of meat, vegetables, etc. ▪ a chicken/veggie *wrap*
4 [*count*] : a treatment for your skin that involves covering your entire body with something (such as wet cloth or seaweed) ▪ I got a ***body wrap*** at the spa.
5 [*count*] : a bandage that you wear around a part of your body to treat or prevent an injury ▪ a leg/elbow *wrap*
it's a wrap *or* ***that's a wrap*** — used to say that the filming of a movie or television show or one of its scenes is finished ▪ *It's a wrap*, folks. We can go home now.
under wraps *informal* : known to only a few people : SECRET ▪ The name of the movie is being ***kept under wraps***.

wrap·around /ˈræpəˌraʊnd/ *adj, always used before a noun* : going all or most of the way around something ▪ *wraparound* sunglasses ▪ a *wraparound* porch ▪ a *wraparound* cover illustration

wrap·per /ˈræpə/ *noun, pl* **-pers** [*count*] : a thin piece of paper, plastic, etc., that covers or surrounds something to protect it ▪ a candy bar *wrapper*

wrapping *noun, pl* **-pings** : a thin piece of paper, plastic, fabric, etc., that covers or surrounds something to protect it [*noncount*] She tore the *wrapping* off the present. [*count*] Some of the mummy's *wrappings* had been removed.

wrapping paper *noun* [*noncount*] : paper that is used to wrap gifts

wrap–up /ˈræpˌʌp/ *noun, pl* **-ups** [*count*] *US* : a brief statement that gives the most important information about what has happened or been done : SUMMARY ▪ a news *wrap-up* — often + *of* ▪ Can you give me a *wrap-up of* the game? — see also *wrap up* at [1]WRAP

wrath /ˈræθ, *Brit* ˈrɒθ/ *noun* [*noncount*] *formal* + *old-fashioned* : extreme anger ▪ the *wrath* of the gods — sometimes used figuratively ▪ These buildings somehow survived the hurricane's *wrath*. ***synonyms*** see [1]ANGER
– **wrath·ful** /ˈræθfəl, *Brit* ˈrɒθfəl/ *adj* [*more ~; most ~*] ▪ *wrathful* deities

wreak /ˈriːk/ *verb* **wreaks; wreaked; wreak·ing** [+ *obj*] : to cause (something very harmful or damaging) ▪ Gangs have been *wreaking* mayhem in the city. — usually + *on* or *upon* ▪ The hurricane *wreaked* terrible damage/destruction *on* coastal cities. ▪ the devastation that alcoholism can *wreak upon* families ▪ The virus ***wreaked havoc on*** my computer. [=the virus caused great damage to my computer] ▪ He swore to ***wreak vengeance/revenge on*** them.

wreath /ˈriːθ/ *noun, pl* **wreaths** /ˈriːðz, ˈriːθs/ [*count*]
1 a : an arrangement of leaves or flowers in the shape of a circle that is worn or placed as a sign of honor or victory ▪ The President laid a *wreath* of flowers on the hero's grave. ▪ The ancient Romans awarded laurel *wreaths* to winners of athletic contests. **b** : an arrangement of leaves, flowers, fruits, etc., in the shape of a circle that is used for decoration ▪ Every December, I put a Christmas *wreath* on my front door.
2 *literary* : something that is shaped like a circle ▪ a *wreath* of flame ▪ a *wreath* of stars

wreath

wreathe /ˈriːð/ *verb* **wreathes; wreathed; wreath·ing** [+ *obj*] *literary* : to surround or cover (something) ▪ Mist *wreathed* the forest. ▪ buildings *wreathed* with ivy — often + *in* ▪ mountaintops *wreathed in* clouds — sometimes used figuratively ▪ She was *wreathed in* glory. ▪ His face was *wreathed in* smiles. [=he was very happy and was smiling a lot]

[1]**wreck** /ˈrɛk/ *noun, pl* **wrecks** [*count*]
1 a : a vehicle, airplane, etc., that has been badly damaged or destroyed ▪ Firefighters pulled him from the (car) *wreck*. **b** : a ruined or destroyed ship : SHIPWRECK ▪ a sunken *wreck*
2 *US* : an accident in which a car, airplane, train, etc., is badly damaged or destroyed ▪ This car has never been in a *wreck*. ▪ a car/train/plane *wreck*
3 *informal* : a person who is very tired, ill, worried, or unhappy ▪ The stress of her final exams made her a *wreck*. ▪ Dad was a ***nervous wreck*** on the day I had my surgery.
4 *informal* : something that is not in good condition ▪ Who would buy this *wreck* of a car? ▪ The house is a *wreck*.

[2]**wreck** *verb* **wrecks; wrecked; wreck·ing** [+ *obj*]
1 : to damage (something) so badly that it cannot be repaired ▪ I *wrecked* my mother's car. ▪ Many houses were *wrecked* by the hurricane. ▪ a *wrecked* car
2 : to ruin or destroy (something) ▪ The affair *wrecked* his marriage. ▪ Even though the rumor was false, it *wrecked* [=*ruined*] her career. ▪ Bad weather *wrecked* our vacation.
3 : to destroy (a ship) by crashing it into something — usual-

ly used as *(be) wrecked* ▪ The ship *was wrecked* off the coast of Ireland.

wreck·age /ˈrɛkɪʤ/ *noun* [*noncount*] : the broken parts of a vehicle, building, etc., that has been badly damaged or destroyed ▪ Workers sifted through the *wreckage* of the building, searching for bodies. ▪ They cleared the *wreckage* from the track.

wrecked *adj, not used before a noun, slang* : very drunk ▪ He came home totally *wrecked* last night.

wreck·er /ˈrɛkɚ/ *noun, pl* **-ers** [*count*]
1 *US* : a truck that takes away cars that are damaged or not working : TOW TRUCK
2 : someone or something that destroys something — used in combination ▪ Lying about your education is a surefire career-*wrecker*. ▪ a ***home-wrecker*** [=someone who has an affair with a married person and causes that person's marriage to fail]

wrecking ball *noun, pl* ~ **balls** [*count*] : a large, heavy ball that is used to knock down buildings ▪ They saved the old factory from the *wrecking ball*. [=from being destroyed]

wren /ˈrɛn/ *noun, pl* **wrens** [*count*] : a small bird with brown feathers and a short tail that points upward — see color picture on page C9

[1]**wrench** /ˈrɛnʧ/ *noun, pl* **wrench·es**
1 [*count*] *US* : a tool consisting of a handle with one end designed to hold, twist, or turn an object (such as a bolt or nut) ▪ an adjustable *wrench* — called also **(*Brit*)** *spanner*; see picture at CARPENTRY; see also MONKEY WRENCH, SOCKET WRENCH
2 [*count*] : a violent twisting or pulling movement — usually singular ▪ He snapped the tree's thick root with a *wrench* of the shovel.
3 [*singular*] *chiefly Brit* : something unpleasant that happens and that causes you to feel emotional pain ▪ It was a *wrench* to say goodbye to all my friends.
throw a wrench into the works US, informal : to damage or change (something) in a way that ruins it or prevents it from working properly ▪ We were going to renew our lease, but the landlord *threw a wrench into the works* [=(*Brit*) *threw a spanner into the works*] by increasing the rent.

[2]**wrench** *verb* **wrenches; wrenched; wrench·ing**
1 : to twist and pull with a sudden violent motion [*no obj*] I tried to *wrench* free from his grip. [+ *obj*] I tried to *wrench* myself free from his grip. — often used figuratively ▪ I have trouble *wrenching* myself away from a good book. ▪ an emotionally *wrenching* experience [=a very sad/painful experience] ▪ a ***heart-wrenching*** story [=a very sad story]
2 [+ *obj*] : to injure (a part of your body) by making a violent twisting motion ▪ He *wrenched* his back when he tried to lift a heavy box. ▪ I *wrenched* [=*sprained*] my knee while playing football.
3 [+ *obj*] : to take (something) by using force ▪ She *wrenched* the toy from his grasp. ▪ The statue was *wrenched* from its pedestal. — often used figuratively ▪ He *wrenched* control of the company (away) from his uncle.

wrest /ˈrɛst/ *verb* **wrests; wrest·ed; wrest·ing** [+ *obj*]
1 : to pull (something) away *from* someone by using violent twisting movements ▪ She *wrested* the gun/knife/weapon (away) *from* her attacker.
2 : to take (something) *from* someone with much effort ▪ He tried to *wrest* control of the company *from* his uncle. ▪ The peasants *wrested* power (away) *from* the nobility.

wres·tle /ˈrɛsəl/ *verb* **wres·tles; wres·tled; wres·tling**
1 a : to fight (someone) by holding and pushing instead of by hitting, kicking, or punching [+ *obj*] She *wrestled* him to the ground. [=she held on to him and forced him to fall to the ground] [*no obj*] — usually + *with* ▪ She *wrestled with* her attacker. **b** : to fight in the sport of wrestling [+ *obj*] They'll be *wrestling* each other for the championship. [*no obj*] They'll be *wrestling* with/against each other for the championship. ▪ I *wrestled* in high school. [=I was a wrestler in high school]
2 : to struggle to move, deal with, or control something [*no obj*] — + *with* ▪ She was *wrestling with* her luggage as she boarded the plane. ▪ She *wrestled with* her conscience. ▪ We *wrestled with* the issue/problem of how to cut costs without laying off workers. [+ *obj*] He finally *wrestled* his drug habit into submission. [=he finally overcame his drug habit]

wres·tler /ˈrɛslɚ/ *noun, pl* **wres·tlers** [*count*] : someone who competes in the sport of wrestling ▪ a professional *wrestler*

wres·tling /ˈrɛslɪŋ/ *noun* [*noncount*] : a sport in which two people try to throw, force, or pin each other to the ground ▪ My favorite sport is *wrestling*. ▪ He was on the *wrestling* team in high school. ▪ a *wrestling* match

wretch /ˈrɛʧ/ *noun, pl* **wretch·es** [*count*]
1 : a very unhappy or unlucky person ▪ The poor *wretch* lost his job.
2 : a very bad or unpleasant person ▪ He's an ungrateful *wretch*.

wretch·ed /ˈrɛʧəd/ *adj* [*more* ~; *most* ~]
1 : very unhappy, ill, etc. ▪ The slums were filled with poor, *wretched* children. ▪ I don't know what's wrong with her, but she looks *wretched*.
2 : very bad or unpleasant ▪ families living in *wretched* poverty ▪ the *wretched* conditions of the refugee camp ▪ How did we get into this *wretched* state of affairs? ▪ *wretched* behavior
3 : very poor in quality or ability ▪ What a *wretched* performance that was. ▪ That movie was positively *wretched*.
— **wretch·ed·ly** *adv* ▪ Her family was *wretchedly* poor. ▪ It's outrageous that they treated you so *wretchedly*. — **wretch·ed·ness** *noun* [*noncount*]

wrig·gle /ˈrɪgəl/ *verb* **wrig·gles; wrig·gled; wrig·gling** [*no obj*]
1 : to twist from side to side with small quick movements like a worm ▪ The children *wriggled* and squirmed in their chairs. ▪ She managed to *wriggle* free of her ropes. ▪ They *wriggled* out of their wet clothes. ▪ I had trouble getting the *wriggling* fish off my hook.
2 *always followed by an adverb or preposition* : to move forward by twisting and turning ▪ The snake *wriggled* across the path and went underneath a bush. ▪ He was able to *wriggle* through the narrow opening.
wriggle out of [*phrasal verb*] ***wriggle out of (something)*** *informal + often disapproving* : to avoid doing (something that you do not want to do) in some clever or dishonest way ▪ She tried to *wriggle out of* the contract. ▪ Don't let him *wriggle out of* paying you for your work.
— **wrig·gly** /ˈrɪgli/ *adj* **wrig·gli·er; -est** ▪ a *wriggly* worm

wring /ˈrɪŋ/ *verb* **wrings; wrung** /ˈrʌŋ/; **wring·ing** /ˈrɪŋɪŋ/ [+ *obj*]
1 : to twist and squeeze (wet cloth, hair, etc.) to remove water ▪ I *wrung* the towel and hung it up to dry. ▪ I *wrung* my hair and wrapped it in a towel. ▪ The rag was **wrung dry**. [=squeezed until almost all of the liquid was gone] — often + *out* ▪ *wring* a sponge *out* ▪ I *wrung out* my wet bathing suit. — sometimes used figuratively ▪ She has been *wrung dry* by bills. [=she has no money left because she used all of it to pay bills]
2 : to get (something) out of someone or something with a lot of effort — + *out of* or *from* ▪ They tried to *wring* [=*squeeze*] every last dollar of profit *out of* the failing company. ▪ I finally managed to *wring* an apology *from* her.
3 : to twist and break (an animal's neck) in order to kill the animal ▪ *wring* a chicken's neck
wringing wet : very wet ▪ His clothes were *wringing wet* from the rain.
wring someone's neck *informal* — used to say that you are very angry with someone ▪ He makes me so mad! I could *wring his neck*!
wring your hands : to twist and rub your hands together because you are nervous or upset ▪ She was *wringing her hands* and pacing back and forth while waiting for her son to call. — see also HAND-WRINGING

wring·er /ˈrɪŋɚ/ *noun, pl* **-ers** [*count*] : a machine used for squeezing water out of clothes that have been washed
through the wringer *informal* : through a series of very difficult or unpleasant experiences ▪ Those poor people have really ***gone/been through the wringer*** lately. ▪ They were ***put through the wringer*** by the adoption agency.

[1]**wrin·kle** /ˈrɪŋkəl/ *noun, pl* **wrin·kles** [*count*]
1 : a small line or fold that appears on your skin as you grow older — usually plural ▪ They claim that this cream will reduce *wrinkles*.
2 : a small fold in the surface of clothing, paper, etc. ▪ *wrinkle*-free pants — usually plural ▪ I ran my hands over my skirt to smooth out the *wrinkles*.
3 *informal* **a** : a surprising or unexpected occurrence in a story or series of events ▪ Here's the latest *wrinkle* in the story—we find out that the villain is actually the hero's father! **b** : a clever technique, trick, or idea ▪ He has added some new *wrinkles* to his game.
iron out the wrinkles *informal* : to fix the small problems in

something ▪ We still have to *iron out* a few more *wrinkles* in the schedule.

– **wrin·kly** /ˈrɪŋkli/ *adj* **wrin·kli·er; -est** [*or more* ~; *most* ~] ▪ *wrinkly* [=*wrinkled*] skin

[2]**wrinkle** *verb* **wrinkles; wrin·kled; wrin·kling**

1 [*no obj*] **:** to develop wrinkles ▪ Linen clothing *wrinkles* easily. ▪ Moisture caused the wallpaper to *wrinkle* and peel. ▪ His brow *wrinkled* as he thought about the question.

2 [+ *obj*] **:** to cause (something) to develop wrinkles ▪ Try not to *wrinkle* your trousers. ▪ She *wrinkled* (up) her nose in disgust.

wrinkled *adj* [*more* ~; *most* ~] **:** having many wrinkles ▪ *wrinkled* [=*wrinkly*] skin ▪ a *wrinkled* face ▪ My shirt is *wrinkled.*

wrist /ˈrɪst/ *noun, pl* **wrists** [*count*] **:** the part of your body where your hand joins your arm ▪ I hurt/sprained/broke my *wrist.* — see pictures at HAND, HUMAN

a slap on the wrist see [2]SLAP

wrist·band /ˈrɪstˌbænd/ *noun, pl* **-bands** [*count*] **:** a band of plastic, paper, cloth, etc., that you wear around your wrist

wrist·watch /ˈrɪstˌwɑːtʃ/ *noun, pl* **-watch·es** [*count*] **:** a watch that you wear on a strap or band around your wrist

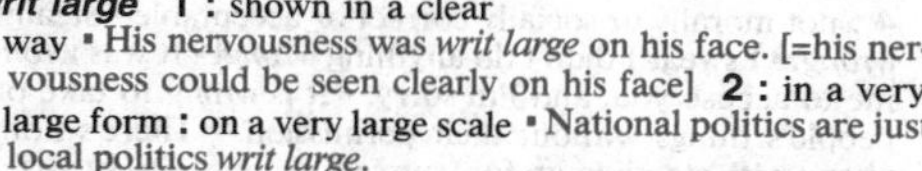
wristwatch

[1]**writ** /ˈrɪt/ *noun, pl* **writs** [*count*] *law* **:** a document from a court ordering someone to do something or not to do something ▪ The judge issued a *writ* of habeas corpus. ▪ He was served with a *writ.*

[2]**writ** *old-fashioned past participle of* WRITE

writ large **1 :** shown in a clear way ▪ His nervousness was *writ large* on his face. [=his nervousness could be seen clearly on his face] **2 :** in a very large form **:** on a very large scale ▪ National politics are just local politics *writ large.*

write /ˈraɪt/ *verb* **writes; wrote** /ˈroʊt/; **writ·ten** /ˈrɪtn̩/; **writ·ing**

1 : to form letters or numbers on a surface with a pen, pencil, etc. [*no obj*] children learning to read and *write* ▪ I don't have anything to *write* with. Could I borrow a pen? [+ *obj*] Please *write* your name at the top of each sheet. ▪ *Write* the number as a decimal instead of as a fraction. ▪ She *wrote* "tag sale" on the sign in big letters. ▪ The note was *written* in blue ink. ▪ I mistakenly *wrote* her name as "Gene" instead of "Jean." ▪ The verb "present" and the noun "present" are *written* [=*spelled*] alike but pronounced differently.

2 [+ *obj*] **a :** to create (a book, poem, story, etc.) by writing words on paper, on a computer, etc. ▪ She *wrote* hundreds of poems during her lifetime. ▪ She *wrote* an essay comparing two poems. ▪ I'm *writing* an article for the school newspaper. ▪ He has *written* several best sellers. **b :** to produce (a written document, agreement, rule, etc.) by writing ▪ She *wrote* [=*drew up*] a contract for me to sign. ▪ I'll *write* you a receipt for your purchase. ▪ I *wrote* (her) a check for $200. ▪ I finally got around to *writing* [=*drafting*] a will. — often + *up* ▪ She *wrote up* a contract for me to sign. ▪ I *wrote up* a review of the art exhibit for the local newspaper. **c :** to create (a piece of music) ▪ He has *written* five symphonies and six concertos. ▪ a performer who *writes* her own songs **d :** to create (a computer program) ▪ I *wrote* a program to keep track of my finances.

3 : to express or state (something) in a book, story, essay, letter, etc. [+ *obj*] Today's homework assignment is to *write* what you thought of the museum. ▪ He *wrote*, "I love you and miss you." ▪ The reporter *wrote* that the strike might last through the weekend. [*no obj*] I'm going to *write* about my cat in my essay.

4 : to use the writing system of a language [*no obj*] + *in* ▪ I can read and *write in* Japanese, but I can't speak it very well. [+ *obj*] I want to learn how to *write* Chinese.

5 : to communicate with someone by sending a letter, e-mail, etc. [*no obj*] I wish you would *write* more often. [=I wish you would send me more letters, e-mails, etc.] — often + *to* ▪ For more information, *write to* the Department of Parks. [+ *obj*] I *wrote* [=*sent*] a letter to him. = I *wrote* him a letter. = (*US*) I *wrote* him.

6 [*no obj*] **:** to do the work of writing books, news articles, stories, etc. **:** to be a writer ▪ He *writes* for the *New York Times.* ▪ I've been *writing* for 20 years.

7 [+ *obj*] *computers* **:** to transfer (information) in a computer to a disk or other device ▪ The data was *written* to/onto a disk.

8 [*no obj*] *of a pen, pencil, etc.* **:** to put marks on paper or another surface ▪ My pen won't *write* smoothly.

have (something) written all over it *informal* **:** to show a certain characteristic very clearly ▪ That proposal *had* "failure" *written all over it.* [=it was obvious that the proposal was going to fail]

nothing to write home about *informal* **:** not very good or appealing **:** ORDINARY ▪ The food at that restaurant is *nothing to write home about.*

write back [*phrasal verb*] ***write back*** *or* ***write (someone) back*** **:** to send someone a letter, e-mail, etc., in response to one that was sent to you ▪ He *wrote back* (to me) as soon as he got my card. ▪ I sent him a letter, but he never *wrote* me *back.*

write down [*phrasal verb*] ***write (something) down*** *or* ***write down (something)*** **:** to write (something) on a piece of paper ▪ I want all of you to *write down* your ideas. ▪ Please *write* your phone number *down* for me.

write in [*phrasal verb*] **1 :** to send a letter to a newspaper, a company, the government, etc., to express an opinion or to ask a question ▪ Dozens of people *wrote in* to the newspaper to complain about the controversial comic strip. ▪ Please *write in* with your comments. **2** ***write (something) in*** *or* ***write in (something)*** **:** to write (something) on a form ▪ She *wrote in* "Latina" under/beside "race or ethnicity." **3** ***write (someone) in*** *or* ***write in (someone)*** *US* **:** to vote for (someone who is not on the official list of candidates) by writing that person's name in a special place on the ballot ▪ Her name wasn't on the ballot, but several hundred voters *wrote* her *in.* — see also WRITE-IN

write into [*phrasal verb*] ***write (something) into (something)*** **:** to add (something new) to a contract, law, etc. ▪ Legislators *wrote* a clause *into* the law that exempts nonprofit agencies. ▪ A bonus was *written into* the contract.

write off [*phrasal verb*] **1** ***write (something) off*** *or* ***write off (something)*** **a :** to say officially that (money that is owed to you) will not be paid or does not need to be paid ▪ The government has agreed to *write off* the debt. ▪ The bank has *written off* the loan. [=has officially said that the money for the loan is lost because the loan will not be repaid] **b :** to take away (an amount) from the total amount that is used to calculate taxes ▪ You might be able to *write off* [=*deduct*] the cost of the computer on your taxes. **2** ***write (someone or something) off*** *or* ***write off (someone or something)*** **:** to consider (someone or something) to be lost, hopeless, unimportant, etc. ▪ I had *written off* [=given up on] college because I couldn't afford to pay tuition. ▪ I *wrote* her *off* as a friend. [=I decided that she was no longer my friend] ▪ I wouldn't *write off* [=*dismiss*] the team just yet. The season still has a long way to go. **3** ***write off for (something)*** *chiefly Brit* **:** to make a request for (something) by sending a letter ▪ She *wrote off for* [=*sent away for*] a free sample.

write out [*phrasal verb*] **1** ***write (something) out*** *or* ***write out (something)*** **a :** to put (something) in writing on a piece of paper ▪ I asked her to *write out* the directions to her house. **b :** to write the required information on (a check, receipt, etc.) ▪ I *wrote out* a check for $200. ▪ The sales clerk *wrote* us *out* an invoice. **2 a** ***write (someone) out of*** **:** to change a document (such as a will) so that (someone) is not included ▪ She *wrote* me *out of* her will. **b** ***write (someone) out of (something)*** *or* ***write out (someone)*** **:** to remove (a character) from a story by having the character die, disappear, etc. ▪ They *wrote* her character *out of* the show at the end of the first season.

write up [*phrasal verb*] **1** ***write (something) up*** *or* ***write up (something)*** **:** to describe (something) in a detailed written account ▪ A music critic *wrote up* the rock concert. — see also WRITE-UP **2** ***write (someone) up*** *or* ***write up (someone)*** *US* **:** to produce an official document that reports (someone) to an authority to be punished ▪ The teacher *wrote up* the boy for throwing food at his classmates. — see also WRITE 2b (above)

write your own ticket *informal* ✧ If you can *write your own ticket*, you can choose to do whatever you want or to go wherever you want because you have excellent or special skills or abilities. ▪ When he graduates, he'll be able to *write his own ticket.*

written in stone see [1]STONE

wrote the book on *informal* — used to say that someone is

an expert on a particular subject ▪ She *wrote the book on* long-distance swimming.

write–in /ˈraɪtˌɪn/ *noun, pl* **-ins** [*count*] *US*
1 : a candidate in an election whose name is not printed on the ballot and whose name must be written on the ballot by voters ▪ Since he couldn't secure his party's nomination, he was forced to run as a *write-in.* ▪ a *write-in* candidate
2 : a vote for someone who is not on an election's official list of candidates ▪ The election commission decided that *write-ins* would not be counted. — see also *write in* at WRITE

writ·er /ˈraɪtɚ/ *noun, pl* **-ers** [*count*]
1 : someone whose work is to write books, poems, stories, etc. ▪ She is my favorite French *writer.* ▪ He's a *writer* of horror stories. ▪ a course on 19th-century *writers* ▪ The magazine is looking for freelance *writers.*
2 : someone who has written something ▪ The *writer* of the best essay will win a prize. ▪ They identified the *writer* of the mysterious letter.

writer's block *noun* [*noncount*] **:** the problem of not being able to think of something to write about or not being able to finish writing a story, poem, etc.

writer's cramp *noun* [*noncount*] **:** pain in your hand or fingers that you get when you have been writing with a pen or pencil for a long time

write–up /ˈraɪtˌʌp/ *noun, pl* **-ups** [*count*] **:** a written description or review of something ▪ There's a *write-up* of the restaurant in the paper. — see also *write up* at WRITE

writhe /ˈraɪð/ *verb* **writhes; writhed; writh·ing** [*no obj*] **:** to twist your body from side to side ▪ She lay on the floor, *writhing* in pain. ▪ a nest of *writhing* snakes

writ·ing /ˈraɪtɪŋ/ *noun, pl* **-ings**
1 [*noncount*] **a :** the activity or work of writing books, poems, stories, etc. ▪ *Writing* usually isn't a lucrative career, but it has been very fulfilling for me. ▪ She quit her job in order to concentrate on (her) *writing.* ▪ He teaches creative *writing* at the university. ▪ Few people nowadays care about the art of ***letter writing***. **b :** the way that you use written words to express your ideas or opinions ▪ The novel's plot is okay, but the *writing* is horrible. ▪ I asked a friend to critique my *writing.* ▪ Her essay was a wonderful piece of *writing.* ▪ She has a unique ***writing style***.
2 : books, poems, essays, letters, etc. [*noncount*] Much of the best Japanese *writing* has not been translated into English. [*plural*] the *writings* of Benjamin Franklin ▪ a book of selected *writings* on moral philosophy
3 [*noncount*] **:** words, numbers, or symbols that have been written or printed on something ▪ Can you read the *writing* on this bottle? ▪ Japanese/Chinese/Arabic *writing* ▪ hieroglyphics and other early *writing* systems
4 [*noncount*] **a :** the activity or skill of forming letters and numbers with a pen, pencil, etc. ▪ She learned *writing* [=learned how to write] at a young age. ▪ Having a broken finger made *writing* difficult. **b :** the particular way in which someone writes letters and numbers **:** HANDWRITING ▪ Whose *writing* is this? ▪ Her *writing* is illegible.
in writing **:** in the form of a letter or a document ▪ The agreement needs to be *in writing* in order for it to be valid. ▪ If they want to buy the house, make sure you get the offer *in writing.*
the writing is on the wall *or* ***see/read the writing on the wall*** see ¹WALL

writing desk *noun, pl* **~ desks** [*count*] **:** a desk with a flat surface for writing on

writing paper *noun* [*noncount*] **:** paper of good quality used for writing letters, notes, etc.

¹written *past participle of* WRITE

²writ·ten /ˈrɪtn̩/ *adj* **:** using writing and not speech ▪ We left *written* instructions for the babysitter. ▪ *written* language ▪ a *written* exam ▪ The landlord must provide the tenant with *written* notice to vacate the property. ▪ a *written* contract ▪ The company issued a *written* statement.

¹wrong /ˈrɑːŋ/ *adj*
1 a : not agreeing with the facts or truth **:** INCORRECT ▪ the *wrong* answer ▪ Their conclusion was *wrong.* ▪ I don't want you to get the *wrong* impression of him. ▪ Don't take/interpret this the *wrong* way, but I think you should start exercising. ▪ Are my actions sending the *wrong* message? ▪ These pages are in the *wrong* order. ▪ I don't understand how I got the answer *wrong.* [=I do not understand how I did not know the right answer] ▪ I got four answers *wrong* on the test. ▪ I think you have dialed the ***wrong number***. [=an incorrect telephone number] — opposite RIGHT **b** *not used before a noun* **:** speaking, acting, or judging in a way that does not agree with the facts or truth ▪ You're *wrong*; the answer is six. ▪ You like baseball, or am I *wrong*? ▪ Am I *wrong* in thinking that she should never have gone? ▪ I think her birthday is May 11th, but I could be *wrong.* ▪ He thinks I can't win, but I'm going to prove him *wrong.* ▪ ***Correct me if I'm wrong***, but isn't tomorrow your birthday? — often + *about* ▪ I was *wrong* [=*mistaken*] *about* the price. It actually costs $30, not $20. — often followed by *to* + *verb* ▪ It is *wrong to assume* that you will be safe if you do that. — opposite RIGHT
2 : not suitable or appropriate for a particular purpose, situation, or person ▪ These shoes are the *wrong* size. ▪ If you're looking to me for advice on love, then you're asking the *wrong* guy. ▪ That was the *wrong* thing to say/do. ▪ He picked the *wrong* time to bring up his salary. ▪ He was the *wrong* person for the job. ▪ I made the *wrong* decision. ▪ We got married for the *wrong* reasons. ▪ It would be *wrong* of me to pressure you into saying yes. ▪ There is nothing *wrong* with being quiet. ▪ We headed off in the *wrong* direction and got lost. ▪ The singer hit a *wrong* note. ▪ She bought the *wrong* kind of rice. ▪ He accidentally pressed the *wrong* button. ▪ They decided that they were *wrong* for each other and broke up. ▪ You are doing it the *wrong* way. ▪ It's not his fault that he was injured. He was just ***in the wrong place at the wrong time***. — opposite RIGHT
3 *not used before a noun* **:** not in a proper, good, or normal state or condition — used to describe a situation in which there is a problem ▪ What's *wrong*? You look unhappy. ▪ She knew something was *wrong* when her friend didn't show up for dinner. — often + *with* ▪ There's something *wrong with* my computer. [=my computer is not working properly] ▪ Nothing is *wrong with* your car. [=your car is working properly] ▪ What's *wrong with* your shoulder? Did you hurt yourself?
4 : not morally or socially correct or acceptable ▪ Stealing is *wrong.* ▪ I swear I didn't do anything *wrong*! ▪ It was *wrong* of me to accuse you, and I'm sorry. ▪ It is *wrong* to take other people's things without their permission. ▪ There's nothing *wrong* with standing up for yourself. — opposite RIGHT
5 *US* — used to refer to the side of something that is not meant to be on top, in front, or on the outside ▪ The CD fell and landed ***wrong side up/down***. ▪ He had his socks on ***wrong side out***. — opposite RIGHT
barking up the wrong tree see ¹BARK
fall into the wrong hands see ¹FALL
get off on the wrong foot see ¹FOOT
get up on the wrong side of the bed see ¹BED
on the wrong track see ¹TRACK
put a foot wrong see ¹FOOT
rub (someone) the wrong way see ¹RUB
the wrong end of the stick see ¹STICK
the wrong horse see ¹HORSE
the wrong side of the tracks see ¹TRACK
– wrong·ly *adv* ▪ She was *wrongly* accused of theft. ▪ They acted *wrongly.* ▪ Many people, ***rightly or wrongly***, believe that the economy will soon improve. **– wrong·ness** *noun* [*noncount*] ▪ I'm not convinced of the *wrongness* of his actions.

²wrong *adv*
1 : in a way that does not agree with the facts or truth **:** in a way that results in an error ▪ I guessed *wrong.* [=*incorrectly*] ▪ I entered the numbers *wrong.* ▪ Her name was spelled *wrong* on the form. — opposite RIGHT
2 : in a way that is not suitable, proper, etc. ▪ You are doing it *wrong.* [=*incorrectly*] ▪ I can't get this to work; could you show me what I did *wrong*? — opposite RIGHT
get (someone or something) wrong **:** to fail to understand (someone or something) correctly ▪ She *got* the instructions *wrong.* ▪ ***Don't get me wrong***—I like his parents. They're just a little too strict. ▪ You've ***got it all wrong***! [=you have misunderstood the situation completely]
go wrong **1 :** to happen or proceed in a way that causes a bad result ▪ We have to figure out what *went wrong* with the experiment. ▪ Everything is *going wrong* for me today. ▪ When she didn't come back, we feared that something had *gone* horribly *wrong.* [=that something very bad had happened] ▪ What could possibly *go wrong*? **2 :** to make a mistake ▪ I followed the instructions to the letter and the computer still doesn't work. Where did I *go wrong*? ▪ "I don't know what to order." "You ***can't go wrong with*** their clam chowder." [=their clam chowder is always a good choice]

³wrong *noun, pl* **wrongs**

1 [*noncount*] : behavior that is not morally good or correct • People who ***do wrong*** [=do bad things] should be punished. • He's old enough to know the difference between right and *wrong*. = He's old enough to know ***right from wrong***. • He is regarded as a hero who can ***do no wrong***. [=who never does anything bad] — opposite RIGHT

2 [*count*] : a harmful, unfair, or illegal act — usually plural • She is seeking compensation for the *wrongs* that she suffered as an employee at that company. • No one has the power to right all *wrongs*. • We discussed the ***rights and wrongs*** of genetic cloning. — opposite RIGHT

do (someone) wrong *informal + old-fashioned* : to treat (someone) badly or unfairly • Her ex-boyfriend *did* her *wrong*.

in the wrong : in the position or situation of being wrong • We had an argument and each of us thinks that the other was *in the wrong*.

two wrongs don't make a right — used to say that if someone hurts you, you should not hurt that person in return

[4]**wrong** *verb* **wrongs; wronged; wrong·ing** [+ *obj*] : to treat (someone) badly or unfairly • We should forgive those who have *wronged* us. • As the *wronged* party, you have the right to sue for damages.

wrong·do·er /ˈrɑːŋˌduːwɚ/ *noun, pl* **-ers** [*count*] : a person who does something that is morally or legally wrong

wrong·do·ing /ˈrɑːŋˌduːwɪŋ/ *noun, pl* **-ings** : behavior that is morally or legally wrong [*noncount*] He denied any *wrongdoing*. • There is no evidence of *wrongdoing* on her part. [=no evidence that she did anything wrong] [*count*] The corporation's *wrongdoings* must be exposed.

wrong·ful /ˈrɑːŋfəl/ *adj* : not legal, fair, or moral • *wrongful* conduct • He is suing his former employer for *wrongful* termination.

— **wrong·ful·ly** *adv* • a *wrongfully* convicted inmate — **wrong·ful·ness** *noun* [*noncount*] • She did not understand the *wrongfulness* of her actions.

wrongful death *noun, pl* ~ **deaths** [*count*] *law* : a death caused by someone's mistake or by someone's improper act • She filed a *wrongful death* suit against the hospital, alleging that its negligence led to her daughter's death.

wrong·head·ed /ˈrɑːŋˈhɛdəd/ *adj* [*more* ~; *most* ~] : having or showing opinions or ideas that are wrong • *wrongheaded* people • a *wrongheaded* approach to dealing with the problem

wrote *past tense of* WRITE

wrought /ˈrɑːt/ *adj, formal + old-fashioned* : carefully formed or worked into shape • carefully *wrought* essays • finely *wrought* woodwork

wrought up *informal + old-fashioned* : very excited or upset • I got *wrought up* [=*worked up*] over nothing.

wrought iron *noun* [*noncount*] : a kind of iron that is often used to make decorative fences, furniture, etc. • an antique *wrought iron* fence • a chair made of *wrought iron*

wrung *past tense of* WRING

wry /ˈraɪ/ *adj* **wry·er; -est** [*or more* ~; *most* ~]

1 : humorous in a clever and often ironic way • His books are noted for their *wry* humor.

2 : showing both amusement and a feeling of being tired, annoyed, etc. • When I asked her how she felt after winning the race, she gave me a ***wry smile/grin*** and said, "Pretty tired."

— **wry·ly** *adv* • She smiled *wryly*. — **wry·ness** *noun* [*noncount*]

wt. *abbr* weight

WTO *abbr* World Trade Organization

wun·der·kind /ˈwʊndɚˌkɪnt/ *noun, pl* **-kinds** *also* **-kind·er** /-ˌkɪndɚ/ [*count*] : someone who achieves success or shows great talent at a young age — usually singular • a musical *wunderkind*

wuss /ˈwʊs/ *also* **wus·sy** /ˈwʊsi/ *noun, pl* **wuss·es** *also* **wus·sies** [*count*] *slang* : a weak or cowardly person • Don't be such a *wuss*.

WV *or* **W VA** *abbr* West Virginia

WW *abbr* World War

www *abbr* World Wide Web

WY *or* **Wyo.** *abbr* Wyoming

WYS·I·WYG /ˈwɪziˌwɪg/ *noun* [*noncount*] *computers* : a display on a computer that shows the exact appearance of a printed document ✧ *WYSIWYG* stands for "what you see is what you get."

[1]**x** *or* **X** /ˈɛks/ *noun, pl* **x's** *or* **xs** *or* **X's** *or* **Xs** /ˈɛksəz/

1 : the 24th letter of the English alphabet [*count*] a word that starts with an *x* [*noncount*] a word that starts with *x*

2 [*count*] : the Roman numeral that means 10 • XX [=20]

3 [*noncount*] *mathematics* **a** — used to represent an unknown quantity • What is the value of *x* in the equation *x* - 4 = 3? **b** — used as a symbol for multiplication • 2 *x* 3 = 6 [=2 times 3 equals 6; 2 multiplied by 3 is 6]

4 [*noncount*] — used as a symbol between the numbers of a measurement • The room is 10' *x* 12'. [=10 feet by 12 feet; two of the room's walls are 10 feet long and two walls are 12 feet long]

5 [*noncount*] : an unknown thing, person, or quantity • Mr. and Mrs. *X* • *x* number of students/people

6 [*noncount*] — used in the phrase ***x, y, and z*** to refer to the first thing in a group of three unnamed things • I hate being told that losing weight is as easy as doing *x, y, and z*.

7 [*count*] — used as a mark at the end of a letter, an e-mail, etc., to represent a kiss • Love, Pat *XXX*

8 [*count*] — used like a signature by a person who cannot write

9 [*count*] — used on a map or picture to show where someone or something is • Look at this map. *X* shows where we are now. • The location of the treasure was marked with an *x*. • *X* marks the spot.

10 [*count*] — used as a mark to show who or what you are voting for or choosing

[2]**x** *verb* **x–es** *also* **x's** *or* **xes** /ˈɛksəz/; **x–ed** *also* **x'd** *or* **xed** /ˈɛkst/; **x–ing** *or* **x'ing** /ˈɛksɪŋ/

x out [*phrasal verb*] ***x (something) out*** *or* ***x out (something)*** : to draw an x or a series of x's through (something) to show that it is wrong or not wanted • *x out* a mistake • One line of the text had been *x-ed out*. [=*crossed out*]

X /ˈɛks/ — used in the past as a special mark to indicate that no one under the age of 17 in the U.S. or 18 in the U.K. was allowed to see a particular movie in a movie theater • The movie was rated *X*. — compare G, NC-17, PG, PG-13, R; see also X-RATED

X chromosome *noun, pl* ~ **-somes** [*count*] : a type of chromosome that is found in pairs in the cells of female mammals and is found with the Y chromosome in the cells of male mammals — compare Y CHROMOSOME

xe·non /ˈziːˌnɑːn/ *noun* [*noncount*] : a chemical element that is a colorless gas and that is used especially in electric lights

xe·no·pho·bia /ˌzɛnəˈfoʊbijə, ˌziːnəˈfoʊbijə/ *noun* [*noncount*] : fear or hatred of strangers or foreigners

— **xe·no·phobe** /ˈzɛnəˌfoʊb, ˈziːnəˌfoʊb/ *noun, pl* **-phobes** [*count*] — **xe·no·pho·bic** /ˌzɛnəˈfoʊbɪk, ˌziːnəˈfoʊbɪk/ *adj* [*more* ~; *most* ~]

Xe·rox /ˈziɚˌɑːks/ *trademark* — used for a machine that makes paper copies of printed pages, pictures, etc.

xe·rox /ˈziɚˌɑːks/ *verb* **-rox·es; -roxed; -rox·ing** : to copy (something, such as a document) by using a special machine (called a copier) [+ *obj*] I'll *xerox* these forms for you. [*no obj*] I'll be *xeroxing* in the library.

xl *or* **XL** *abbr* extra large — usually used for a clothing size • The shirt comes in S, M, L, and *XL*.

Xmas /ˈkrɪsməs, ˈɛksməs/ *noun, pl* **Xmas·es** [*count, noncount*] *informal* : CHRISTMAS — used especially on signs and in advertisements; often used before another noun • The sign read "*Xmas* decorations on sale."

XML /ˌɛksˌɛmˈɛl/ *noun* [*noncount*] : a computer language that is used to clearly mark and organize the different parts

of a document so that it can be read on different computer systems

X-rat·ed /ˈɛksˈreɪtəd/ *adj, of a movie* : having a rating of X : not suitable to be seen by people under age 17 in the U.S. and under 18 in the U.K. because of violence, offensive language, or sexual activity ▪ an *X-rated* movie — often used figuratively ▪ an *X-rated* [=*pornographic*] Web site ▪ *X-rated* language [=obscene or offensive language]

X–ray /ˈɛksˌreɪ/ *noun, pl* **-rays**
1 ***X-rays*** [*plural*] *technical* : powerful invisible rays that can pass through various objects and that make it possible to see inside things (such as the human body)
2 *also* ***x-ray*** [*count*] : an image that is created by using X-rays and that is usually used for medical purposes ▪ The doctor will review the *X-rays* and call you with the results.
3 *also* ***x-ray*** [*count*] : a medical examination that involves using X-rays ▪ After the accident, I went to the hospital for an *X-ray*.
– **X–ray** *adj, always used before a noun* ▪ *X-ray* radiation [=radiation from X-rays] ▪ *X-ray* machines [=machines that use X-rays]

x–ray *or* **X–ray** /ˈɛksˌreɪ/ *verb* **-rays; -rayed; -ray·ing** [+ *obj*] : to examine and make images of (things, such as the bones and organs inside the body) by using X-rays ▪ I had my foot/wrist/chest *x-rayed*. ▪ Your luggage will be *x-rayed* at the airport.

xy·lo·phone /ˈzaɪləˌfoʊn/ *noun, pl* **-phones** [*count*] : a musical instrument that has a set of wooden bars of different lengths that are hit with hammers — see picture at PERCUSSION

y *or* **Y** /ˈwaɪ/ *noun, pl* **y's** *or* **ys** *or* **Y's** *or* **Ys** /ˈwaɪz/
1 : the 25th letter of the English alphabet [*count*] a word that starts with a *y* [*noncount*] a word that starts with *y*
2 [*noncount*] *mathematics* — used to represent especially a second unknown quantity ▪ If x + *y* = 5 and x – *y* = 3, what are the values of x and *y*?
3 [*noncount*] — used in the phrase ***x, y, and z*** to refer to the second thing in a group of three unnamed things ▪ People keep giving me advice about it, saying I should do *x, y, and z*.
4 [*count*] : something that is shaped like a Y ▪ Turn left when you come to the *Y*. [=when the road/path splits like the top half of a Y]
5 ***the Y*** *US, informal* : the YMCA or the YWCA ▪ I'm going to *the Y* after work tonight.

[1]-y *also* **-ey** /i/ *adj suffix*
1 a : full of or having a lot of something ▪ a muddy river [=a river with a lot of mud in it] ▪ dirty hands [=hands with a lot of dirt on them] **b** : having the qualities of something ▪ gooey [=wet and sticky like goo] : made of or seeming to be made of something ▪ waxy **c** : resembling something ▪ icy [=like ice; very cold] ▪ wintry temperatures [=temperatures that are cold like winter temperatures] ▪ a homey atmosphere **d** : very interested in something ▪ outdoorsy [=enthusiastic about activities done outside]
2 a : tending to do something ▪ chatty [=tending to chat] : wanting or needing to do something ▪ sleepy **b** : causing or performing a specified action ▪ a drowsy afternoon [=an afternoon that makes you feel ready to drowse/sleep] ▪ curly hair [=hair that curls]

[2]-y /i/ *noun suffix* : an act of doing something ▪ inquiry [=an act of inquiring]

[3]-y see -IE

YA *abbr* young adult

yacht /ˈjɑːt/ *noun, pl* **yachts** [*count*] : a large boat that is used for racing or pleasure ▪ a sailing *yacht* — see picture at BOAT

yacht·ing /ˈjɑːtɪŋ/ *noun* [*noncount*] : the activity or sport of sailing in a yacht ▪ a *yachting* champion ▪ We ***went yachting*** over the weekend.

yachts·man /ˈjɑːtsmən/ *noun, pl* **-men** /-mən/ [*count*] : a man who owns or sails a yacht

yachts·wom·an /ˈjɑːtsˌwʊmən/ *noun, pl* **-wom·en** /-ˌwɪmən/ [*count*] : a woman who owns or sails a yacht

ya·da ya·da *or* **yad·da yad·da** /ˈjɑːdəˈjɑːdə/ *or* **ya·da ya·da ya·da** *or* **yad·da yad·da yad·da** /ˈjɑːdəˈjɑːdəˈjɑːdə/ *noun* [*noncount*] *US, informal* : talk or language that is boring or that offers little information ▪ They had to listen to the usual *yada yada* about bike safety. — often used as an interjection in place of words that are very dull or not worth saying ▪ It was your typical day: I went to work, came home, had dinner, *yada yada yada*.

[1]ya·hoo /jɑˈhuː/ *interj* — used to express excitement or joy ▪ *Yahoo*! We won!

[2]ya·hoo /ˈjeɪˌhuː, ˈjɑːˌhuː/ *noun, pl* **-hoos** [*count*] *informal* : a person who is very rude, loud, or stupid ▪ Some *yahoo* cut me off in traffic. ▪ A bunch of *yahoos* were making noise outside.

Yah·weh /ˈjɑːˌweɪ/ *noun* [*singular*] — used as the name of God by the ancient Hebrews and in the Old Testament of the Bible

[1]yak /ˈjæk/ *noun, pl* **yaks** *also* **yak** [*count*] : a large wild animal that has long hair and curved horns and that lives in central Asia

yak

[2]yak *verb* **yaks; yakked; yak·king** [*no obj*] *informal* : to talk in a loud way often for a long time ▪ Half the people on the train were *yakking* [=*yammering*] (away) on their cell phones.

y'all /ˈjɑːl/ *US, informal* — used as a contraction of *you all* ▪ How are *y'all* doing tonight? ✧ Like *you-all, y'all* is used mainly in speech in the Southern U.S. to address two or more people.

yam /ˈjæm/ *noun, pl* **yams** [*count*]
1 : a long, thick root of a tropical plant that has rough brown skin and usually white or yellow flesh and that is eaten as a vegetable
2 *US* : SWEET POTATO

yam·mer /ˈjæmɚ/ *verb* **-mers; -mered; -mer·ing** [*no obj*] *informal* : to talk in an annoying way usually for a long time ▪ They're *yammering* (on) about work again.

yang /ˈjɑːŋ, ˈjæŋ/ *noun* [*noncount*] *in Chinese philosophy* : one of the two forces that together form everything that exists : the male principle of the universe that is considered light and active and is associated with heaven — compare YIN

the yin and yang see YIN

[1]yank /ˈjæŋk/ *noun, pl* **yanks** [*count*] : a strong, quick pull ▪ She gave the rope a *yank*. [=she yanked the rope]

[2]yank *verb* **yanks; yanked; yank·ing**
1 : to suddenly pull (something) in a quick, forceful way [+ *obj*] He *yanked* the door shut. [*no obj*] She *yanked* on the dog's leash.
2 [+ *obj*] : to quickly or suddenly remove (something or someone) ▪ The show was *yanked* off the air. [=the show was suddenly canceled; it was suddenly decided that the show would no longer be broadcast]
yank (someone's) chain see [1]CHAIN

Yank /ˈjæŋk/ *noun, pl* **Yanks** [*count*] *informal* : a person from the U.S. : YANKEE

Yan·kee /ˈjæŋki/ *noun, pl* **-kees** [*count*]
1 : a person born or living in the U.S. — often used to show disapproval or as an insult ▪ The protesters held signs that said "*Yankee* Go Home."
2 *US* **a** : a person born or living in the northern U.S. ▪ a Southern girl who married a *Yankee* — sometimes used by people in the southern U.S. to show disapproval or as an insult **b** : a person from New England ▪ a New England *Yan-*

kee • Yankee frugality [=the frugality that is traditionally associated with people from New England]
3 : a soldier who fought on the side of the northern states during the American Civil War

[1]yap /ˈjæp/ *verb* **yaps; yapped; yap·ping** [*no obj*]
1 *of a dog* : to bark in high, quick sounds • The dog was *yapping* all night.
2 *informal* : to talk in a loud and annoying way • Kids were *yapping* in the back of the room. • She seems to spend all her time *yapping* on the phone.

[2]yap *noun, pl* **yaps** [*count*]
1 : a dog's high, quick bark • I heard *yaps* coming from the yard.
2 *US slang* : MOUTH • I told him to shut his *yap*. [=*trap*]

[1]yard /ˈjɑɚd/ *noun, pl* **yards** [*count*]
1 *US* : an outdoor area that is next to a house and is usually covered by grass • Children were playing out in the *yard*. [=(*Brit*) *garden*] • a tree in the back/front *yard*
2 : the land around a building • the prison *yard* [=*grounds*] — see also SCHOOLYARD
3 : an area with buildings and equipment that is used for a particular activity • a rail *yard* [=a place where railroad cars are kept and repaired] — see also BARNYARD, FARMYARD, JUNKYARD, LUMBERYARD, SCRAPYARD, SHIPYARD, STOCKYARD
– compare [2]YARD; see also SCOTLAND YARD

[2]yard *noun, pl* **yards** [*count*] : a unit of measurement equal to 3 feet (0.9144 meters) or 36 inches • We have 10 *yards* of rope. • The football player ran for 35 *yards*. • 40 square *yards* of carpeting • the 100-*yard* dash • a cubic *yard* — abbr. *yd.*
the whole nine yards *chiefly US, informal* : EVERYTHING • I served a huge Thanksgiving dinner: turkey, mashed potatoes, pumpkin pie—*the whole nine yards*. [=all the foods that are traditionally served for Thanksgiving dinner] • If we're going to replace the cabinets, we might as well ***go the whole nine yards*** [=do everything that there is to do] and remodel the entire kitchen.
– compare [1]YARD

yard·age /ˈjɑɚdɪʤ/ *noun* [*noncount*]
1 a : an amount of something measured in yards • fabric *yardage* [=yards of fabric] **b** : the size of something measured in yards • calculating the square *yardage* of the room [=calculating the size of the room in square yards]
2 *American football* : the number of yards a player or team moves the ball down the field • He led the league in rushing/passing *yardage*. • The team lost *yardage* on that play.

yard·er /ˈjɑɚdɚ/ *noun, pl* **-ers** [*count*] : something that is a specified number of yards long — used in combination • The field goal was a 40-*yarder*. [=was 40 yards long]

yard line *noun, pl* **~ lines** [*count*] *American football* : any one of the lines on a football field that are one yard apart and that show the distance to the nearest goal line — often used in combination to refer to a specific yard line • He was tackled on the 20-*yard line*.

yard sale *noun, pl* **~ sales** [*count*] *US* : GARAGE SALE

yard·stick /ˈjɑɚdˌstɪk/ *noun, pl* **-sticks** [*count*]
1 : a long, flat tool that is one yard long and is used to measure things
2 : a rule or specific idea about what is acceptable or desirable that is used to judge or measure something • Some feel that test scores aren't an adequate *yardstick* for judging a student's ability. • Ratings are the *yardstick* by which TV shows are evaluated by networks.

yar·mul·ke /ˈjɑːməkə, ˈjɑɚməlkə/ *noun, pl* **-kes** [*count*] : a small round cap that is worn by some Jewish men — called also *skullcap*

yarn /ˈjɑɚn/ *noun, pl* **yarns**
1 : a long, thin piece of cotton, wool, etc., that is thicker than thread and that is used for knitting and weaving [*noncount*] skeins of *yarn* • The sheep's wool will be spun into *yarn*. [*count*] colorful *yarns* — see picture at SEWING
2 [*count*] : an exciting or interesting story; *especially* : a story that is so surprising or unusual that it is difficult to believe • *yarns* about ghosts and goblins • a storyteller who ***spins yarns*** that will keep any audience riveted

yaw /ˈjɑː/ *noun* [*noncount*] *technical* : movement of an airplane, ship, etc., to the left or right; *especially* : unwanted left or right movement • Sensors measure the pitch and *yaw* of the plane. • The airplane's rudder is used to control *yaw*.
– **yaw** *verb* **yaws; yawed; yaw·ing** [*no obj*] • The plane *yawed* to the left.

[1]yawn /ˈjɑːn/ *verb* **yawns; yawned; yawn·ing** [*no obj*]
1 : to open your mouth wide while taking in breath usually because you are tired or bored • Students were *yawning* in class.
2 *of an opening, hole, etc.* : to be deep, large, etc. • A deep chasm *yawned* [=*gaped*] below us.

[2]yawn *noun, pl* **yawns** [*count*]
1 : an act of opening your mouth wide while taking in breath : an act of yawning • I tried to stifle a *yawn*.
2 *informal* : something that is very boring • The movie was a great big *yawn*. [=was very boring]

yawn·er /ˈjɑːnɚ/ *noun, pl* **-ers** [*count*] *US*
1 : a person who yawns
2 *informal* : something that is very boring • The show was a real *yawner*.

yawn·ing /ˈjɑːnɪŋ/ *adj* : very large or wide open • There was a *yawning* [=*gaping*] hole in the wall. • There is a *yawning* gap between rich and poor. [=the difference between how much money rich people have and poor people have is very great]

yay /ˈjeɪ/ *interj* — used to express joy, approval, or excitement • *Yay*! We won! • You did it! *Yay*! Good for you!

Y chromosome *noun, pl* **~ -somes** [*count*] *biology* : a chromosome that is found with the X chromosome in the cells of male mammals and that is absent from the cells of female mammals — compare X CHROMOSOME

yd. *abbr* yard

[1]ye /ˈjiː/ *pronoun, old-fashioned + literary* : YOU — used especially when speaking to more than one person • "Abandon hope, all *ye* [=all of you] who enter here." —Dante, *The Divine Comedy* (translation) • ". . . Seek and *ye* shall find . . ." —Luke 11:9 KJV

[2]ye /ˈjiː/ *definite article, old-fashioned + literary* : THE — used especially in the names of stores, businesses, etc., to make them seem old-fashioned • *Ye* Olde Tavern

yea /ˈjeɪ/ *noun, pl* **yeas** [*count*] *formal* : a yes vote • We counted seven *yeas* [=*ayes*] and two nays. — compare [2]AYE, [2]NAY

yeah /ˈjɛə/ *adv, informal*
1 : YES • "Are you coming with us?" "*Yeah*, I'm coming." • *Yeah*, I agree with you. • "That looks good." "*Yeah*, I think so too."
2 — used in speech to show that you are surprised by or disagree with what someone has said • "I'm from Maine." "***Oh yeah***? [=*really*?] I didn't know that." • "I'm a better runner than you." "*Oh, yeah*? You think you can beat me?" • "You're a lousy golfer." "*Oh yeah*? I'd like to see you do better."
3 — used in speech to express disbelief • "I met a famous actor yesterday." "***Yeah, right/sure***." [=I do not believe you]

year /ˈjiɚ/ *noun, pl* **years** [*count*]
1 : a unit of time that is equal to 12 months or 365 or sometimes 366 days • I haven't seen her in a *year*. • He quit smoking six *years* ago. • The job pays $45,000 a/per *year*. • She renews her lease every *year*. • We see them once or twice a *year*. • It feels like we've been standing in line for a *year*. • That team hasn't won in *years*. • It's been *years* since I've been on an airplane. • The camp has changed a lot ***over the years***. [=during several/some/many years] • The tree grows taller ***year by year***. = The tree grows taller ***each year***. = The tree grows taller ***as the years go by***. • The park is open ***all year round***. = The park is open the entire *year*. — see also CALENDAR YEAR, DONKEY'S YEARS, FISCAL YEAR, GAP YEAR, LEAP YEAR
2 : the regular period of 12 months that begins in January and ends in December • The work should be done by the end of the *year*. • She was born in the *year* 1967. • The volcano erupted in the *year* 44 B.C. • In what *year* was the car made? • They got married last *year*. [=during the year before this one] • He will retire next *year*. [=during the year after this one] • the movie/teacher/rookie ***of the year*** [=the best movie/teacher/rookie in a specific year]
3 — used to refer to the age of a person • She is 14 *years* old. • the teenage *years* [=the ages 13 through 19] • a six-*year*-old boy • He is ***getting on in years***. [=he is getting old] • She looks ***young/old for her years***. [=she looks younger/older than she is]
4 : a period of time when a particular event, process, activity, etc., happens or is done • The school *year* runs from September to June. [=the school operates from September to June] • The fiscal *year* begins in October and ends in September. • This will be a great *year* [=harvest season] for peaches. • The pitcher is having his best *year* [=*season*] ever. • She took geometry (during) her sophomore *year*. • first- and second-*year* students

glory years see [1]GLORY

in the year of our Lord *formal* — used before a year to say that it is after the birth of Jesus Christ • The couple married on this day *in the year of our Lord* 2005.

never/not in a thousand/million/billion years *informal* — used as a strong way of saying that something is extremely unlikely or impossible • *Never in a million years* did I think she would quit her job. [=I never thought that she would quit her job] • He will never change his mind. *Not in a million years.*

put years on : to cause (someone) to look or feel older • That job has really *put* some *years on* him.

since (the) year one (*US*) *or Brit* ***since the year dot*** *informal* : for a very long time : since a time in the distant past • That monument has been there *since the year one.*

take years off : to cause someone to look or feel younger • Not only has the diet improved how she feels, but it's also *taken years off* (her appearance).

vintage year see [1]VINTAGE

year·book /ˈjiɚˌbʊk/ *noun, pl* **-books** [*count*]
1 : a book about a particular topic (such as sports or news) that is published each year • an auto industry *yearbook*
2 *US* : a book that is published by a school each year and that shows the activities at the school during that year • a high school *yearbook* • her *yearbook* photo • They signed each other's *yearbooks.*

year–end /ˈjiɚˈɛnd/ *adj, always used before a noun* : made or done at the end of the year • The store had a *year-end* sale. • We finished our *year-end* reports.

year·ling /ˈjiɚlɪŋ/ *noun, pl* **-lings** [*count*] : an animal (such as a horse) that is between one and two years old
– yearling *adj* • *yearling* calves

year·long /ˈjiɚˈlɑːŋ/ *adj, always used before a noun* : lasting one year • She went on a *yearlong* sabbatical.

year·ly /ˈjiɚli/ *adj*
1 : happening, done, or made once each year • He went for his *yearly* [=*annual*] checkup. • She renews her lease on a *yearly* basis.
2 : of or relating to one year • your *yearly* income [=the income you receive each year] • the area's *yearly* rainfall
– yearly *adv* • You should get your car inspected *yearly.* [=once each year] • The report is published ***twice yearly.*** [=twice each year]

yearn /ˈjɚn/ *verb* **yearns; yearned; yearn·ing** [*no obj*] : to feel a strong desire or wish *for* something or *to do* something • captives *yearning for* freedom = captives *yearning to be* free • People are *yearning for* a return to normalcy. = People are *yearning to return* to normalcy.
– yearn·ing /ˈjɚnɪŋ/ *noun, pl* **-ings** [*count*] • She had a *yearning* to travel. [=she yearned to travel; she had a strong desire to travel] • our *yearnings* for peace

> ***synonyms*** YEARN, LONG, AND PINE mean to want something very much. YEARN suggests a strong desire for something combined with a feeling of sadness. • They *yearn* for the day when they can be together again. LONG is used like YEARN and may also suggest a desire for something that you can only get or achieve by working hard or being lucky. • She *longs* to be a famous artist. PINE suggests that you grow weak while continuing to want something that you may never have. • He *pines* for his homeland.

year–round /ˈjiɚˈraʊnd/ *adj, always used before a noun* : active, present, or done throughout the year • a *year-round* resort • the island's *year-round* residents • While baseball and football are seasonal, bowling is a *year-round* sport.
– year–round *adv* • The park is open *year-round.* [=all year; throughout the year]

yeast /ˈjiːst/ *noun* [*noncount*] : a type of fungus that is used in making alcoholic drinks (such as beer and wine) and in baking to help make dough rise

yeast infection *noun, pl* **~ -tions** [*count*] *US, medical* : a disease that affects the vagina and that is caused by a fungus — called also (*chiefly Brit*) *thrush*

yeasty /ˈjiːsti/ *adj* **yeast·i·er; -est** [*or more* ~; *most* ~] : full of or resembling yeast • *yeasty* bread dough • The kitchen had a *yeasty* odor.

yech *or* **yecch** /ˈjʌk, ˈjɛk/ *interj, US* — used to express disgust • *Yech!* What a mess!

[1]**yell** /ˈjɛl/ *verb* **yells; yelled; yell·ing**
1 : to say (something) very loudly especially because you are angry, surprised, or are trying to get someone's attention [*no obj*] We saw people *yelling* for help. • She *yelled* [=*shouted*] to her friend across the park. — often + *at* • Stop *yelling at* me! [+ *obj*] I heard someone *yelling* my name. • kids *yelling* [=*shouting*] insults at each other • "Look out!" she *yelled.* — often + *out* • He *yelled out* my name when he saw me.
2 [*no obj*] : to make a sudden, loud cry • The crowd was *yelling* wildly. — often + *out* • She *yelled out* [=*cried out*] in pain.
yell your head off see [1]HEAD
– yell·er *noun, pl* **-ers** [*count*]

[2]**yell** *noun, pl* **yells** [*count*]
1 : a sudden, loud cry — often + *of* • We heard the *yells* [=*shouts*] *of* children coming from the park. • a *yell of* joy/triumph • She let out a *yell.* • (*informal*) ***Give me a yell*** if you need anything. [=call me if you need anything; let me know if you need anything]
2 *US* : a usually rhythmic shout or cheer used especially in schools or colleges to show support for sports teams • the old school *yell*

[1]**yel·low** /ˈjɛloʊ/ *adj* **yel·low·er; -est** [*or more* ~; *most* ~]
1 : having the color of the sun or of ripe lemons • a *yellow* car • The raincoat was *yellow.*
2 *informal* : afraid in a way that makes you unable to do what is right or expected : COWARDLY • He was too *yellow* to stand up and fight.
3 *always used before a noun* : containing news that is meant to shock people and that is not true or is only partly true • ***yellow journalism***

[2]**yellow** *noun, pl* **-lows** : the color of the sun or of ripe lemons [*noncount*] The bridesmaids were dressed in *yellow.* • shades of *yellow* [*count*] a room decorated in *yellows* and greens — see color picture on page C1

[3]**yellow** *verb* **-lows; -lowed; -low·ing** : to become yellow or to cause (something) to become yellow [*no obj*] The paper had *yellowed* with age. [+ *obj*] The leaves were *yellowed* by disease.

yellow–bellied *adj* [*more* ~; *most* ~] *informal + old-fashioned* : not having courage : COWARDLY • You're a *yellow-bellied* traitor!

yellow card *noun, pl* **~ cards** [*count*] *soccer* : a yellow card that a referee holds in the air to indicate that a player has broken the rules of the game and is being officially warned — compare RED CARD

yellow fever *noun* [*noncount*] *medical* : a serious disease that causes fever and often yellowing of the skin and that is passed from one person to another especially by the bite of mosquitoes

yel·low·ish /ˈjɛləwɪʃ/ *adj* : somewhat yellow • a flower with *yellowish* petals • The apple's skin was *yellowish* green.

yellow jacket *noun, pl* **~ -ets** [*count*] *US* : a small flying insect that has yellow marks on its body and that can sting you

yellow pages *noun*
the yellow pages or the Yellow Pages : a phone book or part of a phone book that is printed on yellow paper, that lists the names, addresses, and phone numbers of businesses, organizations, etc., according to what they sell or provide, and that includes advertisements ✧ In British English, *Yellow Pages* is a trademark. — compare WHITE PAGES

yelp /ˈjɛlp/ *verb* **yelps; yelped; yelp·ing** [*no obj*] : to make a quick, high cry or bark • The dog *yelped* in pain.
– yelp *noun, pl* **yelps** [*count*] • She *gave/made a yelp* [=she yelped] when I sprayed her with the hose.

[1]**yen** /ˈjɛn/ *noun, pl* **yen**
1 [*count*] : the basic unit of money of Japan • It costs 300 *yen.*
2 [*count*] : a coin or bill representing one yen • a handful of *yen*
3 ***the yen*** *technical* : the value of the yen compared with the value of the money of other countries • *The yen* fell against the U.S. dollar.
– compare [2]YEN

[2]**yen** *noun* [*singular*] : a strong desire *for* something or *to do* something • I had a *yen* [=*craving*] *for* spicy food. • She has a *yen* [=*longing*] *to travel.* — compare [1]YEN

yeo·man /ˈjoʊmən/ *noun, pl* **-men** [*count*]
1 : an officer in the U.S. Navy who works as a clerk
2 : a farmer in the past who owned a small amount of land
yeoman's work/service *also* ***yeoman work/service*** *US* : very good, hard, and valuable work that someone does especially to support a cause, to help a team, etc. • They've done *yeoman's work* in raising money for the organization.

yep /ˈjɛp/ *adv, informal* : [1]YES • *Yep,* that's right. — compare NOPE

-yer see [2]-ER

Y

[1]yes /ˈjɛs/ *adv*
1 — used to give a positive answer or reply to a question, request, or offer ▪ "Are you ready?" "*Yes*, I am." ▪ "Is the supervisor in today?" "*Yes*." ▪ "I won't tolerate this behavior any longer. Do you understand?" "*Yes*, sir/ma'am." ▪ I asked her to the dance and she said *yes*. ▪ "Would you care for some coffee?" "*Yes*, please/thanks." [=I would like some coffee] ▪ I'll ***say yes to*** anything [=I'll agree to do or accept anything] at this point. ▪ "Are you happy with your job?" "***Yes and no***." [=I'm happy about some parts of my job and unhappy about others]
2 — used to express agreement with an earlier statement or to say that statement is true ▪ *Yes*, I see your point. ▪ "Things could be worse." "*Yes*, that's very true." ▪ *Yes*, such a policy would be helpful. ▪ "The concert was good." "***Yes, but*** it was too crowded."
3 — used to introduce a statement that corrects or disagrees with an earlier negative statement ▪ "She couldn't have meant that." "*Yes*, she did mean it." ▪ "He wasn't even there." "*Yes*, he was!" ▪ "You can't do that!" "Oh, *yes* I can."
4 — used to emphasize a statement or to make it more precise ▪ We are delighted, *yes*, truly delighted to see you! ▪ It was amusing, *yes*, but also very moving.
5 *informal* — used to express excitement, enthusiasm, or relief ▪ "We won!" "*Yes!*"
6 — used to indicate uncertainty or polite interest ▪ *Yes*? Can I help you with anything? ▪ "Mr. Jones?" "*Yes*?" "You have a phone call."
7 — used to show you have remembered something ▪ Where was I? Oh, *yes*. I was going to tell you about the dance.
yes, yes — used to show anger or irritation ▪ "We're leaving in a few minutes. You need to get ready." "*Yes, yes*. I know. I heard you the first time."

[2]yes *noun, pl* **yes·es** *also* **yes·ses** [*count*] : a positive reply : an answer of yes ▪ We need a *yes* to go ahead with the project. ▪ She answered all the questions with *yeses* and nos.

ye·shi·va *or* **ye·shi·vah** /jəˈʃiːvə/ *noun, pl* **-shi·vas** *or* **-shi·vot** /-ˌʃiːˈvoʊt/ [*count*] : a Jewish school for religious instruction

yes–man /ˈjɛsˌmæn/ *noun, pl* **-men** /-ˌmɛn/ [*count*] *disapproving* : a person (especially a man) who agrees with everything that someone says : a person who supports the opinions or ideas of someone else in order to earn that person's approval ▪ corporate *yes-men*

[1]yes·ter·day /ˈjɛstɚˌdeɪ/ *noun, pl* **-days**
1 [*noncount*] : the day before today ▪ *Yesterday*'s game was canceled because of the rain. ▪ *Yesterday* was our anniversary. ▪ She gave birth to a healthy baby boy ***the day before yesterday***. [=two days ago]
2 [*count*] *somewhat formal* : a time in the past : the time of previous years ▪ The radio program features *yesterday's* songs as well as today's. ▪ Today's cars aren't all that different from the models of *yesterday*. ▪ That actor is ***yesterday's news***. [=that actor was popular once, but is not popular now]

[2]yesterday *adv* : on, during, or for the day before today ▪ It rained heavily *yesterday* afternoon. ▪ I mailed the application early/late *yesterday* morning. ▪ It was good to see you *yesterday*. ▪ We met a month ago *yesterday*. [=we met one month and one day ago] ▪ It's been over a year since we met, but it ***seems like only yesterday***. [=it seems as if we just met]
wasn't born yesterday see BORN

yes·ter·year /ˈjɛstɚˌjiɚ/ *noun*
of yesteryear *literary* : of the past : from a long time ago ▪ the values *of yesteryear* ▪ radio shows *of yesteryear*

[1]yet /ˈjɛt/ *adv*
1 a : until now : so far ▪ It's been the hardest year *yet* for our business. [=this is the hardest year our business has ever had] ▪ His latest novel is his best one *yet*. ▪ They haven't done much *yet*. = (less commonly) They haven't *yet* done much. ▪ The team has not *yet* won a game. = The team has not won a game *yet*. = The team has *yet* to win a game. ▪ I haven't read the book *yet*. **b** : at this time : so soon as now ▪ Has the mail arrived *yet*? ▪ Are we there *yet*? ▪ It's not time to eat *yet*. ▪ "Are you ready?" "No, not *yet*." ▪ We don't *yet* know what their plans are. ▪ Hasn't she called *yet*? ▪ Their suggestions won't be implemented, at least not *yet*. ▪ We don't have a firm grasp of the situation *yet*. ▪ Has he left *yet*? = (*US, informal*) Did he leave *yet*?
2 a : in addition — used for emphasis ▪ They made up *yet* another excuse. ▪ It's *yet* one more example of poor sportsmanship. **b** : to a greater extent or degree ▪ The case became *yet* [=*even*] more mysterious as additional facts were revealed.
3 : at a later time ▪ It's still early. He may *yet* join us for dinner. [=there's still a chance that he'll join us for dinner]
4 — used to indicate how long something will last ▪ A nasty cold will probably keep him out of the office for a few days *yet*. [=he will probably be out of the office for a few more days] ▪ It may be some time *yet* before she's ready to date again.
as yet *also* ***as of yet*** : until the present time : so far ▪ He has not *as yet* heard the result. = *As yet* he has not heard the result. [=he has not yet heard the result]
just yet see [2]JUST
the best is yet to come/be see [3]BEST
yet again : for another time : AGAIN ▪ They arrived late *yet again*. [=once again]

[2]yet *conj* — used to introduce a statement that adds something to a previous statement and usually contrasts with it in some way ▪ We thought the idea sounded tempting, *yet* [=*but*] common sense told us it wouldn't work. ▪ She designs simple *yet* [=*but*] elegant clothing. ▪ She played well, *yet* she didn't qualify for the finals. [=although she played well, she didn't qualify for the finals] ▪ Everyone seemed pleased, ***and yet*** I had the feeling that something was wrong.

ye·ti /ˈjɛti/ *noun, pl* **-tis** [*count*] : ABOMINABLE SNOWMAN

yew /ˈjuː/ *noun, pl* **yews**
1 [*count*] : an evergreen tree or bush with stiff needles and small red berries
2 [*noncount*] : the wood of a yew ▪ a bow made of *yew*

Yid·dish /ˈjɪdɪʃ/ *noun* [*noncount*] : a language based on German that is written in Hebrew characters and that was originally spoken by Jews of central and eastern Europe
– Yiddish *adj* ▪ *Yiddish* words/expressions ▪ *Yiddish* culture

[1]yield /ˈjiːld/ *verb* **yields; yield·ed; yield·ing**
1 [+ *obj*] **a** : to produce or provide (something, such as a plant or crop) ▪ The apple/peach trees *yielded* an abundant harvest. ▪ This soil should *yield* good crops. ▪ The seeds *yield* a rich oil. **b** : to produce (something) as a result of time, effort, or work ▪ New methods have *yielded* promising results in the field. ▪ The studies *yielded* clear evidence. — sometimes + *up* ▪ Their research has *yielded up* some surprising results. **c** : to produce (a profit, an amount of money, etc.) ▪ The tax is expected to *yield* millions. ▪ The bond *yields* seven percent annually.
2 [*no obj*] : to agree to do or accept something that you have been resisting : to stop trying to resist or oppose something ▪ After several hours of debate, the opposition *yielded*. — often + *to* ▪ The company refused to *yield to* the protesters' demands. ▪ The architect *yielded to* critics and changed the design. ▪ I finally *yielded to* temptation and had some cake.
3 a [+ *obj*] : to allow (something) to be taken or controlled by another person, group, etc. ▪ Ground troops refused to *yield* [=(more commonly) *surrender*] the fortress to the enemy. — sometimes used figuratively ▪ Despite all my arguments she was unwilling to *yield* the point to me. [=she was unwilling to admit that I was right] **b** *formal* : to give (someone) the chance to speak at a public meeting — + *to* [+ *obj*] I *yield* the floor *to* the Senator from Maine. [*no obj*] I *yield to* the Senator. **c** [*no obj*] : to stop trying to fight someone or something ▪ The enemy refused to *yield*. [=*give up*]
4 [*no obj*] : to bend, stretch, or break because of physical force or pressure ▪ Ripe fruit should *yield* slightly to pressure. [=ripe fruit should be just a little bit soft] ▪ The heavy weight caused the rope to *yield*.
5 *US* : to allow another car or person to go ahead of you or in front of you [*no obj*] The driver failed to *yield* [=(*Brit*) *give way*] and was hit by another car. ▪ You must *yield* to pedestrians in the crosswalk. [+ *obj*] Oncoming traffic must *yield* the right-of-way.

[2]yield *noun, pl* **yields** [*count*]
1 : the amount of something that is produced by a plant, farm, etc. ▪ Our *yield* of wheat increased this year. ▪ The average *yield* per tree is about one bushel.
2 : the profit made from an investment ▪ The *yield* on government bonds is currently seven percent. ▪ stocks with high-percentage *yields*

yield·ing /ˈjiːldɪŋ/ *adj*
1 [*more* ~; *most* ~] : tending to do or willing to do what other people want ▪ She has a gentle, *yielding* temperament.
2 : producing an indicated amount of something — used in combination ▪ a high-*yielding* crop ▪ low-*yielding* securities [=securities that do not produce a high profit]

3 [*more* ~; *most* ~] : bending or stretching easily : not rigid or stiff • The seat was made with a soft and *yielding* material.

yikes /ˈjaɪks/ *interj, informal* — used to express a feeling of fear or surprise • *Yikes*! Is it really midnight already? • *Yikes*, I didn't see you there.

yin /ˈjɪn/ *noun* [*noncount*] *in Chinese philosophy* : one of the two forces that together form everything that exists : the female principle of the universe that is considered dark and passive and is associated with earth — compare YANG

the yin and yang *chiefly US* : the two opposite sides or parts of something • learning about *the yin and yang* of politics

yip /ˈjɪp/ *verb* **yips**; **yipped**; **yip•ping** [*no obj*] *US, of a dog* : to bark in high, quick sounds • We could hear the puppy *yipping* playfully in its kennel.

yip•pee /ˈjɪpi/ *interj, informal + old-fashioned* — used to express delight or joy • *Yippee*! We're on vacation!

YMCA /ˌwaɪˌɛmˌsiːˈeɪ/ *noun*

the YMCA : an international organization originally for young men that provides social programs, a place for athletic activities, etc., for the people in a community • He's a member of *the YMCA*. • We play basketball every weekend at *the YMCA*. [=at the building owned and operated by the YMCA] — often used before another noun • a *YMCA* membership — called also (*US, informal*) *the Y* ✧ *YMCA* is an abbreviation of "Young Men's Christian Association."

yo /ˈjoʊ/ *interj, US, informal* — used especially to attract someone's attention, as a greeting, or in response to a greeting • *Yo*! What's up? • *Yo*! Listen up!

yob /ˈjɑːb/ *noun, pl* **yobs** [*count*] *Brit, informal* : a teenage boy or young man who does noisy and sometimes violent things as part of a group or gang : HOOLIGAN • A couple of *yobs* damaged his car.

[1]**yo•del** /ˈjoʊdl̩/ *verb* **-dels**; *US* **-deled** *or Brit* **-delled**; *US* **-del•ing** *or Brit* **-del•ling** : to sing loudly while changing your voice back and forth between a natural pitch and a higher pitch [*no obj*] The mountaineers were *yodeling*. [+ *obj*] She *yodeled* a song.

– yo•del•er (*US*) *or Brit* **yo•del•ler** /ˈjoʊdlɚ/ *noun, pl* **-ers** [*count*]

[2]**yodel** /ˈjoʊdl̩/ *noun, pl* **yodels** [*count*] : a song, shout, or cry made by yodeling

yo•ga /ˈjoʊgə/ *noun* [*noncount*]

1 : a system of exercises for mental and physical health • She teaches *yoga*. • a *yoga* class/instructor

2 ***Yoga*** : a Hindu philosophy that teaches a person to experience inner peace by controlling the body and mind

yo•gi /ˈjoʊgi/ *noun, pl* **-gis** [*count*]

1 : a person who practices yoga

2 ***Yogi*** : a follower of Yoga

yo•gurt *also Brit* **yo•ghurt** /ˈjoʊgɚt/ *noun, pl* **-gurts** [*count, noncount*] : a food that is made when bacteria is added to milk and that is often flavored and chilled • blueberry *yogurt*

[1]**yoke** /ˈjoʊk/ *noun, pl* **yokes**

1 [*count*] : a bar or frame that is attached to the heads or necks of two work animals (such as oxen) so that they can pull a plow or heavy load

2 [*singular*] *formal + literary* : something that causes people to be treated cruelly and unfairly especially by taking away their freedom — + *of* • The country has struggled to free itself from the *yoke of* foreign rule. • the *yoke of* tyranny

[2]**yoke** *verb* **yokes**; **yoked**; **yok•ing** [+ *obj*] : to connect (two animals) by a yoke • The two oxen were *yoked* together. — often used figuratively • He was *yoked* to his job.

yo•kel /ˈjoʊkəl/ *noun, pl* **-kels** [*count*] *informal* — used as an insulting word for a person who lives in a small town or in the country far away from cities and is regarded as stupid • He dismissed his critics as a bunch of *yokels*.

yolk /ˈjoʊk/ *noun, pl* **yolks** [*count, noncount*] : the yellow part in the center of an egg

Yom Kip•pur /ˌjoʊmkɪˈpuɚ/ *noun* [*noncount*] : a Jewish holiday observed in September or October during which Jewish people do not eat or drink anything and pray to ask for forgiveness for mistakes made during the year

yon /ˈjɑːn/ *adv, old-fashioned + literary* : to that place • They have been traveling ***hither and yon***. [=here and there; traveling to many different places]

yon•der /ˈjɑːndɚ/ *adv, old-fashioned + literary* : at or in that place : over there • the trees over *yonder* • We could see people gathering down *yonder* by the riverbank.

– yonder *adj* • from *yonder* tower [=from the tower over there]

yonks /ˈjɑːŋks/ *noun* [*noncount*] *Brit, informal* : a long period of time • She's lived there for *yonks* [=*ages*] now.

yoof /ˈjuːf/ *noun* [*noncount*] *Brit, informal + humorous* : young people as a group • the nation's *yoof* [=*youth*] • *yoof* culture

yoo–hoo /ˈjuːˌhuː/ *interj, informal* — used to attract someone's attention or to call out to someone • *Yoo-hoo*! We're over here! • *Yoo-hoo*! Is anybody there?

yore /ˈjoɚ/ *noun*

of yore *literary* : of the past • in days *of yore* [=*of old*] • The great composers *of yore* performed for kings and queens.

York•shire pudding /ˈjoɚkʃɚ-/ *noun, pl* ~ **-dings** [*count, noncount*] : a baked British food that is made from eggs, flour, and milk and that is traditionally served with meat

Yorkshire terrier *noun, pl* ~ **-ers** [*count*] : a very small dog with long straight hair that is brown or tan and gray — see picture at DOG

you /ˈjuː, jə/ *pronoun*

1 — used to refer to the person or group of people that is being addressed as the subject of a verb or as the object of a verb or preposition • *You* are absolutely right. • I love *you*. • What did she tell *you*? • *You* have been a pleasure to work with. • *You* can't be serious. • What did *you* mean by that? • How can I help *you*? • I'd like to have a talk with *you*. • I'll meet *you* there. • We will give *you* a few hours to discuss the matter. • Divide it between *you*. [=*yourselves*] • We hope to see *you* both at the party. = We hope to see both of *you* at the party.

2 — used to refer to any person or to people in general • If *you* smoke too much, *you* may harm your lungs. • The work is hard, but after a while, *you* get used to it. • How do *you* change a tire? [=what is the proper way to change a tire?]

3 *informal* — used to address someone directly • "*You* in the red shirt! Come here!" — often used before another noun • *You* fool! • *You* guys crack me up. • Calm down, *you* two.

for you *informal* — used to say that someone has done something that is typical or expected • He's already forgotten he was hurt—that's a child *for you*. [=that's the way children are] — often used to show disapproval • The mayor never responded to our complaints—that's city government *for you*!

you and yours : you and the people in your family or the people you care about • Best wishes to *you and yours* for a joyous holiday season.

you–all /juˈɑːl, ˈjɑːl/ *pronoun, US, informal* — used mainly in speech in the Southern U.S. to address two or more people • How are *you-all* [=*y'all*] doing?

you'd /ˈjuːd, jəd/ — used as a contraction of *you had* or *you would* • If *you'd* [=*you had*] read the note, it would have saved us some trouble. • *You'd* [=*you would*] be surprised how easy it was to assemble.

you–know–what *noun* [*noncount*] *informal*

1 — used in speech to refer to something that is not named but is known to both the hearer and speaker • I've hidden the *you-know-what* in the closet.

2 — used in place of a rude or offensive word in order to express anger or annoyance • He's a complete *you-know-what*. • That's a big pile of *you-know-what*.

you–know–who *noun* [*noncount*] *informal* — used in speech to refer to someone who is not named but is known to both the hearer and speaker • We're planning to throw a party for *you-know-who*.

you'll /ˈjuːl, jəl/ — used as a contraction of *you will* • I hope *you'll* come to the party. • *You'll* love this movie.

[1]**young** /ˈjʌŋ/ *adj* **youn•ger** /ˈjʌŋgɚ/; **-gest** /-gəst/

1 : in an early stage of life, growth, or development : not yet old • mothers with *young* children • a lively *young* colt • a *young* tomato plant • He looks *young* for his age. • A very nice *young* man/woman greeted us at the door. • *Young* people today have a lot of opportunities. • He dreamed of being an artist when he was *young*. • soldiers who died *young* • The movie isn't suitable for *young* viewers. • my *younger* brother • He's still too *young* to buy alcohol legally. • Our *youngest* daughter just started school. • He worked as a farmhand ***in his younger days***. [=when he was younger] • The band members are still ***young at heart***. [=they think and act like young people; they are active and have a lot of energy] • "***When I was young***," the man said, "the world was a different place."

2 : recently formed, produced, started, etc. • a *young* [=*new*] publishing company • a *young* industry • The season is still *young*. • a *young* cheese • *young* wine

not getting any younger *informal + humorous* — used to

Y

say that someone is getting older and may not have much more time to do something ▪ If we really want to see Paris, we should do it soon. We're *not getting any younger*, you know.

the younger **1** — used in comparing the ages of two people who are members of the same family ▪ He's *the younger* of her two brothers. **2** — used to refer to the younger of two people (such as a father and son) who have the same name ▪ the painters Hans Holbein the Elder and his son Hans Holbein *the Younger*

years young *informal* — used to describe an older person's age in a way that is meant to suggest that the person still looks or feels young ▪ She's 60 *years young* today!

you're only young once — used to say that people should enjoy themselves while they are young

²young *noun*

1 ***the young*** **:** young people ▪ music that appeals to *the young* ▪ *The* very *young* and the elderly are particularly sensitive to the disease.

2 *[plural]* **:** young animals, birds, etc. ▪ a robin feeding her *young* ▪ The *young* of a wolf are called pups.

young and old **:** young and old people ▪ The game is played by *young and old* alike. ▪ a story for *young and old* [=a story that will appeal to people of all ages]

young gun *noun, pl* ~ **guns** *[count] informal* **:** a young person who is successful or who is expected to be successful ▪ He's one of the *young guns* at the law firm.

young·ish /ˈjʌŋɪʃ/ *adj* **:** somewhat young ▪ a *youngish* physician

young offender *noun, pl* ~ **-ers** *[count] Brit* **:** a criminal who is under the age of 18

young·ster /ˈjʌŋstɚ/ *noun, pl* **-sters** *[count] somewhat old-fashioned* **:** a young person ▪ As a *youngster*, he was very shy. ▪ bright-eyed *youngsters* interested in learning

your /ˈjoɚ, jɚ/ *adj, always used before a noun, possessive form of* YOU

1 : relating to or belonging to you ▪ *Your* garden is beautiful. ▪ Please wash *your* hands before dinner. ▪ What is *your* new house like? ▪ You forgot *your* wallet at the restaurant. ▪ Don't worry about me—you've got ***your own*** problems. **:** made or done by you ▪ *Your* contributions are valuable. ▪ Did you finish *your* homework? ▪ With *your* permission, we can take a blood test. ▪ You always manage to impress us with *your* ideas.

2 — used to refer to any person or to people in general ▪ She's not *your* [=*a*] typical teenager. ▪ Exercising regularly is good for *your* [=*one's*] health.

3 — used in the titles of royalty, judges, etc. ▪ *Your* Majesty ▪ May we approach the bench, *Your* Honor?

Do not confuse *your* with *you're*.

you're /ˈjoɚ, jɚ/ — used as a contraction of *you are* ▪ *You're* not going fast enough. ▪ She thinks *you're* a nice guy.

Do not confuse *you're* with *your*.

yours /ˈjoɚz/ *pronoun*

1 : that which belongs to you **:** your one **:** your ones ▪ This glass is *yours*. [=this glass belongs to you; it is your glass] ▪ *Yours* is the glass on the left. [=your glass is the one on the left] ▪ My car is old, but *yours* is older. ▪ The responsibility for keeping the apartment clean is *yours*. ▪ All those CDs ***of yours*** take up an awful lot of space. ▪ Is that guy a friend *of yours*? [=your friend] ▪ My wife is a big fan *of yours*.

2 — used at the end of an informal letter ▪ *Yours*, David

3 *old-fashioned* **:** your letter ▪ This is in reply to *yours* of the 24th.

up yours see ³UP

you and yours see YOU

yours ever *or* ***ever yours*** see EVER

yours sincerely *or* ***sincerely yours*** see SINCERELY

yours truly see TRULY

your·self /jɚˈsɛlf/ *pronoun*

1 : the person that is being addressed **a** — used as the object of a verb or preposition when the person being addressed has already been mentioned ▪ You've got to behave *yourself*. ▪ Be careful or you might hurt *yourself*. ▪ When you need to relax, picture/imagine *yourself* at the beach listening to the gentle sound of the waves. ▪ You need to feel good about *yourself*. ▪ You can judge for *yourself*. ▪ You should make a mental note to *yourself*. ▪ You're making a fool/spectacle of *yourself*. **b** — used to emphasize that a particular person already mentioned has done, thought, or said something ▪ You reminded them *yourself*, remember? ▪ If you're not happy with the paint job, you can repaint the whole thing *yourself*. — often used after the noun or pronoun it refers to ▪ You *yourself* reminded them, remember?

2 : your normal or healthy self ▪ You're not *yourself* today. Is something wrong? ▪ You'll feel like *yourself* again after some time away.

be yourself **:** to act or behave as you normally do ▪ If you want to get a girl to like you, the best thing you can do is just *be yourself*.

by yourself **1 :** without any help ▪ You will have to make dinner *by yourself* tonight. ▪ You fixed the car (all) *by yourself*? **2 :** with nobody else ▪ Do you like living *by yourself*? ▪ You're not traveling there *by yourself*.

your·selves /jɚˈsɛlvz/ *pronoun*

1 : those ones that are you **: a** — used as the object of a verb or preposition to refer to a group of people who are being addressed after that group has already been mentioned ▪ You children deserve to buy *yourselves* a treat. ▪ You have a right to be proud of *yourselves*. ▪ You can judge for *yourselves*. **b** — used for emphasis to refer again to a group that is being addressed after that group has already been mentioned ▪ You should have done it *yourselves*. ▪ Did you guys build the house *yourselves*? ▪ Keep in mind that you were young once *yourselves*.

2 : your normal or healthy selves ▪ You'll feel more like *yourselves* after a good rest.

by yourselves **1 :** without any help ▪ I can't believe you fixed the car by *yourselves*. **2 :** with nobody else ▪ You boys aren't old enough to go to the mall *by yourselves*.

youth /ˈjuːθ/ *noun, pl* **youths** /ˈjuːðz/

1 *[noncount]* **:** the time of life when someone is young **:** the time when a young person has not yet become an adult ▪ She had a troubled/privileged *youth*. ▪ He spent his *youth* in the Midwest. ▪ He got into a lot of trouble in his *youth*. ▪ a generation trying to recapture lost *youth* ▪ *youth* groups ▪ (*Brit*) a ***youth club*** [=a club that provides various activities for young people] — see also FOUNTAIN OF YOUTH

2 *[noncount]* **:** the time when something is new and not yet established ▪ when the industry was still in its *youth*

3 *[count]* **:** a teenage boy or young man ▪ a tough-looking *youth* ▪ Four *youths* are suspected of starting the fire.

4 ***the youth*** **:** young people ▪ *the youth* of today ▪ The show sends a strong message to *the youth* of America. ▪ *The* city's *youth* need strong role models.

5 *[noncount]* **:** the quality or state of being young ▪ She's 70 years old but still full of *youth*.

gilded youth see GILD

youth·ful /ˈjuːθfəl/ *adj* [*more* ~; *most* ~]

1 : having or showing the freshness or energy of someone who is young ▪ *youthful* good looks ▪ He's a *youthful* 50-year-old. ▪ My grandparents are still very *youthful*.

2 : having or showing the innocence, hope, lack of knowledge, etc., of someone who is young ▪ *youthful* optimism ▪ *youthful* inexperience

– youth·ful·ly *adv* ▪ a *youthfully* energetic group **– youth·ful·ness** *noun [noncount]*

youth hostel *noun, pl* ~ **-tels** *[count]* **:** HOSTEL

you've /ˈjuːv, jəv/ — used as a contraction of *you have* ▪ I think *you've* solved the problem.

yowl /ˈjawəl/ *verb* **yowls; yowled; yowl·ing** *[no obj]* **:** to make a loud, long cry of grief, pain, or distress ▪ The cat was *yowling* outside. ▪ He was *yowling* in pain.

– yowl *noun, pl* **yowls** *[count]* ▪ He let out a *yowl* when he caught his finger in the door.

¹yo–yo /ˈjoʊˌjoʊ/ *noun, pl* **yo–yos** *[count]* **:** a round toy that has two flat sides with a string attached to its center, that is held in your hand, and that is made to go up and down by unwinding and rewinding the string with a movement of your wrist

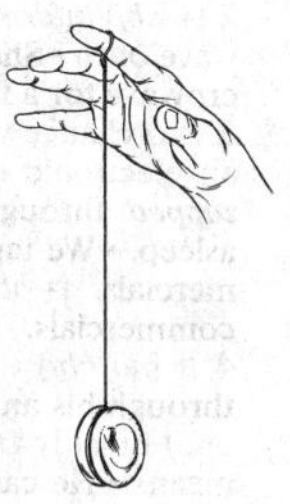

yo-yo

²yo–yo *verb* **yo–yos; yo–yoed; yo–yo·ing** *[no obj]* **:** to move repeatedly and quickly up and down or from a higher level to a lower level ▪ Her weight has *yo-yoed* in recent years. [=she has lost weight and then gained weight again quickly]

yr. *abbr* **1** year **2** your

YT *abbr* Yukon Territory

yu·an /ˈjuːwən/ *noun, pl* **yuan** *[count]* **:** the basic unit of money in China; *also* **:** a coin or bill worth one yuan

yuc·ca /ˈjʌkə/ *noun, pl* **-cas** [*count*] : a type of plant that grows in dry regions and has hard pointed leaves at the base and a long stem with white flowers

yuck /ˈjʌk/ *interj, informal* — used to express disgust • *Yuck*, I hate meat loaf.

yucky *also US* **yuk·ky** /ˈjʌki/ *adj* **yuck·i·er** *also* **yuk·ki·er; -est** [*also more ~; most ~*] *informal*

1 : causing discomfort, disgust, or a strong feeling of dislike : unpleasant and disgusting • The water was dirty and smelled *yucky*. • *yucky* food

2 : having an unpleasant feeling in your stomach : somewhat sick • I felt *yucky* after eating all that cake.

Yule /ˈjuːl/ *noun, pl* **Yules** [*count, noncount*] *old-fashioned* : CHRISTMAS • the *Yule* season

yule log *noun, pl* **~ logs** [*count*] : a large log that is traditionally burned in a fireplace on Christmas Eve

Yule·tide /ˈjuːlˌtaɪd/ *noun, pl* **-tides** [*count, noncount*] *old-fashioned + literary* : the Christmas season • the festive atmosphere of *Yuletide* • *Yuletide* cheer

yum·my /ˈjʌmi/ *adj* **yum·mi·er; -est** [*also more ~; most ~*] *informal* : very pleasing to the taste : DELICIOUS • a *yummy* dessert • He prepared all sorts of *yummy* dishes.

yup /ˈjʌp/ *adv, informal* : YES • "It's cold out, isn't it?" "*Yup*, it sure is."

yup·pie /ˈjʌpi/ *noun, pl* **-pies** [*count*] *often disapproving* : a young college-educated adult who has a job that pays a lot of money and who lives and works in or near a large city • Her friends are just a bunch of *yuppies*. — often used before another noun • her *yuppie* friends

yup·pi·fy /ˈjʌpəˌfaɪ/ *verb* **-fies; -fied; -fy·ing** [+ *obj*] *informal + disapproving* : to change (a city, neighborhood, etc.) so that it is more appealing to young people who make a lot of money : to make (something) appealing to yuppies • a *yuppified* neighborhood/restaurant

YWCA /ˌwaɪˌdʌbəljuˌsiːˈeɪ/ *noun*

the YWCA : an international organization that provides social programs, a place for athletic activities, etc., for the people and especially the women in a community • She's a member of *the YWCA*. • The meeting will be held at *the YWCA*. [=at the building owned and operated by the YWCA] — often used before another noun • a *YWCA* membership — called also (*US, informal*) *the Y* ✧ *YWCA* is an abbreviation of "Young Women's Christian Association."

Z

z *or* **Z** /ˈziː, *Brit* ˈzɛd/ *noun, pl* **z's** *or* **zs** *or* **Z's** *or* **Zs** /ˈziːz, *Brit* ˈzɛdz/

1 : the 26th letter of the English alphabet [*count*] a word that begins with a *z* [*noncount*] a word that begins with *z*

2 ***Z's*** *also* ***Zs*** *or* ***z's*** [*plural*] *US, informal* : SLEEP • I managed to ***catch/get some Z's*** [=get some sleep] on the flight.

3 [*noncount*] — used in the phrase ***x, y, and z*** to refer to the third thing in a group of three unnamed things • She says that I need to do *x, y, and z* before I can be promoted.

from A to Z see [1]A

zaf·tig /ˈzɑːftɪg/ *adj* [*more ~; most ~*] *chiefly US, informal, of a woman* : slightly fat in an attractive way : having a full, rounded figure • The actress playing the lead role was a *zaftig* blonde.

za·ny /ˈzeɪni/ *adj* **za·ni·er; -est** [*also more ~; most ~*] *informal* : very strange and silly • my *zany* [=*wacky*] aunt • He has a *zany* [=*crazy*] sense of humor.

— za·ni·ness /ˈzeɪninəs/ *noun* [*noncount*]

zap /ˈzæp/ *verb* **zaps; zapped; zap·ping** *informal*

1 [+ *obj*] **a :** to attack, destroy, or kill (someone or something) quickly • The flowers were *zapped* by the cold weather. — often used figuratively • The loss on Monday *zapped* [=*killed*] any chance the team had to go on to the finals. • He was *zapped* [=*hit*] with a finance charge because of a single late payment. **b :** to hit (someone or something) with electricity • Lightning *zapped* [=*struck*] the tree. = The tree was *zapped* by lightning. • She won't work with the wiring because she's afraid of getting *zapped*. [=*shocked, electrocuted*] **c :** to shoot (someone or something) with an electric gun, laser, etc. • The aliens in the movie *zapped* people from spaceships. • The doctor *zapped* [=*removed*] a mole on the patient's back with a laser.

2 [+ *obj*] *informal* : to heat or cook (something) in a microwave oven • She reheated her muffin by *zapping* it in the microwave for a few seconds.

3 : to change what you are watching on television by using an electronic device (called a remote control) [*no obj*] I *zapped* through the channels for a while before falling asleep. • We tape the show so we can *zap* through the commercials. [+ *obj*] We tape the show so we can *zap* [=*skip*] the commercials.

4 a [*no obj*] : to move quickly or suddenly • Pain *zapped* through his ankle. **b** [+ *obj*] : to send (something or someone) quickly from one place to another through electronic means • He can *zap* the file to the office from his laptop. • The images can be *zapped* into our homes from anywhere via satellite. • In the movie the hero is *zapped* into the past in a time machine.

zap·per /ˈzæpɚ/ *noun, pl* **-pers** [*count*] *informal*

1 : an electronic device that attracts and kills insects • a bug *zapper*

2 *Brit* : REMOTE CONTROL 1

zeal /ˈziːl/ *noun* [*noncount*] : a strong feeling of interest and enthusiasm that makes someone very eager or determined to do something • She attacked her homework with renewed *zeal* [=*enthusiasm*] after getting her first A. • a politician known for his *zeal* [=*passion*] for reform • religious/entrepreneurial *zeal* • The camp counselors enforced regulations with excessive *zeal*. [=enforced regulations too strictly]

zeal·ot /ˈzɛlət/ *noun, pl* **-ots** [*count*] *often disapproving* : a person who has very strong feelings about something (such as religion or politics) and who wants other people to have those feelings : a zealous person • religious *zealots* [=*fanatics*] • Her father is an exercise *zealot*. [=he is very serious about exercising]

— zeal·ot·ry /ˈzɛlətri/ *noun* [*noncount*] • religious *zealotry*

zeal·ous /ˈzɛləs/ *adj* [*more ~; most ~*] : feeling or showing strong and energetic support for a person, cause, etc. : filled with zeal • *zealous* fans • She was one of the president's most *zealous* [=*ardent*] supporters. • The detective was *zealous* in her pursuit of the kidnappers.

— zeal·ous·ly *adv* • She *zealously* pursued the kidnappers.

— zeal·ous·ness *noun* [*noncount*]

ze·bra /ˈziːbrə, *Brit* ˈzɛbrə/ *noun, pl* **ze·bras** *also* **zebra** [*count*] : an African animal that looks like a horse and has black and white stripes covering its body

zebra

zebra crossing *noun, pl* **~ -ings** [*count*] *Brit* : a path that is painted with stripes on a street or road and that marks the place where people can safely cross : CROSSWALK — compare PELICAN CROSSING

zed /ˈzɛd/ *noun, pl* **zeds** [*count*] *Brit* : the letter *z*

zee /ˈziː/ *noun, pl* **zees** [*count*] *US* : the letter *z*

zeit·geist /ˈzaɪtˌgaɪst/ *noun* [*singular*] : the general beliefs, ideas, and spirit of a time and place • His songs perfectly captured the *zeitgeist* of 1960s America.

Zen /ˈzɛn/ *noun* [*noncount*] : a Japanese form of Buddhism that emphasizes meditation — called also *Zen Buddhism*

ze·nith /ˈziːnəθ, *Brit* ˈzɛnəθ/ *noun* [*singular*]

1 *formal* : the strongest or most successful period of time • At its *zenith* [=*peak*] in the 1980s, the company employed more than 300 people. • That was the *zenith* [=the highest

point] of her career. — opposite NADIR
2 *technical* : the highest point reached in the sky by the sun, moon, etc.

zeph·yr /ˈzɛfɚ/ *noun, pl* **-yrs** [*count*] *literary* : a very slight or gentle wind ▪ a gentle *zephyr*

zep·pe·lin /ˈzɛpələn/ *noun, pl* **-lins** [*count*] : a large aircraft without wings that floats because it is filled with gas and that has a rigid frame inside its body to help it keep its shape — compare AIRSHIP, BLIMP, HOT-AIR BALLOON

¹ze·ro /ˈzirou/ *noun, pl* **ze·ros** *also* **ze·roes**
1 : the number 0 [*count*] One million is a one with six *zeros* [=(*Brit*) *noughts*] after it. [*noncount*] Two minus two equals *zero*.
2 [*noncount*] : the temperature shown by the zero mark on a thermometer ▪ It's supposed to fall below *zero* tonight. ▪ The temperature is 10° above/below *zero*. — see also ABSOLUTE ZERO, SUBZERO
3 [*noncount*] : nothing at all ▪ They are working to reduce the mortality rate to *zero*. ▪ Her contribution to the project was close to *zero*. [=she did almost nothing on the project] ▪ The car can go from *zero* to 60 in 10 seconds. [=from not moving at all to going 60 miles per hour in 10 seconds] ▪ (*informal*) I know *zero* [=*nada, zilch*] about fixing computers. ▪ You'll have to start ***from zero*** [=*from scratch*] if you can't find your notes.
4 [*count*] *informal* : a person who is not important, interesting, popular, etc. — usually singular ▪ Her new boyfriend's a real *zero*. [=*loser*]
— see also GROUND ZERO

²zero *adj* : not any ▪ The economy experienced *zero* [=*no*] inflation last year. ▪ (*informal*) He has *zero* [=*no*] chance of winning. = His chances of winning are *zero*. [=*nonexistent*]

³zero *verb* **zeroes; ze·roed; ze·ro·ing** [+ *obj*] *technical* : to set (a measuring device, such as a scale) so that it reads 0 ▪ *zero* the scale
zero in on [*phrasal verb*] ***zero in on (someone or something)***
1 : to direct all of your attention to (someone or something) ▪ My teacher helped me *zero in on* my problems with algebra. ▪ Scientists are hoping to *zero in on* a cure. **2** : to aim something (such as a gun or camera) directly at (someone or something) ▪ The gunner *zeroed in on* the target. ▪ He *zeroed in on* her with the camera.
zero out [*phrasal verb*] ***zero (something) out*** *or* ***zero out (something)*** *US* : to reduce the amount of (something) to zero ▪ Be sure to *zero out* [=*empty*] the account before you switch banks. : to remove (something) completely ▪ New legislation will *zero out* further funding for the project. [=will completely eliminate further funding for the project] ▪ This program will be *zeroed out* [=*eliminated*] in the budget for next year.

zero gravity *noun* [*noncount*] : a state or condition in which there is no gravity ▪ experiments conducted in *zero gravity*

zero hour *noun* [*noncount*] : the time at which an event (such as a military attack) is scheduled to begin

zero–sum game *noun* [*singular*] : a situation in which one person or group can win something only by causing another person or group to lose it ▪ Dividing up the budget is a *zero-sum game*.

zero tolerance *noun* [*noncount*] : a policy of giving the most severe punishment possible to every person who commits a crime or breaks a rule ▪ The police announced that there will be *zero tolerance* for looters. [=anyone caught looting will be punished as harshly as possible] ▪ The camp has a *zero tolerance* drug and alcohol policy. [=drugs and alcohol are not allowed at the camp and anyone found with drugs or alcohol will be punished]

zest /ˈzɛst/ *noun*
1 a : lively excitement : a feeling of enjoyment and enthusiasm [*noncount*] We'd hoped to recapture some of the *zest* [=*energy*] and enthusiasm of youth at the reunion. [*singular*] She has a real ***zest for life***. [=she enjoys life very much] **b** : a lively quality that increases enjoyment, excitement, or energy [*noncount*] His humor added *zest* to the performance. [*singular*] His humor added a certain *zest* to the performance.
2 [*noncount*] : small pieces of the skin of a lemon, orange, or lime that are used to flavor food ▪ The recipe calls for a tablespoon of lemon *zest*. — compare ²PEEL, RIND
— **zest·ful** /ˈzɛstfəl/ *adj* [*more* ~; *most* ~] ▪ a *zestful* performance — **zest·ful·ly** *adv*

zesty /ˈzɛsti/ *adj* **zest·i·er; -est** [*also more* ~; *most* ~] *chiefly US*
1 : having a strong, pleasant, and somewhat spicy flavor ▪ a *zesty* sauce
2 : lively and pleasing : full of zest ▪ *zesty* humor
— **zest·i·ness** *noun* [*noncount*]

¹zig·zag /ˈzɪgˌzæg/ *noun, pl* **-zags** [*count*] : a line that has a series of short, sharp turns or angles ▪ The kids were running in circles and *zigzags* around the yard. ▪ He's wearing a shirt with red *zigzags* on it. ▪ a *zigzag* pattern

zigzag

²zigzag *verb* **-zags; -zagged; -zag·ging** [*no obj*] : to move along a path that has a series of short, sharp turns or angles ▪ We saw a motorcycle *zigzagging* on the highway. ▪ The player with the ball *zigzagged* back and forth down the field. ▪ A dirt road *zigzags* up the steep hill to our cabin.

zilch /ˈzɪlʧ/ *noun* [*noncount*] *informal* : nothing at all ▪ I know *zilch* about him. ▪ She's done *zilch* [=*nada*] to help me out.

zil·lion /ˈzɪljən/ *noun, pl* **-lions** [*count*] *informal* : a very large number ▪ *zillions* of ants ▪ I have a *zillion* chores to finish before we can leave.

Zim·mer frame /ˈzɪmɚ-/ *trademark, Brit* — used for a metal frame that someone (such as an injured or elderly person) can use for support while walking

zinc /ˈzɪŋk/ *noun* [*noncount*] : a bluish-white metal that is very common and is used especially to make brass and as a protective coating for things made of iron and steel

zine /ˈziːn/ *noun, pl* **zines** [*count*] *informal* : a small magazine that is written by people who are not professional writers and that usually has stories about a particular subject ▪ a punk *zine* ✧ *Zine* is a shortened form of the word *magazine*. — see also FANZINE

¹zing /ˈzɪŋ/ *noun* [*noncount*] *informal* : a quality that makes something exciting, interesting, etc. ▪ They needed to put some *zing* back into their relationship. ▪ A brightly colored scarf can add *zing* [=*interest*] to any basic black outfit. ▪ The chili peppers give the sauce a little extra *zing*.

²zing *verb* **zings; zinged; zing·ing** *informal*
1 [*no obj*] : to move very quickly and make a humming sound ▪ The bullets *zinged* [=*zipped*] past our ears.
2 [+ *obj*] *US, informal* : to insult or criticize (someone) in a sharp, clever, or playful way ▪ The comics spent the evening cracking jokes and *zinging* each other. ▪ His opponent has run television ads *zinging* him.

zing·er /ˈzɪŋɚ/ *noun, pl* **-ers** [*count*] *US, informal* : a quick and clever comment that criticizes or insults someone ▪ The candidate couldn't help getting off a *zinger* or two about his opponent.

zin·nia /ˈzɪnijə/ *noun, pl* **-nias** [*count*] : a plant that is grown in gardens for its brightly colored flowers

Zi·on·ism /ˈzajəˌnɪzəm/ *noun* [*noncount*] : political support for the creation and development of a Jewish homeland in Israel
— **Zi·on·ist** /ˈzajənɪst/ *noun, pl* **-ists** [*count*] — **Zionist** *adj* ▪ the *Zionist* movement

¹zip /ˈzɪp/ *verb* **zips; zipped; zip·ping**
1 : to close, open, or connect something with a zipper [+ *obj*] I helped him *zip* his jacket. ▪ She *zipped* the tent open/closed. [*no obj*] The luggage *zips* open.
2 [+ *obj*] *computers* : to reduce the size of (a file) by using special software : COMPRESS ▪ This kind of file can be *zipped* and unzipped easily.
zip up [*phrasal verb*] **1** ***zip (something) up or zip up (something)*** : to close or connect (something) with a zipper ▪ He *zipped up* his jacket. **2** ***zip (someone) up or zip up (someone)*** : to use a zipper to fasten someone's clothing ▪ Will you *zip* me *up*, please? ▪ I *zipped* her *up* because she couldn't do it herself.
zip your lip *or* ***zip it*** *US, informal* : to stop talking immediately ▪ Tell your sister to *zip her lip*! [=*shut up*] ▪ She angrily told him to *zip it*.
— compare ³ZIP

²zip *noun, pl* **zips** [*count*] *Brit* : ZIPPER ▪ The *zip* was stuck and we couldn't open the suitcase. — compare ⁴ZIP, ⁵ZIP, ⁶ZIP

³zip *verb, always followed by an adverb or preposition* **zips; zipped; zipping** [*no obj*] : to move or act very quickly ▪ We *zipped* [=*rushed*] through the store to find my sister some jeans. ▪ Cars were *zipping* past us on the highway. ▪ The motorcyclist was *zipping* in and out of traffic. — compare ¹ZIP

⁴zip *noun* [*noncount*] *informal*

1 : energy and excitement • The performance seemed to lack *zip*. • We'll try to add a little *zip* [=*zing*] to the usual recipe. • Plant some red flowers to give your garden more *zip*.
2 : speed of movement • The pitcher put some extra *zip* on his fastball. • a car with plenty of *zip*
— compare ²ZIP, ⁵ZIP, ⁶ZIP

⁵zip *noun [noncount] US, informal*
1 : nothing at all • My opinion counts for *zip* around here. • The city council has done *zip* to deal with this problem. • I know *zip* [=*zilch*] about carpentry.
2 : a score of zero • We won the game 7–*zip*. • The final score was 7 to *zip*. [=(*Brit*) *nil*]
— compare ²ZIP, ⁴ZIP, ⁶ZIP

⁶zip *or* **ZIP** /ˈzɪp/ *noun, pl* **zips** *or* **ZIPs** *[count] US* : ZIP CODE — compare ²ZIP, ⁴ZIP, ⁵ZIP

zip code *or* **ZIP code** *noun, pl* **~ codes** *[count] US* : a group of numbers that is used in the U.S. as part of an address to identify a mail delivery area (such as a town or a part of a city) — called also *zip*; compare POSTCODE

zip file *also* **zipped file** *noun, pl* **~ files** *[count] computers* : a computer file in which a large amount of repeated information has been removed to make it smaller

zip·per /ˈzɪpɚ/ *noun, pl* **-pers** *[count] US* : a device that is made of two rows of metal or plastic teeth and another piece that slides over the teeth to make them fit together or come apart and that is used to fasten clothing, open or close bags, etc. • The *zipper* was stuck and we couldn't open the suitcase. • Can you help him with his *zipper*? — called also (*Brit*) *zip*
— **zipper** *verb* **-pers; -pered; -per·ing** [+ *obj*] • She *zippered* [=*zipped*] the bag shut. — **zip·pered** /ˈzɪpɚd/ *adj* • The purse has several *zippered* compartments.

zip·po /ˈzɪpoʊ/ *noun [noncount] US, informal* : nothing at all • I know zilch, nada, *zippo* about wine.

zip·py /ˈzɪpi/ *adj* **zip·pi·er; -est** [*also more ~; most ~*] *informal*
1 : very fast : SPEEDY • a *zippy* little car
2 : appealingly stylish • a *zippy* [=*snappy*] outfit
3 : having a spicy flavor • a *zippy* hot sauce

zit /ˈzɪt/ *noun, pl* **zits** *[count] informal* : a small, red, swollen spot on the skin : PIMPLE

zith·er /ˈzɪðɚ/ *noun, pl* **-ers** *[count]* : a musical instrument that has strings stretched across a shallow wooden box and that is played with your fingers or a pick

zo·di·ac /ˈzoʊdiˌæk/ *noun*
the zodiac : an imaginary area in the sky that the sun, moon, and planets appear to travel through ✧ The zodiac is divided into 12 parts (called star signs or signs of the zodiac) which have special names and symbols and are believed by some people to have influence over people and events.
— **zo·di·a·cal** /zoʊˈdajəkəl/ *adj*

zodiac

zom·bie /ˈzɑːmbi/ *noun, pl* **-bies** *[count]*
1 *informal* : a person who moves very slowly and is not aware of what is happening especially because of being very tired • If I don't go to bed early I'll be a *zombie* tomorrow. • His students usually sat there in the classroom like *zombies*.
2 : a dead person who is able to move because of magic according to some religions and in stories, movies, etc. • a scary film about *zombies* = a scary *zombie* film

zon·al /ˈzoʊnl/ *adj [more ~; most ~]* : relating to or having different areas : divided into zones • We installed a *zonal* heating system in the house.

¹zone /ˈzoʊn/ *noun, pl* **zones** *[count]*
1 : an area that is different from other areas in a particular way • The city is in an earthquake *zone*. [=an area where earthquakes occur] • a pedestrian *zone* [=an area where vehicles are not allowed so that people can walk safely] • a combat/danger/war *zone* • the ***euro zone*** [=the part of Europe that uses the euro as its monetary unit] • He left the car in a ***no-parking zone***. [=an area where parking is not allowed] — see also BUFFER ZONE, COMFORT ZONE, CRUMPLE ZONE, END ZONE, NEUTRAL ZONE, NO-FLY ZONE, RED ZONE, STRIKE ZONE, TIME ZONE, TOWAWAY ZONE, TWILIGHT ZONE
2 : one of the sections in a city or town that is used for a particular purpose • a business/residential *zone* [=*district*]

²zone *verb* **zones; zoned; zon·ing** [+ *obj*] : to officially say that (a section in a city, town, etc.) can be used for a particular purpose (such as business or housing) • The town council voted to *zone* the area for industrial use. — often used as (*be*) *zoned* • This area *is zoned* for residential development. • commercially *zoned* land
zone out [*phrasal verb*] *US, informal* : to stop paying attention because you are tired, bored, etc. • I *zoned out* during the movie. — see also ZONED OUT

zone defense (*US*) *also Brit* **zone defence** *noun [noncount] chiefly US, sports* : a way of playing defense in football, basketball, etc., by having each player on a team guard a certain area of the field or court

zoned out *adj, US, informal* : not thinking clearly or paying attention to what is happening around you because you are tired, drugged, etc. • I was totally *zoned out* and didn't hear what she said. • He was always *zoned out* on drugs back then. — see also *zone out* at ²ZONE

zoning *noun [noncount]* : a system of rules used to control where businesses and homes are built in a city or town • Developers have been frustrated by restrictive *zoning* imposed by state and local governments. • local *zoning* laws • the city's *zoning* board/commission

zonked /ˈzɑːŋkt/ *adj [more ~; most ~] informal* : very tired or affected by alcohol or drugs • Chances are that we'll be too *zonked* [=*exhausted*] from the trip to go out tonight. — often + *out* • After a morning at the beach our kids were *zonked out*. • He was *zonked out* on drugs. • She's becoming known as just another ***zonked-out*** actress.

zoo /ˈzuː/ *noun, pl* **zoos**
1 *[count]* : a place where many kinds of animals are kept so that people can see them — see also PETTING ZOO
2 *[singular] informal* : a place, situation, or group that is crowded, loud, and uncontrolled • The sixth grade classroom was a *zoo* after recess. • The supermarket was a real *zoo* on the night before the storm.

zoo·keep·er /ˈzuːˌkiːpɚ/ *noun, pl* **-ers** *[count]* : a person who takes care of the animals in a zoo

zoological park *noun, pl* **~ parks** *[count] formal* : ZOO 1 — called also *zoological garden*

zo·ol·o·gy /zoʊˈɑːləʤi/ *noun [noncount]* : the branch of science that involves the study of animals and animal behavior
— **zoo·log·i·cal** /ˌzowəˈlɑːʤɪkəl/ *adj* — **zo·ol·o·gist** /zoʊˈɑːləʤɪst/ *noun, pl* **-gists** *[count]*

¹zoom /ˈzuːm/ *verb* **zooms; zoomed; zoom·ing** *[no obj]*
1 *always followed by an adverb or preposition, informal* **a** : to move quickly • Cars were *zooming* [=*speeding*] down the highway. • They got in the car and *zoomed* away. • The group of bicycle racers *zoomed* past. **b** : to move quickly upward • a *zooming* rocket • After her first successful cases she *zoomed* to the top of her profession.
2 *informal* : to increase suddenly • Housing sales have *zoomed* in recent months. — often + *up* • Network executives are hoping to see the ratings *zoom up* overnight.
zoom in [*phrasal verb*] ✧ When a camera or photographer *zooms in*, the lens of the camera is adjusted so that the image seems to be bigger and closer. • The TV cameras *zoomed in*. — often + *on* • The TV cameras *zoomed in on* the winner's face. • I *zoomed in on* her face to show her reaction. — often used figuratively • We're trying to *zoom in*

Z

on the cause of these problems [=to see and understand the exact cause of these problems] before they get worse.

zoom out [*phrasal verb*] ✧ When a camera or photographer *zooms out*, the lens of the camera is adjusted so that the image seems to be smaller and farther away. ▪ The camera *zoomed out* to show a wider view of the scene.

[2]zoom *noun, pl* **zooms**

1 [*count*] : ZOOM LENS ▪ The camera was equipped with a *zoom*.

2 [*singular*] *informal* : the loud sound of a vehicle that is moving very fast ▪ The truck went by with a *zoom*.

zoom lens *noun, pl* ~ **lenses** [*count*] : a camera lens that can make the size of the image become larger and smaller : a camera lens that can zoom in or zoom out — see picture at CAMERA; compare TELEPHOTO LENS

zoot suit /ˈzuːt-/ *noun, pl* ~ **suits** [*count*] : a type of suit for men that was worn in the 1940s and that consisted of a long jacket with wide shoulders and pants that were wide at the top and narrow at the bottom

Zo•ro•as•tri•an•ism /ˌzorəˈwæstrijəˌnɪzəm/ *noun* [*noncount*] : a religion founded by the Persian prophet Zoroaster — **Zo•ro•as•tri•an** /ˌzorəˈwæstrijən/ *adj* — **Zoroastrian** *noun, pl* **-ans** [*count*]

zuc•chi•ni /zuˈkiːni/ *noun, pl* **zucchini** *or* **zuc•chi•nis** [*count, noncount*] *US* : a dark green vegetable that is long and smooth and that has soft skin which can be eaten — called also (*Brit*) *courgette*; see color picture on page C4

Zu•lu /ˈzuːˌluː/ *noun, pl* **-lus**

1 [*count*] : a member of a group of people living mostly in South Africa

2 [*noncount*] : the language of the Zulu people

zwie•back /ˈzwaɪˌbæk, *Brit* ˈzwiːˌbæk/ *noun* [*noncount*] *US* : a dry, hard bread that is eaten especially by young children

zy•de•co /ˈzaɪdəˌkoʊ/ *noun* [*noncount*] : a type of lively popular music originally from southern Louisiana

zy•gote /ˈzaɪˌgoʊt/ *noun, pl* **-gotes** [*count*] *biology* : a cell that is formed when an egg and a sperm combine : a fertilized egg

Geographical Names

Ab·bots·ford /ˈæbətsfəd/ : city in British Columbia, Canada
Ab·er·deen /ˌæbəˈdiːn/ : city in Scotland – **Ab·er·do·ni·an** /ˌæbəˈdounijən/ *adj or noun*
Ab·i·djan /ˌɑːbiˈdʒɑːn/ : city in the Ivory Coast
Ab·i·lene /ˈæbəˌliːn/ : U.S. city, Texas
Ab·kha·zia /ˌæbˈkeɪʒijə/ : area in the Republic of Georgia – **Ab·kha·zian** /ˌæbˈkeɪʒijən/ *adj or noun*
Abu Dha·bi /ˌɑːbuˈdɑːbi/ : city in the United Arab Emirates
Ab·ys·sin·ia /ˌæbəˈsɪnijə/ see ETHIOPIA – **Ab·ys·sin·i·an** /ˌæbəˈsɪnijən/ *adj or noun*
Aca·dia /əˈkeɪdijə/ : early name for Nova Scotia, Canada – **Aca·di·an** /əˈkeɪdijən/ *adj or noun*
Aca·pul·co /ˌɑːkəˈpulkou/ : city in Mexico
Acon·ca·gua /ˌɑːkounˈkɑːgwɑ/ : mountain in Argentina
Ad·dis Aba·ba /ˈɑːdɪsˈɑːbɑˌbɑː/ : city in Ethiopia
Ad·e·laide /ˈædəˌleɪd/ : city in Australia
Aden, Gulf of /ˈɑːdn̩/ – **the Gulf of Aden** : part of the Indian Ocean
Ad·i·ron·dack /ˌædəˈrɑːnˌdæk/ – **the Adirondack Mountains** *also* **the Adirondacks** : mountains in the U.S., in New York
Adri·at·ic /ˌeɪdriˈætɪk/ – **the Adriatic Sea** *also* **the Adriatic** : part of the Mediterranean Sea
Ae·ge·an /ɪˈdʒijən/ – **the Aegean Sea** *also* **the Aegean** : part of the Mediterranean Sea
Af·ghan·i·stan /æfˈgænəˌstæn/ : country in Asia – **Afghan** /ˈæfˌgæn/ *adj or noun* – **Af·ghani** /æfˈgæni/ *adj*
Af·ri·ca /ˈæfrɪkə/ : continent south of the Mediterranean Sea – **African** *adj or noun*
Agra /ˈɑːgrə/ : city in India
Ah·mad·a·bad /ˈɑːmədəˌbɑːd/ : city in India
Ak·ron /ˈækrən/ : U.S. city, Ohio
Al·a·bama /ˌæləˈbæmə/ : state of the U.S. – **Al·a·bam·i·an** /ˌæləˈbæmijən/ *or* **Al·a·bam·an** /ˌæləˈbæmən/ *adj or noun*
Alas·ka /əˈlæskə/
1 : state of the U.S.
2 the Gulf of Alaska : part of the Pacific Ocean
– **Alas·kan** /əˈlæskən/ *adj or noun*
Al·ba·nia /ælˈbeɪnijə/ : country in Europe – **Al·ba·nian** /ælˈbeɪnijən/ *adj or noun*
Al·ber·ta /ælˈbɚtə/ : province of Canada – **Al·ber·tan** /ælˈbɚtn̩/ *adj or noun*
Al·bu·quer·que /ˈælbəˌkɚki/ : U.S. city, New Mexico – **Al·bu·quer·que·an** /ˈælbəˌkɚkijən/ *noun*
Al·ca·traz /ˈælkəˌtræz/ : island in the U.S., in California
Alep·po /əˈlɛpou/ : city in Syria
Aleu·tian /əˈluːʃən/ – **the Aleutian Islands** *also* **the Aleutians** : islands in the U.S., in Alaska
Al·ex·an·dria /ˌælɪgˈzændrijə/
1 : U.S. city, Virginia
2 : city in Egypt
– **Al·ex·an·dri·an** /ˌælɪgˈzændrijən/ *adj or noun*
Al·ge·ria /ælˈdʒirijə/ : country in Africa – **Al·ge·ri·an** /ælˈdʒirijən/ *adj or noun*
Al·giers /ælˈdʒirz/ : city in Algeria – **Al·ge·rine** /ˌældʒəˈrin/ *adj or noun*
Al·lah·a·bad /ˈɑlɑhɑˌbɑd/ : city in India
Al·le·ghe·ny /ˌæləˈgeɪni/
1 the Allegheny River *also* **the Allegheny** : river in the U.S., in Pennsylvania and New York
2 the Allegheny Mountains *also* **the Alleghenies** : mountains in the U.S., in Pennsylvania, Maryland, Virginia, and West Virginia
Al·len·town /ˈælənˌtaun/ : U.S. city, Pennsylvania
Al·ma·ty /ælˈmɑːti/ : city in Kazakhstan
Alps /ˈælps/ – **the Alps** : mountains in Europe – **Al·pine** /ˈælˌpaɪn/ *adj*
Al·sace /ælˈsæs/ : region of France – **Al·sa·tian** /ælˈseɪʃən/ *adj or noun*
Am·a·ril·lo /ˌæməˈrɪlou/ : U.S. city, Texas
Am·a·zon /ˈæməˌzɑːn/ – **the Amazon River** *also* **the Amazon** : river in South America – **Am·a·zo·nian** /ˌæməˈzounijən/ *adj*
Amer·i·ca /əˈmerəkə/
1 : the continent of North America or the continent of South America
2 *or* **the Amer·i·cas** /əˈmerəkəz/ : lands of the Western Hemisphere
3 : UNITED STATES OF AMERICA
– **Amer·i·can** /əˈmerəkən/ *adj or noun*
American Samoa : islands of the U.S., in the Pacific Ocean
Am·ster·dam /ˈæmstəˌdæm/ : city in the Netherlands – **Am·ster·dam·mer** /ˈæmstəˌdæmə/ *noun*
Amu Dar'·ya /ˌɑːmuˈdɑɚjə/ – **the Amu Dar'ya** : river in Asia
Amur /ɑˈmuɚ/ – **the Amur River** *also* **the Amur** : river in Asia
An·a·heim /ˈænəˌhaɪm/ : U.S. city, California
An·a·to·lia /ˌænəˈtoulijə/ see ASIA MINOR – **An·a·to·li·an** /ˌænəˈtoulijən/ *adj or noun*
An·chor·age /ˈæŋkərɪdʒ/ : U.S. city, Alaska
An·da·lu·sia /ˌændəˈluːʒijə/ : region of Spain – **An·da·lu·sian** /ˌændəˈluːʒən/ *adj or noun*
An·da·man Sea /ˈændəmən/ – **the Andaman Sea** : part of the Bay of Bengal
An·des /ˈænˌdiːz/ – **the Andes Mountains** *also* **the Andes** : mountains in South America – **An·de·an** /ˈænˌdijən/ *adj* – **An·dine** /ˈænˌdiːn/ *adj*
An·dor·ra /ænˈdorə/ : country in Europe – **An·dor·ran** /ænˈdorən/ *adj or noun*
Ang·kor /ˈæŋˌkoɚ/ : ruins of old city in Cambodia
An·glia /ˈæŋglijə/ : Latin name of England – **An·gli·an** /ˈæŋglijən/ *adj or noun*
An·go·la /æŋˈgoulə/ : country in Africa – **An·go·lan** /æŋˈgoulən/ *adj or noun*
An·guil·la /æŋˈgwɪlə/ : British island in the West Indies – **An·guil·lan** /æŋˈgwɪlən/ *adj or noun*
An·ka·ra /ˈæŋkərə/ : city in Turkey
An·nam /æˈnæm/ : region of Vietnam – **An·nam·ese** /ˌænəˈmiːz/ *adj or noun*
An·nap·o·lis /əˈnæpəlɪs/ : U.S. city, Maryland
Ann Ar·bor /ˌænˈɑrbɚ/ : U.S. city, Michigan
An·shan /ˈɑːnˈʃɑːn/ : city in China
Ant·arc·tic /ˌæntˈɑɚktɪk/ – **the Antarctic** : Antarctica and the ocean around it
Ant·arc·ti·ca /ˌæntˈɑɚktɪkə/ : continent at the South Pole – **Antarctic** *adj*
An·tie·tam /ænˈtiːtəm/ : creek in the U.S., in Pennsylvania and Maryland
An·ti·gua and Bar·bu·da /ænˈtiːgəəndbɑɚˈbuːdə/ : island country in the West Indies
An·til·les /ænˈtɪliz/ – **the Antilles** : the West Indies except for the Bahamas – **An·til·le·an** /ænˈtɪlijən/ *adj*
Aomen see MACAO
Ap·en·nines /ˈæpəˌnaɪnz/ – **the Apennines** : mountains in Italy – **Ap·en·nine** /ˈæpəˌnaɪn/ *adj*
Ap·pa·la·chia /ˌæpəˈleɪtʃə, ˈlætʃə/ : region of the eastern U.S.
Ap·pa·la·chian /ˌæpəˈleɪtʃijən, ˌæpəˈlætʃijən/ – **the Appalachian Mountains** *also* **the Appalachians** : mountains in North America
Aqa·ba, Gulf of /ˈɑːkɑbə/ – **the Gulf of Aqaba** : part of the Red Sea
Aquid·neck Island /əˈkwɪdˌnɛk/ *or* **Rhode Island** : island in the U.S., in the state of Rhode Island
Aq·ui·ta·nia /ˌækwəˈteɪnjə/ : part of the ancient Roman empire – **Aq·ui·ta·nian** /ˌækwəˈteɪnjən/ *adj or noun*
Ara·bia /əˈreɪbijə/ – **Arabia** *or* **the Arabian Peninsula** : area of southwestern Asia
Ar·a·by /ˈerəbi/ : literary name for Arabia

Ara·fu·ra Sea /orəˈfurɑ/ – **the Arafura Sea** : sea between Australia and New Guinea

Ar·al Sea /ˈerəl/ – **the Aral Sea** : lake between Kazakhstan and Uzbekistan

Ar·a·rat *or* **Mount Ararat** /ˈerəˌræt/ : mountain in Turkey near the border of Iran

Arc·tic /ˈɑɚktɪk/
1 the Arctic Ocean *also* **the Arctic** : ocean north of the Arctic Circle
2 the Arctic : the Arctic Ocean and lands in it
3 the Arctic Archipelago : group of islands of Canada
– **Arctic** *adj*

Are·ci·bo /ˌɑreɪˈsi:boʊ/ : U.S. city, Puerto Rico

Ar·gen·ti·na /ˌɑɚʤənˈti:nə/ : country in South America – **Ar·gen·tine** /ˈɑɚʤənˌtaɪn/ *adj or noun* – **Ar·gen·tin·ean** *or* **Ar·gen·tin·i·an** /ˌɑɚʤənˈtɪnijən/ *adj or noun*

Ar·i·zo·na /ˌerəˈzoʊnə/ : state of the U.S. – **Ar·i·zo·nan** /ˌerəˈzoʊnən/ *or* **Ar·i·zo·nian** /ˌerəˈzoʊnijən/ *adj or noun*

Ar·kan·sas /ˈɑɚkənˌsɑ:; *2 is also* ɑrˈkænzəs/
1 : state of the U.S.
2 the Arkansas River *also* **the Arkansas** : river in the U.S., in Arkansas
– **Ar·kan·san** /ɑɚˈkænzən/ *adj or noun*

Ar·ling·ton /ˈɑɚlɪŋtən/ : U.S. city, Texas

Ar·me·nia /ɑɚˈmi:nijə/ : country in Europe – **Ar·me·nian** /ɑɚˈmi:nijən/ *adj or noun*

Aru·ba /əˈru:bə/ : Dutch island in the Caribbean – **Aru·ban** /əˈru:bən/ *adj or noun*

Ar·vada /ɑɚˈvædə/ : U.S. city, Colorado

As·cen·sion *or* **Ascension Island** /əˈsɛnʃən/ : British island in the Atlantic Ocean

Asia /ˈeɪʒə/ : continent north of the equator – **Asian** /ˈeɪʒən/ *adj or noun*

Asia Minor *or* **Anatolia** : part of Turkey

As·sam /əˈsæm/ : former kingdom; now part of India – **As·sam·ese** /ˌæsəˈmi:z/ *adj or noun*

As·syr·ia /əˈsirijə/ : empire in ancient western Asia – **As·syr·i·an** /əˈsirijən/ *adj or noun*

Ata·ca·ma Desert /ˌætɑˈkɑ:mə/ – **the Atacama Desert** : desert in Chile

Ath·a·bas·ca *also* **Ath·a·bas·ka** /ˌæθəˈbæskə/ – **the Athabasca River** *also* **the Athabaska** : river in Alberta, Canada

Ath·ens /ˈæθənz/
1 : U.S. city, Georgia
2 : city in Greece
– **Athe·nian** /əˈθinijən/ *adj or noun*

At·lan·ta /ətˈlæntə/ : U.S. city, Georgia – **At·lan·tan** /ətˈlæntən/ *adj or noun*

At·lan·tic /ətˈlæntɪk/ – **the Atlantic Ocean** *also* **the Atlantic** : ocean separating North America and South America from Europe and Africa – **Atlantic** *adj*

At·ti·ca /ˈætɪkə/ : state in ancient Greece – **At·tic** /ˈætɪk/ *adj*

Auck·land /ˈɑ:klənd/ : city in New Zealand – **Auck·land·er** /ˈɑ:kləndɚ/ *noun*

Au·gus·ta /ɑˈgʌstə/ : U.S. city, Georgia

Au·ro·ra /əˈrorə/
1 : U.S. city, Colorado
2 : U.S. city, Illinois

Ausch·witz /ˈaʊshˌvɪts/ : site of a Nazi prison in Poland during World War II

Aus·tin /ˈɑ:stən/ : U.S. city, Texas

Aus·tral·asia /ˌɑ:strəˈleɪʒə/ : Australia, Tasmania, New Zealand, and Melanesia – **Aus·tral·asian** /ˌɑ:strəˈleɪʒən/ *adj or noun*

Aus·tra·lia /ɑˈstreɪljə/
1 : continent southeast of Asia
2 : country including the continent of Australia and the island of Tasmania
– **Aus·tra·lian** /ɑˈstreɪljən/ *adj or noun*

Aus·tria /ˈɑ:strijə/ : country in Europe – **Aus·tri·an** /ˈɑ:strijən/ *adj or noun*

Austria–Hungary : former country of central Europe – **Aus·tro–Hun·gar·i·an** /ˈɑ:sˌtroʊˌhʌŋˈgerijən/ *adj or noun*

Aus·tro·ne·sia /ˌɑ:strəˈni:ʒə/ : islands of the southern Pacific Ocean – **Aus·tro·ne·sian** /ˌɑ:strəˈni:ʒən/ *adj or noun*

Ayers Rock /ˈerz/ : large rock formation in central Australia

Azer·bai·jan /ˌæzɚˌbaɪˈʤɑ:n/ : country in Europe and Asia – **Azer·bai·ja·ni** /ˌæzɚˌbaɪˈʤɑ:ni/ *adj or noun*

Azores /ˈeɪˌzorz/ – **the Azores** : Portuguese islands in the Atlantic Ocean – **Azor·e·an** *or* **Azor·i·an** /eɪˈzorijən/ *adj or noun*

Azov, Sea of /ˈɑˌzɑ:f/ – **the Sea of Azov** : part of the Black Sea

Bab·y·lon /ˈbæbəˌlɑ:n/ : city in ancient Asia in Babylonia – **Bab·y·lo·nian** /ˌbæbəˈloʊnjən/ *adj or noun*

Bab·y·lo·nia /ˌbæbəˈloʊnjə/ : country in ancient western Asia – **Bab·y·lo·nian** /ˌbæbəˈloʊnjən/ *adj or noun*

Bac·tria /ˈbæktrijə/ : country in ancient western Asia – **Bac·tri·an** /ˈbæktrijən/ *adj or noun*

Baf·fin /ˈbæfən/
1 Baffin Bay : part of the Atlantic Ocean
2 Baffin Island : island of Canada in the Arctic Archipelago

Bagh·dad /ˈbægˌdæd/ : city in Iraq

Ba·ha·mas /bəˈhɑ:məz/ – **the Bahamas** : island country in the Atlantic Ocean – **Ba·ha·mi·an** /bəˈheɪmijən/ *or* **Ba·ha·man** /bəˈheɪmən/ *adj or noun*

Bah·rain /bɑˈreɪn/ : island country in the Persian Gulf – **Bah·raini** /bɑˈreɪni/ *adj or noun*

Bai·kal, Lake /baɪˈkɑ:l/ : lake in Russia

Ba·ja California /ˈbɑ:ˌhɑ:/ : area of Mexico

Ba·kers·field /ˈbeɪkɚzˌfi:ld/ : U.S. city, California

Ba·ku /bɑˈku:/ : city in Azerbaijan

Bal·e·ar·ic Islands /ˌbæliˈerɪk/ – **the Balearic Islands** : Spanish islands in the Mediterranean Sea

Ba·li /ˈbɑ:li/ : island of Indonesia – **Ba·li·nese** /ˌbɑ:lɪˈni:z/ *adj or noun*

Bal·kan /ˈbɑ:lkən/
1 the Balkan Peninsula : area in southeastern Europe
2 the Balkans : countries in the Balkan Peninsula

Bal·khash, Lake /bælˈkæʃ/ : lake in Kazakhstan

Bal·tic /ˈbɑ:ltɪk/ – **the Baltic Sea** *also* **the Baltic** : part of the Atlantic Ocean – **Baltic** *adj*

Bal·ti·more /ˈbɑ:ltəˌmoɚ/ : U.S. city, Maryland – **Bal·ti·mor·e·an** /ˌbɑ:ltəˈmorijən/ *noun*

Ba·ma·ko /ˌbɑ:mɑˈkoʊ/ : city in Mali

Ban·dung /ˈbɑ:nˌdʊŋ/ : city in Indonesia

Ban·ga·lore /ˈbæŋgəˌloɚ/ : city in India

Bang·kok /ˈbæŋˌkɑ:k/ : city in Thailand

Ban·gla·desh /ˌbɑ:ŋgləˈdɛʃ/ : country in Asia – **Ban·gla·deshi** /ˌbɑ:ŋgləˈdɛʃi/ *adj or noun*

Bar·ba·dos /bɑɚˈbeɪˌdoʊs/ : island country in the West Indies – **Bar·ba·di·an** /bɑɚˈbeɪdijən/ *adj or noun*

Bar·ce·lo·na /ˌbɑrsəˈloʊnə/ : city in Spain

Ba·rents Sea /ˈberənts/ – **the Barents Sea** : part of the Arctic Ocean

Bar·ne·gat Bay /ˈbɑɚnɪˌgæt/ : part of the Atlantic Ocean near the U.S. state of New Jersey

Bar·ran·qui·lla /ˌbɑrɑnˈki:jə/ : city in Colombia

Bar·rie /ˈbæri/ : city in Ontario, Canada

Bar·row, Point /ˈberoʊ/ : most northerly place in the U.S.

Basque Country /ˈbæsk/ : region of Spain – **Basque** *adj or noun*

Bat·on Rouge /ˌbætn̩ˈruʒ/ : U.S. city, Louisiana

Ba·var·ia /bəˈverijə/ : state of Germany – **Ba·var·i·an** /bəˈverijən/ *adj or noun*

Ba·ya·mon /ˌbajəˈmoʊn/ : U.S. city, Puerto Rico

Beau·fort Sea /ˈboʊfɚt/ – **the Beaufort Sea** : part of the Arctic Ocean

Beau·mont /ˈboʊˌmɑ:nt/ : U.S. city, Texas

Beer·she·ba /biɚˈʃi:bə/ : town in Israel

Bei·jing /ˈbeɪˈʤɪŋ/ *or* **Pe·king** /ˈpi:ˈkɪŋ/ : city in China

Bei·rut /beɪˈru:t/ : city in Lebanon

Be·la·rus /ˌbiləˈru:s, ˌbjɛləˈru:s/ : country in Europe – **Be·la·ru·si·an** /ˌbiləˈru:sijən, ˌbjɛləˈru:sijən/ *or* **Be·la·rus·sian** /ˌbiləˈrʌʃən, ˌbjɛləˈrʌʃən/ *adj or noun*

Be·lém /bəˈlɛm/ : city in Brazil

Bel·fast /ˈbɛlˌfæst, *Brit* ˈbɛlˌfɑ:st/ : city in Northern Ireland

Bel·gium /ˈbɛlʤəm/ : country in Europe – **Bel·gian** /ˈbɛlʤən/ *adj or noun*

Bel·grade /ˈbɛlˌgreɪd, ˈbɛlˌgrɑ:d/ : city in Serbia

Be·lize /bəˈli:z/ : country in Central America – **Be·liz·ean** /bəˈli:zijən/ *adj or noun*

Belle·vue /ˈbɛlˌvju:/ : U.S. city, Washington

Be·lo Ho·ri·zon·te /ˌbeɪlouˌorəˈzounti/ : city in Brazil
Ben·gal /bɛnˈgɑːl/ : region divided between Bangladesh and India – **Ben·gal·ese** /ˌbɛŋgəˈliːz/ *adj or noun*
Bengal, Bay of – the Bay of Bengal : part of the Indian Ocean
Be·nin /bəˈniːn/
 1 : country in Africa
 2 the Bight of Benin : part of the Gulf of Guinea
 – **Ben·i·nese** /bəˌnɪnˈiːz/ *adj or noun*
Ben Nev·is /bɛnˈnɛvəs/ : mountain in Scotland
Be·ring /ˈbirɪŋ, ˈberɪŋ/
 1 the Bering Sea : part of the northern Pacific Ocean
 2 the Bering Strait : narrow area of water between North America and Asia near the Bering Sea
Berke·ley /ˈbɚkli/ : U.S. city, California
Ber·lin /bɚˈlɪn/ : city in Germany – **Ber·lin·er** /bɚˈlɪnɚ/ *noun*
Ber·mu·da /bɚˈmjuːdə/ : British islands in the Atlantic Ocean – **Ber·mu·dan** /bɚˈmjuːdn̩/ *or* **Ber·mu·di·an** /bɚˈmjuːdijən/ *adj or noun*
Bes·sa·ra·bia /ˌbɛsəˈreɪbijə/ : region of southeastern Europe – **Bes·sa·ra·bi·an** /ˌbɛsəˈreɪbijən/ *adj or noun*
Beth·le·hem /ˈbɛθlɪˌhɛm/ : town in the West Bank
Bev·er·ly Hills /ˌbɛvɚliˈhɪlz/ : U.S. city, California
Bho·pal /bouˈpɑːl/ : city in India
Bhu·tan /buˈtɑːn/ : country in Asia – **Bhu·ta·nese** /ˌbuːtəˈniːz/ *adj or noun*
Bi·a·fra /biˈɑːfrə/ : region of western Africa – **Bi·a·fran** /biˈɑːfrən/ *adj or noun*
Big Sur /ˈsɚ/ : coastal region in the U.S., in California
Bi·loxi /bəˈlʌksi/ : U.S. city, Mississippi
Bir·ming·ham
 1 /ˈbɚ·mɪŋ·ˌhæm/ : U.S. city, Alabama
 2 /ˈbɚ·mɪŋ·əm/ : city in England
Bis·cay, Bay of /ˈbɪˌskeɪ/ – **the Bay of Biscay** : part of the Atlantic Ocean near Europe
Bis·cayne Bay /bɪˈskeɪn/ : part of the Atlantic Ocean near the U.S. state of Florida
Bi·thyn·ia /bəˈθɪnijə/ : country in ancient Asia Minor – **Bi·thyn·i·an** /bəˈθɪnijən/ *adj or noun*
Black Sea – the Black Sea : sea between Europe and Asia
Blanc, Mont see MONT BLANC
Blue Ridge – the Blue Ridge *also* **the Blue Ridge Mountains** : part of the Appalachian Mountains
Boe·o·tia /biˈouʃijə/ : state of ancient Greece – **Boe·o·tian** /biˈouʃən/ *adj or noun*
Bo·go·tá /ˌbougouˈtɑː/ : city in Colombia
Bo·he·mia /bouˈhimijə/ : region of the Czech Republic – **Bo·he·mi·an** /bouˈhimijən/ *adj or noun*
Boi·se /ˈbɔɪsi/ : U.S. city, Idaho
Bo·liv·ia /bəˈlɪvijə/ : country in South America – **Bo·liv·i·an** /bəˈlɪvijən/ *adj or noun*
Bom·bay /bɑːmˈbeɪ/ *or* **Mum·bai** /ˈmʌmˌbaɪ/ : city in India
Bon·aire /bəˈner/ : Dutch island in the Caribbean Sea
Bon·ne·ville Salt Flats /ˈbɑnəˌvɪl/ : region in the U.S., in Utah
Boo·thia /ˈbuːθijə/ : part of Canada
Bor·neo /ˈborniˌou/ : island divided between Brunei, Indonesia, and Malaysia
Bos·nia and Her·ze·go·vi·na /ˈbɑːznijəəndˌhɛətsəgouˈviːnə/ : country in Europe
Bos·po·rus /ˈbɑːspərəs/ – **the Bosporus** : narrow area of water that connects the Sea of Marmara and the Black Sea
Bos·ton /ˈbɑːstən/ : U.S. city, Massachusetts – **Bos·to·nian** /bɑˈstounijən/ *adj or noun*
Both·nia, Gulf of /ˈbɑːθnijə/ – **the Gulf of Bothnia** : part of the Baltic Sea
Bo·tswa·na /bɑtˈswɑːnə/ : country in Africa
Brah·ma·pu·tra /ˌbrɑːməˈpuːtrə/ – **the Brahmaputra River** *also* **the Brahmaputra** : river in southern Asia
Bramp·ton /ˈbræmptən/ : city in Ontario, Canada
Bra·sí·lia /brəˈzɪljə/ : city in Brazil
Bra·zil /brəˈzɪl/ : country in South America – **Bra·zil·ian** /brəˈzɪljən/ *adj or noun*
Bret·on, Cape /ˌkeɪpˈbrɛtn̩/ : part of Nova Scotia, Canada
Bridge·port /ˈbrɪʤˌport/ : U.S. city, Connecticut
Brigh·ton /ˈbraɪtn̩/ : town in England
Brit·ain /ˈbrɪtn̩/
 1 see GREAT BRITAIN 2
 2 : UNITED KINGDOM
 – **Brit·ish** /ˈbrɪtɪʃ/ *adj or noun*
British Columbia : province of Canada
British Empire – the British Empire : former empire consisting of Great Britain and the areas it controlled
British Isles – the British Isles : Great Britain, Ireland, and nearby islands
Brit·ta·ny /ˈbrɪtəni/ : region of France
Bronx /ˈbrɑːŋks/ – **Bronx** *or* **the Bronx** : part of the U.S. city of New York, in the state of New York
Brook·lyn /ˈbrʊklən/ : part of the U.S. city of New York, in the state of New York
Browns·ville /ˈbraunzˌvɪl/ : U.S. city, Texas
Bru·nei /bruˈnaɪ/ : country in Asia – **Bru·nei·an** /bruˈnajən/ *adj or noun*
Bu·cha·rest /ˈbuːkəˌrɛst/ : city in Romania
Bu·da·pest /ˈbuːdəˌpɛst/ : city in Hungary
Bue·nos Ai·res /ˌbweɪnəsˈeriz/ : city in Argentina
Buf·fa·lo /ˈbʌfəˌlou/ : U.S. city, New York
Bul·gar·ia /ˌbʌlˈgerijə/ : country in Europe – **Bul·gar·i·an** /ˌbʌlˈgerijən/ *adj or noun*
Bur·bank /ˈbɚˌbæŋk/ : U.S. city, California
Bur·gun·dy /ˈbɚgəndi/ : region of France – **Bur·gun·di·an** /bɚˈgʌndijən/ *adj or noun*
Bur·ki·na Fa·so /buɚˈkiːnəˈfɑːsou/ : country in Africa
Bur·ling·ton /ˈbɚlɪntən/ : city in Ontario, Canada
Burma see MYANMAR – **Bur·mese** /ˌbɚˈmiːz/ *adj or noun*
Bur·na·by /ˈbɚnəbi/ : city in British Columbia, Canada
Bu·run·di /bʊˈruːndi/ : country in Africa – **Bu·run·di·an** /bʊˈruːndiən/ *adj or noun*
Busan see PUSAN
By·zan·ti·um /bəˈzæntijəm/ : ancient city on the site of modern Istanbul, Turkey – **Byz·an·tine** /ˈbɪzn̩ˌtiːn/ *adj or noun*
Cab·ot Strait /ˈkæbət/ : narrow area of water connecting the St. Lawrence River with the Atlantic Ocean
Ca·guas /ˈkɑːˌgwɑːs/ : U.S. town, Puerto Rico
Cai·ro /ˈkaɪˌrou/ : city in Egypt – **Cai·rene** /kaɪˈriːn/ *adj or noun*
Ca·la·bria /kəˈleɪbrijə/ : region in southern Italy – **Ca·la·bri·an** /kəˈleɪbrijən/ *adj or noun*
Cal·cut·ta /kælˈkʌtə/ *or* **Kol·ka·ta** /koulˈkɑːtɑ/ : city in India – **Cal·cut·tan** /kælˈkʌtn̩/ *adj or noun*
Cal·e·do·nia /ˌkæləˈdounjə/ : Latin name for Scotland – **Cal·e·do·nian** /ˌkæləˈdounjən/ *adj or noun*
Cal·ga·ry /ˈkælgəri/ : city in Alberta, Canada – **Cal·gar·i·an** /kælˈgerijən/ *noun*
Ca·li /ˈkɑːli/ : city in Colombia
Cal·i·for·nia /ˌkæləˈfoɚnjə/ : state of the U.S. – **Cal·i·for·nian** /ˌkæləˈfoɚnjən/ *adj or noun*
California, Gulf of – the Gulf of California : part of the Pacific Ocean
Cal·va·ry /ˈkælvəri/ : place near ancient Jerusalem
Cam·bo·dia /kæmˈboudijə/ : country in Asia – **Cam·bo·di·an** /kæmˈboudijən/ *adj or noun*
Cam·bridge /ˈkeɪmbrɪʤ/
 1 : U.S. city, Massachusetts
 2 : city in England
Cam·er·oon /ˌkæməˈruːn/ : country in Africa – **Cam·er·oo·nian** /ˌkæməˈruːnijən/ *adj or noun*
Cam·po·bel·lo *or* **Campobello Island** /ˌkæmpəˈbɛˌlou/ : island of New Brunswick, Canada
Cam Ranh Bay /ˈkɑːmˈrɑːn/ : part of the China Sea near Vietnam
Ca·naan /ˈkeɪnən/ : region of ancient southwestern Asia – **Ca·naan·ite** /ˈkeɪnəˌnaɪt/ *adj or noun*
Can·a·da /ˈkænədə/ : country in North America – **Ca·na·di·an** /kəˈneɪdijən/ *adj or noun*
Canal Zone – the Canal Zone *or* **the Panama Canal Zone** : narrow area of land around the Panama Canal
Ca·nary Islands /kəˈneri/ – **the Canary Islands** : Spanish islands in the Atlantic Ocean
Ca·nav·er·al, Cape /kəˈnævrəl/ : part of the U.S., in Florida
Can·cun /ˌkænˈkuːn/ : vacation place in Mexico
Cannes /ˈkæn/ : city in France
Can·ter·bury /ˈkæntɚˌberi, *Brit* ˈkæntəbri/ : city in England

Cape Bret·on Island /keɪpˈbrɛtn̩/ : island of Nova Scotia, Canada
Cape Cor·al /ˈkorəl/ : U.S. city, Florida
Cape Town /ˈkeɪpˌtaʊn/ : city in the Republic of South Africa – **Cape·to·ni·an** /keɪpˈtounijən/ *noun*
Cape Verde /ˈvəd/ : island country in the Atlantic Ocean – **Cape Verd·ean** /ˈvərdijən/ *adj or noun*
Ca·pri /kæˈpriː/ : island of Italy
Ca·ra·cas /kɑˈrɑːkɑs/ : city in Venezuela
Car·diff /ˈkɑədɪf/ : city in Wales
Ca·rib·be·an /ˌkerəˈbijən, kəˈrɪbijən/ – **the Caribbean Sea** *also* **the Caribbean** : part of the Atlantic Ocean – **Caribbean** *adj*
Ca·rin·thia /kəˈrɪnθijə/ : region of Europe – **Ca·rin·thi·an** /kəˈrɪnθijən/ *adj or noun*
Carls·bad Caverns /ˈkɑrəlzˌbæd/ : caves in the U.S., in New Mexico
Ca·ro·li·na /ˌkɑrouˈliːnə/ : U.S. city, Puerto Rico
Ca·ro·li·nas /ˌkerəˈlaɪnəz/ – **the Carolinas** : the U.S. states of North Carolina and South Carolina – **Car·o·lin·i·an** /ˌkerəˈlɪnijən/ *adj or noun*
Car·o·line Islands /ˈkerəˌlaɪn/ – **the Caroline Islands** : islands in the Pacific Ocean
Car·pa·thi·an /kɑəˈpeɪθijən/ – **the Carpathian Mountains** *also* **the Carpathians** : mountains in Europe
Car·roll·ton /ˈkerəltən/ : U.S. city, Texas
Car·thage /ˈkɑəθɪʤ/ : city in ancient northern Africa – **Car·tha·gin·ian** /ˌkɑəθəˈʤɪnjən/ *adj or noun*
Ca·sa·blan·ca /ˌkæsəˈblæŋkə/ : city in Morocco
Cas·cade /kæˈskeɪd/ – **the Cascade Range** *also* **the Cascades** : mountains in the U.S., in Washington, Oregon, and California
Cas·co Bay /ˈkæskou/ : part of the Atlantic Ocean near the U.S. state of Maine
Cas·pi·an /ˈkæspijən/ – **the Caspian Sea** *also* **the Caspian** : salt lake between Europe and Asia
Cas·tile /kæˈstiːl/ : region of Spain – **Cas·til·ian** /kæˈstɪljən/ *adj or noun*
Cat·a·lo·nia /ˌkætəˈlounjə/ : region of Spain – **Cat·a·lo·nian** /ˌkætəˈlounjən/ *adj or noun*
Cats·kill /ˈkætˌskɪl/ – **the Catskill Mountains** *also* **the Catskills** : mountains in the U.S., in New York
Cau·ca·sia /kɑˈkeɪʒə/ : region of southeastern Europe – **Cau·ca·sian** /kɑˈkeɪʒən/ *adj or noun*
Cau·ca·sus Mountains /ˈkɑːkəsəs/ – **the Caucasus Mountains** : mountains between Europe and Asia
Cay·man /keɪˈmæn, ˈkeɪmən/ – **the Cayman Islands** *also* **the Caymans** : British islands in the West Indies
Cedar Rapids : U.S. city, Iowa
Ce·le·bes Sea /ˈsɛləˌbiːz/ – **the Celebes Sea** : part of the Pacific Ocean
Central African Republic – **the Central African Republic** : country in Africa
Central America : narrow area of North America between Mexico and South America – **Central American** *adj or noun*
Cey·lon /sɪˈlɑːn/ : island in the Indian Ocean – **Cey·lon·ese** /ˌseɪləˈniz/ *adj or noun*
Chad /ˈʧæd/ : country in Africa – **Chad·ian** /ˈʧædijən/ *adj or noun*
Chal·dea /kælˈdijə/ : region of ancient southwestern Asia – **Chal·de·an** /kælˈdijən/ *adj or noun* – **Chal·dee** /ˈkælˌdiː/ *noun*
Cham·pagne /ʃæmˈpeɪn/ : region of France
Champlain, Lake /ʃæmˈpleɪn/ : lake in the U.S. between New York and Vermont and in Quebec, Canada
Chan·dler /ˈʧændlɚ/ : U.S. city, Arizona
Chang /ˈʧɑːŋ/ *or* **Yang·tze** /ˈjæŋˈsiː/ – **the Chang River** *or* **the Chang** *or* **the Yangtze River** *or* **the Yangtze** : river in China
Chang·chun /ˈʧɑːŋˈʧʊn/ : city in China
Chang·sha /ˈʧɑːŋˈʃɑː/ : city in China
Charleston /ˈʧɑrəlstən/ : U.S. city, South Carolina
Char·lotte /ˈʃɑələt/ : U.S. city, North Carolina
Chat·ham–Kent /ˈʧætəmˈkɛnt/ : city in Ontario, Canada
Chat·ta·hoo·chee /ˌʧætəˈhuːʧi/ – **the Chattahoochee River** *also* **the Chattahoochee** : river in the southeastern U.S.
Chat·ta·noo·ga /ˌʧætəˈnuːgə/ : U.S. city, Tennessee
Chech·nya /ʧɛʧˈnjɑː/ : part of Russia – **Che·chen** /ʧɪˈʧɛn/ *adj or noun*
Che·lya·binsk /ʧɛlˈjɑːbənsk/ : city in Russia
Cheng·du /ˈʧʌŋˈduː/ : city in China
Chennai see MADRAS
Cher·no·byl /ʧɚˈnoubəl/ : site in Ukraine
Ches·a·peake /ˈʧɛsəˌpiːk/
1 : U.S. city, Virginia
2 **Chesapeake Bay** : part of the Atlantic Ocean near the U.S. states of Virginia and Maryland
Chi·ca·go /ʃəˈkɑːgou/ : U.S. city, Illinois – **Chi·ca·go·an** /ʃəˈkɑːgowən/ *noun*
Chi·chén It·zá /ʧiˌʧenitˈsɑː/ : site of the ruins of an important Mayan city in the Yucatán Peninsula, Mexico
Chi·le /ˈʧɪli/ : country in South America – **Chil·ean** /ˈʧɪlijən/ *adj or noun*
Chil·koot Pass /ˈʧɪlˌkuːt/ – **the Chilkoot Pass** : area between mountains in the U.S. state of Alaska and the Yukon Territory, Canada
Chi·na /ˈʧaɪnə/
1 : country in Asia
2 **the China Sea** : part of the Pacific Ocean
Chit·ta·gong /ˈʧɪtəˌgɑːŋ/ : city in Bangladesh
Chong·qing /ˈʧʊŋˈkɪŋ/ : city in China
Chuk·chi Sea /ˈʧʊkˌʧiː/ – **the Chukchi Sea** : part of the Arctic Ocean
Chu·la Vis·ta /ˌʧuːləˈvɪstə/ : U.S. city, California
Chur·chill /ˈʧɚˌʧɪl/ – **the Churchill River** *also* **the Churchill** : river in Canada
Ci·li·cia /səˈlɪʃijə/ : country in ancient Asia Minor – **Ci·li·cian** /səˈlɪʃən/ *adj or noun*
Cin·cin·nati /ˌsɪnsəˈnæti/ : U.S. city, Ohio – **Cin·cin·nat·i·an** /ˌsɪnsəˈnætijən/ *noun*
Clarks·ville /ˈklɑəksˌvɪl/ : U.S. city, Tennessee
Clear·wa·ter /ˈkliɚˌwɑːtɚ/ : U.S. city, Florida
Cleve·land /ˈkliːvlənd/ : U.S. city, Ohio – **Cleve·land·er** /ˈkliːvləndɚ/ *noun*
Co·lom·bia /kəˈlʌmbijə/ : country in South America – **Co·lom·bi·an** /kəˈlʌmbijən/ *adj or noun*
Col·o·ra·do /ˌkɑːləˈrædou, ˌkɑːləˈrɑːdou/
1 : state of the U.S.
2 **the Colorado River** *also* **the Colorado** : river in the U.S. and Mexico
– **Col·o·rad·an** /ˌkɑːləˈrædən, ˌkɑːləˈrɑːdən/ *or* **Co·lo·ra·do·an** /ˌkɑːləˈrædowən, ˌkɑːləˈrɑːdowən/ *adj or noun*
Colorado Springs : U.S. city, Colorado
Co·lum·bia /kəˈlʌmbiə/
1 : U.S. city, South Carolina
2 **the Columbia River** *also* **the Columbia** : river in the U.S. and Canada
3 **Columbia, District of** see DISTRICT OF COLUMBIA
– **Co·lum·bi·an** /kəˈlʌmbiən/ *adj or noun*
Co·lum·bus /kəˈlʌmbəs/
1 : U.S. city, Ohio
2 : U.S. city, Georgia
Com·o·ros /ˈkɑːməˌrouz/ : island country in the Indian Ocean
Con·cord /ˈkɑːnˌkoɚd/ : U.S. city, California
Co·ney Island /ˈkouni/ : section of the U.S. city of New York, in the state of New York
Con·go /ˈkɑːŋgou/
1 **the Congo River** *also* **the Congo** *also* **the Zaire River** /zɑˈiɚ/ *also* **the Zaire** : river in Africa
2 *or officially* **the Democratic Republic of the Congo** : country in Africa
3 *or officially* **the Republic of the Congo** : country in Africa
– **Con·go·lese** /ˌkɑːŋgəˈliːz/ *adj or noun*
Con·nect·i·cut /kəˈnɛtɪkət/
1 : state of the U.S.
2 **the Connecticut River** *also* **the Connecticut** : river in the northeastern U.S.
Constantinople see ISTANBUL
Co·pen·ha·gen /ˌkoupənˈheɪgən/ : city in Denmark – **Co·pen·ha·gen·er** /ˌkoupənˈheɪgənɚ/ *noun*
Co·quit·lam /kouˈkwɪtləm/ : city in British Columbia, Canada
Coral Springs : U.S. city, Florida

Cór·do·ba /ˈkoɚdəbə/ : city in Argentina
Cor·inth /ˈkorənθ/ : region of ancient Greece – **Co·rin·thi·an** /kəˈrɪnθijən/ *adj or noun*
Co·ro·na /kəˈrounə/ : U.S. city, California
Cor·pus Chris·ti /ˈkorpəsˈkrɪsti/ : U.S. city, Texas
Cor·si·ca /ˈkorsɪkə/ : French island in the Mediterranean Sea – **Cor·si·can** /ˈkorsɪkən/ *adj or noun*
Cos·ta del Sol /ˌkɔstədɛlˈsoul/ : region of Spain
Cos·ta Me·sa /ˈkɑːstəˈmeɪsə/ : U.S. city, California
Cos·ta Ri·ca /ˌkɑːstəˈriːkə/ : country in Central America – **Cos·ta Ri·can** /ˌkɑːstəˈriːkən/ *adj or noun*
Côte d'Ivoire see IVORY COAST
Co·zu·mel /ˌkousuˈmɛl/ : island of Mexico
Crete /ˈkriːt/ : Greek island in the Mediterranean Sea – **Cre·tan** /ˈkriːtn̩/ *adj or noun*
Cri·mea /kraɪˈmijə/ : area of Ukraine – **Cri·me·an** /kraɪˈmijən/ *adj*
Cro·a·tia /krouˈeɪʃə/ : country in Europe – **Croat** /ˈkrouˌæt/ *noun* – **Cro·a·tian** /krouˈeɪʃən/ *adj or noun*
Cu·ba /ˈkjuːbə/ : island country in the West Indies – **Cu·ban** /ˈkjuːbən/ *adj or noun*
Cum·ber·land Gap /ˈkʌmbələnd/ – **the Cumberland Gap** : area between mountains in the U.S. state of Tennessee
Cu·ra·cao /ˌkurəˈsau/ : Dutch island in the Caribbean Sea
Cu·ri·ti·ba /ˌkurəˈtibə/ : city in Brazil
Cush /ˈkʌʃ/ : country in ancient northeastern Africa – **Cush·ite** /ˈkʌʃˌaɪt/ *noun* – **Cush·it·ic** /ˌkʌʃˈɪtɪk/ *adj*
Cy·prus /ˈsaɪprəs/ : island country in the Mediterranean Sea – **Cyp·ri·ot** /ˈsɪprijət/ *or* **Cyp·ri·ote** /ˈsɪpriˌout/ *adj or noun*
Cy·re·na·ica /ˌsirəˈnejəkə/ : region of ancient northern Africa – **Cy·re·na·i·can** /ˌsirəˈnejəkən/ *adj or noun*
Czech·o·slo·va·kia /ˌʧɛkəslouˈvɑːkijə/ : former country in central Europe – **Czecho·slo·vak** /ˌʧɛkəˈslouˌvɑːk/ *adj or noun* – **Czecho·slo·va·ki·an** /ˌʧɛkəslouˈvɑːkijən/ *adj or noun*
Czech Republic /ˈʧɛk/ – **the Czech Republic** : country in Europe
Daegu see TAEGU
Daejeon see TAEJON
Da·kar /dɑˈkɑr/ : city in Senegal
Da·ko·tas /dəˈkoutəz/ – **the Dakotas** : the U.S. states of North Dakota and South Dakota – **Da·ko·tan** /dəˈkoutn̩/ *adj or noun*
Da·lian /ˈdɑːˈljɛn/ : city in China
Dal·las /ˈdæləs/ : U.S. city, Texas – **Dal·las·ite** /ˈdæləˌsaɪt/ *noun*
Dal·ma·tia /dælˈmeɪʃijə/ : region of the Balkan Peninsula – **Dal·ma·tian** /dælˈmeɪʃən/ *adj or noun*
Da·ly City /ˈdeɪli/ : U.S. city, California
Da·mas·cus /dəˈmæskəs/ : city in Syria
Dan·ube /ˈdænˌjuːb/ – **the Danube River** *also* **the Danube** : river in Europe – **Da·nu·bi·an** /dæˈnjuːbijən/ *adj*
Dar es Sa·laam /ˌdɑɚˌɛssəˈlɑːm/ : city in Tanzania
Dar·fur /dɑɚˈfuɚ/ : region of Sudan
Dar·jee·ling /dɑɚˈʤiːlɪŋ/ : city in India
Dar·ling /ˈdɑɚlɪŋ/ – **the Darling River** *also* **the Darling** : river in Australia
Day·ton /ˈdeɪtn̩/ : U.S. city, Ohio
Day·to·na Beach /deɪˈtounə/ : U.S. city, Florida
Dead Sea – the Dead Sea : salt lake between Israel and Jordan
Dear·born /ˈdiɚˌboɚn/ : U.S. city, Michigan
Death Valley : dry valley in the U.S., in California and Nevada
Del·a·ware /ˈdɛləˌwer/
1 : state of the U.S.
2 the Delaware River *also* **the Delaware** : river in the eastern U.S.
3 Delaware Bay : area of the Atlantic Ocean near the U.S. states of New Jersey and Delaware
– **Del·a·war·ean** *or* **Del·a·war·ian** /ˌdɛləˈwerijən/ *adj or noun*
Del·hi /ˈdɛli/ : city in India
Del·mar·va Peninsula /dɛlˈmɑɚvə/ – **the Delmarva Peninsula** : part of the U.S., in the states of Delaware, Maryland, and Virginia
Denali see MCKINLEY, MOUNT
Den·mark /ˈdɛnˌmɑɚk/ : country in Europe – **Dane** /ˈdeɪn/ *noun* – **Dan·ish** /ˈdeɪnɪʃ/ *adj*
Den·ver /ˈdɛnvɚ/ : U.S. city, Colorado
Des Moines /dɪˈmoɪn/ : U.S. city, Iowa
De·troit /dɪˈtroɪt/ : U.S. city, Michigan – **De·troit·er** /dɪˈtroɪtɚ/ *noun*
Dha·ka /ˈdɑːkə/ : city in Bangladesh
Di·jon /diˈʒoun/ : city in France
District of Co·lum·bia /kəˈlʌmbijə/ – **the District of Columbia** : area in the U.S. where the city of Washington is located
Dix·ie /ˈdɪksi/ : the 11 southern states of the U.S. which separated from the U.S. in 1860 and 1861
Dji·bou·ti /ʤəˈbuːti/ : country in Africa
Dnie·per /ˈniːpɚ/ – **the Dnieper River** *also* **the Dnieper** : river in Ukraine, Belarus, and Russia
Dni·pro·pe·trovs'k /dəˌnjɛprəpəˈtrɑːfsk/ : city in Ukraine
Do·de·ca·nese /douˈdɛkəˌniːz/ – **the Dodecanese** : Greek islands in the Aegean Sea
Dom·i·ni·ca /ˌdɑːməˈniːkə/ : island country in the West Indies
Do·min·i·can Republic /dəˈmɪnɪkən/ – **the Dominican Republic** : country in the West Indies – **Dominican** *adj or noun*
Don /ˈdɑːn/ – **the Don River** *also* **the Don** : river in Russia
Do·nets'k /dəˈnjɛtsk/ : city in Ukraine
Do·ver /ˈdouvɚ/ : port in England
Dow·ney /ˈdauni/ : U.S. city, California
Du·bayy /duˈbaɪ/ *or* **Du·bai** : part of the United Arab Emirates
Dub·lin /ˈdʌblən/ : city in Ireland – **Dub·lin·er** /ˈdʌblənɚ/ *noun*
Du·luth /dəˈluːθ/ : U.S. city, Minnesota
Dur·ham /ˈdɚrəm/ : U.S. city, North Carolina
Eastern Hemisphere – the Eastern Hemisphere : the half of the Earth that is east of the Atlantic Ocean
East Sea – the East Sea : Korean name for the Sea of Japan
East Timor : country in Asia
Ec·ua·dor /ˈɛkwəˌdoɚ/ : country in South America – **Ec·ua·dor·an** /ˌɛkwəˈdorən/ *or* **Ec·ua·dor·ean** *or* **Ec·ua·dor·ian** /ˌɛkwəˈdorijən/ *adj or noun*
Ed·in·burgh /ˈɛdn̩ˌbərə/ : city in Scotland
Ed·mon·ton /ˈɛdməntən/ : city in Alberta, Canada – **Ed·mon·to·ni·an** /ˌɛdmənˈtounijən/ *noun*
Egypt /ˈiːʤɪpt/ : country in Africa and the Sinai Peninsula of Asia – **Egyp·tian** /ɪˈʤɪpʃən/ *adj or noun*
Eire see IRELAND 1
Elam /ˈiːləm/ : country in ancient southwestern Asia – **Elam·ite** /ˈiːləˌmaɪt/ *noun*
El·ba /ˈɛlbə/ : Italian island in the Mediterranean Sea
El·bert, Mount /ˈɛlbɚt/ : mountain in the U.S., in Colorado
El·brus, Mount /ɛlˈbruːz/ : mountain in Russia on the border of the Republic of Georgia
El·gin /ˈɛlʤən/ : U.S. city, Illinois
Eliz·a·beth /ɪˈlɪzəbəθ/ : U.S. city, New Jersey
Elles·mere Island /ˈɛlzˌmiɚ/ : island of Canada in the Arctic Archipelago
El·lis Island /ˈɛləs/ : island of the U.S., in New York
El Mon·te /ɛlˈmɑːnti/ : U.S. city, California
El Paso /ɛlˈpæsou/ : U.S. city, Texas – **El Paso·an** /ɛlˈpæsowən/ *noun*
El Sal·va·dor /ɛlˈsælvəˌdoɚ/ : country in Central America – **Sal·va·dor·an** /ˌsælvəˈdorən/ *adj or noun*
En·gland /ˈɪŋglənd/ : part of the United Kingdom – **En·glish** /ˈɪŋglɪʃ/ *adj or noun*
English Channel – the English Channel : part of the Atlantic Ocean between France and the United Kingdom
Equatorial Guinea : country in Africa
Erie /ˈiri/
1 : U.S. city, Pennsylvania
2 Lake Erie : lake in the U.S. and Canada
Er·in /ˈerən/ : literary name for Ireland
Er·i·trea /ˌerəˈtrijə/ : country in Africa – **Er·i·tre·an** /ˌerəˈtrijən/ *adj or noun*
Es·con·di·do /ˌɛskənˈdiːdou/ : U.S. city, California
Es·fa·han /ˌɛsfəˈhɑːn/ : city in Iran

Es·to·nia /ɛˈstounijə/ : country in Europe – **Es·to·nian** /ɛˈstounjən/ *adj or noun*
Ethi·o·pia /ˌiːθiˈoupijə/ *or formerly* **Ab·ys·sin·ia** /ˌæbəˈsɪnjə/ : country in Africa – **Ethi·o·pi·an** /ˌiːθiˈoupijən/ *adj or noun*
Et·na, Mount /ˈɛtnə/ : volcano in Italy, in Sicily
Eu·gene /juˈʤiːn/ : U.S. city, Oregon
Eu·phra·tes /juˈfreɪˌtiːz/ – **the Euphrates River** *also* **the Euphrates** : river in Asia
Eur·asia /juˈreɪʒə/ : land area consisting of Europe and Asia – **Eur·asian** /juˈreɪʒən/ *adj or noun*
Eu·rope /ˈjurəp/ : continent of the Eastern Hemisphere – **European** *adj or noun*
European Union – **the European Union** : an economic, scientific, and political organization of some European countries
Ev·ans·ville /ˈɛvənzˌvɪl/ : U.S. city, Indiana
Ev·er·est *or* **Mount Everest** /ˈɛvrəst/ : mountain in Asia
Ev·er·ett /ˈɛvrət/ : U.S. city, Washington
Ev·er·glades /ˈɛvɚˌgleɪdz/ – **the Everglades** : swamp region of the U.S., in Florida
Faer·oe Islands *or* **Far·oe Islands** /ˈferou/ – **the Faeroe Islands** *or* **the Faroe Islands** *or* **the Faeroes** *or* **the Faroes** : Danish islands in the Atlantic Ocean – **Faero·ese** /ˌferəˈwiːz/ *adj or noun*
Fai·sa·la·bad /ˌfaɪˌsɑːləˈbɑːd/ : city in Pakistan
Falk·land /ˈfɑːklənd/ – **the Falkland Islands** *also* **the Falklands** *or Spanish* **Is·las Mal·vi·nas** /ˌiːslɑsmɑlˈviːnɑːs/ *or* **the Malvinas** : British islands in the Atlantic Ocean near Argentina
Far East – **the Far East** : the countries of eastern Asia and the Malay Archipelago – **Far Eastern** *adj*
Fa·ri·da·bad /fɑˈriːdɑˌbɑːd/ : town in India
Fay·ette·ville /ˈfejətˌvɪl, ˈfɛdvəl/ : U.S. city, North Carolina
Fi·ji /ˈfiːʤi/ : island country in the Pacific Ocean – **Fi·ji·an** /ˈfiːʤijən/ *adj or noun*
Fin·land /ˈfɪnlənd/ : country in Europe – **Finn** /ˈfɪn/ *noun* – **Finn·ish** /ˈfɪnɪʃ/ *adj*
Flan·ders /ˈflændɚz/
1 : region of Belgium and France
2 : region of Belgium
Flint /ˈflɪnt/ : U.S. city, Michigan
Flor·ence /ˈflorəns/ : city in Italy – **Flor·en·tine** /ˈflorənˌtiːn/ *adj or noun*
Flor·i·da /ˈflorədə, ˈflɑrədə/
1 : state of the U.S.
2 **the Straits of Florida** : area of water connecting the Gulf of Mexico and the Atlantic Ocean
3 **the Florida Keys** : group of islands in the U.S., in Florida
– **Flo·rid·i·an** /fləˈrɪdijən/ *or* **Flor·i·dan** /ˈflorədən, ˈflɑrədən/ *adj or noun*
Fon·tana /fɑnˈtænə/ : U.S. city, California
For·ta·le·za /ˌfoɚtəˈleɪzə/ : city in Brazil
Fort Col·lins /ˈkɑːlənz/ : U.S. city, Colorado
Fort Knox /ˈnɑːks/ : military area in the U.S., in Kentucky
Fort Lau·der·dale /ˈlɑːdɚˌdeɪl/ : U.S. city, Florida
Fort Wayne /ˈweɪn/ : U.S. city, Indiana
Fort Worth /ˈwɚθ/ : U.S. city, Texas
France /ˈfræns/ : country in Europe – **French** /ˈfrɛnʧ/ *adj or noun*
Fra·ser /ˈfreɪzɚ/ – **the Fraser River** *also* **the Fraser** : river in British Columbia, Canada
Fre·mont /ˈfriːˌmɑːnt/ : U.S. city, California
French Guiana : part of France in South America
Fres·no /ˈfrezˌnou/ : U.S. city, California
Fro·bi·sher Bay /ˈfroubɪʃɚ/ : part of the Atlantic Ocean near northern Canada
Fu·ji *or* **Mount Fuji** /ˈfuːʤi/ : mountain in Japan
Fu·ku·o·ka /ˌfuːkuˈoukɑ/ : city in Japan
Ful·ler·ton /ˈfulɚtən/ : U.S. city, California
Fun·dy, Bay of /ˈfʌndi/ – **the Bay of Fundy** : area of the Atlantic Ocean between New Brunswick and Nova Scotia, Canada
Fu·shun /ˈfuːˈʃun/ : city in China
Ga·bon /gæˈboun/ : country in Africa – **Gab·o·nese** /ˌgæbəˈniːz/ *adj or noun*
Gads·den Purchase /ˈgædzdən/ – **the Gadsden Purchase** : area of the U.S. purchased in 1853 from Mexico
Gaines·ville /ˈgeɪnzˌvɪl/ : U.S. city, Florida
Ga·lá·pa·gos /gəˈlɑːpəgəs/ – **the Galapagos Islands** *also* **the Galapagos** : islands of Ecuador in the Pacific Ocean
Ga·la·tia /gəˈleɪʃijə/ : country in ancient Asia Minor – **Ga·la·tian** /gəˈleɪʃən/ *adj or noun*
Ga·li·cia /gəˈlɪʃijə/
1 : region in Poland and Ukraine
2 : region in Spain
– **Ga·li·cian** /gəˈlɪʃən/ *adj or noun*
Gal·i·lee /ˈgæləˌliː/
1 : region of Israel
2 **the Sea of Galilee** : lake in Israel on the border of Syria
– **Gal·i·le·an** /ˌgæləˈlijən/ *adj or noun*
Gal·ves·ton Bay /ˈgælvəstən/ : part of the Gulf of Mexico near the U.S. state of Texas
Gam·bia /ˈgæmbijə/ : country in Africa – **Gam·bi·an** /ˈgæmbijən/ *adj or noun*
Gan·ges /ˈgænˌʤiːz/ – **the Ganges River** *also* **the Ganges** : river in India – **Gan·get·ic** /gænˈʤɛtɪk/ *adj*
Garden Grove : U.S. city, California
Gar·land /ˈgɑɚlənd/ : U.S. city, Texas
Gary /ˈgeri/ : U.S. city, Indiana
Gas·co·ny /ˈgæskəni/ : region of France – **Gas·con** /ˈgæskən/ *adj or noun*
Gas·pé Peninsula /gæˈspeɪ/ – **the Gaspé Peninsula** : part of Quebec, Canada – **Gas·pe·sian** /gæˈspiʒən/ *adj or noun*
Gat·i·neau /ˌgætəˈnou/ : town in Quebec, Canada
Gaul /ˈgɑːl/ : country of ancient western Europe
Ga·za Strip /ˈgɑːzə/ – **the Gaza Strip** : area on the eastern coast of the Mediterranean Sea – **Ga·zan** /ˈgɑːzən/ *adj or noun*
Ge·ne·va /ʤəˈniːvə/ : city in Switzerland – **Ge·ne·van** /ʤəˈniːvən/ *adj or noun* – **Gen·e·vese** /ˌʤɛnəˈviːz/ *adj or noun*
Gen·oa /ˈʤɛnowə/ : city in Italy – **Gen·o·ese** /ˌʤenoˈwiːz/ *or* **Gen·o·vese** /ˌʤɛnəˈviz/ *adj or noun*
George·town /ˈʤoɚʤˌtaun/ : section of the U.S. city of Washington, in the District of Columbia
Geor·gia /ˈʤoɚʤə/
1 : state of the U.S.
2 *or* **the Republic of Georgia** : country in Asia on the border with Europe
– **Geor·gian** /ˈʤoɚʤən/ *adj or noun*
Georgian Bay : part of Lake Huron near Ontario, Canada
Ger·ma·ny /ˈʤɚməni/ : country in Europe – **Ger·man** /ˈʤɚmən/ *adj or noun*
Get·tys·burg /ˈgɛtizˌbɚg/ : U.S. town, Pennsylvania
Gha·na /ˈgɑːnə/ : country in Africa – **Gha·na·ian** /gɑˈnejən/ *or* **Gha·ni·an** /ˈgɑːnijən/ *adj or noun*
Gi·bral·tar /ʤəˈbrɑːltɚ/
1 : British colony on the coast of Spain
2 **the Rock of Gibraltar** : part of Gibraltar
– **Gi·bral·tar·i·an** /ʤəˈbrɑːlˈterijən/ *noun*
Gil·bert /ˈgɪlbɚt/ : U.S. town, Arizona
Gil·e·ad /ˈgɪlijəd/ : region of ancient Palestine
Gi·za /ˈgiːzə/ : city in Egypt
Glas·gow /ˈglæˌskou/ : city in Scotland – **Glas·we·gian** /glæsˈwiːʤən/ *adj or noun*
Glen·dale /ˈglɛnˌdeɪl/
1 : U.S. city, Arizona
2 : U.S. city, California
Go·bi /ˈgoubi/ – **the Gobi Desert** *also* **the Gobi** : desert in Mongolia and China
Go·lan Heights /ˈgouˌlɑːn/ – **the Golan Heights** : region of hills in the Middle East
Golden Gate – **the Golden Gate** : area of water connecting San Francisco Bay with the Pacific Ocean
Go·mor·rah /gəˈmorə/ : city in the ancient Middle East
Gond·wa·na·land /gɑnˈdwɑːnəˌlænd/ : a large area of land that is believed to have existed long ago and to have consisted of the lands of the Southern Hemisphere and India
Goth·am /ˈgɑːθəm/ : informal name for the U.S. city of New York, in the state of New York – **Goth·am·ite** /ˈgɑːθəˌmaɪt/ *noun*
Grand Canyon – **the Grand Canyon** : large and deep valley in the U.S., in Arizona

Grand Cou·lee Dam /ˈkuːli/ : dam in the U.S., on the Columbia River in Washington
Grande, Rio see RIO GRANDE
Grand Prairie : U.S. city, Texas
Grand Rapids : U.S. city, Michigan
Great Barrier Reef – the Great Barrier Reef : coral reef off the coast of Australia
Great Basin – the Great Basin : region of the western U.S.
Great Britain
1 : UNITED KINGDOM
2 : island consisting of England, Scotland, and Wales
Greater Antilles – the Greater Antilles : group of islands in the West Indies
Greater Sudbury see SUDBURY, GREATER
Great Lakes – the Great Lakes : Lakes Superior, Michigan, Huron, Erie, and Ontario
Great Plains – the Great Plains : region in the U.S. and Canada
Great Rift Valley – the Great Rift Valley : long valley in Asia and Africa
Great Salt Lake – the Great Salt Lake : lake in the U.S., in Utah
Great Smoky Mountains – the Great Smoky Mountains : mountains in the U.S., in North Carolina and Tennessee
Greece /ˈgriːs/ : country in Europe – **Gre·cian** /ˈgriːʃən/ *adj* – **Greek** /ˈgriːk/ *adj or noun*
Green Bay
1 : U.S. city, Wisconsin
2 : part of Lake Michigan
Green·land /ˈgriːnlənd/ : Danish island in the Atlantic Ocean – **Green·land·er** /ˈgriːnləndɚ/ *noun*
Greens·boro /ˈgriːnzˌbɚroʊ/ : U.S. city, North Carolina
Green·wich /ˈgrɪnɪʤ/ : part of the city of London, in the United Kingdom
Gre·na·da /grəˈneɪdə/ : island country in the West Indies – **Gre·na·dan** /grəˈneɪdən/ *adj or noun* – **Gre·na·di·an** /grəˈneɪdijən/ *adj or noun*
Gresh·am /ˈgrɛʃəm/ : U.S. city, Oregon
Gua·da·la·ja·ra /ˌgwɑːdələˈhɑrə/ : city in Mexico
Gua·de·loupe /ˈgwɑːdəˌluːp/ : French island in the West Indies – **Gua·de·lou·pe·an** /ˌgwɑːdəˈluːpijən/ *noun*
Guam /ˈgwɑːm/ : U.S. island in the Pacific Ocean – **Gua·ma·ni·an** /gwɑˈmeɪnijən/ *adj or noun*
Guang·zhou /ˈgwɑːŋˈʤoʊ/ : city in China
Guan·tá·na·mo Bay /gwɑnˈtɑːnɑˌmoʊ/ : part of the Caribbean Sea near Cuba
Gua·te·ma·la /ˌgwɑːtəˈmɑːlə/ : country in Central America – **Gua·te·ma·lan** /ˌgwɑːtəˈmɑːlən/ *adj or noun*
Gua·ya·quil /ˌgwajəˈkiːl/ : city in Ecuador
Guay·na·bo /gwaɪˈnɑːboʊ/ : U.S. city, Puerto Rico
Guelph /ˈgwɛlf/ : city in Ontario, Canada
Gui·a·na /giˈænə/ : region of South America – **Gui·a·nan** /giˈænən/ *adj or noun*
Guin·ea /ˈgɪni/
1 : country in Africa
2 the Gulf of Guinea : part of the Atlantic Ocean – **Guin·ean** /ˈgɪnijən/ *adj or noun*
Guin·ea–Bis·sau /ˌgɪnibɪˈsaʊ/ : country in Africa
Gui·yang /ˈgweɪˈjɑːŋ/ : city in China
Guj·ran·wala /ˌguːʤrənˈwɑːlə/ : city in Pakistan
Gulf Stream – the Gulf Stream : current of warm water in the Atlantic Ocean
Guy·ana /gaɪˈænə/ : country in South America – **Guy·a·nese** /ˌgajəˈniːz/ *adj or noun*
Gwangju see KWANGJU
Hai·nan /ˈhaɪˈnɑːn/ : island of China
Hai·ti /ˈheɪti/ : country in the West Indies – **Hai·tian** /ˈheɪʃən/ *adj or noun*
Hal·i·fax /ˈhæləˌfæks/ : city in Nova Scotia, Canada – **Hal·i·go·ni·an** /ˌhæləˈgoʊnijən/ *noun*
Ham·burg /ˈhæmˌbɚg, ˈhɑːmˌbuɚg/ : city in Germany – **Ham·burg·er** /ˈhæmˌbɚgɚ, ˈhɑːmˌbuɚgɚ/ *noun*
Ham·il·ton /ˈhæməltən/ : city in Ontario, Canada
Hamp·ton /ˈhæmptən/ : U.S. city, Virginia
Hang·zhou /ˈhɑːŋˈʤoʊ/ : city in China
Ha·noi /hæˈnoɪ/ : city in Vietnam
Ha·ra·re /həˈrɑːˌreɪ/ : city in Zimbabwe
Har·bin /ˈhɑɚbən/ : city in China
Har·lem /ˈhɑɚləm/ : part of the U.S. city of New York, in the state of New York
Har·ris·burg /ˈherəsˌbɚg/ : U.S. city, Pennsylvania
Hart·ford /ˈhɑɚtfɚd/ : U.S. city, Connecticut
Hat·ter·as, Cape /ˈhætərəs/ : part of the U.S., in North Carolina
Ha·vana /həˈvænə/ : city in Cuba
Ha·waii /həˈwaji/
1 : state of the U.S. consisting of a group of islands in the Pacific Ocean
2 : largest island of the state of Hawaii
– **Ha·wai·ian** /həˈwajən/ *adj or noun*
Hay·ward /ˈheɪwɚd/ : U.S. city, California
Heb·ri·des /ˈhɛbrəˌdiːz/ – **the Hebrides** : islands of Scotland in the Atlantic Ocean – **Heb·ri·de·an** /ˌhɛbrəˈdijən/ *adj or noun*
Hel·ve·tia /hɛlˈviːʃijə/ : Latin name for Switzerland
Hen·der·son /ˈhɛndɚsən/ : U.S. city, Nevada
Henry, Cape /ˈhɛnri/ : part of the U.S., in Virginia
Hi·a·le·ah /ˌhajəˈlijə/ : U.S. city, Florida
Hi·ber·nia /haɪˈbɚnijə/ : Latin name for Ireland – **Hi·ber·ni·an** /haɪˈbɚnijən/ *adj or noun*
High·lands /ˈhaɪləndz/ – **the Highlands** : mountains in northern Scotland
Hil·ton Head Island /ˈhɪltn̩ˈhɛd/ : island of U.S., in South Carolina
Hi·ma·la·yas /ˌhɪməˈlejəz/ – **the Himalayas** *or* **the Himalaya** /ˌhɪməˈlejə/ : mountains in Asia – **Hi·ma·la·yan** /ˌhɪməˈlejən/ *adj*
Hin·du Kush /ˈhɪnˌduːˈkʊʃ/ : mountains in Asia
Hi·ro·shi·ma /ˌhirəˈʃiːmə/ : city in Japan
His·pan·io·la /ˌhɪspənˈjoʊlə/ : island divided between Haiti and the Dominican Republic
Ho Chi Minh City /ˈhoʊˌʧiːˈmɪn/ *or formerly* **Sai·gon** /saɪˈgɑːn/ : city in Vietnam
Hok·kai·do /hɑˈkaɪdoʊ/ : island of Japan
Hol·land /ˈhɑːlənd/ see NETHERLANDS – **Hol·land·er** /ˈhɑːləndɚ/ *noun*
Hol·ly·wood /ˈhɑːliˌwʊd/
1 : part of the U.S. city of Los Angeles, in California
2 : U.S. city, Florida
Hon·du·ras /hɑːnˈdɚrəs/ : country in Central America – **Hon·du·ran** /hɑːnˈdɚrən/ *adj or noun*
Hong Kong /ˈhɑːŋˌkɑːŋ/ *or* **Xiang·gang** /ˈʃjɑːŋˌgɑːŋ/ : region of China – **Hong Kong·er** /ˈhɑːŋˈkɑːŋɚ/ *noun*
Ho·no·lu·lu /ˌhɑːnəˈluːlu/ : U.S. city, Hawaii
Hon·shu /ˈhɑːnˌʃuː/ : island of Japan
Hoover Dam /ˈhuːvɚ/ : dam in the U.S. on the Colorado River between Nevada and Arizona
Hous·ton /ˈhjuːstən/ : U.S. city, Texas – **Hous·to·nian** /hjuˈstoʊnijən/ *noun*
How·rah /ˈhaʊrə/ : city in India
Huang Ho /ˈhwɑːŋˈhoʊ/ – **the Huang Ho** : river in China
Hud·son /ˈhʌdsən/
1 the Hudson River *also* **the Hudson** : U.S. river, in New York
2 Hudson Bay : part of the Atlantic Ocean near Canada
Hun·ga·ry /ˈhʌŋgəri/ : country in Europe – **Hun·gar·i·an** /ˌhʌŋˈgerijən/ *adj or noun*
Hun·ting·ton Beach /ˈhʌntɪŋtən/ : U.S. city, California
Hunts·ville /ˈhʌntsˌvɪl/ : U.S. city, Alabama
Hu·ron, Lake /ˈhjɚˌɑːn/ : lake in the U.S. and Canada
Hy·der·a·bad /ˈhaɪdərəˌbæd/
1 : city in India
2 : city in Pakistan
Iba·dan /iˈbɑːdn̩/ : city in Nigeria
Ibe·ria /aɪˈbirijə/ – **Iberia** *or* **the Ibe·ri·an Peninsula** /aɪˈbirijən/ : area of land where Spain and Portugal are located
Ice·land /ˈaɪslənd/ : island country in Europe – **Ice·land·er** /ˈaɪsˌlændɚ/ *noun* – **Ice·lan·dic** /aɪsˈlændɪk/ *adj*
Ida·ho /ˈaɪdəˌhoʊ/ : state of the U.S. – **Ida·ho·an** /ˌaɪdəˈhowən/ *adj or noun*
Il·li·nois /ˌɪləˈnoɪ/ : state of the U.S. – **Il·li·nois·an** /ˌɪləˈnojən/ *adj or noun*

Il·lyr·ia /ɪˈlirijə/ : country in ancient Europe – **Il·lyr·i·an** /ɪˈlirijən/ *adj or noun*
Im·pe·ri·al Valley /ɪmˈpirijəl/ – **the Imperial Valley** : valley in the U.S. and Mexico
In·chon *or* **Incheon** /ˈɪnˌʧʌn/ : city in South Korea
In·de·pen·dence /ˌɪndəˈpɛndənts/ : U.S. city, Missouri
In·dia /ˈɪndijə/ : country in Asia – **In·di·an** /ˈɪndijən/ *adj or noun*
Indian Ocean – the Indian Ocean : ocean east of Africa, south of Asia, west of Australia, and north of Antarctica
In·di·ana /ˌɪndiˈænə/ : state of the U.S. – **In·di·an·an** /ˌɪndiˈænən/ *or* **In·di·an·i·an** /ˌɪndiˈænijən/ *adj or noun*
In·di·a·nap·o·lis /ˌɪndiəˈnæpələs/ : U.S. city, Indiana
In·do·chi·na /ˌɪnˌdoʊˈʧaɪnə/
1 : land area including Myanmar, the Malay Peninsula, Thailand, Cambodia, Laos, and Vietnam
2 : former country of Asia
– **In·do–Chi·nese** /ˌɪnˌdoʊʧaɪˈniz/ *adj or noun*
In·do·ne·sia /ˌɪndəˈniːʒə/ : country in Asia – **In·do·ne·sian** /ˌɪndəˈniːʒən/ *adj or noun*
In·dore /ɪnˈdoɚ/ : city in India
In·dus /ˈɪndəs/ – **the Indus River** *also* **the Indus** : river in Asia
In·gle·wood /ˈɪŋgəlˌwʊd/ : U.S. city, California
Inside Passage – the Inside Passage : shipping route that extends from the U.S. state of Washington, along the coast of Canada, to the U.S. state of Alaska
Io·wa /ˈajəwə/ : state of the U.S. – **Io·wan** /ˈajəwən/ *adj or noun*
Iran /ɪˈrɑːn, ɪˈræn/ : country in Asia – **Ira·ni·an** /ɪˈreɪnijən/ *adj or noun*
Iraq /ɪˈrɑːk, ɪˈræk/ : country in Asia – **Iraqi** /ɪˈrɑːki, ɪˈræki/ *adj or noun*
Ire·land /ˈajɚlənd/
1 *or* **Ei·re** /ˈerə/ : country in Europe
2 : European island in the Atlantic Ocean
3 Northern Ireland see NORTHERN IRELAND
– **Irish** /ˈaɪrɪʃ/ *adj*
Ir·ra·wad·dy /ˌirəˈwɑːdi/ – **the Irrawaddy River** *also* **the Irrawaddy** : river in Myanmar
Ir·tysh /iɚˈtɪʃ/ – **the Irtysh River** *also* **the Irtysh** : river in Asia
Ir·vine /ˈɚˌvaɪn/ : U.S. city, California
Ir·ving /ˈɚvɪŋ/ : U.S. city, Texas
Islas Malvinas see FALKLAND
Is·ra·el /ˈɪzrijəl/
1 : country in Asia
2 : kingdom in ancient Palestine
3 : northern part of the Hebrew kingdom after about 933 B.C.
– **Is·rae·li** /ɪzˈreɪli/ *adj or noun*
Is·tan·bul /ˌɪstənˈbuːl/ *or formerly* **Con·stan·ti·no·ple** /ˌkɑːnˌstæntəˈnoʊpəl/ : city in Turkey
Is·tria /ˈɪstrijə/ – **Istria** *or* **the Istrian Peninsula** : part of Croatia and Slovenia – **Is·tri·an** /ˈɪstrijən/ *adj or noun*
It·a·ly /ˈɪtəli/ : country in Europe – **Ital·ian** /ɪˈtæljən/ *adj or noun*
Itas·ca, Lake /aɪˈtæskə/ : lake in the U.S., in Minnesota
Ivory Coast *or* **Côte d'Ivoire** /ˌkoutdiˈvwɑɚ/ : country in Africa – **Ivor·i·an** /aɪˈvorijən/ *adj or noun* – **Ivory Coaster** *noun*
Iwo Ji·ma /ˌiˌwoʊˈʤiːmə/ : Japanese island in the Pacific Ocean
Iz·mir /ɪzˈmiɚ/ : city in Turkey
Jack·son /ˈʤæksən/ : U.S. city, Mississippi
Jack·son·ville /ˈʤæksənˌvɪl/ : U.S. city, Florida
Ja·kar·ta /ʤəˈkɑɚtə/ : city in Indonesia
Ja·mai·ca /ʤəˈmeɪkə/ : island country in the West Indies – **Ja·mai·can** /ʤəˈmeɪkən/ *adj or noun*
James·town /ˈʤeɪmzˌtaʊn/ : ruins in the U.S. of the first permanent English settlement in America, in Virginia
Ja·pan /ʤəˈpæn/
1 : island country in Asia
2 the Sea of Japan : part of the Pacific Ocean
– **Jap·a·nese** /ˌʤæpəˈniːz/ *adj or noun*
Ja·va /ˈʤɑːvə/ : island of Indonesia – **Ja·van** /ˈʤɑːvən/ *adj or noun* – **Ja·va·nese** /ˌʤɑːvəˈniːz/ *noun*
Jer·i·cho /ˈʤerɪˌkoʊ/ : city in ancient Palestine
Jer·sey /ˈʤɚzi/ : British island in the English Channel – **Jer·sey·ite** /ˈʤɚziˌaɪt/ *noun*
Jersey City : U.S. city, New Jersey
Je·ru·sa·lem /ʤəˈruːsələm/ : city in the Middle East
Ji·lin /ˈʤiːˈlɪn/ : city in China
Ji·nan /ˈʤiːˈnɑːn/ : city in China
Jo·han·nes·burg /ʤoʊˈhænəsˌbɚg/ : city in the Republic of South Africa
Jo·li·et /ˌʤoʊliˈɛt/ : U.S. city, Illinois
Jor·dan /ˈʤoɚdn̩/
1 : country in Asia
2 the Jordan River *also* **the Jordan** : river in Israel and Jordan
– **Jor·da·ni·an** /ʤoɚˈdeɪnijən/ *adj or noun*
Juan de Fu·ca, Strait of /ˌwɑːndəˈfjuːkə/ – **the Strait of Juan de Fuca** : area of water between British Columbia, Canada, and the U.S. state of Washington
Ju·daea *or* **Ju·dea** /ʤʊˈdijə/ : region of ancient Palestine – **Ju·dae·an** *or* **Ju·de·an** /ʤʊˈdijən/ *adj or noun*
Jut·land /ˈʤʌtlənd/ : part of northern Europe
Ka·bul /ˈkɑːbəl, kəˈbuːl/ : city in Afghanistan
Kal·a·ha·ri /ˌkæləˈhɑri/ – **the Kalahari Desert** *also* **the Kalahari** : desert region of southern Africa
Kam·chat·ka Peninsula /kæmˈʧætkə/ : part of eastern Russia
Kan·pur /ˈkɑːnˌpuɚ/ : city in India
Kan·sas /ˈkænzəs/ : state of the U.S. – **Kan·san** /ˈkænzən/ *adj or noun*
Kansas City
1 : U.S. city, Kansas
2 : U.S. city, Missouri
Ka·ra·chi /kəˈrɑːʧi/ : city in Pakistan
Kar·a·ko·ram Pass /ˌkarəˈkorəm/ : area between mountains in Kashmir
Ka·ra Sea /ˈkarə/ – **the Kara Sea** : part of the Arctic Ocean
Ka·re·lia /kəˈriːlijə/ : region of Europe – **Ka·re·lian** /kəˈriːlijən/ *adj or noun*
Karst /ˈkɑɚst/ : area in Slovenia and Italy
Kash·mir /ˈkæʃˌmiɚ/ : region in Asia – **Kash·miri** /kæʃˈmiri/ *adj or noun*
Ka·tah·din, Mount /kəˈtɑːdn̩/ : mountain in the U.S., in Maine
Kau·ai /kaˈwɑːi/ : island of the U.S., in Hawaii
Ka·wa·sa·ki /ˌkɑːwɑˈsɑːki/ : city in Japan
Ka·zakh·stan /ˌkɑːzɑːkˈstɑːn/ : country in Asia – **Ka·zakh** /kəˈzɑːk/ *noun*
Ka·zan' /kəˈzæn/ : city in Russia
Ke·low·na /kəˈloʊnə/ : city in British Columbia, Canada
Ke·no·sha /kəˈnoʊʃə/ : U.S. city, Wisconsin
Ken·tucky /kənˈtʌki/ : state of the U.S. – **Ken·tucki·an** /kənˈtʌkijən/ *adj or noun*
Ken·ya /ˈkɛnjə, ˈkiːnjə/ : country in Africa – **Ken·yan** /ˈkɛnjən, ˈkiːnjən/ *adj or noun*
Ke·wee·naw Peninsula /ˈkiːwəˌnɑː/ – **the Keweenaw Peninsula** : area of the U.S., in Michigan
Khar·kiv /ˈkɑɚkəf/ : city in Ukraine
Khar·toum /kɑɚˈtuːm/ : city in Sudan
Ki·ev /ˈkiːˌɛf, ˈkiːˌɛv/ : city in Ukraine
Ki·lau·ea /ˌkiːˌlɑːˈwejə/ : volcano in the U.S., in Hawaii
Kil·i·man·ja·ro *or* **Mount Kilimanjaro** /ˌkɪləmənˈʤɑroʊ/ : mountain in Tanzania
Kings·ton /ˈkɪŋstən/ : city in Ontario, Canada
Kin·sha·sa /kɪnˈʃɑːsə/ : city in the Democratic Republic of the Congo
Ki·ri·bati /ˈkirəˌbæs/ : island country in the Pacific Ocean
Ki·ta·kyu·shu /kiˌtɑːˈkyuːʃu/ : city in Japan
Kitch·e·ner /ˈkɪʧnɚ/ : city in Ontario, Canada
Klon·dike /ˈklɑːnˌdaɪk/ – **the Klondike** : region of Canada
Knox·ville /ˈnɑːksˌvɪl/ : U.S. city, Tennessee
Ko·be /ˈkoʊbi/ : city in Japan
Ko·la Peninsula /ˈkoʊlə/ – **the Kola Peninsula** : part of northwestern Russia
Kolkata see CALCUTTA
Ko·na /ˈkoʊnɑ/ : area of the U.S., in Hawaii
Ko·rea /kəˈrijə/
1 : area of eastern Asia
2 : North Korea and South Korea

– **Ko·re·an** /kəˈrijən/ *adj or noun*

Ko·so·vo /ˈkɑːsəˌvoʊ, ˈkoʊsəˌvoʊ/ : country in Europe – **Ko·so·var** /ˈkɑːsəˌvɑɚ, ˈkoʊsəˌvɑɚ/ *adj or noun*

Krak·a·tau /ˌkrækəˈtaʊ/ *or* **Krak·a·toa** /ˌkrækəˈtowə/ : volcano in Indonesia

K2 /ˌkeɪˈtuː/ : mountain in Kashmir

Kua·la Lum·pur /ˌkwɑːləˈlʊmˌpʊɚ/ : city in Malaysia

Kun·ming /ˈkʊnˈmɪŋ/ : city in China

Kur·di·stan /ˌkuɚdəˈstæn/ : region of Asia – **Kurd** /ˈkuɚd, ˈkɚd/ *noun* – **Kurd·ish** /ˈkuɚdɪʃ, ˈkɚdɪʃ/ *adj*

Ku·ril *or* **Ku·rile** /ˈkjuɚˌiːl/ – **the Kuril Islands** *or* **the Kurile Islands** *also* **the Kurils** *or* **the Kuriles** : Russian islands in the Pacific Ocean

Ku·wait /kʊˈweɪt/ : country in Asia – **Ku·waiti** /kʊˈweɪti/ *adj or noun*

Kwang·ju *or* **Gwang·ju** /ˈgwɑːŋˌʤuː/ : city in South Korea

Kyo·to /ˈkjoʊˌtoʊ/ : city in Japan

Kyr·gyz·stan /ˌkiɚgɪˈstæn/ : country in Asia

Kyu·shu /ˈkjuːˌʃuː/ : island of Japan

Lab·ra·dor /ˈlæbrəˌdoɚ/ : part of eastern Canada – **Lab·ra·dor·ean** *or* **Lab·ra·dor·ian** /ˌlæbrəˈdorijən/ *adj or noun*

La·co·nia /ləˈkoʊnijə/ : country in ancient Greece – **La·co·nian** /ləˈkoʊnijən/ *adj or noun*

La·fay·ette /ˌlɑːfiˈɛt/ : U.S. city, Louisiana

La·gos /ˈleɪˌgɑːs/ : city in Nigeria

La·hore /ləˈhoɚ/ : city in Pakistan

La Jol·la /ləˈhojə/ : part of the U.S. city of San Diego, in California

Lake·wood /ˈleɪkˌwʊd/ : U.S. city, Colorado

La·nai /ləˈnaɪ/ : island of the U.S., in Hawaii

Lan·cas·ter /ˈlænˌkæstɚ/ : U.S. city, California

Lan·sing /ˈlænsɪŋ/ : U.S. city, Michigan

Lan·zhou /ˈlɑːˈʤoʊ/ : city in China

Laos /ˈlaʊs/ : country in Asia – **Lao·tian** /leɪˈoʊʃən/ *adj or noun*

Lap·land /ˈlæpˌlænd/ : region of northern Europe – **Lap·land·er** /ˈlæpˌlændɚ/ *noun*

La·re·do /ləˈreɪdoʊ/ : U.S. city, Texas

Las Ve·gas /lɑːsˈveɪgəs/ *or informally* **Vegas** : U.S. city, Nevada

Latin America
1 : Spanish America and Brazil
2 : South America and North America south of the U.S.
– **Latin–American** *adj* – **Latin American** *noun*

Lat·via /ˈlætvijə/ : country in Europe – **Lat·vi·an** /ˈlætvijən/ *adj or noun*

Lau·ren·tian Mountains /lɑˈrɛnʃən/ – **the Laurentian Mountains** : hills in eastern Canada

La·val /ləˈvæl/ : city in Quebec, Canada

Law·ton /ˈlɑːtn̩/ : U.S. city, Oklahoma

Leb·a·non /ˈlɛbəˌnɑːn/ : country in Asia – **Leb·a·nese** /ˌlɛbəˈniːz/ *adj or noun*

Le·na /ˈliːnə/ – **the Lena River** *also* **the Lena** : river in Russia

Le·so·tho /ləˈsoʊˌtoʊ, ləˈsuːˌtuː/ : country in Africa

Lesser Antilles – **the Lesser Antilles** : islands in the West Indies

Le·vant /ləˈvænt/ – **the Levant** : countries that border the eastern part of the Mediterranean Sea – **Lev·an·tine** /ˈlɛvənˌtaɪn/ *adj or noun*

Le·vis /ˈliːvəs/ : city in Quebec, Canada

Lex·ing·ton /ˈlɛksɪŋtən/ : U.S. city, Kentucky

Li·be·ria /laɪˈbirijə/ : country in Africa – **Li·be·ri·an** /laɪˈbirijən/ *adj or noun*

Lib·ya /ˈlɪbijə/ : country in Africa – **Lib·y·an** /ˈlɪbijən/ *adj or noun*

Liech·ten·stein /ˈlɪktənˌstaɪn/ : country in Europe – **Liech·ten·stein·er** /ˈlɪktənˌstaɪnɚ/ *noun*

Li·gu·ria /ləˈgjɚriə/ : region of Italy – **Li·gu·ri·an** /ləˈgjɚriən/ *adj or noun*

Li·ma /ˈliːmə/ : city in Peru

Lim·po·po River /lɪmˈpoʊpoʊ/ – **the Limpopo River** : river in Africa

Lin·coln /ˈlɪŋkən/ : U.S. city, Nebraska

Lis·bon /ˈlɪzbən/ : city in Portugal – **Lis·bo·an** /lɪzˈbowən/ *noun*

Lith·u·a·nia /ˌlɪθəˈweɪnijə/ : country in Europe – **Lith·u·a·nian** /ˌlɪθəˈweɪnijən/ *adj or noun*

Lit·tle Rock /ˈlɪtl̩ˌrɑːk/ : U.S. city, Arkansas

Liv·er·pool /ˈlɪvɚˌpuːl/ : city in England – **Liv·er·pud·li·an** /ˌlɪvɚˈpʌdlijən/ *adj or noun*

Li·vo·nia /ləˈvoʊnijə/ : U.S. city, Michigan

Lo·gan, Mount /ˈloʊgən/ : mountain in Canada

Lo·mond, Loch /ˌlɑːkˈloʊmənd/ : lake in Scotland

Lon·don /ˈlʌndən/
1 : city in England
2 : city in Ontario, Canada
– **Lon·don·er** /ˈlʌndənɚ/ *noun*

Long Beach : U.S. city, California

Long Island
1 : island of the U.S., in New York
2 Long Island Sound : part of the Atlantic Ocean between the U.S. states of New York and Connecticut

Lon·gueuil /lɑŋˈgeɪl/ : city in Quebec, Canada

Los An·ge·les /lɑsˈænʤələs/ : U.S. city, California – **An·ge·le·no** /ˌænʤəˈliːnoʊ/ *or* **Los An·ge·le·no** /lɑsˌænʤəˈliːnoʊ/ *noun*

Lou·ise, Lake /luˈiːz/ : lake in Alberta, Canada

Lou·i·si·ana /luˌiːziˈænə/
1 : state of the U.S.
2 the Louisiana Purchase : area of the U.S. purchased from France in 1803
– **Lou·i·si·an·ian** /luˌiːziˈænijən/ *or* **Lou·i·si·an·an** /luˌiːziˈænən/ *adj or noun*

Lou·is·ville /ˈluːwɪˌvɪl/ : U.S. city, Kentucky

Low·ell /ˈlowəl/ : U.S. city, Massachusetts

Lower 48 – **the Lower 48** : the states of the U.S. not including Alaska and Hawaii

Lower Peninsula – **the Lower Peninsula** : part of the U.S., in southern Michigan

Lu·an·da /luˈɑːndə/ : city in Angola

Lub·bock /ˈlʌbək/ : U.S. city, Texas

Luck·now /ˈlʌkˌnaʊ/ : city in India

Lu·dhi·a·na /ˌluːdiˈɑːnə/ : city in India

Lux·em·bourg /ˈlʌksəmˌbɚg/ : country in Europe – **Lux·em·bourg·er** /ˈlʌksəmˌbɚgɚ/ *noun* – **Lux·em·bourg·ian** /ˌlʌksəmˈbɚgijən/ *adj*

Lu·zon /luˈzɑːn/ : island of the Philippines

Lyd·ia /ˈlɪdijə/ : country of ancient Asia Minor – **Lyd·i·an** /ˈlɪdijən/ *adj or noun*

Lynch·burg /ˈlɪnʧˌbɚg/ : U.S. city, Virginia

Ma·cao /məˈkaʊ/ *or Chinese* **Ao·men** /ˈaʊˈmʌn/ : region of China – **Mac·a·nese** /ˌmɑkəˈniːz/ *noun*

Mac·e·do·nia /ˌmæsəˈdoʊnijə/
1 : region of Europe
2 : country in Europe
– **Mac·e·do·nian** /ˌmæsəˈdoʊnjən/ *adj or noun*

Ma·chu Pic·chu /ˌmɑːʧuˈpiːʧu/ : site of the ruins of an Inca city in Peru

Mac·ken·zie /məˈkɛnzi/ – **the Mackenzie River** *also* **the Mackenzie** : river in Canada

Mack·i·nac, Straits of /ˈmækəˌnɑː/ – **the Straits of Mackinac** : area of water in North America that connects Lake Huron and Lake Michigan

Mad·a·gas·car /ˌmædəˈgæskɚ/ : island country in the Indian Ocean – **Mad·a·gas·can** /ˌmædəˈgæskən/ *adj or noun*

Ma·dei·ra /məˈdirə/
1 the Madeira River *also* **the Madeira** : river in Brazil
2 the Madeira Islands : Portuguese islands in the Atlantic Ocean
– **Ma·dei·ran** /məˈdirən/ *adj or noun*

Mad·i·son /ˈmædəsən/ : U.S. city, Wisconsin

Ma·dras /məˈdræs/ *or* **Chen·nai** /ˈʧɛˌnaɪ/ : city in India – **Ma·drasi** /məˈdræsi/ *noun*

Ma·drid /məˈdrɪd/ : city in Spain – **Mad·ri·le·nian** /ˌmædrəˈlɪnijən/ *adj or noun* – **Ma·dri·le·ño** /ˌmɑːdrəˈleɪnjoʊ/ *noun*

Mag·da·len Islands /ˈmægdələn/ : islands of Canada, in Quebec

Ma·gel·lan, Strait of /məˈʤɛlən/ – **the Strait of Magellan** : area of water that connects the Atlantic Ocean with the Pacific Ocean at the southern end of South America

Ma·ghreb *or* **the Maghreb** /ˈmɑːgrəb/ : region of northwestern Africa

Maine /ˈmeɪn/ : state of the U.S. – **Main·er** /ˈmeɪnɚ/ *noun*

Ma·jor·ca /mɑˈʤoɚkə/ : island of Spain in the Mediterranean Sea – **Ma·jor·can** /mɑˈʤoɚkən/ *adj or noun*

Ma·la·wi /mə'lɑːwi/ : country in Africa – **Ma·la·wi·an** /mə'lɑːwiən/ *adj or noun*
Ma·lay Archipelago /mə'leɪ, 'meɪˌleɪ/ – **the Malay Archipelago** : group of islands in southeastern Asia
Ma·lay·sia /mə'leɪʒə/ : country in Asia – **Ma·lay·sian** /mə'leɪʒən/ *adj or noun*
Mal·dives /'mɑːlˌdiːvz/ : island country in the Indian Ocean – **Mal·div·i·an** /mɑl'dɪvijən/ *adj or noun*
Ma·li /'mɑːli/ : country in Africa – **Ma·li·an** /'mɑːlijən/ *adj or noun*
Mal·ta /'mɑːltə/ : island country in the Mediterranean Sea – **Mal·tese** /mɑl'tiːz/ *adj or noun*
Malvinas, Islas see FALKLAND
Man, Isle of /'mæn/ – **the Isle of Man** : island of the United Kingdom – **Manx** /'mæŋks/ *adj or noun*
Ma·naus /mə'naʊs/ : city in Brazil
Man·ches·ter /'mænˌʧɛstɚ, 'mænʧəstɚ/
1 : U.S. city, New Hampshire
2 : city in England
Man·chu·ria /mæn'ʧɚrijə/ : region of northeastern China – **Man·chu·ri·an** /mæn'ʧɚrijən/ *adj or noun*
Man·da·lay /ˌmændə'leɪ/ : city in Myanmar
Man·hat·tan /mæn'hætn̩/ : part of the U.S. city of New York, in the state of New York
Ma·nila /mə'nɪlə/ : city in the Philippines
Man·i·to·ba /ˌmænə'toʊbə/ : province of Canada – **Man·i·to·ban** /ˌmænə'toʊbən/ *adj or noun*
Man·i·tou·lin Island /ˌmænə'tuːlən/ : Canadian island in Lake Huron
Mar·a·cai·bo /ˌmerə'kaɪboʊ/ : city in Venezuela
Mar·i·et·ta /ˌmeri'ɛtə/ : U.S. city, Georgia
Mark·ham /'mɑɚkəm/ : town in Ontario, Canada
Mar·ma·ra, Sea of /'mɑɚmərə/ – **the Sea of Marmara** : sea in Turkey
Mar·seille /mɑɚ'seɪ/ : city in France
Mar·shall /'mɑɚʃəl/ – **the Marshall Islands** *also* **the Marshalls** : islands in the Pacific Ocean – **Mar·shall·ese** /ˌmɑɚʃə'liːz/ *adj or noun*
Mar·tha's Vineyard /'mɑɚθəz/ : island of the U.S., in Massachusetts – **Vine·yard·er** /'vɪnjɚdɚ/ *noun*
Mar·ti·nique /ˌmɑɚtə'niːk/ : French island in the West Indies – **Mar·ti·ni·can** /ˌmɑɚtə'niːkən/ *adj or noun* – **Mar·ti·ni·quais** /ˌmɑɚˌtiːnə'keɪ/ *adj or noun*
Mary·land /'merələnd/ : state of the U.S. – **Mary·land·er** /'merələndɚ/ *noun*
Mash·had /mə'ʃæd/ : city in Iran
Ma·son–Dix·on Line /ˌmeɪsn̩'dɪksən/ – **the Mason–Dixon Line** : boundary between northern and southern states of the U.S.
Mas·sa·chu·setts /ˌmæsə'ʧuːsəts/ : state of the U.S.
Mat·ter·horn /'mætɚˌhoɚn/ – **the Matterhorn** : mountain on the border between Switzerland and Italy
Maui /'mawi/ : island of the U.S., in Hawaii
Mau·na Kea /ˌmaʊnɑ'kejɑ/ : extinct volcano in the U.S., in Hawaii
Mau·na Loa /ˌmaʊnə'lowə/ : volcano in the U.S., in Hawaii
Mau·re·ta·nia /ˌmorə'teɪnijə/ : country of ancient Africa
Mau·ri·ta·nia /ˌmorə'teɪnijə/ : country in Africa – **Mau·ri·ta·ni·an** /ˌmorə'teɪnijən/ *adj or noun*
Mau·ri·tius /moɚ'rɪʃəs/ : island country in the Indian Ocean – **Mau·ri·tian** /moɚ'rɪʃən/ *adj or noun*
May, Cape /'meɪ/ : part of the U.S. state of New Jersey
Ma·ya·guez /ˌmajə'gwez/ : U.S. city, Puerto Rico
Mc·Al·len /mə'kælən/ : U.S. city, Texas
Mc·Kin·ley, Mount /mə'kɪnli/ *or* **De·na·li** /də'nɑːli/ : mountain in the U.S., in Alaska
Mec·ca /'mɛkə/ : city in Saudi Arabia
Me·dan /meɪ'dɑːn/ : city in Indonesia
Me·de·llín /ˌmɛdə'liːn/ : city in Colombia
Me·di·na /mə'diːnə/ : city in Saudi Arabia
Med·i·ter·ra·nean /ˌmɛdətə'reɪnijən/ – **the Mediterranean Sea** *also* **the Mediterranean** : sea between Europe and Africa
Mee·rut /'meɪrət/ : city in India
Me·kong /'meɪ'kɑːŋ/ – **the Mekong River** *also* **the Mekong** : river in Asia
Mel·a·ne·sia /ˌmɛlə'niːʒə/ : islands of the Pacific Ocean – **Mel·a·ne·sian** /ˌmɛlə'niːʒən/ *adj or noun*
Mel·bourne /'mɛlbɚn/ : city in Australia
Mel·ville Island /'mɛlˌvɪl/ : island of Canada in the Arctic Archipelago
Mem·phis /'mɛmfəs/
1 : U.S. city, Tennessee
2 : city in ancient Egypt
Mem·phre·ma·gog, Lake /ˌmɛmfrɪ'meɪˌgɑːg/ : lake on the border between the U.S. state of Vermont and Quebec, Canada
Mer·cia /'mɚʃijə/ : kingdom in ancient England – **Mer·cian** /'mɚʃijən/ *adj or noun*
Me·sa /'meɪsə/ : U.S. city, Arizona
Me·so·amer·i·ca /ˌmɛzowə'merikə/ : region of southern North America – **Me·so·amer·i·can** /ˌmɛzowə'merikən/ *adj*
Mes·o·po·ta·mia /ˌmɛsəpə'teɪmijə/ : region of Asia between the Tigris and Euphrates rivers – **Mes·o·po·ta·mian** /ˌmɛsəpə'teɪmijən/ *adj or noun*
Mes·quite /mə'skiːt/ : U.S. city, Texas
Mex·i·co /'mɛksɪˌkoʊ/
1 : country in North America
2 **the Gulf of Mexico** : part of the Atlantic Ocean
– **Mex·i·can** /'mɛksɪkən/ *adj or noun*
Mi·ami /maɪ'æmi/ : U.S. city, Florida – **Mi·ami·an** /maɪ'æmijən/ *noun*
Mich·i·gan /'mɪʃɪgən/
1 : state of the U.S.
2 **Lake Michigan** : lake in the U.S.
– **Mich·i·gan·der** /ˌmɪʃɪ'gændɚ/ *noun* – **Mich·i·ga·ni·an** /ˌmɪʃə'geɪnijən/ *noun* – **Mich·i·gan·ite** /'mɪʃɪgəˌnaɪt/ *noun*
Mi·cro·ne·sia, Federated States of /ˌmaɪkrə'niːʒə/ – **the Federated States of Micronesia** : island country in the Pacific Ocean – **Mi·cro·ne·sian** /ˌmaɪkrə'niːʒən/ *adj or noun*
Middle East – **the Middle East** : countries of southwestern Asia and northern Africa – **Middle Eastern** *adj* – **Middle Easterner** *noun*
Mid·i·an /'mɪdijən/ : region of ancient Arabia – **Mid·i·an·ite** /'mɪdijəˌnaɪt/ *noun*
Mid·land /'mɪdlənd/ : U.S. city, Texas
Mid·way /'mɪdˌweɪ/ : U.S. islands in the Pacific Ocean
Mid·west /ˌmɪd'wɛst/ – **the Midwest** : region of the U.S. – **Mid·wes·tern** /ˌmɪd'wɛstɚn/ *adj* – **Mid·wes·tern·er** /ˌmɪd'wɛstɚnɚ/ *noun*
Mi·lan /mə'læn, mə'lɑːn/ : city in Italy – **Mil·a·nese** /ˌmɪlə'niːz/ *adj or noun*
Mil·wau·kee /mɪl'wɑːki/ : U.S. city, Wisconsin
Min·ne·ap·o·lis /ˌmɪni'æpələs/ : U.S. city, Minnesota
Min·ne·so·ta /ˌmɪnə'soʊtə/ : state of the U.S. – **Min·ne·so·tan** /ˌmɪnə'soʊtn̩/ *adj or noun*
Mi·nor·ca /mə'norkə/ : island of Spain in the Mediterranean Sea – **Mi·nor·can** /mə'norkən/ *adj or noun*
Minsk /'mɪnsk/ : city in Belarus
Mission Vie·jo /vi'eɪhoʊ/ : U.S. city, California
Mis·sis·sau·ga /ˌmɪsə'sɑːgə/ : city in Ontario, Canada
Mis·sis·sip·pi /ˌmɪsə'sɪpi/
1 : state of the U.S.
2 **the Mississippi River** *also* **the Mississippi** : river in the U.S.
– **Mis·sis·sip·pi·an** /ˌmɪsə'sɪpijən/ *adj or noun*
Mis·sou·ri /mə'zɚri/
1 : state of the U.S.
2 **the Missouri River** *also* **the Missouri** : river in the U.S.
– **Mis·sou·ri·an** /mə'zɚrijən/ *adj or noun*
Mitch·ell, Mount /'mɪʧəl/ : mountain in the U.S., in North Carolina
Mo·bile /moʊ'biːl/ : U.S. city, Alabama
Mo·des·to /mə'dɛstoʊ/ : U.S. city, California
Mo·hen·jo Da·ro /moʊ'hɛnʤoʊ'dɑroʊ/ : prehistoric city in Asia
Mo·ja·ve *or* **Mo·ha·ve** /mə'hɑːvi/ – **the Mojave Desert** *or* **the Mohave Desert** *also* **the Mojave** *or* **the Mohave** : desert in the U.S., in California
Mol·da·via /mɑl'deɪvijə/ : region in Romania and Moldova – **Mol·da·vian** /mɑl'deɪvijən/ *adj or noun*
Mol·do·va /mɑl'doʊvə/ : country in Europe – **Mol·do·van** /mɑl'doʊvən/ *adj or noun*

Mol·o·kai /ˌmɑːləˈkaɪ/ : island of the U.S., in Hawaii

Mo·luc·cas /məˈlʌkəz/ – **the Moluccas** : islands of Indonesia – **Mo·luc·ca** /məˈlʌkə/ *adj* – **Mo·luc·can** /məˈlʌkən/ *adj*

Mo·na·co /ˈmɑːnəˌkoʊ/ : country in Europe – **Mo·na·can** /ˈmɑːnəkən/ *adj or noun* – **Mon·e·gasque** /ˌmɑːnɪˈgæsk/ *adj or noun*

Mon·go·lia /mɑnˈgoʊljə/ : country in Asia – **Mon·go·lian** /mɑnˈgoʊljən/ *adj or noun*

Mon·tana /mɑnˈtænə/ : state of the U.S. – **Mon·tan·an** /mɑnˈtænən/ *adj or noun*

Mont Blanc /ˈmoʊnˈblɑːŋ/ : mountain in France on the Italian border

Mon·te Car·lo /ˌmɑːntiˈkaɚloʊ/ : section of Monaco

Mon·te·ne·gro /ˌmɑːntəˈniːgroʊ/ : country in Europe – **Mon·te·ne·grin** /ˌmɑːntəˈniːgrən/ *adj or noun*

Mon·te·rey /ˌmɑːntəˈreɪ/ : U.S. city, California

Mon·ter·rey /ˌmɑːntəˈreɪ/ : city in Mexico

Mon·te·vi·deo /ˌmɑːntəvəˈdejoʊ/ : city in Uruguay

Mont·gom·ery /məntˈgʌməri/ : U.S. city, Alabama

Mon·tre·al /ˌmɑːntriˈɑːl/ : city in Quebec, Canada – **Mon·tre·al·er** /ˌmɑːntriˈɑːlɚ/ *noun*

Mont·ser·rat /ˌmɑːntsəˈræt/ : British island in the West Indies – **Mont·ser·ra·tian** /ˌmɑːntsəˈreɪʃən/ *noun*

Mo·ra·via /məˈreɪvijə/ : region of the Czech Republic – **Mo·ra·vi·an** /məˈreɪvijən/ *adj or noun*

Mo·re·no Valley /məˈriːnoʊ/ : U.S. city, California

Mo·roc·co /məˈrɑːkoʊ/ : country in Africa – **Mo·roc·can** /məˈrɑːkən/ *adj or noun*

Mos·cow /ˈmɑːˌskaʊ/ : city in Russia – **Mus·co·vite** /ˈmʌskəˌvaɪt/ *adj or noun*

Mo·zam·bique /ˌmoʊzəmˈbiːk/ : country in Africa – **Mo·zam·bi·can** /ˌmoʊzəmˈbiːkən/ *adj or noun*

Mul·tan /mʊlˈtɑːn/ : city in Pakistan

Mumbai see BOMBAY

Mu·nich /ˈmjuːnɪk/ : city in Germany

Mur·cia /ˈmɚʃijə/ : kingdom in ancient Spain – **Mur·cian** /ˈmɚʃijən/ *adj or noun*

Mur·frees·boro /ˈmɚfrizˌbɚroʊ/ : U.S. city, Tennessee

Myan·mar /ˈmjɑːnˌmaɚ/ *or* **Bur·ma** /ˈbɚmə/ : country in Asia

My·sia /ˈmɪʃijə/ : country in ancient Asia Minor

Nab·a·taea *or* **Nab·a·tea** /ˌnæbəˈtijə/ : kingdom in ancient Palestine – **Nab·a·tae·an** *or* **Nab·a·te·an** /ˌnæbəˈtijən/ *adj or noun*

Na·goya /nəˈgojə/ : city in Japan

Nag·pur /ˈnɑːgˌpuɚ/ : city in India

Nai·ro·bi /naɪˈroʊbi/ : city in Kenya

Na·mib·ia /nəˈmɪbijə/ : country in Africa – **Na·mib·ian** /nəˈmɪbijən/ *adj or noun*

Nan·chang /ˈnɑːnˈʧɑːŋ/ : city in China

Nan·jing /ˈnɑːnˈʤɪŋ/ : city in China

Nan·tuck·et /nænˈtʌkət/ : island of the U.S., in Massachusetts

Na·per·ville /ˈneɪpɚˌvɪl/ : U.S. city, Illinois

Na·ples /ˈneɪpəlz/ : city in Italy – **Ne·a·pol·i·tan** /ˌnijəˈpɑːlətən/ *adj or noun*

Nar·ra·gan·sett Bay /ˌnerəˈgænsət/ : part of the Atlantic Ocean

Na·shik /ˈnɑːʃɪk/ : town in India

Nash·ville /ˈnæʃˌvɪl/ : U.S. city, Tennessee

Na·u·ru /nɑˈuːru/ : island country in the Pacific Ocean – **Na·u·ru·an** /nɑˈurəwən/ *adj or noun*

Near East – **the Near East** : countries of northeastern Africa and southwestern Asia – **Near Eastern** *adj*

Ne·bras·ka /nəˈbræskə/ : state of the U.S. – **Ne·bras·kan** /nəˈbræskən/ *adj or noun*

Neg·ev /ˈnɛˌgɛv/ – **the Negev** : desert region of Israel

Ne·gro /ˈneɪˌgroʊ/ – **the Negro River** *also* **the Negro** : river in Colombia and Brazil

Nejd /ˈnɛʤd/ : region of Saudi Arabia

Ne·pal /nəˈpɑːl/ : country in Asia – **Nep·a·lese** /ˌnɛpəˈliːz/ *adj or noun* – **Ne·pali** /nəˈpɑːli/ *adj or noun*

Ness, Loch /ˌlɑːkˈnɛs/ : lake in Scotland

Neth·er·lands /ˈnɛðɚləndz/ *or* **Hol·land** /ˈhɑːlənd/ – **the Netherlands** *or* **Holland** : country in Europe – **Neth·er·land** /ˈnɛðɚlənd/ *adj* – **Neth·er·land·er** /ˈnɛðɚˌlændɚ/ *noun* – **Neth·er·land·ish** /ˈnɛðɚˌlændɪʃ/ *adj*

Ne·va·da /nəˈvædə, nəˈvɑːdə/ : state of the U.S. – **Ne·va·dan** /nəˈvædn̩, nəˈvɑːdn̩/ *adj or noun*

New·ark /ˈnuːwɚk, *Brit* ˈnjuːwək/ : U.S. city, New Jersey

New Bruns·wick /ˈbrʌnzˌwɪk/ : province of Canada

New·cas·tle /ˈnuːˌkæsəl, *Brit* ˈnjuːˌkɑːsəl/ : city in England

New England : region in the U.S. including the states of Maine, New Hampshire, Vermont, Massachusetts, Rhode Island, and Connecticut – **New En·gland·er** /ˌnuːˈɪŋgləndɚ, *Brit* ˌnjuːˈɪŋgləndə/ *noun*

New·found·land /ˈnuːfəndlənd, ˌnuːfəndˈlænd, *Brit* ˈnjuːfəndlənd/ : island of Canada in the Atlantic Ocean – **New·found·land·er** /ˈnuːfəndləndɚ, *Brit* ˈnjuːfəndləndɚ/ *noun*

Newfoundland and Labrador : province of Canada

New Guinea : island divided between Indonesia and Papua New Guinea – **New Guinean** *adj or noun*

New Hamp·shire /ˈhæmpʃɚ/ : state of the U.S. – **New Hamp·shire·man** /ˈhæmpʃɚmən/ *noun* – **New Hamp·shir·ite** /ˈhæmpʃɚˌaɪt/ *noun*

New Ha·ven /ˈheɪvən/ : U.S. city, Connecticut

New Jersey : state of the U.S. – **New Jer·sey·an** /ˈʤɚzijən/ *noun* – **New Jer·sey·ite** /ˈʤɚzijˌaɪt/ *noun*

New Mexico : state of the U.S. – **New Mexican** *adj or noun*

New Or·leans /ˌnuːˈoɚlənz, *Brit* ˌnjuːˈɔːlənz/ : U.S. city, Louisiana – **New Or·lea·nian** /ˌnuːwoɚˈliːnjən, *Brit* ˌnjuwɔːˈliːnjən/ *noun*

New·port News /ˌnuːˌpoɚtˈnuːz, *Brit* ˌnjuːˌpɔːtˈnjuːz/ : U.S. city, Virginia

New World – **the New World** : land of the Western Hemisphere

New York
1 : state of the U.S.
2 *or* **New York City** : U.S. city, in the state of New York – **New York·er** /ˈjoɚkɚ/ *noun*

New Zea·land /ˈziːlənd/ : island country in the Pacific Ocean – **New Zea·land·er** /ˈziːləndɚ/ *noun*

Ni·ag·a·ra Falls /naɪˈægrə/ : waterfalls on the border of the U.S. and Canada

Ni·caea /naɪˈsijə/ : city in ancient Bithynia – **Ni·cae·an** /naɪˈsijən/ *adj or noun* – **Ni·cene** /ˈnaɪˌsiːn/ *adj*

Ni·ca·ra·gua /ˌnɪkəˈrɑːgwə/ : country in Central America – **Ni·ca·ra·guan** /ˌnɪkəˈrɑːgwən/ *adj or noun*

Ni·ger /ˈnaɪʤɚ, niˈʒeɚ/
1 : country in Africa
2 **the Niger River** *also* **the Niger** : river in Africa – **Ni·ger·ien** /ˌnaɪˌʤiriˈɛn/ *adj or noun* – **Ni·ger·ois** /ˌniːʒɚˈwɑː/ *noun*

Ni·ge·ria /naɪˈʤirijə/ : country in Africa – **Ni·ge·ri·an** /naɪˈʤirijən/ *adj or noun*

Nile /ˈnajəl/ – **the Nile River** *also* **the Nile** : river in Africa

Nit·ta·ny Valley /ˈnɪtəni/ : valley in the U.S., in Pennsylvania

Nizh·niy Nov·go·rod /ˈnɪʒniˈnɑːvgəˌrɑːd/ : city in Russia

Nor·folk /ˈnoɚfək/ : U.S. city, Virginia

Nor·man /ˈnoɚmən/ : U.S. city, Oklahoma

North America : continent of the Western Hemisphere – **North American** *adj or noun*

North Car·o·li·na /ˌkerəˈlaɪnə/ : state of the U.S. – **North Car·o·lin·ian** /ˌkerəˈlɪniən/ *adj or noun*

North Da·ko·ta /dəˈkoʊtə/ : state of the U.S. – **North Da·ko·tan** /dəˈkoʊtn̩/ *adj or noun*

Northern Hemisphere – **the Northern Hemisphere** : half of the Earth north of the equator

Northern Ireland : part of the United Kingdom of Great Britain and Northern Ireland

Northern Mar·i·ana Islands /ˌmeriˈænə/ – **the Northern Mariana Islands** : islands of the U.S., in the Pacific Ocean

North Korea see KOREA – **North Korean** *adj or noun*

North Las Vegas : U.S. city, Nevada

North Pole – **the North Pole** : the most northern point on Earth

North Sea – **the North Sea** : part of the Atlantic Ocean

North Slope – **the North Slope** : region of the U.S., in Alaska

North·um·bria /noɚˈθʌmbrijə/ : country in ancient Great Britain – **North·um·bri·an** /noɚˈθʌmbrijən/ *adj or noun*

Northwest Passage – **the Northwest Passage** : sea route between the Atlantic Ocean and the Pacific Ocean along the northern coast of America

Northwest Territories – **the Northwest Territories** : territory of Canada
Nor·walk /ˈnoɚˌwɑːk/ : U.S. city, California
Nor·way /ˈnoɚˌweɪ/ : country in Europe – **Nor·we·gian** /noɚˈwiːʤən/ *adj or noun*
No·va Sco·tia /ˌnoʊvəˈskoʊʃə/ : province of Canada – **No·va Sco·tian** /ˌnoʊvəˈskoʊʃən/ *adj or noun*
No·vo·si·birsk /ˌnoʊvoʊsəˈbiɚsk/ : city in Russia
Nu·bia /ˈnuːbijə, *Brit* ˈnjuːbijə/ : region in Egypt and Sudan – **Nu·bi·an** /ˈnuːbijən, *Brit* ˈnjuːbijən/ *adj or noun*
Null·ar·bor Plain /ˈnʌləˌboɚ/ – **the Nullarbor Plain** : area with no trees in Australia
Nu·mid·ia /nʊˈmɪdijə, *Brit* njʊˈmɪdijə/ : country in ancient Africa – **Nu·mid·i·an** /nʊˈmɪdijən, *Brit* njʊˈmɪdijən/ *adj or noun*
Nu·na·vut /ˈnuːnəˌvuːt/ : territory of Canada
Oa·hu /oʊˈɑːhu/ : island of the U.S., in Hawaii
Oak·land /ˈoʊklənd/ : U.S. city, California
Oak·ville /ˈoʊkˌvɪl/ : town in Ontario, Canada
Ob /ˈɑːb/ – **the Ob River** *also* **the Ob** : river in Russia
Oce·a·nia /ˌoʊʃiˈænijə/ : lands of the central and southern Pacific Ocean – **Oce·a·ni·an** /ˌoʊʃiˈænijən/ *adj or noun*
Ocean·side /ˈoʊʃənˌsaɪd/ : U.S. city, California
Odes·sa /oʊˈdɛsə/ : city in Ukraine
Ohio /oʊˈhajoʊ/
1 : state of the U.S.
2 the Ohio River *also* **the Ohio** : river in the U.S.
– **Ohio·an** /oʊˈhajowən/ *adj or noun*
Okee·cho·bee, Lake /ˌoʊkəˈʧoʊbi/ : lake in the U.S., in Florida
Oke·fe·no·kee /ˌoʊkəfəˈnoʊki/ – **the Okefenokee Swamp** *also* **the Okefenokee** : swamp in the U.S., in Georgia and Florida
Okhotsk, Sea of /oʊˈkɑːtsk/ – **the Sea of Okhotsk** : part of the Pacific Ocean
Oki·na·wa /ˌoʊkəˈnɑːwə/ : Japanese islands in the Pacific Ocean – **Oki·na·wan** /ˌoʊkəˈnɑːwən/ *adj or noun*
Okla·ho·ma /ˌoʊkləˈhoʊmə/
1 : state of the U.S.
2 Oklahoma City : U.S. city, Oklahoma
– **Okla·ho·man** /ˌoʊkləˈhoʊmən/ *adj or noun*
Ola·the /oʊˈleɪθə/ : U.S. city, Kansas
Ol·du·vai Gorge /ˈoʊldəˌvaɪ/ : deep narrow area in Tanzania
Old World – **the Old World** : half of the Earth east of the Atlantic Ocean
Olym·pus *or* **Mount Olympus** /əˈlɪmpəs/ : mountains in Greece
Oma·ha /ˈoʊməˌhɑː/ : U.S. city, Nebraska
Oman /oʊˈmɑːn/
1 : country in Asia
2 the Gulf of Oman : part of the Arabian Sea
– **Omani** /oʊˈmɑːni/ *adj or noun*
Omsk /ˈɑːmsk/ : city in Russia
On·tar·io /ɑnˈterijˌoʊ/
1 : province of Canada
2 : U.S. city, California
3 Lake Ontario : lake in the U.S. and Canada
– **On·tar·i·an** /ɑnˈterijən/ *adj or noun*
Or·ange /ˈɑrɪnʤ, ˈorɪnʤ/
1 : U.S. city, California
2 the Orange River *also* **the Orange** : river in Africa
Or·e·gon /ˈorɪgən/
1 : state of the U.S.
2 the Oregon Trail : route in the U.S. from Missouri to Washington used by pioneers
– **Or·e·go·nian** /ˌorɪˈgoʊnijən/ *adj or noun*
Ori·no·co /ˌoriˈnoʊkoʊ/ – **the Orinoco River** *also* **the Orinoco** : river in Venezuela
Or·lan·do /orˈlændoʊ/ : U.S. city, Florida
Osa·ka /oʊˈsɑːkə/ : city in Japan
Osh·a·wa /ˈɑːʃəˌwə/ : city in Ontario, Canada
Ot·ta·wa /ˈɑːtəˌwə/ : city in Ontario, Canada
Ot·to·man Empire /ˈɑːtəmən/ – **the Ottoman Empire** : former Turkish empire in Europe, Asia, and Africa
Over·land Park /ˈoʊvɚlənd/ : U.S. city, Kansas
Ow·ens·boro /ˈowənzˌbɚroʊ/ : U.S. city, Kentucky
Ox·nard /ˈɑːksˌnɑɚd/ : U.S. city, California
Ozark /ˈoʊˌzɑɚk/ – **the Ozark Plateau** *or* **the Ozark Mountains** *or* **the Ozarks** : mountains in the U.S., in Arkansas – **Ozark·er** /ˈoʊˌzɑɚkɚ/ *noun* – **Ozark·ian** /oʊˈzɑɚkijən/ *adj or noun*
Pa·cif·ic /pəˈsɪfɪk/
1 the Pacific Ocean *also* **the Pacific** : ocean separating North America and South America from Asia and Australia
2 the Pacific Northwest : region of the U.S.
3 the Pacific Rim : countries in or around the Pacific Ocean
– **Pacific** *adj*
Pa·dre Island /ˈpɑːdri/ : island of the U.S., part of the state of Texas, in the Gulf of Mexico
Pa·ki·stan /ˈpækɪˌstæn/ : country in Asia – **Pa·ki·stani** /ˌpækɪˈstæni/ *adj or noun*
Pa·lau /pəˈlaʊ/ : island country in the Pacific Ocean – **Pa·lau·an** /pəˈlawən/ *noun*
Pa·lem·bang /ˌpɑːləmˈbɑːŋ/ : city in Indonesia
Pal·es·tine /ˈpæləˌstaɪn/ : region of ancient Asia – **Pal·es·tin·ian** /ˌpæləˈstɪnjən/ *adj or noun*
Pal·i·sades /ˌpæləˈseɪdz/ – **the Palisades** : cliffs in the U.S., in New York and New Jersey
Palm·dale /ˈpɑːmˌdeɪl/ : U.S. city, California
Pal·o·mar Mountain /ˈpæləˌmɑɚ/ *or* **Mount Palomar** : mountain in the U.S., in California
Pan·a·ma /ˈpænəˌmɑː/
1 : country in Central America
2 the Isthmus of Panama : strip of land connecting North America and South America
3 Panama Canal Zone see CANAL ZONE
– **Pan·a·ma·ni·an** /ˌpænəˈmeɪnijən/ *adj or noun*
Pan·mun·jom /ˌpɑːnˌmʊnˈʤʌm/ : village on the border between North Korea and South Korea
Paph·la·go·nia /ˌpæfləˈgoʊnijə/ : country in ancient Asia Minor
Pa·pua New Guinea /ˈpæpjəwə/ : island country in the Pacific Ocean – **Papua New Guinean** *adj or noun*
Par·a·guay /ˈperəˌgwaɪ/
1 : country in South America
2 the Paraguay River *also* **the Paraguay** : river in South America
– **Par·a·guay·an** /ˌperəˈgwajən/ *adj or noun*
Pa·ra·ná /ˌpɑrɑˈnɑː/ – **the Paraná River** : river in South America
Par·is /ˈperəs/ : city in France – **Pa·ri·sian** /pəˈrɪʒən/ *adj or noun*
Pas·a·de·na /ˌpæsəˈdiːnə/
1 : U.S. city, California
2 : U.S. city, Texas
Pat·a·go·nia /ˌpætəˈgoʊnjə/ : region of South America – **Pat·a·go·nian** /ˌpætəˈgoʊnjən/ *adj or noun*
Pat·er·son /ˈpætɚsən/ : U.S. city, New Jersey
Pat·na /ˈpʌtnə/ : city in India
Peace /ˈpiːs/ – **the Peace River** *also* **the Peace** : river in Canada
Pearl Harbor : part of the Pacific Ocean on the U.S. coast of Oahu, in Hawaii
Pe·cho·ra /pɪˈʧorə/ – **the Pechora River** *also* **the Pechora** : river in Russia
Peking see BEIJING
Pel·o·pon·nese /ˈpɛləpəˌniːz/ – **the Peloponnese** : part of Greece
Pem·broke Pines /ˈpɛmˌbroʊk/ : U.S. city, Florida
Penn·syl·va·nia /ˌpɛnsəlˈveɪnjə/ : state of the U.S. – **Penn·syl·va·nian** /ˌpɛnsəlˈveɪnjən/ *adj or noun*
Pe·nob·scot Bay /pəˈnɑːbˌskɑːt/ : part of the Atlantic Ocean on the U.S. coast of Maine
Pe·o·ria /piˈorijə/
1 : U.S. city, Illinois
2 : U.S. town, Arizona
Perm' /ˈpɚm/ : city in Russia
Per·sian Gulf /ˈpɚʒən/ – **the Persian Gulf** : part of the Arabian Sea
Pe·ru /pəˈruː/ : country in South America – **Pe·ru·vi·an** /pəˈruːvijən/ *adj or noun*
Pe·sha·war /pəˈʃɑːwɚ/ : city in Pakistan
Pe·tra /ˈpiːtrə/ : city in ancient Arabia
Phil·a·del·phia /ˌfɪləˈdɛlfjə/ : U.S. city, Pennsylvania – **Phil·a·del·phian** /ˌfɪləˈdɛlfjən/ *adj or noun*
Phil·ip·pines /ˌfɪləˈpiːnz, ˈfɪləˌpiːnz/ – **the Philippines** : is-

land country in Asia – **Fil·i·pi·no** /ˌfɪləˈpiːnoʊ/ *adj or noun* – **Phil·ip·pine** /ˌfɪləˈpiːn, ˈfɪləˌpiːn/ *adj*

Phoe·ni·cia /fɪˈniːʃijə/ : country in ancient Asia – **Phoe·ni·cian** /fɪˈniːʃən/ *adj or noun*

Phoe·nix /ˈfiːnɪks/ : U.S. city, Arizona

Pied·mont /ˈpiːdˌmɑːnt/ – **the Piedmont** : region of the U.S. – **Pied·mon·tese** /ˌpiːdmənˈtiz/ *adj or noun*

Pikes Peak /ˈpaɪks/ : mountain in the U.S., in Colorado

Pi·nel·las Peninsula /paɪˈnɛləs/ : part of the U.S., in Florida

Pi·sa /ˈpiːzə/ : city in Italy

Pit·cairn Island /ˈpɪtˌkeən/ : British island in the Pacific Ocean – **Pit·cairn·er** /ˈpɪtˌkeənə/ *noun*

Pitts·burgh /ˈpɪtsˌbəg/ : U.S. city, Pennsylvania – **Pitts·burgh·er** /ˈpɪtsˌbəgə/ *noun*

Plac·id, Lake /ˈplæsəd/ : lake in the U.S., in New York

Pla·no /ˈpleɪnoʊ/ : U.S. city, Texas

Platte /ˈplæt/ – **the Platte River** *also* **the Platte** : river in the U.S., in Nebraska

Plym·outh Rock /ˈplɪməθ/ : historic location in the U.S., in Massachusetts

Po·co·no /ˈpoʊkəˌnoʊ/ – **the Pocono Mountains** *also* **the Poconos** : mountains in the U.S., in Pennsylvania

Point Pe·lee /ˌpɔɪntˈpiːli/ : part of Canada, in Ontario on Lake Erie

Po·land /ˈpoʊlənd/ : country in Europe – **Pole** /ˈpoʊl/ *noun* – **Pol·ish** /ˈpoʊlɪʃ/ *adj*

Poly·ne·sia /ˌpɑːləˈniʒə/ : islands of the central and southern Pacific Ocean – **Poly·ne·sian** /ˌpɑːləˈniʒən/ *adj or noun*

Pom·er·a·nia /ˌpɑːməˈreɪnijə/ : region of Europe

Po·mo·na /pəˈmoʊnə/ : U.S. city, California

Pom·peii /pɑmˈpeɪ/ : city in ancient Italy – **Pom·pe·ian** /pɑmˈpejən/ *adj or noun*

Pon·ce /ˈpɑːnseɪ/ : U.S. city, Puerto Rico

Pont·char·train, Lake /ˈpɑːnttʃəˌtreɪn/ : lake in the U.S., in Louisiana

Pon·ti·ac /ˈpɑːntiˌæk/ : U.S. city, Michigan

Port·land /ˈportlənd/ : U.S. city, Oregon – **Port·land·er** /ˈportləndə/ *noun*

Por·to Ale·gre /ˌpoətuwɑˈleɪgri/ : city in Brazil

Ports·mouth /ˈpoətsməθ/ : U.S. city, Virginia

Por·tu·gal /ˈpoətʃɪgəl/ : country in Europe – **Por·tu·guese** /ˈpoətʃɪˌgiːz, ˌpoətʃɪˈgiːz/ *adj or noun*

Po·to·mac /pəˈtoʊmək/ – **the Potomac River** *also* **the Potomac** : river in the U.S.

Prague /ˈprɑːg/ : city in the Czech Republic

Prairie Provinces – **the Prairie Provinces** : the provinces of Alberta, Manitoba, and Saskatchewan, in Canada

Prince Ed·ward Island /ˈɛdwəd/ : province of Canada

Prov·i·dence /ˈprɑːvədəns/ : U.S. city, Rhode Island

Pro·vo /ˈproʊvoʊ/ : U.S. city, Utah

Prud·hoe Bay /ˈpruːdoʊ/ : part of the Beaufort Sea near the U.S. coast of Alaska

Prus·sia /ˈprʌʃə/ : former kingdom in Europe – **Prus·sian** /ˈprʌʃən/ *adj or noun*

Pueb·la /ˈpwɛblɑ/ : city in Mexico

Pueb·lo /ˈpwɛbloʊ, pjuˈɛbloʊ/ : U.S. city, Colorado

Puer·to Ri·co /ˌpoətəˈriːkoʊ, ˌpweətoʊˈriːkoʊ/ : island of the U.S. – **Puer·to Ri·can** /ˌpoətəˈriːkən, ˌpweətoʊˈriːkən/ *adj or noun*

Pu·get Sound /ˈpjuːʤət/ : part of the Pacific Ocean

Pu·ne /ˈpuːnə/ : city in India

Pu·san /ˈpuːˌsɑːn/ *or* **Bu·san** /ˈbuːˌsɑːn/ : city in South Korea

Pyong·yang /ˈpjɑːŋˌjæŋ/ : city in North Korea

Pyr·e·nees /ˈpirəˌniːz/ – **the Pyrenees** : mountains on the border of France and Spain

Qa·tar /ˈkɑːtə/ : country in Arabia – **Qa·tari** /kəˈtɑri/ *adj or noun*

Qing·dao /ˈʧɪŋˈdaʊ/ : city in China

Qi·qi·har /ˈʧiˈʧiˈhɑə/ : city in China

Que·bec /kwɪˈbɛk/
1 : province of Canada
2 : city in the province of Quebec, Canada
– **Que·bec·er** *or* **Que·beck·er** /kwɪˈbɛkə/ *noun*

Queens /ˈkwiːnz/ : part of the U.S. city of New York, in the state of New York

Que·zon City /ˈkeɪˌsɑːn/ : city in the Philippines

Qui·to /ˈkiːtoʊ/ : city in Ecuador

Rai·nier, Mount /rəˈnɪə/ : mountain in the U.S., in Washington

Ra·leigh /ˈrɑːli/ : U.S. city, North Carolina

Ran·cho Cu·ca·mon·ga /ˈrænʧoʊˌkuːkəˈmʌŋgə/ : U.S. city, California

Rangoon see YANGON

Rasht /ˈræʃt/ : city in Iran

Ra·wal·pin·di /ˌrɑːwəlˈpɪndi/ : city in Pakistan

Re·ci·fe /rəˈsiːfi/ : city in Brazil

Red /ˈrɛd/
1 the Red River : river in the U.S.
2 the Red Sea : sea between Arabia and Africa

Re·gi·na /rɪˈʤaɪnə/ : city in Saskatchewan, Canada

Re·no /ˈriːnoʊ/ : U.S. city, Nevada

Ré·union /riˈjuːnjən/ : French island in the Indian Ocean

Rhae·tia /ˈriːʃijə/ : ancient Roman province in Europe

Rhine /ˈraɪn/ – **the Rhine River** *also* **the Rhine** : river in Europe – **Rhen·ish** /ˈrɛnɪʃ/ *adj*

Rhine·land /ˈraɪnˌlænd/ – **the Rhineland** : region of Germany – **Rhine·land·er** /ˈraɪnˌlændə/ *noun*

Rhode Is·land /roʊdˈaɪlənd/ : state of the U.S. – **Rhode Is·land·er** /roʊdˈaɪləndə/ *noun*

Rhodes /ˈroʊdz/ : island of Greece in the Aegean Sea

Rhodesia see ZIMBABWE – **Rho·de·sian** /roʊˈdiːʒən/ *adj or noun*

Ri·al·to /riˈæltoʊ/ : U.S. city, California

Rich·ard·son /ˈrɪʧədsən/ : U.S. city, Texas

Rich·mond /ˈrɪʧmənd/
1 : U.S. city, Virginia
2 : city in British Columbia, Canada

Richmond Hill : town in Ontario, Canada

Ri·deau Canal /rɪˈdoʊ/ – **the Rideau Canal** : canal system in Ontario, Canada

Rio de Ja·nei·ro /ˈrijoʊˌdeɪʒəˈneroʊ/ *or informally* **Rio** : city in Brazil

Rio Grande /ˌrijoʊˈgrænd/ – **the Rio Grande** : river in North America

Riv·er·side /ˈrɪvəˌsaɪd/ : U.S. city, California

Riv·i·era /ˌrɪviˈerə/ – **the Riviera** : coast region in France and Italy

Ri·yadh /riˈjɑːd/ : city in Saudi Arabia

Rob·son, Mount /ˈrɑːbsən/ : mountain in British Columbia, Canada

Roch·es·ter /ˈrɑːʧəstə/ : U.S. city, New York

Rock·ford /ˈrɑːkfəd/ : U.S. city, Illinois

Rocky Mountains /ˈrɑːki/ – **the Rocky Mountains** *also* **the Rock·ies** /ˈrɑːkiz/ : mountains in North America

Ro·ma·nia /roʊˈmeɪnijə/ : country in Europe – **Ro·ma·nian** /roʊˈmeɪnijən/ *adj or noun*

Rome /ˈroʊm/ : city in Italy – **Ro·man** /ˈroʊmən/ *adj or noun*

Ros·tov–on–Don /riˈstɑːfˌɑːnˈdɑːn/ : city in Russia

Rush·more, Mount /ˈrʌʃˌmoə/ : mountain in the U.S., in South Dakota

Rus·sia /ˈrʌʃə/
1 : UNION OF SOVIET SOCIALIST REPUBLICS
2 : country in Europe and Asia
– **Rus·sian** /ˈrʌʃən/ *adj or noun*

Ru·the·nia /ruˈθiːnjə/ : region of Ukraine – **Ru·the·nian** /ruˈθiːnjən/ *adj or noun*

Rwan·da /ruˈɑːndə/ : country in Africa – **Rwan·dan** /ruˈɑːndən/ *adj or noun*

Ryu·kyu Islands /riˈjuːkju/ : Japanese islands in the Pacific Ocean – **Ryu·kyu·an** /riˈjuːkjuwən/ *adj or noun*

Saan·ich /ˈsænɪʧ/ : city in British Columbia, Canada

Sac·ra·men·to /ˌsækrəˈmɛntoʊ/ : U.S. city, California

Sag·i·naw Bay /ˈsægənoʊ/ : part of Lake Huron near the U.S. state of Michigan

Sag·ue·nay /ˈsægəˌneɪ/ : city in Quebec, Canada

Sa·ha·ra /səˈherə/ – **the Sahara** : desert in Africa – **Sa·ha·ran** /səˈherən/ *adj*

Sa·hel /ˈsæhɪl/ – **the Sahel** : southern part of the Sahara

Saigon see HO CHI MINH CITY

Saint Bar·the·le·my /ˌsænbɑətɛɪləˈmiː/ *or informally* **Saint Bart's** /ˌseɪntˈbɑəts/ : French island in the West Indies

Saint Cath·a·rines /ˈkæθrənz/ : city in Ontario, Canada

Saint Clair, Lake /ˈkleɚ/ : lake in the U.S. state of Michigan and Ontario, Canada
Saint Croix /ˈkrɔɪ/ : island of the Virgin Islands of the U.S.
Saint Eu•sta•ti•us /jʊˈsteɪʃəs/ *or informally* **Statia** /ˈsteɪʃə/ : Dutch island in the West Indies
Saint He•le•na /ˌseɪntəˈliːnə/ : British island in the Atlantic Ocean
Saint Hel•ens, Mount /ˈhɛlənz/ : volcano in the U.S., in Washington
Saint–Jean, Lake /ˌseɪntˈʒɑːn/ : lake in Quebec, Canada
Saint John's /ˈʤɑːnz/ : city in Newfoundland and Labrador, Canada
Saint Kitts and Nevis /seɪntˈkɪtsəˈniːvəs/ : island country in the West Indies – **Kit•ti•tian** /kəˈtɪʃən/ *adj or noun* – **Ne•vis•ian** /nəˈvɪʒən/ *adj or noun*
Saint Law•rence /ˈlorəns/
1 the Saint Lawrence River *also* **the Saint Lawrence** : river in Ontario and Quebec, Canada, bordering on the U.S. state of New York
2 the Saint Lawrence Seaway : shipping route in Canada and the U.S.
Saint Lou•is /ˈluwəs/ : U.S. city, Missouri – **Saint Lou•i•san** /ˈluwəsən/ *noun*
Saint Lu•cia /ˈluːʃə/ : island country in the West Indies – **Saint Lu•cian** /ˈluːʃən/ *adj or noun*
Saint Paul /ˈpɑːl/ : U.S. city, Minnesota
Saint Pe•ters•burg /ˈpiːtɚzˌbɚg/
1 : U.S. city, Florida
2 : city in Russia
Saint–Pierre and Miquelon /seɪntˈpirəndˈmɪkəˌlɑːn/ : French islands in the Atlantic Ocean
Saint Si•mons Island /ˈsaɪˈmˈənz/ : island of the U.S., near Georgia in the Atlantic Ocean
Saint Thom•as /ˈtɑːməs/ : U.S. island, in the Virgin Islands
Saint Vin•cent and the Gren•a•dines /seɪntˈvɪnsəntəndðəˌgrɛnəˈdiːnz/ : island country in the West Indies
Sai•pan /saɪˈpæn/ : island in the U.S., in the Northern Mariana Islands
Sa•kha•lin /ˈsækəˌliːn/ : Russian island in the Pacific Ocean
Sa•lem /ˈseɪləm/ : U.S. city, Oregon
Sa•li•nas /səˈliːnəs/ : U.S. city, California
Salt Lake City : U.S. city, Utah
Sal•ton Sea /ˈsɑːltn/ – **the Salton Sea** : salt lake in the U.S., in California
Sal•va•dor /ˈsælvəˌdoɚ/ : city in Brazil
Sal•ween /ˈsælˌwiːn/ – **the Salween River** *also* **the Salween** : river in Asia
Sa•ma•ra /səˈmɑrə/ : city in Russia
Sam•ni•um /ˈsæmnijəm/ : country in ancient Italy – **Samnite** /ˈsæmˌnaɪt/ *adj or noun*
Sa•moa /səˈmowə/
1 : islands in the Pacific Ocean
2 : island country in the Pacific Ocean
– **Sa•mo•an** /səˈmowən/ *adj or noun*
Sa•mos /ˈseɪˌmɑːs/ : Greek island in the Aegean Sea – **Sa•mi•an** /ˈseɪmijən/ *adj or noun*
San An•dre•as Fault /ˌsænænˈdrejəs/ – **the San Andreas Fault** *also* **the San Andreas** : part of the Earth where earthquakes occur in the U.S., in California
San An•to•nio /ˌsænənˈtouniˌoʊ/ : U.S. city, Texas
San Ber•nar•di•no /ˌsænˌbɚnəˈdiːnoʊ/ : U.S. city, California
San Buenaventura see VENTURA
San Di•e•go /ˌsændiˈeɪgoʊ/ : U.S. city, California – **San Di•e•gan** /ˌsændiˈeɪgən/ *adj or noun*
San Fer•nan•do Valley /ˌsænfɚˈnændoʊ/ : valley in the U.S., in California
San Fran•cis•co /ˌsænfrənˈsɪskoʊ/
1 : U.S. city, California
2 San Francisco Bay : part of the Pacific Ocean
– **San Fran•cis•can** /ˌsænfrənˈsɪskən/ *adj or noun*
San Jo•se /ˌsænhoʊˈzeɪ/ : U.S. city, California
San Juan /sænˈwɑːn/ : U.S. city, Puerto Rico
San Ma•ri•no /ˌsænməˈriːnoʊ/ : country in Europe – **Sam•mar•i•nese** /ˌsæmˌmerəˈniːz/ *noun* – **San Mar•i•nese** /ˌsænˌmerəˈniːz/ *adj or noun*
San Ma•teo /ˌsænməˈtejoʊ/ : U.S. city, California
San•ta Ana /ˌsæntəˈænə/ : U.S. city, California
San•ta Bar•ba•ra /ˌsæntəˈbɑɚbrə/ : U.S. city, California
San•ta Clara /ˌsæntəˈklerə/ : U.S. city, California
San•ta Cla•ri•ta /ˌsæntəkləˈriːtə/ : U.S. city, California
San•ta Fe Trail /ˌsæntəˈfeɪ/ – **the Santa Fe Trail** : route in the U.S. from Missouri to New Mexico used by pioneers and traders in the 1800s
San•ta Ro•sa /ˌsæntəˈrouzə/ : U.S. city, California
San•to Do•min•go /ˌsæntədəˈmɪŋgoʊ/ : city in the Dominican Republic
São Pau•lo /ˌsaunˈpaulu/ : city in Brazil
São To•mé and Prín•ci•pe /ˌsauntəmejəndˈprɪnsəpi/ : country in Africa
Sap•po•ro /ˈsɑːpoʊˌroʊ/ : city in Japan
Sar•din•ia /sɑɚˈdɪnijə/ : Italian island in the Mediterranean Sea – **Sar•din•ian** /sɑɚˈdɪnijən/ *adj or noun*
Sas•katch•e•wan /səˈskæʧəwən/ : province of Canada
Sas•ka•toon /ˌsæskəˈtuːn/ : city in Saskatchewan, Canada
Sau•di Arabia /ˈsaudi/ : country on the Arabian Peninsula – **Saudi** *adj or noun* – **Saudi Arabian** *adj or noun*
Sault Sainte Ma•rie Canals /ˌsuːˌseɪntməˈriː/ – **the Sault Sainte Marie Canals** *also* **the Soo Canals** /ˈsuː/ : canals connecting Lake Superior and Lake Huron
Sa•van•nah /səˈvænə/ : U.S. city, Georgia
Sa•voy /səˈvɔɪ/ : region of France – **Sa•voy•ard** /səˈvɔɪˌɑɚd/ *adj or noun*
Sax•o•ny /ˈsæksəni/ : region of Germany – **Sax•on** /ˈsæksən/ *adj or noun*
Scan•di•na•via /ˌskændəˈneɪvijə/
1 : part of Europe
2 : the countries of Denmark, Norway, Sweden, and sometimes also Iceland and Finland
– **Scan•di•na•vian** /ˌskændəˈneɪvijən/ *adj or noun*
Scot•land /ˈskɑːtlənd/ *or Latin* **Cal•e•do•nia** /ˌkæləˈdounjə/ : part of the United Kingdom – **Scot** /ˈskɑːt/ *noun* – **Scotch** /ˈskɑːʧ/ *adj* – **Scots** /ˈskɑːts/ *adj* – **Scot•tish** /ˈskɑːtɪʃ/ *adj*
Scotts•dale /ˈskɑːtsˌdeɪl/ : U.S. city, Arizona
Scyth•ia /ˈsɪθijə/ : area of ancient Europe and Asia – **Scyth•i•an** /ˈsɪθijən/ *adj or noun*
Se•at•tle /siˈætl/ : U.S. city, Washington – **Se•at•tle•ite** /siˈætlˌaɪt/ *noun*
Seine /ˈseɪn, ˈsɛn/ – **the Seine River** *also* **the Seine** : river in France
Se•ma•rang /səˈmɑɚˌɑːŋ/ : city in Indonesia
Sen•dai /ˌsɛnˈdaɪ/ : city in Japan
Sen•e•gal /ˌsɛnɪˈgɑːl/
1 : country in Africa
2 the Senegal River *also* **the Senegal** : river in Africa
– **Sen•e•ga•lese** /ˌsɛnɪgəˈliːz/ *adj or noun*
Seoul /ˈsoʊl/ : city in South Korea
Ser•bia /ˈsɚbijə/ : country in Europe – **Ser•bi•an** /ˈsɚbijən/ *adj or noun*
Ser•en•ge•ti Plain /ˌserənˈgɛti/ – **the Serengeti Plain** : area in Tanzania
Sew•ard Peninsula /ˈsuːwɚd/ – **the Seward Peninsula** : part of the U.S., in Alaska
Sey•chelles /seɪˈʃɛlz/ : island country in the Indian Ocean – **Sey•chel•lois** /ˌseɪʃəlˈwɑː/ *noun*
Shang•hai /ʃæŋˈhaɪ/ : city in China
Shatt al Ar•ab /ˌʃætælˈerəb/ – **the Shatt al Arab** : river in Iraq
Shen•an•do•ah Valley /ˌʃɛnənˈdowə/ – **the Shenandoah Valley** : valley in the U.S., between the Allegheney and Blue Ridge mountains
Shen•yang /ˈʃʌnˈjɑːŋ/ : city in China
Sher•brooke /ˈʃɚˌbrʊk/ : city in Quebec, Canada
Shet•land /ˈʃɛtlənd/ – **the Shetland Islands** *also* **the Shetlands** : islands of Scotland
Shi•jia•zhuang /ˈʃiəˈʤjɑːˈʤwɑːŋ/ : city in China
Shi•ko•ku /ʃiˈkouku/ : island of Japan
Shreve•port /ˈʃriːvˌpoɚt/ : U.S. city, Louisiana
Siam see THAILAND
Si•be•ria /saɪˈbirijə/ : region of Russia – **Si•be•ri•an** /saɪˈbirijən/ *adj or noun*
Sic•i•ly /ˈsɪsəli/ : island of Italy – **Si•cil•ian** /səˈsɪljən/ *adj or noun*
Si•er•ra Le•one /siˌerəliˈoun/ : country in Africa – **Si•er•ra Le•on•ean** /siˌerəliˈounijən/ *adj or noun*

Sier·ra Ne·va·da /siˌerənəˈvædə, siˌerəˈvɑːdə/ – **the Sierra Nevada** : mountain range in the U.S., in California and Nevada
Sik·kim /ˈsɪkəm/ : former country in Asia; now part of India
Si·le·sia /saɪˈliːʒijə/ : region of Europe – **Si·le·sian** /saɪˈliːʒijən/ *adj or noun*
Silicon Valley : region of the U.S., in California
Silk Road *or* **Silk Route** – **the Silk Road** *or* **the Silk Route** : ancient trade route from China to the Mediterranean Sea
Si·mi Valley /siˈmiː/ : U.S. city, California
Si·nai /ˈsaɪˌnaɪ/ – **the Sinai Peninsula** *also* **the Sinai** : land between the Red Sea and the Mediterranean Sea
Sin·ga·pore /ˈsɪŋəˌpoɚ/ : island country in Asia – **Sin·ga·por·ean** /ˌsɪŋəˈporijən/ *adj or noun*
Sioux Falls /ˈsuː/ : U.S. city, South Dakota
Sla·vo·nia /sləˈvounijə/ : region of Croatia – **Sla·vo·ni·an** /sləˈvounijən/ *adj or noun*
Slo·va·kia /slouˈvɑːkijə/ : country in Europe – **Slo·va·ki·an** /slouˈvɑːkijən/ *adj or noun*
Slo·ve·nia /slouˈvinijə/ : country in Europe – **Slo·ve·nian** /slouˈvinijən/ *adj or noun*
Snake /ˈsneɪk/ – **the Snake River** *also* **the Snake** : river in the U.S.
Sod·om /ˈsɑːdəm/ : city in ancient Asia
So·fia /ˈsoufijə/ : city in Bulgaria
Sol·o·mon /ˈsɑːləmən/ – **the Solomon Islands** *also* **the Solomons** : country in the Pacific Ocean
So·ma·lia /souˈmɑːlijə/ : country in Africa – **So·ma·li** /souˈmɑːli/ *noun* – **So·ma·li·an** /souˈmɑːliən/ *adj or noun*
So·nor·an Desert /səˈnorən/ – **the Sonoran Desert** : desert in the U.S. and Mexico
Soo Canals see SAULT SAINTE MARIE
South Africa – **the Republic of South Africa** *or* **South Africa** : country in Africa – **South African** *adj or noun*
South America : continent of the Western Hemisphere – **South American** *adj or noun*
South Bend /ˈbɛnd/ : U.S. city, Indiana
South Car·o·li·na /ˌkerəˈlaɪnə/ : state of the U.S. – **South Car·o·lin·i·an** /ˌkerəˈlɪnijən/ *adj or noun*
South Da·ko·ta /dəˈkoutə/ : state of the U.S. – **South Da·ko·tan** /dəˈkoutn̩/ *adj or noun*
Southern Hemisphere – **the Southern Hemisphere** : half of the Earth south of the equator
Southern Ocean – **the Southern Ocean** : ocean areas surrounding Antarctica
South Korea see KOREA – **South Korean** *adj or noun*
South Pole – **the South Pole** : the most southern point on Earth
South Seas – **the South Seas** : areas of the Atlantic, Indian, and Pacific oceans in the Southern Hemisphere
Soviet Union see UNION OF SOVIET SOCIALIST REPUBLICS
So·we·to /souˈweɪtou/ : area in South Africa – **So·we·tan** /souˈweɪtn̩/ *noun*
Spain /ˈspeɪn/ : country in Europe – **Span·iard** /ˈspænjɚd/ *noun* – **Span·ish** /ˈspænɪʃ/ *adj or noun*
Spanish America : the countries of America where people speak Spanish
Spar·ta /ˈspɑɚtə/ : city in ancient Greece
Spo·kane /spouˈkæn/ : U.S. city, Washington
Spring·field /ˈsprɪŋˌfiːld/
1 : U.S. city, Illinois
2 : U.S. city, Massachusetts
3 : U.S. city, Missouri
Sri Lan·ka /ˌsriːˈlɑːŋkə/ : country in the Indian Ocean, consisting of the island of Ceylon – **Sri Lan·kan** /ˌsriːˈlɑːŋkən/ *adj or noun*
Srp·ska, Re·pu·bli·ka /ˈsɚpskɑ, rɛˈpuːblikɑ/ : region of Bosnia and Herzegovina
Stam·ford /ˈstæmfɚd/ : U.S. city, Connecticut
Stat·en Island /ˈstætn̩/ : part of the U.S. city of New York, in the state of New York
Statia see SAINT EUSTATIUS
Ster·ling Heights /ˈstɚlɪŋ/ : U.S. city, Michigan
Stock·holm /ˈstɑːkˌhoulm/ : city in Sweden
Stock·ton /ˈstɑːktən/ : U.S. city, California
Stone·henge /ˈstounˌhɛnʤ/ : a group of very large stones in England arranged by people in prehistoric times
Styr·ia /ˈstirijə/ : region of Austria
Su·dan /suˈdæn/ : country in Africa – **Su·da·nese** /ˌsuːdəˈniːz/ *adj or noun*
Sud·bury, Greater /ˈsʌdˌberi/ : city in Ontario, Canada
Su·ez Canal /suˈɛz/ – **the Suez Canal** : canal connecting the Red Sea with the Mediterranean Sea
Su·ma·tra /sʊˈmɑːtrə/ : island of Indonesia – **Su·ma·tran** /sʊˈmɑːtrən/ *adj or noun*
Su·mer /ˈsuːmɚ/ : part of ancient Babylonia – **Su·me·ri·an** /suˈmerijən/ *adj or noun*
Sun·belt /ˈsʌnˌbɛlt/ – **the Sunbelt** : region of the southern and southwestern U.S.
Sun·ny·vale /ˈsʌniˌveɪl/ : U.S. city, California
Su·pe·ri·or, Lake /sʊˈpirijɚ/ : lake in the U.S. and Canada
Su·ra·ba·ya /ˌsɚrəˈbajə/ : city in Indonesia
Su·rat /ˈsurət/ : city in India
Su·ri·na·me /ˌsurəˈnɑːmə/ : country in South America – **Su·ri·nam·er** /ˈsurəˌnɑːmɚ/ *noun* – **Su·ri·nam·ese** /ˌsurənəˈmiːz/ *adj or noun*
Sur·rey /ˈsɚri/ : city in British Columbia, Canada
Su·wan·nee /səˈwɑːni/ – **the Suwannee River** *also* **the Suwannee** : river in the U.S., in Georgia and Florida
Swa·zi·land /ˈswɑːziˌlænd/ : country in Africa – **Swa·zi** /ˈswɑːzi/ *adj or noun*
Swe·den /ˈswiːdn̩/ : country in Europe – **Swede** /ˈswiːd/ *noun* – **Swed·ish** /ˈswiːdɪʃ/ *adj*
Swit·zer·land /ˈswɪtsɚlənd/ : country in Europe – **Swiss** /ˈswɪs/ *adj or noun*
Syd·ney /ˈsɪdni/ : city in Australia
Syr·a·cuse /ˈsirəˌkjuːs/ : U.S. city, New York
Syr Dar'·ya /siɚˈdɑɚjə/ – **the Syr Dar'ya** : river in Tajikistan and Kazakhstan
Syr·ia /ˈsirijə/ : country in Asia – **Syr·i·an** /ˈsirijən/ *adj or noun*
Ta·co·ma /təˈkoumə/ : U.S. city, Washington
Tae·gu /ˈteɪgu/ *or* **Dae·gu** /ˈdeɪgu/ : city in South Korea
Tae·jon /ˈteɪˈʤʌn/ *or* **Dae·jeon** /ˈdeɪˈʤʌn/ : city in South Korea
Ta·hi·ti /təˈhiːti/ : French island in the Pacific Ocean
Tahoe, Lake : lake in the U.S., between California and Nevada
Tai·bei /ˈtaɪˈpeɪ, ˈbeɪ/ *or* **Tai·pei** : city in Taiwan
Tai·wan /ˈtaɪˈwɑːn/ : Chinese island off the coast of Asia – **Tai·wan·ese** /ˌtaɪwəˈniːz/ *adj or noun*
Tai·yu·an /ˈtaɪˈjwɛn/ : city in China
Tai·zhong /ˈtaɪˈʤʊŋ/ : city in Taiwan
Ta·jik·i·stan /tɑˌʤɪkɪˈstæn/ : country in Asia – **Ta·jik** /tɑˈʤɪk/ *noun*
Tal·la·has·see /ˌtæləˈhæsi/ : U.S. city, Florida
Tam·pa /ˈtæmpə/
1 : U.S. city, Florida
2 Tampa Bay : part of the Gulf of Mexico
Tan·gan·yi·ka /ˌtæŋgəˈnjiːkə/ : former country in Africa
Tang·shan /ˈdɑːŋˈʃɑːn/ : city in China
Tan·za·nia /ˌtænzəˈnijə/ : country in Africa – **Tan·za·ni·an** /ˌtænzəˈnijən/ *adj or noun*
Tap·pan Zee /ˌtæpənˈziː/ – **the Tappan Zee** : part of the Hudson River in the U.S.
Tash·kent /tæʃˈkɛnt/ : city in Uzbekistan
Tas·ma·nia /tæzˈmeɪnijə/ : island of Australia – **Tas·ma·nian** /tæzˈmeɪnijən/ *adj or noun*
Tbi·li·si /təˈbiːləsi/ : city in the Republic of Georgia
Teh·ran /ˌteɪˈrɑːn, ˌteɪˈræn/ : city in Iran
Tel Aviv /ˌtɛləˈviːv/ : city in Israel
Tem·pe /tɛmˈpiː/ : U.S. city, Arizona
Ten·nes·see /ˌtɛnəˈsiː/ : state of the U.S. – **Ten·nes·se·an** *or* **Ten·nes·see·an** /ˌtɛnəˈsiːjən/ *adj or noun*
Terre·bonne /ˈterəˌbɑːn/ : town in Quebec, Canada
Te·ton /ˈtiːˌtɑːn/ – **the Teton Range** *also* **the Tetons** : mountains in the U.S., in Wyoming
Tex·as /ˈtɛksəs/ : state of the U.S. – **Tex·an** /ˈtɛksən/ *adj or noun*
Thai·land /ˈtaɪˌlænd/ *or formerly* **Si·am** /saɪˈæm/
1 : country in Asia
2 the Gulf of Thailand : part of the South China Sea bordered by Thailand, Cambodia, and Vietnam
– **Thai** /ˈtaɪ/ *adj or noun*

Thames /ˈtɛmz/ – **the Thames River** *also* **the Thames** : river in England
Tha·ne /ˈtɑːnə/ : town in India
Thebes /ˈθiːbz/
1 : city in ancient Egypt
2 : city in ancient Greece
– **The·ban** /ˈθiːbən/ *adj or noun*
Thes·sa·ly /ˈθɛsəli/ : region of Greece
Thomp·son /ˈtɑːmpsən/ : river in British Columbia, Canada
Thousand Oaks : U.S. city, California
Thrace /ˈθreɪs/ : region in the Balkan Peninsula – **Thra·cian** /ˈθreɪʃən/ *adj or noun*
Thunder Bay : city in Ontario, Canada
Thu·rin·gia /θʊˈrɪnʤijə/ : region of Germany
Tian·jin /ˈtjɛnˈʤɪn/ : city in China
Tian Shan /ˈtjɛnˈʃɑːn/ : mountains in Asia
Ti·bet /təˈbɛt/ *or* **Xi·zang** /ˈʃiːˈdzɑːŋ/ : region of China – **Ti·bet·an** /təˈbɛtn/ *adj or noun*
Tier·ra del Fue·go /tiˈerəˌdɛlfuˈeɪgoʊ/ : islands south of South America
Ti·gris /ˈtaɪgrəs/ – **the Tigris River** *also* **the Tigris** : river in Turkey and Iraq
Ti·jua·na /tiˈhwɑːnə/ : city in Mexico on the U.S. border
Ti·mor /ˈtiˌmoɚ/ : island divided between Indonesia and East Timor
Ti·rol *or* **Ty·rol** /təˈroʊl, ˈtaɪˌroʊl/ – **the Tirol** *or* **the Tyrol** : region in Austria and Italy – **Ti·ro·le·an** /təˈroʊlijən/ *or* **Ti·ro·lese** /ˌtirəˈliːz/ *adj or noun*
Ti·ti·ca·ca, Lake /ˌtɪtɪˈkɑːkə/ : lake between Bolivia and Peru
Toa Baja /ˌtowɑˈbɑːhɑ/ : U.S. city, Puerto Rico
To·go /ˈtoʊgoʊ/ : country in Africa – **To·go·lese** /ˌtoʊgəˈliːz/ *adj or noun*
To·kyo /ˈtoʊkiˌoʊ/ : city in Japan – **To·kyo·ite** /ˈtoʊkiˌoʊˌaɪt/ *noun*
To·le·do /təˈliːdoʊ/ : U.S. city, Ohio
Ton·ga /ˈtɑːŋgə/ : island kingdom in the Pacific Ocean – **Ton·gan** /ˈtɑːŋgən/ *adj or noun*
Ton·kin, Gulf of /ˈtɑːŋkən/ – **the Gulf of Tonkin** : part of the South China Sea east of Vietnam
To·pe·ka /təˈpiːkə/ : U.S. city, Kansas
To·ron·to /təˈrɑːntoʊ/ : city in Ontario, Canada – **To·ron·to·ni·an** /təˌrɑːnˈtoʊnijən/ *adj or noun*
Tor·rance /ˈtorəns/ : U.S. city, California
Tran·syl·va·nia /ˌtrænsəlˈveɪnjə/ : region of Romania – **Tran·syl·va·nian** /ˌtrænsəlˈveɪnjən/ *adj or noun*
Trin·i·dad and Tobago /ˈtrɪnəˌdædəndtəˈbeɪgoʊ/ : island country in the West Indies – **To·ba·go·ni·an** /ˌtoʊbəˈgoʊnijən/ *noun* – **Trin·i·da·di·an** /ˌtrɪnəˈdeɪdijən/ *adj or noun*
Trip·o·li /ˈtrɪpəli/ : city in Libya
Tri·po·li·ta·nia /trɪˌpɑːləˈteɪnjə/ : region of Libya
Trois–Ri·vieres /ˌtwɑːrɪˈvjeɚ/ : city in Quebec, Canada
Troy /ˈtroɪ/ : city in ancient Asia Minor
Tuc·son /ˈtuˌsɑːn/ : U.S. city, Arizona
Tul·sa /ˈtʌlsə/ : U.S. city, Oklahoma – **Tul·san** /ˈtʌlsən/ *noun*
Tu·ni·sia /tuˈniːʒə/ : country in Africa – **Tu·ni·sian** /tuˈniːʒən/ *adj or noun*
Tur·key /ˈtɚki/ : country in Asia and Europe – **Turk** /ˈtɚk/ *noun* – **Turk·ish** /ˈtɚkɪʃ/ *adj*
Turk·men·i·stan /tɚkˌmɛnəˈstæn/ : country in Asia – **Turk·men** /ˈtɚkmən/ *adj or noun* – **Turk·me·ni·an** /ˌtɚkˈminijən/ *adj*
Turks and Cai·cos /ˌtɚksəndˈkeɪkəs/ : two groups of British islands in the West Indies
Tus·ca·ny /ˈtʌskəni/ : region of Italy – **Tus·can** /ˈtʌskən/ *adj or noun*
Tu·va·lu /tuˈvɑːlu/ : island country in the Pacific Ocean
Tyre /ˈtajɚ/ : city in ancient Phoenicia – **Tyr·i·an** /ˈtirijən/ *adj or noun*
Tyrol see TIROL – **Ty·ro·le·an** /təˈroʊlijən/ *or* **Ty·ro·lese** /ˌtirəˈliːz/ *adj or noun*
Ufa /uˈfɑː/ : city in Russia
Ugan·da /juˈgændə/ : country in Africa – **Ugan·dan** /juˈgændən/ *adj or noun*
Ukraine /juˈkreɪn/ : country in Europe – **Ukrai·ni·an** /juˈkreɪnijən/ *adj or noun*
Ul·san /ˈuːlsɑːn/ : city in South Korea
Ul·ster /ˈʌlstɚ/ : region of Ireland – **Ul·ster·ite** /ˈʌlstəˌraɪt/ *noun*
Un·gava Peninsula /ˌʌnˈgævə/ – **the Ungava Peninsula** : part of Quebec, Canada
Union of Soviet Socialist Republics *or* **Soviet Union** – **the Union of Soviet Socialist Republics** *or* **the Soviet Union** : former country of Europe and Asia
United Arab Emirates – **the United Arab Emirates** : country in Arabia
United Kingdom of Great Britain and Northern Ireland *or* **United Kingdom** – **the United Kingdom of Great Britain and Northern Ireland** *or* **the United Kingdom** : country in Europe
United Nations – **the United Nations** : political organization with headquarters in the U.S., in New York City
United States of America *or* **United States** – **the United States of America** *or* **the United States** : country in North America – **American** *adj or noun*
Upper Peninsula – **the Upper Peninsula** : area in the U.S., in Michigan
Ural /ˈjurəl/
1 the Ural Mountains *also* **the Urals** : mountains in Russia and Kazakhstan
2 the Ural River *also* **the Ural** : river in Russia and Kazakhstan
Uru·guay /ˈurəˌgwaɪ/
1 : country in South America
2 the Uruguay River : river in South America
– **Uru·guay·an** /ˌurəˈgwajən/ *adj or noun*
Ürüm·qi /uˈrumˈʧi/ : city in China
Utah /ˈjuːˌtɑː/ : state of the U.S. – **Utah·an** /ˈjuːˌtɑːn/ *adj or noun* – **Utahn** /ˈjuːˌtɑːn/ *noun*
Uz·bek·i·stan /ˌuzˌbɛkɪˈstæn/ : country in Asia
Va·do·da·ra /vəˈdoʊdəˌrɑː/ : city in India
Va·len·cia /vəˈlɛnʃijə/ : region of Spain
Val·le·jo /vəˈlejoʊ/ : U.S. city, California
Van·cou·ver /vænˈkuːvɚ/
1 : U.S. city, Washington
2 : island in British Columbia, Canada
3 : city in British Columbia, Canada
Van·u·atu /ˌvænˌwɑːˈtuː/ : island country in the Pacific Ocean
Va·ra·na·si /vəˈrɑːnəsi/ : city in India
Vat·i·can City /ˈvætɪkən/ : independent state within Rome, Italy
Vaughan /ˈvɑːn/ : city in Ontario, Canada
Vegas see LAS VEGAS
Ven·e·zu·e·la /ˌvɛnəˈzweɪlə/ : country in South America – **Ven·e·zu·e·lan** /ˌvɛnəˈzweɪlən/ *adj or noun*
Ven·ice /ˈvɛnəs/ : city in Italy – **Ve·ne·tian** /vəˈniːʃən/ *adj or noun*
Ven·tu·ra /vɛnˈturə/ *or officially* **San Buen·a·ven·tu·ra** /ˌsænˌbwɛnəˌvɛnˈturə/ : U.S. city, California
Ver·mont /vɚˈmɑːnt/ : state of the U.S. – **Ver·mont·er** /vɚˈmɑːntɚ/ *noun*
Ve·su·vi·us *or* **Mount Vesuvius** /vəˈsuːvijəs/ : volcano in Italy
Vi·en·na /viˈɛnə/ : city in Austria – **Vi·en·nese** /ˌvijəˈniːz/ *adj or noun*
Vie·ques /viˈeɪkeɪs/ : island of the U.S., in Puerto Rico
Viet·nam /vijətˈnɑːm/ : country in Asia – **Viet·nam·ese** /vijətnəˈmiz/ *adj or noun*
Vil·la Gus·ta·vo A. Ma·de·ro /ˈvijɑguˈstɑːvoʊˌɑːmɑˈðeɪroʊ/ : city in Mexico
Vir·gin·ia /vɚˈʤɪnjə/
1 : state of the U.S.
2 Virginia Beach : U.S. city, Virginia
– **Vir·gin·ian** /vɚˈʤɪnjən/ *adj or noun*
Vir·gin Islands – **the Virgin Islands** : group of British and U.S. islands in the West Indies
Vi·sa·lia /vaɪˈseɪljə/ : U.S. city, California
Voj·vo·di·na /ˈvoɪvɑˌdiːnə/ : region of Serbia
Vol·ga /ˈvɑːlgə, ˈvoʊlgə/ – **the Volga River** *also* **the Volga** : river in Russia
Vol·go·grad /ˈvɑːlgəˌgræd/ : city in Russia
Wa·co /ˈweɪkoʊ/ : U.S. city, Texas
Wai·ki·ki /ˌwaɪkɪˈkiː/ : section of the U.S. city of Honolulu, in Hawaii

Wake Island /ˈweɪk/ : U. S. island in the Pacific Ocean

Wal·den Pond /ˈwɑːldən/ : pond in the U.S., in Massachusetts

Wales /ˈweɪlz/ : part of the United Kingdom – **Welsh** /ˈwɛlʃ/ *adj or noun*

Wal·lo·nia /wɑˈloʊnijə/ : region of Belgium

War·ren /ˈworən/ : U.S. city, Michigan

War·saw /ˈworˌsɑː/ : city in Poland

Wash·ing·ton /ˈwɑːʃɪŋtən-/

1 : state of the U.S.

2 : city in the U.S. that has the same boundaries as the District of Columbia

– **Wash·ing·to·nian** /ˌwɑːʃɪŋˈtoʊnijən/ *adj or noun*

Wa·ter·bury /ˈwɑːtəˌberi/ : U.S. city, Connecticut

Wa·ter·loo /ˌwɑːtəˈluː/ : city in Ontario, Canada

Wel·land Canal /ˈwɛlənd/ – **the Welland Canal** : canal in Ontario, Canada, connecting Lake Erie with Lake Ontario

West Bank – **the West Bank** : area of the Middle East

West Co·vi·na /koʊˈviːnə/ : U.S. city, California

Western Hemisphere – **the Western Hemisphere** : half of the Earth west of the Atlantic Ocean

Western Sahara *or* **the Western Sahara** : area in Africa – **Western Saharan** *adj*

West In·dies /ˈɪndiz/ – **the West Indies** : islands between southeastern North America and northern South America – **West Indian** *adj or noun*

West·min·ster /ˈwestˌmɪnstə/ : U.S. city, Colorado

West·pha·lia /wɛstˈfeɪljə/ : region of Germany – **West·pha·lian** /wɛstˈfeɪljən/ *adj or noun*

West Valley City : U.S. city, Utah

West Virginia : state of the U.S. – **West Virginian** *adj or noun*

Whit·by /ˈwɪtbi/ : town in Ontario, Canada

Whit·ney, Mount /ˈwɪtni/ : mountain in the U.S., in California

Wich·i·ta /ˈwɪʧəˌtɑː/

1 : U.S. city, Kansas

2 Wichita Falls : U.S. city, Texas

Wil·liams·burg /ˈwɪljəmzˌbəg/ : U.S. city, Virginia

Wind·sor /ˈwɪnzə/ : city in Ontario, Canada

Win·ni·peg /ˈwɪnəˌpɛg/ : city in Manitoba, Canada – **Win·ni·peg·ger** /ˈwɪnəˌpɛgə/ *noun*

Win·ni·pe·sau·kee, Lake /ˌwɪnəpəˈsɑːki/ : lake in the U.S., in New Hampshire

Win·ston–Sa·lem /ˌwɪnstənˈseɪləm/ : U.S. city, North Carolina

Wis·con·sin /wɪˈskɑːnsən/ : state of the U.S. – **Wis·con·sin·ite** /wɪˈskɑːnsəˌnaɪt/ *noun*

Worces·ter /ˈwʊstə/ : U.S. city, Massachusetts

Wu·han /ˈwuˈhɑːn/ : city in China

Wy·o·ming /waɪˈoʊmɪŋ/ : state of the U.S. – **Wy·o·ming·ite** /waɪˈoʊmɪŋˌaɪt/ *noun*

Xi'·an /ˈʃiːˈɑːn/ : city in China

Xianggang see HONG KONG

Xizang see TIBET

Yan·gon /ˌjɑːŋˈgoʊn/ *or formerly* **Ran·goon** /rænˈguːn/ : city in Myanmar

Yangtze see CHANG

Ye·ka·te·rin·burg /jɪˈkætərənˌbəg/ : city in Russia

Yel·low·stone National Park /ˈjɛloʊˌstoʊn/ : national park in the U.S., in Wyoming, Idaho, and Montana

Ye·men /ˈjɛmən/ : country in Arabia – **Ye·me·ni** /ˈjɛməni/ *adj or noun* – **Ye·men·ite** /ˈjɛməˌnaɪt/ *adj or noun*

Yen·i·sey /ˌjɪnɪˈseɪ/ – **the Yenisey River** *also* **the Yenisey** : river in Russia

Ye·re·van /ˌjerəˈvɑːn/ : city in Armenia

Yo·ko·ha·ma /ˌjoʊkoʊˈhɑːmɑ/ : city in Japan

Yon·kers /ˈjɑːŋkəz/ : U.S. city, New York

York /ˈjoək/ : former city in Ontario, Canada

Yo·sem·i·te Falls /joʊˈsɛməti/ : waterfall in the U.S., in California

Yu·ca·tán Peninsula /ˌjuːkəˈtæn/ – **the Yucatan Peninsula** : part of Mexico and Central America

Yu·go·sla·via /ˌjuːgoʊˈslɑːvijə/ : former country in Europe – **Yu·go·slav** /ˌjuːgoʊˈslɑːv/ *or* **Yu·go·sla·vi·an** /ˌjuːgoʊˈslɑːvijən/ *adj or noun*

Yu·kon /ˈjuːˌkɑːn/

1 the Yukon River *also* **the Yukon** : river in the Yukon Territory and Alaska

2 the Yukon Territory : territory of Canada

Zaire see CONGO 1

Zam·be·zi /zæmˈbiːzi/ – **the Zambezi River** *also* **the Zambezi** : river in Africa

Zam·bia /ˈzæmbijə/ : country in Africa – **Zam·bi·an** /ˈzæmbijən/ *adj or noun*

Zan·zi·bar /ˈzænzəˌbɑə/ : island of Tanzania

Zheng·zhou /ˈʤʌŋˈʤoʊ/ : city in China

Zi·bo /ˈdzʌˈboʊ/ : city in China

Zim·ba·bwe /zɪmˈbɑːbwi/ *or formerly* **Rho·de·sia** /roʊˈdiːʒə/ : country in Africa – **Zim·ba·bwe·an** /zɪmˈbɑːbwiən/ *adj or noun*

Zu·rich /ˈzurɪk/ : city in Switzerland – **Zu·rich·er** /ˈzurɪkə/ *noun*

English Grammar Review

This section provides a review of the main elements of English grammar.

THE PARTS OF SPEECH

This dictionary identifies the eight traditional parts of speech. We will look at each of them in turn.

Nouns

Nouns, the largest class of words in English (and in most languages), are the names of things, people, animals, places, qualities, actions, and ideas. A noun that refers to one of these is ***singular***; while a noun that refers to more than one of these is ***plural.*** A noun is usually a single word, but not always: *cake, shoes, school bus,* and *time and a half* are all nouns.

For learners of English, the most important feature of a noun is whether it can be counted. A ***count noun*** is a noun that can be used after *a* or *an* or after a number (or another word that means "more than one"). Count nouns have both singular and plural forms and can be used with both singular and plural verb forms.

> A *letter* for you is on the table. *Letters* for you arrive regularly.
>
> That *man* is his partner. The two *men* are partners in the business.
>
> One *person* came in at noon. A few *people* are going to be late.
>
> Can I use your *cell phone*? Our *cell phones* aren't working here.

Sometimes the plural form of a count noun is the same as its singular form.

> I saw a *deer* in my yard yesterday. There are a lot of *deer* in the woods near my house.

A ***noncount*** (or ***mass***) ***noun*** refers to something that cannot be counted. Noncount nouns are normally not used after the words *a* or *an* or after a number. They have only one form and are used with singular verb forms.

> The *rain* is still coming down heavily.
>
> The *information* was unclear.
>
> Her *despair* now seems even deeper.

A few noncount nouns look like plurals but are used with the singular forms of verbs.

> *Physics* is what he likes best.
>
> The *news* that morning was good.

Gerunds, which are nouns that are identical to the ***present participle*** (*-ing* form) of a verb, are also noncount nouns.

> I enjoy *swimming* more than *running.*
>
> Her *crying* made me sad.

Not all nouns fall into the categories ***count*** and ***noncount.*** Nouns which only ever refer to one thing are called ***singular nouns.***

> *Saturn* is the sixth planet from the sun.
>
> We heard a terrible *din* in the alley.

A ***plural noun*** refers to more than one person or thing, or sometimes to something that has two main parts. Plural nouns have only one form and are used with plural verb forms.

> *Townspeople* are invited to a forum on the project.
>
> These *scissors* are dull.
>
> Her gray *pants* were being cleaned.

A particular noun can have any or all of these kinds of uses.

> [*count*] I've read that book several *times.*
>
> [*noncount*] *Time* seemed to stop when I saw him for the first time.
>
> [*singular*] The *time* is 3:22.
>
> [*plural*] Fuel costs three *times* as much as it did five years ago.

Other categories that can be used to describe nouns include ***common nouns*** and ***proper nouns.*** A common noun refers to a person, place, or thing but is not the name of a particular person, place, or thing. Examples are *animal, sunlight,* and *happiness.* A proper noun is the name of a particular person, place, or thing, and it begins with a capital letter: *Abraham Lincoln, Argentina,* and *World War I* are all proper nouns.

A ***collective noun*** is a noun that names a group of people or things. It is sometimes unclear whether the verb for a collective noun should be singular or plural. In the United States, such nouns as *company, team, herd, public,* and *class,* as well as the names of companies, teams, etc., are treated as singular, but in the United Kingdom they are often treated as plural.

The *jury has* [=(*Brit*) *have*] been seated.

The *crowd was* [=(*Brit*) *were*] restless.

The *committee is* [=(*Brit*) *are*] meeting now.

The British royal family *is* [=(*Brit*) *are*] partly German.

General Electric is [=(*Brit*) *are*] hoping for a contract with Kuwait.

Though English lacks grammatical ***gender*** (masculine, feminine, and neuter categories for words), the actual sex of a person or animal is evident in some nouns (*landlady, husband, bull, queen,* etc.). Feminine gender is often shown by the endings *-ess* and *-woman,* and masculine gender is often shown by the ending *-man.*

Pronouns

A ***pronoun*** is a word that is used instead of a noun or noun phrase. Pronouns refer to either a noun that has already been mentioned or to a noun that does not need to be named specifically.

The most common pronouns are the ***personal pronouns.*** These refer to the person or people speaking or writing (***first person***), the person or people being spoken to (***second person***), or other people or things (***third person***). Several of the personal pronouns have singular and plural forms. Like nouns, personal pronouns can function as either the ***subject*** of a verb or the ***object*** of a verb or preposition. Most of the personal pronouns have different subject and object forms.

	as subject	
	singular	**plural**
1st person	I	we
2nd person	you	you
3rd person	he, she, it	they

	as object	
	singular	**plural**
1st person	me	us
2nd person	you	you
3rd person	him, her, it	them

She likes *him,* but *he* loves *her.*

I sent *them* a wedding gift, and *they* thanked *me.*

We were late, and the train left without *us.*

I, me, you, he, she, him, her, his, we, and *us* can refer to people (most of these can also refer to animals) but not to things. *It* can refer to animals or things. *They* and *them* can refer to people, animals, or things.

The ***interrogative pronouns***—particularly *what, which, who, whom,* and *whose*—introduce questions for which a noun is the answer.

What are you taking?

Which do you prefer?

Who's at the door?

For *whom* are you working?

Whose is this?

(The less common interrogative pronouns include *whoever, whomever, whichever,* and *whatever.*) Interrogative pronouns are neither singular nor plural. *What, which,* and *whose* may also be ***interrogative adjectives***; see p. 1933.

Possessive pronouns refer to things or people that belong to someone. The main possessive pronouns are *mine, yours, his, hers, its, ours,* and *theirs.* Possessive pronouns take the place of a ***possessive adjective*** (see p. 1933) plus a noun.

It's *my book.* = It's *mine.*

That's *his computer.* = That's *his.*

This is *our house.* = This is *ours.*

Which are *your kids*? = Which are *yours*?

See Possession, p. 1948.

The four ***demonstrative pronouns—this, that, these,*** and *those*—distinguish the person or thing being referred to from other people or things. *This* and *these* indicate people or things that are here, nearby, or in the present. *That* and *those* are used to indicate people or things that are not here, not nearby, or in the past or future. The demonstrative pronouns are identical to the ***demonstrative adjectives*** (see p. 1932).

This situation is unfortunate. = *This* is unfortunate.

Who thought of *that* idea? = Who thought of *that*?

These dancers will replace *those* dancers. = *These* will replace *those.*

Relative pronouns introduce ***subordinate clauses.*** (A subordinate clause is part of a sentence that includes a subject and verb but does not form a sentence by itself; see p. 1945.) The main relative pronouns are *that, which, who, whom, what,* and *whose;* others include *whoever, whomever, whatever,* and *whichever.* Relative pronouns are neither singular nor plural.

She liked the students *who* talked in class.

The design *that* Stanley drew was quite odd.

The prizes go to *whoever* finishes first.

Reflexive pronouns refer back to the subject of a sentence or clause and are formed by adding *-self* or *-selves* to a personal pronoun or ***possessive adjective*** (p. 1933).

myself	ourselves
yourself	yourselves
himself, herself, itself	themselves

You think of *yourself* as a good person.

She told *herself* that it would be all right.

We were afraid the *children* might harm *themselves.*

Reflexive pronouns are also sometimes used for emphasis.

I'm sending my brother since *I* can't be there *myself.*

Indefinite pronouns do not refer to a specific person or thing. The most important indefinite pronouns include:

all	everything	nothing
another	few	one
any	less	the other
anybody	little	others
anyone	many	several
anything	more	some
both	most	somebody
each	much	someone
either	neither	something
enough	no one	such
everybody	nobody	
everyone	none	

No one wants to leave yet.

Several of the students hadn't arrived.

He finished his drink and asked for *another.*

They didn't choose *anybody* from my class.

One doesn't like to think of such things.

Most of the indefinite pronouns may also be used as ***indefinite adjectives*** (see p. 1932).

The words *it* and *there* can also be used like pronouns when the rules of grammar require a subject but no noun is actually being referred to. Both are usually used at the beginning of a sentence or clause.

It was almost noon.

It's raining.

It's very odd.

Sunday might be better, but *it* doesn't really matter.

There is some cake left.

There are many reasons to doubt him.

Agreement between a pronoun and the noun or pronoun that it refers to is essential (that is, a pronoun and the noun or pronoun that it refers to must be alike grammatically). There are three kinds of agreement.

First, a personal, possessive, or reflexive pronoun must agree in *person* with the noun or pronoun it refers to. The first person pronouns (*I, me, mine, myself, we, us, ours, ourselves*) can refer only to the person or persons speaking or writing. The second person pronouns (*you, yours, yourself, yourselves*) refer to the person or persons being spoken or written to. The third person pronouns (*he, she, it, they, him, her, them, his, hers, its, theirs, himself, herself, itself, themselves*) refer to everyone and everything else.

We already have *ours.*

You may serve *yourself.*

Second, most pronouns must agree in *number* with the noun or pronoun that they refer to. (Interrogative and relative pronouns do not indicate number.) A singular pronoun must refer to one person or thing, and a plural pronoun must refer to more than one person or thing.

That is the only *choice* we have.

Those are the only *choices* we have.

Finally, a personal pronoun must agree in *gender* with the noun or pronoun that it refers to (that is, a personal pronoun must match the person's sex). Animals are often treated as neuter.

He only drives *his* motorcycle on the weekends.

Antonia joined *her* father for lunch downtown.

The cat crept into the yard for *its* evening meal.

Number and gender together sometimes create a pronoun problem in the third person singular. English has no third person singular personal pronoun that can be used for both male and female people. Traditionally, *he, his, him,* and *himself* have been used when referring to someone whose sex is not known. However, this is now often regarded as sexist. Therefore, "he or she," "his or her," "him or her," and "himself or herself" are now often used instead, and the plural pronouns *they, their, them,* and *themselves* are used even more often.

Anyone can win if *they* buy a ticket. = Anyone can win if *he or she* buys a ticket.

Everyone has to bring *their* own lunch. = Everyone has to bring *his or her* own lunch.

Some people disapprove of using a plural pronoun in such cases because it does not display agreement in number. The use is very common, however, in speech and informal writing.

Pronouns, like nouns, must also agree with their *verbs* in person and number.

It is possible.

We're glad about that.

Since *-body, -one,* and *-thing* are singular forms, the indefinite pronouns *anybody, anyone, anything, everybody, everyone, everything, nobody, no one, nothing, somebody, someone,* and *something* are treated as singular.

Everybody is welcome.

Someone has to tell her.

Everything is fine.

Another, each, either, neither, one, and *(the) other* are also treated as singular.

I have six bowls for sale, and *each costs* $10.

There are two nurses on staff, but *neither is* here right now.

Verbs

This section provides a brief introduction to ***verbs.*** They are discussed at greater length at The English Verb System, p. 1936.

Verbs are words that show an action, occurrence, or state of being. Almost every sentence requires a verb. The basic form of a verb is known as its ***infinitive.***

call	beat
love	go

See Infinitives, p. 1940.

Almost all verbs have two other important forms called ***participles.*** Participles are forms that are used to create several verb ***tenses*** (forms that are used to show when an action happened); they can also be used as ***adjectives.*** The ***present participle*** always ends in *-ing.*

calling	beating
loving	going

(There is also a kind of noun, called a ***gerund,*** that is identical in form to the present participle form of a verb.)

The ***past participle*** usually ends in *-ed.* However, many past participles have irregular endings.

called	beaten
loved	gone

See Participles, p. 1940.

The verb's past tense (see p. 1937) usually has the same *-ed* form as the past participle. For many verbs, however, the past tense is irregular. An irregular past tense is not always identical to an irregular past participle.

called	beat
loved	went

The infinitive form, past tense, and past participle are often called the ***principal parts*** of the verb. Sometimes the present participle is also included in the principal parts. From these, all the tenses and forms of almost any verb can be created. A ***regular verb*** forms its past tense and past participle with *-ed.* An ***irregular verb*** forms either its past tense or its past participle, or both, without *-ed.*

infinitive	**past tense**	**past participle**
call	called	called
love	loved	loved
beat	beat	beaten
go	went	gone

Many common English verbs are irregular. See a list of these at Irregular Verbs, p. 1953.

A ***transitive verb*** is a verb that requires a ***direct object,*** which is a noun, pronoun, or noun phrase that follows it and completes the sentence's meaning by indicating the person or thing that receives the action of the verb.

The kids *like pickles.*

That really *annoys me.*

Have they *sold their house* yet?

An ***intransitive verb*** is not used with a direct object.

Her aunt *died* suddenly last week.

Someone was *coughing* loudly.

A single verb can have both transitive and intransitive uses.

They are *playing* soccer.

They've been *playing* all afternoon.

Transitive verb entries or senses in this dictionary are labeled [*+obj*], while intransitive entries or senses are labeled [*no obj*]. See Transitive and Intransitive Verbs, p. 1941.

In most sentences that contain a transitive verb, the subject is the person or thing that performs the verb's action. However, sometimes the subject is a person or thing that is affected by the action. Sentences of the first type represent ***active voice***; those of the second type represent ***passive voice.***

My grandfather *built* the barn.

The barn *was built* by my grandfather.

See Active and Passive Voice, p. 1941.

A ***linking verb,*** such as *be, seem, look, become,* or *feel,* connects a noun subject with an adjective or with a noun that is not a direct object. The most common linking verb is *be.*

They*'re* tired and hungry.

His father *was* a lawyer.

Some linking verbs involve the five senses. Others involve mental impressions. Still others have the basic meaning "become" or "continue to be."

Her voice *sounded* familiar.

It *feels* cold in here.

She *seems* very nervous.

It *appears* later than it is.

His ears *turned* red.

They *remained* best friends.

The label [*linking verb*] identifies these verbs in this dictionary.

An ***auxiliary verb*** is a verb that is used with another verb to show the verb's tense, to form a question, etc.

The work *was* completed last year.

Where *did* they go?

The rain *has* stopped.

The label [*auxiliary verb*] identifies these verbs in this dictionary. See Auxiliary Verbs, p. 1938.

Modal verbs (also called ***modals, modal auxiliaries,*** and ***modal auxiliary verbs***) are auxiliary verbs like *can, must,* and *might* that are used with another verb to express ideas such as possibility, necessity, and permission.

They *can* leave whenever they want.

She *must* return the key this morning.

It *might* be too late.

The label [*modal verb*] identifies these verbs in this dictionary. See Modal Verbs, p. 1939.

Phrasal verbs are usually two-word verbs made from a one-word verb and an adverb or a preposition. (Occasionally they are three-word verbs that include *both* an adverb and a preposition.) Phrasal verbs have meanings that are quite different from the meaning of the simple verb by itself.

They're driving to Caracas to *pick up* two friends.

The boss told us that we could *knock off* at 4:00.

Tired after the long trip, they *turned in* after dinner.

The label [*phrasal verb*] identifies these verbs in this dictionary. See Phrasal Verbs, p. 1943.

English verbs may use three different ***moods.*** A mood is a set of verb forms that show whether the action or state expressed by the verb is thought of as a fact, a command, or a wish or possibility. The very common ***indicative*** mood is used for ordinary statements.

The strawberries *are* already ripe.

The ***imperative*** mood is used for commands and instructions.

Let me tie your shoe.

Run!

The ***subjunctive*** mood is used to express something different from simple fact, such as wishes, possibilities, or requests.

She would prefer that he *go* alone.

See Mood, p. 1942.

Adjectives

Adjectives describe nouns and pronouns. They may name qualities of all kinds: *huge, red, forty, angry, African, unique, talking, lost, female, rare, thoughtful, ancient, technical, best,* etc.

An adjective usually comes right before a noun.

a high mountain

fifteen people

the dull, heavy beat

When an adjective follows a linking verb such as *be* or *seem,* it is called a ***predicate adjective.***

That building is *huge.*

The workers seem *angry.*

Most adjectives can be used as predicate adjectives. In this dictionary, adjectives that cannot be used as predicate adjectives include the note "*always used before a noun.*" Similarly, the few adjectives that can *only* be used as predicate adjectives are identified with the note "*not used before a noun.*"

Some adjectives describe qualities that can exist in different amounts or degrees. To do this, the adjective will either change in form (usually by adding *-er* or *-est*) or will be used with words like *more, most, very, slightly,* etc.

the *older* girls

the *longest* day of the year

a *very strong* feeling

more expensive than that one

Other adjectives describe qualities that do not vary.

nuclear energy

a *medical* doctor

See Comparison, p. 1949.

The most common of all adjectives are the two (or three) ***articles.*** An article always comes before the noun it describes and before any other adjectives that also describe the noun. Articles are used to show whether or not the noun refers to a specific person or thing. The ***indefinite article*** is *a;* it identifies a single, but not specific, person or thing. *An* is used instead of *a* whenever the word following it begins with a vowel sound.

Are you going to buy *a* house?

The smile is *a* universal sign of pleasure.

It's *an* honor to have been invited.

I've got *an* uncle in Miami.

The ***definite article*** is *the;* it is used to refer to identified or specified people or things, both singular and plural.

Will you be painting *the* house this summer?

He's *the* uncle I was telling you about.

Please put *the* dishes away.

A singular count noun (such as *idea* or *bird*) or singular noun (such as *patter*) is always preceded by a definite or indefinite article or other adjective.

The is used with both count and noncount nouns. It is used when the noun is something that the reader or listener already knows, or something that will be described in the sentence. It is also used when the thing is unique, or when a phrase following the noun distinguishes it from others of its kind.

Give me *the* keys.

That's not *the* subject we were discussing.

The prime minister of Turkey had been invited.

That was *the* news that they wanted to hear.

She's *the* kindest woman I know.

The is not used when a noun is used to refer to a thing in general or to all things of its kind.

I like salsa music.

Cows eat grass.

Water is heavier than oil.

The meaning of these sentences changes if *the* is inserted before the nouns. For example, "I like the salsa music" means "I like the particular salsa music that is playing now."

The is rarely used with proper nouns.

The hotel is on Eighth Avenue. [not *The hotel is on the Eighth Avenue.*]

I caught the fish in Lake Baikal. [not *I caught the fish in the Lake Baikal.*]

However, it is used with some geographical names that end with a general term (such as *River, Bay,* or *Mountains*), and often with proper nouns that occur in the plural.

in *the* Sahara Desert

the Geneva Conventions

The four ***demonstrative adjectives**—this, that, these,* and *those*—are identical to the ***demonstrative pronouns*** (p. 1928). They are used to distinguish the person or thing being described from others of the same category or class. *This* and *these* describe people or things that are nearby, or in the present. *That* and *those* are used to describe people or things that are not here, not nearby, or in the past or future. These adjectives, like *a, an,* and *the,* always come before any other adjectives that modify a noun.

Do you want *this* one here or *that* blue one over there?

She answered *that* question easily, but *these* new questions will be more difficult.

I was happier in *those* early days.

We'll deal with *those* problems when they arise.

An ***indefinite adjective*** describes a whole group or class of people or things, or a person or thing that is not identified or familiar. The most common indefinite adjectives are:

all	half	one, two,
another	least	three, etc.
any	less	other
both	little	several
each	many	some
either	more	such
enough	most	whole
every	much	
few	neither	

Any pen will do.

Some people were unhappy with the decision.

He had *other* reasons.

Adjectives that express amount or number are sometimes called ***quantifiers,*** and many quantifiers are indefinite adjectives. Some of these are used only with count nouns.

both friends

few friends

two friends

several friends

many friends

Others are used only with noncount nouns.

little cash

less cash

much cash

And others can be used with both count and noncount nouns.

all friends/cash

any friends/cash

enough friends/cash

most friends/cash

no friends/cash

some friends/cash

Most indefinite adjectives can also be used as ***indefinite pronouns*** (see p. 1929).

There isn't *any* left.

Some were unhappy with the decision.

Five of them were caught, but three *others* escaped.

The ***interrogative adjectives***—primarily *which, what,* and *whose*—are used to begin questions. They can also be used as ***interrogative pronouns*** (see p. 1928).

Which horse did you bet on? = *Which* did you bet on?

What songs did they sing? = *What* did they sing?

Whose coat is this? = *Whose* is this?

See Questions, p. 1946.

The ***possessive adjectives***—*my, your, his, her, its, our, their*—tell you who has, owns, or has experienced something.

He admired *her* intelligence.

Our cat is 14 years old.

They said *their* trip was wonderful.

See also the discussion of ***possessive pronouns,*** p. 1928.

Proper adjectives are based on proper nouns and start with a capital letter.

The best gift was a box of *French* chocolates.

Charles Dickens wrote during the *Victorian* era.

Their children attended a *Christian* school.

Since English lacks grammatical ***gender,*** adjectives do not change their form to match the gender of a noun.

my *weird* sister

my *weird* brother

Nouns often function like adjectives. When they do, they are called ***attributive nouns.*** Most nouns can be used in this way. When they are, they always precede the nouns they are modifying. A noun used like an adjective does not change its form, except that it usually omits any plural ending.

his *research* paper

the *apartment* building

a *lemon* drink

Two or more attributive nouns may be used together. Unlike other adjectives, they are never separated by commas. When attributive nouns and true adjectives are used together, the true adjectives precede the attributive nouns.

new *work safety* rules

the experienced *summer baseball league* staff

When two or more adjectives are used before a noun, they should be put in proper ***order.*** Any article (*a, an, the*), demonstrative adjective (*that, these,* etc.), indefinite adjective (*another, both,* etc.), or possessive adjective (*her, our,* etc.) always comes first. If there is a number, it comes first or second. As noted above, true adjectives always come before attributive nouns. The ordering of true adjectives will vary, but the following order is the most common: *opinion word* → *size* → *age* → *shape* → *color* → *nationality* → *material.* (In the examples below, only the true adjectives and not the attributive nouns are shown in italics.)

the old Russian coins

those first few words

valuable company phone records

his three clean shirts

brutal young gang members

several large, bluish-green, wooden chairs

Participles are often used like ordinary adjectives. They may come before a noun or after a linking verb. A present participle (an *-ing* word) describes the person or thing that causes something; for example, a *boring* conversation is one that bores you. A past participle (usually an *-ed* word) describes the person or thing who has been affected by something; for example, a *bored* person is one who has been affected by boredom.

They had just watched an *exciting* soccer game.

The instructions were *confusing.*

The *freezing* wind kept everyone indoors all day.

She's *excited* about the trip to North Africa.

Several *confused* students were asking questions about the test.

The lake was *frozen.*

See Participles, p. 1940.

Adverbs

Adverbs usually modify verbs. They may also modify adjectives, other adverbs, phrases, or even entire sentences.

An adverb answers the question "When?" "Where?" "How?" "How much?" "How long?" or "How often?"

The elections are coming *soon.*

They only shopped *locally.*

She was *happily* married to a truck driver.

The roads are *very* steep.

He stopped by *briefly* to say hello.

My son calls me *regularly.*

Most adverbs are formed by adding *-ly* to an adjective. If the adjective already ends in *-y*, the *-y* usually changes to *-i*.

bold / boldly
solid / solidly
interesting / interestingly
heavy / heavily
unnecessary / unnecessarily

Common adverbs that do not end in -ly include:

again	more	today
also	never	too
always	not	very
as	now	well
even	often	when
ever	sometimes	where
here	soon	why
how	then	
just	there	

The words *when, where, why,* and *how* are called ***interrogative adverbs*** when they begin a question.

When did the shooting occur?

Where is the proof?

Why was he so late?

How did they get here?

See Questions, p. 1946.

The ***relative adverbs***—*where, when,* and *why* (*how* is sometimes included as well)—introduce ***subordinate*** (or ***dependent***) ***clauses*** (clauses that do not form simple sentences by themselves; see p. 1945).

This is the house *where* I grew up.

They go to bed *when* they want to.

He wondered *why* the door was open.

See Complex Sentences, p. 1945.

When an adverb modifies a whole sentence or clause, it is called a ***sentence adverb.*** Words such as *fortunately, frankly, hopefully,* and *luckily* are generally used as sentence adverbs and usually express the speaker's feelings about the content of the sentence. Such adverbs normally come at the beginning of a sentence, but may also come in the middle or at the end.

Unfortunately, Friday will be cloudy.

Friday, *unfortunately,* will be cloudy.

Friday will be cloudy, *unfortunately.*

An adverb may not come between a verb and its direct or indirect object.

They *soon* informed the admiral. [<u>not</u> *They informed soon the admiral.*]

The trees were *slowly* losing their leaves. [<u>not</u> *The trees were losing slowly their leaves.*]

Later they bought him a new bike. [<u>not</u> *They bought later him a new bike.*or *They bought him later a new bike.*]

Many adverbs, like many adjectives, describe qualities that can exist in different amounts or degrees.

This time she was working more *carefully.*

The bus arrived *sooner* than they expected.

The most *frequently* used word is probably *the.*

See Comparison, p. 1949.

Many adverbs, such as *past, under, off, along,* and *on,* may also act as ***prepositions*** (see the section immediately below). A few, such as *however, also, thus,* and *nevertheless,* may act as ***conjunctions*** (words that join together other words or groups of words; see p. 1935).

Prepositions

Prepositions, a very important class of words in English, show direction, location, or time, or introduce an object. They are usually followed by an object—a noun, noun phrase, or pronoun. The most common prepositions are:

at	from	on
by	in	to
for	of	with

Also common are:

about	between	outside
above	close to	over
across	down	past
after	during	since
against	except	through
along	inside	toward
among	instead of	under
around	into	until
because of	like	up
before	near	upon
behind	off	within
below	on top of	without
beneath	onto	
beside	out of	

Prepositions typically show how the noun, noun phrase, or pronoun is related to another word in the sentence.

a friend *of* mine
the dress *with* the stripes
hit *by* a car
no one *except* me

The preposition and its object normally form a ***prepositional phrase***; see p. 1944.

A preposition may appear at the end of a sentence or clause, but only when its object comes earlier.

Was he the man she lived *with*?

That isn't what a hammer is *for*.

It's the chair you're sitting *on*.

She just needs someone to talk *to*.

Many prepositions (such as *past, under, off, along,* and *on*) may also act as adverbs. A few (including *before, after, for,* and *since*) may act as conjunctions (words that join together other words or groups of words).

	preposition	**adverb**	**conjunction**
after	I saw them *after* the game.	We were due at noon, but didn't arrive until *after*.	Call me *after* it's over.
for	I baked it *for* you.		It was true, *for* I saw it myself.
since	I've waited *since* noon.	He's never been the same *since*.	It's been years *since* I've sung.
past	Walk *past* the store.	The train had gone *past*.	
off	It fell *off* the bed.	The kids wandered *off*.	

Conjunctions

Conjunctions are words that join together other words or groups of words.

A ***coordinating conjunction*** connects words, phrases, and clauses of equal importance. The main coordinating conjunctions are *and, or,* and *but.*

They bought apples, pears, *and* oranges.

You can wait either on the steps *or* in the car.

Her paintings are pleasant *but* bland.

The dogs barked, *but* he just ignored them.

When placed at the beginning of a sentence, a coordinating conjunction may also link two sentences or paragraphs.

War loomed on the horizon. *But* the country wasn't ready for another war.

She told him that he would have to work to earn her trust. *And* he proceeded to do just that.

A ***subordinating conjunction*** introduces a ***subordinate clause*** (a clause that does not form a simple sentence by itself; see p. 1945) and joins it to a ***main clause*** (a clause that can be used as a simple sentence by itself; see p. 1945).

She waited *until* the students were quiet.

They had been lonely *since* their father left.

See Complex Sentences, p. 1945.

Some conjunctions are used in pairs. The most common pairs are *either . . . or, both . . . and, neither . . . nor,* and *not only . . . but (also).* If verbs follow each conjunction, both verbs must be in the same form.

They could *either* continue searching or go to the police.

Both Clara *and* Jeanette graduated from Stanford.

He could *neither* sing *nor* dance.

Not only the money *but also* the jewelry had been taken.

Some adverbs act like conjunctions by linking either two main clauses separated by a semicolon (;) or two separate sentences. They express some effect that the first clause or sentence has on the second one. The most common adverbs that do this are:

accordingly	meanwhile
afterwards	moreover
also	namely
anyway	nevertheless
besides	nonetheless
consequently	otherwise
finally	regardless
for example	similarly
for instance	so
however	still
incidentally	that is
indeed	therefore
in fact	thus
likewise	

They didn't agree; *however,* each understood the other's opinion.

We'll probably regret it; *still,* we really have no choice.

The team has won its last three games. *Thus,* its record for the year is now 15–12.

Interjections

An interjection is a word or phrase that is grammatically independent and mainly expresses feeling rather than meaning.

Oh, what a beautiful house!

Uh-oh, this looks bad.

Well, it's time to say good night.

Actually, *um,* she's not my girlfriend.

Shoot. I thought I'd fixed that.

Interjections are common in speech and are much more common in electronic messages than in other types of writing.

THE ENGLISH VERB SYSTEM

The following sections discuss in detail all the kinds, forms, and functions of English verbs.

Verb Tenses

Tenses are the different forms used by almost all English verbs to show when an action happened. English verb forms are simple, but the ways that verbs may be combined can be complex.

Present Tenses

The ***present tense*** is used to refer to the period of time that exists now. It always uses the basic form of the verb, called the ***infinitive,*** except in the ***third-person*** singular.

I understand	we understand
you understand	you understand
he/she/it understands	they understand

The third-person singular normally adds *-s* to the infinitive. Verbs ending in *-ch, -s, -sh, -x,* and *-z* add *-es.* In verbs ending in *-y* preceded by a consonant, the *-y* changes to *-ies.* (If a vowel precedes the *-y,* the *-y* does not change.) *Do* changes to *does, go* changes to *goes,* and *have* changes to *has.*

The monument *sits* atop a hill.

She loves him and he *loves* her.

The iguana sometimes *catches* small birds.

The road *crosses* a river.

Her book *mixes* biography and fantasy.

He *relies* on his parents for money.

The dog's barking *annoys* our neighbors.

What *does* she want?

Be is the most irregular of all verbs in the present tense (I *am,* you/we/they *are,* he/she/it *is*).

The present tense is used to talk about something that is true now and most of the time. It is also used for something that happens regularly.

He *lives* in Nigeria.

Baghdad *lies* on the Tigris River.

Do they really *believe* that?

Haste *makes* waste.

She *reads* several books a month.

Buses *come* often on weekdays.

The ***present progressive*** (or ***present continuous***) tense uses *am/are/is* with the ***present participle*** (*-ing* form) of the main verb.

I am coming	we are coming
you are coming	you are coming
he/she/it is coming	they are coming

The present progressive tense indicates that something is happening right now or is continuing to happen.

How many miles *are* you *running* these days?

The engine *is leaking* oil.

The prime minister *is traveling* all this week.

Let's talk later—I*'m eating* lunch.

She's still *sleeping.*

It is also used to talk informally about events in the near future.

We*'re eating* out tonight.

Are you *coming* next week?

Some verbs or senses of verbs always use the present tense in situations where you might expect the present progressive tense. These include most verbs related to the five senses

Do you *hear* it? [*not* *Are you hearing it?*]

This *tastes* funny. [*not* *This is tasting funny.*]

It *feels* heavy. [*not* *It is feeling heavy.*]

and most verbs connected with mental states and functions.

We only *want* peace. [*not* *We're only wanting peace.*]

They *believe* him. [*not* *They're believing him.*]

She *knows* the answer. [*not* *She's knowing the answer.*]

I don't *remember.* [*not* *I'm not remembering.*]

That *seems* strange to me. [*not* *That is seeming strange to me.*]

These verbs also include verbs of possession such as *own, belong,* and *have.*

The company *owns* at least forty stores. [*not* *The company is owning at least forty stores.*]

His aunt *has* a house in the country. [*not* *His aunt is having a house in the country.*]

The label "*not used in progressive tenses*" is used in the book to identify these verbs and verb senses.

Special tenses called the ***perfect tenses*** are used to show a relationship between two different times. The ***present perfect*** tense uses *have/has* with the ***past participle*** (a form usually identical to the past tense that generally expresses completed action).

I have finished	we have finished
you have finished	you have finished
he/she/it has finished	they have finished

The present perfect is used to talk about (1) activities or states that began in the past and are completed at the time of speaking, (2) past activities that have a result in the present, (3) events that have just happened, and (4) events that happened at an unspecified time in the past.

I *have fixed* the radio.

This evidence *has influenced* our decision.

We*'ve eaten* dinner.

She *has decided* not to go to college.

Several adverbs that indicate time—*just, since, already, yet,* and *ever*—are often used with the present perfect to connect the past with the present.

I*'ve just returned* from Memphis.

I saw her Tuesday but I *have*n't *seen* her *since.*

We*'ve already seen* that movie.

Have you *gotten* your grades *yet*?

Did he *ever love* her?

The ***present perfect progressive*** (or ***present perfect continuous***) tense combines *have/has been* and a present participle (*-ing* form).

I have been studying	we have been studying
you have been studying	you have been studying
he/she/it has been studying	they have been studying

The present perfect progressive tense is used to talk about events that began in the past and continue in the present moment.

The war *has been raging* since 1997.

How long *have* you *been waiting*?

We*'ve been painting* the house this weekend.

Have they *been playing* video games all morning?

Past Tenses

The ***past tense*** is used to talk about events that began and ended in the past. The form of a verb in the past tense is the same in the first person, second person, and third person, and in the singular and plural (except in the verb *be*). For regular verbs, the past tense is normally formed by adding *-ed* (or just *-d* if the verb ends in *-e*) to the infinitive. If the verb ends with a short vowel and a single consonant and is accented on the last syllable, its final consonant is doubled. If it ends in *-y*, the *-y* usually changes to *-i*. (If a vowel precedes the *-y*, the *-y* doesn't change.)

talk	The two women *talked* for hours.
wave	He *waved* to the kids from the window.
stop	They *stopped* at the store.
try	Diplomats *tried* to bring the two sides together.

Irregular verbs have an irregular past-tense form.

build	They *built* a new house on the hill.
come	She *came* at six this morning.
go	The taxi *went* the wrong way.
speak	He *spoke* to the governor about it.

See list of Irregular Verbs, p. 1953.

The ***imperfect*** tense (also known as the ***past progressive*** or ***past continuous*** tense) is formed from *was/were* and a present participle (*-ing* form).

I was sleeping	we were sleeping
you were sleeping	you were sleeping
he/she/it was sleeping	they were sleeping

The imperfect tense is used to talk about incomplete actions in the past or about states that continued for a period of time in the past. It is often used in the same sentence with a verb in the past tense.

We *were driving* home and forgot to stop.

I bought it when I *was living* in London.

The ***past perfect*** tense is formed from *had* and a past participle.

I had imagined	we had imagined
you had imagined	you had imagined
he/she/it had imagined	they had imagined

The past perfect is used to refer to an action that was completed by a particular time in the past. Like the imperfect tense, it often is used in sentences with another verb in the past tense.

I *had met* him only once before he moved away.

We *hadn't known* that she had a daughter.

When it is clear what other event is referred to, the clause with the other verb may be omitted.

I *had met* him only once.

We *hadn't known.*

The informal verb *used to,* followed by an infinitive, functions much like the simple past tense. *Used to* refers to something that happened or existed in the past but no longer happens or exists. It refers especially to something that happened repeatedly or to a situation that lasted for a period of time.

This room *used to be* filled with junk.

When they were first in love, they *used to meet* at night down by the river.

The form "use to" is rarely seen in writing but is heard in informal speech, always with *did* or *didn't.*

Did you *use to go out* with Kate?

I *didn't use to like* broccoli, but now I do.

The ***past perfect progressive*** (or ***past perfect continuous***) tense is formed from *had been* and a present participle (*-ing* form).

I had been reading	we had been reading
you had been reading	you had been reading
he/she/it had been reading	they had been reading

The past perfect progressive is somewhat rare. It is generally used in sentences that have another verb.

We *had been living* there a year when the baby was born.

Future Tenses

The ***future tense*** is formed with *will* and an infinitive.

I will arrive	we will arrive
you will arrive	you will arrive
he/she/it will arrive	they will arrive

The future tense predicts a future event or condition.

Christmas *will be* on a Friday this year.

My mother *will retire* in June.

In the first person, the formal *shall* is sometimes used in place of *will.*

I shall [=*will*] inform them immediately.

We shall [=*will*] *expect* a full report from you.

An informal form of the future tense uses *am/are/is going to* instead of *will.* The *going to* future tense is very common in speech.

I am going to arrive	we are going to arrive
you are going to arrive	you are going to arrive
he/she/it is going to arrive	they are going to arrive

I hope my parents *are going to* [=*will*] *like* it.

It*'s going to* [=*will*] *be* hot tomorrow.

The ***future progressive*** (or ***future continuous***) tense is formed with *will be* and a present participle (*-ing* form).

I will be dancing	we will be dancing
you will be dancing	you will be dancing
he/she/it will be dancing	they will be dancing

The future progressive is used to talk about an activity that will be happening in the future, or an activity happening now that will end in the future.

On Friday the committee *will be meeting* again.

We*'ll be staying* here for two weeks.

The ***future perfect*** tense is formed from *will have* and a past participle.

I will have gone	we will have gone
you will have gone	you will have gone
he/she/it will have gone	they will have gone

The future perfect, a rarely used tense, is used to refer to an action that will be completed by a specified time in the future.

By this time tomorrow they *will have arrived.*

She*'ll have left* before the ceremony begins.

The ***future perfect progressive*** (or ***future perfect continuous***) tense is formed from *will have been* and a present participle (*-ing* form).

I will have been skiing	we will have been skiing
you will have been skiing	you will have been skiing
he/she/it will have been skiing	they will have been skiing

The future perfect progressive is very rare. It is used to talk about a time in the future when an activity that began earlier will still be continuing.

In May we *will have been living* here for ten years.

Kinds of Verbs

Action Verbs

Action verbs, as the name suggests, simply express action. Most verbs fall into this category and include such words as *care, drive, think,* and *distinguish.*

The children *ran* across the field.

Can you *build* a fire?

I *think* that's the right answer.

Linking Verbs

Linking verbs connect a subject with an adjective or noun that describes or identifies the subject. They include *act, aggregate, appear, be, become, come, constitute, equal, feel, form, get, go, grow, keep, look, make, measure, prove, remain, represent, seem, smell, sound, stay, taste,* and *turn.*

Today *is* Friday.

It *became* clear that we needed to find another solution.

The tea *tastes* sweet.

All of these can also be used as action verbs. Their linking verb senses are labeled [*linking verb*] in this dictionary.

Auxiliary Verbs

An ***auxiliary verb*** (or ***helping verb***) is used with another verb (or two other verbs) in a verb phrase.

Be, Have,* and *Do

The verbs *be, have,* and *do* are used both as independent verbs and as auxiliary verbs.

Have is used to form all the perfect tenses ("has worked," "had worked," "have been working," etc.), including the modal perfect tenses ("must have worked," etc.). See pp. 1936–37 and 1939 (below).

Be is used to form all the progressive tenses ("is talking," "was talking," "have been talking," etc.) as well as the passive voice ("is pulled," "was pulled," "is being pulled," etc.) and is also used to join *to* infinitives to the subject of a sentence or clause ("she is to retire soon"). See Active and Passive Voice, p. 1941; Infinitives, p. 1940.

Do occurs as an auxiliary verb mainly in negative sentences and in questions. See Negation, p. 1948, and Questions, p. 1946.

Do is also occasionally used for emphasis. In this use, *do* is followed by an infinitive without *to,* just like the modal verbs (see below).

I really *do* want to go.

He *does* talk a lot.

A few jobs *did* need to be finished first.

Do may also substitute for another verb that has just been stated.

This one doesn't look large enough, and neither *does* that one.

Did they succeed? No, they *didn't.*

Her mother worked all day, and so *did* his sister. [=and his sister also worked all day]

Notice that this is possible even when the other verb does not have an auxiliary *do.*

Modal Verbs

A small group of auxiliary verbs, called the ***modal verbs*** (or ***modal auxiliary verbs, modal auxiliaries,*** or simply ***modals***), are only used in combination with ordinary verbs. A modal verb changes the other verb's meaning to something different from simple fact. Modals may express permission, ability, prediction, possibility, or necessity. The principal modal verbs are:

can	ought
could	shall
may	should
might	will
must	would

A few other verbs are closely related to the true modal verbs, especially

had better	need
have to	dare

The modal verbs are different from ordinary verbs in several ways: (1) Modal verbs have no inflections at all; that is, they lack an *-ing* form, an *-ed* form, and even an *-s* form for the third-person singular. (2) A modal verb is always followed by the infinitive form of a verb (unless that verb has already been stated) but never follows another verb. (3) Modal verbs do not follow *to* and are not followed by *to.* (*Ought to,* like the near-modal verb *have to,* is a special case.)

In their simple form, modal verbs normally refer to present or future time.

It *must be* almost 10:00.

He *might call* tomorrow.

That road *can be* dangerous.

The ***modal progressive*** also expresses present or future time, especially in conversation. It is formed with *be* and a present participle (*-ing* form).

See if they're upstairs—they *could be watching* TV.

We *could be going* to El Salvador next year.

Past tense involving modals is usually expressed by the ***modal perfect,*** in which the modal verb is followed by *have* and a past participle.

It *must have happened* last year. [=It's very likely that it happened last year.]

He *might have called* yesterday. [=It's possible that he called yesterday.]

But *will have* or *shall have* with a past participle forms the ordinary future perfect.

By tomorrow he *will have called.*

We *shall* [or *will*] *have left* before September.

Most modal verbs lack a true past tense. However, *could* often functions as the past tense of *can; could* and *might* often function as the past tense of *may;* and *would* often functions as the past tense of both *will* and *shall. Could, might, ought, would,* and *should* keep the same form in the past tense.

I know I *can* take the train if necessary.

I knew I *could* take the train if necessary.

The next few months *could* be difficult.

Everyone knew the next few months *could* be difficult.

He believes that the stock market *may* suffer.

He believed that the stock market *might* suffer.

They think the war *will* be over soon.

They thought the war *would* be over soon.

I think I *shall* stay home.

I thought I *would* stay home.

It *could* take a while.

She said it *could* take a while.

The weatherman says it *might* snow.

The weatherman said it *might* snow.

We realize we *ought* to leave.

We realized we *ought* to leave.

It *would* be better to remain silent.

She said it *would* be better to remain silent.

He thinks we *should* leave.

He thought we *should* leave.

Must is rarely used in the past tense; *have to* is generally used instead.

We all realize that the factory *must* [=*has to*] close.

In 1988 the factory *had to* close.

Had better remains the same in the present and past.

They *had better* get there soon.

They knew they *had better* get there soon.

In the present tense, certain modal verbs often have the same meaning as certain others.

We *might* [=*may, could*] go to the movies tonight.

She *could* [=*might, may*] have stopped there on the way back.

You *can* [=*may*] read for an hour before bedtime.

He *should* [=*ought to*] drive more carefully.

A modal verb has little meaning without another verb. But the other verb is often omitted when it has just been stated, especially in conversation.

"Do you think you'll stay in Paris?" "I might."

"He may go to graduate school." "I think he should."

For more examples, see the individual entries for these verbs. For the use of *will* and *shall* in the future tenses, see p. 1938. See also Questions, p. 1946; Negation, p. 1948; Active and Passive Voice, p. 1941; Conditional Sentences, p. 1950; and Contractions, p. 1957.

Other Verb Forms

Two kinds of verb forms—***infinitives*** and ***participles***—have no tense by themselves. They may be used either (1) in combination with some other verb or (2) as some other part of speech, such as a noun or an adjective.

Infinitives

The infinitive is the basic form of the verb. It is used by itself in the present tense.

I've done everything but *issue* a formal apology.

Usually, however, it is preceded by *to* and follows another verb that expresses tense, person, and number.

I *needed to sleep* a few more hours.

It *was* hard *to see* in the dense fog.

College students *like to party* on weekends.

The infinitive without *to* sometimes follows the verbs *make, do, see, feel, hear,* and *watch.*

We *watched* him *light* the candles one by one.

Please *make* them *stop.*

Did you ever *see* her *dance*?

A few verbs are always followed by an infinitive without *to.* They are *let, have* (when *have* means "to cause, tell, or ask someone to do something"), and the modal verbs.

Don't *let* him *take* my car.

Have her *bring* us the check.

You *must be* here when I get back.

The *to* infinitive can be used as a noun, adjective, or adverb or (more often) in a noun phrase, adjective phrase, or adverb phrase.

noun phrase:	*To learn English* is my main goal.
	Our aim is *to make you feel at home.*
adjective phrase:	Her attempt *to solve the problem* failed.
adverb phrase:	He only wanted *to help his friends.*

In a noun phrase, the *to* infinitive can usually be replaced by a ***gerund*** (a noun in the form of a present participle).

Learning English is my main goal.

Our aim is *making* you feel at home.

Sometimes an adverb or an adverb phrase comes between *to* and the verb, creating a ***split infinitive.*** Some native speakers dislike split infinitives, but they are very common.

Today he expected *to finally meet* the great author.

Participles

The two ***participles*** are required to create verb tenses and are also used as adjectives.

For regular verbs, the ***past participle*** has the same *-ed* form as the past tense. But for most irregular verbs, it has an irregular form that must be memorized. (See list of Irregular Verbs, p. 1953.) Past participles usually express completed action and are used to form three perfect tenses.

present perfect	have/has learned
past perfect	had learned
future perfect	will have learned

(The past participle *been* is also used for the perfect continuous tenses.)

Many past participles are common adjectives.

Some of his friends are *known* criminals.

He noticed her *worried* expression.

My parents are *excited.*

By now they were *drunk.*

The *exhausted* travelers soon went to bed.

This was their first view of the king's *chosen* bride.

The ***present participle*** always ends in *-ing,* and is used to refer to action that is happening at the time of speaking or a time spoken of. It is used to form all the progressive verb tenses.

present progressive:	am/are/is eating
present perfect progressive:	have/has been eating
imperfect:	was/were eating
past perfect progressive:	had been eating
future progressive:	will be eating
future perfect progressive:	will have been eating

They *were eating* lunch when the police arrived.

We *had been hoping* you would come.

She*'ll be running* in the Boston Marathon.

Like many past participles, many present participles also commonly serve as adjectives.

a very *demanding* boss

the *devastating* storm

another *boring* movie

Some verbs can be followed by either a *to* infinitive or a present participle. For a few of these verbs, including *begin, continue, hate, like, love, prefer,* and *start,* the meaning of the sentence does not change.

They *began counting* the ballots. = They *began to count* the ballots.

But for the verbs *forget, remember,* and *stop,* the meaning may change completely.

They stopped *to watch* the horses. [= They stopped because they wanted to watch the horses.]

They stopped *watching* the horses. [= They were watching the horses but then stopped.]

See also Participial Phrases, p. 1944.

Transitive and Intransitive Verbs

A ***direct object*** is the person or thing that receives the action of a verb. An ***indirect object*** is the person or thing that the action is done for or directed to. Objects are always nouns, noun phrases, or pronouns.

Any pronoun object must be in its object form (*me, him, her, us, them,* etc.).

I love *her,* and she loves *me.*

Give *it* to *him.*

A verb that is used with a direct object is called a ***transitive verb.*** A transitive verb may also be used with an indirect object. A verb that is never used with a direct object is an ***intransitive verb.*** One sense of a verb may be transitive while another sense is intransitive.

The trail up the mountain *climbs* steeply.

Both the children like to *climb* trees.

Also, a single sense of a verb can have both transitive and intransitive uses.

He likes to *read* biographies.

He likes to *read.*

In this dictionary, transitive verbs (and uses and senses) have the label [+ *obj*] and intransitive verbs (and uses and senses) have the label [*no obj*].

An indirect object always comes before a direct object. Many common verbs—including *give, take, show, tell, sell, get, buy, explain, make, find, teach, write, do, call, ask, send,* and *bring*—can be used with both direct and indirect objects.

Find *her a chair.* [=Find a chair for her.]

Can you *read me the letter*? [=Can you read the letter to me?]

Who gave *her lawyers the information*? [=Who gave the information to her lawyers?]

He's saving *Caitlin a piece.* [=He's saving a piece for Caitlin.]

As the examples in brackets show, an indirect object can always be replaced by a *to* or *for* phrase that follows the direct object. But note that you cannot say

Find for her a chair.

Find a chair her.

Active and Passive Voice

In a sentence with an action verb (rather than a linking verb) and a direct object, two features tell us who or what is doing the action, and who what is receiving the action. One fea order. The normal word orde *→verb →object.*

The police arrested his wi

The second feature is the form ordinary form of the verb exp

voice; this means that the subject is the one doing the action expressed by the verb. If a verb is instead in the ***passive voice,*** the subject becomes the person or thing that is acted on or affected by the action.

His wife *was arrested* by the police.

Here, the original object ("his wife") has become the subject, and the original subject ("the police") is preceded by "by."

The passive voice is normally formed by using one or more auxiliary verbs and the past participle of the main verb. See the following examples of active and passive voice in several tenses.

present:	Carelessness *causes* many accidents. Many accidents *are caused* by carelessness.
present progressive:	A psychiatrist *is treating* her. She *is being treated* by a psychiatrist.
past:	Elvis *drove* that car. That car *was driven* by Elvis.
imperfect:	Gang members *were watching* the house. The house *was being watched* by gang members.
present perfect:	A 15-year-old *has solved* the puzzle. The puzzle *has been solved* by a 15-year-old.
past perfect:	Thugs *had robbed* him. He *had been robbed* by thugs.
future (*will*):	Jennifer *will return* your car. Your car *will be returned* by Jennifer.
future (*going to*):	That team *isn't going to defeat* Brazil. Brazil *isn't going to be defeated* by that team.

In informal English, *get* is often used instead of *be* to produce the passive. In questions and in most negative statements, *do* must be used as well.

Her talents often *get* [=*are*] *overlooked.*

The dog *got* [=*was*] *fed* earlier.

Did you *get* [=*were you*] *asked* to speak?

The bills *didn't get* [=*weren't*] *paid.*

In a passive sentence, the one doing the action he verb does not have to be identified.

e puzzle *has been solved.*

l *isn't going to be defeated.*

Thus, you may use the passive voice because (1) it is not important to identify the one doing the action, (2) you do not wish to identify the one doing the action, or (3) you do not know the identity of that person or thing.

When the one doing the action of the verb is identified, the passive voice simply changes the emphasis of the sentence.

Federer *was beaten* by a little-known French player.

Mood

English verbs have three possible forms called ***moods,*** which usually indicate whether a sentence (1) states a fact or opinion, (2) gives an order, instruction, or suggestion, or (3) expresses a wish or request or an idea that is not a fact. These are known as the ***indicative,*** the ***imperative,*** and the ***subjunctive.*** (A fourth mood, the ***interrogative,*** is sometimes identified. See Questions, p. 1946.)

Indicative

The ***indicative*** mood is the mood of ordinary sentences that state facts or opinions and of questions that ask about facts or opinions.

Nobody *knows* what happened.

The two countries *were* finally at peace.

They *will meet* in Berlin next week.

I *think* it will work.

What *happened*?

Will it *work*?

Imperative

The ***imperative*** mood is used for orders and instructions, usually without including the subject *you.* An imperative verb is always identical with the verb's infinitive form.

Please *stay* here till I get back.

Cut along the dotted line.

Stop!

Let me see.

Don't open it yet.

Subjunctive

The only mood that is difficult for learners is the ***subjunctive.*** The subjunctive mood is used to express wishes, proposals, suggestions, or imagined situations. The subjunctive verb usually appears in one clause in a sentence while an indicative verb appears in another clause.

Verbs that often (but not always) are followed by a verb in the subjunctive include:

advise	order	require
ask	prefer	suggest
demand	propose	urge
desire	recommend	wish
insist	regret	
intend	request	

He *insisted* that she *stop* smoking.

The governor is *demanding* that he *resign.*

They *asked* that you *be* on time tomorrow.

We *recommend* that he *be punished.*

She *wishes* the teacher *were* more helpful.

The subjunctive forms look like ordinary past and present verb forms; thus, they are often called the ***past subjunctive*** and ***present subjunctive.*** These differ from the simple past and simple present in only two ways: (1) In the present subjunctive, there is no *-s* at the end of the third-person singular (see the first two sentences above). (2) The verb *be* has only two subjunctive forms: *be* for the present subjunctive (as in the third and fourth sentences) and *were* for the past subjunctive (as in the last sentence).

The present subjunctive actually refers mostly to the future. It is generally used in a clause beginning with *that* (though *that* may often be omitted).

She suggested (that) he *arrive* early.

He desires that the carpenter *leave* space for another bookcase.

See Complex Sentences, p. 1945.

The past subjunctive may refer to the present or the past. Like the present subjunctive, it often occurs in a *that* clause.

I wish (that) you *loved* me.

She wishes (that) she *were* younger.

They talked about him as if he *weren't* even in the room.

The English subjunctive has always been used inconsistently. Native English-speakers often use *should* instead of the present subjunctive and use *was* instead of the past subjunctive's *were.*

She suggested (that) he *should arrive* early.

He desires that the carpenter *should leave* space for another bookcase.

She wishes she *was* younger.

They talked about him as if he *wasn't* even in the room.

An important use of the past subjunctive is in clauses beginning with *if.* See Conditional Sentences, p. 1950.

Phrasal Verbs

A phrasal verb looks like an ordinary verb followed by an adverb or a preposition—or sometimes followed by an adverb *and* a preposition. However, its meaning is different from the meaning of the ordinary verb by itself.

turn	The car *turned* left onto a dirt road.
turn up	His brother *turned up* [=arrived] just in time to join them.
turn out	A large crowd *turned out* [=gathered] to see the President.
turn down	She *turned down* [=rejected] several job offers.

The following verbs are the ones that most often form part of phrasal verbs.

break	go	set
bring	hold	sit
carry	look	take
come	make	turn
find	move	work
get	pick	
give	put	

The following adverbs and prepositions are those that most often form part of phrasal verbs.

about	down	out
after	for	over
along	in	through
around/ round	into	to
away	off	up
back	on	with
	onto	

Thus, if you are confused by a sentence, it may help to look for these words. In this book, phrasal verbs are defined in alphabetical order after the main definition(s) of an entry and are labeled [*phrasal verb*].

Phrasal-verb tenses are formed like ordinary verb tenses.

They *hang out* a lot.

He *hung out* all day.

We*'ve been hanging out* for hours.

Some phrasal verbs are transitive and some are intransitive.

When did they *knock down* that house?

What time do you normally *get up*?

Most transitive phrasal verbs can be separated. That is, the direct object may go in the middle of the phrasal verb.

When did they *knock* that house *down*?

If the object is short (one or two words), it usually goes inside the phrasal verb. If it is long, it usually follows the phrasal verb.

She *let* the cat *out.*

She *let out* the children in grades 4 and 5.

If the object is a personal pronoun, it always goes inside.

When did they *knock* it *down*? [*not* *When did they knock down it?*]

She *let* them *out.* [*not* *She let out them.*]

Some transitive phrasal verbs cannot be separated.

We knew we could *count on* Britain. [*not* *We knew we could count Britain on.*]

The examples at the individual dictionary entries will show whether a particular phrasal verb can be separated.

Intransitive phrasal verbs and three-word phrasal verbs cannot be separated.

The truck had *broken down* in Montreal. [*not* *The truck had broken in Montreal down.*]

His sister *took up with* a new boyfriend. [*not* *His sister took up a new boyfriend with.*]

And phrasal verbs in the passive voice are never separated.

The problem had been *worked out* on Friday. [*not* *The problem had been worked on Friday out.*]

The baseball game was *held up* by rain. [*not* *The baseball game was held by rain up.*]

PHRASES, CLAUSES, AND SENTENCES

The basic unit of English expression is the sentence. All sentences contain at least one clause, and phrases are elements of many clauses and sentences.

Phrases

Any group of words that expresses a single idea, functions as a single part of speech, and does not include both a subject and a predicate is a ***phrase.***

A ***noun phrase,*** like a noun, refers to a person, animal, thing, place, quality, action, or idea. Noun phrases answer the question "What?" or "Who?" A ***verb phrase*** expresses an action, an occurrence, or a state of being. An ***adverb phrase*** usually modifies a verb and answers the question "When?" "Where?" "How?" "How much?" "How long?" or "How often?" An ***adjective phrase*** modifies nouns and pronouns and answers the question "What kind?" "How many?" or "Which?"

noun phrase	He was crowned *king of France.*
	A ton of work was waiting for her.
verb phrase	Dinner *was being served.*
	They *had taken off* their shoes.
adverb phrase	It must be done *with care.*
	Last year she married again.
adjective phrase	The article was *rather dull.*
	They played works *by Beethoven.*

While a noun phrase will always have a noun in it, and a verb phrase will always have a verb in it, adverb and adjective phrases sometimes do not have adverbs or adjectives in them. The adverb phrase "with care" in the sentence above is made up of the preposition *with* and the noun *care.* However, since "with care" answers the question "How?" the phrase is an adverb phrase.

Many adverb and adjective phrases begin with either a preposition or a participle. Such phrases are known as ***prepositional phrases*** and ***participial phrases.*** Notice that these terms describe the phrase's first word rather than its function.

Prepositional Phrases

A prepositional phrase is a preposition followed by an object. The object is always a noun or a noun-equivalent: a noun phrase, a pronoun, a gerund, or even a noun clause. A prepositional phrase normally follows the word it modifies.

the causes *of the war*

a gift *to his mother's favorite charity*

nobody *except him*

a good day *for flying*

too late *for the concert we wanted to hear*

A prepositional phrase that acts like an adverb answers the question "When?" "Where?" "How?" "How much?" "How long?" or "How often?"

I sleep late *on Saturdays.*

There's a woman *at the front door.*

They did it *for the money.*

You can eat it *with your hands.*

A prepositional phrase that acts like an adjective describes a noun.

We bought two pounds *of cherries.*

Birds *with colorful feathers* are common here.

The ice *in Antarctica* is more than a mile deep.

Participial Phrases

A participial phrase is a phrase that begins with a participle (a verb form that usually ends in *-ed* or *-ing*) and functions like an adjective.

They were sitting in a wagon *pulled by horses.*

He watched two hawks *flying in opposite directions.*

A woman *believed to be a spy* has just left the building.

Participial phrases, like prepositional phrases, usually, but not always, follow the words they modify.

The guy *sitting by the window* is her boyfriend.

The officer *injured in the accident* was hospitalized.

Lacking a car, she takes the bus to work.

Notice that most participial phrases could instead be included in a subordinate clause beginning with *who, which,* or *that.*

The officer *who was injured in the accident* was hospitalized.

A participial phrase may often be moved within a sentence.

The captain, *seeking to beat the speed record,* had raced through the strait.

Seeking to beat the speed record, the captain had raced through the strait.

Clauses and Sentences

A ***clause*** is a group of words that contains a subject and verb. A ***main*** (or ***independent***) ***clause*** is part of a larger sentence but could be used by itself as a complete sentence. A ***subordinate*** (or ***dependent***) ***clause*** cannot form a complete sentence by itself.

A ***sentence*** expresses a statement, question, command, or wish. It begins with a capital letter and ends with a period, question mark, or exclamation point. Every sentence has two basic parts: a ***subject,*** which is a noun, a noun phrase, or a pronoun that performs the action of the verb; and a ***predicate,*** which contains a verb and usually other words as well and expresses what is said about the subject. (In ***imperative*** sentences, the subject *you* is usually absent but understood; see p. 1942.) The subject normally comes before the predicate, but in questions the verb is normally separate from the rest of the predicate and comes before the subject. A prepositional phrase may sometimes appear before the verb in the normal place of the subject.

She took some coins out of her purse.

Was she the only student there?

Shut up or I'll smack you!

I wish it would stop raining.

She likes hip-hop, he likes reggae, and I like blues.

He knew that the police were looking for him.

In the doorway stood a tall, elegantly dressed man.

A sentence must contain a main clause. Sentences that contain a single clause are called ***simple sentences*** (see the first, second, and seventh sentences above). Sentences that contain two or more main clauses are called ***compound sentences*** (see the third and fifth sentences). Sentences that contain a subordinate clause are called ***complex sentences*** (see the fourth and sixth sentence).

Compound Sentences

In a compound sentence, the main clauses are normally joined with a coordinating conjunction (*and, or, but*) or a semicolon. (For this reason these clauses are sometimes referred to as ***coordinate clauses.***) A comma usually (but not always) precedes the conjunction.

The Senate may vote today, or it may wait till next week.

The rain stopped and the children went back outside.

She liked Toyotas, but he preferred Hondas.

This one is named Lulu; that one is Bobo.

Complex Sentences

A sentence in which the main clause has one or more subordinate clauses is a ***complex sentence.*** A main clause may be joined to a subordinate clause in different ways.

A subordinate clause may begin with a ***subordinating conjunction.*** The most common subordinating conjunctions (some of which are also used as adverbs or prepositions) include:

after	since	where
although	so	whether
because	that	while
before	though	why
how	unless	
if	when	

Show me *how you do that.*

I used to ski *when I lived in Switzerland.*

She doesn't remember *where she left the keys.*

Although it was late, he didn't feel tired.

Stay here *while I go and get some food.*

You'll be assigned to a team *since you didn't choose one.*

Unlike the other subordinating conjunctions, *that* can often be omitted.

The manufacturers claim (*that*) the drug works.

For many more examples, see the individual dictionary entries.

A subordinate clause may also begin with a ***relative pronoun.*** A relative pronoun refers to a noun or noun phrase that was mentioned earlier. The most important relative pronouns are *that, which, who, whom,* and *whose.* (Others include *whatever, whoever, whomever,* and *whichever.*)

Is there a camera *that can take pictures under water*?

They're all good; the question is *which is the best.*

The professor *who won the award* is retiring.

The clerk *whom you spoke to* no longer works here.

Do you know *whose that is*?

Who is more common than *whom* (its object form) at the beginning of a subordinate clause.

Is that the clerk *who* [=*whom*] *you spoke to*?

The relative pronouns *whose* and *which* may also act as ***relative adjectives,*** which are simply adjectives that introduce a subordinate clause.

That's the guy *whose father is an ambassador.*

It wasn't obvious *which road led back to the town.*

Another way to begin a subordinate clause is with a ***relative adverb*** (an adverb that introduces a subordinate clause): *where, when,* or *why.*

They're particularly interested in Angola, *where there are large oil deposits.*

In May, *when the lilacs bloom,* the fragrance is heavenly.

No one really knew *why the marriage had failed.*

Subordinate clauses that modify nouns or verbs (rather than function as objects) may be divided into two categories: ***restrictive clauses*** and ***nonrestrictive clauses.*** A restrictive clause identifies the noun or verb that precedes it and is needed to understand which person or thing is meant.

I preferred the soprano *who sang last year.*

The only thing *that keeps them together* is their son.

A nonrestrictive clause adds information about something but is not needed to understand which person or thing is meant.

She had written two books, *which had been fairly successful.*

My uncle, *who I haven't seen in years,* works for the government.

Nonrestrictive clauses are separated from the rest of the sentence by one or two commas; restrictive clauses are not separated from the rest of the sentence by commas.

Which may refer to an entire main clause.

He moved out of the apartment the next day, *which was fine with her.*

She ignored my advice, *which surprised me.*

When a restrictive clause begins with a relative pronoun or relative adverb, the pronoun or adverb can often be omitted.

The reason (*that*) *he gave* wasn't convincing.

That was the year (*when*) *I went to Romania.*

She just needs a place (*where*) *she can study.*

This is never possible in nonrestrictive clauses, or in clauses where the pronoun is the subject.

He had a magazine, *which he had finished reading.* [not *He had a magazine, he had finished reading.*]

They're the relatives *who raised me.* [not *They're the relatives raised me.*]

A special kind of restrictive clause, known as an ***infinitive clause,*** begins with a *to* infinitive (the basic form of a verb preceded by *to*).

She liked *to hike in the Scottish Highlands.*

It was always fun *to work on puzzles together.*

For more examples, see Infinitives, p. 1940.

Finally, clauses that begin with *if* are known as ***conditional clauses.***

If the day is sunny, the ceremony will be held outdoors.

See Conditional Sentences, p. 1950.

Questions

As stated above, a sentence expresses a statement, wish, command, or question. Sentences that express statements or wishes are ***declarative***; sentences that express commands are ***imperative***; and sentences that express questions are ***interrogative.*** Since questions have a unique form, we will discuss them explicitly here.

Unlike declarative and imperative sentences, which end in either a period or exclamation point, a question ends with a question mark (?).

Questions are used to ask something. Many questions can be answered with either "yes" or "no"; these are called ***yes/no questions.*** All yes/no questions begin with an auxiliary verb or with a form of *be.*

Should that door be open? (No, it shouldn't.)

Did the prime minister speak yesterday? (Yes, she did.)

Has he talked to his doctor? (No, he hasn't.)

May I call you sometime? (Yes, you may.)

Was there enough food? (No, there wasn't.)

Notice that the answers to yes/no questions (such as those in parentheses above) often repeat the auxiliary verb but rarely repeat the main verb except when it is *be*.

Yes/no questions normally look like ordinary declarative sentences with the words in a different order.

(It's late.) Is it late?

(The streets were empty.) Were the streets empty?

(Their prices are high.) Are their prices high?

If the declarative sentence has only one verb and it is not a form of *be*, the question must start with a form of *do* or, in the future tense, *will:* that is, *did* (or *didn't*) for the past tense, *does* or *do* (or *doesn't* or *don't*) for the present tense, and *will* (or *won't*) for the future tense. Since *do* and *will* express the tense, the main verb appears as an infinitive.

(He finally got married.) *Did* he finally *get* married?

(She knows him well.) *Does* she *know* him well?

(They fly north in April.) *Do* they *fly* north in April?

(I will leave tomorrow.) *Will* you *leave* tomorrow?

If the declarative sentence includes an auxiliary verb (*be, have, do,* or a modal verb), that verb is usually moved to the beginning.

(The Yankees are losing.) *Are* the Yankees losing?

(Everyone has gone.) *Has* everyone gone?

(It actually did happen.) *Did* it actually happen?

(He'll be back soon.) *Will* he be back soon?

(That would work better.) *Would* that work better?

(The boys can have those.) *Can* the boys have those?

Must is often replaced by a form of *do* followed by *have to.*

(Every student must take a few science classes.) *Does* every student *have to* take a few science classes?

A question in which *have* or *do* is an independent verb (rather than an auxiliary verb) begins with an auxiliary verb.

(They usually have trouble at customs.) *Do* they usually *have* trouble at customs?

(The hurricane did a lot of damage.) *Did* the hurricane *do* a lot of damage?

Questions that cannot be answered with "yes" or "no" usually begin with an interrogative adjective, adverb, or pronoun: *when, what, where, who, whom, whose, why, which,* or *how.* Such questions do not simply reorder the words of a declarative sentence:

(I liked that one best.) Which one did you like best?

(She wants the blue one.) Which one does she want?

(I'll park the car here.) Where will you park the car?

(Fifteen were missing.) How many were missing?

(They've visited twice.) How often have they visited?

(You should go in an hour.) When should I go?

As shown in these sentences, an auxiliary verb still normally precedes the subject in such questions. But if an interrogative pronoun or adjective (usually *who, what, which,* or *whose*) refers to the subject of the sentence, no auxiliary verb is needed.

Who wants the last beer?

Which was the right answer?

Which cat is sick?

What trail leads down the mountain?

Whose team finally won?

Yes/no questions are often worded negatively (see Negation, p. 1948). Negative questions do not mean that the speaker thinks the answer is "no"; in fact, people usually ask negative questions when they think the answer will be "yes." In negative questions, not follows the auxiliary verb; it is almost always contracted to *-n't.*

Won't it be difficult? (Yes, it probably will.)

Weren't the potatoes good? (Yes, they were delicious.)

Wouldn't they prefer to see a movie? (Yes, they probably would.)

Didn't your friends go with you? (Yes, two of them did.)

A positively worded question usually indicates that the speaker truly has no idea what the answer is.

Will you be at the party? (Yes, I'm planning to go. or No, I have other plans.)

In conversation and informal messages, declarative sentences often end with a short question called a ***tag question.***

We don't have time, do we? [=Do we have time?]

If the main clause is negative, the tag question must be positive. If the main clause is positive, the tag question must be negative. A noun subject in the main clause is replaced by a pronoun in the tag question. If the sentence begins with *there* or *it*, *there* or *it* is repeated in the tag question. The verb in the tag question is always an auxiliary verb. If there is an auxiliary verb in the main clause, it is repeated in the tag question; if the main clause has no auxiliary verb, the tag question uses a form of *do*.

John wouldn't mind, would he? [=Would John mind?]

They'll all be there, won't they? [=Won't they all be there?]

There isn't any tea, is there? [=Is there any tea?]

It was cold, wasn't it? [=Wasn't it cold?]

Elena retired last year, didn't she? [=Didn't Elena retire last year?]

You work in Singapore, don't you? [=Don't you work in Singapore?]

In conversation, a declarative sentence can be turned into a question by simply ending the sentence with rising intonation in the voice. In writing, this is shown by using a question mark rather than a period.

They're going to shut down the company?

OTHER GRAMMAR TOPICS

Possession

The normal way to show possession is to add *-'s* or *-'* to the end of the name or noun. A singular noun normally takes *-'s*. A plural noun that ends in an /s/or /z/sound takes simply *-'*. A noun with an irregular plural takes *-'s*.

the *cat's* tail

Marcos's teacher

the *Beatles'* second drummer

the *children's* cookies

A ***possessive adjective*** (see p. 1933) or ***possessive pronoun*** (p. 1928) can often be used instead of a name or noun.

Lisa took *her* grandmother to the fair.

Our car needs to be replaced.

The dog has lost *its* collar.

The last house on the street is *theirs*.

Yours is newer than *mine*.

Note that the possessive adjective *its* has no apostrophe. *It's* (with an apostrophe) is a contraction of "it is" ("It's getting late") or "it has" ("It's gotten late").

A less common and more formal way to show possession is with *of*. *Of* is normally used when a thing, rather than a person or animal, has possession.

the campus *of the university* =*the university's* campus

the role *of the government* =*the government's* role

Of is rarely used to show possession of something that can be touched or held.

Mrs. Klein's cat [not *the cat of Mrs. Klein*]

Apposition

When two nouns or noun phrases in the same sentence refer to the same thing, the two are said to be in ***apposition*** to one another.

Cairo, *Africa's largest city*, is the cultural center of the Arab world.

A fluent speaker of Finnish, Sirpa was very helpful with the tourists.

The choir performed "Elijah Rock," *a spiritual arranged by Moses Hogan*.

They interviewed *the novelist* J. K. Rowling.

Negation

A negative statement expresses denial or refusal. To ***negate*** a statement is to change its meaning so that it is negative; this process is called ***negation***. A small group of words is used for negation, and all of them start with *n-*.

Not is the most common negating word. It is normally used with a verb as part of a contraction (*isn't*, *shouldn't*, etc.) in spoken English. *Not* can be used to negate nouns, verbs, adjectives, and adverbs.

He *isn't* a *Catholic*.

She's *not going* anywhere.

Those *aren't blue*.

They hoped it *wasn't too* long.

The other negating words are *no, none, nothing, nobody, no one, nowhere,* and *never*.

Nobody told me about it.

There'll be *nothing* left for us.

It *never* happened.

See the individual dictionary entries for many more examples of how these words are used.

Negating a sentence in the simple present or simple past tense requires a form of *do* with *not.*

> These colors *don't* match.
>
> The bus *didn't* arrive on time.

In sentences with modal verbs, *not* follows the modal verb immediately, often forming a contraction.

> It *can't* be true.
>
> The children *shouldn't* stay out too late.
>
> The train *won't* leave until 4:10.

The same is true for the other auxiliary verbs.

> They *aren't* coming this spring.
>
> She *hadn't* traveled in Africa since she was in college.
>
> He *doesn't* work there with us anymore.

Only one negative word is required to make a clause negative. Using two negative words in a clause produces an error called a ***double negative.***

> I *don't* know anything about it. or I know *nothing* about it. [not *I don't know nothing about it.*]

However, a sentence with more than one clause can have more than one negation.

> I've *never* heard that, and I *don't* believe it.
>
> She *won't* tell us who *wasn't* there.

Three common adverbs—*hardly, barely,* and *scarcely*—may have the effect of negation; they should not be used with another negative word.

> I can *barely* hear you. [not *I can't barely hear you.*]
>
> There's hardly any time left. [not *There isn't hardly any time left.*]
>
> She had been gone scarcely five minutes. [not *She hadn't been gone scarcely five minutes.*]

Comparison

In grammar, comparison means stating that something has more or less of a quality or amount than something else has.

Comparisons of Quality

To compare a quality that is possessed by two nouns (or noun phrases or pronouns) or two verbs, we use the ***comparative*** form of an adjective or adverb, which is normally formed by adding *-er* to a one-syllable adjective or adverb and to many two-syllable adjectives and adverbs. If the word ends with a short vowel and a consonant and is accented on the last syllable, the final consonant of the adjective or adverb is usually doubled. If the word ends in a silent *-e,* the *-e* is omitted. If it ends in *-y,* the *y* usually changes to *i.*

smart (adj.)	She's no *smarter* than me.
fat (adj.)	He's *fatter* than he used to be.
late (adj.)	It's *later* than I thought.
early (adj. or adv)	They took an *earlier* train. I arrived *earlier* than they did.

For longer adjectives (including many two-syllable adjectives) and almost all adverbs, the comparative is formed by using *more* or *less* instead.

patriotic (adj.)	He's *more patriotic* than his brother.
traditional (adj.)	Their Easter service is *less traditional* than ours.
readily (adv.)	He responded *less readily* this time than before.
harshly (adv.)	The older kids were punished *more harshly.*

More and *less* are never used with an adjective or adverb with an added *-er* ending.

> This test was *easier* than the last one. [not *This test was more easier than the last one.*]

Notice that *than* always comes between the two items being compared. But if one item was mentioned previously, a *than* phrase may not be needed.

> They drank all the wine almost immediately; the liquor lasted longer.

When comparing three or more things, we use the ***superlative*** form. For a short adjective or adverb, the superlative is normally formed by adding *-est.* For longer words, we instead use *most* or *least. The* almost always precedes a superlative adjective and often precedes a superlative adverb.

smart (adj.)	This paper was written by *the smartest* student.
neurotic (adj.)	She's *the least neurotic* person in the world.
early (adj. or adv.)	They took *the earliest* train. Who got up (*the*) *earliest*?
readily (adv.)	Oranges are *most readily* available in winter here.

Most and *least* are never used before an adjective or adverb with an *-est* ending.

> That was the *hardest* part of the exam. [not *That was the most hardest part of the exam.*]

The normal comparative and superlative forms for adjectives and adverbs are shown at their individual dictionary entries. The labels [*more ~; most ~*] are used for adjectives and adverbs that use *more* and *most* as their comparative and superlative forms. The labels [*also more ~; most ~*] and [*or more ~; most ~*] are used for adjectives and adverbs that can be used with the normal comparative and superlative forms but that often or sometimes use *more* and *most* as their comparative and superlative forms instead.

A few common adjectives and adverbs have irregular comparative and superlative forms.

basic form	comparative	superlative
good (adj.)	better	best
well (adv.)	better	best
bad (adj. or adv.)	worse	worst
badly (adv.)	worse	worst
little (adj. or adv.)	less	least
much (adj. or adv.)	more	most
some (adj.)	more	most
many (adj.)	more	most
far (adj. or adv.)	further/ farther	furthest/ farthest

To say that two qualities are equal, we use *as . . . as* with the adjective or adverb (or the adjective or adverb phrase) between the two words.

She's almost *as old as* her aunt.

My pickup isn't *as easy to drive as* my car.

They're not *as happy with it as* they used to be.

Comparisons of Quantity

To compare the amount or number of things, we use *more, most, less, least,* and other words to modify nouns (rather than adjectives or adverbs). For greater amounts or numbers, we use *more* and *(the) most.* For smaller amounts or numbers, we use *fewer* and *(the) fewest* for count nouns, and *less* and *(the) least* for noncount nouns.

This box holds *more* discs than that one.

Who owns *the most* land?

There were ten *fewer* accidents this year.

February has *the fewest* days.

Kuwait has *less* oil than Iraq.

He always tries to do *the least* work possible.

However, for numbers that are thought of as making up a single sum or a whole, it is normal to use *less* rather than *fewer.*

She had *less* than $30 in her purse.

You can't join if you're *less* than 21 years old.

Because of this, even native English speakers often use *less/fewer* and *least/fewest* inconsistently.

More and *less* can also be used to compare amounts of an activity.

She worries about it *more* than I do.

Each year they travel *less* than the year before.

To say that two quantities are equal, we use *as many . . . as* or *as few . . . as* for count nouns, and *as much . . . as* or *as little . . . as* for noncount nouns.

You don't have *as many cousins as* he does.

I never made *as much money as* she made.

As much as and *as little as* (with no word in the middle) can also be used to compare quantities of an activity.

He doesn't run *as much as* I do.

Conditional Sentences

An important type of ***subordinate clause*** (see p. 1945) begins with the conjunction *if. If* clauses are used to say that something is true or likely or valid only under certain conditions. They are also used for talking about things that failed to happen in the past and things that cannot be true. Since sentences with *if* clauses talk about situations that require certain conditions, they are called ***conditional sentences.***

Conditional sentences may use different combinations of verb tenses. The verb form used in the *if* clause depends on whether the clause is talking about a condition in the past, the present, or the future, or about something that is always true. The verb form in the main clause depends on these same things, and may also depend on which verb form is used in the *if* clause.

The simplest conditional sentences are about the present or the future. They express a result that occurs, or will occur, when the condition in the *if* clause is true.

If it rains today, I'll cut the grass tomorrow.

Sentences of this type generally use the present tense in the *if* clause and the future tense (with either *will* or *going to*) in the main clause. *Unless* can be used instead of *If . . . not.*

We are going to go tomorrow *if the weather is not bad.*

We are going to go tomorrow *unless the weather is bad.*

See the entry for *unless* for more examples.

To speak of a condition that is not true, the *if* clause uses the past subjunctive, and the main clause uses *would.*

If he *were* a better listener, he *would remember* what you said.

I *would order* something if there *were* anything good on the menu.

If you *respected* me, you*'d take off* that ridiculous hat.

To discuss something that failed to happen, or something that is believed to be impossible, the *if* clause uses the past perfect tense, and the main clause uses a modal perfect (see p. 1939).

If it *had snowed* any more, we *couldn't have driven* home.

I *might have called* if I *had known* you were here.

If they *had had* more time, they *would have finished.*

To discuss a future possibility, an *if* clause may use *were to* with the infinitive.

If he *were to die,* who would inherit the house?

Reporting Speech and Writing

There are two ways to report what another person has said or written. One way, called ***direct speech*** or ***quotation,*** repeats the exact language, enclosed in quotation marks.

He added, "I really have to leave soon."

"It's an absolute disaster," she said, "the worst we've ever seen."

The hospital's report began: "The senator's condition has improved slightly overnight."

See also Quotation Marks, p. 1972.

The other way to report what another person has said or written, called ***indirect speech,*** puts the meaning of the person's words, rather than the precise words, into a subordinate clause.

("We have cows and a peach orchard.") She says (that) they have cows and a peach orchard. /She said (that) they had cows and a peach orchard.

As shown by the parentheses around it, the subordinating conjunction *that* often introduces indirect speech but is usually not required. (See Complex Sentences, p. 1945.) Notice that the original speech uses the present tense ("have"), but when the verb used to report the indirect speech is in the past tense, the tense of the indirect speech normally changes also.

The verb used to report indirect speech may be in the present tense when what is being reported was said recently or is from a piece of writing.

("I'm calling them weekly.") He *says* he *is* calling them weekly.

("Home prices have risen 6 percent since last year.") The report *says* (that) home prices have risen 6 percent since last year.

Notice that the verb in the indirect speech does not change.

More commonly, however, the verb used to report indirect speech is in the past tense and causes the verb in the indirect speech to change. The list below shows how the original tense usually changes when it is reported with a verb in the past tense in the normal way.

original tense	**after "said," "asked," etc.**
present	present *or* past
present perfect	past perfect
present progressive	imperfect
future with *will*	*would* + infinitive
future with *be going to*	*was/were going to* + infinitive
past	past *or* past perfect
imperfect	imperfect *or* past perfect progressive
past perfect	(no change)

("She is doing very well.") The teacher *said* (that) she *is* doing very well. The teacher *said* (that) she *was* doing very well.

("We*'ve tried* everything.") They *said* (that) they *had tried* everything.

("When *are* you *coming*?") She *asked* when we *were coming.*

("We *will make* a large profit next year.") The company *said* (that) it *would make* a large profit next year.

("The boat is *going to leave* without us!") He *yelled* that the boat *was going to leave* without us.

("She *failed* her exams last month.") She *told* me (that) she *failed* her exams last month. She *told* me (that) she *had failed* her exams last month.

("He *was sleeping* when I called.") He *said* (that) he *was sleeping* when I called. He *said* (that) he *had been sleeping* when I called.

("They *had left* just a few minutes earlier.") Someone *said* (that) they *had left* just a few minutes earlier.

Notice that in indirect speech a period replaces any question mark or exclamation mark at the end.

Reporting a spoken or written sentence that includes a modal verb requires the following changes.

original	**after "said," "asked," etc.**
can	could
may	might *or* could
must	had to
shall	would
will	would

("Charles *must* go back immediately.") He said that Charles *had to* go back immediately.

("The situation *won't* be getting better soon.") She wrote that the situation *wouldn't* be getting better soon.

However, if the person being quoted spoke recently, or if a document is being quoted, "says," "asks," etc., may be used, in which case the present tense can also be used in the indirect speech.

He *says* that Charles *must* go back immediately.

She *writes* that the situation *won't* be getting better soon.

The other modal verbs (*ought, could, might, should,* and *would*) and the near-modal verb *have to* usually employ the same verb for the past tense.

("I *could* take the job in Uruguay instead.") He said he *could* take the job in Uruguay instead.

("We *have to* make a decision this year.") They told me that they *had to* make a decision this year.

There are three cases in which the tense in indirect speech often does not change: (1) when the speech reported is something that is true all the time, (2) when the speech is reported immediately and concerns something not yet in the past, and (3) when the speech uses the future to make a prediction.

("Global warming *affects* everyone.") He agreed that global warming *affects* everyone.

("The train *is* about to depart.") She just told me the train *is* about to depart.

("She*'ll be* very successful in life.") He said she*'ll be* very successful in life.

Questions in indirect speech are treated in two different ways. For a yes/no question (see p. 1946), the reporting clause begins with *if* or *whether* (these two words have the same meaning in such sentences) and the verb appears in regular sentence order.

("Do you *eat* meat?") She asked *if* I *eat/ate* meat.

("*Can* you stay any longer?") He asked *whether* I *could* stay any longer.

If the question begins with "when," "which," "why," "who," "whose," "what," "where," or "how," the reported question uses the same word but puts the verb after the subject.

("*Where is* my coat?") She asked *where* her coat *was.*

("*How long have* you *lived* here?") He asked me *how* long I *had lived* here.

A command, instruction, or invitation is reported as an infinitive with *to.*

("*Get out.*") He told us *to get out.*

("*Add* a cup of chopped dates.") The instructions said *to add* a cup of chopped dates.

Omitted Words

English sentences usually omit a word when the same word is used either earlier or later in the sentence. The omitted word may be a noun, pronoun, verb, adjective (including an article), adverb, preposition, or conjunction. The word normally would have followed *and, or,* or *but.* (When a noun is omitted, it often would have preceded the conjunction.)

No one could lift the largest (stones) and heaviest stones.

He closed the window and (he) turned out the light.

In the evening she liked to read or (liked to) play the piano.

A horse or (a) cow had knocked down the gate.

The speech was very long and (very) boring.

Most of the oil came from Nigeria or (from) Angola.

They were offered a choice: pasta, (or) potatoes, or rice.

A word should only be omitted when the words that are being linked represent the same part of speech (*largest/heaviest, closed/turned out, horse/cow,* etc.).

Irregular Verbs

The following list shows the infinitive, past-tense, and past-participle forms for the irregular verbs in this dictionary. All verbs with the same final element are grouped together; thus, *outdo, overdo, redo,* and *undo* all appear immediately after *do* rather than in alphabetical order.

A regular English verb forms its past tense and past participle by adding *-ed* to its infinitive: for example, *trust* ("We trust her"), *trusted* ("In those days we trusted her"), *trusted* ("We have always trusted her"). A verb is considered regular if, when the *-ed* is added,

- the infinitive's final consonant is doubled (*stop, stopped, stopped*)
- its final silent *-e* is dropped (*die, died, died*)
- its final *-y* changes to *-i-* (*hurry, hurried, hurried*)
- its final *-c* changes to *-ck-* (*panic, panicked, panicked*)

A verb is considered irregular if

- either the past tense or the past participle lacks *-ed* (*swim, swam, swum; mean, meant, meant*)
- either the past tense or the past participle has a variant form that lacks *-ed* (*burn, burned* or *burnt, burned or burnt*)

INFINITIVE	PAST	PAST PARTICIPLE
be	was, were	been
bear	bore	borne
*forbear	forbore	forborne
beat	beat	beaten *or chiefly US* beat
*browbeat	browbeat	browbeaten
begin	began	begun
bend	bent	bent
*unbend	unbent	unbent
beseech	besought *or* beseeched	besought *or* beseeched
bet	bet *also* betted	bet *also* betted
bid (to express)	bade *or* bid	bidden *or* bid
*forbid	forbade *or* forbad	forbidden
bid (to offer)	bid	bid
*outbid	outbid	outbid
bind	bound	bound
*unbind	unbound	unbound
bite	bit	bitten
bleed	bled	bled
blow	blew	blown
break	broke	broken
*housebreak	housebroke	housebroken
breed	bred	bred
*crossbreed	crossbred	crossbred
*interbreed	interbred	interbred
bring	brought	brought
build	built	built
*rebuild	rebuilt	rebuilt
burn	burned *or* burnt	burned *or* burnt
*sunburn	sunburned *or* sunburnt	sunburned *or* sunburnt
burst	burst *also* bursted	burst *also* bursted

INFINITIVE	PAST	PAST PARTICIPLE
bust	busted *also Brit* bust	busted *also Brit* bust
buy	bought	bought
cast	cast	cast
*broadcast	broadcast	broadcast
*forecast	forecast *also* forecasted	forecast *also* forecasted
*miscast	miscast	miscast
*recast	recast	recast
*telecast	telecast	telecast
*typecast	typecast	typecast
catch	caught	caught
cc	cc'd	cc'd
choose	chose	chosen
cleave (to adhere)	cleaved *or* clove	cleaved
cleave (to split)	cleaved *also* cleft *or* clove	cleaved *also* cleft *or* cloven
cling	clung	clung
clothe	clothed *also* clad	clothed *also* clad
come	came	come
*become	became	become
*overcome	overcame	overcome
cost	cost	cost
creep	crept	crept
cut	cut	cut
*undercut	undercut	undercut
deal	dealt	dealt
dig	dug	dug
dive	dived *or chiefly US* dove	dived *or chiefly US* dove
do	did	done
*outdo	outdid	outdone
*overdo	overdid	overdone
*redo	redid	redone

INFINITIVE	PAST	PAST PARTICIPLE
*undo	undid	undone
draw	drew	drawn
*overdraw	overdrew	overdrawn
*redraw	redrew	redrawn
*withdraw	withdrew	withdrawn
dream	dreamed *or* dreamt	dreamed *or* dreamt
drink	drank	drunk
drive	drove	driven
*test-drive	test-drove	test-driven
dwell	dwelled *or* dwelt	dwelled *or* dwelt
eat	ate	eaten
*overeat	overate	overeaten
fall	fell	fallen
*befall	befell	befallen
feed	fed	fed
*bottle-feed	bottle-fed	bottle-fed
*force-feed	force-fed	force-fed
*overfeed	overfed	overfed
*spoon-feed	spoon-fed	spoon-fed
feel	felt	felt
fight	fought	fought
find	found	found
fit (to be right)	fitted *or chiefly US* fit	fitted *or chiefly US* fit
flee	fled	fled
fling	flung	flung
fly	flew	flown
*overfly	overflew	overflown
forsake	forsook	forsaken
freeze	froze	frozen
*unfreeze	unfroze	unfrozen
get	got	got *or US* gotten
*beget	begot *also* begat	begotten *or* begot
*forget	forgot	forgotten *or* forgot
gild	gilded *or* gilt	gilded *or* gilt
gird	girded *also* girt	girded *also* girt
give	gave	given
*forgive	forgave	forgiven
go	went	gone
*forgo	forwent	forgone
*undergo	underwent	undergone
grind	ground	ground
grow	grew	grown
*outgrow	outgrew	outgrown
*overgrow	overgrew	overgrown
hang (to suspend)	hung *or* hanged	hung *or* hanged
*overhang	overhung	overhung
have	had	had
hear	heard	heard
*mishear	misheard	misheard
*overhear	overheard	overheard
heave	heaved *also* hove	heaved *also* hove
hew	hewed	hewed *or* hewn
hide	hid	hidden *or* hid
hit	hit	hit
*switch-hit	switch-hit	switch-hit
hold	held	held

INFINITIVE	PAST	PAST PARTICIPLE
*behold	beheld	beheld
*uphold	upheld	upheld
*withhold	withheld	withheld
hurt	hurt	hurt
keep	kept	kept
kneel	knelt *also chiefly US* kneeled	knelt *also chiefly US* kneeled
knit	knit *or* knitted	knit *or* knitted
know	knew	known
lay	laid	laid
*inlay	inlaid	inlaid
*mislay	mislaid	mislaid
*overlay	overlaid	overlaid
*underlay	underlaid	underlaid
*waylay	waylaid	waylaid
lead	led	led
*mislead	misled	misled
lean	leaned *or Brit* leant	leaned *or Brit* leant
leap	leapt *or* leaped	leapt *or* leaped
learn	learned *also chiefly Brit* learnt	learned *also chiefly Brit* learnt
leave	left	left
lend	lent	lent
let	let	let
*sublet	sublet	sublet
lie (to recline)	lay	lain
*overlie	overlay	overlain
*underlie	underlay	underlain
light	lighted *or* lit	lighted *or* lit
*spotlight	spotlighted *or* spotlit	spotlighted *or* spotlit
lose	lost	lost
make	made	made
*remake	remade	remade
mean	meant	meant
meet	met	met
mow	mowed	mowed *or* mown
offset	offset	offset
pay	paid	paid
*overpay	overpaid	overpaid
*prepay	prepaid	prepaid
*repay	repaid	repaid
*underpay	underpaid	underpaid
plead	pleaded *or* pled	pleaded *or* pled
prove	proved	proved *or chiefly US* proven
*disprove	disproved *or chiefly US* disproven	disproved *or chiefly US* disproven
put	put	put
*input	inputted *or* input	inputted *or* input
*output	output	output
quit	quit *also* quitted	quit *also* quitted
read	read	read
*lip-read	lip-read	lip-read
*misread	misread	misread
*proofread	proofread	proofread
*reread	reread	reread

INFINITIVE	PAST	PAST PARTICIPLE
*sight-read	sight-read	sight-read
rend	rent *also US* rended	rent *also US* rended
rid	rid *also* ridded	rid *also* ridded
ride	rode	ridden
*override	overrode	overridden
ring (to sound)	rang	rung
rise	rose	risen
*arise	arose	arisen
run	ran	run
*outrun	outran	outrun
*overrun	overran	overrun
*rerun	reran	rerun
saw	sawed	sawed *or Brit* sawn
say	said	said
see	saw	seen
*foresee	foresaw	foreseen
*oversee	oversaw	overseen
seek	sought	sought
sell	sold	sold
*outsell	outsold	outsold
*oversell	oversold	oversold
*resell	resold	resold
*undersell	undersold	undersold
send	sent	sent
set	set	set
*beset	beset	beset
*inset	inset	inset
*reset	reset	reset
*upset	upset	upset
sew	sewed	sewn *or* sewed
shake	shook	shaken
shave	shaved	shaved *or* shaven
shear	sheared	sheared *or* shorn
shed	shed	shed
shine	shone *or chiefly US* shined	shone *or chiefly US* shined
*outshine	outshone *or* outshined	outshone *or* outshined
shit	shit *or* shat	shit *or* shat
shoe	shod *also chiefly US* shoed	shod *also chiefly US* shoed
shoot	shot	shot
*overshoot	overshot	overshot
show	showed	shown *or* showed
shrink	shrank *or* shrunk	shrunk *or* shrunken
shut	shut	shut
sing	sang *or* sung	sung
sink	sank *or* sunk	sunk
sit	sat	sat
*babysit	babysat	babysat
*resit	resat	resat
slay	slew *also* slayed	slain
sleep	slept	slept
*oversleep	overslept	overslept
slide	slid	slid
*backslide	backslid	backslid
sling	slung	slung
slink	slunk *also US* slinked	slunk *also US* slinked

INFINITIVE	PAST	PAST PARTICIPLE
slit	slit	slit
smell	smelled *or Brit* smelt	smelled *or Brit* smelt
smite	smote	smitten
sneak	sneaked *or chiefly US* snuck	sneaked *or chiefly US* snuck
sow	sowed	sown *or* sowed
speak	spoke	spoken
*bespeak	bespoke	bespoken
speed	sped *or* speeded	sped *or* speeded
spell	spelled *or chiefly Brit* spelt	spelled *or chiefly Brit* spelt
*misspell	misspelled *or chiefly Brit* misspelt	misspelled *or chiefly Brit* misspelt
spend	spent	spent
*misspend	misspent	misspent
*outspend	outspent	outspent
*overspend	overspent	overspent
spill	*chiefly US* spilled *or chiefly Brit* spilt	*chiefly US* spilled *or chiefly Brit* spilt
spin	spun	spun
spit (to eject saliva)	spat *or chiefly US* spit	spat *or chiefly US* spit
split	split	split
spoil	spoiled *or chiefly Brit* spoilt	spoiled *or chiefly Brit* spoilt
spread	spread	spread
spring	sprang *or* sprung	sprung
stand	stood	stood
*misunderstand	misunderstood	misunderstood
*understand	understood	understood
*withstand	withstood	withstood
stave	staved *also* stove	staved *also* stove
steal	stole	stolen
stick	stuck	stuck
sting	stung	stung
stink	stank *or* stunk	stunk
strew	strewed	strewed *or* strewn
*bestrew	bestrewed	bestrewn *or* bestrewed
stride	strode	stridden
*bestride	bestrode	bestridden
strike	struck	struck *also* stricken
string	strung	strung
*hamstring	hamstrung	hamstrung
strive	strove *also* strived	striven *or* strived
swear	swore	sworn
*forswear	forswore	forsworn
sweat	sweat *or* sweated	sweat *or* sweated
sweep	swept	swept
swell	swelled	swelled *or* swollen
swim	swam	swum

INFINITIVE	PAST	PAST PARTICIPLE
swing	swung	swung
take	took	taken
*mistake	mistook	mistaken
*overtake	overtook	overtaken
*partake	partook	partaken
*retake	retook	retaken
*undertake	undertook	undertaken
teach	taught	taught
tear (to rip)	tore	torn
tell	told	told
*foretell	foretold	foretold
*retell	retold	retold
think	thought	thought
*rethink	rethought	rethought
thrive	thrived *or old-fashioned* throve	thrived *also old-fashioned* thriven
throw	threw	thrown
*overthrow	overthrew	overthrown
thrust	thrust	thrust
tread	trod *also* treaded	trodden *or* trod

INFINITIVE	PAST	PAST PARTICIPLE
wake	woke *also* waked	woken *or* waked *also* woke
*awake	awoke	awoken
wear	wore	worn
weave	wove *or* weaved	woven *or* weaved
*interweave	interwove	interwoven
wed	wedded *also* wed	wedded *also* wed
weep	wept	wept
wet	wet *or* wetted	wet *or* wetted
win	won	won
wind (to encircle)	wound	wound
*rewind	rewound	rewound
*unwind	unwound	unwound
wring	wrung	wrung
write	wrote	written
*ghostwrite	ghostwrote	ghostwritten
*overwrite	overwrote	overwritten
*rewrite	rewrote	rewritten
*underwrite	underwrote	underwritten

Contractions

English-speakers very often shorten (or *contract*) nine common words in speech. Eight are verbs: *have, has, had, is, am, are, will,* and *would*. One is an adverb: *not*. These words are also often shortened in informal writing. The shortened form of the word is attached to the word that comes before it; in writing, an apostrophe (') takes the place of the omitted letters.

The table below shows how the eight verbs are contracted when they follow a personal pronoun.

I have	**I've**	you have	**you've**	she has	**she's**	they have	**they've**
I had	**I'd**	you had	**you'd**	he had	**he'd**	we had	**we'd**
I am	**I'm**	you are	**you're**	it is	**it's**	we are	**we're**
I will	**I'll**	you will	**you'll**	he will	**he'll**	they will	**they'll**
I would	**I'd**	you would	**you'd**	she would	**she'd**	we would	**we'd**
I would have	**I'd have; I would've**	you would have	**you'd have; you would've**	it would have	**it would've; it'd have**	they would have	**they'd have; they would've**

Note that *-'s* can stand for either *is* or *has*. (It can also form the possessive case, as in "Sarah's dog.") The contracted form *-'d* can stand for either *had* or *would*. In questions, *-'d* sometimes stands for *did* ("Where'd he go?" "Why'd you do it?").

Contractions are commonly formed with other pronouns as well: "Who's that?" "What's happening?" "Someone's coming," "Who'd have guessed it?" "That'll be all," "This'll work." They are also often formed with nouns: "Michael's here," "The coffee's hot," "Time's passing," etc. And they are often used with *here* and *there*: "Here's the book," "There'd be plenty of food."

Contractions are often formed by adding *-'ve* to the modal verbs *would, could, should,* and *might*: "Argentina could've won," "Those should've been better," "I might've known."

The adverb *not* can be shortened to *-n't* and attached to the following verbs:

are	**aren't**	has	**hasn't**	ought	**oughtn't**
can	**can't**	have	**haven't**	should	**shouldn't**
could	**couldn't**	is	**isn't**	was	**wasn't**
did	**didn't**	might	**mightn't**	were	**weren't**
do	**don't**	must	**mustn't**	will	**won't**
does	**doesn't**	need	**needn't**	would	**wouldn't**
had	**hadn't**				

Note that *will/won't* is the only irregular example.

The contraction *let's* (*let us*) is common even in formal writing. *Ain't* (*am not, are not, is not, have not, has not*) is common in very informal speech but never used in formal writing. *Y'all* (*you all*) is common in speech in the American South.

In American writing that is intended to represent very informal speech, the final *-g* in words ending in *-ing* may be replaced with an apostrophe: *seein', hopin', movin'*, etc. Other shortenings of single words include *'em* (*them*) and *'n'* (*and*).

Writing that imitates very informal speech may include words that represent combinations of two words without an apostrophe, including:

betcha (bet you)
coulda (could have)
dunno (don't know)
gimme (give me)
gonna (going to)
gotcha (got you)
gotta (got to)
kinda (kind of)
lemme (let me)
shoulda (should have)
sorta (sort of)
wanna (want to)
whatcha (what are you, what do you, what have you)
woulda (would have)

Prefixes and Suffixes

Learning the common English prefixes and suffixes can help you to better understand and remember the meaning of many English words. **For other common English word parts, see English Word Roots, page 1960.**

PREFIXES

PREFIX	MEANING	EXAMPLES
a-	*on, in; in (such a) state or manner*	abed, afire, aloud
a-, an-	*not; without*	asexual
ante-	*before*	antedate, anteroom
anti-	*against, opposite*	antidote, anticlimax
arch-	*chief, extreme*	archbishop, archenemy
be-	*cause to be; treat as; about; thoroughly*	befoul, befriend, bemoan, bejeweled, beloved
bi-	*two; every other; twice a*	bicycle, bipartisan, biweekly, biannual
co-	*with, together*	coexist, coauthor
counter-	*opposite, against*	counterclockwise, counteract
de-	*do the opposite of; remove from; reduce*	deactivate, defrost, devalue
dis-	*exclude, not*	disbar, disagreeable
em-, en-	*put into or onto; cause to be or have; thoroughly*	endanger, empower, enslave, entangle
ex-	*former*	ex-husband, ex-president
extra-	*outside, beyond*	extracurricular, extraterrestrial
hyper-	*very, too much*	hypercritical, hyperactive, hypertension
hypo-	*under, down, below normal*	hypothermia, hypoallergenic
in-	*not*	incapable, inconsistent
inter-	*between, among*	intermarry, international
intra-	*within, inward*	intracellular, intravenous
meta-	*change; beyond*	metamorphosis, metaphysics
mis-	*bad, wrongly*	mistake, mislead
neo-	*new*	neoclassical, neo-Nazi
non-	*not*	nonalcoholic, nontoxic
out-	*more than*	outgrow, outnumber
over-	*go beyond; too much, very*	overachieve, overambitious
para-	*assisting; resembling; beyond*	paralegal, paramilitary, paranormal
post-	*after, later*	postdate, postpone
pre-	*before*	prehistoric, premature
pro-	*favoring, supporting*	pro-American
re-	*again, back*	retell, recall
retro-	*back, behind, backward*	retroactive, retrofit
semi-	*twice a; half; partly, partial*	semiannual, semicircle, semiconsciousness
sub-	*under; division*	subsoil, substandard, subtopic
super-	*more than*	superhighway, superhuman
trans-	*through, across, beyond*	transaction, transparent, transport
tri-	*three*	triangle, tricycle
ultra-	*beyond, extremely*	ultrabright, ultramodern
un-	*not; contrary to; reverse; remove*	unable, unethical, unfold, untie
under-	*below; too low or little*	underlying, underpaid
uni-	*one, single*	unilateral

SUFFIXES

SUFFIX	MEANING	EXAMPLES
-ability, -ibility	*capacity, fitness*	adaptability, compatibility
-able, -ible	*tending to, fit for*	agreeable, collectible
-age	*action; condition; place of*	breakage, bondage, orphanage
-al	*relating to; action*	fictional, rehearsal
-ance	*action or process*	performance, acceptance
-ancy	*quality or state*	infancy, pregnancy
-ant	*one that does; doing or acting*	assistant, coolant, hesitant
-ar, -ary	*of, relating to; one that relates to*	molecular, budgetary, revolutionary
-ation	*action or process*	flirtation, memorization
-ative	*relating to, made to, tending to*	creative, informative, talkative
-dom	*realm, state*	kingdom, freedom
-ee	*one who does or receives*	escapee, trainee
-eer	*one who does or makes*	auctioneer, profiteer
-en	*cause to be or to have*	sharpen, lengthen
-ence, -ency	*action, quality*	emergence, fluency
-er	*one that has, is, does, or is connected with*	double-decker, foreigner, reporter, prisoner
-ette	*little one; female*	cigarette, majorette
-ful	*characterized by; amount that fills*	peaceful, helpful; cupful
-fy	*cause to become*	simplify, purify
-hood	*condition, quality*	childhood, likelihood
-ide	*chemical compound*	cyanide, peroxide
-ie	*little one; one that is or relates to*	birdie, cutie, druggie
-ion	*act or process; state or condition*	ignition; perfection
-ish	*almost, approximately*	greenish
-ism	*practice, doctrine*	criticism, egotism
-ist	*one who is; relating to*	bicyclist, hairstylist, elitist
-istic, -istical	*relating to, characterized by*	altruistic, egotistical
-ite	*one who is from; one who supports*	suburbanite, Reaganite
-itis	*disease, inflammation*	arthritis, bronchitis
-ity	*state, degree*	capacity, density
-ize	*treat like, become like*	idolize, crystallize
-less	*not having, doing, or becoming*	witless, childless, tireless
-let	*small one*	booklet, droplet
-like	*resembling*	apelike, childlike
-ment	*action or process; result; condition*	development, entertainment, excitement
-ness	*condition, quality*	alertness, goodness
-or	*one that does*	actor, professor
-ory	*relating to; place of*	illusory, observatory
-ous	*full of; having or containing*	glamorous, poisonous
-ship	*condition; skill; position, status*	friendship, penmanship, professorship
-some	*characterized by; group of (so many)*	awesome, foursome
-ure	*act, process; group of people*	exposure, legislature
-ward	*toward*	westward, upward
-y	*characterized by*	dirty, icy, sleepy

English Word Roots

Most words in English are based on Greek and Latin. By learning the common Greek and Latin roots (basic words or word parts from which other words are formed), you can better understand and remember the meaning of many English words. The most useful roots are listed below. For other common English word parts, see Prefixes and Suffixes, page 1958.

ROOT	MEANING	EXAMPLES
acer, acr	*sharp, sour*	acerbic, acrimony
acro	*height, beginning*	acrobatics, acronym
aer	*air*	aerate, aerobic, aerodynamic
algia	*pain*	neuralgia, nostalgia
ambi, amphi	*on both sides, around*	ambidextrous, ambience, amphitheater
ann, enn	*year*	annual, anniversary, biennial, millennium
anthrop	*humankind*	anthropoid, philanthropy
antiqu	*old*	antiquarian, antiquity
aqu	*water*	aquarium, aquatic
arm	*weapon*	armor, disarming
art	*skill*	artifact, artisan
aster, astr	*star, outer space*	asterisk, asteroid, astronomy
aud	*hearing*	audience, inaudible
auto	*self*	autonomy, automated
avi	*bird*	aviary, aviation
bell	*war*	bellicose, rebellion
bene	*good*	beneficial, benevolent
bio	*life*	biosphere, symbiosis
cant	*sing*	cantata, descant
capit	*head*	capital, decapitate
carn	*flesh*	carnivore, carnal
cav	*hollow*	cavernous, cavity, excavate
cent	*hundred*	centigrade, centipede
centr, center	*middle of a circle*	epicenter, egocentric
chron	*time*	chronicle, chronological
clam, claim	*shout, cry out*	clamor, acclaim, exclamation
clar	*clear*	clarion, clarify
corp	*body*	corporation, corpse
cred	*believe*	credit, incredible
crypt	*hidden*	cryptic, cryptography, encrypt
culp	*guilt*	culprit, culpable
cycl	*circle*	cyclone, recycle
de	*down, away*	dejected, descent
dec	*ten*	decade, decimal
demo	*people*	democracy, demographic
derm	*skin*	dermatitis, hypodermic
dic	*speak*	diction, edict
doc, doct	*teach*	docile, doctrine
dol	*grief*	condolence, doleful
don	*give*	donation, condone
dur	*hard, lasting*	duress, durable, endure
dyna	*power, energy*	dynamite, dynasty
emia	*blood*	anemia, leukemia
equ	*equal*	equator, equanimity
err	*wander, stray*	error, erratic
exo	*outside*	exodus, exorcist
femin	*female*	effeminate, feminist
fid	*faith*	confidence, infidel
fig	*shape, mold*	effigy, disfigure
fil	*son*	affiliate, filial
fin	*end, boundary*	final, finish
flor	*flower*	flora, floral
flu	*flow*	fluid, fluent, affluence
form	*shape*	conform, formation
fort	*strong*	fortress, fortitude
gen	*be born*	genealogy, generate
grad	*step, degree*	downgrade, gradually
graph	*write*	autograph, graphic
grat	*pleasing*	gratify, ingratitude
gyn	*woman*	gynecology, misogynist
hom, homo	*same*	homogeneous, homogenized
hydr	*water*	dehydrated, hydrant
junct	*join*	conjunction, adjunct
jur	*swear; right, law*	juror, injury, perjure
juven	*youth*	juvenile, rejuvenate
lat	*side, wide*	bilateral, latitude
liber	*free*	liberal, liberate
lith	*stone*	megalith, lithography
luc	*light, shine*	lucid, elucidate
lum	*light*	luminescent, illuminate
macro	*large*	macrobiotic, macrocosm
mal	*bad*	malpractice, malevolent

ROOT	MEANING	EXAMPLES
mania	*mental disorder*	egomaniac, kleptomania
manu	*hand*	manual, manuscript
mar	*sea*	maritime, submarine
medi	*middle*	intermediate, medium
mega	*large*	megadose, megaphone
mens	*measure*	dimension, immense
metr	*measure*	isometric, symmetrical
micro	*small*	microchip, microscopic
mill	*thousand; a thousandth*	millennium, milligram
mono	*one, only*	monorail, monotonous
mor, mort	*death*	immortal, mortician
multi	*many*	multiple, multiply
mut	*change*	mutate, transmute
nau	*ship*	nautical, nauseous
neg	*denial, refusal*	negative, neglect
neur	*nerve*	neurologist, neurotic
nom	*name*	nominate, misnomer
nov	*new*	innovative, novelty
nul	*nothing*	annulment, nullify
numer	*number*	enumerate, numerous
nym	*name, word*	anonymous, pseudonym
oid	*appearance, form*	asteroid, ovoid
omni	*all*	omnipotent, omnivore
orth, ortho	*straight, right*	orthodontics, orthodox
paleo	*old*	Paleolithic, paleontology
pan	*all, whole*	panacea, pandemonium
par	*equal*	compare, parallel
part	*part*	apartment, particle
path	*suffering*	empathy, pathetic
phil	*love*	bibliophile, philosophy
phob	*fear*	phobic, technophobia
phon	*sound, voice*	telephone, symphony
phos, phot	*light*	phosphorescent, photograph
plac	*please, soothe*	placid, implacable
plen	*full*	plentiful, replenish
polis, polit	*city, citizen*	metropolis, political
poly	*many*	polygamy, polyglot
popul	*people*	populated, popularize
port	*carry*	deport, export
pot	*power*	potent, despot
prim	*first*	primary, primitive
prop	*own*	proprietor, property
psych	*mind, soul*	psychic, psychological

ROOT	MEANING	EXAMPLES
put	*think, believe*	impute, reputation
quad, quart	*four*	quadrangle, quarterly
quint	*five*	quintet, quintuplet
rect	*straight, right*	correction, rectify
reg	*rule*	regulate, irregular
rota	*wheel*	rotary, rotation
sacr, sanct	*holy*	sacrosanct, sanctuary
san	*health*	sanitize, insanity
sci	*know, understand*	science, prescient
scop	*look, view*	colonoscopy, horoscope
scrib, scrip	*write*	inscription, prescribe
sect	*cut*	section, dissect
sent, sens	*feel, sense*	sentimental, sensual
serv	*keep*	conservative, preserve
sign	*sign, mark*	designate, signature
simil, simul	*like, make like*	facsimile, simulate
sol	*sun*	solar, parasol
somn	*sleep*	insomniac, somnolent
son	*sound*	sonata, supersonic
spir	*breath, spirit*	dispiriting, inspirational, respiratory
strat	*layer*	stratosphere, stratified
surg	*rise*	insurgency, upsurge
sym, syn	*with*	sympathy, synchronize
tele	*distant*	telephoto, telepathic
tempor	*time*	temporal, contemporary
ten, tenu	*hold; thin*	tenant, attenuate
term, termin	*limit, bound*	interminable, terminal
terr	*earth, land*	subterranean, territory
therm, thermo	*heat*	thermal, thermostat
top	*place*	topical, topography
tract	*drag, pull, draw*	attractive, retract
urb	*city*	urban, suburb
ver	*truth*	verify, veracity
verb	*word*	verbal, verbatim
vest	*clothe*	divest, transvestite
vid, vis	*see, sight*	evidence, video, visionary
vir	*man*	virile, virtuoso
viv, vit	*life, live*	survivor, vital
voc	*speaking, calling*	vocal, vocation
volu, volv	*roll, turn around*	evolution, revolve

Words That Are Often Confused

Because English has a large vocabulary and English spelling is difficult, even native speakers sometimes write a word that looks and sounds similar to the word they are thinking of but has a different meaning. The words below are the ones that native speakers most often confuse.

The definitions that are shown here are very short. You can find full definitions for these words in the dictionary.

When a word is commonly used as two different parts of speech, labels indicate which these are: (*n*) noun, (*pron*) pronoun, (*vb*) verb, (*adj*) adjective, (*adv*) adverb, (*prep*) preposition, (*conj*) conjunction.

See also Spelling Rules, p. 1965.

accede to agree
exceed to go beyond

accent (*vb*) to stress; (*n*) emphasis
ascend to climb
ascent climb
assent to agree

accept to receive, to agree to
except not including

access (*n*) ability to enter; (*vb*) to enter
excess extra amount

adapt to adjust, to change
adept skilled
adopt to take as your own

addition something added
edition book or newspaper

adjoin to be next to
adjourn to end a meeting

adverse not good
averse against, opposed

advice suggestions
advise to give advice

affect to influence
effect result

allude to talk about, to refer
elude to avoid

allusion hint, reference
illusion false idea or picture

anecdote brief story
antidote medicine for poison

any more additional
anymore now, still

assure to give confidence to
ensure to make certain
insure to make certain, to prepare for when a bad thing happens

aural relating to hearing
oral relating to the mouth, spoken

base foundation, bottom
bass musical instrument, deep voice, fish

born starting to live
borne carried

brake (*n*) device for stopping; (*vb*) to slow or stop
break to crack, to destroy

breadth width
breath air from your mouth
breathe to take air into your mouth

bridal relating to a bride
bridle straps that are put on a horse's head

capital city that is the center of government
capitol government building
Capitol U.S. Congress building in Washington, D.C.

casually in a relaxed way
casualty someone who is injured or killed

cite to quote
sight ability to see, something that you see
site location, set of Web pages

climactic relating to a high point
climatic relating to weather

collaborate to work together
corroborate to say or show that something is true

collision act of hitting
collusion act of working together to hurt someone

complement (*n*) remaining part; (*vb*) to complete
compliment to praise

confidant someone who is trusted with secrets
confident certain, sure of your own abilities

conscience awareness of right and wrong
conscious mentally awake

consul diplomat
council group that meets for special purposes
counsel (*vb*) to give advice; (*n*) lawyer

credible believable
creditable deserving praise

currant fruit
current (*n*) stream; (*adj*) happening now

decent good, satisfactory
descent downward movement
dissent difference of opinion

decree official order
degree extent

defuse to make less harmful
diffuse to spread out or scatter

deluded believing false things
diluted lessened in strength

depraved corrupted
deprived poor

desert (*n*) dry region; (*vb*) to leave
dessert sweet food following a meal

detract to reduce
distract to draw attention away

device tool
devise to invent, to create

e.g. for example
i.e. that is, namely

elicit to bring out
illicit not lawful

eligible entitled, qualified
illegible not readable

eminent well-known, prominent
imminent ready to happen

envelop to surround
envelope paper holder for a letter

every day each day
everyday ordinary

flaunt to display
flout to defy

flounder to struggle helplessly
founder to sink

formally in a formal manner
formerly earlier

forth forward, onward
fourth 4th

gait manner of walking
gate entrance

gorilla large ape
guerrilla non-army fighter

hardy strong, tough
hearty loud and happy, healthy

hoard treasure, hidden supply
horde crowd

incite to cause bad actions
insight wisdom, ability to understand

incredible unbelievable, amazing
incredulous amazed

ingenious very clever
ingenuous innocent and sincere

inherent natural and basic
inherit to receive from someone who has died

it's it is, it has
its belonging to it

lead (*vb*) to guide; (*n*) heavy metal
led guided

liable likely, exposed to risk
libel to make false statements about

loose not attached, free to move
lose to misplace, to fail to win

martial military
marital relating to marriage

medal metal piece resembling a coin
meddle to interfere

median (*adj*) in the middle of a group of numbers; (*n*) something in the middle of a range
medium (*adj*) not large or small; (*n*) way of communicating

miner mine worker
minor (*adj*) not important; (*n*) young person

moral good, ethical
morale emotional state

peace state of calm
piece part, unit

pear fruit
peer (*vb*) to look closely; (*n*) person of equal rank
pier a place for a boat to stop

pedal foot lever
peddle to sell

perpetrate to be guilty of
perpetuate to make something continue

persecute to be unfair or cruel to
prosecute to sue or charge legally

personal private, individual
personnel group of employees

plain ordinary, not fancy
plane airplane, flat surface

pole long thin piece of wood or metal
poll sampling of opinion

pore to read carefully
pour to empty from a container

pray to speak to God
prey (*n*) victim; (*vb*) to hunt

precede to come before
proceed to move forward, to continue

preposition part of speech
proposition proposal, suggestion

principal (*adj*) main, primary; (*n*) school leader, main performer
principle basic rule or law

quiet noiseless
quite very, rather

rain water falling from the sky
reign (*n*) rule; (*vb*) to govern
rein (*n*) strap used to guide a horse, restraint; (*vb*) to restrain

raise to lift, to increase
raze to tear down

reality state of being real
realty real estate

respectfully with respect
respectively in the order mentioned

resume to start again
résumé summary of a career

right (*adj*) correct; (*n*) privilege
rite ceremony

role part, function
roll to turn over many times

shone past tense of *shine*
shown past participle of *show*

sit to rest, to be located
set (*vb*) to place, to apply; (*n*) group, collection

stationary not moving
stationery writing paper

statue piece of sculpture
stature height, importance
statute law

tack small nail, course of action
tact social sensitivity

tenant person renting a house or apartment
tenet belief, principle

than compared to
then at that time

their belonging to them
there in that place
they're they are

thorough complete
through (prep) by way of; (*adj*) finished

to toward
too also, very
two 2

track path, footprints
tract piece of land

waist middle of a body
waste (*vb*) to use carelessly; (*n*) garbage

waive to give up willingly
wave to motion with the hand

wander to walk without a particular purpose or direction

wonder (*vb*) to question, to feel surprise; (*n*) amazement

weather rain, snow, wind, etc.
whether if

were past tense of *are*
we're we are
where (*adv*) at what place; (*conj*) in the place

who's who is, who has
whose of whom

your belonging to you
you're you are

Spelling Rules

Since English evolved from many different sources, English words can be difficult to spell, even for native English-speakers.

Regular and irregular spellings for pluralized nouns, comparative and superlative forms of adjectives, verb tenses, and adverbs ending in *-ly* are shown at the entries in this dictionary. Here we provide the basic rules that determine most of these spellings along with some other general rules for spelling English words.

Nouns

- Most regular plurals are formed by simply adding *-s: car, cars.*
- For nouns ending in *-s, -x, -z, -ch,* or *-sh,* add *-es: loss, losses; box, boxes; blitz, blitzes; lunch, lunches; dish, dishes.*
- For nouns ending in *-y,* change the *y* to *i* and add *-es: academy, academies.* For nouns ending in a *-y* that comes after a vowel, add *-s: alley, alleys.*
- For a few nouns ending in *-f* or *-fe,* change the *-f* or *-fe* to *-ves: calf, calves; elf, elves; half, halves; hoof, hooves; knife, knives; leaf, leaves; life, lives; loaf, loaves; self, selves; shelf, shelves; thief, thieves; wife, wives; wolf, wolves.*
- For some nouns ending in an *-o* that comes after a consonant, form the plural by adding *-es: cargo, cargoes; echo, echoes; hero, heroes; motto, mottoes; potato, potatoes; tomato, tomatoes.*
- For some nouns of Latin origin ending in *-a,* add *-e: larva, larvae; vertebra, vertebrae.* For some nouns of Latin origin ending in *-um,* replace the *-um* with *-a: bacterium, bacteria; quantum, quanta.* For some nouns of Latin origin ending in *-us,* replace the *-us* with *-i: alumnus, alumni; fungus, fungi.*
- For words of Greek origin ending in *-is,* substitute *-es: analysis, analyses; basis, bases; crisis, crises; oasis, oases.*
- For many animals, use the same spelling for both singular and plural forms: *moose, moose; sheep, sheep.*
- Some plural forms of nouns are completely irregular: *foot, feet; mouse, mice; goose, geese.*

Adjectives

- To form regular comparatives and superlatives of one-syllable adjectives and some two-syllable adjectives, add *-er* and *-est: warm, warmer, warmest; clever, cleverer, cleverest.* Do not double a final *-e: nice, nicer, nicest.*
- When a final *-y* follows a consonant, form the comparative and superlative by changing the *y* to *i* and adding *-er* and *-est: lazy, lazier, laziest.*
- When a one-syllable word ends in a consonant that follows a single vowel, double the consonant before adding *-er* or *-est: mad, madder, maddest.*
- When forming an adjective by adding the suffix *-able* to a verb, remove the verb's final *-e: cure, curable; advise, advisable.* Do not remove the *-e* when it comes after *c* or *g: enforce, enforceable; manage, manageable.* When the word ends in *-y,* change the *y* to *i: deny, deniable; rely, reliable.*

Verbs

- To form the present-tense third-person singular form of regular verbs, simply add *-s: work, works.* Add *-es* for verbs ending in *-s, -x, -z, -ch,* or *-sh: bless, blesses; fix, fixes; buzz, buzzes; teach, teaches; wish, wishes.*
- For almost all verbs ending in an *-e* that comes after a consonant, remove the *e* before adding *-ed* or *-ing: arrange, arranged, arranging.*
- For regular verbs ending in a vowel followed by *-e,* form the past tense by removing the *e* before adding *-ed: agree, agreed; lie, lied; hoe, hoed; argue, argued.*
- For regular verbs ending in a *-y* that comes after a consonant, form the past tense and past participle by changing the *y* to *i* and adding *-ed: carry, carried.*
- For verbs ending in *-ac* or *-ic,* add *-k* when forming the past tense, past participle, and present participle: *traffic, trafficked, trafficking.*
- For verbs ending in a consonant following a single vowel and stressed on the final syllable, double the final consonant (except *v, w, x,* and *y*) when forming the tenses: *admit, admitted, admitting; grab, grabbed, grabbing; hum, hummed, humming.*

Adverbs

- Form most adverbs by simply adding *-ly* to an adjective: *tight, tightly.*
- When the adjective ends in *-y,* change the *y* to *i* and add *-ly: dreamy, dreamily; merry, merrily.*
- When the adjective ends in *-ic,* add *-ally* in almost all cases: *academic, academically; artistic, artistically; athletic, athletically.*
- When the adjective ends in *-ll,* remove one *l* before adding *-ly: full, fully.*

Other Rules

- The letters *j, q, x,* and *y* are never doubled in English words, and *a, h, i, k, u, v,* and *w* are almost never doubled. (Exceptions: *aardvark, bazaar; hitchhike, roughhouse, withhold; shiitake, skiing; jackknife, knickknack; continuum, muumuu, vacuum; divvy, savvy; glowworm, powwow.*)
- English words never end in *j* or *q,* and they almost never end in *v.*
- The letter *q* is always followed by *u* in English words: *quick, mystique.*
- When *i* and *e* come together to produce an /iː/ sound, the *e* normally follows the *i: believe, cookie, piece.* (Exceptions: *caffeine, leisure, protein, seize, weird.*) When both letters follow *c,* the *i* normally follows the *e: ceiling, receive, conceit.* (People commonly use a rhyme to remember the rule: "*i* before *e* except after *c.*")
- When *i* and *e* come together to produce an /eɪ/ sound, the *i* follows the *e: eighty, freight, neighbor, weigh.*
- When *i* and *e* come together following a *c* that is pronounced /ʃ/, the *i* comes before the *e: ancient, sufficient.*
- When a prefix is added to a word, the spelling of the original word does not change: *read, reread; spell, misspell; necessary, unnecessary.*
- If a word ends with a silent *-e,* the *-e* is dropped before adding a suffix that begins with a vowel: *sense, sensory; race, racism.* The final *-e* is kept if it comes after a soft *c* or *g: notice, noticeable; change, changeable.* (Exception: The *-e* is generally dropped before *-ing: notice, noticing; change, changing.*)
- The letter *c* produces the /s/sound only before the vowels *e, i,* and *y: center, cinema, cycle.* It produces the /k/ sound elsewhere: *act, cause, corner, cut.* (Exceptions: *Celt, soccer.*)
- The letter *g* produces the /ʤ/ sound only before the vowels *e, i,* and *y: genius, giant, Gypsy.* (Exception: *margarine.*)

Words Often Misspelled

The following list includes many of the words most often misspelled by native English-speakers. (See also Words Often Confused, p. 1962.)

absence
accelerate
accidentally
accommodate
accumulate
achieve
acquire
acquit
already
amateur
appearance
argument
basically
believe
broccoli
business
calendar
category
cemetery
commemorate
committee
consensus
deceive
definite
description
despair
desperate
development
disappear
discipline
dissipate
ecstasy
embarrass
exaggerate
exceed
existence
February
finally
foreign
forty
gauge
government
grammar
harass
height
humorous
independent
inoculate
insistent
intelligent
irresistible
led
library
lightning
liquefy
maintenance
marriage
memento
millennium
minuscule
mischievous
misspell
necessary
occasion
occurred
parallel
phenomenon
possession
privilege
pursue
receipt
receive
recommend
rein
repetition
restaurant
rhythm
seize
separate
sergeant
siege
successful
supersede
surprise
threshold
tomorrow
weird
withhold
yield

American vs. British Spelling

British spelling differs from American spelling in a few ways, mostly because of the spelling reforms that Noah Webster carried out in the U.S. beginning in the 1780s. Several common differences are shown below.

-e- /-ae-: In words derived from Greek, British English often uses the Greek spelling *-ae-:*

AMERICAN	BRITISH
anemia	anaemia
eon	aeon
orthopedics	orthopaedics
primeval	primaeval

-e- /-oe-: In words derived from Greek, British English often uses the Greek spelling *-oe-:*

AMERICAN	BRITISH
diarrhea	diarrhoea
gonorrhea	gonorrhoea
homeopathic	homoeopathic
maneuver	manoeuvre

-er /-re: The *-er/-re* difference is seen at the ends of many words:

AMERICAN	BRITISH
center	centre
fiber	fibre
meter	metre
theater	theatre

-l- /-ll-: In British English, the final *-l* of a verb is doubled when *-ed* or *-ing* is added at the end, even when the stress does not fall on the last syllable:

AMERICAN	BRITISH
counseled	counselled
dialed	dialled
equaling	equalling
traveling	travelling

-or- /-our-: The spelling *-our-* in words in British English often appears as *-or-* in words in American English, especially in an unstressed final syllable:

AMERICAN	BRITISH
color	colour
favorite	favourite
honor	honour
humor	humour

-ze /-se: Words that end in *-ize* and *-yze* in American English are often spelled *-ise* and *-yse* in British English:

AMERICAN	BRITISH
analyze	analyse
criticize	criticise
memorize	memorise
paralyze	paralyse

Unlike abbreviations in American English, an abbreviation in British English usually does not have a period at the end if its last letter is the same as the last letter of the word being abbreviated: *Mr./Mr* (for *Mister*), *St./St* (for *Saint* or *Street*), *Dr./Dr* (for *Doctor*), *Ltd.* (for *Limited*), etc.

Many other spelling differences affect only individual words.

AMERICAN	BRITISH
airplane	aeroplane
jewelry	jewellery
jail	gaol
tire	tyre

The Spelling of Different Sounds in English

In English pronunciation, many individual sounds may be spelled in several ways. The following list shows, in **boldface** type, the most common ways of spelling each sound, followed by an example. If you know how a word is pronounced but are not sure how to spell it, this list may help you to find it in the dictionary.

Some words may be pronounced in different ways. When a word appears in *italics* below, this means that the sound being illustrated is not used in every pronunciation of the word.

Sometimes a sound is pronounced in a word but is not represented by any letter in that word. In such cases, a dash (–) appears where the boldface spelling of the sound would be, and the word's full pronunciation is shown, as in the last two entries at /ə/:

–	chasm /ˈkæzəm/
–	McCoy /məˈkoɪ/

A dash and the full pronunciation of a word are also shown when it is difficult to know which letter or letters represent a particular sound in the word, as in the last entry at /ʧ/:

–	nature /ˈneɪʧɚ/

Vowels and Diphthongs

Sound	Spelling	Example
/ə/	**a**	abut
	e	silent
	i	marinate
	o	hillock
	u	circus
	y	physician
	ah	cheetah
	ai	captain
	ea	ocean
	eo	luncheon
	ia	collegiate
	io	cushion
	ou	famous
	–	chasm /ˈkæzəm/
	–	McCoy /məˈkoɪ/
/ʌ/	**u**	humdrum
	o	above
	ou	rough
/ɚ, ɚr/	**er**	fern
	ir	bird
	ur	fur
	or	world
	ar	liar
	re	ogre
	ear	earth
	eur	chauffeur
	our	journal
	err	*err*
	irr	*squirrel*
	urr	hurry

Sound	Spelling	Example
/æ/	**a**	mat
/eɪ, ej/	**a**	fade
	ai	main
	ay	day
	ea	steak
	ei	vein
	ey	prey
/ɑ, ɑ:/	**o**	cot
	au	sausage
	aw	saw
	a	father
	ah	shah
/aʊ, aw/	**ou**	loud
	ow	now
/ɛ/	**e**	bet
	ea	bread
/i, i:/	**e**	me
	i	ski
	y	pretty
	ea	easy
	ee	see
	ei	receive
	ey	key
	ie	grief
/ɪ/	**i**	tip
	y	myth

Sound	Spelling	Example
/aɪ, aj/	**i**	fine
	y	sly
	ie	lie
	ye	dye
/oʊ, ow/	**o**	bone
	oa	coat
	oe	doe
	oh	oh
	ou	boulder
	ow	know
/oɪ, oj/	**oi**	coin
	oy	boy
/u, u:/	**u**	flu
	o	do
	eu	rheumatism
	ew	crew
	oo	school
	ou	youth
	ue	blue
/ʊ/	**u**	pull
	oo	wood
	o	woman
	ou	could
/iɚ, ir/	**er**	serious
	ir	emir
	ear	hear
	eer	beer
	eir	weird
	ier	pier

/eɚ, er/	**ar**	bare
	er	there
	air	air
	ear	bear
	eir	their
	err	*err*
/ɑɚ, ɑr/	**ar**	farther
	or	sorry
/oɚ, or/	**or**	port
	ar	war
	oar	boar
	oor	door
	our	pour
/uɚ, ur/	**ur**	lure
	oor	boor
	our	tour

Consonants

/b/	**b**	baby
	bb	rubber
/ʧ/	**ch**	rich
	c	cello
	ti	question
	tch	match
	–	nature /ˈneɪʧɚ/
/d/	**d**	did
	dd	odd
	ed	crazed
/f/	**f**	fan
	ff	offer
	gh	laugh
	ph	telephone
/g/	**g**	go
	gg	egg
	gh	ghost
	gu	guide
	–	example /ɪgˈzæmpəl/
/h/	**h**	hat
/ʤ/	**g**	gem
	j	joy
	dg	budget
	di	soldier
	dj	adjective
	gg	exaggerate
	gi	region
	–	graduation /grædʒəˈweɪʃən/
/k/	**c**	fact
	k	take
	q	aqua
	cc	soccer
	ch	*schism*
	ck	pick
	cq	acquisition
	–	tax /ˈtæks/
/l/	**l**	low
	ll	dollar
/l̩/	**al**	pedal
	el	betel
	ol	idol
	yl	vinyl
	le	battle
/m/	**m**	me
	mb	comb
	mm	dummy
	mn	autumn
/n/	**n**	no
	gn	sign
	kn	knot
	mn	mnemonic
	nn	banner
/n̩/	**an**	Satan
	en	sudden
	in	satin
	on	cotton
	un	bosun
/ŋ/	**n**	ink
	ng	sing
/p/	**p**	stop
	pp	supper
/r/	**r**	red
	rh	rhyme
	rr	arrive
	wr	write
/s/	**s**	say
	c	race
	ss	mass
	sc	fascinate
	–	tax /ˈtæks/
/ʃ/	**sh**	shy
	c	oceanic
	s	sugar
	ch	machine
	ci	special
	sc	fascism
	se	*nauseous*
	ss	tissue
	ti	nation
	sch	schist
	sci	conscious
	ssi	mission
/t/	**t**	eat
	tt	mattress
	ed	cracked
/θ/	**th**	thin
/ð/	**th**	this
/v/	**v**	very
	vv	savvy
/w/	**w**	way
	wh	whale
	u	persuade
	–	choir /ˈkwajɚ/
	–	one /ˈwʌn/
	–	patois /ˈpæˌtwɑː/
	–	strenuous /ˈstrɛnjəwəs/
/j/	**y**	yard
	i	opinion
	–	beauty /ˈbjuːti/
	–	cute /ˈkjuːt/
	–	feud /ˈfjuːd/
	–	few /ˈfjuː/
	–	strenuous /ˈstrɛnjəwəs/
	–	unit /ˈjuːnət/
/z/	**s**	days
	z	zone
	x	xylophone
	zz	buzz
	–	example /ɪgˈzæmpəl/
/ʒ/	**si**	vision
	zi	glazier
	–	azure /ˈæʒɚ/
	–	measure /ˈmɛʒɚ/

Handbook of Style

This section deals with the elements of written English that do not include grammar, spelling, or choice of words. It discusses the use of punctuation, capital letters, and italic type, and the special problems in writing compounds, abbreviations, and numbers.

Punctuation

Apostrophe ’

1. The apostrophe is used with nouns and some pronouns to show that a person or thing belongs to someone or something. This form of a noun or pronoun is called the *possessive* (see Possession, page 1948). If the noun or pronoun is singular, the possessive is formed by adding *-’s*.

the dog’s owner

someone’s idea

If a noun is plural, the possessive is usually formed by adding just an apostrophe.

most birds’ eggs

the Johnsons’ house

2. The apostrophe is used in contractions and numbers to show that some letters or digits have been omitted.

didn’t [=did not]

they’re [=they are]

the ’80s and ’90s [=the 1980s and 1990s]

3. The apostrophe is used in the plurals of letters and numbers, and often in the plurals of abbreviations.

two A’s
a row of 8’s
several NGO’s *or* several NGOs

Brackets (*or* Square Brackets) [ ]

Brackets are used around words or letters that have been added to quoted text.

His letter of November 2 ends: “By the way, did B[eaverbrook] mention it?”

“In my Father’s house are many mansions [i.e., rooms].”

See also Parentheses, p. 1972.

Colon :

1. The colon introduces a word or phrase that gives more detail about the word or phrase that comes before it. When a full sentence follows the colon, its first word is often capitalized.

That year she took up a new sport: tennis.

They had reached a decision: The defendant was guilty.

2. The colon introduces a list or series.

Five of the crew members chose to go: Crawford, Sunshine, King, Gilbert, and Loretucci.

3. The colon may introduce quotations.

His father had followed Emerson’s rule: “Never read any book that is not a year old.”

Together the class recited the well-known lines from Shakespeare:

This happy breed of men, this little world,
This precious stone set in the silver sea,
This blessed plot, this earth, this realm, this England

4. The colon separates titles from subtitles.

the biography *Einstein: His Life and Universe*

Comma ,

1. The comma separates independent clauses joined by *and, or, but, so, yet, for,* or *nor.*

The bar was closing, and the last two customers were finishing their drinks.

The trial had lasted nine months, but the jury needed only four hours to reach its verdict.

2. The comma separates adverbial words, clauses, and phrases from the rest of a sentence.

In fact, no one seemed to have heard of him.

They concluded, however, that she had told the truth.

Having lost five games, we were almost desperate.

The storm, after a short pause, revived with even greater fury.

3. The comma is used after words and phrases that introduce examples.

First she called two friends, Soraya and Magda.

4. The comma separates words and phrases in a series. (Some writers always omit the comma before *and* and *or.*)

Geese, ducks, and chickens shared the large pen.

He had already showered, shaved, and dressed.

There were no sheets, blankets, or pillows.

5. The comma usually separates two or more ordinary adjectives that come before a noun.

the shiny, orange fabric

her cool, formal, elegant style

If the first adjective applies to everything that follows it, the comma is omitted.

her first major defeat

the only clean plate

a good used car

6. A comma usually separates a word or phrase from a noun that it identifies or defines and that comes immediately before or after it. If the word or phrase comes in the middle of a sentence, another comma separates it from the rest of the sentence.

We visited Gettysburg, site of the famous Civil War battle.

One of the book's authors, Julia Child, went on to become a television icon.

7. The comma usually separates a direct quotation from a phrase (such as "he said" or "Jane replied") that shows who is being quoted. A comma at the end of a quotation is always placed inside the quotation marks. Commas are not used after question marks or exclamation points.

Kate whispered, "It's time to go."
"I suspect," Gregory observed, "that we'll see them again."
"Would anyone like some salad?" she asked.

"Go to bed right now!" he shouted.

8. The comma is used before a short question (called a tag question) that sometimes occurs in conversation at the end of a sentence.

"We can't stay here, can we?"

"It's almost lunchtime, isn't it?"

9. The comma usually divides the digits of a number into groups of three. See Numbers, p. 1975.

Dash —

1. The dash marks a sudden change or break in a sentence.

All the younger officers would remain loyal to the new ruler—or perhaps they wouldn't.

He'd always done every job they had asked him to—even the most ridiculous ones—and he'd had enough.

2. The dash may introduce a phrase that defines a word that precedes it.

The marriage was annulled—that is, declared invalid.

3. The dash, like the colon, may introduce a list:

Her duties were the ordinary ones—cleaning, cooking, shopping, and sometimes looking after the children.

Ellipsis . . .

1. The ellipsis indicates that words have been omitted from a quoted sentence. The second and third examples below are shortened versions of the first.

"Is it so bad, then, to be misunderstood? Pythagoras was misunderstood, and Socrates, and Jesus, and Luther, and Copernicus, and Galileo, and Newton, and every pure and wise spirit that ever took flesh. To be great is to be misunderstood."

"Is it so bad, then, to be misunderstood? Pythagoras was misunderstood, and Socrates, and Jesus, . . . To be great is to be misunderstood."

"Is it so bad, then, to be misunderstood? . . . To be great is to be misunderstood."

2. The ellipsis indicates a pause or an unfinished sentence in speech.

"Are you . . . Are the two of you . . . in love?"

Exclamation Point !

1. The exclamation point ends a sentence, word, or phrase that expresses strong emotion (such as surprise or anger).

The jewels were gone!

Excellent!

Absolutely not!

2. The exclamation point may end a word or phrase that interrupts a sentence to express a strong emotion.

The children—thank God!—weren't there when it happened.

Hyphen -

1. The hyphen is often used to link words to form a compound. (See Compounds, p. 1973.)

a cost-effective program

three light-years

an up-to-date list

2. The hyphen is used in spelled-out numbers.

forty-one years old

his forty-first birthday

3. The hyphen is used between numbers and dates, with the meaning "to" or "up to and including." (In printed material, a slightly longer dash is used.)

pages 112–18

served as secretary-general 1995–99

Vacation dates are Dec. 20–Jan. 12.

4. The hyphen is used between two nouns or numbers, with the meaning "to," "and," or "versus." (In printed material, a slightly longer dash is used.)

a New York–Paris flight

the last Sampras–Agassi match

a final score of 7–2

5. The hyphen is used to divide a word at the end of a line.

In 1975 smallpox was declared completely eradicated by the World Health Organization.

6. The hyphen separates a prefix from a capitalized word, and may separate a suffix from a word that is more than two syllables long.

anti-American

industry-wide

Parentheses (*or* Brackets) ( )

1. Parentheses are used around words, phrases, clauses, and sentences that give examples, explanations, or additional facts. Within a sentence, a phrase in parentheses may end with an exclamation point, a question mark, or quotation marks; it may not end with a period except after an abbreviation.

The government believes this is unnecessary. (We're hoping that will change.)

Four computers (all outdated models) were replaced.

His prose was awkward (he had never really learned to shape a good paragraph), and he struggled with even the simplest writing tasks.

The music there is always extremely loud (are all young people deaf?).

On bad days he yells a lot ("No one here knows how to do their job!"), but he's usually pleasant enough.

There were photos of most of the major stars of the 1950s (Doris Day, Humphrey Bogart, Marlon Brando, Marilyn Monroe, etc.).

2. Parentheses are used around numbers or letters that indicate individual items in a series within a sentence.

They were concerned about three security issues: (1) ports, (2) air flights, and (3) national borders.

Period (*or* Full Stop) .

1. The period ends a sentence or sentence fragment that is not a question or an exclamation.

Few travelers ever dared to enter the forest.

Tell me about it.

Unlikely. In fact, impossible.

Only one period comes at the end of a sentence, even if the sentence ends with a quoted sentence or an abbreviation.

She especially liked the sentence, "Leda Rubin has been the true spirit of Blake Business Machines, Inc."

2. A period ends most abbreviations, especially in American writing.

Peter R. Addington, Jr.	vegetables, grains, etc.
Dr. Rosenberg	Sept. 16
11 p.m.	American Dental Assn.

See Abbreviations, p. 1975.

Question Mark ?

A question mark ends a direct question, but not an indirect question.

Was anyone seen on the street after midnight?

"Was anyone seen on the street after midnight?" she asked.

She asked whether anyone had been seen on the street after midnight.

Quotation Marks, Double (*or* Inverted Commas) " "

1. Quotation marks are used around direct quotations, but not indirect quotations.

"I'm leaving," she whispered. "This meeting could go on forever."

She whispered that she was leaving.

2. Quotation marks are used around words or phrases borrowed from others.

The military term "collateral damage" often refers to the deaths of civilians.

3. Quotation marks are used around titles of songs, poems, stories, essays, and articles.

"Over the Rainbow" was chosen by Americans as the most beloved song of the 20th century.

Frost's most famous poem is "Stopping by Woods on a Snowy Evening."

The first detective story was probably Poe's "The Murders in the Rue Morgue."

Thoreau's essay "Civil Disobedience" was studied by Mohandas Gandhi and Martin Luther King.

The article was published in the *New Yorker* as "The Coming Wars."

4. Quotation marks are used with other punctuation marks as follows:

A period or comma at the end of a quotation is placed inside the quotation marks.

He smiled and said, "I'm happy for you."

"That's ridiculous," she said quickly.

A colon or semicolon is placed outside the quotation marks.

Medals were given to the three "most promising scholars": Hernández, Jeffries, and Yomuro.

She called it her "little house in the country"; to us it looked like a palace.

A dash, question mark, or exclamation point is placed inside the quotation marks when it punctuates the quoted matter only, but outside the quotation marks when it punctuates the larger sentence.

"I can't see how—" he started to say.

He told everyone to bring beach sandals—he called them "flip-flops"—and an umbrella.

She collapsed in her seat with a stunned "Good God!"

"Has anyone seen Emily?" she asked.

What does he mean by "personal reasons"?

Quotation Marks, Single (*or* Inverted Commas) ' '

1. Single quotation marks are used around a quotation within another quotation.

"I heard him say 'Don't be late,' and then the door closed."

2. Often in British writing, single quotation marks are used around ordinary quoted material, and double quotation marks are used around a quotation within another quotation.

'I heard him say "Don't be late," and then the door closed.'

Semicolon ;

1. The semicolon joins two closely related main clauses. It is used especially when the second clause is introduced by an adverb or a short phrase, such as *however, indeed, thus, in that case, as a result, on the other hand, for example,* or *that is.*

Mix the milk and flour; add the eggs and beat well.

The job won't be easy; however, it has to be done.

The boat was two hours late; as a result, they missed their train.

He worried about his wife; that is, he worried that she would worry about him.

2. The semicolon separates phrases or items in a series when they contain commas.

It includes $22 million in land, buildings, and equipment; $34 million in stocks and bonds; and $8 million in cash.

3. The semicolon is placed outside quotation marks and parentheses.

The ambassador again demanded "complete autonomy"; the demand was again rejected.

My mother enjoyed his stories (and even his jokes); my father asked him questions about his work.

Slash (*or* Oblique) /

1. The slash usually substitutes for *or* or *and/or.*

in his/her case

the social/cultural background

2. The slash may replace *to* or *and* or a hyphen.

2008/09 (*or* 2008–09)

the May/June issue (*or* the May–June issue)

3. The slash is used with numerals in dates and fractions.

8/15/08

a 7/8-mile course

2 3/16 inches wide

4. The slash means *per* or *to* when used in a ratio, or when used between units of measure.

their price/earnings ratio

400,000 tons/year [=tons per year]

29 mi/gal [=miles per gallon]

a 50/50 split

5. The slash punctuates a few abbreviations.

w/o [=without]

c/o [=care of]

Compounds

Compounds are words that are made up of two or more words. Compounds may be closed, with no space between the words (for example, *airport, bypass*), hyphenated (*late-night, air-conditioning*), or open (*black market, love affair*). Compounds may be nouns (for example, *sailboat*), verbs (*ice-skate*), adjectives (*all-night*), or any other part of speech. Many common compounds are listed in this dictionary; however, new compounds may be invented by writers for a single use. If a compound is not found in a dictionary, it should either be hyphenated or left open.

1. Compound nouns that consist of longer words are usually left open.

computer program

employment agency

costume designer

2. Compounds that act as adjectives before a noun are usually hyphenated, but not when the individual words of the compound are capitalized.

a made-up excuse

higher health-care costs

the Civil War era

a New York restaurant

3. A compound adjective that follows a noun is usually not hyphenated unless it consists of a noun followed by an adjective.

Her fame was well deserved.

Aluminum is rust-resistant.

Capitals and Italics

Beginnings

1. The first word of a sentence or sentence fragment is capitalized.

They make a desert and call it peace.

So many men, so many opinions.

Bravo!

2. The first word of a sentence that is a direct quotation is normally capitalized. If a quoted sentence is interrupted, the second part does not begin with a capital.

She replied, "All he ever wanted was a home he could call his own."

"All he ever wanted," she replied, "was a home he could call his own."

3. The first word of a complete sentence within a sentence is usually capitalized.

As they say, "In unity is strength."

The basic rule is, When in doubt, spell it out.

My first thought was, Who's responsible for this?

4. The first word of a line of poetry is traditionally capitalized, though in modern poetry it is often not capitalized. The poem's original capitalization should not be changed.

Go, and catch a falling star,
Get with child a mandrake root,
Tell me, where all past years are,
Or who cleft the Devil's foot.
—John Donne

Proper Nouns and Adjectives

1. Names of people and places, organizations and their members, conferences and councils, and historical periods and events are capitalized.

Noah Webster	the Yalta Conference
Madrid	the Bronze Age
the United Nations	World War I

2. Nouns and adjectives for languages, nationalities, peoples, religious groups, and tribes are capitalized.

Latin and Greek	the Asian continent
Spanish nouns	Asians and Africans
most Spaniards	Muslims
a few Hispanics	a Muslim prayer
Hispanic culture	an Apache
Islam	Apache warriors

3. Adjectives that are formed from people's names and other proper nouns are usually capitalized.

Elizabethan England

the Trojan War

a Himalayan expedition

4. Titles that come before the name of a person are generally capitalized. Titles that are separated from the name by a comma, and titles that are used alone, usually are not capitalized.

President Lincoln

King Henry VIII

Henry VIII, king of England

President Rodríguez

Astropha's president, Salma Rodríguez

Astropha Corp.'s president was there.

5. Words of family relationship are capitalized when used before, or in place of, a person's name.

Uncle Fred's car

on Mother's birthday

6. Words for the supreme being are capitalized.

Allah	the Almighty
Jehovah	in the eyes of God

7. Names of days of the week, months, and holidays and holy days are capitalized, but not names of seasons.

Tuesday	Hanukkah
August	Easter
New Year's Day	winter
Ramadan	

8. Words in titles of books, magazines, newspapers, plays, movies, artworks, and musical compositions are capitalized, except for articles (*a, an, the*), conjunctions (*and, but, or,* etc.), and short prepositions (*by, of, from,* etc.). A title's first word is always capitalized. The entire title is set in italics.

J. R. R. Tolkien's *The Lord of the Rings*

reading *National Geographic*

the *New York Times*

Lawrence of Arabia, starring Peter O'Toole

Rodin's sculpture *The Thinker*

a production of Mozart's *The Marriage of Figaro*

Titles of newspaper and magazine articles, short stories, and songs are capitalized in the same way, but enclosed in quotation marks rather than italicized.

an article entitled "Solving the Housing Crisis"

Chekhov's famous story "The Black Monk".

"La Marseillaise" is France's national anthem.

9. Trademarks and brand names are capitalized.

Coke	Levi's	Velcro

Other Styling Conventions

1. Italics are often used for letters that are referred to as letters, words that are referred to as

words, and numerals that are referred to as numerals.

The *g* in *align* is silent.

Data may be treated as either a singular or a plural noun.

The first *2* and the last *0* are hard to read.

2. Italics are used for emphasis.

He wasn't *the* vice president, merely *a* vice president.

"We're leaving *right now*!"

Abbreviations

The rules listed below are generally followed in American writing. Though these rules are often followed in British writing as well, many British publications omit the periods from most abbreviations (for example, *Mr, Mrs, Ms, Dr, Ltd, etc, eg*).

1. A period ends most abbreviations that are formed by omitting letters of a single word. However, former abbreviations of this kind that are now considered words do not use a period.

cont. [=continued] lab [=laboratory]
Oct. [=October] gym [=gymnasium]
Dr. [=Doctor] ad [=advertisement]

2. Periods are usually omitted from abbreviations made up of single first letters that are capitalized. Uncapitalized abbreviations usually keep their periods.

GOP [=Grand Old Party]
PR [=public relations]
CEO [=chief executive officer]
AM *or* a.m. [=ante meridiem]

3. A few abbreviations are punctuated with slashes.

c/o [=care of] w/o [=without]

5. When an abbreviation with a period ends a sentence, its period becomes the sentence's final period.

Renata Shortlidge is employed by Briggs & Strahan Ltd.

5. Abbreviations are capitalized if the words they represent are capitalized.

22° F [=Fahrenheit]
the IRS [=Internal Revenue Service]
on Jan. 6 [=January]

6. Abbreviations are usually all-capitalized when they represent the first letters of uncapitalized words.

IQ [=intelligence quotient]
FYI [=for your information]

7. Most abbreviations that are formed from first letters and pronounced as words are capitalized.

NATO [=North Atlantic Treaty Organization]
NASCAR [=National Association for Stock Car Auto Racing]

8. Abbreviations of given names are followed by a period.

J. Edgar Hoover
T. S. Eliot
V. S. Naipaul

9. The courtesy titles *Mr., Mrs.,* and *Ms.* occur only as abbreviations today. When followed by a name, *Doctor* is usually abbreviated, and *Professor, Reverend, Senator,* and *Representative* are often abbreviated.

Ms. Rachel A. Downs
Dr. Paul Lazare
Prof. (*or* Professor) Henry Keys
Sen. (*or* Senator) Lee Gross

10. Abbreviations are usually made plural by adding *-s* or *-'s*.

yrs. [=years] PCs *or* PC's
figs. [=figures] PhDs
HMOs

11. Possessives of abbreviations are formed like ordinary possessives, by adding *-'s* to singular nouns and an apostrophe to plural nouns.

the CEO's speech Brown Bros.' ads
Apex Co.'s profits HMOs' lobbyists

Numbers

1. Numbers from one to nine are generally spelled out; numbers greater than nine are generally shown as figures.

The museum has eight rooms of paintings, containing a total of 155 works.

They sold 700 TV sets during the 10-day sale.

Higher numbers that are not meant to be literal are spelled out.

She had told him a thousand times. [=she had told him many times]

Some writers instead spell out all the numbers from one to ninety-nine, as well as approximate numbers consisting of a whole number plus *hundred, thousand,* etc.

The island is 161 miles long and only two miles wide.

In the course of four hours, she signed twenty-five hundred copies of her book.

For very large round numbers, it is common to spell out only the word *million, billion,* etc.

Profits for the year exceeded $7 million.

More than 3.5 billion people live in poverty.

2. If a number begins a sentence, it is written out.

> Sixty-two new bills will be brought before the committee.

3. Numbers of more than three digits are normally written with a comma before each group of three. Commas are not used in street addresses, page numbers, or year numbers.

2,241 cases	2305 Sunset Blvd.
a fee of $12,250	on page 1121
population: 3,466,000	the events of 1985

4. In full dates, commas are generally used before and after the year in American-style dates (which list the month first, followed by the day and year).

> On August 8, 1920, the entire building was destroyed by fire.

British-style dates (which list the day first, followed by the month and year) do not require a comma.

> On 8 August 1920 the entire building was destroyed by fire.

Common First Names

The list below shows the common first names used in the United States, the United Kingdom, Canada, and Australia. Common nicknames are shown in parentheses next to the formal name. Many names that are widely used as nicknames may also be given at birth as legal names; such names appear more than once in this list.

FEMALE

Alice
Amanda (Mandy)
Amy
Andrea (Andy)
Angela (Angie)
Ann, Anne (Annie)
Anna
Annie
Ashley
Barbara (Barb, Bobbi, Babs)
Betty
Beverly (Bev)
Bonnie
Brenda
Caitlin
Carol
Carolyn, Caroline (Lyn)
Catherine (Cathy, Kate, Katie, Kay)
Charlotte (Lottie)
Cheryl
Chloe
Christina (Chris, Tina, Chrissie, Christie)
Christine (Chris, Tina, Chrissie, Christie)
Claire
Cynthia (Cindy, Cyndi)
Deborah, Debra (Deb, Debbie, Debby)
Denise (Denny)
Diana (Di)
Diane (Di)
Donna
Doris (Dot, Dottie)
Dorothy (Dot, Dottie)
Edith (Edie)
Elizabeth (Liz, Beth, Betsy, Ellie, Betty, Bette, Liza, Bess, Eliza)
Ellie
Emily (Emmy)
Emma
Erin
Evelyn (Evie)
Florence (Flo)
Frances (Francie, Fran, Franny)
Georgia
Gloria
Grace (Gracie)
Hannah
Heather
Helen
Irene
Jacqueline (Jackie)
Jane (Janie)
Janet (Jan, Nettie)
Janice (Jan)
Jean (Jeannie)
Jennifer (Jen, Jenny, Jenna)
Jessica (Jessie)
Joan (Joanie)
Joyce
Judith (Judy)
Julia
Julie
Karen
Katherine, Kathryn (Kathy, Kate, Katie, Kay)
Kathleen (Kathy, Kate, Katie, Kay)
Kathy (Kate, Katie, Kay)
Kelly
Kimberly (Kim)
Laura
Lauren
Lillian (Lil)
Lily
Linda
Lisa
Lois
Lori
Louise (Lou)
Lucy
Madison (Maddy)
Margaret (Meg, Maggie, Peggy, Peg, Marge)
Maria
Marie
Marilyn (Lyn)
Martha (Marty)
Mary
Megan, Meghan
Melissa (Missy, Lissa)
Michelle (Shelly, Shelley, Shell)
Mildred (Millie)
Nancy (Nan)
Nicola (Nicki, Nicky, Nikki)
Nicole (Nicki, Nicky, Nikki)
Norma
Olivia
Pamela (Pam, Pammy)
Patricia (Pat, Patty, Trish, Tricia)
Paula
Phyllis
Rachel
Rebecca (Becky, Becca)
Robin, Robyn
Rose (Rosie)
Ruby
Ruth (Ruthie)
Samantha (Sammy, Sam)
Sandra (Sandy)
Sara, Sarah (Sally)
Sharon (Shari)
Shirley (Shirl)
Sophie
Stephanie (Steph, Stephie)
Susan (Sue, Susie, Suzy)
Tammy
Teresa, Theresa (Terry, Terri, Tess)
Tina
Virginia (Ginny)
Wanda

MALE

Aaron
Adam
Alan, Allan (Al)
Albert (Al, Bert)
Alexander (Alex, Alec, Sandy)
Andrew (Andy)
Anthony (Tony)
Antonio (Tony)
Arthur (Art, Artie)
Benjamin (Ben, Benny)
Billy
Bobby
Brandon
Brian
Bruce
Carl
Carlos
Charles (Chuck, Charlie, Chip)
Chris
Christopher (Chris)
Clarence
Colin
Connor, Conor
Craig
Daniel (Dan, Danny)
David (Dave)
Dennis (Denny)
Donald (Don, Donnie, Donny)
Douglas (Doug, Dougie)
Dylan
Earl
Edward (Ed, Ted, Eddie, Teddy)
Eric (Rick, Ricky)
Ernest (Ernie)
Ethan
Eugene (Gene)
Frank (Frankie)
Fred (Freddy)
Gary
George
Gerald (Jerry, Gerry)
Gregory (Greg)
Harold (Hal, Harry)
Harry
Henry (Harry, Hank)
Howard (Howie)
Ian
Jack (Jackie)
Jacob (Jake, Jack)
James (Jim, Jimmy, Jamie)
Jason
Jeffrey (Jeff)
Jeremy (Jerry)
Jerry
Jesse
Jimmy
Joe
John (Jack, Johnny)
Johnny
Jonathan (Jon)
Jordan (Jordy)
José
Joseph (Joe, Joey)
Joshua (Josh)
Juan
Justin
Keith
Kenneth (Ken, Kenny)
Kevin
Lachlan
Larry
Lawrence (Larry)
Liam
Logan
Louis (Lou)
Luke
Mark
Martin (Marty)
Matthew (Matt, Matty)
Michael (Mike)
Nathan (Nate)
Nicholas (Nick, Nicky)
Oliver (Ollie)
Patrick (Pat, Rick, Ricky, Paddy)
Paul
Peter (Pete)
Philip, Phillip (Phil)
Ralph
Randy
Raymond (Ray)
Richard (Dick, Rich, Richie, Rick, Ricky)
Robert (Bob, Bobby, Robbie, Rob, Bert, Robin)
Roger
Ronald (Ron, Ronnie)
Roy
Russell (Russ, Rusty)
Ryan
Samuel (Sam, Sammy)
Scott (Scottie, Scotty)
Sean, Shawn
Stephen, Steven (Steve, Stevie)
Steve (Stevie)
Terry
Thomas (Tom, Tommy)
Timothy (Tim, Timmy)
Todd
Tyler
Victor (Vic)
Walter (Walt, Wally)
Wayne
William (Bill, Billy, Will, Willie, Liam)
Willie

Money

CURRENCY

About half of all English-speaking countries use currencies based on their own *dollar* ($), divided into 100 *cents* (¢). The other half use non-dollar currencies, also divided into 100 units.

United States

The basic unit of U.S. currency is the U.S. dollar. Bills are issued with values of $1, $2, $5, $10, $20, $50, and $100, although the $2 bill is rarely used. All bills are the same size and have traditionally all been the same green color. The basic color of the bills continues to be green, but some now include other colors as well. U.S. coins are issued with values of 1¢ (a *penny*), 5¢ (a *nickel*), 10¢ (a *dime*), 25¢ (a *quarter*), 50¢ (a *half-dollar*), and $1, although the 50¢ and $1 coins are rarely used. A coin's size does not indicate its value; the dime is smaller than the penny and nickel, and the dollar is smaller than the half-dollar. A dollar is often informally called a *buck*.

United Kingdom

The unit of British currency is the pound (£), which is divided into 100 pence (p). Coins are issued with values of 1p (a *penny*), 2p, 5p, 10p, 50p, £1, and £2. Bills, or *notes*, are issued with values of £5, £10, £20, and £50, although the £50 note is rarely used. Informally, a pound is often called a *quid*, a £10 note is often called a *tenner*, a £5 note is often called a *fiver*, and pence (pennies) are usually called simply "p" ("I need another 50p"). A coin's size does not indicate its value; the £1 coin is smaller than the 50p, 10p, and 2p coins.

Canada

The Canadian currency unit is the Canadian dollar. There are $5, $10, $20, $50, and $100 bills, each with its own color. The $1 coin is often called the *loonie* (the bird on the coin is a loon), and the $2 coin is often called the *toonie*. Smaller coins are valued at 1¢ (*penny*), 5¢ (*nickel*), 10¢ (*dime*), 25¢ (*quarter*), and 50¢ (*50-cent piece*), although the 50¢ coin is rarely used. A coin's size does not indicate its value; the $2 coin, $1 coin, and 50-cent piece are all similar in size, and the dime is smaller than the penny and nickel.

Australia

Australia's currency unit is the Australian dollar. The currency consists of coins of 5¢, 10¢, 20¢, 50¢, $1, and $2, and *notes* (bills) in various colors with values of $5, $10, $20, $50, and $100. A coin's size does not indicate its value; the $1 and $2 coins are smaller than the 20¢ and 50¢ coins.

CARDS AND CHECKS

Credit cards are plastic cards issued by banks and other institutions. You can use them to pay for items and services, but only up to the amount of your *credit limit*, which is usually somewhat higher than the amount in your *bank account*. When the bill arrives each month, you may pay all of what you owe. If you instead choose to pay smaller amounts of money for several months until the full *balance* has been paid, an *interest fee* may be added. The interest fee depends on the *interest rate* of the particular credit card; interest rates can vary a great deal.

You must go through an application process to get an ordinary credit card. Although getting a card does not cost anything, some credit cards require you to pay an annual *fee*. Some of these cards have no credit limit but require you to pay the entire amount you owe when the bill arrives. If you fail to pay on time, a large fee will be charged.

Credit cards may be used to get *loans*, or *cash advances*. However, the interest rate for cash advances is higher than the card's ordinary interest rate. Also, interest begins to be charged immediately, rather than after the first bill arrives.

Debit cards are issued by banks. When you use a debit card to pay for something, you *swipe* your card through an electronic device and type your personal identification number, or *PIN*. The money is then immediately removed from your bank account and given to the person or company you are paying.

ATM cards, or *cash cards*, are issued by banks. By using the card and typing in your PIN at an *ATM* (*automated teller machine*), or *cashpoint*, at any time of day, you can *withdraw* money from your account, *deposit* money into the account, find out what your balance is, and make loan *payments*.

Today, a single card issued by a bank usually serves as a credit card, debit card, and ATM card combined.

A *check* (or *cheque*) is a piece of paper that you use to pay for items and services. A check tells your bank to pay a certain amount of money to the person or company you have written the check to. Anyone with a *checking account* at a bank may write checks. In some countries, you must show a special *cheque card* or a credit card whenever you write a check for someone. If your checking account does not contain enough money to *cover* the amount of a check that you have written, the check will *bounce* and you will have to pay a fee to the bank and write another check.

Numbers

CARDINAL NUMBERS

0	zero *also Brit* nought	15	fifteen	100	one hundred *or* a hundred
1	one	16	sixteen	101	one hundred (and) one
2	two	17	seventeen	102	one hundred (and) two
3	three	18	eighteen	200	two hundred
4	four	19	nineteen	300	three hundred
5	five	20	twenty	1,000	one thousand *or* a thousand
6	six	21	twenty-one	1,001	one thousand (and) one
7	seven	22	twenty-two	1,002	one thousand (and) two
8	eight	30	thirty	2,000	two thousand
9	nine	40	forty	100,000	one hundred thousand
10	ten	50	fifty	1,000,000	one million
11	eleven	60	sixty		
12	twelve	70	seventy		
13	thirteen	80	eighty		
14	fourteen	90	ninety		

ORDINAL NUMBERS

1st	first	15th	fifteenth	90th	ninetieth
2nd	second	16th	sixteenth	100th	one-hundredth
3rd	third	17th	seventeenth	101st	one hundred (and) first
4th	fourth	18th	eighteenth	102nd	one hundred (and) second
5th	fifth	19th	nineteenth	200th	two hundredth
6th	sixth	20th	twentieth	300th	three hundredth
7th	seventh	21st	twenty-first	1,000th	(one) thousandth
8th	eighth	22nd	twenty-second	1,001st	one thousand (and) first
9th	ninth	30th	thirtieth	1,002nd	one thousand (and) second
10th	tenth	40th	fortieth	2,000th	two thousandth
11th	eleventh	50th	fiftieth	100,000th	one hundred thousandth
12th	twelfth	60th	sixtieth	1,000,000th	one millionth
13th	thirteenth	70th	seventieth		
14th	fourteenth	80th	eightieth		

For numbers above a million, different words were used in American English and British English in the past. However, the American terms are now in official use in the United Kingdom. As a result, both the American terms and the older British terms are found in British English.

	American	British
1,000,000,000	billion	billion *or* thousand million
1,000,000,000,000	trillion	trillion *or* million million *or* billion
1,000,000,000,000,000	quadrillion	quadrillion *or* thousand billion *or* trillion

Numbers that are actual amounts of money, objects, people, etc., are usually spoken using the words shown above. For example, "304 cows" is spoken as "three hundred (and) four cows," and "$1,500" is spoken as "one thousand, five hundred dollars" or "fifteen hundred dollars."

Other types of numbers, such as numbers that are used for identification, in addresses, or in series, are often spoken in different ways. Any of the following may occur in speech: (1) zero may be spoken as "oh" (that is, the same as the letter O); (2) "hundred" may be omitted; (3) each digit may be pronounced separately; (4) the first two digits of a four-digit number may be spoken as if they were a complete number. For example:

109	"one oh nine"
234	"two thirty-four" *or* "two three four"
2012	"twenty twelve" *or* "two oh one two"
3104	"thirty-one oh four" *or* "three one oh four"

ROMAN NUMERALS

Roman numerals were first used by the ancient Romans but are still sometimes used by English speakers to suggest age and tradition or for certain purposes. They are often used on monuments and on clocks; in numbered outline lists; at the beginning of paragraphs in complex documents; in copyright dates; for numbering sports events such as the Olympic Games; and for identifying kings, queens, popes, and children with the same name as others who came earlier.

1	I	10	X	70	LXX	600	DC
2	II	11	XI	80	LXXX	900	CM
3	III	12	XII	90	XC	1000	M
4	IV	20	XX	100	C	1492	MCDXCII
5	V	21	XXI	101	CI	1558	MDLVIII
6	VI	30	XXX	200	CC	1943	MCMXLIII
7	VII	40	XL	300	CCC	2020	MMXX
8	VIII	50	L	400	CD		
9	IX	60	LX	500	D		

FRACTIONS AND DECIMALS

Simple fractions are often spelled out in print.

1/10	one tenth *or* a tenth
1/5	one fifth *or* a fifth
1/4	one fourth *or* a fourth, one quarter *or* a quarter
1/3	one third *or* a third
3/8	three eighths
2/5	two fifths
1/2	one half *or* a half
3/4	three quarters
7/8	seven eighths
11/10	eleven tenths
1 1/2	one and a half *or* one and one half
12 1/4	twelve and a quarter *or* twelve and one quarter

The words in spelled-out fractions may be connected with hyphens: *one-tenth, three-quarters, one-and-a-half*, etc.

Decimal numbers are never spelled out in print. When they are spoken, the decimal point is always called "point," and each digit after the point is named separately.

.25	"point two five"
10.30	"ten point three zero"
42.597	"forty-two point five nine seven"
2.5 million	"two point five million"

Weights and Measures

U.S. and British Systems

Unit	Equivalents in Other Units of Same System	Metric Equivalent
	WEIGHT	
ton	2,000 pounds, 20 hundredweight (*US*)	0.907 metric ton
	2,240 pounds, 20 hundredweight (*Brit*)	1.016 metric tons
hundredweight	100 pounds, 0.05 ton (*US*)	45.359 kilograms
	112 pounds, 0.05 ton (*Brit*)	50.802 kilograms
stone (*Brit*)	14 pounds	6.350 kilograms
pound	16 ounces, 7,000 grains	0.4536 kilogram
ounce	437.5 grains, 0.0625 pound	28.350 grams
grain	0.002286 ounce	0.0648 gram
	CAPACITY	
	U.S. liquid measure	
gallon	4 quarts, 231 cubic inches	3.785 liters
quart	2 pints, 57.75 cubic inches	0.946 liter
pint	16 fluid ounces, 28.875 cubic inches	0.473 liter
cup	8 fluid ounces, 14.438 cubic inches	0.237 liter
fluid ounce	1.805 cubic inches	29.573 milliliters
	British imperial liquid measure	
gallon	4 quarts, 277.420 cubic inches	4.546 liters
quart	2 pints, 69.355 cubic inches	1.136 liters
pint	20 fluid ounces, 34.678 cubic inches	568.26 milliliters
fluid ounce	1.734 cubic inches	28.412 milliliters
	LENGTH	
mile	1,760 yards, 5,280 feet	1.609 kilometers
yard	3 feet, 36 inches	0.9144 meter
foot	12 inches, 0.333 yard	30.48 centimeters
inch	0.083 foot, 0.028 yard	2.54 centimeters
	AREA	
square mile	640 acres	2.590 square kilometers
acre	4,840 square yards, 43,560 square feet	0.405 hectare, 4,047 square meters
square yard	9 square feet, 1,296 square inches	0.836 square meter
square foot	144 square inches, 0.111 square yard	0.093 square meter
square inch	0.0069 square foot, 0.00077 square yard	6.452 square centimeters
	VOLUME	
cubic yard	27 cubic feet, 46,656 cubic inches	0.765 cubic meter
cubic foot	1,728 cubic inches, 0.0370 cubic yard	0.028 cubic meter
cubic inch	0.00058 cubic foot, 0.000021 cubic yard	16.387 cubic centimeters

Metric System

Unit	Equivalent in Base Unit	U.S. Equivalent		
WEIGHT				
metric ton	1,000,000 grams	1.10 tons		
kilogram	1,000 grams	2.20 pounds		
gram		0.035 ounce		
centigram	0.01 gram	0.15 grain		
milligram	0.001 gram	0.015 grain		
CAPACITY				
		cubic	***U.S. liquid***	***Brit. imperial liquid***
kiloliter	1,000 liters	1.31 cubic yards	264.17 gallons	880.28 quarts
liter		61.02 cubic inches	1.06 quarts	0.88 quart
centiliter	0.01 liter	0.61 cubic inch	0.34 fluid ounce	0.352 fluid ounce
milliliter	0.001 liter	0.061 cubic inch	0.034 fluid ounce	0.035 fluid ounce
LENGTH				
kilometer	1,000 meters	0.62 mile		
meter		39.37 inches		
centimeter	0.01 meter	0.39 inch		
millimeter	0.001 meter	0.039 inch		
micrometer	0.000001 meter	0.000039 inch		
AREA				
square kilometer	1,000,000 square meters	0.39 square mile		
hectare	10,000 square meters	2.47 acres		
square meter		1.196 square yards		
square centimeter	0.0001 square meter	0.16 square inch		
VOLUME				
cubic meter		1.31 cubic yards		
cubic decimeter	0.001 cubic meter	61.02 cubic inches		
cubic centimeter	0.000001 cubic meter	0.061 cubic inch		

Dates

In the U.S., full dates are normally written in the order *month-day-year,* with commas before and after the year.

The *Titanic* sank on April 15, 1912.

In Britain, Australia, and Canada, month and day are usually in the opposite order, and no commas are used.

The *Titanic* sank on 15 April 1912.

The same order used for full dates is also used when a date is written entirely in numbers. Thus, 6/8/08 means June 8, 2008, in the U.S., but in Britain and usually in Australia and Canada, 6/8/08 means August 6, 2008. Because of this difference, dates should never be written entirely in numbers when their meaning might be unclear. The International Organization for Standardization (ISO) has called for an all-numbers style in the order *year-month-day;* thus, June 8, 2008, would be abbreviated as 2008-06-08. The ISO style is widely used in technical contexts in all four countries.

In dates that include only the month and year, commas are omitted.

In October 2008 the factory closed.

In informal speech and writing, *of* is often inserted between the month and year.

We sold the house in January of 2001.

Century numbers may be either spelled out or written in digits.

in the nineteenth [*or* 19th] century

a 16th- [*or* sixteenth-] century painting

Decades are often called by a short name.

a song from the sixties [*or* '60s *or* Sixties]

The abbreviations *B.C., B.C.E.,* and *C.E.* are placed after the date; *A.D.* is usually placed before a specific date.

1792–1750 B.C. *or* 1792–1750 B.C.E.

22 C.E. *or* A.D. 22

All four abbreviations follow the word *century.*

the 4th century A.D. *or* the 4th century C.E.

In speech, people often omit the word *hundred* from the names of years.

814: "eight fourteen" / "eight hundred fourteen"

1492: "fourteen ninety-two" / "fourteen hundred ninety-two"

1801: "eighteen-oh-one" / "eighteen hundred and one" / "eighteen one"

2013: "two thousand thirteen" / "two thousand and thirteen" / "twenty thirteen"

In both speech and writing, ordinal numbers (*1st, 2nd, 3rd, 4th,* etc.) are often used instead of cardinal numbers (*1, 2, 3, 4,* etc.), especially for dates that lack a year.

The package arrived on December 4th. = The package arrived on the 4th of December.

Holidays

This table shows the most important religious and nonreligious holidays in four English-speaking countries.

The abbreviation *(g)* marks public holidays set by the government. In the United States, these holidays are official only for employees of the federal government (although they are also observed by many businesses). In Canada and Australia, some government holidays are not observed in all provinces or states.

Most holidays associated with a particular date, such as Christmas, are celebrated on that date even when the actual holiday from work falls on the closest weekday. Some, such as Valentine's Day, St. Patrick's Day, Halloween, and Guy Fawkes Day, are almost never holidays from work.

UNITED STATES

New Year's Day, January 1 (g)
Martin Luther King Day, third Monday in January (g)
Valentine's Day, February 14
Washington's Birthday (Presidents' Day), third Monday in February (g)
St. Patrick's Day, March 17
Easter, first Sunday after first full moon after March 20
Mother's Day, second Sunday in May
Memorial Day, last Monday in May (g)
Father's Day, third Sunday in June
Independence Day, July 4 (g)
Labor Day, first Monday in September (g)
Columbus Day, second Monday in October (g)
Halloween, October 31
Veterans Day, November 11 (g)
Thanksgiving, fourth Thursday in November (g)
Christmas, December 25 (g)

UNITED KINGDOM

New Year's Day, January 1 or following Monday (g)
Valentine's Day, February 14
St. Patrick's Day, March 17
Early May Bank Holiday, first Monday in May (g)
Mother's Day, third Sunday before Easter
Good Friday, two days before Easter (g)
Easter, first Sunday after first full moon after March 20
Easter Monday, day after Easter (g)
Spring Bank Holiday, last Monday in May (g)
Father's Day, third Sunday in June
Summer Bank Holiday, last Monday in August (g)
Guy Fawkes Day, November 5
Remembrance Sunday, Sunday nearest November 11
Christmas, December 25 or following Monday (g)
Boxing Day, December 26 or first weekday after Christmas holiday (g)

CANADA

New Year's Day, January 1 (g)
Valentine's Day, February 14
St. Patrick's Day, March 17
Good Friday, two days before Easter (g)
Easter, first Sunday after first full moon after March 20
Easter Monday, day after Easter (g)
Mother's Day, second Sunday in May
Victoria Day, Monday before May 25 (g)
Father's Day, third Sunday in June
Canada Day, July 1; if Sunday, moved to Monday (g)
Labour Day, first Monday in September (g)
Thanksgiving Day, second Monday in October (g)
Remembrance Day, November 11 (g)
Christmas, December 25 or following Monday (g)
Boxing Day, December 26 or first weekday after Christmas holiday (g)

AUSTRALIA

New Year's Day, January 1 or following Monday (g)
Australia Day, January 26 or following Monday (g)
Valentine's Day, February 14
St. Patrick's Day, March 17
Good Friday, two days before Easter (g)
Easter, first Sunday after first full moon after March 20
Easter Monday, day after Easter (g)
Anzac Day, April 25; if Sunday, moved to Monday (g)
Mother's Day, second Sunday in May
Queen's Birthday, second Monday in June (g)
Father's Day, first Sunday in September
Remembrance Day, November 11
Christmas, December 25 or following Monday (g)
Boxing Day, December 26 or first weekday after Christmas holiday (g)

Envelope Addresses

The first two or three lines of an address on an envelope have the same general elements in the United States, the United Kingdom, Canada, and Australia. The first line shows the name of the person receiving the letter, and the next line consists of a street address or post-office box number, as appropriate. In most cases, the street address has a street number followed by the street name. Additional information, such as the person's title or the company's name (for example, Universal Metrics, Inc.) can be entered on additional lines above the street address. The elements of the remaining address lines in each country are discussed below.

United States The name of the city or town, the two-letter state abbreviation, and the five-digit zip code are written on the same line. Every address has a unique four-digit number that is attached to the zip code (for example, 77269-2501), but these numbers are not used frequently.

Elizabeth Kingston Murray
Universal Metrics, Inc.
357 East Madison St.
Houston, TX 77269
U.S.A.

United Kingdom The city or town name is written in all capital letters. The postcode consists of numbers and capital letters and is entered on its own line with one space between its two parts. A county name, not written in all capital letters, may be included on its own line below the postcode but is usually omitted. The name of the specific country within the United Kingdom—England, Scotland, Wales, or Northern Ireland—may appear in place of "United Kingdom" or "UK" as the last line of the address.

Mr. G. B. Robinson
Universal Metrics Ltd.
29 Edgbaston Park Rd.
BIRMINGHAM
B15 2RT
England

Canada The name of the city or town, the two-letter province or territory abbreviation, and the postal code should be written on the same line. The six-character postal code consists of letters and numbers with one space between its two parts.

Jane MacAllister
Universal Metrics, Ltd.
249 Adelaide St. E., Suite 203
Toronto, ON M5A 1N1
Canada

Australia The city, town, or post-office name is followed by the state or territory abbreviation and the four-digit postcode, with one or two spaces between each of these parts. There is no punctuation on this line, and all letters are capitalized. When a country name is entered on the last line, it should be written in all capital letters.

Mr. Roger Lewis
Universal Metrics Pty. Ltd.
166 Kent Street, Level 9
SYDNEY NSW 2001
AUSTRALIA

STANDARD STATE AND PROVINCE ABBREVIATIONS

United States: States and Territories

(Official abbreviations are listed in the middle column. Traditional abbreviations are listed in the right-hand column.)

Alabama	AL	Ala.
Alaska	AK	Alas.
American Samoa	AS	—
Arizona	AZ	Ariz.
Arkansas	AR	Ark.
California	CA	Cal.
Colorado	CO	Colo.
Connecticut	CT	Conn.
Delaware	DE	Del.
District of Columbia	DC	D.C.
Florida	FL	Fla.
Georgia	GA	Ga.
Guam	GU	—
Hawaii	HI	—
Idaho	ID	—
Illinois	IL	Ill.
Indiana	IN	Ind.
Iowa	IA	Ia.
Kansas	KS	Kan.
Kentucky	KY	Ky.
Louisiana	LA	La.
Maine	ME	Me.
Maryland	MD	Md.
Massachusetts	MA	Mass.
Michigan	MI	Mich.
Minnesota	MN	Minn.
Mississippi	MS	Miss.
Missouri	MO	Mo.
Montana	MT	Mont.
Nebraska	NE	Neb.
Nevada	NV	Nev.
New Hampshire	NH	N.H.
New Jersey	NJ	N.J.
New Mexico	NM	N.M.
New York	NY	N.Y.
North Carolina	NC	N.C.
North Dakota	ND	N.D.
Northern Mariana Islands	MP	—
Ohio	OH	O.
Oklahoma	OK	Okla.
Oregon	OR	Ore.
Pennsylvania	PA	Pa.
Puerto Rico	PR	P.R.
Rhode Island	RI	R.I.
South Carolina	SC	S.C.
South Dakota	SD	S.D.
Tennessee	TN	Tenn.
Texas	TX	Tex.
Utah	UT	—
Vermont	VT	Vt.
Virgin Islands	VI	V.I.
Virginia	VA	Va.
Washington	WA	Wash.
West Virginia	WV	W.Va.
Wisconsin	WI	Wisc.
Wyoming	WY	Wyo.

United Kingdom

Though all four countries of the United Kingdom are divided into counties, counties are usually omitted from postal addresses.

Australia: States and Territories

Australian Capital Territory	ACT
New South Wales	NSW
Northern Territory	NT
Queensland	QLD
South Australia	SA
Tasmania	TAS
Victoria	VIC
Western Australia	WA

Canada: Provinces and Territories

Alberta	AB
British Columbia	BC
Manitoba	MB
New Brunswick	NB
Newfoundland and Labrador	NL
Northwest Territories	NT
Nova Scotia	NS
Nunavut	NU
Ontario	ON
Prince Edward Island	PE
Quebec	QC
Saskatchewan	SK
Yukon Territory	YT

General

Several other abbreviations are standard in addresses in all four countries.

Street	St.
Avenue	Ave.
Road	Rd.
Drive	Dr.
Boulevard	Blvd.
North	N.
South	S.
East	E.
West	W.

E-Mail, Letters, Memos, and Résumés

E-Mail

Almost all business correspondence today uses e-mail.

Business e-mails should always include a subject line. This may let the other person know whether the message is urgent, and it will be valuable whenever either person needs to find the message in the future. When you answer a business e-mail, you should normally retain the subject line of the e-mail that you are answering.

Use the CC box to send copies to other people in your office who might be interested in the message. If you want to send a copy to someone without showing that person's name to the other people who receive the message, use the BCC box instead.

E-mail greetings, even in business correspondence, are usually quite informal. When writing to someone you do not know, always begin with "Dear Mr." or "Dear Ms." (for example, "Dear Mr. Nast:"). Business relationships in the U.S. now often become friendly and informal quickly, however. When the other person sends you an e-mail and signs it with his or her first name by itself, or uses your first name by itself in the greeting (for example, "Dear Martin,"), you may generally feel free to address him or her in that same way in your next e-mail. You may feel comfortable using "Hi" ("Hi Martin,") soon afterward. If the other person has a higher title than you, however, it is often better to remain formal in all your correspondence with him or her.

The language in the rest of the e-mail may also become quite informal. However, always be careful about using humor, since it often will not be understood properly.

A message should normally be limited to one subject. If you have two subjects to discuss, it is best to send two separate e-mails (with different subject lines). Keeping messages limited to one subject will make it easier for both you and the other person to file and find them.

If someone has written to you about several different subjects in a single e-mail, it may be best to write each separate response after the appropriate paragraph in the other person's message.

Use asterisks to emphasize a word or phrase (for example, "I meant the *Philips* account, not the Phillips account"). Using all capital letters ("I meant the PHILIPS account . . . ") can seem rude; any other kind of unusual type (such as boldface, italic, or underlining) may disappear when the message is sent.

Most business e-mails include a special ending (called a *complimentary close*) before the writer's name at the end. Somewhat formal ways of ending an e-mail include "Sincerely yours," "Yours sincerely," and "Best regards"; less formal options include "Sincerely," "Yours," and "Best." If you know someone well, your first name by itself may be enough, and very informal e-mails even omit the name. However, it is generally best to include at least an informal ending and your first name.

From: charlotte_gates@kestrel.com
To: mbkim@lakeland.com
CC: efrost@kestrel.com; nnmarkova@kestrel.com
Subject: Lunch meeting

Dear Meg:

After so many phone conversations, it was delightful to finally meet over lunch on Tuesday. (And what a great lunch it was!)

If my notes are correct, my responsibilities at this point are basically as follows:

Review the Tomkins manuscript with an eye to its textbook potential.
Get a final decision from Ken Pascal on whether we'll be entering the bidding for the Perez translation.
Sound out WideWorld about a distribution arrangement for the Ghost Riders series.

Please let me know if I've forgotten anything. Otherwise, I'll be in touch to inform you of any progress.

Best regards,
Charlotte Gates

Letters

Business letters are usually more formal than e-mails. All business letters employ very similar formats.

Business letters are normally written on the company's official stationery (or *letterhead*). Any business letter that is not written on company letterhead should include the writer's address at the top, without the writer's name. The date comes next. Below the date comes the name and address of the person you are writing to, exactly as they will appear on the envelope (see Envelope Addresses, p. 1986). This is followed by the greeting (or *salutation*), which always begins with "Dear." When you write to a company or organization and you do not know the name of a particular person to address, you can address the company, organization, or department in general (for example, "Dear Merriam-Webster:").

Business letters end with a complimentary close, the writer's signature, the typed name, and often the writer's title. The common endings for letters, both formal and less formal, are mostly the same as those for e-mails.

Below is a sample letter from a retail hardware business.

May 7, 2008

Mr. David Lindberg
Credit Manager
Harkins Hardware
100 Lake Street
Smithville, UT 84103

Dear Mr. Lindberg:

After meeting with you and inspecting your exhibit of fine carpenters' tools at the BTSE Convention in San Francisco last week, we have decided that we would like to carry your entire line of tools on a locally exclusive basis.

Please consider this letter an application for a charge account in the $5,000-$10,000 range. Credit references will be supplied upon request.

We are delighted to have the opportunity to handle the exclusive Harkins franchise in the Carson City area, and we look forward to building a healthy and profitable business relationship.

Very truly yours,

Howard Perretta

Howard Perretta
Vice President, Sales